R BK 791.43   T866W   1983
WHO WAS WHO ON SCREEN
                                   /TRUITT, EV
3   1983   65.00   FV

3000 664804 30018
St. Louis Community College

W9-DIU-066

R 791.43 T866w 1983   FV
TRUITT
WHO WAS WHO ON SCREEN
                              65.00

For Reference

Not to be taken from this room

WITHDRAWN

 St. Louis Community
College

Library

5801 Wilson Avenue
St. Louis, Missouri 63110

Who
Was
Who
On
Screen

Who Was Who On Screen

Third Edition

Evelyn Mack Truitt

R.R. BOWKER COMPANY
New York & London, 1983

Published by R.R. Bowker Co.
1180 Avenue of the Americas, New York, N.Y. 10036
Copyright © 1983 by Evelyn Mack Truitt
All rights reserved

Printed and bound in the United States of America

ISBN 0-8352-1578-4

For Berry
1951-1978

PREFACE

The first edition of *Who Was Who on Screen* covered over 6,000 screen personalities, primarily American, British, and French, who died between the years 1920 and 1971; the second edition was revised to span the years 1905 and 1975, which included some 9,000 names. This, the third edition, totals more than 13,000 entries and covers the years 1905 to 1982, and represents primarily American, British, French and German screen personalities.

This book is concerned with the players—not only the greats and the near-greats, but the bit players in important features and the headliners in lesser known films. Also listed are persons who, while they appeared at least briefly on screen, are better known for other achievements—fighters Joe Louis and James T. Corbett, Senator Everett Dirkson, artist Pablo Picasso, golfer Bobby Jones, athlete Jim Thorpe, and authors Somerset Maugham and George Bernard Shaw, for example, plus would you believe King Victor Emmanuel II, of all people. Animal performers are not forgotten and the efforts of Rin Tin Tin (Jr. and Sr.), Trigger, Petey, Flipper, Tony the Wonder Horse, and others are recognized.

Because screen appearances are what this book is all about, directors, producers, and other behind-the-scenes luminaries are included only if they also appeared in front of the camera. Marriage and family data have usually been included only if industry-related or relevant to a well known performer's career.

For ease of reference, performers are listed alphabetically. Each entry is comprised of a brief biographical sketch, together with a full list of screen credits, if available, rather than the summary or highlighted version found in most reference works.

For consistency, *Film Daily* (through 1970) and the *International Motion Picture Almanac* (1971 through 1981) have been used for release dates, thus avoiding the discrepancy between East Coast vs. West Coast and foreign opening dates. Because early films seldom exceeded four reels in length, shorts are distinguished from features only after 1920. For the purposes of this book, a short is defined as a film of less than five reels and a feature as one of five reels or more.

In its coverage of both well-remembered and obscure performers, this book brings together information from hundreds of sources. This information has been carefully cross-checked to assure accuracy, and vital records and living sources have been consulted wherever possible to resolve conflicting or inadequate data. The keen memory of J. Patrick O'Malley, in one instance, helped make it possible to distinguish his films from those of Patrick O'Malley; Brenda Forbes helped determine in which films her mother, Mary Forbes, appeared, rather than Mary Elizabeth Forbes; and without the assistance of Frances Delmar, widow of Victor Daniels (Chief Thundercloud), and Anne Bauer, widow of Scott T. Williams, (the other Chief Thundercloud), it would not have been possible to accurately credit each actor. Where name duplications or similarities could not be resolved, screen credits are not given and this is noted in the individual entries.

The cataloging of foreign film credits presents a special problem for several reasons: the limited availability of source material, the discrepancy between foreign and U.S. release dates, and title changes or translations. British films, more than most, particularly in the early years, undergo a variety of title changes before being imported to Hollywood. Therefore, in many instances, the listing of the original British title and release date is followed by the title and date of release in the United States. Foreign language films, if released in the United States, are listed primarily by their retitled or translated names.

Films that have been made for television are purposely not included in this work even though they may be a feature film in length. Many of these TV originated projects have been released abroad and frequently with a title change. I have attempted to weed out these disparate films, and hopefully, I have succeeded.

Every effort has been made to provide you—whether film scholar or film buff—with as comprehensive, functional, and reliable a book as possible. Conflicting data have been noted along with the verifiable information. Since mystery—sometimes intended, sometimes merely clouded by the past—continues to surround many performers, additional or supplementary information is welcome and can be submitted via the publisher.

For those who may have the Second Edition of *Who Was Who on Screen,* you will recall I made note of a special *Who Was Who on Screen* fan who was most supportive of my efforts, offering invaluable data and encouragement. The expertise that Barry Brown shared made the second endeavor a more thorough work.

It is an impossible task to research and finalize a book such as this without the benefit of true and dedicated assistance. I must confess I could not have assembled this myriad of data without the untiring and capable help of Elaine Langwell Decker, Sue Fisher, Jackie Bristol, Chris Burns, and of course my friend, research assistant, and film historian, Carol Cullen. They truly worked above and beyond the call of duty. Words of thanks are inadequate. And, I must again thank my dear friend, Charles Pollock, who convinced me to get the initial project from the hobby stage to reference book status.

E.M.T.

ACKNOWLEDGEMENTS

Since publication of prior editions of *Who Was Who on Screen,* I have been the happy recipient of countless letters from a variety of people offering suggestions and advising me of their interest and support. It is mind-boggling to think of the time and effort these people have spent to provide me with extensive additional information or miscellaneous corrections. I will forever be grateful to them for their contributions on my behalf: Scott Cohen, Robert Evans, Mike Lackey, Jim Lacy, Ivan Marinov, Bob Nitsche, Scott Palmer, Rob Pinsel, John Rengstorff, Glenn Shipley, Bob Tamkin, Michael Thornton, Lillian Tudiver, Zoe Voigtsberg Truitt, Roi Uselton, William Wilson, and Bill and Marcia Lawhead, who are truly film credit specialists; Bill Doyle, who continued where Barry stopped; Leonard Maltin, for his invaluable assistance in correctly identifying "Our Gang" participants; plus Sam Gill and Anthony Slide of the Academy of Motion Picture Arts & Sciences Library.

WHO WAS WHO ON SCREEN

AABEL, HANK
Died: Dec., 1961, Oslo, Norway. Screen actor.

Appeared in: **1933** En Glad Gutt.

AANDY, K (aka JAIDEV)
Born: 1904. Died: May 19, 1980, Tellicherry, N. Kerala, India. Screen actor.

Appeared in: **1932** Marthanda Varma.

AASEN, JOHN
Born: 1887, Minnesota. Died: Aug. 1, 1938, Mendocino, Calif. Screen actor and circus giant.

Appeared in: **1923** Why Worry? **1927** Legionnaires in Paris; Two Flaming Youths. **1928** Should Married Men Go Home?

ABBAS, HECTOR
Born: Nov. 9, 1884, Amsterdam, Holland. Died: Nov. 11, 1942, England? Screen and stage actor.

Appeared in: **1919** The First Men in the Moon. **1920** Fate's Plaything. **1922** A Prince of Lovers (US 1927 and aka Life of Lord Byron). **1923** The Wandering Jew. **1928** Bolibar. **1930** The School for Scandal. **1931** Madame Guillotine. **1937** The Man Who Made Diamonds. **1941** Old Mother Riley's Circus.

ABBE, CHARLES S.
Born: 1860. Died: June 16, 1932, Darien, Conn. (blood poisoning). Stage and screen actor.

Appeared in: **1915** Niobe. **1921** Cappy Ricks; The Conquest of Canaan. **1922** Back Home and Broke. **1923** Homeward Bound. **1924** West of the Water Tower.

ABBE, JAMES
Born: 1883, Alfred, Me. Died: Nov. 11, 1973, San Francisco, Calif. Screen actor, radio and television columnist, journalist and photographer.

Appeared in: **1923** The White Sister (only film).

ABBEY, MAY
Born: 1872, Hartford, Conn. Died: Aug. 20, 1952, New York, N.Y. ("fell or jumped" from building). Screen and stage actress. Married to actor George Lessey (dec. 1947). Appeared in films for Edison, Colonial, and Eastern.

Appeared in: **1917** The Spy.

ABBOTT, AL
Born: 1884. Died: Sept. 4, 1962, Reseda, Calif. (heart attack). Screen and vaudeville actor.

Appeared in: **1929** Small Town's Ramblers (short).

ABBOTT, BUD (William A. Abbott)
Born: Oct. 2, 1896, Asbury, N.J. Died: Apr. 24, 1974, Woodland Hills, Calif. (cancer). Screen, stage, television, radio, vaudeville and burlesque actor. Married to burlesque actress Betty Pratt (dec. 1981). Was part of comedy team of Abbott and Costello. For films they appeared in together see Lou Costello (dec. 1959).

Appeared in (without Costello): **1946** The Ghost Steps Out. **1950** The Real McCoy. **1967** Voice only used for cartoon shorts.

ABBOTT, DOROTHY
Died: Dec. 5, 1968. Screen actress.

Appeared in: **1946** The Razor's Edge. **1948** The Night Has a Thousand Eyes. **1949** Neptune's Daughter; Red, Hot and Blue; Take Me Out to the Ball Game. **1950** A Life of Her Own; The Petty Girl; Where Danger Lives. **1952** The Las Vegas Story. **1955** Love Me or Leave Me; Rebel Without a Cause. **1956** Everything but the Truth. **1957** Gunfight at the OK Corral; Jailhouse Rock. **1959** Pillow Talk. **1960** The Apartment; Pepe. **1962** Sergeants Three; That Touch of Mink. **1963** A Gathering of Eagles.

ABBOTT, FRANK
Born: 1879. Died: 1957, Los Angeles, Calif. Screen actor. Entered films during early silents.

Appeared in: **1925** The Wild Bull's Lair.

ABBOTT, GREGORY M.
Born: 1900. Died: Sept. 25, 1981, Riverdale, N.Y. Screen actor, radio and television announcer, pianist and singer.

ABBOTT, GYPSY
Born: 1895, Atlanta, Ga. Died: July 23, 1952, Hollywood, Calif. Screen actress. Divorced from film director Henry King.

Appeared in: **1913** Vengeance is Mine. **1914** The Man Who Could Not Lose. **1917** Lorelei of the Sea. **1919** Some Liar. **1926** The Wicked City.

ABBOTT, JAMES FRANCIS
Born: 1873. Died: Jan. 19, 1954, North Hollywood, Calif. Screen actor.

ABBOTT, MARION
Born: 1867, Danville, Ky. Died: Jan. 15, 1937, Philadelphia, Pa. (pneumonia). Screen and stage actress.

Appeared in: **1921** Tol'able David. **1923** The Backbone.

ABBOTT, MERRIEL
Born: 1893. Died: Nov. 6, 1977, Chicago, Ill. Screen actress and dancer. Founder of the Merriel Abbott Dancers.

Appeared in: **1931** Night Club Revels (short). **1932** Smiling Faces; The Milky Way (short). **1940** Love Thy Neighbor. **1943** Swing Fever.

ABE, UTAKA
Born: 1896, Japan. Died: Jan. 1977, Tokyo, Japan (heart ailment). Screen actor and film director.

ABEL, ALFRED
Born: Mar. 12, 1880, Leipzig, Germany. Died: Dec. 12, 1937. Screen actor and film producer. Known as "The Louis Stone of German pictures."

Appeared in: **1913** Der Niegeküsste Mund; Sodoms Ende. **1914** Venetianische Nacht; Weisse Rosen. **1915** Die Geschichte der Stillen Mühle. **1917** Es Werde Licht. **1918** Colomba; Sundiege Mutter (Sinning Mothers). **1919** Rausch; Kameraden; Lache Bajazzo; Das Laster; Sundiege Eltern. **1920** Das Tagebuch Meiner Frau. **1921** Die em Schatten Gehen; Die Frau ohne Seele; Grausige Nächte; Die Rote Mühle; Der Streik der Diebe; Irrende Seelen (aka Sklaven der Sinne and aka Der Idiot); Sappho (US 1922). **1922** Doktor Mabuse, der Spieler (Dr. Mabuse, the Gambler—US 1927); Der Brennende Acker; Die Flamme; Das Phantom; Der Falsche Dimitri; Fra Diavolo; Die Intriguen der Madame de la Pommeraye; Bigamie; Menschenopfer; Die Nacht der Medici. **1923** Die Buddenbrooks; Die Finanzen des

1

Grossherzogs (The Grand Duke's Finances); Arme Sünderin; Im Rausche der Leidenschaft; Das Spiel der Liebe; Die Prinzessin Suwarin (US 1925). **1924** Die Frau im Feuer; Dudu, ein Menschenschicksal; Versuchung; Mensch Gegen Mensch; Das Spiel mit dem Schicksal. **1925** Der Bankraub Unter den Linden; Die Feuertänzerin; Der Herr Generaldirektor. **1926** Metropolis (US 1927); Eine Dubarry von Heute; Der Gardeoffizier; Die Lachende Grille; Menschen Untereinander; Tragödie einer Ehe; Die Tragödie eines Verlorenen. **1927** Das Tanzende Wien; Das Geheimnis von Genf; Jahrmarkt des Lebens; Ein Tag der Rosen im August . . . da hat die Garde Fortgemusst; Laster der Menschheit (Lusts of Mankind). **1928** L'Argent; Rasputins Liebesabenteuer (aka Rasputin und die Frauen); Ariadne im Hoppegarten; Heut' Spielt der Strauss; Mein Herz ist eine Jazzband; Eine Nacht in Yoshiwara; Wer das Scheiden hat Erfunden. **1929** Cagliostro; Narkose; Strauss, the Waltz King; Ehe in Not; Giftgas. **1930** Sei Gegrüsst, Du mein Schönes Sorrent; Dolly Macht Karriere (Dolly's Career, aka Dolly's Way to Stardom—US 1931). **1931** Der Herzog von Reichstadt; Das Schicksal der Renate Langen (The Fate of the Renata Lancer—US 1933, and aka Sein Letzter Brief); Die Koffer des Herrn O. F. (The Luggage of Mr. O. F.); Der Kongress Tanzt (Congress Dances—US 1932); Meine Frau, die Hochstaplerin; 1914, die Letzten Tage vor dem Weltbrand (The Last Days Before the War—US 1932); Mary, das Ekel; Der Herr Bueroovorsteher (US 1932). **1932** Das Madel von Montparnasse; Das Schone Abenteuer; Jonny Stiehlt Europa; Der Weisse Daemon (The White Demon, aka Rauschgift); Kampf; Spione im Savoy-Hotel (aka Die Galavorstellung der Fratellinis—US 1933). **1933** Manloescu, der Furst der Diebe; Brennendes Geheimnis; Die Frau von der Man Spricht; Wege zur Guten Ehe; Die Kleine Schwindlerin; Salon Dora Green (House of Dora Green—US 1937, and aka Die Falle). **1934** Eine Siebzehnjaehrige; Die Liebe Siegt. **1935** Viktoria. **1936** Kater Lampe; Ein Seltsamer Gast (US 1937); Maris die Magd (US 1937); Das Hofkonzert; Und Du, Mein Schatz, Faehrst Mit; Spiel an Bord; Skandal um die Fledermaus. **1937** Ich Moecht' so Gern mit Dir Allein Sein; Millionen Erbschaft; Unter Ausschluss der Offentlichkeit; Sieben Ohrfeigen (Seven Slaps, aka Boxes on the Ears—US 1938). **1938** Frau Sylvelin. **1940** Alle Stehen Kopf (General Confusion).

ABELES, EDWARD

Born: 1870. Died: July 10, 1919, New York, N.Y. (pneumonia). Stage and screen actor.

Appeared in: **1914** Brewster's Millions; Ready Money. **1915** After Five; Under Two Flags. **1918** Opportunity.

ABINGDON, WILLIAM L.

Born: May 2, 1859, Tewcester-Hertheontes, England. Died: May 17, 1918, New York, N.Y. Screen actor. Father of stage director William Abingdon.

Appeared in: **1914** Manon Lescaut. **1916** Panthea. **1918** Fedora.

ABLE, WILL B.

Born: 1924, Providence, R.I. Died: Nov. 18, 1981, St Louis, Mo. (viral infection). Screen, stage actor, dancer and comic. Married to Graziella Able with whom he toured on stage. Performed with "George White's Scandals."

Appeared in: **1968** The Night They Raided Minsky's.

ABRAHAMIAN, AROUSIAK (Arousiak Hashashian)

Born: 1890, Ankara, Turkey. Died: July 2, 1973, Philadelphia, Pa. Screen actress. Mother of actor Val Avery.

ABRIL, DOROTHY

Born: 1897, Paterson, N.J. Died: Apr. 28, 1977, Hollywood, Calif. Screen actress. Married to stuntman Harvey Parry.

Appeared in: **1915** The Golden Chance; The Secret Sin. **1916** The Clown. **1917** The Little American; The Hostage.

ABURTO, ARMANDO

Born: 1910, Mexico. Died: July 1, 1955, Mexico City, Mexico. Screen and stage actor.

ACE, JANE (Jane Sherwood)

Born: 1900. Died: Nov. 11, 1974, New York, N.Y. Screen and radio actress. Married to writer Goodman Ace.

Appeared in: **1935** Easy Aces (short); an RKO short.

ACKER, JEAN (aka MRS. JEAN ACKER VALENTINO)

Born: 1893, Trenton, N.J. Died: Aug. 16, 1978, Los Angeles, Calif. Screen, stage and vaudeville actress. Divorced from actor Rudolph Valentino (dec. 1926).

Appeared in: **1915** Are You a Mason? **1919** Lombardi, Ltd.; Checkers. **1920** Help Wanted—Male; The Ladder of Lies; The Round Up; Arabian Knight. **1921** Brewster's Millions; Wealth; See My Lawyer; The Kiss. **1922** Her Own Money. **1923** The Woman in Chains. **1925** Braveheart. **1927** The Nest. **1931** The Girl Habit. **1935** No More Ladies. **1937** Vogues of 1938. **1939** Good Girls Go to Paris. **1940** Remember the Night; My Favorite Wife. **1944** The Thin Man Goes Home. **1945** Masquerade in Mexico; Spellbound. **1951** The Mating Season. **1952** Something to Live For.

ACKERMAN, WALTER

Born: 1881. Died: Dec. 12, 1938, Hollywood, Calif. Screen actor. Entered films in 1907.

Appeared in: **1925** Rugged Water. **1926** Man of the Forest. **1927** Aflame in the Sky; Back to God's Country. **1929** Bride of the Desert.

ACORD, ART

Born: 1890, Stillwater, Minn. Died: Jan. 4, 1931, Chihuahua, Mexico (suicide—poison). Screen actor. Entered films in 1912. Divorced from actresses Edythe Sterling and Louise Lorraine (dec. 1981).

Appeared in: **1914** The Squaw Man. **1915** A Man Afraid of His Wardrobe. **1917** Cleopatra. **1918** Headin' South. **1920** The Moon Riders (serial). **1921** The White Horseman (serial); Winners of the West (serial). **1922** In the Days of Buffalo Bill (serial). **1923** The Oregon Trail (serial). **1924** Fighting for Justice; Looped for Life. **1925** The Scrappin' Kid; The Call of Courage; Three in Exile; The Circus Cyclone; Pals; Triple Action; The Wild Girl. **1926** Lazy Lightning; The Man From the West; The Ridin' Rascal; Rustler's Ranch; The Set-Up; The Silent Guardian; Sky High Corral; The Terror; Western Pluck. **1927** Hard Fists; Loco Luck; Set Free; Spurs and Saddles; The Western Rover. **1928** Two Gun O'Brien. **1929** The Arizona Kid; Bullets and Justice; Fighters of the Saddle; An Oklahoma Cowboy; The White Outlaw; Wyoming Tornado.

ACOSTA, RODOLFO

Born: 1920, Mexico. Died: Nov. 7, 1974, Woodland Hills, Calif. Screen, stage and television actor.

Appeared in: **1948** The Fugitive. **1950** One Way Street; Poncho Villa Returns. **1951** The Bullfighter and the Lady (aka Torero). **1952** Yankee Buccaneer; Horizons West. **1953** Destination Gobi; Wings of the Hawk; Appointment in Honduras; City of Bad Men; San Antone; Hondo. **1954** Drum Beat; Passion. **1955** A Life in the Balance; The Littlest Outlaw. **1956** Bandido; The Proud Ones. **1957** The Tijuana Story; Apache Warrior; Last Stagecoach West; Trooper Hook. **1958** From Hell to Texas. **1960** Flaming Star (aka Black Star, Flaming Heart, Flaming Lance); Walk Like a Dragon; Let No Man Write My Epitaph. **1961** One-Eyed Jacks; The Second Time Around; Posse from Hell; The Last Rebel; How the West Was Won. **1963** Savage Sam. **1964** Rio Conchos. **1965** The Sons of Katie Elder; The Reward; The Greatest Story Ever Told. **1966** Return of the Seven. **1967** Valley of Mystery. **1968** Dayton's Devils. **1969** Impasse; Young Billy Young. **1970** Flap (aka Nobody Loves Flapping Eagle); The Great White Hope.

ACTON, WALLACE

Born: 1905. Died: Sept. 2, 1980, Anaheim, Calif. (lung cancer). Screen and stage actor.

Appeared in: **1952** The Marrying Kind.

ACUFF, EDDIE

Born: 1908, Caruthersville, Mo. Died: Dec. 17, 1956, Hollywood, Calif. (heart attack). Stage and screen actor.

Appeared in: **1934** Here Comes the Navy. **1935** I Found Stella Parish; Shipmates Forever; Miss Pacific Fleet. **1936** The Petrified Forest; The Black Legion; Crash Donovan; Boulder Dam; The Law in Her Hands; Jail Break; The Case of the Velvet Claws; The Golden Arrow; The Walking Dead. **1937** Talent Scout; The Go-Getter; The Outer Gate; They Won't Forget; The Singing Marine; Love Is On the Air; Without Warning; The Missing Witness; Hollywood Hotel; Back in Circulation; What Price Vengeance; Laughing at Trouble; Guns of the Pecos; Behind Prison Bars. **1938** Young Fugitives; His Exciting Night; How to Watch Football (short); Four Daughters; Smashing the Rackets; Law of the Underworld; She Loved a Fireman; Ladies in Distress; Rhythm of the Saddle; The Invisible Menace. **1939** When Tomorrow Comes; Society Smugglers; Hero for a Day; The Roaring Twenties; The Phantom Creeps (serial); Blondie Meets the Boss; Help Wanted (short); The Mysterious Miss X; Rough Riders' Roundup; Two Bright

Boys; Cowboy Quarterback; Meet Doctor Christian; Backfire; Lawyer Woman. **1940** Ma, He's Making Eyes at Me; The Fighting 69th; Oh Johnny How You Can Love; Dr. Kildare's Crisis; The Green Hornet Strikes Again (serial); Charlie Chan in Panama; Shooting High; Cafe Hostess; One Night in the Tropics; The Boys from Syracuse. **1941** Six Lessons from Madame La Zonga; High Sierra; Jungle Girl (serial); Dr. Kildare's Wedding Day; Robin Hood of the Pecos; Texas Rangers Ride Again; Blondie Goes Latin; The Great American Broadcast; The People vs. Dr. Kildare; Here Comes Happiness; Rags to Riches; Blondie for Victory; Hellzapoppin. **1942** Yankee Doodle Dandy; Bells of Capistrano; Dr. Gillespie's New Assistant; Pardon My Sarong; Mr. District Attorney in the Carter Case; The Traitor Within; The Lady is Willing; Dr. Kildare's Victory; Mississippi Gambler; Girl Trouble; War Against Mrs. Hadley; Army Surgeon. **1943** Daredevils of the West (serial); He Hired the Boss; Headin' for God's Country; Guadalcanal Diary; Flesh and Fantasy. **1944** Rainbow Island; See Here, Private Hargrove; Wing and a Prayer; Carolina Blues; South of Dixie; Weekend Pass; In the Meantime, Darling; It Happened Tomorrow. **1945** Without Love; Between Two Women; San Antonio; On Stage Everybody; Sergeant Mike; The Frozen Ghost; The Hidden Eye; She Gets Her Man; Don Juan Quilligan; Diamond Horseshoe; Honeymoon Ahead; Her Lucky Night; Leave It to Blondie; Shadow of Terror; Jungle Captive. **1946** Cinderella Jones; Nick Carter, Detective (serial); Danger Woman; The Notorious Lone Wolf; Flying Serpent; Wake Up and Dream; Night Train to Memphis. **1947** Wyoming; Bandits of Dark Canyon; Blondie's Holiday; Buck Privates Come Home; Bells of San Angelo; Helldorado; Blondie's Big Moment; Swing the Western Way; Blondie in the Dough; Slippy McGee. **1948** Blondie's Reward; G-Men Never Forget (serial). **1949** Blondie's Big Deal; Blondie's Secret.

ADAIR, JACK
Born: 1894. Died: Sept. 22, 1940, Hollywood, Calif. Screen actor.

Appeared in: **1935** Peter Ibbetson. **1936** Lady Be Careful. **1937** 52nd Street; Manhattan Merry-Go-Round.

ADAIR, JEAN
Born: 1873. Died: May 11, 1953, New York, N.Y. Screen, stage, and vaudeville actress.

Appeared in: **1922** In the Name of the Law. **1933** Advice to the Lovelorn. **1944** Arsenic and Old Lace. **1946** Something in the Wind. **1947** Living in a Big Way.

ADAIR, JOHN
Born: 1885. Died: Jan. 22, 1952, New York. Screen, stage, radio and television actor.

Appeared in: **1936** Muss 'Em Up. **1940** The Ramparts We Watch.

ADAIR, ROBERT
Born: Jan. 3, 1900, San Francisco, Calif. Died: Aug. 10, 1954, London, England. Screen, stage, television and vaudeville actor.

Appeared in: **1925** Raffles. **1930** Journey's End. **1933** King of the Jungle; The Kiss Before the Mirror. **1934** Where Sinners Meet; Limehouse Blues; The Crusades. **1935** Bride of Frankenstein; The Last Outpost; Peter Ibbetson; The Girl Who Came Back. **1936** Empty Saddles. **1937** The Prince and the Pauper. **1948** Noose (aka The Silk Noose—US 1950). **1951** There is Another Sun (aka Wall of Death—US 1955). **1953** Park Plaza (aka Norman Conquest—US); There Was a Young Lady. **1954** Eight O'Clock Walk (US 1955).

ADALBERT, MAX (Max Krampf)
Born: 1874, Danzing, Germany. Died: Sept. 7, 1933, Munich, Germany. Stage and screen actor.

Appeared in: **1915** Der Schirm mit dem Schwan. **1919** Konig Nicolo oder So Ist das Leben; Die Verfuhrten. **1920** Der Dummkopf. **1921** Der Mude Tod (aka Between Worlds/Destiny); Dr. Mabuse der Spieler (Dr. Mabuse, the Gambler—US 1927). **1922** Die Flamme; Lebenshunger; Sein Ist das Gericht. **1925** Vorderhaus und Hinterhaus. **1930** Das Gestohlene Gesicht; Hans in Allen Gasen. **1931** Die Schlacht von Bademunde; Der Hauptmann von Kopenick (Captain of Koepenick); Das Ekel; Mein Leopold; Hurra! Ein Junge!; Der Herr Finanzdirektor; Kyritz—Pyritz; Drei Tage Mittelarrest (Three Days in the Guard-House); Der Hellseher (aka Mein Herz Sehnt Sich Nach Liebe). **1932** Ein Toller Einfall (A Mad Idea); Der Schutzenkonig; Die Galavorstellung der Fratellinis (aka Spione im Savoy-Hotel). **1933** Lachende Erben. **1934** Tante Gusti Kommandiert. Other German film: So Und Die Drei.

ADAM, JEAN-FRANCOIS (Jean Francis Adam)
Born: 1936. Died: Oct. 14, 1980, Paris, France (suicide). Screen actor, film and stage director.

Appeared in: **1962** L'amour a Vingt Ans (aka Love at Twenty—US 1963). **1968** Baisers Voles (aka Stolen Kisses—US). **1975** Le Secret (The Secret). **1979** Passe Ton Bacd'Abord.

ADAM, RONALD
Born: 1896, Worcestershire, England. Died: Mar. 27, 1979, London, England. Screen, television actor, playwright, author and theatrical manager. Son of stage actors Blake Adams (dec. 1913) and Mona Robin (dec.).

Appeared in: **1938** The Drum (aka Drums—US film debut); Strange Boarders. **1939** Inspector Hornleigh; The Missing People (US 1944); Hell's Cargo (aka Dangerous Cargo—US 1940); At the Villa Rose (aka House of Mystery—US 1941); Meet Maxwell Archer (aka Maxwell Archer, Detective—US 1942); Too Dangerous to Live. **1942** The Foreman Went to France (aka Somewhere in France—US 1943). **1943** Escape to Danger (US 1944). **1945** Journey Together (US 1946). **1946** Green for Danger (US 1947). **1947** Take My Life (US 1948); Fame is the Spur (US 1949); The Phantom Shot. **1948** Counterblast. **1949** All Over the Town; Christopher Columbus; That Dangerous Age (aka If This be Sin—US 1950); Under Capricorn; Obsession (aka The Hidden Room—US 1950); Bonnie Prince Charlie (US 1952). **1950** Shadow of the Past; My Daughter of Joy (aka Operation X—US 1951); Seven Days to Noon. **1951** Laughter in Paradise; The Late Edwina Black (aka Obsessed—US); The Lavender Hill Mob; The Adventures (aka The Great Adventure—US 1951); Captain Horatio Hornblower. **1952** Angels One Five (US 1954); Circumstantial Evidence. **1953** Malta Story (US 1954); Flannelfoot. **1954** To Dorothy a Son (aka Cash on Delivery—US 1956); The Black Knight; Front Page Story (US 1955); The Million Pound Note (aka Man With a Million—US); Johnny on the Spot; Escape by Night. **1956** Tons of Trouble; Assignment Redhead (aka Million Dollar Manhunt—US 1962); Lust for Life; Reach for the Sky (US 1957). **1957** Carry on Admiral (aka The Ship was Loaded—US 1959); Kill Me Tomorrow (US 1958); The Surgeon's Knife; Inside Information; Seawife. **1958** The Golden Disc (aka The Inbetween Age—US). **1959** Carlton Browne of the F.O. (aka Man in a Cocked Hat—US 1960); Please Turn Over (US 1960). **1961** Offbeat (US 1966); Three on a Spree. **1962** Postman's Knock. **1963** The Haunting. **1964** The Tomb of Ligeia (US 1965). **1966** Who Killed the Cat? **1970** Song of Norway.

ADAMS, BARTON
Born: 1900. Died: July 9, 1970, Hollywood, Calif. Screen actor and film director.

Appeared in: **1923** The Glimpses of the Moon.

ADAMS, CLAIRE
Born: Sept. 24, 1900, Winnipeg, Canada. Died: Sept. 25, 1978, Melbourne, Australia. Screen actress. Entered films in 1918.

Appeared in: **1920** Riders of the Dawn; Dwelling Place of Light; The Money Changers; The Penalty; The Great Lover. **1921** The Lure of Egypt; The Killer; The Man of the Forest; The Mysterious Rider; A Certain Rich Man; The Spenders. **1922** Do and Dare; The Gray Dawn; Golden Dreams; Just Tony; Heart's Haven; When Romance Rides. **1923** Brass Commandments; The Clean Up; Legally Dead; The Scarlet Car; Where the North Begins; Stepping Fast. **1924** The Girl in the Limousine; Missing Daughters; The Night Hawk; Oh, You Tony!; The Brass Bowl; The Fast Set; Daddies; Honor Among Men; Helen's Babies. **1925** The Wheel; The Devil's Cargo; Souls for Sables; Men and Women; The Kiss Barrier; The Big Parade. **1926** The Sea Wolf; Yellow Fingers. **1927** Married Alive; Combat.

ADAMS, CONSTANCE
Born: 1893. Died: July 17, 1960, Hollywood, Calif. Screen actress. Married to producer/director Cecil B. DeMille (dec. 1959).

Appeared in silent films

ADAMS, EDITH
Born: 1879. Died: Jan. 10, 1957, New York, N.Y. Screen and stage actress.

ADAMS, ERNEST S.
Born: 1885. Died: Nov. 26, 1947, Hollywood, Calif. Screen and stage actor.

Appeared in: **1919** A Regular Girl. **1924** Curlytop; Hutch of the U.S.A.; The Beloved Brute. **1925** The Best People; The Pony Express; Where the Worst Begins. **1926** Hair Trigger Baxter; The Jazz Girl; Pals in Paradise; The Valley of Bravery; The Black Bird. **1927** Jewels of Desire; The Main Event; Men of Daring; The Gay Defender; Nevada; Melting Millions (serial). **1928** So This is Love; Stool Pigeon; What a Night; A Woman's Way; Tenth Avenue. **1929** One Splendid Hour; The Saturday Night Kid. **1930** The Fighting Legion; Shadow Ranch; The Storm; For the Defense. **1931** Fair Warning; The Galloping Ghost (serial); The Gang Buster; The Tip Off. **1932** Merrily We Go to Hell; The Hurrican Express (serial); Panama Flo; The Big Broadcast; Hold

'Em Jail. **1933** West of Singapore; Breed of the Border; Secrets of Hollywood; She Done Him Wrong; Operator 13. **1934** Here Comes the Groom; We're Not Dressing; The Law of the Wild (serial); The Lost Jungle (serial); Good Dame. **1935** Men of the Hour; The Miracle Rider (serial); Ruggles of Red Gap; The Perfect Clue. **1936** Three on the Trail; Hopalong Cassidy Returns; The Invisible Ray; My Man Godfrey. **1937** San Quentin; Hopalong Rides Again; Stars over Arizona; Colorado Kid; Two Gun Law; The Man Who Cried Wolf. **1938** The Purple Vigilantes; The Painted Trail; You and Me; The Cowboy and the Lady. **1939** Trigger Pals; Tower of London; The Lone Ranger Rides Again (serial); Mandrake the Magician (serial). **1940** The Man with Nine Lives; Enemy Agent. **1941** The Invisible Ghost; The Man Who Came to Dinner; Road Agent; Bury Me Not on the Lone Prairie; The Sea Wolf; Sea Raiders (serial). **1942** Pride of the Yankees; Cactus Makes Perfect (short); Alias Boston Blackie. **1943** Keep 'Em Sluggin'; The Phantom (serial). **1944** Adventures of Mark Twain; Jack London; Lake Placid Serenade; The Princess and the Pirate. **1945** Jungle Captive; Patrick the Great; Rhapsody in Blue; Jungle Raiders (serial); Brenda Starr, Reporter (serial). **1946** Hop Harrigan (serial); King of the Forest Rangers (serial); The Blue Dahlia. **1947** Trail Street; Son of Zorro (serial); The Black Widow (serial); The Perils of Pauline; The Pretender; Buck Privates Come Home. **1948** Return of the Bad Men.

ADAMS, HOWARD
Born: 1909. Died: Sept. 29, 1936, Chicago, Ill. (plane crash). Screen actor, film director and radio announcer.

ADAMS, ISABEL
Born: 1856. Died: Sept. 22, 1936, Englewood, N.J. Screen and stage actress.

ADAMS, JEFF (Carol Wayne Adams)
Born: 1936. Died: May 21, 1967, Hawthorne, Calif. (plane crash). Screen, stage and television actor.

ADAMS, JIMMY (James B. Adams)
Born: 1890. Died: Dec. 19, 1933, Glendale, Calif. (heart attack). Screen and radio actor.

Appeared in: **1924** Hold Your Breath; Triumph. **1925** Stop Flirting. **1926** Her Man O'War. **1928** The Farmer's Daughter. **1929** Office Scandal. **1930** The Grand Parade; High C's (short). **1931** Rough Seas (short). **1932** The Tobasco Kid (short). **1933** The following shorts: Sherman Said It; Midsummer Mush; Arabian Tights.

ADAMS, JOHN WOLCOTT
Born: 1874, Worcester, Mass. Died: June 3, 1925, New York, N.Y. (appendicitis). Artist, illustrator and screen actor.

Appeared in: **1913** Saved by Parcel Post.

ADAMS, KATHRYN
Born: 1894. Died: Feb. 17, 1959, Hollywood, Calif. Screen actress.

Appeared in: **1915** The Shooting of Dan McGrew. **1917** Baby Mine. **1919** A Gentleman of Quality; A Rogues Romance. **1920** The Forbidden Woman; The Best of Luck; 813. **1921** The Silver Car. **1922** The Man from Downing Street. **1924** Borrowed Husbands. **1925** Pampered Youth. **1931** The Squaw Man. **1939** Fifth Avenue Girl. **1940** Argentine Nights; If I Had My Way; Ski Patrol; Black Diamonds; Love, Honor and Oh, Baby! **1941** The Invisible Woman; Bachelor Daddy; Meet the Chump; Unfinished Business; Saboteur; Sky Raiders (serial); Arizona Cyclone; Bury Me Not on the Lone Prairie; Model Wife; Rawhide Rangers. **1942** You're Telling Me. **1946** Blonde for a Day.

ADAMS, LESLIE
Born: 1887. Died: Mar. 26, 1936, New York, N.Y. Screen, stage, vaudeville and burlesque actor.

Appeared in: **1934** Crime without Passion.

ADAMS, LIONEL
Born: 1866. Died: Aug. 10, 1952, New York, N.Y. Screen and stage actor.

Appeared in: **1915** The Mystery of Mary; The Lady of the Lighthouse. **1916** The Closed Road. **1919** The Sacred Flame. **1920** Yes or No; Fantomas (serial). **1923** Success. **1924** Janice Meredith.

ADAMS, MARY
Died: Nov. 30, 1973. Screen actress.

Appeared in: **1944** Irish Eyes are Smiling. **1948** Hazard; The Night Has a Thousand Eyes; For the Love of Mary. **1951** Starlift. **1952** Bugles in the Afternoon. **1954** Her Twelve Men; Executive Suite. **1956** Rebel in Town; The Mountain. **1957** Blood of Dracula. **1962** The Clown and the Kid. **1963** Diary of a Madman.

ADAMS, MAUDE PIERCE *See* ALLEN, MAUDE

ADAMS, NICK (Nicholas Aloysius Adamshock)
Born: July 10, 1932, Nanticoke, Pa. Died: Feb. 5, 1968, Beverly Hills, Calif. (drug overdose). Screen and television actor. Nominated for 1963 Academy Award for Best Supporting Actor in Twilight of Honor.

Appeared in: **1952** Somebody Loves Me. **1955** Rebel Without a Cause; Strange Lady in Town; Picnic; The Jagged Edge; Mr. Roberts. **1956** Our Miss Brooks; The Last Wagon; A Strange Adventure; Frankenstein Meets the Giant Devil Fish. **1957** Fury at Showdown. **1958** No Time for Sergeants; Teacher's Pet; Sing, Boy, Sing. **1959** The FBI Story; Pillow Talk. **1962** The Interns; Hell Is for Heroes. **1963** Twilight of Honor; The Hook. **1964** The Young Lovers. **1965** Die, Monster, Die; Young Dillinger. **1966** Invasion of the Astro Monsters (aka Battle of the Astros, Invasion of the Astros and Monster Zero—US 1970); Frankenstein Conquers the World; Don't Worry, We'll Think of a Title. **1968** Fever Heat; Mission Mars.

ADAMS, SAM
Born: 1871. Died: Mar. 24, 1958. Screen actor.

Appeared in: **1932** Golden West; Million Dollar Legs. **1933** Love is Dangerous; Man of Sentiment; Love is Like That; Dirty Work (short). **1934** Washee Ironee (short). **1935** Treasure Blues (short). **1936** Hill Tillies (short). **1937** Pick a Star; Million Dollar Racket.

ADAMS, STANLEY
Born: 1915. Died: Apr. 27, 1977, Santa Monica, Calif. (suicide—gun). Screen, television actor, screenwriter and television writer.

Appeared in: **1936** In His Steps. **1937** Every Day's a Holiday. **1941** Road Show. **1954** The Atomic Kid. **1955** Hell's Horizon; Hell on Frisco Bay. **1956** The Bold and the Brave. **1957** Trooper Hook; Valerie; Hell Bound; Hell Ship Mutiny. **1958** I Married a Woman. **1959** High School Big Shot. **1960** North to Alaska; The Wizard of Baghdad; Studs Lonigan. **1961** The Young Savages; Breakfast at Tiffany's; Pirates of Tortuga; The Outsider. **1962** The Errand Boy; Requiem for a Heavyweight; 13 West Street. **1963** Critic's Choice; Lilies of the Field. **1964** A House is Not a Home; Wild and Wonderful. **1965** Ship of Fools; When the Boys Meet the Girls. **1966** Nevada Smith. **1967** Double Trouble; Thunder Alley. **1970** The Grasshopper; Machismo—40 Graves for 40 Guns; Move. **1974** The Nine Lives of Fritz the Cat; Act of Vengeance. **1976** Dixie Dynamite; Woman in the Rain.

ADAMS, STELLA
Died: Sept. 17, 1961. Screen actress and comedienne.

Appeared in: **1907** The Power of the Sultan. **1915** Jimmy's Little Kid; Almost a King; All in the Same Boat. **1916** A Seminary Scandal. **1926** Uppercuts (short); Honeymoon Hospital (short). **1928** Me, Gangster. **1932** Bachelor Mother. **1933** The Vampire Bat; Sister to Judas; Sing, Sinner, Sing; The Whirlwind.

ADAMS, TOMMYE (Abigail Adams)
Died: Feb. 13, 1955. Screen actress.

Appeared in: **1942** Moonlight Masquerade. **1943** Let's Face It; Old Acquaintance; Tahiti Honey. **1944** I Love a Soldier; Here Come the Waves; Bowery to Broadway. **1945** Our Vines Have Tender Grapes; Over 21. **1948** Trapped by Boston Blackie.

ADAMS, VIRGINIA
Died: May 13, 1961. Silent screen actress.

ADAMS, WILLIAM PERRY
Born: 1887, Tiffin, Ohio. Died: Sept. 29, 1972, New York. Screen, stage, radio, television actor and stage director. Married to actress Eleanor Wells.

Appeared in: **1945** The House on Ninety-Second Street. **1959** Odds Against Tomorrow.

ADAMSON, JAMES (William James Adamson)
Born: June 12, 1896, Calif. Died: Jan. 29, 1956, Los Angeles, Calif. (heart attack). Black screen actor.

Appeared in: **1933** Lone Cowboy. **1935** Hands Across the Table. **1942** Jungle Siren. **1944** Double Indemnity. **1948** A Letter to Three Wives. **1951** Bomba and the Elephant Stampede; The Lion Hunters. **1952** African Treasure. **1953** Safari Drums. **1954** The Golden Idol. **1956** Lord of the Jungle.

ADDYMAN, ELIZABETH
Born: England. Died: England. Screen and stage actress. Married to actor Arthur Brough (dec. 1978).

ADESON, MARTIN
Born: 1867, New York. Died: Jan. 18, 1936. Screen actor.

Appeared in: **1929** When Knights Were Bold. **1933** The King's Cup.

ADLER, CELIA (Celia Feinman Adler)
Born: 1890. Died: Jan. 31, 1979, Bronx, N.Y. Screen and stage actress. Daughter of stage actress Dinah Shtettin (dec.) and actor Jacob P. Adler (dec. 1926). For additional family information see Jacob P. Adler listing. Divorced from actor Lazar Freed (dec.), and theatrical manager Jack Cone. Later married to businessman Nathan Forman. Known as the "First Lady of the Yiddish Theatre."

Appeared in: **1937** Where Is My Child? **1969** The Golden Age of Second Avenue.

ADLER, DR. HARRY (Emil Harry Adler)
Born: 1883. Died: May 5, 1944, San Francisco, Calif. (heart attack). Screen actor and nightclub entertainer.

ADLER, JACOB P. (Jacob Pavlovitch Adler)
Born: Feb. 12, 1855, Odessa, Russia. Died: Apr. 1, 1926, New York, N.Y. Yiddish screen, stage actor and stage producer. Married to stage actress Sophia Oberlander (aka Sonyz Michelson—dec. 1885); father of stage actor Abram (Abe) Adler. Divorced from stage actress Dinah Shtettin (dec.); father of actress Celia Feinman Adler (dec. 1979). Married to stage actress Sarah Heine (dec. 1953); father of actors Jay (dec. 1978), Luther, Stella, Julia, Florence, Frances and Charles Adler.

Appeared in: **1914** Michael Strogoff.

ADLER, JAY
Born: 1896. Died: Sept. 24, 1978, Woodland Hills, Calif. Screen actor. Son of actors Jacob P. (dec. 1926) and Sarah Heine Adler (dec. 1953). For additional family information see Jacob P. Adler listing.

Appeared in: **1938** No Time to Marry. **1950** Cry Danger. **1951** The Mob. **1952** The Bad and the Beautiful; Assignment Paris; My Six Convicts; Dreamboat; Scandal Sheet. **1953** 99 River Street; Vice Squad; The Juggler. **1954** Down Three Dark Streets; The Long Wait. **1955** Illegal; Lucy Gallant; The Big Combo; Man With the Gun. **1956** The Killing; The Catered Affair; Lust for Life. **1957** Sweet Smell of Success; Crime of Passion; Hell on Devil's Island. **1958** Seven Guns to Mesa. **1959** Curse of the Undead; The Brothers Karamazov; The Story on Page One. **1962** Belle Sommers. **1963** Dime With a Halo. **1965** The Family Jewels. **1970** Brother, Cry for Me. **1974** Grave of the Vampire.

ADLON, LOUIS
Died: Mar. 31, 1947, Los Angeles, Calif. (heart attack). Screen actor.

Appeared in: **1938** Dramatic School. **1939** Confessions of a Nazi Spy. **1940** Mystery Sea Raider. **1942** Iceland. **1943** First Comes Courage. **1945** Counter-Attack.

ADOLFI, JOHN G. (aka JOHN ADOLPHI)
Born: Feb. 19, 1888, New York. Died: May 11, 1933, Canoe River, British Columbia (stroke). Screen, stage actor and film director. Entered films as an actor in 1909 and became director approximately 1912.

Appeared in: **1909** Napoleon, The Man of Destiny. **1912** Apartment No. 13; His Day.

ADOREE, RENEE (Renee LaFonte)
Born: Sept. 30, 1898, Lille, France. Died: Oct. 5, 1933, Tujunga, Calif. (tuberculosis). Screen actress and circus performer.

Appeared in: **1920** The Strongest. **1921** Made in Heaven. **1922** Daydreams; Monte Cristo; Honor First; Mixed Faces; A Self-Made Man; West of Chicago. **1923** The Eternal Struggle; The Six-Fifty. **1924** The Bandolero; Defying the Law; A Man's Mate; Women Who Give.

1925 The Big Parade; Exchange of Wives; Excuse Me; Parisian Nights; Man and Maid. **1926** Tin Gods; La Boheme; Blarney; The Exquisite Sinner; The Flaming Forest; The Black Bird. **1927** Mr. Wu; On Ze Boulevard; The Show; Back to God's Country; Heaven on Earth. **1928** Forbidden Hours; The Cossacks; Show People; A Certain Young Man; The Mating Call; The Michigan Kid; The Spieler. **1929** The Pagan; His Glorious Night; Tide of Empire. **1930** The Spoiler; The Singer of Seville; Redemption; Call of the Flesh.

ADRIAN, MAX (Max Cavendish)
Born: Nov. 1, 1903, Ireland. Died: Jan. 19, 1973, Surrey, England. Screen, stage and television actor.

Appeared in: **1934** The Primrose Path; Eight Cylinder Love. **1936** A Touch of the Moon; To Catch a Thief; The Happy Family; Nothing Like Publicity. **1937** Why Pick on Me?; Macushla (US 1940); When the Devil Was Well. **1938** Merely Mr. Hawkins. **1941** Kipps (aka The Remarkable Mr. Kipps—US 1942); Penn of Pennsylvania (aka The Courageous Mr. Penn—US 1944). **1942** The Young Mr. Pitt; Talk About Jacqueline. **1945** Henry V (US 1946). **1950** Her Favourite Husband (aka The Taming of Dorothy—US). **1951** Pool of London. **1952** The Pickwick Papers (US 1953). **1964** Dr. Terror's House of Horrors (US 1965). **1966** The Deadly Affair (US 1967). **1967** The Terronauts. **1970** Julius Caesar; The Music Lovers. **1971** The Devils; The Boy Friend.

AFRIQUE (Alexander Witkin)
Born: 1907, South Africa. Died: Dec. 17, 1961, London, England. Stage and screen actor, vocalist and impersonator.

Appeared in: **1936** Grand Finale; Digging for Gold. **1937** Let's Make a Night of It. **1939** Discoveries.

AGADATI, BARUCH
Born: 1895. Died: Jan. 18, 1976. Screen actor and film director. Starred in Hebrew-language films.

AGAR, JANE
Born: 1889. Died: June 10, 1948, Lakewood, Ohio. Screen and stage actress. Appeared in silent films.

AGEE, JAMES
Born: Nov. 27, 1909, Knoxville, Tenn. Died: May 16, 1955, New York, N.Y. (heart attack). Film critic, screen actor and screenwriter.

Appeared in: **1949** The Quiet One (narrator). **1952** Face to Face. **1953** The Bride Comes to Yellow Sky.

AGUGLIA, MIMI
Born: 1885, Italy. Died: July 31, 1970, Woodland Hills, Calif. Stage and screen actress.

Appeared in: **1924** The Last Man on Earth. **1933** El Eltimo Varon Sobre la Tierra; Su Ultimo Amor. **1934** Tres Amores. **1941** The Lady Escapes. **1944** The Navy Way. **1945** The Shanghai Gesture. **1945** A Bell for Adano. **1946** The Time, the Place and the Girl. **1947** Carnival in Costa Rica; Captain from Castile; Unconquered; The Outlaw. **1948** Cry of the City. **1949** We Were Strangers; That Midnight Kiss. **1950** Black Hand; Deported; The Man Who Cheated Himself; Right Cross. **1951** Cuban Fireball. **1952** When in Rome. **1955** The Rose Tattoo. **1957** The Brothers Rico.

AGUIRRE, MANUEL B.
Born: 1907, Mexico. Died: Dec. 3, 1957, Mexico City, Mexico. Screen actor.

AHEARNE, TOM
Born: 1906, Boston, Mass. Died: Jan. 5, 1969, New York, N.Y. (influenza). Screen, stage and television actor.

Appeared in: **1949** Project X; The Window. **1950** Cry Murder. **1951** Mister Universe. **1968** Three in the Attic.

AHERNE, PATRICK
Born: 1901, Ireland. Died: Sept. 30, 1970, Hollywood, Calif. (cancer). Screen, stage and television actor. Brother of actor Brian Aherne. Married to actress Rene Houston.

Appeared in: **1924** The Cost of Beauty. **1926** Blinkeyes; The Ball of Fortune; Thou Fool; Horsey series including The Game Chicken. **1927** A Daughter in Revolt; The Silver Lining; Carry On!; Huntingtower. **1928** Virginia's Husband; Love's Option (aka A Girl of Today); W. W. Jacobs Stories series including Double Dealing. **1929** Auld Lang Syne; City of Play; The Inseparables. **1932** Come Into My Parlour. **1933** The Pride of the Force; Oh What a Duchess! (aka My Old Duchess). **1934** The Outcast; Falling in Love (aka Trouble Ahead—US); Eight

Cylinder Love; The Return of Bulldog Drummond. **1935** The Stoker. **1936** Polly's Two Fathers. **1939** Q Planes (aka Clouds Over Europe—US); Ask a Policeman. **1943** Warn that Man; Thursday's Child. **1947** Green Dolphin Street. **1948** The Paradine Case. **1952** Bwana Devil. **1953** Botany Bay; Rogue's March; The Royal African Rifles. **1956** The Court Jester; The Man Who Knew Too Much.

AHLERS, ANNY
Born: 1906, Hamburg, Germany. Died: Mar. 14, 1933, London, England. Screen and stage actress.

Appeared in: **1931** Der Wahre Jakob. **1936** Die Marquise von Pompadour.

AHLM, PHILIP E.
Born: 1905. Died: July 5, 1954, Hollywood, Calif. (shot). Screen actor.

AHMED, RAJU
Born: 1937, India. Died: Dec. 12, 1972, Dacca, Bangladesh. Screen, radio and television actor.

AHN, PHILIP
Born: Mar. 29, 1911, Los Angeles, Calif. Died: Feb. 28, 1978, Los Angeles, Calif. (lung cancer). Screen and television actor. Entered films as an extra.

Appeared in: **1936** The General Died at Dawn (film debut); Stowaway. **1937** Thank You Mr. Moto; Something to Sing About; China Passage; Daughter of Shanghai. **1938** Roaring Timber; Charlie Chan in Honolulu; Hawaii Calls; Red Barry (serial). **1939** King of Chinatown; Disputed Passage; Barricade. **1941** Passage from Hong Kong; They Met in Bombay. **1942** China Girl; A Yank on the Burma Road; Across the Pacific; We Were Dancing; Let's Get Tough. **1943** They Got Me Covered; The Amazing Mrs. Holliday; China; Adventures of Smilin' Jack (serial); Adventures of the Flying Cadets (serial). **1944** The Keys of the Kingdom; Dragon Seed; The Story of Dr Wassell; The Purple Heart. **1945** They Shall Have Faith; Back to Bataan; Betrayal from the East; China Sky; China's Little Devils; Blood on the Sun; God is My Co-Pilot. **1947** Intrigue; Chinese Ring; Singapore; The Red Hornet. **1948** Rogues' Regiment; The Creeper; Woman in the Night; The Miracle of the Bells; The Cobra Strikes. **1949** State Department File—649; Boston Blackie's Chinese Venture; Impact. **1950** The Big Hangover; Halls of Montezuma. **1951** China Corsair; The Sickle or the Cross; I Was an American Spy; Secrets of Monte Carlo. **1952** Red Snow; Japanese War Bride; Target: Hong Kong; Battle Zone; Macao. **1953** Battle Circus; Fair Wind to Java; China Venture; His Majesty O'Keefe. **1954** The Shanghai Story; Hell's Half Acre. **1955** The Left Hand of God; Love is a Many Splendored Thing. **1956** Around the World in 80 Days. **1957** Battle Hymn; The Way to the Gold. **1958** Hong Kong Confidential. **1959** Never so Few. **1960** The Great Imposter; Yesterday's Enemy. **1961** One-Eyed Jacks. **1962** A Girl Named Tamiko; Confessions of an Opium Eater. **1963** Diamond Head; Shock Corridor. **1966** Paradise—Hawaiian Style. **1967** Thoroughly Modern Millie. **1973** The World's Greatest Athlete; Johnathan Livingston Seagull (voice). **1975** Voodoo Heartbeat.

AICKEN, ELINOR
Born: 1834, England. Died: May 5, 1914, England? Screen and stage actress.

Appeared in: **1911** Richard III.

AIMOS, RAYMOND
Born: 1889, La Fere, France. Died: 1944, Paris, France. Screen actor.

Appeared in: **1922** Vingt Ans Apres. **1931** Les Croix de Bois. **1933** Quatorze Juillet; Le Paquebot Tenacity. **1934** Dernier Milliardaire. **1935** Escape from Yesterday. **1936** Mayerling; The Golem; They Were Five. **1938** Katia; Port of Shadows; SOS Mediterranean; Ultimatum. **1939** Dede de Montmartre. **1940** De Mayerling a Sarajevo. **1942** Lumiere d'Ete. **1943** Les Petites du Quai aux Fleurs. **1959** The French Way.

AINLEY, HENRY H.
Born: Aug. 21, 1879, Morley, England. Died: Oct. 31, 1945, London, England. Stage and screen actor. Father of actor Richard Ainley (dec. 1967).

Appeared in: **1914** A Bachelor's Love Story; She Stoops to Conquer; Called Back. **1915** The Prisoner of Zenda; Rupert of Hentzau (US 1916); Sweet Lavender; The Outrage; Iris; The Great Adventure; Brother Officers; Jelf's (aka A Man of His Word—US). **1916** The Marriage of William Ashe; Sowing the Wind; The Manxman. **1919** Quinneys. **1920** Build Thy House. **1921** Money; The Prince and the Beggarmaid. **1923** The Royal Oak; Sally Bishop. **1926** The Inscrutable Drew, Investigator (series). **1929** Armistice (narration). **1932** The First Mrs. Fraser. **1933** The Good Companions (narration). **1936** As You Like It. **1941** Battle of the Books (short-narration).

AINLEY, RICHARD (aka RICHARD RIDDLE)
Born: Dec. 22, 1910, Stanmore, Middlesex, England. Died: May 18, 1967, London, England. Screen, stage and radio actor. Son of actor Henry Ainley (dec. 1945). Divorced from stage actresses Ethel Glendinning and Betzi Beaton. Married to Rowena Woolf. Occasionally used the name of Richard Riddle on stage.

Appeared in: **1936** As You Like It. **1937** The Gang Show; Our Fighting Lady (aka Torpedoed—US 1939); The Frog (US 1939). **1938** Lily of Laguna; Old Iron. **1939** There Ain't No Justice; An Englishman's Home (aka Madmen of Europe—US); A Stolen Life. **1940** Lady with Red Hair. **1941** Singapore Woman; Bullets for O'Hara; The Smiling Ghost; Shining Victory. **1942** White Cargo. **1943** Three Hearts for Julie; I Dood It; Above Suspicion. **1949** Passage to Hong Kong.

AINSLEY, NORMAN
Born: May 4, 1881, Edinburgh, Scotland. Died: Jan. 23, 1948, Hollywood, Calif. Screen and stage actor.

Appeared in: **1930** Scotland Yard. **1933** International House; Horseplay. **1934** The Gay Bride; The Notorious Sophie Lang. **1935** Bride of Frankenstein; The Man Who Reclaimed His Head. **1936** Too Many Parents; Modern Times; Drawing Roomers; Tale of Two Cities; Lost Horizon; Sworn Enemy; Libeled Lady; Captains Courageous. **1937** Shall We Dance; The Shadow Strikes. **1940** Adventure in Diamonds. **1941** The Lady Eve. **1943** The Good Fellows. **1944** Man in Half Moon Street. **1945** Kitty. **1946** Cluny Brown.

AINSWORTH, SIDNEY (aka SYDNEY AINSWORTH)
Born: 1872, Manchester, England. Died: May 21, 1922, Madison, Wis. Screen and stage actor. Entered films in 1909.

Appeared in: **1915** The White Sister. **1916** The Strange Case of Mary Page (serial). **1919** A Man and His Money; The Crimson Gardenia; Heartsease; The Girl from Outside. **1920** Madame X. **1921** Boys Will Be Boys; Hold Your Horses; The Invisible Power; A Poor Relation; Doubling for Romeo. **1922** Mr. Barnes of New York.

AITKEN, FRANK "SPOTTISWOODE"
Born: 1869, Edinburgh, Scotland. Died: Feb. 26, 1933, Los Angeles, Calif. Screen and stage actor.

Appeared in: **1911** The Battle. **1915** Birth of a Nation. **1916** Intolerance; The Americano. **1919** Captain Kidd, Jr.; The White Heather; Hay Foot, Straw Foot; Her Kingdom of Dreams. **1920** Nomads of the North. **1921** At the End of the World; Beyond; Reputation; The Unknown Wife. **1922** A Dangerous Game; Man of Courage; Manslaughter; Monte Cristo; One Wonderful Night; The Price of Youth; The Snowshoe Trail; The Trap; The Young Rajah. **1923** Around the World in 18 Days (serial); The Love Pirate; Merry-Go-Round; Six Days. **1924** The Fire Patrol; Lure of the Yukon; Gerald Cranston's Lady; Triumph; Those Who Dare. **1925** The Eagle; The Coast Patrol; Accused; The Goose Woman. **1926** The Power of the Weak; The Two-Gun Man. **1927** God's Great Wilderness; Roaring Fires.

AKED, MURIEL
Born: Nov. 9, 1887, Bingley, Yorkshire, England. Died: Mar. 23, 1955, Settle, Yorkshire, England. Stage and screen actress. Entered films approx. 1920.

Appeared in: **1922** A Sister to Assist 'Er. **1926** Bindle Series, including Bindle's Cocktail. **1930** Bed and Breakfast; The Middle Watch. **1932** Goodnight Vienna (aka Magic Night—US); The Mayor's Nest; Her First Affaire; Rome Express. **1933** Yes, Madam; The Good Companions; Trouble; Friday the Thirteenth (US 1934); No Funny Business. **1934** The Queen's Affair (aka Runaway Queen—US 1935); Evensong; Josser on the Farm; The Night of the Party; Autumn Crocus. **1935** Can You Hear Me Mother? **1936** Don't Rush Me!; Fame; Public Nuisance No. 1; Royal Eagle. **1937** Mr. Stringfellow Says No. **1939** The Girl Who Forgot; The Silent Battle (aka Continental Express—US 1942). **1941** Cottage to Let (aka Bombsight Stolen—US). **1943** The Life and Death of Colonel Blimp (aka Colonel Blimp—US 1945); The Demi Paradise (aka Adventure for Two—US 1945). **1944** 2,000 Women. **1945** They; The Wicked Lady (US 1946). **1947** Just William's Luck. **1948** William Comes to Town; So Evil My Love; It's Hard to be Good (US 1950); Accidental Spy (reissue of Mr. Stringfellow Says No—1937); A Sister to Assist 'Er (and 1922 version). **1950** The Happiest Days of Your Life. **1951** Flesh and Blood; The Wonder Kid. **1953** The Story of Gilbert and Sullivan (aka The Great Gilbert and Sullivan—US).

AKERS, HENRY CARL "HANK"
Born: 1908. Died: Aug. 22, 1967, Hollywood, Fla. Screen actor and stand-in for Johnny Weismuller.

AKST, HARRY
Born: Aug. 15, 1894. Died: Mar. 31, 1963, Hollywood, Calif.
Composer and screen actor.

Appeared in: **1929** Show of Shows. **1931** June Moon. **1933** 42nd Street.

ALADDIN (Aladdin Abdullah Achmed Anthony Pallante)
Born: 1913, New York. Died: June 9, 1970, Van Nuys, Calif. (heart disease). Screen, radio, television actor and comic singer.

ALARIE, AMANDA
Born: 1889, Canada? Died: Dec. 9, 1965. Screen actress.

ALBACH-RETTY, ROSA
Born: 1875, Austria. Died: Aug. 26, 1980, Baden, Austria. Screen and stage actress.

Appeared in: **1948** The Mozart Story.

ALBANESI, MEGGIE (Margherita Albanesi)
Born: Oct. 8, 1899, London, England. Died: Dec. 9, 1923, England. Screen and stage actress.

Appeared in: **1918** The Better 'Ole, Or the Romance of Old Bill (aka Carry On—US). **1919** Darby and Joan; Mr. Wu. **1920** The Great Day (US 1921). **1921** The Skin Game (stage and film versions).

ALBERG, SOMAR
Born: 1908, Canada. Died: May 31, 1977, Pound Ridge, N.Y. (heart attack). Screen actor. Married to film producer Mildred Freed Alberg.

Appeared in: **1955** The Shrike (stage and film versions).

ALBERNI, LUIS
Born: 1887, Spain. Died: Dec. 23, 1962, Hollywood, Calif. Stage and screen actor.

Appeared in: **1921** Little Italy. **1922** The Man from Beyond. **1923** The Bright Shawl; The Valley of Lost Souls. **1930** The Santa Fe Trail. **1931** I Surrender Dear (short); Men in Her Life; Side Show; Svengali; Monkey Business in Africa (short); The Mad Genius; The Last Flight; I Like Your Nerve; Sweepstakes; Children of Dreams. **1932** Trouble in Paradise; Hombres Em Mi Vida; Girl in the Tonneau; Woman in Room 13; First in War (short); The Cohens and the Kellys in Hollywood; Working Wives; Hypnotized; Guilty or Not Guilty; Crooner; The Kid from Spain; Manhattan Parade; Week-End Marriage; Cock of the Air; Big Stampede; A Parisian Romance; High Pressure. **1933** Lady Killer; Flying Down to Rio; California Weather (short); The Last Trail; Topaze; Artists Muddles (short); Sherman Said It (short); Child of Manhattan; Men Must Fight; I Love that Man; The Spinx; When Ladies Meet; Trick for Trick; California Trial; The Man From Monterey; Above the Clouds. **1934** The Black Cat; The Captain Hates the Sea; When Strangers Meet; Goodbye Love; La Ciudad de Carton; Count of Monte Cristo; La Buenaventura; I Believed in You; Glamour; One Night of Love. **1935** Ticket or Leave It (short); Love Me Forever; Bad Boy; Roberta; The Gilded Lily; Goin' to Town; The Winning Ticket; Let's Live Tonight; In Caliente; The Gay Deception; Music is Magic; Metropolitan; Public Opinion; Manhattan Moon. **1936** Colleen; Anthony Adverse; Dancing Pirate; Ticket to Paradise; Follow Your Heart; Hat's Off. **1937** Sing and Be Happy; Two Wise Maids; Manhattan Merry-Go-Round; When You're in Love; Under Suspicion; The King and the Chorus Girl; The Great Garrick; Easy Living; Hitting a New High; Madame X. **1938** I'll Give a Million; Love on Toast. **1939** The Great Man Votes; Naughty but Nice; The Housekeeper's Daughter. **1940** The Lone Wolf Meets a Lady; Enemy Agent; Public Deb No. 1; Scatterbrain; Santa Fe Trail. **1941** They Met in Argentina; The Lady Eve; They Met in Bombay; Road to Zanzibar; San Antonio Rose; World Premier; Babes on Broadway; That Hamilton Woman. **1942** Mexican Spitfire's Elephant; Obliging Young Lady; Two Weeks to Live. **1943** You're a Lucky Fellow, Mr. Smith; Here Comes Kelly; Submarine Base; Nearly Eighteen; Here Comes Elmer; Harvest Melody; My Son, the Hero. **1944** Rainbow Island; Henry Aldrick Plays Cupid; When the Lights Go on Again; In Society; Men on Her Mind; Voice in the Wind; Machine Gun Mama. **1945** A Bell for Adano. **1946** In Fast Company. **1947** Night Song. **1950** Captain Carey, U.S.A.; When Willie Comes Marching Home. **1952** What Price Glory. **1956** The Ten Commandments.

ALBERS, HANS
Born: 1892, Hamburg, Germany. Died: July 24, 1960, Munich, Germany. Screen, stage, vaudeville and circus actor.

Appeared in: **1911** Im Grossen Augenblick; Der Mut zur Sünde; Baronchen auf Urlaub; Die Sünden der Väter; Zigeunerblut. **1912** Komödianten (aka Komedianter); Die Macht des Goldes (aka Gulden Magt); Der Totentanz (aka Dodedansen); Wenn die Maske Fällt (aka Naar Masken Falder); Zu Tode Gehetzt (aka Dodens Gaade). **1917** Mut Zur Sünde; Rache des Gefallenen; Rauschgold. **1918** Baronesschen auf Straufurlaub; 1001 Nacht (1001 Nights). **1919** Die Prinzessin von Urbino; Der Furst. **1920** Berlin W. (aka Der Weg ins Verderben Fuhrt); Die Marquise von O. **1921** Die Grosse und die Kleine Welt; Der Falschspieler; Madeleine. **1922** Menschenopfer; Die Geliebte des Königs; Der Böse Geist Lumpazivagabundus; Der Falsche Dimitri; Söhne der Nacht; Der Tiger des Zirkus Farius; Versunkene Welten. **1923** Fraulein Raffke; Lydia Sanin; Das Testament des Joe Sievers. **1924** Auf Befehl der Pompadour; Die Venus vom Montmarte (US 1925); Das Schöne Abenteuer; Gehetzte Menschen; Guillotine; Taumel; Ein Sommernachtstraum (US 1925). **1925** Der König und das Kleine Mädchen; Der Mann aus dem Jenseits (aka Feldgrau); Halbseide; Luxusweibchen (aka Ein Zeitbild Berlin-W); Mein Freund—der Chauffeur (My Friend, the Chauffeur); Der Bankraub Unter den Linden (aka Der Herr auf der Galgenleiter); Athleten; Vorderhaus und Hinterhaus; Die Gesunkenen (The Sunken). **1926** An der Schönen Blauen Donau; Bara en Danserska; Der Lachende Eheman; Der Prinz und die Tänzerin (aka Der Prinz und die Drei Probier-Mamsells); Die Frau, die Nacht "Nein" Sagen Kann; Die Versunkene Flotte; Die Seeschlacht Beim Skagerak; Die Villa im Tiergarten (aka Die Dame aus der Cittage-Villa); Die Warenhausprinzessin; Eine Dubarry von Heute; Es Blasen die Trompeten (aka Husarenliebe); Ich Hatt' Einen Kameraden; Jagd auf Menschen; Nixchen; Schatz, Mach Kasse; Deutsche Herzen am Deutschen Rhein (aka Liebe und Heimat); Die Drei Mannequins; Nur eine Tänzerin; Der Soldat der Marie; Wir sind von K. und K. Infanterie-Regiment; Küssen ist Keine Sünde (aka Die Letzte Einquartierung). **1927** Es Zogen Drei Burschen; Der Goldene Abgrund; Die Dollarprinzessin und Ihre Sechs Freier (aka Kie Liebeszentrale); Die Glühende Gasse; Drei Seelen—ein Gedanke; Eine Kleine Freundin Braucht Jeder Mann; Ein Perfekt Gentleman (The Perfect Gentleman); Der Grösste Gauner des Jahrhunderts; Primanerliebe; Rinaldo Rinaldini (aka Abenteuer Eines Heimgekehrten). **1928** Das Fraulein aus Argentinien (aka Das Madchen Argentinien); Der Rote Kreis (aka Rund um Europa); Dornenweg Einer Furstin (aka Zerstorte Heimat); Frauenarzt Dr. Schafer (aka Der Frauenarzt); Herr Meister und Frau Meisterin; Heut War Ich bei der Frieda; Prinzessin Olala; Rasputin's Liebesabenteuer (aka Rasputin und die Frauen); Saxophon-Susie; Weib in Flammen (aka Die Geschichte Einer Leidenschaft); Wer das Scheiden Hat Erfunden (aka Die Juwelen der Furstin Ljuba). **1929** Ja, Ja, Die Frauen Sind Meine Schwache Seite; Mascottchen (aka Bist du es Lachendes Gluck); Mobliette Zimmer (aka Der Sturmfreie Junggeselle); Drei Machen ihr Gluck (aka Teure Heimat); Vererbte Triebe; Der Kampf ums Neue Geschlecht (aka Erbsunde). **1930** Hans in Allen Gassen; Der Blaue Engel (The Blue Angel); Die Nacht Gehoert Uns (The Night Belongs to Us—US 1932). **1931** Bomben Auf Monte Carlo (Monte Carlo Madness); Der Draufganger (The Daredevil); Der Sieger (The Victor); Drei Tage Liebe (Three Days of Love). **1932** Liebe ist Lieb (Love is Love); Koenigin der Unterwelt; Heut' Kommt's Drauf An (US 1933); Quick, Koenig der Clowns (US 1933); Der Weisse Dämon (The White Demon, aka Rauschgift); F. P. 1 Antwortet Nicht (F. P. 1 Does Not Answer). **1933** Ein Gewisser Herr Gran; Flüchtlinge (Refugees—German propaganda film). **1934** Gold; Peer Gynt (US 1939). **1935** Henker, Frauen und Soldaten (Hangman, Women and Soldiers—US 1940). **1936** Casanova; Mord im Savoy (Savoy-Hotel 217); Unter Heissem Himmel. **1937** Der Mann, der Sherlock Holmes War; Die Gelbe Flagge. **1938** Fahrendes Volk (aka Gehetzter Gaukler); Sergeant Berry. **1939** Zwei Lustige Abenteurer (Two Merry Adventurers; Wasser für Canitoga. **1940** Trenck, der Pandur; Ein Mann auf Abwegen. **1941** Carl Peters (German propaganda film). **1942** Munchhausen (US 1943). **1944** Grosse Freiheit Nr. 7 (aka La Paloma). **1945** Shiva und die Galgenblume. **1947** ... und Über uns der Himmel. **1950** City of Torment; Föhn; Vom Teufel Gejagt. **1951** Blaubart. **1952** Nachts auf den Strassen. **1953** Käpt'n Bay-Bay; Jonny Rettet Nebrador; The White Hell of Pitz Palu. **1954** Auf der Reeperbahn Nachts um Halb Eins; An Jedem Finger Zehn. **1955** Der Letzte Mann (The Last Laugh). **1956** Vor Sonnenuntergang (US 1961); I Fidenzati Della Morte. **1957** Das Herz von St. Pauli; Der Tolle Bomberg. **1958** Das Gab's Nur Einmal; Der Mann im Strom; Dreiaehn Alte Esel; 13 Kleine Esel und der Sonnenhof. **1960** Kein Engel ist so Rein.

ALBERT, CARLOS
Born: 1902, Argentina. Died: Feb. 23, 1980, Hollywood, Calif. Screen and stage actor. Married to musical partner Rosa Albert.

ALBERT, DAN
Born: 1890, Nashville, Tenn. Died: Aug., 1919, Nashville, Tenn. Screen actor.

ALBERT, ELSIE
Born: Nov. 20, 1888, North Caldwell, N.J. Died: Oct. 7, 1981, Ore. Screen and stage actress.

Appeared in: **1912** Leg and Legacy. **1914** Winning a Prize; The Wayward Son. **1921** Welcome Children.

ALBERTSON, ARTHUR W.
Born: Jan. 6, 1891, Waycross, Georgia. Died: Oct. 20, 1926, New York, N.Y. Stage and screen actor. Married to actress Esther Howard (dec. 1965).

Appeared in: **1916** It Happened in Honolulu. **1917** The Argyle Case.

ALBERTSON, FRANK
Born: Feb. 2, 1909, Fergus Falls, Minn. Died: Feb. 29, 1964, Santa Monica, Calif. Screen, stage and television actor. Entered films in 1922.

Appeared in: **1928** Prep and Pep; The Farmer's Daughter. **1929** Salute; Words and Music; Blue Skies; Happy Days. **1930** Son of the Gods; The Big Party; Born Reckless; Men without Women; So This Is London; Wild Company; Just Imagine; Spring Is Here. **1931** The Connecticut Yankee; The Brat; The Tiger's Son; Big Business Girl; Old Greatheart; Traveling Husbands. **1932** Lost Special (serial); The Cohens and the Kellys in Hollywood; Way Back Home; Huddle. **1933** King for a Night; Ann Carver's Profession; Dangerous Crossroads; Midshipman Jack; Ever in My Heart; Racing Youth; Impossible Lover; Air Mail; Billion Dollar Scandal; The Cohens and the Kellys in Trouble; Rainbow Over Broadway. **1934** The Last Gentleman; The Life of Vergie Winters; Bachelor of Arts; Hollywood Hoodlum; Enter Madame. **1935** Doubting Thomas; Alice Adams; Ah, Wilderness; Personal Maid's Secret; East of Java; Kind Lady; Waterfront Lady. **1936** The Farmer in the Dell; Fury; The Plainsman. **1937** Navy Blue and Gold. **1938** Hold That Kiss; Spring Madness; The Shining Hour; Mother Carey's Chickens; Fugitives for a Night; Room Service. **1939** Bachelor Mother. **1940** Framed; Dr. Christian Meets the Women; The Ghost Comes Home; When the Daltons Rode; Behind the News. **1941** Man-Made Monster; Louisiana Purchase; Ellery Queen's Penthouse Mystery; Citadel of Crime; Flying Cadets; Father Steps Out; City Limits; Burma Convoy. **1942** Wake Island; Underground Agent; Shepherd of the Ozarks; The Man From Headquarters; Junior G-Men of the Air (serial); City of Silent Men. **1943** Keep 'Em Slugging; Here Comes Elmer; O, My Darling Clementine; Mystery Broadcast. **1944** And the Angels Sing; I Love a Soldier; Rosie the Riveter. **1945** Arson Squad; How Do You Do? **1946** They Made Me a Killer; Gay Blades; It's A Wonderful Life; Ginger. **1947** Killer Dill; The Hucksters. **1948** Shed No Tears. **1956** Nightfall. **1957** The Enemy Below. **1958** The Last Hurrah. **1960** Psycho. **1961** Girl on the Run; Man-Trap. **1962** Don't Knock the Twist. **1963** Johnny Cool; Bye Bye Birdie.

ALBERTSON, JACK
Born: 1907, Malden, Mass. Died: Nov. 25, 1981, Hollywood Hills, Calif. (cancer). Screen, stage, vaudeville, television and burlesque actor. Brother of actress Mabel Albertson (dec. 1982). Won 1968 Academy Award for Best Supporting Actor in "The Subject Was Roses."

Appeared in: **1937** Rebecca of Sunnybrook Farm. **1947** Miracle on 34th Street. **1954** Top Banana. **1955** Bring Your Smile Along. **1956** The Harder They Fall; Over-Exposed; The Eddie Duchin Story; The Unguarded Moment; You Can't Run Away from It. **1957** Don't Go Near the Water; Man of a Thousand Faces; Monkey on My Back. **1958** Teacher's Pet. **1959** Never Steal Anything Small; The Shaggy Dog. **1961** Lover, Come Back; The George Raft Story. **1962** Who's Got the Action?; Period of Adjustment; Convicts Four; Days of Wine and Roses. **1963** Son of Flubber. **1964** Kissin' Cousins; The Patsy; Roustabout; A Tiger Walks. **1965** How to Murder Your Wife. **1967** The Flim Flam Man. **1968** How to Save a Marriage—and Ruin Your Life; The Subject was Roses (stage and film versions). **1969** Changes; Justine. **1970** Rabbit, Run. **1971** Willy Wonka and the Chocolate Factory. **1972** The Poseidon Adventure. **1981** Dead and Buried.

ALBERTSON, LILLIAN
Born: Aug. 6, 1881, Neblesville, Ind. Died: Aug. 24, 1962, Los Angeles, Calif. Screen, stage actress, stage producer and talent coach.

Appeared in: **1952** The Greatest Show on Earth.

ALBRIGHT, BOB "OKLAHOMA"
Born: 1884. Died: Apr. 30, 1971, Hollywood, Calif. (heart attack). Screen, stage, vaudeville actor and orchestra leader.

Appeared in: **1929** Oklahoma Bob Albright and His Rodeo Do Flappers (short).

ALBRIGHT, HARDIE (Hardy Albrecht)
Born: Dec. 16, 1903, Charleroi, Pa. Died: Dec. 7, 1975, Mission Viejo, Calif. (heart failure). Screen, stage, television actor and writer. Divorced from actress Martha Sleeper and later married to Arnita Wallace.

Appeared in: **1931** Hush Money; Heartbreak; Hotel Continental;

Young Sinners; Skyline. **1932** Three on a Match; The Purchase Price; Jewel Robbery; The Crash; A Successful Calamity; Cabin in the Cotton; This Sporting Age; So Big; Match King. **1933** The Working Man; Song of Songs; Three-Cornered Moon; The House on 56th Street. **1934** Crimson Romance; The Scarlet Letter; The Ninth Guest; White Heat; Nana; Beggar's Holiday; Two Heads on a Pillow; Silver Streak; Sing Sing Nights. **1935** Red Salute; Women Must Dress; Calm Yourself; Ladies Love Danger; Champagne for Breakfast. **1940** Ski Patrol; Granny Get Your Gun; Carolina Moon. **1941** Flight from Destiny; Marry the Boss's Daughter; Men of Timberland; Bachelor Daddy. **1942** The Pride of the Yankees; The Loves of Edgar Allen Poe; Lady in a Jam. **1944** Army Wives. **1945** Jade Mask; Sunset in Eldorado; Captain Tugboat Annie. **1946** Angel on My Shoulder. **1947** The Gangster. **1957** Mom and Dad.

ALCALDE, MARIO
Born: 1927. Died: Apr. 22, 1971, Los Angeles, Calif. (cancer). Screen, stage and television actor.

Appeared in: **1956** Crowded Paradise. **1960** All the Young Men. **1964** Dead Ringer. **1969** Hail, Hero!

ALCOCK, DOUGLAS
Born: 1908. Died: Oct. 14, 1970, Cinecitta, Italy (heart attack). Screen, stage actor and film director.

ALDEA, MERCEDES
Born: Spain. Died: Oct. 28, 1954, Sabadell, Spain (killed when struck by airplane propeller while filming What Never Dies). Screen actress.

ALDEN, BETTY
Born: 1898. Died: Apr., 1948, Beverly Hills, Calif. Screen and stage actress.

Appeared in: **1930** Lightnin'. **1934** The Fugitive and the Lady; The Fountain. **1935** The Nut Farm; Carnival. **1937** Captains Courageous.

ALDEN, ERIC
Born: 1908. Died: Feb. 28, 1962, Los Angeles, Calif. Screen and stage actor.

Appeared in: **1934** Scarlet Empress. **1936** Little Lord Fauntleroy. **1941** Broadway Limited. **1953** Pony Express; Arrowhead; Flight to Tangier. **1956** That Certain Feeling; The Court Jester. **1957** Fear Strikes Out. **1958** The Buccaneer.

ALDEN, MARY (Mary Maguire Alden)
Born: 1883, New Orleans, La. Died: July 2, 1946, Woodland Hills, Calif. Screen and stage actress.

Appeared in: **1914** The Little Country House; The Old Maid; The Second Mrs. Roebuck. **1915** Birth of a Nation. **1916** The Good-Bad Man; Hell-to-Pay; Austin. **1919** The Unpardonable Sin; The Naulahka. **1920** Milestone; Honest Hutch. **1921** The Old Nest; Snowblind; Trust Your Wife; Parted Curtains; The Witching Hour. **1922** Man with Two Mothers; A Woman's Woman; The Bond Boy; The Hidden Woman; Notoriety. **1923** Pleasure Mad; The Eagle's Feather; The Empty Cradle; Has the World Gone Mad!; The Steadfast Heart; The Tents of Allah. **1924** Babbitt; A Fool's Awakening; Painted People; The Beloved Brute; When a Girl Loves; Soiled. **1925** Faint Perfume; The Happy Warrior; Siege; Under the Rouge; The Plastic Age; The Unwritten Law. **1926** April Fool; Brown of Harvard; The Earth Woman; Lovely Mary. **1927** The Potters; The Joy Girl; Twin Flappers. **1928** Ladies of the Mob; The Cossacks; Fools for Luck; Sawdust Paradise; Someone to Love. **1929** Girl Overboard. **1932** Hell's House; Strange Interlude.

ALDERSON, ERVILLE
Born: 1883. Died: Aug. 4, 1957, Glendale, Calif. Screen actor.

Appeared in: **1921** The Good-Bad Wife. **1923** The Exciters; The White Rose. **1924** America; Isn't Life Wonderful. **1925** Sally of the Sawdust. **1926** The White Black Sheep. **1927** The Girl from Chicago; The Heart of Maryland; The Price of Honor; Salvation Jane. **1928** A Thief in the Dark; The Fortune Hunter; Fazil; Fleetwing. **1929** Speakeasy. **1930** The Bad Man; Guilty?; Redemption; The Dawn Trail. **1931** Too Many Cooks; The Lash; Arrowsmith; Shanghaied Love. **1932** Alias the Doctor; Cabin in the Cotton; They Call It Sin; I Am a Fugitive from a Chain Gang. **1933** State Fair; To the Last Man. **1934** Lazy River; The Scarlet Empress. **1935** Square Shooter; The County Chairman; Woman Wanted; Pursuit; Public Opinion; The Virginia Judge; Seven Keys to Baldpate. **1936** Educating Father; Career Woman; Jungle Princess. **1937** The Mighty Treve; Small Town Boy. **1938** Love Finds Andy Hardy; Gold is Where You Find It; Marie Antoinette. **1939** Jesse James; Mr. Smith Goes to Washington; Romance of the Redwoods;

Andy Hardy Gets Spring Fever; The Hardys Ride High; Outside These Walls; Nancy Drew—Trouble Shooter; Vitaphone short. **1940** Santa Fe Trail; Dr. Kildare Goes Home; The Grapes of Wrath. **1941** High Sierra; H. M. Pulham, Esq.; Honky Tonk; The Last of the Duanes; Tobacco Road; Sergeant York; Bad Men of Missouri; Parachute Battalion. **1942** The Commandos Strike at Dawn; My Favorite Blonde; The Postman Didn't Ring; The Loves of Edgar Allan Poe; You Can't Escape Forever; Careful, Soft Shoulders; The Vanishing Virginian. **1943** Arizona Trail; First Comes Courage. **1944** And the Angels Sing; Heavenly Days; Rationing; Man from Frisco. **1945** Incendiary Blonde; Along Came Jones. **1946** The Magnificent Doll; The Spiral Staircase. **1947** The Bishop's Wife; Pursued; Smash-Up, the Story of a Woman. **1948** Shanghai Chest; The Feathered Serpent; Station West; Blood on the Moon. **1949** Mr. Whitney Had a Notion (short). **1950** Summer Stock. **1952** Something to Live For. **1957** The Spirit of St. Louis.

ALDERSON, FLOYD T. *See* WALES, WALLY

ALDRICH, MARISKA
Born: Mar. 27, 1881, Mass. Died: Sept. 28, 1965, Los Angeles, Calif. (acute intestinal obstruction). Opera singer and screen actress.

Appeared in: **1934** Bottoms Up; Evelyn Prentice; Lady by Choice. **1936** Under Your Spell; Camille. **1937** Maytime; I'll Take Romance; Live, Love and Learn; The Emperor's Candlesticks. **1938** Bluebeard's Eighth Wife. **1939** At the Circus; The Women; The Forgotten Woman. **1941** You're the One. **1945** Song of the Sarong.

ALDRIDGE, ALFRED
Born: 1876, New Orleans, La. Died: May 4, 1934, Hollywood, Calif. Stage and screen actor.

Appeared in: **1921** It Can Be Done.

ALERME, ANDRE
Born: 1887, France. Died: 1960, France? Screen actor.

Appeared in: **1933** Mam'zelle Nitouche. **1936** Pension Mimesas; La Kermosse Heroique. **1938** Avocate d'Amour. **1939** Mademoiselle ma Mere. **1940** The Man of the Hour. **1941** The Man Who Seeks the Truth. **1942** Four Flights to Love. **1945** The Barge-Keeper's Daughter. **1946** Symphonie d'Amour. **1947** The Blue Veil. **1948** Passionnelle. **1950** Noah's Ark; Hoboes in Paradise.

ALEXANDER, A. L.
Born: 1906, Boston, Mass. Died: Feb. 24, 1967. Screen actor, radio announcer and screenwriter.

Appeared in: **1934** War Is a Racket. **1937** Private Life of the Gannets (short).

ALEXANDER, ALEX
Born: 1911, Brooklyn, N.Y. Died: Apr. 24, 1977, New York, N.Y. Screen, stage and television actor. Do not confuse with film producer or musician with same name.

ALEXANDER, BEN (Nicholas Benton Alexander)
Born: May 26, 1911, Goldfield, Nev. Died: June, 1969, Westchester, Calif. (natural causes). Screen, television actor, radio emcee and announcer.

Appeared in: **1916** Each Pearl a Tear (film debut). **1918** Hearts of the World. **1919** The Turn in the Road; The White Heather. **1921** The Heart Line. **1922** In the Name of the Law. **1923** Penrod and Sam; Boy of Mine. **1924** Jealous Husbands; A Self-Made Failure. **1925** Pampered Youth; Flaming Love; The Shining Adventure; Frivolous Sal. **1926** Scotty of the Scouts (serial); The Highbinders. **1927** Fighting for Fame (serial). **1930** All Quiet on the Western Front. **1931** A Wise Child; Many a Slip; Are These Our Children?; Mystery Ship; Suicide Fleet. **1932** The Strange Love of Molly Louvain; Tom Brown of Culver; The Vanishing Frontier; High Pressure. **1933** What Price Innocence?; This Day and Age; Stage Mother. **1934** Once to Every Woman; The Most Precious Thing in Life; The Life of Vergie Winters. **1935** Reckless Roads; Splendor; Grand Old Girl; Annapolis Farewell; Born to Gamble; The Fire Trap. **1936** Hearts in Bondage. **1937** Red Lights Ahead; The Outer Gate; Behind Prison Bars; Western Gold. **1938** The Spy Ring; Mr. Doodle Kicks Off. **1939** Convicts' Code. **1940** The Leather Pushers. **1954** Dragnet. **1957** Pay the Devil; Man in the Shadow.

ALEXANDER, C. K.
Born: 1923, Cairo, Egypt. Died: Sept. 2, 1980, New York, N.Y. (cancer). Screen, stage, television actor, stage director and producer.

ALEXANDER, CHICK
Born: England. Died: Oct., 1969, London, England. Screen and stage actor.

ALEXANDER, CLAIRE
Born: 1898. Died: Nov. 16, 1927, Alhambra, Calif. (double pneumonia). Screen actress. One of the first Mack Sennett bathing beauties and was in early Keystone films.

Appeared in: **1917** Jerry's Big Mystery; Jerry's Brilliant Scheme; Jerry's Triple Alliance; Jerry's Romance; Minding the Baby; Be Sure You're Right; The Lady Detective; The Ransom; Jerry's Picnic; Jerry's Finishing Touch; Jerry Joins the Army; Jerry's Master Stroke; Jerry and the Bully; Jerry's Soft Snap; Jerry's Lucky Day; Jerry and the Vampire; Jerry's Running Fight; Jerry's Victory; Jerry and the Burglars; Jerry Takes Gas; Jerry's Boarding House; Jerry's Best Friend. **1920** The Fatal Sign (serial).

ALEXANDER, EDWARD
Born: 1888. Died: Aug. 15, 1964, Dearborn, Ohio (heart attack). Screen actor and film producer. Entered films in 1910.

Appeared in: **1915** The Terror of the Fold; Bait; Curse of the Black Pearl. **1917** Chosen Prince (aka The Friendship of David and Jonathan); North of 53. **1918** The Wild Strain. **1919** The Island of Intrigue. **1920** The Heart of Youth.

ALEXANDER, FRANK "FATTY"
Born: 1879. Died: Sept. 8, 1937, North Hollywood, Calif. Screen actor. Entered films in 1913 with Keystone.

Appeared in: **1923** Cyclone Jones. **1925** SOS Perils of the Sea. **1926** Oh, What a Night! **1927** Play Safe.

ALEXANDER, GEORG (Werner Louis Georg Luddeckens)
Born: 1889, 1892 or 1895?, Hannover, Germany. Died: 1945, Berlin, Germany. Screen and stage actor. Entered films in 1919.

Appeared in: **1919** Fahrt ins Blaue; Die Platonische Ehe. **1920** Falscher Start; Der Mann ohne Namen (The Man Without a Name). **1921** Das Madchen aus der Fremde. **1922** Der Film ohne Name; Lady Hamilton; Das Madchen aus dem Goldenen Western; Das Spiel mit dem Weibe; Stubbs, der Detektiv; Die Tanzerin des Konigs; Vanina oder die Galgenhochzeit; Der Frauenkonig. **1923** Die Frau mit den Millionen; Liebe macht Blind (Love Makes One Blind); Das Milliardensouper; Das Paradies im Schnee. **1924** Die Grosse Unbekannte; Komodianten des Lebens; Mein Leopold; Das Schone Abenteuer; Die Schonste Frau der Welt. **1925** Eifersucht (Jealousy); Herrn Filip Collins Abenteuer; Der Herr ohne Wohnung; Husarenfieber. **1926** Gasthaus zur Ehe; Die Insel der Verbotenen Kusse; Die Kleine vom Variete; Die Muhle von Sanssouci; Nanette macht Alles; Die Welt will Belogen Sein; Coloialskandal (aka Liebe im Rausch). **1927** Die Dame mit dem Tigerfell; Die Dollarprinzessin und Ihre sechs Freier; Eins plus Eins Gleich Drei; Flucht vor Blonde; Die Frau Ohne Namen; Die Indiskrete Frau; Die Jagd nach der Braut; Der Kampf um den Mann; Der Orlow; Venus in Frack. **1928** Dyckerpott's Erben; Er geht Rechts-Sie Geht Links; Die Grosse Abenteurerin; Leontines Ehemanner; Liebe im Schnee; Die Lustigen Vagabunden; Mikosch Rucht; Prinzessin Olala; Sechs Madchen Suchten Nachtquartier; Unmoral; Was Ist los mit Nanette. **1929** Autobus Nr. 2; Die Garde-Diva; Der Leutnant ihrer Majestat; Das Recht auf Liebe; Schwarzwaldmadel; Ehestreik. **1930** Die Singende Stadt; Liebeswalzer (Love Waltz); Zartlichkeit; Leutnant Warst du Einst bei den Husaren; Geld auf der Strasse. **1931** Die Brautigamswitwe (Bridegroom for Two); Der Liebesexpress; Wiener Liebschaften Trara um Liebe; Opernredoute; Der Verjungte Adolar; Die Fledermaus; Hurraein Junge!; Nitouche; Ehe G.m.b.H. **1932** Das Testament der Cornelius Gulden; Wie sag' ich's Meinem Mann; Durchlaucht Amusiert Sich; Ein Bisschen Liebe für Dich; Flucht nach Nizza (Ein Ganz Verflixter Kerl); Wenn die Liebe Mode Macht; Moderne Mitgift; Liebe, Scherz und Ernst. **1933** Und wer Kusst Mich?; Mein Liebster Ist ein Jagersmann; Madame Wunscht Keine Kinder; Eine Frau wie Du; Der Zarewitsch; Ist Mein; Mann Nicht Fabelhaft?; Liebe Muss Verstanden Sein. **1934** Das Blumenmadchen vom Grande-Hotel; Zigeunerblut; Der Doppelganger; G'schichten aus dem Wienerwald; Die Englische Heirat; Alles Hort auf Mein Kommando. **1935** Tanzmusik; Der Alte und der Junge Konig; Ein Falscher Fullziger; Ein Idealer Gatte; Der Schlafwagenkontrolleur; Ein Madel aus Guter Familie; Ein Teufelskerl; Der Vogelhandler; Rendezvous am Rhein. **1936** Martha; Das Frauenparadies; Das Schloss in Flandern; Donaumelodien; Madchen in Weiss; Eskapade. **1937** Abenteuer in Warschau; Eine Nacht mit Hindernissen; Die Fledermaus (and 1931 verison); Krach und Gluck bei Kunnemann; Hahn im Korb; Karussell; Zwei mal Zwei im Himmelbett. **1938** Verliebtes Abenteuer; Das Madchen von Gestern Nacht; Der Fall Deruga; Gelt Fallt vom Himmel; Heimat; Die Frau am Scheidewege; Kleiner Mann; Ganz Gross; Unsere Kleine Frau; Gastspiel im Paradies. **1939** Wenn Manner Verreisen; Leinen an Steuer; Der Arme Millionar; Die Kluge Schwiegermutter. **1940** Was Will Brigitte?; Der Kleinstadtpoet. **1941** Das Himmelblaue Abendkleid; Oh Diese Manner; Frau Luna; Frauen sind doch Bessere Diplomaten. **1942** Ein Zug Fahrt Ab. c. **1943** Abenteuer im Grandhotel; Die Beiden Schwestern; Und die Musik Spielt Dazu. **1944** Die Frau Meiner Traume; Der Meisterdetektiv.

ALEXANDER, JAMES "JIMMY" (James Burnel Alexander)
Born: Apr. 25, 1902, Indiana. Died: Jan. 31, 1961, Hollywood, Calif. (diabetes, arteriosclerosis). Screen, stage and television actor. Do not confuse with James Alexander who appeared in later films.

Appeared in: **1952** Jack and the Beanstalk. **1955** Las Vegas Shakedown; Treasure of Ruby Hills.

ALEXANDER, JANET
Born: Ewell, England. Died: June 28, 1961, England? Screen and stage actress. Married to actor Lauderdale Maitland (dec. 1929).

Appeared in: **1916** Queen of the Wicked; What's Bred ... Comes Out in the Flesh; A Fallen Star; The Treasure of Heaven. **1917** A Strong Man's Weakness (aka The Will of the People); For All Eternity; The Village Blacksmith. **1918** The Secret Woman. **1919** Queen's Evidence; God's Clay; I Hear You Calling Me. **1920** The Hour of Trial. **1922** The Romance of British History series including The Threefold Tragedy. **1923** Wonder Women of the World series including Henrietta Maria, or The Queen of Sorrow and Empress Josephine, or Wife of a Demigod. **1926** Screen Playets series including: Miss Bracegirdle Does Her Duty; Back to the Trees. **1928** Not Quite a Lady. **1929** The Lily of Killarney; High Seas. **1930** No Exit; The Compulsory Husband.

ALEXANDER, JOHN
Born: 1865. Died: Apr. 5, 1951, Ontario, Calif. Screen and stage actor. In recent years a stand-in for Guy Kibbee and Donald Meek. Do not confuse with John Alexander born in 1897 (dec. 1982).

ALEXANDER, KATHERINE
Born: 1898. Died: Jan., 1981. Screen actress.

Appeared in: **1933** Should Ladies Behave? **1934** Death Takes a Holiday; Operator 13; The Barretts of Wimpole Street; The Painted Veil. **1935** Enchanted April; After Office Hours; Cardinal Richlieu; Ginger; The Girl from Tenth Avenue; Splendor; Alias Mary Dow; She Married Her Boss. **1936** Moonlight Murder; Sutter's Gold; The Devil is a Sissy; Reunion. **1937** As Good as Married; The Girl from Scotland Yard; Stage Door; That Certain Woman; Double Wedding. **1938** Rascals. **1939** The Great Man Votes; Broadway Serenade; Three Sons; In Name Only; The Hunchback of Notre Dame. **1940** Anne of Windy Poplars; Dance, Girl, Dance. **1941** Sis Hopkins; Playgirl; Angels with Broken Wings; Small Town Deb. **1942** On the Sunny Side; Now, Voyager; The Vanishing Virginian. **1943** The Human Comedy. **1945** Kiss and Tell. **1948** For the Love of Mary. **1949** John Loves Mary.

ALEXANDER, LOIS A.
Born: 1891, Warsau, Indiana. Died: May 3, 1968, Washington, D.C. (stroke). Screen, television actress and dancer. Do not confuse with silent screen actress "Baby" Lois Alexander.

ALEXANDER, MARA (Mara Levine)
Born: Feb. 7, 1914, New York. Died: May 23, 1965, San Francisco, Calif. (pneumonia). Stage and screen actress.

Appeared in: **1939** The Rains Came.

ALEXANDER, MURIEL (Muriel Marsh)
Born: Sept. 12, 1898, Cape Town, South Africa or Dublin, Ireland. Died: Mar., 1975, Johannesburg, South Africa. Screen and stage actress.

Appeared in: **1920** The Skin Game (stage and film versions). **1921** The Scallywag.

ALEXANDER, RENE
Died: 1914, France. Screen actor.

Appeared in: **1915** The Old Thespian.

ALEXANDER, ROSS
Born: July 27, 1907, Brooklyn, N.Y. Died: Jan. 2, 1937, Los Angeles, Calif. (suicide—gun). Screen and stage actor. Married to actress Anna Nagel (dec. 1966).

Appeared in: **1932** The Wiser Sex. **1934** Flirtation Walk; Gentlemen Are Born; Loudspeaker Lowdown; Social Register. **1935** A Midsummer Night's Dream; Captain Blood; We're in the Money; Shipmates Forever; Going Highbrow; Maybe It's Love. **1936** Brides Are Like That; I Married a Doctor; Boulder Dam; China Clipper; Hot Money; Here Comes Carter! **1937** Ready, Willing and, Able.

ALEXANDER, SARA
Born: 1839. Died: Dec. 24, 1926, New York, N.Y. Screen and stage actress.

ALEXANDER, SUZANNE
Died: Sept. 21, 1975. Screen actress.

Appeared in: **1953** Cat Women of the Moon. **1954** Down Three Dark Streets; Princess of the Nile. **1955** The Girl in the Red Velvet Swing.

ALEXANDER THE GREAT
Died: Aug., 1933, Bridgeport, Ohio (old age and excessive heat). Stage and screen animal performer (German police dog).

Appeared in 241 films.

ALEXANDRE, ROLAND
Born: 1937, France. Died: Feb., 1956, France? Screen actor.

Appeared in: **1952** The Perfectionist. **1954** House of Ricordi (US 1956).

ALGARO, GABRIEL
Born: 1888. Died: Oct., 1951, Sargozza, Spain. Screen, stage actor and film director.

ALGIER, SIDNEY H.
Born: Dec. 5, 1889, Shamokin, Pa. Died: Apr. 24, 1945, West Los Angeles, Calif. (heart attack). Screen, stage, vaudeville, burlesque actor, film director and screenwriter. Entered films as an actor in 1915.

ALI, GEORGE
Born: 1866. Died: Apr. 26, 1947, Freeport, N.Y. Screen actor and animal impersonator.

Appeared in: **1924** Peter Pan.

ALIPPI, ELIAS
Died: May 4, 1942, Buenos Aires, Argentina. Screen actor.

Appeared in: **1939** Viento Norte (North Wind); Cadetes de San Martin. **1940** Asi es Vida (Such Is Life). **1942** Viejo Hucha.

ALLAIRE, JOSIAH
Born: 1865. Died: Oct. 8, 1935. Screen actor. Appeared in silent films made in Ft. Lee, N.J.

ALLEN, BEBE *See* BEBE, ALLEN

ALLBEURY, DAISY
Born: 1885. Died: Oct. 20, 1961, London, England. Screen film extra.

ALLBRITTON, LOUISE
Born: July 3, 1920, Oklahoma City, Okla. Died: Feb. 16, 1979, Puerto Vallarta, Mexico (cancer). Screen, stage and television actress.

Appeared in: **1942** Parachute Nurse (film debut); Pittsburgh; Danger in the Pacific; Who Done It?; Not a Ladies' Man. **1943** It Comes Up Life; Good Morning, Judge; Fired Wife; Son of Dracula. **1944** Her Primitive Man; This is the Life; San Diego, I Love You; Bowery to Broadway; Follow the Boys. **1945** The Men in Her Diary; That Night With You. **1946** Tangier. **1947** The Egg and I. **1948** Don't Trust Your Husband; Sitting Pretty; Walk a Crooked Mile; An Innocent Affair. **1949** The Doolins of Oklahoma.

ALLEBORN, AL
Born: 1892. Died: June 14, 1968, Hollywood, Calif. (leukemia). Retired studio executive and former assistant director who entered films as a stuntman.

ALLEGRET, MARC
Born: 1900, France. Died: Nov. 3, 1973, Paris, France. Screen actor, film director and screenwriter.

Appeared in: **1960** Et Mourir de Plaisir (aka Blood and Roses—US 1961).

ALLEN, ALFRED
Born: 1866, Alfred, N.Y. Died: June 18, 1947. Screen actor.

Appeared in: **1916** The Yoke of Gold; The Unattainable; The Price of Victory; A Child of Mystery. **1917** The Price of a Good Time (aka The Whim). **1918** The Lion's Claw (serial). **1919** The Red Glove (serial). **1920** An Old Fashioned Boy. **1921** The New Disciple; O'Malley of the Mounted; The Sage Hen. **1922** The Pride of Palomar; Colleen of the Pines; Shattered Idols. **1923** Desert Driven; A Gentleman of Leisure; The Grub Stake; The Miracle Baby; A Noise in Newboro; Shootin' for Love. **1924** Abraham Lincoln; Stolen Secrets; A Girl of the Limberlost. **1925** Bustin' Thru; Dangerous Innocence; Speed. **1926** The Mystery Club; Rolling Home. **1927** Singed; The Outlaw Dog; The Golden Yukon; Out All Night; The Magic Garden. **1928** Anybody Here Seen Kelly?; Hot News; The Fifty-Fifty Girl; Under the Tonto Rim. **1929** The Flying Fleet; Sunset Pass.

ALLEN, ARTHUR B.
Born: 1881. Died: Aug. 25, 1947, New York, N.Y. Screen, stage actor and radio emcee.

Appeared in: **1937** Ebb Tide. **1940** Our Town; Rangers of Fortune.

ALLEN, BAMBI (Rosalie Erbsen)
Born: 1938. Died: Jan. 21, 1973. Screen and television actress.

Appeared in: **1968** Someone. **1969** The Ribald Tales of Robin Hood; The Fabulous Bastard from Chicago; The Hanging of Jake Ellis; Satan's Sadists; Wild Outtakes. **1970** Angels Die Hard!; The Bang Bang Gang; Hell's Bloody Devils; How to Succeed with Sex.

ALLEN, BEBE (aka BEBE ALLAN)
Died: Oct. 11, 1978. Screen actress.

Appeared in: **1957** Operation Mad Ball. **1962** State Fair.

ALLEN, DOROTHY
Born: 1896. Died: Sept. 30, 1970, N.Y. Screen and stage actress.

Appeared in: **1921** Beyond Price; The Power Within; Dynamite Allen. **1922** The Broken Silence; Free Air. **1923** If Winter Comes. **1924** Youth for Sale; The Hoosier Schoolmaster. **1925** Pearl of Love; School for Wives.

ALLEN, ESTELLE
Born: Jan. 5, 1893, Portland, Ore. Died: July 14, 1940. Screen actress.

Appeared in: **1913** The Flotsam; Highland Romance.

ALLEN, ETHAN
Born: 1882. Died: Aug. 21, 1940, Hollywood, Calif. Screen, stage actor, film director and screenwriter.

Appeared in: **1930** The Border Legion. **1931** The Flood. **1939** Trigger Pals.

ALLEN, FRED (John Florence Sullivan)
Born: May 31, 1894, Cambridge, Mass. Died: Mar. 17, 1956, New York, N.Y. (heart attack). Screen, stage, vaudeville actor, columnist, radio emcee and film director. Billed in vaudeville as "Fred St. James," "Freddie James, World's Worst Juggler" and "Paul Huckle, European Entertainer," In 1927 was part of emcee team "Allen and York."

Appeared in: **1929** Fred Allen's Prize Playettes (short). **1930** The Still Alarm (short). **1935** Thanks a Million. **1938** Sally, Irene and Mary. **1940** Love Thy Neighbor. **1945** It's in the Bag (aka The Fifth Chair). **1952** We're Not Married; O. Henry's Full House. **1956** Fabulous Hollywood (film clips).

ALLEN, GRACIE (Grace Ethel Cecile Rosale Allen)
Born: July 26, 1906, San Francisco, Calif. Died: Aug. 28, 1964, Los Angeles, Calif. (heart attack). Screen, vaudeville, radio and television actress. Married to actor George Burns and was half of comedy team "Burns and Allen." She was known as "the smartest dumbbell in the history of show business."

Appeared with Burns in: **1929** Lamb Chops (short). **1930** The following shorts: Insurance, Pulling a Bone, Fit to Be Tied. **1931** Burns and Allen (short); The Antique Shop (short); Once over Lightly (short); One Hundred Percent Service (short). **1932** The Big Broadcast of 1932; Oh, My Operation (short); The Babbling Book (short); Hollywood on Parade #2 (short). **1933** International House; College Humor; Walking the Baby (short); Let's Dance (short). **1934** Six of a Kind; Many Happy Returns; We're Not Dressing; College Rhythm. **1935** Love in Bloom; Here Comes Cookie; The Big Broadcast of 1936. **1936** College Holiday; The Big Broadcast of 1937. **1937** A Damsel in Distress. **1938** College Swing. **1939** Honolulu. **1944** Hollywood on Parade. **1954** Hollywood Grows Up (film clips); Hollywood Fathers (film clips); Appeared without Burns in: **1939** Gracie Allen Murder Case. **1941** Mr. and Mrs. North. **1944** Two Girls and a Sailor.

ALLEN, HARRY R.
Born: July 10, 1883, Australia. Died: Dec. 4, 1951, United States. Screen actor.

Appeared in: **1923** The Last Moment. **1924** The Enchanted Cottage. **1926** Corporal Kate; Ella Cinders. **1927** The Silent Hero; The Scorcher; Turkish Delight. **1928** The Adorable Cheat; Two Lovers; The Singapore Mutiny; Sweet Sixteen. **1929** Strange Cargo; In Old California. **1930** Dawn Patrol; Headin' North; Hell Harbor; Hell's Island; Sunny; Second Honeymoon. **1931** Chances; Rich Man's Folly. **1932** Texas Pioneers. **1933** Fourth Horseman. **1934** Bombay Mail. **1935** The Silver Streak; Anna Karenina. **1936** The White Angel; The White Legion. **1937** California Straight Ahead. **1938** Outside of

Paradise. **1939** The Little Princess. **1940** Moon Over Burma. **1943** Buckskin Frontier; Forever and a Day. **1944** The Hour Before Dawn; The Lodger. **1947** The Swordsman; Thunder in the Valley; Bob, Son of Battle.

ALLEN, HUGH (Hugh Clifford Allen)
Born: Nov. 19, 1886, Canada. Died: Sept. 13, 1966, Los Angeles, Calif. (suicide—jumped from building). Screen actor. Do not confuse with actor Hugh Allan, born 1903.

ALLEN, JANE MARIE
Born: 1916. Died: Feb. 16, 1970, Santa Monica, Calif. Screen actress and dancer.

ALLEN, JOE
Born: 1888. Died: Jan. 31, 1955, Hollywood, Calif. (cancer). Screen actor.

ALLEN, JOSEPH
Born: 1840. Died: Jan. 12, 1917. Screen actor. Appeared in Essanay Film Co. films.

ALLEN, JOSEPH, JR.
Born: Mar. 30, 1918, Boston, Mass. Died: Nov. 9, 1962, Patchogue, N.Y. Screen, stage and television actor. Son of actor Joseph Allen, Sr. (dec. 1952).

Appeared in: **1936** Motor Madness. **1939** Death of a Champion; Lucky Night; Our Leading Citizen. **1942** Who Is Hope Schuyler?; Death of Champion; Right to the Heart; It Happened in Flatbush; The Night before the Divorce. **1946** Dangerous Money. **1947** Big Town after Dark; I Cover Big Town; Road to the Big House. **1948** Big Town Scandal; The Time of Your Life. **1951** The Wild Blue Yonder. **1953** Valley of the Headhunters. **1954** Gunfighters of the Northwest (serial); Cannibal Attack.

ALLEN, JOSEPH, SR.
Born: 1872. Died: Sept. 9, 1952, Newton, Mass. Screen and stage actor. Father of actor Joseph Alllen, Jr. (dec. 1962).

Appeared in: **1912** Essaney films. **1929** Seven Keys to Baldpate. **1934** Gambling.

ALLEN, KENNETH
Born: 1904. Died: Jan. 15, 1976, Alameda, Calif. (Parkinson's Disease). Screen, stage actor, and stuntman.

Appeared in: **1930** Just Imagine.

ALLEN, LESTER
Born: 1891, England. Died: Nov. 6, 1949, Hollywood, Calif. (struck by auto). Screen, stage, vaudeville, minstrel, burlesque, circus actor and film director.

Appeared in: **1930** Leave It to Lester. **1932-33** Paramount shorts. **1943** The Heat's On. **1945** The Great Flamario; The Dolly Sisters. **1946** The Dark Mirror. **1948** Crime on Their Hands (short); The Pirate; That Lady in Ermine. **1949** Ma and Pa Kettle.

ALLEN, MAUDE (Maude Allen Giannone aka MAUDE PIERCE ADAMS)
Died: Nov. 7, 1956, Washington. Screen and stage actress.

Appeared in: **1930** La Grande Mare (The Big Pond). **1931** The Smiling Lieutenant. **1935** The Cowboy Millionaire; It's in the Air; Whispering Smith Speaks. **1936** Showboat; The Captain's Kid. **1937** Secret Valley. **1938** Painted Desert. **1939** The Women. **1940** Adventures of Red Ryder (serial); Danger Ahead; Black Diamonds. **1942** Juke Box Jennie; I Married an Angel.

ALLEN, PHYLLIS
Born: 1861. Died: Mar. 26, 1938, Los Angeles, Calif. Screen and vaudeville actress.

Appeared in: **1914** Caught in a Cabaret (reissued as The Jazz Waiter); The Property Man; The Rounders; Dough and Dynamite (reissued as The Doughnut Designers); Gentlemen of Nerve (reissued as Some Nerve); Fatty's Jonah Day; Getting Acquainted. **1915** Giddy, Gay and Ticklish (reissued as A Gay Lothario); Gussle's Wayward Path; Fickle Fatty's Fall; A Submarine Pirate; A Movie Star; The Judge.

ALLEN, RICCA (Rica Allen)
Born: June 9, 1863, Victoria, British Columbia, Canada. Died: Sept 13, 1949. Screen and stage actress. Sister of actress Ray Allen.

Appeared in: **1915** Runaway June (serial). **1920** Song of the Soul;

Headin' Home. **1921** Silas Marner; Handcuffs and Kisses; The Oath. **1923** The Empty Cradle. **1925** The Mad Dancer. **1929** Close Harmony; Show Boat. **1931** Ten Cents a Dance. **1934** The Pursuit of Happiness. **1936** The Trail of the Lonesome Pine. **1938** Blockade.

ALLEN, ROSE (Carrie Allen)
Born: 1885. Died: May 3, 1977, Hollywood, Calif. Silent screen actress. Mother of actress Ann Doran.

ALLEN, SAM
Born: 1861, Md. Died: Sept. 13, 1934, Los Angeles, Calif. Screen and stage actor. Entered films with Biograph in 1910.

Appeared in: **1921** The Conflict. **1922** Forget-Me-Not; The Son of the West; Confidence. **1923** Are You a Failure?; The Virginian. **1925** Timber Wolf; Bashful Buccaneer; Midnight Limited. **1926** The Call of the Klondike; Man Rustlin'; The Sea Beast. **1927** Blackjack; Death Valley; Mother; Woman's Law. **1928** Burning Bridges. **1930** The Sea Wolf. **1934** The Last Round-Up.

ALLEN, VIOLA
Born: Oct. 27, 1869, Huntsville, Ala. Died: May 9, 1948, New York, N.Y. Screen and stage actress. Daughter of stage actor C. Leslie Allen (dec.).

Appeared in: **1915** The White Sister.

ALLENBY, FRANK (Frank Gatehouse)
Born: Dec. 22, 1898, Hobart, Tasmania. Died: May 29, 1953, England. Screen and stage actor.

Appeared in: **1937** The Return of the Scarlet Pimpernel (US 1938). **1949** Madame Bovary. **1950** The Flame and the Arrow. **1951** Soldiers Three.

ALLENBY, THOMAS
Born: 1861, Australia. Died: Dec. 19, 1933, Hollywood, Calif. Screen actor.

ALLERTON, LITTLE HELEN (aka HELEN KILDUFF aka HELEN SCHWEISTHAL)
Born: 1888. Died: Nov. 4, 1959, Golf, Ill. Screen, stage and vaudeville actress. Appeared in vaudeville as part of "May and Kilduff" team. Entered films with Essanay and Selig Studios in Chicago and appeared in films from 1910 to 1916.

ALLGOOD, SARA
Born: Oct. 31, 1883, Dublin, Ireland. Died: Sept. 13, 1950, Woodland Hills, Calif. (heart attack). Screen and stage actress. Nominated for 1941 Academy Award as Best Supporting Actress for How Green Was My Valley.

Appeared in: **1929** Blackmail (film debut); Juno and the Paycock (aka The Shame of Mary Boyle—US). **1932** The World, the Flesh and the Devil. **1933** The Fortunate Fool. **1934** Irish Hearts (aka Norah O'Neale—US); Lily of Killarney (aka Bride of the Lake—US). **1935** The Passing of the Third Floor Back; Lazybones; Peg of Old Drury (US 1936); Riders to the Sea. **1936** Pot Luck; Southern Roses; It's Love Again. **1937** Storm in a Teacup; The Sky's the Limit; Kathleen Mavourneen (aka Kathleen—US 1938). **1938** The Londonderry Air. **1939** On the Night of the Fire (aka The Fugitive—US 1940). **1941** That Hamilton Woman; How Green Was My Valley; Dr. Jekyll and Mr. Hyde; Lydia. **1942** The War Against Mrs. Hadley; Roxie Hart; This Above All; It Happened in Flatbush; Life Begins at 8:30. **1943** City Without Men. **1944** The Lodger; Between Two Worlds; Jane Eyre; Keys of the Kingdom. **1945** The Strange Affair of Uncle Harry. **1946** Cluny Brown; Kitty; The Spiral Staircase. **1947** Mother Wore Tights; The Fabulous Dorseys; Ivy; Mourning Becomes Electra; My Wild Irish Rose. **1948** One Touch of Venus; The Man from Texas; The Girl from Manhattan; The Accused. **1949** Challenge to Lassie. **1950** Sierra; Cheaper by the Dozen.

ALLISON, STEVE
Born: 1916. Died: Mar. 6, 1969, Hollywood, Calif. (lung cancer). Screen actor, radio emcee and singer.

Appeared in: **1957** The Burglar.

ALLISTER, CLAUD (Claud Palmer)
Born: Oct. 3, 1893, London, England. Died: July 26, 1970, Santa Barbara, Calif. Screen and stage actor. Entered films in 1929.

Appeared in: **1929** The Trial of Mary Dugan; Bulldog Drummond; Three Live Ghosts; Charming Sinners. **1930** Monte Carlo; The Floradora Girl; The Czar of Broadway; Slightly Scarlet; In the Next Room; Such Men Are Dangerous; Murder Will Out; Ladies Love

Brutes. **1931** On the Loose (short); Captain Applejack; Reaching for the Moon; Meet the Wife; Papa Loves Mamma; I Like Your Nerve; Rough-House Rhythm (short); Platinum Blonde. **1932** The Midshipman; Two White Arms (aka Wives Beware—US 1933); Diamond Cut Diamond (aka Blame the Woman—US); The Return of Raffles. **1933** The Medicine Man; That's My Wife; Excess Baggage. **1934** The Lady is Willing; Those Were the Days; The Return of Bulldog Drummond; The Private Lives of Don Juan. **1935** The Dark Angel; Three Live Ghosts (and 1929 version). **1936** Dracula's Daughter; Yellowstone. **1937** Bulldog Drummond at Bay; Danger—Love at Work; Radio Parade of 1937; The Awful Truth; Let's Make a Night of It (US 1938). **1938** Men Are Such Fools; Storm Over Bengal; Kentucky Moonshine; The Blonde Cheat. **1939** Arrest Bulldog Drummond; Captain Fury. **1940** Lillian Russell. **1941** Never Give a Sucker an Even Break; Charley's Aunt; The Reluctant Dragon; A Yank in the RAF; Confirm or Deny. **1943** Forever and a Day; Hundred Pound Widow. **1944** Kiss the Bride Goodbye. **1945** Don Chicago; Dumb Dora Discovers Tobacco. **1946** Gaiety George (US 1948). **1947** Fag End (reissue of Dumb Dora Discovers Tobacco—US 1945). **1948** Quartet (US 1949). **1949** Ichbod and Mr. Toad. **1951** Hong Kong. **1953** Kiss Me, Kate; Down Among the Sheltering Palms.

ALLMAN, RAY FRANCIS
Died: June 24, 1978. Screen actor.

ALLWYN, ASTRID
Born: 1909 or 1911. Died: Mar. 31, 1978, Los Angeles, Calif. (cancer). Screen, stage actress and singer. Mother of actress Melinda Fee.

Appeared in: **1932** Lady With a Past; Love Affair; Night Mayor; Girl from Calgary; Bachelor Mother. **1933** The Iron Master; He Couldn't Take It; Only Yesterday. **1934** Mystery Liner; Beggers in Ermine; All of Me; Monte Carlo Nights; Servant's Entrance; The White Parade. **1935** One More Spring; It's a Small World; Accent on Youth; Way Down East; Hands Across the Table. **1936** Charlie Chan's Secret; Follow the Fleet; Star for a Night; Dimples; Flying Hostess; Stowaway. **1937** Murder Goes to College; Woman Wise; Venus Makes Trouble; It Could Happen to You; Love Takes Flight; The Westland Case. **1938** International Crime. **1939** Love Affair; Miracles for Sale; Honeymoon in Bali; Mr. Smith Goes to Washington; Reno. **1940** The Lone Wolf Strikes; The Leather Pushers; Meet the Missus; Gangs of Chicago. **1941** City of Missing Girls; Melody for Three; Puddin'head; Unexpected Uncle; No Hands on the Clock. **1943** Hit Parade of 1943.

ALLYN, ALYCE
Died: Feb. 11, 1976, Santa Monica, Calif. Screen and television actress.

Appeared in: **1959** Operation Dames. **1962** The Manchurian Candidate. **1969** The Wild Bunch.

ALLYN, LILLY (Elizabeth A. Tatu)
Born: 1866. Died: May 5, 1944, Philadelphia, Pa. Screen, stage, vaudeville actress and light opera performer.

ALMAR THE CLOWN See MARX, ALBERT A.

ALONSO, JULIO
Born: 1906. Died: Feb. 9, 1955, Hollywood, Calif. Screen actor. Brother of actor Gilbert Roland.

ALSACE, GENE
Born: 1903. Died: June 16, 1967. Screen actor.

Appeared in: **1936** Treachery Rides the Range. **1940** The Golden Trail; Arizona Frontier; Adventures of Red Ryder (serial). **1941** Rolling Home to Texas; The Pioneers; Arizona Bound; Wanderers of the West; Ridin' the Cherokee Trail; Dynamite Canyon; The Driftin' Kid.

ALSEN, ELSA
Born: 1881, Obra, Poland. Died: Jan. 31, 1975, New York, N.Y. Screen actress and opera singer.

Appeared in: **1930** The Rogue Song.

ALSTRUP, CARL
Born: 1877. Died: 1942. Stage and screen actor.

Appeared in: **1911** The Actor as Soldier; Buttons and Hooks; His First Monacle; The Twins.

ALTHOFF, CHARLES R.
Born: 1890. Died: Oct. 14, 1962, Irvington, N.J. Screen, vaudeville and radio actor.

Appeared in: Along Came Ruth (short).

ALTHOUSE, EARL F.
Born: 1893. Died: Feb. 6, 1971, Gladwyne, Pa. Screen cowboy actor. Entered films with Lubin Studios.

ALTON, ROBERT
Born: Jan. 28, 1906, Bennington, Vt. Died: June 12, 1957, Los Angeles, Calif. (kidney ailment). Screen actor, film, dance director and composer.

Appeared in: **1941** Two-Faced Woman.

ALTSCHUK, MAE See COSTELLO, MRS. MAE

ALVARADO, DON (Jose Paige)
Born: Nov. 4, 1900, Albuquerque, N.M. Died: Mar. 31, 1967, Los Angeles, Calif. (cancer). Screen and television actor. Also known professionally as Don Page.

Appeared in: **1925** The Pleasure Buyers; Satan in Sables; The Wife Who Wasn't Wanted. **1926** A Hero of the Big Snows; The Night Cry; His Jazz Bride. **1927** Loves of Carmen; Breakfast at Sunrise; Drums of Love; The Monkey Talks. **1928** The Battle of the Sexes; No Other Woman; The Scarlet Lady; Driftwood. **1929** Rio Rita; The Apache; The Bridge of San Luis Rey. **1930** Free and Easy; The Bad One; Forever Yours. **1931** Beau Ideal; Captain Thunder; Reputation. **1932** The Bachelor's Affair; La Cucaracha; Lady With a Past; The King Murder. **1933** Under Secret Orders; Contraband; Black Beauty; Morning Glory. **1934** Demon for Trouble; No Sleep on the Deep (short); Once to Every Bachelor. **1935** The Devil Is a Woman; Red Wagon; I Live for Love; Sweet Adeline. **1936** Rosa de Francia; Federal Agent; Rio Grande Romance; Put on the Spot; Rose of the Rancho; Spy 77. **1937** Nobody's Baby; The Lady Escapes; Love Under Fire. **1938** Rose of the Rio Grande. **1939** Cafe Society. **1940** One Night in the Tropics. **1949** The Big Steal.

AMARANTE, ESTEVAO
Born: 1890. Died: Jan., 1952, Oporto, Portugal. Stage and screen actor. During 1930's did first talkies in Portuguese language for Paramount in Paris.

AMATO, GIUSEPPE (Giuseppe Vasaturo)
Born: 1899, Italy. Died: Feb. 3, 1964, Rome, Italy (heart attack). Screen actor, film producer/director and screenwriter.

AMATO, PASQUALE
Born: 1879, Naples, Italy. Died: Aug. 13, 1942, Jackson Heights, N.Y. Opera singer and screen actor.

Appeared in: **1928** Glorious Betsy.

AMAYA, CARMEN
Born: 1913. Died: Nov. 19, 1963, Bagur, Spain (kidney ailment). Screen, stage actress and flamenco dancer.

Appeared in: **1936** Maria De La O. **1944** Follow the Boys; Knickerbocker Holiday. **1945** See My Lawyer (with her dancing company). **1963** Los Tarantos (US 1964).

AMBLER, JOSS
Born: 1900, England. Died: 1959. Screen actor.

Appeared in: **1937** Captain's Orders; The Last Curtain. **1938** Meet Mr. Penny; Break the News (US 1941); The Citadel; The Claydon Treasure Mystery. **1939** Trouble Brewing; Come on George; Secret Journey (aka Among Human Wolves—US 1940). **1940** Contraband (aka Blackout—US); Fingers. **1941** Penn of Pennsylvania (aka The Courageous Mr. Penn—US 1944); Once a Crook; The Black Sheep of Whitehall. **1942** The Big Blockade; The Peterville Diamond; Gert and Daisy Clean Up; Flying Fortress; The Next of Kin (US 1943); Much Too Shy. **1943** Happidrome; The Silver Fleet (US 1945); Rhythm Serenade; Battle for Music; Somewhere in Civvies; Headline. **1944** The Halfway House (US 1945); A Canterbury Tale; Candles at Nine; Give Me the Stars. **1945** The Agitator; Here Comes the Sun. **1946** The Years Between (US 1947). **1947** Mine Own Executioner (US 1949). **1952** Ghost Ship; Who Goes There! (aka The Passionate Sentry—US 1957). **1953** The Captain's Paradise. **1954** The Harrassed Hero. **1955** Miss Tulip Stays the Night. **1956** The Long Arm (aka The Third Key—US 1957); The Feminine Touch (aka The Gentle Touch—US 1957); Soho Incident (aka Spin a Dark Web—US).

AMES, ADRIENNE
Born: Aug. 3, 1909, Fort Worth, Tex. Died: May 31, 1947, New York, N.Y. (cancer). Screen, stage actress and radio commentator. Sister of actress Linda March (dec. 1933) and Gladys McClure (dec. 1933). Divorced from actor Bruce Cabot (dec. 1972).

Appeared in: **1931** Girls About Town; Twenty-Four Hours; The Road to Reno. **1932** Husband's Holiday; Two Kinds of Women; Merrily We Go to Hell; Sinners in the Sun. **1933** Broadway Bad; The Death Kiss; From Hell to Heaven; A Bedtime Story; Disgraced; The Avenger. **1934** You're Telling Me; George White's Scandals. **1935** Abdul the Damned; Black Sheep; La Fiesta de Santa Barbara (short); Gigolette; Woman Wanted; Harmony Lane; Ladies Love Danger. **1938** Slander House; City Girl; Fugitives for a Night. **1939** Zero Hour; Panama Patrol.

AMES, GERALD
Born: Sept. 12, 1881, Blackheath, England. Died: July, 1933, London, England (accident—fall). Screen, stage actor and film director.

Appeared in: **1914** The King's Minister; The Kitchen Countess; The Cage; The Revenge of Thomas Atkins; England's Menace; The Fringe of War; She Stoops to Conquer; The Black Spot; A Highwayman's Honour; The Difficult Way; On His Majesty's Service (aka A Message from the Sky—US). **1915** Rupert of Hentzau (US 1916); The Prisoner of Zenda; The Middleman; "1914"; The King's Outcast (aka His Vindication—US); Brother Officers; The Christian; The Sons of Satan; Whoso Diggeth a Pit; The Shulamite; The Derby Winner; Love in a Wood; Jelf's (aka A Man of His Word—US). **1916** Arsene Lupin; The Princess of Happy Chance; You; The Game of Liberty (aka Under Suspicion—US); Paste; Me and Me Moke (aka Me and My Pal—US); The Greater Need; The Morals of Weybury (aka The Hypocrites); When Knights Were Bold; The King's Daughter. **1917** A Gamble for Love; The Ragged Messenger; Masks and Faces. **1918** Adam Bede; Boundary House; A Fortune at Stake; Missing the Tide; A Peep Behind the Scenes; Red Pottage; A Turf Conspiracy. **1919** Sunken Rocks; The Nature of the Beast; Comradeship (aka Comrades in Arms); The Forest on the Hill; The Irresistible Flapper; Possession; Sheba. **1920** Alf's Button; The Amazing Quest of Ernest Bliss (serial); Anna the Adventuress; Aylwin; Helen of Four Gates; John Forest Finds Himself; Mrs. Erricker's Reputation. **1921** Wild Heather; Tansy; Mr. Justice Raffles. **1923** The Loves of Mary Queen of Scots (aka Marie, Queen of Scots); A Royal Divorce; Within the Maze; The Woman Who Obeyed; God's Prodigal. **1924** Fights Through the Ages (series). **1926** The Little People. **1927** The King's Highway. **1928** A Light Woman; The Rising Generation.

AMES, HARRY
Born: 1893. Died: Aug. 11, 1969, Hollywood, Calif. Screen and stage actor.

AMES, JIMMY
Born: 1915. Died: Aug. 14, 1965, Hollywood, Calif. (heart attack). Screen and television actor.

Appeared in: **1941** Love Crazy. **1942** Panama Hattie; The Tuttles of Tahiti; Woman of the Year. **1946** Daughter of Don Q (serial); Whistle Stop; The Kid from Brooklyn; The Best Years of Our Lives. **1947** Forever Amber; Daisy Kenyon; Ride the Pink Horse. **1948** Silver River; Smart Woman; River Lady; Calamity Jane and Sam Bass. **1949** The Lucky Stiff.

AMES, PERCY
Born: 1874, England. Died: Mar. 29, 1936, New York, N.Y. Screen and stage actor.

Appeared in: **1923** Adam and Eva. **1925** Soul Fire. **1934** Gambling.

AMES, ROBERT
Born: Mar. 23, 1898, Hartford, Conn. Died: Nov. 27, 1931, New York, N.Y. (bladder hemorrhage). Stage and screen actor. Entered films in 1925.

Appeared in: **1925** Without Mercy; The Wedding Song. **1926** Three Faces East; The Crown of Lies. **1929** Voice of the City; Marianne; Rich People; Black Waters; Nix on Dames; The Trespasser. **1930** Holiday; Madonna of the Streets; Double Cross Roads; Not Damaged; A Lady to Love; War Nurse. **1931** Rebound; Millie; Behind Office Doors; Smart Woman; Rich Man's Folly. **1932** The Slippery Pearls (short).

AMMON, ALICIA
Born: 1886, London, England. Died: Feb. 24, 1980, North Vancouver, British Columbia, Canada. Screen, stage, radio, television actor, stage producer and radio writer.

Appeared in: **1969** That Cold Day in the Park. **1975** Russian Roulette.

AMORES, ADELINA
Born: 1883, Spain. Died: Mar. 10, 1958, Madrid, Spain. Screen and stage actress.

AMUANARRIZ, RAUL CANCIO
Born: 1911, Spain. Died: Oct. 23, 1961, Madrid, Spain. Screen and stage actor who appeared in more than 100 Spanish films.

ANALLA, ISABEL
Born: 1920. Died: Jan. 17, 1958, San Francisco, Calif. (cancer). Screen and television actress.

Appeared in: **1957** Pal Joey; Kiss Them for Me. **1958** Vertigo.

ANDERS, GLENN
Born: 1889, Los Angeles, Calif. Died: Oct. 26, 1981, Englewood, N.J. Screen and stage actor.

Appeared in: **1930** Laughter. **1934** By Your Leave. **1941** Nothing But the Truth. **1948** The Lady from Shanghai. **1950** Nancy Goes to Rio. **1951** M; Behave Yourself; Tarzan's Peril.

ANDERSON, AUDLEY (Audley Lloyd Anderson)
Born: Mar. 5, 1885, Louisiana. Died: Dec. 19, 1966, Hollywood, Calif. (pulmonary edema). Screen actor.

Appeared in: **1957** Outlaw's Son.

ANDERSON, BRUCE
Born: England? Died: Nov. 29, 1973. Screen actor. Do not confuse with actor Bruce Anderson (dec. 1979).

Appeared in: **1952** Cry, the Beloved Country (aka African Fury—US). **1969** 2,000 Weeks (US 1970).

ANDERSON, BRUCE
Born: 1906. Died: Sept. 14, 1979, Johannesburg, South Africa. Screen, stage, radio actor, radio producer and singer.

ANDERSON, CLAIRE
Born: 1896, Detroit, Mich. Died: Mar. 23, 1964, Venice, Calif. Screen actress. Was one of the original Mack Sennett beauties.

Appeared in: **1916** Cinders of Love; The Lion and the Girl; A Male Governess; Bath Tub Perils; She Loved a Sailor. **1917** A Clever Dummy; Her Finishing Touch; The Late Lamented; The Hidden Spring. **1920** The Palace of Darkened Windows. **1921** The Road Demon; When We Were Twenty-One; Who Am I; The Servant in the House. **1922** The Yellow Stain. **1923** The Clean-Up. **1925** The Meddler.

ANDERSON, DALLAS
Born: 1875, Grieff, Scotland. Died: Nov. 16, 1934, Richmond, Va. Screen actor.

Appeared in: **1920** Branded; The Edge of Youth; The Fall of a Saint; The Forbidden Twins; Walls of Prejudice. **1921** Serving Two Masters.

ANDERSON, EDDIE "ROCHESTER"
Born: Sept. 18, 1905, Oakland, Calif. Died: Feb. 28, 1977, Woodland Hills, Calif. (heart attack). Black screen, vaudeville, radio and television actor. Son of minstrel performer Big Ed and circus performer Ella Mae Anderson. Appeared in vaudeville with his brother Cornelius in a song and dance team.

Appeared in: **1932** What Price Hollywood? **1936** Green Pastures; Transient Lady; Three Men on a Horse; Rainbow on the River. **1937** Melody for Two; Bill Cracks Down; On Such a Night; White Bondage; One Mile from Heaven; Over the Goal. **1938** Reckless Living; Gold Diggers in Paris; You Can't Take It With You; Going Places; Exposed; Thanks for the Memory; Jezebel; Kentucky. **1939** Honolulu; You Can't Cheat an Honest Man; Man About Town; Going Places; Gone With the Wind; Man Benny Rides Again; Love Thy Neighbor. **1941** Topper Returns; Kiss the Boys Goodbye; Birth of the Blues. **1942** Tales of Manhattan; Star Spangled Rhythm. **1943** Cabin in the Sky; The Meanest Man in the World; What's Buzzin' Cousin? **1944** Broadway Rhythm. **1945** Brewster's Millions; The Sailor Takes a Wife; I Love a Bandleader. **1946** The Show-Off. **1963** It's a Mad, Mad, Mad, Mad World.

ANDERSON, GENE
Born: 1931, London, England. Died: May 5, 1965, London, England (cerebral hemorrhage). Screen, stage and television actress. Married to actor Edward Judd.

Appeared in: **1953** Background (aka Edge of Divorce); The Intruder (US 1955). **1956** Doublecross. **1957** Yangtse Incident (aka Battle Hell—US); The Long Haul. **1960** The Shakedown. **1961** The Day the Earth Caught Fire (US 1962). **1962** The Break (US 1963).

ANDERSON, GEORGE
Born: 1891. Died: Aug. 28, 1948, Los Angeles, Calif. Screen and stage actor.

Appeared in: **1937** Under Suspicion. **1938** Born to Be Wild. **1939**

Million Dollar Legs; Our Neighbors, The Carters; King of Chinatown; The Lady's from Kentucky; Union Pacific; A Woman Is the Judge. **1940** Santa Fe Marshal; Hidden Gold; The Secret Seven. **1942** The Major and the Minor; The Palm Beach Story. **1943** Dixie; Henry Aldrich Haunts a House. **1944** Destination Tokyo; Henry Aldrich Plays Cupid; Wilson; Murder, My Sweet. **1945** Mildred Pierce; Nob Hill. **1946** Road to Utopia; The Killers; The Bride Wore Boots. **1947** Blaze of Noon. **1956** The Bottom of the Bottle.

ANDERSON, GILBERT M. "BRONCHO BILLY" (Max Aronson)
Born: Mar. 21, 1882, Little Rock, Ark. Died: Jan. 20, 1971, South Pasadena, Calif. Screen, stage, vaudeville, television actor, film director and screenwriter. In 1907 he co-founded Essanay Film Manufacturing Co. Won 1958 Special Academy Award for his pioneer contribution to the film industry. He appeared in "Broncho Billy" series, beginning in 1908 with The Bandit Makes Good; "Snakeville Comedy" series, beginning in 1911; and "Alkali Ike" series, beginning in 1912.

Appeared in: **1902** The Messenger Boy's Mistake (film debut). **1903** The Great Train Robbery. **1907** An Awful Skate. **1908** The Bandit Makes Good. **1909** The Heart of a Cowboy; The Indian Trailer; A Western Maid; The Ranchman's Rival; The Spanish Girl; His Reformation; Judgment; The Best Man Wins; A Tale of the West; The Black Sheep; A Mexican's Gratitude. **1910** Away Out West; The Cowboy and the Squaw; The Cowpuncher's Ward; The Flower of the Ranch; The Forest Ranger; The Mistaken Bandit; The Outlaw's Sacrifice; The Ranch Girl's Legacy; The Ranchman's Feud; The Sheriff's Sacrifice; The Bandit's Wife; Western Chivalry; Take Me Out to the Ball Game; The Bad Man's Last Deed; The Unknown Claim; Trailed by the West; The Desperado; Under Western Skies; The Dumb Half Breed's Defense; The Deputy's Love Affair; The Millionaire and the Girl; An Indian Girl's Love; The Pony Express Rider; The Tout's Remembrance; Patricia of the Plains; The Bearded Bandit; A Cowboy's Mother-in-Law; Pals of the Range; The Silent Message; A Westerner's Way; The Marked Trail; A Western Woman's Way; A Cowboy's Vindication; The Tenderfoot Messenger; A Gambler of the West; The Bad Man's Christmas; Broncho Billy's Redemption. **1911** The Girl from the Triple X; Last Round-Up; The Cowboy Coward; When Love and Honor Called; A Girl of the West; The Border Ranger; The Two Reformations; The Bad Man's Downfall; On the Desert's Edge; The Romance of Bar O; The Faithful Indian; A Thwarted Vengeance; Across the Plains; Carmenita the Faithful; The Sheriff's Chum; The Indian Maiden's Lesson; The Puncher's New Love; The Lucky Card; The Infant at Snakeville; The Tribe's Penalty; The Sheriff's Brother; The Hidden Mine; The Corporation and the Ranch Girl; The Count and the Cowboy; The Outlaw and the Child; Broncho Billy's Adventure. **1912** Broncho Billy's Outwitted; The Outlaw's Sacrifice; The Shotgun Ranchman; The Tomboy on Bar Z; The Ranch Girl's Trail; The Mother of the Ranch; An Indian Friendship; Cutting California Redwoods; Broncho Billy's Heart; The Dance at Silver Gulch; Broncho Billy's Mexican Wife; The Boss of the Katy Mine; Western Girls; Broncho Billy's Promise; The Prospector; The Sheriff's Luck; The Sheriff's Inheritance; The Reward for Broncho Billy; The Smuggler's Daughter; Alkali Ike Plays the Devil; Alkali Ike Stung!; Alkali Ike's Boarding House; Alkali Ike's Pants; Love on Tough Luck Ranch; Alkali Ike's Close Shave; Alkali Ike's Motorcycle. **1913** Oath; Alkali Ike's Misfortunes; Alkali Ike's in Jayville; Alkali Ike's Homecoming; Alkali Ike's Auto; Broncho Billy and the Maid; Broncho Billy and the Outlaw's Mother; Broncho Billy's Gun Play; The Sheriff's Child; The Making of Broncho Billy; The Sheriff's Story; Broncho Billy's Last Deed; Broncho Billy's Ward; Broncho Billy and the Squatter's Daughter; Broncho Billy and the Step-Sisters; Broncho Billy's Sister; Broncho Billy's Gratefulness; Broncho Billy's Way; The Sheriff's Honeymoon; Broncho Billy's Secret; Broncho Billy's First Arrest; Broncho Billy's Squareness; Broncho Billy's Christmas Deed; The Three Gamblers. **1914** The Treachery of Broncho Billy's Pal; Broncho Billy and the Rattler; Broncho Billy's True Love; Broncho Billy's Close Call; Broncho Billy Gun-Man; Broncho Billy's Sermon; Broncho Billy's Leap; Broncho Billy's Cunning; Broncho Billy's Duty; Broncho Billy's Jealousy; Broncho Billy and the Mine Shark; Broncho Billy Outlaw; Red Riding Hood of the Hills; Broncho Billy's Punishment; Broncho Billy and the Sheriff; The Redemption of Broncho Billy; Snakeville's New Doctor; Broncho Billy Guardian; Broncho Billy and the Bad Man; Broncho Billy and the Settler's Daughter; Broncho Billy and the Red Man; The Calling of Jim Barton; The Interference of Broncho Billy; Broncho Billy's Bible; Broncho Billy and the Sister; The Good-for-Nothing; Broncho Billy and the Claim Jumpers; Broncho Billy and athe Escaped Bandit. **1915** Broncho Billy and the Land Grabber; Broncho Billy and the Lumber King; Broncho Billy and the Posse; Broncho Billy Evens Matters; Broncho Billy's Love Affair; Broncho Billy Well Repaid; Broncho Billy's Marriage; Broncho Billy and the False Note; Broncho Billy and the Vigilante; Broncho Billy's Parents; Broncho Billy's Protege; Broncho

Billy's Sentence; Broncho Billy's Teachings; Broncho Billy and the Baby; Broncho Billy Begins Life Anew; Broncho Billy Sheepman; Broncho Billy's Brother; Broncho Billy's Greaser Deputy; Broncho Billy's Surrender; Broncho Billy's Word of Honor; Broncho Billy's Vengeance; Broncho Billy's Cowardly Brother; Broncho Billy Steps In. **1918** Shootin' Mad. **1965** The Bounty Killer.

ANDERSON, IVIE
Born: 1909, Gilroy, Calif. Died: Dec. 28, 1949, Los Angeles, Calif. Black singer and screen actress.

Appeared in: **1937** A Day at the Races; The Hit Parade.

ANDERSON, JAMES
Born: 1872. Died: Mar. 22, 1953, Glasgow, Scotland (burns received in fire). Screen, stage and radio actor.

Appeared in: **1925** The Freshman. **1926** Butterflies in the Rain; The College Boob; Flying High. **1928** Fleetwing. **1929** Welcome Danger. **1930** The Runaway Bride. **1941** Sergeant York. **1949** Whiskey Galore (aka Tight Little Island—US and Mad Little Island).

ANDERSON, JAMES "JIM"
Born: 1921. Died: Sept. 14, 1969, Billings, Mont. Screen actor. Entered films in 1951.

Appeared in: **1951** Hunt the Man Down; Along the Great Divide; Five. **1952** The Last Musketeer; Duel at Silver Creek; Ruby Gentry. **1953** China Venture; The Great Jesse James Raid; Flight to Tangier. **1954** Drums Across the River; Dragnet; Riot in Cell Block 11. **1955** An Annapolis Story; The Violent Men; The Marauders; Seven Angry Men. **1956** Fury at Gunsight Pass; Running Target; The Rawhide Years. **1957** The Big Land. **1958** I Married a Monster from Outer Space; The Thing That Couldn't Die. **1962** To Kill a Mockingbird; The Connection; Pressure Point. **1965** The Brig. **1969** Take the Money and Run. **1970** The Ballad of Cable Hogue; Little Big Man.

ANDERSON, JOAN
Died: May 14, 1974. Screen actress.

Appeared in: **1963** Lonnie.

ANDERSON, LAWRENCE
Born: 1893, London, England. Died: Mar. 28, 1939, London, England (pneumonia). Stage and screen actor. Entered films in 1920.

Appeared in: **1921** Innocent; Bluff. **1922** The Recoil. **1932** Threads. **1933** The Stickpin; Mayfair Girl; The Fire Raisers; The Right to Live. **1934** Nell Gwyn. **1936** Living Dangerously; His Lordship (aka Man of Affaires—US 1937). **1937** O.H.M.S. (aka You're in the Army Now—US); Make Up; Gangway. **1938** Let's Make a Night of It.

ANDERSON, LILLIAN
Born: Aug. 6, 1881, Indiana. Died: Aug. 25, 1962, Los Angeles, Calif. Screen actress and drama coach.

ANDERSON, MARGARET
Born: 1884. Died: Apr. 22, 1922. Screen and stage actress.

ANDERSON, MARY
Born: July 28, 1859, Sacramento, Calif. Died: May 29, 1940, Worcestershire, England. Screen, stage actress and playwright. Do not confuse with U.S. actress Mary Anderson.

ANDERSON, RUTH
Born: 1923, Lakewood, Ohio. Died: June 22, 1980, Santa Monica, Calif. Screen, stage actress, film director and screenwriter. Married to screenwriter John W. Bloch.

ANDERSON, WARNER
Born: Mar. 10, 1911, Brooklyn, N.Y. Died: Aug. 26, 1976, Santa Monica, Calif. Screen, stage and television actor. Entered films in 1915 at age four.

Appeared in: **1943** Destination Tokyo. **1945** Dangerous Partners; Objective Burma; Abbott and Costello in Hollywood; Her Highness and the Bellboy; Weekend at the Waldorf. **1946** Bad Bascomb; My Reputation; Three Wise Fools; Faithful in My Fashion. **1947** The Arnelo Affair; The Beginning or the End; Dark Delusion; High Wall; Song of the Thin Man. **1948** Alias a Gentleman; 10th Avenue Angel; Command Decision. **1949** The Lucky Stiff; The Doctor and the Girl. **1950** Destination Moon. **1951** Detective Story; The Blue Veil; Santa Fe; Go for Broke; Bannerline; Only the Valiant. **1953** The Last Posse; The Star; A Lion Is in the Street. **1954** The Yellow Tomahawk; The Caine Mutiny; Drum Beat. **1955** Blackboard Jungle; Lawless Street; Violent Men (aka Rough Company). **1958** The Line-up. **1961** Armored Command. **1964** Rio Conchos.

ANDERSON, WILLIAM "CAT" (William Alonzo Anderson)
Born: 1917. Died: Apr. 30, 1981, Norwalk, Calif. (cancer). Black trumpet player, band leader, screen and television actor.

Appeared in: **1972** Lady Sings the Blues.

ANDRA, FERN (aka FERN ANDRE)
Born: Feb. 24, 1893, Watseka, Ill. Died: Feb. 8, 1974, Aiken, S.C. (cancer). Screen, stage, vaudeville actress, film director, producer and screenwriter. Appeared in German, British and U.S. films. Entered films in Vienna.

Appeared in: **1915** Eine Motte Flog zum Licht; Zwei Freude. **1916** Ernst ist das Leben; Little Eve Edgarton. **1917** Des Lebens Ungemischte Freude (serial); Uncle Tom's Cabin. **1918** Um Krome und Peitsche. **1919** Gebannt und Erloest. **1920** Genuine; Madame Recamier; Die Nacht der Koenigin Isabeau. **1921** Die Treibende Kraft. **1923** L'Incubo di Za-La-Vie; Der Rote Reiter; Zalamort (aka Der Traum der Zalavie). **1924** L'Ergastolano Innocente; Die Liebe ist der Frauen Macht (aka Kabale und Liebe im Zirkus). **1925** ... und es Lockt ein Ruf aus Suendiger Welt. **1926** Frauen der Leidenschaft. **1927** Funkzauber. **1928** Spangles; The Burgomaster of Stilemonde. **1930** The Lotus Lady; Eyes of the World.

ANDRE, CHARLES
Died: 1966. Screen actor.

Appeared in: **1942** Seven Days' Leave. **1945** Paris Underground. **1949** The Secret of St. Ives. **1951** On the Riviera. **1953** I Confess.

ANDRE, GABY
Died: Aug. 9, 1972, Rome, Italy (cancer). Screen actress. Mother of actress Carol Andre.

Appeared in: **1939** Fin du Jour (End of a Day). **1950** Please Believe Me; Hoboes in Paradise; Highway 301. **1952** The Green Glove; L'Ingiusta Condanna (Guilt Is Not Mine—US 1968). **1957** The Life and Music of Giuseppe Verdi. **1958** Incognito; The Crawling Terror. **1959** The Cosmic Monsters (aka Strange World of Planet X). **1960** Goliath and the Dragon. **1962** East of Kilimanjaro (aka La Grande Caccia (The Big Hunt) and The Big Search). **1970** Pussycat, Pussycat, I Love You. Other foreign films: Stage Door; Paradise Lost; The Heir of Mondesir; Strange Suzy; L'Ange de la Nuit; Un Seul Amour; $2,000,000 Bank Robbery; The Victim; Angel of Sin; Donatella; Verde; Moglie e Amante.

ANDRE, GWILI
Born: 1908, Copenhagen, Denmark. Died: Feb. 5, 1959, Venice, Calif. (apartment fire). Screen actress.

Appeared in: **1932** The Roar of the Dragon; Secrets of the French Police. **1933** No Other Woman. **1937** The Girl Said No; Meet the Boy Friend. **1941** A Woman's Face. **1942** The Public Be Damned; The Falcon's Brother.

ANDRE, MONYA (Monya Andree)
Died: Jan. 5, 1981, Los Angeles, Calif.? Screen actress.

Appeared in: **1925** The Police Patrol. **1934** Search for Beauty. **1937** Guilding the Lily (short).

ANDREWS, ADORA
Born: 1872, Denver, Colo. Died: Sept. 18, 1956, Rye, N.Y. Screen and stage actress.

Appeared in: **1932** Smiling Faces.

ANDREWS, BART
Died: July 31, 1969, New York, N.Y. Screen actor.

Appeared in: **1965** Superman vs. the Gorilla Gang (short). **1966** Rocketman Flies Again (short).

ANDREWS, LAVERNE
Born: July 6, 1915, Minneapolis, Minn. Died: May 8, 1967, West Los Angeles, Calif. (cancer). Screen, radio, television actress and vaudeville singer. One of the "Andrews Sisters" trio.

Appeared in: **1940** Argentine Nights. **1941** Buck Privates; In the Navy; Hold That Ghost; Private Buckaroo. **1942** What's Cookin'?; Give Out, Sisters. **1943** How's About It?; Always a Bridesmaid. **1944** Swingtime Johnny; Moonlight and Cactus; Follow the Boys; Hollywood Canteen. **1945** Her Lucky Night. **1946** Make Mine Music. **1947** Road to Rio. **1948** Melody Time.

ANDREWS, LOIS (Lorraine Gourley)
Born: Mar. 24, 1924, Huntington Park, Calif. Died: Apr., 1968, Encino, Calif. (lung cancer). Stage and screen actress. Divorced from entertainer George Jessel (dec. 1981).

Appeared in: **1943** Dixie Dugan; Roger Touhy, Gangster. **1949** Rustlers. **1950** The Desert Hawk. **1951** Meet Me After the Show.

ANDREWS, ORVILLE
Born: Nebr. Died: Mar. 29, 1968, Hartford, Conn. Screen, television actor and radio comedy singer.

ANDREWS, STANLEY
Born: 1892. Died: June 23, 1969, Los Angeles, Calif. Screen and television actor.

Appeared in: **1935** All the King's Horses; Private Worlds; People Will Talk; The Crusades; Nevada; Wanderer of the Wasteland; Drift Fence; Hold 'Em Yale; Escape from Devil's Island; The Big Broadcast of 1936; She Gets Her Man; Alias Mary Dow; Goin' to Town. **1936** Wild Brian Kent; Desire; Foolproof (short); In His Steps; Happy Go Lucky. **1937** John Meade's Woman; High, Wide and Handsome; The Devil's Playground; Easy Living; The Man Who Found Himself; Nancy Steele Is Missing; She's Dangerous; The Man Who Cried Wolf. **1938** The Buccaneer; Cocoanut Grove; Spawn of the North; The Mysterious Rider; Prairie Moon; When G-Men Step In; Blondie; Adventure in Sahara; Alexander's Ragtime Band; I'll Give a Million; Kentucky; The Lone Ranger (serial); Stablemates; Forbidden Valley. **1939** Andy Hardy Gets Spring Fever; Mr. Smith Goes to Washington; Homicide Bureau; Beau Geste; Union Pacific; Geronimo. **1940** King of the Royal Mounted (serial); The Blue Bird; Little Old New York; Brigham Young—Frontiersman; Kit Carson. **1941** In Old Colorado; Play Girl; Meet John Doe; Strange Alibi; Mr. and Mrs. North; Wild Geese Calling; Time Out for Rhythm. **1942** Valley of the Sun; North to the Klondike; The Fleet's In; Reap the Wild Wind; The Major and the Minor; Canal Zone; My Gal Sal; The Postman Didn't Ring; Ten Gentlemen from West Point. **1943** Daredevils of the West (serial); Crash Dive. **1944** Murder, My Sweet; Tucson Raiders; Princess and the Pirate; Sensations of 1945; Follow the Boys; Lake Placid Serenade; The Hitler Gang. **1945** Keep Your Powder Dry; Practically Yours; Trail to Vengeance; Road to Utopia. **1946** The Virginian; California; Til the Clouds Roll By. **1947** Desire Me; Road to Rio; Easy Come, Easy Go; Trail Street; Robin Hood of Texas; Michigan Kid. **1948** Adventures of Frank and Jesse James (serial); The Return of Wildfire; Last of the Wild Horses; State of the Union; Sinister Journey; The Dead Don't Dream; The Valiant Hombre; Dock of New Orleans; The Paleface; Northwest Stampede; My Dear Secretary; The Fuller Brush Man. **1949** Blondie's Big Deal; Brothers in the Saddle; Man from Colorado; Trail of the Yukon; The Last Bandit; Brimstone; Tough Assignment. **1950** Colt 45; Where Danger Lives; Across the Badlands; Arizona Cowboy; Blonde Dynamite; Mule Train; The Nevadan; Outcast of Black Mesa; Salt Lake Raiders; Short Grass; Streets of Ghost Town; Trigger, Jr.; Two Flags West; Tyrant of the Sea; Under Mexicali Stars; West of Wyoming. **1951** The Lemon Drop Kid; Al Jennings of Oklahoma; Saddle Legion; Silver Canyon; Utah Wagon Train; Vengeance Valley. **1952** The Bad and the Beautiful; The Greatest Show on Earth; Carson City; Fargo; Kansas Territory; The Man from Black Hills; Montana Belle; Talk About a Stranger; Thundering Caravans; Waco. **1953** Canadian Mounties vs. Atomic Invaders (serial); Appointment in Honduras; Dangerous Crossing. **1954** Dawn at Socorro; Southwest Passage; The Steel Cage. **1955** Treasure of Ruby Hills. **1956** Frontier Gambler.

ANDREWS, TOD
Born: 1920. Died: Nov. 6, 1972, Beverly Hills, Calif. (heart attack). Screen, stage and television actor.

Appeared in: **1941** Murder in the Big House; Dive Bomber; They Died With Their Boots On. **1942** The Male Animal; Now Voyager. **1943** Heaven Can Wait. **1950** Outrage. **1956** Between Heaven and Hell. **1957** From Hell It Came. **1965** In Harm's Way. **1968** Hang 'Em High. **1969** Changes. **1970** Beneath the Planet of the Apes.

ANDREYER, YVETTE
Born: 1892. Died: 1962. Screen actress. Appeared in Gaument Film Co. films.

Appeared in: **1948** Un Ami Viendra ce Soir (A Friend Will Come Tonight).

ANGELI, PIER (Anna Maria Pierangeli)
Born: June 19, 1932, Sardinia, Italy. Died: Sept. 10, 1971, Beverly Hills, Calif. (overdose of drugs). Screen, stage and television actress. Twin sister of actress Marisa Pavan. Divorced from singer/actor Vic Damone.

Appeared in: **1951** Teresa; The Light Touch. **1952** The Devil Makes Three; Tomorrow Is Too Late. **1953** The Story of Three Loves (aka Equilibrium); Sombrero. **1954** Flame and the Flesh; The Silver Chalice. **1956** Port Afrique; Somebody Up There Likes Me. **1957** The Vintage. **1958** Merry Andrew. **1960** S.O.S. Pacific; The Angry Silence. **1961** Sodoma e Gomorra (Sodom and Gomorrah—US 1963 and aka Last Days of Sodom and Gomorrah). **1962** White Slave Ship. **1964** Banco a Bangkok (aka OSS 17 and Shadow of Evil—US 1967). **1965** The Battle of the Bulge. **1966** Spy in Your Eye. **1968** Rey de Africa (aka King of Africa and One Step to Hell—US 1969); Kol Mamzer Melech (aka Every Bastard a King—US 1970). **1970** Nelle Piege Carne; Addio Alexandra (aka Love Me, Love My Wife); Octamon.

ANGELO, JEAN
Born: 1888. Died: Nov. 26, 1933, Paris, France. Screen and stage actor.

Appeared in: **1928** Une Java. **1929** Nana; La Vierge Folle. **1930** The Strange Case of District Attorney M. **1932** L'Atlantide.

ANGOLD, EDIT (Edit Goldstandt)
Born: 1895, Berlin, Germany. Died: Oct. 4, 1971, Los Angeles, Calif. Screen, stage, radio and television actress.

Appeared in: **1944** Tomorrow the World! (stage and film version). **1946** Suspense. **1949** Ringside; Tough Assignment. **1950** The Secret Fury; The White Tower; Molly (aka The Goldbergs, film and radio versions). **1951** The Great Caruso. **1952** Woman in the Dark. **1953** Murder Without Tears. **1956** The Birds and the Bees. **1957** Bernardine. **1958** A Certain Smile. **1959** The Blue Angel. **1960** G.I. Blues.

ANKRUM, MORRIS (Morris Nussbaum aka STEPHEN MORRIS)
Born: Aug. 28, 1897, Danville, Ill. Died: Sept. 2, 1964, Pasadena, Calif. (trichinosis). Screen, stage actor and film director.

Appeared in: **1933** Reunion in Vienna. **1936** Hopalong Cassidy Returns; Trail Dust. **1937** Borderland; Hills of Old Wyoming; North of the Rio Grande; Rustler's Valley. **1940** Buck Benny Rides Again; Knights of the Range; The Showdown; Three Men from Texas; Light of the Western Stars; Cherokee Strip. **1941** I Wake Up Screaming; This Woman Is Mine; The Roundup; In Old Colorado; Border Vigilantes; Wide Open Town; Doomed Caravan; Pirates on Horseback; Road Agent; The Bandit Trail. **1942** Tales of Manhattan; Ten Gentlemen from West Point; The Loves of Edgar Allen Poe; The Omaha Trail; Time to Kill; Tennessee Johnson. **1943** Let's Face It; Reunion in France; Swing Fever; Dixie Dugan; The Heavenly Body. **1944** Thirty Seconds Over Tokyo; See Here Private Hargrove; Marriage Is a Private Affair; Barbary Coast Gent; Meet the People; Rationing; Gentle Annie; The Thin Man Goes Home; plus the following shorts: Dark Shadows; Radio Bugs; and Return from Nowhere. **1945** The Hidden Eye. **1946** The Postman Always Rings Twice; Undercurrent; The Harvey Girls; Courage of Lassie; Little Mr. Jim; Cockeyed Miracle; Lady in the Lake; The Mighty McGurk. **1947** Undercover Maisie; Cynthia; Good News; Desire Me; High Wall; Sea of Grass. **1948** The Fabulous Fraud (short); Joan of Arc; For the Love of Mary; Fighting Back; Bad Men of Tombstone. **1949** We Were Strangers; Colorado Territory; Slattery's Hurricane. **1950** Borderline; Chain Lightning; The Damned Don't Cry; Redhead and the Cowboy; Rocketship XM; In a Lonely Place; Short Grass; Southside 1-000. **1951** Tomorrow Is Another Day; My Favorite Spy; Fighting Coast Guard; Along the Great Divide; The Lion Hunters; Flight to Mars. **1952** The Raiders; The Man Behind the Gun; Hiawatha; Mutiny; Red Planet Mars; Son of Ali Baba; Fort Osage. **1953** Arena; Devil's Canyon; The Moonlighter; Invaders from Mars; Fort Vengeance; Sky Commando; Mexican Manhunt. **1954** Vera Cruz; Southwest Passage; Apache; The Three Young Texans; Taza, Son of Cochise; Silver Lode; Drums Across the River; The Steel Cage; Cattle Queen of Montana; Two Guns and a Badge; The Outlaw Stallion; The Saracen Blade. **1955** Chief Crazy Horse; The Eternal Sea; The Silver Star; Tennessee's Partner; No Man's Woman; Crashout; Jupiter's Darling; Abbott and Costello Meet the Mummy; Jujin Yukiotoko (Half Human). **1956** Fury at Gunsight Pass; Quincannon, Frontier Scout; Earth vs. The Flying Saucers; Death of a Scoundrel; Walk the Proud Land; When Gangland Strikes. **1957** Omar Khayyam; Hell's Crossroads; Drango; Zombies of Mora-Tau; Kronos; The Giant Claw; Beginning of the End. **1958** Badman's Country; Tarawa Beachhead; From the Earth to the Moon; Twilight for the Gods; Young and Wild; The Saga of Hemp Brown; Frontier Gun; How to Make a Monster; Giant From Unknown. **1961** The Most Dangerous Man Alive; The Little Shepherd of Kingdom Come. **1963** The Man With the X-Ray Eyes.

ANSELMI, ROSINA
Born: 1880, Italy. Died: May 23, 1965, Cantania, Sicily. Stage and screen actress.

Appeared in: **1935** The Rich Uncle; L'Eredita dello Zio; L'Aria del

Continente (Continental Atmosphere—US 1939); Milizia Territoriale. **1937** El Feroce Saladino; Signora Fortuna (Lady Luck); Gat Ci Cova; Lasciate Ogni Speranza. **1939** El Marchese De Rivolito (The Marquis of Rivolito); L'Ha Fatto Una Signora (A Woman Did It); Re di Danari (Money King). **1940** El Paraninfo (The Matchmaker).

ANSON, A. E.
Born: Sept. 14, 1879, England. Died: June 25, 1936, Monrovia, Calif. Stage and screen actor. Son of actor George W. Anson (dec. 1920).

Appeared in: **1931** Arrowsmith; The Road to Singapore.

ANSON, GEORGE WILLIAM
Born: Nov. 25, 1847, Montrose, Scotland. Died: Aug. 2, 1920, England? Screen actor. Father of Actor A. E. Anson (dec. 1936).

Appeared in: **1914** The Builder of Bridges. **1920** The Magic Skin (aka Desire).

ANSON, LAURA
Born: 1892. Died: July 15, 1968, Woodland Hills, Calif. Screen actress. Married to actor Philo McCullough. She was a leading lady of Roscoe "Fatty" Arbuckle.

Appeared in: **1921** The Easy Road; Crazy to Marry; The Little Clown. **1922** Bluebeard, Jr.; If You Believe It, It's So; The Great Alone. **1923** Flames of Passion; Skid Proof; The Call of the Canyon; The Silent Partner; The Way of the Transgressor.

ANTHONY, JACK (John Anthony Herbertson)
Born: 1901, Scotland. Died: Feb. 28, 1962, Dunbar, Scotland (coronary thrombosis). Screen, stage, vaudeville and radio actor.

ANTHONY, JOHN J.
Died: July 6, 1970, San Francisco, Calif. (heart attack). Screen and radio actor.

Appeared in: **1967** Divorce American Style.

ANTONY, P. J.
Born: 1924, India. Died: Apr., 1979, Madras, India. Screen actor, film director, playwright, singer, lyricist and harmonium player.

ANTRIM, HARRY
Born: 1895, Chicago, Ill. Died: Jan. 18, 1967, Hollywood, Calif. (heart attack). Screen, stage, television and vaudeville actor.

Appeared in: **1947** Miracle on 34th Street (film debut). **1948** The Luck of the Irish; Larceny; Let's Live a Little; Words and Music; Act of Violence. **1949** Free for All; Johnny Allegro; Thelma Jordan (aka File on Thelma Jordan); Intruder in the Dust; Prison Warden; The Heiress; Chicago Deadline; Ma and Pa Kettle. **1950** Devil's Doorway; I'll Get By; Outside the Wall; No Man of Her Own; Side Street; There's A Girl in My Heart. **1951** Appointment with Danger; Night Into Morning; Meet Me After the Show; Tommorow is Another Day; Follow the Sun; Mr. Belvedere Rings the Bell; I'll See You in My Dreams. **1952** The Lion and the Horse; Mutiny. **1954** The Bounty Hunter. **1955** A Lawless Street. **1956** The Solid Gold Cadillac. **1958** Teacher's Pet. **1959** Gunmen from Laredo. **1965** The Monkey's Uncle.

AOKI, TSURU
Born: Sept. 9, 1892, Tokyo, Japan. Died: Oct. 18, 1961, Tokyo, Japan (acute peritonitis). Screen and stage actress. Married to actor Sessue Hayakawa (dec. 1973).

Appeared in: **1914** The Typhoon; The Wrath of the Gods (aka The Destruction of Sakura-Jima); The Vigil. **1916** Alien Souls; The Honorable Friend. **1917** Each to His Kind; The Call of the East. **1918** The Bravest Way; His Birth Right. **1919** Bonds of Honor; A Heart in Pawn; The Courageous Coward; The Gray Horizon (aka A Dead Line); The Dragon Painter; The Rajah's Amulet (reissue of 1917 Each To His Kind). **1920** The Breath of the Gods. **1921** Black Roses. **1922** Night Life in Hollywood; Five Days to Live. **1923** La Bataille. **1924** The Danger Line; The Great Shan; Sen Yan's Devotion. **1960** Hell to Eternity.

APFEL, OSCAR C.
Born: Cleveland, Ohio. Died: Mar. 21, 1938, Hollywood, Calif. (heart attack). Screen, stage actor, film, stage director and stage producer. Entered films with Edison and Reliance in 1911.

Appeared in: **1922** Ten Nights in a Bar Room; Auction of Souls; The Man Who Paid; The Wolf's Fangs. **1923** A Man's Man; In Search of a Thrill; The Social Code. **1924** The Heart Bandit; Trail of the Law. **1925** Borrowed Finery; The Thoroughbred; The Sporting Chance. **1926** Perils of the Coast Guard; Somebody's Mother; The Call of the

Klondike; The Last Alarm; Midnight Limited; Race Wild. **1927** When Seconds Count; Cheaters; Code of the Country. **1928** The Valley of Hunted Men; The Heart of Broadway; Romance of the Underworld. **1929** Marianne; Not Quite Decent; True Heaven; Halfway to Heaven; Smiling Irish Eyes; Hurdy Gurdy. **1930** The Texan; Misbehaving Ladies; The Spoilers; Virtuous Sin; The Right to Love; Man Trouble; Abraham Lincoln. **1931** Men in Her Life; Huckleberry Finn; Helping Grandma (short); Five-Star Final; Finger Points; Wicked; Big Business Girl; The Maltese Falcon; Sidewalks of New York; The Bargain; Sooky; Inspiration. **1932** State's Attorney; High Pressure; Woman from Monte Carlo; Hot Saturday; Shopworn; East Side; Cardigan's Last Case; The Silent Voice; Business and Pleasure; Woman in Room 13; You Said a Mouthful; Heart of New York; It's Tough To Be Famous; Old Greatheart; The World and the Flesh; Alias the Doctor; When a Fellow Needs a Friend; Two Against the World; Mad Masquerade; Sporting Widow; Way Back Home; The Man Who Played God; Make Me a Star; Hell's Highway; False Faces; Madame Racketeer. **1933** Pick Up; Story of Temple Drake; Tomorrow at Seven; Emergency Call; One Man's Journey; Before Dawn; Ladies Must Love; Only Yesterday; The Bowery; The World Changes; Hold the Press. **1934** Fifteen Wives; The Old-Fashioned Way; Take the Stand; I Am a Thief; Romance in Manhattan; Beloved; Madame Spy; It Happened One Day (short); You Said a Hateful (short); The House of Rothschild; Are We Civilized?; White Lies; Whirlpool. **1935** Border Town; Two Faces; Death Flies East; The Nut Farm; Mary Jane's Pa; The Man on the Flying Trapeze; Cappy Ricks Returns; O'Shaughnessey's Boy; His Night Out; Another Face; The Fire Trap. **1936** Murder at Glen Athol; Sutter's Gold; Bridge of Sighs; Every Saturday Night; The Criminal Within; Hearts in Bondage; Bulldog Edition; And Sudden Death; Hollywood Boulevard; We Who Are About to Die; The Plot Thickens; Crack-Up. **1937** Fifty Roads to Town; The Soldier and the Lady; Conquest; Shadows of the Orient; History Is Made at Night; Trouble in Morocco; Jim Hanvey-Detective; The Toast of New York.

APOLLON, DAVID "DAVE"
Born: 1898, Kiev, Russia. Died: May 30, 1972, Las Vegas, Nev. (heart attack). Screen actor and orchestra leader.

Appeared in: **1937** Merry-Go-Round of 1938.

APPEL, ANNA
Born: 1888. Died: Nov. 19, 1963, New York, N.Y. Screen, stage and television actress.

Appeared in: **1926** Broken Hearts. **1929** Ad Musal (The Eternal Prayer). **1932** The Heart of New York; Symphony of Six Million; Faithless. **1937** Green Fields; The Singing Blacksmith.

APPLEGARTH, JONAS
Born: 1920. Died: July 23, 1965, Bashaw, Alberta, Canada (auto accident). Screen actor.

Appeared in: **1954** Saskatchewan. **1955** Battle Cry. **1959** The Sheriff of Fractured Jaw.

APPLEGATE, HAZEL
Born: 1886. Died: Oct. 30, 1959, Chicago, Ill. Screen actress. Entered films in Chicago with Essaney.

APPLEWHITE, "RIC" (Eric Leon Applewhite)
Born: 1897. Died: May 29, 1973, Miami, Fla. Screen and television actor.

Appeared in: **1954** Dial M for Murder. **1961** X-15.

AQUISTAPACE, JEAN
Born: 1882, France. Died: Oct. 20, 1952, Nice, France. Screen actor and opera singer. Appeared in a number of French films.

ARASHI, KANJURO
Born: 1903, Japan. Died: Oct. 21, 1980, Japan? Screen actor.

Appeared in: **1968** Higashi Shinkai (aka East China Sea—US 1969); Kamigami no Fukaki Yokubo (aka Deep Desire of Gods, and aka Kuragejima—Legends from a Southern Island—US 1970). **1970** Zato Ichi to Yojimbo (Zatoichi Meets Yojimbo).

ARBENZ, ARABELLA
Born: 1945. Died: Oct. 5, 1965, Bogota, Colombia (suicide—gun). Screen actress.

Appeared in: A Pure Soul (played dual lead role, in Mexico and N.Y., in the experimental film).

ARBUCKLE, ANDREW
Born: Sept. 5, 1884 or 1887, Galveston, Texas. Died: Sept. 21, 1939, Los Angeles, Calif. Screen, stage and vaudeville actor.

Appeared in: **1915** Old Heidelberg. **1916** Big Tremaine; Little Mary Sunshine; Matrimonial Martyr. **1917** Happiness; Peggy Leads the Way. **1919** Romance of Happy Valley; A White Man's Chance; John Petticoats; The Hoodlum. **1920** Pinto. **1921** Light in the Clearing; Son of the Wallingford; Mother O'Mine. **1922** Caught Bluffing; The Deuce of Spades; Quincy Adams Sawyer; Saved by Radio. **1923** The Spider and the Rose. **1924** Name the Man; Clean Heart; The Dangerous Coward. **1926** The Fighting Boob. **1927** Hazardous Valleys. **1928** Jazz Mad.

ARBUCKLE, MACKLYN
Born: July 9, 1866, San Antonio, Tex. Died: Apr. 1, 1931, Waddington, N.Y. Screen and stage actor.

Appeared in: **1915** The County Chairman. **1922** The Prodigal Judge; Squire Phin; Welcome to Our City; Mr. Potter of Texas; Mr. Bingle; The Young Diana. **1923** Broadway Broke. **1924** Yolanda; Janice Meredith. **1925** That Old Gang of Mine; Lure of the Track; The Thoroughbred. **1926** The Gilded Highway.

ARBUCKLE, ROSCOE "FATTY"
Born: Mar. 24, 1887, San Jose, Calif. Died: June 29, 1933, New York, N.Y. (heart attack). Screen, stage, vaudeville, burlesque actor, film director and producer. Directed under name of William Goodrich. Married to actress Addie McPhail. Divorced from actresses Doris Deane (dec. 1974) and Minta Durffee (dec. 1975).

Appeared in: **1909** Ben's Kid; Mrs. Jones' Birthday; Making It Pleasant for Him. **1910** The Sanitarium. **1913** Alas! Poor Yorick; The Gangsters (aka The Feud); Passions, He Had Three (aka He Had Three and Possums, He Had Three); Help! Help! Hydrophobia!; The Waiters' Picnic; A Bandit; Peeping Pete; For the Love of Mabel; The Telltale Light; A Noise from the Deep; Love and Courage; Professor Bean's Removal; The Riot; Mabel's New Hero (aka Fatty and the Bathing Beauties); Fatty's Day Off; Mabel's Dramatic Career (aka Her Dramatic Debut); The Gypsy Queen; The Fatal Taxicab (aka The Faithful Taxicab); When Dreams Come True; Mother's Boy (aka Mother's Boys); Two Old Tars (aka The Sea Dogs); A Quiet Little Wedding; The Speed Kings; Fatty at San Diego (aka A Jealous Husband); Wine (aka Wine Making); Fatty Joins the Force; The Woman Haters (aka The Woman Hater); Ride for a Bride; Fatty's Flirtation (aka The Masher); His Sister's Kids; He Would a Hunting Go. **1914** A Misplaced Foot; The Under Sheriff; A Flirt's Mistake; In the Clutches of the Gang; Rebecca's Wedding Day; A Robust Romeo; Twixt Love and Fire; A Film Johnnie (aka Movie Nut; Million Dollar Job); Tango Tangles (aka Charlie's Recreation; Music Hall); Her Favorite Pastime (aka The Bonehead; Charlie Is Thisty); A Rural Demon; Barnyard Flirtations; Chicken Chaser (aka New Yard Lovers); A Suspended Ordeal; The Water Dog (aka The Rescue); The Alarm (aka Fireman's Picnic); The Knockout (aka Counted Out; The Pugilist); Fatty and the Heiress; Fatty's Finish; Love and Bullets (aka The Trouble Mender); A Rowboat Romance; The Sky Pirate; Those Happy Days; That Minstrel Man; Those Country Kids; Fatty's Gift; The Masquerader (aka Putting One Over; The Female Impersonator; The Picnic; His New Profession; Charlie at the Studio; Charlie the Actor); A Brand New Hero; The Rounders (aka Revelry; Two of a Kind; Oh, What a Night); Lover's Luck; Fatty's Debut (aka Fatty Butts In); Fatty Again (aka Fatty the Fourflusher); Their Ups and Downs; Zip, the Dodger; Lovers' Post Office; An Incompetent Hero; Fatty's Jonah Day (aka Fatty's Hoodoo Day); Fatty's Wine Party; The Sea Numphs; Leading Lizzie Astray; Shotguns That Kick; Fatty's Magic Pants (aka Fatty's Suitless Day); Fatty and Minnie-He-Haw. **1915** Mabel and Fatty's Wash Day; Fatty and Mabel's Simple Life; Fatty and Mabel at the San Diego Exposition; Mabel, Fatty and the Law; Fatty's New Role; Mabel and Fatty's Married Life; Fatty's Reckless Fling; Fatty's Chance Acquaintance; Love in Armor; That Little Band of Gold; Fatty's Faithful Fido (aka Fatty's Fatal Fido); When Love Took Wings; Wished on Mabel; Mabel and Fatty Viewing the World's Fair at San Francisco; Mabel's Wilful Way; Miss Fatty's Seaside Lovers; The Little Teacher (aka Small Town Bully); Fatty's Plucky Pup (aka Foiled by Fido); Fatty's Tintype Tangle; Fickle Fatty's Fall; The Village Scandal; Fatty and the Broadway Stars. **1916** Fatty and Mabel Adrift; He Did and He Didn't; The Bright Lights (aka The Lure of Broadway); His Wife's Mistake; The Other Man; The Waiters' Ball; A Reckless Romeo; A Creampuff Romance. **1917** The Butcher Boy; The Rough House; His Wedding Night; Oh, Doctor!; Fatty at Coney Island; A Country Hero. **1918** Out West; The Bell Boy; Moonshine; Good Night, Nurse!; The Cook; The Sheriff; United States Fourth Liberty Loan Drive; Canadian Victory Loan Drive; Camping Out; The Pullman Porter; Love; The Bank Clerk; A Desert Hero; Back

Stage; The Hayseed. **1920** The Garage; The Round Up; The Life of the Party. **1921** Brewster's Millions; The Dollar a Year Man; The Traveling Salesman; Gasoling Gus; Crazy to Marry; Leap Year (aka This is So Sudden; Skirt Shy); Freight Prepaid (aka The Fast Freight; Handle with Care). **1923** Hollywood. **1925** Go West. **1932** Hey, Pop (short). **1933** The following shorts: Buzzin' Around; How've You Bean?; Close Relations; In the Dough; Tomalio. **1951** Memories of Famous Hollywood comedians (film clips). **1960** When Comedy Was King (doc.). **1961** Days of Thrills and Laughter (doc.).

ARBURY, GUY
Born: 1907. Died: Dec. 26, 1972, New York, N.Y. (stab wounds). Screen, stage and television actor.

Appeared in: **1970** Kremlin Letter. **1971** They Might Be Giants. **1972** Lady Liberty.

ARCARO, FLAVIA
Born: 1876. Died: Apr. 8, 1937, New York, N.Y. Screen, stage and vaudeville actress.

ARCHAINBAUD, GEORGE
Born: May 7, 1890, Paris, France. Died: Feb. 20, 1959, Beverly Hills, Calif. (heart attack). Screen, stage actor, film, television director and film producer.

ARCHER, ANNE
Born: 1912. Died: Aug. 5, 1959, Los Angeles, Calif. Screen actress.

Appeared in: **1944** Cover Girl.

ARCHER, LOUIS A. "LOU"
Born: 1874. Died: Aug., 1922, Hollywood, Calif. Screen actor.

Appeared in: **1926** Lightning Reporter. **1927** Babe Comes Home; Duty's Reward.

ARDELL, JOHN E.
Born: 1881. Died: Apr. 26, 1949, Hollywood, Calif. (monoxide gas). Screen actor.

ARDELL, LILLIAN
Died: Mar. 15, 1950, New York, N.Y. Screen and stage actress.

Appeared in: **1926** Rainbow Riley. **1931** Alice in Wonderland. **1937** The Good Earth.

ARDEN, EDDIE
Born: 1908. Died: June 23, 1952, Hollywood, Calif. (heart attack). Stage and screen actor.

ARDEN, EDWIN
Born: Feb. 13, 1864, St. Louis, Mo. Died: Oct. 2, 1918, New York, N.Y. (heart attack). Screen and stage actor.

Appeared in: **1915** Eagle's Nest; The New Exploits of Elaine (serial); The Beloved Vagabond; Simon, the Jester; The Grey Mask. **1917** The Iron Heart. **1918** Virtuous Wives. **1919** Ruling Passions.

ARDEN, JANE
Born: 1905. Died: Mar. 21, 1981, Studio City, Calif. Screen actress, film director, screenwriter and author.

Appeared in: **1926** The Escape. **1968** Separation.

ARDEN, VICTOR
Born: 1893, Ill. Died: July 30, 1962, New York, N.Y. Screen actor, orchestra leader, musician and radio performer.

ARENA, MAURIZIO
Born: 1933, Italy. Died: Nov. 1979, Rome, Italy (apparent heart attack). Screen and television actor.

Appeared in: **1957** It Happened in the Park; Un Angel Paso Sobre Brooklyn (aka The Man Who Wagged His Tail—US 1961). **1958** Belle Ma Povere (Poor But Beautiful—US). **1960** Holiday Island. **1963** Marschier oder Krepier (aka Commando—US 1964). **1965** Bambole (The Dolls, aka Treatise on Eugenics); La Fuga (US 1966). **1966** El Sigillo de Pechino (aka Die Holle von Macao and aka The Corrupt Ones—US 1967). **1969** Les Hommes de Las Vegas (They Came to Rob Las Vegas—US and aka Radiografia d'un Colpo d'oro). **1972** Er Piu (The Greatest). **1975** To Love Ophelia. **1976** Romolo and Remo.

ARENA, RODOLFO
Born: 1911, Brazil. Died: Aug. 31, 1980, Rio de Janeiro, Brazil (heart attack). Screen, stage actor and circus performer.

Appeared in: **1964** Asfalto Selvagem (aka Lollipop—US 1966). **1980** Summer Showers; Bye-Bye Brazil; Sao Bernardo.

ARENAS, MIGUEL
Born: 1902, Alicante, Spain. Died: Nov. 3, 1965, Mexico City, Mexico (heart attack). Screen and stage actor.

Appeared in: **1933** In Fraganti. **1936** Mas Alla de la Muerta. **1937** El Misterio del Rostro Palido. **1938** No Basta ser Madre (Motherhood Is Not Enough); Abnegacion. **1939** Un Domingo en la Tarde (On a Sunday Afternoon); Maria. **1940** Herencia Macabra (A Macabre Legacy); Vivire Otra Vez (I Shall Live Again); El Conde de Monte Cristo. **1944** La Dama de las Camelias. **1951** Toast to Love.

AREOLA, ARMANDO
Born: 1905, Mexico. Died: Nov., 1978, Mexico City, Mexico. Screen and stage actor.

AREY, WAYNE
Born: Apr. 12, 1880, Rock Falls, Ill. Died: July 1, 1937, New York, N.Y. Screen and stage actor.

Appeared in: **1917** Hinton's Double; The Woman in White; It Happened to Adele; War and the Woman.

ARGYLE, PEARL
Born: Nov. 7, 1910, Johannesburg, South Africa. Died: Jan. 29, 1947, New York, N.Y. (cerebral hemorrhage). Screen, stage actress and ballet dancer. Married to screen actor/director Curtis Bernhardt.

Appeared in: **1934** Chu Chin Chow. **1936** Things to Come.

ARLEDGE, JOHN (Johnson Lundy Arledge)
Born: Mar. 12, 1906, Crockett, Tex. Died: May 15, 1947. Screen, stage and vaudeville actor.

Appeared in: **1930** The King of Jazz. **1931** Young Sinners; Daddy Long Legs; Heartbreak; Spider. **1932** Careless Lady; Huddle; Week Ends Only. **1933** Jimmy and Sally. **1934** Olsen's Big Moment; Flirtation Walk. **1935** Devil Dogs of the Air; Mary Jane's Pa; Old Man Rhythm; Shipmates Forever. **1936** We're Only Human; You May Be Next; Two in Revolt; Murder on a Bridle Path; Don't Turn 'Em Loose; The Big Game. **1937** Saturday's Heroes; County Fair; The Big City. **1938** Prison Nurse; Numbered Woman; Campus Confessions. **1939** All Women Have Secrets; Twelve Crowded Hours; Gone With the Wind; You Can't Cheat an Honest Man; 6,000 Enemies. **1940** Son of Roaring Dan; The Fighting 69th; The Grapes of Wrath; Strange Cargo; Ski Patrol; Flight Angels; City of Conquest. **1941** Cheers for Miss Bishop. **1947** I Wonder Who's Kissing Her Now; Dark Passage.

ARLEN, BETTY
Born: 1904. Died: 1966. Screen actress. Was a Wampas Baby Star of 1925.

ARLEN, JUDITH (Laurette Rutherford)
Born: Mar. 18, 1914, Hollywood, Calif. Died: June 5, 1968. Screen actress. Was a Wampas Baby Star of 1934. Sister of actress Ann Rutherford. Daughter of opera singers Juan Gilberti and Pauline Daly (aka Actress Mary Lou Mansfield).

Appeared in: **1934** Kiss and Make Up; Young and Beautiful.

ARLEN, RICHARD (Cornelius Van Mattimore aka VAN MATTIMORE)
Born: Sept. 1, 1898, Charlottesville, Va. Died: Mar. 28, 1976, North Hollywood, Calif. (emphysema). Screen, stage, radio and television actor. Divorced from actresses Ruth Austin and Jobyna Ralston (dec. 1967). Married to Margaret Kinsella. Entered films in 1920 as Van Mattimore.

Appeared in: **1923** Vengeance of the Deep. **1925** In the Name of Love. **1926** Behind the Front; The Enchanted Hill; Padlocked. **1927** Wings; Rolled Stockings; The Blood Ship; Figures Don't Lie; Sally in Our Alley; She's a Sheik. **1928** Feel My Pulse; Ladies of the Mob; Beggars of Life; Manhattan Cocktail; Under the Tonto Rim. **1929** Thunderbolt; The Man I Love; Dangerous Curves; The Virginian; The Four Feathers. **1930** Burning Up; Dangerous Paradise; Light of the Western Stars; Paramount on Parade; Border Legion; Santa Fe Trail; Sea God; Only Saps Work. **1931** The Conquering Horde; Gun Smoke; The Lawyer's Secret; Caught; Touchdown. **1932** Guilty as Hell; Hot Saturday; The All-American; Tiger Shark; Wayward; The Sky Bride. **1933** Lives of a Bengal Lancer; College Humor; Hell and High Water; I Cover the Waterfront; Three-Cornered Moon; Island of Lost Souls; Song of the Eagle; Golden Harvest; Alice in Wonderland. **1934** Come on Marines; She Made Her Bed; Ready for Love. **1935** Helldorado; Let 'Em Have It; Three Live Ghosts. **1936** The Calling of Dan Matthews; The Mine With the Iron Door; Secret Valley; You May Be Next. **1937** Artists and Models; The Great Barrier (aka Silent Barriers—US); Murder in Greenwich Village. **1938** Straight, Place and Show; Call of

the Yukon; No Time to Marry. **1939** Legion of Lost Flyers; Missing Daughters; Mutiny on the Blackhawk; Tropic Fury. **1940** The Man from Montreal; Hot Steel; Danger on Wheels; The Leather Pushers; Black Diamonds; The Devil's Pipeline. **1941** Riders of the Desert; Mutiny in the Arctic; Power Dive; Flying Blind; A Dangerous Game; Forced Landing; Lucky Devils; Men of the Timberland. **1942** Torpedo Boat; Wildcat; Wrecking Crew. **1943** Aerial Gunner; Alaska Highway; Submarine Alert; Minesweeper. **1944** Timber Queen; Storm Over Lisbon; The Lady and the Monster; That's My Baby! **1945** The Big Bonanza; Identity Unknown; The Phantom Speaks. **1946** Accomplice; The French Key. **1947** Buffalo Bill Rides Again. **1948** The Return of Wildfire; When My Baby Smiles at Me; Speed to Spare. **1949** Grand Canyon. **1950** Kansas Raiders. **1951** Flaming Feather; Silver City. **1952** Blazing Forest; Hurricane Smith. **1953** Devil's Canyon; Sabre Jet. **1955** Stolen Time (aka Blonde Blackmailer—US 1958); Devil's Harbor. **1956** Hidden Guns; The Mountain. **1959** Warlock. **1960** Raymie. **1961** The Last Time I Saw Archie. **1963** The Crawling Hand; Cavalry Command; The Young and the Brave; Shepherd of the Hills (aka Thunder Mountain). **1964** The Best Man; Law of the Lawless. **1965** Young Fury; Black Spurs; The Human Duplicators; The Bounty Killer; Town Tamer. **1966** Apache Uprising; Johnny Reno; To the Shores of Hell; Waco; Road to Nashville. **1967** Fort Utah; Hostile Guns; Red Tomahawk; Rogue's Galley. **1968** Buckskin (aka The Frontiersman). **1970** Sex and the College Girl. **1971** A Whale of a Time. **1976** Won Ton Ton, the Dog Who Saved Hollywood.

ARLEY, CECILE See ARNOLD, CECILE

ARLISS, FLORENCE
Died: Mar. 11, 1950, London, England. Screen actress. Married to actor George Arliss (dec. 1946).

Appeared in: **1921** The Devil; Disraeli. **1929** Disraeli (and 1921 version). **1932** The Millionaire. **1933** The King's Vacation. **1934** The House of Rothschild.

ARLISS, GEORGE
Born: Apr. 10, 1868, London, England. Died: Feb. 5, 1946, London, England (bronchial trouble). Screen and stage actor. Married to actress Florence Arliss (dec. 1950). Won 1929-30 Academy Award for Best Actor in Disraeli (1929) and nominated for 1929-30 Academy Award for Best Actor in The Green Goddess (1930).

Appeared in: **1921** The Devil; Disraeli. **1922** Man Who Played God. **1923** The Green Goddess; The Ruling Passion. **1924** $20 a Week. **1929** Disraeli (and 1921 version). **1930** The Green Goddess (and 1923 version); Old English. **1931** The Millionaire; Alexander Hamilton. **1932** Man Who Played God (and 1922 version); A Successful Calamity. **1933** The Working Man; A King's Vacation; Voltaire; The Adopted Father. **1934** The House of Rothschild; The Last Gentleman. **1935** The Tunnel (aka Transatlantic Tunnel—US); Cardinal Richelieu; The Guv'nor (aka Mr. Hobo—US 1936); Iron Duke. **1936** His Lordship (aka Man of Affairs—US 1937); East Meets West. **1937** Dr. Syn.

ARMAND, TEDDY V. (Edwin C. Winscott)
Born: 1874. Died: July 12, 1947, Los Angeles, Calif. Screen and stage actor.

ARMENDARIZ, PEDRO
Born: May 9, 1912, Mexico City, Mexico. Died: June 18, 1963, Los Angeles, Calif. (cancer and suicide—gun). Screen and stage actor. Father of actor Pedro Armendariz, Jr.

Appeared in: **1936** Rosario. **1937** Jalisco Nunca Pierde (Jalisco Never Loses). **1938** Mi Candidato (My Candidate). **1939** El Indio, La China Hilaria. **1940** Los Olvidados de Dios (Those Forgotten by God); La Reina del Rio (The Queen of the River). **1941** Isle of Passion (aka Passion Island—US 1943). **1943** Maria Candeleria (US 1944); Guadalajara; The Life of Simon Bolivar. **1944** Tierra de Passiones. **1945** Flor Sylvestre. **1947** The Fugitive; Juan Charasqueado. **1948** The Pearl; Three Godfathers; Fort Apache; Maclovia. **1949** La Masquereda; Tulsa; We Were Strangers; Enamorada. **1950** The Torch. **1951** Ella y Yo. **1952** Lucretia Borgia. **1954** Border River; Lovers of Toledo; El Bruto; Both Sides of the Law. **1955** The Littlest Outlaw; Diane. **1956** Viva Revolution; Sins of the Borgias; The Conqueror. **1957** The Big Boodle (aka A Night in Havana); Manuela (aka Stowaway Girl—US). **1958** Conqueror of the Desert. **1959** The Little Savage; The Wonderful Country. **1960** Soldiers of Pancho Villa. **1961** Beyond All Limits (aka Flowers of Mayo); La Cucaracha; Francis of Assisi. **1962** La Bandida (The Bandit). **1963** My Son, the Hero (aka The Titans); Captain Sinbad. **1964** From Russia with Love.

ARMENGOD, RAMON

Born: 1910, Vera Cruz, Mexico. Died: Oct. 31, 1976, near Chilpancingo, Guerrero, Mexico (auto accident). Screen, radio actor and vocalist.

Appeared in: **1936** Que Hago con la Criatura?; La Familia Dressel; Hoy Comienza la Vida. **1938** Alma Jarocha. **1939** Nobleza Rancher (Rural Chivalry). **1940** Un Viejo Amor (An Old Love); Herencia Macabra (A Macabre Legacy; Vivire Otra Vez (I Shall Live Again).

ARMETTA, HENRY

Born: July 4, 1888, Palermo, Italy. Died: Oct. 21, 1945, San Diego, Calif. (heart attack). Screen, stage and television actor.

Appeared in: **1923** The Silent Command. **1928** Street Angel. **1929** Lady of the Pavements; In Old Arizona; Homesick; Love, Live and Laugh; Jazz Heaven. **1930** A Lady to Love; The Climax; The Little Accident; Lovin' the Ladies; Romance; Sins of the Children; Die Sehnsucht Jeder Frau. **1931** Strangers May Kiss; A Tailor Made Man; Five and Ten; Hush Money; The Unholy Garden; Speak Easily. **1932** Scarface; Arsene Lupin; The Passionate Plumber; The Doomed Battalion; Impossible Lover; Tiger Shark; Weekends Only; Penalty of Fame; Central Park; Cauliflower Alley; Steady Company; Huddle; They Just Had to Get Married; Prosperity; Farewell to Arms; Uptown New York; Okay, American; Men of America; **1932-33** Universal shorts. **1933** Fra Diavolo (The Devil's Brother); The Cohens and the Kellys in Trouble; Her First Mate; Too Much Harmony; Laughing at Life; Deception; What! No Beer?; So This Is Africa; Don't Bet on Love. **1934** Cat and the Fiddle; Cross Country Cruise; One Night to Love; Viva Villa!; Poor Rich; Hide-Out; Embarrassing Moments; Gift of Gab; Two Heads on a Pillow; Wake up and Dream; Imitation of Life; The Merry Widow; The Man Who Reclaimed His Head; Kiss and Make Up; Cheating Cheaters; Romance in the Rain; Let's Talk It Over; Universal shorts. **1935** Straight from the Heart; Vanessa, Her Love Story; Night Life of the Gods; After Office Hours; I've Been Around; Dinky; Princess Ohara; Unknown Woman; Three Kids and a Queen; The Show Goes On; Magnificent Obsession; Manhattan Moon. **1936** Let's Sing Again; The Crime of Dr. Forbes; Poor Little Rich Girl; The Magnificent Brute; Two in a Crowd. **1937** Top of the Town; Make a Wish; Manhattan Merry-Go-Round; Seventh Heaven. **1938** Everybody Sing; Speed to Burn; Road Demon; Submarine Patrol. **1939** Fisherman's Wharf; The Lady and the Mob; My Pop; Winner Take All; I Stole a Million; The Outsider; Dust Be My Destiny; The Escape. **1940** Three Cheers for the Irish; We Who Are Young; You're Not So Tough; The Man Who Talked Too Much. **1941** Caught in the Act; The Big Store; Slick Chick; Stage Door Canteen; Good Luck, Mr. Yates. **1943** Thank Your Lucky Stars. **1944** Allergic to Love; The Ghost Catchers. **1945** Penthouse Rhythm; A Bell for Adano; Col. Effingham's Raid; Anchors Aweigh.

ARMITAGE, BUFORD

Born: 1898, Greeneville, Tenn. Died: Nov. 3, 1978, Mt. Kisco, N.Y. Screen, stage, vaudeville actor and stage manager. Married to actress Claire Waring.

Appeared in: **1931** Stolen Heaven.

ARMITAGE, WALTER W.

Born: 1907, South Africa. Died: Feb. 22, 1953, New York, N.Y. Screen, stage actor, playwright and screenwriter.

Appeared in: **1931** The Love Habit. **1934** Bombay Mail; Where Sinners Meet; British Agent.

ARMONTEL (Roland Armontel)

Born: France. Died: Mar. 8, 1980, France? Screen actor.

Appeared in: **1947** Man About Town. **1950** The Scandals of Clochmerle. **1951** Face to the Wind; The Lovers of Verona; Minne; Oh, Amelia. **1957** Pantaloons; Razzi. **1958** Senechal the Magnificent; Les Tricheurs (The Cheaters—US 1961). **1962** Le Diable et les Dix Commandments (The Devil and the Ten Commandments—US 1963).

ARMSTRONG, BILLY

Born: 1891, Bristol, England. Died: Mar. 1, 1924, England? Screen and stage actor.

Appeared in: **1915** The Tramp; By the Sea; Work; A Woman; The Bank; Shanghaied. **1916** A Lover's Might. **1917** A Royal Rogue; A Shanghaied Jonah; Hula Hula Land. **1920** Down on the Farm. **1921** Skirts; Love, Honor and Behave.

ARMSTRONG, CLYDE

Born: 1879. Died: Sept. 30, 1937, N.Y. Screen, stage and vaudeville actor.

ARMSTRONG, LOUIS "SATCHMO" (Daniel Louis Armstrong)

Born: July 4, 1900, New Orleans, La. Died: July 6, 1971, Queens, N.Y. Black screen, stage, television actor and jazz trumpeter. Winner of Down Beat Hall of Fame Award in 1952.

Appeared in: **1930** Ex-Flame. **1932** Paramount shorts. **1936** Pennies from Heaven. **1937** Artists and Models; Every Day's a Holiday. **1938** Going Places; Doctor Rhythm. **1940** The Philadelphia Story. **1943** Cabin in the Sky. **1944** Jam Session; Atlantic City. **1945** Pillow to Post. **1947** New Orleans. **1948** A Song Is Born. **1951** Glory Alley; The Strip; Here Comes the Groom. **1954** The Glenn Miller Story. **1956** High Society. **1957** The Five Pennies; The Beat Generation. **1960** Jazz on a Summer's Day. **1961** Paris Blues. **1965** When the Boys Meet the Girls (aka Girl Crazy). **1966** A Man Called Adam. **1969** Hello, Dolly; On Her Majesty's Secret Service.

ARMSTRONG, R. L. "TEX"

Born: 1925. Died: Mar. 10, 1978, Burbank, Calif. Screen and television actor.

Appeared in: **1960** The Fugitive Kind. **1962** To Kill a Mockingbird. **1966** The Black Klansman; Dimension 5; Fireball 500. **1968** The Destructors; The Money Jungle; Panic in the City. **1972** Ulzana's Raid; J. W. Coop. **1976** The Missouri Breaks. **1978** Goin' South.

ARMSTRONG, ROBERT

Born: Nov. 20, 1896, Saginaw, Mich. Died: Apr. 20, 1973, Santa Monica, Calif. Screen, stage, television and vaudeville actor. Divorced from actresses Ethel Kent (dec. 1952) and Gladys Dubois and later married to Louise Armstrong.

Appeared in: **1927** The Main Event (film debut). **1928** Celebrity; The Baby Cyclone; A Girl in Every Port; Square Crooks; The Cop; The Leopard Lady; Show Folks; Ned McCobb's Daughter. **1929** Big News; The Leatherneck; The Woman from Hell; The Shady Lady; Oh, Yeah!; The Racketeer. **1930** Dumbbells in Ermine; Be Yourself!; Danger Lights; Big Money. **1931** Easy Money; Paid; Iron Man; The Tip-Off; Suicide Fleet; Ex-Bad Boy. **1932** Panama Flo; The Lost Squadron; Is My Face Red?; Radio Patarol; The Most Dangerous Game; Hold 'Em Jail; The Penguin Pool Murder. **1933** Blind Adventure; The Billion Dollar Scandal; King Kong; Fast Workers; I Love that Man; Son of Kong; Above the Clouds. **1934** Flirting with Danger; Search for Beauty; Palooka; She Made Her Bed; The Hell Cat; Kansas City Princess; Manhattan Love Song. **1935** Sweet Music; G Men; Gigolette; Little Big Shot; Remember Last Night; The Mystery man. **1936** The Ex-Mrs. Bradford; Dangerous Waters; Public Enemy's Wife; Without Orders; All-American Chump. **1937** Nobody's Baby; Three Legionnaires; It Can't Last Forever; The Girl Said No. **1938** She Loved a Fireman; The Night Hawk; There Goes My Heart. **1939** Unmarried; Call a Messenger; The Flying Irishman; Man of Conquest; Winter Carnival; Flight at Midnight. **1940** Enemy Agent; Forgotten Girls; Framed; Behind the News. **1941** Mr. Dynamite; The Bride Wore Crutches; Dive Bomber; Sky Raiders (serial); Outside the Law; San Francisco Docks; Citadel of Crime. **1942** Gang Busters (serial); My Favorite Spy; It Happened in Flatbush; Baby Face Morgan; Let's Get Tough. **1943** The Kansan; The Mad Ghoul; Adventures of Flying Cadets (serial); Around the World. **1944** Action in Arabia; Mr. Winkle Goes to War; Goodnight, Sweetheart; The Navy Way; Belle of the Yukon. **1945** The Royal Mounted Rides Again (serial); Blood on the Sun; The Falcon in San Francisco; Gangs of the Waterfront; Arson Squad. **1946** Decoy; Criminal Court; Gay Blades; G.I. War Brides; Blonde Alibi. **1947** The Sea of Grass; The Fugitive; The Fall Guy; Exposed. **1948** The Paleface; Return of the Bad Men. **1949** The Lucky Stiff; Might Joe Young; Streets of San Francisco; The Crime Doctor's Diary; Captain China. **1950** Sons of New Mexico; Destination Big House. **1952** The Pace That Thrills. **1955** Las Vegas Shakedown. **1956** The Peacemaker. **1957** The Crooked Circle. **1963** Johnny Cool. **1964** For Those Who Think Young.

ARMSTRONG, WILL H.

Born: 1869. Died: July 28, 1943, Hollywood, Calif. Screen and vaudeville actor.

Appeared in: **1927** Clancy's Kosher Wedding; A Boy of the Streets.

ARNA, LISSY

Born: Germany. Died: Jan. 22, 1964, Berlin, Germany (cancer). Screen and television actress. Entered films in German silents and entered U.S. films in 1930.

Appeared in: **1928** The Physician. **1929** The Prince of Rogues. **1930** Der Tanz Geht Weiter (Those Who Dance). **1931** Beyond Victory. **1932** Der Ungetreue Eckehart. **1933** Theodor Koerner. **1937** Die Schwedende Jungfrau. Other German films: The Yellow Flag; Mountains in Flames.

ARNAUD, YVONNE
Born: Dec. 20, 1892, Bordeaux, France. Died: Sept. 20, 1958, London, England. Screen, stage, televison actress and pianist.

Appeared in: **1920** The Magic Skin (aka Desire); The Temptress. **1930** Canaries Sometimes Sing (stage and film versions); On Approval (stage and film versions). **1931** Tons of Money. **1933** A Cuckoo in the Nest. **1934** Princess Charming (US 1935); Lady in Danger. **1935** Widow's Might; Stormy Weather (US 1936). **1936** The Improper Duchess; The Gay Adventure. **1940** Neutral Port. **1942** Tomorrow We Live (aka At Dawn We Die—US 1943). **1946** Woman to Woman. **1947** The Ghosts of Berkeley Square. **1958** My Uncle.

ARNHEIM, GUS
Born: 1899. Died: Jan. 19, 1955, Beverly Hills, Calif. (heart attack). Screen, television actor, bandleader and songwriter.

Appeared with his orchestra in: **1928** Gus Arnheim and His Ambassadors (short); Gus Arnheim and His Cocoanut Grove Orchestra (short). **1929** Broadway; Half Marriage; Street Girl; Gus Arnheim and His Ambassador Hotel Orchestra (short). **1934** Gift of Gab. **1937** Paramount short.

ARNO, SIG (Siegfried Arno)
Born: 1895, Hamburg, Germany. Died: Aug. 17, 1975, Woodland Hills, Calif. (Parkinson's disease). Screen, stage actor and cabaret performer.

Appeared in: **1925** Pandora's Box; Manon Lescaut. **1933** The Big Attraction. **1935** The Star Maker. **1940** A Little Bit of Heaven; The Mummy's Hand; Diamond Frontier; Dark Streets of Cairo; The Great Dictator. **1941** Hellzapoppin; Raiders of the Desert; This Thing Called Love; New Wine; Two Latins from Manhattan; Gambling Daughters; It Started With Eve. **1942** Pardon My Sarong; Tales of Manhattan; Juke Box Jenny; Palm Beach Story; The Devil With Hitler; Two Yanks in Trinidad. **1943** The Crystal Ball; Larceny With Music; His Butler's Sister; Taxi, Mister. **1944** The Angels Sing; Once Upon a Time; Song of the Open Road; Up in Arms. **1945** A Song to Remember; Roughly Speaking; Bring on the Girls. **1946** One More Tomorrow. **9149** The Great Lover; Holiday in Havana. **1950** Duchess of Idaho; The Toast of New Orleans. **1951** On Moonlight Bay. **1952** Diplomatic Courier. **1953** Fast Company; The Great Diamond Robbery.

ARNOLD, CECILE (aka CECILE ARLEY)
Died: 1931, Hong Kong (influenza). Screen actress. Was a Sennett bathing beauty.

Appeared in: **1914** The Face on the Barroom Floor; The Masquerader; Those Love Pangs; Dough and Dynamite; Getting Acquainted; His Prehistoric Past. **1915** Gussle's Day of Rest; A Game Old Knight. **1916** His Last Scent.

ARNOLD, EDWARD (Guenther Schneider)
Born: Feb. 18, 1890. Died: Apr. 26, 1956, Encino, Calif. (cerebral hemorrhage). Screen, stage and televison actor and author. Father of actor Edward Arnold, Jr. Entered films in 1915 with Essanay.

Appeared in: **1916** The Primitive Strain. **1927** Sunrise—a Song of Two Humans. **1932** Man of the Nile; Rasputin and the Empress; The White Sister; Afraid to Talk; Okay America; Three on a Match. **1933** Whistling in the Dark; I'm No Angel; Gennie Gerhardt; The Barbarian; Her Bodyguard; Secret of the Blue Room; Roman Scandals. **1934** The President Vanishes; Unknown Blonde; Thirty Day Princess; Madame Spy; Million Dollar Ransom; Hide-Out; Sadie McKee; Wednesday's Child. **1935** Remember Last Night?; Biography of a Bachelor Girl; The Glass Key; Crime and Punishment; Diamond Jim; Cardinal Richelieu. **1936** Meet Nero Wolf; Sutter's Gold; Come and Get It. **1937** The Toast of New York; Easy Living; Blossoms on Broadway; John Meade's Woman. **1938** The Crowd Roars; You Can't Take It With You. **1939** Idiot's Delight; Mr. Smith Goes to Washington; Let Freedom Ring; Man About Town. **1940** Slightly Honorable; Johnny Apollo; The Earl of Chicago; Lillian Russell. **1941** Unholy Partners; All That Money Can Buy; Meet John Doe; The Penalty; The Lady from Cheyenne; Johnny Eager; Nothing But the Truth; Design for Scandal. **1942** The War Against Mrs. Hadley; Eyes in the Night. **1943** The Youngest Profession. **1944** Kismet; Mrs. Parkington; Standing Room Only; Janie; Main Street after Dark. **1945** The Hidden Eye; Weekend at the Waldorf. **1946** Janie Gets Married; Ziegfeld Follies; Three Wise Fools; No Leave, No Love; My Brother Talks to Horses; The Mighty McGurk. **1947** Dear Ruth; The Hucksters. **1948** Three Daring Daughters; The Big City; Wallflower. **1949** John Loves Mary; Command Decision; Big Jack; Take Me Out to the Ball Game; Johnny Eager; Honest John (Horner); Dear Wife. **1950** Annie Get Your Gun; The Yellow Cab Man; The Skipper Surprised His Wife. **1951** Dear Brat. **1952** Belles on Their Toes; The

Devil and Daniel Webster (reissue and retitle of All That Money Can Buy—1941). **1953** Man of Conflict; Money From Home; City That Never Sleeps. **1954** Living It Up. **1956** Miami Expose; The Huston Story; The Ambassador's Daughter. **1974** That's Entertainment (film clips).

ARNOLD, JESSIE (Jessie Gertrude Arnold)
Born: June 29, 1877, Mich. Died: June 10, 1971, Los Angeles, Calif. (heart attack). Screen actress.

Appeared in: **1916** A Social Slave; The Masked Woman; Cross Purposes; He Became a Regular Fellow; Mixed Blood; Circumstantial Justice; The Light of Love; The Losing Winner; The Pointed Finger. **1921** The Idol of the North. **1923** Playing With Souls. **1930** Brothers. **1932** Stranger in Town; Hot Saturday. **1933** The Bitter Tea of General Yen. **1934** We Live Again. **1935** Carnival; Southern Exposure (short); The Four-Star Boarder (short). **1938** Three Comrades. **1940** Two Girls on Broadway; The Ape; The Haunted House. **1941** Three Girls About Town. **1942** You're Telling Me. **1945** Boston Blackie Booked on Suspicion; Kiss and Tell. **1946** The Strange Woman; The Jolson Story; The Hoodlum Saint. **1947** Trail Street; A Likely Story. **1948** The Lady from Shanghai; Tenth Avenue Angel. **1949** Air Hostess; The Stratton Story; The Reckless Moment. **1951** Golden Girl.

ARNOLD, LOIS
Born: 1877, St. Augustine, Fla. Died: Jan. 26, 1947, Philadelphia, Pa. Screen, stage and vaudeville actress. Appeared in Biograph, Thanhouser, Famous Players, Fox and Frohman films.

ARNOLD, MABEL
Born: 1889. Died: Jan. 7, 1964, Hollywood, Calif. Screen actress.

ARNOLD, MARCELLA
Born: 1911. Died: Mar. 3, 1937, Pasadena, Calif. (auto accident). Screen actress.

Appeared in: **1928** Trial Marriage. **1929** Unguarded Girls.

ARNOLD, PHIL
Born: 1909, Hackensack, N.J. Died: May 9, 1968, Van Nuys, Calif. Screen, stage, television and vaudeville actor.

Appeared in: **1939** King of the Turf. **1940** Drafted in the Depot (short). **1941** Sis Hopkins. **1942** Men of San Quentin. **1947** Buffalo Bill Rides Again. **1949** I Cheated the Law. **1951** G.I. Jane; Yes Sir, Mr. Bones; Kentucky Jubilee. **1953** The Jazz Singer; plus the following shorts: Tricky Dicks; Pardon My Backfire; and Rip, Sew and Stitch. **1954** The Big Chase; Money From Home; A Star Is Born; So You Want to Be Your Own Boss (short). **1955** It's Always Fair Weather; The Court Martial of Billy Mitchell; Illegal. **1957** Jet Pilot; My Gun Is Quick. **1958** Damn Yankees. **1960** Studs Lonigan. **1962** The Errand Boy. **1963** The Three Stooges Go Around the World in a Daze; Under the Yum Yum Tree. **1964** Robin and the Seven Hoods; Three Nuts in Search of a Bolt; The Candidate; What a Way to Go. **1965** Zebra in the Kitchen. **1966** Hold On! **1967** The Cool Ones; Good Times. **1968** Skiddo.

ARNOLD, SETH
Born: 1885, London, England. Died: Jan. 3, 1955, New York, N.Y. Screen, stage actor and stage director.

Appeared in: **1949** Lost Boundaries.

ARNOLD, WILLIAM R. "BILLY"
Born: 1883. Died: July 20, 1940, Hollywood, Calif. (streptococcus infection). Screen, stage and vaudeville actor.

Appeared in: **1931** Oh! Oh! Cleopatra (short); Gun Smoke; The Vice Squad; Rich Man's Folly. **1932** The Crowd Roars. **1934** Thirty Day Princess; In Love With Life; Cain and Mabel. **1935** The Bride Comes Home; Magnificent Obsession; Splendor; Rendezvous at Midnight. **1936** Love Before Breakfast; Big Brown Eyes. **1937** Four Days' Wonder. **1938** The Overland Express. **1939** St. Louis Blues. **1940** Edison, The Man; The Great Dictator.

ARNOUX, ROBERT
Born: 1900, France. Died: Mar. 15, 1964, France? Screen actor.

Appeared in: **1935** Lilliom. **1939** Mademoiselle ma Mere. **1940** Whirlpool. **1950** Between Eleven and Midnight. **1951** Au Grand Balcon. **1953** The Night Is My Kingdom. **1957** Four Bags Full; Deadlier Than the Male. **1961** Il Suffit d'Aimer (aka Bernadette of Lourdes—US 1962).

ARNST, BOBBE
Died: Oct. 11, or Nov. 25, 1980. Screen actress and dancer. Divorced from actor Johnny Weismuller.

Appeared in: **1914** Perils of Pauline (serial). **1916** The Iron Claw (serial). **1929** The Night Club. **1934** Wine, Women and Song.

ARQUETTE, CLIFF (aka CHARLEY WEAVER)
Born: Dec. 28, 1905, Toledo, Ohio. Died: Sept. 23, 1974, Burbank, Calif. (heart attack). Screen, vaudeville, radio and television actor.

Appeared in: **1940** Comin' 'Round the Mountain. **1965** Saturday Night Bath in Apple Valley. **1966** Don't Worry, We'll Think of a Title; Appeared in vaudeville as part of "Three Public Enemies" team.

ARRAS, HARRY
Born: 1882. Died: Jan. 28, 1942, Hollywood, Calif. (heart attack). Screen actor. Entered films approximately 1918.

Appeared in: **1922** Blind Circumstances. **1942** Escape from Crime.

ARRUZA, CARLOS "EL CICLON"
Born: 1920, Mexico. Died: May 20, 1966, Mexico (auto accident). Matador and screen actor.

Appeared in: Mi Reino por un Torero (My Kingdom for a Bullfighter, film debut). **1957** Torero! **1960** The Alamo.

ARSHANSKY, MICHAEL
Born: 1896, Moscow, Russia. Died: June 30, 1978, New York, N.Y. Screen, stage actor, ballet dancer and makeup artist.

Appeared in: **1939** The Wizard of Oz. **1946** Night and Day.

ARTAUD, ANTONIN
Born: 1896, Marseille, France. Died: Mar. 4, 1948, Ivry-sur-Seine, France (cancer). Screen, stage actor, film director, screenwriter and author.

Appeared in: **1927** Napoleon (US 1929). **1928** La Passion de Jeanne d'Arc (The Passion of Joan of Arc—US 1929). **1934** Le Serment.

ARTEMAL, TALAT
Born: 1902, Turkey. Died: Aug., 1957, Bolu, Turkey (heart attack). Stage and screen actor.

ARTHUR, JOHNNY (John Lennox Arthur Williams)
Born: May 10, 1883, Scottsdale, Pa. Died: Dec. 31, 1951, Woodland Hills, Calif. (heart disease). Screen and stage actor. Appeared in silent "Christie" comedies.

Appeared in: **1923** The Unknown Purple. **1924** Mlle. Midnight; Daring Love. **1925** The Monster. **1928** On Trial. **1929** The Desert Song; The Gamblers; Show of Shows; Divorce Made Easy; Lover's Delight; Adam's Eve; The Aviator; Stimulation (short). **1930** Cheer Up and Smile; Personality; She Couldn't Say No; Scrappily Married; Down With Husbands; Paper Hanging (short); Bridal Night (short). **1931** Penrod and Sam, Going Wild; It's a Wise Child. **1933** Convention City; Easy Millions. **1934** Twenty Million Sweethearts; Many Happy Returns; Hell in Heaven. **1935** Anniversary Trouble (short); Traveling Saleslady; Doubting Thomas; The Ghost Walks; It's in the Air; The Bride Comes Home; Crime and Punishment; Too Tough to Kill. **1936** Freshmen Love; Murder of Dr. Harrigan; The King Steps Out; All Amerian Toothache (short); Stage Struck. **1937** The Hit Parade; Exiled to Shanghai; Pick a Star; Night 'n' Gales (short); Make a Wish; Blossoms on Broadway; It Had to Happen Out West; Something to Sing About. **1938** Danger on the Air; Feed 'Em and Weep (short). **1940** Road to Singapore. **1941** Mountain Moonlight. **1942** Shepherd of the Ozarks. **1943** The Nazty Nuissance; The Masked Marvel (serial); Henry Aldrich Gets Glamour.

ARTHUR, JULIA
Born: Mar. 3, 1869, Hamilton, Ontario, Canada. Died: Mar. 28, 1950, Boston, Mass. Stage and screen actress.

Appeared in: **1918** The Common Cause; The Woman the Germans Shot.

ARUNDALE, SYBIL (Sybil Kelly)
Born: June 20, 1882, England. Died: Sept. 5, 1965, London, England. Screen, stage and vaudeville actress.

Appeared in: **1917** Tom Jones. **1918** God and the Man. **1919** The Chinese Puzzle. **1930** Loose Ends.

ARUNDELL, EDWARD "TEDDY"
Born: Devonshire, England. Died: Nov. 5, 1922, London, England. Screen and stage actor.

Appeared in: **1916** The Lyons Mail. **1918** The Greatest Wish in the World; Nelson; The Splendid Coward. **1919** God's Good Man; The Romance of Lady Hamilton; Mr. Wu; Comradeship (aka Comrades in Arms); The Swindler; The Elusive Pimpernel. **1920** General Post; The Amateur Gentleman; At the Villa Rose; The Hundredth Chance; The Duchess of Seven Dials; Bleak House; London Pride; A Question of Trust. **1921** Greatheart; The Amazing Partnership; Kipps; The Tragedy of a Comic Song; The River of Stars; The Mystery of Mr. Bernard Brown; General John Regan; A Gentleman of France; The Woman of His Dream. **1922** The Pointing Finger; While London Sleeps (aka Cocaine); Lamp in the Desert (US 1923); The Passionate Friends; False Evidence; A Lost Leader; The Further Adventures of Sherlock Holmes series including: Charles Augustus Milverton; The Abbey Grange; The Norwood Builder; The Reigate Squires; The Second Stain; The Red Circle; The Six Napoleons; Black Peter; The Bruce Partington Plans; The Golden Pince-Nez. **1923** Through Fire and Water.

ARVAN, JAN
Born: 1913. Died: May 24, 1979, Los Angeles, Calif. (heart attack). Screen, stage, television actor and stage director.

Appeared in: **1953** How to Marry a Millionaire. **1954** The Other Woman. **1955** The Cobweb. **1957** Istanbul; 20 Million Miles to Earth. **1958** Curse of the Faceless Man. **1960** Noose for a Gunman; The Sign of Zorro; Three Came to Kill; Gunfighters of Abilene. **1961** Frontier Uprising. **1963** Island of Love. **1964** The Brass Bottle. **1966** The Spy With My Face. **1972** The Poseidon Adventure. **1977** The Other Side of Midnight.

ARVIDSON, LINDA (Linda Johnson)
Born: 1884. Died: July 26, 1949, New York, N.Y. Screen, stage actress and author. Divorced from film producer David Wark Griffith (dec. 1948).

Appeared in: **1908** When Knighthood Was in Flower; When Knights Were Bold; A Calamitous Elopement; Balked at the Altar; Where Breakers Roar; An Awful Moment; The Adventures of Dollie; The Greaser's Gauntlet; The Man and the Woman; The Barbarian, Ingomar; The Planter's Wife; The Curtain Pole. **1909** Edgar Allan Poe; The Cricket on the Hearth; Lines of White on a Sullen Sea; At the Altar; The Cord of Life; The Salvation Army Lass; Tragic Love; Politician's Love Story; The Deception; A Drunkard's Reformation; Her First Biscuits; A Convict's Sacrifice; The Mills of the Gods; 1776, or The Hessian Renegades; Comata, the Sioux; Pippa Passes; The Death Disc. **1910** The Unchanging Sea; The Broken Doll; White Roses. **1919** Enoch Arden; Fisher Folks; Heartbeats of Long Ago.

ASCHE, OSCAR
Born: 1871, England. Died: Mar. 23, 1936, London, England. Screen, stage actor, playwright and screenwriter. Married to actress Lily Brayton (dec. 1953).

Appeared in: **1914** Kismit. **1933** Don Quixote (US 1934); My Lucky Star. **1934** Two Hearts in Waltztime. **1935** Scrooge; The Private Secretary. **1936** Eliza Comes to Stay; Robber Symphony (US 1937).

ASCHER, ANTON
Born: 1868. Died: Sept. 30, 1928, New York, N.Y. (cancer). Screen and stage actor. Appeared in early Famous Players, Peerless and Universal films.

ASH, ARTY
Born: 1893, England. Died: Feb. 6, 1954, England? Screen and stage actor.

Appeared in: **1929** Josser (short). **1931** The Love Race. **1933** Soldiers of the King (aka The Women in Command—US 1934).

ASH, RUSSELL (Russell Harvey Ash)
Born: Dec. 12, 1910, Ohio. Died: June 3, 1974, Los Angeles, Calif. (cancer). Screen actor. Entered films in 1937.

Appeared in: **1956** Around the World in 80 Days.

ASH, SAMUEL HOWARD
Born: 1884. Died: Oct. 20, 1951, Hollywood, Calif. Screen and stage actor.

Appeared in: **1929** Unmasked. **1933** Girl Without a Room; Lady Killer; Operator 13. **1934** Kiss and Make Up. **1935** Four Hours to Kill; Paris in the Spring; Millions in the Air; The Man Who Broke the Bank at Monte Carlo; Broadway Gondolier; Hands Across the Table. **1936** A Man Betrayed; Ace Drummon (serial). **1937** Love is News; The King and the Chorus Girl. **1938** Alexander's Ragtime Band; Juvenile Court; You and Me. **1941** West Point Widow. **1943** The Dancing Master; The Heat's On. **1944** Cover Girl. **1945** Dick Tracey; The Stork Club. **1947** The Secret Life of Walter Mitty; Desire Me; Saddle Pals. **1948** Hazard. **1949** Oh, You Beautiful Doll. **1951** Along the Great Divide; The Mating Season.

ASHE, WARREN
Born: New York. Died: Sept. 19, 1947, Madison, Conn. (auto accident). Screen, stage and radio actor.

Appeared in: **1940** Military Academy. **1941** Here Comes Mr. Jordan; The Face Behind the Mask; Naval Academy; Harmon of Michigan. **1942** The Lady has Plans; Bombay Clipper; Smith of Minnesota. **1943** One Dangerous Night; What's Buzzin' Cousin?; Destroyer. **1946** Boston Blackie and the Law. **1947** Monsieur Verdoux.

ASHER, MAX
Born: 1880. Died: Apr. 15, 1957, Hollywood, Calif. Screen actor.

Appeared in: **1913** Mike and Jake at the Beach; The Cheese Special; Lazy Louis; Mike and Jake in the Wild West; Mike and Jake in Mexico; Mike and Jake as Heroes; Mike and Jake as Pugilists; Mike and Jake at College; Mike and Jake Among the Cannibals; Jake and Mike go Fishing; The Stingers Stung, or Mike and Jake in the Oil Fields. **1914** Love Disguised; The Tender-Hearted Sheriff; In the Clutch of Circumstance; Mike Searches for His Long-Lost Brother; Across the Court; In the Clutches of the Villain; Their First Anniversary; The Diamond Nippers; Love and Electricity; Love and Graft; O, What's the Use?; Well! Well! Well!; The Mystery of a Taxicab; In the Year 2014; A Freak Temperance Wave; Love and Politics. **1915** Lady Baffles and Detective Duck; Saved by a Shower; Back to School Days; Schultz's Lady Friend; Wedding Bells Shall Ring; The Way He Won the Widow; The Fatal Kiss; Over the Bounding Waves; No Babies Allowed; A Millionaire for a Minute; Pete's Awful Crime; Dad's Awful Deed; Chills and Chickens; Their Bewitched Elopement; A Dip in the Water; When Hiram Went to the City; At the Beach Incognito; He Couldn't Fool His Mother-in-Law; The Sign of the Sacred Safety Pin; A Day at the San Diego Fair; Hiram's Inheritance; The Lover's Lucky Predicament; When Schultz Led the Orchestra; How Billy Got His Raise; At the Bingville Barbecue; The Mechanical Man; Mrs. Prune's Boarding House; The Opera Singer's Romance; Slightly Mistaken; The Ore Mystery; Lemonade Aids Cupid. **1916** You Want Something. **1917** Suds of Love; A Wise Dummy; Kicked in the Kitchen; Rainstorms and Brainstorms. **1918** Maimed in the Hospital. **1919** A Yankee Princess. **1921** Rip Van Winkle; The Silver Car. **1922** The Ladder Jinx. **1923** The Courtship of Miles Standish. **1924** Trigger Finger; The Shooting of Dan McGrew. **1925** Heir-Loons; The Snob Buster. **1926** Beyond the Rockies; The Carnival Girl; The Call of the Wilderness; What Happened to Jane (series); We're in the Navy Now. **1927** Avenging Fangs; Galloping Fury; Painting the Town; She's My Baby; Lost at the Front. **1928** Burning Up Broadway. **1929** Show Boat; Kid's Clever. **1930** Trigger Tricks; Sweethearts on Parade. **1931** Bag O' Tricks; Talking Picture Epics (short). **1933** The Perils of Pauline (serial). **1934** Little Man, What Now?

ASHFORD, EMMETT L.
Born: Nov. 23, 1916, Los Angeles, Calif. Died: Mar. 1, 1980, Marina Del Rey, Calif. (heart attack). Baseball umpire and screen actor.

Appeared in: **1976** The Bingo Long Traveling All Stars and Motor Kings.

ASHLEY, ARTHUR H.
Born: 1886, New York. Died: Dec. 28, 1970, East Islip, N.Y. Screen actor and film director.

Appeared in: **1916** The Summer Girl; The Struggle. **1917** The Iron Ring; Rasputin, the Black Monk; Shall We Forgive Her? **1918** Broken Ties. **1919** The American Way; The Praise Agent; Forest Rivals. **1922** Breaking Home Ties.

ASHLEY, BEAULAH
Died: July 6, 1965, Hollywood, Calif. Screen actress.

ASHLEY, FRANKIE See HORNE, EDNA

ASHTON, DORRIT
Born: 1873. Died: July 25, 1936, Los Angeles, Calif. Screen, stage and vaudeville actress. Entered films in 1915 with American Films. Married to actor Charles Newton (dec. 1926).

ASHTON, HERBERT, JR.
Born: Sept. 25, 1902, San Francisco, Calif. Died: Aug. 13, 1960, San Francisco, Calif. Screen actor, stage director and author. Son of screen actors Herbert Ashton, Sr. (dec. 1930) and Lily Branscombe (dec.).

Appeared in: **1928** Me, Gangster. **1930** Brothers. **1931** It's a Wise Child.

ASHTON, HERBERT, SR.
Born: 1872, New York, N.Y. Died: Jan. 31, 1930. Screen and stage actor. Father of actor Herbert Ashton, Jr. (dec. 1960). Married to actress Lily Branscombe (dec.).

ASHTON, SYLVIA
Born: 1880. Died: Nov. 17, 1940, Los Angeles, Calif. Screen and stage actress.

Appeared in: **1917** The Nick of Time Baby; Her Fame and Shame; Secrets of a Beauty. **1919** The Lottery Man; For Better, For Worse; Peggy Does her Darndest; Men, Women and Money; Don't Change Your Husband; Why Change Your Wife?; Jenny Be Good; Sweet Lavender; Conrad in Quest of His Youth. **1921** The Blushing Bride; Garments of Truth; Her Sturdy Oak; Hold Your Horses; The Love Charm; Sham; The Love Special; A Prince There Was. **1922** Manslaughter; Is Matrimony a Failure?; For the Defense; Borderland; Saturday Night; Our Leading Citizen; A Daughter of Luxury; Youth to Youth; While Satan Sleeps. **1923** Desire; The White Flower; Souls for Sale. **1924** Greed. **1926** Dancing Days. **1927** Cheating Cheaters; Red Signals; Woman's Wares. **1928** Bachelor's Paradise; The Head Man; The Leopard Lady; Ladies' Night in a Turkish Bath; Queen Kelly; The Barker; The Crash.

ASHTON, VERA
Died: Apr. 28, 1965, Hollywood, Calif. Screen actress. Doubled for Viola Dana in silent films and also appeared in talkies.

ASHWELL, LENA (Lena Pocock)
Born: Sept. 28, 1872, England. Died: Mar. 13, 1957, London, England. Screen, stage actress, film producer, playwright and author.

Appeared in: **1916** Lady Windermere's Fan.

ASKAM, EARL
Born: 1899. Died: Apr. 3, 1940, Los Angeles, Calif. (heart attack). Stage and screen actor.

Appeared in: **1930** Madam Satan. **1936** Flash Gordon (serial); Empty Saddles; Cain and Mabel; Trail Dust. **1938** Pride of the West. **1940** Northwest Mounted Police; Pioneer of the West.

ASKAM, PERRY
Born: Aug. 31, 1898, Seattle, Wash. Died: Oct. 22, 1961, San Francisco, Calif. Screen, stage actor and opera singer.

Appeared in: **1930** Sweet Kitty Bellairs (film debut). **1935** The Crusaders.

ASQUITH, ANTHONY
Born: 1902, London, England. Died: Feb. 20, 1968, London, England. Screen actor, film director and screenwriter. Son of first Earl of Oxford, British W.W. I Prime Minister.

Doubled in blonde wig for Phyliss Neilson Terry in: **1926** Boadicea.

ASTAIRE, ADELE (Adele Marie Austerlitz)
Born: Sept. 10, 1898, Omaha, Neb. Died: Jan. 25, 1981, Phoenix, Ariz. (stroke). Screen and stage actress. Sister of actor Fred Astaire with whom she appeared on stage.

Appeared in: **1915** Fanchon, the Cricket. **1931** A Vitaphone short.

ASTAN, LAURENCE See ASTANGOV, MIKHAIL

ASTANGOV, MIKHAIL (aka LAURENCE ASTAN)
Born: 1901, Russia. Died: Apr. 21, 1965, Moscow, Russia. Stage and screen actor. Winner of three Stalin Awards.

Appeared in: **1937** Prisoners. **1949** The First Front. **1950** The Victors and the Vanquished. **1953** Sadko (rereleased as The Magic Voyage of Sinbad—US 1962); Maximba.

ASTHER, NILS
Born: Jan. 17, 1897, Hellerup, Denmark or Malmo, Sweden. Died: Oct. 13, 1981, near Stockholm, Sweden. Screen, stage and television actor. Divorced from actress Vivian Duncan.

Appeared in: **1916** Vingarina. **1917** Hittebarnet. **1918** Himmelskibet; De Mystiske Fodspor; Solen, der Draebte. **1920** Gyurkovicsarna. **1922** Vem Domer. **1923** Norrtullsligan; Der Geheimnis der Herzogin. **1924** Carl XII's Kurir; Wienerbarnet. **1925** Briefe, die ihn Nicht Erreichten; Finale der Liebe. **1926** Der Mann Seiner Frau; Der Goldene Schmetterling; Die Drei Kuckusuhren; Das Suesse Maedel; Die Versunkene Flotte (aka Die Schlacht am Skagerrack). **1927** Gauner im Frack; Der Mann mit der Flaschen Banknote; Hotellratten; Topsy and Eva; Sorrel and Son. **1928** The Blue Danube; Laugh, Clown, Laugh; The Cossacks; Loves of an Actress; The Cardboard Lover; Our Dancing Daughters; Dream of Love. **1929** Wild Orchids; The Single Standard; The Hollywood Revue of 1929; The Wrath of the Sea. **1930** The Sea Bat; King of Jazz. **1932** But the Flesh is Weak; Letty Lynton;

The Washington Masquerade. **1933** Storm at Daybreak; The Right to Romance; The Bitter Tea of General Yen; If I Were Free. **1934** By Candlelight; Madame Spy; The Crime Doctor; The Love Captive; Love Time. **1935** Abdul the Damned. **1936** The Marriage of Corbal (aka Prisoner of Corbal—US 1939); Guilty Melody. **1937** Make Up. **1938** Tes Leaves in the Wind (aka Hate in Paradise). **1941** The Man Who Lost Himself; Forced Landing; Dr. Kildare's Wedding Day; Flying Blind; The Night of January 16th. **1942** The Night Before the Divorce; Sweater Girl; Night Monster. **1943** Submarine Alert; Mystery Broadcast. **1944** The Hour Before the Dawn; The Man in Half Moon Street; Bluebird; Alaska. **1945** Son of Lassie; Jealousy; Love, Honor and Goodbye. **1948** The Feathered Serpent. **1950** Aquel Hombre de Tanger (That Man from Tangier—US 1953). **1960** Naer Morkret Faller. **1961** Svenska Floyd. **1962** Vita Frun. **1963** Gudrun (aka Suddenly a Woman!—US 1967).

ASTOR, GERTRUDE

Born: Nov. 9, 1887, Lakewood, Ohio. Died: Nov. 9, 1977, Woodland Hills, Calif. (stroke). Screen, stage and television actress.

Appeared in: **1917** The Gray Ghost (serial). **1918** The Lion's Claw (serial). **1919** The Lion Man (serial). **1920** Burning Daylight; The Great Lover; Branding Iron; Occasionally Yours. **1921** The Concert; Lucky Carson; Her Mad Bargain; Who Am I?; Through the Back Door; The Spenders. **1922** Beyond the Rocks; Hurricane's Gas; The Impossible Mrs. Bellew; The Kentucky Derby; The Ninety and Nine; Seeing's Believing; Skin Deep; You Never Know; The Wall Flower. **1923** Alice Adams; Flaming Youth; Hollywood; Rupert of Hentzau; The Ne'er-Do-Well; The Wanters; The Six-Fifty. **1924** Daring Love; The Ridin' Kid from Powder River; Broadway or Bust; Robes of Sin; The Silent Watcher; Secrets; The Torrent. **1925** Borrowed Finery; Easy Money; The Charmer; Kentucky Pride; Pursued; The Reckless Sex; Satan in Sables; Stage Struck; Ship of Souls; The Verdict; The Wife Who Wasn't Wanted; Laughing Ladies (short). **1926** The Boy Friend; The Country Beyond; Dame Chance; Kiki; Don Juan's Three Nights; Sin Cargo; The Old Soak; The Strong Man; plus the following shorts: Tell 'Em Nothing; Dizzy Daddies; Wife Tamers. **1927** The Cat and the Canary; The Cheerful Fraud; Ginsberg the Great; Pretty Clothes; The Irresistible Lover; Shanghaied; The Small Bachelor; The Taxi Dancer; Uncle Tom's Cabin; Oh, What a Man (short). **1928** The Butter and Egg Man; The Cohens and the Kellys in Paris; Five and Ten Cent Annie; The Naughty Duchess; Hit of the Show; Rose Marie; Stocks and Blondes; Family Group (short). **1929** The Fall of Eve; Frozen Justice; Synthetic Sin; Twin Beds; Two Weeks Off; Untamed. **1930** Be Yourself!; Dames Ahoy!; Cheer Up and Smile; plus the following shorts: The Doctor's Wife; and Pathe, Folly, and Manhattan Comedies, second series. **1931** Are You There?; Hell Bound; Finger Prints (serial); Come Clean (short). **1932** They Never Come Back; Western Limited. **1933** I Have Lived; Carnival Lady; Wine, Women and Song. **1934** Guilty Parents; plus the following shorts: Washee Ironee; The Chases of Pimple Street; I'll Take Vanilla. **1935** Northern Frontier; Four Hours to Kill; Okay Toots (short); Manhattan Monkey Business (short). **1936** Empty Saddles; Camille. **1937** All Over Town. **1939** The Cat and the Canary (and 1927 version). **1941** How Green Was My Valley. **1942** Rough on Rents (short). **1948** My Dear Secretary; Joe Palooka in Winner Take All; Music Man. **1950** Father Makes Good. **1961** All in a Night's Work. **1962** The Man Who Shot Liberty Valance.

ASTOR, JUNIE

Born: 1918, France. Died: Aug. 23, 1967, Avalon, France (auto accident). Screen actress.

Appeared in: **1937** The Lower Depths; Club des Femmes (Girls' Club). **1939** Entente Cordiale. **1940** Il Carnevale di Venezia (The Carnival of Venice). **1948** L'Eternel Retour (The Eternal Return).

ATCHLEY, HOOPER

Born: 1887, Tenn. Died: Nov. 16, 1943, Hollywood, Calif. (suicide—gun). Screen and stage actor.

Appeared in: **1929** Love at First Sight. **1930** The Santa Fe Trail. **1931** Millie; Men in Her Life; The Secret Witness; Branded Men; Sundown Trail; Clearing the Range; Arizona Terror; Ladies' Man. **1932** Hell's House; Trouble in Paradise; Rasputin and the Empress; Lawyer Man; Hat Check Girl; The Phantom President. **1933** The Sphinx; Gambling Ship; Big Time or Bust; Gun Justice; Speed Wings; The Three Musketeers (serial); Fighting for Justice; After Tonight. **1934** Mystery Mountain (serial); Prescott Kid; Chained. **1935** Hot Money (short); Behind the Green Lights; The Sagebrush Troubadour; Two for Tonight; Star of Midnight; Law Beyond the Range; Rumba. **1936** The Return of Jimmy Valentine; Hearts in Bondage; Navy Born; Roarin' Lead!; Bulldog Courage; Ace Drummond (serial). **1937** A Day at the Races; Portia on Trial; Saratoga; The Firefly; Last Train from Madrid;

One Hundred Men and a Girl. **1938** Little Tough Guy; Penny's Picnic (short); The Old Barn Dance; Cipher Bureau; Hunted Men; Mr. Wong, Detective; Trade Winds; Having a Wonderful Time; Bluebeard's Eighth Wife. **1939** Think First (short); Chicken Wagon Family; Mountain Rhythm; East Side of Heaven; Pirates of the Skies. **1940** The Gay Caballero; Adventures of Red Ryder (serial); I Love You Again. **1941** In the Navy; Dick Tracy vs. Crime, Inc. (serial); The Little Foxes; Honky Tonk; The Corsican Brothers; Design for Scandal; Repent at Leisure. **1942** Are Husbands Necessary?; Rings on Her Fingers; In Old California; Fingers at the Window; Gentlemen Jim. **1943** Honeymoon Lodge; Mission to Moscow; G-Men vs. the Black Dragon (serial); The Song of Bernadette; Sweet Rosie O'Grady.

ATES, ROSCOE

Born: Jan. 20, 1892. Died: Mar. 1, 1962, Hollywood, Calif. (lung cancer). Screen, stage, vaudeville and television actor. Married to actress Barbara Ray (dec. 1955). Father of actress Dorothy Ates (dec. 1982).

Appeared in: **1929** South Sea Rose. **1930** The Lone Star Ranger; Billy the Kid; The Big House; Caught Short; Love in the Rough; City Girl. **1931** The Great Lover; Cimarron; A Free Soul; The Champ; Politics; Too Many Cooks; Cracked Nuts. **1920** Shampoo the Magician (short); Freaks; Ladies of the Jury; Rainbow Trail; The Optimist; Roadhouse Murder; Young Bride; Deported; The Big Shot; Come on Danger; Hold 'Em Jail. **1933** Renegades of the West; What! No Beer?; Lucky Devils; The Scarlet River; Past of Mary Holmes; Cheyenne Kid; Golden Harvest; Alice in Wonderland. **1934** Woman in the Dark; She Made Her Bed; Merry Wives of Reno. **1935** The People's Enemy, a Vitaphone short. **1936** God's Country and the Woman; Fair Exchange. **1937** Universal and Columbia shorts. **1938** Riders of the Black Hills; The Great Adventures of Wild Bill Hickok (serial). **1939** Three Texas Steers; Gone With the Wind. **1940** Rancho Grande; A Cowboy from Sundown; Fireman, Save My Choo Choo (short); Untamed; Captain Caution; Chad Hannah. **1941** I'll Sell My Life; Mountain Moonlight; Bad Men of Missouri; Robin Hood of the Pecos; One Foot in Heaven; Reg'lar Fellers. **1942** Sullivan's Travels; Palm Beach Story; Affairs of Mimi Valentine. **1946** Colorado Serenade; Down Missouri Way; Driftin' River; Stars Over Texas. **1947** Wild Country; West to Glory; Range Beyond the Blue. **1948** Black Hills; Inner Sanctum; Tumblewood Trail. **1949** Thunder in the Pines. **1950** Hills of Oklahoma; Father's Wild Game. **1951** Honeychile. **1952** The Blazing Forest. **1953** The Stranger Wore a Gun; Those Redheads from Seattle; Lucy Gallant; Abbott and Costello Meet the Keystone Kops. **1956** The Kettles in the Ozarks; Meet Me in Las Vegas; Come Next Spring. **1957** The Birds and the Bees; The Big Caper; Short Cut to Hell. **1961** The Silent Call; The Ladies' Man.

ATKINS, ALFRED

Born: 1900. Died: May 10, 1941, London, England (air raid). Screen and stage actor.

ATKINS, ROBERT

Born: Aug. 10, 1886, Dulwich, England. Died: Feb. 9, 1972, London, England. Screen, stage actor and stage director.

Appeared in: **1935** Peg of Old Drury (US 1936). **1936** The Cardinal; Everything Is Thunder. **1942** The Great Mr. Handel (US 1943). **1946** A Matter of Life and Death (aka Stairway to Heaven—US). **1949** Black Magic; That Dangerous Age (aka If this Be Sin—US 1950). **1951** The House in the Square (aka I'll Never Forget You—US).

ATKINSON, EVELYN

Born: 1900. Died: Dec. 16, 1954, Seattle, Wash. Screen and stage actress.

Appeared in: **1926** The Boy Friend.

ATKINSON, FRANK

Born: Mar. 19, 1893, Blackpool, England. Died: Feb. 23, 1963, Pinner, England. Screen, stage, vaudeville, television actor, circus performer and screenwriter. Married to actress Jeanne D'Arcy. Entered films in U.S.

Appeared in: **1931** Ladies' Man; Along Came Youth; Ambassador Bill. **1932** The Woman in Room 13; The Man from Yesterday; Devil's Lottery; Sherlock Holmes. **1933** The Right to Live; Sailor's Luck; Pleasure Cruise; Cavalcade. **1934** The Great Defender; The Third Clue; Rolling in Money; Freedom of the Seas; The Path of Glory. **1935** Barnacle Bill; Death Drives Through; Night Mail; Play Up the Band; The Morals of Marcus (US 1936); Be Careful Mr. Smith. **1936** Shipmates O' Mine; The Limping Man; A Woman Alone (aka Two Who Dared—US 1937). **1937** A Romance in Flanders (aka Lost on the Western Front—US 1940); Knights for a Day; The Schooner Gang; The Green Cockatoo (US 1947 aka Four Dark Hours). **1938** I've Got a Horse. **1939** Ten Days in Paris (aka Missing Ten Days—US); Two Days to Live; The Body Vanishes. **1942** Mrs. Miniver; Hard Steel. **1948** The Last Load. **1953** Time Bomb (aka Terror on a Train—US). **1954** Lease of Life; The Green Buddha (US 1955). **1955** Track the Man Down; Before I Wake (aka Shadow of Fear—US 1956). **1956** Wicked as They Come (US 1957); Three Men in a Boat (US 1958). **1957** At the Stroke of Nine (US 1958); High Flight (US 1958); Cat Girl; Just My Luck. **1959** Left, Right and Centre (US 1961). **1960** Trouble with Eve (aka In Trouble with Eve—US 1964). **1961** The Kitchen.

ATKINSON, GEORGE A.
Born: Dec. 15, 1877, Liverpool, England. Died: May 1, 1968, Woodland Hills, Calif. (arteriosclerosis). Screen actor, screenwriter and film critic.

Appeared in: **1921** The Conquering Power. **1923** Times Have Changed. **1924** Racing for Life. **1928** The Crimson Canyon.

ATKINSON, MAUDE
Born: 1885, England. Died: Mar. 7, 1944, North Hollywood, Calif. Screen actress.

ATKINSON, ROSALIND
Born: Apr. 11, 1900, Wellington, New Zealand. Died: 1977, Northwood, Middlesex, England. Screen and stage actress.

Appeared in: **1963** Tom Jones. **1964** The Pumpkin Eater.

ATMAR, ANN
Born: Mar. 10, 1939, Tex. Died: Oct. 14, 1966, Hollywood, Calif. (suicide). Screen and television actress.

Appeared in: **1959** Street Fighter. **1961** A Cold Wind in August. **1966** Incubus.

ATWATER, BARRY
Born: May 16, 1918, Denver, Colo. Died: May 24, 1978, Los Angeles, Calif. (cancer). Screen, stage and television actor.

Appeared in: **1956** The Wrong Man; The Scarlet Hour; The Rack; Nightmare; Man from Del Rio; Everything But the Truth. **1957** Hard Man; The True Story of Jesse James. **1958** As Young as We Are. **1959** Pork Chop Hill; Vice Raid; Porgy and Bess. **1961** Battle at Bloody Beach. **1962** Sweet Bird of Youth. **1963** Captain Newman, M.D. **1969** The 1,000 Plane Raid.

ATWELL, ROY
Born: 1880, Syracuse, N.Y. Died: Jan. 6, 1962, New York. Screen, stage, vaudeville and radio actor.

Appeared in: **1922** The Heart Specialist; South of Suva; Red Hot Romanace; Grand Larceny; Don't Get Personal. **1923** Souls for Sale. **1926** The Outsider. **1933** A Universal short; Strike Me Pink. **1936** The Harvester. **1937** Varsity Show; Behind the Mike. **1942** The Fleet's In. **1956** People Are Funny; Gentleman Joe Palooka.

ATWILL, LIONEL (Lionel Alfred Willian Atwill)
Born: Mar. 1, 1885, Croydon, England. Died: Apr. 22, 1946, Pacific Palisades, Calif. (pneumonia). Screen and stage actor. Divorced from Mary Louise Cromwell Stolesbury and actress Phyllis Relph and Elsie Mac Kay (dec. 1928). Later married to writer Paula Pruter.

Appeared in: **1918** Eve's Daughter. **1919** The Marriage Price. **1921** The Highest Bidder; Indiscretion. **1928** Lionel Atwell in the Actors Advice to his Son (short); The White Faced Fool (short). **1932** Silent Witness; Mystery of the Wax Museum; Dr. X. **1933** Solitaire Man; The Sphinx; Song of Songs; Secret of the Blue Room; Vampire Bat; Secret of Madame Blanche; Murders in the Zoo. **1934** Beggars in Ermine; Nana; The Firebird; Age of Innocence; One More River; Stamboul Quest. **1935** The Devil Is a Woman; Mark of the Vampire; Captain Blood; Murder Man; The Man Who Reclaimed His Head; Rendezvous; Lives of a Bengal Lancer. **1936** Lady of Secrets; 'Til We Meet Again; Absolute Quiet. **1937** High Command; Last Train from Madrid; The Road Back; Lancer Spy; The Wrong Road; The Great Garrick. **1938** The Three Comrades; The Great Waltz. **1939** The Mad Empress; The Sun Never Sets; The Gorilla; The Hound of the Baskervilles; The Three Musketeers; Son of Frankenstein; Mr. Moto Takes a Vacation; Balalaika; The Secret of Dr. Kildare. **1940** Johnny Apollo; Boom Town; Charlie Chan's Murder Cruise; The Girl in 313; The Great Profile; Charlie Chan in Panama. **1941** Man-Made Monster. **1942** Strange Case of Dr. X; Cairo; Night Monster; Junior G-Men of the Air (serial); Pardon My Sarong; Sherlock Holmes and the Secret Weapon; The Mad Doctor of Market Street; The Ghost of Frankenstein; To Be or Not to Be. **1943** Captain America (serial); Frankenstein Meets the Wolf Man. **1944** Raiders of Ghost City (serial); Secrets of Scotland Yard; Lady in the Death House. **1945** House of Dracula; Fog Island; Crime, Inc.; House of Frankenstein. **1946** Lost City of the Jungle (serial); Genius at Work. **1953** Return of Captain America (reissued serial).

AUBERT, LOUIS
Born: 1878, France. Died: June 2, 1944, Berne, Switzerland. Screen actor and film producer.

AUBREY, GEORGES
Born: 1928, Verviers, Belgium. Died: Nov. 1, 1975, Brussels, Belgium (acute bronchitis). Stage and screen actor.

Appeared in: **1966** Le Depart (US 1968). **1975** On the Tip of the Lips.

AUBREY, WILL
Born: 1894, Lithuania. Died: Jan. 3, 1958, San Francisco, Calif. Screen, vaudeville actor and radio emcee. Entered films in 1927 and appeared in Vitaphone shorts.

Appeared in: **1934** The Thin Man. **1936** After the Thin Man.

AUBURN, JOY *See* MC CORMICK, ALYCE

AUDRAN, EDMOND
Born: 1919. Died: July, 1951, Lyons, France (injuries from auto accident). Screen actor, dancer and choreographer.

Appeared in: **1948** The Red Shoes. **1951** Tales of Hoffman.

AUER, ANNA *See* BAKER, ANNA

AUER, FLORENCE
Born: 1880, Albany, N.Y. Died: May 14, 1962, New York, N.Y. Screen, stage actress and screenwriter. Entered films in 1908 with Biograph.

Appeared in: **1912** His Auto's Maiden Trip. **1922** Fair Lady. **1925** The Beautiful City; Heart of a Siren; That Royal Girl. **1942** I Married an Angel. **1943** The North Star; Hangmen Also Die. **1944** Abroad With Two Yanks. **1945** Adventure. **1946** The Black Angel; The Chase; Wife Wanted. **1947** It Happened on Fifth Avenue; The Bishop's Wife; Nightmare Alley. **1948** State of the Union; Eight-Ball Andy (short); Michael O'Halloran; The Loves of Carmen. **1949** Bad Boy; Knock on Any Door; Hold That Baby; Madame Bovary. **1950** Blonde Dynamite. **1951** Love Nest. **1954** Silver Lode. **1956** Andy Goes Wild (short); Pardon My Nightshirt (short).

AUER, MISCHA (Mischa Ounskowski)
Born: Nov. 17, 1905, St. Petersburg, Russia. Died: Mar. 5, 1967, Rome, Italy (heart attack). Screen, stage and television actor. Nominated for 1936 Academy Award for Best Supporting Actor in My Man Godfrey.

Appeared in: **1928** Something Always Happens (film debut). **1929** Marquis Preferred. **1930** Just Imagine; The Benson Murder Case; Inside the Lines; Paramount on Parade. **1931** This Unholy Garden; Delicious; Women Love Once; The Yellow Ticket. **1932** Call Her Savage; Western Code; Rasputin and the Empress; No Greater Love; The Midnight Patrol; Scarlet Dawn. **1933** Tarzan the Fearless (serial); Infernal Machine; Dangerously Yours; Sucker Money; Corruption; After Tonight; Cradle Song; Girl Without a Room; Woman Condemned. **1934** Crosby Case; Wharf Angel; Bulldog Drummond Strikes Back; Stamboul Quest. **1935** Anna Karenina; The Adventures of Rex and Rinty (serial); Lives of a Bengal Lancer; I Dream Too Much; The Crusaders; Clive of India; Mystery Woman; Murder in the Fleet. **1936** We're Only Human; The House of a Thousand Candles; One Rainy Afternoon; The Gay Desperado; Sons O' Guns; The Princess Comes Across; My Man Godfrey; Winterset; That Girl from Paris; Tough Guy. **1937** Three Smart Girls; We Have Our Moments; Top of the Town; One Hundred Men and a Girl; Prescription for Romance; Pick a Star; Marry the Girl; Merry-Go-Round of 1938; Vogues of 1938. **1938** It's All Yours; Rage of Paris; Service De Luxe; Little Tough Guys in Society; Sweethearts; You Can't Take It With You. **1929** East Side of Heaven; Unexpected Father; Destry Rides Again. **1940** Seven Sinners; Trail of the Vigilantes; Alias the Deacon; Sandy Is a Lady; Margie; Spring Parade; Public Deb No. 1. **1941** Moonlight in Hawaii; Sing Another Chorus; Cracked Nuts; Flame of New Orleans; Hold That Ghost; Hellzapoppin'. **1942** Don't Get Personal. **1943** Twin Beds; Around the World. **1944** Up in Mabel's Room; Lady in the Dark. **1945** A Royal Scandal; Czarina; And Then There Were None; Brewster's Millions. **1946** She Wrote the Book; Sentimental Journey. **1947** For You I Die. **1948** Sofia. **1952** Song of Paris (aka Bachelor in Paris—US 1953); Fame and the Devil; The Sky Is Red. **1953** Confidential Report. **1957** The Monte Carlo Story. **1958** Foxiest Girl in Paris; Mam'zelle Pigalle; That Naughty Girl. **1960** Au Pied, au Cheval et par Sputnik (A Dog, A Mouse and a Sputnik); Futures Vedettes (aka School for Love—US). **1962** We Joined the Navy; Mr. Arkadin. **1963** Ladies First; Dynamite Girl. **1966** Arrivederci, Baby!; The Christmas That Almost Wasn't.

AUERBACH, ARTHUR
Born: 1903, N.Y. Died: Oct. 3, 1957, Van Nuys, Calif. (heart attack). Screen, stage, television and radio actor.

Appeared in: **1937** An MGM short.

AUERBACH, HENRY L.
Died: Aug. 22, 1916, Oakland, Calif. Screen, stage and vaudeville actor.

AUG, EDNA
Born: 1878, Cincinnati, Ohio. Died: Nov. 30, 1938, Willow, N.Y. Screen, stage and vaudeville actress.

AUGUST, EDWIN (Edwin August Philip Von der Butz)
Born: 1883. Died: Mar. 4, 1964, Hollywood, Calif. Screen, stage actor, film director and author. Brother of actor Hal August (dec. 1918). Entered films in 1908 with Biograph.

Appeared in: **1910** The Fugitive; Simple Charity; Winning Back His Love; His Daughter; Madame Rex. **1911** A Tale of the Wilderness; A Blot on the 'Scutcheon. **1912** The Girl and Her Trust; The Lesser Evil; The Old Actor; The School Teacher and the Waif; The Sands of Dee. **1918** The Lion's Claw (serial). **1921** The Idol of the North. **1922** The Blonde Vampire. **1925** Scandal Sheet. **1929** Side Street. **1930** Romance of the West. **1942** Over My Dead Body. **1947** The Exile.

AUGUST, HAL
Born: 1890. Died: Sept. 21, 1918, Great Lakes, Ill. Screen actor. Brother of actor Edwin August (dec. 1964).

Appeared in: **1914** The Romance of an Actor. **1916** Beyond the Trail.

AUGUSTINE, WILLIAM
Died: July, 1934, Eaton, Ohio. Screen actor.

Appeared in: **1934** Six of a Kind; Little Man What Now?; Bachelor Bait; Poisoned Ivory (short).

AULT, MARIE (Marie Cragg)
Born: Sept. 2, 1870, Wigan, England. Died: May 9, 1951, London, England. Screen and stage actress.

Appeared in: **1922** Class and No Class; The Wee MacGregor's Sweetheart; A Prince of Lovers (US 1927 aka Life of Lord Byron); The Grass Orphan; If Four Walls Told. **1923** Paddy-the-Next-Best-Thing; The Monkey's Paw; The Starlit Garden; Woman to Woman (US 1924). **1924** The Colleen Bawn; The Prude's Fall. **1925** The Rat; Children of the Night Series #2. **1926** The Triumph of the Rat; The Lodger (aka The Case of Jonathan Drew—US 1928); Mademoiselle from Armentieres. **1927** A Daughter in Revolt; Roses of Picardy; Hindle Wakes (aka Fanny Hawthorne—US 1929); The Rolling Road; The Silver Lining; Madame Pompadour. **1928** Dawn; Virginia's Husband; Yellow Stockings; Troublesome Wives (aka Summer Lightning); Life (aka Juan Jose); Victory; God's Clay; Hell Cat. **1929** Kitty; Little Miss London; The Return of the Rat; Downstream; The Alley Cat. **1931** Third Time Lucky; The Speckled Band; Contraband Love; Peace and Quiet. **1932** Little Fella. **1933** Money for Speed; Daughters of Today; Their Night Out; Maid Happy. **1935** Windfall; Swinging the Lead; Lend Me Your Wife. **1936** Tropical Trouble. **1941** Major Barbara; Love on the Dole. **1942** The Missing Million. **1943** We Dive at Dawn. **1944** It Happened One Sunday. **1945** They Knew Mr. Knight. **1948** The Three Weird Sisters. **1949** Madness of the Heart (US 1950). **1951** Cheer the Brave.

AUSTIN, ALBERT
Born: 1882. Died: Aug. 17, 1953, North Hollywood, Calif. Screen actor, film director and screenwriter. Entered films in 1910.

Appeared in: **1916** The Rink. **1917** The Cure. **1921** The Kid; My Boy. **1922** Trouble. **1923** A Prince of a King. **1925** Keep Smiling.

AUSTIN, CHARLES
Born: 1878. Died: Jan. 14, 1944, London, England. Screen and stage actor.

Appeared in: **1937** Another Dawn.

AUSTIN, GENE (Eugene Lucas)
Born: 1901. Died: Jan. 24, 1972, Palm Springs, Calif. (cancer). Screen actor, singer and songwriter.

Appeared in: **1933** Melody Cruise. **1934** Belle of the Nineties; Sadie McKee; Gift of Gab. **1935** RKO Headliners short. **1936** Klondike Annie; RKO Headliner short. **1940** My Little Chickadee. **1944** Moon Over Las Vegas.

AUSTIN, JERE
Born: 1876. Died: Nov. 12, 1927, Hollywood, Calif. (cancer). Screen actor.

Appeared in: **1914** The School for Scandal; Nina of the Theatre; The Lynbrook Tragedy. **1915** The White Goddess; Unfaithful to His Trust. **1916** The Romance of the Hollow Tree; For Uncle Sam's Navy. **1918** Resurrection; Fedora. **1919** The Woman on the Index. **1927** King of Kings.

AUSTIN, JOHANNA (Anna R. Austin)
Born: 1853. Died: June 1, 1944, Hollywood, Calif. Screen actress. Appeared in early Edison Co. films.

AUSTIN, LOIS
Born: 1909. Died: Apr. 26, 1957, Hollywood, Calif. (cachexia). Screen actress. Married to film director Charles Barton.

Appeared in: **1941** In the Navy; Father Takes a Wife; Melody for Three. **1942** Swamp Woman; Down Texas Way. **1946** The Spider Woman Strikes Back; Centennial Summer; Tomorrow is Forever; Deception; Without Reservations. **1947** The Trap; Ivy; The Voice of the Turtle; The Unfaithful. **1948** Smart Woman; Letter from an Unknown Woman; Family Honeymoon; Winter Meeting; The Golden Eye (aka The Mystery of the Golden Eye). **1949** Night Unto Night; Henry, the Rainmaker; The Barkleys of Broadway; It's a Great Feeling. **1950** Father Makes Good; The Fuller Brush Girl. **1951** On Moonlight Bay. **1952** Night Stage to Galveston. **1957** Mom and Dad.

AUSTIN, RICHARD
Born: 1941, New York? Died: July 1, 1974, Hawthorne, Calif. (auto accident). Black screen actor and stuntman.

AUSTIN, STEPHEN E.
Born: 1891. Died: May 12, 1955, Dallas, Tex. (heart attack). Screen and radio actor.

AVALIER, DON
Died: May 29, 1973. Screen actor.

Appeared in: **1954** Playgirl.

AVERY, CHARLES (Charles Bradford Avery)
Born: 1873, Chicago, Ill. Died: July 23, 1926, Hollywood, Calif. Screen, stage actor and film director. One of Sennett's original seven Keystone Kops.

Appeared in: **1913** A Deaf Burglar; Cohen's Outing; The Telltale Light. **1915** Submarine Pirate. **1925** Fighting Ranger (serial). **1927** The Rambling Ranger; The Western Rover.

AVERY, FRED "TEX"
Born: 1909, Dallas, Tex. Died: Aug. 26, 1980, Burbank, Calif, (cancer). Film animator and screen actor.

Appeared in: **1975** Bugs Bunny Superstar.

AVERY, PATRICIA
Born: 1902. Died: 1973. Screen actress. Was a Wampas Baby Star of 1927. Married to art director Merrill Pye.

Appeared in: **1927** A Light in the Window; Annie Laurie; Night Life. **1928** Alex the Great.

AVERY, TOL
Born: 1915. Died: Aug. 27, 1973, Calif. (heart attack). Screen and television actor.

Appeared in: **1950** Where Danger Lives. **1951** His Kind of Woman. **1952** Scarlet Angel. **1955** It Came from Beneath the Sea; I'll Cry Tomorrow. **1956** All That Heaven Allows. **1957** The Unholy Wife; Pal Joey. **1958** Buchanan Rides Alone; The Case Against Brooklyn. **1961** Twist Around the Clock; The George Raft Story; Man-Trap. **1963** Ticklish Affair. **1964** A Tiger Walks. **1965** Satan Bug. **1966** Follow Me, Boys!. **1967** Hotel. **1969** A Dream of Kings. **1970** W.U.S.A.

AYE, MARYON (aka MARION AYE)
Born: 1906. Died: July 21, 1951, Hollywood, Calif. (suicide—poison). Screen and stage actress. Was a Wampas Baby Star of 1922.

Appeared in: **1921** Montana Bill; The Vengeance Trail. **1923** The Meanest Man in the World; The Eternal Three. **1924** The Last Man on Earth; The Roughneck. **1926** Irene.

AYERTON, ROBERT
Died: May 18, 1924. Screen and stage actor.

Appeared in: **1919** A Regular Girl. **1921** You Find It Everywhere.

AYLESWORTH, ARTHUR
Born: Aug. 12, 1884, Apponaug, R.I. Died: June 26, 1946. Screen actor.

Appeared in: **1932-33** Paramount shorts. **1934** Babbitt; St. Louis Kid; Gentlemen Are Born; Six Day Bike Rider; Dames; Midnight Alibi; The Dragon Murder Case; The Key; Desirable; The Man With Two Faces; Case of the Howling Dog; British Agent. **1935** I Am a Thief; The Secret Bride; The Nitwits; Men Without Names; The Man on the Flying Trapeze; The Big Broadcast of 1936; The Virginia Judge; Escape from Devil's Island; Forced Landing. **1936** Rose of the Rancho; Woman Trap; The Petrified Forest; King of the Pecos; Next Time We Love; Girl of the Ozarks; Love Begins at Twenty; Arizona Raiders; Down the Ribber (short); To Mary With Love; Mister Cinderella; Dimples; The Man I Marry; The Plot Thickens; The President's Mystery. **1937** The Life of Emile Zola; Sandflow; Marked Woman; Fifty Roads to Town; That Man's Here Again; I Cover the War; Slave Ship; Escape by Night; Marry the Girl. **1938** Boys Town; Test Pilot; Of Human Hearts; Blockade; Outside the Law; Spawn of the North. **1939** In Name Only; The Oklahoma Kid; King of the Underworld; Jesse James; The Return of the Cisco Kid; 6,000 Enemies; Beau Geste; Drums Along the Mohawk; What a Life; The Return of Dr. X; Dust Be My Destiny. **1940** Northwest Passage; Little Old New York; The Grapes of Wrath; Edison the Man; Young People; Brigham Young—Frontiersman; The Westerner. **1941** High Sierra; Shadow of the Thin Man; Sergeant York; Dancing on a Dime; The Smiling Ghost. **1942** Roxie Hunt; Moontide; Sin Town; Scattergood Rides High. **1944** The Adventures of Mark Twain; Home in Indiana; Roger Touhy Gangster. **1945** Scared Stiff; Christmas in Connecticut.

AYLING, ROBERT
Died: Aug. 28, 1919, New York, N.Y. Screen actor.

AYLMER, DAVID
Born: 1933. Died: July 20, 1964, London, England (suicide). Screen, stage and television actor. Son of actor Felix Aylmer (dec. 1979) and actress Cecily Byrne (dec. 1975).

Appeared in: **1957** Yangtse Incident (aka Battle Hell—US). **1958** Gideon's Day (aka Gideon of Scotland Yard—1959); The Man Who Wouldn't Talk (US 1960). **1962** The Iron Maiden (aka The Wingin' Maiden—US 1963).

AYLMER, SIR FELIX (Felix Edward Aylmer-Jones)
Born: Feb. 21, 1889, Corsham, Wilts, England. Died: Sept. 2, 1979, Sussex, England. Screen, stage, television actor and author. Father of actor David (dec. 1964) and Jennifer Aylmer. Married to actress Cecily Byrne (dec. 1975). Made Commander of the Order of the British Empire in 1965.

Appeared in: **1930** Escape; The Temporary Widow. **1932** The World, the Flesh and the Devil. **1933** Home Sweet Home; The Ghost Camera; The Wandering Jew (US 1935). **1934** My Old Dutch; Doctor's Orders; The Path of Glory; Night Club Queen; Whispering Tongues. **1935** Her Last Affaire; Checkmate; Old Roses; Hello Sweetheart (aka The Butter and Egg Man—US); The Divine Spark; The Ace of Spades; The Iron Duke; The Clairvoyant, She Shall Have Music (US 1942). **1936** The Man in the Mirror (US 1937); As You Like It; Dusty Ermine (aka Hideout in the Alps—US 1938); Seven Sinners (aka Doomed Cargo—US); Royal Eagle; Tudor Rose (aka Nine Days a Queen—US); In the Soup; The Improper Duchess; Jack of All Trades (aka The Two of Us—US 1937). **1937** Sensation; The Mill on the Floss (US 1939); Dreaming Lips; The Frogs (US 1939); The Vicar of Bray; Glamorous Night; Action for Slander (US 1938); Victoria the Great; The Rat; The Live Wire. **1938** Bank Holiday (aka Three on a Weekend—US); Just Like a Woman; Break the News (US 1941); Kate Plus Ten; Sixty Glorious Years (aka Queen of Destiny—US); I've Got a Horse. **1939** Spies of the Air (US 1940); Young Man's Fancy (US 1943). **1940** Night Train to Munich (aka Gestapo and aka Night Train—US); The Briggs Family; Dr. O'Dowd; Charley's (Big Hearted) Aunt; Saloon Bar (US 1944); The Case of the Frightened Lady—US 1941); The Girl in the News (US—1941). **1941** The Ghost of St Michael's; The Saint's Vacation; Spellbound (aka The Spell of Amy Nugent—US); Atlantic Ferry (aka Sons of the Sea—US); Once a Crook; Major Barbara; The Seventh Survivor; I Thank You; Hi Gang!; Black Sheep of Whitehall; South American George. **1942** The Peterville Diamond; The Young Mr. Pitt; Sabotage at Sea; Uncensored (US 1944). **1943** Escape to Danger (US 1944); The Life and Death of Colonel Blimp (aka Colonel Blimp—US 1945); Thursday's Child; The Demi-Paradise (aka Adventure for Two—US 1945). **1944** Time Flies; Mr. Emmanuel (US 1945); English Without Tears (aka Her Man Gilbey—US 1949). **1945** Henry V (US 1946); Julius Caesar (short); The Way to the Stars (aka Johnny in the Clouds—US); The Wicked Lady (US 1946). **1946** Laughing Lady (US 1950); The Magic Bow (US 1947); The Years

Between (US 1947). **1947** Green Fingers; The Man Within (aka The Smugglers—US 1948); The October Man (US 1948); A Man About the House (US 1949); The Ghosts of Berkeley Square. **1948** Hamlet; The Calendar; Quartet (US 1949); Alice in Wonderland (US 1951). **1949** Edward My Son; Christopher Columbus; Prince of Foxes. **1950** Trio; Your Witness (aka Eye Witness—US); So Long at the Fair (US 1951); She Shall Have Murder. **1951** The House in the Square (aka I'll Never Forget You—US); The Lady With the Lamp; Quo Vadis. **1952** Ivanhoe. **1953** The Man Who Watched Trains Go By (aka Paris Express—US); The Master of Ballantrae. **1954** The Love Lottery; Knights of the Round Table; The Angel Who Pawned Her Harp (US 1956). **1956** Anastasia; Loser Takes All (US 1957). **1957** Saint Joan. **1958** I Accuse!; The Two-Headed Spy (US 1959); Separate Tables. **1959** The Mummy; The Doctor's Dilemma. **1960** Never Take Sweets from a Stranger (aka Never Take Candy form a Stranger—US 1961); The Hands of Orlac; From the Terrace; Exodus. **1961** Macbeth (US 1963). **1962** The Boys (US 1963); The Road to Hong Kong. **1963** The Running Man; The Chalk Garden (stage and film versions, US 1964). **1964** Masquerade (US 1965); Becket. **1968** The Decline and Fall ... of a Birdwatcher (US 1969); Hostile Witness.

AYNESWORTH, ALLAN (E. Abbot-Anderson)
Born: Apr. 14, 1864, Sandhurst, England. Died: Aug. 22, 1959, Camberley, Surrey, England. Screen, stage and vaudeville actor.

Appeared in: **1922** Flames of Passion; The Game of Life. **1931** Brown Sugar; The Calendar (aka Bachelor's Folly—US 1932). **1933** Just Smith. **1934** Little Friend; Love, Life and Laughter. **1935** The Iron Duke; Brewster's Millions. **1949** The Last Days of Dolwyn (aka Woman of Dolwyn—US).

AYRES, AGNES (Agnes Hinkle)
Born: Apr. 4, 1898, Carbondale, Ill. Died: Dec. 25, 1940, Los Angeles, Calif. (cerebral hemorrhage). Screen, stage, radio, and vaudeville actress.

Appeared in: **1915** His New Job. **1917** The Dazzling Miss Davison; The Debt. **1920** The Furnace; Held by the Enemy; Go and Get It. **1921** Affairs of Anatole; Forbidden Fruit; The Sheik; Cappy Ricks; The Love Special; Too Much Speed. **1922** Clarence; The Ordeal; The Lane That Had No Turning; Bought and Paid For; Borderland; A Daughter of Luxury. **1923** The Ten Commandments; Tess of the Storm Country; Racing Hearts; The Heart Raider; Hollywood; The Marriage Maker. **1924** The Story Without a Name; When a Girl Loves; Bluff; Don't Call It Love; The Guilty One; Worldly Goods. **1925** Tomorrow's Love; Morals for Men; The Awful Truth. **1926** The Son of the Sheik; Her Market Value. **1928** The Lady of Victories (short); Into the Night. **1929** Bye, Bye, Buddy; The Donovan Affair; Broken Hearted; Eve's Love Letters. **1936** Small Town Girl. **1937** Morning Judge (short); Souls at Sea.

AYRES, MITCHELL "MITCH"
Born: 1911, Milwaukee, Wis. Died: Sept. 5, 1969, Las Vegas, Nev. (auto accident). Orchestra leader and screen actor.

Appeared in: **1944** Swingtime Johnny; Moonlight and Cactus; Lady, Let's Dance!

AYRES, ROBERT
Born: 1914, Mich. Died: Nov. 5, 1968, Hemel Hempstead, England (heart attack). Screen, stage and television actor.

Appeared in: **1949** They Were Not Divided. **1951** The Black Widow (US 1954); To Have and To Hold. **1952** 24 Hours in a Woman's Life (aka Affair in Monte Carlo). **1953** The Mask; Cosh Boy (aka The Slasher—US). **1954** A Prize of Gold; River Beat. **1955** Contraband Spain; It's Never Too Late. **1956** The Baby and the Battleship; Depraved. **1957** Time Lock (US 1959); The Story of Esther Costello; The Cat Girl; Operation Murder. **1958** A Night to Remember. **1959** First Man into Space; John Paul Jones. **1962** The Road to Hong Kong; Two and Two Make Six. **1963** The Sicilians. **1965** The Heroes of Telemark (US 1966). **1968** Battle Beneath the Earth. **1969** Isadora (aka The Loves of Isadora—US).

AYRES, SYDNEY
Died: Sept. 9, 1916, Oakland, Calif. Screen actor, screenwriter and film producer.

Appeared in: **1911** Captain Brand's Wife; Blackbeard; The Heart of John Barlow. **1912** The Foreign Spy. **1913** Trapped in a Forest Fire; An Innocent Informer. **1914** The Power of Light; The Rose of San Juan; Destinies Fulfilled; The Son of Thomas Gray; The Cricket on the Hearth; The Crucible; The Turning Point; The Last Supper; The Story of the Olive. **1915** Fifty Years Behind; The Stranger; Around the Corner; The Honor of Kenneth McGrath; On Desert Sands; The Love

That Lasts; Love and Handcuffs; The Law o' The Parent; The Hearts of Fate; Haunting Winds; Every Man's Money; The Shot; The Vengeance of Guido; A Pure Gold Partner; The Man From Argentine; Honor Thy Husband; His Good Name; The Mirror of Justice; The Third Partner. **1919** The Stolen Melody; As in a Dream; The String of Conscience.

AYRTON, RANDLE
Born: Aug. 9, 1869, Chester, England. Died: May 28, 1940, Stratford-on-Avon, England. Screen, stage actor and stage producer.

Appeared in: **1923** Chu Chin Chow (US 1925). **1926** The Little People; Nell Gwyn. **1927** Passion Island; One of the Best. **1928** Eileen of the Trees (aka Glorious Youth—US). **1929** The Hate Ship; The Manxman. **1930** Two Worlds; Dreyfus (aka The Dreyfus Case—US). **1936** Talk of the Devil (US 1937); Debt of Honor.

BABBITT, ORRIN
Born: 1883. Died: July 5, 1941, Warwick, R.I. Silent screen actor.

BABCOCK, THEODORE
Died: Sept. 7, 1930. Screen actor.

Appeared in: **1921** The Silver Lining. **1923** The Silent Command. **1925** The Shock Punch; The Sky Raider.

BABIN, HOWARD A.
Born: 1913. Died: Jan. 28, 1980, Los Angeles, Calif. (cancer). Screen and vaudeville actor. Divorced from actress Dorothy Burr, with whom he appeared in vaudeville in an act billed as "Dot and Dash."

Appeared in: **1944** Adventure in Music.

"BABY LAURENCE" (Lawrence Jackson)
Born: 1921, Baltimore, Md. Died: Apr. 2, 1974, New York, N.Y. (cancer). Black screen, stage, vaudeville, television actor and tap dancer.

BACCALONI, SALVATORE
Born: 1900, Rome, Italy. Died: Dec. 31, 1969, New York, N.Y. Screen actor and operatic comedian.

Appeared in: **1956** Full of Life (film debut). **1958** Rock-A-Bye Baby; Merry Andrew. **1961** Operation Bottleneck; Fanny. **1962** The Pigeon That Took Rome.

BACCHIOCCHI, NORMAN
Born: 1943. Died: May, 1978. Screen actor.

Appeared in: **1972** The Godfather.

BACH See PASQUIER, CHARLES "BACH"

BACH, REGINALD
Born: Sept. 3, 1886, Shepperton, England. Died: Jan. 6, 1941, New York, N. Y. (pneumonia). Screen, stage actor, stage producer and director.

Appeared in: **1919** The Chinese Puzzle. **1920** Once Aboard the Lugger; The Amazing Quest of Mr. Ernest Bliss series; Daily Jesters series including: Whispering Gables. **1921** The Will. **1923** Wonder Women of the World series including: Madame Recamier, or, The Price of Virtue; Empress Josephine, or, Wife of Demigod. **1925** A Romance of Mayfair; We Women. **1931** Hobson's Choice; The Girl in the Night. **1932** The Hound of the Baskervilles; Let Me Explain, Dear; Account Rendered. **1934** The Scoop.

BACH, MRS. RUDI
Died: Apr. 11, 1960, Buffalo, N.Y. Stage and screen actress.

BACKUS, GEORGE
Born: 1858. Died: May 22, 1939, Merrick, N.Y. Screen, stage actor and playwright.

Appeared in: **1916** The Habit of Happiness. **1921** The Price of Possession. **1923** The Exciters. **1924** Her Own Free Will; The Warrens of Virginia.

BACLANOVA, OLGA
Born: 1899?, Moscow, Russia. Died: Sept. 6, 1974, Vevey, Switzerland. Screen, stage, radio actress and ballet dancer. Married to actor Nicholas Soussanin (dec. 1975); married to theatre owner Richard Davis.

Appeared in: **1927** The Dove (film debut). **1928** The Street of Sin; Forgotten Faces; Docks of New York; Avalanche; Three Sinners; The Man Who Laughs. **1929** A Dangerous Woman; The Wolf of Wall Street; The Man I Love. **1930** Are You There?; Cheer Up and Smile. **1931** The Great Lover. **1932** Downstairs; Freaks. **1933** The Billion Dollar Scandal. **1935** Broadway Brevities (short); a Universal short. **1943** Claudia.

BACON, BESSIE (Bessie Bacon Allen)
Born: 1886. Died: Dec. 7, 1952, Los Angeles, Calif. Screen actress and writer.

BACON, DAVID (David Gaspar Griswold Bacon)
Born: Mar. 24, 1914, Jamaica Plains, Mass. Died: Sept. 13, 1943, Los Angeles, Calif. (stab wounds). Screen actor. Married to actress Greta Keller (dec. 1977).

Appeared in: **1942** Ten Gentlemen from West Point. **1943** The Masked Marvel (serial); Crash Dive; Gals Inc.

BACON, FAITH
Born: 1909. Died: Sept. 26, 1956, Chicago, Ill. (suicide—jump from window). Screen and vaudeville actress.

Appeared in: **1938** Prison Train.

BACON, FRANK
Born: 1864, Marysville, Calif. Died: Nov. 19, 1922, Chicago, Ill. (heart attack). Stage and screen actor. Married to stage actress Jane Bacon (dec. 1956). Father of actor Lloyd Bacon (dec. 1955).

Appeared in: **1915** The Silent Voice.

BACON, IRVING
Born: Sept. 6, 1893, St Joseph, Mo. Died: Feb. 5, 1965, Hollywood, Calif. Screen, stage and television actor. Entered films in 1913 with Mack Sennett.

Appeared in: **1927** California or Bust. **1928** Head Man; The Goodbye Kiss. **1929** Half Way to Heaven; Side Street; Dane and Arthur series; Louise Fazenda series; Two Sisters; The Old Barn (short); The Saturday Night Kid. **1930** Street of Chance. **1931** Sing Baby, Sing (short); Alias the Bad Man; Branded Men. **1932** I Am a Fugitive from a Chain Gang; Union Depot; No One Man; This Is the Night; Gentleman for a Day; Central Park; File 113; Million Dollar Legs. **1933** Sitting Pretty; He Learned About Women; Hello, Everybody!; Private Detective 62; Big Executive. **1934** Shadows of Sing Sing; You Belong to Me; Hat, Coat and Glove; Ready for Love; The Pursuit of Happiness; Lone Cowboy; Miss Fane's Baby Is Stolen; Six of a Kind; It Happened One Night; The Hell Cat; No Ransom. **1935** Tuned Out (short); West of the Pecos; Powdersmoke Range; Here Comes Cookie; Private Worlds; Goin' to Town; The Glass Key; The Virginia Judge; Ship Cafe; Two-Fisted; It's a Small World; Diamond Jim; Manhattan Moon; Bright Leaves; Millions in the Air. **1936** The Bride Walks Out; Trail of the Lonesome Pine; Rhythm on the Range; Petticoat Fever; Earthworm Tractors; Drift Fence; Hollywood Boulevard; Lady Be Careful; Murder with Pictures; Wives Never Know; Valiant is the Word for Carrie; Hopalong Cassidy Returns; It's a Great Life; Big Town Girl; Three Cheers for Love; The Big Broadcast of 1937. **1937** True Confession; Let's Make a Million; Interns Can't Take Money; Exclusive; Seventh Heaven; Arizona Mahoney; Big City; Marry the Girl; It's Love I'm After. **1938** Letter of Introduction; Every Day's a Holiday; Sweethearts; Strange Faces; Passport Husband; Blondie; Mr. Moto's Gamble; The Big Broadcast of 1938; The Texans; There Goes My Heart; The Cowboy and the Lady; You Can't Take it with You; Midnight Intruder; Exposed; The First Hundred Years; The Chaser; Tip-Off Girls; Sing, You Sinners; Spawn of the North; Kentucky Moonshine; The Amazing Dr. Clitterhouse; The Sisters. **1939** Too Busy to Work; Blondie Meets the Boss; Hollywood Slaves; Tailspin; Lucky Night; Second Fiddle; Hollywood Cavalcade; Gone With the Wind; I Stole a Million; Blondie Takes a Vacation; Rio; Blondie Brings up Baby; The Gracie Allen Murder Case; The Oklahoma Kid; Torchy Runs for Mayor. **1940** Lillian Russell; Love, Honor and Oh, Baby!; Indianapolis Speedway; Heaven with a Barbed Wire Fence; The Grapes of Wrath; The Man Who Wouldn't Talk; Young People; Dr. Ehrlich's Magic Bullet; Blondie on a Budget; Manhattan Heartbeat; The Return of Frank James; Gold Rush Maisie; The Howards of Virginia; Dreaming Out Loud; Blondie Has Servant Trouble; Michael Shayne, Private Detective; Star Dust; You Can't Fool Your Wife; Blondie Plays Cupid. **1941** Skylark; Blondie Goes Latin; She Couldn't Say No; Western Union; Ride on, Vaquero; Caught in the Draft; Accent on Love; Too Many Blondes; Moon over Her Shoulder; It Started with Eve; Never Give a Sucker an Even Break; Blondie in Society; Remember the Day; Meet John Doe; A Girl, A Guy and a Gob; Great Guns; Henry Aldrich for President; Cadet Girl; Tobacco Road. **1942** Lady in a Jam; They Died with Their Boots On; The Bashful Bachelor; Pardon My Sarong; Through Different Eyes; Juke Girl; Young America; Give Out, Sister; Between Us Girls; Get Hep to Love; Blondie for Victory; Holiday Inn; Footlight Serenade. **1943** Gung Ho!; It's a Great Life; Footlight Glamour; Shadow of a Doubt; Johnny Come Lately; Hers to Hold; Follow the Band; King of the Cowboys; Two Weeks to Live; Happy Go Lucky; So's Your Uncle; The Good Fellows; In Old Oklahoma; Action in the North Atlantic; The

Desperados; Stranger in Town; Dixie Dugan. **1944** Casanova Brown; The Story of Dr. Wassell; Weekend Pass; Chip off the Old Block; Her Primitive Man; Since You Went Away; Heavenly Days; Pin Up Girl; Wing and a Prayer. **1945** Weekend at the Waldorf; Under Western Skies; Roughly Speaking; Patrick the Great; Out of This World; Guest Wife; Hitchhike to Happiness. **1946** Night Train to Memphis; One Way to Love; Wake Up and Dream. **1947** Dear Ruth; My Brother Talks to Horses; Saddle Pals; Monsieur Verdoux; The Bachelor and the Bobby-Soxer. **1948** Albuquerque; Moonrise; Adventures in Silverado; State of the Union; The Velvet Touch; Good Sam; Rocky; Family Honeymoon. **1949** Night unto Night; John Loves Mary; The Green Promise; The Big Cat; Dynamite; It's a Great Feeling; Manhandled; Woman in Hiding. **1950** Wabash Avenue; Born to Be Bad; Emergency Wedding; Dear Wife; Sons of New Mexico. **1951** Here Comes the Groom; Honeychile; Cause for Alarm; Katie Did It; Desert of Lost Men. **1952** O. Henry's Full House; Room for One More. **1953** Fort Ti; Devil's Canyon; Kansas Pacific; Sweethearts on Parade. **1954** Ma and Pa Kettle at Home; Black Horse Canyon; Duffy of San Quentin; A Star is Born; The Glenn Miller Story. **1955** Run for Cover; At Gunpoint. **1956** Hidden Guns; The Dakota Incident. **1958** Ambush at Cimarron Pass; Fort Massacre.

BACON, LLOYD
Born: Jan. 16, 1890, San Jose, Calif. Died: Nov. 15, 1955, Burbank, Calif. (cerebral hemorrhage). Screen, stage, vaudeville actor and film director. Entered films with Essanay Co. Son of stage actress Jane (dec. 1956) and actor Frank Bacon (dec. 1922).

Appeared in: **1915** Broncho Billy and the Lumber King; Broncho Billy Misled; Wine, Women and Song; Snakeville's Champion; Broncho Billy's Cowardly Brother; The Burglar's Grandfather; Broncho Billy and the Cardsharp; A Quiet Little Game; Broncho Billy Begins Life Anew; A Christmas Revenge. **1917** His Thankless Job; A Hotel Disgrace; His Fatal Move; His Taking Ways; A Dark Room Secret. **1919** Square Deal Sanderson. **1921** The Great Profit; Hands Off; Hearts and Masks; The Road Demon. **1922** Smudge.

BACON, MABEL (aka MABEL MC KERRON)
Born: Feb.8, 1894, Prescott, Ariz. Died: Nov. 3, 1950, Los Angeles, Calif. (cancer). Screen and stage actress. Sister of actress Mary Bacon. Mother of prominent La Jolla attorney, C. Neil Ash.

Appeared in: **1914** When the Cook Fell In. **1915** Cora.

BACON, WALTER SCOTT
Born: 1891. Died: Nov. 7, 1973, Hollywood, Calif. (heart attack). Screen actor and assistant film director. Married to actress Sybil Bacon.

BACUS, LUCIA *See* SEGAR, LUCIA

BADDELEY, ANGELA (Madeleine Angela Clinton-Baddeley)
Born: July 4, 1904, London, England. Died: Feb. 22, 1976, London, England. Screen, stage and television actress. Sister of actress Hermione Baddeley. Divorced from Stephen Kerr Thomas. Married to actor-director Glen Byam Shaw.

Appeared in: **1931** The Speckled Band; Ghost Train (US 1932). **1932** The Safe; Arms and the Man. **1934** Those Were the Days. **1948** Quartet (US 1949). **1957** No Time for Tears. **1963** Tom Jones.

BADGELY, HELEN
Died: Oct. 25, 1977. Screen actress.

Appeared in: **1914** A Dog's Love. **1915** Two-Cent Mystery; Milestone of Life.

BADGLEY, FRANK C.
Born: Jan. 1, 1895, Ottawa, Canada. Died: 1955. Screen, stage, vaudeville actor, film director, writer and newsman. Entered films in 1919 with D. W. Griffith.

Appeared in: **1920** Way Down East. **1921** The Ghost in the Garret; Scrambled Wives.

BAER, ARTHUR "BUGS"
Born: 1886, Philadelphia, Pa. Died: May 17, 1969, New York, N.Y. (cancer). Screen actor and newspaper columnist.

Appeared in: **1924** The Great White Way. **1926** Oh, Baby! **1930** They Learned About Women.

BAER, MARY *See* BEAR, MARY

BAER, MAX
Born: 1909. Died: Nov. 21, 1959, Hollywood, Calif. (heart attack). Screen, stage, radio and vaudeville actor and former heavyweight boxing champion of the world. Divorced from actress Dorothy Dunbar.

Appeared in: **1933** The Prizefighter and the Lady. **1938** Fisticuffs (short). **1942** The Navy Comes Through. **1943** Ladies' Day; Buckskin Frontier. **1944** The Iron Road. **1949** Africa Screams; Bride for Sale. **1950** Riding High. **1951** Skipalong Rosenbloom. **1956** The Harder They Fall. **1957** Utah Blaine. **1958** Once upon a Horse; Over She Goes.

BAER, THAIS
Born: 1929. Died: Sept. 8, 1930, Painted Desert, Ariz. Fourteen-month-old baby girl making fourth screen appearance when she died during filming of Painted Desert.

Appeared in: **1931** Painted Desert.

BAGDAD, WILLIAM
Died: Nov. 20, 1975. Screen actor.

Appeared in: **1967** She Freak. **1968** The Girl in Gold Boots; The Astro-Zombies; Head.

BAGDASARIAN, ROSS S. (aka DAVID SEVILLE)
Born: 1920. Died: Jan. 16, 1972, Beverly Hills, Calif. (natural causes). Composer, orchestra leader and screen actor.

Appeared in: **1952** Viva Zapata. **1953** Destination Gobi. **1954** Alaska Seas; Rear Window. **1956** Three Violent People; The Proud and the Profane. **1957** The Devil's Hairpin. **1958** The Deep Six. **1959** Stalag 17.

BAGGETT, LYNNE
Born: 1928. Died: Mar. 22, 1960, Hollywood, Calif. (overdose of barbiturates). Screen actress. Divorced from film producer Sam Spiegel.

Appeared in: **1941** Manpower. **1943** Air Force; Thank Your Lucky Stars. **1944** The Adventures of Mark Twain; Hollywood Canteen. **1945** Mildred Pierce. **1946** The Time of Their Lives; Janie Gets Married; Night and Day; The Time, the Place and the Girl. **1950** D.O.A.; Flame and the Arrow. **1951** The Mob.

BAGGOT, KING
Born: 1874, St. Louis, Mo. Died: July 11, 1948, Los Angeles, Calif. (stroke). Screen, stage actor, film director and screenwriter. Entered films in 1910 as an actor.

Appeared in: **1911** The Scarlet Letter. **1912** Lady Audley's Secret. **1913** Dr. Jekyll and Mr. Hyde; Ivanhoe. **1914** The Secret of the Air (aka Across the Atlantic—US). **1915** The Corsican Brothers. **1916** Lovely Mary. **1918** The Eagle's Eye (serial). **1920** Dwelling Place of Light; The Cheater; The Hawk's Trail (serial). **1921** Moonlight Follies; Snowy Baker; The Shadow of Lightning Ridge; The Fighting Breed; The Butterfly Girl; The Girl in the Taxi. **1922** Going Straight. **1923** His Last Race; The Thrill Chaser. **1925** Tumbleweeds. **1926** Lovely Mary. **1927** The Notorious Lady. **1930** Once a Gentleman; The Czar of Broadway. **1931** Scareheads; Sweepstakes. **1932** The Big Flash (short); Fame Street. **1934** The Black Cat; Romance in the Rain; Beloved. **1935** It Happened in New York; Father Brown, Detective; I've Been Around; Mississippi; Chinatown Squad; She Gets Her Man. **1936** Next Time We Love. **1941** Come Live with Me. **1945** Abbott and Costello in Hollywood.

BAGLEY, SAM (Samuel Borken)
Born: 1903. Died: July 3, 1968, Hollywood, Calif. (heart ailment). Screen actor. Entered films approx. 1930.

Appeared in: **1955** The Lieutenant Wore Skirts.

BAGNI, JOHN
Born: 1911. Died: Feb. 13, 1954, Hollywood, Calif. (heart attack). Screen, stage actor, radio and television writer.

Appeared in: **1941** Adventures of Captain Marvel (serial); Aloma of the South Seas; New York Town. **1942** Junior G-Men of the Air (serial); Bombay Clipper; The Jungle Book; The Tuttles of Tahiti; Perils of Nyoka (serial). **1943** The North Star; Mug Town; The Phantom (serial). **1944** Captain America (serial); Cobra Woman; Passage to Marseille; The Bridge of San Luis Rey. **1945** A Bell for Adano; Counter-Attack. **1946** The Phantom Thief. **1947** The Senator was Indiscreet; The Pretender. **1948** Casbah. **1950** Captain China.

BAILEY, ALBERT
Born: 1891. Died: July 31, 1952, Hollywood, Calif. (suicide—gun). Western screen actor and trainer of film horses.

BAILEY, BILL
Born: 1912. Died: Dec. 12, 1978, Philadelphia, Pa. Black screen, stage, vaudeville, television actor, tap dancer and nightclub entertainer. Brother of actress/singer Pearl Bailey. Do not confuse with actor William Norton Bailey (dec. 1962).

Appeared in: **1943** Cabin in the Sky. **1947** Robin Hood in Texas. **1974** The Groove Tube.

BAILEY, EDWARD LORENZ
Born: 1883. Died: Oct. 16, 1951, Lima, Ohio. Stage and screen actor.

BAILEY, EDWIN B.
Born: 1873. Died: July 22, 1950, Santa Monica, Calif. Screen, stage and vaudeville actor. Married to actress Grace Lockwood (dec. 1955).

BAILEY, FRANKIE (Frankie Walters)
Born: 1859, New Orleans, La. Died: July 8, 1953, Los Angeles, Calif. Screen, stage and burlesque actress. Known at the turn of the century as "The Girl with the Million Dollar Legs." Entered films in 1922.

Appeared in: **1923** The Famous Mrs. Fair. **1925** Flower of the Night; Thank You. **1926** The Crown of Lies.

BAILEY, JACK (John Wesley Bailey III)
Born: 1908, Hampton, Iowa. Died: Feb. 1, 1980, Santa Monica, Calif. (pneumonia complications). Screen, stage, radio, television actor and author.

Appeared in: **1950** Mrs. O'Malley and Mr. Malone. **1974** How to Seduce a Woman.

BAILEY, JAMES "BULLET"
Born: 1950, Australia. Died: Apr., 1981, Puunene, Maui (plane accident while filming stunt). Screen, television actor and stuntman.

Appeared in: **1978** The Wild Geese.

BAILEY, RAYMOND
Born: 1905, San Francisco, Calif. Died: Apr. 15, 1980, Irvine, Calif. (heart attack). Screen, stage and television actor. Entered films during silents.

Appeared in: **1939** Secret Service of the Air; S.O.S. Tidal Wave; Hell's Kitchen; Flight at Midnight; Daredevils of the Red Circle (serial). **1955** Picnic; The Girl in the Red Velvet Swing; The Return of Jack Slade. **1956** The Girl He Left Behind; Outside the Law; I've Lived Before; The Great American Pastime. **1957** The Incredible Shrinking Man; Band of Angels. **1958** Underwater Warrior; The Lineup; No Time for Sergeants; Vertigo; I Want to Live!; Darby's Rangers; The Space Children; Lafayette Escadrille. **1959** Al Capone. **1960** The Gallant Hours; Wake Me When It's Over; From the Terrace. **1961** The Absent-Minded Professor. **1962** Five Weeks in a Balloon. **1974** Herbie Rides Again.

BAILEY, WILLIAM (William Norton Bailey)
Born: 1886. Died: Nov. 8, 1962, Hollywood, Calif. Screen actor and film director. Do not confuse with actor Bill Bailey (dec. 1978).

Appeared in: **1912** The Fall of Montezuma; The Penitent. **1913** For Old Times Sake; Dear Old Girl; The Snare. **1916** A Million a Minute. **1918** The Eagle's Eye (serial). **1920** The Phantom For (serial). **1921** The Yellow Arm (serial). **1923** Is Money Everything? **1924** Three O'Clock in the Morning; The Cyclone Rider; The Desert Hawk; The Uninvited Guest; Against All Odds; The Flaming Forties; Gold Heels; Winner Take All. **1925** Big Pal; My Neighbor's Wife; Bustin' Thru; The Desert Flower; Fighting Youth; Lazybones; Top Hand; You're Fired. **1926** House Without a Key (serial); Queen O'Diamonds; The Stolen Ranch; Fighting Jack; Lightning Bill; Lash of the Law; Ranson's Folly. **1927** Melting Millions (serial); Wild Beauty; High School Hero; The Fighting Three. **1928** Waterfront; The Flyin' Cowboy; The Lone Patrol; Burning Bridges; Hit of the Show; Man in the Rough; The Stronger Will; The Way of the Strong. **1929** The Aviator. **1930** Back Pay; Today. **1932** Central Park; The Midnight Patrol. **1933** The Lone Avenger. **1934** Search for Beauty; Manhattan Melodrama. **1935** Living on Velvet; Straight from the Heart; George White's Scandals; Thunder Mountain; One Hour Late. **1936** Charlie Chan's Secret; Too Many Parents. **1938** Arsene Lupin Returns. **1944** National Velvet; Movie Pests (short). **1947** The Egg and I. **1948** Family Honeymoon. **1949** The Gal Who Took the West; Flamingo Road; Brand of Fear; Across the Rio Grande. **1950** Father of the Bride; Lightning Guns. **1951** Al Jennings of Oklahoma; Captain Video (serial); Three Desperate Men. **1952** Clash by Night. **1955** Tall Man Riding. **1957** Gunfight at the O.K. Corral; A Hatful of Rain.

BAINBRIDGE, WILLIAM (William Herbert Bainbridge)
Born: Mar. 21, 1853, England. Died: Oct. 24, 1931. Screen actor.

Appeared in: **1915** Chimmie Fadden Out West. **1916** God's Country and the Woman. **1917** The Promise; Under Handicap; The Desire of the Moth. **1918** Broadway Scandal; The Kaiser, The Beast of Berlin. **1919** False Faces; Desert Gold; The Heart o' the Hills. **1920** The Furnace; In Folly's Trail. **1921** Passion Fruit; The Saphead; The Offshore Pirate; Bonnie May; The Whistle. **1922** His Back Against the Wall; Under Two Flags. **1924** The White Panther. **1928** Quick Triggers.

BAINES, BEULAH
Born: 1905. Died: Aug. 16, 1930, Banning, Calif. Screen and stage actress.

Appeared in: **1921** The Charm School. **1923** The Trail of the Lonesome Pine.

BAINTER, FAY
Born: Dec. 7, 1891, Los Angeles, Calif. Died: Apr. 16, 1968, Los Angeles, Calif. Screen, stage and television actress. Mother of actor Reginald Venable (dec. 1974). Won 1938 Academy Award for Best Supporting Actress in Jezebel and was nominated for Best Actress in White Banners—did not win. A change in the Academy Awards nominating and voting rules was made because of confusion of her two nominations in 1938. Also nominated for 1961 Academy Award for Best Supporting Actress in The Children's Hour.

Appeared in: **1934** This Side of Heaven (film debut). **1937** The Soldier and the Lady; Make Way for Tomorrow; Quality Street. **1938** Mother Carey's Chickens; Jezebel; White Banners; The Arkansas Traveler; The Shining Hour. **1939** Daughters Courageous; The Lady and the Mob; Yes, My Darling Daughter; Our Neighbors, the Carters. **1940** A Bill of Divorcement; Our Town; Young Tom Edison; Maryland. **1941** Babes on Broadway; Love Crazy. **1942** Journey for Margaret; Mrs. Wiggs of the Cabbage Patch; The War Against Mrs. Hadley; Woman of the Year. **1943** Cry Havoc; The Human Comedy; Salute to the Marines; Presenting Lily Mars; The Heavenly Body. **1944** Three is a Family; Dark Waters. **1945** State Fair. **1946** The Virginian; The Kid from Brooklyn. **1947** The Secret Life of Walter Mitty; Deep Valley. **1948** June Bride; Give My Regards to Broadway. **1951** Close to My Heart. **1953** The President's Lady. **1961** The Children's Hour. **1962** Bon Voyage.

BAIR, STEWART
Born: 1903. Died: May 20, 1977. Screen, television actor and singer.

BAIRD, CORA
Born: 1913. Died: Dec. 7, 1967, New York, N.Y. Screen, stage and television actress. Partner in puppet team of Bil and Cora Baird.

BAIRD, DOROTHEA
Born: May 20, 1875, Teddington, England. Died: Sept. 24, 1933, Broadstairs, England. Screen and stage actress. Mother of actress Elizabeth Irving. Married to actor H. B. Irving (dec. 1919). Do not confuse with actress Dorothy Baird (aka Dorothy Vernon—dec. 1970).

Appeared in: **1917** Motherhood. **1924** Conductor 1492.

BAIRD, DOROTHY See VERNON, DOROTHY

BAIRD, LEAH
Born: c. 1891. Died: Oct. 3, 1971, Hollywood, Calif. (anemia). Screen, stage actress, screenwriter and film producer. Entered films with Vitagraph in New York.

Appeared in: **1912** The Gamblers; Stenographers Wanted; Chumps; The Black Sheep; The Extension Table; The Foster Child; The Miracle; The Way of a Man; Counsel for the Defense; Working for Hubby; The Nipper's Lullaby; Adventure of the Italian Model; Lord Browning and Cinderella; The Dawning; The Red Barrier; The Days of Terror; All for a Girl. **1913** Bunny and the Bunny Hug (aka Bunny Dips into Society); Red and White Roses; Ivanhoe; Sue Simpkins' Ambition; The Anarchist; Mr. and Mrs. Innocence Abroad; The Two Purses; A Woman; The Birthday Gift; The Locket; A Soul in Bondage; A Vampire of the Desert; The Heart of Mrs. Robbins; My Lady Idleness; Time is Money; Cutey and the Chorus Girls; Hearts of the First Empire. **1914** The Secret of the Air (aka Across the Atlantic—US); Neptune's Daughter; The Old Rag Doll; The Price of Sacrilege; The Flaming Diagram; Fine Feathers Make Fine Birds; The Man Who Knew; Love and a Lottery Ticket; His Last Chance; His Dominant Passion; Out of the Far East; The Upper Hand; Love or a Throne; Watch Dog of the Deep. **1915** Tried for His Own Murder; The Ruling Power; Dorothy; Saints and Sinners; The Gods Redeem; A Question of Right or Wrong; The Romance of a Handkerchief. **1916** The Eyes of Love; The Primal Instinct; The Bond of Blood; Would You Forgive Her? **1917** A Sunset; The Old Toymaker; The Devil's Pay Day; One Law for Both; The Doctor's Deception; A Woman of Clay; Sins of Ambition. **1918** Wolves of Kultur (serial); The Fringe of Society; Moral Suicide. **1919** The Echo of Youth; As a Man Thinks. **1921** The Heart Line. **1922** Don't Doubt Your Wife; When the Devil Drives; The Bride's Confession; When Husbands Deceive. **1923** Destroying Angel; Is Divorce a Failure?; The Miracle Makers. **1924** The Law Demands; The Radio Flyer. **1925** The Unnamed Woman. **1941** Bullets for O'Hara. **1942** Lady Ganster; Yankee Doodle Dandy. **1943** Air Force. **1946** My Reputation. **1956** Around the World in 80 Days.

BAIRD, STEWART
Born: 1881, Boston, Mass. Died: Oct. 28, 1947, New York, N.Y. (heart attack). Screen and stage actor.

Appeared in: **1915** The Moth and the Flame; The Incorrigible Dukane; The Runaway Wife.

BAJOR, GOZI
Born: 1896, Hungary. Died: Feb. 12, 1951, Budapest, Hungary ("self-administered overdose of morphine"). Screen and stage actress.

Appeared in: **1938** Ket Fogoly (Two Prisoners).

BAKER, ANNA (Anna Auer)
Born: 1860. Died: Apr. 2, 1944, Fort Lee, N.J. Screen and stage actress. Married to actor Willis Baker (dec. 1932).

BAKER, ART
Born: 1898, New York, N.Y. Died: Aug. 26, 1966, Los Angeles, Calif. (heart attack). Screen, radio and television actor.

Appeared in: **1937** Artists and Models. **1938** Trade Winds (voice). **1944** Once Upon a Time. **1945** Spellbound. **1946** Abie's Irish Rose. **1947** The Beginning of the End; Dark Delusion; Daisy Kenyon; The Farmer's Daughter. **1948** Silver River; A Southern Yankee; Walk a Crooked Mile; The Decision of Christopher Blake; State of the Union; The Walls of Jericho. **1949** Easy Living; Take One False Step; Any Number Can Play; Night Unto Night; Massacre River; Cover Up; Impact; Task Force. **1950** The Underworld Story; Hot Rod. **1951** Here Comes the Groom; Cause for Alarm; Only the Valiant. **1954** Living It Up. **1955** Artists and Models. **1960** Twelve Hours to Kill. **1961** Voyage to the Bottom of the Sea. **1962** Swingin' Along. **1965** Young Dillinger. **1966** The Wild Angels.

BAKER, BELLE
Born: 1895, New York, N.Y. Died: Apr. 29, 1957, Los Angeles, Calif. (heart attack). Screen, stage, vaudeville and television actress.

Appeared in: **1929** Song of Love. **1944** Atlantic City.

BAKER, BOB (Leland T. Weed)
Born: Nov. 8, 1901, Forest City, Iowa. Died: Aug. 29, 1975, Prescott, Ariz. (stroke). Screen actor and singing cowboy.

Appeared in: **1937** Courage of the West. **1938** Guilty Trails; Prairie Justice; Western Trails; Border Wolves; The Last Stand; Outlaw Express; Black Bandit; Singing Outlaw. **1939** Honor of the West; Desperate Trails; Oklahoma Frontier. **1940** Chip of the Flying U; West of Carson City; Riders of Pasco Basin; Bad Man from Red Butte. **1942** Overland Mail (serial). **1943** Wild Horse Stampede. **1944** Mystery Man.

BAKER, EDDIE (Edward King)
Born: Nov. 17, 1897, Davis, W.Va. Died: Feb. 4, 1968, Hollywood, Calif. Screen actor. Entered films as a prop boy with Biograph in 1914. Was one of the original Keystone Kops and appeared in early "Joker" comedies, "Gale Henry" comedies, Hal Roach films and Christie shorts.

Appeared in: **1924** Hold Your Breath. **1929** All at Sea. **1930** The Big Kick (short). **1931** City Lights; Monkey Business; plus the following shorts: One of the Smiths; Call a Cop; and Come Clean. **1932** The following shorts: Free Eats; Choo Choo; Now We'll Tell One; and Too Many Women. **1933** The following shorts: Beauty and the Bus; Kickin' the Crown Around; Sons of the Desert; His Silent Racket; Arabian Tights; Midsummer Mush; Tired Feet; Knight Duty; Tired for Life; and Feeling Rosy. **1934** Elmer and Elsie; Babes in Toyland (aka The March of the Wooden Soldiers); plus the following shorts: Them Thar Hills; It Happened One Day; Something Simple; The Chases of Pimple Street; and Petting Preferred. **1950** Revenge Is Sweet (reissue of Babes in Toyland—1934). **1955** Land of Fury.

BAKER, ELSIE
Born: 1893, Chicago, Ill. Died: Aug. 16, 1971, Hollywood, Calif. (heart attack). Screen, stage, vaudeville, radio and television actress. Made stage debut at age of ten months.

Appeared in: **1952** No Room for the Groom.

BAKER, FAY
Born: 1894. Died: Nov. 13, 1954, New York, N.Y. (heart attack). Screen, stage and vaudeville actress. Married to stage actor John Kirk (dec. 1948).

Appeared in: **1946** Notorious. **1950** Chain Lightning. **1951** The House on Telegraph Hill.

BAKER, FLOYD
Born: 1906. Died: Mar. 17. 1943, Hollywood, Calif. Screen actor.

BAKER, FRANK
Born: 1894, Australia. Died: Dec. 30, 1980, Woodland Hills, Calif. Screen actor. Entered films in Australia in 1912.

Appeared in: **1924** The Diamond Bandit; Lash of the Whip. **1925** Red Blood and Blue; Scar Hanan. **1926** The Gallant Fool. **1927** Wolf's Trail. **1928** The Bushranger; Call of the Heart; A Million for Love. **1935** The New Adventures of Tarzan. **1936** Mary of Scotland. **1938** The Baroness and the Butler; Four Men and a Prayer; Tarzan and the Green Goddess. **1939** Arrest Bulldog Drummond. **1940** A Chump at Oxford. **1961** Two Rode Together. **1963** Donovan's Reef. **1975** Defiance.

BAKER, FRANK "HOME RUN" (John Franklin Baker)
Born: Mar. 13, 1883, Trappe, Md. Died: June 28, 1963, Trappe, Md. Baseball player and screen actor. Do not confuse with actor Frank Baker (dec. 1980).

Appeared in: **1913** The Short Stop's Double.

BAKER, JOSEPHINE
Born: June 3, 1906, St. Louis, Mo. Died: Apr. 12, 1975, Paris, France (cerebral hemorrhage). Black screen, stage actress and singer-dancer. Divorced from painter Count Heno Abatino and orchestra leader Jo Bouillon.

Appeared in: **1923** Black Shadows (documentary). **1944** Moulin Rouge. **1959** The French Way. **1975** Black Shadows on the Silent Screen (documentary-rerelease of 1923 film).

BAKER, LEE
Born: 1876, Ovid, Mich. Died: Feb. 24, 1948, Los Angeles, Calif. Screen and stage actor.

Appeared in: **1923** The Fighting Blade. **1925** Soul Fire. **1947** Mourning Becomes Electra.

BAKER, MARK
Born: England. Died: June 20, 1972, England? Screen actor.

Appeared in: **1954** Make Me an Offer (US 1956); Orders are Orders. **1955** Joe MacBeth (US 1956). **1957** Across the Bridge; After the Ball; The Flying Scot (aka Mailbag Robbery—US 1958). **1958** Floods of Fear (US 1959); The Man Inside. **1960** Never Take Sweets from a Stranger (aka Never Take Candy from a Stranger—US 1961).

BAKER, PHIL
Born: Aug. 24, 1898, Philadelphia, Pa. Died: Dec. 1, 1963, Copenhagen, Denmark. Screen, stage, radio and vaudeville actor. Appeared in vaudeville with Ben Bernie (dec. 1943) as part of "Bernie and Baker" team.

Appeared in: **1929** A Bad Boy from a Good Family (short); In Spain (short). **1934** Gift of Gab. **1938** The Goldwyn Follies; Start Cheering. **1943** The Gang's All Here. **1944** Take It or Leave It.

BAKER, SIR STANLEY
Born: Feb. 28, 1928, Glamorgah, Wales. Died: June 28, 1976, Malaga, Spain (lung cancer). Screen, stage, television actor and film producer. Made Commander of the Order of the British Empire in 1976.

Appeared in: **1943** Undercover (film debut, aka Underground Guerillas—US 1944). **1949** All Over Town. **1950** Your Witness (aka Eye Witness—US); Lili Marlene (US 1951). **1951** The Rossiter Case; Cloudburst (US 1952); Captain Horatio Hornblower RN; Home to Danger. **1952** Whispering Smith Hits London (aka Whispering Smith Versus Scotland Yard—US). **1953** The Cruel Sea; The Red Beret (aka Paratrooper—US 1954); The Tell-Tale Heart (short). **1954** Hell Below Zero; The Good Die Young; The Young Lovers (aka Chance

Meeting—US 1955); Beautiful Stranger (aka Twist of Fate—US); Knights of the Round Table. **1955** Richard III (US 1956); Helen of Troy. **1956** Child in the House; A Hill in Korea (aka Hell in Korea—US 1957); Checkpoint (US 1957); Alexander the Great. **1957** Hell Drivers (US 1958); Campbell's Kingdom (US 1958). **1958** Violent Playground; Sea Fury. **1959** The Angry Hills; Yesterday's Enemy; Jet Storm (US 1961); Blind Date. **1960** Hell is a City; The Criminal (aka The Concrete Jungle—US 1962). **1961** The Guns of Navarone; Sodoma e Gomorra (Sodom and Gomorrah—US 1963, aka The Last Days of Sodom and Gomorrah). **1962** The Man Who Finally Died (US 1967); Eva (US 1964); A Prize of Arms. **1963** Zulu (US 1964); In the French Style. **1965** Sands of the Kalahari; Dingaka. **1967** Accident; Robbery; One of Them is Brett (voice, short). **1968** Girl with a Pistol. **1969** Where's Jack? **1970** The Games; The Last Grenade; Perfect Friday. **1971** The Butterfly Affair (aka Popsy Pop). **1972** Innocent Bystanders. **1977** Zorro.

BAKER, WILLIAM
Died: Dec. 21, 1916, New York, N.Y. Screen actor.

BAKER, WILLIS
Born: 1851, Circleville, Ohio. Died: Apr. 20, 1932, Hackensack, N.J. Screen actor. Married to actress Anna Baker (dec. 1944).

BAKUNAS, A. J.
Born: 1951. Died: Sept. 22, 1978, Lexington, Ky. (injuries sustained during stunt). Screen actor and stuntman.

Appeared in: **1978** Hooper. **1980** Steel.

BALACHOVA, TANIA
Born: 1902, France. Died: Aug., 1973, France? Screen and stage actress.

BALCH, JOSEPH "SLIM" (Joseph I. Balch)
Born: Dec. 31, 1898, Kansas. Died: Jan. 30, 1967, Woodland Hills, Calif. (pneumonia). Screen actor.

Appeared in: **1937** Hollywood Cowboy.

BALDRA, CHARLES M.
Born: 1899, Albany, Ore. Died: May 14, 1949, Hollywood, Calif. (train-auto accident). Stage and screen actor. Entered films in 1920.

Appeared in: **1936** The Law-less Nineties.

BALDWIN, GEORGE
Died: Feb. 28, 1923, Manila, Philippine Islands (poisoned). Screen and vaudeville actor.

BALDWIN, KITTY
Born: 1853. Died: June 27, 1934, Buffalo, N.Y. Stage and screen actress.

Appeared in: **1915** Are You a Mason?

BALDWIN, WALTER S.
Born: 1887. Died: Jan. 27, 1977, Santa Monica, Calif. (pneumonia). Screen, stage, vaudeville and television actor.

Appeared in: **1941** All That Money Can Buy; The Devil Commands; Look Who's Laughing. **1942** Harvard, Here I Come; Scattergood Rides High. **1943** A Stranger in Town; Happy Land. **1944** Home in Indiana; Mr. Winkle Goes to War; Since You Went Away; Dark Mountain; I'm from Arkansas; Together Again. **1945** Bring on the Girls; Captain Eddie; Why Girls Leave Home; State Fair. **1946** Johnny Comes Flying Home; Sing While You Dance; The Best Years of Our Lives. **1947** The Unsuspected; Mourning Becomes Electra. **1948** Winter Meeting; Albuquerque; Return of the Bad Men; Cry of the City; Rachel and the Stranger. **1949** Special Agent; The Gay Amigo; Calamity Jane and Sam Bass; Come to the Stable; Thieves' Highway. **1950** Storm Warning; Cheaper by the Dozen; Stella; The Jackpot. **1951** Rough Riders of Durango; A Millionaire for Christy; The Racket; I Want You. **1952** The Winning Team; Carrie; Something for the Birds; The Devil and Daniel Webster (reissue and retitle of All That Money Can Buy—1941). **1953** Ride, Vaquero; Scandal at Scourie. **1954** The Long, Long Trailer; Living It Up; Destry. **1955** Interrupted Melody; The Desperate Hours. **1956** Glory; You Can't Run Away from It. **1960** Oklahoma Territory. **1964** Cheyenne Autumn. **1968** Rosemary's Baby. **1969** Hail, Hero!

BALFOUR, LORNA
Born: 1913, England. Died: Mar. 2, 1932, Hollywood, Calif. (complications following surgery). Stage and screen actress.

Appeared in: **1931** Merely Mary Ann.

BALIEFF, NIKITA
Born: 1877. Died: Sept. 3, 1936, New York, N.Y. Screen and stage actor.

Appeared in: **1936** Once in a Blue Moon.

BALIN, MIREILLE
Born: 1911, France. Died: Nov. 8, 1968, Paris, France. Screen actress.

Appeared in: **1933** Don Quixote. **1936** Pepe Le Moko. **1938** Gueurde d'Amour. **1940** The Kiss of Fire.

BALL, SUZAN (Susan Ball)
Born: Feb 3, 1933, Buffalo, N.Y. Died: Aug. 5, 1955, Beverly Hills, Calif. (cancer). Screen actress. Married to actor Richard Long (dec. 1974). Injured her right knee while filming East of Sumatra in 1952; injury developed into cancer.

Appeared in: **1952** Untamed Frontier (film debut); Yankee Buccaneer. **1953** East of Sumatra; City Beneath the Sea. **1954** War Arrow. **1955** Chief Crazy Horse.

BALLANTINE, E. J.
Born: 1888, Edinburgh, Scotland. Died: Oct. 20, 1968, London, England. Stage and screen actor.

Appeared in: **1943** The Moon Is Down. **1944** Tampico. **1947** Boomerang.

BALLANTYNE, NELL
Died: Feb. 19, 1959, Glasgow, Scotland. Screen, stage and radio actress.

Appeared in: **1954** Scotch on the Rocks. **1958** Rockets Galore. **1959** The Bridal Path.

BALLARD, ELMER
Born: 1879, N.Dak. Died: June 5, 1947. Screen, stage, vaudeville and radio actor.

Appeared in: **1929** Alibi; Thunderbolt. **1930** Her Private Affair; The Fall Guy; Little Caesar; Doorway to Hell; Square Dice; The Squealer. **1931** City Sentinels; Consolation Marriage. **1934** Green Eyes.

BALLIN, MRS. MABLE
Born: 1885. Died: July 24, 1958, Santa Monica, Calif. Screen actress.

Appeared in: **1917** The Spreading Dawn; For Valour; Just What Bobby Wanted; When Bobby Broke His Arm. **1921** East Lynne; Pagan Love; Jane Eyre; The Journey's End. **1922** Other Women's Clothes; Married People. **1923** Vanity Fair; Souls for Sale. **1925** Barriers Burned Away; Beauty and the Bad Man; Code of the West; Riders of the Purple Sage; The Shining Adventure.

BALLISTA, LUIGI "GIGI"
Born: Florence, Italy. Died: Aug. 2, 1980, Rome, Italy (natural causes). Screen actor.

Appeared in: **1966** Signore e Signori (aka The Birds, the Bees and the Italians—US 1967); Le Fate (aka The Queens—US 1968). **1967** L'immortale (aka The Climax—US). **1969** The Secret of Santa Vittoria. **1974** Stavinsky. **1976** The Sunday Woman. **1977** Madame Kitty. **1978** Midnight Express.

BALLOU, MARION
Born: 1871. Died: Mar. 25, 1939, Hollywood, Calif. Screen and stage actress.

Appeared in: **1930** Night Work; The Big Pond. **1933** Little Women; Cradle Song. **1935** David Copperfield; The Melody Lingers On. **1936** Camille. **1937** Portia on Trial. **1938** Holiday.

BALPETRE, ANTOINE
Born: 1898, France. Died: 1963, France? Screen actor.

Appeared in: **1945** Dawn Over France. **1947** Carnival of Sinners. **1949** Le Corbeau (The Raven). **1950** Tainted. **1953** Justice is Done. **1954** Diary of a Country Priest. **1956** The Snow was Black. **1957** We Are All Murderers; I Vampiri (The Vampires, aka The Devil's Commandment—US). **1958** Rouge et Noir (The Red and the Black); Le Cas du Dr. Laurent (The Case of Dr. Laurent). **1960** Katia (aka Magnificent Sinner—US 1963); Une Fille Pour L'ete (A Mistress for the Summer—US 1964). **1961** Le Cave se Rebiffe (aka Money, Money, Money, and aka The Counterfeiters of Paris—US 1962); Le Mains d'Orlac (The Hands of Orlac—US 1964). **1962** La Chambre Ardente (The Ardent Room, aka The Burning Court—US 1963).

BALTZELL, DEBORAH
Born: 1956. Died: Oct. 24, 1981, Los Angeles, Calif. (heart attack). Screen, stage and television actress.

Appeared in: **1980** Altered States.

BAMATTRE, MARTHA
Born: 1892. Died: July 12, 1970, Glendale, Calif. Screen and stage actress. Entered films in 1927.

Appeared in: **1939** Everything Happens at Night. **1942** Reunion in France. **1947** Golden Earrings. **1951** An American in Paris. **1955** To Catch a Thief.

BANCROFT, CHARLES (Fred Bently)
Born: 1911. Died: May 17, 1969, Woodland Hills, Calif. (cancer). Screen actor. Entered films approx. 1930.

BANCROFT, GEORGE
Born: Sept. 30, 1882, Philadelphia, Pa. Died: Oct. 2, 1956, Santa Monica, Calif. Screen and stage actor. Nominated for 1928/29 Academy Award for Best Actor in Thunderbolt.

Appeared in: **1921** The Journey's End. **1922** Driven; The Prodigal Judge. **1924** The Deadwood Coach; Teeth. **1925** The Pony Express; Code of the West; The Rainbow Trail; The Splendid Road. **1926** Old Ironsides; The Enchanted Hill; The Runaway; Sea Horses. **1927** White Gold; Underworld; The Rough Riders; Tell It to Sweeney; Too Many Crooks. **1928** The Dragnet; The Docks of New York; The Showdown. **1929** The Wolf of Wall Street; Thunderbolt. **1930** The Mighty; Ladies Love Brutes; Derelict; Nuits de Chicago (French release of Underworld—1927); Paramount on Parade. **1931** Scandal Sheet; Rich Man's Folly; The Skin Game. **1932** The World and the Flesh; Lady and Gent. **1933** Blood Money; Hello, Everybody!; A Lady's Profession; Under the Tonto Rim; Sunset Pass; Mama Loves Papa; This Day and Age; Turn Back the Clock; Love, Honor and Oh, Baby!; Tillie and Gus. **1934** Elmer and Elsie; Miss Fane's Baby is Stolen; Journal of a Crime; Many Happy Returns; Merry Widow; She Loves Me Not; The Cat's Paw; Ladies Should Listen; College Rhythm. **1936** Mr. Deeds Goes to Town; Hell Ship Morgan; Wedding Present. **1937** John Meade's Woman; Racketeers in Exile. **1938** A Doctor's Diary; Submarine Patrol; Angels with Dirty Faces. **1939** Stagecoach; Each Dawn I Die; Rulers of the Sea; Espionage Agent. **1940** Green Hell; When the Daltons Rode; Northwest Mounted Police; Little Men; Young Tom Edison. **1941** Texas; The Bugle Sounds. **1943** Whistling in Dixie; Syncopation.

BANDINI, LORENZO
Born: Dec. 21, 1936, Barce, Cyrenaica, N. Africa. Died: May 10, 1967, Monaco (burns from car crash). Race car driver and screen actor.

Appeared in: **1966** Grand Prix.

BANDO, MITSUGORO
Died: Jan. 16, 1975, Kyoto, Japan (food poisoning). Screen and Kabuki actor.

BANDO, TSUMASBURO
Born: 1898, Japan. Died: July, 7, 1953, Kyoto, Japan (cerebral hemorrhage). Screen and Kabuki actor. Entered films approx. 1923.

BANGHART, KENNETH
Born: 1910, Paramus, N.J. Died: May 25, 1980, Delray Beach, Fla. Screen, stage actor, stage producer, drama critic, radio and television reporter.

Appeared in: **1968** Wild in the Streets.

BANJAMIN, GLADYS (Gladys Lanphere)
Died: 1948. Screen actress.

BANKHEAD, TALLULAH
Born: Jan. 31, 1902, Huntsville, Ala. Died: Dec. 12, 1968, New York, N.Y. (double pneumonia). Screen, stage, radio and television actress. Divorced from actor John Emory (dec. 1964).

Appeared in: **1918** When Men Betray; Thirty a Week. **1919** The Trap. **1928** His House in Order. **1929** Her Cardboard Lover. **1931** Tarnished Lady; The Cheat; My Sin. **1932** Thunder Below; The Devil and the Deep; Faithless; Make Me a Star (guest without billing). **1943** Stage Door Canteen. **1944** Lifeboat. **1945** A Royal Scandal. **1953** Main Street to Broadway. **1965** Fanatic (aka Die! Die! My Darling—US). **1966** The Daydreamer (voice only).

BANKS, LESLIE
Born: June 9, 1890, Liverpool, England. Died: Apr. 21, 1952, London, England. Screen, stage actor, stage director and stage producer.

Appeared in: **1932** The Most Dangerous Game (film debut aka The Hounds of Zaroff). **1933** Strange Evidence; The Fire Raisers. **1934** Night of the Party; Red Ensign (aka Strike!—US); I Am Suzanne; The Man Who Knew Too Much. **1935** Sanders of the River; The Tunnel (aka Transatlantic Tunnel—US). **1936** The Three Maxims (aka The Show Goes On—US 1938); Debt of Honor. **1937** Fire Over England; Farewell Again (aka Troopship—US 1938); Wings of the Morning; The First and the Last (aka 21 Days Together—US 1940). **1939** Jamaica Inn; Dead Man's Shoes; The Arsenal Stadium Mystery; Sons of the Sea; Guide Dogs for the Blind (short). **1940** The Door with Seven Locks (aka Chamber of Horrors—US 1941); Neutral Port; Busman's Honeymoon (aka Haunted Honeymoon—US). **1941** Cottage to Let (aka Bombsight Stolen—US); Ship with Wings (US 1942); Give Us More Ships (short). **1942** The Big Blockade; Went the Day Well? (aka 48 Hours—US 1944). **1945** Henry V (US 1946). **1947** Mrs. Fitzherbert (US 1950). **1949** The Small Back Room (US 1952). **1950** Your Witness (aka Eye Witness—US); Madeleine.

BANKS, MONTY (Mario Bianchi aka MONTAGUE BANKS)
Born: 1897, Casene, Italy. Died: Jan. 7, 1950, Arona, Italy (heart attack). Screen, stage actor, film director and film producer. Married to actress Gracie Fields (dec. 1979). Divorced from actress Gladys Frazin (dec. 1939). Appeared in early Mack Sennett films.

Appeared in: **1921** Monty Banks series. **1924** Racing Luck. **1925** Keep Smiling. **1926** Atta Boy. **1927** Flying Luck; Horse Shoes; Play Safe. **1928** Adam's Apple (aka Honeymoon Ahead—US); Weekend Wives (US 1929); A Perfect Gentleman. **1929** Atlantic. **1930** The Compulsory Husband. **1932** Tonight's the Night; For the Love of Mike. **1933** You Made Me Love You. **1934** The Girl in Possession; Church Mouse (US 1935). **1935** So You Won't Talk; Man of the Moment. **1936** Honeymoon Merry-Go-Round (aka Olympic Honeymoon). **1941** Blood and Sand. **1945** A Bell for Adano. **1961** Days of Thrills and Laughter (doc.).

BANKS, PERRY
Born: Apr. 24, 1877, Victoria, British Columbia, Canada. Died: Oct. 10, 1934, Santa Barbara, Calif. Screen, stage, vaudeville actor and circus performer.

Appeared in: **1916** Other Side of the Door; Overalls. **1917** Melissa of the Hills; The Sea Master. **1919** A Sporting Chance; Six Feet Four; Eva in Exile. **1920** House of Toys; The Virtuous Outcast (aka Faith).

BANNER, JOHN
Born: 1910, Austria. Died: Jan. 28, 1973, Vienna, Austria (abdominal hemorrhage). Screen, stage and television actor.

Appeared in: **1942** Once Upon a Honeymoon; Seven Miles from Alcatraz. **1943** The Moon Is Down; Tonight We Raid Calais; The Fallen Sparrow. **1946** Tangier; Black Angel; Rendezvous. **1948** My Girl Tisa; To the Victor; The Argyle Secrets. **1949** Guilty of Treason. **1950** King Solomon's Mines. **1953** The Juggler. **1954** Executive Suite. **1955** The Rains of Ranchipur. **1958** The Beast of Budapest. **1959** The Blue Angel. **1960** The Story of Ruth. **1961** Operation Eichmann; 20,000 Eyes. **1962** Hitler; The Interns. **1963** The Yellow Canary. **1964** 36 Hours. **1968** The Wicked Dreams of Paula Schulz. **1970** Togetherness.

BANNERMAN, MARGARET (Margaret Le Grand)
Born: Dec. 5, 1896, Toronto, Canada. Died: Apr. 25, 1976, Englewood, N.J. Screen and stage actress.

Appeared in: **1917** Justice; Flames; Mary Girl; The Gay Lord Quex. **1918** Hindle Wakes; Goodbye. **1919** Her Secret. **1920** Lady Audley's Secret. **1922** The Grass Orphan. **1932** Two White Arms (aka Wives Beware—US 1933); Lilly Christine. **1934** Over the Garden Wall; The Great Defender. **1935** I Give My Heart. **1946** Cluny Brown. **1947** The Home Stretch.

BANNISTER, HARRY
Born: 1889, Holland, Mich. Died: Feb. 26, 1961, N.Y. Screen, stage and television actor. Divorced from actress Ann Harding (dec. 1981).

Appeared in: **1921** The Porcelain Lamp. **1929** Her Private Affair. **1930** The Girl of the Golden West. **1931** Suicide Fleet; Husband's Holiday. **1961** Girl on the Run.

BANNISTER, KATHERINE
Died: Oct. 16, 1919, Chicago, Ill. (injuries from auto accident). Screen actress.

BANVARD, FIFI
Born: 1901. Died: June 24, 1962, Sydney, Australia (heart attack). Screen actress. Mack Sennett Bathing Beauty.

BANZET, JANET
Died: July 29, 1971, New York, N.Y. Screen actress.

Appeared in: **1964** Lilith. **1966** Teen Age Gang Debs. **1967** To Turn a Trick; Teach Me How to Do It; Cool It, Baby; Mini-Skirt Love; Julie Is No Angel; Venus in Furs. **1968** Come Play with Me.

BAO, MIGUEL GOMEZ
Born: Argentina. Died: 1961, Argentina. Screen actor.

Appeared in: **1939** Madreselva (Honeysuckle).

BAPTISTA, CARLOS
Born: 1900. Died: Jan. 7, 1950, Lisbon, Portugal. Screen and stage actor.

BARA, LORO
Born: Cincinnati, Ohio. Died: Aug. 4, 1965, Los Angeles, Calif. Screen actress and screenwriter. Sister of actress Theda Bara (dec. 1955).

Appeared in: **1925** The Unchastened Woman.

BARA, THEDA (Theodosia Goodman aka THEODOSIA DE COPPETT)
Born: 1890, Cincinnati, Ohio. Died: Apr. 7, 1955, Los Angeles, Calif. (cancer). Screen and stage actress. Sister of actress Loro Bara (dec. 1965). Married to actor and director Charles J. Brabin (dec. 1957).

Appeared in: **1915** The Two Orphans; The Clemenceau Case; The Stain; A Fool There Was; Sin; Carmen; Kreutzer Sonata; The Devil's Daughter; Lady Audley's Secret; The Galley Slave. **1916** Romeo and Juliet; Destruction; The Light; Gold and the Woman; The Serpent; The Eternal Sappho; East Lynne; Her Double Life; Under Two Flags; The Vixen. **1917** Cleopatra; Camille; Heart and Soul; The Tiger Woman; The Darling of Paris; Her Greatest Love. **1918** Salome; When a Woman Sins; The Forbidden Path; The She Devil; Rose of the Blood; Madame DuBarry; The Soul of Buddha; Under the Yoke. **1919** Kathleen Mavourneen; La Belle Russe; The Light; When Men Desire; The Siren's Song; A Woman There Was; The Lure of Ambition. **1921** The Prince of Silence; Her Greatest Love. **1923** The Hunchback of Notre Dame. **1925** The Unchastened Woman. **1926** Madame Mystery; The Dancer of Paris.

BARAGREY, JOHN
Born: April, 1919, Haleyville, Ala. Died: Aug. 4, 1975, New York, N.Y. (cerebral hemorrhage). Screen, stage and television actor. Married to actress Louise Larabee.

Appeared in: **1948** The Loves of Carmen; The Saxon Charm; The Creeper; The Fabulous Fraud (short). **1949** Shockproof. **1950** Four Days Leave. **1955** Tall Man Riding. **1956** Pardners. **1958** The Colossus of New York. **1959** The Fugitive Kind. **1965** Daikaiju Gamma Ray (aka Gamma Ray the Invisible—US 1966).

BARBANELL, FRED
Born: 1931. Died: Sept. 11, 1959, Hollywood, Calif. (following surgery). Screen and television actor.

BARBAT, PERCY (Percy Dewitt Barbat)
Born: 1883. Died: June 20, 1965, San Antonio, Tex. Screen, vaudeville and radio actor.

Appeared in: **1925** Peter Pan. **1934** Tubal-Cain. **1964** No Man's Land.

BARBEE, JOHN
Born: 1893. Died: Apr. 20, 1981, Los Angeles, Calif. Screen, stage, vaudeville and television actor. Appeared in early Vitagraph films.

"BARBETTE" (Vander Barbette)
Born: 1906, Round Rock, Tex. Died: Aug. 5, 1973, Austin, Tex. Screen actor and circus performer.

Appeared in: **1932** Le Sang d'un Poete (Blood of a Poet).

BARBIER, GEORGE W.
Born: Nov. 9, 1865, Philadelphia, Pa. Died: July 19, 1945, Los Angeles, Calif. (heart attack). Stage and screen actor.

Appeared in: **1924** Monsieur Beaucaire. **1930** The Big Pond; The Sap from Syracuse. **1931** The Smiling Lieutenant; 24 Hours; Girls about Town; Touchdown. **1932** Skyscraper Souls; Evenings for Sale; No Man of Her Own; No One Man; Strangers in Love; The Broken Wing; One Hour with You; The Strange Case of Clara Deane; Million Dollar Legs; Madame Racketeer; The Phantom President; The Big Broadcast. **1933** Hello, Everybody!; Mama Loves Papa; Sunset Pass; Under the Tonto Rim; This Day and Age; Tillie and Gus; Turn Back the Clock; A Lady's

Profession; Love, Honor and Oh, Baby! **1934** Miss Fane's Baby is Stolen; Many Happy Returns; Ladies Should Listen; She Loves Me Not; College Rhythm; Elmer and Elsie; The Notorious Sophie Lang; Journal of a Crime; The Merry Widow. **1935** McFadden's Flats; Hold 'Em Yale; The Crusades; Here Comes Cookie; Millions in the Air; Life Begins at 40; Broadway Gondolier; Old Man Rhythm; The Cat's Paw. **1936** The Milky Way; Preview Murder Mystery; Wife vs. Secretary; The Princess Comes Across; Spendthrift; Early to Bed; Three Married Men. **1937** On the Avenue; Waikiki Wedding; Hotel Haywire; It's Love I'm After; A Girl With Ideas. **1938** Tarzan's Revenge; Little Miss Broadway; My Lucky Star; Hold That Coed; Straight, Place and Show; Thanks for Everything; Hold That Kiss; Sweethearts; The Adventures of Marco Polo. **1939** Wife, Husband and Friend; SOS Tidal Wave; News is Made at Night; Smuggled Cargo; Remember? **1940** Village Barn Dance; The Return of Frank James. **1941** Repent at Leisure; The Man Who Came to Dinner; Million Dollar Baby; Marry the Boss's Daughter; Weekend in Havana. **1942** The Magnificent Dope; Thunder Birds; Song of the Islands; Yankee Doodle Dandy. **1943** Hello, Frisco, Hello. **1944** Weekend Pass. **1945** Blonde Ransom; Her Lucky Night.

BARBOUR, DAVE (David Michael Barbour)
Born: May 28, 1912, New York, N.Y. Died: Dec. 11, 1965, Hollywood, Calif. (hemorrhaged ulcer). Jazz musician, composer and screen actor. Divorced from singer Peggy Lee.

Appeared in: **1950** Secret Fury.

BARBOUR, EDWIN WILBOUR
Died: Sept. 14, 1914. Screen actor and screenwriter. Appeared in early Lubin films.

BARBOUR, JOYCE
Born: Mar. 27, 1901, Birmingham, England. Died: Mar. 14, 1977, England? Screen and stage actress. Married to actor Richard Bird.

Appeared in: **1932** Diamond Cut Diamond. **1936** Sabotage (aka The Woman Alone—US 1937). **1938** Housemaster (US 1939). **1944** Don't Take It to Heart (US 1949). **1964** The Main Chance (US 1966).

BARCENA, CATALINA
Born: 1896, Spain. Died: Aug. 3, 1978, Spain. Screen and stage actress.

Appeared in: **1933** Primavera en Otono; Mama; Viuda Romantica; Io ... Tu ... Y ... (I ... Thou ... and She). **1934** La Ciudad de Carton. **1935** Julieta Compra un Hijo (Julieta Buys a Baby).

BARCLAY, DELANCEY
Born: New York, N.Y. Died: Dec. 10, 1917, New York, N.Y. Screen actor.

BARCLAY, DON (Don Van Tassel Barclay)
Born: 1892, Ashland, Ore. Died: Oct. 16, 1975, Palm Springs, Calif. Screen, stage actor and artist. Member of Hal Roach's "All Star" trio of the mid-1930s. Do not confuse with British stage actor (dec. 1977).

Appeared in: **1914** The Cannon Ball (aka The Dynamiter). **1915** That Little Band of Gold (aka For Better or Worse); The Wrong Address. **1918** All Stuck Up; Check Your Hat, Sir? **1933** Air Fright (short); Backs to Nature (short); Beauty and the Bus (short). **1934** Honkey Donkey (short); Soup and Fish (short); Maid in Hollywood (short). **1935** Frisco Kid. **1936** Man Hunt; Black Legion; Treachery Rides the Range; The Murder of Dr. Harrigan; The Lion's Den; Bengal Tiger; The White Legion. **1937** Fugitive in the Sky; Navy Spy; Border Phantom; Sweetheart of the Navy; I Cover The War. **1938** The Spy Ring; Accidents Will Happen; Thunder in the Desert; Outlaw Express. **1939** The Oklahoma Kid. **1940** Badlands of Dakota. **1941** Bedtime Story. **1942** Blondie's Blessed Event; The Falcon's Brother; Mexican Spitfire Sees a Ghost; Sing Your Worries Away; The Big Street. **1943** White Savage; After Midnight with Boston Blackie; Frankenstein Meets the Wolfman; Good Morning, Judge. **1944** Shine On Harvest Moon; In Society. **1946** My Darling Clementine. **1948** Whispering Smith; The Sainted Sisters; Mr. Perrine and Mr. Traill. **1949** Father was a Fullback. **1955** The Long Gray Line. **1961** The Hundred and One Dalmatians (voice). **1964** Mary Poppins. **1968** Half a Sixpence.

BARCROFT, ROY (Howard H. Ravenscroft)
Born: Sept. 7, 1902, Crab Orchard, Nebr. Died: Nov. 28, 1969, Woodland Hills, Calif. (cancer). Screen, stage and television actor.

Appeared in: **1932** Mata Hari (film debut); A Woman Commands. **1937** S.O.S. Coastguard (serial); Join the Marines; Dick Tracy (serial); Rosalie. **1938** The Crowd Roars; Blondes at Work; Heroes of the Hills; Stranger from Arizona; The Frontiersman; Flaming Frontiers. **1939** Silver on the Sage; Mexicali Rose; The Renegade Trail; The Phantom Creeps (serial); The Oregon Trail (serial); Crashing Thru; They All

Came Out; Daredevils of the Red Circle (serial); Another Thin Man. **1940** Winners of the West; Santa Fe Trail; East of the River; Flash Gordon Conquers the Universe (serial); Deadwood Dick (serial); The Green Hornet Strikes Again (serial); Rancho Grande; Hidden Gold; Bad Men from Red Butte; Yukon Flight; Stage to Chino; Ragtime Cowboy Joe; Trailing Double Trouble; The Showdown. **1941** Pals of the Pecos; The Bandit Trail; Wide Open Town; Jessie James at Bay; Outlaws of the Cherokee Trail; The Masked Rider; West of Cimarron; King of the Texas Rangers (serial); Riders of Death Valley; Sheriff of Tombstone; White Eagle; Riders of the Bad Lands; They Died With Their Boots On; Sky Raiders (serial). **1942** The Valley of Vanishing Men (serial); The Lone Rider in Cheyenne; Nazi Agent; Northwest Rangers; Tennessee Johnson; Stardust on the Sage; Dawn on the Great Divide; Land of the Open Range; West of the Law; Romance on the Range; Sunset on the Desert; Below the Border; Sunset Serenade; Pirates of the Prairie. **1943** Hoppy Serves a Writ; False Colors; Riders of the Rio Grande; Cheyenne Roundup; Calling Wild Bill Elliott; Carson City Cyclone; The Stranger from Pecos; Bordertown Gun Fighters; Wagon Tracks West; Raiders of Sunset Pass; The Old Chisholm Trail; Sagebrush Law; The Masked Marvel (serial); Chatterbox; Dr. Gillespie's Criminal Case; Idaho; In Old Oklahoma (aka War of the Wildcats); Man from Music Mountain; Overland Mail Robbery; Six-Gun Gospel. **1944** The Fighting Seabees; Man from Frisco; Rosie the Riveter; Storm Over Lisbon; Tucson Raiders (voice); Call of the South Seas; The Girl Who Dared; The Laramie Trail; Hidden Valley Outlaws; Code of the Prairie; Lights of Old Santa Fe; Stagecoach to Monterey; Firebrands of Arizona; Sheriff of Sundown; Cheyenne Wildcat; Haunted Harbor (serial). **1945** Wagon Wheels Westward; The Vampire's Ghost; Marshal of Laredo; The Big Bonanza; Bells of Rosarito; Sunset in El Dorado; Dakota; Along the Navajo Trail; Manhunt of Mystery Island (serial); The Purple Monster Strikes (serial); Santa Fe Saddlemates; The Lone Texas Ranger; Colorado Pioneers; Trail of Kit Carson; Topeka Terror; Corpus Christi Bandits. **1946** The Plainsman and the Lady; Crime of the Century (voice); Daughter of Don Q (serial); Home on the Range; The Phantom Rider (serial); Alias Billy the Kid; Sun Valley Cyclone; My Pal Trigger; Night Train to Memphis; Traffic in Crime; Stagecoach to Denver. **1947** Oregon Trail Scouts; The Web of Danger; Stage Coach to Reno; Vigilantes of Boomtown; Spoilers of the North; Rustlers of Devil's Canyon; Springtime in the Sierras; Wyoming; Marshal of Cripple Creek; Blackmail; Along the Oregon Trail; The Wild Frontier; Bandits of Dark Canyon; Last Frontier Uprising; The Fabulous Texan; Jesse James Rides Again (serial); Son of Zorro (serial). **1948** The Bold Frontiersman; Old Los Angeles; The Main Street Kid; Madonna of the Desert; Lightnin' in the Forest; Oklahoma Badlands; Secret Service Investigator; The Timber Trail; Train to Alcatraz; Out of the Storm; Eyes of Texas; Sons of Adventure; Grand Canyon Trail; Renegades of Sonora; Desperadoes of Dodge City; Marshal of Amarillo; Sundown at Santa Fe; G-Men Never Forget (serial); The Gallant Legion. **1949** The Far Frontier; Sheriff of Wichita; Prince of the Plains; Frontier Investigator; Law of the Golden West; South of Rio; Down Dakota Way; San Antone Ambush; Ranger of Cherokee Strip; Outcasts of the Trail; Powder River Rustlers; Ghost of Zorro (serial); Federal Agents vs. Underworld, Inc. (serial); The Duke of Chicago. **1950** Desperadoes of the West (serial); Gunman of Abilene; Radar Patrol vs. Spy King (serial, voice); The James Brothers of Missouri (serial); Woman From Headquarters (voice); Pioneer Marshal; The Arizona Cowboy; The Vanishing Westerner; Rock Island Trail; Federal Agent at Large; Code of the Silver Sage; Salt Lake Raiders; The Savage Horde; Vigilante Hideout; Rustlers on Horseback; West of the Great Divide; Surrender; The Missourians; Under Mexicali Skies; North of the Great Divide; Tyrant of the Sea. **1951** Wells Fargo Gunmaster; In Old Amarillo; Insurance Investigator; Night Riders of Montana; The Dakota Kid; Rodeo King and the Senorita; Fort Dodge Stampede; Arizona Manhunt; Utah Wagon Train; Street Bandits; Honeychile; Pals of the Golden West; Flying Disc Men from Mars (serial); Desert of Lost Men; Rhythm Inn; Don Daredevil Rides Again (serial); Pirates Harbor (rerelease of Haunted Harbor serial, 1941); Government Agents vs. Phantom Legion (serial, voice). **1952** Tropical Heat Wave; Radar Men from the Moon (serial); Leadville Gunslinger; Oklahoma Annie; Hoodlum Empire; Border Saddlemates; Wild Horse Ambush; Black Hills Ambush; Thundering Caravans; Oklahoma Plains; Desperadoes' Outpost; Ride the Man Down; The WAC from Walla Walla; South Pacific Trail; Captive of Billy the Kid; Montana Belle. **1953** Marshal of Cedar Creek; Down Laredo Way; Iron Mountain Trail; Bandits of the West; Savage Frontier; Old Overland Trail; El Paso Stampede; Shadows of Tombstone. **1954** The Desperado; Two Guns and a Badge; Rogue Cop; The Man With the Steel Whip (serial). **1955** Man Without a Star; Okalhoma; The Spoilers; Commando Cody (serial); The Cobweb. **1956** Gun Brothers; The Last Hunt. **1957** Gun Duel in Durango; Band of Angels; The Kettles on Old MacDonald's Farm; Domino Kid; Last Stagecoach West. **1959** Escort West; Ghost of Zorro. **1960** Freckles; Ten Who Dared. **1961** When the

Clock Strikes. **1962** Six Black Horses. **1965** Superman vs. the Gorilla Gang (short). **1966** Gunpoint; Texas Across the River; Billy the Kid vs. Dracula; Destination Inner Space. **1967** The Way West. **1968** Bandolero! **1969** Gaily, Gaily; The Reivers.

BARD, BEN
Born: Jan. 23, 1893, Milwaukee, Wis. Died: May 17, 1974, Los Angeles, Calif. (cerebral thrombosis). Screen and stage actor. Married to actress Ruth Roland (dec. 1937).

Appeared in: **1926** My Own Pal (film debut); Sandy. **1927** Seventh Heaven; The Secret Studio; Two Girls Wanted; Love Makes 'Em Wild. **1928** Come to My House; Dressed to Kill; No Other Woman; Arizona Wildcat; Fleetwing. **1929** Romance of the Underworld; Love and the Devil; The Champion Golfer (short). **1930** Born Reckless; Night Work; Reno; Vacation Loves (short). **1931** The Bat Whispers. **1933** Meet the Baron. **1934** Hollywood Party. **1943** The Leopard Man; The Ghost Ship; The Seventh Victim. **1944** Youth Runs Wild. **1946** Black Angel. **1951** I Can Get It for You Wholesale.

BARD, MARIA (aka MIGO BARD)
Born: July 7, 1901, Switzerland. Died: Apr., 1944, Germany. Screen and stage actress. Married to actor Werner Krauss (dec. 1959).

Appeared in: **1924** NJU (aka Husbands or Lovers—US 1927). **1932** Mensch Ohne Namen (Man Without a Name). **1933** Berlin-Alexanderplatz. **1938** Liebe im Gleitflug (Love in Stunt Flying). Other film: Emperor of America.

BARDETTE, TREVOR
Born: 1902. Died: Nov. 28, 1977. Screen and stage actor.

Appeared in: **1937** They Won't Forget; The Great Garrick; Borderland; White Bondage. **1938** Mystery House; In Old Mexico; Topa Topa. **1939** Let Freedom Ring; The Oklahoma Kid; Charlie Chan at Treasure Island; Overland With Kit Carson (serial). **1940** Girl from Havana; The Westerner; The Refugee; Abe Lincoln in Illinois; The Dark Command; Wagons Westward; Three Faces West; Killers of the Wild; Young Buffalo Bill; Winners of the West (serial). **1941** Romance of the Rio Grande; Topper Returns; Mystery Ship; Doomed Caravan; Buy Me That Town; Wild Bill Hickok Rides; Red River Valley; Jungle Girl (serial). **1942** Flight Lieutenant; Henry and Dizzy; Apache Trail; The Secret Code (serial). **1943** The Moon is Down; Deerslayer. **1944** None Shall Escape; The Whistler; Tampico; The Black Parachute; U-Boat Prisoner. **1945** Counter-Attack; Dick Tracy. **1946** The Hoodlum Saint; The Big Sleep; Man Who Dared; Sing While You Dance. **1947** The Sea of Grass; Slave Girl; Wyoming; The Last Round-Up; Marshal of Cripple Creek; Ramrod. **1948** Secret Service Investigator; Alias a Gentleman; Sword of the Avenger; Adventures in Silverado; The Return of the Whistler; Black Eagle; Sundown at Sante Fe; Marshal of Amarillo. **1949** The Blazing Trail; Renegades of the Sage; Sheriff of Wichita; Hellfire; Song of India; Omoo-Omoo, the Shark God; The Wyoming Bandit; San Antone Ambush; Deadly as the Female; Apache Chief. **1950** The Palomino; Hills of Oklahoma; A Lady Without Passport. **1951** The Texas Rangers; Gene Autry and the Mounties; Fort Savage Raider; Fort Dodge Stampede; The Barefoot Milkman; Lorna Doone. **1952** Lone Star; The San Francisco Story; Montana Territory. **1953** Ambush at Tomahawk Gap; Thunder Over the Plains; Bandits of the West; The Desert Song; The Outlaw Stallion. **1954** Red River Shore; Destry. **1955** Run for Cover; The Man from Bitter Ridge. **1956** Red Sundown; The Rack. **1957** Shoot-Out at Medicine Bend; The Monolith Monsters; Dragoon Wells Massacre; The Hard Man. **1958** Thunder Road; The Saga of Hemp Brown. **1959** The Mating Game. **1963** Papa's Delicate Condition. **1964** The Raiders. **1969** Mackenna's Gold.

BARKER, ADELLA
Born: 1867. Died: Sept. 29, 1930, Amityville, N.Y. Screen, stage and vaudeville actress.

Appeared in: **1916** Romeo and Juliet. **1917** Red, White and Blue Blood.

BARKER, BRADLEY
Born: 1883, Hempstead, N.Y. Died: Sept. 29, 1951, New York, N.Y. Screen, radio actor, film producer and animal imitator (original screen voice of Leo the Metro lion).

Appeared in: **1919** Erstwhile Susan. **1920** The Master Mind. **1921** Coincidence; Devotion; God's Crucible. **1922** Insinuation; The Secrets of Paris. **1923** Adam and Eva; The Fair Cheat; The Fighting Blade; The Leavenworth Case; Twenty-One. **1924** The Man Without a Heart; Plaything of Desire; Into the Net (serial). **1925** The Crackerjack; The Early Bird; Ermine and Rhinestones; The Live Wire; The Police Patrol. **1926** The Brown Derby; Rainbow Riley. **1927** Combat; His Rise to Fame; The Potters; Rubber Heels. **1928** The Ape; Inspiration.

BARKER, CORINNE
Born: 1893. Died: Aug. 6, 1928, New York, N.Y. Screen actress.

Appeared in: **1918** Money Mad; Why I Would Not Marry; Peck's Bad Girl. **1919** One Week of Life; The Peace of Roaring River; The Climbers; The Golden Shower; The Broken Melody. **1920** The Restless Sex; The Silent Barrier. **1921** Enchantment; Why Girls Leave Home.

BARKER, FLORENCE
Born: Nov. 22, 1891, Calif. Died: Feb. 15, 1913, Los Angeles, Calif. (pneumonia). Screen actress.

Appeared in: **1908** An Awful Moment. **1909** A Fool's Revenge; The Girls and Daddy. **1910** Faithful; The Dancing Girl of Butte; Her Terrible Ordeal; The Newlyweds; The Last Deal; The Call; The Oath and the Man; His Sister-in-Law; The Love of Lady Irma; The Kid; Up a Tree; An Affair of Hearts; ; The Implement; A Knot in the Plot; A Child's Impulse; A Child's Faith; The Tenderfoot's Triumph. **1911** A Wreath of Orange Blossoms; The Diamond Star; Priscilla and the Umbrella. **1912** That Jane Shore; His Madonna; The Burglar and the Rose; Just a Woman; What the Milk Did; The Golden Rule; Two Women; On the Danger Line; A Dreamland Tragedy; The First Glass.

BARKER, LEX (Alexander Crichlow Barker, Jr.)
Born: May 8, 1919, Rye, N.Y. Died: Apr. 11, 1973, New York, N.Y. (heart attack). Screen, stage and television actor. Divorced from Constance Thurlow, Irene Labhart, Maria del Carmen Cervera and actresses Lana Turner and Arlene Dahl. Won Germany's Bambi Award for Best Foreign Actor of 1966. Was the 10th actor to portray "Tarzan" in film series.

Appeared in: **1945** Doll Face (film debut). **1946** Two Guys from Milwaukee; Do You Love Me? **1947** Under the Tonto Rim; Crossfire; The Farmer's Daughter; Dick Tracy Meets Gruesome; Unconquered. **1948** The Velvet Touch; Return of the Badmen; Mr. Blandings Builds His Dream House. **1949** Tarzan's Magic Fountain. **1950** Tarzan and the Slave Girl. **1951** Tarzan's Peril (aka Tarzan and the Jungle Goddess). **1952** Tarzan's Savage Fury (aka Tarzan, the Hunted); Battles of Chief Pontiac. **1953** Tarzan and the She-Devil; Thunder Over the Plains; The Last of the Renegades. **1954** The Yellow Mountain. **1955** The Man from Bitter Ridge; Duel on the Mississippi; Mystery of the Black Jungle; Black Devils of Kali. **1956** Away All Boats; The Price of Fear. **1957** The Deerslayer; The Girl in Black Stockings; War Drums; The Girl in the Kremlin; Jungle Heat. **1958** Female Friends (aka The Strange Awakening—US 1960). **1959** Mission in Morocco; Terror of the Red Mask; Capitano Fuoco; La Scimitarra del Saraceno (aka La Vengeance du Sarrasin and The Pirate and the Slave Girl—US 1961). **1960** Robin Hood and the Pirates; Pirates of the Barbary Coast; Caravane pour Zagota; La Dolce Vita (US 1961). **1961** Marco Polo; Il Secreto Dello Sparviera Nero (The Secret of the Black Falcon); Im Stahlnetz des Dr. Mabuse (The Return of Dr. Mabuse—US 1966). **1962** Die Unsichtbaren Krallen des Dr. Mabuse (The Invisible Dr. Mabuse—US 1965). **1963** Le Tresor du lac d'Argent (Treasure of Silver Lake—US 1965); Breakfast in Bed; Knight of the 100 Faces; Son of the Red Corsair; Winnetou I Teil (aka Apache Gold—US 1965). **1964** Winnetou II Teil (aka Last of the Renegades—US 1966); Old Shatterhand (aka Shatterhand—US 1967); Captain Falcon; Goddess of Vengeance (aka Kali-Yug or Kali-Yug, Goddess of Vengeance). **1965** Die Holle von Manitoba (aka A Place Called Glory—US 1966); Winnetou III Teil (aka The Desperate Trail—US 1967); Code 7, Victim 5. **1966** The Apaches' Last Battle; 24 Hours to Kill; Savage Kurdistan (aka Attacks of the Kurds); "3." **1967** Sept Fois Femme (Woman Times Seven); Die Schlangengrube und das Pendel (aka The Blood Demon—US 1969). **1968** The Longest Day in Kansas City; Devil May Care.

BARKER, REGINALD
Born: 1886, Bothwell, Scotland. Died: Feb. 23, 1945, Los Angles, Calif. (heart attack). Screen, stage actor, film and stage director. Entered films as an actor in 1913.

BARLOW, REGINALD
Born: 1866, Mass. Died: July 6, 1943, Hollywood, Calif. Screen, stage and minstrel actor. Entered films temporarily in 1916 and permanently in 1931. Married to actress Zelma Rose (dec. 1933).

Appeared in: **1925** Clothes Make the Pirate. **1932** The Woman from Monte Carlo; The Washington Masquerade; Age of Consent; If I Had a Million; Night Court; World and the Flesh; Wet Parade; Blessed Event; I Am a Fugitive from a Chain Gang; Sinners in the Sun; Mata Hari; This Reckless Age; Alias the Doctor; Afraid to Talk; Horse Feathers. **1933** His Private Secretary; The Big Cage; Grand Slam; Flying Down to Rio. **1934** You Can't Buy Everything; Romance in Manhattan; Half a Sinner. **1935** The Werewolf of London; Captain Blood; Cardinal Richelieu; Strangers All; The Bride of Frankenstein;

Mutiny Ahead. **1936** Little Lord Fauntleroy; The Last of the Mohicans; O'Malley of the Mounted; Lloyds of London. **1937** It Happened Out West. **1939** Rovin' Tumbleweeds; The Witness Vanishes; The Man in the Iron Mask. **1940** The Courageous Dr. Christian.

BARNARD, IVOR
Born: June 13, 1887, London, England. Died: June 30, 1953, England? Screen and stage actor.

Appeared in: **1920** The Skin Game. **1931** The Skin Game (and 1920 version); Sally in Our Alley. **1932** Blind Spot. **1933** The Roof; The Good Companions; Illegal; Sleeping Car; Waltz Time; The Crime at Blossoms; The Wandering Jew (US 1935). **1934** Princess Charming (US 1935); The Wigan Express (aka Death at Broadcasting House); Brides to Be; Love, Life and Laughter. **1935** The Village Squire; The Guv'nor (aka Mister Hobo—US 1936); Foreign Affaires; The Price of Wisdom; Some Day. **1936** Dreams Come True; The House of the Spaniard. **1937** Double Exposures; Secret Lives (aka I Married a Spy—US 1938); Farewell to Cinderella; The Mill on the Floss (US 1939); Storm in a Teacup; Victoria the Great; What a Man! **1938** Pygmalion; Everything Happens to Me. **1939** Cheer Boys Cheer; The Stars Look Down (US 1941); Eye Witness; Oh Dear Uncle! **1941** The Saint's Vacation. **1943** The Silver Fleet (US 1945); Undercover (aka Undercover Guerillas—US 1944); Escape to Danger (US 1944). **1944** Hotel Reserve (US 1946); Don't Take It to Heart (US 1949). **1945** Great Day (US 1946); Murder in Reverse (US 1946); Perfect Strangers (aka Vacation from Marriage—US). **1946** Caesar and Cleopatra; Appointment With Crime (US 1950); Great Expectations (US 1949). **1947** So Well Remembered; Mrs. Fitzherbert (US 1950). **1948** Esther Waters; London Belongs to Me (aka Dulcimer Street—US); Oliver Twist (US 1951). **1949** The Queen of Spades (US 1950); Paper Orchid. **1950** Madeleine. **1952** Hot Ice; Time Gentlemen, Please! **1953** Sea Devils; Malta Story (US 1954); Beat the Devil (US 1954).

BARNARD, MAE *See* GISH, MARY

BARNELL, NORA ELY
Born: 1882. Died: July 10, 1933, Los Angeles, Calif. (cerebral hemorrhage). Screen actress and casting director. Entered films as an actress with Thomas Ince.

BARNES, BARRY K. (Nelson Barnes)
Born: Dec. 27, 1906, Chelsea, England. Died: Jan. 12, 1965, London, England. Screen and stage actor. Married to actress Diana Churchill.

Appeared in: **1936** Dodging the Dole. **1937** The Return of the Scarlet Pimpernel (US 1938). **1938** Who Goes Next?; This Man is News; You're the Doctor; Prison Without Bars (US 1939); The Ware Case (US 1939). **1939** Spies of the Air (US 1940); This Man in Paris; The Midas Touch. **1940** Two for Danger; Law and Disorder; The Girl in the News (US 1941). **1946** Bedelia (US 1947). **1947** Dancing With Crime.

BARNES, EDNA REMING
Born: 1883. Died: Mar. 7, 1935, Los Angeles, Calif. (cancer). Screen character actress.

BARNES, FLORENCE "PANCHO" (Florence Lowe)
Born: 1902, Calif. Died: Mar., 1975, Boron, Calif. Screen stunt pilot.

Appeared in: **1929** Hell's Angels.

BARNES, FRANK (Richard Allen)
Born: 1875. Died: Nov. 1, 1940, Bronx, N.Y. Stage and screen actor. Entered films prior to 1917.

Appeared in: **1927** The General.

BARNES, GEORGE
Born: 1890. Died: Nov. 18, 1949, Hollywood, Calif. (cancer). Screen and stage actor.

Appeared in: **1903** The Great Train Robbery.

BARNES, GEORGE E.
Born: 1879. Died: Mar. 3, 1926, Honolulu, Hawaii (cerebral hemorrhage). Screen and vaudeville actor. Toured in act billed as "Barnes and West." Do not confuse with cinematographer of same name.

BARNES, J. H.
Born: Feb. 26, 1850, England. Died: Nov. 10, 1925, England? Screen, stage actor and writer.

Appeared in: **1913** Hamlet (US 1915).

BARNES, JUSTUS D.
Born: 1862. Died: Feb. 6, 1946, Weedsport, N.Y. Screen and stage actor.

Appeared in: **1915** The Country Girl.

BARNES, MAC M.
Died: Jan. 10, 1923, Los Angeles, Calif. Screen actor.

Appeared in: **1921** Get-Rich-Quick Wallingford; Experience; The Sign on the Door.

BARNES, T. ROY
Born: Aug. 11, 1880, Lincolnshire, England. Died: Mar. 30, 1937, Hollywood, Calif. Screen, stage and vaudeville actor. Appeared in vaudeville with his wife, Bessie Crawford, in an act billed as "Package of Smiles."

Appeared in: **1920** Scratch My Back; So Long Letty. **1921** See My Lawyer; Exit the Vamp; Her Face Value; A Kiss in Time. **1922** The Old Homestead; Is Matrimony a Failure?; Don't Get Personal; Too Much Wife. **1923** Adam and Eva; The Go-Getter; Hollywood; Souls for Sale. **1924** The Great White Way; Butterfly; Reckless Romance; Young Ideas. **1925** Seven Chances; The Crowded Hour; The Price of Pleasure; The Re-Creation of Brian Kent. **1926** Dangerous Friends; Ladies of Leisure; A Regular Scout; The Unknown Cavalier. **1927** Body and Soul; Chicago; Smile, Brother, Smile; Tender Hour. **1928** A Blonde for a Night; The Gate Crasher. **1929** Sally; Dangerous Curves. **1930** Wide Open; Caught Short. **1931** Alpha; Women of All Nations. Prior - to **1933** the following shorts: How's My Baby; His Error; Carnival Revue. **1934** Kansas City Princess; It's a Gift. **1935** Village Tale; The Virginia Judge; Doubting Thomas; The Four-Star Boarder (short).

BARNES, V. L.
Born: 1870. Died: Aug. 9, 1949, Los Angeles, Calif. Screen actor.

Appeared in: **1921** Cold Steel. **1924** Crossed Trails. **1925** Peggy of the Secret Service. **1926** The Fighting Cheat.

BARNET, BORIS
Born: 1902, Russia. Died: 1965, Russia? Screen actor and film director.

Appeared in: **1946** Dark is the Night. **1949** Secret Agent.

BARNET, SAMUEL *See* BERNARD, SAM

BARNETT, CHESTER A.
Born: 1885. Died: Sept. 22, 1947, Jefferson City, Mo. (pneumonia). Screen and stage actor.

Appeared in: **1912** The Girl in the Next Room; Her Dressmaker's Bills; The Gypsy Flirt; Locked Out; A Tangled Marriage. **1913** Where Charity Begins; Pearl's Mistake; Dress Reform; The Woman and the Law; His Rich Uncle; Robert's Lesson; Girls Will Be Boys; The Cabaret Singer; Hubby's New Coat; The Convict's Daughter; A Woman's Revenge; Pearl's Hero. **1915** Trilby. **1916** La Boheme. **1919** The Wishing Ring.

BARNETT, GRIFF
Born: 1885. Died: Jan. 12, 1958, Hollywood, Calif. (heart condition and pneumonia). Screen actor.

Appeared in: **1941** The Lady from Cheyenne. **1942** Stardust on the Sage. **1943** Shadows on the Sage. **1946** Danger Woman; Without Reservation; Duel in the Sun; To Each His Own. **1947** Suddenly It's Spring; Unconquered; Possessed; Gunfighters; Cass Timberlane; Wild Harvest; The Millerson Case; Daisy Kenyon. **1948** Saigon; Fighting Father Dunne; Fury at Furnace Creek; The Walls of Jericho; Tap Roots; For the Love of Mary; Apartment for Peggy. **1949** Criss Cross; The Doolins of Oklahoma; Mother is a Freshman; Pinky. **1950** Customs Agent; No Man of Her Own; Peggy; Sierra. **1951** Hometown Story; Cattle Drive; Passage West; Two of a Kind; When I Grow Up. **1952** Scandal Sheet; The Sellout. **1953** Angel Face. **1957** The Spirit of St. Louis.

BARNETT, LADY ISOBEL
Born: 1918, England. Died: Oct., 1980, Crossington, England. Screen, stage and television actress.

BARNETT, VINCENT "VINCE"
Born: July 4, 1902, Pittsburgh, Pa. Died: Aug. 10, 1977, Encino, Calif. (heart ailment). Screen, stage, vaudeville and television actor. Son of stage actor Luke Barnett (dec.).

Appeared in: **1929** Wide Open; All's Quiet on the Western Front. **1930**

Dancing Sweeties; Night Work; Queen of Scandal; One Heavenly Night; A Royal Flush (short). **1931** Scratch as Catch Can (short). **1932** Tiger Shark; Scarface; The Night Mayor; Rackety Rax; Flesh; Horse Feathers. **1933** The Death Kiss; Heritage of the Desert; Fast Workers; Made on Broadway; Sunset Pass; The Big Cage; Girl in 419; Man of the Forest; The Prizefighter and the Lady; I Cover the Waterfront; Air Maniacs (short). **1934** The Ninth Guest; Madame Spy; The Affairs of Cellini; Thirty Day Princess; Now I'll Tell; She Loves Me Not; Take the Stand; Young and Beautiful; Kansas City Princess; Crimson Romance; Hell in the Heavens; Super-Stupid (short); Two Lame Ducks (short). **1935** No Ransom; Black Fury; Princess O'Hara; Champagne for Breakfast; Don't Bet on Blondes; Silk Hat Kid; Streamline Express; I Live My Life; Riffraff; Springfield Rifle; Just Another Murder (short). **1936** Dancing Feet; Captain Calamity; Down to the Sea; Yellow Cargo; I Cover Chinatown; The Brain Busters (short). **1937** The Woman I Love; A Star is Born; Bank Alarm. **1938** The Headleys at Home. **1939** Ride 'Em Cowgirl; Exile Express; Overland Trail. **1940** Heroes of the Saddle; East Side Kids; Boys of the City; Seven Sinners; Sierra Sue. **1941** A Dangerous Game; Paper Bullets; Puddin'head; Jungle Man; I Killed That Man. **1942** Stardust on the Sage; Klondike Fury; Girl's Town; The Corpse Vanishes; Baby Face Morgan; Foreign Agent; Bowery at Midnight; Prison Girls; X Marks the Spot; Queen of Broadway. **1943** The Crime Smasher; Kid Dynamite; Captive Wild Woman; Danger! Women at Work; Petticoat Larceny; Torando. **1944** Leave It to the Irish; Sweethearts of the U.S.A. **1945** High Powered; Thrill of a Romance; River Gang. **1946** The Falcon's Alibi; The Virginian; Sensation Hunters; No Leave, No Love; The Killers; Bowery Bombshell; Swell Guy. **1947** I Cover Big Town; Shoot to Kill; Brute Force; Gas House Kids go West; Little Miss Broadway; Joe Palooka in the Knockout; Big Town After Dark; High Wall. **1948** Big Town Scandal; Thunder in the Pines. **1949** Loaded Pistols; Knock on Any Door; Deputy Marshal; Sweet Cheat (short). **1950** International Burlesque; Mule Train; Border Treasure. **1951** Kentucky Jubilee. **1952** Carson City; Red Planet Mars; Springfield Rifle. **1954** The Human Jungle. **1957** The Quiet Gun. **1959** The Rookie. **1965** Dr. Goldfoot and the Bikini Machine; Zebra in the Kitchen. **1967** The Big Mouth. **1975** Summer School Teachers; Crazy Mama.

BARONCELLI, JACQUES DE
Born: 1881, France. Died: Jan. 12, 1951, Paris, France (heart attack). Screen actor, film producer and director.

BAROUX, LUCIEN
Born: 1889, Toulouse, France. Died: May 21, 1968, Toulouse, France. Screen and stage actor.

Appeared in: **1931** Un Soir de Rafle (Night Raid). **1932** Levy and Co. **1933** Le Petit Ecart. **1934** Ces Messieurs de la Sande. **1935** Bacara; Charlemagne. **1936** Le Mioche. **1937** Les Mysteres de Paris; L'Enfant de Troupe. **1938** Forty Little Mothers. **1939** Champs Elysees; Behind the Facade. **1943** Fire in the Straw. **1944** 32 Rue de Montmarte; Moulin Rouge. **1952** The French Way; Father's Dilemma. **1953** Naughty Martine. **1958** Lovers and Thieves. **1962** Le Diable et les Dix Commandments (The Devil and the Ten Commandments—US 1963).

BARR, BYRON
Born: 1917. Died: Nov. 3, 1966. Screen actor. Do not confuse with actor Gig Young who appeared in early films under his real name, Byron Barr.

Appeared in: **1940** Misbehaving Husbands. **1941** Navy Blues. **1942** The Man Who Came to Dinner; You're in the Army Now. **1944** Double Indemnity. **1945** Follow That Woman; Tokyo Rose; Love Letters; The Affairs of Susan. **1946** They Made Me a Killer. **1947** Seven Were Saved; Big Town. **1948** The Pitfall; The Main Street Kid. **1949** Down Dakota Way; Thelma Jordan (aka File on Thelma Jordan). **1950** There's a Girl in My Heart; Tarnished; Covered Wagon Raiders (aka Covered Wagon Raid); Paid in Full.

BARR, JEANNE
Born: 1932. Died: Aug. 10, 1967, New York, N.Y. Screen, stage and television actress.

Appeared in: **1960** The Fugitive Kind. **1962** Long Day's Journey into Night. **1964** Lilith.

BARR, LEONARD (Leonard Barri)
Born: 1903. Died: Nov. 22, 1980, West Hollywood, Calif. (stroke). Screen, vaudeville, television actor, dancer and nightclub entertainer.

Appeared in: **1971** Diamonds are Forever. **1973** The Sting. **1978** Record City. **1979** Skatetown U.S.A. **1981** Under the Rainbow.

BARRAT, ROBERT (Robert H. Barrat)
Born: July 10, 1891, New York, N.Y. Died: Jan. 7, 1970, Hollywood, Calif. Screen, stage and television actor.

Appeared in: **1933** Mayor of Hell; Baby Face; The Picture Snatcher; The Silk Express; Heroes for Sale; The Kennel Murder Case; Wild Boys of the Road; Lily Turner; King of the Jungle; I Loved a Woman; The Secrets of the Blue Room; From Headquarters; Ann Carver's Profession. **1934** Dark Hazard; Massacre; Wonder Bar; Fog Over Frisco; Friends of Mr. Sweeney; Dames; Here Comes the Navy; A Very Honorable Guy; Midnight Alibi; Hi, Nelli; Gambling Lady; Upper World; The Dragon Murder Case; Housewife; Return of the Terror; Big-Hearted Herbert; The St. Louis Kid; I Sell Anything; The Firebird. **1935** Devil Dogs of the Air; Captain Blood; Moonlight on the Prairie; While the Patient Slept; Bordertown; The Florentine Dagger; Stranded; Dr. Socrates; Village Tale; Special Agent; Dressed to Thrill; The Murder Man; I Am a Thief. **1936** The Last of the Mohicans; Exclusive Story; The Country Doctor; I Married a Doctor; Sons O'Guns; Draegerman Courage; Charge of the Light Brigade; God's Country and the Woman; The Black Legion; Trail of the Lonesome Pine; Trailin' West; Mary of Scotland. **1937** Mountain Justice; Life of Emile Zola; Confessions; Love is on the Air; The Barrier. **1938** Bad Man of Brimstone; Penitentiary; The Texans; Charlie Chan in Honolulu; Breaking the Ice; Shadows Over Shanghai; The Buccaneer; Forbidden Valley. **1939** Colorado Sunset; Allegheny Uprising; Conspiracy; Bad Lands; The Cisco Kid and the Lady; The Return of the Cisco Kid; Man of Conquest; Heritage of the Desert; Union Pacific. **1940** The Man from Dakota; Northwest Passage; Laddie, Go West; Captain Caution; Fugitive from a Prison Camp. **1941** Parachute Battalion; Riders of the Purple Sage; They Met in Argentina. **1942** The Girl from Alaska; American Empire; Fall In. **1943** Johnny Come Lately; The Bomber's Moon; They Came to Blow Up America; A Stranger in Town; Dr. Paul Joseph Goebbels. **1944** The Adventures of Mark Twain; Enemy of Women. **1945** They Were Expendable (He portrayed General Douglas MacArthur as he did in American Guerilla in the Philippines—1950); Road to Utopia; Grissly's Millions; Dakota; The Great John L; Strangler of the Swamp; San Antonio; Wanderer of the Wasteland. **1946** The Magnificent Doll; Dangerous Millions; Sunset Pass; Just Before Dawn; The Time of Their Lives. **1947** Sea of Grass; Fabulous Texan; Road to Rio. **1948** Joan of Arc; I Love Trouble; Relentless; Bad Men of Tombstone. **1949** Riders of the Range; The Lone Wolf and His Lady; Canadian Pacific; Song of India; The Doolins of Oklahoma. **1950** An American Guerilla in the Philippines; Baron of Arizona; Davy Crockett, Indian Scout; The Kid from Texas; Double Crossbones. **1951** Darling, How Could You; Distant Drums; Flight to Mars; The Pride of Maryland. **1952** Denver and the Rio Grande; Son of Ali Baba. **1953** Cow Country. **1955** Tall Man Riding.

BARRETT, CHARLES C.
Born: 1871. Died: Feb. 11, 1929, Baltimore, Md. Screen, stage, vaudeville and burlesque actor.

BARRETT, EDITH
Born: 1913, Roxbury, Mass. Died: Feb. 22, 1977, Albuquerque, N.Mex. (heart attack). Screen, stage and television actress. Divorced from actor Vincent Price.

Appeared in: **1941** Ladies in Retirement (film debut); Lady for a Night. **1942** Give Out, Sisters; Get Hep to Love. **1943** I Walked With a Zombie; Always a Bridesmaid; The Ghost Ship; The Song of Bernadette. **1944** Jane Eyre; Strangers in the Night. **1945** Molly and Me; Keys of the Kingdom; That's the Spirit. **1948** Ruthless. **1949** The Lady Gambles. **1952** Holiday for Sinners. **1953** The Ghost Ship (and 1943 version). **1956** The Swan. **1958** In Love and War.

BARRETT, GENTRY (Gentry Wickizer)
Born: Apr. 11, 1892, Calif. Died: Oct. 10, 1956, Los Angeles, Calif. Screen actress.

BARRETT, GEORGE (Charles Frederick Barrett)
Born: 1869, Leeds, England. Died: June 13, 1935, England? Screen and stage actor.

BARRETT, IVY RICE
Born: 1898. Died: Nov. 8, 1962, Hollywood, Calif. Screen and stage actress. In Sennett films as a bathing beauty from 1915 to 1920.

BARRETT, JANE
Born: May 7, 1923, Highgate, London, England. Died: July 20, 1969, England. Screen, stage and television actress.

Appeared in: **1938** The Citadel (film debut); Mr. Sheffington. **1946** The Captive Heart (US 1947). **1948** Colonel Bogey. **1949** Eureka Stockade. **1952** Time Gentlemen Please! **1953** The Sword and the Rose. **1956** Bond of Fear.

BARRETT, MINNETTE
Born: 1884, Gainesville, Ga. Died: June 20, 1964, Whitestone, N.Y. Screen, stage and vaudeville actress.

Appeared in: **1916** The Ragamuffin.

BARRETT, PAT
Born: 1889. Died: Mar. 25, 1959. Screen and radio actor.

Appeared in: **1940** Comin' Round the Mountain.

BARRETT, RICE See CROSTHWAITE, IVY

BARRETT, TONY
Born: May 24, 1916, New York, N.Y. Died: Nov. 16, 1974, Los Angeles, Calif. (cancer). Screen, radio actor, screenwriter and television writer-producer. Married to writer Steffi Barrett.

Appeared in: **1946** The Falcon's Adventure; San Quentin; Seven Keys to Baldpate; Under the Tonto Rim; Wild Horse Mesa. **1947** Born to Kill; Dick Tracy's Dilemma; Dick Tracy Meets Gruesome. **1948** Western Heritage; Mystery in Mexico. **1949** Impact; Flame of Youth. **1950** Prisoners in Petticoats. **1955** It's a Dog's Life.

BARRI, MARIO
Died: Nov. 21, 1963, Manila, Philippine Islands. Screen actor and film producer.

Appeared in: **1956** Huk. **1961** The Steel Claw. **1962** Out of the Tiger's Mouth; No Man Is An Island; Samar. **1964** A Yank in Viet-Nam.

BARRIE, SIR JAMES MATTHEW
Born: May 9, 1860, Kirriemuir, Scotland. Died: June 19, 1937, London, England (bronchial pneumonia). Playwright, novelist and screen actor.

Appeared in: **1918** Masks and Faces.

BARRIE, JOHN
Born: 1917, England. Died: Mar. 24, 1980, York, England. Screen, stage and television actor.

Appeared in: **1961** Victim (US 1962). **1962** Life for Ruth (aka Walk in the Shadow—US 1966); The Wild and the Willing (aka Young and Willing—US 1964). **1963** Lancelot and Guinevere (aka The Sword of Lancelot—US). **1968** The File of the Golden Goose (US 1969). **1969** The Oblong Box (aka Edgar Allen Poe's The Oblong Box—US). **1970** Patton; Song of Norway.

BARRIE, WENDY (Wendy Jenkins)
Born: Apr. 18, 1912, Hong Kong or May 8, 1919, London, England. Died: Feb. 2, 1978, Englewood, N.J. Screen, stage, radio and television actress.

Appeared in: **1932** Wedding Rehearsal; Collision; The Barton Mystery; Where is This Lady?; Threads; The Callbox Mystery. **1933** Cash (aka For Love or Money—US 1934); The House of Trent; The Private Life of Henry VIII; This Acting Business; It's a Boy! (US 1934). **1934** Without You; The Man I Want; Murder at the Inn; Give Her a Ring; Freedom of the Seas; There Goes Susie (aka Scandals of Paris—US 1935). **1935** It's a Small World; College Scandal; Big Broadcast of 1936; Millions in the Air; A Feather in Her Hat. **1936** Love on a Bet; Speed; Ticket to Paradise; Under Your Spell. **1937** Breezing Home; Prescription for Romance; What Price Vengeance; Wings Over Honolulu; Dead End; A Girl With Ideas. **1938** I am the Law. **1939** The Saint Strikes Back; Hound of the Baskervilles; Five Came Back; Newsboy's Home; Pacific Liner; The Witness Vanishes; Day-Time Wife. **1940** Women in War; The Saint Takes Over; Cross-Country Romance; Men Against the Sky; Who Killed Aunt Maggie? **1941** The Saint in Palm Springs; A Date With the Falcon; The Gay Falcon; Repent at Leisure; Public Enemies. **1943** Eyes of the Underworld; Forever and a Day; Submarine Alert. **1954** It Should Happen to You.

BARRIER, EDGAR
Born: Mar. 4, 1907, New York, N.Y. Died: June 20, 1964, Hollywood, Calif. (heart attack). Screen and stage actor.

Appeared in: **1940** Escape; Comrade X. **1941** The Penalty; They Dare Not Love. **1942** Eagle Squadron; Danger in the Pacific; Arabian Nights; Journey Into Fear. **1943** Adventures of Smilin' Jack (serial); We've Never Been Licked; Flesh and Fantasy; Phantom of the Opera. **1944** The Cobra Woman; Secrets of Scotland Yard. **1945** Nob Hill; A Game of Death (US 1946); Song of Mexico. **1946** Cornered; Tarzan and the Leopard Woman. **1948** Adventures in Silverado; Rocky; To the Ends of the Earth; Port Said; Macbeth; Rogues' Regiment. **1949** The Secret of St. Ives. **1950** Last of the Buccaneers; The Squared

Circle; Cyrano de Bergerac. **1951** The Whip Hand; Hurricane Island. **1953** Count the Hours; The Stand at Apache River; Destination Gobi; The Prince of Pirates; Eyes of the Jungle; The Golden Blade. **1954** Silver Lode; The Sarecen Blade; Princess of the Nile. **1956** Rumble on the Docks. **1957** The Giant Claw. **1959** Juke Box Rhythm. **1961** On the Double; Snow White and the Three Stooges; Pirates of Tortuga. **1963** Irma la Douce.

BARRINGER, BARRY (A. B. Barringer)
Born: June 25, 1888, Mobile, Ala. Died: May 21, 1938, Los Angeles, Calif. Screen actor, screenwriter and director. Entered films as an actor during silents.

BARRINGER, NED (Spencer Edward (Ned) Barringer)
Born: 1883. Died: Feb. 13, 1976, Leavenworth, Kan. (cancer). Screen, stage, radio actor and screenwriter.

BARRINGTON, HERBERT (Herbert Barrington Hollingsworth)
Born: 1872. Died: Oct. 26, 1933, Tarrytown, N.Y. Screen and stage actor. Entered films in Yonkers, N.Y. with Pilot Films.

Appeared in: **1912** Souls in the Shadow. **1913** The Streets of New York; Hoodman Blind. **1915** The Undying Fire; Jean the Faithful; The Girl and the Matinee Idol; The Woman Who Paid. **1916** Broken Chains; The Way of the World. **1917** Maternity; Shall We Forgive Her? **1918** The Spurs of Sybil; His Royal Highness.

BARRINGTON, RUTLAND (George Rutland Fleet)
Born: Jan. 15, 1853, Penge, England. Died: May 31, 1922, England. Screen, stage actor and author.

Appeared in: **1916** The Girl Who Loves a Soldier; Still Water Runs Deep.

BARRIS, HARRY
Born: Nov. 24, 1905, New York, N.Y. Died: Dec. 14, 1962, Burbank, Calif. (cancer). Screen actor, singer and songwriter. Member of "The Rhythm Boys" singing group. Divorced from singer Lois Whiteman and later married to Esther Margie Barris. Father of singer Marti Barris.

Appeared in: **1930** Two Plus Fours (short). **1931** The Spirit of Notre Dame. **1932** Now's the Time (short); He's a Honey (short); That Rascal (short). **1934** Hollywood Party. **1935** Every Night at Eight; Love Me Forever; After the Dance. **1936** The Man I Marry; Showboat. **1937** Something to Sing About; Double or Nothing. **1938** Trade Winds; Cowboy from Brooklyn. **1939** Some Like It Hot; The Shining Hour. **1940** Rhythm on the River. **1941** Blondie Goes Latin; Birth of the Blues. **1942** Footlight Serenade; Priorities on Parade; The Fleet's In. **1943** The Youngest Profession; Dixie; Happy-Go-Lucky. **1944** And the Angels Sing; Here Come the Waves; Practical Joker (short). **1945** Weekend at the Waldorf; Anchors Aweigh; Penthouse Rhythm; Steppin' in Society. **1946** Young Widow; The Blue Dahlia. **1947** Pet Peeves (short). **1948** You Were Meant for Me. **1950** A Life of Her Own; Three Little Words.

BARRIS, HERBIE
Born: 1909. Died: Dec. 28, 1977, Las Vegas, Nev. Screen, burlesque actor and nightclub entertainer.

Appeared in: **1961** Kiss Me, Baby.

BARRISCALE, BESSIE
Born: 1884, New York. Died: June 30, 1965, Kentfield, Calif. Screen, stage and vaudeville actress. Married to actor/director Howard Hickman (dec. 1940).

Appeared in: **1914** The Making of Bobby Burnit; The Rose of the Rancho. **1916** Home, Plain Jane; Not My Sister. **1917** Wooden Shoes. **1919** A Trick of Fate. **1921** The Broken Gate; The Breaking Point. **1923** Girl of the Golden West. **1928** Show Folks. **1933** Secrets; Above the Clouds. **1934** Beloved. **1935** The Man Who Reclaimed His Head.

BARRON, FREDERICK C.
Born: 1888, Melbourne, Australia. Died: Oct. 9, 1955, Central Islip, N.Y. Screen, stage and television actor. Entered films in U.S. in 1898.

BARRON, MARCUS
Born: 1869, England. Died: Mar. 15, 1944, England? Screen and stage actor.

Appeared in: **1934** Loyalties; Waltzes for Vienna (aka Strauss's Great Waltz—US 1935).

BARROWS, HENRY A.
Born: Apr. 29, 1875, Saco, Maine. Died: Mar. 25, 1945. Screen and stage actor. Entered films in 1913.

Appeared in: **1916** Fires of Conscience. **1917** The World Apart; The Heir of the Ages; The Bride's Silence; Charity Castle; Her Country's Call; The Sunset Trail; Lost in Transit; The Stainless Barrier. **1919** The Lion Man (serial). **1920** The Veiled Mystery (serial). **1921** Tiger True; It Can Be Done. **1922** The Great Night; Putting It Over; Rent Free; The Law and the Woman; A Tailor Made Man; Yellow Men and Gold; The Woman's Side; The Wise Kid. **1923** Broadway Gold; The Footlight Ranger; Jazzmania; Long Live the King; The Shock. **1924** The Reckless Age; Between Friends; Captain Blood; The Marriage Cheat; Sporting Youth; The Sea Hawk. **1925** Cobra; Drusilla With a Million; His Majesty, Bunker Bean; The Man on the Box; Crack O'Dawn. **1926** Footloose Widows; The Little Irish Girl; The Lost Express; Mistake Orders; Oh, What a Nurse!; Skinner's Dress Suit; Atta Boy. **1927** All Aboard; Horse Shoes; The Sunset Derby; The Lost Limited; White Pants Willie; Three's a Crowd; The Return of the Riddle Rider (serial). **1928** A Perfect Gentleman; The Wright Idea; Burning Brides; Women Who Dare. **1929** Some Mother's Boy; The Drake Case. **1930** The Kibitzer. **1931** Guilty Hands.

BARROWS, JAMES O.
Born: 1853. Died: Dec. 7, 1925, Hollywood, Calif. (heart attack). Screen and stage actor.

Appeared in: **1921** Silent Years. **1922** Pawned; The Pride of Palomar; When Love Comes; The Call of Home; Hurricane's Gal; White Shoulders. **1923** The Old Fool; Cause for Divorce; Shadows of the North; Stephen Steps Out. **1924** Her Night of Romance; The Tomboy; The Gaiety Girl; The Signal Tower; Young Ideas. **1925** The Goose Woman; Daddy's Gone A-Hunting; The Price of Pleasure. **1926** The Sea Beast.

BARRY, DONALD "RED" (Donald Barry de Acosta)
Born: 1911, Houston, Tex. Died: July 17, 1980, North Hollywood, Calif. (suicide—gun shot). Screen, stage, radio actor and film director.

Appeared in: **1936** Night Waitress (film debut). **1937** The Woman I Love. **1938** Sinners in Paradise; The Crowd Roars; The Duke of West Point; Young Dr. Kildare; Think It Over (short). **1939** Calling All Marines; Days of Jesse James; Saga of Death Valley; Wyoming Outlaw; S.O.S. Tidal Wave; Only Angels Have Wings; Calling Dr. Kildare; Panama Patrol. **1940** Ghost Valley Raiders; One Man's Law; The Tulsa Kid; Frontier Vengeance; Texas Terrors; Adventures of Red Ryder (serial); Jack Pot (short). **1941** The Phantom Cowboy; Wyoming Wildcat; Two-Gun Sheriff; Desert Bandit; Kansas Cyclone; The Apache Kid; Death Valley Outlaws; A Missouri Outlaw. **1942** Remember Pearl Harbor; Jesse James, Jr.; Stagecoach Express; Arizona Terrors; The Cyclone Kid; The Sombrero Kid; Outlaws of Pine Ridge. **1943** The Sundown Kid; Dead Man's Gulch; Carson City Cyclone; The Black Hills Express; Fugitive from Sonora. **1944** The Purple Heart; California Joe; Outlaws of Santa Fe; My Buddy. **1945** The Chicago Kid; Bells of Rosarita. **1946** The Last Crooked Mile; Out California Way; The Plainsman and the Lady. **1947** That's My Gal. **1948** Madonna of the Desert; Slippery McGee; Lightin' in the Forest; Train to Alcatraz. **1949** Square Dance Jubilee; Tough Assignment; The Dalton Gang; Red Desert; Ringside. **1950** Gunfire; Border Rangers; Train to Tombstone; Everybody's Dancing. **1954** Jesse James' Women; Untamed Heiress. **1955** The Twinkle in God's Eye; I'll Cry Tomorrow. **1956** Seven Men from Now. **1957** Gun Duel in Durango. **1958** Frankenstein—1970; China Doll. **1959** The Last Mile; Warlock; Born Reckless; The Big Operator. **1960** Walk Like a Dragon. **1961** Buffalo Gun. **1962** Walk on the Wild Side; The Errand Boy. **1963** Twilight of Honor. **1964** Law of the Lawless; The Carpetbaggers; Iron Angel. **1965** Convict Stage; Fort Courageous; Town Tamer; War Party. **1966** Alvarez Kelly; Apache Uprising. **1967** Fort Utah; Hostile Guns; Red Tomahawk. **1968** Bandolero!; Shalako; The Shakiest Gun in the West. **1970** The Cockeyed Cowboys of Calico County; Rio Lobo; Dirty Dingus Magee. **1975** Whiffs. **1977** Orca. **1978** Hot Lead and Cold Feet; Buckstone County Prison; One Man Jury.

BARRY, FERN (Fern Barry Hill)
Born: 1909. Died: Sept. 9, 1981, Burbank, Calif. (cancer). Screen and television actress.

Appeared in: **1957** Three Brave Men; Funny Face. **1962** The Chapman Report.

BARRY, JOE
Died: July 8, 1974. Screen actor. Do not confuse with assistant film director Joe Barry.

Appeared in: **1955** Man With the Gun. **1958** Bell, Book and Candle.

BARRY, LEON *See* BARY, LEON

BARRY, ROBERT
Born: 1901. Died: Mar. 21, 1931, Santa Monica, Calif. (auto accident). Screen actor.

BARRY, TOM (Hal Donahue)
Born: 1884. Died: Nov. 7, 1931, Hollywood, Calif. (heart trouble). Screen, stage, vaudeville actor, playwright, screenwriter and newspaperman.

Appeared in: **1931** The Cisco Kid (his only film).

BARRY, VIOLA
Born: 1894. Died: Apr. 2, 1964, Hollywood, Calif. Screen, stage actress, screenwriter, stage producer and stage director.

Appeared in: **1913** The Mothering Heart. **1920** Sea Wolf.

BARRYE, EMILY
Born: 1896. Died: Dec. 15, 1957, Hollywood, Calif. Screen actress. Entered films in 1915 with Universal.

Appeared in: **1924** Fast and Fearless. **1925** The Bloodhound; Border Intrigue; Fast Fightin'. **1926** The Bonanza Buckaroo; Speedy Spurs; Volcano. **1927** King of Kings. **1929** The Godless Girl.

BARRYMORE, DIANA (Diana Blanche Barrymore Blythe)
Born: Mar. 3, 1921, New York, N.Y. Died: Jan. 25, 1960, New York, N.Y. (natural causes). Screen, stage actress and author. Married to actor Rober Wilcox (dec. 1955). Divorced from actor Bramwell Fletcher and tennis pro John Howard. Daughter of actor John Barrymore (dec. 1942) and Blanche Oelrichs who wrote under the pen name of Michael Strange. Regarding family, see John Barrymore.

Appeared in: **1941** Manpower. **1942** Eagle Squadron; Between Us Girls; Nightmare. **1943** Fired Wife; Frontier Badman; When Ladies Fly. **1944** The Ghost Catchers; Ladies Courageous; The Adventures of Mark Twain; Hollywood Canteen. **1950** D.O.A.; Flame and the Arrow. **1951** The Mob.

BARRYMORE, ETHEL (Ethel Blythe)
Born: Aug. 15, 1879, Philadelphia, Pa. Died: June 18, 1959, Beverly Hills, Calif. (heart condition). Screen, stage and television actress. Mother of actress Ethel Barrymore Colt (aka Louisa Kinlock) dec. 1977. Regarding family, see John Barrymore. Won 1944 Academy Award for Best Supporting Actress in None But the Lonely Heart. Nominated for 1946 Academy Award for Best Supporting Actress in The Spiral Staircase, in 1947 for The Paradine Case and in 1949 for Pinky.

Appeared in: **1914** The Nightingale (film debut). **1915** The Final Judgement. **1916** Kiss of Hate. **1917** The Awakening of Helen Ritchie; The Lifted Veil; The Call of Her People; The White Raven; The American Widow. **1918** Our Mrs. McChesney; The Whirlpool. **1919** The Divorcee. **1932** Rasputin and the Empress. **1933** All at Sea (short). **1935** Peter Ibbetson. **1944** None But the Lonely Heart. **1946** The Spiral Staircase. **1947** Night Song; Moss Rose; The Farmer's Daughter. **1948** Portrait of Jenny; The Paradine Case; Moonrise. **1949** Pinky; The Great Sinner; That Midnight Kiss; The Red Danube. **1951** Kind Lady; The Secret of Convict Lake; Daphne, the Virgin of the Golden Laurels (narr.). **1952** Deadline U.S.A.; Just for You; It's a Big Country. **1953** The Story of Three Loves; Main Street to Broadway. **1954** Young at Heart. **1957** Johnny Trouble. **1974** That's Entertainment (film clips).

BARRYMORE, JOHN (John Blythe)
Born: Feb. 15, 1882, Philadelphia, Pa. Died: May 29, 1942, Los Angeles, Calif. Screen, stage and television actor. Son of stage actor Maurice Barrymore (dec. 1905) and stage actress Georgia Drew (dec.). Brother of actor Lionel Barrymore (dec. 1954) and actress Ethel Barrymore (dec. 1959). Father of actress Diana Barrymore (dec. 1960) and actor John Drew Barrymore, Jr. Divorced from Blanche Oelrichs (aka Michael Strange) and actresses Katherine Harris (dec. 1927), Dolores Costello (dec. 1979) and Elaine Barry.

Appeared in: **1908** The Boys of Company B. **1914** The Man from Mexico; An American Citizen. **1915** The Dictator; Incorrigible Dukane; Are You a Mason? **1916** The Lost Bridegroom; The Red Widow. **1917** Raffles; The Empress. **1918** On the Quiet; Here Comes the Bride. **1919** Test of Honor. **1920** Dr. Jekyll and Mr. Hyde. **1921** The Lotus Eaters. **1922** Sherlock Holmes. **1924** Beau Brummel. **1926** The Sea Beast; When a Man Loves; Don Juan. **1927** The Beloved Rogue. **1928** Tempest. **1929** The Show of Shows; Eternal Love; General Crack. **1930** Moby Dick; The Man from Blankley's; Handsome Gigolo, Poor Gigolo. **1931** Svengali; The Mad Genius. **1932** Arsene Lupin; Rasputin and the Empress; A Bill of Divorcement; Grand Hotel; State's Attorney. **1933** Dinner at Eight; Counsellor at Law; Reunion in Vienna; Topaze; Night Flight. **1934** Long Lost Father; Twentieth Century. **1936** Romeo and Juliet. **1937** Maytime; True Confession; Night Club Scandal; Bulldog Drummond Comes Back; Bulldog Drummond's Revenge. **1938** Bulldog Drummond's Peril;

Romance in the Dark; Spawn of the North; Marie Antoinette; Hold That Co-ed. **1939** The Great Man Votes; Jesse James; Midnight. **1940** The Great Profile. **1941** The Invisible Woman; Playmates; World Premiere.

BARRYMORE, LIONEL (Lionel Blythe)
Born: Apr. 28, 1878, Philadelphia, Pa. Died: Nov. 15, 1954, Van Nuys, Calif. (heart attack). Screen, stage, radio, vaudeville actor, film producer and screenwriter. Divorced from Doris Rankin (dec. 1946). Married to stage actress Irene Fenwick. Acted from wheelchair from 1940 due to the effects of arthritis and hip injury. Regarding family, see John Barrymore. Won 1930/31 Academy Award for Best Actor in A Free Soul.

Appeared in: **1908** The Paris Hat. **1911** Fighting Blood; The Battle. **1912** Friends; The One She Loved; The Musketeers of Pig Alley; Gold and Glitter; My Baby; The Informer; The New York Hat; My Hero; Oil and Water; The Burglar's Dilemma; A Cry for Help; The God Within; Fate; An Adventure in the Autumn Woods. **1913** The Sheriff's Baby; The Perfidy of Mary; A Misunderstood Boy; The Wanderer; The House of Darkness; Just Gold; The Yaqui Cur; The Ranchero's Revenge; A Timely Interception; Death's Marathon; Judith of Bethulia. **1915** The Exploits of Elaine; The Romance of Elaine; The Yellow Streak. **1916** The Brand of Cowardice; The Quitter. **1917** His Father's Son. **1918** The Yellow Ticket. **1920** The Copperhead; The Master Mind. **1921** Jim the Penman; The Devil's Garden; The Great Adventure. **1922** The Face in the Fog; Unseeing Eyes. **1924** I Am the Man; America; Decameron Nights (US 1928); Wedding Women. **1925** The Little Colonel; The Wrongdoers; Wildfire; The Iron Man; Fifty-Fifty; The Girl Who Wouldn't Work; Children of the Whirlwind. **1926** The Bells; The Splendid Road; The Barrier; The Temptress; Brooding Eyes; The Lucky Lady; Paris at Midnight. **1927** Love; The Show; The Thirteenth Hour; Body and Soul; Women Love Diamonds. **1928** The River Woman; Drums of Love; Sadie Thompson; Alias Jimmy Valentine; The Lion and the Mouse; Road House; West of Zanzibar. **1929** Stark Mad; The Mysterious Island; The Hollywood Revue of 1929. **1930** Free and Easy. **1931** Jackie Cooper's Christmas Party (short); A Free Soul; Guilty Hands; The Yellow Ticket (and 1918 version). **1932** Mata Hari; Broken Lullaby; Grand Hotel; Rasputin and the Empress; Arsene Lupin; Washington Masquerade; The Man I Killed. **1933** Sweepings; One Man's Journey; Christopher Bean; Should Ladies Behave?; Reunion in Vienna; Dinner at Eight; The Stranger's Return; Night Flight; Looking Forward. **1934** Treasure Island; This Side of Heaven; The Girl from Missouri; Carolina. **1935** Mark of the Vampire; David Copperfield; The Return of Peter Grimm; Ah, Wilderness!; Public Hero Number One; The Little Colonel. **1936** The Devil Doll; The Gorgeous Hussy; The Road to Glory; The Voice of Bugle Ann; Camille. **1937** A Family Affair; Saratoga; Captains Courageous; Navy Blue and Gold. **1938** Young Doctor Kildare; You Can't Take It With You; A Yank at Oxford; Test Pilot. **1939** Let Freedom Ring; Calling Dr. Kildare; The Secret of Dr. Kildare; On Borrowed Time. **1940** Dr. Kildare Goes Home; Dr. Kidare's Strangest Case; Dr. Kildare's Crisis. **1941** The Bad Man; The Penalty; The People vs. Dr. Kildare; Lady Be Good; Dr. Kildare's Victory; Dr. Kildare's Wedding Day; Invisible Woman. **1942** Dr. Gillespie's New Assistant; Calling Dr. Gillespie; Tennessee Johnson. **1943** Dr. Gillespie's Criminal Case; Thousands Cheer; A Guy Named Joe; The Last Will and Testament of Tom Smith (short). **1944** Three Men in White; Since You Went Away; Dragon Seed (narr.); Between Two Women. **1945** Valley of Decision. **1946** Duel in the Sun; It's a Wonderful Life; The Secret Heart; Three Wise Fools. **1947** Dark Delusion; Cynthia. **1948** Key Largo. **1949** Down to the Sea in Ships; Malaya; Some of the Best (documentary). **1950** Right Cross. **1951** Bannerline. **1952** Lone Star. **1953** Main Street to Broadway. **1964** Big Parade of Comedy (documentary). **1974** That's Entertainment (film clips).

BARSTOW, MARGARET
Died: Feb. 7, 1973. Screen actress.

Appeared in: **1955** Artists and Models.

BARTELL, RICHARD
Born: 1898. Died: July 22, 1967, Woodland Hills, Calif. (cancer). Screen and stage actor.

Appeared in: **1941** Design for Scandal. **1942** My Sister Eileen; Sabotage Squad. **1944** The Very Thought of You; Goodnight, Sweetheart. **1945** Rhapsody in Blue; Spellbound. **1950** The Glass Menagerie. **1951** Abbot and Costello Meet the Invisible Man; The Enforcer. **1953** The Vanquished.

BARTELS, LOUIS JOHN
Born: 1895, Bunker Hill, Ill. Died: Mar. 4, 1932, Hollywood, Calif. (stomach disorder). Stage and screen actor.

Appeared in: **1927** Broadway Nights; Dance Magic. **1929** The Canary Murder Case; Nothing But the Truth. **1930** The Floradora Girl; The Cohens and the Kellys in Africa; Sin Takes a Holiday. **1931-32** Pathe shorts. **1931** The Prodigal. **1932** The Big Shot.

BARTER, TEDDY
Born: 1889. Died: Oct. 10, 1939, Hollywood, Calif. (auto accident). Screen actor and stage manager.

BARTET, JULIA (Jeanne Julia Bartet)
Born: Oct. 28, 1854, Paris, France. Died: Nov., 1941, Paris, France. Screen and stage actress.

Appeared in: **1908** Le Retour d'Ulysse.

BARTHELMESS, CAROLINE See HARRIS, CAROLINE

BARTHELMESS, RICHARD
Born: May 9, 1897, New York, N.Y. Died: Aug. 17, 1963, Southampton, N.Y. (cancer). Screen actor and film producer. Son of actress Caroline Harris (dec. 1937). Nominated for 1927/28 Academy Award for Best Actor in The Noose and in The Patent Leather Kid.

Appeared in: **1916** War Brides. **1917** The Seven Swans; Bab's Burglar; The Eternal Sin. **1918** Hit-the-Trail-Haliday; Rich Man, Poor Man. **1919** The Girl Who Stayed Home; Three Men and a Girl; I'll Get Him Yet; Scarlet Blossoms; Boots; The Hope Chest; Peppy Poppy. **1920** The Love Flower; Way Down East; The Idol Dancer. **1921** Experience; Tol'able David. **1922** The Seventh Day; Sonny; The Bond Boy; Just a Song at Twilight. **1923** The Bright Shawl; Fury; Twenty-One; The Fighting Blade. **1924** The Enchanted Cottage; Classmates. **1925** Soul Fire; Shore Leave; The Beautiful City; New Toys. **1926** Ranson's Folly; Just Suppose; The White Black Sheep; The Amateur Gentleman. **1927** The Drop Kick; The Patent Leather Kid. **1928** Wheel of Chance; Out of the Ruins; Scarlet Seas; Little Shepherd of Kingdom Come; The Noose. **1929** Weary River; Drag; Young Nowheres; The Show of Shows; Adios. **1930** The Dawn Patrol; Son of the Gods. **1931** The Lash; The Last Flight; The Finger Points. **1932** The Cabin in the Cotton; Alias the Doctor; Cock of the Air; The Putter (short); The Slippery Pearls (short). **1933** Central Airport; Heroes for Sale. **1934** Massacre; A Modern Hero; Midnight Alibi. **1935** Four Hours to Kill. **1936** Spy of Napoleon (US 1934). **1939** Only Angels Have Wings. **1940** The Man Who Talks Too Much. **1942** The Mayor of 44th Street; The Spoilers. **1963** The Great Chase (film strip); Hallelujah the Hills (film clip from Way Down East).

BARTHOLOMEW, AGNES
Born: Scotland. Died: Sept. 10, 1955, Glasgow, Scotland. Stage and screen actress. Married to actor Holmes Herbert (dec. 1956).

Appeared in: **1955** A Man Called Peter.

BARTLETT, CLIFFORD
Born: 1903, England. Died: Dec. 25, 1936, London, England (influenza). Screen and stage actor.

BARTLETT, ELISE
Died: 1944, Daytona Beach, Fla. Screen actress. Divorced from actor Joseph Schildkraut (dec. 1964) and Horace Liveright. Later married to Michel Picard.

Appeared in: **1927** The Angel of Broadway; Harp in Hock. **1929** Show Boat. **1930** Oh! Sailor Behave! **1931** Hot Heiress.

BARTON, BUZZ
Born: 1914. Died: Nov. 20, 1980, St Louis, Mo.? Screen actor.

Appeared in: **1927** The Boy Rider; The Slingshot Kid. **1928** Wizard of the Saddle; The Little Buckaroo; The Pinto Kid; The Bantam Cowboy; Rough Ridin' Red; Young Whirlwind; The Fightin' Redhead; Orphan of the Sage. **1929** The Freckled Rascal; The Vagabond Cub; The Little Savage; Pals of the Prairie. **1930** Canyon Hawks; The Lone Defender (serial). **1931** Cyclone Kid; Riders of the Cactus. **1932** Human Targets; Tangled Fortunes. **1935** Fighting Pioneers; Powdersmoke Range; Saddle Aces. **1936** Feud of the West; The Riding Avenger; Romance Rides the Range. **1938** Phantom Gold. **1967** In the Heat of the Night.

BARTON, CHARLES T.
Born: May 25, 1902, Sacramento, Calif. Died: Dec. 5, 1981, Burbank, Calif. (heart attack). Screen, stage, vaudeville actor, film, television director and cameraman. Married to actress Julie Gibson.

Appeared in: **1939** Beau Geste.

BARTON, DORA (Dora Brookbank)
Born: c. 1884, London, England. Died: Sept. 13, 1966, London, England. Screen and stage actress.

Appeared in: **1928** Zero; Glorious Youth (aka Eileen of the Trees). **1929** The Bondman.

BARTON, HOMER
Born: 1880, Mexico, Mo. Died: Oct. 29, 1935, New York, N.Y. (complication of diseases). Screen and stage actor.

Appeared in: **1931** The Last Straw (short).

BARTON, J. THORNTON
Born: Aug. 6, 1892, San Francisco, Calif. Died: May 3, 1970. Screen, stage and vaudeville actor.

Appeared in: **1918** Empty Pockets. **1921** Virgin Paradise.

BARTON, JAMES
Born: Nov. 1, 1890, Gloucester, N.J. Died: Feb. 19, 1962, Mineola, N.Y. (heart attack). Screen, vaudeville and burlesque actor.

Appeared in: **1923** Why Women Re-Marry. **1930** The Underdog (short). **1935** Captain Hurricane; His Family Tree. **1938** Universal short. **1941** The Shepherd of the Hills. **1944** Lifeboat. **1948** The Time of Your Life; Yellow Sky. **1950** The Dungeon; Daughter of Rosie O'Grady; Wabash Avenue. **1951** Here Comes the Groom; The Scarf; Golden Girl. **1956** The Naked Hills. **1957** Quantez. **1961** The Misfits.

BARTON, JOAN
Born: 1925. Died: May, 1977, Dallas, Tex. (heart attack). Screen, radio, television actress and singer. Married to bandleader Jerry Gray (dec. 1976).

Appeared in: **1945** State Fair (voice). **1946** Gilda (voice); Romance of the West; Lone Star Moonlight. **1947** Angel and the Badman; Cigarette Girl. **1948** Strange Gamble; Mary Lou.

BARTON, JOE
Born: 1883. Died: July 5, 1937, Los Angeles, Calif. (following surgery). Screen actor. Entered films approx. 1930.

Appeared in: **1933** Lone Cowboy. **1935** McFadden's Flats.

BARTON, JOHN
Born: May 1, 1872, Germantown, Pa. Died: Dec. 23, 1946, New York, N.Y. Screen, stage and vaudeville actor. Married to Anne Ashley (dec. 1947) with whom he appeared in vaudeville in an act billed as "Barton and Ashley."

Appeared in: **1946** Scarlet Street.

BARTOSCH, CHESTER
Born: 1899. Died: Oct. 31, 1967, San Diego, Calif. (heart ailment). Screen and television actor.

BARTRAM, GUS M.
Born: 1890. Died: Oct. 7, 1951, Traverse City, Mich. Screen and vaudeville actor.

BARTY, JACK
Born: 1889, London, England. Died: Nov. 25, 1942, Streatham, London, England. Screen, stage, vaudeville actor, screenwriter and film producer.

Appeared in: **1933** This is the Life (US 1935). **1934** My Song Goes Round the World; plus the following shorts: Maid in Hollywood; Babes in the Goods; and Oliver the Eighth. **1935** In Town Tonight. **1936** All In; It's in the Bag. **1937** Take a Chance; Talking Feet. **1938** Stepping Toes. **1939** What Would You Do Chums?

BARUA, PRAMATESH CHANDRA
Born: 1903, Gauripur, India. Died: 1951, India? Screen actor, film producer, film director and screenwriter.

BARY, LEON (aka LEON BARRY)
Born: 1880, Paris, France. Died: 1954, France. Screen, stage actor and film director.

Appeared in: **1916** The Shielding Shadow (serial). **1917** The Mystery of the Double Cross (serial); The Seven Pearls (serial). **1920** Kismet. **1921** The Three Musketeers; The Lure of the Jade. **1922** The Call of Home; June Madness; The Galloping Kid; Suzanna. **1923** The White Flower; Bucking the Barrier; The King of Wild Horses; The W's Virgin; The Grail; The Temple of Venus. **1924** George Washington, Jr.; The Lightning Rider. **1925** Midnight Molly. **1929** The Iron Mask. **1930** Le Secret du Docteur.

BARZELL, WOLFE
Born: 1897, Poland. Died: Feb. 14, 1969, off Acapulco, Mexico (heart attack). Screen and stage actor.

Appeared in: **1957** Street of Sinners. **1958** Frankenstein's Daughter. **1959** The Blue Angel. **1961** Homicidal; Atlantis, The Lost Continent. **1962** The Scarface Mob. **1963** Love With the Proper Stranger. **1964** Judith. **1965** Mordei Haor (aka Sands of Beersheba—US 1966).

BASCH, FELIX
Born: 1889. Died: May 17, 1944, Los Angeles, Calif. Screen actor, film producer and director.

Appeared in: **1942** Destination Unknown; Desperate Journey; Once Upon a Honeymoon; Pacific Rendezvous; Enemy Agents Meet Ellery Queen. **1943** Hitler—Dead or Alive; Mission to Moscow; The Falcon in Danger; Bomber's Moon; Hostages; The Cross of Lorraine; Chitnicks; Desert Song. **1944** Woman in Bondage; Uncertain Glory.

BASKCOMB, A. W.
Born: July 5, 1880, London, England. Died: Dec. 10, 1939, London, England. Screen and stage actor. Brother of actor Lawrence Baskcomb (dec. 1962).

Appeared in: **1932** The Lodger (aka The Phantom Fiend—US 1935); The Midshipmaid. **1933** The Good Companions.

BASKCOMB, LAWRENCE
Born: Oct. 13, 1883, London, England. Died: Feb. 12, 1962, England? Screen, stage and television actor. Brother of actor A. W. Baskcomb (dec. 1939).

Appeared in: **1930** Escape (film debut); Extravagance. **1938** Drums.

BASKETT, JAMES
Born: 1904, Indianapolis, Ind. Died: Sept. 9, 1948, Los Angeles, Calif. (heart ailment). Black screen, stage and radio actor. Won 1946 Special Academy Award for his performance as Uncle Remus in Song of the South.

Appeared in: **1938** Policy Man. **1939** Straight to Heaven; Gone Harlem. **1940** Comes Midnight. **1943** Revenge of the Zombies. **1946** Song of the South.

BASSERMANN, ALBERT
Born: Sept. 7, 1865, Mannheim, Germany. Died: May 15, 1952, Zurich, Switzerland (heart attack). Stage and screen actor. Married to actress Else Bassermann-Schiff (dec. 1961). Nominated for 1940 Academy Award for Best Supporting Actor in Foreign Correspondent.

Appeared in: **1913** Der Andere; Der König. **1919** Eine Schwache Stunde. **1921** Das Weib des Pharao (The Loves of Pharaoh, aka Pharaoh's Wife). **1922** Christoph Columbus; Frauenopfer; Lukrezia Borgia. **1923** Erdgeist (Earth Spirit). **1924** Helena. **1925** Briefe, die ihn Nicht Erreichten; Der Herr Generaldirektor. **1926** Wenn das Herz der Jugend Spricht. **1928** Fräulein Else. **1929** Napoleon auf St. Helena. **1930** Dreyfus (US 1931); Alraune. **1931** Vorunter-Suchung (Inquest); 1914, die Letzten Tage vor dem Weltbrand (1914: The Last Days Before the War); Zum Goldenen Anker; Gefahren der Liebe. **1933** Kadetten; Ein Gewisser Herr Gran (US 1934). **1934** Alraune. **1938** Letzte Liebe (Last Love). **1939** Le Famille Lefrancois (aka Heroes of the Marne). **1940** The Story of Dr. Ehrlich's Magic Bullet; Foreign Correspondent; A Dispatch from Reuters; Moon Over Burma; This Man Reuter; Knute Rockne, All American; Escape. **1941** The Shanghai Gesture; The Great Awakening; New Wine; A Woman's Face. **1942** The Moon and Sixpence; Invisible Agent; Once Upon a Honeymoon; Fly by Night; Desperate Journey. **1943** Good Luck, Mr. Yates; Passport to Heaven; Reunion in France. **1944** Madame Curie; Since You Went Away. **1945** Rhapsody in Blue. **1946** Strange Holiday; The Searching Wind. **1947** Private Affairs of Bel Ami; Escape Me Never. **1948** The Red Shoes.

BASSERMANN-SCHIFF, ELSE
Born: Jan. 14, 1878, Leipzig, E.Germany. Died: May 30, 1961, Baden-Baden, W.Germany. Screen, stage actress, author and playwright. Married to actor Albert Bassermann (dec. 1952).

Appeared in: **1938** Letzte Liebe (Last Love). **1940** Escape. **1941** Captain of Koepenick. **1942** Desperate Journey. **1944** Madame Curie. **1945** Rhapsody in Blue.

BASSETT, RUSSELL
Born: 1846, Milwaukee, Wis. Died: May, 2, 1918, New York, N.Y. (brain hemorrhage). Screen and stage actor. Married to stage actress Carlotta E. M. Basset (dec. 1952) and father of actor Albert Bassett.

Appeared in: **1911** The Best Man Wins. **1912** Young Wild West Leading a Raid. **1913** The New Clerk. **1914** The Eagle's Mate; Behind the Scenes; Such a Little Queen; Those Persistent Old Maids; One of the Finest; What a Baby Did. **1915** Sold; Jim the Penman; Little Pal; The Commanding Officer; The Fatal Card; Masquerades; May Blossom; The Morals of Marcus; The Heart of Jennifer. **1916** Hulda from Holland; Less Than the Dust; The Quest of Life; A Coney Island Pricess; Diplomacy. **1917** The Public Be Damned; Broadway Jones; The Honeymoon; Seven Keys to Baldpate. **1918** Hit the Trail Holiday. **1919** The Traveling Salesman.

BASSETT, TONY (Albert Anthony Bassett)
Born: 1885. Died: Aug, 4, 1955, Hollywood, Calif. Screen and vaudeville actor.

BATALOV, NIKOLAI
Born: 1898, Russia. Died: 1937, Russia? Screen actor and film director.

Appeared in: **1924** Aelita. **1926** Mother. **1927** Bed and Sofa. **1931** Road to Life. **1933** Horizon; The Wandering Jew. **1935** Tovaristschi.

BATCHOFF, PIERRE
Born: 1906, France. Died: Apr. 13, 1932, France? Screen actor.

Appeared in: **1927** The Education of the Prince; Napoleon; The Best Hour of the Day. **1930** The Chess Player. **1933** Love in Morocco.

BATEMAN, VICTORY
Born: 1866. Died: Mar. 2, 1926, Los Angeles, Calif. (bronchial asthma). Stage and screen actress.

Appeared in: **1916** Romeo and Juliet. **1921** The Idle Rich; Keeping Up With Lizzie; A Trip to Paradise. **1922** Captain Fly-By-Night; A Girl's Desire; If I Were Queen. **1923** Can a Woman Love Twice?; The Eternal Three; Human Wreckage. **1924** Tess of the D'Urbervilles; The Turmoil.

BATES, BARBARA
Born: Aug. 6, 1925, Denver, Colo. Died: Mar. 18, 1969, Denver, Colo. Screen actress.

Appeared in: **1945** Salome, Where She Danced; This Love of Ours. **1946** A Night in Paradise; Strange Holiday. **1947** The Fabulous Joe. **1948** Johnny Belinda; June Bride. **1949** The House Across the Street; One Last Fling; The Inspector General. **1940** All About Eve; Quicksand; Cheaper By the Dozen. **1951** The Secret of Convict Lake; I'd Climb the Highest Mountain; Let's Make It Legal. **1952** Belles on Their Toes; The Outcasts of Poker Flat. **1953** All Ashore; The Caddy. **1954** Rhapsody. **1956** House of Secrets. **1957** Town on Trial; Triple Deception. **1958** Campbell's Kingdom; Apache Territory.

BATES, BLANCHE
Born: 1873, Portland, Ore. Died: Dec. 25, 1941, San Francisco, Calif. (following stroke). Stage and screen actress.

Appeared in: **1914** The Seats of the Mighty. **1918** The Border Legion.

BATES, FLORENCE (Florence Rabe)
Born: Apr. 15, 1888, San Antonio, Tex. Died: Jan. 31, 1954, Burbank, Calif. (heart attack). Screen, stage, television actress and attorney.

Appeared in: **1937** The Man in Blue. **1940** Rebecca; Calling All Husbands; Son of Monte Cristo; Hudson's Bay; Kitty Foyle. **1941** Kathleen; Road Show; Love Crazy; The Chocolate Soldier; Strange Alibi; The Devil and Miss Jones. **1942** The Tuttles of Tahiti; The Moon and Sixpence; My Heart Belongs to Daddy; Mexican Spitfire at Sea; We Were Dancing. **1943** Slightly Dangerous; His Butler's Sister; They Got Me Covered; Mister Big; Heaven Can Wait; Mr. Lucky; Whistle Stop at Eaton Falls. **1944** Since You Went Away; The Mask of Dimitrios; Kismit; The Belle of the Yukon; The Racket Man. **1945** Saratoga Trunk; Tahiti Nights; Tonight and Every Night; San Antonio; Out of This World. **1946** Cluny Brown; Claudia and David; The Diary of a Chambermaid; Whistle Stop; The Time, the Place and the Girl. **1947** The Brasher Doubloon; Love and Learn; Desire Me; The Secret Life of Walter Mitty; The High Window. **1948** Texas, Brooklyn and Heaven; Winter Meeting; A Letter to Three Wives; The Inside Story; River Lady; My Dear Secretary; Portrait of Jennie; I Remember Mama. **1949** The Judge Steps Out; The Girl from Jones Beach; On the Town. **1950** Belle of Old Mexico; County Fair. **1951** The Second Woman; Lullaby of Broadway; The Tall Target; Havana Rose; Father Takes the Air. **1952** San Francisco Story; Les Miserables. **1953** Paris Model; Main Street to Broadway.

BATES, GRANVILLE

Born: 1882, Chicago, Ill. Died: July 8, 1940, Hollywood, Calif. (heart attack). Screen and stage actor.

Appeared in: **1929** Jealousy. **1930** The Sap from Syracuse. **1931** The Smiling Lieutenant. **1934** Midnight; Warner Bros. newspaper shorts. **1935** Woman Wanted; Pursuit; O'Shaughnessey's Boy. **1936** Here Comes Trouble; Poppy; Chatterbox; 13 Hours by Air; The Plainsman; The Captain's Kid; Times Square Playboy; Sing Me a Love Song; Beloved Enemy; Under Suspicion. **1937** The Life of Emile Zola; Breezing Home; Wings Over Honolulu; Make Way for Tomorrow; When's Your Birthday?; Let's Get Married; It Happened in Hollywood; Green Light; They Won't Forget; The Perfect Specimen; Larceny on the Air; Nancy Steel is Missing; Waikiki Wedding; Wells Fargo; Mountain Justice; Back in Circulation. **1938** The Jury's Secret; Youth Takes a Fling; Mr. Chump; Go Chase Yourself; The Affairs of Annabel; A Man to Remember; Next Time I Marry; Gold Is Where You Find It; Romance on the Run; Cowboy from Brooklyn; Garden of the Moon; Hard to Get. **1939** Eternally Yours; At the Circus; The Great Man Votes; Blackwell's Island; Twelve Crowded Hours; Naughty But Nice; Pride of the Blue Grass; Our Neighbors, the Carters; Fast and Furious; Internationally Yours; Sweepstakes Winner; Of Mice and Men; Charlie McCarthy, Detective; Indianapolis Speedway; Jesse James. **1940** Millionaire Playboy; Thou Shalt Not Kill; My Favorite Wife; The Mortal Storm; Private Affairs; Men Against the Sky; Flowing Gold; Brother Orchid.

BATES, LESLIE A. (aka LES BATES)

Born: 1877. Died: Aug. 8, 1930, Hollywood, Calif. (auto accident). Screen actor.

Appeared in: **1921** A Broken Doll. **1922** Belle of Alaska; Big Stakes; Deserted at the Altar; My Dad; Strength of the Pines. **1923** Blood Test; Vanity Fair. **1924** Martyr Sex; Shackles of Fear. **1925** Once in a Lifetime; Triple Action. **1926** Beyond All Odds; Blue Blazes; In Search of a Hero; Lure of the West; The Texas Streak; While London Sleeps. **1927** Irish Hearts. **1928** Buck Privates; The Glorious Trail. **1930** The Fighting Legion; Mountain Justice.

BATES, LOUISE EMERALD

Born: Dec. 28, 1886. Died: Jun. 11, 1972. Appeared in Mutual Comedies produced by the Thanhouser Co.

BATES, MICHAEL

Born: 1920, India. Died: Jan. 11, 1978, London, England (cancer). Screen, stage and television actor.

Appeared in: **1954** Carrington, V.C. (aka The Court Martial—US 1955). **1958** Dunkirk. **1959** I'm All Right Jack (US 1960). **1967** Bedazzled; Here We Go Round the Mulberry Bush (US 1968). **1968** Don't Raise the Bridge, Lower the River; Hammerhead; Salt and Pepper. **1969** Battle of Britain; Oh! What a Lovely War. **1970** Patton; The Engagement. **1971** A Clockwork Orange. **1973** No Sex Please, We're British. **1976** The Bawdy Adventures of Tom Jones.

BATIE, FRANKLYN A.

Born: 1880, Norwich, N.Y. Died: Dec. 31, 1949, Norwich, N.Y. Screen, stage and vaudeville actor.

Appeared in: **1930** Big Boy.

BATLEY, ERNEST G.

Died: c. 1917. Screen actor, producer, director and screenwriter. Married to film producer/director Ethyle Batley (dec. 1917). Father of actress Dorothy Batley.

Appeared in: **1910** The Drawn Blind. **1912** A Child's Strategy; The Heavenly Twins; Peggy Gets Rid of the Baby; Through the Flames. **1913** Peggy as Peacemaker; The Broken Chisel (aka Escape from Broadmoore—US); Through the Clouds; A Tragedy in the Alps; The Child Mother (aka The Little Mother); Guy Fawkes and the Gunpowder; The Two Father Christmasses; There's Good in the Worst of Us; The Battle of Waterloo; In Fate's Grip; Bess the Detective's Daughter (aka to Save Her Dad). **1914** The Tattooed Will; The Midnight Wedding; The Master Crook Turns Detective; The Master Crook Outwitted by a Child; An Englishman's Home; Retribution; The Price of Her Silence. **1915** Dewdrop Braves the Floods of Maidenhead; Honour Among Thieves; Instruments of Fate; Bulldog Grit; Remember Belgium; Across the Wires.

BATTIER, ROBERT

Born: 1887. Died: Dec. 16, 1946, Hollywood, Calif. Screen actor.

Appeared in: **1937** Love and Hisses.

BATTY, ARCHIBALD

Born: 1887. Died: Nov. 24, 1961, Budleigh, Salterton, England. Screen, stage actor and playwright.

Appeared in: **1938** I See Ice; The Drum (aka Drums—US). **1939** Four Feathers.

BAUCOM, EARL

Born: 1911. Died: Mar. 16, 1981, Glendale, Calif. Screen, radio and television actor.

BAUDIN, GINETTE

Born: 1921, France. Died: Mar., 1971, France. Screen, stage actress, dancer and singer.

Appeared in: La Briseur de Chaines; L'Escalier sans Fin; Seul Dans le Nuit; Une Femme par Jour; Les Amants Maudits; Lady Paname.

BAUER, DAVID

Born: 1918, Chicago, Ill. Died: Feb. 13, 1973, London, England. Screen, stage and television actor. Married to singer Stella Tanner.

Appeared in: **1963** Man in the Middle (aka The Winston Affair—US 1964); Live It Up (aka Sing and Swing—US 1964); Walk a Tightrope (US 1964). **1965** The Spy Who Came in from the Cold. **1967** Danger Route (US 1968); The Double Man; Torture Garden (US 1968). **1968** Inspector Clouseau; The Mercenaries (aka Dark of the Sun—US). **1969** Crooks and Coronets (aka Sophie's Place—US 1970); Royal Hunt of the Sun. **1970** Patton; Tropic of Cancer.

BAUERSFELD, MARJORIE "MIRANDY"

Born: 1890, Springfield, Mo. Died: July 22, 1974, Santa Barbara, Calif. Screen, stage, radio and television actress. Appeared in Mack Sennett comedies.

Appeared in: **1940** Comin' Round the Mountain.

BAUM, MRS. H. WILLIAM (Doris Doscher)

Born: 1882. Died: Mar. 9, 1970, Farmingdale, N.Y. Screen and radio actress. Was the model for the U.S. Liberty 25-cent piece.

Appeared in: **1915** Birth of a Nation.

BAUM, HARRY

Born: 1916. Died: Jan. 31, 1974, Hollywood, Calif. (heart attack). Screen actor, stand-in and stuntman. Son of actress Lily Teitelbaum.

BAUMER, JACQUES

Born: 1885, France. Died: 1951, France. Screen actor.

Appeared in: **1939** Heart of Paris; Crime in the Maginot Line; Rasputin; Entente Cordiale. **1940** Daybreak. **1942** The Great Temptation. **1944** 32 Rue de Montmartre. **1947** Colonel Chabert. **1948** En Scene; Private Life of an Actor. **1949** Strangers in the House. **1950** The Cheat. **1951** Ma Pomme. **1952** A Simple Case of Money.

BAUR, ESPERANZA

Born: 1926, Mexico. Died: Mar. 11, 1961, Mexico City, Mexico (heart attack). Screen actress. Divorced from actor John Wayne (dec. 1979).

Appeared in: **1937** Jalisco Nunca Pierde (Jalisco Never Loses). **1943** Guadalajara; El Conde de Monte Cristo.

BAUR, HARRY

Born: 1881, France. Died: Apr. 8, 1943, Paris, France. Screen, stage and radio actor.

Appeared in: **1913** Shylock. **1923** La Voyante. **1932** David Golder. **1933** Poil de Carotte; Les Trois Mousquetaires; The Red Head. **1934** Golgotha. **1935** Moscow Nights (US 1938); Le Cap Perdu; Les Miserables; Crime et Chatiment (Crime and Punishment); Cette Vielle Canaille; Taras Bulba. **1936** I Stand Condemned. **1937** The Golem; The Life and Loves of Beethoven; Le Juif Polonaise. **1938** Un Carnet de Bal; Dark Eyes; Rothschild; The Rebel Son; Moscow Nights; Rasputin. **1939** A Man and His Wife. **1941** Volpone; Hatred; The Mad Empress.

BAXLEY, JACK (Andrew J. Baxley)

Born: 1886. Died: Dec. 10, 1950, Los Angeles, Calif. Screen actor.

Appeared in: **1928** Neighbors (short). **1935** Our Little Girl. **1937** Woman Chases Man; A Night at the Movies (short). **1938** International Crime. **1939** The Gracie Allen Murder Case. **1942** City of Silent Men; Prison Girls. **1943** True to Life; What a Man! **1947** The Last Round-Up.

BAXTER, ALAN
Born: Nov. 19, 1908, East Cleveland, Ohio. Died: May 8, 1976, Woodland Hills, Calif. (cancer). Screen, stage, radio, television actor, playwright and screenwriter. Married to Barbara Williams (dec.) and actress Christy Palmer.

Appeared in: **1935** Mary Burns, Fugitive. **1936** Big Brown Eyes; The Case Against Mrs. Ames; Big Town Girl; Ramona; Trail of the Lonesome Pine; Parole!; 13 Hours by Air. **1937** Breezing Home; Night Key; Men in Exile; It Could Happen to You; The Last Gangster. **1938** Wide Open Faces; I Met My Love Again; Gangs of New York. **1939** Boy Slaves; Off the Record; My Son is a Criminal; Let Us Live; Each Dawn I Die. **1940** Santa Fe Trail; Free, Blonde and 21; The Lone Wolf Strikes; Abe Lincoln in Illinois; Escape to Glory (aka Submarine Zone—US 1941). **1941** Under Age; Rags to Riches; Bad Men of Missouri; Borrowed Hero; Shadow of the Thin Man; Pittsburgh Kid. **1942** Prisoner of Japan; Saboteur; China Girl. **1943** The Human Comedy; Behind Prison Walls; Pilot No. 5; Submarine Base; Women in Bondage; Stand By All Networks. **1944** Winged Victory. **1948** Close-Up; Prairie. **1949** The Set Up. **1957** The True Story of Jesse James; End of the Line. **1958** The Restless Years; Voice in the Mirror. **1959** Face of a Fugitive. **1960** The Mountain Road. **1961** Judgment at Nuremburg. **1966** This Property is Condemned. **1967** Welcome to Hard Times. **1969** Paint Your Wagon. **1970** Chisum.

BAXTER, GEORGE (George David Baxter)
Born: Apr. 8, 1905, Paris, France. Died: Sept. 10, 1976, New York, N.Y. Screen, stage, radio and television actor.

Appeared in: **1929** Marianne (film debut); The Careless Age. **1930** The Right to Love. **1932** A Woman Commands. **1933** Dinner at Eight. **1934** Thirty Day Princess; The Great Flirtation; Sing Sing Nights. **1935** Spanish Cape Mystery; Restless Knights (short); China Girl. **1948** Sofia. **1949** Son of Billy the Kid. **1951** Prairie Roundup; The Lady and the Bandit. **1952** Big Jim McLain; Actors and Sin. **1953** Island in the Sky; Champ for a Day; Flight Nurse; Hot News; Lili. **1958** Legion of the Doomed. **1959** The Purple Gang. **1964** Lady in the Cage.

BAXTER, JAMES C. "JIMMY"
Born: 1923. Died: Apr. 20, 1969, Dallas, Tex. Screen actor and singer.

Appeared in: **1935** The Dark Angel.

BAXTER, LORA
Born: 1908. Died: June 16, 1955, New York, N.Y. Screen, stage, vaudeville, television actress and screenwriter.

BAXTER, MARIAN (aka MARIAN MONTGOMERY)
Born: 1897. Died: Feb. 7, 1973, Woodland Hills, Calif. Screen actress. Mother of Baby Peggy (Diana Serrs Cary), film moppet of silents. Married to actor Jack Montgomery (dec. 1962).

BAXTER, WARNER
Born: Mar. 29, 1891, Columbus, Ohio. Died: May 7, 1951, Beverly Hills, Calif. Screen and stage actor. Married to actress Winifred Bryson. Won 1928/29 Academy Award for Best Actor for In Old Arizona.

Appeared in: **1914** Her Own Money. **1918** All Woman. **1919** Lombardi, Ltd. **1921** Cheated Hearts; First Love; The Love Charm; Sheltered Daughters. **1922** If I Were Queen; The Girl in His Room; A Girl's Desire; The Ninety and Nine; Her Own Money (and 1914 version). **1923** Blow Your Own Horn; In Search of a Thrill; St. Elmo. **1924** Alimony; Christine of the Hungry Heart; The Female; The Garden of Weeds; His Forgotten Wife; Those Who Dance. **1925** The Golden Bed; The Air Mail; The Awful Truth; The Best People; Rugged Water; A Son of His Father; Welcome Home. **1926** Mannequin; Miss Brewster's Millions; Mismates; Aloma of the South Seas; The Great Gatsby; The Runaway. **1927** The Telephone Girl; The Coward; Drums of the Desert; Singed. **1928** Danger Street; Three Sinners; Ramona; Craig's Wife; The Tragedy of Youth; A Woman's Way. **1929** Linda; Far Call; Through Different Eyes; Behind That Curtain; Romance of the Rio Grande; In Old Arizona; West of Zanzibar; Happy Days. **1930** The Arizona Kid; Such Men Are Dangerous; Renegades. **1931** The Cisco Kid; Squaw Man; Doctor's Wives; Their Mad Moment; Daddy Long Legs; Surrender. **1932** Six Hours to Live; Man About Town; The Slippery Pearls (short); Amateur Daddy. **1933** Paddy, the Next Best Thing; Forty-Second Street; Dangerously Yours; I Loved You Wednesday; Penthouse. **1934** Stand Up and Cheer; Broadway Bill; As Husbands Go; Such Women Are Dangerous; Grand Canary; Hell in the Heavens. **1935** Under the Pampus Moon; One More Spring; La Fiesta de Santa Barbara (short); King of Burlesque. **1936** The Prisoner of Shark Island; Road to Glory; To Mary, With Love; White Hunter; Robin Hood of El Dorado. **1937** Slave Ship; Vogues of 1938; Wife, Doctor and Nurse. **1938** Kidnapped; I'll Give a Million. **1939** Wife, Husband and Friend; Barricade; The Return of the Cisco Kid. **1940** Earthbound. **1941** Adam Had Four Sons. **1943** Crime Doctor; Crime Doctor's Strangest Case. **1944** Lady in the Dark; Shadows in the Night. **1945** The Crime Doctor's Courage; The Crime Doctor's Warning. **1946** Just Before Dawn; The Crime Doctor's Man Hunt. **1947** The Millerson Case; The Crime Doctor's Gamble. **1948** A Gentleman from Nowhere. **1949** Prison Warden; The Devil's Henchman; The Crime Doctor's Diary. **1950** State Penitentiary.

BAY, TOM (aka TOMMY BAY)
Born: 1901. Died: Oct. 12, 1933, Burbank, Calif. (shooting). Screen actor.

Appeared in: **1922** The Better Man Wins. **1926** The Dead Line; The Devil's Gulch; The Fighting Boob; The Valley of Bravery. **1927** Drifting On; Tearin' Into Trouble; White Pebbles. **1928** Desperate Courage; Devil's Tower; Lightnin' Shot; Mystery Valley; Painted Trail; Trail Riders; Trailin' Back. **1929** The Oklahoma Kid; Pioneers of the West; Code of the West; Fighters of the Saddle; The Fighting Terror; The Lone Horseman. **1930** The Parting of the Trails.

BAYER, CHARLES W.
Born: 1893. Died: Nov. 28, 1953, Hollywood, Calif. (cancer). Screen actor. Entered films with Vitagraph.

BAYLIFF, W. LANE
Born: Apr. 6, 1870, London, England. Died: Feb., 1938, Australia. Screen and stage actor.

BAYNTON, HENRY
Born: Sept. 23, 1892, Warwick, England. Died: Jan. 2, 1951, London, England. Screen and stage actor.

Appeared in: **1917** Auld Lang Syne.

BEACH, CORRA
Died: Oct. 5, 1963, North Hollywood, Calif. Screen, stage, vaudeville actress, stage producer and screenwriter. Married to actor Walter Shumway (dec. 1965).

Appeared in: **1919** What Becomes of the Children?

BEAL, FRANK
Born: 1864. Died: Dec. 20, 1934, Hollywood, Calif. Screen actor and film director. Married to actress Louise Lester (dec. 1952) and father of actor/director Scott Beal (dec. 1973) and actress Dolly Beal.

Appeared in: **1922** A Question of Honor. **1923** Playing It Wild; Soft Boiled; When Odds Are Even. **1924** The Arizona Express; The Cyclone Rider; Hook and Ladder; The Lone Chance. **1925** The Best Bad Man; The Golden Strain; Marraige in Transit. **1926** The Dead Line; Man Four Square. **1927** The Final Extra; Galloping Fury; The Stolen Bride. **1928** The Danger Rider; Women Who Dare. **1929** Broken Barriers; The Big Diamond Robbery; Senor Americano. **1930** Wide Open. **1931** Everything's Rosie (short); Cimarron.

BEAL, ROYAL
Born: 1900. Died: May 20, 1969, Keene, N.H. (cancer). Screen, stage and television actor. Married to actress Edna Bennett (dec. 1976).

Appeared in: **1949** Lost Boundaries; Death of a Salesman. **1953** The Joe Lewis Story. **1959** Anatomy of a Murder.

BEAL, SCOTT
Born: 1890. Died: July 10, 1973, Hollywood, Calif. (cancer). Screen actor, film director and cameraman. Son of actress Louise Lester (dec. 1952) and film director Frank Beal (dec. 1934). Brother of actress Dolly Beal. Entered films with Selig in 1910.

BEALE, KEN
Born: 1932. Died: June 20, 1979, Bronx, N.Y. (lymphoma). Screen, radio actor, author, story editor and magician.

Appeared in: **1963** Man Outside. **1967** Beware the Black Widow.

BEAMISH, FRANK
Born: 1881, Memphis, Tenn. Died: Oct. 3, 1921, New York, N.Y. Stage and screen actor.

Appeared in: **1922** The Blonde Vampire; The Faithless Sex.

BEAR, MARY (aka MARY BAER)
Born: Mar. 10, 1910. Died: Dec. 9, 1972. Stage and screen actress. Married to actor Don Shelton (dec. 1976).

Appeared in: **1948** That Lady in Ermine. **1949** Bride for Sale. **1950** Mother Didn't Tell Me; Singing Guns; Stella.

BEARD, MATTHEW, JR. "STYMIE"

Born: Jan. 1, 1925, Los Angeles, Calif. Died: Jan. 8, 1981, Los Angeles, Calif. (stroke). Black screen and television actor. Appeared as "Stymie" in Our Gang Comedies.

Appeared in: **1927** Uncle Tom's Cabin (film debut); My Best Girl. **1929** Hallelujah; Show Boat; Hearts in Dixie. **1930** Mamba; Teacher's Pet (short); School's Out (short). **1931** The following shorts: Helping Grandma; Love Business; Little Daddy; Bargain Days; Fly My Kite; Big Ears; Shiver My Timbers; Dogs is Dogs. **1932** The following shorts: Readin' and Writin'; Free Eats; Spanky; Choo Choo; Pooch; Hook and Ladder; Free Wheeling; Birthday Blues; A Lad an' a Lamp. **1933** The following shorts: Fish Hooky; Forgotten Babies; Kid from Borneo; Mush and Milk; Bedtime Worries; Wild Poses. **1934** Kid Millions; plus the following shorts: Mike Fright; Hi Neighbor; For Pete's Sake; First Round-Up; Honkey Donkey; Washee Ironee; Shrimps for a Day; The Cracked Iceman; Four Parts. **1935** Captain Blood; Beginner's Luck (short); Teacher's Beau (short). **1936** Rainbow on the River. **1937** Reunion in Rhythm (short). **1938** Jezebel; Kentucky; Beloved Brat. **1939** Way Down South. **1940** Broken Strings; The Return of Jesse James. **1945** Fallen Angel. **1974** Truck Turner. **1978** The Buddy Holly Story.

BEATON, MARY (Mary Louise Beaton)

Died: Jan. 25, 1962. Screen actress.

Appeared in: **1920** Clothes. **1921** The Man Who; A Message from Mars.

BEATTY, MRS. CLYDE (Harriet Beatty)

Died: Oct. 25, 1950, Kosciusko, Miss. (heart attack). Screen, vaudeville actress and circus performer. Married to actor Clyde Beatty (dec. 1965).

Appeared in: **1940** Cat College (short).

BEATTY, CLYDE R.

Born: June 10, 1903, Chillicothe, Ohio. Died: July 19, 1965, Ventura, Calif. (cancer). Screen actor, circus performer, animal trainer and circus owner. Married to actress Harriett Beatty (dec. 1950).

Appeared in: **1933** The Big Cage. **1934** The Lost Jungle (serial). **1936** Darkest Africa (serial). **1937** Paramount short. **1940** Cat College (short). **1949** Africa Screams. **1954** Ring of Fear.

BEATTY, GEORGE

Born: Sept. 5, 1895, Steubenville, Ohio. Died: Aug. 6, 1971, Hollywood, Calif. (stroke). Screen, stage, vaudeville, radio actor, screenwriter and radio writer.

Appeared in: **1943** Hi' Ya, Sailor; Crazy Horse. **1944** Johnny Doesn't Live Here.

BEATTY, MAY

Born: 1881, Christchurch, New Zealand. Died: Apr. 1, 1945, Covina, Calif. Screen and stage actress. Married to actor William Lauri (dec.).

Appeared in: **1930** The Benson Murder Case; The Boudoir Diplomat. **1931** Ex-Flame. **1934** The Little Minister; Horse Play. **1935** Night Life of the Gods; Becky Sharp; Mad Love; Here Comes the Band; The Girl Who Came Back; Bonnie Scotland. **1936** Sylvia Scarlet; Little Lord Fauntleroy; Show Boat; Private Number; Lloyds of London. **1937** Call It a Day; Four Days' Wonder; She Loved a Fireman. **1938** If I Were King. **1939** The Women; Eternally Yours; We Are Not Alone; The Adventures of Sherlock Holmes; Union Pacific. **1940** Queen of the Mob; Pride and Prejudice; My Son, My Son. **1941** I Wake Up Screaming (aka Hot Spot). **1943** The Crystal Ball; Lassie Come Home; Forever and a Day.

BEAUBIEN, JULIEN (Julien A. Dolenzai)

Born: 1896. Died: Oct. 18, 1947, Long Branch, N.J. Screen and stage actress.

Appeared in: **1919** The Winning Stroke; Checkers. **1923** Main Street.

BEAUDET, LOUISE

Born: 1862. Died: Dec. 31, 1947, New York. Screen, stage, opera and vaudeville actress.

Appeared in: **1913** Sauce for the Goose; Which? **1914** Jerry's Uncle's Namesake. **1915** The Battle Cry of Peace; A Price for Folly; On Her Wedding Night. **1916** The Law Decides. **1917** The Price She Paid. **1921** Her Lord and Master. **1923** The Gold Diggers. **1925** Sally.

BEAUDINE, WILLIAM, SR.

Born: Jan. 15, 1892, New York, N.Y. Died: Mar. 18, 1970, Canoga Park, Calif. (complications of uremic poisoning). Screen actor, director and television director. Father of film producer William Beaudine, Jr. Entered films in 1909 as an actor and turned director in 1914.

Appeared in: **1909** Pippa Passes. **1910** The Broken Doll. **1912** A Close Call.

BEAUMONT, CHARLES

Born: 1929. Died: Feb. 21, 1967, Woodland Hills, Calif. (rare disease of nervous system). Screen actor, screenwriter, television writer and author.

Appeared in: **1962** The Intruder.

BEAUMONT, DIANA MURIEL

Born: May 8, 1909, London, England. Died: June 21, 1964, London, England. Screen and stage actress. Married to actor Gabriel Toyne (dec. 1963).

Appeared in: **1928** Adam's Apple (aka Honeymoon Ahead—US, film debut). **1931** Alibi; The Old Man. **1932** A Lucky Sweep. **1933** Mannequin. **1934** Autumn Crocus. **1935** A Real Bloke; Birds of a Feather. **1936** The Secret Voice; They Didn't Know; While London Sleeps. **1937** Stage Struck. **1938** Black Limelight (US 1939); Luck of the Navy (aka North Sea Patrol—US 1940). **1939** Murder in Soho (aka Murder in the Night—US 1940); Old Mother Riley MP. **1940** Let George Do It. **1941** Hi Gang! **1942** Let the People Sing. **1943** Millions Like Us. **1944** Out of Chaos. **1952** Home at Seven (aka Murder on Monday—US 1953); Stolen Face. **1958** I Was Monty's Double (aka Hell, Heaven or Hoboken).

BEAUMONT, HARRY

Born: Feb. 10, 1888, Abilene, Kans. Died: Dec. 22, 1966, Santa Monica, Calif. Screen actor, film director and screenwriter.

Appeared in: **1912** How Father Accomplished His Work; Linked Together; Their Hero; The Butler and the Maid; How the Boys Fought the Indians; Uncle Mun and the Minister; Annie Crawls Upstairs; The Totville Eye; The Third Thanksgiving. **1913** Leonie; False to Their Trust; The Photograph and the Blotter; The Elder Brother; The Golden Wedding; Mother's Lazy Boy; It Wasn't Poison After All; For Her; Over the Back Fence. **1914** Treasure Trove; The Witness to the Will; A Transplanted Prairie Flower; Who Goes There?; The Ever-Gallant Marquis; The Shattered Tree. **1915** The Stoning; Poisoned by Jealousy; A Thorn Among Roses; Jack Kennerd, Coward; That Heavenly Cook. **1916** Putting It Over; The Grouch; His Little Wife; The Discards.

BEAUMONT, LUCY

Born: May 18, 1873, Bristol, England. Died: Apr. 24, 1937, New York, N.Y. Screen, stage and radio actress.

Appeared in: **1923** Ashes of Vengeance; Enemies of Children; Lucretia Lombard; Cupid's Fireman. **1924** The Family Secret; The Last of the Duanes; Good Bad Boy. **1925** The Man Without a Country; The Trouble With Wives. **1926** The Greater Glory; The Old Soak; The Fighting Failure; Men of the Night; Torrent. **1927** The Beloved Rogue; Closed Gates; The Love Wager; Resurrection; Hook and Ladder No. 9; Stranded; Savage Passions. **1928** Stool Pigeon; The Crowd; A Bit of Heaven; Branded Man; The Little Yellow House; Outcast Souls; Comrades. **1929** The Greyhound Limited; Knights Out (short); One Splendid Hour; The Ridin' Demon; Hard Boiled Rose; The Girl in the Show; Sonny Boy. **1931** A Free Soul; Caught Plastered; Get Rich Quick Wallingford. **1932** Union Depot; Three Wise Girls; Parlor, Bedroom and Wrath (short); Cheaters at Play; Midnight Lady; Movie Crazy; Thrill of Youth. **1934** His Double Life. **1935** False Pretenses; Temptation. **1936** The Devil Doll. **1937** The Maid of Salem.

BEAUMONT, VERTEE

Born: 1889. Died: June 27, 1934, Hollywood, Calif. (heart disease). Screen, stage and vaudeville actress. Married to stage actor Jack Arnold (dec.) with whom she appeared in vaudeville as part of "Beaumont and Arnold" team.

BEAUMONT, VICTOR

Born: England. Died: 1977, England. Screen and stage actor.

Appeared in: **1957** Man from Tangier (aka Thunder Over Tangier—US). **1958** I Was Monty's Double (aka Hell, Heaven or Hoboken). **1959** The Night We Dropped a Clanger (aka Make Mine a Double—US 1961). **1960** The Criminal (aka The Concrete Jungle—US 1962). **1962** Freud. **1963** Master Spy (US 1964); The Bay of Saint-Michel (aka Pattern for Plunder—US 1964). **1964** Le Train (The Train—US 1965). **1965** The Heroes of Telemark (US 1966). **1968** Attack on the Iron Coast; Where Eagles Dare (US 1969). **1970** The Kremlin Letter.

BEAVERS, LOUISE
Born: 1898, Cincinnati, Ohio. Died: Oct. 26, 1962, Hollywood, Calif. (heart attack). Black screen, television and minstrel actress. Entered films in 1924.

Appeared in: **1927** Uncle Tom's Cabin. **1929** Election Day (short); The Glad Rag Doll; Gold Diggers of Broadway; Barnum Was Right; Coquette; Nix on Dames; Wall Street. **1930** Second Choice; Recaptured Love; Back Pay; Wide Open; She Couldn't Say No; Safety in Numbers. **1931** Millie; Heaven on Earth; Don't Bet on Women; Party Husbands; Reckless Living; Sundown Trail; Annabell's Affairs; Six Cylinder Love; Good Sport; Up for Murder; Girls About Town. **1932** Midnight Lady; The Strange Love of Molly Louvain; Hell's Highway; You're Telling Me (short); Ladies of the Big House; Old Man Minick; The Expert; Freaks; Night World; Street of Women; What Price Hollywood?; Unashamed; Young America; Divorce in the Family; Wild Girl; Too Busy to Work; It's Tough to Be Famous; We Humans; Jubilo. **1933** 42nd Street; Hold Your Man; The Big Cage; In the Money; Girl Missing; What Price Innocence; Her Bodyguard; Bombshell; Her Splendid Folly; Notorious But Nice; Pick Up; She Done Him Wrong; A Shriek in the Night. **1934** West of the Pecos; Glamour; I Believed in You; I Give My Love; Merry Wives of Reno; A Modern Hero; Registered Nurse; Imitation of Life; I've Got Your Number; Bedside; The Merry Frinks; Cheaters; Hat, Coat and Glove; Dr. Monica. **1935** Annapolis Farewell. **1936** Bullets or Ballots; General Spanky; Wives Never Know; Rainbow on the River. **1937** Make Way for Tomorrow; Wings Over Honolulu; Love in a Bungalow; The Last Gangster. **1938** Scandal Sheet; Peck's Bad Boy With the Circus; The Headleys at Home; Life Goes On; Brother Rat; Reckless Living. **1939** Reform School; The Lady's from Kentucky; Reform School; Made for Each Other. **1940** I Want a Divorce; Women Without Names; Parole Fixer; No Time for Comedy. **1941** Kisses for Breakfast; Shadow of the Thin Man; The Vanishing Virginian; Sign of the Wolf; Belle Starr; Virginia. **1942** Young America; Holiday Inn; Reap the Wild Wind; The Big Street; Seven Sweethearts (aka Tulip Time); Tennessee Johnson. **1943** Good Morning, Judge; DuBarry Was a Lady; All By Myself; There's Something About a Soldier; Jack London; Top Man. **1944** South of Dixie; Dixie Jamboree; Follow the Boys; Barbary Coast Gent. **1945** Delightfully Dangerous. **1946** Lover Come Back; Young Widow. **1947** Banjo. **1948** Mr. Blandings Builds His Dream House; For the Love of Mary; Good Sam. **1949** Tell It to the Judge. **1950** My Blue Heaven; Girls' School; The Jackie Robinson Story. **1952** Colorado Sundown; I Dream of Jeannie; Never Wave at a WAC. **1956** Goodbye, My Lady; You Can't Run Away From It; Teenage Rebel. **1957** Tammy and the Bachelor. **1958** The Goddess. **1960** The Facts of Life; All the Fine Young Cannibals.

BEBAN, GEORGE
Born: 1873, San Francisco, Calif. Died: Oct. 5, 1928, Los Angeles, Calif. (fall from horse). Screen, stage, vaudeville, minstrel actor, screenwriter and film director. Married to actress Edith McBride (dec. 1927). Father of actor George Beban, Jr.

Appeared in: **1915** The Alien. **1916** Pasquale. **1917** Lost in Transit. **1921** One Man in a Million. **1922** The Sign of the Rose (stage and film versions). **1924** The Greatest Love of All. **1926** The Loves of Ricardo. **1928** The Loves of Ricardo (and 1926 version).

BECH, LILI
Born: 1885, Denmark. Died: 1939, Sweden. Stage and screen actress. Married to actor Victor Seastrom (dec. 1960).

Appeared in: The Talisman; The Gardener; The Black Masks; The Vampire; The Child; Because of Her Love; The Stormy Petrel; Children of the Street; Daughter of the High Mountain; When Artists Love; One Out of Many; Expiated Guilt; The Playmates; His Wife's Past; Ace of Thieves; The Dagger; The Mine-Pilot; The Governor's Daughters; Ships That Meet; She Was Victorious; The Wings; The Gold Spider; Therese.

BECHTEL, WILLIAM A. "BILLY"
Born: 1867, Germany. Died: Oct. 27, 1930, Hollywood, Calif. Stage and screen actor. Entered films approx. 1907.

Appeared in: **1921** Idle Hands. **1924** Meddling Women. **1929** Spite Marriage; Jazz Age. **1930** The Social Lion; Die Sehnsucht jeder Frau.

BECK, DANNY
Born: 1904. Died: Nov. 8, 1959, Hollywood, Calif. Screen actor.

Appeared in: **1941** Birth of the Blues. **1946** Mr. Hex. **1947** Hard Boiled Mahoney. **1957** Man of a Thousand Faces.

BECK, JAMES
Born: 1932. Died: Aug. 6, 1973, London, England. Screen, stage and television actor.

Appeared in: **1958** The Bonnie Parker Story. **1959** Hound-Dog Man; Paratroop Command. **1970** I Am a Groupie.

BECK, NELSON C.
Born: 1887. Died: Mar. 3, 1952, Hollywood, Calif. (overdose of sleeping pills). Screen actor.

BECKER, JACQUES
Born: 1906, Paris, France. Died: 1960, Paris, France. Screen actor, screenwriter and film director.

Appeared in: **1932** Boudu Sauve des Eaux (Boudu Saved from Drowning). **1937** La Grande Illusion (The Grand Illusion—US 1938).

BECKETT, SCOTTY (Scott Hastings Beckett)
Born: Oct. 4, 1929, Oakland, Calif. Died: May 10, 1968, Los Angeles, Calif. Screen, radio and television actor. Was in "Our Gang" films during early 1930s at age of three.

Appeared in: **1933** Gallant Lady. **1934** Stand Up and Cheer; I Am Suzanne; Sailor Made Widow; Whom the Gods Destroy; George White's Scandals; plus the following shorts: Mike Fright; Hi Neighbor; For Pete's Sake; First Round-Up; Honkey Donkey; Washee Ironee; Mama's Little Pirates; Shrimps for a Day. **1935** Dante's Inferno; Pursuit; I Dream Too Much; plus the following shorts: Anniversary Trouble; Beginner's Luck; Teacher's Beau; Sprucin' Up; Little Papa; Our Gang Follies of 1936. **1936** Anthony Adverse; Charge of the Light Brigade; The Case Against Mrs. Ames; The Lucky Corner (short). **1937** Life Begins With Love; Conquest. **1938** Marie Antoinette; Listen, Darling; You're Only Young Twice; The Devil's Party; Four's a Crowd; Marie Walewska; Bad Man from Brimstone. **1939** The Flying Irishman; Mickey the Kid; Our Neighbors, the Carters; The Escape; Days of Jesse James; Blind Alley; plus the following shorts: Cousin Wilbur; Dog Daze; Royal Rodeo. **1940** Street of Memories; Gold Rush Maisie; My Favorite Wife; The Blue Bird; My Son, My Son. **1941** Aloma of the South Seas; Father's Son; The Vanishing Virginian; King's Row. **1942** Between Us Girls; It Happened in Flatbush. **1943** Heaven Can Wait; Good Luck, Mr. Yates; The Youngest Profession. **1944** Ali Baba and the Forty Thieves; The Climax. **1945** Junior Miss; Circumstancial Evidence. **1946** The Jolson Story; My Reputation; White Tie and Tails; Her Adventurous Night. **1947** Cynthia; Dangerous Years. **1948** Michael O'Halleran; A Date With Judy. **1949** Battleground. **1950** Nancy Goes to Rio; The Happy Years; Louisa. **1951** Corky of Gasoline Alley. **1952** Savage Triangle. **1953** Hot News. **1956** Three for Jamie Dawn. **1957** The Oklahomans. **1974** That's Entertainment (film clips).

BECKINSALE, RICHARD
Born: 1948, England. Died: Mar. 19, 1979, Sunningdale, England (heart attack). Screen, stage and television actor. Married to actress Judy Loe.

BECKLEY, TONY
Born: 1932, Southhampton, England. Died: Apr. 19, 1980, Los Angeles, Calif. (cancer). Screen, stage and television actor.

Appeared in: **1962** A Kind of Loving. **1966** Campanadas a Medianoche (Chimes at Midnight, aka Falstaff—US 1967). **1967** The Penthouse. **1968** The Lost Continent; The Long Day's Dying. **1969** The Italian Job. **1974** In the Devil's Garden; Gold. **1978** The Revenge of the Pink Panther. **1979** When a Stranger Calls.

BECKWITH, REGINALD
Born: Nov. 2, 1908, York, England. Died: June 26, 1965, Bourne End, England. Screen, stage, television actor, stage director, playwright and screenwriter.

Appeared in: **1941** Freedom Radio (aka A Voice in the Night—US). **1948** Scott of the Antarctic (US 1949). **1950** Miss Pilgrim's Progress; The Body Said No! **1951** Mr. Drake's Duck; Circle of Danger; Another Man's Poison (US 1952). **1952** Whispering Smith Hits London (aka Whispering Smith vs. Scotland Yard—US); Brandy for the Parson; You're Only Young Twice!; Penny Princess. **1953** The Titfield Thunderbolt; Innocents in Paris (US 1955); Genevieve (US 1954). **1954** Don't Blame the Stork; The Million Pound Note (aka Man With a Million—US); Fast and Loose; The Runaway Bus; Lease on Life (US 1955); Men of Sherwood Forest (US 1956); Aunt Clara. **1955** The Lyons in Paris; Break in the Circle (US 1957); They Can't Hang Me; A Yank in Ermine. **1956** The March Hare; It's a Wonderful World (US 1961); A Touch of the Sun; Charley Moon. **1957** Carry On Admiral (aka The Ship Was Loaded—US 1959); These Dangerous Years (aka Dangerous Youth—US 1958); Light Fingers; Lucky Jim; Night of the Demon (aka Curse of the Demon—US 1958). **1958** Up the Creek; Law and Disorder; Next to No Time (US 1960); Rockets Galore (aka Mad Little Island—US). **1959** The Captain's Table (US 1960); The Horse's Mouth; The 39 Steps (US 1960); The Ugly Duckling; The Navy Lark; Friends and Neighbors (US 1963); Desert Mice; Expresso Bongo. **1960** Bottoms Up!; Dentist in the Chair (US

1961); Doctor in Love (US 1962); There Was a Crooked Man (US 1962). **1961** The Girl on the Boat; Five Golden Hours; Double Bunk; Dentist on the Job (aka Get On With It!—US 1963); The Day the Earth Caught Fire (US 1962). **1962** Hair of the Dog; The Prince and the Pauper; Night of the Eagle (aka Burn Witch Burn—US); The Password is Courage (US 1963). **1963** The King's Breakfast; Just for Fun; Lancelot and Guinevere (aka Sword of Lancelot—US); The VIPS; Doctor in Distress (US 1964); Never Put It in Writing (US 1964). **1964** Mister Moses (US 1965); A Shot in the Dark; The Yellow Rolls Royce (US 1965). **1965** How To Undress in Public Without Undue Embarassment; Gonks Go Beat; The Amorous Adventures of Moll Flanders; Where the Spies Are; The Secret of My Success; Thunderball; The Big Job.

BECKWITH, ROGER See VON BRINCKEN, WILHELM

BECWAR, GEORGE (George Jerome Becwar)
Born: Sept. 16, 1917, Ill. Died: July 9, 1970, Santa Monica, Calif. (heart attack). Screen and television actor.

Appeared in: **1956** Bride of the Monster. **1958** Attack of the Fifty-Foot Woman; War of the Colossal Beast.

BEDOYA, ALFONSO
Born: 1904, Vicam, Sonora, Mexico. Died: Dec. 15, 1957, Mexico City, Mexico. Screen actor.

Appeared in: **1948** The Treasure of the Sierra Madre (Hollywood film debut); Angel of the Amazon; The Pearl; Angel in Exile. **1949** Border Incident; Streets of Laredo. **1950** Fortunes of Captain Blood; The Black Rose. **1951** The Man in the Saddle. **1952** California Conquest; Stronghold. **1953** Sombrero; The Strange Wore a Gun. **1954** Ricochet Romance; Border River; The Black Pirates; Both Sides of the Law. **1955** Ten Wanted Men. **1958** The Big Country.

BEECHER, ADA
Born: 1862. Died: Mar. 30, 1935, Hollywood, Calif. Screen actress.

BEECHER, EGON
Born: 1880. Died: Aug. 13, 1946, Los Angeles, Calif. Screen and stage actor. Entered films in 1933.

BEECHER, JANET (J. B. Meysenburg)
Born: 1884, Jefferson City, Mo. Died: Aug. 6, 1955, Washington, Conn. Screen and stage actress.

Appeared in: **1933** Gallant Lady. **1934** The Last Gentleman; The Mighty Barnum; The President Vanishes; Once a Gentleman. **1935** Let's Live Tonight; Village Tale; The Dark Angel; So Red the Rose. **1936** Love Before Breakfast; I'd Give My Life; The Longest Night. **1937** Good Old Soak; Give Till It Hurts (short); The Thirteenth Chair; Between Two Women; Big City; My Dear Miss Aldrich; Beg, Borrow or Steal; Rosalie. **1938** Judge Hardy's Children; Yellow Jack; Woman Against Woman; Say It in French. **1939** The Story of Vernon and Irene Castle; I Was a Convict; Man of Conquest; Career; Laugh It Off. **1940** Slightly Honorable; The Gay Caballero; All This and Heaven Too; Bitter Sweet; The Mark of Zorro. **1941** The Man Who Lost Himself; The Lady Eve; A Very Young Lady; West Point Widow; The Parson of Panamint; For Beauty's Sake. **1942** Hi, Neighbor; Silver Queen; Reap the Wild Wind; Men of Texas; Mrs. Wiggs of the Cabbage Patch; Henry Aldrich Gets Glamour.

BEECROFT, VICTOR R.
Born: 1887, London, England. Died: Mar. 25, 1958, Newport News, Va. Screen, stage, television and radio actor.

Appeared in: **1915** A Dawn of Tomorrow.

BEERBOHM, LADY See KAHN, FLORENCE

BEERS, FANNIE (Frances Culver Beers)
Born: Apr. 15, 1870, Pa. Died: Aug. 26, 1951, Puente, Calif. Screen and stage actress.

BEERY, NOAH, SR.
Born: Jan. 17, 1884, Kansas City, Mo. Died: Apr. 1, 1945, Los Angeles, Calif. (heart attack). Screen and stage actor. Brother of actors William C. (dec. 1949) and Wallace Beery (dec. 1949) and father of actor Noah Beery, Jr. Married to actress Marguerita Lindsay (dec. 1955).

Appeared in: **1918** The Mormon Maid. **1919** The Red Lantern; In Mizzoura; The Woman Next Door; Louisiana. **1920** The Sea Wolf; The Mark of Zorro; The Fighting Shepherdess; Go and Get It; Dinty. **1921** Beach of Dreams; Bits of Life; The Call of the North; Lotus Blossom; Bob Hampton of Placer. **1922** I Am the Law; The Heart Specialist; The Lying Truth; Omar the Tentmaker; Good Men and True; Flesh and Blood; Belle of Alaska; Ebb Tide; The Crossroads of New York; The

Power of Love; Youth to Youth; Tillie; Wild Honey. **1923** The Spoilers; Wandering Daughters; When Love Comes to Hades; Dangerous Trails; The Call of the Canyon; The Destroying Angel; Stephen Steps Out; Stormswept; To the Last Man; Forbidden Lover; His Last Race; Main Street; Hollywood; Quicksands; The Spider and the Rose; Soul of the Beast; Tipped Off. **1924** The Heritage of the Desert; North of 36; The Female; The Fighting Coward; Lily of the Dust; Wanderer of the Wasteland; Welcome Stranger. **1925** The Coming of Amos; East of Suez; Lord Jim; The Thundering Herd; Contraband; The Light of Western Stars; Old Shoes; The Spaniard; Wild Horse Mesa; The Vanishing American. **1926** Beau Geste; The Crown of Lies; Padlocked; Paradise; The Enchanted Hill. **1927** The Rough Riders; The Dove; Evening Clothes; The Love Mart. **1928** Two Lovers; Beau Sabreaur; Hellship Bronson. **1929** False Feathers; Noah's Ark; Passion Song; Linda; Careers; Two O'Clock in the Morning; The Isle of Lost Ships; Four Feathers; Love in the Desert; The Show of Shows; The Godless Girl; Glorifying the American Girl. **1930** Murder Will Out; Sin Flood; Song of the Flame; The Way of All Men; Under a Texas Moon; Golden Dawn; Big Boy; El Dorado; Isle of Escape; The Love Trader; Renegades; Tol'able David; Oh Sailor, Behave!; Mammy. **1931** Bright Lights; Honeymoon Lane; Lost Men; Millionaire; In Line of Duty; Soldiers Plaything; Homicide Squad; Shanghai Love; Riders of the Purple Sage. **1932** The Devil Horse (serial); Stranger in Town; The Stoker; No Living Witness; Big Stampede; Long Loop Laramie; The Drifter; The Kid from Spain; Out of Singapore. **1933** Fighting With Kit Carson (serial); The Flaming Signal; Cornered; Man of the Forest; Easy Millions; Sunset Pass; She Done Him Wrong; To the Last Man (and 1923 version); Laughing at Life; The Woman I Stole. **1934** David Harum; Kentucky Kernels; Madame Spy; Happy Landing; The Trail Beyond; Caravan; Mystery Liner; Cockeyed Cavalier; The Thundering Herd (and 1925 version). **1935** Sweet Adeline. **1936** King of the Damned; The Crimson Circle; The Avenging Hand; Strangers on a Honeymoon (US 1937); Live Again; The Marriage of Corbal (aka Prisoner of Corbal—US 1939); Someone at the Door. **1937** Our Fighting Navy (aka Torpedoed—US 1939); The Frog; Zorro Rides Again (serial). **1938** Bad Man of Brimstone; The Girl of the Golden West; Panamints Bad Man. **1939** Mexicali Rose; Mutiny on the Blackhawk. **1940** A Little Bit of Heaven; The Tulsa Kid; Pioneers of the West; Grandpa Goes to Town; Adventures of Red Ryder (serial). **1941** A Missouri Outlaw. **1942** Overland Mail (serial); Isle of Missing Men; Tennessee Johnson. **1943** Clancy Street Boys; Salute to the Marines. **1944** Block Busters; Barbary Coast Gent; The Million Dollar Kid; Gentle Annie; The Honest Thief. **1945** This Man's Navy; Sing Me a Song of Texas.

BEERY, WALLACE
Born: Apr. 1, 1885, Kansas City, Mo. Died: Apr. 15, 1949, Los Angeles, Calif. (heart attack). Screen, stage, circus actor and film director. Entered films with Essaney in 1913. Brother of actors William C. (dec. 1949) and Noah Beery, Sr. (dec. 1946). Divorced from Areta Gillman and actress Gloria Swanson. Nominated for 1929/30 Academy Award for Best Actor in The Big House. Won a 1934 foreign award for Viva Villa! and won 1931/32 Academy Award for Best Actor in The Champ.

Appeared in: **1914** The Plum Tree; Fable of the Bush League Lover Who Failed to Qualify; "Sweedie" series. **1916** A Dash of Courage; Teddy at the Throttle. **1917** Cactus Nell. **1919** The Unpardonable Sin; The Love Burglar; The Life Line; Victory. **1920** Behind the Door; Virgin of Stamboul; The Mollycoddle. **1921** The Four Horsemen of the Apocalypse; The Last of the Mohicans; A Tale of Two Worlds; The Golden Snare; The Last Trail; The Rookie's Return. **1922** Only a Shop Girl; The Sagebrush Trail; Hurricane's Gal; Robin Hood; Wild Honey; I Am the Law; The Man from Hell's River; The Rosary; Trouble. **1923** The Three Ages; Patsy; Ashes of Vengeance; White Tiger; The Spanish Dancer; Richard the Lion-Hearted; Drifting; The Eternal Struggle; Bavu; The Flame of Life; The Drums of Jeopardy; Stormswept. **1924** The Signal Tower; The Red Lily; Another Man's Wife; Dynamite Smith; Madonna of the Streets; The Sea Hawk; Unseen Hands. **1925** The Lost World; The Wanderer; Rugged Water; Adventure; The Devil's Cargo; The Great Divide; The Pony Express; So Big; Coming Through; The Night Club; In the Name of Love; Let Women Alone. **1926** Old Ironsides; Behind the Front; We're in the Navy Now; Volcano. **1927** We're in the Air Now; Fireman, Save My Child; Casey at the Bat. **1928** The Big Killing; Partners in Crime; Wife Savers; Beggars of Life. **1929** Stairs of Sand; River of Romance; Chinatown Nights. **1930** The Big House; Min and Bill; Way for a Sailor; A Lady's Morals; Billy the Kid; Derelict; Soul Kiss. **1931** Jackie Cooper's Christmas Party (short); The Champ; Jenny Lind; The Secret Six; Hell Divers; Stolen Jools (short). **1932** Grand Hotel; Flesh; The Slippery Pearls (short); Tugboat Annie; Dinner at Eight; The Bowery. **1934** Treasure Island; Viva Villa!; The Mighty Barnum. **1935** China Seas; West Point of the Air; O'Shaughnessy's Boy; Ah, Wilderness! **1936** A Message to Garcia; Old Hutch. **1937** Slave Ship; Good Old

Soak. **1938** Stablemates; Bad Man from Brimstone; Port of Seven Seas. **1939** Stand Up and Fight; Thunder Afloat; Sergeant Madden. **1940** Two Gun Cupid; Wyoming; The Man from Dakota; Twenty-Mule Team. **1941** Barnacle Bill; The Bugle Sounds; The Bad Man. **1942** Jackass Mail. **1943** Salute to the Marines. **1944** Barbary Coast Gent; Rationing; Gold Town; The Honest Thief; Airship Squadron. **1945** This Man's Navy. **1946** The Mighty McGurk; Bad Bascomb. **1948** A Date With Judy; Alias a Gentleman. **1949** Big Jack. **1960** When Comedy Was King (documentary). **1964** Big Parade of Comedy (documentary). **1974** That's Entertainment (film clips).

BEERY, WILLIAM C.
Born: 1879, Clay County, Mo. Died: Dec. 25, 1949, Beverly Hills, Calif. Screen, stage actor and circus performer. Brother of actors Wallace (dec. 1949) and Noah Berry, Sr. (dec. 1946). Appeared in Mack Sennett films.

Appeared in: Soldiers of Fortune.

BEGGS, LEE
Born: 1871. Died: Nov. 18, 1943, New York, N.Y. Screen, stage actor and film director. Father of actor Malcolm Lee Beggs (dec. 1956).

Appeared in: **1911** His Musical Soul. **1912** A Terrible Lesson; Mignon; A Solax Celebration; The Gold Brick; Making an American Citizen; Father and the Boys; Phantom Paradise; Canned Harmony; The Equine Spy; The Idol Worshipper; Billy's Shoes; Saved by a Cat; The Child of the Tenements; Mickey's Pal; The Wooing of Alice; The Detective Dog; For the Love of the Flag. **1914** Eats; Father's Timepiece; The Egyptian Mummy. **1915** Forcing Dad's Consent; A Mix-Up in Dress-Suit Cases; The Green Cat. **1921** The Iron Trail. **1924** America; Janice Meredith; Playing for Desire. **1926** Stepping Along. **1934** Tailspin Tommy (serial).

BEGGS, MALCOLM LEE
Born: 1907. Died: Dec. 10, 1956, Chicago, Ill. (beaten to death). Screen, stage, television actor and stage director. Son of actor/director Lee Beggs (dec. 1943) and actress Doris Singleton.

Appeared in: **1952** It Grows on Trees; Love Island. **1953** Botany Bay; Houdini. **1958** Edge of Fury.

BEGLEY, ED
Born: Mar. 25, 1901, Hartford, Conn. Died: Apr. 28, 1970, Hollywood, Calif. (heart attack). Screen, stage, radio and television actor. Won 1962 Academy Award for Best Supporting Actor in Sweet Bird of Youth.

Appeared in: **1947** Boomerang; The Web; The Roosevelt Story (narr.); Big Town. **1948** Sorry, Wrong Number; Sitting Pretty; Deep Waters; The Street With No Name. **1949** It Happens Every Spring; The Great Gatsby; Tulsa. **1950** Stars in My Crown; Saddle Tramp; Dark City; Backfire; Wyoming Mail; Convicted. **1951** The Lady from Texas; You're in the Navy Now (aka U.S.S Teakettle); On Dangerous Ground. **1952** Boots Malone; Lone Star; Deadline U.S.A.; The Turning Point; What Price Glory. **1956** Patterns. **1957** Twelve Angry Men. **1959** Odds Against Tomorrow. **1961** The Green Helmet. **1962** Sweet Bird of Youth. **1964** The Unsinkable Molly Brown. **1966** The Oscar. **1967** The Warning Shot; Billion Dollar Brain. **1968** Firecreek; A Time to Sing; Hang 'Em High; Wild in the Streets. **1969** The Monitors. **1970** The Dunwich Horror. **1971** Road to Salina.

BEHRENS, FREDERICK
Born: 1854. Died: Jan. 5, 1938, Los Angeles, Calif. Screen and stage actor.

BEHRLE, FRED
Born: 1891, San Diego, Calif. Died: May 20, 1941, San Fernando Valley, Calif. (heart attack). Screen actor. Entered films with Vitagraph Co.

Appeared in: **1923** The Midnight Alarm. **1927** Through Thick and Thin. **1929** Big News. **1941** Texas.

BEIR, FRED
Born: 1927. Died: June 3, 1980, Hollywood, Calif. (cancer). Screen and television actor.

Appeared in: **1957** The Violators. **1979** A Perfect Couple.

BELA, NICHOLAS
Born: July 18, 1900, Budapest, Hungary. Died: Nov. 18, 1963, New York, N.Y. (heart attack). Screen, stage actor, stage director and screenwriter.

Appeared in: **1928** The Night Watch. **1929** Adoration. **1930** The Princess and the Plumber; Little Caesar; Such Men Are Dangerous. **1931** Public Enemy; Gentleman's Fate; Dracula. **1940** Lady in Question.

BELASCO, ARTHUR J. B.
Born: 1888. Died: Nov. 8, 1979, Los Angeles, Calif. Screen, stage actor, and songwriter.

Appeared in: **1927** The Sea Captain (short—narrator). **1933** Penthouse. **1935** Mutiny on the Bounty.

BELASCO, DAVID
Born: July 25, 1854, San Francisco, Calif. Died: May 14, 1931, New York, N.Y. Screen actor, stage producer, screenwriter, playwright and author. Brother of actor Walter Belasco (dec. 1939).

Appeared in: **1914** The Prologue of a Good Little Devil. **1919** A Star Overnight.

BELASCO, GENEVIEVE
Born: 1871, London, England. Died: Nov. 17, 1956, New York, N.Y. Screen, stage and radio actress.

Appeared in: **1923** Ten Commandments. **1924** The Sainted Devil.

BELASCO, WALTER
Born: 1876, Vancouver, British Columbia, Canada. Died: June 21, 1939, San Francisco, Calif. Screen and stage actor. Brother of actor David Belasco (dec. 1931).

Appeared in: **1915** Putting One Over on Ignatz. **1916** Good Morning, Judge. **1917** A Jewel in Pawn; A Romany Rose; The Car of Chance; Little Mariana's Triumph.

BELCHER, ALICE
Born: 1880. Died: May 9, 1939, Hollywood, Calif. Screen and stage actress.

Appeared in: **1922** Second Hand Rose. **1936** Mistaken Orders; Pals First. **1927** Blondes By Choice. **1928** The Cowboy Kid.

BELCHER, CHARLES M.
Born: 1872, San Francisco, Calif. Died: Dec. 10, 1943, Hollywood, Calif. Screen and stage actor.

Appeared in: **1921** The Three Musketeers. **1922** Blood and Sand; Rose O' the Sea; The Woman He Married. **1923** Rosita. **1924** Fools in the Dark; The Thief of Bagdad. **1925** Never too Late; Ben Hur. **1926** The Black Pirate; Midnight Faces; The Devil's Gulch; Modern Youth. **1927** The King of Kings. **1928** A Thief in the Dark.

BELCHER, FRANK H.
Born: 1869, San Francisco, Calif. Died: Feb. 27, 1947, Brentwood, N.Y. Stage and screen actor.

Appeared in: **1916** Gloria's Romance. **1921** Coincidence.

BELL, DAVID SCOTT
Born: 1958. Died: Dec. 27, 1980, North Hollywood, Calif. (shot). Screen actor.

BELL, DIANA
Born: Queensland, Australia. Died: Oct. 30, 1965, Melbourne, Australia. Screen, stage and television actress.

BELL, DIGBY VALENTINE
Born: 1851, Milwaukee, Wis. Died: June 20, 1917, New York, N.Y. Screen, stage and vaudeville actor.

Appeared in: **1914** The Education of Mr. Pipp.

BELL, F. G. (Fred Gatenby Bell)
Born: 1879, England. Died: Dec. 10, 1930, New York, N.Y. Screen and stage actor. Married to stage actress Gladys Hopton (dec.).

Appeared in: **1915** An Enemy to Society.

BELL, GASTON
Born: 1877, Boston, Mass. Died: Dec. 11, 1963, Woodstock, N.Y. Screen and stage actor. Appeared in silent films.

BELL, GENEVIEVE
Born: 1895. Died: Oct. 3, 1951, Los Angeles, Calif. (after surgery). Screen actress. Entered films during silents.

Appeared in: **1943** So's Your Uncle. **1944** Follow the Boys. **1945** Don Juan Quillan; Her Lucky Night. **1951** The Blue Veil. **1952** Something to Live For; Macao; Phone Call from a Stranger.

BELL, GEORGE O.
Died: Oct. 2, 1969. Screen actor.

Appeared in: **1948** The Loves of Carmen. **1957** Shoot Out at Medicine Bend.

BELL, HANK (Henry Bell)
Born: 1892. Died: Feb. 4, 1950, Hollywood, Calif. (heart attack). Screen actor.

Appeared in: **1923** Don Quickshot of the Rio Grande. **1925** The Pony Express; Gold and Grit. **1926** Double Daring; The Terror; Twin Triggers; Ace of Action; The Scrappin' Kid. **1927** Soda Water Cowboy; Code of the Cow Country; Between Dangers. **1928** Saddle Mates. **1929** The Fighting Terror; The Last Roundup; 'Neath Western Skies. **1930** Trails of Peril; Abraham Lincoln; Min and Bill. **1932** Beyond the Rockies. **1933** Fiddlin' Buckaroo; Young Blood; Terror Trail. **1935** Westward Ho. **1936** Red River Valley; Comin' Round the Mountain; Disorder in the Court (short); Three Troubledoers (short); The Trail of the Lonesome Pine. **1927** Goofs and Saddles (short). **1938** Colorado Trail; The Man from Music Mountain; The Renegade Ranger; The Girl of the Golden West. **1939** Oklahoma Frontier; Spoilers of the Range; Geronimo; Teacher's Pest (short). **1940** My Little Chickadee. **1941** Border Vigilantes. **1942** Valley of the Sun. **1943** The Ox-Bow Incident. **1944** Mystery Man. **1945** Flame of the Barbary Coast, Salome, Where She Danced; She Gets Her Man; Along Came Jones. **1946** Rustler's Roundup; The Plainsman and the Lady; Duel in the Sun. **1949** Loaded Pistols. **1950** Fancy Pants.

BELL, JAMES
Born: Dec. 1, 1891, Suffolk, Va. Died: Oct. 26, 1973. Screen and stage actor.

Appeared in: **1932** I Am a Fugitive from a Chain Gang. **1933** King's Vacation; Infernal Machine; Private Detective 62; Day of Reckoning; White Woman; Storm at Daybreak. **1935** The Lives of a Bengal Lancer. **1943** I Walked With a Zombie; My Friend Flicka; Gangway for Tomorrow; The Leopard Man; So Proudly We Hail! **1944** I Love a Soldier; Step Lively; Secret Mission. **1945** Thunderhead—Son of Flicka; Blood on the Sun; The Girl of the Limberlost. **1946** The Spiral Staircase; The Unknown. **1947** Dead Reckoning; Blind Spot; The Sea of Grass; Brute Force; Romance of Rosy Ridge; Driftwood; Driftwood; Killer McCoy; Philo Vance's Secret Mission; The Millerson Case. **1948** I, Jane Doe; Sealed Verdict; Black Eagle. **1949** Streets of Laredo; Roughshod. **1950** Dial 1119; The Company She Keeps; Buckaroo Sheriff of Texas; The Violent Hour. **1951** The Dakota Kid; Flying Leathernecks; Arizona Manhunt; Red Mountain. **1952** Japanese War Bride; Wild Horse Ambush; Ride the Man Down; Million Dollar Mermaid. **1953** Devil's Canyon; All the Brothers Were Valiant; The Last Posse. **1953** The Glenn Miller Story; Riding Shotgun; Crime Wave; About Mrs. Leslie; Black Tuesday. **1955** Marty; Strategic Air Command; Lay That Rifle Down; Teen-age Crime Wave; Sincerely Yours; A Lawless Street; Texas Lady; Stranger on Horseback. **1956** Huk; Four Girls in Town; The Search for Bridey Murphy; Tribute to a Bad Man. **1957** The Lonely Man; Back From the Dead; Johnny Trouble; The Tin Star. **1958** In Love and War. **1959** The Oregon Trail; 30. **1961** Claudelle Inglish; Posse from Hell. **1963** Twilight of Honor.

BELL, LOLA
Born: Russia. Died: Jan. 6, 1967, Hollywood, Calif. Screen, stage and television actress.

BELL, MARY
Died: Dec. 16, 1973. Screen and stage actress.

Appeared in: **1955** The Shrike. **1956** Crowded Paradise.

BELL, MONTA
Born: Feb. 5, 1891, Washington, D.C. Died: Feb. 4, 1958, Hollywood, Calif. Screen, stage actor, screenwriter, film producer and film director. Divorced from screen actress Betty Lawford (dec. 1960).

Appeared in: **1923** The Pilgrim.

BELL, RALPH W.
Born: 1883. Died: July 14, 1936, San Francisco, Calif. (pneumonia). Screen, stage actor and stage director.

Appeared in: **1930** Clancy in Wall Street; Cock O' The Walk. **1931** Connecticut Yankee.

BELL, REX
Born: Oct. 16, 1905, Chicago, Ill. Died: July 4, 1962, Las Vegas, Nev. (coronary occlusion). Screen actor. Married to actress Clara Bow (dec. 1965) and was Lieutenant Governor of Nevada from 1954 to 1962.

Appeared in: **1928** Wild West Romance; The Girl-Shy Cowboy; The Cowboy Kid. **1929** Taking a Chance; Joy Street; Pleasure Crazed; Salute; They Had to See Paris; Happy Days. **1930** Courage; True to the Navy; Harmony at Home; Lightnin'. **1931** Battling with Buffalo Bill (serial). **1932** Forgotten Women; Law of the Sea; From Broadway to Cheyenne; The Man from Arizona; Arm of the Law; Crashin'

Broadway; Diamond Trail; Lucky Larrigan; The Fighting Texans. **1935** Fighting Pioneers; Fun Fire; Saddle Acres. **1936** Too Much Beef; The Idaho Kid; West of Nevada; Men of the Plains; Stormy Trails. **1942** Tombstone, the Town Too Tough to Die; Dawn on the Great Divide. **1952** Lone Star.

BELL, RODNEY
Born: 1916. Died: Aug. 3, 1968. Screen actor.

Appeared in: **1945** The Strange Affair of Uncle Harry; An Angel Comes to Brooklyn; Scarlet Street. **1946** Centennial Summer; Live Wires. **1947** My Wild Irish Rose; Blondie's Holiday. **1951** Meet Me After the Show; So You Want to Be a Handyman (short); So You Want to Be a Paperhanger (short); So You Want to Be a Plumber (short); Close to My Heart. **1952** Something for the Birds; So You Want to Get It Wholesale (short); So You're Going to the Dentist (short). **1953** The Hitchhiker; So You Want a Television Set (short). **1954** So You're Having Neighbor Trouble (short); So You Want to Be Your Own Boss (short); So You're Taking in a Roomer (short). **1946** The Phantom from 10,000 Leagues. **1958** The Missouri Traveler; Wink of an Eye. **1960** The Rookie. **1961** Go Naked in the World.

BELL, RUTH
Born: 1907. Died: June 17, 1933, Los Angeles, Calif. (suicide—poison). Screen actress.

BELLAMY, GEORGE
Born: 1866, Bristol, England. Died: Dec. 26, 1944, England? Screen and stage actor.

Appeared in: **1911** Her Mother's Image; Wanted—a Husband; An Act of Kindness. **1912** Love Conquers Crime; The Mexican's Love Affair; His Duty. **1914** The King's Minister; The Cage; England Expects; Called Back; A Christmas Carol; Clancarty; For the Empire (aka For Home and Country—US); Two Little Britons; The Two Columbines; The Third String; The Bosun's Mate; Duty; Her Children; England's Menace; The Revenge of Mr. Thomas Atkins. **1915** The Middleman; The Devil's Bondsman (aka The Scorpion's Sting—US); Rupert of Hentau (US 1916); The Sons of Satan; The Heart of a Child (US 1916); The Derby Winner; The Third Generation; Jeff's (aka A Man of His Word—US); Brother Officers; The Prisoner of Zenda; The Christian. **1916** The Hard Way; Honour in Pawn; The Answer; Fatal Fingers; A Mother's Influence. **1917** The Mother of Dartmoor; Quicksands (aka Broken Barrier); Auld Land Syne. **1919** Sweet and Twenty; Forgive Us Our Trespasses. **1920** True Tilda; Lady Noggs—Peeress; Lorna Doone; The Black Sheep; The Scarlet Wooing; Judge Not; The Edge of Youth; Little Dorrit; The Woman of the Iron Bracelets; Ernest Maltravers; Enchantment; The Glad Eye; Uncle Dick's Darling; The Town of Crooked Ways. **1921** The Old Country; The Way of a Man; Four Just Men; Moth and Rust; The Princess of New York; In His Grip. **1922** A Lost Leader; A Romance of Old Bagdad; The House of Peril; The Truants; The Doddington Diamonds; Open Country; Was She Justified?; The Further Adventures of Sherlock Holmes series including: The Six Napoleons. **1924** The Mating of Marcus; Not for Sale. **1926** The Happy Rascals series; White Heat; Screen Playlets series including: Miss Bracegirdle Does Her Duty and Back to the Tress. **1927** Mr. Nobody. **1928** The Intruder; Valley of the Ghosts; Not Quite a Lady. **1929** Red Aces. **1931** Midnight; Stepping Stones; Immediate Possession; The Officer's Mess. **1933** Mixed Doubles.

BELLANDE, EDWARD A.
Born: Dec. 19, 1897, Ocean Springs, Miss. Died: Nov. 17, 1976, Los Angeles, Calif. (cardiac arrest). Business executive, aviation pioneer and film stunt flyer.

BELLEW, COSMO KYRLE
Born: 1886. Died: Jan. 25, 1948, Hollywood, Calif. Screen and stage actor. Son of actor Kyrle Bellew (dec. 1911).

Appeared in: **1926** Summer Bachelors. **1927** The Magic Flame. **1928** Black Butterflies; Midnight Life; Hit of the Show. **1929** The Devil's Apple Tree; Strange Cargo; Disraeli. **1930** Lummox. **1931** The Lady Who Dared. **1932** The Love Contract. **1934** Beloved; Norah O'Neill. **1935** Splendor.

BELLEW, H. KYRLE
Born: 1857, Calcutta, India. Died: Nov. 3, 1911, Salt Lake City, Utah (pneumonia). Stage and screen actor. Father of actor Cosmo Kyrle Bellew (dec. 1948).

Appeared in: **1904** A Gentleman of France.

BELMAR, HENRY
Born: 1849. Died: Jan. 12, 1931, New Castle, Pa. Screen, stage actor, playwright and stage producer. Appeared in silents. Married to actress Laurel Love (dec.).

BELMONT, JOE A.
Born: 1860. Died: Mar. 28, 1930, Toledo, Ohio. Screen actor double and circus acrobat. Do not confuse with screen actor Joseph Belmont.

BELMONT, JOSEPH "BALDY"
Born: Aug. 18, 1874, Port Huron or St. Clair, Mich. Died: May 16, 1939. Screen, stage, vaudeville actor, film director and screenwriter. Appeared in "Baldy" Belmont and Sennett Comedies.

Appeared in: **1916** A Bath House Blunder; The Love Comet; A La Cabaret; Wings and Wheels; Better Late Than Never; Dollars and Sense. **1917** Skidding Hearts; Oriental Love. **1919** The Star Boarder; Never too Old; No Mother to Guide Him. **1920** White Youth; Don't Weaken. **1925** Too Much Youth. **1926** Prowlers of the Night; Young April. **1927** The King of Kings; Blondes by Choice. **1929** The Black Pearl; Painted Faces.

BELMONT, MICHAEL
Born: 1915. Died: Nov. 9, 1941, Beverly Hills, Calif. (injuries—fall from horse). Screen actor.

BELMONT, RALF
Born: 1892. Died: Sept. 21, 1964, Hollywood, Calif. (struck by car). Screen actor.

BELMONTE, HERMAN
Born: 1891. Died: Sept. 15, 1975, Woodland Hills, Calif. (stroke). Screen actor, dance director and dancer.

BELMORE, ALICE
Born: 1870, London, England. Died: July 31, 1943, New York, N.Y. Screen and stage actress. Daughter of stage actors George (dec.) and Alice Cooke Belmore (dec.).

Appeared in: **1915** The Girl Who Took the Wrong Turning; The Shop Soiled Girl. **1916** The Female Swindler; The Girl Who Wrecked His Home.

BELMORE, BERTHA
Born: Dec. 22, 1882, Manchester, England. Died: Dec. 14, 1953, Barcelona, Spain. Screen and stage actress.

Appeared in: **1934** Going Gay; Are You a Mason?; Over the Garden Wall. **1935** Give Her a Ring; So You Won't Talk; You Never Can Tell; In the Soup. **1936** Broken Blossoms. **1938** Let's Make a Night of It; Over She Goes. **1939** Discoveries; The Midas Touch; Yes, Madam. **1941** She Couldn't Say No; Pirates of the Seven Seas.

BELMORE, DAISY (Daisy Garstin)
Born: June 30, 1874, London, England. Died: Dec. 12, 1954, New York, N.Y. (heart attack). Stage and screen actress. Entered films with Famous Players in N.Y. in 1912.

Appeared in: **1928** We Americans. **1930** Seven Days' Leave; Alias French Gertie; Scarlet Pages; All Quiet on the Western Front; Way for a Sailor. **1931** Fifty Million Frenchmen; My Past; Born to Love; Dracula. **1936** Sylvia Scarlett.

BELMORE, LIONEL
Born: 1867, England. Died: Jan. 30, 1953, Woodland Hills, Calif. Screen and stage actor.

Appeared in: **1920** Jes' Call Me Jim; Madame X. **1921** Courage; A Shocking Night; Guile of Women; Moonlight Follies; Two Minutes to Go; The Stings of the Lash. **1922** Oliver Twist; The Barnstormer; The Galloping Kid; Iron to Gold; Head Over Heels; Enter Madame; The Kentucky Derby; Kindred of the Dust; The World's Champion; Peg O' My Heart. **1923** Within the Law; Jazzmania; Forgive and Forget; Red Lights; Quicksands; Railroaded. **1924** A Boy of Flanders; A Lady of Quality; The Sea Hawk; Try and Get It; A Fool's Awakening; The Man Who Fights Alone; Racing Luck; The Silent Watcher. **1925** Madame Behave; Without Mercy; Eve's Secret; Never the Twain Shall Meet; The Storm Breaker. **1926** Bardelys the Magnificent; The Return of Peter Grimm; The Black Bird; The Checkered Flag; Shipwrecked; Stop, Look and Listen. **1927** The Student Prince in Old Heidelberg; Sorrell and Son; Roaring Fires; Winners of the Wilderness; The Sunset Derby; The Demi-Bride; The Dice Woman; The King of Kings; The Tender Hour; Wide Open. **1928** The Play Girl; Rose Marie; The Circus Kid; The Matinee Idol; The Wife's Relations; The Good-Bye Kiss; Heart Trouble. **1929** The Redeeming Sin; The Love Parade; The Yellowback; The Unholy Night; Evidence; From Headquarters; Stark Mad. **1930** Love Comes Along; The Rogue Song; Hell's Island; Monte Carlo; Sweet Kitty Bellairs; The Boudoir Diplomat; Queen of Scandal; Playing Around; One Heavenly Night; Captain of the Guard. **1931** Ten Nights in a Barroom; Shanghai Love; Frankenstein; Alexander

Hamilton. **1932** The Sign of the Cross; So Big; Vanity Fair; Police Court; Malay Nights. **1933** Cavalcade; The Vampire Bat; Oliver Twist (and 1922 version); The Constant Wife; Warrior's Husband. **1934** Cleopatra; The Count of Monte Cristo; Caravan; I Am Suzanne; Jane Eyre. **1935** The Man Who Reclaimed His Head; Mutiny on the Bounty; Red Morning; Dressed to Kill; Forced Landing; Vanessa, Her Love Story; Hitch Hike Lady; Bonnie Scotland; Cardinal Richelieu; Clive of India. **1936** Little Lord Fauntleroy; The Last of the Mohicans; Mary of Scotland. **1937** It's Love I'm After; Maid of Salem; The Prince and the Pauper; The Toast of New York. **1938** Service de Luxe; The Adventures of Robin Hood; If I Were King; Pie a la Maid (short). **1939** Tower of London; Son of Frankenstein. **1940** My Son, My Son; Diamond Frontier.

BELOKUROV, VLADIMIR V.
Born: 1904, Russia. Died: Jan. 30, 1973, Moscow, Russia. Screen and stage actor.

Appeared in: **1932** House of Death. **1937** Paris Commune. **1941** Wings of Victory. **1963** Optimisticheskaya Tragediya (The Optimistic Tragedy—US 1964).

BELSON, EDWARD
Born: 1898. Died: Dec. 1, 1975, Hollywood, Calif. (kidney failure). Screen actor. Married to former dancer Billie Belson.

BELTRAN, RAYMOND "RAY"
Born: 1892. Died: Oct. 17, 1967. Screen actor.

Appeared in: **1941** This Woman Is Mine. **1945** Masquerade in Mexico. **1949** The Cowboy and the Indians. **1953** Treasure of the Goldon Condor.

BELTRI, RICARDO
Born: 1899, Mexico. Died: June, 1962, Mexico City, Mexico. Screen and stage actor. Appeared in silents.

BELWIN, ALMA
Born: c. 1894, San Francisco, Calif. Died: May 3, 1924, Boston, Mass. Stage and screen actress.

Appeared in: **1915** The Ivory Snuff Box.

BENADERET, BEA
Born: Apr. 4, 1906, New York, N.Y. Died: Oct 13, 1968, Los Angeles, Calif. (cancer). Screen, stage, television and radio actress.

Appeared in: **1946** Notorious. **1949** On the Town. **1952** For the First Time. **1959** Plunderers of Painted Flats. **1962** Tender Is the Night.

BEN-AMI, JACOB
Born: 1890, Minsk, Russia. Died: July 22, 1977, New York, N.Y. Screen, stage actor, film, stage director. Founder of the Yiddish Art Theater. Married to stage actress Slava Estrin (dec. 1966).

Appeared in: **1933** The Wandering Jew. **1969** The Golden Age of Second Avenue.

BENARD, RAY *See* CORRIGAN, RAYMOND "CRASH"

BEN-ARI, RAKIN
Born: 1904, Russia. Died: Jan. 2, 1968, Moscow, Russia. Screen, stage actor and stage director.

Appeared in: **1959** Gangster Story.

BENASSI, MEMO
Born: 1886, Italy. Died: Feb. 24, 1957, Bologna, Italy. Stage and screen actor.

Appeared in: **1936** La Signora di Tutti. **1937** Signora Paradiso. **1939** Scipio Africanus. **1948** Rossini.

BENCHLEY, ROBERT
Born: Sept. 15, 1889, Worcester, Mass. Died: Nov. 21, 1945, New York, N.Y. (cerebral hemorrhage). Screen, radio actor, writer, critic and film director. Father of screenwriter Nathaniel Benchley (dec. 1981). Won 1935 Academy Award for his short, How to Sleep.

Appeared in: **1928** The Sex Life of the Polyp; The Treasurer's Report (short); The Spellbinder (short). **1929** The following shorts: Lesson No. 1; Furnace Trouble; Stewed, Fried and Boiled. **1932** Sport Parade. **1933** Headline Shooter; Dancing Lady; Your Technocracy and Mine (short). **1934** Rafter Romance; Social Register. **1935** China Seas; How to Sleep (short); How to Break 90 at Croquet (short). **1936** Piccadilly Jim; plus the following shorts: How to Behave; How to Train a Dog;

How to Vote; How to Be a Detective. **1937** Live, Love and Learn; plus the following shorts: Broadway Melody of 1938; The Romance of Digestion; How to Start the Day; A Night at the Movies. **1938** The following shorts: How to Figure Income Tax; Music Made Simple; An Evening Alone; How to Raise a Baby; The Courtship of the Newt; How to Read; How to Watch Football; Opening Day; Mental Poise. **1939** The following shorts: How to Sub-Let; An Hour for Lunch; Dark Magic; Home Early; How to Eat; The Day of Rest; See Your Doctor. **1940** Hired Wife; Foreign Correspondent; plus the following shorts: That Interior Feeling; Home Movies; The Trouble With Husbands. **1941** Nice Girl?; The Reluctant Dragon; You'll Never Get Rich; Three Girls About Town; Bedtime Story; plus the following shorts: Waiting for Baby; Crime Control; The Forgotten Man; How to Take a Vacation. **1942** Take a Letter, Darling; The Major and the Minor; I Married a Witch; plus the following shorts: But Nerves; The Witness; Keeping in Shape; The Man's Angle. **1943** Flesh and Fantasy (narr.); Young and Willing; The Song of Russia; The Sky's the Limit; My Tomato (short); No News Is Good News (short). **1944** Her Primitive Man; The National Barn Dance; See Here, Private Hargrove; Practically Yours; Janie; Important Business (short); Why, Daddy? (short). **1945** Pan-Americana; It's in the Bag; Weekend at the Waldorf; Kiss and Tell; Duffy's Tavern; Stork Club; The Road to Utopia; Boogie Woogie (short); I'm a Civilian Here Myself (short). **1946** The Bride Wore Boots; Snafu; Janie Gets Married; Blue Skies. **1964** Big Parade of Comedy (documentary).

BENDA, WLADYSLAW T.
Born: 1875, Poland. Died: Nov. 30, 1948, Newark, N.J. (heart attack). Artist, screen actor, playwright and writer.

Appeared in: **1926** The American Venus.

BENDER, CHIEF (Charles Albert Bender)
Born: May 5, 1883, Brainerd, Minn. Died: May 22, 1954. Professional baseball player and screen actor.

Appeared in: **1911** The Baseball Bug.

BENDER, RUSSELL "RUSS" (Russell Richard Bender, Jr.)
Born: Jan. 1, 1910, New York, N.Y. Died: Aug. 16, 1969, Woodland Hills, Calif. Screen, television actor and screenwriter.

Appeared in: **1956** It Conquered the World. **1957** The Amazing Colossal Man; Badlands of Montana; Dragstrip Girl; Invasion of the Saucer Men; The Joker Is Wild; Motorcycle Gang. **1958** Hot Rod Gang; I Bury the Living; War of the Colossal Beast; Suicide Battalion. **1959** Ghost of Dragstrip Hollow; Compulsion; No Name on the Bullet. **1960** Vice Raid. **1961** Anatomy of a Psycho; The Purple Hills; The Little Shepherd of Kingdom Come. **1962** Air Patrol; Panic in Year Zero!; That Touch of Mink. **1963** A Gathering of Eagles. **1964** Raiders from Beneath the Sea; The Strangler. **1965** The Satan Bug; Wild on the Beach; The End of the World (rerelease of Panic in Year Zero!—1962). **1966** The Navy vs. the Night Monsters. **1967** Devil's Angels. **1968** Maryjane; The Young Animals (aka Born Wild).

BENDIX, WILLIAM
Born: Jan. 14, 1906, New York, N.Y. Died: Dec. 14, 1964, Los Angeles, Calif. (lobar pneumonia and complications). Screen, stage, television and radio actor. Nominated for 1942 Academy Award for Best Supporting Actor in Wake Island.

Appeared in: **1941** Woman of the Year (film debut). **1942** Brooklyn Orchid; Wake Island; The Glass Key; Star Spangled Rhythm; Who Done It? **1943** The McGuerins from Brooklyn; Guadalcanal Diary; China; The Crystal Ball; Taxi, Mister; Hostages. **1944** Lifeboat; The Hairy Ape; Abroad With Two Yanks; Greenwich Village; Skirmish on the Home Front (short). **1945** It's in the Bag; Don Juan Quilligan; A Bell for Adano. **1946** The Blue Dahlia; Two Years Before the Mast; Sentimental Journey; The Dark Corner; White Tie and Tails. **1947** Blaze of Noon; The Web; I'll Be Yours; Calcutta; Where There's Life; Variety Girl. **1948** Race Street; The Babe Ruth Story; The Time of Your Life. **1949** Life of Riley; Streets of Laredo; Cover Up; The Big Steal; Connecticut Yankee in King Arthur's Court; Johnny Holiday. **1950** Gambling House; Kill the Umpire. **1951** Submarine Command; Detective Story. **1952** Macao; Blackbeard the Pirate; A Girl in Every Port. **1954** Dangerous Mission. **1955** Crash Out. **1956** Battle Stations. **1958** The Deep Six. **1959** Idle on Parade; The Rough and the Smooth (aka Portrait of a Sinner—US 1961). **1962** Boy's Night Out. **1963** The Young and the Brave; For Love or Money. **1964** Law of the Lawless (aka Invitation to a Hanging); The Phony American. **1965** Young Fury; Johnny Nobody.

BENEDICT, BROOKS
Born: Feb. 6, (?), New York, N.Y. Died: Jan. 1, 1968. Screen and stage actor.

Appeared in: **1923** Cupid's Fireman. **1924** The Only Woman. **1925** The Freshman; His Master's Voice; The Love Gamble; Shoes. **1926** College Days; Going the Limit; Ranson's Folly; Tramp, Tramp, Tramp; Why Girls Go Back Home; Officer of the Day. **1927** Backstage; Casey Jones; The Drop Kick; The Gorilla; The Kid Sister; Orchids and Ermine; Lost at the Front; White Flannels; Three's a Crowd. **1928** The Cowboy Kid; Moran of the Marines; Speedy. **1929** Clear the Decks; The Sophomore; The Garden of Eatin'. **1930** Derelict; The Office Wife; Recaptured Love; The Street of Chance; The Widow from Chicago. **1931** Six Cylinder Love (stage and film version); Gun Smoke; Reckless Living. **1932** Girl Crazy; What Price Hollywood? **1933** No Other Woman; Pick Up; Cheating Blondes; Don't Bet on Love; Sons of the Desert. **1934** Belle of the Nineties; Picture Brides. **1935** G-Men; Murder on a Honeymoon; Hot Money (short); Slightly Static (short). **1936** Showboat; Follow the Fleet; Vamp Till Ready (short); Early to Bed; Life Hesitates at 40 (short). **1937** Midnight Madonna; Love Takes Flight; Pick a Star. **1938** Bringing Up Baby. **1939** Laugh It Off. **1940** I Take This Oath; Enemy Agent. **1941** I Wake Up Screaming (aka Hot Spot). **1943** The Iron Major; Hi'Ya, Chum; Jack London. **1944** Bowery to Broadway. **1946** The Man Who Dared; Out California Way; Murder in the Music Hall. **1947** Three on a Ticket. **1951** The People Against O'Hara. **1952** The Las Vegas Story. **1958** Houseboat.

BENEDICT, JEAN
Born: 1876. Died: July 28, 1943, Woodland Hills, Calif. Screen and stage actress. Married to actor Kingsley Benedict.

Appeared in: **1938** A Slight Case of Murder; The Patient in Room 18; Blondes at Work; Little Miss Thoroughbred; Fools for Scandal.

BENEDICT, KINGSLEY
Born: Nov. 14, 1882, Buffalo, N.Y. Died: Nov. 27, 1951, Woodland Hills, Calif. Screen, stage actor, screenwriter and playwright.

Appeared in: **1917** The Mystery Ship (serial). **1919** Who Will Marry Me? **1921** The Stampede; The Secret of the Hills. **1922** Gay and Devilish; The Kentucky Derby. **1923** A Man of Action. **1924** Riders of the Plains (serial). **1925** White Thunder. **1927** Fast and Furious. **1930** Terry of the Times (serial). **1932** The Last Mile.

BENELL, JOHN THOMAS
Born: 1915. Died: Aug. 12, 1940, Beverly Hills, Calif. Screen and stage actor.

BENGE, MRS. SARAH L.
Born: 1883. Died: Jan. 27, 1954. Screen and stage actress. Married to actor Wilson Benge (dec. 1955).

BENGE, WILSON
Born: 1875, Greenwich, London, England. Died: July 1, 1955, Hollywood, Calif. Screen, stage actor and stage producer. Married to actress Sarah L. Benge (dec. 1954).

Appeared in: **1922** Robin Hood. **1923** Ten Commandments. **1925** Lady Windermere's Fan; Alias Mary Flynn; The Road to Yesterday. **1926** A Trip to Chinatown; The Midnight Message. **1927** King of Kings; Fast and Furious; The Lone Eagle. **1928** Anybode Here Seen Kelly?; A Gentleman Preferred; Freedom of the Press; That's My Daddy. **1929** A Most Immoral Lady; Bulldog Drummond; Untamed; This Thing Called Love. **1930** Raffles; Her Wedding Night; Charley's Aunt; The Bat Whispers. **1931** Men in Her Life; Platinum Blonde. **1932** Cynara. **1933** Song of Songs; Big Executive; By Appointment Only. **1934** Twin Husbands; Bulldog Drummond Strikes Back. **1935** A Feather in Her Hat; Cardinal Richelieu; The Ghost Walks; False Pretenses. **1936** Dancing Feet; Murder at Glen Athol. **1937** The Shadow Strikes; Easy Living; Mr. Boggs Steps Out; Oh, Doctor!; The Man Who Cried Wolf. **1938** The Adventures of Robin Hood; Trade Winds. **1940** Green Hell. **1941** The Lady Eve; The Man Who Lost Himself; Nothing But the Truth. **1942** You're Telling Me; The Palm Beach Story; Miss Annie Rooney; The Pied Piper. **1944** The Lodger; The White Cliffs of Dover; Mrs. Parkington; Gaslight. **1945** Pursuit of Algiers; Tonight and Every Night; The House of Fear. **1948** The Three Musketeers. **1950** Emergency Wedding. **1951** Kind Lady; Royal Wedding. **1952** Million Dollar Mermaid. **1955** The Scarlet Coat.

BENGLIA, HABIB
Born: 1895, France. Died: 1961, France? Screen actor.

Appeared in: **1958** The Roots of Heaven.

BENHAM, DOROTHY
Born: Sept. 6, 1910, Boston, Mass. Died: Sept. 19, 1956, Watertown, Wis. (Hodgkin's disease). Screen actress. Daughter of actor Harry Benham (dec. 1969) and actress Ethyle Cook (dec. 1949). Sister of actor Leland Benham.

Appeared in: **1912** The Wrecked Taxi; Don't Pinch My Pup; The Country's Prize Baby. **1915** Mr. Meeson's Will; The Commuted Sentence. **1916** The Path of Happiness.

BENHAM, HARRY
Born: Feb. 26, 1886, Valparaiso, Ind. Died: July 17, 1969, Sarasota, Fla. Stage and screen actor. Entered films with Thanhouser in 1911. Married to actress Ethyle Cook (dec. 1949) and father of actress Dorothy Benham (dec. 1956) and actor Leland Benham (dec. 1976).

Appeared in: **1911** One Flag at Last; Their Burglar; The Tomboy. **1912** Dr. Jekyll and Mr. Hyde; Her Ladyship's Page; When a Count Counted. **1913** For Another's Sin; The Head of the Ribbon Counter; The Girl of the Cabaret; Louie the Life Saver. **1914** Henry's Waterloo; The Runaway Princess; Zudora, the Twenty Million Dollar Mystery (serial). **1915** The Country Girl; The Heart of Princess Mirsari; The Girl of the Sea; A Freight Car Honeymoon; Daughters of Kings; When the Fleet Sailed; When Hungry Hamlet Fled; The Scoop at Belleville; Helen's Babies; His Two Patients; Madam Blanche. **1916** The Man Inside; The Doll Doctor; The Capital Prize; Mignonette; Through Flames to Love; Her Wonderful Secret; Peggy and the Law; Clever Mrs. Carter; The Little Gray Mouse; The Intruder; A College Boomerang; Love's Masquerade; The Angel of the Attic; The Heart Wrecker; The Girl Who Didn't Tell; Pamela's Past; Toto of the By-Ways; Path to Happiness; Mischief Makers. **1917** The Outsider; Souls United; When Thieves Fall Out; The Dancers Peril; Warfare of the Flesh; When You and I Were Young. **1918** Cecilia of the Pink Roses; Convict 993; The Frame-Up. **1920** Polly with a Past; The Dangerous Paradise; The Prey. **1921** Hush Money. **1922** The Road to Mandalay; The Town That Forgot God; Your Best Friend.

BENHAM, JOAN
Born: England? Died: June 13, 1981, England? Screen actress.

Appeared in: **1952** The Pickwick Papers (US 1953). **1953** Innocents in Paris (US 1955). **1955** King's Rhapsody (US 1956); The Man Who Loved Redheads. **1956** Loser Takes All (US 1957). **1958** The Whole Truth. **1959** The Bridal Path. **1962** I Thank a Fool. **1963** The Wild Affair (US 1966); Tamahine (US 1964); The V.I.P.'s; Ladies Who Do. **1964** Murder Ahoy. **1969** The Magic Christian (US 1970). **1970** Perfect Friday. **1978** The Greek Tycoon. **1979** Fiona.

BENHAN, LELAND
Born: 1907, Boston, Mass. Died: Sept. 26, 1976. Screen actor. Son of actors Harry Benhan (dec. 1969) and Ethyle Cook (dec. 1949). Entered films as a child actor.

Appeared in: **1916** The Path to Happiness.

BENJAMIN, JIM
Born: 1947. Died: June 21, 1978, Los Angeles, Calif. (murdered—shot). Screen, stage and television actor. Do not confuse with assistant director of same name.

Appeared in: **1979** Penitentiary.

BENKHOFF, FITA
Born: 1908, Dortmund, Germany. Died: 1967, Munich, Germany. Screen and stage actress.

Appeared in: **1924** Mutter und Kind (Mother and Child). **1934** Was bin ich ohne Dich; Schwarzer Jaeger Johanna; Ein Kind, ein Hund, ein Vagabund (aka Vielleicht War's nur ein Traum); Gold; Die Beiden Seehunde (aka Seine Hoheit der Dienstmann); Alte Kameraden (aka Das Faehnlein der Versprengten); Das Erbe von Pretoria; Ein Maedel Wirbelt Durch die Welt; Der Meisterboxer (aka Pantoffelhelden); Charleys Tante (Charley's Aunt); Krach um Jolanthe; Heina im Mond. **1935** Liebeslied; Henker, Krauen und Soldaten; Die Werft zum Grauen Hecht; Amphitryon (aka Aus den Wolken komt das Glueck); Der Ammenkoenig (aka Das Tal des Lebens). **1936** Moral, Diener Lassen Bitten; Die Un-Erhoerte Frau (aka Ich Kenne Dich Nicht Mehr); Boccaccio; Der Schuechterne Casanova; Strassenmusik. **1937** Petermann ist Dagegen; Capriolen; Manege; Heiratsschwindler (aka Die Rote Muetze); Wenn Frauen Schweigen. **1938** Diskretion—Ehrensache; Schuesse in Kabine 7; Spassvoegel; Lauter Luegen; Die Werf zum Graven Hecht (The Gray Pikes Wharf); Liebe im Gleitflug (Love in Stunt Flying). **1939** Schneider Wibbel; Opernball (Opera Ball); Drunter und Drueber; Die Goldene Maske. **1940** Ihr Privatsekretaer; Casanova Heiratet; Was Wird Hier Gespilet?; Das Fraeulein von Barnhelm; Was Will Brigitte?; Henker Fraven und Soldaten (Hangmen, Women and Soldiers). **1941** Frau Luna; Immer nur Du. **1942** So ein Fruechtchen; Meine Freudin Josefine. **1943** Johann. **1944** Ich Brauche Dich; Freitag, der 13; Ich hab' von Dir Getraeumt. **1945** Der Scheiterhaufen. **1948** Morgen ist Alles Besser; Die Zeit mit Dir. **1949** Der Biberpelz; Krach im Hinterhaus. **1950** Kein Engel ist so Rein; Melodie des Schicksals; Taxi-Kitty. **1951** Das Gestohlene Jahr; Die Mitternachtsvenus; Hilfe, ich bin Unsichtbar; Die Frauen des Herrn S.; Durch Dick und Duenn. **1952** In Muenchen Steht ein Hofbrauehaus; Die Diebin von Bagdad; Pension Schoeller; Tanzende Sterne; Wenn Abends die Heide Trauemt. **1953** Von der Liebe Reden wir Spaeter; Das Singende Hotel; Fanfaren der Ehe; Muss man Sich Gleich Scheiden Lassen? **1954** Der Raub der Sabinerinnen; Fraeulein vom Amt; Auf der Reeperbahn Nachts um Halb Eins; Maxie. **1955** Der Hauptmann und Sein Held; Der Himmel ist nie Ausverkauft; Ein Herz Voll Musik; Wenn der Vater mit dem Sohne; Drei Maedels vom Rhein. **1956** Dany, Bitte Schreiben Sie; Der Erste Fruehlingstag; Der Bettelstudent (The Beggar Student—US 1958); Opernball (Opera Ball, and 1939 version); Wenn wir Alle Engel Waeren; Familie Schimek. **1957** Zwei Herzen Voller Seligkeit; ... und die Liebe Lacht Dazu; Wenn Frauen Schwindeln (aka Europas Neue Musikparade). **1958** Majestaet auf Abwegen. **1959** Liebe, Luft und Lauter Luegen; Immer die Maedchen; Ein Sommer, den man nie Vergisst (aka Traenen in Deinen Augen). **1960** Ingeborg. **1961** Bei Pichler Stimmt die Kasse Nicht. **1963** Liebe Will Gelernt Sein.

BENNER, YALE DESPIN
Born: 1875, New York. Died: Sept. 29, 1952. Screen and stage actor.

Appeared in: **1916** The Pillory. **1917** A Wife by Proxy. **1922** The Man Beyond.

BENNETT, ALMA
Born: 1904, Seattle, Wash. Died: Sept. 16, 1958. Screen actress.

Appeared in: **1922** Flaming Hearts; Without Compromise; Smiling Jim. **1923** The Face on the Barroom Floor; The Grail; Man's Size; Three Jumps Ahead. **1924** The Cyclone Rider; Lilies of the Field; Triumph; The Dawn of a Tomorrow; Why Men Leave Home; The Silent Watcher. **1925** The Lost World; The Light of Western Stars; A Fool and His Money; The Price of Success. **1926** Brooding Eyes; Don Juan's Three Nights; The Silent Lover; The Thrill Hunter. **1927** Long Pants; Orchids and Ermine; Compassion. **1928** The Goodbye Kiss; The Grain of Dust; The Head of the Family. **1929** My Lady's Past; New Orleans; Painted Faces; Two Men and a Maid; Girl Crazy (short); Midnight Daddies. **1930** Woman Who Was Forgotten; Hail the Princess (short); Jack White talking shorts.

BENNETT, BARBARA
Born: 1911. Died: Aug. 8, 1958, Montreal, Canada (heart attack). Stage and screen actress. Sister of actresses Constance (dec. 1965) and Joan Bennett. Daughter of actor Richard Bennett (dec. 1944) and actress Adrianne Morrison (dec. 1940). Divorced from singer Morton Downey. Married to actor Addison "Jack" Randall (dec. 1945).

Appeared in: **1916** The Valley of Decision. **1927** Black Jack. **1929** Syncopation; Mother's Boy. **1930** Love Among the Millionaires.

BENNETT, BELLE
Born: 1891, Milaca, Minn. Died: Nov. 4, 1932, Los Angeles, Calif. Screen, stage and vaudeville actress.

Appeared in: **1916** Sweet Kitty Bellairs. **1917** Fuel of Life. **1918** A Soul in Trust. **1920** The Courage of Marge O'Doone. **1922** Flesh and Spirit; Robin Hood; Your Best Friend. **1924** In Hollywood with Potash and Perlmutter. **1925** Stella Dallas; Playing With Souls; East Lynne; His Supreme Moment; If Marriage Fails. **1926** The Lily; Reckless Lady; Fourth Commandment; The Amateur Gentleman. **1927** Wild Geese; Mother; Way of All Flesh. **1928** The Devil's Skipper; The Devil's Trademark; The Sporting Age; Mother Machree; Battle of the Sexes; The Power of Silence. **1929** The Iron Mask; Molly and Me; My Lady's Past; Big Money; Fashions in Love. **1930** Their Own Desire; Courage; Recaptured Love; Night Work; One Romantic Night; The Woman Who Was Forgotten. **1932** The Big Shot.

BENNETT, BILLIE (Emily Haynie)
Born: Oct. 23, 1875, Evansville, Ind. Died: May 19, 1951, Los Angeles, Calif. (cerebral hemorrage). Screen actress.

Appeared in: **1915** The Best of Enemies. **1916** Cinders of Love; His Last Laugh; Hearts and Sparks. **1920** Courage of Marge O'Doone. **1921** Crossing Trails; The Parish Priest. **1922** Robin Hood; Penrod. **1923** Within the Law; Blood Test. **1924** Call of the Mate; The Martyr Sex; Crossed Trails. **1925** The Fighting Smile; Galloping Jinx; Lady Windermere's Fan; The Wyoming Wildcat; The Wall Street Whiz. **1926** Ransom's Folly; The Amateur Gentleman; Memory Lane. **1927** The Claw; The Slaver; Marriage; The Sonora Kid. **1928** The Tragedy of Youth. **1929** Fashions in Love; My Lady's Past. **1930** One Romantic Night; Night Work; Big Money.

BENNETT, CHARLES
Died: July, 1925, New York, N.Y. (hemorrhage). Screen actor and scenery designer.

BENNETT, CHARLES J.
Born: 1891. Died: Feb. 15, 1943, Hollywood, Calif. Screen actor. Divorced from actress Boots Mallory (dec. 1958).

Appeared in: **1914** Tillie's Punctured Romance. **1919** The Adventures of Ruth (serial). **1922** The Top of New York. **1924** America. **1937** The Man Who Cried Wolf. **1939** Gunga Din. **1941** Confirm or Deny; Man Hunt; Citizen Kane. **1942** Captains of the Clouds.

BENNETT, CONSTANCE
Born: Oct. 22, 1905, New York, N.Y. Died: July 24, 1965, Ft. Dix, N.J. (cerebral hemorrhage). Screen, stage actress and film producer. Daughter of actor Richard Bennett (dec. 1944) and actress Adrianne Morrison (dec. 1940). Sister of actresses Barbara (dec. 1958) and Joan Bennett. Married to John Coulter. Divorced from Chester Moorhead, Philip Plant, film producer Marquis de la Falaise de la Coudray and actor Gilbert Roland.

Appeared in: **1916** The Valley of Decision. **1922** Reckless Youth; What's Wrong With Women?; Evidence. **1924** Cytherea; The Forbidden Way; Into the Net. **1925** My Wife and I; Sally, Irene and Mary; The Pinch Hitter; Code of the West; The Goose Hangs High; The Goose Woman; My Son; Wandering Fires. **1926** Should a Woman Tell; Married. **1929** This Thing Called Love. **1930** Three Faces East; Common Clay; Rich People; Sin Takes a Holiday; Son of the Gods. **1931** The Common Law; The Easiest Way; Born to Love; Bought. **1932** What Price Hollywood?; Lady With a Past; Two Against the World; Rockabye. **1933** Our Betters; Bed of Roses; After Tonight. **1934** The Affairs of Cellini; Moulin Rouge; Outcast Lady. **1935** After Office Hours. **1936** Everything Is Thunder; Ladies in Love. **1937** Topper. **1938** Merrily We Live; Service de Luxe; Topper Takes a Trip. **1939** Tail Spin. **1940** Escape to Glory (aka Submarine Zone). **1941** Two-Faced Woman; Law of the Tropics; Wild Bill Hickok Rides. **1942** Sin Town; Madame Spy. **1945** Madame Pimpernel; Paris Underground. **1946** Centennial Summer. **1947** The Unsuspected. **1948** Smart Woman; Blonde Ice. **1949** Angel on the Amazon. **1951** As Young As You Feel. **1954** It Should Happen to You. **1966** Madame X.

BENNETT, EDNA
Born: 1900. Died: June 9, 1976, Keene, N.H. Screen and stage actress. Married to actor Royal Beal (dec. 1969).

Appeared in: **1930** The Big Fight. **1932** Ladies of the Big House.

BENNETT, ENID
Born: Jan. 2, 1895, Australia. Died: May 14, 1969, Malibu, Calif. (heart attack). Stage and screen actress. Entered Films in 1917. Sister of actress Marjorie Bennett (dec. 1982). Married to actor/director Fred Niblo, Sr. (dec. 1948) and later married to producer Sidney Franklin.

Appeared in: **1917** Princess in the Dark. **1918** The Biggest Show on Earth; The Vamp; Fuss and Feathers. **1919** The Haunted Bedroom; Stepping Out. **1920** The Woman and the Suitcase; Hairpins. **1921** Her Husband's Friend; Keeping Up With Lizzie; Silk Hosiery. **1922** Robin Hood; The Bootlegger's Daughter; Scandalous Tongues. **1923** The Bad Man; The Courtship of Miles Standish; Strangers of the Night; Your Friend and Mine. **1924** The Sea Hawk; The Red Lily; A Fool's Awakening. **1926** A Woman's Heart. **1927** The Wrong Mr. Wright. **1929** Good Medicine. **1931** Skippy; Waterloo Bridge; Sooky. **1939** Meet Dr. Christian; Intermezzo: A Love Story. **1940** Strike Up the Band.

BENNETT, FRANK
Born: 1891. Died: Apr. 29, 1957. Screen actor. Entered films during the silents. Married to actress Billie West (dec. 1967).

Appeared in: **1955** The Far Horizon.

BENNETT, HAROLD
Born: 1899, England. Died: Sept. 15, 1981, London, England (cancer). Screen, stage and television actor.

BENNETT, JOE (Joseph Bennett Aldert)
Born: 1889, Charleston, S.C. Died: Aug. 31, 1967, Amityville, N.Y. Screen, vaudeville, minstrel actor and dancer. Appeared in vaudeville as part of "The Dark Clouds" team with Edward Richards and later in a vaudeville act billed as "The Georgia Trio," both blackface acts.

Appeared in: **1937** Something to Sing About.

BENNETT, JOSEPH
Born: 1896, Los Angeles, Calif. Died: Dec. 4, 1931, Hollywood, Calif. Screen actor. Entered films in 1917.

Appeared in: **1921** Love Never Dies; The Night Horsemen; A Daughter of the Law; The Home Stretch. **1922** Elope If You Must. **1924** Barbara Frietchie; The Breed of the Border; Trigger Finger; Flashing Spurs. **1925** Cold Nerve. **1926** The Sign of the Claw; The Man in the Shadow. **1927** God's Great Wilderness; Shooting Straight; Men of Daring; Straight Shootin'; Wolf's Trail; Three Miles Up; Somewhere in Sonora; The Valley of Hell. **1928** The Shepherd of the Hills; Vultures of the Sea (serial); Won in the Clouds. **1929** The Lariat Kid. **1930** After the Fog.

BENNETT, LEE
Born: 1911. Died: Oct. 10, 1954, Chicago, Ill. Screen, radio actor, singer and orchestra leader.

Appeared in: **1937** Hold 'Em Navy. **1942** Girl Trouble. **1944** Follow the Boys. **1947** The Last Round-Up; Spirit of West Point. **1948** Coroner Creek. **1950** At War With the Army. **1951** The Dakota Kid; Three Desperate Men (aka Three Outlaws).

BENNETT, MICKEY
Born: 1915, Victoria, B.C., Canada. Died: Sept. 6, 1950, Hollywood, Calif. (heart attack). Screen actor and assistant film director.

Appeared in: **1922** The Man Who Played God; Reported Missing. **1923** Big Brother; The Empty Cradle; The Last Moment; Loyal Wives; Marriage Morals. **1924** The New School Teacher; Second Youth. **1926** Big Pal; The Cohens and the Kellys; Grabbing Grabbers (short); It's the Old Army Game; There Ain't No Santa Claus (short); Honesty—The Best Policy. **1927** A Boy of the Streets; Babe Comes Home; Slaves of Beauty. **1928** Tillie's Punctured Romance; United States Smith; The Vanishing West (serial); The Head of the Family. **1929** The Dummy; Footlights and Fools; The Ghost Talks. **1930** Strictly Modern; Swing High; Father's Son. **1931** Big Business Girl. **1932** Laughter in Hell. **1933** The Mayor of Hell.

BENNETT, RAY
Born: 1895. Died: Dec. 17, 1957, Hollywood, Calif. (heart attack). Screen actor.

Appeared in: **1932** Texas Trail; Public Cowboy No. 1. **1938** The Old Barn Dance; Prairie Moon. **1940** Hidden Gold. **1942** The Spoilers; Call of the Canyon. **1946** Gun Town. **1948** Black Bart; Hollow Triumph; Canon City; Northwest Stampede. **1949** Red Canyon; Samson and Delilah; Son of Surrender; Rimfire; Ma and Pa Kettle; The Dalton Gang. **1950** Fancy Pants; Winchester 73. **1951** Apache Drums. **1952** Carson City; The Man from Black Hills; Waco. **1953** The Redhead from Wyoming. **1956** The Wrong Man; Giant. **1957** African Manhunt.

BENNETT, RED (William Houghton)
Born: 1873. Died: May 10, 1941, Hollywood, Calif. Screen actor.

BENNETT, RICHARD
Born: May 21, 1873, Deacon's Mills, Cass County, Ind. Died: Oct. 22, 1944, Los Angeles, Calif. (heart attack). Screen, stage and vaudeville actor. Divorced from actress Adrianne Morrison (dec. 1940). Father of actresses Constance (dec. 1965), Barbara (dec. 1958) and Joan Bennett.

Appeared in: **1915** Damaged Goods. **1923** The Eternal City. **1924** Youth for Sale. **1925** Lying Wives. **1928** The Home Towners. **1931** Five and Ten; Arrowsmith; Bought. **1932** No Greater Love; Strange Justice; This Reckless Age; If I Had a Million; Madame Racketeer. **1933** The Woman Accursed; The Song of Songs; Big Executive. **1934** Nana. **1935** 18 Minutes; This Woman is Mine. **1942** Journey Into Fear; The Magnificent Ambersons.

BENNETT, SAM
Born: 1887. Died: Aug. 25, 1937, Hollywood, Calif. Screen and stage actor.

BENNETT, TOMMY
Died: Oct., 1943. Screen actor.

BENNETT, VIVIENNE
Born: July 29, 1905, Poole, Dorset, England. Died: Nov. 11, 1978, London, England. Screen, stage, television actress and dancer. Divorced from actor Godfrey Kenton.

BENNETT, WILDA
Born: 1884. Died: Dec. 20, 1967, Winnemucca, Nev. Screen and stage actress.

Appeared in: **1935** Back in Circulation. **1939** What a Life; The Women. **1940** Those Were the Days.

BENNISON, ANDREW
Born: 1887. Died: Jan. 7, 1942, Oxnard, Calif. Screen, stage actor, screenwriter and film director.

BENNISON, LOUIS
Born: 1884. Died: June 9, 1929, New York, N.Y. (suicide—gun). Screen actor and playwright.

Appeared in: **1921** Lavender and Old Lace.

BENNY, JACK (Benjamin Kubelsky)
Born: Feb. 14, 1894, Waukegan, Ill. Died: Dec. 26, 1974, Holmby Hills, Calif. (stomach cancer). Screen, stage, burlesque, vaudeville, radio, television actor, film producer, violinist and orchestra leader. Married to actress Mary Livingstone.

Appeared in: **1928** Bright Moments (short). **1929** Hollywood Revue of 1929. **1930** Chasing Rainbows (aka Road Show); The Medicine Man; The Song Writers Revue (short); plus Paramount shorts. **1931** Taxi Tangle (short). **1933** Mr. Broadway. **1934** Transatlantic Merry-Go-Round. **1935** Broadway Melody of 1936; It's in the Air. **1936** The Big Broadcast of 1937; College Holiday. **1937** Artists and Models. **1938** Artists and Models Abroad. **1939** Man About Town. **1940** Love Thy Neighbor; Buck Benny Rides Again. **1941** Charley's Aunt (aka Charley's American Aunt). **1942** George Washington Slept Here; To Be or Not to Be. **1943** The Meanest Man in the World. **1944** Hollywood Canteen. **1945** The Horn Blows at Midnight; It's in the Bag (aka The Fifth Chair). **1946** Without Reservations. **1949** The Great Lover. **1952** Somebody Loves Me. **1954** Susan Slept Here. **1957** Beau James. **1962** Gypsy. **1963** It's a Mad, Mad, Mad, Mad World. **1967** A Guide for the Married Man.

BENOIT, VICTOR L.
Born: 1877, Ottawa, Canada. Died: Jan. 16, 1943, Newburgh, N.Y. Screen and stage actor. Appeared in early Pathe Co. films.

BENSON, JOHN WILLIAM
Born: 1862. Died: July 12, 1926, New York, N.Y. (complications of diseases). Screen, stage and vaudeville actor.

BENSON, JULIETTE V. P.
Born: 1875. Died: Dec. 22, 1962, Hollywood, Calif. Screen actress. Entered films approx. 1933.

BENSON, LADY CONSTANCE (Gertrude Constance Samwell aka CONSTANCE FEATHERSTONHAUGH)
Born: 1860, England. Died: Jan. 19, 1946, England? Screen and stage actress. Married to actor Sir Frank Benson (dec. 1939).

Appeared in: **1911** Julius Caesar; Macbeth; Taming of the Shrew; Richard III.

BENSON, MAY
Died: Sept. 29, 1916. Stage and screen actress.

Appeared in: **1915** Mariana.

BENSON, SANDFORD
Born: 1914. Died: Feb. 4, 1935, Hollywood, Calif. (injuries from auto accident). Stage and screen actor.

BENSON, SIR FRANK P.
Born: Nov. 4, 1858, Alresford, England. Died: Dec. 31, 1939, London, England. Screen and stage actor. Married to actress Lady Constance Benson, aka Constance Featherstonhaugh (dec. 1946).

Appeared in: **1911** Richard III; Julius Caesar; Taming of the Shrew. **1923** Becket.

BENT, BUENA
Born: London, England. Died: Dec. 17, 1957, England? Screen, stage and television actress.

Appeared in: **1921** The Lunatic at Large. **1923** The Pipes of Pan. **1924** Reveille. **1925** Mr. Preedy and the Countess.

BENT, MARION
Born: Dec. 23, 1879, Bronx, N.Y. Died: July 28, 1940, Bronx, N.Y. Screen, stage actress and dancer. Married to Pat Rooney II (dec. 1962). Mother of Pat Rooney III (dec. 1979).

Appeared in: **1914** I'll Get You Yet.

BENT, PHILIP
Born: 1941. Died: June 12, 1966, La Jolla, Calif. (plane crash). Screen actor.

Appeared in: **1966** How to Stuff a Wild Bikini; Dr. Goldfoot and the Bikini Machine.

BENTLEY, ALICE
Born: 1892, Scranton, Pa. Died: Sept. 3, 1956, Long Island, N.Y. (stroke). Screen and stage actress. Mother of actor Spencer Bentley.

Appeared in: **1916** Gloria's Romance.

BENTLEY, GRENDON
Born: Apr. 8, 1877, Bromyard, England. Died: Apr. 27, 1956, England? Screen and stage actor.

Appeared in: **1913** Hamlet.

BENTLEY, IRENE (Alexina Bentley)
Born: Nov. 12, 1904, New York, N.Y. Died: Nov., 1965, Palm Beach, Fla. (heart attack). Screen actress. Divorced from Kenneth Niemann (dec.); stockbroker George S. Kent (dec.) and actor Richard C. Hemingway (dec.). Do not confuse with musical comedy actress (dec. 1940).

Appeared in: **1933** My Weakness. **1934** Smoky; Frontier Marshall. **1935** Folies Bergere.

BENTLEY, ROBERT
Born: 1895. Died: Apr. 19, 1958, Benton Harbor, Mich. Screen, stage and radio actor.

Appeared in: **1921** The Power Within. **1923** None So Blind. **1924** The New School Teacher.

BENTON, BESSIE
Died: Jan., 1917, Los Angeles, Calif. Screen actress.

BENTON, CURTIS (Horatio Curtis Benton)
Born: Aug. 26, 1880, Toledo, Ohio. Died: Sept. 13, 1938, Van Nuys, Calif. (cerebral hemorrage). Screen, stage actor, screenwriter and author.

Appeared in: **1915** The Pursuit Eternal; Conscience. **1916** Twenty Thousand Leagues Under the Sea; Jealousy. **1917** The Siren. **1932** Fireman Save My Child.

BENTON, STEVE
Born: 1897. Died: Aug. 4, 1976, Hollywood, Calif. (heart failure). Screen actor and stuntman.

Appeared in: **1955** Picnic. **1956** You Can't Run Away From It.

BEN-YOSSEF, AVRAHAM
Born: 1907, Besarabia, Rumania. Died: Dec. 1, 1980, Tel Aviv, Israel. Screen and stage actor. Brother of actor Nathan Kogan.

BERANGER, GEORGE (George Andre de Beranger)
Born: Mar. 27, 1895, Sydney, Australia. Died: 1973. Screen, stage actor and film director.

Appeared in: **1915** Birth of a Nation; The Stab. **1916** The Half-Breed; Flirting With Fate; Pillars of Society; Manhattan Madness; The Good-Bad Man; Should She Have Told?; In the Dead O'Night; Mixed Blood. **1917** Those Without Sin. **1918** Sandy; A Bum Bomb. **1923** The Leopardess; Dulcy; The Bright Shawl; The Extra Girl; Ashes of Vengeance; Tiger Rose; The Man Life Passed By. **1924** Beau Brummel. **1925** Grounds for Divorce; Beauty and the Bad Man; Are Parents People?; A Woman's Faith; The Man in Blue; Confessions of a Queen. **1926** The Grand Duchess and the Waiter; So This Is Paris; The Bat; Miss Brewster's Millions; The Popular Sin; The Eagle of the Sea; Fig Leaves; The Lady of the Harem. **1927** Altars of Desire; Paradise for Two; If I Were Single; The Small Bachelor. **1928** Powder My Back; Beware of Bachelors; Five and Ten-Cent Annie. **1929** Stark Mad; Strange Cargo; The Glad Rag Doll. **1930** Lillies of the Field; The Boudoir Diplomat. **1931** Annabelle's Affair; Surrender; Ladies of the Jury. **1933** Mama Loves Papa. **1934** Young and Beautiful; Kiss and Make Up. **1935** Dangerous; The Pay-Off. **1936** The Story of Louis Pasture; Snowed Under; Love Before Breakfast; The Noise; Walking on Air; Down the Stretch; Colleen; Hot Money; King of Hockey. **1937** Cafe Metropole; Wake Up and Live; I'll Take Romance; Hollywood Round-Up; Gilding the Lily (short). **1939** Beauty for the Asking. **1940** He Stayed for Breakfast. **1941** Our Wife; She Knows All the Answers. **1942** Over My Dead Body. **1945** Saratoga Trunk. **1947** Nightmare Alley. **1948** Unfaithfully Yours; Road House. **1949** Dancing in the Dark.

BERANGERE, MME.
Born: France. Died: Nov., 1928, Paris, France. Screen actress.

BEREGI, OSCAR, JR.
Born: 1918, Hungary. Died: Nov. 1, 1976, Los Angeles, Calif. (heart attack). Screen and television actor. Son of actor Oscar Beregi, Sr. (dec. 1965).

Appeared in: **1953** Call Me Madam; Desert Legion; Tonight We Sing. **1960** Oscar Wilde. **1961** The Fiercest Heart; Operation Eichmann. **1963** Police Nurse. **1964** The Incredible Mr. Limpet; My Fair Lady. **1965** 36 Hours; Morituri (aka The Saboteur: Code Name—Morituri); Ship of Fools. **1968** Panic in the City. **1970** The Great White Hope; The Christine Jorgenson Story. **1972** Everything You Always Wanted to Know About Sex. **1974** Young Frankenstein; The Testament of Dr. Mabuse.

BEREGI, OSCAR, SR.
Born: 1875, Hungary. Died: Oct. 18, 1965, Hollywood, Calif. Hungarian screen and stage actor. Father of actor Oscar Beregi, Jr. (dec. 1976).

Appeared in: **1926** Butterflies in the Rain; The Love Thief; The Flaming Forest. **1927** Camille; Moon of Israel. **1933** A Key Balvany (A Blue Idol). **1934** Iza Neni; Rakoczi Indulo.

BERENDT, RACHEL (Monique Arkell)
Born: Paris, France. Died: Jan. 19, 1957, Paris, France. Screen actress. Divorced from actor Pierre Fresnay (dec. 1975).

Appeared in: **1932** Paris—Beguin.

BERENSON, ABE
Born: Oct. 20, 1909, New Orleans, La. Died: Dec. 7, 1977, New Orleans, La. Screen actor, theater owner, exhibitor and attorney.

Appeared in: **1950** Panic in the Streets.

BERESFORD, HARRY
Born: Nov. 4, 1864, London, England. Died: Oct. 4, 1944, Los Angeles, Calif. Screen, stage actor, screenwriter and novelist.

Appeared in: **1926** The Quarterback. **1931** Charlie Chan Carries On; Sob Sister; Heaven on Earth; Sooky; Finn and Hattie; Scandal Sheet; Up Pops the Devil; The Secret Call. **1932** Ambition; High Pressure; Scandal for Sale; So Big; Strange Love of Molly Louvain; Prosperity; Dr. X; The Match King; Dance Team; Forgotten Commandments; The Sign of the Cross. **1933** Little Women; Lady Killer; Murders in the Zoo; The Mind Reader; I Cover the Waterfront; Dinner at Eight; Night Flight; Bureau of Missing Persons; Ever in My Heart; College Coach. **1934** Friends of Mr. Sweeney; Cleopatra; The Little Minister; Fashions of 1934; The Merry Frinks. **1935** Seven Keys to Baldpate; Anna Karenina; David Copperfield; A Dog of Flanders; I'll Love You Always; Page Miss Glory; I Found Stella Parrish. **1936** Klondike Annie; Follow the Fleet; Grand Jury; Postal Inspector; In His Steps. **1937** The Prince and the Pauper; The Go-Getter; She's No Lady; She Asked For It; They Won't Forget. **1939** Newsboys' Home. **1944** The Sign of the Cross (revised version of 1932 film).

BERG, GERTRUDE (Gertrude Edelstein)
Born: Oct. 3, 1900, New York, N.Y. Died: Sept. 14, 1966, N.Y. (heart ailment). Screen, stage, television, radio actress, author and screenwriter.

Appeared in: **1951** Molly. **1953** Main Street to Broadway.

BERG, STINA
Born: 1869, Sweden. Died: 1930, Sweden. Screen actress.

Appeared in: The Tyrannical Fiance; On the Fateful Roads of Life; The Modern Suffragette; People of the Border; Halfbreed; The Birthday Present; King Solomon's Judgement; The Way to the Man's Heart; The Chamberlain; Children of the Street; Expiated Guilt; The Playmates; Revenge Is Sweet; Keep to Your Trade; The Consequences of Jealousy; His Wedding Night; Her Royal Highness; The Lucky Brooch; Love and Journalism; The Million Inheritance; Sir Arne's Treasure (1919); Erotikon; Mrs. Anderson's Charlie; Gunnar Hede's Saga; The Norrtull Gang; Constable Paulus's Easter Bomb; Her Little Majesty; Two Kings; Ebberod's Bank; The Gyurkovics Girls; The Queen of Pellagonia; His English Wife; Sealed Lips; Sin (1928); Jansson's Temptation; Say It With Music; People of Norrland; For Her Sake; Gentlemen in Uniform; Charlotte Lowenskold; Motley Leaves; 33.333.

BERGEN, EDGAR (Edgar John Berggren)
Born: Feb. 16, 1903, Chicago, Ill. Died: Sept. 30, 1978, Las Vegas, Nev. (heart attack). Ventriloquist, screen, stage, radio, television actor, screenwriter and nightclub entertainer. Married to model Frances

Westerman. Father of actress Candice Bergen. Won 1937 Special Academy Award.

Appeared in: **1930** The Office Scandal (short); The Operation (short). **1931** The Eyes Have It (short); Donkey Business (short). **1933** Africa Speaks English (short). **1937** Double Talk (short). **1938** Letter of Introduction; The Goldwyn Follies. **1939** Charlie McCarthy, Detective; You Can't Cheat an Honest Man. **1941** Look Who's Laughing. **1942** Here We Go Again. **1943** Stage Door Canteen. **1944** Song of the Open Road. **1947** Fun and Fancy Free. **1948** I Remember Mama. **1950** Charlie McCarthy and Mortimer Snerd in Sweden (short); Captain China. **1965** One Way Wahine. **1967** Don't Make Waves. **1970** The Phynx.

BERGER, GUSTAV
Born: 1910. Died: Oct. 18, 1958, New York, N.Y. Screen and stage actor. Married to actress Fania Rubina.

Appeared in: **1939** My Son. **1950** God, Man and the Devil.

BERGER, NICOLE
Born: 1934, France. Died: Apr. 9, 1967, Rougen, France (following auto accident). Screen, stage and television actress.

Appeared in: **1955** The Game of Love. **1956** Bold Adventure. **1957** Julietta. **1958** He Who Must Die; Premier Mai (The First Day of May). **1959** Filles de la Nuit (Girls of the Night). **1960** The Siege of Sidney Street (US 1961); The Chasers (aka Les Dragueurs (The Dredgers)). **1962** La Denounciation (The Denunciation—aka The Immoral Moment—US 1967); Love Is My Profession; Shoot the Piano Player. **1963** The Girl from Flanders; Char de Poule (aka Highway Pick Up—US 1965). **1968** La Permission (aka The Story of a Three Day Pass—US).

BERGERE, DOROTHY
Born: 1898. Died: July 12, 1979, Harrison, N.J. Screen and stage actress.

Appeared in: **1919** Daddy Long Legs.

BERGERE, RAMONA
Born: 1902. Died: Apr. 26, 1941, Glendale, Calif. Screen actress.

BERGERE, VALERIE
Born: Feb. 2, 1875, Alsace-Lorraine, France. Died: Sept. 16, 1938, Hollywood, Calif. Screen, stage and vaudeville actress.

Appeared in: **1937** The Singing Marine; It's Love I'm After.

BERGMAN, HENRI
Born: 1859. Died: Jan. 9, 1917, New York, N.Y. Screen and stage actor. Do not confuse with actor Henry Bergman (dec. 1946).

Appeared in: **1915** The House of Tears. **1916** Kiss of Hate; In the Diplomatic Service.

BERGMAN, HENRY
Born: 1870, San Francisco, Calif. Died: Oct. 22, 1946, Hollywood, Calif. (heart attack). Screen actor, circus and opera performer, screenwriter and assistant film director. Entered films with Pathe-Lehrman in 1913.

Appeared in: **1915** His New Job; A Night Out; The Champion; In the Park; The Jitney Elopement; The Tramp; By the Sea; Work; A Woman; The Bank; Shanghaied; A Night in the Show. **1916** Carmen; Police; Triple Trouble; The Floorwalker; The Fireman; The Vagabond; One A.M.; The Count; The Pawnshop; Behind the Screen; The Rink. **1917** Easy Street; The Cure; The Immigrant; The Adventurer. **1918** A Dog's Life; The Bond; Shoulder Arms. **1919** Synnyside; A Day's Pleasure. **1920** The Idle Class. **1921** The Kid. **1922** Pay Day; The Pilgrim. **1923** A Woman of Paris. **1925** The Gold Rush. **1928** The Circus. **1931** City Lights. **1936** Modern Times. **1940** The Great Dictator.

BERGMAN, TEDDY *See* REED, ALAN

BERGULAND, CHRIS
Born: 1926. Died: Feb. 23, 1958, Chicago, Ill. Screen actor.

BERISTAIN, LEOPOLDO
Born: 1883, Mexico. Died: Jan. 5, 1948, Tijuana, Mexico (diabetes). Screen actor.

Appeared in: **1939** Mexico Lindo.

BERISTAIN, LUIS
Born: 1918, Mexico. Died: Apr. 1, 1962, Mexico City, Mexico (heart attack). Screen and television actor.

Appeared in: **1955** This Strange Passion. **1962** El Angel Exterminador (The Exterminating Angel—US 1967).

BERK, SARA
Born: 1898. Died: Apr. 21, 1975, New York, N.Y. (heart attack). Screen actress.

Appeared in: **1962** Light Fantastic.

BERKELEY, ARTHUR
Born: 1896. Died: July 29, 1962, Hollywood, Calif. Screen actor.

Appeared in: **1957** Teenage Monster.

BERKELEY, BUSBY (William Berkeley Enos, Jr.)
Born: Nov. 29, 1895, Los Angeles, Calif. Died: Mar. 14, 1976, Palm Springs, Calif. Screen, stage actor, film producer and director, stage producer and director. Son of actress Gertrude Berkeley (dec. 1946) and film director William Berkeley Enos, Sr. (dec.). Divorced from actress Esther Muir, Myra Steffens, Marge Pemberto, actress Merna Kennedy (dec. 1944), actress Claire James, and later married to Etta Judd.

Appeared in: **1935** A Trip Through a Hollywood Studio (short). **1970** The Phynx.

BERKELEY, GERTRUDE
Born: 1865. Died: June 15, 1946, Hollywood, Calif. Screen and stage actress. Mother of film producer/actor Busby Berkeley (dec. 1976). Married to film director William Berkeley Enos, Sr. (dec.).

Appeared in: **1916** War Brides. **1918** Song of Songs; Just Sylvia. **1919** The Way of a Woman; Break the News to Mother. **1921** Suspicious Wives.

BERKELEY, REGINALD
Born: Aug. 18, 1890, London, England. Died: Mar. 30, 1936, Hollywood, Calif. Screen actor, screenwriter and author.

BERKES, JOHN PATRICK "JOHNNY"
Born: 1897. Died: July 5, 1951, Hollywood, Calif. Screen and stage actor.

Appeared in: **1936** Calling All Tars (short). **1941** Dr. Kildare's Wedding Day; Shadow of the Thin Man; Corsican Brothers. **1942** Madame Spy; Arabian Nights; Woman of the Year. **1944** Lost in a Harem; Christmans Holiday; Shine On Harvest Moon. **1945** Honeymoon Ahead; Our Vines Have Tender Grapes; A Tree Grows in Brooklyn. **1946** The Killers; Blonde Alibi; A Night in Paradise. **1947** The Corpse Came C.O.D.; The Egg and I. **1948** Station West; Romance on the High Seas. **1949** My Dream Is Yours. **1950** Branded. **1951** Journey Into Light; The Big Carnival.

BERLE, SANDRA (Sarah Glanz)
Born: 1877, New York, N.Y. Died: May 31, 1954, New York, N.Y. (cerebral hemorrhage). Screen and television actress. An occasional extra at Biograph Studios in youth. Mother of actor Milton Berle and often in his various acts, and mother of performer Rosalind Berle (dec. 1977).

BERLEY, ANDRE
Born: France. Died: Nov. 27, 1936, France? Screen actor.

Appeared in: **1929** The Passion of Joan of Arc. **1930** Big House; Le Petit Cafe; Si L'Empereur Savait Ca. **1931** Buster Se Marie (aka Parlor, Bedroom and Bath—US). **1932** Tu Seras Duchesse. **1934** The Merry Widow. **1935** Avec L'Assurance.

BERLINER, MARTIN
Born: 1896, Germany. Died: Jan. 26, 1966, Berlin, Germany (heart attack). Screen, stage and television actor.

Appeared in: **1962** The Counterfeit Traitor. **1963** Die Dreigroschenoper (Three Penny Opera).

BERN, PAUL (Paul Levy)
Born: 1889, Wandabeck, Germany. Died: Sept. 4, 1932, Beverly Hills, Calif. (suicide—gun). Screen, stage actor, film producer, film director and screenwriter. Married to actress Jean Harlow (dec. 1937).

BERNARD, ADOLPH See REINOLD, BERNARD

BERNARD, AL
Born: 1888. Died: Mar. 6, 1949, New York, N.Y. Screen, television, radio, vaudeville, minstrel actor, singer, author and songwriter.

BERNARD, BARNEY
Born: Aug. 17, 1877, Rochester, N.Y. Died: Mar. 21, 1924, New York, N.Y. (bronchial pneumonia). Screen, stage and vaudeville actor. He and Alexander Carr (dec. 1946) created the roles of Potash and Perlmutter on stage.

They appeared in: **1923** Potash and Perlmutter.

BERNARD, DOROTHY
Born: 1890. Died: Dec. 14, 1955, Hollywood, Calif. (heart attack). Screen and stage actress. Married to actor A. H. Van Buren (dec. 1965).

Appeared in: **1909** The Cricket on the Hearth; "Jonesy" series. **1910** Fate's Turning. **1911** The Failure; Sunshine Through the Dark; A Tale of the Wilderness; A Sister's Love; A Blot on the 'Scutcheon; The Root of Evil. **1912** The Girl and Her Trust; The Female of the Species; A Siren of Impulse; The Goddess of Sagebrush Gulch; His Lesson; Heaven Avenges. **1916** A Man of Sorrow. **1918** Little Women; Les Miserables. **1921** The Wild Goose. **1946** Kitty.

BERNARD, HARRY
Born: 1870. Died: Mar. 25, 1929, New York, N.Y. ("complication of diseases"). Screen, stage and vaudeville actor. Brother of actors Sam (dec.1950), and Richard (dec. 1925), and stage actor Louis Bernard. Do not confuse with screen actor Harry Bernard (dec. 1940).

BERNARD, HARRY
Born: Jan. 13, 1878, San Francisco, Calif. Died: Nov. 4, 1940, Hollywood, Calif. (cancer). Screen and vaudeville actor. Appeared in Keystone films in 1915. Do not confuse with actor dec. 1929.

Appeared in: **1915** Crossed Love and Swords; Dirty Work in a Laundry; The Battle of Ambrose and Walrus; Our Daredevil Chief. **1928** Two Tars (short). **1929** The following shorts: Berth Marks; Liberty; Wedding Again; That's My Wife; Men O'War; A Perfect Day. **1930** The following shorts: Night Owls; Blotto; Another Fine Mess. **1931** The following shorts: Laughing Gravy; Bargain Days; Shiver My Timbers; Dogs Is Dogs; The Pip from Pittsburgh; Rough Seas; One of the Smiths; The Panic Is On; Skip the Maloo!; The Hasty Marriage; High Gear; Call a Cop; Mama Loves Papa; The Kickoff. **1932** The following shorts: Any Old Port; Readin' and Writin'; Free Eats; Choo Choo; A Lad an' a Lamp; Pooch; In Walked Charley; Young Ironsides; Mr. Bride; Love Pains; The Knock-Out; Too Many Women; Sneak Easily. **1933** The following shorts: Maids a la Mode; The Bargain of the Century; Forgotten Babies; Kid from Borneo; Bedtime Worries; The Midnight Patrol; Fallen Arches; The Silent Racket; Sherman Said It; Luncheon at Twelve. **1934** Sons of the Desert; plus the following shorts: Three Chumps Ahead; The Live Ghost; Hi Neighbor; The Cracked Iceman; Another Wild Idea; Something Simple; You Said a Hatefull; The Chases of Pimple Street. **1935** Ruggles of Red Gap; plus the following shorts: Top Flat; Sprucin' Up; Okay Toots!; Poker at Eight; Southern Exposure; Manhattan Monkey Business. **1936** Swing Time; The Bohemian Girl; Our Relations; plus the following shorts: On the Wrong Trek; Life Hesitates at 40; Neighborhood House. **1937** Way Out West; New Faces of 1937. **1938** Trade Winds. **1939** Rattling Romeo (short). **1940** Saps at Sea. **1941** They Meet Again; That Hamilton Woman. **1942** The Mad Doctor of Market Street; Captains of the Clouds.

BERNARD, LOIS
Born: 1898. Died: Apr. 25, 1945, Los Angeles, Calif. (suicide—jumped from building). Screen actress. Married to actor Joseph Bernard.

BERNARD, PAUL
Born: France. Died: May, 1958, Paris, France. Stage and screen actor.

Appeared in: **1936** Pension Mimosas. **1947** Panic. **1948** Les Maudits (The Damned); Un Ami Viendra Ce Soir (A Friend Will Come Tonight). **1954** Caroline Cherie. **1956** Les Dames du Bois du Boulogne (Women of the Bois du Boulogne).

BERNARD, PETER
Born: 1888, U.S. Died: Dec. 22, 1960, Huddersfield, England. Screen, vaudeville actor, vocalist and songwriter.

BERNARD, RICHARD "DICK"
Born: 1865. Died: Dec. 25, 1925, New York, N.Y. Screen, stage and vaudeville actor. For family information see Harry Bernard (dec. 1929) listing.

Appeared in: **1926** Bluebeard's Seven Wives.

BERNARD, SAM
Born: 1889. Died: July 5, 1950, Hollywood, Calif. Screen and stage actor. Brother of Louis and actors Harry (dec. 1929) and Richard "Dick" Bernard (dec. 1925).

Appeared in: **1931** Wanted By the Police; Prison Train. **1941** Tumbledown Ranch in Arizona. **1942** Let's Get Tough; Today I Hang; Smart Alecks; Baby Face Morgan; Ice Capades Revue. **1943** The Crime Smashers. **1945** Thoroughbreds. **1948** The Vicious Circle; When My Baby Smiles at Me. **1940** The Big Sombrero.

BERNARD, SAM (aka SAMUEL BARNET)

Born: 1863, Birmingham, England. Died: May 16, 1927, on board ship in the Atlantic (apoplexy). Screen, stage and vaudeville actor. Entered films with Triangle Film Corp. in 1915. Appeared in vaudeville under name of Samuel Barnet.

Appeared in: **1915** Fatty and the Broadway Stars. **1916** Because He Loved Her; The Great Pearl Tangle.

BERNARDI, NERIO

Born: 1899. Died: Jan. 12, 1971. Screen actor.

Appeared in: **1922** Nero. **1923** The Shepherd King. **1935** Il Delitto di Mastrovanni. **1936** Tempo Massimo; Fiat Voluntas Dei. **1937** Loyalty of Love. **1938** Adventura di Giacomo Casanova. **1939** Il Corsaro Nero (The Black Corsair). **1948** La Traviata (The Lost One). **1950** Heart and Soul. **1952** Never Take No for an Answer; I Cadetti di Guascogna. **1953** Fanfan the Tulip; The Young Caruso. **1954** Theodora, Slave Empress. **1959** Ballerina e Buon Dio (aka Ballerina and the Good God and Angel in a Taxi—US 1963). **1960** La Donna dei Faraoini (The Pharaoh's Woman—US 1961); Les Nuits de Raspoutine (The Night They Killed Rasputin—US 1962); Le Passage du Rhin (Tomorrow Is My Turn—US 1962); Prisoner of the Volga. **1961** La Guerra di Trois (aka The Trojan Horse—US 1962); Tesco Contro il Minotauro (aka The Minotaur—The Wild Beast of Crete and The Minotaur—US); Liane Die Weisse Sklavin (Nature Girl and the Slaver and The White Slave). **1962** La Leggenda di Enea (The Avenger—US 1964); Col Ferro e Col Fuoco (aka Daggers of Blood and Invasion 1700—US 1965). **1963** Giulio Caesare il Conquistatore delle Gallie (aka Caeser the Conqueror—US). **1964** Ercole Contro Molock (Conquest of Mycene—US 1965). **1966** Se Tutte le Donne del Mondo (Kiss the Girls and Make Them Die—US 1967).

BERNES, MARK

Born: 1912, Russia. Died: Aug. 25, 1969, Moscow, Russia. Screen, television actor and singer.

Appeared in: **1943** Diary of a Nazi. **1944** Two Soldiers. **1945** The Ural Front. **1946** The Turning Point. **1952** Taras Shevchenko. **1953** Maxima. **1955** The Boys from Leningrad; The Frigid Sea. **1957** School of Courage. **1965** Zvonyat Otkrdyte Dver (aka The Girl and the Burglar—US 1967).

BERNHARDT, RUSS

Born: 1925. Died: Oct. 9, 1978, San Jose, Calif. (heart attack). Screen, stage, radio, television actor, writer and press agent. Married to actress Clarisa Bernhardt.

BERNHARDT, SARAH (Rosalie Bernard)

Born: Oct. 22, 1844, Paris, France. Died: Mar. 26, 1923, Paris, France (uremic poisoning and weak heart). Screen, stage and vaudeville actress.

Appeared in: **1900** Hamlet (title role). **1910** La Dame aux Camelias (Camille—US 1912); Queen Elizabeth. **1915** Sarah Bernhardt at Home; Jeanne Dore. **1917** Mothers of France. **1931** Stars of Yesterday (short—film clips). **1950** Paris, 1900 (documentary).

BERNIE, BEN (Benjamin Anzelvitz)

Born: 1891, Bayonne, N.J. Died: Oct. 20, 1943, Hollywood, Calif. Screen, vaudeville, radio actor and bandleader. Appeared in vaudeville with Phil Baker (dec. 1963) as part of "Bernie and Baker" team.

Appeared in: **1930** Ben Bernie and His Orchestra (short). **1934** Shoot the Works. **1935** Stolen Harmony. **1937** Wake Up and Live; Love and Hisses.

BERNIVICI, COUNT (aka COUNT BERNAVICI aka COUNT BERNI VICI)

Born: 1884. Died: July 12, 1966, Hollywood, Calif. Screen and vaudeville actor.

BERNOUDY, JANE

Born: Aug. 19, 1893, New Castle, Colo. Died: Oct. 28, 1972, Canoga Park, Calif. Screen actress. Appeared in early Bisen Co. films.

Appeared in: **1917** Who Said Chicken?

BERNSTEIN, ISADORE

Born: Nov., 1877, New York, N.Y. Died: Oct. 18, 1944. Screen actor, screenwriter and writer.

Appeared in: **1914** The Great Universal Mystery.

BERRELL, GEORGE (aka GEORGE BURRELL)

Born: 1849, Philadelphia, Pa. Died: Apr. 20, 1933. Screen and stage actor.

Appeared in: **1916** The People vs. John Doe. **1917** The Girl in the Garret; Swede Hearts; Double Suspicion; The Lair of the Wolf. **1920** The City of Masks. **1921** The Fire Eater; The Girl from God's Country; The Barbarian. **1922** Tracks. **1923** The Grub Stake; Crimson Gold. **1925** The Everlasting Whisper; The Trail Rider. **1926** The Sea Beast. **1927** Black Jack.

BERRY, ALINE

Born: 1905. Died: Apr. 3, 1967, Hollywood, Calif. (heart attack). Screen, stage and radio actress.

Appeared in: **1925** Soul Fire.

BERRY, ARTHUR NELSON

Born: 1887. Died: June 12, 1945, Hollywood, Calif. Screen and vaudeville actor. Married to actress Elizabeth Berry with whom he appeared in vaudeville.

BERRY, JAMES

Born: May 11,1883, Manchester, England. Died: Aug. 1, 1915, England? Screen and stage actor. Do not confuse with U.S. actor James J. Berry (dec. 1969).

Appeared in: **1911** Richard III.

BERRY, JAMES J.

Born: 1914. Died: Jan. 28, 1969, New York, N.Y. Screen actor.

Appeared in: **1941** Lady Be Good.

BERRY, JULES (Jules Peaufichet)

Born: 1883, France. Died: Apr. 25, 1951, Paris, France (heart ailment). Stage and screen actor.

Appeared in: **1929** Crossroads; Le Four Se Leve. **1940** Daybreak. **1942** Les Visiteurs du Soir. **1944** 32 Rue de Montmartre. **1947** Etoile Sans Lumiere (Star Without a Light); The Devil's Own Envoy; La Symphonie Fantastique. **1954** Dreams of Love. **1964** The Crime of Monsieur Lange.

BERRY, MADY

Born: 1887, France. Died: 1965, France? Screen actress.

Appeared in: **1932** Le Roi des Resquilleurs. **1935** Le Maternelle. **1937** Le Juif Polonais. **1938** Ballerina. **1940** Daybreak. **1941** Personal Column. **1945** Ces Dames aux Chapeaux Verts (The Ladies in the Green Hats). **1949** Twilight. **1950** Gates of the Night. **1960** The Ostrich Has Two Eggs.

BERRY, NYAS

Born: 1915. Died: Oct. 6, 1951. Screen actor and dancer. Brother of actor-dancer Walter Berry with whom he appeared in an act billed as "The Berry Brothers."

Appeared in: **1936** San Francisco. **1941** Lady Be Good. **1942** Panama Hattie. **1949** You're My Everything.

BERRY, WILLIAM HENRY

Born: Mar. 23, 1870, London, England. Died: May 2, 1951, London, England. Screen, stage and radio actor. Married to stage actress Kitty Hanson (dec. 1947) and later married to Agnes Lydon.

Appeared in: **1934** Mister Cinders. **1935** Royal Cavalcade (aka Regal Cavalcade—US). **1936** Once in a Million (aka Weekend Millionaire—US 1937).

BERTRAM, VEDAH (Adele Buck)

Born: Dec. 4, 1891, Boston, Mass. Died: Aug. 27, 1912, Oakland, Calif. (appendicitis). Screen actress. Entered films with Essanay in 1911.

Appeared in: **1912** Broncho Billy's Adventure; The Bandit's Child; A Road Agent's Love; Broncho Billy and the Bandits; Broncho Billy and the Indian Maid; A Moonshiner's Heart; On the Cactus Trail; The Smuggler's Daughter; Broncho Billy's Gratitude; The Desert Sweethearts; Broncho Billy's Pal; The Deputy's Love Affair; Western Hearts; Broncho Billy Outwitted.

BERTRAM, WILLIAM (Benjamin Switzer)

Born: Jan. 19, 1880, Walkerton, Ont., Canada. Died: May 1, 1933, Los Angeles, Calif. Screen, stage actor, film, stage director and screenwriter. Entered films in 1903 with Pathe.

Appeared in: **1922** The Long Chance. **1924** The Dramatic Life of

Abraham Lincoln; The Smoking Trail. **1925** Fangs of Fate. **1926** Twisted Triggers; Under Fire. **1927** The Swift Shadow; Wanted—A Coward. **1928** The Boss of Rustler's Room; Little Shepherd of Kingdom Come. **1930** Spurs. **1931** Trails of the Golden West; Lightnin' Smith's Return.

BERTRAND, MARY
Born: 1881. Died: May 12, 1955, Woodland Hills, Calif. Screen actress. Appeared in silents.

Appeared in: **1942** The Wife Takes a Flyer.

BESOZZI, NINO
Born: Italy. Died: Feb., 1971, Italy. Screen actor.

Appeared in: **1935** Il Serpente a Sonagli. **1936** Vivere (To Live). **1937** Tre Anni Senza Donna; Destino di Donna; Trenta Second d'Amore; I Due Misantropi; Nina Non Far La Stupida. **1938** Come le Foglie (Like the Leaves); Amore in Quarantena (Love in Quarantine); Duetta Vagabondo (Vagabond Duet); La Donna Bianca (The White Woman aka The Lady in White—US 1948). **1939** Eravamo Sette Sorelle (We Were Seven Sisters); Ho Perduto Mio Marito (I Have Lost My Husband). **1940** Amicizia (Friendship). **1948** Rossini. **1960** Holiday Island.

BESSENT, MARIE
Born: 1898. Died: Oct. 12, 1947, Los Angeles, Calif. Screen, stage and vaudeville actress. Double for actress Mabel Normand.

BESSERER, EUGENIE
Born: 1870. Died: May 30, 1934, Los Angeles, Calif. Screen and stage actress. Entered films in 1910.

Appeared in: **1912** The Millionaire Vagabond; The Count of Monte Cristo. **1913** The Governor's Daughter; Diverging Paths; Love Before Ten; The Spanish Parrott-Girl; Women—Past and Present; Phantoms. **1914** Memories. **1915** The Ingratitude of Liz Taylor. **1918** Little Orphan Annie. **1921** Molly O; The Sin of Martha Queed; The Light in the Clearing; The Breaking Point; Good Women; What Happened to Rosa? **1922** The Hands of Nara; June Madness; The Rosary; Penrod; The Stranger's Banquet. **1923** Anna Christie; Her Reputation; Enemies of Children; The Rendezvous; The Lonely Road. **1924** Bread; The Price She Paid. **1925** A Fool and His Money; Friendly Enemies; Bright Lights; The Circle; Confessions of a Queen; The Coast of Folly; Wandering Footsteps. **1926** The Millionaire Policeman; The Skyrocket. **1927** The Jazz Singer; When a Man Loves; Flesh and the Devil; The Fire Brigade; Captain Salvation; Slightly Used; Wandering Girls. **1928** The Yellow Lily; Two Lovers; Drums of Love; Lilac Time. **1929** Seven Faces; The Bridge of San Luis Rey; A Lady of Chance; Madame X; Fast Company; Illusion; Thunderbolt; Mister Antonio; Speedway; Whispering Winds. **1930** In Gay Madrid; A Royal Romance. **1933** To the Last Man.

BEST, DOLLY
Born: 1899. Died: Oct. 6, 1968, Los Angeles, Calif. Screen and stage actress. Appeared in silents.

BEST, EDNA (Edna Hove)
Born: Mar. 3, 1900, Hove, Sussex, England. Died: Sept. 18, 1974, Geneva, Switzerland. Screen, stage and television actress. Divorced from actors Seymour Beard and Herbert Marshall (dec. 1966) and later married to agent Nat Wolff (dec.). Mother of actress Sarah Best Marshall.

Appeared in: **1921** Tilly of Bloomsbury. **1923** A Couple of Down and Outs. **1930** Sleeping Partners; Loose Ends; Escape; Beyond the Cities. **1931** Michael and Mary (US 1932); The Calendar (aka Bachelor's Folly—US 1932). **1932** The Faithful Heart (aka Faithful Hearts—US 1933). **1934** The Key (aka High Peril); The Man Who Knew Too Much. **1938** South Riding; Prison Without Bars (US 1939). **1939** Intermezzo; A Love Story. **1940** The Swiss Family Robinson; A Dispatch from Reuters (aka This Man Reuter). **1947** The Ghost and Mrs. Muir; The Late George Apley. **1948** The Iron Curtain.

BEST, WILLIE (aka "SLEEP 'N EAT")
Born: May 27, 1916, Miss. Died: Feb. 27, 1962, Woodland Hills, Calif. (cancer). Black screen and television actor.

Appeared in: **1931** Up Pops the Devil. **1932** The Monster Walks. **1934** Little Miss Marker; Kentucky Kernels; several RKO shorts. **1935** West of the Pecos; Murder on a Honeymoon; The Nitwits; The Arizonian; Hot Tip; The Littlest Rebel. **1936** Murder on the Bridle Path; The Bride Walks Out; Mummu's Boys; Racing Lady; Make Way for a Lady; Thank You, Jeeves!; General Spanky; Two in Revolt; Down the Stretch. **1937** Meet the Misses; Breezing Home; The Lady Fights Back;

Super Sleuth; Saturday's Heroes. **1938** Vivacious Lady; Gold Is Where You Find It; Merrily We Live; Goodbye Broadway; Blondie; Youth Takes a Fling. **1939** Nancy Drew—Trouble Shooter; Mr. Moto Takes a Vacation; The Covered Trailer; At the Circus. **1940** Money and Women; Who Killed Aunt Maggie?; I Take This Woman; The Ghost Breakers. **1941** Road Show; High Sierra; The Lady from Cheyenne; Nothing But the Truth; Flight from Destiny; Scattergood Baines; Highway West; The Smiling Ghost. **1942** Juke Girl; Whispering Ghosts; Busses Road; The Hidden Hand; Scattergood Survives a Murder; The Body Disappears; A-Haunting We Will Go. **1943** Dixie; Cabin in the Sky; Thank Your Lucky Stars; The Kansan; Cinderella Swings It. **1944** Adventures of Mark Twain; Home in Indiana; The Girl Who Dared. **1945** The Monster of the Apes (serial); Hold That Blonde; The Red Dragon; Pillow to Post. **1946** The Bride Wore Boots; The Face of Marble; Dangerous Money. **1947** The Red Stallion; Suddenly It's Spring. **1948** The Smart Woman; Half Past Midnight; The Shanghai Chest. **1949** Jiggs and Maggie in Jackpot Jitters; The Hidden Hand. **1950** High and Dizzy (short). **1951** South of Caliente.

BETTAC, ULRICH
Born: 1898, Germany. Died: Apr., 1959, Germany? Screen and stage actor.

Appeared in: **1954** Ewiger Walzer (The Eternal Waltz—US 1959).

BETTS, JANE
Died: Apr. 24, 1976. Screen actress.

BETTS, WILLIAM E.
Born: 1856. Died: Apr. 6, 1929, New York, N.Y. (pneumonia and heart disease). Stage and screen actor.

Appeared in: **1924** A Sainted Devil.

BETZ, AUDREY
Died: May 21, 1974. Screen actress.

Appeared in: **1947** Monsieur Verdoux. **1965** The Outlaws is Coming.

BETZ, CARL
Born: Mar. 9, 1921, Pittsburgh, Pa. Died: Jan. 18, 1978, Los Angeles, Calif. (lung cancer). Screen, stage, radio and television actor.

Appeared in: **1953** The President's Lady; Powder River; Inferno; Vickie; Dangerous Crossing; City of Bad Men. **1966** Spinout. **1975** The Meal.

BETZ, MATTHEW (Matthew Von Betz)
Born: 1881, St. Louis, Mo. Died: Jan. 26, 1938, Los Angeles, Calif. Screen, stage and vaudeville actor.

Appeared in: **1915** The Parson of Pine Mountain. **1917** A Social Climber; An Actress's Romance; The Evil Sag; The Love of Princess Olga. **1921** Salvation Nell; Burn 'Em Up Barnes; The Single Track. **1922** My Old Kentucky Home; Boomerang Bill. **1923** The Self-Made Wife; Let's Go; Sawdust; Luck. **1924** Those Who Dance; The Heart Bandit; Love's Whirlpool; The Only Woman; The Siren of Seville. **1925** The Way of a Girl; The Lighthouse By the Sea; My Lady's Lips; The White Desert; The Unholy Three; Lights of Old Broadway; White Fang. **1926** The Flame of the Yukon; The Exquisite Sinner; Oh, What a Nurse!; The Little Irish Girl; Shipwrecked. **1927** The Patent Leather Kid; Broadway After Midnight. **1928** The Wedding March; Sins of the Fathers; The Big City; Shepherd of the Hills; The Terror; The Crimson City; Telling the World. **1929** Girls Gone Wild; Fugitives; The Girl in the Glass Case. **1930** The Big House; Shooting Straight; The Squealer; See America Thirst; Her Man. **1931** Salvation Nell (and 1921 version); Side Show. **1932** The Hurricane Express (serial); The Big Flash (short); The Fighting Marshal; Alias Mary Smith; Dynamite Denny; From Broadway to Cheyenne; Speed Madness; Gold. **1933** Tarzan the Fearless (serial); Knight Dry (short); Western Code; Via Pony Express; The Big Chance; Silent Men; Under Secret Orders; State Trooper; The Whirlwind; I Have Lived. **1934** Fighting Rookie; Circus Hoodoo (short); The Woman Who Dared; Countess of Monte Cristo; The House of Rothschild. **1935** Men of the Night; Mississippi; On Probation; Let 'Em Have It; The Tin Man (short); Reckless Roads; Mutiny Ahead; The Girl Who Came Back. **1936** The Black Coin (serial); Just My Luck; The Last Assignment; Racing Blood; Florida Special. **1937** Jail Bait (short); Outcast. **1938** Fury Below.

BEVAN, BILLY (William Bevan Harris)
Born: Sept. 29, 1897, Orange, Australia. Died: Nov. 26, 1957, Escondido, Calif. Screen, stage actor and opera singer.

Appeared in the following shorts, unless otherwise noted: **1920** Let 'Er Go; The Quack Doctor; It's a Boy; My Goodness; Love, Honor and Behave (feature); A Fireside Brewer. **1921** A Small Town Idol (feature); Be Reasonable; By Heck; Astray from the Steerage. **1922** Duck Hunter; On Patrol; Oh, Daddy; Gymnasium Jim; Ma and Pa; When Summer Comes; The Crossroads of New York. **1923** Nip and Tuck; Sinbad the Sailor; The Extra Girl. **1924** One Spooky Night; Wall Street Blues; Lizzies of the Field; Wandering Waistlines; The Cannon Ball Express; The White Sin. **1925** Honeymoon Hardships; Giddap; The Lion's Whiskers; Butter Fingers; Skinners in Silk; Super-Hooper-Dyne Lizzies; Sneezing Beezers; The Iron Nag; Over There-Abouts; From Rags to Britches. **1926** Whispering Whiskers; Trimmed in Gold; Circus Today; Wandering Willies; Hayfoot, Strawfoot; Fight Night; Muscle Bound Music; Ice Cold Cocos; A Sea Dog's Tale; Hubby's Quiet Little Game; Masked Mamas; Hoboken to Hollywood; The Divorce Dodger; Flirty Four-Flushers. **1927** Should Sleepwalkers Marry?; Peaches and Plumbers; A Small Town Princess; The Bull Fighter; Cured in the Excitement; The Golf Nut; Gold Digger of Weepah; Easy Pickings. **1928** The Beach Club; The Best Man; The Bicycle Flirt; His Unlucky Night; Caught in the Kitchen ("Tired Businessman's" series); Motorboat Mamas; Motoring Mamas; Hubby's Latest Alibi; Hubby's Weekend Trip; The Lion's Roar; His New Steno; Riley the Cop. **1929** Calling Hubby's Bluff; Button My Back; Foolish Husbands; Pink Pajamas; Don't Get Jealous. The following are features unless so noted: **1929** High Voltage; Sky Hawk. **1930** Scotch (short); Journey's End; For the Love O' Lil; Temptation; Peacock Alley. **1931** Transatlantic. **1932** Sky Devils; Spot on the Rug; Honeymoon Beach; The Silent Witness; Vanity Fair; Payment Deferred; Honeymoon Beach (short). **1933** Alice in Wonderland; Big Squeal (short); Looking Forward; Midnight Club; Too Much Harmony; A Study in Scarlet; Cavalcade; Luxury Liner; Peg O' My Heart; The Way to Love. **1934** The Lost Patrol; Shock; Caravan; Limehouse Blues. **1935** Mystery Woman; Black Sheep; The Last Outpost; A Tale of Two Cities; The Song and Dance Man; Lloyds of London; Private Number; Dracula's Daughter; Piccadilly Jim; God's Country and the Woman. **1937** Slave Ship; Another Dawn; The Sheik Steps Out; The Wrong Road. **1938** The Young in Heart; Bringing Up Baby; The Mysterious Mr. Moto; Girl of the Golden West; Shadows Over Shanghai. **1939** Pack Up Your Troubles; Captain Fury; Let Freedom Ring; Grand Jury Secrets; We Are Not Alone. **1940** Earl of Chicago; The Long Voyage Home; Tin Pan Alley. **1941** Suspicion; Shining Victory; Dr. Jekyll and Mr. Hyde; Confirm or Deny. **1942** I Married a Witch; Mrs. Miniver; The Man Who Wouldn't Die; London Blackout Murders; Counter Espionage. **1943** Forever and a Day; The Return of the Vampire; Young and Willing. **1944** The Lodger; National Velvet; The Invisible Man's Revenge; South of Dixie. **1945** The Picture of Dorian Gray; Tonight and Every Night. **1946** Cluny Brown; Devotion; Terror By Night. **1947** Moss Rose; It Had to Be You; Swordsman. **1948** The Black Arrow; Let's Live a Little. **1949** The Secret of St. Ives; The Secret Garden. **1950** Rogues of Sherwood Forest; Fortunes of Captain Blood. **1960** When Comedy Was King (documentary). **1963** Thirty Years of Fun (documentary).

BEVANI, ALEXANDER
Born: 1863. Died: Feb. 24, 1938, Los Angeles, Calif. Screen, vaudeville actor and opera singer.

Appeared in: **1925** The Phantom of the Opera.

BEVANS, CLEM
Born: 1880, Cozaddle, Ohio. Died: Aug. 11, 1963, Woodland Hills, Calif. Screen, stage, television and vaudeville actor.

Appeared in: **1935** Way Down East (film debut). **1936** Rhythm on the Range. **1937** Riding on Air; Big City; Idol of the Crowds. **1938** Boy Meets Girl; Miracle Money (short); Of Human Hearts; Young Fugitives; Comet Over Broadway; Tom Sawyer, Detective; Hold That Coed. **1939** The Oklahoma Kid; Dodge City; Help Wanted (short); Ambush; Zenobia; Hell's Kitchen; Night Work; Thunder Afloat; Main Street Lawyer; The Cowboy Quarterback. **1940** Abe Lincoln in Illinois; Go West; Young Tom Edison; 20 Mule Team; Half a Sinner; The Captain Is a Lady; Untamed; Girl from God's Country; Calling All Husbands; Granny Get Your Gun. **1941** Sergeant York; She Couldn't Say No; Midnight Angel; The Parson of Panamint; The Smiling Ghost. **1942** Tombstone, the Town Too Tough to Die; The Forest Rangers; Captains of the Clouds; Mrs. Wiggs of the Cabbage Patch; Saboteur. **1943** The Human Comedy; The Kansan; Lady Bodyguard; Happy Go Lucky; The Woman of the Town. **1944** Night Club Girl. **1945** Grissly's Millions; Captain Eddie. **1946** Wake Up and Dream; Gallant Bess; The Yearling. **1947** The Yankee Fakir; The Millerson Case; Mourning Becomes Electra. **1948** Texas, Brooklyn and Heaven; Highway 13; Portrait of Jenny; The Paleface; The Relentless. **1949** Loaded Pistols; Big Jack; Streets of Laredo; Rim of the Canyon; The Gal Who Took the West; Deputy Marshal; Moonrise; Tell It to the Judge. **1950** Joe Palooka Meets Humphrey; Harvey. **1951** Gold Raiders; Silver City Bonanza; Man in the Saddle. **1952** Captive of Billy the Kid; Hangman's Knot. **1953** The Stranger Wore a Gun. **1954** Boy from Oklahoma. **1955** The Twinkle in God's Eye; Ten Wanted Men; The Kentuckian. **1956** Davy Crockett and the River Pirates.

BEVANS, LIONEL
Born: 1884. Died: Feb. 17, 1965, Los Angeles, Calif. Screen, stage actor and stage director.

BEVANS, PHILIPPA
Born: 1913, London, England. Died: May 10, 1968, New York, N.Y. Screen, stage and television actress.

Appeared in: **1962** The Notorious Landlady. **1964** The World of Henry Orient. **1966** The Group. **1968** Madigan.

BEYER, CHARLES WALTER (aka CHARLES BYER)
Born: Feb. 28, 1895, Newark, N.J. Died: Nov. 28, 1953, Hollywood, Calif. Screen, stage, vaudeville actor and talent agent. Entered films with Vitagraph Co.

Appeared in: **1921** Ten Nights in a Bar Room. **1922** How Women Love; The Man Who Paid. **1923** Lost in a Big City; Unseeing Eyes. **1924** Trail of the Law; Youth for Sale; Week End Husbands. **1925** A Man Must Live; The Unguarded Hour; The Pace That Thrills; The Shock Punch. **1927** Shanghai Bound; Cabaret; New York. **1928** Dead Man's Curve; A Horseman of the Plains; Red Riders of Canada; Alex the Great; Beautiful but Dumb; Clothes Make the Woman; Taxi 13. **1929** Romance of the Rio Grande; Side Street; Red Hot Speed; The Delightful Rogue; Molly and Me.

BIANCHETTI, SUZANNE
Born: 1894, Paris, France. Died: 1936, Paris, France. Screen actress.

Appeared in: **1921** Les Mysteres de Paris (The Mysteries of Paris); Le Pere Goriot. **1922** Jocelyn. **1925** Madame Sans-Gene. **1927** Napoleon; Loves of Cassanova (US 1929). **1930** Verdun Vision d'Histoire. **1935** L'Appel du Silence; La Violetera.

BIANCHI, GEORGIO
Born: 1904. Died: Feb. 9, 1968, Rome, Italy. Screen actor, film director and film producer.

Appeared in: **1932** Il Miracolo di Sant' Antonio.

BIANCO, ERNESTO (Oscar Ernesto Pericoro)
Born: 1923. Died: Oct. 2, 1977, Buenos Aires, Argentina (heart attack). Screen and stage actor.

Appeared in: **1964** Demonio en la Sangre (Demon in the Blood); La Herencia (The Inheritance).

BIAS, CHESTER
Born: 1917. Died: Mar. 1, 1954, Woodland Hills, Calif. Screen actor.

BIBERMAN, ABNER
Born: Apr. 1, 1909, Milwaukee, Wis. Died: June 20, 1977, San Diego, Calif. Screen, stage actor, film, stage, television director, screenwriter, television writer and author.

Appeared in: **1939** Another Thin Man; Panama Patrol; Panama Lady; Balalaika; The Rains Came; Gunga Din; The Roaring Twenties. **1940** Enemy Agent; South of Karanga; Girl from Havana; South of Pago-Pago; His Girl Friday; Zanzibar. **1941** Singapore Woman; South of Tahiti; The Devil Pays Off; This Woman is Mine; Gay Vagabond. **1942** Whispering Ghosts; Beyond the Blue Horizon; Broadway; Little Tokyo; U.S.A.; King of the Mounties (serial). **1943** The Leopard Man; Submarine Alert; The Bridge of San Luis Rey. **1945** Salome, Where She Danced; Keys of the Kingdom; Betrayal from the East; Back to Bataan; Captain Kidd. **1946** Strange Conquest. **1950** Winchester '73. **1951** Roaring City. **1952** Viva Zapata. **1954** Knock on Wood; Elephant Walk; The Golden Mistress.

BIBERTI, LEOPOLD
Born: 1894, Switzerland. Died: Nov. 24, 1969, Mindes, West Germany. Screen and stage actor.

Appeared in: **1945** The Last Chance. **1950** Four Day's Leave. **1959** The Sins of Rose Bernd.

BIBY, EDWARD
Born: 1885. Died: Oct. 3, 1952, Los Angeles, Calif. Screen actor.

Appeared in: **1937** The Life of Emile Zola. **1946** Night and Day. **1947** The Strange Woman. **1950** Dear Wife.

BICE, ROBERT (Robert Lee Bice)
Born: Mar. 4, 1914, Dallas, Tex. Died: Jan. 8, 1968, Hollywood, Calif. Screen, radio, television actor, radio writer and screenwriter. Married to actress Andre Stuart.

Appeared in: **1943** The Ghost Ship. **1944** Dragon Seed. **1947** Red

Stallion. **1948** Canon City. **1949** In this Corner; Theives' Highway; Bandit King of Texas. **1950** Under Mexicali Stars; Bells of Coronado. **1951** Government Agents vs. Phantom Legion (serial); Al Jennings of Oklahoma; Gunplay. **1952** Night Stage to Galveston; Junction City; Red Snow; Captain Pirate; Hiawatha. **1953** Captive Women; Tarzan and the She Devil; Paris Model; The Star of Texas; On Top of Old Smoky; The Marksman; Bandits of the West; Border City Rustlers. **1954** The Wild One; The Adventures of Hajji Baba; The Steel Cage. **1955** Three for the Show; Foxfire; Teenage Crime Wave; Dial Red O; The Big Bluff; Bowery to Bagdad; The Gun That Won the West. **1958** It!; The Terror From Beyond Space; Spacemaster X-7.

BICKEL, GEORGE L.
Born: 1863, Saginaw, Mich. Died: June 5, 1941, Los Angeles, Calif. Screen, stage, circus and vaudeville actor. Entered films approx. 1915 with Edison Feature Film Co.

Appeared in: **1929** Beneath the Law (short); In Holland (short). **1930** Soup to Nuts; Maybe It's Love; Recaptured Love. **1931** One Heavenly Night. **1932** The Man I Killed; Dancers in the Dark.

BICKFORD, CHARLES
Born: Jan. 1, 1889, Cambridge, Mass. Died: Nov. 9, 1967, Los Angeles, Calif. (emphysema). Screen, stage, television and burlesque actor. Married to actress Beatrice Loring. Nominated for 1943 Academy Award for Best Supporting Actor in Song of Bernadette, in 1947 for The Farmer's Daughter, and in 1948 for Johnny Belinda.

Appeared in: **1929** Dynamite (film debut); South Sea Rose; Hell's Heroes. **1930** Anna Christie; The Sea Bat; The Passion Flower. **1931** The Squaw Man; East of Borneo; The Pagan Lady; River End; Men in Her Life. **1932** Ambition; Scandal for Sale; Vanity Street; The Last Man; Thunder Below; Devil and the Deep; Panama Flo. **1933** No Other Woman; Song of the Eagle; This Day and Age; White Woman. **1934** Little Miss Marker; Red Wagon (US 1935); A Wicked Woman. **1935** Under Pressure; A Notorious Gentleman; The Farmer Takes a Wife; East of Java; The Littlest Rebel. **1936** Red Wagon; Rose of the Rancho; The Plainsman; Pride of the Marines. **1937** High, Wide and Handsome; Thunder Trail; Night Club Scandal; Daughter of Shanghai. **1938** Gangs of New York; Valley of the Giants; The Storm. **1939** Stand Up and Fight; Street of Missing Men; Mutiny in the Big House; Romance of the Redwoods; Our Leading Citizens; One Hour to Live; Of Mice and Men. **1940** Thou Shalt Not Kill; Girl from God's Country; South To Karango; Queen of the Yukon. **1941** Burma Convoy; Riders of Death Valley (serial). **1942** Reap the Wild Wind; Tarzan's New York Adventure. **1943** The Song of Bernadette; Mr. Lucky. **1944** Wing and a Prayer. **1945** Fallen Angel; Captain Eddie. **1946** Duel in the Sun. **1947** The Farmer's Daughter; The Woman on the Beach; Brute Force. **1948** The Babe Ruth Story; Johnny Belinda; Four Faces West; Command Decision. **1949** Guilty of Treason; Roseanna McCoy; Whirlpool. **1950** Branded; Riding High. **1951** The Raging Tide; Elopement; Jim Thorpe All-American. **1952** Man of Bronze. **1953** The Last Posse. **1954** A Star is Born. **1955** Prince of Players; Not as a Stranger; The Court-Martial of Billy Mitchell. **1956** You Can't Run Away from It. **1957** Mister Cory. **1958** The Big Country. **1960** The Unforgiven. **1962** Days of Wine and Roses. **1966** A Big Hand for the Little Lady.

BIEGEL, ERWIN
Born: 1896. Died: May 24, 1954, Berlin, Germany (heart ailment). German screen and stage actor.

Appeared in: **1938** Wenn Du eine Schwiegermutte hast (When You Have a Mother-in-Law). **1949** Palace Scandal. **1952** The Berliner. **1953** Das Tanzende Herz (The Dancing Heart—US 1958).

BIGARD, BARNEY (Leon Albany Bigard)
Born: Mar. 3, 1906. Died: June 27, 1980, Culver City, Calif. (cancer). Jazz clarinetist and screen actor.

Appeared in: **1947** New Orleans. **1958** St. Louis Blues.

BIG MAYBELLE (Mabel Smith)
Born: 1924, Jackson, Tenn. Died: Jan. 23, 1972, Cleveland, Ohio. Black jazz singer and screen actress.

Appeared in: **1960** Jazz on a Summer's Day.

BILDT, PAUL
Born: 1885, Germany. Died: Mar. 16, 1957, Berlin, Germany. Stage and screen actor.

Appeared in: **1927** Slums of Berlin. **1933** The Rebel. **1935** Schwarzer Jaeger Johanna; Die Toerichte Jungfrau. **1939** Der Schritt vom Were (The Fatal Step). **1940** The Dreyfus Case. **1948** Razzia. **1949** Somewhere in Berlin; The Affair Blum. **1950** Our Daily Bread. **1956** As Long As You're Near Me; Anastasia. **1958** International Counterfeiters. **1959** Himmel Ohne Sterne (Sky Without Stars).

BILLIMORIA, EDDIE
Born: 1910, India. Died: Feb. 18, 1981, Bombay, India. Screen actor. Brother of actor Dinshaw Billimoria.

Appeared in the following silents: The Punjab Mail; Vanishing Hope.

BILLINGS, BENJAMIN
Born: 1903. Died: May 3, 1923, Los Angeles, Calif. (auto accident). Screen actor.

BILLINGS, ELMO
Born: 1913. Died: Feb. 6, 1964, Los Angeles, Calif. (stroke). Screen actor. Freckle-faced urchin of early "Our Gang" comedies.

Appeared in: **1925** Locked Doors; The Midnight Flyer. **1927** Tumbling River.

BILLINGS, GEORGE A.
Born: Nov. 22, 1870. Died: Apr. 15, 1934, West Los Angeles, Calif. Screen and stage actor.

Appeared in: **1924** Barbara Frietchie; Abraham Licoln. **1925** The Man Without a Country. **1926** Hands Up!; The Greater Glory. **1929** Woman to Woman. **1930** Night Work; The Third Alarm; Traffic (short); "Folly Comedies" second series. **1933** King for a Night. **1934** As the Earth Turns; The Pursuit of Happiness. **1935** The Gilded Lily.

BILLINGS, TED
Born: 1880. Died: July 5, 1947. Screen actor.

Appeared in: **1935** The Bride of Frankenstein.

BINDER, SYBILLA
Born: 1900, Vienna, Austria. Died: June 30, 1962, Dusseldorf, Germany. Screen and stage actress.

Appeared in: **1942** Thunder Rock (US 1944). **1945** The Man from Morocco (US 1946). **1948** Blanche Fury; Broken Journey (US 1949); Against the Wind (US 1949). **1950** Golden Salamander.

BING, GUS (aka GEORGE BINGHAM)
Born: 1893. Died: Aug. 4, 1967, Los Angeles, Calif. (leukemia). Screen, stage, vaudeville and burlesque actor. Brother of actor Herman Bing (dec. 1947).

BING, HERMAN
Born: Mar. 30, 1889, Germany. Died: Jan. 9, 1947, Los Angeles, Calif. (suicide—gun). Screen actor, film producer and opera performer. Brother of actor Gus Bing (dec. 1967).

Appeared in: **1929** A Song of Kentucky; Married in Hollywood. **1930** Show Girl in Hollywood; The Three Sisters; Menschen Hinter Gettern. **1931** The Great Lover; The Guardsman; Women Love Once. **1932** Big City Blues; Silver Dollar; Hypnotized; Jewel Robbery; Flesh. **1933** Lady Killers; Barbary Coast; Chance at Heaven; The Nuisance; Dinner at Eight; The Bowery; My Lips Betray; Fits in a Fiddle (short); Footlight Parade; The Great Jasper; The College Coach. **1934** Manhattan Melodrama; Evelyn Prentice; The Hide-Out; Embarrassing Moments; Love Time; The Crimson Romance; When Strangers Meet; The Mighty Barnum; Mandalay; Melody in Spring; The Merry Widow; Manhattan Love Song; I'll Tell the World; The Black Cat; Twentieth Century. **1935** Night Is Young; It Happened in New York; Thunder in the Night; Hands Across the Table; Great Hotel Murder; Redheads on Parade; Call of the Wild; The Florentine Dagger; Don't Bet on Blondes; Calm Yourself; In Caliente; Every Night at Eight; His Family Tree; Three Kids and a Queen; Fighting Youth; A Thousand Dollars a Minute; The Misses Stooge (short). **1936** Laughing Irish Eyes; The Music Goes 'Round; Tango; Come Closer Folks; Rose Marie; The Great Ziegfeld; Three Wise Guys; Human Cargo; Dimples; The King Steps Out; Adventure in Manhattan; Champagne Waltz; That Girl from Paris. **1937** Maytime; Beg, Borrow or Steal. **1938** Every Day's a Holiday; Paradise for Three; Vacation from Love; The Great Waltz; Sweethearts; Bluebeard's Eighth Wife; Four's a Crowd. **1940** Bitter Sweet. **1941** Captains of Koepenick. **1942** The Devil With Hitler. **1945** Where Do We Go from Here? **1946** Rendezvous 24; Night and Day.

BINGHAM, GEORGE *See* BING, GUS

BINGHAM, STANLEY J.
Born: Apr. 28, 1880, Cleveland, Ohio. Died: Jan. 9, 1962. Screen actor.

Appeared in: **1920** Sand. **1921** Three Word Brand; A Midnight Bell. **1922** When Romance Rides; Alias Julius Caesar; A Tailor Made Man. **1923** Courtship of Miles Standish; Thru the Flames; Robin Hood, Jr. **1924** The White Panther; After a Million; Call of the Mate.

BINNEY, FAIRE
Born: Aug. 24, 1900, Pa. or N.Y.C. Died: Aug. 28, 1957 (pneumonia). Screen actress. Sister of actress Constance Binney.

Appeared in: **1918** Sporting Life; Woman. **1919** Here Comes the Bride; Open Your Eyes. **1920** Madonnas and Men; The Blue Pearl; The Wonder Man. **1921** A Man's Home; The Frontier of the Stars; The Girl from Porcupine. **1922** What Fools Men Are; A Wide-Open Town. **1923** Loyal Lives. **1924** The Man Without a Heart; Second Youth; The Speed Spook. **1925** The Lost Chord. **1951** Love Nest. **1952** Monkey Business.

BINNS, GEORGE H.
Born: 1886, England. Died: Oct. 27, 1918, Glendale, Calif. (Spanish influenza, pneumonia). Screen actor.

Appeared in: **1916** Tubby Turns the Tables; The Telephone Belle. **1917** The Late Lamented; A Dog's Own Tale; The Camera Cure; Innocent Sinners; His Marriage Failure; His Bitter Fate; An Innocent Villain; Their Domestic Deception; His Baby Doll.

BIRCH, FRANK
Born: Dec. 5, 1889, London, England. Died: Feb. 14, 1956, England? Screen, stage actor and film director. Married to Hon. Vera Benedicta.

Appeared in: **1935** Jubilee Window; School for Stars. **1937** Jump for Glory (aka When Thief Meets Thief—US); The Academy Decides; Double Exposures (reissued as Alibi Breaker); Twin Faces; Victoria the Great. **1938** The Challenge (US 1939). **1952** Lady in the Fog (aka Scotland Yard Inspector—US).

BIRCH, PAUL
Died: May 24, 1969. Screen and stage actor.

Appeared in: **1952** Assignment Paris. **1953** The War of the Worlds. **1954** Ride Clear of Diablo. **1955** Rebel Without a Cause; Apache Woman; Strange Lady in Town; The Fighting Chance; Five Guns West. **1956** The Fastest Gun Alive; Beast With 1,000,000 Eyes; When Gangland Strikes; The White Squaw; Everything But the Truth. **1957** Gun for a Coward; Not of This Earth; The Twenty-Seventh Day; The Tattered Dress; Joe Dakota. **1958** The World Was His Jury; Gunman's Walk; Wild Heritage; The Gun Runners; Queen of Outer Space. **1959** Gunmen from Laredo. **1960** The Dark at the Top of the Stairs; Pay or Die; Portrait in Black. **1961** Two Rode Together. **1962** The Man Who Shot Liberty Valence; A Public Affair. **1963** The Raiders; It's a Mad, Mad, Mad, Mad World. **1967** Welcome to Hard Times; A Covenant With Death.

BIRCH, WYRLEY (Ernest Wyrley Birch)
Born: May 7, 1883, Montreal, Canada. Died: Feb. 7, 1959. Screen actor.

Appeared in: **1935** Awakening of Jim Burke; Air Hawks; The Last Days of Pompeii; Grand Exit; Guard That Girl; After the Dance. **1936** The Music Goes 'Round; Mr. Deeds Goes to Town; Trapped by Television; Blackmailer; Panic on the Air. **1947** The Boomerang.

BIRELL, TALA (Natalie Bierl)
Born: Sept. 10, 1908, Vienna or Bucharest, Rumania? Died: 1959, Europe. Screen and stage actress.

Appeared in: **1932** The Doomed Battalion. **1933** Nagana; The Black Pearl. **1934** The Captain Hates the Sea; Let's Fall in Love. **1935** Let's Live Tonight; Air Hawks; Crime and Punishment. **1936** The Lone Wolf Returns; The White Legion. **1937** She's Dangerous; As Good as Married. **1938** Bringing Up Baby; Invisible Enemy; Josette. **1942** Seven Miles from Alcatraz. **1943** Isle of Forgotten Sins; Women in Bondage; China; The Song of Bernadette. **1944** The Purple Heart; The Monster Maker; Make Your Own Bed; Til We Meet Again; Mrs. Parkington. **1945** Jungle Queen (serial); The Frozen Ghost. **1946** The Power of the Whistler; Dangerous Millions. **1947** Song of Love; Philo Vance's Secret Mission; Philo Vance's Gamble. **1948** Women in the Night; Homicide For Three.

BIRKETT, VIVA
Born: 1887, England. Died: June 27, 1934, London, England. Screen and stage actress. Married to actor Philip Merivale (dec. 1946).

Appeared in: **1927** The Prince of Lovers.

BISHOP, ALFRED
Born: Feb. 7, 1848, Liverpool, England. Died: May 22, 1928, London, England. Screen and stage actor. Brother of actress Kate Bishop (dec. 1923).

Appeared in: **1914** The Brass Bottle.

BISHOP, CHESTER
Born: 1858. Died: May 23, 1937, Los Angeles, Calif. Screen and stage actor.

Appeared in: **1923** Lights Out. **1924** Missing Daughters.

BISHOP, RICHARD
Born: 1898. Died: May 28, 1956, Sharon, Conn. Screen, stage, radio and television actor.

Appeared in: **1942** Native Land. **1948** Call Northside 777. **1951** Teresa. **1955** The Long Gray Line.

BISHOP, STARK, JR.
Born: 1932. Died: July 9, 1945, Hollywood, Calif. Screen actor.

BISHOP, WILLIAM
Born: July 16, 1917, Oak Park, Ill. Died: Oct. 3, 1959, Malibu, Calif. (cancer). Screen, stage, television and radio actor.

Appeared in: **1943** Serving Shift Maisie; A Guy Named Joe. **1946** Pillow to Post. **1947** Romance of Rosy Ridge; Song of the Thin Man; Devil Ship. **1948** Thunderhoof; Untamed Breed; Coroner Creek; Adventures in Silverado; Port Said; Black Eagle. **1949** Walking Hills; Anna Lucasta. **1950** The Tougher They Come; Harriet Craig; Killer That Stalked New York. **1951** Lorna Doone; The Texas Ranger; The Frogmen; Baseball Fix. **1952** Cripple Creek; Breakdown; The Raiders; The Redhead from Wyoming. **1953** Gun Belt. **1954** Overland Pacific. **1955** Top Gun; Wyoming Renegades. **1956** The White Squaw; The Boss. **1957** The Phantom Stagecoach; Short Cut to Hell. **1959** The Oregon Trail.

BITTNER, WILLIAM W.
Born: 1866. Died: July 6, 1918, New York, N.Y. Screen and stage actor.

Appeared in: **1917** Runaway Romany. **1918** My Four Years in Germany.

BJORNE, HUGO
Born: 1886, Sweden. Died: Feb. 14, 1966, Stockholm, Sweden. Screen, stage, radio and television actor. Married to actress Gerda Bjorne.

Appeared in: **1912** Lojen ock Tarar (film debut). **1938** Karl Fredrik Reigns; Sun Over Sweden; Frun Tillhanda (Servant Girl). **1944** Himlaspelet. **1947** Torment. **1948** Crime and Punishment.

BLACK, BILL
Born: 1927. Died: Oct. 21, 1965, Memphis, Tenn. Screen actor and musician. Leader of "Bill Black's Combo."

Appeared in: **1961** Teenage Millionaire.

BLACK, MAURICE
Born: 1891, Warsaw, Poland. Died: Jan. 18, 1938, Hollywood, Calif. Stage and screen actor. Entered films approx. 1923.

Appeared in: **1928** Marked Money. **1929** Leaping Love (short); Broadway Babies; Dark Streets; The Carnation Kid. **1930** Common Clay; Numbered Men; The Chumps (short); Little Caesar; Playing Around; The Street of Chance; Live and Learn; Brothers; The Sea God; Framed; The Runaway Bride. **1931** Front Page; Oh! Oh! Cleopatra (short); Women Go On Forever; Smart Money; Sob Sister; While Paris Sleeps. **1932** Shame of a Nation; Scarface; Rasputin and the Empress; The King Murder; High Pressure; Dancers in the Dark; The Strange Love of Molly Louvain; Scarlet Dawn. **1933** Picture Snatcher; The Cohens and the Kellys in Trouble; Grand Slam; A Shriek in the Night; I Cover the Waterfront; Flying Down to Rio; Ship of Wanted Men; Murder on the Campus. **1934** Sixteen Fathoms Deep; The Great Barnum; Twin Husbands; Wake Up and Dream; West of the Pecos; Down to Their Last Yacht. **1935** Bride of Frankenstein; The Crusaders; Bonnie Scotland; Stars Over Broadway. **1936** Laughing Irish Eyes. **1937** Three Legionnaires; The Californian; Adventure's End; The Firefly.

BLACKFORD, MARY
Born: 1914, Philadelphia, Pa. Died: Sept. 24, 1937, Santa Monica, Calif. (results of auto accident). Screen actress.

Appeared in: **1933** The Sweetheart of Sigma Chi.

BLACKHAWK, LAWRENCE
Born: 1888. Died: Aug., 1978, (natural causes). Screen actor.

BLACKMAN, DON
Born: 1912. Died: Sept. 11, 1977, San Fernando, Calif. (massive heart attack). Black screen, stage, television actor and lightweight boxing champ.

Appeared in: **1952** Bomba and the Jungle Girl. **1953** Desert Legion; Valley of the Headhunters; Mississippi Gambler; Jungle Drums of Africa (serial). **1954** The Egyptian; Black Tuesday; On the Waterfront. **1956** Santiago.

BLACKMER, SIDNEY (aka SYDNEY BLACKMER)
Born: July 13, 1896, Salisbury, N.C. Died: Oct. 5, 1973, New York, N.Y. (cancer). Screen, stage, television, radio and vaudeville actor. Divorced from actress Lenore Ulric and married to actress Suzanne Kaaren.

Appeared in: **1914** Perils of Pauline (film debut). **1927** Million Dollar Mystery (serial). **1929** A Most Immoral Lady. **1930** The Love Racket; Strictly Modern; Kismet; Sweethearts and Wives; The Bad Man; Mother's Cry; Little Caeser; One Adventurous Night. **1931** Woman Hungry; It's a Wise Child; The Lady Who Daréd; Daybreak; Once a Sinner. **1933** From Hell to Heaven; Cocktail Hour; The Deluge; The Wrecker. **1934** The Count of Monte Cristo; Goodbye Love; This Man Is Mine; Down to Their Last Yacht; Transatlantic Merry-Go-Round; The President Vanishes. **1935** Forced Landing; False Pretenses; A Notorious Gentleman; The Little Colonel; The Firetrap; Behind Green Lights; Great God Gold; Smart Girl; Streamline Express; The Girl Who Came Back. **1936** Woman Trap; Florida Special; Early to Bed; Missing Girls; The President's Mystery; Heart of the West. **1937** A Doctor's Diary; John Meade's Woman; House of Secrets; Girl Overboard; Shadows of the Orient; The Last Gangster; Charlie Chan at Monte Carlo; Thank You, Mr. Moto; This Is My Affair; Doctor and Nurse; Heidi; The Women Men Marry; Michael O'Halloran. **1938** Straight, Place and Show; Speed to Burn; Suez; Sharpshooters; While New York Sleeps; Orphans of the Streets; Trade Winds; In Old Chicago. **1939** The Convict's Code; Unmarried; Law of the Pampas; Trapped in the Sky; Fast and Loose; Within the Law; It's a Wonderful World; Hotel for Women. **1940** Maryland; I Want a Divorce; Third Finger, Left Hand; Framed; Dance, Girl, Dance. **1941** Cheers for Miss Bishop; The Great Swindle; Rookies on Parade; Love Crazy; Ellery Queen and the Perfect Crime; The Officer and the Lady; The Feminine Touch; Murder Among Friends; Angels With Broken Wings; Down Mexico Way; Obliging Young Lady. **1942** Always in My Heart; Nazi Agent; Sabotage Squad; Quiet Please, Murder; Gallant Lady; Prison Girls; The Panther's Claw. **1943** Murder in Times Square; In Old Oklahoma; I Escaped from the Gestapo. **1944** The Lady and the Monster; Buffalo Bill; Wilson; Broadway Rhythm. **1946** Duel in the Sun. **1948** My Girl Tisa; A Song Is Born (narr.); The Hero (narr.). **1950** Farewell to Yesterday. **1951** Saturday's Hero; People Will Talk. **1952** Washington Story; The San Francisco Story. **1954** Johnny Dark; The High and the Mighty. **1955** The View from Pompey's Head (aka Secret Interlude). **1956** Accused of Murder; High Society; Beyond a Reasonable Doubt. **1957** Tammy and the Bachelor. **1965** Joy in the Morning; How to Murder Your Wife. **1967** A Covenant With Death. **1969** Rosemary's Baby.

BLACKMORE, E. WILLARD
Born: 1870. Died: Nov. 20, 1949, East St. Louis, Mo. Screen and stage actor. Aided Thomas A. Edison in making the first talking film.

BLACKMORE, HARRY D.
Born: 1859. Died: Feb. 14, 1936, Bay Shore, N.Y. Screen actor.

Appeared in: **1915** Always in the Way.

BLACKTON, J. STUART
Born: Jan. 5, 1875, Sheffield, England. Died: Aug. 13, 1941, Hollywood, Calif. (auto accident). Screen actor, film director, producer and screenwriter. One of founders of Vitagraph Pictures. Worked with Thomas Edison on first ten films ever made—he drew sketches. Divorced from Isabelle Mabel MacArthur (dec. 1925). Married to actress Paula Dean (aka Paula Hunt (dec. 1930)); Married to Helen Stahle (dec.) and later married to actress Evangeline Russell (dec. 1966). Father of songwriter Marian Constance and actors Violet Virginia (dec. 1973), James, Jr. (dec. 1968) and Charles Stuart Blackton.

Appeared in: **1902** The Twentieth Century Tramp (aka Happy Hooligan and His Airship). **1912** A Vitagraph Romance.

BLACKTON, JAMES STUART, JR.
Born: Nov. 6, 1897. Died: Dec. 16, 1968. Screen actor. Son of actor J. Stuart Blackton (dec. 1941) and Isabelle MacArthur (dec. 1925). Brother of screenwriter Marian Blackton and half brother of actress Violet (dec. 1973) and actor Charles Blackton. Entered films as a child actor with Vitagraph Company.

BLACKTON, PAULA *See* DEAN, PAULA

BLACKTON, VIOLET VIRGINIA
Born: 1912. Died: Mar. 28, 1973. Screen actress. Daughter of J. Stuart Blackton (dec. 1941) and actress Paula Hunt (dec. 1930). Half sister of actor J. Stuart Blackton, Jr. (dec. 1968), screenwriter Marian Constance Blackton and actor Charles Blackton. Appeared in films as a child actress with her half brother J. Stuart Blackton, Jr. in Vitagraph films.

Appeared in: **1922** The Glorious Adventure. **1923** The Virgin Queen.

BLACKWELL, CARLYLE
Born: 1888, Troy, Pa. Died: June 17, 1955, Miami, Fla. Screen, stage actor, stage and film producer. Entered films in 1909 with Vitagraph. Married to actress Ruth Hartman (dec. 1956). Father of actor Carlyle Blackwell, Jr. (dec. 1974).

Appeared in: **1909** Uncle Tom's Cabin. **1910** A Dixie Mother. **1911** Slim Jim's Last Chance; Slabsides; The Love of Summer Morn; Over the Garden Wall; The Wasp; The Alpine Lease; The Temptation of Rodney Vane. **1912** A Bell of Penance; The Russian Peasant; A Princess of the Hills; The Adventures of American Joe; The Mexican Revolutionist; The Stolen Invention; The Outlaw; Saved By Telephone; The Badge of Courage; The Suffragette Sheriff; Fantasca the Gypsy. **1913** Perils of the Sea. **1914** Such a Little Queen; The Spitfire; The Key to Yesterday. **1915** The Secret Orchard; The Case of Becky. **1916** A Woman's Way. **1917** The Burglar. **1918** His Royal Highness; The Road to France. **1920** The Restless Sex. **1923** Bulldog Drummond; The Virgin Queen; The Beloved Vagabond; Good for Nothing. **1924** The Shadow of Egypt. **1925** Monte Carlo; Racing Dramas (shorts); She. **1926** The Steve Donoghue series including: Riding for a King and Beating the Book. **1927** One of the Best; The Rolling Road. **1928** The Wrecker (US 1929); The Crooked Billet. **1930** Beyond the Cities. **1944** Destination Tokyo; Follow the Boys.

BLACKWELL, CARLYLE, JR.
Born: 1913. Died: Sept. 20, 1974, North Hollywood, Calif. Screen and television actor. Son of actor Carlyle Blackwell (dec. 1955).

Appeared in: **1935** Old Man Rhythm; The Goose and the Gander. **1936** The Calling of Dan Matthews; Romeo and Juliet. **1937** Thrill of a Lifetime. **1941** All-American Co-Ed. **1944** The Doughgirls; Ladies Courageous; The Imposter; The Story of Dr. Wassell; Destination Tokyo. **1945** Docks of New York. **1947** The Beginning or the End.

BLACKWOOD, BONNIE
Born: 1909. Died: Feb. 18, 1949, Burbank, Calif. Screen and stage actress.

BLACKWOOD, DIANA
Died: Mar., 1961, London, England. Screen, stage and television actress.

BLADE, AUGUSTA
Born: 1871. Died: Nov. 9, 1953, Copenhagen, Denmark. Screen and stage actress.

Appeared in early films for Great Northern Film Company of Denmark.

BLAGOI, GEORGE
Born: 1898, Russia. Died: June 23, 1971, Hollywood, Calif. Screen actor. Married to actress Tina Blagoi.

Appeared in: **1926** Into Her Kingdom. **1928** Four Sons. **1935** Crime and Punishment.

BLAINE, JOAN
Died: Apr. 19, 1949, New York. Screen, stage and radio actress.

BLAIR, DAVID (David Butterfield)
Born: July 27, 1932, Halifax, Yorkshire, England. Died: Apr. 1, 1976, London, England. Screen actor, ballet dancer and choreographer. Married to British ballerina Maryon Lane.

Appeared in: **1950** The Happy Years. **1963** An Evening with the Royal Ballet (US 1965). **1966** Romeo and Juliet.

BLAIR, ELLA S.
Born: 1895. Died: Dec. 11, 1917, New York, N.Y. Screen actress.

BLAISDELL, WILLIAM
Died: Jan. 1, 1931, Brooklyn, N.Y. Screen and stage actor. Married to stage actress Clara Lavine (dec. 1948).

Appeared in: **1924** Racing Luck. **1927** The Yankee Clipper.

BLAISE, PIERRE
Born: 1951. Died: Aug. 31, 1975, near Montauban, France (auto accident). Screen actor.

Appeared in: **1974** Lacombe, Lucien (film debut).

BLAISELL, CHARLES "BIG BILL"
Born: 1874. Died: May 10, 1930, Hollywood, Calif. Screen and vaudeville actor. Appeared in early Christie Comedies.

BLAKE, AL (Alva D. Blake aka A. D. BLAKE)
Born: 1877, Manitou, Colo. Died: Nov. 5, 1966, Los Angeles, Calif. (heart attack). Screen actor.

Appeared in: **1916** The Trap; The Jungle Flashlight; Father of Her Child; Where Are My Children?

BLAKE, ANNE
Died: Feb. 17, 1973. Screen actress.

Appeared in: **1951** The Second Mate. **1956** Murder Reported (US 1960). **1957** The Curse of Frankenstein; The Secret Place (US 1958). **1958** Orders to Kill. **1961** Taste of Fear (aka Scream of Fear—US); The Curse of the Werewolf; Saturday Night and Sunday Morning. **1965** The Spy Who Came In From the Cold. **1966** Sky West and Crooked (aka Gypsy Girl—US 1966). **1970** The Private Life of Sherlock Holmes.

BLAKE, MADGE
Born: 1900. Died: Feb. 19, 1969, Pasadena, Calif. (heart attack). Screen and television actress.

Appeared in: **1949** Adam's Rib. **1950** Between Midnight and Dawn; A Life of Her Own. **1951** Finders Keepers; The Prowler; Queen for a Day; An American in Paris. **1952** The Bad and the Beautiful; It Grows on Trees; Singin' in the Rain; Something for the Birds. **1953** Tumbleweed; Dangerous Crossing. **1954** Brigadoon; Rhapsody; The Long, Long Trailer; Fireman, Save My Child. **1956** The Solid Gold Cadilac; Please Murder Me; Glory. **1957** Loving You. **1960** Please Don't Eat the Daisies. **1962** Sergeants Three. **1966** Batman; Follow Me, Boys!

BLAKE, MARIE (Edith Blossom Mac Donald aka EDITH ROCK aka BLOSSOM MACDONALD)
Born: 1896. Died: Jan. 14, 1978, Woodland Hills, Calif. Screen, stage, vaudeville and television actress. Sister of actress Jeanette MacDonald (dec. 1965). Married to vaudevillian Clarence Rock (dec. 1960) with whom she appeared in vaudeville.

Appeared in: **1936** San Francisco. **1937** Mannequin. **1938** Love Finds Andy Hardy; Young Dr. Kildare; Rich Man-Poor Girl; Dramatic School. **1939** Calling Dr. Kildare; The Secret of Dr. Kildare; The Women; Judge Hardy and Son; Alfalfa's Aunt (short); Blind Alley. **1940** Dr. Kildare Goes Home; Dr. Kildare's Strange Case; Dr. Kildare's Crisis; They Knew What They Wanted; A Child is Born; Home Movies (short). **1941** The People vs. Dr. Kildare; Dr. Kildare's Wedding Day; Dr. Kildare's Victory; Here Comes Happiness; Remember the Day; Small Town Deb; Blue, White and Perfect. **1942** Dr. Gillespie's New Assistant; I Married a Witch; Give Out, Sisters; The Major and the Minor. **1943** Dr. Gillespie's Criminal Case; Good Morning Judge; Campus Rhythm. **1944** Between Two Women; Gildersleeve's Ghost; South of Dixie; Sensations of 1945; Radio Bugs (short). **1945** Pillow to Post; Abbott and Costello in Hollywood. **1946** Gentleman Joe Palooka. **1947** Dark Delusion; Mourning Becomes Electra. **1948** An Innocent Affair; The Snake Pit. **1949** Alimony; Angels in Disguise. **1950** Sons of New Mexico. **1951** The F.B.I. Girl; Love Nest. **1952** The Brigand. **1953** Small Time Girl. **1960** From the Terrace.

BLAKE, PAUL
Died: Jan. 28, 1960, London, England. Stage and screen actor.

Appeared in: **1937** Cafe Colette. **1940** The Lilac Domino.

BLAKECLOCK, ALBAN
Died: Dec. 6, 1966, London, England. Screen, stage, radio and television actor.

Appeared in: **1952** Murder in the Cathedral.

BLAKENEY, OLIVE
Born: Aug. 21, 1903, Newport, Ky. Died: Oct. 21, 1959, Hollywood, Calif. Stage and screen actress. Married to actor Bernard Nedell (dec. 1972).

Appeared in: **1934** Mr. What's His Name (film debut); Her Imaginary Lover; Leave It to Blanche; Give Her a Ring. **1935** Hello Sweetheart (aka The Butter and Egg Man—US); Come Out of the Pantry. **1936** Excuse My Glove; The Three Maxims (aka The Show Goes On—US 1938); Two's Company. **1937** Don't Get Me Wrong; Gangway. **1940** Third Finger, Left Hand. **1941** Billy the Kid; Two-Faced Woman; That Uncertain Feeling; Glamour Boy. **1942** Are Husbands Necessary?; Henry and Dizzy; Henry Aldrich, Editor; Random Harvest. **1943** Henry Aldrich Haunts a House; Henry Aldrich Gets Glamour; Henry Aldrich Swings It. **1944** Allergic to Love; Henry Aldrich Plays Cupid; Henry Aldrich's Little Secret; Henry Aldrich, Boy Scout; The Ghost Catchers; Experiment Perilous. **1945** Nob Hill; Dakota; Leave Her to Heaven. **1946** Sentimental Journey; The Strange Woman. **1947** Time Out of Mind. **1948** Sealed Verdict. **1954** Roogie's Bump. **1957** The Green-Eyed Blonde; Three Brave Men. **1958** I Want to Live!; Auntie Mame.

BLANCARD, RENE
Born: 1897, France. Died: Nov. 5, 1965, Paris, France. Screen actor.

Appeared in: **1947** La Cage aux Rossignols (A Cage of Nightingales); Au Bonheur des Dames (Shop-Girls of Paris). **1948** Jenny Lamour. **1951** Marie Du Port. **1952** Under the Paris Sky. **1954** Marchandes d'Illusions (Nights of Shame—US 1961). **1955** To Catch a Thief. **1958** The Lovemaker; Diary of a Bad Girl. **1959** Julie La Rouge (Julie the Redhead—US 1963). **1960** Sin and Desire; La Verite (The Truth—US 1961).

BLANCHAR, PIERRE
Born: 1893, Philippeville, Algeria. Died: Nov. 21, 1963, Paris, France. Screen and stage actor.

Appeared in: **1923** Jocelyn. **1929** La Marche Nuptiale. **1930** The Chess Player. **1931** L'Atlantide. **1932** La Courtourierre de Luneville. **1933** Le Diable en Bouteille. **1934** Crime et Chatiment (Crime and Punishment). **1935** Cette Vieille Canaille. **1936** A Royal Divorce. **1937** The Late Mattia Pascal; L'Affaire du Courrier de Lyon (US 1938); Mademoiselle Docteur. **1938** Un Carnet de Bal; The Volga Boatman. **1940** Two Women. **1942** Poncarral. **1944** La Dame de Pique. **1946** La Symphonie Pastorale (US 1948). **1948** They Are Not Angels; Street of Shadows. **1958** Riff Raff Girls (US 1962 aka Rififi for Girls and Rififi Among the Women). **1963** Magnificent Sinner.

BLANCHARD, HARRY
Born: 1876. Died: Apr. 27, 1944, Hollywood, Calif. Screen and vaudeville actor. Do not confuse with film sound engineer of same name. Appeared in Harold Lloyd films.

BLANCHARD, MARI
Born: 1927. Died: May 10, 1970, Woodland Hills, Calif. (cancer). Screen and television actress.

Appeared in: **1951** On the Riviera; Ten Tall Men; No Questions Asked; The Unknown Man; The Overland Telegraph. **1952** The Brigand; Assignment—Paris; Back at the Front. **1953** Abbott and Costello Go to Mars; The Veils of Bagdad. **1954** Destry; Rails Into Laramie; Black Horse Canyon. **1955** The Return of Jack Slade; Son of Sinbad; The Crooked Web. **1956** Stagecoach to Fury; The Cruel Tower. **1957** Jungle Heat; She Devil. **1958** Machete; No Place to Land. **1962** Don't Knock the Twist. **1963** Twice Told Tales; McLintock.

BLANCHE, FRANCIS
Born: 1922, France. Died: July 7, 1974, France. Screen actor and songwriter.

Appeared in: **1954** Ah! Les Belles Bacchantes (aka Peek-a-Boo—US 1961). **1959** La Jument Verte (The Green Mare—US 1961). **1960** La Francaise et l'Amour (Love and the Frenchwoman—US 1961); L'Ours (The Bear—US 1963); Babette Goes to War; Au Pied, Au Cheval, et Par Spoutnik (A Dog, A Mouse and a Sputnik). **1961** Les Menteurs (The Liars—US 1964 aka Twisted Lives). **1962** Le Septieme Jure (The Seventh Juror—US 1964); Les Petits Matins (Early Mornings); La Planque (The Hideout). **1963** Dragees au Poivre (Sweet and Sour—US 1964); Un Drole de Paroissien (aka Deo Gratias, The Funny Parishioner); Heaven Sent (aka Thank Heaven for Small Favors—US 1965); Les Tontons Flingueurs (The Gentlemen Gunmen). **1964** La Chasse a l'Homme (Male Hunt—US 1965); Les Barbouzes (aka The Great Spy Chase—US 1966); Les Plus Belles Escroqueries du Monde (The Beautiful Swindlers—US 1967); La Tulipe Noire (The Black Tulip). **1967** Belle de Jour (US 1968); La Grande Sauterelle (aka Femmina—US 1968); Le Plus Vieux Metier du Monde (The Oldest Profession—US 1968).

BLANCKE, KATE (aka KATE BLANKE)
Born: 1860, Cheltenham, England. Died: June 24, 1942, East Islip, N.Y. Screen and stage actress.

Appeared in: **1915** Should a Mother Tell?; The Whirl of Life. **1916** The Pretenders; The Brand of Cowardice. **1917** The End of the Tour; Sowers and Reapers; Duchess of Doubt. **1921** The Old Oaken Bucket; Without Limit; Why Girls Leave Home. **1922** The Streets of New York. **1923** As a Man Lives; The Silent Command. **1924** Trouping with Ellen.

BLAND, JOYCE
Born: 1906, England. Died: Aug. 24, 1963, Bournemouth, England. Screen and stage actress.

Appeared in: **1932** Goodnight Vienna (aka Magic Night—US). **1935** The Right Age to Marry. **1936** A Touch of the Moon; Spy of Napoleon (US 1939). **1937** Dreaming Lips. **1938** Sixty Glorious Years (aka Queen of Destiny—US); The Citadel.

BLANDICK, CLARA
Born: 1881, aboard American ship in harbor of Hong Kong, China. Died: Apr. 15, 1962, Hollywood, Calif. (suicide). Stage and screen actress.

Appeared in: **1911** The Maids' Double. **1914** Mrs. Black Is Back. **1916** The Stolen Triumph. **1929** Men Are Like That; Poor Aubrey. **1930** Wise Girls; Burning Up; The Girl Said No; Sins of the Children; Romance; Last of the Duanes; Tom Sawyer. **1931** Once a Sinner; The Easiest Way; Dance, Fools, Dance; Inspiration; Drums of Jeopardy; Daybreak; It's a Wise Child; Laughing Sinners; I Take This Woman; Bought; Murder at Midnight; Huckleberry Finn; New Adventures of Get-Rich-Quick Wallingford; Posessed. **1932** Shopworn; The Strange Case of Clara Deane; The Pet Parade; Life Begins; Two Against the World; The Expert; Three on a Match; Rockabye. **1933** Bitter Tea of General Yen; Child of Manhattan; The Mind Reader; Three-Cornered Moon; One Sunday Afternoon; Turn Back the Clock; Charlie Chan's Greatest Case; Ever in My Heart. **1934** The President Vanishes; Broadway Bill; Jealousy; Beloved; As the Earth Turns; Harold Teen; The Show-Off; The Girl from Missouri; Sisters Under the Skin; Fugitive Lady. **1935** The Winning Ticket; Straight from the Heart; Princess O'Hara; Party Wire. **1936** Fury; Transient Lady; The Trail of the Lonesome Pine; Anthony Adverse; The Case of the Velvet Claws; Hearts Divided; The Gorgeous Hussy; In His Steps; Make Way for a Lady. **1937** A Star Is Born; Wings Over Honolulu; The Road Back; The League of Frightened Men; Small Town Boy; You Can't Have Everything; Her Husband's Secretary. **1938** My Old Kentucky Home; Tom Sawyer, Detective; Professor Beware; Swing, Sister, Swing; Crime Ring. **1939** Drums Along the Mohawk; Swanee River; I Was a Convict; Adventures of Huckleberry Finn; The Wizard of Oz; The Star Maker. **1940** Alice in Movieland; Tomboy; Anne of Windy Poplars; Dreaming Out Loud; Youth Will Be Served; Northwest Mounted Police. **1941** The Big Store; Enemy Within; Private Nurse; One Foot in Heaven; It Started with Eve; The Nurse's Secret; The Wagons Roll at Night. **1942** Lady in a Jam; Gentleman Jim; Rings on Her Fingers. **1943** Heaven Can Wait; DuBarry Was a Lady; Dixie. **1944** Shadow of Suspicion; Can't Help Singing. **1945** Frontier Gal. **1946** She-Wolf of London; Pillow of Death; People are Funny; Claudia and David; So Goes My Love; A Stolen Life. **1947** Philo Vance Returns; Life With Father. **1948** Bride Goes Wild. **1949** Mr. Soft Touch; Roots in the Soil. **1950** Love That Brute; Key to the City.

BLANEY, MAY
Born: 1874, England. Died: Feb. 10, 1953, Wepener, Orange Free State, South Africa. Stage and screen actress.

BLANKE, KATE See BLANCKE, KATE

BLANKMAN, GEORGE
Born: 1877. Died: Mar. 13, 1925, Los Angeles, Calif. Screen actor.

Appeared in: **1925** Don Q.

BLATCHFORD, WILLIAM
Born: 1886, Pittsburgh, Pa. Died: Dec. 30, 1936, Los Angeles, Calif. Stage and screen actor.

Appeared in: **1934** The Old Fashioned Way.

BLEDSOE, JULES
Born: 1899. Died: July 14, 1943, Hollywood, Calif. Black screen, stage actor and singer.

Appeared in: **1929** Show Boat. **1942** Drums of the Congo.

BLEIBTREAU, HEDWIG
Born: 1868, Austria. Died: Jan. 24, 1958, Vienna, Austria. Screen and stage actress.

Appeared in: **1924** Die Kurtisane von Venedig (aka Das Nackte Weib). **1930** Das Lied ist aus. **1931** Tänzerinnen für Süd-Amerika Gesucht. **1932** Scampolo, ein Kind der Strasse; Der Prinz von Arkadien. **1933** Ein Maedel der Strasse. **1935** Pygmalion; Es Flüstert die Liebe. **1936** Das Mädchen Irene (US 1937). **1937** Die Ganz Grossen Torheiten. **1938** 13 Stühle; Der Spieler (aka Roman eines Spielers); Das Leben Kann so Schön Sein (aka Ultimo). **1939** Hotel Sacher; Waldrausch (Forest Fever—US 1940); Maria Ilona (US 1940). **1940** Wiener G'schichten (Vienna Tales); Wunschkonzert; Alles Scheindel; Meine Tochter Lebt in Wien; Der Ungetreue Ekkehart; Herzensfreud—Herzensleid; Fahrt ins Leben. **1941** Dreimal Hockzeit; Aufruhr im Damenstift. **1942** Sommerliebe; Wiener Blut; Frauen sind Keine Engle. **1943** Ein Mann für Meine Frau. **1945** Wiener Mädeln. **1947** Wiener Melodien. **1948** Alles Lüge; Dern Engel mit der Posaune. **1949** The Third Man (US 1950). **1950** Grosstadtnacht. **1952** Gefangene Seele.

BLEICH, JUDAH
Born: 1901, Austria. Died: May 31, 1961, Tel Aviv, Israel. Screen, stage actor and stage director.

Appeared in: **1930** Ewige Naranim (Eternal Fools). **1933** Victims of Persecution. **1937** The Cantor's Son.

BLETCHER, WILLIAM "BILLY"
Died: Jan. 5, 1979, Los Angeles, Calif. Screen, vaudeville actor and voice for Disney animation. Married to Arline Bletcher, former Ziegfeld performer and film extra. Father of Barbara Bletcher, film extra. Voice of The Big Bad Wolf in "Three Little Pigs" cartoon.

Appeared in: **1922** Billy Jim; Turn to the Right. **1925** The Wild Girl. **1926** The Silent Guardian; The Dude Cowboy. **1927** Better Days; One Hour of Love; Two Girls Wanted; Wolves of the Air. **1928** Daredevil's Reward; The Cowboy Kid. **1930** Dancing Sweeties; Top Speed; The Man Hunter. **1931** Branded Man. **1932** Boiling Point; The Dentist (short). **1933** A Lady's Profession; Diplomaniacs; Air Freight (short). **1934** Texas Ranger; The following shorts: First Round-Up; Maid in Hollywood; One Horse Farmers; Punch Drunks. **1935** One Hour Late; The following shorts: The Tin Man; Twin Triplets; Teacher's Beau; The Lost City (serial). **1936** Divot Diggers (short); All-American Toothache (short). **1937** High, Wide and Handsome; Lash of the Penitentes. **1940** Buck Benny Rides Again; Melody Ranch. **1941** Come Back, Miss Phipps; Robot Wrecks (short). **1942** Even as I.O.U. (short). **1943** Chatterbox. **1944** Boss of Rawhide. **1951** Navy Bound.

BLICH, CATTO (Katherine Friedman)
Born: 1891, Germany. Died: June 8, 1926, Hollywood, Calif. Screen actress.

BLICK, NEWTON
Born: 1899, Bristol, England. Died: Oct., 1965, Dublin, Ireland. Screen, stage and television actor.

Appeared in: **1954** Carrington VC (aka Court-Martial—US 1955). **1956** The Feminine Touch (aka The Gentle Touch—US 1957); Charlie Moon; The Long Arm (aka The Third Key—US 1957). **1957** Town on Trial; Barnacle Bill (aka All at Sea—US 1958). **1958** The Gypsy and the Gentleman; Bachelor of Hearts (US 1962). **1960** Man in the Moon (US 1961). **1961** Flame in the Streets (US 1962). **1962** Term of Trial (US 1963). **1963** Ring of Spies (aka Ring of Treason—US 1964). **1965** Lord Jim. **1966** Morgan—A Suitable Case for Treatment (aka Morgan—US).

BLINN, BENJAMIN F.
Born: 1872. Died: Apr. 28, 1941, Hollywood, Calif. Screen and stage actor.

Appeared in: **1923** Danger. **1925** Quicker'n Lightnin'.

BLINN, GENEVIEVE (Genevieve Namary)
Born: St. John, New Brunswick, Canada. Died: July 20, 1956, Ross, Calif. Screen and stage actress.

Appeared in: **1921** Queen of Sheba; Crazy to Marry; Don't Tell Everything; The Witching Hour. **1922** If I Were Queen; The Call of Home. **1924** Abraham Lincoln. **1930** Common Clay.

BLINN, HOLBROOK
Born: 1872, San Francisco, Calif. Died: June 24, 1928, Crota, N.Y. (fall from horse). Screen, stage actor and film producer.

Appeared in: **1915** The Boss; McTeague; The Butterfly on the Wheel.

1916 The Weakness of Man; Husband and Wife. **1921** Power. **1923** The Bad Man; Rosita. **1924** Janice Meredith; Yolanda. **1925** Zander the Great; The New Commandment. **1926** The Unfair Sex. **1927** The Masked Woman; The Telephone Girl.

BLISS, LELA
Born: May 11, 1896. Died: May 15, 1980, Woodland Hills, Calif. Screen, stage, vaudeville, television actress and stage producer. Married to Harry Hayden (dec. 1955).

Appeared in: **1938** Home on the Rage (short). **1944** Since You Went Away. **1946** The Dark Mirror. **1947** Miracle on 34th Street; Gas House Kids Go West; When a Girl's Beautiful. **1948** Give My Regards to Broadway; The Snake Pit. **1949** Intruder in the Dust. **1950** To Please a Lady. **1951** Ghost Chasers. **1952** Army Bound. **1955** The Big Tip-Off.

BLOCKER, DAN
Born: 1929, Texas. Died: May 13, 1972, Hollywood, Calif. (pulmonary embolus). Screen, stage and television actor.

Appeared in: **1957** Outer Space Jitters (short). **1961** The Errand Boy. **1963** Come Blow Your Horn. **1968** Lady in Cement. **1970** The Cockeyed Cowboys of Calico County.

BLOMFIELD, DEREK
Born: 1920. Died: July 23, 1964, Brittany, France. Screen, stage, television actor and playwright. Entered films in 1932.

Appeared in: **1935** Emil and the Detectives (aka Emil—US 1938); Turn of the Tide. **1936** Shipmates O'Mine. **1941** Ghost of St. Michael's. **1942** Alibi. **1950** Night and the City. **1953** The Floating Dutchman. **1954** Hobson's Choice. **1956** It's Great to Be Young (US 1958); It's a Wonderful World (US 1961). **1957** Carry on Admiral (aka The Ship Was Loaded—US 1959). **1964** East of Sudan.

BLONDELL, JOAN (Rose Joan Blondell)
Born: Aug. 30, 1906 or 1909, New York, N.Y. Died: Dec. 25, 1979, Santa Monica, Calif. (leukemia). Screen, stage, vaudeville, television actress and author. Daughter of vaudeville actors Ed and Kathryn Blondell (dec.). Divorced from cinematographer George Barnes, actor Dick Powell (dec. 1963), and film producer Mike Todd (dec. 1958). Mother of director/actor Norman Powell, Ellen Pamela Powell and Michael Todd. Sister of actress Gloria Blondell. Nominated for 1951 Academy Award as Best Supporting Actress in the Blue Veil.

Appeared in: **1930** Sinner's Holiday (film debut); Steel Highway; How I Play Golf—Trouble Shots (short); The Office Wife. **1931** Illicit; Millie; My Past; Big Business Girl; Public Enemy; God's Gift to Women; Other Men's Women; The Reckless Hour; Night Nurse; Larceny Lane; Blonde Crazy. **1932** The Greeks had a Word for Them; Union Depot; The Crowd Roars; Famous Ferguson Case; Make Me a Star; Miss Pinkerton; Big City Blues; Three on a Match; Central Park; Lawyer Man. **1933** Broadway Bad; Blondie Johnson; Gold Diggers of 1933; Goodbye Again; Footlight Parade; Havana Widows; Convention City. **1934** I've Got Your Number; Smarty; He Was Her Man; Dames; Kansas City Princess. **1935** Traveling Saleslady; Broadway Gondolier; We're in the Money; Miss Pacific Fleet. **1936** Colleen; Sons O' Guns; Bullets or Ballots; Stage Struck; Three Men on a Horse; Gold Diggers of 1937. **1937** The King and the Chorus Girl; Back in Circulation; The Perfect Specimen; Stand-In. **1938** There's Always a Woman. **1939** Off the Record; East Side of Heaven; The Kid from Kokomo; Good Girls Go to Paris; The Amazing Mr. Williams. **1940** Two Girls on Broadway; I Want a Divorce. **1941** Topper Returns; Model Wife; Three Girls About Town; Lady For a Night. **1943** Cry Havoc. **1945** A Tree Grows in Brooklyn; Don Juan Quilligan; Adventure. **1947** Nightmare Alley; The Corpse Came C.O.D.; Christmas Eve. **1950** For Heaven's Sake. **1951** The Blue Veil. **1956** The Opposite Sex. **1957** Lizzie; This Could be the Night; The Desk Set; Will Success Spoil Rock Hunter?. **1961** Angel Baby. **1964** Advance to the Rear. **1965** The Cincinnati Kid. **1966** Ride Beyond Vengeance; Paradise Road. **1967** Waterhole #3. **1968** Kona Coast; Stay Away, Joe. **1969** Big Daddy. **1970** The Phynx. **1978** Grease. **1979** The Champ; Opening Night; The Glove.

BLOOD, ADELE
Born: Apr. 23, 1886 or 1888, San Francisco, Calif. Died: Sept. 13, 1936, Yonkers, N.Y. (self-inflicted gun shot). Screen, stage and vaudeville actress. Mother of actress Dawn Hope.

Appeared in: **1916** The Devil's Toy.

BLOOM, ROBERT "BOBBY" MARTIN
Born: 1946. Died: Feb. 28, 1974, West Hollywood, Calif. (shot—murder or suicide?). Screen actor and composer.

BLORE, ERIC
Born: Dec. 23, 1887, London, England. Died: Mar. 2, 1959, Hollyood, Calif. (heart attack). Screen, stage actor and songwriter. Married to actress Clara Mackin (dec. 1973).

Appeared in: **1920** A Night Out and a Day In. **1926** The Great Gatsby. **1930** Laughter. **1931** My Sin; Tarnished Lady. **1933** Flying Down to Rio. **1934** Gay Divorcee (stage and film versions); Limehouse Blues. **1935** Folies-Bergere; The Good Fairy; Diamond Jim; The Casino Murder Case; I Live My Life; Top Hot; I Dream Too Much; Old Man Rhythm; To Beat the Band; Seven Keys to Baldpate; Glitter; Behold My Wife. **1936** Two in the Dark; The Ex-Mrs. Bradford; Swing Time; Smartest Girl in Town; Sons O' Guns; Piccadilly Jim. **1937** The Soldier and the Lady; Quality Street; Shall We Dance?; Breakfast for Two; Hitting a New High; It's Love I'm After; Michael Strogoff. **1938** The Joy of Living; Swiss Miss; A Desperate Adventure. **1939** $1,000 a Touchdown; Island of Lost Men; A Gentleman's Gentleman. **1940** The Man Who Wouldn't Talk; The Lone Wolf Meets a Lady; The Boys from Syracuse; Earl of Puddlestone; South of Suez. **1941** Road to Zanzibar; The Lone Wolf Keeps a Date; The Lady Eve; The Lone Wolf Takes a Chance; Red Head; New York Town; Lady Scarface; Three Girls About Town; Confirm or Deny; The Shanghai Gesture; Sullivan's Travels; Secrets of the Lone Wolf. **1942** The Moon and Sixpence; Counter Espionage. **1943** Forever and a Day; Submarine Base; Holy Matrimony; One Dangerous Night; Passport to Suez; The Sky's the Limit; Happy Go Lucky. **1944** San Diego, I Love You. **1945** Penthouse Rhythm; Easy to Look At; Men in Her Diary. **1946** Kitty; The Notorious Lone Wolf; Abie's Irish Rose; Two Sisters from Boston. **1947** Winter Wonderland; The Lone Wolf in London; The Lone Wolf in Mexico; Love Happy. **1948** Romance on the High Seas. **1949** Adventures of Ichabod and Mr. Toad (voice). **1950** Fancy Pants. **1952** Babes in Bagdad. **1955** Bowery to Bagdad.

BLUE, BEN (Ben Bernstein)
Born: Sept. 12, 1901, Montreal, Canada. Died: Mar. 7, 1975, Los Angeles, Calif. Screen, stage, vaudeville, radio and television actor. Married to actress Axie Dunlap. Divorced from Mary Blue.

Appeared in: **1926** Vitaphone shorts. **1927** The Arcadians. **1932** Strange Innertube (short); What Price Taxi (short). **1933** Wreckety Wreck (short); Call Her Sausage (short); College Rhythm. **1934** A Vitaphone short. **1936** College Holiday; Follow Your Heart. **1937** Top of the Town; High, Wide and Handsome; Turn Off the Moon; Artists and Models; Thrill of a Lifetime. **1938** College Swing; The Big Broadcast of 1938; Cocoanut Grove. **1939** Paris Honeymoon. **1942** Panama Hattie; For Me and My Gal. **1943** Thousands Cheer. **1944** Two Girls and a Sailor; Broadway Rhythm. **1945** Badminton (short). **1946** Two Sisters from Boston; Easy to Wed. **1947** My Wild Irish Rose. **1948** One Sunday Afternoon (aka The Strawberry Blonde). **1963** It's a Mad, Mad, Mad, Mad World. **1966** The Russians Are Coming, The Russians Are Coming. **1967** A Guide for the Married Man; The Busy Body. **1968** Where Were You When the Lights Went Out?

BLUE, MONTE
Born: Jan. 11, 1890, Indianapolis, Ind. Died: Feb. 18, 1963, Milwaukee, Wis. (coronary attack). Screen actor, screenwriter, and circus performer. Entered films as a screenwriter and stuntman with Griffith.

Appeared in: **1915** Birth of a Nation. **1916** Intolerance. **1917** Wild and Wooly; The Man from Painted Post. **1918** Till I Come Back to You. **1919** In Mizzoura; Every Woman; Pettigrew's Girl. **1920** Jucklins; Something to Think About. **1921** Moonlight and Honeysuckle; The Affairs of Anatole; A Broken Doll; A Perfect Crime; The Kentuckians. **1922** Orphans of the Storm; Peacock Alley; My Old Kentucky Home. **1923** Loving Lies; Defying Destiny; Main Street; Lucretia Lombard; Brass; The Tents of Allah; The Purple Highway. **1924** Being Respectable; Revelation; The Lover of Camille; The Marraige Circle; Daddies; The Dark Swan; Daughters of Pleasure; Her Marriage Vow; How to Educate a Wife; Mademoiselle Midnight. **1925** Kiss Me Again; Red Hot Tires; Hogan's Alley; The Limited Mail; Recompense. **1926** Across the Pacific; So This Is Paris; The Man Upstairs; Other Women's Husbands. **1927** Bitter Apples; The Black Diamond Express; Brass Knuckles; The Brute; The Bush Leaguer; Wolf's Clothing; One-Round Hogan. **1928** Across the Atlantic; White Shadows of the South Seas. **1929** Tiger Rose; Conquest; From Headquarters; The Greyhound Limited; No Defense; Skin Deep; The Show of Shows. **1930** Isle of Escape; Those Who Dance. **1931** The Flood. **1932** The Stoker; The Valley of Adventure. **1933** The Nectors; Her Forgotten Past; The Intruder; Officer 13. **1934** The Last Round-Up; Come On Marines!; The Thundering Herd; Student Tour; Wagon Wheels; College Rhythm. **1935** Hot Off the Press; Trails of the Wild; Nevada; G-Men; Lives of a Bengal Lancer; Wanderer of the Wasteland; On Probation. **1936** Ride, Ranger, Ride; Undersea Kingdom (serial); Treachery Rides the

Range; Mary of Scotland; Song of the Gringo; Desert Gold. **1937** Secret Agent X-9 (serial); The Outcasts of Poker Flat; Rootin' Tootin' Rhythm; Thunder Trail; Souls at Sea; High, Wide and Handsome. **1938** Hawk of the Wilderness (serial); Tom Sawyer, Detective; Spawn of the North; Big Broadcast of 1938; The Mysterious Rider; Illegal Traffic; Wild Bill Hickok (serial); Born to the West; Rebellious Daughters; Cocoanut Grove. **1939** Union Pacific; Dodge City; Geronimo; Frontier Pony Express; Days of Jesse James; Juarez; Port of Hats; Our Leading Citizen. **1940** Road to Singapore; Northwest Mounted Police; A Little Bit of Heaven; Mystery Sea Rider; Young Bill Hickok; Texas Rangers Ride Again. **1941** King of the Texas Rangers (serial); The Great Train Robbery; Arkansas Judge; Law of the Timber; Riders of Death Valley (serial) Scattergood Pulls the Strings; New York Town; Sunset in Wyoming; Bad Man of Deadwood. **1942** I Married a Witch; Reap the Wild Wind; Gentleman Jim; Sullivan's Travels; The Palm Beach Story; The Road to Morocco; North to the Klondike; Secret Enemies; Across the Pacific; Panama Hattie. **1943** Thank Your Lucky Stars; Truck Busters; Edge of Darkness; Northern Pursuit; Mission to Moscow; Secret Enemies; Thousands Cheer. **1944** The Mask of Dimitrios; The Conspirators; Passage to Marseille; The Adventures of Mark Twain. **1945** Saratoga Trunk; San Antonio. **1946** Cinderella Jones; Shadow of a Woman; Two Sisters from Boston; Easy to Wed; Never Say Goodbye. **1947** The Unfaithful; Bells of San Fernando; Life With Father; Speed to Spare; That Way With Women; Cheyenne; Possessed; My Wild Irish Rose. **1948** The Adventures of Don Juan; Silver River; Two Guys from Texas; Key Largo; Johnny Belinda. **1949** The Younger Brothers; Ranger of Cherokee Strip; Flaxy Martin; Homicide; South of St. Louis. **1950** Dallas; This Side of The Law; The Tomahawk Trail; The Blonde Bandit; Backfire; Montana; The Iroquois Trail. **1951** The Sea Hornet; Warpath; Snake River Desperadoes; Three Desperate Men; Gold Raiders. **1952** Rose of Cimarron; Hangman's Knot. **1953** The Last Posse.

BLUETTE, ISA
Born: 1898, Italy. Died: Nov. 10, 1939, Turin, Italy. Screen and stage actor.

BLUM, MAX
Born: 1874. Died: Jan. 10, 1944, Hollywood, Calif. Screen actor.

Appeared in: Torrid Zone.

BLUM, SAMMY
Born: 1889, New York, N.Y. Died: June 1, 1945, Hollywood, Calif. (heart attack). Screen and stage actor. Entered films in 1905.

Appeared in: **1925** Galloping Jinx. **1926** The Winning of Barbara Worth; Black Paradise; Siberia. **1927** Smile, Brother, Smile; The Wheel of Destiny. **1929** Rio Rita; The Delightful Rogue; The Prince of Hearts. **1930** More Sinned Against Than Usual (short); The Grand Parade; Party Girl. **1931** Iron Man. **1932** Night World. **1935** Alias Mary Dow. **1936** Under Your Spell; Criminals of the Air. **1937** Lodge Night (short). **1944** Nevada; The Falcon in Hollywood. **1945** West of the Pecos; George White's Scandals; plus the following shorts: Alibi Baby; Sleepless Tuesday; What, No Cigarettes?; It's Your Move; Let's Go Stepping.

BLYDEN, LARRY (Ivan Lawrence Blieden)
Born: June 23, 1925, Houston, Tex. Died: June 6, 1975, Agadir, Morocco (auto accident). Screen, stage, television and radio actor, stage director and producer. Divorced from actress Carol Haney (dec. 1962).

Appeared in: **1957** The Bachelor Party; Kiss Them for Me. **1970** On a Clear Day You Can See Forever.

BLYSTONE, JOHN G.
Born: Dec. 2, 1892, Rice Lake, Wis. Died: Aug. 6, 1938, Beverly Hills, Calif. (heart attack). Screen actor and film director.

Appeared in: **1914** Passing of the Beast; The Wheel of Life; A Wife on a Wager.

BLYSTONE, STANLEY "STAN" (William Stanley Blystone)
Born: Aug. 1, 1894, Wis. Died: July 16, 1956, Hollywood, Calif. (heart attack). Screen and television actor.

Appeared in: **1924** Darwin Was Right; Excitement. **1925** Under the Rouge. **1927** The Circus Ace. **1928** Four Sons; Wildcat Valley (short); Always a Gentleman (short); His Maiden Voyage (short); Ladies Preferred (short). **1929** Synthetic Sin; Through Different Eyes; Waltzing Around (short). **1930** The Fighting Legion; Parade of the West; Young Eagles; The Laurel-Hardy Murder Case (short). **1931** Dancing Dynamite; Man from Death Valley; Sundown Trail. **1932** Galloping Through; Honor of the Mounted; Sunkissed Sweeties

(short); The Golden West; Hold 'Em Jail. **1933** Dancing Lady; Strange People; Man of Action; Infernal Machine; Cross Fire; Lucky Larrigan; The Fighting Parson. **1934** Manhattan Melodrama; Burn 'Em Up Barnes (serial and feature); We're Not Dressing; Lemon Drop Kid; Hips, Hips Hooray; In Old Santa Fe; Sons of the Desert. **1935** G-Men; The Three Musketeers; Fighting Pioneers; Ladies Crave Excitement; Smart Girl; Code of the Mounted; Trail's End; Saddle Aces; The Ivory Handled Gun; The Phantom Empire (serial); Restless Knights (short) A Night at the Opera. **1936** Strike Me Pink; Modern Times; Ace Drummond (serial); The Vigilantes Are Coming (serial); Here Comes Trouble; The Riding Avenger; Half-Shot Shooters (short); False Alarms (short). **1937** Love in a Bungalow; The Life of Emile Zola; Second Honeymoon; Edgar and Goliath (short); Armored Car; Goofs and Saddles (short); Two Wise Maids; Windjammer; Galloping Dynamite; Headin' East; Boots and Saddles. **1938** California Frontier; Stranger from Arizona; Swiss Miss. **1939** The Lone Ranger Rides Again (serial); Trigger Pals; Crashing Through; Three Texas Steers; Torture Ship; Mr. Moto Takes a Vacation. **1940** Ma, He's Making Eyes at Me; Captain Caution; The Tulsa Kid; A Chump at Oxford; Remedy for Riches; Pony Post. **1941** King of the Texas Rangers (serial); Sea Raiders (serial); Tall, Dark and Handsome; Sunset in Wyoming; Buck Privates; I Wake Up Screaming (aka Hot Spot); Holt of the Secret Service (serial); Appointment for Love. **1942** Roxie Hart; Through Different Eyes; Piano Mooner (short); Jesse James, Jr.; Even as I.O.U. (short); Carry Harry (short). **1943** Spook Luder (short); Three Little Twerps (short). **1945** Navajo Kid. **1946** King of the Forest Rangers (serial); Six Gun Man; Moon Over Montana; Magnificent Doll. **1947** The Perils of Pauline; Road to Rio; Suddenly It's Spring; The Sea Hound (serial); Out West (short). **1948** The Paleface; I, Jane Doe; Eyes of Texas; I Wouldn't Be in Your Shoes. **1949** Samson and Delilah; Calamity Jane and Sam Bass; Master Minds; Ride, Ryder, Ride; Deputy Marshal; Rustlers; Loaded Pistols; Powder River Rustlers. **1950** Desperadoes of the West (serial); Six Gun Mesa; County Fair; Square Dance Katy; Slap Happy Sleuths (short). **1951** Santa Fe; Silver Canyon. **1952** Road Agent; Carson City. **1953** Jack McCall, Desperado; Abbott and Costello Go to Mars; A Perilous Journey. **1954** Living It Up. **1955** A Lawless Street; You're Never Too Young. **1956** Pardners.

BLYTHE, BETTY (Elizabeth Blythe Slaughter)
Born: Sept. 1, 1893, Los Angeles, Calif. Died: Apr. 7, 1972, Woodland Hills, Calif. Screen and stage actress. Married to film director Paul Scardon (dec. 1954). In 1938 was presented a Special Academy Award for her pioneer contributions to the motion picture industry. Entered films with Vitagraph Studios.

Appeared in: **1916** Slander. **1917** His Own People. **1918** Miss Ambition; Over the Top; Tangled Lives; The Green God. **1919** Dust of Desire; Undercurrent. **1920** Nomads of the North; Silver Horde; Third Generation. **1921** Charge It; Just Outside the Door; Mother O'Mine; The Queen of Sheba; The Truant Husband; Disraeli. **1922** Fair Lady; His Wife's Husband; How Women Love. **1923** Darling of the Rich; Sinner or Saint; Truth About Wives; Chu Chin Chow (US 1925). **1924** In Hollywood with Potash and Perlmutter; The Spitfire; The Breath of Scandal; The Folly of Vanity; The Recoil; Southern Love (aka A Woman's Secret—US). **1925** She; Speed; Percy. **1927** Snowbound; Eager Lips; A Million Bid; The Girl from Gay Paree. **1928** Sisters of Eve; Domestic Troubles; Glorious Betsy; Into No Man's Land; Daughters of Israel. **1929** Stolen Love. **1931** Stars of Yesterday (short). **1932** Tom Brown of Culver; Lena Rivers; Back Street. **1933** Pilgrimage; Only Yesterday; Before Midnight. **1934** The Scarlet Letter; Ever Since Eve; Money Means Nothing; Badge of Honor; Girl of the Limberlost; Two Heads on a Pillow; Night Alarm. **1935** Anna Karenina; I've Been Around; Cheers of the Crowd; The Perfect Clue; The Spanish Cape Mystery. **1936** Murder at Glen Athol; The Gorgeous Hussy; Yours for the Asking; Rainbow on the River. **1938** Man-Proof; Romance of the Limberlost; Gangster's Boy. **1940** Misbehaving Husbands; Earl of Puddlestone. **1941** Our Wife; Honky Tonk; Federal Fugitives; Top Sergeant Mulligan; Tuxedo Junction. **1942** The Miracle Kid; House of Errors; Dawn on the Great Divide; Piano Mooner (short). **1943** Girls in Chains; Bar 20; Sarong Girl; Spotlight Scandals; Where Are Your Children?; Farmer for a Day (short). **1944** The Chinese Cat. **1945** They Were Expendable; Adventure; Her Highness and the Bellboy; Docks of New York; Abbott and Costello in Hollywood. **1946** The Hoodlum Saint; Undercurrent; The Postman Always Rings Twice; Joe Palooka, Champ; The Undercover Woman. **1947** Song of Love. **1948** Luxury Liner; Letter from an Unknown Woman; Jiggs and Maggie in Society; Madonna of the Desert. **1949** The Lonesome Trail; The Barkleys of Broadway; Jackpot Jitters (aka Maggie and Jiggs in Jackpot Jitters). **1950** Jiggs and Maggie Out West. **1951** The Hollywood Story. **1956** Lust for Life. **1957** Helen Morgan Story. **1964** My Fair Lady.

BO, ARMANDO
Born: 1915, Argentina. Died: Oct 8, 1981, Buenos Aires, Argentina. Screen actor, film director, film producer and screenwriter. Married to actress Isabel Sarli.

Appeared in: **1959** Sabaleros (aka Put Up or Shut Up—US 1968). **1960** ...Y el Demonio Creo a los Hombres (aka Heat—US 1970). **1964** Lujuria Tropical (aka Tropical Ecstacy—US 1970). **1966** La Tentacion Desnuda (Naked Temptaton, aka Woman and Temptation—US 1967). **1967** La Mujer de mi Padre (aka Muhair—US 1970). **1968** Fuego (US 1969).

BOARDMAN, THELMA (Thelma Hubbard)
Born: Canal Zone. Died: Apr. 21, 1978, Los Angeles, Calif. Screen, stage, radio actress and playwright. Married to actor True Boardman (do not confuse with actor True Boardman, dec. 1918). Was the voice of "Minnie Mouse" during the 1940's.

BOARDMAN, TRUE (William True Boardman)
Born: Apr. 21, 1882, Oakland, Calif. Died: Sept. 28, 1918, Norwalk, Calif. Screen and stage actor. Married to actress Virginia True Boardman (dec. 1971). Starred in "Stingaree" series; "The Girl from Frisco" series; "The Social Pirates" series; "The Hazards of Helen" series from 1915-1917.

Appeared in: **1911** The New Editor. **1912** The Outlaw's Sacrifice. **1914** The Calling of Jim Barton; The Conquest of Man; Broncho Billy and the Sheriff; Single-Handed; Sophie Gets Stung. **1915** When Thieves Fall Out; Broncho Billy's Sentence; The False Clue; The Dream Seekers; Mysteries of the Grand Hotel; The Man in Irons; Stingaree; A Voice in the Wilderness; The Pitfall; An Enemy of Mankind; A Bushranger at Bay. **1916** On the Brink of War; The Purification of Mulfera; The Moth and the Star; The Villain Worshipper; The Duel in the Desert; The Darkest Hour; The Trapping of Peeler White; The Record Run; The Race for a Siding; The Governor's Special; The Fighting Heiress; The Oil Field Plot; The Turquoise Mine Mystery; Tigers Unchained; The Treasure of Cibola; The Web of Guilt; The Reformation of Dog Hole; The Yellow Hand; The Harvest of Gold; A Battle in the Dark; Mystery of the Brass Bound Chest; The Fight for Paradise Valley; The Son of Cain; The Witch of the Dark House; The Poisoned Dart; The Stain of Chuckawalla. **1917** The False Prophet; The Resurrection of Gold Bar; Wolf of Los Alamos; The Homesteader's Feud; The Jackaroo; The Fugitive Passenger; The Tracking of Stingaree. **1919** Tarzan of the Apes; Molly Go Get 'Em; The Doctor and the Woman.

BOARDMAN, VIRGINIA TRUE
Born: 1889. Died: June 10, 1971, Hollywood, Calif. Screen and stage actress. Entered films in 1911 with Selig Studios in Chicago. Appeared on stage as Virginia Eames. Married to actor True Boardman (dec. 1918).

Appeared in: **1922** The Village Blacksmith; Where Is My Wandering Boy Tonight?; A Blind Bargain; Penrod; The Third Alarm. **1923** The Town Scandal; The Barefoot Boy; The Gunfighter; Pioneer Trails; Three Jumps Ahead; The Mailman; Michael O'Halloran. **1924** Girl of the Limberlost; The Tomboy. **1925** The Home Maker; The Red Rider. **1926** The Test of Donald Norton. **1927** Down the Stretch; King of the Jungle (serial); Speedy Smith. **1929** The Lady Lies. **1931** Scareheads. **1933** One Year Later. **1934** The Road to Ruin; "Baby Burlesque" series. **1936** The Fugitive Sheriff.

BODEL, BURMAN
Born: 1911. Died: July 17, 1969, Calif. Stage and screen actor.

BOEHLER, GEORGE (George Henry Boehler)
Born: Jan. 2, 1892, Lawrenceburg, Ind. Died: June 23, 1958, Lawrenceburg, Ind. Baseball player and screen actor.

Appeared in: **1929** Fast Company.

BOEHN, KARL
Born: 1894, Graz, Austria. Died: Aug. 14, 1981, Salzburg, Austria (stroke). Symphony, opera conductor and screen actor. Father of actor Karlheinz Boehn.

BOESE, JOACHIM
Born: 1933, Germany. Died: Apr. 25, 1971, Germany? (auto accident). Stage and screen actor.

BOESEN, WILLIAM
Born: 1924. Died: Mar. 25, 1972, New York, N.Y. Screen and stage actor.

Appeared in: **1969** Putney Swope. **1971** The Gang Who Couldn't Shoot Straight.

BOETIGER, JULIA
Born: 1852. Died: Oct. 28, 1938, Los Angeles, Calif. Screen actress.

BOGART, HUMPHREY (Humphrey DeForest Bogart)
Born: Dec. 25, 1899, New York, N.Y. Died: Jan. 14, 1957, Los Angeles, Calif. (cancer). Screen and stage actor. Married to actress Lauren Bacall. Divorced from actresses Helen Menken (dec. 1966), Mary Phillips (dec. 1975) and Mayo Methot (dec. 1951). Nominated for 1943 Academy Award for Best Actor in Casablanca and in 1954 for The Caine Mutiny. Won 1951 Academy Award for Best Actor in The African Queen.

Appeared in: **1930** A Devil With Women (film debut); Broadway's Like That (short); Up the River. **1931** Body and Soul; Bad Sister; Women of All Nations; A Holy Terror. **1932** Love Affair; Big City Blues; Three on a Match. **1934** Midnight. **1935** Black Fury. **1936** The Petrified Forest (stage and film versions); Two Against the World; Bullets or Ballots; China Clipper; Isle of Fury. **1937** The Great O'Malley; Black Legion; San Quentin; Marked Woman; Kid Galahad; Dead End; Stand-In. **1938** Swing Your Lady; Men Are Such Fools; Crime School; The Amazing Dr. Clitterhouse; Racket Busters; Angels With Dirty Faces. **1939** King of the Underworld; You Can't Get Away With Murder; Dark Victory; The Oklahoma Kid; The Return of Dr. X; The Roaring Twenties; Invisible Stripes; Arizona Kid. **1940** Virginia City; It All Came True; Brother Orchid; They Drive By Night. **1941** High Sierra; The Wagons Roll At Night; The Maltese Falcon. **1942** All Through the Night; The Big Shot; Across the Pacific; In This Our Life (unbilled). **1943** Casablanca; Action in the North Atlantic; Thank Your Lucky Stars; Sahara. **1944** Passage to Marseille. **1945** Conflict; To Have and Have Not; Hollywood Victory Canteen (short). **1946** Message from the Front (short); The Big Sleep; Two Guys from Milwaukee (unbilled). **1947** The Two Mrs. Carrolls; Dead Reckoning; Dark Passage; Always Together. **1948** The Treasure of Sierra Madre; Key Largo. **1949** Knock on Any Door; Tokyo Joe. **1950** Chain Lightning; In a Lonely Place. **1951** The Enforcer; Sirocco; Saving Bond (short); The African Queen. **1952** Road to Bali (film clip); Deadline—U.S.A. **1953** Battle Circus. **1954** Beat the Devil; The Caine Mutiny; Sabrina; The Barefoot Contessa; Love Lottery (unbilled). **1955** We're No Angels; The Desperate Hours; The Left Hand of God. **1956** The Harder They Fall. **1982** Dead Men Don't Wear Plaid (film clips).

BOHANNON, E. J. "BO"
Born: 1896. Died: Feb. 14, 1966, Sacramento, Calif. Screen actor and stuntman.

BOHN, MERRITT F.
Born: 1905. Died: Dec. 11, 1978, Torrence, Calif. (pneumonia following stroke). Screen, stage and television actor.

Appeared in: **1960** The Story of Ruth. **1961** The Young Savages; By Love Possessed. **1962** Kid Galahad; The Manchurian Candidate. **1965** How to Murder Your Wife; Wild Seed; Zebra in the Kitchen. **1966** Lord Love a Duck; Nevada Smith. **1968** Sol Madrid.

BOHNEN, MICHAEL
Born: May 2, 1887, Cologne, Germany. Died: Apr. 26, 1965, Berlin, Germany (heart attack). Screen actor and opera singer. Entered films in 1919. Divorced from singer Mary Lewis, later married to dancer La Jana (dec. 1940) and later married to singer Ingeborg Behrend.

Appeared in: **1929** Sajenko the Soviet. **1930** Zwei Kravatten (Two Neckties). **1933** Viktoria und Ihr Husar (Victoria and Her Hussar); Wiener Blut. **1934** Gold. **1936** The Private Life of Louis XIV. **1937** August der Starke. **1938** Solo Per Te (Only for Thee). **1939** Das Unsterbliche Herz (The Immortal Heart).

BOHNEN, ROMAN
Born: Nov. 24, 1894, St. Paul, Minn. Died: Feb. 24, 1949, Hollywood, Calif. (heart attack). Screen and stage actor.

Appeared in: **1937** 52nd Street; Vogues of 1938. **1939** Of Mice and Men. **1940** The Living Dead. **1941** They Dare Not Love; The Bugle Sounds; Appointment for Love; So Ends Our Night. **1942** Young America; The Hard Way; Grand Central Murder; Affairs of Jimmy Valentine. **1943** Edge of Darkness; Mission to Moscow; The Mask of Dimitrios; The Song of Bernadette. **1944** The Hitler Gang; None But the Lonely Heart; The Hairy Ape. **1945** A Bell for Adano; Counter-Attack. **1946** Deadline at Dawn; The Hoodlum Saint; Mr. Ace; The Strange Love of Martha Ivers; Miss Susie Slagle's; Two Years Before the Mast; California; The Best Years of Our Lives. **1947** Brute Force; For You I Die; Winter Wonderland; Song of Love. **1948** Arch of Triumph; Joan of Arc; Open Street; The Night Has a Thousand Eyes. **1949** Kazan; Mr. Soft Touch.

BOLAND, EDDIE
Born: 1883, San Francisco, Calif. Died: Feb. 3, 1935, Santa Monica, Calif. (heart attack). Screen actor. Entered films in 1913.

Appeared in: **1922** Oliver Twist. **1923** Within the Law; Long Live the King. **1924** Little Robinson Crusoe. **1926** Hard Boiled; Unknown Dangers; A Gentleman Roughneck. **1927** Sunrise; The Kid Brother. **1928** Manhattan Knights; shorts prior to 1929: Nobody's Business; Nothing Matters; Who's My Wife? **1929** Last Performance. **1930** Wings of Adventure; City Girl. **1931** The Miracle Woman. **1932** Mother-In-Law's Day (short); Giggle Water (short); Vanity Street. **1933** I Have Lived.

BOLAND, MARY
Born: Jan. 28, 1880, Philadelphia, Pa. Died: June 23, 1965, New York, N.Y. Screen, stage and television actress.

Appeared in: **1916** The Edge of the Abyss (film debut); The Stepping Stone. **1918** His Temporary Wife. **1931** Personal Maid; Secrets of a Secretary. **1932** If I Had a Million; The Night of June Thirteen; Trouble in Paradise; Evening for Sale; Night after Night. **1933** Mama Loves Papa; Three-Cornered Moon; The Solitaire Man. **1934** Six of a Kind; Stingaree; Down to Their Last Yacht; Four Frightened People; Melody in Spring; Here Comes the Groom; The Pursuit of Happiness. **1935** People Will Talk; Two for Tonight; The Big Broadcast of 1936; Ruggles of Red Gap. **1936** Wives Never Know; Early to Bed; College Holiday; A Son Comes Home. **1937** Marry the Girl; There Goes the Groom; Mama Runs Wild; Danger—Love at Work. **1938** Little Tough Guys in Society; Artists and Models Abroad. **1939** The Magnificent Fraud; The Women; Boy Trouble; Night Work. **1940** He Married His Wife; The Hit Parade of 1941; One Night in the Tropics; New Moon; Pride and Prejudice. **1944** Nothing But Trouble; In Our Time. **1945** Forever Yours; The Right to Live; They Shall Have Faith. **1948** Julia Misbehaves. **1950** Guilty Bystander.

BOLD, DAVEY
Born: 1923, Chicago, Ill. Died: July 16, 1978, Omaha, Neb. (heart attack). Screen, television actor and comic.

Appeared in: **1961** Hoodlum Priest.

BOLDER, ROBERT "BOBBIE"
Born: 1859, London, England. Died: Dec. 10, 1937, Beverly Hills, Calif. Screen and stage actor.

Appeared in: **1919** Strictly Confidential. **1921** The Fighting Lover; The Silent Call; Black Beauty; The House That Jazz Built; The Marriage of William Ash; Beyond the Rocks; The Lane That Had No Turning. **1923** Grumpy; The Christian; The Love Piker. **1924** Abraham Lincoln; Captain Blood; What Three Men Wanted; Vanity's Price; The Sea Hawk. **1925** Raffles, the Amateur Cracksman; Stella Maris; The Handsome Brute; Blue Blood. **1926** Butterflies in the Rain. **1927** The Wise Wife; Woman's Wares; Tarzan and the Golden Lion. **1929** The Tip Off. **1930** Grumpy (and 1923 version); Lady of Scandal; Charlie's Aunt. **1931** Get-Rich-Quick Wallingford; The Miracle Woman; East Lynne. **1935** The Great Impersonation.

BOLES, JIM (James Boles, Jr.)
Born: Feb. 28, 1914, Lubbock, Tex. Died: May 26, 1977, Sherman Oaks, Calif. (heart seizure). Screen, stage, radio and television actor. Married to actress Athena Lorde (dec. 1973). Father of actors Eric, Sue, and Barbara Boles. Approximately 1946 dubbed English voices in foreign films.

Appeared in: **1950** The Tattooed Stranger. **1951** The Man with My Face. **1957** Naked in the Sun. **1960** The Pusher. **1962** The Most Wanted Man in the World. **1964** Fate is the Hunter; He Rides Tall. **1965** Fluffy; The Greatest Story Ever Told; John Goldfarb, Please Come Home. **1966** The Trouble with Angels; A Big Hand for the Little Lady; The Ghost and Mr. Chicken. **1967** The Reluctant Astronaut; Waterhole #3; The Karate Killers. **1968** With Six You Get Eggroll; The Shakiest Gun in the West; P.J. **1969** Angel in my Pocket; The Love God. **1970** WUSA; When the Lines Goes Through. **1971** Skin Game; Le Mans. **1973** Are Eli and Rodger of the Skies; Doctor Death; Seeker of Souls. **1974** The White Dawn (narrator); Deadly Honeymoon. **1975** Once is not Enough; The Apple Dumpling Gang.

BOLES, JOHN
Born: Oct., 1895, Greenville, Tex. Died: Feb. 27, 1969, San Angelo, Tex. (heart attack). Screen and stage actor. During W.W.I he was a U.S. spy in Germany, Bulgaria and Turkey.

Appeared in: **1925** So This Is Marraige; Excuse Me. **1927** The Love of Sunya. **1928** Shepherd of the Hills; Bride of the Colorado; What Holds Men?; We Americans; The Water Hole; Virgin Lips; Man-Made Woman. **1929** The Desert Song; The Last Warning; Rio Rita; Scandal;

Romance of the Underworld; She Goes to War. **1930** Song of the West; Captain of the Guard; Queen of Scandal; King of Jazz; One Heavenly Night. **1931** Seed; Good Sport; Resurrection; Frankenstein. **1932** Careless Lady; Back Street; Six Hours to Live. **1933** Hollywood on Parade (short); Child of Manhattan; My Lips Betray; Only Yesterday; Beloved. **1934** I Believed in You; Age of Innocence; Bottoms Up; Stand Up and Cheer; Life of Vergie Winters; The White Parade; Music in the Air; Wild Gold. **1935** Orchids to You; Curly Top; Redheads on Parade; The Littlest Rebel; Masquerade (aka Escapade). **1936** Rose of the Rancho; A Message to Garcia; Craig's Wife. **1937** As Good as Married; Stella Dallas; Fight for Your Lady. **1938** Romance in the Dark; She Married an Artist; Sinners in Paradise. **1942** Road to Happiness; Between Us Girls. **1943** Thousands Cheer. **1952** Babes in Bagdad.

BOLEY, MAY
Born: Washington, D.C. Died: Jan. 7, 1963, Hollywood, Calif. (cancer). Screen and stage actress.

Appeared in: **1928** The Wagon Show. **1929** Dangerous Curves; Dance of Life; Beneath the Law (short); Hail the Princess; Woman from Hell. **1930** Lillies of the Field; Moby Dick; Children of Pleasure. **1931** Going Wild. **1932** A Woman Commands; The Expert. **1933** Advice to the Lovelorn. **1934** The Mighty Barnum. **1935** The Informer. **1936** Without Orders. **1937** Ready, Willing and Able; Tovarich. **1938** Reckless Living; Cowboy from Brooklyn; Prison Farm. **1939** Persons in Hiding; Death of a Champion; Undercover Doctor; The Women. **1941** Skylark.

BOLGER, ROBERT "BO" (Robert Erin Bolger)
Born: 1937. Died: Aug. 23, 1969, Oceanside, Calif. (killed while skydiving). Screen, television actor and stuntman.

BOMBARD, LOTTIE GERTRUDE
Born: 1908. Died: Nov., 1913, Saranac Lake, N.Y. Child actress featured in Pathe films.

BONANOVA, FORTUNIO
Born: Jan. 13, 1893, Palma de Mallorca, Spain. Died: Apr. 2, 1969, Woodland Hills, Calif. (cerebral hemorrhage). Screen, stage, television actor, opera singer and playwright.

Appeared in: **1924** Don Juan (film debut). **1932** Careless Lady; A Successful Calamity. **1936** El Desaparecido; Podoroso Caballer. **1938** Tropic Holiday; Romance in the Dark; Bulldog Drummond in Africa. **1939** La Immaculada. **1940** I Was an Adventuress; Down Argentine Way. **1941** They Met in Argentina; Moon Over Miami; A Yank in the R.A.F; Two Latins from Manhattan; Mr. and Mrs. North; Obliging Young Lady; Citizen Kane; That Night in Rio; Blood and Sand. **1942** Sing Your Worries Away; Girl Trouble; Larceny, Inc; The Black Swan. **1943** The Sultan's Daughter; For Whom the Bell Tolls; Five Graves to Cairo. **1944** Double Indemnity; My Best Gal; Ali Baba and the Forty Thieves; Falcon in Mexico; Mrs. Parkington; Brazil; Going My Way. **1945** Where Do We Go From Here?; A Bell for Adano; Hit the Hay; Man Alive; The Red Dragon. **1946** Monsieur Beaucaire. **1947** Rose of Santa Rosa; Fiesta; The Fugitive. **1948** Bad Men of Tombstone; Angel on the Amazon; Romance on the High Seas; Adventures of Don Juan. **1949** Whirlpool. **1950** Nancy Goes to Rio; September Affair. **1951** Havana Rose. **1953** So This Is Love; Conquest of Cochise; Second Chance; Thunder Bay; The Moon Is Blue. **1955** New York Confidential; Kiss Me Deadly. **1956** Jaguar. **1957** An Affair to Remember. **1958** The Saga of Hemp Brown. **1959** Thunder in the Sun. **1963** The Running Man. **1967** The Million Dollar Collar.

BOND, FRANK G. (Franklin G. Bond)
Born: 1886, Salina, Kans. Died: Oct. 4, 1929, New York, N.Y. Screen and stage actor.

Appeared in: **1915** One Night Stand. **1925** Hogan's Alley; Three Weeks in Paris. **1927** Tell it to Sweeney.

BOND, JACK (Alfred Welch)
Born: 1899. Died: Apr. 29, 1952, Hollywood, Calif. Screen and stage actor.

Appeared in: **1944** Since You Went Away. **1946** The Kid from Brooklyn; Duel in the Sun.

BOND, JOHNNY
Born: 1915. Died: June 12, 1978, Burbank, Calif. Screen, radio, television actor and songwriter.

Appeared in: **1941** Stick to Your Guns. **1944** Arizona Trail; Since You Went Away; Kansas City Kitty; Marshall of Gunsmoke; Oklahoma Raiders. **1946** Gallant Bess. **1947** Swing the Western Way; Song of the Wasteland.

BOND, LYLE
Born: 1917. Died: Apr. 14, 1972, San Diego, Calif. (heart attack). Screen, radio, television actor, newscaster and television sportscaster.

BOND, WARD
Born: Apr. 9, 1903, Denver, Colo. Died: Nov. 5, 1960, Dallas, Tex. (heart attack). Screen, stage and television actor. Entered films in 1928 while attending U.S.C.

Appeared in: **1929** Salute (film debut); Words and Music. **1930** Born Reckless; The Big Trail. **1931** Arrowsmith. **1932** High Speed; White Eagle; Rackety Rax; Flesh; Hello Trouble; Virtue. **1933** Obey the Law; The Sundown Rider; Heroes for Sale; Wild Boys of the Road; When Strangers Marry; The Wrecker; Whirlpool; Unknown Valley; Police Car 17. **1934** Chained; Straightaway; Most Precious Thing in Life; Tall Timber; The Fighting Code; The Voice in the Night; A Man's Game; The Crime of Helen Stanley; Girl in Danger; The Human Side; Kid Millions; Against the Law; The Poor Man; The Frontier Marshal; It Happened One Night; The Defense Rests; The Fighting Ranger; Here Comes the Groom. **1935** G-Men; Western Courage; Men of the Night; Justice of the Range; Too Tough to Kill; Devil Dogs of the Air; Little Big Shot; The Crimson Trail; She Gets Her Man; His Night Out; Black Fury; Fighting Shadows; Guard That Girl; Murder in the Fleet; Headline Woman; Waterfront Lady; The Informer. **1936** Fury; Cattle Thief; Pride of the Marines; Avenging Waters; Muss 'Em Up; The Bride Walks Out; Second Wife; Without Orders; Crash Donovan; Conflict; They Met in a Taxi; The Man Who Lived Twice; The Legion of Terror; The Leathernecks Have Landed. **1937** The Wildcatter; A Fight to the Finish; You Only Live Once; Dead End; Park Avenue Logger; The Devil's Playground; 23 1/2 Hours' Leave; Night Key; Escape By Night. **1938** Bringing Up Baby; Hawaii Calls; Born to Be Wild; Flight Into Nowhere; Reformatory; Gun Law; The Law West of Tombstone; Professor Beware; Mr. Moto's Gamble; Submarine Patrol; Prison Break; Numbered Woman; Over the Wall; The Amazing Dr. Clitterhouse. **1939** Confessions of a Nazi Spy; Son of Frankenstein; Mr. Moto in Danger Island; They Made Me a Criminal; Made for Each Other; Dodge City; Waterfront; Gone With the Wind; Trouble in Sundown; The Return of the Cisco Kid; Frontier Marshal (and 1934 version); The Girl from Mexico; The Kid from Kokomo; The Oklahoma Kid; Drums Along the Mohawk; Dust Be My Destiny; Young Mr. Lincoln. **1940** Heaven With a Barbed Wire Fence; Virginia City; The Cisco Kid and the Lady; The Grapes of Wrath; Little Old New York; Santa Fe Trail; Buck Benny Rides Again; The Mortal Storm; Kit Carson; The Long Voyage Home. **1941** The Shepherd of the Hills; A Man Betrayed; Sergeant York; Manpower; Doctors Don't Tell; Swamp Water; Wild Bill Hickok Rides; Tobacco Road; The Maltese Falcon. **1942** In This Our Life; The Falcon Takes Over; Gentleman Jim; Sin Town; Ten Gentlemen from West Point. **1943** Slightly Dangerous; They Came to Blow Up America; Cowboy Commandos; Hello, Frisco, Hello; Hitler, Dead or Alive; A Guy Named Joe. **1944** Home in Indiana; The Sullivans; Tall in the Saddle. **1945** Dakota; They Were Expendable. **1946** Canyon Passage; My Darling Clementine; It's a Wonderful Life. **1947** The Fugitive; Unconquered. **1948** Fort Apache; The Time of Your Life; Joan of Arc; Tap Roots; Three Godfathers. **1950** Riding High; Wagonmaster; Singing Guns; Kiss Tomorrow Goodbye; Dodge City; Great Missouri Raid. **1951** Operation Pacific; Only the Valiant; On Dangerous Ground. **1952** The Quiet Man; Hellgate; Thunderbirds. **1953** Blowing Wild; The Moonlighter; Hondo. **1954** Gypsy Colt; The Bob Mathias Story; Johnny Guitar. **1955** Mr. Roberts; A Man Alone; The Long Gray Line. **1956** The Searchers; Dakota Incident; Pillars of the Sky. **1957** Halliday Brand; The Wings of Eagles. **1958** China Doll. **1959** Rio Bravo; Alias Jesse James.

BONDHILL, GERTRUDE (Gertrude Schafer)
Born: 1880. Died: Sept. 15, 1960, Chicago, Ill. Screen, stage and radio actress. Appeared in early silents made at Essanay Studios in Chicago.

BONDI, BEULAH (Beulah Bondy)
Born: May 3, 1892, Chicago, Ill. Died: Jan. 11, 1981, Woodland Hills, Calif. (pulmonary complications). Screen, stage and television actress.

Appeared in: **1931** Street Scene (film debut); Arrowsmith. **1932** Rain. **1933** The Stranger's Return; Christopher Bean. **1934** Finishing School; Two Alone; Registered Nurse; Ready for Love. **1935** The Good Fairy; Bad Boy. **1936** The Moon's Our Home; The Case Against Mrs. Ames; Hearts Divided; The Trail of the Lonesome Pine; The Gorgeous Hussy; The Invisible Ray. **1937** Make Way for Tomorrow; Maid of Salem. **1938** Of Human Hearts; The Buccaneer; Vivacious Lady; The Sisters. **1939** Mr. Smith Goes to Washington; On Borrowed Time; The Upper-Pup. **1940** Our Town; The Captain is a Lady; Remember the Night. **1941** One Foot in Heaven; The Shepherd of the Hills; Penny Serenade. **1943** Watch on the Rhine; Tonight We Raid Calais. **1944** I Love a Soldier; She's a Soldier, Too; Our Hearts Were Young and Gay; And

Now Tomorrow; The Very Thought of You. **1945** Back to Bataan; The Southerner. **1946** It's a Wonderful Life; Breakfast in Hollywood; Sister Kenny. **1947** High Conquest. **1948** So Dear to My Heart; The Sainted Sisters; The Snake Pit. **1949** The Black Book; Reign of Terror; The Life of Riley; Mr. Soft Touch. **1950** The Baron of Arizona; The Furies. **1952** Lone Star. **1953** Latin Lovers. **1954** Track of the Cat. **1956** Back from Eternity. **1957** The Unholy Wife. **1959** The Big Fisherman; A Summer Place. **1961** Tammy Tell Me True. **1962** The Wonderful World of the Brothers Grimm. **1963** Tammy and the Doctor.

BONELLI, RICHARD (Richard Bunn)
Born: Feb. 6, 1889, Port Byron, N.Y. Died: June 7, 1980, Los Angeles, Calif. Screen, radio, television actor, opera singer and teacher. Divorced from singer Pauline Cornelys (dec.). Married to Mona Chapman Wood. Appeared in one of the first sound films—Fox Movietone short.

Appeared in: **1935** Enter Madame. **1941** There's Magic in Music (aka The Hard Boiled Canary).

BONHAM, JOHN "BONZO"
Born: 1948, England. Died: Sept. 25, 1980, near Windsor, England. Musician (drummer) and screen actor. Leader of rock group "Led Zeppelin."

Appeared in: **1974** Son of Dracula. **1976** The Song Remains the Same.

BONIFACE, SYMONA
Born: 1894. Died: Sept. 2, 1950, Woodland Hills, Calif. Screen, stage actress, stage producer and playwright. Daughter of stage actor George C. Boniface and stage actress Nona Ferner. Married to actor Frank Pharr Sims.

Appeared in: **1932** Strictly Unreliable (short). **1934** Washee Ironee (short). **1936** Girls Dormitory. **1938** Ankles Away (short). **1940** Ninotchka; A-Plumbing We Will Go (short); No Census, No Feeling (short). **1941** The following shorts: All the World's a Stooge; An Ache in Every Stake; In the Sweet Pie and Pie. **1942** Unexpected Riches (short). **1943** Spook Louder (short). **1944** Mrs. Parkington; Crash Goes the Hash (short). **1945** Her Highness and the Bellboy; Micro Phonies (short). **1946** G.I. Wanna Go Home (short). **1947** Half-Wits Holiday (short). **1949** Who Done It (short); Vagabond Loafers (short). **1950** Rogues of Sherwood Forest; Pirates of High Seas (serial). **1951** The Pest Man Wins (short). **1955** Bedlam in Paradise (short). **1956** Scheming Schemers (short). **1958** Pies and Guys (short).

BONIFANT, CARMEN
Born: 1890, Mexico. Died: Aug. 1, 1957, Mexico City, Mexico. Screen actress.

BONILLAS, MYRNA
Born: 1890. Died: Nov. 13, 1959, Hollywood, Calif. (heart attack). Screen actress.

Appeared in: **1922** Shackles of Gold; A Stage Romance. **1923** The Custard Cup. **1927** The Claw; The Gingham Girl. **1930** Lummox; Asi es la Vida.

BONN, FERDINAND
Born: Germany. Died: Sept. 24, 1933, Berlin, Germany (stroke). Screen actor.

Appeared in: **1929** Strauss, the Waltz King.

BONN, FRANK
Born: 1873. Died: Mar. 4, 1944, Los Angeles, Calif. Screen actor.

Appeared in: **1926** Old Ironsides.

BONN, WALTER
Born: 1889. Died: Sept. 8, 1953, Hollywood, Calif. Screen and stage actor.

Appeared in: **1935** The Man Who Broke the Bank at Monte Carlo. **1937** Thin Ice. **1938** The Girl of the Golden West; Three Comrades; International Crime; Cipher Bureau. **1940** The Man I Married. **1941** Man Hunt. **1942** Once Upon a Honeymoon. **1943** Around the World; We've Never Been Licked. **1945** A Song to Remember; Counter-Attack; Where Do We Go from Here? **1946** The Razor's Edge. **1948** All My Sons.

BONNARD, MARIO
Born: 1889, Italy. Died: Mar. 22, 1965, Rome, Italy (heart attack). Screen actor, film director and screenwriter. Entered films as an actor and director in 1909.

BONNER, ISABEL
Born: 1908. Died: July 1, 1955, Los Angeles, Calif. (brain hemorrhage). Screen, stage, television and radio actress.

Appeared in: **1955** The Shrike.

BONNER, JOE
Born: 1882. Died: Apr. 13, 1959. Screen actor.

Appeared in: **1922** The Man Who Waited; Affinities. **1923** Slow as Lightning. **1924** Western Grit. **1927** Face Value; Is Your Daughter Safe?

BONNIER, JO (Joakim Bonnier)
Born: Jan 31, 1930, Stockholm, Sweden. Died: June 12, 1972, Le Mans, France (auto race crash). Auto racer and screen actor.

Appeared in: **1966** Grand Prix.

BONOMO, JOE
Born: Dec. 25, 1902, Coney Island, N.Y. Died: Mar. 28, 1978, Hollywood, Calif. Screen actor, stuntman, professional strongman and daredevil. Entered films in 1911.

Appeared in: **1922** A Light in the Dark. **1923** The Hunchback of Notre Dame; Beasts of Paradise (serial); The Eagle's Talons (serial). **1924** The Iron Man (serial); Wolves of the North (serial). **1925** The Great Circus Mystery (serial); Perils of the Wild (serial). **1926** You Never Know Women; The Flaming Frontier. **1927** The King of Kings; The Golden Stallion (serial); Heroes of the Wild (serial); Sea Tiger. **1928** The Chinatown Mystery (serial); Vamping Venus; Noah's Ark. **1929** Phantoms of the North; Courtin' Wildcats. **1931** The Phantom of the West (serial); The Vanishing Legion (serial). **1932** The Lost Special (serial); The Last Frontier (serial); Sign of the Cross. **1933** Island of Lost Souls.

BONSTELLE, HELEN
Born: 1918. Died: July 26, 1979, New York, N.Y. Screen and stage actress. Married to actor Robert Fitzsimmons.

BONUCCI, ALBERTO
Born: 1919, Italy. Died: Apr. 7, 1969, Rome, Italy (heart attack). Screen actor and film director.

Appeared in: **1954** Fugitive in Trieste. **1956** The Magnificent Seven (Japan). **1961** Neapolitan Carousel; Blood and Roses. **1963** Love and Larceny. **1966** The Little Nuns. **1967** The Taming of the Shrew. Other Italian Films: The Tenor from Oklahoma; Walter and His Cousins.

BOOKER, HARRY
Born: 1850. Died: June 28, 1924, San Diego, Calif. Screen, vaudeville actor and film director. Played in vaudeville as part of "Canfield and Booker" team. Entered films with Mack Sennett in Keystone comedies.

Appeared in: **1915** The Great Vacuum Robbery; Her Painted Hero; A Game Old Night. **1916** The Feathered Nest (aka Girl Guardian—reissued 1920 as Only a Farmer's Daughter); Her Marble Heart; The Judge; His Hereafter (aka Murray's Mix-Up); Maid Mad (aka The Fortune Teller); A Love Riot; Pills or Peril; Bombs. **1917** Maggie's First False Step; Her Fame and Shame; Her Torpedoed Love; She Needed a Doctor; His Uncle Dudley. **1921** Skirts. **1922** The Hottentot.

BOONE, RICHARD
Born: June 18, 1917, Los Angeles, Calif. Died: Jan. 10, 1981, St. Augustine, Fla. (cancer). Screen, stage and television actor.

Appeared in: **1950** Halls of Montezuma. **1951** Call Me Mister; The Desert Fox. **1952** Kangaroo; Pony Soldier; Way of a Gaucho; Return of the Texan; Red Skies of Montana; Smoke Jumpers. **1953** Man on a Tightrope; City of Bad Men; The Robe; Beneath the 12-Mile Reef; Vicki. **1954** The Seige at Red River; The Raid; Dragnet. **1955** Man Without a Star; Ten Wanted Men; Robber's Roost. **1956** Battle Stations; Star in the Dust; Away All Boats. **1957** Lizzie; The Tall T; The Garment Jungle. **1958** I Bury the Living. **1960** The Alamo. **1961** A Thunder of Drums. **1964** Rio Conchos. **1965** The War Lord. **1967** Hombre. **1968** Kona Coast. **1969** The Arrangement; The Night of the Following Day. **1970** Madron; The Kremlin Letter. **1971** Big Jake. **1975** Against a Crooked Sky. **1976** The Shootist. **1978** God's Gun; The Big Sleep.

BOOT, GLADYS
Born: 1890. Died: Oct. 16, 1964, London, England. Screen, stage and television actress.

Appeared in: **1949** The Blue Lagoon. **1956** Murder Reported. **1958** Gypsy and the Gentleman; Harry Black and the Tiger; Virgin Island (US 1960).

BOOTH, ELMER (W. Elmer Booth)
Born: Dec. 9, 1882, Los Angeles, Calif. Died: June 16, 1915, Los Angeles, Calif. (auto accident). Screen actor.

Appeared in: **1912** Brutality; So Near, Yet So Far; The Narrow Road; Gold and Glitter; In the North Woods; An Unseen Enemy; The Musketeers of Pig Alley; An Interrupted Elopement. **1913** The Unwelcome Guest; Drink's Lure. **1914** Mrs. Black Is Back. **1915** Mr. Wallack's Wallet; A Chase By Moonlight; Mixed Values; Ethel's Deadly Alarm Clock; Gasoline Gus; Beppo the Barber; Two Daughters of Eve.

BOOTH, HELEN
Died: Feb. 5, 1971, England. Screen, stage and television actress.

Appeared in: **1967** The Family Way.

BOOTH, NESDON (Nesdon Foye Booth)
Born: Sept. 1, 1918, Baker, Ore. Died: Mar. 25, 1964, Hollywood, Calif. (heart attack). Screen, stage and television actor.

Appeared in: **1949** City Across the River (film debut). **1952** The Girl in White; Sally and Saint Anne. **1953** The Glass Wall; I Love Melvin; Executive Suite. **1954** Rogue Cop. **1955** I'll Cry Tomorrow; Pete Kelly's Blues; I Died a Thousand Times. **1956** He Laughed Last; The Price of Fear; These Wilder Years. **1957** The Shadow on the Window; Funny Face; Reform School Girl; Escape from Red Rock; Mister Cory; The Brothers Rico. **1958** Cattle Empire; Space Master X-7; Damn Yankees; Too Much, Too Soon; Sing, Boy, Sing. **1959** Rio Bravo; The Big Circus; The FBI Story; Yellowstone Kelly. **1960** Bells Are Ringing; Let No Man Write My Epitaph; The Rise and Fall of Legs Diamond. **1961** The Wackiest Ship in the Army; Claudelle Inglish; Gun Street; Ada; One-Eyed Jacks. **1962** Walk on the Wild Side; Jumbo. **1963** Critic's Choice. **1964** What a Way to Go! **1965** The Greatest Story Ever Told.

BOOTH, SYDNEY BARTON
Born: Jan. 29, 1877, Boston, Mass. Died: Feb. 5, 1937, Stanford, Conn. (cerebral hemorrhage). Screen and stage actor.

Appeared in: **1911** The Three Musketeers.

BORDAS, EMILIA F.
Born: 1874, Spain. Died: 1958, Madrid, Spain. Stage and screen actress.

BORDEAUX, JOE (aka JOE BORDEAU)
Born: 1894. Died: Sept. 10, 1950, Hollywood, Calif. Screen actor. Entered films with Keystone in 1913.

Appeared in: **1916** Fatty and Mabel Adrift; The Other Man; The Moonshiners; The Waiter's Ball; Bright Lights. **1929** Hurricane. **1930** The Man Hunter. **1932** High Speed. **1935** Miss Pacific Fleet. **1936** The Lucky Corner (short); On the Wrong Trek.

BORDEN, EDDIE
Born: 1888, Deer Lodge, Tenn. Died: July 1, 1955, Hollywood, Calif. Screen, stage and vaudeville actor. Entered films in 1921.

Appeared in: **1922** Back Home and Broke. **1925** Bad Boy (short). **1926** Hold Everything (short); Battling Butler. **1927** The Show Girl; One Chance in a Million. **1928** The Dove. **1930** The Rampant Age; Rough Romance. **1932** Breach of Promise. **1933** California Weather (short); Flying Down to Rio; Knee Deep in Music (short); Jungle Bride. **1934** Belle of the Nineties; Derby Decade (short); The Chases of Pimple Street (short). **1935** The Devil Is a Woman. **1936** Early to Bed; Conflict. **1938** Give Me a Sailor. **1939** St. Louis Blues; The Day the Bookies Wept. **1940** A Chump at Oxford; Secrets of a Model. **1941** Obliging Young Lady. **1943** Unlucky Dog (short). **1948** The Time of Your Life. **1949** The Red Pony.

BORDEN, EUGENE
Born: Mar. 21, 1897, Paris, France. Died: July 21, 1972. Screen and stage actor.

Appeared in: **1917** Draft 258. **1921** The Barricade; The Porcelain Lamp. **1922** Forget Me Not. **1924** Revelation. **1925** Blue Blood. **1926** The Jade Cup. **1928** Gentlemen Prefer Blondes. **1929** Hold Your Man; Rampant Age. **1930** The Woman Racket; Rough Romance. **1935** Goin' to Town. **1936** Conflict. **1937** I Met Him in Paris; Charlie Chan on Broadway; The Firefly; Thin Ice; Cafe Metropole. **1939** Midnight; Charlie Chan in the City of Darkness. **1940** Hudson's Bay; The Mark of Zorro. **1941** Obliging Young Lady; Charlie Chan in Rio; Scotland Yard. **1942** Dr. Renault's Secret. **1943** Song of Bernadette; Mission to Moscow; Adventure in Iraq. **1944** Mrs. Parkington; Till We Meet Again; Dark Waters; Our Hearts Were Young and Gay. **1945** A Song to Remember; Dakota; To Have and Have Not; The Caribbean Mystery. **1946** The Searching Wind; Do You Love Me?; So Dark the Night; The Thrill of Brazil; The Return of Monte Cristo. **1947** The Foxes of Harrow; The Perils of Pauline; The Lost Moment; Cigarette Girl; Jewel of Brandenburg; The Bishop's Wife. **1948** Glamour Girl; Saigon. **1950** Under My Skin; All About Eve; Last of the Buccaneers. **1951** Silver Canyon; An American in Paris; On the Riviera. **1952** The Big Sky; Happy Time. **1953** Titanic; Saginaw Trail; A Blueprint for Murder. **1954** Jubilee Trail. **1955** The Far Country; Pirates of Tripoli. **1956** The Best Things in Life Are Free. **1957** The Spirit of St. Louis; The Tarnished Angels. **1958** The Fly; Me and the Colonel; The Perfect Furlough. **1960** Can-Can. **1961** The Devil at 4 O'Clock. **1963** A New Kind of Love. **1965** Boeing Boeing.

BORDEN, OLIVE (Sybil Trinkle)
Born: July 14, 1907, Richmond, Va. Died: Oct. 1, 1947, Los Angeles, Calif. (stomach ailment). Screen actress. Entered films as a Sennett bathing beauty in 1922 and was one of the twelve Wampas Baby Stars of 1925.

Appeared in: **1925** Dressmaker from Paris; The Happy Warrior; The Overland Limited. **1926** Three Bad Men; Fig Leaves; Yellow Fingers; The Country Beyond; My Own Pal; The Yankee Senor. **1927** Monkey Talks; The Joy Girl; Come To My House; Pajamas; The Secret Studio. **1928** The Albany Night Boat; Sinners in Love; Gang War; Stool Pigeon; Virgin Lips. **1929** The Eternal Woman; Love in the Desert; Half Marriage; Dance Hall. **1930** Wedding Rings; The Social Lion; Hello Sister. **1933** Hotel Variety.

BORDONI, IRENE
Born: 1895, Ajaccio, Corsica. Died: Mar. 19, 1953, New York, N.Y. Screen, stage, radio and vaudeville actress.

Appeared in: **1929** Paris (film debut); The Show of Shows. **1936** A Vitaphone short. **1942** Louisiana Purchase (stage and film versions).

BORELL, LOUIS
Born: Oct. 6, 1906, Amsterdam, Holland. Died: Apr., 1973, Amsterdam, Holland. Screen, stage and television actor.

Appeared in: **1936** The Crosspatch; The Avenging Hand; House Broken. **1937** Head Over Heels in Love; Over the Moon. **1938** Queer Cargo. **1941** Pirates of the Seven Seas. **1942** London Blackout Murders. **1943** Paris After Dark. **1944** A Night of Adventure.

BORELLI, ADA
Born: 1882, Italy. Died: May 21, 1964, Milan, Italy. Screen and stage actress. Appeared in silent films.

BORELLI, LYDA
Born: 1888, Genoa, Italy. Died: June 2, 1959, Rome, Italy. Screen and stage actress.

Appeared in: **1913** Ma l'Amore Mio Non Muore (My Love Never Dies); Memorie Dell 'Altro. **1914** La Donna Nuda. **1915** Il Bosco Dacr; Fior di Male; Rapsodia Satanica; Marcia Nuziale (Wedding March). **1916** La Falena; Malombra; Madame Tallian. **1917** Carnevalesca (Carnival); Il Dramma di una Notte; La Storia dei Tredici. Other Italian film: Vergine Folle (Foolish Virgin).

BORELLO, MARCO
Born: 1899. Died: Jan. 21, 1966, Santa Cruz, Calif. Screen actor and stuntman. Appeared in silents.

BOREO, EMIL
Born: 1885. Died: July 27, 1951, New York, N.Y. Screen, stage and vaudeville actor.

Appeared in: **1938** The Lady Vanishes. **1947** Carnegie Hall.

BORG, VEDA ANN
Born: Jan. 15, 1915, Boston or Roxbury, Mass? Died: Aug. 16, 1973, Hollywood, Calif. Screen actress. Divorced from film director Andrew McLaglen.

Appeared in: **1936** Three Cheers for Love (film debut). **1937** Back in Circulation; Men in Exile; Marry the Girl; Public Wedding; Kid Galahad; The Singing Marine; San Quentin; Confession; It's Love I'm After; Submarine D-1; The Missing Witness; The Case of the Stuttering Bishop; Varsity Show. **1938** Alcatraz Island; She Loved A Fireman; Over the Wall. **1939** The Law Comes to Texas. **1940** Bitter Sweet; Cafe Hostess; Behind the News; A Miracle on Main Street; I Take This Oath; Dr. Christian Meets the Women; Laughing at Danger; Glamour for Sale; Melody Ranch; The Shadow (serial). **1941** Arkansas Judge; The Penalty; The Pittsburgh Kid; Honky Tonk; The Corsican Brothers; Down in San Diego; The Get-Away. **1942** Two Yanks in

Trinidad; Duke of the Navy; I Married an Angel; About Face; She's In the Army; Lady in a Jam. **1943** Something to Shout About; Murder in Times Square; The Isle of Forgotten Sins; Revenge of the Zombies; The Girl from Monterey; The Unknown Guest; False Faces. **1944** Standing Room Only; The Big Noise; Irish Eyes Are Smiling; The Falcon in Hollywood; Smart Guy; Detective Kitty O'Day; Marked Trails; The Girl Who Dared. **1945** Rough, Tough and Ready (aka Men of the Deep); Don Juan Quilligan; Love, Honor and Goodbye; What a Blonde; Fog Island; Bring on the Girls; Scared Stiff; Nob Hill; Dangerous Intruder; Jungle Raiders (serial); Mildred Pierce. **1946** Avalanche; Life With Blondie; Accomplice; Wife Wanted; The Fabulous Suzanne; I Love My Husband, But! (short). **1947** Mother Wore Tights; Blonde Savage; Big Town; The Pilgrim Lady; The Bachelor and the Bobby-Soxer. **1948** Julia Misbehaves; Chicken Every Sunday. **1949** One Last Fling; Forgotten Women; Mississippi Rhythm. **1950** Kangaroo Kid; Rider from Tucson. **1952** Aaron Slick from Punkin Crick; Big Jim McLain; Hold That Line. **1953** Mister Scoutmaster; Three Sailors and a Girl; Hot News; A Perilous Journey. **1954** Bitter Creek. **1955** I'll Cry Tomorrow; You're Never Too Young; Guys and Dolls; Love Me or Leave Me. **1956** Frontier Gambler. **1958** The Naked Gun; The Fearmakers. **1959** Thunder in the Sun. **1960** The Alamo.

BORGATO, AGOSTINO
Born: 1871, Venice, Italy. Died: Mar. 14, 1939, Hollywood, Calif. (heart attack). Screen actor. Entered films in 1913.

Appeared in: **1925** The Street of Forgotten Men. **1926** The Love Thief. **1927** Magic Flame; Kiss in a Taxi; Helen of Troy; Hula; Fashions for Women; Horse Shoes. **1928** A Perfect Gentleman. **1929** Romance of the Rio Grande; She Goes to War; Hot for Paris. **1930** Behind the Make-Up; Redemption. **1931** The Maltese Falcon; Transgression. **1932** Bird of Paradise. **1937** The Firefly.

BORGSTROM, HILDA
Born: 1871, Sweden. Died: Jan. 2, 1953, Stockholm, Sweden. Stage and screen actress.

Appeared in: **1912** En Sommarsaga (film debut). **1939** Du Fria, Du Gamla (Thou Old, Thou Free); Familjen Andersson (The Anderson Family). **1948** Musik I Morker (Night Is My Future—US 1963).

BORING, EDWARD
Died: Jan. 18, 1923, New York, N.Y. Screen and stage actor.

Appeared in: **1916** A Daughter of the Gods. **1921** The Passion Flower. **1922** A Stage Romance. **1923** The Custard Cup.

BORIS, ANTHONY H.
Born: 1915. Died: Aug. 12, 1954, Grand Rapids, Mich. Screen actor.

BORLAND, BARLOWE
Born: Aug. 6, 1877, Scotland. Died: Aug. 31, 1948, Woodland Hills, Calif. Screen actor.

Appeared in: **1924** The Man Who Fights Alone. **1934** The Little Minister. **1935** A Tale of Two Cities; Bonnie Scotland. **1936** Mary of Scotland; Lloyds of London; College Holiday; The Witness Chair. **1937** King of the Gamblers; Blonde Trouble; Easy Living; Night Club Scandal; Thunder Trail; Murder Goes to College; Sophie Lang Goes West. **1938** Bluebeard's Eighth Wife; Dangerous to Know; Gun Packer; College Swing; Tip-Off Girls. **1939** King of the Turf; The Hound of the Baskervilles; The Witness Vanishes; At the Circus. **1940** Tom Brown's School Days.

BOROS, FERIKE
Born: 1880, Nagvarad, Hungary. Died: Jan. 16, 1951, Hollywood, Calif. Screen, stage actress and playwright.

Appeared in: **1930** Born Reckless; Little Caesar; Ladies Love Brutes. **1931** Bought; Gentleman's Fate; Svengali. **1932** The World and the Flesh; Huddle. **1933** Humanity; Rafter Romance. **1934** Eight Girls in a Boat; The Fountain. **1935** Symphony of Living. **1937** Make Way for Tomorrow. **1939** Love Affair; Stronger Than Desire; Bachelor Mother; Fifth Avenue Girl; Dust Be My Destiny; Rio; The Light That Failed. **1940** Lillian Russell; Argentine Nights; Three Cheers for the Irish; La Conga Nights; Girl from God's Country; Christmas in July. **1941** Sleepers West; Caught in the Draft; Private Nurse. **1942** Once Upon a Honeymoon; The Pied Piper; The Talk of the Town. **1943** Margin for Error; Princess O'Rourke. **1944** The Doughgirls. **1945** This Love of Ours; A Tree Grows in Brooklyn. **1946** Specter of the Rose.

BORZAGE, DANIEL "DANNY"
Born: 1897. Died: June 17, 1975, Los Angeles, Calif. Screen actor and musician. Brother of director-actor Frank Borzage (dec. 1962).

Appeared in: **1943** True to Life. **1952** What Price Glory. **1955** Mister Roberts. **1957** The Wings of Eagles. **1958** The Last Hurrah. **1961** Two Rode Together. **1963** McLintock! **1964** Cheyenne Autumn.

BORZAGE, FRANK
Born: Apr. 23, 1893, Salt Lake City, Utah. Died: June 19, 1962, Hollywood, Calif. (cancer). Screen, stage actor and film director. Divorced from actress Rena Rogers (dec. 1966). Brother of actor Daniel Borzage (dec. 1975).

Appeared in: **1914** The Typhoon. **1915** His Mother's Portrait; The Hammer; In the Switch Tower; The Spark in the Embers; Her Alibi; The Girl of the Sea; A Friend in Need; Alias James—Chauffeur; Touring With Tillie; One to the Minute; Anita's Butterfly; Almost a Widow; Cupid Beats Father; Two Hearts and a Thief; The Papered Door; Settled Out of Court; Nobody's Home; The Pitch of Chance; Aloha Oe; The Cactus Blossom; The Clean-Up. **1916** That Gal of Burk's; Immediate Lee; Land O'Lizards; Mammy's Rose; The Forgotten Prayer; The Courtin' of Calliope Clew; Nugget Jim's Partner. **1917** A Mormon Maid; A School for Husbands; Fear Not. **1918** The Curse of Iku. **1922** Hair Trigger Casey (reissue of Immediate Lee—1916). **1957** Jeanne Eagles.

BORZAGE, WILLIAM
Died: June 7, 1973. Screen actor.

Appeared in: **1973** House of Usher.

BOS, ANNIE
Born: 1887. Died: Aug. 3, 1975. Screen actress. One of the top stars of Dutch silent films.

BOSHELL, ADA
Born: 1854. Died: Mar. 31, 1924, Philadelphia, Pa. Screen and stage actress. Married to stage actor James A. Boshell (dec).

Appeared in: **1915** Not Guilty.

BOSSE, HARRIET
Born: 1878, Norway. Died: Nov., 1961, Oslo, Norway. Screen and stage actress.

BOSSICK, BERNARD B.
Born: 1918. Died: Nov. 10, 1975, Hollywood, Calif. (heart attack). Screen actor, film producer, director and television writer.

Appeared in: **1970** The Golden Box.

BOSTON, NELROY BUCK
Born: 1911. Died: Feb. 28, 1962, Van Nuys, Calif. (auto accident). Stage and screen actor. Entered films approx. 1940.

BOSWELL, CONNEE
Born: Dec. 3, 1907, New Orleans, La. Died: Oct. 10, 1976, New York, N.Y. (cancer). Screen, stage, vaudeville, radio actress, and singer. Was member of singing team "Boswell Sisters" with Martha (dec. 1958) and Helvetia.

Appeared in: **1932** A Paramount short; Big Broadcast. **1934** Trans-atlantic Merry-Go-Round; Moulin Rouge; Radio Star series. **1937** Artists and Models; It's All Yours. **1941** Kiss the Boys Goodbye. **1942** Syncopation. **1946** Swing Parade of 1946. **1958** Senior Prom.

BOSWELL, MARTHA
Born: 1905. Died: July 2, 1958, Peekskill, N.Y. Screen, stage, radio actress and singer. Was one of the three singing Boswell Sisters including Connee (dec. 1976) and Helrvetia Boswell.

Appeared in: **1932** The Big Broadcast; Universal shorts; a Paramount short. **1934** Moulin Rouge; Transatlantic Merry-Go-Round; Radio Star. **1937** A Paramount short.

BOSWORTH, HOBART
Born: Aug. 11, 1867, Marietta, Ohio. Died: Dec. 30, 1943, Glendale, Calif. (pneumonia). Screen, stage actor, film producer, director and screenwriter. Formed Bosworth Film Company approx. 1913.

Appeared in: **1908** The Roman. **1909** The Sultan's Power. **1912** The Count of Monte Cristo. **1913** Sea Wolf. **1914** The Country Mouse; Odessy of the North. **1916** Joan the Woman; Oliver Twist. **1917** The Little American. **1919** The Border Legion. **1920** Behind the Door. **1921** The Foolish Matrons; The Brute Master; Below the Surface; His Own Law; A Thousand to One; Blind Hearts; The Cup of Life. **1922** The Sea Lion; White Hands; The Stranger's Banquet. **1923** Man Alone; The Common Law; The Eternal Three; Little Church Around the Corner; In the Place of the King; Vanity Fair; The Man Life Passed By; Rupert of Hentzua; Souls for Sale. **1924** Captain January; Bread; The Silent Watcher; Name the Man; Hearts of Oak; Nellie, the Beautiful Cloak Model; Sundown; Through the Dark; The Woman on the Jury. **1925** The Big Parade; Zander the Great; My Son; Chickie;

The Half-Way Girl; Winds of Chance; The Golden Strain; If I Marry Again. **1926** Steel Preferred; The Nervous Wreck; Spangles; The Far Cry. **1927** The Blood Ship; Annie Laurie; My Best Girl; Three Hours. **1928** Chinese Parrott; Annapolis; Hangman's House; After the Storm; Freckles; The Sawdust Paradise; The Smart Set; A Man of Peach (short). **1929** The Show of Shows; Hurricane; King of the Mountain; A Woman of Affairs; Eternal Love; General Crack. **1930** Just Imagine; The Office Wife; Sit Tight; The Third Alarm; DuBarry, Woman of Passion; The Devil's Holiday; Mammy; Abraham Lincoln; A Man of Peace. **1931** Dirigible; Shipmates; This Modern Age; Fanny Foley Herself; Bad Timber. **1932** Carnival Boat; No Greater Love; Phantom Express; The Miracle Man; County Fair. **1933** Divine Love; Last of the Mohicans; Lady for a Day. **1934** Music in the Air; Whom the Gods Destroy. **1935** The Crusades; Keeper of the Bees; Steamboat 'Round the Bend. **1936** General Spanky (short). **1937** Portia on Trial. **1938** The Secret of Treasure Island (serial); Wolves of the Sea. **1941** One Foot in Heaven; Law of the Tropics. **1942** Sin Town; I Was Framed; Bullet Scars; They Died With Their Boots On.

BOTELER, WADE
Born: 1891, Santa Ana, Calif. Died: May 7, 1943, Hollywood, Calif. (heart attack). Screen, stage actor and screenwriter.

Appeared in: **1919** Twenty-Three and a Half Hours' Leave; An Old-Fashioned Boy. **1921** Blind Hearts; One Man in a Million; Stranger Than Fiction; Ducks and Drakes; Fifty Candles; The Home Stretch. **1922** At the Sign of the Jack O'Lantern; Second Hand Rose; Ridin' Wild; Afraid to Fight; The Lying Truth; The Woman's Side; Deserted at the Altar; While Satan Sleeps; Through a Glass Window; The Unfoldment; Don't Shoot; The Great Night. **1923** Going Up; A Man of Action; The Ghost Patrol; Around the World in 18 Days (serial); Alias the Night Wind (serial). **1924** Through the Dark; The Whipping Boss; Never Say Die; The Phantom Horseman. **1925** Capital Punishment; Introduce Me; Seven Keys to Baldpate; Marriage in Transit; Winds of Chance; Havoc; Jimmie's Millions; The Last Edition. **1926** Hold That Lion; That's My Baby. **1927** Let It Rain; High School Hero; Soft Cushions. **1928** Let 'Er Go Gallagher; Sporting Goods; Warming Up; Just Married; A Woman Against the World; The Toilers; The Baby Cyclone; Top Sergeant Mulligan; The Crash. **1929** Close Harmony; The New Halfback (short); Big News; The Leatherneck; The Godless Girl. **1930** Navy Blues; The Devil's Holiday; Soldiers and Women; Way of All Men; College Lovers; Top Speed; Derelict. **1931** Painted Desert; Blonde Crazy; Beyond Victory; Fainting Lover (short); Kick In; Silence; Twenty-Four Hours; Bad Company; Penrod and Sam; The Way Back Home; Local Boy Makes Good. **1932** Silver Dollar; For the Love of Ludwig (short); Night Mayor; Painted Woman; Speed Madness; Manhattan Tower; Central Park; Death Kiss; The Man Who Played God. **1933** Duck Soup; End of the Trail; Come On Danger; She Done Him Wrong; Speed Demon; Humanity; This Day and Age; College Humor; Unknown Valley; King for a Night. **1934** The St. Louis Kid; The Man With Two Faces; Manhattan Melodramma; Chained; Melody in Spring; Charlie Chan's Courage; A Man's Game; Among the Missing; Belle of the Nineties; The Richest Girl in the World; The Crosby Case; Operator 13; Fugitive Lady. **1935** Bordertown; Love in Bloom; Goin' to Town; The Leather Necker (short); Baby Face Harrington; O'Shaughnessey's Boy; Black Fury; The Goose and the Gander; Headline Woman; The Three Musketeers; Cheers of the Crowd; Freckles; Melody Trail; Streamline Express. **1936** Three Smart Girls; Whipsaw; Riff Raff; Exclusive Story; The Return of Jimmy Valentine; The President's Mystery; The Country Gentleman; Here Comes Trouble; Charlie Chan at the Circus; Human Cargo; The Bride Walks Out; Alibi for Murder; Poppy. **1937** The Great Hospital Mystery; The Frame-Up; A Fight to the Finish; The Mandarin Mystery; You Only Live Once; Hold 'Em Navy; 52nd Street; Dead Yesterday; Find the Witness; Jim Hanvey—Detective; Dangerous Holiday; Youth On Parole; It Can't Last Forever; Borrowing Trouble; Second Honeymoon; Green Light; Breezing Home; The Last Gangster. **1938** Angels With Dirty Faces; A Slight Case of Murder; The Amazing Dr. Clitterhouse; Letter of Introduction; Red Barry (serial); Passport Husband; The Marines Are Here; Little Miss Roughneck; In Old Chicago; Peck's Bad Boy with the Circus; Spawn of the North; Valley of the Giants; Billy the Kid Returns. **1939** Code of the Streets; When Tomorrow Comes; The Roaring Twenties; Blackmail; Dog Daze (short); Southward Ho!; Sabotage; The Man from Down Under; Days of Jesse James; Everything's on Ice; Missing Daughters; The Mysterious Miss X; Thunder Afloat; Ambush; Chicken Wagon Family. **1940** Ma, He's Making Eyes at Me; The Green Hornet (serial); The Green Hornet Strikes Again (serial); Double Alibi; Torrid Zone; Gaucho Serenade; Three Faces West; Castle on the Hudson; Young Buffalo Bill; Hot Steel; The Leather Pushers; The Howards of Virginia; Under Texas Skies; Till We Meet Again; My Little Chickadee; Three Cheers for the Irish. **1941** Six Lessons from Madame La Zonga; The Strawberry Blonde; High Sierra; Love Crazy; The Singing Hill; The Kid from Kansas; The Body

Disappears; Where Did You Get That Girl?; A-Hunting We Will Go; Shanghai Alibi; It Started With Eve; Kathleen. **1942** Don Winslow of the Navy (serial); The Forest Rangers; Blue, White and Perfect; Bombay Clipper; Ride 'Em Cowboy; I Was Framed; Escape from Crime; Moonlight in Havana; Mississippi Gambler; I Married a Witch; Gentleman Jim. **1943** It Ain't Hay; Hi, Buddy; The Good Fellows; Find the Blackmailer; Hit the Ice; Eyes of the Underworld. **1944** The Last Ride.

BOTHWELL, JOHN F.
Born: 1921. Died: Mar. 7, 1967, Long Branch, N.J. Screen actor.

BOTKIN, PERRY, SR.
Born: 1907. Died: Oct. 14, 1973, Van Nuys, Calif. Guitarist, songwriter and screen actor.

Appeared in: **1941** Birth of the Blues.

BOTTOMLEY, ROLAND
Born: Sept. 23, 1880, Liverpool, England. Died: Jan. 5, 1947, New York, N.Y. Screen and stage actor.

Appeared in: **1916** The Tricksters; The Grip of Evil (serial). **1917** The Neglected Wife (series). **1921** The Charming Deceiver; The Devil; A Man's Home. **1923** Does It Pay?; Modern Marriage. **1924** The Dawn of a Tomorrow. **1925** Enticement; Raffles, the Amateur Cracksman.

BOUCHER, VICTOR
Born: France. Died: Feb. 22, 1942, France. Screen and stage actor.

Appeared in: **1931** La Douceur D'Aimer. **1939** Ils Etaient Neufs Celibataires (Nine Bachelors—US 1942).

BOUCHEY, WILLIS "BILL" (William Bouchey)
Born: 1895 or 1900. Died: Sept. 28, 1977, Burbank, Calif. Screen, stage, radio and television actor.

Appeared in: **1951** Elopement. **1952** Don't Bother to Knock; Red Planet Mars; Just for You; Assignment-Paris; Million Dollar Mermaid; Deadline U.S.A. **1953** Gun-Belt; Pickup on South Street; Dangerous Crossing; Big Heat; The President's Lady. **1954** Battle of Rogue River; Fireman, Save My Child; Suddenly; Drum Beat; The Bridges at Toko-Ri. **1955** Battle Cry; The Long Gray Line; I Cover the Underworld; Big House, USA: The McConnell Story; The Spoilers; Hell on Frisco Bay; Violent Men (aka Rough Company). **1956** Forever Darling; Johnny Concho; Magnificent Roughnecks; Pillars of the Sky. **1957** The Night Runner; Mister Cory; The Wings of the Eagles; Last of the Badmen; The Garment Jungle; Beau James; Zero Hour!; Last Stagecoach West. **1958** Darby's Rangers; The Sheepman; The Last Hurrah. **1959** No Name on the Bullet. **1960** Sergeant Rutledge. **1961** Two Rode Together; You Have to Run Fast; Pocketful of Miracles. **1962** Panic in Year Zero!; Saintly Sinners; Incident in an Alley; The Man Who Shot Liberty Valance. **1963** How the West was Won. **1964** Where Love Has Gone; Cheyenne Autumn. **1965** McHale's Navy Joins the Air Force. **1966** Follow Me, Boys! **1969** The Love God; Support Your Local Sheriff!; Young Billy Oung. **1970** Dirty Dingus Magee.

BOUCICAULT, DION G.
Born: 1859, England? Died: June 25, 1929, Hurley, Berkshire, England. Screen, stage actor, stage director and playwright. Son of stage actor/playwright Dion Boucicault (dec. 1890) and stage actress Agnes Kelly Robertson (dec. 1916). Brother of actress Nina (dec. 1950), stage actor Aubrey (dec. 1913) and actress Eva Boucicault. Married to actress Irene Vanbrugh (dec. 1949).

Appeared in: **1917** Masks and Faces.

BOUCICAULT, NINA
Born: 1867, England. Died: Aug. 4, 1950, Ealing, England. Screen and stage actress. Daughter of stage actor/playwright Dion Boucicault (dec. 1890) and stage actress Agnes Kelly Robertson (dec. 1916). Sister of actor Dion G. (dec. 1929), stage actor Aubrey (dec. 1913) and actress Eva Boucicault.

Appeared in: **1923** Daddy-the-Next-Best-Thing. **1924** Miriam Rozella. **1937** Juggernaut.

BOUCICAULT, RENEE
Born: 1898. Died: July, 3, 1935, New York, N.Y. (pneumonia). Screen actress. Daughter of stage actor Aubrey Boucicault (dec. 1913). Divorced from Clarel L. Sellye and stage actor Alexander E. Marks (aka Al Hill and Howard Boucicault).

Appeared in: **1916** His Picture in the Paper.

BOUCOT, LOUIS
Born: 1889. Died: Mar. 30, 1949, Paris, France. Screen and stage actor.

BOULTON, MATTHEW
Born: Jan. 20, 1893, Lincoln, England. Died: Feb. 12, 1962. Screen, stage actor and screenwriter.

Appeared in: **1927** His Rest Day. **1930** The Man from Chicago (US 1931); Bed and Breakfast. **1931** Potiphar's Wife (aka Her Strange Desire—US 1932); Third Time Lucky; Keepers of Youth; Creeping Shadows (aka The Limping Man—US 1932); The Flying Fool; The Ghost Train. **1936** Sabotage (aka The Woman Alone—US). **1937** Night Must Fall; The Thirteenth Chair; The Firefly. **1938** Bulldog Drummond's Peril; Lord Jeff; Bulldog Drummond in Africa. **1940** Adventure in Diamonds; Phantom Raiders; Mystery Sea Raider. **1941** Dangerously They Live; Rage in Heaven; They Met in Bombay. **1942** Journey for Margaret; Counter-Espionage; The Undying Monster. **1944** The White Cliffs of Dover; Secrets of Scotland Yard; The Man in Half-Moon Street; Nothing But Trouble. **1945** Molly and Me; The Brighton Strangler; The Woman in Green; Love Letters. **1947** Ivy; Stallion Road; Bulldog Drummond Strikes Back. **1948** Tarzan and the Mermaids; The Woman in White; Enchantment. **1949** The Secret Garden; Barbary Pirate. **1952** Last Train from Bombay.

BOURBON, DIANA
Born: 1900. Died: Mar. 19, 1978, Los Angeles, Calif. (cancer). Screen, stage, radio, television actress, radio producer, drama critic, stage production coordinator and agency executive.

Appeared in: **1964** My Fair Lady.

BOURCHIER, ARTHUR
Born: June 22, 1863, Speen, Berkshire, England. Died: Sept. 14, 1927, Johannesburg, S. Africa. Screen, stage actor and film producer. Divorced from actress Violet Vanbrugh (dec. 1942) and later married to stage actress Kyrle Bellow (dec.). Father of actress Prudence Vanbrugh.

Appeared in: **1911** Henry VIII. **1913** Macbeth. **1920** The Great Day (US 1921).

BOURKE, FAN
Born: 1886, Brooklyn, N.Y. Died: Mar. 9, 1959, Norwalk, Conn. Screen, stage, vaudeville actress and screenwriter. Entered films in 1915.

Appeared in: **1930** Lummox.

BOURNE, ADELINE
Born: 1872, India. Died: Feb. 8, 1965, England. Screen and stage actor.

Appeared in: **1913** Hamlet (US 1915).

BOURNE, WILLIAM PAYNE
Born: 1936. Died: Oct. 8, 1972, Hollywood, Calif. (suicide—gun). Screen actor and screenwriter.

BOURNEUF, PHILIP
Born: 1908, Somerville, Mass. Died: Mar. 23, 1979, Santa Monica, Calif. Screen, stage and television actor. Divorced from actress Frances Reid.

Appeared in: **1944** Winged Victory. **1948** Joan of Arc. **1951** The Big Night. **1953** Thunder in the East. **1956** Beyond a Reasonable Doubt; Everything but the Truth. **1962** Hemingway's Adventures of a Young Man. **1966** Chamber of Horrors. **1969** The Arrangement. **1970** The Molly Maguires.

BOURVIL (Andre Raimbourg)
Born: 1913, Normandy, France. Died: Sept. 23, 1970, Paris, France. Screen, stage and radio actor.

Appeared in: **1945** La Ferme du Pendu. **1946** Pas Si Bete. **1947** Blanc Comme Neige. **1948** Le Coeur Sur la Maine. **1949** Miguette et Sa Mere. **1950** Le Rosier de Madame Husson. **1951** Garou-Garou au Passe-Murail-le; Seul dans Paris; Miquette; Mr. Peek-A-Boo. **1952** The Price. **1953** Le Trois Mousquetaires (The Three Musketeers—US 1954). **1954** Le Cadet Rousselle; Poisson d'Avril. **1955** Les Hussards. **1956** La Traversee de Paris (The Crossing of Paris—aka Four Bags Full—US 1957). **1957** Le Chanteur de Mexico. **1959** La Jumet Verte (The Green Mare—US 1961); The Mirror Has Two Faces. **1960** Crazy for Love. **1962** Tout l'Or du Monde; The Longest Day. **1963** Les Culottes Rouges (The Red Pants); Les Bonnes Causes (The Good Causes); Heaven Sent. **1964** La Cuisine au Beurre (Cooking With Butter); Don't Tempt the Devil. **1965** Les Grandes Gueles (The Wild Guys—US 1969); The Secret Agents; Thank Heaven for Small Favors; My Wife's Husband. **1966** La Grande Vadrouille (The Big Spree); The Dirty Game; The Sucker. **1967** Don't Look Now (US 1969). **1968** Le Verveau (The Brain—US 1969). **1969** Monte Carlo or Bust; L'Albero di Natale (The Christmas Tree); Those Daring Young Men in Their Jaunty Jalopies. Other French films: The Atlantic Wall; Le Corniaud (The Dumbbell).

BOVY, BERTHE
Born: 1887, Belgium. Died: Feb. 26, 1977. Screen and stage actress.

Appeared in: **1949** Man to Men. **1952** L'Armoire Volante (The Cupboard was Bare).

BOW, CLARA
Born: Aug. 25, 1905, Brooklyn, N.Y. Died: Sept. 27, 1965, Los Angeles, Calif. (heart attack). Screen actress. Married to Rex Bell, former actor and Lt. Gov. of Nevada (dec. 1962). She was known as the "It" Girl.

Appeared in: **1922** Beyond the Rainbow. **1923** Enemies of Women; Down to the Sea in Ships; The Daring Years; Maytime. **1924** Black Oxen; Black Lightning; Grit; Daughters of Pleasure; Poisoned Paradise; Empty Hearts; This Woman; Wine. **1925** Helen's Babies; Free to Love; Keeper of the Bees; The Plastic Age; Kiss Me Again; The Scarlet West; Capital Punishment; The Primrose Path; Eve's Lover; The Adventurous Sex; The Best Bad Men; Lawful Cheaters; My Lady's Lips; Parisian Love. **1926** The Ancient Mariner; Dancing Mothers; Kid Boots; Fascinating Youth; My Lady of Whims; Mantrap; Two Can Play; The Runaway; The Shadow of the Law. **1927** Hula; Rough House Rosie; Get Your Man; Children of Divorce; It; Wings. **1928** Red Hair; The Fleet's In; Three Week Ends; Ladies of the Mob. **1929** Dangerous Curves; The Saturday Night Kid; The Wild Party. **1930** Love Among the Millionaires; Paramount on Parade; True to the Navy; Her Wedding Night. **1931** Kick In; No Limit. **1932** Call Her Savage. **1933** Hoopla.

BOWERS, JOHN
Born: Dec. 25, 1899, Garrett, Ind. Died: Nov. 17, 1936, Santa Monica, Calif. (drowned). Screen and stage actor. Entered films in 1916. Divorced from actress Marguerite de la Motte (dec. 1950).

Appeared in: **1916** Hulda from Holland; Madame X. **1919** Sis Hopkins; Through the Wrong Door; Strictly Confidential. **1921** Roads of Destiny; The Silent Call; The Sky Pilot; The Ace of Hearts; Bits of Life; Godless Men; The Night Rose; An Unwilling Hero; The Poverty of Riches. **1922** Quincy Adams Sawyer; Affinities; South of Suva; The Bonded Woman; The Golden Gift. **1923** Lorna Doone; The Woman of Bronze; Desire; The Barefoot Boy; What a Wife Learned; Crinoline and Romance; The Destroying Angel; Divorce; Richard, the Lion-Hearted. **1924** When a Man's a Man; Code of the Wilderness; The White Sin; Those Who Dare; Empty Hearts; So Big. **1925** Confessions of a Queen; Chickie; Flattery; Daughters Who Pay; Off the Highway; The People vs. Nancy Preston. **1926** Pals in Paradise; The Danger Girl; Whispering Smith; Hearts and Fists; Rocking Moon; Laddie. **1927** The Dice Woman; For Ladies Only; Ragtime; The Heart of the Yukon; Heroes in Blue; Opening Night; Three Hours; Jewels of Desire. **1929** Skin Deep; Say It With Songs. **1931** Mounted Fury.

BOWERS, LYLE
Born: 1896. Died: Mar. 8, 1943, Hollywood, Calif. Screen actor. Entered films approx. 1923.

BOWES, MAJOR EDWARD
Born: 1874, San Francisco, Calif. Died: June 13, 1946, Rumson, N.J. Screen, radio actor and composer. Married to actress Margaret Illington (dec. 1934). Began radio career in 1925 and originated Major Bowes Amateur Radio Hour in 1934.

Appeared in: **1936** Amateur Parade (short); Amateur Theatre of the Air (short). Other shorts he appeared in are as follows: Musical Varieties; Variety Review; Radio Revels; Stars of Tomorrow; Harmony Broadcast and Melody Maker.

BOWKER, ALDRICH
Born: 1875, Mass. Died: Mar. 21, 1947, Los Angeles, Calif. (artereosclerosis). Screen actor.

Appeared in: **1939** Torchy Plays with Dynamite; Nancy Drew—Trouble Shooter; The Dead End Kids on Dress Parade (aka On Dress Parade); Angels Wash Their Faces; Everybody's Hobby; Pride of the Bluegrass; Joe and Ethel Turp Call on the President; No Place to Go; Waterfront. **1940** Abe Lincoln in Illinois; Susan and God; Those Were the Days. **1941** Romance on the Rio Grande; Meet John Doe; Pot O' Gold; The Wagons Roll at Night. **1942** I Was Framed; I Married a Witch; Mississippi Gambler.

BOWLES, DONALD
Died: Oct. 3, 1921, Los Angeles, Calif. (tuberculosis). Screen and stage actor.

Appeared in: **1915** Rhoda's Burglar.

BOWMAN, LAURA
Born: 1881. Died: Mar. 29, 1957. Black screen actress. Married to stage actor Sidney Kirkpatrick (dec. 1930).

Appeared in: **1933** Voodoo Drums. **1935** Lem Hawkins Confession. **1938** God's Step Children. **1939** Birthright. **1940** Son of Ingagi. **1945** Miss Susie Slagle's.

BOWMAN, LEE
Born: Dec. 28, 1914, Cincinnati, Ohio. Died: Dec. 25, 1979, Brentwood, Calif. (heart attack). Screen, stage, radio and television actor.

Appeared in: **1936** Three Men in White (film debut). **1937** I Met Him in Paris; Interns Can't Take Money; Last Train From Madrid; This Way Please; Sophie Lang Goes West. **1938** Having a Wonderful Time; A Man to Remember; Tarnished Angel; Next Time I Marry; The First Hundred Years. **1939** Society Lawyer; Stronger Than Desire; Fast and Furious; Dancing Co-Ed; The Lady and the Mob; Miracles For Sale; Love Affair; The Great Victor Herbert. **1940** Florian; Wyoming; Gold Rush Maisie; Third Finger, Left Hand. **1941** Buck Privates; Model Wife; Washington Melodrama; Married Bachelor; Design for Scandal. **1942** Kid Glove Killer; We Were Dancing; Pacific Rendezvous; Tish. **1943** Bataan; Three Hearts for Julia. **1944** Cover Girl; The Impatient Years. **1945** Tonight and Every Night. **1946** Walls Came Tumbling Down; She Wouldn't Say Yes. **1947** Smash-Up, The Story of a Woman. **1949** My Dream is Yours; There's a Girl in My Heart. **1950** The House by the River. **1964** Youngblood Hawke.

BOWMAN, LEWIS EDWARD
Born: 1886. Died: 1961. Screen actor and stuntman. Appeared in silents.

BOWMAN, PALMER
Born: 1883. Died: Sept. 25, 1933, Chicago, Ill. (heart disease). Screen, stage, vaudeville actor, film director and screenwriter. Appeared in early Selig and Essanay Company productions.

BOWMAN, WILLIAM J.
Born: 1876, Bakersville, N.Y. Died: Jan. 1, 1960. Screen, vaudeville actor, film director and film producer.

Appeared in: **1912** The Merchant of Venice.

BOWSER, CHARLES
Died: Mar. 17, 1917. Screen actor. Appeared in Peerless-Brady World Film Company films.

Appeared in: **1917** Yankee Pluck.

BOYCE, GEORGE
Born: 1899. Died: Feb. 14, 1977, Woodland Hills, Calif. Screen, vaudeville actor, dancer and choreographer.

Appeared in: **1954** Three Ring Circus. **1955** The Seven Little Foys. **1965** How to Stuff a Wild Bikini.

BOYCE, JACK
Born: 1885. Died: Dec. 13, 1923, New York, N.Y. Screen and stage actor.

BOYD, ADA
Born: 1890. Died: Mar. 25, 1978, Great Barrington, Mass. Silent screen actress. Was a Mack Sennet Bathing Beauty.

BOYD, BETTY
Born: May 11, 1908, Kansas City, Mo. Died: Sept. 16, 1971. Screen and stage actress. Was a Wampas Baby Star in 1929. Appeared in Educational Comedies in the '20's.

Appeared in: **1914** In a Persian Garden. **1928** Pirates Beware. **1929** The Godless Girl; The Right Bed. **1930** French Kisses; The Green Goddess; Lilies of the Field; Paradise Island; Under a Texas Moon; A Royal Romance; Vacation Loves (short). **1931** Maid to Order; Along Came Youth. **1933** Gun Law. **1934** An Old Gypsy Custom (short).

BOYD, BILL "COWBOY RAMBLER"
Born: 1910. Died: Dec. 7, 1977, Dallas, Tex. Country singer, screen and radio actor.

Appeared in: **1941** Texas Manhunt.

BOYD, BLANCHE "DEEDEE"
Born: 1889. Died: Apr. 14, 1959, Laguna Beach, Calif. (heart attack). Stage and screen actress.

BOYD, DAVID AMOS

Born: 1896. Died: Oct. 12, 1977, Whittier, Calif. Screen, stage and vaudeville actor.

Appeared in: **1962** Jumbo (aka Billy Rose's Jumbo).

BOYD, STEPHEN (William Millar)

Born: July 4, 1928, near Belfast, Ireland. Died: June 2, 1977, Northridge, Calif. (heart attack). Screen, stage, radio and television actor.

Appeared in: **1955** An Alligator Named Daisy (US 1957). **1956** A Hill in Korea (aka Hell in Korea—US 1957); The Man Who Never Was. **1957** Seven Thunders (aka The Beasts of Marseilles—US 1959); Island in the Sun; Seven Waves Away (aka Abandon Ship!—US). **1958** The Bravados. **1959** The Best of Everything; Ben Hur; Woman Obsessed. **1961** The Big Gamble. **1962** Jumbo (aka Billy Rose's Jumbo); The Inspector (aka Lisa—US). **1963** Venere Imperial (Venus). **1964** The Third Secret; The Fall of the Roman Empire. **1965** Genghis Khan. **1966** The Bible; Fantastic Voyage; The Oscar; The Poppy is also a Flower. **1967** The Caper of the Golden Bulls; Assignment K (US 1968). **1968** Shalako. **1969** Slaves. **1973** A Man Called Noon. **1974** Marta; Kill Kill Kill; Those Dirty Dogs. **1976** Evil in the Deep. **1977** The Squeeze; The Devil Has Seven Faces; Impossible Love; One Man Against the Organization.

BOYD, WILLIAM

Born: June 5, 1895, Hedrysburg, Ohio. Died: Sept. 12, 1972, South Laguna, Calif. (combination of Parkinson's disease and congestive heart failure). Screen and television actor. Married to Grace Bradley. Divorced from actresses Ruth Miller, Elinor Fair and Dorothy Sebastian (dec. 1957). Star of "Hopalong Cassidy" film and television series. Entered films in 1915.

Appeared in: **1918** Old Wives for New. **1920** Why Change Your Wife? **1921** Brewster's Millions; Moonlight and Honeysuckle; A Wise Fool; Exit the Vamp. **1922** Bobbed Hair; Nice People; On the High Seas; Manslaughter; The Young Rajah. **1923** Enemies of Children; The Temple of Venus; Michael O'Halloran; Hollywood. **1924** Tarnish; Changing Husbands; Triumph. **1925** Forty Winks; The Road to Yesterday; The Midshipman; Golden Bed. **1926** The Last Frontier; Her Man O'War; The Volga Boatman; Steel Preferred; Eve's Leaves. **1927** King of Kings; Wolves of the Air; Two Arabian Knights; Dress Parade; Jim the Conqueror; Yankee Clipper. **1928** The Night Flyer; Power; The Cop; Skyscraper. **1929** High Voltage; Lady of the Pavements; The Flying Fool; The Leatherneck; Wolf Song. **1930** Those Who Dance; His First Command; Officer O'Brien; The Frame (short). **1931** Suicide Fleet; The Painted Desert; Beyond Victory; Gang Buster; Big Gambler. **1932** The Wiser Sex; Carnival Boat; Painted Woman; Sky Devils; Madison Square Garden. **1933** Men of America; Midnight Warning; Lucky Devils; Emergency Call; The Great Decision. **1934** Cheaters; Flaming Gold. **1935** Night Life of the Gods; Hopalong Cassidy (aka Hopalong Cassidy Enters); The Eagle's Brood; Bar 20 Rides Again; Racing Luck; Port of Lost Dreams. **1936** Call of the Prairie; Three on the Trail; Heart of the West; Hopalong Cassidy Returns; Trail Dust; The Last Frontier; Federal Agent; Burning Gold; Go Get 'Em Haines. **1937** Borderland; Borrowed Trouble; North of the Rio Grande; Rustler's Valley; Hopalong Rides Again; Texas Trail; Partners of the Plains; Hills of Old Wyoming; Men Have to Fight. **1938** Cassidy of Bar 20; Heart of Arizona; Bar 20 Justice; Pride of the West; In Old Mexico; The Sunset Trail; Deputy Sheriff; The Frontiersman. **1939** Range War; Law of the Pampas; Silver on the Sage; Renegade Trail. **1940** Santa Fe Marshall; The Showdown; Hidden Gold; Stagecoach War; Three Men from Texas; War Along the Stage Trail. **1941** Doomed Caravan; In Old Colorado; Border Vigilantes; Pirates on Horseback; Wide Open Town; Twilight on the Trail; Riders of the Timberline; Stick to Your Guns; Outlaws of the Desert (aka Arabian Desert Outlaws); Secrets of the Wasteland. **1942** Undercover Man. **1943** Border Patrol; The Leather Burners; Lost Canyon; Hoppy Serves a Writ; Colt Comrades; Bar 20; False Colors; Riders of the Deadline. **1944** Forty Thieves; Mystery Man; Texas Masquerade; Lumberjack; Frontier Marshal in Prairie Pals. **1946** The Devil's Playground; Fool's Gold; The Unexpected Guest. **1947** Dangerous Venture; Hoppy's Holiday; The Marauders. **1948** Silent Conflict; Sinister Journey; The Dead Don't Dream; Borrowed Trouble; False Paradise; Strange Gamble. **1952** The Greatest Show on Earth.

BOYD, WILLIAM "STAGE"

Born: 1890. Died: Mar. 20, 1935, Hollywood, Calif. (liver ailment). Screen, stage actor. Do not confuse with William "Hopalong Cassidy" Boyd (dec. 1972). Divorced from stage actress Clara Joel.

Appeared in: **1930** The Locked Door; The Spoilers; Derelict. **1931** Gun Smoke; City Streets; The Road to Reno. **1932** The False Madonna; State's Attorney. **1933** The House on 56th Street; Oliver Twist; The Chief; Laughing at Life. **1934** Transatlantic Merry-Go-Round. **1935** The Lost City (serial).

BOYER, CHARLES

Born: Aug. 28, 1899, Figeac, France. Died: Aug. 26, 1978, Phoenix, Ariz. (suicide—overdose of barbiturates). Screen, stage, radio and television actor. Married to actress Pat Patterson (dec. Aug. 24, 1978). Won 1969 Special Academy Award. Entered films in 1920.

Appeared in: **1930** The Big House. **1931** Buster se Marie (French Version of Parlor, Bedroom and Bath); Magnificent Lie; Tumultes. **1932** Man from Yesterday; Red Headed Woman; Tempest. **1933** The Only Girl (French and English versions aka Heart Song—US 1934); F.P.1; L'Impervier. **1934** Caravan; The Battle (French and English versions aka Thunder in the East—US). **1935** Private Worlds; Break of Hearts; Shanghai; Liliom. **1936** Le Bonheur; Garden of Allah. **1937** History is Made at Night; Mayerling; Tovarich; Conquest. **1938** Algiers; Orage. **1939** Love Affair; When Tomorrow Comes; Li Corsaille. **1940** All This and Heaven Too; Les Amoureaux. **1941** The Trial of Mary Dugan; Back Street; Hold Back the Dawn; Appointment for Love. **1942** Tales of Manhattan. **1943** The Constant Nymph; Flesh and Fantasy; Hara-Kiri (reissue of The Battle—1934). **1944** Gaslight; Together Again. **1945** Confidential Agent. **1946** Cluny Brown. **1947** A Woman's Vengeance. **1948** Arch of Triumph. **1951** The 13th Letter; First Legion. **1952** The Happy Time. **1953** Thunder in the East (1934 Version). **1954** Earrings of Madame De. **1955** The Cobweb. **1956** Around the World in 80 Days. **1957** La Parisienne; Maxime (US 1962); The Buccaneer. **1959** Paris Palace Hotel (aka Paris Hotel). **1961** Fanny. **1962** Julia, Du Bist Zauberhaft (Julia, You Are Adorable and aka Adorable Julia—US 1964); The Four Horseman of the Apocalypse; Les Demons de Minuit. **1963** Love is a Ball. **1965** A Very Special Favor. **1966** How to Steal a Million; Is Paris Burning? **1967** Barefoot in the Park; Casino Royale. **1969** Le Rouble a Deux Faces (aka The Day the Hot Line Got Hot—US); Madwoman of Chaillot; The April Fools. **1973** Lost Horizon. **1974** Stavisky. **1976** A Matter of Time.

BOYLE, JOHN W.

Born: 1881, Memphis, Tenn. Died: Sept. 28, 1959, Hollywood, Calif. Screen actor, film director and cameraman.

Appeared in: **1917** Kick In.

BOYNE, CLIFTON

Born: 1874, England. Died: Dec. 16, 1945, England? Screen and stage actor.

Appeared in: **1922** The Crimson Circle.

BOYNE, SUNNY (Hazel Boyne)

Born: 1883, Boston, Mass. Died: Aug. 27, 1966, Van Nuys, Calif. Screen actress and dancer.

Appeared in: **1941** All That Money Can Buy. **1950** The Secret Fury; Where Danger Lives; Born to Be Bad. **1951** That's My Boy. **1952** The Devil and Daniel Webster (reissue of All That Money Can Buy—1941); One Minute to Zero. **1958** King Creole.

BOYNE, EVA LEONARD *See* LEONARD-BOYNE, EVA

BOYNTON, CHARLES "TED"

Born: 1921. Died: Sept. 19, 1968. Screen and television actor.

BOZO THE CLOWN *See* COOPER, EDWIN

BOZYK, MAX (aka MAX BOZHYK)

Born: 1899. Died: Apr. 5, 1970, Town Hall, N.Y. (heart attack). Yiddish stage and screen actor. Married to actress Reizel Bozyk with whom he appeared in an act billed as "Max and Reizel Bozyk."

Appeared in: **1937** Yiddle With His Fiddle; Der Purimspieler. **1938** The Dybbuk; Tkies Khal (The Vow); Mamele (Little Mothers). **1939** A Brivele der Mamen (A Letter to Mother). **1950** God, Man and Devil; Catskill Honeymoon.

BRABIN, CHARLES J.

Born: Apr. 17, 1882, Liverpool, England. Died: Nov. 4, 1957, Santa Monica, Calif. (heart attack). Screen actor, film director and screenwriter. Married to Theda Bara (dec. 1955). Entered films with Edison in 1908 as an actor.

Appeared in: **1917** Adopted Son.

BRACE, NORMAN C.

Born: 1892. Died: June 20, 1954, New York, N.Y. Screen, stage actor, film and stage director. Appeared in early silent films.

BRACEY, CLARA T. (aka CLARA BRACY)

Born: 1847. Died: Feb. 22, 1941, Los Angeles, Calif. Screen, stage actress and stage producer. Married to concert tenor Henry Bracey (dec. 1917). Mother of actor Sidney Bracey (dec. 1942). Made early films with Kinemacolor and later Biograph.

Appeared in: **1909** Eloping With Auntie; The Awakening. **1910** Three Sisters; A Decree of Destiny. **1924** Her Night of Romance.

BRACEY, SIDNEY (aka SIDNEY BRACY)

Born: 1877, Melbourne, Australia. Died: Aug. 5, 1942, Hollywood, Calif. Screen and stage actor. Son of actress Clara T. Bracey (dec. 1941) and concert tenor Henry Bracey (dec. 1917). Entered films in 1910.

Appeared in: **1914** Zudora (The Twenty Million Dollar Mystery—serial). **1920** The Invisible Ray (serial). **1921** An Amateur Devil; The Outside Woman; Passion Fruit; Crazy to Marry; The March Hare; Morals. **1922** Manslaughter; The Dictator; The Radio King (serial); Is Matrimony a Failure?; Midnight; One Wonderful Night. **1923** Merry-Go-Round; Nobody's Bride; The Wild Party; The Social Buccaneer (serial); Ruggles of Red Gap. **1924** Being Respectable; By Divine Right; Her Night of Romance; So This Is Marriage?; Why Men Leave Home. **1925** Her Market Value; The Merry Widow; Wandering Footsteps; A Slave of Fashion. **1926** A Man Four-Square; The Mystery Club; The Black Bird; My Official Wife; You Never Know Women. **1927** Birds of Prey; Painting the Town; The Thirteenth Juror; The Woman on Trial. **1928** Show People; Haunted House; The Cameraman; Queen Kelly; The Wedding March; Win That Girl; Home James, Man-Made Women. **1929** His Captive Woman; Sioux Blood; The Bishop Murder Case. **1930** Second Floor Mystery; Anybody's Woman; Outside the Law; Monte Carlo; Redemption. **1931** Ten Cents a Dance; What a Bozo (short); Thundering Tenors (short); The Avenger; Parlor, Bedroom and Bath; Lion and the Lamb; A Dangerous Affair; Subway Express; Shanghaied Love; The Deceiver. **1932** The Air Mail Mystery (serial); The Monster Walks; The Greeks Had a Word for Them; Tangled Destinies; No More Orchids; Little Orphan Annie. **1933** Flying Down to Rio; Little Giant; The Phantom of the Air (serial); The Intruder; Corruption; Broken Dreams. **1934** The Vanishing Shadow (serial); The Poor Rich; The Ninth Guest; Many Happy Returns. **1935** I've Been Around; Anna Karenina. **1936** Magnificent Obsession; Second Childhood (short); Sutter's Gold; Isle of Fury; Preview Murder Mystery. **1937** The Prince and the Pauper; The Firefly; A Girl With Ideas; Three Smart Boys (short). **1938** Boy Meets Girl; The Amazing Dr. Clitterhouse; Mr. Chump; Dawn Patrol; The Baroness and the Butler; Merrily We Live; My Bill. **1939** On Trial; Smashing the Money Ring; Everybody's Hobby; Sweepstakes Winner; We Are Not Alone; Dark Victory. **1940** My Love Came Back; Devil's Island; Tugboat Annie Sails Again; A Child is Born. **1941** Bullets for O'Hara; Shadows on the Stairs. **1942** The Gay Sisters.

BRACKEN, BERTRAM

Born: 1879, San Antonio, Tex. Died: Nov. 1, 1952, Los Angeles, Calif. Screen actor, film director and screenwriter. Entered films as an actor in 1910.

BRADBURY, JAMES, JR.

Born: Oct. 5, 1894, New York, N.Y. Died: June 21, 1936, Los Angeles, Calif. (suicide-burns). Screen actor. Son of actor James Bradbury, Sr. (dec. 1940).

Appeared in: **1921** Bits of Life. **1924** Classmates. **1925** Fear-Bound. **1926** Exclusive Rights; Kentucky Handicap; The Little Giant. **1927** Hidden Aces; Let it Rain; The Drop Kick; The Wreck; She's a Sheik. **1928** Code of the Air; Flying Romeos; Hellship Bronson; The Glorious Trail; Walking Back; Waterfront. **1929** Alibi; Anne Against the World; Cheyenne; Half Marriage; In Old Arizona; Smilin' Guns; Scarlet Seas. **1930** Man Trouble; The Rogue Song; Last of the Duanes. **1931** The Cisco Kid; Monkey Business; Soul of the Slums. **1932** Gorilla Ship. **1933** Between Fighting Men.

BRADBURY, JAMES, SR.

Born: Oct. 12, 1857, Old Town, Maine. Died: Oct. 12, 1940, Clifton, Staten Island, N.Y. Screen and stage actor. Father of actor James Bradbury, Jr. (dec. 1936).

Appeared in: **1924** Manhattan. **1926** Fascinating Youth; The High Flyer. **1927** The Blood Ship; The Fair Co-Ed; Babe Comes Home; The Circus Ace; Romantic Rogue; The Racing Fool. **1928** Skinner's Big Idea; Blockade; Waterfront; Scarlet Seas; Hot Heels; The Leopard Lady; Walking Back; Midnight Madness. **1929** Tide of the Empire; Woman from Hell. **1930** The Matrimonial Bed; Tol'able David; Abraham Lincoln. **1934** The Silver Streak.

BRADBURY, SAXE

Born: 1943. Died: Nov 13, 1976, Ariz. (plane crash). Screen actor.

Appeared in: **1977** The Turning Point.

BRADFORD, LANE

Born: 1923. Died: June 7, 1973, Honolulu, Hawaii (cerebral hemorrhage). Screen and television actor. Son of actor John Merton (dec. 1959) and brother of actor Robert La Varre.

Appeared in: **1946** Silver Range; Ghost Town Renegades; Pioneer Justice. **1947** Prairie Raiders; Riders of the Lone Star; Black Hills; Shadow Valley; Swing the Western Way; Return of the Lash. **1948** Adventures of Frank and Jesse James (serial); The Hawk of Powder River; Black Hills; Tornado Ridge; Check Your Guns; Frontier Agent; Sundown at Santa Fe. **1949** The Far Frontier; The Wyoming Bandit; South of Rio; San Antone Ambush; Prince of the Plains; Law of the Golden West; Bandit King of Texas; The Fighting Redhead; Death Valley Gunfighter. **1950** The Invisible Monster (serial); The James Brothers of Missouri (serial); The Desert Hawk; Bells of Coronado; Frisco Tornado; Hills of Oklahoma; The Missourians; The Old Frontier; Cowboy and the Prizefighter; Code of the Silver Sage. **1951** Don Daredevil Rides Again (serial); Stage from Blue River; Whistling Hills; Texas Lawmen; The Lady from Texas; Lawless Cowboys. **1952** African Treasure; Dead Man's Trail; Desperados' Outpost; Fort Osage; Texas City; Waco; Gunman; Kansas Territory; The Man from the Black Hills; The Lusty Men; Night Raiders; The Raiders; Rose of Cimarron; Zombies of the Stratosphere (serial); Target; Desert Passage. **1953** Savage Frontier; Son of Belle Starr. **1954** The French Line; Man With the Steel Whip (serial); Drums Across the River; The Forty-Niners; Ride Clear of Diablo; The Golden Idol. **1955** The Spoilers. **1956** The Rawhide Years; The Conqueror; Showdown at Abilene. **1957** Shoot-Out at Medicine Bend; Apache Warrior; The Phantom Stagecoach. **1958** The Lone Ranger and the Lost City of Gold; Satan's Satellites; Toughest Gun in Tombstone. **1963** The Gun Hawk. **1964** A Distant Trumpet. **1965** Shenandoah; The Slender Thread. **1968** Journey to Shiloh.

BRADFORD, MARSHALL

Born: 1896. Died: Jan. 11, 1971, Hollywood, Calif. (heart attack). Screen, stage and television actor.

Appeared in: **1949** White Heat; Western Renegades. **1950** Texas Dynamo. **1951** The Magnificent Yankee; Ghost Chasers; Night Raiders of Montana; Colorado Ambush. **1952** The Bad and the Beautiful; Hellgate. **1954** The Bounty Hunter; Yukon Vengeance. **1957** Shoot-Out at Medicine Bend; Band of Angels; I Was a Teenage Frankenstein. **1958** Teenage Caveman. **1959** A Summer Place. **1962** Terror at Black Falls. **1965** Shenandoah.

BRADLEY, AMANDA

Died: Dec. 13, 1916, New York, N.Y. (auto accident). Screen actress.

BRADLEY, BENJAMIN R.

Born: 1898. Died: Sept. 29, 1950, St. Louis, Mo. (heart disease and complications). Screen actor and magician. Appeared in silents.

BRADLEY, HARRY C.

Born: Apr. 15, 1869, San Francisco, Calif. Died: Oct. 18, 1947, Hollywood, Calif. (heart attack). Screen and stage actor.

Appeared in: **1931** The Smiling Lieutenant. **1933** Lady Killer; Dancing Lady; Frozen Assets (short); I Love That Man; This Day and Age; I Have Lived. **1934** It Happened One Night; Heat Lightning; The Merry Frinks; The Last Gentleman; City Limits; White Lies. **1935** Love in Bloom; Private Worlds; Way Down East. **1936** Cain and Mabel; It Had to Happen; Three of a Kind; Gold Diggers of 1937; Don't Get Personal; Next Time We Love; Rhythm of the Range; Come and Get It; The Country Doctor. **1937** New Faces of 1937; Trouble at Midnight. **1938** Women Are Like That; The Little Adventuress; I Am The Law; The Jury's Secret. **1939** The Roaring Twenties; When Tomorrow Comes. **1940** Flash Gordon Conquers the Universe (serial); Slightly Tempted. **1941** The Big Store; The Invisible Woman. **1942** Busses Roar; Hi, Neighbor; Get Hep to Love; Mrs. Wiggs of the Cabbage Patch. **1943** Henry Aldrich Gets Glamour; Dixie. **1944** Bowery to Broadway; Henry Aldrich's Little Secret; Make Your Own Bed; Henry Aldrich Plays Cupid.

BRADLEY, LOVYSS

Born: 1906. Died: June 21, 1969, Woodland Hills, Calif. (cancer). Screen and television actress.

Appeared in: **1947** They Won't Believe Me. **1950** Outrage. **1951** Golden Girl; The Blue Veil. **1968** Up Tight.

BRADLEY, TRUMAN

Born: 1905. Died: July 28, 1974, Los Angeles, Calif. Screen, television, radio actor and sports announcer.

Appeared in: **1938** Vacation from Love; Spring Madness; Young Doctor Kildare. **1939** The Hardys Ride High; On Borrowed Time; Money to Loan (short); Help Wanted (short). **1940** Millionaires in Prison; Yesterday's Heroes; Northwest Passage; A Night at Earl Carroll's. **1941** Murder Among Friends; Dead Men Tell; Keep 'Em Flying; Charlie Chan in Rio; Last of the Duanes; Mob Town; Burma Convoy. **1942** Treat 'Em Rough; Night Before the Divorce; Lone Star Ranger; Bombay Clipper. **1945** The Horn Blows at Midnight. **1947** I Wonder Who's Kissing Her Now.

BRADSHAW, EUNICE
Born: 1893. Died: 1973. Screen actress. Appeared in silent films.

BRADSHAW, LIONEL M.
Born: May 10, 1892, Lima, Ohio. Died: Dec. 17, 1918, Los Angeles, Calif. (Spanish influenza). Stage and screen actor.

Appeared in: **1915** The Black Box; Carmen. **1916** Peg O' the Ring (series); Lady Raffles Returns.

BRADY, ALICE
Born: Nov. 2, 1892, New York, N.Y. Died: Oct. 28, 1939, New York, N.Y. (cancer). Screen and stage actress. Daughter of stage producer William A. Brady and dancer Rose Marie Rene. Divorced from actor James Lyon Crane (dec. 1968). Won 1937 Academy Award for Best Supporting Actress for In Old Chicago and nominated for 1936 Academy Award for Best Supporting Actress for My Man Godfrey.

Appeared in: **1914** As Ye Sow. **1915** The Boss; The Cup of Chance; The Lure of Woman. **1916** La Boheme; Bought and Paid For; The Guilded Cage; The Rack; The Ballet Girl; The Woman in 47; Then I'll Come Back to You; Tangled Fates; Miss Petticoats. **1917** Betsy Ross; A Woman Alone; A Hungry Heart; The Dancer's Peril; Darkest Russia; Maternity; The Divorce Game; A Self-Made Widow; A Maid of Belgium. **1918** Woman and Wife; Her Silent Sacrifice; The Knife; The Spurs of Sybil; At the Mercy of Men; The Trap; The Whirlpool; The Death Dance; The Ordeal of Rosetta; The Better Half; In the Hollow of Her Hand; Her Great Chance. **1919** The Indestructible Wife; The World to Live In; Marie, Ltd; The Redhead; His Bridal Night. **1920** Fear Market; The New York Idea; Sinners; A Dark Lantern. **1921** Out of the Chorus; Little Italy; The Land of Hope; The Dawn of the East; Hush Money. **1922** Anna Ascends; Missing Millions. **1923** The Leopardess; The Snow Bride. **1933** When Ladies Meet; Beauty for Sale; Broadway to Hollywood; Stage Mother; Should Ladies Behave? **1934** Miss Fane's Baby is Stolen; The Gay Divorcee; False Faces. **1935** Gold Diggers of 1935; Let 'Em Have It; Lady Tubbs; Metropolitan. **1936** The Harvester; My Man Godfrey; Go West, Young Man; Mind Your Own Business. **1937** Three Smart Girls; One Hundred Men and a Girl; Mama Steps Out; Call It a Day; In Old Chicago; Mr. Dodd Takes the Air; Merry-Go-Round of 1938. **1938** Joy of Living; Goodbye Broadway. **1939** Zenobia; Young Mr. Lincoln.

BRADY, EDWARD J.
Born: 1888, New York, N.Y. Died: Mar. 31, 1942, Hollywood, Calif. (heart attack). Screen, stage and vaudeville actor.

Appeared in: **1915** Who Pays?; Neal of the Navy (serial). **1919** The Great Radium Mystery (serial). **1921** The Rough Diamond; The Silent Call; Cheated Love; The Kiss. **1922** The Old Homestead; The Pride of Palomar; Over the Border; The Siren Call; Boy Crazy; If You Believe It, It's So; A Question of Honor. **1923** To the Last Man; The Broken Wing; Racing Hearts; The Trail of the Lonesome Pine; The Eternal Struggle. **1924** The Dancing Cheat; The Fighting American; The Rose of Paris; The Price She Paid; Stolen Secrets; Fool's Highway. **1925** Marry Me; The Thundering Herd; A Child of the Prairie; Flower of Night. **1926** Three Faces East; Whispering Canyon. **1927** The Rose of Kildare; Hoof Marks; Lost at the Front; King of Kings; Clancy's Kosher Wedding. **1928** Harold Teen; The Noose; Do Your Duty; The Code of the Scarlet; The Bushranger; Dressed to Kill. **1929** The Delightful Rogue; Stewed, Fried and Boiled (short); Alibi. **1930** The Texan; City Girl; Cameo Kirby. **1931** The Squaw Man; The Sin of Madelon Claudet; Shanghaied Love; The Conquering Horde. **1932** Union Depot; The Night Club Lady. **1933** The Lone Avenger; Son of Kong. **1934** Redhead; In a Pig's Eye (short). **1935** It's a Small World. **1936** Fury; Klondike Annie. **1938** The Buccaneer; Blockade; If I Were King. **1939** The Oklahoma Kid; Union Pacific; Stagecoach. **1940** North West Mounted Police; Shooting High; Saps at Sea (short). **1941** Billy the Kid. **1942** Reap the Wild Wind; The Forest Rangers. **1943** The Outlaw.

BRADY, FRED (Frederick Kress)
Born: Mar. 29, 1912, New York, N.Y. Died: Nov. 11, 1961, Los Angeles, Calif. (heart failure). Screen actor and screenwriter.

Appeared in: **1943** Stage Door Canteen; Swing Shift Maisie. **1944** Why, Daddy? (short); Three Is a Family; Dancing in Manhattan. **1946** Meet Me on Broadway; The Cat Creeps; Little Miss Big; Slightly Scandalous.

BRADY, PAT
Born: Dec. 31, 1914, Toledo, Ohio. Died: Feb. 27, 1972, Green Mountain Falls, Colo. Screen, stage, television actor and musician. Member of the "Sons of the Pioneers" singing group.

Appeared in: **1938** West of Cheyenne. **1939** Man from Sundown. **1940** Two-Fisted Rangers; The Durango Kid. **1943** Song of Texas; The Man from Music Mountain. **1949** Down Dakota Way; The Golden Stallion. **1950** Bells of Coronado; Trigger, Jr.; Twilight in the Sierras. **1951** South of Caliente.

BRADY, VERONICA
Born: 1890, Dublin, Ireland. Died: Jan. 19, 1964, Twickenham, England. Screen and stage actress.

Appeared in: **1934** Love, Life and Laughter; What Happened to Harkness. **1935** Birds of a Feather.

BRAGA, EURICO
Born: 1894, Rio de Janeiro, Brazil. Died: Nov. 19, 1962, Lisbon, Portugal (cancer). Screen, stage actor and newspaper columnist.

BRAGAGLIA, ARTURO
Born: 1892, Italy. Died: Jan. 21, 1962, Rome, Italy. Screen actor. Brother of film director Carlo Ludovico Bragaglia.

Appeared in: **1940** Il Documento Fatale. **1948** Four Steps in the Clouds. **1951** Miracolo a Milano (Miracle in Milan). **1953** Ring Around the Clock; L'Ennemi Public No. 1 (aka The Most Wanted Man in the World—US 1962). **1957** Les Week-ends de Neron (aka Nero's Mistress—US 1962).

BRAHAM, HARRY
Born: 1874, London, England. Died: Sept. 21, 1923, Staten Island, N.Y. Stage and screen actor. Appeared in Griffith films.

BRAHAM, HORACE
Born: 1893. Died: Sept. 7, 1955, New York, N.Y. Screen, stage, radio and television actor. Married to actress Gladys Feldman (dec. 1974).

Appeared in: **1922** The Prodigal Judge. **1923** Sinner or Saint.

BRAHAM, LIONEL
Born: 1879, England. Died: Oct. 6, 1947, Hollywood, Calif. (heart attack). Screen and stage actor.

Appeared in: **1916** Diane the Huntress. **1925** I'll Show You the Town. **1926** Skinner's Dress Suit; Don Juan. **1927** Night Life; Out All Night. **1936** As You Like It. **1937** Personal Property; The Prince and the Pauper; Wee Willie Winkie. **1938** A Christmas Carol. **1939** The Little Princess. **1948** Macbeth.

BRAITHWAITE, DAME LILIAN
Born: 1873, England. Died: Sept. 17, 1948, London, England (heart attack). Screen and stage actress. Was made Dame Commander of the Order of the British Empire in 1943. Married to actor Gerald Lawrence (dec. 1957).

Appeared in: **1915** The World's Desire (aka The Lord Gave); The Climax (aka Motherhood). **1917** The Woman Who Was Nothing; Dombey and Son; Justice; The Gay Lord Quex; Masks and Faces. **1918** Because. **1919** The Chinese Puzzle. **1920** General Post; Castles in Spain; Garry Owen. **1921** Mary-Find-The-Gold. **1927** Downhill (aka When Boys Leave Home—US 1928). **1931** Carnival (aka Venetian Nights—US); Man of Mayfair. **1932** The Chinese Puzzle (and 1919 version). **1947** A Man About the House (US 1949).

BRAMBLE, A. V.
Born: Portsmouth, England. Died: 1955?, England. Screen, stage actor, film director and screenwriter.

Appeared in: **1914** The Loss of the Birkenhead; The Suicide Club; Beautiful Jim (aka The Price of Justice—US); The Bells of Rheims; It's a Long, Long Way to Tipperary; Her Luck in London; The Courage of a Coward; The Idol of Paris; The Sound of Her Voice; In the Days of Trafalgar (aka Black-eyed Susan and aka The Battling British—US). **1915** There's Good in Everyone; A Honeymoon for Three; Midshipman Easy; London's Yellow Peril; Florence Nightingale; The Lord Gave (aka The World's Desire); From Shopgirl to Duchess; Another Man's Wife; Her Nameless Child; Wild Oats; Shadows; Grip; At the Torrent's Mercy; Motherhood (aka The Climax); Yvonne; Strategy (aka Society Crooks); The Mystery of a Hansom Cab. **1916** A Soldier and a Man; Fatal Fingers; Jimmy; The Blind Man of Verdun. **1916** Nearer My God to Thee; When Paris Sleeps; The Laughing Cavalier; Broken Threads. **1918** The Hanging Judge; Towards the Light; Film Tags series including: The Message. **1923** Becket. **1927** The Rolling Road. **1952** Outcast of the Islands.

BRANDON, ARTHUR F.
Born: 1925. Died: June 27, 1975, near Barton, Vt. (heart attack). Screen, stage actor and composer.

Appeared in: **1938** Life Goes On.

BRANDON, DOLORES
Born: 1917. Died: Aug. 9, 1959, Hollywood, Calif. Screen and vaudeville actress.

BRANDON, FLORENCE
Born: 1879. Died: Oct. 11, 1961, London, England. Screen and stage actress. Appeared in silents.

BRANDON, FRANCIS
Born: 1886. Died: Oct. 3, 1924, Bronx, N.Y. Stage and screen actor.

BRANDON-THOMAS, AMY (Amy Marguerite Brandon-Thomas)
Born: Mar. 9, 1890, London, England. Died: May 9, 1974, London, England. Screen and stage actress. Sister of actor Jevan Brandon-Thomas.

Appeared in: **1930** Mystery at the Villa Rose. **1934** Java Head (US 1935). **1935** Vintage Wine.

BRANDT, C. EDWIN
Born: 1871. Died: Jan. 8, 1939, New York, N.Y. Screen and stage actor.

Appeared in: **1914** The Million Dollar Robbery.

BRANDT, CHARLES
Born: 1864. Died: June 9, 1924, Philadelphia, Pa. Screen and stage actor.

Appeared in: **1912** A Matter of Business; A Child's Devotion; The Heavenly Voice. **1913** The Power of the Cross; The District Attorney's Conscience; The Insurance Agent; Dr. Maxwell's Experiment; John Arthur's Trust; A Timely Rescue; Annie Rowley's Fortune; When John Brought Home His Wife; The Sea Eternal; The School Principal. **1914** The Fortune Hunter; A Daughter of Fire. **1915** The Sporting Duchess; The District Attorney; The Great Ruby Mystery; The Rights of Man; Think, Mothers; Sweeter Than Revenge; The Road of Strife (serial). **1916** The Soul Market; Friday the Thirteenth. **1919** The Misfit Earl. **1920** The Master Mind.

BRANDT, LOUISE
Born: 1877. Died: July 13, 1959, San Diego, Calif. Screen actress.

BRANNIGAN, OWEN
Born: 1909, England. Died: May 9, 1973, Newcastle, England. Screen, stage actor and singer.

Appeared in: **1953** The Story of Gilbert and Sullivan (aka Gilbert and Sullivan—US).

BRANSCOMBE, LILY
Died: Date Unknown. Screen actress. Married to actor Herbert Ashton, Sr. (dec. 1930). Mother of actor Herbert J. Ashton, Jr. (dec. 1960).

BRASFIELD, ROD
Died: Sept. 12, 1958. Screen and radio actor.

Appeared in: **1956** A Face in the Crowd. **1958** Country Music Holiday.

BRASSELLE, KEEFE (John D. Brasselli)
Born: Feb. 7, 1923, Elyria, Ohio. Died: July 7, 1981, Downey, Calif. (cirrhosis of the liver). Screen, vaudeville actor, film director, television producer and writer.

Appeared in: **1944** Janie (film debut). **1945** The River Gang. **1947** Railroaded. **1949** Not Wanted. **1950** Dial 1119; Never Fear; The Young Lovers. **1951** A Place in the Sun; Bannerline; The Unknown Man; It's a Big Country. **1952** Skirts Ahoy! **1953** The Eddie Cantor Story. **1954** The Three Young Texans. **1955** Mad at the World; Bring Your Smile Along. **1956** Battle Stations. **1957** The Fighting Wildcats; West of Suez. **1972** Black Gunn. **1975** If You Don't Stop It ... You'll Go Blind.

BRASSENS, GEORGES
Born: 1921, Sete, France. Died: Oct. 30, 1981, Sete, France (cancer). Screen actor, writer, singer and songwriter.

Appeared in: **1957** Porte Des Lilas. **1958** Gates of Paris.

BRASSEUR, PIERRE (Pierre Espinasse)
Born: 1903, Paris, France. Died: Aug. 14, 1972, Italy. Screen and stage actor, playwright, screenwriter, film director and stage producer. Married to actress Odette Joyeux and father of actor Claude Brasseur.

Appeared in: **1928** Claudine a l'Ecole. **1933** Cafe de Paris. Other films prior to 1936: Circulez; Papa Sans le Savoir; Vainqueur; La Reve Blonde; Moi et l'Imperatrice; Voyage de Noce; Chanson d'une Nuit; Le Sexe Faible; Incognito; Garnison Amoureuse; Oncle de Pekin; Je Suis un As; Patte de Mouche; Debauche. **1938** Le Quai des Brumes (The Foggy Quay). **1939** Mademoiselle ma Mere; Port of Shadows; Last Desire. **1940** Claudine. **1942** Lumiere d'ete. **1944** Les Enfants du Paradis (The Children of Paradise—US 1947). **1946** Jericho; Les Portes de la Nuit (Gates of the Night—US 1950). **1950** Julie de Carneilhan; Noah's Ark. **1951** The Lovers of Verona; Barbe Bleu (Bluebeard). **1953** Le Plaisir (aka House of Pleasure and The House of Madame Tellier); Maitre Apres Dieu (aka Skipper Next to God). **1954** Dirty Hands. **1955** Portes des Lilas. **1957** Oasis. **1958** Gates of Paris. **1959** The Processors; Sans Famille. **1960** Candide (US 1962); Il Bell'Antonio (Bell Antonio—US 1962); Cartagine en Flamme (Carthage in Flames—US 1961); Where the Hot Wind Blows (aka Le Legge—The Law); Les Yeux Sans Visage (aka The Horror Chamber of Dr. Faustus—US 1962). **1962** Le Crime ne Paie Pas (Crime Does Not Pay). **1963** Les Bonnes Causes (The Good Causes aka Don't Tempt the Devil—US 1964). **1964** Liola (aka A Very Handy Man—US 1966). **1965** Deux Heures a Tuer; La Metamorphose des Cloportes (Cloportes—US 1966). **1966** Un Monde Nouveau (A Young World—US); Le Roi de Coeur (King of Hearts—US 1967). **1968** Les Oiseux vont Mourir au Perou (Birds in Peru).

BRASWELL, CHARLES
Born: 1925. Died: May 17, 1974, Bronx, N.Y. Screen and stage actor.

Appeared in: **1957** Bail Out at 43,000. **1960** Pretty Boy Floyd. **1970** The Only Game in Town.

BRATANOV, IVAN
Born: 1920, Bulgaria. Died: 1968, Bulgaria. Screen actor.

Appeared in: **1954** Septembrists (Septemvriitsi); Pessen za Choveka (Song for Man). **1955** Nespokoen Pat (Troubled Road). **1956** Dimitrovgradtsi (People of Dimitrovgrad). **1960** Parvi Urok (First Lesson); Stubenskite Lipi (The Stoublen Lindens). **1967** Nai Dalgata Nosht (The Longest Night).

BRAVO, JAMIE
Born: 1932. Died: Feb. 2, 1970, Zacatecas, Mexico (auto accident). Matador and screen actor.

Appeared in: **1965** Love Has Many Faces.

BRAWN, JOHN P.
Born: 1869, New York, N.Y. Died: June 16, 1943, New York, N.Y. Stage and screen actor.

BRAY, JOHN F.
Born: 1906. Died: May 3, 1955, Gladewater, Tex. Screen actor.

Appeared in: **1948** Paleface. **1949** Mr. Belvedere Goes to College. **1951** Here Comes the Groom. **1952** Viva Zapata!

BRAYFIELD, GEORGE
Died: Feb. 17, 1968. Screen actor. Appeared in early westerns.

BRAYTON, LILY
Born: June 23, 1876, Hindley, Lancs, England. Died: Apr. 30, 1953, Dawlish, England. Screen, stage actress and stage producer. Married to actor/producer Oscar Asche (dec. 1936) and later married to Douglas Chalmers Watson.

Appeared in: **1914** Kismet.

BRAZZI, LYDIA
Born: 1925, Italy. Died: Apr. 21, 1981, Rome, Italy (cancer). Screen and television actress. Married to actor Rossano Brazzi.

Appeared in: **1966** Caccia alla Volpe (After the Fox); Il Natale che Quasi non Fu (aka The Christmas That Almost Wasn't—US).

BREAKSTON, GEORGE P.
Born: Jan. 22, 1920, Paris, France. Died: May 21, 1973, Paris, France. Screen, stage, television, radio actor, film director, producer and screenwriter.

Appeared in: **1933** Wild Boys of the Road. **1934** It Happened One Night; No Greater Glory; Mrs. Wiggs of the Cabbage Patch; A Successful Failure; Great Expectations. **1935** The Dark Angel; The Return of Peter Grimm; Life Returns. **1936** Second Wife; Boulder Dam. **1938** Love Finds Andy Hardy; A Criminal Is Born (short). **1939** Jesse James; Andy Hardy Gets Spring Fever; Boy Slaves; Swanee River. **1940** Judge Hardy and Son; Andy Hardy Meets the Debutante; Grapes of Wrath. **1941** Life Begins for Andy Hardy; Andy Hardy's Private Secretary. **1942** The Courtship of Andy Hardy; Men of San Quentin.

BREAMER, SYLVIA
Born: 1903. Died: June 7, 1943, New York, N.Y. Screen actress.

Appeared in: **1918** We Can't Have Everything; The Common Cause; Missing. **1921** The Devil; Not Guilty; Doubling for Romeo; The Roof Tree; A Poor Relation. **1922** Wolf Law; Money to Burn; The Man Who Married His Own Wife; The Man With Two Mothers; The Man Unconquerable; Calvert's Valley; The Face Between; Money to Burn; Sherlock Brown. **1923** Bavu; The First Degree; Flaming Youth; The Barefoot Boy; Her Temporary Husband; The Girl of the Golden West; Thundergate. **1924** Lillies of the Field; Woman on the Jury; Reckless Romance; Robes of Sin. **1925** Too Much Youth; Women and Gold. **1926** Up in Mabel's Room; Lightning Reporter. **1936** Too Many Parents.

BRECHER, EGON
Born: Feb. 16, 1880, Czechoslovakia. Died: Aug. 12, 1946, Hollywood, Calif. (heart attack). Screen, stage actor and stage director.

Appeared in: **1929** The Royal Box. **1933** To the Last Man. **1934** As the Earth Turns; No Greater Glory; Many Happy Returns; The Black Cat; Now and Forever. **1935** Break of Hearts; Black Fury; The Florentine Dagger; Here's to Romance. **1936** One in a Million; Charlie Chan's Secret; Boulder Dam; Till We Meet Again; Sins of Man; Ladies in Love; The White Angel; Stolen Holiday; Alibi for Murder. **1937** The Life of Emile Zola; The Black Legion; Heidi; I Met Him in Paris; Love Under Fire; Thin Ice. **1938** Arsene Lupin Returns; I'll Give a Million; Suez; Cocoanut Grove; You and Me; Spawn of the North; The Spy Ring; Invisible Enemy. **1939** We Are Not Alone; Confessions of a Nazi Spy; While America Sleeps (short); Devil's Island; The Three Musketeers; Nurse Edith Cavell; Judge Hardy and Son; Juarez; Angels Wash Their Faces. **1940** All This and Heaven Too; Dr. Ehrlich's Magic Bullet; A Dispatch from Reuters; Pound Foolish (short); Four Sons; The Man I Married; I Was An Adventuress. **1941** Manhunt; Out of Darkness (short); Kings Row; They Dare Not Love; Underground; Manpower. **1942** All Through the Night; Isle of Missing Men; For a Common Defense (short); Berlin Correspondent. **1944** The Desert Hawk (serial); The Seventh Cross; The Hairy Ape; U-Boat Prisoner. **1945** A Royal Scandal; White Pongo. **1946** Temptation; Sister Kenny; The Wife of Monte Cristo; OSS; So Dark the Night.

BRECKNER, GARY
Born: 1896. Died: June 25, 1945, Redlands, Calif. (auto accident). Screen, stage and radio actor.

Appeared in: **1937** Wake Up and Live; Love and Hisses. **1938** Thanks for Everything; Rebecca of Sunnybrook Farm. **1940** Johnny Apollo. **1941** The Great American Broadcast.

BREEDEN, JOHN NORTON
Born: May 3, 1904, San Francisco, Calif. Died: Sept 9, 1977, San Francisco, Calif. Screen and stage actor. Entered films in 1929.

Appeared in: **1929** Masquerade; Joy Street; Salute; The Shannons of Broadway; Movietone Follies of 1929. **1931** Beloved Bachelor. **1932** False Madonna; Madame Racketeer.

BREEN, HURLEY "RED"
Born: 1913. Died: Sept. 8, 1963, Hollywood, Calif. Screen actor and boxer. Double for James Cagney.

Appeared in: **1952** Boots Malone.

BREEN, JOHN P.
Died: Aug., 1972. Screen actor.

Appeared in: **1956** The Man in the Gray Flannel Suit.

BREEN, MARGARET
Died: Dec. 5, 1960, Santa Monica, Calif. Screen, stage and vaudeville actress. Was part of the "Breen Family" vaudeville act.

Appeared in: **1930** Heads Up.

BREESE, EDMUND
Born: June 18, 1871, Brooklyn, N.Y. Died: Apr. 6, 1936, New York, N.Y. (peritonitis). Screen, stage actor and playwright. Entered films in 1914.

Appeared in: **1915** The Song of the Wage Slave. **1916** The Spell of the Yukon. **1921** Burn 'Em Up Barnes. **1922** Beyond the Rainbow; Sure-Fire Flint; The Curse of Drink. **1923** Luck; The Little Red Schoolhouse; You are Guilty; Bright Lights of Broadway; The Fair Cheat; Jacqueline of Blazing Barriers; Marriage Morals. **1924** Three O'Clock in the Morning; The Early Bird; The Shooting of Dan McGrew; Damaged Hearts; Restless Wives; Playthings of Desire; The

Sixth Commandment; The Speed Spook; Those Who Judge. **1925** The Police Patrol; Wildfire; The Live Wire. **1926** Stepping Along; Woman Handled; The Brown Derby; The Highbinders. **1927** Paradise for Two; Back to Liberty; Home Made. **1928** Finders Keepers; Burning Daylight; Perfect Crime; The Wright Idea; On Trial; The Haunted House. **1929** Sonny Boy; Fancy Baggage; Conquest; Girls Gone Wild; From Headquarters; The Gamblers; The Hottentot; Girl Overboard; In the Headlines. **1930** Hold Everything; The Sea Bat; Rough Waters; Top Speed; Tol'able David; All Quiet on the Western Front; Kismet; The Czar of Broadway; Playboy of Paris. **1931** Bright Lights; Playthings of Hollywood; Oh! Oh! Cleopatra (short); Public Defender; Wicked; Chinatown After Dark; Mother's Millions; Millie; The Last Parade; Defenders of the Law; Young Sinners; The Good Bad Girl; The Painted Desert; Platinum Blonde; Morals for Women; Bad Girl. **1932** The Hurricane Express (serial); Cross Examination; The Hatchet Man; Mata Hari; Police Court; The Reckoning; Love Bound; Drifting Souls; Alias Mary Smith; Cabin in the Cotton; Golden West; Madame Butterfly; The Match King. **1933** Women Won't Tell; Billion Dollar Scandal; International House; Laughing at Life; Man of Sentiment; Ladies Must Love; Duck Soup; Above the Clouds. **1934** Come on Marines; Beloved; Treasure Island; Broadway Bill; The Dancing Man; Lost in the Stratosphere. **1935** The Marriage Bargain.

BREL, JACQUES
Born: 1929, Brussels, Belgium. Died: Oct. 9, 1978, Paris, France (cancer). Screen actor, film director, composer and singer.

Appeared in: **1975** Jacques Brel is Alive and Well and Living in Paris; A Pain in the A... **1976** Money, Money, Money.

BRENDEL, EL (Elmer G. Brendel)
Born: Mar. 25, 1890, Philadelphia, Pa. Died: Apr. 9, 1964, Hollywood, Calif. (heart attack). Screen, stage, vaudeville and television actor. Married to Sophie Flo Bert with whom he appeared in vaudeville. Entered films in 1926.

Appeared in: **1926** The Campus Flirt; You Never Know Women. **1927** Ten Modern Commandments; Too Many Crooks; Wings; Arizona Bound; Rolled Stockings. **1929** The Cock-Eyed World; Sunny-Side Up; Frozen Justice; Hot for Paris; Beau Night (short). **1930** Happy Days; The Big Trail; The Golden Calf; Just Imagine; New Movietone Follies of 1930. **1931** Mr. Lemon of Orange; Spider; Delicious; Women of All Nations; Six Cylinder Love. **1932** West of Broadway; Disorderly Conduct; Handle With Care. **1933** Hot Pepper; My Lips Betray; The Last Trail. **1934** The Meanest Gal in Town; Olsen's Big Moment. **1935** What! No Men (short); Broadway Brevities (short). **1936** Career Woman; Lonesome Trailer (short); God's Country and the Woman. **1937** The Holy Terror; Blonde Trouble. **1938** Happy Landing; Little Miss Broadway; Valley of Giants. **1939** Code of the Streets; House of Fear; Risky Business; Spirit of Culver; Call of a Messenger. **1940** If I Had My Way; Captain Caution; Gallant Sons. **1943** A Rookie's Cookie (short). **1944** I'm from Arkansas; Machine Gun Mama; Defective Detectives (short); Mopey Dope (short). **1945** Pistol Packin' Nitwits (short); Snooper Service (short). **1949** The Beautiful Blonde from Bashful Bend. **1953** Paris Model. **1956** The She-Creature.

BRENDLIN, ANDRE
Born: 1911, France. Died: Oct. 6, 1934, Marne, France (drowned). Screen actor.

BRENEMAN, TOM
Born: 1902. Died: Apr. 28, 1948, Encino, Calif. Screen actor and radio emcee of "Breakfast in Hollywood."

Appeared in: **1946** Breakfast in Hollywood.

BRENNAN, JAY
Born: 1883. Died: Jan. 14, 1961, Brooklyn, N.Y. Screen, vaudeville actor and screenwriter.

Appeared in: **1943** Follies Girl.

BRENNAN, JOHN E.
Born: 1865, Springfield, Mass. Died: Dec. 27, 1940, Los Angeles, Calif. (heart attack). Screen actor.

Appeared in: **1912** Strong Armed Nellie; The Landlubber; The Chaperon Gets a Ducking. **1916** Vindication.

BRENNAN, ROBERT
Born: 1892. Died: Apr. 17, 1940, Los Angeles, Calif. Stage and screen actor. Entered films during silents.

BRENNAN, WALTER

Born: July 25, 1894, Swampscott or Lynn, Mass.? Died: Sept. 21, 1974, Oxnard, Calif. (emphysema). Screen, stage, vaudeville and television actor. Father of Arthur, Ruth and film producer Walter Brennan, Jr. Won 1936 Academy Award for Best Supporting Actor in Come and Get It; in 1938 for Kentucky; and in 1940 for The Westerner. Nominated for 1941 Academy Award for Best Supporting Actor in Sergeant York. Entered films as an extra in the early 1920s.

Appeared in: **1927** The Ridin' Rowdy; Tearin' Into Trouble. **1928** Ballyhoo Buster. **1929** The Lariat Kid; The Long, Long Trail; Shannons of Broadway; Smilin' Guns; One Hysterical Night. **1930** The King of Jazz. **1931** Scratch as Catch Can (short); Dancing Dynamite; Neck and Neck. **1932** Twin Lips and Juleps or Southern Love and Northern Exposure (short); The Airmail Mystery (serial); The Iceman's Ball (short); Law and Order; Texas Cyclone; Two-Fisted Law; All American. **1933** The Phantom of the Air (serial); One Year Later; Parachute Jumper; Man of Action; Fighting for Justice; Sing, Sinner, Sing; Strange People. **1934** Woman Haters (short); Good Dame; Half a Sinner. **1935** Hunger Pains (short); Restless Knights (short); The Wedding Night; Northern Frontier; Lady Tubbs; The Man on the Flying Trapeze; Barbary Coast; Seven Keys to Baldpate; Law Beyond the Range; Bride of Frankenstein; Metropolitan; Bric-a-Brac (short). **1936** Three Godfathers; These Three; Come and Get It; Fury; Banjo on My Knee; The Moon's Our Home; The Prescott Kid. **1937** When Love Is Young; The Affairs of Cappy Ricks; Wild and Wooly; She's Dangerous. **1938** The Adventures of Tom Sawyer; The Buccaneer; Kentucky; The Texans; Mother Carey's Chickens; The Cowboy and the Lady. **1939** Stanley and Livingstone; The Story of Vernon and Irene Castle; They Shall Have Music; Joe and Ethel Turp Call on the President. **1940** The Westerner; Northwest Passage; Maryland. **1941** Sergeant York; Meet John Doe; Swampwater; This Woman Is Mine; Nice Girl?; Rise and Shine. **1942** The Pride of the Yankees; Stand By for Action. **1943** The North Star; Slightly Dangerous; Hangmen Also Die; The Last Will and Testament of Tom Smith (short). **1944** The Princess and the Pirate; To Have and Have Not; Home in Indiana. **1945** Dakota. **1946** My Darling Clementine; Centennial Summer; A Stolen Life; Nobody Lives Forever. **1947** Driftwood. **1948** Scudda Hoo! Scudda Hay!; Red River; Blood on the Moon. **1949** Brimstone; The Green Promise; Task Force; The Great Dan Patch. **1950** Curtain Call at Cactus Creek; Ticket to Tomahawk (aka The Sheriff's Daughter); Singing Guns; Surrender; The Showdown. **1951** Best of the Bad Men; The Wild Blue Yonder; Along the Great Divide. **1952** Lure of the Wilderness; Return of the Texan. **1953** Sea of Lost Ships. **1954** Drums Across the River; Four Guns to the Border; Bad Day at Black Rock. **1955** The Far Country; At Gunpoint. **1956** Glory; Come Next Spring; Good-Bye My Lady; The Proud Ones. **1957** Tammy and the Bachelor; The Way to Gold; God Is My Partner. **1959** Rio Bravo. **1962** How the West Was Won; Shoot Out at Big Sag. **1964** Those Calloways. **1966** The Oscar. **1967** The Gnome-Mobile; Who's Minding the Mint? **1968** The One and Only, Genuine, Original Family Band. **1969** Support Your Local Sheriff. **1973** The Love Bug Rides Again.

BRENNEN, CLAIRE

Born: 1934. Died: Nov. 27, 1977, Hollywood, Calif. (cancer). Screen and television actress.

Appeared in: **1961** The Touchables. **1967** She Freak. **1970** The Traveling Executioner. **1973** Walking Tall. **1974** The Domino Principle. **1977** The Choirboys.

BRENON, HERBERT

Born: Jan. 13, 1880, Dublin, Ireland. Died: June 21, 1958, Los Angeles, Calif. Screen, stage, vaudeville actor, film director, film producer and screenwriter. Brother of actress Roma Brenon (dec. 1927). Married to Helen Oberg (dec.) with whom he appeared in vaudeville.

Appeared in: **1911** Blind Musician; The Strike. **1913** Ivanhoe. **1914** The Secret of the Air (aka Across the Atlantic—US). **1915** The Heart of Maryland; Two Orphans.

BRENON, JULIET

Born: 1897. Died: Nov. 18, 1979, New York, N.Y. Screen and stage actress. Married to stage designer Cleon Throckmorton (dec.).

Appeared in: **1925** The Street of Forgotten Men. **1926** A Kiss for Cinderella.

BRENON, ROMA

Born: 1870, Rome, Italy. Died: Oct. 9, 1927, New York, N.Y. Screen, stage and vaudeville actress. Sister of actor/director Herbert Brenon (dec. 1958).

BRENT, EVELYN (Mary Elizabeth Riggs aka DOROTHY RIGGS aka BETTY RIGGS)

Born: Oct. 20, 1899, Tampa, Fla. Died: June 4, 1975, Los Angeles, Calif. (heart attack). Screen, stage and television actress. Entered films as an extra with World Film Studio in 1914. Was a Wampas Baby Star of 1923. Divorced from director/producer Harry Edwards and Bernard P. Fineman. Later married vaudeville actor Harry Fox (dec. 1959).

Appeared in: **1914** A Gentleman from Mississippi; The Heart of a Painted Woman; The Pit. **1915** The Shooting of Dan McGrew. **1916** Lure of Heart's Desire; The Soul Market; The Spell of the Yukon; The Iron Woman; Playing With Fire; The Weakness of Strength. **1917** The Millionaire's Double; Who's Your Neighbor?; To the Death; Raffles, the Amateur Cracksman. **1918** Daybreak. **1919** Fool's Gold; The Other Man's Wife; Help, Help, Police; The Glorious Lady; Into the River; The Border River. **1920** The Shuttle of Life; The Law Divine. **1921** Demos (aka Why Men Forget—US); The Door That Has No Key (US 1922); Sybil; Sonia (aka The Woman Who Came Back—US 1922); Laughter and Tears; Circus Jim. **1922** Trapped by the Mormons; The Spanish Jade; The Experiment; Married to a Mormon; Pages of Life. **1923** Held to Answer; Loving Lies. **1924** The Arizona Express; The Cyclone Rider; The Dangerous Flirt; The Desert Outlaw; The Lone Chance; My Husband's Wives; The Plunderer; Silk Stocking Sal; The Shadow of the East (aka Shadow of the Desert and Shadows of the East). **1925** Alias Mary Flynn; Broadway Lady; Forbidden Cargo; Lady Robinhood; Midnight Molly; Smooth as Satin; Three Wise Crooks (aka Three of a Kind). **1926** The Flame of the Argentine; The Imposter; The Jade Cup; Love 'Em and Leave 'Em; Queen of Diamonds; Secret Orders. **1927** Blind Alley; Love's Greatest Mistake; Underworld; Women's Wares. **1928** Beau Sabreur; The Drag Net; His Tiger Lady; The Last Command; The Mating Call; A Night of Mystery; The Showdown; Interference; The Mormon Peril (reissue of Trapped by the Mormons—1922); Broadway; Darkened Rooms; Fast Company; Why Bring That Up?; Woman Trap. **1930** Framed; Madonna of the Streets; Paramount on Parade; The Silver Horde; Slightly Scarlet; Nuits de Chicago (French release of Underworld—1927). **1931** Traveling Husbands; Mad Parade (aka Forgotten Women); The Pagan Lady. **1932** High Pressure; Attorney for the Defense; The Crusader. **1933** The World Gone Mad (aka The Public Be Damned). **1935** Home on the Range; The Nitwits; Symphony of Living. **1936** It Couldn't Have Happened; The President's Mystery (aka One for All); Hopalong Cassidy Returns; Penthouse Party (aka Without Children); Song of the Trail. **1937** Jungle Jim (serial); King of the Gamblers; Night Club Scandal; Daughter of Shanghai (aka Daughter of the Orient); Last Train from Madrid. **1938** Tip-Off Girls; Law West of Tombstone; Mr. Wong, Detective; Sudden Bill Dorn; Speed Limited. **1939** Daughter of the Tong; Juarez and Maximilian (aka The Mad Empress); Panama Lady. **1940** The Fighting 69th; Adventure in Diamonds; 'Til We Meet Again. **1941** Emergency Landing; Dangerous Lady; Wide Open Town; Forced Landing; Holt of the Secret Service (serial); Ellery Queen and the Murder Ring. **1942** Wrecking Crew; The Pay-Off; Westward Ho! **1943** Silent Witness (aka Attorney for the Defense); The Seventh Victim; Spy Train. **1944** Bowery Champs. **1946** Raiders of the South. **1947** Robin Hood of Monterey. **1948** The Mystery of the Golden Eye (aka The Golden Eye); Stage Struck. **1950** Again, Pioneers.

BRENT, GEORGE (George Nolan)

Born: Mar. 15, 1904, Dublin, Ireland. Died: May 26, 1979, Solana Beach, Calif. (natural causes). Screen, stage and television actor. Divorced from actresses Ruth Chatterton (dec. 1961), Helen Nolan, Constance Worth (dec. 1963), Ann Sheridan (dec. 1967) and model Janet Michaels (dec. 1974). Father of actor Barry and interior designer Suzanne Brent.

Appeared in: **1930** Under Suspicion. **1931** The Lightning Warrior (serial); Fair Warning; Once a Sinner; Charlie Chan Carries On; Ex-Bad Boy; Homicide Squad. **1932** The Rich Are Always With Us; So Big; Week-End Marriage; Purchase Price; Miss Pinkerton; The Crash; They Call It Sin. **1933** Luxury Liner; 42nd Street; The Keyhole; Lilly Turner; Baby Face; Female From Headquarters. **1934** Housewife; Desirable; Stamboul Quest; The Painted Veil. **1935** The Right to Live; Living on Velvet; Stranded; Front Page Woman; Special Agent; The Goose and the Gander; In Person. **1936** Snowed Under; The Golden Arrow; The Case Against Mrs. Ames; Give Me Your Heart; More Than A Secretary; God's Country and the Woman. **1937** The Go-Getters; Mountain Justice; Submarine D-1. **1938** Gold is Where You Find It; Jezebel; Racket Busters; Secrets of an Actress. **1939** The Old Maid; The Rains Came; Wings of the Navy; Dark Victory. **1940** The Fighting 69th; Adventure in Diamonds; 'Til We Meet Again; The Man Who Talked Too Much; South of Suez. **1941** The Great Lie; Honeymoon for Three; They Dare Not Love; International Lady. **1942** In This Our Life; Twin Beds; The Gay Sisters; You Can't Escape

Forever; Silver Queen. **1944** Experiment Perilous. **1945** The Affairs of Susan. **1946** Temptation; Lover Come Back; The Spiral Staircase; My Reputation; Tomorrow is Forever. **1947** Slave Girl; The Corpse Came C.O.D.; Christmas Eve; Out of the Blue. **1948** Luxury Liner; Angel on the Amazon. **1949** Red Canyon; Bride for Sale; Illegal Entry; The Kid from Cleveland. **1951** F.B.I. Girl. **1952** Montana Belle; The Last Page (aka Manbait—US). **1953** Tangier Incident; Mexican Manhunt. **1956** Death of a Scoundrel. **1978** Born Again.

BRENT, ROMNEY (Romulo Larraide)
Born: Jan. 26, 1902, Saltillo, Mexico. Died: Sept. 24, 1976, Mexico City, Mexico. Screen, stage actor, stage director, stage producer, playwright and screenwriter. Married to actress Gina Malo (dec. 1963).

Appeared in: **1927** Cradle Snatchers. **1936** East Meets West. **1937** The Dominant Sex; Secretary in Trouble; Dinner at the Ritz; Under the Red Robe; Head Over Heels (aka Head Over Heels in Love—US); Dreaming Lips; Schools for Husbands (US 1939). **1939** On the Night of the Fire (aka The Fugitive—US 1940). **1940** Let George Do It. **1948** The Adventures of Don Juan. **1951** The Wind is My Lover (aka Gypsy Fury and Singoalla the Saga of Singoalla). **1957** Don't Go Near the Water. **1958** Screaming Mimi. **1960** The Sign of Zorro.

BREON, EDMUND (E. McLaverty)
Born: Dec. 12, 1882, Hamilton, Scotland. Died: 1951. Screen and stage actor.

Appeared in: **1930** The Dawn Patrol; On Approval. **1931** The Love Habit; Uneasy Virtue; I Like Your Nerve; Born to Love; Chances. **1932** Women Who Play; Wedding Rehearsal; Leap Year. **1933** Waltz Time; No Funny Business; Three Men in a Boat. **1934** Mister Cinders; The Private Life of Don Juan. **1935** The Divine Spark; Night Mail; The Scarlet Pimpernel; She Shall Have Music (US 1942). **1936** Love in Exile; Strangers on a Honeymoon (US 1937). **1937** Keep Fit; The Return of the Scarlet Pimpernel (US 1938); French Leave. **1938** A Yank at Oxford; Dangerous Medicine; Owd Bob (aka To the Victor—US); Premiere (aka One Night in Paris—US 1940); Crackerjack (aka The Man With a Hundred Faces—US); Luck of the Navy (aka North Sea Patrol—US 1940); Many Tanks Mr. Atkins. **1939** The Outsider (US 1940); Goodbye, Mr. Chips. **1940** Gentleman of Venture (aka It Happened to One Man—US 1941). **1944** Casanova Brown; Man in Half Moon Street; Hour Before the Dawn; Our Hearts Were Young and Gay; Gaslight. **1945** Saratoga Trunk; The Corn Is Green; Woman in the Window. **1946** Devotion; Six Gun Man; Outlaw of the Plains; Dressed to Kill; Sherlock Holmes and the Secret Code. **1947** The Imperfect Lady. **1948** Julia Misbehaves; Forever Amber; Hills of Home. **1949** Rope of Sand; Challenge to Lassie; Enchantment. **1951** Sons of the Musketeers. **1952** At Sword's Point.

BRERTON, TYRONE
Born: 1894. Died: Apr. 25, 1939, Hollywood, Calif. Screen actor.

Appeared in: **1925** Secrets of the Night. **1928** The Canyon of Adventure. **1931** Cimarron.

BRESSART, FELIX
Born: 1880, Eydtkuhnen, Germany. Died: Mar. 17, 1949, Los Angeles, Calif. (leukemia). Stage and screen actor.

Appeared in: **1928** Liebe im Kuhstall. **1930** Es Gibt eine Frau, die Dich Niemals Vergisst; Eine Freundin so Goldig wie Du (US 1931); Die Zaertlichen Verwandten; Die Drei; von der Tankstelle (US 1931); Der Keusche Joseph; Drei Tage Mittelarrest (Three Days in the Guardhouse—US 1933); Der Sohn der Weissen Berge (US 1933, aka Das Geheimnis von Zermatt); Das Alte Lied (US 1931, aka Zu Jedem Kommt Einmal die Liebe). **1931** Nie Wieder Liebe (No More Love); Hirsekorn Greift Ein (US 1932); Trara um Liebe; Der Herr Buerovorsteher (US 1932); Der Schrecken der Garnison (US 1932); Der Wahre Jakob (aka Das Maedchen vom Variete); Die Privaetsekretarin (Private Secretary). **1932** Holzapfel Weiss Alles (US 1933); Goldblondes Maedchen, ich Schenk' ich Mein Herz—Ich bin ja so Verliebt ... (aka Der Glueckszylinder—US 1934). **1933** Und wer Kuesst Mich? (US 1935). **1939** Swanee River; Ninotchka; Three Smart Girls Grow Up; Bridal Suite. **1940** Third Finger, Left Hand; The Shop Around the Corner; Edison the Man; Bitter Sweet; It All Came True; Comrade X. **1941** Married Bachelor; Kathleen; Mr. and Mrs. North; Blossoms in the Dust; Ziegfeld Girl; Escape. **1942** Iceland; Crossroads; To Be or Not to Be. **1943** Song of Russia; Three Hearts for Julia; Above Suspicion. **1944** The Seventh Cross; Greenwich Village; Secrets in the Dark; Blonde Fever. **1945** Dangerous Partners, Without Love. **1946** I've Always Loved You; Ding Dong Williams; The Thrill of Brazil; Her Sister's Secret. **1947** Concerto. **1948** A Song is Born; Portrait of Jennie. **1949** Take One False Step; My Friend Irma.

BREWER, MONTE
Born: 1934. Died: Apr. 21, 1942, Hollywood, Calif. (stomach ailment). Screen actor and radio singer.

Appeared in: **1941** Mr. Dynamite.

BREYER, MAGGIE
Born: 1845, Fort Recovery, Ohio. Died: Mar. 11, 1931, Indianapolis, Ind. Screen and stage actress.

Appeared in: **1916** The Sunbeam.

BRIAN, DONALD
Born: 1871, St. Johns, Newfoundland, Canada. Died: Dec. 22, 1948, Great Neck, N.Y. Screen, stage actor and singer. Married to actress Virginia O'Brien.

Appeared in: **1915** The Voice in the Fog. **1916** The Smugglers. **1929** America's Foremost Musical Comedy Star (short). **1930** My Mistake (short). **1931** Squaring the Triangle (short).

BRIANT, GEORGE HAMILTON
Born: 1922. Died: Oct. 22, 1946, near San Antonio, Tex. (died during filming of Blaze at Noon in air accident). Screen actor and stunt flyer.

Appeared in: **1947** Blaze at Noon.

BRICE, BETTY (aka ROSETTA BRICE)
Born: 1892, Sunbury, Pa. Died: Feb. 15, 1935, Van Nuys, Calif. Stage and screen actress. Married to concert singer John L. Pratt.

Appeared in: **1914** The Fortune Hunter. **1921** The Spenders. **1922** The Green Temptation; Heart's Haven. **1924** Beau Brummell.

BRICE, FANNY (Fanny Borach)
Born: Oct. 29, 1891, New York, N.Y. Died: May 29, 1951, Beverly Hills, Calif. (cerebral hemorrhage). Screen, stage, radio, vaudeville and burlesque actress. Sister of actor Lew Brice (dec. 1966). Divorced from Nick Arnstein and producer Billy Rose (dec. 1966).

Appeared in: **1928** My Man (film debut). **1929** The Man from Blankleys'. **1930** Be Yourself. **1936** The Great Ziegfeld. **1938** Everybody Sing. **1946** Ziegfeld Follies.

BRICE, LEW
Born: 1894. Died: June 16, 1966, Hollywood, Calif. (heart attack). Screen and vaudeville actor. Brother of actress Fannie Brice (dec. 1951).

Appeared in: **1926** Lew Tyler's Wives; Partners Again. **1929** Happy Days. **1930** The Window Cleaners (short). **1932** Two Seconds.

BRICKER, BETTY
Born: 1890. Died: Feb. 15, 1954, Hollywood, Calif. Screen actress. Entered films approx. 1914.

BRICKERT, CARLTON
Born: 1891. Died: Dec. 23, 1943, New York, N.Y. Screen, stage and radio actor.

Appeared in: **1921** The Rider of the King Log. **1923** You Are Guilty.

BRICKLEY, CHARLES E.
Born: 1891. Died: Dec. 28, 1949, New York, N.Y. (heart attack). Professional athlete and screen actor.

Appeared in: **1915** The Hero of the Gridiron.

BRICKMAN, ELSIE
Born: 1893. Died: Apr. 22, 1950, Los Angeles, Calif. Silent screen actress.

BRIDGE, ALAN "AL"
Born: Feb. 26, 1891, Pa. Died: Dec. 27, 1957. Screen actor.

Appeared in: **1931** Ridin' Fool; Rider of the Plains; Rose of the Rio Grande; God's Country and the Man. **1932** Galloping Thru; Spirit of the West; Wyoming Whirlwind; A Man's Land; The Forty-Niners; The Hurricane Express (serial). **1933** Drum Taps; When a Man Rides Alone; Cowboy Counsellor; Sucker Money; Sunset Pass; Black Beauty; Lone Avenger; Cheyenne Kid; Son of the Border; Fighting Texans. **1934** Thundering Herd; Public Stenographer; Mystery Mountain (serial). **1935** Melody Trail; The Good Fairy; Burn 'Em Up Barnes (serial); New Frontier; Valley of Wanted Men; A Night at the Opera; Alias Mary Dow. **1936** And So They Were Married; Ace Drummond (serial); The Adventures of Frank Merriwell (serial); Call of the Prairie; Fast Bullets; The Lawless Nineties; Public Enemy's

Wife; Three Mesquiteers; The Trail Dust. **1937** Jungle Jim (serial); Borderland; Western Gold; Two-Gun Law; Woman Chases Man; Springtime in the Rockies; The Go-Getter; The Awful Truth; Wild West Days (serial). **1938** Jezebel; The Great Adventures of Wild Bill Hickok (serial); Two-Gun Justice; Highway Patrol; Little Miss Roughneck; Adventure in Sahara; Down in Arkansas; Colorado Trail; Crime School. **1939** Blue Montana Skies; Man from Sundown; Romance of the Redwoods; No Place to Go; Blazing Six Shooters; Pioneers of the Frontier; Christmas in July; The Oklahoma Kid. **1940** My Little Chickadee; The Courageous Dr. Christian. **1941** The Lady from Cheyenne; Law of the Range; The Little Foxes; The Kid's Last Ride; Sullivan's Travels; Road to Zanzibar; Honolulu Lu. **1942** Talk of the Town; In This Our Life; The Saboteur; The Mad Doctor of Market Street; Lady in a Jam; Reap the Wild Wind; Fighting Bill Fargo; Bad Men of the Hills; Bells of Capistrano. **1943** Tenting Tonight on the Old Camp Grounds; Seeing Nellie Home (short). **1944** The Miracle of Morgan's Creek; Hail the Conquering Hero; The Unwritten Code; The Princess and the Pirate. **1945** They Were Expendable; Road to Utopia; Saratoga Trunk; Thunderhead; Son of Flicka; A Tree Grows in Brooklyn; A Guy, a Gal and a Pal; The Jade Mask. **1946** The Virginian; The Falcon's Alibi; My Pal Trigger; Below the Deadline; Singin' in the Corn; Cowboy Blues; The Sin of Harold Diddlebock; Cross My Heart; Shadows Over Chinatown; Miss Susie Slagle's; California. **1947** Down to Earth; Road to Rio; Nora Prentiss; The Hal Roach Comedy Carnival; Alias Mr. Twilight; Robin Hood of Texas; Last Days of Boot Hill; Black Gold. **1948** Silver River; Unfaithfully Yours; That Wonderful Urge; Fury at Furnace Creek. **1949** Trail of the Yukon; The Beautiful Blonde from Bashful Bend; The Devil's Henchman. **1950** The Traveling Saleswoman; The Tougher They Come. **1951** Oh, Susanna; All That I Have; Mad Wednesday. **1952** The Last Musketeer; We're Not Married. **1953** Iron Mountain Trail. **1954** Hell's Outpost; Jubilee Trail.

BRIDGE, LOIE
Born: 1890. Died: Mar. 8, 1974, Glendale, Calif. (natural causes). Screen, stage and television actress.

Appeared in: **1932** Single-Handed Sanders; Wyoming Whirlwind. **1935** A Night at the Opera. **1943** O, My Darling Clementine. **1947** Life With Father. **1949** Riders of the Whistling Pines; Riders of the Sky.

BRIGGS, HAL
Born: 1881. Died: Apr. 28, 1925, Rockville, N.Y. (heart failure). Screen actor and film director.

BRIGGS, HARLAN
Born: 1880. Died: Jan. 26, 1952, Woodland Hills, Calif. (stroke). Screen and stage actor.

Appeared in: **1936** The Garden of Allah; After the Thin Man; Dodsworth; Mad Holiday; Happy-Go-Lucky; Easy Money. **1937** Behind the Mike; Marked Woman; Maytime; A Family Affair; Easy Living; Interns Can't Take Money; Live, Love and Learn; Beg, Borrow or Steal; Riding on Air; Exclusive. **1938** That's My Story; Reckless Living; The Missing Guest; Opening Day (short); Dynamite Delaney; One Wild Night; You and Me; Meet the Girls; Quick Money; Trouble at Midnight; Having a Wonderful Time; A Man to Remember. **1939** Made for Each Other; Calling Dr. Kildare; Tell Me No Tales; Flight at Midnight; The Mysterious Miss X; The Wizard of Oz; Mr. Smith Goes to Washington; Maisie; Blondie Takes a Vacation. **1940** Abe Lincoln in Illinois; Young As You Feel; The Man Who Wouldn't Talk; The Bank Dick; My Little Chickadee; Charlie Chan's Murder Cruise. **1941** Paris Calling; Among the Living; One Foot in Heaven. **1942** The Remarkable Andrew; The Vanishing Virginian; Tennessee Johnson. **1943** Lady Bodyguard. **1945** State Fair. **1946** Canyon Passage; Do You Love Me?; The Magnificent Doll; A Stolen Life. **1947** Cynthia; Ladies' Man. **1948** A Double Life. **1949** Rusty Saves a Life. **1952** Carrie.

BRIGGS, MATT
Born: 1883. Died: June 10, 1962, Seattle, Wash. Screen and stage actor.

Appeared in: **1933** Advice to the Lovelorn. **1934** Hips, Hips, Hooray; Born to Be Bad. **1943** The Ox-Bow Incident; The Dancing Master; Meanest Man in the World. **1944** Roger Touhy, Gangster; Coney Island; Buffalo Bill. **1948** The Babe Ruth Story.

BRIGGS, OSCAR
Born: 1877, Wis. Died: Jan. 17, 1928, Hollywood, Calif. (paralysis—stroke). Screen, stage and vaudeville actor.

BRIGHTON, ALBERT
Born: 1876. Died: July 11, 1911, Grassmere, N.Y. (drowned while filming). Stage and screen actor. Entered films with Edison Co.

BRILL, PATTI (Patricia Brilhante aka PATSY PAIGE)
Born: Mar. 8, 1923, San Francisco, Calif. Died: Jan. 18, 1963, Calif. Screen, stage actress and dancer.

Appeared in: **1928** Lillies of the Field. **1929** The Vagabond Lover. **1938** Mad About Music. **1939** 1,000 Men and a Girl. **1940** Best Foot Forward. **1942** Star Spangled Rhythm; The Petty Girl. **1943** Mexican Spitfire's Blessed Event; Gildersleeve's Bad Day; Government Girl; Tender Comrade; Lady of Burlesque; Henry Aldrich Gets Glamour; Adventures of a Rookie; Salute for Three; The Falcon Strikes Back; The Falcon and the Co-eds. **1944** The Falcon in Hollywood; Nevada; The Falcon Out West; Music in Manhattan; Girl Rush; Cocktails for Two. **1945** Pan-Americana; Sing Your Way Home. **1946** Live Wires. **1947** Hard Boiled Mahoney. **1949** Incident. **1955** Not As a Stranger.

BRINDLEY, MADGE
Died: Aug. 28, 1968, near Brighton, England (auto accident). Screen and stage actress.

Appeared in: **1949** The Spider and the Fly (US 1952). **1954** Hobson's Choice. **1955** The Ladykillers (US 1956). **1956** The Feminine Touch (aka The Gentle Touch—US 1957). **1957** The Long Haul. **1969** A Nice Girl Like Me.

BRINDMOUR, GEORGE
Born: 1870. Died: July 21, 1941, Los Angeles, Calif. Screen and vaudeville actor. Married to Helen Hilliard with whom he appeared in vaudeville. He was known as the "Handcuff King."

BRINKMAN, ERNEST
Born: 1872. Died: Dec. 28, 1938, Los Angeles, Calif. Screen, stage and vaudeville actor. Married to Mary Steele with whom he appeared in vaudeville in an act billed as "Brinkman and the Steele Sisters."

BRINLEY, CHARLES "CHARLIE" E.
Born: Nov. 15, 1880, Yuma, Arizona. Died: Feb. 17, 1946, Los Angeles, Calif. Screen actor.

Appeared in: **1914** Tray of Hearts. **1916** Liberty. **1917** The Red Ace (serial); Patra. **1921** The Beautiful Gambler; Go Straight; "If Only" Jim; Tiger True. **1922** Morals of Lady Letty; Hills of Missing Men. **1923** In the Days of Daniel Boone (serial). **1924** The Western Wallop; California in '49; Days of '49 (serial); Riders of the Plains (serial). **1925** White Outlaw; The Fighting Smile; Hidden Loot; Idaho (serial); The Mystery Box (serial). **1926** Desert Valley. **1930** Covered Wagon Trails; Beau Bandit; The Dawn Trail. **1933** Treason. **1934** Fighting Code; Wharf Angel; Dawn Trail. **1935** Crimson Trail; Outlaw Deputy. **1937** It Happened in Hollywood.

BRISCOE, LOTTIE
Born: 1881. Died: Mar. 19, 1950, New York, N.Y. Screen, stage and radio actress.

Appeared in: **1911** Getting Sister Married. **1912** An Amateur Iceman; The Sporting Editor; The Heavenly Voice; The Country School Teacher; The Samaritan of Coogan's Tenement; A Little Family Affair; A Child's Devotion; A Leap Year Lottery Prize; The Violin's Message; The Wooden Bowl; A Bachelor's Waterloo; Her Gift; The Spoiled Child; The Power of Conscience; A College Girl; A Matter of Business; In After Years; The Convalescent. **1913** His Better Self; Two Boys; John Arthur's Trust; The Sea Eternal; Her Husband's Wife; The District Attorney's Conscience; Annie Rowley's Fortune; Dr. Maxwell's Experiment; The Artist's Romance; The School Principal; The Gift of the Storm; A Timely Rescue; When John Brought Home His Wife; The Power of the Cross; The Pawned Bracelet; His Niece from Ireland; A Jealous Husband; The Insurance Agent. **1914** The Beloved Adventurer (serial); Lord Algy; The Girl from the West; The Question and Answer Man; The Shadow of Tragedy; The Parasite. **1915** Comrade Kitty; Who Violates the Law; When Father Interfered; Her Martyrdom; On the Road to Reno; The Cornet; Winning Winsome Winnie; Socially Ambitious; Country Blood; The Last Rose. **1918** The House of Mirth.

BRISSAC, VIRGINIA
Died: 1979. Screen actress.

Appeared in: **1935** Honeymoon Limited (screen debut). **1936** Murder by an Aristocrat; The Big Noise. **1937** Torchy Blaine, The Adventurous Blonde; White Bondage. **1938** Secrets of a Nurse. **1909** Dark Victory; Woman Doctor; Jesse James; The Forgotton Woman; Parents on Trial. **1940** Chad Hanna; Remember the Night; Little Old New York; Black Friday; It's a Date; Alias thhe Deacon; The Ghost Breakers; Wagons Westward; Hired Wife; Strike up the Band; Always a Bride; Little Orvie; The House Across the Bay. **1941** The Great Lie; Washington Melodrama; The Nurse's Secret; Bad Men of Missouri;

Dressed to Kill; The Little Foxes; Appointment for Love; One Foot in Heaven; They Died With Their Boots On. **1942** The Mummy's Tomb; Tough as They Come; Lady Gangster; The Big Shot. **1943** Crime Doctor's Strangest Case; Mug Town; Moonlight in Vermont. **1944** Phantom Lady; This is the Life; Sing, Neighbor, Sing. **1945** The Scarlet Clue; G.I. Honeymoon; Night Club Girl; Captain Eddie; Three's a Crowd; Bewitched; Why Girls Leave Home; The Daltons Ride Again; A Tree Grows in Brooklyn. **1946** The Mysterious Mr. Valentine; Renegrades; Hot Cargo; The Mysterious Mr. M (serial). **1947** Captain From Castile; Monsieur Verdoux. **1948** The Mating of Millie; Summer Holiday; Old Los Angeles; Live Today for Tomorrow; An Act of Murder; The Snake Pit; The Untamed Breed. **1949** The Doolins of Oklahoma; Harriet Craig; Edge of Doom. **1951** Operation Pacific; Two of a Kind; Warpath. **1952** Woman of the North Country. **1954** About Mrs. Leslie; The Bandits of Corsica; Executive Suite. **1955** Rebel Without a Cause.

BRISSON, CARL (Carl Brisson Peterson)
Born: Dec. 24, 1893, Copenhagen, Denmark. Died: Sept. 24, 1958, Copenhagen, Denmark (jaundice). Screen, stage actor and singer. Married to actress Cleo Willard (dec. 1975). Father of film producer Frederick Brisson.

Appeared in: **1917** De Mysteske Fodspor. **1927** The Ring. **1928** Hjaratas Triumf. **1929** The Manxman; The American Prisoner; Chelsea Nights (short). **1930** Knowing Men; Song of Soho. **1933** Prince of Arcadia. **1934** Two Hearts in Waltztime. **1935** All the King's Horses; Ship Cafe.

BRISSON, CLEO (Cleo Willard)
Born: 1894, Denmark. Died: Nov. 28, 1975, Copenhagen, Denmark. Screen, stage actress and singer. Married to actor Carl Brisson (dec. 1958). Mother of producer Frederick Brisson.

BRISTER, ROBERT S.
Born: 1889. Died: Mar. 2, 1945, Hollywood, Calif. Screen, stage and radio actor.

Appeared in: **1937** Night Club Scandal. **1938** Dangerous to Know.

BRITT, ELTON (James Britt Baker)
Born: July 7, 1912, Marshall, Ark. Died: June 23, 1972, Connellsville, Pa. Country singer, screen, television and radio actor.

Appeared in: **1949** Laramie.

BRITTON, BARBARA (Barbara Brantingham)
Born: 1921, Long Beach, Calif. Died: Jan. 17, 1980, New York, N.Y. (cancer). Screen, stage and television actress. Mother of actress Christina Britton.

Appeared in: **1941** Louisiana Purchase; Secret of the Wastelands. **1942** Reap the Wild Wind; Wake Island; Mrs. Wiggs of the Cabbage Patch; The Fleet's In. **1943** So Proudly We Hail; Young and Willing. **1944** Till We Meet Again; The Story of Mr. Wassell. **1945** Captain Kidd; The Great John L. **1946** The Return of Monte Cristo; The Virginian; The Fabulous Suzanne; They Made Me a Killer. **1947** Gunfighters. **1948** Albuquerque; Mr. Reckless; The Untamed Breed. **1949** I Shot Jesse James; Cover Up; Loaded Pistols. **1950** Bandit Queen; Champagne for Caesar. **1952** Bwana Devil; The Raiders; Ride the Man Down. **1954** Dragonfly Squadron. **1955** Ain't Misbehavin'; The Spoilers; Night Freight.

BRITTON, EDNA
Born: June 28, 1887. Died: Aug. 5, 1960, Mansfield, Mass. Screen actress.

Appeared in: **1919** The Master Mystery (serial).

BRITTON, ETHEL
Born: 1915. Died: Feb. 26, 1972, New York, N.Y. Screen, stage and television actress. Married to stage producer/director Frank McCoy (dec. 1947).

Appeared in: **1956** Patterns.

BRITTON, HUTIN "NELLIE"
Born: Apr. 24, 1876, Reading, England. Died: Sept 3, 1965, England? Screen and stage actress. Married to actor Matheson Lang (dec. 1948).

Appeared in: **1923** The Wandering Jew (stage and film versions).

BRITTON, KEITH (Eli Britza)
Born: Aug. 3, 1919, Pa. Died: Oct. 23, 1970, Woodland Hills, Calif. (heart disease). Screen actor.

Appeared in: **1949** Flamingo Road. **1956** Storm Fear.

BRITTON, MILT (Milton Levy)
Born: 1894, Winston-Salem, N.C. Died: Apr. 29, 1948, New York, N.Y. (heart attack). Screen, stage, vaudeville actor and bandleader. His band was known as "America's Craziest Orchestra," "The Brown Derby Band" and "The Mad Musical Maniacs."

Appeared in: **1933** Moonlight and Pretzels. **1935** Sweet Music. **1937** A Vitaphone short. **1945** Riding High.

BRITTON, PAMELA
Born: 1923. Died: June 17, 1974, Arlington Heights, Ill. (brain tumor). Screen, stage and television actress. Daughter of radio actress Ethel Owens.

Appeared in: **1945** Anchors Aweigh. **1946** A Letter for Evie. **1949** D.O.A. **1950** Key to the City; Watch the Birdie. **1969** If It's Tuesday, This Must Be Belgium. **1970** Suppose They Gave a War and Nobody Came?

BRITTONE, MOZELLE
Born: 1912. Died: May 18, 1953, Los Angeles, Calif. (heart attack). Screen actress and columnist. Married to actor Alan Dinehart (dec. 1944) and Thomas W. Gosser (dec.).

Appeared in: **1934** The Fighting Rangers.

BROAD, KID (William M. Thomas)
Born: Mar. 3, 1878, Cornwall, England. Died: June 11, 1947, New York, N.Y. Boxer and screen actor.

Appeared in: **1921** The Man Worth While. **1924** The Great White Way.

BROADLEY, EDWARD
Died: Nov. 24, 1947, New York, N.Y. Stage and screen actor.

Appeared in: **1938** The Jury's Secret; Women Are Like That.

BROCHARD, JEAN
Born: 1893, France. Died: June, 1972, France? Screen actor.

Appeared in: **1945** Jericho. **1947** Angel and Sinner. **1948** A Lover's Return; Who Killed Santa Claus. **1950** Dieu a Besom des Hommes (aka God Needs Men and aka Isle of Sinners—US 1951). **1952** A Simple Case of Money; Under the Paris Sky. **1955** Dr, Knock; Diabolique; La Mome Pigalle (The Maiden—US 1961). **1956** Vitelleni (aka The Young and the Passionate—US). **1957** Pot Bouille (aka House of Lovers and aka Lovers of Paris—US 1958). **1959** The Law is the Law; The Virtuous Bigamist; Rafles sur la Ville (Sinners of Paris—US); Ein Engel auf Erden (Angel on Earth—US 1966).

BROCK, TONY
Died: Nov. 26, 1924, New York, N.Y. (auto accident while filming stunt in The Great Circus Mystery). Screen actor.

Appeared in: **1925** The Great Circus Mystery (serial).

BROCKBANK, HARRISON
Born: 1867, Liverpool, England. Died: Nov. 30, 1947, New York, N.Y. Screen and stage actor.

BROCKWELL, GLADYS
Born: 1894, Brooklyn, N.Y. Died: July 2, 1929, Hollywood, Calif. (peritonitis as result of auto accident injuries). Stage and screen actress.

Appeared in: **1915** Double Trouble. **1916** She-Devil; Sins of the Parent. **1918** The Devil's Wheel. **1921** The Sage Hen. **1922** Paid Back; Double Stakes; Oliver Twist. **1923** The Drug Traffic; Penrod and Sam; The Darling of New York; His Last Race; The Hunchback of Notre Dame. **1924** So Big; The Foolish Virgin; Unmarried Wives. **1925** The Ancient Mariner; Chickie; Stella Maris; The Necessary Evil; The Reckless Sex; The Splendid Road. **1926** The Carnival Girl; Spangles; Her Sacrifice; The Skyrocket; Twinkletoes; The Last Frontier. **1927** Seventh Heaven; The Satin Woman; The Country Doctor; Long Pants; Man, Woman and Sin. **1928** The Law and the Man; My Home Town; Lights of New York; Home Towners; Woman Disputed; Hollywood Bound. **1929** From Headquarters; Hard-Boiled Rose; The Hottentot; The Argyle Case; The Drake Case.

BRODERICK, HELEN
Born: 1891, Philadelphia, Pa. Died: Sept. 25, 1959, Beverly Hills, Calif. Screen, stage, vaudeville and radio actress. Mother of actor Broderick Crawford.

Appeared in: **1924** High Speed. **1926** The Mystery Club. **1930** Nile Green (short); For Art's Sake (short). **1931** Fifty Million Frenchmen; The Spirits of 76th Street (short); Court Plastered (short). **1932** Cold

Turkey (short). **1935** Top Hat; To Beat the Band. **1936** Love on a Bet; Murder on the Bridle Path; The Bride Walks Out; Swing Time; Smartest Girl in Town. **1937** We're on the Jury; Meet the Missus; The Life of the Party. **1938** She's Got Everything; Radio City Revels; The Rage of Paris; The Road to Reno; Service Deluxe. **1939** Stand Up and Fight; Honeymoon in Bali; Naughty But Nice. **1940** The Captain Is a Lady; No, No, Nanette. **1941** Virginia; Father Takes a Wife; Nice Girl. **1942** Are Husbands Necessary? **1943** Stage Door Canteen. **1944** Her Primitive Man; Three Is a Family; Chip Off the Old Block. **1945** Love, Honor and Goodbye. **1946** Because of Him.

BRODERICK, JOHNNY
Born: 1894. Died: Apr. 14, 1977, Port Charlotte, Fla. Screen, stage vaudeville actor and composer. Married to actress Charlotte Arren with whom he appeared in vaudeville in an act billed as "Arren & Broderick." Do not confuse with actor John C. Broderick.

Appeared in: **1929** Broadway Melody. **1935** A Vitaphone Short.

BRODIE, BUSTER
Born: 1886. Died: Apr. 9, 1948, Hollywood, Calif. (heart attack). Screen, stage and vaudeville actor. Entered films approx. 1926.

Appeared in: **1927** All Aboard. **1932** The Island of Lost Souls. **1944** Lady in the Dark. **1945** George White's Scandals.

BRODY, ANN (Ann Brody Goldstein)
Born: Aug. 29, 1884, Poland. Died: July 16, 1944, New York, N.Y. Screen and stage actress. Entered films with Vitagraph Co. in 1912.

Appeared in: **1916** The Suspect. **1919** A Girl at Bay. **1921** Shams of Society. **1923** Lost in a Big City. **1924** A Sainted Devil. **1925** The Manicure Girl; Red Love. **1926** Too Much Money. **1927** Alias the Lone Wolf; Clancy's Kosher Wedding; Jake the Plumber; Heroes in Blue. **1928** Turn Back the Hours; My Man. **1929** Betrayal; Times Square; So This Is College; The Case of Lena Smith; The Wolf Song; Alpine Tale; The Man from Blankley's. **1930** Fall Guy; A Royal Romance; Playing Around. **1931** Oh! Oh! Cleopatra (short); Drums of Jeopardy. **1932** The Drifter; Lawyer Man; Heart of New York. **1933** High Gear; Bloody Money. **1934** Money Means Nothing.

BROGAN, HARRY
Born: 1905, Ireland. Died: May 20, 1977, Dublin, Ireland. Screen, stage, radio and television actor.

Appeared in: **1959** Home is the Hero (US 1961); Shake Hands With the Devil; Broth of a Boy. **1960** The Poacher's Daughter; A Terrible Beauty (aka The Night Fighters—US); The Seige of Sidney Street (US 1961). **1962** The Quare Fellow. **1963** Never Put it in Writing (US 1964). **1964** Girl with Green Eyes. **1965** The Face of Fu Manchu; Young Cassidy.

BROKAW, CHARLES
Born: 1898. Died: Oct. 23, 1975, New York, N.Y. Screen and stage actor.

Appeared in: **1926** Fascinating Youth. **1937** Behind the Mike; I Cover the War; Idol of the Crowd; Behind Prison Bars. **1938** The Buccaneer; Air Devils; Convicts at Large. **1940** Murder in the Air.

BROKENSHIRE, NORMAN (Norman Ernest Brokenshire)
Born: June 10, 1898, Murchenson, Ontario, Canada. Died: May 4, 1965, Ronkonkom, N.Y. (heart failure). Screen and radio actor.

Appeared in: **1929** Glorifying the American Girl. **1930** The Figlet (short). **1932** The Big Broadcast. **1935** Soviet Russia Thru the Eyes of an American (narrator).

BROMBERG, J. EDWARD
Born: Dec. 25, 1903, Temesvar, Hungary. Died: Dec. 6, 1951, London, England (natural causes). Screen and stage actor.

Appeared in: **1936** Under Two Flags; Reunion; Stowaway; Sins of Man; The Crime of Dr. Forbes; Girl's Dormitory; Star for a Night; Ladies in Love. **1937** Fair Warning; That I May Live; Seventh Heaven; Charlie Chan on Broadway; Second Honeymoon. **1938** Mr. Moto Takes a Chance; The Baroness and the Butler; One Wild Night; Four Men and a Prayer; Sally, Irene and Mary; Rebecca of Sunnybrook Farm; I'll Give a Million; Suez. **1939** Wife, Husband and Friend; Hollywood Cavalcade; Jesse James; The Mark of Zorro. **1941** Hurricane Smith; Midnight Angel; Dance Hall. **1942** Life Begins at Eight-Thirty; Invisible Agent; Pacific Blackout; Reunion in France; Tennessee Johnson; The Devil Pays Off; Halfway to Shanghai. **1943** Sons of Dracula; Lady of Burlesque; Phantom of the Opera. **1944** Chip Off the Old Block; A Voice in the Wind. **1945** Salome, Where She Danced; The Missing Corpse; Easy to Look At; Pillow of Death. **1946** Tangier; The Walls Came Tumbling Down; Cloak and Dagger. **1947** Queen of the Amazon. **1948** Arch of Triumph; A Song is Born. **1949** I Shot Jesse James. **1950** Guilty Bystander.

BROMLEY-DAVENPORT, ARTHUR (aka ARTHUR BROMLEY DAVENPORT)
Born: Oct. 29, 1867, Baginton, Warwickshire, England. Died: Dec. 15, 1946, England? Screen and stage actor.

Appeared in: **1924** Eugene Aram; What the Butler Saw. **1925** The Impatient Patient; An Inconvenient Infant; Somebody's Darling. **1927** Roses of Picardy; The Glad Eye; The Fake; The Flight Commander; A Sister to Assist 'Er. **1928** The Blue Peter; Glorious Youth (aka Eileen of the Trees); Spangles. **1929** The American Prisoner. **1930** Too Many Crooks; Leave it to Me. **1931** Captivation; Glamour. **1932** Mr. Bill the Conqueror (aka The Man Who Won—US 1933); Self-Made Lady; Flat No. 9; Money Means Nothing (US 1934); The Return of Raffles; A Face at the Window; Lord Camber's Ladies. **1933** The Iron Star; The Melody Maker; Little Miss Nobody; The Wishbone; A Shot in the Dark (US 1935); Enemy of the Police; The Pointing Finger. **1934** Lily of Killarney (aka The Bride of the Lake—US); The Warren Case; Love, Life and Laughter; Lost in the Legion. **1935** Vintage Wine; So You Won't Talk? **1936** The Mysterious Mr. Davis (aka My Partner Mr. Davis). **1938** Owd Bob (aka To the Victor—US); Second Thoughts. **1939** Jamaica Inn. **1941** Old Mother Riley's Ghosts; Love on the Dole. **1942** The Young Mr. Pitt. **1943** The Crime of Peter Frame (reissue of Second Thoughts—1938).

BRONSON, BETTY (Elizabeth Ada Bronson)
Born: Nov. 17, 1907, Trenton, N.J. Died: Oct. 19, 1971, Pasadena, Calif. Screen, stage and television actress.

Appeared in: **1922** Anna Ascends. **1923** Java Head; His Children's Children; Twenty-One. **1924** The Great White Way; The Eternal City. **1925** Are Parents People?; Not So Long Ago; The Golden Princess; Peter Pan. **1926** The Cat's Pajamas; Everybody's Acting; A Kiss for Cinderella; Paradise; Ben Hur. **1927** Brass Knuckles; Paradise for Two; Open Range; Ritzy. **1928** The Singing Fool; The Companionate Marriage (aka The Jazz Bride). **1929** Bellamy Trial; Sonny Boy; One Stolen Night. **1930** The Medicine Man; A Modern Sappho; The Locked Door. **1931** Lover Come Back. **1932** The Midnight Patrol. **1937** Yodelin' Kid from Pine Ridge (aka The Hero of Pine Ridge). **1961** Pocketful of Miracles. **1962** Who's Got the Action? **1964** The Naked Kiss. **1968** Blackbeard's Ghost. **1971** Evel Knievel.

BROOK, CLIVE (Clifford Hardman Brook)
Born: June 1, 1887, London, England. Died: Nov. 17, 1974, London, England. Screen, stage, television actor and film director. Married to actress Mildred Evelyn. Father of actress Faith and actor/playwright Clive Lyndon Brook.

Appeared in: **1920** Trent's Last Case; Kissing Cup's Race. **1921** Her Penalty; The Loudwater Mystery; Daniel Deronda; A Sportsman's Wife; Sonia (aka The Woman Who Came Back—US 1922); Christie Johnstone. **1922** Tense Moments with Great Authors series including: Vanity Fair and A Tale of Two Cities; Master Song Scenes series including: Whispering and The Sheik; Famous Poems by George R. Sims series including: Sir Rupert's Wife and The Parson's Wife; Tense Moments from Opera Series including: Rigoletto and La Traviata; Shirley; Married to a Mormon; The Experiment; A Debt of Honour; Love and a Whirlwind. **1923** Through Fire and Water; This Freedom; Out to Win; The Reverse of the Medal; The Royal Oak; Woman to Woman (US 1924). **1924** The Money Habit; The White Shadow (aka White Shadows—US); The Recoil (aka Recoil); The Wine of Life; The Passionate Adventure; Human Desires; Christine of the Hungry Heart; The Mirage. **1925** When Love Grows Cold; Enticement; Declasse (aka The Social Exile); Playing With Souls; If Marriage Fails; The Woman Hater; Compromise; Seven Sinners; The Home Maker; The Pleasure Buyers. **1926** Three Faces East; Why Girls Go Back Home; For Alimony Only; You Never Know Women; The Popular Sin. **1927** Afraid to Love; Barbed Wire; Underworld; Hula; The Devil Dancer; French Dressing. **1928** Midnight Madness; The Yellow Lily; The Perfect Crime; Forgotten Faces. **1929** Interference; A Dangerous Woman; The Four Feathers; Charming Sinners; Return of Sherlock Holmes; The Laughing Lady. **1930** Slightly Scarlet; Paramount on Parade; Sweethearts and Wives; Anybody's Woman. **1931** Scandal Sheet; East Lynne; Tarnished Lady; The Lawyer's Secret; Silence; Twenty-Four Hours (aka The Hours Between); Husband's Holiday. **1932** Shanghai Express; The Man from Yesterday; The Night of June 13th; Sherlock Holmes; Make Me a Star (cameo appearance). **1933** Cavalcade; Midnight Club; Gallante Lady. **1934** If I Were Free (aka Behold, We Live); Where Sinners Meet (aka The Dover Road); Let's Try Again (aka The Marriage Symphony). **1935** The Love Affair of the Dictator (aka The Dictator and The Loves of a Dictator—US); Dressed to Thrill. **1936** The Lonely Road (aka Scotland Yard Commands—US 1937); Love in Exile. **1937** Action for Slander (US 1938). **1938** The Ware Case (US 1939). **1940** Return to Yesterday; Convoy (US 1941). **1941** Freedom Radio (aka A Voice in the Night—US); Breach of

Promise (aka Adventure in Blackmail—US 1943). **1943** The Flemish Farm; The Shipbuilders; For the Love of a Queen (rerelease of The Love Affair of a Dictator—1935). **1944** On Approval (US 1945). **1963** The List of Adrian Messenger.

BROOKE, CLAUDE
Born: 1853. Died: Dec. 14, 1933, Leonia, N.J. Screen and stage actor.

Appeared in: **1922** Silver Wings. **1923** Does It Pay? **1924** Pied Piper Malone; Classmates. **1926** Great Gatsby; Sorrows of Satan; God Save Me Twenty Cents.

BROOKE, CLIFFORD
Born: 1872, England. Died: Dec. 28, 1951, Santa Monica, Calif. (injuries sustained after struck by auto). Screen and stage actor. Entered films approx. 1939.

Appeared in: **1940** The Sea Hawk. **1941** They Met in Bombay; A Woman's Face. **1944** Wilson. **1945** Captain Kidd; Hangover Square; Molly and Me; The Suspect. **1946** Three Strangers; Black Beauty. **1948** The Woman in White. **1950** Where Danger Lives. **1951** The First Legion.

BROOKE, E. H.
Born: 1876, England. Died: Jan. 18, 1929, England? Screen and stage actor. Son of stage actor E. H. Brook (dec. 1884) and stage actress Mrs. E. H. Brook (dec. 1915).

Appeared in: **1916** Still Waters Run Deep.

BROOKE, (MRS.) MYRA
Born: 1865. Died: Feb. 9, 1944, Amityville, N.Y. Screen and stage actress.

BROOKE, RALPH (Ralph Tweer Brooks)
Born: 1920. Died: Dec. 4, 1963, Hollywood, Calif. Screen, stage actor, screenwriter and film producer/director. Entered films with the Max Reinhardt Co. in Hollywood.

Appeared in: **1935** A Shot in the Dark; Strange Wives; Naughty Marietta. **1936** Libeled Lady; Love Before Breakfast. **1937** Make Way for Tomorrow. **1939** Irving Berlin's Second Fiddle. **1940** Love, Honor and Oh, Baby! **1941** Mr. and Mrs. Smith. **1942** The Saboteur; You're Telling Me. **1944** Thirty Seconds Over Tokyo; Wing and a Prayer; The Thin Man Goes Home. **1945** The Affairs of Susan; Without Love; Between Two Women. **1946** Smooth as Silk; Her Adventurous Night. **1947** Song of Scheherazade. **1948** One Touch of Venus; A Letter to Three Wives. **1950** Mystery Submarine. **1953** The Charge at Feather River. **1954** Jubilee Trail. **1960** The Third Voice.

BROOKE, TYLER (Victor Huge de Biere)
Born: 1891, New York, N.Y. Died: Mar. 2, 1943, North Hollywood, Calif. (suicide—carbon monoxide poisoning). Screen and stage actor.

Appeared in: **1927** Rich But Honest; Stage Madness; The Cradle Snatchers. **1928** Fazil; None But the Brave. **1929** Dynamite; Van Bibber Fox comedies. **1930** Playboy of Paris; Madame Satan; The Furies; The Divorcee; Monte Carlo; Lillies of the Field. **1931** The Magnificent Lie; Oh! Oh! Cleopatra (short); A Dangerous Affair. **1932** Love Me Tonight. **1933** Hallelujah, I'm a Bum; Child of Manhattan; Morning Glory. **1934** Blind Date; Belle of the Nineties; Imitation of Life. **1935** Call of the Wild; Reckless; Times Square Lady; Here Comes the Band. **1936** Next Time We Love; The Poor Little Rich Girl; To Mary—With Love; Two in a Crowd. **1937** This Is My Affair; You Can't Have Everything. **1938** Tom Sawyer, Detective; Bluebeard's Eighth Wife; In Old Chicago; Alexander's Ragtime Band. **1940** Tin Pan Alley; Little Old New York; One Night in the Tropics. **1941** Lydia; Two Latins from Manhattan. **1942** Lucky Legs; I Married an Angel; The McGuerins from Brooklyn.

BROOKE, VAN DYKE (aka VAN DYKE BROOKS)
Born: Detroit, Mich. Died: Sept. 17, 1921, Saratoga Springs, N.Y. Screen, stage actor, film director, stage director and screenwriter. Entered films with Vitagraph.

Appeared in: **1911** Captain Barnacle's Courtship; My Old Dutch; Captain Barnacle's Baby; Captain Barnacle, Diplomat. **1912** The First Violin; Captain Barnacle, Reformer; For the Honor of the Family; The Law or the Lady; Winning Is Losing; The Diamond Brooch; On the Pupil of His Eye; Captain Barnacle's Legacy; The Old Silver Watch; Nemesis; Counsel for the Defense; Dr. Lafleur's Theory; The Foster Child; The Spider's Web; Their Golden Anniversary; Flirt or Heroine; Lord Browning and Cinderella; Captain Barnacle's Waif; O'Hara, Squatter and Philosopher; Mrs. 'Enry 'Awkins; Mrs. Lirriper's Lodger. **1913** O'Hara and the Youthful Prodigal; A Modern Psyche; O'Hara as Guardian Angel; Ida's Christmas; O'Hara Helps Cupid; An

Elopement at Home; Fanny's Conspiracy; O'Hara's Godchild; The Mouse and the Lion; Wanted: A Strong Hand; Tim Grogan's Foundling; An Old Man's Love Story; Better Days. **1914** A Wayward Daughter; His Little Page; The Memories in Men's Souls; Politics and the Press; Under False Colors; Goodbye Summer; Fogg's Millions; Officer John Donovan; The Vavasour Ball. **1915** The Romance of a Handkerchief; Dorothy; The Fortune Hunter; A Question of Right or Wrong; Elsa's Brother; Saints and Sinners; A Daughter's Strange Inheritance. **1916** The Primal Instinct; The Bond of Blood; Would You Forgive Her? **1919** The Moonshine Trail. **1921** Midnight Bell; The Passionate Pilgrim; The Son of Wallingford; The Crimson Cross; Straight Is the Way.

BROOK-JONES, ELWYN
Born: Dec. 11, 1911, Borneo. Died: Sept. 4, 1962, Reading, England. Screen, stage and television actor.

Appeared in: **1941** Pimpernel Smith (aka Mister V—US 1942); Dangerous Moonlight (aka Suicide Squadron—US 1942). **1942** Tomorrow We Live (aka At Dawn We Die—US 1943). **1943** The Night Invader. **1947** Odd Man Out. **1948** The Three Weird Sisters; Good Time Girl (US 1950); It's Hard to Be Good (US 1950); Bonnie Prince Charlie (US 1952). **1951** I'll Get You for This (aka Lucky Nick Cain—US); Life in Her Hands; The Wonder Kid. **1952** Judgment Deferred; The Night Won't Talk. **1953** Three Steps in the Dark. **1954** Beau Brummel; The Harrassed Hero. **1955** The Gilded Cage. **1956** Assignment Redhead (aka Million Dollar Manhunt—US 1962). **1957** Rogue's Yarn. **1958** The Duke Wore Jeans. **1959** Passport to Shame (aka Room 43—US); The Ugly Duckling. **1961** The Pure Hell of St. Trinians.

BROOKS, ALAN (Irving Hayward)
Born: 1888. Died: Sept., 1936, Saranac, N.Y. Screen, vaudeville actor, stage and vaudeville producer.

Appeared in: **1926** Red Dice; Young April; Pals in Paradise. **1927** King of Kings; Home Struck; Ladies Beware; Shanghaied; South Sea Love. **1929** Mr. Intruder (short); The Hole in the Wall. **1932-33** Paramount shorts. **1937** The League of Frightened Men.

BROOKS, GERALDINE (Geraldine Stroock)
Born: Oct. 29, 1925, New York, N.Y. Died: June 19, 1977, Riverhead, N.Y. (cancer). Screen, stage and television actress. Sister of actress Gloria Stern. Married to author Budd Schulberg.

Appeared in: **1947** Cry Wolf (film debut); Possessed. **1948** This Side of the Law; Embraceable You; Live Today for Tomorrow; An Act of Murder. **1949** The Younger Brothers; Reckless Moment; Challenge to Lassie. **1950** I Dreamed of Paradise. **1952** Green Glove; Streets of Sorrow. **1953** Volcano; 1957 Street of Sinners. **1966** Johnny Tiger. **1975** Mr. Ricco.

BROOKS, HANK
Died: Dec. 3, 1925, Los Angeles, Calif. Screen actor. Entered films with Sennett in 1915.

BROOKS, JESSE LEE
Born: 1894. Died: Dec. 13, 1944, Hollywood, Calif. (heart attack). Black screen and stage actor.

Appeared in: **1937** Dark Manhattan; Two-Gun Man from Harlem. **1938** Life Goes On; Spirit of Youth. **1939** Gang War; Midnight Shadow. **1940** Mystery in Swing; Am I Guilty?; Broken Strings; Four Shall Die. **1941** Sullivan's Travels. **1942** Drums of the Congo; Jungle Siren. **1945** Wilson; The Lost Weekend.

BROOKS, PAULINE
Born: 1913. Died: June 7, 1967, Glendale, Calif. (cancer). Stage and screen actress.

Appeared in: **1933** Beauty for Sale. **1934** Student Tour. **1935** Age of Indiscretion; Make a Million; Alibi Ike.

BROOKS, RANDY
Born: 1918. Died: Mar. 21, 1967, Springvale, Maine (result of smoke inhalation). Band leader; trumpeter and screen actor. Do not confuse with screen actor with same name. Divorced from swing orchestra leader Ina Ray Hutton.

Appeared in: **1945** A Columbia short (with his orchestra).

BROOME, GEORGE B. "BEN"
Born: 1894. Died: Aug. 7, 1979, Providence, R.I. Stunt pilot and screen actor.

BROPHY, EDWARD
Born: Feb. 27, 1895, New York, N.Y. Died: May 30, 1960, Los Angeles, Calif. Screen actor. Entered films in 1919.

Appeared in: **1920** Yes or No (film debut). **1927** West Point. **1929** The Cameraman. **1930** Our Blushing Brides; Free and Easy; Those French Girls; Paid; Doughboys; Remote Control. **1931** Parlor, Bedroom and Bath; A Dangerous Affair; A Free Soul; The Champ. **1932** Speak Easily; Freaks; Flesh; The Big Shot. **1933** What, No Beer?; Broadway to Hollywood. **1934** Hide-Out; Death on the Diamond; Evelyn Prentice; I'll Fix It; The Thin Man; Paris Interlude. **1935** I Live My Life; $1,000 a Minute; Naughty Marietta; The Whole Town's Talking; Shadow of Doubt; Mad Love; China Seas; People Will Talk; She Gets Her Man; Remember Last Night?; Show Them No Mercy. **1936** Mr. Cinderella; The Soldier and the Lady; Strike Me Pink; Woman Trap; The Case Against Mrs. Ames; Spendthrift; Wedding Present; All American Chump; Kelly the Second; Here Comes Trouble; Career Woman; Great Guy. **1937** Hideaway Girl; Michael Strogoff; The Great Gambini; Blossoms on Broadway; Varsity Show; Jim Hanvey—Detective; The Hit Parade; Oh, Doctor!; The Last Gangster; The Girl Said No; The River of Missing Men; Trapped by G-Men. **1938** A Slight Case of Murder; Romance on the Run; Come On, Leathernecks!; Gambling Ship; Hold That Kiss; Vacation from Love; Passport Husband; Pardon Our Nerve; Golddiggers in Paris. **1939** You Can't Cheat an Honest Man; For Love or Money; Society Lawyer; The Kid from Kokomo; Golden Boy; The Amazing Mr. Williams; Kid Nightingale. **1940** The Big Guy; Dance, Girl, Dance; Sandy Gets Her Man; Calling Philo Vance; Alias the Deacon; Golden Gloves; The Great Profile. **1941** Sleepers West; A Dangerous Game; The Invisible Woman; Dumbo (voice); Thieves Fall Out; Nine Lives Are Not Enough; Steel Against the Sky; The Bride Came C.O.D.; Buy Me That Town; The Gay Falcon. **1942** Broadway; Lady Bodyguard; Air Force; Madame Spy; One Exciting Night; Destroyer; Larceny, Inc.; All Through the Night. **1944** It Happened Tomorrow; A Night of Adventure; The Thin Man Goes Home; Cover Girl. **1945** I'll Remember April; Wonder Man; See My Lawyer; The Falcon in San Francisco; Penthouse Rhythm. **1946** Swing Parade of 1946; Girl on the Spot; The Falcon's Adventure; Sweetheart of Sigma Chi. **1947** It Happened on 5th Avenue. **1949** Arson, Inc. **1951** Pier 23; Danger Zone; Roaring City. **1956** Bundle of Joy. **1958** The Last Hurrah.

BROSIG, EGON
Born: 1890, Germany. Died: May 23, 1961, Berlin, Germany. Screen, stage and radio actor.

Appeared in the following German films: The Old and the Young King; The Strange Adventures of Mr. Fridolin; The Cold Heart; The Subject.

BROSKE, OCTAVIA
Born: June 4, 1886, Pa. Died: Mar. 19, 1967. Screen actress.

Appeared in: **1920** She Loves and Lies. **1921** The Great Adventure.

BROTHER BONES *See* DAVIS, FREEMAN

BROTT, ROBERT
Born: 1881. Died: Aug. 15, 1933, Welfare Island, N.Y. Screen, stage and vaudeville actor.

Appeared in: **1917** Pearl of the Army (serial).

BROUGH, ARTHUR
Born: 1905, England. Died: May 28, 1978, Folkestone, England. Screen, stage and television actor. Married to actress Elizabeth Addyman (dec.).

Appeared in: **1959** The Night We Dropped a Clanger (aka Make Mine a Double—US 1961). **1960** The Challenge (aka It Takes a Thief—US 1962).

BROUGH, MARY
Born: Apr. 16, 1863, London, England. Died: Sept. 30, 1934, London, England (heart trouble). Screen and stage actress.

Appeared in: **1914** The Brass Bottle; The Bosun's Mate; A Christmas Carol; Lawyer Quince; Mrs. Scrubbs' Discovery; Beauty and the Barge. **1915** His Lordship. **1917** Masks and Faces. **1920** Fordington Twins; John Forest Finds Himself; Judge Not; London Pride; The Amazing Quest Ernest Bliss (serial); The Law Divine; Enchantment. **1921** Squibs; The Will; The Adventures of Mr. Pickwick; The Bachelor's Club; The Diamond Necklace; Demos (aka Why Men Forget—US); The Golden Dawn; The Old Wives' Tale; The Night Hawk (aka The Haven); The Tinted Venus; All Sorts and Conditions of Men. **1922** A Sister to Asssist 'Er; Squibs Wins the Calcutta Sweep; Tit for Tat. **1923** Lights of London; The School for Scandal; Lily of the Alley; Married Love (aka Married Life and Maisie's Marriage). **1924**

The Alley of Golden Hearts; His Grace Gives Notice; Not for Sale; The Passionate Adventure; Tons of Money. **1925** The Only Way. **1926** Safety First. **1927** A Sister to Assist 'Er (and 1922 version). **1928** Dawn; The Passing of Mr. Quin; The Physician (US 1929); Sailors Don't Care; Wait and See; When We Were Young series including: Nursery Chairs and The King's Breakfast. **1929** The Broken Melody; Master and Man. **1930** Rookery Nook (aka One Embarassing Night—US); On Approval. **1931** Tons of Money (and 1924 version). **1932** A Night Like This; Thark. **1933** Turkey Time; A Cuckoo in the Nest; Up to the Neck.

BROWER, OTTO
Born: Dec. 2, 1895, Grand Rapids, Mich. Died: Jan. 25, 1946, Hollywood, Calif. (heart failure). Screen actor and film director.

Appeared in: **1922** On the High Seas. **1923** All the Brothers Were Valiant.

BROWER, ROBERT
Born: July 14, 1850, Point Pleasant, N.Y. Died: Dec. 8, 1934, West Hollywood, Calif. Screen, stage actor and screenwriter.

Appeared in: **1911** Foul Play; How Mrs. Murray Saved the American Army; A Conspiracy Against the King; The Reform Candidate; The Living Peach; The Bo'sun's Watch; John Brown's Heir; Uncle Hiram's List; The Trapper's Five Dollar Bill; The New Church Carpet; The Captain of Fort Ticonderoga; Maiden of the Piefaced Indians; The Hair Restorer and the Indians; His First Trip; The Declaration of Independence; The Three Musketeers; A Cure for Crime; The Death of Nathan Hale. **1912** The Third Thanksgiving; How the Boys Fought the Indians; For the Commonwealth; The Convict's Parole; Blinks and Jinks; Attorneys at Law; The Bank President's Son; The Sunset Gun; The Usurer's Grip; Helping John; The Father; The Harbinger of Peace; Under False Colors; A Baby's Shoe; The Dam Builder. **1919** The Lottery Man; Hawthorne of the U.S.A.; The Beauty Market. **1920** City Sparrow; Held by the Enemy; A Cumberland Romance; Jack Straw; The Jucklins. **1921** The Faith Healer; The Little Minister; The Lost Romance; What Every Woman Knows. **1922** Fools First; Is Matrimony a Failure?; The Man Who Saw Tomorrow; Singed Wings; Thirty Days. **1923** Adam's Rib; Long Live the King; Racing Hearts. **1924** Riders Up. **1925** Fifth Avenue Models; The Thoroughbred. **1926** The Honeymoon Express; Wild Oats Lane. **1927** The Gay Defender; The Last Trail. **1928** Beggars of Life. **1930** Abraham Lincoln.

BROWER, THOMAS L.
Died: July 19, 1937. Screen actor.

Appeared in: **1927** Hook and Ladder No. 9; Not for Publication. **1933** Crossfire. **1936** The Lawless Nineties; Love Begins at 20; The Singing Vagabond.

BROWN, ADA
Born: 1891. Died: Mar. 31, 1950, Kansas City, Mo. Black screen, stage actress and singer.

Appeared in: **1943** Stormy Weather.

BROWN, ALFRED C.
Born: 1897. Died: Jan. 28, 1978, London, England (apparent heart attack). Screen, stage and television actor. Do not confuse with U.S. actor Alfred Brown.

BROWN, BARBARA
Born: 1907. Died: July 7, 1975. Screen actress.

Appeared in: **1941** Three Girls About Town; Melody Lane; Bachelor Daddy. **1942** The Wife Takes a Flyer; You Were Never Lovelier. **1943** Moonlight in Vermont; Reveille With Beverly; Falcon and the Co-eds; Wedtime Stories (short); Mission to Moscow; Never a Dull Moment; Top Man. **1944** The Sullivans; Janie; The Ghost That Walks Alone; Hey, Rookie; The Doughgirls; Hollywood Canteen. **1945** Roughly Speaking; Pillow to Post; Too Young to Know; Mildred Pierce. **1946** Janie Gets Married; Personality Kid; White Tie and Tails; The Beast With Five Fingers. **1947** That Way With Women; High Barbaree; Love and Learn; That Haggen Girl. **1948** Arthur Takes Over; Wallflower. **1949** Henry, the Rainmaker; Miss Mink of 1949; Yes, Sir, That's My Baby; Leave It to Henry. **1950** Ma and Pa Kettle Go to Town; Father Makes Good; Born Yesterday; Father's Wild Game. **1951** Ma and Pa Kettle Back on the Farm; Home Town Story; Father Takes the Air; The Lady and the Bandit. **1952** Jack and the Beanstalk; The Brigand; You for Me. **1953** Ma and Pa Kettle on Vacation. **1955** Sincerely Yours; Annapolis Story; My Sister Eileen. **1970** The Red, White and Black.

BROWN, BARRY (Donald Barry Brown)
Born: Apr. 19, 1951, San Jose, Calif. Died: June 25, 1978, Los Angeles, Calif. (self-inflicted gunshot wounds). Screen, stage, television actor, film producer, playwright and author. Brother of actress Marilyn Brown.

Appeared in: **1970** Halls of Anger. **1972** Bad Company. **1974** Daisy Miller; The Ultimate Thrill.

BROWN, BLY
Born: 1898. Died: Dec. 19, 1950, Los Angeles, Calif. Screen and stage actress.

BROWN, CHARLES D.
Born: July 1, 1887, Council Bluffs, Iowa. Died: Nov. 25, 1948, Hollywood, Calif. (heart ailment). Screen and stage actor.

Appeared in: **1921** The Man of Stone; The Way of a Maid. **1929** The Dance of Life; Dangerous Curves. **1931** The Road to Reno; Twenty-Four Hours; Murder by the Clock; Touchdown. **1933** The Woman I Stole. **1934** Tailspin Tommy (serial); It Happened One Night. **1936** Golddiggers of 1937. **1937** Thoroughbreds Don't Cry. **1938** Think It Over (short); Island in the Sky; Mr. Moto's Gamble; Speed to Burn; Inside Story; Up the River; Exposed; Algiers; Duke of West Point; Shopworn Angel; The Crowd Roars; Barefoot Boy; Five of a Kind. **1939** Tell No Tales; Mr. Moto in Danger Island; Charlie Chan in Reno; Hotel for Women; Kid Nightingale; Smashing the Money Ring; Ice Follies of 1939; Little Accident; Disbarred. **1940** Know Your Money (short); Brother Orchid; Pier 13; The Santa Fe Trail; The Grapes of Wrath; He Married His Wife; Sailor's Lady. **1941** Maisie Was a Lady; Glamour Boy; Tall, Dark and Handsome; Reaching for the Sun; International Lady. **1942** Fingers at the Window; Roxie Hart; Sweater Girl. **1943** A Lady Takes a Chance. **1944** Up in Arms; The Fighting Seabees; The Contender; Jam Session; Secret Command. **1945** Having a Wonderful Crime; Don Juan Quilligan; Apology for Murder; Sunbonnet Sue. **1946** Danger Woman; The Bride Wore Boots; Notorious; In Fast Company; Wake Up and Dream; The Killers; Just Before Dawn; The Last Crooked Mile; The Big Sleep; Night Editor; The Strange Loves of Martha Ivers. **1947** Smash-Up; The Story of a Woman; Merton of the Movies; The Senator Was Indiscreet. **1948** On Our Merry Way; A Miracle Can Happen; In This Corner. **1949** Follow Me Quietly. **1951** Sealed Cargo.

BROWN, EVERETT
Died: Oct. 14, 1953. Black screen actor.

Appeared in: **1927** South Sea Love. **1931** Danger Island (serial). **1932** Hell's Headquarters. **1933** Nagana. **1935** Murder for Dr. Harrigan; The Payoff; Black Fury. **1939** Gone With the Wind. **1940** Zanzibar; Congo Maisie. **1953** White Witch Doctor.

BROWN, FRED G.
Born: 1878, London, England. Died: 1944, Toronto, Canada. Screen actor.

Appeared in: **1917** She Needed a Doctor. **1920** Empty Arms. **1923** That Woman; Little Old New York; Under the Red Robe.

BROWN, HALBERT W.
Born: 1865. Died: Oct. 24, 1942, New York, N.Y. Screen actor.

Appeared in: **1921** The Black Panther's Cub.

BROWN, HARRY W. (Harry William Brown)
Born: Feb. 27, 1918. Died: May 26, 1966, Pacoima, Calif. (lung cancer). Screen actor.

Appeared in: **1954** The Bounty Hunter.

BROWN, HELEN "MINA"
Born: 1916. Died: Sept. 9, 1974, Calif. (cancer). Screen and television actress.

Appeared in: **1935** Diamond Jim; Tailspin Tommy and the Great Air Mystery (serial). **1936** Three Godfathers; Collegiate; Big Brown Eyes; To Mary—With Love. **1937** This Is My Affair. **1939** Hidden Power; Should a Girl Marry; Hotel for Women; When Tomorrow Comes. **1940** Untamed; Babies for Sale; Out West With the Peppers; Five Little Peppers in Trouble. **1941** Mr. District Attorney. **1943** She's for Me. **1944** Tampico. **1946** Danny Boy. **1947** Nora Prentiss; Curley. **1948** The Walls of Jericho; All My Sons. **1949** Holiday Affair; Arctic Manhunt; Dancing in the Dark; The Set-Up. **1950** Key to the City; Shadow on the Wall; Molly (aka The Goldbergs). **1951** Al Jennings of Oklahoma; As Young as You Feel; The Company She Keeps. **1952** Something to Live For; Dreamboat. **1953** Shane. **1954** Executive Suite. **1955** Strategic Air Command; Teen-Age Crime Wave. **1958** Houseboat; The Missouri Traveler. **1960** Dark at the Top of the Stairs. **1962** That Touch of Mink.

BROWN, HORACE
Born: 1905, Richmond, Va. Died: Nov. 9, 1972, Long Beach, Calif. Screen actor. Married to actress Marion Davies (dec. 1961).

Appeared in: **1968** The Destructors.

BROWN, JOE E. (Joseph Even Brown)
Born: July 28, 1892, Holgate, Ohio. Died: July 6, 1973, Brentwood, Calif. Screen, stage, circus, vaudeville actor and author.

Appeared in: **1928** Crooks Can't Wait (film debut); Me, Gangster; Road House; Dressed to Kill; The Circus Kid; Hit of the Show; Take Me Home; Burlesque; Don't Be Jealous. **1929** In Old Arizona; Sunny Side Up; Molly and Me; Sally; My Lady's Past; On With the Show; Painted Faces; The Cock-Eyed World; The Ghost Talks; Protection. **1930** How to Play Golf—Trouble Shots (short); Up the River; Maybe It's Love; Song of the West; Born Reckless; City Girl; Hold Everything; The Lottery Bride; Top Speed. **1931** Going Wild; Local Boy Makes Good; Broad-Minded; Sit Tight. **1932** The Tenderfoot; Fireman, Save My Child; The Slippery Pearls (short); You Said a Mouthful; The Putter (short); Hollywood on Parade #8 (short); Elmer the Great; Son of a Sailor. **1934** The Circus Clown; Six Day Bike Rider; A Very Honorable Guy. **1935** A Midsummer Night's Dream; Alibi Ike. **1936** Bright Lights; Polo Joe; Sons O'Gun; Earthworm Tractors. **1937** Fit for a King; When's Your Birthday?; Riding on Air (aka All Is Confusion). **1938** Flirting With Fate; The Gladiator; Wide Open Faces. **1939** Beware Spooks!; $1,000 a Touchdown. **1940** So You Won't Talk. **1942** Shut My Big Mouth; The Daring Young Man; Joan of the Ozarks. **1943** Chatterbox. **1944** Pin-Up Girl; Hollywood Canteen; Casanova in Burlesque. **1947** Riding on Air. **1949** The Tender Years. **1951** Showboat; Memories of Famous Hollywood Comedians (short—narrator). **1954** Hollywood Fathers (short). **1956** Around the World in 80 Days. **1959** Some Like It Hot. **1963** A Comedy of Terrors (doc.); It's a Mad, Mad, Mad, Mad World.

BROWN, JOEY (Josephine Brown)
Born: 1892, Chicago, Ill. Died: Apr. 26, 1976, Ibiza, Spain. Screen, stage, television actress and singer.

Appeared in: **1929** Strange Cargo; Tonight at Twelve. **1958** The Man Inside. **1961** The Roman Spring of Mrs. Stone.

BROWN, JOHN
Died: May 16, 1957. Screen and radio actor. Do not confuse with actor John Brown who entered films during the 1950's.

Appeared in: **1944** Casanova Brown.

BROWN, JOHNNY MACK
Born: Sept. 1, 1904, Dothan, Ala. Died: Nov. 14, 1974, Woodland Hills, Calif. (cardiac condition). Screen actor and All American college football player.

Appeared in: **1927** The Bugle Call; Fair Co-Ed. **1928** Our Dancing Daughters; Divine Woman; Soft Living; Square Crooks; Play Girl; Annapolis; Lady of Chance. **1929** Woman of Affairs; Coquette; The Valiant; Single Standard; Hurricane; Jazz Heaven. **1930** Undertow; Montana Moon; Billy the Kid. **1931** Secret Six; Great Meadow; Lasca of the Rio Grande; Last Flight; Laughing Sinners. **1932** Flames; 70,000 Witnesses; Vanishing Frontier; Malay Nights. **1933** Saturday's Millions; Female; Son of a Sailor; Fighting With Kit Carson (serial); Hollywood on Parade. **1934** Marrying Widows; Three on a Honeymoon; Belle of the Nineties; Cross Streets; Against the Law. **1935** St. Louis Woman; Between Men; Courageous Avenger; The Rustlers of Red Dog (serial); The Right to Live. **1936** The Desert Phantom; Rogue of the Range; Every Man's Law. **1937** Lawless Land; Bar Z Bad Man; Guns in the Dark; A Lawman Is Born; Boothill Brigade; Wells Fargo; Wild West Days (serial). **1938** Born to the West; Flaming Frontiers (serial). **1939** Desperate Trails; Oklahoma Frontier; The Oregon Trail (serial). **1940** Chip of the Flying U; West of Carson City; Riders of Pasco Basin; The Bad Man from Red Butte; Son of Roaring Dan; Ragtime Cowboy Joe; Law and Order; Pony Post. **1941** Law of the Range; The Masked Rider; Man from Montana. **1942** Ride 'Em Cowboy; Arizona Cyclone; Fighting Bill Fargo; Stagecoach Buckaroo; The Silver Bullet; Deep in the Heart of Texas; The Boss of Hangtown; Little Joe, the Wrangler. **1943** Tenting Tonight on the Old Camp Ground; The Old Chisholm Trail; Cheyenne Roundup; The Ghost Rider; The Stranger from Pecos; Lone Star Trail. **1944** Range Law; Land of the Outlaws; Raiders of the Border; West of the Rio Grande; Partners of the Trail; Law Men. **1945** They Shall Have Faith; Law of the Valley; Flame of the West. **1946** Drifting Along; The Haunted Mine; Under Arizona Skies; Shadows on the Range; Raiders of the South; Gentleman from Texas; Trigger Fingers; Silver Range. **1947** Land of the Lawless; Valley of Fear; Trailing Danger; The Law Comes to Gunsight; Flashing Guns; Prairie Express; Code of the

Saddle; Gun Talk. **1948** Triggerman; Frontier Agent; Overland Trails; Cross Trails; The Fighting Ranger; Backtrail; The Sheriff of Medicine Bow; Hidden Danger; Gunning for Justice. **1949** Stampede; Trails End; Law of the West; Western Renegades; West of El Dorado; Range Justice. **1950** Over the Border; West of Wyoming; Short Grass; Six Gun Mesa; Outlaw Gold; Law of the Panhandle. **1951** Man from Sonora; Blazing Bullets; Colorado Ambush; Montana Desperado; Texas Lawmen; Whistling Hills. **1952** Man from the Black Hills; Canyon Ambush; Dead Man's Trail; Texas City. **1954** Hollywood Fathers (short). **1965** Requiem for a Gunfighter; The Bounty Killer. **1966** Apache Uprising.

BROWN, MAXINE VELENA
Born: 1897, Denver, Colo. Died: Dec. 28, 1956, Alameda, Calif. (burns). Screen, stage, vaudeville and radio actress. Divorced from vaudeville performer George Maines. Married to actor Clarence Willard. Appeared in Famous and Warner films.

BROWN, MELVILLE
Born: 1888, Portland, Ore. Died: Jan. 31, 1938, Hollywood, Calif. (heart attack). Screen, stage, vaudeville actor, film, stage director and screenwriter. Entered films in 1916.

BROWN, MILTON "MILT"
Born: 1896. Died: Mar. 29, 1948, Hollywood, Calif. Screen actor, assistant film director and cameraman.

Appeared in: **1913** A Frontier Wife; An Indian's Gratitude; An Indian's Honor; The Long Portage. **1914** The Only Son. **1915** The Arab. **1921** Cold Steel. **1923** Ruggles of Red Cap; King's Creek Law. **1924** The Breaking Point. **1929** Points West. **1930** Mounted Stranger. **1932** Local Bad Man.

BROWN, PAMELA (aka PAMELA BROWNE)
Born: July 8, 1917, London, England. Died: Sept. 18, 1975, London, England. Screen, stage and television actress. Do not confuse with Pamela Brown, writer/producer, etc., born 1924.

Appeared in: **1942** One of Our Aircraft Is Missing. **1945** I Know Where I'm Going (US 1947). **1951** The Tales of Hoffman. **1952** The Second Mrs. Tanqueray (US 1954). **1953** Personal Affair (US 1954). **1955** Richard III (US 1956). **1956** Lust for Life. **1959** The Scapegoat. **1963** Cleopatra. **1964** Becket. **1965** Gonks Go Beat. **1966** A Funny Thing Happened on the Way to the Forum. **1967** Half a Sixpence (US 1968). **1968** Secret Ceremony. **1970** Wuthering Heights; On a Clear Day You Can See Forever. **1972** Lady Caroline Lamb.

BROWN, PHIL
Died: July 11, 1973. Screen actor. Do not confuse with screen child actor Philip Brown.

Appeared in: **1941** I Wanted Wings; H. M. Pulham, Esq. **1942** Calling Dr. Gillespie; Pierre of the Plains; Hello Annapolis. **1944** Weird Woman; The Impatient Years. **1945** Jungle Captive; Over 21; State Fair. **1946** Without Reservations; The Killers. **1947** Johnny O'Clock. **1948** If You Knew Susie; The Luck of the Irish. **1949** Moonrise. **1950** The Hidden Room (aka Obsession). **1955** The Green Scarf. **1958** The Camp on Blood Island. **1959** John Paul Jones. **1962** The Counterfeit Traitor. **1965** The Bedford Incident. **1966** The Boy Cried Murder. **1969** The Adding Machine; Operation Cross Eagles. **1970** Land Raiders; Tropic of Cancer. **1971** Valdez Is Coming.

BROWN, RAYMOND "RAY"
Born: Aug. 16, 1880, Champaign, Ill. Died: July 30, 1939, Los Angeles, Calif. Screen and stage actor. Entered films in 1929.

Appeared in: **1933** My Woman. **1934** Jealousy; It's the Cats (short); I'll Fix It; Blind Date; Whom the Gods Destroy; White Lies; Successful Failure; Mystery Liner. **1935** She Gets Her Man; Magnificent Obsession; Million Dollar Baby; Baby Face Harrington; The Flame Within; Dr. Socrates; Moonlight on the Prairie. **1936** Fury; Bullets or Ballots; The Story of Louis Pasteur; Laughing Irish Eyes; Comin' 'Round the Mountain; Down the Stretch; The Magnificent Brute; Career Woman. **1937** Black Aces; The Holy Terror; Two Wise Maids; We Have Our Moments; Parole Rackets; Back in Circulation. **1938** Gold Is Where You Find It. **1939** They Made Me a Criminal; King of the Underworld; The Family Next Door.

BROWN, RONALD C.
Born: 1911. Died: Oct. 27, 1962, Hollywood, Calif. Screen actor and dancer. Entered films approx. 1937.

BROWN, RUSS
Born: May 30, 1892, Philadelphia, Pa. Died: Oct. 19, 1964, Englewood, N.J. Screen, stage and vaudeville actor. Divorced from screen actress Gertrude Whitaker. Appeared in vaudeville in an act with Bert Wheeler and later with Gertrude Whitaker in an act billed as "Brown and Whitaker."

Appeared in: **1928** "Brown and Whitaker" appeared in the following shorts: A Laugh or Two; In the Park. Brown later appeared in:. **1933** Moulin Rouge; My Woman. **1934** The Love Captive; Let's Talk It Over. **1958** South Pacific; Damn Yankees. **1959** Anatomy of a Murder; It Happened to Jane. **1962** Advise and Consent. **1963** The Cardinal.

BROWN, SYDNEY
Born: 1899. Died: Mar. 1, 1979, Sudbury, Ontario, Canada (heart attack). Screen, stage, radio and television actor.

Appeared in: **1958** Wolf Dog. **1961** 1 + 1 (Exploring the Kinsey Reports). **1964** The Luck of Ginger Coffey. **1969** Change of Mind.

BROWN, TROY, JR.
Died: Nov. 18, 1944. Screen actor.

Appeared in: **1936** Can This Be Dixie? **1937** Second Honeymoon; Nothing Sacred. **1940** Dreaming Out Loud.

BROWN, VIRGINIA FAIRE *See* FAIRE, VIRGINIA BROWN

BROWN, WALLY
Born: Oct. 9, 1904, Malden, Mass. Died: Nov. 13, 1961, Los Angeles, Calif. Screen, vaudeville, radio and television actor. Was part of film comedy team of "Brown and Carney" with Alan Carney.

Appeared in: **1943** Petticoat Larceny; Radio Runaround (short); Mexican Spitfire's Blessed Event; The Seventh Victim; Gangway for Tomorrow; Around the World. **1944** The Girl in the Case. **1946** From This Day Forward; Notorious; Vacation in Reno. **1948** Family Honeymoon; Backstage Follies (short); Bachelor Blues (short). **1949** Come to the Stable. **1951** As Young as You Feel. **1954** The High and the Mighty. **1956** The Wild Dakotas. **1957** The Joker Is Wild; Untamed Youth. **1958** The Wink of an Eye; The Left-Handed Gun. **1959** The Best of Everything; Westbound; Holiday for Lovers. **1961** The Absent Minded Professor. Brown and Carney films: **1943** The Adventures of a Rookie (their film debut together) and Rookies in Burma. **1944** Girl Rush; Seven Days Ashore; Step Lively. **1945** Radio Stars on Parade; Zombies on Broadway. **1946** Genius at Work.

BROWNE, E. MARTIN
Born: Jan. 29, 1900, Zeals, England. Died: Apr. 27, 1980, London, England. Screen, stage actor and stage director. Married to actress Henzie Raeburn (dec. 1973) and later to Audrey Rideout.

BROWNE, EARLE
Born: 1872. Died: Nov. 28, 1944, Hollywood, Calif. Screen and stage actor.

Appeared in: **1922** Sherlock Holmes. **1926** Sparrows. **1927** Love of Sunya. **1929** The Iron Mask; The Locked Door; The Taming of the Shrew. **1930** DuBarry, Woman of Passion. **1932** Mr. Robinson Crusoe.

BROWNE, IRENE
Born: 1893, London, England. Died: July 24, 1965, London, England (cancer). Screen and stage actress.

Appeared in: **1929** The Letter. **1933** Cavalcade (stage and film versions); Berkeley Square; My Lips Betray; Peg O' My Heart; Christopher Strong. **1936** The Amateur Gentleman. **1938** Pygmalion. **1941** The Prime Minister; Kipps (aka The Remarkable Mr. Kipps—US 1942). **1947** Meet Me at Dawn (US 1948). **1948** The Red Shoes; Quartet. **1950** Madeleine. **1951** The House in the Square (aka I'll Never Forget You—US). **1953** The Gay Duellist (rerelease of Meet Me at Dawn—1947). **1957** Barnacle Bill (aka All at Sea—US 1958). **1958** Rooney. **1959** Serious Charge (aka Immoral Charge—US 1962). **1963** The Wrong Arm of the Law. **1964** A Touch of Hell (rerelease of Serious Charge—1959).

BROWNE, LAIDMAN
Born: Sept. 13, 1896, Newcastle, England. Died: Sept. 11, 1961, Bournemouth, England. Screen, stage, radio and television actor. Entered films in 1936.

Appeared in: **1953** Ghost Ship.

BROWNE, LUCILLE (aka LUCILLE BROWN)
Born: 1907, Memphis, Tenn. Died: May 10, 1976, Los Angeles, Calif. Screen and stage actress. Married to actor James Flavin (dec. Apr. 1976).

Appeared in as Brown: **1921** The Sport of the Gods. **1927** The King of Kings; as Browne: **1930** Soup to Nuts; Last of the Duanes. **1931** Battling with Buffalo Bill (serial); Danger Island (serial); As Young as You Feel. **1932** The Airmail Myster (serial); Cannonball Express; Girls About Town. **1933** Mystery Squadron (serial); King of the Arena; The Devil's Brother; The Moonshiner's Daughter or Abroad in Old Kentucky (short—one title); Double Harness. **1934** The Law of the Wild (serial); Hide-Out; The Brand of Hate (as Brown). **1935** On Probation; Rainbow Valley; Tumbling Tumbleweeds; Secrets of Chinatown; Western Frontier. **1947** Wife to Spare (short). **1950** No Sad Songs for Me.

BROWNE, W. GRAHAM
Born: 1870, Ireland. Died: Mar. 11, 1937, London, England (pneumonia). Stage and screen actor. Married to actress Marie Tempest (dec. 1942).

Appeared in: **1915** Mrs. Plumb's Pudding. **1934** The Lady Is Willing. **1937** Moonlight Sonata.

BROWNELL, JOHN C.
Born: 1877. Died: Aug. 27, 1961, Starksboro, Vt. Screen, stage actor and screenwriter.

Appeared in: **1914** The Mad Man's Ward.

BROWNING, ALAN
Born: 1926. Died: Sept. 7, 1979, Stockport, England. Screen, stage and television actor. Married to actress Pat Phoenix.

Appeared in: **1964** Guns at Batasi. **1970** Julius Caesar.

BROWNING, TOD
Born: July 12, 1882, Louisville, Ky. Died: Oct. 6, 1962, Hollywood, Calif. (cancer). Screen, stage actor, film director and screenwriter. Married to actress Alice Browning.

Appeared in: **1914** Billy Takes a Lady to Lunch; Bill Saves the Day; The Deceiver; An Interrupted Seance; A Race for a Bride; The White Slave Catchers; Bill Squares It With the Boss. **1915** Cupid and the Pest; Bill and Ethel at the Ball. **1916** Intolerance. **1964** Big Parade of Comedy (doc.).

BROWNING, WILLIAM E.
Born: 1871. Died: Dec. 21, 1930, Middle Village, N.Y. Screen, stage and radio actor.

Appeared in: **1929** Applause; plus numerous shorts.

BROWNLEE, FRANK
Born: Oct. 11, 1874, Dallas, Tex. Died: Feb. 10, 1948. Screen actor.

Appeared in: **1919** Brass Buttons; Miss Adventure; The Brute Breaker. **1920** Shore Acres; Riders of the Dawn; The Lincoln Highwayman; The Man Who Dared; Under Crimson Skies; The Valley of Tomorrow; Hearts Are Trumps. **1921** His Own Law; The Hole in the Wall; Love Never Dies; Soul and Body; The Whistle. **1922** The Face Between; Fools of Fortune. **1923** Boston Blackie; Nobody's Bride; Romance Land; Sawdust. **1924** The Beloved Brute. **1925** The Desert Flower; The Ridin' Streak; Straight Through. **1926** The Social Highwayman; King of the Pack. **1927** Wanted—A Coward; Sailors Beware. **1928** Sawdust Paradise; Midnight Rose. **1929** Beggars of Life. **1931** The Vanishing Legion (serial); The Lightning Warrior (serial); The Galloping Ghost (serial); Rough Seas (short). **1932** Pack Up Your Troubles; Tombstone Canyon. **1933** The Midnight Patrol (short); Terror Trail. **1935** Man's Best Friend. **1941** Lucky Devils; South of Tahiti. **1942** Ice Capades Revue.

BRUCE, BELLE
Died: June 15, 1960. Screen actress.

Appeared in: **1917** The Great Secret (serial).

BRUCE, BETTY
Born: 1920. Died: July 18, 1974, New York, N.Y. Screen, stage actress, singer, dancer.

Appeared in: **1962** Gypsy (stage and film versions). **1963** Island of Love (aka Not on Your Life). **1969** Potpourri.

BRUCE, BEVERLY
Died: July, 1925, Bryn Mawr, Calif. Screen, stage and vaudeville actress.

Appeared in: **1920** Empty Arms.

BRUCE, CLIFFORD
Born: 1885, Toronto, Canada. Died: Aug. 27, 1919, West Camp, N.Y. Screen and stage actor.

Appeared in: **1914** A Page From Yesterday; The Perils of Pauline (serial). **1915** A Woman's Past; A Fool There Was; Lady Audley's Secret; Princess Romanoff. **1916** The Fourth Estate; The Devil at His Elbow; The Weakness of Strength. **1917** The Siren; The Barricade; Blue Jeans; Seven Deadly Sins; Passion. **1918** The Winding Trail; A Weaver of Dreams; Breakers Ahead; Riders of the Night. **1919** The Racing Strain; Woman! Woman!

BRUCE, DAVID (Andrew McBroom)
Born: Jan. 6, 1914, Kankakee, Ill. Died: May 3, 1976, Hollywood, Calif. (heart attack). Screen, stage and television actor. Father of actress Amanda McBroom. Entered films in 1940.

Appeared in: **1940** The Man Who Talked Too Much; The Sea Hawk; River's End; A Dispatch from Reuters; Santa Fe Trail. **1941** Flight from Destiny; Singapore Woman; The Smiling Ghost; The Sea Wolf; Sergeant York; The Body Disappears. **1942** Flying Tigers. **1943** Gung Ho!; How's About That?; Honeymoon Lodge; Corvette K-225; She's For Me; Calling Dr. Death; The Mad Ghoul. **1944** Ladies Courageous; Christmas Holiday; Can't Help Singing; Allergic to Love; Moon Over Las Vegas; South of Dixie. **1945** Lady on a Train; Salome, Where She Danced; That Night With You. **1946** Susie Steps Out. **1948** Racing Luck. **1949** Prejudice; Joe Palooka in the Big Fight. **1950** Young Daniel Boone; The Great Plane Robbery; Hi-Jacked; Timber Fury; Revenue Agent; Pygmy Island. **1951** Pier 23. **1954** The Iron Glove; Cannibal Attack; Masterson of Kansas. **1976** Moving Violation.

BRUCE, KATE
Born: 1858. Died: Apr. 2, 1946. Screen actress. Entered films in 1908.

Appeared in: **1908** In Old Kentucky; An Awful Moment. **1909** A Corner in Wheat; At the Altar; The Golden Louis; Choosing a Husband; The Girl and the Daddy; In the Hempen Bag. **1910** The Two Brothers; A Gold Necklace; The Fugitive; The Rocky Road; A Romance of the Western Hills; Willful Peggy; Examination Day at School; The Fugitive Waiter. **1911** How She Triumphed. **1912** The Spirit Awakened; The Painted Lady; The Leading Man; Home Folks; An Indian Summer; The Punishment; One Is Business, the Other Is Crime; The Informer; A Dash Through the Clouds; The Would-Be Shriner. **1913** Death's Marathon; My Hero; Just Gold; Look Up; The Yaqui Cur; A Tender-Hearted Boy; The Sheriff's Baby. **1914** Judith of Bethulia; The Battle at Firebrush Gulch; A Nest Unfeathered; The Scar; Her Mother's Weakness; A Soldier Boy. **1915** Betty of Greystone; Suzan Rocks the Boat; Gretchen the Greenhorn; The Microscope Mystery. **1917** Betsy's Burglar. **1918** Hearts of the World; The Hun Within. **1919** A Romance of Happy Valley; The Girl Who Stayed at Home; Scarlet Days. **1920** Mary Ellen Comes to Town; Flying Pat; The Idol Dancer; Way Down East; Jacqueline of the Blazing Barriers. **1921** The City of Silent Men; Orphans of the Storm; Experience. **1923** The White Rose. **1924** His Darker Self. **1925** I Want My Man. **1927** A Bowery Cinderella; Ragtime; The Secret Studio.

BRUCE, LENNY (Leonard Alfred Schneider)
Born: 1926, Mineola, N.Y. Died: Aug. 3, 1966, Hollywood, Calif. (drug overdose). Nightclub comic, screenwriter and screen actor. Divorced from actress Honey Harlow.

Appeared in: **1953** Dance Hall Racket. **1967** Lenny Bruce (aka Lenny Bruce Concert). **1974** Lenny Bruce Performance Film.

BRUCE, NIGEL
Born: Feb. 4, 1895, Ensenada, Mexico. Died: Oct. 8, 1953, Santa Monica, Calif. (heart attack). Screen, stage and radio actor. Married to actress Violet Campbell (dec. 1970). Best known for his long film and radio portrayal as Dr. Watson in "Sherlock Holmes" series.

Appeared in: **1929** Red Aces. **1930** Escape; Birds of Prey (aka The Perfect Alibi—US 1931); The Squeakers. **1931** The Calendar (aka Bachelor's Folly—US 1932). **1932** Lord Camber's Ladies; I Was a Spy (US 1934); The Midshipmaid. **1933** Channel Crossing (US 1934). **1934** Stand Up and Cheer; Coming Out Party; Murder in Trinidad; The Lady is Willing; Springtime for Henry; Treasure Island. **1935** Jalna; She; The Man Who Broke the Bank at Monte Carlo; The Scarlet Pimpernel; Becky Sharp. **1936** Follow Your Heart; Make Way for a Lady; The Man I Marry; The Trail of the Lonesome Pine; The Charge of the Light Brigade; The White Angel; Under Two Flags. **1937** Thunder in the City; The Last of Mrs. Cheyney. **1938** The Baroness and the Butler; Kidnapped; Suez. **1939** The Adventures of Sherlock Holmes; The Hound of the Baskervilles; The Rains Came. **1940** Adventures in Diamonds; Lillian Russell; A Dispatch from Reuters; Hudson's Bay; The Blue Bird; Rebecca; Susan and God. **1941** Play

Girl; Free and Easy; The Chocolate Soldier; This Woman Is Mine; Suspicion. **1942** Roxie Hart; Eagle Squadron; Sherlock Holmes and the Voice of Terror; Journey for Margaret; Sherlock Holmes and the Secret Weapon; This Above All. **1943** Sherlock Holmes in Washington; Forever and a Day; Sherlock Holmes Faces Death; Crazy House; Lassie, Come Home. **1944** The Scarlet Claw; The Pearl of Death; Follow the Boys; Sherlock Holmes and the Spider Woman; Gypsy Wildcat; Frenchman's Creek. **1945** Son of Lassie; The House of Fear; The Corn Is Green; Pursuit to Algiers; The Woman in Green. **1946** Terror By Night; Dressed to Kill; Two Mrs. Carrolls. **1947** Exile. **1948** Julia Misbehaves. **1950** Vendetta. **1951** Hong Kong; B'wana Devil; Limelight. **1954** World for Ransom.

BRUCE, PAUL
Died: May 2, 1971, Hollywood, Calif. (heart attack). Screen, stage and television actor.

Appeared in: **1967** The Born Losers. **1969** The Harem Bunch or War and Piece (aka Dessert Odyssey).

BRUCE, TONIE EDGAR See EDGAR-BRUCE, TONI

BRUCE, TONY
Born: 1910, England. Died: Mar. 3, 1937, England? Screen and stage actor.

Appeared in: **1931** Tell England (aka The Battle of Gallipoli).

BRUGGEMAN, GEORGE
Born: Nov. 1, 1904, Belgium. Died: June 9, 1967, North Hollywood, Calif. Screen actor.

Appeared in: **1933** I'm No Angel. **1942** The Forest Rangers. **1945** Song of the Sarong. **1952** What Price Glory? **1954** Demetrius and the Gladiators. **1956** Around the World in 80 Days. **1962** Bachelor Flat. **1963** Forty Pounds of Trouble; Wives and Lovers.

BRULE, ANDRE
Born: 1879, Bordeau, France. Died: Feb. 14, 1953, Paris, France. Screen, stage actor, film producer, stage producer and screenwriter.

Appeared in: **1909** Werther.

BRUNDAGE, BERTHA
Born: 1860. Died: May 7, 1939, Long Beach, Calif. Screen actress.

BRUNDAGE, MATHILDE
Born: 1871, Louisville, Ky. Died: May 6, 1939. Screen actress.

Appeared in: **1914** The Crucible. **1915** Wormwood; Dr. Rameau; Emmy of Stork's Nest; The Corsican Brothers. **1916** The Lords of High Decision; Half a Rogue; The City of Illusion. **1917** Wife Number Two; Thou Shalt Not Steal; Bridges Burned; The Soul of a Magdalen; The Little Terror; Enlighten Thy Daughter; Reputation. **1921** The Good-Bad Wife; The Lady from Longacre; Hail the Woman; Lovetime; My Boy; No Defense; The Rage of Paris; The Unknown Wife; Too Much Married. **1922** Conquering the Woman; Don't Doubt Your Wife; A Front Page Story; A Self-Made Man; Shirley of the Circus; The Primitive Lover. **1923** Blinky; Fashion Row; Refuge; Strangers of the Night; The Midnight Guest. **1924** One Glorious Night; Oh, You Tony!; Westbound. **1925** Anything Once; Seven Sinners; Border Intrigue; The Charmer; The Spaniard. **1926** Men of the Night; Racing Romance; Midnight Limited; The Midnight Message; Coming an' Going; Dangerous Friends; Cupid's Knockout. **1927** The Denver Dude; Tongues of Scandal; Silver Comes Through. **1928** That's My Daddy; Love Me and the World Is Mine.

BRUNEL, ADRIAN
Born: Mar., 1892, Brighton, England. Died: 1958, England? Screen actor, film producer, screenwriter and singer.

Appeared in: **1923** The Man Without Desire. **1924** Crossing the Great Sagrada; Lovers in Araby; The Pathetic Gazette.

BRUNETTE, FRITZI
Born: 1890. Died: Sept. 28, 1943, Hollywood, Calif. Screen and stage actress.

Appeared in: **1912** A Waiter of Weight; The Consequences; The Foolishness of Oliver; It Happened Thus; The Professor's Dilemma. **1913** The Hypocrite; The Lie; Sunny Smith; The Grouch; The Appeal; The Ring of Sorrow; For the Sins of Another. **1916** Unto Those Who Sin; At Piney Ridge. **1919** The Woman Thou Gavest Me. **1920** The Devil to Pay; Live Sparks; Thirty Thousand Dollars. **1921** The Butterfly Girl; Sure Fire; The Man from Lost River; Tiger True; Discontented Wives; A Wife's Awakening. **1922** Give Me My Son; Bells of San Juan; The Boss of Camp 4; While Satan Sleeps; The Crusader; The Other Side. **1923** The Footlight Ranger; Cause for Divorce. **1925** Camille of the Barbary Coast; The Pace That Thrills. **1928** Driftwood. **1937** Maid of Salem. **1942** You're Telling Me.

BRUNETTI, MIRO
Born: 1908, Italy. Died: July 3, 1966, Hollywood, Calif. Screen actor. Married to actress Argentina Brunetti.

BRUNIUS, JACQUES (Jacques-Bernard Brunius)
Born: 1906, Paris, France. Died: Apr. 24, 1967. Screen actor, film director and screenwriter.

Appeared in: **1930** L'Age d'Or (The Age of Gold—US 1964). **1932** L'Affaire est Dans le Sac. **1935** Le Crime de M. Lange. **1936** Une Partie de Campagne (US 1937). **1951** The Lavender Hill Mob. **1952** 24 Hours of a Woman's Life (aka Affair in Monte Carlo—US 1953); South of Algiers (aka The Golden Mask—US 1954). **1953** Sea Devils; Always a Bride (US 1954); Laughing Anne (US 1954). **1954** Forbidden Cargo (US 1956). **1955** To Paris With Love; The Cockleshell Heroes (US 1956). **1956** House of Secrets (aka Triple Deception—US 1957); The Lieutenant Wore Skirts; Wicked As They Come (US 1957). **1957** True as Turtle; Dangerous Exile (US 1958). **1958** Orders to Kill. **1961** The Greengage Summer (aka Loss of Innocence—US). **1964** The Yellow Rolls-Royce (US 1965). **1965** Return from the Ashes.

BRUNIUS, JOHN W.
Born: 1884, Stockholm, Sweden. Died: Dec. 16, 1937, Sweden? Screen actor and director.

Appeared in: **1918** Masterkatten i Stovlar (Puss in Boots). **1930** Roeda Dagen (Red Day); Longing For the Sea. **1937** Happy Vestkoping.

BRUNIUS, PAULINE
Born: 1881, France. Died: 1954, France? Screen actress.

Appeared in: **1922** Give Me My Son. **1932** Charlotte Loewenskoeld. **1938** Karl Fredrik Reigns.

BRUNO, JOE
Born: 1922. Died: June 9, 1977. Screen actor.

BRUNOT, ANDRE
Born: 1880, France. Died: Aug. 6, 1973, Paris, France. Screen and stage actor.

Appeared in: **1939** The Curtain Rises. **1940** Hotel du Nord. **1941** Personal Column. **1948** Portrait of Innocence. **1957** The Virtuous Scoundrel. **1958** Rouge et Noir (The Red and the Black). **1960** Picnic on the Grass. **1962** Maxine.

BRUNSKILL, MURIEL
Born: 1900, England. Died: Feb. 20, 1980, London, England. Opera singer and screen actress. Married to conductor Robert Ainsworth (dec. 1947).

Appeared in: **1953** Gilbert and Sullivan.

BRUNTON, DOROTHY
Born: Oct. 14, 1893, Melbourne, Australia. Died: June 5, 1977, Sydney, Australia. Screen and stage actress.

Appeared in: **1934** Clara Gibbings.

BRUNTON, WILLIAM "BILLIE"
Born: Mar. 13, 1883, Canada. Died: Feb. 19, 1965. Screen, stage and vaudeville actor. Married to actress Luella Maxam (dec. 1970).

Appeared in: **1916** Whispering Smith; Medicine Bend. **1917** The Railroad Raiders (serial); The Lost Express (serial). **1918** The Squaw Man; Cruise of the Make Believe. **1919** Valley of the Giants; As the Sun Went Down. **1920** The Tiger Band (serial). **1921** The Mad Marriage. **1922** The Lady From Longacre.

BRYAN, ARTHUR Q.
Born: 1899. Died: Nov. 30, 1959, Hollywood, Calif. Screen, television and radio actor.

Appeared in: **1932** The Big Shop; Fast Life; The Mummy. **1933** 20,000 Years in Sing Sing; Tonight Is Ours; Gabriel Over the White House; The Silk Empress; Mayor of Hell; Private Detective 62; College Coach. **1934** House of Rothschild; Two Alone; Fog Over Frisco; The Notorious Sophie Lang; The Man With Two Faces; That's Gratitude!; The President Vanishes; Marie Gallante. **1935** Secret Brides; The Casino Murder Case; Shadow of a Doubt; The Whole Town's Talking; Oil for the Lamps of China; Murder in the Fleet. **1936** Prisoner of Shark Island. **1939** Little Accident. **1940** Road to Singapore; South of the Boudoir (short); Millionaire Playboy. **1941** Devil Bat. **1943** Swing Out the Blues. **1944** Mopey Dope (short); I'm from Arkansas. **1946** Idea Girl; Dark Horse. **1947** Road to Rio. **1949** Samson and Delilah. **1954** Broken Lance. **1955** Hell's Outpost. **1956** The Lieutenant Wore Skirts.

BRYAN, GEORGE
Born: 1910. Died: June 27, 1969, New York. Radio announcer, screen and radio actor.

Appeared in: **1948** Will It Happen Again? (narrator). **1957** Lost Continent (narrator). **1961** Ritual of Love (narrator).

BRYAN, JACKSON "JACK" LEE
Born: 1909. Died: Sept. 14, 1964, Hollywood, Calif. (following surgery). Screen, stage and television actor.

BRYANT, CHARLES
Born: 1879, England. Died: Aug. 7, 1948, Mt. Kisco, N.Y. Screen, stage actor, film director and stage producer. Divorced from actress Alla Nazimova (dec. 1945).

Appeared in: **1918** Eye for Eye; Revelation. **1919** The Brat; Out of the Fog; The Red Lantern. **1920** Stronger Than Death; Heart of a Child.

BRYANT, J. V.
Born: May 26, 1889, Ayr, Scotland. Died: Mar. 2, 1924, ›England? Screen and stage actor.

Appeared in: **1915** Sweet Lavender.

BRYANT, MARGUERITE
Died: Jan., 1951, Brooklyn, N.Y. Screen and stage actress. Appeared in silents.

BRYANT, MARIE
Born: 1919, New Orleans, La. Died: May 23, 1978, Los Angeles, Calif. (cancer). Black screen, stage, television actress, band singer and choreographer.

Appeared in: **1948** The Twisted Road; They Live By Night. **1950** Wabash Avenue. **1952** Return of Gilbert and Sullivan. **1955** Cross-Up.

BRYANT, NANA
Born: 1888, Cincinnati, Ohio. Died: Dec. 24, 1955, Hollywood, Calif. Screen, stage and television actress.

Appeared in: **1935** Guard That Girl (film debut); Crime and Punishment; Unknown Woman; One Way Ticket; A Feather in Her Hat. **1936** Lady of Secrets; The Blackmailer; The Lone Wolf Returns; You May Be Next; The King Steps Out; The Man Who Lived Twice; Theodora Goes Wild; Pennies from Heaven; Meet Nero Wolf; Panic on the Air. **1937** Let's Get Married; The League of Frightened Men; The Devil Is Driving; Counsel for Crime. **1938** Man Proof; Midnight Intruder; Mad About Music; The Adventures of Tom Sawyer; Sinners in Paradise; Swing, Sister, Swing; Give Me a Sailor; Always in Trouble; Out West With the Hardys; Peck's Bad Boy With the Circus. **1939** Espionage Agent; Streets of Missing Men; Parents on Trial; Our Neighbors, the Carters. **1940** Brother Rat and the Baby; If I Had My Way; A Little Bit of Heaven; Father Is a Prince. **1941** Thieves Fall Out; Nice Girl?; One Foot in Heaven; Public Enemies; The Corsican Brothers. **1942** Youth on Parade; Thunder Birds; Calling Dr. Gillespie; Get Hep to Love; The Reluctant Dragon (voice); Madam Spy. **1943** The West Side Kid; Hangmen Also Die; Get Going; The Song of Bernadette; Princess O'Rourke. **1944** The Adventures of Mark Twain; Take It or Leave It; Bathing Beauty; Jungle Woman; Marriage Is a Private Affair. **1945** Black Market Babies; Weekend at the Waldorf; Brewster's Millions. **1946** The Virginian; The Runaround. **1947** The Perfect Marriage; Millie's Daughter; Big Town; The Big Fix; Possessed; Her Husband's Affair; The Hal Roach Comedy Carnival; The Unsuspected; The Fabulous Joe. **1948** On Our Merry Way; Stage Struck; The Eyes of Texas; Lady at Midnight; Dangerous Years; Return of October; Inner Sanctum. **1949** Hideout; State Department File-649; Ladies of the Chorus; The Lady Gambles. **1950** Let's Dance; Key to the City; The Blonde Bandit; Modern Marriage; Harvey. **1951** Follow the Sun; Bright Victory; Only the Valiant. **1954** About Mrs. Leslie; The Outcast; Geraldine. **1955** The Private War of Major Benson.

BRYANT, ROBIN
Born: 1926, Evanston, Ill. Died: Jan. 18, 1976, Arlington, Tex. Screen, stage and radio actress.

Appeared in: **1947** Boomerang; The Senator Was Indiscreet. **1948** A Portrait of Jenny.

BRYDONE, ALFRED (Alfred Brydone Boark)
Born: Dec. 9, 1863, Edinburgh, Scotland. Died: Nov. 26, 1920, England? Screen and stage actor.

Appeared in: **1911** Richard III.

BUCHANAN, EDGAR (William Edgar Buchanan)
Born: Mar. 20, 1903, Humansville, Mo. Died: Apr. 4, 1979, Palm Desert, Calif. Screen, television actor and dentist.

Appeared in: **1940** My Son is Guilty (film debut); Three Cheers for the Irish; The Sea Hawk; Too Many Husbands; Tear Gas Squad; The Doctor Takes a Wife; When the Daltons Rode. **1941** Submarine Zone (aka Escape to Glory); You Belong to Me; Her First Beau; Richest Man in Town; Penny Serenade; Texas. **1942** Tombstone, The Town too Tough to Die; The Talk of the Town. **1943** Good Luck, Mr. Yates; Destroyer; City Without Men; The Desperadoes. **1944** Bride by Mistake; The Impatient Years; Strange Affair; Buffalo Bill. **1945** The Fighting Guardsman. **1946** Abilene Town; The Bandit of Sherwood Forest; Perilous Holiday; Renegades; If I'm Lucky; The Walls Came Tumbling Down. **1947** The Sea of Grass; Framed; The Swordsman. **1948** The Untamed Breed; The Black Arrow; Adventures in Silverado; Best Man Wins; The Wreck of the Hesperus; Coroner Creek; The Man From Colorado. **1949** Any Number Can Play; Lust for Gold; The Walking Hills; Red Canyon. **1950** The Big Hangover; The Great Missouri Raid; Cargo to Capetown; Devil's Doorway; Cheaper By the Dozen. **1951** Rawhide; The Cave of the Outlaws; Flaming Feather; Silver City. **1952** The Big Trees; Toughest Man in Arizona; Wild Stallion. **1953** It Happens Every Thursday; Shane. **1954** Dawn at Socorro; Destry; Human Desire; Make Haste to Live; She Couldn't Say No. **1955** The Lonesome Trail; Rage at Dawn; Wichita. **1956** Come Next Spring. **1957** Spoilers of the Forest. **1958** The Sheepman; Day of the Bad Man. **1959** Four Fast Guns; Edge of Eternity; Hound-Dog Man; It Started With a Kiss; King of the Wild Stallions. **1960** Chartroose Caboose; Cimarron; Stump Run. **1961** The Comancheros; Tammy, Tell Me True. **1962** The Devil's Partner; Ride the High Country. **1963** McLintock!; Move Over, Darling; A Ticklish Affair; Donovan's Reef. **1965** The Rounders; The Man From Button Willow (voice only). **1966** Gunpoint. **1967** Welcome to Hard Times. **1969** Angel in My Pocket. **1974** Benji.

BUCHANAN, JACK
Born: Apr. 2, 1891, Glasgow, Scotland. Died: Oct. 20, 1957, London, England (spinal arthritis). Screen, stage, television actor, screenwriter, stage director, film producer and director.

Appeared in: **1917** Auld Lang Syne. **1919** Her Heritage. **1923** The Audacious Mr. Squire. **1925** Bulldog Drummond's Third Round (aka The Third Round); Settled Out of Court (aka Evidence Enclosed); The Happy Ending. **1927** Confetti. **1928** Toni. **1929** Paris; The Show of Shows. **1930** The Glee Quartette (short); Monte Carlo. **1931** Man of Mayfair. **1932** Goodnight Vienna (aka Magic Night—US). **1933** Yes Mr. Brown; That's a Good Girl. **1935** Brewster's Millions; Come Out of the Pantry. **1936** When Knights Were Bold (US 1942); This'll Make You Whistle (US 1938); Limelight (aka Backstage—US). **1937** Smash and Grab; The Sky's the Limit. **1938** Break the News (US 1941); Cavalcade of the Stars. **1939** The Gang's All Here (aka The Amazing Mr. Forrest—US); The Middle Watch. **1940** Bulldog Sees It Through. **1952** Giselle (short—voice). **1953** The Bank Wagon. **1955** Josephine and Men; As Long as They're Happy (US 1957). **1957** The French Are a Funny Race (aka The French They Are a Funny Race). **1974** That's Entertainment (film clips).

BUCHANAN, MEG (Margaret Buchanan)
Born: Scotland. Died: July, 1970, Uddingston, Scotland. Screen, stage and radio actress.

Appeared in: **1952** The Brave Don't Cry. **1954** The Maggie (aka High and Dry—US).

BUCHANAN, STUART
Born: 1894. Died: Feb. 4, 1974, Cleveland, Ohio. Screen, radio actor, radio, television director and announcer. One of the founders of American Federation of Radio Artists.

Appeared in: **1937** Snow White and the Seven Dwarfs (voice of Grumpy).

BUCK, ELIZABETH
Born: 1912. Died: Mar. 31, 1934, Van Nuys, Calif. (hit by auto). Screen dancer.

BUCK, FORD (Ford Lee Washington)
Died: Jan. 31, 1955, New York, N.Y. Black screen, stage and radio comedian.

BUCK, FRANK
Born: Mar. 17, 1888, Gainesville, Tex. Died: Mar. 25, 1950, Houston, Tex. (lung ailment). Screen actor, circus performer, film director and producer.

Appeared in: **1932** Bring 'Em Back Alive. **1934** Wild Cargo. **1935** Fang and Claw. **1937** Jungle Menace (serial). **1943** Jacare. **1949** Africa Screams.

BUCK, INEZ
Born: 1890, Oetrichs, S.Dak. Died: Sept. 6, 1957, Oakland, Calif. Screen and stage actress. Entered films with Lubin Studios.
Appeared in: **1915** Sorrows of Happiness.

BUCK, NELL ROY
Born: 1911. Died: Feb. 28, 1962, Van Nuys, Calif. (auto accident). Screen and stage actor.
Appeared in: **1922** Forever.

BUCKLAND, VEDA
Born: Apr. 25, 1882, Montreal, Canada. Died: May 20, 1941. Screen actor.
Appeared in: **1930** The Texan; This Mad World; The Right to Love. **1932** Sinners in the Sun. **1933** Doctor Bull. **1935** Mystery of Edwin Drood.

BUCKLER, HUGH
Born: 1870, Southgate, England. Died: Oct., 1936, Lake Malibu, Calif. (auto accident). Screen and stage actor. Father of actor John Buckler (dec. 1936).
Appeared in: **1919** The Garden of Resurrection. **1920** Duke's Son; The Lure of the Crooning Water. **1931** A Gentleman of France; The Place of Honour. **1923** Guy Fawkes. **1936** Crash Donovan; The Last of the Mohicans; The Jungle Princess. **1937** Lost Horizon.

BUCKLER, JOHN
Born: 1896, London, England. Died: Oct. 30, 1936, Lake Malibu, Calif. (auto accident). Stage and screen actor. Son of actor Hugh Buckler (dec. 1936).
Appeared in: **1935** David Copperfield; Eight Bells; Black Room Mystery. **1936** Tarzan Escapes; The Unguarded Hour.

BUCKLEY, FLOYD
Born: 1874. Died: Nov. 14, 1956, New York, N.Y. (heart attack). Screen, stage, vaudeville, radio actor, film producer, director and stuntman.
Appeared in the following serials: **1914** Exploits of Elaine. **1916** Pearl of the Army. **1917** The Fatal Ring; Patria; The Seven Pearls. **1918** The House of Hate. **1919** The Fatal Fortune; The Master Mystery.

BUCKLEY, JOSEPH
Born: 1875. Died: Dec. 2, 1930, Van Nuys, Calif. Screen actor.

BUCKO, BUCK
Born: 1892. Died: Aug. 6, 1962, Yakima, Wa. Screen, television actor and stuntman. Entered films in 1921.
Appeared in: **1930** Code of the West.

BUCKSTONE, ROWLAND
Born: Mar. 29, 1860, Syndeham, Kent, England. Died: Sept. 13, 1922, London, England. Screen and stage actor.

BUFFALO, BILL, JR. *See* WILSEY, JAY
Appeared in: **1916** An Enemy to the King.

BUCQUET, HAROLD S.
Born: 1891, England. Died: Feb. 13, 1946, Hollywood, Calif. Screen actor and film director. Entered films as an extra.

BUDLONG, JACK
Born: 1911. Died: July 30, 1941, Hollywood, Calif. (injuries received while filming "They Died With Their Boots On"). Screen actor.

BUEHLER, ARTHUR
Born: 1894. Died: Dec. 1, 1962, Los Angeles, Calif. Screen actor.

BUEL, KENNAN
Born: 1873, Kentucky. Died: Nov. 5, 1948, New York, N.Y. Screen actor and film director. Appeared in early Kalen Film Company films.

BUFFALO BILL *See* CODY, COLONEL WILLIAM FREDERICK

BUFFALO MAN, FRANK WHITE
Born: 1903. Died: Mar. 18, 1977, Milwaukee, Wis. Screen actor. Grandson of Chief Sitting Bull (dec. 1890).
Appeared in: **1970** A Man Called Horse.

BUFFINGTON, SAM
Born: 1932. Died: May 15, 1960. Screen actor.
Appeared in: **1957** Invasion of the Saucer Men. **1958** The Brothers Karamazov; The Light in the Forest; The Rawhide Trail; Damn Citizen; Unwed Mother. **1959** Blue Denim; They Came to Cordura.

BUHLER, RICHARD
Born: 1876, Washington, D.C. Died: Mar. 27, 1925, Washington, D.C. Screen and stage actor. Entered films with Lubin Co. in 1913.
Appeared in: **1915** The Rights of Man; A Man's Making. **1916** Gods of Fate.

BUKHARI, MANSOOR S.
Born: 1957. Died: Apr., 1979, Bombay, India (result of burns while filming). Screen actor and stuntman.

BULGAKOV, LEO
Born: Mar. 22, 1889, Moscow, Russia. Died: July 20, 1948, Binghamton, N.Y. Screen, stage actor, stage director, film producer and director.
Appeared in: **1943** This Land Is Mine; For Whom the Bell Tolls. **1944** Song of Russia; And Now Tomorrow. **1945** A Royal Scandal.

BULLOCK, DICK
Died: Dec. 1, 1971, Kans. (hit by auto). Screen actor/stuntman.
Appeared in: **1969** Hell's Belles. **1972** The Culpepper Cattle Company; Bad Company.

BUMP, EDMOND
Born: 1877. Died: Nov. 6, 1938, Hollywood, Calif. Stage and screen actor.

BUMPAS, H. W. "BOB"
Born: 1911. Died: Dec. 9, 1959, Gulf of Mexico (airline crash). Screen, stage, television actor, screenwriter and radio writer.
Appeared in: **1951** The Big Carnival.

BUNCE, ALAN
Born: 1903, Westfield, N.J. Died: Apr. 27, 1965, New York, N.Y. Screen, stage, radio and television actor.
Appeared in: **1930** She's My Weakness. **1959** The Last Mile. **1960** Sunrise at Campobello. **1961** Homicidal.

BUNKER, RALPH
Born: 1889, Boston, Mass. Died: Apr. 28, 1966, New York, N.Y. (stroke). Screen and stage actor.
Appeared in: **1931** Scrambled Wives. **1922** That Woman. **1924** Another Scandal. **1936** The Ghost Goes West. **1947** The Hucksters. **1948** The Naked City.

BUNNY, GEORGE
Born: 1870, New York, N.Y. Died: Apr. 16, 1952, Hollywood, Calif. (heart attack). Screen and stage actor. Brother of actor John Bunny (dec. 1915).
Appeared in: **1921** "If Only" Jim; Danger Ahead. **1922** The Super Sex. **1925** The Dark Angel; The Lost World; Enticement; Lights of Old Broadway. **1926** Thrilling Youth. **1927** Tender Hour; Laddie Be Good. **1928** Breed of the Sunsets; Heroes in Blue; The Love Mart. **1929** The Man and the Moment; The Locked Door.

BUNNY, GEORGE
Born: 1893. Died: Dec. 8, 1958, Hollywood, Calif. (apartment house fire). Screen actor. Son of actor John Bunny (dec. 1915). Brother of actor John Bunny, Jr. (dec. 1971). Do not confuse with actor George Bunny (dec. 1952).

BUNNY, JOHN
Born: Sept. 21, 1863, New York, N.Y. Died: Apr. 26, 1915, Brooklyn, N.Y. (Bright's disease). Screen, stage, vaudeville actor and stage director. Brother of actor George Bunny (dec. 1952). Father of actors George (dec. 1958) and John Bunny (dec. 1971). Entered films with Vitagraph in 1910. He made 260 shorts with Flora Finch (dec. 1940) between 1910 and 1915. They appeared as Mr. and Mrs. Bunny and/or Mr. and Mrs. Brown, and fans referred to these shorts as "Bunnygraphs," "Bunnyfinches" and "Bunnyfinchgraphs." See Flora Finch regarding the films they appeared in together.

Other films he appeared in: **1910** Jack Fat and Jim Slim at Coney Island (film debut); He Who Laughs; Cupid and the Motor Boat. **1911** Doctor Cupid; A Queen for a Day; Captain Barnacle's Courtship; The Widow Visits Springtown; An Unexpected Review; Winsor McCay's Drawings; In the Arctic Night; The Return of "Widow" Pogson's Husband; Treasure Trove; Intrepid Davy; The Wrong Patient; Her Sister's Children; Ups and Downs; Kitty and the Cowboys; Madge of the Mountains; The Gossip; In the Clutches of a Vapor Bath; The

Leading Lady; Vanity Fair; The Old Doll; The Latent Spark; The Hundred Dollar Bill; Captain Barnacle's Baby; The Tired Absent-Minded Man; Her Hero; The Missing Will; Hypnotizing the Hypnotist; A Slight Mistake; Bachelor Buttons. **1912** The Suit of Armor; The First Violin; His Mother-in-Law; The Unknown Violinist; Burnt Cork; Leap Year Proposals; Chased By Bloodhounds; A Persistent Lover; Lovesick Maidens of Cuddleton; Cork and Vicinity; Ida's Christmas; The Troublesome Stepdaughters; Chumps; Who Stole Bunny's Umbrella?; Captain Jack's Dilemma; Captain Barnacle's Messmate; I Deal, the Diver; The Honeymooners; Mr. Bolter's Infatuation; At Scrogginess Corner; Captain Jenks' Diplomacy; Working for Hubby; Who's to Win?; An Eventful Elopement; Bunny of the Derby; Bunny and the Dogs; Michael McShane, Matchmaker. **1913** Mr. Bolter's Niece; The Three Black Bags; Ma's Apron Strings; And His Wife Came Back; The Man Higher Up; Seeing Double; Bunny and the Bunny Hug (aka Bunny Dips Into Society); A Millinary Bomb; John Tobin's Sweetheart; Autocrat of Flapjack Junction; Bunny's Mistake; Bunny for the Cause; Flaming Hearts; Suspicious Henry; Bunny Blarneyed; The Fortune; Bunny's Honeymoon; Bunny Versus Cutey; Bunny as a Reporter; His Tired Uncle; One Good Joke Deserves Another; The Pirates; Pickwick Papers series including: The Honourable Event, The Adventure of Westgate Seminary and the Adventure of the Shooting Party. **1914** The Misadventures of a Mighty Monarch; Bunny's Mistake; Mr. Bunny in Disguise; Pigs Is Pigs; The Locked House; Personal Introductions; Bachelor Buttons; Bunny Attempts Suicide; Love, Luck and Gasoline; Setting the Style; Sheep's Clothing. **1915** Bunny at Bunnyland; To John Bunny's.

BUNNY, JOHN FRANCIS, JR.
Born: 1895. Died: Apr. 16, 1971, Hollywood, Calif. Screen actor. Son of actor John Bunny (dec. 1915). Brother of actor George (dec. 1958). Appeared in early silents.

BUNSTON, HERBERT
Born: 1874. Died: Feb. 27, 1935, Los Angeles, Calif. (heart attack). Screen and stage actor.

Appeared in: **1929** The Last of Mrs. Cheyney. **1930** The Lady of Scandal. **1931** Dracula; Always Good-Bye; Once a Lady. **1932** Charlie Chan's Chance; File No. 113. **1933** Trick for Trick. **1934** Long Lost Father; Doctor Monica; The Richest Girl in the World; The Little Minister. **1935** A Shot in the Dark; Cardinal Richelieu; After Office Hours; Clive of India.

BUQUOR, ROBERT
Born: 1935. Died: July 27, 1966, Malibu, Calif. (parachute failed to open while filming Don't Make Waves). Screen actor/stuntman.

Appeared in: **1967** Don't Make Waves.

BURANI, MICHELETTE
Born: 1882, Paris, France. Died: Oct. 27, 1957, Eastchester, N.Y. Screen, stage, opera, radio and television actress.

Appeared in: **1926** Aloma of the South Seas. **1935** Enter Madame; The Gilded Lily. **1936** Give Us This Night. **1938** Fools for Scandal; Everybody Sing.

BURBANK, GOLDIE
Born: 1880. Died: Mar. 1, 1954, Toledo, Ohio. Screen and vaudeville actress. Appeared in vaudeville as part of "Melville Sisters" and later as part of "Sutherland Sisters" acts. Was in films from 1910 to 1913.

BURCH, BETTY EVANS
Born: 1888. Died: May 30, 1956, Pasadena, Calif. Screen actress.

BURCH, JOHN
Born: Aug. 17, 1896, Chicago, Ill. Died: July 29, 1969, Honolulu, Hawaii. Screen actor, film and television director.

Appeared in: **1925** White Fang. **1947** Great Expectations.

BURCHILL, WILLIAM
Born: England. Died: Apr. 1, 1930, England? Screen and stage actor.

Appeared in: **1920** Lady Audley's Secret; The Manchester Man.

BURGESS, DOROTHY
Born: Mar. 4, 1907, Los Angeles, Calif. Died: Aug. 20, 1961. Screen and stage actress.

Appeared in: **1929** In Old Arizona; Pleasure Crazed; Protection; Song of Kentucky; Beyond Victory. **1930** Recaptured Love; Swing High; Lasca of the Rio Grande; Cleopatra; The Voice of Hollywood (short series in 1930 and 1931). **1931** Oh! Oh! Cleopatra (short). **1932** The Stoker; Malay Nights; Taxi; Play Girl; Out of Singapore. **1933** Strictly Personal; Ladies They Talk About; What Price Decency; I Love That Man; Hold Your Man; It's Great to Be Alive; The Important Witness; Easy Millions; Rusty Rides Alone; Headline Shooter; Ladies Must Love; From Headquarters. **1934** Fashions of 1934; Orient Express; Miss Fane's Baby Is Stolen; A Modern Hero; Black Moon; The Circus Clown; Registered Nurse; Affairs of a Gentleman; Hat, Coat and Glove; Friends of Mr. Sweeney; Gambling. **1935** Village Tale; Manhattan Butterfly. **1940** I Want a Divorce; The Lady in Question. **1941** Lady For a Night. **1942** The Lone Star Ranger. **1943** Man of Courage; Girls in Chains.

BURGESS, GLADYS
Born: 1900, England? Died: Jan. 22, 1933, New York, N.Y. Screen and stage actress.

BURGESS, HAZEL
Born: 1910. Died: Dec. 11, 1973, Hollywood, Calif. (following surgery). Screen actress. Entered films in 1936 as an extra and stand-in.

BURGESS, HELEN
Born: 1918. Died: Apr. 7, 1937, Beverly Hills, Calif. (lobar pneumonia). Stage and screen actress.

Appeared in: **1936** The Plainsman. **1937** A Doctor's Diary; King of Gamblers; A Night of Mystery.

BURGESS, MAYNARD
Born: 1901. Died: May 5, 1976, Niagara Falls, N.Y. Screen actor and stage director.

Appeared in: **1930** The Forest Ring.

BURGESS, WILLIAM
Born: 1867. Died: Oct. 30, 1948. Screen actor.

Appeared in: **1935** The Story of Louis Pasteur. **1936** After the Thin Man. **1937** Wild Money.

BURGHER, FAIRFAX
Born: 1897. Died: Sept. 29, 1965, New York, N.Y. Screen and stage actor.

BURIAN, VLASTA
Born: 1891. Died: Feb. 5, 1962, Prague, Czechoslovakia. Screen and stage actor. Barred from appearing in public for ten years after W.W. II for allegedly collaborating with Nazis.

Appeared in: **1931** Versuchen Sie Meine Schwester. **1932** Der Falsche Felmarschall. **1934** Der Adjutant Seiner Hoheit. **1937** The Inspector General.

BURKE, BILLIE (Mary William Ethelberg Appleton Burke)
Born: Aug. 7, 1885, Washington, D.C. Died: May 14, 1970, Los Angeles, Calif. Screen, stage, radio and television actress. Daughter of circus clown Billy Burke (dec.). Married to stage producer Flo Ziegfeld (dec. 1932). Nominated for 1938 Academy Award for Best Supporting Actress for Merrily We Live.

Appeared in: **1915** Peggy. **1916** Gloria's Romance (serial). **1917** The Land of Promise; The Mysterious Miss Terry; Arms and the Girl; The Runaway. **1918** Eve's Daughter; Let's Get a Divorce; In Pursuit of Polly; The Make-Believe Wife. **1919** Good Gracious, Annabelle; Wanted—A Husband; The Misleading Widow; Sadie Love. **1920** Away Goes Prudence. **1921** The Education of Elizabeth; Frisky Mrs. Johnson. **1930** Ranch House Blues (short). **1932** A Bill of Divorcement. **1933** Dinner at Eight; Only Yesterday; Christopher Strong. **1934** Forsaking All Others; Finishing School; We're Rich Again; Where Sinners Meet. **1935** Becky Sharp; Society Doctor; After Office Hours; Doubting Thomas; She Couldn't Take It; Splendor; A Feather in Her Hat. **1936** Craig's Wife; My American Wife; Piccadilly Jim. **1937** Topper; Navy, Blue and Gold; The Bride Wore Red; Parnell. **1938** Merrily We Live; Everybody Sing; The Young in Heart. **1939** The Wizard of Oz; Topper Takes a Trip; Bridal Suite; Remember?; Eternally Yours; Zenobia. **1940** The Captain Is a Lady; The Ghost Comes Home; And One Was Beautiful; Irene; Dulcy; Hullabaloo. **1941** Topper Returns; The Man Who Came to Dinner; Wild Man of Borneo; One Night in Lisbon. **1942** In This Our Life; They All Kissed the Bride; Girl Trouble; What's Cooking?. **1943** Hi Diddle Diddle; So's Your Uncle; Gildersleeve on Broadway; You're a Lucky Fellow, Mr. Smith. **1944** Laramie Trail. **1945** Swing Out, Sister; The Cheaters. **1946** Breakfast in Hollywood; The Bachelor Daughter. **1948** Silly Billy (short); Billie Gets Her Man (short). **1949** The Barkleys of Broadway. **1950** Father of the Bride; Three Husbands; The Boy from Indiana; And Baby Makes Three. **1951** Father's Little Dividend; Darling, How Could You. **1953** Small Town Girl. **1959** The Young Philadelphians. **1960** Sgt. Rutledge; Pepe.

BURKE, J. FRANK
Born: Apr., 1867, Hartland, Vt. Died: Jan. 23, 1918, Los Angeles, Calif. (arteriosclerosis). Screen, stage and vaudeville actor.

Appeared in: **1915** The Ace of Hearts; The Toast of Death; Aloha Oe. **1916** The Beckoning Flame; The Waifs; The No-Good Guy; The Vagabond Prince; The Dawn Maker. **1917** The Iced Bullet; Bawbs o' Blue Ridge; Princess of the Dark; The Square Deal Man. **1918** The Bargain.

BURKE, JAMES
Born: 1886, New York, N.Y. Died: May 28, 1968, Los Angeles, Calif. Screen, stage and vaudeville actor. Married to actress Elinor Durkin (dec.); they appeared in vaudeville together in an act billed as "Burke and Durkin."

Appeared in: **1929** Tete-a-Tete in Songs (short with Durkin). **1932** Hollywood Handicap. **1933** The Kennel Murder Case; Torch Singer; A Lady's Profession; Girl in 419; College Humor; To the Last Man; Lady Killer. **1934** Good Dame; Little Miss Marker; Wharf Angel; City Limits; Treasure Island; Scarlet Empress; Love Time; The Lemon Drop Kid; Lady By Choice; Six of a Kind; It's a Gift; It Happened One Night. **1935** Rumba; The Case of the Missing Man; Hot Money (short); Ruggles of Red Gap; Mystery Man; Mississippi; Dinky; Call of the Wild; Make a Million; Here Comes Cookie; Affairs of Susan; Coronado; Frisco Waterfront; Man on the Flying Trapeze; Welcome Home; Broadway Gondolier; So Red the Rose. **1936** Trail of the Lonesome Pine; Rhythm on the Range; 36 Hours to Kill; Can This Be Dixie; Song and Dance Man; Dancing Feet; The Leathernecks Have Landed; Klondike Annie; Forgotten Faces; Old Dutch; The Great Guy. **1937** Champagne Waltz; Laughing at Trouble; Dead End; High, Wide and Handsome; The Perfect Specimen; Life Begins With Love. **1938** The Mad Miss Manton; Dawn Patrol; The Joy of Living; Flight Into Nowhere; Affairs of Annabel; Men With Wings; Orphans of the Street; Little Orphan Annie. **1939** Dodge City; I'm from Missouri; The Saint Strikes Back; Within the Law; On Borrowed Time; Beau Geste; At the Circus; Fast and Furious. **1940** The Way of All Flesh; No Time for Comedy; The Cisco Kid and the Lady; Double Alibi; Charlie Chan's Murder Cruise; Buck Benny Rides Again; Opened By Mistake; The Saint Takes Over; The Golden Fleecing; Little Nellie Kelly; Ellery Queen, Master Detective. **1941** The Maltese Falcon; Pot O' Gold; Ellery Queen's Penthouse Mystery; Ellery Queen and the Perfect Crime; Ellery Queen and the Murder Ring; Reaching for the Sun; Million Dollar Baby. **1942** Are Husbands Necessary?; Close Call for Ellery Queen; It Happened in Flatbush; Enemy Agents Against Ellery Queen; Army Surgeon; All Through the Night. **1943** A Night to Remember; Riding High; No Place for a Lady; Dixie. **1944** Casanova Brown; Three Men in White. **1945** Anchors Aweigh; The Horn Blows at Midnight; I Love a Bandleader; Shady Lady; How Do You Do. **1946** Young Widow; Two Years Before the Mast; Bowery Bombshell; California; The Virginian. **1947** The Gashouse Kids in Hollywood; Easy Come, Easy Go; Philo Vance's Gamble; Body and Soul; Down to Earth; Nightmare Alley; Blaze of Noon. **1948** Texas, Brooklyn and Heaven; The Timber Trail; Night Wind; June Bride. **1949** Shamrock Hill. **1950** Mrs. O'Malley and Mr. Malone; Copper Canyon. **1951** His Kind of Woman; Raton Pass; The Last Outpost. **1952** We're Not Married; Denver and Rio Grande; Lone Star. **1953** Arrowhead. **1954** Lucky Me. **1955** You're Never Too Young. **1956** The Birds and the Bees. **1957** Public Pigeon No. 1; The Unholy Wife. **1962** Geronimo. **1965** The Hallelujah Trail.

BURKE, JOSEPH
Born: 1884, New York, N.Y. Died: Dec. 17, 1942, New York, N.Y. Screen, stage and vaudeville actor. Do not confuse with actor Joe Burke.

Appeared in: **1918** Kidnapped; Independence, By Gosh. **1920** The Fortune Teller; Heritage; The Perfect Woman. **1921** Worlds Apart; Princess Jones; The Wakefield Case. **1922** The Prophet's Paradise. **1923** His Children's Children; The White Rose. **1924** The Law and the Lady; Two Shall Be Born; Pied Piper Malone; West of the Water Tower. **1925** The Adventurous Sex; The Fool; Lucky Devil; The Pinch Hitter; Share and Share Alike; Too Many Kisses. **1926** Fascinating Youth; Striving for Fortune; The Kick-Off. **1928** Hangman's House; Manhattan Knights; Obey Your Husband; South of Panama. **1929** The Royal Rider; The Show of Shows.

BURKE, KATHLEEN
Born: Sept. 5, 1913, Hammond, Ind. Died: Apr. 9, 1980, Chicago, Ill. Screen actress.

Appeared in: **1933** Island of Lost Souls (film debut); Murders in the Zoo; Sunset Pass; Torch Singer; Mad Game. **1934** Good Dame; Bulldog Drummond Strikes Back; School for Girls; Six of a Kind. **1935** Nevada; Rocky Mountain; Awakening Mystery of Jim Burke; Mutiny Ahead; Beauty's Daughter; The Lives of a Bengal Lancer; The Last Outpost. **1936** Craig's Wife. **1937** The Sheik Steps Out; Boy of the Streets. **1938** Rascals.

BURKE, MARTIN
Born: 1895. Died: Sept. 18, 1978, Palm Springs, Calif. Boxer and screen actor. Father of actor Paul Burke.

Appeared in: **1976** One Summer Love.

BURKE, THOMAS F.
Died: Mar. 25, 1941, Los Angeles, Calif. Screen actor.

Appeared in: **1932** Carmen. **1938** Kathleen; Father O'Flynn.

BURKE, TOM
Born: 1890, Leigh, Lancashire, England. Died: Sept. 14, 1969, Carshalton, England. Screen actor and opera singer.

Appeared in: **1935** Father O'Flynn (US 1938). **1937** Kathleen Mavourneen (aka Kathleen—US 1938). **1938** My Irish Molly (aka Little Miss Molly—US 1940).

BURKHARD, CHARLES
Died: Feb., 1927. Screen actor.

BURKHARD, MONTE
Died: Aug., 1976. Screen actor.

Appeared in: **1960** Flaming Star (aka Black Star, Flaming Heart and Flaming Lance). **1961** Gun Fight.

BURKHARDT, HARRY
Born: Sept. 27, 1890, Boston, Mass. Died: Sept. 18, 1943, Los Angeles, Calif. Screen and stage actor.

Appeared in: **1915** The Soul of Broadway; The Closing Net; The Right of Way. **1916** The Ruling Passion; The Marble Heart; The Masked Rider; The Prima Donna's Husband; The Stolen Triumph; The Ruling Claw (serial). **1921** A Millionaire for a Day. **1930** Captain of the Guard. **1934** Are We Civilized?

BURLANDO, CLAUDE
Born: 1918. Died: Sept. 25, 1938, Hollywood, Calif. (traffic injuries). Screen actor and extra.

BURMASTER, AUGUSTA
Born: 1860, Hamburg, Germany. Died: Mar. 28, 1934, Los Angeles Calif. Screen actress.

Appeared in: **1915** Stop Thief. **1917** Mary Moreland. **1929** The Greene Murder Case.

BURNABY, DAVE "DAVY"
Born: Apr. 7, 1881, Buckland Herts, England. Died: Apr. 18, 1949, Angmering, Sussex, England. Screen, stage, radio actor, songwriter and author.

Appeared in: **1929** The Co-Optimists (US 1930). **1933** Just My Luck; The Wishbone; That's My Wife; Cleaning Up; Three Men In a Boat; Strike It Rich; A Shot In the Dark (US 1935); The Right to Live. **1934** On the Air; Murder At the Inn; The Man I Want; Keep It Quiet; How's Chances; Are You A Mason?; Radio Parade of 1935 (US 1935); Screen Vaudeville Number One (short). **1935** Equity Musical Revue series; Dandy Dick; Boys Will Be Boys; While Parents Sleep; We've Got to Have Love; When the Cat's Away. **1936** The Marriage of Corbal (aka Prisoner of Corbal—US 1939). **1937** Feather Your Nest; Leave It to Me; Song of the Forge; Calling All Stars; Talking Feet. **1938** Chips; Many Tanks Mr. Atkins; Second Best Bed; Kicking the Moon Around. **1939** The Diplomatic Lover (reissue of 1934 How's Chances); Come On George.

BURNE, NANCY
Born: 1913, England. Died: Mar. 25, 1954, Maidstone, England. Screen, stage and vaudeville actress.

Appeared in: **1933** Facing the Music (US 1934); The Love Nest; Little Napoleon. **1934** Song at Eventide; Irish Hearts (aka Norah O'Neale—US); The Warren Case. **1935** Trust the Navy; Lend Me Your Husband; Old Roses; Once a Thief; Royal Eagle. **1936** A Wife or Two; Reasonable Doubt; Skylarks. **1937** Thunder in the City; Knights for a Day; When the Poppies Bloom Again; Feather Your Nest. **1938** John Halifax, Gentleman. **1939** Flying Fifty Five.

BURNETT, AL
Born: 1906, England. Died: Apr. 19, 1973, London, England. Screen actor and comedian.

Appeared in: **1959** Sweet Beat (aka The Amorous Sex—US 1962).

BURNETT, CHESTER ARTHUR *See* HOWLIN' WOLF

BURNETTE, "SMILEY" (Lester Alvin Burnett)
Born: Mar. 18, 1911, Summum, Ill. Died: Feb. 16, 1967, Los Angeles, Calif. (leukemia). Screen, television, radio actor and songwriter. Married to screenwriter Dallas McDonald (dec. 1976). Entered films in 1934. Appeared in Roy Rogers, Gene Autry and Charles Starrett (as Durango Kid) series.

Appeared in: **1934** In Old Santa Fe; Mystery Mountain (serial). **1935** The Adventures of Rex and Rinty (serial); Tumbling Tumbleweeds; Waterfront Lady; Melody Trail; Sagebrush Troubadour; The Singing Vagabond; The Phantom Empire (serial); Hitch Hike Lady; Rex and Rinty; Streamline Express; Harmony Lane. **1936** Undersea Kingdom (serial); Doughnuts and Society; Hearts in Bondage; Oh, Susannah; Ride, Ranger, Ride; Comin' 'Round the Mountain; Red River Valley; The Singing Cowboy; Guns and Guitars; A Man Betrayed; The Border Patrolman. **1937** The Old Corral; The Big Show; Round Up Time in Texas; Springtime in the Rockies; Larceny on the Air; Dick Tracy (serial); Git Along Little Dogies; Rootin' Tootin' Rhythm; Yodelin' Kid from Pine Ridge; Meet the Boy Friend; Public Cowboy No. 1; Manhattan Merry-Go-Round; Boots and Saddles. **1938** Prairie Moon; The Old Barn Dance; Hollywood Stadium Mystery; Under Western Stars; Gold Mine in the Sky; Man from Music Mountain; Billy the Kid Returns; Rhythm of the Saddle; Western Jamboree. **1939** Home on the Prairie; Blue Montana Skies; Mountain Rhythm; Colorado Sunset; In Old Monterey; Rovin' Tumbleweeds; South of the Border; Mexicali Rose. **1940** Rancho Grande; Men With Steel Faces; Gaucho Serenade; Carolina Moon; Ride, Tenderfoot, Ride. **1941** Ridin' on a Rainbow; Back in the Saddle; The Singing Hill; Sunset in Wyoming; Under Fiesta Stars; Down Mexico Way; Sierra Sue. **1942** Cowboy Serenade; Heart of the Rio Grande; Home in Wyomin'; Stardust on the Sage; Call of the Canyon; Bells of Capistrano; Heart of the Golden West. **1943** Beyond the Last Frontier; Idaho; King of the Cowboys; Silver Spurs. **1944** Beneath Western Skies; The Laramie Trail; Call of the Rockies; Code of the Prairie; Pride of the Plains; Bordertown Trail; Firebrands of Arizona. **1946** The Desert Horseman; The Fighting Frontiersman; The Galloping Thunder; Gunning for Vengeance; Land Rush; Roaring Rangers; Two-Fisted Stranger; Hunting West. **1947** The Lone Hand Texan; Terror Trail; West of Dodge City; Law of the Canyon; Prairie Riders; Riders of the Lone Star; South of Chisholm Trail. **1948** Buckaroo from Powder River; Last Days of Boot Hill; Phantom Valley; Six-Gun Law; West of Sonora; Whirlwind Raiders; Trail to Laredo. **1949** Quick on the Trigger; Laramie; Eldorado Pass; Desert Vigilante; Challange of the Range; Horsemen of the Sierras; Blazing Trail; South of Death Valley; Bandits of El Dorado; Renegades of the Sage. **1950** Outcast of Black Mesa; Texas Dynamo; Trail of the Rustlers; Streets of Ghost Town; Across the Badlands; Raiders of Tomahawk Creek; Lightning Guns; Frontier Outpost. **1951** Whirlwind; Riding the Outlaw Trail; Prairie Roundup; Snake River Desperadoes; Fort Savage Raider; Bonanza Town; Cyclone Fury; The Kid from Amarillo; Pecos River. **1952** Smoky Canyon; The Hawk of Wild River; The Kid from Broken Gun; The Rough, Tough West; Junction City; Laramie Mountains. **1953** Winning of the West; Goldtown Ghost Riders; On Top of Old Smoky; Pack Train; Saginaw Trail; Last of the Pony Riders.

BURNEY, HAL (Harold Burmeister)
Born: 1900. Died: Nov. 11, 1933, Eureka, Calif. Screen, stage, vaudeville and radio actor.

BURNHAM, NICHOLAS
Born: 1860. Died: Jan. 30, 1925, Bernardsville, N.Y. Screen and stage actor.

Appeared in: **1920** Uncle Sam of Freedom Ridge.

BURNS, BOB "BAZOOKA"
Born: Aug. 2, 1890, Van Buren, Ark. Died: Feb. 2, 1956, San Fernando Valley, Calif. Screen, vaudeville, radio and carnival actor. Known as "The Arkansas Philosopher."

Appeared in: **1931** Quick Millions. **1935** The Phantom Empire (aka Radio Ranch and Men With Steel Faces); The Singing Vagabond; The Courageous Avenger; Restless Knights (short). **1936** Rhythm on the Range; Guns and Guitars. **1937** The Big Broadcast of 1937; Waikiki Wedding; Wells Fargo; Git Along Little Dogies; Public Cowboy No. 1; Yodelin' Kid from Pine Ridge; Hit the Saddle; Mountain Music. **1938** The Arkansas Traveler; Tropic Holiday; Radio City Revels. **1939** New Frontier; Our Leading Citizen; I'm From Missouri; Rovin' Tumbleweed. **1940** Alias the Deacon; Comin' Round the Mountain; Prairie Schooner. **1942** Call of the Canyon; The Hillbilly Deacon. **1944** Belle of the Yukon; Mystery Man. **1947** Twilight on the Rio Grande; Saddle Pals.

BURNS, BOBBY (Harry M. Berman)
Born: Sept. 16, 1896, London, England. Died: Feb. 15, 1955, San Francisco, Calif. Screen actor, orchestra leader and composer.

BURNS, CLYDE
Born: 1885. Died: Oct. 29, 1964, Palm Springs, Calif. Screen actor.

BURNS, DAVID
Born: June 22, 1901, New York, N.Y. Died: Mar. 12, 1971, Philadelphia, Pa. (heart attack). Screen, stage and television actor.

Appeared in: **1939** The Saint in London. **1954** Knock on Wood; Deep in My Heart. **1960** Let's Make Love. **1967** The Tiger Makes Out. **1970** More. **1971** Who Is Harry Kellerman and Why Is He Saying Those Terrible Things About Me?

BURNS, DOROTHY *See* VERNON, DOROTHY

BURNS, EDDIE
Died: Sept. 1, 1957. Screen actor. Do not confuse with actor with similar name Edmund (aka Edward and Ed) Burns (dec. 1980).

BURNS, EDMUND J. (aka EDWARD BURNS aka ED BURNS)
Born: Sept. 27, 1892, Philadelphia, Pa. Died: Apr. 2, 1980, Balboa, Calif. Screen, stage actor and casting manager.

Appeared in: **1916** The Ruling Passion. **1917** The Slave; Her Hour. **1918** Diamonds and Pearls (aka The Hour Glass); The Danger Mark; Love Watches; The Soap Girl; The Wasp. **1919** Male and Female; Made in America; A Marriage for Convenience; Miss Adventure; The Love Burglar. **1920** Eyes of the Heart. **1921** Outlawed; Open Shutters; The Girl From God's Country; To Please One Woman; Children of the Night; Hickville to Broadway; Fifty Candles. **1922** East is West; The Freshie; Blaze Away; The Green Temptation; The Dangerous Age; The Lavender Bath Lady; Lights of the Desert; The Woman's Side. **1923** Jazzmania; Scars of Jealousy; The Country Kid; Thundering Dawn. **1924** 40-Horse Hawkins; Broadway After Dark; The Humming Bird; The Guilty One; Abraham Lincoln; Those Who Dare. **1925** The Manicure Girl; Two-Fisted Jones; Hell's Highroad; Fightin' Odds; Simon the Jester; The Million Dollar Handicap; The Knockout Kid; O.U. West. **1926** Forlorn River; Whispering Wires; Made for Love; The Lodge in the Wilderness; Out of the Storm; Sunny Side Up; Paris at Midnight. **1927** Poor Girls; The Princess from Hoboken; The Shamrock and the Rose; On Guard (serial). **1928** The Chinese Parrot; Phyllis of the Follies; Ransom. **1929** Children of the Ritz; Hard to Get; She Goes to War; Tanned Legs. **1930** After the Fog; The Love Racket; Under the Greenwood Tree. **1931** Sea Devils; Devil Plays. **1932** Western Limited; Air Mail. **1933** The Death Kiss; Dangerously Yours; When a Man Rides Alone; Rusty Rides Alone. **1936** Hollywood Boulevard.

BURNS, FRED
Born: 1878, Fort Keogh, Mont. Died: July 18, 1955. Screen actor.

Appeared in: **1915** The Birth of a Nation. **1916** Ben Blair; Sold for Marriage. **1917** Sunlight's Last Raid; Vengeance and the Woman (serial); The Fighting Trail (serial). **1918** Bound in Morocco; Eyes of the World. **1920** Ruth of the Rockies (serial). **1921** Shadows of Conscience. **1923** Cyclone Jones. **1924** The Breed of the Border; The Western Wallop. **1925** O.U. West; Speed Wild; The Demon Rider; Triple Action. **1926** The Outlaw Express; The Unknown Cavalier; The Haunted Range; Wild to Go; Without Orders. **1927** The Galloping Gobs; The Overland Stage. **1929** California Mail; Rio Rita. **1930** Parade of the West; Mounted Stranger; Mountain Justice; Headin' North; Men Without Law; The Land of the Missing Men; Sunrise Trail; Branded; Freighters of Destiny. **1932** Partners; The Saddle Buster. **1933** Law and the Lawless; Trailing North; Dude Bandit; Flaming Guns; War of the Range. **1934** Texas Tornado. **1936** The Trail of the Lonesome Pine; Too Much Beef. **1937** Springtime in the Rockies. **1939** In Old Monterey; Rovin' Tumbleweeds; The Arizona Kid; Days of Jesse James. **1940** Gaucho Serenade; Colorado; Thundering Frontier. **1941** Ridin' the Cherokee Trail. **1942** Stardust on the Stage; Sunset on the Desert; Sons of the Pioneers.

BURNS, HARRY
Born: 1885. Died: July 9, 1948, Santa Monica, Calif. (heart attack). Screen, stage and vaudeville actor. Married to actress Helen Lockwood (dec. 1946).

Appeared in: **1935** A Vitaphone short. **1936** Hot Money. **1937** Two Wise Maids. **1939** Kid Nightingale. **1940** Northwest Mounted Police. **1941** Redhead. **1942** Tortilla Flat; What's the Matador (short). **1943** G-Men vs. the Black Dragon (serial).

BURNS, HARRY
Born: 1885. Died: Jan. 9, 1939, Los Angeles, Calif. (heart attack). Screen actor and film director. Married to actress Dorothy Vernon and father of actor Bobby Vernon (dec. 1939).

BURNS, IRVING
Born: 1914. Died: Sept. 21, 1968, Hollywood, Calif. (heart attack). Screen actor.

BURNS, JAMES "JIM"
Died: July 16, 1975. Screen actor.

Appeared in: **1925** O. U. West.

BURNS, LULU *See* JENKS, LULU BURNS

BURNS, NAT (Nat Burden Haines)
Born: 1887, Philadelphia, Pa. Died: Nov. 8, 1962, New York, N.Y. Screen, stage and television actor.

BURNS, NEAL
Born: June 26, 1891, Bristol, Tenn. or Pa. Died: Oct. 3, 1969, Los Angeles, Calif. (cancer). Screen and stage actor. Appeared in Christie and Education Comedies.

Appeared in: **1915** When Hubby Grew Jealous; Molly's Malady. **1917** Doing His Bit; Bucking Broadway. **1918** Sauce for the Goose. **1920** Darn That Stocking; Mary's Ankle. **1924** Hot Water (short). **1927** Mad Scrambles (short); French Fried (short). **1928** Hot Scotch (short); Slick Slickers (short); Loose Change (short); Just the Type (short). **1929** Divorce Made Easy. **1930** Johnny's Weekend (short); Don't Leave Home (short). **1931** Sob Sister. **1933** Kickin' the Crown Around. **1934** Six of a Kind; Men in Black (short); Ocean Swells (short).

BURNS, PAUL E.
Born: Jan. 26, 1881. Died: May 17, 1967, Van Nuys, Calif. (heart attack). Screen and television actor.

Appeared in: **1920** The Mollycoddle. **1930** Framed; Hell Harbor. **1932** Renegades. **1939** The Return of the Cisco Kid; Rose of Washington Square; Jesse James. **1940** Shooting High; Little Orvie; New Moon; Chad Hanna; Seventeen. **1941** Men of Timberland; Bell Starr; Swamp Water; The Last of the Duanes; Wild Geese Calling; Wild Bill Hickok Rides. **1942** The Saboteur; Mystery of Marie Roget; Timber; The Mummy's Tomb. **1943** Dixie Dugan; Crash Dive; The Ox-Bow Incident; The Meanest Man in the World; Sweet Rosie O'Grady. **1944** Dragon Seed; Barbary Coast Gent; Seventh Cross. **1945** State Fair; Fallen Angel; The Royal Mounted Rides Again (serial); Dakota; The Southerner; The Clock; Along Came Jones. **1946** The Hoodlum Saint; Crime Doctor's Man Hunt; Mysterious Intruder; Night Editor; Devil's Mask; Gallant Journey; Sing While You Dance; Shadowed; My Pal Trigger. **1947** Desperate; Saddle Pals; Framed (and 1930 version); Smokey River Serenade; Exposed; Blind Sport; Unconquered. **1948** The Paleface; Letter from an Unknown Woman; On Our Merry Way; Fifth Avenue Angel; Relentless; Hollow Triumph. **1949** Johnny Allegro; Look for the Silver Lining; I Married a Communist; Arctic Manhunt; Cover Up; Hideout; Lust for Gold; Anna Lucasta. **1950** Summer Stock; Dear Wife; Young Man With a Horn; Montana; Father Makes Good; It's a Small World; Sunset in the West; Tarnished; The Woman on Pier 13. **1951** The Big Gusher; Frenchie; Santa Fe; Storm Warning; Vengeance Valley; Silver City. **1952** The Lusty Men; Son of Paleface; Sound Off. **1955** Man With the Golden Arm. **1956** Fury at Gunsight Pass. **1958** Gunman's Walk. **1959** Face of a Fugitive. **1960** Spartacus; Guns of the Timberland. **1961** A Pocketful of Miracles. **1964** Stage to Thunder Rock. **1967** Barefoot in the Park.

BURNS, ROBERT E.
Born: 1885. Died: Mar. 14, 1957. Screen actor and screenwriter. Do not confuse with actors with variations of the same name.

BURNS, ROBERT PATRICK
Born: 1929. Died: June 8, 1955, Los Angeles, Calif. Screen actor.

Appeared in: **1935** Teacher's Beau (short).

BURNS, ROBERT PAUL "BOBBY"
Born: 1878, Philadelphia, Pa. Died: Jan. 16, 1966. Screen, stage, vaudeville actor and film director. Do not confuse with other actors of the same name.

BURNS, WILLIAM JOHN
Born: Oct. 19, 1861, Baltimore, Md. Died: Apr. 14, 1932, Sarasota, Fla. (heart attack). Detective and screen actor.

Appeared in: **1914** The Five Million Dollar Counterfeiting Plot.

BURNSIDE, WILLIAM WESLEY, JR.
Born: 1927. Died: Mar. 25, 1976, Burbank, Calif. (auto accident). Screen, television actor and stuntman.

Appeared in: **1963** The Ugly American; Donovan's Reef. **1968** The Impossible Years.

BURR, EDMUND
Died: July 16, 1975. Screen actor.

Appeared in: **1928** Chinese Parrot. **1931** Sea Devils; Devil Plays. **1932** Western Limited; Air Mail; Death Kiss.

BURR, EUGENE "GENE"
Born: Leavenworth, Kans. Died: June 7, 1940, Los Angeles, Calif. (pulmonary edema). Screen actor.

Appeared in: **1917** Fanatics; Fuel of Life. **1918** Captain of His Soul; Old Hartwell's Cab; Modern Sphinx; The Painted Lily; Alias Mary Brown; The Atom; Daughter Angele; An Heiress for a Day; Nancy Comes Home. **1919** The Girl With No Regrets; Restless Souls; The Final Closeup. **1920** The Son of Tarzan (serial). **1921** Her Face Value. **1922** Life's Greatest Question; The Broadway Madonna. **1923** Bell Boy 13; Jungle Trail of the Son of Tarzan.

BURRELL, GEORGE *See* BERRELL, GEORGE

BURROUGH, TOM
Born: 1869, Clinton County, Ill. Died: Sept. 8, 1929. Stage and screen actor.

Appeared in: **1916** Caprice of the Mountains; Unwelcome Mother; Sins of Men. **1917** Miss U.S.A. **1921** Heedless Moths.

BURROUGHS, ERIC
Died: Aug., 1960, New York. Stage and screen actor.

Appeared in: **1959** Odds Against Tomorrow.

BURT, BENNY (Benny Sachs)
Born: 1900, Chicago, Ill. Died: May 27, 1980, Hollywood, Calif. (kidney failure). Screen, vaudeville and burlesque actor.

Appeared in: **1937** Pick a Star; Sweetheart of the Navy; Sea Racketeers. **1938** Hawaiian Buckaroo; Long Shot. **1951** Cry Danger. **1952** Boots Malone; The Steel Trap. **1957** Chicago Confidential. **1960** The Apartment.

BURT, FREDERIC
Born: Feb. 12, 1876, Onarga, Ill. Died: Oct. 2, 1943, Twenty-Nine Palms, Calif. Screen and stage actor. Entered films in 1930. Married to actress Helen Ware (dec. 1939).

Appeared in: **1930** The Shadow of the Law; The Eyes of the World; Outside the Law. **1931** Cimarron; The Yellow Ticket; The Cisco Kid; The Royal Bed; Up for Murder.

BURT, LAURA
Born: 1872. Died: Oct. 17, 1952. Screen and stage actress. Married to actor Henry Stanford (dec. 1921).

Appeared in: **1905** The House Thief.

BURT, WILLIAM P. (William Presley Burt)
Born: Feb. 11, 1873, St. Peter, Minn. Died: Feb. 23, 1955, Denver, Colo. Screen, stage, minstrel, circus actor, film director, radio and screenwriter. Entered films with the Thanhouser Picture Co. in 1915.

Appeared in: **1920** Pirate Gold (serial). **1927** King of Kings. **1928** The Leopard Lady; Night of Mystery. **1930** Girl of the Port; Danger Lights; Midnight Mystery; Rogue of the Rio Grande. **1931** Sally of the Subway; Cimarron. **1933** Her Splendid Folly. **1940** Oh, Johnny, How You Can Love.

BURTIS, JAMES
Born: May 12, 1893. Died: July 24, 1939, Calif. Screen actor.

Appeared in: **1930** Jazz Cinderella; Ladies in Love. **1931** The Tip Off; The Lawless Woman. **1932** The Hurricane Express (serial); The Crowd Roars; Strangers of the Evening. **1933** The Bargain of the Century (short); Trick for Trick; One Sunday Afternoon. **1934** The St. Louis Kid; Here Comes the Navy; Here Comes the Groom; Burn 'Em Up Barnes (serial); Hips Hips Hooray; Twentieth Century; Young and Beautiful; The Case of the Howling Dog. **1935** Mystery Man; Wings in the Dark; The Farmer Takes a Wife; One Hour Late; Rumba; Mister Dynamite; Keeper of the Bees; Stormy; $1,000 a Minute; Sprucin' Up (short); Bonnie Scotland. **1936** The Return of Jimmy Valentine; Dancing Feet; Ghost Patrol; General Spanky; The Criminal Within. **1937** Arizona Mahoney; That Man's Here Again. **1938** The Texans. **1939** St. Louis Blues.

BURTON, BLANCHE
Died: July 26, 1934, New York, N.Y. Screen and stage actress. Married to actor Sir Guy Standing, Sr. (dec. 1937).

BURTON, CHARLOTTE
Born: 1882. Died: Mar. 28, 1942, Los Angeles, Calif. (heart attack). Screen actress. Entered films in 1911 with American Film Mfg. Co.

Appeared in: **1913** Trapped in a Forest Fire. **1915** The Diamond from the Sky (serial); A Man's Way. **1916** The Sequel to the Diamond from the Sky (serial).

BURTON, CLARENCE
Born: May 10, 1882, Fort Lyons, Mo. Died: Dec. 2, 1933, Hollywood, Calif. (heart attack). Screen and stage actor. Entered films in 1912.

Appeared in: **1916-17** American Film Mfg. Co. films. **1921** Miss Lulu Bett; Forbidden Fruit; Crazy to Marry; Fool's Paradise; High Gear Jeffrey; The Lost Romance; The Love Special. **1922** Manslaughter; The Ordeal; The Beautiful and Damned; The Crimson Challenge; One Glorious Day; The Law and the Woman; A Daughter of Luxury; Her Husband's Trademark; Her Own Money; The Impossible Mrs. Bellew; The Man Unconquerable. **1923** The Ten Commandments; Adam's Rib; Mr. Billings Spends His Dime; Sixty Cents an Hour; Garrison's Finish; Hollywood; Nobody's Money; Salomy Jane; The Satin Girl. **1924** The Navigator; No More Women; Bluff; The Guilty One; Mine with the Iron Door. **1925** The Coming of Amos; Flyin' Thru; The Wedding Song; The Million Dollar Handicap; The Road to Yesterday; Savages of the Sea. **1926** The Danger Girl; The Nervous Wreck; Red Dice; Three Faces East; Shipwrecked; The Warning Signal. **1927** King of Kings; The Angel of Broadway; Chicago; The Fighting Eagle; The Yankee Clipper; A Harp in Hock; Rubber Tires. **1928** Stool Pigeon; Submarine; Square Crooks; Midnight Madness; Stand and Deliver. **1929** Godless Girl; Barnum Was Right; Dynamite. **1930** The Unholy Three; Love Trader; The Love Racket; Only Saps Work. **1932** The Sign of the Cross. **1944** The Sign of the Cross (revised version of 1932 film).

BURTON, DAVID
Born: May 22, 1877, Odessa, Russia. Died: Dec., 1963, New York, N.Y. Screen, stage actor, film director and stage director.

Appeared in: **1915** The Galloper. **1930** Free and Easy.

BURTON, FREDERICK
Born: Oct. 20, 1871, Indianapolis, Ind. Died: Oct. 23, 1957, Woodland Hills, Calif. Screen, stage actor and opera performer.

Appeared in: **1919** Anne of Green Gables. **1920** The Fortune Teller; Yes or No; Heliotrope. **1921** Bits of Life; If Women Only Knew; The Education of Elizabeth. **1922** The Man She Brought Back; Anna Ascends; Back Home and Broke. **1923** Broadway Broke; The Fighting Blade. **1924** The Rejected Woman. **1925** Back to Life. **1927** Running Wild. **1930** The Big Trail. **1931** Sweepstakes; Secret Service; An American Tragedy. **1932** I Am a Fugitive from a Chain Gang; Silver Dollar; Woman from Monte Carlo; Fireman Save My Child; Alias the Doctor; Mata Hari; The Wet Parade; State's Attorney; Okay America; One Way Passage; Too Busy to Work. **1933** No Other Woman; Broadway Baby; The Working Man; Golden Harvest; Counsellor-at-Law. **1934** Smarty; Love Birds; Belle of the Nineties; Flirtation Walk. **1935** The Farmer Takes a Wife; Transient Lady; McFadden's Flats; Shipmates Forever. **1936** The Calling of Dan Matthews; Theodora Goes Wild; Everybody's Old Man; Mummy's Boys; The Voice of Bugle Ann. **1937** The Man in Blue; Love is News; Nancy Steele Is Missing; The Duke Comes Back. **1938** Jezebel; I Am the Law; Air Devil; The Saint in New York; My Lucky Star; Kentucky. **1939** Inside Information; Hollywood Cavalcade; Old Maid; Mr. Smith Goes to Washington; Silver on the Sage; Confessions of a Nazi Spy. **1940** The Man from Dakota; Go West Brigham Young. **1941** Andy Hardy's Private Secretary; Bowery Boys; Washington Melodrama. **1942** Silver Queen; Babes on Broadway; Tennessee Johnson; Gentleman After Dark. **1944** Town Went Wild; Casanova Brown. **1946** Miss Susie Slagle's.

BURTON, GEORGE H.
Born: 1900. Died: Dec. 8, 1955, Los Angeles, Calif. (heart attack). Bird trainer, screen, stage and television actor.

Appeared in: **1934** In Old Santa Fe. **1935** Ruggles of Red Gap; The Miracle Rider (serial). **1937** Come On Cowboys. **1947** Bill and Coo.

BURTON, LANGHORNE
Born: Dec. 25, 1880, Somersby, England. Died: Dec. 6, 1949, England? Screen and stage actor.

Appeared in: **1914** Turtle Doves; Bootle's Baby; The Difficult Way; The King's Minister; Liberty Hall. **1916** The Treasure of Heaven. **1917** The Profligate; Tom Jones; Auld Robin Gray; Daddy. **1918** God and the Man. **1919** The Impossible Woman; Sweet and Twenty. **1920** The Amateur Gentleman; Two Little Wooden Shoes; At the Villa Rose; Little Dorrit; By Berwin Banks; The Children of Gibeon; The Temptress; A Man's Shadow. **1921** Appearances; Moth and Rust; Beside the Bonnie Brier Bush (aka The Bonnie Briar Bush—US). **1924** Who is the Man?; Sexton Blake series including: Blake the Lawbreaker; Sexton Blake, Gambler; The Clue of the Second Goblet. **1926** Marriage License.

BURTON, MARTIN
Born: 1905, Mitchell, Ind. Died: Aug. 4, 1976, Santa Monica, Calif. Screen, stage actor and stage producer.

Appeared in: **1931** Ladies Man. **1933** When Ladies Meet; Hotel Variety; Broken Dreams.

BURTON, NED
Born: c. 1850. Died: Dec. 11, 1922, New York, N.Y. Screen, stage and vaudeville actor.

Appeared in: **1921** Jim the Penman. **1922** Back Home and Broke.

BURTON, ROBERT
Born: Aug. 13, 1895. Died: Sept. 29, 1964, Woodland Hills, Calif. (lung cancer). Screen actor.

Appeared in: **1952** The Bad and the Beautiful; Fearless Fagan; Everything I Have Is Yours; My Man and I; Sky-Full of Moon; Desperate Search; Above and Beyond. **1953** Latin Lovers; Code Two; The Band Wagon; The Girl Who Had Everything; A Slight Case of Larceny; Cry of the Hunted; Fast Company; All the Brothers Were Valiant; Inferno; The Big Heat; Confidentially Connie; Taza, Son of Cochise. **1954** Hit the Deck; Rogue Cop; Riot in Cell Block 11; The Siege of Red River; Broken Lance. **1955** The Road to Denver; Soldier of Fortune; Count Three and Pray; Lay That Rifle Down; The Left Hand of God; The Last Command; A Man Called Peter. **1956** Reprisal!; The Brass Legend; Slander; Ransom; Jubal; The Rack. **1957** Three Brave Men; No Down Payment; The Spirit of St. Louis; The Hired Gun; The Tall T; Domino Kid; The Hard Man; I Was a Teenage Frankenstein. **1958** Man or Gun; Mardi Gras; Too Much, Too Soon. **1959** The Story on Page One; The Thirty Foot Bride of Candy Rock; Compulsion; A Private's Affair. **1960** Seven Days from Sundown; Wake Me When It's Over; Gallant Hours. **1961** The Young Savages. **1962** Sweet Bird of Youth; The Invasion of the Animal People; Jumbo; Bird Man of Alcatraz; Manchurian Candidate. **1963** The Slime People.

BURTON, WILLIAM H.
Born: 1845. Died: Mar. 15, 1926, New York, N.Y. Screen and stage actor.

Appeared in: **1923** Radio Mania. **1924** Born Rich. **1925** Makers of Men.

BURTWELL, FREDERICK
Born: England. Died: Nov. 16, 1948, England? Screen actor.

Appeared in: **1932** Down Our Street. **1933** Just My Luck. **1935** Inside the Room. **1936** Twelve Good Men; Rembrandt; Laburnum Grove (US 1941); Midshipman Easy (aka Men of the Sea—US); Educated Evans. **1937** Dr. Syn; Feather Your Nest; Gypsy; French Love; The Vulture; It's Not Cricket. **1938** Almost a Honeymoon; I See Ice; Many Thanks to Mr. Atkins; Everything Happens to Me. **1939** Murder Will Out; A Girl Must Live (US 1941); His Brothers Keeper. **1942** Much Too Shy; This Was Paris. **1943** The Silver Fleet (US 1945); The Shipbuilders; The Dark Tower; We Dive at Dawn; There's a Future in It. **1945** They Knew Mr. Knight; I'll Be Your Sweetheart. **1946** The Laughing Lady (US 1950); Gaiety George (aka Showtime—US 1948). **1947** Uncle Silas (aka The Inheritance—US 1951); Nicholas Nickleby.

BUSBY, AMY
Born: 1872, Rochester, N.Y. Died: July 13, 1957, East Stroudsberg, Pa. Stage and screen actress.

BUSCAGLIONE, FRED
Born: 1921, Italy. Died: Feb. 3, 1960, Rome, Italy (auto accident). Screen, stage actor, singer and composer.

Appeared in: I Ragazzi del Juke Box (The Jukebox Boys); A Qualcuno Piace Fred (Someone Likes Fred).

BUSCH, ERNST
Born: 1900, Kiel, Germany. Died: June 8, 1980, East Berlin, East Germany. Screen, stage actor and ballad singer.

Appeared in: **1929** Katherina Knie. **1931** Gassenhauer; Die Dreigroschenoper (The Threepenny Opera, aka The Beggar's Opera); Niemandsland (No Man's Land, aka Hell on Earth—US 1934); Die Koffer des Herrn O. F. (The Luggage of Mr. O. F., aka Thirteen Trunks of Mr. O. F.—US); Kameradschaft (US 1932). **1932** Kuhle Wampe (aka Wem Gehoert die Welt, aka Wither Germany—US); Razzia in St. Pauli; Strafsache van Geldern; Die Zwei vom Suedexpress; Eine von Uns (US 1937). **1933** Das Meer Ruft. **1935** Kaempfer (US 1936). **1961** Mutter Courage und Ihre Kinder.

BUSCH, MAE
Born: Jan. 20, 1891, Melbourne, Australia. Died: Apr. 19, 1946, Woodland Hills, Calif. Screen, stage and vaudeville actress. Entered films with Mack Sennett.

Appeared in: **1915** A One Night Stand; Settled at the Seaside; The Rent Jumpers; A Rascal of Wolfish Ways (reissued as A Polished Villain); The Best of Enemies; A Favorite Fool. **1916** The Worst of Friends; Because He Loved Her; Better Late Than Never (aka Getting Married); Wife and Auto Trouble; A Bath House Blunder; Sisters of Eve. **1919** The Grim Game. **1920** The Devil's Passkey. **1921** The Love Charm; A Parisian Scandal. **1922** Foolish Wives; Brothers Under the Skin; Her Own Money; Only a Shop Girl; Pardon My Nerve! **1923** The Christian; Souls for Sale. **1924** Broken Barriers; Bread; Married Flirts; Nellie, the Beautiful Cloak Model; The Shooting of Dan McGrew; Name the Man; A Woman Who Sinned; The Triflers. **1925** Camille of the Barbary Coast; The Unholy Three; Frivolous Sal; Time, the Comedian. **1926** Nutcracker; Fools of Fashion; The Miracle of Life. **1927** San Francisco Nights; Tongues of Scandal; The Truthful Sex; Love 'Em and Weep (short); Husband Hunters; Perch of the Devil. **1928** Fazil; The Beauty Shoppers; Sisters of Eve; Black Butterflies; While the City Sleeps. **1929** Alibi; Unaccustomed As We Are (short); A Man's Man. **1930** Young Desire. **1931** Defenders of the Law; Wicked; plus the following shorts: Fly My Kite; Chickens Come Home; Come Clean. **1932** Their First Mistake (short); Without Honor; Man Called Back; Doctor X; Heart Punch; Scarlet Dawn; Rider of Death Valley; Racing Strain. **1933** Women Won't Tell; Blondie Won't Tell; Blondie Johnson; Sucker Money; Lilly Turner; Cheating Blondes; Secrets of Hollywood; Picture Brides; Dance, Girl, Dance (short); Sons of the Desert. **1934** Going Bye Bye (short); The Live Ghost (short); Beloved; The Road to Ruin; I Like It That Way; Oliver the Eighth (short); Them Thar Hills (short). **1935** Tit for Tat (short); The Fixer Uppers (short); Affairs of Susan; Stranded. **1936** The Clutching Hand (serial); The Bohemian Girl. **1937** Marie Antoinette; Daughter of Shanghai. **1938** The Buccaneer; Prison Farm; Nancy Drew, Detective. **1940** Ziegfeld Girl; Women Without Names. **1942** Hello, Annapolis; The Mad Monster. **1945** Stork Club; Masquerade in Mexico. **1946** The Blue Dahlia; The Bride Wore Boots; Cross My Heart. **1947** Ladies' Man.

BUSH, ANITA
Born: Washington, D.C. Died: Feb. 16, 1974, New York. Black screen, stage and vaudeville actress. Appeared in vaudeville as part of "Williams and Walker" team.

Appeared in: **1921** The Crimson Skull. **1923** The Bull Doggers.

BUSH, GEORGE
Born: 1858, Janesville, Wis. Died: Nov. 23, 1937, Culver City, Calif. Screen actor.

Appeared in: **1938** The Adventures of Tom Sawyer.

BUSH, PAULINE
Born: May 22, 1886, Lincoln, Nebr. Died: Nov. 1, 1969, San Diego, Calif. (pneumonia). Screen actress. Divorced from film director Allan Dwan (dec. 1981).

Appeared in: **1911** The Brand of Fear; The Poisoned Flume; The Sheriff's Sister; Objection Over-ruled. **1912** The Thief's Wife; A Life For a Kiss; An Innocent Grafter; Maiden and Men; A Bad Investment; The Outlaw Colony; The Jealous Rage; The Reformation of Sierra Smith; The Power of Love; The Agitator; The Ranchman's Marathon; The Promise; The New Cowpuncher; The Haters; The Brand; The Man and the Maid; Fidelity; Under False Pretenses; Nell of the Pampas; Driftwood; The Land of Death; Her Mountain Home; The Coward; The Girl of the Manor; The Pensioners; For the Good of Her Men; The Intrusion at Lompoc; The Stranger at Coyote. **1913** The Embezzler; Love Is Blind; An Eastern Flower; The Angel of the Canyon; The Lamb, the Woman, the Wolf; The End of the Feud; Red Margaret—Moonshiner; The Lie; The Wishing Seat; The Wall of Money; The Spirit of the Flag; Jewels of Sacrifice. **1914** The Honor of the Mounted; Remember Mary Magdalen; Discord and Harmony; The Menace of Carlotta (aka Carlotta, the Bead Stringer); The Tragedy of Whispering Creek; The Unlawful Trade; The Higher Law; The Cross; Her Bounty; The Hopes of Blind Alley; The Forbidden Room; The Oubliette; Richelieu; The Pipes of Pan; Virtue Is Its Own Reward; Lights and Shadows; A Night of Thrills; The Sin of Olga Brandt. **1915** Star of the Sea; The Measure of a Man; The Threads of Fate; The Girl Who Couldn't Go Wrong; Such Is Life; Where the Forest Ends; Outside the Gates; The Desert Breed; The Maid of the Mist; The Grind; Girl of the Night; For Cash; An Idyll of the Hills; The Stronger Mind; Steady Company; The Chimney's Secret; The Trap; Her Escape. **1916** The Capture of Rattlesnake Ike. **1917** Double Revenge; Nature's Calling; The Old Sheriff; The Man Who Saved the Day; Bloodhounds of the North. **1924** The Enemy Sex.

BUSHMAN, FRANCIS X. (Francis Xavier Bushman)
Born: Jan. 10, 1883, Baltimore, Md. Died: Aug. 23, 1966, Pacific Palisades, Calif. (heart attack due to fall). Screen, stage, radio and television actor. Divorced from Josephine Fladune (dec. 1964). Father of Bruce, Virginia, Lenore, Josephine and actor Ralph (Francis X. Bushman, Jr.) (dec. 1978). Divorced from actress Beverly Bayne (dec. 1982). Father of Richard Stansbury Bushman (dec. 1960s). Married to Norma Emily Atkins (dec. 1956) and later married to Ivy Milicent Richardson. Entered films with Essanay in 1911.

Appeared in: **1911** His Friend's Wife; The Rosary; Her Dad the Constable; God's Inn by the Sea; The New Manager; The Gordian Knot; Fate's Funny Frolic; The Burglarized Burglar; Saved from the Torrents; The Dark Romance of a Tobacco Tin; Live, Love and Believe; Lost Years; A False Suspicion; Bill Bumper's Bargain; He Fought for the U.S.A.; The Madman; The Goodfellow's Christmas. **1912** Alias Billy Sargent; The Mail Order Bride; The Melody of Love; Tracked Down; The Little Black Box; Out of the Depths; At the End of the Trail; Lonesome Robert; Wapatia, the Greek Singer; Out of the Night; The Eye That Never Sleeps; The Laurel Wreath of Fame; The Passing Shadow; Return of William Marr; Billy and the Butler; White Roses; The Butterfly Net; Signal Lights; The Understudy; Her Hour of Triumph; The New Church Organ; Twilight; The Old Wedding Dress; The Fall of Montezuma; Neptune's Daughter; The Voice of Conscience; The End of the Feud; The Warning Hand; Chains; When Wealth Torments; The House of Pride; The Penitent; The Iron Heel; The Virtue of Rags; The Magic Wand; A Good Catch. **1913** The Spy's Defeat; Sunlight; When Soul Meets Soul; The Thirteenth Man; The Farmer's Daughter; The Discovery; A Mistaken Accusation; The Pathway of Years; White Rose; Let No Man Put Asunder; A Brother's Loyalty; The Motor Buccaneers; The Whip Hand; The Power of Conscience; The Right Way; For Old Times Sake; Tony the Fiddler; Dear Old Girl; The Way Perilous; The Toll of the Marshes; The Little Substitute; The Stigma. **1914** The Hour and the Man; Hearts and Flowers; Through the Storm; The Girl at the Curtain; Dawn and Twilight; Mongrel and Master; The Other Girl; Shadows; The Three Scratch Clue; The Spirit of the Madonna; A Man for a Hat; The Mystery of Room 643; Ashes of Hope; In the Moon's Ray; The Voice in the Wilderness; Ambushed; The Woman Scorned; The Shanty at Trembling Hill; The Elder Brother; Fingerprints; The Countess; Trinkets of Tragedy; A Night With a Million; Night Hawks; His Stolen Fortune; The Masked Wrestler; The Plum Tree; Sparks of Fate; A Splendid Dishonor; The Other Man; In the Glare of the Lights; The Private Officer; The Unplanned Elopement; Scars of Possession; The Prince Party; Fable of the Bush League Lover Who Failed to Qualify; Every Inch a King; The Battle of Love; Any Woman's Choice; One Wonderful Night; Blood Will Tell; Under Royal Patronage. **1915** Graustark; The Return of Richard Neal; The Silent Voice; Dear Old Girl; The Ambition of the Baron; Thirteen Down; The Accounting; Stars Their Courses Change; The Gallantry of Jimmy Rogers; The Great Silence; The Slim Princess; Providence and Mrs. Urmy; The Second in Command; Pennington's Choice; Thirty. **1916** Man and His Soul; The Wall Between; A Million a Minute; A Virginia Romance; In the Diplomatic Service; Romeo and Juliet; The Great Secret (serial). **1917** Red, White and Blue Blood; The Secret Seven (serial); Adopted Son; Their Compact. **1918** Under Suspicion; The Brass Check; With Neatness and Dispatch; Cyclone Higgens D.D.; A Pair of Cupids; The Poor Rich Man; Social Quicksands. **1919** God's Outlaw; Daring Hearts. **1920** Smiling All the Way. **1923** Modern Marriage. **1925** The Masked Bride. **1926** Ben Hur; The Marriage Clause. **1927** The Lady in Ermine; The Thirteenth Juror; The Flag. **1928** The Grip of the Yukon; Midnight Life; Say It With Sables; The Charge of the Gauchos. **1930** The Call of the Circus; The Dude Wrangler; Once a Gentleman. **1931** Spell of the Circus (serial); The Galloping Ghost (serial); Ben Hur (rerelease of 1926 film). **1932** Watch Beverly. **1933** The Three Musketeers (serial). **1936** Hollywood Boulevard. **1937** Dick Tracy (serial). **1941** Mr. Celebrity. **1942** Silver Queen. **1944** Wilson. **1951** David and Bathsheba; Hollywood Story. **1952** The Bad and the Beautiful; Apache Country. **1954** Sabrina. **1957** The Story of Mankind. **1959** Twelve to the Moon. **1962** The Phantom Planet. **1965** Peer Gynt. **1966** The Ghost in the Invisible Bikini.

BUSHMAN, FRANCIS X., JR. (Ralph E. Bushman aka RALPH BUSHMAN)
Born: May 1, 1903, Md. Died: Apr. 16, 1978, Los Angeles, Calif. (respiratory failure). Screen and stage actor. Son of Francis X. Bushman, Sr. (dec. 1966), and Josephine Fladune (dec. 1964).

Appeared in: **1920** It's a Great Life. **1923** The Man Who Passed By; Our Hospitality. **1925** Never Too Late; Always in the Lead; Who's Your Friend; The Pride of the Force. **1926** Brown of Harvard; Dangerous Traffic; Eyes Right; Midnight Faces. **1927** The Understanding Heart. **1928** Marlie, The Killer; Four Sons; The Scarley Arrow (serial); Haunted Island (serial). **1929** Father's Day. **1930** They

Learned About Women; Call of the Circus; The Girl Said No; Dude Wrangler; Richest Man in the World; Way Out West; Sins of the Children. **1931** Cyclone Kid; Spell of the Circus (serial). **1932** Human Targets; Tangled Fortunes; The Last Frontier (serial). **1933** The Three Musketeers (serial). **1934** Viva Villa! **1936** Caryl of the Mountains.

BUSHMAN, RALPH *See* BUSHMAN, FRANCIS X., JR.

BUSLEY, JESSIE
Born: 1869, Albany, N.Y. Died: Apr. 20, 1950, New York, N.Y. Stage and screen actress.

Appeared in: **1930** Seeing Off Service (short); Home Made (short). **1931** Personal Maid. **1938** Brother Rat. **1939** King of the Underworld. **1940** It All Came True; Brother Rat and a Baby; Escape to Glory (aka Submarine Zone).

BUSQUETS, JOAQUIN
Born: 1875, Mexico. Died: Dec. 4, 1942, Mexico City, Mexico. Screen, radio actor and radio producer. Entered films during silents.

Appeared in: **1934** La Sangre Manda; Enemigos. **1935** Tierra, Amor y Dolor. **1936** La Mujer del Puerto. **1937** El Misterio del Rostro Palido; La Gran Cruz (The Heavy Cross).

BUSSEY, HANK
Born: 1891. Died: Jan. 14, 1971, Hollywood, Calif. Screen, stage and vaudeville actor. Member of vaudeville team of "Bussey and Case."

BUSTER, BUDD (Budd Leland Buster aka BUD BUSTER aka GEORGE SELK)
Born: June 14, 1891, Colo. Died: Dec. 22, 1965, Los Angeles, Calif. (heart attack). Screen actor.

Appeared in: **1935** The Cyclone Ranger; The Texas Rambler; The Vanishing Riders. **1936** Blazing Justice; Desert Guns; Desert Justice; The Riding Avenger; Cavalry; Headin' for the Rio Grande. **1937** Arizona Days; Sing, Cowboy, Sing; The Gun Ranger; Old Louisiana; The Trusted Outlaw; Drums of Destiny; Colorado Kid; Hit the Saddle. **1938** Code of the Rangers; Paroled—to Die; Thunder in the Desert; Song and Bullets; Desert Patrol; Stranger from Arizona; Frontier Scout. **1939** Dick Tracy's G-Men (serial); Zorro's Fighting Legion (serial); Daughter of the Tong. **1940** King of the Royal Mounted (serial); The Courageous Dr. Christian; Straight Shooter; Covered Wagon Trails; Murder on the Yukon; I Take This Oath; Marked Men; West of Pinto Basin. **1941** Billy the Kid's Fighting Pals; Secret Evidence; The Lone Rider in Ghost Town; Texas Marshal; Gangs of Sonora; Thunder Over the Prairie; The Lone Star Vigilantes; Sierra Sue; Billy the Kid Wanted; West of Cimarron. **1942** Heart of the Rio Grande; Call of the Canyon; Westward, Ho; West of Tombstone; Billy the Kid Trapped; The Yukon Patrol; Down Rio Grande Way; Billy the Kid's Smoking Guns; Texas Bataan. **1943** The Old Chisholm Trail; Cheyenne Roundup; Cowboy Commandos; Daredevils of the West (serial); The Black Trail; Santa Fe Scouts. **1944** Trail of Terror; Wolves of the Range; Frontier Outlaws; Hidden Valley Outlaws; Call of the South Seas; Trigger Trail; Brand of the Devil; Guns of the Law; Thundering Gun Slingers; The Pinto Bandit; Outlaw Roundup; Wild Horse Phantom; Riders of the Santa Fe; Saddle Leather Law. **1945** Salome, Where She Danced; Secret Agent X-9 (serial); Navajo Kid; Border Badmen; Jungle Raiders (serial). **1946** Six-Gun Man; The Flying Serpent; Gentlemen With Guns; Ambush Trail; Home on the Alamo; Terrors on Horseback; Sheriff of Redwood Valley; Texas Panhandle; Outlaw of the Plains; Terror Trail; Rainbow Over the Rockies; Songs of the Sierras. **1947** Vigilantes of Boomtown; The Wild Frontier; Shadow Valley; Cheyenne Takes Over. **1948** The Westward Trail. **1949** Loaded Pistols. **1953** City of Bad Men; It Came From Outer Space. **1954** Riding Shotgun; The Bounty Hunter; Trader Tom of the China Seas (serial). **1955** I'll Cry Tomorrow; Battle Cry. **1957** The Vampire; The Spirit of St. Louis. **1958** Gun Fever. **1959** Bus Stop. **1960** Elmer Gantry; Guns of the Timberland.

BUTCHER, ERNEST
Born: 1885. Died: June 8, 1965, London, England. Screen, stage and radio actor. Divorced from actress Muriel George (dec. 1965) and later remarried to actress Miss Brough.

Appeared in: **1935** Key to Harmony; Wedding Eve; The Small Man; Lieutenant Darling, RN. **1937** Overcoat Sam; Talking Feet; Song of the Road. **1938** Stepping Toes. **1939** Me and My Pal. **1940** Pack Up Your Troubles; Old Mother Riley in Business. **1942** Variety Jubilee. **1943** The Tawny Pipit (US 1947); It's in the Bag; When We Are Married. **1944** Candles at Nine; It Happened One Sunday. **1945** Men of the Mines. **1946** The Years Between (US 1947); Appointment With Crime (US 1950). **1947** Dear Murderer (US 1948); While I Live. **1948** My Brother Jonathan (US 1949). **1949** Meet Simon Cherry. **1950** Highly Dangerous (US 1951). **1953** Time Bomb (aka Terror on a Train—US); Background (aka Edge of Divorce). **1959** The Desperate Man.

BUTI, CARLO
Born: 1902. Died: Nov. 16, 1963, Florence, Italy. Screen actor and singer.

Appeared in: **1938** I Due Gemelli (The Twins). **1939** Per Uomini Soli (For Men Only).

BUTLER, BARBARA
Born: 1902, Ogdensburg, N.Y. Died: Jan. 4, 1975. Screen actress.

Appeared in: **1916** A Woman's Way. **1919** The American Way; Phil-for-Short. **1920** The Flapper. **1922** Beyond the Bend; Missing Millions. **1923** This Wife Business.

BUTLER, CHARLES
Born: 1856. Died: Aug. 17, 1920, New York, N.Y. Screen and stage actor.

Appeared in: **1915** Zaz.

BUTLER, DAVID (David Wayne Butler)
Born: Dec. 17, 1895, San Francisco, Calif. Died: June 15, 1979, Arcadia, Calif. (heart ailment). Screen, stage actor, film director, film producer, television director and screenwriter. Son of actor Fred Butler (dec. 1929) and stage actress Adele Belgrade (dec.). Entered films in 1913 as an actor.

Appeared in: **1918** The Greatest Thing in Life. **1919** The Girl Who Stayed Home; Upstairs and Down; Nugget Nell; Bonnie Bonnie Lassie; The Other Half. **1920** Fickle Women; The County Fair; Don't Ever Marry. **1921** The Sky Pilot; Girls Don't Gamble; Making the Grade; Smiling All the Way. **1922** Conquering the Woman; The Milky Way; The Village Blacksmith; According to Hoyle; The Wise Kid; Bing Bang Boom. **1923** Poor Men's Wives; Temple of Venus; Cause for Divorce; The Fog; The Hero; Hoodman Blind; Mary of the Movies; A Noise in Newboro. **1924** In Hollywood with Potash and Perlmutter; Arizona Express. **1925** The Narrow Street; Code of the West; Private Affairs; Tracked in the Snow Country; His Majesty, Bunker Bean; The Man on the Box; Havoc; Wages for Wives; The Gold Hunters; The People vs. Nancy Preston; The Blue Eagle; The Phantom Express. **1926** The Quarterback; The Plastic Age; Oh Baby!; Meet the Prince; The Sap; Woman Power. **1927** Seventh Heaven; Nobody's Widow; Girl in the Rain; The Rush Hour. **1929** Salute. **1949** It's a Great Feeling.

BUTLER, EDDIE
Born: 1888. Died: May 31, 1944, Hollywood, Calif. Screen actor.

Appeared in: **1936** Bullets or Ballots.

BUTLER, FRANK
Born: Dec. 28, 1890, Oxford, England. Died: June 10, 1967, Hollywood, Calif. Screen, stage actor and screenwriter. Was in early "In-Law" series.

Appeared in: **1921** The Sheik; The Great Moment. **1922** A Tailor-Made Man; Beyond the Rocks; My American Wife. **1923** The Self-Made Wife; The Tiger's Claw; Bluebeard's Eighth Wife; The Call of the Wild. **1924** The King of the Wild Horses. **1925** Tol'able Romeo (short); Compromise; Satan in Sables. **1926** Made for Love; The Passionate Quest; The Fighting Buckaroo; Thirty Below Zero. **1947** Variety Girl.

BUTLER, FRED J. (Alfred Joline Butler)
Born: 1864. Died: Feb. 22, 1929, Los Angeles, Calif. (kidney trouble). Screen, stage actor, film director, film producer, and stage director. Married to stage actress Adele Belgrade (dec.). Father of actor and director David Butler (dec. 1979).

Appeared in: **1916** Susan Rocks the Boat. **1917** The Price She Paid. **1921** Making the Grade. **1922** The Dictator; According to Hoyle. **1923** Racing Hearts; Three Wise Fools. **1924** Bluff; Welcome Stranger; The Brass Bowl; Gold Heels; The Battling Fool. **1925** Marriage in Transit; Red Blood and Blue.

BUTLER, JAMES "JIMMY"
Born: 1921. Died: Feb. 18, 1945, France (killed in action, W.W.II). Screen actor. One of the original "Dead End Kids."

Appeared in: **1933** Only Yesterday; Beloved. **1934** No Greater Glory; Romance in Manhattan; Mrs. Wiggs of the Cabbage Patch; Manhattan Melodrama; I'll Fix It. **1935** When a Man's a Man; Laddie; Dinky; The Dark Angel. **1936** Battle of Greed; Stella Dallas; County Fair. **1937** Wells Fargo. **1938** Boys Town. **1939** Call a Messenger; The Escape; Nurse Edith Cavell; Winter Carnival. **1940** Military Academy. **1941** Naval Academy. **1942** Tough as They Come.

BUTLER, JOHN A. (aka JOHNNY BUTLER)
Born: 1884. Died: Oct. 9, 1967. Screen actor.

Appeared in: **1922** John Smith. **1923** Wet Gold. **1936** Make Way for a Lady. **1937** Some Blondes Are Dangerous; Expensive Husbands. **1938** Accidents Will Happen; Exposed; What Price Safety (short); How to Watch Football (short); Opening Day (short); Mental Poise (short). **1939** Torchy Runs for Mayor; The Day of Rest (short); Think First (short); Money to Loan (short). **1940** We Who Are Young; That Inferior Feeling (short). **1941** Mob Town. **1942** Joe Smith, American. **1947** The Senator Was Indiscreet; Dream Girl. **1948** Silent Conflict; Sinister Journey. **1949** That Wonderful Urge; It Happens Every Spring. **1950** The Yellow Cab Man; Convicted; Code of the Silver Sage; Branded. **1951** Strangers on a Train. **1952** The Pride of St. Louis. **1953** The Farmer Takes a Wife.

BUTLER, LOUISE (Estelle Louise Fiske)
Died: Dec. 8, 1958, Chicago, Ill. Stage and screen actress.

BUTLER, ROYAL "ROY" (Royal Edwin Butler)
Born: May 4, 1895, Atlanta, Ga. Died: July 28, 1973, Desert Hot Springs, Calif. Screen, stage and vaudeville actor. Entered films in 1911 with Photo Drama Co.

Appeared in: **1941** Sierra Sue. **1942** Home in Wyomin'; Heart Burn (short); House of Errors. **1943** Frontier Law; The Old Chisholm Trail. **1944** Bowery to Broadway. **1945** Renegades of the Rio Grande. **1946** The Hoodlum Saint. **1947** Land of the Lawless; Gun Talk. **1948** Overland Trails; Range Renegades. **1949** Sky Liner; Deputy Marshal; Stallion Canyon. **1950** Bandit Queen; Fast on the Draw; Indian Territory; One Too Many. **1951** Vengeance Valley; Fingerprints Don't Lie; Gene Autry and the Mounties; Texans Never Cry. **1952** Night Raiders. **1953** The Girl Who Had Everything.

BUTLER, WILLIAM J. "DADDY"
Born: 1860. Died: Jan. 27, 1927, Staten Island, N.Y. Screen and stage actor.

Appeared in: **1909** 1776, or The Hessian Renegades; In Old Kentucky; One Night and Then— **1910** The Purgation; A Flash of Light; The Usurer. **1911** The Two Sides; A Romany Tragedy; The Last Drop of Water; Fighting Blood; The Unveiling; Dan the Dandy; A Blot on the 'Scutcheon. **1912** Man's Lust for Gold. **1913** The Hero of Little Italy; A Timely Interception. **1917** The Great Secret (serial).

BUTT, JOHNNY "TOM"
Born: England. Died: 1930, England? Screen and stage actor.

Appeared in: **1906** Hoaxing the Professor. **1909** The Fatal Appetiser; The Escapades of Teddy Bear; What Happened to Brown. **1910** The Devoted Ape; Twixt Red Man and White; Prison Reform. **1911** Exceeding His Duty; A Touch of Hydrophobia. **1912** Plot and Pash; The Emperor's Message. **1913** The Burglar at the Ball; Love and a Burglar; Father's Little Flutter; The Law in Their Own Hands; Professor Longhead's Burglar Trap; David Copperfield; Puzzled; On the Brink of the Precipice. **1914** Follow Your Leader; Judged by Appearance; Once Upon the Lugger; Simpkins' Little Swindle; Simpkins' Sunday Dinner; Simpkins Get the War Scare; War's Grim Reality; The Chimes; The Bridge Destroyer; Simpkins, Special Constable. **1915** Sister Susie's Sewing Shirts for Soldiers; Who Stole Pa's Purse; Slips and Slops; Phyllis and the Foreigner; Far From the Madding Crowd. **1916** The Grand Babylon Hotel; Who's Your Friend?; Miggles Maid; Trelawney of the Wells; 'Orace's Ordeal; I Do Like a Joke; The Exploits of Tubby (series). **1917** Carrots; The American Heiress; The Man Behind "The Times"; Neighbours; The Joke That Failed. **1920** Three Men in a Boat. **1922** The Head of the Family; The Skipper's Wooing; No. 7, Brick Row. **1923** The Convert; The Constable's Move; An Odd Reak; The Last Adventures of Sherlock Holmes series including: The Cardboard Box. **1924** Lawyer Quince; The Prehistoric Man; Sen Yen's Devotion; The Further Mysteries of Dr. Fu Manchu series including: The Coughing Horror. **1925** The Gold Cure. **1926** Every Mother's Son; Nell Gwynne; Second to None; Nelson. **1927** Passion Island; Carry On. **1928** The Hellcat; Q-Ships. **1929** A Peep Behind the Scenes; The Last Post; The Clue of the New Pin; The Informer; Blackmail. **1930** A Sister to Assist 'Er.

BUTTERFIELD, EVERETT
Born: 1885, Portland, Maine. Died: Mar. 6, 1925, New York, N.Y. Screen actor.

Appeared in: **1915** The Magic Skin.

BUTTERFIELD, HERBERT
Born: 1896. Died: May 2, 1957, Los Angeles, Calif. Screen and television actor.

Appeared in: **1950** Never Fear; The Young Lovers. **1951** House on Telegraph Hill. **1953** A Blueprint for Murder. **1954** Shield for Murder. **1956** The Ten Commandments.

BUTTERWORTH, CHARLES
Born: July 26, 1896, South Bend, Ind. Died: June 14, 1946, Los Angeles, Calif. (auto accident). Screen, stage, vaudeville and radio actor.

Appeared in: **1930** Life of the Party (film debut); Illicit. **1931** Side Show; The Bargain; The Mad Genius. **1932** Beauty and the Boss; Love Me Tonight; The Slippery Pearls (short); Manhattan Parade. **1933** The Nuisance; Penthouse; My Weakness. **1934** The Cat and the Fiddle; Hollywood Party; Student Tour; Forsaking All Others; Bulldog Drummond Strikes Back; Ruggles of Red Gap. **1935** The Night Is Young; Baby Face Harrington; Orchids to You. **1936** The Magnificent Obsession; The Moon's Our Home; Half Angel; We Went to College; Rainbow on the River. **1937** Swing High, Swing Low; Every Day's a Holiday. **1938** Thanks for the Memory. **1939** Let Freedom Ring. **1940** Second Chorus; The Boys from Syracuse. **1941** Blonde Inspiration; Sis Hopkins; There's Nothing to It (short); Road Show. **1942** Love Me Tonight; Night in New Orleans; Give Out, Sisters; What's Cooking? **1943** Always a Bridesmaid; The Sultan's Daughter; This Is the Army. **1944** Bermuda Mystery; Follow the Boys; Dixie Jamboree.

BUTTERWORTH, PETER
Born: 1919, England. Died: Jan. 16, 1979, Coventry, England (heart attack). Screen, stage and television actor. Married to actress Janet Brown.

Appeared in: **1948** William Comes to Town. **1949** The Adventures of Jane; Murder at the Windmill (aka Murder at the Burlesque—US). **1950** Miss Pilgrim's Progress; Paul Temple's Triumph (US 1951); The Body Said No! **1951** Old Mother Riley's Jungle Treasure; Mr. Drake's Duck; Appointment With Venus (aka Island Rescue—US 1952); The Case of the Missing Scene. **1952** Penny Princess (US 1953); Saturday Island (aka Island of Desire—US). **1953** Watch Out! (short); A Good Pull-Up (short); Will Any Gentleman? (US 1955). **1954** Five O'Clock Finish. **1955** That's an Order (short); Black in the Face. **1956** Fun at St. Fanny's. **1958** Tom Thumb. **1960** The Spider's Web. **1961** Murder She Said; The Day the Earth Caught Fire (US 1962). **1962** Kill or Cure; Fate Takes a Hand; Win Now—Pay Later. **1963** Doctor in Distress (US 1964). **1964** Never Mention Murder. **1965** The Amorous Adventures of Moll Flanders. **1967** Danny the Dragon (short); Follow That Camel (US 1968); Carry On Doctor. **1968** Prudence and the Pill. **1970** Carry on Henry. **1976** Robin and Marian; The Ritz. **1979** The Great Train Robbery.

BUTTERWORTH, WALTER T.
Born: 1893. Died: Mar. 10, 1962, Hollywood, Calif. Screen, stage and vaudeville actor.

BUZZI, PIETRO
Died: Feb. 16, 1921, Los Angeles, Calif. Screen actor and opera performer. Entered films approx. 1910.

BYER, CHARLES See BEYER, CHARLES WALTER

BYERS, NANCY
Born: 1900. Died: Nov. 14, 1980. Silent screen actress.

BYFORD, ROY
Born: 1873. Died: Jan. 31, 1939, London, England. Screen and stage actor.

Appeared in: **1905** The Village Blacksmith. **1916** The Little Damozel; On the Banks of Allen Water. **1918** The Happy Warrior. **1920** The Twelve Pound Look. **1921** The Night Hawk (aka The Haven); The Double Event. **1922** Treasure Trove; The Spanish Jade; A Master of Craft; Perpetua (aka Love's Boomerang—US). **1923** The Gems of Literature series including Falstaff the Tavern King. **1924** Tons of Money. **1935** Immortal Gentleman. **1937** Museum Mystery. **1938** Horse Sense.

BYINGTON, SPRING
Born: Oct. 17, 1893, Colorado Springs, Colo. Died: Sept. 7, 1971, Hollywood, Calif. Screen, stage, radio and television actress. Nominated for 1938 Academy Award for Best Supporting Actress in You Can't Take It With You.

Appeared in: **1931** Papa's Slay Ride (short). **1933** Little Women. **1935** Mutiny on the Bounty; The Werewolf of London; Love Me Forever; Orchids to You; Way Down East; Ah, Wilderness; Broadway Hostess; The Great Impersonation. **1936** The Charge of the Light Brigade; Every Saturday Night; Educating Father; Back to Nature; The Voice of Bugle Ann; Palm Springs; Stage Struck; The Girl on the Front Page; Dodsworth; Theodora Goes Wild. **1937** The Road Back; Green Light; Penrod and Sam; Off to the Races; Big Business; Hot Water; Borrowing Trouble; Hotel Haywire; It's Love I'm After; Clarence; A Family

Affair. **1938** You Can't Take It With You; Love on a Budget; A Trip to Paris; Safety in Numbers; The Buccaneer; Penrod and His Twin Brother; Jezebel; Down on the Farm; The Adventures of Tom Sawyer. **1939** Everybody's Baby; The Jones Family in Hollywood; Quick Millions; The Story of Alexander Graham Bell; Chicken Wagon Family; Too Busy to Work; Jones Family at the Grand Canyon. **1940** A Child Is Born; The Bluebird; On Their Own; My Love Came Back; Lucky Partners; Laddie; Young As You Feel; The Ghost Comes Home. **1941** Arkansas Judge; Meet John Doe; The Devil and Miss Jones; When Ladies Meet; Ellery Queen and the Perfect Crime; The Vanishing Virginian. **1942** Roxie Hart; Once Upon a Thursday; The War Against Mrs. Hadley; Rings on Her Fingers; The Affairs of Martha. **1943** Heaven Can Wait; Presenting Lily Mars; The Heavenly Body. **1944** I'll Be Seeing You. **1945** The Thrill of a Romance; Captain Eddie; Salty O'Rourke; The Enchanted Cottage; A Letter for Evie. **1946** Dragonwyck; Meet Me on Broadway; Little Mr. Jim; Faithful in My Fashion; My Brother Talks to Horses. **1947** Living in a Big Way; Singapore; It Had to Be You; Cynthia; The Rich Full Life. **1948** B. F's Daughter. **1949** The Big Wheel; In the Good Old Summertime. **1952** Please Believe Me; Devil's Doorway; Louisa; Walk Softly, Stranger; The Skipper Surprised His Wife; The Reformer and the Redhead (voice only). **1951** Angels in the Outfield; Bannerline; According to Mrs. Hoyle. **1952** No Room for the Groom; Because You're Mine. **1954** The Rocket Man. **1960** Please Don't Eat the Daisies.

BYLES, BOBBY
Born: 1931. Died: Aug. 26, 1969, Hollywood, Calif. (heart attack). Screen and television actor.

Appeared in: **1958** Onionhead. **1964** War Is Hell.

BYRAM, RONALD
Born: Brisbane, Australia. Died: Apr., 1919, Calgary, Canada. Stage and screen actor.

Appeared in: **1919** Out of the Shadow; A Gentleman of Quality.

BYRD, RALPH
Born: Apr. 22, 1909, Dayton, Ohio. Died: Aug. 18, 1952, Tarzana, Calif. (heart attack). Screen and television actor. Starred as Dick Tracy in film and television series.

Appeared in: **1936** You May Be Next; Hell-Ship Morgan; Border Caballero; Swing Time. **1937** S.O.S. Coast Guard (serial); Motor Madness; The Trigger Trio; Paid to Dance; Blake of Scotland Yard (serial); Dick Tracy (serial); Criminals of the Air. **1938** Down in "Arkensaw"; Born to Be Wild; Army Girl; Dick Tracy Returns (serial). **1939** Mickey, the Kid; Dick Tracy's G-Men (serial); Fighting Thoroughbreds; S.O.S. Tidal Wave. **1940** The Mark of Zorro; Play Girl; Misbehaving Husbands; The Howards of Virginia; Drums of the Desert; The Golden Fleecing; The Son of Monte Cristo; Dark Streets of Cairo; Northwest Mounted Police. **1941** Dr. Kildare's Wedding Day; Life Begins for Andy Hardy; Dick Tracy vs. Crime, Inc. (serial); The Penalty; Desperate Cargo; A Yank in the RAF. **1942** Broadway Big Shot; Jungle Book; Careful, Soft Shoulders; Time to Kill; Moontide; Duke of the Navy; Ten Gentlemen from West Point; Manilla Calling. **1943** Margin for Error; They Came to Blow Up America; Guadalcanal Diary. **1944** Four Jills in a Jeep; Tampico. **1947** The Vigilante (serial); Dick Tracy's Dilemma; Dick Tracy Meets Gruesome; Stallion Road; Mark of the Claw. **1948** Jungle Goddess; Thunder in the Pines; Canon City; Stage Struck; The Argyle Secrets. **1950** Radar Secret Service; The Redhead and the Cowboy. **1951** Close to My Heart. **1952** Dick Tracy vs. The Phantom Empire (serial).

BYRENS, MYER
Born: 1840. Died: June 29, 1933, Los Angeles, Calif. Screen and stage actor.

BYRNE, CECILY
Born: Birmingham, England. Died: June 30, 1975, England? Screen and stage actress. Married to actor Felix Aylmer (dec. 1979). Mother of actor David (dec. 1964) and Jennifer Aylmer.

Appeared in: **1934** Loyalties.

BYRNE, DONN
Born: 1889, New York, N.Y. Died: June 18, 1928, Brandon, Cork, Ireland (auto accident). Screen actor and writer.

Appeared in: **1928** Hangman's House.

BYRNE, EDDIE
Born: 1911, Dublin, Ireland. Died: Apr. 6, 1981, Dublin, Ireland. Screen, stage and vaudeville actor.

Appeared in: **1947** Odd Man Out; Hungry Hill; Captain Boycott. **1949**

Saints and Sinners. **1951** Lady Godiva Rides Again (US 1954). **1952** Time, Gentleman Please; The Gentle Gunman (US 1953). **1953** Annapurna (narrator); The Square Ring (US 1955); Albert R.N. (US 1955). **1954** Happy Ever After (aka Tonight's the Night—US); Beautiful Stranger (aka Twist of Fate—US); Trouble in the Glen; The Sea Shall Not Have Them (US 1955); The Divided Heart (US 1955). **1955** A Kid for Two Farthings (US 1956); Three Cases of Murder. **1956** Reach for the Sky (US 1957); It's Great to be Young (US 1958). **1957** Zarak; The Admirable Crichton (aka Paradise Lagoon—US); The Man in the Sky (aka Decision Against Time—US); Seven Waves Away (aka Abandon Ship!—US); Face in the Night (aka Menace in the Night—US 1958); These Dangerous Years (aka Dangerous Youth—US 1958). **1958** Dunkirk; Rooney; Wonderful Things!; Floods of Fear (US 1959). **1959** The Mummy; The Scapegoat; Jack the Ripper (US 1960). **1960** The Shakedown; Jackpot; The Bulldog Breed. **1961** Johnny Nobody (US 1965); The Mark. **1962** The Pot Carriers; The Break (US 1963); Locker Sixty-Nine; The Punch and Judy Man (US 1963); Mutiny on the Bounty. **1963** The Running Man; The Cracksman. **1964** Devils of Darkness (US 1965). **1966** Island of Terror (US 1967). **1967** Mr. Ten Percent. **1968** Gold is Where You Find It. **1969** I Can't ... I Can't (aka Wedding Night—US 1970); Where's Jack?; Guns in the Heather; Sinful Davey. **1973** The Mackintosh Man. **1977** Star Wars.

BYRNES, NANCY ROSENBLUTH
Born: 1915. Died: June 15, 1962, Union, N.J. Screen actress and singer.

BYROADE, GEORGE
Born: 1883. Died: Mar. 5, 1975. Screen stuntman and stand-in.

BYRON, A. S. "POP"
Born: 1877. Died: Feb. 6, 1964. Screen actor.

Appeared in: **1932** The Big Shot; You Said a Mouthful; The Fast Life; The Mummy. **1933** One Sunday Afternoon. **1934** Wharf Angel; The Countess of Monte Cristo; Menace. **1935** Two for Tonight; The Bride Comes Home. **1936** The Milky Way; Walking on Air. **1939** The Star Maker.

BYRON, ARTHUR
Born: Apr. 3, 1872, Brooklyn, N.Y. Died: July 17, 1943, Hollywood, Calif. Screen and stage actor.

Appeared in: **1929** A Family Affair (short). **1932** Twenty Thousand Years in Sing Sing; The Mummy; Fast Life. **1933** Gabriel Over the White House; Tonight Is Ours; Silk Express; Mayor of Hell; Private Detective 62; College Coach. **1934** The Man With Two Faces; Marie Galante; Two Alone; Notorious Sophie Lang; The House of Rothschild; The President Vanishes; Stand Up and Cheer; The Secret Bride; Fog Over Frisco. **1935** The Whole Town's Talking; Shadows of Doubt; The Casino Murder Case; Murder in the Fleet; Oil for the Lamps of China. **1936** The Prisoner of Shark Island.

BYRON, KATY (Catherine Byron)
Born: 1918. Died: Feb. 22, 1970, New Haven, Conn. Screen and radio actress. Married to radio producer-director Edward A. Byron (dec.).

Appeared in: **1929** A Funny Affair (short). **1933** The Mummy. **1960** Othello.

BYRON, PAUL
Born: 1891. Died: May 12, 1959, San Diego, Calif. Screen and stage actor. Entered films with Universal in 1915.

BYRON, ROYAL JAMES
Born: 1887. Died: Mar. 4, 1943, Trenton, N.J. Screen, stage and vaudeville actor. Entered films with Vitagraph.

Appeared in: **1926** The Palm Beach Girl. **1930** Unmasked.

BYSTROM, WALTER E.
Born: 1894. Died: Sept. 13, 1969, San Diego, Calif. Screen actor. Entered films as an extra before joining Sennett as a Keystone Kop.

CABANNE, WILLIAM CHRISTY
Born: 1888, St. Louis, Mo. Died: Oct. 15, 1950, Philadelphia, Pa. (heart attack). Film director, screen, stage actor, and screenwriter.

Appeared in: **1909** The Cord of Life; One Touch of Nature; The Song of the Shirt. **1912** Under Burning Skies; The Punishment; A Temporary Truce; A String of Pearls. **1913** Judith of Bethulia. **1942** Reap the Wild Wind.

CABARET TESS See WHEELER, TERESA

CABOT, BRUCE (Jacques Etienne Pellissier de Bujac)
Born: Apr. 20, 1904, Carlsbad, N. Mex. Died: May 3, 1972, Woodland Hills, Calif. (lung and throat cancer). Screen, stage and television actor. Divorced from Grace Mary Mather Smith and actresses Adrienne Ames (dec. 1947) and Franchesca de Scaffa.

Appeared in: **1931** Confessions of the Coed. **1932** Lady With a Past; What Price Hollywood?; Roadhouse Murder. **1933** Lucky Devils; King Kong; Great Jasper; Midshipman Jack; Ann Vickers; Disgraced!; Flying Devils. **1934** Redhead; Shadows of Sing Sing; Murder on the Blackboard; Finishing School; His Greatest Gamble; Night Alarm; Their Big Moment. **1935** Men of the Night; Without Children; Let 'Em Have It!; Show Them No Mercy. **1936** Don't Gamble with Love; Legion of Terror; Three Wise Guys; Fury; Sinner Take All; The Last of the Mohicans; Don't Turn 'Em Loose; The Big Game; Robin Hood of Eldorado; Penthouse Party. **1937** Love Takes Flight; Bad Guy. **1938** Bad Man of Brimstone; Sinners in Paradise; Smashing the Rackets; 10th Avenue Kid. **1939** You and Me; Homicide Bureau; Dodge City; Traitor Spy (aka The Torso Murder Mystery—US 1940); Mickey the Kid; Mystery of White Room. **1940** My Son Is Guilty; Susan and God; Captain Caution; Girls Under 21. **1941** The Flame of New Orleans; Wild Bill Hickok Rides; Sundown. **1942** Pierre of the Plains; Silver Queen. **1943** The Desert Song. **1945** Divorce; Salty O'Rourke; Fallen Angel. **1946** Smoky; The Avalanche. **1947** The Angel and the Badman; Gunfighters (aka The Assassin). **1948** The Gallant Legion. **1949** Sorrowful Jones. **1950** Fancy Pants; Rock Island Trail (aka Transcontinental Express). **1951** Best of the Badmen. **1952** Lost in Alaska; Kid Monk Baroni. **1955** El Mantello Rosso (The Red Cloak—US 1961). **1956** Il Tesoro di Rommel (Rommel's Treasure—US 1963). **1958** The Quiet American; The Sheriff of Fractured Jaw. **1959** The Love Specialist; John Paul Jones; Goliath and the Barbarian. **1961** The Comancheros. **1962** Hatari!. **1963** McLintock! **1964** Law of the Lawless. **1965** In Harm's Way; Cat Ballou; Black Spurs; Town Tamer. **1966** The Chase. **1967** The War Wagon. **1968** The Hellfighters; The Green Berets. **1969** The Undefeated; A Hall of Mirrors. **1970** WUSA; Chisum. **1971** Big Jake; Diamonds are Forever.

CABOT, ELLIOT
Born: 1899. Died: June 17, 1938, New York, N.Y. (results of a fall). Screen and stage actor.

Appeared in: **1923** Puritan Passions.

CABOT, SEBASTIAN
Born: July 6, 1918, London, England. Died: Aug. 23, 1977, Victoria, B.C. Canada (stroke). Screen, stage, radio and television actor.

Appeared in: **1946** Othello. **1947** Dual Alibi. **1949** Teheran (aka The Plot to Kill Roosevelt—US); Third Time Lucky (US 1950); Old Mother Riley's New Adventure; Dick Barton Strikes Back; The Adventures of Jane; The Spider and the Fly (US 1952). **1950** Midnight Episode (US 1951); Old Mother Riley, Headmistress (US 1951). **1951** Old Mother Riley's Jungle Treasure; The Wonder Kid. **1952** Ivanhoe; Babes in Baghdad. **1953** Heights of Danger (US 1962); Always a Bride (US 1954); The Captain's Paradise. **1954** Romeo and Juliet; The Love Lottery. **1956** Westward Ho the Wagons! **1957** Johnny Tremain; Dragoon Wells Massacre; Omar Khyyam; Black Patch. **1958** Terror in a Texas Town; In Love and War. **1959** The Angry Hills; Say One for Me; Los Misterios del Rosario (aka The Redeemer—US—voice). **1960** Seven Thieves; The Time Machine. **1963** Twice Told Tales; The Sword in the Stone (voice). **1965** The Family Jewels. **1967** The Jungle Book (voice); Winnie the Pooh (narrator).

CADELL, JEAN
Born: Sept. 13, 1884, Edinburgh, Scotland. Died: Sept. 24, 1967, London, England. Screen, stage and television actress.

Appeared in: **1912** David Garrick. **1915** The Man Who Stayed at Home. **1920** Alf's Button; Anna the Adventuress. **1923** The Naked Man. **1930** The Loves of Robert Burns. **1932** Two White Arms (aka Wives Behave—US 1933); Fires of Fate (US 1933). **1933** Timbuctoo. **1934** Little Friend; The Luck of a Sailor. **1935** David Copperfield. **1937** Love from a Stranger; Whom the Gods Love (aka Mozard—US 1940). **1938** Pygmalion. **1939** Confidential Lady. **1941** Quiet Wedding. **1942** Young Mr. Pitt. **1943** Dear Octopus (aka The Randolph Family—US 1945). **1945** I Know Where I'm Going (US 1947). **1947** Jassy (US 1948). **1949** That Dangerous Age (aka If This be Sin—US 1950); Marry Me (US 1951); Whisky Galore (aka Tight Little Island—US and Mad Little Island). **1950** Madeleine; The Reluctant Widow (US 1951); No Place for Jennifer (US 1951). **1951** The Late Edwina Black (aka Obsessed—US). **1952** I'm a Stranger. **1953** Meet Mr. Lucifer. **1956** Keep It Clean. **1957** The Little Hut; The Surgeon's Knife; Let's Be Happy. **1958** Rockets Galore (aka Mad Little Island—US). **1959** Upstairs and Downstairs (US 1961); Serious Charge (aka Immoral Charge—US 1962). **1960** A Taste of Money. **1964** A Touch of Hell (rerelease of Serious Charge-1959).

CAHILL, LILLY
Born: 1886. Died: July 20, 1955, San Antonio, Tex. Screen, stage and television actress. Married to actor Blandon Tynan (dec. 1967).

Appeared in: **1910** The Fugitive. **1931** My Sin. **1939** So This Is London (US 1940).

CAHILL, MARIE
Born: 1874, Brooklyn, N.Y. Died: Aug. 23, 1933, N.Y. (heart trouble). Screen, stage and vaudeville actress.

Appeared in: **1915** Judy Forgot. **1917** Gladys' Day Dreams and three two-reel comedies.

CAHILL, THOMAS M.
Born: 1889, Chillicothe, Ohio. Died: Apr. 3, 1953, near Washington, D.C. Screen, stage, television actor, and newspaper reporter.

Appeared in government-made short documentary films.

CAHOON, MILLIAN BENEDICT
Born: 1860. Died: Jan. 28, 1951, Darien, Conn. Screen and stage actor.

CAIN, ROBERT
Born: 1887. Died: Apr. 27, 1954, New York, N.Y. Screen, stage, television and radio actor.

Appeared in: **1916** My Lady Incog. **1918** He Comes Up Smiling. **1919** In Mizzoura; Male and Female. **1921** The Witching Hour; Man-Woman-Marriage. **1922** The Impossible Mrs. Bellew; The Crossroads of New York; Burning Sands; Reported Missing. **1923** Children of Jazz; Hollywood; Drums of Fate; Racing Hearts; The Tiger's Claw. **1924** Three Weeks; Conductor 1492; Soiled; The Rose of Paris. **1925** The Everlasting Whisper; The Golden Bed; When the Door Opened; Every Man's Wife; Wings of Youth. **1926** The Danger of Paris; Too Much Money; The Wilderness Woman. **1927** Husband Hunters; Rich Men's Sons.

CAINE, GEORGIA
Born: 1876, San Francisco, Calif. Died: Apr. 4, 1964, Hollywood, Calif. Screen and stage actress.

Appeared in: **1930** Good Intentions; Night Work. **1933** The Cradle Song. **1934** Evelyn Prentice; Call It Luck; Love Theme; I Am Suzanne; Once to Every Woman; Count of Monte Cristo; The Crusades; The White Angel. **1935** Dante's Inferno; The Crusades; She Married Her Boss; Hooray for Love. **1936** One Rainy Afternoon; Camille; Sing Me a Love Song; Navy Born. **1937** Time Out for Romance; It's Love I'm After; Bill Cracks Down; The Affairs of Cappy Ricks. **1938** Jezebel; Women Are Like That; His Exciting Night. **1939** Dodge City; Juarez; No Place to Go; Honeymoon in Bali; Tower of London. **1940** A Child is Born; All This and Heaven Too; Remember the Night; Babes for Sale; Nobody's Children; The Lone Wolf Meets a Lady; Christmas in July. **1941** You Belong to Me; Manpower; The Nurse's Secret; The Great Lie; Ridin' on a Rainbow; Hurry, Charlie, Hurry. **1942** Hello, Annapolis; The Wife Takes a Flyer; Yankee Doodle Dandy; Gentleman Jim; Are Husbands Necessary? **1943** The Sky's the Limit. **1944** The Miracle of Morgan's Creek; Hail the Conquering Hero. **1945** Mr. Skeffington. **1947** Nora Prentiss; Mad Wednesday; A Double Life. **1948** Give My Regards to Broadway; Unfaithfully Yours. **1949** The Beautiful Blonde from Bashful Bend; Bride for Sale.

CAINE, HENRY
Born: June 19, 1888, Seamington Spa, England. Died: July 9, 1962, Hayle, Cornwall, England. Screen and stage actor. Entered films in 1930.

Appeared in: **1931** Dreyfus (aka The Dreyfus Case—US); The Ghost Train (US 1933). **1949** That Dangerous Age (aka If This Be Sin—US 1950). **1954** The Green Scarf (US 1955). **1957** The Curse of Frankenstein.

CAINES, ELEANOR
Born: Philadelphia, Pa. Died: June 2, 1913, Philadelphia, Pa. Screen actress.

Appeared in: **1910** The Sheriff's Capture. **1912** Just Pretending.

CAIRNES, SALLY
Born: 1920. Died: Feb. 9, 1965, Hollywood, Calif. Screen actress and singer.

Appeared in: **1941** Look Who's Laughing; Playmates; Father Takes a Wife. **1943** Hit Parade of 1943. **1944** Cover Girl.

CAIROLI, CHARLIE, SR.
Born: 1910, Italy. Died: Feb. 17, 1980, Blackpool, England. Screen actor and circus clown. Father of circus clown Charlie Cairoli, Jr.

Appeared in: **1961** Io Amo, Tu Ami (I Love, You Love—US 1962).

CAITS, JOSEPH
Born: 1889. Died: Mar. 9, 1957, New York, N.Y. Screen, stage and vaudeville actor. Appeared in vaudeville with his brother Louis in an act billed as "The Caits Brothers."

Appeared in: **1936** After the Thin Man. **1937** Hollywood Cowboy; Youth on Parole. **1938** The Secret of Treasure Island (serial); A Slight Case of Murder; Reformatory. **1939** Lady and the Mob; Babes in Arms. **1940** Brother Orchid.

CALDARA, ORME
Born: 1875. Died: Oct. 21, 1925, Saranac Lake, N.Y. Screen and stage actor.

Appeared in: **1917** The Spreading Dawn.

CALDER, KING
Born: 1900. Died: June 28, 1964, Los Angeles, Calif. (heart attack). Screen, stage and television actor. Married to actress Ethel Wilson (dec. 1980).

Appeared in: **1956** Timetable; On the Threshold of Space; The Rains of Ranchipur. **1958** Hong Kong Confidential; Mardi Gras. **1960** Three Came to Kill. **1961** Everything's Ducky. **1964** Ready for the People.

CALDWELL, JACK
Died: Oct. 21, 1944, Honolulu, Hawaii. Screen actor.

CALDWELL, ORVILLE R.
Born: Feb. 28, 1896, Oakland, Calif. Died: Sept. 24, 1967, Santa Rosa, Calif. Screen and stage actor.

Appeared in: **1923** The French Doll; The Lonely Road; The Six-Fifty; The Scarlet Lily. **1924** Daughters of the Night. **1925** Sackcloth and Scarlet. **1926** The Wives of the Prophet; Flame of the Argentine. **1927** The Harvester; Judgment of the Hills. **1928** The Patsy; The Little Yellow House. **1938** Just Around the Corner; The Last Warning; Boys Town.

CALHERN, LOUIS (Carl Henry Vogt)
Born: Feb. 19, 1895, Brooklyn, N.Y. Died: May 12, 1956, Tokyo, Japan (heart attack). Screen, stage, vaudeville and burlesque actor. Divorced from actresses Ilka Chase (dec. 1978), Julia Hoyt (dec. 1955), Natalie Schaefer and Marianne Stewart. Nominated for 1950 Academy Award for Best Actor in The Magnificent Yankee.

Appeared in: **1921** The Blot; Too Wise Wives; What's Worth While? **1922** Woman, Wake Up! **1923** The Last Moment. **1931** Stolen Heaven; Road to Singapore; Larceny Lane; Blonde Crazy. **1932** Okay, America; They Call It Sin; Night After Night; Afraid to Talk. **1933** Strictly Personal; 20,000 Years In Sing Sing; Frisco Jenny; The Woman Accused; Diplomaniacs; The World Gone Mad; Duck Soup. **1934** The Affairs of Cellini; The Count of Monte Cristo; The Man with Two Faces. **1935** The Arizonian; The Last Days of Pompeii; Woman Wanted; Sweet Adeline. **1936** The Gorgeous Hussy. **1937** Her Husband Lies; The Life of Emile Zola. **1938** Fast Company. **1939** Juarez; 5th Avenue Girl; Charlie McCarthy, Detective. **1940** I Take This Woman; Dr. Erlich's Magic Bullet. **1943** Up in Arms; Nobody's Darling; Heaven Can Wait. **1944** The Bridge of San Luis Rey. **1946** Notorious. **1948** Arch of Triumph. **1949** The Red Danube; The Red Pony. **1950** Annie Get Your Gun; The Asphalt Jungle; Two Weeks with Love; Devil's Doorway; A Life of Her Own; Nancy Goes to Rio. **1951** The Man with a Cloak; The Magnificent Yankee (stage and film versions). **1952** The Invitation; The Washington Story; We're Not Married; The Prisoner of Zenda. **1953** Julius Caesar; Confidentially Connie; Remains to Be Seen; Main Street to Broadway; Latin Lovers. **1954** Executive Suite; The Student Prince; Men of the Fighting Lady; Betrayed; Athena; Rhapsody. **1955** High Society; The Blackboard Jungle; The Prodigal. **1956** Forever, Darling; The Teahouse of the August Moon.

CALHOUN, ALICE
Born: Nov. 24, 1904, Cleveland, Ohio. Died: June 3, 1966, Los Angeles, Calif. (cancer). Screen actress. Entered films with Vitagraph in N.Y.

Appeared in: **1920** Captain Swift; Human Collateral; Deadline at Eleven. **1921** The Charming Deceiver; Closed Doors; Peggy Puts It Over; Princess Jones. **1922** Angel of Crooked Street; Girl in His Room; The Little Minister; Matrimonial Web; The Rainbow; A Girl's Desire; Little Wildcat; Blue Blood. **1923** The Man from Brodney; The Man Next Door; The Midnight Alarm; One Stolen Night; Masters of Men; Pioneer Trails. **1924** Between Friends; Code of the Wilderness; Flowing Gold. **1925** Pampered Youth; The Other Woman's Story; The Part Time Wife; The Everlasting Whisper; The Happy Warrior; The Man on the Box. **1926** Flying High; Hero of the Big Snows; The Power of the Weak; Kentucky Handicap; Tentacles of the North. **1927** The Down Grade; Savage Passions; The Trunk Mystery; Hidden Aces; In the First Degree; Isle of Forgotten Women. **1929** Bride of the Desert.

CALHOUN, RICHARD
Born: 1899. Died: Apr. 11, 1977, Los Angeles, Calif. Circus performer, screen and vaudeville actor. Entered films with Mack Sennett as an extra.

CALL, JOHN
Born: 1907. Died: Apr. 3, 1973, New York, N.Y. Screen and stage actor.

Appeared in: **1952** Hangman's Knot; Boots Malone; Fearless Fagan; Indian Uprising; Youn Man With Ideas. **1954** The Long, Long Trailer. **1964** Santa Claus Conquers the Martians.

CALLAGAN, MARGARET
Born: 1890. Died: Nov. 29, 1947, New York, N.Y. Screen and stage actress. Married to stage producer Lucien Self.

CALLAHAN, BILLY
Born: 1911. Died: Feb. 21, 1964, Queens, N.Y. (heart attack). Screen and vaudeville actress. Appeared in vaudeville with Louise Brooks in an act billed as "Brooks and Callahan." Doubled for Thelma Todd.

CALLAHAN, CHARLES S. "CHUCK"
Born: 1891. Died: Nov. 12, 1964, New York, N.Y. Screen, stage, radio, television and vaudeville actor. Brother of actor Bobby Callahan (dec. 1938), with whom he appeared in vaudeville in an act billed as "Bob and Chuck Callahan."

Appeared in: **1937** Grips, Grunts and Groans (short).

CALLAHAN, ROBERT "BOBBY"
Born: 1896. Died: May 15, 1938, West Los Angeles, Calif. Screen and vaudeville actor. Brother of actor Chuck Callahan (dec. 1964) with whom he appeared in vaudeville in an act billed as "Bob and Chuck Callahan."

Appeared in: **1929** The Champion Golfer (short). **1930** Wild Company. **1934** Men in Black (short). **1937** Battle of Greed.

CALLAS, MARIA (Maria Anna Sofia Cecilia Kalogeropoulos)
Born: Dec. 3, 1923, New York, N.Y. Died: Sept. 16, 1977, Paris, France (heart attack). Opera singer and screen actress.

Appeared in: **1971** Medea (film debut).

CALLEIA, JOSEPH (Joseph Spurin-Calleia)
Born: Aug. 4, 1897, Malta. Died: Oct. 31, 1975, Malta. Screen, stage actor, singer and screenwriter.

Appeared in: **1931** His Woman. **1935** Public Hero No. 1; Riffraff. **1936** Exclusive Story; Tough Guy; Sworn Enemy; His Brother's Wife; Sinner Take All; After the Thin Man. **1937** Man of the People. **1938** Bad Man of Brimstone; Algiers; Marie Antoinette; Four's a Crowd. **1939** Juarez; The Gorilla; Five Came Back; Golden Boy; Full Confession. **1940** My Little Chickadee; Wyoming. **1941** The Monster and the Girl; Sundown. **1942** The Glass Key; Jungle Book. **1943** For Whom the Bell Tolls; The Cross of Lorraine. **1944** The Conspirators. **1946** Gilda; Deadline at Dawn. **1947** The Beginning of the End; Lured. **1948** The Noose Hangs High; Four Faces West. **1950** Palomino; Captain Carey, U.S.A.; Branded; Vendetta. **1951** Valentino; The Light Touch. **1952** Yankee Buccaneer; The Iron Mistress; When in Rome. **1953** The Caddy. **1955** Underwater; The Treasure of Pancho Villa; The Littlest Outlaw. **1956** Hot Blood; Serenade. **1957** Wild Is the Wind. **1958** Touch of Evil; The Light in the Forest. **1959** Cry Tough. **1960** The Alamo. **1963** Johnny Cool.

CALLEY, ROBERT (Robert Starr Calley)
Born: 1889, Oakland, Calif. Died: May 6, 1977, Kansas City, Mo. Screen actor, stage director/manager and production manager. Entered films as an extra during silent films.

CALLIER, FELICITAS
Born: 1905. Died: Oct. 1, 1967, Hollywood, Calif. (cancer). Screen actress. Married to film director Fred Frank (dec.) and later married to Paul Callier.

CALLIS, DAVID
Born: 1888. Died: Sept. 10, 1934, Los Angeles, Calif. Screen and stage actor.

Appeared in: **1929** The Sin Sister; What's Your Racket?

CALMETTES, ANDRE
Born: Apr. 18, 1861, Paris, France. Died: 1942, France? Screen actor and film director.

CALTHROP, DION (Dion Clayton Calthrop)
Born: May 2, 1878, London, England. Died: Mar. 7, 1937, England. Screen, stage actor, novelist, artist and designer. Brother of actor Donald Calthrop (dec. 1940). Son of stage actor John Clayton Calthrop (dec. 1888) and stage actress Eva Boucicault (dec.).

CALTHROP, DONALD
Born: Apr. 11, 1888, England. Died: July 15, 1940, England (heart attack). Screen and stage actor. Son of stage actor John Clayton Calthrop (dec.) and stage actress Eva Boucicault. Brother of actor Dion Calthrop (dec. 1937).

Appeared in: **1916** Wanted a Widow; Altar Chains. **1917** Masks and Faces; The Gay Lord Quex. **1918** Nelson; Goodbye. **1928** Shooting Stars. **1929** Atlantic; Blackmail; The Clue of the New Pin; The Flying Squad; Up the Poll (short); Juno and the Paycock (aka The Shame of Mary Boyle—US). **1930** Two Worlds; Murder; Loose Ends; Elstree Calling; Almost a Honeymoon (US 1931); Song of Soho; The Night Porter; Spanish Eyes; We Take Off Our Hats; Star Impersonations (short); The Cockney Spirit in the War series including All Riot on the Western Front and The Cockney Spirit in the War. **1931** The Ghost Train (US 1933); Uneasy Virtue; Cape Forlorn (aka The Love Storm—US); The Bells; Many Waters. **1932** Money for Nothing; Rome Express; Fires of Fate (US 1933); Number Seventeen. **1933** Friday the Thirteenth (US 1934); The Acting Business; F.P.T; Orders Is Orders (US 1934); I Was a Spy; Early to Bed; Sorrell and Son (US 1934). **1934** Red Ensign (aka Strike!—US); Nine Forty-Five; It's a Cop. **1935** Man of the Moment; Scrooge; The Phantom Light; The Clairvoyant; The Divine Spark. **1936** The Man Behind the Mask; Broken Blossoms (US 1937); The Man Who Changed His Mind (aka The Man Who Lived Again—US). **1937** Cafe Colette (aka Danger in Paris—US); Dreaming Lips; Fire Over England; Love from a Stranger. **1939** Shadow of Death. **1940** Band Wagon; Let George Do It. **1941** Major Barbara.

CALVERT, CATHERINE (Catherine Cassidy)
Born: 1891, Baltimore, Md. Died: Jan. 18, 1971, Uniondale, N.Y. Screen and stage actress.

Appeared in: **1918** A Romance of the Underworld. **1919** Fires of Faith; The Career of Catherine Bush. **1920** Dead Men Tell No Tales. **1921** The Heart of Maryland; Moral Fibre; You Find It Everywhere. **1922** That Woman; The Green Caravan. **1923** The Indian Love Lyrics; Out to Win.

CALVERT, MRS. CHARLES
Born: 1835, England. Died: Sept. 20, 1921, London, England. Screen, stage actress and playwright. Daughter of stage actor James Biddles (dec.). Married to stage actor Charles Calvert (dec. 1879). Mother of Leonard, Alexander, actor Louis (dec. 1923) and stage actor Cecil G. Calvert (dec.).

Appeared in: **1911** Henry VIII.

CALVERT, EDDIE
Born: 1922, Lancashire, England. Died: Aug. 7, 1978, Johannesburg, S. Africa (heart attack). Trumpet player, screen and television actor.

Appeared in: **1956** Beyond Mombasa (US 1957). **1964** Mishpahat Simchon (aka The Simchon Family—US 1969).

CALVERT, ELISHA H.
Born: June 27, 1873, Alexandria, Va. Died: Oct. 5, 1941, Hollywood, Calif. Screen, stage, vaudeville actor, film director and producer. Married to actress Lillian Drew (dec. 1924).

Appeared in: **1911** The Love Test (film debut). **1912** The House of Pride; Giuseppe's Good Fortune. **1913** The Boomerang; Tapped Wires; The Sign; The Love Theft; Broken Threads United; The Heart of the Law; In Convict Garb; The Pay-as-You-Enter Man; The Melburn Confession; Seeing Is Believing; The Heiress; Bill Mixes With His Relations; The Unknown; The Misjudging of Mr. Hubby; The Little Mother; Love Through a Lens; The Road of Transgression; Odd Knots; The Hero-Coward; Hypnotism in Hicksville; What George Did; The Price of Gold; The Rival Salesman. **1914** Trinkets of Tragedy; Under Royal Patronage; The Grip of Circumstance; The Counter-Melody; One Wonderful Night; Ashes of Hope. **1923** The Silent Partner. **1924** Bluff; The Only Woman; Why Men Leave Home; Inez from Hollywood. **1925** Havoc; Sally; East of Suez; The Talker. **1926** Ella Cinders; The Girl from Montmarte. **1927** Melting Millions (serial); The First Auto; Lonesome Ladies; The Wizard; Rookies. **1928** Moran of the Marines; The Man Without a Face (serial); The Legion of the Condemned; Let 'Er Go Gallagher; Why Sailors Go Wrong; Prop and Pep. **1929** The Greene Murder Case; Darkened Rooms; The Mighty; The Virginian; Dark Street; The Studio Murder Mystery; The

Canary Murder Case; Fast Company; The Love Parade; Thunderbolt. **1930** Half Shot at Sunrise; Behind the Makeup; The Benson Murder Case; The Border Legion; The Kibitzer; Ladies Love Brutes; A Man from Wyoming; Men Are Like That; Only the Brave; The Widow from Chicago; The Social Lion; Peacock Alley. **1932** Beyond Victory; Horse Feathers. **1933** Wild Horse Mesa; The Mysterious Rider; Duck Soup. **1934** Here Comes the Groom; The Mighty Barnum. **1935** Rumba. **1936** The Glory Trail.

CALVERT, LOUIS
Born: 1859, England. Died: July 9, 1923, England? Screen and stage actor. Son of actress Mrs. Charles Calvert (dec. 1921). Brother of stage actor Cecil G. (dec.) and Charles Calvert (dec. 1879). Father of actress Patricia Calvert.

Appeared in: **1913** David Garrick.

CALVIN, HENRY (Wimberly Calvin Goodman, Jr.)
Born: 1918, Dallas, Tex. Died: Oct. 6, 1975, Dallas, Tex. (cancer). Screen, television, radio and stage actor.

Appeared in: **1956** The Broken Star; Crime Against Joe. **1960** Toby Tyler; The Sign of Zorro. **1961** Babes in Toyland. **1965** Ship of Fools.

CALVIN, LESTER (Leslie Calvin Vesey)
Born: 1890, Iowa. Died: May 30, 1978, Orlando, Fla. Screen, stage and vaudeville actor. Entered films in 1917 as an extra for Universal Pictures.

CAMACHO, LEW
Born: 1932. Died: Apr. 24, 1974, Ventura County, Calif. (heart attack). Screen and stage actress.

Appeared in: **1972** The New Centurions.

CAMBRIDGE, GODFREY (Godfrey MacArthur Cambridge)
Born: Feb. 26, 1929 or 1933, New York, N.Y. Died: Nov. 29, 1976, Burbank, Calif. (heart attack). Black screen, stage, television actor and nightclub comedian. Divorced from actress Barbara Ann Tee.

Appeared in: **1959** The Last Angry Man. **1963** Gone are the Days! **1964** Troublemaker. **1967** The President's Analyst; The Busy Body. **1968** The Biggest Bundle of Them All; Bye Bye Braverman. **1970** Watermelon Man (aka Night the Sun Came Out); Cotton Comes to Harlem. **1972** Come Back Charleston Blue; The Biscuit Eater. **1975** Whiffs; Friday Foster.

CAMELIA, MURIEL
Born: 1913. Died: Nov. 15, 1925, Miami, Fla. (motor bus accident). Screen and stage actress. Appeared in D.W. Griffith films.

CAMERON, BRUCE (Paul Brachard, Jr.)
Born: 1910. Died: Apr. 10, 1959, Los Angeles, Calif. Screen actor and circus acrobat.

Appeared in: **1943** Riding High.

CAMERON, DONALD
Born: 1889. Died: July 11, 1955, West Cornwall, Conn. Screen and stage actor.

Appeared in: **1921** The Education of Elizabeth.

CAMERON, GENE
Died: Nov. 16, 1928, Yuma, Ariz. Screen actor.

Appeared in: **1922** The Sign of the Rose. **1923** An Old Sweetheart of Mine. **1924** Circe, The Enchantress. **1925** Excuse Me. **1926** The Midnight Kiss. **1927** Chain Lightning; The Gay Retreat.

CAMERON, HUGH
Born: 1879, Duluth, Minn. Died: Nov. 9, 1941, New York, N.Y. Screen and stage actor.

Appeared in: **1921** Cappy Ricks. **1923** Homeward Bound. **1924** Pied Piper Malone. **1925** The Man Who Found Himself. **1927** For the Love of Mike. **1921** One Heavenly Night; Papa's Slay Ride (short). **1932** The Emergency Case. **1939** One Third of a Nation; Back Door to Heaven.

CAMERON, RUDOLPH "RUDY" (Rudolph Cameron Brennan)
Born: Oct. 24, 1894, Washington, D.C. Died: Feb. 17, 1958, Los Angeles, Calif. (hemorrhage). Screen and stage actor.

Appeared in: **1917** The More Excellent Way; Clover's Rebellion. **1918** My Husband's Friend. **1922** Rose o' the Sea. **1923** Shattered Faith. **1927** For the Love of Mike. **1928** Coney Island; Three-Ring Marriage. **1930** Song of the West; Queen High. **1935** The Man Who Reclaimed His Head; The Gilted Lily.

CAMP, SHEPPARD
Born: 1882, West Point, Ga. Died: Nov. 20, 1929, Hollywood, Calif. (injuries from fall). Screen and stage actor.

Appeared in: **1929** The Greene Murder Case. **1930** Playing Around; Song of the Flame.

CAMPBELL, ALAN
Born: 1905. Died: June 14, 1963, West Hollywood, Calif. Screen, stage actor and screenwriter. Married to writer Dorothy Parker (dec. 1967).

CAMPBELL, COLIN
Born: 1883, Falkirk, Scotland. Died: Mar. 27, 1966, Woodland Hills, Calif. Screen, stage actor and film producer. Entered films in 1915. Do not confuse with film director Colin Campbell (dec. 1928).

Appeared in: **1915** Tillie's Tomato Surprise; Toodles, Tom and Trouble; Bing Bang Brothers. **1916** Belinda's Bridal Breakfast. **1920** Nothing But the Truth. **1921** Where Lights Are Low; The Girl from Nowhere; The Man of Stone. **1922** Cardigan. **1925** The White Monkey. **1930** Big Boy; The Road to Singapore; Unwanted; The Gay Diplomat. **1931** The Deceiver. **1933** Alice in Wonderland. **1934** Eight Girls in a Boat. **1938** The Secret of Treasure Island (serial). **1941** San Francisco Docks. **1942** Life Begins at 8:30; Mrs. Miniver; This Above All; The War Against Mrs. Hadley. **1944** Jane Eyre; National Velvet; The Lodger. **1945** Sabrina; The Fatal Witness; Scotland Yard Investigator. **1947** Ivy; Love from a Stranger; Moss Rose; The Wife of Monte Cristo; Exposed; The Two Mrs. Carrolls. **1948** Texas, Brooklyn and Heaven. **1949** The Fan; Mr. Belvedere Goes to College; Adventure of Icabod and Mr. Toad (voice). **1955** Abbott and Costello Meet the Keystone Kops. **1954** Sabrina. **1960** The Lost World. **1963** The Three Stooges Go Around the World in a Daze; The Leather Boys (US 1965). **1964** My Fair Lady; Saturday Night Out; The High Bright Sun (aka McGuire Go Home!—US 1966).

CAMPBELL, ERIC (Eric Alfred Campbell)
Born: Apr. 26, 1879, Scotland. Died: Dec. 20, 1917, Los Angeles, Calif. (auto accident). Screen, stage actor and screenwriter.

Appeared in: **1914** Between Showers; Cruel, Cruel Love; Mabel At the Wheel; Caught In a Cabaret; The Fatal Mallet; Her Friend the Bandit; The Knockout. **1916** The Floorwalker; The Fireman; The Vagabond; The Count; The Pawnshop; The Rink; Behind the Screen. **1917** Easy Street; The Cure; The Immigrant; The Adventurer. **1963** 30 Years of Fun (documentary).

CAMPBELL, FLORA "FLO"
Born: 1911. Died: Nov. 6, 1978, Stamford, Conn. (cancer). Screen, stage, radio and television actress.

Appeared in: **1930** His Public (short).

CAMPBELL, FRANK
Born: 1847. Died: Apr. 30, 1934, Hollywood, Calif. Screen and stage actor.

Appeared in: **1929** Frozen River.

CAMPBELL, GILLY (William Gilthorpe Campbell)
Born: Feb. 13, 1907, Kansas City, Kans. Died: Feb. 21, 1973, Los Angeles, Calif. Professional baseball player and screen actor.

Appeared in: **1942** Pride of the Yankees.

CAMPBELL, MARGARET
Born: 1873. Died: June 27, 1939, Los Angeles, Calif. (murdered—hammer attack; son confesssed to crime). Screen actress. Divorced from actor Josef Swickard (dec. 1940).

Appeared in: **1921** Lying Lips; Eden and Return; The Girl in the Taxi. **1922** Don't Shoot; Confidence; The Top O' the Morning. **1923** The Clean Up; Legally Dead; His Mystery Girl. **1924** The Dangerous Blonde; The Fast Worker. **1925** Home Maker. **1926** The Better Man; Monte Carlo; The Lady from Hell. **1927** Children of Divorce; Wages of Conscience. **1929** One Hysterical Night. **1930** Take the Heir. **1933** Hello, Everybody!

CAMPBELL, MAY *See* FOSTER, MAY

CAMPBELL, MRS. PATRICK (Beatrice Stella Tanner)
Born: Feb. 9, 1865, Kensington, London, England. Died: Apr. 10, 1940, Pau, France. Screen and stage actress. Sister of stage actress Stella Patrick Campbell (dec. 1940).

Appeared in: **1930** The Dancers (film debut). **1934** Riptide; Outcast Lady; One More River. **1935** Pygmalion; Crime and Punishment.

CAMPBELL, PHOEBE HARRIET
Born: 1902. Died: June 21, 1978, Los Angeles, Calif. Screen actress and talent agent. Sister of stage actor Stafford Cherry Campbell (dec.).

CAMPBELL, VIOLET (Violet Shelton)
Born: 1893. Died: Jan. 3, 1970, London, England. Screen and stage actress. Married to actor Nigel Bruce (dec. 1953).

Appeared in: **1941** Suspicion (her only film).

CAMPBELL, WEBSTER (William Webster Campbell)
Born: 1893, Kansas City, Mo. Died: Aug. 28, 1972, Liberty, Kans. Screen actor, film director, screenwriter and author. Divorced from actress Corinne Griffith (dec. 1979). Married to Beatrice Campbell.

Appeared in: **1914** The Secret Marriage. **1915** Oh, Daddy and Kay-Bee films. **1917** Transgression; The Clock Struck One; Satan's Private Door; The Fettered Woman; Local Color; The Renaissance at Charleroi. **1918** The Love Doctor; The Count and the Wedding; The Girl of Today. **1920** Human Collateral; The Tower of Jewels. **1921** It Isn't Being Done This Season. **1930** The Love Racket; In the Next Room.

CAMPEAU, FRANK
Born: Dec. 14, 1864, Detroit, Mich. Died: Nov. 5, 1943, Woodland Hills, Calif. Screen and stage actor.

Appeared in: **1915** Jordan In a Hard Road. **1917** A Modern Musketeer; Reaching for the Moon; Man from Painted Post. **1918** Mr. Fix-It; He Comes Up Smiling; Bound in Morocco; Light of the Western Stars; Headin' South; Arizona. **1919** When the Clouds Roll By; Cheating Cheaters; The Knickerbocker Buckaroo; His Majesty the American. **1920** The Life of the Party. **1921** The Kid; The Killer; For Those We Love. **1922** The Sin of Martha Queed; The Crimson Challenge; Just Tony; The Lane That Had No Turning; The Yosemite Trail; The Trap; Skin Deep. **1923** Isle of Lost Ships; To the Last Man; Modern Matrimony; North of Hudson Bay; Quicksands; The Spider and the Rose; Three Who Paid. **1924** Hoodman Blind; Those Who Dance; The Alaskan; Not a Drum Was Heard. **1925** Battling Bunyon; Heir-Looms; Coming Through; The Man from Red Gulch; The Saddle Hawk; The Pleasure Buyers; Manhattan Madness; The Golden Cocoon. **1926** The Three Bad Men; The Frontier Trail; No Man's Gold; Sea Horses; Whispering Wires. **1927** The First Auto; Let It Rain; The Heart of the Yukon. **1928** Across the Border (short); The Candy Kid. **1929** In Old Arizona; In the Headlines; Sea Fury; Points West; The Gamblers; Frozen River; Say It With Songs. **1930** Hideout; The Last of the Duanes; Abraham Lincoln; Captain Thunder; The People Versus (short); Lightnin'; Trifles (short); Danger (short). **1931** Fighting Caravans; Soldier's Plaything; Lasco of the Rio Grande. **1932** Girl of the Rio; White Eagle; The Dove. **1933** Smoky. **1935** Hopalong Cassidy. **1936** Everyman's Law; Empty Saddles. **1937** Black Aces. **1938** Border Wolves; The Painted Trail; Marie Antoinette.

CAMPTON, MISS
Died: Nov. 21, 1930, Paris, France. Screen and stage actress. Married to stage manager Paul Derval.

CANE, CHARLES
Born: 1899. Died: Nov. 30, 1973, Woodland Hills, Calif. Screen actor.

Appeared in: **1932** Jewel Robbery. **1933** The Mayor of Hell. **1942** Lady in a Jam; The Big Street; All Through the Night; The Man in the Trunk; Bells of Capistrano; Beyond the Blue Horizon. **1943** Always a Bridesmaid; Hello, Frisco, Hello; Henry Aldrich Haunts a House; Gildersleeve's Bad Day; Dixie; True to Life. **1944** Mrs. Parkington; Casanova Brown; The Hairy Ape; The Lady and the Monster. **1945** Billy Rose's Diamond Horseshoe; Nob Hill; Circumstantial Evidence; Don Juan Quilligan. **1946** The Kid From Brooklyn; Crime of the Century; Valley of the Zombies; It Shouldn't Happen to a Dog. **1947** Dead Reckoning; The Guilt of Janet Ames. **1948** Fighting Mad; Tenth Avenue Angel; Adventures in Silverado; Bodyguard. **1949** The Gal Who Took the West; The Dark Past; Prison Warden; Streets of San Francisco; Calamity Jan and Sam Bass. **1950** Born Yesterday; Southside 1-1000; The Blonde Bandit. **1951** Soldiers Three; Belle le Grand; Native Son. **1952** Scandal Sheet; Lone Star; Models, Inc.; Ruby Gentry. **1953** A Perilous Journey; No Escape. **1954** She Couldn't Say No. **1955** Marty; Prince of Players; Revenge of the Creature. **1956** The Birds and the Bees. **1957** Gun Battle at Monterey. **1961** The Gambler Wore a Gun.

CANFIELD, WILLIAM F.
Died: Feb. 14, 1925, New York, N.Y. Screen, stage and vaudeville actor.

CANN, ALEXANDER
Born: 1903, Canada. Died: Dec. 21, 1977, Sydney, Australia. Screen actor, film producer, correspondent and cameraman.

Appeared in: **1970** Ned Kelly.

CANNON, ESMA
Born: England. Died: 1972, England? Screen actress.

Appeared in: **1939** I Met a Murderer. **1944** Don't Take it to Heart (US 1949). **1947** The Years Between; Jassy (US 1948); Holiday Camp (US 1948). **1950** Last Holiday; Guilt is my Shadow (US 1954); Double Confession (US 1948). **1954** The Sleeping Tiger. **1956** Sailor Beware! (aka Panic in the Parlor—US 1957);Three Men in a Boat (US 1958). **1959** Jack the Ripper (US 1960). **1960** No Kidding (aka Beware of Children—US 1961); Carry on Constable (US 1961); Doctor in Love (US 1962); The Flesh and the Fiends (aka Mania—US 1961). **1961** Raising the Wind (aka Roommates—US 1962); What a Carve Up! (aka No Place Like Homicide—US 1962); Carry on Regardless (US 1963); In the Doghouse (US 1964). **1962** The Fast Lady (US 1965); We Joined the Navy. **1963** Nurse on Wheels (US 1964); Hide and Seek (US 1964); Carry on Cabby (aka Call Me a Cab—US 1967).

CANNON, RAYMOND
Born: Long Hollow, Tenn. Died: June 7, 1977, Hollywood, Calif. (cancer). Screen, stage actor, film director and screenwriter.

Appeared in: **1920** Mary Ellen Comes to Town. **1921** Chickens; Penny of Top Hill Trail. **1922** His Back Against the Wall; The Unfoldment; Watch Your Step. **1923** Mary of the Movies; The Printer's Devil.

CANOVA, LEON "ZEKE"
Born: Dec. 31, 1898, Fla. Died: Aug. 9, 1980, Los Angeles, Calif. (cardiac arrest). Screen, stage actor and opera singer. Brother of actors Pete (dec. 1947), Judy and Anne Canova.

Appeared in: **1935** In Caliente; Broadway Gondolier. **1937** Thrill of a Lifetime.

CANOVA, PETE
Died: 1947, Calif? (heart attack). Screen actor. Brother of actors Leon "Zeke" (dec. 1980), Judy and Anne Canova.

Appeared in: **1935** In Caliente; Broadway Gondolier.

CANSINO, EDUARDO
Born: 1895. Died: Dec. 24, 1968, Pompano Beach, Fla. Screen actor/dancer. Brother of dancer Elisa Cansino, father of actress Rita Hayworth and actor Eduardo Cansino, Jr. (dec. 1974). Leader of the "Dancing Cansino" group.

Appeared in: **1926** A Vitagraph short. **1936** The Dancing Pirate. **1953** Miss Sadie Thompson; The Mississippi Gambler; Salome.

CANSINO, EDUARDO, JR.
Born: 1920. Died: Mar. 11, 1974, Hollywood, Calif. (cancer). Screen actor/dancer. Brother of actress Rita Hayworth and son of actor Eduardo Cansino, Sr. (dec. 1968).

Appeared in: **1926** Vitagraph short. **1953** The Great Adventures of Captain Kidd (serial).

CANSINO, RAFAEL
Born: 1888. Died: Mar. 18, 1941, Hollywood, Calif. Dancer, screen and stage actor.

CANTER, LYNN *See* CASTILE, LYNN

CANTER, NELLIE BELL
Born: 1902. Died: May 1, 1981, Pittsburgh, Pa. Screen actress. Appeared in silent films for Universal.

CANTOR, CHARLES
Born: 1898. Died: Sept. 11, 1966, Hollywood, Calif. (heart attack). Screen, stage and radio actor. Brother of actor Nat Cantor (dec. 1956).

Appeared in: **1954** Duffy's Tavern. **1952** Stop, You're Killing Me.

CANTOR, EDDIE (Edward Israel Iskowitz)
Born: Jan. 31, 1892, New York, N.Y. Died: Oct. 10, 1964, Beverly Hills, Calif. (heart attack). Screen, stage, vaudeville, burlesque, radio, television actor and screenwriter. Received a 1956 Special Academy Award for distinguished service to the film industry. Married to actress Ida Cantor (dec. 1962).

Appeared in: **1926** Kid Boots (film debut). **1927** Special Delivery; Follies. **1929** Glorifying the American Girl. **1930** Insurance (short); Whoopee. **1931** Palmy Days. **1932** The Kid from Spain. **1933** Roman Scandals. **1934** The Hollywood Gad-About (short); Screen Snapshots #11 (short); Kid Millions. **1936** Strike Me Pink. **1937** Ali Baba Goes to Town. **1940** Forty Little Mothers. **1943** Thank Your Lucky Stars. **1944** Hollywood Canteen; Show Business. **1945** Rhapsody in Blue. **1948** If You Knew Susie. **1952** The Story of Will Rogers.

CANTOR, HERMAN
Born: 1896. Died: Oct. 12, 1953, Jersey City, N.J. Screen actor.

Appeared in: **1948** Trouble Makers. **1951** Two Tickets to Broadway. **1952** Road to Bali.

CANTOR, IDA (Ida Tobias)
Born: 1892, New York, N.Y. Died: Aug. 8, 1962, Beverly Hills, Calif. (heart attack). Screen actress. Married to actor Eddie Cantor (dec. 1964).

Appeared in: **1953** The Eddie Cantor Story (cameo).

CANTOR, NAT
Born: 1897. Died: Mar. 15, 1956, Queens, N.Y. Screen, stage, vaudeville, burlesque, radio and television actor. Brother of screen actor Charles Cantor (dec. 1966).

CANTWAY, FRED R.
Born: 1883. Died: Mar. 12, 1939, Hollywood, Calif. Screen and stage actor.

CANTZEN, CONRAD
Born: 1867, New Orleans, La. Died: June 28, 1945, New York, N.Y. Screen and stage actor.

Appeared in: **1915** The Melting Pot.

CANZONERI, TONY
Born: Nov. 6, 1908, Slidell, La. Died: Dec. 10, 1959. Professional boxer and screen actor.

Appeared in: **1933** Mr. Broadway. **1949** Ringside.

CAPOZZI, ALBERTO
Born: 1885, Italy. Died: 1945, Italy. Screen actor.

Appeared in: **1908** Grandmother's Lamp; The Mysterious Piano; Perjury. **1947** Marco Visconti.

CAPP, AL (Alfred Gerald Caplin)
Born: Sept. 28, 1909, New Haven, Conn. Died: Nov. 5, 1979, Cambridge, Mass (emphysema). Cartoonist, screen, radio, television actor and screenwriter. Creator of Li'l Abner Cartoon Strip.

Appeared in: **1956** That Certain Feeling.

CAPRICE, JUNE
Born: Nov. 19, 1899. Died: Nov. 9, 1936, Los Angeles, Calif. Screen actress. Married to actor and film director Harry Millarde (dec.).

Appeared in: **1916** Caprice of the Mountains. **1917** A Modern Cinderella; Unknown 274. **1918** The Camouflage Kiss; Blue-Eyed Mary; Miss Innocence; The Heart of Romance. **1921** Rogues and Romance.

CARBALLO, RICHARD "DICK"
Born: 1937. Died: Apr. 27, 1980, New York, N.Y. Screen, stage, television actor, cameraman and stuntman.

Appeared in: **1970** Guess What We Learned in School Today? (aka Guess What!?! and I Ain't no Buffalo). **1978** Slow Dancing in the Big City. **1979** The Wanderers.

CARD, KATHRYN
Born: 1893. Died: Mar. 1, 1964, Costa Mesa, Calif. (heart attack). Screen, stage, radio and television actress.

Appeared in: **1945** Kiss and Tell. **1946** It Shouldn't Happen to a Dog; Undercurrent. **1947** The Hucksters; Born to Kill; That Hagen Girl. **1948** Three Daring Daughters; The Sainted Sisters. **1949** The Reckless Moment; The Dark Past; A Kiss for Corliss; Mother Is a Freshman. **1950** Harriet Craig; The Skipper Surprised His Wife. **1951** Never Trust a Gambler. **1952** Paula; The Girl in White; You for Me; The Model and the Marriage Broker; The Pride of St. Louis. **1953** Remains to Be Seen; It Happens Every Thursday. **1954** Woman's World; A Star is Born. **1955** Daddy Long Legs. **1956** Hollywood or Bust; The Birds and the Bees. **1958** Home Before Dark; Good Day for a Hanging. **1960** Please Don't Eat the Daisies; Because They're Young. **1962** Walk on the Wild Side. **1964** The Unsinkable Molly Brown.

CARDWELL, JAMES (Albert James Cardwell)
Born: Nov. 21, 1921, Camden, N.J. Died: Feb. 4, 1954, Hollywood, Calif. (suicide—gun). Screen actor.

Appeared in: **1944** The Sullivans; Sweet and Low Down. **1945** The Shanghai Cobra; Voice of the Whistler. **1946** Canyon Passage; Fear; A

Walk in the Sun; Behind the Mask; The Missing Lady. **1947** Devil on Wheels. **1948** Harpoon; He Walked by Night. **1949** Daughter of the Jungle; Down Dakota Way; San Antone Ambush; Tokyo Joe; And Baby Makes Three. **1950** Arizona Cowboy.

CARELL, ANNETTE
Died: Oct. 20, 1967, London, England. Screen, stage and television actress. Appeared in U.S., British and German films.

Appeared in: **1953** Martin Luther. **1962** The Tell-Tale Heart. **1965** Darling. **1967** Our Mother's House; The Vulture.

CARELSEN, FIE
Born: 1890. Died: July 21, 1975. Dutch screen and stage actor.

CARETTE (Julien Carette)
Born: Dec. 23, 1897, France. Died: July 20, 1966, Paris, France (burns). Screen and stage actor.

Appeared in: **1932** L'Affaire est dans le Sac; L'Amour a l'Americaine; Les Gaites de l'Escadron. **1933** Adieu les Beaux Jours; Le Billet de Mille; Georges et Georgette; Je te Confie ma Femme; Gonzague; Moi et l'Imperatrice; Ganster Malgre; Le Greluchon Delicat. **1934** Quadrille d'Amour; La Marraine; Paris-Camargue; Marinella. **1935** Fanfare d'Amour; Et Moi j'te Dis Qu'elle t'a Fait d' L'Oeil; Fernand le Noceur; Dora Nelson; Les Soeurs Hortensias; Une Nuit de Noce. **1936** Mon Coeur t'appelle; Adventure a Paris; Les Rois du Sport. **1937** Gribouille; La vie Est Belle; 27 Rue de la Paix; La Grand Illusion. **1938** Cafe de Paris; Entree des Artistes; La Marseillaise; La Bete Humaine; La Route Enchantee; L'accroche-coeur. **1939** Le Monde Tremblera; Sixieme Etage; Tempete sur Paris; Menaces; La Famille Duraton; Je Chante; Battements des Coeur; Derriere la Facade; La Regle du Jeu; Le Reciff de Corail. **1940** 24 Heures de Perm; Soyez les Bienvenus. **1941** Parade en Sept Nuits; Fromont Jeune et Risler Aine. **1942** Fou d'amour; Une Etoile au Soleil; Croisteres Siderales; Lettres d'amour; Monsieur des Lourdines. **1943** Coup de Tete; Adieu Leonard; Service de Nuit; Bonsoir Mesdames, Bonsoir Messieurs; Le bal des Passants. **1944** L'enquete sur le 58; Le Merle Blanc. **1945** Impasse; Sylvie et le Fantome. **1946** Les Portes de la Nuit; Histoire de Chanter; Monsieur Ludovic; L'ampir Autor de la Maison; Le Chateau de la Derniere Chance. **1947** La Mannequin Assassine; La Fleur de l'age. **1948** Une si Jolie Petite Plage. **1949** Branquigno!, Amedee; Premieres Armes; Le 84 Prend des Vacances; La Marie du Port; Occupe-toi d'Armelie; Ronde de Nuit; Oh, Amelia. **1950** Sans Laisser d'Addresse. **1951** L'auberge Rouge (The Red Inn—US 1954); Pour l'amour du Ciel; Ovvero E' piu Facile Che un Cammello; Rome-Paris-Rome Ovvero Signori in Carrozza!. **1952** Drole de Noce; Agence Matrimoniale. **1953** Au Diable la Vertue; La Fete a Henriette; Gli Uomini che Mascalzoni; Le Bon Dieu sans Confession. **1954** Chateaux en Espagne; Sur le Banc; Pas de Coup dur Par Johnny; Si Paris Nous Etait Conte; Ces Sacrees Vacances; Elena et les Hommes. **1955** La Mome Pigalle (aka The Maiden—US 1961). **1956** Coup dur Chez les Mous; Je Reviendrai a Kandara; Paris-Palace-Hotel. **1957** Crime et Chatiment. **1959** La Jument Verte (The Green Mare—US 1961); The Mirror Has Two Faces; Archimede, Le Clochard (Magnificient Tramp—US 1962). **1961** Rules of the Game. Other French film: A Nous la Liberte.

CAREW, ARTHUR EDMUND (aka ARTHUR EDMUND CAREWE)
Born: 1894, Trebeizond, Armenia. Died: Apr. 23, 1937, Santa Monica, Calif. Screen and stage actor.

Appeared in: **1920** Rio Grande. **1921** Bar Nothin'; Her Mad Bargain; The Easy Road; Sham; The Mad Marriage. **1922** The Ghost Breaker; His Wife's Husband; My Old Kentucky Home; The Prodigal Judge. **1923** Trilby; Refuge; Daddy. **1924** The Song of Love; The Price of a Party. **1925** Sandra; Phantom of the Opera; The Only Thing; The Boomerang; A Lover's Oath. **1926** The Torrent; The Silent Lover; Diplomacy; Volcano. **1927** Uncle Tom's Cabin; A Man's Past; The Cat and the Canary; The Claw. **1930** The Matrimonial Bed; Sweet Kitty Bellairs; The Life of the Party. **1931** God's Gift to Women; The Gay Diplomat. **1932** Doctor X. **1933** The Mystery of the Wax Museum. **1935** Thunder in the Night. **1936** Charlie Chan's Secret.

CAREW, HELEN
Died: Mar. 7, 1980. Screen and stage actress.

Appeared in: **1947** Boomerang. **1963** All the Way Home.

CAREW, JAMES
Born: Feb. 5, 1876, Goshen, Ind. Died: Apr. 4, 1938, London, England. Screen, stage and radio actor. Entered films in England. Married to actress Ellen Terry (dec. 1928).

Appeared in: **1913** The Fool; The Suffragette. **1914** The Flight of

Death; The Rajah's Tiara; The Corner House Burglary. **1915** The Polo Champion. **1917** Justice; The Profit and the Loss. **1919** Sheba; The Kinsman; The Forest on the Hill; The Nature of the Beast; Spinner O'Dreams; Sunken Rocks; Twelve: Ten. **1920** Alf's Button; Anna the Adventuress; Helen of Four Gates; Mrs. Erricker's Reputation. **1921** Dollars in Surrey; Mr. Justice Raffles; The Narrow Valley; Tansy; Wild Heather. **1923** The Naked man; Mist in the Valley; Comin' Thro' the Rye; Strangling Threads. **1924** Eugene Aram; The Love Story of Aliette Brunton; Owd Bob; The Wine of Life. **1925** Children of the Night (series); Satan's Sister. **1926** One Colombo Night. **1927** A Woman Redeemed; The House of Marney; The King's Highway; One of the Best. **1928** Love's Option (aka A Girl of Today); A Window in Piccadilly (aka Lady of the Lake—US 1930). **1929** The City of Play; High Seas; High Treason. **1931** To Oblige a Lady; Mischief; Guilt. **1932** Brother Alfred. **1933** You Made Me Love You; Mayfair Girl. **1934** Freedom of the Seas; Too Many Millions. **1935** Come Out of the Pantry; The Mystery of the Mary Celeste (aka Phantom Ship—US 1937); Oh! What a Night!; All at Sea; Who's Your Father?; Royal Cavalcade (aka Regal Cavalcade—US). **1936** The Improper Duchess; Living Dangerously; David Livingston; Murder at the Cabaret; Midnight at Madame Tussaud's (aka Midnight at the Wax Museum—US); Not Wanted on Voyage (aka Treachery on the High Seas— US 1939); You Must Get Married. **1937** Rhythm Racketeer; Thunder in the City; Wings Over Africa; Strange Experiment; Jericho (aka Dark Sands—US 1938). **1938** Glamour Girl.

CAREW, ORA (Ora Whytock)
Born: 1893, Salt Lake City, Utah. Died: Oct. 26, 1955, Los Angeles, Calif. Screen, stage and vaudeville actress. Entered films with Sennett in 1915.

Appeared in: **1915** Saved by the Wireless; The Martyrs of the Alamo. **1916** A La Cabaret; The Torrent of Vengeance; Dollars and Sense (aka The Twins); Love Comet; Wings and Wheels. **1917** Her Circus Knight (aka The Circus Girl); Oriental Love; Skidding Hearts. **1918** Too Many Millions; Go West Young Man. **1919** The Terror of the Range (serial); Loot; Under Suspicion. **1920** The Peddler of Lies. **1921** The Big Town Roundup; Little Fool; Ladyfingers; Alias Ladyfingers; A Voice in the Dark; After Your Own Heart. **1922** Sherlock Brown; Beyond the Crossroads; The Girl from Rocky Point; Smiles Are Trumps; Smudge. **1924** Paying the Limit; Getting Her Man; Three Days to Live; Waterfront Wolves; The Torrent. **1925** Cold Fury.

CAREWE, EDWIN (Jay J. Fox)
Born: Mar. 5, 1883, Gainesville, Tex. Died: Jan. 22, 1940, Los Angeles, Calif. (heart attack). Screen, stage actor, film, stage director and film producer. Entered films as an actor with Lubin Company in 1910. Father of actress Rita Carewe (dec. 1955).

Appeared in: **1916** The Snow Bird.

CAREWE, RITA (Violette Carewe aka RITA MASON)
Born: 1908. Died: Oct. 22, 1955, Torrance, Calif. Screen actress. Daughter of actor/director Edwin Carewe (dec. 1940).

Appeared in: **1925** Joanna. **1926** High Steppers. **1928** Revenge; Ramona; The Stronger Will. **1930** Radio Kisses (short).

CAREY, EDWARD F.
Born: 1905. Died: Oct. 30, 1979, New Rochelle, N.Y. Police inspector and screen actor.

Appeared in: **1973** The Seven Ups; Badge #73.

CAREY, HARRY
Born: Jan. 16, 1878, New York, N.Y. Died: Sept. 21, 1947, Brentwood, Calif. (coronary thrombosis). Screen, stage actor and playwright. Father of actor Harry Carey, Jr. Married to actress Olive Golden. Nominated for 1939 Acadamy Award for Best Supporting Actor in Mr. Smith Goes to Washington.

Appeared in: **1912** An Unseen Enemy; The Musketeers of Pig Alley; In the Aisles of the Wild; Friends; Heredity; The Informer; The Unwelcome Guest; An Adventure in the Autumn Woods. **1913** Love in an Apartment Hotel; Broken Ways; The Sheriff's Baby; The Ranchero's Revenge; The Left Handed Man; The Hero of Little Italy; Olaf—An Atom; Judith of Bethulia. **1915** Graft (serial). **1917** Straight Shooting. **1919** The Outcasts of Poker Flat; The Blind Husband. **1921** Freeze-Out; Hearts Up; If Only Jim; Sundown Slim; The Wallop; West Is West; The Fox; Desperate Trails. **1922** Man to Man; Good Men and True; Kickback. **1923** Canyon of the Fools; Crashin' Thru; Desert Driven; Miracle Baby. **1924** The Lightning Rider; The Night Hawk; The Man from Texas; Tiger Thompson; Roaring Rails; The Flaming Forties. **1925** Beyond the Border; Soft Shoes; The Texas Trail; Silent Sanderson; Bad Lands; The Prairie Pirate; The Man From Red Gulch;

Wanderer. **1926** The Frontier Trail; Satan Town; Driftin' Thru; The Seventh Bandit. **1927** Slide, Kelly, Slide; A Little Journey. **1928** Trail of '98; The Border Patrol; Burning Bridges. **1931** Cavalier of the West; Trader Horn; Bad Company; The Vanishing Legion (serial); Across the Line; Double Sixes; Horsehoofs; The Hurricane Rider; Border Devils. **1932** Without Honor; Law and Order; The Devil Horse (serial); Last of the Mohicans (serial); Night Rider. **1933** Man of the Forest; Sunset Pass. **1934** Thundering Herd. **1935** Rustler's Paradise; Powdersmoke Range; Barbary Coast; The Last of the Clintons; Wild Mustang; The Last Outpost; Wagon Trail. **1936** The Last Outlaw; The Prisoner of Shark Island; Little Miss Nobody; Sutter's Gold; Valiant Is the Word for Carrie; The Accusing Finger; The Age of Innocence; I Sell Anything; The Three Mesquiteers; The Man Behind the Mask; Ghost Town. **1937** Kid Galahad; Born Reckless; Souls at Sea; Border Cafe; Annapolis Salute; Danger Patrol; Aces Wild. **1938** The Port of Missing Girls; You and Me; King of Alcatraz; Sky Giant; The Law West of Tombstone; Gateway. **1939** Burn 'Em Up O'Connor; Mr. Smith Goes to Washington; Street of Missing Men; Inside Information; Code of the Streets. **1940** They Knew What They Wanted; My Son Is Guilty; Outside the 3-Mile Limit; Beyond Tomorrow. **1941** Shepherd of the Hills; Sundown; Among the Living; Parachute Battalion. **1942** The Spoilers. **1943** Air Force; Happy Land. **1944** The Great Moment. **1945** China's Little Devils. **1946** Duel in the Sun. **1947** Sea of Grass; The Angel and the Badman. **1948** So Dear to My Heart; Red River.

CAREY, LEONARD
Born: 1887, England. Died: Sept. 11, 1977, Woodland Hills, Calif. Screen and stage actor.

Appeared in: **1930** Laughter. **1931** Honor Among Lovers. **1932** Nice Women; This Reckless Age; Merrily We Go to Hell. **1933** Infernal Machine; The Avenger; Bombshell; Worst Woman in Paris. **1934** Smarty; His Greatest Gamble; The Age of Innocence; I Sell Anything; The Little Minister. **1935** Hold 'Em Yale; Our Little Girl; Ladies Love Danger; Ginger. **1936** Bunker Bean. **1937** The Last of Mrs. Cheyney; Angel; Hitting a New High. **1939** The Lone Wolf Spy Hunt; Fast and Loose; The Zero Hour; Five Little Peppers. **1940** Rebecca; Private Affairs; Sing, Dance, Plenty Hot; Hired Wife. **1941** Private Nurse; Mountain Moonlight; Accent on Love; Moon Over Her Shoulder; Tuxedo Junction. **1942** Give Out, Sisters. **1943** Heaven Can Wait. **1949** Slightly French. **1951** Kind Lady. **1952** The Snows of Kilimanjaro. **1953** Thunder in the East.

CARIN, VICTOR
Born: 1933, Scotland. Died: Jan. 2, 1981, Edinburgh, Scotland (cancer). Screen, stage, radio, television actor and playwright.

CARLE, RICHARD (Charles Nicholas Carleton)
Born: July 7, 1871, Somerville, Mass. Died: June 28, 1941, North Hollywood, Calif. (heart attack). Screen, stage actor and playwright.

Appeared in: **1925** Zander the Great; The Mad Marriage; The Coming of Amos. **1926** Eve's Leaves. **1927** Soft Cushions; The Understanding Heart; Stranded (short); While the City Sleeps; Habeus Corpus (short); Sunny California (short); The Worrier (short). **1929** It Can Be Done; Madame X; His Glorious Night. **1930** Brothers; The Grand Parade; A Lady to Love; Free and Easy. **1931** Flying High. **1932** One Hour With You; Fireman, Save My Child!; Night of June 13th; other shorts prior to 1933: Rich Uncles; Hold the Babies; Some Babies. **1933** Private Jones; Man Hunt; Diplomaniacs; Morning Glory; Ladies Must Love; Golden Harvest. **1934** Hollywood Party (short); The Witching Hour; Wake Up and Dream; Caravan; Beloved; Last Round Up; Old Fashioned Way; Harold Teen; George White Scandals; Such Woman Are Dangerous; Sing and Like It; Affairs of a Gentleman. **1935** Life Returns; Home on the Range; The Ghost Walks; When a Man's a Man; The Gay Deception; Love in Bloom; Here Comes Cookie; The Bride Comes Home; Night Life of the Gods; Baby Face Harrington; Moonlight on the Prairie; Dangerous. **1936** San Francisco; Little Red Schoolhouse; Easy to Take; The Man I Marry; College Holiday; The Trail of the Lonesome Pine; Love Before Breakfast; Nevada; Anything Goes; The Case against Mrs. Ames; Drift Fence; Spendthrift; The Texas Rangers; The Arizona Raiders; Let's Sing Again; One Rainy Afternoon; Three of a Kind. **1937** She's Dangerous; Top of the Town; She Asked For It; Outcast; Arizona Mahoney; True Confession; The Man in Blue; Love in a Bungalow; Racketeers in Exile; It's All Yours; I'll Take Romance; Rhythm in the Clouds; 45 Fathers. **1939** Persons in Hiding; It's a Wonderful World; Undercover Doctor; Maisie; Ninotchka; Remember? **1940** Ma, He's Making Eyes at Me; Parole Fixer; Lillian Russell; The Great McGinty; Comin' Round the Mountain; One Night in the Tropics; Seven Sinners; The Golden Fleecing; The Ghost Comes Home. **1941** A Dangerous Game; That Uncertain Feeling; Buy Me That Town; Moonlight in Hawaii; New Wine; The Devil and Miss Jones; My Life with Caroline; Million Dollar Baby.

CARLES, ROMEO
Born: 1896, France. Died: Sept., 1971, France. Screen actor.

Appeared in: Chouchou; Bancede Princess; Au Fil des Ondes.

CARLETON, CLAIRE
Born: 1913, New York, N.Y. Died: Dec. 11, 1979, Northridge, Calif. (cancer). Screen and stage actress.

Appeared in: **1940** Melody and Moonlight; Grand Ole Opry; Girl From Havana; The Crooked Road; Sing, Dance, Plenty Hot. **1941** Petticoat Politics; The Great Train Robbery. **1943** Lady Of Burlesque; Gildersleeve on Broadway; Rookies in Burma. **1944** A Night of Adventure; My Pal, Wolf. **1945** Frontier Girl. **1946** A Close Call for Boston Blackie; Gun Town; That Texas Jamboree; The Missing Lady; Vacation in Reno; Crime Doctor's Manhunt. **1947** Too Many Winners. **1948** A Double Life; Ruthless; The Time of Your Life. **1949** Crime Doctor's Diary; Bad Men of Tombstone; It's a Great Feeling; Red Light; Shockproof. **1950** Born Yesterday; Wabash Avenue. **1951** The Son of Dr. Jekyll; Two of a Kind; Honeychile; Death of a Salesman. **1952** Bal Tabarin; The Fighter (aka The First Time); Ride the Man Down. **1954** Witness to Murder. **1956** Accused of Murder; The Black Sleep. **1957** The Buster Keaton Story; The Careless Years; My Gun is Quick; Reform School Girl. **1958** Fort Massacre; Unwed Mother. **1959** The Miracle of the Hills. **1961** The Devil's Partner.

CARLETON, GEORGE
Born: 1885. Died: Sept. 23, 1950, Hollywood, Calif. (heart attack). Screen and stage actor.

Appeared in: **1941** Whistling in the Dark; The People vs. Dr. Kildare; Life Begins for Andy Hardy. **1942** The Fleet's In; This Land is Mine; Just Off Broadway; Tennessee Johnson; The Great Gildersleeve; Over My Dead Body. **1943** Gildersleeve on Broadway; Henry Aldrich Haunts a House. **1944** And Now Tomorrow; Henry Aldrich's Little Secret. **1945** Wilson; The Purple Monster Strikes (serial); Boston Blackie Booked on Suspicion; A Tree Grows in Brooklyn. **1946** The Magnificent Doll; Temptation; Sioux City Sue. **1947** Blaze of Noon; The Last Round-Up; Ladies Man. **1948** A Foreign Affair; You Gotta Stay Happy. **1949** Prince of the Plains; Calamity Jane and Sam Bass; Move Over, My Darling.

CARLETON, LLOYD B.
Born: 1872. Died: Aug. 8, 1933, N.Y. Screen, stage actor, and film director.

Appeared in: **1910** The Fugitive. **1927** Tongues of Scandal.

CARLETON, WILL C.
Born: 1871. Died: Sept. 21, 1941, Los Angeles, Calif. Stage and screen actor and screenwriter. Appeared in silents.

CARLETON, WILLIAM P.
Born: 1873. Died: Apr. 6, 1947, Hollywood, Calif. (injuries from auto accident). Screen and stage actor.

Appeared in: **1921** A Wife's Awakening; Behind Masks; Good Women; Morals; The Inside of the Cup; Straight from Paris; What No Man Knows. **1922** Bobbed Hair; The Danger Point; Our Leading Citizen; The Law and the Woman; The Worldly Madonna; Domestic Relations. **1923** Homeward Bound; Sinner of Saint; The Truth About Wives; The Tie That Binds. **1924** Half-a-Dollar Bill. **1932** Charlie Chan's Chance. **1933** Girl Without a Room; Ann Vickers. **1935** Rendezvous at Midnight; The Perfect Clue. **1936** The Bohemian Girl; The Border Patrolman. **1938** La Zandunga.

CARLETON, WILLIAM T.
Born: 1859, England. Died: Sept. 28, 1930, St. John, New Brunswick, Canada. Screen, stage actor and stage director.

Appeared in: **1909** Lines of White On a Sullen Sea. **1916** Gloria's Romance; Pearl of the Army. **1917** A Daughter of Maryland. **1918** Eye for Eye; The Danger Mark. **1919** Home Wanted; His Father's Wife; Me and Capt. Kidd; A Society Exile. **1920** The Copperhead; The Amateur Wife. **1921** The Inside of the Cup; Sinners; Straight From Paris; Good Women.

CARLIE, EDWARD
Born: 1878. Died: Nov. 25, 1938, Hollywood, Calif. (heart attack). Screen and vaudeville actor.

Appeared in: **1924** Racing Luck. **1939** I'm from Missouri (died while dancing during filming).

CARLINI, PAOLO
Born: 1926, Italy. Died: Nov. 7, 1979, Rome, Italy (cerebral hemorrhage). Screen, stage and television actor.

Appeared in: **1948** Baron Carlo Mazza (film debut). **1953** Roman Holiday; La Gioconda (US 1958). **1960** It Started in Naples. **1968** Cronaca di Anna Magdalena Bach (Chronicle of Anna Magdalena Bach—US 1969). **1973** The Slave.

CARLISLE, ALEXANDRA (Alexandra Swift)
Born: Jan. 15, 1886, Yorkshire, England. Died: Apr. 21, 1936, New York, N.Y. Stage and screen actress.

Appeared in: **1924** Half a Sinner.

CARLISLE, ELSIE
Born: 1900, England. Died: Sept. 6, 1977, London, England. Singer, screen and radio actress.

Appeared in: **1933** Radio Parade.

CARLSON, JOAN *See* MC AVOY, JOAN

CARLSON, RICHARD
Born: 1912, Albert Lea, Minn. Died: Nov. 24, 1977, Encino, Calif. (cerebral hemmorhage). Screen, stage actor, film director, stage director, stage producer and playwright.

Appeared in: **1938** The Young in Heart (film debut); The Duke of West Point. **1939** Little Accident; Winter Carnival; These Glamour Girls; Dancing Co-ed. **1940** The Howards of Virginia; Beyond Tomorrow; Too Many Girls; No, No, Nanette; The Ghost Breakers. **1941** West Point Widow; Hold That Ghost; Back Street; The Little Foxes. **1942** Fly by Night; Once Upon a Thursday; Highways by Night; White Cargo; My Heart Belongs to Daddy. **1943** A Stranger in Town; The Man from Down Under; Young Ideas; Presenting Lily Mars. **1947** So Well Remembered. **1948** Behind Locked Doors; The Spiritualist. **1950** Sound of Fury (aka Try and Get Me); King Solomon's Mines. **1951** A Millionaire for Christy; The Blue Veil; Valentino. **1952** Flat Top; Retreat Hell!; Whispering Smith Versus Scotland Yard. **1953** Seminole; The Magnetic Monster; All I Desire; It Came from Outer Space; The Maze. **1954** Riders to the Stars; Creature from the Black Lagoon; The Cowboy. **1955** The Last Command; Bengazi. **1956** Three for Jamie Dawn. **1957** The Helen Morgan Story. **1960** Tormented. **1966** Kid Rodelo. **1968** The Power. **1969** The Valley of Gwangi.

CARLTON, HARRY
Born: 1860. Died: Jan. 31, 1922, Boston, Mass. Screen and stage actor.

CARLYLE, FRANCIS
Born: 1868. Died: Sept. 15, 1916. Screen actor. Appeared in early Lubin Co. films.

Appeared in: **1914** Perils of Pauline (serial).

CARLYLE, HELEN
Born: Oct. 18, 1893. Died: June 30, 1933, Hollywood, Calif. (complications of ailments). Screen and stage actress.

Appeared in: **1932** Forgotten Commandments.

CARLYLE, RICHARD
Born: May 21, 1879, Guelph, Ontario, Canada. Died: June 12, 1942, San Fernando, Calif. Stage and screen actor. Married to stage actress Mirza Marston. Entered films in 1913.

Appeared in: **1920** The Copperhead. **1921** The Inside of the Cup; Out of the Chorus; Ten Nights in a Barroom. **1922** Women Men Marry; Back Home and Broke. **1923** Haldane of the Secret Service. **1927** Shootin' Irons. **1928** Brotherly Love; Lingerie. **1929** Taking a Chance; The Valiant; Children of the Ritz; The Girl in the Show; It Can Be Done; In Old California; Hearts in Dixie. **1930** Guilty?; Mountain Justice; Playing Around; Tol'able David; Hideout; The Girl of the Golden West; Kismet. **1931** West of Broadway; Oh! Oh! Cleopatra (short); Quick Trigger Lee. **1932** Saddle Buster; Unholy Love. **1933** Midnight Club. **1935** When a Man's a Man; Sons of Steel; Public Opinion; Happiness C.O.D. **1936** The Country Doctor.

CARLYLE, RITA
Died: Sept., 1949, Banning, Calif. Screen and stage actress.

Appeared in: **1930** Brothers. **1933** Midnight Club. **1934** Limehouse Blues; Menace.

CARMEN, SYBIL
Born: 1900, France. Died: Apr. 15, 1929, Paris, France (heart desease). Screen actress.

Appeared in: **1921** Experience.

CARMI, MARIA
Born: 1880, Germany. Died: Aug., 1957, Myrtle Beach, S.C. Screen actress. Appeared in early UFA films.

CARMICHAEL, HOAGY (Hoagland Howard Carmichael)
Born: Nov. 22, 1899, Bloomington, Ind. Died: Dec. 27, 1981, Rancho Mirage, Calif. (heart attack). Screen, radio, television actor, composer and author. Divorced from Ruth M. Meinardi and later married to actress Wanda McKay.

Appeared in: **1944** To Have and Have Not. **1945** Johnny Angel. **1946** The Best Years of our Lives; Canyon Passage. **1947** Night Song. **1949** Johnny Holiday. **1950** Young Man with a Horn. **1942** Belles on Their Toes; Las Vegas Story. **1955** Timberjack.

CARMICHAEL, MYRA
Died: Oct. 22, 1974. Screen actress.

CARMINATI, TULLIO (Count Tullio Carminati de Brambilla)
Born: Zara, Dalmatia, Italy. Died: Feb. 26, 1917, Rome, Italy (stroke). Screen and stage actor.

Appeared in: **1926** The Bat; The Dutchess of Buffalo. **1927** Stage Madness; Honeymoon Hate. **1928** Three Sinners. **1933** Gallant Lady. **1934** Moulin Rouge; One Night of Love. **1935** Let's Live Tonight; Paris in Spring. **1936** The Three Maxims; The Wedding March; London Melody (aka Girl in the Street—US 1938); Sunset in Vienna (aka Suicide Legion—US 1940); La Marcia Nuzialf. **1938** The Show Goes On. **1940** Safari. **1949** The Golden Madonna. **1952** Beauty and the Devil. **1953** Roman Holiday; The Secret Conclave. **1956** War and Peace. **1960** A Breath of Scandal. **1961** El Cid. **1962** Le Mercenaire (aka Swordsman of Siena—US); Hemingway's Adventures of a Young Man. **1963** The Cardinal.

CARNERA, PRIMO
Born: Oct. 25, 1906, Sequals, Italy. Died: June 29, 1967, Sequals, Italy (liver ailment). World heavyweight boxing champion, circus performer, wrestler and screen actor.

Appeared in: **1933** Mr. Broadway; The Prizefighter and the Lady. **1949** Mighty Joe Young; Iron Crown. **1954** Prince Valiant; Casanova's Big Night. **1956** A Kid for Two Farthings. **1960** Hercules Unchained.

CARNEY, ALAN (David Bougal)
Born: Dec. 22, 1911, Brooklyn, N.Y. Died: May 2, 1973, Inglewood, Calif. (heart attack). Screen, stage and vaudeville actor. Partner in vaudeville and film comedy team of "Brown and Carney" with Wally Brown (dec. 1961).

Appeared in: **1941** Convey. **1942** In Which We Serve. **1943** Mr. Lucky; Adventures of a Rookie (with Brown); Rookies in Burma (with Brown); Around the World; Mexican Spitfire's Blessed Event; Gangway For Tomorrow; Gildersleeve's Bad Day. **1944** Step Lively; The Girl Rush; Seven Days Ashore. **1945** Radio Stars on Parade; Zombies on Broadway. **1946** Genius at Work; Vacation in Reno. **1947** The Pretender. **1949** Hideout. **1959** Lil' Abner. **1960** North to Alaska. **1961** The Absent-Minded Professor; Double Trouble. **1962** Swingin' Along. **1963** Son of Flubber; It's a Mad, Mad, Mad, Mad World. **1965** Sylvia. **1967** Monkeys, Go Home!; The Adventures of Bullwhip Griffin. **1968** Blackbeard's Ghost. **1973** The Love Bug Rides Again.

CARNEY, DON "UNCLE DON" (Howard Rice)
Born: 1897. Died: Jan. 14, 1954, Miami, Fla. (heart trouble). Screen, stage, radio and vaudeville actor. Appeared in films briefly prior to 1928.

CARNEY, GEORGE
Born: Nov. 21, 1887, Bristol, England. Died: Dec. 9, 1947. Screen, stage and vaudeville actor.

Appeared in: **1916** Some Waiter! **1933** The Television Follies; Commissionaire. **1934** Say It With Flowers; Music Hall; Lest We Forget; Hyde Park; Flood Tide; Night Club Queen; Easy Money; A Glimpse of Paradise. **1935** A Real Bloke; The Small Man; Variety; The City of Beautiful Nonsense; Windfall; Cock O' the North. **1936** Land Without Music (aka Forbidden Music—US 1938); It's in the Bag; Tomorrow We Live. **1937** Dreaming Lips; Father Steps Out; Little Miss Somebody; Lancashire Luck; Beauty and the Barge. **1938** Easy Riches; Weddings are Wonderful; Paid in Error; Kicking the Moon Around; Miracles Do Happen; Consider Your Verdict. **1939** Come on George; A Window in London (aka Lady in Distress—US 1941); The Stars Look Down (US 1941); Young Man's Fancy (US 1943). **1940** Convoy (US 1941); The Briggs Family. **1941** Love on the Dole; The Common Touch; Kipps (aka The Remarkable Mr. Kipps—US 1942). **1942** Thunder Rock (US 1944); In Which We Serve; Hard Steel; Unpublished Story; Rose of Tralee. **1943** When We Are Married; The Night Invader; Schweik's New Adventures. **1944** Tawny Pipit (US 1947); Welcome Mr. Washington. **1945** Waterloo Road (US 1949); The Agitator; I Know Where I'm Going (US 1947). **1946** Spring Song (aka Springtime—US); Woman to Woman; Wanted for Murder. **1947** The Root of All Evil; The Little Ballerina (US 1951); Brighton Rock; Fortune Lane. **1948** Good Time Girl (US 1950).

CARNEY, HARRY (Harry Howell Carney)
Born: 1910, Boston, Mass. Died: Oct. 8, 1974, New York, N.Y. Black musician and screen actor.

Appeared in: **1937** The Hit Parade. **1943** Reveille With Beverly.

CAROL, DIANE
Born: 1940. Died: Sept. 30, 1966. Screen actress.

CAROL, JOHN
Born: 1910, England. Died: Oct., 1968, London, England. Screen and stage actor. Do not confuse with U.S. actor John Carroll.

Appeared in: **1937** We Live and Learn; The Windmill; The Perfect Crime. **1938** The Dark Stairway. **1943** The Silver Fleet (US 1945); The Dummy Talks. **1945** Pink String and Sealing Wax (US 1950). **1947** It Always Rains on Sunday (US 1949). **1949** The Spider and the Fly (US 1952).

CAROL, MARTINE (Marie-Louise de Mourer aka MARYSE MOURER)
Born: 1921, France. Died: Feb. 6, 1967, Monte Carlo (heart attack). Screen, stage and radio actress. Known on stage as Catherine Arley and appeared in "Caroline" film series as Carol Martine.

Appeared in: **1943** La Femme aux Loups. **1944** The Wolf Farm. **1945** Bifur III; L'extravagante Mission; Trente et Quarante. **1946** En Etes-Vous Bien Sur? **1947** La Fleur de l'age ou L'ile des Enfants Perdus; Voyage. **1948** Les Souvenirs ne Sont pas a Vendre. **1949** Les Amants de Verone (Lovers of Verone—US 1954); Je n'Aime que Toi. **1950** Une Nuit de Noces; Mefiez-vous des Blondes; Caroline Cherie (US 1954); Nous Irons a Paris. **1951** El Deseo y el Amor; Nana (US 1957). **1952** Adorable Creature (US 1956); A Night with Caroline; Les Belles de Nuit (Beauties of the Night—US 1954). **1953** Un Caprice de Caroline Cherie; Lucrece Borgia; Destinees Destini di Donne; The Bed (US 1955). **1954** Secrets d'Alcove; Il Letto Della Pompadour; La Spiaggia (The Beach); Madam DuBarry. **1956** Le Carnet du Major Thompson; Defendo il Mio Amour (Defend My Love—US 1959); Around the World in 80 Days; Austerlitz. **1957** Le Passager Clandestin; The French Are a Funny Race (US 1958); Action of the Tiger. **1958** Sins of the Borgias; The Foxiest Girl in Paris (aka Nathalie). **1959** Ten Seconds to Hell. **1960** The Sins of Lola Montes; La Francoise et l'Amour (Love and the Frenchwoman—US 1961). **1961** Violent Summer; Vanina, Vanina; La Cave Se Rebiffe (The Sucker Strikes Back—aka The Counterfeiters of Paris and Money, Money, Money—US 1962). **1963** Operation Gold Ingot. **1966** Hell Is Empty.

CARPENTER, GLORIA
Born: 1927. Died: Sept. 11, 1958, Hollywood, Calif. Screen actress.

CARPENTER, HORACE B.
Born: 1875. Died: May 21, 1945, Hollywood, Calif. (heart attack). Screen, stage actor and screenwriter. Entered films with Famous Players-Lasky Co.

Appeared in: **1914** The Call of the North; The Man from Home; The Virginian. **1915** The Arab; Carmen; The Golden Chance. **1916** Maria Rosa. **1917** Joan the Woman. **1923** King's Creek Law. **1924** Headin' Through; The Silent Stranger; Travelin' Fast. **1928** Texas Tommy. **1929** False Feathers; Riders of the Rio Grande; West of the Rockies; Bride of the Desert. **1930** South of Sonora. **1934** In Old Santa Fe. **1937** Range Defenders; Git Along Little Dogies; The Big Show; Gunsmoke Ranch. **1939** Rovin' Tumbleweeds. **1944** Belle of the Yukon.

CARPENTER, PAUL
Born: 1921, Montreal, Canada. Died: June 12, 1964, London, England. Screen, television actor and singer with Ted Heath's band. Married to actress Kim Parker.

Appeared in: **1946** School for Secrets. **1948** Uneasy Terms. **1949** Landfall. **1953** Albert RN (aka Break to Freedom—US 1955). **1954** The House Across the Lake (aka Heatwave—US); Face the Music (aka The Black Glove—US); Five Days (aka Paid to Kill—US); Duel in the Jungle; The Young Lovers (aka Chance Meeting—US 1955); The Stranger Came Home (aka The Unholy Four—US); The Sea Shall Not Have Them (US 1955); Diplomatic Passport; Johnny on the Spot. **1955** Shadow of a Man; One Jump Ahead; The Hornet's Nest; Stock Car. **1956** Fire Maidens from Outer Space; The Iron Petticoat; The Narrowing Circle; Women Without Men (aka Blonde Bait—US); Behind the Headlines. **1957** No Road Back; Action Stations (aka Hi-Jack); Murder Reported (US 1960); The Hypnotist (aka Scotland Yard Dragnet—US 1958); Black Ice (US 1958). **1958** Undercover Girl; Intent to Kill. **1959** Jet Storm (US 1961). **1960** Date at Midnight. **1962** Dr. Crippen (US 1964). **1963** Call Me Bwana; Panic (US 1966). **1964** First Men on the Moon; The Beauty Jungle (aka Contest Girl—US 1966). **1965** Miss Tulip Stays the Night.

CARPENTIER, GEORGES
Born: Jan. 12, 1894, Lens, France. Died: Oct. 28, 1975, Paris, France. Professional heavyweight fighter, screen and vaudevill actor.

Appeared in: **1912** The Romance of Carpentier (film debut). **1913** Carpentier vs. Bombadier Wells Fight. **1920** The Wonder Man; Le Match Criqui-Ledoux. **1922** A Gypsy Cavalier (aka My Lady April). **1928** La Symphonie Pathetique. **1929** The Show of Shows. **1930** Hold Everything; Georges Carpentier in Naughty But Nice (short). Other French films: The Adventures of a Champion; The Treasure of Keriolet.

CARR, ALEXANDER
Born: 1878, Rimni, Russia. Died: Sept. 19, 1946, Los Angeles, Calif. Screen, stage, burlesque actor and circus performer. Married to stage actress Helen Ryan (dec. 1938). He was "Perlmutter" in the "Potash and Perlmutter" series on screen and stage with Barnie Bernard (dec. 1924).

Appeared in: **1923** Potash and Perlmutter. **1924** In Hollywood with Potash and Perlmutter. **1926** Partners Again; The Beautiful Cheat; April Fool. **1929** The End of the World (short). **1932** Uptown New York; No Greater Love; Hypnotized; Pathe comedies. **1933** The Death Kiss; Constant Woman; Her Splendid Folly; Out All Night. **1934** I Hate Women. **1940** Christmas in July.

CARR, GEORGIA
Born: 1925. Died: July 4, 1971, Los Angeles, Calif. (stroke). Black singer, screen, stage and television actress. Sang with bands during 1950s and early 1960s.

Appeared in: **1957** Will Success Spoil Rock Hunter? **1964** Handle With Care.

CARR, GERALDINE
Born: 1917. Died: Sept. 2, 1954, near Hollywood, Calif. (auto accident). Screen and television actress.

Appeared in: **1950** The Great Jewel Robbery; The Company She Keeps. **1952** The Sniper. **1954** The Long, Long Trailer.

CARR, GINNA
Born: 1937. Died: July 13, 1972, Hollywood, Calif. (cancer). Screen, stage and burlesque actress. Married to comedian Joey Faye. Daughter of vaudeville performers known as "The Dancing Alexanders."

CARR, GLADYS
Born: 1890. Died: Sept. 26, 1940, Hollywood, Calif. Screen and stage actress.

Appeared in: **1915** At Bay.

CARR, JACK
Born: 1899. Died: Feb. 2, 1968, Calexico, Calif. Screen and television actor. Do not confuse with black actor Jack Carr (dec. 1951).

Appeared in: **1933** She Done Him Wrong. **1938** Personal Secretary. **1944** The Princess and the Pirate. **1957** Chicago Confidential. **1958** Seven Guns to Mesa; Bullwhip; Toughest Gun in Tombstone. **1960** Platinum High School.

CARR, JACK
Died: 1951. Black screen actor. Do not confuse with Jack Carr (dec. 1968).

CARR, JANE (Rita Brunstrom)
Born: Aug. 1, 1909, Whitley Bay, Northumberland, England. Died: Sept. 29, 1957. Screen and stage actress.

Appeared in: **1931** Stolen Heaven. **1932** Let Me Explain Dear; Love Me, Love My Dog. **1933** Taxi to Paradise; Orders is Orders (US 1934); Dick Turpin. **1934** On the Air; Oh No Doctor!; Murder at the Inn; Night Club Queen; Keep It Quiet; The Outcast; Those Were the Days; The Church Mouse (US 1935); Lord Edgware Dies; Youthful Folly. **1935** The Ace of Spades; The Triumph of Sherlock Holmes; Night Mail; Hello Sweetheart; Get Off My Foot. **1936** The Interrupted Honeymoon; Millions; It's You I Want. **1937** The Lilac Domino; Little Miss Somebody; Melody and Romance; Captain's Orders. **1942** Sabotage at Sea; Lady from Lisbon. **1949** It's Not Cricket. **1953** The Saint's Return (aka The Saint's Girl Friday—US). **1954** Thirty-Six Hours (aka Terror Street—US).

CARR, JOE "FINGERS" (Louis Busch)
Born: July 18, 1910, Louisville, Ky. Died: Sept. 19, 1979, Camarillo, Calif. (auto accident). Pianist, composer and screen actor. Divorced from actress Janet Blair and singer Margaret Whiting. Later married to Nina Archambeau.

Appeared in: **1951** Hue and Cry; The Galloping Major.

CARR, LUELLA
Died: Jan. 16, 1937, Los Angeles, Calif. Screen actress.

Appeared in: **1921** Home-Keeping Hearts.

CARR, MARY K. (Mary Kennevan)
Born: 1874, Philadelphia, Pa. Died: June 24, 1973, Woodland Hills, Calif. Stage and screen actress. Married to actor/producer William Carr (dec. 1937). Mother of directors Thomas and Stephen Carr.

Appeared in: **1919** Mrs. Wiggs of the Cabbage Patch. **1920** Over the Hill. **1921** Thunderclap. **1922** Silver Wings. **1923** Broadway Broke; Loyal Lives; The Darling Years; You Are Guilty; The Custard Cup; On the Banks of the Wabash; Three O'Clock in the Morning. **1924** Damaged Hearts; On the Stroke of Three; Roulette; East of Broadway; For Sale; Why Men Leave Home; The Woman on the Jury; The Mine with the Iron Door; Painted People; A Self-Made Failure; The Spirit of the USA; Three Woman. **1925** Red Kimona; The Wizard of Oz; Big Pal; Hogan's Alley; The Re-creation of Brian Kent; A Slave of Fashion; Capital Punishment; Drusilla with a Million; Easy Money; The Fighting Cub; Flaming Waters; Go Straight; Gold Hunters; His Master's Voice; The Night Ship; The Parasite. **1926** Atta Boy; The Night Patrol; The Night Watch; Stop, Look and Listen; Dame Chance; Whom Shall I Marry?; The Wise Guy; Frenzied Flames; Her Own Story; The False Alarm; The Hidden Way; The King of the Turf; The Midnight Message; Pleasures of the Rich; Somebody's Mother. **1927** Blonde or Brunette; Special Delivery; The Show Girl; Better Days; Paying the Price; The Swell-head; False Morals; The Fourth Commandment; God's Great Wilderness; On Your Toes; Jesse James. **1928** Love Over Night; Lights of New York; A Million for Love. **1929** Sailor's Holiday; Some Mother's Boy. **1930** Just Imagine; Second Wife; Hot Curves; Ladies in Love; The Utah Kid; The Midnight Special. **1931** Morals for Women; Primrose Path; Law of the Tongs; Kept Husbands; Beyond Victory; Honeymoon Lane; One Good Turn (short); Stout Hearts and Willing Hands (short). **1932** The Fighting Marshall; Pack Up Your Troubles. **1933** The Moonshiners Daughter or Aboard in Old Kentucky (short); Forbidden Trails; Gun Law; Police Call. **1934** The Gay Bride; Love Past Thirty; Change of Heart; Loud Speaker. **1935** The World Accuses; Fighting Lady; I Don't Remember (short). **1939** East Side of Heaven. **1940** Manhattan Heartbeat. **1941** Model Wife. **1942** Eagle Squadron. **1956** Friendly Persuasion. **1957** Dino.

CARR, MICHAEL (Michael Cohen)
Born: Mar. 17, 1900, Leeds, Yorkshire, England. Died: Sept. 16, 1968, London, England. Screen actor and composer. Do not confuse with Michael Carr, US actor.

Appeared in: **1937** Let's Make a Night of It.

CARR, NAT
Born: Aug. 12, 1886, Russia. Died: July 6, 1944, Hollywood, Calif. Screen, stage, vaudeville, burlesque actor and screenwriter.

Appeared in: **1925** His People. **1926** The Cohens and the Kellys; Private Izzy Murphy; Millionaires; Kosher Kitty Kelly; April Fool; Her Big Night; The Mystery Club; Watch Your Wife. **1927** The Jazz Singer; The Love Thrill; Popular Comedian (short). **1929** Madonna of the Sleeping Cars; Wall Street; "Ginsburg" series including One Gun Ginsburg, Gunboat Ginsburg and General Ginsburg. **1930** Red Heads; The Talk of Hollywood; plus the following shorts: Traffic; Two Plus Fours. **1931** Fifty Million Frenchmen; His People; plus the following shorts: Night Class; Campus Champs; Open House; Humanette. **1932** Union Depot; High Pressure. **1933** Knee Deep in Music (short); What Fur (short); The Merchant of Menace (short); Big Time or Bust. **1934** Wrong Direction (short); Hey Nanny (short). **1935** Pardon My Scotch (short). **1936** Next Time We Love. **1937** Portia on Trial. **1938** Comet Over Broadway; Torchy Gets Her Man. **1939** The Roaring Twenties; Dodge City; On Trial; Everybody's Hobby; Torchy Plays with Dynamite. **1940** King of the Lumberjacks; Granny Get Your Gun. **1941** Manpower.

CARR, PERCY
Born: 1865, England. Died: Nov. 22, 1926, Saranac Lake, N.Y. Screen and stage actor.

Appeared in: **1922** One Exciting Night. **1923** The Ragged Edge.

CARR, SADE (Sade Latham)
Born: 1889, London, England. Died: Nov. 17, 1940, Carmel, Calif. Stage and screen actress. Appeared in early Essaney films.

CARR, WILLIAM
Born: 1892. Died: Mar. 12, 1945, Hollywood, Calif. Screen and stage actor. Do not confuse with other actors of same name.

CARR, WILLIAM
Born: 1867. Died: Feb. 13, 1937, Los Angeles, Calif. Screen actor and film director. Entered films as an actor with Lubin Company in 1907. Married to actress Mary Carr (dec. 1973).

Appeared in: **1921** Get-Rich-Quick Wallingford.

CARR, WILLIAM A.
Born: 1880. Died: May 3, 1939, Los Angeles, Calif. Screen and stage actor. Do not confuse with other actors of the same name.

CARRE, BARTLETT A.
Born: July 10, 1897, Melrose, Mass. Died: Apr. 26, 1971, Hollywood, Calif. (respiratory ailment). Screen actor, stuntman, assistant film production manager.

Appeared in: **1924** Behind Two Guns. **1925** Flying Hoofs.

CARRICO, CHARLES
Born: 1888. Died: Jan. 18, 1967, Desert Hot Springs, Calif. Screen actor. Appeared in films during the 1920s.

CARRIGAN, THOMAS J. (aka THOMAS J. CORRIGAN)
Born: 1886. Died: Oct. 2, 1941, Lapeer, Mich. (cerebral hemorrhage). Stage and screen actor. Entered films during experimental days with Powers in New York and later with Selig. Divorced from stage actress Mabel Taliaferro (dec. 1979).

Appeared in: **1911** Two Orphans; Cinderella. **1919** Checkers. **1921** Room and Board. **1923** Crooked Alley; Salomy Jane; You Can't Fool Your Wife. **1925** The Making of O'Malley. **1927** Wings. **1932** The Big Broadcast.

CARRILLO, LEO
Born: Aug. 6, 1881, Los Angeles, Calif. Died: Sept. 10, 1961, Santa Monica, Calif. (cancer). Screen, stage and vaudeville actor.

Appeared in: **1927** The following shorts: Italian Humorist; At the Ballgame. **1928** The Dove; plus the following shorts: The Hell Gate of Soissons; The Foreigner. **1929** Mister Antonio. **1931** Lasca of the Rio Grande; Homicide Squad; Guilty Generation; Hell Bound. **1932** Lost Men; Broken Wings; Second Fiddle; Cauliflower Alley; Girl of the Rio. **1933** Parachute Jumper; City Streets; Deception; Men Are Such Fools; Moonlight and Pretzels; Obey the Law; Racetrack; Before Morning. **1934** The Barretts of Wimpole Street; Band Plays On; Four Frightened People; The Gay Bride; Manhattan Melodrama; Viva Villa. **1935** If You Could Only Cook; In Caliente; Love Me Forever; La Fiesta de Santa Barbara (short); The Winning Ticket. **1936** The Gay Desperado; It Had to Happen; Moonlight Murder. **1937** The Barrier; History Is Made at Night; Hotel Haywire; I Promise to Pay; Manhattan Merry-Go-Round; 52nd Street. **1938** Arizona Wildcat; Blockade; Flirting with Fate; Girl of the Golden West; Little Miss Roughneck; Too Hot to Handle; City Streets. **1939** The Girl and the Gambler; Society Lawyer; Chicken Wagon Family; Rio; Fisherman's Wharf. **1940** Twenty-Mule Team; One Night in the Tropics; Wyoming; Captain Caution; Bad Man of Wyoming; Lillian Russell. **1941** Horror Island; Riders of Death Valley (serial); Tight Shoes; The Kid from Kansas; Road Agent; Barnacle Bill. **1942** What's Cooking?; Unseen Enemy; Escape from Hong Kong; Men of Texas; Top Sergeant; Danger in the Pacific; Timber; Sin Town; American Empire. **1943** Crazy House; Screen Snapshot #5 (short); Frontier Badmen; Larceny with Music; Follow the Band; Phantom of the Opera. **1944** Babes on Swing Street; Bowery to Broadway; The Ghost Catchers; Gypsy Wildcat; Merrily We Sing; Moonlight and Cactus. **1945** Crime, Inc.; Mexicana; Under Western Skies. **1947** The Fugitive. **1948** So Evil My Love; The Valiant Hombre. **1949** The Gay Amigo; The Darling Caballero; Satan's Cradle. **1950** The Girl from San Lorenzo; Pancho Villa Returns. **1964** Big Parade of Comedy (doc.).

CARRINGTON, EVELYN
Born: 1876. Died: Nov. 21, 1942, Hollywood, Calif. Screen and stage actress.

Appeared in: **1920** In Search of a Sinner. **1921** Salvation Nell. **1937** Living on Love.

CARRINGTON, FRANK
Born: 1902. Died: July 3, 1975, Millburn, N.J. Screen, stage actor and stage producer.

CARRINGTON, HELEN
Born: 1895. Died: Oct. 22, 1963, Morristown, N.J. Screen and stage actress.

Appeared in: **1930** Heads Up; Queen High (stage and film versions).

CARRINGTON, MURRAY
Born: Mar. 13, 1885, Upper Norwood, England. Died: Dec. 2, 1941, England? Screen and stage actor. Son of stage actress Cecil Cromwell (dec. 1913).

Appeared in: **1911** Richard III. **1915** In Search of a Husband.

CARROLL, DEE (Betty Jean Marsh)
Born: 1926. Died: Apr. 28, 1980, Burbank, Calif (following surgery). Screen actress.

Appeared in: **1956** A Day of Fury. **1965** Inside Daisy Clover. **1967** Hotel; The Gnome-Mobile; A Guide for the Married Man. **1969** Sweet Charity. **1970** Lost Flight; The Christine Jorgensen Story; Cheyenne Social Club; Airport. **1974** The Terminal Man; Busting; Uptown Saturday Night. **1975** The Prisoner of Second Avenue. **1980** The Stunt Man.

CARROLL, EARL
Born: Sept. 16, 1893, Pittsburgh, Pa. Died: June 17, 1948, Mt. Carmel, Pa. (plane crash). Stage, film producer, playwright and screen actor. Married to actress Marcelle Hontabat (dec. 1936).

Appeared in: **1941** A Night at Earl Carroll's.

CARROLL, JOHN (Julian La Faye)
Born: July 17, 1907, New Orleans, La. Died: Apr. 24, 1979, Hollywood, Calif. (leukemia). Screen, stage actor, film director, film producer and singer.

Appeared in: **1935** Hi, Gaucho (film debut). **1936** Muss 'Em Up; Murder on a Bridle Path. **1937** We Who Are About to Die; Zorro Rides Again (serial). **1938** Rose of the Rio Grande; I am a Criminal. **1939** Only Angels Have Wings; Wolf Call. **1940** Congo Maisie; Phantom Raiders; Hired Wife; Susan and God; No, No Nanette; Go West. **1941** This Woman is Mine; Lady Be Good; Sunny. **1942** Pierre of the Plains; Rio Rita; Flying Tigers. **1943** Hit Parade of 1943; The Youngest Profession. **1945** Bedside Manner; A Letter for Evie. **1947** Fiesta; Wyoming; The Fabulous Texan. **1948** I, Jane Doe; The Flame; Los Angeles; Angel in Exile. **1949** Change of Heart (re-release of Hit Parade of 1943). **1950** The Avengers; Surrender; Hit Parade of 1951. **1951** Belle Le Grande. **1953** The Farmer Takes a Wife; Geraldine. **1955** Touch and Go (aka The Light Touch—US 1956). **1957** Decision at Sundown; Two Grooms for a Bride. **1958** Rock Baby, Rock It. **1959** The Plunderers of Painted Flats.

CARROLL, LEO G.
Born: 1892, Weedon, Northants, England. Died: Oct. 16, 1972, Hollywood, Calif. Screen, stage and television actor.

Appeared in: **1934** Sadie McGee; Outcast Lady; Stamboul Quest; Barretts of Wimpole Street. **1935** Murder on a Honeymoon; The Right to Live; Clive of India; The Casino Murder Case. **1937** London by Night. **1938** A Christmas Carol. **1939** Wuthering Heights; The Private Lives of Elizabeth and Essex; Bulldog Drummond's Secret Police; Charlie Chan in City in Darkness; Tower of London. **1940** Charlie Chan's Murder Cruise; Rebecca; Waterloo Bridge. **1941** Suspicion; Scotland Yard; Bahama Passage; This Woman Is Mine. **1945** Spellbound; The House on 92nd Street. **1947** Forever Amber; Time Out of Mind; Song of Love. **1948** So Evil My Love; Enchantment; The Paradine Case. **1950** Father of the Bride; The Happy Years. **1951** The First Legion; The Desert Fox; Strangers on a Train. **1952** The Snows of Kilimanjaro; Rogue's March; The Bad and the Beautiful. **1953** Treasure of the Golden Condor; Young Bess. **1955** Tarantula; We're No Angels. **1956** The Swan. **1959** North by Northwest. **1961** One Plus One (Exploring the Kinsey Reports); The Parent Trap. **1963** The Prize. **1965** That Funny Feeling. **1966** The Spy With My Face; One of Our Spies Is Missing; One Spy Too Many. **1969** From Nashville With Music.

CARROLL, NANCY (Ann Veronica La Hiff)
Born: Nov. 19, 1906, New York, N.Y. Died: Aug. 6, 1965, New York, N.Y. (natural causes). Screen, stage and television actress. Married to C. H. J. Groen. Divorced from playwright Jack Kirkland and magazine editor Bolton Mallory. Nominated for 1929-30 Academy Award for Best Actress in The Devil's Holiday.

Appeared in: **1927** Ladies Must Dress (film debut). **1928** Chicken a la King; Abie's Irish Rose; Easy Come, Easy Go; The Water Hole; Manhattan Cocktail. **1929** The Shopworn Angel; The Wolf of Wall Street; The Sin Sister; Close Harmony; The Dance of Life; Illusion; Sweetie. **1930** Dangerous Paradise; The Devil's Holiday; Honey; Paramount on Parade; Follow Thru; Laughter; Two Against Death. **1931** Revolt; Stolen Heaven; Personal Maid; The Night Angel. **1932** The Man I Killed; Broken Lullaby; Wayward; Scarlet Dawn; Hot Saturday; Under Cover Man. **1933** I Love That Man; Child of

Manhattan; The Woman Accused; The Kiss Before the Mirror. **1934** Transatlantic Merry-Go-Round; Jealousy; Springtime for Henry; Broken Melody. **1935** I'll Love You Always; After the Dance; Atlantic Adventure. **1938** There Goes My Heart; That Certain Age.

CARROLL, PEGGY (Peggy Mitchell aka JEAN STEVENS)
Born: 1915. Died: Mar. 3, 1981, Los Angeles, Calif. Screen, stage actress, dancer and choreographer. Daughter of actress Virginia Mitchell (aka Virginia Reed). Sister of actress Mary Carroll Rasset and lyricist Diane Carroll.

Appeared in: **1940** The Durango Kid. **1943** A Lady Takes a Chance. **1945** Mexicana; Over 21.

CARROLL, WILLIAM A.
Born: 1876. Died: Jan. 26, 1928, Glendale, Calif. (cancer). Stage and screen actor. Entered films with Selig and Vitagraph.

Appeared in: **1912** Black Sheep. **1916-1918** American Film Mfg. Co. films. **1919** Bill Henry; Trail of the Octopus (serial). **1920** The Branded Four (serial); The Screaming Shadow (serial). **1921** Fifty Candles. **1922** A Motion to Adjourn; Confidence; Chain Lighting; Remembrance; Yellow Men and Gold; Gas, Oil and Water. **1924** North of 36; Women First; Alimony; Wanderer of the Wasteland; K—The Unknown; Stolen Secrets; Sporting Youth. **1925** The Unwritten Law; The Ancient Highway; I'll Show You the Town. **1926** Born to the West; College Days; Joselyn's Wife; The Fighting Edge. **1927** Snowbound; Beauty Shoppers.

CARRON, GEORGE
Born: 1930, Canada. Died: Apr. 23, 1970, Montreal, Canada (heart attack). Screen, stage, television and radio actor.

Appeared in the following Canadian films: Footsteps in the Snow; Entre la Mer et l'Eau Douce.

CARRUTHERS, BRUCE C.
Born: 1901, Bedeque, Prince Edward Island, Canada. Died: Jan. 1, 1954, Woodland Hills, Calif. Screen actor and film technical advisor.

Appeared in: **1951** Gene Autry and the Mounties.

CARSEY, MARY
Born: 1938. Died: Aug. 27, 1973, Dallas, Tex. Screen, stage, television actress, model and stage producer.

Appeared in: **1964** The Pink Panther.

CARSON, JACK
Born: Oct. 27, 1910, Carmen, Canada. Died: Jan. 2, 1963, Encino, Calif. (cancer). Screen, stage, television and vaudeville actor. Brother of actor Robert Carson (dec. 1979). Married to Sandra Tucker. Divorced from actress Lola Albright and singer Kay St. Germain.

Appeared in: **1937** Stage Door (film debut); Stand-In; A Rented Riot (short); You Only Live Once; On Again, Off Again; Too Many Wives; Music for Madame; It Could Happen to You; High Flyers; The Toast of New York; Reported Missing. **1938** The Girl Downstairs; Condemned Woman; The Saint in New York; Vivacious Lady; Mr. Doodle Kicks Off; Crashing Hollywood; Bringing Up Baby; She's Got Everything; Night Spot; Go Chase Yourself; Law of the Underworld; This Marriage Business; Maid's Night Out; Having a Wonderful Time; Carefree; Everybody's Doing It; Quick Money. **1939** Fifth Avenue Girl; Destry Rides Again; The Kid from Texas; Mr. Smith Goes to Washington; Legion of Lost Flyers; The Escape; The Honeymoon's Over. **1940** The Girl in 313; I Take This Woman; Shooting High; Young As You Feel; Enemy Agent; Parole Fixer; Typhoon; Alias the Deacon; Queen of the Mob; Sandy Gets Her Man; Love Thy Neighbor; Lucky Partners. **1941** Mr. and Mr. Smith; Love Crazy; The Bride Came C.O.D.; Navy Blues in the Night; The Strawberry Blonde. **1942** Larceny, Inc.; Wings for the Eagle; Gentleman Jim; The Hard Way; The Male Animal. **1943** Thank Your Lucky Stars; Princess O'Rourke. **1944** The Dough Girls; Make Your Own Bed; Hollywood Canteen; Shine on Harvest Moon; Arsenic and Old Lace; Road to Glory (short). **1945** Mildred Pierce; Roughly Speaking. **1946** The Time, the Place and the Girl; One More Tomorrow; Two Guys from Milwaukee. **1947** Love and Learn; Royal Flush. **1948** Two Guys from Texas; April Showers; Always Together; Romance on the High Seas. **1949** It's a Great Feeling; John Loves Mary; My Dream Is Yours. **1950** Bright Leaf; The Good Humor Man. **1951** Mister Universe; The Groom Wore Spurs. **1953** Dangerous When Wet. **1954** Red Garters; Phffft; A Star Is Born. **1955** Ain't Misbehaving. **1956** The Bottom of the Bottle; Magnificent Roughnecks. **1957** The Tattered Dress; The Tarnished Angels. **1958** Rally 'Round the Flag, Boys!; Cat On A Hot Tin Roof. **1960** The Bramble Bush; Circus of Horrors. **1961** The Big Bankroll; King of the Roaring 20's. **1962** Sammy the Way-Out Seal.

CARSON, JAMES B.
Born: 1885. Died: Nov. 18, 1958, Los Angeles, Calif. Screen, stage and vaudeville actor.

Appeared in: **1930** Everything Happens to Me (short). **1933** Moonlight and Pretzels. **1935** Harmony Lane; Coronado. **1937** The Firefly. **1938** Secrets of an Actress; Crime School; The Girls Downstairs. **1939** The Gracie Allen Murder Case; Disputed Passage.

CARSON, ROBERT
Born: 1910. Died: June 2, 1979, Atascadero, Calif. (stroke). Screen, television actor and writer. Brother of actor Jack Carson (dec. 1963).

Appeared in: **1939** Dick Tracy's G-Men. **1941** Jungle Man. **1942** Phantom Killer. **1950** Country Fair; The Fighting Stallion; Indian Territory; Mule Train; Radar Secret Service. **1952** For Men Only; Actors and Sin; Red Snow; Greatest Show on Earth. **1953** Murder Without Tears; Three Sailors and a Girl. **1955** You're Never too Young; Gang-Busters. **1956** The Birds and the Bees.

CARSTENS, LINA
Born: 1883, Germany. Died: Sept. 21, 1978, Germany? Screen and stage actress.

Appeared in: **1938** Der Zerbrechene Krug (The Broken Jug). **1951** The Last Illusion. **1954** Angelika. **1956** Kleines Zelt und Grosse Liebe (aka Two in a Sleeping Bag—US 1964). **1959** Ein Mann Geht Durch die Wand (aka The Man who Walked Through the Wall—US 1964); Himmel Ohne Sterne (Sky Without Stars). **1961** Die Wahrheit Uber Rosemarie (The Truth About Rosemarie—aka Love Now Pay Later and aka She Walks by Night—US). **1964** I Was All His.

CARTER, BEN F.
Born: Feb. 10, 1911, Fairfield, Iowa. Died: Dec. 11, 1946. Black screen, radio actor and singer. Do not confuse with musician Benny Carter.

Appeared in: **1935** Ben Carter and his Pickaninny Choir (short). **1937** Adventures End. **1939** Gone With the Wind; Little Old New York. **1940** Maryland; Tin Pan Alley; Chad Hanna; South to Karanga; Earl of Puddlestone; Safari. **1941** Sleeps West; Ride on Vaquero; Dressed to Kill; Reap the Wild Wind; Young America; Born to Sing; Her Cardboard Lover; Happy Go Lucky. **1943** Crash Drive. **1944** Bowery to Broadway; Dixie Jamboree. **1945** The Scarlet Clue; Dark Alibi; Lady on a Train. **1946** The Harvey Girls.

CARTER, BOAKE
Born: Baku, Russia. Died: Nov. 16, 1944, Hollywood, Calif. Radio announcer and screen actor.

Appeared in: **1937** The Dead March (narrator).

CARTER, CHARLES CALVERT
Born: 1859. Died: Aug. 29, 1932, Long Beach, Calif. (heart ailment). Screen actor. Entered films in 1912.

Appeared in: **1921** The Smart Set; Lying Lips. **1923** The Bolted Door; Slave of Desire. **1924** Abraham Lincoln. **1929** Broadway Fever.

CARTER, FRANK
Died: May 9, 1920, Grantville, Md. Screen actor.

Appeared in: **1922** Foolish Lives.

CARTER, HUBERT
Born: 1869, Great Horton Yorks, England. Died: Mar. 26, 1934, England? Screen and stage actor.

Appeared in: **1923** The Beloved Vagabond.

CARTER, MRS. LESLIE (Caroline Louise Dudley)
Born: June 10, 1862, Lexington, Ky. Died: Nov. 12, 1937, Los Angeles, Calif. (heart disease). Screen, stage and vaudeville actress.

Appeared in: **1915** The Heart of Maryland (stage and film versions); Du Barry (stage and film versions). **1934** The Vanishing Pioneer. **1935** Rocky Mountain Mystery.

CARTER, LOUISE
Born: 1875, Denison, Iowa. Died: Nov. 10, 1957, Hollywood, Calif. Screen, stage actress and playwright.

Appeared in: **1924** The Truth About Women. **1925** The Lost Chord; Scandal Street; The Substitute Wife. **1926** Striving for Fortune; In Borrowed Plumes. **1930** Back Pay. **1931** All Gummed Up (short). **1932** Blondie of the Follies; Hell's Highway; Broken Lullaby; The Strange Case of Clara Deane; Madame Butterfly; Week-End Marriage; Two Against the World; The Last Mile; Tess of the Storm Country. **1933**

Jennie Gerhardt; This Day and Age; Pilgrimage; East of Fifth Avenue; Beauty for Sale; The Right to Romance; The Monkey's Paw. **1934** Beloved; You're Telling Me; Ready for Love. **1935** Straight From the Heart; The Mystery of Edwin Drood; Paddy O'Day; Reckless Roads. **1936** Rose of the Rancho. **1937** Angel; The Last Train From Madrid. **1938** Inside Story. **1939** Nancy Drew and the Hidden Staircase.

CARTER, MONTE
Born: 1886, San Francisco, Calif. Died: Nov. 14, 1950, San Francisco, Calif. Screen, stage, burlesque, vaudeville actor, film director and stage director.

Appeared in: **1928** Midnight Life. **1929** Melody Lane. **1931** Street Scene; The Vice Squad. **1934** Redhead. **1935** Make a Million; Confidential. **1936** Give Us This Night. **1937** Million Dollar Racket.

CARTIER, INEZ GIBSON
Born: 1918. Died: Aug. 4, 1970, Hollywood, Calif. Screen actress and film stunt pilot.

CARTON, PAULINE
Born: 1885 , France. Died: June 17, 1974, France? Screen and stage actress.

Appeared in: **1927** The Living Dead Man. **1931** The Parisian. **1937** Desire; Quadrille; Meet Miss Mozart. **1938** Story of a Cheat; Indiscretions; The Pearls of the Crown; Forty Little Mothers. **1939** The Affair la Font. **1940** Louise. **1948** Private Life of an Actor. **1951** La Poison; Miquette. **1952** The Prize; Armoire Volante (The Cupboard Was Bare). **1956** Fruits of Summer. **1957** The Virtuous Scoundrel. **1958** Lovers and Thieves. **1960** Au Pied, au Chevel et par Sputnik (aka A Dog, a Mouse and a Sputnik).

CARUSO, ENRICO
Born: Feb. 25, 1873, Naples, Italy. Died: Aug. 2, 1921, Naples, Italy (peritonitis). Opera singer and screen actor.

Appeared in: **1917** Webb Singing Pictures. **1918** My Cousin; The Splendid Romance (not released).

CARUSO, MARIA
Born: 1923. Died: June 13, 1979, Las Vegas, Nev. Screen, stage actress and singer.

Appeared in: **1944** The Song of Bernadette.

CARUTH, BURR
Born: June 15, 1865, Ill. Died: June 2, 1953. Screen actor.

Appeared in: **1934** The Double Door; Ready for Love; The Pursuit of Happiness. **1936** The Harvester; The Cowboy and the Kid. **1937** Ghost Town Gold; Gunsmoke Ranch; Too Tough to Handle. **1938** Under Western Stars. **1939** Invitation to Happiness; New Frontier. **1940** Rocky Mountain Rangers; Konga—the Wild Stallion. **1941** Ridin' on a Rainbow; The Phantom Cowboy. **1943** Calling Wild Bill Elliott. **1944** The Adventures of Mark Twain.

CARVAL, CLAUDE
Born: 1921, France. Died: July, 1972, France. Screen and stage actor.

CARVER, KATHRYN (aka KATHRYN HILL)
Born: 1906, New York, N.Y. Died: July 17, 1947, Elmhurst, N.Y. (gastric ulcer). Screen actress. Appeared under both names. Divorced from actor Adolphe Menjou (dec. 1963).

Appeared in: **1925** When Loves Grows Cold. **1926** The Wanderer; The Yankee Senor. **1927** Beware of Widows; Service for Ladies; Serenade. **1928** His Private Life; Outcast. **1929** No Defense.

CARVER, LOUISE (Louise Spilger Murray)
Born: June 9, 1869, Davenport, Iowa. Died: Jan. 18, 1956, Hollywood, Calif. Screen, stage, opera and vaudeville actress. Appeared in Mark Sennett silent films. Married to actor Tom Murray (dec. 1935).

Appeared in: **1923** The Extra Girl; Main Street; Scaramouche. **1924** The Breed of the Border. **1926** A Blonde's Revenge; A Harem Knight; Shameful Behavior? **1927** Blondes By Choice; Backstage; The Fortune Hunter. **1929** The Redeeming Sin; The Sap; Must We Marry?; Tonight at Twelve; The Bride's Relations (short); Wolves of the City. **1930** Back Pay; The Man from Blankley's; Big Trail. **1931** One of the Smiths (short); Side Show. **1932** Week-end Marriage; The Monkey's Paw. **1933** Roman Scandals; Hallelujah, I'm a Bum. **1934** Kid Millions. **1935** Every Night at Eight; Southern Exposure (short); I'm a Father (short). **1937** Dizzy Doctors (short); Lodge Night (short). **1941** Some More of Samoa (short).

CARVER, LYNN (Virginia Reid Sampson)
Born: Sept. 13, 1909. Died: Aug. 12, 1955, New York, N.Y. Screen, stage and television actress.

Appeared in: **1935** Strangers All; Roberta; Old Man Rhythm; To Beat the Band. **1937** Maytime; The Bride Wore Red; Madame X. **1938** Young Dr. Kildare; Everybody Sing; A Christmas Carol. **1939** Huckleberry Finn; Calling Dr. Kildare; Within the Law. **1940** Sporting Blood; A Door Will Open; Broadway Melody of 1940; Pound Foolish (short); Dulcy; Bitter Sweet. **1941** Mr. District Attorney in the Carter Case; County Fair; Blood and Sand; Charley's Aunt; Sucker List (short). **1942** Man from Cheyenne; Yokel Boy; Sunset on the Desert. **1943** The Human Comedy; Bataan; Tennessee Johnson. **1944** Law of the Valley. **1945** Flame of the West. **1946** Drifting Along. **1948** Crossed Trails.

CARVER, NOBLE
Born: 1896, Barren County, Ky. Died: Mar. 15, 1978, Tompkinsville, Ky. Country western performer and screen actor. Appeared in films as one of the "Log Cabin Boys."

CARVILL, HENRY J.
Born: 1867, London, England. Died: Mar. 11, 1941, United States. Screen and stage actor.

Appeared in: **1918** To Hell With the Kaiser. **1919** Our Teddy. **1920** If I Were King; The Branded Woman; Guilty of Love; The Fortune Teller. **1921** The Black Panther's Cub; Disraeli. **1922** Shackles of Gold. **1929** Disraeli (and 1921 version).

CASADESUS, MATHILDE
Born: May 15, 1921, Paris, France. Died: Aug. 30, 1965, Minorco Island, Spain (heart attack). Screen and stage actress.

Appeared in: **1943** La Boite aux Reves. **1945** Le Part de L'ombre. **1946** L'ediota. **1948** Marlene. **1949** Au Royaume des Cieux; Branguignol. **1950** Boniface Sonnambule. **1951** Le Plaisir. **1953** La Dame aux Camelias. **1955** Gervaise (US 1957). **1956** Ce soir les Jupons Volent. **1960** Candide (US 1962); Meutre en 45 Tours (Murder at 45 R.P.M.—US 1965). **1962** Love Is My Profession. **1963** Five Miles to Midnight. Other French film: L'Air de Paris.

CASALEGGIO, GIOVANNI
Born: 1880, Italy. Died: Nov. 11, 1955, Turin, Italy. Italian screen actor and film director.

Appeared in: **1913-1914** Cabiria.

CASALS, PABLO (Pau Carlos Salvador Defillo de Casals)
Born: Dec. 29, 1876, Vendrell, Spain. Died: Oct. 22, 1973, Rio Pedras, Puerto Rico (heart attack). Cellist, conductor, composer and screen actor. Divorced from soprano Susan Metcalfe. Married to Marta Montanez.

Appeared in: **1958** Windjammer.

CASANAVE, CHARLES
Born: 1895, Chicago, Ill. Died: May 7, 1958, Rye, N.Y. (heart attack). Screen actor.

CASE, PAUL
Born: 1895. Died: Mar. 29, 1933, Los Angeles, Calif. (injuries from fall from horse). Screen actor.

CASEY, DOLORES (Margaret Dolores Katherine Casey)
Born: 1917, New York, N.Y. Died: May 11, 1945, Hollywood, Calif. Screen actress.

Appeared in: **1936** Big Brown Eyes. **1937** Artists and Models Abroad. **1938** Cocoanut Grove; Doctor Rhythm.

CASEY, KENNETH
Born: 1899, N.Y. Died: Aug. 10, 1965, Newburg, N.Y. (heart condition). Screen actor and songwriter.

Appeared in: **1911** Daddy's Boy and Mammy; Wig-Wag; The Little Spy. **1912** How Tommy Saved His Father; The Higher Mercy; Xenophon, A Story of the Circus; Tom Tillin's Baby; Bumps; Ingenuity; The Eavesdroppers; Fate's Awful Jest; An Innocent Theft; The Man Under the Bed; A Juvenile Love Affair; The Old Silver Watch. **1913** When Bobby Forgot; In the Shadow. **1919** Heartsease. **1935** An MGM short.

CASEY, LESLIE J.
Born: 1891, Australia. Died: Feb. 18, 1942, New York, N.Y. Screen actor, playwright and production manager.

Appeared in: **1921** Little Miss Hawkshaw; Bucking the Line. **1922** The World's Champion; Captain Kidd (serial). **1923** Stormy Seas; One Million in Jewels.

CASEY, STUART F.
Born: 1896, London, England. Died: Jan. 23, 1948, Saratoga, N.Y. Stage and screen actor.

Appeared in: **1935** Reckless; The Age of Indiscretion; Captain Blood.

CASH, WILLIAM F.
Born: c. 1880. Died: Apr. 15, 1963, New York, N.Y. (stroke). Stage and screen actor.

CASHER, IZADORE (aka ISIDORE CASHIER)
Born: 1887, Russia. Died: Apr. 15, 1948, Savannah, Ga. (heart ailment). Yiddish screen and stage actor.

Appeared in: **1926** Broken Hearts. **1937** Green Fields. **1939** The Light Ahead.

CASHMAN, HARRY
Died: Dec. 14, 1912, Chicago, Ill. Screen actor.

Appeared in: **1911** Her Dad, the Constable; Bill Bumper's Bargain. **1912** The Fall of Montezuma; Neptune's Daughter; The Tale of a Cat; The Voice of Conscience; The Iron Heel; The Warning Hand; The End of a Feud; Almost a Man; When a Man's Married; Down Jayville Way; Sunshine; The Moving Finger; The Eye That Never Sleeps; Lonesome Robert; Getting a Hired Girl. **1913** The Farmer's Daughter.

CASNER, LUCKY
Born: 1925, Miami, Fla. Died: Apr. 10, 1965, Le Mans, France (auto race crash). Airplane pilot, race driver and screen actor.

Appeared in: **1961** The Green Helmet.

CASON, JOHN L.
Died: July 7, 1961. Screen actor.

Appeared in: **1941** Buck Privates. **1947** The Last Round-Up. **1949** Ringside; Rimfire; The Blazing Trail; Red Desrt; Tough Assignment; The Big Sombrero; Range Land. **1950** Desperadoes of the West (serial); Crooked River; Redwood Forest Trail; Fast on the Draw; Marshal of Heldorado; West of the Brazos; Colorado Ranger; Traveling Saleswoman; Streets of Ghost Town; Hostile Country; Rustlers on Horseback. **1951** Don Daredevil Rides Again (serial); Prairie Round-up; Savage Raider. **1952** The Hawk of Wild River; Black Hills Ambush; Wagon Team; Voodoo Tiger. **1953** Jungle Drums of Africa (serial); From Here to Eternity; Gun Fury; The Lost Planet (serial); Savage Frontier. **1954** Saskatchewan; Red River Shore. **1955** Wyoming Renegades; Count Three and Pray. **1956** He Laughed Last; Over-Exposed. **1957** Don't Go Near the Water; The Storm Rider. **1958** Snowfire. **1960** Cimarron.

CASS, GUY (Caster Abney Gay, Jr.)
Born: 1921. Died: Sept. 28, 1959, near Hollywood, Calif. (auto accident). Screen actor.

CASS, MAURICE
Born: Oct. 12, 1884, Vilna, Luthuania. Died: June 8, 1954, Hollywood, Calif. (heart attack). Screen, stage actor and playwright.

Appeared in: **1923** Experimental picture (sound-on-film) by Dr. Lee De Forest, exhibited at Rivoli Theatre in N.Y. **1930** Wife vs. Secretary. **1932** Something to Live For. **1935** Two for Tonight; Millions in the Air; Whispering Smith Speaks. **1936** The Big Broadcast of 1937; Arbor Day (short); Professional Soldier; Everybody's Old Man; Pepper; Charlie Chan at the Oepra; Give Us This Night; Champagne Waltz. **1937** The Firefly; Last Train from Madrid; Maytime; Women of Glamour; This Is My Affair; The Lady Escapes; She Had to East; Thin Ice; Wife, Doctor and Nurse; Danger—Love at Work; Life Begins in Collge; Ali Baba Goes to Town; Big Town Girl; Exiled to Shanghai. **1938** Making the Headlines; The Lone Wolf in Paris; Gangs of New York; Walking Down Broadway; The Baroness and the Butler; When Were You Born?; Josette; Sunset Trail; Gold Diggers in Paris; A Desperate Adventure; Exposed; Breaking the Ice. **1939** Second Fiddle; Mr. Smith Goes to Washington. **1940** The Lady With Red Hair; No, No Nanette; Florian. **1941** Weekend in Havanna; Chocolate Soldier; Charley's Aunt; Glamour Boy (short); Blood and Sand. **1942** Blondie Goes to College; My Heart Belongs to Daddy. **1943** Mission to Moscow. **1944** Up in Arms; Mrs. Parkington. **1945** Federal Operator 99 (serial); She Gets Her Man; Easy to Look At; Hit the Hay; Paris Underground; Her Lucky Night; Wonder Man. **1946** Idea Girl; The Notorious Lone Wolf; Angel on My Shoulder; Catman of Paris; Spook Busters. **1947** Springtime in the Rockies; High Conquest; Spoilers of the North; Saddle Pals. **1948** The Girl from Manhattan; Song of My Heart. **1949** Sorrowful Jones; Once More My Darling. **1952** We're Not Married. **1953** So You Want to be a Musician (short).

CASSADY, JAMES (James H. Cassidy)
Born: 1869, Philadelphia, Pa. Died: Mar. 23, 1928, Spokane, Wash. Screen actor.

Appeared in: **1915** Siren of Corsica.

CASSADY, SED ONSTOTT
Born: 1923. Died: Feb. 15, 1980, Simi Valley, Calif. (heart attack). Screen and television actor. Married to actress Rosemary Marsh.

Appeared in: **1948** Blood on the Moon (film debut).

CASSEL, SID
Born: 1897, Leeds, England. Died: Jan. 17, 1960, Hollywood, Calif. Screen, stage and television actor.

CASSIDY, BILL (William E. Cassidy)
Born: 1876. Died: Apr. 6, 1943, Cincinnati, Ohio. Screen and stage actor.

Appeared in: **1915** Birth of a Nation. **1916** Intolerance.

CASSIDY, ED (Edward Cassidy)
Born: 1893. Died: Jan. 19, 1968, Woodland Hills, Calif. Screen actor.

Appeared in: **1935** Toll of the Desert; Commodore. **1937** Borderland; Hit the Saddle; Come On, Cowboys; Arizona Days; Hittin' the Trail; Tex Rides With the Boy Scouts. **1938** Border Wolves; Outlaw Express; Frontier Town; The Purple Vigilantes; Man from Music Mountain; Cassidy of Bar 20; Rawhide; The Mexicali Kid; Starlight Over Texas. **1939** Wild Horse Canyon; Silver on the Sage; Mountain Rhythm; Rovin' Tumbleweeds; Desperate Trails; Cowboys from Texas; Son of Frankenstein. **1940** Deadwood Dick (serial); Riders of Pasco Basin; Ragtime Cowboy Joe; Gaucho Serenade. **1941** Wide Open Town; Robbers of the Range; Wyoming Wildcat; Ridin' on a Rainbow; The Gang's All Here; Bury Me Not on the Lone Prairie. **1942** House of Errors; The Mad Monster; Stardust on the Sage; Pirates of the Prairie. **1943** Thundering Trails; Cowboys in the Clouds; The Avenging Rider. **1944** Boss of Rawhide; Brand of the Devil; Frontier Outlaws; Fuzzy Settles Down; The Great Mike; The Pinto Bandit; Saddle Leather; Rustlers' Hideout; Trigger Law; Tucson Raiders; The Whispering Skull; Marked for Murder. **1945** The Daltons Ride Again; Manhunt of Mystery Island (serial); Along the Navajo Trail; Arson Squad; Corpus Christi Bandits; The Gangster's Den; Sheriff of Cimarron; Stagecoach Outlaws; Sunset in Eldorado; Three in the Saddle. **1946** Alias Billy the Kid; Ambush Trail; Days of Buffalo Bill; Trigger Fingers; The El Paso Kid; The Navajo Kid; Prairie Badmen; Roaring Rangers; Roll on Texas Moon; Sun Valley Cyclone. **1947** Jesse James Rides Again (serial); Homesteaders of Paradise Valley; Oregon Trail Scouts; Son of Zorro (serial); Valley of Fear; Stagecoach to Denver; Buffalo Bill Rides Again; Border Feud; The Beginning or the End. **1948** The Bold Frontiersman; Desperadoes of Dodge City. **1949** Roughshod; Take Me Out to the Ball Game. **1950** Fence Riders; Trail of Robin Hood; Buckaroo Sheriff of Texas. **1951** Belle Le Grande; Million Dollar Pursuit. **1952** Desperadoes' Outpost; Black Hills Ambush; Night Raiders; And Now Tomorrow; Talk About a Stranger. **1956** The First Traveling Saleslady.

CASSIDY, FRANK
Born: 1921. Died: Mar. 7, 1978, Washington, D.C. (heart attack). Screen, stage, television actor and executive director of Kennedy Center.

CASSIDY, JACK (John Edward Joseph Cassidy)
Born: Mar. 5, 1927, Queens, N.Y. Died: Dec. 12, 1976, West Hollywood, Calif. (burned to death). Screen, stage, television actor and playwright. Divorced from actresses Evelyn Ward and Shirley Jones. Father of Patrick, Ryan and actors David and Shaun Cassidy.

Appeared in: **1961** Look in Any Window. **1962** The Chapman Report. **1964** F.I.I. Code 98. **1967** A Guide for the Married Man. **1970** The Cockeyed Cowboys of Calico County; Mr. Magoo's Holiday Festival (voice). **1971** Bunny O'Hare. **1975** The Eiger Sanction. **1976** W. C. Fields and Me. **1978** The Private Files of J. Edgar Hoover.

CASSIDY, TED
Born: 1933. Died: Jan. 16, 1979, Los Angeles, Calif. (complications after open heart surgery). Screen, stage, radio, television actor and screenwriter.

Appeared in: **1969** Butch Cassidy and the Sundance Kid; McKenna's Gold. **1973** The Slams. **1975** Poor Pretty Eddie. **1976** Harry and Walter Go to New York. **1977** The Last Remake of Beau Geste. **1978** Going Coconuts. **1979** Sunshine Run.

CASSIN, BILLIE See CRAWFORD, JOAN

CASSON, SIR LEWIS
Born: 1876. Died: May 16, 1969, London, England. Screen, stage, television actor, stage producer and director. Married to actress Dame Sybil Thorndyke (dec. 1976) and father of actors John and Christopher and actresses Ann and Mary Casson.

Appeared in: **1930** Escape. **1933** Crime on the Hill. **1936** Rhodes of Africa (aka Rhodes—US); Calling the Tune. **1937** Victoria the Great. **1938** South Riding; Sixty Glorious Years (aka Queen of Destiny—US). **1951** Men of the Sea. **1959** Shake Hands With the Devil.

CASTAGNA, JOE
Born: 1934. Died: Aug. 22, 1970, Los Angeles, Calif. (heart attack). Screen actor and stuntman.

Appeared in: **1957** Johnny Trouble. **1969** That Tender Touch.

CASTIGLIONI, IPHIGENE
Born: 1901. Died: July 30, 1963, Hollywood, Calif. Screen, stage and television actress.

Appeared in: **1935** Story of Louis Pasteur. **1937** Life of Emile Zola; Maytime. **1950** September Affair. **1953** Greatest Show on Earth. **1954** Three Coins in the Fountain; Rear Window. **1955** Conquest of Space. **1957** Funny Face; Wild Is the Wind; Valerie. **1964** Back Street; Comancheros. **1962** Rome Adventure.

CASTILE, LYNN (aka LYNN CANTER)
Born: 1898. Died: Apr. 8, 1975, Los Angeles, Calif. Screen, stage, radio actress and singer.

Appeared in: **1948** Marshal of Amarillo.

CASTLE, DON
Born: Sept. 29, 1917, Beaumont, Tex. Died: May 26, 1966, Hollywood, Calif. (overdose of medication). Screen actor.

Appeared in: **1938** Young Dr. Kildare; Love Finds Andy Hardy (film debut); Rich Man, Poor Girl; Out West With the Hardys. **1939** The Hardys Ride High; These Glamour Girls. **1940** Susan and God; Northwest Passage; I Take This Woman. **1941** Power Dive; World Premiere. **1942** Tombstone, the Town Too Tough To Die. **1947** Born to Speed; The Invisible Wall; The Guilty; High Tide; Roses Are Red. **1948** Perilous Waters; I Wouldn't Be in Your Shoes; Strike It Rich; Who Killed "Doc" Robbin? **1949** Stampede. **1950** Motor Patrol. **1957** The Big Land; Gunfight at the O.K. Corral.

CASTLE, IRENE (Irene Foote)
Born: 1893, New Rochelle, N.Y. Died: Jan. 25, 1969, Eureka Springs, Ark. Screen, stage actress and dancer. Married to Vernon Castle (dec. 1918) with whom she appeared on stage and screen.

Appeared in: **1914** Mr. and Mr. Vernon Castle Before the Camera (with Vernon Castle). **1915** The Whirl of Life (with Vernon Castle). **1917** Patria (serial); Vengenace is Mine; Sylvia of the Secret Service; Stranded in Arcady; The Mark of Cain; Convict 999. **1918** The Hillcrest Mystery; The First Law; The Mysterious Client; The Girl from Bohemia; The Common Cause. **1919** The Firing Line; The Invisible Bond. **1920** The Amateur Wife. **1921** The Broadway Bride. **1922** French Heels; No Trespassing; Slim Shoulders. **1924** Broadway After Dark.

CASTLE, LILLIAN
Born: 1865. Died: Apr. 24, 1959, Los Angeles, Calif. Screen and vaudeville actress.

Appeared in: **1935** Confidential; Straight from the Heart. **1947** The Exile; When a Girl's Beautiful. **1949** The Set-Up.

CASTLE, NICK
Born: Mar. 21, 1910, Brooklyn, N.Y. Died: Aug. 28, 1968, Los Angeles, Calif. (heart attack). Screen, vaudeville dancer, film and television dance director.

Appeared in: **1955** Artists and Models.

CASTLE, PEGGY (aka PEGGIE CASTLE)
Born: Dec. 22, 1926, Appalachia, Va. Died: Aug. 11, 1973, Hollywood, Calif. (cirrhosis of the liver and heart condition). Screen and television actress. Divorced from film producer William McGarry.

Appeared in: **1947** When a Girl's Beautiful. **1949** Mr. Belvedere Goes to College. **1950** I Was a Shoplifter; Shakedown; Woman in Hiding; Buccaneer's Girl. **1951** Bright Victory; Payment on Demand (aka Story of Divorce); Air Cadet; The Prince Who Was a Thief; The Golden Horde. **1952** Invasion USA; Harem Girl; Wagons West. **1953** I, The Jury; 99 River Street; Cow Country; Son of Belle Starr. **1954** The

Long Wait; Jesse James' Women; The White Orchid; The Yellow Tomahawk; Overland Pacific; Southwest Passage. **1955** Finger Man; Target Zero; Tall Man Riding. **1956** Two Gun Lady; Miracle in the Rain; Oklahoma Woman; Quincannon—Frontier Scout. **1957** Beginning of the End; The Counterfeit Plan; Hell's Crossroads; Back from the Dead (aka Bury Me Dead). **1958** The Seven Hills of Rome.

CASTLE, VERNON
Born: May 2, 1887, England. Died: Feb. 15, 1918, Houston, Tex. (plane crash). Screen, stage actor and dancer. Married to Irene Castle (dec. 1969) with whom he appeared on stage and screen.

Appeared in: **1914** Mr. and Mrs. Vernon Castle Before the Camera (with Irene Castle). **1915** The Whirl of Life (with Irene Castle).

CASTLE, WILLIAM (William Schloss)
Born: Apr. 24, 1914, New York, N.Y. Died: May 31, 1977, Los Angeles, Calif. (heart attack). Screen, stage, television actor, film director, film producer and screenwriter.

Appeared in: **1937** The Man Who Cried Wolf. **1940** The Lady in Question; He Stayed for Breakfast. **1968** Rosemary's Baby. **1975** Shampoo; The Day of the Locust.

CASTLETON, BARBARA
Born: 1896, Little Rock, Ark. Died: 1981. Screen and stage actress.

Appeared in: **1916** Daughter of the Gods. **1917** Parentage; Her Good Name; On Trial; God's Man; Sins of Ambition. **1918** For the Freedom of the World; Empty Pockets; Heart of a Girl; Just Sylvia. **1919** The Silver King; The Man Who Turned White. **1920** Out of the Storm (aka The Tower of Ivory); Dangerous Days; Branding Iron; Dangerous Hours. **1921** Shams of Society; The Child Thou Gavest Me. **1922** False Fronts; My Friend, the Devil; The Streets of New York; What's Wrong with the Women? **1923** The Net.

CASTRO, STEVEN
Born: 1864. Died: Nov. 19, 1952, Hollywood, Calif. Screen cowboy actor and rodeo rider.

CATLETT, WALTER
Born: Feb. 4, 1889, San Francisco, Calif. Died: Nov. 14, 1960, Woodland Hills, Calif. (stroke). Screen, stage, opera, vaudeville actor and screenwriter.

Appeared in: **1924** Second Youth. **1926** Summer Bachelors. **1929** Married in Hollywood; Why Leave Home?; The Gay Nineties. **1930** The Floradora Girl; Let's Go Places; Happy Days; The Big Party; The Golden Calf; Stage Struck; Aunts in the Pants. **1931** Front Page; Cock of the Air; Platinum Blonde; Yellow; Camping Out (short); Palmy Days; Gold Fish Bowl; The Maker of Men. **1932** The Expert; It's Tough to Be Famous; Big City Blues; The Penalty of Fame; Sky Devils; Back Street; Rain; Free, White and 21; Rockabye; Okay Ameria; Sport Parade. **1933** Private Jones; Only Yesterday; Mama Loves Papa; Arizona to Broadway. **1934** Unknown Blonde; The Captain Hates the Sea; Olsen's Big Moment; Lightning Strikes Twice. **1935** Every Night at Eight; A Tale of Two Cities; Affair of Susan. **1936** I Loved a Soldier; Mr. Deeds Goes to Town; We Went to College; Follow Your Heart; Sing Me A Love Song; Cain and Mable; Banjo on My Knee. **1937** Four Days' Wonder; On the Avenue; Love is News; Wake Up and Live; Love Under Fire; Danger—Love at Work; Varsity Show; Every Day's a Holiday; Come Up Smiling. **1938** Bringing Up Baby; Going Places. **1939** Kid Nightingale; Exile Express; Zaza. **1940** Pop Always Pays; Remedy for Riches; Comin' 'Round the Mountain; Spring Parade; Half a Sinner; Pinocchio (voice); Li'l Abner; The Quarterback. **1941** You're the One; Honeymoon for Three; Horror Island; It Started with Eve; Wild Man of Borneo; Million Dollar Baby; Hello Sucker; Manpower; Mad Men of Missouri; Unfinished Business; Steel Against the Sky; Wild Bill Hickok Rides. **1942** Star Spangled Rhythm; My Gal Sal; Maisie Gets Her Man; Yankee Doodle Dandy; Give Out Sisters; Heart of the Golden West; Between Us Girls. **1943** West Side Kid; Hit Parade of 1943; How's About It?; Cowboy in Manhattan; Get Going; They Got Me Covered; Fired Wife; His Butler's Sister. **1944** Her Primitive Man; Pardon My Rhythm; The Ghost Catchers; Hat Check Honey; Up in Arms; Lady, Let's Dance!; Three Is a Family; Hi, Beautiful; My Gal Loves Music; Lake Placid Serenade. **1945** The Man Who Walked Alone; I Love a Bandleader. **1946** Riverboat Rhythm; Slightly Scandalous. **1947** I'll Be Yours. **1948** Mr. Reckless; Are You With It?; The Boy with Green Hair. **1949** Henry, the Rainmaker; Look for the Silver Lining; Dancing in the Dark; The Inspector General; Leave It to Henry. **1950** Father Makes Good; Father's Wild Game. **1951** Father Takes the Air; Honeychile; Here Comes the Groom. **1956** The Gay Nineties; Davy Crockett and the River Pirates; Friendly Persuasion. **1957** Beau James.

CATO, MINTO
Born: 1900. Died: Oct. 26, 1979, New York, N.Y. Black screen, stage actress and opera singer.

CAULKINS, RUFUS
Died: July 15, 1935, Los Angeles, Calif. (auto accident). Screen actor.

CAVALIERI, LINA
Born: Dec. 25, 1874, Rome, Italy. Died: Feb. 8, 1944, near Florence, Italy. Screen, opera and stage actress.

Appeared in: **1914** Manon Lescaut. **1917** The Eternal Temptress. **1918** A Woman of Impulse. **1919** The House of Granada; Two Brides; Mad Love.

CAVANAGH, PAUL
Born: Dec. 8, 1895, Chislehurst, Kent, England. Died: Mar. 15, 1964. Screen, stage, radio actor and author.

Appeared in: **1928** Tesha; Two Little Drummer Boys. **1929** A Woman in the Night; The Runaway Princess. **1930** Stricly Unconventional; Grumpy; The Storm; The Devil to Pay; The Virtuous Sin. **1931** Born to Love; Unfaithful; Transgression; Always Goodbye; The Squaw Man. **1932** Heartbreak; Tonight is Ours; The Devil's Lottery; The Crash; A Bill of Divorcement. **1933** The Sin of Nora Moran; The Kennel Murder Case. **1934** Tarzan and His Mate; Shoot the Works; Menance; The Notorious Sophie Lang; Curtain at Eight; Uncertain Lady; Escapade; One Exciting Adventure. **1935** Goin' to Town; Splendor; Wings in the Dark; Without Regret; Thunder in the Night. **1936** Champagne Charlie; Crime Over London (US 1938). **1937** A Romance in Flanders (aka Lost on the Western Front—US 1940); Cafe Colette (aka Danger in Paris—US). **1939** Reno; Within the Law; The Under-pup. **1940** I Take This Woman. **1941** The Case of the Black Parrot; Maisie Was a Lady; Shadows on the Stairs; Passage from Hong Kong. **1942** Eagle Squadron; Captains of the Clouds; The Strange Case of Dr. Rx; Pacific Rendezvous; The Hard Way; The Gorilla Man. **1943** Adventures in Iraq. **1944** The Scarlet Claw; Maisie Goes to Reno; Marriage is a Private Affair; The Man in Half Moon Street. **1945** The House of Fear; The Woman in Green. **1946** Night and Day; Night in Paradise; The Verdict; Club Havana; Humoresque. **1947** Ivy; Dishonored Lady. **1948** The Black Arrow; The Babe Ruth Story; The Secret Beyond the Door; You Gotta Stay Happy. **1949** Madame Bovary. **1950** The Iroquois Trail; Hit Parade of 1951; Rogues of Sherwood Forest; Hi-Jacked. **1951** Desert Fox; All That I Have; The Strange Door; Hollywood Story; The Son of Dr. Jekyll; Tales of Robin Hood; The Highwayman. **1952** The Golden Hawk; Plymouth Adventure. **1953** The Mississippi Gambler; House of Wax; The All American; The Bandits of Corsica; Flame of Calcutta; Port Sinister; Charade. **1954** The Raid; Casanova's Big Night; The Iron Glove; Magnificent Obsession; The Law vs. Billy the Kid; Khyber Patrol. **1955** The Purple Mask; The King's Thief; The Prodigal; The Scarlet Coat; Diane. **1956** Francis in the Haunted House; Blonde Bait. **1957** She-Devil; God is My Partner; The Man Who Turned to Stone. **1958** In the Money. **1959** The Four Skulls of Jonathan Drake; The Beat Generation.

CAVANAGH, PETER
Born: 1915, England. Died: Feb. 23, 1981, London, England. Screen, stage, vaudeville, radio actor and singer.

CAVANAUGH, HOBART
Born: 1887, Virginia City, Nev. Died: Apr. 27, 1950, Woodland Hills, Calif. Screen, stage and vaudeville actor.

Appeared in: **1928** San Francisco Nights. **1929** Sympathy (short). **1930** The Poor Fish (short); The Headache Man (short). **1932** Close Friends (short). **1933** State Fair; Footlight Parade; Picture Snatcher; Death Watch; Study in Scarlet; Gold Diggers of 1933; Goodbye Again; Mary Stevens, M.D; The Mayor of Hell; Private Detective 62; Kennel Murder Case; From Headquarters; Broadway Thru a Keyhole; Lilly Turner; Havana Widows; Convention City; Headline Shooter; No Marriage Ties; The Devil's Mate; My Woman; I Cover the Waterfront. **1934** Wonder Bar; Mandalay; The Firebird; Dark Hazard; I Sell Everything; Madame Du Barry; I am a Thief; St. Louis Kid; Housewife; A Lost Lady; Fashions of 1934; Kansas City Princess; Moulin Rouge; Hi Nellie; Easy to Love; I've Got Your Number; Harold Teen; Jimmy the Gent; Merry Wives of Reno; The Key; A Very Honorable Guy; A Modern Hero; Now I'll Tell. **1935** Wings in the Dark; While the Patient Slept; Captain Blood; Broadway Breveties (short); Don't Bet on Blondes; We're in the Money; Border Town; Broadway Gondolier; Page Miss Glory; Dr. Socrates; A Midsummer Night's Dream; I Live for Love. **1936** The Lady Consents; Love Letters of a Star; Colleen; Love Begins at Twenty; Two Against the World; Hearts Divided; Sing Me a Love Song; Cain and Mabel; Here Comes Carter; The Golden Arrow; Stage Struck; Wife vs. Secretary. **1937** The Great O'Malley; Three Smart Girls; Mysterious Crossing; The Mighty Treve; Night Key; Girl Overboard; Love in a Bungalow; Reported Missing. **1938** Strange Faces; That's My Story; Cowboy from Brooklyn; Orphans of the Street. **1939** Zenobia; Career; Tell No Tales; Chicken Wagon

Family; Reno; That's Right, You're Wrong; The Covered Trailer; The Day of Rest (short); See Your Doctor (short); The Honeymoon's Over; Adventures of Jane Arden; Rose of Washington Square. **1940** You Can't Fool Your Wife; A Child Is Born; Home Movies (short); I Stole a Million; Shooting High; An Angel from Texas; Street of Memories; Stage to Chino; Public Deb. No. 1; The Great Plane Robbery; Santa Fe Trail; Charter Pilot; Love, Honor and Oh Baby!; The Ghost Comes Home; Hired Wife. **1941** Playmates; Skylark; Our Wife; Horror Island; Meet the Chump; Thieves Fall Out; Land of the Open Range; I Wanted Wings. **1942** The Remarkable Andrew; A Tragedy at Midnight; Jackass Mail; Whistling in Dixie; Stand by for Action; My Favorite Spy; The Magnificent Dope. **1943** Skylark; Dangerous Blondes; The Meanest Man in the World; The Kansan; Gildersleeve on Broadway; Man from Down Under. **1944** The Immortal Blacksmith (short); Louisiana Hayride; Sweet Rosie O'Grady; Jack London; Kismet. **1945** House of Fear; Roughly Speaking; Don Juan Quilligan; I'll Remember April; Lady on a Train. **1946** Cinderella Jones; The Spider Woman Strikes Back; Faithful in My Fashion; Black Angel; Little Iodine; Margie. **1947** Driftwood. **1948** Best Man Wins; You Gotta Stay Happy; Up in Central Park; The Inside Story. **1949** A Letter to Three Wives. **1950** Stella.

CAVANAUGH, JAMES
Born: 1912. Died: Sept. 30, 1981, Long Beach, Calif. Screen, stage, vaudeville, television actor, singer and burlesque entertainer.

Appeared in: **1957** The Joker is Wild. **1964** Vengeance.

CAVANNA, ELISE
Born: 1902. Died: May 12, 1963, Hollywood, Calif. (cancer). Screen, stage actress, author and painter.

Appeared in: **1926** Love 'Em and Leave 'Em. **1931** A Melon-Drama (short). **1932** The Dentist (short). **1933** The Barber Shop (short); The Pharmacist (short). **1934** You're Telling Me. **1938** Three Loves Has Nancy; I Met My Love Again; Everybody Sing. **1946** Ziegfeld Follies.

CAVEN, ALLAN
Born: Mar. 25, 1880, Concord, Calif. Died: Jan. 19, 1941, Hollywood, Calif. Stage and screen actor. Entered films in 1919.

Appeared in: **1921** The Primal Law. **1923** When Odds are Even. **1927** London After Midnight; Shanghai Bound. **1928** The Terrible People (serial); The Man Who Laughs. **1929** Leave It to Gerry; The Million Dollar Collar. **1931** City Lights. **1934** Opened by Mistake (short); The Mighty Barnum. **1935** Thicker Than Water (short). **1936** Rebellion. **1937** Hit the Saddle; Old Louisiana; Nation Aflame. **1938** I Am A Criminal. **1939** Dick Tracy's G-Men (serial); Mr. Smith Goes to Washington.

CAVENDER, GLEN W.
Born: 1884. Died: Feb. 9, 1962, Hollywood, Calif. Screen, actor and film director. One of the original Keystone Kops.

Appeared in: **1915** Fickle Fatty's Fall; A Submarine Pirate. **1916** Fatty and Mable Adrift; Because He Loved Her; The Village Blacksmith; The Surf Girl. **1917** A Dog Catcher's Love; The Pawnbroker's Heart. **1921** Hearts of Youth; The Primal Law; Skirts; Little Miss Hawkshaw; Straight From the Shoulder; What Love Will Do. **1922** Iron to Gold. **1923** Main Street. **1925** Keep Smiling; Manhattan Madness. **1927** The General. **1929** Ships of the Night. **1935** G-Men. **1938** Penrod's Double Trouble. **1940** The Man I Married. **1942** Yankee Doodle Dandy.

CAVENDISH, DAVID
Born: 1891. Died: Oct. 8, 1960, Hollywood, Calif. (heart attack). Screen and stage actor.

Appeared in: **1942** Random Harvest. **1945** Wilson. **1946** Lady in the Lake. **1947** The Exile; Ivy; Forever Amber; Love From a Stranger; The Homestretch; Life With Father. **1949** Madame Bovary.

CAVENDISH, JUNE
Died: Feb. 22, 1976, Los Angeles, Calif. (leukemia). Screen actress.

CAVENS, FRED (Frederic Adolphe Cavens)
Born: Aug. 30, 1882. Died: Apr. 30, 1962, Woodland Hills, Calif. (uremia). Screen actor, stuntman and fencing master.

Appeared in: **1922** The Three-Must-Get-Theres. **1927** King of Kings. **1933** Breed of the Border. **1937** Cape Metropole. **1938** Artists and Models Abroad; Kidnapped. **1939** The Man in the Iron Mask. **1952** Lydia Bailey. **1954** The French Line.

CAWTHORN, JOSEPH
Born: Mar. 29, 1868, N.Y. Died: Jan. 21, 1949, Beverly Hills, Calif. (stroke). Stage and screen actor. Married to actress Queenie Vass (dec. 1960).

Appeared in: **1927** Very Confidential; Two Girls Wanted; The Secret Studio. **1928** Silk Legs; Hold 'Em Yale. **1929** Street Girl; Jazz Heaven; Dance Hall; The Taming of the Shrew; Speakeasy. **1930** Dixiana; The Princess and the Plumber. **1931** Kiki; The Runaround; Peach O'Reno; A Tailor Made Man. **1932** White Zombie; Love Me Tonight; They Call It Sin. **1933** Whistling in the Dark; Blondie Johnson; Grand Slam; Men Are Such Fools; Made on Broadway; Best of Enemies; Broken Dreams; Radio short. **1934** Housewife; Young and Beautiful; The Human Side; Lazy River; The Last Gentleman; Twenty Million Sweethearts; Glamour; Music in the Air; The Cat and the Fiddle. **1935** Adeline; Maybe It's Love; Go Into Your Dance; Sweet Music; Page Miss Glory; Bright Lights; Harmony Lane; Gold Diggers of 1935; Naughty Marietta; Smart Girl. **1936** Freshman Love; Hot Money; The Great Ziegfeld; One Rainy Afternoon; Brides Are Like That; Crime Over London. **1940** Lillian Russell; Scatterbrain. **1941** So Ends the Night. **1942** The Postman Didn't Ring.

CAZALE, JOHN
Born: 1936, Boston, Mass. Died: Mar. 12, 1978, New York, N.Y. (cancer). Screen and stage actor.

Appeared in: **1972** The Godfather. **1974** The Godfather Part II; The Conversation. **1975** Dog Day Afternoon. **1978** The Deer Hunter.

CAZENUVE, PAUL
Born: France. Died: June 22, 1925, Hollywood, Calif. Screen, stage actor and film director.

Appeared in: **1921** Big Town Ideas; The Queen of Sheba. **1923** Six Days; The French Doll.

CEBALLOS, LARRY (Hilarion Ceballos)
Born: Oct. 21, 1887, Iquique, Chile. Died: Sept., 1978, Los Angeles, Calif. (cancer). Screen, stage actor, film producer, dance director and circus performer. Son of circus performers Sarah Fergus (dec.) and Teodulo R. Ceballos (dec).

CEBOTARI, MARIA
Born: 1911, Australia. Died: June 9, 1949, Vienna, Austria. Screen actress and opera singer.

Appeared in: **1938** Solo Per To (aka Only for Thee). **1939** Ueber Alles die Treue. **1940** Life of Giuseppe Verdi. **1941** The Dream of Butterfly.

CECCARELLI, VINCENZO
Born: 1889. Died: Aug. 8, 1969, Los Angeles, Calif. Screen actor and singer.

CECIL, EDWARD
Born: Sept., 1888, San Francisco, Calif. Died: Dec. 13, 1940, Los Angeles, Calif. Screen, stage and vaudeville actor.

Appeared in: **1918** The Man Who Wouldn't Tell. **1921** Big Game; The Greater Claim; Parted Curtains; There Are No Villains; The Off-Shore Pirate. **1922** The Guttersnipe; The Love Gambler; My Wild Irish Rose; The Top of New York. **1923** The Scarlet Car. **1924** Wolves of the North (serial); The Sword of Valor. **1925** The Phantom of the Opera; Hidden Loot; Secrets of the Night; What Happened to Jones? **1926** Vanishing Millions (serial); The Crown of Lies; The Stolen Ranch; The Smoke Eaters. **1927** Woman's Law; Hoof Marks; Cheaters; The Desert of the Lost. **1928** Jazzland; The Sky Rider; Saddle Mates; A Midnight Adventure. **1929** Silent Sentinel; The Black Book (serial). **1930** Guilty?; Lotus Lady. **1931** Resurrection.

CECIL, MARY
Born: 1885, N.Y. Died: Dec. 21, 1940, New York, N.Y. (pneumonia). Screen, stage and radio actress.

Appeared in: **1939** The Women (stage and film versions).

CECIL, NORA
Died: 1954? Screen actress.

Appeared in: **1918** Prunella. **1925** The Deadwood Coach; His Majesty Bunker Bean. **1927** The Devil Dancer. **1928** The Fortune Hunter; The Cavalier. **1930** Seven Days' Leave; Little Accident; Only Saps Work. **1931** Street Scene; Caught Plastered. **1933** Peg O' My Heart; Doctor Bull; Design for Living. **1934** Once to Every Woman; You're Telling Me; The Old Fashioned Way. **1935** Car 99. **1936** Dancing Pirate. **1937** Easy Living. **1938** King of Alcatraz. **1939** What a Life. **1946** The Missing Lady. **1947** Mourning Becomes Electra.

CEDAR, DAYNA
Died: June 10, 1974. Screen actress.

CEDAR, IVAN

Died: Nov., 1937, Tucson, Ariz. (auto accident). Screen actor and stuntman.

CELESTE, OLGA

Born: 1887, Sweden. Died: Aug. 31, 1969, Burbank, Calif. (heart attack after treatment for pneumonia). Screen, circus, vaudeville actress and animal trainer.

Appeared in: **1934** Cleopatra.

CELLI, FAITH

Born: Nov. 27, 1888, Kensington, London, England. Died: Dec. 27, 1942, Ascot, England. Screen and stage actress.

Appeared in: **1920** The Bump (short).

CELLIER, FRANK

Born: Feb. 23, 1884, Surbiton, Surrey, England. Died: Sept. 27, 1948, London, England. Screen and stage actor. Divorced from actress Florence Glossop-Harric (dec. 1931).

Appeared in: **1931** Her Reputation; Tin Gods. **1933** The Golden Cage; Soldiers of the King (aka The Woman in Command—US 1934); Doss House; Hearts of Oak; The Fire Raisers. **1934** Colonel Blood. **1935** Lorna Doone; The Love Affair of the Dictator (aka The Dictator and the Loves of a Dictator—US); The 39 Steps; The Guv'nor (aka Mister Hobo—US 1936); The Passing of the Third Floor Back. **1936** Rhodes of Africa (aka Rhodes—US); Tudor Rose (aka Nine Days a Queen—US); The Man Who Changed His Mind (aka The Man Who Lived Again—US). **1937** O.H.M.S. (aka You're in the Army Now—US); Take My Tip; Action for Slander (US 1938); Non-Stop New York. **1938** Kate Plus Ten; Sixty Glorious Years (aka Queen of Destiny—US); A Royal Divorce; The Ware Case (US 1939). **1939** The Midas Touch. **1941** Quiet Wedding; Love on the Dole; Ships with Wings (US 1942); The Black Sheep of Whitehall; Cottage to Let (aka Bombsight Stolen—US); Jennie (US 1943). **1942** The Big Blockade. **1944** Give Us the Moon. **1946** Quiet Weekend (US 1948); The Magic Blow (US 1947). **1948** Easy Money (US 1949); The Blind Goddess (US 1949).

CENNERAZZO, ARMANDO

Born: 1886, Italy. Died: Jan. 10, 1962, New York, N.Y. Screen, stage actor and stage director. Appeared in silent films.

CERF, KURT

Born: 1910, Germany. Died: Oct. 27, 1979, Wilmington, Del. (massive stroke). Screen, stage actor and drama teacher.

CERVAL, CLAUDE

Born: 1921, France. Died: July, 1972, France? Screen and stage actor.

Appeared in: **1955** Bob le Flambeur (Bob the Gambler; aka Fever Heat—US 1961). **1957** Marchands de Filles (Sellers of Girls—US 1967; aka Girl Merchants). **1958** Le Beau Serge (Handsome Serge). **1959** Les Cousins (The Cousins). **1960** Les Jeux de L'Amour (The Love Game); Classe tous Risques (The Big Risk—US 1963). **1962** Le Crime ne Paie Pas (Crime Does Not Pay). **1963** Melodie en Sous-Sol (aka Any Number Can Win—US); Ophelia; Le Glaive et la Balance (The Sword and the Balance; aka Two are Guilty—US 1964). **1965** Les Chiens dans la Nuit (aka The Girl Can't Stop—US 1966). **1966** Du Rififi a Paname (aka The Upper Hand—US 1967). **1967** Belle de Jour (US 1968); La Peur et L'Amour (aka La Peur et Le Derir; aka Love + Fear + Torment; aka Fear and Love; aka Torment—US); Une Femme aux Abois (aka The Slave—US). **1969** La Voie Lactee (The Milky Way—US). **1970** Borsalino.

CERVI, GINO

Born: May 3, 1901, Bologna, Italy. Died: Jan. 3, 1974, Punta Ala, Italy (pulmonary stroke). Screen, stage, television actor, stage director, stage producer and political figure. Father of film producer Tonino Cervi.

Appeared in: **1934** Frontier (film debut). **1935** Amore; Aldebaran. **1936** I Due Sergenti. **1937** Gli Uomini non Sono Ingrati; Voglio Vivere Con Letizia; Il Ponto di Vetro. **1938** L'Argine (The River Bank); Ettore Fieramosca. **1939** Un Matrimonio Ideale (An Ideal Marriage). **1940** Un Aventura di Salvator Rosa (An Adventure of Salvator Rosa). **1942** Four Steps in the Clouds (US 1948). **1947** Fabiola (US 1951); Revenge. **1948** Anna Karenina; Eternal Melodies; The Spirit and the Flesh; Iron Crown (US 1949); His Young Wife. **1950** My Widow and I. **1951** Women Without Names. **1952** Little World of Don Camillo (US 1953—first of the Don Camillo series); Les Miserables; Malia; The Cliff of Sin; O.K. Nero (US 1953). **1953** Tre Storie Proibite (Three Forbidden Stories); Maddalena (US 1955); Queen of Sheba; Strange Deception (aka The Forbidden Christ). **1954** Indiscretion of an American Wife. **1955** Moglie per una Notte (Wife for a Night—US 1957). **1956** The Return of Don Camillo. **1958** Los Amantes del Desierto (aka Amanti del Desierto and La Figlia Dello Sceicco aka Desert Warrior—US 1961). **1959** The Naked Maja; Sans Famille; Sign of the Gladiator. **1960** L'Assedio di Siracusa (Siege of Syracuse—US 1962 aka Archimede); Femme di Lusso (Love, the Italian Way—US 1964); Gli Inamorati (Wild Love—US 1962); Agguato a Tangier (Trapped in Tangiers aka Ambush in Tangiers). **1961** La Rivolta degli Schiavi (The Revolt of the Slaves). **1962** Le Crime ne Paie Pas (Crime Does Not Pay). **1963** La Smania Addosso (The Eye of the Needle—US 1965). **1964** Becket; Volles Herz und Leere Taschen (A Full Heart and Empty Pockets).

CESANA, RENZO

Born: Oct. 30, 1907. Died: Nov. 8, 1970, Hollywood, Calif. (lung cancer). Screen and television actor.

Appeared in: **1950** A Lady Without a Passport; Stromboli. **1951** Mark of the Renegade; Try and Get Me. **1952** California Conquest. **1959** For the First Time; The Naked Maja. **1960** Fast and Sexy. **1961** Francis of Assisi. **1965** The Art of Love. **1966** Three on a Couch.

CESAR, M.

Died: Sept., 1921. Screen actor.

CEVERT, FRANCOIS (Albert Francois Cevert)

Born: Feb. 25, 1944, Paris, France. Died: Oct. 6, 1973, Watkins Glen, N.Y. (auto crash). Auto racer and screen actor.

Appeared in: **1975** One by One (documentary).

CHABRIER, MARCEL

Born: 1888, France. Died: Aug. 18, 1946, Piedmont, Canada (drowned). Screen, stage, radio actor and painter.

Appeared in: **1943** Le Pere Chopin.

CHADWICK, HELENE

Born: Nov. 25, 1897, Chadwick, N.Y. Died: Sept. 4, 1940, Los Angeles, Calif. (injuries from fall). Screen and stage actress. Divorced from film director William Wellman (dec. 1975). Entered films in 1916.

Appeared in: **1917** The Angel Factory. **1918** The Naulahka. **1919** Heartsease. **1920** Scratch My Back; Cupid; The Cowpuncher; Long Arm of Mannister; The Cup of Fury. **1921** The Sin Flood; From the Ground Up; Godless Men; The Old Nest; Dangerous Curve Ahead; Made in Heaven. **1922** Yellow Men and Gold; Glorious Fool; Dust Flower; Brothers Under the Skin. **1923** Quicksands; Gimme. **1924** Her Own Free Will; Reno; The Border Legion; Her Dark Swan; Love of Women; The Masked Dancer; The Naked Truth; Trouping with Ellen; Why Men Leave Home. **1925** Re-Creation of Brian Kent; The Woman Hater; The Golden Cocoon. **1926** Dancing Days; Hard Boiled; Pleasures of the Rich; The Still Alarm. **1927** The Rose of Kildare; The Bachelor's Baby; Stage Kisses; Stolen Pleasures. **1928** Modern Mothers; Say It With Sables; Women Who Dare. **1929** Father and Son; Confessions of a Wife. **1930** Men Are Like That. **1931** Bad Sister; Hell Bound. **1934** School for Girls. **1935** Frisco Kid; Mississippi; Mary Burns, Fugitive.

CHALFANT, FRANK E.

Born: 1922. Died: Jan. 3, 1981, Los Angeles, Calif. (heart attack). Screen and television actor. Married to actress Margarita Moya. Entered films approximately 1942.

CHALIAPIN, FEODOR

Born: Feb. 13, 1873, Kazan-Kazan, Russia. Died: Apr. 12, 1938, Paris, France (anemia brought on by kidney ailment). Screen, opera and vaudeville actor. Father of actors Feodor, Jr. and Irina Chaliapin (dec. 1978).

Appeared in: **1933** Don Quixote.

CHALIAPIN, IRINA

Born: Russia. Died: Oct. 11, 1978, Moscow, Russia. Screen and stage actress. Daughter of actor/singer Feodor Chaliapin, Sr. (dec. 1938). Sister of actor Feodor Chaliapin, Jr.

CHALMERS, THOMAS

Born: Oct. 20, 1890, New York, N.Y. Died: June 12, 1966, Greenwich, Conn. Screen, opera, television, radio actor, film director and producer of industrial and documentary films.

Appeared in: **1923** Puritan Passions. **1927** Blind Alleys. **1938** The Rivers (narrator). **1961** Romanoff and Juliet. **1963** All the Way Home. **1964** The Outrage.

CHALZEL, LEO
Born: 1901. Died: July 16, 1953, Westport, Conn. (heart ailment). Screen, stage, vaudeville and television actor.

Appeared in: **1934** Men in White; Come on Marines.

CHAMBERLIN, FRANK
Born: 1870. Died: Aug. 29, 1935, Los Angeles, Calif. Cowboy screen actor and songwriter.

CHAMBERLIN, J. RAYMOND
Born: 1886. Died: Dec. 2, 1957, Norristown, Pa. Screen actor and film director. Appeared in early Lubin Co. films.

CHAMBERLIN, RILEY C.
Born: 1854, Grand Rapids, Mich. Died: Jan. 24, 1917, New Rochelle, N.Y. Stage and screen actor. Entered films with Thanhouser in 1912.

Appeared in: **1912** Why Tom Signed the Pledge; Old Dr. Judd; Conductor 786; Now Watch the Professor; Please Help the Pope; Six-Cylinder Elopement; Dottie the Dancer; In a Garden; Brains vs. Brawn. **1913** Rosie's Revenge; Waiting for Hubby; The Official Goat Protector; What Might Have Been; How Philmy Won His Sweetheart. **1914** Mrs. Pinkhurst's Proxy; Coals of Fire; The Strategy of Conductor 786; The Benevolence of Conductor 786; The Touch of a Little Hand. **1915** Capers of College Chaps; Film Favorite's Finish; Madame Blanche—Beauty Doctor; Tracked Through the Snow; P. Henry Jenkins and Mars; Freddie Fink's Flirtation; Three Roses; Truly Rural Types; Help! Help!; That Poor Damp Cow; Biddy Brady's Birthday Coos; The Car Conductor; Simon's Swimming Soul-Mate; The Dead Man's Keys; When William's Whiskers Worked; The Conductor's Classy Chassis; Clarence Cheats at Croquet; Una's Useful Uncle; Cousin Clare's Cook Book; Bing-Bang Brothers; Tille the Terrible Typist; The Dog Catcher's Bride; The Actor and the Rube. **1916** Ruining Randall's Reputation; The Optimistic Oriental Occults; The Sailor's Smiling Spirit; Dad's Darling Daughters; Lucky Larry's Lady Love; Snow Storm and Sunshine; Grace's Gorgeous Gown; Maud Muller Modernized; Theodore's Thirst; Perkins' Peace Party; The Kiddie's Captain Kidd; Politickers; Prudence the Pirate; Doughnuts.

CHAMBERS, J. WHEATON
Born: 1888. Died: Jan. 31, 1958, Hollywood, Calif. Screen and stage actor. Entered films in 1929.

Appeared in: **1936** The Story of Louis Pasteur. **1940** Slightly Honorable; Drums of Fu Manchu (serial); Adventures of Red Ryder (serial). **1942** Reap the Wild Wind; Even as I.O.U. (short); The Wife Takes a Flyer; They All Kissed the Bride; Life Begins at 8:30. **1943** Beyond the Last Frontier; This Land is Mine. **1944** The Falcon Out West; Tall in the Saddle; Girl Rush; Nevada. **1945** The Clock; The Purple Monster Strikes (serial); That's the Spirit; Marshal of Laredo. **1946** The Crimson Ghost (serial); South of Monterey; People are Funny; Murder in the Music Hall; Tangier. **1947** Always Together; Son of Zorro (serial); Monsieur Verdoux; Good News; Body and Soul; Possessed; Song of Love; Crime Doctor's Gamble. **1948** The Pirate. **1949** The Great Sinner; Samson and Delilah; The Barkleys of Broadway; Deputy Marshal; I Can't Remember (short); Not Wanted; Mississippi Rhythm. **1950** Baron of Arizona; Between Midnight and Dawn; Peggy; The Secret Fury. **1951** The Magnificent Yankee; The Unknown Man; Lorna Doone; The Prowler; The Well; The Cimarron Kid; The Day the Earth Stood Still. **1952** Wagons West; Slaves of Babylon; Ma and Pa Kettle at the Fair. **1954** The Big Chase. **1955** East of Eden. **1956** The Peacemaker.

CHAMBERS, LESTER
Born: 1876. Died: Jan. 27, 1947, New York, N.Y. Screen and stage actor.

Appeared in: **1915** Divorced.

CHAMBERS, MARGARET
Died: Oct. 6, 1965, Hollywood, Calif. Screen actress.

Appeared in: **1916** The Woman in the Case. **1929** Woman to Woman.

CHAMBERS, MARIE
Born: 1889. Died: Mar. 21, 1933, Paris, France. Screen actress.

Appeared in: **1925** That Royal Girl.

CHAMBERS, RALPH
Born: 1892. Died: Mar. 10, 1968. Screen actor.

Appeared in: **1924** Another Scandal. **1957** The Pajama Game.

CHAMBLISS, WOODROW
Born: 1915. Died: Jan. 8, 1981, Ojai, Calif. (cancer). Screen, stage and television actor. Married to actress Elika Chambliss.

Appeared in: **1957** 3:10 to Yuma (film debut). **1965** Wild Seed. **1971** The Wild Country; Glen and Randa. **1974** Face to the Wind. **1975** The Devil's Rain. **1978** Sergeant Pepper's Lonely Heart's Club Band.

CHAMPION ("World's Wonder Horse")
Horse screen performer. Collective name for three horses used by actor Gene Autry in Westerns from early 1930s through early 1950s. Champion, Jr. (#2) is still alive.

CHAMPION #1 (Lindy)
Born: May 20, 1927. Died: c. 1944. Horse screen performer. Appeared in exhibitions.

Appeared in: **1933** Whirlwind. **1935** Tumbling Tumbleweeds; The Phantom Empire. **1936** The Big Show; The Singing Cowboy; Red River Valley; Comin' Round the Mountain; Guns and Guitars. **1937** The Old Corral; Round-up Time in Texas. **1938** Prairie Moon.

CHAMPION #3 (aka LITTLE CHAMP)
Died: 1976. Horse screen and television performer. Appeared in exhibitions. Son of Champion, Jr. (#2).

Appeared in: **1948** The Strawberry Roan (film debut). **1950** Mule Train; Beyond the Purple Hills.

CHAMPION, GOWER
Born: June 22, 1919, Geneva, Ill. Died: Aug. 25, 1980, New York, N.Y. (Waldenstrom's disease). Screen, stage, vaudeville, television actor, film director, stage director and choreographer. Divorced from actress Marge (Belcher) Champion with whom he appeared on stage and film, and Karla Champion.

Appeared in: **1946** Til the Clouds Roll By. **1950** Mr. Music. **1951** Showboat. **1952** Lovely to Look At; Everything I Have Is Yours. **1953** Give a Girl a Break. **1955** Three for the Show; Jupiter's Darling.

CHAN, MRS. PON Y.
Born: 1870. Died: Apr. 1, 1958, Hollywood, Calif. Screen character actress.

Appeared in: **1944** The Story of Dr. Wassell; Keys of the Kingdom. **1946** Anna and the King of Siam. **1948** Saigon.

CHANCE, ANNA
Born: Oct. 25, 1884, Oxford, Md. Died: Sept. 11, 1943, Hollywood, Calif. Screen, stage and vaudeville actress. Married to actor Charles Grapewin (dec. 1956) with whom she appeared in Christie Comedies. Entered films in 1929.

Appeared in: **1929** Jed's Vacation; Ladies' Choice; That Red Headed Hussy. Prior to 1930 was in The Wanderlust (short).

CHANCE, FRANK (Frank Leroy Chance)
Born: Sept. 19, 1879, Fresno, Calif. Died: Sept. 14, 1924. Professional baseball player and screen actor.

Appeared in: **1913** Baseball's Peerless Leader.

CHANDLER, ANNA
Born: 1887. Died: July 10, 1957, El Sereno, Calif. Screen, vaudeville actress and singer.

Appeared in: **1928** Popular Songs (short). **1932** The Big Broadcast. **1942** Tennesse Johnson.

CHANDLER, EDWARD "EDDIE"
Born: Mar., 1894, Wilton Junction, Iowa. Died: Mar. 23, 1948. Screen and vaudeville actor. Do not confuse with actor Edward S. Chandler.

Appeared in: **1925** Marriage in Transit. **1926** Flaming Fury; Flashings Fangs. **1927** Flying Luck; Through Thick and Thin. **1928** Young Whirlwind. **1929** Hurricane; She Goes to War. **1930** Dixiana; Borrowed Wives. **1932** Carnival Boat; High Speed. **1933** State Trooper. **1934** Girl in Danger; It Happened One Night; Name the Woman. **1935** Unknown Woman; Desert Trail; His Night Out; Car 99. **1936** Stage Struck; Wild Brian Kent; Here Comes Carter!; The Bohemian Girl. **1937** Over the Goal. **1938** She Loved a Fireman; Gold Is Where You Find It; Over the Wall; Penrod and His Twin Brother. **1939** Gone With the Wind; The Roaring Twenties; Torchy Blane in Chinatown; Help Wanted (short). **1940** Double Alibi; A Fugitive from Justice; Slightly Honorable. **1941** The Big Store. **1944** Charlie Chan in the Secret Service.

CHANDLER, HELEN

Born: Feb. 1, 1906, Charleston, S.C. Died: Apr. 30, 1965, Hollywood, Calif. (following surgery). Stage and screen actress. Divorced from actor Branwell Fletcher and writer Cyril Hume.

Appeared in: **1927** The Joy Girl; The Music Master. **1929** Salute; Mother's Boy; The Sky Hawk. **1930** Outward Bound; Rough Romance; Mother's Cry. **1931** Dracula; Fanny Foley Herself; Daybreak; Salvation Nell; The Last Flight. **1932** A House Divided; Cock of the Air; Vanity Street; Behind Jury Doors. **1933** Goodbye Again; Alimony Madness; Dance Hall Hostess; The Worst Woman in Paris?; Christopher Strong. **1934** Long Lost Father; Lover Divine; Midnight Alibi; Unfinished Symphony. **1935** Radio Parade of 1935; It's a Bet. **1938** Mr. Boggs Steps Out.

CHANDLER, HOWARD

Died: Jan., 1933, San Antonio, Tex. Rodeo performer and screen actor.

CHANDLER, JAMES ROBERT

Born: 1860. Died: Mar. 17, 1950, East Islip, N.Y. Screen and stage actor.

Appeared in: **1921** Home Stuff. **1925** Hurricane Horseman. **1927** Hawk of the Hills (serial). **1928** Quick Triggers. **1929** Hawk of the Hills (rerelease of 1927 serial as a feature film).

CHANDLER, JEFF (Ira Grossel)

Born: Dec., 1918, Brooklyn, N.Y. Died: June 17, 1961, Culver City, Calif. (blood poisoning following surgery). Screen, stage and radio actor. Nominated for 1950 Academy Award for Best Supporting Actor for Broken Arrow.

Appeared in: **1947** Johnny O'Clock; The Invisible Wall; The Roses Are Red. **1949** Sword in the Desert; Mr. Belvedere Goes to College; Abandoned. **1950** Deported; Two Flags West; Broken Arrow. **1951** The Iron Man; The Bird of Paradise; Flame of Araby; Smuggler's Island. **1952** The Battle at Apache Pass; Red Ball Express; Yankee Buccaneer; Meet Danny Wilson (unbilled); Because of You. **1953** East of Sumatra; The Great Sioux Uprising; War Arrows. **1954** The Sign of the Pagan; Taza, Son of Cochise (unbilled); Yankee Pasha. **1955** Foxfire; Female on the Beach; The Spoilers. **1956** Away All Boats; Pillars of the Sky; Toy Tiger. **1957** Man in the Shadow; Jeanne Eagles; The Tattered Dress; Drango; Pay the Devil. **1958** The Lady Takes a Flyer; Raw Wind in Eden. **1959** Ten Seconds to Hell; Stranger in My Arms; The Jayhawkers; Thunder in the Sun. **1960** A Story of David; The Plunderers. **1961** Mad Dog Coll; Return to Peyton Place. **1962** Merrill's Marauders.

CHANDLER, JOAN

Born: 1924. Died: May 11, 1979, New York, N.Y. Screen and stage actress. Divorced from actor David McKay and Dr. Charles C. Hogan.

Appeared in: **1948** The Street With No Name; Rope. **1949** Humoresque. **1958** Dragstrip Riot; How to Make a Monster. **1978** Wishbone Cutter.

CHANDLER, LANE R. (aka ROBERT CHANDLER OAKES)

Born: June 4, 1899, S.Dak. Died: Sept. 14, 1972, Hollywood, Calif. (cardiovascular disease). Screen actor.

Appeared in: **1927** Open Range. **1928** Love and Learn; The Legion of the Condemned; Red Hair; The Big Killing; The First Kiss. **1929** The Studio Murder Mystery; The Single Standard; The Forward Pass. **1930** Rough Waters; Firebrand Jordan; Beyond the Law; The Lightning Express (serial). **1931** The Reckless Rider; Primrose Path; Under Texas Skies; The Hurricane Horseman. **1932** Cheyenne Cyclone; Wyoming Whirlwind. **1933** Trouble Busters; War of the Range; Sagebrush Trail; Corruption; Via Pony Express; The Devil's Brother. **1934** Texas Tornado. **1936** Hearts in Bondage; Winds of the Wasteland; Idaho Kid; Stormy Trails; The Lawless Nineties; The Bohemian Girl; The Return of Jimmy Valentine; Undersea Kingdom (serial); The Black Coin (serial). **1937** Sea Racketeers; Sing While You're Able; Law of the Ranger; Heroes of the Alamo. **1938** Alcatraz Island; Come on Rangers; She Loved a Fireman; Heart of Arizona; Campus Confessions; Two Gun Justice (serial?); The Lone Ranger (serial); Many Sappy Returns (short); Mutts to You (short). **1939** The Man in the Iron Mask; Outpost of the Mounties. **1940** Man from Montreal; Hi-Ho Silver; Northwest Mounted Police; The Great Plane Robbery; Pioneers of the West; Deadwood Dick (serial). **1942** Sundown Jim. **1943** Tenting Tonight on the Old Campground; Ridin' High; Behind Prison Walls. **1944** Men on Her Mind; Law of the Saddle; The Great Mike; Trigger Trail; Rustler's Hideout; Laura; Trigger Law; Silver City Kid; Riders of the Santa Fe; Sagebrush Heroes. **1945** Along Came Jones; The Spider; Manhunt of Mystery Island (serial). **1946** Little Giant; Behind Green Lights; Idea Girl; Gunning for Vengence; Terror Train; Two-Fisted Stranger. **1947**

The Vigilantes Return; Pursued; Song of My Heart. **1948** Northwest Stampede; Campus Sleuth; Money Madness; Belle Starr's Daughter. **1949** Samson and Delilah; Riders of the Whistling Pines. **1950** Montana; Outcast of Black Mesa. **1951** Prairie Roundup; The Well. **1952** The Lion and the Horse; The San Francisco Story; The Hawk of Wild River. **1953** The Charge at Feather River; Thunder Over the Plains; Take Me to Town. **1954** Both Sides of the Law; Living It Up; Border River; Return to Treasure Island. **1955** Shotgun; Prince of Players; Tall Man Riding; Creature With the Atom Brain; The Indian Fighter. **1956** The Lone Ranger. **1957** The Storm Rider. **1958** Quantrill's Raiders. **1960** Noose for a Gunman. **1961** The Little Shepherd of Kingdom Come. **1965** Requiem for a Gunfighter.

CHANEY, CREIGHTON See CHANEY, LON, JR.

CHANEY, FRANCES (Frances Cleveland Bush aka CLEVA CREIGHTON)

Born: 1889, Oklahoma. Died: Nov. 21, 1967, Sierra Madre, Calif. (stroke). Stage and screen actress. Divorced from actor Lon Chaney, Sr. (dec. 1930) and mother of Lon Chaney, Jr. (dec. 1973).

Appeared in: **1950** The Underworld Story (aka The Whipped). **1951** When I Grow Up.

CHANEY, LON, JR. (Creighton T. Chaney aka CREIGHTON CHANEY)

Born: Feb. 10, 1905, Oklahoma City, Okla. Died: July 12, 1973, San Clemente, Calif. Screen, stage and television actor. Son of actor Lon Chaney (dec. 1930) and actress Frances Chaney (dec. 1967). Married to model Patsy Beck. Entered films in 1932 as a stuntman.

Appeared in: **1932** The Last Frontier (serial); Bird of Paradise; Girl Crazy. **1933** Son of the Border; The Three Musketeers (serial); Lucky Devils; Scarlet River. **1934** Girl O' My Dreams; Sixteen Fathoms Deep; The Life of Vergie Winters. **1935** Accent on Youth; Captain Hurricane; Hold 'Em Yale; Shadow of Silk Lennox; The Marriage Bargain; Scream in the Night. **1936** Ace Drummond (serial); The Singing Cowboy; Rhythm on the Range; Undersea Kingdom (serial); Killer at Large. **1937** The Old Corral; Life Begins in College; Angel's Holiday; Wild and Woolly; Midnight Taxi; Wife, Doctor and Nurse; Charlie Chan on Broadway; Secret Agent X-9 (serial); The Lady Escapes; Love and Hisses; One Mile From Heaven; Second Honeymoon; That I May Live; City Girl; Slave Ship; Born Reckless; Thin Ice. **1938** Mr. Moto's Gamble; Passport Husband; Road Demon; Josette; Alexander's Ragtime Band; Straight, Place and Show; Walking Down Broadway; Submarine Patrol; Speed to Burn; Happy Landing. **1939** Jesse James; Union Pacific; Frontier Marshal; Charlie Chan in City in Darkness; Of Mice and Men. **1940** One Million B.C.; Northwest Mounted Police. **1941** Man-Made Monster (aka The Electric Man); Billy the Kid; Badlands of Dakota; The Wolf Man; Too Many Blondes; San Antonio Rose; Riders of Death Valley (serial). **1942** North of the Klondike; The Ghost of Frankenstein; The Mummy's Tomb; The Overland Mail (serial). **1943** Crazy House; Frankenstein Meets the Wolf Man; Son of Dracula; Frontier Badmen; Calling Dr. Death; Eyes of the Underworld. **1944** Ghost Catchers; Weird Woman; Cobra Woman; The Mummy's Ghost; Dead Man's Eyes; Follow the Boys; The Mummy's Curse. **1945** House of Frankenstein; Here Come the Co-Eds; The Frozen Ghost; Strange Confession; The Daltons Ride Again; House of Dracula; Pillow of Death. **1947** My Favorite Brunette. **1948** Abbott and Costello Meet Frankenstein; Albuquerque; 16 Fathoms Deep (rerelease of 1934 film); The Counterfeiters. **1949** There's a Girl in My Heart; Captain China. **1950** Once a Thief. **1951** Inside Straight; Only the Valiant; Behave Yourself; Flame of Araby; Bride of the Gorilla. **1952** Thief of Damascus; High Noon; Springfield Rifle; The Black Castle; The Bushwackers. **1953** A Lion in the Streets; Raiders of the Seven Seas. **1954** The Black Pirates; The Boy From Oklahoma; Jivaro; Casanova's Big Night; Passion; The Big Chase. **1955** Big House U.S.A.; Not As a Stranger; I Died a Thousand Times; The Indian Fighter; The Silver Star. **1956** Manfish; Pardners; The Black Sleep; The Indestructible Man; Daniel Boone—Trail Blazer. **1957** Cyclops. **1958** Money, Women and Guns; The Defiant Ones. **1959** La Casa del Terror (aka Face of the Screaming Werewolf—US 1965); The Alligator People; No. 13 Demon Street (aka The Devil's Messenger—US 1962). **1961** Rebellion in Cuba (aka Chivato). **1963** The Haunted Palace. **1964** Witchcraft; Stage to Thunder Rock; Law of the Lawless (aka Invitation to a Hanging and the Day of the Hanging); Long Rifle and the Tomahawk; The Pathfinder and the Mohicans. **1965** Black Spurs; Young Fury; Town Tamer. **1966** Johnny Reno; Apache Uprising. **1967** Dr. Terror's Gallery of Horrors (aka The Blood Suckers and Return From the Past); Welcome to Hard Times; Hillbillys in a Haunted House; The Vulture. **1968** Spider Baby (aka Cannibal Orgy, or the Maddest Story Ever Told and The Liver Eaters); Buckskin (aka The Frontiersman). **1969** Fireball Jungle (aka Jungle Terror). **1971** Dracula vs. Frankenstein.

CHANEY, LON, SR. (Alonzo Chaney)
Born: Apr. 1, 1883, Colorado Springs, Colo. Died: Aug. 26, 1930, Los Angeles, Calif. Screen, stage actor, film director, screenwriter and stage producer. Father of actor Lon Chaney, Jr. (dec. 1973). Divorced from actress Frances Chaney (aka Cleva Creighton)(dec. 1967).

Appeared in: **1913** Poor Jake's Demise; The Sea Urchin; The Trap; Almost an Actress; Back to Life; Red Margaret, Moonshiner; Bloodhounds of the North. **1914** The Lie; The Honor of the Mounted; Remember Mary Magdalen; Discord and Harmony; The Menace to Carlotta; The Embezzler; The Lamb, the Woman, the Wolf; The End of the Feud; The Tragedy of Whispering Creek; The Unlawful Trade; The Forbidden Room; The Old Cobbler; A Ranch Romance; Her Grave Mistake; By the Sun's Rays; The Oubliette; The Higher Law; A Miner's Romance; Her Bounty; The Pipes of Pan; Richelieu; Virtue Is Its Own Reward; Her Life's Story; Lights and Shadows; The Lion, the Lamb, the Man; A Night of Thrills; Her Escape; Where the Forest Ends. **1915** The Sin of Olga Brandt; Star of the Sea; Threads of Fate; The Measure of a Man; When the Gods Played a Badger Game; Such is Life; Where the Forest Ends; All For Peggy; The Desert Breed; Outside the Gates; The Grind; Maid of the Mist; The Girl of the Night; The Stool Pigeon; An Idyll of the Hills; For Cash; The Stronger Mind; The Oyster Dredger; Steady Company; The Violin Maker; The Trust; Bound on the Wheel; Mountain Justice; Quits; The Chimney's Secret; The Pine's Revenge; The Fascination of the Fleur de Lis; Alas and Alac; A Mother's Atonement; Lon of the Lone Mountain; The Millionaire Paupers; Father and the Boy; Under a Shadow; Stronger Than Death. **1916** The Grip of Jealousy; Dolly's Scoop; Tangled Hearts; The Gilded Spider; Bobbie of the Ballet; Grasp of Greed; The Mark of Cain; If My Country Should Call; Place Beyond the Winds; Felix on the Job; The Price of Silence; The Piper's Price. **1917** Hell Morgan's Girl; The Mask of Love; The Girl in the Checkered Coat; The Flashlight Girl; A Doll's House; Fires of Rebellion; Vengeance of the West; The Rescue; Triumph; Pay Me; The Empty Gun; Anything Once; Bondage; The Scarlet Car. **1918** The Grand Passion; Broadway Love; The Kaiser, the Beast of Berlin; Fast Company; A Broadway Scandal; That Devil Bateese; The Talk of the Town; Riddle Gawne; Danger—Go Slow. **1919** The Wicked Darling; The False Faces; A Man's Country; Paid in Advance; The Miracle Man; When Bearcat Went Dry; Victory. **1920** Daredevil Jack; Treasure Island; The Gift Supreme; Nomads of the North; The Penalty. **1921** Outside the Law; The Ace of Hearts; Bit of Life; For Those We Love; The Night Rose. **1922** The Trap; Quincy Adams Sawyer; Shadows; A Blind Bargain; Flesh and Blood; Voices of the City; The Light in the Dark; Oliver Twist. **1923** The Hunchback of Notre Dame; The Shock; All the Brothers Were Valiant; While Paris Sleeps. **1924** He Who Gets Slapped; The Next Corner. **1925** The Phantom of the Opera; The Tower of Lies; The Monster; The Unholy Three. **1926** The Black Bird; The Road to Mandalay; Tell It to the Marines. **1927** Mr. Wu; The Unknown; Mockery; London After Midnight. **1928** The Big City; Laugh, Clown, Laugh; While the City Sleeps; West of Zanzibar. **1929** The Thunder; Where East Is East. **1930** The Unholy Three (and 1925 version).

CHANEY, NORMAN "CHUBBY"
Born: Jan. 18, 1918, Baltimore, Md. Died: May 30, 1936, Baltimore, Md. (glandular trouble). Screen actor. Entered the "Our Gang" series in 1926 and appeared in part of Joe Cobb until he outgrew his role in 1934.

Appeared in: **1929** The following shorts: Railroadin'; Lazy Days; Boxing Days; Moan and Groan. **1930** The following shorts: Shivering Shakespeare; The First Seven Years; When the Wind Blows; Bear Shooters; A Tough Winter; Pups Is Pups; Teacher's Pet; School's Out. **1931** The following shorts: Helping Grandma; Love Business; Little Daddy; Bargain Days; Fly My Kite; The Stolen Jools (short).

CHANRAL, MARCELLE
Born: 1903, France. Died: 1960, France? Screen actress.

Appeared in: **1932** Au Nom de la Loi (In the Name of the Law). **1935** L' Ordonnance (The Orderly). **1939** Rasputin. **1942** The Great Temptation.

CHAPIN, ALICE
Born: 1858. Died: July 6, 1934, (injuries from a fall). Screen and stage actress.

Appeared in: **1921** Anne of Little Smoky. **1924** Argentine Love; Daughters of the Night; Manhattan; Youth for Sale. **1925** The Crowded Hour; The Pearl of Love.

CHAPIN, BENJAMIN (Benjamin Chester Chapin)
Born: 1875. Died: June 2, 1918, New York, N.Y. (tuberculosis). Screen actor. Famous for his Abraham Lincoln impersonation.

Appeared in: **1917** The Lincoln Cycle films including: My Mother; My Father; Myself; The Call to Arms.

CHAPIN, HARRY
Born: Dec. 7, 1942, Greenwich Village, N.Y. Died: July 16, 1981, Jericho, L.I., N.Y. (auto accident). Screen, stage actor, film director, film producer, folk-rock musician, songwriter, screenwriter and playwright. Son of musician Jim Chapin.

CHAPLIN, CHARLES, JR.
Born: 1925, Beverly Hills, Calif. Died: Mar. 20, 1968, Hollywood, Calif. (blood clot). Screen, stage and television actor. Son of actor Charles Chaplin (dec. 1977) and actress Lita Grey Chaplin.

Appeared in: **1952** Limelight. **1954** Follow the Hunter; Fangs of the Wild. **1958** High School Confidential. **1959** Night of the Quarter Moon; The Beat Generation; Girls' Town; The Big Operator.

CHAPLIN, CHARLIE (Sir Charles Spencer Chaplin)
Born: Apr. 16, 1889, London, England. Died: Dec. 25, 1977, Corsiersur-Vevey, Switzerland. Screen, stage, vaudeville actor, film producer, film director, screenwriter and author. Son of vaudeville actor Charles Spencer Chaplin (dec. 1901) and music hall soubrette Lily Harley (dec. 1928). Half-brother of actor Sydney Chaplin (dec. 1956), and Wheeler Dryden. Divorced from actresses Mildred Harris (dec. 1944), Lita Grey, and Paulette Goddard. Later married to actress Oona O'Neill. Father of actors Charles, Jr. (dec. 1968), Sydney, and Geraldine Chaplin, and Josephine, Christopher, Jane Eugene, Michael, Victoria and Annette-Emilie Chaplin. Won Special Academy Award in 1928 and 1971. Was made Commander of the Order of the British Empire in 1975. Co-founder of United Artists.

Appeared in: **1914** Making a Living; Kid Auto Races at Venice; Mabel's Strange Predicament; Between Showers; A Film Johnnie; Tango Tangles; His Favorite Pastime; Cruel, Cruel Love; The Star Boarder; Mabel at the Wheel; Twenty Minutes of Love; Caught in a Cabaret; Caught in the Rain; The Fatal Mallet; Her Friend the Bandit; The Knockout; Mabel's Busy Day; Mabel's Married Life; Laughing Gas; The Property Man; The Face on the Barroom Floor; Recreation; The Masquerader; His New Profession; The Rounders; The New Janitor; Those Love Pangs; Dough and Dynamite; Gentlemen of Nerve; His Musical Career; His Trysting Place; Tillie's Punctured Romance; Getting Acquainted; His Prehistoric Past. **1915** His New Job; A Night Out; The Champion; In the Park; The Jitney Elopement; The Tramp; By the Sea; Work; A Woman; The Bank; Shanghaied; A Night in the Snow; His Regeneration. **1916** Carmen (aka Charlie Chaplin's Burlesque on Carmen); Police; The Floorwalker; The Fireman; The Vagabond; One A.M; The Count; The Pawnshop; Behind the Screen; The Rink. **1917** Easy Street; The Cure; The Immigrant; The Adventurer. **1918** How to Make Movies; Triple Trouble; A Dog's Life; The Bond (aka Charlie Chaplin in a Library Loan Appeal); Shoulder Arms. **1919** A Day's Pleasure; Sunnyside. **1921** The Kid; The Idle Class. **1922** Pay Day; Nice and Friendly; The Pilgrim. **1923** Souls for Sale; A Woman of Paris. **1925** The Gold Rush. **1928** The Circus; Show People. **1931** City Lights. **1936** Modern Times. **1940** The Great Dictator. **1947** Monsieur Verdoux. **1952** Limelight. **1957** A King in New York (US 1973). **1960** When Comedy Was King (documentary). **1961** Days of Thrills and Laughter (documentary). **1963** Thirty Years of Fun (documentary). **1964** The Chaplin Revue (documentary). **1966** Countess from Hong Kong; Chaplin's Art of Comedy (documentary). **1974** The Gentleman Tramp (film clips).

CHAPLIN, SYDNEY (Sydney Hawkes)
Born: Mar. 17, 1885, Capetown, S. Africa. Died: Apr. 16, 1956, Nice, France. Screen, stage actor and film producer. Half brother of actor Charles Chaplin (dec. 1977). Entered films with Sennett.

Appeared in: **1914** Fatty's Wine Party; Tillie's Punctured Romance; Gussle, the Golfer (in which he appeared as "Gussle" in the series). **1915** Hushing the Scandal (reissued as Friendly Enemies); A Steel Rolling Mill; The United States Army in San Francisco; Giddy, Gay and Ticklish (aka A Gay Lothario); That Springtime Feeling; Gussle's Day of Rest; Gussle's Wayward Path; Gussle Rivals Jonah; Gussle's Backward Way; Gussle Tied to Trouble; A Lover's Lost Control (aka Looking Them Over); A Submarine Pirate. **1918** Shoulder Arms; A Dog's Life. **1921** King, Queen, Joker. **1922** Pay Day. **1923** Her Temporary Husband; The Rendezvous; The Pilgrim. **1924** The Perfect Flapper; Galloping Fish. **1925** The Man on the Box; Charley's Aunt. **1926** Oh, What a Nurse; The Better 'Ole. **1927** The Missing Link. **1928** A Little Bit of Fluff (aka Skirts—US); The Fortune Hunter. **1955** Land of Pharaohs. **1963** Thirty Years of Fun (doc.).

CHAPMAN, BLANCHE
Born: 1851, Covington, Ky. Died: June 7, 1941, Rutherford, N.J. Screen, stage and radio actress. Appeared in silents and talking films.

CHAPMAN, EDWARD

Born: Nov. 1, 1901, Harrogate, Yorkshire, England. Died: Aug. 9, 1977, Brighton, England (heart attack). Screen, stage and television actor.

Appeared in: **1929** Juno and the Paycock (film debut—US 1930). **1930** Murder; Caste. **1931** Tilly of Bloomsbury; The Skin Game. **1932** The Flying Squad; Happy Ever After. **1934** The Queen's Affair (aka Runaway Queen—US 1935); Guest of Honour; Blossom Time (aka April Romance—US 1937); Girls Will Be Boys (US 1935); Mister Cinders; The Church Mouse (US 1935). **1935** The Divine Spark. **1936** Things to Come; Someone at the Door; The Man Who Could Work Miracles (US 1937); Rembrandt. **1937** Who Killed John Savage? **1938** Marigold; Premiere (aka One Night in Paris—US 1940); The Citadel. **1939** There Ain't No Justice; Inspector Hornleigh on Holiday; Poison Pen; The Nursemaid Who Disappeared; Four Just Men (aka The Secret Four—US 1940). **1940** The Proud Valley (US 1941); Now You're Talking; The Briggs Family; Law and Disorder; Convoy (US 1941); Goofer Troubel (short). **1941** Inspector Hornleigh Goes To It (aka Mail Train—US); Turned Out Nice Again; Jeannie (US 1943); Ships With Wings (US 1942); Eating Out With Tommy (short). **1942** They Flew Alone (aka Wings and the Woman— US). **1945** Journey Together (US 1946). **1947** The October Man (US 1948); It Always Rains on Sunday (US 1949). **1948** Mr. Perrin and Mr. Traill. **1949** The History of Mr. Polly (US 1951). **1950** Gone to Earth (aka The Wild Heart—US 1952); Madeleine; Night and the City; Man on the Run (US 1951); The Spider and the Fly (US 1952). **1951** The Magic Box (US 1952). **1952** Folly to be Wise; The Ringer; The Card (aka The Promoter—US); Mandy (aka Crash of Silence—US 1953); His Excellency (US 1956). **1953** A Day to Remember (US 1955); The Intruder (US 1955). **1954** The Crowded Day; The End of the Road (US 1957). **1955** The Love Match; A Yank in Ermine. **1956** Lisbon; X the Unknown (US 1957); Bhowani Junction. **1957** Doctor at Large; Just My Luck. **1958** The Square Peg; Innocent Sinners; The Young and the Guilty. **1959** The Rough and the Smooth (aka Portrait of a Sinner—US 1961). **1960** Oscar Wilde; School for Scoundrels; The Bulldog Breed. **1963** A Stitch in Time (US 1967); Hide and Seek (US 1964). **1965** Joey Boy; The Early Bird.

CHAPMAN, EDYTHE

Born: Oct. 8, 1863, Rochester, N.Y. Died: Oct. 15, 1948, Glendale, Calif. Screen and stage actress. Married to actor James Neill (dec. 1931).

Appeared in: **1915** The Golden Chance. **1916** Public Opinion; The Plough Girl; Oliver Twist. **1917** The Mormon Maid; The Little American; The Evil Eye. **1918** The Whispering Chorus; Say! Young Fellow; Bound in Morocco. **1919** Everywoman. **1920** Huckleberry Finn; Double Dyed Deceiver. **1921** Alias Ladyfingers; Ladyfingers; Bits of Life; The Night Rose; Bunty Pulls the Strings; Dangerous Curves Ahead; Just Out of College; One Wild Week; A Tale of Two Worlds; A Wife's Awakening. **1922** Manslaughter; Beyond the Rocks; Her Husband's Trademark; Youth to Youth; My Amerian Wife; North of the Rio Grande; The Sleepwalker; Saturday Night; Tailor-Made Man. **1923** The Ten Commandments; Divorce; The Miracle Makers; The Girl I Loved; Hollywood. **1924** Chastity; Broken Barriers; Worldly Goods; The Breaking Point; Daughters of Pleasure; The Shadow of the East; The Wise Virgin. **1925** Lightnin'; Soul Mates; Classified; Havoc; The Pride of the Force; Daddy's Gone A-Hunting; In the Name of Love; Lazybones; Learning to Love. **1926** Faithful Wives; The Runaway; Three Faces East; One Minute to Play. **1927** King of Kings; American Beauty; The Student Prince in Old Heidelberg; The Crystal Cup; Naughty but Nice. **1928** Man Crazy; Happiness Ahead; Shepherd of the Hills; The Count of Ten; Love Hungry; Three Week Ends; The Little Yellow House; Sally's Shoulders. **1929** Twin Beds; Synthetic Sin; The Idle Rich. **1930** Double Cross Roads; Take the Heir; Navy Blues; Up the River; Man Trouble.

CHAPMAN, THOMAS H. (Maj. Gen.)

Born: 1896. Died: June 7, 1969, Boerne, Tex. Screen actor and pilot.

Appeared in: **1927** Wings (flew the plane in Buddy Rogers' role).

CHARBENEAU, OSCAR

Died: Sept., 1915, Los Angeles, Calif. (killed while on film location). Screen actor.

CHARLEE See SCOTT, LINDA

CHARLES, LEON

Born: May 4, 1915, Brooklyn, N.Y. Died: Aug. 14, 1981, Los Angeles, Calif. Screen, stage, television actor and dialog coach.

Appeared in: **1981** Delusion.

CHARLES, LEWIS

Born: 1916. Died: Nov. 9, 1979, Los Angeles, Calif. (cancer). Screen, stage, vaudeville, television actor and ballroom dancer.

Appeared in: **1950** Panic in the Streets. **1955** Finger Man; To Catch a Thief; The Rose Tattoo. **1956** Bigger Than Life. **1957** The Sweet Smell of Success; Monkey on My Back; Undersea Girl. **1958** Party Girl. **1959** Al Capone. **1960** 48 Hours to Live. **1962** Birdman of Alcatraz; The Three Stooges Meet Hercules; Who's Got the Action. **1963** Soldier in the Rain; Island of Love. **1964** A House Is Not A Home. **1966** Our Man Flint. **1969** Topaz. **1965** The Human Factor.

CHARLESON, MARY

Born: May 18, 1893, Dunganon, Ireland. Died: Dec. 3, 1961, Woodland Hills, Calif. Screen and stage actress. Married to actor Henry B. Walthall (dec. 1936).

Appeared in: **1912** Bill Wilson's Gal; When California Was Young; The Spirit of the Range; Timid May; Natoosa. **1913** A Bit of Blue Ribbon; The Winning Hand; Matrimonial Maneuvers; The Whispered Word; A Corner in Crooks; The Two Brothers; The Transition; The Actor; Bedelia Becomes a Lady; After the Honeymoon; The Silver Skull; A Matter of Matrimony; The Deceivers; The Spell. **1914** Etta of the Footlights; Iron and Steel; The Acid Test; The Honeymooners; Her Great Scoop (aka Her Biggest Scoop); The Barnes of New York; The Evil Men Do; The Education of Aunt Georgiana; Dr. Smith's Baby. **1915** The Raven; Road of Strife (serial); What Happened to Jones?; The Iron Hand of Law; The Sacrifice; The Call of Motherhood; Polly of the Pots and Pans; Think, Mothers; Sealed Lips; Tony and Marie; Greater Love; Cutting Down Expenses; When Youth is Ambitious; The Silent Accuser. **1916** Passers By; The Country God Forgot; A Prince Chap. **1917** The Truant Souls; Little Shoes; The Saint's Adventure; Satan's Private Door. **1918** His Robe of Honor; With Hoops of Steel; Humdrum Brown. **1919** The Long Lane's Turning; Upstairs and Down. **1920** Human Stuff.

CHARLESTON, HELEN

Died: Dec. 22, 1978, Los Angeles, Calif. (cerebral hemorrhage). Screen, vaudeville and television actress. Sister of vaudeville actor Milton Charleston with whom she appeared in an act billed as the "Dancing Charlestons."

CHARLESWORTH, JOHN

Born: 1935, England. Died: Apr. 2, 1960, Birmingham, England. (suicide). Screen, stage and television actor.

Appeared in: **1951** Scrooge; Tom Brown's Schooldays; The Magic Box (US 1952). **1954** The Horse's Mouth; John of the Fair. **1956** Yield to the Night (aka Blonde Sinner—US); A Question of Adultery (US 1959). **1957** Yangtse Incident (aka Battle Hell—US). **1958** The Man Upstairs (US 1959). **1959** Blue Peter; The Angry Silence (US 1960).

CHARLOT, ANDRE

Born: July 26, 1882, Paris, France. Died: May 20, 1956, Woodland Hills, Calif. Screen, stage, radio actor, stage producer and manager.

Appeared in: **1942** Here We Go Again; The Falcon's Brother; Arabian Nights. **1943** The Constant Nymph; The Falcon Strikes Back; Above Suspicion; The Fallen Sparrow; The Man from Down Under; They Came to Blow Up America; Melody Parade; The Song of Bernadette; The Heavenly Body. **1944** Action in Arabia; Summer Storm. **1945** Delightfully Dangerous; This Love of Ours; Paris Underground; The Dolly Sisters. **1946** The Razor's Edge; Temptation. **1947** The Foxes of Harrow; · Mourning Becomes Electra. **1948** Saigon; Julia Misbehaves. **1949** I Was a Male War Bride; The Great Sinner; That Forsyte Woman. **1950** Annie Get Your Gun. **1951** Flame of Araby; Here Comes the Groom. **1955** Interrupted Melody.

CHARON, JACQUES

Born: 1920, Paris, France. Died: Oct. 15, 1975, Paris, France (heart attack). Screen, stage actor, film and stage director.

Appeared in: **1950** The Paris Waltz. **1960** The Would-Be Gentleman. **1962** Cartouche (US 1964). **1963** In the French Style. **1968** A Flea in Her Ear.

CHARRIERE, HENRI

Born: 1907. Died: July 29, 1973, Madrid, Spain (throat cancer). Author and screen actor.

Appeared in: **1974** Popsy Pop.

CHARSKY, BORIS

Born: May 28, 1893, Petrograd, Russia. Died: June 1, 1956, Hollywood, Calif. Screen and stage actor.

Appeared in: **1928** The Red Dance. **1929** Captain Lash.

CHARTERS, SPENCER
Born: 1875, Ducannon, Pa. Died: Jan. 25, 1943, Hollywood, Calif. (suicide—pills and carbon monoxide). Stage and screen actor.

Appeared in: **1923** Little Old New York. **1924** Janice Meredith. **1930** Whoopee (stage and film version). **1931** Lonely Wives; The Front Page; Traveling Husbands; Palmy Days; The Bat Whispers. **1932** The Fabulous Ferguson Case; Movie Crazy; Central Park; Hold 'Em Jail; The Match King; The Tenderfoot; Jewel Robbery; The Crooked Circle. **1933** Lady Killer; 20,000 Years in Sing Sing; Broadway Bad; So This is Africa; Gambling Ship; Female; The Kennel Murder Case. **1934** Southern Style (short); The Firebird; Wake Up and Dream; The St. Louis Kid; It's a Gift; Million Dollar Ransom; Blind Date; Wonder Bar; Pursuit of Happiness; Fashions of 1934; The Circus Clown; Hips, Hips Hooray; Half a Sinner; Loud Speaker. **1935** Star of Midnight; $1000 a Minute; Alibi Ike; Murder on a Honeymoon; In Person; The Nut Farm; The Ghost Walks; The Raven; Welcome Home; Don't Bet on Blondes; The Goose and the Gander; Whispering Smith Speaks. **1936** F-Man; Colleen; Postal Inspector; The Farmer in the Dell; The Lady from Nowhere; Love on a Bet; Murder on the Bridle Path; Career Woman; Banjo on My Knee; Preview Murder Mystery; The Moon's Our Home; 'Til We Meet Again; Spendthrift; Don't Get Personal; The Mine with the Iron Door; Mr. Deeds Goes to Town; The Harvester; All American Chump; Libeled Lady; Fugitive in the Sky. **1937** The Perfect Specimen; Dangerous Number; Wells Fargo; The Mighty Treve; Girl Loves Boy; Venus Makes Trouble; The Prisoner of Zenda; Behind the Mike; The Hurricane; Four Days' Wonder; Back in Circulation; Fifty Roads to Town; Wife, Doctor and Nurse; Danger—Love at Work; Big Town Girl; Checkers; Pick a Star; Mountain Music; Mr. Boggs Steps Out. **1938** Four's a Crowd; Vivacious Lady; The Joy of Living; Forbidden Valley; Mr. Chump; The Texans; Five of a Kind; In Old Chicago; One Wild Night; Three Blind Mice; Inside Story; Professor Beware; Breaking the Ice; The Road to Reno; Lady Behave; Crime School. **1939** Dodge City; Woman Doctor; I'm from Missouri; Women in the Wind; Young Mr. Lincoln; Second Fiddle; Drums Across the Mohawk; Yes, My Darling Daughter; Topper Takes a Trip; The Covered Trailer; The Flying Irishman; In Name Only; They Made Her a Spy; Two Thoroughbreds; The Hunchback of Notre Dame; Exile Express; They Asked For It; The Under-Pup; Unexpected Father; Jesse James. **1940** Kitty Foyle; Virginia City; Friendly Neighbors; Maryland; The Refuge; Remember the Night; He Married His Wife; Our Town; Alias the Deacon; The Girl from God's Country; The Golden Fleecing; Meet the Missus; Blondie Plays Cupid; Santa Fe Trail. **1941** Bedtime Story; Moon over Miami; Tobacco Road; Glamour Boy; Petticoat Politics; High Sierra; So Ends Our Night; She Couldn't Say No; The Lady from Cheyenne; Mr. District Attorney in the Carter Case; Midnight Angel; Look Who's Laughing; Man at Large; The Singing Hill. **1942** Pride of the Yankees; The Remarkable Andrew; Born to the Heart; The Night Before the Divorce; The Postman Didn't Ring; The Affairs of Jimmy Valentine; Scattergood Survives a Murder; Juke Girl; Pacific Blackout; Yankee Doodle Dandy. **1944** Arsenic and Old Lace.

CHASE, ARLINE
Born: 1900. Died: Apr. 19, 1926, Sierra Madre, Calif. (tuberculosis). Screen, vaudeville actress and dancer. Was a Mack Sennett bathing beauty.

CHASE, CHARLEY (Charles Parrott)
Born: Oct. 20, 1893, Baltimore, Md. Died: June 20, 1940, Hollywood, Calif. (heart attack). Screen, stage, vaudeville actor, and film director. Under name of Charles Parrott he was a film producer, director and screenwriter. Brother of actor and director James Parrot (dec. 1939). Entered films in 1912.

Appeared in: **1914** Our Country Cousin; The Knock-Out (reissued as The Pugilist); Mabel's New Job; The Masquerader; Her Last Chance; His New Profession (reissued as the Good-For-Nothing); The Rounders; Dough and Dynamite (reissued as the Doughnut Designer); Gentlemen of Nerve (reissued at Some Nerve); Cursed By His Beauty; Tillie's Punctured Romance. **1915** Love in Armor; Only a Farmer's Daughter; Hash House Mashers; Settled at the Seaside; Love, Loot and Crash; A Versatile Villain; His Father's Footsteps; The Rent Jumpers; The Hunt. **1917** Her Torpedoed Love; Chased Into Love. **1918** Hello Trouble (short). **1919** Ship Ahoy (short). **1920** Kids Is Kids (short). **1923** Long Live the King. **1924** His Wooden Wedding (short). **1925** Appeared in the following shorts: The Rat's Knuckles; Hello Baby; Fighting Fluid; The Family Entrance; Bad Boy; Is Marriage the Bunk; Big Red Riding Hood; Looking for Sally; What Price Goofy; Isn't Life Terrible; Innocent Husbands; No Father to Guide Him; Hard Boiled; The Caretaker's Daughter; The Uneasy Three; His Wooden Wedding. **1927** One Mama Man; The Call of the Cuckoo (short). **1929** Modern Love; You Can't Buy Love!; plus the following shorts: The Big Squawk; Leaping Love; Snappy Sneezer; Crazy Feet; Stepping Out;

Great Gobs. **1930** The following shorts: The Real McCoy; Whispering Whoopee; All Teed Up; Fifty Million Husbands; Fast Work; Girl Shock; Dollar Dizzy; Looser Than Loose; High C's. **1931** The following shorts: Thundering Tenors; The Pip from Pittsburgh; Rough Seas; One of the Smiths; The Panic Is On; Skip the Maloo!; What a Bozo!; The Hasty Marriage. **1932** The following shorts: The Tabasco Kid; The Nickel Nurser; In Walked Charley; First In War; Young Ironsides; Girl Grief; Now We'll Tell One; Mr. Bride. **1933** Sons of the Desert; plus the following shorts: Fallen Arches; Nature in the Wrong; His Silent Racket; Arabian Tights; Sherman Said It; Midsummer Mush; Luncheon at Twelve. **1934** The following shorts: The Cracked Iceman; Four Parts; I'll Take Vanilla; Another Wild Idea; It Happened One Day; Something Simple; You Said a Hateful; Fate's Fathead; The Chases of Pimple Street. **1935** The following shorts: Okay Toots!; Poker at Eight; Southern Exposure; The Four-Star Boarder; Nurse to You; Manhattan Monkey Business; Public Ghost No. 1. **1936** Kelly the Second; plus the following shorts: Life Hesitates at Forty; The Count Takes the Count; Vamp Till Ready; On the Wrong Trek; Neighborhood House. **1937** The following shorts: The Grand Hooters; From Bad to Worse; The Wrong Miss Wright; Calling All Doctors; The Big Squirt; Man Bites Lovebug. **1938** The following shorts: Time Out for Trouble; The Mind Needer; Many Sappy Returns; The Nightshirt Bandit; Pie a la Maid. **1939** The following shorts: Mutiny on the Body; The Sap Takes Rap; The Chump Takes a Bump; Rattling Romeo; Skinny the Moocher; Teacher's Pest; The Awful Goof. **1940** The following shorts: The Heckler; South of the Boudoir; His Bridal Fright. **1957** The Golden Age of Comedy (documentary). **1960** When Comedy Was King (documentary). **1961** Days of Thrills and Laughter (documentary). **1963** Thirty Years of Fun (documentary). **1965** Laurel and Hardy's Laughing 20's (documentary). **1968** The Further Perils of Laurel and Hardy (documentary).

CHASE, COLIN (Colin Collings)
Born: 1886. Died: Apr. 24, 1937, Los Angeles, Calif. (paralysis attack). Screen and stage actor.

Appeared in: **1923** Bucking the Barrier; Snowdrift. **1924** The Iron Horse. **1926** Silver Fingers. **1927** King of Kings. **1929** The Air Legion; Big News; The Godless Girl. **1930** Renegades; The Lone Star Ranger. **1935** The Cyclone Ranger; The Vanishing Riders.

CHASE, GEORGE WASHINGTON
Born: 1890, Spokane, Wash. Died: July 29, 1918, Woodhaven, N.Y. Screen and stage actor.

Appeared in: **1915** Between Father and Son. **1916** Four Narratives. **1917** Doing Her Bit; Flame of the Yukon; Flying Colors.

CHASE, HAL (Harold W. Chase)
Born: Feb. 13, 1883, Los Gatos, Calif. Died: May 18, 1947, Colusa, Calif. (kidney ailment). Professional baseball player and screen actor.

Appeared in: **1911** Hal Chase's Home Run.

CHASE, ILKA
Born: Apr. 8, 1905, New York, N.Y. Died: Feb. 15, 1978, Mexico City, Mexico (internal hemorrhage—results of a fall). Screen, stage, radio, television actress, playwright and novelist. Divorced from actor Louis Calhern (dec. 1956) and William B. Murray. Later married to Dr. Norton S. Brown.

Appeared in: **1929** Careless Age; Paris Bound; Red Hot Rhythm; Why Leave Home; South Sea Rose; Rich People. **1930** Let's Go Places; The Big Party; Fast and Loose; The Florodora Girl; The Golden Calf; On Your Back; Free Love. **1931** Once a Sinner; Woman Pursued; Gay Diplomat. **1932** Animal Kingdom. **1936** Soak the Rich; The Lady Consents. **1939** Stronger Than Desire. **1942** Now Voyager. **1943** No Time for Love. **1948** Miss Tatlock's Millions. **1954** It Should Happen to You; Johnny Dark. **1955** The Big Knife. **1960** Ocean's 11.

CHASEN, DAVE
Born: July 18, 1899, Odessa, Russia. Died: June 16, 1973, Los Angeles, Calif. (cancer). Restaurateur, stage, vaudeville and screen actor.

Appeared in: **1930** Rain or Shine. **1935** Millions in the Air; Old Man Rhythm; Warner Bros. shorts. **1937** Arizona Mahoney.

CHATTERTON, RUTH
Born: Dec. 24, 1893, New York, N.Y. Died: Nov. 24, 1961, Norwalk, Conn. Screen, stage actress, film producer, and novelist. Married to stage actor Barry Thomson (dec. 1960). Divorced from actors Ralph Forbes (dec. 1951) and George Brent (dec. 1979). Nominated for 1928/29 Academy Award for Best Actress in Madame X and in 1929/30 for Sarah and Son.

Appeared in: **1928** Sons of the Fathers (film debut). **1929** The Doctor's

Secret; Madame X; Charming Sinners; The Dummy; The High Road. **1930** The Laughing Lady; Sarah and Son; The Right to Love; Paramount on Parade; The Lady of Scandal; Anybody's Woman. **1931** Once a Lady; Unfaithful; Magnificent Lie. **1932** The Rich Are Always With Us; Tomorrow and Tomorrow; The Crash. **1933** Frisco Jenny; Female; Lilly Turner. **1934** Journal of a Crime. **1936** Dodsworth; Girl's Dormitory; The Lady of Secrets. **1938** The Rat; A Royal Divorce.

CHATTERTON, THOMAS "TOM"
Born: Feb. 12, 1881, Geneva, N.Y. Died: Aug. 17, 1952, Hollywood, Calif. Screen and stage actor.

Appeared in: **1915** American Film Mfg. Co. and Kay-Bee films. **1916** The Secret of the Submarine. **1921** The Price of Silence. **1931** The Galloping Ghost (serial). **1936** The Boss Rider of Gun Creek. **1937** A Fight to the Finish; Sandflow. **1938** Hawk of the Wilderness (serial); Sudden Bill Dorn; Under Western Stars. **1939** The Oklahoma Kid; Laugh It Off; Dodge City; Arizona Legion; Rovin' Tumbleweeds. **1940** Covered Wagon Days; The Trail Blazers; Drums of Fu Manchu (serial); Son of Roaring Dan; Pony Post; Flash Gordon Conquers the Universe (serial). **1941** Outlaws of the Cherokee Trail. **1942** Overland Mail (serial); Raiders of the Range; Reap the Wild Wind. **1943** Santa Fe Scouts. **1944** Captain America (serial); Zorro's Black Whip (serial). **1947** Smash-Up, The Story of a Woman. **1948** Family Honeymoon. **1949** Gun Law Justice; Highway 13.

CHATTON, SYDNEY
Born: 1918, Bolton, England. Died: Oct. 6, 1966, Berkeley, Calif. (coronary). Screen, stage, radio and television actor. Known as "the man of 1,000 voices."

Appeared in: **1938** The Rangers Roundup. **1957** Loving You. **1958** Once Upon a Horse.

CHAUFFARD, JACQUES-RENE
Born: 1920, France. Died: Nov., 1972, France? Screen and stage actor.

Appeared in: **1960** Et Mourir de Plaisir (aka Blood and Roses—US 1961).

CHAUTARD, EMILE
Born: 1881, Paris, France. Died: Apr. 24, 1934, Westwood, Calif. (organic trouble). Screen, stage actor and film director. Entered films in Paris in 1907.

Appeared in: **1926** Bardely's, the Magnificent; The Flaming Forest; My Official Wife; Broken Hearts of Hollywood; Paris at Midnight. **1927** Blonde or Brunette; Now We're in the Air; Seventh Heaven; Upstage; Whispering Sage. **1928** Love Mart; Lilac Time; Out of the Ruins; Caught in the Fog; The Olympic Hero; Adoration; The Noose; His Tiger Lady. **1929** Times Square; Marianne; South Sea Rose; Tiger Rose; The House of Horrors. **1930** Just Like Heaven; Morocco; A Man from Wyoming; Estrellados (Spanish version of Free and Easy); Contre-Enquete; L'Enigmatique Monsieur Parkes. **1931** Le Petit Cafe; Road to Reno. **1932** Cock of the Air; Blonde Venus; Man from Yesterday; Shanghai Express. **1933** The Three Musketeers (serial); California Trail; The Devil's in Love; Design for Living. **1934** Man of Two Worlds; Wonder Bar.

CHAUVEL, CHARLES E.
Born: 1897. Died: Nov. 11, 1959, Sydney, Australia. Screen actor, screenwriter, film producer and film director. Worked as an extra in Hal Roach comedies during the 1920s.

CHEATHAM, JACK (John Preston Cheatham)
Born: Dec. 28, 1894, Miss. Died: Mar. 30, 1971, La Mirada, Calif. (heart failure). Screen actor.

Appeared in: **1934** The St. Louis Kid; Jealousy; Something Simple (short). **1935** Fighting Pilot; Gunners and Guns; His Fighting Blood. **1936** Next Time We Love. **1937** Paid to Dance; Bank Alarm. **1941** Holt of the Secret Service. **1942** Broadway Big Shot; Men of San Quentin; Quiet Please—Murder; The Saboteur. **1945** They Were Expendable; Secret Agent X-9 (serial). **1946** The Killers; Girl on the Spot. **1947** Hard Boiled Mahoney; The Secret Life of Walter Mitty. **1948** Tenth Avenue Angel.

CHECCHI, ANDREA
Born: Oct. 21, 1916, Italy. Died: Mar. 31, 1974, Rome, Italy (rare virus infection). Screen, stage, television actor and painter.

Appeared in: **1933** 1860 (film debut). **1938** Luciano Serra. **1939** Grandi Magazzini (US 1941); Piccolo Hotel; L'Assedio Dell'Alcazar (Siege of Alcazar). **1940** Ragazza che Dorme; Senza Cielo. **1941** Ore 9 Lezione di Chimica; Via delle Cinque Lune. **1942** Malombra; Giacomo L'Idealista. **1943** Tempesta sul Golfo; La Velle del Diavolo. **1945** Due

Lettere; Un Americano in Vacanza. **1946** Le Vie del Peccato; Roma Citta Libera; La Notte Porta Consiglio; L'Ultimo Amore. **1947** Caccia Tragica (Tragic Hunt—US 1948). **1948** Eleanora Duse. **1949** Le Mura di Malapaga (The Walls of Malapaga—US 1950); El Grido Della Terra (The Earth Cries Out). **1950** Atto D'Accusa. **1951** L'Eroe Sono Io; Altri Tempi (Times Gone By—US 1953). **1952** La Signora Senza Camelie. **1953** Amori di Mezzo Secolo; Pieta per chi Cade. **1954** Casa Ricordi (House of Ricordi—US 1956); Tempi Nostri; Siluri Umani. **1955** Operazione Notte; Buonanotte Avvocato. **1956** Il Tesoro di Rommel (Rommel's Treasure—US 1963); I Quattro del Getto Tonante; Parola di Ladro. **1959** Il Nemico di Mia Moglie (My Wife's Enemy—US 1967). **1960** L'Assassino (aka The Lady Killer of Rome—US 1965). **1963** Finche dura la Tempesta (aka Beta Som and Torpedo Bay—US 1964). **1965** Italiano Brava Gente; Made in Italy (US 1967). **1967** Quien Sabe? (aka A Bullet for the General—US 1968). **1968** El Che Guevara (US 1969).

CHEFEE, JACK (aka JACK CHEFE)
Born: Apr. 1, 1894, Kiev, Russia. Died: Dec. 1, 1975, Hollywood, Calif. Stage and screen actor.

Appeared in: **1917** Veiled Lady. **1919** Tailor Made Romance. **1921** Who's Who. **1928** Runaway Girls. **1929** Alibi; Madame X; Men Without Women; Redeeming Sin. **1930** Son of the Gods; Her Wedding Night. **1931** Hot and Bothered (short); Lonely Wives; Nice Women. **1932** Last Ride; One Hour With You. **1936** My Man Godfrey. **1937** We Have Our Moments. **1939** The Flying Deuces. **1940** The Perfect Snob. **1941** Louisiana Purchase; Captain of Koepenick. **1942** Tales of Manhattan; The Big Street. **1943** Dixie Dugan. **1944** Bermuda Mystery; That's My Baby!; Sensations of 1945; Sudan; Dick Tracy; Rhapsody in Blue. **1945** It's a Pleasure. **1946** The Big Sleep; Tangier; Her Sister's Secret; The Postman Always Rings Twice. **1947** Lured. **1948** Appointment with Murder; Arch of Triumph; Larceny; Saigon. **1949** Illegal Entry; Holiday Affair; Everybody Does It. **1950** Spy Hunt; Born to be Bad. **1951** Double Dynamite (aka It's Only Money); Payment on Demand (aka The Story of a Divorce); Target Unknown; Magic Carpet. **1952** On the Riviera. **1953** Gentlemen Prefer Blondes. **1954** The French Line; So You Want to Go to a Nightclub (short). **1956** Around the World in 80 Days. **1957** Funny Face.

CHEF MILANI (Joseph L. Milani)
Born: 1892. Died: Nov. 30, 1965, San Juan Capistrano, Calif. (auto accident). Television and radio cooking-show host and screen actor.

Appeared in: **1943** Government Girl; The Seventh Victim. **1944** Hollywood Canteen; None But the Lonely Heart; To Have and Have Not. **1945** Adventure.

CHEIREL, JEANNE (Jeanne Leriche)
Born: Mar. 18, 1869, Paris, France. Died: Nov. 2, 1934, Paris, France. Screen, stage and vaudeville actress.

Appeared in: **1909** Le bal Noir. **1922** Crainquebille. **1931** Hardi les Gars!; Ma Tante d'Honfleur. **1932** La Petite de Montparnasse. **1933** Les Deux "Monsieurs" de Madame; Touchons du Bois; Le Sexe Faible; Je te Confie ma Femme; Les Surprises du Sleeping. **1934** Le Voyage de Monsieur Perrichon; Miquette et sa Mere; La Jeune Fille d'une Nuit; Les Filles de la Concierge; Le Monde ou l'on S'ennuie.

CHEKHOV, MICHAEL
Born: Aug. 29, 1891, Leningrad, Russia. Died: Sept. 30, 1955, Beverly Hills, Calif. Screen, stage actor, film and stage director. Nephew of author Anton Chekhov. Nominated for 1945 Academy Award for Best Supporting Actor in Spellbound.

Appeared in: **1944** In Our Time; Song of Russia. **1945** Spellbound. **1946** Specter of the Rose. **1947** Cross My Heart. **1948** Texas, Brooklyn and Heaven; Arch of Triumph. **1952** Holiday for Sinners; The Invitation. **1954** Rhapsody.

CHEKHOVA, OLGA
Born: 1897, Russia. Died: Mar. 9, 1980, Munich, West Germany. Screen and stage actress.

Appeared in: **1929** Moulin Rouge; Pawns of Passion; His Latest Excellency; City of Temptation.

CHENE, ETHEL
Born: 1900. Died: Aug. 31, 1972, (auto accident). Silent screen actress.

CHERKASSOV, NIKOLAI
Born: 1903, Russia. Died: Sept. 14, 1966. Screen actor.

Appeared in: **1937** Baltic Deputy; Peter the First. **1938** Ski Battalion. **1939** Friends; Captain Grant's Children; The Man with the Gun; Alexander Nevsky; Lenin in 1918; The Conquests of Peter the Great.

1941 General Suvorov. **1942** Ivan the Terrible Part I (US 1947); In the Name of Life. **1948** Spring. **1949** The First Front. **1950** Ivan Pavlov. **1951** Moussorgsky. **1954** Rimsky Korsakov. **1959** Ivan the Terrible Part II. **1961** Don Quixote.

CHEROCK, CLARENCE "SHORTY"
Born: 1916, Minneapolis, Minn. Died: Feb. 26, 1980, Los Angeles, Calif. (cancer). Jazz trumpeter, bandleader and screen actor.

CHERRY, CHARLES
Born: 1872, Greenwich, Kent, England. Died: Sept. 2, 1931, England? Screen and stage actor.

Appeared in: **1920** Passers-by.

CHERRY, MALCOLM
Born: 1879. Died: Apr. 13, 1925. Screen actor and author.

Appeared in: **1916** Far From the Maddening Crowd. **1921** The Call of Youth.

CHERRYMAN, REX
Born: 1898. Died: Aug. 10, 1928, Le Havre, France (septic poisoning). Screen and stage actor.

Appeared in: **1920** Madame Peacock. **1921** Camille. **1923** The Sunshine Trail.

CHESEBRO, GEORGE (George Newell Chesebro)
Born: July 29, 1888, Minneapolis, Minn. Died: May 28, 1959, Hermosa Beach, Calif. (arteriosclerosis). Screen and stage actor.

Appeared in: **1918** Hands Up (serial). **1920** Wanted at Headquarters; The Lost City (serial). **1921** The Recoil; The Diamond Queen (serial); The Hope Diamond Mystery (serial). **1922** Blind Circumstances; Diamond Carlisle; For Love of Service; The Hate Trail; The Menacing Pact. **1924** Safe Guarded. **1925** Wolf Blood. **1926** Money to Burn; Rustler's Ranch; The Block Signal; Hearts and Spangles; The Mile-a-Minute Man. **1927** Mountains of Manhattan; The Silent Avenger. **1929** Should a Girl Marry?; Handcuffed; Show Boat; Brothers. **1931** Air Police; Sheriff's Secret; First Aid; Sky Spider; Lariats and Six Shooters. **1932** 45 Calibre Echo; Mark of the Spur; Behind Stone Walls; County Fair; Gorilla Ship; Tex Takes a Holiday; Fighting Camp. **1933** Lucky Larrigan. **1934** The Law of the Wild (serial); Mystery Ranch; Rawhide Mail; Fighting Hero; In Old Santa Fe; Mystery Mountain. **1935** Unconquered Bandit; Danger Ahead; Tumbling Tumbleweeds; Wild Mustang; Never Too Late; Man from Guntown; Confidential. **1936** Robinson Crusoe of Clipper Island (serial); The Lawless Nineties; The Return of Jimmy Valentine; Caryl of the Mountains; The Speed Reporter; Roamin' Wild; Trail Dust; Gallant Defender; Red River Valley. **1937** SOS Coast Guard (serial); The Game that Kills; Borderland; Hills of Old Wyoming; Roarin' Lead; Two-Fisted Sheriff; Springtime in the Rockies. **1938** The Great Adventures of Wild Bill Hickok (serial); Outlaws of Sonora; The Purple Vigilantes; The Mexicali Kid; Starlight Over Texas. **1939** The following serials: Daredevils of the Red Circle; Flying G-Men; Mandrake the Magician. **1940** Frontier Crusader; Land of Six Guns; Wild Horse Range; Gun Code; The Kid from Santa Fe; West of Pinto Basin. **1941** Billy the Kid; Trail of the Silver Spurs; Billy the Kid's Fighting Pals; Law of the Wild; The Lone Rider in Ghost Town; The Pioneers; Wrangler's Roost; The Medico of Painted Springs; The Lone Rider Ambushed. **1942** Perils of the Royal Mounted (serial); The Valley of Vanishing Men (serial). **1943** Two-Fisted Justice; Fugitive of the Plains; The Renegade; Black Market Rustlers. **1944** The Drifter; Arizona Whirlwind; Boss of Rawhide; Thundering Gunslingers. **1946** Badmen's Territory; Gentlemen with Guns; Sun Valley Cyclone; That Texas Jamboree; Days of Buffalo Bill; Two Fisted Stranger; Gunning for Vengeance; Texas Panhandle; Overland Riders; The Fighting Frontiersman; South of the Chisholm Trail; Singin' in the Corn; Terror Trail; Landrush; Daughter of Don Q (serial). **1947** The Vigilante (serial); Stage Coach to Denver; The Lone Hand Texan; Vigilantes of Boomtown; Over the Santa Fe Trail; West of Dodge City; Wyoming; Song of the Wasteland; Riders of the Lone Star; Law of the Canyon; Black Hills; Return of the Lash; Shadow Valley; The Fighting Vigilantes; Cheyenne Takes Over; Stage to Mesa City; Code of the Plains; Homesteaders of Paradise Valley; Out West (short). **1948** Adventures of Frank and Jesse James (serial); Tornado Range; Black Hills; Check Your Guns; West of Sonora. **1949** Death Valley Gunfighter; Trails End; Desert Vigilante; Challenge of the Range; Renegades of the Sage; Horseman of the Sierra. **1950** Gunslingers; Gunmen of Abilene; Salt Lake Raiders; Hostile Country; Texas Dynamo; Streets of Ghost Town; West of the Brazos; Marshal of Heldorado; Colorado Ranger; Crooked River; Fast on the Draw; Tornado; Lightning Guns; Trail of Robin Hood; Frisco Tornado. **1951** Blonde Atom Bomb (short); Night Riders of Montana; Snake River Desperadoes; Kentucky Jubilee; Cyclone Fury; The Kid from Amarillo. **1952** Montana Territory; Junction City. **1953** Last of the Comanches; Winning of the West. **1954** Pals and Gals (short).

CHESHIRE, HARRY V. "PAPPY"
Born: 1892. Died: June 16, 1968. Screen actor.

Appeared in: **1940** Barnyard Follies. **1942** Hi, Neighbor. **1943** Swing Your Partner; O, My Darling Clementine. **1944** Sing, Neighbor, Sing. **1946** It's a Wonderful Life; The Best Years of Our Lives; Smooth as Silk; Child of Divorce; Affairs of Geraldine; Traffic in Crime; If I'm Lucky; Sioux City Sue. **1947** Nightmare Alley; The Homestretch; The Hucksters; I Wonder Who's Kissing Her Now; The Invisible Wall; Shoot to Kill; Springtime in the Sierras; Sport of Kings; Tender Years; The Flame; Luckiest Guy in the World (short). **1948** Slippy McGee; Black Eagle; 16 Fathoms Deep; Incident; Moonrise; Adventures of Gallant Bess; For the Love of Mary; Racing Luck. **1949** The Lady Takes a Sailor; Bride for Sale; Anna Lucasta; Sand; Riders of the Whistling Pines; It Happens Every Spring; Miss Grant Takes Richmond; I Married a Communist; Fighting Man of the Plains; Brimstone. **1950** Paid in Full; A Woman of Distinction; County Fair; Girls' School; The Woman on Pier 13; No Sad Songs for Me; Lucky Losers; Lonely Hearts Bandits; Chain Gang; The Arizona Cowboy; Square Dance Katy. **1951** Blue Blood; Thunder in God's Country. **1952** Here Come the Nelsons; Phone Call from a Stranger; The Sniper; Dreamboat. **1954** Flesh and Fury; Fireman Save My Child; Pride of the Blue Grass; Dangerous Mission. **1955** Seven Little Foys. **1956** The Boss; The First Traveling Saleslady. **1957** Loving You; My Man Godfrey; Lure of the Swamp; The Restless Breed. **1958** The Big Country. **1960** From the Terrace; Heller in Pink Tights; Let's Make Love. **1961** The Errand Boy.

CHESNEY, ARTHUR
Born: 1882, England. Died: Aug. 27, 1949, London, England. Stage and screen actor. Brother of actor Edmund Gwenn (dec. 1959). Divorced from actress Estelle Winwood.

Appeared in: **1920** The Lure of Crooning Water. **1926** The Lodger. **1931** French Leave. **1933** Fires of Fate. **1934** Sensation; Sorrell and Son. **1936** O.H.M.S. (aka You're in the Army Now—US 1937). **1938** Girl in the Street.

CHESTER, ALMA
Born: 1871. Died: Jan. 22, 1953, Monterey, Calif. Screen and stage actress.

Appeared in: **1931** Beloved Bachelor. **1934** Dude Ranger. **1935** A Feather in Her Hat.

CHESTER, BETTY
Born: Oct. 12, 1895, Torquay, England. Died: Jan. 11, 1943, Lisbon, Portugal. Screen and stage actress.

Appeared in: **1929** The Co-Optimists (US 1930). **1932** Tell Me Tonight (aka Be Mine Tonight—US 1933).

CHESTER, BROCK
Born: Mar. 10, 1947, Wichita, Kans. Died: Apr. 28, 1971. Screen and television actor.

CHESTER, VIRGINIA E.
Born: Aug. 27, 1896, San Francisco, Calif. Died: July 28, 1927, Oakland, Calif. (pulmonary tuberculosis). Screen actress.

Appeared in: **1915** Hash House Mashers.

CHEVALIER, ALBERT
Born: Mar. 21, 1861, London, England. Died: July 10, 1923, London, England. Screen, stage, vaudeville actor, playwright, stage, film producer and screenwriter.

Appeared in: **1915** The Middleman; The Bottle; My Old Dutch. **1916** The Fallen Star.

CHEVALIER, GUS
Born: 1887, England. Died: Nov. 20, 1947, London, England. Screen and stage actor.

Appeared in: **1937** Carry on London; Footlights. **1938** Two Men in a Box; Revue Parade.

CHEVALIER, MAURICE (Maurice Auguste Chevalier)
Born: Sept. 12, 1888, Menilmontante, France. Died: Jan. 1, 1972, Paris, France (heart attack following kidney surgery). Screen, stage, television actor and writer. Divorced from actress Yvonne Vallee. Nominated for 1929/30 Acadmey Award for Best Actor in The Love Parade and The Big Pond. In 1958 received Special Academy Award for his contributions to the world of entertainment for more than half a century.

Appeared in: **1908** Trop Credule. **1911** Un Mariee qui se Fait Attendre; La Mariee Recalcitrante; Par Habitude. **1914** La Valse Renversante. **1917** Une Soiree Mondaine. **1921** Le Mauvais Garcon. **1922** Gonzague; Le Match Crique-Ledoux (short). **1923** Jim Bougne Boxeur; L'Affaire de la Rue de Lourcine; Par Habitude (and 1911 version). **1928** Bonjour New York! **1929** Innocents of Paris; The Love Parade. **1930** The Big Pond; Playboy of Paris; Le Grande Mere; Paramount on Parade. **1931** The Smiling Lieutenant; Le Petit Cafe; El Cliente Seductor (short); The Stolen Jools (short—aka The Slippery Pearls). **1932** One Hour With You; Love Me Tonight; Toboggan (short—aka Battling Georges); Make Me a Star. **1933** A Bedtime Story; The Way to Love. **1935** Folies Bergere. **1936** The Beloved Vagabond (US 1937); L'Homme du Jour (The Man of the Hour—US 1940); Avec le Sourir (With a Smile—US 1939). **1938** Break the News (US 1941). **1941** Personal Column. **1945** Le Silence est D'Or (Man About Town—US 1947). **1947** The Little Cafe. **1949** Le Roi (aka A Royal Affair—US 1950). **1950** Ma Pomme (aka Just Me); Paris 1900 (doc.). **1953** Un Siecle d'Amour; Schlager Parade. **1955** Cento Anni d'Amour; J'Avais Sept Filles (My Seven Little Sins—US 1956). **1957** Love in the Afternoon; The Happy Road; Rendezvous avec Maurice Chevalier. **1958** Gigi. **1959** Count Your Blessings. **1960** Can-Can; A Breath of Scandal; Pepe; Un, Deux, Trois, Quatre! (narr.; aka Black Tights—US 1962). **1961** Fanny. **1962** In Search of the Castaways; Jessica. **1963** A New Kind of Love. **1964** Panic Button; I'd Rather Be Rich. **1967** Monkeys, Go Home!. **1970** The Aristocats (sang). **1972** Le Chagrin et la Pitie (The Sorrow and the Pity—documentary). **1976** Singing Under the Occupation (documentary).

CHIEF BLACK HAWK (Elmer Attean)
Died: May 15, 1975. Screen actor.

Appeared in: **1922** Suzanna. **1927** Painted Ponies.

CHIEF DAN GEORGE (Geswanouth Slaholt)
Born: July 24, 1899, North Vancouver, British Columbia, Canada. Died: Sept. 23, 1981, Vancouver, British Columbia, Canada. Screen, stage and television actor. Nominated for 1970 Academy Award as Best Supporting Actor in "Little Big Man."

Appeared in: **1969** Smith! **1970** Little Big Man. **1974** Harry and Tonto; The Bears and I. **1975** Alien Thunder. **1976** Shadow of the Hawk; The Outlaw Josey Wales. **1979** Americathon. **1980** Spirit of the Wind.

CHIEF EDWARD LITTLE
Born: 1868. Died: Jan. 10, 1928, Detroit, Mich. Screen actor. Chippewa Indian who appeared in Buffalo Bill Wild West Shows, etc.

CHIEF HENRY "RED EAGLE" PERLEY (aka HENRY PERLEY)
Born: 1885. Died: Nov., 1972, Greenville, Maine. Screen actor.

CHIEF JACK
Born: 1877. Died: Jan. 9, 1943, Los Angeles, Calif. Screen and vaudeville actor.

CHIEF JOHN BIG TREE (Isaac Johnny John)
Born: 1865. Died: July, 1967, Onondaga Reservation, N.Y. Screen actor. Posed for artist James Fraser for the profile which became the famous Indian head nickel.

Appeared in: **1922** The Primitive Lover. **1923** The Huntress. **1924** The Iron Horse. **1925** The Red Rider. **1926** The Desert's Toll; The Frontier Trail; Ranson' Folly. **1927** Painted Ponies; Winners of the Wilderness; The Fontiersman; Spoilers of the West. **1928** Wyoming. **1929** The Overland Telegraph; Sioux Blood. **1935** The Singing Vagabond. **1937** Lost Horizon; Hills of Old Wyoming. **1939** Destiny Rides Again; Stagecoach; Susannah of the Mounties; Drums Along the Mohawk. **1940** Brigham Young, Frontiersman; Hudson's Bay. **1941** Western Union; Las Vegas Nights. **1947** Unconquered. **1949** She Wore a Yellow Ribbon. **1950** Devil's Doorway.

CHIEF MANY TREATIES (William Hazlett)
Born: 1875. Died: Feb. 29, 1948, Los Angeles, Calif. (heart attack). Screen actor and rodeo performer.

Appeared in: **1937** Drums of Destiny. **1941** Go West Young Lady. **1948** Black Bart.

CHIEF NIPO STRONGHEART (Nee-hah-pouw Tah-che-num)
Born: May 15, 1891, Yakima (Indian reservation), Wash. Died: Dec. 30, 1966, Woodland Hills, Calif. Screen and stage actor. Entered films with Lubin Co. in 1905.

Appeared in: **1925** Braveheart; The Road to Yesterday. **1926** The Last Frontier. **1947** Canyon Passage; Black Passage; Black Gold. **1950** The

Outriders; Young Daniel Boone. **1951** The Painted Hills; Across the Wide Missouri; Westward the Women. **1952** Lone Star; Pony Soldier. **1953** Charge at Feather River; Take the High Ground. **1954** Rose Marie. **1955** Foxfire; Seven Cities of Gold. **1960** Ten Who Dared. **1963** Savage Sam.

CHIEF RED FOX (Willian Red Fox)
Born: 1871. Died: Mar. 1, 1976, Corpus Christi, Tex. Screen, vaudeville, television actor and Wild West Shows.

CHIEF RUNNING HORSE (Edward Sorocki)
Born: 1901. Died: Mar. 30, 1977. Screen actor.

CHIEF STANDING BEAR
Died: Feb., 1939. Screen actor.

Appeared in: **1930** Santa Fe Trail. **1931** Conquering Horde. **1935** The Miracle Rider (serial).

CHIEF THUNDERBIRD
Born: 1867, near Tongue River, Mont. Died: Apr. 6, 1946, Calif. Screen, vaudeville and radio actor.

Appeared in: **1923** Covered Wagon. **1931** Battling With Buffalo Bill (serial). **1934** Laughing Boy. **1935** Annie Oakley. **1936** Silly Billies. **1937** Wild West Days (serial). **1944** The Falcon Out West. **1947** Perils of Pauline (serial).

CHIEF THUNDERCLOUD (Victor Daniels)
Born: Apr. 12, 1889, Muskogee, Okla. Died: Nov. 30, 1955, Ventura, Calif. (cancer). Screen, radio actor, singer and rodeo performer. Married to singer/dancer Frances Delmar. Entered films as stuntman in 1929.

Appeared in: **1935** Rustler's Paradise; The Singing Vagabond; The Farmer Takes a Wife. **1936** Ride, Ranger, Ride; For the Service; Ramona; Silly Billies; The Plainsman. **1937** Wild West Days (serial); Renfrew of the Royal Mounted. **1938** The Lone Ranger (serial); The Great Adventures of Wild Bill Hickok (serial); Flaming Frontier (serial). **1939** The Cat and the Canary; Geronimo; Union Pacific; The Lone Ranger Rides Again (serial). **1940** Young Buffalo Bill; Hi-Yo Silver; Typhoon; Wyoming; Norhtwest Mounted Police; Hudson's Bay; Murder on the Yukon. **1941** Western Union; Silver Stallion. **1942** My Gal Sal; Shut My Big Mouth; King of the Stallions. **1943** Daredevils of the West (serial). **1944** The Falcon Out West; Black Arrow (serial); Fighting Seabees; Buffalo Bill; "The Trail Blazers" series, incl. Sonora Stage-Coach; An Outlaw Trail. **1946** The Phantom Rider (serial); Romance of the West; Badman's Territory. **1947** The Senator Was Indiscreet; Unconquered. **1948** Blazing Across the Pecos; Renegade Girl. **1949** Ambush; Call of the Forest. **1950** Colt .45; Ticket to Tomahawk; The Traveling Saleswoman; Indian Territory; Davy Crockett—Indian Scout; I Killed Geronimo. **1951** Santa Fe. **1952** Bufalo Bill in Tomahawk Territory; The Half-Breed.

CHIEF THUNDERCLOUD (Scott T. Williams)
Born: Dec. 20, 1898, Cedar, Mich. Died: Jan. 31, 1967, Chicago, Ill. Screen and radio actor. Was great, great, great grandson of Chief Pontiac of the Ottawa Tribe. Portrayed "Tonto" on early Lone Ranger radio program and appeared in numerous western films during the 1930s but should not be confused with Victor Daniels, also known as "Chief Thundercloud."

CHIEF YOWLACHIE (Daniel Simmons)
Born: Aug. 15, 1891, Wash. Died: Mar. 7, 1966, Los Angeles, Calif. (pneumonia). Screen actor.

Appeared in: **1925** Tonio, Son of the Sierras. **1926** Ella Cinders; Moran of the Mounted; Forlorn River; War Paint. **1927** The Red Raiders; Sitting Bull at the Spirit Lake Massacre. **1929** The Glorious Trail; Hawk of the Hills; The Invaders. **1930** The Girl of the Golden West; The Santa Fe Trail. **1940** Northwest Mounted Police; Winners of the West (serial). **1941** White Eagle (serial). **1942** King of the Stallions; Ride 'Em Cowboy. **1946** Canyon Passage. **1947** The Hucksters; Bowery Buckaroos; The Senator Was Indiscreet. **1948** Red River; The Paleface; You Gotta Stay Happy. **1949** El Paso; Ma and Pa Kettle; Mrs. Mike; The Cowboy and the Indians; My Friend Erma; Yellow Sky. **1950** A Ticket to Tomahawk; My Friend Erma Goes West; Winchester '73; Annie Get Your Gun; Cherokee Uprising; Indian Terrority. **1951** The Painted Hills; Warpath. **1952** Buffalo Bill; Son of Geronimo (serial). **1953** The Pathfinder. **1954** Rose Marie; Gunfighters of the Northwest (serial). **1956** Hollywood or Bust. **1957** The Spirit of St. Louis. **1960** Heller in Pink Tights.

CHILDERS, NAOMI
Born: Nov. 15, 1893, Pottstown, Penn. Died: May 9, 1964, Hollywood, Calif. Screen actress.

Appeared in: **1913** Their Mutual Friend. **1914** The Ageless Sex; The Rose and the Thorn; The Wrong Flat. **1915** The Island of Regeneration; Dust of Egypt; The Price of Fame; Anselo Lee. **1916** The Devil's Prize. **1919** Lord and Lady Algy. **1920** Earthbound. **1921** Hold Your Horses; Courage. **1922** Mr. Barnes of New York. **1923** Success. **1924** Restless Wives; Virtuous Liars. **1934** White Heat; The Mighty Barnum. **1944** Mrs. Parkington. **1945** Weekend at the Waldorf. **1947** Sea of Grass.

CHILDS, GILBERT
Born: 1866, England. Died: Sept. 24, 1931, London, England. Screen, stage and vaudeville actor.

Appeared in: **1929** The Co-Optimists (US 1930—film and stage version).

CHILDS, MONROE (J. Monroe Rothschild)
Born: 1891. Died: Nov. 7, 1963, Santa Monica, Calif. Screen and stage actor.

CHINNAPPA, P. U.
Died: Sept. 23, 1951. South Indian screen actor.

CHIRELLO, GEORGE "SHORTY"
Born: 1897. Died: Feb. 9, 1963, Honolulu, Hawaii. Screen actor. Formerly Orsen Welles' cook and chauffeur.

Appeared in: **1948** Macbeth.

CHIRGWIN, GEORGE H.
Born: Dec. 13, 1854, London, England. Died: Nov. 14, 1922, England? Screen and stage actor.

Appeared in: **1917** Blind Boy.

CHISHOLM, ROBERT
Born: Apr. 18, 1898, Melbourne, Australia. Died: Nov. 4, 1960. Screen and stage actor.

Appeared in: **1930** The Lottery Bride; The Big Pond. **1938** Father O'Flynn.

CHITTISON, HERMAN
Died: Mar. 8, 1967, Cleveland, Ohio. Screen, radio actor and jazz pianist.

Appeared in: French film Pepe Le Moko.

CHITTY, ERIK (Eric)
Born: England. Died: July, 1977, England? Screen actor.

Appeared in: **1950** Eye Witness. **1955** Raising a Riot (US 1957); Footsteps in the Fog. **1957** After the Ball. **1959** Left, Right and Centre (US 1961). **1960** The Day They Robbed the Bank of England. **1964** The Horror Of It All; First Men In the Moon. **1976** The Seven-Per-Cent Solution.

CHIVVIS, CHIC
Born: 1884. Died: Oct. 26, 1963, Hollywood, Calif. Screen actor and stuntman. Entered films during silents.

CHRISTENSEN, BENJAMIN
Born: 1879, Viborg, Denmark. Died: 1959, Sweden?. Screen, stage actor, film director and screenwriter. Appeared in U.S., Danish, German and Swedish films.

Appeared in: **1926** Chained.

CHRISTIAN, JOHN
Born: 1884. Died: Aug. 29, 1950, Hollywood, Calif. Screen and stage actor.

Appeared in: **1945** Mildred Pierce. **1946** Cinderella Jones.

CHRISTIANO, ELEANOR IRENE
Born: 1912. Died: 1932. Screen, stage actress and dancer.

CHRISTIANS, MADY
Born: 1900, Vienna, Austria. Died: Oct. 28, 1951, South Norwalk, Conn. (cerebral hemorrhage). Screen, stage and radio actress. Appeared in U.S., Austrian, German, French and British films.

Appeared in: **1916** Adrey. **1917** Die Krone von Kertzyna. **1920** Der Mann ohne Namen (Man Without a Name). **1921** Es Leuchtet die Liebe; Das Weib des Pharao (The Loves of Pharaoh, aka Pharaoh's Wife). **1922** Kinder der Zeit; Malmaison. **1923** Die Buddenbrooks; Der Verlorene Schuh; Der Wetterwart; Das Speil der Königin (aka Ein Glas Wasser); Die Finanzen des Grossherzogs (The Grand Duke's Finances). **1924** Mensch Gegen Mensch; Soll und Haban. **1925** Die vom Niederrhein; Der Abenteurer; Der Farmer aus Texas; Die Verrufenen (aka Der Fuenfte Stand, and aka Slums of Berlin—US 1929); Ein Walzertraun (Waltz Dream—US 1926). **1926** Die Geschiedene Frau; Nanette Macht Alles; Die Welt Will Belogen Sein; Wien, wie es Weint und Lacht; Zopf und Schwert; Die Koenigin vom Moulin-Rouge. **1927** Grand Hotel ...!; Heimweh; Koenigin Luise (Queen Luise); Der Sohn der Hagar (Out of the Mist). **1928** Fraeulein Chauffeur; Eine Frau von Format; Priscillas Fahrt ins Glueck (Princess Priscilla's Fortnight, aka The Runaway Princess—US 1929). **1929** Das Brennende Herz; Meine Schwester und Ich; Dich Hab' ich Geliebt. **1930** Because I Love You; The Burning Heart; Leutnant Warst Du Einst bei den Husaren (US 1932). **1931** Die Frau, von der Man Spricht (US 1933); Das Schicksal der Renate Langen (The Fate of the Renata Lancer—US 1933, aka Sein Letzter Brief). **1932** Friederike (US 1933); Der Schwartze Husar (The Black Hussar). **1933** Manolescu, der Fuerst der Diebe; Salon Dora Green (House of Dora Green—US 1937); Ich und die Kaiserin (US 1935); One Year Later; The Only Girl (aka Heart Song—US 1934). **1934** Wicked Woman. **1935** Escapade; Ship Cafe. **1936** Come and Get It. **1937** Seventh Heaven; Heidi; The Woman I Love. **1943** Tender Comrade. **1944** Address Unknown. **1948** All My Sons; Letter from an Unknown Woman; Other European films: Cinderella; Glass of Water; Finances of the Archduke; Queen Louise; Duel; Meet My Sister; Mon Amour.

CHRISTIANS, RUDOLPH
Born: 1869. Died: Feb. 7, 1921, Pasadena, Calif. (pneumonia). Screen actor.

Appeared in: **1922** Foolish Wives.

CHRISTIE, GEORGE (George Stuart Christie)
Born: 1873, Philadelphia, Pa. Died: May 20, 1949, Tom's River, N.J. Stage and screen actor.

Appeared in: **1917** Duchess of Doubt; Sowers and Reapers.

CHRISTY, BILL
Born: 1925. Died: Feb. 25, 1946, Los Angeles, Calif. (form of paralysis). Screen and radio actor.

Appeared in: **1944** Song of the Open Road. **1946** Live Wires; Behind the Mask.

CHRISTY, IVAN
Born: 1888. Died: May 9, 1949, Burbank, Calif. (heart attack). Screen actor.

Appeared in: **1921** Rainbow. **1922** Island Wives; The Madness of Love. **1926** Man of the Forest. **1927** Nevada; The Mysterious Rider. **1929** Seven Footprints to Satan. **1930** Son of the Gods.

CHRISTY, KEN
Born: 1895. Died: July 23, 1962, Hollywood, Calif. Screen, stage, vaudeville, radio and television actor.

Appeared In: **1940** Dr. Kildare Goes Home; plus the following shorts: He Asked For It; Tattle Television; Soak the Old; You the People. **1941** Six Lessons from Madame La Zonga; Whistling in the Dark; Design for Scandal; Ball of Fire; Shadow of the Thin Man; I Love You Again; Burma Convoy; Harmon of Michigan; plus the following shorts: I'll Fix That; A Panic in the Parlor; Whispers. **1942** Arabian Nights; Blondie Goes to College; The Big Shop; Manila Calling; Just Off Broadway; Top Sergeant; Dear! Dear! (short); Bells of Capistrano (short). **1943** Gildersleeve on Broadway; He Hired the Boss; Secrets of the Underworld; Gildersleeve's Bad Day; Hit the Ice. **1944** Wilson; Say Uncle (short); The Big Noise. **1947** Cass Timberlane. **1948** Sitting Pretty; Give My Regards to Broadway; Scudda Hoo! Scudda Hay! **1949** The Devil's Henchman; Trapped. **1950** The Jackpot; Sunset Boulevard; No Way Out; Cheaper by the Dozen. **1951** A Place in the Sun; Call Me Mister. **1952** Ace in the Hole (aka The Big Carnival); The Model and the Marriage Broker. **1955** My Sister Eileen; Inside Detroit. **1956** Blackjack Ketchum, Desperado; The Werewolf. **1957** Fury at Showdown; Outlaw's Son; Utah Blaine; Escape from San Quentin.

CHRISTY, TED
Born: 1911. Died: Sept. 11, 1976, Woodland Hills, Calif. Screen actor and stuntman.

CHUMAN, HOWARD
Died: Mar. 27, 1978. Screen actor.

Appeared in: **1950** Three Came Home; The Halls of Montezuma. **1951** Secrets of Monte Carlo. **1952** Mara Maru. **1953** Forbidden.

CHURCH, ESME
Born: Feb. 10, 1893, England. Died: May 31, 1972, Quenington, England. Screen, stage actress and stage director.

Appeared in: **1934** Autumn Crocus; Mister Cinders. **1935** Old Roses. **1951** Men of the Sea.

CHURCHILL, BERTON
Born: 1876, Toronto, Canada. Died: Oct. 10, 1940, New York, N.Y. (uremic poisoning). Stage and screen actor.

Appeared in: **1923** Six Cylinder Love. **1924** Tongues of Flame. **1929** Nothing But the Truth. **1930** Five Minutes from the Station (short). **1931** Secrets of a Secretary; Air Eagles; A Husband's Holiday. **1932** The Rich Are Always With Us; Cabin in the Cotton; The Dark Horse; Taxi!; Impatient Maiden; Two Seconds; Week Ends Only; Crooked Circle; Silver Dollar; Big Stampede; Okay America; Laughter in Hell; Washington Parade; Fast Companions; Afraid to Talk; It's Tough to be Famous; The Mouthpiece; The Wet Parade; The Information Kid; Faith; If I Had a Million; Common Ground; Forgotten Million; American Madness; False Faces; Scandal for Sale; I Am a Fugitive from a Chain Gang; Madame Butterfly. **1933** Ladies Must Love; From Hell to Heaven; Employees' Entrance; The Mysterious Rider; Billion Dollar Scandal; Elmer the Great; Private Jones; Her First Mate; Only Yesterday; The Little Giant; Heroes for Sale; The Big Brain; Golden Harvest; Master of Men; The Avenger; Doctor Bull; College Coach; So This Is Africa. **1934** The Girl Is Mine; King of the Ritz; Dizzy Dames; Life Is Worth Living; Men of Steel; Men in White; If I Was Rich; Alias the Deacon; Bachelor of Arts; Dames; Take the Stand; Kid Millions; Lillies of Broadway; Friends of Mr. Sweeney; Hi, Nellie; Babbitt; The Menace; Half a Sinner; Let's Be Ritzy; Judge Priest; Frontier Marshall; Helldorado; Sing Sing Nights; Red Head; Strictly Dynamite; Bachelor Bait; Murder in the Private Car. **1935** The County Chairman; $10 Raise; Steamboat 'Round the Bend; A Night at the Ritz; Page Miss Glory; I Live for Love; Vagabond Lady; The Rainmakers; Colorado; Speed Devils; The Spanish Cape Mystery. **1936** Colleen; You May Be Next; Three of a Kind; Dimples; Under Your Spell; Bunker Bean; Racing Lady; Parole; The Dark Hour. **1937** You Can't Beat Love; Quick Money; Parnell; The Singing Marine; He Couldn't Say No; Wild and Wooly; Racing Lady; Public Wedding; Sing and Be Happy. **1938** Wide Open Faces; Meet the Mayor; In Old Chicago; Four Men and a Prayer; Kentucky Moonshine; The Cowboy and the Lady; Ladies in Distress; Down in "Arkansaw"; Danger on the Air; Sweethearts. **1939** Daughters Courageous; Should Husbands Work?; Angels Wash Their Faces; Hero for a Day; On Your Toes; Stagecoach. **1940** Brother Rat and a Baby; I'm Nobody's Sweetheart Now; Saturday's Children; Twenty-Mule Team; Turnabout; Cross-Country Romance; The Way of All Flesh; Public Deb. No. 1.

CIANELLI, ALMA
Born: 1892. Died: June 23, 1968, Villa San Pietro, Italy (stroke). Stage and screen actress. Married to actor Eduardo Cianelli (dec. 1969).

CIANELLI, EDUARDO
Born: 1887, Naples, Italy. Died: Oct. 8, 1969, Rome, Italy (cancer). Screen, stage, opera, television actor and playwright. Married to actress Alma Cianelli (dec. 1968).

Appeared in: **1933** Reunion in Vienna. **1935** The Scoundrel. **1936** Winterset (stage and film versions). **1937** Criminal Lawyer; The Marked Woman; Super Sleuth; Hitting a New High; The League of Frightened Men; On Such a Night; Girl from Scotland Yard. **1938** Law of the Underworld; Blind Alibi. **1939** Angels Wash Their Faces; Society Lawyer; Risky Business; Bulldog Drummond's Bride; Gunga Din. **1940** Forgotten Girls; Outside the Three-Mile Limit; Strange Cargo; Zanzibar; Foreign Correspondent; The Mummy's Hand; Mysterious Dr. Satan (serial). **1941** Ellery Queen's Penthouse Mystery; They Met in Bombay; I Was a Prisoner on Devil's Island; Paris Calling; Sky Raiders (serial). **1942** Dr. Broadway; You Can't Escape Me Forever; Cairo. **1943** Adventures of the Flying Cadets (serial); Flight for Freedom; The Constant Nymph; They Got Me Covered; For Whom the Bell Tolls. **1944** The Mask of Dimitrios; Storm over Lisbon; The Conspirators; Passage to Marseille. **1945** A Bell for Adano; The Crime Doctor's Warning; Incendiary Blonde; Dillinger. **1946** Gilda; The Wife of Monter Cristo; Joe Palooka, Champ; Heartbeat; Perilous Holiday. **1947** Seven Keys to Baldpate; The Lost Moment; Crime Dotor's Gamble; Miracles Can Happen; I Love Trouble; California. **1948** On Our Merry Way; To the Victor; Rose of Santa Rosa; The Creeper. **1949** Prince of Foxes. **1950** Rapture. **1951** The People Against O'Hara; Fugitive Lady. **1953** Volcano. **1954** The City Stands Trial; Voice of Silence. **1955** The Stranger's Hand; Mambo; Helen of Troy. **1957** Love Slaves of the Amazon. **1958** Houseboat; Attila; The Monster from Green Hell. **1962** Forty Pounds of Trouble. **1963** Ship of Condemned Women. **1964** The Visit. **1966** Dr. Satan's Robot; The Chase. **1968** The Brotherhood. **1969** Mackenna's Gold; The Secret of Santa Vittoria; Boot Hill.

CIERKES, VINCENT "DANTINI THE MAGNIFICENT"
Born: 1906. Died: Mar. 14, 1979, Baltimore, Md. Screen, vaudeville actor, film producer, magician, nightclub and carnival entertainer. Entered films in 1920's as an extra.

CIGOLI, EMILIO
Born: 1909. Died: Nov. 7, 1980. Screen actor and singer.

Appeared in: **1947** Shoe-Shine. **1959** Il Momento Piu Bello (The Most Wonderful Moment). **1960** Lettere di una Novizia (Letter from a Novice, aka Rita—US 1963). **1974** Giuseppe Verdi.

CIMARA, LUIGI
Born: 1890, Italy. Died: Jan. 26, 1962, Rome, Italy. Screen actor.

Appeared in: **1936** Il re Burlone. **1937** Loyalty of Love. **1938** Il Destino. **1947** Anything for a Song.

CIOLLI, AUGUSTA
Born: 1901. Died: Feb. 3, 1967, New York, N.Y. Screen and stage actress.

Appeared in: **1955** Marty. **1960** Fast and Sexy. **1963** Love With The Proper Stranger.

CIRILLO, MICHAEL (Michael Anthony Cirillo)
Born: Apr. 20, 1903, Mass. Died: Aug. 29, 1968, South Pasadena, Calif. (heart attack). Screen and vaudeville actor. Brother of actor Tony Cirillo (dec. 1968).

Appeared in: **1956** Around the World in 80 Days.

CIRILLO, TONY (Anthony John Cirillo)
Born: Nov. 14, 1910, Mass. Died: Nov. 16, 1968, Los Angeles, Calif. (perontonitis). Screen, vaudeville actor and film extra. Brother of actor Michael Cirillo (dec. 1968).

CISAR, GEORGE
Died: June 13, 1979. Screen actor.

Appeared in: **1949** Johnny Holiday. **1955** Teenage Crime Wave. **1956** Emergency Hospital; Nightfall; The Werewolf. **1957** The Brothers Rico; The Buckskin Lady; Chicago Confidential; Don't Knock the Rock; The Abductors. **1958** Jet Attack. **1959** Edge of Eternity; The Giant Leeches; Vice Squad. **1962** Married Too Young. **1966** Billy The Kid vs. Dracula. **1970** ... Tick ... Tick ... Tick.

CITARELLA, JEAN G. See GABRIELL, JEAN

CLAIR, RENE (Rene Chomette)
Born: Nov. 11, 1898, Paris, France. Died: Mar. 15, 1981, Neuilly, France. Screen actor, film director, film producer, screenwriter and author.

Appeared in: **1920-1922** Les Deux Gamines; Parisette; L'Orpheline. **1963** En Compagnie de Max Linder (with Max Linder—narrator).

CLAIRE, GERTRUDE
Born: 1852. Died: Apr. 28, 1928, Los Angeles, Calif. Screen and stage actress.

Appeared in: **1911** A True Western. **1919** Stepping Out; Widow by Proxy. **1920** The Cradle of Courage. **1921** The Fox; Hail the Woman; Greater Than Love; Things Men Do; The Sin of Martha Queed; The Invisible Power; Society Secrets. **1922** The Crusader; Human Hearts; Forget-Me-Not; The Adventures of Robinson Crusoe (serial); Environment; The Super-Sex; Ridin' Wild; Oliver Twist. **1923** Itching Palms; Double Dealing. **1924** Daughters of Today; The Heart Bandit; Wine of Youth; Ladies to Board. **1925** The Wedding Song; Romance Road; The Goose Hangs High; Her Sister from Paris; His Majesty, Bunker Bean; The Storm Breaker; Tumbleweeds. **1926** The Little Irish Girl; Out of the West. **1927** We're All Gamblers; Married Alive. **1928** Red Head.

CLAIRE, HELEN
Born: 1906, Union Springs, Ala. Died: Jan. 13, 1974, Birmingham, Ala. Screen, stage, radio and television actress. She was a commentator for Fox Movietone Newreels 1937-1949.

CLAPHAM, CHARLIE
Born: 1884, England. Died: July 28, 1959, St. Leonards-on-Sea, England. Screen, radio actor and music hall entertainer. Appeared in music hall act billed as "Clapham and Dwyer."

Appeared in: **1933** Hello Radio.

CLARANCE, ARTHUR
Born: 1883. Died: Oct. 26, 1956, Newcastle, England. Screen, stage, vaudeville and television actor.

CLARE, MADELYN
Born: 1894, Cleveland, Ohio. Died: Sept. 20, 1975, Raleigh, N.C. Screen actress. Married to Thomas Dixon (dec.) who wrote "The Klansman," the source for the film Birth of a Nation.

Appeared in: **1920** The Discarded Woman. **1921** If Women Only Knew; The Misleading Widow. **1922** False Fronts; Young America. **1923** Mark of the Beast; The Supreme Passion.

CLARE, MARY
Born: July 17, 1894, London, England. Died: Aug. 30, 1970, London, England. Screen and stage actress.

Appeared in: **1920** The Black Spider; The Skin Game. **1922** A Prince of Lovers (US 1927 aka The Life of Lord Byron); A Gipsy Cavalier (aka My Lady April). **1923** Becket; Lights of London. **1927** Packing Up. **1928** The Constant Nymph; The Princess in the Tower. **1929** The Feather. **1931** Hindle Wakes; Many Waters; Bill's Legacy; Keepers of Youth; Gipsy Blood (aka Carmen—US 1932); Shadows; The Outsider. **1933** The Constant Nymph (and 1928 version). **1934** Say It With Flowers; Jew Suess (aka Power—US); Night Club Queen. **1935** Lorna Doone; A Real Blocke; The Gov'nor (aka Hobo—US 1936); Line Engaged; The Clairvoyant; The Passing of the Third Floor Back. **1937** The Mill On the Floss (US 1939); Young and Innocent (aka A Girl Was Young—US 1938); The Rat. **1938** The Challenge (US 1939); The Citadel; Climbing High (US 1939); The Lady Vanishes. **1939** A Girl Must Live (US 1941); There Ain't No Justice; Mrs. Pym of Scotland Yard; On the Night of the Fire (aka The Fugitive—US 1940). **1940** Old Bill and Son; The Briggs Family; Miss Grant Goes to the Door. **1941** The Patient Vanishes (US 1947 aka This Man Is Dangerous). **1942** The Next of Kin; The Night Has Eyes (aka Terror House—US 1943). **1943** The Hundred Pound Window. **1944** One Exciting Night (aka You Can't Do Without Love—US 1946); Fiddler's Three. **1946** London Town (aka My Heart Goes Crazy—US 1953). **1947** Mrs. Fitzherbert (US 1950). **1948** Oliver Twist (US 1951); The Three Weird Sisters; My Brother Jonathan (US 1949); Esther Waters. **1949** Cardboard Cavalier. **1950** Portrait of Clare; The Black Rose. **1952** Penny Princess (US 1953); Hindle Wakes (aka Holiday Week—US). **1953** Moulin Rouge; The Beggar's Opera. **1955** Mambo. **1960** The Price of Silence.

CLARE, PHYLLIS
Born: Sept. 12, 1908, London, England. Died: Nov. 1, 1947, England? Screen and stage actress.

Appeared in: **1931** The Gangbuster. **1932** Roadhouse Murder. **1933** Just My Luck; The Love Nest; The Flaw; Aunt Sally (aka Along Came Sally—US 1934). **1934** Romance in Rhythm; Clive of India. **1935** The Stoker. **1936** His Brother's Wife; Hot News. **1938** Convicted; Women Are Like That. **1939** Manhattan Shakedown.

CLARENCE
Born: 1960. Died: July 12, 1969, California. Screen and television animal performer. Know as "Clarence the Cross-Eyed Lion."

Appeared in: **1965** Clarence the Cross-Eyed Lion.

CLARENCE, O. B. (Oliver B. Clarence)
Born: Mar. 25, 1870, London, England. Died: Oct. 2, 1955. Screen and stage actor.

Appeared in: **1914** Liberty Hall. **1920** London Pride; The Little Hour of Peter Wells. **1930** The Man from Chicago (US 1931). **1931** Keepers of Youth; The Bells. **1932** Where Is This Lady? The Barton Mystery; The Flag Lieutenant; Goodnight Vienna (aka Magic Night—US). **1933** Perfect Understanding; Discord; The Only Girl (aka Heart Song—US 1934); A Shot in the Dark (US 1935); I Adore You; Eyes of Fate; His Grace Gives Notice; Soldiers of the King (aka The Woman in Command—US 1934); Falling For You; Excess Baggage. **1934** The Feathered Serpent; Song at Eventide; The Great Defender; Father and Son; The King of Paris; The Silver Spoon; The Double Event; Lady in Danger. **1935** The Scarlet Pimpernel; Barnacle Bill; Squibs; The Private Secretary; Captain Bill; No Monkey Business. **1936** Seven Sinners (aka Doomed Cargo—US); East Meets West; All In; King of Hearts; The Cardinal. **1937** The Return of the Scarlet Pimpernel (US 1938); The Mill on the Floss (US 1939). **1938** It's In the Air (aka George Takes the Air—US 1940); Pygmalion; Old Iron. **1939** Me and My Pal; Black Eyes. **1940** Return to Yesterday; Spy For a Day; Saloon Bar (US 1944); Old Mother Riley in Business. **1941** Quiet Wedding; Inspector Hornleigh Goes To It (aka Mail Train—US); Turned Out Nice Again; Penn of Pennsylvania (aka The Courageous Mr. Penn—US 1944); Old Mother Riley's Circus. **1942** Front Line Kids. **1944** On Approval (US 1945). **1945** A Place of One's Own (US 1949). **1946** Great Expectations (US 1947). **1947** While the Sun Shines; Uncle Silas (aka The Inheritance—US 1951). **1948** Meet Me at Dawn.

CLARENS, HENRY F.
Born: 1860. Died: Dec. 19, 1928, New York, N.Y. Screen and stage actor.

CLARGES, VERNER
Born: 1848. Died: Aug. 11, 1911, New York, N.Y. Screen and stage actor. Entered films with Biograph.

Appeared in: **1909** The Better Way; 1776, or the Hessian Renegades; In Old Kentucky; The Face at the Window. **1910** A Flash of Light; As the Bells Rang Out!; Little Angels of Luck. **1911** His Trust Fulfilled; Swords and Hearts.

CLARIOND, AIME
Born: 1894, France. Died: Jan. 1, 1960, France? Screen actor.

Appeared in: **1935** Sans Famille. **1936** Le Prince Jean. **1937** Lucrezia Borgia. **1938** The Lie of Nina Petrovna. **1939** Boys' School; Katia; Entente Cordiale. **1940** Mayerling to Sarajevo. **1942** 32 Rue de Montmartre. **1947** Colonel Chabert; The Blue Veil; Midnight in Paris. **1948** Mlle. Desiree; Monsieur Vincent. **1949** The Wicked Duchess; The Eternal Husband. **1951** My First Love. **1957** Deadlier Than the Male. **1958** Nathalie (aka Foxiest Girl in Paris). **1959** The Possessors. **1960** Une Fille Pour L'ete (A Mistress for the Summer—US 1964).

CLARK, ANDREW J. "ANDY"
Born: Mar., 1903, New York, N.Y. Died: Nov. 16, 1960, New Rochelle, N.Y. Screen, stage and vaudeville actor. Entered films with Edison in 1913 and starred in "Andy" series.

Appeared in: **1913** It Wasn't Poison After All; Greedy George; Mr. Newcomb's Necktie. **1914** The Adventures of Andy Clark; Andy Goes on the Stage; Andy the Actor; Andy Plays Cupid; One Touch of Nature; The New Partner; Andy and the Red; Andy Gets A Job; Getting Andy's Goat; Andy Plays Hero; Making A Convert. **1925** The Sporting Chance. **1926** The Shamrock Handicap. **1927** One Round Hogan; Wings. **1928** Beggars of Life. **1929** Rio Rita; The Man I Love. **1930** Hit the Deck.

CLARK, BILL
Died: June 6, 1973 (injuries received in plane crash). Screen actor and stuntman.

Appeared in: **1954** The Wild One; The Robe. **1955** The Tall Men. **1958** The Young Lions. **1959** Day of the Outlaw. **1965** Young Fury.

CLARK, BOBBY
Born: 1923. Died: July 10, 1976, Chicago, Ill. (heart attack). Screen actor and marionettist. Do not confuse with comic actor Bobby Clark (dec. 1960).

CLARK, BOBBY (Robert Edwin Clark)
Born: June 16, 1888, Springfield, Ohio. Died: Feb. 12, 1960, New York, N.Y. (heart attack). Screen, stage, vaudeville, minstrel, circus and burlesque actor. Was partner with Paul McCullough (dec. 1936) in comedy team of "Clark and McCullough."

Together they appeared in the following shorts: **1928** Clark and McCullough in the Interview; Clark and McCullough in the Honor System. **1929** The Bath Between; The Diplomats; Waltzing Around; In Holland; Belle of Samoa; Beneath the Law; The Medicine Men; Music Fiends; Knights Out; All Steamed Up; Hired and Fired; Detectives Wanted. **1931** False Roomers; Chesterfield Celebrities; A Melon-Drama; Scratch as Catch Can. **1932** The Iceman's Ball; The Millionaire Cat; Jitters the Butler. **1933** Hokus Focus; The Druggist's Dilemma; The Gay Nighties; Fits in a Fiddle; Kickin' the Crown Around; Snug in the Jug. **1934** Hey, Nanny Nanny; In the Devil's Doghouse; Bedlam of Beards; Love and Hisses; Odor in the Court; Everything's Ducky; In a Pig's Eye. **1935** Flying Down to Zero; Alibi Bye Bye. **1938** Clark appeared without McCullough in The Goldwyn Follies (feature).

CLARK, BUDDY
Died: Oct. 1, 1949, Beverly Hills, Calif. (plane crash). Screen, radio actor and singer. Married to model Nedra Clark. Do not confuse with other actors-entertainers with same name.

Appeared in: **1942** Seven Days' Leave.

CLARK, CHARLES DOW
Born: 1870. Died: Mar. 26, 1959, N.Y. Screen and stage actor.

Appeared in: **1924** The Confidence Man. **1925** Old Home Week. **1930** The Bat Whispers. **1932** Ladies of the Jury; The Half-Naked Truth. **1933** Quiet, Please (short).

CLARK, CLIFF
Born: 1893. Died: Feb. 8, 1953, Hollywood, Calif. (heart attack). Screen, vaudeville and television actor.

Appeared in: 1937 Mountain Music. 1938 Mr. Moto's Gamble; Time Out for Murder; The Patient in Room 18; While New York Sleeps; Inside Story; Kentucky; Cocoanut Grove. 1939 They Made Me a Criminal; Within the Law; Honolulu; It's A Wonderful World; Miracles for Sale; Fast and Furious; Joe and Ethel Turp Call on the President; Young Mr. Lincoln; Missing Evidence; Dust Be My Destiny; Help Wanted (short). 1940 Jack Pot (short); Slightly Honorable; Grapes of Wrath; Double Alibi; Black Diamonds; Honeymoon Deferred; Three Cheers for the Irish; Cross Country Romance; Stranger on the Third Floor; Wagon Train. 1941 Blue, White and Perfect; Dangerously They Live; The Sea Wolf; Law of the Tropics; Nine Loves Are Not Enough; Strange Alibi; Washington Melodrama; Manpower; Golden Hoofs; The Wagons Roll at Night. 1942 Madam Spy; Joe Smith, American; Kid Glove Killer; Tennessee Johnson; Babes on Broadway; Jail House Blues; Fingers at the Window; Monkey; Who Is Hope Schuyler?; Secret Enemies; Henry Aldrich, Editor; The Falcon's Brother; Army Surgeon; The Mummy's Tomb; Taxi, Mister? 1943 Ladies' Day; The Falcon Strikes Back; The Falcon in Danger; The Falcon and the Co-eds. 1944 Barbary Coast Gent; The Falcon Out West; In the Meantime, Darling; The Missing Juror. 1947 It Had to Be You; Mister District Attorney; Cass Timberlane; Philo Vance's Gamble; Bury Me Dead; Buck Private Come Home. 1948 Fort Apache; I, Jane Doe; Deep Waters; Trouble Makers; Borrowed Trouble; False Paradise. 1949 Fighting Man of the Plains; Flaming Fury; Home of the Brave; Homicide; Powder River Rustlers; The Stratton Story; Post Office Investigator; Crime Doctor's Diary. 1950 The Men; Desperadoes of the West (serial); Try and Get It; Vigilante Hideout; The Man; The Cariboo Trail; Gunfighter. 1951 My Forbidden Past; Joe Palooka in the Triple Cross; Operation Pacific; Saddle Legion; The Second Woman; Cavalry Scout; Warpath. 1952 High Noon; The Pride of St. Louis; The Sniper; The Big Sky; It Grows on Trees; Cripple Creek. 1953 South Sea Woman.

CLARK, E. HOLMAN
Born: Apr. 22, 1864, East Hothley, Sussex, England. Died: Sept. 7, 1925, London, England. Screen, stage actor and stage producer.

Appeared in: 1913 A Message from Mars. 1923 The Naked Man.

CLARK, EDDIE (Edward Clark)
Born: 1879. Died: Nov. 18, 1954, Hollywood, Calif. (heart attack). Screen, stage, television actor and playwright.

Appeared in: 1926 Millionaires; Broken Hearts of Hollywood; Private Izzy Murphy. 1927 Finger Prints; The Gay Old Bird; Sally in Our Alley; Hills of Kentucky. 1928 Marriage by Contract. 1929 Unmasked; Silks and Saddles. 1930 Bitter Friends (short); Carnival Revue (short). 1941 Ball of Fire; Swamp Water. 1942 The Male Animal. 1946 The Falcon's Alibi. 1947 The Senator Was Indiscreet; My Wild Irish Rose. 1948 Give My Regards to Broadway. 1949 Abandoned; Amazon Quest; Oh, You Beautiful Doll. 1950 Branded; Dancing in the Dark; Petty Girl; A Ticket to Tomahawk. 1951 Strangers on a Train; Little Egypt; Bedtime for Bonzo; Million Dollar Pursuit; Mr. Belvedere Rings the Bell; Savage Drums; Rhubarb. 1952 Here Come the Nelsons; Thundering Caravan. 1953 Flame of Calcutta; It Happens Every Thursday; Topeka; Money From Home. 1954 Hell's Outpost. 1955 Crashout; East of Eden.

CLARK, ETHEL (Ethel Schneider)
Born: 1916. Died: Feb. 18, 1964, Hollywood, Calif. Screen, vaudeville and television actress.

Appeared in: 1938 The Headleys at Home.

CLARK, FRANK
Died: Apr. 10, 1945, Woodland Hills, Calif. Stage and screen actor. Do not confuse with actors Frank M. or Frank H. Clark.

CLARK, FRED (Frederic Leonard Clark)
Born: Mar. 9, 1914, Lincoln, Calif. Died: Dec. 5, 1968, Santa Monica, Calif. (liver ailment). Screen, stage, television and radio actor. Married to Gloria Glaser. Divorced from actress Benay Venuta.

Appeared in: 1947 Ride the Pink Horse; The Unsuspected. 1948 Fury at Furnace Creek; Mr. Peabody and the Mermaid; Cry of the City; Hazard; Two Guys from Texas. 1949 The Younger Brothers; Task Force; Alias Nick Beal; The Lady Takes a Sailor; White Heat; Flamingo Road. 1950 The Eagle and the Hawk; Return of the Frontiersman; The Jackpot; Mrs. O'Malley and Mr. Malone; Sunset Boulevard; Dynamite Pass; Treasure Island. 1951 The Lemon Drop Kid; Hollywood Story; Meet Me After the Show; A Place in the Sun.

1952 Three for Bedroom C; Dreamboat. 1953 The Stars Are Singing; How to Marry a Millionaire; Here Come the Girls; The Caddy. 1954 Living It Up. 1955 How to Be Very, Very Popular; The Court-Martial of Billy Mitchell; Daddy Long Legs; Abbott and Costello Meet the Keystone Kops. 1956 The Solid Gold Cadillac; Miracle in the Rain; The Birds and the Bees; Back from Eternity. 1957 The Fuzzy Pink Nightgown; Joe Butterfly; Don't Go Near the Water. 1958 Mardi Gras; Auntie Mame. 1959 The Mating Game; It Started With a Kiss. 1960 Risate di Gioia (aka The Passionate Thief—US 1963); Bells Are Ringing; Visit to a Small Planet. 1962 Hemingway's Adventures of a Young Man; Boys' Night Out; Zotz! 1963 Move Over, Darling. 1964 John Goldfarb, Please Come Home. 1965 Sergeant Deadhead; When the Boys Meet the Girls; Dr. Goldfoot and the Bikini Machine; The Curse of the Mummy's Tomb. 1967 War Italian Style. 1968 The Horse in the Gray Flannel Suit; Skidoo; Eve. 1969 I Sailed to Tahiti With an All Girl Crew.

CLARK, HARRY
Born: 1911. Died: Feb. 28, 1956, New York, N.Y. Screen and stage actor.

Appeared in: 1941 Ice Capades. 1953 Taxi.

CLARK, HARVEY (aka HARVEY CLARKE)
Born: 1886, Boston, Mass. Died: July 19, 1938, Hollywood, Calif. (heart attack). Screen, stage and vaudeville actor. Entered films with New York Motion Picture Co. in 1916.

Appeared in: 1916 The Innocence of Lizette; The Gentle Intruder; The Frame-Up; The Voice of Love; Periwinkle. 1917 New York Luck; Snap Judgment. 1918-20 American Film Mfg. Co. films. 1921 The Kiss; High Gear Jeffrey; Payment Guaranteed; The Servant in the House; Her Face Value. 1922 Don't Shoot; Alias Julius Caesar; The Gray Dawn; Mixed Faces; Money to Burn; Elope If You Must; The Men of Zanzibar; Thelma; The Woman He Loved; Shattered Idols. 1923 In the Palace of the King; The Man Who Won; Brass; Second Hand Love. 1924 Secrets; He Who Gets Slappped; The Man Who Came Back; The Roughnecks. 1925 Havoc; The Arizona Romeo; Blue Blood; The Man Without a Country; Marriage in Transit. 1926 Black Paradise; The Frontier Trail; The Flying Horseman; The Dixie Merchant; Midnight Lovers; The Cowboy and the Countess; The Silver Treasure; The Palace of Pleasure. 1927 Rose of the Golden West; Get Your Man; Putting Pants on Phillip (short); The Magic Flame; Camille; In Old Kentucky; McFadden's Flats; The Understanding Heart. 1928 A Woman Against the World; Tragedy of Youth; Ladies Night in a Turkish Bath; Floating College; The Toilers; Beautiful But Dumb; The Head Man; The Night Bird; The Olympic Hero. 1929 His Lucky Day; The Rainbow; Seven Keys to Baldpate. 1930 Man Trouble; Going Wild; Anybody's Woman; Up the River; What a Man. 1931 Millie; The Deceiver; Cracked Nuts. 1932 The Big Shot; Red Headed Woman; Down to Earth. 1933 Strictly Personal; West of Singapore; I Love That Man; A Shriek in the Night; Alice in Wonderland; Picture Brides. 1934 Charlie Chan's Courage; Peck's Bad Boy; Countess of Monte Cristo. 1936 Three Godfathers; Grand Jury; Sitting on the Moon; The Singing Cowboy; Empty Saddles. 1937 History Is Made at Night; Dance, Charlie, Dance; Dangerous Holiday; It's Love I'm After; Blonde Trouble; Partners of the Plains. 1938 Mother Carey's Chickens; Spawn of the North; What Price Safety (short).

CLARK, HELEN
Born: 1895, New York. Died: Jan. 9, 1974, Los Gatos, Calif. Screen, stage actress and dancer. Married to composer-conductor Frank E. Tours (dec.).

CLARK, IVAN-JOHN
Died: 1967. Screen actor.

CLARK, JOHN J. (aka JACK CLARK)
Born: 1877. Died: Apr. 12, 1947, Hollywood, Calif. Screen, stage actor, film director and stage producer. Entered films with Kalem in 1907.

Appeared in: 1913 In the Power of a Hypnotist; The Wives of Jamestown; Lady Peggy's Escape; When Men Hate; A Daughter of the Confederacy; In the Clutches of the Ku Klux Klan. 1914 Come Back to Erin; Rory O'More; His Brother's Wife. 1915 The Smuggler's Class; The Woman-Hater's Baby. 1927 Pajamas. 1928 Love and Learn. 1929 Howdy, Broadway. 1934 The Return of Chandu (serial). 1935 Home on the Range.

CLARK, JOHNNY
Born: Aug. 10, 1916, Hampton, Iowa. Died: July 3, 1967, Hollywood, Calif. (heart attack). Screen, stage, television actor and composer.

Appeared in: 1941 Las Vegas Nights. 1943 Jive Junction. 1944 Hey Rookie; Weekend Pass; The Sultan's Daughter; Irish Eyes Are Smiling. 1947 The Locket.

CLARK, LES
Born: 1907. Died: Mar. 24, 1959, London, England (heart attack). Screen and vaudeville actor.

Appeared in: **1946** Do You Love Me? **1947** The Walls of Jericho; You Were Meant For Me. **1950** When Willie Comes Marching Home. **1952** Somebody Loves Me. **1954** The Country Girl; White Christmas.

CLARK, MARGUERITE
Born: Feb. 22, 1887, Avondale, Ohio. Died: Sept. 25, 1940, New York, N.Y. (pneumonia as a result of a cerebral hemorrhage). Stage and screen actress. Entered films with Famous Players.

Appeared in: **1914** Wildflower (film debut); The Crucible; The Pretty Sister of Jose; Gretna Green. **1915** Still Waters; The Prince and the Pauper; The Goose Girl; Morals of Marcus. **1916** Molly Make-Believe; Little Lady Eileen; Miss George Washington; Silks and Satins; Out of the Drifts. **1917** The Seven Sisters; The Amazons; The Seven Swans; Snow White. **1918** Out of a Clear Sky; Rich Man, Poor Man; Uncle Tom's Cabin. **1919** Mrs. Wiggs of the Cabbage Patch; Girls, Come Out of the Kitchen; Widow by Proxy; Luck in Pawn; Three Men and a Girl; Prunella. **1920** All-of-a-Sudden Peggy. **1921** Scrambled Wives.

CLARK, PAUL
Born: 1927. Died: May 20, 1960, Santa Barbara, Calif. (auto accident). Screen, stage and television actor.

Appeared in: **1938** Boy Meets Girl; How to Raise a Baby (short).

CLARK, ROGER W.
Born: 1909. Died: Oct. 13, 1978, Los Angeles, Calif. (stroke). Screen, stage actor, stage producer and writer.

Appeared in: **1941** You Belong to Me. **1942** The Lady is Willing; The Man Who Returned to Life; Two Yanks in Trinidad; The Wife Takes a Flyer; Meet the Stewarts; They All Kissed the Bride. **1943** Girls in Chains; Swing Your Partner; So This is Washington. **1944** Pin-Up Girl; The Eve of St. Mark; Sweet and Lowdown; Faces in the Fog; Something for the Boys. **1945** A Song for Miss Julie. **1946** Detour. **1958** Lost Lagoon. **1961** Angel Baby. **1962** Advise and Consent.

CLARK, STEPHEN "STEVE" (Elmer Stephen Clark)
Born: Feb. 26, 1891, Davis County, Ind. Died: June 29, 1954, Van Nuys, Calif. (heart disease). Screen actor and film director. Do not confuse with actors with same name.

CLARK, T. C.
Born: 1882. Died: Oct. 4, 1954, Hollywood, Calif. (heart attack). Screen actor.

CLARK, WALLIS
Born: Mar. 2, 1889, Essex, England. Died: Feb. 14, 1961. Screen actor.

Appeared in: **1932** I Am a Fugitive From a Chain Gang; Madame Butterfly; Hell's House; The Final Edition; Alias the Doctor; Shopworn; Attorney for the Defense; Okay America; My Pal the King; The Night Mayor. **1933** Hidden Gold; Double Harness; The World Gone Mad; Bureau of Missing Persons; Ever in My Heart; Police Car 17; Lady for a Day; Luxury Liner; They Just Had to Get Married; The Working Man; The Kiss Before the Mirror; The World Changes. **1934** Cheating Cheaters; Beloved; Massacre; A Woman's Man; I've Got Your Number; It Happened One Night; The Life of Vergie Winters; I'll Fix It. **1935** Bordertown; It Happened in New York; Chinatown Squad; Mutiny on the Bounty. **1936** Postal Inspector; The Unguarded Hour; Parole; Missing Girls; Come Closer Folks; Great Guy; Easy Money. **1937** The Wildcatter; The Last of Mrs. Cheyney; I Promise to Pay; Big Business; She Had to Eat; Woman in Distress; River of Missing Men. **1938** The Higgins Family. **1939** Blondie Meets the Boss; Main Street Lawyer; Allegheny Uprising; I Stole a Million; Smuggled Cargo. **1940** The Big Guy. **1941** Penny Serenade; Murder By Invitation. **1942** The Remarkable Andrew; Yankee Doodle Dandy; Gentleman Jim. **1943** You're a Lucky Fellow Mr. Smith. **1944** Follow the Boys; Mrs. Parkington; Uncertain Glory. **1945** Mildred Pierce; Without Love; San Antonio. **1949** Free For All. **1950** Kim. **1951** Criminal Lawyer.

CLARK, WALLY
Died: Jan. 30, 1920, Philadelphia, Pa. Screen and stage actor.

CLARKE, BETTY ROSS See ROSS, BETTY

CLARKE, DOWNING GEORGE
Born: Birmingham, England. Died: Aug. 17, 1930, New Haven, Conn. Screen and stage actor.

Appeared in: **1916** The Vixen. **1917** The Tiger Woman. **1920** The Stealers. **1921** The Ghost in the Garret; Know Your Men. **1922** When Knighthood Was in Flower. **1923** Human Wreckage. **1924** Sandra; America; Monsieur Beaucaire. **1925** The Fool. **1932** Okay America; Here's George.

CLARKE, FRANK
Born: Dec. 29, 1898, Paso Robles, Calif. Died: June 12, 1948, near Los Angeles, Calif. (plane crash). Stunt pilot and screen actor. Do not confuse with actors with same name.

Appeared in: **1920** The Lost City (serial). **1921** The Diamond Queen (serial). **1927** Wings. **1928** Eagle of the Night. **1930** Hell's Angels.

CLARKE, GAGE (aka GAGE CLARK)
Born: Mar. 3, 1900, Michigan. Died: Oct. 23, 1964, Woodland Hills, Calif. (lung cancer). Screen, stage and television actor.

Appeared in: **1956** The Bad Seed (film debut); Nightmare. **1957** The Invisible Boy; Fury at Showdown; Valerie. **1958** The Return of Dracula; I Want to Live; The Brothers Karamazov. **1960** Pollyanna; Midnight Lace. **1961** The Great Imposter; The Absent Minded Professor. **1965** The Monkey's Uncle.

CLARKE, GEORGE
Born: Apr. 11, 1888, Bromley, Middlesex, England. Died: Dec. 21, 1946, London, England. Screen, stage and vaudeville actor.

Appeared in: **1930** His First Car. **1932** Here's George.

CLARKE, GORDON B.
Born: 1907. Died: Jan. 11, 1972, New York, N.Y. (coronary). Screen, stage and television actor.

Appeared in: **1950** Under My Skin. **1954** Paris Playboys. **1956** The Wrong Man. **1957** A Hatful of Rain. **1960** From the Terrace. **1961** The Hustler; The Last Gunfighter.

CLARKE, REDFIELD
Born: Peru, N.Y. Died: Oct. 23, 1928, Detroit, Mich. Screen and stage actor.

Appeared in: **1915** A Fool There Was; Emmy of Stork's Nest; The Woman Pays. **1917** The Greatest Power; Pardners. **1924** $20.00 A Week.

CLARKE, WESTCOTT B.
Born: Sept. 27, 1886, Jerey City, N.J. Died: Jan. 26, 1959. Screen and stage actor.

Appeared in: **1922** North of the Rio Grande. **1923** Why Women Remarry; Safety Last. **1924** The Breaking Point; Abraham Lincoln. **1927** Finnegan's Ball. **1929** The Trial of Mary Dugan; Father and Son.

CLARKE-SMITH, D. A. (Douglas A. Clarke-Smith)
Born: 1888, Montrose, Scotland. Died: Mar. 12, 1959, Withyham, Sussex, England. Screen, stage and television.

Appeared in: **1929** Atlantic. **1931** Peace and Quiet; Bracelets; Shadows; Michael and Mary (US 1932); The Old Man. **1932** Help Yourself; A Voice Said Goodnight; The Frightened Lady (aka Criminal at Large—US 1933); Illegal; White Face; A Letter of Warning. **1933** I'm an Explosive; The Thirteenth Candle; The Good Companions; Sleeping Car; Waltz Time; Follow the Lady; Head of the Family; The Ghoul; Mayfair Girl; The Laughter of Fools; Skipper of the Osprey; Friday the Thirteenth; Turkey Time; Smithy. **1934** Flat No. 3; A Cup of Kindness; Warn London; Passing Shadows; The Perfect Flaw; Money Mad; Sabotage (aka Menace and When London Sleeps—US); The Man Who Knew Too Much; The Feathered Serpent; Keep It Quiet; Designing Women. **1935** Lorna Doone; Key to Harmony; Royal Cavalcade (aka Regal Cavalcade—US—narration). **1936** Murder by Rope; The Happy Family; Southern Roses. **1937** Cafe Colette (aka Danger in Paris—US); Little Miss Somebody; Splinters in the Air; Dangerous Fingers (aka Wanted by Scotland Yard—US). **1938** Weddings Are Wonderful; I've Got a Horse. **1939** Flying Fifty Five. **1951** Quo Vadis. **1952** The Pickwick Papers (US 1953); Something Money Can't Buy. **1953** The Sword and the Rose. **1956** The Man Who Never Was; The Baby and the Battleship.

CLARY, CHARLES
Born: Mar. 24, 1873, St. Charles, Ill. Died: Mar. 24, 1931, Los Angeles, Calif. Screen and stage actor.

Appeared in: **1910** The Englishman and the Girl. **1911** Two Orphans; Maud Muller; How They Stopped the Run on the Bank; Lost in the Jungle; Back to the Primitive. **1912** The Other Woman; The Law of the North; The Last Dance; The Adopted Son; Officer Murray; The Girl at the Cupola; The Coming of Columbus; Sons of the Northwoods; An Unexpected Fortune; When the Heart Rules; The Devil, the Servant and the Man; The Fire-Fighter's Love; The Three Valises; A Detective's Strategy. **1913** The Lesson; The Adventures of Kathlyn (serial). **1914** The Tradegy That Lived; The Woman of It; Her Sacrifice; The Story of the Blood Red Rose; The Carpet of Bagdad. **1915** The Way of a Woman's Heart; The Fortunes of Marian; At the Stroke of the Angelus; His Guiding Angel; A Day That Is Dead; Children of the Sea. **1916** Joan the Woman. **1917** DuBarry. **1920** Street Called Straight; Woman in Room 13. **1921** A Connecticut Yankee at King Arthur's Court; Don't Neglect Your Wife; The Hole in the Wall; Opened Shutters; The Sea Lion; Sunset Jones. **1922** The Rosary; The Flaming Hour; Hate; Heroes and Husbands; Rich Men's Wives; Skin Deep; Two Kinds of Women; Very Truly Yours. **1923** The Last Hour; Michael O'Halloran; Money! Money! Money!; Nobody's Money; Prodigal Daughters; Thundering Dawn; Six Days; Cause for Divorce; In the Palace of the King. **1924** Behind the Curtain; The Breath of Scandal; Empty Hands; Flames of Desire; In Fast Company; On Time; The Whispered Name. **1925** An Enemy of Men; The Golden Bed; Jimmie's Millions; The Kiss Barrier; Seven Days; Speed Wild; Super Speed; She Wolves; Three Keys; The Unwritten Law. **1926** Beverly of Graustark; The Auction Block; The Blind Goddess; The Blue Streak; Modern Youth; Red Dice; Satan Town; Thrilling Youth; Whispering Wires. **1927** The Magic Garden; Man Power; Pretty Clothes; See You in Jail; Smile, Brother, Smile; What Price Love; When a Man Loves; His Foreign Wife; King of Kings; Land of the Lawless. **1928** The Big Hop; Jazz Mad; Nameless Men; The Power of the Press; A Woman Against the World. **1929** The Exalted Flapper; Eyes of the Underworld; Sailor's Holiday; Prisoners; Wolves of the City; Trial Marriage. **1930** Kismet; Lucky Larkin; Night Work.

CLAUDIUS, DANE
Born: 1874. Died: Apr. 26, 1946, Los Angeles, Calif. Screen, stage and vaudeville actor. Entered films approx. 1930.

CLAYTON, BOB
Born: 1922. Died: Nov. 1, 1979, New York, N.Y. (cardiac arrest). Screen, television actor, television announcer and dance instructor.

Appeared in: **1951** Disc Jockey. **1960** The Bell Boy.

CLAYTON, DONALD
Born: 1890. Died: Jan. 18, 1964. Screen actor.

CLAYTON, ETHEL
Born: 1884, Champaign, Ill. Died: June 11, 1966, Oxnard, Calif. Stage and screen actress. Entered films in 1909. Divorced from actor Ian Keith (dec, 1969).

Appeared in: **1912** Her Own Money. **1914** Mazie Puts One Over; The Fortune Hunter. **1915** The College Widow; The Great Divide. **1916** A Woman's Way; Oliver Twist. **1918** The Girl Who Came Back. **1919** Pettigrew's Girl; The Woman Next Door; Men, Women and Money; A Sporting Chance; Maggie Pepper. **1921** Sham; City Sparrow; Price of Possession; Sins of Rosanne; Wealth; Beyond. **1922** The Cradle; Exit the Vamp; For the Defense; Her Own Money (and 1912); If I Were Queen. **1923** Can A Woman Love Twice; The Remittance Woman. **1925** Lightnin'; The Mansion of Aching Hearts; Wings of Youth. **1926** The Bar-C Mystery (serial and feature film); His New York Wife; Risky Business; Sunny Side Up. **1927** The Princess on Broadway; The Princess from Hoboken. **1928** Mother Machree. **1930** The Call of the Circus; Hit the Deck. **1932** Thrill of Youth; The All-American; Hotel Continental; Crooked Circle. **1933** Whispering Shadows (serial); Private Jones; Secrets. **1937** Souls at Sea; Artists and Models; Easy Living; Hold 'Em Navy. **1938** The Big Broadcast of 1938; Men With Wings; Say It In French; The Buccaneer; Cocoanut Grove; Tom Sawyer, Detective; If I Were a King. **1939** Ambush; The Sap Takes a Rap (short); Artists and Models Abroad. **1941** West Point Widow. **1942** Lucky Jordan; The Major and the Minor. **1943** Dixie; Lady Bodyguard; True to Life. **1947** The Perils of Pauline.

CLAYTON, GILBERT
Born: Dec. 18, 1860, Polo, Ill. Died: Mar. 1, 1950. Screen and stage actor. Entered films in 1920.

Appeared in: **1920** The Mark of Zorro. **1921** Across the Divide; Habit; The Three Musketeers. **1923** Blood and Sand; When Love Comes. **1924** Main Street; Trilby. **1925** Below the Line. **1926** Partners Again; The Silver Treasure; Ben Hur.

CLAYTON, HAZEL *See* HILLIARD, MRS. MACK

CLAYTON, LOU (Louis Finkelstein)
Born: 1887, Brooklyn, N.Y. Died: Sept. 12, 1950, Santa Monica, Calif. (cancer). Screen and vaudeville actor. Appeared in vaudeville with partners Jimmy Durante (dec. 1980) and Eddie Jackson (dec. 1980) in an act billed as "Clayton, Jackson and Durante."

Appeared in: **1930** Roadhouse Nights.

CLAYTON, MARGUERITE
Born: 1894 or 1896?, Salt Lake City, Utah. Died: Dec. 20, 1968. Screen and stage actress.

Appeared in: **1912** When Love and Honor Called; Last Round-Up; The Cowboy Coward. **1913** The Doctor's Duty; The Three Gamblers; Why Broncho Billy Left Bear Country; Bonnie of the Hills; The Struggle. **1914** The Promise Land; The Warning; Snakeville's New Doctor; Broncho Billy and Sheriff; Broncho Billy Puts One Over; Broncho Billy and the Guesser; Broncho Billy—Favorite; A Snakeville Romance. **1915** A Daughter of the City; An Unexpected Romance; The Convict's Threat; Broncho Billy Misled; Suppressed Evidence; A Christmas Revenge. **1916** Is Marriage Sacred?; The Promise Land; Putting It Over; Prince of Graustark. **1917** The Dream Doll; The Clock Struck One; Two-Bit Seats; Star Dust; The Long Green Trail. **1918** Hit-the-Trail Haliday. **1919** The New Moon. **1920** Bride 13 (serial); Pleasure Seekers. **1921** Dangerous Toys; Forbidden Love; The Inside of the Cup. **1922** The Curse of Drink. **1923** Canyon of the Fools; Desert Driven; Men in the Raw; What Love Will Do. **1924** Idle Tongues; The Circus Cowboy; The Dawn of a Tomorrow; Flashing Spurs; The Street of Tears; Tiger Thompson. **1925** Barriers of the Law; Wolf Blood; Straight Through. **1926** The Palm Beach Girl; Sky High Corral; The Power of the Weak. **1927** Twin Flappers. **1928** Inspiration.

CLEARY, LEO THOMAS
Born: 1895. Died: Apr. 11, 1955, Hollywood, Calif. (uremic poisoning). Screen and radio actor.

Appeared in: **1940** You Can't Fool Your Wife. **1949** Johnny Holiday; The Red Menace. **1950** Bells of Coronado; State Penitentiary. **1952** The Price of St. Louis. **1954** The Human Jungle.

CLEARY, PEGGY
Born: 1892. Died: Jan. 10, 1972, Los Angeles, Calif. Screen actress and writer. Appeared in D. W. Griffith films.

CLEGG, VALCE V.
Born: 1888. Died: July 29, 1947, Hollywood, Calif. Screen and stage actor.

Appeared in: **1926** Lucky Stars.

CLEMENT, CLAY
Born: 1888, Greentree, Ky. Died: Oct. 20, 1956, Watertown, N.Y. Screen, stage and television actor. Entered films approx. 1914.

Appeared in: **1930** Curses (short); Keeping Company (short). **1932** Washington Merry-Go-Round; False Faces; Evenings for Sale. **1933** Tonight Is Ours; Past of Mary Holmes; Second Hand Wife; Hold Me Tight; Bureau of Missing Persons; Son of a Sailor; The World Changes. **1934** The St. Louis Kid; The Thin Man; I've Got Your Number; Wonder Bar; Journal of a Crime; I Sell Anything; Let's Be Ritzy; The Personality Kid. **1935** Sweet Music; Murder in the Clouds; Don't Bet on Blondes; Dinky; Chinatown Squad; Streamline Express; Confidential; Whipsaw. **1936** The Leavenworth Case; The Leathernecks Have Landed; Heart in Bondage; It Had to Happen; Let's Sing Again; Two Against the World; Nobody's Fool. **1937** Bad Guy; Give Till It Hurts (short); Rosalie. **1938** A Trip to Paris; Arson Gang Busters; Numbered Woman. **1939** The Roaring Twenties; Allegheny Uprising; Society Smugglers; Each Dawn I Die; Disbarred; Off the Record. **1940** Passport to Alcatraz; I'm Still Alive. **1947** Boomerang.

CLEMENT, DONALD
Born: 1941, Wantagh, N.Y. Died: July 28, 1970, New York, N.Y. (electrocuted). Screen and stage actor.

Appeared in: **1970** Tell Me That You Love Me, Junie Moon.

CLEMENTE, ROBERTO (Roberto Walker Clemente)
Born: Aug. 8, 1934, Carolina, Puerto Rico. Died: Dec. 31, 1972, San Juan, Puerto Rico (plane crash). Baseball player and screen actor.

Appeared in: **1968** The Odd Couple.

CLEMENTE, STEVE (Steve Clemento Morro aka STEVE CLEMENTS and STEVE CLEMENTO)
Born: Nov. 22, 1885, Mexico. Died: May 7, 1950, Los Angeles, Calif. (cerebral hemorrhage). Screen actor and circus performer.

Appeared in: **1919** Lightning Bryce (serial). **1920** Thunderbolt Jack (serial). **1921** Sure Fire; Outlawed; Cyclone Bliss. **1922** Two Fisted Jefferson. **1923** The Double-O; The Forbidden Trail. **1924** Fast and Fearless; Crashin' Through. **1925** The Rainbow Trail. **1926** The Temptress; The Combat; Davy Crockett at the Fall of the Alamo; Chip of the Flying U; Riding Romance. **1928** The Sideshow. **1932** The Most Dangerous Game. **1933** King Kong. **1936** The Vigilantes Are Coming (serial). **1937** It Happened Out West; Hills of Wyoming.

CLEMENTO, STEVE *See* CLEMENTE, STEVE

CLEMENTS, DUDLEY
Born: Mar. 31, 1889, New York, N.Y. Died: Nov. 4, 1947, New York, N.Y. (heart ailment). Screen and stage actor.

Appeared in: **1930** The Three Sailors (short). **1931** Court Plastered (short); The Spirits of 76th Street (short). **1932** Speaking Out of Turn (short); The Bitter Half (short). **1937** The Outcasts of Poker Flat; You Can't Buy Luck; New Faces of 1937; The Toast of New York; The Big Shot; Hideaway; Too Many Wives; Night Club Scandal; The Woman I Love; Man Who Found Himself; Take the Heir.

CLEMENTS, STANLEY
Born: July 16, 1926, Long Island, N.Y. Died: Oct. 16, 1981, Pacoima, Calif. (emphysema). Screen, radio and television actor. Divorced from Gloria Grahame (dec. 1981) and later married to Maria Welek.

Appeared in: **1941** Tall, Dark and Handsome; Accent on Love; Down in San Diego. **1942** Smart Alecks; Right to the Heart; 'Neath Brooklyn Bridge; On the Sunny Side. **1943** The More the Merrier; Sweet Rosie O'Grady; Ghosts on the Loose. **1944** Going My Way; Gal in the Case. **1945** Salty O'Rourke; See My Lawyer. **1948** Racing Luck; Joe Palooka in Winner Take All; Canon City; The Babe Ruth Story; Hazard; Big Town Scandal. **1949** Johnny Holiday; Mr. Soft Touch; Bad Boy. **1950** Military Academy; Destination Murder. **1951** Pride of Maryland. **1952** Boots Malone; Jet Job; Army Bound. **1953** White Lightning; Off Limits; Hot News. **1954** The Rocket Man. **1955** Robber's Roost; Air Strike. **1956** Wiretappers; Fighting Trouble; Hot Shots. **1957** Spook Chasers; Hold That Hypnotist; Looking for Danger; Up in Smoke. **1958** In the Money; A Nice Little Bank That Should Be Robbed. **1961** The Devil's Partner; Sniper's Ridge. **1962** Saintly Sinners. **1963** Tammy and the Doctor; It's a Mad, Mad, Mad, Mad World. **1965** That Darn Cat. **1968** Panic in the Street. **1978** Hot Lead and Cold Feet.

CLEMENTS, STEVE See CLEMENTE, STEVE

CLEMONS, CHARLES D.
Born: 1874. Died: Aug. 30, 1947, Cincinnati, Ohio. Screen, stage and vaudeville actor.

CLEMONS, JAMES K.
Born: 1883. Died: June 5, 1950, Hollywood, Calif. Screen and stage actor.

Appeared in: **1943** Dixie.

CLERGET, PAUL
Born: 1867, France. Died: Dec. 4, 1935, Paris, France. Screen and stage actor.

Appeared in: **1918** Woman. **1920** My Lady's Garter.

CLERMONT, HARVEY
Born: 1907. Died: Jan. 28, 1978, Marina del Rey, Calif. (heart attack). Silent screen actor and casting director.

CLEVELAND, ANNA
Born: 1880. Died: Jan. 7, 1954, Manhasset, N.Y. Screen and stage actress.

CLEVELAND, GEORGE
Born: 1883, Sydney, Nova Scotia. Died: July 15, 1957, Burbank, Calif. (heart attack). Screen, stage, vaudeville, television actor, film producer and film director. Son of actress Lavinia Cleveland (dec. 1950).

Appeared in: **1934** Mystery Line; Blue Steel; City Limits; Monte Carlo Nights; The Man from Utah; Star Packer; School for Girls. **1935** She Gets Her Man; Make a Million; His Night Out; The Keeper of the Bees; The Spanish Cape Mystery; Forced Landing. **1936** Robinson Crusoe of Clipper Island (serial); I Conquer the Sea; Foolproof (short); Revolt of the Zombies; North of Nome; Don't Get Personal; Rio Grande Romance; Brilliant Marriage; Put on the Spot. **1937** Behind the Mike; A Girl With Ideas; Night Key; Prescription for Romance; Breezing Home; Paradise Express; The River of Missing Men; Boy of the Streets; Swing It, Professor; The Adventure's End. **1938** The Lone Ranger (serial); Rose of the Rio Grande; Romance of the Limberlost; Under the Big Top; Ghost Town Riders; The Port of Missing Girls. **1939** The Sap Takes a Rap (short); Home on the Prairie; Streets of New York; Wolf Call; Stunt Pilot; Mutiny in the Big House; Overland Mail. **1940** Midnight Limited; Tomboy; The Haunted House; Drum of Fu Manchu (serial); Queen of the Yukon; The Ol' Swimmin' Hole; Pioneers of the West; Hi-Yo Silver!; One Man's Law; Blazing Six Shooters; West of Abilene; Chasing Trouble; Konga; The Wild Stallion; The Ape. **1941** A Girl, a Guy and a Gob; Sucker List (short); All That Money Can Buy; Nevada City; Sunset in Wyoming; Two in a Taxi; Obliging Young Lady; Here Is a Man; Man at Large; Look Who's Laughing; Playmates. **1942** The Big Street; Call Out the Marines; Seven Miles from Alcatraz; Valley of the Sun; The Spoilers; Hold 'Em

Jail (short); Mail Trouble (short); My Favorite Spy; The Falcon Takes Over; The Mexican Spitfire's Elephant; Army Surgeon; The Traitor Within; Valley of the Giants; Powder Town; Highway by Night. **1943** Cowboy in Manhattan; Woman of the Town; Johnny Come Lately; Ladies Day; The Man from Music Mountain; Drums of Fu Manchu. **1944** It Happened Tomorrow; Abroad With Two Yanks; Alaska; Yellow Rose of Texas; Home in Indiana; Can't Help Singing; My Best Gal; When the Lights Go On Again; My Pal Wolf. **1945** Song of the Sarong; It's in the Bag; Dakota; Senorita from the West; She Wouldn't Say Yes; Pillow of Death; Sunbonnet Sue; Her Highness and the Bellboy. **1946** Little Giant; Wake Up and Dream; The Runaround; Angel On My Shoulder; Step By Step; Wild Beauty; Courage of Lassie; The Show-off. **1947** Mother Wore Tights; I Wonder Who's Kissing Her Now; The Wistful Widow of Wagon Gap; Easy Come, Easy Go; My Wild Irish Rose. **1948** Alburquerque; Fury at Furnace Creek; Miraculous Journey; The Plunderers; A Date With Judy. **1949** Kazan; Miss Grant Takes Richmond; Home in San Antone; Rimfire. **1950** Boy from Indiana; Please Believe Me; Trigger, Jr.; Frenchie. **1951** Flaming Feather; Fort Defiance. **1952** Cripple Creek; Carson City; Wac from Walla Walla; The Devil and Daniel Webster (reissue and retitle of All That Money Can Buy). **1953** San Antone; Affair With a Stranger; Walking My Baby Back Home. **1954** Outlaw's Daughter; Fireman Save My Child; Racing Blood; Untamed Heiress.

CLEVELAND, LAVINIA
Born: 1857. Died: May 10, 1950, Stockton, Calif. Screen and stage actress. Mother of actor George Cleveland (dec. 1957).

CLIFF, LADDIE (Laddie Perry)
Born: Sept. 3, 1891, Bristol, England. Died: Dec. 8, 1937, London, England. Screen, stage actor and stage producer. Divorced from Mary E. Parker (dec. 1980) and later married to actress Phyllis Monkman (dec. 1976).

Appeared in: **1922** The Card. **1927** On With the Dance series. **1929** The Co-Optimists (US 1930). **1933** Sleeping Car. **1934** Happy. **1936** Sporting Love. **1937** Over She Goes.

CLIFFE, H. COOPER
Born: 1862, Oxford, England. Died: May 1, 1939, New York, N.Y. (pneumonia). Screen, stage and radio actor.

Appeared in: **1921** The Woman God Changed; Love's Redemption. **1922** Missing Millions. **1923** His Children's Children. **1924** Monsieur Beaucaire.

CLIFFORD, CAL
Born: 1904. Died: July 10, 1978, Hollywood, Calif. (heart attack). Screen, radio television actor and trumpeter. Father of actor-singer Mike Clifford.

CLIFFORD, CARMEN
Born: 1922, Pa. Died: Feb. 15, 1981, Philadelphia, Pa. (cancer). Screen, stage, television actress, dancer and choreographer.

CLIFFORD, JACK (Virgil James Montani)
Born: 1880. Died: Nov. 10, 1956, New York, N.Y. Screen, stage actor and boxer. Divorced from actress Evelyn Nesbit Thaw (dec. 1967).

Appeared in: **1926** Sweet Adeline. **1931** Skippy. **1932** The Lost Special (serial). **1933** One Sunday Afternoon; One Track Minds (short). **1934** The Poor Rich. **1935** Man from Guntown; One Way Ticket. **1936** Speed; King of the Pecos; The Gallant Defender; Dimples; Timothy's Quest. **1937** Racketeers in Exile; High, Wide and Handsome; Midnight Madonna. **1938** Colorado Trail. **1940** Murder on the Yukon Flight. **1941** Six Lessons from Madame La Zonga; Confession of Boston Blackie; Beyond the Sacramento; The Bandit Trail. **1942** Sea Raiders (serial). **1944** The Old Texas Trail. **1945** Salome, Where She Dance; Secret Agent X-9 (serial); Senorita from the West; Honeymoon Ahead; Rockin' in the Rockies. **1946** The Blue Daklia; Badmen's Territory; The Harvey Girls; Canyon Passage. **1947** Ladies' Man; My Favorite Brunette. **1948** I, Jane Doe; Danger of the Canadian Mounted (serial).

CLIFFORD, KATHLEEN
Born: Feb. 16, 1887, Charlottesville, Va. Died: Jan. 11, 1962, Hollywood, Calif. Screen, stage and vaudeville actress.

Appeared in: **1917** Who Is "Number One"? (serial). **1920** When the Clouds Roll By. **1921** Cold Steel. **1922** Kick In. **1923** Richard, the Lion-Hearted. **1924** No More Women. **1925** The Love Gamble; Sporting Life. **1928** Excess Baggage.

CLIFFORD, LARRY
Died: Feb. 9, 1955. Screen actor.

CLIFFORD, WILLIAM
Born: June 27, 1887, New Orleans, La. Died: Dec. 23, 1941, Los Angeles, Calif. Screen and stage actor. Do not confuse with producer William H. Clifford.

Appeared in: 1913 Sheridan's Ride. 1914 Cast Adrift in the South Seas; A Romance of Hawaii; Olana of the South Sea; Rescued by Wireless; The Vagabond Soldiers; The Lure of the Geisha. 1915 Rosemary. 1916 The Hidden Law; The Bait; Highlights and Shadows; A Siren of the Jungle; The Lion Nemesis; Clouds in Sunshine Valley; The Ostrich Tip; Destiny's Boomerang; Fate's Decision; After the Battle; The Star of India; The Good for Nothing Brat; The Trap; The Jungle Flashlight. 1917 Snow White; The Square Deceiver. 1918 Broadway Bill; The Landlopers. 1919 Gambling in Souls; A Man of Honor. 1921 The Mask; Sowing the Wind; Parted Curtains. 1923 Ashes of Vengeance. 1924 Stepping Lively. 1927 Out of the Past; Three Miles Up.

CLIFT, MONTGOMERY
Born: Oct. 17, 1920, Omaha, Nebr. Died: July 23, 1966, New York, N.Y. (heart attack). Stage and screen actor. Nominated for 1948 Academy Award for Best Actor in The Search, in 1951 for A Place in the Sun and in 1953 for From Here to Eternity. Nominated for 1961 Academy Award for Best Supporting Actor in Judgment at Nuremberg.

Appeared in: 1948 Red River; The Search. 1949 The Heiress. 1950 The Big Lift. 1951 A Place in the Sun. 1953 I Confess; From Here to Eternity. 1954 Indiscretion of an American Wife. 1957 Raintree County. 1958 The Young Lions; Lonelyhearts. 1959 Suddenly Last Summer. 1960 Wild River. 1961 The Misfits; Judgment at Nuremberg. 1962 Freud. 1966 The Defector.

CLIFTON, ELMER
Born: 1893, Chicago, Ill. Died: Oct. 15, 1949, Los Angeles, Calif. (cerebral hemorrhage). Screen, stage actor, film producer, film director and screenwriter.

Appeared in: 1915 Birth of a Nation. 1916 Intolerance. 1919 The Fall of Babylon.

CLIFTON, EMMA BELL (Emma MacGrew)
Born: Nov. 1, 1874, Pa. Died: Aug. 3, 1922, Los Angeles, Calif. (heart attack). Screen actress and screenwriter.

Appeared in: 1914 Between Showers.

CLIFTON, HERBERT
Born: 1884, London, England. Died: Sept. 26, 1947, Hollywood, Calif. (after major operation). Screen and stage actor.

Appeared in: 1935 False Pretenses. 1937 High Flyers; She's Got Everything. 1942 This Above All; Mrs. Miniver. 1947 Ivy.

CLIFTON-JAMES, M. E.
Born: 1898. Died: May 8, 1963, Worthing, England. Screen, stage actor, screenwriter and author. He impersonated Field Marshal Montgomery so well he was used by British Intelligence to confuse the Germans during W.W.II.

Appeared in: 1948 Blanche Fury. 1959 I Was Monty's Double (which he also wrote).

CLINE, EDDIE (Edward Francis Cline)
Born: Nov. 7, 1892, Kenosha, Wis. Died: May 22, 1961, Hollywood, Calif. Screen actor, film director and screenwriter. Entered films as an actor with Keystone in 1913.

Appeared in: 1921 The Haunted House.

CLINTON-BADDELEY, V. V.
Born: 1900. Died: Aug. 6, 1970, London, England. Screen, stage actor, screenwriter and radio writer.

CLITHEROE, JIMMY
Born: 1923, England. Died: June 6, 1973, England? Screen actor.

Appeared in: 1967 Jules Verne's Rocket to the Moon (aka Those Fantastic Flying Fools and Blast-Off—US).

CLIVE, COLIN (Colin Clive Greig)
Born: Jan. 20, 1900, St. Malo, France. Died: June 25, 1937, Los Angeles, Calif. (pulmonary and intestinal ailment). Stage and screen actor. Married to actress/playwright Jeanne de Casalis (dec. 1966).

Appeared in: 1930 Journey's End. 1931 The Stronger Sex; Frankenstein. 1932 Lily Christine. 1933 Christopher Strong; Looking Forward. 1934 Jane Eyre; The Key; One More River. 1935 Bride of Frankenstein; Clive of India; The Hands of Orlac; The Right to Live; The Widow From Monte Carlo; The Girl from 10th Avenue; Mad Love; The Man Who Broke the Bank of Monte Carlo. 1937 History is Made at Night; The Woman I Love.

CLIVE, E. E. (Edward E. Clive)
Born: Aug. 28, 1883, Monmouthshire, Wales. Died: June 6, 1940, North Hollywood, Calif. (heart attack). Screen, stage actor, film producer and film director. Appeared as "Tenny" in the Bulldog Drummond series, 1937-1939. Married to actress Eleanor Ellis (dec. 1982).

Appeared in: 1933 The Invisible Man. 1934 The Gay Divorce; The Poor Rich; Tin Pants; Bulldog Drummond Strikes Back; Charlie Chan in London; One More River; Long Lost Father; Riptide; Service; Bulldog Drummond. 1935 The Man Who Broke the Bank at Monte Carlo; The Gold Diggers of 1935; Atlantic Adventure; Father Brown, Detective; Sylvia Scarlett; The Widow From Monte Carlo; The Mystery of Edwin Drood; The Bride of Frankenstein; Remember Last Night?; We're in the Money; Stars Over Broadway; A Tale of Two Cities; Captain Blood. 1936 Showboat; Little Lord Fauntleroy; Love Before Breakfast; Dracula's Daughter; The Unguarded Hour; Trouble For Two; Piccadilly Jim; All American Chump; Libeled Lady; Tarzan Escapes; Camille; The Golden Arrow; Isle of Fury; Charge of the Light Brigade; Cain and Mabel; Palm Springs; Tickets to Paradise; Lloyds of London; The Dark Hour. 1937 They Wanted to Marry; Maid of Salem; Bulldog Drummond Escapes; Bulldog Drummond Comes Back; Bulldog Drummond's Revenge; Ready, Willing and Able; On the Avenue; Love Under Fire; Danger—Love at Work; Personal Property; Night Must Fall; The Emperor's Candlesticks; Live, Love and Learn; Beg, Borrow or Steal. 1938 Bulldog Drummond's Peril; Bulldog Drummond in Africa; Arsene Lupin Returns; The First Hundred Years; The Last Warning; Kidnapped; Gateway; Submarine Patrol. 1939 We Are Not Alone; Mr. Moto's Last Warning; Arrest Bulldog Drummond; The Little Princess; I'm From Missouri; Bulldog Drummond's Secret Police; Bulldog Drummond's Bride; Man About Town; The Hound of the Baskervilles; Rose of Washington Square; The Adventures of Sherlock Holmes; The Honeymoon's Over; Bachelor Mother; Mr. and Mrs. Bulldog Drummond; Raffles. 1940 Foreign Correspondent; Pride and Prejudice; Earl of Chicago; Congo Maisie.

CLIVE, HENRY (Henry Clive O'Hara)
Born: Oct. 3, 1883, Melbourne, Australia. Died: Dec. 12, 1960, Hollywood, Calif. (lung cancer). Screen, stage, vaudeville actor, commercial artist and magician.

Appeared in: 1917 The Fighting Odds. 1921 Heedless Moths; The Oath. 1923 Obey the Law.

CLIVE, VINCENT
Born: Upper Norwood, England. Died: Apr. 11, 1943, England. Screen and stage actor.

Appeared in: 1913 The Eleventh Commandment. 1914 The Ring and the Rajah.

CLOINGER, RALPH
Born: Apr. 20, 1888, Tex. Died: June 17, 1962. Screen actor.

Appeared in: 1922 Monte Cristo. 1923 The Man Who Won; Hearts Aflame. 1927 Winds of the Pampas.

CLOSE, IVY
Born: 1890. Died: Dec. 4, 1968, Goring, England. Screen actress. Entered films with Britain's Hepworth Co. Mother of British film director Ronald Neame.

Appeared in: 1912 Sleeping Beauty; Dream Paintings; The Lady of Shallot; Pygmalion and Galatea; The Legend of King Cophetua. 1913 Mifanwy—A Tragedy; La Cigale. 1914 The Lure of London; Ghosts; The Hon. William's Donah; The Terrible Twins; Ivy's Elopement; Two Elderly Cupids; The Girl from the Sky. 1915 The Haunting of Silas P. Gould; Darkest London, or The Dancer's Romance. 1916 The Girl and the Terror; Peaches and Ponies; Doing the Demonstrator; He Wrote Poetry; Meter in the Kitchen; The Stolen Jail; That Pesky Parrot; The Mysterious Double; The Battered Bridegroom; Rival Artist. 1917 The Ware Case; The House Opposite; The Adventures of Dick Dolan; The Women's Land Army. 1918 Adam Bede; A Peep Behind the Scenes; Nelson; Missing the Tide. 1919 Darby and Joan; The Irresistible Flappper; The Flag Lieutenant; Her Cross. 1920 The Worldings; La Roue. 1922 Expiation; Was She Justified? 1929 The Jolly Peasant.

CLOSE, JOHN
Died: Dec. 18, 1964. Screen actor.

Appeared in: **1950** Where the Sidewalk Ends. **1951** Jim Thorpe—All American; Belle Le Grand; The Guy Who Came Back; Korea Patrol; The Girl on the Bridge. **1952** Pat and Mike; Sailor Beware; We're Not Married; You For Me; Red Skies of Montana. **1953** The Farmer Takes a Wife; Above and Beyond; Torpedo Alley; Gentlemen Prefer Blondes; Fangs of the Arctic. **1954** Francis Joins the WACS; Finger Man; Sudden Danger. **1957** Chain of Evidence; Three Brave Men; The Storm Rider; Beginning of the End. **1958** Outcasts of the City; Street of Darkness. **1959** The Purple Gang. **1960** Pay or Die. **1962** Convicts 4. **1963** The Slime People.

CLOUD, MABEL C.
Died: June, 1921, Newkirk, Okla. Screen and stage actress.

CLOUZOUT, VERA
Died: Dec. 15, 1960, Paris, France (possible heart attack). Screen actress. Married to film director Henri Georges Clouzout (dec. 1977).

Appeared in: **1955** Diabolique. **1956** Wages of Fear. **1957** Les Espions.

CLOVELLY, CECIL
Born: 1891, England. Died: Apr. 25, 1965, New York, N.Y. Screen, stage actor and film director.

Appeared in: **1930** The Forest Ring. **1950** So Young, So Bad. **1951** Two Gals and a Guy.

CLUNES, ALEC S.
Born: May 17, 1912, Brixton, London, England. Died: Mar. 13, 1970, London, England (lung ailment). Screen, stage actor, stage producer and stage director. Son of stage actor Alexander Sheriff Sydney Clunes and stage actress Georgina Sumner Clunes.

Appeared in: **1940** Convoy; Sailors Three (aka Three Cockeyed Sailors—US 1941). **1941** Saloon Bar (US 1944). **1942** One of Our Aircraft is Missing. **1949** Now Barabbas. **1953** Melba. **1955** Adventures of Quentin Durward; Richare III (US 1956). **1956** Tiger in the Smoke. **1962** Tomorrow at Ten (US 1964).

CLUTE, CHESTER L.
Born: 1891. Died: Apr. 5, 1956, Woodland Hills, Calif. (heart attack). Screen actor. Married to actress Eleanor Hicks (dec. 1936).

Appeared in: **1930** The Jay Walker (short). **1931** The Antique Shop (short). **1932** The Babbling Book (short). **1933** Walking the Baby (short). **1937** Dance, Charlie, Dance; The Great Garrick; He Couldn't Say No; Navy Blues; The Wrong Road; Exclusive; There Goes My Girl; Living on Love. **1938** Change of Heart; Touchdown Army; Rascals; Pardon Our Nerve; Comet Over Broadway; Annabel Takes a Tour; Service DeLuxe; Mr. Chump. **1939** Dodge City; I Was a Convict; Dancing Co-ed; Laugh It Of; Too Busy to Work; East Side of Heaven. **1940** My Favorite Wife; The Doctor Takes a Wife; Hired Wife; Millionaires in Prison; Dance, Girl, Dance; Too Many Girls; Love Thy Neighbor. **1941** Manpower; Footlight Fever; Wedding Worries (short); She Couldn't Say No; Hold Back the Dawn; Sun Valley Serenade; Scattergood Meets Broadway; Niagra Falls; The Perfect Snob; The Man Who Came to Dinner. **1942** The Lady is Willing; The Gun for Hire; Larceny, Inc.; The Wife Takes a Flyer; Yankee Doodle Dandy; Just Off Broadway; The Forest Rangers; My Favorite Spy; George Washington Slept Here; Star Spangled Rhythm. **1943** Chatterbox; The Desperadoes; Someone to Remember; The Good Fellows; So's Your Uncle; Here Comes Elmer; Crazy House. **1944** Lake Placid Serenade; Arsenic and Old Lace; Radio Bugs (short); Nothing But the Truth; Bermuda Mystery; Hat Check Honey; Rationing; San Diego, I Love You; The Reckless Age; Johnny Doesn't Live Here Anymore. **1945** The Clock; She Gets Her Man; She Went to the Races; Saratoga Trunk; Let's Go Stepping (short); Guest Wife; The Man Who Walked Alone; Anchors Aweigh; Arson Squad; Blonde Ransom; Mildred Pierce; Earl Carroll Vanities. **1946** Angel on My Shoulder; Cinderella Jones; One Exciting Week; Social Terrors (short); Spook Busters. **1947** Easy Come, Easy Go; Suddenly It's Spring; Hit Parade of 1947; Web of Danger; Joe Palooka in the Knockout; The Crimson Key; Host to a Ghost (short); Something in the Wind. **1948** On Our Merry Way; Mary Lou; Winner Take All; The Strange Mrs. Crane; Train to Alcatraz; Jiggs and Maggie in Court; Blondie's Reward. **1949** Master Minds; Square Dance Jubilee; Ringside; Blondie's Big Deal. **1950** Luck Losers; Joe Palooka in Humphrey Takes a Chance; Mary Ryan, Detective. **1951** Kentucky Jubilee; Punchy Pancho (short); So You Want to Be a Bachelor (short); Stop That Cab. **1952** Colorado Sundown.

CLUZETTI, JULES
Born: 1861. Died: Apr. 27, 1927, New Orleans, La. Screen and stage actor.

Appeared in: **1915** The Reformer; Zabliltsky's Waterloo.

CLYDE, ANDY
Born: Mar. 25, 1892, Blairgowrie, Scotland. Died: May 18, 1967, Los Angeles, Calif. Screen, stage and television actor. Brother of actor David Clyde (dec. 1945) and actress Jean Clyde (dec. 1962). Married to actress Elsie Maud Tarron, Mack Sennett bathing beauty. Appeared in numerous westerns including several Hopalong Cassidy series films.

Appeared in: **1926** The following shorts: Whispering Whiskers; Circus Today; Ice Cold Cocos; A Sea Dog's Tale. **1928** Branded Man; The Goodbye Kiss; Blindfold (short). **1929** Should a Girl Marry?; Ships of the Night; Midnight Daddies; plus the following shorts: The Lunkhead; The Golfers; A Hollywood Star; Clancy at the Bat; The New Halfback; Uppercut O'Brien; The Bride's Relations; The Old Barn; Whirls and Girls; The Bee's Buzz; The Big Palooka; Girl Crazy; The Barber's Daughter; The Constable. **1930** The following shorts: Scotch; Sugar Plum Papa; Match Play; Fat Wives for Thin; Campus Crushes; The Chumps; Goodbye Legs; Hello Television; Average Husband; Vacation Loves; Radio Kisses; The Bluffer; Grandma's Girl; Take Your Medicine; Don't Bite Your Dentist; Racket Cheers; Bulls and Bears. **1931** The following shorts: Speed; Taxi Troubles; Half Holiday; No, No, Lady; The College Vamp; The Dog Doctor; Just a Bear; In Conference; The Cow-Catcher's Daughter; Ghost Parade; Monkey Business in Africa; Fainting Lover; Too Many Husbands; The Cannonball; All-American Kickback; Great Pie Mystery. **1932** Million Dollar Legs; plus the following shorts: Shopping With Wifie; Heavens! My Husband; Speed in the Gay Nineties; The Boudoir Butler; Alaska Love; Her Royal Shyness; The Giddy Age; Sunkissed Sweeties; For the Love of Ludwig; A Fool About Women; Boy Oh Boy; The following shorts: Artist's Muddles; Feeling Rosy; Loose Relations; Big Squeal; Dora's Dunkin' Donuts; His Weak Moment; Frozen Assets. **1934** The Little Minister; plus the following shorts: Super Snooper; Hello Prosperity; Half-Baked Relations; An Old Gyspy Custom; In the Dog House. **1935** Romance in Manhattan; McFadden's Flats; The Village Tale; Annie Oakley; plus the following shorts: I'm A Father; Old Sawbones; Tramp, Tramp, Tramp; Alimony Aches; It Always Happens; Hot Paprika. **1936** Yellow Dust; Straight From the Shoulder; Two In a Crowd; Red Lights Ahead; plus the following shorts: Caught in the Act; Share the Wealth; Peppery Salt; Mister Smarty; Am I Having Fun; Love Comes to Mooneyville. **1937** The Barrier; plus the following shorts: Knee Action; Stuck in the Sticks; My Little Feller; Lodge Night; Gracie at the Bat; He Done His Duty. **1938** The following shorts: The Old Raid Mule; Jump, Chum, Jump; Ankles Away; Soul of a Heel; Not Guilty Enough; Home on the Rage. **1939** It's a Wonderful World; Bad Lands; plus the following shorts: Swing, You Swingers; Boom Goes the Groom; Now It Can Be Sold; Trouble Finds Andy Clyde; All-American Blondes; Andy Clyde Gets Spring Chicken. **1940** Cherokee Strip; Three Men From Texas; Abe Lincoln in Illinois; Hopalong Cassidy; plus the following shorts: Mr. Clyde Goes to Broadway; Money Squawks; Boobs in the Woods; Fireman, Save My Choo Choo; A Bundle of Bliss. **1941** Doomed Caravan; In Old Colorado; Pirates on Horseback; Men of Action; Wide Open Town; Riders of the Timberline; Twilight on the Trail; Stick to Your Guns; Secret of the Wastelands; Outlaws of the Desert; Border Vigilantes; plus the following shorts: The Watchman Takes a Wife; Ring and the Belle; Yankee Doodle Andy; Host to a Ghost; Lovable Trouble. **1942** Undercover Man; This Above All; plus the following shorts: Sappy Birthday; How Spry I Am; All Work and No Pay; Sappy Pappy. **1943** Lost Canyon; Border Patrol; The Leather Burners; Hoppy Serves a Writ; Missing Men; False Colors; Bar 20; Sunset Riders; Colt Comrades; plus the following shorts: Wolf in Thief's Clothing; A Maid Made Mad; Farmer for a Day; He Was Only Feudin'. **1944** Texas Masquerade; Riders of the Deadline; Lumberjack; Forty Thieves; Mystery Man; plus the following shorts: His Tale Is Told; You Were Never Uglier; Gold Is Where You Lose It; Heather and Yon'. **1945** Roughly Speaking; Son of the Prairie; plus the following shorts: A Miner Affair; Spook to Me; Two Local Yokels. **1946** The Devil's Playground; Fool's Gold; The Green Years; That Texas Jamboree; Throw a Saddle on a Star; The Plainsman and the Lady; Unexpected Guest; plus the following shorts: The Blonde Stayed On; Andy Plays Hooky. **1947** The Marauders; Hoppy's Holiday; Dangerous Venture; plus the following shorts: Two Jills and a Jack; Wife to Spare. **1948** Strange Gamble; The Dead Don't Dream; Silent Conflict; False Paradise; plus the following shorts: Eight-Ball Andy; Go Chase Yourself; Sinister Journey; Borrowed Trouble. **1949** Crashing Thru; Riders of the Dusk; Shadows of the West; Haunted Trails; Range Land; Sunk in the Sink (short). **1950** Gunslingers; Silver Raiders; Fence Riders; Arizona Territory; Outlaws of Texas; Cherokee Uprising; plus the following shorts: Marinated Mariner; A Blunderful Time. **1951** Abilene Trail; Blonde Atom Bomb (short). **1952** A Blissful Blunder (short); Hooked and Rooked (short). **1953** The following shorts: Fresh Painter; Pardon My Wrench; Love's A-Poppin'; Oh, Say, Can You Sue. **1954** Two April Fools (short). **1955** Caroline Cannonball; The Road to Denver; plus the following shorts: Scratch, Scratch, Scratch; One Spooky Night. **1956** Andy Goes Wild (short); Pardon My Nightshirt (short). **1960** When Comedy Was King (documentary). **1963** Thirty Years of Fun (documentary); The Sound of Laughter (documentary).

CLYDE, DAVID

Born: 1855. Died: May 17, 1945, San Fernando Valley, Calif. Screen actor. Married to actress Fay Holden (dec, 1973). Brother of actor Andy (dec. 1967) and actress Jean Clyde (dec. 1962).

Appeared in: **1935** Cardinal Richelieu; Hard Rock Harrigan; The Man on the Flying Trapeze; Bonnie Scotland. **1936** Suzy. **1937** Lost Horizon; Fury and the Woman; Another Dawn; Love Under Fire. **1938** If I Were King; Bulldog Drummond's Peril; Kidnapped. **1939** We Are Not Alone; Arrest Bulldog Drummond; Bulldog Drummond's Secret Police; Death of a Champion; Captain Fury; Ruler of the Sea. **1940** The Philadelphia Story. **1941** Smilin' Through; Blossoms in the Dust; The Feminine Touch; H. M. Pulham, Esq. **1942** Son of Fury; Nightmare; Random Harvest; Mrs. Miniver; The Gay Sisters; Now, Voyager; Eagle Squadron. **1944** Jane Eyre; Frenchman's Creek; None But the Lonely Heart; The Hour Before the Dawn; The Lodger; The Scarlet Claw. **1945** The Lost Weekend; Molly and Me; Love Letters; Molly, Bless Her; The House of Fear. **1946** Two Years Before the Most.

CLYDE, JEAN

Born: 1889. Died: July, 1962, Helensburgh, Scotland. Screen actress. Sister of actors Andy (dec. 1967) and David Clyde (dec. 1945).

CLYMER, BETH

Born: 1887. Died: Jan. 14, 1952, Woodland Hills, Calif. (heart attack). Screen actress.

COAD, ALAN

Born: 1913, South Australia. Died: Feb. 21, 1980, Sydney, Australia. Screen, radio actor and opera singer.

COATES, PAUL

Born: 1921. Died: Nov. 17, 1968, West Hollywood, Calif. (heart attack). Columnist, television commentator and screen actor. Do not confuse with singer Richard Paul Coates (dec. 1972).

Appeared in: **1957** The Tijuana Story.

COATS, THOMAS J. "TOMMY"

Born: 1901. Died: June 6, 1954, Los Angeles, Calif. Screen actor.

Appeared in: **1943** Fugitive From Sonora. **1946** Sioux City Sue; The Phantom Rider (serial). **1948** Grand Canyon Trail. **1949** San Antone Ambush.

COBB, EDMUND F.

Born: 1892, Albuquerque, New Mexico. Died: Aug. 15, 1974, Woodland Hills, Calif. (heart attack). Screen and stage actor. Entered films in 1910.

Appeared in: **1915** Fifty-Fifty; The Destroyer; The Second Son; The Papered Door; Ties That Meet; Mind Over Motor; Brought Home; Tish's Spy; The Circular Path. **1916** Once a Thief; Captain Jinks of the Horse Marines; The Face in the Mirror; The War Bride of Plumville; The Condemnation; A Little Volunteer; The Promise Land; Money to Burn. **1917** Moral Courage. **1918** Social Briars. **1920** Wolves of the Street; Desert Scorpion. **1921** Finders Keepers; Out of the Depths. **1923** The Law Rustlers; Battling Bates; At Devil's Gorge; The Miracle Baby; Riders of the Range; Playing It Wild; The Sting of the Scorpion. **1924** A Rodeo Mix-Up; Western Yesterday; Blasted Hopes; Days of '49 (serial); Cupid's Rustler; California in '49 (feature made of Days of '49 serial); Midnight Shadows; Range Blood; Western Feuds. **1925** The Burning Trail. **1926** General Custer at Little Big Horn; The Galloping Cowboy; The Terror; Looking for Trouble; The Scrappin' Kid; Fighting With Buffalo Bill (serial). **1927** Fangs of Destiny; Wolf's Trail. **1928** Call of the Heart; The Fighting Redhead; The Hound of Silver Creek; The Four-Footed Ranger; Young Whirlwind. **1929** A Final Reckoning (serial). **1930** Beyond the Rio Grande; The Indians Are Coming (serial). **1931** Law of the Rio Grande. **1932** Human Targets; Lone Trail; Tangled Fortunes; Rider of Death Valley; Heroes of the West (serial); The Lost Special (serial). **1933** Clancy of the Mounted (serial); Gordon of Ghost City (serial); Fourth Horseman; Deadwood Pass; Rusty Rides Alone. **1934** Mystery Mountain (serial); Tracy Rides; Racketeer Roundup; Tailspin Tommy (serial); The Law of the Wild (serial); The Red Rider (serial); The Vanishing Shadow (serial). **1935** Rustlers of Red Dog (serial); Stormy; Rustler's Paradise; The Miracle Rider; The Westerner; Gunners and Guns. **1936** The Fugitive Sheriff; Darkest Africa (serial); Ace Drummond (serial); Showboat; The Adventures of Frank Merriwell (serial). **1937** Zorro Rides Again (serial); The Mighty Treve; Springtime in the Rockies; Sergeant Murphy; Cherokee Strip. **1938** Wild Horse Rodeo; I'm from the City; Outlaws of the Prairie; Cattle Raiders; West of Cheyenne; Law of the Plains; Colorado Trail; Call of the Rockies; South of Arizona; Fighting Devil Dogs (serial). **1939** Zorro's Fighting Legion (serial); Twelve Crowded Hours; Blue Montana Skies; West of Santa Fe; Spoilers of the Range; Western Caravans; Riders of Black River; Outpost of the Mounties; Stranger from Texas. **1940** West of Carson City; One Man's Law; Prairie Schooners; Melody Ranch; How High is Up? (short); Deadwood Dick; Blazing Six Shooters; Winners of the West (serial); Pony Post. **1941** Citizen Kane; Prairie Stranger; The Son of Davy Crockett; The Medico of Painted Springs; Wyoming Wildcat; Back in the Saddle; I Was a Prisoner on Devil's Island; Texas; North from the Lone Star; So You Won't Squawk (short); The Wildcat of Tucson; The Return of Daniel Boone; The Lone Star Vigilantes; Man from Montana. **1942** Two Yanks in Trinidad; Down Rio Grande Way; Heart of the Rio Grande; Stardust on the Sage; Westward Ho; Deep in the Heart of Texas; The Glass Key; Alias Boston Blackie. **1943** Silver City Raiders; Fighting Devil Dogs; The Old Chisholm Trail; Riding Through Nevada; Mission to Moscow; The Ghost Rider; The Stranger from Pecos; Frontier Fury; Jack London. **1944** Law Men; House of Frankenstein; Outlaws of Santa Fe; West of the Rio Grande; Raiders of the Border; Call of the Rockies (and 1938 version); Song of the Range; The Old Texas Trail; Cyclone Prairie Rangers; The Missing Juror; Double Indemnity. **1945** Secret Agent X-9 (serial); The Man from Oklahoma; The Falcon in San Francisco; Law of the Valley. **1946** The Falcon's Alibi; Song of Arizona; Days of Buffalo Bill; Galloping Thunder; Roaring Rangers; The El Paso Kid; Sun Valley Cyclone; Last Frontier Uprising; Red River Renegades; Rustler's Round-Up; Santa Fe Uprising; Rio Grande Raiders; The Scarlet Horseman (serial); The Phantom Thief. **1947** Son of Zorro (serial); Brute Force; The Homestretch; Jesse James Rides Again (serial); The Vigilante (serial); Robin Hood of Texas; Stage Coach to Denver; Oregon Trail Scouts; The Wistful Widow of Wagon Gap; Flashing Guns; Law of the Canyon; Riders of the Lone Star; Land of the Lawless; Buffalo Bill Rides Again. **1948** Pride of Virginia; The Bold Frontiersman; River Lady; Feudin', Fussin' and A-Fightin'; Carson City Raiders; The Far Frontier; Hidden Danger; The Mystery of the Golden Eye; G-Men Never Forget (serial); Fury at Furnace Creek; The Street With No Name; Family Honeymoon. **1949** Red Canyon; Take One False Step; The Daring Caballero; Sheriff of Wichita; The Wyoming Bandit; Gun Law Justice; San Antone Ambush. **1950** The Girl from San Lorenzo; Arizona Cowboy; Comanche Territory; The Vanishing Westerner; Bells of Coronado; Hills of Oklahoma; Frisco Tornado; Desperadoes of the West (serial); The James Brothers of Missouri (serial); Winchester 73. **1951** Detective Story; Government Agents vs. Phantom Legion (serial); Blazing Bullets; Montana Desperado. **1952** Something for the Birds; Confidence Girl; Ma and Pa Kettle at the Fair; Carson City; The Redhead from Wyoming. **1953** All I Desire; Canadian Mounties vs. Atomic Invaders (serial). **1954** Man With the Steel Whip (serial); The Egyptian; Ma and Pa Kettle at Home; Broken Lance; River of No Return. **1955** The Girl in the Red Velvet Swing; Lucy Gallant; The Violent Men; How to Be Very, Very Popular. **1956** The True Story of Jesse James; Hidden Guns; The Oklahoma Woman. **1957** The Amazing Colossal Man; Dragstrip Girl; Motorcycle Gang. **1958** The Last Hurrah. **1962** Tales of Terror; The Underwater City. **1965** The Bounty Killer; Requiem for a Gunfighter. **1966** Johnny Reno.

COBB, IRVIN S.

Born: June 23, 1876, Paducah, Ky. Died: Mar. 11, 1944, New York, N.Y. Screen, radio actor, humorist, playwright, novelist, screenwriter and newspaperman.

Appeared in: **1914** Our Mutual Girl # 33. **1915** The Arab. **1921** Pardon My French; Peck's Bad Boy. **1922** The Five Dollar Baby. **1924** The Great White Way. **1927** Turkish Delight. **1932** An Old City Speaks (short—narr.). **1934** Judge Priest; a series of MGM shorts. **1935** Steamboat 'Round the Bend; La Fiesta de Santa Barbara (short). **1936** Everybody's Old Man; Pepper. **1938** Hawaii Calls; The Arkansas Traveler; The Young in Heart.

COBB, LEE J. (Leo Jacoby)

Born: Dec. 8, 1911, New York, N.Y. Died: Feb. 11, 1976, Woodland Hills, Calif. (heart attack). Screen, stage, radio and television actor. Divorced from actress Helen Beverly. Later married to Mary Hirsch. Nominated for 1954 Academy Award as Best Supporting Actor for On the Waterfront and in 1958 for The Brothers Karmazov.

Appeared in: **1937** North of the Rio Grande (film debut); Ali Baba Goes to Town; Rustler's Valley. **1938** Danger on the Air. **1939** Golden Boy (and stage version); The Phantom Creeps (serial). **1941** This Thing Called Love; Men of Boys Town; Paris Calling. **1943** Song of Bernadette; The Moon is Down; Tonight We Raid Calais; Buckskin Frontier. **1944** Winged Victory. **1946** Anna and the King of Siam. **1947** Boomerang; Captain from Castile; Johnny O'Clock. **1948** Call Northside 777; The Luck of the Irish; The Dark Past; Miracle of the Bells. **1949** Thieves' Highway. **1950** The Man who Cheated Himself. **1951** Sirocco; Family Secret. **1952** The Fighter (aka The First Time). **1953** The Tall Texan. **1954** Yankee Pasha; On the Waterfront; Gorilla at Large; Day of Triumph. **1955** The Road to Denver; The Left Hand of God; The Racers. **1956** The Man in the Gray Flannel Suit; Miami Expose. **1957** Three Faces of Eve; Twelve Angry Men; The Garment Jungle. **1958** The Brothers Karamazov; Man of the West; Party Girl. **1959** The Trap; Green Mansions; But Not For Me. **1960** Exodus. **1962** How the West Was Won; Four Horsemen of the Apocalypse. **1963** Come Blow Your Horn. **1966** Our Man Flint. **1967** In Like Flint. **1968** Coogan's Bluff; Il Giono'della Civetta (aka La Maffia Fait la Loi and aka Mafia—US 1970). **1969** MacKenna's Gold; They Came to Rob Las Vegas. **1970** The Liberation of L. B. Jones; Macho Callahan. **1971** Lawman. **1973** The Exorcist; The Man Who Loved Cat Dancing; La Polizia sta a Guardare (The Police Look On). **1974** Venditore di Palloncini (The Balloon Vender). **1975** Mark il Poliziotto (Mark of the Cop); Ultimatum alla Citta; That Lucky Touch. **1976** Mafia. **1977** Ultimatum.

COBB, TY (Tyrus Raymond Cobb)
Born: Dec. 18, 1886, Narrows, Georgia. Died: July 17, 1961, Atlanta, Ga. Professional baseball player and screen actor.

Appeared in: **1916** Somewhere in Georgia. **1942** The Ninth Inning. **1951** Angels in the Outfield.

COBORN, CHARLES (Colin Whitton McCallum)
Born: 1852, England. Died: Nov. 23, 1945, London, England. Screen, revue, stage actor and songwriter. Do not confuse with U.S. actor Charles Coburn.

Appeared in: **1934** Say It With Flowers. **1936** Pictorial Revue; Old Timers. **1943** Variety Jubilee.

COBURN, CHARLES DOUVILLE
Born: June 19, 1877, Savannah, Ga. Died: Aug. 30, 1961, N.Y. (heart ailment). Screen, stage, radio, television actor, stage producer and stage director. Won 1943 Academy Award for Best Supporting Actor in The More the Merrier and was nominated for 1941 Best Supporting Actor in The Devil and Miss Jones and in 1946 for The Green Years. Married to stage actress Ivah Wills (dec, 1937) and later to Winifred Natzka.

Appeared in: **1933** Boss Tweed. **1935** The People's Enemy. **1938** Idiot's Delight; Bachelor Mother; The Story of Alexander Graham Bell; Stanley and Livingstone; Made for Each Other; In Name Only. **1940** Road to Singapore; Edison the Man; The Captain Is a Lady; Three Faces West; Florian; Refugee. **1941** The Devil and Miss Jones; H. M. Pulham, Esq; The Lady Eve; Our Wife; Unexpected Uncle; Kind's Row. **1942** In This Our Life; George Washington Slept Here. **1943** The More the Merrier; The Constant Nymph; Heaven Can Wait; Princess O'Rourke; My Kindgdom for a Cook. **1944** Since You Went Away; Knickerbocker Holiday; Wilson; The Impatient Years; Together Again. **1945** A Royal Scandal; Colonel Effingham's Raid; Shady Lady; Over 21; Rhapsody in Blue. **1946** The Green Years; Man of the Hour. **1947** Lured; Personal Column. **1948** B. F.'s Daughter; Green Grass of Wyoming; Rose of Singapore; The Paradine Case. **1949** The Doctor and the Girl; Everybody Does It; The Gal Who Took the West; Impact; Yes Sir, That's My Baby. **1950** Louisa; Mr. Music; Peggy. **1951** The Highwayman; Oh Money, Money. **1952** Monkey Business; Has Anybody Seen My Gal?; Alma Mater. **1953** Gentlemen Prefer Blondes; Trouble Along the Way. **1954** The Rocket Man; The Long Wait. **1955** How to Be Very, Very Popular. **1956** Around the World in 80 Days; The Power and the Prize. **1957** How to Murder a Rich Uncle; Town on Trial; The Story of Mankind; Uncle George. **1959** The Remarkable Mr. Pennypacker; Stranger in My Arms; John Paul Jones. **1960** Pepe. **1974** That's Entertainment (film clip).

COBURN, DOROTHY "DOTTIE"
Born: June 8, 1905, Great Falls, Mont. Died: May 15, 1978, Los Angeles, Calif. (emphysema). Screen actress and stuntwoman. Daughter of film producer Wallace Coburn (dec.). Entered films in 1926.

Appeared in: **1927** Hats Off (short). **1928** The following shorts: Battle of the Century; Putting Pants on Philip; Finishing Touch; That Night; Do Gentlemen Snore. **1965** Laurel and Hardy's Laughing 20's.

COCAINE
Died: c. 1973 (euthanasia). Screen and television animal performer (horse).

Appeared in: **1949** Three Godfathers; The Fighting Kentuckian; She Wore a Yellow Ribbon. **1950** Rio Grande. **1953** Hondo. **1959** Rio Bravo; The Horse Soldiers. **1960** The Alamo. **1961** The Comancheros. **1962** The Man Who Shot Liberty Valance. **1963** McClintock; How the West Was Won. **1965** The Sons of Katie Elder. **1967** El Dorado; The War Wagon.

COCHRAN, EDDIE
Born: 1939, England? Died: Apr. 17, 1960, Bath, England (auto accident). Singer and screen actor.

COCHRAN, JACQUELINE
Born: 1906, Fla.? Died: Aug. 9, 1980, Coachella Valley, Calif. Stunt pilot and screen actress.

COCHRAN, STEVE (Robert Alexander Cochran)
Born: May 25, 1917, Eureka, Calif. Died: June 15, 1965, Pacific Ocean, off coast of Guatemala (acute infectious edema which caused swelling in a lung). Screen and stage actor. Divorced from singer Fay McKenzie and artist Florence Lockwood. Married to actress Jonna Jensen.

Appeared in: **1943** Stage Door Canteen. **1945** Boston Blackie Booked on Suspicion; Boston Blackie's Rendezvous; The Gay Senorita; Wonder Man. **1946** The Kid from Brooklyn; The Best Years of Our Lives; The Chase. **1947** Copacabana. **1948** A Song Is Born. **1949** White Heat. **1950** The Big Stickup; The West Point Story; The Damned Don't Cry; Storm Warning; Dallas; Highway 301. **1951** Raton Pass; The Tanks Are Coming; Jim Thorpe—All American; Inside the Walls of Folsom Prison; Tomorrow Is Another Day. **1952** The Lion and the Horse; Operation Secret. **1953** The Desert Song; She's Back on Broadway; Back To God's Country; Shark River. **1954** Private Hell 36; Rummelplatz Der Liebe (The Carnival Story). **1956** Come Next Spring; Slander. **1957** The Weapon; Il Grido (aka The Outcry—US 1962). **1958** I, Mobster; Quantrill's Raiders. **1959** The Big Operator; The Beat Generation (aka This Rebel Age). **1961** The Deadly Companions. **1963** Of Love and Desire. **1966** Mozambique. **1967** Tell Me in Sunlight.

COCHRANE, FRANK
Born: Oct. 28, 1882, Durham, England. Died: 1962, London, England. Screen, stage and radio actor.

Appeared in: **1930** The Yellow Mast. **1934** Chu-Chin-Chow. **1935** McGlusky the Sea Rover (aka Hell's Cargo—US 1938). **1936** The Tenth Man (US 1937). **1937** Bulldog Drummond at Bay; Jericho (aka Dark Sands—US 1938). **1938** Queer Cargo (aka Pirates of the Seven Seas—US). **1953** Ali Baba Nights.

COCKELBERG, LOUIS J.
Born: 1880. Died: July 7, 1962, Hollywood, Calif. Screen actor.

COCTEAU, JEAN (Clement Eugene Jean Maurice Cocteau)
Born: July 5, 1889, Maisons-Laffitte, France. Died: Oct. 11, 1963, Milly, France (heart attack). Screen, stage actor, film director, producer, screenwriter, playwright, musician and poet.

Appeared in: **1952** The Strange Ones. **1957** 8 x 8. **1960** Le Testament D'Orphee (The Testament of Orpheus—US 1962). **1963** Egypte O Egypte (narration). **1976** Singing Under the Occupation (documentary).

CODE, GRANT HYDE
Born: 1896. Died: June 28, 1974, New York, N.Y. Screen, stage, television actor and dancer.

Appeared in: **1961** The Young Doctors. **1962** The Miracle Worker.

CODEE, ANN
Born: 1890, Belgium. Died: May 18, 1961, Hollywood, Calif. (heart attack). Screen, television and vaudeville actress. Married to actor Frank Orth (dec. 1962). Appeared in vaudeville with her husband in an act billed "Codee and Orth."

Appeared with Orth as a team in the following shorts: **1929** A Bird in the Hand; Zwei Und Fierzigste Strasse; Stranded in Paris; Music Hath Charms; Meine Frau (Meet the Wife). **1930** Taking Ways; Imagine My Embarrassment. **1931** On the Job; Sleepy Head; Dumb Luck; The Bitter Half. Appeared without Orth in: **1935** Gaucho; Under the Pampas Moon. **1936** Hi, Gaucho; Brilliant Marriage. **1937** Expensive Husbands. **1938** Jezebel. **1939** The Roaring Twenties. **1940** Drums of the Desert; Captain Caution; Arise My Love. **1941** Come Live With Me; Charlie Chan in Rio. **1942** Woman of the Year; Reunion in France; Army Surgeon. **1943** The Youngest Profession; Paris After Dark; Tonight We Raid Calais; Old Acquaintance. **1944** Mrs. Parkington; Mr. Skeffington; The Mummy's Curse; Bathing Beauty. **1945** Secret Agent X-9 (serial); Hangover Square; This Love of Ours; Tonight and Every Night; Kitty; The Clock; Her Highness and the Bellboy. **1946** Till the Clouds Roll By; Holiday in Mexico; It's Great to Be Young; So Dark the Night. **1947** Unfinished Dance; The Other Love. **1948** Rose of Santa Rosa. **1949** That Midnight Kiss. **1950** The Secret Fury; Under My Skin; When Willie Comes Marching Home. **1951** An American in Paris; Detective Story; Go for Broke; Mr. Imperium; The Lady Pays Off; On the Riviera. **1952** What Price Glory. **1953** Kiss Me, Kate; Dangerous When Wet; War of the Worlds. **1954** So This Is Paris. **1955** Daddy Long Legs; Interrupted Melody. **1958** Kings Go Forth. **1960** Can-Can.

CODRE, DIDI
Born: Geneva, Switzerland. Died: July 2, 1981, San Francisco, Calif. Screen, stage, radio and television actress.

CODY, BILL, SR. (William Frederick Cody, Sr.)
Born: 1891. Died: Jan. 24, 1948, Santa Monica, Calif. Screen actor and rodeo performer. Father of actor Bill Cody, Jr.

Appeared in: **1924** Border Justice. **1925** Cold Nerve; Dangerous Odds; Riders of Mystery; The Fighting Sheriff; The Fighting Smile; Love on the Rio Grande; Moccasins. **1926** The Galloping Cowboy; King of the Saddle. **1927** Laddie Be Good; The Arizona Whirlwind; Born to Battle; Gold from Weepah. **1928** Price of Fear. **1929** Wolves of the City; Slim Fingers; Eyes of the Underworld; Tip Off. **1931** Under Texas Skies; Dugan of the Bad Lands; The Montana Kid; Oklahoma Jim. **1932** Texas Pioneers; Ghost City; Law of the North; Mason of the Mounted; Land of Wanted Men. **1934** Frontier Days. **1935** The Cyclone Ranger; The Texas Rambler; The Vanishing Riders; Six-Gun Justice; Lawless Border. **1936** Outlaws of the Range; Blazing Justice. **1938** Girl of the Golden West. **1939** Stagecoach; The Fighting Cowboy; The Fighting Gringo. **1948** Joan of Arc.

CODY, COLONEL WILLIAM FREDERICK (aka BUFFALO BILL)
Born: Feb. 26, 1846, Scott County, Iowa. Died: Jan. 10, 1917, Denver, Colo. Circus, rodeo performer and screen actor.

Appeared in: **1902** Parade of Buffalo Bill's West. **1911** Buffalo Bill Wild West and Pawnee Bill Far East. **1912** The Life of Buffalo Bill. **1914** The Indian Wars. **1915** Patsy of the Circus.

CODY, EMMETT F. (Emmett Francis Cody)
Born: 1920. Died: 1960. Screen actor.

Appeared in: **1944** Keys to the Kingdom; Our Hearts Were Young and Gay. **1945** Lady on the Train; State Fair. **1946** The Harvey Girls.

CODY, GENE
Born: 1894, Baltimore, Md. Died: July 10, 1976, Atlanta, Ga. Screen, stage, radio actor and stuntman. Appeared in early Keystone Kop Films.

Appeared in: **1915** Birth of a Nation. **1927** Ben Hur. **1973** Payday.

CODY, HARRY (Van Doak Covington)
Born: 1896. Died: Oct. 22, 1956, Hollywood, Calif. Screen and stage actor.

Appeared in: **1951** Callaway Went Thataway; People Against O'Hara. **1952** Singin' in the Rain. **1954** The Vanquished.

CODY, LEW (Lewis J. Cody)
Born: Feb. 22, 1887, Waterville, Maine. Died: May 31, 1934, Beverly Hills, Calif. (heart disease). Screen, stage, vaudeville actor and film producer. Married to actress Mabel Norman (dec. 1930) and divorced from actress Dorothy Dalton (dec. 1972).

Appeared in: **1915** A Branded Soul; Comrade John. **1917** Treasure of the Sea. **1918** The Demon; For Husbands Only; The Mating. **1919** Don't Change Your Husband; The Life Line; Our Better Selves. **1920** The Beloved Chester. **1921** Sign of the Door. **1922** Dangerous Pastime; The Secrets of Paris; The Valley of Silent Men. **1923** Within the Law; Rupert of Hentzau; Jacqueline of Blazing Barriers; Lawful Larceny; Souls for Sale. **1924** Reno; Husbands and Lovers; Defying the Law; Nellie, the Beautiful Cloak Model; Revelation; The Woman on the Jury; The Shooting of Dan McGrew; Three Women. **1925** The Tower of Lies; Man and Maid; Exchange of Wives; His Secretary; Slave of Fashion; So This Is Marriage?; Time, the Comedian. **1926** The Gay Deceiver; Monte Carlo. **1927** On Ze Boulevard; Adam and Evil; The Demi-Bride; Tea for Three. **1928** Beau Broadway; Wickedness Preferred; The Baby Cyclone. **1929** A Single Man. **1930** What a Widow. **1931** Dishonored; Stout Hearts and Willing Hands (short); Not Exactly Gentlemen; Common Law; Three Girls Lost; X Marks the Spot; Beyond Victory; Sweepstakes; Woman of Experience; Meet the Wife; Sporting Blood; Divorce Among Friends. **1932** The Tenderfoot; 70,000 Witnesses; The Crusader; Madison Square Garden; Unwritten Law; Undercover Man; File 113; A Parisian Romance. **1933** I Love That Man; Wine, Women and Song; By Appointment Only; Sitting Pretty. **1934** Private Scandal; Shoot the Works.

COEDEL, LUCIEN
Born: 1905. Died: Oct., 1947, France (fell from train). Screen actor.

Appeared in: **1946** Resistance; Releton d'Execution; Carmen. **1947** The Bellman. **1948** The Idiot; Portrait of Innocence. **1949** Strangers in the House; Counter Investigation.

COFFER, JACK
Born: 1939. Died: Feb. 18, 1967, Encino, Calif. (results of auto accident). Screen actor and stuntman.

Appeared in: **1967** The Way West.

COFFEY, JOHN
Born: 1909. Died: Mar. 25, 1944, Hollywood, Calif. Screen actor.

Appeared in: **1944** Since You Went Away; Sensations of 1945; Meet the People.

COFFIN, C. HAYDEN
Born: Apr. 22, 1862, Manchester, England. Died: Dec. 8, 1935, London, England. Screen and stage actor.

Appeared in: **1916** It's Always the Woman. **1917** Queen of My Heart.

COFFIN, HANK
Born: 1904, Lakeport, Calif. Died: Sept. 17, 1966, Los Angeles, Calif. Screen, television actor and stunt flyer.

Appeared in: **1930** Dawn Patrol; Hell's Angels.

COGAN, ALMA
Born: 1933. Died: Oct. 26, 1966. Screen actress.

COGAN, FANNY HAY
Born: 1866, Philadelphia, Pa. Died: May 18, 1929, N.Y. (heart disease). Screen, stage actress and opera performer. Often called "the mother of the movies."

COGDELL, JOSEPHINE
Born: 1901. Died: May 2, 1969, N.Y. Screen actress and ballet dancer. Appeared as a Mack Sennett bathing beauty.

COGGIN, BARBARA
Born: 1940. Died: Jan. 19, 1981, New York, N.Y. Screen and stage actress. Married to film publicist James Butler.

COGHLAN, CHARLES F.
Died: Mar. 18, 1972, Hershey, Pa. Screen, stage, vaudeville actor, stage producer and director.

Appeared in: **1921** Jim the Penman.

COGHLAN, KATHERINE
Born: 1889. Died: Sept. 21, 1965, Hollywood, Calif. (cancer). Screen actress (film extra 1919-20). Mother of actor Junior Coghlan.

COGHLAN, ROSE
Born: 1850, Peterborough, England. Died: Apr. 2, 1932, Harrison, N.Y. (cerebral hemorrhage). Screen and stage actress.

Appeared in: **1912** As You Like It. **1915** The Sporting Duchess. **1922** The Secrets of Paris; Beyond the Rainbow. **1923** Under the Red Rose. **1932** Hot Saturday. **1933** Jennie Gerhardt. **1934** Finishing School.

COGLEY, NICHOLAS "NICK" (Nicholas P. J. Cogley)
Born: 1869, N.Y. Died: May 20, 1936, Santa Monica, Calif. (following operation). Screen, stage actor and film director. Entered films with Selig.

Appeared in: **1913** Mabel's Heroes; Mother's Boy. **1915** Peanuts and Bullets; A Lucky Leap; Saved by the Wireless. **1916** Dizzy Heights and Daring Hearts; Hearts and Sparks; A La Cabaret; Dollars and Sense (sometimes referred to as The Twins). **1917** Her Circus Knight (sometimes referred to as The Circus Girl); Oriental Love. **1919** Toby's Bow. **1920** Jes' Call Me Jim. **1921** Beating the Game; Boys Will Be Boys; Guile of Women; The Old Nest; An Unwilling Hero. **1922** The Marriage Chance; One Clear Call; Restless Souls. **1923** Crinoline and Romance; Desire. **1924** Abraham Lincoln. **1927** The Missing Link; The Heart of Maryland; In Old Kentucky; Hey! Hey! Cowboy. **1928** Abie's Irish Rose. **1930** Ranch House Blues; The Cohens and the Kellys in Africa. **1933** Cross Fire.

COHAN, GEORGE M.
Born: July 4, 1878, Providence, R.I. Died: Nov. 3, 1942, New York, N.Y. (cancer). Screen, stage, vaudeville, radio actor, songwriter, stage producer, screenwriter and playwright. Appeared in vaudeville as "The Cohan Mirthmakers." Divorced from actress Ethel Levey (dec. 1955).

Appeared in: **1917** Seven Keys to Baldpate; Broadway Jones. **1918** Hit-the-Trail-Haliday. **1932** The Phantom President. **1934** Gambling.

COHN, JULIA
Born: Apr. 9, 1902, New York, N.Y. Died: Apr. 10, 1975, New York, N.Y. (heart attack). Screen, stage actress and attorney.

Appeared in: **1967** The Producers.

COLBOURNE, MAURICE
Born: Sept. 24, 1894, Cuddington, Cheshire, England. Died: Sept. 22, 1965. Screen, stage, television actor and stage director.

Appeared in: **1924** Monsieur Beaucaire. **1925** The Swan. **1953** King of the Khyber Rifles. **1956** Brothers in Law.

COLBURN, CARRIE
Born: 1859. Died: May 23, 1932, New York, N.Y. Screen and stage actress.

Appeared in: **1924** A Society Scandal.

COLBY, BARBARA
Born: July 2, 1940, New York, N.Y. Died: July 24, 1975, Palms, Calif. (murdered—shot). Screen, stage and television actress.

Appeared in: **1968** Petulia. **1974** California Split; The Memory of Us. **1975** Rafferty and the Gold Dust Twins.

COLBY, HERBERT
Born: 1839. Died: Feb. 6, 1911, Brooklyn, N.Y. Screen actor.

COLCORD, MABEL
Born: 1872, San Francisco, Calif. Died: June 6, 1952, Los Angeles, Calif. Stage and screen actress.

Appeared in: **1933** Little Women. **1934** Sadie McKee. **1935** The Irish in Us; No More Ladies; David Copperfield; Reckless. **1936** Camile; The Story of Louis Pasteur; The Law in Her Hands; Three Married Men. **1937** The Great O'Malley. **1938** Holiday; Out West with the Hardys; The Cowboy and the Lady. **1939** The Women. **1942** Invisible Agent.

COLE, BRIAN
Born: 1944, Portland, Ore. Died: Aug. 2, 1972, Hollywood, Calif. Screen actor, writer and singer. He was a member of the "Association" rock group.

COLE, BUDDY (Edwin LeMar Cole)
Born: Dec. 15, 1916, Irving, Ill. Died: Nov. 5, 1964, Hollywood, Calif. (heart attack). Screen, radio actor, pianist, composer and musical arranger.

Appeared in: **1949** Johnny Holiday. **1954** A Star Is Born.

COLE, CHARLOTTE RENE
Born: 1869, Pa. Died: Oct. 2, 1956, Port Chester, N.Y. Screen and radio actress.

COLE, "COZY" (William R. Cole)
Born: 1910, East Orange, N.J. Died: Jan. 29, 1981, Columbus, Ohio (cancer). Black screen, stage actor and musician.

Appeared in: **1954** The Glenn Miller Story.

COLE, FRED
Born: 1901. Died: Sept. 20, 1964, Hollywood, Calif. Screen actor.

Appeared in: **1924** Dangerous Blonde. **1925** Daring Days; Secrets of the Night; Two-Fisted Jones.

COLE, JACK
Born: 1914. Died: Feb. 17, 1974, Los Angeles, Calif. Screen, stage actor, dancer and choreographer.

Appeared in: **1941** Moon Over Miami. **1944** Kismet. **1957** Designing Woman. **1966** The Case of the Stripping Wives.

COLE, JOHNNY
Died: Mar. 25, 1974. Screen actor.

COLE, LESTER
Born: 1900. Died: Mar. 4, 1962, New York, N.Y. Screen, stage actor and singer.

Appeared in: **1929** Desert Song; Painted Faces. **1930** Love at First Sight.

COLE, MARY KEITH
Born: 1914. Died: Mar. 16, 1975, San Jose, Calif. Screen, stage, vaudeville actress and singer.

Appeared in: **1938** He Loved an Actress.

COLE, NAT "KING" (Nathaniel Adams Coles)
Born: Mar. 17, 1919, Montgomery, Ala. Died: Feb. 15, 1965, Santa Monica, Calif. (lung cancer). Black screen, television actor, singer and composer.

Appeared in: **1945** See My Lawyer. **1949** Make Believe Ballroom. **1953** The Blue Gardenia; Small Town Girl. **1955** Kiss Me Deadly. **1956** The Scarlet Hour. **1957** Istanbul; China Gate. **1958** St. Louis Blues. **1959** The Night of the Quarter Moon. **1965** Cat Ballou.

COLEAN, CHUCK
Born: 1908. Died: Jan. 8, 1971, Hollywood, Calif. (cancer). Screen actor, extra, stuntman and assistant film director.

COLEBY, A. E.
Born: England. Died: July, 1930, England? Screen actor, film director and screenwriter.

Appeared in: **1907** Serving a Summons. **1908** For Baby's Sake; A Fight for Honour; His Wedding Morn; A Traitor to His King. **1909** Boxing Fever. **1910** 'Twixt Red Man and White; Vice Versa; A Bolt from the Blue; A Rake's Romance. **1912** The Widow's Legacy. **1915** The Lure of Drink; The Fighting Cobbler (aka The Cobbler). **1916** Kent the Fighting Man; The Treasure of Heaven. **1917** A Pit-Boy's Romance; A Strong Man's Weakness (aka The Will of the People); The Village Blacksmith; Holy Orders; For All Eternity. **1918** Matt; The Secret Woman; The Great Game. **1920** The Way of the World; The Call of the Road. **1921** The Right to Live. **1922** The Peacemaker; Long Odds. **1924** The Great Prince Shan. **1925** The Call of the Road (reissue of 1920 film).

COLEE, FOREST R.
Born: 1893. Died: Feb. 10, 1962, Calif. Screen actor.

Appeared in: **1950** Colt .45.

COLEMAN, CHARLES
Born: Dec. 22, 1885, Sydney, Australia. Died: Mar. 8, 1951, Woodland Hills, Calif. (stroke). Screen, stage and television actor.

Appeared in: **1923** Big Dan; Second Hand Love. **1924** That French Lady; The Vagabond Trail. **1926** Sand. **1928** Good Morning, Judge; That's My Daddy. **1930** What a Man; Lawful Larceny; Once a Gentleman. **1931** Beyond Victory; Bachelor Apartment. **1932** The Heart of New York; Play Girl; Merrily We Go to Hell; Winner Take All; Jewel Robbery. **1933** Diplomaniacs; Midnight Club; Gallant Lady; Sailor Be Good. **1934** The Gay Divorcee; Embarrassing Moments; Born to Be Bad; The Merry Frinks; Housewife; Million Dollar Ransom; Down to Their Last Yacht. **1935** Becky Sharp; The Goose and the Gander; His Family Tree; Magnificent Obsession; Gold Diggers of 1935. **1936** Fury; Born to Dance; Colleen; Her Master's Voice; Don't Get Personal; Everybody's Old Man; The Poor Little Rich Girl; Mummy's Boys; Walking on Air; Lloyds of London. **1937** Love is News; Too Many Wives; There Goes My Girl; Fight for Your Lady; Three Smart Girls; The Go-Getter; Captains Courageous; Shall We Dance; One Hundred Men and a Girl. **1938** Alexander's Ragtime Band; Penrod and His Twin Brother; Little Miss Broadway; Gateway; The Rage of Paris; That Certian Age; Little Orphan Annie. **1939** Mexican Spitfire; You Can't Cheat an Honest Man; First Love; Raffles; In Name Only. **1940** The Westerner; Mexican Spitfire Out West. **1941** Buck Privates; Free and Easy; It Started With Eve; Maisie Was a Lady. **1942** Lady in a Jam; Twin Beds; Almost Married; Miss Annie Rooney; Between Us Girls; Highways by Night; Arabian Nights; Design for Scandal. **1943** Air Raid Wardens; It Ain't Hay; It Comes Up Love; Pittsburgh; She's for Me; Girl Crazy. **1944** Lady in the Dark; Mrs. Parkington; Once Upon a Time; Frenchman's Creek; In Society; The Whistler. **1945** The Picture of Dorian Gray; Missing Corpse; Stork Club; Diamond Horseshoe; Kitty; Earl Carroll Vanities; Anchors Aweigh. **1946** Monsieur Beaucaire; Cluny Brown; In High Gear; Oh, Professor, Behave (short); Magnificent Rogue; The Runaround; Never Say Goodbye; Ziegfeld Follies. **1947** Pilgrim Lady; The Imperfect Lady; Ladies' Man; Lured; Variety Girl; Love from a Stranger. **1948** Trouble Makers. **1949** My Friend Irma; Oil's Well That Ends Well (short). **1950** Texas Tough Guy (short).

COLEMAN, CLAUDIA
Born: 1889, Atlanta, Ga. Died: Aug. 17, 1938, Hollywood, Calif. Screen, stage and vaudeville actress.

Appeared in: **1927** Putting It On (short). **1933** Operator 13; I Cover the Waterfront; Warrior's Husband; Son of the Border; Frisco Jenny; Let's Live Tonight. **1934** The Merry Widow; Big Hearted Herbert. **1936** Human Cargo; King of Burlesque; Little Miss Nobody; The Country Beyond; Lady from Nowhere; Under Your Spell; Navy Born. **1937** They Won't Forget; You Can't Have Everything. **1938** Penrod and His Twin Brother; Test Pilot; Keep Smiling.

COLEMAN, EMIL
Born: 1893, Russia. Died: Jan. 26, 1965, New York, N.Y. (kidney infection). Bandleader and screen actor.

Appeared in: **1935** Melody Masters (short). **1945** Nob Hill.

COLEMAN, THOMAS
Born: 1897. Died: Jan. 28, 1959, Hollywood, Calif. Screen and television actor.

Appeared in: **1939** Stanley and Livingstone. **1946** The Magnificent Doll; Spook Busters. **1957** Top Secret Affair.

COLEMAN, VINCENT (aka WILLIE B. COLEMAN)
Born: Feb. 16, 1900, La. Died: Oct. 26, 1971, Los Angeles, Calif. Screen and stage actor.

Appeared in: **1918** The Scarlet Trail. **1919** Should a Husband Forgive. **1920** Partners of the Night. **1921** Good References; Princess Jones; The Magic Cup; Such a Little Queen. **1922** Divorce Coupons; Fascination. **1923** Has the World Gone Mad!; The Purple Highway; Salome.

COLEMAN, WARREN R.
Born: 1901. Died: Jan. 13, 1968, Martha's Vineyard, Mass. Black screen, stage, television, radio actor, film director, stage director, film and stage producer. Played "Kingfish" on "Amos 'n Andy" radio show.

COLEMAN, WILLIE B. *See* COLEMAN, VINCENT

COLERIDGE, ETHEL (Ethel Coleridge-Tucker)
Born: Jan. 14, 1883, South Molton, Devon, England. Died: Aug. 15, 1976, London, England. Screen and stage actress.

Appeared in: **1930** Rookery Nook (aka One Embarrassing Night—US). **1948** The Fallen Idol (US 1949).

COLES, RUSSELL
Born: 1909. Died: Sept. 26, 1960, Hollywood, Calif. (heart attack). Screen actor.

Appeared in: **1940** The Bank Dick.

COLL, OWEN G.
Born: 1879. Died: Feb. 7, 1960, Long Island, N.Y. Screen, stage and television actor.

COLLEANO, BONAR, JR. (Bonar Sullivan)
Born: Mar. 14, 1923, New York, N.Y. Died: Aug. 17, 1958, Birkenhead, England (auto accident). Screen, stage, vaudeville, radio actor and circus performer. Member of the Colleano circus family. Married to actress Susan Shaw (dec. 1978). Father of actor Mark Colleano.

Appeared in: **1944** Starlight Serenade. **1945** The Way to the Stars (aka Johnny in the Clouds—US). **1946** Wanted For Murder; A Matter of Life and Death (aka Stairway to Heaven—US). **1947** While the Sun Shines (US 1950). **1948** One Night With You; Good Time Girl (US 1950); Merry-Go-Round; Sleeping Car to Trieste (US 1949). **1949** Once a Jolly Swagman (aka Maniacs on Wheels—US 1951); Give Us This Day (aka Salt to the Devil—US). **1950** Dance Hall. **1951** Pool of London; A Tale of Five Cities (aka A Tale of Five Women—US 1952). **1952** Eight Iron Men. **1953** Is Your Honeymoon Really Necessary? **1954** Escape by Night; Flame and the Flesh; The Sea Shall Not Have Them (US 1955); Time Is My Enemy (US 1957). **1955** Joe Macbeth (US 1956). **1956** Stars In Your Eyes. **1957** Zarak; Interpol (aka Pickup Alley—US); Fire Down Below. **1958** No Time to Die (aka Tank Force—US); Them Nice Americans; The Man Inside.

COLLIER, CONSTANCE (Laura Constance Hardie)
Born: Jan. 22, 1878, Windsor, England. Died: Apr. 25, 1955, New York, N.Y. Screen, stage, radio actress, stage producer, director, playwright and screenwriter. Married to actor Julian L'Estrange (dec. 1918).

Appeared in: **1915** Intolerance (film debut). **1916** The Code of Marcia Gray; Macbeth. **1919** The Impossible Woman. **1920** Bleak House. **1922** The Bohemian Girl. **1933** Our Betters; Dinner at Eight. **1935** Anna Karenina; Peter Ibbetson; Shadow of Doubt. **1936** The Bohemian Girl; Professional Soldier; Girls' Dormitory; Little Lord Fauntleroy. **1937** Thunder in the City; Wee Willie Winkie; She Got What She Wanted; Stage Door; Clothes and the Woman; A Damsel in Distress. **1939** Zaza. **1940** Susan and God; Half a Sinner. **1945** Weekend at the Waldorf. **1946** Kitty; Monsieur Beaucaire; Dark Corner. **1947** The Perils of Pauline. **1948** An Ideal Husband; Rope; The Girl from Manhattan. **1949** Whirlpool.

COLLIER, SHIRLEE
Died: Feb. 19, 1972. Screen actress.

Appeared in: **1943** Two Tickets to London. **1948** Enchantment. **1951** Kind Lady.

COLLIER, WILLIAM, SR.
Born: Nov. 12, 1866, New York, N.Y. Died: Jan. 13, 1944, Beverly Hills, Calif. (pneumonia). Screen, stage actor, film dialog director and playwright. Son of stage actor Edmund Collier (dec.) and actress Henrietta Engel (dec.). Father of actor William "Buster" Collier, Jr. Married to stage actress Louise Allen (dec. 1909) and later to actress Paula Marr (dec. 1960).

Appeared in: **1915** Fatty and the Broadway Stars. **1916** Better Late Than Never (working title Getting Married); Plain Jane; Wife and Auto Trouble. **1920** The Servant Question. **1930** Happy Days; High Society Blues; Free and Easy; She's My Weakness; Up the River; Harmony at Home. **1931** Mr. Lemon of Orange; The Seas Beneath; The Brat; Six Cylinder Love; Annabel's Affairs. **1932** After Tomorrow; Hot Saturday; Washington Masquerade; Madison Square Garden; Stepping Sisters. **1934** A Succesful Failure; All of Me; The Crosby Case; Cheaters. **1935** The Murder Man; Annapolis Farewell; The Bride Comes Home. **1936** Love on a Bet; Give Us This Night; Valiant Is the Word for Carrie; Cain and Mabel. **1938** Josette; Thanks for the Memory; Say It in French. **1939** I'm From Missouri; Invitation to Happiness; Television Spy; Disputed Passage; Persons in Hiding. **1940** A Miracle on Main Street. **1941** The Hard-Boiled Canary; There's Magic in Music.

COLLINGE, PATRICIA
Born: Sept. 20, 1894, Dublin, Ireland. Died: Apr. 10, 1974, New York, N.Y. (heart attack). Screen, stage, television actress, playwright and author. Nominated for 1941 Academy Award for Best Supporting Actress in the Little Foxes.

Appeared in: **1941** The Little Foxes (stage and film versions). **1943** Shadow of a Doubt; Tender Comrade. **1944** Casanova Brown. **1951** Teresa. **1952** Washington Story. **1959** The Nun's Story.

COLLINS, BLANCHE M.
Born: 1910. Died: Mar. 30, 1968, Los Angeles, Calif. Screen and stage actress. Appeared in films 1929-1938.

COLLINS, C. E.
Born: July 23, 1873, Missouri. Died: Apr. 15, 1951. Screen and stage actor. Entered films in 1917.

Appeared in: **1917** Flame of the Yukon. **1920** Kismet. **1921** Four Horsemen of the Apocalypse; Conquering Power. **1923** The Hunchback of Notre Dame.

COLLINS, EDDIE (Edward Bernard Collins)
Born: 1884. Died: Sept. 2, 1940, Arcadia, Calif. (heart attack). Stage and screen actor.

Appeared in: **1938** In Old Chicago (film debut); Penrod and His Twin Brother; Sally, Irene and Mary; Kentucky Moonshine; Alexander's Ragtime Band; Little Miss Broadway; Always in Trouble; Up the River; Charlie Chan in Honolulu. **1939** Charlie Chan in Reno; News Is Made at Night; Stop, Look and Love; Quick Millions; Drums Along the Mohawk; Young Mr. Lincoln; Hollywood Cavalcade. **1940** The Blue Bird; The Return of Frank James.

COLLINS, EDDY (Edward Collins)
Born: 1866. Died: Dec. 17, 1916, Hollywood, Calif. (suicide—leap from building). Screen and vaudeville actor.

COLLINS, G. PAT (George Pat Collins)
Born: Dec. 16, 1895, Brooklyn, N.Y. Died: Aug. 5, 1959, Los Angeles, Caiif. (cancer). Screen, stage and television actor.

Appeared in: **1928** The Racket. **1929** Half Marriage. **1930** All Quiet on the Western Front; Manslaughter; Be Yourself!; Big Money; Only Saps Work. **1931** The Vice Squad. **1932** I Am a Fugitive From a Chain Gang; Central Park; Hold 'Em Jail. **1933** Hard to Handle; The Mayor of Hell; 20,000 Years in Sing Sing; Parachute Jumper; Girl Missing; Picture Snatcher; The Silk Express; Heroes for Sale; Fog. **1934** Manhattan Melodrama; Keep 'Em Rolling; The Crime Doctor; The Big Shakedown; A Very Honorable Guy; The Personality Kid. **1935** Black Fury; Alibi Ike; West Point of the Air; Baby Face Harrington; West of the Pecos; Mr. Dynamite. **1938** What Price Safety (short). **1939** Charlie McCarthy, Detective. **1940** Brother Orchid. **1948** Scudda Hoo! Scudda Hay! **1949** Flaming Fury; I Married a Communist; White Heat. **1950** Indian Territory; The Woman on Pier 13. **1952** The Wild North (aka The Big North). **1953** Above and Beyond. **1955** Ten Wanted Men; A Lawless Street; Betrayed Women; The Big Tip-Off; The Naked Street; Night Freight. **1956** Yaqui Drums.

COLLINS, JOSE
Born: May 23, 1887, London, England. Died: Dec. 6, 1958, London, England. Screen, stage and vaudeville actress.

Appeared in: **1916** The Light That Failed. **1919** Nobody's Child. **1920** The Sword of Damocles.

COLLINS, LAURA
Born: 1951. Died: Sept., 1977, Los Angeles, Calif. Screen actress.

COLLINS, MAE
Born: 1906, New York, N.Y. Died: May 6, 1955, Fairfield, Conn. (heart ailment). Screen and stage actress.

Appeared in: **1921** The Shark Master; All Fair in Love; Red Hot Romance; Little Eva Ascends.

COLLINS, MONTE F., JR. "MONTY" (Monte Francis Collins, Jr.)
Born: Dec. 3, 1898, New York, N.Y. Died: June 1, 1951, North Hollywood, Calif. (heart attack). Screen, stage, vaudeville actor, film producer, director and screenwriter.

Appeared in: **1920** Forty-five Minutes from Broadway (film debut as an extra). **1921** Old Swimmin' Hole; Nineteen and Phyllis; The Cup of Life; The Man from Lost River; Midnight Bell; My Best Girl. **1922** My Wife's Relations (short); At the Sign of the Jack O'Lantern; The Man With Two Mothers; Come on Over. **1923** Big Dan; Long Live the King; Our Hospitality; The Old Fool. **1924** Men; A Boy of Flanders; Pride of Sunshine Alley; Tiger Love. **1925** All Around Frying Pan; That Man Jack!; Cold Nerve; The Desert Flower; Tumbleweeds; plus a series of Fox short comedies. **1926** The Loves of Ricardo; The Cowboy and the Countess. **1927** King of Kings; Painting the Town. **1928** Arizona Wildcat. **1929** Why Bring That Up?; The Talkies; Romance Deluxe; plus the two following shorts: The Madhouse; Ticklish Business. **1930** The following shorts: Hail the Princess; Peace and Harmony; How's My Baby; His Error; French Kisses. **1931** Peach O'Reno. **1932** Girl Crazy; plus the following shorts: Show Business; Anybody's Goat; It's a Cinch; Keep Laughing; Hollywood Handicap; Hollywood Runaround; Sunkissed Sweeties. **1933** The Gay Nighties (short). **1934** The following shorts: Woman Haters; Love and Hisses; In a Pig's Eye; Hey Nanny Nanny. **1935** Gobs of Trouble (short); The Mystery Man; Flying Down to Zero (short). **1936** Rent Free (short). **1937** Hollywood Round-Up; Columbia shorts. **1938** Wild Bill Hickok (serial); Sue My Lawyer (short); The Missing Links (short). **1939** Moochin' Through Georgia (short); Boom Goes the Groom (short); The Gracie Allen Murder Case. **1940** The Heckler (short); Cold Turkey (short); Benny Rides Again. **1941** She's Oil Mine (short); General Nuisance (short); Kathleen. **1942** Cactus Makes Perfect (short); What Makes Lizzy Dizzy? (short). **1943** My Tomato (short).

COLLINS, PAMELA (Pamela Ray Collins)
Born: Nov. 29, 1948, Virginia. Died: Sept. 20, 1974, Beverly Hills, Calif. (suicide—pills). Screen actress.

Appeared in: **1968** Finders Keepers, Lovers Weepers. **1970** Substitution. **1973** Sweet Sugar; So Long, Blue Boy.

COLLINS, RAY
Born: 1890, Sacramento, Calif. Died: July 11, 1965, Santa Monica, Calif. (emphysema). Screen, stage, television, radio and vaudeville actor.

Appeared in: **1940** The Grapes of Wrath. **1941** Citizen Kane. **1942** The Magnificent Ambersons; Highways by Night; Commandos Strike at Dawn; The Big Street; The Navy Comes Through. **1943** The Crime Doctor; The Human Comedy; Slightly Dangerous; Salute to the Marines; Whistling in Brooklyn. **1944** Eve of St. Mark; See Here, Private Hargrove; Barbary Coast Gent; Shadows in the Night; The Seventh Cross; The Hitler Gang; Can't Help Singing. **1945** Roughly Speaking; The Hidden Eye; Leave Her to Heaven; Miss Susie Slagle's. **1946** Badman's Territory; Boys' Ranch; Crack-Up; The Return of Monte Cristo; The Best Years of Our Lives; Two Years Before the Mast; Night in Paradise; Up Goes Maisie; Three Wise Fools. **1947** The Red Stallion; The Bachelor and the Bobby-Soxer; The Senator Was Indiscreet; The Swordsman. **1948** Homecoming; Good Sam; For the Love of Mary; The Man from Colorado; A Double Life. **1949** Red Stallion in the Rockies; Hideout; Francis; The Fountainhead; The Heiress; It Happens Every Spring; Free For All; Command Decision. **1950** Kill the Umpire!; Paid in Full; The Reformer and the Redhead; Summer Stock. **1951** Ma and Pa Kettle Back on the Farm; I Want You; You're in the Navy Now (aka U.S.S. Teakettle); Reunion in Reno; The Racket; Vengeance Valley. **1952** The Invitation; Young Man with Ideas; Dreamboat. **1953** Ma and Pa Kettle at the Fair; Ma and Pa Kettle on Vacation; The Desert Song; Column South; The Kid from Left Field; Bad for Each Other. **1954** Rose Marie; Athena. **1955** The Desperate Hours; Texas Lady. **1956** Never Say Goodbye; The Solid Gold Cadillac. **1957** Spoilers of the Forest. **1958** Touch of Evil. **1961** I'll Give My Life.

COLLINS, RUSSELL
Born: Oct. 11, 1897. Died: Nov. 14, 1965, West Hollywood, Calif. (heart attack). Screen, stage and television actor.

Appeared in: **1948** Close-Up. **1949** The Walking Hills; Shockproof. **1953** Destination Gobi; Miss Sadie Thompson; Niagara. **1955** Canyon Crossroads; The Last Frontier; Bad Day at Black Rock; Soldier of Fortune. **1957** Raintree County; The Enemy Below. **1958** The Matchmaker; God's Little Acre. **1959** The Rabbit Trap. **1964** Fail Safe. **1965** Those Calloways; When the Boys Meet the Girls.

COLLINS, S. D. J.
Born: 1907. Died: Dec. 28, 1947, Leavenworth, Kans. (heart ailment). Screen actor and circus performer.

Appeared in: **1935** A Night at the Opera.

COLLINS, TOM
Died: June 17, 1973. Screen actor.

Appeared in: **1939** Fast and Loose; Tell No Tales; These Glamour Girls; Burn 'Em Up O'Connor; Money to Loan (short). **1940** Dr. Kildare's Strangest Case; Dr. Kildare Goes Home. **1941** Dancing on a Dime.

COLLUM, JOHN
Born: 1926. Died: Aug. 28, 1962, Hollywood, Calif. Screen actor.

Appeared in: **1940** Tom Brown's School Days.

COLLYER, JUNE (Dorothea Heermance)
Born: Aug. 19, 1907. Died: Mar. 16, 1968, Los Angeles, Calif. (bronchial pneumonia). Screen, stage and television actress. Married to actor Stuart Erwin (dec. 1967).

Appeared in: **1927** East Side, West Side (film debut). **1928** Me, Gangster; Four Sons; Hangman's House; Woman Wise. **1929** Red Wine; Let's Make Whoopee; Not Quite Decent; Illusion; River of Romance; The Love Doctor; The Pleasant Sin. **1930** Extravagance; Charley's Aunt; A Man from Wyoming; Sweet Kitty Bellaire; Toast of the Legion; Three Sisters; Beyond Victory. **1931** Damaged Love; The Brat; Honeymoon Lane; Kiss Me Again; Drums of Jeopardy; Alexander Hamilton; Dude Ranch. **1933** Revenge at Monte Carlo; Before Midnight. **1934** Cheaters; Lost in the Stratosphere. **1935** The Ghost Walks; Murder by Television.

COLMAN, IRENE
Born: 1915, Nashua, N.H. Died: July 19, 1975, Santa Monica, Calif. (leukemia). Screen actress.

Appeared in: **1934** Bottoms Up; Stand Up and Cheer; Springtime for Henry; Change of Heart; Jealousy; The Fugitive Lady. **1935** Broadway Melody of 1936. **1936** Three Men on a Horse; Gold Diggers of 1937; Stage Struck After the Thin Man. **1939** Hero for a Day. **1940** North West Mounted Police. **1941** The Corsican Brothers; Affectionately Yours; Model Wife; Never Give a Sucker an Even Break.

COLMAN, RONALD
Born: Feb. 9, 1891, Richmond-Surrey, England. Died: May 19, 1958, Santa Barbara, Calif. (lung infection). Screen, stage, television and radio actor. Divorced from actress Victoria Maud (aka Thelma Ray) and married to actress Benita Hume (dec. 1967). Nominated for 1929/30 Academy Award for Best Actor in Bulldog Drummond and Condemned and again in 1942 for Random Harvest. Won 1947 Academy Award for Best Actor in A Double Life.

Appeared in: **1919** The Toilers; Sheba; The Snow in the Desert. **1920** Anna the Adventuress; The Black Spider; A Son of David. **1921** Handcuffs or Kisses. **1923** The White Sister; The Eternal City. **1924** Romola; $20 a Week; Heart Trouble; Her Night of Romance; Tarnish. **1925** The Sporting Venus; Stella Dallas; The Dark Angel; His Supreme Moment; Her Sister from Paris; Lady Windermere's Fan; A Thief in Paradise. **1926** Beau Geste; Kiki; The Winning of Barbara Worth. **1927** The Magic Flame; The Night of Love. **1928** Two Lovers. **1929** The Rescue; Condemned; I Have Been Faithful; Bulldog Drummond. **1930** Raffles; The Devil to Pay. **1931** Arrowsmith; The Unholy Garden. **1932** Cynara. **1933** The Masquerader. **1934** Bulldog Drummond Strikes Back. **1935** Clive of India; The Man Who Broke the Bank at Monte Carlo; A Tale of Two Cities. **1936** Under Two Flags. **1937** Lost Horizon; The Prisoner of Zenda. **1938** If I Were King. **1939** The Light That Failed. **1940** Lucky Partners. **1941** My Life With Caroline. **1942** Random Harvest; Talk of the Town. **1944** Kismet. **1947** A Double Life; The Late George Apley. **1950** Champagne for Caesar. **1956** Around the World in 80 Days. **1957** The Story of Mankind.

COLMANS, EDWARD
Died: May 25, 1977. Screen actor.

Appeared in: **1951** Sirocco. **1952** Thief of Damascus; The Iron Mistress; California Conquest. **1953** Conquest of Cochise; Prince of Pirates. **1954** The Secret of the Incas. **1955** Headline Hunters. **1957** Hell on Devil's Island. **1958** The Gun Runners. **1960** The Third Voice. **1963** Diary of a Madman.

COLT, ETHEL BARRYMORE (aka LOUISE KINLOCK)
Born: Apr. 20, 1912, Mamaroneck, N.Y. Died: May 22, 1977, New York, N.Y. Screen, stage and vaudeville actress. Daughter of actress Ethel Barrymore (dec. 1959). Mother of actor John Miglietta.

COLT, SAM
Born: 1873. Died: Jan. 1, 1933, N.Y. (pneumonia). Screen and stage actor.

Appeared in: **1914** The Old Fogey; Soldiers of Fortune.

COLUMBO, RUSS (Ruggerio de Rudolpho Columbo)
Born: Jan. 14, 1908, Philadelphia, Pa. Died: Sept. 2, 1934, Hollywood, Calif. (accidentally shot). Screen, radio actor, singer and songwriter.

Appeared in: **1929** Wolf Song; The Street Girl; Dynamite; The Wonders of Women. **1931** Hellbound. **1933** That Goes Double (short); Broadway Thru a Keyhole. **1934** Moulin Rouge; Wake Up and Dream.

COLVIG, VANCE D. "PINTO"
Born: 1892, Jacksonville, Ore. Died: Oct. 3, 1967, Woodland Hills, Calif. Screen, stage actor and songwriter. Known as the "Dean of Hollywood Voice Men." Entered films with Sennett in 1923. He created the voices of "Goofy," "Pluto," and "Grumpy" in Snow White and the Seven Dwarfs (1937) and was the voice of "Bozo the Clown" on Capitol Records.

COLVIN, WILLIAM G.
Born: 1876, Sligo, Ireland. Died: Aug. 10, 1930, Los Angeles, Calif. Screen and stage actor.

COMANCHE, LAURENCE "TEX"
Born: 1908. Died: Oct. 10, 1932, Hollywood, Calif. (suicide or accident—gun shot wounds). Screen actor and Indian film extra.

COMANT, MATHILDA
Born: 1888, France. Died: June 22, 1938, Hollywood, Calif. Screen and stage actress.

Appeared in: **1923** Rosita. **1924** The Thief of Baghdad; Mademoiselle Midnight. **1925** If Marriage Fails; The Enchanted Hill. **1926** Paris at Midnight; The Sea Beast; The Girl from Montmartre; Puppets. **1927** Loves of Carmen. **1928** A Woman's Way; Streets of Shanghai; Ramona. **1930** Romance; Call of the Flesh. **1931** The Lady Who Dared; The Cuban Love Song; The Lash. **1932** L'Athlete Incomplete. **1933** Design for Living. **1934** A Torch Tango (short). **1935** Le Chanteur de Seville; Here's to Romance; Escapade. **1936** Poor Little Rich Girl; God's Country and the Woman; Anthony Adverse. **1937** The Go-Getter.

COMBER, BOBBIE (Edmund Comber)
Born: Jan. 8, 1890, Bury St. Edmunds, England. Died: Mar. 2, 1942, Wales (heart attack). Screen, stage and radio actor.

Appeared in: **1930** Elstree Calling. **1931** Hot Heir. **1932** Brother Alfred. **1933** Sleeping Car; The Fortunate Fool. **1934** There Goes Susie (aka Scandals of Paris—US 1935); Lilies of the Field. **1935** The Ace of Spades; Lazybones; Be Careful Mr. Smith. **1936** Don't Rush Me; Sporting Love; Excuse My Glove. **1938** The Singing Cop.

COMFORT, JANE
Born: 1889, England. Died: Dec. 4, 1979, London, England. Screen and stage actress.

COMINGORE, DOROTHY (Linda Winters)
Born: 1913. Died: Dec. 30, 1971, Stonington, Conn. Screen and stage actress.

Appeared in: **1938** Comet Over Broadway; Prison Train; Campus Cinderella. **1939** Good Girls Go to Paris; Scandal Sheet; Cafe Hostess; Blondie Meets the Boss; The Awful Goof; Trade Winds; Mr. Smith Goes to Washington. **1940** Pioneers of the Frontier; Rockin' Through the Rockies (short); The Hecklers (short); Street of Missing Women. **1941** Citizen Kane. **1944** The Hairy Ape. **1949** Any Number Can Play. **1952** The Big Night.

COMMERFORD, THOMAS (aka THOMAS COMBERFORD)
Born: 1855, New York. Died: Feb. 17, 1920. Screen actor.

Appeared in: **1911** Two Orphans. **1912** The Miller of Burgundy; A Heart in Rags; The Girl at the Cupola. **1913** The Boomerang; Broken Threads United; A False Order; The Ex-Convict; A Lucky Mistake; What's the Matter With Father?; Homespun; A Midnight Bell. **1914** Under Royal Patronage; The Other Man; The Grip of Circumstance; One Wonderful Night; The Fable of the Family That Did Too Much for Nellie; The Private Officer; The Great Game. **1915** The White Sister; Graustark; Countess Veschi's Jewels; Mr. Buttles; Thirteen Down; The Surprise of My Life; The Little Straw Wife; A Night Given Over to Revelry; The Longer Voyage; The Call of Yesterday; Caught; On the Little Mill Trace; The Little Deceiver; The Greater Courage. **1916** The Sting of Victory; Is Marriage Sacred (series); The Romance of Billy Goat Hill; Our People; The Three Scratch Clue; His Little Wife; It Never Could Happen; What I Said, Goes; A Failure at Fifty. **1917** The Fable of the Uplifter and His Dandy Little Opus.

COMPSON, BETTY
Born: Mar. 18, 1897, Beaver, Utah. Died: Apr. 18, 1974, Glendale, Calif. Screen, stage, television actress and film producer. Divorced from actor/director James Cruze (dec. 1942) and business manager Irving Weinberg. Married to Silvius Jack Gall (dec. 1962). Nominated for 1928-29 Academy Award for Best Actress in The Barker.

Appeared in: **1915-1916** Wanted—a Leading Lady (film debut); Their Quiet Honeymooon; Where the Heater Blooms; Love and a Savage; Some Chaperone; Jed's Trip to the Fair; Mingling Spirits; When the Losers Won; Her Steady Carfare; A Quiet Supper for Four; Her Friend; The Doctor; When Lizzie Disappeared; Cupid Trims His Lordship; The Deacon's Waterloo; Love and Vaccination; He Almost Eloped; The Janitor's Busy Day; A Leap Year Tangle; Eddie's Night Out; The Newylwed's Mix-up; Lem's College; Career; Potts Bungles Again; He's a Devil; The Wooing of Aunt Jemima; Her Celluloid Hero; All Over a Stocking; Almost a Widow; Wanted—A Husband. **1916-1918** His Baby; The Making Over of Mother; A Brass-Buttoned Romance; Some Kid; Hist at 6 O'Clock; Cupid's Uppercut; Out for the Coin; Her Crooked Career; Her Friend the Chauffeur; Small Change; Hubby's Night Out; A Bold Bad Knight; As Luck Would Have It; Suspended Sentence; His Last Pill; Those Wedding Bells; Almost a Scandal; Down by the Sea; Won in a Cabaret; Crazy by Proxy; Betty's Big Idea; Love and the Locksmiths; Almost a Bigamist; Almost Divorced; Betty Wakes Up; Their Seaside Tangle; Nearly a Papa; Cupid's Camouflage; Many a Slip; Whose Wife?; Betty's Adventure; All Dressed Up; Somebody's Baby; A Seminary Scandal. **1918** The Sheriff; Border Raiders. **1919** The Terror of the Range (serial); The Prodigal Liar; Light of Victory; The Little Diplomat; The Devil's Trail; The Miracle Man. **1921** Prisoners of Love; At the End of the World; Ladies Must Live; For Those We Love. **1922** The Little Minister; The Law and the Woman; The Green Temptation; Over the Border; Always the Woman; The Bonded Woman; To Have and To Hold; Kick In. **1923** The White Flower; The Rustle of Silk; The Woman With Four Faces; Hollywood; The Royal Oak; The Prude's Fall; Woman to Woman (US 1924). **1924** The Stranger; Miami; The Enemy Sex; The White Shadow (aka White Shadow—US); Ramshackle House; The Female; The Garden of Weeds; The Fast Set. **1925** Locked Doors; New Lives for Old; Eve's Secret; Beggar on Horseback; Paths to Paradise; The Pony Express. **1926** The Palace of Pleasure; The Counsel for Defense; The Wise Guy; The Belle of Broadway. **1927** Twelve Miles Out; The Ladybird; Say It With Diamonds; Temptations of a Shop Girl; Cheating Cheaters. **1928** Love Me and the World is Mine; Big-City; The Masked Angel; The Desert Bride; Life's Mockery; The Docks of New York; Court Martial; The Barker; Scarlet Seas. **1929** Weary River; On With the Show; The Time, the Place and the Girl; Street Girl; The Great Gabbo; Skin Deep; Woman to Woman (and 1923 version); The Show of Shows. **1930** Blaze O' Glory; The Case of Sergeant Grischa; Isle of Escape; The Midnight Mystery; The Czar of Broadway; Inside the Lines; Those Who Dance; The Spoilers; She Got What She Wanted; The Boudoir Diplomat. **1931** The Lady Refuses; Virtuous Husband; Three Who Loved; The Gay Diplomat. **1932** The Silver Lining; Guilty or Not Guilty. **1933** West of Singapore; Destination Unknown; Notorious But Nice. **1935** False Pretenses. **1936** Laughing Irish Eyes; The Millionaire Kid; The Dragnet; August Weekend; Hollywood Boulevard; Bulldog Edition; Killer at Large. **1937** Circus Girl; Two Minutes to Play; Federal Bullets. **1938** Blondes at Work; A Slight Case of Murder; The Port of Missing Girls; Torchy Blane in Panama; Two Gun Justice; Under the Big Top. **1939** News is Made at Night; The Mystic Circle Murder; Cowboys from Texas. **1940** Strange Cargo; Mad Youth; Laughing at Danger. **1941** Mr. and Mrs. Smith; The Invisible Ghost; The Roar of the Press. **1943** Danger! Women at Work; Her Adventurous Night. **1946** Claudia and David. **1947** Hard Boiled Mahoney; Second Chance. **1948** Here Comes Trouble.

COMPTON, BETTY
Born: 1907, Isle of Wight. Died: July 12, 1944, N.Y. Screen, stage actress, singer and dancer. Divorced from James J. Walker, former Mayor of New York (dec. 1946).

Appeared in: **1930** The Legacy (short). **1934** A British International film.

COMPTON, FAY
Born: Sept. 18, 1894, London, England. Died: Dec. 12, 1978, England. Screen, stage, radio and television actress. Daughter of stage actors Edward Compton (dec. 1918), and Virginia Bateman (dec. 1940). Married to actors H. G. Pelissier (dec. 1913) and Lauri de Frece (dec. 1921). Divorced from actors Leon Quartermaine (dec. 1967) and Ralph Michael (aka Ralph Champion Shotter). Mother of stage/film director Anthony Pelissier.

Appeared in: **1914** She Stoops to Conquer. **1917** The Labour Leader; One Summer's Day. **1920** Judge Not. **1921** The Old Wives' Tale; A Woman of No Importance. **1922** The House of Peril; A Bill for Divorcement; Diana of the Crossways. **1923** This Freedom; The Loves of Mary, Queen of Scots (aka Mary, Queen of Scots). **1924** The Eleventh Commandment; Claude Duval. **1925** The Happy Ending; Settled Out of Court (aka Evidence Enclosed). **1926** London Love. **1927** Robinson Crusoe; Somehow Good. **1928** Zero. **1929** Fashions in Love. **1931** Cape Forlorn (aka The Love Storm—US); Tell England (aka The Battle of Gallipoli—US); Uneasy Virtue. **1934** Song of Eventide; Autumn Crocus; Waltzes from Vienna (aka Strauss's Great Waltz—US 1935). **1936** Wedding Group (aka Wrath of Jealousy—US). **1937** The Mill on the Floss (US 1939). **1938** Cavalcade of the Stars. **1939** So This is London (US 1940). **1941** The Prime Minister (US 1942). **1947** Odd Man Out; Nicholas Nickleby. **1948** Esther Waters; London Belongs to Me (aka Dulcimer Street— US). **1949** Britannia Mews (aka Forbidden Street—US). **1951** Blackmailed; Laughter in Paradise. **1952** A Lady Possessed. **1954** Aunt Clara. **1955** Othello. **1956** Doublecross. **1957** Town on Trial; The Story of Esther Costello. **1963** The Haunting. **1969** I Start Counting. **1970** The Virgin and the Gypsy.

COMPTON, FRANCIS
Born: 1885, San Francisco, Calif. Died: Sept. 17, 1964, Noroton, Conn. Screen actor.

Appeared in: **1936** Soak the Rich. **1941** Rage in Heaven; Mr. and Mrs. Smith. **1958** Witness for the Prosecution.

COMPTON, MADGE
Born: England. Died: 1970, England. Screen and stage actress. Divorced from actor George Graves (dec. 1949). Later married to Gerald Lawrence (dec.).

Appeared in: **1943** Dear Octopus (aka The Randolph Family—US 1945).

COMPTON, VIOLA
Born: 1886, London, England. Died: Apr. 7, 1971, Birchington, England. Screen and stage actress. Sister of actress Fay Compton.

Appeared in: **1932** Looking on the Bright Side. **1933** The Good Companions; The Medicine Man; The Shadow (US 1936); Excess Baggage. **1936** Under Proof; The Big Noise; Find the Lady; Happy Days are Here Again; Servants All; The Man in the Mirror (US 1937).

CONCHITA (Maria de la Concepcion Conchita Serafina Bacigalupi)
Born: 1861. Died: June 13, 1940, South Colby, Wash. Screen and stage actress.

Appeared in: **1936** Three on the Trail.

CONDE, JOHNNY
Born: 1895. Died: Dec. 5, 1960, Hollywood, Calif. (heart attack). Screen actor.

CONDON, JACKIE
Born: Mar. 25, 1918, Los Angeles, Calif. Died: Oct. 13, 1977, Inglewood, Calif. (cancer). Screen actress.

Appeared in: **1919** Hoodlum; Daddy Longlegs. **1921** Little Lord Fauntleroy; The Love Light. **1920** Pollyanna. **1922** Our Gang; Fire Fighters; Young Sherlocks; One Terrible Day; A Quiet Street; Saturday Morning. **1923** The Big Show; The Cobbler; The Champeen; Boys to Beard; A Pleasant Journey; Giants vs. Yanks; Back Stage; Dogs of War; Lodge Night; Stage Fright; July Days; Sunday Calm; No Noise; Derby Days. **1924** Tire Trouble; Big Business; The Buccaneers; Seein' Things; Commencement Day; It's a Bear; Cradle Robbers; Jubile, Jr.; High Society; The Sun Down Limited; Every Man For Himself; The Mysterious Mystery. **1925** The Big Town; Circus Fever; Dog Days; The Love Bug; Ask Grandma; Shootin' Injuns; Official Officers; Mary—Queen of Tots; Boys Will Be Boys; Better Movies.

CONE, MIKE "ZETS"
Born: 1910. Died: Jan. 4, 1969, North Miami Beach, Fla. (cancer). Screen, television actor and musician.

CONKLIN, CHARLES "HEINIE"
Born: 1880. Died: July 30, 1959, Hollywood, Calif. Screen actor.

Appeared in: **1923** The Day of Faith. **1924** The Cyclone Rider; Find Your Man; George Washington, Jr.; Troubles of a Bride. **1925** Below the Line; A Fool and His Money; Hogan's Alley; Clash of the Wolves; Red Hot Tires; Seven Sinners. **1926** The Fighting Edge; Hardboiled; The Man Upstairs; More Pay—Less Work; Whispering Wires; Fig Leaves; Honesty—the Best Policy; The Night Cry; The Sap; Ruggles of Red Gap. **1927** Beware of Widows; Ham and Eggs at the Front; Cheaters; Drums of the Desert; Silk Stockings. **1928** The Air Circus; Beau Broadway; Feel My Pulse; A Horseman of the Plains; A Trick of Hearts. **1929** The Show of Shows; Side Street; Tiger Rose. **1930** Duckling Duty (short); All Quiet on the Western Front. **1932** Trailing the Killer; Young Ironsides (short). **1933** She Done Him Wrong; Riders of Destiny. **1934** Most Precious Thing in Life. **1935** Girl from 10th Avenue; Ruggles of Red Gap; Steamboat 'Round the Bend; plus the following shorts: Old Sawbones; Tramp, Tramp, Tramp. **1936** Modern Times; Rhythm on the Range; Wedding Present. **1937** A Girl With Ideas; Oh, Doctor! **1938** Strange Faces; Passport Husband; Little Miss Broadway. **1939** Hollywood Cavalcade; Newsboys' Home; Big Town Czar. **1940** Dr. Christian Meets the Women; The Heckler (short); The Courageous Dr. Christian; Margie. **1941** Caught in the Draft. **1942** You're Telling Me; Even as I.O.U. (short); Hold 'Em Jail (short). **1943** Three Little Twerps (short). **1944** Lost in a Harem; plus the following shorts: His Tale is Told; Movie Pests. **1945** Song of the Prairie; Senorita from the West; She Gets Her Man. **1947** Wife to Spare (short). **1948** Family Honeymoon; Fifth Avenue Angel. **1949** Loaded Pistols. **1950** Joe Palooka in Humphrey Takes a Chance; County Fair. **1954** Pals and Gals (short). **1955** Abbott and Costello Meet the Keystone Kops.

CONKLIN, CHESTER
Born: Jan. 11, 1888, Oskaloosa, Iowa. Died: Oct. 11, 1971, Woodland Hills, Calif. Screen, stage, vaudeville and circus actor. Entered films in 1913 with Majestic and later appeared in several Keystone Kop comedies.

Appeared in: **1913** Amborse-Walrus series. **1914** Making a Living (reissued as A Busted Johnny); Mabel's Strange Predicament; Between Showers; Tango Tangles; Mabel at the Wheel (reissued as His Daredevil); Twenty Minutes of Love; Caught in a Cabaret (reissued as The Jazz Waiter); Mabel's Busy Day; Mabel's New Job; The Face on the Barroom Floor (reissued as The Ham Artist); Those Love Pangs; The Love Thief; Dough and Dynamite (reissued as The Doughnut Designers); Gentlemen of Nerve (reissued as Some Nerve); Curses! They Remarked; How Heroes Are Made; His Taking Ways; A Colored Girl's Love; Wild West Love. **1915** Hushing the Scandal (reissued as Friendly Enemies); Hash House Mashers; Love, Speed and Thrills; The Home Breakers (reissued as Other People's Wives); Caught in a Park; A Bird's a Bird; A One Night Stand; Hearts and Planets; Ambrose's Sour Grapes; Droppington's Devilish Dream; Droppington's Family Tree; Do-Re-Me-Fa; A Hash House Fraud; The Cannon Ball (reissued as The Dynamiter); When Ambrose Dared Walrus; The Battle of Ambrose and Walrus; Saved By the Wireless; The Best of Enemies. **1916** Dizzy Heights and Daring Hearts; Cinders of Love; Bucking Society; His First False Step; A Tugboat Romeo. **1917** The Pullman Bride; Dodging His Doom; A Clever Dummy; The Pawnbroker's Heart. **1919** Uncle Tom's Cabin. **1920** "Sunshine" comedies; Chicken a la Cabaret. **1921** Skirts. **1923** Anna Christie; Desire; Souls for Sale; Tea With a Kick. **1924** Galloping Fish; Another Man's Wife; The Fire Patrol; North of Nevada; Greed. **1925-26** 12 "Blue-Ribbon" comedies (shorts). **1925** A Woman of the World; Battling Bunyon; The Great Love; The Masked Bride; Where Was I?; The Winding Stair; The Great Jewel Robbery; My Neighbor's Wife; One Year to Live; The Phantom of the Opera; The Pleasure Buyers; Under the Rouge; The Gold Rush. **1926-27** Series of shorts for Tennek Film Corp. **1926** The Wilderness Woman; A Social Celebrity; Say It Again; We're in the Navy Now; Behind the Front; The Duchess of Buffalo; Fascinating Youth; The Lady of the Harem; The Nervous Wreck; Midnight Lovers. **1927** Cabaret; Rubber Heels; Kiss in a Taxi; Tell It to Sweeney; McFadden's Flats. **1928** Two Flaming Youths; Fools for Luck; Gentlemen Prefer Blondes; Tillie's Punctured Romance; Varisty; The Big Noise; Trick of Hearts; The Haunted House; Feel My Pulse; Horseman of the Plains; Beau Broadway. **1929** Marquis Preferred; The House of Horror; Stairs of Sand; The Studio Murder Mystery; Sunset Pass; The Virginian; Shanghai Rose; Show of Shows; Taxi Thirteen; Fast Company; plus several Hal Roach shorts. **1930** Swing High; The Master Sweeper (short); The Love Trader. **1930-31** Six shorts for Paramount. **1931** The New Yorker; Her Majesty, Love; Stout Hearts and Willing Hands (short). **1933** Halleluja, I'm a Bum. **1935** A Vitaphone short. **1936** Call of the Prairie; Modern Times; The Preview Murder Mystery. **1937** Hotel Haywire; Forlorn River. **1938** Flatfoot Stooges (short); Every Day's a Holiday. **1939** Zenobia; The Teacher's Pet (short); Hollywood Cavalcade. **1940** The Great Dictator; Li'l Abner. **1941** Goodnight Sweetheart; Harmon of Michigan; Dutiful But Dumb (short). **1942** Sullivan's Travels; Piano Mooner (short); Sons of the Pioneers. **1943** Three Little Twerps (short); Phony Express (short). **1944** Can't Help Singing; The Miracle of Morgan's Creek; Adventures of Mark Twain; Knickerbocker Holiday; Sunday Dinner for a Soldier; Hail the Conquering Hero. **1945** Micro Phonies (short); Abbott and Costello in Hollywood. **1946** She Wrote the Book; Smooth as Silk; The Best Years of Our Lives; Little Giant. **1947** Perils of Pauline; Springtime in the Sierras. **1948** Isn't It Romantic? **1949** Jiggs and Maggie in Jackpot Jitters; The Beautiful Blonde from Bashful Bend; The Golden Stallion. **1950** Fancy Pants; Let's Dance; Joe Palooka in Humphrey Takes a Chance. **1952** Son of Paleface. **1953** So You Want To Be a Musician (short). **1955** Apache Woman; Beast With a Million Eyes. **1958** Rock-a-Bye Baby. **1960** When Comedy Was King (documentary). **1962** Paradise Alley. **1966** A Big Hand for the Little Lady.

CONKLIN, FRANCES (Frances Elizabeth Conklin)
Born: July 18, 1893, San Francisco, Calif. Died: June 27, 1935, Los Angeles, Calif. (Murdered—shot). Screen actress.

CONKLIN, FREDERICK MEADE
Born: 1874. Died: Jan. 22, 1929, Long Island, N.Y. (pneumonia). Screen and stage actor.

CONKLIN, WILLIAM
Born: Brooklyn, N.Y. Died: Mar. 21, 1935, Hollywood, Calif. (paralytic stroke). Screen, stage actor and film producer. Entered films in 1915.

Appeared in: **1915** Neal of the Navy (serial). **1917** Joan the Woman; Law of the Land. **1919** Hay Foot, Straw Foot; Red Hot Dollars. **1920** The Woman in the Suitcase; Hairpins. **1921** Beau Revel; Blind Hearts; The Lure of Youth; The Other Woman. **1922** Iron to Gold; The Unfoldment; Up and Going; When Husbands Deceive; The Woman He Married. **1923** Daytime Wives; The Darlings of New York; The Lone Star Ranger; The Lonely Road; The Man Alone; The Meanest Man in the World; Three Who Paid. **1924** The Goldfish; Never Say Die; Stolen Secrets. **1925** Counsel for the Defense; Fifth Avenue Models; A Gentleman Roughneck; The Man Without a Country; Ports of Call; The Rag Man; Winds of Chance. **1926** Faithful Wives; Old Ironsides; Sweet Rosie O'Grady. **1927** Outlaws of Red River; Rose of the Golden West; Tumbling River. **1928** Life's Crossroads. **1929** The Divine Lady; Shanghai Rose.

CONLAN, FRANK (Peter Murphy)
Born: July 22, 1874 or 1890?, Ireland. Died: Aug. 24, 1955, East Islip, N.Y. Screen and stage actor.

Appeared in: **1922** Bought and Paid For (film debut). **1935** The Scoundrel. **1940** Chad Hanna; Angels Over Broadway. **1941** Billy the Kid; Here is a Man; Lydia; All That Money Can Buy. **1943** The Crystal Ball. **1945** Strangler of the Swamp. **1949** Reign of Terror; The Black Book. **1950** Perfect Strangers. **1952** The Devil and Daniel Webster (reissue of 1941 film All That Money Can Buy).

CONLEY, HARRY J.
Born: 1885. Died: June 23, 1975, Cleveland, Ohio (heart attack). Screen, stage and vaudeville actor.

Appeared in: **1928** The Bookworm (short). **1930** Slick as Ever (short).

CONLEY, LIGE
Born: 1899. Died: Dec. 11, 1937, Hollywood, Calif. (hit by auto). Screen actor. Entered films in silents with Sennett.

Appeared in: **1928** The Charge of the Gauchos.

CONLEY, WILLIAM "BING"
Died: July 23, 1962. Screen actor.

Appeared in: **1940** My Little Chickadee. **1949** The Big Steal.

CONLIN, JIMMY (aka JIMMY CONLON)
Born: Oct. 14, 1884, Camden, N.J. Died: May 7, 1962, Encino, Calif. Screen, stage, vaudeville and television actor. Married to actress Myrtle Glass with whom he appeared in vaudeville as "Conlin and Glass."

Appeared in: **1928** Sharps and Flats (film debut); Lights of New York. **1933** Footlight Parade; 20,000 Years in Sing Sing; College Humor. **1934** 365 Nights in Hollywood; She Learned About Sailors; Now I'll

Tell; Cross Country Cruise; City Limits. **1935** The Bride Comes Home. **1936** And Sudden Death; Rose Bowl. **1937** Find the Witness; The Bad Man Who Found Himself; The Adventurous Blonde. **1938** The Big Broadcast of 1938; Mannequin; Crashing Hollywood; Torchy Blande in Panama; Broadway Musketeers; Cocoanut Grove. **1939** Idiot's Delight; $1000 a Touchdown; No Place to Go. **1940** Calling Philo Vance; Second Chorus; The Great McGinty. **1941** Obliging Young Lady; Ridin' on a Rainbow; Sullivan's Travels. **1942** Woman of the Year; The Lady Is Willing; The Remarkable Andrew; The Forest Rangers; The Palm Beach Story; The Man in the Trunk. **1943** Old Acquaintance; Dixie; Hitler's Madness; Petticoat Larceny; Jitterbugs; Taxi, Mister? **1944** And the Angels Sing; Lost in a Harem; Town Went Wild; Hail the Conquering Hero; Summer Storm; Army Wives; Ali Baba and the Forty Thieves; Miracle of Morgan's Creek. **1945** Bring on the Girls; What, No Cigarettes? (short); Don Juan Quilligan; An Angel Comes to Brooklyn; Fallen Angel; Picture of Dorian Gray. **1946** Cross My Heart; Blue Skies; Whistle Stop. **1947** Mad Wednesday; It's a Joke, Son; Dick Tracy's Dilemma; Rolling Home; Seven Keys to Baldpate; The Hucksters; Mourning Becomes Electra. **1948** Hazard. **1949** Prejudice; Knock on Any Door; Tulsa. **1950** Operation Haylift; Sideshow; The Great Rupert. **1953** It Happens Every Thursday; The Seven Little Foys. **1959** Anatomy of a Murder; The 30 Foot Bride of Candy Rock.

CONLISS, EDWARD B.
Born: 1901. Died: Aug. 3, 1981, Toledo, Ohio. Screen actor, circus and burlesque performer. Known as "Zam Zam, the Clown of a Thousand Laughs."

Appeared in: **1920** Convict 13.

CONNELLY, BOBBY (Robert J. Connelly)
Born: Apr. 4, 1909. Died: July 5, 1922, Lynbrook, N.Y. (enlarged heart and bronchitis). Screen and vaudeville actor. Brother of actress Helen Connelly. Entered films at age of three for Kalem in 1912.

Appeared in: **1913** Love's Sunset. **1914** Happy-Go-Lucky; Bunny's Mistake; Street Singer; Goodness Gracious!; The Heart of Sonny Jim; Carpenter; The Circus and the Boy; The Cave Dwellers. **1915** The Professor's Romance; The Night Before Christmas; The Island of Regeneration; To Cherish and Protect; Sonny Jim at the Mardi Gras; The Faith of Sonny Jim; Sonny Jim and the Great American Game; One Plus One Equals One; Sonny Jim's First Love Affair; The Turn of the Road; Old Good-for-Nothin'; A Case of Eugenics; Sonny Jim and the Amusement Co., Ltd.; Bobby's Bargain; Jim and the Family Party; The Third Party; The Prince in Disguise. **1916** A Prince in a Pawnshop; Salvation Jane; The Suspect; Fathers of Men; From Out of the Past; The Writing on the Wall; Her Bad Quarter of an Hour; The Rookie; The Law Decides. **1917** The Soul Master; Intrigue; Her Right to Live; Just What Bobby Wanted; Bobby's Secret; When Bobby Broke His Arm; Bobby and the Helping Hand; Bobby of the Home Defenders; Bobby and the Fairy; Bobby and Company; Bobby Takes a Wife; Bobby's Country Adventure; Bobby the Magician; To the Rescue. **1918** Out of a Clear Sky; A Youthful Affair; The Seal of Silence. **1919** What Love Forgives; The Unpardonable Sin. **1920** Other Men's Shoes; Humoresque. **1921** The Old Oaken Bucket. **1922** A Wide-Open Town; Wildness of Youth.

CONNELLY, EDWARD J.
Born: 1855, New York. Died: Nov. 21, 1928, Hollywood, Calif. (influenza). Screen and stage actor.

Appeared in: **1914** The Good Little Devil (film debut). **1917** The Great Secret (serial). **1920** Shore Acres; The Willow Tree. **1921** The Four Horsemen of the Apocalypse; Camille; The Conquering Power; The Conflict. **1922** Quincy Adams Sawyer; Kisses; Love in the Dark; Seeing's Believing; Red Hot Romance; The Prisoner of Zenda; Turn to the Right; Trifling Women. **1923** Desire; Where the Pavement Ends; Slave of Desire; Her Fatal Millions; Scaramouche. **1924** The Beauty Prize; Revelation; Sinners in Silk; So This Is Marriage; A Fool's Awakening. **1925** Sun-Up; The Only Thing; The Denial; The Unholy Three; The Merry Widow. **1926** The Gay Deceiver; Bardely's, the Magnificent; Brown of Harvard; The Torrent. **1927** Lovers?; Winners of the Wilderness; The Show; The Student Prince. **1928** Brotherly Love; Across to Singapore; Forbidden Hours; The Mysterious Lady. **1929** The Desert Rider.

CONNELLY, ERWIN
Born: 1873. Died: Feb. 12, 1931, Los Angeles, Calif. (auto accident injuries). Screen, stage and vaudeville actor. Married to actress Jan Connelly (dec. 1925) and together they appeared in vaudeville.

Appeared in: **1922** The Man from Beyond. **1924** Sherlock, Jr. **1925** Beggar on Horseback; Marry Me; Seven Chances; When Husbands Flirt. **1926** The Blind Goddess; The Crown of Lies; The Danger Girl; The Fire Brigade; Kiki; Shipwrecked; The Son of the Sheik; The Winning of Barbara Worth. **1927** Cheating Cheaters; Rubber Tires.

CONNELLY, JANE

Died: Oct. 25, 1925, Los Angeles, Calif. (result of a nervous breakdown). Screen and vaudeville actress. Married to actor Erwin Connelly (dec. 1931) and together they appeared in vaudeville.

Appeared in: **1922** The Man from Beyond. **1924** Sherlock, Jr.

CONNELLY, MARC

Born: Dec. 30, 1890, McKeesport, Pa. Died: Dec. 21, 1980, New York, N.Y. Screen, stage actor, film director, stage director and screenwriter.

Appeared in: **1922** Devil's Angel. **1957** The Spirit of St. Louis. **1960** Tall Story (film and stage version).

CONNESS, ROBERT

Born: 1868, La Salle County, Ill. Died: Jan. 15, 1941, Portland, Maine. Screen, stage and vaudeville actor. Married to actress Helen Strickland (dec. 1938).

Appeared in: **1911** His Misjudgment. **1916** The Witching Hour; The Martyrdom of Philip Strong; A Message to Garcia. **1917** The Rainbow; The Master Passion; The Ghost of Old Morro.

CONNOLLY, WALTER

Born: Apr. 8, 1887, Cincinnati, Ohio. Died: May 28, 1940, Beverly Hills, Calif. (stroke). Screen and stage actor.

Appeared in: **1930** Many Happy Returns (short). **1932** Washington Merry-Go-Round; Plainsclothes Man; No More Orchids; Man Against Woman. **1933** Lady for a Day; Master of Men; East of Fifth Avenue; A Man's Castle; Paddy the Next Best Thing; The Bitter Tea of General Yen. **1934** Eight Girls in a Boat; It Happened One Night; Twentieth Century; Whom the Gods Destroy; Broadway Bill; Lady by Choice; White Lies; Once to Every Woman; Servants' Entrance; Captain Hates the Sea; Many Happy Returns. **1935** So Red the Rose; She Couldn't Take It; Father Brown, Detective; One Way Ticket. **1936** Soak the Rich; The Music Goes 'Round; The King Steps Out; Libeled Lady. **1937** The Good Earth; Nancy Steele Is Missing; Let's Get Married; The League of Frightened Men; First Lady; Nothing Sacred. **1938** Start Cheering; Penitentiary; Four's a Crowd; Too Hot to Handle. **1939** The Girl Downstairs; Those High Gray Walls; Good Girls Go to Paris; Bridal Suite; Coast Guard; The Adventures of Huckleberry Finn; Fifth Avenue Girl; The Great Victor Herbert.

CONNOR, EDRIC

Born: 1915, Mayaro, Trinidad. Died: Oct. 16, 1968, London, England (stroke). Black screen, stage, radio, television actor, singer, author and film producer. Entered films in 1952.

Appeared in: **1952** Cry, The Beloved Country (aka African Fury—US). **1954** East of Zanzibar. **1956** Moby Dick. **1957** Fire Down Below; Seven Thunders (aka The Beasts of Marseilles—US 1959). **1958** Virgin Island (US 1960); The Vikings. **1961** King of Kings. **1963** Four for Texas. **1968** Nobody Runs Forever (aka The High Commissioner—US); Only When I Larf.

CONQUEST, ARTHUR

Born: 1875, London, England. Died: Dec. 6, 1945, London, England. Screen and stage actor. Brother of stage actors George (dec. 1926), Fred (dec. 1941), Daisy (dec. 1889), Laura, Ada, Louisa, Lydia and Edna Conquest. Married to actress Lottie Hallett (dec.). Father of actress Elizabeth (Betty) Conquest.

Appeared in: **1902** Bluebeard. **1913** Will Evans Harnessing a Horse. **1914** Building a Chicken House; Moving a Piano; The Jockey; The Showman's Dream; Tincture of Iron.

CONRAD, EDDIE

Born: 1891. Died: Apr. 27, 1941, Los Angeles, Calif. Screen, stage and vaudeville actor.

Appeared in: **1927** Broadway's Favorite Comedian (short). **1929** Blaze O' Glory. **1934** Done in Oil (short). **1935** Every Night at Eight; I Live for Love; Stars Over Broadway; The Melody Lingers On. **1936** Sleepy Time (short); Big Brown Eyes; Hot Money. **1938** Boy Meets Girl; Happy Landing; Romance in the Dark; Always Goodbye; I'll Give a Million; Gateway; Just Around the Corner; Topper Takes a Trip. **1939** Midnight. **1940** Saps at Sea; I Was an Adventuress; Foreign Correspondent; Lucky Partners; Down Argentine Way; Chad Hanna; Behind the News. **1941** You're the One; That Night in Rio; West Point Widow; Hurry, Charlie, Hurry; Angels With Broken Wings; The Great American Broadcast; Road to Zanzibar.

CONROY, FRANK

Born: Oct. 14, 1890, Derby, England. Died: Feb. 24, 1964, Paramus, N.Y. (heart ailment). Screen, stage and television actor.

Appeared in: **1930** The Royal Family of Broadway. **1931** Bad Company; Possessed; Hell Divers. **1932** Manhattan Parade; West of Broadway; Grand Hotel; Disorderly Conduct. **1933** Midnight Mary; Night Flight; Ann Carver's Profession; Ace of Aces; The Kennel Murder Case. **1934** Little Miss Marker; Keep 'Em Rolling; The Crime Doctor; The White Parade; The Little Minister; Frontier Marshal; Such Women Are Dangerous; The Cat and the Fiddle. **1935** Call of the Wild; Last Days of Pompeii; Show Them No Mercy; Charlie Chan in Egypt; West Point of the Air; I Live My Life. **1936** The White Angel; Stolen Holiday; Meet Nero Wolfe; Nobody's Fool; The Gorgeous Hussy; Charlie Chan at the Opera. **1937** Love Is News; Wells Fargo; That I May Live; Nancy Steele Is Missing; Big Business; This Is My Affair; The Emperor's Candlesticks; The Last Gangster; Music for Madame. **1941** This Woman Is Mine. **1942** Adventures of Martin Eden; Crossroads; The Loves of Edgar Allen Poe. **1943** The Ox-Bow Incident; Crash Dive; Lady of Burlesque. **1947** That Hagen Girl. **1948** For the Love of Mary; Sealed Verdict; Rogues' Regiment; Naked City; All My Sons; The Snake Pit. **1949** The Threat. **1951** The Day the Earth Stood Still; Lightning Strikes Twice. **1959** The Last Mile; Compulsion; The Young Philadelphians. **1960** The Bramble Bush.

CONROY, THOM

Born: 1911. Died: Nov. 16, 1971, Hollywood, Calif. (heart attack). Screen and stage actor.

Appeared in: **1951** Ten Tall Men. **1955** Man With the Gun. **1961** The Young Savages; The Manchurian Candidate. **1963** The Ugly American. **1964** Robin and the 7 Hoods; Seven Days in May. **1965** The Hallelujah Trail; Marriage on the Rocks; None But the Brave. **1966** Assault on a Queen; Seconds. **1968** Swimmer.

CONSTANDUROS, MABEL (Mabel Tilling)

Born: 1880, London, England. Died: Feb. 8, 1957, England? Screen, stage, radio actress, screenwriter, playwright and radio writer.

Appeared in: **1933** Radio Parade. **1935** The Hope of His Side (aka Where's George). **1942** Salute John Citizen; Rose of Tralee. **1944** Medal for the General; My Ain Folk. **1946** Caravan (US 1947); The Gay Intruders. **1947** The White Unicorn (aka Bad Sister—US 1948). **1948** Easy Money (US 1949).

CONSTANT, MAX

Born: France. Died: May, 1943, Mojave Desert, Calif. (died during flying test for Air Force). Screen actor.

Appeared in: **1923** Trilby.

CONTE, RICHARD (Nicholas Conte)

Born: Mar. 24, 1914, Jersey City, N.J. Died: Apr. 15, 1975, Los Angeles, Calif. (heart attack and paralyzing stroke). Screen, stage and television actor. Divorced from actress Ruth Strome and later married to actress Shirley Garner (aka Colleen Conte).

Appeared in: **1939** Heaven With a Barbed Wire Fence. **1943** Guadalcanal Diary. **1944** The Purple Heart. **1945** A Bell for Adano; Captain Eddie; A Walk in the Sun; The Spider. **1946** Somewhere in the Night; 13 Rue Madeleine. **1947** The Other Love. **1948** Call Northside 777; Cry of the City; Appointment With Murder. **1949** Thieve's Highway; Big Jack; House of Strangers; Whirlpool. **1950** The Sleeping City; Under the Gun. **1951** Hollywood Story; The Raging Tide. **1952** Thief of Damascus; The Fighter (aka The First Time); The Raiders. **1953** Desert Legion; The Blue Gardenia; Slaves of Babylon. **1954** Highway Dragnet; A Race for Life. **1955** Target Zero; The Big Combo; Bengazi; New York Confidential; The Big Tip-Off; I'll Cry Tomorrow. **1956** Full of Life. **1957** The Brothers Rico; Little Red Monkey (aka The Case of the Red Monkey—US). **1958** This Angry Age. **1959** They Came to Cordura. **1960** Ocean's Eleven; Pep. **1963** Who's Been Sleeping in My Bed? **1964** The Eyes of Annie Jones; Circus World. **1965** Synanon; Stay Tuned for Terror; The Greatest Story Ever Told. **1966** Assault on a Queen. **1967** Tony Rome; Hotel. **1968** Lady in Cement. **1969** Operation Cross Eagle. **1970** Explosion (aka The Blast). **1972** The Godfather.

CONTI, ALBERT (Albert De Conti Cadassamare)

Born: Jan. 29, 1887, Trieste, Austria. Died: Jan. 18, 1967, Hollywood, Calif. (stroke). Screen actor. Entered films in 1922.

Appeared in: **1923** Merry-Go-Round (film debut). **1925** The Merry Widow; Eagle. **1926** The Blonde Saint; Old Loves and New; Watch Your Wife. **1927** Slipping Wives (short); Camille; The Devil Dancer; South Sea Love. **1928** The Chinese Parrot; Love Me and the World Is Mine; Stocks and Blondes; Plastered in Paris; Legion of the

Condemned; Magnificent Flirt; Dry Martini; Alex the Great; Show People; Tempest. **1929** Making the Grade; The Exalted Flapper; Jazz Heaven; Captain Lash; Lady of the Pavements; Saturday's Children; He Loved the Ladies. **1930** Such Men Are Dangerous; Oh, For a Man!; The Melody Man; One Romantic Night; Morocco; Sea Legs; Madame Satan; Average Husband (short); Monte Carlo; Our Blushing Brides. **1931** This Modern Age; Reputation; Gang Busters; Strangers May Kiss; Just a Gigolo; Heartbreak. **1932** Shopworn; Doomed Battalion; The Giddy Age (short); As You Desire Me; Night Club Lady; Freaks; Lady With a Past; Second Fiddle. **1933** Gigolettes of Paris; Topaze; Men Are Such Fools; Love Is Dangerous; Love Is Like That; Shanghai Madness; Torch Singer. **1934** Love Time; Beloved; Elmer and Elsie. **1935** Goin' to Town; The Night Is Young; Hands Across the Table; Mills of the Gods; Symphony of Living; Diamond Jim; The Crusades; Here's to Romance. **1936** Next Time We Love; Three Smart Girls; The Case Against Mrs. Ames; Fatal Lady; Hollywood Boulevard; One in a Million; Collegiate. **1937** Dangerously Yours; Cafe Metropole. **1938** Always Goodbye; Gateway; Suez. **1942** My Gal Sal.

CONTRERAS, MIGUEL
Born: 1905, Sonora, Mexico. Died: Dec. 30, 1956, Culver City, Calif. Screen, stage, television actor, film director and film producer.

Appeared in: **1954** Secret of the Incas.

CONWAY, CURT
Born: 1915, Boston, Mass. Died: Apr. 11, 1974, Los Angeles, Calif. (heart attack). Screen, stage actor, film, stage and television director. Divorced from actress Sandra Francis (dec. 1981) and later married to Gail Burton.

Appeared in: **1947** Gentleman's Agreement; Singapore. **1948** A Double Life; The Naked City; The Saxon Charm; Casbah; Raw Deal. **1949** Illegal Entry; A Woman's Secret; The Lady Gambles. **1958** The Goddess; Wind Across the Everglades. **1961** Run Across the River. **1963** Hud. **1964** Invitation to a Gunfighter. **1970** Macho Callahan. **1972** The Man.

CONWAY, JACK
Born: Ireland. Died: May, 1951, Forest Hills, N.Y. Screen and vaudeville actor. Appeared in early Paramount pictures.

CONWAY, JACK
Born: July 17, 1887, Graceville, Minn. Died: Oct. 11, 1952, Pacific Palisades, Calif. Screen, stage actor and film director.

Appeared in: **1909** Her Indian Hero. **1914** The Old Arm Chair. **1919** Restless Souls.

CONWAY, JOSEPH
Born: c. 1889, Philadelphia, Pa. Died: Feb. 28, 1959, Philadelphia, Pa. Screen actor and circus owner. Appeared in early silents made in Philadelphia.

CONWAY, MORGAN
Born: 1900. Died: Nov. 16, 1981, Livingston, N.J. Screen and stage actor.

Appeared in: **1934** Happy Landing; Looking for Trouble. **1938** Sinners in Paradise; Illegal Traffic; Nurse from Brooklyn; Crime Ring. **1939** Blackwell's Island; Charlie Chan in Reno; Off the Record; Secret Service of the Air; Grand Jury Secrets; The Spellbinder; Television Spy; The Kid from Kokomo. **1940** Millionaires in Prison; Sued for Libel; A Fugitive from Justice; Three Cheers for the Irish; The Saint Takes Over; Brother Orchid. **1942** Sing Your Worries Away; Bells of Capistrano. **1943** Tornado; Jack London. **1945** Dick Tracy. **1946** Vacation in Reno; Dick Tracy vs. Cueball; The Truth About Murder; Badman's Territory.

CONWAY, PATRICK "PAT" (Patrick Douglas Conway)
Died: Apr. 24, 1981. Screen actor.

Appeared in: **1952** Above and Beyond; The Invitation. **1955** An Annapolis Story. **1956** Screaming Eagles; Flight to Hong Kong. **1957** The Deadly Mantis; Destination 60,000; Undersea Girl. **1962** Geronimo. **1966** Brighty of the Grand Canyon.

CONWAY, TOM (Thomas Charles Sanders)
Born: 1904, St. Petersburg, Russia. Died: Apr. 22, 1967, Culver City, Calif. (liver ailment). Screen, television and radio actor. Brother of actor George Sanders (dec. 1972).

Appeared in: **1940** Sky Murder. **1941** Wild Man of Borneo; The People vs. Dr. Kildare; Tarzan's Secret Treasure; Mr. and Mrs. North; The Trial of Mary Dugan; Free and Easy; The Bad Man; Lady Be Good. **1942** Mrs. Miniver; Grand Central Murder; Rio Rita; The Falcon's

Brother; The Cat People. **1943** The Falcon in Danger; The Falcon and the Co-eds; The Seventh Victim; The Falcon Strikes Back; I Walked With a Zombie; One Exciting Night. **1944** The Falcon in Mexico; The Falcon Out West; A Night of Adventure; The Falcon in Hollywood. **1945** Two O'Clock Courage; The Falcon in San Francisco; One Exciting Month. **1946** Criminal Court; The Falcon's Adventure; The Falcon's Alibi; Whistle Stop; Runaway Daughters. **1947** Repeat Performance; Fun on a Weekend; Lost Honeymoon. **1948** One Touch of Venus; 13 Lead Soldiers; The Challenge; Bungalow 13; Checkered Coat. **1949** I Cheated the Law. **1950** The Great Plane Robbery. **1951** Painting the Clouds With Sunshine; The Bride of the Gorilla; Triple Cross. **1952** Confidence Girl. **1953** Tarzan and the She-Devil; Peter Pan (voice); Park Plaza 605 (aka Norman Conquest—US); Paris Model. **1954** Three Stops to Murder; Prince Valiant. **1955** Barbados Quest (aka Murder on Approval—US 1956). **1956** The Last Man to Hang; Operation Murder; Breakaway; Death of a Scoundrel; The She-Creature; Murder on Approval. **1957** Voodoo Woman. **1959** The Atomic Submarine; Rocket to the Moon. **1960** 12 to the Moon. **1961** One Hundred and One Dalmatians (voice). **1964** What a Way to Go.

CONWAY, WILLIAM
Born: 1876. Died: Oct. 13, 1924, New York, N.Y. Screen and stage actor.

CONYERS, JOSEPH (Joseph O'Connor)
Born: 1854. Died: June 25, 1920, New York, N.Y. Screen and stage actor.

Appeared in: **1913** Our New Minister.

COOGAN, GENE B.
Died: Jan. 21, 1972, Los Angeles, Calif. (results of a fire). Screen, television actor and stuntman. Married to actress Linda Landi.

Appeared in: **1939** The Story of Alfred Nobel (short). **1952** Plymouth Adventure. **1961** Gun Fight.

COOGAN, JACK, SR. (John Coogan)
Born: 1880, Syracuse, N.Y. Died: May 4, 1935, near San Diego (auto accident). Screen, stage and vaudeville actor. Father of actor Jackie Coogan. Married to vaudeville actress Lillian Dolliver.

Appeared in: **1921** The Kid.

COOK, AL
Born: 1882. Died: July 6, 1935, Santa Monica, Calif. Screen actor.

Appeared in: **1916** Fighting Blood. **1927** The Telephone Girl. **1929** As You Like It; Meet the Quince; Love's Labor Found; They Shall Not Pass Out; Eventually, But Not Now; The Captain of the Roll. **1930** The Sleeping Cutie; Lost and Found; Old Vamps for New; The Setting Son; The Dear Slayer; Cash and Merry; Land of the Sky Blue Daughters. **1937** The Man Who Cried Wolf.

COOK, DONALD
Born: Sept. 26, 1901, Portland, Ore. Died: Oct. 1, 1961, New Haven, Conn. (heart attack). Screen, stage, television, radio and vaudeville actor.

Appeared in: **1930** Roseland (short). **1931** Practice Shots (short); Eastside; The Silent Voice; Mad Genius; The Unfaithful; Party Husband; Side Show; The Public Enemy. **1932** Heart of New York; New Morals of Old; The Conquerors; So Big; Washington Merry-Go-Round; The Man Who Played God; The Trial of Vivienne Ware; The Unfaithful; The Penguin Pool Murder; Safe in Hell. **1933** Frisco Jenny; Kiss Before the Mirror; Jennie Gerhardt; The Circus Queen Murder; Private Jones; Baby Face; The World Changes; The Woman I Stole; Brief Moment. **1934** The Lost Lady; Fury of the Jungle; Fog; The Ninth Guest; Jealousy; The Most Precious Thing in Life; Whirlpool; Viva Villa. **1935** The Night Is Young; Ladies Love Danger; Behind the Evidence; Fugitive Lady; Gigolette; Confidential; The Casino Murder Case; Here Comes the Band; Motive for Revenge; Murder in the Fleet; The Spanish Cape Mystery. **1936** Ring Around the Moon; Girl from Mandalay; Can This Be Dixie?; Ellis Island; The Calling of Dan Matthews; The Leavenworth Case; Showboat. **1937** Circus Girl; Two Wise Maids; Beware of Ladies. **1944** Bowery to Broadway; Murder in the Blue Room; Patrick the Great. **1945** Blonde Ransom; Here Come the Co-eds. **1950** Our Very Own.

COOK, ETHYLE
Born: Aug. 4, 1880, Lynn, Mass. Died: Apr. 20, 1949, Waukesha, Wis. Screen actress. Married to actor Harry Benham (dec. 1969) and mother of actress Dorothy (dec. 1956) and actor Leland Benham (dec. 1976).

Appeared in: **1914** A Dog's Love. **1915** The Game; Their Last

Performance; Mr. Meeson's Will; All Aboard; A Call from the Dead; The Necklace of Pearls; The Commuted Sentence; His Vocation. **1916** John Brewster's Wife. **1917** Her Life and His; When Love Was Blind. **1918** Convict 993.

COOK, JOE (Joseph Lopez)
Born: 1890, Evansville, Ind. Died: May 16, 1959, Clinton Hollows, N.Y. Screen, stage and vaudeville actor. Do not confuse with film director Joe Cook.

Appeared in: **1930** Rain or Shine (stage and film versions—film debut). **1933** Hold Your Horses. **1935** An Educational short. **1948** You Gotta Stay Happy. **1964** The Sound of Laughter (documentary).

COOK, KEN
Born: 1914. Died: Dec. 28, 1963, Hollywood, Calif. (heart attack). Stage and screen actor.

COOK, LILLIAN
Born: 1898, Hot Springs, Ark. Died: Mar. 14, 1918, New York, N.Y. Screen and stage actress.

Appeared in: **1915** Their Last Performance; The Cotton King; Mother. **1916** A Woman's Power (aka Code of the Mountains); Camille; As in a Looking Glass; The Spirit of the Game; The Common Law. **1917** The Submarine Eye; Betsy Ross; Rasputin, the Black Monk; Darkest Russia; The Corner Grocer; Her Hour; The Honeymoon. **1918** The Blue Bird; The Devil's Playground.

COOK, LUCIUS (Lucius Moore Cook)
Born: July 23, 1891, New York. Died: June 2, 1952, Los Angeles, Calif. (arteriosclerosis). Screen actor, stage director and drama coach.

Appeared in: **1951** Goodbye, My Fancy. **1952** Lone Star.

COOK, MARY
Died: May 27, 1944, Hollywood, Calif. Screen actress, singer, and dancer. Divorced from actor Elisha Cook, Jr.

Appeared in: **1941** Moonlight in Hawaii; Melody Lane. **1942** Ride 'Em Cowboy.

COOK, ROSS
Born: 1898. Died: Jan. 2, 1930. Screen pilot.

Appeared in: **1930** Hell's Angels.

COOK, WARREN
Born: 1879. Died: May 2, 1939, New York, N.Y. Screen and stage actor.

Appeared in: **1920** The Flapper; My Lady's Garter; Lady Rose's Daughter. **1921** Conceit; The Fighter; The Girl from Nowhere; Is Life Worth Living?; The Last Door; The Man of Stone; Suspicious Wives; Worlds Apart. **1922** John Smith; Slim Shoulders. **1923** The Broken Violin; Dark Secrets; Fog Bound; The Silent Command. **1924** His Darker Self; The Truth About Women. **1925** Shore Leave; The Knockout; Wild, Wild Susan. **1926** Lew Tyler's Wives. **1927** The Lunatic at Large.

COOKE, BALDWIN G. "BALDY" (Baldwin Gardner Cooke)
Born: Mar. 10, 1888, New York. Died: Dec. 31, 1953, Los Angeles, Calif. Screen actor.

Appeared in: **1929** The following shorts: Berth Marks; Men O'War; Perfect Day; The Hoose Gow. **1930** The following shorts: Teacher's Pet; Blotto; Below Zero; The Big Kick. **1931** The following shorts: The Pip From Pittsburg; Call a Cop; Bargain Days; Be Big; Chickens Come Home; Beau Hunks. **1932** The following shorts: Choo Choo; Country Hospital; Scram; Young Ironsides. **1933** The following shorts: Fish Hooky; Twice Two. **1934** The following shorts: Going Bye Bye; Another Wild Idea; The Live Ghost. **1936** The Bohemian Girl; Our Relations. **1939** Auto Antics (short).

COOKE, SAM
Born: 1932. Died: Dec. 10, 1964, Los Angeles, Calif. (shot). Black screen actor and singer.

COOKE, STANLEY
Born: Jan. 16, 1868, Liverpool, England. Died: Jan. 6, 1931, England? Screen and stage actor.

Appeared in: **1929** Alf's Button.

COOKE, STEPHEN BEACH
Born: 1898. Died: Sept. 16, 1948, Cooperstown, N.Y. Screen and stage actor.

COOKSEY, CURTIS
Born: 1892. Died: Apr. 19, 1962, Hollywood, Calif. (cancer—suicide). Screen and stage actor.

Appeared in: **1915** The Dawn of Courage; The Old and the New. **1916** My Partner; The Coward's Code. **1920** The Silver Horde. **1922** A Virgin's Sacrifice. **1932** The Misleading Lady. **1952** Because You're Mine; The Girl in White; Young Man With Ideas; Scaramouche. **1953** Taxi. **1956** Storm Center; Death of a Scoundrel.

COOKSON, MAURINE
Died: Jan. 8, 1981, Williamstown, Mass. Screen and stage actress.

Appeared in: **1936** The Great Ziegfeld.

COOKSON, S. A.
Born: 1869, England. Died: Feb. 27, 1947, England? Screen and stage actor.

Appeared in: **1911** Henry VIII.

COOLEY, CHARLES (Charles Cali)
Born: 1903, Cleveland, Ohio. Died: Nov. 15, 1960, Hollywood, Calif. (rare blood disease). Screen, television and vaudeville actor.

Appeared in: **1947** My Favorite Brunette. **1949** Sorrowful Jones. **1950** Fancy Pants. **1951** The Lemon Drop Kid. **1952** Son of Paleface; Sound Off.

COOLEY, FRANK L.
Born: 1870, Natchez, Miss. Died: July 6, 1941, Hollywood, Calif. Screen, stage actor and film director. Entered films with Keyston Company in 1912.

Appeared in: **1926** First Year; More Pay—Less Work. **1927** Wanted—A Coward. **1928** Honor Bound.

COOLEY, HALLAM "HAL"
Born: Feb. 8, 1895 or 1888, Brooklyn, N.Y. Died: Mar. 20, 1971, Tiburon, Calif. Screen and stage actor.

Appeared in: **1916** The Courtesan. **1917** A Dog Catcher's Love. **1918** The Deciding Kiss; Bull's Eye (serial). **1919** Daddy Long Legs; One of the Finest; Upstairs; Girl From Outside; Happy Through Marriage; Girl Dodger; More Deadly Than the Male. **1920** An Old Fashioned Boy; Pinto; Long Arm of Mannister; A Light Woman; Beware of the Bride; Leave it to Me; Trumpet Island. **1921** The Foolish Age; The Daughter of the Don; Ten Dollar Raise; The Tom Boy; Playing With Fire; What Do Men Want? **1922** Beauty's Worth; Her Night of Nights; Confidence; The Kingdom Within; The Man With Two Mothers; Money to Burn; Rose O' the Sea; Up and At 'Em; The Wise Kid; One Week of Love. **1923** Going Up; Are You a Failure?; Dollar Devils. **1924** The White Sin; The Painted Flapper; Never Say Die; Sporting Youth. **1925** Headlines; Seven Days; Free to Love; The Monster; Stop Flirting; Some Pun'kins; The Thoroughbred. **1926** Forever After; Ladies at Play. **1927** Wedding Bells; Naughty But Nice; Ladies Must Dress. **1928** Her Wild Oat; The Little Wildcat. **1929** In the Headlines; Fancy Baggage; The Little Wild Cat; Black Waters; Paris Bound; Stolen Kisses; Tonight at Twelve. **1930** So Long Letty; Back Pay; What Men Want; Holiday; Soup to Nuts; Wedding Rings; Oh, Sailor, Behave. **1931** Too Many Cooks; Sporting Blood. **1933** Frisco Jenny.

COOLEY, JAMES R.
Born: 1880. Died: Nov. 5, 1948, Hollywood, Calif. Screen and stage actor.

Appeared in: **1916** The Eternal Sopho. **1917** A Tale of Two Nations. **1924** The Song of Love. **1934** The Mighty Barnum.

COOLEY, SPADE (Donnell C. Cooley)
Born: 1910, Grand, Okla. Died: Nov. 23, 1969, Oakland, Calif. (heart attack). Bandleader, screen and television actor.

Appeared in: **1943** Chatterbox; The Silent Bandit. **1944** The Singing Sheriff. **1945** Rockin' in the Rockies; Outlaws of the Rockies. **1946** Texas Panhandle. **1947** Vacation Days. **1949** Square Dance Jubilee; The Kid from Gower Gulch; Border Outlaw; I Shot Billy the Kid. **1950** Everybody's Dancin'. **1951** Casa Manana.

COOLIDGE, PHILIP
Born: Aug. 25, 1908, Concord, Mass. Died: May 23, 1967, Hollywood, Calif. (cancer). Screen, stage and television actor.

Appeared in: **1947** Boomerang. **1956** The Shark Fighters. **1957** Slander. **1958** I Want to Live! **1959** The Tingler; It Happened to Jane; The Mating Game; North by Northwest. **1960** Because They're Young; The Bramble Bush; Inherit the Wind. **1962** Bon Voyage! **1964** Hamlet. **1965** The Greatest Story Ever Told. **1966** The Russians Are Coming, The Russians Are Coming. **1968** Never a Dull Moment.

COOMBE, CAROL (Gwendoline Alice Coombe)
Born: Sept. 20, 1911, Perth, Australia. Died: Oct. 4, 1966, London, England. Screen and stage actress.

Appeared in: **1931** The Ghost Train (US 1933); The Rasp. **1932** Help Yourself; The Strangler. **1933** Double Bluff; My Lucky Star. **1935** The Man Without a Face. **1949** Woman to Woman.

COOMBS, JACK "COLBY JACK"
Born: 1883, LeGrand, Iowa. Died: Apr. 15, 1957, Palestine, Tex. (heart attack). Professional baseball player and screen actor.

Appeared in: **1911** The Baseball Bug.

COONS, JOHNNY
Born: 1917. Died: July 6, 1975. Screen and television actor.

Appeared in: **1969** Tell Them Willie Boy Is Here.

COONTZ, WILLARD "BILL"
Born: 1916. Died: Apr. 7, 1978, Van Buren, Ark. (cancer). Screen, television actor and stuntman.

Appeared in: **1954** The Lawless Rider. **1956** Hidden Guns. **1957** Raiders of Old California. **1958** Frankenstein's Daughter; The Littlest Hobo; The Lone Texan; No Place to Land. **1961** Bloodlust. **1978** Convoy.

COOPER, ASHLEY
Born: 1882, Australia. Died: Jan. 3, 1952, New York, N.Y. Screen, stage and vaudeville actor. Father of actress Dulcie Cooper (dec. 1981).

Appeared in: **1921** Partners of the Tide; Shadows of Conscience. **1922** Gay and Devilish; The Hands of Nara; The Son of the Wolf; Tillie. **1923** Desert Driven; Robin Hood, Jr. **1924** The Torrent. **1926** Paradise.

COOPER, CLANCY
Born: 1907. Died: June 14, 1975, Hollywood, Calif. (heart attack). Screen, stage, television actor and stage director. Married to author Elizabeth Cooper.

Appeared in: **1941** High Sierra. **1942** The Secret Code (serial); Native Land; Flight Lieutenant; Unseen Enemy; The Man Who Returned to Life; West of Tombstone. **1943** Redhead from Manhattan; Riding Through Nevada; Girls in Chains; Dead Man's Gulch; Frontier Fury; Deerslayer. **1944** Haunted Harbour (serial); The Whistler; Timber Queen; Sundown Valley; Riding West; Cyclone Prairie Rangers. **1945** Mildred Pierce; Abbott and Costello in Hollywood; Enchanted Forest; Without Love. **1946** Dragonwyck; The Best Years of Our Lives; Courage of Lassie; The Wife of Monte Cristo; Somewhere in the Night; Centennial Summer; It Shouldn't Happen to a Dog. **1947** A Really Important Person (short); Her Husband's Affair. **1948** The Sainted Sisters; Lulu Belle; The Man from Texas. **1949** Whirlpool; Song of Surrender; Mr. Belvedere Goes to College; Prison Warden. **1950** The Great Rupert; Mary Ryan, Detective; Where the Sidewalk Ends. **1951** Distant Drums. **1952** The Man Behind the Gun; The Wild North; Deadline U.S.A.; Lydia Bailey. **1953** All the Brothers Were Valiant; The Silver Whip. **1954** Living It Up. **1955** Artists and Models. **1956** Somebody Up There Likes Me. **1957** The True Story of Jesse James; Oh, Men! Oh, Women! **1958** A Time to Love and a Time to Die. **1959** The Sheriff of Fractured Jaw. **1961** Wild Youth. **1962** Incident in an Alley; Saintly Sinners.

COOPER, CLAUDE
Born: 1881. Died: July 20, 1932, Laurelton, N.Y. (heart attack). Screen, stage actor and film director.

Appeared in: **1915** The Country Girl. **1921** A Heart to Let; The Plaything of Broadway. **1924** Daughters of the Night. **1932** The Struggle.

COOPER, DOUG
Born: 1921. Died: Aug. 1, 1977, Hollywood, Calif. (complications following heart surgery). Screen actor and talent agent.

COOPER, DULCIE
Born: 1904, Australia. Died: Sept. 3, 1981, New York, N.Y. Screen, stage and television actress. Daughter of actor Ashley Cooper (dec. 1952).

Appeared in: **1921** Charge It; Desert Blossoms; Live and Let Live; What No Man Knows. **1922** Do and Dare; The Hands of Nara. **1932** Face on the Barroom Floor.

COOPER, EDWARD
Born: England. Died: July, 1956, Surrey, England. Screen and stage actor. Married to actress Ethel Griffies (dec. 1975). Do not confuse with British entertainer Edward Cooper (dec. 1945).

Appeared in: **1933** Officer 13; The Working Man; Female; Diplomaniacs. **1935** Clive of India; The Perfect Gentleman. **1936** To Mary—With Love. **1937** On the Avenue. **1938** Rascals. **1939** Wife, Husband and Friend. **1941** Marry the Boss's Daughter. **1944** Bermuda Mystery; Enter Arsene Lupin. **1945** Kitty.

COOPER, FREDERICK
Born: 1890, London, England. Died: Jan., 1945, England? Screen and stage actor.

Appeared in: **1937** Jericho (aka Dark Sands—US 1938). **1942** Unpublished Story; Thunder Rock (US 1944); The Great Mr. Handel (US 1943). **1943** Warn That Man. **1945** They Knew Mr. Knight; Henry V (US 1946).

COOPER, GARY (Frank James Cooper)
Born: May 17, 1901, Helena, Mont. Died: May 13, 1961, Hollywood, Calif. (cancer). Screen, television actor and film producer. Made one television special. Married to actress Veronica Balfe who acted under the name of Sandra Shaw. Won 1941 Academy Award for Best Actor in Sergeant York, and in 1952 for High Noon. Nominated for 1936 Academy Award as Best Actor in Mr. Deeds Goes to Town; in 1942 for the Pride of the Yankees and in 1943 For Whom The Bell Tolls.

Appeared in: **1925** The Lucky Horseshoe; The Vanishing American; The Eagle; The Enchanted Hill; Watch Your Wife; Tricks. **1926** Three Pals; Lightning Justice; The Winning of Barbara Worth. **1927** Arizona Bound; Nevada; The Last Outlaw; Wings; Children of Divorce; It. **1928** Beau Sabreur; The Legion of the Condemned; Doomsday; The First Kiss; Lilac Time; Half a Bride. **1929** Shopworn Angel; The Wolf Song; The Betrayal; The Virginian. **1930** Only the Brave; Paramount on Parade; The Texan; Seven Days' Leave; A Man from Wyoming; The Spoilers; Morocco. **1931** Fighting Caravans; City Streets; I Take This Woman; His Woman. **1932** The Devil and the Deep; Make Me a Star; If I Had a Million; A Farewell to Arms. **1933** Today We Live; One Sunday Afternoon; Design for Living; Alice in Wonderland; The Eagle and the Hawk. **1934** The Hollywood Gad-about (short); Operator 13; Now and Forever. **1935** La Fiesta de Santa Barbara (short); The Wedding Night; Lives of a Bengal Lancer; Peter Ibbetson. **1936** Desire; Mr. Deeds Goes to Town; The General Died at Dawn; Hollywood Boulevard; The Plainsman. **1937** Souls at Sea. **1938** The Adventures of Marco Polo; Bluebeard's Eighth Wife; The Cowboy and the Lady. **1939** Beau Geste; The Real Glory. **1940** The Westerner; Northwest Mounted Police. **1941** Meet John Doe; Sergeant York; Ball of Fire. **1942** The Pride of the Yankees. **1943** For Whom the Bell Tolls. **1944** The Story of Dr. Wassell; Casanova Brown. **1945** Along Came Jones; Saratoga Trunk. **1946** Cloak and Dagger. **1947** Unconquered; Variety Girl. **1948** Good Sam. **1949** The Fountainhead; It's a Great Feeling; Task Force. **1950** Bright Leaf; Dallas. **1951** You're in the Navy Now (aka U.S.S. Teakettle); Starlift; It's a Big Country; Distant Drums. **1952** High Noon; Springfield Rifle. **1953** Return to Paradise; Blowing Wild. **1954** Garden of Evil; Vera Cruz. **1955** The Court-Martial of Billy Mitchell. **1956** Friendly Persuasion. **1957** Love in the Afternoon. **1958** Glamourous Hollywood (short); Ten North Fredrick; Man of the West. **1959** The Hanging Tree; They Came to Cordura; The Wreck of the Mary Deare; Alias Jesse James. **1961** The Naked Edge.

COOPER, GEORGE
Born: Dec. 18, 1892, Newark, N.J. Died: Dec. 9, 1943. Screen and stage actor. Entered films in 1908. Do not confuse with other actors George Cooper or George A. Cooper.

COOPER, GEORGIA (aka GEORGIE COOPER)
Born: 1882. Died: Sept. 3, 1968, Holywood, Calif. Screen and stage actress. Married to actor Landers Stevens (dec. 1940) and mother of actor/director George Stevens (dec. 1975).

Appeared in: **1928** The Question of Today (short). **1934** Desirable. **1936** Theodora Goes Wild. **1937** Four Days' Wonder; Hollywood Hotel; It's Love I'm After; Paid to Dance. **1938** The Sister; Racket Busters. **1939** Homicide Bureau. **1941** Father Takes a Wife. **1944** Music in Manhattan.

COOPER, DAME GLADYS
Born: Dec. 18, 1888, Lewisham, England. Died: Nov. 17, 1971, Henley-on-Thames, England (pneumonia). Screen, stage, television actress, stage producer and author. Was made a Dame Commander of the Order of the British Emmpire in 1967. Divorced from Herbert Buckmaster and Sir Neville Pearson and later married to actor Philip Merivale (dec. 1946). Mother of actors John Merivale and John

Buckmaster, actress Sally Cooper and Joan Buckmaster. Nominated for 1942 Academy Award for Best Supporting Actress in Now Voyager; in 1943 for The Song of Bernadette and in 1964 for My Fair Lady.

Appeared in: **1913** The Eleventh Commandment (film debut). **1914** Dandy Donovan, the Gentleman Cracksman. **1916** The Real Thing At Last. **1917** The Sorrows of Satan; Masks and Faces; My Lady's Dress. **1920** Unmarried. **1922** Headin' North; The Bohemian Girl. **1923** Bonnie Prince Charlie. **1935** The Iron Duke. **1938** The Seventh Commandment. **1940** Kitty Foyle; Rebecca. **1941** That Hamilton Woman (aka Lady Hamilton); The Black Cat; The Gay Falcon. **1942** This Above All; Eagle Squadron; Now Voyager. **1943** The Song of Bernadette; Forever and a Day; Mr. Lucky; Princess O'Rourke. **1944** The White Cliffs of Dover; Mrs. Parkington. **1945** The Valley of Decision; Love Letters. **1946** The Green Years; The Cockeyed Miracle. **1947** Green Dolphin Street; Beware of Pity; The Bishop's Wife. **1948** The Pirate; Homecoming. **1949** Madame Bovary; The Secret Garden. **1951** Thunder on the Hill. **1952** At Sword's Point (aka Sons of the Musketeers). **1955** The Man Who Loved Redheads. **1958** Separate Tables. **1963** The List of Adrian Messenger. **1964** My Fair Lady. **1967** The Happiest Millionaire. **1969** A Nice Girl Like Me.

COOPER, HARRY
Born: 1882. Died: Aug. 28, 1957, Hollywood, Calif. Screen, vaudeville actor, stuntman and double. Appeared in vaudeville with his wife in an act billed "Cooper and Valli." Entered films as a stunt man with Vitagraph.

Appeared in: **1937** Golf Mistakes (short).

COOPER, MELVILLE G.
Born: Oct. 15, 1896, Birmingham, England. Died: Mar. 29, 1973, Woodland Hills, Calif. (cancer). Stage and screen actor. Divorced from Gladys Grice and actress Rita Page and later married to Elizabeth Sutherland (dec. 1960).

Appeared in: **1931** Blood Coffee; The Calendar (aka Bachelor's Folly—US 1932). **1932** Two White Arms (aka Wives Beware—US 1933). **1933** Leave It to Me; Forging Ahead; To Brighton With Gladys. **1934** The Private Life of Don Juan. **1935** The Scarlet Pimpernel; The Bishop Misbehaves. **1936** The Gorgeous Hussy. **1937** The Last of Mrs. Cheyney; Thin Ice; The Great Garrick; Tovarich. **1938** Women Are Like That; The Adventures of Robin Hood; Gold Diggers in Paris; Four's a Crowd; Garden of the Moon; Hard to Get; Dramatic School; Comet Over Broadway; Dawn Patrol. **1939** I'm From Missouri; Blind Alley; Thin Ice; The Sun Never Sets; Two Bright Boys. **1940** Too Many Husbands; Rebecca; Pride and Prejudice; Murder Over New York. **1941** The Lady Eve; Submarine Zone; Scotland Yard; The Flame of New Orleans; You Belong to Me. **1942** Once Upon a Thursday (aka Affairs of Martha); This Above All; Life Begins at Eight-Thirty; Random Harvest. **1943** The Immortal Sergeant; Hit Parade of 1943; Holy Matrimony; My Kingdom for a Cook. **1946** Heartbeat; 13 Rue Madeleine. **1947** The Imperfect Lady. **1948** Enchantment. **1949** The Red Danube; And Baby Makes Three; Love Happy. **1950** Father of the Bride; Pretty Girl; Let's Dance; The Whipped (aka Underworld Story). **1952** Return of Gilbert and Sullivan. **1954** It Should Happen to You. **1955** Moonfleet; The King's Thief; Diane. **1956** Around the World in 80 Days; Bundle of Joy. **1957** The Story of Mankind. **1958** From the Earth to the Moon.

COOPER, MERIAN C.
Born: Oct. 24, 1893, Jacksonville, Fla. Died: Apr. 21, 1973, Coronado, Calif. (cancer). Film director, producer, screenwriter, cinematographer, author and screen actor. Married to actress Dorothy Jordan. In 1952 he received a Special Academy Award for his innovations in the film industry.

Appeared in: **1925** Grass.

COOPER, MIRIAM
Born: 1892, Baltimore, Md. Died: Apr. 12, 1976, Charlottesville, Va. (stroke). Screen actress and author. Divorced from actor, film director and film producer Raoul Walsh (dec. 1980).

Appeared in: **1911** A Blot on the Scutcheon. **1912** Victim of Circumstances; Battle of Pottsburgh Bridge; Tide of Battle; War's Havoc; The Drummer Girl of Vicksburg; The Colonel's Escape; The Bugler of Battery B; The Soldier Brothers of Susannah; The Seigh of Petersburg; The Darling of the CSA; Saved from the Court Martial; A Railroad Lochnivar; His Mother's Picture; The Girl in the Caboose; The Pony Express Girl; Battle in the Virginia Hills; The Water Right War; The Battle of Wits; A Race for Time. **1913** A Sawmill Hazard; A Desperate Chance; The Turning Point; A Treacherous Shot; The Farm Bully; The Toll Gate Raiders; Infamous Don Miguel; Captured

by Strategy. **1914** Birth of a Nation; The Stolen Radium; For His Master; Home Sweet Home; A Diamond in the Rough; The Gunman; The Dishonored Medal; The Odalisque; The Double Deception. **1915** The Fatal Black Bean; His Return; The Burned Hand. **1916** Intolerance. **1917** The Honor System; The Silent Lie; The Innocent Sinner; Berated. **1918** The Woman and the Law; The Prussian Cur. **1919** Evangaline; Should a Husband Forgive? **1920** The Deep Purple; The Oath; Serenade. **1922** Kindred of the Dust. **1923** Is Money Everything; The Girl Who Came Back; Daughters of the Rich; Her Accidental Husband; After the Ball; The Broken Wing.

COOPER, RICHARD
Born: July 16, 1893, Harrow-on-the-Hill, England. Died: June 18, 1947, England? Screen and stage actor. Entered films in 1929.

Appeared in: **1930** Mystery at the Villa Rose; House of the Arrow; Bed and Breakfast; The Last Hour; Lord Richard in the Pantry; Kissing Cup's Race; Enter the Queen. **1931** Black Coffee; Once Bitten; The Officer's Mess; Rodney Steps In; The Other Mrs. Phipps. **1932** The First Mrs. Fraser; Double Dealing. **1933** Home Sweet Home; Mannequin. **1934** The Black Abbot; The Four Masked Men; Lord Edgeware Dies. **1935** Annie, Leave the Room; Three Witnesses; That's My Uncle; The Ace of Spades. **1937** The Angelus (aka Who Killed Fen Markham?). **1939** Shipyard Sally.

COOPER, TEX
Born: 1877. Died: Mar. 29, 1951, Hollywood, Calif. Screen actor. Entered films in 1916.

Appeared in: **1921** The Man Worthwhile. **1939** The Oklahoma Kid. **1945** Pistol Packin' Nitwits (short).

COOPER, WYATT
Born: Sept. 3, 1927, near Quitman, Mass. Died: Jan. 5, 1978, New York, N.Y. (heart ailment). Screen, stage actor, screenwriter and author. Married to Gloria Vanderbilt.

Appeared in: **1961** Sanctuary.

COOTE, BERT
Born: 1868, England. Died: Sept. 1, 1938, London, England. Stage and screen actor.

COPAS, COWBOY
Born: 1914, Muskogee, Okla. Died: Mar. 5, 1963, near Camden, Tenn. (plane crash). Screen actor and singer.

Appeared in: **1949** Square Dance Jubilee.

COPEAU, JACQUES
Born: 1879, Paris, France. Died: Oct. 20, 1949, Beaune, France. Screen, stage actor, stage producer, director and playwright.

Appeared in: **1937** Razumov. **1938** The Courier of Lyons. **1939** The Affair Laflont.

COPELAND, NICHOLAS W. "NICK"
Born: 1895. Died: Aug. 17, 1940, Los Angeles, Calif. Screen, stage and vaudeville actor and screenwriter.

Appeared in: **1934** Manhattan Love Song; The Hell Cat; Twentieth Century; Here Comes the Navy; Student Tour. **1935** The Case of the Curious Bride; Miss Pacific Fleet; The Goose and the Gander; Murder in the Clouds. **1936** Man Hunt; Neighborhood House; The Legion of Terror; More Than a Secretary. **1937** True Confession; Lodge Night (short); Midnight Madonna. **1938** The Main Event; Romance in the Dark; Juvenile Court; Who Killed Gail Preston? **1939** Tell No Tales. **1940** Enemy Agent.

COPPEN, HAZEL
Born: 1925. Died: Apr. 8, 1975, London, England. Screen, stage and radio actress.

Appeared in: **1948** The Naked City.

COQUELIN, BENOIT CONSTANT
Born: 1841, Boulogne-sur-Mer, France. Died: Jan. 27, 1909, Ont-aux-Dames, France. Screen actor.

COQUELINE, JEAN
Born: 1865, France. Died: Oct. 3, 1944, France? Screen actor and film director.

Appeared in: **1936** Faisons un Reve.

CORBE, EDUARDO
Born: 1878, Cuba. Died: Aug. 29, 1967, Cuba. Screen and television actor.

CORBETT, BEN "BENNY"

Born: 1892, Hudson, Ill. Died: May 19, 1961, Hollywood, Calif. Screen actor. Entered films approx. 1915. Doubled for actors William Duncan and Antonio Moreno.

Appeared in: **1919** Lightning Bryce (serial). **1921** Black Sheep. **1922** The Heart of a Texan; The Kingfisher's Roost; Lure of Gold; Rangeland; South of Northern Lights; West of the Pecos. **1923** Don Quickshot of the Rio Grande; The Red Warning. **1924** The Man from Wyoming; The Phantom Horseman; The Riddle Rider (serial). **1925** The Circus Cyclone; Daring Days; The Outlaw's Daughter. **1926** Law of the Snow Country; Shadows of Chinatown; Without Orders. **1927** The Border Cavalier; The Man from Hardpan; Somewhere in Sonora; One Glorious Scrap. **1928** The Black Ace; The Boss of Rustler's Roost; The Bronc Stomper; The Fearless Rider; A Made-to-Order Hero; Put 'Em Up; Quick Triggers; Arizona Cyclone; The Mystery Rider (serial). **1929** Forty-Five Calibre War; The Royal Rider. **1930** Bar-L Ranch; Beau Bandit; The Lonesome Trail; Phantom of the Desert; Ridin' Law; Romance of the West; Westward Bound. **1933** Strawberry Roan. **1934** The Last Round-Up; Girl Trouble. **1936** For the Service; Empty Saddles. **1937** Texas Trail. **1938** Gold Mine in the Sky; Lightning Carson Rides Again. **1939** Straight Shootin'; Racketeers of the Range. **1942** Ghost Town Law. **1943** Hoppy Serves a Writ. **1946** Fool's Gold; The Bandit of Sherwood Forest. **1947** Pursued. **1948** Blood on the Moon. **1950** Colt .45; Cody of the Pony Express (serial); County Fair. **1953** The Charge at Feather River.

CORBETT, JAMES J.

Born: 1867. Died: Feb. 18, 1933, Bayside, N.Y. (cancer of liver). Heavyweight boxing champion, screen, stage and vaudeville actor. Divorced from actress Olive Lake.

Appeared in: **1894** Corbett and Peter Courteney made the first fight film for Edison. **1913** The Man from the Golden West. **1915** The Lady and the Burglars. **1919** The Midnight Man (serial). **1920** The Prince of Avenue A. **1922** The Beauty Shop. **1924** Broadway After Dark. **1929** Happy Days; James J. Corbett and Neil O'Brien (short). **1930** At the Round Table (short). **1942** Gentleman Jim (film clips). **1968** The Legendary Champions (doc.).

CORBETT, JEAN

Born: 1912. Died: Feb. 22, 1978, Philadelphia, Pa. Screen and television actress. Sister of actress Joan Corbitt.

Appeared in: **1953** The Robe. **1957** The Young Stranger.

CORBETT, LEONORA

Born: June 28, 1908, London, England. Died: July 29, 1960, Vleuten, Holland. Screen, stage actress and film producer.

Appeared in: **1932** Love on Wheels. **1933** The Constant Nymph; Friday the 13th (US 1934). **1934** Lady in Danger; Warn London; Wild Boy. **1935** Royal Cavalcade (aka Regal Cavalcade—US); Heart's Desire. **1936** Living Dangerously; The Happy Family. **1937** Farewell Again (aka Troopship—US 1938); The Price of Folly. **1938** Night Alone; Anything to Declare? **1940** Under Your Hat; Fingers.

CORBETT, MARY

Born: 1926. Died: Apr. 28, 1974, New York, N.Y. Screen, stage and television actress.

Appeared in: **1948** Portrait of Jenny.

CORBIN, ANDY

Died: Aug. 13, 1973. Screen actor.

CORBIN, VIRGINIA LEE

Born: Dec. 5, 1910, Prescott, Ariz. Died: June 5, 1942, Winfield, Ill. (heart disease). Screen and stage actress.

Appeared in: **1917** Aladdin and the Wonderful Lamp; Jack and the Beanstalk. **1923** Enemies of Children. **1924** Broken Laws; The Chorus Lady; The City That Never Sleeps; Sinners in Silk; Wine of Youth. **1925** The Cloud Rider; The Handsome Brute; Headlines; Lillies of the Streets; North Star; Three Keys. **1926** The Honeymoon Express; Hands Up!; Ladies at Play; The Whole Town's Talking. **1927** Driven from Home; No Place to Go; The Perfect Sap; Play Safe. **1928** Bare Knees; The Head of the Family; Jazzland; The Little Snob. **1929** Footlights and Fools; Knee High. **1931** Morals for Women; X Marks the Spot; Shotgun Pass.

CORDER, LEETA

Born: 1890. Died: Aug. 10, 1956, New York, N.Y. (cancer). Screen, stage, opera and radio actress.

CORDING, HARRY

Born: Apr. 29, 1891, England. Died: Sept. 1, 1954, Sun Valley, Calif. Screen actor. Entered films in 1921.

Appeared in: **1925** The Knockout. **1927** Black Jack. **1928** Daredevil's Reward; The Patriot; Sins of the Fathers. **1929** The Rescue; The Squall; The Isle of Lost Ships; Christina. **1930** Captain of the Guard; Rough Romance; Bride of the Regiment. **1931** The Right of Way; The Conquering Horde; Honor of the Family. **1932** File No. 113; The World and the Flesh; Forgotten Commandments; Cabin in the Cotton. **1933** Captured; To the Last Man. **1934** Great Expectations; The Black Cat. **1935** The Crusades; Peter Ibbetson; Captain Blood; The Man Who Reclaimed His Head; Strange Wives; Anna Karenina; Mutiny on the Bounty; Charlie Chan in Paris. **1936** The Country Doctor; Road Gang; Sutter's Gold; The White Angel; Daniel Boone. **1937** The Prince and the Pauper. **1938** Crime School; The Adventures of Robin Hood; Valley of the Giants; Painted Desert; The Adventures of Marco Polo. **1939** We Are Not Alone; The Light That Failed; Destry Rides Again; Tower of London; Son of Frankenstein; The Sun Never Sets; Each Dawn I Die; The Hound of the Baskervilles; The Adventures of Sherlock Holmes. **1940** King of the Royal Mounted (serial); Passport to Alcatraz; The Great Plane Robbery; Trial of the Vigilantes; The Sea Hawk; The Invisible Man Returns; Law and Order. **1941** The Lady from Cheyenne; Mutiny in the Arctic; The Wolf Man. **1942** Overland Mail (serial); Arabian Nights; Tennessee Johnson; Yukon Patrol; Ride 'Em Cowboy; Sherlock Holmes and the Secret Weapon; Son of Fury; Road to Morocco. **1944** The Hour Before Dawn; The Great Alaskan Mystery (serial); Ali Baba and the Forty Thieves; Gypsy Wildcat; Mrs. Parkington; Lost in a Harem. **1945** The House of Fear; Sudan; San Antonio. **1946** Dressed to Kill; Fool's Gold; The Bandit of Sherwood Forest; Terror by Night; A Night in Paradise. **1947** Forever Amber; Slave Girl; The Marauders; Dangerous Venture. **1948** A Woman's Vengeance; That Lady in Ermine; Red River; Tap Roots; Kiss the Blood Off My Hands. **1949** Rope of Sand; Samson and Delilah; The Fighting O'Flynn; Bad Men of Tombstone; Secret of St. Ives. **1950** Fortunes of Captain Blood; Last of the Buccaneers. **1951** Mask of the Avenger; Santa Fe; Al Jennnings of Oklahoma. **1952** Road to Bali; Ma and Pa Kettle at the Fair; The Big Trees; Against All Flags; Brave Warrior; Cripple Creek; Night Stage to Galveston. **1953** Treasure of the Golden Condor; Abbott and Costello Meet Dr. Jekyll and Mr. Hyde; Titanic. **1954** Man in the Attic; Demetrius and the Gladiators; Killer Leopard; Jungle Gents. **1955** East of Eden.

CORDON, NORMAN

Born: 1904, Washington, N.C. Died: Mar. 1, 1964, Chapel Hill, N.C. Screen actor and singer.

Appeared in: **1935** Educational shorts.

CORDY, HENRY (Henry Korn)

Born: 1908. Died: Nov. 27, 1965, New York, N.Y. (heart ailment). Screen actor and opera performer.

Appeared in: **1941** The Great American Broadcast; Unfinished Business.

CORDY, RAYMOND (Raymond Cordiaux)

Born: 1898, France. Died: 1956. Screen actor.

Appeared in: **1931** Le Million; A Nous la Liberte. **1933** La Quatorze Juillet. **1934** Le Dernier Milliardaire. **1937** Ignace. **1938** The Slipper Episode; They Were Five. **1942** Les Inconnus dans la Maison. **1946** Le Silence Est d'Or. **1947** Retour a l'Aube (She Returned at Dawn); Man About Town. **1949** Le Beaute du Diable (Beauty and the Devil—US 1952). **1954** A Nous la Liberte (rerelease of 1931 film). **1955** Les Grandes Maneuvers (The Grand Maneuver—US 1956). **1958** The Girl in the Bikini. **1960** Sin and Desire (aka l'Epave—The Wreck).

COREEN, MARCELLE (aka MARCELLE IMHOF)

Born: 1888. Died: Jan. 15, 1977, Hollywood, Calif. Screen and vaudeville actress. Married to actor Roger Imhof (dec. 1958) with whom she appeared in vaudeville.

Appeared in: **1930** Rural Hospitality (short). **1948** Jiggs and Maggie in Society. **1949** Maggie and Jiggs in Jackpot Jitters.

COREY, ARTHUR H.

Born: Mar. 22, 1889, New York, N.Y. Died: Mar. 26, 1950, Hollywood, Calif. Screen actor.

COREY, JOSEPH (Joseph Martorano)

Born: 1927. Died: Aug. 30, 1972, Los Angeles, Calif. (heart attack). Screen and television actor.

Appeared in: **1956** Gaby. **1957** The Delicate Delinquent.

COREY, MILTON R., SR.
Born: 1879. Died: Oct. 23, 1951, Washington, Mass. Screen actor and minister. Father of actor Wendell Corey (dec. 1968).

Appeared in: **1950** The Great Missouri Raid. **1951** Rawhide.

COREY, WENDELL
Born: Mar. 20, 1914, Dracut, Mass. Died: Nov. 9, 1968, Woodland Hills, Calif. (liver ailment). Screen, stage and television actor. Son of actor Milton Corey (dec. 1951).

Appeared in: **1947** Desert Fury (film debut); I Walk Alone. **1948** Man-Eater of Kumaon; The Search; Sorry, Wrong Number; The Accused. **1949** Holiday Affair; Thelma Jordan (aka File on Thelma Jordan); Any Number Can Play. **1950** No Sad Songs for Me; Harriet Craig; The Great Missouri Raid; The Furies; There's a Girl in My Heart. **1951** The Wild Blue Yonder; Rich, Young and Pretty. **1952** My Man and I; The Wild North; Carbine Williams. **1953** Laughing Anne (US 1954); Jamaica Run. **1954** Fireman Save My Child; Rear Window; Laughing Anne; Hell's Half Acre. **1955** The Big Knife. **1956** The Killer Is Loose; The Bold and the Brave; The Rack; The Rainmaker. **1957** Loving You. **1958** The Light in the Forest. **1959** Giant Leeches; Alias Jesse James. **1964** Blood on the Arrow. **1965** Broken Sabre. **1966** Women of the Prehistoric Planet; Waco; Picture Mommy Dead; Agent for H.A.R.M. **1967** Cyborg 2087; Red Tomahawk. **1968** The Astro Zombies; Buckskin. **1969** Young Billy Young.

CORLEY, ROBERT
Died: Nov. 18, 1971. Screen, radio and television actor.

Appeared in: **1965** Forty Acre Feud; The Legend of Blood Mountain.

CORNELL, KATHARINE
Born: Feb. 16, 1893, Berlin, Germany. Died: June 9, 1974, Vineyard Haven, Mass. Stage, radio, television, screen actress and stage producer. Married to stage director Guthrie McClintic (dec. 1961).

Appeared in: **1943** Stage Door Canteen. **1954** The Unconquered (narr.—aka Helen Keller in Her Story).

CORNELL, R. C. "DUFFY" (Roscoe Conkling Cornell)
Born: 1885. Died: Apr. 28, 1967, Hollywood, Calif. Screen actor. Managing editor of "Daily Variety." Appeared as himself in an MGM short.

CORNER, JAMES W.
Born: 1919. Died: Dec. 2, 1944, Germany (killed in action). Screen and stage actor.

Appeared in: **1939** Winter Carnival; What a Life.

CORNER, SALLY
Born: 1894. Died: Mar. 5, 1959, Hollywood, Calif. (heart attack). Screen and stage actress.

Appeared in: **1949** Task Force; Abandoned Woman; Once More, My Darling. **1950** Harvey; Two Flags West. **1951** The Company She Keeps. **1952** Scarlet Angel. **1953** The Robe. **1954** A Man Called Peter. **1957** The True Story of Jesse James.

CORNWALL, ANNE
Born: Jan. 17, 1897, Brooklyn, N.Y. Died: Mar. 2, 1980. Screen and stage actress.

Appeared in: **1918** The Knife; Prunella. **1919** Indestructible Wife; The World to Live In; Copperhead; The Firing Line. **1920** Everything but the Truth; The Path She Chose; Girl in the Rain; La, La, Lucille. **1922** Her Gilded Cage; The Seventh Day; To Have and to Hold. **1923** Dulcy; The Gold Diggers; Only 38. **1924** The Arizona Express; 40-Horse Hawkins; The Roughneck. **1925** Introduce Me; Keep Smiling; The Rainbow Trail; The Wrongdoers. **1926** The Splendid Crime; The Flaming Frontier; Racing Blood; Under Western Skies. **1927** The Heart of the Yukon; Chicken Feathers; Eyes of the Totem; College. **1928** Fighting Fanny. **1930** The Baby Bandit (short); The Widow From Chicago.

CORRELL, CHARLES J.
Born: Feb. 3, 1890, Peoria, Ill. Died: Sept. 26, 1972, Chicago, Ill. (heart attack). Screen, stage, radio actor and circus performer. Married to dancer Alyce Mercedes McLaughlin (dec. 1937). Was partner with Freeman Gosden in team of "Amos and Andy" on radio.

Appeared in: **1930** Check and Double Check (with Gosden). **1936** The Big Broadcast.

CORRIGAN, CHARLES
Born: 1894. Died: Apr. 4, 1966, New York, N.Y. Screen and stage actor.

Appeared in: **1939** The Roaring 20's.

CORRIGAN, D'ARCY
Born: Jan. 2, 1870, Country Cork, Ireland. Died: Dec. 25, 1945, U.S.? Screen actor.

Appeared in: **1925** Double Action Daniels; The Merry Widow; Lady Robin Hood. **1926** Ella Cinders; Exit Smiling. **1927** Wild Geese; Tarzan and the Golden Lion. **1929** The Last Warning. **1930** The Man from Blankley's. **1932** Murders in the Rue Morgue; Law and Order. **1935** The Informer. **1936** The Plough and the Stars; Mary of Scotland. **1937** All Over Town. **1938** A Christmas Carol. **1939** The Man in the Iron Mask; The Great Commandment.

CORRIGAN, EMMETT
Born: 1867, Amsterdam, Holland. Died: Oct. 29, 1932, Los Angeles, Calif. Stage and screen actor.

Appeared in: **1923** The Rendezvous. **1924** The Turmoil. **1928** The Lion and the Mouse. **1930** Soldiers and Women. **1931** An American Tragedy; Corsair. **1932** The Beast of the City; The World and the Flesh; The Night Mayor; Man Against Woman; Silver Dollar. **1933** The Bitter Tea of General Yen.

CORRIGAN, JAMES
Born: 1871. Died: Feb. 28, 1929, Los Angeles, Calif. Screen and stage actor.

Appeared in: **1921** Brester's Millions; Lavender and Old lace; Peck's Bad Boy; The Sky Pilot. **1922** A Front Page Story. **1923** April Showers; Divorce; Her Reputation. **1924** The Law Forbids; The Man from Wyoming; The White Sin. **1925** Durand of the Bad Lands; A Slave of Fashion. **1926** The Auction Block. **1927** Johnny Get Your Hair Cut.

CORRIGAN, LLOYD
Born: Oct. 16, 1900, San Francisco, Calif. Died: Nov. 5, 1969, Woodland Hills, Calif. Screen, television actor, film director and screenwriter. Entered films as an actor approx. 1925 and then turned to writing and directing. Son of actress Lillian Elliott (dec. 1959).

Appeared in: **1925** The Splendid Crime. **1939** The Great Commandment. **1940** Queen of the Mob; Sporting Blood; Jack Pot (short); Captain Caution; Return of Frank James; Dark Streets of Cairo; Lady in Question; High School; Young Tom Edison; Two Girls on Broadway; Public Deb No. 1; The Ghost Breakers. **1941** Mexican Spitfire's Baby; Whistling in the Dark; Kathleen; Confessions of Boston Blackie; A Girl, a Guy and a Gob; Men of Boys Town. **1942** Tennessee Johnson; London Blackout Murders; Bombay Clipper; North of the Klondike; Treat 'Em Rough; The Great Man's Lady; The Wife Takes a Flyer; The Mystery of Marie Roget; Maisie Gets Her Man; Lucky Jordan; Man Trap. **1943** Captive Wild Woman; Stage Door Canteen; Nobody's Darling; Tarzan's Desert Mystery; Hitler's Children; Secrets of the Underworld; King of the Cowboys; Song of Nevada. **1944** Passport to Adventure; Rosie the Riveter; Gambler's Choice; Goodnight, Sweetheart; Reckless Age; Lights of Old Santa Fe; The Thin Man Goes Home; Since You Went Away. **1945** Bring on the Girls; Boston Blackie Booked on Suspicion; The Fighting Guardsman; Lake Placid Serenade; Crime Doctor's Courage. **1946** She-Wolf of London; The Bandit of Sherwood Forest; Two Smart People; Lady Luck; The Chase; Alias Mr. Twilight. **1947** Stallion Road; Blaze of Noon; Shadowed; Ghost Goes Wild. **1948** Adventures of Casanova; Mr. Reckless; The Bride Goes Wild; A Date With Judy; Strike It Rich; Homicide for Three; The Big Clock; Return of October. **1949** Home in San Antone; Blondie Hits the Jackpot; Dancing in the Dark; Girl from Jones Beach. **1950** Father Is a Bachelor; And Baby Makes Three; When Willie Comes Marching Home; My Friend Irma Goes West. **1951** Her First Romance; The Last Outpost; Sierra Passage; Ghost Chasers; New Mexico; Cyrano de Bergerac. **1952** Son of Paleface; Rainbow 'Round My Shoulder; Sound Off. **1953** The Stars Are Singing; Marry Me Again. **1954** Return from the Sea; The Bowery Boys Meet the Monsters. **1955** Paris Follies of 1956. **1956** Hidden Guns. **1962** The Manchurian Candidate. **1963** It's a Mad, Mad, Mad, Mad World.

CORRIGAN, RAYMOND "CRASH" (Raymond Benard aka RAY BENARD)
Born: Feb. 14, 1907, Milwaukee, Wis. Died: Aug. 10, 1976, Brookings Harbor, Ore. (heart attack). Screen, television actor and stuntman. Entered films in 1932 as a stuntman.

Appeared in: **1933** Night Flight. **1935** The Singing Vagabond; Night Life of the Gods. **1936** Country Gentleman; The Leathernecks Have Landed; The Three Mesquiteers; Undersea Kingdom (serial); Darkest Africa (serial); The Vigilantes Are Coming (serial). **1937** Join the Marines; Ghost Town Gold; Roarin' Lead; Riders of the Whistling Skull; Hit the Saddle; Gunsmoke Ranch; Come on Cowboys; Range Defenders; Heart of the Rockies; The Trigger Trio; The Painted

Stallion (serial). **1938** Wild Horse Rodeo; The Purple Vigilantes; Call of the Mesquiteers; Outlaws of Sonora; Riders of the Black Hills; Overland Stage Raiders; Pals of the Saddle; Red River Range; Heroes of the Hills; Santa Fe Stampede. **1939** The Night Riders; Three Texas Steers; Wyoming Outlaw; New Frontier. **1940** The Range Busters; Trailing Double Trouble; West of Pinto Basin. **1941** Trail of the Silver Spurs; Tumbledown Ranch in Arizona; Wrangler's Roost; The Kid's Last Ride; Fugitive Valley; Saddle Mountain Round-Up. **1942** Rock River Renegades; Boot Hill Bandits; Texas Trouble Shooters. **1943** Cowboy Commandos; Black Market Rustlers. **1945** The White Gorilla. **1949** Zamba. **1953** Killer Ape. **1955** Apache Ambush. **1957** Zombies of Mora-Tau; Domino Kid. **1958** It! The Terror From Beyond Space. **1969** The Ribald Tales of Robin Hood (aka Robin Hood).

CORRIGAN, THOMAS J. *See* CARRIGAN, THOMAS J.

CORTES, ARMAND (aka ARMAND CORTEZ)
Born: Aug. 16, 1880, Nimes, France. Died: Nov. 19, 1948, San Francisco, Calif. Stage and screen actor.

Appeared in: **1914** House of Bondage. **1915** How Molly Malone Made Good. **1916** Yellow Menace (serial). **1917** Seven Keys to Baldpate; Her Better Self. **1920** Taking the Count; Return of Tarzan; His Temporary Wife. **1921** The Matrimonial Web; The Scarab Ring. **1924** Wages of Virtue; Galloping Hoofs (serial). **1925** The Crowded Hour. **1926** The Palm Beach Girl. **1927** The Music Master; Rubber Heels. **1938** Bluebeard's Eighth Wife.

CORTEZ, LEON
Born: 1898, England. Died: Dec. 31, 1970, Brighton, England. Screen, television, radio and vaudeville actor.

Appeared in: **1944** Can't Help Singing. **1963** I Could Go on Singing.

CORTEZ, RICARDO (Jake Krantz)
Born: Sept. 19, 1899, Vienna, Austria. Died: Apr. 28, 1977, New York, N.Y. Screen actor and film director. Brother of cinematographer Stanley Cortez. Divorced from actress Alma Rubens (dec. 1931) and Christine Coniff Lee (dec.). Married to Margaret Cortez.

Appeared in: **1923** The Call of the Canyon; Hollywood; Children of Jazz; Sixty Cents an Hour. **1924** Argentine Love; The Bedroom Window; Feet of Clay; The Next Corner; The City That Never Sleeps; The Society Scandal; This Woman. **1925** In the Name of Love; Not So Long Ago; The Spainard; The Swan; The Pony Express. **1926** Volcano; The Torrent; The Cat's Pajamas; The Eagle of the Sea; The Sorrows of Satan. **1927** By Whose Hand?; Mockery; New York; The Private Life of Helen of Troy. **1928** The Gun Runner; The Grain of Dust; Excess Baggage; Prowlers of the Sea; Ladies of the Nightclub. **1929** New Orleans; The Lost Zeppelin; Midstream; The Phantom in the House; The Younger Generation. **1930** Her Man; Montana Moon; Illicit. **1931** Big Business Girl; Ten Cents a Dance; Behind Office Doors; Bad Company; Maltese Falcon; Reckless Living; White Shoulders; Transgression. **1932** No One Man; Men of Chance; Symphony of Six Million; Is My Face Red?; Thirteen Women; The Phantom of Crestwood; Flesh. **1933** Broadway Bad; Midnight Mary; Big Executive; Torch Singer; House on 56th Street; Lady of the Night. **1934** Big Shakedown; Wonder Bar; Mandalay; Man With Two Faces; Hat, Coat and Glove; A Lost Lady; The Firebird. **1935** I Am a Thief; Shadow of Doubt; White Cockatoo; Manhattan Moon; Special Agent; Frisco Kid. **1936** Manhunt; The Murder of Dr. Harrigan; The Walking Dead; Postal Inspector; The Case of the Black Cat; Talk of the Devil (US 1937). **1937** Her Husband Lies; The Californian; West of Shanghai. **1939** Mr. Moto's Last Warning; Charlie Chan in Reno. **1940** Murder Over New York. **1941** A Shot in the Dark; Romance of the Rio Grande; World Premiere; I Killed That Man. **1942** Who is Hope Schuyler?; Rubber Racketeers; Tomorrow We Live. **1944** Make Your Own Bed. **1946** The Inner Circle; The Locket. **1947** Blackmail. **1948** Mystery in Mexico. **1950** Bunco Squad. **1958** The Last Hurrah.

CORTHELL, HERBERT
Born: 1875, Boston, Mass. Died: Jan. 23, 1947, Hollywood, Calif. Screen and stage actor.

Appeared in: **1924** Classmates; Second Youth. **1933** The Cohens and the Kellys in Trouble; Only Yesterday; Lone Cowboy. **1934** Bombay Mail; There Ain't No Justice; Let's Talk It Over; Uncertain Lady. **1935** The Fire Trap. **1936** The Story of Louis Pasteur; Dancing Feet. **1937** Renfrew of the Royal Mounted; Man in Blue; Blazing Barriers. **1938** Sing You Sinners. **1939** Fifth Avenue Girl; Career; House of Fear; Espionage. **1941** Citizen Kane. **1942** Duke of the Navy.

CORY, ROBERT
Born: 1883. Died: Nov. 9, 1955, Hollywood, Calif. (cancer). Screen and stage actor. Entered films approx. 1925.

Appeared in: **1940** Hudson's Bay. **1945** The Coin is Green.

COSGRAVE, JACK *See* COSGROVE, JACK

COSGRAVE, LUKE
Born: Aug. 6, 1862, Ballaghdreen, County Mayo, Ireland. Died: June 28, 1949, Woodland Hills, Calif. Stage and screen actor. Entered films in 1923.

Appeared in: **1923** Hollywood; The Light That Failed. **1924** The Border Legion; Code of the Sea; Flaming Barriers; Merton of the Movies. **1925** Contraband; Durand of the Bad Lands; Welcome Home. **1926** Rocking Moon; Sir Lumberjack. **1927** Jewels of Desire. **1928** Gentlemen Prefer Blondes; The Mating Call; The Red Mark. **1929** The Duke Steps Out. **1930** Men on Call; Lightin'. **1931** Not Exactly Gentlemen; The Squaw Man. **1932** Sinners in the Sun. **1935** Steamboat 'Round the Bend. **1940** Comin' 'Round the Mountain.

COSGROVE, JACK (aka JACK COSGRAVE)
Born: Sept. 29, 1875, Pa. Died: Jan. 27, 1975. Screen actor.

Appeared in: **1918** Hearts of the World. **1921** Girls Don't Gamble; Making the Grade; Smiling All the Way; There are no Villians. **1922** Monte Cristo.

COSGROVE, ROBERT
Born: 1900. Died: Sept., 1960, Saranac Lake, N.Y. (tuberculosis—heart attack). Screen actor.

COSIMA, RENEE
Born: 1926, France. Died: Sept. 1, 1981, France. Screen actor.

Appeared in: **1949** Les Enfants Terrible (aka The Strange Ones—US 1952). **1957** Marchands de Filles (Sellers of Girls—US 1967, aka Girl Merchants). The following French films: Au Royaume des Cieux; Gibier de Potence; Adieu Paris; Un Tresor de Femme; Les Naufrageurs; Cause Toujours mon Lapin.

COSMO, TOM "CRAZY CUE" (Thomas Anthony DiCosimo)
Born: 1915. Died: Oct. 16, 1978, New York, N.Y. Billiard Player, screen and vaudeville actor.

Appeared in: **1961** The Hustler.

COSSAEUS, SOPHIE
Born: 1893, Wiesbaden, Germany. Died: Sept. 23, 1965, Frankfurt-Main, Germany. Screen, stage, television, radio actress and dancer.

COSSAR, JOHN HAY
Born: 1865, London, England. Died: Apr. 28, 1935, Hollywood, Calif. Screen, stage and vaudeville actor.

Appeared in: **1914** His Stolen Fortune; The Other Man. **1919** The Highest Trump. **1921** Hearts and Masks; Made in Heaven; The Night Rose; The Poverty of Riches; That Something. **1922** Doubling for Romeo; Grand Larceny; Thorns and Orange Blossoms; Watch Your Step; When Husbands Deceive. **1923** The Steel Train (serial); Fools and Riches; The Hunchback of Notre Dame. **1924** The Fast Express (serial); The Great Diamond Mystery. **1926** The Sap. **1927** Melting Millions (serial); Web of Fate; Woman's Law. **1929** The Fire Detective (serial).

COSSART, ERNEST
Born: Sept. 24, 1876, Cheltenham, England. Died: Jan. 21, 1951, New York, N.Y. Screen and stage actor.

Appeared in: **1916** The Strange Case of Mary Page (serial). **1935** The Scoundrel; Accent on Youth; Two for Tonight. **1936** Desire; Big Broadcast of 1937; Palm Springs; My American Wife; Murder With Pictures; Champagne Waltz; The Great Ziegfeld. **1937** Three Smart Girls; Top of the Town; As Good as Married; The Lady Fights Back; Angel. **1938** A Letter of Introduction. **1939** Zaza; Tower of London; The Light That Failed; Lady of the Tropics; The Magnificent Fraud; Three Smart Girls Grow Up; Never Say Die. **1940** A Bill of Divorcement; Kitty Foyle; Tom Brown's School Days. **1941** Kings Row; Charley's Aunt; One Foot in Heaven; Skylark. **1944** Knickerbocker Holiday; Casanova Brown. **1945** The Girl of the Limberlost; Love Letters; Tonight and Every Night. **1946** Cluny Brown; The Jolson Story. **1947** Love from a Stranger. **1949** John Loves Mary.

COSTA, SAM
Born: 1910, England. Died: Sept. 22, 1981, London, England (cancer). Screen, stage, radio actor and singer.

Appeared in: **1951** One Wild Oat. **1952** The Pickwick Papers (US 1953). **1956** One Wish Too Many (US 1962).

COSTA, SEBASTIANO
Born: 1876. Died: July 18, 1935, New Rochelle, N.Y. (heart attack). Screen actor.

COSTE, MAURICE R.
Born: 1875. Died: Mar. 22, 1963, Chatham, Ont., Canada. Screen and stage actor.

COSTELLO, DELMAR
Born: 1906. Died: July 29, 1961. Screen actor.

Appeared in: **1934** Four Frightened People. **1954** Elephant Walk; Secret of the Incas. **1955** Hell's Island.

COSTELLO, DOLORES
Born: Sept. 17, 1905, Pittsburg, Pa. Died: Mar. 1, 1979, Fallbrook, Calif. Screen, stage actress and model. Daughter of actor Maurice Costello (dec. 1950) and actress Mae Altschuk Costello (dec. 1929). Sister of actress Helene Costello (dec. 1957). Divorced from John Barrymore (dec. 1942) and Dr. John Vrywink. Mother of actress Dolores Ethel Mae and actor John Blythe Barrymore, Jr.

Appeared in: **1911** The Meeting of the Ways; His Sister's Children. **1912** A Juvenile Love Affair; Wanted a Grandmother; Ida's Christmas; A Reformed Santa Claus; Vultures and Doves. **1913** The Hindoo Charm. **1914** Too Much Burglar; Some Steamer Scooping; The Evil Men Do; Etta of the Footlights. **1923** The Glimpses of the Moon; Lawful Larceny. **1925** Bobbed Hair; Greater Than a Crown. **1926** The Little Irish Girl; Mannequin; Bride of the Storm; The Sea Hunt; The Sea Beast. **1927** A Million Bid; The Third Degree; When a Man Loves; The Heart of Maryland; The College Widow; Old San Francisco. **1928** Tenderloin; Glorious Betsy. **1929** The Redeeming Sin; Glad Rag Doll; Noah's Ark; The Show of Shows; Hearts in Exile; Madonna of Avenue A. **1930** Second Chance. **1931** Expensive Woman. **1936** Little Lord Fauntleroy; Yours for the Asking. **1938** The Beloved Brat; Breaking the Ice. **1939** Outside These Walls; Whispering Enemies; The King of the Turf. **1942** The Magnificent Ambersons. **1943** This is the Army.

COSTELLO, DON
Born: 1901. Died: Oct. 24, 1945, Hollywood, Calif. Screen and stage actor.

Appeared in: **1939** Another Thin Man. **1940** Joe and Ethel Turp Call on the President; One Crowded Night. **1941** Sleepers West; Ride on Vaquero; I'll Wait for You; Here Comes Mr. Jordan; Unholy Partners; Whistling in the Dark. **1942** Johnny Eager; Joe Smith, American; A-Haunting We Will Go; Just Off Broadway. **1943** A Night to Remember; Truck Busters; Air Raid Wardens; Crime Doctor; A Lady Takes a Chance. **1944** Mystery Man; Texas Masquerade; The Whistler. **1945** Nob Hill; Incendiary Blonde; The Red Dragon; Here Come the Co-Eds. **1946** The Blue Dahlia; Along Came Jones.

COSTELLO, HELENE
Born: June 21, 1903, New York, N.Y. Died: Jan. 26, 1957, Los Angeles, Calif. (pneumonia, tuberculosis and narcotics). Screen and stage actress. Entered films with Vitagraph in 1912. Was a 1927 Wampas Baby Star. Sister of actress Dolores Costello (dec. 1979) and daughter of actor Maurice Costello (dec. 1950) and actress Mae Altschuk (dec. 1929). Divorced from actor Lovell Sherman (dec. 1934) and artist George Lee Le Blanc.

Appeared in: **1912** Two Women and Two Men; The Night Before Christmas; The First Violin; The Black Sheep; Wanted—A Grandmother; She Never Knew; Lulu's Doctor; In the Garden Fair; The Church Across the Way. **1913** The Mystery of the Stolen Child; The Other Woman; Heartbroken Shep. **1914** The Memories That Count; My Official Wife. **1925** The Man on the Box; Bobbed Hair; Ranger of the Big Pines. **1926** Wet Paint; Don Juan; The Honeymoon Express; The Love Toy; Millionaires; While London Sleeps. **1927** In Old Kentucky; Good Time Charley; Heart of Maryland; The Broncho Twister; Finger Prints. **1928** Burning Up Broadway; Comrades; The Circus Kid; The Midnight Taxi; Fortune Hunter; Lights of New York; Husbands for Rent; Phantom of the Turf. **1929** Broken Barriers; The Fatal Warning (serial); When Dreams Come True; Show of Shows. **1935** Riffraff.

COSTELLO, LOU (Louis Francis Cristillo)
Born: Mar. 6, 1906, Paterson, N.J. Died: Mar. 3, 1959, Los Angeles, Calif. (heart attack). Screen, stage, burlesque, vaudeville and radio actor. Was part of the comedy team "Abbott and Costello" with Bud Abbot (dec. 1974).

Together they appeared in: **1940** One Night in the Tropics. **1941** Buck Privates; In the Navy; Hold That Ghost; Keep 'Em Flying. **1942** Ride 'Em Cowboy; Rio Rita; Hold Your Horses; Who Done It?; Pardon My Sarong. **1943** It Ain't Hay; Hit the Ice. **1944** Lost in a Harem; In Society. **1945** Here Come the Co-Eds; The Naughty Nineties; Abbott and Costello in Hollywood. **1946** Little Giant; The Time of Their Lives. **1947** Buck Privates Come Home; The Wistful Widow of Wagon

Gap. **1948** The Noose Hangs High; Abbott and Costello Meet Frankenstein; Mexican Hayride. **1949** Abbott and Costello Meet the Killer, Boris Karloff; Africa Screams. **1950** Abbott and Costello in the Foreign Legion. **1951** Abbott and Costello Meet the Invisible Man; Comin' 'Round the Mountain. **1952** Jack and the Beanstalk; Lost in Alaska; Abbott and Costello Meet Captain Kidd; News of the Day (MGM short (newsreel) for promotion of U.S. Bonds). **1953** Abbott and Costello Go to Mars; Abbott and Costello Meet Dr. Jekyll and Mr. Hyde. **1954** Hollywood Grows Up (short). **1955** Abbott and Costello Meet the Keystone Kops; Abbott and Costello Meet the Mummy. **1956** Dance With Me, Henry. **1959** The 30-Foot Bride of Candy Rock (without Abbott). **1964** Big Parade of Comedy (doc.). **1965** The World of Abbott and Costello (doc.).

COSTELLO, MRS. MAE (aka MAE ALTSCHUK)
Born: 1882, Brooklyn, N.Y. Died: Aug. 2, 1929 (heart disease). Screen actress. Married to actor Maurice Costello (dec. 1950). Mother of actresses Dolores (dec. 1979) and Helene (dec. 1957) Costello.

Appeared in: **1911** Her Crowning Glory. **1912** Diamond Cut Diamond; The Mills of the Gods.

COSTELLO, MAURICE
Born: 1877, Pittsburgh, Pa. Died: Oct. 30, 1950, Hollywood, Calif. (heart ailment). Screen, stage and vaudeville actor. Entered films with Edison in 1905. Divorced from actress Mae Altschuk (dec. 1929) and stage actress Ruth Reeves. Father of actresses Dolores and Helene (dec. 1957) Costello.

Appeared in: **1910** The New Stenographer. **1911** A Tale of Two Cities. **1912** The Spider's Crime; The Night Before Christmas; As You Like It. **1913** The Adventure of the Ambassador's Disappearance. **1914** Mr. Barnes of New York. **1915** The Man Who Couldn't Beat God; Tried for His Own Murder. **1916** The Crown Prince's Double; The Crimson Stain Mystery (serial). **1918** Cap'n Abe's Niece. **1919** The Cambric Mask. **1920** Deadline at Eleven; Human Collateral. **1921** Conceit. **1922** Determination. **1923** None So Blind; Glimpses of the Moon; Fog Bound; Man and Wife. **1924** Virtuous Liars; Love of Women; Let No Man Put Asunder; The Story Without a Name; Week-End Husbands; The Law and the Lady; Heart of Alaska; Roulette. **1925** The Mad Marriage. **1926** Wives of the Prophet; The Last Alarm. **1927** Johnny Get Your Hair Cut; The Shamrock and the Rose; Camille; Spider Webs; Wolves of the Air. **1928** The Wagon Show; Eagle of the Night (serial); Black Feather. **1936** Hollywood Boulevard. **1938** There's That Woman Again. **1939** Mr. Smith Goes to Washington; Andy Hardy Gets Spring Fever; Rovin' Tumbleweeds. **1940** A Little Bit of Heaven; Third Finger Left Hand. **1941** Here Comes Mr. Jordan; Lady from Louisiana. **1942** Reap the Wild Wind. **1943** DuBarry Was a Lady. **1944** The Climax.

COSTELLO, WILLIAM A.
Born: 1898. Died: Oct. 9, 1971, San Jose, Calif. Screen, radio actor, musician and singer. Voice of "Popeye the Sailor Man."

Appeared in: **1927** King of Kings. **1930** Border Romance. **1935** Melody Trail. **1938** The Port of Missing Girls; Wanted by the Police. **1939** Balalaika.

COTSWORTH, STAATS
Born: Feb. 17, 1908, Oak Park, Ill. Died: Apr. 9, 1979, New York, N.Y. Screen, stage, radio, television actor and painter. Married to Muriel Kirkland (dec. 1968) and actress Josephine Hutchinson.

Appeared in: **1957** Peyton Place. **1971** They Might Be Giants.

COTTO DEL VALLE, LUIS
Born: 1913. Died: Mar., 1971, Mexico City, Mexico. Screen and stage actor.

COTTON, BILLY (William Edward Cotton)
Born: 1900, England. Died: Mar. 25, 1969, London, England (heart attack). Bandleader, screen, radio and television actor.

Appeared in: **1921** The Old Next.

COTTON, FRED AYRES
Born: 1907, Hastings, Nebr. Died: Jan. 29, 1964, New York, N.Y. Screen and stage actor.

COTTON, GEORGE
Born: 1903, Grand Rapids, Mich. Died: May 26, 1975, Lisbon, Portugal. Screen, stage and television actor.

Appeared in: **1964** The Curse of the Living Corpse.

COTTON, LARRY
Born: 1912. Died: Jan. 12, 1977, Hollywood, Calif. Screen actor and vocalist.

Appeared in: **1941** Pot O'Gold.

COTTON, LUCY (Lucy Cotton Magraw)
Born: 1891. Died: Dec. 12, 1948, Miami Beach, Fla. (suicide—overdose of sleeping pills). Stage and screen actress.

Appeared in:**1910** The Fugitive. **1921** The Devil; Whispering Shadows; The Man Who.

COTTON, RICHARDSON
Died: Sept. 24, 1916, Ephraim, Wisc. (hit by auto). Screen actor.

Appeared in: **1915** Hearts and Roses; A Mansion of Tragedy; The Lighthouse by the Sea. **1916** Pieces of the Game; Folly; A Man's Work; The Danger Line; Once a Thief; Our People; The Sting of Victory.

COTTS, CAMPBELL
Born: 1903, England? Died: Feb. 19, 1964, London, England. Screen and stage actor.

Appeared in: **1949** Stop Press; Dear Mr. Prohack (US 1950). **1950** Last Holiday; The Angel With the Trumpet. **1951** Encore (US 1952). **1952** The Hour of 13. **1955** Barbados Quest (aka Murder on Approval—US 1956). **1956** Three Men in a Boat (US 1958). **1957** Doctor at Large; The Good Companions (US 1958); Just My Luck.

COUGHLIN, KEVIN
Born: 1946, New York. Died: Jan. 19, 1976, Los Angeles, Calif. (hit-and-run accident). Screen, stage and television actor.

Appeared in: **1956** Storm Center (film debut). **1958** The Defiant Ones. **1959** Happy Anniversary. **1966** Duel at Diablo. **1968** Wild in the Streets; Mary Jane; The Young Runaways. **1969** The Gay Deceivers.

COULTER, FRAZER
Born: 1849, Smith Falls, Ont., Canada. Died: Jan. 26, 1937, East Islip, N.Y. Screen and stage actor.

Appeared in: **1921** His Brother's Keeper; Love's Redemption. **1923** The Heart Raider; The Governor's Lady. **1926** The Prince of Tempters.

COUNTESS DUCELLA
Born: Buffalo, N.Y. Died: Nov. 28, 1921, Los Angeles, Calif. Screen actress.

Appeared in: **1917** The Honor System; Devil's Payday; The Man Who Took a Chance. **1919** Sue of the South.

COURT, ALFRED C.
Born: 1886, Australia. Died: Dec. 31, 1953, Hollywood, Calif. Stage and screen actor.

COURTENAY, WILLIAM
Born: 1875, Worcester, Mass. Died: Apr. 20, 1933, Rye, N.Y. (severe cold and heart weakness). Stage and screen actor. Married to stage actress Virginia Harned (dec. 1946).

Appeared in: **1894** Miss Jerry. **1917** Kick In. **1929** Evidence; The Show of Shows; The Sacred Flame. **1930** The Way of All Men; Three Faces East.

COURTLEIGH, STEPHEN
Died: 1968. Screen actor.

Appeared in: **1955** Yellowneck. **1960** North to Alaska.

COURTLEIGH, WILLIAM, JR.
Born: June 28, 1892, Buffalo, N.Y. Died: Mar. 13, 1918, Philadelphia, Pa. (pneumonia). Stage and screen actor. Married to actress Ethel Flemming.

Appeared in: **1914** The Nightingale; The Better Man. **1915** Neal of the Navy (serial); Souls in Pawn; Life's Crucible. **1916** The Innocent Lie; Out of the Drifts; Cinders; The Sheriff of Pine Mountain. **1917** Miss U.S.A.; The Heart of a Lion. **1918** By Right of Purchase. **1919** Eyes of Youth.

COURTLEIGH, WILLIAM, SR.
Born: 1869, Guelph, Ont., Canada. Died: Dec. 27, 1930, Rye, N.Y. Screen actor.

Appeared in: **1920** Madame X. **1922** Handle With Care; Ashes; Any Night; Midnight.

COURTNEIDGE, DAME CICELY
Born: Apr. 1, 1893, Sydney, Australia (New South Wales). Died: Apr. 26, 1980, London, England. Screen, stage, vaudeville actress and author. Married to actor Jack Hulbert (dec. 1978). Was made Dame Commander of the Order of the British Empire in 1972.

Appeared in: **1930** Elstree Calling. **1931** The Ghost Train (US 1933). **1932** Jack's the Boy (aka Night and Day—US 1933); Happy Ever After. **1933** Aunt Sally (aka Along Came Sally—US 1934); Soldiers of the King (aka The Woman in Command—US 1934); Falling For You. **1935** Everybody Dance. **1937** Take My Tip. **1940** Under Your Hat. **1947** The Imperfect Lady. **1960** The Spider's Web. **1962** The L-Shaped Room (US 1963). **1965** Those Magnificent Men in Their Flying Machines. **1966** The Wrong Box.

COURTNEY, INEZ
Born: Mar. 12, 1908, New York. Died: Apr. 5, 1975, Neptune, N.J. Screen and stage actress.

Appeared in: **1930** Loose Ankles; Not Damaged; Song of the Flame; Spring is Here; Hold Your Man; Sonny. **1931** Hot Heiress; Bright Lights. **1932** Big City Blues. **1933** The World Gone Mad; Cheating Blondes; I Love That Man. **1934** Jealousy; The Captain Hates the Sea; It's the Cat's (short); Broadway Bill. **1935** Carnival; The Girl Friend; Millions in the Air; I'm a Father (short); Sweepstake Annie; Break of Hearts; Another Face; The Raven; Ship Cafe; The Affair of Susan; Magnificent Obsession. **1936** Dizzy Dames; Let's Sing Again; Suzy; It Couldn't Have Happened; Wedding Present; Brilliant Marriage. **1937** The Hurricane; Time Out for Romance; The Hit Parade; MGM short; Armored Car; Clarence; Partners in Crime; The Thirteenth Man; The Thirteenth Chair. **1938** Letter of Introduction; Having a Wonderful Time; Crime Ring; Five of a Kind. **1939** When Tomorrow Comes; Blondie Meets the Boss; Beauty for the Asking; Missing Evidence. **1940** The Shop Around the Corner; The Farmer's Daughter; Turnabout.

COURTNEY, OSCAR W.
Born: 1877. Died: June 13, 1962, Chicago, Ill. Screen and vaudeville actor. Entered films with Essanay in 1912.

COURTRIGHT, CLYDE
Born: 1885. Died: Dec. 6, 1967, Santa Cruz, Calif. Screen actor. Stand-in for Gary Cooper and Charles Bickford.

COURTRIGHT, WILLIAM "UNCLE BILLY"
Born: Mar. 10, 1848, New Milford, Ill. Died: Mar. 6, 1933, Ione, Calif. Screen, stage and minstrel actor. Entered films in 1910.

Appeared in: **1920** Peaceful Valley. **1921** The Rookie's Return; The Speed Girl; Extravagance; R.S.V.P.; The Lure of Youth; The Millionaire. **1922** At the Sign of the Jack O'Lantern; The Deuce of Spades; A Man of Action; The Sunset Trail; The Man Under Cover. **1923** The Girl I Loved; Bell Boy 13. **1924** The Heart Buster; George Washington, Jr. **1925** Are Parents People?; Some Pun'kins; Thank You; The Trouble With Wives; All Around the Frying Pan. **1926** For Wives Only; The Grand Duchess and the Waiter; Atta Boy; The Two Gun Man; A Regular Scout; The Tough Guy; Lone Hand Saunders; Hands Across the Border. **1927** Don Mike; Arizona Nights; Jesse James; My Best Girl; Silver Comes Thru; The Poor Nut. **1928** The Pioneer Scout; Kit Carson; Sunset Legion.

COVENTRY, FLORENCE
Born: 1874, New Brunswick, Canada. Died: Nov. 22, 1939, New York, N.Y. Screen and stage actress.

Appeared in: **1914** The Long Way. **1915** The Danger Signal. **1916** Devil's Prayer Book.

COVERT, EARL L.
Born: 1910. Died: Mar. 8, 1975, Long Beach, Calif. Screen actor and signer.

COWAN, JEROME (Jerome Palmer Cowan)
Born: Oct. 6, 1897, New York, N.Y. Died: Jan. 24, 1972, Encino, Calif. Screen, stage, vaudeville, burlesque and television actor.

Appeared in: **1936** Beloved Enemy. **1937** Vogues of 1938; You Only Live Once; Shall We Dance; New Faces of 1937; The Hurricane. **1938** The Goldwyn Follies; There's Always a Woman. **1939** The Old Maid; St. Louis Blues; The Gracie Allen Murder Case; Exile Express; The Great Victor Herbert; East Side of Heaven; The Saint Strikes Back; She Married a Cop. **1940** Torrid Zone; Wolf of New York; Ma, He's Making Eyes at Me; Meet the Wildcat; City for Conquest; Melody Ranch; Victory; The Quarterback; Street of Memories; Castle on the Hudson; Framed. **1941** High Sierra; Rags to Riches; The Roundup;

Affectionately Yours; One Foot in Heaven; Kiss the Boys Goodbye; Kisses for Breakfast; The Maltese Falcon; Out of the Fog; Singapore Woman; The Great Lie; Mr. and Mrs. North; Too Many Blondes. **1942** The Girl from Alaska; Frisco Lil; Moontide; Through Different Eyes; Joan of Ozark; Who Done It?; A Gentleman at Heart; Street of Chance; The Bugle Sounds. **1943** The Song of Bernadette; Ladies' Day; Crime Doctor; No Place for a Lady; Mission to Moscow; Hi Ya, Sailor!; Silver Spurs; Find the Blackmailer; Crime Doctor's Strangest Case. **1944** Sing a Jingle; Minstrel Man; Guest in the House; Crime by Night; South of Dixie; Mr. Skeffington. **1945** Fog Island; Divorce; Getting Gertie's Garter; Behind City Lights; Crime Doctor's Courage; Blonde Ransom; Hitchhike to Happiness; G.I. Honeymoon; Jungle Captive. **1946** My Reputation; One Way to Love; Claudia and David; Murder in the Music Hall; One Exciting Week; Blondie Knows Best; Mr. Ace; Deadline at Dawn; Deadline for Murder; A Night in Paradise; The Kid from Brooklyn; The Perfect Marriage. **1947** Blondie's Holiday; Blondie's Anniversary; Blondie's Big Moment; Driftwood; Flight to Nowhere; Riffraff; The Unfaithful; Miracle on 34th Stret; Cry Wolf; Blondie in the Dough. **1948** So This Is New York; Blondie's Reward; Wallflower; Arthur Takes Over; June Bride; Night Has a Thousand Eyes; Dangerous Year. **1949** Blondie Hits the Jackpot; Blondie's Secret; Blondie's Big Deal; Scene of the Crime; Always Leave Them Laughing; The Girl from Jones Beach; The Fountainhead. **1950** The West Point Story; Young Man With a Horn; Dallas; Joe Palooka Meets Humphrey; The Fuller Brush Girl; Peggy; When You're Smiling. **1951** Disc Jockey; The Fat Man; Criminal Lawyer. **1953** The System. **1959** Have Rocket, Will Travel. **1960** Private Property; Visit to a Small Planet. **1961** All in a Night's Work; Pocketful of Miracles. **1963** Critic's Choice; Black Zoo. **1964** The Patsy; John Goldfarb, Please Come Home. **1966** Frankie and Johnny; Penelope. **1967** The Gnome-Mobile. **1969** The Comic (aka Billy Bright).

COWAN, LYNN F.
Born: June 8, 1894, Iowa Falls, Iowa. Died: Aug. 29, 1973, Pensacola, Fla. Pianist, singer, composer, vaudeville and screen actor.

Appeared in: **1925** The Compromise. **1926** The Social Highwayman.

COWARD, SIR NOEL (Noel Pierce Coward)
Born: Dec. 16, 1899, Teddington-on-the-Thames, England. Died: Mar. 26, 1973, Port Maria, Jamaica (heart attack). Screen, stage, television actor, film director, producer, stage producer, composer, playwright, screenwriter and author. In 1942 received a Special Academy Award for outstanding production achievement for In Which We Serve.

Appeared in: **1918** Hearts of the World (film debut). **1935** The Scoundrel. **1942** In Which We Serve. **1950** The Astonished Heart. **1956** Around the World in 80 Days. **1960** Our Man in Havana; Surprise Package. **1964** Paris When It Sizzles. **1965** Bunny Lake is Missing. **1968** Boom! **1969** The Italian Job.

COWELLS, MABEL
Died: Date unknown. Screen actress. Mother of actress Sally Banks (dec. 1977).

COWIE, LAURA
Born: Apr. 7, 1892, Aberdeen, Scotland. Died: Feb. 11, 1969, England? Screen and stage actress. Married to stage producer/playwright John Hastings Turner.

Appeared in: **1916** The Vicar of Wakefield.

COWL, GEORGE
Born: Feb. 24, 1878, Blackpool, England. Died: Apr. 4, 1942, United States? Screen actor.

Appeared in: **1916** The Closed Road. **1921** The Plaything of Broadway. **1922** The Glory of Clementine; Pink Gods. **1923** The Prisoner; Fashionable Fakers. **1924** Secrets. **1926** Broadway Madness. **1928** The Adventurer; Court-Martial. **1930** Jazz Cinderella. **1933** Secrets of Hollywood.

COWL, JANE
Born: 1887, Boston, Mass. Died: June 22, 1950, Santa Monica, Calif. (cancer). Screen, stage actress and playwright.

Appeared in: **1915** The Garden of Lies. **1917** The Spreading Dawn. **1943** Stage Door Canteen. **1949** Once More, My Darling; Come Be My Love. **1950** No Man of Her Own; The Secret Fury. **1951** Payment on Demand.

COWLES, JULES
Born: 1878, Farmington, Conn. Died: May 22, 1943, Hollywood, Calif. Screen actor.

Appeared in: **1921** The Idol of the North; Tangled Trails; God's

Crucible. **1922** The Bootleggers. **1923** Lost in a Big City; The Ne'er-Do-Well. **1924** The Love Bandit; High Speed. **1925** Seven Chances; The Lost World; Lord Jim. **1926** Man Rustlin'; Money to Burn; The Scarlet Letter; The Ace of Clubs. **1927** The Road to Romance. **1928** Bringing Up Father; Dog Law; Why Sailors Go Wrong; Terror; Isle of Lost Men; Thundergod. **1929** Sal of Singapore; The Leatherneck. **1930** His First Command; One Hysterical Night. **1931** Heaven on Earth. **1932** Heroes of the West (serial). **1933** Cross Fire; The Fighting Parson. **1934** The Scarlet Letter (and 1926 version); The Pursuit of Happiness. **1935** Mississippi; Barbary Coast. **1941** Billy the Kid. **1943** Air Raid Wardens.

COWLEY, ERIC
Born: July 11, 1886, Southsea, England. Died: Sept. 8, 1948, England. Screen actor.

Appeared in: **1933** The Jewel.

COWPER, WILL C. (William C. Cowper)
Born: 1853, Manchester, England. Died: June 13, 1918. Screen and stage actor.

Appeared in: **1913** Gold is Not All. **1915** Emmy of Stork's Nest; A Yellow Streak; An Enemy of Society. **1916** Dimples.

COX, ROBERT
Born: 1895. Died: Sept. 8, 1974, Phoenix, Ariz. Screen actor and assistant film director. Was one of the original Keystone Kops and appeared in nearly 300 one-reelers.

Appeared in: **1934** Young Eagles (serial).

COX, TOM (Thomas Sinclair Cox)
Born: 1892. Died: Dec. 6, 1914, La Crescenta, Calif. Screen actor. Appeared in Kalem films.

COX, WALLY (Wallace Maynard Cox)
Born: Dec., 1924, Detroit, Mich. Died: Feb. 15, 1973, Los Angeles, Calif. (heart attack). Screen, stage, radio, television actor and author.

Appeared in: **1962** State Fair. **1963** Spencer's Mountain. **1964** Fate Is the Hunter. **1965** The Bedford Incident; Morituri; The Yellow Rolls-Royce. **1967** A Guide for the Married Man. **1968** The One and Only, Genuine, Original Family Band. **1970** The Boatniks; The Cockeyed Cowboys of Calico County (aka A Woman for Charlie); Up Your Teddy Bear.

COXEN, EDWARD ALBERT
Born: 1884. Died: Nov. 21, 1954, Hollywood, Calif. Screen and stage actor.

Appeared in: **1912** Where the Road Forks; Hypnotized. **1913** The Spartan Girl of the West; A Divorce Scandal; The End of Black Bart. **1914** The Dream Child; Daylight; Her Fighting Chance; Sheltering an Ingrate; Jim; A Modern Freelance; The Ruin of Manley; Down by the Sea; The Little House in the Valley; Lodging for a Night; The Hermit; The Shriner's Daughter; In the Firelight; False Gods; This is the Life. **1915** The Resolve; The Guiding Light; The Forecast; Comrades Three; It Was Like This; On Secret Service; Out of the Ashes; The Clean-Up; The Water Carrier of San Juan; The Sting of It; A Broken Genius; Spider Barlow Cuts In. **1916** The Profligate; A Woman's Daring; The Voice of Love; The Franchise; Ruth Ridley's Return; The Key; Citizens All; The Happy Masquerader; Bonds of Deception; In the Shuffle; The Trail of the Thief; The Suppressed Order. **1917** Madam Who; A Man's Man. **1918** Carmen of the Klondike; Honor's Cross; A Law Unto Herself; Blindfolded. **1921** Desperate Trails; No Man's Woman. **1922** Nine Points of the Law; The Stranger of the Hills; The Veiled Woman. **1923** A Man's Man; Scaramouche; Temporary Marriage; Our Hospitality; The Flying Dutchman; Foolish Mothers. **1924** Flashing Spurs; Singer Jim McKee; One Glorious Night. **1925** Cold Nerve; The Man Without a Country. **1926** The Man in the Shadow. **1927** The Web of Fate; Galloping Fury; God's Great Wilderness. **1930** The Spoilers. **1933** King of the Arena; Cross Fire; The Fighting Parson. **1934** Wheels of Destiny; Gun Justice; Smoking Guns; The Scarlet Letter (and 1926 version); The Pursuit of Happiness. **1935** Barbary Coast; Mississippi. **1943** Air Raid Wardens.

COY, JOHNNIE
Born: 1921. Died: Nov. 4, 1973, Barbados. Screen and stage actor.

Appeared in: **1945** Bring on the Girls; Duffy's Tavern; That's the Spirit; On Stage Everybody. **1946** Earl Carroll Sketchbook. **1947** Ladies' Man. **1954** Top Banana.

COY, WALTER
Born: Jan. 31, 1906, Great Falls, Mont. Died: Dec. 11, 1974. Screen, stage and vaudeville actor.

Appeared in: **1935** Paradise Lost. **1936** Love Letters of a Star; Case of Clyde Griffith. **1950** Barricade; Tyrant of the Sea; Saddle Tramp; Under Mexicali Skies; Colt .45. **1951** FBI Girl. **1952** The Lusty Men; Flat Top. **1953** So Big. **1954** Sign of the Pagan. **1955** Cult of the Cobra; Wichita; Running Wild. **1956** The Searchers; On the Threshold of Space; Pillars of the Sky; The Young Guns. **1957** Johnny Tremaine. **1958** Juvenile Jungle. **1959** Gunmen from Laredo; The Gunfight at Dodge City. **1961** Five Guns to Tombstone; Gun Fight.

COYAN, BETTY
Born: 1901. Died: Feb. 10, 1935, Council Bluffs, Iowa. Screen actress. Entered films approx. 1921.

COYLE, MARION J.
Born: 1897. Died: May, 23, 1981, North Hollywood, Calif. Screen, radio actress and musician.

Appeared in: **1927** College.

COYLE, WALTER V.
Born: 1888. Died: Aug. 3, 1948, Freeport, N.Y. Screen and stage actor.

COYNE, JEANNE
Born: 1923. Died: May 10, 1973, Los Angeles, Calif. Screen, stage actress and film production assistant. Married to actor Gene Kelly.

Appeared in: **1953** Kiss Me Kate.

CRABTREE, PAUL
Born: 1919. Died: Mar., 1979, Hershey, Pa. (heart attack). Screen, stage actor, stage director, television director, screenwriter, playwright and television writer. Married to actress/director Mary Evelyn Ducey.

Appeared in: **1966** Country Boy. **1967** Track of Thunder.

CRADDOCK, CLAUDIA
Born: 1889. Died: Dec. 17, 1945, Hollywood, Calif. Screen actress.

Appeared in: **1933** A Lady's Profession.

CRAFT, LYNNE
Died: Mar. 20, 1975. Screen actress and film extra.

Appeared in: **1956** Around the World in 80 Days.

CRAFTS, GRIFFIN
Born: 1900. Died: Aug. 7, 1973, New York, N.Y. (cancer). Screen, stage and radio actor.

Appeared in: **1960** I Passed for White.

CRAIG, ALEC
Born: 1885, Scotland. Died: June 25, 1945, Glendale, Calif. Screen and stage actor.

Appeared in: **1934** The Little Minister. **1935** Old Homestead; Vanessa, Her Love Story; Sweepstakes Annie; Mutiny on the Bounty. **1936** Winterset; Mary of Scotland (stage and film versions). **1937** That Girl from Paris; Hideaway; The Man Who Found Himself; The Woman I Love; China Passage; There Goes My Girl; Super Sleuth; She's Got Everything. **1938** If I Were King; Crashing Hollywood; Wise Girl; Double Danger; Vivacious Lady. **1939** Confessions of a Nazi Spy; Ruler of the Seas; Night Work; They Made Her a Spy; Charlie McCarthy, Detective. **1940** Abe Lincoln in Illinois; Phantom Raiders; Tom Brown's School Days; Golden Gloves; Stranger on the Third Floor. **1941** All That Money Can Buy; Shining Victory; A Date With the Falcon; Three Girls About Town; Mr. and Mrs. Smith. **1942** Life Begins at Eight-Thirty; Roxie Hart; Random Harvest; Mrs. Miniver; The Night Before the Divorce; Cat People; Tennessee Johnson; Wrecking Crew. **1943** Action in the North Atlantic; Appointment in Berlin; Holy Matrimony; Lassie Come Home; Northern Pursuit. **1944** Sherlock Holmes and the Spider Woman; Callng Dr. Death; Jane Eyre; The White Cliffs of Dover; National Velvet; Bring on the Girls; The Ghost Chasers. **1945** Kitty; Love Letters; A Tree Grows in Brooklyn; Serenade for Murder. **1946** Three Strangers; Girl on the Spot. **1952** The Devil and Daniel Webster (reissue of 1941 All That Money Can Buy).

CRAIG, BLANCHE (Blanche Sanderson)
Born: Jan. 6, 1866, Cutler, Maine. Died: Sept. 23, 1940, Los Angeles, Calif. Screen, stage and vaudeville actress.

Appeared in: **1913** Eagle's Mate; Cinderella. **1916** Hulda From

Holland. **1918** Come On In; I Want to Forget. **1921** The Magic Cup; Room and Board. **1922** The Good Provider. **1923** Modern Marriage; Loyal Lives. **1924** Two Shall Be Born. **1925** The Making of O'Malley; The Fool; The Police Patrol; The Wrongdoers. **1926** Then Came the Woman. **1928** Beyond London's Lights; The Wright Idea. **1929** Darkened Rooms; Dynamite. **1930** Navy Blues. **1935** Peter Ibbetson.

CRAIG, CAROLYN
Born: Oct. 29, 193?, Long Island, N.Y. Died: Dec. 11, 1970. Screen, stage and television actress.

Appeared in: **1956** Giant (film debut). **1957** Portland Expose; Fury at Sundown; Gunsight Ridge. **1958** Apache Territory; House on Haunted Hill. **1960** Studs Lonigan.

CRAIG, MRS. CHARLES G.
Born: 1869. Died: July 21, 1925, Los Angeles, Calif. Screen and stage actress.

Appeared in: **1924** Barriers Burned Away; The Age of Innocence; Name the Man.

CRAIG, EDITH
Born: 1908. Died: Mar. 2, 1979, Tenafly, N.J. Screen, stage, television actress and writer. Do not confuse with English actress Edith Craig (dec. 1947).

Appeared in: **1924** The Desert Sheik. **1935** Harmony Lane. **1936** Love on a Bet. **1937** Behind the Headlines; The Outcasts of Poker Flats; The Singing Marine. **1938** Condemned Woman; Smashing the Rackets.

CRAIG, EDITH
Born: Dec. 9, 1869, England. Died: Mar. 27, 1947, Small Hythe, Kent, England. Screen, stage actress, film director and stage director. Do not confuse with U.S. actress (dec. 1979). Daughter of actress Dame Ellen Terry (dec. 1928). Sister of actor Edward Gordon Craig (dec. 1966).

Appeared in: **1935** Harmony Lane; Home Work (short). **1937** Behind the Headlines. **1938** Smashing the Rackets.

CRAIG, EDWARD GORDON
Born: Jan. 16, 1872, England. Died: July 29, 1966, Vence, France. Screen, stage actor, stage designer and author. Son of actress Dame Ellen Terry (dec. 1928) and Edward William Godwin. Brother of actress Edith Craig (dec. 1947).

CRAIG, FRANCES B.
Born: c. 1869. Died: July 22, 1925, Los Angeles, Claif. Stage and screen actress.

CRAIG, GODFREY
Born: 1915. Died: May 26, 1941, Los Angeles, Calif. Screen actor. Appeared in "Our Gang" comedies.

CRAIG, JOHN
Born: 1868, Columbia County, Tenn. Died: Aug. 23, 1932, Woodmere, N.Y. (heart attack). Screen and stage actor. Do not confuse with actor John Craig in later films.

CRAIG, MAY
Born: 1889, Ireland. Died: Feb. 8, 1972, Dublin, Ireland. Stage and screen actress.

Appeared in: **1952** The Quiet Man. **1957** The Rising of the Moon (aka A Minute's Wait). **1961** Johnny Nobody (US 1965). **1964** Girl With Green Eyes. **1965** Young Cassidy.

CRAIG, NELL
Born: 1891. Died: Jan. 5, 1965, Hollywood, Calif. Screen and stage actress. Entered films in 1913. Appeared in Essanay films in 1914.

Appeared in: **1914** The Shanty at Trembling Hill. **1915** The Return of Richard Neal; In the Palace of the King; The Primitive Strain. **1921** The Queen of Sheba. **1922** The Flirt; Remembrance. **1923** The Abysmal Brute. **1924** A Boy of Flanders; Abraham Lincoln. **1931** Cimarron; Consolation Marriage. **1935** The Man Who Reclaimed His Head; She Gets Her Man; Goin' to Town; Hands Across the Table. **1936** Klondike Annie; The Big Broadcast of 1937; Palm Springs. **1937** Paid to Kill. **1938** There's That Woman Again; Who Killed Gail Preston?; The Big Broadcast of 1938. **1939** Homicide Bureau; Another Thin Man; The Women; Calling Dr. Kildare; The Secret of Dr. Kildare. **1940** Dr. Kildare Goes Home; Dr. Kildare's Strangest Case; Dr. Kildare's Crisis; Kitty Foyle; I Love You Again. **1941** Glamour Boy; Dr. Kildare's Wedding Day; Dr. Kildare's Victory; The People vs. Dr. Kildare. **1942** Calling Dr. Gillespie; Dr. Gillespie's New Assistant. **1943** Three Hearts for Julia; Henry Aldrich Gets Glamour. **1944**

Practically Yours; Henry Aldrich Plays Cupid; Our Hearts Were Young and Gay; Between Two Women; Three Men in White. **1945** Out of This World. **1946** Our Hearts Were Growing Up. **1947** Dark Delusion; Possessed; Blaze of Noon.

CRAIG, RICHY, JR.
Born: 1902. Died: Nov. 28, 1933, New York, N.Y. Screen, stage, vaudeville and radio actor.

Appeared in: **1932-33** "Vitaphone Big Star" comedies and "Big V" comedies.

CRAMER, EDD
Born: 1924. Died: Dec. 21, 1963, New York, N.Y. Screen, stage and television actor.

Appeared in: **1954** On the Waterfront.

CRAMER, RICHARD (Richard Earl Cramer aka RYCHARD CRAMER)
Born: July 2, 1889, Bryan, Ohio. Died: Aug. 9, 1960, Los Angeles, Calif. (Laennec's cirrhosis). Screen and stage actor.

Appeared in: **1929** Big News; Illusion; Kid Gloves. **1930** Those Who Dance; Captain of the Guard; Sweet Mama; Hell's Island; Murder on the Roof; Big Money. **1931** Ladies' Man; Platinum Blonde; An American Tragedy; Painted Desert; Air Police; In Line of Duty; Night Boat; Dancing Dynamite; Neck and Neck; Lariats and Six Shooters; Pocatello Kid. **1932** The Strange Love of Molly Louvain; The Tenderfoot; 45 Calibre Echo; Pack Up Your Troubles; Scram! (short); Unexpected Father; His Royal Shyness (short). **1933** Fourth Horseman; The Fatal Glass of Beer (short); Private Jones; Storm at Daybreak. **1934** The Vanishing Shadow (serial); The Red Rider (serial); The Law of the Wild (serial); Hollywood Party; Rawhide Mail. **1935** She Gets Her Man; Danger Ahead; Judgment Book; Riddle Ranch. **1936** The Black Coin (serial); Frontier Justice; Just My Luck; O'Malley of the Mounted; The Speed Reporter; Three Godfathers; Sutter's Gold; The Red Rider; Spanish Cape Mystery; Cappy Ricks Returns; Speed Demon; Rio Grande Romance. **1937** Courage of the West; Woman Chases Man; The Trusted Outlaw; Where Trails Divide; Night Club Scandal; Crusade Against the Rackets. **1938** Rangers Roundup; Clipped Wings; Thunder in the Desert; Song and Bullets; Phantom Ranger; Knight of the Plains. **1939** Dodge City; In Old Montana; The Flying Deuces. **1940** Saps at Sea; Arizona Frontier; Northwest Passage. **1941** Double Trouble. **1942** Broadway Big Shot; Rock River; Renegades; This Time for Keeps; Eagle Squadron; The Phantom Plainsman. **1945** Song of Old Wyoming. **1946** Scarlet Street. **1951** Santa Fe.

CRAMER, SUSANNE
Born: 1938, Germany. Died: Jan. 7, 1939, Hollywood, Calif. (pneumonia). Screen and television actress. Appeared in U.S., German and French films.

Appeared in: **1956** Kleines Gelt und Grosse Liebe (aka Two in a Sleeping Bag—US 1964). **1957** Every Second Counts. **1958** Wie ein Sturmwind (Tempestuous Love); Schwarze Nylons—Heisse Nachate (aka All Bad and aka Indecent—US 1962). **1959** Vacanzie a Lzchia (Holiday Island). **1964** Bedtime Story. **1968** Waylaid Women (reissue of 1958 Schwarze Nylons).

CRAMPTON, HOWARD
Died: June 15, 1922. Screen actor.

Appeared in: **1916** Black Orchids. **1917** The Gray Ghost (serial); The Voice on the Wire (serial). **1918** Humdrum Brown. **1919** Trail of the Octapus (serial). **1920** Someone in the House; Hearts are Trumps; The Screaming Shadow (serial). **1921** The Bronze Bell. **1922** The Man Who Married His Own Wife; Nan of the North (serial).

CRANDALL, EDWARD
Born: 1904, Brooklyn, N.Y. Died: May 9, 1968, Palm Beach, Fla. Screen, stage actor and playwright.

Appeared in: **1929** Glorifying the American Girl. **1931** Over the Hill. **1932** Dance Team.

CRANE, BOB
Born: July 13, 1929, Waterbury, Conn. Died: June 29, 1978, Scottsdale, Ariz. (murder—beaten). Screen, stage, radio and television actor. Divorced from Anne Terzain. Married to actress Patricia Olson.

Appeared in: **1961** Mantrap; Return to Peyton Place. **1968** The Wicked Dreams of Paula Schultz. **1974** Superdad. **1976** Gus.

CRANE, DIXIE
Born: 1888. Died: Nov. 18, 1936, Hollywood, Calif. Screen and vaudeville actress. Appeared with her husband Henry Johnson in a vaudeville act billed as "Johnson and Crane." She appeared in early Lasky films.

CRANE, ETHEL G.
Died: Oct., 1930, San Bernardino, Calif. (suicide—poison). Screen actress.

CRANE, FRANK HALL
Born: 1873, San Francisco, Calif. Died: Sept. 1, 1948, Hollywood, Calif. Screen, stage actor and film director.

Appeared in: **1910** The Vicar of Wakefield. **1922** A Girl's Desire; Little Wildcat. **1926** My Old Dutch. **1928** Bitter Sweets. **1929** The Man From Nevada. **1932** Mason of the Mounted. **1934** Mystery Ranch. **1936** The Speed Reporter.

CRANE, JAMES LYON
Born: Aug 9, 1889, Rantoul, Ill. Died: June 3, 1968. Screen and stage actor. Divorced from actress Alice Brady (dec. 1939).

Appeared in: **1919** His Bridal Night; Misleading Widow; Sadie Love; Wanted a Husband. **1920** Sinners; A Dark Lantern. **1929** The Drake Case. **1930** One Night at Susie's. **1931** Dude Ranch; The Mummy. **1932** Two Kinds of Women; Lady and Gent. **1934** Good Dame. **1940** The Mummy's Hand. **1950** A Lady Without a Passport.

CRANE, LLOYD See HALL, JON

CRANE, MAE
Born: 1925. Died: Apr. 15, 1969, Port Washington, N.Y. (lung ailment). Screen, stage, radio and television actress.

Appeared in: **1967** The Producers. **1968** For Love of Ivy; No Way to Treat a Lady.

CRANE, NORMA (Norma Anna Bella Zuckerman)
Born: 1931, New York, N.Y. Died: Sept. 28, 1973, West Los Angeles, Calif. (cancer). Stage and screen actress. Divorced from writer Herb Sargent.

Appeared in: **1956** Tea and Sympathy. **1961** All in a Night's Work. **1966** Penelope. **1968** The Sweet Ride. **1970** They Call Me Mr. Tibbs. **1971** Fiddler on the Roof.

CRANE, OGDEN
Born: Sept. 1, 1873, Brooklyn, N.Y. Died: May 14, 1940, West Hollywood, Calif. Screen and stage actor.

Appeared in: **1919** The Paliser Case; The Valley of the Giants; Soldiers of Fortune; The Hornet's Net; Jinx. **1920** The Dwelling Place of Light. **1921** The Greater Profit; See My Lawyer; The Invisible Fear.

CRANE, RICHARD O.
Born: 1918. Died: Mar. 9, 1969, San Fernando Valley, Calif. (heart attack). Screen and television actor.

Appeared in: **1940** Susan and God. **1941** In the Navy; The Saint in Palm Springs; Keep 'Em Flying. **1942** Eagle Squadron; The Phantom Plainsman; This Time for Keeps. **1943** So Proudly We Hail!; Someone to Remember; Riders of the Deadline; Happy Land. **1944** Wing and a Prayer; None Shall Escape. **1945** Captain Eddie. **1946** Scarlet Street; Johnny Comes Flying Home; Behind Green Lights. **1948** Angel on the Amazon; Arthur Takes Over; Waterfront at Midnight; Campus Honeymoon; Triple Threat. **1949** Dynamite. **1950** A Lady Without a Passport. **1951** The Last Outpost; Mysterious Island (serial); Man in the Saddle. **1952** Thundering Caravans; Leadville Gunslinger. **1953** The Great Adventures of Captain Kidd (serial); Winning of the West; The Neanderthal Man; The Woman They Almost Lynched. **1955** No Man's Woman; The Eternal Sea. **1956** The Eddy Duchin Story. **1957** Bailout at 43,000. **1958** The Deep Six. **1959** Battle Flame; The Alligator People. **1960** Thirteen Fighting Men. **1961** The Boy Who Caught a Crook. **1962** The Devil's Partner. **1963** House of the Damned. **1964** Surf Party.

CRANE, WARD
Born: 1891, Albany, N.Y. Died: July 21, 1928, Saranac Lake, N.Y. (pneumonia). Screen actor.

Appeared in: **1921** Heedless Moths. **1922** Broadway Rose; French Heels; No Trespassing; Destiny's Isle. **1923** Enemies of Children; Pleasure Mad; The Famous Mrs. Fair; Within the Law; The Meanest Man in the World. **1924** Sherlock, Jr.; Empty Hands; Bread; Gambling Wives. **1925** How Baxter Butted In; The Crimson Runner; The Mad

Whirl; The Million Dollar Handicap; Classified; Borrowed Finery; The Phantom of the Opera; Peacock Feathers. **1926** Boy Friend; Risky Business; Upstage; That Model from Paris; The Blind Goddess; The Flaming Frontier; The Sporting Lover; Under Western Skies. **1927** The Lady in Ermine; The Auctioneer; Beauty Shoppers; The Rush Hour; Down the Stretch. **1928** Honeymoon Flats.

CRANE, WILLIAM H.
Born: 1892. Died: Jan. 22, 1957, Scranton, Pa. Screen and stage actor.

CRANE, WILLIAM H.
Born: 1845, Leicester, Mass. Died: Mar. 7, 1928, Hollywood, Calif. (general breakdown). Screen and stage actor.

CRAVAT, NOEL
Born: 1910. Died: Feb. 20, 1960, Hollywood, Calif. (after surgery). Screen actor.

Appeared in: **1942** Junior G-Men of the Air (serial). **1943** G-Men vs. the Black Dragon (serial). **1944** Ali Baba and the Forty Thieves. **1946** The Killers. **1947** Sweet Genevieve; Three on a Ticket; The Razor's Edge. **1948** The Iron Curtain. **1949** The Mutineers. **1952** Radar Men from the Moon (serial). **1953** South Sea Women; The 5,000 Fingers of Dr. T. **1954** Captain Kidd and the Slave Girl (serial). **1956** Flight to Hong Kong.

CRAVEN, FRANK
Born: 1875, Boston, Mass. Died: Sept. 1, 1945, Beverly Hills, Calif. (heart ailment). Screen, stage actor, film director, playwright and screenwriter.

Appeared in: **1928** We Americans. **1929** The Very Idea. **1932** The Putter (short). **1933** State Fair. **1934** That's Gratitude; He Was Her Man; Let's Talk It Over; City Limits; Funny Thing Called Love. **1935** Barbary Coast; Car 99; Vagabond Lady. **1936** Small Town Girl; The Harvester. **1937** Penrod and Sam; Blossoms on Broadway. **1938** You're Only Young Once; Penrod and His Twin Brother. **1939** Our Neighbors, the Carters; Miracles for Sale. **1940** Dreaming Out Loud; City for Conquest; Our Town. **1941** The Lady from Cheyenne; The Richest Man in Town. **1942** In This Our Life; Pittsburgh; Girl Trouble; Through Different Eyes. **1943** Son of Dracula; Harrigan's Kid; Jack London; The Human Comedy; Keeper of the Flame. **1944** Destiny; My Best Gal; They Shall Have Faith. **1945** The Right to Live; Colonel Effingham's Raid.

CRAWFORD, ANNE (Imelda Crawford)
Born: Nov. 22, 1920, Haifa, Israel. Died: Oct. 17, 1956, London, England. Screen, stage and television actress.

Appeared in: **1942** They Flew Alone (film debut—aka Wings and the Woman—US); The Peterville Diamond. **1943** The Dark Tower; Millions Like Us; Headline; The Hundred Pound Window; The Night Invader. **1944** 2,000 Women. **1945** They Were Sisters (US 1946). **1946** Caravan (US 1947); Bedelia (US 1947). **1947** Master of Bankdam. **1948** Daughter of Darkness; Night Beat; The Blind Goddess (US 1949). **1950** Tony Draws a Horse (US 1951); Trio. **1951** Thunder on the Hill. **1953** Street Corner. **1954** Knights of the Round Table; Mad About Men.

CRAWFORD, BESSIE
Born: 1882. Died: Nov. 11, 1943, Hollywood, Calif. (heart attack). Screen, stage and vaudeville actress. Married to screen actor T. Roy Barnes (dec. 1937) and appeared with him in a vaudeville act billed as "Barnes and Crawford."

CRAWFORD, CLIFTON
Born: 1875, Edinburgh, Scotland. Died: June 3, 1920, London, England. Screen, stage and vaudeville actor.

Appeared in: **1915** The Galloper.

CRAWFORD, HOWARD MARION
Born: 1914. Died: Nov. 24, 1969, London, England (overdose of sleeping pills). Screen, stage, radio and television actor.

Appeared in: **1935** Forever England (aka Brown on Resolution and Born for Glory—US). **1938** 13 Men and a Gun. **1941** Freedom Radio (aka A Voice in the Night—US). **1945** The Rake's Progress (aka Notorious Gentleman—US 1946). **1949** The Hasty Heart. **1951** Mr. Drake's Duck; The Man in the White Suit (US 1952). **1952** His Excellency (US 1956); Where's Charley? **1953** Top of the Form. **1954** Don't Blame the Stork; West of Zanzibar; Five Days (aka Paid to Kill—US); The Rainbow Jacket. **1956** Reach for the Sky (US 1957); The Silken Affaire. **1957** The Birthday Present; Don Kikhot (Don Quixote—US 1961—dubbed English voioce); The Man in the Sky (aka

Decision Against Time—US); The Tyburn Case. **1958** Gideon's Day (aka Gideon of Scotland Yard—US 1959); The Silent Enemy; Next to No Time (US 1960); Virgin Island (US 1960); Nowhere to Go (US 1959). **1959** Model for Murder; Life in Danger (US 1964). **1960** Foxhole in Cairo (US 1961). **1962** Lawrence of Arabia. **1963** Man in the Middle (US 1964); Tamahine (US 1964). **1965** The Face of Fu Manchu. **1966** The Brides of Fu Manchu. **1967** Vengeance of Fu Manchu (US 1968); The Singing Princess (voice); Smashing Times. **1968** The Charge of the Light Brigade; The Blood of Fu Manchu (aka Kiss and Tell—US 1969).

CRAWFORD, (CAPTAIN) JACK (John Wallace Crawford)
Born: Mar. 4, 1847, County Donegal, Ireland. Died: Feb. 27, 1917, Ireland? Screen actor, playwright and military officer.

Appeared in: **1914** The Poet Scout's Pledge.

CRAWFORD, JESSE
Born: 1895, Woodland Hills, Calif. Died: May 27, 1962, Los Angeles, Calif. (stroke). Organist, screen and radio actor.

Appeared in: **1934** Organ Festival.

CRAWFORD, JIMMY
Born: 1910. Died: Jan. 27, 1980, New York, N.Y. Jazz Drummer and screen actor.

Appeared in: **1954** His Majesty O'Keefe. **1962** Play it Cool (US 1963).

CRAWFORD, JOAN (Lucille Fay Le Sueur aka BILLIE CASSIN)
Born: Mar. 23, 1906, San Antonio, Tex. Died: May 10, 1977, New York, N.Y. (heart attack). Screen, stage, television actress, dancer and author. Sister of actor Hal Le Sueur (dec. 1963). Divorced from actors Douglas Fairbanks, Jr., Franchot Tone (dec. 1968) and Philip Terry. Married to industrialist Alfred Steele (dec. 1959). Won 1945 Academy Award for Best Actress in "Mildred Pierce." Nominated for 1947 Academy Award for Best Actress in "Possessed" and in 1952 for "Sudden Fear." Was a 1926 Wampas Baby Star. Entered films in 1925.

Appeared in: **1925** Pretty Ladies; Old Clothes; The Only Thing; Sally, Irene and Mary. **1926** The Boob; Paris; Tramp, Tramp, Tramp. **1927** Spring Fever; The Taxie Dancer; Twelve Miles Out; The Understanding Heart; Winners of the Wilderness; The Unknown. **1928** Across to Singapore; Dream of Love; Four Walls; The Law of the Range; Our Dancing Daughters; Rose-Marie; West Point; Voices Across the Sea (short). **1929** The Duke Steps Out; The Hollywood Revue of 1929; Our Modern Maidens; Untamed. **1930** Montana Moon; Our Blushing Brides; Paid. **1931** Dance, Fools, Dance; Laughing Sinners; This Modern Age; Possessed. **1932** Grand Hotel; Letty Lynton; Rain; The Slippery Pearls (short). **1933** Today We Live; Dancing Lady. **1934** Sadie McKee; Chained; Forsaking All Others. **1935** No More Ladies; I Live My Life. **1936** The Gorgeous Hussy; Love on the Run. **1937** The Last of Mrs. Cheyney; The Bride Wore Red; Mannequin; Maytime. **1938** The Shinning Hour. **1939** Ice Follies of 1939; The Women. **1940** Strange Cargo; Susan and God. **1941** A Woman's Face; When Ladies Meet. **1942** They All Kissed the Bride (aka Reunion in France). **1943** Above Suspicion. **1944** Hollywood Canteen. **1945** Mildred Pierce. **1946** Humoresque. **1947** Possessed (and 1931 version). **1947** Daisy Kenyon. **1949** Flamingo Road; It's a Great Feeling. **1950** The Damned Don't Cry; Harriet Craig. **1951** Goodbye, My Fancy. **1952** This Woman is Dangerous; Sudden Fear. **1953** Torch Song. **1954** Johnny Guitar. **1955** Female on the Beach; Queen Bee; Hollywood Mothers (short). **1956** Autumn Leaves. **1957** The Story of Esther Costello; The Golden Virgin. **1959** The Best of Everything. **1962** What Ever Happened to Baby Jane? **1963** The Caretakers. **1964** Strait Jacket; Big Parade of Comedy (documentary). **1965** I Saw What You Did. **1968** Beserk. **1970** Trog. **1976** That's Entertainment, Part 2. **1980** Dead Men Don't Wear Plaid (film clips).

CRAWFORD, KATHRYN
Born: Oct. 5, 1908, Wellsboro, Pa. Died: Dec. 7, 1980, Pasadena, Calif. (cancer). Screen and stage actress.

Appeared in: **1929** Red Hot Rhythm; Modern Love; The Kid's Clever; King of the Rodeo. **1930** Senor Americano; Hide-Out; Mountain Justice; The Climax; The King of Jazz; Safety in Numbers; Hit the Deck; The Concentratin' Kid. **1931** Flying High. **1932** Emma; New Morals for Old. **1933** Skyway. **1941** City of Missing Girls.

CRAWFORD, NAN
Born: 1893, Richmond, Va. Died: July 4, 1975, Inglewood, Calif. Screen, stage, vaudeville and radio actress. Married to actor Henry Hollingsworth (dec. 1947) with whom she appeared in vaudeville in an act billed as "Hollingsworth and Crawford."

Appeared in: **1929** Bedtime (short with "Hollingsworth and Crawford").

CRAWFORD, SAM (Samuel Earl Crawford)
Born: Apr. 18, 1880, Wahoo, Nebr. Died: June 15, 1968, Hollywood, Calif. Baseball player and screen actor.

Appeared in: **1927** College.

CRAWFORD, TIMOTHY S.
Born: 1904. Died: June 13, 1978, Reno, Nev. Screen, stage actor and organist. Appeared in silent films.

CRAWLEY, CONSTANCE
Born: Mar. 30, 1879, England. Died: Mar. 18, 1919, Los Angeles, Calif. (asthma). Screen actress and screenwriter.

Appeared in: **1913** Pelleas and Melisande; Jedediah's Daughter. **1914** Thais. **1915** The Alternative; The Wrath of Haddon Towers. **1916** Revelations; Lord Loveland Visits America; Powder; Embers.

CRAWLEY, SAYRE
Born: England. Died: Mar. 7, 1948, New York, N.Y. Screen and stage actor.

CREAMER, CHARLES
Born: 1894. Died: July 22, 1971, Hollywood, Calif. (heart attack). Screen actor, extra and stand-in for Walter Brennan.

CREED, CATHERINE
Born: 1891, St. Louis, Mo. Died: Nov. 20, 1978, Las Vegas, Nev. Screen, stage, vaudeville, radio, television actress, dancer, singer and night-club entertainer. Married to vaudeville entertainer Chic Johnson (dec. 1962).

CREGAR, LAIRD
Born: 1913, Philadelphia, Pa. Died: Dec. 9, 1944, Los Angeles, Calif. (heart attack). Screen and stage actor.

Appeared in: **1940** Granny Get Your Gun; Oh Johnny, How You Can Love; Hudson's Bay. **1941** Blood and Sand; Charley's Aunt; I Wake Up Screaming. **1942** Rings on Her Fingers; This Gun for Hire; Joan of Paris; Black Swan; Ten Gentlemen from West Point. **1943** Heaven Can Wait; Holy Matrimony; Hello, Frisco, Hello. **1944** The Lodger. **1945** Hangover Square.

CREHAN, JOSEPH
Born: July 12, 1886, Baltimore, Md. Died: Apr. 15, 1966, Hollywood, Calif. Screen, stage and television actor.

Appeared in: **1916** Under Two Flags. **1931** Stolen Heaven. **1933** Hold the Press. **1934** Here Comes the Navy; It Happened One Night; The Man With Two Faces Against the Law; Jimmy the Gent; Identity Parade; Before Midnight; The Line-Up; The Hell Cat. **1935** Devil Dogs of the Air; Don't Bet on Blondes; Strange Wives; Go into Your Dance; Black Fury; The Traveling Saleslady; Bright Lights; The Case of the Lucky Legs; Shipmates Forever; Man of Iron; The Payoff; Oil for the Lamps of China; Stranded; Page Miss Glory; Front Page Woman; Alibi Ike; Special Agent; Dinky; Frisco Kid. **1936** Brides Are Like That; The Singing Kid; Bengal Tiger; Murder of Dr. Harrigan; Road Gang; God's Country and the Woman; King of Hockey; Smart Blonde; Gold Diggers of 1937; Here Comes Carter; Murder by an Aristocrat; Boulder Dam; The Law in Her Hands; Jail Break; Anthony Adverse; Bullets or Ballots; Earthworm Tractors; China Clipper; Cain and Mabel; Down the Stretch; Trailin' West. **1937** Draegerman Courage; Don't Pull Your Punches; Kid Galahad; Her Husband's Secretary; Once a Doctor; Midnight Court; Talent Scout; The Go-Getter; This Is My Affair; Born Reckless; My Girl; Midnight Madonna; The Wrong Road; The Duke Comes Back; Mama Runs Wild; Here's Flash Casey; Guns of the Pecos; Girls Can Play; Outlaws of the Orient; The Case of the Stuttering Bishop. **1938** Bluebeard's Eighth Wife; A Criminal Is Born (short); Midnight Intruder; The Goldwyn Follies; Happy Landing; Alexander's Ragtime Band; The Arkansas Traveler; Illegal Traffic; Billy the Kid Returns; Night Spot; Four's a Crowd; Crime Takes a Holiday; Woman Against Woman; The Kid Comes Back. **1939** Newsboys' Home; Dodge City; We Are Not Alone; Navy Secrets; Star Maker; Society Lawyer; Tell No Tales; Maisie; Babes in Arms; Hollywood Cavalcade; Behind Prison Gates; Private Detective; Geronimo; The Roaring Twenties; The Return of Dr. X; Whispering Enemies; You Can't Get Away With Murder; Pride of the Navy; Stanley and Livingstone; Union Pacific. **1940** Jack Pot (short); Emergency Squad; Music in My Heart; The Secret Seven; The House Across the Bay; City for Conquest; Gaucho Serenade; Brother Orchid. **1941** They Died With Their Boots On; Sealed Lips; Andy Hardy's Private Secretary; Nine Lives Are Not Enough; Doctors Don't Tell; Texas; The Case of the Black Parrot; Washington Melodrama; Scattergood Baines; Manpower; Love Crazy; Here Comes Happiness; Nevada City. **1942** Gang Busters (serial); Treat 'Em Rough; The

Courtship of Andy Hardy; Cadets on Parade; Larceny, Inc; To the Shores of Tripoli; Murder in the Big House; Men of Texas; Hello, Annapolis; Girl Trouble; You Can't Escape Forever; Gentleman Jim. **1943** Flesh and Fantasy; Old Acquaintance; Eyes of the Underworld; Mystery Broadcast; Hit the Ice; Mission to Moscow; Hands Across the Border; The Desert Song. **1944** The Great Alaskan Mystery (serial); When the Lights Go on Again; Roger Touhy, Gangster; Phantom Lady; The Navy Way; Shine on Harvest Moon; The Adventures of Mark Twain; Black Magic; One Mysterious Night. **1945** The Royal Mounted Rides Again (serial); Adventures; The Missing Juror; The Chicago Kid; I Love a Mystery; Brewster's Millions; Man Alive; Dick Tracy; Youth on Trial; Captain Tugboat Annie. **1946** The Mysterious Mr. M. (serial); Cinderella Jones; The Brute Man; A Guy Could Change; Girl on the Spot; The Big Sleep; Deadline at Dawn; Dick Tracy vs. Cueball; The Shadow Returns; O.S.S.; Phantom Thief; Behind the Mask; Night Train to Memphis; The Falcon's Adventure; Dangerous Money; The Virginian. **1947** The Sea of Grass; Monsieur Verdoux; The Trespasser; Philo Vance's Gamble; The Foxes of Harrow; Louisiana; Dick Tracy Meets Gruesome; Night Time in Nevada. **1948** Blondie's Secret; Triple Threat; The Enchanted Valley; The Hunted; April Showers; Silver Rider; Adventures in Silverado; Homicide for Three; The Countess of Monte Cristo; Street Corner; Bad Men of Tombstone; Sundown at Santa Fe; The Story of Life. **1949** Red Desert; The Last Bandit; The Duke of Chicago; Prejudice; Alias the Champ; Ringside; Alimony; State Department File 649; Amazon Quest. **1950** The Arizona Cowboy; Square Dance Katy; The Tougher They Come; Triple Trouble. **1951** Pride of Maryland; Roadblock; Hometown Story. **1952** Deadline U.S.A. **1953** Crazylegs. **1954** Highway Dragnet. **1961** Judgment at Nuremburg.

CREIGHTON, CLEVA See CHANEY, FRANCES

CREMIEUX, HENRI
Born: 1896, France. Died: May 10, 1980, France? Screen actor.

Appeared in: **1946** Stormy Waters. **1950** Orpheus. **1951** Mr. Peek-a-Boo. **1954** Paris Incident. **1955** Holiday for Henrietta. **1958** La Moucharde (aka Woman of Sin—US 1961). **1959** The Law is the Law. **1960** Le Testament d'Orphee (Testament of Orpheus—US 1962); Nude in a White Car; The Earliest Profession; La Corde Raide (The Tight Rope, aka Lovers on a Tightrope—US 1962). **1962** Le Septieme Jure (The Seventh Juror—Us 1964). **1963** Le Glaive et la Balance (aka Two Are Guilty—US 1964). **1964** Anatomy of a Marriage. **1967** Les Demoiselles de Rochefort (The Young Girls of Rochefort—US 1968).

CRESSALL, MAUD
Born: Dec. 5, 1886, Demerara, British Guiana. Died: May, 1962, England? Screen and stage actress.

Appeared in: **1920** The Barton Mystery. **1921** The Tinted Venus. **1923** Mist in the Valley; The Naked Man.

CRETINETTI See DEED, ANDRE

CREWS, KAY C.
Born: 1901. Died: Nov. 29, 1959, San Antonio, Tex. Screen, stage and vaudeville actress. Appeared in silent films.

CREWS, LAURA HOPE
Born: 1880, San Francisco, Calif. Died: Nov. 13, 1942, New York, N.Y. Screen and stage actress.

Appeared in: **1915** The Fighting Hope. **1929** Charming Sinners. **1932** Rockabye; New Morals for Old. **1933** Out All Night; The Silver Cord; I Love You Wednesday; Blind Adventure; If I Were Free; Female; Ever in My Heart. **1934** Rafter Romance; Age of Innocence. **1935** Behold My Wife; The Flame Within; Lightning Strikes Twice; Escapade; The Melody Lingers On. **1936** Her Master's Voice (stage and film versions); Camille. **1937** The Road Back; Confession; Angel. **1938** Dr. Rhythm; The Sisters; Thanks for the Memory. **1939** Idiot's Delight; Gone With the Wind; Remember?; Reno; The Rains Came; Starmaker. **1940** The Lady With Red Hair; The Bluebird; I'm Nobody's Sweetheart Now; Girl from Avenue A. **1941** The Man Who Came to Dinner; The Flame of New Orleans. **1942** One Foot in Heaven.

CRIDER, DOROTHY ELLEN
Born: 1918. Died: July 3, 1980, Woodland Hills, Calif. Screen, stage and television actress.

Appeared in: **1952** The Greatest Show on Earth. **1956** The Ten Commandments.

CRIMMINS, DANIEL "DAN" (Alexander M. Lyons)
Born: 1863, Liverpool, England. Died: July 11, 1945, U.S. Screen, stage and vaudeville actor. Father of actor Dan Crimmins, Jr.

Appeared in: **1914** Officer Kate; Second Sight. **1915** The Commuters. **1916** Ambition. **1919** The Garage; Johnny Get Your Gun; Under the Top; You're Fired. **1920** Pink Tights. **1921** Colorado; Straight from the Shoulder. **1923** Desert Driven. **1924** The Midnight Express; Women First. **1925** Not So Long Ago; Pretty Ladies. **1926** Peril of the Rail. **1929** Smiling Irish Eyes. **1932** White Zombie. **1935** Vagabond Lady. **1936** The Jungle Princess.

CRINLEY, WILLIAM A.
Died: Jan. 1, 1927, Hollywood, Calif. (following operation). Screen actor and film director.

Appeared in: **1921** Big Town Round-Up.

CRIPPS, KERNAN (John Kernan Cripps)
Born: July 8, 1886, Connecticut. Died: Aug. 12, 1953, Calif. Screen actor.

Appeared in: **1929** Alibi. **1930** Those Who Dance. **1934** I Hate Women. **1935** Nothern Frontier; Wilderness Mail; Stone of Silver Creek; Smart Girl; Mary Burns, Fugitive; The Lone Wolf Returns. **1936** And So They Were Married; The Cowboy and the Kid. **1937** Hit the Saddle; Swing It, Sailor. **1938** Strange Faces. **1939** Newsboys' Home; Society Smugglers; Hero for a Day. **1940** Oh, Johnny, How You Can Love; Gaucho Serenade. **1941** The Invisible Woman. **1942** The Saboteur; Sin Town; You're Telling Me. **1943** Henry Aldrich Haunts a House. **1944** Double Indemnity. **1945** Hold That Blonde; The Scarlet Clue. **1946** The Strange Love of Martha Ivers. **1947** California; My Wild Irish Rose; The Last Round-Up; Blondie in the Dough. **1950** Mary Ryan, Detective.

CRISMAN, ARLINE C.
Died: May 10, 1956, Hollywood, Calif. Screen actress.

CRISP, DONALD
Born: 1880, Aberfeddy, Scotland. Died: May 25, 1974, Van Nuys, Calif. Screen, opera, stage actor, film director, producer, stage director and magazine writer. Married to screenwriter Jane Murfin (dec. 1957). Won 1941 Academy Award for Best Supporting Actor in How Green Was My Valley.

Appeared in: **1910** Fate's Turning; The Two Paths. **1911** The Battle. **1914** The Battle of the Sexes; The Escape; Home Sweet Home. **1915** Birth of a Nation. **1919** Broken Blossoms. **1921** Beside the Bonnie Briar Bush (aka The Bonnie Briar Bush—US). **1925** Don Q.; Son of Zorro. **1926** The Black Pirate. **1928** The River Pirate; The Viking. **1929** The Pagan; Trent's Last Case; The Return of Shelock Holmes. **1930** Scotland Yard. **1931** Svengali; Kick In. **1932** Red Dust; Passport to Hell. **1933** Broadway Bad. **1934** The Little Minister; The Crime Doctor; The Life of Vergie Winters; The Key; What Every Woman Knows. **1935** Vanessa, Her Love Story; Laddie; Oil for the Lamps of China; Mutiny on the Bounty. **1936** Mary of Scotland; Beloved Enemy; The White Angel; Charge of the Light Brigade; A Woman Rebels. **1937** The Great O'Malley; Parnell; The Life of Emile Zola; Confession; That Certain Woman. **1938** Sergeant Murphy; Dawn Patrol; Jezebel; The Sisters; The Beloved Brat; The Amazing Dr. Clitterhouse; Valley of the Giants; Comet Over Broadway. **1939** Juarez; The Old Maid; The Oklahoma Kid; Wuthering Heights; Daughters Courageous; The Private Lives of Elizabeth and Essex. **1940** The Story of Dr. Ehrlich's Magic Bullet (aka Dr. Ehrlich's Magic Bullet); Brother Orchid; City for Conquest; Knute Rockne—All American; The Sea Hawk. **1941** Dr. Jekyll and Mr. Hyde; How Green Was My Valley; Shining Victory. **1942** The Battle of Midway (narrator); The Gay Sisters. **1943** Lassie Come Home; Forever and a Day. **1944** National Velvet; The Adventures of Mark Twain; The Uninvited. **1945** The Valley of Decision; Son of Lassie. **1947** Ramrod. **1948** Whispering Smith; Hills of Home. **1949** Challenge to Lassie. **1950** Bright Leaf. **1951** Home Town Story. **1954** Prince Valiant. **1955** The Man from Laramie; The Long Gray Line. **1957** Drango. **1958** Saddle the Wind; The Last Hurrah. **1959** A Dog of Flanders. **1960** Pollyanna. **1961** Greyfriar's Bobby. **1963** Spencer's Mountain.

CRISS, SONNY (William Criss)
Born: 1927, Memphis, Tenn. Died: Nov. 19, 1977, Los Angeles, Calif. (shot—"possible suicide"). Black screen, radio, television actor and saxophonist.

CRITTENDEN, THROCKWOOD DWIGHT
Born: Sept. 27, 1878, Oakland, Calif. Died: Feb. 17, 1938, Los Angeles Calif. (gun shot—homicide). Screen and stage actor.

Appeared in: **1916** Home. **1917** The Gray Ghost (serial). **1918** Thais. **1919** The Veiled Adventure; Miracle Man; The Hoodlum. **1920** Cup of Fury; Pinto; The Star Rover; The Tiger Band (serial). **1921** Bob Hampton of Placer; Tale of Two Worlds; The Old Nest; High Heels. **1922** Woman's Side; Hottentot. **1923** Pioneer Trails. **1924** The Fast Worker.

CROCKER, HARRY
Born: July 2, 1893, San Francisco, Calif. Died: May 23, 1958. Screen, stage actor and assistant film director.

Appeared in: **1927** Tillie the Toiler; Becky; Sally in our Alley; South Sea Love. **1928** The Circus. **1942** A Night for Crime; Gentleman Jim. **1944** A Song for Miss Julie. **1945** The Great John L. **1949** Dancing in the Dark.

CROCKETT, CHARLES B.
Born: 1872, Md. Died: June 12, 1934, Los Angeles, Calif. Screen and stage actor.

Appeared in: **1924** Sundown; The Millionaire Cowboy. **1925** The Dressmaker from Paris; The Vanishing American; Daddy's Gone A-Hunting; Winds of Chance. **1926** Into Her Kingdom. **1927** The Princess from Hoboken; Arizona Bound; The Gingham Girl. **1930** Abraham Lincoln; Ex-Flame. **1931** Guilty Hands.

CROCKETT, DICK (Richard)
Born: 1915. Died: Jan., 1979, Los Angeles, Calif. (cancer). Screen actor.

Appeared in: **1945** This Man's Navy. **1948** Panhandle. **1950** Wabash Avenue. **1951** Gold Raiders. **1953** All Ashore; Cruisin' Down the River; Topeka. **1954** Drive a Crooked Mile. **1956** Davy Crockett and the River Pirates; Over-Exposed. **1957** Baby Face Nelson; Operation Mad Ball; Mister Cory. **1958** Escape from Red Rock; The Perfect Furlough; Street of Darkness. **1959** It Happened to Jane; Operation Petticoat. **1960** High Time; Breakfast at Tiffany's. **1962** The Notorious Landlady; Days of Wine and Roses; Experiment in Terror. **1963** Soldier in the Rain. **1964** The Pink Panther. **1965** The Great Race. **1966** Batman; What Did You Do in the War, Daddy? **1967** Gunn. **1968** The Party. **1970** Darling Lili; The Moonshine War. **1976** The Pink Panther Strikes Again.

CROCKETT, JOHN
Died: Feb. 22, 1922, Los Angeles, Calif. Screen actor.

Appeared in: **1918** Hobbs in a Hurry. **1920** The Slim Princess. **1921** The Four Horsemen of the Apoclypse.

CROKER-KING, CHARLES H.
Born: Apr. 30, 1873, Rock Helm, Yorkshire, England. Died: Oct. 25, 1951, England? Screen and stage actor.

Appeared in: **1936** The White Angel; The Crime of Dr. Forbes; Lloyds of London.

CROLIUS, GLADYS
Born: 1893. Died: Apr. 5, 1972, Hollywood, Calif. Screen actress. Married to actor Harry Tyler (dec. 1961).

Appeared in: **1929** Shannons of Broadway.

CROLLA, HENRI
Born: 1920, France. Died: 1960, Paris, France. Guitarist, composer and screen actor.

CROMWELL, JOHN
Born: 1914. Died: Sept. 1, 1979, London, England. Screen, stage, television actor, playwright and author. Do not confuse with actor/ director of same name (dec. Sept. 26, 1979).

CROMWELL, JOHN (Elwood Dager Cromwell)
Born: Dec. 23, 1887, Toledo, Ohio. Died: Sept 26, 1979, Santa Barbara Calif. (pulmonary embolism). Screen, stage actor, film director, stage director, stage producer and playwright. Divorced from stage actresses Alice Lindahl, Marie Goff, and Kay Johnson (dec. 1975). Later married to actress Ruth Nelson. Father of actor James Cromwell. Do not confuse with actor/playwright of same name (dec. Sept. 1, 1979). Entered films in 1928 as an actor.

Appeared in: **1929** Mighty. **1957** Top Secret Affair. **1977** Three Women. **1978** A Wedding.

CROMWELL, RICHARD (Roy Radabaugh)
Born: Jan. 8, 1910, Los Angeles, Calif. Died: Oct. 11, 1960, Hollywood, Calif. Stage and screen actor. Divorced from actress Angela Lansbury.

Appeared in: **1930** Tol'able David (film debut); King of Jazz. **1931** Fifty Fathoms Deep; Shanghaied Love; Are These Our Children?; Maker of Men. **1932** Strange Love of Molly Louvain; The Age of Consent; Emma; Tom Brown of Culver; That's My Boy. **1933** This Day and Age; Above the Clouds; Hoopla. **1934** Among the Missing; When Strangers Meet; The Most Precious Thing in Life; Name the Woman; Carolina. **1935** Life Begins at 40; Lives of a Bengal Lancer; McFadden's Flats; Unknown Woman. **1936** Poppy. **1937** Our Fighting Navy (aka Torpedoed—US 1939); The Road Back; The Wrong Road. **1938** Jezebel; Come On, Leathernecks; Storm Over Bengal. **1939** Mr. Lincoln; Torpedoed. **1940** Enemy Agent; The Villain Still Pursued Her; Village Barn Dance. **1941** Riot Squad; Parachute Battalion. **1942** Baby Face Morgan. **1943** The Crime Doctor. **1948** Bungalow 13.

CROSBY, BING (Harry Lissis Crosby)
Born: Mar. 2, 1903?, Tacoma, Wash. Died: Oct. 14, 1977, Madrid, Spain (heart attack). Screen, stage, vaudeville, radio, television actor, singer and writer. Married to actress Dixie Lee (dec. 1952) and later married to actress Kathryn Grant. Father of actor/singers Gary, Philip and Dennis (twins) and Lindsay Crosby plus Harry, Nathaniel and actress Mary Frances Crosby. Won 1944 Academy Award for Best Actor in "Going My Way" and nominated for 1945 Academy Award as Best Actor in "The Bells of St. Mary's" and in 1954 for "The Country Girl." Was leader of "Bing Crosby and the Rhythm Boys" musical group.

Appeared in: **1930** King of Jazz; Two Plus Fours (short); Ripstitch the Tailor (short). **1931** Confessions of a Co-Ed; Reaching for the Moon; The following shorts: Billboard Girl; Dreamhouse; Sing, Bing, Sing; Bring on Bing. **1932** The Big Broadcast of 1932; Hollywood on Parade (short); Just One More Chance (short). **1933** College Humor; Going Hollywood; Too Much Harmony; Please (short); Blue of the Night (short). **1934** We're Not Dressing; She Loves Me Not; Just an Echo (short); I Surrender Dear (short); Here is My Heart. **1935** Mississippi; Two for Tonight; The Big Broadcast of 1936; Star Night at the Coconut Grove (short). **1936** Rhythm on the Range; Pennies from Heaven. **1937** Waikiki Wedding; Double or Nothing; Swing with Bing (short). **1938** Doctor Rhythm; Sing You Sinners; Don't Hook Now (short). **1939** East Side of Heaven; Paris Honeymoon; The Star Maker. **1940** If I Had My Way; Rhythm on the River; Road to Singapore. **1941** Road to Zanzibar; Birth of the Blues; Angels of Mercy (short); The Road to Victory (short). **1942** Road to Morocco; Holiday Inn; My Favorite Blonde (unbilled); Star Spangled Rhythm. **1943** Dixie. **1944** Going My Way; Princess and the Pirate (unbilled); Here Come the Waves. **1945** Out of This World (voice); The Bells of St. Mary's; Duffy's Tavern; Road to Utopia; The following shorts: All-Star Bond Rally; Hollywood Victory Caravan. **1946** Blue Skies. **1947** Welcome Stranger; Road to Rio; Variety Girl; My Favorite Brunette (unbilled). **1948** The Emperor Waltz; A Connecticut Yankee in King Arthur's Court; Top O' the Morning; The Adventures of Ichabod and Mr. Toad (voice). **1950** Mr. Music; Riding High. **1951** Here Comes the Groom. **1952** Just for You; Road to Bali; The Greatest Show on Earth (unbilled); Son of Paleface (unbilled). **1953** Little Boy Lost; Scared Stiff (unbilled). **1954** White Christmas; The Country Girl. **1956** High Society; Anything Goes; Bing Presents Oreste (short). **1957** Man on Fire. **1958** Showdown at Ulcer Gulch (short). **1959** Alias Jesse James (unbilled); Say One for Me. **1960** High Time; Let's Make Love (as himself). **1962** The Road to Hong Kong. **1963** The Sound of Laughter (documentary). **1964** Robin and the Seven Hoods. **1966** Stagecoach; Cinerama's Russian Adventure (narration). **1968** Bing Crosby's Washington State (Short). **1974** That's Entertainment.

CROSBY, JULIETTE
Born: 1896. Died: May 1, 1969, Plainville, Conn. Screen and stage actress.

Appeared in: **1929** Charming Sinners; Paris Bound.

CROSBY, MARSHAL
Born: 1883, Australia. Died: Jan. 3, 1954, Port Macquarie, N.S.W., Australia (heart attack). Screen, stage, radio and vaudeville actor.

Appeared in: **1946** The Overlanders. **1947** Pacific Adventure. **1952** Kangaroo. Other Australian film: Eureka Stockade.

CROSBY, WADE
Born: 1905, Cedar Rapids, Iowa. Died: Oct. 1, 1975, Newport Beach, Calif. (grand mal seizure). Screen, stage actor and art director.

Appeared in: **1938** Marie Antoinette (film debut); The Affairs of Annabel; Ride a Crooked Mile. **1940** Arizona; Wagon Train. **1941** They Died With Their Boots On; Citadel of Crime; Sign of the Wolf. **1942** Twin Beds; Shepherd of the Ozarks. **1943** The Sundown Kid; Headin' for God's Country; The Woman of the Town. **1946** A Night in Paradise; Traffic in Crime. **1947** Sinbad the Sailor; Dick Tracy's Dilemma; The Wistful Widow of Wagon Gap; Along the Oregon Trail. **1948** Under California Skies; The Timber Trail; Angel's Alley; The Paleface. **1949** The Black Book; Rose of the Yukon. **1950** Hit Parade of 1951; Tales of Robin Hood. **1951** Valley of Fire. **1952** Invasion USA. **1953** Old Overland Trail; Prisoners of the Casbah. **1973** Westworld. **1975** Airport; The Hindenberg.

CROSBY, WARREN L.
Born: 1930. Died: Apr. 24, 1968, Wilmington, Del. (results of auto accident). Screen actor, stuntman and special effects man.

Appeared in: **1958** Tank Battalion. **1966** The Blue Max.

CROSMAN, HENRIETTA
Born: 1861, Wheeling, W.Va. Died: Oct. 31, 1944, Pelham Manor, N.Y. Screen and stage actress.

Appeared in: **1914** The Unwelcome Mrs. Hatch. **1915** How Molly Made Good. **1923** Broadway Broke. **1925** Wandering Fires. **1930** The Roy Family of Broadway. **1933** Pilgrimage. **1934** Among the Missing; Carolina; Three on a Honeymoon; Such Women Are Dangerous; Menace; The Curtain Falls. **1935** Elinor Norton; The Right to Live; The Dark Angel. **1936** Hitchhike to Heaven; Charlie Chan's Secret; The Moon's Our Home; Girl of the Ozarks; Follow Your Heart. **1937** Personal Property.

CROSS, ALFRED FRANCIS
Born: 1891. Died: Jan. 28, 1938, San Diego, Calif. (heart attack). Screen, stage actor and stage director. Entered films approx. 1920.

Appeared in: **1931** Smart Woman.

CROSS, JAMES "STUMP"
Born: 1920. Died: Jan. 25, 1981, New York, N.Y. Screen, stage, vaudeville and radio actor. Appeared with Eddie Hartman (dec.) in an act billed as "Stump and Stumpy," later with Harold Cromer, who replaced Hartman. Do not confuse with actor Jimmy Cross (dec. 1981).

Appeared in: **1942** Ship Ahoy. **1943** This is the Army (film and stage versions).

CROSS, JIMMY
Born: 1907. Died: June 14, 1981, Los Angeles, Calif. (stroke). Screen, stage, vaudeville, television actor, dancer and writer.

Appeared in: **1946** Behind Green Lights. **1948** French Leave. **1951** G.I. Jane; Leave it to the Marines. **1957** The Amazing Colossal Man. **1960** Squad Car. **1961** Everything's Ducky. **1964** Three Nuts in Search of a Bolt. **1965** Day of the Nightmare. **1967** A Guide for the Married Man.

CROSS, LEACH (Louis Cross Wallach)
Born: Feb. 12, 1886, New York, N.Y. Died: Sept. 7, 1957, New York, N.Y. Prizefighter, boxing judge and screen actor.

Appeared in: **1920** The Vanishing Dagger (serial). **1926** The Prince of Broadway.

CROSS, MILTON J.
Born: Apr. 16, 1897, New York, N.Y. Died: Jan. 3, 1975, New York, N.Y. (heart attack). Radio commentator, singer and screen actor. Known as the "Voice of the Metropolitan."

Appeared in: **1937** A Warner Bros. short. **1950** Grounds for Marriage (narrator).

CROSSE, RUPERT
Born: 1928. Died: Mar. 5, 1973, Nevis, West Indies (cancer). Black screen and television actor. Nominated for 1969 Academy Award for Best Supporting Actor in The Reivers.

Appeared in: **1961** Shadows. **1962** Too Late Blues. **1963** Twilight of Honor. **1965** Wild Seed. **1966** To Trap a Spy. **1967** Waterhole #3. **1969** The Reivers.

CROSSLEY, SID (aka SYD CROSSLEY)
Born: Nov. 18, 1885, London, England. Died: Nov., 1960, Troon, England. Screen actor and music hall comedian.

Appeared in: **1925** Keep Smiling; North Star. **1926** The Golden Web; The Unknown Soldier; One Hour Married. **1927** Ain't Love Funny?;

Jewels of Desire; Romantic Rogue; Play Safe; The Blood Ship; The Gorilla. **1928** A Perfect Gentleman; That Certain Thing; Fangs of the Wild; The Circus Kid; The Cowboy Kid; Into No Man's Land. **1929** The Younger Generation; Atlantic; Hate Ship; Just for a Song; The Fatal Warning (serial). **1930** Suspense; The Middle Watch; Man from Chicago; All of a Tremble; Flying Fool; Never Trouble Trouble. **1931** Men Like These; Tonight's the Night. **1932** For the Love of Mike; Letting in the Sunshine; Leave It to Me. **1933** The Medicine Man; Excess Baggage; The Umbrella; Meet My Sister; You Made Me Love You; The Bermondsey Kid. **1934** Those Were the Days; Over the Garden Wall; Night Club Queen; Give Me a Ring; Gay Love; It's a Bet; Eighteen Minutes; Dandy Dick; Radio Parade of 1935. **1935** Me and Marlborough; Royal Cavalcade; Jimmy Boy; Honeymoon for Three; The Deputy Drummer; Music Hath Charms; Another Spot of Bother; Cheer Up; The Ghost Goes West; One Good Turn; Public Nuisance No. 1; Queen of Hearts; Man Behind the Mask; Royal Romance. **1936** Two's Company; Everything Is Rhythm. **1937** Man in the Mirror; Silver Blaze; Sensation; The Gang Show; Old Mother Riley. **1938** Young and Innocent (aka The Girl Was Young); We're Going to Be Rich; The Return of Carol; Everything Happens to Me; His Lordship Goes to Press; Peter's Pence; Save a Little Sunshine; Penny Paradise. Other British films: Romantic Rhythm; Paybox Adventure; Boys Will Be Girls; Sporting Love; Keep Your Seats, Please; Cotton Queen; The Limping Man; Ghosts Alive; Full Steam Ahead; Feather Your Nest; Double Alibi; Lucky Jade; Pearls Bring Tears; Racketeer Rhythm; Dark Stairway; Sweet Devil; Little Dolly Daydream; Open House; He Was Her Man.

CROSTHWAITE, IVY (aka RICE BARRETT)
Born: 1898, San Diego, Calif. Died: Nov. 8, 1962, Los Angeles, Calif. Screen actress. Was a Sennett Bathing Beauty.

Appeared in: **1915** The Beauty Bunglers; Fickle Fatty's Fall; Fatty and the Broadway Stars. **1916** By Stork Delivery. **1917** Brainstorm; A Bath House Tangle.

CROUCH, WORTH
Born: 1917. Died: Feb. 6, 1943, Calabasas, Calif. Screen actor and stuntman.

Appeared in: **1943** We've Never Been Licked (died on location during filming).

CROWE, EILEEN
Born: 1899. Died: May 8, 1978, Dublin, Ireland. Screen and stage actress. Married to actor F. J. McCormick (aka Peter Judge, dec. 1947).

Appeared in: **1936** The Plough and the Stars. **1944** Going My Way. **1947** Hungry Hill. **1949** Top of the Morning. **1952** The Quiet Man; Steel Town. **1957** The Rising of the Moon. **1959** Home is the Hero (US 1961); Shake Hands With the Devil. **1960** A Terrible Beauty (aka The Night Fighters—US). **1964** Girl With Green Eyes.

CROWELL, BURT (Walter J. Crowley)
Born: 1873. Died: Mar. 26, 1946, Chicago, Ill. Screen, stage and vaudeville actor. Appeared in vaudeville with his wife Ann as "Crowell and Gardner."

CROWELL, JOSEPHINE (Josephine Bonaparte Crowell)
Born: Canada. Died: July 27, 1932, Amityville, N.Y. Screen and stage actress.

Appeared in: **1915** The Birth of a Nation. **1916** As in a Looking Glass; Little School Ma'am; Intolerance. **1917** Rebecca of Sunnybrook Farm; Betsey's Burglar. **1918** Hearts of the World. **1919** Peppy Polly; Flames of the Flesh; The Greatest Question; Puppy Love; House of Intrigue; Joselyn's Wife. **1920** Held by the Enemy; Crooked Streets; White Lies; Half a Chance. **1921** Bunty Pulls the Strings; The Snob; Don't Neglect your Wife; Home Stuff; Live and Let Live. **1922** A Homespun Vamp; Lights of the Desert; Minnie; Shattered Idols; Seeing's Believing; The Birth of a Nation. **1923** Rupert of Hentzau; Ashes of Vengeance; Main Street; Nobody's Money; Yesterday's Wife. **1924** Flowing Gold; Hot Water. **1925** The Sporting Venus; Welcome Home; The Merry Widow; New Brooms; The Splendid Crime. **1926** Mantrap; Padlocked; Bred in Old Kentucky; Yellow Fingers. **1927** Fighting Love; For Wives Only; The Kings of Kings; The Man Who Laughs. **1965** Laurel and Hardy's Laughing 20's (film clips).

CROY, HOMER
Born: Mar. 11, 1883, near Maryville, Mo. Died: May 24, 1965, New York, N.Y. (heart attack). Novelist, screen actor and screenwriter.

Appeared in: **1915** In the Land of the Mikado with Homer Croy.

CRUME, CAMILLA
Born: 1874. Died: Mar. 20, 1952, Norwalk, Conn. Screen, stage and radio actress. Appeared in early films made at Vitaphone Studios, Brooklyn, N.Y.

CRUSTER, AUD (Cruster Aud Olsen)
Born: 1889. Died: May 18, 1938, Moline, Ill. Screen and vaudeville actor.

Appeared in: **1926** Kid Boots.

CRUTE, SALLY (Sally C. Kirby)
Born: 1886. Died: Aug. 12, 1971, Miami, Fla. Screen actress.

Appeared in: **1915** While the Tide Was Rising. **1916** Helen of the Chorus. **1920** The Garter Girl. **1921** It Isn't Being Done This Season; Perjury. **1923** Broadway Broke; His Children's Children; The Tents of Allah. **1925** The Half-Way Girl; A Little Girl in a Big City; Ermine and Rhinestones.

CRUZE, JAMES (Jens Cruz Bosen)
Born: Mar. 27, 1894, Ogden, Utah. Died: Aug. 3, 1942, Los Angeles, Calif. Screen, stage, vaudeville actor, film director, producer and screenwriter. Divorced from actresses Margarite Snow (dec. 1958) and Betty Compson (dec. 1974).

Appeared in: **1911** The Higher Law. **1912** Lucille; Dr. Jekyll and Mr. Hyde; On Probation; Cross Your Heart; For Sale—A Life; Rejuvenation; Miss Robinson Crusoe; The Thunderbolt; The Other Half; Whom God Hath Joined; But the Greatest of These is Charity; Love's Miracle; A Militant Suffragette; The Ring of a Spanish Grandee; Put Yourself in His Place; Miss Arabella Smith; Jess; Called Back. **1913** The Silver-Tongued Doctor; A Poor Relation; The Tiniest of Stars; The Ward of the King; The Plot Against the Governor; The Idol of the Hour; The Lost Combination; Her Sister's Secret; Tannhauser; The Marble Heart; A Girl Worth While; Cymbeline; The Snare of Fate; Good Morning, Judge. **1914** The Leak in the Foreign Office; From Wash to Washington; A Debut in the Secret Service; A Mohammedan Conspiracy; The Million Dollar Mystery (serial); Joseph in the Land of Egypt; Zudora—The Twenty Million Dollar Mystery (serial).

CRUZE, MAE
Born: 1891. Died: Aug. 16, 1965, Hollywood, Calif. Screen actress. Entered films in silents.

Appeared in: **1964** Mary Poppins.

CULLEY, FREDERICK
Born: Mar. 9, 1879, Warwickshire, Plymouth, England. Died: Nov. 3, 1942, England? Screen and stage actor.

Appeared in: **1930** Enter the Queen. **1931** Madame Guillotine. **1933** The Private Life of Henry VIII. **1934** Colonel Blood. **1935** Peg of Old Drury (US 1936). **1936** Annie Laurie; Talk of the Devil (US 1937); Conquest of the Air. **1937** Our Fighting Navy (aka Torpedoed—US 1939); Knight Without Armour; The Rat. **1938** The Drum; Sword of Honour; The Four Feathers. **1942** The Young Mr. Pitt.

CULLINGTON, MARGARET
Born: 1891. Died: July 18, 1925, Hollywood, Calif. Screen actress. Appeared in early "Christie" comedies.

Appeared in: **1921** The Son of Wallingford; The Mad Marriage. **1923** Wolves of the Border. **1924** Excitement; The Breathless Moment; That Wild West.

CULLISON, WEBSTER
Born: Feb. 18, 1880, Baltimore, Md. Died: July 7, 1938, Glendale, Calif. Screen, stage actor, film director, stage director and writer.

Appeared in: **1912** The Silent Signal. **1924** The Air Hawk.

CULLY, ZARA BROWN
Born: 1892, Worcester, Mass. Died: Feb. 28, 1978, Los Angeles, Calif. (cancer). Black screen, stage, television actress, stage producer and playwright.

Appeared in: **1969** The Learning Tree. **1970** The Liberation of L. B. Jones; The Great White Hope. **1971** Brother John. **1974** Sugar Hill. **1975** Darktown Strutters.

CUMMING, RUTH
Born: 1904. Died: Aug. 11, 1967, New York, N.Y. Screen, stage actress and opera performer.

CUMMINGS, CATHERINE
Born: 1871, Grantsburg, Ill. Died: July 10, 1950, Hollywood, Calif. (heart attack). Screen actress. Married to actor Richard H. Cummings (dec. 1938). Appeared in Biograph Company films.

CUMMINGS, FRANCES
Died: Aug. 12, 1923, New York, N.Y. (cancer). Screen and stage actress. Appeared in early Lupin Film Company and Famous Players production.

CUMMINGS, GEORGE F.
Born: July 4, 1880, Richmond, Va. Died: Mar. 11, 1946. Screen actor.

Appeared in: **1913** Nathan Hale. **1915** The Passer-By. **1916** Romeo and Juliet. **1917** Awakening of Helen Ritchie; The Argyle Case. **1920** Alias Jimmy Valentine. **1922** Man's Law and God's. **1924** The Whipping Boss.

CUMMINGS, IRVING, SR.
Born: Oct. 9, 1888, New York, N.Y. Died: Apr. 18, 1959, Hollywood, Calif. (heart attack). Screen, stage actor and film director. Entered films as an actor in 1909.

Appeared in: **1913** Ashes; The Man from Outside; Duty and the Man; The Tangled Web; The Woman Who Knew; London Assurance; The Bells; The Open Road. **1914** The Million Dollar Mystery (serial); The Messenger of Death; Jane Eyre; Broken Paths; The Finger of Fate; The Varsity Race; The Sword of Damocles; The Resurrection. **1915** The Diamond From the Sky (serial); The Lure of the Mask; The Silent Witness (serial). **1916** The Hidden Scar; Pamela's Past. **1918** Merely Players; The Heart of a Girl. **1919** Her Code of Honor; Some Bride; The Unveiling Hand; Men, Women and Money; Everywoman. **1920** The Thirteenth Commandment. **1921** The Saphead. **1925** As Man Desires. **1936** Girl's Dormitory. **1941** The Devil and Mrs. Jones.

CUMMINGS, RICHARD H.
Born: 1858. Died: Dec. 25, 1938, Los Angeles, Calif. Screen, stage, vaudeville and minstrel actor. Married to actress Catherine Cummings (dec. 1950). Entered films with Tannhauser Co. in 1912.

Appeared in: **1915** Birth of a Nation. **1917** Reaching for the Moon. **1921** Red Courage; The Bride's Play; Partners of Fate; No Woman Knows; The Tomboy. **1922** Great Alone; The Top O' the Morning; Wolf Law. **1923** Thundergate; Itching Palms. **1925** Thank You. **1926** The Galloping Cowboy. **1930** The Social Lion.

CUMMINGS, ROBERT
Born: Feb. 22, 1867, Richmond, Va. Died: July 22, 1949. Stage and screen actor. Do not confuse with actor Robert "Bob" Cummings.

Appeared in: **1916** Romeo and Juliet; Bought. **1917** The Awakening of Helena Richie; Betsy Ross; A Rich Man's Plaything.

CUMMINGS, VICKI
Born: 1919, Northampton, Mass. Died: Nov. 30, 1969, New York, N.Y. Screen, stage and television actress.

Appeared in: **1951** I Can Get It for You Wholesale. **1962** The Time and the Touch.

CUMPSON, JOHN R.
Born: 1868. Died: Mar. 15, 1913, New York, N.Y. (pneumonia—diabetes). Screen actor.

Appeared in: **1908** A Calamitous Elopement; Monday Morning in a Coney Island Police Court; A Smoked Husband; Mr. Jones at the Ball. **1909** Mrs. Jones Entertains; The Cord of Life; At the Altar; Mr. Jones has a Card Party; His Wife's Mother; Jones and the Lady Book Agent; Her First Biscuits. **1911** A Famous Duel; His First Trip; The Escaped Lunatic; The Daisy Cowboys; Maiden of the Piefaced Indians; The Summer Girl; Mae's Suitors; The Kid from Klondyke; John Brown's Heir; Ludwig from Germany; The Troubles of a Bulter; An International Heartbreaker. **1912** The Flag of Distress; The Broken Lease; Mr. Smith, Barber; A Piece of Ambergris; A Millionaire for a Day; Breach of Promise; The Maid's Stratagem; How Shorty Won Out; Portugee Joe; A Case of Dynamite; Ferdie's Family Feud; Chappie the Chaperon; Her Diary; An Exciting Outing; Curing Hubby.

CUNARD, GRACE (Harriet Mildred Jefferies)
Born: 1893, Columbus, Ohio. Died: Jan. 19, 1967, Woodland Hills, Calif. (cancer). Screen and stage actress. Married to actor Joe Moore (dec. 1926) and later married to actor Jack Shannon (dec. 1968). Sister of actress Myna Seymour.

Appeared in: **1912** Custer's Last Fight; The Duke's Plan. **1913** The Favorite Son; Captain Billy's Mate; The She Wolf; From Dawn Till Dark. **1914** Be Neutral; The Bride of Mystery; In the Fall of '64; Lady Raffles; Lucille Love, Girl of Mystery (serial); The Madcap of Queen of Gretzhoffen; The Mystery of the White Car; The Mysterious Hand; The Mysterious Leopard Lady; The Mysterious Rose; The Phantom of the Violin; Washington at Valley Forge; A Wartime Reformation; The Unsigned Agreement. **1915** And They Called Him Hero; The Broken Coin (serial); The Campbells Are Coming; The Doorway of Destruction; The Heart of Lincoln; The Hidden City; The Lumber Yard Gang; Nabbed; One Kind of a Friend; 3 Bad Men and a Girl; An Outlaws's Honor. **1916** The Bandit's Wager; Behind the Mask; Brennon O' the Moor; Born of the People; The Elusive Enemy; Her Better Self; Her Sister's Sin; The Heroine of San Juan; His Majesty Dick Turpin; Lady Raffles Returns; The Mad Hermit; The Madcap Queen of Crona; Phamtom Island; The Adventures of Pet O' the Ring (serial); The Powder Trail; The Princely Bandit; The Purple Mask (serial); The Sham Reality. **1917** Circus Sarah; Her Western Adventure; In Treason's Grasp; The Puzzle Woman; Society's Driftwood; True to Their Colors; Unmasked. **1918** Hell's Carter; The Spawn. **1919** After the War; Elmo the Mighty (serial). **1920** A Daughter of the Law; Gasoline Buckaroo; The Man Hater; The Woman of Mystery. **1922** The Girl in the Taxi; A Dangerous Adventure (serial); The Heart of Lincoln (reissue of 1915 film). **1924** The Last Man on Earth; Emblems of Love. **1925** The Kiss Barrier; Outwitted. **1926** Exclusive Rights; Fighting With Buffalo Bill (serial); The Winking Idol (serial). **1927** Blake of Scotland Yard (serial); The Denver Dude; The Return of Riddle Rider (serial); The Rest Cure. **1928** The Haunted Island (serial); The Masked Angel; The Price of Fear; The Chinatown Mystery (serial). **1929** The Ace of Scotland Yard (serial); Untamed. **1930** A Lady Surrenders. **1931** Ex-Bad Boy; Resurrection. **1933** Ladies They Talk About. **1934** The Man Who Reclaimed His Head. **1935** The Bride of Frankenstein; Alias Mary Dow. **1937** Wings Over Honolulu. **1943** The North Star. **1944** The Climax; Casanova Brown. **1946** Magnificent Doll.

CUNARD, MYRA
Born: Dec. 16, 1894, Columbus, Ohio. Died: Aug. 2, 1978, Woodland Hills, Calif. Screen, television actress and circus performer.

Appeared in: **1915** The Broken Coin (serial). **1916** The Sign of the Poppy. **1917** Won by Grit; The Daring Change.

CUNEO, LESTER
Born: 1888, Indian Territory, Okla. Died: Nov. 1, 1925. Screen and stage actor. Married to actress Francelia Billington.

Appeared in: **1914** The Other Man; A Splendid Dishonor; The Private Officer. **1915** Pennington's Choice; Thirteen Down; Graustark; The Silent Voice. **1916** A Virginia Romance; Mr. Forty-Four; Big Tremaine. **1917** Pidgin Island; The Haunted Pajamas; Under Handicap; Paradise Garden; The Square Deceiver. **1920** Are All Men Alike?; The Terror; Food for Scandal. **1921** The Ranger and the Law. **1922** Blazing Arrows; Blue Blazes; The Masked Avenger; Silver Spurs; Trapped in the Air. **1923** The Eagle's Feather; Fighting Jim Grant; The Vengeance of Pierre; The Zero Hour. **1924** Lone Hand Texas; Ridin' Fool; Western Grit. **1925** Hearts of the West; Range Vultures; Two Fisted Thompson; Western Promise.

CUNINGHAM, PHILLIP (Philip Harold Boosey)
Born: Aug. 12, 1865, London, England. Died: Jan. 10, 1928, England? Screen and stage actor.

CUNNINGHAM, ALOYSIUS
Died: July 27, 1936, Pottsville, Pa. (heart attack). Stage and screen actor.

CUNNINGHAM, ARTHUR
Born: 1888, San Francisco, Calif. Died: Nov. 29, 1955, San Francisco, Calif. Screen, stage and vaudeville actor.

Appeared in: **1915** Biddy Brady's Birthday; Busted But Benevolent; A Cunning Canal-Boat; Hattie the Hair Heiress; Pansy's Prision Pies; A Perplexing Puzzle; The Villainous Vegetable Vender.

CUNNINGHAM, CECIL
Born: Aug. 2, 1888, St. Louis, Mo. Died: Apr. 17, 1959, Woodland Hills, Calif. (arteriosclerosis). Screen, stage, vaudeville and radio actress.

Appeared in: **1930** Their Own Desire; Anybody's Woman; Playboy of Paris; Paramount on Parade. **1931** Susan Lenox, Her Fall and Rise; Age for Love; Monkey Business; Safe in Hell; Mata Hari; Trouble from Abroad (short). **1932** Never the Twins Shall Meet (short); It's Tough to be Famous; The Rich Are Always With Us; The Candid Camera (short); Blonde Venus; If I Had a Million; Baby Face; Impatient Maiden; Those We Love; Love is a Racket; Love Me Tonight. **1933**

From Hell to Heaven; Ladies They Talk About; The Druggist's Dilemma (short). **1934** Manhattan Love Song; The Life of Vergie Winters; Return of the Terror; We Live Again; Bottoms Up. **1935** People Will Talk. **1936** Come and Get It; Mr. Deeds Goes to Town. **1937** Swing High—Swing Low; King of Gamblers; Artists and Models; This Way Please; The Awful Truth; Night Club Scandal; Daughter of Shanghai. **1938** College Swing; Scandal Sheet; Four Men and a Prayer; Kentucky Moonshine; You and Me; Wives Under Suspicion; Girl's School; Blonde Cheat; Marie Antoinette. **1939** The Family Next Door; It's a Wonderful World; Winter Carnival; Lady of the Tropics; Laugh It Off. **1940** Lillian Russell; The Captain is a Lady; New Moon; The Great Profile; Kitty Foyle; Play Girl. **1941** Back Street; Repent at Leisure; Blossoms in the Dust; Hurry, Charlie, Hurry. **1942** Cowboy Serenade; The Wife Takes a Flyer; Cairo; The Hidden Hand; Twin Beds. **1943** Above Suspicion; In Old Oklahoma; DuBarry Was a Lady. **1945** Wonder Man; Saratoga Trunk; The Horn Blows at Midnight. **1946** My Reputation. **1948** The Bride Goes Wild.

CUNNINGHAM, GEORGE
Born: 1904. Died: May 1, 1962, Los Angeles, Calif. Screen actor and dancer.

Appeared in: **1929** Broadway Melody (film debut); The Hollywood Revue of 1929; Our Modern Maidens; Thunder.

CUNNINGHAM, JACK
Born: 1912, England. Died: Jan. 13, 1967, London, England. Screen and stage actor. Do not confuse with U.S. actor with same name.

Appeared in: **1961** The Snake Woman. **1962** The Quare Fellow. **1963** Billy Liar!

CUNNINGHAM, JOE (Joseph A. Cunningham)
Born: June 22, 1890, Philadelphia, Pa. Died: Apr. 3, 1943, Los Angeles, Calif. (coronary occlusion). Screen, radio actor, screenwriter and cartoonist.

Appeared in: **1936** The Country Gentlemen; Hot Money. **1937** Prescription for Romance; Kid Galahad; Sensation; Fugitive in the Sky. **1938** Torchy Blane in Panama; Torchy Gets Her Man; Going Places; Four's a Crowd; Blondes at Work. **1939** They Drive by Night; Torchy Runs for Mayor; Torchy Plays With Dynamite; Blackwell's Island; Secret Service of the Air. **1940** It's in the Air. **1941** Tom, Dick and Harry. **1942** The Affairs of Jimmy Valentine; Dudes Are Pretty People; The Navy Comes Through; Broadway; Talk of the Town; I Live on Danger.

CUNNINGHAM, ZAMAH
Born: 1893. Died: June 2, 1967, New York, N.Y. Screen, stage, vaudeville and television actress. Entered films with Griffith.

Appeared in: **1948** Dream Girl. **1950** Key to the City. **1953** Here Come the Girls. **1965** Baby, The Rain Must Fall.

CURCI, GENNARO (Baron Gennaro Mario Curci)
Born: Sept. 19, 1888, Italy. Died: Apr. 13, 1955, Los Angeles, Calif. (cerebral thrombosis). Screen actor and opera performer. Married to actress Elvira Curci.

Appeared in: **1935** The Melody Lingers On. **1937** Manhattan Merry-Go-Round; I Met Him in Paris; I'll Take Romance. **1939** Juarez; Midnight.

CURLEY, LEO
Born: Apr. 2, 1878, New York, N.Y. Died: Apr. 11, 1960, Woodland Hills, Calif. (arteriosclerosis). Screen actor. Married to actress Lucille Husting (dec. 1972).

Appeared in: **1935** Speed Devils. **1949** Johnny Holiday. **1952** Something for the Birds. **1953** The Robe; The President's Lady; City of Bad Men. **1954** The Bounty Hunter.

CURRAN, J. P.
Died: Jan. 11, 1919, Sawtelle, Calif. Screen actor.

Appeared in Ince Film Company films.

CURRAN, THOMAS A.
Born: 1880. Died: Jan. 24, 1941, Hollywood, Calif. (pneumonia). Screen and stage actor.

Appeared in: **1928** The Black Pearl. **1929** Object Alimony; Anne Against the World; Ships of the Night; Two Sisters; Must We Marry?; Trial of Mary Dugan; Wolf of Wall Street; The Phantom in the House. **1930** Morocco; The Kibitzer; Worldly Goods. **1931** Dishonored; Mother and Son; Forgotten Women; The Ghost City. **1932** Dance Team; Charlie Chan's Chance; Lost Squadron; Lady With a Past. **1935** The Cowboy Millionaire. **1940** Her First Romance. **1941** Citizen Kane.

CURRIE, CLIVE
Born: Mar. 26, 1877, Birmingham, England. Died: May 25, 1935, London, England. Screen and stage actor.

Appeared in: **1932** Money Means Nothing (US 1934); Goodnight Vienna (aka Magic Night—US).

CURRIE, FINLAY
Born: Jan. 20, 1878, Edinburgh, Scotland. Died: May 9, 1968, Gerrads Cross, England. Screen, stage, minstrel and television actor. Married to stage actress Maude Courtney (dec. 1959).

Appeared in: **1931** The Old Man. **1932** Rome Express; The Frightened Lady (aka Criminal at Large—US 1933). **1933** Excess; The Good Companions; Orders is Orders (US 1934). **1934** Princess Charming (US 1935); Little Friend; Gay Love; Mister Cinders; My Old Dutch. **1935** The Big Splash. **1936** The Improper Duchess; The Gay Adventure. **1937** Wanted; Glamorous Night; Command Performance; Catch as Catch Can; The Edge of the World (US 1938); Paradise for Two (aka The Gaiety Girls—US 1938). **1938** The Claydon Treasure Mystery; Around the Town; Follow Your Star. **1939** Hospital Hospitality. **1941** 49th Parallel (aka The Invaders—US 1942). **1942** Thunder Rock (US 1944); The Day Will Dawn (aka The Avengers—US). **1943** The Bells Go Down; Warn That Man; They Met in the Dark (US 1945); The Shipbuilders; Undercover (aka Undercover Guerillas—US 1944). **1945** Theatre Royal. **1945** Don Chicago; I Know Where I'm Going (US 1947). **1946** The Trojan Brothers; Great Expectations (US 1947); Woman to Woman; Spring Song (aka Springtime—US); School for Secrets. **1947** The Brothers (US 1948); Atlantic Episode (rerelease of 1943 Catch as Catch Can). **1948** My Brother Jonathan (US 1949); So Evil My Love; Mr. Perrin and Mr. Traill; Bonnie Prince Charlie (US 1952); Sleeping Car to Trieste (US 1949). **1949** The History of Mr. Polly (US 1951). **1950** Treasure Island; My Daughter Joy (aka Operation X—US 1951); Trio; The Black Rose; The Mudlark. **1951** Quo Vadis; People Will Talk. **1952** Kangaroo; Ivanhoe; Walk East on Beacon; Stars and Stripes Forever. **1953** Treasure of the Golden Condor; Rob Roy the Highland Rogue. **1954** The End of the Road (US 1959); Beau Brummel; Make Me an Offer (US 1956); Captain Lightfoot. **1955** Third Party Risk (aka The Deadly Game—US); Footsteps in the Fog; King's Rhapsody (US 1956). **1956** Around the World in 80 Days. **1957** Zarak; Seven Waves Away (aka Abandon Ship!—US); Saint Joan; The Little Hut; Campbell's Kingdom (US 1958); Dangerous Exile (US 1958). **1958** The Naked Earth; 6.5 Special; Corridors of Blood (US 1963). **1959** Ben Hur; Solomon and Sheba; Tempest. **1960** The Angel Wore Red; The Adventures of Huckleberry Finn; Kidnapped; Hand in Hand (US 1961); Giuseppe Vinduto dai Fratelli (Joseph Sold by His Brothers aka The Story of Joseph and His Brethren—US 1962). **1961** Five Golden Hours; Francis of Assisi. **1962** Calling All Cars (reissue of 6.5 Special—1958); The Inspector (aka Lisa—US); The Amorous Prawn (aka The Playgirl and the War Minister—US 1963); Go to Blazes. **1963** Billy Liar!; The Three Worlds of Thomasina; Cleopatra. **1964** Who Was Maddox?; The Fall of the Roman Empire. **1965** The Battle of the Villa Fiorita; Bunny Lake is Missing.

CURRIER, FRANK
Born: 1857, Norwich, Conn. Died: Apr. 22, 1928, Hollywood, Calif. (blood poisoning). Screen and stage actor. Married to stage actress Ada Dow (dec. 1926).

Appeared in: **1914** Midst Woodland Shadows. **1915** The Juggernaut. **1918** With Neatness and Dispatch. **1919** Her Kingdom of Dreams; Should Women Tell? **1921** Clay Dollars; The Rookie's Return; Smiling All the Way; The Lotus Eater; Man Who; A Message from Mars; Without Limit. **1922** The Woman Who Fooled Herself; Why Announce Your Marriage?; The Lights of New York; Reckless Youth; My Old Kentucky Home; The Snitching Hour. **1923** The Tents of Allah; Children of Jazz; The Fog; The Victor; The Go-Getter; The Darling of New York; Desire; Stephen Steps Out. **1924** The Red Lily; Being Respectable; The Family Secret; The Heart Buster; The Sea Hawk; The Rose of Paris; Revelation; The Story Without a Name; The Trouble Shooter. **1925** Graustark; Lights of Old Broadway; The White Desert; The Great Love; Too Many Kisses. **1926** The Big Parade; Ben Hur; La Boheme; Men of Steel; The First Year; Tell It to the Marines; The Exquisite Sinner. **1927** Annie Laurie; The Callahans and the Murphys; Rookies; California; The Enemy; Winners of the Wilderness; Foreign Devils. **1928** Across to Singapore; Easy Come, Easy Go; Telling the World; Riders of the Dark.

CURRY, DORA DEAN
Born: 1911. Died: July 1, 1931, U.S. (pneumonia). Screen, stage actress and ballet dancer.

CURRY, ELIZABETH
Born: 1918. Died: Aug. 25, 1935, Los Angeles, Calif. (auto accident). Screen, stage actress and dancer.

CURRY, MASON

Born: 1909, Port Williams, Novia Scotia, Canada. Died: Apr. 1, 1980, Mobile, Ala. Screen and television actor.

Appeared in: **1960** The Apartment. **1961** Sniper's Ridge. **1967** Valley of the Dolls. **1973** The Exorcist.

CURTIS, ALAN (Harry Ueberroth)

Born: July 24, 1909, Chicago, Ill. Died: Feb. 1, 1953, New York, N.Y. (kidney operation). Screen actor. Divorced from screen actresses Ilona Massey (dec. 1974) and Betty Sundmark (dec. 1959).

Appeared in: **1936** The Smartest Girl in Town; Winterset; Walking on Air. **1937** The Firefly; Between Two Women; Bad Gun; China Passage; Don't Tell the Wife. **1938** Mannequin; Yellow Jack; Shopworn Angel; Duke of West Point. **1939** Good Girls Go to Paris; Sergeant Madden; Burn 'Em Up O'Connor; Hollywood Cavalcade. **1940** Four Sons. **1941** Come Live With Me; New Wine; High Sierra; We Go Fast; Buck Privates; The Great Awakening. **1942** Remember Pearl Harbor. **1943** Crazy House; Two Tickets to London; Hitler's Madman; Gung Ho!. **1944** Destiny; Phantom Lady; The Invisible Man's Revenge; Follow the Boys. **1945** Frisco Sal; Shady Lady; The Naughty Nineties; See My Lawyer; The Daltons Ride Again. **1946** Inside Job. **1947** Flight to Nowhere; Renegade Girl; Philo Vance's Secret Mission; Philo Vance's Gamble. **1948** Enchanted Valley. **1949** Captain Sorocco; Pirates of Capri; Apache Chief. **1950** The Masked Pirate.

CURTIS, BEATRICE (Beatrice White)

Born: 1901. Died: Mar. 26, 1963, Los Angeles, Calif. Screen and vaudeville actress. Divorced from actor Harry Fox (dec. 1959) with whom she appeared in vaudeville.

Together they made the following two shorts: **1929** The Fox and the Bee. **1930** The Play Boy. She appeared without Fox in: **1934** Most Precious Thing in Life. **1936** Mr. Deeds Goes to Town; Theodora Goes Wild; And So They Were Married. **1937** Paid to Dance; Girls Can Play; Lost Horizon. **1939** Good Girls Go to Paris; Homicide Bureau; The Lone Wolf Spy Hunt.

CURTIS, DICK

Born: May 11, 1902, Newport, Ky. Died: Jan. 3, 1952, Hollywood, Calif. Screen and stage actor.

Appeared in: **1918** The Unpardonable Sin (film debut as an extra). **1930** Shooting Straight. **1932** Girl Crazy. **1933** King Kong. **1934** Wilderness Mail; Racing Luck; Burning Gold; Silver Streak; Mutiny Ahead. **1935** Code of the Mounted; Fighting Trooper; Lion's Den; Northern Frontier. **1936** Ghost Patrol; The Wildcat Trooper. **1937** Paid to Dance; The Shadow. **1938** Penitentiary; Women in Prison; The Main Event; Adventure in Sahara; Rawhide; Time Out For Trouble (short); Flat Foot Stooges (short). **1939** Mandrake the Magician (serial); Overland With Kit Carson (serial); Flying G-Men (serial); West of Santa Fe; Spoilers of the Range; Western Caravans; Taming of the West; Behind Prison Gates; Riders of Black River; The Man They Could Not Hang; Outpost of the Mounties; The Stranger From Texas; plus the following shorts: Three Little Sew and Sews; We Want Money; Oily to Bed—Oily to Rise; The Awful Goof; Boom Goes the Groom; Now It Can Be Sold; Trouble Finds Andy Clyde; All-American Blondes; We Want Our Mummy; Yes, We Have No Bonanza. **1940** Terry and the Pirates (serial); Boom Town; Blazing Six-Shooters; Bullets for Rustlers; Pioneers of the Frontier; Two-Fisted Rangers; Texas Stagecoach; Three Men from Texas; Ragtime Cowboy Joe; Men Without Souls; My Son Is Guilty; You Nazty Spy (short). **1941** Billy the Kid; Stick to Your Guns; The Roundup; Across the Sierras; Mystery Ship; I Was A Prisoner on Devil's Island. **1942** Two Yanks in Trinidad; Arizona Cyclone; Men of San Quentin; City of Silent Men; The Power of God; Jackass Mail. **1943** Pardon My Gun; Jack London; Salute to the Marines; Cowboy in the Clouds; Higher Than a Kite (short). **1944** Spook Town; Crash Goes the Hash (short). **1945** Wagon Wheels Westward; Song of the Prairie; Singing Guns; Hidden Trails; Shotgun Rider; plus the following shorts: Snooper Service; Pistol Packin' Nitwits; The Last Installment. **1946** Scarlet Street; Wild Beauty; Bandit of Sherwood Forest; California Gold Rush; Traffic in Crime; Song of Arizona; Abilene Town; Santa Fe Uprising; Three Troubledoers (short). **1947** Wyoming. **1949** Navajo Trail Raiders. **1950** The Jackpot; Wabash Avenue; Covered Wagon Raid; The Vanishing Westerner. **1951** Roar of the Iron Horse (serial); The Red Badge of Courage; Lorna Doone; Rawhide; Whirlwind; Government Agents vs. Phantom Legion (serial); Three Arabian Nuts (short); Don't Throw That Knife (short). **1952** Rose of Cimmaron; My Six Convicts.

CURTIS, HOWARD

Born: 1927. Died: Sept. 2, 1979, Lake Elsinore, Calif. (free-fall jump accident). Screen actor and stuntman.

Appeared in: **1961** Black Sunday. **1964** Pajama Party. **1965** The Great Race. **1969** Butch Cassidy and the Sundance Kid. **1970** Lost Flight. **1976** Swashbuckler. **1977** The Deep. **1979** Moonraker.

CURTIS, JACK

Born: May 28, 1880, Calif. Died: Mar. 16, 1956, Hollywood, Calif. Screen actor. Do not confuse with former child actor Jack Curtis or Jack B. Curtis (dec. 1970).

Appeared in: **1915** Graft (serial); The Case of the First Born. **1916** The Torrent of Vengeance; The Iron Rivals; The Yaqui; Two Men of Sandy Bar; The Iron Hand; Her Great Part; The Romance of Billy Goat Hill; The Girl of Lost Lake; The Way of the World; The Secret of the Swamp; The End of the Rainbow; It Happened in Honolulu. **1917** A Prairie Romeo; Broadway, Arizona; Until They Get Me; The Firefly of Tough Luck; Southern Justice; Up or Down; God's Crucible. **1918** The Hard Rock Breed; The Golden Fleece; My Husband's Friend; Wolves of the Border; The Last Rebel; Marked Cards; Little Red Decides. **1919** Treat 'Em Rough; Hell Roarin' Reform; The Coming of the Law; The Pest. **1920** The Hell-Ship. **1921** The Big Punch; Steelheart; The Torrent; Beach of Dreams; Flowers of the North; An Unwilling Hero; The Servant in the House; The Sea Lion. **1922** Caught Bluffing; The Long Chance; The Silent Vow; Two Kinds of Women; Western Speed; His Back to the Wall; The Stranger's Banquet. **1923** Reno; The Spoilers; Quicksands; Times Have Changed; Canyon of the Fools; Dangerous Trails; The Day of Faith; Masters of Men; Soft Boiled. **1924** Captain Blood; Fighter's Paradise. **1925** Greed; Baree, Son of Kazan; The Shadow on the Wall; Free and Equal; The Wedding Song. **1926** The Texas Streak; Through Thick and Thin; Hearts and Fists. **1927** Brass Knuckles; Jaws of Steel; Wolf's Clothing. **1928** Scarlet Seas. **1929** The Phantom in the House; The Show of Shows. **1930** Moby Dick; Under a Texas Moon; Mammy; The Love Trader; The Love Racket; The Dawn Trail; Hold Everything. **1934** The Mighty Barnum. **1935** Westward Ho; Bride of Frankenstein. **1936** Trail of the Lonesome Pine. **1945** Song of the Sarong.

CURTIS, JACK B.

Born: 1926. Died: Sept. 25, 1970, New York, N.Y. Screen, radio actor, film producer and director. Son of agent Jack Curtis and vaudeville actress Mabel Ford. Frequently served as voice of Italian actor/director Vittorio de Sica in American release of Italian films. Do not confuse with actor Jack Curtis (dec. 1956).

CURTIS, JOHN W.

Born: 1846. Died: July 21, 1925, New York, N.Y. Screen actor.

CURTIS, SPENCER M.

Born: 1856. Died: July 13, 1921, Long Beach, Calif. Screen and stage actor.

CURTIS, WILLA PEARL

Born: Mar. 21, 1896, Tex. Died: Dec. 19, 1970, Los Angeles, Calif. (cerebral arteriosclerosis and diabetes). Black screen actress.

Appeared in: **1938** The Toy Wife. **1942** Unexpected Riches (short). **1944** Tale of a Dog (short). **1945** The Lost Weekend; The Valley of Decision. **1951** Native Son; The Mating Season; Prince of Peace (aka The Lawton Story). **1955** Queen Bee.

CURTIZ, MICHAEL (Mihaly Kertesz)

Born: Dec. 24, 1888, Budapest, Hungary. Died: Apr. 11, 1962, Hollywood, Calif. Film director, screen, stage actor, film producer and screenwriter.

Appeared in: **1949** It's a Great Feeling.

CURWEN, PATRIC

Born: Dec. 14, 1884, London, England. Died: May 31, 1949, England. Screen, stage, radio actor and screenwriter.

Appeared in: **1931** The Ringer (US 1932). **1933** Loyalties (US 1934). **1935** Mimi. **1944** Don't Take it to Heart (US 1949).

CURZON, GEORGE

Born: Oct. 18, 1896, Amersham, England. Died: May 10, 1976, London, England. Screen, stage and television actor. Son of actress Ellis Jeffreys.

Appeared in: **1930** Escape. **1931** Chin Chin Chinaman (aka Boat from Shanghai—US 1932). **1932** The Impassive Footman (aka Woman in Bondage—US); After the Ball (US 1933); Her First Affair; Murder at Covent Garden. **1933** Strange Evidence; Trouble. **1934** The Scotland Yard Mystery (aka The Living Dead—US); Java Head (US 1935); The Man Who Knew Too Much (US 1935). **1935** Lorna Doone; Admirals All; Sexton Blake and the Mademoiselle; Sexton Blake and the Bearded Doctor; Two Hearts in Harmony; Widow's Might. **1936** White Angel; Whom the Gods Love (US 1940). **1937** Young and Innocent (aka A Girl Was Young—US 1938). **1938** Sexton Blake and the Hooded Terror; Strange Boarders; A Royal Divorce. **1939** The

Mind of Mr. Reeder (aka The Mysterious Mr. Reeder—US 1940); Jamaica Inn; Q Planes (aka Clouds Over Europe—US). **1947** Uncle Silas (aka The Inheritance—US 1951). **1948** The First Gentleman (aka Affairs of a Rogue—US 1949). **1949** For Them That Trespass (US 1950); That Dangerous Age (aka If This Be Sin—US 1950). **1952** Sing Along With Me. **1953** The Cruel Sea. **1958** Harry Black (aka Harry Black and the Tiger—US). **1964** Woman of Straw.

CUSACK, MAUREEN (Maureen Kiely)
Born: 1920. Died: Dec. 18, 1977, Dublin, Ireland (heart aliment). Screen and stage actress. Married to actor Cyril Cusack. Mother of Niamh, producer/director Paul, and actresses Sinead and Sorcha Cusack.

Appeared in: **1947** Odd Man Out.

CUSCADEN, SARAH D.
Born: 1873. Died: Oct. 18, 1954, Hollywood, Calif. Screen actress.

CUSHMAN, NANCY
Born: 1914, Brooklyn, N.Y. Died: Sept. 26, 1979, New York, N.Y. Screen, stage and television actress.

Appeared in: **1968** The Swimmer.

CUSTER, BOB (aka RAYMOND GLENN)
Born: Oct. 18, 1898, Frankfort, Ky. Died: Dec. 27, 1974, Torrance, Calif. (natural causes). Screen actor.

Appeared in: **1924** Trigger Finger. **1925** The Bloodhound; A Man of Nerve; Galloping Vengeance; No Man's Law; That Man Jack!; The Texas Bearcat; The Ridin' Streak; The Range Terror; Flashing Spurs. **1926** The Fighting Boob; Hair Trigger Baxter; Beyond the Rockies; The Border Whirlwind; Man Rustlin'; Dead Line; The Dude Cowboy; The Devil's Gulch. **1927** The Terror of Bar X; Bulldog Pluck; Galloping Thunder; Cactus Trails; The Fighting Hombre; Ladies at Ease. **1928** The Manhattan Cowboy; On the Divide; The Silent Trail. **1929** Arizona Days; The Law of the Mounted; Headin' Westward; West of Santa Fe; Texas Tommy; The Oklahoma Kid; The Last Roundup; The Fighting Terror; Riders of the Rio Grande. **1930** Code of the West; O'Malley Rides Alone; Covered Wagon Trails; The Parting of the Trails. **1931** Quick Trigger Lee; Riders of the North; Son of the Plains; Law of the Rio Grande; Headin' for Trouble; Under Texas Skies. **1932** Mark of the Spur; Scarlet Band. **1934** The Law of the Wild (serial). **1936** Ambush Valley.

CUTELLI, COUNT GAETANO
Died: July 16, 1944, Seattle, Wash. Screen actor. Voice of many animal characters in cartoon comedy films.

CUTLER, KATE
Born: Aug. 14, 1870, London, England. Died: May 14, 1955, England? Screen and stage actress.

Appeared in: **1929** Dark Red Roses. **1930** Such is the Law. **1932** Wedding Rehearsal. **1933** To Brighton with Gladys. **1935** Come Out of the Pantry; Moscow Nights (aka I Stand Condemned—US 1936). **1936** When Knights Were Bold. **1938** Pygmalion.

CUTTING, RICHARD H. "DICK"
Born: Oct. 31, 1912, Mass. Died: Mar. 7, 1972, Woodland Hills, Calif. (kidney disease and uremia). Screen actor and newswriter. Married to actress Edwina Booth.

Appeared in: **1953** War Paint; City of Bad Men; The Great Jesse James Raid; Shotgun; Law and Order; The Man from the Alamo. **1954** Magnificent Obsession; Black Widow; Shield for Murder; The Law vs. Billy the Kid; Taza, Son of Cochise; Drive a Crooked Mile. **1955** Prince of Players; The Left Hand of God; Seminole Uprising; Chicago Syndicate; Good Morning, Miss Dove; The Vagabond King; The Private War of Major Benson; You're Never Too Young; The Gun that Won the West. **1956** The Eddy Duchin Story; The Mountain; You Can't Run Away From It; Showdown at Abilene; The Fastest Gun Alive; Outside the Law. **1957** House of Numbers; Top Secret Affair; The Story of Mankind; Attack of the Crab Monster; The Night Runner; Rock All Night; Teenage Doll; The Girl in Black Stockings; The Monolith Monsters; War Drums. **1958** The World Was His Jury; Ride a Crooked Trail; The Last of the Fast Guns; The Law and Jake Wade; Monster on the Campus; South Pacific. **1959** Rally Round the Flag, Boys; A Nice Little Bank that Should be Robbed. **1960** Gunfighters of Abilene. **1963** The Raiders. **1967** The Ride to Hangman's Tree.

CUTTS, PATRICIA (aka PATRICIA WAYNE)
Born: July 20, 1926, London, England. Died: Sept. 6, 1974, London, England (suicide—overdose of pills). Screen, stage and television actress. Daughter of film director Jack Graham Cutts (dec.).

Appeared in: **1932** Self Made Lady (film debut). **1947** Just William's Luck (US 1948). **1950** Your Witness (aka Eye Witness—US). **1951** The Long Dark Hall. **1953** Those People Next Door. **1954** The Happiness of 3 Women. **1955** The Man Who Loved Redheads. **1958** Merry Andrew. **1959** North by Northwest; The Tingler; Battle of the Coral Sea. **1971** Private Road.

CYBULSKI, ZBIGNIEW
Born: 1927, Poland. Died: Jan. 8, 1967, Wroclaw, Breslau, Poland (accidental fall). Screen and stage actor.

Appeared in: **1954** A Generation. **1958** Popiol i Diament (Ashes and Diamonds—US 1961). **1959** The Eighth Day of the Week; Pociag (aka Baltic Express—US 1962). **1962** La Poupee (aka He, She or It—US 1963); L'amour a Vingt Ans (Love at Twenty—US 1963). **1963** Milczenie (Silence); Jak byc Kochanna (How to be Loved—US 1965). **1964** Att Alska (To Love). **1965** Salto (US 1966); Rekopis Znaleziony w Saragoissie (aka Adventures of a Noble Man and Manuscript Found in Saragossa aka The Saragossa Manuscript—US 1966). **1967** Jowita (Jovita—US 1970).

DA CUNHA, JOSE
Born: 1889, Portugal. Died: Sept. 25, 1956, Lisbon, Portugal. Screen, stage actor and stage manager.

DADE, FRANCES
Born: Feb. 14, 1910, Philadelphia, Pa. Died: Jan. 21, 1968, Philadelphia, Pa. Screen and stage actress.

Appeared in: **1930** Grumpy; Raffles; He Knew Women. **1931** Dracula; Mother's Millions; Daughter of the Dragon; Range Law; Seed. **1932** Pleasure; Big Town.

DAGET, ROBERT (Robert True Daget)
Died: July 20, 1975, Westboro, Mass. Screen, stage, television actor and stage producer.

Appeared in: **1961** The Hustler.

DAGOVER, LIL (Marta Maria Liletts, r.n. Marie Antonia Siegelinde Martha Seubert)
Born: 1887, 1894, or 1897, Madiven, Java. Died: Jan. 23, 1980, West Germany. Screen and stage actress. Married to stage actor Fritz Daghofer (dec. 1936).

Appeared in: **1919** Harakiri; Das Kabinett des Dr. Caligari (The Cabinet of Dr. Caligari); Die Spinnen (The Spiders). **1920** Das Geheimnis von Bombay; Der Richter von Zalamea; Spiritismus; Die Toteninsel. **1921** Die Jagd Nach dem Tode; Das Medium; Der Muede Tod (aka Between Worlds—US 1924, and aka Destiny). **1922** Dr. Mabuse der Spieler (Dr. Mabuse, the Gambler—US 1927); Luise Millerin (aka Kabale und Liebe); Macht der Versuchung (US 1925); Tiefland. **1923** Liebe Macht Blind (Love Makes One Blind—US 1928); Die Prinzessin Suwarin; Seine Frau, die Unbekannte (aka Wilbur Crawford's Wundersames Abenteuer). **1924** Komoedie des Herzens. **1925** Der Demuetige und die Saengerin; Tartueff (aka Tartuffe, the Hypocrite—US 1927); Zur Chronik von Grieshuus (Chronicles of the Grey House, aka At the Grey House—US 1927). **1926** Die Brueder Schellenberg (aka Two Brothers—US 1928); Nur Eine Taenzerin; Der Veilchenfresser. **1927** Discord; Der Anwalt des Herzens; Orientexpress. **1928** Beyond the Wall; Der Geheime Kurier; Ungarische Rhapsodie (Hungarian Rhapsody—US 1929). **1929** Es Fluestert de Nacht ...; Spielereien Einer Kaiserin; Der Guenstling von Schoenbrunn. **1930** Va Banque; Hungarian Nights; Das Alte Lied (aka Zu Jedem Kommt Einmal die Liebe—US 1931); Der Weisse Teufel (The White Devil—US 1931); Es Gibt Eine Frau, die Dich Niemals Vergisst; Die Grosse Sehnsucht. **1931** Der Kongress Tanzt (Congress Dances—US 1932); Elisabeth von Oesterreich; Der Fall des Generalstabs—Oberst Redl. **1932** Das Abenteuer der Thea Roland (aka Das Abenteuer Einer Schoenen Frau); Die Taenzerin von Sanssouci; Barberina. **1933** Madame Blaubart; Der Storch Hat uns Getraut; Johannisnacht (US 1935). **1934** Ich Heirate Meine Frau; Der Fluechtling aus Chikago (US 1936); Eine Frau, die Weiss was sie Will (US 1936). **1935** Der Vogelhaendler; Lady Windermeres Fascher; Der Hoehere Befehl. **1936** Schlussakkord; August der Starke (US 1937); Fridericus (US 1939); Das Maedchen Irene (US 1937); Das Schoenheitspflaesterchen. **1937** Streit um den Knaben Jo (Strife Over the Boy Jo—US 1938); Die Kreutzersonate (aka Kreutzer Sonata—US 1938). **1938** Dreiklang; Maja Zwischen Zwei Ehen; Raetsel um Beate. **1939** Umwege zum Glueck. **1940** Friedrich Schiller (aka Der Triumph

Eines Genies); Bismarck. **1942** Wien 1910. **1944** Musik in Salzburg. **1948** Die Soehne des Herrn Gaspary. **1949** Man Spielt Nicht mit der Liebe. **1950** Vom Teufel Gejagt; Es Kommt ein Tag. **1953** Rote Rosen, Rote Lippen, Roter Wein; Koenigliche Hoheit. **1954** Schloss Hubertus. **1955** Der Fischer von Heiligensee (The Fisherman from Heiligensee, aka The Big Barrier—US 1958); Ich Weiss, Wofuer ich Lebe; Die Barrings; Rosen im Herbst (aka Effi Briest). **1956** Meine 16 Soehne; Kronprinz Rudolfs Letzte Liebe. **1957** Bekenntnisse des Hochstaplers Felix Krull; Unter Palmen am Blauen Meer. **1959** Die Buddenbrooks (US 1962). **1960** A Day Will Come. **1961** Die Seltsame Graefin. **1974** The Pedestrian. **1976** End of the Game. **1979** The Spiders (and 1919 version).

DAHLENE, DELORYS
Born: 1897. Died: Oct. 25, 1976, Chula Vista, Calif. Screen and radio actress. Married to actor Barney O'Hagan (dec. 1961), with whom she appeared as part of the "O'Hagans Comedy Singing and Dancing Team."

DAHLQUIST, LASSE
Born: 1910, Sweden. Died: Oct. 13, 1979, Stockholm, Sweden. Screen, stage actress, screenwriter and songwriter.

DAHMER, WAYNE
Born: 1937, Canada. Died: Sept. 25, 1980, Hollywood, Calif. (heart attack). Screen and television actor.

Appeared in: **1958** Run Silent, Run Deep.

DAI, LIN
Born: 1931, China. Died: July 17, 1964, Hong Kong, China ("accident?"). Screen actress. Entered films approximately 1950.

Appeared in: **1964** The Last Woman of Shang.

DAILEY, DAN (Dan Dailey, Jr.)
Born: Dec. 14, 1915, New York, N.Y. Died: Oct. 16, 1978, Hollywood, Calif. (anemia). Screen, stage, television actor, minstrel player and burlesque performer. Brother of actors Irene and Ben Daily. Nominated for 1947 Academy Award as Best Actor in Mother Wore Tights.

Appeared in: **1940** The Captain Is a Lady; Susan and God; The Mortal Storm; Hullabaloo; Dulcy. **1941** Ziegfeld Girl; Washington Melodrama; Lady Be Good; The Wild Man of Borneo; The Get-Away; Down in San Diego; Moon Over Her Shoulder. **1942** Panama Hattie; Timber; Give Out, Sisters; Sunday Punch; Mokey. **1947** Mother Wore Tights. **1948** You Were Meant for Me; Chicken Every Sunday; Give My Regards to Broadway; When My Baby Smiles at Me. **1949** You're My Everything. **1950** Ticket to Tomahawk; When Willie Comes Marching Home; My Blue Heaven. **1951** I Can Get It for You Wholesale; Call Me Mister. **1952** The Pride of St. Louis; What Price Glory?; Meet Me at the Fair. **1953** The Girl Next Door; Taxi; The Kid from Left Field. **1954** There's No Business Like Show Business. **1955** It's Always Fair Weather. **1956** The Best Things in Life Are Free; Meet Me in Las Vegas. **1957** The Wings of Eagles; Oh, Men! Oh, Women!; The Wayward Bus. **1958** Underwater Warrior. **1960** Pepe. **1962** Hemingway's Adventures of a Young Man.

DAILEY, JOHN HAMMOND
Died: Jan. 14, 1940, New York, N.Y. Screen and stage actor.

Appeared in: **1933** Counsellor-at-Law.

DAILEY, JOSEPH
Born: 1862, New York. Died: Sept. 23, 1940, Englewood, N.J. Screen and stage actor.

DAIX, DAISY (Denis Cariveac)
Born: 1930, Belgium. Died: Aug. 16, 1950, suburbs of Asnieres, France (auto accident). Screen and stage actress.

DALBERT, SUZANNE
Born: May 12, 1927. Died: Dec. 31, 1970. Screen actress.

Appeared in: **1948** Sorry Wrong Number; The Accused. **1949** Trail of the Yukon. **1950** Mark of the Gorilla; Breakthrough. **1951** Target Unknown; The Lady and the Bandit. **1953** The 49th Man.

D'ALBIE, JULIAN
Born: 1892, Ireland. Died: Apr. 6, 1978, London, England. Screen, stage, radio and television actor. Married to actress Rosemary Scott.

Appeared in: **1947** So Well Remembered. **1949** Edward My Son. **1950** The Woman in Question (aka Five Angels on Murder—US 1953). **1951** The Lady With the Lamp. **1953** The Gay Adventure. **1955** Room in the House. **1958** Corridors of Blood (US 1963). **1959** The Night We Dropped a Clanger (aka Make Mine a Double—US 1961). **1970** One More Time.

D'ALBROOK, SIDNEY (aka Sidney Dalbrook)
Born: May 3, 1886, Chicago, Ill. Died: May 30, 1948, Los Angeles, Calif. (heart attack). Screen, stage and vaudeville actor.

Appeared in: **1914** The Bond Sinister. **1915** A Mystery of the Mountains; County Twenty. **1916** His Little Story. **1917** Draft 258. **1918** Under Suspicion; Heart of the Wilds. **1919** The Fatal Fortune (serial); Three Men and a Girl; The Lost Battalion. **1920** Parlor, Bedroom and Bath; The Flaming Clue; Mutiny of the Elsinore. **1921** Big Game; A Motion to Adjourn; The Right of Way; The Son of Wallingford. **1922** Across the Continent; I Can Explain; The Fighting Guide; Little Miss Smiles; Over the Border; West of Chicago; Yankee Doodle, Jr. **1923** Bucking the Barrier; The Call of the Wild; Tea—With a Kick. **1924** THe King of Wild Horses. **1925** Without Mercy. **1926** So This is Paris. **1927** Chicago; King of Kings; The Princess from Hoboken. **1928** The Matinee Idol. **1929** The Spirit of Youth. **1930** Party Girl; Renegades; Midnight Mystery. **1931** Bat Whispers; Chances. **1932** Arlene Lupin. **1935** Barbary Coast. **1937** Maid of Salem; Prescription for Romance. **1939** The Amazing Mr. Williams. **1940** Third Finger-Left Hand. **1947** Sea of Grass; The Perils of Pauline; Desire Me. **1948** Julia Misbehaves; The Sainted Sisters.

DALBY, AMY
Born: c. 1888, England. Died: 1969. Screen actress.

Appeared in: **1945** The Wicked Lady (US 1946). **1953** The Straw Man. **1958** The Man Upstairs (US 1959). **1962** The Lamp in Assassin Mews. **1963** The Haunting. **1964** Topkapi. **1965** The Secret of My Success. **1966** Who Killed the Cat?; The Spy With a Cold Nose. **1967** Smashing Time.

D'ALCY, JEANNE
Born: Mar. 20, 1865, Vaujours, France. Died: 1956, France? Screen, stage actress and film director.

Appeared in: **1898** Pygmalion and Galatea. **1899** Cinderella. **1902** The Trip to the Moon. **1904** Faust and Margerite.

DALE, CHARLES (Charles Marks)
Born: 1881, New York, N.Y. Died: Nov. 16, 1971, Teaneck, N.J. Screen, vaudeville and television actor. Partner of Joesph Smith (dec. 1981) in vaudeville team of "Smith and Dale." Was the "Dr. Kronkhite" of the team. The team was originally called "Charlie Marks (Dale) and Joe Seltzer (Smith)" but they changed it to just "Smith and Dale."

Appeared in: **1929** Knights in Venice (short). **1931** Manhattan Parade. **1932** The Heart of New York. **1939** Mutiny on the Body (short). **1951** Two Tickets to Broadway.

DALE, DOROTHY
Born: 1883. Died: May 13, 1957, Hollywood, Calif. (fire). Screen actress and stand in for Mabel Normand. Her husband, Dr. Jacob Hyman (dec. 1944), had at one time been a partner with Harry Houdini in an act billed the "Houdini Brothers."

Appeared in: **1923** The Ten Commandments. The makeup with which she painted herself bronze for role of an Egyptian girl caused severe facial scars and she then went into retirement.

DALE, DOROTHY
Born: 1925. Died: Aug. 1, 1937, (heart ailment). Child screen and stage actress. Appeared in shorts.

DALE, ELDRIDGE LYON
Born: c. 1878. Died: Oct. 6, 1950, Los Angeles, Calif. Screen extra and stand-in.

DALE, ESTHER
Born: 1886, Beaufort, S.C. Died: July 23, 1961, Hollywood, Calif. Stage and screen actress. Married to producer/writer Arthur Beckhard.

Appeared in: **1934** Crime without Passion (film debut). **1935** The Great Impersonation; I Dream Too Much; Curly Top; In Old Kentucky; Private Worlds; The Wedding Night. **1936** Lady of Secrets; Fury; The Magnificent Brute; The Case Against Mrs. Ames; Timothy's Quest; Hollywood Boulevard; The Farmer in the Dell. **1937** Wild Money; On Such a Night; Of Human Hearts; The Awful Truth; Damaged Goods; Dead End; Easy Living; Outcast. **1938** Condemned Women; Girls on Probation; Prison Farm; Stolen Heaven; 6,000 Enemies. **1939** Made for Each Other; Broadway Serenade; Big Town Czar; Tell No Tales; Blackmail; Swanee River; The Women. **1940** Convicted Woman; Village Barn Dance; And One Was Beautiful; Opened by Mistake; Women Without Names; Untamed; Laddie; Blondie Has Servant Trouble; A Child is Born; Love Thy Neighbor; Arise, My Love; The Mortal Storm. **1941** Mr. and Mrs. Smith; There's Magic in Music;

Aloma of the South Seas; Unfinished Business; All-American Co-ed; Dangerously They Live; Back Street. **1942** Blondie Goes to College; Ten Gentlemen from West Point; Wrecking Crew. **1943** Hello, Frisco, Hello; The Amazing Mrs. Holiday; Swing Your Partner; Murder in Times Square; North Star; Old Acquaintance. **1945** Out of this World; Behind City Lights; Bedside Manner; On Stage, Everybody. **1946** A Stolen Life; Margie; My Reputation; Smoky. **1947** The Egg and I; The Unfinished Dance. **1948** A Song is Born. **1949** Anna Lucasta; Holiday Affair; Ma and Pa Kettle. **1950** Ma and Pa Kettle Go to Town; No Man of Her Own; Surrender; Walk Softly, Stranger. **1951** On Moonlight Bay; Too Young to Kiss. **1952** Ma and Pa Kettle at the Fair; Monkey Business. **1955** Ma and Pa Kettle at Waikiki; Betrayed Women. **1957** The Oklahoman. **1960** North to Alaska.

DALE, JEAN (Jean Dale Crane)
Born: 1911, Canton, S.D. Died: Oct. 6, 1981, Carmel, Calif. Screen, stage actress and stage director.

Appeared in: **1937** Missing Witness.

DALE, MARGARET
Born: Mar. 6, 1880, Philadelphia, Pa. Died: Mar. 23, 1972, New York, N.Y. Screen and stage actress. Do not confuse with English dancer, Margaret Dale.

Appeared in: **1921** Disraeli. **1922** One Exciting Night. **1924** Second Youth; Week-End Husbands. **1934** The Man with Two Faces.

DALE, PEGGY (Margaret Dale Dudley)
Born: Dec. 25, 1903, New York, N.Y. Died: June 6, 1967, Hollywood, Calif. (suicide—pills). Screen actress.

Appeared in: **1929** Desert Song. **1934** The Mighty Barnum.

DALEY, CASS (Katherine Daley)
Born: July 17, 1915, Philadelphia, Pa. Died: Mar. 23, 1975, Hollywood, Calif. (results of an accidental fall). Screen, stage, vaudeville and radio actress.

Appeared in: **1941** The Fleet's In. **1942** Star Spangled Rhythm. **1943** Riding High; Crazy House. **1945** Out of This World; Duffy's Tavern. **1947** Ladies' Man. **1951** Here Comes the Groom. **1954** Red Garters. **1967** The Spirit is Willing. **1970** Norwood; The Phynx.

DALEY, JACK
Born: Aug. 29, 1882. Died: Aug. 28, 1967, El Cajon, Calif. Screen and stage actor. Do not confuse with actor Jack Daly (dec. 1968).

Appeared in: **1930** The Sap from Syracuse. **1935** O'Shaughnessy's Boy. **1936** Fury; Klondike Annie; Next Time We Love. **1937** Parole Racket; A Girl With Ideas; Man Who Cried Wolf; Artists and Models. **1938** Goodbye Broadway; Kathleen; Born to the West. **1939** Mutiny in the Big House. **1940** I Love You Again. **1941** Arizona Bound. **1942** West of the Law; Down Texas Way. **1943** The Ghost Rider. **1945** Within These Walls. **1949** Chicken Every Sunday. **1950** Tea for Two; Summer Stock. **1951** Royal Wedding. **1952** Carson City; Scarlet Angel.

D'ALGY, ANTOINE "TONY" (Antonio D'Algy)
Born: 1905, Spain. Died: Apr. 29, 1977. Screen and stage actor. Brother of actress Helene D'Algy.

Appeared in: **1924** Meddling Women; The Sainted Devil; The Rejected Woman. **1925** Soul Mates. **1926** The Boob; The Gay Deceiver; Monte Carlo. **1933** Toda una Vida.

DALL, JOHN (John Dall Thompson)
Born: 1918. Died: Jan. 15, 1971, Beverly Hills, Calif. (heart attack). Screen, stage and television actor. Nominated for 1945 Academy Award for Best Supporting Actor in The Corn Is Green.

Appeared in: **1939** For the Love of Mary. **1945** The Corn Is Green. **1947** Something in the Wind. **1948** The Rope; Another Part of the Forest. **1949** Deadly Is the Female. **1950** Gun Crazy; The Man Who Cheated Himself. **1960** Spartacus. **1961** Atlantis, the Lost Continent.

DALLIMORE, MAURICE
Born: June 23, 1912, England. Died: Feb. 20, 1973, Los Angeles, Calif. (Laennec's cirrhosis). Screen and television actor.

Appeared in: **1962** Tender Is the Night; Lad a Dog. **1963** The Three Stooges Go Around the World in a Daze. **1965** The Collector. **1966** Not With My Wife, You Don't.

DALROY, HARRY "RUBE"
Born: 1879. Died: Mar. 8, 1954, Hollywood, Calif. Western screen actor. Known as the "Mayor of Gower Gulch."

Appeared in: **1923** Stormy Seas.

DALSACE, LUCIEN
Born: 1893. Died: July, 1980, Hay-les-Roses, France. Screen actor. Entered films during the silents.

DALTON, CHARLES
Born: Aug. 29, 1864, England. Died: June 11, 1942, Stanford, Conn. Screen and stage actor.

Appeared in: **1917** Fighting Odds. **1921** The Wakefield Case.

DALTON, DOROTHY
Born: Sept. 22, 1893, Chicago, Ill. Died: Apr. 12, 1972, Scarsdale, N.Y. Screen, stage and vaudeville actress. Divorced from actor Lew Cody (dec. 1934). Married to stage producer Arthur Hammerstein (dec. 1955).

Appeared in: **1914** Pierre of the Plains. **1915** The Disciple. **1916** D'Artagnan; Civilization's Child; The Raiders; The Captive God; The Jungle Child; The Vagabond Prince; The Female of the Species; The Weaker Sex; A Gamble in Souls. **1917** The Flame of the Yukon; Wild Winship's Widow; Chicken Casey; Back of the Man; The Dark Road; Ten of Diamonds; The Price Mark; Love Letters. **1918** Vive la France; Quicksand; Flare-Up Sal; Love Me; Unfaithful; The Tyrant Fear; The Mating of Marcella; The Kaiser's Shadow; Green Eyes; Hard Boiled. **1919** The Home Breaker; Market of Souls; Other Men's Wives; Extravagance; The Lady of Red Butte; L'Apache. **1920** Black is White; Dark Mirror; Half an Hour; His Wife's Friend; The Romantic Adventuress; Guilty of Love. **1921** Fool's Paradise; Behind Masks; The Idol of the North. **1922** Moran of the Lady Letty; The Crimson Challange; The Woman Who Walked Alone; The Siren Call; On the High Seas. **1923** Fog Bound; The Law and the Lawless; Dark Secrets. **1924** The Moral Sinner; The Lone Wolf.

DALTON, EMMET
Died: July 13, 1937, Los Angeles, Calif. Onetime real "badman" of the Old West and member of the "Dalton Gang" with his brothers Robert (dec. 1892) and Grattan (dec. 1892) Dalton. He was a horse thief, train robber and screen actor.

Appeared in: **1916** The Dalton Boys. **1918** Beyond the Law.

DALTON, IRENE
Born: 1901. Died: Aug. 15, 1934, Chicago, Ill. Screen and stage actress. Divorced from screen actor Lloyd Hamilton (dec. 1935).

Appeared in: **1922** "Christie" comedies. **1923** Bluebeard's Eighth Wife; Children of Jazz.

DALY, ARNOLD
Born: Oct. 4, 1875, Brooklyn, N.Y. Died: Jan. 13, 1927, New York, N.Y. (burned to death). Screen, stage and vaudeville actor.

Appeared in: **1915** The Exploits of Elaine (serial); The Romance of Elaine (serial). **1916** The New Exploits of Elaine (serial). **1924** For Another Woman. **1926** In Borrowed Plumes.

DALY, HERBERT
Born: 1902. Died: Mar. 12, 1940, New York, N.Y. Screen and stage actor.

Appeared in: **1932** Air Mail.

DALY, JACK
Died: June 2, 1968. Screen actor. Do not confuse with actor Jack Daley (dec. 1967).

Appeared in: **1949** Search for Danger. **1950** Mr. 880; Once a Thief; Champagne for Caesar; For Heaven's Sake. **1951** Pickup; Badman's Gold. **1952** Here Come the Nelsons; No Room for the Groom. **1953** Phantom from Space. **1954** The Big Chase; Killers from Space; The Snow Creature. **1955** The Big Bluff; I'll Cry Tomorrow. **1956** The Opposite Sex; Meet Me in Las Vegas. **1957** Raintree County; The Spirit of St. Louis; The Young Stranger. **1959** North by Northwest; The Return of the Fly; Inside the Mafia. **1962** Lad: A Dog.

DALY, JAMES
Born: Oct. 23, 1918, Wisconsin Rapids, Wis. Died: July 2, 1978, Nyack, N.Y. (heart attack). Screen, stage and television actor. Divorced from actress Mary Hope Newell. Father of Pegeen, Glyn, Timothy and actress Tyne Daly.

Appeared in: **1955** The Court Martial of Billy Mitchell. **1957** The Young Stranger. **1960** I Aim at the Stars. **1968** Planet of the Apes. **1969** The Big Bounce. **1970** Five Man Army.

DALY, JAMES L.
Born: 1852. Died: Nov. 10, 1933, Philadelphia, Pa. (heart trouble). Stage and screen actor. Married to screen actress Clara Lamber (dec. 1921). Appeared in silents.

DALY, MARK
Born: Aug. 23, 1887, Edinburgh, Scotland. Died: Sept. 27, 1957. Screen, stage, vaudeville and radio actor.

Appeared in: **1931** East Lynne on the Western Front; The Beggar-Student. **1932** The Third String. **1933** Up For the Derby; Doss House; The Private Life of Henry VIII; A Cuckoo in the Nest. **1934** The River Wolves; There Goes Susie (aka Scandals of Paris—US 1935); Say It With Flowers; By-Pass to Happiness; Music Hall; Flood Tide. **1935** That's My Uncle; Jubilee Window; The Small Man; A Real Bloke. **1936** The Ghost Goes West; The Man Who Could Work Miracles (US 1937); The Captain's Table; Shipmates O' Mine. **1937** Wings of the Morning; Wanted; Knight Without Armour; Good Morning Boys (aka Where There's a Will—US); Captain's Orders; Command Performance. **1938** Break the News (US 1941); Lassie From Lancashire; Follow Your Star. **1939** Q Planes (aka Clouds Over Europe—US); Ten Days in Paris (aka Missing Ten Days—US); Hoots Mon! **1942** The Big Blockade; The Next of Kin (US 1943). **1946** The Voyage of Peter Joe series. **1947** Stage Frights. **1948** Bonnie Prince Charlie. **1949** Three Bags Full; The Romantic Age (aka Naughty Arlette—US 1951). **1953** Alf's Baby. **1954** Lease of Life; Don't Blame the Stork; The Delavine Affair. **1956** The Dynamiters; The Feminine Touch (aka The Gentle Touch—US 1957). **1957** You Pay Your Money; The Tommy Steele Story (aka Rock Around the World—US).

DALY, PAT (Gordon C. Munger)
Born: 1891. Died: Nov. 19, 1947, Detroit, Mich. Screen, stage, minstrel, vaudeville and radio actor. Appeared in vaudeville with his wife, Genevieve, in an act billed as "Pat and Genevieve Daly."

Appeared in: **1938** A Slight Case of Murder.

D'AMBRICOURT, ADRIENNE
Born: 1888, France. Died: Dec. 6, 1957, Hollywood, Calif. (heart attack). Stage and screen actress.

Appeared in: **1924** Wages of Virtue; The Humming Bird. **1926** God Gave Me Twenty Cents. **1929** Footlights and Fools; The Trial of Mary Dugan. **1930** L'Enigmatique Monsieur Parkes (Mysterious Mr. Parkes); The Bad One; What a Widow! **1931** Le Proces de Mary Dugan; Quand on est Belle; Svengali; This Modern Age; Transgression; The Men in Her Life. **1933** Eagle and the Hawk; Disgraced!; Design for Living; Gallant Lady. **1934** Marie Galante; Caravan; The Cat and the Fiddle; The Way to Love. **1935** It Happened in New York; Goin' to Town; Peter Ibbetson. **1936** Valiant is the Word for Carrie; San Francisco; Sylvia Scarlet. **1937** We Have Our Moments; Live, Love and Learn; Seventh Heaven; Mama Steps Out. **1938** Artists and Models Abroad. **1939** Bulldog Drummond's Bride; Pack Up Your Troubles; Charlie Chan in City in Darkness; Nurse Edith Cavell; The Story of Vernon and Irene Castle. **1940** Two Girls on Broadway. **1941** Two-Faced Woman. **1942** Syncopation; The Pied Piper. **1943** The Song of Bernadette. **1944** To Have and Have Not; Experiment Perilous; The White Cliffs of Dover. **1945** Paris Underground; This Love of Ours; Saratoga Trunk. **1946** A Night in Casablanca; The Return of Monte Cristo; So Dark the Night. **1952** Million Dollar Mermaid; Bal Tabarin. **1955** The Purple Mask. **1957** Les Girls.

DAMEREL, DONNA
Born: 1913. Died: Feb. 15, 1941, Englewood, N.J. (childbirth). Screen and radio actress. Married to international swimming champion Peter J. Fick. Daughter of actress Myrtle Vail (dec. 1978) with whom she appeared on radio and film as "Marge" in the "Myrt and Marge" series.

Appeared in: **1934** Myrt and Marge.

DAMIA (Marie-Louise Damien)
Born: 1889, France. Died: Jan. 30, 1978, St. Cloud, France. Screen actress, singer and music hall performer. Known as the "Tragedienne of Song."

Appeared in: **1938** Pearls of the Crown.

DAMON, LES
Born: 1909. Died: July 20, 1962. Screen actor.

DAMPIER, CLAUDE (Claude Cowan)
Born: 1879, Clapham, England. Died: Jan. 1, 1955, London, England (pneumonia). Screen, stage and radio actor.

Appeared in: **1930** Claude Deputises (short). **1934** Radio Parade of 1935 (US 1935). **1935** So You Won't Talk; White Lilac; Boys Will Be Boys; No Monkey Business; She Shall Have Music (US 1942). **1936** King of the Castle; Public Nuisance No. 1; She Knew What She Wanted; Such is Life; All In; Valiant is the Word for Carrie. **1937** Wanted; Mr. Stringfellow Says No; Sing as You Swing; Riding High (aka Remember When). **1940** The Backyard Front (short). **1944** Don't Take it to Heart (US 1949). **1946** Wot! No Gangsters? **1948** Accidental Spy (reissue of Mr. Stringfellow Says No—1937). **1954** Meet Mr. Malcolm.

DAMROSCH, WALTER (Walter Johannes Damrosch)
Born: Jan. 30, 1862, Breslau, Prussia (now Wroclaw, Poland). Died: Dec. 22, 1950, New York, N.Y. Musician, conductor and screen, radio actor.

Appeared in: **1939** The Star Maker. **1947** Carnegie Hall.

DAN, ZHAO (Zhao Fengao)
Born: 1914, China. Died: Oct. 10, 1980, Peking, China (cancer). Screen, stage actor, screenwriter and author. Entered films as a child actor.

Appeared in: **1928** Street Angel. **1939** Crossroads. **1965** Red Crag.

DANA, CLARA L.
Born: c. 1878. Died: June 23, 1956, Los Angeles, Calif. Silent screen actress.

DANA, DICK (Samuel Critcherson)
Born: 1901. Died: July 10, 1976, Ridgewood, N.J. Screen, stage and television actor.

Appeared in: **1954** Top Banana.

DANDRIDGE, DOROTHY
Born: Nov. 9, 1922, Cleveland, Ohio. Died: Sept. 8, 1965, West Hollywood, Calif. (drug overdose—"probable accident"). Black screen, stage and vaudeville actress. Nominated for 1954 Academy Award for Best Actress in Carmen Jones.

Appeared in: **1937** A Day at the Races. **1940** Four Shall Die. **1941** Lady from Louisiana; Sundown; Sun Valley Serenade; Bahama Passage. **1942** Lucky Jordan; Drums of the Congo. **1943** Moo Cow Boogie; Hit Parade of 1943. **1944** Since You Went Away; Atlantic City. **1945** Pillow to Post. **1947** Flamingo; Ebony Parade. **1951** Tarzan's Peril; Jungle Queen; Harlem Globetrotters. **1953** Bright Road; Remains to Be Seen. **1954** Carmen Jones. **1957** The Happy Road; Island in the Sun. **1958** The Decks Ran Red. **1959** Porgy and Bess; Tamango. **1960** Moment of Danger (aka Malaga—US 1962).

DANDY, JESS (Jesse A. Danzig)
Born: 1871, Rochester, N.Y. Died: Apr. 15, 1923, Brookline, Mass. (septicemia). Screen and stage actor. Appeared in early Keystone films.

DANE, KARL
Born: Oct. 12, 1886, Copenhagen, Denmark. Died: Apr. 15, 1934, Los Angeles, Calif. (suicide—gun). Screen and stage actor.

Appeared in: **1925** The Big Parade; His Secretary; Lights of Old Broadway; The Everlasting Whisper. **1926** Bardely's, The Magnificent; The Son of the Sheik; The Scarlet Letter; Monte Carlo; War Paint. **1927** The Red Mill; Rookies; Slide, Kelly, Slide. **1928** The Trail of 98; Show People; The Enemy; Alias Jimmy Valentine; Circus Rookies; Detectives; Baby Mine; Brotherly Love. **1929** Speedway; The Hollywood Revue of 1929; All at Sea; China Bound; The Duke Steps Out; The Voice of the Storm. **1930** The Big House; Navy Blues; Montana Moon; Free and Easy; Numbered Men; Billy the Kid. **1933** A Paramount Short; Whispering Shadows (serial). **1964** Big Parade of Comedy (documentary). **1967** Show People (reissue of 1928 film).

DANEGGER, THEODOR
Born: 1891. Died: Oct. 11, 1959, Vienna, Austria. Screen, stage actor and opera performer.

Appeared in: **1935** Ehestreik. **1936** The Royal Waltz; Weiberregiment. **1940** Drei Vater um Anna (Three Fathers for Anna).

DANERI, JULIE
Born: 1914, Mexico. Died: Aug. 28, 1957, Mexico City, Mexico. Mexican screen and stage actor.

DANFORTH, WILLIAM
Born: 1888. Died: Aug. 9, 1958. Screen actor. Do not confuse with stage actor of same name (dec. 1941).

Appeared in: **1937** The Girl Said No.

D'ANGELO, CARLO
Born: 1919, Italy? Died: May, 1973, Bologna, Italy. Screen, stage and television actor.

Appeared in: **1954** Fugitive in Trieste. **1957** I Vampiri (aka The Vampires—The Devil's Commandment—US). **1959** La Grande Guerra (The Great War—US 1961). **1960** Hercules Unchained. **1961** David and Goliath. **1962** Rosmunda e Alboino (aka Rosamund and Alboino—Sword of the Conqueror); Nefertite, Regina del Nilo (aka Queen of the Nile—US 1964). **1966** Secret Agent Super Dragon.

DANIEL, BILLY (William Baker)
Born: July 4, 1912, Fort Worth, Texas. Died: May 15, 1962, Beverly Hills, Calif. (coronary attack). Screen, stage actor and dancer. Do not confuse with singer Billy Daniels.

Appeared in: **1937** Hold 'Em, Navy (film debut). **1944** Lady in the Dark; Frenchman's Creek. **1950** My Blue Heaven. **1953** Scared Stiff. **1960** The Alamo.

DANIELL, HENRY (Charles Henry Daniel)
Born: Mar. 5, 1894, London, England. Died: Oct. 31, 1963, Santa Monica, Calif. Screen and stage actor.

Appeared in: **1929** Jealousy (film debut); The Awful Truth. **1930** Last of the Lone Wolf. **1934** The Path of Glory. **1936** The Unguarded Hour; Camille. **1937** Under Cover of Night; The Thirteenth Chair; The Firefly; Madame X. **1938** Holiday; Marie Antoinette. **1939** We Are Not Alone; Private Lives of Elizabeth and Essex. **1940** The Sea Hawk; The Great Dictator; The Philadelphia Story; All This and Heaven Too. **1941** A Woman's Face; Dressed to Kill; Four Jacks and a Jill; The Feminine Touch. **1942** Sherlock Holmes and the Voice of Terror; Reunion; Castle in the Desert; The Great Impersonation; Nightmare. **1943** Mission to Moscow; Sherlock Holmes in Washington; Watch on the Rhine. **1944** Jane Eyre; The Suspect. **1945** Captain Kidd; Hotel Berlin; The Woman in Green; The Body Snatcher. **1946** The Bandit of Sherwood Forest. **1947** Song of Love; The Exile. **1948** Siren of Atlantis; Wake of the Red Witch. **1950** Secret of St. Ives. **1954** The Egyptian. **1955** The Prodigal; Diane. **1956** The Man in the Gray Flannel Suit; Lust for Life. **1957** The Story of Mankind; Les Girls; The Sun Also Rises; Mr. Cory; Witness for the Prosecution. **1958** From the Earth to the Moon. **1959** The Four Skulls of Jonathan Drake. **1961** The Comancheros; Voyage to the Botton of the Sea. **1962** Five Weeks in a Balloon; The Notorious Landlady; Mutiny on the Bounty; The Chapman Report; Madison Avenue. **1964** My Fair Lady.

DANIELS, BEBE (Virginia Daniels)
Born: Jan. 14, 1901, Dallas, Tex. Died: Mar. 16, 1971, London, England (cerebral hemorrahage). Screen, stage, radio, televison actress and stage producer. Entered films at age seven. Daughter of actress Phyllis Griffin Daniels (dec. 1959). Married to actor Ben Lyon (dec. 1979). Mother of actors Richard and Barbara Lyon.

Appeared in: **1908** A Common Enemy (film debut). **1916-1917** "Lonesome Luke" series. **1919** Everywoman; Male and Female; Captain Kidd's Kids. **1920** The Fourteenth Man; Oh Lady, Lady; You Never Can Tell; Sick Abed; Why Change Your Wife?; The Dancin' Fool; Feet of Clay. **1921** The Affairs of Anatol; Ducks and Drakes; She Couldn't Help It; The March Hare; One Wild Week; Speed Girl; Two Weeks With Pay. **1922** Nice People; The Game Chicken; Nancy from Nowhere; North of the Rio Grande; Pink Gods; Singed Wings. **1923** Sinners in Heaven; The Exciters; Glimpses of the Moon; His Children's Children; The World's Applause. **1924** Dangerous Money; The Heritage of the Desert; Monsieur Beaucaire; Daring Youth; Argentine Love; Unguarded Women. **1925** The Splendid Crime; Wild, Wild Susan; The Manicure Girl; Miss Bluebeard; The Crowded Hour; Lovers in Quarantine. **1926** Stranded in Paris; The Campus Flirt; Mrs. Brewster's Millions; The Palm Beach Girl; Volcano. **1927** She's a Sheik; Swim, Girl, Swim; Senorita; A Kiss in a Taxi. **1928** Feel My Pulse; The Fifty-Fifty Girl; What a Night!; Hot News; Take Me Home. **1929** Rio Rita. **1930** Love Comes Along; Alias French Gertie; Dixiana; Lawful Larceny. **1931** Reaching for the Moon; My Past; The Maltese Falcon; Honor of the Family. **1932** Silver Dollar; The Slippery Pearls (short); Radio Girl (short). **1933** The Song You Gave Me (US 1934); Hollywood on Parade (short); Forty-Second Street; Cocktail Hour; Counsellor-at-Law. **1934** Registered Nurse. **1935** Music Is Magic; The Return of Carol Deane (US 1939). **1936** Not Wanted on Voyage (aka Treachery on High Seas—US 1939); A Southern Maid. **1941** Hi, Gang! **1954** Life with the Lyons (aka Family Affair—US). **1955** The Lyons in Paris (aka Mr. and Mrs. in Paree).

DANIELS, FRANK
Born: 1860, Dayton, Ohio. Died: Jan. 12, 1935, West Palm Beach, Fla. Screen and stage actor. Entered films with Vitagraph in 1915.

Appeared in: **1915** Crooky Scruggs. **1916** Mr. Jack's Hat and the Cat; Mr. Jack, a Doctor by Proxy; Mr. Jack Goes Into Business; Dear Percy; His Dukeship, Mr. Jack; Kernel Nutt the Janitor; Kernel Nutt's One Hundred Dollar Bill; Kernel Nutt Wins a Wife; Kernel Nutt, the Footman; Kernel Nutt in Mexico; Kernel Nutt's Musical Shirt; Kernel Nutt Flirts With Wife; Kernel Nutt and Prince Tango; Kernel Nutt, the Piano Tuner.

DANIELS, HANK (Henry Hartog Daniels)
Born: Jan. 27, 1919, New Jersey. Died: Dec. 21, 1973, Los Angeles, Calif. (heart attack). Screen actor.

Appeared in: **1944** Meet Me in St. Louis. **1945** Anchors Aweigh; The Chicago Kid; Bewitched. **1946** The Green Years; In Old Sacramento. **1948** The Burning Cross.

DANIELS, HAROLD
Born: 1903, Buffalo, N.Y. Died: Dec. 27, 1971, Hollywood, Calif. (died during surgery). Screen actor, television, film producer, director, screenwriter and writer for television.

Appeared in: **1936** Hi, Gaucho; Trail Dust. **1937** Hollywood Cowboy. **1940** Oklahoma Renegades; Secret of a Model; Dangerous Wheels. **1941** Keep 'Em Flying; U.S. Army short (c. 1941). **1942** Bombay Clipper.

DANIELS, VICTOR See CHIEF THUNDERCLOUD

DANIELS, WALTER
Born: 1875. Died: Mar. 30, 1928, Los Angeles, Calif. Screen and vaudeville actor. Appeared in vaudeville with his wife, Mina Daniels.

Appeared in: **1927** The Dove. **1928** Stolen Love; Rough Ridin' Red. **1929** The Jazz Age; The Vagabond Club.

DANILO, DON See DEWEY, ELMER

DANIS, IDA
Born: France. Died: Apr. 9, 1921, Nice, France (consumption). Screen actress.

Appeared in: **1921** La Roue.

D'ANNUNZIO, LOLA
Born: c. 1903. Died: June 5, 1956. Screen actress.

Appeared in: **1957** The Wrong Man.

DANSEY, HERBERT (Count Berte Danyell Tassinari)
Born: Mar. 6, 1870, Rome, Italy. Died: May 30, 1917, New York, N.Y. Screen and stage actor.

Appeared in: **1915** For Her People.

DANSON, LINDA
Died: Mar. 14, 1975. Screen actress.

Appeared in: **1954** The Adventures of Haji Baba.

DANTE (Harry A. Jansen)
Born: 1884. Died: June 15, 1955, near Northridge, Calif. (heart attack). Screen, stage, vaudeville, burlesque, circus, radio and television actor. Billed as "Dante, King of Magicians."

Appeared in: **1942** A-Haunting We Will Go. **1954** The Golden Coach.

DANTE, LIONEL
Born: 1907. Died: July 30, 1974, Hollywood, Calif. (heart attack). Screen, stage and television actor.

Appeared in: **1947** Road to Rio.

DARBAUD, MONIQUE
Born: 1924, France. Died: Feb., 1971, France? Screen and stage actress.

DAR BOGGIE, HENRY
Died: Jan. 11, 1976. Screen actor.

Appeared in: **1954** Forever Female.

D'ARCY, CAMILLE
Born: 1879. Died: Sept. 26, 1916, Chicago, Ill. Screen actress.

Appeared in: **1915** The White Sister; A Daughter of the City; Third Hand High; The Strength of the Weak; The Snow Burner; The Cave on Thunder-Cloud; Tish's Spy; The Circular Path; The Reaping; The Fable of the Escape of Arthur and the Salvation of Herbert; The Fable of the Low Down Expert on the Subject of Babies. **1916** Captain Jinks of the Horse Marines; Putting It Over; The Grouch; The Prince Chap; The Pacifist.

D'ARCY, ROY (Roy F. Guisti)
Born: Feb. 10, 1894, San Francisco, Calif. Died: Nov. 15, 1969, Redlands, Calif. Screen, stage and vaudeville actor.

Appeared in: **1925** The Merry Widow; Graustark; The Masked Bride; Pretty Ladies. **1926** Beverly of Graustark; La Boheme; The Temptress;

Bardely's, The Magnificent; The Gay Deceiver; Monte Carlo. **1927** On Ze Boulevard; Lovers?; Winners of the Wilderness; Buttons; Valencia; The Road to Romance; Adam and Evil; Frisco Sally Levy. **1928** Beyond the Sierras; Riders of the Dark; Beware of Blondes; Domestic Meddlers; The Actress; Forbidden Hours. **1929** A Woman of Affairs; Stolen Kisses; The Last Warning; Girls Gone Wild; Woman from Hell; The Black Watch. **1930** Romance. **1931** Masquerade (short). **1932** The Shadow of the Eagle (serial); Gay Buckaroo; File 113; Discarded Lovers; From Broadway to Cheyenne; Sherlock Holmes; Lovebound. **1933** Whispering Shadows (serial); Flying Down to Rio. **1934** Orient Express. **1935** Outlawed Guns; Kentucky Blue Streak. **1936** Revolt of the Zombies; Hollywood Boulevard; Captain Calamity. **1939** Chasing Danger.

DARDEN, ANNE (Anne-Marie Thirion)
Born: 1932, Belgium? Died: Nov. 29, 1977, Brussels, Belgium (heart attack). Screen, stage and radio actress.

Appeared in: **1963** Le Prostitution (The Prostitution—US 1967). **1968** To Be a Woman.

DARE, DORRIS (Dorris Prince)
Born: 1899. Died: Aug. 16, 1927, Los Angeles, Calif. Screen and stage actress.

Appeared in: **1919** The Mystery of 13 (serial). **1923** Tango Cavalier. **1925** Fightin' Odds.

DARE, HELENA
Died: Aug. 3, 1972. Screen actress.

Appeared in: **1948** Open Secret. **1950** Cody of the Pony Express (serial). **1952** Buffalo Bill in Tomahawk Territory.

DARE, PHYLLIS
Born: Aug. 15, 1890, London, England. Died: Apr. 27, 1975, Brighton, England. Screen, stage and television actress. Sister of actress Zena Dare (dec. 1975).

Appeared in: **1913** The Argentine Tango and Other Dances. **1916** Dr. Wake's Patient. **1923** The Common Law. **1933** Crime on the Hill. **1936** Debt of Honour. **1938** Marigold.

DARE, VIRGINIA
Died: July 8, 1962, Hillywood, Calif. Screen, stage and television actress.

Appeared in: **1911** Aunt Huldah—The Matchmaker.

DARE, ZENA
Born: Feb. 4, 1887, London, England. Died: Mar. 11, 1975, London, England. Screen, stage and vaudeville actress. Sister of actress Phyllis Dare (dec. 1975).

Appeared in: **1921** No. 5, John Street. **1929** A Knight in London. **1937** Over the Moon (US 1940). **1938** The Return of Carol Deane.

DARIEN, FRANK, JR.
Born: New Orleans, La. Died: Oct. 20, 1955, Hollywood, Calif. Screen and stage actor. Entered films approx. 1912.

Appeared in: **1914** D. W. Griffith productions. **1915** "Mack Sennett" comedies. **1931** Five Star Final; I Take This Woman; Cimarron; Bad Girl; Big Business Birl; June Moon. **1932** The Miracle Man; Prosperity; Now We'll Tell One (short); The Big Shot; Okay America. **1933** Hello, Everybody!; Professional Sweetheart; Big Executive; From Headquarters. **1934** The Man With Two Faces; Marie Galante; Service With a Smile (short); Fashions of 1934; Journal of a Crime. **1935** Behind the Evidence; The Perfect Clue; The Little Colonel; Nurse to You (short); Here Comes Cookie. **1936** Brides Are Like That. **1937** On the Avenue; The Life of Emile Zola; Jim Hanvey, Detective; The River of Missing Men; Trapped by G-Men. **1938** Cassidy of Bar 20; Western Jamboree; Love Finds Andy Hardy; Long Shot; Prison Break. **1939** At the Circus; Sabotage; Maisie; Dark Victory; When Tomorrow Comes. **1940** Lillian Russell; The Grapes of Wrath; Arizona. **1941** Under Fiesta Stars; King of the Texas Rangers (serial); Hellzapoppin; Bedtime Story. **1942** The Gay Sisters; Hello, Frisco, Hello; Tales of Manhattan; Syncopation. **1943** The Outlaw; Old Acquaintance; The Gang's All Here; Get Hep to Love. **1944** Bowery to Broadway. **1945** Abbott and Costello in Hollywood; The Last Installment (short); Kiss and Tell; The Clock; Counter-Attack. **1946** Claudia and David; The Fabulous Suzanne; Bad Bascombe; A Likely Story. **1947** Merton of the Movies; Woman on the Beach; Magic Town. **1948** Belle Starr's Daughter; You Gotta Stay Happy. **1950** The Flying Saucer.

DARIN, BOBBY (Robert Walden Cassotto)
Born: May 14, 1936, Bronx, N.Y. Died: Dec. 20, 1973, Hollywood, Calif. (following heart surgery). Screen, television actor, singer and songwriter. Divorced from actress Sandra Dee. Married to Andrea Joy Yeager. Nominated for 1963 Academy Award for Best Supporting Actor in Captain Newman, M.D.

Appeared in: **1960** Pepe. **1961** Come September. **1962** Pressure Point; If A Man Answers; Too Late Blues; State Fair; Hell Is for Heroes. **1963** Captain Newman, M.D. **1965** That Funny Feeling. **1967** Gunfight in Abilene; Stranger in the House. **1968** Cop-Out. **1969** The Happy Ending.

DARK, CHRISTOPHER
Died: Oct. 8, 1971, Hollywood, Calif. (heart attack). Screen, stage and television actor.

Appeared in: **1953** Raiders of the Seven Seas; The Steel Lady. **1954** Suddenly. **1955** Diane. **1956** World Without End; Johnny Concho. **1957** The Halliday Brand; Baby Face Nelson. **1958** Day of the Bad Man; Wild Heritage. **1959** The Rabbit Trap. **1960** Platinum High School. **1965** None But the Brave. **1968** The Private Navy of Sgt. O'Farrell.

DARKCLOUD, BEULAH (Beulah T. Filson)
Died: Jan. 2, 1946, Thermolite, Calif. Screen actress. Entered films with D. W. Griffith in 1912.

Appeared in: **1922** The Crimson Challenge.

DARLEY, BRIAN
Born: 1859. Died: Feb. 25, 1924, New York, N.Y. Screen and stage actor.

Appeared in: **1921** The Highest Bidder. **1922** The Ruling Passion.

DARLING, CANDY (James Slattery)
Born: 1948. Died: Mar. 21, 1974, New York (cancer/pneumonia). Screen, stage actor and female impersonator. Known as one of Andy Warhol's "Superstars."

Appeared in: **1968** Flesh. **1970** Brand X. **1971** Andy Warhol's Women (aka Women in Revolt). **1972** Lady Liberty.

DARLING, IDA
Born: 1875. Died: June 5, 1936, Hollywood, Calif. Screen and stage actress.

Appeared in: **1914** The Nightingale. **1918** Mrs. Dane's Defence; The Girl of Today. **1921** Society Snobs; Nobody; Wedding Bells. **1922** Destiny's Isle; The Exciters. **1923** The Ruling Passion. **1924** Meddling Women. **1925** The Sky Raider; Heart of a Sire. **1926** Irene; Stranded in Paris. **1927** Singed. **1928** The House of Scandal; A Woman Against the World. **1929** Love in the Desert. **1930** Lummox. **1934** Here Comes the Navy; The Mighty Barnum. **1935** The Girl Who Came Back.

DARLING, RUTH
Died: Sept. 11, 1918, San Francisco, Calif. (auto accident). Screen actress.

Appeared in: **1916** Manhattan Madness; Fifty-Fifty; Intolerance.

DARMOND, GRACE
Born: 1898, Toronto, Canada. Died: Oct. 8, 1963, Los Angeles, Calif. (lung ailment). Screen and stage actress.

Appeared in: **1916** The Shielding Shadow (serial). **1917** In the Balance; An American Live Wire; The Seal of Silence; The Girl in His House; A Diplomatic Mission; The Man Who Wouldn't Tell. **1919** The Highest Trump. **1920** Below the Surface; The Hawk's Trail (serial). **1921** The Hope Diamond Mystery (serial); The Beautiful Gambler; See My Lawyer; White and Unmarried. **1922** A Dangerous Adventure (serial and feature film); Handle With Care; The Song of Life; I Can Explain. **1923** The Midnight Guest; Gold Madness; Daytime Wives. **1924** Alimony; The Gaiety Girl; Discontented Husbands. **1925** Flattery; Where the Worst Begins; The Great Jewel Robbery. **1926** Honesty—The Best Policy; Her Big Adventure; The Marriage Clause; The Night Patrol; Midnight Thieves; Her Man O'War. **1927** Wide Open; Hour of Reckoning; Wages of Conscience. **1941** Our Wife.

DARNELL, JEAN (Jean Jarratt Darnell)
Born: 1889, Sherman, Tex. Died: Jan. 20, 1961, Dallas, Tex. Screen actress. Entered films with Thannhouser Company.

Appeared in: **1912** The Truant's Doom; The Thunderbolt. **1914** Sisters. **1916** The Woman Who Did Not Care.

DARNELL, LINDA
Born: Oct. 16, 1921, Dallas, Tex. Died: Apr. 10, 1965, Chicago, Ill. (fire burns). Screen, stage and television actress. Divorced from film cameraman Pererell Marley, Philip Liebman and Merle Ray Robertson.

Appeared in: **1939** Hotel for Women; Daytime Wife. **1940** Star Dust; Mark of Zorro; Brigham Young—Frontiersman; Chad Hanna. **1941** Blood and Sand; Rise and Shine. **1942** The Loves of Edgar Allan Poe. **1943** City Without Men; The Song of Bernadette. **1944** Buffalo Bill; It Happened Tomorrow; Summer Storm; Sweet and Low Down. **1945** Hangover Square; All-Star Bond Rally (short); Fallen Angel; The Great John L; Stange Confession. **1946** My Darling Clementine; Centennial Summer; Anna and the King of Siam. **1947** Forever Amber. **1948** Unfaithfully Yours; The Walls of Jericho; A Letter to Three Wives. **1949** Slattery's Hurricane; Everybody Does It. **1950** No Way Out; Two Flags West. **1951** The 13th Letter; The Guy Who Came Back; The Lady Pays Off. **1952** Blackbeard the Pirate; Saturday Island (aka Island of Desire—US); Night Without Sleep. **1953** Second Chance. **1954** This Is My Love. **1955** Oli Ultimi Cinque Minute (The Last Five Minutes). **1956** Dakota Incident; Angels of Darkness. **1957** Zero Hour. **1963** El Valle de las Espados (Valley of the Swords—aka The Castillan—US). **1965** Black Spurs.

DARNLEY, HERBERT
Born: 1872, England. Died: Feb. 7, 1947, London, England. Screen, stage, vaudeville actor and playwright.

Appeared in: **1908** Napoleon and the English Sailor.

D'ARNO, ALBERT
Died: Dec. 19, 1977. Screen actor.

Appeared in: **1943** Mission to Moscow. **1953** Flight to Tangier. **1954** Alaska Seas. **1957** Funny Face. **1961** Mr. Sardonicus.

DARNOLD, BLAINE A.
Born: 1886. Died: Mar. 11, 1926, Kansas City, Mo. (pneumonia). Screen, stage and vaudeville actor.

DARO, BARON GINO
Born: 1892. Died: Nov. 28, 1977, San Diego, Calif. (heart attack). Screen and vaudeville actor.

Appeared in: **1952** Moulin Rouge. **1961** A Raisin in the Sun.

DARRELL, J. STEVAN
Born: 1905. Died: Aug. 14, 1970, Hollywood, Calif. Screen, stage, radio and television actor.

Appeared in: **1938** Angels With Dirty Faces (film debut). **1939** Women in the Wind; Code of the Secret Service. **1945** The Bull Fighters; Lightning Raiders; Nothing But Trouble. **1946** The Bride Wore Boots; Gentlemen With Guns; Terrors on Horseback; Roll On, Harvest Moon. **1947** Cheyenne; On the Old Spanish Trail; Helldorado; Valley of Fear; Riders of the Lone Star; Song of My Heart; Under Colorado Skies. **1948** I Wouldn't Be In Your Shoes; Carson City Raiders; The Timber Trail; West of Sonoma; Overland Trail; Cowboy Cavalier; Son of God's Country; Adventures of Frank and Jesse James (serial). **1949** The Gal Who Took the West; Ghost of Zorro (serial); Crashing Thru; Challenge of the Range; Abandoned; Frontier Outpost; Riders of the Sky; The Blazing Trail; Outcasts of the Trail. **1950** Winchester '73; The Arizona Cowboy; The Blazing Sun; David Harding; Counterspy; Cow Town Under Mexicali Skies. **1951** Along the Great Divide; Rough Riders of Durango; Pecos River. **1953** The Girl in the Red Velvet Swing; Thunder Over the Plains. **1954** Dangerous Mission; Cannibal Attack; The Law vs. Billy the Kid. **1955** Good Morning Miss Dove; Prince of Players; Treasure of Ruby Hills; The Tall Men. **1956** The Ten Commandments; Red Sundown. **1957** Utah Blaine; The Monolith Monsters; Joe Dakota. **1959** These Thousand Hills; Warlock; Timbuktu.

DARRO, FRANKIE (Frank Johnson aka FRANKIE DARROW)
Born: Dec. 22, 1918, Chicago, Ill. Died: Dec. 25, 1976, Huntington Beach, Calif. (heart attack). Screen, stage and television actor. Divorced from actress Aloha Wray (dec. 1968). Later married to Dorothy Darro.

Appeared in: **1924** So Big; Half-a-Dollar Bill; Judgment of the Storm; Racing for Life; Roaring Rails; The Signal Tower. **1925** Confessions of a Queen; The Fearless Lover; Women and Gold; The Cowboy Musketeer; Fighting the Flames; Her Husband's Secret; The Wyoming Wildcat; Wandering Footsteps; The Phantom Express; The People vs. Nancy Preston; The Midnight Flyer; Let's Go Gallagher. **1926** The Arizona Streak; Hearts and Spangles; Memory Lane; Wild to Go; The Thrill Hunter; Born to Battle; The Carnival Girl; The Cowboy Cop;

Mike; The Masquerade Bandit; Kiki; Out of the West; Tom and His Pals; Red Hot Hoofs. **1927** The Desert Pirate; Little Mickey Grogan; Cyclone of the Range; The Flying U Ranch; Her Father Said No; Judgement of the Hills; Lightning Lariats; Long Pants; Tom's Gang; Moulders of Men. **1928** When the Law Rides; Tyrant of Red Gulch; The Avenging Rider; The Circus Kid; Phantom of the Range; Terror Mountain; The Texas Tornado. **1929** Blaze O' Glory; The Pride of Pawnee; The Rainbow Man; Gun Law; Idaho Red; Trail of the Horse Thieves. **1931** Mad Genius; The Lightning Warrior (serial); The Vanishing Legion. **1932** Way Back Home; Three on a Match; The Devil Horse (serial); Cheyenne Cyclone; Amateur Daddy. **1933** Wolf Dog (serial); Tugboat Annie; Mayor of Hell; Wild Boys of the Road; Laughing at Life; Hollywood on Parade #8 (short). **1934** Little Men; No Greater Glory; The Merry Frinks; Big Race; Broadway Bill. **1935** Burn 'Em Up Barnes (serial and feature); The Pay-Off; Red Hot Tires; Unwelcome Stranger; Stranded; Three Kids and a Queen; Phantom Empire (serial); Men of Action; Valley of Wanted Men. **1936** Born to Fight; Racing Blood; The Ex-Mrs. Bradford; Charlie Chan at the Race Track; Mind Your Own Business. **1937** Young Dr. Dynamite; A Day at the Races; Thoroughbreds Don't Cry; Saratoga; Anything for a Thrill; Headliner Crasher; Tough to Handle. **1938** The Great Adventures of Wild Bill Hickok (serial); Juvenile Court; Wanted by the Police. **1939** Tough Kid; Irish Luck; Boy's Reformatory. **1940** Chasing Trouble; Men With Steel Faces; On the Spot; Laughing at Danger. **1941** Up in the Air; The Gang's All Here; You're Out of Luck; Let's Go Collegiate; Tuxedo Junction. **1942** Junior G-Men of the Air (serial). **1946** Freddie Steps Out; High School Hero; Junior Prom. **1947** Vacation Days; That's My Man; Sarge Goes to College. **1948** Pride of Virginia (aka Heart of Virginia); Angel's Alley; Trouble Makers. **1949** Fighting Fools; Hold That Baby! **1950** Sons of New Mexico; Wyoming Mail; Riding High. **1951** Across the Wide Missouri; Pride of Maryland. **1953** Two Gun Marshal. **1954** The Lawless Rider. **1959** Operation Petticoat. **1964** The Carpetbaggers. **1969** Hook, Line and Sinker.

DARVAS, LILI
Born: Apr. 10, 1902, Budapest, Hungary. Died: July 22, 1974, New York, N.Y. Screen, stage, radio and televison actress. Married to actor/playwright Ferenc Molnar (dec. 1952).

Appeared in: **1935** Tagebuch der Geliebten. **1938** The Affairs of Maupassant. **1956** Meet Me in Las Vegas. **1960** Cimarron. **1973** Love.

DARVI, BELLA (Bayla Wegier)
Born: Oct. 23, 1928, Sosnowiec, Poland. Died: Sept. 11, 1971, Monte Carlo, Monaco (suicide—gas). Screen and television actress.

Appeared in: **1954** Hell and High Water; The Egyptian. **1955** The Racers; Je Suis un Sentimental. **1959** Sinners of Paris. **1965** Lipstick.

DARWELL, JANE (Patti Woodward)
Born: Oct. 15, 1880, Palmyra, Mo. Died: Aug. 13, 1967, Woodland Hills, Calif. (heart attack). Screen, stage and television actress. Won 1940 Academy Award for Best Supporting Actress in The Grapes of Wrath.

Appeared in: **1914** Rose of the Rancho (film debut); The Only Son; Brewster Millions; The Master Mind. **1915** After Five. **1930** Tom Sawyer. **1931** Huckleberry Finn; Fighting Caravans. **1932** Ladies of the Big House; Hot Saturday; Back Street; No One Man. **1933** Good Housewrecking (short); Jennie Gerhardt; Air Hostess; Women Won't Tell; One Sunday Afternoon; Design for Living; Emergency Call; Before Dawn; Only Yesterday; He Couldn't Take It; Bondage; Child of Manhattan; Murders in the Zoo; Roman Scandals. **1934** Wonder Bar; Fashions of 1934; Jimmy the Gent; Embarrassing Moments; Heat Lightning; Gentlemen Are Born; Blind Date; Once to Every Woman; The Most Precious Thing in Life; Happiness Ahead; The Scarlet Empress; The White Parade; Bright Eyes; Change of Heart; Let's Talk It Over; Desirable; Wake Up and Dream; The Firebird; David Harum; Journal of a Crime; Million Dollar Ransom; One Night of Love. **1935** Tomorrow's Youth; Beauty's Daughter; One More Spring; Life Begins at Forty; Curly Top; McFadden's Flats; Paddy O'Day; Navy Wife; Metropolitan. **1936** We're Only Human; Captain January; The Country Doctor; Little Miss Nobody; The First Baby; Private Number; The Poor Little Rich Girl; White Fang; Star for a Night; Ramona; Craig's Wife. **1937** The Great Hospital Mystery; Love Is News; Dead Yesterday; Nancy Steele Is Missing; Fifty Roads to Town; Slave Ship; Wife, Doctor and Nurse; Dangerously Yours; The Singing Marine; Laughing at Trouble. **1938** Little Miss Broadway; Five of a Kind; Change of Heart (and 1934 version); Battle of Broadway; Three Blind Mice; Time Out for Murder; Inside Story; Up the River; The Jury's Secret. **1939** Jesse James; Unexpected Father; The Zero Hour; Grand Jury Secrets; The Rains Came; Gone With the Wind; 20,000 Men a Year. **1940** The Grapes of Wrath; Brigham Young—Frontiersman; A Miracle on Main Street; Youth Will Be Served; Chad Hanna;

Untamed. **1941** Here Is a Man; All That Money Can Buy; Private Nurse; Small Town Deb. **1942** On the Sunny Side; Highways by Night; The Great Gildersleeve; All Through the Night; Battle of Midway (documentary); The Loves of Edgar Allan Poe; It Happened in Flatbush; Young America; Men of Texas. **1943** A Family Feud (short); Gildersleeve's Bad Day; The Ox-Bow Incident; Tender Comrade; Stagedoor Canteen; Government Girl. **1944** She's a Sweetheart; Music in Manhattan; Double Indemnity; The Impatient Years; Reckless Age; Sunday Dinner for a Soldier. **1945** Captain Tugboat Annie; I Live in Grosvenor Square (aka A Yank in London—US 1946). **1946** My Darling Clementine; Three Wise Fools; Dark Horse. **1947** The Red Stallion; Keeper of the Bees. **1948** The Time of Your Life; Train to Alcatraz; Three Godfathers. **1949** Red Canyon. **1950** Red-Wood Forest Trail; Surrender; Three Husbands; The Second Face; Father's Wild Game; Wagonmaster; Caged; The Daughter of Rosie O'Grady. **1951** Fourteen Hours; Excuse My Dust; Journey into Light; The Lemon Drop Kid. **1952** We're Not Married; The Devil and Daniel Webster (reissue and retitle of All That Money Can Buy, 1941). **1953** It Happens Every Thursday; The Sun Shines Bright; Affair With a Stranger; The Bigamist. **1955** Hit the Deck; A Life at Stake. **1956** There's Always Tomorrow; Girls in Prison. **1958** The Last Hurrah. **1959** Hound-Dog Man. **1964** Mary Poppins.

DASH, PAULY (Paul Walter Dashiff)
Born: 1918, Brooklyn, N.Y. Died: Feb. 2, 1974, Miami Beach, Fla. (cancer). Screen and stage actor.

Appeared in: **1964** It's Hot on Sin Island; Sextet. **1966** The Hot Pearl Snatch. **1968** Lady in Cement; I Am for Sale.

DASHIELL, WILLARD
Born: 1867. Died: Apr. 19, 1943, Holyoke, Mass. Screen, stage, vaudeville actor, playwright and lawyer. Entered films during silents.

Appeared in: **1931** The Cheat. **1934** War is a Racket.

DA SILVA, HENRY
Born: 1881, Lisbon, Portugal. Died: June 6, 1947, Los Angeles, Calif. Screen actor.

DASSIN, JOSEPH "JOE"
Born: 1938, New York. Died: Aug. 21, 1980, Papeete, Tahiti (heart attack). Screen, stage actor, stage director and singer. Son of actor/director Jules Dassin and musician Beatrice Launer.

Appeared in: **1964** Topkapi. **1965** Lady L (US 1966).

DASTAGIR, SABU See SABU

DATE, KESHAVRAO
Born: 1939, India. Died: Sept. 13, 1971, Bombay, India. Screen and stage actor.

DAUBE, HARDA (Belle Daube)
Born: 1888, Northampton, England. Died: May 25, 1959, Hollywood, Calif. Screen and stage actress.

Appeared in: **1919** The Virtuous Vamp. **1933** Tailspin Tommy (serial). **1949** Joe Palooka in the Big Fight; Dancing in the Dark; My Dream is Yours.

DAUFEL, ANDRE (David Van Offel)
Born: 1919, England. Died: Apr. 22, 1975, Brussels, Belgium. Screen, stage actor, stage director and playwright.

DAUMERY, CARRIE "MADAME"
Born: Mar. 24, 1863, Brussels, Belgium. Died: July 1, 1938. Screen and stage actress.

Appeared in: **1920** Garden of Eden; The Man Who Laughs. **1921** The Conquering Power. **1924** The Rose of Paris; Forbidden Paradise; Dorothy Vernon of Hadden Hall. **1925** Lady Windemere's Fan. **1926** Paris at Midnight; The Greater Glory; The Lucky Lady; The Love Thief; Young April. **1929** Hearts in Exile; The Last Warning; General Crack. **1930** Cameo Kirby. **1931** War Mamas (short). **1934** Grand Canary.

DAUNT, WILLIAM
Born: Aug. 21, 1893, Dublin, Ireland. Died: Oct. 1, 1938, England? Screen and stage actor.

Appeared in: **1931** The Wrong Mr. Perkins. **1934** Night Club Queen. **1935** Variety.

DAUPHIN, CLAUDE (Claude LeGrand Franc-Nohain)
Born: Aug. 19, 1903, Corbeil, France. Died: Nov. 17, 1978, Paris, France. Screen, stage and television actor. Brother of actor Jean Nohain (dec. 1981). Divorced from actresses Rosine Derean, Maria Mauban and Norma Eberhardt. Entered films in 1930.

Appeared in: **1938** Entree des Artistes (aka The Curtain Rises—US 1939); The Slipper Episode. **1939** Affair Lafont (aka The Conflict—US); Battement de Coeur (Heartbeat—US). **1942** Les Deux Timides. **1944** English Without Tears (aka Her Man Gilbey—US 1949). **1949** Deported; L'Affaire. **1952** Casque d'Or; April in Paris; Le Plaisir (aka The Mask—US 1954). **1953** Innocents in Paris (US 1955); Little Boy Lost; L'Erentaile (aka Naughty Martine). **1954** Phantom of the Rue Morgue. **1958** The Quiet American. **1961** The Full Treatment (aka Stop Me Before I Kill!—US). **1962** Tiara Tahiti (US 1963); Le Diable et Les Dix Commandments (The Devil and the Ten Commandments—US 1963). **1963** Symphonie pour un Messacre (Symphony for a Massacre—US 1965). **1964** La Rancune (aka The Visit—US); La Bonne Soupe (The Good Soup, aka Careless Love). **1965** Lady L (US 1966); Compartiment Tueurs (aka The Sleeping Car Murders—US 1966). **1966** Grand Prix; Is Paris Burning? **1967** Two for the Road; The Other One. **1968** Barbarella. **1969** Hard Contract; The Madwoman of Chaillot. **1975** Rosebud. **1976** The Wild Goose Chase; Rum Runner; The Tenant.

DAVENPORT, ALICE (Alice Shepard)
Born: 1853 or 1864?, New York, N.Y. Died: June 24, 1936, Los Angeles, Calif. Screen and stage actress. Divorced from actor Harry Davenport (dec. 1949) and mother of actresses Dorothy (dec. 1977) and Ann Davenport (dec. 1968).

Appeared in: **1911** The Best Man Wins. **1912** The Love Trail; Drummer's Vacation; Mabel's Lovers. **1913** The Telltale Light; Cohen's Outing; John Brown's Luck. **1914** Making a Living; Mabel's Strange Predicament; The Star Boarder; Caught in a Cabaret; Caught in the Rain; Mabel's New Job. **1915** My Valet; The Home Breakers; Ambrose's Fury; Fickle Fatty's Fall; Stolen Magic. **1916** Perils of the Park; A Love Riot; Wife and Auto Trouble; The Snow Cure; The Worst of Friends; Fido's Fate. **1917** Secrets of a Beauty Parlour; A Maiden's Trust; Maggie's First False Step. **1918** Little Red Decides; Her Blighted Love. **1921** Skirts. **1924** The Legend of Hollywood. **1930** The Dude Wrangler.

DAVENPORT, ANN
Died: Jan. 28, 1968, Hollywood, Calif. Screen actress. For family information see Harry Davenport listing.

DAVENPORT, ARTHUR BROMLEY See BROMLEY-DAVENPORT, ARTHUR

DAVENPORT, DORIS
Born: 1917, Moline, Ill. Died: June 18, 1980, Santa Cruz, Calif. Screen actress.

Appeared in: **1934** Kid Millions. **1940** The Westerner; Behind the News.

DAVENPORT, DOROTHY (aka MRS. WALLACE REID)
Born: 1896. Died: Oct. 12, 1977, Woodland Hills, Calif. Screen actress, film producer and screenwriter. Daughter of actors Harry (dec. 1949) and Alice Davenport (dec. 1936). Married to actor Wallace Reid, Sr. (dec. 1923). Mother of actor Wallace Reid, Jr. For further family information see Harry Davenport listing.

Appeared in: **1911** The Best Man Wins. **1920** The Fighting Chance. **1921** Every Woman's Problem. **1922** Night Life in Hollywood; The Masked Avenger. **1923** Human Wreckage. **1924** Broken Laws. **1925** Red Kimono. **1927** The Satin Woman. **1928** Hellship Bronson.

DAVENPORT, EDGAR LOOMIS
Born: Feb. 7, 1862, Roxbury, Mass. Died: July 25, 1918, Boston, Mass. Screen and stage actor. Brother of stage actress Fanny Davenport (dec.). Father of actor Harry Davenport (dec. 1949).

Appeared in: **1916** Dorian's Divorce; The Blindness of Love; Upheaval.

DAVENPORT, HARRY
Born: Jan. 19, 1866, New York, N.Y. Died: Aug. 9, 1949, Los Angeles, Calif. (heart attack). Screen, stage actor and film director. Son of stage actor Edgar Loomis Davenport (dec. 1918). Divorced from actress Alice Davenport (dec. 1936). Father of actresses Ann (dec. 1968) and Dorothy Davenport (dec. 1977). Married to actress Phyllis Rankin (dec. 1934). Father of actor Arthur Rankin (dec. 1947), actress Kate (dec. 1954), Fanny, and stage manager E. L. Davenport (dec. 1977) Entered films in 1912.

Appeared in: **1930** Her Unborn Child. **1931** My Sin. **1932** His Woman. **1933** Get That Venus. **1934** Three Cheers for Love. **1935** The Scoundrel. **1936** Three Men on a Horse; The Case of the Black Cat;

King of Hockey. **1937** Fly-Away Baby; The Life of Emile Zola; Under Cover of Night; Her Husband's Secretary; White Bondage; They Won't Forget; Mr. Dodd Takes the Air; First Lady; The Perfect Specimen; Paradise Express; As Good as Married; Armored Car; Wells Fargo; Fit for a King. **1938** Marie Antoinette; Gold Is Where You Find It; Saleslady; The Sisters; Long Shot; The First Hundred Years; The Cowboy and the Lady; Reckless Living; The Rage of Paris; Tailspin; Young Fugitives; You Can't Take It With You; The Higgins Family; Orphans of the Street. **1939** Made for Each Other; My Wife's Relatives; Should Husbands Work?; The Covered Trailer; Money to Burn; Exile Express; Death of a Champion; The Story of Alexander Graham Bell; Juarez; Gone With the Wind; The Hunchback of Notre Dame. **1940** The Story of Dr. Ehrlich's Magic Bullet; Granny Get Your Gun; Too Many Husbands; Grandpa Goes to Town; Earl of Puddlestone; Lucky Partners; I Want a Divorce; All This and Heaven Too; Foreign Correspondent. **1941** That Uncertain Feeling; I Wanted Wings; Hurricane Smith; The Bride Came C.O.D.; One Foot in Heaven; Kings Row. **1942** Son of Fury; Larceny, Inc,; Ten Gentlemen from West Point; Tales of Manhattan. **1943** Headin' for God's Country; We've Never Been Licked; Riding High; The Ox-Bow Incident; Shantytown; The Amazing Mrs. Holliday; Gangway for Tomorrow; Government Girl; Jack London; Princess O'Rourke. **1944** Meet Me in St. Louis; The Impatient Years; The Thin Man Goes Home; Kismet. **1945** Music for Millions; The Enchanted Forest; Too Young to Know; This Love of Ours; She Wouldn't Say Yes. **1946** Courage of Lassie; A Boy, a Girl and a Dog; Faithful in My Fashion; Three Wise Fools; GI War Brides; Lady Luck; Claudia and David; Pardon My Past; Adventure. **1947** The Farmer's Daughter; That Hagen Girl; Stallion Road; Keeper of the Bees; Sport of Kings; The Fabulous Texan; The Bachelor and the Bobbysoxer. **1948** Three Daring Daughters; The Man from Texas; For the Love of Mary; That Lady in Ermine; The Decision of Christopher Blake. **1949** Down to the Sea in Ships; Little Women; Tell It to the Judge; That Forsyte Woman. **1950** Riding High (and 1943 version).

DAVENPORT, HARRY J.
Born: 1858. Died: Feb. 20, 1929, Glendale, Calif. (complication of diseases). Screen actor. Married to actress Milla Davenport (dec. 1936).

DAVENPORT, HAVIS
Born: 1933. Died: July 23, 1975, Hollywood, Calif. Screen and television actress.

Appeared in: **1954** Rear Window.

DAVENPORT, HELENE (Cleo Boone)
Born: 1865. Died: May 31, 1928, New York ("complication of diseases"). Screen, stage and vaudeville actress. Divorced from stage actor W. H. Davenport (dec.), and later married to stage manager Harry Hardy (dec.).

Appeared in: **1911** Ever the Accuser.

DAVENPORT, KATE
Born: 1896. Died: Dec. 7, 1954, Hollywood, Calif. Screen actress. Daughter of actor Harry Davenport (dec. 1949). For family information see Harry Davenport listing.

Appeared in: **1916** The Supreme Temptation. **1921** Sentimental Tommy.

DAVENPORT, KENNETH
Born: 1879. Died: Nov. 10, 1941, Los Angeles, Calif. (heart attack). Stage and screen actor.

Appeared in: **1921** The Nut.

DAVENPORT, MILLA
Born: 1871, Sicily, Italy. Died: May 17, 1936, Los Angeles, Calif. Screen, stage, vaudeville and burlesque actress. Married to screen actor Harry J. Davenport (dec. 1929). Entered films approx. 1911.

Appeared in: **1919** Daddy Long Legs; In Mizzoura. **1920** Stronger Than Death; The Forbidden Woman; You Never Can Tell. **1921** Rip Van Winkle; Why Trust Your Husband; The Girl from God's Country; The Man from Lost River; Patsy. **1922** The Worldly Madonna; The Man Who Waited. **1923** The Christian; Dulcy. **1924** Daddies; The Red Lily; The Shooting of Dan McGrew; The Right of the Strongest. **1925** Wild West (serial); Dangerous Innocence. **1926** Crossed Signals; The Road to Glory. **1927** Hey! Hey! Cowboy; King of Kings. **1928** Sins of the Fathers; The Danger Rider. **1929** The Girl from Woolworth's. **1932** Merrily We Go To Hell. **1934** In Love With Life. **1935** The Wedding Night; Here Comes Cookie. **1936** Human Cargo.

DAVENPORT, WILLIAM
Born: 1867. Died: May 11, 1941, Philadelphia, Pa. Screen and stage actor. Appeared in early Edison, Lubin and Biograph Co. films.

DAVES, DELMER (Delmer Lawrence Daves)
Born: July 24, 1904, San Francisco, Calif. Died: Aug. 17, 1977, La Jolla, Calif. Screen actor, film director, film producer, screenwriter and commercial artist. Married to writer Mary Lou Lawrence.

Appeared in: **1929** The Duke Steps Out. **1930** The Bishop Murder Case; Good News.

DAVEY, NUNA (Margaret Symonds)
Born: Dec. 19, 1902, Cawnpore, India. Died: Dec. 11, 1977, London, England. Screen and stage actress. Married to actor Gerald Cross.

DAVID, THAYER (David Thayer Hersey)
Born: 1927, Medford, Mass. Died: July 17, 1978, New York, N.Y (heart attack). Screen, stage and television actor. Divorced from actress Valerie French.

Appeared in: **1957** Baby Face Nelson. **1958** A Time to Love and a Time to Die; Wolf Cry. **1960** Journey to the Center of the Earth; The Story of Ruth. **1970** House of Dark Shadows; Little Big Man. **1972** Save the Tiger. **1975** The Eiger Sanction; Hearts of the West. **1976** Rocky; The Duchess and the Dirtwater Fox; Pepper. **1977** House Calls.

DAVID, WILLIAM
Born: 1882, Vicksburg, Miss. Died: Apr. 10, 1965, East Islip, N.Y. Screen and stage actor.

Appeared in: **1922** Outcast; Received Payment. **1923** Fog Bound.

DAVIDOFF, SERAFIN
Died: Apr., 1975. Screen extra.

Appeared in: **1956** Around the World in 80 Days.

DAVIDS, HEINTJE
Born: 1888. Died: Feb. 14, 1975. Dutch film actress.

DAVIDSON, BING (aka JAMES B. DAVIDSON)
Born: 1939. Died: July 18, 1965, San Francisco, Calif. (fall from hotel window). Screen actor. Also in films as James B. Davidson.

DAVIDSON, DORE
Born: 1850. Died: Mar. 7, 1930 (complication of diseases). Screen, stage actor, stage producer and playwright.

Appeared in: **1920** Humoresque. **1922** The Rosary; Your Best Friend; The Good Provider; The Light in the Dark. **1923** Broadway Broke; The Purple Highway; Success; None So Blind. **1924** The Great White Way; Welcome Stranger; Grit. **1925** The Royal Girl. **1927** The Music Master; East Side, West Side.

DAVIDSON, JAMES B. *See* DAVIDSON, BING

DAVIDSON, JO "SKIPPER" (Joseph Davidson)
Born: 1904. Died: Apr. 3, 1981, Brooklyn, N.Y. (heart attack). Screen and stage actor.

Appeared in: **1976** Next Stop Greenwich Village. **1978** Annie Hall. **1981** Eyewitness.

DAVIDSON, JOHN
Born: Dec. 25, 1886, New York. Died: Jan. 15, 1968, Los Angeles, Calif. (heart failure). Screen and stage actor. Do not confuse with singer/actor John Davidson.

Appeared in: **1914** The Genius Pierre. **1915** Green Cloak; Sentimental Lady; Danger Signal. **1916** Romeo and Juliet; The Wall Between; A Million a Minute; Caravan; Pawn of Fate. **1919** Black Circle; Forest Rivals; Through the Toils. **1920** The Great Lover. **1921** The Bronze Bell; Cheated Love; Fool's Paradise; The Idle Rich; No Woman Knows. **1922** Saturday Night; The Woman Who Walked Alone; Under Two Flags. **1923** His Children's Children. **1924** Monsieur Beaucaire; Ramshackle House. **1929** Kid Gloves; The Rescue; Queen of the Night Clubs; Skin Deep; The Time, the Place and the Girl; The Thirteenth Chair. **1930** The Life of the Party. **1932** Arsene Lupin; Docks of San Francisco; Six Hours to Live. **1933** Behind Jury Doors; Dinner at Eight; The Mad Game. **1934** The Perils of Pauline (serial); Burn 'Em Up Barnes (serial and feature film); Lightning Strikes Twice; Tailspin Tommy (serial); Bombay Mail; Hold That Girl; Murder in Trinidad; Hollywood Hoodlum. **1935** A Tale of Two Cities; The Call of the Savage (serial); Behind the Green Lights; Last Days of Pompeii; A Shot in the Dark. **1938** Fighting Devil Dogs (serial); Mr. Moto Takes a Vacation. **1939** Mr. Moto's Last Warning; Duel Personalities (short); Arrest Bulldog Drummond. **1940** King of the Royal Mounted (serial). **1941** Adventures of Captain Marvel (serial); Dick Tracy vs. Crime, Inc. (serial); Devil Bat. **1942** Perils of Nyoka (serial); The Yukon Patrol. **1943** Secret Service in Darkest Africa (serial). **1944** Captain America (serial); The Chinese Cat; Call of the Jungle. **1945** The Purple

Monster Strikes (serial); Where Do We Go from Here? **1946** Smooth as Silk; Shock; Sentimental Journey. **1947** Suddenly, It's Spring; Daisy Kenyon. **1948** A Letter to Three Wives; Bungalow 13; That Wonderful Urge; The Luck of the Irish. **1949** Slattery's Hurricane; Oh, You Beautiful Doll. **1951** Half Angel. **1954** Prince Valiant.

DAVIDSON, MAX

Born: 1875, Berlin, Germany. Died: Sept. 4, 1950, Woodland Hills, Calif. Screen and stage actor. Entered films in 1913.

Appeared in: **1915** Love in Armor. **1916** The Village Vampire (working title The Great Leap). **1921** The Idle Rich; No Woman Knows. **1922** Remembrance; The Light That Failed; Second Hand Rose. **1923** The Extra Girl; The Rendezvous; The Ghost Patrol; The Darling of New York. **1924** Fool's Highway; Untamed Youth; Hold Your Breath. **1925** Old Clothes; Hogan's Alley; The Rag Man; Justice of the Far North. **1926** Into Her Kingdom; Sunshine of Paradise Alley; The Johnstown Flood. **1927** Hotel Imperial; Pleasure Before Business; Cheaters; Hats Off (short); The Call of the Cuckoo (short). **1928** The following shorts: Pass the Gravy; Should Women Drive?; Tell It to the Judge; That Night. **1929** Moan and Groan, Inc. (short); So This Is College; Hurdy Gurdy (short). Shorts prior to 1930: Dumb Daddies; Blow by Blow. **1930** The Shrimp (short). **1931** Oh! Oh! Cleopatra (short). **1932** Docks of San Francisco; Daring Danger. **1933** The Cohens and the Kellys in Trouble; Hokus Focus (short); The World Gone Wrong. **1935** Southern Exposure (short). **1936** Roamin' Wild. **1937** The Girl Said No. **1939** Union Pacific. **1940** The Mortal Storm; No Census, No Feeling (short). **1942** Reap the Wild Wind; The Great Commandment. **1965** Laurel and Hardy's Laughing 20's (documentary).

DAVIDSON, WILLIAM B.

Born: June 16, 1888, Dobbs Ferry, N.Y. Died: Sept. 28, 1947, Santa Monica, Calif. (following surgery). Screen and stage actor. Entered films with Vitagraph in 1914.

Appeared in: **1915** For the Honor of the Crew. **1916** The Price of Malice; Her Debt of Honor; Dorian's Divorce; The Child of Destiny; The Pretenders; In the Diplomatic Service. **1917** White Raven; The Call of Her People; Modern Cinderella; Her Second Husband; The Greatest Power; Lady Barnacle; A Magdalene of the Hills; Mary Lawson's Secret; More Truth than Poetry; American Maid. **1918** Friend Husband; In Pursuit of Polly; Persuasive Peggy; Our Little Wife. **1920** Partners of the Night. **1921** Nobody; Conceit; The Girl from Nowhere. **1922** Destiny's Isle. **1923** Salomy Jane; Adam and Eva. **1924** The Storm Daughter. **1925** Hearts and Spurs; Ports of Call; Women and Gold; Recompense. **1927** The Cradle Snatchers; The Lash (short); Gentlemen of Paris; The Last Trail; Love Makes 'Em Wild. **1928** Sharp Tools (short); Good Morning, Judge; The Gaucho. **1929** Queen of the Night Clubs; Ain't It the Truth (short); The Carnation Kid; Woman Trap; Painted Faces. **1930** Fat Wives for Thin (short); Sunny; A Man from Wyoming; Hell's Angels; Playboy of Paris; Captain Applejack; The Silver Horde; Hook, Line and Sinker; Oh, For a Man!; The Costello Case; Men Are Like That; For the Defense; How I Play Golf; The Feathered Serpent; Blaze O'Glory; Scarlet Face; Letters (short). **1931** Dishonored; Half Holiday (short); No Limit; The Secret Call; Vice Squad; Graft. **1932** The Menace; The 13th Guest; Her Mad Night; Guilty or Not Guilty; Sky Devils; Scarface; Guilty as Hell; The Animal Kingdom. **1933** Dangerously Yours; Hello Everybody!; The Intruder; I'm No Angel; Sitting Pretty; Meet the Baron; Lady Killer; Torch Singer; Billion Dollar Scandal. **1934** Imitation of Life; The Big Shakedown; Housewife; Circus Clown; Friends of Mr. Sweeney; Dragon Murder Case; The Lemon Drop Kid; St. Louis Kid; Massacre; Fog Over Frisco; Laughing Boy; The Secret Bride. **1935** In Person; Straight from the Heart; Roberta; Sweet Music; Bordertown; Devil Dogs of the Air; A Night at the Ritz; Oil for the Lamps of China; Special Agent; Dangerous; Go Into Your Dance; In Caliente; The Crusaders; Woman Wanted; Show Them No Mercy; Bright Lights. **1936** Road Gang; The Singing Kid; Murder by an Aristocrat; The Big Noise; Earthworm Tractors; Gold Diggers of 1937; Mind Your Own Business. **1937** Easy Living; Behind the Mike; Marked Woman; Midnight Court; Ever Since Eve; Marry the Girl; Sergeant Murphy; Hollywood Hotel; Let Them Live; The Road Back; The Affairs of Cappy Ricks; Paradise Isle; Something to Sing About; It Happened in Hollywood. **1938** Racket Busters; The Jury's Secret; Cocoanut Grove; Mr. Doodle Kicks Off; Blockade; Cowboy from Brooklyn; Illegal Traffic. **1939** Wings of the Navy; When Tomorrow Comes; On Trial; Indianapolis Speedway; Private Detectives; Hidden Power; Each Dawn I Die; Smashing the Money Ring; The Honeymoon's Over; They Made Me a Criminal; On the Record; Dust Be My Destiny; Honeymoon in Bali. **1940** The Lady With Red Hair; Tin Pan Alley; Three Cheers for the Irish; Florian; Lillian Russell; Half a Sinner; My Love Came Back; The Girl in 313; Sailor's Lady; Maryland; Hired Wife; Seven Sinners; A Night at Earl Carroll's; Sandy Gets Her Man; My Little Chickadee. **1941** Remember the Day; Week-end in Havana;

San Francisco Docks; In the Navy; The Lady from Cheyenne; Thieves Fall Out; Hold That Ghost; Highway West; Three Sons O' Guns; Keep 'Em Flying; Sun Valley Serenade. **1942** In This Our Life; Juke Girl; The Magnificent Dope; Over My Dead Body; The Male Animal; Larceny, Inc.; Yankee Doodle Dandy; Tennessee Johnson; Gentleman Jim; Affairs of Jimmy Valentine; Careful, Soft Shoulders. **1943** Happy Go Lucky; Mission to Moscow; Calaboose; Truck Busters; Murder on the Waterfront; The Good Fellows; Slick Chick. **1944** Allergic to Love; Since You Went Away; Greenwich Village; The Imposter; In Society; Shine on Harvest Moon; Song of Nevada. **1945** Swing Out, Sister; They Were Expendable; Saratoga Trunk; Blonde Ransom; The Man Who Walked Alone; Tell It to the Judge; Circumstantial Evidence; See My Lawyer. **1946** Blonde Alibi; My Darling Clementine; The Cat Creeps; Ding Dong Williams; The Plainsman and the Lady; The Notorious Lone Wolf. **1947** Dick Tracey's Dilemma; That's My Man; That Hagen Girl; My Wild Irish Rose; The Farmer's Daughter.

DAVIDT, MICHAEL

Born: 1877. Died: Mar. 15, 1944, Hollywood, Calif. Screen actor.

DAVIES, BETTY ANN

Born: Dec. 24, 1910, London, England. Died: May 14, 1955, Manchester, England (following appendectomy). Screen and stage actress.

Appeared in: **1933** Oh What a Duchess! (aka My Old Duchess). **1934** Death at Broadcasting House; Youthful Folly. **1935** Joy Ride; Play Up the Band. **1936** Chick; Radio Lover; She Knew What She Wanted; Tropical Trouble; Excuse My Glove. **1937** Merry Comes to Town; Under a Cloud; Lucky Jade. **1938** Silver Top; Mountains of Mourne. **1941** Kipps (aka The Remarkable Mr. Kipps—US 1942); I Bet. **1947** It Always Rains on Sunday (US 1949). **1948** Escape; To the Public Danger. **1949** The Passionate Friends (aka One Woman's Story—US); The History of Mr. Polly (US 1951); Now Barabbas; Which Will You Have? (aka Barabbas the Robber—US). **1950** The Blue Lamp; Trio; The Man in Black; The Woman With No Name (aka Her Panelled Door—US 1951); Sanitarium. **1951** Outcast of the Islands. **1952** Meet Me Tonight. **1953** Cosh Boy (aka The Slasher—US); Grand National Night (aka Wicked Wife—US 1955); Tonight at 8:30. **1954** Children Galore; The Belles of St Trinian's (US 1955). **1955** Murder by Proxy (aka Blackout—US). **1956** Alias John Preston.

DAVIES, DAVID

Died: May, 1920, Chicago, Ill. Screen, stage and vaudeville actor.

DAVIES, GEORGE

Born: 1891. Died: Mar., 1960, Edinburgh, Scotland. Screen, stage, radio and television actor.

DAVIES, HOWARD

Born: May 18, 1879, Liverpool, England. Died: Dec. 30, 1947, Los Angeles, Calif. Screen, stage and vaudeville actor.

Appeared in: **1916** Davy Crockett; American Beauty; Making of Maddalena; The Intrigue; Call of the Cumberlands. **1917** Her Own People; Sapho. **1918** His Birthright; Boston Blackie's Little Pal. **1919** It's a Bear; A Sporting Chance; A White Man's Chance. **1920** One Hour Before Dawn; Dice of Destiny. **1922** The Sin Flood. **1926** Infatuation. **1927** The Return of the Riddle Rider (serial); The Phantom Buster. **1928** The Avenging Shadow. **1929** The White Outlaw. **1940** My Son, My Son.

DAVIES, LILIAN

Born: Jan. 18, 1895, Lymouth, North Devon, England. Died: Mar. 3, 1932, England? Screen and stage actress.

Appeared in: **1930** Just for a Song.

DAVIES, MARION

Born: Jan. 3, 1897. Died: Sept. 22, 1961, Hollywood, Calif. (cancer). Screen actress. Sister of actress Reine Davies. Married to actor Horace Brown (dec. 1972).

Appeared in: **1917** Runaway Romany (film debut). **1918** Cecilia of the Pink Roses. **1919** The Cinema Murder; The Dark Star; The Belle of New York. **1920** The Restless Sex; April Folly. **1921** Enchantment; Buried Treasure. **1922** The Bride's Play; Beauty Worth; When Knighthood Was in Flower; The Young Diana; Daughter of Luxury. **1923** Little Old New York; Adam and Eva. **1924** Janice Meredith; Yolanda. **1925** Lights of Old Broadway; Zander the Great. **1926** Beverly of Graustark. **1927** Quality Street; The Fair Co-ed; The Red Mill; Tillie the Toiler. **1928** The Cardboard Lover; The Patsy; Show People. **1929** The Hollywood Revue of 1929; Marianne; The Gay Nineties. **1930** Not So Dumb; The Floradora Girl. **1931** Jackie Cooper's Christmas Party (short); It's a Wise Child; Five and Ten;

Bachelor Father. **1932** Polly of the Circus; Blondie of the Follies; The Dark Horse. **1933** Peg O' My Heart. **1934** Operator Thirteen; Going Hollywood. **1935** Page Miss Glory. **1936** Hearts Divided; Cain and Mabel. **1937** Ever Since Eve. **1964** Big Parade of Comedy (documentary). **1967** Show People (reissue of 1928 film).

DAVIES, RUPERT
Born: 1916, Liverpool, England. Died: Nov. 22, 1976, London, Enland (cancer). Screen, stage and television actor.

Appeared in: **1955** The Dark Avenger (aka The Warriors—US). **1957** The Traitors (aka The Accursed—US 1958). **1958** Sea Fury (US 1959); The Key. **1959** Bobbikins (US 1960); Sapphire; John Paul Jones' Violent Moment (US 1966). **1960** The Criminal (aka The Concrete Jungle—US 1962). **1964** The Uncle (US 1966). **1965** The Spy Who Came In From the Cold. **1966** The Brides of Fu Manchu. **1968** Witchfinder General (aka the Conqueror Worm—US); Dracula Has Risen from the Grave (US 1969); Curse of the Crimson Altar (aka The Crimson Cult—US 1970). **1969** The Oblong Box (aka Edgar Allen Poe's The Oblong Box—US); Submarine X-1. **1971** Waterloo; Zeppelin. **1975** Frightmare.

DAVIS, ALLAN
Born: Aug. 30, 1913, London, England. Died: Dec. 11, 1943, Los Angeles, Calif. Screen, stage actor and stage director.

Appeared in: **1932** All American. **1935** Frisco Kid; Magnificent Obession. **1936** Under Your Spell. **1937** Marked Woman; Penrod and Sam; The Barrier. **1938** Swing Sister, Swing; Gold is Where You Find It; Over the Wall. **1939** Wings of the Navy; King of the Underworld; Big Town Czar. **1940** The Big Guy; Arise, My Love.

DAVIS, ANNA
Born: 1890. Died: May 5, 1945, Hollywood, Calif. Screen actress.

DAVIS, BOB "ALABAM"
Born: 1910. Died: Sept. 22, 1971, Hollywood, Calif. (heart attack). Screen actor and sometime stand-in for Franchot Tone.

Appeared in: **1936** Postal Inspector. **1940** The Mortal Storm. **1941** King of the Texas Rangers (serial). **1949** Knock on Any Door. **1951** The Lion Hunters. **1952** Red Ball Express. **1953** Jungle Drums of Africa (serial).

DAVIS, BOYD
Born: June 19, 1885, Santa Rosa, Calif. Died: Jan. 25, 1963, Hollywood, Calif. Screen and stage actor. Entered films in 1925.

Appeared in: **1932** Smiling Faces. **1941** You'll Never Get Rich; Two Latins from Manhattan. **1942** Hello, Annapolis; Harvard Here I Come; Star Spangled Rhythm; Blondie Goes to College; Once Upon a Honeymoon. **1943** So Proudly We Hail!; The Ghost Ship. **1944** Standing Room Only. **1945** Hold That Blond; Saratoga Trunk; Captain Eddie; Youth on Trial; Colonel Effingham's Raid. **1946** Terror by Night; The Unknown; Smooth as Silk; The Secret Heart; Night and Day. **1947** My Favorite Brunette; Blondie in the Dough; The Senator Was Indiscreet. **1948** The Wreck of the Hesperus; They Live by Night (aka The Twisted Road, and aka Your Red Wagon); A Foreign Affair; For the Love of Mary. **1949** Samson and Delilah; Ma and Pa Kettle. **1950** Girl's School; Perfect Strangers; Let's Dance. **1952** At Sword's Point.

DAVIS, CONRAD
Born: Feb. 29, 1915. Died: Dec. 22, 1969, Los Angeles, Calif. Screen actor.

DAVIS, DANNY
Born: 1929. Died: Feb. 10, 1970, N.Y. (struck by a car). Stage and screen actor, comedian/comedy writer.

Appeared in: **1946** The Bamboo Blonde.

DAVIS, EDWARDS
Born: 1871, Santa Clara, Calif. Died: May 16, 1936, Hollywood, Calif. Screen, stage and vaudeville actor.

Appeared in: **1920** The Invisible Ray (serial). **1921** The Right Way; Shams of Society; The Plaything of Broadway; The Silver Lining. **1924** Tainted Money; The Sea Hawk; Good Bad Boy; Hook and Ladder; The Woman on the Jury; On the Stroke of Three; The Only Woman; The Price She Paid; Stolen Secrets. **1925** The Best People; Flattery; Joanna; The Splendid Road; Part Time Wife; Not So Long Ago; Her Husband's Secret; The Charmer; Contraband; A Fool and His Money; My Neighbor's Wife. **1926** The Amateur Gentleman; High Steppers; Tramp, Tramp, Tramp; Butterflies in the Rain. **1927** A Hero on Horseback; The Life of Riley; A Reno Divorce; Face Value; Marriage;

Singed; Winds of the Pampas. **1928** The Sporting Age; Happiness Ahead; The Power of the Press. **1929** A Song of Kentucky. **1930** The Love Racket; Love in the Rough; Madam Satan; Madonna of the Streets. **1933** Hello, Everybody!

DAVIS, FAY
Born: Dec. 15, 1872, Boston, Mass. Died: Feb. 26, 1945, London, England. Screen and stage actress. Married to actor Gerald Lawrence (dec. 1957).

Appeared in: **1914** Enoch Arden. **1915** The Little Minister.

DAVIS, FREEMAN (aka BROTHER BONES)
Born: 1903. Died: June 14, 1974, Long Beach, Calif. Screen actor and whistler/entertainer.

Appeared in: **1941** Pot of Gold. **1951** Yes Sir, Mr. Bones.

DAVIS, REV. GARY
Born: 1896. Died: May 5, 1972, Hammonton, N.J. (heart attack). Black screen actor, gospel and blues singer.

Appeared in: **1970** Black Roots (documentary).

DAVIS, GEORGE
Born: 1889, Amsterdam, Holland. Died: Apr. 19, 1965, Woodland Hills, Calif. (cancer). Screen and vaudeville actor. Appeared in U.S., French, German, English and Italian films.

Appeared in: **1924** Sherlock, Jr.; He Who Gets Slapped. **1926** Into Her Kingdom. **1927** The Magic Flame. **1928** The Circus; The Wagon Show; The Awakening; the following shorts: Going Places; Leaping Luck; Who's Lyin'. **1929** 4 Devils; Broadway; The Kiss; Devil May Care. **1930** Men of the North; A Lady to Love; Not So Dumb; Die Sennsucht Jeder Frau; Le Petit Cafe; Le Spectre Vert (The Unholy Night). **1931** Parlor, Bedroom and Bath; Laugh and Get Rich; Strangers May Kiss; Private Lives. **1932** Arsene Lupin; The Man from Yesterday; Broken Lullaby; Love Me Tonight; Under-cover Man. **1934** The Scarlet Empress; The Black Cat. **1935** The Good Fairy. **1936** Next Time We Love; Desire; Angel. **1937** We Have Our Moments; History is Made at Night; I Met Him in Paris; Thin Ice; Charlie Chan at Monte Carlo; Conquest; You Can't Have Everything. **1938** The Baroness and the Butler; Passport Husband; Always Goodbye; Hunted Men. **1939** Topper Takes a Trip; Bulldog Drummond's Bride; Everything Happens at Night; Charlie Chan in City in Darkness; Ninotchka. **1940** Arise, My Love; Chad Hanna. **1941** Unfinished Business; That Hamilton Woman. **1945** This Love of Ours; The Dolly Sisters; See My Lawyer. **1946** The Kid from Brooklyn; If I'm Lucky. **1947** Mother Wore Tights; The Razor's Edge; Crime Doctor's Gamble. **1948** Arch of Triumph. **1949** Madame Bovary; Everybody Does It. **1950** Wabash Avenue. **1951** On the Riveria; Secrets of Monte Carlo; The Lady Says No; An American in Paris. **1952** The Snows of Kilimanjaro. **1953** Lili; Gentlemen Prefer Blondes. **1957** Les Girls. **1958** Ten North Frederick. **1963** Come Blow Your Horn. Other foreign films: Louis the Fox (English, French, German, and Italian versions); The Little Cafe (French version); The Queen's Husband (French version).

DAVIS, GEORGIA See SKELTON, GEORGIA

DAVIS, HAL
Born: 1910. Died: Jan. 4, 1960, Lancaster, Calif. (heart attack). Screen actor, choreographer and dancer.

Appeared in: **1927** The Bandit's Son. **1930** Case of Sergeant Grischa.

DAVIS, HARRY
Born: 1874. Died: Apr. 4, 1929, New York, N.Y. (heart disease). Screen and stage actor.

Appeared in: **1925** Old Clothes. **1926** Devil's Dice; Unknown Treasures; Whispering Canyon; Dangerous Friends; Lightning Reporter. **1927** The Blood Ship; Burning Gold. **1928** Runaway Girls; Crashing Through.

DAVIS, JACK
Died: 1968. Screen actor.

Appeared in: **1946** Up Goes Maisie; Behind Green Lights; Somewhere in the Night; Talk About a Lady; Strange Triangle; Night Editor; Gallant Bess; Secret of the Whistler; Shadowed. **1947** Sea of Grass; Blondie's Big Moment; The Millerson Case. **1948** Silver River. **1956** Crowded Paradise. **1967** The Gnome-Mobile.

DAVIS, JAMES GUNNIS
Born: 1874, Sunderland, England. Died: Mar. 23, 1937, Los Angeles, Calif. Stage and screen actor. Entered films in 1912.

Appeared in: **1921** A Certain Rich Man; The Secret of the Hills. **1922**

The Gray Dawn. **1923** The Midnight Alarm; Refuge; Chastity. **1924** Jealous Husbands; The Trouble Shooter. **1925** Lord Jim; Winds of Chance; His Lucky Horseshoe. **1927** Twinkle Toes; The Notorious Lady. **1928** Lilac Time. **1930** Headin' North. **1931** A Melon Drama (short); East Lynne; Charlie Chan Carries On. **1934** One More River. **1935** The Bride of Frankenstein.

DAVIS, JEFF (Jefferson Davis)
Born: 1884, Cincinnati, Ohio. Died: Apr. 5, 1968, Cincinnati, Ohio. Screen actor and self-proclaimed "Hobo King."

Appeared in: **1915** The Bridge of Sighs.

DAVIS, JIM (James Davis)
Born: Aug. 26, 1915, Edgerton, Mo. Died: Apr. 26, 1981, Northridge, Calif. (following surgery). Screen and television actor.

Appeared in: **1940** Safari. **1941** King of the Zombies. **1942** White Cargo; Keep 'Em Smiling (short). **1944** Cyclone Prairie Rangers. **1945** What Next, Corporal Hargrove? **1946** Gallant Bess. **1947** The Beginning of the End; The Fabulous Texan; The Romance of Rosy Ridge. **1948** Winter Meeting. **1949** Red Stallion in the Rockies; Hellfire; Brimstone; Yes Sir, That's My Baby; Mississippi Rhythm. **1950** The Savage Horde; Hi-Jacked; The Cariboo Trail; Square Dance Katy; The Showdown; California Passage. **1951** Little Big Horn; Three Desperate Men; Oh, Susanna; Calvary Scout; Silver Canyon; The Sea Hornet. **1952** The Big Sky; The Iron Mistress; Rose of Cimarron; Woman of the North Country; Ride the Man Down. **1953** The Woman They Almost Lynched; The President's Lady. **1954** Jubilee Trail; The Outcast; The Outlaw's Daughter; The Big Chase. **1955** The Last Command; Hell's Outpost; Timberjack; The Vanishing American. **1956** The Wild Dakotas; Blonde Bait; The Bottom of the Bottle; The Maverick Queen; Frontier Gambler. **1957** Lure of the Swamp; The Restless Breed; The Badge of Marshal Brennan; Duel of Apache Wells; The Quiet Gun; Apache Warrior; Raiders of Old California; Last Stagecoach West. **1958** Toughest Gun in Tombstone; Flaming Frontier; The Monster from Green Hell; Wolf Dog. **1959** Alias Jesse James. **1960** Lust to Kill; Noose for a Gunman. **1961** Frontier Uprising; The Gambler Wore a Gun. **1964** Iron Angel. **1965** Zebra in the Kitchen. **1966** Jesse James Meets Frankenstein's Daughter. **1967** Fort Utah; El Dorado. **1968** The Road Hustlers; They Ran for Their Lives. **1969** Five Bloody Graves; The Ice House (aka Love in Cold Blood and aka The Passion Pit). **1970** Monty Walsh; Rio Lobo. **1971** Dracula vs. Frankenstein. **1974** The Parallax View. **1977** The Choirboys. **1978** Comes a Horseman. **1980** The Day Time Ended.

DAVIS, JOAN
Born: June 29, 1907, St. Paul, Minn. Died: May 23, 1961, Palm Springs, Calif. (heart attack). Screen, radio and televison actress. Mother of actress Beverly Wills (dec. 1963).

Appeared in: **1935** Way Up Thar (short); Millions in the Air. **1937** The Holy Terror; On the Avenue; Time Out for Romance; The Great Hospital Mystery; Life Begins in College; Wake Up and Live; Thin Ice; Sing and Be Happy; Angel's Holiday; Love and Hisses; Nancy Steele Is Missing; You Can't Have Everything. **1938** Sally, Irene and Mary; Josette; My Lucky Star; Just Around the Corner; Hold That Co-ed. **1939** Day-Time Wife; Tail Spin; Too Busy to Work. **1940** Free, Blonde and 21; Manhattan Heartbeat; Sailor's Lady. **1941** Sun Valley Serenade; For Beauty's Sake; Two Latins from Manhattan; Hold That Ghost. **1942** Sweetheart of the Fleet; Yokel Boy. **1943** He's My Guy; Two Senoritas From Chicago; Around the World. **1944** Beautiful But Broke; Kansas City Kitty; Show Business. **1945** She Gets Her Man; George White's Scandals. **1946** She Wrote the Book. **1948** If You Knew Susie. **1949** Make Mine Laughs. **1950** Love That Brute; Traveling Saleswoman. **1951** The Groom Wore Spurs. **1952** Harem Girl. **1963** The Sound of Laughter (documentary).

DAVIS, KARL "KILLER"
Born: 1906. Died: May 30, 1979, Chicago, Ill. Screen, radio actor, country music singer, songwriter and musician.

Appeared in: **1951** Fingerprints Don't Lie; Mask of the Dragon. **1952** Young Man With Ideas. **1953** The Lost Planet (serial); Salome; Siren of Bagdad. **1954** The Egyptian; Demetrius and the Gladiators. **1955** Timberjack; Creature With the Atom Brain; Pirates of Tripoli; The Road to Denver. **1957** Apache Warrior; Zombies of Mora-Tau. **1958** The Bonnie Parker Story; Man or Gun.

DAVIS, MILDRED
Born: Jan. 1, 1900, Brooklyn, N.Y. Died: Aug. 18, 1969, Santa Monica, Calif. (heart attack). Screen actress. Married to actor Harold Lloyd (dec. 1971) and mother of actor Harold Lloyd, Jr. (dec. 1971).

Appeared in: **1916** Marriage a la Carte. **1919** His Royal Slyness; From Hand to Mouth. **1921** Among Those Present; Sailor-Made Man. **1922** Grandma's Boy; Doctor Jack. **1923** Condemned; Safety Last; Temporary Marriage. **1927** Too Many Crooks.

DAVIS, OWEN JR.
Born: 1907, New York, N.Y. Died: May 21, 1949, Long Island South, N.Y. (drowned—accident). Screen, stage and radio actor. Son of writer Owen Davis.

Appeared in: **1929** They Had to See Paris. **1930** Good Intentions; All Quiet on the Western Front. **1936** Bunker Bean; Murder on the Bridle Path; Special Investigator; Grand Jury; The Plot Thickens. **1937** It Could Happen to You; The Woman I Love. **1938** Touchdown Army. **1939** These Glamour Girls. **1940** Thou Shalt Not Kill; Knute Rockne—All American; Henry Goes to Arizona.

DAVIS, ROGER
Born: 1884. Died: Mar. 3, 1980, Woodland Hills, Calif. (cancer). Screen and stage actor. Do not confuse with other actors with the same name.

Appeared in: **1926** A Social Celebrity. **1929** The Woman Tamer (short). **1930** Are You There? **1938** Youth Takes a Fling. **1948** Miss Tatlock's Millions. **1949** Adam's Rib. **1952** Pat and Mike; The Belle of New York.

DAVIS, RUFE (Rufus Davidson)
Born: 1908, Dinson, Okla. Died: Dec. 13, 1974, Torrance, Calif. Screen, stage, radio and television actor.

Appeared in: **1937** Vitaphone shorts; Mountain Music; This Way Please; Blossoms on Broadway. **1938** Big Broadcast of 1938; Dr. Rhythm; Cocoanut Grove. **1939** Ambush; Some Like It Hot. **1940** Under Texas Skies; The Trail Blazers; Lone Star Raiders; Barnyard Follies. **1941** Prairie Pioneers; Pals of the Pecos; Saddlemates; Gangs of Sonora; Outlaws of the Cherokee Trail; Gauchos of El Dorado; West of Cimarron; Prairie Schooners. **1942** Code of the Outlaw; Westward, Ho; The Phantom Plainsmen; Riders of the Range. **1944** Jamboree. **1945** Radio Stars on Parade. **1948** The Strawberry Roan. **1952** Joe Palooka in the Triple Cross. **1969** Angel in My Pocket.

DAVIS, SPENCER
Born: Tennessee. Died: Sept. 13, 1976, New York, N.Y. Screen, stage and television actor.

Appeared in: **1956** The Wrong Man. **1964** Pie in the Sky; The World of Henry Orient. **1966** Terror in the City. **1973** The Way We Were.

DAW, EVELYN
Born: 1912, Geddes, S.Dak. Died: Nov. 29, 1970, San Diego, Calif. Screen, stage and opera actress.

Appeared in: **1937** Something to Sing About. **1938** Panamint's Bad Man.

DAWKINS, ERMA
Died: Oct. 13, 1972, Raleigh, N.C. Screen actress. Appeared in early Biograph Co. films.

DAWN, GLORIA
Born: 1929. Died: Apr. 2, 1978, Sydney, Australia (cancer). Screen, stage and vaudeville actress. Married to juggler/compere Frank Cleary. Mother of actress Donna Lee.

DAWN, ISABEL
Born: Oct. 20, 1905, Evansville, Ind. Died: June 29, 1966, Woodland Hills, Calif. (pulmonary infection). Screen, stage actress and screenwriter.

DAWSON, FRANK
Born: 1870. Died: Oct. 11, 1953, Hollywood, Calif. Screen actor.

Appeared in: **1934** Flirtation Walk; Double Door. **1935** My Marriage; The Last Outpost; Broadway Hostess. **1936** Rhythm on the Range; Private Number; Ladies in Love. **1937** A Day at the Races. **1938** Four Men and a Prayer; I'll Give a Million. **1939** The Adventures of Sherlock Holmes; Beau Geste; Cafe Society. **1940** The Blue Bird. **1941** Scotland Yard. **1942** They All Kissed the Bride. **1943** What A Woman; Crash Dive. **1944** Bermuda Mystery; Woman in the Window. **1945** Wilson.

DAWSON, IVO
Born: 1880, Rutlandshire, England. Died: Mar. 7, 1934, United States? Screen and stage actor.

Appeared in: **1918** Out of the Night. **1919** Miracle of Love. **1920** Footlights and Shadows; Love Without Questions. **1921** The Great Adventure; The Money Maniac; The Princess of New York. **1930** The Hate Ship; After the Verdict.

DAY, DULCIE
Born: 1911. Died: Dec. 1, 1954, Woodland Hills, Calif. Screen actress and singer.

Appeared in: **1934** Jealousy. **1946** Girl on the Spot. **1948** Hollow Triumph. **1950** The Jackpot. **1952** Something to Live For; Carrie. **1954** Deep in My Heart.

DAY, EDITH
Born: 1896, Minneapolis, Minn. Died: May 1, 1971, London, England. Stage and screen actress.

Appeared in: **1918** The Grain of Dust; A Romance of the Air.

DAY, JOSETTE
Born: 1914, France. Died: June 29, 1978, Paris, France. Screen actress. Divorced from film director Marcel Pagnol.

Appeared in: **1932** Allo Berlin, Ici Paris. **1936** Le Barbier de Seville (The Barber of Seville). **1937** Lucrezia Borgia; Club de Femmes. **1940** The Man of the Hour; La Fille du Puistier (The Well Digger's Daughter). **1941** The Mad Emperor. **1945** The Barge-Keeper's Daughter; La Belle et la Bete (Beauty and the Beast). **1948** Les Parents Terribles (aka The Storm Within—US 1950). **1950** Four Days Leave. **1951** Stolen Affections.

DAY, JULIETTE
Born: 1894, Boston, Mass. Died: Sept. 18, 1957, Huntington, N.Y. Screen and stage actress.

Appeared in: **1917** The Rainbow Girl; The Calendar Girl; Betty and Buccaneers.

DAY, MARIE L.
Born: 1855, Troy, N.Y. Died: Nov. 7, 1939, Cleveland, Ohio (pneumonia). Stage and screen actress.

Appeared in: **1922** Timothy's Quest. **1923** The Ragged Edge. **1938** Mother Cary's Chickens.

DAYKARHANOVA, TAMARA
Born: 1889, Russia. Died: Aug. 2, 1980, Englewood, N.J. Screen, stage, television actress and drama coach.

Appeared in: **1965** Andy. **1969** A Dream of Kings. **1977** The Three Sisters.

DAYTON, FRANK
Born: 1865, Boston, Mass. Died: Oct. 17, 1924, New York, N.Y. Stage and screen actor.

Appeared in: **1912** Lonesome Robert; Return of William; Signal Lights; The Fall of Montezuma; The Warning Hand. **1913** The Spy's Defeat; The Fall of the Marshes. **1915** Graustark; The Strange Case of Mary Page; The Great Silence.

DAZE, MERCEDES
Born: 1892. Died: Mar. 18, 1945, Los Angeles, Calif. Screen and stage actress.

DEAGAN, CHARLES
Born: 1880. Died: July 19, 1932, New York, N.Y. (heart failure). Screen, vaudeville and radio actor.

Appeared in vaudeville as part of "Charles and Madeline Dunbar" team.

DE ALBA, CARLOS
Born: 1925. Died: Oct., 1960, Mexico City; Mexico (after brain surgery). Screen and television actor.

DEAN, BARNEY
Born: 1904, Russia. Died: Aug. 31, 1954, Santa Monica, Calif. (cancer). Screen, vaudeville actor and screenwriter. Appeared in vaudeville with Sid Tarradasch as the "Dean Bros."

Appeared in: **1938** Thanks for the Memory. **1942** Star Spangled Rhythm. **1945** Duffy's Tavern. **1947** Variety Girl.

DEAN, BASIL
Born: Sept. 27, 1888, Croydon, London, England. Died: Apr. 22, 1978, London, England. Screen, stage actor, film director, film producer, stage director, stage producer, screenwriter, playwright and author. Divorced from Esther Van Gruisen, Lady Mercy Gerville, and actress Victoria Hopper.

DEAN, FABIAN (Gibilaro)
Born: 1930. Died: Jan. 15, 1971, Hollywood, Calif. Screen and television actor.

Appeared in: **1962** Fallguy. **1967** The Ride to Hangman's Tree; The Reluctant Astronaut. **1968** Candy; Single Room Furnished. **1970** The Computer Wore Tennis Shoes.

DEAN, IVOR
Born: 1917, England. Died: Aug. 10, 1974, Truro, Cornwall, England (heart failure). Screen and television actor. Married to actress Patricia Hamilton.

Appeared in: **1966** Theatre of Death (aka Blood Fiend—US 1967). **1967** The Sorcerers (US 1968); Stranger in the House (aka Cop-Out—US 1968). **1968** Decline and Fall of a Bird Watcher (US 1969); The File of the Golden Goose (US 1969); Where Eagles Dare (US 1969). **1969** The Oblong Box (aka Edgar Allan Poe's "The Oblong Box"); Crooks and Coronets (aka Sophie's Place—US 1970).

DEAN, JACK (John Wooster Dean)
Born: 1875, Washington. Died: June 23, 1950, New York, N.Y. Screen and stage actor. Married to actress Fannie Ward (dec. 1952).

Appeared in: **1915** The Cheat. **1916** Tennessee's Pardner; Witchcraft; The Years of the Locust. **1917** Betty to the Rescue; Her Strange Wedding; Unconquered; The Crystal Gazer; The Winning of Sally Temple; A School for Husbands. **1918** The Yellow Ticket. **1919** Sealed Hearts.

DEAN, JAMES (James Byron Dean)
Born: Feb. 8, 1931, Marion, Ind. Died: Sept. 30, 1955, near Paso Robles, Calif. (auto accident). Screen, stage and television actor. Nominated for 1955 Academy Award for Best Actor in East of Eden and in 1956 for Giant.

Appeared in: **1951** Fixed Bayonets; Sailor Beware. **1952** Has Anybody Seen My Girl. **1955** East of Eden; Rebel Without a Cause. **1956** Giant.

DEAN, JULIA
Born: May 12, 1878, St. Paul, Minn. Died: Oct. 17, 1952, Hollywood, Calif. Screen and stage actress.

Appeared in: **1915** How Molly Made Good; Judge Not. **1916** Matrimony. **1917** Rasputin; The Black Monk. **1942** The Cat People. **1944** Experiment Perilous; The Curse of the Cat People. **1946** Do You Love Me?; O.S.S. **1947** Magic Town; Nightmare Alley; Out of the Blue. **1948** The Emperor Waltz. **1949** Easy Living; Rimfire; Red Desert; Ringside; Treasure of Monte Cristo; Grand Canyon. **1950** Girl's School. **1951** People Will Talk; Elopement. **1952** You for Me; At Sword's Point.

DEAN, LOUIS
Born: 1876, Wilmington, Del. Died: Apr. 8, 1933, Honolulu, Hawaii (heart attack). Screen, stage actor and stage director. Married to actress Virginia Duncan.

Appeared in: **1916** Romeo and Juliet. **1917** The Tiger Woman; Darling of Paris. **1918** My Four Years in Germany; The Common Cause. **1919** Moonshine Trail; Sealed Hearts. **1920** Blood Barrier; Man and His Woman. **1922** Cardigan; Married People; The Woman Who Fooled Herself; Dawn of Revenge. **1923** For You, My Boy.

DEAN, MAN MOUNTAIN (Frank S. Leavitt)
Born: 1890. Died: May 29, 1953, Norcross, Ga. Screen actor and wrestler.

Appeared in: **1933** Private Life of Henry VIII (doubled for Charles Laughton). **1935** Reckless; We're in the Money. **1937** Three Legionaires; Big City. **1938** The Gladiator. **1949** Mighty Joe Young. **1955** The Woman for Joe; Man of the Moment.

DEAN, MAY
Died: Sept. 1, 1937, N.Y. Screen and stage actress.

Appeared in: **1923** Riders of the Range. **1935** Mississippi. **1937** A Damsel in Distress.

DEAN, NELSON (Nelson S. Whipple)
Born: 1882. Died: Dec. 19, 1923, Detroit, Mich. (apoplexy). Screen and stage actor.

DEAN, PAULA (Paula Hillburn aka PAULA HUNT)
Born: Aug. 1, 1881, Ga. Died: Mar. 27, 1930, Los Angeles, Calif. (cancer). Screen actress. Married to actor/director J. Stuart Blackton (dec. 1941). For family information see J. Stuart Blackton listing.

Appeared in: **1924** Monsieur Beaucaire. **1925** Raffles, the Amateur Cracksman.

DEAN, RALPH
Born: 1868. Died: Sept. 15, 1923, New York, N.Y. Screen, stage actor and film director.

DEAN, ROSE
Born: 1892. Died: Oct. 6, 1952, Hollywood, Calif. Screen actress.

DEAN, RUBY
Born: 1887. Died: Feb. 23, 1935, Cleveland, Ohio. Screen and vaudeville actress.

DE ANDA, AGUSTIN
Born: 1935, Mexico. Died: May 29, 1960, Mexico (murdered). Screen actor. Son of actor/producer Raoul de Anda. Entered films in 1952 with his father in a series of "Charro Negro" pictures.

DEANE, DORIS (aka DORRIS DEANE)
Born: 1901. Died: Mar. 24, 1974, Los Angeles, Calif. Screen actress. Divorced from actor Fatty Arbuckle (dec. 1933).

Appeared in: **1921** The Shark Master. **1922** The Half Breed.

DE ANGELIS, JEFFERSON
Born: Nov. 30, 1859, San Francisco, Calif. Died: Mar. 20, 1933, Orange, N.J. Screen and stage actor.

Appeared in: **1915** The Funny Side of Jealousy; Beware the Dog.

DEARHOLT, ASHTON
Born: Milwaukee, Wis. Died: Apr. 27, 1942. Screen actor and film producer. Divorced from actresses Helene Rosson and Florence Gilbert.

Appeared in: **1919** The Light. **1917** The Marked Heart; The Bride's Silence; Charity Castle; The Calendar Girl; Her Country's Call; Peggy Leads the Way. **1918** Beloved Rogue; Cabaret Girl; The Girl in the Dark; The Bride's Awakening; The Brass Buller (serial). **1919** Pitfalls of a Big City. **1920** Out of the Storm; Luck of Geraldine Laird; Slam Bang Jim; The Branded Four (serial). **1921** A Yankee Go-Getter. **1922** The Price of Youth; Impulse; The Sheriff of Sun-Dog. **1923** The Law Rustlers; At Devil's Gorge; Battling Bates; The Sting of the Scorpion. **1924** Cupid's Rustler; The Cowboy Prince; The Diamond Bandit; Lash of the Whip; The Lash of Pinto Pete; Western Feuds; A Rodeo Mixup; Western Yesterdays. **1926** West of the Law; Baited Trap. **1927** A Racing Romeo.

DEARING, EDGAR (aka EDGAR DEERING)
Born: May 4, 1893, Ceres, Calif. Died: Aug. 17, 1974, Woodland Hills, Calif. (lung cancer). Screen, stage and television actor.

Appeared in: **1927** The Second Hundred Years; Call of the Cuckoos. **1928** Leave 'Em Laughing; Their Purple Moment; Two Tars. **1929** The Jazz Age; The Locked Door. **1930** Free and Easy; Big Money; A Man from Wyoming; Abraham Lincoln; plus the following shorts: Live and Learn; Rich Uncles; Two Plus Fours. **1932** Horse Feathers. **1933** The Midnight Patrol. **1934** Thirty Day Princess; Cleopatra. **1935** The Crusades; The Nitwits; The Rainmakers; Lightning Strikes Twice. **1936** The Sky Parade; The Bride Walks Out; Swing Time; The Count Takes the Count (short); Down the Ribber (short); After the Thin Man. **1937** Saratoga; The Awful Truth; It Happened in Hollywood; They Gave Him a Gun; Love is News; Married Before Breakfast; Big City. **1938** Thanks for Everything; Border G-Man; Every Day's a Holiday. **1939** Honolulu; The Gracie Allen Murder Case; Twelve Crowded Hours; Blondie Meets the Boss; Torchy Plays With Dynamite; Some Like It Hot; Nick Carter, Master Detective. **1940** Go West; One Night in the Tropics; Little Orvie; Cross Country Romance; When the Daltons Rode; No Time for Comedy; Sailor's Lady; A Little Bit of Heaven; Lucky Partners; Hudson's Bay. **1941** Remember the Day; Design for Scandal; Kisses for Breakfast; Maisie Was a Lady; Pot O' Gold; Shadow of the Thin Man; The Big Store; Hold That Ghost; Caught in the Draft; Niagara Falls. **1942** Star Spangled Rhythm; Henry Aldrich, Editor; A Hunting We Will Go; Miss Annie Rooney; Wings for the Eagle; A Gentleman After Dark; Sullivan's Travels. **1943** Henry Aldrich Haunts a House; Henry Aldrich Swings It; The Good Fellows. **1944** Ghost Catchers; The Big Noise; In Society; Strange Affair; Seven Doors to Death; Bowery to Broadway; And the Angels Sing. **1945** Swing Out, Sister; Her Lucky Night; Don't Fence Me In; Scarlet Street; Road to Utopia. **1947** The Bishop's Wife; Variety Girl; Wild Harvest; Unconquered. **1948** The Return of the Whistler; Out of the Storm. **1949** Boston Blackie's Chinese Venture; Prison Warden; Sorrowful Jones. **1950** Fancy Pants; Right Cross; Raiders of Tomahawk Creek; Lightning Guns. **1951** As You Were (aka Present Arms); Silver Canyon; Riding the Outlaw Trail; Pecos River; Santa Fe. **1952** Carson City; The Kid from Broken Gun; My Wife's Best Friend. **1953** It Came from Outer Space. **1954** Her Twelve Men; Ma and Pa Kettle at Home. **1960** Pollyanna.

DEARLY, MAX
Born: 1874, France. Died: June 2, 1943, Paris, France. Screen and stage actor.

Appeared in: **1934** Madame Bovary. **1935** Le Dernier Milliardaire. **1936** Les Miserables. **1939** Ils Etaient Neufs Celibataires (Nine Bachelors—US 1942). **1940** Claudine. **1941** They Met on Skis.

DEASE, BOBBY (Robert C. McCahan)
Born: 1899. Died: Feb. 22, 1958, Reading, Pa. Screen actor.

Appeared in: **1939** Some Like It Hot. **1940** Dancing Co-ed.

DEASE, JOHN
Born: 1906, Upper Burma. Died: Feb. 1, 1979, Sydney, Australia (stroke). Screen, radio and television actor.

Appeared in: **1947** Pacific Adventure. **1970** Ned Kelly. **1979** Newsfront.

DE AUBRY, DIANE (Diane Rubini)
Born: 1890, Sault Ste. Marie, Mich. Died: May 24, 1969, Los Angeles, Calif. (heart attack). Screen, stage and vaudeville actress. Entered films with Biograph and World Films.

DEBALZAC, JEANNE
Born: France. Died: May, 1930, Paris, France. Screen actress.

DE BANZIE, BRENDA
Born: 1915, Manchester, England. Died: Mar. 5, 1981, Maywards Heath, Sussex, England. Screen, stage and television actress. Entered films in 1939 as an extra.

Appeared in: **1951** The Long Dark Hall. **1952** I Believe in You (US 1953). **1953** A Day to Remember (US 1955). **1954** Hobson's Choice; What Every Woman Wants; The Purple Plain (US 1955); Happiness of Three Woman. **1955** Doctor at Sea (US 1956); As Long as They're Happy (US 1957); A Kid for Two Farthings (US 1956). **1956** The Man Who Knew Too Much; House of Secrets (aka Triple Deception—US 1957). **1959** Too Many Crooks; Passport to Shame (aka Room 43—US); The 39 Steps (US 1960). **1960** The Entertainer. **1961** Come September; The Mark; Flame in the Streets (US 1962). **1962** I Thank a Fool; A Pair of Briefs (US 1963). **1964** The Pink Panther. **1967** Pretty Polly (aka A Matter of Innocence—US 1968).

DE BEAUSSET, MICHAEL
Died: Nov. 24, 1974. Screen actor.

Appeared in: **1964** Honeymoon of Horror. **1966** The Devil's Sisters. **1968** Mission Mars; The Hooked Generation. **1970** Darker Than Amber.

DE BECKER, HAROLD
Born: 1889, England. Died: July 23, 1947, Hollywood, Calif. Screen, stage and radio actor. Son of stage actress Kate De Becker (dec. 1946). Brother of actress Marie De Becker (dec. 1946).

Appeared in: **1942** Sherlock Holmes and the Secret Weapon; Eagle Squadron; This Above All. **1943** Sherlock Holmes Faces Death. **1944** The Lodger; The Pearl of Death. **1945** The Woman in Green; The Picture of Dorian Gray; Two O'Clock Courage. **1946** Cluny Brown.

DE BECKER, MARIE
Born: 1881. Died: Mar. 23, 1946, Hollywood, Calif. (heart attack). Screen and stage actress. Daughter of stage actress Kate De Becker (dec. 1946). Sister of actor Harold De Becker (dec. 1947).

Appeared in: **1942** Mrs. Miniver; Random Harvest. **1944** The Hour Before the Dawn; Sherlock Holmes and the Spider Woman; None But the Lonely Heart. **1946** Devotion.

DE BELLEVILLE, FREDERICK
Born: Feb. 17, 1857, Liege, Belgium. Died: Feb. 25, 1923, New York, N.Y. Screen and stage actor.

Appeared in: **1915** A Daughter of the People.

DEBLASIO, GENE (aka HOUSTON SAVOY aka HOUSTON SAVAGE)
Born: 1940. Died: Nov. 3, 1971, Arkansas (auto accident). Screen, stage and television actor.

Appeared in: **1970** The Losers.

DEBOZOKY, BARBARA (Barbara Springer)
Born: Nov. 10, 1871, Hungary. Died: Nov. 29, 1937, Los Angeles, Calif. (cancer). Stage and screen actress.

DE BRAY, HAROLD
Born: 1874. Died: Oct. 31, 1932, Los Angeles, Calif. (heart disease). Screen actor.

DE BRAY, HENRI
Born: 1889. Died: Apr. 5, 1965, Nottingham, England. Screen, stage, television actor and dancer.

DE BRAY, YVONNE
Born: 1889, France. Died: Feb. 1, 1954, Paris, France (heart aliment). Screen and stage actress.

Appeared in: **1944** The Eternal Return. **1949** Gigi; Les Parents Terribles (aka The Storm Within—US 1950). **1950** Olivia. **1952** Nous Sommes Tous Les Assassins. **1954** Caroline Cherie.

DE BRUGH, AIMEE
Born: Aberdeen, Scotland. Died: Apr. 2, 1946, England? Screen and stage actress. Divorced from actor Leon Quartermaine (dec. 1967), and later married to Gilbert Frankau.

Appeared in: **1912** Witch of the Welsh Mountains.

DE BRULIER, NIGEL
Born: 1878, England. Died: Jan. 30, 1948. Screen actor.

Appeared in: **1915** Ghost. **1916** Intolerance. **1917** 'Twixt Death and Dawn (serial); The Mystery Ship (serial); A Prince for a Day. **1918** Me und Gott; Kulter. **1919** The Mystery of 13 (serial); Sahara. **1920** Virgin of Stamboul. **1921** Cold Steel; The Devil Within; The Four Horsemen of the Apocalypse; His Pajama Girl; That Something; The Three Musketeers; Without Benefit of Clergy. **1922** A Doll's House; Omar the Tentmaker. **1923** Salome; The Eleventh Hour; The Hunchback of Notre Dame; Rupert of Hentzau; St. Elmo. **1924** A Boy of Flanders; Mademoiselle Midnight; Three Weeks; Wild Oranges. **1925** The Ancient Mariner; A Regular Fellow. **1926** Ben-Hur; Don Juan; The Greater Glory; Yellow Fingers. **1927** The Beloved Rogue; Patent Leather Kid; Soft Cushions; Surrender; Wings. **1928** The Divine Sinner; The Gaucho; Loves of an Actress; Me; Gangster; Two Lovers. **1929** Noah's Ark; The Iron Mask; Thru Different Eyes; The Wheel of Life. **1930** Golden Dawn; The Green Goddess; Moby Dick; Redemption. **1931** Song of India. **1932** Miss Pinkerton; Rasputin and the Empress. **1933** I'm No Angel; Life in the Raw. **1935** Charlie Chan in Egypt; The Three Musketeers (and 1921 version). **1936** San Francisco; Half Angel; Down to the Sea; Mary of Scotland; The Garden of Allah; The White Legion. **1937** Zorro Rides Again (serial); The Californians. **1939** The Hound of the Baskervilles; Mutiny in the Big House; The Man in the Iron Mask; The Mad Empress. **1940** Viva Cisco Kid; One Million B.C.; Heaven With a Barbed Wire Fence. **1941** For Beauty's Sake; Adventure of Captain Marvel (serial). **1943** Tonight We Raid Calais; Adventures of Smilin' Jack (serial).

DEBUCOURT, JEAN
Born: 1894, France. Died: Mar., 1958, Paris, France. Screen and stage actor.

Appeared in: **1922** Le Petit Chose. **1933** Mistigri. **1934** L'Agonie des Aigles. **1936** Le Prince Jean. **1937** Mayerling; The Life and Loves of Beethoven. **1940** Mayerling to Sarajevo. **1946** Le Diable au Corps. **1948** The Eagle Has Two Heads; The Idiot; Not Guilty; Monsieur Vincent. **1949** Man to Men; Woman Who Dared; Devil in the Flesh; Love Story; Occupe-Toi D'Amelie. **1950** Tainted. **1951** The Secret of Mayerling; Nana (US 1957). **1953** Justice Is Done; Fanfan La Tulipe (Fanfan the Tulip); Seven Deadly Sins. **1954** Desperate Decision; The Golden Coach. **1956** The Doctors; La Lumiere d'en Face (The Light Across the Street). **1958** Inspector Maigret. **1959** Proces au Vatican (Trial at the Vatican aka Miracle of Saint Theresa—US).

DE CAMP, FRANK
Born: 1865, London, England. Died: Dec. 18, 1919, England? Screen and stage actor.

Appeared in: **1916** Ambition. **1921** Suspicious Wives.

DE CAMP, GAYLE S.
Died: Dec. 30, 1976, Orlando, Fla. (heart attack). Screen actor, film director, film producer and stuntman. Entered films as an extra with RKO.

DE CARDO, WALTON FAY
Born: 1901. Died: Jan. 26, 1953, Burbank, Calif. Screen and stage actor.

DECARLOS, PERLA GRANDA
Born: 1903, Nicaragua. Died: June 8, 1973, Woodhaven, N.Y. Screen, stage and vaudeville actress. Married to actor Jack DeCarlos (dec.) with whom she appeared in a vaudeville act billed as "The DeCarlos."

Appeared in: **1933** Flying Down to Rio.

DE CASALIS, JEANNE (De Casalis de Pury)
Born: May 22, 1897, Basutoland, South Africa. Died: Aug. 19, 1966, London, England. Screen, stage, radio actress and playwright. Married to actor Colin Clive (dec. 1937).

Appeared in: **1925** Settled Out of Court (aka Evidence Enclosed). **1927** The Glad Eye; The Arcadians. **1928** Zero. **1930** Infatuation; Knowing Men. **1932** Nine 'Till Six. **1933** Radio Parade; Mixed Doubles. **1934** Nell Gwyn. **1938** Just Like a Woman. **1939** Jamaica Inn; The Girl Who Forgot. **1940** Charley's (Big Hearted) Aunt; Sailors Three (aka The Cockeyed Sailors—US 1941). **1941** Cottage to Let (aka Bombsight Stolen—US); Those Kids from Town. **1942** The Fine Feathers. **1943** They Met in the Dark (US 1945). **1944** Medal for the General. **1946** This Man Is Mine. **1947** The Turners of Prospect Road. **1948** Woman Hater (US 1949). **1950** The Twenty Questions Murder Mystery.

DE CASTREJON, BLANCA
Born: 1916, Mexico. Died: Dec. 26, 1969, Mexico City, Mexico. Screen and stage actress.

Appeared in: **1963** Signs of the Zodiac.

DECHAMPS, CHARLES
Born: 1890, France. Died: 1958, France? Screen actor.

Appeared in: **1939** Indiscretions. **1951** Oh, Amelia.

DE CICCO, PASQUALE "PAT"
Born: 1910. Died: Oct. 24, 1978, New York, N.Y. (cancer). Screen actor, film producer and theatrical agent. Divorced from artist and designer Gloria Vanderbilt.

Appeared in: **1935** Night Life of the Gods.

DECKER, HOWARD
Born: 1940. Died: Jan. 22, 1981, Eureka, Calif. Screen actor, stuntman and assistant film director. Entered films as a stuntman in 1960.

DECKER, JOHN
Born: Nov. 8, 1895, San Francisco, Calif. Died: June 7, 1947, Hollywood, Calif. (hemorrhage). Artist/painter employed to do stand-in-painting for actors playing role of artists. Was a pal of numerous famous Hollywood film personalities.

Appeared in: **1952** Cruise of the ZACA (Travelogue).

DECKER, KATHRYN BROWNE
Born: Richmond, Va. Died: Feb. 13, 1919, Colombo, Ceylon. Screen and stage actress.

Appeared in: **1915** The Prima Donna's Husband; The Beloved Vagabond; The Fifth Commandment; The Closing Net. **1917** The Pride of the Clan.

DECOMBIE, GUY
Born: France. Died: Aug., 1964, France? Screen actor.

Appeared in: **1936** Le Crime de Monsieur Lange. **1950** Francois Villon. **1952** Jour de Fete. **1957** The Winner's Circle. **1958** Inspector Maigret. **1959** Les Quarte Cents Coups (The 400 Blows); Les Cousins (The Cousins). **1961** Fever Heat.

DE COPPETT, THEODOSIA See BARA, THEDA

DE CORDOBA, PEDRO
Born: Sept. 28, 1881, New York, N.Y. Died: Sept. 17, 1950, Sunland, Calif. (heart attack). Screen, stage and radio actor. Married to stage actress Antoinette Glover (dec. 1921) and later married to Eleanor Mary Nolan.

Appeared in: **1915** Carmen. **1916** Temptation; Maria Rosa. **1917** Runaway Romany. **1919** The New Moon. **1920** The World and His Wife; Barbary Sheep. **1921** The Inner Chamber. **1922** The Young Diana; Just a Song at Twilight; When Knighthood Was in Flower. **1923** I Will Repay (aka Swords and the Woman—US 1924); The Enemies of Women; The Purple Highway. **1924** The Bandolero; The Desert Sheik. **1925** The New Commandment. **1933** Through the Centuries. **1935** The Crusades; Captain Blood; Professional Soldier. **1936** Ramona; Rose of the Rancho; Moonlight Murder; Trouble for Two; The Devil Doll; His Brothers's Wife; Anthony Adverse; The Garden of Allah. **1937** Firefly; Maid of Salem; Damaged Goods; Girl Loves Boy. **1938** International Settlement; Keep Smiling; Heart of the North; Storm Over Bengal. **1939** Chasing Danger; The Light That Failed; Juarez; Winner Take All; Man of Conquest; Law of the Pampas; Range War; Charlie Chan in the City in Darkness. **1940** My Favorite Wife; South of Pago-Pago; Earthbound; The Mark of Zorro; Devil's Island;

Before I Hang; The Sea Hawk; The Ghost Breakers. **1941** Paris Calling; Romance of the Rio Grande; Phantom Submarine; Blood and Sand; The Corsican Brothers; Aloma of the South Seas. **1942** Saboteur; The Son of Fury; Shut My Big Mouth. **1943** Tarzan Triumphs; The Song of Bernadette; Background to Danger; For Whom the Bell Tolls. **1944** Kismet; The Falcon in Mexico; Uncertain Glory; Tahiti Nights. **1945** Club Havana; Keys of the Kingdom; San Antonio; The Cisco Kid; In Old New Mexico; Picture of Dorian Gray. **1946** A Night in Paradise; Cuban Pete; A Scandal in Paris; Swamp Fire. **1947** Green Dolphin Street; The Beast With Five Fingers; Carnival in Costa Rica; Robin Hood of Monterey. **1948** Adventures of Don Juan; Time of Your Life; Mexican Hayride. **1949** Omoo Omoo the Shark God; The Daring Caballero; Daughter of the West; Samson and Delilah. **1950** Comanche Territory; The Lawless; When the Redskins Rode. **1951** Crisis.

DE CORDOVA, ARTURO (Arturo Garcia)
Born: May 8, 1907, Merida, Yucatan, Mexico. Died: Nov. 3, 1973, Mexico City, Mexico. Screen actor. Won Mexico's 1938, 1939 and 1940 motion picture industry Actor's Award.

Appeared in: **1934** Jealousy (film debut); Cielito Lindo (US 1936); La Zundunga; La Noche de Los Amayas; The Son's Command; Refugiados en Madrid; Miracle of Main Street. **1936** Celos. **1937** Esos Hombres. **1938** Ave sin Rumbo (Wandering Bird); Hombres de Mar (Men of the Sea). **1939** La Casa del Orgro (The House of the Ogre). **1940** Alexandra; Mientras Mexico Duerme (While Mexico Sleeps); Odio (Hate); La Bestia Negra (The Black Beast); El Conde de Monte Cristo (The Count of Monte Cristo—US 1943). **1941** Night of the Mayas. **1943** For Whom the Bell Tolls; Hostages; Rurales. **1944** Frenchman's Creek. **1945** A Medal for Benny; Incendiary Blonde; Duffy's Tavern; Masquerade in Mexico; La Selva de Fuego. **1946** Cinco Rostras de Mujer. **1947** New Orleans; The Flame. **1948** Adventures of Casanova. **1951** El. **1952** Stronghold; Reportaje. **1954** Kill Him for Me. **1955** This Strange Passion. **1962** Assassino (Assassins—aka The Violent and the Dammed); The New Invisible Man.

DECORDOVA, LEANDER
Born: 1878, Jamaica. Died: Sept. 19, 1969. Screen, stage actor and film director.

Appeared in: **1939** Zorro's Fighting Legion (serial); Midnight. **1947** Danger Street; Big Town. **1948** Casbah; Albuquerque.

DE CORDOVA, RUDOLPH
Born: 1860, Kingston, Jamica. Died: Jan. 11, 1941, London, England. Screen, stage actor, screenwriter, playwright and author. Married to stage actress/playwright Alicia Ramsey (dec. 1933).

Appeared in: **1922** The Glorious Adventure.

DE CORSIA, TED
Born: 1904. Died: Apr. 11, 1973, Encino, Calif. (natural causes). Screen, vaudeville, radio and television actor.

Appeared in: **1948** The Naked City; The Lady from Shanghai. **1949** The Life of Riley; Neptune's Daughter; It Happens Every Spring; Mr. Soft Touch. **1950** The Outriders; Cargo to Capetown; Three Secrets. **1951** The Enforcer (aka Murder, Inc.); Vengeance Valley; Inside the Walls of Folsom Prison; New Mexico; A Place in the Sun; Win, Place and Show. **1952** The Turning Point; Captain Pirate; The Savage. **1953** Man in the Dark; Ride, Vaquero!; Hot News. **1954** Crime Wave; 20,000 Leagues Under the Sea. **1955** The Big Combo; Kismet; Man With the Gun. **1956** The Steel Jungle; Slightly Scarlet; The Conqueror; The Killing; Dance With Me Henry; The Kettles in the Ozarks; Mohawk; Showdown at Abilene. **1957** Gunfight at the O.K. Corral; The Midnight Story; The Joker is Wild; Baby Face Nelson; The Lawless Eighties; Gun Battle at Monterey; Man on the Prowl. **1958** The Buccaneer; Enchanted Island; Handle With Care. **1959** Inside the Mafia. **1960** Spartacus; From the Terrace; Noose for a Gunman; Oklahoma Territory. **1962** It's Only Money. **1964** Blood on the Arrow; The Quick Gun. **1966** Nevada Smith. **1967** The King's Pirate. **1968** Five Card Stud. **1970** The Delta Factor.

DE COSTA, MORRIS (Morris Miller)
Born: 1890. Died: Oct. 6, 1957, Phoenixville, Pa. Screen and vaudeville actor and xylophonist. Appeared in silent films.

DECOY, ROBERT
Died: 1975. Black screen actor and writer.

Appeared in: **1964** Looking for Love.

DECTREAUX, EVELYN
Born: 1902. Died: Aug. 28, 1952, Santa Monica, Calif. Screen actress.

DE DIEGO, JULIO
Born: 1900, Spain. Died: Aug. 22, 1979, Sarasota, Fla. (cancer). Screen actor and artist. Divorced from actresses Rosalind Mallery and Gypsy Rose Lee (dec. 1970).

Appeared in: The Buccaneer.

DEE, FREDDIE (Freddie De Piano)
Born: 1924. Died: Apr. 27, 1958, Hollywood, Calif. Screen actor.

DEE, GEORGE
Died: Aug. 24, 1974, Calif.? Screen actor.

Appeared in: **1953** Gentlemen Prefer Blondes. **1955** We're No Angels. **1957** Funny Face.

DEED, ANDRE (Andre Chapuis aka CRETINETTI)
Born: 1884, Le Havre, France. Died: 1938, Paris, France. Screen, stage actor, singer, acrobat and music hall performer.

Appeared in: **1905** Boireau Demenage. **1907** Le Chevalier Mysters; Bureau Demanage; Les Apprentisages de Boireau. **1908** L'Homme Singe. **1909** Cretinetti alla Guerra. **1913** Boireau Domestique. **1915** Cretinetti e le Donne. **1928** Graine au Vent.

DEELEY, J. BERNARD "BEN"
Born: 1878. Died: Sept. 23, 1924, Hollywood, Calif. (pneumonia). Screen, stage and vaudeville actor. Divorced from actress Barbara La Marr (dec. 1925) with whom he had appeared in vaudeville.

Appeared in: **1919** Victory. **1921** Kazan; Molly O; Sowing the Wind. **1922** The Crossroads of New York. **1923** The Acquittal; Lights Out. **1924** Passions Pathway; Winner Take All; The Cycle Rider. **1925** Never the Twain Shall Meet.

DEEN, NEDRA (Elizabeth Ann Deen)
Born: Shreveport, La. Died: Dec. 29, 1975, Los Angeles, Calif. (cerebral hemorrhage). Screen, stage and television actress.

Appeared in: **1972** Conquest of the Planet of the Apes.

DEER, DIANE (aka DIANE DEERING)
Born: 1894. Died: May 30, 1979, New York, N.Y. Screen, stage, vaudeville actress and singer. Mother of producer/director Chris Christenberry.

Appeared in: **1921** Hurricane Hutch (serial).

DEERING, JOHN
Born: 1905. Died: Jan. 28, 1959, Hollywood, Calif. (cerebral hemorrhage). Screen, radio and television actor.

Appeared in: **1932** Forgotten Commandments. **1934** Most Precious Thing in Life. **1939** The Roaring Twenties; Confessions of a Nazi Spy.

DEETER, JASPER
Born: 1895, Mechanicsburg, Pa. Died: May 31, 1972, Media, Pa. Screen, stage actor, stage director, producer and drama coach.

Appeared in: **1959** 4D Man.

DEFERAUDY, MAURICE
Born: 1859, France. Died: May 12, 1932, France. Screen and stage actor.

DE FILIPPO, PEPPINO
Born: Aug. 24, 1903, Naples, Italy. Died: Jan. 26, 1980, Rome, Italy (heart and respiratory ailments). Screen, stage, vaudeville, television actor, stage director, playwright and impresario. Brother of actor, film director, film producer, screenwriter and author Eduardo De Filippo.

Appeared in: **1934** Il Capello a tre Punte (The Three Cornered Hat). **1937** Una Commedia Fra I Pazzi. **1940** Sono Stato Io (It Was I). **1949** The Peddler and the Lady. **1950** Escape Into Dreams. **1951** Luci del Varieta (Variety Lights—US 1965). **1952** The Bad Woman. **1954** Un Giorno in Pretura (A Day in Court—US 1963). **1959** Vacanzie a Izchia (aka Holiday Island—US 1960). **1960** Il Mattatore (aka Love and Larceny—US 1963); Fast and Sexy. **1962** Boccaccio '70.

DE FILIPPO, TITINA
Born: 1898, Italy. Died: 1963, France? Screen actress.

Appeared in: **1954** Side Street Story. **1957** Toto, Vittorio e la Dottoressa (aka The Lady Doctor—US 1963). **1958** Le Chair et Le Diable (The Flesh and the Devil, aka Flesh and Desire—US).

DEFOE, ANNETTE
Born: 1889. Died: Aug. 7, 1960, U.S. Screen actress.

Appeared in: **1917** Social Pirates (short). **1922** One Clear Call.

DE FOREST, HAL (Aloysius J. De Sylva)
Born: 1862. Died: Feb. 16, 1938, New York, N.Y. (heart attack). Screen, stage actor and stage director.

Appeared in: **1916** Daughter of the Gods (his only film).

DE FRECE, LAURI
Born: 1880, Liverpool, England. Died: Aug. 25, 1921, Deauville, England. Screen and stage actor. Married to actress Fay Compton (dec. 1978).

Appeared in: **1917** The Labour Leader. **1918** All the Sad World Needs.

DEGA, IGOR
Died: July 5, 1976, Burbank, Calif. (heart attack). Screen actor and dancer. Divorced from actress Ann Dvorak (dec. 1979), and dancer Mimi Dega.

Appeared in: **1947** My Wild Irish Rose.

DE GRASSE, JOSEPH
Born: 1873, Bathurst, New Brunswick, Canada. Died: May 25, 1940, Eagle Rock, Calif. (heart attack). Screen, stage actor, screenwriter, screen director and newspaperman. Brother of actor Sam De Grasse (dec. 1953). Entered films in 1910 as an actor.

Appeared in: **1924** So Big. **1928** The Cowboy Kid.

DE GRASSE, SAM
Born: 1875, Bathurst, New Brunswick, Canada. Died: Nov. 29, 1953, Hollywood, Calif. (heart attack). Screen actor. Brother of screen actor/director Joseph De Grasse (dec. 1940). Entered films in 1912.

Appeared in: **1916** The Good Bad Man; Birth of a Nation. **1917** Wild and Wooly. **1919** Sis Hopkins; Blind Husbands. **1920** The Devil's Pass Key. **1921** Courage; A Wife's Awakening; The Cheater Reformed. **1922** Robin Hood; Forsaking All Others. **1923** Circus Days; A Prince of a King; Slippy McGee; The Spoilers; Tiger Rose; The Courtship of Miles Standish; The Dancer of the Nile; In the Palace of the King. **1924** Painted People; The Virgin; Pagan Passions; A Self-Made Failure. **1925** One Year to Live; Sun-Up; Sally, Irene and Mary. **1926** Mike; Love's Blindness; The Black Pirate; Her Second Chance; Broken Hearts of Hollywood; The Eagle of the Sea. **1927** King of Kings; Captain Salvation; The Country Doctor; The Fighting Eagle; When a Man Loves; The Wreck of the Hesperus. **1928** Dog Law; The Racket; The Man Who Laughs; Honor Bound; Our Dancing Daughters; The Farmer's Daughter. **1929** Silks and Saddles; Last Performance; Wall Street. **1930** Captain of the Guard.

DE GREY, SYDNEY (Sidney de Gray)
Born: June 16, 1886, England. Died: June 30, 1941, Calif. Screen actor.

Appeared in: **1920** Jes' Call Me Jim; The Chorus Girl's Romance; The Mark of Zorro. **1921** The Innocent Cheat. **1922** Blood and Sand; The Half Breed; One Wonderful Night. **1923** The Oregon Trail (serial); Rouged Lips; The Love Brand; Other Men's Daughters; Single Handed; Trifling With Honor; The Wild Party. **1924** My Man; Wine of Youth; The King of Wild Horses; Cheap Kisses. **1925** Brand of Cowardice; Amerian Pluck; Steel of the Royal Mounted. **1926** Forest Havoc; The Amateur Gentleman; The Silver Treasure. **1927** Closed Gates; Bitter Apples; Naughty Nanette. **1930** Just Imagine; Three Sisters. **1932** Gay Buckaroo. **1934** Beggars in Ermine. **1935** Slightly Static (short). **1937** Hotel Haywire.

DEGUINGAND, PIERRE
Born: France. Died: June, 1964, France? Screen actor.

Appeared in: **1928** L'Equipage. **1929** The Last Flight. **1932** La Chance; Le Bal. **1938** The Call.

DE HAVEN, CARTER, JR.
Born: Dec. 23, 1910, New York, N.Y. Died: Mar. 1, 1979, Encino, Calif. Screen, stage actor, film director and film producer. Son of actors Flora Parker (dec. 1950) and Carter De Haven, Sr. (dec. 1977). Brother of David and actress Gloria De Haven.

Appeared in: **1930** Courage. **1940** The Great Dictator.

DE HAVEN, CARTER, SR.
Born: 1886, Chicago, Ill. Died: July 20, 1977, Woodland Hills, Calif. Screen, stage, vaudeville actor, film produceer, stage director, stage producer, screenwriter and playwright. Brother of actress Rose De Haven (dec. 1972). Divorced from actress Flora Parker (dec. 1950) with whom he appeared on stage and screen as "Mr. and Mrs. Carter De Haven." Father of David and actors Carter, Jr. (dec. 1979) and Gloria De Haven.

Appeared in: **1915** College Orphan. **1916** From Broadway to a Throne; Youth of Fortune; Timothy Dobbs, That's Me (series). **1917** A Gentleman of Nerve; His Little Roommate; Kicked Out; Where Are My Trousers?; The Losing Winner. **1919** In a Pinch. **1920** Twin Beds; Hoodooed (series). **1921** Girl in the Taxi; Marry the Poor Girl; My Lady Friends. **1923** Their First Vacation (series). **1925** The Thoroughbred. **1962** The Notorious Landlady. **1963** 30 Years of Fun (documentary).

DE HAVEN, FLORA (Flora Parker aka MRS. CARTER DE HAVEN, SR.)
Born: 1883, Perth, Amboy, N.J. Died: Sept. 9, 1950, Hollywood, Calif. Screen, stage and vaudeville actress. Divorced from actor Carter DeHaven (dec. 1977) with whom she appeared in "Mr. and Mrs. Carter DeHaven" comedy series. Mother of David and actors Carter, Jr. (dec. 1979) and Gloria DeHaven.

Appeared in: **1915** College Orphan. **1916** The Madcap; Youth of Fortune. **1919** Close to Nature; Why Divorce? **1920** Twin Beds; plus the following shorts: Beating Cheaters; Teasing the Soil; Excess Baggage; What Could Be Sweeter; Hoodooed. **1921** The Girl in the Taxi; Marry the Poor Girl; My Lady Friends. **1923** A Ringer for Dad.

DE HAVEN, MRS. CARTER, SR. *See* DE HAVEN, FLORA

DE HAVEN, ROSE
Born: 1881. Died: July 23, 1972, Hollywood, Calif. (heart ailment). Screen and stage actress. Sister of actor Carter De Haven, Sr. (dec. 1977).

DEHELLY, JEAN
Born: 1896, France. Died: 1964, France? Screen actor.

Appeared in: **1961** Graziella.

DEIGHTON, MARGA ANN
Died: Apr. 10, 1971. Screen actress.

Appeared in: **1939** Stagecoach. **1960** Seven Thieves.

DEININGER, DIANE
Born: 1894. Died: Nov. 24, 1978, Los Angeles, Calif. (heart attack). Screen and television actress.

Appeared in: **1963** Who's Got the Action? **1975** The Psychic Killer.

DE JONGE, HARRY
Died: Mar. 13, 1927, Chicago, Ill. Screen actor and film director.

Appeared in: **1914** The Eugenic Boy.

DE KEREKJARTO, DUCI
Born: 1901. Died: Jan. 3, 1962, Hollywood, Calif. (heart attack). Concert violinist and screen actor.

Appeared in prior to 1933: Metro Movietone short. **1951** Rich, Young and Pretty.

DEKKER, ALBERT (Albert Ecke)
Born: Dec. 20, 1904, Brooklyn, N.Y. Died: May 5, 1968, Hollywood, Calif. ("accidental death" per coroner). Screen, stage and television actor. Divorced from actress Esther Guerini. Served in California Legislature 1944 to 1946 as the Democratic Assemblyman of 57th District.

Appeared in: **1937** The Great Garrick. **1938** Marie Antoinette; The Last Warning; She Married an Artist; The Lone Wolf in Paris; Extortion. **1939** Paris Honeymoon; Never Say Die; Hotel Imperial; The Great Commandment; Beau Geste; The Man in the Iron Mask. **1940** Rangers of Fortune; Seven Sinners; Dr. Cyclops; Strange Cargo. **1941** You're the One; Blonde Inspiration; Reaching for the Sun; Buy Me That Town; Honky Tonk; Among the Living. **1942** The Lady Has Plans; Yokel Boy; The Forest Rangers; Night in New Orleans; Wake Island; Once Upon a Honeymoon; Star Spangled Rhythm. **1943** The Woman of the Town; In Old Oklahoma; Buckskin Frontier; The Kansan. **1944** Experiment Perilous; The Hitler Gang (narr.). **1945** Incendiary Blonde; Salome, Where She Danced; Hold That Blonde. **1946** Suspense; The French Key; Two Years Before the Mast; The Killers. **1947** California; Slave Girl; The Fabulous Texan; The Pretender; Gentleman's Agreement; Wyoming; Cass Timberlane. **1948** Fury at Furnace Creek; Lulu Belle. **1949** Bride of Vengeance; Tarzan's Magic Fountain; Search for Danger. **1950** Destination Murder; The Kid from Texas; The Furies. **1951** As Young as You Feel. **1952** Wait 'til the Sun Shines, Nellie. **1954** The Silver Chalice. **1955** East of Eden; Kiss Me Deadly; Illegal. **1957** She Devil. **1958** Machete. **1959** The Sound and the Fury; These Thousand Hills; Middle of the Night; The Wonderful Country; Suddenly, Last Summer. **1965** Daikaiju Gamera (Gammera the Invincible—US 1966). **1967** Come Spy With Me. **1969** The Wild Bunch.

DE KOCK, HUBERT
Born: 1863. Died: Nov. 25, 1941, Montrose, Calif. Screen, stage and vaudeville actor.

DE KOVA, FRANK
Born: 1910. Died: Oct. 15, 1981, Sepulveda, Calif. Screen, stage and television actor.

Appeared in: **1951** The Mob. **1952** Viva Zapata!; The Big Sky; Holiday for Sinners. **1953** The Robe; Raiders of the Seven Seas; Split Second; Fighter Attack; The Desert Song; King of the Khyber Rifles; Arrowhead; All the Brothers Were Valiant. **1954** They Rode West; Drum Beat; Passion. **1955** Strange Lady in Town; Hold Back Tomorrow; Shack Out on 101; The Man from Laramie. **1956** The Lone Ranger; The Ten Commandments; Santiago; Pillars of the Sky; Reprisal; The White Squaw. **1957** Run of the Arrow; Ride Out for Revenge. **1958** Machine Gun Kelly; Cowboy; The Brothers Karamazov; Apache Territory; Appointment With a Shadow; Teenage Caveman. **1959** Day of the Outlaw. **1960** The Rise and Fall of Legs Diamond. **1961** Atlantis, the Lost Continent; Portrait of a Mobster. **1962** The Scarface Mob; Follow That Dream. **1965** The Greatest Story Ever Told; The Sword of Ali Baba; Those Calloways. **1967** The Legend of the Boy and the Eagle (narrator). **1972** The Mechanic (aka Killer of Killers). **1973** Heavy Traffic; The Slams. **1974** Baby Needs a New Pair of Shoes. **1975** Johnny Firecloud.

DE KOWA, VIKTOR (Viktor Kowarzik)
Born: Mar. 8, 1904, near Goerlitz, Germany. Died: Apr. 8, 1973, Berlin, Germany (cancer). Screen, stage actor, film, stage and television director. Married to actress Michi Tanaka. Entered films in 1931.

Appeared in: **1931** Der Wahre Jakob. **1932** Der Stolz der 3 Kompagnie. **1934** Tannenberg; Der Junge Baron Neuhaus. **1935** Lockvogel; Die Finanzen des Grossherzogs (The Grand Duke's Finances). **1936** Das Schloss im Suden; Madonna, Wo Bist Du?; Pappi; Ein Lieb Geht um die Welt. **1937** Zwei im Sonnenschein. **1938** Herzensdieb (Heart Thief); Mit Versiegelter Order (Under Sealed Orders). **1951** The Joseph Schmidt Story. **1957** Des Teufels General (The Devil's General). **1958** Ein Liebesgeschichte (A Love Story). **1959** Das Madchen Scampolo (The Girl Scampolo); Embezzled Heaven. **1964** The House in Montevideo (aka Montevideo).

DE LACEY, JOHN
Born: 1872, New York, N.Y. Died: Dec. 18, 1924, New York, N.Y. (heart disease). Screen and stage actor.

Appeared in: **1916** Price of Malice. **1917** Broadway Jones; The Auction Block; Small Town Girl. **1918** Wanted for Murder; Queen of the Seas; The Cavell Case; Peg of the Pirates. **1919** The Unpardonable Sin; Prunella.

DE LA CRUZ, JOE (Jose De La Cruz)
Born: 1892. Died: Dec. 14, 1961. Screen actor.

Appeared in: **1922** The Bearcat. **1924** Western Yesterdays. **1930** A Devil With Women; Call of the West; Hell's Heroes. **1932** Trailing the Killer. **1933** Law and the Lawless. **1934** Four Frightened People. **1935** Unconquered Bandit; Lawless Border. **1936** Magnificent Obsession. **1939** Oklahoma Frontier. **1957** The Black Scorpion.

DELAMARE, GIL
Born: France. Died: June, 1966, near Paris, France. Screen actor and stuntman.

Appeared in: **1955** One Step to Eternity. **1960** Amazing Mr. Callaghan. **1964** That Man from Rio. **1966** Man from Cocody; Up to His Ears.

DE LA MOTHE, LEON
Born: 1880. Died: June 12, 1943, Woodland Hills, Calif. Screen actor and film director.

Appeared in: **1919** The Red Glove (serial). **1924** The Desert Hawk. **1925** Ridin' Wild; Northern Code. **1926** Desperate Chance; Cyclone Bob. **1928** Trailin' Back; Painted Trail; Trail Riders.

DE LA MOTTE, MARGURIETE
Born: June 22, 1902, Duluth, Minn. Died: Mar. 10, 1950, San Francisco, Calif. (cerebral thrombosis). Screen actress. Entered films in 1919. Married to actor John Bowers (dec. 1936).

Appeared in: **1919** Arizona. **1920** Mark of Zorro. **1921** The Three Musketeers; The Nut; Ten Dollar Raise. **1922** The Jilt; Shadows; Shattered Idols; Fools of Fortune. **1923** Desire; The Famous Mrs. Fair; What a Wife Learned; Just Like a Woman; Richard the Lion-Hearted;

Scars of Jealousy; A Man of Action; Wandering Daughters. **1924** The Beloved Brute; The Clean Heart; Behold This Woman; When a Man's a Man; Those Who Dare; East of Broadway; In Love With Love; Gerald Cranston's Lady. **1925** The People vs. Nancy Preston; Off the Highway; Cheaper to Marry; Flattery; Daughters Who Pay; Children of the Whirlwind; The Girl Who Wouldn't Work. **1926** The Unknown Soldier; Red Dice; Fifth Avenue; Hearts and Fists; The Last Frontier; Meet the Prince; Pals in Paradise. **1927** Broadway Madness; Held by the Law; Ragtime; The Kid Sister; His Final Extra. **1929** Montmartre Rose; The Iron Mask. **1930** Shadow Ranch. **1934** A Woman's Man. **1940** 'Til We Meet Again. **1942** Reg'lar Fellers; Overland Mail (serial).

DE LANDA, JUAN
Born: 1894, Motrico, Spain. Died: Feb. 18, 1968, Motrico, Spain. Screen actor and opera performer.

Appeared in: **1935** Se ha Fugado un Preso. **1938** The Penitentiary. **1947** The King's Jester. **1952** Brief Rapture. **1953** Devotion. **1954** Beat the Devil.

DELANEY, CHARLES
Born: Aug., 1892, New York, N.Y. Died: Aug. 31, 1959, Hollywood, Calif. Screen, stage, vaudeville and television actor.

Appeared in: **1922** Solomon in Society. **1923** The Devil's Partner. **1924** Emblems of Love; Those Who Dance; Barbara Frietchie. **1925** Accused; Sporting Life; Enemies of Youth. **1926** College Days; The Jade Cup; The Night Watch; Flaming Fury; Satan Town; The Sky Pirate; The Silent Power. **1927** The Main Event; Frisco Sally Levy; The Thirteenth Hour; Husband Hunters; Mountains of Manhattan; Lovelorn; The Silent Avenger; The Tired Business Man. **1928** Women Who Dare; The Cohens and the Kellys in Paris; Branded Man; After the Storm; The Air Circus; Home, James; The Show Girl; Stool Pigeon; The Adventurer; Do Your Duty; The River Woman; Outcast Souls. **1929** The Faker; Hard to Get; Girl from Woolworth's; The Clean-Up; Broadway Babies. **1930** The Man Hunter; Lonesome Trail; Kathleen Mavoureen; Around the Corner; Millie; Air Police; Playthings of Hollywood; Hell Bent for Frisco. **1932** Big Timber; Hearts of Humanity; Midnight Morals. **1933** Officer 13; Elmer the Great; Corruption; The Important Witness. **1934** Fighting Trooper; Big Time or Bust. **1935** What Price Crime?; Captured in Chinatown; Trails of the Wild. **1936** The Millionaire Kid; Below the Deadline. **1937** Bank Alarm; The Gold Racket. **1941** I'll Fix That (short). **1945** Blonde Ransom. **1950** Kansas Raiders. **1952** The Half-Breed. **1953** Winning of the West. **1954** The Bounty Hunter. **1959** Running Target. **1960** The Beatniks.

DELANEY, JERE A.
Born: 1888. Died: Jan. 2, 1954, Forest Hills, N.Y. Screen and stage actor. Married to stage actress Mary O'Moore (dec. 1980).

Appeared in: **1928** Lights of New York. **1929** Rubeville. **1954** On the Waterfront.

DELANEY, LEO
Born: 1885, Swanton, Vt. Died: Feb. 4, 1920, New York, N.Y. Screen actor.

Appeared in: **1911** Their Charming Mama; Vanity Fair; As You Like It; The Stumbling Block. **1912** The Love of John Ruskin; The Awakening of Bianca; The Mills of the Gods; Old Love Letters; The Days of Terror; The Light of St. Bernard; The Unknown Violinist; None But the Brave Deserve the Fair; The Extension Table; At Scorgineses Corner; A Lively Affair; Fate's Awful Jest; Her Boy. **1913** His Life for His Emperor; Bunny and the Bunny Hug.

DELANEY, MAUREEN (aka MAUREEN DELANY)
Born: 1888, Kilkenny, Ireland. Died: Mar. 27, 1961, London, England. Screen and stage actress.

Appeared in: **1947** Odd Man Out; Captain Boycott; Under Capricorn. **1948** Another Shore. **1952** The Holly and the Ivy (US 1953). **1956** The Long Arm (aka The Third Key—US 1957); Jacqueline. **1957** The Rising of the Moon; The Story of Esther Costello (aka Golden Virgin—US); The Scamp. **1958** Tread Softly Stranger (US 1959). **1959** The Doctor's Dilemma.

DE LANGE, BOB
Born: 1916, Holland. Died: Dec. 27, 1978, Holland? Screen actor.

Appeared in: **1958** Spy in the Sky.

DE LANGE, EDDIE
Born: 1904, Long Island City, N.Y. Died: July 16, 1949, Hollywood, Calif. Orchestra leader, screen actor, stuntman and composer. Stunted for Reginald Denny whom he resembled.

Appeared in: **1930** Half Shot at Sunrise.

DELANNOY, MONIQUE
Born: 1937, Belgium. Died: Apr. 25, 1979, Belgium (cancer). Screen and televison actress. Married to actor David Lachterman.

Appeared in: **1977** March or Die.

DELANO, GWEN
Born: 1882. Died: Nov. 20, 1954, Hollywood, Calif. Screen, stage, radio and television actress. Appeared in silents.

DELARGO, CELIA
Born: 1901. Died: Oct. 3, 1927, San Francisco, Calif. Screen actress.

DELARO, HATTIE
Born: 1861, Brooklyn, N.Y. Died: Apr. 18, 1941, New York. Screen, stage and vaudeville actress.

Appeared in: **1915** Old Homestead. **1916** Eternal Sapho; Scarlet Runner; Kennedy Square; Blindness of Love; The Quitter; The Upheaval. **1917** The Awakening of Helena Ritchie. **1918** Resurrection; Marriage. **1919** Mind the Paint Girl; False God. **1921** You Find It Everywhere. **1922** Cardigan; The Ragged Edge. **1924** Judith Meredith.

DE LA VEGA, ALFREDO GOMEZ
Born: 1897, Mexico. Died: Jan. 15, 1958, Mexico City, Mexico. Screen and stage actor.

DE LA VEGA, CARMEN
Died: Sept. 29, 1977. Screen actress.

DE LAY, MEL
Born: 1900. Died: May 3, 1947, Saugus, Calif. (heart attack—collapsed on location). Screen actor and film director. Entered films as an actor in 1923.

DE LEO, DON
Born: 1905. Died: Aug. 14, 1979, New York, N.Y. Screen, stage and television actor.

Appeared in: **1948** The Incident. **1951** The Mob; The Desert Fox. **1953** Salome. **1959** Happy Anniversary. **1961** The Hustler. **1962** Night of Evil. **1967** The Incident (and 1948 version).

DE LEON, ARISTIDES
Born: 1904. Died: July 23, 1954, New York, N.Y. Screen, stage, radio and television actor.

DELEON, RAOUL
Born: June 19, 1905, New York, N.Y. Died: Jan. 6, 1972, Los Angeles, Calif. (heart disease). Screen actor.

Appeared in: **1960** The Third Voice. **1962** Advise and Consent. **1964** The Pleasure Seekers.

DELEVANTI, CYRIL
Born: 1887, England. Died: Dec. 13, 1975, Hollywood, Calif. (lung cancer). Screen, stage and television actor.

Appeared in: **1931** Devotion. **1938** Red Barry (serial). **1940** A Dispatch from Reuters. **1941** Man Hunt. **1942** Journey for Margaret; Night Monster. **1943** Adventures of Smilin' Jack (serial). **1944** The Lodger; The Invisible Man's Revenge. **1945** Jade Mask; The Phantom of 42nd Street; Captain Tugboat Annie; This Love of Ours; Kitty. **1946** Deception; The Shadow Returns; I'll Be Yours. **1947** Forever Amber. **1948** The Emperor Waltz. **1951** David and Bathsheba. **1952** The Voice of Merrill. **1955** Land of the Pharoahs. **1957** Les Girls; Trooper Hook. **1958** Ride Out for Revenge. **1963** Bye Bye Birdie. **1964** Mary Poppins; Dead Ringer; Night of the Iguana. **1965** The Greatest Story Ever Told. **1967** Counterpoint; Oh Dad, Poor Dad, Mamma's Hung You in the Closet and I'm Feelin' So Sad. **1968** The Killing of Sister George. **1971** Bedknobs and Broomsticks. **1973** Soylent Green. **1974** Black Eye.

DELF, HARRY
Born: 1891. Died: Feb. 7, 1964, New York, N.Y. (heart attack). Screen actor, playwright, songwriter, dancer and comedian. Brother of stage actress Juliette Delf (dec.).

Appeared in: **1928** Harry Delf, the Popular Broadway Comedian (short); Soup (short); Giving In (short).

DELGADO, MARIA
Born: 1906. Died: June 24, 1969, Hollywood, Calif. Screen actress. Mother of actress Rosita Delva. Entered films approximately 1932.

Appeared in: **1956** Around the World in 80 Days.

DELGADO, ROGER
Born: 1920. Died: June 19, 1973, Turkey (auto accident). Screen, stage and television actor.

Appeared in: **1953** Star. **1955** Third Party Risk (aka Deadly Game—US). **1956** Storm Over the Nile; Battle of the River Plate (aka Pursuit of the Graf Spee—US 1957). **1957** Stowaway Girl; Man in the Shadow; Manuela. **1958** Sea Fury (US 1959). **1959** First Man Into Space. **1960** The Stranglers of Bombay. **1961** The Terror of the Tongs; The Singer Not the Song (US 1962). **1962** The Road to Hong Kong; In Search of the Castaways. **1963** The Mind Benders; The Running Man; Hot Enough for June (aka Agent 8 3/4—US 1965). **1965** Masquerade. **1966** Khartoum. **1967** The Mummy's Shroud. **1969** The Assassination Bureau. **1970** Underground.

DELIGHT, JUNE
Born: 1898, Rochester, N.Y. Died: Oct. 3, 1975, Carmel, Calif. Screen, stage, vaudeville actress and dancer.

Appeared in: **1920** Huckleberry Finn. **1923** The Ten Commandments.

DE LIGUORO, RINA
Born: 1893, Italy. Died: Apr., 1966, Rome, Italy. Screen actress.

Appeared in: **1923** Messalina. **1928** The Mystic Mirror. **1929** Loves of Casanova. **1930** Romance. **1963** The Leopard.

DE LIMUR, JEAN
Born: 1887, Vannes, Brittany, France. Died: June 5, 1976, Paris, France. Screen actor, film director and screenwriter.

Appeared in: **1922** The Worldly Madonna. **1924** The Arab.

DE LINDA, JUAN
Born: 1893, Motrice, Spain. Died: Feb. 17, 1968, Motrice, Spain. Screen actor.

Appeared in: **1979** The Penitentiary.

DELINSKY, VICTOR A.
Born: 1883. Died: May 8, 1951, Hollywood, Calif. (injuries from auto accident). Screen actor and stand-in for Adolphe Menjou.

Appeared in: **1927** King of Kings. **1935** Strange Wives.

DELL, CLAUDIA
Born: Jan. 10, 1910, San Antonio, Tex. Died: Sept. 5, 1977, Hollywood, Calif. Screen actress.

Appeared in: **1930** Sweet Kitty Bellairs; Big Boy. **1931** Sit Tight; Fifty Million Frenchmen; Bachelor Apartment; The Confessions of a Co-ed; Leftover Ladies; Sporting Chance. **1932** Scandal for Sale; The Midnight Lady; Destry Rides Again; Heart of Humanity; Guilty or Not Guilty; The Slippery Pearls (short). **1933** Midnight Warning; Big Bluff. **1934** Cleopatra; Woman Who Dared; Woman Condemned; Mama's Little Pirates (short). **1935** Lady in Scarlet; The Lost City (serial); Trail's End; Midnight Phantom; Anniversary Trouble (short). **1936** Yellow Cargo; Ghost Patrol. **1937** A Bride for Henry. **1938** Algiers; Angels With Dirty Faces; Juarez and Maximilian. **1943** Spotlight Scandals. **1944** Black Magic; Call of the Jungle.

DELL, DOROTHY (Dorothy Goff)
Born: Jan. 30, 1915, Hattiesburg, Miss. Died: June 8, 1934, Pasadena, Calif. (auto accident). Screen and stage actress.

Appeared in: **1934** Wharf Angel; Little Miss Marker; Shoot the Works.

DELL, RUPERT L.
Born: 1881, Oxfordshire, England. Died: Oct. 25, 1945, Los Angeles, Calif. Screen and stage actor.

DEL MAR, CLAIRE (Clare Eloise Mohr)
Born: 1901. Died: Jan. 10, 1959, Carmel, Calif. (murdered). Screen actress.

Appeared in: **1921** The Four Horsemen of the Apocalypse. **1927** The Jazz Singer. **1928** The Wedding March.

DELMAR, EDDIE (Robert Frandsen)
Born: 1886. Died: Mar. 2, 1944, Hollywood, Calif. Screen actor.

DELMONT, EDOUARD
Born: 1893, France. Died: 1955, France? Screen actor.

Appeared in: **1936** Les Amours de Toni. **1939** Le Famille Lefrancois (aka Heroes of the Marne); Heartbeat; Harvest; Port of Shadows. **1944** Three Hours. **1949** The Wench. **1951** Passion of Life. **1955** The Sheep Has Five Legs; Letters from My Windmill. **1956** The Return of Don Camillo. **1968** Toni (reissue of 1936 film Les Amours de Toni).

DELMONTE, JACK
Born: 1889. Died: June 8, 1973, New York, N.Y. Screen, stage and television actor.

DELMORE, RALPH
Born: Dec. 18, 1853. Died: Dec. 18, 1923, New York, N.Y. Screen and stage actor.

Appeared in: **1916** The Hand of Peril.

DELPHIN (Jules Sirveaux)
Born: 1882, France. Died: 1938, France. Dwarf screen and stage actor.

Appeared in: **1933** Zero de Conduite. **1935** La Kermesse Heroique. **1939** The Devil is an Empress.

DEL RIO, JACK
Died: Oct. 13, 1978. Screen actor.

Appeared in: **1950** Between Midnight and Dawn. **1955** We're No Angels.

DELTGEN, RENE
Born: 1909 or 1912, Esch-sur Alzette, Luxembourg. Died: Jan. 28, 1979, Cologne, West Germany (cancer). Screen and television actor.

Appeared in: **1935** Das Maedchen Johanna. **1936** Einer zu Viel an Bord; Port Arthur; Savoy-Hotel 217; Unter Heissem Himmel. **1937** Starke Herzen; Urlaub auf Ehrenwort. **1938** Schwarzfahrt ins Glueck (aka Die Kleine Suenderin (The Little Sinner)); Geheimzeichen LB 17; Ab Mitternacht; Kautschuk; Nordlicht. **1939** Der Gruene Kaiser; Kongo-Express (Congo Express—US 1940); Die Gruene Hoelle (The Green Hall). **1940** Das Leichte Maedchen; Achtung! Feind Hoert Mit!; Drei Codonas. **1941** Mein Leben fuer Irland; Spaehtrupp Hallgarten. **1942** Dr. Crippen an Bord; Fronttheater; Das Grosse Spiel; Anschlag auf Baku; Wen die Goetter Lieben (aka The Mozart Story—US 1948). **1943** Wenn der Junge Wein Blueht; Zirkus Renz; Kolberg. **1944** Das Hochzeitshotel; Zwischen Nacht und Morgen (aka Augen der Liebe); Sommernaechte. **1945** Wir Beiden Liebten Katharina; Der Stumme Gast. **1949** Nachtwache; Tromba, the Tiger Man (US 1952). **1950** Tobias Knopp, Abenteuer eines Junggesellen (voice); Export in Blond. **1951** Torreani. **1952** Das Letzte Rezept; Unter den Tausend Laternen. **1953** Weg ohne Umkehr; Keepers of the Night; Sterne Ueber Colombo. **1954** Die Gefangene des Maharadscha; Der Mann Meines Lebens; Der Letzte Sommer; Fruehlingslied; Phantom des Grossen Zeltes; Desires. **1955** Vom Himmel Gefallen (Special Delivery); Hotel Adlon; No Way Back. **1956** Ohne Dich wird es Nacht (Without You It is Night); Circus Girl. **1957** Koenigin Luise. **1959** Der Tiger von Eschnapur (The Tiger of Bengal, aka Das Indische Grabmal und aka Journey to the Lost City—US 1960); The House of Intrigue (aka London Calling North Pole). **1962** Die Blonde Frau des Maharadscha. **1964** Die Goldene Goettin vom Rio Beni (aka Golden Goddess of Rio Beni). **1965** Neues vom Hexer. **1966** Der Arzt Stellt Fest (aka The Doctor Says No—US 1967).

DE LULLO, GIORGIO
Born: 1921, Italy. Died: July 10, 1981, Rome, Italy (liver ailment). Screen, stage actor and stage director.

Appeared in: **1949** Professor, My Son. **1950** Heart and Soul. **1963** Il Processo di Verona (The Verona Trial).

DEL VAL, JEAN (Jean Gauthier)
Born: 1892, France. Died: Mar. 13, 1975, Pacific Palisades, Calif. (heart attack). Screen and televison actor.

Appeared in: **1924** A Sainted Devil. **1925** Fifty-Fifty; The Iron Man; A Man of Iron. **1927** Back to Liberty. **1930** Sea Legs. **1931** Women Men Marry; The Magnificent Lie. **1932** The Passionate Plumber. **1938** Blockheads. **1939** The Flying Deuces. **1940** Mystery Sea Raider; Arise, My Love; Drums of the Desert; Hudson's Bay; The Mark of Zorro; Brother Orchid. **1941** Paris Calling; Sergeant York; Outlaws of the Desert. **1942** Secret Agent of Japan; The Pied Piper; The Lady Has Plans; Gentleman Jim. **1943** For Whom the Bell Tolls; Paris After Dark; Mission to Moscow; Wintertime; The Song of Bernadette. **1944** Tampico; Passage to Marseilles; Irish Eyes Are Smiling; Uncertain Glory. **1945** The Spider; Molly and Me. **1946** So Dark the Night; 13 Rue Madeleine; The Razor's Edge; Gilda. **1947** The Foxes of Harrow; Life With Father; The Crime Doctor's Gamble; The Return of Monte Cristo. **1948** Repeat Performance; Siren of Atlantis. **1949** The Great Sinner; The Secret of St. Ives. **1950** Last of the Buccaneers; Under My Skin. **1953** The Hitch-Hiker; Little Boy Lost; Gentlemen Prefer Blondes. **1955** Pirates of Tripoli; Duel on the Mississippi. **1956** Anything Goes. **1957** Funny Face; The Sad Sack. **1960** Can-Can. **1961** The Devil at 4 O'Clock. **1966** Fantastic Voyage. **1967** Wait Until Dark.

DELYSIA, ALICE
Born: Mar. 3, 1889, Paris, France. Died: Feb. 9, 1979, Brighton, England. Screen, stage actress and singer.

Appeared in: **1916** She. **1934** Evensong.

DEMAIN, GORDON (aka GORDON D. WOOD)
Born: 1897. Died: Mar. 5, 1954. Screen actor. Married to actress Octavia Handford (dec. 1978).

Appeared in: **1929** The Marriage Playground; Why Leave Home? **1930** Headin' North; Men Are Like That; Young Eagles. **1931** Mata Hari; Rider of the Plains; Ridin' Fool; Rose of the Rio Grande; Son of the Plains; Ships of Hate. **1932** No Living Witness; Heart Punch; Honor of the Mounted; Galloping Thru; Two-Fisted Justice; Single-Handed Sanders. **1933** The Three Musketeers (serial); Cowboy Counsellor; Western Code; Behind Jury Doors; High Gear; Dude Bandit; Fighting Texans; Devil's Mate; The Fugitive; Rainbow Ranch; Lucky Larrigan; Return of Casey Jones. **1934** Chained; The Gay Bride; Beggars in Ermine; Mystery Liner; Lucky Texan. **1935** Port of Lost Dreams; Behind the Evidence; Lawless Frontier. **1937** The Painted Stallion (serial). **1941** International Lady; Thundering Hoofs; Honky Tonk.

DE MARCO, TONY
Born: 1898, Buffalo, N.Y. Died: Nov. 14, 1965, Palm Beach, Fla. (cerebral homorrhage). Screen actor and dancer.

Appeared in: **1938** The Shining Hour. **1943** The Gang's All Here. **1944** Greenwich Village.

DEMAREST, RUBIN
Born: 1886. Died: Sept. 20, 1962, Hollywood, Calif. (cerebral homorrhage). Screen and television actor. Brother of screen actor William Demarest.

Appeared in: **1939** The Gracie Allen Murder Case. **1941** A Girl, a Guy and a Gob.

DE MARNEY, DERRICK
Born: Sept. 21, 1906, London, England. Died: Feb. 18, 1978, London, England. Screen, stage actor, film director and film producer. Brother of actor Terence De Marney (dec. 1971).

Appeared in: **1928** The Adventurous Youth; The Forger; The Little Drummer Boys; Valley of the Ghosts. **1931** Shadows; Stranglehold. **1933** Laughter of Fools. **1934** Music Hall. **1935** Immortal Gentleman; Once in a New Moon; Windfall. **1936** Things to Come; Cafe Mascot; Land Without Music (aka Forbidden Music—US 1938). **1937** Young and Innocent (aka A Girl Was Young—US 1938; Victoria the Great. **1938** Sixty Glorious Years (aka Queen of Destiny—US); Pearls of the Crown. **1939** The Lion Has Wings (US 1940); Flying Fifty Five; The Spider. **1940** Three Silent Men; The Second Mr. Bush. **1941** Dangerous Moonlight (aka Suicide Squadron—US 1942). **1942** The First of the Few (aka Spitfire—US 1943). **1945** Latin Quarter. **1946** Franzy. **1947** Uncle Silas (aka The Inheritance—US 1951). **1948** Sleeping Car to Trieste (US 1949). **1950** She Shall Have Murder. **1954** Meet Mr. Callaghan. **1956** The March Hare; Private's Progress. **1963** Doomsday at Eleven. **1966** The Projected Man (US 1967).

DE MARNEY, TERRENCE
Born: Mar. 1, 1909. Died: May 25, 1971, London, England (accidental subway fall). Screen, stage, radio, television actor and stage director. Brother of actor Derrick DeMarney (dec. 1978). Married to Diana Hope Dunbar and later to actress Beryl Meason (dec. 1965).

Appeared in: **1931** The Eternal Feminine. **1932** The Merry Men of Sherwood; Heroes of the Mine. **1933** Eyes of the Fate; Little Napoleon. **1934** The Unholy Quest. **1935** Immortal Gentleman; The Mystery of the Mary Celeste (aka Phantom Ships—US 1937). **1936** Born That Way. **1937** The House of Silence. **1939** I Killed the Count (aka Who is Guilty?—US 1940). **1947** Duel Alibi. **1949** No Way Back. **1954** The Silver Chalice. **1955** Desert Sands; Target Zero. **1956** 23 Paces to Baker Street; Pharaoh's Curse. **1957** My Gun Is Quick. **1959** The Wreck of the Mary Deare. **1960** Spartacus; The Secret of the Purple Reef. **1961** On the Double. **1962** Confessions of an Opium Eater. **1965** Monster of Terror (aka Die, Monster, Die—US). **1966** Death Is a Woman (aka Love Is a Woman—US 1967); The Hand of Night (US 1968). **1968** Separation; The Strange Affair; All Neat in Black Stockings.

DE MAX, EDOUARD (aka M. DE MAX)
Born: Feb. 14, 1869, Jassy, Romania. Died: Oct. 28, 1924, Paris, France. Screen and stage actor.

DE MILLE, CECIL B.
Born: Aug. 12, 1881, Ashfield, Mass. Died: Jan. 21, 1959, Los Angeles, Calif. (heart disease). Film producer, director, screen, stage, radio actor and playwright. Brother of film director/producer William C. De Mille (dec. 1955). Married to actress Constance Adams (dec. 1960).

Appeared in: **1925** Hollywood. **1930** Free and Easy. **1931** The Squaw Man. **1935** Hollywood Extra Girl (short). **1937** The Last Train from Madrid. **1942** Star Spangled Rhythm. **1947** Variety Girl. **1949** History Brought to Life (short—narrator). **1950** Sunset Boulevard. **1952** Son of Paleface. **1957** The Heart of Show Business (narrator).

DE MILLE, WILLIAM C.
Born: July 25, 1878, Washington, D.C. Died: Mar. 8, 1955, Playa Del Rey, Calif. Playwright, screenwriter, film producer, director and one-time screen actor. Brother of film director/producer Cecil B. De Mille (dec. 1959).

DEMOTT, JOHN A.
Born: 1912. Died: Mar. 19, 1975, San Diego, Calif. (heart failure). Screen actor and television producer. One of the original members of "Our Gang" comedies.

DEMPSEY, CLIFFORD
Born: 1865. Died: Sept. 4, 1938, Atlantic Highlands, N.J. Stage and screen actor.

Appeared in: **1929** Salute; The Ghost Talks; Knights Out (short); Happy Days; The Valiant. **1930** Only Saps Work; Soup to Nuts. **1931** Too Many Cooks; Everything's Rosie. **1932** Guilty as Hell; Blonde Venus.

DEMPSEY, PAULINE
Born: 1868. Died: 1923, Harlem, N.Y. Screen actress.

Appeared in: **1920** The Good-Bad Wife. **1921** Women Men Love. **1922** Destiny's Isle; Broadway Rose. **1923** Modern Marriage.

DEMPSEY, THOMAS
Born: 1862. Died: Oct. 7, 1947, Hollywood, Calif. Screen, stage and vaudeville actor. Entered films during early 1920s and played for a number of years in Sennett comedies.

Appeared in: **1927** The Bush Leaguer. **1930** Goodbye Legs (short). **1932** A Fool About Women (short). **1934** Elmer and Elsie. **1936** Share the Wealth (short); Peppery Salt (short). **1937** Stuck in the Sticks (short). **1939** Maid to Order (short). **1940** Trailer Tragedy (short).

DE NEEF, DINY
Born: 1927, Holland. Died: June 28, 1978, Holland? Screen actress.

DENIAUD, YVES
Born: 1901, France. Died: 1959, France? Screen actor.

Appeared in: **1936** Le Crime de Monsieur Lange (The Crime of Monsieur Lange). **1948** Blind Desire. **1952** A Simple Case of Money. **1955** Dr. Knock. **1958** La Moucharde (aka Woman of Sin—US 1961).

DENISON, EDWIN
Born: 1863. Died: Jan. 26, 1928. Screen actor.

Appeared in: **1917** Seven Swans.

DENNIS, CRYSTAL
Born: 1893. Died: Dec. 16, 1973. Screen actress.

DENNIS, JOHN (John F. Sheehan)
Born: 1920. Died: July 30, 1973, Los Angeles, Calif. (shot). Screen and stage actor.

Appeared in: **1953** From Here to Eternity. **1955** The Naked Secret; Target Zero; Conquest of Space; Pete Kelly's Blues; Battle Taxi; The Return of Jack Slade. **1956** Calling Homicide. **1957** My Gun is Quick. **1958** Too Much, Too Soon; Frankenstein—1970; Violent Road; Hell's Highway. **1959** Revolt in the Big House. **1961** The Touchables. **1962** Convicts Four. **1965** Tickle Me; Quick, Before It Melts. **1966** Mister Buddwing; Lt. Robin Crusoe, U.S.N.; The Oscar. **1968** Never a Dull Moment. **1970** All the Loving Kinfolk; Fandango. **1972** Conquest of the Planet of the Apes. **1973** The Slams. **1974** Earthquake; Garden of the Dead.

DENNIS, NADINE
Born: 1896. Died: Aug. 11, 1979, Studio City, Calif. (heart attack). Silent screen actress. Sister of actresses Marjean Dennis and Kay Ramsey.

DENNIS, NICHOLAS "NICK"
Born: 1904. Died: Nov. 14, 1980, Los Angeles, Calif. (heart arrest). Screen, stage and television actor.

Appeared in: **1951** A Streetcar Named Desire; Ten Tall Men; Take Care of My Little Girl; Sirocco. **1952** Anything Can Happen; Eight Iron Men; The Iron Mistress. **1953** Man in the Dark?; The Glory Brigade. **1955** East of Eden; Top of the World; Kiss Me Deadly; The Big Knife. **1956** Hot Blood. **1957** Slaughter on Tenth Avenue. **1959** Alaska Passage. **1960** Spartacus. **1962** Too Late Blues; Birdman of Alcatraz. **1963** Four for Texas. **1966** Gunpoint. **1968** The Legend of Lylah Clare. **1969** The Good Guys and the Bad Guys.

DENNIS, RUSSELL
Born: 1916. Died: May 29, 1964, N.Y. (heart attack). Screen actor and physician.

Appeared in: **1951** Bright Victory.

DENNISTON, REYNOLDS
Born: 1881, Dunedin, New Zealand. Died: 1943, New York, N.Y. Screen and stage actor.

Appeared in: **1936** Love Letters of a Star.

DENNY, REGINALD (Reginald Leigh Daymore)
Born: Nov. 20, 1891, Richmond, Surrey, England. Died: June 16, 1967, Surrey, England (stroke). Screen, stage actor and screenwriter. Entered films in England in 1914. Starred in 24 "Leather Pusher" series (shorts) from 1922 to 1924.

Appeared in: **1920** 49 East. **1921** Footlights; Disraeli; The Iron Trail; Tropical Love; Paying the Piper; The Prince of Possession. **1922** The Kentucky Derby; Sherlock Holmes; plus the following "Leather Pusher" shorts: Let's Go; Round Two; Payment Through the Nose; A Fool and His Money; The Taming of the Shrew; Whipsawed; plus the following "New Leather Pusher" series shorts: Young King Cole; He Raised Kane; Chichasha Bone Crusher; When Kane Met Abel. **1923** The Abysmal Brute; The Thrill Chaser; plus the following "New Leather Pusher" series shorts: Strike Father, Strike Son; Joan of Newark; The Wandering Two; The Widower's Mite; Don Coyote; Something for Nothing; Columbia the Gem and the Ocean; Barnaby's Grudge; That Kid from Madrid; He Loops to Conquer. **1924** Sporting Youth; Captian Fearless; The Fast Worker; The Reckless Age; Oh, Doctor!; plus the following "New Leather Pusher" series shorts: Girls Will Be Girls; A Tough Tenderfoot; Swing Bad the Sailor; Big Boy Blue. **1925** Where Was I?; California Straight Ahead; I'll Show You the Town; Skinner's Dress Suit. **1926** Take It From Me; Rolling Home; What Happened to Jones? **1927** The Cheerful Fraud; On Your Toes; Out All Night; Fast and Furious; Jaws of Steel. **1928** The Night Bird; That's My Daddy; Good Morning, Judge. **1929** Clear the Decks; His Lucky Day; Red Hot Speed. **1930** Madam Satan; What a Man!; Embarrassing Moments; Those Three French Girls; Oh, for a Man!; One Hysterical Night; A Lady's Morals. **1931** Private Lives; Kiki; Parlor, Bedroom and Bath; Stepping Out. **1932** Strange Justice. **1933** The Iron Master; The Barbarian; Only Yesterday; The Big Bluff. **1934** Fog; Of Human Bondage; The Richest Girl in the World; The World Moves On; Dancing Man; One More River; We're Rich Again; The Lost Patrol; The Little Minister. **1935** Lottery Lover; No More Ladies; Vagabond Lady; Anna Karenina; Here's to Romance; Midnight Phantom; Remember Last Night?; The Lady in Scarlet. **1936** The Rest Cure; The Preview Murder Mystery; Romeo and Juliet; It Couldn't Have Happened; Two in a Crowd; More Than a Secretary; Penthouse Party. **1937** Join the Marines; Bulldog Drummond Escapes; The Great Gambini; Let's Get Married; Bulldog Drummond Comes Back; Bulldog Drummond's Revenge; Beg, Borrow or Steal; Women of Glamour; Jungle Menace (serial). **1938** Bulldog Drummond's Peril; Bulldog Drummond in Africa; Blockade; Four Men and a Prayer; Everybody's Baby. **1939** Bulldog Drummond's Bride; Bulldog Drummond's Secret Police; Arrest Bulldog Drummond. **1940** Spring Parade; Seven Sinners; Rebecca. **1941** One Night in Lisbon; Appointment for Love; International Squadron. **1942** Eyes in the Night; Sherlock Holmes and the Voice of Terror; Thunder Birds; Over My Dead Body; Captains of the Clouds. **1943** The Ghost Ship; The Crime Doctor's Strangest Case. **1944** Song of the Open Road. **1945** Love Letters. **1946** Tangier; The Locket. **1947** Escape Me Never; My Favorite Brunette; The Macomber Affair; Christmas Eve; The Secret Life of Walter Mitty. **1948** Mr. Blandings Builds His Dream House. **1950** The Iroquois Trail. **1953** Abbott and Costello Meet Dr. Jekyll and Mr. Hyde; Fort Vengeance; Hindu (aka Sadaka—US 1955). **1954** Bengal Brigade; The Snow Creature; World for Ransom. **1955** Escape to Burma. **1956** Around the World in 80 Days. **1957** Street of Sinners. **1959** Fort Vengeance. **1964** Advance to the Rear. **1965** Cat Ballou. **1966** Assault on a Queen; Batman.

DE NORMAND, GEORGE
Born: New York, N.Y. Died: Dec. 23, 1976, Woodland Hills, Calif. (cancer). Screen, television actor, film director and stuntman. Married to screenwriter Wanda Tuchock.

Appeared in: **1934** Pirate Treasure (serial). **1935** Melody Trail. **1937** The Painted Stallion (serial). **1942** West of the Law; Stardust on the Sage. **1943** The Ghost Rider; The Ghost Ship. **1945** Law of the Valley. **1947** Brick Bradford (serial). **1949** The Lost Tribe; The Gay Amigo; Satan's Cradle. **1950** Over the Border; Fence Riders; Gunslingers; Silver Raiders; Outlaw Gold; Outlaw of Texas; Six Gun Mesa. **1955** King of the Carnival (serial). **1961** A Raisin in the Sun. **1962** The Underwater City; Advice and Consent. **1968** The Money Jungle.

DENT, JOSEPHINE
Born: England. Died: Aug. 18, 1978, England? Screen and stage actress.

DENT, VERNON
Born: 1900, San Jose, Calif. Died: Nov. 5, 1963, Hollywood, Calif. Screen actor and screenwriter. Appeared in early Mann comedies, Mack Sennett and educational comedies.

Appeared in: **1921** Hail the Woman. **1923** The Extra Girl; Soul of the Beast. **1925** Remember When? **1926** A Dead Dog's Tale; Flirty Four-Flushers. **1927** His First Flame. **1928** Golf Windows; plus the following shorts: The Beach Club; The Best Man; The Bicycle Flirt; The Campus Carmen. **1929** Ticklish Business; The Talkies; plus the following shorts: The Old Barn; Girl Crazy; The Barber's Daughter. **1930** Johnny's Week End; Midnight Daddies; and the following shorts: Goodbye Legs; Take Your Medicine. **1931** Passport to Paradise; Fainting Lover (short); The Cannonball (short). **1932** Daring Danger; Texas Cyclone; Riding Tornado; Million Dollar Legs; plus the following shorts: The Big Flash; The Iceman's Ball; Hollywood Handicap; For the Love of Ludwig; Sunkissed Sweeties; A Fool About Women. **1933** The following shorts: Tired Feet; The Hitch Hiker; Knight Duty; Tied for Life; Marriage Humor; Hooks and Jabs; Roaming Romeo; Artist's Muddles; Three Little Swigs; On Ice. **1934** Manhattan Melodrama; You're Telling Me; plus the following shorts: Good Morning, Eve; Circus Hoodoo; Petting Preferred. **1935** I Don't Remember (short); Tuned Out (short); Tars and Stripes (short). **1936** San Francisco; plus the following shorts: Slippery Silks; Share the Wealth; Half-Shot Shooters. **1937** The Awful Truth; Easy Living; The Shadow; plus the following shorts: Dizzy Doctors; Back to the Woods; Calling All Doctors; Gracie at the Bat. **1938** Who Killed Gail Preston?; Juvenile Court; Thanks for the Memory; Reformatory; plus the following shorts: Sue My Lawyer; Wee Wee, Monsieur; Tassels in the Air; Mutts to You; Time Out For Trouble; The Mind Needer; Many Sappy Returns; A Doggone Mixup; The Old Raid Mule; Ankles Away; Home on the Rage. **1939** Mr. Smith Goes to Washington; Stanley and Livingstone; Beasts of Berlin; plus the following shorts: Teacher's Pest; Three Little Sew and Sews; A-Ducking They Did Go; Yes, We Have No Bonanza. **1940** The Lady in Question; plus the following shorts: From Nurse to Worse; Nutty But Nice; No Census, No Feeling; How High Is Up; The Heckler; His Bridal Fright; Cold Turkey; Mr. Clyde Goes to Broadway; A Bundle of Bliss; Pardon My Berth Marks. **1941** San Antonio; plus the following shorts: In the Sweet Pie and Pie; So Long, Mr. Chumps; Dutiful But Dumb; I'll Never Heil Again; An Ache in Every Stake; Ring and the Bell; Yankee Doodle Andy; Lovable Trouble; So You Won't Squawk. **1942** House of Errors; plus the following shorts: Loco Boy Makes Good; Cactus Makes Perfect; Even As I.O.U.; Tireman, Spare My Tires; Sappy Birthday; All Work and No Pay; Sappy Pappy; Matri-Phony. **1943** The following shorts: Blitz on the Fritz; Back from the Front; A Maid Made Mad; His Tale is Told; They Stooge to Conga; Higher Than a Kite. **1944** Mrs. Parkington; plus the following shorts: Crash Goes the Hash; Busy Buddies; Idle Roomers; No Dough, Boys; To Heir is Human; Defective Detectives; Snooper Service. **1945** She Gets Her Man; Rockin' in the Rockies; plus the following shorts: Three Pests in a Mess; Booby Dupes; Idiots Deluxe. **1946** The Harvey Girls; Renegades; plus the following shorts: A Bird in the Head; Beer Barrel Polecats; The Blonde Stayed On. **1947** It Had to Be You; Wild Harvest; plus the following shorts: Two Jills and a Jack; Half-Wits Holiday; Out West. **1948** The following shorts: Squareheads of the Round Table; Heavenly Daze; Mummu's Dummies; It's Great to Be Young; Eight-Ball Andy; Fiddlers Three. **1949** Make Believe Ballroom; plus the following shorts: Malice in the Palace; Hocus Pocus; Fuelin' Around. **1950** Punchy Cowpunchers (short); Studio Stoops (short). **1951** Bonanza Town; plus the following shorts: The Tooth Will Out; Three Arabian Nuts; The Pest Man Wins; Scrambled Brains. **1952** The following shorts; A Missed Fortune; Listen Judge; Gents in a Jam. **1953** Booty and the Beast (short); Rip Sew and Stitch (short). **1954** Musty Musketeers (short); Pal and Gals (short). **1955** Bedlam in Paradise (short). **1956** Hot Stuff (short). **1957** Andy Goes Wild (short). **1957** Gun A-Poppin (short). **1960** When Comedy Was King (documentary). **1963** Thirty Years of Fun (documentary).

DENTON, CRAHAN
Born: 1914. Died: Dec. 4, 1966, Piedmont, Calif. (heart attack). Screen, stage and television actor.

Appeared in: **1959** Great St. Louis Robbery. **1961** The Parent Trap; The Young One. **1962** To Kill a Mockingbird; Birdman of Alcatraz. **1963** Captain Newman, M.D.; Hud. **1965** Bus Riley's Back in Town.

DENTON, GEORGE
Born: 1865. Died: Mar. 12, 1918, New York, N.Y. (accidental asphyxiation). Stage and screen actor.

DENVER, MARYESTHER
Born: 1918. Died: June 3, 1980, Hollywood, Calif. Screen and television actress.

Appeared in: **1959** Born to be Loved. **1962** The Interns. **1963** Under the Yum Yum Tree. **1966** The Fortune Cookie; The Russians are Coming, the Russians are Coming. **1968** Project X.

DE OLIVEIRA, ANGENOR *See* CARTOLA

DEPARIS, WILBUR
Born: 1901, Indiana. Died: Jan. 3, 1973, New York, N.Y. Bandleader, trombonist, screen and television actor.

Appeared in: **1958** Windjammer (with his New Orleans Jazz Band).

DEPP, HARRY
Born: 1886. Died: Mar. 31, 1957, Hollywood, Calif. Screen actor.

Appeared in: **1916** Honest Thieves; A Male Governess; The Haunted House. **1917** Her Candy Kid; The Book Worm Turns; Her Birthday Knight; Skirt Strategy; The Girl and the Ring; A Janitor's Vengeance; Her Widow's Might; Half and Half; A Dark Room Secret; A Love Case. **1922** Quncy Adams Sawyer. **1923** His Last Race; Nobody's Money. **1924** Inez from Hollywood. **1926** When the Wife's Away. **1934** One Hour Late. **1935** Barbary Coast. **1936** The Big Broadcast of 1937; Desire. **1937** Bill Cracks Down; Swing It, Professor; The Go-Getter. **1938** Pals of the Saddle. **1939** Made for Each Other. **1940** The Mortal Storm. **1941** Blues in the Night. **1942** Priorities on Parade; The Magnificent Dope; Heart of the Rio Grande. **1944** Black Magic; The Lady and the Monster. **1945** Leave Her to Heaven. **1946** Two Smart People; Lady Luck.

DEPPE, HANS
Born: 1898, Berlin, Germany. Died: Sept. 23, 1969, West Berlin, Germany (diabetes). Screen, stage, television actor and film director.

Appeared in: **1933** Ein Tuer geht Auf. **1934** Der Stern von Valencia. **1935** Der Schimmelreiter (The Rider of the White Horse). **1958** The Berliner.

DE PUTTI, LYA
Born: 1901, Budapest, Hungary. Died: Nov. 27, 1931, New York, N.Y. (pneumonia after operation). Screen, stage and vaudeville actor. Entered films in 1921 and appeared in German, British and U.S. films.

Appeared in: **1921** Das Indische Grabmal (The Indian Tomb, including Die Sendung des Yoghi and Der Tiger von Eschnapur). **1922** Der Brennende Acker; Ilona; Othello; Phantom (US 1925). **1923** Die Fledermaus; SOS die Insel der Traenen; Die Schlucht des Todes (aka Pampasreiter); Thamar, das Kind der Berge. **1924** Komoedianten; Malva; Claire (aka Die Geschichte Eines Jungen Maedchens). **1925** Im Namen des Kaisers; Vareite (Variety); Eifersucht (Jealousy—US 1928). **1926** Junges Blut; Manon Lescaut; God Gave Me Twenty Cents; The Sorrows of Satan; The Prince of Tempters. **1927** The Heart Thief. **1928** Midnight Rose; Buck Privates; The Scarlet Lady; Charlott Etwas Verrueckt. **1929** The Informer.

DE QUICK, ALFO
Born: 1901, Belgium. Died: May 23, 1978, Belgium? Screen actor and opera singer.

DERAVENNE, CAROLINE MARIE
Born: 1883. Died: May 8, 1962. Screen actress.

DE RAVENNE, RAYMOND
Born: 1904. Died: Oct. 14, 1950, Hollywood, Calif. (heart attack). Screen actor.

Appeared in: **1938** Romance in the Dark; Artists and Models Abroad. **1947** The Perils of Pauline. **1950** Mister 880.

DERBA, MIMI (Hermina Perez de Leon)
Born: 1894, Mexico. Died: July, 1953, Mexico City, Mexico (lung trouble). Stage and screen actress.

Appeared in: **1935** Martin Garatuza. **1936** So Juana Ines de La Cruz. **1938** Abnegacion. **1945** Flor Sylvestre.

DEREN, MAYA
Born: 1908, Russia. Died: 1961. Screen actress, film director, dancer and author.

Appeared in: **1943** Meshes of the Afternoon. **1944** At Land. **1961** Maeva (narrator).

DERMO, PIERRE (Leopold Molders)
Born: 1911, United States. Died: June 15, 1976, Liege, Belgium. Screen and stage actor.

DE ROCHE, CHARLES
Born: 1880, France. Died: Feb. 2, 1952, Paris, France. Screen, stage actor and stage producer.

Appeared in: **1923** Hollywood; The Law of the Lawless; The Ten Commandments; The Cheat; The Marriage Maker. **1924** Love and Glory; Shadows of Paris; The White Moth. **1925** Madame Sans Gene.

DE ROSAS, ENRIQUE
Born: Argentina. Died: Jan. 20, 1948, near Buenos Aires, Argentina. Screen, stage, radio actor and circus performer.

Appeared in: **1937** Sandflow. **1939** We Are Not Alone.

DERWENT, CLARENCE
Born: Mar. 23, 1884, London, England. Died: Aug. 6, 1959, New York, N.Y. Screen, stage actor and film director.

Appeared in: **1918** Men Who Have Made Love to Me. **1931** The Night Angel. **1939** Stanley and Livingston; The Story of Vernon and Irene Castle. **1940** British Intelligence. **1958** Uncle Vanya (stage and film version).

DESAI, V. H.
Born: India. Died: c. 1950, India? Screen actor.

Appeared in: **1943** Gyandev of India.

DES AUTELS, VAN
Born: 1911. Died: Sept. 2, 1968, Los Angeles, Calif. Screen, radio and television actor.

Appeared in: **1953** The Robe; How to Marry a Millionaire. **1955** Inside Detroit; The Crooked Web.

DE SEGUROLA, ANDREAS (Count Andreas Perello de Segurola)
Born: 1875, Madrid, Spain. Died: Jan. 23, 1953, Barcelona, Spain. Screen, stage actor and opera performer.

Appeared in: **1927** The Love of Sunya. **1928** The Red Dance; Glorious Betsy; My Man; Bringing Up Father; The Cardboard Lover. **1929** Behind Closed Doors; Careers; General Crack. **1930** Mamba; The Man From Blankleys; Son O' My Heart. **1933** Cascarrabia; Su Eltimo Amor; El Principe Gondolero. **1934** La Ciudad de Carton; Ganaderos del Amore; Dos Mas Uno Dos; One Night of Love; We're Rich Again. **1935** Public Opinion.

DESFIS, ANGELO
Born: 1888. Died: July 28, 1950, Hollywood, Calif. Screen and stage actor. Appeared in silents and talkies.

DESHON, FLORENCE
Born: 1894, Tacoma, Wash. Died: Feb. 4, 1922, New York, N.Y. (accidental gas asphyxiation). Screen and stage actress.

Appeared in: **1917** The Auction Block. **1918** Clutch of Circumstance; Love Watches; The Other Man; The Desired Woman; A Bachelor's Children; The Golden Goal; One Thousand Dollars. **1919** The Cambric Mask. **1920** Dangerous Days; Duds; Dollars and Sense; Deep Waters; Twins of Suffering Creek; The Loves of Letty; The Cup of Fury. **1921** The Roof Tree.

DE SICA, VITTORIO
Born: July 7, 1901, Sora, Italy. Died: Nov. 13, 1974, Paris, France. Screen, stage, television actor, film director, producer, screenwriter and singer. Divorced from actress Giuditta Rissoni (dec. 1977). Married to actress Maria Mercader. Nominated for 1957 Academy Award for Best Supporting Actor for A Farewell to Arms.

Appeared in: **1932** Gli Uomini che Mascalzoni! (What Rascals Men Are!—film debut); Due Cuori Felici (Two Happy Hearts). **1933** Passa L'Ammore. **1935** Lohengrin; Non Ti Conosco Piu; Dario un Milione (I'll Give a Million). **1936** Ma Non e una Cosa Seria; L'Uomo Che Sorride; Questi Ragazzi; Amo Te Sola; Tempo Massimo; La Canzione del Sole. **1937** Il Signor Max; Napoli di Altri Tempi; Le Dame e i Cavalieri. **1938** Hanno Rapito un Uoma (They Have Kidnapped a Man); L'Orologio a Cucu (The Cuckoo Clock); Partire (Departure); Giochi di Societa (Society Games); Le Due Madri (The Two Mothers—US 1940). **1940** Due Dozzine di Rose Scarlette (Two Dozen Red Roses). **1941** Grandi Magazzini. **1942** Un Garibaldino in Convento. **1949** Lost in the Dark. **1950** Peddlin' in Society; Escape Into Dreams; Heart and Soul; My Widow and I. **1951** Doctor, Beware; Miracolo a Milano (Miracle in Milan); Altri Tempi (Times Gone By—US 1953). **1954** Pare, Amore e Gelosia (Bread, Love and Jealousy); The Earrings of Madame De; Hello Elephant; Pane, Amore e Fantasia (Bread, Love and Dreams). **1955** Gran Varieta; The Bed (aka The Divorce); Frisky; Too Bad She's Bad. **1957** Gold of Naples (aka The Gambler); The Miller's Beautiful Wife; Scandal in Sorrento; It Happened in the Park; A Farewell to Arms; The Monte Carlo Story; Les Week-ends de Neron (aka Nero's Mistress—US 1962 and Nero's Big Weekend); Toto Vittorio de la Dottoressa (aka The Lady Doctor—US 1963). **1958** A Plea for Passion (aka The Bigamist). **1959** Il Moralista (The Moralist—US 1964); Patri e Figli (Fathers and Sons, aka The Tailor's Maid); Anatomy of Love; Souvenier D'Italie (Souvenir of Italy, aka It Happened in Rome); Il Generale Della Rovere (General Della Rovere); Ballerina e Buon Dio (aka Angel in a Taxi—US 1963); Il Nemico di Mia Moglie (My Wife's Enemy—US 1967). **1960** Austerlitz; Always Victorious; It Started in Naples; The Angel Wore Red; Fast and Sexy; Vacanzie a Izchia (Holiday Island); The Millionairess (US 1961). **1961** The Wonders of Aladdin. **1962** La Fayette (Lafayette—US 1963); Eva (US 1963). **1965** The Amorous Adventures of Moll Flanders. **1966** After the Fox. **1968** The Biggest Bundle of Them All; The Shoes of the Fisherman. **1969** If It's Tuesday, This Must Be Belgium. **1974** Dracula.

DE SILVA, FRANK
Born: 1890, India. Died: Mar. 20, 1968, New York, N.Y. (throat cancer). Screen, stage and television actor.

DE SILVA, FRED F.
Born: Feb. 7, 1885, Lisbon, Portgual. Died: Feb. 16, 1929. Screen, stage, vaudeville actor and stage director.

Appeared in: **1920** Kismet. **1921** Thunder Island. **1922** The Fighting Guide. **1924** The Sea Hawk; Excitement; Passion's Pathway. **1925** The Rainbow Trail; Idaho (serial); Durand of the Bad Lands. **1926** The Bar-C Mystery (serial and feature film); Buffalo Bill of the U.P. Trail; Prisoners of the Storm.

DESJARDINS, MAXINE
Born: 1861, France. Died: Oct. 1, 1936, Venice, Italy. Screen and stage actor.

Appeared in: **1920** J'Accuse (I Accuse—US 1921). **1922** The Three Musketeers. **1928** The Legion of Terror. **1929** The Soul of France. **1931** Le Mystere de la Chambre Jaune.

DESLYS, GABY
Born: 1884, Marseilles, France. Died: Feb. 11, 1920, Paris, France (cancer of the throat). Screen and stage actor.

Appeared in: Rosy Rapture. **1915** Her Triumph. **1918** Infatuation.

DESMOND, ETHEL
Born: 1874. Died: Feb. 5, 1949, San Bernardino, Calif. Screen, stage and vaudeville actress.

DESMOND, LUCILLE
Born: 1894. Died: Nov. 20, 1936, Los Angeles, Calif. Screen actress.

DESMOND, WILLIAM
Born: Jan., 1878, Dublin, Ireland. Died: Nov. 3, 1949, Los Angeles, Calif. (heart attack). Screen, stage and vaudeville actor. Married to actress Mary McIvor (dec. 1941).

Appeared in: **1915** Peggy (film debut). **1916** Not My Sister; The Captive God. **1917** Paws of the Bear. **1918** An Honest Man; The Sudden Gentleman; Society for Sale; The Pretender; Deuce Duncan. **1920** The Prince and Betty; The Man From Make Believe; Twin Beds. **1921** The Child Thou Gavest Me; Dangerous Toys; Women Men Love; Don't Leave Your Husband; The Parish Priest; Fighting Mad. **1922** Perils of the Yukon; Night Life in Hollywood. **1923** The Extra Girl; McGuire of the Mounted; Shadows of the North; Beast of Paradise (serial); The Phantom Fortune (serial); Around the World in 18 Days (serial). **1924** The Breathless Moment; The Riddle Rider (serial); Big Timber; The Sunset Trail; Measure of a Man. **1925** Barriers of the Law; Duped; Outwitted; Straight Through; The Meddler; Ace of Spades (serial); Blood and Steel; The Burning Trail; Ridin' Pretty. **1926** The Winking Idol (serial); Strings of Steel (serial). **1927** The Return of the Riddle Rider (serial); Red Clay; Tongues of Scandal. **1928** The Vanishing Rider (serial); The Mystery Rider (serial); The

Devil's Trade-Mark. **1929** No Defense. **1931** Hell Bent for Frisco; First Aid; Oklahoma Jim; Battling With Buffalo Bill (serial); The Phantom of the West (serial); The Vanishing Legion (serial). **1932** The Jungle Mystery (serial); The Last Frontier (serial); Scarlet Week-End; Heroes of the West (serial). **1933** Flying Fury; Rustler's Round-Up; Laughing at Life; The Phantom of the Air (serial); Mr. Broadway; Fargo Express; Strawberry Roan; Clancy of the Mounted (serial); Gordon of Ghost City (serial); The Three Musketeers (serial). **1934** Perils of Pauline (serial); Pirate Treasure (serial); Frontier Days; Bordered Guns; The Red Rider (serial); Tailspin Tommy (serial); The Vanishing Shadow (serial); Rawhide Terror. **1935** Rustlers of Red Dog (serial); Roaring West (serial); Courage of the North; Powdersmoke Range; Frisco Kid; Cowboy and the Bandit; Cyclone of the Saddle; Rough Riding Range; Timber Terrors (stage and film versions); The Ghost Rider; Gun Fire; The Phantom Cowboy; Born to Battle; Defying the Law; Devil's Canyon; Five Bad Men; Nevada. **1936** Treachery Rides the Range; Custer's Last Stand (serial); The Black Coin (serial); The Vigilantes Are Coming (serial); Song of the Saddle; Cavalry; Hollywood Boulevard; Song of the Gringo; Headin' for the Rio Grande. **1937** Arizona Days. **1940** A Little Bit of Heaven; Winners of the West (serial). **1941** Bury Me Not on the Lone Prairie; Sky Raiders (serial). **1943** The Lone Star Trail. **1944** The Climax; Bowery to Broadway. **1945** Frontier Gal; Song of the Sarong; The Naughty Nineties.

DESMONDE, JERRY
Born: July 20, 1908, Middlesbrough, England. Died: Feb. 11, 1967, London, England. Screen, stage and television actor.

Appeared in: **1946** London Town (aka My Heart Goes Crazy—US 1953). **1949** Cardboard Cavalier. **1953** Alf's Baby; Malta Story (US 1954); Trouble in Store. **1954** The Angel Who Pawned Her Harp (US 1956). **1955** Man of the Moment. **1956** Ramsbottom Rides Again; Up in the World. **1957** A King in New York (US 1973). **1959** Follow a Star (US 1961). **1961** Carry On Regardless (US 1963). **1962** A Kind of Loving. **1963** The Stolen Hours; A Stitch in Time (US 1967). **1964** The Beauty Jungle (aka Contest Girl—US 1966). **1965** The Early Bird.

DESOTO, HENRY
Born: 1888. Died: Sept. 9, 1963. Screen actor.

Appeared in: **1942** Seven Day's Leave. **1946** Somewhere in the Night; The Dark Horse; Scarlet Street.

DESPRES, SUZANNE
Born: Dec. 16, 1875, Verdun, France. Died: July, 1951, France? Screen and stage actress.

Appeared in: **1935** Maria Chapdelaine. **1938** L'Equipage (aka Flight Into Darkness). **1940** Louise.

DES ROCHES, CECILIA *See* TOTO, BILLIE

DE STAFINI, HELEN
Born: 1880. Died: Jan. 8, 1938, Hollywood, Calif. Screen and stage actress. Married to screen actor Joseph de Stafini.

DESTE, LULI (Luli Kollsman and Luli Hohenberg)
Born: 1902, Vienna, Austria. Died: July 7, 1951, New York, N.Y. Stage and screen actress and author.

Appeared in: **1937** Thunder Over the City; Thank You, Madame. **1938** She Married an Artist. **1940** Ski Patrol; South to Karanga. **1941** The Case of the Black Parrot; Outlaws of the Desert.

DESTINN, EMMY
Born: Feb. 20, 1878, Prague, Czechoslovakia. Died: Jan. 28, 1930, Budweis, Czechoslovakia (stroke). Screen actress and opera performer.

Appeared in: **1914** The Lion's Bride.

DE TELLIER, MARIETTE
Born: 1891, France. Died: Dec. 11, 1957, Cincinnati, Ohio. Screen actress. Appeared in silents.

DE TOLLY, DEENA
Born: Russia. Died: Jan. 23, 1976, Hollywood, Calif. (stroke). Screen actress and dancer.

DEUTSCH, ERNST
Born: 1891, Germany. Died: Mar. 22, 1969, Berlin, Germany. Stage and screen actor.

Appeared in: **1917** Die Rache der Toten. **1919** Der Galeerensträfling; Die Geisha und der Samurai; Gerechtigkeit; Monika Vogelsang. **1920** Das Frauenhaus von Brescia; Der Golem wie er in die Welt Kam; Judith Trachtenberg; Die Tochter des Henkers; Von Morgens bis Mitternacht (From Morn to Midnight). **1921** Brennendes Land; Hannerl und ihr Liebhaber. **1922** Die Dame und der Landstreicher; Herzog Ferrantes Ende; Der Kampf ums Ich; Sein ist das Gericht. **1923** Die Pagode; Das Alte Gesetz (The Ancient Law); Mutter, Dein Kind Ruft (aka Brennende Geheimnis). **1924** Soll und Haben. **1926** Dagfin. **1927** Das Frauenhaus von Rio; Artisten; Zwei Unterm Himmelszelt. **1939** Nurse Edith Cavell. **1940** The Man I Married. **1941** So Ends Our Night. **1948** Der Prozess. **1949** The Third Man (US 1950). **1951** K—Das Haus des Schweigens. **1952** Wenn Abends die Heide Träumt; Symphonie Wien. **1958** Sebastian Kneipp.

DEUTSCH, LOU
Born: 1898. Died: Oct. 11, 1968, Calif. Screen actor. Appeared mostly in westerns.

DEVAL, MARGUERITE
Born: 1878, France. Died: Dec. 18, 1955, Paris, France. Screen and stage actress.

Appeared in: **1940** The Man of the Hour. **1942** Nine Bachelors. **1949** Marked Girls. **1953** The Spice of Life.

DE VALDEZ, CARLOS J.
Born: Mar. 19, 1894, Arica, Peru. Died: Oct. 30, 1939, Encino, Calif. Stage and screen actor.

Appeared in: **1934** Little Man, What Now?. **1935** Bonnie Scotland; Robin Hood of Eldorado. **1936** Men in Exile; The Beloved Rogue; Littlest Diplomat. **1937** Conquest; Drums of Destiny; Lancer Spy. **1938** Blockade; Romance in the Dark; Girl from Mexico; Suez; The Girl and the Gambler; The Llano Kid. **1939** Juarez. **1940** British Intelligence.

DEVAULL, WILLIAM P.
Born: 1871. Died: June 4, 1945, Hollywood, Calif. Screen and vaudeville actor.

Appeared in: **1915** Birth of a Nation. **1921** Hole in the Wall. **1922** White Shoulders. **1923** Around the World in 18 Days (serial); Kentucky Days; Tea With a Kick. **1925** Lights of Old Broadway. **1927** In the First Degree.

DE VERA, CRIS (Cristobal Masilongan)
Born: 1925. Died: June 25, 1974, Manilla, Philippines (kidney ailment). Screen, stage, radio and television actor. Known as the "Man With a Thousand Voices."

Appeared in: **1950** An American Guerrilla in the Philippines.

DEVERE, ARTHUR
Born: 1883. Died: Sept. 23, 1961, Brussels, Belgium. Screen, stage and vaudeville actor.

Appeared in: **1936** La Kermesse Heroique. **1939** The End of a Day. **1945** Goupi Mains-Rouges (It Happened at the Inn). Other French films: Un de la Legion; Midnight Circuit.

DEVERE, FRANCESCA "FRISCO"
Born: 1891. Died: Sept. 11, 1952, Port Townsend, Wash. (heart attack). Stage and screen actress. Appeared in Keystone comedies and Mack Sennett productions.

DEVERE, MARGARET
Born: 1889. Died: Oct. 24, 1918, New York, N.Y. (Spanish influenza). Screen actress.

DEVEREAUX, JACK
Born: 1882. Died: Jan. 19, 1958, New York, N.Y. Screen and stage actor. Married to stage actress Louise Drew (dec. 1954). Father of actor John Drew Devereaux.

Appeared in: **1916** The Sentimental Lady. **1917** Her Father's Keeper; America—That's All. **1920** Romero's Dad. **1922** Superstition.

DEVERELL, JOHN W.
Born: May 30, 1880, England. Died: Mar. 2, 1965, Haywards Heath, England. Stage and screen actor.

Appeared in: **1930** Children of Chance. **1931** Alibi. **1932** Monte Carlo Madness. **1934** The Path of Glory. **1935** Marry the Girl; The Divine Spark.

DE VERNON, FRANK
Born: 1845. Died: Oct. 19, 1923, New York, N.Y. Screen and stage actor.

Appeared in: **1921** The Black Panther's Cub; The Man Worth While. **1923** Under the Red Robe. **1924** Cain and Mabel; Yolande.

DEVESTEL, GUY
Died: Apr. 28, 1973. Screen actor.

Appeared in: **1949** Secret of St. Ives. **1950** The Toast of New Orleans. **1953** South Sea Woman. **1955** To Catch a Thief. **1964** Wild and Wonderful.

DEVI, PROVA
Born: India. Died: Nov. 8, 1952, India. Screen actress.

DEVINE, ANDY (Andrew Devine)
Born: Oct. 7, 1905, Flagstaff, Ariz. Died: Feb. 18, 1977, Orange, Calif. (leukemia). Screen, stage, radio, television actor and professional football player. Noted for his role as "Jingles" in the Wild Bill Hickock television series. Entered films as an extra in 1926.

Appeared in: **1928** We Americans; Red Lips. **1929** Naughty Baby; Hot Stuff. **1931** Spirit of Notre Dame; The Criminal Code; Danger Island (serial). **1932** Destry Rides Again; Law and Order; Three Wise Girls; The Impatient Maiden; Information Kid; Man Wanted; The Man from Yesterday; Radio Patrol; Tom Brown of Culver; Fast Companions; The All-American; Dangerous Brunette. **1933** The Cohens and Kellys in Trouble; Song of the Eagle; The Big Cage; Midnight Mary; Doctor Bull; Saturday's Millions; Chance at Millions; Lady of the Night. **1934** The Poor Rich; Stingaree; Let's Talk It Over; The Upper World; The Gift of Gab; Million Dollar Ransom; The President Vanishes; Wake Up and Dream; Hell in the Heavens. **1935** Hold 'Em Yale; Straight from the Heart; The Farmer Takes a Wife; Chinatown Squad; Fighting Youth; Way Down East; Coronado. **1936** Small Town Girl; Romeo and Juliet; The Big Game; Yellowstone; Flying Hostess. **1937** Mysterious Crossing; A Star is Born; The Road Back; Double or Nothing; You're a Sweetheart. **1938** In Old Chicago; Dr. Rhythm; Yellow Jack; The Storm; Strange Faces; Swing That Cheer; Men With Wings; Personal Secretary. **1939** Stagecoach; Never Say Die; The Spirit of Culver; Geronimo; Mutiny on the Blackhawk; Legion of Lost Flyers; Tropic Fury. **1940** The Man from Montreal; Little Old New York; Buck Benny Rides Again; Danger on Wheels; Torrid Zone; Hot Steel; When the Daltons Rode; The Leather Pushers; Black Diamonds; The Devil's Pipeline; Trail of the Vigilantes. **1941** A Dangerous Game; Lucky Devils; The Flame of New Orleans; Mutiny in the Arctic; Men of the Timberland; Badlands of Dakota; South of Tahiti; Road Agent; Raiders of the Desert; The Kid from Kansas. **1942** Unseen Enemy; North to the Klondike; Escape from Hong Kong; Danger in the Pacific; Between Us Girls; Sin Town; Top Sergeant. **1943** Rhythm of the Islands; Frontier Badmen; Corvette K-225; Crazy House. **1944** Ali Baba and the Forty Thieves; Follow the Boys; Ghost Catchers; Babes of Swing Street; Bowery to Broadway. **1945** Sundan; Frisco Sal; That's the Spirit; Frontier Gal. **1946** Canyon Passage. **1947** The Marauders; Slave Girl; Springtime in the Sierras; Bells of San Angelo; The Michigan Kid; On the Old Spanish Trail; The Vigilantes Return; The Fabulous Texan. **1948** The Gay Ranchero; Old Los Angeles; Under California Skies; Eyes of Texas; Grand Canyon Trail; Nighttime in Nevada; The Far Frontier; The Gallant Legion. **1949** The Last Bandit. **1950** Traveling Saleswoman; Never a Dull Moment. **1951** New Mexico; The Red Badge of Courage; Slaughter Trail. **1952** Montana Belle. **1953** Island in the Sky; Border City Rustlers; Six Gun Decision; Two-Gun Marshal. **1954** Thunder Pass. **1955** Pete Kelly's Blues. **1956** Around the World in 80 Days. **1960** The Adventures of Huckleberry Finn. **1961** Two Rode Together. **1962** The Man Who Shot Liberty Valance; How the West Was Won. **1963** It's a Mad, Mad, Mad, Mad World. **1965** Zebra in the Kitchen. **1968** The Ballad of Josie; The Road Hustlers. **1970** The Phynx; Myra Breckenridge. **1977** A Whale of a Tale.

DEVINE, GEORGE
Born: Nov. 20, 1910, London, England. Died: Jan. 20, 1966, England. Screen, stage actor, stage producer and director.

Appeared in: **1939** The Silent Battle (aka Continental Express—US 1942). **1952** The Card (aka The Promoter—US). **1953** The Beggar's Opera (US—1954). **1954** The Million Pound Note (aka Man With a Million—US). **1957** Time Without Pity. **1959** Look Back in Anger. **1963** Tom Jones.

DEVLIN, JOE A.
Born: 1899. Died: Oct. 1, 1973, Burbank, Calif. Screen, stage and television actor.

Appeared in: **1938** Angels With Dirty Faces. **1939** Another Thin Man; The Roaring Twenties; The Oklahoma Kid; Torchy Runs for Mayor; King of the Underworld; No Place to Go. **1940** A Fugitive From Justice; Half a Sinner; The Green Hornet Strikes Again (serial). **1941** Manpower; Shadow of the Thin Man; Whistling in the Dark; Unholy Partners; They Died With Their Boots On. **1942** Syncopation; The Devil With Hitler; Shepherd of the Ozarks. **1943** They Got Me Covered; The Phantom (serial); Taxi, Mister; That Nazty Nuisance; Hi

Diddle Diddle. **1944** Sensations of 1945; Dixie Jamboree; Delinquent Daughters; My Buddy; The Miracle of Morgan's Creek; See Here, Private Hargrove; Gambler's Choice; Johnny Doesn't Live Here Anymore. **1945** Without Love; Boston Blackie's Rendezvous; Mr. Skeffington; Bedside Manner; Captain Eddie; The Shanghai Cobra; Brenda Starr, Reporter (serial); Abbott and Costello in Hollywood. **1946** Criminal Court; Bringing Up Father; Trouble or Nothing (short); Oh, Professor, Behave (short); San Quentin; Scarlet Street. **1947** That Way With Women; Body and Soul; Shoot to Kill. **1948** Blood on the Moon. **1949** A Kiss in the Dark. **1951** Stop That Cab; Double Dynamite (aka It's Only Money); All That I Have. **1954** Bitter Creek; Silver Lode. **1955** Abbott and Costello Meet the Keystone Kops. **1956** Shake, Rattle and Rock. **1957** Up in Smoke. **1958** In the Money. **1959** Darby O'Gill and the Little People. **1967** Good Times.

DEVOE, BERT
Born: 1884. Died: Jan. 17, 1930, Steelton, Pa. (cancer). Screen and vaudeville actor. Toured in vaudeville with Lew Worth. Appeared in early Mack Sennett comedies.

Appeared in: **1924** Shackles of Fear.

DEVORE, DOROTHY (Alma Inez Williams)
Born: Sept. 1899, Fort Worth, Tex. Died: Sept. 10, 1976, Woodland Hills, Calif. Screen, stage, vaudeville actress, film producer and singer. Was a Wampas Baby Star of 1923. Billed in vaudeville as "Dorothy Devore Revue." Appeared in early Christie Comedies.

Appeared in: **1921** The Magnificent Brute; 45 Minutes from Broadway. **1923** When Odds are Even. **1924** Hold Your Breath; The Narrow Street; The Tomboy. **1925** A Broadway Butterfly; Fighting the Flames; How Baxter Butted In; His Majesty, Bunker Bean; The Prairie Wife; Who Cares?; Three Weeks in Paris. **1926** The Gilded Highway; The Man Upstairs; Money to Burn; Senor Daredevil; The Social Highwayman. **1927** The First Night; Better Days; Mountains of Manhattan; The Wrong Mr. Wright. **1928** No Babies Wanted. **1930** Take the Heir.

DEWAN, KARAN
Born: 1917, India. Died: Aug. 2, 1979, Bombay, India (stroke). Screen actor.

Appeared in: Rattan.

DE WARFAZ, GEORGE
Born: Dec. 2, 1889, Spain. Died: Oct. 14, 1959, England. Screen, stage actor and stage producer.

Appeared in: **1930** A Warm Corner; French Leave; At the Villa Rose (aka Mystery at the Villa Rose—US). **1931** Captivation; A Gentleman of Paris. **1932** Nine Till Six; It's a King. **1948** Sleeping Car to Trieste (US 1949). **1954** Beau Brummel.

DE WEESE, FRANK
Born: 1903. Died: Apr. 15, 1928, Salina, Kans. (sceptic poisoning). Screen actor.

Appeared in: **1926** The Quarterback. **1927** New York.

DEWEY, EARL S.
Born: June 2, 1881, Manhattan, Kans. Died: Feb. 5, 1950, Hollywood, Calif. Screen, stage and vaudeville actor. Married to Billie Rogers with whom he appeared in vaudeville. Appeared in "Pathe Folly" comedies, first series.

Appeared in: **1929** Fancy That (short); So This Is Marriage (short). **1940** Howards of Virginia; Arizona. **1941** H. M. Pulham, Esq.; Design for Scandal. **1942** I Married an Angel; This Gun for Hire; Between Us Girls. **1943** Seeing Nellie Home (short); Shadow of a Doubt. **1944** Say Uncle (short); Adventures of Mark Twain; Louisiana Hayride; The Imposter. **1945** Wilson; Rogues Gallery; Captain Eddie; George White's Scandals; Blonde Ransom. **1946** Deception. **1947** Tycoon. **1948** The Gallant Legion. **1950** All the King's Men.

DEWEY, ELMER (aka DON DANILO)
Born: 1884. Died: Oct. 28, 1954, Hollywood, Calif. (heart attack). Screen actor.

Appeared in: **1921** Bring Him In; Girls Don't Gamble. **1922** Taking Chances. **1926** Shadows of Chinatown; The Escape. **1927** Million Dollar Mystery.

DEWHURST, WILLIAM
Born: 1888. Died: Oct. 26, 1937, London, England (heart failure). Stage and screen actor.

Appeared in: **1937** A Woman Alone; Victoria the Great; Non-Stop New York; Dark Journey; Bulldog Drummond at Bay; Dinner at the Ritz. **1938** Sailing Along. **1939** Sabotage. **1940** 21 Days Together.

DE WILDE, BRANDON (Andre Brandon de Wilde)
Born: Apr. 9, 1942, Brooklyn N.Y. Died: July 6, 1972, Denver, Colo. (auto accident). Screen, stage and television actor. Son of stage actor Frederic (dec. 1980) and actress Eugenia de Wilde. Nominated for 1953 Academy Award for Best Supporting Actor for Shane.

Appeared in: **1952** The Member of the Wedding (stage and flim versions—film debut). **1953** Shane. **1956** The Day They Gave Babies Away; Goodbye, My Lady. **1957** Night Passage. **1958** The Missouri Traveler. **1959** Blue Denim. **1962** All Fall Down. **1963** Hud. **1964** Those Calloways. **1965** In Harm's Way. **1967** The Trip. **1969** God Bless You, Uncle Sam. **1970** The Deserter. **1972** Wild in the Sky.

DEWITT, ALAN "BOOMIE"
Born: 1924, Canton, Ohio. Died: June 2, 1976, Los Angeles, Calif. (heart attack). Screen, stage, television actor and stage director.

Appeared in: **1962** Tales of Terror. **1963** The Comedy of Terrors. **1965** The Graveside Story (rerelease of The Comedy of Terrors, 1963). **1967** Luv. **1970** Angels Die Hard. **1976** Alex and the Gypsy.

DE WITT, GEORGE
Born: 1923. Died: July 14, 1979, Miami, Fla. (heart attack). Screen, television actor and comedian. Divorced from actress Claire Kelly.

Appeared in: **1959** A Hole in the Head. **1974** Lenny.

DE WOLFE, BILLY (William Andrew Jones)
Born: 1907, Wollaston, Mass. Died: Mar. 5, 1974, Los Angeles, Calif. (cancer). Screen, stage, vaudeville, television actor and dancer.

Appeared in: **1943** Dixie (film debut). **1945** Miss Susie Slagle's; Duffy's Tavern. **1946** Blue Skies; Our Hearts Were Growing Up. **1947** Dear Ruth; The Perils of Pauline; Variety Girl. **1948** Isn't It Romantic. **1949** Dear Wife. **1950** Tea for Two. **1951** Dear Brat; The Lullaby of Broadway. **1953** Call Me Madam. **1965** Billie. **1973** The World's Greatest Athlete.

DE WOLFE, ELSIE (aka LADY MENDL)
Born: Dec. 20, 1865, New York, N.Y. Died: July 12, 1950, Versailles, France. Screen and stage actress. Married to British diplomat Sir Charles Mendl.

Appeared in: **1920** Democracy, the Vision Restored.

DEXTER, AUBREY (Douglas Peter Jonas)
Born: Mar. 29, 1889, London, England. Died: May, 1958, England? Screen and stage actor. Entered films in 1927.

Appeared in: **1952** Angel Street. **1957** The Prince and the Showgirl; The Counterfiet Plan.

DEXTER, ELLIOTT
Born: 1870, Galveston, Tex. Died: June 23, 1941, Amityville, N.Y. Screen and vaudeville actor. Divorced from actress Marie Doro (dec. 1956).

Appeared in: **1915** The Masqueraders. **1916** The Heart of Nora Flynn; The Lash; Diplomacy. **1917** A Romance of the Redwoods; Castles for Two; The Rise of Jennie Cushing. **1918** Woman and Wife. **1919** Don't Change Your Husband; For Better, For Worse; The Squaw Man; Maggie Pepper; We Can't Have Everything. **1920** Behold My Wife; Something to Think About. **1921** The Witching Hour; Forever; The Affairs of Anatol; Don't Tell Everything. **1922** Grand Larceny; Enter Madam; The Hands of Nara. **1923** Adam's Rib; Mary of the Movies; Only 38; Souls for Sale; Broadway Gold; The Common Law; Flaming Youth; An Old Sweetheart of Mine. **1924** The Fast Set; Age of Innocence; By Divine Right; For Woman's Favor; The Triflers; The Spitfire. **1925** Capital Punishment; The Verdict; Wasted Lives. **1926** Stella Maris.

DHELIA, FRANCE
Born: France. Died: May, 1964, France? Screen actress.

Appeared in: **1931** Mephisto.

DIAL, PATTERSON
Born: 1903, Madison, Fla. Died: Mar. 23, 1945. Screen actress. Married to actor Rupert Hughes (dec. 1956).

Appeared in: **1921** Tol'able David; Get-Rich-Quick Wallingford. **1922** The Seventh Day; Sonny. **1923** Fury; The Silent Partner; Reno. **1924** Happiness; Secrets; Married Flirts; A Lady of Quality; Man's Mate.

DICENTA, MANUEL
Born: 1904, Spain. Died: Nov. 19, 1974, Madrid, Spain (cardiac-respiratory insufficiency). Screen, stage and television actor. Son of actress Consuelo Badillo and playwright Joaquin Dicenta.

Appeared in: **1938** Morena Clara.

DICKERSON, HENRY (Dudley Henry Dickerson)
Born: Nov. 27, 1906, Oklahoma. Died: Sept. 23, 1968, Lynwood, Calif. (cerebral thrombosis). Black screen actor.

Appeared in: **1935** The Virginia Judge. **1936** The Green Pastures. **1939** Some Like It Hot. **1941** The Man Who Came to Dinner; Borrowed Hero. **1943** Gung Ho! **1944** The Adventures of Mark Twain; Allergic to Love; Ever Since Venus. **1946** Without Reservations; Dangerous Money. **1950** Peggy. **1956** Scheming Schemers (short). **1959** The Alligator People.

DICKERSON, JENNIE
Born: 1855, Newburgh, N.Y. Died: Aug. 14, 1943, Philadelphia, Pa. Screen, stage actress and opera signer.

Appeared in: **1915** Stop Thief!

DICKEY, PAUL
Born: May 12, 1885, Chicago, Ill. Died: Jan. 8, 1933, N.Y. (heart disease). Screen, stage actor, screenwriter, playwriter and stage director.

Appeared in: **1922** Robin Hood.

DICKINSON, HAL
Born: 1914. Died: Nov. 18, 1970, Santa Barbara, Calif. Screen, stage and radio actor and vocalist. Married to vocalist Paula Kelly. Founder and leader of "The Modernaires" singing group.

Appeared in: **1949** Home in San Antone. **1954** The Glenn Miller Story.

DICKINSON, HOMER
Born: 1890. Died: June 6, 1959, Hollywood, Calif. Screen, stage and vaudeville actor. Appeared in vaudeville from 1914 to 1926 with his wife, Florence Tempest and her sister in an act billed as "Sunshine and Tempest."

Appeared in: **1928** Broadway's Smart Musical Comedy Star (short).

DICKSON, DONALD
Born: 1911, Pittsburgh, Pa. Died: Sept. 20, 1972, Brooklyn, N.Y. Screen, radio actor and opera baritone.

Appeared in: **1944** Up in Arms.

DICKSON, GLORIA (Thais Dickerson)
Born: Aug. 13, 1916, Pocatello, Idaho. Died: Apr. 10, 1945, Hollywood, Calif. (asphyxiation from fire). Stage and screen actress.

Appeared in: **1936** They Won't Forget (film debut). **1938** Gold Diggers in Paris; Secrets of an Actress; Racket Busters; Heart of the North. **1939** Private Detective; No Place to Go; Cowboy Quarterback; On Your Toes; Waterfront; They Made Me a Criminal. **1940** I Want a Divorce; King of the Lumberjacks; Tear Gas Squad; This Thing Called Love. **1941** The Big Boss; Mercy Island. **1942** Affairs of Jimmy Valentine. **1943** The Crime Doctor's Strangest Case; Power of the Press; Lady of Burlesque. **1944** Crime Doctor; Rationing.

DICKSON, LAMONT
Died: May 7, 1944. Screen actor.

Appeared in: **1931** Almost a Honeymoon.

DICKSON, LYDIA
Born: Apr. 17, 1887, Missouri. Died: Apr. 2, 1928, Hollywood, Calif. Screen and stage comedienne and actress.

Appeared in: **1928** Don't Marry; Square Crooks.

DIDRICKSON, BABE (Mildred Ella Didrickson)
Born: June 16, 1914, Port Arthur, Tex. Died: Sept. 27, 1956, Galveston, Tex. (cancer). Professional athlete and screen actress. Married to professional wrestler George Zaharias.

Appeared in: **1952** Pat and Mike.

DIDWAY, ERNEST
Born: 1872. Died: Jan. 3, 1939, Los Angeles, Calif. Screen and stage actor. Entered films approx. 1932.

DIE ASTA *See* NIELSEN, ASTA

DIEHL, KARL LUDWIG
Born: 1897, Germany. Died: Mar., 1958, Oberbayern, West Germany. Stage and screen actor.

Appeared in: **1924** Die Tragödie der Enterbten. **1929** Masken. **1930** Rosenmontag (Rose Monday—US 1931); Zärtlichkeit; Liebeswalzer

(US 1931); Der Greifer (Night Birds); Aschermittwoch (Ash Wednesday—US 1935). **1931** Die Königin einer Nacht; Der Zinker; Täter Gesucht; Im Geheimdienst; Schatten der Manege. **1932** Scampolo, ein Kind der Strasse; Das Geheimnis um Johann Ort (aka Ein Liebesroman im Hause Hasburg—US 1936); Rasputin (aka Der Dämon der Frauen); Die Unsichtbare Front; Zwei in Einem Auto; Schuss im Morgengrauen (US 1934); Koenigin der Unterwelt; Zirkus Leben. **1933** Ein Maedel der Strasse; Volldampf Voraus; Spione am Werk. **1934** Die Freundin Eines Grossen Mannes; Ein Mann will Nach Deutschland; Abenteuer im Südexpress. **1935** Episode (US 1937); Der Hohere Befehl (US 1936); Ein Idealer Gatte (US 1937); Der Grüne Domino; Der Stählerne Strahl. **1936** Spy 77; Die Ganze Welt Dreht Sich um Liebe; Es Geht um Mein Leben (My Life Is at Stake—US 1938); Die Leuchten des Kaisers; Seine Tochter ist der Peter (His Daughter Is Peter—US 1938). **1937** Andere Welt; Liebe Kann Lügen; Liebe Geht Seltsame Wege. **1938** Der Mann, der Nicht Nein Sagen Konnte. **1939** Ein Hoffnungsloser Fall; Der Schritt vom Wege (The False Step, aka Effie Briest). **1940** Der Fuchs von Glenarvon. **1941** Die Schwedische Nachtigall; Annelie (aka Die Geschichte eines Lebens); Was Geschah in Dieser Nacht?; Der 5. Juni. **1942** Die Entlassung. **1943** Nacht ohne Abschied; Die Hochstaplerin. **1945** Wo ist Herr Belling?; Ruf an das Gewissen (aka Ruf des Gewissens). **1949** Die Reise nach Marrakesch. **1951** Das Seltsame Leben des Herrn Bruggs. **1952** Bis wir uns Wiederseh'n. **1953** Geliebtes Leben. **1954** Eine Liebesgeschichte; Der Mann Meines Lebens. **1955** Die Stadt ist Voller Geheimnisse; Des Teufels General (The Devil's General—US 1957); Es Geschah am 20. Juli (Jackpot Mutiny); Banditen der Autobahn; Ein Herz Bleibt Allein (aka Mein Leopold). **1956** Meine 16 Söhne. **1958** The Story of Vickie.

DIERKES, JOHN
Born: Feb. 10, 1908. Died: Jan. 8, 1975, Hollywood, Calif. (emphysema). Screen and television actor.

Appeared in: **1948** Macbeth. **1950** Three Husbands. **1951** The Red Badge of Courage; Silver City. **1952** Les Miserables; Plymouth Adventure. **1953** Abbott and Costello Meet Dr. Jekyll and Mr. Hyde; Shane; The Moonlighter; The Vanquished; A Perilous Journey. **1954** Hell's Outpost; The Naked Jungle; Silver Lode; Prince Valiant; The Desperado; Passion; The Raid. **1955** Betrayed Women; The Vanishing American; Not as a Stranger. **1956** Jubal. **1957** Valerie; The Buckskin Lady; Daughter of Dr. Jekyll; Duel at Apache Wells. **1958** The Buccaneer; The Left-Handed Gun; Blood Arrow; The Rawhide Trail. **1959** Hanging Tree; The Oregon Trail. **1960** The Alamo. **1961** The Comancheros; One-Eyed Jacks. **1962** The Premature Burial; Convicts 4. **1963** The Haunted Palace; Johnny Cool; "X" The Man with the X-Ray Eyes. **1973** Oklahoma Crude.

DIESEL, GUSTAV
Born: 1900, Vienna, Austria. Died: Mar. 20, 1948, Vienna, Austria. Screen, stage actor and film director.

Appeared in: **1924** Ssanin. **1925** Im Banne der Kralle; Die Rache der Pharaonen. **1928** Abwege; Der Lebende Leichnam; Sensations-Prozess; Die Buechse der Pandora (Pandora's Box). **1929** That Murder in Berlin; Die Drein um Edith; Die Ehe; Frauen am Abgrund; Der Mann, der Nicht Liebt; Mutterliebe (Mother Love—US 1931). **1930** Menschen Hinter Gettern; Moral um Mitternacht; Hans in Allen Gassen; Die Grosse Sehnsucht; Die Weisse Hoelle von Piz Palue (The White Hell of Pitz Palu); Leutnant Warts Du Einst bei den Husaren (US 1932); Westfront 1918 (aka Vier von der Infanterie aka Comrades of 1918—US 1931). **1931** The Living Corpse; Das Gelbe Haus des King-Fu. **1932** Teilnehmer Antwortet Nicht; Eine von Uns; Die Naechte von Port Said; Die Herrin von Atlantis; Der Goldene Gletscher (aka Herrgottsgrenadiere). **1933** Roman Einer Nacht (US 1934); S.O.S. Eisberg; Das Testament des Dr. Mabuse (The Testament of Dr. Mabuse). **1934** Die Weisse Majestaet (The White Majesty—US 1939). **1935** Der Daemon des Himalaya; Alles um Eine Frau (aka Kameraden). **1936** Die Biebe des Maharadscha; Schatten der Vergangenheit (Shadows of the Past—US 1940); Moskau—Shanghai (aka Der Weg Nach Shanghai). **1937** Gilgi Eine von Uns; Starke Herzen. **1938** Der Tiger von Eschnapur (The Indian Tomb); Kautschuk; Fortsetzung Folgt. **1939** Die Gruene Hoelle (The Green Hell); Amore Sulle Alpi; Ich Verweigere die Aussage; Ich bin Sebastian Ott; Der Gruene Kaiser. **1940** Herz ohne Heimat; Stern von Rio. **1941** Komoedianten; Menschen im Sturm; Clarissa. **1944** Nora; Kolberg; Ein Blick Zurueck (aka Am Vorabend). **1945** Ruf am das Gewissen (aka Ruf des Gewissens). **1948** Der Prozess.

DIETERLE, WILLIAM (Wilhelm Dieterle)
Born: July 15, 1893, Rheinpfalz, Germany. Died: Dec. 9, 1972, Ottobrunn, West Germany. Screen actor, film director, producer, and screenwriter. Married to stage actress Charlotte Hagenbruch (dec.). Directed German and U.S. films.

Appeared in: **1913** Fiesco. **1918** Der Rattenfaenger von Hameln (The Pied Piper of Hamelin). **1921** Die Geirerwally; Die Hintertreppe (Backstairs). **1922** Lucrezia Borgia; Frauenopfer; Der Graf von Charolais; Malmaison; Tiefland; Fraulein Julie (Lady Julia). **1923** Boheme; Der Zweite Schuss; Die Pagode; Die Gruene Manuela; Die Ausstrelbung; Der Mensch am Wege. **1924** Carlos und Elisabeth; Das Wachsfiguerenkabinett (The Waxworks); Moderne Ehen; Mutter und Kind (Mother and Child). **1925** Wetterleuchten; Lena Warnstetten; Sumpf und Moral; Der Hahn im Korb; Die Blumenfrau vom Potsdamer Platz; Die vom Niederrhein; Die Dame aus Berlin (US 1926); Die Gesunkenen (US 1926); Der Rosa Diamant. **1926** Die Foersterchristel; Qualen der Nacht; Zopf und Schwert; Faust; Hoelle der Liebe; Die Flucht in den Zirkus; Der Jaeger von Fall; Der Pfarrer von Kirchfeld; Die vom Schicksal Verfolgten (US 1927); Wie Bleibe ich Jung und Schoen (US 1927); Familie Schimek (aka Wiener Herzen). **1927** Unter Ausschluss der Oeffentlichkeit; Der Zigeunerbaron; Ich Habe im Mai von der Liebe Getraeumt; Violantha (US 1928); Frau Sorge (US 1928); Am Rande der Welt; Liebesreigen; Petronella; Der Mann, der Nicht Lieben Darf; Heimweh (Homesickness); Die Weber (The Weavers). **1928** Geschlecht in Fesseln (Sex in Fetters); Der Heilige und ihr Narr; Ritter der Nacht. **1929** Fruehlingsrauschen; Ich Lebe fuer Dich; Ludwig der Zweite, Koenig von Bayern; Das Schweigen im Walde. **1930** Der Tanz Geht Weiter (Those Who Dance); Eine Stunde Glueck; Die Maske Faellt (Way of All Men). **1931** Daemon des Meeres (Moby Dick).

DIETL, FRANK H.
Born: Nov. 15, 1875, Lakeville, Ind. Died: Jan. 24, 1925. Screen actor.

Appeared in: **1915** Neal of the Navy.

DIEUDONNE, ALBERT
Born: 1892, France. Died: Mar. 19, 1976, France? Screen actor.

Appeared in: **1929** Napoleon.

DIEUDONNE, HELENE
Born: 1887, France. Died: Sept., 1980, Chaumont-en-Vexin, France. Screen, stage and television actress. Daughter of stage actor Alfred Dieudonne (dec.).

Appeared in: **1961** Le Belle Americaine; Paris Blues; Le Cave se Rebiffe (aka Money, Money, Money and aka The Counterfeiters of Paris—US 1962). **1962** Un Singe en Hiver (A Monkey in Winter—US 1963); Therese Desqueyroux (aka Therese—US 1963). **1966** A Ravishing Idiot. **1975** Don't Cry With Your Mouth Full.

DIGAETANO, ADAM
Born: 1907. Died: Apr. 30, 1966, Hollywood, Calif. (coronary ailment). Screen actor and dancer. Married to actress Jayne DiGaetano with whom he appeared as part of "Jayne and Adam DiGaetano" dance team.

Appeared in: **1946** Night and Day.

DIGGES, DUDLEY
Born: 1879, Dublin, Ireland. Died: Oct. 24, 1947, New York, N.Y. (stroke). Screen, stage actor and screen dialogue director.

Appeared in: **1929** Condemned. **1930** Outward Bound. **1931** Upper Underworld; The Maltese Falcon; The Ruling Voice; Alexander Hamilton; Devotion; Honorable Mr. Wong. **1932** The Hatchet Man; The Strange Case of Clara Deane; Roar of the Dragon; The First Year; Tess of the Storm Country. **1933** The King's Vacation; The Mayor of Hell; Silk Express; The Narrow Corner; Emperor Jones; Before Dawn; The Invisible Man. **1934** Fury of the Jungle; Caravan; The World Moves On; Massacre; What Every Woman Knows. **1935** I Am a Thief; A Notorious Gentleman; Mutiny on the Bounty; China Seas; The Bishop Misbehaves. **1936** Three Live Ghosts; The Voice of Bugle Ann; The Unguarded Hour; The General Died at Dawn; Valiant Is the Word for Carrie. **1937** Love Is News. **1939** The Light That Failed. **1940** The Fight for Life; Raffles. **1942** Son of Fury. **1946** The Searching Wind.

DIGGINS, EDDIE (Edward Ayer Diggins)
Born: Jan. 8, 1903, San Francisco, Calif. Died: Mar. 26, 1927, Hollywood, Calif. (stabbed). Screen actor.

Appeared in: **1925** The Goat Getter. **1926** One Punch O'Day.

DIGNAM, BASIL
Born: England. Died: Jan. 31, 1979, England. Screen actor. Brother of actor Mark Dignam.

Appeared in: **1955** Touch and Go (aka The Light Touch—US 1956). **1956** His Excellency; The Intimate Stranger (aka Finger of Guilt—US); Brothers In Law; The Narrowing Circle. **1957** Depraved;

Yangtse Incident (aka Battle Hell—US); Three Sundays to Live; You Pay Your Money; Son of a Stranger. **1958** Up the Creek; The Safecracker; A Cry From the Streets (US 1959); Corridors of Blood (US 1963); Carry on Sergeant (US 1959). **1960** Suspect (aka The Risk—US 1961). **1961** The Secret Partner; Gorgo. **1962** Life for Ruth (aka Walk in the Shadow—US 1966); Il Dominatore dei Sette Mari (aka Seven Seas to Calais—US 1963). **1963** Ring of Spies (aka Ring of Treason—US 1964); Master Spy (US 1964); Heavens Above!; 80,000 Suspects. **1965** Rotten to the Core; The Amorous Adventures of Moll Flanders; Where the Spies Are. **1966** The Jokers (US 1967). **1967** Assignment K (US 1968); I'll Never Forget What's 'is Name (US 1968). **1968** Twisted Nerve (US 1969). **1969** Laughter in the Dark. **1970** The Games; The Great White Hope.

DIGNT, KENNETH "KEN"
Born: England. Died: Apr. 28, 1978, England? Screen, stage and television actor.

Appeared in: **1965** Rotten to the Core.

DI GOLCONDA, LIGIA
Born: 1884, Mexico. Died: Jan., 1942, Mexico City, Mexico. Mexican screen actor.

DIKKERS, PIM
Born: 1918, Holland. Died: Nov. 29, 1978, Holland. Screen actor.

DILL, MAX M.
Born: 1878. Died: Nov. 21, 1949, San Francisco, Calif. Screen, stage and vaudeville actor. Was partner with Clarence Kolb (dec. 1964) in vaudeville team billed as "Kolb and Dill."

The team appeared in: **1916** a series of comedies. **1917** Glory; Mutual Star; Beloved Rogues.

DILLARD, BURT
Born: 1909. Died: June 19, 1960, Ruidoso Downs, N.Mex. (heart attack). Screen actor, stuntman and horse trainer.

Appeared in: **1935** Rainbow Valley. **1951** Three Desperate Men (aka Three Outlaws).

DILLARD, CHARLES "ART"
Died: Mar. 3, 1960, Chatsworth, Calif. (heart attack). Screen actor.

Appeared in: **1936** Ghost Patrol. **1937** Yodelin' Kid from Pine Ridge. **1938** Gold Mine in the Sky. **1941** Sierra Sue. **1950** Vigilante Hideout. **1952** Leadville Gunslinger.

DILLIGIL, AVNI
Born: 1909, Turkey. Died: June, 1971, Ankara, Turkey (heart attack). Stage and screen actor.

DILLON, DICK (Kenneth Bowstead)
Born: 1896. Died: 1961, Boston, Mass. Screen and vaudeville actor. Known in vaudeville as part of "Dean and Dillon" act with Bob Dean.

Appeared in: **1914** Perils of Pauline (serial).

DILLON, EDWARD "EDDIE"
Born: 1880, N.Y. Died: July 11, 1933, Hollywood, Calif. (heart attack). Screen, stage actor and film director.

Appeared in: **1908** The Feud and the Turkey; The Reckoning; After Many Years; The Welcome Burglar; The Salvation Army Lass; The Fight For Freedom; The Black Viper. **1909** As the Bells Rang Out; The Sorrows of the Unfaithful; Examination Day at School; Muggsy Becomes a Hero; The Fugitive; His Sister-in-Law; The Brahma Diamond; The Little Teacher. **1910** Fisher Folks; The Oath and the Man; A Lucky Toothache; Waiter No. 5; White Roses. **1911** The Miser's Heart; Sunshine Through the Dark; Through His Wife's Picture; Priscilla's Engagement Kiss; Priscilla's April Fool Joke; The Spanish Gypsy; Priscilla and the Umbrella; Misplaced Jealousy; The Crooked Road; Dave's Love Affair; The Delayed Proposal; A Convenient Burglar. **1912** The Spirit Awakened; With a Kodak; A Voice From the Deep; Blind Love; A Limited Divorce; At the Basket Picnic; His Auto's Maiden Trip; The Leading Man; An Interrupted Elopement. **1913** Love in an Apartment Hotel; An Indian's Loyalty; Judity of Bethulia. **1915** Faithful to the Finish. **1926** The Skyrocket. **1928** Lilac Time. **1929** The Broadway Melody; Hot for Paris. **1930** Caught Short; Whispering Whoopee (short); Fifty Million Husbands (short). **1931** Sob Sister; Thundering Tenors (short). **1932** The Trial of Vivienne Ware; Sherlock Holmes; The Nickel Nurser (short); Young Ironsides (short).

DILLON, GEORGE "TIM"
Born: 1888. Died: Oct. 22, 1965, Burbank, Calif. Screen actor.

Appeared in: **1951** The Mudlark.

DILLON, JOHN FRANCIS
Born: Nov. 28, 1884, New York, N.Y. Died: Apr. 4, 1934, Beverly Hills, Calif. (heart attack). Screen, stage actor, and film director. Divorced from stage actress Maud Housley and later married to actress Edith Hallor (dec. 1971). Father of actor Anthony Dillon and film editor John Dillon II.

Appeared in: **1914** Dough and Dynamite; The Rajah's Vow; The Key to Yesterday; The Magnet; Bess the Detectress or, The Old Mill at Midnight; Willie Walrus, Detective; Willie Walrus and the Baby; A Dramatic Mistake; The New Janitor. **1915** The Comeback; His Guiding Angel; Molly's Malady; He Fell in a Cabareta; A Desert Honeymoon; Love in a Hospital; Henry's Little Kid; Where the Deacon Lives; When His Lordship Proposed; Wanted: A Chaperone; A Maid by Proxy (aka A Maid and a Man); Almost a King; It Might Have Been Serious; Down On the Farm; Taking Her Measure; It Happened On a Friday; Kids and Corsets; His Only Pants; A Mixed-Up Elopement; All in the Same Boat; When Cupid Crossed the Bay; With Father's Help; Too Many Crooks; It Happened While He Fished; Dan Cupid, Fixer; Getting in Wrong. **1916** Paddy's Political Dream; The Lion-Hearted Chief; More Truth Than Poetry; Love, Dynamite and Baseballs. **1917** A Bachelor's Finish; Hobbled Hearts; A Berth Scandal; Her Finishing Touch; A Dishonest Burglar; Twin Troubles; Wheels and Woe; Aired in Court; His Sudden Rival; A Warm Reception; His Taking Ways; A Hotel Disgrace. **1919** Green-Eyed Johnny; A Burglar by Proxy. **1921** Cappy Ricks; The Journey's End. **1922** Without Compromise. **1923** Double Dealing. **1926** The Test of Donald Norton. **1927** Smile, Brother, Smile; Temptations of a Shopgirl.

DILLON, JOHN T. (aka JACK DILLON)
Born: 1866. Died: Dec. 29, 1937, Los Angeles, Calif. (pneumonia). Screen and stage actor. Do not confuse with screen actor and film dirctor John Francis Dillon (dec. 1934) who also appeared in films as Jack Dillon.

Appeared in: **1910** The Iconoclast; The Oath and the Man; Examination Day at School; Waiter No. 5; His Sister-in-Law; White Roses; The Fugitive; A Lucky Toothache. **1911** Priscilla's Engagement; Her Wedding Ring; Priscilla's April Fool Joke; The Spanish Gypsy; Priscilla and the Umbrella; Misplaced Jealousy; The Crooked Road; Dave's Love Affair; The Delayed Proposal; A Convenient Burglar; A Decree of Destiny; The Chief's Daughter; A Dutch Gold Mine; The Jealous Husband; Out From the Shadow. **1912** The Musketeers of Pig Alley. **1913** Love in an Apartment Hotel; The Sheriff's Baby; Her Mother's Oath; Three Friends. **1914** Birth of a Nation. **1915** The Keeper of the Flock. **1916** Seven Days. **1921** The Family Closet. **1922** For His Sake. **1924** Stepping Lively; Tiger Thompson. **1925** Midnight Molly. **1928** Bitter Sweets. **1929** In Old Arizona. **1931** The Cisco Kid.

DILLON, JOHN WEBB
Born: 1877. Died: Dec. 20, 1949, Hollywood, Calif. Screen and stage actor.

Appeared in: **1916** Romeo and Juliet; One Day. **1917** The Darling of Paris; Heart and Soul; The Tiger Woman; The Phantom Call. **1918** The Queen of Hearts. **1920** Trailed by Three (serial). **1921** Jane Eyre; The Inner Chamber; The Mountain Woman; Perjury. **1922** Speed (serial); Married People; The Mohican's Daughter. **1923** The Exiles; No Mother to Guide Her. **1924** Rip Roarin' Roberts. **1925** The Air Mail; The Vanishing American; The Devil's Cargo; The Phantom Express. **1926** The Seventh Bandit; House Without a Key (serial); Snowed In (serial). **1927** A Bowery Cinderella; Wolf's Clothing. **1928** Dry Martini. **1929** The Black Book (serial). **1930** Girl of the Port; In the Next Room. **1933** The Diamond Trail. **1934** Carolina. **1935** She Couldn't Take It. **1946** The Secret Heart.

DILLON, JOSEPHINE
Born: 1884. Died: Nov. 10, 1971, Verdugo City, Calif. Screen actress and drama coach. Divorced from actor Clark Gable (dec. 1960).

Appeared in: **1944** The Lady and the Monster.

DILLON, MRS. STELLA
Born: 1878. Died: Apr. 28, 1934, Los Angeles, Calif. Screen actress.

DILLON, THOMAS PATRICK "TOM"
Born: 1896. Died: Sept. 15, 1962, Hollywood, Calif. Screen, stage, circus and vaudeville actor.

Appeared in: **1944** Going My Way; Whistling in Brooklyn; Thin Man Goes Home; The Invisible Man's Revenge; She's a Soldier, Too. **1945** Mildred Pierce; Pursuit to Algiers; Captain Eddie. **1946** The Virginian; Dressed to Kill; The Kid from Brooklyn; Black Beauty; The Well-

Groomed Bride; The Strange Love of Martha Ivers; Scarlet Street; Duel in the Sun; The Postman Always Rings Twice. **1947** The Exile; Forever Amber; The Unfinished Dance; My Favorite Brunette. **1948** Kiss the Blood Off My Hands; Tenth Avenue Angel; My Girl Tisa. **1949** Saints and Sinners. **1950** Woman on the Run. **1952** Million Dollar Mermaid. **1956** The Catered Affair; The Search for Bridey Murphy; The Oklahoma Woman. **1960** North to Alaska. **1963** Night Tide.

DILLON, TIM
Born: 1888. Died: Oct. 22, 1965, Burbank, Calif. Screen actor. Member of the Keystone Kops.

DILLSON, CLYDE (aka CLYDE DILSON)
Born: 1900. Died: Jan. 25, 1957. Screen actor.

Appeared in: **1929** Unmasked. **1935** Let 'Em Have It; Men Without Names; King Solomon of Broadway. **1936** You May Be Next; Thirteen Hours By Air; Florida Special. **1937** There Goes My Girl; Midnight Madonna; Under Suspicion; The Duke Comes Back. **1938** Secrets of a Nurse. **1939** Big Town Czar. **1940** Andy Hardy Meets Debutante. **1941** Up in the Air; Naval Academy.

DILSON, JOHN H.
Born: 1891. Died: June 1, 1944, Ventura, Calif. Screen and stage actor.

Appeared in: **1935** Twin Triplets (short); Cheers of the Crowd; Every Night at Eight; The Girl Who Came Back; Cyclone on Horseback. **1936** Great Guy; Next Time We Love; The Country Doctor; The Case of the Velvet Claws; The Public Pays (short); Robinson Crusoe of Clipper Island (serial). **1937** Dick Tracy (serial); Easy Living; Escape by Night. **1938** Who Killed Gail Preston?; Women in Prison; A Clean Sweep (short); Major Difficulties (short). **1939** At the Circus; Lady of the Tropics; When Tomorrow Comes; Women in the Wind; Fixer Dugan; Forgotten Women; Racketeers of the Range; A Woman is the Judge; Laugh It Off; Ring Madness (short); Weather Wizards (short). **1940** Adventures of Red Ryder (serial); Drums of Fu Manchu (serial); Girls Under 21; Pioneers of the West; King of the Royal Mounted (serial); The Westerner; The Man With Nine Lives; Johnny Apollo; I Love You Again; No, No Nanette. **1941** Footsteps in the Dark; Unholy Partners; International Lady; Shadow of the Thin Man; Obliging Young Lady; Confirm or Deny; The Wagons Roll at Night; Citizen Kane; Father Steps Out; Dick Tracy vs. Crime Inc. (serial); Father's Son; Man Made Monster; Naval Academy; I'll Fix That (short); Sunset in Wyoming; Andy Hardy's Private Secretary. **1942** They All Kissed the Bride; You Can't Escape Forever; Madame Spy; Pittsburgh; Footlight Serenade. **1943** You're a Lucky Fellow, Mr. Smith; Mission to Moscow; Lady Bodyguard.

DIMBLEBY, RICHARD
Born: May 25, 1913, England. Died: Dec. 22, 1965, London, England (cancer). Screen, television, radio actor, news commentator, author and publisher.

Appeared in: **1936** Strange Cargo (US 1940). **1950** The Twenty Questions Murder Mystery. **1958** Rockets Galore. **1959** Libel.

DIME, JAMES "JIMMY"
Born: 1898. Died: May 11, 1981, Woodland Hills, Calif. Screen actor.

Appeared in: **1927** The King of Kings. **1928** Stand and Deliver. **1933** White Woman. **1949** Down to the Sea in Ships.

DINEHART, ALAN
Born: Oct. 3, 1889, Missoula, Mont. Died: July 17, 1944, Hollywood, Calif. Screen, stage, vaudeville actor and playwright. Divorced from stage actress Louise Dyer (dec. 1934). Married to actress Mozelle Britton (dec. 1953).

Appeared in: **1931** Sob Sister; Girls About Town; Good Sport; The Brat; Wicked. **1932** The Trial of Vivienne Ware; Disorderly Conduct; Street of Women; Bachelor's Affairs; Almost Married; Week Ends Only; Penalty of Fame; Silver Dollar; Washington Merry-Go-Round; Rackety Rax; Devil Is Driving; Okay America; Lawyer Man. **1933** Sweepings; As the Devil Commands; Supernatural; Her Bodyguard; The Sin of Nora Moran; A Study in Scarlet; No Marriage Ties; Bureau of Missing Persons; I Have Lived; Dance, Girl, Dance; The World Changes. **1934** Cross Country Cruise; The Crosby Case; The Love Captive; A Very Honorable Guy; Jimmy the Gent; Baby, Take a Bow; Fury of the Jungle; The Cat's Paw. **1935** Dante's Inferno; Lottery Lover; $10 Raise; In Old Kentucky; Redheads on Parade; Thanks a Million; Your Uncle Dudley; The Pay-Off. **1936** It Had to Happen; Everybody's Old Man; The Country Beyond; Human Cargo; The Crime of Dr. Forbes; Charlie Chan at the Race Track; Star for a Night; King of the Royal Mounted; Reunion; Parole; Born to Dance. **1937**

Fifty Roads to Town; King of the Turf; Step Lively, Jeeves!; Woman Wise; Midnight Taxi; This Is My Affair; Danger—Love at Work; Ali Baba Goes to Town; Big Town Girl. **1938** Love on a Budget; Rebecca of Sunnybrook Farm; Up the River; The First Hundred Years. **1939** Hotel for Women; Money to Loan (short); Fast and Loose; House of Fear; Two Bright Boys; Second Fiddle; Everything Happens at Night. **1940** Slightly Honorable. **1942** Girl Trouble. **1943** The Heat's On; Sweet Rosie O'Grady; It's a Great Life; Fired Wife; What a Woman. **1944** Johnny Doesn't Live Here Anymore; Moon Over Las Vegas; The Whistler; Oh, What a Night; Seven Days Ashore; Minstrel Man; A Wave, a Wac and a Marine.

DINESEN, ROBERT
Born: Oct. 23, 1874, Copenhagen, Denmark. Died: c. 1940. Screen actor and film director.

Appeared in: **1911** The Abyss; The Four Devils. **1912** The Governor's Daughter; Help.

DINGLE, CHARLES W.
Born: Dec. 28, 1887, Wabash, Ind. Died: Jan. 19, 1956, Worcester, Mass. Screen, stage, radio and television actor.

Appeared in: **1939** One Third of a Nation. **1941** Unholy Partners; The Little Foxes; Johnny Eager. **1942** Calling Dr. Gillespie; Are Husbands Necessary?; Tennessee Johnson; Somewhere I'll Find You; George Washington Slept Here; The Talk of the Town. **1943** Someone to Remember; She's for Me; Edge of Darkness; Lady of Burlesque. **1944** Home in Indiana; National Barn Dance; Practically Yours; The Song of Bernadette; Together Again. **1945** A Medal for Benny; Guest Wife; Here Come the Co-eds; Three's a Crowd; A Song to Remember. **1946** Cinderella Jones; Sister Kenny; Centennial Summer; Three Wise Fools; Wife of Monte Cristo; The Beast With Five Fingers; Duel in the Sun. **1947** My Favorite Brunette; Welcome Stranger; The Romance of Rosy Ridge. **1948** If You Knew Susie; State of the Union; A Southern Yankee; The World and His Wife. **1949** Big Jack. **1952** Never Wave at a WAC. **1953** Call Me Madam; President's Lady; Half a Hero. **1955** The Court Martial of Billy Mitchell.

DIONE, ROSE
Born: 1875, Paris, France. Died: Jan. 29, 1936, Los Angeles, Calif. Screen and stage actress.

Appeared in: **1919** The World and Its Women. **1920** The Great Lover; Suds; The Woman and the Puppet. **1921** Be My Wife; Little Lord Fauntleroy; Silent Years; The Blushing Bride; Silk Hosiery; Cheated Love. **1922** Omar the Tent Maker; Golden Dreams. **1923** Salome; Drifting; The French Doll; Scaramouche; Trilby. **1924** Shadows of Paris; The Lover of Camille; Inez from Hollywood; Beau Brummell; Try and Get It; Rose of Paris. **1925** Fifth Avenue Models; One Year to Live. **1926** Mlle. Modiste; Paris; The Duchess of Buffalo; Fools of Fashion; Love's Blindness. **1927** When a Man Loves; The Beloved Rogue; Camille; Old San Francisco; Ragtime; Polly of the Movies. **1928** Bringing Up Father; The Mad Hour; His Tiger Lady; Out of the Ruins; The Red Mark. **1929** Naughty Baby; Hearts in Exile; One Stolen Night. **1930** Women Everywhere; On Your Back; Isle of Escape. **1931** Salvation Nell. **1932** Back Street; Freaks; King Murder.

DIONNE, EMELIE
Born: May 28, 1934, Callander, Ontario, Canada. Died: Aug. 6, 1954 (epileptic seizure). Screen actress. One of the Dionne quintuplets. Daughter of actor Oliva Dionne (dec. 1979). For family information see Oliva Dionne listing.

Appeared in: **1936** Reunion; The Country Doctor; Going on Two (short); Pathe shorts. **1938** Five of a Kind; Quintupland (short).

DIONNE, MARIE
Born: May 28, 1934, Callander, Ontario, Canada. Died: Feb. 27, 1970. Screen actress. One of the Dionne quintuplets. Daughter of Oliva Dionne (dec. 1979). For family information see Oliva Dionne listing.

Appeared in: **1936** Reunion; The Country Doctor; Going on Two (short); Pathe shorts. **1938** Five of a Kind; Quintupland (short).

DIONNE, OLIVA
Born: 1908, Canada. Died: Nov. 15, 1979, near North Bay, Ontario, Canada. Screen actor. Father of Dionne Quintuplets: Emilie (dec. 1954), Marie (dec. 1970), Annette Allard, Cecile Langlois, and Yvonne.

Appeared in: **1936** Going on Two; Pathe shorts.

DIRKSEN, EVERETT (Everett McKinley Dirksen)
Born: Jan. 4, 1896, Pekin, Ill. Died: Sept. 7, 1969, Washington, D.C. (lung cancer). United States Senator, author and screen actor.

Appeared in: **1969** The Monitors.

DITRICHSTEIN, LEO
Born: Jan. 6, 1865, Temesbar, Hungary. Died: June 28, 1928, Vienna, Austria (heart trouble). Screen, stage actor and playwright.

Appeared in: **1915** How Molly Made Good.

DITT, JOSEPHINE
Born: Sept. 7, 1868, Chicago, Ill. Died: Oct. 18, 1939, Hollywood, Calif. Screen actress.

Appeared in: **1914** Her Fighting Chance; False Gods.

DIX, BILLY (William H. Dixon)
Born: Sept. 4, 1911, Miami, Okla. Died: Mar. 22, 1973. Screen actor and rodeo performer. Do not confuse with actor William Dix.

Appeared in: **1945** Sunset in El Dorado. **1946** West of the Alamo; Rainbow Over the Rockies; Raiders of the South; Silver Range. **1947** Song of the Sierras. **1950** Buckaroo Sheriff of Texas. **1952** The Lion and the Horse. **1953** Arena. **1956** Meet Me in Las Vegas; The Lonely Man; The Wild Dakotas. **1966** Tribute to a Bad Man.

DIX, DOROTHY
Born: Feb. 27, 1892, London, England. Died: Jan., 1970, England? Screen, stage and vaudeville actress. Divorced from actor Jameson Thomas (dec. 1939), T. Vezey-Strong, and Roy Clark.

Appeared in: **1930** Dollar Dizzy (short). **1931** Nevada Buckaroo. **1932** The First Mrs. Fraser. **1933** Drum Taps. **1934** Wheels of Destiny; plus the following shorts: Trimmed in Furs; Super Snooper; The Gold Ghost. **1936** Sunset of Power; Guns and Guitars.

DIX, LILLIAN
Born: 1864. Died: Oct. 10, 1922, New York, N.Y. Screen, stage and vaudeville actress. Married to actor William H. Thompson (dec. 1923). Appeared in early Kalem, Famous Players, Peerless and Kleine Film Co. films.

DIX, MAE
Born: 1895, Lake Ann, Mich. Died: Oct. 21, 1958, Los Angeles, Calif. (burns in apartment fire). Screen, stage, burlesque and vaudeville actress. Entered films as an extra with Biograph in 1913.

DIX, RICHARD (Ernest Carlton Brimmer)
Born: Aug. 8, 1894, St. Paul, Minn. Died: Sept. 20, 1949, Los Angeles, Calif. (heart trouble). Screen and stage actor. Father of actor Robert Dix. Nominated for 1930/1931 Academy Award for Best Actor in Cimarron.

Appeared in: **1921** The Sin Flood; The Old Nest; All's Fair in Love; Not Guilty; The Poverty of Riches; Dangerous Curve Ahead. **1922** Yellow Men and Gold; The Glorious Fool; The Bonded Woman; The Wallflower; Fools First. **1923** Quicksands; Racing Hearts; The Woman With Four Faces; The Christian; The Call of the Canyon; The Ten Commandments; Souls for Sale; To the Last Man. **1924** Manhattan; Sinners in Heaven; Icebound; Iron Horse; The Stranger; Unguarded Women. **1925** The Vanishing American; Too Many Kisses; The Shock Punch; The Lucky Devil; A Man Must Live; Men and Women; The Lady Who Lied. **1926** Woman-handled; The Quarterback; Let's Get Married; Fascinating Youth; Say It Again. **1927** Paradise for Two; Knock-Out Reilly; Manpower; Shanghai Bound; Quicksands (and 1923 version). **1928** The Gay Defender; Sporting Goods; Easy Come, Easy Go; Warming Up; Moran of the Marines. **1929** Nothing But the Truth; The Wheel of Life; The Love Doctor; Redskin; Seven Keys to Baldpate. **1930** Lovin' the Ladies; Shooting Straight. **1931** Cimarron; The Public Defender; Young Donovan's Kid; Secret Service. **1932** Slippery Pearls (short); The Lost Squadron; Roar of the Dragon; Hell's Highway; The Conquerors; Liberty Road. **1933** No Marriage Ties; The Great Jasper; Day of Reckoning; The Ace of Aces. **1934** Stingaree; West of the Pecos; His Greatest Gamble; I Won a Medal. **1935** Trans-Atlantic Tunnel; The Arizonian. **1936** Yellow Dust; Special Investigator; Devil's Squadron. **1937** Once a Hero; The Devil's Playground; The Devil Is Driving; It Happened in Hollywood. **1938** Blind Alibi; Sky Giant. **1939** Man of Conquest; Reno; Twelve Crowded Hours; Here I Am a Stranger. **1940** The Marines Fly High; Men Against the Sky; Cherokee Strip. **1941** The Roundup; Badlands of Dakota. **1942** American Empire; Tombstone, the Town Too Tough to Die. **1943** The Iron Road; Buckskin Frontier; Top Man; The Kansan; Eyes of the Underworld; The Ghost Ship. **1944** The Mark of the Whistler; The Whistler. **1945** The Power of the Whistler. **1946** The Voice of the Whistler; The Mysterious Intruder; The Secret of the Whistler. **1947** The 13th Hour.

DIXEY, HENRY E.
Born: 1859, Boston, Mass. Died: Feb. 25, 1943, Atlantic City, N.J. (struck by bus). Stage and screen actor. Entered films with Universal in 1915.

DIXIT
Born: India. Died: June 29, 1949, India. Screen actor.

DIXON, CHARLOTTE L.
Died: 1970, West Palm Beach, Fla. Screen actress.

Appeared in: **1915** Birth of a Nation.

DIXON, CONWAY
Born: 1874, England. Died: Jan. 17, 1943, London, England (heart attack). Stage and screen actor.

Appeared in: **1935** The Triumph of Sherlock Holmes. **1937** The Mutiny of Elsinore (US 1939). **1938** Sixty Glorious Years (aka Queen of Destiny—US).

DIXON, DENVER (Victor Adamson)
Born: 1890, Kansas City, Mo. Died: Nov. 9, 1972, Hollywood, Calif. (heart attack). Screen, vaudeville actor, film director and producer. Father of film producer-director Al Adamson.

Appeared in: **1915** Birth of a Nation. **1919** The Squaw Man. **1922** The Lone Rider. **1936** Guns and Guitars. **1937** Way Out West. **1938** The Old Barn Dance. **1947** Unconquered **1949** Riders in the Sky. **1969** Five Bloody Graves.

DIXON, HENRY
Born: 1871. Died: May 3, 1943, Hollywood, Calif. Screen, vaudeville actor and burlesque producer.

DIXON, JAMES "JIM"
Born: 1949. Died: Mar. 13, 1974, Inyo County, Calif. (plane crash). Screen and television actor.

Appeared in: **1968** Ice Station Zebra.

DIXON, JEAN
Born: July 14, 1896, Waterbury, Conn. Died: Feb. 12, 1981, New York, N.Y. Screen and stage actress. Entered films in 1929.

Appeared in: **1929** The Lady Lies. **1930** Two Rounds of Love (short). **1933** The Kiss Before the Morror. **1934** Sadie McKee. **1935** Mister Dynamite; I'll Love You Always; She Married Her Boss. **1936** The Magnificent Brute; My Man Godfrey; To Mary, With Love. **1937** You Only Live Once; Swing High, Swing Low. **1938** Joy of Living; Holiday.

DIXON, LEE
Born: Jan. 22, 1914, Brooklyn, N.Y. Died: Jan. 8, 1953, New York, N.Y. Screen, stage and vaudeville actor.

Appeared in: **1936** Gold Diggers of 1937. **1937** Ready, Willing and Able; The Singing Marine; Variety Show. **1947** Angel and the Badman.

DIXON, PAUL (Gregory Schleier)
Born: 1918. Died: Dec. 28, 1974, Cincinnati, Ohio (ruptured heart artery). Screen and television actor. Known on television as "The Mayor of Kneesville."

Appeared in: **1951** Disc Jockey.

DOBBINS, EARL E.
Born: 1911. Died: Feb. 9, 1949, Los Angeles, Calif. (result of knife wound). Screen actor and stuntman.

DOBLE, BUDD
Born: Oct. 10, 1841, Philadelphia, Pa. Died: Mar. 29, 1926, Puente, Calif. (stroke). Screen actor and harness race driver.

Appeared in: **1913** Budd Doble Comes Back.

DOBLE, FRANCES
Died: Dec., 1969, England. Stage and screen actress.

Appeared in: **1927** The Vortex (US 1928). **1928** The Constant Nymph. **1929** Dark Red Roses.

DOBSON, EDWARD
Died: Feb. 7, 1925, San Jose, Calif. Screen actor.

DOCKSON, EVELYN
Born: 1888. Died: May 20, 1952, Burbank, Calif. (cancer). Screen and vaudeville actress.

Appeared in: **1936** The Great Ziegfeld. **1943** Let's Face It; The Heavenly Body.

DOCKSTADER, LEW (George Alfred Clapp)
Born: 1856, Hartford, Conn. Died: Oct. 26, 1924, New York, N.Y. (bone tumor). Screen, Stage, vaudeville actor and minstrel player.

Appeared in: **1914** Dan.

DODD, CLAIRE
Born: 1909?, New York, N.Y. Died: Nov. 23, 1973, Beverly Hills, Calif. (cancer). Screen and stage actress.

Appeared in: **1930** Whoopee; Our Blushing Brides. **1931** An American Tragedy; The Secret Call; Working Girls; Girls About Town; Up Pops the Devil; The Lawyer's Secret; Road to Reno. **1932** Under Eighteen; Two Kinds of Women; Alias the Doctor; The Broken Wing; Man Wanted; This is the Night; Guilty as Hell; Crooner; The Match King; Lawyer Man; Dancers in the Dark. **1933** Parachute Jumper; Hard to Handle; Blondie Johnson; Ex-Lady; Elmer the Great; Ann Carver's Profession; Footlight Parade; My Woman. **1934** Massacre; Gambling Lady; Journal of a Crime; The Personality Kid; Babbit; I Sell Anything; Smarty. **1935** Roberta; The Case of the Curious Bride; The Glass Key; Don't Bet on Blondes; The Goose and the Gander; The Pay-Off; Secret of the Chateau. **1936** The Singing Kid; Murder By An Aristocrat; The Case of the Velvet Claws; Navy Born; Two Against the World; A Vitaphone short. **1937** The Women Men Marry. **1938** Romance in the Dark; Fast Company; Three Loves Has Nancy; Charlie Chan in Honolulu. **1939** Woman Doctor. **1940** If I Had My Way; Slightly Honorable. **1941** The Black Cat; In the Navy. **1942** The Mad Doctor of Market Street; Don Winslow of the Navy (serial); Mississippi Gambler.

DODD, MRS. ELAN E.
Born: 1868. Died: Mar. 12, 1935, Brooklyn, N.Y. Screen actress. Entered films with Vitaphone.

DODD, JIMMIE
Born: 1910, Cincinnati, Ohio. Died: Nov. 10, 1964, Honolulu, Hawaii. Screen, television actor and songwriter.

Appeared in: **1940** Those Were the Days; Law and Order. **1941** The Richest Man in Town. **1942** Snuffy Smith; Hillbilly Blitzkrieg; Yard Bird; Flying Tigers; Valley of Hunted Men. **1943** Thundering Trails; The Blocked Trail; Keep 'Em Slugging; Shadows on the Sage; Riders of the Rio Grande. **1944** Hi, Beautiful!; Moon Over Las Vegas; Twilight on the Prairie; Janie. **1945** Penthouse Rhythm; The Crimson Canary; China's Little Devils; Men in Her Diary. **1946** Young Widow. **1947** Living in a Big Way; Rolling Home; Buck Privates Come Home; The Tender Years; Song of My Heart. **1948** The Noose Hangs High; Daredevils of the Clouds; You Gotta Stay Happy; Sleep, My Love; Easter Parade. **1949** Flaming Fury; Post Office Investigator; Incident. **1950** Singing Guns. **1951** Al Jennings of Oklahoma; The Second Woman; G.I. Jane. **1952** The Winning Team; The Lusty Men. **1954** Phffft.

DODD, MOLLY
Born: c. 1925. Died: Mar. 26, 1981, Santa Monica, Calif. Screen, stage and television actress. Married to screenwriter Henry Farrell.

Appeared in: **1971** What's The Matter With Helen? **1978** Harper Valley PTA.

DODD, REV. NEAL
Born: Sept. 6, 1878, Fort Madison, Iowa. Died: May 26, 1966, Los Angeles, Calif. Screen actor, film director and religious advisor. Known as the "Padre of Hollywood." Entered films in 1920.

Appeared in: **1924** The Only Woman. **1926** Lost at Sea. **1927** Tillie's Punctured Romance. **1930** Anna Christie. **1932** Merrily We Go to Hell. **1933** Employee's Entrance. **1934** It Happened One Night; You Belong to Me; Gambling Lady. **1935** Strange Wives; Hold 'Em Yale. **1937** The Man Who Cried Wolf; She's Dangerous. **1939** Mr. Smith Goes to Washington. **1940** Santa Fe Trail. **1941** Unfinished Business. **1942** They All Kissed the Bride. **1946** The Killers; Easy to Wed; Scarlet Street; Blue Skies. **1947** The Secret Life of Walter Mitty. **1948** Sorry, Wrong Number. **1950** Louisa. **1951** Here Comes the Groom.

DODDS, CHUCK
Born: 1936. Died: Oct. 11, 1967, Hollywood, Calif. (leukemia). Screen actor and nightclub singer.

DODDS, JACK
Born: 1927. Died: June 2, 1962, Hollywood, Calif. (cancer). Screen, stage, television actor and dancer.

Appeared in: **1962** State Fair.

DODGE, ROGER (Roger Pryor Dodge)
Born: 1898, Paris, France. Died: June 2, 1974, New York, N.Y. Screen actor, choreographer and stage producer.

Appeared in: **1935** A Universal short.

DODSON, JON (Dodson Blunt)
Died: 1964. Black screen actor and singer. Member of "The King's Men" quartet.

Appeared in: **1929** Sweetie. **1930** Only the Brave. **1939** St. Louis Blues.

DODSON, WILLIAM T.
Born: 1892. Died: Sept. 17, 1933, Hollywood, Calif. Screen actor and stuntman.

DODSWORTH, JOHN (John Cecil Dodsworth)
Born: Sept. 17, 1910, England. Died: Sept. 11, 1964, Los Angeles, Calif. (suicide—asphyxiation). Screen actor.

Appeared in: **1952** Storm Over Tibet; The Snows of Kilimanjaro; Bwana Devil; Rogue's March. **1953** Loose in London; The Maze. **1954** Bengal Brigade. **1955** Untamed. **1958** In the Money.

DOLAN, JOHN
Born: 1930. Died: Mar. 9, 1974, Woodland Hills, Calif. Screen actor and stuntman.

DOLAN, MICHAEL J.
Born: 1884, Ireland. Died: Oct. 21, 1954, Dublin, Ireland. Screen and stage actor.

Appeared in: **1949** Saints and Sinners. **1951** A Christmas Carol. **1952** You Can't Beat the Irish.

DOLENZ, GEORGE
Born: Jan. 5, 1908, Trieste, Italy. Died: Feb. 8, 1963, Hollywood, Calif. (heart attack). Screen, stage and television actor.

Appeared in: **1941** The Unexpected Uncle (film debut); Faculty Row. **1943** Fired Wife; The Strange Death of Adolf Hitler; She's for Me; Moonlight in Vermont; Calling Dr. Death; Young Ideas. **1944** In Society; The Climax; Enter Arsene Lupin; Bowery to Broadway. **1945** The Royal Mounted Rides Again (serial); Song of the Sarong; Easy to Look At. **1946** Idea Girl; A Night in Paradise; Girl on the Spot. **1947** Song of Scheherazade. **1950** Vendetta. **1952** My Cousin Rachel. **1953** Thunder Bay; Scared Stiff; Wings of the Hawk. **1954** The Last Time I Saw Paris; Sign of the Pagan. **1955** The Racers; A Bullet for Joey; The Purple Mask. **1957** Sad Sack. **1959** Timbuktu. **1961** Look in Any Window. **1962** The Four Horsemen of the Apocalypse.

DOLLARHIDE, ROSS, JR.
Born: 1922. Died: Sept. 8, 1977 (accident while filming). Screen actor and stuntman.

DOLLY, JENNY (Janszieka Deutsch)
Born: Oct. 25, 1892, Hungary. Died: June 1, 1941, Hollywood, Calif. (suicide—hanging). Screen, stage and vaudeville actress. She and her twin sister Rosie Dolly (dec. 1970) were known as the famous dancing "Dolly Sisters." Divorced from actor Harry Fox (dec. 1959).

Appeared in: **1915** The Call of the Dance. **1918** The Million Dollar Dollies.

DOLLY, LADY
Born: 1876. Died: Sept. 5, 1953, Hollywood, Calif. Screen actress (midget performer). Was also stand-in for child actors.

DOLLY, ROSIE (Roszicka Deutsch)
Born: Oct. 25, 1892, Hungary. Died: Feb. 1, 1970, New York, N.Y. (heart failure). Screen, stage and vaudeville actress. She and her sister Jenny Dolly (dec. 1941) were known as the famous dancing "Dolly Sisters."

Appeared in: **1915** Dance of Creations; The Lily and the Rose. **1918** The Million Dollar Dollies.

DOMBRE, BARBARA
Born: 1950. Died: Jan. 3, 1973, U.S. Stage and screen actress.

Appeared in: **1969** Heaven with a Gun.

DOMGRAF-FASSBENDER, WILLI
Born: 1898, Germany. Died: Feb. 13, 1978, Germany? Screen actor and opera singer.

Appeared in: **1932** Theodor Koerner (US 1933); Die Verkaufte Braut (US 1934). **1935** Aufforderung Zum Tanz (Invitation to Dance). **1949** Figaros Hochzeit (The Marriage of Figaro—US).

DOMINGUEZ, BEATRICE
Died: Feb. 27, 1921, Los Angeles, Calif. (after operation complications). Screen actress.

Appeared in: **1920** The Moon Riders (serial). **1921** The White Horseman (serial); The Fire Cat; The Four Horsemen of the Apocalypse.

DOMINGUEZ, JOE (Jose J. Dominguez)
Born: Mar. 19, 1894, Mexico. Died: Apr. 11, 1970, Woodland Hills, Calif. Screen actor.

Appeared in: **1932** Riders of the Desert; Mason of the Mounted. **1939** Mexicali Rose. **1940** Geronimo; Gaucho Serenade. **1941** Outlaws of the Rio Grande. **1942** Undercover Man. **1944** The Story of Dr. Wassell. **1945** The Bull Fighters. **1949** The Streets of Laredo; The Big Sombrero. **1950** One Way Street; Dallas; Bandit Queen. **1952** Blackbeard the Pirate; Rancho Notorious. **1953** Ride, Vaquero; Son of Belle Starr; The Hitch-Hiker. **1954** Jubilee Trail; Gypsy Colt; Green Fire. **1956** The Broken Star. **1957** The Ride Back. **1958** Man of the West. **1961** One-Eyed Jacks. **1968** I Love You, Alice B. Toklas.

DOMINQUE, IVAN
Born: 1928, Antwerp, Belgium. Died: Apr. 3, 1973, Ghent, Belgium. Screen, stage actor and composer. Son of writer Evelyne Pollet.

Appeared in: Princess of Cleves.

DON, DAVID L.
Born: 1867, Utica, New York. Died: Oct. 27, 1949, New York, N.Y. Screen actor.

Appeared in: **1915** Love and Swords. **1916** Half a Million; Romance of a Beanery; Limberger's Victory; No Place Like Jail; The Butler; Otto the Bell Boy; Skirts and Cinders; Frilby Frilled; Otto the Artist; Otto the Reporter; Otto the Salesman; Otto the Sleuth; Otto the Hero; Otto the Cobbler; Otto the Gardener; Otto's Vacation; Otto's Legacy; Otto the Traffic Cop. **1918** The Hidden Truth.

DONAHUE, JACK (John J. Donahue)
Born: 1892. Died: Oct. 1, 1930, New York, N.Y. (heart disease). Stage, burlesque, vaudeville actor, stage producer, and playwright. Appeared in vaudeville with his wife in a team billed "Donahue and Stewart."

DONAHUE, VINCENT
Born: 1918, Portland, Maine. Died: Feb. 10, 1976, New York, N.Y. (stabbed to death). Screen and stage actor.

Appeared in: **1948** Joan of Arc; Beyond Glory.

DONAHUE, WILLIAM FRANCIS "RED"
Born: 1895. Died: May 21, 1981, Alturas, Calif. Screen, stage and vaudeville actor.

Appeared in: **1937** Mountain Music. **1942** Ten Gentlemen from West Point. **1946** Little Giant.

DONALDSON, ARTHUR
Born: 1869 or 1875, Norsholm, Sweden. Died: Sept. 28, 1955, Long Island, N.Y. Screen, stage actor, film producer, stage director, stage producer and singer.

Appeared in: **1915** The Hearts of Men; Babbling Tongues; The Ghost of the Twisted Oaks. **1916** A Woman's Honor. **1917** For France; The Danger Trail; I Will Repay; Enlighten Thy Daughter; Who Goes There. **1918** Over the Top. **1919** The Captain's Captain; Miss Dulcie from Dixie; Fighting Destiny; Daring Hearts; Coax Me; The Undercurrent; Mind the Paint Girl; The ABC of Love. **1921** The Silver Lining; The Passionate Pilgrim; Rider of the King Log; Gilded Lies; Is Life Worth Living?; Wise Husbands. **1922** Find the Woman; Orphans of the Ghetto; When Knighthood Was in Flower. **1924** America; Yolanda; For Woman's Favor; The Bandolero. **1925** Down Upon the Suwannee River; School for Wives; The Swan; Fifty-Fifty. **1926** Love 'Em and Leave 'Em. **1927** The Winning Oar; The Broadway Drifter.

DONALDSON, JACK
Born: 1910. Died: June 20, 1975, Woodland Hills, Calif. (stroke). Screen, stage actor and theatrical agent.

DONAT, ROBERT
Born: Mar. 18, 1905, Manchester, England. Died: June 9, 1958, London, England (respiratory ailment, asthma). Screen, stage actor and film director. Won 1939 Academy Award for Best Actor in Goodbye, Mr. Chips and nominated for 1938 Academy Award for Best Actor in The Citadel. Divorced from Ella Annesley Voysey and later married to actress Renee Asherson.

Appeared in: **1932** Men of Tomorrow (film debut); That Night in London (aka Overnight—US 1934). **1933** Cash (aka For Love or Money—US 1934); The Private Life of Henry VIII. **1934** The Count of Monte Cristo. **1935** The 39 Steps. **1936** The Ghost Goes West. **1937** Knight Without Armour. **1938** The Citadel. **1939** Goodbye, Mr. Chips. **1942** The Young Mr. Pitt. **1943** Adventures of Tartu (aka Tartu—US). **1945** Perfect Strangers (aka Vacation from Marriage—US). **1947**

Captain Boycott. **1948** The Winslow Boy (US 1950). **1950** The Cure for Love. **1951** The Magic Box (US 1952). **1954** Lease of Life. **1956** Stained Glass at Fairford (short—voice only). **1958** The Inn of the Sixth Happiness.

DONAT, SANDRA See FRANCIS, SANDRA

DONATH, LUDWIG
Born: 1900, Vienna, Austria. Died: Sept. 29, 1967, New York, N.Y. (leukemia). Screen, stage and television actor.

Appeared in: **1942** The Secret Code (serial); Enemy Agents Meet Ellery Queen; Lady from Chungking. **1943** Margin for Error (voice); Hangmen Also Die; The Strange Death of Adolf Hitler; Hostages. **1944** The Story of Dr. Wassell; The Seventh Cross; The Hitler Gang; Tampico. **1945** The Master Race; Counter-Attack. **1946** Blondie Knows Best; Gilda; The Jolson Story; The Devil's Mask; Prison Ship; Renegades; Return of Monte Cristo. **1947** Cigarette Girl; Assignment to Treasury. **1948** Sealed Verdict; To the Ends of the Earth. **1949** The Fighting O'Flynn; The Great Sinner; There's a Girl in My Heart; The Lovable Cheat. **1950** The Killer That Stalked New York; Mystery Submarine; Jolson Sings Again. **1951** Journey into Light; Sirocco; The Great Caruso. **1952** My Pal Gus. **1953** Sins of Jezebel; The Veils of Bagdad. **1966** Torn Curtain; Death Trap.

DONATI, MARIA
Born: 1902, Mexico. Died: Nov. 4, 1966, Mexico. Screen actress.

Appeared in: **1947** La Vita Ricominicia (Life Begins Anew). **1948** Angelina. **1952** Tears of Blood.

DONER, MAURICE
Born: 1905. Died: Feb. 21, 1971, Hollywood, Calif. Screen, stage and television actor.

Appeared in: **1949** Flame of Youth. **1952** Assignment—Paris. **1956** Congo Crossing. **1957** The Enemy Below. **1966** Torn Curtain.

DONER, ROSE
Born: 1905. Died: Aug. 15, 1926, New York, N.Y. (following operation for appendicitis). Screen, stage, vaudeville actress and dancer. Appeared in vaudeville with her brother and sister, Ted and Kitty Donner.

DONER, TED
Born: July 17, 1896, Chicago, Ill. Died: June, 1969. Screen, stage and vaudeville actor.

Appeared in: **1928** Broadway's Favorite Dancing Man (short).

DONLAN, JAMES
Born: 1889. Died: June 7, 1938, Hollywood, Calif. (heart attack). Screen and stage actor. Father of actress Yolanda Donlan.

Appeared in: **1929** Wise Girls; Big News. **1930** Night Work; The Bishop Murder Case; Beau Bandit; Remote Control; Sins of the Children. **1931** Good Bad Girl; Five Star Final; A Free Soul; The Front Page; Dance, Fools, Dance. **1932** The Half-Naked Truth; Back Street. **1933** The Working Man; They Just Had to Get Married; College Humor; Design for Living; The Avenger. **1934** A Very Honorable Guy; The Cat's Paw; Now I'll Tell; Hi, Nellie!; Belle of the Nineties. **1935** Dr. Socrates; The Man Who Reclaimed His Head; Under Pressure; The Daring Young Man; The Whole Town's Talking; Traveling Saleslady; The Case of the Curious Bride; We're Only Human. **1936** The Ex-Mrs. Bradford; The Plot Thickens; Crash Donovan; Murder on the Bridle Path. **1937** Oh, Doctor!; Music for Madame; This is My Affair; It Happened in Hollywood. **1938** Every Day's a Holiday; Professor Beware.

DONLEVY, BRIAN
Born: Feb. 9, 1899, Portadown County, Armagh, Ireland. Died: Apr. 5, 1972, Woodland Hills, Calif. (throat cancer). Screen, stage and television actor. Divorced from singer Marjorie Lane. Married to Lillian Lugosi. Nominated for 1939 Academy Award as Best Supporting Actor in Beau Geste.

Appeared in: **1923** Jamestown. **1924** Damaged Hearts; Monsieur Beaucaire. **1925** School for Wives. **1926** A Man of Quality. **1929** Mother's Boy; Gentlemen of the Press. **1932** A Modern Cinderella. **1934** The Milky Way. **1935** Barbary Coast; Mary Burns, Fugitive; Another Face. **1936** Strike Me Pink; Thirteen Hours by Air; High Tension; Crack-Up; Human Cargo; 36 Hours to Kill; Half Angel. **1937** Born Reckless; This is My Affair; Midnight Taxi. **1938** In Old Chicago; Sharpshooters; Battle of Broadway; We're Going to be Rich. **1939** Jesse James; Destry Rides Again; Beau Geste; Union Pacific; Behind Prison Gates; Alleghany Uprising. **1940** The Great McGinty; When the Daltons Rode; Brigham Young—Frontiersman. **1941** I Wanted Wings; South of Tahiti; Birth of the Blues; Billy the Kid; Hold Back the

Dawn. **1942** Wake Island; The Great Man's Lady; A Gentleman After Dark; The Remarkable Andrew; The Glass Key; Two Yanks in Trinidad; Stand By For Action; Cargo of Innocents; Nightmare. **1943** Hangmen Also Die; The City That Stopped Hitler—Heroic Stalingrad (narrator). **1944** An American Romance; The Miracle of Morgan's Creek. **1945** Duffy's Tavern. **1946** Our Hearts Were Growing Up; The Virginian; Two Years Before the Mast; Canyon Passage. **1947** Song of Scheherazade; Killer McCoy; Kiss of Death; The Beginning or the End; The Trouble With Women; Heaven Only Knows. **1948** A Southern Yankee; Command Decision. **1949** Impact; The Lucky Stiff. **1950** Kansas Raiders; Shakedown. **1951** Slaughter Trail; Fighting Coast Guard. **1952** Hoodlum Empire; Ride the Man Down. **1953** The Woman They Almost Lynched. **1955** The Big Combo; The Quatermass Experiment (aka The Creeping Unknown—US 1956). **1956** A Cry in the Night. **1957** Quatermass II (aka Enemy from Space—US). **1958** Cowboy; Escape from Red Rock. **1959** Never so Few; Juke Box Rhythm. **1961** The Girl in Room 13. **1962** The Pigeon That Took Rome; The Errand Boy. **1965** Curse of the Fly; How to Stuff a Wild Bikini; The Fat Spy. **1966** Waco. **1967** Hostile Guns; Gammera the Invincible. **1968** Arizona Bushwackers; Five Golden Dragons. **1969** Pit Stop. **1982** Dead Men Don't Wear Plaid (film clips).

DONLIN, MIKE
Born: May 30, 1877, Peoria, Ill. Died: Sept. 24, 1933, Los Angeles, Calif. Screen, stage, vaudeville actor and baseball player.

Appeared in: **1923** Woman Proof; Railroaded; The Unknown Purple. **1924** Oh, Doctor; Flaming Barriers; Hit and Run; The Trouble Shooter. **1925** Raffles; Fifth Avenue Models; The Unnamed Woman. **1926** The Sea Beast; Her Second Chance; Ella Cinders; The Fighting Marine (serial and feature film). **1927** The General; Slide, Kelly, Slide. **1928** Riley the Cop; Beggars of Life; Warming Up. **1929** Below the Deadline; Thunderbolt; Noisy Neighbors. **1930** Her Man; Born Reckless; Hot Curves. **1931** Arrowsmith; Iron Man; The Tip Off. **1933** Air Hostess; High Gear.

DONNELLY, DOROTHY
Born: 1880, New York, N.Y. Died: Jan. 3, 1928, New York, N.Y. (pneumonia). Screen, stage actress and playwright.

Appeared in: **1916** Madame X.

DONNELLY, JAMES
Born: 1865, Boston, Mass. Died: Apr. 13, 1937, Hollywood, Calif. Screen and stage actor.

Appeared in: **1916** The Snow Cure; Bubbles of Trouble. **1917** She Needed a Doctor. **1921** Black Beauty. **1922** A Girl's Desire.

DONNELLY, LEO
Born: 1878. Died: Aug. 21, 1935, Atlantic City, N.J. Screen, stage and vaudeville actor, and screenwriter.

Appeared in: **1923** Potash and Perlmutter. **1930** Roadhouse Nights; Stepping Out (short); The Music Racket (short).

DONOHUE, JOSEPH
Born: 1884. Died: Oct. 25, 1921, Brooklyn, N.Y. Screen and vaudeville actor.

Appeared in: **1917** Within the Law. **1920** Over the Hill.

DONOVAN, RICHARD
Born: 1920. Died: Apr. 25, 1980, Los Angeles, Calif. (heart attack). Screen actor, journalist and television writer.

DONSKOY, MARK (Mark Semonovitch Donskoy)
Born: Mar. 6, 1901, Russia. Died: Mar., 1981, Moscow, Russia. Screen actor, film director, film producer, screenwriter and author.

Appeared in: **1926** The Prostitute.

DOOLEY, BILLY
Born: Feb. 8, 1893, Chicago, Ill. Died: Aug. 4, 1938, Hollywood, Calif. (heart attack). Screen, stage and vaudeville actor. Entered films with Al Christie.

Appeared in: **1925** A Goofy Gob (short). **1928** The following shorts: Campus Cuties; Sea Sword; The Dizzy Diver; A Gallant Gob; Oriental Hugs and Water Bugs. **1934** The Fugitive Lady. **1936** Sleepy Time (short); Anything Goes. **1938** Go Chase Yourself; Call of the Yukon; The Marines Are Here.

DOOLEY, JOHNNY (John D. Dool)
Born: 1887, Glasgow, Scotland. Died: June 7, 1928, Yonkers, N.Y. (intestinal trouble). Screen, stage and vaudeville actor. Son of circus performer Robert Rogers Dooley (dec.). Brother of stage actors William (dec. 1921) and J. Gordon (dec. 1930) and actress Ray Dooley.

Appeared in: **1921** Skinning Skinners. **1922** When Knighthood Was in Flower. **1924** Yolanda. **1927** East Side, West Side.

DOONAN, GEORGE
Born: 1897, England. Died: Apr. 17, 1973, London, England. Screen, stage and vaudeville actor. Father of actors Patrick (dec. 1958) and Tony Doonan.

DOONAN, PATRICK
Born: 1927. Died: Mar. 10, 1958, London, England (suicide—gas). Screen and stage actor. Son of actor George Doonan (dec. 1973) and brother of actor Anthony Doonan.

Appeared in: **1948** Once a Joly Swagman (aka Maniacs on Wheels—US 1951). **1949** Train of Events (US 1952); A Run for Your Money (US 1950); All Over Town. **1950** The Blue Lamp; Blackout; Highly Dangerous (US 1951). **1951** The Lavender Hill Mob; Calling Bulldog Drummond; The Man in the White Suit (US 1952); High Treason (US 1952); Appointment With Venus (aka Island Rescue—US 1952). **1952** The Gift Horse (aka Glory at Sea—US 1953); I'm a Stranger; The Gentle Gunman (US 1953). **1953** The Net (aka Project M7—US); The Red Beret (aka Paratrooper—US 1954); Wheel of Fate. **1954** What Every Woman Wants; Seagulls Over Sorrento (aka Crest of the Wave—US). **1955** John and Julie (US 1957); Cockleshell Heroes (US 1956).

DOORENBOS, J. P. J. H. CLINGE
Born: 1885, Holland. Died: May 11, 1978, Holland? Screen actor and cabaret entertainer.

DORALDINA
Born: 1888. Died: Feb. 13, 1936, Los Angeles, Calif. (heart attack). Screen actress and stage dancer.

Appeared in: **1918** The Naulahka. **1921** Passion Fruit; Woman Untamed.

DORETY, CHARLES R.
Born: May 20, 1898, San Francisco, Calif. Died: Apr. 2, 1957, Hollywood, Calif. Screen, circus, vaudeville actor, film director and film producer.

Appeared in: **1931** La Senorita de Chicago (short—Spanish version of The Pip from Pittsburgh). **1934** Men in Black (short); Three Little Pigskins (short). **1935** The following shorts: Uncivil Warriors; I'm a Father; Sawbones. **1936** Ants in the Pantry (short); Movie Maniacs (short).

DORHAM, KENNY (McKinley Howard Dorham)
Born: Aug. 30, 1924, Fairfield, Tex. Died: Dec. 5, 1972, New York, N.Y. (kidney disorder). Composer, jazz trumpeter and screen actor.

Appeared in: **1959** Witness in the City; Les Liasons Dangerouses (Dangerous Liaisons).

DORIAN, CHARLES
Born: 1893. Died: Oct. 21, 1942, Albuquerque, N.Mex. (heart attack). Screen, vaudeville actor and assistant film director. Entered films in 1917.

DORLEAC, FRANCOISE
Born: 1941, France. Died: June 26, 1967, Nice, France (auto accident). Screen actress. Sister of actress Catherine Deneuve.

Appeared in: **1957** Mensonges. **1958** The Door Slams. **1959** Les Loups Dans la Berbaries. **1960** Ce Soir ou Jamais; Les Portes Claquent. **1961** Le Jeu de la Verite; A D'Autres Amours; La Gamberge; Tout L'Or de Monde; Payroll; La Fille aux Yeux D'Or (The Girl With the Golden Eyes—US 1962). **1962** Arsene Lupin Contre Arsene Lupin (Arsene Lupin Against Arsene Lupin). **1964** La Ronde (Circle of Love—US 1965); La Peau Douce (The Soft Skin); L'Homme de Rio (That Man from Rio). **1965** Genghis Khan. **1966** Cul-de-Sac; Where the Spies Are. **1967** Les Demoiselles de Rochefort (The Young Girls of Rochefort—US 1968); Billion Dollar Brain.

DORN, PHILIP (Fritz Van Dungen)
Born: 1902, Scheveningen, Holland. Died: May 9, 1975, Woodland Hills, Calif. (heart attack). Screen and stage actor.

Appeared in: **1940** Ski Patrol (film debut); Enemy Agent; Escape; Diamond Frontier. **1941** Tarzan's Secret Treasure; Ziegfeld Girl; Underground. **1942** Random Harvest; Calling Dr. Gillespie; Reunion. **1943** Chetniks; Paris After Dark. **1944** Passage to Marseilles; Blonde Fever. **1945** Escape in the Desert. **1946** I've Always Loved You; Concerto. **1948** I Remember Mama. **1949** The Fighting Kentuckian; Panther's Moon. **1950** Spy Hunt. **1951** Sealed Cargo. **1956** Salto Mortale.

DORO, MARIE (Marie K. Steward)
Born: 1882, Duncannon, Pa. Died: Oct. 9, 1956, New York, N.Y. (heart ailment). Screen and stage actress. Divorced from actor Elliott Dexter (dec. 1941).

Appeared in: **1915** The Morals of Marcus (film debut); The White Pearl. **1916** The Heart of Nora Flynn; Oliver Twist (stage and film versions); Diplomacy; The Wood Nymph. **1917** Lost and Won; Castles for Two. **1919** The Mysterious Princess; A Sinless Sinner (aka Midnight Gambols—US 1920); Twelve Ten. **1920** Maid of Mystery. **1922** The Stronger Passion. **1923** Sally Bishop.

DORR, HARRY LESTER (aka LESTER DORR)
Born: May 8, 1893, Mass. Died: Aug. 25, 1980, Los Angeles, Calif. (pneumonia). Screen actor.

Appeared in: **1930** All Stuck Up. **1931** Riders of the Purple Sage. **1934** Washee Ironee (short); You Said a Hateful (short). **1935** The following shorts: Thicker Than Water; Poker at Eight; Southern Exposure; The Four-Star Boarder. **1936** The Following Shorts: Neighborhood House; The Lucky Corner; Pinch Singer; On the Wrong Trek. **1937** Cash and Carry (short); Hollywood Cowboy; Criminals of the Air; Hollywood Round-Up. **1938** The Main Event. **1939** Help Wanted (short); Duel Personalities (short). **1940** Danger Ahead. **1941** South of Panama. **1942** The Secret Code (serial); Meet the Mob. **1943** The Masked Marvel (serial). **1945** The Jade Mask. **1946** The Shadow Returns; Bowery Bombshell. **1947** The Vicious Circle; Robin Hood of Texas. **1950** Covered Wagon Raiders; The Blonde Bandit. **1951** Flying Disc Man from Mars; Night Riders of Montana. **1954** Killers from Space; Three Ring Circus. **1955** The Girl Rush. **1958** Hot Rod Gang; Missile Monsters. **1959** Vice Raid; Arson for Hire. **1967** Hotel. **1975** At Long Last Love.

DORREE, BABETTE "BOBBIE"
Born: 1906, Vienna, Austria. Died: Jan. 10, 1974, Woodland Hills, Calif. (cancer). Screen actress and professional skater.

DORSAY, EDMUND
Born: 1897. Died: June 12, 1959, New York, N.Y. Screen, stage, vaudeville and television actor. Appeared in silents.

D'ORSAY, LAWRENCE
Born: 1860, England. Died: Sept. 13, 1931, London, England. Screen and stage actor.

Appeared in: **1918** Ruggles of Red Gap. **1922** The Bond Boy. **1923** His Children's Children. **1924** The Side Show of Life. **1925** Miss Bluebeard. **1926** The Sorrows of Satan.

DORSCH, KAETHE
Born: Dec. 29, 1889, Neumarkt, Germany. Died: Dec., 1957, Vienna, Austria. Stage and screen actress.

Appeared in: **1917** Der Blusenkoenig; Die Memoiren des Satans. **1918** Die Blaue Mauritius. **1920** Gefesselte Menschen; Klatsch. **1922** Fraulein Julie (Lady Julia). **1924** Paragraph 144 (aka Muss die Frau Mutter Werden?). **1930** Die Lindenwirtin (US 1931). **1931** Drei Tage Liebe (Three Days of Love). **1936** Eine Frau Ohne Bedeutung (US 1938); Savoy-Hotel 217. **1938** Yvette. **1939** Irrtum des Herzens; Morgen Werde ich Verhaftet; Mutterliebe (Mother Love—US 1940). **1940** Trenck, der Pandur. **1941** Komoedianten. **1945** Die Fahrt ins Glueck. **1947** Singende Engel (Singing Angel—US 1952). **1949** Der Bagnostraefling; Das Kuckucks-Ei. **1950** Regine.

DORSEY, JIMMY (James Francis Dorsey)
Born: 1904, Shenandoah, Pa. Died: June 12, 1957, New York, N.Y. (cancer). Bandleader and screen actor. Brother of bandleader and actor Tommy Dorsey (dec. 1956). Son of bandmaster Thomas F. Dorsey, Sr. (dec. 1942).

Appeared in: **1940** Paramount short. **1942** The Fleet's In. **1943** I Dood It. **1944** Lost in a Harem; Four Jills in a Jeep; Hollywood Canteen. **1947** The Fabulous Dorseys. **1949** Make Believe Ballroom.

DORSEY, TOMMY (Thomas Francis Dorsey)
Born: 1905, Mahanoy Plane, Pa. Died: Nov. 26, 1956, Greenwich, Conn. (choked while asleep). Bandleader and screen actor. Brother of bandleader and actor Jimmy Dorsey (dec. 1957). Son of bandmaster Thomas F. Dorsey, Sr. (dec. 1942).

Appeared in: **1941** Las Vegas Nights. **1942** Ship Ahoy. **1943** Du Barry Was a Lady; Presenting Lily Mars; Girl Crazy; I Dood It. **1944** Broadway Rhythm. **1947** The Fabulous Dorseys. **1948** A Song Is Born.

DORZIAT, GABRIELLE
Born: 1880, Epernay, Marne, France. Died: Nov. 30, 1979, Biarritz, France. Screen and stage actress.

Appeared in: **1937** Mayerling. **1938** The Life of Nina Petrovna; Forty Little Mothers; La Vierge Folle. **1939** La Fin du Jour (The End of a Day). **1940** Mayerling to Sarajevo. **1941** Hatred; The Man Who Seeks the Truth. **1944** 32 Rue de Montmartre; Falbalas. **1945** Drame de Shanghai (The Shanghai Drama). **1946** Paris Frills. **1947** Her First Affair (aka Children of Paradise); Monsieur Vincent (US 1948). **1948** Ruy Blas. **1949** Une Grande Fille Toute Simple (Just a Big Simple Girl). **1950** Manon; Les Parents Terribles (aka The Storm Within). **1951** Dream Ballerina. **1952** Tomorrow is Too Late; The French Way. **1953** Act of Love; Little Boy Lost; So Little Time. **1958** Mitsou. **1960** Katia (aka Magnificent Sinner—US 1963). **1962** Gigot; Un Singe en Hiver (Monkey in Winter—US 1963).

DOTY, WESTON AND WINSTON
Born: 1915. Died: Jan. 2, 1934, Calif. (both drowned in flood). Twin screen actors.

Appeared in: **1925** Peter Pan; four "Our Gang" comedies. Winston appeared in: **1922** Firefighters (short); One Terrible Day (short). **1923** A Pleasant Journey (short); Lodge Night (short).

DOUCET, CATHERINE
Born: 1875, Richmond, Va. Died: June 24, 1958, New York, N.Y. Screen and stage actress.

Appeared in: **1934** As Husbands Go; Wake Up and Dream; Little Man, What Now?; The Party's Over; Servant's Entrance. **1935** Rendezvous at Midnight; Age of Indiscretion; Accent on Youth; Millions in the Air. **1936** These Three; The Golden Arrow; Poppy; The Longest Night; The Luckiest Girl in the World. **1937** When You're in Love; Oh, Doctor; Jim Harvey—Detective; Man of the People. **1941** Nothing But the Truth; It Started With Eve. **1942** There's One Born Every Minute. **1948** Hollow Triumph; The Dude Goes West. **1949** Family Honeymoon. **1951** Detective Story.

DOUCET, M. PAUL
Born: 1886, France. Died: Oct. 10, 1928, N.Y. (septic poisoning). Stage and screen actor.

Appeared in: **1921** Tropical Love. **1922** Polly of the Follies. **1923** The Leavenworth Case. **1924** America. **1925** Heart of a Siren; The Little French Girl. **1927** The Broadway Drifter.

DOUGHERTY, JOE
Born: 1898. Died: Apr. 19, 1978, Los Angeles, Calif. (heart condition). Screen actor and makeup artist. Married to actress Louise Frye. Entered films as an extra in 1948.

DOUGHERTY, VIRGIL JACK
Born: 1895. Died: May 16, 1938, Hollywood, Calif. (suicide—carbon monoxide). Screen actor. Married to actress Barbara Lamar (dec. 1925).

Appeared in: **1921** The Greater Claim. **1922** Impulse; Second Hand Rose; Chain Lightning. **1923** Money! Money! Money! **1924** Girl of the Limberlost. **1925** The Burning Trail; The Meddler. **1926** The Runaway Express. **1927** Arizona Bound; Special Delivery; Down the Stretch; The Lure of the Night Club. **1928** Gypsy of the North; Into No Man's Land. **1929** The Body Punch. **1937** Yodelin' Kid from Pine Ridge.

DOUGLAS, BYRON
Born: 1865. Died: Apr. 21, 1935, New York, N.Y. Screen and stage actor.

Appeared in: **1920** Held by the Enemy. **1921** Dynamite Allan; Know Your Man; Beyond Price. **1923** Under the Red Robe; The Silent Command; The Net. **1924** It Is the Law. **1925** That Devil Quemado; Two-Fisted Jones; Marriage in Transit. **1927** The Perfect Sap; The Coward; Dead Man's Curve; Ladies Beware; Red Clay. **1928** Man, Woman and Wife. **1929** Born to the Saddle; The Drake Case. **1931** Secret Service.

DOUGLAS, DON (Douglas Kinleyside)
Born: 1905, New York or London, England. Died: Dec. 31, 1945, Los Angeles, Calif. (complications after emergency appendectomy). Screen, stage actor and opera performer.

Appeared in: **1929** Great Gabbo; Tonight at Twelve. **1930** Ranch House Blues. **1932** Love in High Gear. **1933** He Couldn't Take It. **1934** Jimmy the Gent; A Woman's Man; Tomorrow's Children; Men in White. **1937** Headin' East. **1938** The Spider Web (serial); Judge Hardy's Children; Law of the Texan; Alexander's Ragtime Band; Orphans of the Street; Fast Company; Come Across (short); The Crowd Roars; The Gladiator; Convicted; Smashing the Rackets. **1939** Jesse James; Fast and Loose; Within the Law; Zero Hour; The House of Fear; Mr. Moto in Danger Island; Forgotten Victory (short); The Dead End Kids on Dress Parade (aka On Dress Parade); Fugitive at Large; Manhattan Shakedown; Sabotage; The Mysterious Miss X; Wings of the Navy. **1940** A Fugitive from Justice; Calling Philo Vance; Gallant Sons; Deadwood Dick (serial); Charlie Chan in Panama; I Love You Again. **1941** Andy Hardy's Private Secretary; Sergeant York; Flight Command; Sleepers West; Dead Men Tell; Murder Among Friends; The Great Swindle; The Get-Away; Hold Back the Dawn; Night of January 16th; Mercy Isalnd; Melody Lane; Cheers for Miss Bishop; Whistling in the Dark. **1942** On the Sunny Side; Tales of Manhattan; Now, Voyager; Little Tokyo, U.S.A.; Juke Box Jenny; A Daring Young Man. **1943** The Meanest Man in the World; He's My Guy; Wintertime; Appointment in Berlin; Action in the North Atlantic; Behind the Rising Sun; The More the Merrier; The Crystal Ball. **1944** The Falcon Out West; Heavenly Days; Murder, My Sweet; Show Business; Tall in the Saddle. **1945** Grissly's Millions; A Royal Scandal; Tarzan and the Amazons; Tokyo Rose; Club Havana. **1946** The Strange Mr. Gregory; The Truth About Women; Gilda.

DOUGLAS, DORIS
Born: 1918. Died: May 30, 1970. Screen actress.

DOUGLAS, FREDERICK C.
Born: 1867, Newark, N.J. Died: July 17, 1929, Hollywood, Calif. Screen and stage actor. Entered films in 1923.

DOUGLAS, GILBERT
Born: 1881, Southampton, England. Died: Oct. 11, 1959, Philadelphia, Pa. Screen and stage actor.

Appeared in: **1918** Five Thousand an Hour. **1919** Good Gracious Annabelle! **1923** Dulcy.

DOUGLAS, KEITH See KENNEDY, DOUGLAS

DOUGLAS, KENT See MONTGOMERY, DOUGLAS

DOUGLAS, MELVYN (Melvyn Hesselberg)
Born: Apr. 5, 1901, Macon, Ga. Died: Aug. 4, 1981, New York, N.Y. (pneumonia/cardiac complications). Screen, stage, television actor, stage director and stage producer. Married to actress Helen Gahagan (dec. 1980). Won 1970 Academy Award Nomination for Best Actor in I Never Sang For My Father. Won 1963 Academy Award as Best Supporting Actor in Hud, and again in 1979 in Being There.

Appeared in: **1931** Tonight or Never (film debut). **1932** The Broken Wing; The Wiser Sex; As You Desire Me; The Old Dark House; Prestige. **1933** Counsellor-At-Law; The Vampire Bat; Nagana. **1934** Dangerous Corner; Woman in the Dark. **1935** The People's Enemy; Annie Oakley; She Married Her Boss; Mary Burns, Fugitive. **1936** The Lone Wolf Returns; Theodora Goes Wild; The Gorgeous Hussy; And So They Were Married. **1937** Angel; I Met Him in Paris; I'll Take Romance; Captains Courageous; Women of Glamour. **1938** Arsene Lupin Returns; Fast Company; That Certain Age; The Shining Hour; The Toy Wife; There's Always a Woman. **1939** Ninotchka; There's That Woman Again; Tell No Tales; Good Girls Go to Paris; The Amazing Mr. Williams. **1940** He Stayed for Breakfast; Too Many Husbands; Third Finger, Left Hand. **1941** That Uncertain Feeling; A Woman's Face; Two-Faced Woman; Our Wife; This Thing Called Love. **1942** We Were Dancing; They All Kissed the Bride. **1943** Three Hearts for Julia. **1947** Sea of Grass; The Guilt of Janet Ames; The Long Denial. **1948** My Own True Love; Mr. Blandings Builds His Dream House. **1949** The Great Sinner; A Woman's Secret. **1951** My Forbidden Past; On the Loose. **1960** Inherit the Wind. **1962** Billy Budd. **1963** Hud. **1964** The Americanization of Emily; Advance to the Rear; The Best Man; Big Parade of Comedy (documentary). **1965** Rapture. **1967** Hotel. **1970** I Never Sang For My Father. **1972** One Is a Lonely Number; The Candidate. **1976** The Tenant. **1977** Twilight's Last Gleaming. **1979** The Seduction of Joe Tynan; The Changling; Being There. **1980** Tell Me A Riddle. **1981** Ghost Story; French Kiss (aka Act of Deceit).

DOUGLAS, MILTON
Born: 1906. Died: Sept. 5, 1970. Screen actor, dancer and singer.

Appeared in: **1930** Viennese Nights. **1934** Three Little Pigskins (short).

DOUGLAS, PAUL
Born: Apr. 11, 1907, Philadelphia, Pa. Died: Sept. 11, 1959, Hollywood, Calif. (heart attack). Screen, stage, television and radio actor. Married to actress Jan Stering; divorced from Elizabeth Farnesworth, Sussie Welles, Geraldine Higgins and actress Virginia Field.

Appeared in: **1948** A Letter to Three Wives (film debut). **1949** It Happens Every Spring; Everybody Does It; Twelve O'Clock High. **1950** Panic in the Streets; The Big Lift; Love That Brute. **1951** Angels in the Outfield; Fourteen Hours; The Guy Who Came Back; Rhubarb (unbilled). **1952** We're Not Married; When in Rome; Clash By Night; Never Wave at a WAC. **1953** Forever Female. **1954** The Maggie (aka High and Dry—US); Executive Suite; Green Fire. **1955** Joe Macbeth (US 1956). **1956** Solid Gold Cadillac; The Gamma People; The Leather Saint. **1957** This Could Be the Night; Beau James. **1959** The Mating Game.

DOUGLAS, TOM
Born: 1896, Louisville, Ky. Died: May 4, 1978, Cuernavaca, Mexico (heart attack). Screen, stage actor and interior decorator.

Appeared in: **1921** Footfalls. **1922** The Country Flapper; Free Air. **1930** The Cheerleader (short). **1931** Road to Reno. **1932** Guilty or Not Guilty; Sky Bride; Broken Lullaby. **1933** West of Singapore.

DOUGLAS, VALERIE
Born: 1938, England. Died: Mar. 2, 1969, England. Screen and stage actress.

DOUGLAS, WALLY See FROES, WALTER J.

DOUGLASS, AMY
Born: 1903. Died: Mar. 5, 1980, Los Angeles, Calif. Screen and stage actress.

Appeared in: **1964** The Unsinkable Molly Brown. **1977** Close Encounters of the Third Kind.

DOVEY, ALICE
Born: 1885, England. Died: Jan. 11, 1969, Tarzana, Calif. Stage and screen actress. Entered films with Famous Players-Lasky in 1915. Married to stage actor and playwright Jack Hazzard.

DOVZHENKO, ALEXANDER (aka ALEXANDER DOVJHENKO)
Born: 1894. Died: 1956. Screen actor, film director, film producer and screenwriter.

Appeared in: **1929** Arsenal. **1930** Earth. **1932** Ivan. **1935** Aerograd. **1947** Life in Blossom.

DOWLAN, WILLIAM C.
Born: 1882, St. Paul, Minn. Died: Nov. 6, 1947. Screen actor and film director.

Appeared in: **1915** Under the Crescent (serial). **1916** Drugged Waters.

DOWLING, CONSTANCE
Born: 1920, New York, N.Y. Died: Oct. 28, 1969, Los Angeles, Calif. (cardiac arrest). Stage and screen actress.

Appeared in: **1944** Knickerbocker Holiday; Up in Arms. **1946** The Black Angel; Blackie and the Law; The Well-Groomed Bride. **1947** Blind Spot. **1948** The Flame. **1950** Her Wonderful Lie; Mad About Opera. **1951** Stormbound. **1952** A Voice in Your Heart; Miss Italy. **1953** Duel Without Honor. **1954** Gog. **1955** Othello.

DOWLING, EDDIE "EDWARD" (Joseph Nelson Goucher)
Born: Dec. 9, 1894, Woonsocket, R.I. Died: Feb. 18, 1976, Smithfield, R.I. Screen, stage, radio actor, film producer, stage director, stage producer, screenwriter, playwright and singer. Married to actress Ray Dooley.

Appeared in: **1929** The Rainbow Man. **1930** Blaze O'Glory. **1931** Honeymoon Lane.

DOWLING, JOAN
Born: Jan., 1928, England. Died: Mar. 31, 1954, London, England (found dead in gas-filled room). Screen and stage actress. Married to actor Harry Fowler.

Appeared in: **1947** Hue and Cry (film debut—US 1950). **1948** Bond Street (US 1950); No Room at the Inn. **1949** A Man's Affair; For Them That Trespass (US 1950); Train of Events (US 1952); Landfall. **1950** Murder Without Crime (US 1951). **1951** The Magic Box (US 1952); Pool of London. **1952** 24 Hours of a Woman's Life (aka Affair in Monte Carlo—US 1953); Women of Twilight (aka Twilight Women—US 1953).

DOWLING, JOSEPH J.
Born: 1848. Died: July 10, 1928, Hollywood, Calif. Screen actor. Achieved fame as the "Miracle Man."

Appeared in: **1915** The Coward. **1919** The Miracle Man. **1920** The Kentucky Colonel. **1921** Fightin' Mad; The Lure of Egypt; The Spenders; The Other Woman; The Beautiful Liar; Breaking Point; The Sin of Martha Queed; A Certain Rich Man; The Grim Comedian; His Nibs; Little Lord Fauntleroy. **1922** If You Believe It, It's So; The Infidel; Quincy Adams Sawyer; The Girl Who Ran Wild; Half Breed; The Pride of Palomar; One Clear Call; The Trail of the Axe; The Danger Point. **1923** The Christian; A Man's Man; The Spider and the Rose; Dollar Devils; Tiger Rose; The Courtship of Miles Standish; Enemies of Children; The Girl Who Came Back. **1924** Those Who Dare; One Night in Rome; The Gaiety Girl; Tess of the D'Urbervilles; Untamed Youth; Her Night of Romance; The Law Forbids; Unseen Hands; Women Who Give; Free and Equal (reissue and retitle to The Coward, 1915). **1925** Lorraine of the Lions; Confessions of a Queen; Lord Jim; The Golden Princess; Flower of Night; New Lives for Old. **1926** The Rainmaker; The Little Irish Girl; Why Girls Go Back Home; Two Gun Man.

DOWNES, OLIN
Born: 1886. Died: Aug. 22, 1955, New York, N.Y. (heart attack). Screen actor and writer.

Appeared in: **1947** Carnegie Hall. **1948** First Opera Film Festival (narr.).

DOWNING, HARRY
Born: 1894. Died: Jan. 9, 1972, Boston, Mass. (cancer). Screen and vaudeville actor.

Appeared in: High Up and Low Down (short). **1928** Lights of New York.

DOWNING, JOSEPH
Born: 1903. Died: Oct. 16, 1975, Canoga Park, Calif. (heart attack). Screen and stage actor.

Appeared in: **1935** Dr. Socretes; Case of the Lucky Legs. **1937** Borrowing Trouble. **1938** I Am the Law; A Slight Case of Murder; Wide Open Faces; The Devil's Party; Lady in the Morgue; Danger on the Air; The Night Hawk; Angels With Dirty Faces; Racket Busters; What Price Safety (short). **1939** Another Thin Man; You Can't Get Away With Murder; The Forgotten Woman; Each Dawn I Die; Smashing the Money Ring; Missing Evidence; Torchy Runs for Mayor; Invisible Stripes. **1940** The Secret Seven (short); Oh, Johnny, How You Can Love; Jack Pot (short); Sandy Is a Lady. **1941** Sealed Lips; Double Date; San Francisco Docks; Strange Alibi; Belle Starr; Unholy Partners; Johnny Eager; Flight from Destiny. **1942** Lucky Jordan; Larceny, Inc; The Big Shot; You Can't Escape Forever; My Gal Sal. **1953** Las Vegas Shakedown. **1956** Fighting Trouble. **1957** Slaughter on Tenth Avenue.

DOWNING, ROBERT
Born: 1915. Died: June 15, 1975, Denver, Colo. Screen, stage, television actor and drama critic.

Appeared in: **1954** On the Waterfront. **1961** Splendor in the Grass. **1968** No More Excuses.

DOWNING, WALTER
Born: 1874. Died: Dec. 21, 1937, Hollywood, Calif. Screen actor. Entered films in 1915.

Appeared in: **1924** Pied Piper Malone. **1935** Mary Burns, Fugitive; One More Spring.

DOWNS, CATHY
Born: Mar. 3, 1924, Port Jefferson, N.Y. Died: Dec. 8, 1978, Los Angeles, Calif.? Screen actress. Divorced from actor Joe Kirkwood, Jr. and Robert Brunson.

Appeared in: **1945** State Fair; Diamond Horseshoe; The Dolly Sisters. **1946** North of the Border; My Darling Clementine; The Dark Corner. **1947** For You I Die. **1948** Panhandle; The Noose Hangs High. **1949** Massacre River. **1950** Short Grass; The Sundowners. **1951** Joe Palooka in Triple Cross. **1952** Gobs and Gals. **1953** Bandits of the West. **1955** The Big Tip-Off. **1956** Kentucky Rifle; She-Creature; The Phantom from 10,000 Leagues; Oklahoma Woman. **1957** The Amazing Colossal Man. **1958** Missile to the Moon.

DOWSEY, ROSE WALKER See WALKER, ROSE

DOYLE, BRENDA
Born: 1933, Ireland. Died: Nov. 12, 1981, Dublin, Ireland (road accident). Screen and stage actress. Divorced from director Vincent Dowling. Mother of actress Barbara Doyle.

Appeared in: **1967** Ulysses.

DOYLE, BUDDY
Born: 1901. Died: Nov. 9, 1939, New York, N.Y. (appendix operation). Screen and stage actor.

Appeared in: **1927** Take in the Sun (short); Georginia (short). **1929** At a Talkie Studio (short). **1936** The Great Ziegfeld.

DOYLE, JOHN T.
Born: 1873. Died: Oct. 16, 1935, New York, N.Y. Screen, stage actor and playwright.

Appeared in: **1929** Mother's Boy. **1931** His Woman. **1934** Gambling.

DOYLE, LEN
Born: 1893. Died: Dec. 6, 1959, Port Jervis, N.Y. Screen, stage, radio and television actor, stage director and stage producer.

Appeared in: **1962** Dead to the World.

DOYLE, MAXINE
Born: Jan. 1, 1915, San Francisco, Calif. Died: May 8, 1973, Studio City, Calif. (cancer). Screen, stage and radio actress. Married to film director William Witney.

Appeared in: **1934** The Key; Student Tour; 6-Day Bike Rider; Babbitt; Service With a Smile (short); Good Morning, Eve (short). **1935** The Mystery Man; Born to Gamble. **1936** Rio Grande Romance; Put on the Spot. **1937** Round-Up Time in Texas; Come On, Cowboys; SOS Coast Guard (serial); Thanks for Listening. **1938** Fury Below. **1943** G-Men vs. the Black Dragon (serial). **1944** Sing, Neighbor, Sing; The Lady and the Monster; Man from Frisco.

DOYLE, PATRICIA
Born: 1915. Died: Sept. 22, 1975, Los Angeles, Calif. (cancer). Screen actress and dancer. Married to film producer-director Robert Wise.

Appeared in: **1940** Grapes of Wrath. **1941** All That Money Can Buy.

DOYLE, REGINA
Born: 1907. Died: Sept. 30, 1931, Hollywood, Calif. (auto accident). Screen actress.

DRAIN, KATE See LAWSON, KATE

DRAINIE, JOHN
Born: 1916. Died: Oct. 30, 1966, Toronto, Ontario, Canada (cancer). Screen, television and radio actor.

Appeared in: **1963** The Incredible Journey.

DRAKE, JOSEPHINE S.
Died: Jan. 7, 1929, New York, N.Y. (pneumonia). Screen and stage actress.

Appeared in: **1926** The Song and Dance Man; A Social Celebrity; The Palm Beach Girl.

DRAKE, STEVE (Dale Laurence Fink)
Born: 1923. Died: Dec. 19, 1948, Burbank, Calif. (auto accident). Screen actor.

Appeared in: **1947** Pioneer Justice; Black Hills.

DRANE, SAM DADE
Died: Aug. 15, 1916, New York, N.Y. Stage and screen actor.

Appeared in: **1916** The Crisis.

DRANEM
Born: 1869, France. Died: Oct. 13, 1935, Paris, France. Stage and screen actor.

Appeared in: **1932** Il est Charmant (He Is Coming); Miche. **1935** Soir de Reveillon.

DRANGE, EMILY
Born: 1898. Died: Dec. 30, 1961, Torrance, Calif. Screen and stage actress. Married to actor Lynne Overman (dec. 1943).

DRAPER, JOSEPH
Born: 1907. Died: June 30, 1962, New York, N.Y. Black screen, stage and television actor. Do not confuse with actor with same name (dec. 1978).

DRAPER, JOSEPH
Born: Aug. 30, 1912, Czechoslovakia. Died: Aug. 18, 1978, North Hollywood, Calif. (heart disease). Screen and television actor. Do not confuse with actor with same name (dec. 1962).

DRAPER, "OLD COLONEL" (Col. T. Waln-Morgan Draper)
Born: c. 1855. Died: Nov. 8, 1915. Screen actor. Entered films with Thanhouser.

DRAYTON, ALFRED (Alfred Varick)
Born: Nov. 1, 1881, Brighton, England. Died: Apr. 25, 1949, London, England. Screen and stage actor.

Appeared in: **1915** Iron Justice. **1919** A Little Bit of Fluff. **1920** The Honeypot; A Temporary Gentleman; The Winning Goal. **1921** The Adventures of Sherlock Holmes series including: A Scandal in Bohemia; Love Song. **1930** The Squeaker; The "W" Plan (US 1931). **1931** The Calendar (aka Bachelor's Folly—US); The Happy Ending; Brown Sugar. **1932** Lord Babs. **1933** Friday the Thirteenth; The Little Damozel; Falling for You; It's a Boy (US 1934). **1934** Jack Ahoy!; Red Ensign (aka Strike!—US); Radio Parade of 1935 (US 1935); Lady in Danger. **1935** The Love Affair of the Dictator (aka The Dictator and The Loves of a Dictator—US); Oh Daddy!; First a Girl; Look Up and Laugh; Me and Marlborough. **1936** The Crimson Circle; Tropical Trouble. **1937** Aren't Men Beasts! **1939** So This Is London (US 1940). **1941** Banana Ridge. **1942** The Big Blockade; Women Aren't Angels. **1944** Don't Take It to Heart (US 1949); The Halfway House (US 1945). **1945** They Knew Mr. Knight. **1947** Nicholas Nickleby. **1948** Things Happen at Night.

DRAYTON, NOEL
Born: 1913, Capetown, South Africa. Died: Dec. 7, 1981, Sedona, Ariz. Screen and television actor.

Appeared in: **1950** Under My Skin. **1952** Plymouth Adventure; Blackbeard the Pirate. **1953** Botany Bay. **1954** Elephant Walk; Knock on Wood. **1955** The Virgin Queen. **1956** The Court Jester. **1957** Zero Hour!; Across the Bridge. **1958** Hong Kong Confidential. **1962** A Public Affair. **1969** The Wrecking Crew.

DRESDEL, SONIA (Lois Obee)
Born: 1909, Yorkshire, England. Died: Jan. 18, 1976, Canterbury, England. Screen, stage and television actress.

Appeared in: **1945** The World Owes Me a Living. **1947** While I Live. **1948** The Fallen Idol (US 1949); This Was a Woman (US 1949). **1950** Clouded Yellow (US 1952). **1951** The Third Visitor. **1956** Now and Forever. **1960** The Trials of Oscar Wilde (aka The Man With the Green Carnation—US, aka The Green Carnation). **1962** The Break (US 1963). **1972** Lady Carolyn Lamb.

DRESSER, LOUISE (Louise Kerlin)
Born: Oct. 5, 1880, Evansville, Ind. Died: Apr. 24, 1965, Woodland Hills, Calif. (intestinal obstruction). Screen, stage and vaudeville actress. Divorced from actor Jack Norworth (dec. 1959) and later married actor and singer Jack Gardner (dec. 1950). During the first presentation of the Academy Awards she received a "Citation of Merit," and was nominated for 1927/28 Academy Award for Best Actress in A Ship Comes In.

Appeared in: **1922** Enter Madame; Burning Sands; The Glory of Clementina. **1923** The Fog; Prodigal Daughters; Ruggles of Red Gap; Salomy Jane; Woman Proof; To the Ladies. **1924** The City That Never Sleeps; Cheap Kisses; What Shall I Do?; The Next Corner. **1925** The Eagle; The Goose Woman; Enticement; Percy. **1926** The Blind Goddess; Padlocked; Everybody's Acting; Gigolo; Broken Hearts of Hollywood; Fifth Avenue. **1927** The Third Degree; The White Flannels; Mr. Wu. **1928** The Air Circus; A Ship Comes In; The Garden of Eden; Mother Knows Best. **1929** The Madonna of Avenue A; Not Quite Decent. **1930** This Mad World; Mammy; Lightnin'; The Three Sisters. **1931** Caught. **1932** Stepping Sisters. **1933** Doctor Bull; Song of the Eagle; Cradle Song; State Fair. **1934** Hollywood on Parade (short); Servants Entrance; Girl of the Limberlost; David Harum; The Scarlet Empress; The World Moves On. **1935** The County Chairman. **1937** Maid of Salem.

DRESSLER, MARIE (Leila Koerber)
Born: Nov. 9, 1869, Coburg, Canada. Died: July 28, 1934, Santa Barbara, Calif. (cancer). Screen, stage, vaudeville actress and circus performer. Divorced from stage actor James Hoeppert (dec.). Some reference sources indicate she was married to J. H. Dalton, but this has never been confirmed. Won 1930/31 Academy Award for Best Actress for Min and Bill (1930) and was nominated for 1931/32 Academy Award for Best Actress in Emma (1932).

Appeared in: **1914** Tillie's Punctured Romance (film debut). **1915** Tillie's Tomato Surprise; Tillie's Nightmare. **1917** The Scrublady. **1918** The Red Cross Nurse; The Agonies of Agnes. **1927** The Callahans and the Murphys; Breakfast at Sunrise; The Joy Girl. **1928** Bringing Up Father; The Patsy. **1929** The Divine Lady; The Vagabond

Lovers; The Hollywood Revue of 1929; Road Show. **1930** Chasing Rainbows; One Romantic Night; Let Us Be Gay; Derelict; Voice of Hollywood (short); Anna Christie; Caught Short; The Swan; March of Time; Call of the Flesh; The Girl Said No; Min and Bill. **1931** Reducing; Politics. **1932** Jackie Cooper's Christmas Party (short); Emma; Prosperity. **1933** Tugboat Annie; Dinner at Eight; Singer of Seville; Christopher Bean. **1964** Big Parade of Comedy (documentary).

DREW, ANN
Born: 1891, New York, N.Y. Died: Feb. 6, 1974, Miami, Fla. Screen actress. Entered films with D. W. Griffith in 1909.

Appeared in: **1921** His Brother's Keeper. **1923** Riders of the Range. **1927** The Red Raiders; Winds of the Pampas.

DREW, DELPHINE
Died: Mar. 16, 1979, Los Angeles, Calif. Screen actress and attorney.

Appeared in: **1935** Tailspin Tommy in The Great Air Mystery (serial).

DREW, GLADYS RANKIN
Died: Jan. 9, 1914, New York, N.Y. Screen, stage actress and playwright. Married to actor Sidney Drew (dec. 1919) with whom she appeared on stage as his comedy partner. Mother of actor S. Ranklin Drew (dec. 1918). She was daughter of actor McKee Rankin (dec.) and actress Kitty Blanchard (dec.).

DREW, LILLIAN
Born: 1883 or 1886, Chicago, Ill. Died: Feb. 4, 1924, Chicago, Ill. Screen, stage and vaudeville actress. Married to actor Elisha H. Calvert (dec. 1941). Entered films with Essanay Film Co. in 1912.

Appeared in: **1914** One Wonderful Night. **1915** Jane of the Seil. **1916** His Moral Code; Money to Burn. **1923** Children of Jazz.

DREW, LOWELL
Born: 1882. Died: Oct. 14, 1942. Screen actor.

Appeared in: **1929** The Green Murder Case. **1935** Les Miserables. **1937** Hotel Haywire.

DREW, MARGARET
Born: 1886. Died: Mar. 30, 1963, London, England. Screen and stage actress.

DREW, PHILIP YALE
Born: 1880. Died: July 2, 1940. Screen actor.

Appeared in: **1920** The Hobo of Pizen City; Tex of the Timberlands; The Hold-Up Man; His Pal's Gal.

DREW, S. RANKIN (Sidney Rankin Drew)
Born: 1892, New York, N.Y. Died: May 19, 1918, France (shot down in plane during combat). Screen, stage actor and film director. Son of actor Sidney Drew (dec. 1919) and actress Gladys Rankin Drew.

Appeared in: **1913** His Tired Uncle; The Penalties of Reputation; My Lady Idleness; The Glove; An Unwritten Chapter; A Game of Cards. **1914** Mr. Barnes of New York. **1917** The Girl Philippa.

DREW, SIDNEY
Born: Aug. 28, 1864, New York, N.Y. Died: Apr. 9, 1919, New York, N.Y. (uremia, heart disease). Screen, stage, vaudeville actor, film director and producer. Married to actress Gladys Rankin Drew (dec. 1914) with whom he appeared on stage as part of a comedy team. Later married to actress Lucille McVey (dec. 1925) who appeared on film with him in a series of "Mr. and Mrs. Sidney Drew" comedies between 1914 and 1919. Father of actor S. Rankin Drew (dec. 1918). He was member of Drew-Barrymore theatrical family.

Appeared in: **1911** When Two Hearts Are Won. **1913** A Regiment of Two; Jerry's Mother-in-Law; Beauty Unadorned; A Lesson in Jealousy; Why I Am Here; Sweet Deception; The Late Mr. Jones; The Master Painter; The Feudists. **1914** Innocent But Awkward; A Horeshoe—For Luck; Auntie's Portrait; Jerry's Uncle's Namesake; Good Gracious; A Florida Enchantment; Too Many Husbands; A Model Young Man; The Royal Wild West; Who's Who in Hogg's Hollow; Never Again. **1915** Wanted—A Nurse; Story of a Glove; A Safe Investment; Following the Scent; Boobley's Baby; A Case of Eugenics; The Fox Trot Finesse; The Home Cure; Romantic Reggie; When Two Play a Game; The Honeymoon Baby; Miss Sticky—Moufie-Kiss; The Combination; The Hair of Her Head; The Profesor's Romance; Unlucky Louey; Their Night Out; The Cub and the Daisy Chain; Playing Dead; The Professor's Painless Cure; Mr. and Mrs. Drew in Their Agreement; Back to the Primitive. **1916** Childhood's Happy Days; At the Count of Ten; At a Premium; Taking a Rest; A Telegraphic Tangle; Too Clever By Half. **1917** How John Came Home; Diplomatic Henry; Rooney's Sad Case; By Might of His Right; All for the Love of a Girl; His Wife Knew About It; Beautiful Thoughts; Is Christmas a Bore?; The Hypochondriac; Cave Man's Bluff; His Perfect Day; The Pest; Blackmail; Locked Out; High Cost of Living; Awakening of Helen Minor; Handy Henry; Putting It Over on Henry; One of the Family; Her Lesson; Nothing to Wear; Her Anniversaires; Wages No Object; Too Much Henry; The Spirit of Merry Christmas; The Unmarried Look; Shadowing Henry; Rubbing It In; Her Obsession; Reliable Henry; The Matchmakers; Lest We Forget; Mr. Parker—Hero; Henry's Ancestors; His Ear for Music; Her Economic Independence; Her First Game; The Patriot; Music Hath Charm; His Curiosity; The Joy of Freedom; Double Life; The Dentist; Hist ... Spies!; Twelve Good Hens and True; As Others See Us; A Lady in the Library; Duplicity; Help; Number One; Nobody Home; His Deadly Calm; The Rebellion of Mr. Minor; Borrowing Trouble; His Rival; Their First; A Close Resemblance. **1918** Before and After Taking; Gas Logic; His First Love; Special Today; Romance and Rings; Why Henry Left Home. **1919** Squared; Once a Man; A Sisterly Scheme.

DREW, (MRS.) SIDNEY (Lucille McVey)
Born: Apr. 18, 1890, Sedalia, Mo. Died: Nov. 3, 1925, Hollywood, Calif. Screen, stage actress, film producer, director and screenwriter. She also appeared under her real name, Lucille McVey and as Jane Morrow. Was second wife of film actor Sidney Drew (dec. 1919) and appeared with him in a series of comedies between 1914 and 1919.

Appeared in: **1914** Too Many Husbands. **1915** The Story of a Glove; Miss Sticky—Moufie-Kiss; A Safe Investment. **1916** At the Count of Ten; Childhood's Happy Days. **1917** Cave Man's Bluff; His Perfect Day; The Pest; Blackmail; Her Obsession; Reliable Henry; Locked Out; High Cost of Living; Awakening of Helen Minor; Putting It Over on Henry; Handy Henry; One of the Family; Safety First; Her Lesson; Nothing to Wear; Her Anniversaires; Tootsie; The Hypochondriac; The Matchmakers; Lest We Forget; Mr. Parker, Hero; Henry's Ancestors; His Ear for Music; Her Economic Independence; Her First Game; The Patriot; Music Hath Charms; Rubbing It In; His Curiosity; The Joy of Friends!; His Double Life; The Dentist; Hist ... Spies!; Twelve Good Hens and True; His Deadly Calm; Rebellion of Mr. Minor; A Close Resemblance; As Others See Us; Too Much Henry; Wages No Object; The Spirit of Merry Christmas; The Unmarried Look; Shadowing Henry. **1918** A Youthful Affair; Duplicity. **1919** Romance and Rings; Once a Mason; A Sisterly Scheme; Bunkered; The Amateur Liar; Harold and the Saxons.

DREYER, DAVE
Born: 1894. Died: Mar. 2, 1967, New York, N.Y. Screen, vaudeville actor, composer, pianist and music publisher.

Appeared in: **1929** Tin Pan Alley (short).

DREYFUSS, MICHAEL
Born: 1928. Died: Mar. 30, 1960, New York, N.Y. Screen, stage, television, radio actor and television director.

Appeared in: **1956** Patterns.

DRIGGERS, DONALD CLAYTON
Born: 1893. Died: Nov. 19, 1972, Birmingham, Ala. Screen actor. Entered films as an extra in 1927.

Appeared in: **1941** Sergeant York; Love Crazy; The Badlands of Dakota. **1942** Reap the Wild Wind; Woman of the Year. **1947** Pirates of Monterey.

DRISCOLL, BOBBY (Robert Driscoll)
Born: Mar. 3, 1937, Cedar Rapids, Iowa. Died: Mar., 1968, New York, N.Y. (occlusive coronary arteriosclerosis—hardening of the arteries). Screen actor. Won 1947 juvenile Academy Award for So Dear to My Heart and in 1949 for The Window.

Appeared in: **1943** Lost Angel (film debut). **1944** The Sullivans; Sunday Dinner for a Soldier. **1945** Big Bonanza; From This Day Forward; Identity Unknown. **1946** Miss Susie Slagle's; O.S.S.; So Goes My Love. **1947** So Dear to My Heart. **1948** Song of the South; If You Knew Susie; Melody Time. **1949** The Window. **1950** Treasure Island. **1951** When I Grow Up. **1952** The Happy Time. **1953** Peter Pan (voice). **1955** Scarlet Coat. **1958** Party Chasers.

DRISCOLL, SAM W.
Born: 1868. Died: Dec. 13, 1956, Hollywood, Calif. Screen actor and musician.

Appeared in: **1935** Mutiny on the Bounty.

DROESHOUT, ADRIAN
Born: 1897, New York. Died: Dec. 26, 1965, Los Angeles, Calif. Screen actor and publicist. Divorced from actress Frances Woodward.

DROHAN, BENNY (Benjamin V. Drohan)
Born: 1895. Died: Apr. 24, 1972, Boston, Mass. Screen, vaudeville actor and composer. Married to singer/dancer Marty Dupree, with whom he toured with the USO.

Appeared in: **1939** Winter Carnival.

DROUET, ROBERT
Born: 1870. Died: Aug. 17, 1914, New York, N.Y. Screen actor. Entered films with Biograph.

Appeared in: **1913** On the Dumb Waiter. **1914** The Inspector's Story; Cricket on the Hearth.

DRUBIN, CHARLES
Born: 1894. Died: Sept. 23, 1976, Woodland Hills, Calif. Screen actor.

DRUCE, HUBERT
Born: 1870, Richmond, England. Died: Apr. 6, 1931, New York, N.Y. (pneumonia). Stage and screen actor and stage producer.

Appeared in: **1917** Please Help Emily. **1918** Dodging a Million. **1928** Return of Sherlock Holmes. **1930** Laughing Lady. **1931** The Night Angel.

DRUM, JAMES
Born: 1918. Died: Nov. 28, 1976, Hollywood, Calif. (emphysema). Screen actor.

Appeared in: **1960** Studs Lonigan. **1975** Swiss Bank Account.

DRUMGOLD, GEORGE C.
Born: 1894, Los Angeles, Calif. Died: Apr. 9, 1948, Ft. Lauderdale, Fla. Screen actor and film director.

Appeared in: **1920** Go Get It. **1921** Through the Back Door. **1922** Penrod; Fools First; Minnie; The Lying Truth. **1925** Waking Up the Town.

DRUMIER, JACK
Born: 1869. Died: Apr. 22, 1929, Clearwater, Fla. (pneumonia). Screen, stage and vaudeville actor.

Appeared in: **1917** The Adventures of Carol; The Volunteer. **1921** You Find It Everywhere; The Girl from Porcupine. **1922** The Broken Silence; The Splendid Lie; Shadows of the Sea. **1924** Emblems of Love. **1925** The Pinch Hitter; Enemies of Youth.

DRURY, NORMA
Died: Feb., 1978. Screen actress.

Appeared in: **1937** Stage Door. **1941** That Hamilton Woman. **1942** The Mystery of Marie Roget.

DRYDEN, LEO
Born: 1864, England. Died: Apr. 21, 1939, London, England. Screen, stage actor and composer.

Appeared in: **1928** The Lady of the Lake (US 1930).

DRYDEN, WHEELER
Born: Aug. 31, 1892, Brixton, London, England. Died: Sept. 30, 1957, Los Angeles, Calif. Screen and stage actor.

Appeared in: **1921** False Women. **1922** Penrod. **1928** Skirts. **1947** Monsieur Verdoux. **1952** Limelight.

DUANE, JACK *See* PADJAN, JACK

DUARTE, MARIA EVA "EVITA"
Born: May 7, 1919, Los Toldos, Argentina. Died: July 26, 1952, Buenos Aires, Argentina (cancer). Screen and radio actress. Married to Argentine president Juan Peron (dec.).

Appeared in: **1937** Segundos Afuera. **1940** La Carga de los Valientes; El Mos Infeliz del Pueblo. **1941** Una Novia en Apuros. **1944** La Cabalgata del Circo. **1945** La Prodiga.

DUBIN, AL (Alexander Dubin)
Born: June 10, 1890, Zurich or Berne?, Switzerland. Died: Feb. 11, 1945, New York, N.Y. Screen actor, lyricist and composer.

Appeared in: **1933** 42nd Street. **1934** A Very Honorable Guy. **1935** Go Into Your Dance.

DU BOIS, JEAN
Born: 1888, Sumatra, West Indonesia. Died: Oct. 28, 1957, Denver, Colo. (cancer). Screen actor. Entered films as a cameraman in 1925.

DUBOIS, LOUIS-ALEXIS
Born: 1933, Belgium. Died: Jan. 11, 1978, Brussels, Belgium (suicide). Screen, stage, television actor and comedian.

DUBOSC, ANDRE
Born: 1865, France. Died: 1935, France? Screen actor.

Appeared in: **1933** Mistigri. **1935** La Dame aux Camelis. **1931** Mayerling.

DUBOSC, GASTON
Born: 1860, France. Died: Aug., 1941, France. Screen actor.

Appeared in: **1934** Le Serment. **1938** The Pearls of the Crown. **1940** Mayerling to Sarajevo. **1941** The King.

DUBOV, PAUL
Died: Sept. 20, 1979, Encino, Calif. (cancer). Screen, stage actor, television producer, television writer and novelist. Married to television writer Gwen Bagni.

Appeared in: **1942** Bombay Clipper; North to the Klondike; Girl's Town; Escape from Hong Kong; Danger in the Pacific; Boss of Big Town; Who Done It? **1943** Follow the Band; It Ain't Hay. **1950** Cyrano De Bergerac; Triple Trouble. **1951** Suicide Attack (narrator); Sunny Side of the Street. **1952** Deadline U.S.A. **1953** The Jury (aka I, the Jury). **1955** Mad at the World; Cell 2455, Death Row; Apache Woman; Abbott and Costello Meet the Keystone Kops. **1956** He Laughed Last; Shake, Rattle and Rock; The She-Creature; That Certain Feeling. **1957** Voodoo Woman; Forty Guns; China Gate; The Brothers Rico. **1959** The Atomic Submarine; The Crimson Kimono; Tokyo After Dark; Verboten!. **1960** Ma Barker's Killer Brood; The Purple Gang. **1961** Underworld, U.S.A. **1962** The Underwater City; The Scarface Mob. **1963** Shock Corridor; Irma La Douce.

DUCHAMPS, MARCEL (Henri Robert Marcel Duchamps)
Born: July 28, 1887, Blainsville, Normandy, France. Died: Oct. 2, 1968, Neuilly, France. Artist and screen actor.

Appeared in: **1957** 8 x 8. **1968** Grimaces.

DUCHESS, OLGA (Eva Liminana)
Born: 1899, Mexico. Died: Oct., 1953, Mexico City, Mexico. Screen actress, film producer and screenwriter. Divorced from Argentinian actor Jose Bohr. Appeared in Spanish language films made in both U.S. and Mexico.

DUCHIN, EDDY
Born: Apr. 1, 1909, Cambridge, Mass. Died: Feb. 9, 1951, New York, N.Y. (leukemia). Pianist, bandleader and screen actor. Married to actress Marjorie Oelrichs (dec. 1937). Father of pianist Eddy Duchin, Jr. Part of two piano team with Nat Brandwynne (dec. 1978).

Appeared in: **1932** Mr. Broadway. **1935** Coronado. **1937** Hit Parade.

DU COUNT, GEORGE
Born: Mar. 3, 1898, Kavkaz, Georgia, Russia. Died: 1960, Russia? Screen actor and opera singer.

Appeared in: **1936** White Fang; The Gay Desperado. **1938** Anesthesia (short).

DUDGEON, ELSPETH (aka JOHN DUDGEON)
Born: Dec. 4, 1871. Died: Dec. 11, 1955. Screen actress.

Appeared in: **1932** The Old Dark House. **1934** The Moonstone. **1935** Vanessa, Her Love Story; Becky Sharpe; The Last Outpost; Magnificent Obsession; The Night Is Young. **1936** Camille; Show Boat; Sylvia Scarlett; Give Me Your Heart. **1937** The Prince and the Pauper; Sh! The Octopus; The Great Garrick. **1938** Mystery House; Fools for Sale; Movie House. **1939** Bulldog Drummond's Secret Police; Calling Dr. Kildare. **1940** Pride and Prejudice; Raffles; Foreign Correspondent. **1942** Random Harvest; Now, Voyager; Nightmare. **1943** Family Troubles (short); The Heavenly Body. **1944** The Canterville Ghost. **1946** Devotion. **1947** If Winter Comes; Time Out of Mind; Yankee Fakir; Bulldog Drummond Strikes Back. **1948** The Paradine Case; Julia Misbehaves. **1949** The Great Sinner; Lust for Gold.

DUDLAH, DAVID (David Wiliford Kelly)
Born: 1892. Died: Feb. 26, 1947, Memphis, Tenn. Screen and carnival actor.

DUDLEY, BERNARD
Born: 1878, London, England. Died: Oct., 1964, London, England. Screen, stage actor and singer.

Appeared in: **1918** The Great Imposter; A Romany Lass (US 1919). **1919** The Man Who Forgot. **1920** Brenda of the Barge. **1923** Men Who Forget.

DUDLEY, ETHLYN (Ethyl Sloat)
Died: Apr. 28, 1977, Alameda, Calif. Screen and stage actress.

DUDLEY, JOHN (John Stuart Dudley)
Born: 1894. Died: May 1, 1966, Wilmington, N.C. Screen actor, screenwriter, playwright and lawyer.

Appeared in: **1956** Baby Doll. **1957** A Face in the Crowd.

DUDLEY, ROBERT Y.
Born: Sept. 13, 1875, Cincinnati, Ohio. Died: Nov. 12, 1955, San Clemente, Calif. Screen and stage actor. Entered films in 1920. Founder of the "Troupers Club of Hollywood."

Appeared in: **1921** The Traveling Salesman. **1922** Making a Man; The Ninety and Nine. **1923** Sixty Cents an Hour; The Tiger's Claw; The Day of Faith; Nobody's Bride. **1924** Flapper Wives; On the Stroke of Three. **1926** The Marriage Clause. **1927** Broadway Madness; The Lure of the Night Club. **1928** Skinner's Big Idea; On Trial; Fools for Luck; Baby Cyclone; The Night Flyer. **1929** Mysterious Island; Big News; Shanghai Rose. **1930** Wide Open. **1932** Three Wise Girls. **1935** Frisco Kid; Goin' to Town. **1936** The Prisoner of Shock Island. **1937** Springtime in the Rockies; The Toast of New York. **1941** Skylark; The Lady Eve; Citizen Kane; All That Money Can Buy. **1942** Sullivan's Travels; Palm Beach Story; Tennessee Johnson. **1944** Belle of the Yukon; The Big Noise; Casanova Brown; It Happened Tomorrow. **1945** Col. Effingham's Raid. **1947** Mad Wednesday; Mourning Becomes Electra; Living in a Big Way; Magic Town. **1949** Portrait of Jennie. **1952** The Devil and Daniel Webster (reissue and retitle of All That Money Can Buy, 1941).

DUEL, PETER (Peter Deuel)
Born: 1940, Rochester, N.Y. Died: Dec. 31, 1971, Hollywood, Calif. (gunshot—suicide?). Screen and television actor. Brother of actor Geoffrey Deuel.

Appeared in: **1961** W.I.A.—Wounded in Action. **1968** The Hell With Heroes. **1969** Generation; Cannon for Cordoba.

DUFF, WARREN
Born: May 17, 1904, San Francisco, Calif. Died: Aug. 5, 1973, Los Angeles, Calif. (cancer). Screen, stage actor, screenwriter, television writer, stage and screen producer.

DUFFIELD, BRAINERD
Born: 1917, Boston, Mass. Died: Apr. 5, 1979, Hollywood, Calif. (heart attack). Screen, stage actor, screenwriter, playwright and radio writer.

Appeared in: **1948** Macbeth. **1949** Jigsaw.

DUFFIELD, HARRY S.
Born: 1850. Died: Oct. 13, 1921, Los Angeles, Calif. Screen and stage actor.

Appeared in: **1921** For Those We Love; Face of the World; Smiling All the Way; A Wise Fool.

DUFFY, HENRY
Born: 1890, Chicago, Ill. Died: Nov. 18, 1961, Hollywood, Calif. (cancer). Screen, stage actor and stage producer.

DUFFY, JACK
Born: Sept. 4, 1882, Pawtucket, R.I. Died: July 23, 1939, Hollywood, Calif. Screen, stage, vaudeville actor and make-up artist.

Appeared in: **1924** The Brass Bowl; Reckless Romance. **1925** Madame Behave; Stop Flirting. **1926** Ella Cinders. **1927** No Control. **1928** Harold Teen; plus the following shorts: Hot Scotch; Long Hose; Say Uncle. **1929** Loose Change (short); Divorce Made Easy; Sally. **1930** The Skin Game (short). **1931** Heaven on Earth. **1933** Alice in Wonderland. **1935** Here Comes Cookie; plus the following shorts: Keystone Hotel; Pop Goes the Easel; Restless Knights. **1936** Wild Brian.

DUFRAINE, ROSA
Born: 1901. Died: Apr. 29, 1935, Duarte, Calif. Screen actress.

DUGAN, TOM (Thomas J. Dugan)
Born: 1889, Dublin, Ireland. Died: Mar. 6, 1955, Redlands, Calif. (auto accident). Screen, stage and vaudeville actor.

Appeared in: **1926** Early to Wed. **1927** By Whose Hand?; Swell Head; My Friend from India; The Kid Sister; The Small Bachelor. **1928** Soft Living; Shadows of the Night; The Barker; Broadway Daddies; Sharp Shooters; Dressed to Kill; Melody of Love; Midnight Taxi; Lights of New York. **1929** Broadway Babies; Drag; The Drake Case; The Million Dollar Collar; Kid Gloves; Sonny Boy; Hearts in Exile. **1930** They Learned About Women; The Bad One; Night Work; The Medicine Man; She Who Gets Slapped; Surprise. **1931** Bright Lights; Woman

Hungry; Star Witness; The Hot Heiress; plus the following serials: The Vanishing Legion; The Phantom of the West; The Galloping Ghost. **1932** Big Timber; Wide Open Spaces (short); Dr. X; Big City Blues; Pride of the Legion; Blessed Event. **1933** Grand Slam; Skyway; Trick for Trick; The Sweetheart of Sigma Chi; Don't Bet on Love. **1934** Palooka; A Woman's Man; No More Women; The Circus Clown; Let's Talk It Over; Girl O' My Dreams; The President Vanishes. **1935** The Bride Comes Home; The Gilded Lady; One New York Night; Poker at Eight (short); Chinatown Squad; The Case of the Missing Man; Affair of Susan; Princess O'Hara; Three Kids and a Queen; Murder in the Fleet. **1936** Don't Get Personal; Divot Diggers (short); The Calling of Dan Matthews; Pennies from Heaven; Wife vs. Secretary; Neighborhood House; Mister Cinderella. **1937** Nobody's Baby; Pick a Star; True Confession; She Had to Eat. **1938** Sing You Sinners; There's That Woman Again; Four Daughters. **1939** When Tomorrow Comes; The Lone Wolf Spy Hunt; I'm from Missouri; Mystery of the White Room; The Lady and the Mob; House of Fear; Missing Evidence; $1000 a Touchdown; Laugh It Off; The Housekeeper's Daughter. **1940** Too Many Husbands; The Farmer's Daughter; The Fighting 69th; Isle of Destiny; The Ghost Breakers; Cross Country Romance; Half a Sinner; So You Won't Talk; A Little Bit of Heaven; Star Dust. **1941** Dive Bomber; Navy Blues; Ringside Maisie; Where Did You Get That Girl?; Ellery Queen's Penthouse Mystery; The Monster and the Girl; You're the One; A Dangerous Game; Tight Shoes; The Richest Man in Town; We Go Fast; Ellery Queen and the Murder Ring; The Bugle Sounds; Texas. **1942** The Glass Key; The Major and the Minor; Captains of the Clouds; Yokel Boy; A Haunting We Will Go; To Be or Not to Be; Yankee Doodle Dandy; Moontide; Meet the Stewarts; Star Spangled Rhythm. **1943** Coney Island; Bataan; Johnny Come Lately. **1944** Bermuda Mystery; Gambler's Choice; In Society; Greenwich Village; Hi, Beautiful!; Home in Indiana; Moon Over Las Vegas; Swingtime Johnny; Ghost Catchers; Up in Arms. **1945** Don Juan Quilligan; Eadie Was a Lady; Earl Carroll Vanities; See My Lawyer; The Kid Sister; The Man Who Walked Alone; Tell It to a Star; Trail of Kit Carson; Her Highness and the Bellboy. **1946** Cross My Heart; The Best Years of Our Lives; Bringing Up Father; Hoodlum Saint; Johnny Comes Flying Home; The Shadow Returns; Accomplice; It Shouldn't Happen to a Dog. **1947** The Perils of Pauline; Merton of the Movies; The Fabulous Dorseys; The Pilgrim Lady; Good News; Ladies' Man; The Senator Was Indiscreet. **1948** Half Past Midnight; Texas, Brooklyn and Heaven. **1949** It's a Great Feeling; On the Town; Take Me Out to the Ball Game. **1950** Dear Wife. **1951** Painting the Clouds With Sunshine; The Lemon Drop Kid. **1952** Belle of New York. **1955** Crashout. **1968** The Further Perils of Laurel and Hardy (documentary).

DUGGAN, JAN
Born: Dallas, Tex. Died: Mar., 1977, Los Angeles, Calif. Screen and stage actress.

Appeared in: **1934** The Old Fashioned Way; Wagon Wheels. **1935** County Chairman; Mississippi; Alimony Aches (short). **1936** Drift Fence; Easy to Take. **1937** Wife, Doctor and Nurse; Mountain Music; A Damsel in Distress. **1938** Kentucky Moonshine; Midnight Intruder; Scandal Street; One Wild Night; Thanks for Everything; Inside Story. **1939** The Story of Alexander Graham Bell; The House of Fear. **1941** The Big Store; Richest Man in Town. **1942** Dudes are Pretty People. **1943** The Meanest Man in the World.

DUGGAN, TOM (Thomas Duggan Goss)
Born: 1915, Chicago, Ill. Died: May 29, 1969, Los Angeles, Calif. (auto accident injuries). Screen, radio, television actor and newscaster. Divorced from actress Ann Duggan Goss. Do not confuse with actors Tom Dugan (dec. 1955) or Thomas Duggan.

DUKE, ROBERT
Died: Mar. 8, 1979, Katonah, N.Y. (emphysema). Screen and stage actor.

Appeared in: **1945** An Angel Comes to Brooklyn. **1950** Time Running Out.

DUKELAN, GEORGE WASHINGTON "SLIM JIM"
Born: 1845, Smith Falls, Ontario, Canada. Died: Jan. 9, 1933, Amityville, N.Y. Black screen, stage, vaudeville actor and minstrel player.

DUKES, RONNIE
Born: 1932, England. Died: June 6, 1981, Jersey, England (heart attack). Screen and stage actor.

DULAC, ARTHUR
Born: 1910, France. Died: Sept. 18, 1962, Hollywood, Calif. (coronary thrombosis). Screen actor.

Appeared in: **1938** Artists and Models Abroad. **1950** Mister 880. **1953** Little Boy Lost. **1954** The French Line. **1958** The Fury.

DULIEN, TOBE (Tobie Ella Dulien)
Born: July 2, 1893, Latvia. Died: Nov. 27, 1969, Los Angeles, Calif. (heart attack). Screen and television actress.

DULL, ORVILLE O. "BUNNY"
Born: Apr. 25, 1890, Lima, Ohio. Died: Dec. 29, 1978, Los Angeles, Calif. (heart problem). Screen actor, film director and film producer. Appeared in films for the original Thomas H. Inge Co.

DULLIN, CHARLES
Born: 1885, Yennes, France. Died: 1949, Paris, France. Screen, stage actor and stage producer.

Appeared in: **1921** Le Miracle des Loups (The Miracle of the Wolves—US 1925). **1925** Joueur D'Echecs (The Chessplayer—US 1930). **1927** Maldone (Misdeal). **1933** Les Miseables. **1937** Mademoiselle Docteur. **1938** The Courier of Lyons. **1939** Volpone. **1947** Les Jeux sont Faits; Que des Orfevres. **1948** Jenny Lamour. **1949** Chips Are Down.

DULLZELL, PAUL
Born: June 15, 1879, Boston, Mass. Died: Dec. 21, 1961, New York, N.Y. Screen, stage actor and stage director. Former president of Associated Actors and Artists of America.

DUMAURIER, SIR GERALD
Born: Mar. 26, 1873, Hampstead, London, England. Died: Apr. 11, 1934, London, England (following operation for internal disorder). Screen, stage actor, author and stage producer. Married to stage actress Muriel Beaumont.

Appeared in: **1917** Justice; Masks and Faces; Everybody's Business. **1920** Unmarried. **1930** Escape. **1932** Lord Camber's Ladies. **1933** I Was a Spy (US 1934). **1934** Jew Suess (aka Power—US); Catherine the Great; The Scotland Yard Mystery (aka The Living Dead—US).

DUMBRILLE, DOUGLASS
Born: 1890, Hamilton, Ont., Canada. Died: Apr. 2, 1974, Woodland Hills, Calif. (heart attack). Screen, stage and television actor. Married to stage actress Jessie Lawson (dec. 1958) and later married to actress Patricia Mowbray.

Appeared in: **1931** His Woman; Monkey Business. **1932** I Am a Fugitive from a Chain Gang; That's My Boy; The Wiser Sex; Blondie of the Follies; Laughter in Hell. **1933** Hard to Handle; Baby Face; King of the Jungle; Heroes for Sale; Convention City; Female; The World Changes; Silk Express; Voltaire; Smoke Lightning; Rustlers' Round-Up; Lady Killer; The Big Brain; The Man Who Dared; The Way to Love; Elmer the Great; Laughter in Hell. **1934** Massacre; Fog Over Frisco; Harold Teen; Journal of a Crime; The Secret Bride; Operator 13; Broadway Bill; Hi, Nellie; Treasure Island. **1935** Love Me Forever; Cardinal Richelieu; Peter Ibbetson; Lives of a Bengal Lancer; Naughty Marietta; Crime and Punishment; Air Hawks; Secret Bride; Unknown Woman; Public Menace. **1936** Calling of Dan Matthews; The Lone Wolf Returns; The Music Goes 'Round; Mr. Deeds Goes to Town; You May Be Next; End of the Trail; The Witness Chair; M'Liss; The Princess Comes Across. **1937** A Woman in Distress; A Day at the Races; Ali Baba Goes to Town; The Firefly; The Emperor's Candlesticks; Counterfeit Lady. **1938** Stolen Heaven; The Buccaneer; Mysterious Rider; Storm Over Bengal; Crime Takes a Holiday; Fast Company; Sharpshooters; Kentucky. **1939** Thunder Afloat; Charlie Chan at Treasure Island; Mr. Moto in Danger Island; The Three Musketeers; Charlie Chan in City in Darkness; Rovin' Tumbleweeds; Captain Fury; Tell No Tales. **1940** Virginia City; Slightly Honorable; The Catman of Paris; South of Pago Pago; Michael Shayne, Private Detective. **1941** Murder Among Friends; The Big Store; The Roundup; Washington Melodrama; Ellery Queen and the Perfect Crime. **1942** Stand By For Action; King of the Mounties (serial); I Married an Angel; Ride 'Em Cowboy; Castle in the Desert; A Gentleman After Dark; Ten Gentlemen from West Point. **1943** False Colors; DuBarry Was a Lady. **1944** Jungle Woman; Lost in a Harem; Forty Thieves; Lumberjack; Uncertain Glory; Gypsy Wildcat. **1945** Road to Utopia; The Frozen Ghost; Jungle Queen (serial); The Daltons Ride Again; Flame of the West. **1946** The Cat Creeps; Pardon My Past; Spook Busters; Night in Paradise; Monsieur Beaucaire; The Catman of Paris; Under Nevada Skies. **1947** Christmas Eve; Dishonored Lady; Blonde Savage; The Fabulous Texan; It's a Joke; Dragnet. **1948** Last of the Wild Horses. **1949** Alimony; Tell It to the Judge; Riders of the Whistling Pines; Dynamite; Joe Palooka in the Counterpunch; The Lone Wolf and His Lady. **1950** Her Wonderful Lie; Riding High; Buccaneer's Girl; Abbott and Costello in the Foreign Legion; The Kangaroo Kid; Rapture; The Savage Horde. **1951** A Millionaire for Christy. **1952** Scaramouche; Sky Full of Moon; Son of Paleface; Apache War Smoke; Sound Off. **1953** Julius Caesar; Captain John

Smith and Pocahontas; Plunder of the Sun. **1954** World for Ransom; Lawless Rider. **1955** Jupiter's Darling; Sky Full of Moon. **1956** The Ten Commandments; Shake, Rattle and Roll. **1958** The Buccaneer. **1962** Air Patrol. **1963** Johnny Cool. **1964** Shock Treatment.

DUMKE, RALPH
Born: 1899. Died: Jan. 4, 1964, Sherman Oaks, Calif. Screen, stage, radio and vaudeville actor.

Appeared in: **1949** All the King's Men. **1950** Where Danger Lives; Mystery Street; The Breaking Point; The Fireball. **1951** When I Grow Up; The Mob; The Law and the Lady. **1952** The San Francisco Story; Boots Malone; Carbine Williams; We're Not Married; Holiday for Sinners; Hurricane Smith. **1953** Lili; Hannah Lee; Mississippi Gambler; Massacre Canyon; The President's Lady. **1954** She Couldn't Say No; Alaska Seas; They Rode West; Rails Into Laramie. **1955** Daddy Long Legs; Artists and Models; Violent Saturday; Hell's Island; They Came from Another World. **1956** Francis in the Haunted House; Forever Darling; When Gangland Strikes; Invasion of the Body Snatchers; Solid Gold Cadillac. **1957** The Buster Keaton Story; Loving You. **1960** Elmer Gantry; Wake Me When It's Over. **1961** All in a Night's Work.

DUMONT, GORDON
Born: 1894, Milwaukee, Wis. Died: Mar., 1966, Hollywood, Calif. Screen actor.

Appeared in: **1921** A Certain Rich Man. **1924** Phantom Justice.

DUMONT, J. M. (Jean M. Dumont)
Born: 1879, Paris, Ky. Died: Dec. 19, 1959. Screen actor.

Appeared in: **1919** The Miracle Man; Midnight Romance. **1920** The City of Masks; Jack Straw; Young Mrs. Winthrop; Always Audacious. **1921** Dollar a Year Man; Wealth; Stranger Than Fiction.

DUMONT, MARGARET
Born: 1889. Died: Mar. 6, 1965, Los Angeles, Calif. (heart attack). Screen, stage and television actress. Won 1937 Screen Actor Guild Award for A Day at the Races.

Appeared in: **1929** The Cocoanuts. **1930** Animal Crackers. **1931** Girl Habit. **1933** Duck Soup. **1934** Gridiron Flash; Fifteen Wives; Kentucky Kernels. **1935** A Night at the Opera; Orchids to You; Rendezvous. **1936** Song and Dance Man; Anything Goes. **1937** A Day at the Races; The Life of the Party; High Flyers; Youth on Parole; Wise Girl. **1938** Dramatic School. **1939** The Women; At the Circus. **1941** The Big Store; Never Give a Sucker an Even Break; For Beauty's Sake. **1942** Born to Sing; Sing Your Worries Away; Rhythm Parade; About Face. **1943** The Dancing Masters. **1944** Bathing Beauty; Seven Days Ashore; Up in Arms. **1945** The Horn Blows at Midnight; Diamond Horseshoe; Sunset in El Dorado. **1946** The Little Giant; Susie Steps Out. **1952** Three for Bedroom C. **1953** Stop, You're Killing Me. **1956** Shake, Rattle and Roll. **1958** Auntie Mame. **1962** Zotz! **1964** What a Way to Go.

DUNBAR, BLANCHE
Born: 1894. Died: Mar. 7, 1926, Hollywood, Calif. Screen actress. Married to actor David Dunbar (dec. 1953). Appeared in American Film Co. films.

DUNBAR, CHARLES
Died: Feb. 22, 1971. Screen actor.

Appeared in: **1933** What! No Beer?

DUNBAR, DAVID
Born: Sept. 14, 1893, West Maitland, N.S.W., Australia. Died: Nov. 7, 1953, Woodland Hills, Calif. Screen actor.

Appeared in: **1924** Trail Dust; The Fortieth Door (serial and feature); Leatherstocking (serial); North of 36. **1925** The Bloodhound; Fair Play; The Cowboy Musketeer; Ridin' the Wind; Galloping Vengeance; A Man of Nerve. **1926** The Galloping Cowboy; The Non-Stop Flight; Beyond the Rockies. **1927** King of Kings; The Boy Rider; The Broncho Buster; Gold from Weepah; The Arizona Whirlwind; The Fighting Hombre. **1929** Plunging Hoofs. **1930** The Return of Dr. Fu Manchu. **1935** The Great Impersonator. **1938** Kidnapped. **1942** Mrs. Miniver. **1947** If Winter Comes. **1948** Summer Holiday. **1950** Young Man With a Horn.

DUNBAR, HELEN
Born: 1868. Died: Aug. 28, 1933, Los Angeles, Calif. Screen, stage and vaudeville actress.

Appeared in: **1912** Billy and the Butler; The Magic Wand; The

Warning Hand; When Wealth Torments; The Virtue of Rags; Lonesome Robert. **1913** The Fall of the Marshes; Sunlight. **1914** His Stolen Fortune; One Wonderful Night; Any Woman's Choice. **1915** Graustark; The Silent Voice; Pennington's Choice. **1916** A Million a Minute; A Virginia Romance. **1917** The Great Secret (serial). **1918** The Squaw Man; Cyclone Higgins. **1920** Behold My Wife. **1921** Her Winning Way; The House That Jazz Built; Sham; The Great Moment; Sacred and Profane Love; The Little Clown. **1922** Beyond the Rocks; The Impossible Mrs. Bellew; The World's Champion; A Homespun Vamp; The Law and the Woman; Man of Courage; Thirty Days. **1923** Hollywood; The Call of the Canyon; The Cheat. **1924** Changing Husbands; This Woman; The Fighting Coward; Three Weeks. **1925** Siege; The Reckless Sex; Rose of the World; Compromise; The Man Without a Conscience; The Woman Hater; His Majesty, Bunker Bean; Lady Windermere's Fan; New Lives for Old; She Wolves. **1926** Meet the Prince; Stranded in Paris; His Jazz Bride; Fine Manners; The Man Upstairs.

DUNCAN, ARCHIE
Born: May 26, 1914, Glasgow, Scotland. Died: July 24, 1979, Leytonstone, England. Screen, stage and television actor. Entered films in 1948.

Appeared in: **1948** Operation Diamond (film debut). **1949** Floodtide; The Bad Lord Byron (US 1952). **1950** The Gorbals Story. **1951** Green Grow the Rushes. **1952** The Brave Don't Cry. **1953** Counterspy (aka Undercover Agent—US); Street Corner (aka Both Sides of the Law—US 1954); Rob Roy, the Highland Rogue. **1954** Trouble in the Glen. **1957** Saint Joan. **1958** Harry Black and the Tiger. **1959** John Paul Jones. **1960** The Boy and the Pirates. **1961** Tess of the Storm Country. **1962** Postman's Knock. **1963** Lancelot and Guinevere (aka The Sword of Lancelot—US); The Mouse on the Moon. **1964** The Horror of It All. **1968** The Man Outside. **1969** Ring of Bright Water. **1976** The Wilby Conspiracy.

DUNCAN, BOB
Born: Dec. 7, 1904, Topeka, Kans. Died: Mar. 13, 1967, North Hollywood, Calif. (suicide—gun). Screen actor and television director.

Appeared in: **1944** End of the Road. **1945** The Cisco Kid Returns; Weekend at the Waldorf. **1946** Caravan Trail; Up Goes Maisie. **1947** Border Feud; The Sea Hound (serial). **1949** The Fighting Redhead. **1950** Law of the Panhandle. **1953** The Marshal's Daughter. **1957** The Parson and the Outlaw. **1963** Black Gold.

DUNCAN, BUD (Albert Edward Duncan)
Born: Oct. 31, 1883, New York, N.Y. Died: Nov. 25, 1960, Los Angeles, Calif. (circulatory failure). Screen, stage, vaudeville actor and author. Partner with Lloyd Hamilton (dec. 1935) in vaudeville and film team of "Ham and Bud."

Appeared in: **1913** His Nobs, the Plumber; Teddy Loosebelt from Africa; The Rube Boss. **1914** Dad's Terrible Match; The Winning Whiskers; Ham at the Garbageman's Ball; Ham, the Piano Mover. **1915** Cookey's Adventure; A Melodious Mix-Up; Ham in the Harem; Ham and the Jitney Bus; The Merry Moving Men; Ham at the Fair; The Phoney Cannibal; Ham's Easy Eats; Rushing the Lunch Counter; Ham, the Detective; The Liberty Party; Ham in the Nut Factory; Romance a la Carte; Double Crossing Marmaduke; Foiled; Queering Cupid; Adam's Ancestors; The Knaves and the Kight; Minnie the Tiger; Only a Country Girl; Hoodoo's Busy Day; A Bargain in Brides; Oh, Doctor; The Bandits of Macaroni Mountains; The Hypnotic Monkey; Whitewashing William; Diana of the Farm; The Missing Mummy; The Caretaker's Dilemma; Ham's Harrowing Duel; Ham Among the Redskins; The Pollywog's Picnic; Lotta Cain's Ghost; Ham at the Beach; Mixing It Up; Nearly a Bride; Raskey's Road Show; The Spook Raisers; The Toilers; In High Society. **1916** Guardian Angels; Snoop Hounds; The Tale of a Coat; Artful Artists; Wurr-Wurra; Ham Takes a Chance; A Molar Mix-Up; Ham the Diver; Winning the Widow; Ham Agrees With Sherman; Ham and the Hermit's Daughter; Maybe Moonshine; For Sweet Charity; From Altar to Halter; Millionaires By Mistake; Ham and Preparedness; Ham's Waterloo; Ham's Busy Day; A Bunch of Flivvers; Ham the Explorer; The Beggar of His Child; Ham and the Masked Marvel; The Tank Town Troupe; Midnight at the Old Mill; The Alaskan Mouse Hount; The Peach Pickers; The Baggage Smashers; The Great Detective; Ham's Whirlwind Finish; Good Evening, Judge; Ham's Strategy; Star Boarders; Ham in the Drugstore; Ham the Fortune Teller; Patented By Ham; One Step Too Far; The Mud Cure; The Bogus Booking Agents; The Love Magnet; A Sauerkraut Symphony; Bumping the Bumps. **1917** Rival Romeos; Cupid's Caddies; The Blundering Blacksmiths; Safety Pin Smugglers; A Flyer in Flapjacks; Efficiency Experts; Experts; Bulls or Bullets?; The Bogus Bride; Hard Times in Hardscrapple; The Deadly Doughnut; A Misfit Millionaire;

A Menagerie Mixup; A Day Out of Jail; Seaside Romeos; Doubles and Troubles. **1918** Rig Roaring Rivals; The Curse of the Make-Believes; Wooing of Coffee Cake Cate. **1919** Maggie Pepper. **1927** The Haunted Ship. **1942** Snuffy Smith, Yard Bird; Hillbilly Blitzkrieg.

DUNCAN, EVELYN
Born: Jan. 21, 1893, Los Angeles, Calif. Died: June 8, 1972, Bellflower, Calif. Screen, stage and vaudeville actress. Sister of singers Rosetta (dec. 1959) and Vivian Duncan (The Duncan Sisters Trio).

Appeared in: **1915** Peer Gynt. **1929** Imperfect Ladies.

DUNCAN, KENNE (Kenneth D. MacLachlan)
Born: Feb. 17, 1902, Chatham, Ont., Canada. Died: Feb. 5, 1972, Hollywood, Calif. (stroke). Screen, stage actor and stuntman.

Appeared in: **1930** The Man from Wyoming; Derelict. **1931** No Limit. **1933** Shadow River. **1935** Charing Cross Road. **1936** Racetrack Racketeer; Under Cover; Cross My Heart; Make Up. **1937** Colorado Kid. **1938** Flash Gordon's Trip to Mars (serial); Frontier Scout; Mars Attacks the World; The Spider's Web (serial). **1939** Roll, Wagons, Roll; Fighting Thoroughbreds; Buck Rogers (serial). **1941** Outlaws of the Rio Grande; Buck Privates; King of the Texas Rangers (serial); Adventures of Captain Marvel (serial); The Spider Returns (serial). **1942** Perils of Nyoka (serial); Westward, Ho; Code of the Outlaw; Man With Two Lives; Isle of Missing Men; Law and Order; Texas to Bataan. **1943** The Batman (serial); The Avenging Rider; The Sundown Kid; Border Buckaroos; Fugitive from Sonora; Daredevils of the West (serial). **1944** Sheriff of Las Vegas; End of the Road; Haunted Harbor (serial); Storm Over Lisbon; Trail of Terror; Beneath Western Skies; The Tiger Woman (serial); Wolves of the Range; Outlaws of Santa Fe; Pride of the Plains; Mojave Firebrand; Hidden Valley Outlaws; Vigilantes of Dodge City; Stagecoach to Monterey; Sheriff of Sundown; Cheyenne Wildcat. **1945** A Sporting Chance; Road to Alcatraz; The Chicago Kid; The Master Key (serial); Trail of Kit Carson; Manhunt of Mystery Island (serial); The Purple Monster Strikes (serial). **1946** Drifting Along; Sioux City Sue; The Crimson Ghost (serial); Home on the Range; Rainbow Over Texas; Sheriff of Redwood Valley; Sun Valley Serenade; California Gold Rush; My Pal Trigger; The Phantom Rider (serial); Man from Rainbow Valley; Night Train to Memphis; Roll on Texas Moon; Santa Fe Uprising; Rio Grande Raiders; Red River Renegades; The Mysterious Mr. Valentine; Conquest of Cheyenne; Code of the Saddle; The Scarlet Horseman (serial). **1947** Twilight on the Rio Grande. **1948** Hidden Danger. **1949** Riders of the Sky; Deputy Marshall; Across the Rio Grande; Crashing Thru; Gun Runner; Law of the West; Range Land; West of El Dorado; Roaring Westward (aka Boom Town Badmen); Shadow of the West; Stampede; Range Justice; Lawless Code. **1950** Surrender; Davy Crockett, Indian Scout; The Blazing Sun (aka The Blazing Hills); Mule Train; Radar Secret Service; Sons of New Mexico; Indian Territory; Code of the Silver Sage. **1951** Hills of Utah; Badman's Gold; Nevada Badmen; Whirlwind; Silver Canyon; Pirate's Harbor (rerelease and retitle of 1944 serial, Haunted Harbor). **1953** On Top of Old Smoky; Pack Train. **1954** The Lawless Rider. **1955** Hell's Horizon. **1956** Flesh and the Spur. **1957** Revolt at Fort Laramie. **1958** The Astounding She Monster. **1959** A Date With Death; Night of the Ghouls (aka Revenge of the Dead). **1960** Natchez Trace. **1961** The Sinister Urge.

DUNCAN, LEE
Died: Sept. 20, 1960, Riverside, Calif. (heart attack). Screen actor and film dog trainer. Discovered Rin Tin Tin.

Appeared in: **1939** Hollywood Cavalcade.

DUNCAN, MALCOLM
Born: 1872. Died: May 2, 1942, Bay Shore, N.Y. Screen and stage actor.

Appeared in: **1915** The Spendthrifts.

DUNCAN, ROSETTA
Born: 1900, Los Angeles, Calif. Died: Dec. 4, 1959, Acero, Ill. (auto accident injuries). Screen, stage and vaudeville actress. Sister of Vivian and Evelyn Duncan (dec. 1972). Entered films in 1926.

Appeared in: **1927** Two Flaming Youths; Topsy and Eva. **1929** It's a Great Life. **1935** Broadway Brevities (short).

DUNCAN, WILLIAM A.
Born: 1880. Died: Feb. 8, 1961, Hollywood, Calif. Screen, stage actor and film director. Entered films in 1910. Married to actress Edith Johnson with whom he appeared in film serials.

Appeared in: **1917** Vengeance and the Woman (serial); The Fight Trail (serial). **1918** A Fight for Millions (serial). **1919** Man of Might (serial); Smashing Barriers (serial); Perils of Thunder Mountain (serial). **1920**

The Silent Avenger (serial). **1921** Fighting Fate (serial); Where Men Are Men; Steelheart. **1922** No Defense; The Silent Vow; When Danger Smiles; The Fighting Guide. **1923** The Steel Trail (serial); Smashing Barriers (1919 serial rereleased as feature film); Playing It Wild. **1924** The Fast Express (serial); Wolves of the North (serial).

DUNCAN, WILLIAM CARY
Born: Feb. 6, 1874, North Brookfield, Mass. Died: Nov. 12, 1945, North Brookfield, Mass. (heart ailment). Screen actor, playwright, author, screenwriter and lyricist. Entered films with Famous Players in 1929.

Appeared in: **1935** Nevada. **1936** Three on the Trail. **1937** Hopalong Rides Again; Thunder Trail. **1938** Bar 20 Justice; The Frontiersman. **1939** Law of the Pampas. **1940** The Farmer's Daughter. **1941** Texas Rangers Ride Again.

DUNDEE, JIMMY
Born: 1901. Died: Nov. 20, 1953, Woodland Hills, Calif. (leukemia). Screen actor, stuntman, boxer and auto racer.

Appeared in: **1934** The Mighty Barnum. **1935** Dr. Socrates. **1938** You and Me; The Buccaneer. **1940** Murder Over New York; Northwest Mounted Police. **1942** Sullivan's Travels. **1944** Hail the Conquering Hero; Going My Way; I Love a Soldier; Here Comes the Waves. **1945** A Medal for Benny; Bring on the Girls; Incendiary Blonde; The Stork Club; The Bells of St. Mary's; Road to Utopia. **1946** Angel on My Shoulder; The Blue Dahlia. **1947** Suddenly It's Spring. **1948** The Sainted Sisters; Saigon; Whispering Smith. **1949** Red, Hot and Blue; Bride of Vengeance; My Fried Irma. **1950** My Friend Irma Goes West; At War With the Army; Branded; Fancy Pants; Where Danger Lives. **1951** Two Tickets to Broadway; Sailor Beware. **1952** The Greatest Show on Earth; Somebody Love Me; My Son John.

DUNHAM, PHILLIP "PHIL" (Phillip Gray Dunham)
Born: Apr. 23, 1885, London, England. Died: Sept. 5, 1972, Los Angeles, Calif. Screen, stage and vaudeville actor.

Appeared in: **1915** Flirtation a la Carte; Dad's Dollars and Dirty Doings; Gaby's Gasoline Glide; Spring Fever; Lizzie's Lingering Love; Shooting His 'Art Out. **1916** Limburger Cyclone; Phil's Busy Days. **1917** On the Trail of the Lonesome Pill; Faking Fakers; After the Balled-Up Ball; Even as Him and Her; The Joy Riders; Love and Blazes; A Good Little Bad Boy; Dry Goods and Damp Deeds; Chicken Chased and Henpecked; Nabbing a Noble; Defective Detectives; Summer Boarders. **1918** Playthings; Kidder and Co. **1919** In Bad All Around; Man Hunters. **1920** All for the Dough Bag. **1921** Two Minutes to Go; Punch of the Irish (short). **1922** Alias Julius Caesar; The Barnstormer; The Deuce of Spades. **1923** The Dangerous Maid; Robin Hood, Jr. **1931** Scratch as Catch Can (short). **1932** Jitters the Butler (short); Hurry Call. **1933** Fighting Parson; Fugitive; Rainbow Ranch. **1934** Bandits and Ballads (short); Perfectly Mismated (short); Everything Ducky (short); Search for Beauty; Down to Their Last Yacht. **1935** She Gets Her Man; I'm a Father (short). **1936** The Case Against Mrs. Ames; Big Brown Eyes; Hair-Trigger Casey; Idaho Kid; Cavalcade of the Wests; Romance Rides the Range. **1937** Beware of Ladies; Aces Wild; Navy Spy; Bank Alarm. **1938** Fury Below. **1939** Our Leading Citizen. **1940** West of the Pinto Basin. **1941** Miss Polly. **1942** Code of the Outlaw. **1945** Sudan. **1946** Undercurrent; Two Smart People. **1952** The Bad and the Beautiful. **1953** Hold Your Temper (short).

DUNKINSON, HARRY (Harry Leopold Dunkinson)
Born: Dec. 16, 1876, New York, N.Y. Died: Mar. 14, 1936. Screen, stage and vaudeville actor.

Appeared in: **1916** The Misleading Lady; The Strange Case of Mary Page (serial). **1917** The Edge of the Law. **1918** Selfish Yates; The Brass Bullet (serial). **1919** The Forbidden Room; The Rebellious Bride; Love is Love;; Chasing Rainbows; Don't Change Your Husband. **1920** The Willow Tree; Officer 666; Prairie Trails; Beware of the Bride. **1921** The Tomboy; The Blushing Bride; Big Town Round-Up; The Duke of Chimney Butte; The Primal Law; Trailin'; A Ridin' Romeo; Why Trust Your Husband?; The Law Trail. **1922** The Fast Mail. **1923** Bag and Baggage; Gentle Julia; Soft Boiled; Mine to Keep; The Sting of the Scorpion. **1924** The Diamond Bandit; Lash of the Whip; The Last Man on Earth. **1925** The Desert's Price. **1926** Mulhall's Great Catch; Doubling With Danger. **1927** Smile, Brother, Smile; Silver Valley. **1931** False Roomers (short). **1932** Amateur Daddy. **1933** Design for Living. **1934** Going Bye-Bye (short); Another Wild Idea (short). **1935** George White's 1935 Scandals. **1936** Nevada.

DUNLAP, FLORENCE
Born: 1883. Died: May 3, 1977, New York, N.Y. Screen and stage actress.

Appeared in: **1966** The Group. **1967** The Producers. **1968** The Night They Raided Minsky's. **1973** The Way We Were.

DUNN, EDWARD F. "EDDIE"
Born: 1896. Died: May 5, 1951, Hollywood, Calif. Screen actor.

Appeared in: **1928** The Fleet's In. **1929** The Saturday Night Kid; plus the following shorts: Bouncing Babies; The Hoose Gow; Sky Boy. **1930** Headin' North; True to the Navy; The Land of Missing Men; plus the following shorts: Another Fine Mess; Whispering Whoopee; Looser Than Loose; The Head Guy; The Fighting Parson. **1931** The Gang Buster; plus the following shorts: A Melon-Drama; False Roomers; The Pajama Party; Skip the Maloo!; The Hasty Marriage; Love Fever. **1932** The Big Broadcast; In Walked Charley (short). **1933** The following shorts: Me and My Pal; The Midnight Patrol; Asleep in the Fleet; Fallen Arches; Sherman Said It. **1935** G-Men; Car 99; Here Comes Cookie; The Bride Comes Home; Powder Smoke Range. **1936** The Big Broadcast of 1937; Go West, Young Man; The Preview Murder Mystery; plus the following shorts: Locks and Bonds; Dumb's the Word; Tramp Trouble. **1938** The Sky Parade; The Bride Walks Out; Rascals; Give Me a Sailor; plus the following shorts: Kennedy's Castle; Beaux and Errors; A Clean Sweep; His Pest Friend. **1939** Let Freedom Ring; Hollywood Calvacade; Three Smart Girls Grow Up; Tail Spin; Wrong Room (short); Of Mice and Men; Charlie McCarthy, Detective; Hero for a Day. **1940** On Their Own; The Great Profile; Mexican Spitfire Out West; The Great Dictator; One Night in the Tropics. **1941** Sea Raiders (serial); In the Navy; The Saint in Palm Springs; The Gay Falcon; Billy the Kid. **1942** Lady in a Jam; Mississippi Gambler; The Falcon's Brother; Invisible Agent; Ride 'Em Cowboy; Mexican Spitfire at Sea. **1943** Hit the Ice; The Falcon in Danger; Hello, Frisco, Hello; Dixie Dugan; Let's Face It. **1944** Bowery to Broadway; Cover Girl; I Love a Soldier; Standing Room Only; Three Men in White; Bermuda Mystery; Dead Man's Eyes; Henry Aldrich's Little Secret; Army Wives; Nothing But Trouble; Lost in a Harem. **1945** Frontier Gal; Wonder Man; George White's Scandals; State Fair; See My Lawyer; Here Come the Co-eds; Patrick the Great; Salome, Where She Danced; Senorita from the West. **1946** The Phantom Thief; Canyon Passage; Boston Blackie and the Law; The Dark Horse; Centennial Summer; Bowery Bombshell. **1947** Scareheads; Buck Privates Come Home; The Flame; Television Turmoil (short); Deep Valley; Born to Speed. **1948** Sleep, My Love; Call Northside 777; Lightning in the Forest; Big Punch; Homicide for Three; Checkered Coat. **1949** Incident; I Shot Jesse James; Whirlpool; Mother Is a Freshman. **1950** Mary Ryan, Detective; Lonely Hearts; Bandits; Buckaroo Sheriff of Texas; The Secret Fury; Summer Stock.

DUNN, EMMA
Born: 1875, Cheshire, England. Died: Dec. 14, 1966, Los Angeles, Calif. Screen and stage actress. Entered films in 1919.

Appeared in: **1920** Old Lady 31. **1924** Pied Piper Malone. **1929** Side Street. **1930** The Texan; Broken Dishes; Manslaughter. **1931** Too Young to Marry; Big Business Girl; The Prodigal; Compromised; Bad Comany; Morals of Women; Bad Sister; This Modern Age; The Guilty Generation. **1932** We Three; Wet Parade; The Man I Killed; The Cohens and the Kellys in Hollywood; Hell's House; Letty Lynton; It's Tough to Be Famous; Blessed Event; Broken Lullaby; Under Eighteen. **1933** Grand Slam; Hard to Handle; Man of Sentiment; Elmer, the Great; Private Jones; It's Great to Be Alive; Walls of Gold. **1934** Dark Hazard; The Quitter; Doctor Monica. **1935** This Is the Life; George White's Scandals of 1935; The Glass Key; Keeper of the Bees; The Little Big Shop; Ladies Crave Excitement; Another Face; Seven Keys to Baldpate; The Crusades. **1936** The Harvester; Second Wife; Mr. Deeds Goes to Town. **1937** Waikiki Wedding; When You're in Love; The Emperor's Candlesticks; Madame X; The Hideaway; Varsity Show; Circus Girl. **1938** The Cowboy from Brooklyn; Thanks for the Memory; The Cowboy and the Lady; Lord Jeff; Three Loves Has Nancy; Duke of West Point; Young Dr. Kildare. **1939** Calling Dr. Kildare; The Secret of Dr. Kildare; Hero for a Day; The Llano Kid; Son of Frankenstein; Each Dawn I Die. **1940** High School; Little Orvie; Dr. Kildare's Stangest Case; Dr. Kildare Goes Home; You Can't Fool Your Wife; Half a Sinner; One Crowded Night; Dance, Girl, Dance; Yesterday's Heroes; The Great Dictator. **1941** The Penalty; Scattergood Baines; Scattergood Pulls the Strings; Scattergood Meets Broadway; Mr. and Mrs. Smith; Dr. Kildare's Wedding Day; Ladies in Retirement; Rise and Shine. **1942** The Postman Didn't Ring; The Talk of the Town; Babes on Broadway; When Johnny Comes Marching Home; I Married a Witch. **1943** The North Star; Hoosier Holiday; Minesweeper; The Cross of Lorraine. **1944** The Bridge of San Luis Rey; It Happened Tomorrow; Are These Our Parents?; My Buddy. **1945** The Horn Blows at Midnight. **1946** The Hoodlum Saint; Night Train from Memphis. **1947** Life With Father; Mourning Becomes Electra. **1948** Woman in White.

DUNN, HARVEY B.
Born: Aug. 19, 1894, South Dakota. Died: Feb. 21, 1968, Hollywood, Calif. (cirrhosis of liver). Screen actor.

Appeared in: **1951** Vengeance Valley. **1954** Sabrina; The Bounty Hunter. **1956** Bride of the Monster. **1959** Teenagers from Outer Space; The Remarkable Mr. Pennypacker.

DUNN, HERBERT STANLEY
Born: 1892, Brooklyn, N.Y. Died: Apr. 14, 1979, Costa Mesa, Calif. (stroke). Screen, stage actor and property master. Appeared in films from 1913-1915 as the "Cisco Kid."

DUNN, J. MALCOLM
Born: England. Died: Oct. 10, 1946, Long Island, N.Y. Screen, stage and radio actor.

Appeared in: **1920** Dr. Jekyll and Mr. Hyde. **1921** The Magic Cup; Dawn of the East. **1926** Sandy. **1930** The Sap from Syracuse; Absent Minded (short).

DUNN, JACK (John Edward Powell Dunn)
Born: Mar. 28, 1917, Tunbridge Wells, England. Died: July 16, 1938, Los Angeles, Calif. (tularemia). Ice skater and screen actor. Won male figure skating title at 1936 Olympic Games.

DUNN, JAMES (James Howard Dunn)
Born: Nov. 2, 1901, New York, N.Y. Died: Sept. 1, 1967, Santa Monica, Calif. Screen, stage and television actor. Married to singer Edna Rush. Divorced from Edna O'Lier and actress Frances Gifford. Won 1945 Academy Award for Best Supporting Actor in A Tree Grows in Brooklyn.

Appeared in: **1931** Bad Girl; Over the Hill; Sob Sister. **1932** Society Girl; Handle With Care; Dance Team; Walking Down Broadway. **1933** Jimmy and Sally; Sailor's Luck (aka Hello Sister); Hold Me Tight; Arizona to Broadway; Take a Chance; The Girl in 419. **1934** Hold That Girl; Change of Heart; Baby Takes a Bow; Have a Heart; She Learned About Sailors; 365 Nights in Hollywood; Bright Eyes; Stand Up and Cheer. **1935** George White's Scandals of 1935; The Daring Young Man; Welcome Home; The Pay-Off; Bad Boy. **1936** Don't Get Personal; Hearts in Bondage; Come Closer Folks; Two-Fisted Gentlemen. **1937** Mysterious Crossing; We Have Our Moments; Living on Love; Venus Makes Trouble. **1938** Shadows Over Shanghai. **1939** Pride of the Navy. **1940** Son of the Navy; Mercy Plane; A Fugitive from Justice; Hold That Woman. **1942** The Living Ghost. **1943** The Ghost and the Guest; Government Girl. **1944** Leave It to the Irish. **1945** The Caribbean Mystery; A Tree Grows in Brooklyn. **1946** That Brennan Girl. **1947** Killer McCoy. **1948** Texas, Brooklyn and Heaven. **1950** The Golden Gloves Story. **1951** A Wonderful Life. **1960** The Bramble Bush. **1962** Hemingway's Adventures of a Young Man. **1966** The Oscar.

DUNN, JOHN J.
Born: 1906, Binghamtom, N.Y. Died: Apr. 2, 1938, Bluefield, W.Va. (pneumonia). Screen, stage and radio actor.

Appeared in: **1917** The Seven Pearls (serial).

DUNN, LIAM
Born: 1917. Died: Apr. 11, 1976, Granda Hills, Calif. (emphysema). Screen and television actor.

Appeared in: **1970** Catch-22. **1972** Charley and the Angel; What's Up Doc? **1973** The World's Greatest Athlete. **1974** Blazing Saddles; Young Frankenstein; Bank Shot; Herbie Rides Again. **1975** Peeper. **1976** Gus; Silent Movie; At Long Last Love.

DUNN, MICHAEL (Gary Neil Miller)
Born: Oct. 20, 1934, Shattuck, Okla. Died: Aug. 29, 1973, London, England. Screen, stage and television actor. Nominated for 1965 Academy Award for Best Supporting Actor in Ship of Fools.

Appeared in: **1965** Ship of Fools. **1967** You're a Big Boy Now; Without Each Other. **1968** Madigan; No Way to Treat a Lady; Boom! **1969** Justine; Fight for Rome (Pt. 1). **1971** Murders in the Rue Morgue. **1973** House of Freaks.

DUNN, RALPH
Born: 1902. Died: Feb. 19, 1968. Screen actor.

Appeared in: **1932** The Crowd Roars. **1936** Bullets or Ballots. **1937** The Game That Kills. **1938** A Slight Case of Murder; Alexander's Ragtime Band; The Tenth Avenue Kid; Numbered Woman; Come On Leathernecks. **1939** Tail Spin; The Return of the Cisco Kid; The Lone Ranger Rides Again (serial); Scouts to the Rescue (serial); Desperate Trails; Rose of Washington Square; One Hour to Live; Newsboys' Home. **1940** The Fighting 69th; Brigham Young—Frontiersman; The Grapes of Wrath; The Green Hornet (serial). **1941** The Lady from Cheyenne; Sun Valley Serenade; Manpower; Mr. and Mrs. Smith; I Wake Up Screaming (aka Hot Spot). **1942** Seven Days Leave; You're Telling Me; The Saboteur; Boston Blackie Goes Hollywood; Blondie Goes to College; Sing Your Worries Away; Moontide. **1943** He Hired the Boss; Always a Bridesmaid. **1944** U-Boat Prisoner; Follow the

Boys; Bowery to Broadway; Government Girl; Laura; The Hairy Ape; Roger Touhy, Gangster; Wilson; Dark Mountain. **1945** Circumstantial Evidence; Within These Walls; Along Came Jones; Love, Honor and Goodbye; An Angel Comes to Brooklyn; Dick Tracy; Hold That Blonde; Saratoga Trunk; Penthouse Rhythm. **1946** The Bandit of Sherwood Forest; Little Giant; Murder is My Business; Larceny in Her Heart; The Missing Lady; Genius at Work; Nobody Lives Forever; Gas House Kids; Lady Chasers. **1947** Three on a Ticket; Too Many Winners; News Hounds; Dragnet; Road to Rio; Nora Prentiss; Possessed. **1948** The Babe Ruth Story; Jinx Money; The Mystery of the Golden Eye; King of the Gamblers; Lady at Midnight; Train to Alcatraz; Incident. **1949** Whirlpool; The Lost Tribe. **1950** The Asphalt Jungle; Mary Ryan, Detective; Singing Guns; The Great Plane Robbery. **1951** A Place in the Sun. **1953** Taxi. **1956** Crowded Paradise. **1957** The Pajama Game. **1960** From the Terrace. **1964** Black Like Me.

DUNN, ROBERT "BOBBY"
Born: 1891, Milwaukee, Wis. Died: Mar. 24, 1937, Hollywood, Calif. (heart attack). Screen actor.

Appeared in: **1920** "Mirthquake" comedies. **1921** Skirts. **1926** The Thrill Hunter; When the Wife's Away. **1928** The Upland Rider. **1929** The Wagon Master; Captain Cowboy; 'Neath Western Skies; Code of the West; The Racketeer; Riders of the Storm; The Royal Rider. **1930** Half Pint Polly (short); Call of the Desert; Canyon Hawks; Trails of Peril; The Parting of the Trails; Parade of the West; The Canyon of Missing Men; The Cry Baby (short). **1932** The Big Flash (short); The Dentist (short). **1933** Me and My Pal (short); Loon Relations (short). **1934** Them Thar Hills (short). **1935** One More Spring; Tit for Tat (short); The Fixer-Uppers (short). **1936** The Bohemian Girl; Our Relations; plus the following shorts: The Lucky Day; Arbor Day; Neighborhood House. **1949** Lost Boundaries. **1951** The Whistle at Eaton Falls. **1952** Walk East on Beacon.

DUNN, REV. ROBERT H.
Born: 1896. Died: Feb. 11, 1960, Portsmouth, N.H. Screen actor and clergyman.

DUNNE, CHARLES
Died: Sept. 16, 1951, "Heartbreak Ridge," Korea (killed in action). Screen actor.

DUNNE, MICHAEL See DUNNE, STEVE

DUNNE, STEVE (Stephen Dunne aka MICHAEL DUNNE)
Born: 1918, Mass. Died: Aug. 27, 1977. Screen and radio actor.

Appeared in: **1946** Shock; Colonel Effingham's Raid; Doll Face; Junior Miss. **1947** When a Girl's Beautiful; The Son of Rusty; Mother Wore Tights. **1948** Whirlwind Raiders; The Return of October; The Dark Past. **1949** Law of the Barbary Coast; The Crime Doctor's Diary; Miss Grant Takes Richmond; The Big Sombrero; Rusty Saves a Life. **1950** The Underworld Story (aka The Whipped). **1952** Lady Possessed; The WAC from Walla Walla; Above and Beyond. **1956** Cha-Cha-Cha Boom. **1957** 10,000 Bedrooms. **1958** I Married a Woman; Home Before Dark. **1961** Explosive Generation. **1962** Hand of Death. **1974** Superdad.

DUNROBIN, LIONEL CLAUDE
Born: 1875. Died: Aug. 15, 1950, Hollywood, Calif. (suicide). Screen actor.

DUNSKUS, ERICH
Born: 1890, Germany. Died: Nov. 25, 1967, Hagen, West Germany. Screen, stage and television actor.

Appeared in: **1940** Gluck auf den Lande (Rural Happiness). **1950** Girls Behind Bars. **1954** A Prize of Gold.

DUNSMUIR, ALEXANDER
Born: 1877, Scotland. Died: July 30, 1938, Los Angeles, Calif. (auto crash injuries). Screen actor.

DUNTON, HELEN
Died: Nov., 1920, San Francisco, Calif. (suicide). Screen actress.

DU PEA, TATZUMBIE
Born: July 26, 1849, California. Died: Feb. 28, 1970, Los Angeles, Calif. (heart failure). American Indian screen actress.

Appeared in: **1931** Cimarron. **1934** Laughing Boy. **1940** 20 Mule Team. **1942** Tortilla Flat. **1944** Buffalo Bill. **1950** Across the Wide Missouri.

DU PONT, PATRICIA (aka MISS DU PONT)
Born: 1894, Frankfort, Ky. Died: Feb. 5, 1973. Screen and stage actress.

Appeared in: **1921** The Rage of Paris. **1922** False Kisses; The Golden Gallows; Foolish Wives; Shattered Dreams; A Wonderful Wife. **1923** The Common Law; The Broken Wing; The Man from Brodney's; Brass. **1924** So This Is Marriage; One Night in Rome; Sinners in Silk; What Three Men Wanted. **1925** Raffles, the Amateur Cracksman; Three Keys; Defend Yourself; Accused; A Slave of Fashion. **1926** Good and Naughty; Mantrap; That Model from Paris. **1928** Wheel of Destiny.

DUPRAY, GASTON
Born: 1885, Belgium. Died: Dec. 12, 1976, Brussels, Belgium. Screen and stage actor.

Appeared in: **1929** Atlantis (film debut). **1931** L'Amour Maitre des Choses. **1934** Le Roi des Champs-Elysees (The Champ of the Champs-Elysees). **1938** The Story of a Cheat.

DUPREE, GEORGE
Born: 1874, Cincinnati, Ohio. Died: July 29, 1951, New York. Screen and stage actor. Brother of actress Jeannette Dupree (dec.).

Appeared in: **1918** Woman the Germans Shot. **1919** The Avalanche; Thirteenth Chair. **1920** Great Lover; Inner Voice. **1921** Bachelor Apartments.

DUPREE, MINNIE
Born: 1873, San Francisco, Calif. Died: May 23, 1947, New York, N.Y. Stage and screen actress.

Appeared in: **1929** Night Club. **1938** The Young in Heart. **1940** Anne of Windy Poplars.

DUPREZ, FRED
Born: Sept. 6, 1884, Detroit, Mich. Died: Oct. 27, 1938, aboard ship bound for England (heart attack). Screen, stage, radio and vaudeville actor. Father of actress June Duprez.

Appeared in: **1933** Heads We Go (aka The Charming Deceiver—US); Oh What a Duchess! (aka My Old Duchess); Meet My Sister. **1934** Without You; Love, Life and Laughter; Danny Boy. **1935** Dance Band; No Monkey Business; Dark World. **1936** Ball at Savoy; A Wife or Two; Queen of Hearts; The Big Noise; Gypsy Melody; International Revue; Hearts of Humanity; You Must Get Married; Reasonable Doubt; All that Glitters. **1937** Cafe Colette (aka Danger in Paris—US); Head Over Heels (aka Head Over Heels in Love—US); Kathleen Mavourneen (aka Kathleen—US 1938); Knights for a Day; Okay for Sound. **1938** Hey! Hey! U.S.A.; Take Off That Hat.

DU PUIS, ARTHUR (Adolph Arthur Pierre Piete Du Puis)
Born: Mar. 29, 1901, Canada. Died: Apr. 8, 1952, Los Angeles, Calif. Screen actor, stuntman and makeup artist.

Appeared in: **1936** The Last of the Mohicans. **1937** Love is News. **1940** The Mark of Zorro; Strange Cargo. **1941** A Date With the Falcon; Rage in Heaven. **1950** Gambling House; Where Danger Lives; Never a Dull Moment. **1951** The Racket; An American in Paris. **1952** Macao; Clash by Night; Carson City; At Sword's Point.

DUPUIS, PAUL
Born: 1914, Canada. Died: Jan. 23, 1976, St. Saureun, Canada. Screen and televison actor.

Appeared in: **1945** Johnny Frenchman (US 1946). **1946** The Laughing Lady (US 1950). **1947** The White Unicorn (aka Bad Sister—US 1948). **1948** Against the Wind (US 1949); Sleeping Car to Trieste (US 1949). **1949** Madness of the Heart (US 1950); Passport to Pimlico; The Romantic Age (aka Naughty Arlette—US 1951); The Reluctant Widow (US 1951).

DURAN, VAL
Born: 1896. Died: Feb. 1, 1937, Los Angeles, Calif. (influenza). Screen actor.

Appeared in: **1936** The General Died at Dawn. **1937** Join the Marines; The Lost Horizon.

DURAND, EDOUARD
Born: 1871, France. Died: July 31, 1926, Port Chester, N.Y. (stroke). Screen and stage actor.

Appeared in: **1922** Anna Ascends. **1923** Potash and Perlmutter. **1924** The Lone Wolf. **1925** The King on Main Street; The Sky Raider.

DURAND, JEAN
Born: 1882, Paris, France. Died: 1946, Paris, France. Screen actor and film director.

DURANTE, CHECCO
Born: 1892, Italy. Died: Jan. 7, 1976, Heart ailment. Screen actor. Married to actress Annita Durante.

Appeared in: **1951** Luci del Varieta (Variety Lights—US 1965).

DURANTE, JIMMY (James Francis Durante)
Born: Feb. 10, 1893, New York, N.Y. Died: Jan. 28, 1980, Santa Monica, Calif. (pneumonitis). Screen, stage, vaudeville, radio, television actor and songwriter. Married to singer Jeanne Olson (dec. 1943) and later married to Marjorie Little. Appeared in vaudeville with partners Lou Clayton (dec. 1950) and Eddie Jackson (dec. 1980) in an act billed as "Clayton, Jackson and Durante." Entered films in 1929.

Appeared in: **1930** Roadhouse Nights. **1931** The Cuban Love Song; The New Adventures of Get-Rich-Quick Wallingford. **1932** The Passionate Plumber; Speak Easily; Blondie of the Follies; Her Cardboard Lover; The Phantom President; The Wet Parade. **1933** Hell Below; Broadway to Hollywood; Meet the Baron; What! No Beer? **1934** Hollywood Party; She Learned About Sailors; Strictly Dynamite; George White's Scandals; Student Tour; Joe Palooka. **1935** Carnival. **1936** One in a Million. **1938** Start Cheering; Sally, Irene and Mary; Little Miss Broadway; Forbidden Music. **1940** Melody Ranch. **1941** You're in the Army Now; The Man Who Came to Dinner. **1944** Music for Millions; Two Girls and a Sailor. **1946** Two Sisters From Boston; Ziegfeld Follies. **1947** It Happened in Brooklyn; This Time for Keeps. **1948** On an Island With You. **1950** The Milkman; The Great Rupert; Yellow Cab Man. **1960** Pepe. **1962** Jumbo. **1963** It's a Mad, Mad, Mad, Mad World. **1964** Big Parade of Comedy. **1974** That's Entertainment (film clips).

DURFEE, MINTA
Born: 1890, Los Angeles, Calif. Died: Sept. 9, 1975, Woodland Hills, Calif. (congestive heart failure). Screen, television and vaudeville actress. Divorced from actor Fatty Arbuckle (dec. 1933).

Appeared in: **1913** His Wife's Mistake. **1914** A Misplaced Foot; A Busted Johnny (aka Making a Living); A Film Johnnie; Twenty Minutes of Love; The Jazz Waiter (aka Caught in a Cabaret); Our Country Cousin; The Pugilist (aka The Knock-out); The Masquerader; The Rounders; Among the Mourners; Leading Lizzie Astray; Tillie's Punctured Romance; Fattie and Minnie-He-Haw; Cruel, Cruel Love. **1915** Love, Speed and Thrills; Colored Villainy; Fatty's Spooning Day (aka Mabel, Fatty and the Law); Other People's Wives (aka The Home Breakers); Hearts and Planets; Our Daredevil Chief; Court House Crooks; A Desperate Scoundrel (aka Dirty Work in a Laundry); Fickle Fatty's Fall. **1916** The Great Pearl Tangle; Ambrose's Cup of Woe; His Wife's Mistakes; The Other Man. **1918** Mickey; The Cabaret. **1925** Bright Lights. **1926** Skinner's Dress Suit. **1935** Naughty Marietta. **1941** Rolling Home to Texas; How Green Was My Valley. **1942** The Miracle Kid. **1954** Rose Marie. **1956** Hollywood or Bust. **1957** Will Success Spoil Rock Hunter?; An Affair to Remember. **1958** King Creole. **1963** It's a Mad, Mad, Mad, Mad World. **1964** The Unsinkable Molly Brown. **1971** What's the Matter With Helen?; Willard.

DURHAM, LEWIS
Born: New Oxford, Pa. Died: Oct. 16, 1937. Screen actor.

Appeared in: **1916** Law Unto Himself; The Conscience of John David. **1917** One Shot Ross. **1919** The Flame of the Desert.

DURIEUX, TILLA (Ottilie Godeffroy)
Born: 1881, Vienna, Austria. Died: Feb. 21, 1971, Berlin, Germany (after operation necessitated by fall). Screen, stage and television actress.

Appeared in: **1957** The Last Bridge.

DURKIN, ELEANOR
Died: prior to 1968. Screen and vaudeville actress. Married to actor James Burke (dec. 1968) and appeared with him in vaudeville in an act billed as "Burke and Durkin."

Appeared in: **1929** A Tete-A-Tete in Songs (short). **1942** Are Husbands Necessary?

DURKIN, JAMES PETER
Born: 1879. Died: Mar. 12, 1934, Los Angeles, Calif. Screen and stage actor.

Appeared in: **1930** Derelict; Shadow of the Law. **1933** The Big Cage; The Secret of the Blue Room. **1934** Uncertain Lady; Wild Girl; Nice Women; Alexander Hamilton; Vice Squad; Gun Smoke; Conquering Horde; Heat Lightning; Perils of Pauline (serial); The Vanishing Shadow (serial).

DURKIN, JUNIOR (Trent Junior Durkin)
Born: 1915, New York, N.Y. Died: May 4, 1935, near San Diego, Calif. (auto accident). Screen and stage actor.

Appeared in: **1930** Fame (film debut); Tom Sawyer; Santa Fe Trail; Recaptured Love; The Law Rides West. **1931** The Conquering Horde; Huckleberry Finn. **1932** Hell's House. **1933** Manhunt. **1934** Little Men; Big Hearted Herbert.

DURNING, BERNARD J.
Born: 1893. Died: Aug. 29, 1923, New York, N.Y. (typhoid). Screen actor and film director. Married to actress Shirley Mason (dec. 1979).

Appeared in: **1919** Blackie's Redemption. **1921** Devil Within; Seeds of Vengeance.

DURST, EDWARD
Born: 1917. Died: Mar. 10, 1945, Hollywood, Calif. Screen and stage actor.

Appeared in: **1944** Days of Glory.

DURYEA, DAN
Born: Jan. 23, 1907, White Plains, N.Y. Died: June 7, 1968, Los Angeles, Calif. (cancer). Screen, stage and television actor. Father of actor Peter and manager Richard Duryea.

Appeared in: **1941** The Little Foxes; Ball of Fire. **1942** Pride of the Yankees; That Other Woman. **1943** Sahara. **1944** Woman in the Window; Ministry of Fear; Main Street After Dark; Mrs. Parkington; None But the Lonely Heart; The Man from Frisco. **1945** Scarlet Street; Lady on a Train; Along Came Jones; The Great Flamarion; Valley of Decision. **1946** White Tie and Tails; Black Angel. **1948** Larceny; Another Part of the Forest; Black Bart; River Lady. **1949** Criss Cross; Manhandled; Too Late for Tears; Johnny Stool-Pigeon. **1950** One Way Street; Winchester 73; The Underworld Story. **1951** Al Jennings of Oklahoma; Chicago Calling. **1953** Thunder Bay; Sky Commando. **1954** Ride Clear of Diablo; World for Ransom; Thirty Six Hours (aka Terror Street—US); Rails Into Laramie; This Is My Love; Silver Lode. **1955** The Marauders; Foxfire. **1956** Battle Hymn; Storm Fear. **1957** The Burglar; Slaughter on Tenth Avenue; Night Passage. **1958** Kathy O'. **1960** Platinum High School; Rich, Young and Deadly. **1962** Six Black Horses. **1964** He Rides Tall; Taggart; Walk a Tightrope. **1965** Flight of the Phoenix; The Faceless Men; The Bounty Killer. **1966** Il Fiume di Dollari (A River of Dollars aka The Hills Run Red—US 1967); Incident at Phantom Hill; Five Golden Dragons (US 1968). **1968** The Bamboo Saucer.

DURYEA, GEORGE *See* KEENE, TOM

DUSE, ELEANORA
Born: 1858, Vigerano, Italy. Died: Apr. 23, 1924, Pittsburgh, Pa. Screen and stage actress.

Appeared in: **1916** Cenere. **1927** Madre.

DUTT, NARGIS (Fatima Rashid)
Born: 1928, India. Died: May 3, 1981, Bombay, India. Screen actress. Married to actor/producer/director Sunil Dutt.

DUVAL, JOE (Jose DuVal)
Born: 1907. Died: Apr. 22, 1966. Screen and radio actor.

Appeared in: **1951** The Girl on the Bridge. **1963** The Cardinal.

DUVAL, JUAN
Died: 1954. Screen actor.

Appeared in: **1930** One Mad Kiss. **1933** Flying Down to Rio; California Trail. **1935** Bordertown. **1936** The Black Coin (serial). **1940** Rhythm of the Rio Grande; Arise, My Love. **1946** Trail to Mexico. **1948** The Loves of Carmen; The Feathered Serpent. **1949** The Big Steal; Neptune's Daughter. **1950** The Palomino. **1953** The Big Sombrero.

DUVALEIX, CHRISTIAN
Born: 1923, France. Died: July 28, 1979, France. Screen, stage actor, and music hall performer.

Appeared in: **1941** The King. **1952** The Prize. **1957** Crazy in the Noodle. **1964** Paris When It Sizzles. **1968** Isadora.

DUVALLES (Frederic Duvalles)
Born: 1895, France. Died: Feb., 1971, France. Screen and stage actor.

Appeared in: **1932** Paris-Mediterranee. **1933** On Demande un Compagnon. **1963** The Burning Court.

DUVERNET, PAULETTE
Born: 1910, France. Died: Mar. 21, 1933, Paris, France. Screen and stage actress.

DUXBURY, ELSPETH
Born: 1912, India. Died: Mar. 10, 1967, London, England. Screen, stage and television actress.

Appeared in: **1960** Make Mine Mink. **1966** The Great St. Trinian's Train Robbery (US 1967).

DVORAK, ANN (Ann McKin)
Born: Aug. 2, 1912, New York, N.Y. Died: Dec. 10, 1979, Honolulu, Hawaii. Screen, stage actress and writer. Divorced from actors Leslie Fenton and Igor Dega (dec. 1976), and producer Nicholas H. Wade.

Appeared in: **1929** The Hollywood Revue of 1929. **1930** Way Out West; Free and Easy. **1931** The Guardsman; This Modern Age. **1932** Sky Devils; The Crowd Roars; Scarface (aka Scarface, the Shame of a Nation); Love is a Racket; Strange Love of Molly Louvain; Stranger in Town; Crooner; Three on a Match. **1933** The Way to Love; College Coach. **1934** Massacre; Heat Lightning; Side Streets; Friends of Mr. Sweeney; Midnight Alibi; Housewife; Gentlemen Are Born; I Sell Anything; Murder in the Clouds. **1935** A Trip Through a Hollywood Studio (short); Sweet Music; G-Men; Dr. Socrates; Bright Lights; Thanks a Million; Follies Bergere. **1936** We Who Are About to Die. **1937** Racing Lady; Midnight Court; The Case of the Stuttering Bishop; Manhattan Merry-Go-Round; She's No Lady. **1938** Gangs of New York; Merrily We Live. **1939** Blind Alley; Stronger Than Desire. **1940** Girls of the Road; Street of Missing Women; Cafe Hostess. **1942** This Was Paris; Squadron Leader (US 1943). **1943** Escape to Danger (US 1944). **1945** Flame of the Barbary Coast; Masquerade in Mexico. **1946** Abilene Town; The Bachelor's Daughters. **1947** The Private Affairs of Bel Ami; The Long Night; Out of the Blue. **1948** The Walls of Jericho. **1950** Our Very Own; A Life of Her Own; The Return of Jesse James; Mrs. O'Malley and Mr. Malone. **1951** I Was an American Spy; The Secret of Convict Lake.

DWIGGINS, JAY
Died: Sept. 8, 1919. Screen actor.

Appeared in: **1914** Bunny's Little Brother. **1915** A Mistake in Typesetting; Mr. Jarr and Gertrude's Beaux; A Disciple of Plato; The Smoking Out of Bella Butts; The Lady of Shalott; The Capitulation of the Major; They Loved Him So; Whose Husband?; Strictly Neutral; War; The Starring of Flora Finchurch; The Kidnapped Stockbroker; Sis; Old Good-for-Nothin'; A Queen for an Hour; The Reward; Brown's Summer Boarders; The Dust of Egypt; A Man's Sacrifice; Sonny Jim's First Love Affair; Heredity. **1916** By Love Redeemed; A Film Exposure. **1917** A Finished Product; His Uncle Dudley; Whose Baby? **1918** He Comes Up Smiling; Bound in Morocco. **1919** His Majesty, the American; The Poor Boob; In for Thirty Days; Whitewashed Walls; The Man Who Turned White. **1920** Everywoman.

DWIRE, EARL
Born: 1884. Died: Jan. 16, 1940, Carmichael, Calif. Screen actor.

Appeared in: **1931** Dugan of the Bad Lands. **1932** Law of the West; Man from Hell's Edges; Son of Oklahoma. **1933** Galloping Romeo; Riders of Destiny; Sagebrush Trail. **1934** West of the Divide; The Lucky Texan; Randy Rides Alone; The Star Packer; Trail Beyond; Lawless Frontier. **1935** Unconquered Bandit; Wagon Trail; Fighting Pioneers; Smokey Smith; Rider of the Law; Saddle Acres; Between Men; Last of the Clintons; Toll of the Desert. **1936** Millionaire Kid; Caryl of the Mountains; Desert Justice; Roamin' Wild; The Last Assignment; The Speed Reporter; Cavalcade of the West; Sundown Saunders; Headin' for the Rio Grande; Stormy Trails; The Gun Ranger. **1937** The Mystery of the Hooded Horseman; Arizona Days; Trouble in Texas; The Trusted Outlaw; Riders of the Rockies; Hittin' the Trail; Riders of the Dawn; Galloping Dynamite; Atlantic Flight; Trouble at Midnight; Git Along, Little Dogies. **1938** Accidents Will Happen; Under Western Stars; Trouble at Midnight; The Purple Vigilantes; The Old Barn Dance; The Daredevil Drivers; Two-Gun Justice; Man from Music Mountain; Six Shootin' Sheriff; Mysterious Rider; Angels With Dirty Faces; Gold Mine in the Sky. **1939** Each Dawn I Die; The Star Maker; The Arizona Kid; On Trial. **1940** King of the Lumberjacks; His Girl Friday; Flash Gordon Conquers the Universe (serial).

DWYER, JOHN T.
Born: 1877. Died: Dec. 7, 1936, New York, N.Y. Screen, stage and radio actor.

Appeared in: **1920** Over the Hill to the Poor House. **1926** Jack O'Hearts; The Man in the Shadow.

DWYER, RUTH "JACKIE"
Born: 1898, Brooklyn, N.Y. Died: Mar. 2, 1978, Woodland Hills, Calif. Screen and stage actress.

Appeared in: **1919** The Lurking Peril (serial). **1920** The Evil Eye (serial); The Stealers. **1921** Clay Dollars. **1923** Second Hand Love; His Mystery Girl. **1924** After a Million; Broadway or Bust; Cornered; Dark Stairways; Jack O' Clubs; The Covered Trail; The Reckless Age. **1925** Seven Chances; The Canvas Kisser; Crack O' Dawn; The Fear Fighter; The Gambling Fool; Going the Limit; White Fang. **1926** Stepping Along; The Brown Derby; A Man of Quality. **1927** The Patent Leather Kid; White Pants Willie; The Lost Limited; The Racing Fool; The Nest; A Hero for a Night. **1928** A Perfect Gentleman; Sailors' Wives; Alex the Great.

DYALL, FRANKLIN
Born: Feb. 3, 1874, Liverpool, England. Died: May 8, 1950, Worthing, England. Screen, stage, radio actor and stage producer. Divorced from Mary Phyllis Logan and later married to actress Mary Merrall (dec. 1973). Father of actor Valentine Dyall.

Appeared in: **1919** The Garden of Resurrection. **1927** Easy Virtue (US 1928). **1929** Atlantic. **1931** Alibi; The Ringer (US 1932); A Night in Montmartre; Creeping Shadows (aka The Limping Man—US 1932); A Safe Affair. **1932** Men of Steel. **1933** Called Back; The Private Life of Henry VIII. **1935** The Iron Duke; The Case of Gabriel Perry. **1936** Conquest of the Air. **1939** All at Sea. **1943** Yellow Canary (US 1944). **1948** Bonnie Prince Charlie (US 1952).

DYCE, HAMILTON
Died: Jan. 8, 1972. Screen actor.

Appeared in: **1961** Whistle Down the Wind (US 1962). **1963** The Double (US 1967); Master Spy (US 1964). **1964** Becket. **1965** King Rat. **1966** Sky West and Crooked (aka Gypsy Girl); The Wrong Box. **1969** Two Gentlemen Sharing.

D'YD, JEAN
Born: France. Died: May, 1964, France. Screen actress.

Appeared in: **1929** The Passion of Joan of Arc. **1938** Rothschild. **1939** Entente Cordiale. **1940** SOS Mediterranean. **1948** The Room Upstairs; L'Eternal Retour (The Eternal Return). **1955** Martin Roumagnac; Chiens Perdus San Collier.

DYER, BOB (James Robert Dyer)
Born: 1900. Died: Nov. 19, 1965, Hollywood, Calif. Screen actor. Entered films approx. 1930.

DYER, JOHN E.
Born: 1884. Died: Oct. 11, 1951, Detroit, Mich. Screen and vaudeville actor.

DYER, WILLIAM J. "BILLY"
Born: 1881. Died: Dec. 23, 1933. Screen actor. Father of actor William Dyer, Jr.

Appeared in: **1916** Broken Fetters. **1917** Triumph. **1919** Trail of the Octopus (serial); Who Will Marry Me?; A Little White Savage; Man's Desire. **1920** The Branded Four (serial); The Screaming Shadow (serial); Courage of Marge O'Doone. **1921** Cupid's Brand; The Sheriff of Hope Eternal; Cyclone Bliss; Fightin' Mad. **1922** The Crow's Nest; The Silent Call; Don't Shoot; Gun Shy. **1923** Pioneer Trails; Wild Bill Hickok; Quicksands; Scaramouche; Tea With a Kick; Wolves of the Border. **1924** Singer Jim McKee; The Measure of a Man; The Martyr Sex; Marry in Haste; Women First. **1926** The Man in the Saddle; Looking for Trouble. **1927** Hands Off; The Fighting Three; Gun Gospel. **1928** Desert of the Lost. **1930** Code of Honor; Overland Bound.

DYKES, JIMMY (James Joseph Dykes)
Born: Nov. 10, 1896, Philadelphia, Pa. Died: June 15, 1976, Philadelphia, Pa. Baseball player, coach, manager and screen actor.

Appeared in: **1949** The Stratton Story.

EADIE, DENNIS
Born: Jan. 14, 1869, Glasgow, Scotland. Died: June 10, 1928, England. Screen and stage actor.

Appeared in: **1915** The Man Who Stayed Home. **1916** Disraeli (US 1917).

EAGAN, EVELYN
Born: 1908. Died: July 17, 1946, Hollywood, Calif. Screen actress.

EAGELS, JEANNE
Born: 1894, Kansas City, Mo. Died: Oct. 3, 1929, New York, N.Y. Screen and stage actress. Nominated for 1928/29 Academy Award for Best Actress in The Letter.

Appeared in: **1916** The World and the Woman. **1917** Fires of Youth; Under False Colors. **1918** The Cross Bearer. **1927** Man, Woman and Sin. **1929** The Letter; Jealousy.

EAGER, JOHNNEY (John Tanner)
Born: 1930. Died: Sept. 8, 1963, Hollywood, Calif. Screen, stage and television actor.

Appeared in: **1963** Four for Texas.

EAGLE, FRANCIS SITTING (aka SITTING EAGLE)
Died: 1977. Screen actor and Wild West Shows.

EAGLE, JAMES "JIMMY" (James Crump Eagle)
Born: Sept. 10, 1907, Virginia. Died: Dec. 15, 1959, Los Angeles, Calif. (cirrhosis of liver). Screen actor.

Appeared in: **1928** Crooks Can't Win; Hey Rube! **1929** Half Marriage. **1930** Abraham Lincoln; The Big Fight; Son of the Gods. **1932** Thirteenth Guest; Parisian Romance; You Said a Mouthful; Gambling Sex. **1933** The Penal Code; From Hell to Heaven; She Done Him Wrong; Story of Temple Drake; To the Last Man. **1934** Manhattan Melodrama; Massacre; He Was Her Man; Opened by Mistake (short). **1935** Sunset Range; Rocky Mountain Mystery; Charlie Chan in Egypt. **1936** Ace Drummond (serial); I'd Give My Life; Down the Stretch; Racing Blood. **1938** Eagle Squadron; The Painted Trail; All-American Sweetheart; Heroes of the Hills. **1950** When Willie Comes Marching Home.

EAGLE EYE *See* ENS, WILLIAM

EAMES, CLARE
Born: 1896, Hartford, Conn. Died: Nov. 8, 1930, London, England. Stage and screen actress.

Appeared in: **1924** Dorothy Vernon of Haddon Hall. **1929** The Three Passions.

EARL, CATHERINE V.
Born: 1886. Died: Aug. 14, 1946, Hollywood, Calif. (heart attack). Stage and screen actress.

EARL, KATHLEEN
Born: 1913. Died: May 21, 1954, Hollywood, Calif. Screen and stage actress.

EARLCOTT, GLADYS
Died: May 18, 1939, Los Angeles, Calif. Stage and screen actress.

EARLE, BLANCHE "BONNIE"
Born: 1883. Died: Jan. 22, 1952, Woodland Hill, Calif. (heart attack). Screen actress. Married to silent film director William P. S. Earle (dec. 1973).

Appeared in: **1915** Battle Cry of Peace. **1917** Within the Law.

EARLE, DOROTHY
Died: 1958. Screen actress. Married to screen actor Gabby Hayes (dec. 1969).

Appeared in: **1927** Out of the Night; Pioneers of the West.

EARLE, EDWARD
Born: July 16, 1882, Toronto, Canada. Died: Dec. 15, 1972, Woodland Hills, Calif. Screen, stage and vaudeville actor.

Appeared in: **1915** Greater Than Art; The Working of a Miracle; The Bedouin's Sacrifice; Olive and the Heirloom; Olive is Dismissed; The Lesson of the Flames; Olive's Opportunities; Olive's Manufactured Mother; Olive's Other Self. **1916** Ranson's Folly. **1917** For France. **1918** The Blind Adventure; One Thousand Dollars; Transients in Arcadia. **1919** Buried Treasure; His Bridal Night; Miracle of Love. **1920** Law of the Yukon. **1921** East Lynne; Passion Fruit. **1922** False Fronts; The Man Who Played God; The Streets of New York. **1923** Broadway Broke; None So Blind; You Are Guilty. **1924** The Dangerous Flirt; The Lure of Love; How to Educate a Wife; Gambling Wives; The Family Secret. **1925** Her Market Value; The Lady Who Lied; The Splendid Road; Why Women Love. **1926** The Greater Glory; A Woman's Heart; Irene; Pals First. **1927** Twelve Miles Out; Spring Fever. **1928** Runaway Girls; The Wind. **1929** The Hottentot; Kid Gloves; Spite Marriage; Smiling Irish Eyes. **1930** In the Next Room; Phantom of the Desert. **1931** Stout Hearts and Willing Hands (short); Woman of Experience; Second Honeymoon. **1932** Forgotten Women. **1933** Revenge at Monte Carlo; Alimony Madness. **1934** Here Comes the Navy; Ticket to a Crime; Little Miss Marker; Mystery Mountain (serial); He Was Her Man. **1935** Revenge Rider; Fighting Lady; Chinatown Squad; Mutiny Ahead; Magnificent Obsession. **1936** Life Hesitates at 40 (short); The Case Against Mrs. Ames; Dangerous Waters; Love Before Breakfast. **1937** Love in a Bungalow; Headline Crasher; Find the Witness; The Frame Up; Artists and Models; A Day at the Races; History is Made at Night. **1938** When G-Men Step In; Her Jungle Love; The Marines Are Here; Riders of the Black Hills; The Headleys at Home; I Am a Criminal; The Duke of West Point; Start Cheering; Give Me a Sailor; Men With Wings; Judge Hardy's Children. **1939** Newsboys' Home; Mandrake the Magician (serial); When Tomorrow Comes; In Old Monterey; Honolulu; East Side of Heaven. **1940** The Green Hornet (serial); Seventeen; Sued for Libel; On Their Own; Angels Over Broadway; She Knew All the Answers; Johnny Eager. **1941** Ride, Kelly, Ride; Scattergood Baines; Blue, White and Perfect; Border Vigilantes; Great Guns. **1943** Two Weeks to Live; Alaska Highway; Bordertown Gun Fighters; The Good Fellows; Jack London; The Dancing Masters; Slightly Dangerous; The Heat's On; What a Woman! **1944** Casanova Brown; The Story of Dr. Wassell; Maisie Goes to Reno; She's a Soldier Too; Practically Yours; Black Magic; I Accuse My Parents; Nothing But Trouble; Ghost Catchers. **1945** Circumstantial Evidence; Captain Tugboat Annie; The Cisco Kid in Old Mexico. **1946** The Harvey Girls; Dark Alibi; The Devil's Mask; Accomplice; The Postman Always Rings Twice; The Best Years of Our Lives. **1947** The Homestretch; Ride the Pink Horse; Beginning or the End. **1948** Command Decision; River Lady; Night Has a Thousand Eyes. **1949** That Midnight Kiss; The Gal Who Took the West. **1950** Blondie's Hero; When You're Smiling; Beware of Blondie; Annie Get Your Gun. **1951** The Texas Rangers; Flight to Mars. **1952** Hangman's Knot. **1953** The Mississippi Gambler; It Happens Every Thursday; Stranger Wore a Gun. **1955** A Man Called Peter; One Desire. **1956** Francis in the Haunted House; The Ten Commandments.

EARLE, JACK (Jacob Ehrlich)
Born: 1906, Denver, Colo. Died: July 18, 1952, El Paso, Tex. Screen actor and circus performer.

Appeared in: **1924** Jack and the Beanstalk.

EARLE, JOSEPHINE
Born: Feb. 23, 1892, Brooklyn, N.Y. Died: Aug., 1929, Brooklyn, N.Y. Screen and stage actress. Entered films with Vitagraph.

Appeared in: **1916** The Blue Envelope; Dollar and the Law; The Scarlet Runner (serial); Footlights of Fate (aka Joan Thursday). **1917** Indiscretion. **1920** Branded; The Edge of Youth; The Fall of a Saint; Walls of Prejudice. **1921** The Way of a Man; Serving Two Masters. **1923** The Hotel Mouse; The Knock-Out; Woman to Woman (US 1924). **1930** Raise the Roof.

EARLE, WILLIAM P. S.
Born: 1884, New York, N.Y. Died: 1973, Los Angeles, Calif. Screen actor, film director, screenwriter and playwright. Married to actress Blanche "Bonnie" Earle (dec. 1952) and later married to actress Evangeline Russell (dec. 1966).

EARLY, MARGO
Born: 1918. Died: Jan. 13, 1936, Santa Monica, Calif. (auto accident). Screen actress.

Appeared in: **1934** Operator 13. **1935** Naughty Marietta.

EARLY, MARGOT
Born: 1915. Died: Jan. 13, 1936, Hollywood, Calif. (auto crash). Screen actress.

Appeared in: **1934** Operator 13. **1935** Naughty Marietta.

EARLY, PEARL M.
Born: 1879, Wooster, Ohio. Died: June 17, 1960, Oceanside, Calif. Screen and vaudeville actress. Toured in vaudeville with her husband John Early in an act billed as "Early & Laight."

Appeared in: **1942** My Favorite Blonde. **1945** This Love of Ours.

EASON, MYLES
Born: May 7, 1915, Tatura, Victoria, Australia. Died: Jan. 8, 1977, Grand Cayman Island (heart attack). Screen, stage and television actor.

Appeared in: **1959** The Rough and the Smooth (aka Portrait of a Sinner US 1961).

EASON, REEVES B. "BREEZY"
Born: 1886, Fryors Point, Miss. Died: June 9, 1956, Sherman Oaks, Calif. (heart attack). Screen, stage, vaudeville actor, film producer, director and screenwriter. Divorced from actress Jimsy Maye (dec. 1968). Father of actor Breezy Eason (dec. 1921).

Appeared in: **1912** The Law of the Wilds. **1915** The Echo; When Empty Hearts are Filled; In the Purple Hills. **1916** The Better Woman. **1928** The Danger Rider.

EASON, REEVES "BREEZY", JR.
Born: 1913. Died: Oct. 24, 1921, Hollywood, Calif. (struck by auto). Screen actor. Son of actor Eason Reeves (dec. 1956). Entered films with Universal.

Appeared in: **1920** Two Kinds of Love. **1921** The Big Adventure; The Fox; Sure Fire.

EAST, ED
Born: 1896, Bloomington, Ind. Died: Jan. 18, 1952, New York, N.Y. (heart attack). Screen, stage, vaudeville, radio actor, and pianist. Appeared in vaudeville with Ralph Dumke.

Appeared in: **1937** Educational short. **1938** Universal short. **1949** Jackpot Jitters. **1951** Stop That Cab.

EAST, JOHN M.
Born: 1861. Died: Aug. 18, 1924, London, England. Screen and stage actor.

Appeared in: Little Lord Fauntleroy.

EASTON, SIDNEY
Died: 1971. Black screen actor.

Appeared in: **1931** His Woman. **1932** Wayward. **1940** Sunday Sinners; Paradise in Harlem. **1941** Murder on Lenox Ave. **1946** Fight That Ghost. **1947** Killer Diller. **1948** Boarding House Blues.

EATON, ELWYN
Born: 1864, England. Died: Apr. 30, 1937, Los Angeles, Calif. Screen actor.

EATON, EVELYN
Born: 1924. Died: June 17, 1964, Los Angeles, Calif. Screen, stage and television actress. Married to announcer, Eddie King.

Appeared in: **1949** Mr. Belvedue Goes to College; Flying Fools.

EATON, JAMES (James Latessa)
Born: Oct. 2, 1934, Ohio. Died: May 8, 1964, West Hollywood, Calif. (suicide—barbiturate poisoning). Screen and television actor.

EATON, JAY
Born: 1900. Died: Feb. 5, 1970, Hollywood, Calif. (heart attack). Screen actor. Entered films in 1919.

Appeared in: **1921** Where Lights Are Low. **1928** Lady Be Good; Man-Made Woman; The Noose; Three-Ring Marriage. **1929** Synthetic Sin. **1932** Merrily We Go to Hell; Winner Take All. **1933** The Cocktail Hour. **1934** The Affairs of Cellini; Jimmy the Gent. **1935** A Night at the Opera; Southern Exposure (short); Living on Velvet; The Wedding Night; The Gilded Lily. **1936** And So They Were Married; Under Your Spell; Libeled Lady; Criminals of the Air. **1937** Paid to Dance; Toast of New York. **1941** Love Crazy. **1946** The Kid from Brooklyn. **1947** The Unfaithful. **1952** Carrie.

EATON, MABEL
Died: Jan. 10, 1916, Chicago, Ill. Screen actress. Divorced from actor William Farnum (dec. 1953).

Appeared in: **1914** The Fable of the Good Fairy.

EATON, MARY
Born: 1901, Norfold, Va. Died: Oct. 10, 1948, Hollywood, Calif. (heart attack). Stage and screen actress. Married to screen actor Eddie Lawton.

Appeared in: **1923** His Children's Children. **1924** Broadway After Dark. **1929** The Cocoanuts; Glorifying the American Girl.

EBELE, EDWARD, SR.
Born: 1862. Died: Feb. 19, 1936, Hollywood, Calif. Screen actor.

Appeared in: **1935** The Wedding Night.

EBERG, VICTOR
Born: 1925, Mexico? Died: Feb. 26, 1972, Hollywood, Calif. (sclerosis of the liver). Screen and television actor.

Appeared in: **1969** Butch Cassidy and the Sundance Kid.

EBERLE, RAY
Born: 1919. Died: Aug. 25, 1979, Douglasville, Ga. (heart attack). Screen, stage actor and singer. Brother of singer Bob Eberly (dec. 1981).

Appeared in: **1943** Mister Big. **1944** This is the Life.

EBERLY, BOB (Robert Eberly)
Born: 1918, Mechanicsville, N.Y. Died: Nov. 17, 1981, Glen Burnie, Md. (cancer). Screen, radio, television actor and band vocalist. Brother of actor/singer Ray Eberle (dec. 1979). Married to actress Florine Callahan.

Appeared in: **1942** The Fleet's In. **1943** I Dood It.

EBERT, BERNIE
Born: 1915. Died: Jan. 13, 1969, Hollywood, Calif. (heart attack). Screen, stage, television actor and television producer, director.

EBI, EARL
Born: June 25, 1903, Fresno, Calif. Died: Jan. 24, 1973, Encino, Calif. (heart attack). Screen, stage actor, film producer, director, television producer, radio producer and director.

Appeared in: **1935** Mary Burns, Fugitive. **1936** The Singing Cowboy; Hearts in Bondage; Long Before Breakfast.

EBURNE, MAUDE
Born: 1875. Died: Oct. 8, 1960, Hollywood, Calif. Screen and stage actress. Married to stage producer Gene Hill (dec. 1932).

Appeared in: **1931** Lonely Wives; Bought; The Man in Possession; Larceny Lane; Blonde Crazy; The Bat Whispers; The Guardsman; Her Majesty; Love; Indiscreet. **1932** Under Eighteen, Panama Flo; Polly of the Circus; The Passionate Plumber; Woman from Monte Carlo; The Trial of Vivienne Ware; First Year; Stranger in Town; This Reckless Age. **1933** Vampire Bat; Ladies They Talk About; Ladies Must Love; Robbers' Roost; Shanghai Madness; The Warrior's Husband; My Lips Betray; Big Executive; East of Fifth Avenue; Havana Widows. **1934** Fog; When Strangers Meet; Here Comes the Navy; Return of the Terror; Lazy River; Love Birds. **1935** Maybe It's Love; Happiness C.O. D.; Ruggles of Red Gap; Party Wire; Don't Bet on Blondes. **1936** Doughnuts and Society; Reunion; Man Hunt; The Leavenworth Case; Poppy; Valiant Is the Word for Carrie. **1937** Champagne Waltz; When's Your Birthday?; Hollywood Cowboy; Fight for Your Lady; Live, Love and Learn; Paradise Express. **1938** Riders of the Black Hills. **1939** The Amazing Mr. Williams; Exile Empress; My Wife's Relatives; Mountain Rhythm; Meet Dr. Christian; Sabotage; The Covered Trailer. **1940** Li'l Abner; Colorado; The Courageous Dr. Christian; Dr. Christian Meets the Women; Remedy for Riches; The Border Legion. **1941** Melody for Three; They Meet Again; Glamour Boy; West Point Widow; Among the Living; You Belong to Me. **1942** I Married an Angel; Henry and Dizzy; To Be or Not to Be; Almost Married; Henry Aldrich, Editor; The Boogie Men Will Get You. **1943** Lady Bodyguard. **1944** Henry Aldrich Plays Cupid; The Princess and the Pirate; Rosie the Riveter; The Suspect; Goodnight, Sweetheart; The Town Went Wild; Bowery to Broadway; I'm from Arkansas. **1945** Man from Oklahoma; Hitchhike to Happiness; Leave It to Blondie. **1947** Slippery Magee; Mother Wore Tights. **1948** The Plunderers. **1949** Arson, Inc. **1951** Prince of Peace (aka The Lawton Story).

EBY-ROCK, HELYN
Born: 1896. Died: July 20, 1979, Woodland Hills, Calif. (heart attack). Screen, stage, vaudeville and television actress.

Appeared in: **1933** Ann Vickers.

ECCLES, JANE
Born: 1896. Died: July, 1966, London, England. Screen, stage and television actress.

Appeared in: **1959** Look Back in Anger.

ECHOLS, J. KERMIT
Born: 1921, Sandusky, Ohio. Died: Jan. 4, 1978, Atlanta, Ga. Screen, stage, television actor, film producer, film director and screenwriter.

Appeared in: **1952** Wait Till the Sun Shines Nellie. **1957** The Delinquents; The James Dean Story. **1974** The Longest Yard; The Cockfighter. **1976** Grizzly.

ECKERLEIN, JOHN E.
Born: 1884, N.Y. Died: Sept. 9, 1926, New York, N.Y. Screen and vaudeville actor.

Appeared in: **1923** Little Old New York.

ECKHARDT, OLIVER J.
Born: 1873. Died: Sept. 15, 1952, Hollywood, Calif. Screen actor.

Appeared in: **1925** Sporting Life. **1927** The Last Trail. **1928** The Cavalier. **1930** The Lone Star Ranger. **1936** The Cowboy and the Kid; Desire; Empty Saddles.

ECKLES, LEWIS C. "LEW"
Born: 1888. Died: Mar. 26, 1950, Kansas City, Mo. (heart attack). Screen and stage actor. Married to actress Cara Louise Field.

Appeared in: **1945** The House on Ninety-Second Street. **1948** Call Northside 777.

ECKLUND, CAROL
Born: 1934. Died: Nov. 4, 1939 (burns). Five-year-old screen actress.

EDDY, MRS. AUGUSTA ROSSNER
Born: 1860. Died: Sept. 21, 1925, New York, N.Y. Screen and stage actress.

EDDY, DOROTHY
Born: 1907. Died: June 10, 1959, Brooklyn, N.Y. Screen and vaudeville actress. One of the "Four Eddy Sisters," of vaudeville and film fame.

EDDY, LEO (Leo Eddy Schapiro)
Born: 1907. Died: July 3, 1978, North Hollywood, Calif. Screen actor.

EDDY, NELSON
Born: June 29, 1901, Providence, R.I. Died: Mar. 6, 1967, Miami, Fla. (stroke). Screen, radio, opera and television actor.

Appeared in: **1933** Broadway to Hollywood; Dancing Lady. **1934** Student Tour. **1935** Naughty Marietta. **1936** Rose Marie. **1937** Maytime; Rosalie. **1938** The Girl of the Golden West; Sweethearts. **1939** Let Freedom Ring; Balalaika. **1940** Bitter Sweet; New Moon. **1941** The Chocolate Soldier. **1942** I Married an Angel. **1943** The Phantom of the Opera. **1944** Knickerbocker Holiday. **1946** Never Say Goodbye; Nobody Lives Forever; Willy, The Operatic Whale (voice only); Make Mine Music (voice only). **1947** End of the Rainbow; Northwest Outpost. **1974** That's Entertainment (film clips).

EDELSTEIN, "DAD"
Born: 1845. Died: June, 1927, Sydney, Australia. Screen actor.

EDESON, ROBERT
Born: 1868, New Orleans, La. Died: Mar. 24, 1931, Hollywood, Calif. (heart attack). Stage and screen actor. Divorced from actress Mary Newcomb (dec. 1967).

Appeared in: **1914** The Call of the North; Where the Trail Divides. **1915** How Molly Made Good. **1916** The Light That Failed. **1921** Extravagance. **1922** Any Night; The Prisoner of Zenda; Sure-Fire Flint. **1923** The Spoilers; Has the World Gone Mad?; Luck; The Silent Partner; Souls for Sale; The Ten Commandments; The Tie That Binds; To the Last Man; You Are Guilty. **1924** Feet of Clay; The Bedroom Window; Don't Call It Love; Mademoiselle Midnight; Men; Missing Daughters; Thy Name Is Woman; Triumph; Welcome Stranger. **1925** Blood and Steel, Braveheart; The Danger Signal; Go Straight; The Golden Bed; Hell's Highroad; Keep Smiling; Locked Doors; Men and Women; The Prairie Pirate; The Rag Man; The Scarlet West. **1926** The Blue Eagle; The Clinging Vine; Eve's Leaves; Her Man O'War; The Volga Boatman; Whispering Smith. **1927** King of Kings; Altars of Desire; The Heart Thief; His Dog; The Night Bride; The Rejuvenation of Aunt Mary. **1928** Tenth Avenue; Marriage by Contract; Chicago; The Home Towners; The Man Higher Up; The Power of the Press; Beware of Blondes; A Ship Comes In; Walking Back. **1929** George Washington Cohen; Marianne; The Little Wildcat; The Doctor's Secret; A Most Immoral Lady; Romance of the Rio Grande; Dynamite. **1930** Danger Lights; Big Money; Little Johnny Jones; Way of All Men; Cameo Kirby; Pardon My Gun; Swing High; A Devil with Women. **1931** Aloha; The Lash.

EDGAR, MARRIOTT (George Marriott Edgar)
Born: Oct. 5, 1880, Colvend, Kercudbright, England. Died: May 4, 1951, London, England. Screen, stage, vaudeville actor and writer.

Appeared in: **1932** Here's George.

EDGAR-BRUCE, TONI (Sybil Etonia Bruce)
Born: June 4, 1892, London, England. Died: Mar. 28, 1966, Chertsey, England. Screen, stage and radio actress. Daughter of stage actor/manager Edgar Bruce (dec.).

Appeared in: **1920** Duke's Son (aka Squandered Lives—US). **1922** The Further Adventures of Sherlock Holmes series including Charles Augustus Milverton. **1930** A Warm Corner. **1932** Brother Alfred; Diamond Cut Diamond (aka Blame the Woman—US); Mr. Bill the Conqueror (aka The Man Who Won—US 1933); Lucky Girl. **1933** Letting in the Sunshine; The Melody Maker; As Good as New; Leave It to Me; Falling for You; Heads We Go (aka The Charming Deceiver—US); The Private Life of Henry VIII. **1934** Whispering Tongues; The Broken Melody; Lilies of the Field. **1935** Handle with Care; Night Mail; Mr. What's-His-Name; Captain Bill. **1936** The Last Waltz. **1937** Behind Your Back; Boys Will be Girls. **1938** Scruffy; The Citadel. **1939** Too Dangerous to Live. **1942** Gert and Daisy Clean Up; The First of the Few (aka Spitfire—US 1943); Somewhere on Leave. **1944** Heaven is Round the Corner. **1945** Waltz Time. **1952** Derby Day (aka Four Against Fate—US 1955).

EDGARD, LEWIS
Born: 1878. Died: Dec. 8, 1917, New York, N.Y. Screen and stage actor.

Appeared in: **1915** The Family Divided; In the Palace of the King.

EDISS, CONNIE
Born: Aug. 11, 1871, Brighton, Sussex, England. Died: Apr. 18, 1934, London, England. Screen and stage actress.

Appeared in: **1930** A Warm Corner.

EDLER, CHARLES
Born: 1877. Died: Mar. 29, 1942, Santa Monica, Calif. Screen and stage actor.

Appeared in: **1921** The Magnificent Brute; That Girl Montana. **1922** The Sign of the Rose.

EDMONSON, WILLIAM
Born: 1903, Spokane, Wa. Died: May 28, 1979, Los Angeles, Calif. Black screen, stage, radio, television and concert singer.

Appeared in: **1927** The Millionaire. **1928** The Midnight Ace; Thirty Years Later. **1960** The Wizard of Bagdad. **1962** Five Weeks in a Balloon. **1968** The Secret War of Harry Frigg.

EDMUNDSEN, AL
Born: 1896, Pueblo, Colo. Died: May 11, 1954. Screen and stage actor.

Appeared in: **1915** The Butterfly; Just Jim. **1922** Foolish Wives. **1923** Merry Go Round.

EDNEY, FLORENCE
Born: June 2, 1879, London, England. Died: Nov. 24, 1950, New York, N.Y. Screen and stage actress.

Appeared in: **1916** Who's Guilty; Hazel Kirke.

EDSTROM, KATHERINE
Born: 1901. Died: June 2, 1973, Hollywood, Fla. Screen, stage and television actress. Once billed as "Queen of the Alligator Wrestlers." She appeared in early silents.

EDWARDS, ALAN
Born: June 3, 1900, New York, N.Y. Died: May 8, 1954, Los Angeles, Calif. Stage and screen actor. Entered films with Edison Co. in 1912. Married to actress Nita Pike (dec. 1954).

Appeared in: **1921** A Virgin Paradise. **1933** The White Sister; Clear All Wires; Looking Forward; Stage Mother; Life in the Raw. **1934** The Show Off; The Frontier Marshall; Hold That Girl. **1935** If You Could Only Cook; Women Must Dress. **1936** Ring Around the Moon; Forgotten Faces; Make Way for a Lady. **1937** Forty Naughty Girls. **1938** Little Tough Guy. **1939** For Love or Money; Laugh it Off; South of the Border. **1941** Mr. District Attorney. **1945** Thoroughbreds; Junior Miss. **1946** Mr. Ace. **1947** The Lone Wolf in Mexico.

EDWARDS, CHARLES (Charles E. Virian)
Born: 1898. Died: Aug. 18, 1978, Hollywood, Calif. Screen, vaudeville, television actor, nightclub, songwriter, pianist and singer.

Appeared in: **1924** The Truth About Women.

EDWARDS, CLIFF "UKELELE IKE"
Born: June 14, 1895, Hannibal, Mo. Died: July 17, 1971, Hollywood, Calif. Screen, stage, vaudeville actor and singer. Divorced from singer Irene Wiley and actress Nancy Dover.

Appeared in: **1929** The Hollywood Revue of 1929; So This Is College?; Marianne; What Price Glory? **1930** Montana Moon; Dogway Melody (short); Way Out West; Romeo in Pajamas; Those Three French Girls;

Good News; Forward March; The Lullaby; Dough Boys; Lord Byron of Broadway; War Babies. **1931** Parlor, Bedroom and Bath; The Great Lover; The Sin of Madelon Claudet; Dance, Fools, Dance!; Stepping Out; The Prodigal; Shipmates; Sidewalks of New York; Laughing Sinners; Hell Divers. **1932** Young Bride; The Big Shot; Fast Life; Love Starved. **1933** Flying Devils; Take a Chance; MGM short. **1934** George White's Scandals. **1935** George White's 1935 Scandals; Red Salute. **1936** The Man I Marry. **1937** They Gave Him a Gun; Between Two Women; Saratoga; Bad Guy; The Women Men Marry; MGM short. **1938** The Girl of the Golden West; The Bad Man of Braimstone; The Little Adventuress. **1939** Maisie; Smuggled Cargo; Royal Rodeo (short); Gone With the Wind. **1940** High School; His Girl Friday; Pinocchio (voice of Jiminy Cricket); Millionaires in Prison; Flowing Gold; Friendly Neighbors. **1941** The Monster and the Girl; She Couldn't Say No; Power Dive; Knockout; International Squadron; Thunder Over the Prairie; Prairie Stranger. **1942** West of Tombstone; Sundown Jim; Lawless Plainsmen; Riders of the Northland; Bad Men of the Hills; Seven Miles to Alcatraz; Pirates of the Prairie; Overland to Deadwood; American Empire; Bandit Ranger. **1943** Fighting Frontier; The Falcon Strikes Back; Salute for Three; The Avenging Rider. **1947** Fun and Fancy Free (voice); The Man from Button Willow (voice). **1974** That's Entertainment (film clips).

EDWARDS, EDNA PARK
Born: 1895, Pittsburgh, Pa. Died: June 5, 1967, Burbank, Calif. Screen, stage, vaudeville actress and radio writer.

EDWARDS, ELEANOR
Born: 1883, N.Y. Died: Oct. 22, 1968, Los Angeles, Calif. Stage and screen actress. Married to actor Snitz Edwards (dec. 1937). Entered films in 1922.

EDWARDS, GUS (Gus Simon)
Born: Aug. 18, 1881, Germany. Died: Nov. 7, 1945, Los Angeles, Calif. Screen, stage, vaudeville, radio actor, songwriter and film producer.

Appeared in: **1929** The Hollywood Revue of 1929. **1932** Screen Songs (short). **1933** Screen Songs (short); Mr. Broadway.

EDWARDS, HENRY
Born: Sept. 18, 1882, Weston-Supern-Mare, England. Died: Nov. 2, 1952, Chobham, England. Screen, stage actor, film director, screenwriter and stage producer.

Appeared in: **1914** Clancarty; A Bachelor's Love Story. **1915** Lost and Won (aka Odds Against); The Man Who Stayed at Home; A Welsh Singer; Far from the Madding Crowd; Alone in London; My Old Dutch. **1916** Doorsteps; Grim Justice; East is East. **1917** Merely Mrs. Stubbs; Dick Carson Wins Through (aka The Failure); The Cobweb; Broken Threads; Nearer My God to Thee. **1918** The Refugee; Tares; The Hanging Judge; The Touch of a Child; Towards the Light; "Film Tags" series including: A New Version, The Message, Against the Grain, Anna, Her Savings Saved, The Poet's Windfall and The Secret; Heppworth. **1919** Her Dearest Possession; The City of Beautiful Nonsense; The Kinsman; Possession; Broken in the Wars. **1920** Aylwin; John Forrest Finds Himself; A Temporary Vagabond; The Amazing Quest of Mr. Ernest Bliss (serial). **1921** The Lunatic at Large; The Bargain. **1922** Simple Simon; Tit for Tat. **1923** Lily of the Alley; Boden's Boy; The Naked Man. **1924** The World of Wonderful Reality. **1926** The Flag Lieutenant. **1927** The Fake; Further Adventures of the Flag Lieutenant; Fear. **1929** Ringing the Changes; The Three Kings. **1930** The Call of the Sea. **1931** The Girl in the Night. **1932** The Flag Lieutenant (and 1926 version). **1933** General John Regan. **1935** Scrooge. **1937** Captain's Orders; High Treason; Juggernaut. **1941** Spring Meeting; East of Piccadilly (aka The Strangler—US 1942). **1946** Green for Danger (US 1947); Magic Bow (US 1947). **1947** Take My Life (US 1948). **1948** Quartet (US 1949); Woman Hater (US 1949); London Belongs to Me (aka Dulcimer Street—US); Lucky Mascot (aka The Brass Monkey—US 1951); Oliver Twist (US 1951). **1949** Dear Mr. Prohack (US 1950); All Over Town. **1950** Trio; Madeleine; Golden Salamander; Double Confession (US 1953); The Verger. **1951** The Lady with the Lamp; The Magic Box (US 1952); The Rossiter Case; White Corridors. **1952** Something Money Can't Buy; Never Look Back. **1953** The Long Memory.

EDWARDS, JAMES
Born: 1912, Ind. Died: Jan. 4, 1970, San Diego, Calif. (heart attack). Black screen, stage and television actor.

Appeared in: **1949** Man Handled; The Set-Up; Home of the Brave. **1951** The Steel Helmet; Bright Victory. **1952** The Member of the Wedding. **1953** The Joe Louis Story. **1954** The Caine Mutiny. **1955** African Manhunt; Seven Angry Men; The Phoenix City Story. **1956** Battle Hymn. **1957** Men in War. **1958** Anna Lucasta; Fraulein; Tarzan's Fight for Life. **1959** Night of the Quarter Moon; Pork Chop Hill; Blood and Steel. **1962** The Manchurian Candidate. **1965** The Sandpiper. **1968** The Young Runaways; Coogan's Bluff. **1970** Patton.

EDWARDS, JOAN
Born: 1921. Died: Aug. 27, 1981, New York, N.Y. (heart attack). Screen, radio actress, songwriter and singer.

Appeared in: **1947** Hit Parade of 1947.

EDWARDS, JOHN
Born: 1869, Boston, Mass. Died: Oct. 16, 1929. Screen and stage actor. Do not confuse with film director John Edwards.

EDWARDS, JULIA
Born: 1883. Died: Apr. 16, 1976, Stockton, Calif. Screen, vaudeville actress, burlesque and circus performer.

EDWARDS, LEE
Died: Mar. 3, 1978. Screen actor.

Appeared in: **1958** Invisible Avenger. **1962** Bourbon Street Shadows.

EDWARDS, MATTIE
Born: 1886. Died: June 26, 1944, Los Angeles, Calif. Screen actress. Entered films approx. 1924.

Appeared in: **1936** Give Us This Night.

EDWARDS, NATE
Born: 1902. Died: Sept. 12, 1972, Hollywood, Calif. Screen actor, film extra, stuntman, casting director and production manager.

EDWARDS, NEELY (Cornelius Limbach)
Born: Sept. 16, 1889, Delphos, Ohio. Died: July 10, 1965, Woodland Hills, Calif. Screen, stage and vaudeville actor. Married to actress Marguerite Snow (dec. 1958). Was half of hoofer-comedy team known as "The Hall Room Boys."

Appeared in: **1921** Brewster's Millions; The Little Clown. **1922** The Green Temptation. **1925** I'll Show You the Town. **1926** Footloose Widows; Made for Love. **1927** The Princess on Broadway. **1928** Excess Baggage; Sunny California (short). **1929** Dynamite; Gold Diggers of Broadway; Show Boat. **1930** Scarlet Pages; plus the following shorts: Her Relatives, The Window Cleaners, The Milky Way. **1931** The Hangover (short). **1932** The following shorts: Junior, The Weekend. **1933** Diplomaniacs; Love, Honor and Oh, Baby! **1935** Broadway Melody of 1936. **1939** Mr. Moto in Danger Island; For Love or Money. **1942** Sin Town. **1943** Strictly in the Groove. **1945** George White's Scandals.

EDWARDS, SARAH
Born: 1883. Died: Jan. 7, 1965, Hollywood, Calif. Screen, stage and vaudeville actress.

Appeared in: **1929** Glorifying the American Girl. **1934** Smarty. **1935** Ruggles of Red Gap; The World Accuses; Welcome Home; The Dark Angel; Two-Fisted. **1936** The Golden Arrow; Earthworm Tractors; Palm Springs; Early to Bed; Colleen; Stage Struck; Theodora Goes Wild; The Great Ziegfeld. **1937** Second Honeymoon; We're on the Jury; It's Love I'm After; Hollywood Hotel. **1938** Touchdown Army; A Doggone Mixup (short); Women are Like That; The Shining Hour; Three Loves Has Nancy; Fools for Scandal. **1939** Boy Trouble; Meet Dr. Christian; The Shop Around the Corner. **1940** Young People; Strike Up the Band; Mr. District Attorney; Arise, My Love. **1941** Footsteps in the Dark; The Invisible Woman; Kitty Foyle; Bedtime Story; Hot Spot (aka I Wake Up Screaming); One Foot in Heaven; Three Girls About Town; Meet John Doe; Glamour Boy; Sunset in Wyoming; All That Money Can Buy. **1942** Rings on Her Fingers; Dudes are Pretty People; The Forest Rangers; Scattergood Survives a Murder; Twin Beds; My Favorite Blonde; Reap the Wild Wind. **1943** All By Myself; Happy Go Lucky; Dixie Dugan; Calaboose. **1944** Storm Over Lisbon; The Little Cynic (short); Henry Aldrich's Little Secret; The Big Noise; Where are Your Children?; Henry Aldrich Plays Cupid; The Thin Man Goes Home; You Can't Ration Love; Rationing. **1945** Two O'Clock Courage; The Corn is Green; Abbott and Costello in Hollywood; Mother-in-Law's Day (short); Saratoga Trunk. **1946** It's a Wonderful Life; Girl on the Spot; The Hoodlum Saint; Easy to Wed; Undercurrent. **1947** The Bishop's Wife. **1948** Good Sam; Isn't It Romantic?; Family Honeymoon. **1950** Petty Girl; The Fuller Brush Girl; The Glass Menagerie. **1951** Honeychile. **1952** The Devil and Daniel Webster (reissue and retitle of All That Money Can Buy, 1941); Carson City.

EDWARDS, SNITZ
Born: 1862, Hungary. Died: May 1, 1937, Los Angeles, Calif. (arthritis). Stage and screen actor. Entered films in 1920. Married to actress Eleanor Edwards (dec. 1968).

Appeared in: **1920** The City of Masks. **1921** The Charm School;

Cheated Love; Ladies Must Live; The Love Special; No Woman Knows. **1922** The Ghost Breaker; The Gray Dawn; Human Hearts; June Madness; Love Is an Awful Thing; Rags to Riches; Red Hot Romance. **1923** Children of Jazz; Hollywood; The Huntress; Modern Matrimony; Rosita; Souls for Sale; Tea with a Kick. **1924** The Thief of Bagdad; Hill Billy; In Fast Company; Inez from Hollywood; Passion's Pathway; Tarnish; Tiger Love; The Tornado; A Woman Who Sinned. **1925** Seven Chances; Heir-Loons; A Lover's Oath; Old Shoes; The Phantom of the Opera; The White Desert. **1926** Battling Butler; April Fool; The Clinging Vine; The Cruise of the Jasper B; The Lady of the Harem; The Sea Wolf; Volcano; The Wanderer. **1927** Red Mill; College; Night Life. **1929** A Dangerous Woman; The Mysterious Island; The Phantom of the Opera (and 1925 version). **1931** Right of Way; Sit Tight; Public Enemy.

EDWARDS, TED (M. E. Barrell)
Born: 1883. Died: Sept. 29, 1945, Los Angeles, Calif. Screen and vaudeville actor. In Mack Sennett comedies and an original Keystone Kop.

Appeared in: **1924** Fires of Youth.

EDWARDS, VIRGINIA
Died: Mar. 7, 1964, Hollywood, Calif. Screen, stage actor, playwright and drama coach.

Appeared in: **1932** Silver Dollar.

EDWARDS, WALTER
Born: Michigan. Died: Apr., 1920, Honolulu, Hawaii. Screen, stage actor and film director. Entered films as an actor with Broncho Film Company.

Appeared in: **1916** Honor's Alter. **1917** The Relic; Conscience.

EGAN, MISHKA
Born: 1891. Died: Feb. 15, 1964, Hollywood, Calif. Screen and vaudeville actor.

Appeared in: **1946** The Hoodlum Saint. **1949** Holiday Affair. **1957** An Affair to Remember.

EGBERT, ALBERT
Born: England. Died: Mar. 18, 1942, England? Screen actor and music hall performer. Brother of actor Seth Egert. Appeared in W. P. Kelline films in 1902.

Appeared in: **1915** Bill's Monickee. **1916** The Dustman's Outgoing. **1927** The Further Adventures of the Flag Lieutenant.

EGGENTON, JOSEPH
Born: 1870. Died: June 3, 1946, Hollywood, Calif. Screen and stage actor.

Appeared in: **1940** The Doctor Takes a Wife; You'll Find Out. **1941** Lady from Cheyenne. **1943** The Moon is Down.

EGLEVSKY, ANDRE
Born: 1917, Moscow, Russia. Died: Dec. 4, 1977, Elmira, N.Y. (heart attack). Screen actor and classical dancer.

Appeared in: **1952** Limelight.

EGLI, JOSEPH E.
Born: 1900. Died: Aug. 2, 1974, Calif. Film casting director and screen extra. Entered films as an extra with Carl Laemmle.

EHFE, WILLIAM (William Carl Ehfe)
Born: June 19, 1887, Payette, Idaho. Died: Aug. 1, 1940, Los Angeles, Calif. (heart ailment). Screen actor.

Appeared in: **1912** Tempest-Tossed. **1913** The Bully. **1914** Love vs. Duty; The Raiders. **1915** The End of the Road; Scandals; Secretary of Frivolous Affairs. **1917** The Best Man. **1919** Code of the Yukon.

EICHBERG, RICHARD
Born: 1888, Berlin, Germany. Died: May 8, 1952, Munich, Germany. Screen actor, film producer, director and screenwriter. Married to actress Lee Parry and later married to actress Kitty Jantzen.

EILERS, SALLY (Dorothea Sally Eilers)
Born: Dec. 11, 1908, New York, N.Y. Died: Jan. 5, 1978, Woodland Hills, Calif. (heart attack). Screen and stage actress. Divorced from actor Hoot Gibson (dec. 1962), movie producer Harry Joe Brown, naval aviator Howard Barney, and married to television director John

Hollingworth Morse. Enterd films in 1926. Was a Wampas Baby Star in 1928.

Appeared in: **1927** Sunrise—A Song of Two Humans; Slightly Used. **1928** Dry Martini; Goodbye Kiss; Trial Marriage. **1929** Sailor's Holiday; Broadway Babies; The Long, Long Trail; The Show of Shows. **1930** Doughboys; She Couldn't Say No; Trigger Tricks; Let Us Be Gay; Roaring Ranch. **1931** The Black Camel; Parlor, Bedroom and Bath; Reducing; Clearing the Range; Quick Millions; Bad Girl; Holy Terror; Over the Hill. **1932** Hat Check Girl; Dance Team; Disorderly Conduct. **1933** I Spy; State Fair; Bad Boy; Second Hand Wife; Sailor's Luck; Made on Broadway; Central Airport; Hold Me Tight; Walls of Gold. **1934** She Made Her Bed; Three on a Honeymoon; Morning After. **1935** Carnival; Alias Mary Dow; Pursuit; Remember Last Night? **1936** Don't Get Personal; Strike Me Pink; Florida Special; Without Orders; Talk of the Devil (US 1937). **1937** We Have Our Moments; Danger Patrol; Lady Behave. **1938** Nurse from Brooklyn; Everyody's Doing It; Condemned Woman; Tarnished Angel. **1939** They Made Her a Spy; Full Confession. **1941** I Was a Prisoner on Devil's Island. **1943** First Aid (short). **1944** A Wave, a Wac and a Marine. **1945** Strange Illusion. **1948** Coroner Creek. **1950** Stage to Tucson.

EINHORN, LIZZIE
Born: 1857. Died: Jan. 14, 1945, New York, N.Y. Screen actress. Married to film director Ivan Abramson (dec.). Appeared in silent films.

EINSTEIN, HARRY See PARKYAKARKUS

EISSA, MICKEY
Born: 1900. Died: Aug. 14, 1962, Hermosa Beach, Calif. Screen actor.

Appeared in: **1941** Riders of the Timberline; Stick to Your Guns; Outlaws of the Desert.

EKBORG, LARS
Born: 1926, Upsala, Sweden. Died: 1969, Sweden. Screen and stage actor.

Appeared in: **1939** U-Boat. **1958** Blonde in Bondage. **1965** Wedding—Swedish Style. Other Swedish films: Backyard; Mrs. Anderson's Charlie; Poker; When Lilacs Blossom; Meeting Life; Wingbeats in the Night; Summer with Monika; The Lunchbreak Cafe; Yellow Squadron; In Smoke and Dancing; Dangerous Freedom; Blocked Rails; The Dance Hall; Violence; Private Entrance; Little Fridolf and I; Stage Entrance; The Flame; A Guest in One's Own Home; Never in Your Life; Lights at Night; Little Fridolf Becomes a Grandfather; No Tomorrow; Fridolf is Rebellious; The Love Game; A Thief in the Bedroom; Three Wishes; Ticket to Paradise; Siska; Swedish Portraits; To Go Ashore; Stimulantia; The Murderer—an Ordinary Person; Duet for Cannibals; Ansiket (The Face and aka The Magician).

EKELUND, CARYLL N.
Born: May 6, 1935, Cottonwood, Calif. Died: Nov. 3, 1939, Los Angeles, Calif. (burns). Screen actress.

Appeared in: **1940** The Blue Bird.

EKMAN, GOESTA
Born: 1887, Sweden. Died: Jan. 12, 1938, Stockholm, Sweden. Screen and stage actor.

Appeared in: **1926** Faust. **1928** Heart of a Clown; Discord; A Husband by Proxy. **1930** The Last Night; For Her Sake. **1931** Brokiga Blad. **1933** Charles XII. **1934** Kaera Slaekten. **1935** Swedenhielms; The Noble Prize Winner. **1937** Intermezzo.

EKMAN, JOHN
Born: 1880, Stockholm, Sweden. Died: 1949, Sweden? Screen and stage actor.

Appeared in: **1919** The Song of the Scarlet Flower. **1928** Sin. **1938** Baldwin's Wedding. **1943** Lasse-Maja. Other Swedish films: The Death Ride Under the Big Top; The Black Masks; A Secret Marriage; Lady Marion's Summer Flirtation; The Voice of Blood; Love Stronger than Hate; The Brothers; People of the Border; Half-Breed; The Miracle; Do Not Judge; Children of the Street; Daughter of the High Mountain; Hearts that Meet; The Strike; His Wife's Past; The Ace of Thieves; The Fight for the Rembrandt Painting; His Father's Crime; Judas Money; Madame de Thebes; The Avenger; The Governor's Daughters; Sea Vultures; Old Age and Folly; The Lucky Brooch; The Hermit's Wife; At Eleventh Hour; Who Fired?; The Jungle Queen's Jewels; Slave to Yourself; The Living Mummy; The Outlaw and His Wife; The Executioner; Family Traditions; The Phantom Carriage (aka They Shall Bear Witness); For High Ends; The Suitor from Roads; Johan Ulfstjerna; The Norrtull Gang; The Young Count Takes the Girl and the Prize; Kalle Utter; A Merchant House in the Archipelago; The

Ingmar Inheritance; The Girls at Slovik; What Woman Wants; Black Rudolf; The Secret of the Paradise Hotel; The Atlantic Adventure; Synnove Solbakken; The Song of the Scarlet Flower; Outlawed; 33,333; Bombi Bitt and I; Baldevin's Wedding; His Grace's Will; The Gentleman Gangster; The Fight Goes On; Scanian Guerilla; General von Dobeln; Count the Happy Moments Only; The Rose of Thistle Island; Black Roses; The Serious Game; Don't Try It With Me; The Evening of the Fair; Lars Hard; Janne Vangman's New Adventures; Tall Lasse from Delsbo; To Joy.

EKSTROM, MARTA
Born: 1899, Sweden. Died: Jan. 26, 1952, Stockholm, Sweden. Screen and stage actress.

Appeared in: **1938** John Ericsson Victor of Hampton Roads. **1949** Katrina.

ELAM, LINDA
Born: Aug. 10, 1947. Died: July 1, 1974, Hawthorne, Calif. (auto accident). Black screen actress.

ELBA, MARTA
Born: 1920, Cuba. Died: Apr. 19, 1954, Mexico City, Mexico (cancer). Screen, stage actress and newspaper columnist.

ELDER, DOTTIE
Born: 1929. Died: Nov. 28, 1965, Hollywood, Calif. (heart attack). Screen and televison actress.

ELDER, RICHARD LT. COL.
Born: 1911. Died: Oct. 4, 1963, Fort Huachuca, Ariz. (heart attack). Screen and radio actor.

ELDER, RUTH
Born: Sept. 8, 1905, Anniston, Ala. Died: Oct. 9, 1977, San Francisco, Calif. Screen, vaudeville actress and aviatrix.

Appeared in: **1928** Moran of the Marines (film debut). **1929** Winged Horseman. **1938** Bringing Up Baby. **1939** The Women.

ELDREDGE, RUTH See MEAKIN, RUTH

ELDRIDGE, ANNA MAE
Born: 1894. Died: Apr. 17, 1950, Van Nuys, Calif. Screen actress. Appeared in silents.

ELDRIDGE, CHARLES
Born: 1854, Saratoga Springs, N.Y. Died: Oct. 29, 1922, New York, N.Y. (cancer). Stage and screen actor.

Appeared in: **1912** The Old Kent Road; The Spider Web; The Picture Idol; Who's to Win; Half a Hero; The Professor and the Lady; The Crossroads; The Little Minister; She Cried; The Red Barrier; As You Like It; An Elephant on their Hands; Reincarnation of Komar; The Model for St. John. **1918** Sporting Life. **1921** Ashamed of Parents; Made in Heaven. **1922** No Trespassing. **1925** Hearts and Spurs.

ELDRIDGE, JOHN (John Eldredge)
Born: Aug. 30, 1904, San Francisco, Calif. Died: Sept. 23, 1961, Laguna Beach, Calif. (heart attack). Screen, stage and television actor.

Appeared in: **1934** Flirtation Walk; The Man with Two Faces. **1935** Dangerous; Dr. Socrates; The Goose and the Gander; The Girl from Tenth Avenue; Snowed Under; Man of Iron; Oil for the Lamps of China; The Woman in Red; The White Cockatoo. **1936** The Murder of Dr. Harrigan; Follow Your Heart; His Brother's Wife; Murder by an Aristocrat. **1937** Fair Warning; Charlie Chan at the Olympics; The Go-Getter; The Holy Terror; Mr. Dodd Takes the Air; Mysterious Crossing; One Mile from Heaven; Sh! the Octopus. **1938** Blind Alibi; Women Are Like That; They're Always Caught (short); Persons in Hiding. **1939** King of Underworld; Private Detective; Television Spy; Undercover Doctor. **1940** Always a Bride; The Devil's Pipeline; Dr. Kildare's Strangest Case; The Marines Fly High; Son of Roaring Dan. **1941** It Started with Eve; Life Begins for Andy Hardy; Flight from Destiny; The Black Cat; Blossoms in the Dust; High Sierra; Horror Island; Mr. District Attorney in the Carter Case. **1942** Madame Spy; The Mad Doctor of Market Street. **1944** Beautiful but Broke; Bermuda Mystery; Song of Nevada. **1945** Bad Men of the Border; Dangerous Passage; Eve Knew Her Apples; Dangerous Partners. **1946** Up Goes Maisie; Lost City of the Jungle (serial); Swing Parade of 1946; Dark Alibi; Passkey to Danger; Little Miss Big; Temptation; Circumstantial Evidence; The French Key; I Ring Doorbells; Live Wires; There Goes Maisie. **1947** Backlash; Seven Were Saved; Second Chance; The Fabulous Joe. **1948** Angels' Alley; California's Gold; Jinx Money; Whispering Smith. **1949** The Sickle or the Cross; Sky Dragon; Square Dance Jubilee; Stampede; Top of the Morning. **1950** Champagne for Caesar; Lonely Hearts Bandits; Rustlers on Horseback; Unmasked.

1951 Night into Morning; An American in Paris; All That I Have; Insurance Investigator; Rhythm Inn; Street Bandits. **1953** Loophole. **1955** Toughest Man Alive. **1956** Meet Me in Las Vegas; The First Traveling Saleslady. **1957** Raintree County. **1958** I Married a Monster from Outer Space. **1960** Freckles. **1961** Five Guns to Tombstone.

ELINE, MARIE
Died: Jan. 3, 1981, Longview, Wa. Screen, stage and vaudeville actress. Sister of actress Grace Elines with whom she appeared in vaudeville.

ELINOR, CARLI D.
Born: Sept. 21, 1890, Bucharest, Rumania. Died: Oct. 20, 1958, Hollywood, Calif. (heart attack). Screen actor and musician. Entered films during the silents.

Appeared in: **1945** Weekend at the Waldorf; Thrill of a Romance. **1946** Gilda. **1953** Ma and Pa Kettle on Vacation.

ELISCU, FERNANDA
Died: 1968. Stage and screen actress.

Appeared in: **1936** Winterset. **1943** The Song of Bernadette. **1944** Uncertain Glory. **1945** Her Highness and the Bellboy. **1946** Gilda. **1947** Desire Me. **1948** Berlin Express. **1950** The Harbor of Missing Men. **1952** Viva Zapata! **1953** Remains to be Seen. **1954** Charge of the Lancers.

ELIZONDO, JOAQUIN
Born: 1896. Died: June 15, 1952, Hollywood, Calif. Screen actor and dancer. Formerly Mae Murray's dancing partner.

Appeared in: **1947** Twilight on the Rio Grande.

ELLERY, ARTHUR
Born: 1870. Died: Aug. 27, 1945, Elizabeth, N.J. Screen and stage actor. Appeared in early Lubin films.

Appeared in: **1912** Locked Out.

ELLINGFORD, WILLIAM
Born: 1863. Died: May 20, 1936, Los Angeles, Calif. Screen and stage actor.

Appeared in: **1927** Hands Off.

ELLINGTON, "DUKE" (Edward Kennedy Ellington)
Born: Apr. 29, 1899, Washington, D.C. Died: May 24, 1974, New York, N.Y. (lung cancer—pneumonia). Black screen, radio actor, bandleader and composer. Married to dancer Evie Ellis Ellington (dec. 1976) and father of bandleader Mercer Ellington.

Appeared in: **1929** Black and Tan (short). **1930** Check and Double Check. **1934** Murder at the Vanities (short). **1937** The Hit Parade; New Faces of 1937. **1943** Reveille with Beverly; Cabin in the Sky. **1959** Anatomy of a Murder. **1961** Paris Blues; Twist all Night. **1966** Assault on a Queen. **1969** Adalen 31; Change of Mind.

ELLINGWOOD, HELMERT
Born: 1907. Died: Oct. 13, 1971. Screen actor.

Appeared in: **1945** Objective Burma. **1947** Pursued.

ELLIOTT, BERT (Berton Rex Elliot)
Born: Mar. 15, 1929, Michigan. Died: July 3, 1972, Valinda, Calif. (suicide—hanging). Screen actor.

ELLIOTT, CASSANDRA (Ellen Naomi Cohen aka "MAMA" CASS ELLIOTT)
Born: 1941, Arlington, Va. Died: July 29, 1974, London, England (heart attack/obesity). Singer, screen and television actress. Divorced from singer James Hendricks and Baron Donald von Wiedenman.

Appeared in: **1969** Monterey Pop. **1970** Monte Walsh; Pufnstuf.

ELLIOTT, DEL B.
Born: 1879. Died: Jan. 22, 1945, San Francisco, Calif. Screen and stage actor.

Appeared in: **1929** The Desert Song.

ELLIOTT, DICK (Richard Damon Elliott)
Born: Apr. 30, 1886, Mass. Died: Dec. 22, 1961, Burbank, Calif. Screen, stage and televison actor.

Appeared in: **1933** Picture Snatcher. **1934** Gift of Gab; We're Rich Again; Shivers (short). **1935** Sprucin' Up (short); Annie Oakley; It Happened in New York; Dr. Socrates; Break of Hearts. **1936** The

Princess Comes Across; Go West, Young Man; The Prisoner of Shark Island; Brilliant Marriage; Her Master's Voice; Neighborhood House (short). **1937** China Passage; Quick Money; The Outcasts of Poker Flat. **1938** Campus Confessions; Penitentiary; Under Western Stars; Every Day's a Holiday. **1939** Another Thin Man; Frontiers of '49; Nancy Drew and the Hidden Staircase; Let Us Live; The Story of Alexander Graham Bell; Boy Trouble; Mr. Smith Goes to Washington; Sudden Money; Truth Aches (short); Home Boner (short). **1940** Behind the News; Flight Angels; Melody Ranch; Florian; Li'l Abner; One Man's Law; The Mortal Storm. **1941** One Foot in Heaven; The Wagons Roll at Night; The Pittsburgh Kid; Top Sgt. Mulligan; Up in the Air; Sunset in Wyoming. **1942** Keeper of the Flame; The Man from Headquarters; Scattergood Survives a Murder; Sweetheart of the Fleet; We Were Dancing; The Magnificent Ambersons; I Married an Angel. **1943** The Outlaw; Henry Aldrich Gets Glamour; Wintertime; After Midnight With Boston Blackie; Laugh Your Eyes Away. **1944** Adventures of Mark Twain; Silent Partners; Girl in the Case; Henry Aldrich Plays Cupid; Hi, Beautiful; Whispering Footsteps; Goin' to Town; When Strangers Marry; Show Business. **1945** Diamond Horseshoe; Adventures of Kitty O'Day; The Clock; Gangs of the Waterfront; Christmas in Connecticut; Saratoga Trunk; plus the following shorts: You Drive Me Crazy, Mother-in-Law's Day, Purity Squad. **1946** Partners in Time; Rainbow Over Texas; That Texas Jamboree; Hot Cargo; High School Hero; Dangerous Money; Ginger; The Kid from Brooklyn; Trouble or Nothing (short); Follow That Blonde (short); Her Sister's Secret; My Reputation; The Blue Dahlia; The Dark Horse. **1947** Magic Town; Copacabana; Television Turmoil (short); For the Love of Rusty; Heading for Heaven. **1948** Main Street Kid; The Dude Goes West; Homicide for Three; Slippy McGee; The Paleface; The Sainted Sisters. **1949** Flamingo Road; Feudin' Rhythm; Night Unto Night; Rose of the Yukon; Trail of the Yukon. **1950** Across the Badlands; A Modern Marriage; Rock Island Trail; Western Pacific Agent. **1951** Fort Defiance; Honeychile. **1952** High Noon; Montana Belle. **1954** Witness to Murder. **1956** Don't Knock the Rock. **1957** The Joker is Wild; New Day at Sundown; Up in Smoke. **1958** In the Money.

ELLIOTT, GERTRUDE (Gertrude Dermott)
Born: 1874, Rockland, Maine. Died: Dec. 24, 1950, Kent, England. Stage and screen actress. Married to actor Sir Johnston Forbes-Robertson (dec. 1937). Mother of actress Jean Forbes-Robertson (dec. 1962). Sister of actress Maxine Elliott (dec. 1940).

Appeared in: **1913** Hamlet (US 1915). **1917** Masks and Faces.

ELLIOT, GORDON *See* ELLIOTT, WILLIAM "WILD BILL"

ELLIOTT, JOHN H.
Born: July 5, 1876, Keosauqua, Iowa. Died: Dec. 12, 1956, Los Angeles, Calif. (heart attack). Stage and screen actor.

Appeared in: **1920** Homer Comes Home; A Master Stroke; Held in Trust; Are All Men Alike? **1921** Her Winning Way. **1923** The Eagle's Feather; The Spoilers. **1926** Christine of the Big Tops; Racing Blood; What Happened to Jones. **1927** Horse Shoes; Million Dollar Mystery. **1929** Only the Brave; The Phantom in the House. **1930** For the Defense; The Rampant Age; The Widow from Chicago. **1931** Conquering Horde. **1932** Galloping Thru; Two-Faced Justice; Single-Handed Sanders; Riders of the Desert; Week-ends Only; Texas Pioneers; From Broadway to Cheyenne; Call Her Savage. **1933** Lucky Larrigan; Gallant Fool. **1934** Murder in the Museum; Green Eyes; Cowboy Holiday; Ticket to a Crime; Carolina; Sons of the Desert. **1935** Danger Ahead; Sunset Range; Red Hot Tires; Make a Million; Unconquered Bandit; Fighting Pioneers; What Price Crime?; Captured in Chinatown; Saddle Aces; Rider of the Law; Trails of the Wild; Midnight Phantom; Lawless Border; Skull and Crown. **1936** Frontier Justice; Millionaire Kid; Roamin' Wild; Avenging Waters; Rogues Tavern; Kelly of the Secret Service; Roaring Guns; The Clutching Hand (serial); Prison Shadows; The Fugitive Sheriff; Ambush Valley. **1937** Death in the Air; Headin' East. **1938** Cassidy of Bar 20; Heart of Arizona; Hold that Co-Ed. **1939** Charlie Chan at Treasure Island; Jesse James. **1940** The Tulsa Kid; Gun Code; Lone Star Raiders. **1941** Citizen Kane; Tumble Down Ranch in Arizona; Texas Marshal; Gentleman from Dixie; The Kid's Last Ride; The Apache Kid; Land of the Open Range; Come on Danger. **1942** The Magnificent Ambersons; I Married an Angel; The Mad Monster; Rock River Renegades; Pirates of the Prairie; Perils of the Royal Mounted (serial). **1943** Raiders of San Joaquin; You're a Lucky Fellow Mr. Smith; Tenting Tonight on the Old Camp Grounds; Two-Fisted Justice. **1944** Bowery to Broadway; Law of the Saddle; Oklahoma Raiders; Fuzzy Settles Down; Wild Horse Phantoms. **1945** Allotment Wives; Escape in the Fog; Hollywood and Vine; Jungle Raiders (serial). **1946** Badman's Territory; Nora Prentiss; Frontier Gunlaw; The Devil's Mask. **1947** Cry Wolf; Law of the Lash; News Hounds; The Fighting Vigilantes. **1948** The Countess of Monte Cristo; I Wouldn't Be in Your Shoes; Angels' Alley. **1950** The Arizona Cowboy. **1956** Perils of the Wilderness (serial).

ELLIOTT, LESTER
Born: 1888. Died: Nov. 9, 1954, Van Nuys, Calif. (heart attack). Screen and stage actor.

ELLIOTT, LILLIAN
Born: 1875. Died: Jan. 15, 1959, Hollywood, Calif. (stroke). Screen and stage actress. Mother of actor Lloyd Corrigan (dec. 1969).

Appeared in: **1921** Lavender and Old Lace; Too Much Married. **1924** The Chorus Lady; One Glorious Night. **1925** Old Clothes; Proud Flesh; Sally, Irene and Mary. **1926** The City; The Family Upstairs; Partners Again. **1927** Ankles Preferred; King of Kings. **1930** Her Wedding Night; Liliom; The Swellhead. **1931** The Single Sin; Thundering Tenors (short); The Hasty Marriage (short). **1932** The Man I Killed; Free Eats (short); Now We'll Tell One (short); Polly of the Circus. **1934** Trumpet Blows; Palsie Walsie (short). **1935** Alias Mary Dow; I'm a Father (short). **1938** The Jury's Secret; Wanted by the Police. **1939** When Tomorrow Comes; Tough Kid. **1940** On the Spot. **1942** Road to Happiness. **1965** Laurel and Hardy's Laughing 20's (documentary).

ELLIOTT, MADGE
Born: May 12, 1898, Kensington, England. Died: Aug. 8, 1955, New York, N.Y. Screen, stage, television actress and dancer. Married to actor Cyril Ritchard (dec. 1977).

Appeared in: **1927** On With the Dance (series).

ELLIOTT, MAXINE (Jessica Dermott)
Born: Feb. 5, 1873, Rockland, Maine. Died: Mar. 5, 1940, Juan Les Pins, France (heart ailment). Stage and screen actress. Sister of actress Gertrude Elliott (dec. 1950). Divorced from stage actor Nat Goodwin.

Appeared in: **1917** Fighting Odds. **1919** The Eternal Magdalene. **1937** Live, Love and Learn.

ELLIOTT, MILTON "SKEETS"
Born: 1896, Gadsden, Ala. Died: Aug. 2, 1920, Los Angeles, Calif. (airplane accident during filming of The Skywayman). Screen actor and stunt flier.

Appeared in: **1920** The Skywayman.

ELLIOTT, ROBERT
Born: Oct. 9, 1879, Ohio. Died: Nov. 15, 1951. Screen actor. Married to stage actress Ruth Elliott (dec. 1971).

Appeared in: **1917** The Mirror; Mary Moreland; The Dazzling Miss Davison; Motherhood; The Debt. **1919** Checkers. **1921** Lonely Heart; Money Maniac; A Virgin Paradise. **1922** The Broken Silence; Fair Lady; A Pasteboard Crown; Without Fear. **1923** Man Wife. **1928** Happiness Ahead; Light of New York; Obey Your Husband; Romance of the Underworld. **1929** The Lone Wolf's Daughter; Protection; Thunderbolt. **1930** How I Play Golf—Chip Shots (short); Captain Thunder; The Divorcee; The Doorway to Hell; Hide-Out; Kathleen Mavoureen; Men of the North; Sweet Mama. **1931** The Finger Points; The Maltese Falcon; The Star Witness; Five Star Final; Murder at Midnight; The Midnight Patrol; White Eagle; Madison Square Garden; The Phantom of Crestwood; Rose of the Rio Grande; Conquering Horde; The Montana Kid; Secret Menace; Mother and Son; Oklahoma Jim. **1932** Galloping Thru; Riders of the Desert; Call Her Savage; Broadway to Cheyenne; Two-Fisted Justice; Single-Handed Sanders; Week-ends Only; Texas Pioneers. **1933** Self Defense; Crime of the Century; Return of Casey Jones; Heroes for Sale; Lady Killer. **1934** Girl of the Limberlost; Transatlantic Merry-Go-Round; Gambling Lady; Woman Who Dared; Twin Husbands. **1935** The World Accuses; Black Sheep; Times Square Lady; Port of Lost Dreams; Circumstantial Evidence. **1938** I'd Give My Life. **1939** Trade Winds. **1939** The Roaring Twenties; I Stole a Million; Mickey the Kid; Gone With the Wind; The Saint Strikes Back. **1940** Half a Sinner. **1945** Captain Tugboat Annie. **1946** The Devil's Playground; Nick Carter, Detective (serial).

ELLIOTT, WILLIAM
Born: 1880. Died: Feb. 5, 1932, New York, N.Y. Screen, stage actor and stage manager.

Appeared in: **1918** Hearts of the World.

ELLIOTT, WILLIAM "WILD BILL" (Gordon Elliott)
Born: 1904, Pattonsburg, Mo. Died: Nov. 26, 1965, Las Vegas, Nev. (cancer). Screen, stage and television actor.

Appeared in: **1927** The Private Life of Helen of Troy. **1928** Valley of Hunted Men; The Arizona Wildcat; Beyond London's Lights. **1929** Passion Song; Restless Youth; Broadway Scandals; Napoleon, Jr. **1930** The Great Divide; She Couldn't Say No; Sunny; The Midnight Mystery. **1931** City Streets; Delicious; The Magnificent Lie; Palmy Days; Convicted. **1932** Merrily We go to Hell; Lady With a Past; Night After Night; One Hour With You; Vanity Fair; The Rich are Always

With Us; Jewel Robbery; Crooner. **1933** Private Detective 62; The Keyhole; The Little Giant; Gold Diggers of 1933. **1934** Registered Nurse; Wonder Bar; Twenty Million Sweethearts; Case of the Howling Dog; Here Comes the Navy; A Modern Hero. **1935** Dr. Socrates; Dangerous; Broadway Hostess; Secret Bride; Go Into Your Dance; A Night at the Ritz; Alibi Ike; Broadway Gondolier; Bright Lights; I Live for Love; Stars Over Broadway; The Story of Louis Pasteur; Ceiling Zero; While the Patient Slept; The Traveling Saleslady; Devil Dogs of the Air; The Woman in Red; G-Men; The Girl from Tenth Avenue; The Goose and the Gander; Moonlight on the Prairie; Man of Iron; Gold Diggers of 1935. **1936** The Murder of Dr. Harrigan; Murder bu an Aristocrat; Down the Stretch; The Case of the Velvet Claws; Trailin' West; Polo Joe; The Case of the Black Cat; The Walking Dead; The Singing Kid; The Big Noise; Two Against the World; Bullets or Ballots; Romance in the Air. **1937** Roll Along, Cowboy; You Can't Have Everything; Melody for Two; Midnight Court; Fugitive in the Sky; Guns of the Pecos; Speed to Spare; Love Takes Flight; Wife, Doctor and Nurse; Swing It, Professor; Boots and Saddles; Boy of the Streets. **1938** The Great Adventures of Wild Bill Hickok (serial); In Early Arizona; The Devil's Party; Tarzan's Revenge; Lady in the Morgue; Valley of Hunted Men. **1939** The Taming of the West; Lone Star Pioneers; The Law Comes to Texas; Overland with Kit Carson (serial); Frontiers of '49. **1940** Man from Tumbleweed; Prairie Schooners; The Return of Wild Bill; Pioneers of the Frontier. **1941** Return of Daniel Boone; Where Did You Get That Girl?; Roaring Frontiers; Beyond the Sacramento; The Wildcat of Tucson; North from the Lone Star; Hands Across the Rockies; Across the Sierras; The Lone Star Vigilantes; The Son of Davy Crockett; King of Dodge City. **1942** Valley of Vanishing Men (serial); Bullets for Bandits; Vengeance of the West; The Devil's Trail; North of the Rockies; Prairie Gunsmoke. **1943** Calling Wild Bill Elliott; Bordertown Gun Fighters; The Man from Thunder River; Wagon Tracks West; Death Valley Manhunt. **1944** Marshall of Reno; Hidden Valley Outlaws; Cheyenne Wildcat; Vigilantes of Dodge City; Mojave Firebrand; Sheriff of Las Vegas; Tucson Raiders; Overland Mail Robbery; The San Antonio Kid. **1945** The Great Stagecoach Robbery; Lone Texas Ranger; Phantom of the Plains; Bells of Rosarita; Colorado Pioneers; Marshall of Laredo; Wagon Wheels Westward. **1946** Sun Valley Cyclone; Sheriff of Redwood Valley; Conquest of Cheyenne; California Gold Rush; In Old Sacramento; The Plainsman and the Lady. **1947** Wyoming; The Fabulous Texan. **1948** The Gallant Legion; In Old Los Angeles. **1949** The Last Bandit; Hellfire. **1950** The Savage Horde; The Showdown. **1952** The Maverick; The Longhorn; Waco; Vengeance Trail; Kansas Territory; Fargo. **1953** The Homesteaders; Revel City; Vigilante Terror; Topeka. **1954** Bitter Creek; The Forty-Niners. **1955** Dial Red O; Sudden Danger. **1956** Calling Homicide. **1957** Footsteps in the Night; Chain of Evidence.

ELLIS, DIANE
Born: Dec. 20, 1909, Los Angeles, Calif. Died: Dec. 16, 1930, Madras, India. Screen actress.

Appeared in: **1927** Paid to Love; The Cradle Snatchers; Chain Lightning; Is Zat So?; Hook and Ladder No. 9. **1928** Happiness Ahead. **1929** The Leatherneck; High Voltage. **1930** Laughter.

ELLIS, EDWARD
Born: 1871, Coldwater, Mich. Died: July 26, 1952, Hollywood, Calif. Screen and stage actor.

Appeared in: **1921** The Frontier of the Stars. **1932** I Am a Fugitive from a Chain Gang. **1933** Girl Missing; From Headquarters; Without Glory; After Tonight; Strictly Personal. **1934** Madame Spy; Hi, Nellie; The Ninth Guest; The Last Gentleman; Trumpet Blows; The President Vanishes; The Thin Man. **1935** The Return of Peter Grimm; Wanderer of the Wasteland; Village Tale; Transient Lady; The Black Sheep. **1936** Chatterbox; The Lady Consents; Winterset; Fury; The Texas Rangers. **1937** Maid of Salem; Midnight Madonna; Let Them Live; The Man in Blue. **1938** Little Miss Broadway; A Man to Remember. **1939** Man of Conquest; Main Street Lawyer; Career; Three Sons; Remember. **1942** A Man Betrayed; Steel Against the Sky. **1942** The Omaha Trail.

ELLIS, EVELYN
Born: 1894. Died: June 5, 1958, Saranac Lake, N.Y. (heart ailment). Screen, stage and television actress.

Appeared in: **1948** The Lady from Shanghai. **1953** The Joe Louis Story. **1955** Interrupted Melody.

ELLIS, FRANK B.
Died: Feb. 24, 1969. Screen actor.

Appeared in: **1920** Elmo, the Fearless (serial). **1923** King's Creek Law. **1924** Bringin' Home the Bacon. **1925** The Desert Demon; The Fighting Sheriff; Tearin' Loose. **1926** Ace of Action; The Outlaw

Express; Speedy Spurs; Vanishing Hoofs; Without Orders. **1927** Code of the Cow Country. **1928** Yellow Contraband; The Valley of Hunted Men. **1929** Law of the Mounted; Texas Tommy. **1930** Trails of Danger. **1933** Treason. **1934** In Old Santa Fe; Mystery Mountain. **1935** The Phantom Empire. **1936** Lawless Riders; Comin' Round the Mountain. **1937** Public Cowboy Number One; Git Along, Little Dogies; Springtime in the Rockies; Hopalong Rides Again; Riders of the Whistling Skull; Range Defenders; Gun Lords of Stirrup Basin; Boothill Brigade; Two Fisted Sheriff; **1938** Western Jamboree; Border Wolves. **1939** In Old Monterey; Roll, Wagons, Roll; Rovin' Tumbleweeds; Ride 'Em Cowgirl. **1940** Westbound Stage; Marshal of Mesa City. **1941** Outlaws of the Rio Grande; Wranglers' Roost; The Bandit Trail; The Kid's Last Ride; Man from Montana; Thundering Hoofs; Land of the Open Range; Billy the Kid Wanted; The Loan Rider Fights Back. **1942** Stardust on the Sage; Billy the Kid's Smoking Guns; Phantom Killer; Texas to Bataan. **1943** Two Fisted Justice; Fugitive of the Plains; Black Market Rustlers. **1944** Trail of Terror; Law of the Saddle; Arizona Whirlwind; Westward Bound; Outlaw Roundup; Oath of Vengeance; Wild' Horse Phantom. **1946** Son of the Guardsman (serial); Ambush Trail; Gentlemen With Guns; Overland Riders; Prairie Badmen; The Fighting Frontiersman; Stage to Mesa City. **1947** Out West (short). **1948** The Westward Trail; Deadline. **1950** Beyond the Purple Hills; Indian Territory; Cowboy and the Prizefighter; Cody of the Pony Express (serial). **1951** Roar of the Iron Horse (serial). **1952** The Old West; Blackhawk (serial); King of the Congo (serial). **1953** The Stranger Wore a Gun. **1954** Silver Lode.

ELLIS, JEANNIE MAE
Born: 1888. Died: Aug. 20, 1972, Santa Monica, Calif. Screen actress. Entered films in 1942 as an extra.

ELLIS, LILLIAN
Born: 1911, Denmark. Died: Feb. 21, 1951, Copenhagen, Denmark. Screen, radio and television actress.

Appeared in: **1929** Strauss, the Waltz King. **1932** Kyritz-Pyritz; Schoen Ist die Manoeverzeit. **1933** Die Frau von der Man Spricht.

ELLIS, PATRICIA (Patricia Leftwich)
Born: May 20, 1916, Birmingham, Mich. Died: Mar. 26, 1970, Kansas City, Mo. Stage and screen actress. She was a Wampas Baby Star of 1932. Daughter of actor/film producer Alexander Leftwich (dec. 1947).

Appeared in: **1932** Three on a Match; Central Park. **1933** Forty-Second Street; Hollywood on Parade (short); Picture Snatcher; Elmer the Great; The King's Vacation; The Narrow Corner; Convention City; The World Changes. **1934** Harold Teen; Melody for Two; St. Louis Kid; Easy to Love; Big Hearted Herbert; The Circus Clown; Here Comes the Groom; Let's Be Ritzy; Affairs of a Gentleman. **1935** While the Patient Slept; Bright Lights; The Case of the Lucky Legs; The Pay Off; A Night at the Ritz; Stranded; Hold 'Em Yale. **1936** Sing Me a Love Song; Freshman Love; Snowed Under; Boulder Dam; Love Begins at Twenty; Down the Stretch; Postal Inspector. **1937** Venus Makes Trouble; Step Lively, Jeeves!; Rhythm in the Clouds; Paradise for Two (aka The Gaity Girls—US 1938); Melody for Two. **1938** The Lady in the Morgue; Blockheads; Romance on the Run. **1939** Back Door to Heaven; Fugitives at Large.

ELLIS, ROBERT "BOBBY"
Born: 1933. Died: Nov. 23, 1973, Los Angeles, Calif. (kidney failure). Screen, radio and television actor. Played "Henry Aldrich" on the radio and television series. Entered films in 1938.

Appeared in: **1948** The Babe Ruth Story; April Showers. **1949** A Kiss for Corliss; The Green Promise; Easy Living; El Paso. **1950** Walk Softly, Stranger. **1951** Call Me Mister. **1952** Retreat, Hell! **1953** Niagara. **1955** The McConnell Story. **1956** Pillars of the Sky. **1958** Space Master X-7. **1959** Gidget.

ELLIS, ROBERT J.
Born: Sept. 5, 1888, Pasadena, Calif. Died: May 20, 1935, Hollywood, Calif. Screen actor and art director. Do not confuse with actor Robert Ellis (dec. 1974).

ELLIS, ROBERT REEL
Born: June 27, 1892, Brooklyn, N.Y. Died: Dec. 29, 1974, Santa Monica, Calif. (cardiac arrest). Screen, stage actor and screenwriter. Divorced from actresses May Allison and Vera Reynolds (dec. 1962). Later married to screenwriter Helen Logen.

Appeared in: **1919** Louisiana; Upstairs and Down. **1921** Handcuffs or Kisses; Ladies Must Live. **1922** The Woman Who Fooled Herself; Anna Ascends; Hurricane's Gal; The Dangerous Little Demon; Wild Honey; The Infidel; Love's Masquerade. **1923** The Wild Party; The

Wanters; Dark Secrets; The Flame of Life; Mark of the Beast. **1924** A Cafe in Cairo; For Sale; The Law Forbids; On Probation; Lover's Lane; Silk Stocking Gal. **1925** Forbidden Cargo; Lady Robinhood; Northern Code; Capital Punishment; Defend Yourself; The Part Time Wife; Speed. **1926** S.O.S. Perils of the Sea; Brooding Eyes; The Girl From Montmartre; Devil's Dice; Ladies of Leisure; Whispering Canyon. **1927** The Lure of the Night Club; Ragtime. **1928** Varsity; Freedom of the Press; Law and the Man; The Law's Lash; Marry the Girl. **1929** Restless Youth; Tonight at Twelve; The Love Trap; Broadway; Night Parade. **1930** The Squealer; Undertow; What Men Want. **1931** The Last Parade; The Good Bad Girl; Murder at Midnight; Aloha; Caught Cheating; The Fighting Sheriff; Dancing Dynamite; Is There Justice?; The Devil Plays; Mounted Fury. **1932** American Madness; The Last Man; White Eagle; The Deadline; One Man Law; Behind Stone Walls; Fighting Fools; Phantom Express; Daring Danger; From Broadway to Cheyenne; All American; The Penal Code; Women Won't Tell; Come on Danger?; A Man's Land; Slightly Married. **1933** Officer 13; Speed Demon; Reform Girl; Constant Woman; Treason; Soldiers of the Storm; Thrill Hunter; The Sphinx; Police Call; The Important Witness; Only Yesterday; Notorious But Nice; **1934** Dancing Man; Madame Spy; Girl of the Limberlost. I've Got Your Number;

ELLISON, EDITH
Born: Oct. 31, 1864, Boston, Mass. Died: July 29, 1944. Screen actress.

ELLISSEN, ISABEL *See* RALEIGH, SABA

ELLISTON, GRACE
Born: 1878, Memphis, Tenn. Died: Dec. 14, 1950, Lenox, Mass. Screen and stage actress.

Appeared in: **1916** The Black Fear.

ELLSLER, EFFIE
Born: 1855, Philadelphia, Pa. Died: Oct. 9, 1942, Hollywood, Calif. (heart attack). Stage and screen actress.

Appeared in: **1926** Old Ironsides. **1927** Honeymoon Hate. **1928** The Actress. **1929** Woman Trap. **1930** Song O' My Heart; The Lady of Scandal. **1931** The Front Page; Up Pops the Devil; Daddy Long Legs. **1933** Doctor Bull; Second Hand Wife; The Girl in 419; The Chief. **1934** Hold That Girl. **1935** The Whole Town's Talking; Black Fury; We're Only Human. **1936** Drift Fence; Camille.

ELLSWORTH, JACK HERSCHEL
Born: 1911. Died: Aug. 19, 1949, Hollywood, Calif. Screen actor.

ELMAN, HARRY "ZIGGY"
Born: May 26, 1914, Philadelphia, Pa. Died: June 25, 1968, Van Nuys, Calif. Bandleader, musician, screen actor and composer.

Appeared in: **1955** The Benny Goodman Story.

ELMAN, MISCHA
Born: Jan. 20, 1891, Tainoye, Russia. Died: Apr. 5, 1967, New York, N.Y. (heart attack). Concert violinist and screen actor.

ELMER, BILLY (William E. Johns)
Born: 1870. Died: Feb. 24, 1945, Hollywood, Calif. Screen, stage and vaudeville actor.

Appeared in: **1913** The Squaw Man. **1914** The Virginian; Rose of the Rancho. **1915** The Arab; Kindling; Carmen; The Unafraid; The Girl of the Golden West; The Captive. **1917** Joan the Woman. **1921** The Foolish Age; The Road Demon. **1922** The Bootlegger's Daughter; Pawned. **1923** In Search of a Thrill. **1924** Battling Mason; The Whipping Boss. **1942** Reap the Wild Wind; The Magnificent Ambersons.

ELMORE, BRUCE (Alfred G. Kennedy)
Born: 1885. Died: May 15, 1940, New York, N.Y. Screen and stage actor.

ELSIE, LILY
Born: Apr. 18, 1886, Wortley, England. Died: Dec. 16, 1962, Palehouse Common, Sussex, England. Screen, stage and vaudeville actress.

Appeared in: **1919** Comradeship.

ELSOM, ISOBEL (aka ISOBEL REED and ISOBEL HARBORD)
Born: Mar. 16, 1893, Cambridge, England. Died: Jan. 12, 1981, Woodland Hills, Calif. Screen, stage and television actress. Divorced from director/actor Maurice Elvey (dec. 1967).

Appeared in: **1915** A Prehistoric Love Story. **1916** Milestones. **1918** The Way of the Eagle; The Elder Miss Blossom; Tinker, Tailor, Soldier, Sailor; Onward Christian Soldiers; The Man Who Won; God Bless Our Red, White and Blue. **1919** Mrs. Thompson; Edge O'Beyond; A Member of Tattersalls; Linked By Fate; In Bondage (aka Faith); Quinneys. **1920** Aunt Rachel; Nance. **1921** For Her Father's Sake. **1922** A Debt of Honour; Dick Turbin's Ride to New York; The Game of Life. **1923** Just a Mother; The Sign of Four; The Wandering Jew; The Love Story of Ailette Brunton; Harbour Lights. **1924** Who Is the Man? **1925** The Last Winess. **1926** Human Law; The Tower of London (short); Glamis Castle (short). **1927** Dance Magic. **1931** The Other Woman; Stranglehold. **1932** Illegal. **1933** The Thirteenth Candle. **1934** The Primrose Path. **1941** Ladies in Retirement. **1942** Eagle Squadron; The War Against Mrs. Hadley; Seven Sweethearts; You Were Never Lovlier. **1943** Forever and a Day; First Comes Courage; My Kingdom for a Cook. **1944** Casanova Brown; Between Two Worlds. **1945** The Unseen. **1946** Of Human Bondage; Two Sisters from Boston. **1947** Ivy; Love from a Stranger; Monsieur Verdoux; The Two Mrs. Carrolls; The Ghost and Mrs. Muir; Escape Me Never. **1948** Smart Woman. **1949** The Secret Garden. **1950** Her Wonderful Lie. **1954** Deep in My Heart; Desiree. **1955** The King's Thief; Love is a Many Splendored Thing. **1956** Over-Exposed; 23 Paces to Baker Street; Lust for Life. **1957** The Guns of Fort Petticoat. **1958** Rock-a-Bye Baby. **1959** The Miracle; The Young Philadelphians. **1961** The Second Time Around. **1962** The Errand Boy. **1963** Who's Minding the Store? **1964** My Fair Lady; The Pleasure Seekers.

ELTINGE, JULIAN (Bill Dalton)
Born: 1883, Butte, Mont. Died: Mar. 7, 1941, New York, N.Y. (cerebral hemorrhage). Screen, stage and vaudeville actor.

Appeared in: **1915** How Molly Made Good. **1917** The Countess Charming; The Clever Mrs. Carfax. **1918** Over the Rhine; Widows Might; War Relief. **1922** The Isle of Love. **1925** Madame Behave. **1940** If I Had My Way.

ELTON, EDMUND
Born: Feb. 5, 1871, England. Died: Jan. 4, 1962, United States? Screen actor.

Appeared in: **1937** Stella Dallas. **1939** Should a Girl Marry. **1940** Thou Shalt Not Kill; Abe Lincoln in Illinois. **1941** Back in the Saddle.

ELVEY, MAURICE (William Seward Folkard)
Born: Nov. 11, 1887, Yorkshire, England. Died: Aug. 28, 1967, Brighton, England. Screen, stage actor, film director, film producer and stage director. Divorced from actresses Isobel Elsom (dec. 1981) and Philippa Preston.

Appeared in: **1913** The Fallen Idol; Maria Marten; Or, The Murder in the Red Barn. **1914** The Cup Final Mystery.

ELVIDGE, JUNE C.
Born: 1893, St. Paul, Minn. Died: May 1, 1965, Eatontown, N.J. Screen, stage and vaudeville actress.

Appeared in: **1915** The Lure of a Woman. **1916** La Boheme; The Almighty Dollar; The World Against Him. **1917** The Tenth Case; The Family Hour; Shall We Forgive Her?; The Page Mystery; The Price of Pride; The Crimson Dove; The Guardian; The Marriage Market; Rasputin, the Black Monk; A Girl's Folly; Youth; A Square Deal. **1918** The Strong Way; The Power and the Glory; Broken Ties; The Oldest Law; The Way Out; The Cabaret; A Woman of Redemption; The Beautiful Mrs. Reynolds; Joan of the Woods; Stolen Order. **1919** Love and the Woman; The Poison Pen. **1921** Fine Feathers. **1922** Beauty's Worth; Beyond the Rocks; Forsaking All Others; The Impossible Mrs. Bellew; The Man Who Saw Tomorrow; The Power of a Lie; Quincy Adams Sawyer; Thelma; The Woman Conquers. **1923** The Prisoner; Temptation. **1924** Chalk Marks; Pagan Passions; Painted People; The Right of the Strongest; The Torrent.

ELWELL, GEORGE (Edmund George Elwell)
Born: 1896. Died: Nov. 3, 1916, Los Angeles, Calif. (heart attack). Screen actor.

Appeared in: **1916** The Raiders.

ELY, HARRY R.
Born: 1883, July 15, 1951. Died: July 15, 1951, Hollywood, Calif. Silent screen actor.

ELY, S. GILBERT
Born: 1858. Died: May, 1920, Osgood, Ind. Screen actor and film director.

Appeared in: **1914** A Recent Confederate Victory. **1915** Belle of Barnegat; The Inevitable Penalty.

EMDEN, MARGARET
Born: England. Died: Feb. 13, 1946, England. Screen and stage actress. Entered films in 1916 with London Film Company.

Appeared in: **1931** Bracelets.

EMERICK, BESSE
Born: 1875, Rochester, Ind. Died: Dec. 13, 1939, Boston, Mass. Screen actress.

Appeared in: **1917** The Black Stork. **1922** Welcome to Our City.

EMERICK, ROBERT
Born: 1916, Tacoma, Wash. Died: June 1, 1973, San Diego, Calif. (heart attack). Screen, radio, television actor and drama coach.

Appeared in: **1970** Guess What We Learned in School Today? (aka Guess What? and I Ain't No Buffalo); Joe.

EMERSON, EDWARD
Born: 1910. Died: Apr. 11, 1975, Bronx, N.Y. (cancer). Screen, stage and television actor.

Appeared in: **1936** I Cover Chinatown. **1937** Behind the Criminal (short). **1942** Road to Morocco. **1943** What a Woman!; So Proudly We Hail; Dixie. **1944** Dragon Seed. **1945** There Goes Kelly; Road to Utopia.

EMERSON, ERIC
Born: 1945. Died: May 28, 1975. Screen and stage actor.

Appeared in: **1966** The Chelsea Girls. **1968** Lonesome Cowboys; The Mine Blowers. **1972** Heat.

EMERSON, HOPE
Born: Oct. 29, 1897, Hawarden, Iowa. Died: Apr. 25, 1960, Hollywood, Calif. (liver ailment). Screen, stage, television and radio actress. Nominated for 1950 Academy Award for Best Supporting Actress in Caged.

Appeared in: **1932** Smiling Faces. **1948** Cry of the City; That Wonderful Urge. **1949** House of Strangers; Adam's Rib; Dancing in the Dark; Roseanne McCoy; Thieves' Highway. **1950** Caged; Copper Canyon; Double Crossbones. **1951** Belle Le Grande. **1952** Westward the Women. **1953** Lady Wants Mink; Champ for a Day; A Perilous Journey. **1954** Casanova's Big Night. **1955** Untamed. **1956** The Day They Gave Babies Away. **1957** Guns of Fort Petticoat; All Mine to Give. **1958** Rock-A-Bye Baby.

EMERSON, JOHN (Clifton Paden)
Born: May 29, 1874, Sandusky, Ohio. Died: Mar. 7, 1956, Pasadena, Calif. Screen, stage actor, playwright, screenwriter, film, stage producer and film director. Married to authoress Anita Loos.

Appeared in: **1914** The Conspiracy; Bachelor's Romance. **1915** The Failure; Ghosts. **1916** The Flying Torpedo.

EMERTON, ROY (Hugh Fitzroy Emerton)
Born: Oct. 9, 1893, Burford, Oxfordshire, England. Died: Nov. 30, 1944, England. Screen and stage actor. Married to actress Catherine Lacey (dec. 1979). Entered films in 1930.

Appeared in: **1931** Shadows. **1932** That Night in London (aka Overnight—US 1934); The Sign of the Four. **1934** The Lash; Java Head (US 1935). **1935** The Triumph of Sherlock Holmes; Lorna Doone. **1936** Tudor Rose (aka Nine Days a Queen—US); Everthing is Thunder. **1937** The Gang Show; The Great Barrier (aka Silent Barriers—US); Big Fella; The Last Adventurers; Dr. Syn. **1938** Convict 99; The Drum (aka Drums—US). **1939** Home From Home; The Good Old Days. **1940** Busman's Honeymoon (aka Haunted Honeymoon—US); The Case of the Frightened Lady (aka The Frightened Lady—US 1941); The Thief of Bagdad. **1941** Old Mother Riley's Circus. **1942** The Young Mr. Pitt. **1943** The Man in Gray (US 1945). **1944** Welcome Mr. Washington; Time Flies. **1945** Henry V (US 1946).

EMERY, GILBERT
Born: 1882. Died: Dec. 31, 1934, Los Angeles, Calif. Screen and stage actor. Entered films in 1924.

EMERY, GILBERT (Arthur MacArthur)
Born: 1875, Naples, N.Y. Died: Oct. 26, 1945. Screen, stage actor and screenwriter. Entered films in 1920.

Appeared in: **1921** Cousin Kate. **1929** Behind That Curtain; Sky Hawk. **1930** Happy Days; Sarah and Son; Prince of Diamonds; Let Us Be Gay; A Lady's Morals; Soul Kiss. **1931** A Royal Bed; Scandal Sheet; The Lady Refuses; Ladies' Man; Party Husband; Upper Underworld; Rich Man's Folly; The Ruling Voice. **1932** Man Called Back; A Farewell to Arms. **1933** Gallant Lady. **1934** Coming Out Party; All of Me; The House of Rothschild; Where Sinners Meet; One More River; Now and Forever; Grand Canary; I Believed in You; Whom the Gods Destroy. **1935** Clive of India; Man Who Reclaimed His Head; Night Life of the Gods; Let's Live Tonight; Cardinal Richelieu; Goin' to Town; Reckless Roads; Ladies Crave Excitement; Harmony Lane; Without Regret; Peter Ibbetson; Magnificent Obsession. **1936** Wife vs. Secretary; Dracula's Daughter; Bullets or Ballots; The Girl on the Front Page; Little Lord Fauntleroy. **1937** The Life of Emile Zola; Double or Nothing; Souls at Sea. **1938** Making the Headlines; The House of Mystery; The Buccaneer; Lord Jeff; A Man to Remember; Storm Over Bengal; Always Goodbye. **1939** The Saint Strikes Back; Juarez; The Lady's from Kentucky; Nurse Edith Cavell. **1940** Raffles; The House of the Seven Gables; Anne of Windy Poplars; The Rivers End; South of Suez. **1941** That Hamilton Woman; Rage in Heaven; Adam Had Four Sons; Scotland Yard; A Woman's Face; Singapore Woman; New Wine; Sundown. **1942** King of the Royal Mounted (serial); The Remarkable Andrew; Escape from Hong Kong; The Loves of Edgar Allan Poe. **1943** Sherlock Holmes in Washington. **1944** The Return of the Vampire; Between Worlds. **1945** The Brighton Strangler.

EMERY, JOHN
Born: 1905, New York, N.Y. Died: Nov. 16, 1964, New York, N.Y. Screen, stage and televison actor. Divorced from actress Tallulah Bankhead (dec. 1968).

Appeared in: **1937** The Road Back. **1941** Here Comes Mr. Jordan; The Corsican Brothers. **1942** Two Yanks in Trinidad; Ship Ahoy; Eyes in the Night; George Washington Slept Here. **1943** Assignment in Brittany. **1944** Mademoiselle Fifi. **1945** Spellbound; Blood on the Sun; The Spanish Main. **1947** The Voice of the Turtle. **1948** Joan of Arc; The Woman in White; The Gay Intruders; Let's Live Again. **1950** Dakota Lil; Rocket Ship X-M; Frenchie; Double Crossbones. **1951** Joe Palooka in the Triple Cross. **1954** The Mad Magician. **1955** A Lawless Street. **1956** Forever Darling; The Girl Can't Help It. **1957** Kronos. **1958** Ten North Frederick. **1964** Youngblood Hawke.

EMERY, KATHERINE
Born: 1907, Ala. Died: Feb. 7, 1980, Portland, Maine (pulmonary illnesses). Screen and stage actress.

Appeared in: **1942** Eyes in the Night. **1945** Isle of the Dead. **1946** The Locket; The Walls Came Tumbling Down. **1947** The Private Affairs of Bel Ami. **1948** Chicken Every Sunday. **1949** Strange Bargain. **1951** Payment On Demand. **1952** Untamed Frontier; Hiawatha. **1953** The Maze. **1955** The Intruder. **1962** Kid Galahad.

EMERY, POLLIE
Born: May 10, 1875, Bolton, Lancashire, England. Died: Oct. 31, 1958, England? Screen and stage actress. Daughter of stage actor Frank Emery (dec. 1910).

Appeared in: **1916** The Persecution of Bob Pretty. **1919** Patricia Brent, Spinster. **1920** Watch Your Step; The Case of Lady Camber; Nothing Else Matters. **1922** If Four Walls Told; A Sister to Assist 'Er (and 1927 and 1930 version); A Will and a Way; Treasure Trove; The Pauper Millionaire; Perpetua (aka Love's Boomerang—US). **1923** Beautiful Kitty. **1924** The Alley of the Golden Hearts. **1925** The Impatient Patient. **1926** Screen Playlets series including: Cash on Delivery. **1927** A Sister To Assist 'Er (and 1922 and 1930 version). **1930** A Sister to Assist 'Er (and 1922 and 1927 versions).

EMERY, WINIFRED
Born: Aug. 1, 1862, Manchester, England. Died: July 15, 1924, England? Screen and stage actress. Daughter of stage actor Samuel Anderson Emery (dec. 1881). Married to actor Cyril Maude (dec. 1951).

Appeared in: **1917** Masks and Faces.

EMMET, KATHERINE
Died: June 6, 1960, N.Y. Screen, stage and radio actress.

Appeared in: **1921** Orphans of the Storm; Paying the Piper. **1929** Hole in the Wall. **1931** The Night Angel.

EMMETT, FERN
Born: Mar. 22, 1896, Oakland, Calif. Died: Sept. 3, 1946, Hollywood, Calif. Screen and stage actress. Married to actor Henry Roquemore (dec. 1943).

Appeared in: **1930** Bar L Ranch; Ridin' Law; The Land of Missing Men; Romance of the West; Second Honeymoon; Westbound; Skip the Maloo! (short). **1932** The following shorts: A Fool About Women;

Boy, Oh, Boy; Anybody's Goat; Bridge Wives; Mother's Holiday. **1933** His Weak Moment (short); Frozen Assets (short); East of Fifth Avenue; The Vampire Bat; Hello Everybody; The Trail Drive. **1934** City Limits; An Old Gypsy Custom (short). **1935** Behind the Green Lights; Motive for Revenge; Smart Girl; Melody Trail; Southern Exposure (short); The E-Flat Man (short). **1936** The Trail of the Lonesome Pine; The Harvester; M'Liss; Three on a Limb (short); Don't Turn 'Em Loose; Ticket to Paradise; The Oregon Trail; Swing Time. **1937** A Girl With Ideas; Girls Can Play; Paradise Express; Dangerous Holiday; Riders of the Whistling Skull; Come on Cowboys; Calling All Doctors (short); Hillbilly Goat (short). **1938** Scandal Sheet; Hunted Men; Overland Stage Raiders; You and Me. **1939** Desperate Trails; Pirates of the Skies; Made for Each Other; The Rains Came; They Shall Have Music; Disputed Passage; In Love Only; Romance of the Potato (short). **1940** Star Dust; South of Suez; Half a Sinner; The Lady in Question; Arise, My Love; Lucky Partners. **1941** You're in the Army Now; She Knew All the Answers; A Girl, a Guy and a Gob; Kathleen; Glamour Boy; All That Money Can Buy; Scattergood Baines; Love Crazy. **1942** Broadway; In Old California; Careful, Soft Shoulders; Henry Aldrich, Editor; The Great Man's Lady; Woman of the Year; Valley of the Sun. **1943** Keep 'Em Slugging; Gildersleeve's Bad Day; First Comes Courage. **1944** Johnny Doesn't Live Here Anymore; Cover Girl; Once Upon a Time; Together Again; Can't Help Singing; San Diego, I Love You; Henry Aldrich's Little Secret. **1945** A Song to Remember; Pillow of Death. **1946** The Kid from Brooklyn. **1952** The Devil and Daniel Webster (reissue and retitle of All That Money Can Buy, 1941).

EMMONS, LARRY
Died: May 27, 1978. Screen actor.

EMMONS, LOUISE
Born: 1852. Died: Mar. 6, 1935, Hollywood, Calif. Screen actress. Entered films in 1909.

Appeared in: **1931** Heaven on Earth.

EMNEY, FRED, JR.
Born: 1900, London, England. Died: Dec. 25, 1980, Bognor Regis, England. Screen, stage, radio and television actor. Son of actor Fred Emney, Sr. (dec, 1917). Brother of actress Joan Emney.

Appeared in: **1935** Brewster's Millions; Come Out of the Kitchen. **1937** Let's Make a Night of It (US 1938). **1938** Yes, Madam? **1939** Just William; The Middle Watch. **1942** Let the People Sing. **1962** The Fast Lady (US 1965). **1964** Father Came Too (US 1966, aka We Want to Live Alone). **1968** Bunny Lake is Missing; Those Magnificent Men in Their Flying Machines. **1968** Oliver! **1969** Lock up Your Daughters!; The Italian Job; The Magic Christian (US 1970).

EMNEY, FRED, SR.
Born: Mar. 5, 1865, Islington, England. Died: Jan. 7, 1917, England? Screen and stage actor. Father of actress Blanche Emney and actor Fred Emney, Jr. (dec. 1980). Entered films with British Actors' Film Company in 1915.

EMPEY, ARTHUR GUY
Born: 1884. Died: Feb. 22, 1963, Wadsworth, Kans. Screen actor, author, screenwriter, film director and film producer (President of Guy Empey Pictures Corp.).

Appeared in: **1918** Over the Top. **1919** The Undercurrent. **1921** Millionaire for a Day.

EMPRESS, MARIE
Born: England. Died: 1919, Atlantic Ocean (drowned—fell overboard on voyage to United States). Screen and vaudeville actress.

Appeared in: **1915** Old Dutch; When We Were Twenty-One.

ENDOR, CHICK
Born: England. Died: 1941, England. Screen actor and nightclub entertainer.

Appeared in: **1935** Two Hearts in Harmony.

ENDRESSE, CLARA
Born: 1896, Mont. Died: Dec. 2, 1979, Los Angeles, Calif. Screen actress. Entered films in the 1920's.

ENFIELD, HUGH *See* REYNOLDS, CRAIG

ENGEL, ALEXANDER
Born: 1902. Died: Aug., 1968, Saarbruecken, Germany. Screen, stage and television actor.

Appeared in: **1934** Eines Prinzen Junge Liebe. **1936** Einer zu viel an Bord. **1952** The Merry Wives of Windsor. **1958** A Time to Love and a Time to Die. **1959** Taiga. **1960** Hamlet (US 1968). **1961** Im Stahinetz des Dr. Mabuse (Return of Dr. Mabuse—US 1966). **1963** Der Henker von London (The Mad Executioners—US 1965).

ENGEL, ROY
Born: Sept. 13, 1913, Mo. Died: Dec. 29, 1980, Burbank, Calif. (meningitis). Screen and radio actor.

Appeared in: **1949** D.O.A. (film debut). **1950** The Flying Saucer; Outrage; Rogue River. **1951** The Man From Planet X; The Well; Chicago Calling; The Sellout. **1952** Strange Fascination; Breakdown. **1953** Vicki. **1954** Dragon's Gold. **1955** A Bullet for Joey; The Naked Dawn; Thy Neighbor's Daughter; Love Me or Leave Me. **1956** Three Violent People; Frontier Gambler. **1957** Not of This Earth; The Storm Rider; Death in Small Doses; Escape from San Quentin; All Mine to Give. **1958** Satan's Satellites; Joy Ride; Some Came Running. **1960** Spartacus; A Dog's Best Friend. **1961** The Sergeant Was a Lady; The Flight That Disappeared. **1962** The Three Stooges in Orbit. **1963** It's a Mad, Mad, Mad, Mad World. **1964** Your Cheatin' Heart. **1972** Skyjacked; Silent Running. **1977** Kingdom of the Spiders.

ENGLAND, DAISY
Born: 1862, England. Died: Mar. 7, 1943, England. Screen and stage actress.

Appeared in: **1922** Head of the Family.

ENGLAND, PAUL
Born: 1893. Died: Nov. 21, 1968, Devonshire, England. Screen, radio actor and singer.

Appeared in: **1934** Charlie Chan in London; Love Time. **1939** Disputed Passage. **1954** Knock on Wood.

ENGLE, BILLY
Born: 1889. Died: Nov. 28, 1966, Hollywood, Calif. (heart attack). Screen and burlesque actor. Entered films in 1919 and appeared in Christie comedies during the 1920's.

Appeared in: **1926** Red Hot Leather. **1927** The Cat and the Canary; The Western Whirlwind. **1933** Knight Duty (short). **1934** Midnight Intruder. **1935** I'm a Father (short); Uncivil Warriors (short); Big Broadcast of 1936; It's a Gift. **1936** Wedding Present. **1938** Test Pilot; Tom Sawyer, Detective. **1939** Hero for a Day. **1940** Our Neighbors—the Carters. **1941** Glamour Boy. **1942** Mrs. Miniver. **1945** Frontier Gal. **1946** The Best Years of Our Lives; Along Came Jones. **1947** The Wistful Widow of Wagon Gap. **1948** The Paleface. **1949** Red, Hot and Blue.

ENGLE, MARIE
Born: 1902. Died: Mar. 23, 1971, Hollywood, Calif. (stroke). Screen and vaudeville actress. Married to actor Tom Dugan (dec. 1955) and they appeared in vaudeville in an act billed as "Dugan and Engle."

Appeared in: **1947** Swing the Western Way.

ENGLISCH, LUCIE
Born: 1897, Baden, Austria. Died: Oct., 1965, Erlangen, Germany (liver ailment). Screen actress.

Appeared in: **1929** Alimente; Die Nacht Gehoert Uns; Ruhiges Heim mit Kuechenbenutzung. **1930** Der Witwenball; Ein Walzer im Schlafcoupe; Zweimal Hochzeit; Kasernenzauber; Komm' zu mir zum Rendezvous; Das Lockende Ziel (US 1933); Das Rheinlandmaedel (US 1931); Zwei Menschen (US 1931); Drei Tage Mittelarrest (Three Days in the Guardhouse—US 1933). **1931** Keine Feier ohne Meyer (US 1932); Der Schrecken der Garnison (US 1932); Dienst ist Dienst (US 1932); Um Eine Nasenlaenge; Mein Leopold (US 1932); Reserve hat Ruh (US 1932); So'n Windhund!; Schuberts Fruehlingstraum (US 1932). **1932** Der Ungetreue Eckehart; Die Graefin von Monte Christo (The Countess of Monte Christo); Hurra! Ein Junge!; Ballhaus Goldener Engel; Annemarie, die Braut der Kompanie (US 1934); Aus Einer Kleinen Residenz. **1933** Die Kalte Mamsell (US 1935); Heimat am Rhein (US 1934); Gretel Zieht das Grosse Los (US 1935); Die Unschuld vom Lande (US 1933). **1934** Wenn ein Maedel Hochzeit Macht; Meine Frau, die Schuetzenkoenigin (US 1935). **1935** Der Unbekannte Gast (The Unknown Guest); Der Kampf mit dem Drachen; Der Mutige Seefahrer (US 1936); Ein Falscher Fuffziger (US 1937). **1936** Die Ahnungslose Engel; Wo die Lerche Singt; Du Kannst Nicht Treu Sein; Der Lachende Dritte (US 1938); Der Postillon von Lonjumeau (US 1937, aka Der Koenig Laechelt—Paris Lacht). **1937** So Weit Geht die Liebe Nicht; Pat und Patachon im Paradies; Die Verschwundene Frau; Ihr Leibhusar; Die Landstreicher (The Hoboes—US 1938); Eine Nacht mit Hindernissen (aka Der Klapperstorchverband). **1938** Dir Gehoert Mein Herz; Die Unruhigen Maedchen; Unsere Kleine Frau; Immer, Wenn ich Gluecklich Bin; Kleines Bezirksgericht (Little Country Court—US 1939). **1939** Dinghort Mein Herz (My Heart Belongs to Thee); Solo per Danne; Der Kampf mit dem Dralhen (The Fight With the Dragon); Premiere der Butterfly; Rheinische Brautfahrt. **1940** Our Little Wife;

Walzerlange (Waltz Melodies); Weltrekord im Seitensprung; Der Ungetreue Eckehart (and 1932 version); Herzensfreud—Herzensleid. **1941** Was Geschah in Dieser Nacht; Tanz mit dem Kaiser. **1942** Ein Zug Faehrt Ab; So Ein Fruechtchen; Drei Tolle Maedels. **1943** Fahrt ins Arbenteuer; Ein Walzer mit Dir. **1944** Spiel; Die Heimlichen Braeute. **1945** Philine; Die Kreuzlschreiber. **1950** Der Theodor im Fussballtor; Alles fuer die Firma; Es Liegt was in der Luft; So Sind die Frauen (aka Der Dorfmonarch); Schwarzwaldmaedel. **1951** Durch Dick und Duenn; Wildwest in Oberbayern; Drei Kavaliere. **1952** Das Weisse Abenteuer; Der Eingebildete Kranke; Moenche, Maedchen und Panduren; Mikosch Rueckt Ein; Karneval in Weiss; Der Mann in der Wanne. **1953** Fiakermilli—Liebling von Wien; Der Keusche Josef; Tante Jutta aus Kalkutta; Die Nacht ohne Moral; Auf der Gruenen Wiese; Die Fuenf Karnickel. **1954** Der Treue Husar; Der Engel mit dem Flammenschwert; ...und Ewig Bleibt die Liebe. **1955** Die Heilige Luege; Oh Diese "Lieben" Verwandten; Liebe ist ja nur ein Maerchen; Der Jaeger vom Roteck; Seine Tochter ist der Peter. **1956** 1A in Oberbayern; Zwei Bayern in St. Pauli; Johannisnacht; Wo der Wildbach Rauscht; Der Glockengiesser von Tirol; 11A in Berlin; Die Magd von Heiligenblut; Familie Schimek. **1957** Vater Macht Karriere; Tante Wanda aus Uganda; Ober Zahlen!; Hoch Droben auf dem Berg; Die Fidelen Detektive; Jungfrauenkrieg; Der Wilderer vom Silberwald; Zwei Bayern im Urwald; Liebe—wie die Frau sie Wuenscht; Der Pfarrer von St. Michael. **1958** Heiratskandidaten; Hallo Taxi; Graefin Mariza; Wehe, Wenn sie Losgelassen; Die Singenden Engel von Tirol (aka Sagja, Mutti). **1959** Herrn Josefs Letzte Liebe; Hubertusjagd; Peter Voss, der Held des Tages. **1961** Drei Weisse Birken. **1962** Schwarze Rose, Rosemarie.

ENGLISH, HARRY
Born: 1861. Died: Apr. 3, 1939, Englewood, N.J. Screen, stage and vaudeville actor.

Appeared in: **1915** Playing Dead.

ENNIS, SKINNAY
Born: 1907. Died: June 2, 1963, Los Angeles, Calif. (suffocation). Bandleader, radio and screen actor.

Appeared in: **1938** College Swing. **1939** Blondie Meets the Boss.

ENRIGHT, FLORENCE
Died: Apr. 3, 1961, Hollywood, Calif. Screen, stage actress, and drama coach. Entered films in 1931.

Appeared in: **1931** Women Love Once; Street Scene; Possessed. **1932** Nice Women. **1934** Six of a Kind; Gift of Gab.

ENRIGHT, JOSEPHINE
Born: 1904. Died: Feb. 24, 1976, Hollywood, Calif. Screen, stage and radio actress.

ENS, WILLIAM (aka EAGLE EYE)
Born: 1877, Ft. Thomas, Ariz. Died: Jan. 17, 1927, Los Angeles, Calif. (homicide). Screen actor and stuntman.

Appeared in: **1916** The Beast. **1917** Honor System. **1921** The Fire Cat; The Magnificent Brute; Wolves of the North; Serenade. **1922** The Son of the Wolf; The Pride of Palomar. **1924** The Shooting of Dan McGrew; Lure of the Yukon.

ENSERRO, MICHAEL "MIKE" (Michael T. Enserro)
Born: Oct. 5, 1918, Soldier, Pa. Died: Mar. 4, 1981, New York, N.Y. (heart attack). Screen, stage and television actor.

Appeared in: **1958** Never Love a Stranger. **1962** Two for the Seesaw. **1963** The Cardinal; Love With the Proper Stranger. **1965** A Thousand Clowns.

ENSTEDT, HOWARD
Born: May 7, 1906, Ill. Died: Dec. 13, 1928. Screen and stage actor.

Appeared in: **1926** Rolling Home; The Radio Detective (serial) (with "the Boy Scouts").

ENTRATTER, JACK
Born: Feb. 28, 1913, New York, N.Y. Died: Mar. 11, 1971, Las Vegas, Nev. (cerebral hemorrhage). Veteran hotel man, showman and screen actor. Married to Dorothy Entratter (dec.) and later married and divorced actress Corinne Cole.

Appeared in: **1960** Pepe.

ENTWISTLE, HAROLD (Charles H. Entwistle)
Born: Sept. 5, 1865, London, England. Died: Apr. 1, 1944, Hollywood, Calif. Screen, stage actor and film director. Entered films in 1910.

Appeared in: **1917** One of Many. **1919** The Divorcee; The Woman Under Oath. **1932** Two Against the World. **1933** Our Betters; She Done Him Wrong. **1934** Jimmy the Gent; The Journal of a Crime. **1935** Goin' to Town; Vanessa, Her Love Story; Paris in Spring; Mutiny on the Bounty; The Perfect Gentleman; Two Sinners. **1936** Sylvia Scarlett; Romeo and Juliet; The Suicide Club. **1937** Easy Living. **1938** Marie Antoinette. **1939** The Light That Failed.

ENTWISTLE, PEG (Lillian Millicent Entwistle)
Born: 1908, London, England. Died: Sept. 18, 1932, Hollywood, Calif. (suicide—leap off "Hollywoodland" sign). Screen and stage actress.

Appeared in: **1932** Thirteen Women.

EPAILLY, JULIES
Born: France. Died: Apr. 29, 1967, Central Islip, N.Y. Screen and stage actor.

Appeared in: **1931** Honor Among Lovers.

EPPERSON, DON
Born: 1938. Died: Mar. 17, 1973, Cottonwood, Ariz. (auto accident). Screen, television actor, singer and assistant film director.

Appeared in: **1969** Wild Wheels. **1970** Cain's Way. **1971** The Female Bunch; Big Jake. **1973** Oklahoma Crude.

ERASTOFF, EDITH
Born: 1887, Helsinki, Finland. Died: 1945, Finland? Screen actress.

Appeared in: **1919** The Song of the Scarlet Flower. Other Finish films: A People of the Border; A Hero in Spite of Himself; The First Prize; The Avenger; Old Age and Folly; Mrs. B's Lapse; Terje Vigen; The Architect of One's Own Fortune; The Secret of the Inn; Chanson Triste; The Outlaw and His Wife; For High Ends; Johan Ulfsjerna.

ERBY, MORRIS
Died: Jan. 9, 1979. Screen actor.

Appeared in: **1966** A Man Called Adam. **1969** The Lost Man.

ERIC, FRED
Born: 1874, Peru, Ind. Died: Apr. 17, 1935, New York, N.Y. Screen and stage actor. Appeared in Frohman, Pathe, Thanhouser and World films.

Appeared in: **1915** Builder of Bridges. **1916** The Jester. **1917** Woman and the Beast. **1923** Columbus; Skid Proof.

ERICKSON, CHRIS
Born: 1945. Died: Feb. 11, 1971 (auto accident). Screen actor. Son of actor Leif Erickson.

ERICKSON, KNUTE
Born: 1871, Norrkoping, Sweden. Died: Jan. 1, 1946, Los Angeles, Calif. Screen, stage, radio and televison actor. Entered films in 1920.

Appeared in: **1921** The Conflict; Gasoline Gus. **1922** They Like 'Em Rough. **1924** Fair Week. **1925** The Commandment; Johnny Get Your Hair Cut. **1928** The Fourflusher; Scarlet Seas; Waterfront. **1929** The Squall; Twin Beds; Illusion. **1930** The Spoilers. **1932** His Royal Shyness (short). **1933** The Bitter Tea of General Yen. **1936** The Clutching Hand (serial).

ERISTOFF, NESTOR
Born: 1870, Russia. Died: Oct. 24, 1961, Hollywood, Calif. Screen actor.

ERMELLI, CLAUDIO (Ettore Foa)
Born: 1892, Turin, Italy. Died: Oct. 29, 1964, Rome, Italy. Stage and screen actor. Entered films in 1932.

Appeared in: **1949** The Golden Madonna. **1953** Roman Holiday. **1957** A Farewell to Arms. **1960** It Started in Naples.

ERNSTER, DEZSO
Born: 1899, Hungary. Died: Feb. 15, 1981, Zurich, Switzerland. (cancer). Screen actor and opera singer.

Appeared in: **1956** Don Giovanni.

ERROL, LEON
Born: July 3, 1881, Sydney, Australia. Died: Oct. 12, 1951, Los Angeles, Calif. (heart attack). Screen, stage and vaudeville actor. Entered films in 1924. Married to dancer Stella Chatelaine (dec. 1946). Was Lord Epping in the "Mexican Spitfire" features of the early 1940's.

Appeared in: **1924** Yolanda. **1925** Sally; Clothes Make the Pirate. **1927** The Lunatic at Large. **1930** How I Play Golf—The Mashie Niblick (short); Only Saps Work; Let's Merge (short); Paramount on Parade; Queen of Scandal; One Heavenly Night. **1931** Fin and Hattie; Her Majesty, Love. **1933** Alice in Wonderland; plus the following shorts: Poor Fish; Three Little Swigs; Hold Your Temper. **1934** We're Not Dressing; The Captain Hates the Sea; The Notorious Sophie Lang; plus the following shorts: Perfectly Mismated; No More Bridge; Autobuyography; Service With a Smile; Good Morning, Eve; Fixing a Stew; One Too Many. **1935** Princess O'Hara; Coronado; plus the following shorts: Hit and Rum; Salesmanship Ahoy; Home Work; Honeymoon Bridge; Counselitis; Vitaphone shorts. **1936** The following shorts: Down the Ribber; Wholesailing Along; One Live Ghost; Columbia shorts. **1937** Make a Wish; plus the following shorts: Wrong Romance; Should Wives Work?; A Rented Riot. **1938** The following shorts; Dummy Owner; His Pest Friend; Berth Quakes; The Jitters; Stage Fright; Major Difficulties. **1939** The Girl from Mexico; Career; Dancing Co-ed; Mexican Spitfire; plus the following shorts: Crime Rave; Home Boner; Moving Vanities; Ring Madness; Wrong Room; Truth Aches. **1940** Pop Always Pays; Mexican Spitfire Out West; The Golden Fleecing; plus the following shorts: Scrappily Married; Bested by a Beard; He Asked for It; Tattle Television. **1941** Six Lessons from Madame La Zonga; Where Did You Get That Girl?; Hurry, Charlie, Hurry; Mexican Spitfire's Baby; Never Give a Sucker an Even Break; Melody Lane; plus the following shorts: The Fired Man; When Wifie's Away; A Polo Phony; A Panic in the Parlor; Man I Cured; Who's a Dummy? **1942** Moonlight in Hawaii; Mexican Spitfire at Sea; Mexican Spitfire Sees a Ghost; Mexican Spitfire's Elephant; plus the following shorts: Home Work (and 1935 version); Wedded Blitz; Framing Father; Hold 'Em Jail; Mail Trouble; Deal! Deer!; Pretty Dolly. **1943** Strictly in the Groove; Follow the Band; Mexican Spitfire's Blessed Event; Gals, Inc; Higher and Higher; Cross Your Fingers; Cowboy in Manhattan; Cocktails for Two; plus the following shorts: A Family Feud; Double Up; Gem Jams; Radio Runaround; Seeing Nellie Home; Cutie on Duty; Wedtime Stories. **1944** Hat Check Honey; The Invisible Man's Revenge; Slightly Terrific; Babes on Swing Street; Twilight on the Prairie; plus the following shorts: Price Unlimited; Say Uncle; Poppa Knows Worst; Girls, Girls, Girls; Triple Trouble; He Forgot to Remember. **1945** She Gets Her Man; Panamericana; Under Western Skies; Mama Loves Papa; What a Blonde; plus the following shorts: Birthday Blues; Let's Go Stepping; Beware of Redheads; Double Honeymoon; It Shouldn't Happen to a Dog. **1946** Riverboat Rhythm; Joe Palooka, Champ; Gentleman Joe Palooka; plus the following shorts: Maid Trouble; Oh, Professor, Behave; Twin Husbands; I'll Take Milk; Follow That Blonde. **1947** Joe Palooka in the Knockout; plus the following shorts: Borrowed Blonde; Wife Tames Wolf; In Room 303; Hired Husband; Blondes Away; The Spook Speaks. **1948** Joe Palooka in the Big Fight; Joe Palooka in the Counterpunch; Make Mine Laughs; plus the following shorts: Bet Your Life; Don't Fool Your Wife; Secretary Trouble; Bachelor Blues; Uninvited Blonde; Backstage Follies. **1949** The following shorts: Dad Always Pays; Cactus Cut-Up; I Can't Remember; Oil's Well That Ends Well; Sweet Cheat; Shocking Affair. **1950** Joe Palooka in Humphrey Takes a Chance; Joe Palooka Meets Humphrey; plus the following shorts: High and Dizzy; Texas Tough Guy; Spooky Wooky. **1951** Footlight Varieties; plus the following shorts: Chinatown Chump; Punchy Pancho; One Wild Night; Deal Me In; Lord Epping Returns; Too Many Wives.

ERSKINE, WALLACE
Born: 1862, England. Died: Jan. 6, 1943, Massapequa, L.I., N.Y. Screen and stage actor.

Appeared in: **1921** Perjury. **1923** The Ragged Edge.

ERWAY, BEN
Born: 1893, Reno, Nev. Died: Feb. 6, 1981, Sun City, Calif. Screen and stage actor. Married to actress Gladys George (dec. 1954).

Appeared in: **1942** Mountain Rhythm. **1943** Mission to Moscow. **1944** Tampico. **1947** The Bishop's Wife. **1948** Lulu Belle. **1949** Shep Comes Home; Rimfire; Sand.

ERWIN, JUNE
Born: 1918. Died: Dec. 28, 1965, Carmichael, Calif. Screen actress. Appeared in "Our Gang" comedies.

ERWIN, PEE WEE
Born: May 30, 1913, Fall City, Nebr. Died: June 20, 1981, Teaneck, N.J. Screen, radio actor and jazz trumpet player.

ERWIN, ROY (LeRoy Franklin Erwin)
Born: 1925. Died: June 18, 1958, Rosarito Beach, Baja, Calif. (heart attack). Screen, television actor and television writer.

ERWIN, STUART
Born: Feb. 14, 1902, Squaw Valley, Calif. Died: Dec. 21, 1967, Beverly Hills, Calif. (heart attack). Screen, stage and television actor. Married to actress June Collyer (dec. 1968). Nominated for 1936 Academy Award for Best Supporting Actor in Pigskin Parade.

Appeared in: **1928** Mother Knows Best (film debut). **1929** Happy Days; The Exalted Flapper; New Year's Eve; Dangerous Curves; This Thing Called Love; Cockeyed World; Speakeasy; Hold Your Man; Sweetie; The Sophomore; The Trespasser; Thru Different Eyes. **1930** Men Without Women; Young Eagles; Dangerous Nan McGrew; Love Among the Millionaires; Playboy of Paris; Only Saps Work; Along Came Youth; Paramount on Parade; Maybe It's Love. **1931** No Limit; Up Pops the Devil; Dude Ranch; Working Girls; The Magnificent Lie. **1932** Two Kinds of Women; Make Me a Star; The Big Broadcast; Hollywood on Parade (short); The Misleading Lady; Strangers in Love. **1933** The Crime of the Century; He Learned About Women; Face in the Sky; International House; Under the Tonto Rim; Stranger's Return; Day of Reckoning; Going Hollywood; Before Dawn; Make Me a Star; Hold Your Man. **1934** Palooka; Viva Villa!; The Band Plays On; Chained; Bachelor Bait; The Party's Over; Have a Heart. **1935** Ceiling Zero; After Office Hours; Three Men on a Horse. **1936** Exclusive Story; Pigskin Parade; Absolute Quiet; Women Are Trouble; All American Chump. **1937** Dance, Charlie, Dance; Slim; Second Honeymoon; Checkers; Small Town Boy; I'll Take Romance. **1938** Three Blind Mice; Passport Husband; Mr. Boggs Steps Out. **1939** Hollywood Cavalcade; The Honeymoon's Over; Back Door to Heaven; It Could Happen to You. **1940** Our Town; When the Daltons Rode; A Little Bit of Heaven; Sandy Gets Her Man. **1941** The Bride Came C.O.D.; Cracked Nuts. **1942** Drums of the Congo; Adventures of Martin Eden; Blondie for Victory; Through Different Eyes. **1943** He Hired the Boss. **1944** The Great Mike. **1945** Pillow to Post. **1947** Killer Dill; Heaven Only Knows; Heading for Heaven. **1948** Strike It Rich. **1950** Father Is a Bachelor. **1953** Mainstreet to Broadway. **1960** For the Love of Mike; When Comedy was King (documentary). **1963** Son of Flubber. **1964** The Misadventures of Merlin Jones.

ESCANDE, MAURICE
Born: 1893, France? Died: Feb. 11, 1973, Paris, France. Screen and stage actor.

Appeared in: **1933** Les Trois Mousquetaires. **1937** Lucrezia Borgia. **1947** The Queen's Necklace. **1949** Man to Men. **1963** Les Animaux (The Animals—US 1965).

ESCUDERO, VICENTE
Born: 1889, Spain. Died: Dec. 4, 1980, Barcelona, Spain. Screen actor and dancer.

Appeared in: **1935** Here's to Romance.

ESDALE, CHARLES
Born: 1873. Died: July 10, 1937, New York, N.Y. (complication of diseases). Screen and stage actor.

Appeared in: **1925** Soul Fire. **1926** Summer Bachelors.

ESMELTON, FREDERICK "FRED"
Born: June 22, 1872, Melbourne, Australia. Died: Oct. 23, 1933, Los Angeles, Calif. Screen, stage actor and stage director.

Appeared in: **1919** The Avalanche. **1923** Can a Woman Love Twice?; Three Wise Fools; Boston Blackie; The Custard Cup; Dulcy; The Darling of New York; The Rustle of Silk. **1924** Conductor 1492. **1925** Lady of the Night; Smooth as Satin; Red Hot Tires; Raffles, the Amateur Cracksman. **1926** California Straight Ahead; Kid Boots. **1927** Shield of Honor; The Gay Defender. **1928** Romance of a Rogue; The Baby Cyclone; The Chinese Parrot; Two Lovers; The Michigan Kid. **1931** Born to Love.

ESSEN, VIOLA
Born: 1925. Died: Jan. 16, 1970. Screen actress and dancer. Divorced from actor Gabriel Dell.

Appeared in: **1946** Specter of the Rose.

ESSER, PETER
Born: 1896, Germany. Died: June 23, 1970, Dusseldorf, Germany. Screen and stage actor.

Appeared in: **1956** Die Trapp-Familie (The Trapp Family—US 1961). **1961** King in Shadow.

ESSER, WRIGHT (Karl Wright Esser)
Born: 1907, England. Died: Aug. 12, 1976, Honolulu, Hawaii. Screen, stage actor, stage producer and stage director.

Appeared in: **1949** The Great Lover. **1963** Memento Mei.

ESSLER, FRED
Born: 1896. Died: Jan. 17, 1973, Woodland Hills, Calif. Screen and television actor.

Appeared in: **1943** Mission to Moscow; Gildersleeve on Broadway; Behind the Rising Sun; Up in Arms. **1944** Mask of Demitrios; Passage to Marseille. **1945** Captain Eddie; Where Do We Go From Here?; Saratoga Trunk; What Next, Corporal Hargrove? **1946** Scarlet Street; Temptation; Faithful In My Fashion. **1948** Every Girl Should Be Married. **1950** The Toast of New Orleans; The White Tower; The Admiral Was a Lady; Messenger of Peace. **1953** Houdini. **1955** The Girl in the Red Velvet Swing. **1956** Hot Rod Girl; The First Traveling Saleslady. **1957** My Man Godfrey. **1958** Ten North Frederick. **1962** That Touch of Mink. **1964** The Unsinkable Molly Brown. **1966** The Money Trap.

ESTABROOK, HOWARD
Born: 1884, Detroit, Mich. Died: July 16, 1978, Woodland Hills, Calif. Screen, stage, vaudeville actor, film director, stage director, screenwriter, playwright and television writer.

Appeared in: **1914** Officer 666. **1915** Who's Guilty. **1916** The Mysteries of Myra (serial).

ESTEE, ADELYN
Born: 1871. Died: June 3, 1941, Los Angeles, Calif. Screen, vaudeville actress and opera performer.

ESTUDILLO, LEO B.
Born: 1900, San Diego, Calif. Died: Sept. 21, 1957, San Francisco, Calif. Screen actor and trick rider.

ETCHEPARA, PIERRE
Born: 1891, France. Died: 1944, France? Screen actor.

Appeared in: **1932** Tu Seras Duchesse.

ETHIER, ALPHONSE
Born: 1875, Springville, Utah. Died: Jan. 4, 1943, Hollywood, Calif. Screen and stage actor.

Appeared in: **1910** Thelma. **1918** The Forbidden Path. **1921** A Message from Mars; The Frontier of the Stars. **1924** The Moral Sinner; The Alaskan; The Lone Wolf. **1925** Contraband; The Midnight Flyer; Gold and the Girl; The People vs. Nancy Preston. **1926** Breed of the Sea; The Lone Wolf Returns. **1927** Cheaters; Alias the Lone Wolf; The Fighting Eagle. **1928** Say It With Sables; Shadows of the Night. **1929** The Donovan Affair; In Old Arizona; Hardboiled; Smoke Bellew. **1930** The Storm; His First Command; Lightnin'; The Big Trail. **1931** Fair Warning; Transgression; Honor of the Family. **1932** Rebecca of Sunnybrook Farm; Law and Order; Wild Girl; The Match King. **1933** Men of America; Ex-Lady; Baby Face. **1934** Voice in the Night; British Agent; No More Women. **1935** Border Town; Secret of the Chateau; Red Morning; The Crusades. **1936** The Story of Louis Pasteur; Boss Rider of Gun Creek. **1938** The Baroness and the Butler; Sunset Trail.

ETTING, RUTH
Born: Nov. 23, 1896, David City, Nev. Died: Sept. 24, 1978, Colorado Springs, Colo. Screen, stage and radio actress.

Appeared in: **1928** Ruth Etting Paramount Movietone (short). **1929** Ruth Etting The Book of Lovers (short). **1930** One Good Turn (short). **1931** The following shorts: Freshman Love; Radio Salutes; Words and Music; Seasons Greetings; Old Lace. **1933** Roman Scandals; The following shorts: Bye-Gones; Along Came Ruth; Crashing the Gate; Knee-Deep in Music; California Weather. **1934** Hips Hips Hooray; Gift of Gab; The following shorts: Hollywood on Parade; A Torch Tango; Derby Decade; The Song of Fame; Southern Style; Bandits and Ballots. **1935** The following shorts: No Contest; An Old Spanish Onion; Ticket or Leave It; Tuned Out. **1936** The following shorts: Aladdin from Manahattan; Melody in May; Sleepy Time.

EUARD, OPAL
Born: 1895, Ill. Died: May 13, 1980, Los Angeles, Calif. Screen, stage, television actress and drama teacher.

Appeared in: **1960** Studs Lonigan. **1961** The Two Little Bears.

EUSTACHE, JEAN
Born: 1939, France. Died: Nov. 4, 1981, Paris, France (suicide). Screen actor, film director and screenwriter.

Appeared in: **1967** Le Week-end (Weekend—US 1968). **1977** The American Friend.

EUSTREL, ANTONY
Born: Oct. 12, 1904, London, England. Died: July 2, 1979, Woodland Hills, Calif. Screen, stage and television actor.

Appeared in: **1937** Under the Red Robe. **1938** The Revenge of General Ling. **1943** The Adventures of Tartu; The Silver Fleet (US 1945). **1946** Caesar and Cleopatra. **1952** The Story of Robin Hood and His Merry Men. **1953** Devil's Plot; Titanic; The Robe; East of Sumatra; Captain John Smith and Pocahontas. **1954** King Richard and the Crusaders. **1963** The Three Stooges Go Around the World in a Daze. **1964** The Unsinkable Molly Brown; Goodbye Charley; What a Way to Go. **1967** Games; Fitzwilly.

EVANS, BOB (Robert D. Evans)
Born: 1904. Died: Mar. 21, 1961, Hollywood, Calif. (heart attack). Screen actor. Do not confuse with ventriloquist, screen actor nor film executive with same name.

Appeared in: **1937** Kid Galahad. **1938** Fisticuffs (short). **1941** The Flame of New Orleans. **1956** Around the World in 80 Days.

EVANS, BRANDON
Born: 1878. Died: Apr. 3, 1958, Santa Monica, Calif. Screen actor.

Appeared in: **1933** The Emperor Jones. **1937** Windjammer.

EVANS, BRUCE
Born: 1903. Died: Feb. 9, 1978, Sweden, Maine. Screen, stage actor, film director, film producer, stage director and screenwriter.

Appeared in: **1938** Hellzapoppin. **1939** Back Door to Heaven.

EVANS, CECILIA
Born: 1902. Died: Nov. 11, 1960, San Rafael, Calif. Screen and stage actress. Entered films with Sennett.

Appeared in: **1924** Worldly Goods. **1925** Blue Blood; The Goose Hangs High; Heir-Loons; The Talker. **1926** The Family Upstairs; Whispering Wires. **1927** Prince of Headwaiters.

EVANS, CHARLES EVAN
Born: 1857, Rochester, N.Y. Died: Apr. 16, 1945, Santa Monica, Calif. Screen, stage actor and stage producer. Married to actress Helena Phillips Evans (dec. 1955).

Appeared in: **1929** The Greene Murder Case; Disraeli; Happy Days. **1932** The Man Who Played God; The Expert. **1933** The King's Vacation; The Working Man. **1934** Peck's Bad Boy; The House of Rothschild. **1935** Clive of India; Cardinal Richelieu. **1946** The Dark Mirror; Without Reservations.

EVANS, DOUGLAS "DOUG"
Born: 1904, Va. Died: Mar. 25, 1968, Hollywood, Calif. Screen, stage and radio actor.

Appeared in: **1937** Public Cowboy No. 1. **1940** The Green Hornet (serial). **1947** The Crimson Key; Dangerous Venture. **1949** King of the Rocket Men (serial); Powder River Rustlers; The Golden Stallion; Hideout. **1950** No Sad Songs for Me; North of the Great Divide; At War With the Army; Rustlers on Horseback; Champagne for Caesar; Lucky Losers. **1951** Sky High; Horsie; Leave It to the Marines; Let's Go Navy. **1952** Actors and Sin. **1953** City of Bad Men. **1954** The Eddie Cantor Story. **1956** The Birds and the Bees. **1957** Short Cut to Hell; The Female Animal. **1965** The Family Jewels; I Saw What You Did. **1966** The Oscar. **1968** Panic in the City.

EVANS, DAME EDITH
Born: Feb. 8, 1888, London, England. Died: Oct. 14, 1976, Cranbrook, Kent, England. Screen, stage and television actress. In 1946 was created a Dame Commander of the Order of the British Empire. Nominated for 1963 Academy Award for Best Supporting Actress in Tom Jones; in 1964 for The Chalk Garden and in 1967 as Best Actress for The Whisperers.

Appeared in: **1915** A Welsh Singer. **1916** East is East. **1949** The Queen of Spades (US 1950); The Last Days of Dolwyn (aka Woman of Dolwyn—US). **1952** The Importance of Being Earnest. **1959** Look Back in Anger; The Nun's Story. **1963** Tom Jones. **1964** The Chalk Garden. **1965** Young Cassidy. **1966** The Whisperers (US 1967). **1967** Fitzwilly. **1968** Prudence and the Pill. **1969** David Copperfield; The Madwoman of Chaillot; Crooks and Coronets (aka Sophie's Place—US 1970). **1970** Scrooge. **1973** A Doll's House. **1974** Craze. **1976** The Slipper and the Rose (The Story of Cinderella). **1977** The Abbess of Philadelphia (aka Nasty Habits—US).

EVANS, EDITH
Born: 1894. Died: Oct. 12, 1962, Madison, N.J. Screen actress. Appeared in silents. Do not confuse with Dame Edith Evans, English actress.

EVANS, EVAN

Born: 1901, Birkenhead, England. Died: Jan. 3, 1954, New York, N.Y. (heart ailment). Opera singer and screen actor. Appeared during the 1930's in film/musical shorts.

Appeared in: **1941** How Green Was My Valley.

EVANS, FRED "PIMPLE"

Born: 1889, England. Died: 1951, England? Screen actor, film director, screenwriter, burlesque and circus performer. Appeared in burlesque with his brother Joe Evans (dec. 1967).

Appeared in: **1910** A Costly Gift; The Last of the Dandy; Prison Reform; As Prescribed by a Doctor; The Marriage of Muggins VC and a Further Exploit. **1911** Charley Smiler Joins the Boy Scouts; Charley Smiler Takes Brain Food; Charley Smiler Competes in a Cycle Race; Charley Smiler Takes Up Ju-Jitsu; Charley Smiler Is Robbed (aka Charley Smiler Loses His Watch—US); Charley Smiler Is Stage Struck (aka Smiler Has Stage Fever—US); Stop the Fight. **1912** Cowboy Mad (with Joe); Pimple Does the Turkey Trot; The Taming of Big Ben; Pimple and the Snake; The Whisling Bet (with Joe); Grand Harlequinade (with Joe); Pimple Gets A Quid (with Joe); Pimple Wins a Bet (with Joe); Pimple's Fire Brigade (with Joe); Pimple as a Cinema Actor; Pimple as a Ballet Dancer; Pimple as a Rent Collector; Fred's Police Force (with Joe); Fifty Years After; A Novel Burglary; Wanted a Wife and Child; The Little General. **1913** Pimple Goes A-Busking; The Adventures of Pimple—Pimple PC; Pimple, Detective; Pimple Writes a Cinema Plot; Pimple and the Gorilla; Miss Pimple, Suffragette; Pimple Meets Captain Scuttle (with Joe); Adventures of Pimple—The Indian Massacre; Pimple's Complaint; Two to One on Pimple; Pimple's Motor Trap (with Joe); Pimple's Sporting Chance (with Joe); Pimple Takes a Picture; Pimple Gets the Sack; Adventures of Pimple—The Battle of Waterloo (with Joe); Pimple's Rest Cure; Pimple's Wonderful Gramophone; Pimple Joins the Army; A Bathroom Problem; A Tragedy in Pimple's Life; Dick Turpin's Ride to Yorke; Pimple's Motor Bike; Pimple Does the Hat Trick; Pimple's Wife; Pimple's Inferno; Pimple Goes Fishing; When Pimple Was Young; Pimple the Sport; Pimple Gets the Jumps; Once Upon a Time (with Joe); Slippery Pimple; Lieutenant Pimple on Secret Service; How Pimple Saved Kissing Cup; Pimple's Great Bull Fight; Pimple's Midnight Ramble; What Happened to Pimple—The Suicide; Pimple's New Job. **1914** Pimple's Humanity; Lieutenant Pimple and the Stolen Submarine; What Happened to Pimple—The Gentleman Burglar (with Joe); When Pimple Was Young—His First Sweetheart; Pimple Elopes; Lieutenant Pimple's Dash for the Pole (with Joe); When Pimple Was Young—Young Pimple's Schooldays; Pimple and Galatea; Pimple in the Grip of the Law; What Happened to Pimple—In the Hands of the London Crook; The House of Distemperley; Young Pimple and His Little Sister; Pimple Goes to Paris; The Battle of Gettysownback; Lieutenant Pimple's Sealed Orders; The Whitewashers (with Joe); How Pimple Won the Derby; Pimple's Burglar Scare; Lieutenant Pimple Goes to Mexico (with Joe); Pimple 'Midst Raging Beasts; Stolen Honours (with Joe); Pimple in Society (with Joe); Pimple's Advice; Pimple's Trousers; Pimple Turns Honest; Pimple, Anarchist; Broncho Pimple; Pimple, Counter Jumper; Pimple's Vengeance; Pimple Pinched (with Joe); Pimple's Last Resource; Pimple Beats Jack Johnson; Pimple's Escape from Portland; Lieutenant Pimple, Gunrunner; Pimple, MP; Pimple's Proposal; Pimple's Charge of the Light Brigade; Lieutenant Pimple and the Stolen Invention; Pimple Enlists; Pimple's Great Fire; Pimple, Special Constable; Pimple's Prison; Lieutenant Pimple, King of Cannibal Islands; Pimple's Leap to Fortune; The Clowns of Europe (with Joe); Inspector Pimple; How Lieutenant Pimple Captured the Kaiser; Pimple and the Stolen Plans (with Joe); Pimple on Football; The Adventures of Pimple—The Spiritualist (with Joe); The Adventures of Pimple—Trilby (aka Tribly by Pimple and Co., with Joe). **1915** Pimple's Ivanhoe (reissue of 1913 film); Mrs. Raffles Nee Pimpie (with Joe); Pimple in the Kilties; Judge Pimple (with Joe); Sexton Pimple; Flash Pimple the Master Crook (with Joe); Pimple's Storyette; Pimple's Dream of Victory; Pimple, The Bad Girl of the Family (with Joe); Pimple, Child Stealer; Pimple Copped (with Joe); Pimple's Million Dollar Mystery (aka Flivver's Famous Cheese Hound—US); Pimple's The Man Who Stayed at Home; Pimple's Past (aka Flivver's Terrible Past—US); Pimple's The Case of Johnny Walker; Pimple Three Weeks Without the Option; Pimple's Royal Divorce; Pimple's Peril; Pimple's Art of Mystery (aka Flivver's Art of Mystery—US); Pimple's Rival; Pimple's Dilemma (aka Flivver's Dilemma—US); Liza's Legacy; Pimple's Holiday; Tally Ho! Pimple; Pimple's Scrap of Paper; The Kaiser Captures Pimple; The Smugglers; For Her Brother's Sake; Driven by Hunger; Pimple's Boy Scout; Mademoiselle Pimple; Pimple's Burlesque of the Still Alarm (aka Flivver's Still Alarm—US); Pimple Has One; Pimple's Good Turn (aka Flivver's Good Turn—US, with Joe); Pimple Up the Pole; Pimple's Three; Pimple's Road to Ruin; Pimple Explains; Aladdin; War Pimple (W) Right?; Pimple's Uncle; Pimple Sees Ghosts; Pimple

Acts; Pimple Will Treat; Pimple's Artful Dodge; Pimple Gets the Hump; Some Fun; A Study in Skarlit; Ragtime Cowboy Pimple; Pimple's Willit-Wasit-Isit; Pimple's Some Burglar; Pimple's Motor Tour; Pimple's Three O'Clock Rage. **1916** How Lieutenant Pimple Captured the Kaiser (reissue of 1914 film); How Pimple Saved Kissing Cup (reissue of 1913 film); Pimple Beats Jack Johnson (reissue of 1914 film); The Adventures of Pimple—The Spiritualist (reissue of 1914 film); Pimple's Great Adventure; Pimple's Crime; Pimple's Part; Pimple Ends It; Pimple's Zeppelin Scare; Pimple's Double (with Joe); Pimple's Pink Forms; Pimple Splits the Difference; Pimple's Arm of the Law; Pimple—Himself and Others; Pimple Poor but Dishonest; Pimple as Hamlet; Pimple's A Woman in the Case (with Joe); Diamond Cut Diamond; Pimple's Tenth Commandment; Pimple's Silver Lagoon; Some Monkey Business (aka Pimple's Monkey Business, with Joe); Pimple's Clutching Hand; The Merry Wives of Pimple (aka Pimple's Merry Wives); Pimple's Nautical Story. **1917** Lieutenant Pimple's Sealed Orders (reissue of 1914 film); Pimple's The Whip; Pimple's Senseless Censoring; Pimple's Motor Tour; Pimple's Mystery of the Closed Door; Some Dancer; Saving Raffles (with Joe); Pimple's Tableaux Vivants; Oliver Twisted; Pimple-His Voluntary Corps; Pimple's Romance; Pimple's Pitter-Patter; Pimple's Lady Godiva; Pimple's The Woman Who Did. **1918** Rations; Pimple's Better 'Ole (with Joe); Inns and Outs (with Joe). **1919** Pimple's The Whip (reissue of 1917 film). **1920** Pimple's Topical Gazette (with Joe). **1922** Pimple's Three Musketeers.

EVANS, HELEN ST. CLAIR

Born: 1905. Died: June 6, 1927, Hollywood, Calif. Screen actress.

EVANS, HELENA PHILLIPS

Born: 1875. Died: July 24, 1955, Santa Monica, Calif. (heart attack). Stage and screen actress. She appeared as both Helena Phillips and Helena Evans. Married to actor Charles E. Evans (dec. 1945).

Appeared in: **1921** My Lady's Latchkey. **1929** The Greene Murder Case. **1932** Two Seconds; Life Begins. **1933** The King's Vacation; Voltaire; Design for Living. **1934** Elmer and Elsie; I'll Fix It; Kiss and Make Up. **1935** College Scandal. **1938** Nancy Drew, Detective; My Bill. **1939** 6,000 Enemies. **1942** The Remarkable Andrew. **1947** My Favorite Brunette.

EVANS, HERBERT

Born: Apr. 16, 1883, London, England. Died: Feb. 10, 1952, San Gabriel, Calif. Stage and screen actor. Entered films in 1914.

Appeared in: **1927** The Devil Dancer. **1928** Speedy; Beyond London Lights; The Naughty Duchess. **1930** Way for a Sailor. **1933** Reunion in Vienna; Secrets; One Year Later; Brief Moment. **1934** The Gay Bride; Service With a Smile (short). **1935** The Glass Key; Peter Ibbetson. **1936** The Charge of the Light Brigade; And Sudden Death. **1937** Angel; High Flyers. **1938** The Adventures of Robin Hood; Everybody's Doing It; Dawn Patrol; The Mysterious Mr. Moto; Gangster's Boy. **1939** Susannah of the Mounties; The Adventures of Sherlock Holmes; The Rains Came; The Kid from Kokomo; Man About Town. **1940** Susan and God; The Blue Bird. **1941** How Green Was My Valley; One Night in Lisbon; Man Hunt. **1942** Journey for Margaret; Miss Minerver. **1943** Gildersleeve on Broadway. **1944** Abroad With Two Yanks; The White Cliffs of Dover; Up in Arms; None But the Lonely Heart; Her Primitive Man. **1945** The Corn Is Green. **1946** Pardon My Past; Bringing Up Father; Kitty. **1947** Ivy; Banjo; Fun on a Weekend; Singapore; Night Song. **1948** Hot Scots (short). **1949** Sky Liner; The Great Sinner; Who Done It? (short); Vagabond Loafers (short).

EVANS, JACK

Born: 1893. Died: Mar. 14, 1950, Hollywood, Calif. (heart attack). Screen actor.

Appeared in: **1922** The Hidden Woman. **1936** Guns and Guitars. **1937** Stuck in the Sticks (short).

EVANS, JOE

Born: 1891, England. Died: 1967, England? Screen actor, film director and screenwriter. Brother of actor Fred Evans (dec. 1951) with whom he appeared in burlesque and films. See Fred Evans for films they appeared in together. Do not confuse with U.S. actor (dec. 1973).

Appeared in: Who Will Marry Martha; Pearls of Death; The Terrible Two; The Terrible Two on the Mash; The Fiery Deeds of the Terrible

Two; The Terrible Two on the Warpath; The Terrible Two on the Twist; The Terrible Two on the Stage; The Terrible Two on the Wait; The Terrible Two on the Wangle; The Terrible Two in Luck; The Terrible Two, Kidnappers. **1915** The Terrible Two Abroad; The Terrible Two—A.B.S.; Mr. and Mrs. Piecan—The Giddy Husband; Piecan's Tonic; Ye Olde Waxworks by the Terrible Two; The Terrible Two Had; Poor Old Piecan; When the Germans Came; Lynxeye Trapped; Arabella Meets Rattles; Shells, More Shells; Joey's 21st Birthday. **1916** West End Pals; Joey's Aunt; Joey's Permit; Joey's High Jinks; Joey's Night Escapade; Joey's Apache Mania; Silas at the Seaside; Joey's Automatic Furniture; Joey's Dream; Joey's Liar Meter; A Boarding House Scandal; Joey The Showman; Joey's Pluck; Joey's Black Defeat; Joey Walks in His Sleep.

EVANS, JOE
Born: 1916. Died: Sept. 12, 1973, Woodland Hills, Calif. Screen and vaudeville actor. Appeared in vaudeville and films in a dance act with George Boyce.

Appeared in: **1954** Three Ring Circus (with Boyce). **1955** The Seven Little Foys (with Boyce).

EVANS, MADGE
Born: July 1, 1909, Manhattan, N.Y. Died: Apr. 26, 1981, Oakland, N.J. (cancer). Screen, stage, radio and television actress. Married to playwright Sidney Kingsley. Entered films in 1914 with World Film Corp.

Appeared in: **1915** Zaza; The Seven Sisters. **1916** The Revolt; The Hidden Scar; Broken Chains; Seventeen; Husband and Wife; Sudden Riches. **1917** The Little Patriot; The Adventures of Carol; The Beloved Adventuress; The Little Duchess; The Burglar; The Volunteer; The Web of Desire; Corner Grocer; Maternity. **1918** True Blue; Gates of Gladness; Golden Wall; The Power and the Glory; Stolen Orders; Neighbors; Wanted—A Mother. **1919** Love Nest; Home Wanted. **1923** On the Banks of the Wabash. **1924** Classmates. **1931** Sporting Blood; Son of India; Guilty Hands; Heartbreak. **1932** Lovers Courageous; Are You Listening?; The Greeks Had a Word for Them; Huddle; Fast Life; The Sign of the Cross; West of Broadway. **1933** Dinner at Eight; Broadway to Hollywood; Hell Below; Hallelujah, I'm a Bum; Made on Broadway; The Nuisance; The Mayor of Hell; Beauty for Sale; Day of Reckoning. **1934** The Show-Off; The Fugitive Lovers; Death on the Diamond; Grand Canary; Paris Interlude; Stand Up and Cheer; What Every Woman Knows. **1935** David Copperfield; Helldorado; Calm Yourself; Age of Indiscretion; Men Without Names; Trans-Atlantic Tunnel. **1936** Piccadilly Jim; Moonlight Murder; Exclusive Story; Pennies from Heaven. **1937** The Thirteenth Chair; Espionage. **1938** Sinners in Paradise; Army Girl. **1957** Hell Bound.

EVANS, NANCY
Died: July 29, 1963, Los Angeles, Calif. (cancer). Screen and stage actress. Married to actor/agent Jack Stuart-Fife.

Appeared in: **1944** Mr. Winkle Goes to War. **1945** Weekend at the Waldorf. **1946** The Stranger; Strange Triangle; My Reputation. **1947** Life With Father; The Homestretch. **1948** Family Honeymoon. **1956** The Peacemaker.

EVANS, PAULINE
Born: 1917. Died: Jan. 22, 1952, Calexico, Calif. Screen actress.

Appeared in: **1938** The Sisters. **1941** She Wouldn't Say No.

EVANS, RENEE
Born: 1908. Died: Dec. 22, 1971, Hollywood, Calif. (heart condition). Screen, stage actress and dancer. Married to stage actor John Alban and mother of stage actress Diane Alban.

Appeared in: **1933** 42nd Street. **1947** Ivy.

EVANS, REX
Born: 1903, England. Died: Apr. 3, 1969, Glendale, Calif. Screen and stage actor.

Appeared in: **1933** Along Came Sally. **1936** Camille. **1937** The Prince and the Pauper; The Wrong Road. **1939** Zaza. **1940** The Philadelphia Story; Adventure in Diamonds; I'm Nobody's Sweetheart Now. **1941** The Shanghai Gesture; The Flame of New Orleans; Suspicion; A Woman's Face. **1942** Keeper of the Flame; The Great Impersonation. **1943** Frankenstein Meets the Wolf Man. **1944** Higher and Higher; The Thin Man Goes Home; Ali Baba and the Forty Thieves. **1945** The Picture of Dorian Gray; Weekend at the Waldorf; Swing Out, Sister; Pursuit to Algiers. **1946** Till the Clouds Roll By; A Night in Paradise; Cluny Brown. **1947** Dangerous Millions. **1949** Adam's Rib. **1952** Captain Pirate. **1953** Loose in London; Jamaica Run. **1954** Knock on Wood; A Star Is Born; It Should Happen to You. **1956** The Birds and the Bees; Lust for Life. **1957** Merry Andrew. **1958** The Matchmaker. **1960** Midnight Lace. **1961** On the Double; All in a Night's Work.

EVANS, WILL
Born: May 29, 1872, London, England. Died: Apr. 11, 1931, London, England. Screen, stage actor, circus performer, author, playwright, songwriter and screenwriter. Son of circus performer Frederick William Evans (dec.). Brother of actress Winifred Evans.

Appeared in: **1899** They Do Such Things at Brighton; The Musical Eccentric (aka Will Evans the Living Catherine Wheel); Let 'Em All Come. **1900** The Rats. **1907** Will Evans: On the Doorstep; Novelette; The Jockey. **1913** Will Evans Harnessing a Horse. **1914** Building a Chicken House; The Jockey; Moving a Piano; The Showman's Dream; Tincture of Iron. **1915** Some Fun; A Study of Skarlit.

EVANSON, EDITH
Died: Nov. 29, 1980. Screen actress.

Appeared in: **1941** Life With Henry. **1942** Orchestra Wives; Girl Trouble; Woman of the Year. **1943** Bomber's Moon; Reunion in France. **1945** The Jade Mask. **1946** The Notorious Lone Wolf. **1947** Singapore. **1948** You Gotta Stay Happy; Rope; I Remember Mama. **1950** The Damned Don't Cry; Perfect Strangers; The Magnificent Yankee; The Redhead and the Cowboy. **1951** The Day the Earth Stood Still; Bomba and the Elephant Stampede. **1953** Shane; It Happens Every Thursday; Down Among the Sheltering Palms. **1954** Desiree. **1956** The Leather Saint; Storm Center. **1957** Drango; The Young Stranger; The Quiet Gun. **1960** Toby Tyler. **1964** Twice Told Tales (aka Rappaccini's Daughter).

EVELYN, CLARA (Clara Evelyn Smith)
Born: Jan. 1, 1886, London, England. Died: May 22, 1980, London, England. Screen, stage, television actress and pianist.

EVELYN, JUDITH (J. E. Allen)
Born: 1913. Died: May 7, 1967, New York, N.Y. (cancer). Screen, stage, television and radio actress.

Appeared in: **1951** The Thirteenth Letter. **1954** The Egyptian; Rear Window. **1955** Female on the Beach. **1956** Hilda Crane; Giant. **1958** The Brothers Karamazov; Twilight for the Gods. **1959** The Tingler.

EVELYNNE, MAY
Born: 1856. Died: Apr. 3, 1943, Los Angeles, Calif. Screen and stage actress.

EVEREST, BARBARA
Born: June 9, 1890, London, England. Died: Feb. 9, 1968, London, England. Screen, stage, television and radio actress.

Appeared in: **1916** The Man Without a Soul (aka I Believe—US 1917); The Morals of Weybury (aka The Hypocrites). **1919** Not Guilty; The Lady Clare; Whosoever Shall Offend; Till Our Ship Comes In (series). **1920** Calvary; The Joyous Adventures of Aristide Pujol; Testimony. **1921** The Bigamist. **1922** The Persistent Lovers; Fox Farm; A Romance of Old Bagdad. **1932** Lily Christine; When London Sleeps; The Lodger (aka The Phantom Fiend—US 1935); There Goes the Bride (US 1933); The World, The Flesh and the Devil. **1933** The Umbrella; The Wandering Jew; Love's Old Sweet Song; She Was Only a Village Maiden; The Lost Chord; The Road. **1934** Passing Shadows; The Warren Case. **1935** Scrooge; The Passing of the Third Floor Back. **1936** Love in Exile; Man Behind the Mask. **1937** Death Croons the Blues; Jump for Glory (aka When Thief Meets Thief—US); Old Mother Riley. **1939** Discoveries; Trunk Crime (aka Design for Murder—US 1940); Meet Maxwell Archer (aka Maxwell Archer, Detective—US 1942); Inquest. **1940** The Second Mr. Bush; Bringing It Home. **1941** He Found a Star; This Man is Dangerous (aka The Patient Vanishes—US 1947); Telefootlers; The Prime Minister. **1942** Commandos Strike at Dawn. **1943** Mission to Moscow; Phantom of the Opera. **1944** Jane Eyre; The Univited; Gaslight. **1945** The Valley of Decision; The Fatal Witness. **1946** Wanted for Murder. **1947** Frieda. **1949** Children of Chance. **1950** Madeleine; Tony Draws a Horse (US 1951). **1954** An Inspector Calls. **1958** The Safecracker. **1959** Upstairs and Downstairs (US 1961). **1961** Dangerous Afternoon; El Cid. **1962** The Damned (aka These Are The Damned—US 1964); The Man Who Finally Died (US 1967). **1963** Nurse on Wheels (US 1964). **1965** Rotten to the Core. **1969** Franchette—Les Intrigues.

EVERETT, TIMMIE
Born: 1938. Died: Mar. 4, 1977, New York, N.Y. (heart attack). Screen, stage, television actor, stage director and choreographer.

Appeared in: **1962** The Music Man.

EVERS, ERNEST P.
Born: 1874. Died: July 22, 1945, Hollywood, Calif. Screen and stage actor. Entered films approx. 1915.

EVERTON, PAUL
Born: 1869. Died: Feb. 26, 1948, Woodland Hills, Calif. (heart attack). Screen and stage actor.

Appeared in: **1917** Motherhood; The Debt; The Mirror. **1918** The Eagle's Eye (serial). **1921** Cappy Ricks; City of Silent Men; The Conquest of Canaan; Proxies; The Silver Lining. **1923** The Little Red Schoolhouse. **1925** That Royle Girl. **1937** They Won't Forget; The Life of Emile Zola; The Great Garrick. **1938** Reformatory; Touchdown Army; Midnight Intruder; The Beloved Brat; Merrily We Live; Outside the Law; Orphans of the Street; Gun Law; Strange Case of Dr. Meade. **1939** Topper Takes a Trip; Stand Up and Fight; Whispering Enemies; Trapped in the Sky; Maisie; Joe and Ethel Turp Call on the President; The Great Man Votes. **1940** Arise, My Love; Mexican Spitfire Out West; You the People (short); Pound Foolish (short); Prairie Law. **1941** Unfinished Business. **1942** Tennessee Johnson. **1945** Leave Her to Heaven.

EYSOLDT, GERTRUD
Born: 1871, Germany. Died: Jan. 6, 1955, Ohlstadt, West Germany. Screen, stage actress and stage director.

Appeared in: **1953** Keepers of the Night.

EYTHE, WILLIAM (William John Joseph Eythe)
Born: Apr. 7, 1918, Mars, Pa. Died: Jan. 26, 1957, Los Angeles, Calif. (acute hepatitis). Screen, stage, radio, television actor, stage producer and stage director. Divorced from actress Buff Cobb.

Appeared in: **1943** The Ox-Bow Incident (film debut); The Song of Bernadette. **1944** The Eve of St. Mark; Wilson; A Wing and a Prayer. **1945** Czarina; The House on 92nd Street; A Royal Scandal; Colonel Effingham's Raid. **1946** Centennial Summer; Man of the Hour. **1948** Meet Me at Dawn; Mr. Reckless. **1949** Special Agent. **1950** Customs Agent.

FABER, LESLIE
Born: Aug. 30, 1879, Newcastle-on-Tyne, England. Died: Aug. 5, 1929, London, England (pneumonia). Screen and stage actor. Divorced from Winifred Arthur-Jones and later married to stage actress Gladys Gray.

Appeared in: **1929** The Three Passions; White Cargo (US 1930).

FABRE, SATURNIN
Born: 1884, France. Died: Oct. 24, 1961, Paris, France. Screen and stage actor.

Appeared in: **1932** Paris-Bequin. **1936** Les Petits. **1937** Pepe le Moko (US 1941). **1938** Generals Without Buttons. **1939** Ils Etaient Neufs Celibataires (Nine Bachelors—US 1942). **1940** The Mayor's Dilemma. **1942** The Pasha's Wives. **1948** Un Ami Viendra Ce Soir (A Friend Will Come Tonight). **1950** Gates of the Night; The Scandals of Clochemerle; Ignace. **1951** Miquette. **1952** The French Way (US 1959). **1953** L'ennemi Public No. 1 (aka The Most Wanted Man in the World—US 1962). **1955** Holiday for Henrietta.

FABREGAS, VIRGINIA
Born: 1870, Vautepec, Morelos, Mexico. Died: Nov. 17, 1950, Mexico City, Mexico. Stage and screen actress. Made Spanish language films in Hollywood in 1919 and 1937-38.

Appeared in: **1934** La Sangre Manda. **1938** Abnegacion.

FABRIZI, MARIO
Born: 1925. Died: Apr. 5, 1963, London, England. Screen, stage and television actor.

Appeared in: **1962** Postman's Knock; On the Beat; Operation Snatch; Ring-A-Ding Rhythm! **1963** The Punch and Judy Man.

FADDEN, GENEVIEVE
Born: Oakdale, Calif. Died: Mar. 28, 1959, Santa Monica, Calif. Screen, stage and vaudeville actress. Married to actor Tom Fadden.

FADDEN, TOM
Born: 1895. Died: Apr. 14, 1980, Vero Beach, Fla. Screen, stage, vaudeville and television actor.

Appeared in: **1939** I Stole a Million; Destry Rides Again. **1940** Winners of the West (serial); Congo Maisie; Zanzibar; The Captain is a Lady. **1941** The Shepherd of the Hills; Kiss the Boys Goodbye. **1942** Sundown Jim; The Lone Star Ranger; The Remarkable Andrew; Wings for the Eagle; Pardon My Sarong; The Night Before the Divorce. **1943** Edge of Darkness; Riding High; The Good Fellows; Frontier Badman; A Lady Takes a Chance; Northern Pursuit; In Society. **1944** The Hairy

Ape; Henry Aldrich's Little Secret; Three Little Sisters; Tomorrow the World!; The Naughty Nineties. **1945** The Royal Mounted Rides Again (serial); Murder, He Says; State Fair. **1946** The Big Sleep. **1947** Cheyene; Dragnet; That Hagen Girl. **1948** A Miracle Can Happen; State of the Union; The Inside Story; The Dude Goes West. **1949** Bad Men of Tombstone. **1950** Singing Guns. **1951** Drums in the Deep South. **1953** Kansas Pacific. **1955** Thy Neighbor's Daughter; The Tall Men; Prince of Players; They Came From Another World. **1956** Invasion of the Body Snatchers. **1957** Baby Face Nelson. **1959** Edge of Eternity. **1960** Toby Tyler. **1961** Pocketful of Miracles. **1962** Paradise Alley. **1969** Flareup; They Shoot Horses, Don't They? **1970** Dirty Dingus Magee. **1977** Empire of the Ants.

FAGAN, BARNEY
Born: Jan. 12, 1850, Boston, Mass. Died: Jan. 12, 1937, Bayshore, New York. Screen and stage actor.

Appeared in: **1930** MGM short.

FAHEY, MYRNA
Born: 1939. Died: May 6, 1973, Santa Monica, Calif. Screen and television actress.

Appeared in: **1957** Jeanne Eagles. **1959** Face of a Fugitive; The Story on Page One. **1960** The House of Usher.

FAHRNEY, MILTON H.
Born: 1871. Died: Mar. 27, 1941, Culver City, Calif. (heart attack). Screen, stage actor and film director. Entered films in 1907.

Appeared in: **1924** Not Built for Runnin'; Yankee Speed. **1926** Chasing Trouble. **1927** In the First Degree. **1929** Untamed.

FAIN, JOHN
Born: 1915, Jonesville, La. Died: Jan. 2, 1970, Malibu, Calif. (hit by car). Screen actor.

Appeared in: **1963** Beach Party. **1964** Pajama Party.

FAIR, ELINOR
Born: Dec. 21, 1903, Richmond, Va. Died: Apr. 26, 1957, Seattle, Wash. Screen, stage and vaudeville actress. Divorced from actor William Boyd (dec. 1972). She was a Wampas Baby Star of 1924.

Appeared in: **1919** Miracle Man. **1920** Kismet; Broadway and Home. **1921** Cold Steel; It Can Be Done; Through the Back Door. **1922** The Able-minded Lady; Big Stakes; Dangerous Pastime; White Hands. **1923** Driven; The Eagle's Feather; Has the World Gone Mad!; The Mysterious Witness; One Million in Jewels. **1924** The Law Forbids. **1925** Flyin' Thru; Gold and the Girl; Timber Wolf; Trapped; The Wife Who Wasn't Wanted. **1926** Bachelor Brides; The Volga Boatman. **1927** Jim the Conquerer; My Friend from India; The Yankee Clipper. **1928** Let 'Er Go Gallegher. **1929** Sin Town. **1932** 45 Caliber Echo; Night Rider. **1934** The Scarlet Empress.

FAIR, VIRGINIA
Born: 1899. Died: Sept. 8, 1948, Hollywood, Calif. Screen actress. Do not confuse with actress Virginia Brown Faire (dec. 1980).

FAIRBANKS, DOUGLAS, SR. (Douglas Elton Ullman)
Born: May 23, 1883, Denver, Colo. Died: Dec. 12, 1939, Santa Monica, Calif. (heart attack). Screen, stage actor and film director. Won Photoplay 1922 Medal of Honor for Robin Hood. Divorced from Beth Sully and actress Mary Pickford (dec. 1979). Married to Lady Sylvia Ashley (dec. 1977). Father of actor Douglas Fairbanks, Jr.

Appeared in: **1915** The Lamb (film debut); His Picture in the Papers; Double Trouble. **1916** Reggie Mixes In; The Americano; The Matrimaniac; Manhattan Madness; The Good Bad Man; Flirting With Fate; Half Breed; American Aristocracy; The Habit of Happiness. **1917** In Again, Out Again; Wild and Wooly; Down to Earth; The Man from Painted Post; Reaching for the Moon. **1918** Headin' South; Mr. Fix-It; Say! Young Fellow; War Relief; Bound in Morocco; He Comes Up Smiling; Arizona. **1919** Knickerbocker Buckaroo; His Majesty the American; Modern Musketeers. **1920** Where the Clouds Roll By; The Mollycoddle; The Mark of Zorro. **1921** The Nut; The Three Musketeers. **1922** Robin hood. **1924** The Thief of Bagdad. **1925** Don Q. **1926** The Black Pirate. **1927** The Gaucho; Show People. **1929** The Iron Mask; Taming of the Shrew. **1931** Reaching for the Moon (and 1917 version); Around the World in 80 Minutes. **1932** Mr. Robinson Crusoe. **1934** The Private Life of Don Juan. **1961** Days of Thrills and Laughter (documentary). **1963** The Great Chase (documentary). **1973** Sky High (documentary). **1974** That's Entertainment (film clips).

FAIRBANKS, FLOBELLE
Born: 1910. Died: Jan. 5, 1969, New York, N.Y. (heart attack). Screen actress.

Appeared in: **1925** Stella Dallas. **1926** Eyes Right! **1927** The Love of Sunya; The Climbers; Sorrell and Son; What Happened to Father.

FAIRBANKS, FRED T.
Born: 1871. Died: May 15, 1927, Coney Island, N.Y. (tuberculosis). Screen and stage actor.

FAIRBANKS, WILLIAM
Born: May 24, 1894, St. Louis, Mo. Died: Apr. 1, 1945, Los Angeles, Calif. (lobar pneumonia). Screen and stage actor.

Appeared in: **1921** Broadway Buckaroo; Go Get Him; A Western Adventurer; Montana Bill. **1922** Fighting Hearts; Hell's Border; The Clean Up; Peaceful Peters; A Western Demon. **1923** Sheriff of Sun Dog; Sun Dog Trail; The Devil's Dooryard; Law Rustlers; Spawn of the Desert. **1924** The Battling Fool; Border Women; Women First; The Beautiful Sinner; Call of the Mate; The Cowboy and the Flapper; Do It Now; Down by the Rio Grande; The Fatal Mistake; A Fight for Honor; Her Man; Man from God's Country; Marry in Haste; The Martyr Sex; The Other Kind of Love; Racing for Life; Tainted Money; That Wild West; The Torrent. **1925** The Fearless Lover; A Fight to the Finish; Fighting Youth; The Great Sensation; The Handsome Brute; New Champion; Speed Mad. **1926** Flying High; The Mile-a-Minute Man; The Winning Wallop; Vanishing Millions (serial). **1927** When Danger Calls; Catch-As-Catch-Can; The Down Grade; One Chance in a Million; Spoilers of the West; Through Thick and Thin. **1928** Wyoming; Under the Black Eagle; The Vanishing West (serial).

FAIRBROTHER, SYDNEY
Born: July 31, 1872, England. Died: Jan. 4, 1941, London, England. Screen and stage actress.

Appeared in: **1915** Iron Justice. **1916** The Game of Liberty (aka Under Suspicion—US); The Mother of Dartmoor; A Mother's Influence; Frailty (aka Temptation's Hour); Me and Me Moke (aka Me and M'Pal—US). **1917** Auld Lang Syne. **1919** In Bondage (aka Faith). **1920** Laddie; The Children of Gibeon; A Temporary Gentleman. **1921** The Bachelor's Club; The Rotters; The Golden Dawn. **1923** Maisie's Marriage (aka Married Love and Married Life); Love, Life and Laughter (aka Tip Toes); Heartstrings; The Beloved Vagabond; The Rest Cure; Don Quixote; Sally Bishop. **1924** Reveille; Pett Ridge Stories (series). **1925** Mrs. May Comedies (series). **1926** Nell Gwynne. **1927** The Silver Lining; Confetti; My Lord the Chauffeur. **1931** The Other Mrs. Phipps. **1932** Murder on the Second Floor; The Third String; Postal Orders; A Letter of Warning; Double Dealing; Down Our Street; Insult; The Return of Raffles; Lucky Ladies; The Temperence Fete. **1933** Excess Baggage; Home Sweet Home. **1934** The Spotting series including: A Touching Story; The Crucifix; Chu Chin Chow; Gay Love. **1935** Brewster's Millions; The Private Secretary; The Last Journey (US 1936). **1936** All In; Fame. **1937** Dreaming Lips; King Solomon's Mines; Paradise for Two (aka The Gaiety Girls—US 1938); Rose of Tralee (US 1938). **1938** Make it Three; Little Dolly Daydream.

FAIRE, VIRGINIA BROWN (Virginia LaBiuna)
Born: June 26, 1904, Brooklyn, N.Y. Died: June 30, 1980, Laguna Beach, Calif. Screen and radio actress. Divorced from Jack Daughterty and film producer Howard "Duke" Worne (dec. 1933). Later married to businessman William Bayer. Won Motion Picture Classic Fame and Fortune Contest in 1919.

Appeared in: **1921** Without Benefit of Clergy; Doubling for Romeo; Fightin' Mad. **1922** Omar the Tentmaker; Monte Cristo. **1923** Stormswept; The Cricket on the Hearth; Shadows of the North; Vengeance of the Deep. **1924** Romance Ranch; The Lightning Rider; Welcome Stranger; Thundergate; The Air Hawk. **1925** Peter Pan; Recompense Friendly Enemies; Proud Heart; The Calgary Stampede; His People; The Thoroughbred. **1926** Racing Romance; Wings of the Storm; Chip of the Flying U.; The Temptress; The Wolf Hunters; Broadway Billy; Desert Valley; The Mile-a-Minute Man; Frenzied Flames. **1927** Tracked by the Police; White Flannels; Gun Gospel; Hazardous Valley; Pleasure Before Business; The Devil's Masterpiece. **1928** The Body Punch; A Race for Life; The Chorus Kid; The House of Shame; Undressed; Queen of the Chorus; The Canyon of Adventure; Danger Patrol. **1929** Burning the Wind; The Donovan Affair; The Devil's Chaplain; Handcuffed; Untamed Justice. **1930** Murder on the Roof; The Lonesome Trail; Trails of Peril; Breed of the West. **1931** Hell's Valley; Secret Menace; Alias the Bad Man. **1932** Last Ride; Lone Trail; Tex Takes a Holiday. **1934** West of the Divide; Tracy Rides.

FAIRFAX, BETTY
Born: England. Died: 1962, Los Angeles, Calif. Screen, stage actress and talent agent. Married to actor Keith Kenneth (dec. 1966).

Appeared in: **1946** Sister Kenny; Cluny Brown. **1947** The Private Affairs of Bel Ami; Imperfect Lady. **1948** The Paradise Case; The Black Arrow. **1951** Lorna Doone. **1962** The Notorious Landlady.

FAIRFAX, JAMES
Born: 1897, England. Died: May 8, 1961, Papeete, Tahiti (heart attack). Screen, television and vaudeville actor.

Appeared in: **1948** If Winter Comes; The Challenge. **1949** Mrs. Mike. **1950** Tyrant of the Sea; Customs Agent; Fortunes of Captain Blood. **1951** Royal Wedding. **1952** Last Train from Bombay. **1953** Loose in London; White Goddess; Abbott and Costello Meet Dr. Jekyll & Mr. Hyde. **1962** Mutiny on the Bounty (died while filming).

FAIRFAX, LETTICE
Born: Mar. 26, 1876, England. Died: Dec. 25, 1948, England? Screen and stage actress.

Appeared in: **1915** Brother Officers.

FAIRMAN, AUSTIN
Born: Mar. 4, 1892, London, England. Died: Mar. 26, 1964, Dedham, Mass. Screen, stage, radio actor and playwright. Married to actress Hilda Moore (dec. 1929).

Appeared in: **1930** Her Hired Husband. **1931** The Grand Dame (short). **1938** The Adventures of Robin Hood; Bulldog Drummond's Peril. **1940** British Intelligence.

FALCONETTI, RENEE
Born: 1901, France. Died: Dec. 12, 1946, Buenos Aires, Argentina. Screen and stage actress.

FALCONI, ARMANDO
Born: 1872, Italy. Died: Sept. 10, 1954, Milan, Italy. Screen and stage actor. Son of stage actors Pietro Falconi (dec.) and Adelaide Negri (dec.).

Appeared in: **1932** Rubacuori. **1933** Passa L'Amore. **1936** Il Re Burlone. **1939** Lo Zio d'America (The Uncle from America). **1940** Il Documente Fatale. **1948** Rossini; The Spirit and the Flesh.

FALCONI, ARTURO
Born: Italy. Died: Nov. 12, 1934, Italy? Screen actor.

Appeared in: **1932** La Vecchia Signora; Il Cappelle a Tre Punte (US 1936).

FALKENSTEIN, JULIUS
Born: 1879, Germany. Died: Dec. 9, 1933, Germany? Screen actor.

Appeared in: **1925** Ein Walzertraum (The Waltz Dream—US 1926). **1929** His Late Excellency; Meistersinger; Beautiful Blue Danube; Dancing Vienna. **1930** Nur am Rhein (US 1931); Brand in der Oper (US 1932); Die Lustigen Musikanten (US 1933). **1931** Luegen auf Ruegen; Inquest; Voruntersuchung; Der Wahre Jakob (aka Das Maedchen vom Variete); Nie Wieder Liebe (US 1932); Sein Scheidungsgrund (US 1932); Stuerme der Leidenschaft (US 1932); Ein Ausgekochter Junge (US 1932). **1932** Secrets of the Orient; Die Csikos Baroness; Liebe ist Liebe; Week-End Im Paradies; Mensch Ohne Namen (Man Without a Name); Drunter und Drueber; Holzapfel weiss Alles (US 1933); Marion, das Gehoert Sinch Nicht (US 1934). **1933** Ich und die Kaiserin; Lachende Erben; Die Kalte Mamsell (US 1935). **1934** Heart Song; Wenn Herzen Sich Finden.

FALLON, CHARLES (Charles Ludovic Van Der Belen)
Born: 1885, Antwerp, Belgium. Died: Mar. 11, 1936, Hollywood, Calif. (heart attack). Screen, stage actor, film producer, and film director.

Appeared in: **1935** Alias Mary Dow; Ruggles of Red Gap; The Man Who Broke the Bank at Monte Carlo. **1936** Next Time We Love.

FALLON, GABRIEL
Born: 1899, Dublin, Ireland. Died: June 10, 1980, Dublin, Ireland. Screen, stage actor, stage director, playwright, critic, author and university lecturer.

Appeared in: **1938** Men of Ireland.

FANNING, FRANK B.
Born: 1880. Died: Mar. 3, 1934, Los Angeles, Calif. Screen and stage actor.

Appeared in: **1922** The Masked Avenger. **1930** Guilty. **1934** The St. Louis Kid. **1935** The Case of the Curious Bride.

FAREBROTHER, VIOLET
Born: Aug. 22, 1888, Grimsby, Lincs, England. Died: Sept. 27, 1969, Eastbourne, Sussex, England. Stage and screen actress.

Appeared in: **1911** Richard III (stage and film versions). **1927**

Downhill (aka When Boys Leave Home—US 1928); Easy Virtue (US 1928). **1930** At the Villa Rose (aka Mystery at the Villa Rose—US); Murder. **1933** Enemy of the Police; This Acting Business. **1934** Nine Forty-Five; The Official Wife. **1935** It's a Bet; Mr. Cohen Takes a Walk (US 1936). **1936** Where's Sally? **1937** It's Not Crickett; Change for a Sovereign; Les Perles de la Couronne. **1945** The Voice Within. **1948** Cup-Tie Honeymoon; Look Before You Love. **1955** Man of the Moment; The Woman for Joe. **1957** Fortune is a Woman (aka She Played With Fire—US 1958). **1958** The Solitary Child.

FARFAN, MARIAN
Born: 1913. Died: Apr. 3, 1965, Hollywood, Calif. Screen actress.

FARFARIELLO (Edward Migliaccio)
Born: 1881, Salerno, Italy. Died: Mar. 28, 1946, N.Y. Screen, vaudeville and radio actor. Appeared in several Hollywood shorts.

FARINA See HOSKINS, ALLEN

FARINA, NINO (Giuseppe Farina)
Born: Oct. 10, 1908, Turin, Italy. Died: June, 1966, near Chambery, France (auto accident). Auto racer, screen actor and attorney.

Appeared in: **1966** Grand Prix.

FARINA, RICHARD
Born: 1937, New York, N.Y. Died: Apr. 30, 1966, Carmel, Calif. (motorcycle accident). Novelist, singer and screen actor. Married to actress Mimi Baez.

Appeared in: **1967** Festival.

FARLEY, DOT (Dorothea Farley)
Born: Feb. 6, 1881, Chicago, Ill. Died: May 2, 1971, South Pasadena, Calif. Screen, stage actress and screenwriter.

Appeared in: **1910** Romantic Redskins. **1912** At the Basket Picnic; A Wife Wanted; Perils of the Plains; Raiders on the Mexican Border. **1913** A Life in the Balance. **1914** Soul Mates; Her Bandit Sweetheart; The Toll of the Warpath; How Johanna Saved the Home. **1915** Buy, Buy Baby; Her New Job; Wheeled Into Matrimony; Oh, You Female Cop; Married in Disguise; She Couldn't Get Away From It; When Quality Meets; Aunt Matilda Outwitted; The Poor Fixer; Sammy's Scandalous Schemes. **1917** The House of Terrible Scandals. **1918** Wooing of Coffee Cake Kate. **1921** Home Talent; A Small Town Idol. **1922** Young Sherlock (short); The Crossroads of New York. **1923** Pitfalls of a Big City; The Acquittal; Boy of Mine; Tea—With a Kick. **1924** The Enemy Sex; The Fatal Mistake; Listen Lester; So Big; The Signal Tower; Vanity's Pride. **1925** The Wild Goose Chaser; Border Intrigue; Lure of the Track; My Son; Rugged Water; A Woman of the World. **1926** Brooding Eyes; The Family Upstairs; The Grand Duchess and the Waiter; Honesty—The Best Policy; The Little Irish Girl; Memory Lane; Money Talks; The Still Alarm; Young April; Weak But Billing (short). **1927** The Girl from Everywhere (short); All Aboard; The Climbers; His First Flame; The King of Kings; The Lost Limited; McFadden's Flats; Nobody's Widow; The Overland Stage; The Shamrock and the Rose; Yours to Command; The Tired Business Man. **1928** The Bicycle Flirt (short); The Girl From Nowhere (short); Black Feather; Celebrity; The Code of Scarlet; Lady Be Good; The Head Man; Should a Girl Marry? **1929** Divorce Made Easy; Why Leave Home?; Marquis Preferred; Whirls and Girls (short); The Bee's Buzz (short). **1930** Harmony at Home; The Little Accident; Road to Paradise; The Third Alarm; Swell People (short). **1931** Dancing Dynamite; Law of the Tongs; plus the following shorts: The Dog Doctor; Lemon Meringue; Thanks Again; Camping Out. **1932** While Paris Sleeps; plus the following shorts: Bon Voyage; Mother-in-Law's Day; Giggle Water; The Golf Chump; Parlor, Bedroom and Wrath; Fish Feathers. **1933** The following shorts: Art in the Raw; The Merchant of Menace; Good Housewrecking; Quiet, Please; What Fur; Grin and Bear It. **1934** Love Past Thirty; Down to Their Last Yacht; Mr. Average Man series; plus the following shorts: Love on a Ladder; Wrong Direction; In-Laws Are Out; A Blasted Event; Poisoned Ivory; Fixing a Stew. **1935** Diamond Jim; False Pretenses; plus the following shorts: Tramp Tramp Tramp; South Seasickness; Bric-a-Brac; Sock Me to Sleep; Edgar Hamlet; In Love at 40; Happy Tho Married. **1936** The following shorts: Will Power; Gasoloons; High Beer Pressure; Dummy Ache. **1937** Too Many Wives; A Rented Riot (short). **1938** Stranger from Arizona; Lawless Valley; Road to Reno. **1939** The Women. **1941** Obliging Young Lady. **1942** Cat People; plus the following shorts: Heart Burn; Inferior Decorator; Cooks and Crooks; Two for the Money; Rough on Rents; Duck Soup. **1943** The following shorts: Hold Your Temper; Indian Signs; Hot Foot; Not On My Account; Unlucky Dog. **1944** Hail the Conquering Hero; San Fernando Valley; plus the following shorts: Prunes and Politics; Radio Rampage; Feather Your Nest. **1945** The following shorts: Sleepless Tuesday; What, No Cigarettes?; It's Your Move; The Big Beef; Mother-in-Law's Day (and

1932 version). **1946** The following shorts: Trouble or Nothing; Wall Street Blues; Motor Maniacs; Noisy Neighbors; I'll Build It Myself; Social Terrors. **1947** They Won't Believe Me; plus the following shorts: Do or Diet; Heading for Trouble; Host to a Ghost; Television Turmoil; Mind Over Mouse. **1948** Variety Time; plus the following shorts: Brother Knows Best; No More Relatives; How to Clean House; Home Canning; Contest Crazy.

FARLEY, FREDERICK
Born: 1913, England. Died: July 23, 1978, London, England. Screen, stage actor and stage producer.

Appeared in: **1959** Nebo Zovyot (Battle Beyond the Sun—US 1963).

FARLEY, JAMES LEE "JIM"
Born: Jan. 8, 1882, Waldron, Ark. Died: Oct. 12, 1947, Pacoima, Calif. Screen and stage actor.

Appeared in: **1919** Nugget Nell. **1921** That Something; The Devil Within; Bar Nothin'; The One-Man Trail; Bucking the Line. **1922** Gleam O'Dawn; Travelin' On; When Danger Smiles; Boy Crazy; Little Wildcat; My Wild Irish Rose. **1923** Trifling With Honor; The Woman With Four Faces; Wild Bill Hickok. **1924** The City That Never Sleeps. **1925** A Son of His Father. **1926** The Lodge in the Wilderness. **1927** King of Kings; The Tired Business Man; The General. **1928** The Racket; Shady Lady; The Grip of the Yukon; Mad Hour; The Perfect Crime; A Woman Against the World. **1929** Weary River; In Old Arizona; Hunted; The Voice of the City; The Dance of Life; The Godless Girl; Courtin' Wildcats; Dynamite. **1930** Lucky Larkin; Danger Lights. **1931** Fighting Caravans; Three Rogues. **1932** Scandal for Sale. **1934** Here Comes the Groom. **1935** Frisco Kid; Hold 'Em Yale; Down to Their Last Yacht; Midnight Phantom; Westward Ho. **1936** High Treason; Captain January; Dancing Pirate; Song of the Saddle; The Bride Walks Out. **1937** The Girl With Ideas; Breezing Home; Mannequin; City of Havens; The Californian. **1938** Gold Is Where You Find It; Angels With Dirty Faces; Quick Money. **1939** Dodge City; I Stole a Million; The Forgotten Woman. **1940** East Side Kids. **1941** My Life With Caroline; World Premiere; Sky Raiders (serial); Glamour Boy; Badlands of Dakota; Among the Living; All That Money Can Buy. **1942** This Gun for Hire; Quiet Please, Murder; The Silver Bullet; You Can't Escape Forever. **1943** What a Man!; Hot Foot (short). **1944** Hail the Conquering Hero; San Fernando Valley; The Adventures of Mark Twain; Gambler's Choice. **1945** Leave Her to Heaven; They Were Expendable; The Cisco Kid in Old New Mexico. **1946** The Kid from Brooklyn. **1947** Ladies' Man. **1952** The Devil and Daniel Webster (retitle and reissue of All That Money Can buy, 1941).

FARMER, CHARLES A
Born: 1883. Died: Oct. 2, 1946, Los Angeles, Calif. Screen actor.

FARMER, FRANCES
Born: Sept. 19, 1914, Seattle, Wash. Died: Aug. 1, 1970, Indianapolis, Ind. (cancer). Screen, stage, radio and television actress. Divorced from actor Leif Erickson and Alfred Lobley (dec.). Married to Leland Mikesell.

Appeared in: **1936** Come and Get It; Too Many Parents; Border Flight; Rhythm on the Range. **1937** Ebb Tide; The Toast of New York; Exclusive. **1938** Ride a Crooked Mile. **1940** South of Pago Pago; Flowing Gold. **1941** Badlands of Dakota; World Premiere; Among the Living. **1942** Son of Fury. **1958** The Party Crashers.

FARNUM, DUSTIN
Born: 1874, Hampton Beach, Maine. Died: July 3, 1929, New York, N.Y. (kidney trouble). Screen, stage and vaudeville actor. Brother of actor William Farnum (dec. 1953).

Appeared in: **1913** The Squaw Man. **1914** The Virginian. **1915** Cameo Kirby; Captain Courtesy; The Gentlemen from Indiana. **1916** The Iron Strain; David Garrick; Davy Crockett. **1917** The Scarlet Pimpernell; The Spy; North of 53. **1918** Light of the Western Stars. **1919** A Man's Fight; A Man in the Open; The Corsican Brothers. **1920** Big Happiness. **1921** The Primal Law; The Devil Within; Call of the North. **1922** Strange Idols; Iron to Gold; The Yosemite Trail; While Justice Waits; The Trail of the Axe; Oathbound; Three Who Paid. **1923** The Virginian; Bucking the Barrier; The Buster; The Grail; The Man Who Won. **1924** Kentucky Days; My Man. **1926** The Flaming Frontier.

FARNUM, FRANKLYN
Born: 1876, Boston, Mass. Died: July 4, 1961, Hollywood, Calif. (cancer). Screen and stage actor.

Appeared in: **1916** A Stranger from Somewhere; Little Partner. **1917** The Devil's Pay Day; The Man Who Took a Chance; Bringing Home

Father; Anything Once; The Winged Mystery; The Scarlet Car; The Car of Chance. **1918** The Fighting Grin; The Empty Cab; The Rough Lover; Fast Company; $5,000 Reward; In Judgment Of. **1919** Go Get 'Em Garringer. **1920** Vanishing Trails (serial). **1921** The Fighting Stranger; The Hunger of the Blood; The White Masks; The Struggle; The Last Chance; The Raiders. **1922** Cros Roads; Gold Grabbers; Angel Citizens; Gun Shy; Texas; Smiling Jim; So This Is Arizona; When East Comes West; Trail's End; The Firebrand. **1923** The Man Getter; It Happened Out West; Wolves of the Border. **1924** A Desperate Adventure; Two Fisted Tenderfoot; Battling Brewster; Calibre 45; Baffled; Courage; Crossed Trails; Western Vengeance. **1925** Border Intrigue; The Drug Store Cowboy; The Gambling Fool; The Bandit Tamer; Double-Barreled Justice; Rough Going; Two Gun Sap. **1930** Beyond the Rio Grande; Beyond the Law. **1931** Hell's Valley; Battling With Buffalo Bill (serial); Not Exactly Gentlemen; Three Rogues; Leftover Ladies; Oklahoma Jim. **1932** Human Targets; Mark of the Spur; Honor of the Bad Man; The Texas Bad Man. **1934** Frontier Days; Honor of the Range. **1935** Hopalong Cassidy; The Crusades; The Ghost Riders; Powdersmoke Range; Gold Diggers of 1935. **1936** The Clutching Hand (serial); The Plainsman; Undersea Kingdom (serial); Charlie Chan at the Circus; Frontier Justice; Preview Murder Mystery. **1937** The Life of Emile Zola. **1938** Romance of the Rockies; Prison Train. **1939** Hollywood Cavalcade; Stagecoach. **1940** The House Across the Bay; Tin Pan Alley. **1941** Belle Starr. **1942** Stardust on the Sage; Silver Queen. **1944** Saddle Leather Law. **1945** Saratoga Trunk; Dick Tracy; The Stork Club. **1946** Sister Kenny. **1947** The Perils of Pauline; Honeymoon. **1948** Silver River; I Remember Mama; Johnny Belinda; Assigned to Danger. **1949** Bride of Vengeance. **1950** Colt .45; Dear Wife; Destination Murder; Sunset Boulevard. **1951** Here Comes the Groom; The Mating Season. **1952** Carrie; Somebody Loves Me; My Pal Gus. **1953** Meet Me at the Fair; Affair With a Stranger; The Stranger Wore a Gun. **1955** East of Eden; Guys and Dolls; Ten Wanted Men. **1956** Beyond a Reasonable Doubt; The Ten Commandments; Around the World in 80 Days. **1957** Oh, Men! Oh, Women!; Pal Joey. **1958** King Creole; Rock-a-Bye Baby.

FARNUM, WILLIAM
Born: July 4, 1876, Boston, Mass. Died: June 5, 1953, Los Angeles, Calif. (cancer). Screen and stage actor. Brother of actor Dustin Farnum (dec. 1929). Divorced from actress Mable Eaton (dec. 1916).

Appeared in: **1913** The Redemption of David Corson. **1914** The Spoilers (small part in 1942 remake); The Sign of the Cross. **1915** The Plunderer; The Nigger. **1916** A Man of Sorrow. **1917** A Tale of Two Cities; The Heart of a Lion; The Conqueror. **1918** Les Miserables; Rough and Ready. **1919** The Last of the Duanes; The Man Hunter; The Lone Star Ranger. **1920** The Adventurer; Drag Harlan; If I Were King. **1921** His Greatest Sacrifice; The Scuttlers; Perjury. **1922** A Stage Romance; Shackles of Gold; Without Compromise; Moonshine Valley. **1923** The Gun Fighter; Brass Commandments. **1924** The Man Who Fights Alone. **1927** Ben Hur. **1930** If I Were King (and 1920 version); DuBarry, Woman of Passion. **1931** The Painted Desert; Oh! Oh! Cleopatra (short); Ten Nights in a Bar Room; A Connecticut Yankee; Pagan Lady. **1932** The Drifter; Mr. Robinson Crusoe; Law of the Sea; Wide Open Spaces (short). **1933** Supernatural; Marriage on Approval; Another Language; Flaming Guns. **1934** Cleopatra; Brand of Hate; Happy Landing; The Count of Monte Cristo; School for Girls; Good Dame; The Scarlet Letter; Are We Civilized?; The Silver Streak. **1935** The Crusades; The Eagles' Brood; Powdersmoke Range; Between Men. **1936** Undersea Kingdom (serial); Custer's Last Stand (serial); The Vigilantes Are Coming (serial); The Last Assignment; The Cluthcing Hand (serial). **1937** Git Along Little Dogies; Public Cowboy No. 1; Maid of Salem. **1938** The Lone Ranger (serial); The Secret of Treasure Island (serial); Santa Fe Stampede; If I Were King (and 1920 and 1930 versions); Shine on Harvest Moon. **1939** Mexicali Rose; Colorado Sunset; Rovin' Tumbleweeds; South of the Border. **1940** Adventures of Red Ryder (serial); Convicted Woman; Hi-Yo Silver; Kit Carson. **1941** Cheers for Miss Bishop; A Woman's Face; Gangs of Sonora; The Corsican Brothers; Last of the Duanes. **1942** Men of Texas; The Lone Star Ranger; Today I Hang; The Silver Bullet; Deep in the Heart of Texas; The Boss of Hangtown Mesa; American Empire; The Spoilers (and 1914 version); Tennessee Johnson. **1943** Frontier Badmen; Hangmen Also Die. **1944** The Mummy's Curse. **1945** Captain Kidd. **1946** God's Country. **1947** Perils of Pauline; Rolling Home. **1948** My Dog Shep. **1949** Bride of Vengeance; Daughter of the West. **1950** The Undersea Kingdom (serial). **1951** Samson and Delilah. **1952** Jack and the Beanstalk; Lone Star.

FARQUHARSON, ROBERT
Born: 1878. Died: Jan. 11, 1966, Ticiono, Switzerland. Screen, stage and radio actor.

Appeared in: **1931** Captivation. **1933** The Man They Couldn't Arrest.

FARR, CHICK
Born: England? Died: Feb. 28, 1948, London, England. Screen, stage actor and music hall entertainer. Member of vaudeville team "Far and Farland."

FARR, FRANKIE (Frankie Farinacci)
Born: 1903, Albany, N.Y. Died: Mar. 20, 1953, Tulsa, Okla. Screen actor.

Appeared in: **1936** The Great Ziegfeld. **1939** Gone With the Wind.

FARR, KARL
Born: Texas. Died: Sept. 20, 1961. Screen actor, singer and musician. One of the original members of "Sons of the Pioneers" singing group.

Appeared in: **1946** My Pal Trigger.

FARR, PATRICIA
Born: 1915. Died: Feb. 23, 1948, Burbank, Calif. Screen actress.

Appeared in: **1931** The Secret Call; Silence. **1933** I Loved You Wednesday; My Weakness. **1934** I Am Suzanne; Stand Up and Cheer; Tailspin Tommy (serial). **1935** Orchids to You; Helldorado. **1936** Lady Luck; Three of a Kind; Speed to Spare. **1937** Girls Can Play; Criminals of the Air; All American Sweetheart. **1938** Lady Behave; Trade Winds. **1941** Mr. and Mrs. Smith; West Point Story; Sky Lark. **1942** This Gun for Hire; To the Shores of Tripoli.

FARR, THOMAS "HUGH"
Born: 1904. Died: Mar. 17, 1980, Wyo. Screen actor, singer and musician. One of the original "Sons of the Pioneers" singing group.

FARRAND, JAN
Born: 1928. Died: Nov. 4, 1980, New York, N.Y. Screen and stage actor.

Appeared in: **1968** The Detective.

FARRAR, GERALDINE
Born: 1882. Died: Mar. 11, 1967, Conn. Opera and screen actress. Divorced from actor Lou Tellegen (dec. 1934).

Appeared in: **1915** Carmen. **1916** Temptation; Maria Rosa. **1917** The Devil Stone; Joan, the Woman; The Woman God Forgot. **1918** The Hell Cat; The Turn of the Wheel. **1919** The World and Its Women; The Stranger Vow; Flame of the Desert; Shadows. **1920** The Woman and the Puppet. **1921** Riddle Woman.

FARRAR, GWEN
Born: July 14, 1899, London, England. Died: Dec. 25, 1944, London, England. Screen, stage, radio actress and music hall entertainer.

Appeared in: **1935** She Shall Have Music (US 1942).

FARRAR, MARGARET
Born: 1901. Died: Aug. 9, 1925, Los Angeles, Calif. (suicide—poison). Screen actress.

FARRAR, STANLEY
Born: 1911. Died: Apr. 5, 1974, Mendocino, Calif. (heart attack). Screen, stage, radio and television actor.

Appeared in: **1953** Perils of the Jungle. **1955** How to Be Very, Very Popular. **1957** Badlands of Montana; Portland Expose. **1959** Face of a Fugitive.

FARRELL, CHARLES "SKIP" (Charles Farrell Fielder)
Born: 1919. Died: May 8, 1962, Hollywood, Calif. (heart attack). Screen, radio, television actor and singer. Do not confuse with US actor born in 1902 nor Irish actor born in 1905.

Appeared in: **1950** Night and the City. **1957** Morning Call. **1958** The Strange Case of Dr. Manning. **1959** The Sheriff of Fractured Jaw. **1960** Hidden Homicide.

FARRELL, EVE
Born: New Orleans, La. Died: Jan. 31, 1972, Los Angeles, Calif. Screen actress.

Appeared in: **1938** Dynamite Delaney.

FARRELL, GLENDA
Born: June 30, 1904, Enid, Okla. Died: May 1, 1971, New York, N.Y. Screen, stage and television actress. Mother of actor Tommy Farrell. Starred in several "Torchy Blane" series films.

Appeared in: **1929** Lucky Boy. **1930** Little Caesar; The Lucky Break (short). **1932** Life Begins (film and stage versions); I Am a Fugitive from a Chain Gang; The Match King; Three on a Match; Scandal for Sale; Night Nurse. **1933** The Mayor of Hell; Central Airport; The Keyhold; Girl Missing; Mary Stevens, M.D.; Bureau of Missing Persons; Gambling Ship; Lady for a Day; Man's Castle; Havana Widows; Grand Slam; The Mystery of the Wax Museum. **1934** The Big Shakedown; Dark Hazard; The Personality Kid; Hi, Nellie!; Merry Wives of Reno; Kansas City Princess; I've Got Your Number; Heat Lightning. **1935** Go Into Your Dance; In Caliente; Traveling Saleslady; Gold Diggers of 1935; We're in the Money; Little Big Shot; Miss Pacific Fleet; The Secret Bride. **1936** Snowed Under; The Law in Her Hands; Smart Blonde; Here Comes Carter!; Gold Diggers of 1937; High Tension; Nobody's Fool. **1937** Dance, Charlie, Dance; Fly Away Baby; The Adventurous Blonde; Hollywood Hotel; Breakfast for Two; You Live and Learn. **1938** Stolen Heaven; Prison Break; The Road to Reno; Exposed; Blondes at Work; Torchy Gets Her Man. **1939** Torchy Blane in Chinatown; Torchy Runs for Mayor. **1941** Johnny Eager. **1942** A Night for Crime; The Talk of the Town; Twin Beds. **1943** Klondike Kate; City Without Men. **1944** Ever Since Venus. **1947** Heading for Heaven. **1948** I Love Trouble; Mary Lou; Lulu Belle. **1952** Apache War Smoke. **1953** Girls in the Night. **1954** Secret of the Incas; Susan Slept Here. **1955** The Girl in the Red Velvet Swing. **1959** Middle of the Night. **1964** The Disorderly Orderly; Kissin' Cousins. **1968** Dead Heat. **1970** Tiger by the Tail.

FARRELL, JOHN W.
Born: 1885. Died: July 8, 1953, Brooklyn, N.Y. Screen, stage, vaudeville and television actor. Appeared in vaudeville with his wife Josephine Saxton in an act billed as "Saxton & Farrell."

Appeared in: **1947** Desert Fury. **1949** Portrait of Jenny.

FARRELL, PAUL
Born: Sept 1, 1893, Dublin, Ireland. Died: June, 1975, England? Screen and stage actor.

Appeared in: **1957** The Rising of the Moon. **1958** Alive and Kicking (US 1964); She Didn't Say No (US 1962). **1959** Shake Hands With the Devil. **1960** The Seige of Sydney Street (US 1961); The Poacher's Daughter. **1964** Becket. **1968** Hot Millions. **1970** Brotherly Love.

FARRELL, VESSIE
Born: 1890. Died: Sept. 30, 1935, Los Angeles, Calif. Screen and stage actress.

Appeared in: **1935** The Healer.

FARREN, GEORGE FRANCIS
Born: 1858. Died: Apr. 21, 1935, New York, N.Y. Screen and stage actor.

Appeared in: **1917** The Cinderella Man.

FARREN, MARY
Born: 1908. Died: May 9, 1977, Norwalk, Conn. (cancer). Screen and stage actress. Daughter of actor George Farren (dec.). Married to actor Paul Jones.

Appeared in: **1929** Glorifying the American Girl; The following shorts: Ripley's Believe It or Not—1930; Ripley's Believe It or Not—1931; Ripley's Believe It or Not—1932.

FARRINGTON, ADELE
Born: 1867, Brooklyn, N.Y. Died: Dec. 19, 1936, Los Angeles, Calif. Screen, stage and vaudeville actress. Divorced from actor Hobart Bosworth (dec. 1943).

Appeared in: **1914** The Country Mouse. **1917** American Film Mfg. Co. films. **1918** Wild Youth; Such a Little Pirate. **1919** In Old Kentucky. **1920** The Girl in the Web; The Mollycoddle. **1921** Black Beauty; The Charm School; The Child Thou Gavest Me; A Connecticut Yankee at King Arthur's Court; Her Mad Bargain; The Spenders. **1922** The Bachelor Daddy; Bobbed Hair; The Cradle; Little Wildcat; The Ordeal; A Question of Honor. **1923** Bag and Baggage; A Gentleman of Leisure; The Man Next Door; One Stolen Night; The Scarlet Lily. **1924** Along Came Ruth. **1926** The Shadow of the Law; The Traffic Cop.

FARRINGTON, BETTY
Born: Nov. 17, 1885. Died: Dec. 22, 1967. Screen actress.

Appeared in: **1929** The Fall of Eve. **1930** Anybody's War. **1933** Knee-Deep in Music (short). **1934** Down to Their Last Yacht. **1935** One Hour Late. **1936** Theodora Goes Wild; Trail of the Lonesome Pine. **1939** Made For Each Other. **1940** Our Neighbors the Carters. **1941** The Saint in Palm Springs; Footsteps in the Dark; Whistling in the Dark. **1942** Home In Wyomin'; Ice-Capades Revue; Stardust on

the Sage. **1943** Henry Aldrich Gets Glamour; True to Life. **1944** Henry Aldrich Plays Cupid; Double Indemnity; Our Hearts Were Young and Gay; The Uninvited (voice). **1945** The Dolly Sisters; George White's Scandals. **1947** My Favorite Brunette. **1949** Samson and Delilah. **1950** Father of the Bride; Two Weeks With Love.

FARRINGTON, FRANK
Born: 1874. Died: May 27, 1924, Los Angeles, Calif. Screen actor.

Appeared in: **1914** The Million Dollar Mystery (serial); Zudora—The Twenty Million Dollar Mystery (serial). **1923** The Clean Up; The Courtship of Miles Standish. **1924** The Man Who Fights Alone.

FASSEN, ALEX
Born: 1894, Holland. Died: Sept. 4, 1981, Laren, Holland. Screen, stage, radio and television actor.

FATIMA, "LA BELLE"
Born: 1880, Syria. Died: Mar. 14, 1921, Venice, Calif. (heart attack). Screen, stage actress and dancer. Appeared in shorts made at the St. Louis World's Fair.

FAULKNER, RALPH C.
Born: 1890, San Antonio, Tex. Died: Aug. 21, 1948, Washington, D.C. Screen, vaudeville actor, impersonator, cartoonist and reporter.

Appeared in: **1917** War and the Woman. **1918** The Prussian Cur. **1921** Anne of Little Smoky. **1923** April Showers. **1924** Loving Lies. **1925** My Neighbor's Wife. **1928** God of Mankind. **1925** The Three Musketeers. **1937** The Prisoner of Zenda. **1939** The Star Maker.

FAUST, HAZEL LEE
Born: 1910. Died: Dec. 11, 1973. Screen actress.

FAUST, MARTIN J.
Born: Jan. 16, 1886, Poughkeepsie, N.Y. Died: July 20, 1943, Los Angeles, Calif. Screen and stage actor. Entered films in 1908.

Appeared in: **1910** A Winter's Tale. **1921** Hell Bound. **1923** Big Brother; Under the Red Robe; The Silent Command; The Tents of Allah. **1924** I Am the Man; Yolanda. **1925** North Star. **1947** Chain Lightning; Spider Webs. **1928** Hello Cheyenne. **1929** Caress. **1934** Six of a Kind. **1938** If I Were King. **1939** Hero for a Day. **1941** Paris Calling; Saddlemates. **1943** Larceny With Music; The Fallen Sparrow; The North Star (and 1925 version); Hold Your Temper (short); This Is the Army. **1944** Ali Baba and the Forty Thieves.

FAUSTMAN, ERIK "HAMPE"
Born: 1919, Stockholm, Sweden. Died: 1961, Sweden? Screen actor, film director and screenwriter.

Appeared in: **1939** They Staked Their Lives. **1945** Crime and Punishment. **1946** When Meadows Bloom. **1949** Vagabond Blacksmiths; Katrina. **1960** Die Sista Stegen (A Matter of Morals—US 1961); Other Swedish films: We Need Each Other; Lars Hard; A Woman on Board; Ride Tonight; Women in Prison; A Spring in Arms; There Burned a Flame; Darling I Surrender; His Excellency; My People Are Not Yours; When the Door was Closed; Never in Your Life.

FAVERSHAM, WILLIAM
Born: Feb. 12, 1868, London, England. Died: Apr. 7, 1940, Bay Shore, N.Y. (coronary embolism). Screen and stage actor. Married to Marian Merwin (dec.), stage actress Julie Opp (dec. 1921) and Edith Campbell (dec.). Father of William, Jr. and actor Philip Faversham (dec. 1982).

Appeared in: **1919** The Silver King. **1920** The Man Who Lost Himself; The Sin That Was His. **1924** The Sixth Commandment. **1934** Lady by Choice. **1935** Becky Sharp; Secret of the Chateau; Mystery Woman. **1937** Arizona Days.

FAVOR, EDWARD M.
Born: 1856. Died: Jan. 10, 1936, Brooklyn, N.Y. Screen and stage actor.

Appeared in: **1915** The Deceivers.

FAWCETT, GEORGE D.
Born: Aug. 25, 1860, Alexandria, Va. Died: June 6, 1939, Nantucket Island, Mass. (heart ailment). Screen and stage actor. Married to actress Percy Haswell (dec. 1945) who also appeared in films as Mrs. George Fawcett.

Appeared in: **1915** The Majesty of the Law (film debut). **1917** Panthea; The Cinderella Man. **1918** The Great Love; Hearts of the World. **1919** The Girl Who Stayed at Home; The Hope Chest; A Romance of Happy

Valley; I'll Get Him Yet; Nobody Home; Turning the Tables; Scarlet Days; The Greatest Question. **1920** Two Weeks; The Branded Women; Little Miss Rebellion. **1921** Burn 'Em Up Barnes; Chivalrous Charley; Hush Money; Lessons in Love; Little Italy; Nobody; Paying the Piper; Sentimental Tommy; Such a Little Queen; The Way of a Maid. **1922** Beyond the Rainbow; The Curse of Drink; Destiny's Isle; Ebb Tide; His Wife's Husband; Isle of Doubt; John Smith; Manslaughter; The Old Homestead; Polly of the Follies. **1923** Salomy Jane; The Drums of Fate; His Children's Children; Hollywood; Java Head; Just Like a Woman; Mr. Billings Spends His Dime; Only 38; The Woman With Four Faces. **1924** West of the Water Tower; The Bedroom Window; The Breaking Point; Broken Barriers; Code of the Sea; Her Love Story; In Every Woman's Life; Pied Piper Malone; Tess of the D'Urbervilles; Triumph. **1925** A Lost Lady; The Merry Widow; The Circle; The Fighting Cub; Go Straight; The Home Maker; Joanna; The Mad Whirl; 9 3/5 Seconds; Peacock Feathers; The Price of Pleasure; Some Pun'kins; Souls for Sables; The Sporting Venus; Thank You; Up the Ladder; The Verdict; The Sporting Chance. **1926** The Flaming Frontier; Flesh and the Devil; Man of the Forest; Men of Steel; Out of the Storm; The Son of the Sheik; There You Are; Two Can Play; Under Western Skies. **1927** Captain Salvation; Duty's Reward; The Enemy; Hard-Boiled Haggerty; The Little Firebrand; Love; Painting the Town; The Private Life of Helen of Troy; Rich Men's Sons; Riding to Fame; See You in Jail; Snowbound; Spring Fever; Tillie the Toiler; The Valley of the Giants. **1928** Prowlers of the Sea; Tempest; The Wedding March. **1929** Little Wildcat; Fancy Baggage; His Captive Woman; Tide of Empire; Lady of the Pavements; Innocents of Paris; Four Feathers; The Gamblers; Wonder of Women; Hot for Paris; Hearts in Exile; Men Are Like That; The Prince of Hearts. **1930** The Great Divide; Once a Gentleman; Ladies of Leisure; Wild Company; Swing High; Hello Sister; The Bad One. **1931** Drums of Jeopardy; Woman of Experience; Personal Maid.

FAWCETT, JAMES
Born: 1905. Died: June 9, 1942, San Fernando Valley, Calif. (auto accident). Film stuntman and vaudeville acrobat.

FAWCETT, WILLIAM
Died: Jan. 25, 1974. Screen actor.

Appeared in: **1946** Stars Over Texas; The Michigan Kid; Driftin' River; Tumbleweed Trail. **1947** Wild Country; Black Hills; Green Dolphin Street; The High Wall; Ghost Town Renegades; Justice. **1948** Live Today for Tomorrow; Words and Music; An Act of Murder; The Tioga Kid; Check Your Guns. **1949** Barbary Coast; The Kid from Texas; Ride, Ryder Ride!; Roll, Thunder, Roll; Barbary Pirate; Batman and Robin (serial); Adventures of Sir Galahad (serial). **1950** Tyrant of the Sea; State Penitentiary; Cody of the Pony Express (serial); Pirates of the High Seas (serial); Chain Gang; Ace in the Hole. **1951** Comin' Round the Mountain; Valley of Five; Hollywood Story; Wanted—Dead or Alive; Honeychile; Oklahoma Annie; Hills of Utah; The Magic Carpet; The Mating Season; Captain Video (serial); Montana Incident (aka Gun Smoke Range). **1952** The Longhorn; Roar of the Iron Horse (serial); King of the Congo (serial); Springfield Rifle; The Lion and the Horse; Kansas Territory; Barbed Wire; Jungle Jim in the Forbidden Land; Montana Incident; Blackhawk (serial). **1953** The Star of Texas; The Homesteaders; The Marksman; Has Anybody Seen My Gal?; Sweetheart Time; The Raiders; A Man's Country; Canadian Mounties vs Atomic Invaders (serial). **1954** Dawn at Socorro; The Law vs Billy the Kid; Alaska Seas; Riding with Buffalo Bill (serial). **1955** Seminole Uprising; Pirates of Tripoli; Tall Man Riding; Lay That Rifle Down; Timberjack; The Spoilers; Gang-Busters. **1956** The Kettles in the Ozarks; Dakota Incident; Cattle King; The Proud Ones; Canyon River. **1957** The Storm Rider; The Tijuana Story; Band of Angels; Tension at Table Rock; The First Traveling Saleslady. **1958** No Time for Sergeants; Damn Yankees. **1959** The Wild and the Innocent; Good Day for a Hanging. **1960** The Walking Target. **1961** Claudelle Inglish; The Comancheros. **1962** The Interns; Saintly Sinners; Gypsy; Music Man. **1963** The Wheeler Dealers. **1964** Sex and the Single Girl; The Quick Gun. **1965** Dear Brigitte; King Rat. **1966** Jesse James Meets Frankenstein's Daughter. **1967** Hostile Guns; Adventures of Batman and Robin (rerelease of 1949 serial Batman and Robin); The Gnome-Mobile. **1968** Blackbeard's Ghost.

FAX, JESSLYN
Died: Feb. 16, 1975. Screen actress.

Appeared in: **1954** Rear Window. **1955** How to Be Very, Very Popular; Kiss Me Deadly. **1957** An Affair to Remember. **1958** The Man Who Died Twice. **1962** The Music Man; Paradise Alley. **1963** Four For Texas. **1965** The Family Jewels. **1966** The Ghost and Mr. Chicken; Three on a Couch. **1967** The Gnome-Mobile (voice only). **1969** Angel in My Pocket; The Love God?

FAY, BRENDAN
Born: 1921. Died: Feb. 7, 1975, Brooklyn, N.Y. (heart attack). Screen and stage actor.

Appeared in: **1960** Juke Box Racket. **1961** The Hustler. **1974** Man on a Swing.

FAY, ELFIE
Born: 1881. Died: Sept. 18, 1927, Hollywood, Calif. Screen and stage actress.

FAY, FRANK
Born: Nov. 17, 1894, San Francisco, Calif. Died: Sept. 25, 1961, Santa Monica, Calif. Screen, stage, vaudeville, radio actor and stage producer. Divorced from actress Barbara Stanwyck.

Appeared in: **1929** Show of Shows (film debut). **1930** The Matrimonial Bed; Under a Texas Moon. **1931** Bright Lights; God's Gift to Women; Stout Hearts and Willing Hands (short). **1932** The Slippery Pearls (short); Fool's Advice. **1935** Stars Over Broadway. **1937** Nothing Sacred. **1938** Meet the Mayor. **1940** I Want a Divorce; They Knew What They Wanted; A WAC in His Life. **1943** Spotlight Scandals. **1951** Love Nest; When Worlds Collide; Stage from Blue River.

FAY, GABY See HOLDEN, FAY

FAY, JACK
Born: 1903. Died: Nov. 15, 1928, Los Angeles, Calif. (after effects of injuries from explosion at Fox Studios while filming What Price Glory, 1926). Screen actor.

FAY, OLIVE
Born: 1925. Died: Nov. 23, 1977, Los Angeles, Calif. Screen and vaudeville actress. Entered films as a child actress.

FAY, WILLIAM GEORGE
Born: Nov. 12, 1872, Dublin, Ireland. Died: Oct. 27, 1947, London, England. Screen, stage actor, film producer and stage producer. Was co-founder of Abbey Theatre, Dublin.

Appeared in: **1918** Doing Her Bit (film debut). **1933** The Blarney Stone. **1934** General John Regan. **1935** Dark World. **1936** The Show Goes On; Storm in a Teacup. **1937** Kathleen Mavoureen; My Last Curtain. **1938** My Irish Molly. **1941** Spellbound. **1947** Odd Man Out; The Patient Vanishes.

FAYE, HERBIE
Born: 1899. Died: June 28, 1980, Las Vegas, Nev. Screen, stage, vaudeville and television actor.

Appeared in: **1954** Top Banana. **1955** The Shrike. **1956** The Harder They Fall. **1959** Never Steal Anything Small. **1962** Requiem for a Heavyweight. **1963** The Thrill of It All; Come Blow Your Horn. **1964** The Disorderly Orderly. **1965** The Family Jewels. **1966** The Fortune Cookie. **1967** Enter Laughing; Thoroughly Modern Millie. **1968** The Night They Raided Minskys; Blackbeard's Ghost. **1969** Angel in My Pocket; The Love God? **1980** Melvin and Howard.

FAYE, IRMA
Born: 1913. Died: May 17, 1976, Burbank, Calif.? Screen, stage actress and burlesque entertainer. Sister of actress Valerie Cost.

FAYE, JULIA
Born: Sept. 24, 1896, Richmond, Va. Died: Apr. 6, 1966, Santa Monica, Calif. (cancer). Screen actress. Entered films in 1916.

Appeared in: **1915** The Lamb. **1916** His Auto Ruination; His Last Laugh; A Lover's Might. **1917** The Woman God Forgot. **1918** The Whispering Chorus; Old Wives for New; Till I Come Back to You; The Squaw Man; Mrs. Leffingwell's Boots; Sandy. **1919** Stepping Out; Male and Female; Don't Change Your Husband. **1920** The Life of the Party; Something to Think About. **1921** Affairs of Anatol; Fool's Paradise; Forbidden Fruit; The Great Moment; The Snob. **1922** Manslaughter; Nice People; Saturday Night. **1923** The Ten Commandments; Adam's Rib; Hollywood; Nobody's Money. **1924** Feet of Clay; Changing Husbands; Don't Call It Love; Triumph. **1925** The Golden Bed; Hell's Highroad; The Road to Yesterday. **1926** Volga Boatman; Corporal Kate; Meet the Prince; Bachelor Brides. **1927** King of Kings; The Yankee Clipper; His Dog; The Main Event; The Fighting Eagle. **1928** Chicago; Turkish Delight. **1929** The Godless Girl; Dynamite. **1930** Not So Dumb; The Squaw Man (and 1918 version). **1933** Only Yesterday. **1936** 'Til We Meet Again. **1938** You and Me. **1939** Union Pacific. **1940** North West Mounted Police; Reap the Wild Wind; Remember the Night. **1943** So Proudly We Hail! **1944** Casanova Brown; The Story of Dr. Wassell. **1945** Masquerade in

Mexico. **1946** California; The Perils of Pauline; Welcome Stranger. **1947** Unconquered; Blaze of Noon; Easy Come, Easy Go; I Cover Big Town. **1948** Night Has a Thousand Eyes. **1949** Red, Hot and Blue; A Connecticut Yankee in King Arthur's Court. **1950** Sunset Boulevard; Copper Canyon. **1951** Samson and Delilah; Here Comes the Groom. **1952** The Greatest Show on Earth. **1956** The Ten Commandments (and 1923 version). **1958** Buccaneer.

FAYLAUER, ADOLPH
Born: 1884. Died: Jan. 11, 1961, Los Angeles, Calif. (heart attack). Screen actor.

Appeared in: **1929** The Dream Melody.

FAZENDA, LOUISE
Born: June 17, 1889, Lafayette, Ind. Died: Apr. 17, 1962, Beverly Hills, Calif. (cerebral hemorrhage). Screen and vaudeville actress. Married to film producer Hal Wallis.

Appeared in: **1913** The Cheese Special; Mike and Jake at the Beach. **1915** The Great Vacuum Robbery; Wilful Ambrose; Ambrose's Fury; Ambrose's Lofty Perch; A Bear Affair; Crossed Love and Swords; A Versatile Villain; A Hash House Fraud; Fatty's Tin Type Tangle; A Game Old Knight. **1916** His Hereafter (working title Murray's Mix-Up); The Judge; A Love Riot; Her Marble Heart; The Feathered Nest; Maid Mad (working title The Fortune Teller); Bombs. **1917** The Summer Girls; Maggie's First False Step; Her Fame and Shame; Her Torpedoed Love; The Betrayal of Maggie; His Precious Life. **1920** Down on the Farm. **1922** Quincy Adams Sawyer; The Beauty Shop. **1923** Beautiful and Damned; Main Street; The Fog; The Gold Diggers; Mary of the Movies; The Old Fool; The Spider and the Rose; The Spoilers; Tea With a Kick; The Wanters. **1924** Abraham Lincoln; Being Respectable; Galloping Fish; Listen, Lester; This Woman; True As Steel. **1925** Bobbed Hair; The Lighthouse by the Sea; A Broadway Butterfly; Cheaper to Marry; Compromise; Declasse; Grounds for Divorce; Hogan's Alley; The Love Hour; The Night Club; The Price of Pleasure. **1926** The Bat; Footloose Widows; Loose Ankles; Ladies at Play; The Lady of the Harem; Millionaires; Miss Nobody; The Old Soak; The Passionate Quest. **1927** The Cradle Snatchers; Babs Comes Home; Finger Prints; The Gay Old Bird; The Red Mill; A Sailor's Sweetheart; Simple Sis; A Texas Steer. **1928** The Terror; Tillie's Punctured Romance; Domestic Troubles; Five and Ten-Cent Annie; Heart to Heart; Outcast; Pay As You Enter; Riley the Cop; Vamping Venus. **1929** The Desert Song; Hot Stuff; The House of Horror; On With the Show; Noah's Ark; Stark Mad; Hard to Get; The Show of Shows. **1930** No, No, Nanette; Rain or Shine; Gold Diggers of Broadway; Viennese Nights; Loose Ankles (and 1926 version); Leathernecking; Wide Open; Bride of the Regiment; Broadway Hoofer; High Society Blues; Spring Is Here. **1931** Practice Shots (short); Gun Smoke; Cuban Love Song; Mad Parade; Newly Rich. **1932** The Slippery Pearls (short); Forbidden Adventure; Racing Youth; Unwritten Law; Once in a Lifetime. **1933** Alice in Wonderland; Universal shorts. **1934** Wonder Bar; Caravan; Mountain Music. **1935** Bad Boy; The Casino Murder Case; The Winning Ticket; Broadway Gondolier; The Widow From Monte Carlo. **1936** Doughnuts and Society; Colleen; I Married a Doctor. **1937** Ready, Willing and Able; Ever Since Eve; First Lady; The Road Back; Merry-Go-Round of 1938. **1938** Swing Your Lady. **1939** Down on the Farm (and 1920 version); The Old Maid.

FEALY, MARGARET
Born: 1866, Memphis, Tenn. Died: Feb. 11, 1955. Screen and stage actress. Mother of actress Maude Fealy.

Appeared in: **1929** The Love Parade. **1930** The Return of Dr. Fu Manchu. **1932** Cross Examination. **1940** Mad Youth.

FEALY, MAUDE
Born: 1881. Died: Nov. 9, 1971, Woodland Hills, Calif. Screen and stage actress. Reportedly appeared in roles in every DeMille film after the advent of sound movies, including the producer's last The Ten Commandments (1956).

Appeared in: **1916** Pamela's Past. **1931** Laugh and Get Rich. **1938** The Buccaneer. **1939** Union Pacific. **1943** This Land is Mine. **1947** The Unfaithful. **1948** Summer Holiday. **1956** The Ten Commandments.

FEATHERSTONE, EDDIE See FETHERSTON, EDDIE

FEATHERSTONE, VANE (Vane Featherstonhaugh)
Born: Dec. 16, 1864, London, England. Died: Nov. 6, 1948, England? Screen and stage actress.

Appeared in: **1914** The Brass Bottle.

FEATHERSTONHAUGH, CONSTANCE See BENSON, LADY CONSTANCE

FEE, VICKIE (Astrid Victoria Fee)
Born: 1947. Died: Dec. 13, 1975, Santa Monica, Calif. Screen actress. Daughter of actress Astrid Allwyn and sister of actress Melinda Fee.

Appeared in: **1966** Out of Sight.

FEILER, HERTA
Born: 1916. Died: Nov. 4, 1970, Munich, Germany. Screen actress.

Appeared in: **1939** Manner Mussen so Sein (Men Are That Way).

FEINDT, JUERGEN
Born: 1935, Germany. Died: Sept. 9, 1978, Black Forest, West Germany (plane crash). Screen, stage, television actor, opera singer, choreographer and dancer.

Appeared in: **1963** Die Dreigroschenoper (Three Penny Opera—US 1964).

FELDARY, ERIC
Born: 1920, Budapest, Hungary. Died: Feb. 25, 1968, Los Angeles, Calif. (fire burns). Screen and stage actor.

Appeared in: **1941** Hold Back the Dawn. **1943** Hostages; For Whom the Bell Tolls. **1944** The Master Race; U-Boat Prisoner. **1945** Salome, Where She Danced. **1947** High Conquest; Golden Earrings. **1948** I, Jane Doe; 16 Fathoms Deep. **1951** Sealed Cargo. **1954** The Iron Glove. **1956** Magnificent Roughnecks. **1962** Tender Is the Night.

FELDMAN, ANDREA (Andrea Whips)
Died: Aug. 8, 1972, New York, N.Y. (suicide—jumped from building). Screen actress.

Appeared in: **1963** Cleopatra. **1970** Imitation of Christ; Groupies; Trash.

FELDMAN, EDYTHE A.
Born: 1913. Died: Feb. 28, 1971, Miami Beach, Fla. Screen, stage and television actress.

Appeared in: **1969** Midnight Cowboy.

FELDMAN, GLADYS
Born: 1892. Died: Feb. 12, 1974, New York, N.Y. Screen, stage and radio actress. Married to actor Horace Braham (dec. 1955).

Appeared in: **1921** Shams of Society. **1924** West of the Water Tower.

FELIPE, ALFREDO
Born: 1931. Died: 1958, Lisbon, Portugal. Screen and radio actor. Known as the Portuguese "Fernandel."

FELIX, GEORGE
Born: 1866. Died: May 12, 1949, New York, N.Y. Screen, stage, and vaudeville actor. Married to actress Lydia Berry (dec.) with whom he appeared in vaudeville.

Appeared in: **1916** Haystacks and Steeples.

FELLOWES, ROCKLIFFE
Born: 1885, Ottawa, Canada. Died: Jan. 30, 1950, Los Angeles, Calif. (heart attack). Screen and stage actor.

Appeared in: **1917** The Easiest Way. **1918** Friendly Husbands. **1920** In Search of a Sinner; Yes or No. **1921** Bits of Life; The Price of Possession. **1922** Island Wives; The Stranger's Banquet. **1923** Boy of Mine; Penrod and Sam; The Remittance Woman; The Spoilers; Trifling with Honor. **1924** The Border Legion; The Signal Tower; The Garden of Weeds; Borrowed Husbands; Cornered; Flapper Wives; Missing Daughters. **1925** The Golden Princess; Rose of the World; East of Suez; Declasse; Without Mercy; Counsel for the Defense. **1926** Syncopating Sue; Honesty—the Best Policy; The Road to Glory; Rocking Moon; Silence. **1927** The Understanding Heart; Third Degree; The Crystal Cup; The Taxi Dancer; The Satan Woman. **1929** The Charlatan. **1930** Outside the Law. **1931** Vice Squad; Monkey Business. **1932** Hotel Continental; Huddle; Renegades of the West; All American; Lawyer Man; 20,000 Years in Sing Sing; Ladies of the Big House. **1933** Rusty Rides Again; The Phantom Broadcast. **1934** Back Page.

FELLOWS, ROBERT (Robert Fellowes)
Born: Aug. 23, 1903, Los Angeles, Calif. Died: May 11, 1969, Hollywood, Calif. (heart attack). Screen, stage actor, film director and film producer.

FELLS, GEORGE (George Flevitsky)
Born: 1902. Died: May 10, 1960, N.Y. Screen, stage, radio actor and screenwriter.

FELTON, HAPPY (Francis J. Felton, Jr.)
Born: 1908. Died: Oct. 21, 1964, New York, N.Y. Screen, stage, television, vaudeville and circus actor. Was part of "Adele Jason and The Boys" vaudeville act.

Appeared in: **1943** Swing Shift Maisie; Whistling in Brooklyn; A Guy Named Joe.

FELTON, VERNA
Born: July 20, 1890, Salinas, Calif. Died: Dec. 14, 1966, North Hollywood, Calif. (stroke). Screen, stage, television and radio actress. Married to actor Lee Millar (dec. 1941). Mother of actor Lee Millar, Jr. (dec. 1980).

Appeared in: **1940** Northwest Passage; If I Had My Way. **1941** Dumbo (voice only). **1946** She Wrote the Book. **1948** The Fuller Brush Man. **1949** Cinderella (voice only). **1950** Buccaneer's Girl; The Gunfighter. **1951** Alice in Wonderland; Little Egypt; New Mexico. **1952** Belles on Their Toes; Don't Bother to Knock. **1955** Picnic; The Lady and the Tramp (voice only). **1957** The Oklahoman; Taming Sutton's Gal. **1959** Sleeping Beauty (voice only). **1960** Guns of the Timberland. **1965** The Man From Button Willow. **1967** Jungle Book (voice only).

FENIMORE, FORD (Ford Fenimore Hoft)
Died: Apr. 20, 1941, El Paso, Tex. Screen and stage actor. Appeared in early Griffith films.

FENNER, WALTER S.
Born: 1882, Akron, Ohio. Died: Nov. 7, 1947, Los Angeles, Calif. (diabetes). Screen actor.

Appeared in: **1930** The Sap from Syracuse. **1935** Speed Devils. **1936** Mixed Magic. **1939** Juarez; Mountain Rhythm; A Woman is the Judge; Torchy Runs for Mayor. **1940** You Can't Fool Your Wife. **1942** True to the Army; The Jungle Book; Henry Aldrich-Editor. **1943** G-Men vs the Black Dragon (serial); Henry Aldrich Gets Glamour; Sweet Rosie O'Grady; Guadalcanal Diary. **1944** Lost Angel; Henry Aldrich Plays Cupid. **1945** The Shanghai Cobra; Miss Susie Slagle's.

FENTON, FRANK (Frank Fenton-Morgan)
Born: Apr. 9, 1906, Hartford, Conn. Died: July 24, 1957, Los Angeles, Calif. Screen, stage, television actor and screenwriter.

Appeared in: **1942** The Navy Comes Through. **1943** Claudia; Lady of Burlesque. **1944** Buffalo Bill; The Big Noise; Secret Command. **1945** Destiny; Hold That Blonde; This Man's Navy. **1946** If I'm Lucky; It's a Wonderful Life; Magic Town. **1947** Philo Vance's Secret Mission; Hit Parade of 1947. **1948** A Foreign Affair; Red River; Mexican Hayride; Hazard; Relentless. **1949** The Clay Pigeon; The Doolins of Oklahoma; The Golden Stallion; Joe Palooka in the Big Fight; Ranger of Cherokee Strip; Rustlers. **1950** Modern Marriage; Sideshow; Trigger, Jr; Tripoli; Rogue River; Wyoming Mail; The Lawless. **1951** Texans Never Cry; The Man With a Cloak; Silver City. **1953** Eyes of the Jungle; Island in the Sky; Vicki. **1956** Emergency Hospital; Fury at Gunsight Pass; The Naked Hills. **1957** Hell Bound.

FENTON, LESLIE C. (Leslie Carter Fenton)
Born: 1902, England. Died: Mar. 25, 1978, Montecito, Calif. Screen, stage actor, film director and film producer. Divorced from actress Ann Dvorak (dec. 1979). Later married to Marcela Zabala Howard.

Appeared in: **1925** The Ancient Mariner; East Lynne; Havoc; Lazybones; Thunder Mountain. **1926** What Price Glory; Black Paradise; Going Crooked; Sandy; The Shamrock Handicap; The Road to Glory. **1927** The Last Performance; An Old Flame. **1928** The First Kiss; The Showdown; The Dragnet; The Gateway of the Moon. **1929** Broadway; A Dangerous Woman; Dynamite; Girls Gone Wild; Paris Bound; Woman Trap; The Office Scandal; The Man I Love. **1931** An American Tragedy; Public Enemy; Pagan Lady; Man Who Came Back; The Guilty Generation; Kick In; Murder at Midnight. **1932** Hatchet Man; Strange Love of Molly Louvain; Thunder Below; Famous Ferguson Case; Airmail. **1933** F.P.1; Night Flight; Lady Killer. **1934** I Believed in You; Take the Stand; Fugitive Road; Marie Galante; White Lies. **1935** Casino Murder Case; Strange Wives; Stolen Harmony; Star of Midnight; Chinatown Squad; Men Without Names; East of Java.

FENTON, LUCILLE
Born: c. 1916. Died: Oct. 17, 1966, London, England. Screen and stage actress.

Appeared in: **1948** Citizen Saint. **1964** I'd Rather Be Rich.

FENTON, MABEL
Born: 1868, Van Buren County, Mich. Died: Apr. 19, 1931, Hollywood, Calif. Screen, stage, vaudeville and burlesque actress. Married to actor Charles Ross (dec. 1918).

Appeared in: **1915** How Molly Made Good.

FENTON, MARK
Born: 1870. Died: July 29, 1925, Los Angeles, Calif. (surgery complications after auto accident). Screen actor.

Appeared in: **1915** The Black Box (serial). **1916** The Adventures of Peg O' the Ring (serial). **1919** The Mystery of 13. **1920** Behold My Wife. **1921** The Conquering Power; The Four Horsemen of the Apocalypse; Life's Darn Funny; The Unknown; The Wallop. **1922** Headin' West; Little Eva Ascends; Too Much Business; The Village Blacksmith; The Yellow Stain. **1923** Alias the Night Wind; Speed King. **1924** American Manners; The Battling Fool; Black Lightning; A Fool's Awakening; Name the Man; The Passing of Wolf MacLean; The Spirit of the U.S.A. **1925** Brand of Cowardice; The Storm Breaker.

FENWICK, IRENE (Irene Frizzel)
Born: 1887, Chicago, Ill. Died: Dec. 24, 1936, Beverly Hills, Calif. Screen and stage actress. Married to actor Lionel Barrymore (dec. 1954).

Appeared in: **1915** The Spendthrift; The Commuters. **1916** A Coney Island Princess; Child of Destiny.

FEODOROFF, LEO
Born: 1867, Odessa, Russia. Died: Nov. 23, 1949, Long Beach, N.Y. (auto accident injuries). Screen, stage actor and opera performer.

Appeared in: **1926** God Gave Me Twenty Cents. **1927** The Music Master. **1928** Laugh, Clown, Laugh.

FERGUSON, AL
Born: Apr. 19, 1888, Rosslarre, Ireland. Died: Dec. 4, 1971, Calif. Screen actor. Entered films in 1910.

Appeared in: **1920** The Lost City. **1921** High Gear Jeffrey; Sunset Jones; Miracles of the Jungle (serial). **1922** Smiling Jim; The Timber Queen (serial). **1923** Flames of Passion; The Power Divine; The Range Patrol; The Way of the Transgressor. **1924** The Trail of Vengeance; Driftwood; Shackles of Fear; Harbor Patrol. **1925** The Fighting Romeo; Phantom Shadows; Scarlet and Gold. **1926** Baited Trap; A Captain's Courage; Hi-Jacking Rustlers; West of the Law; Tentacles of the North; The Wolf Hunters. **1927** Fangs of Destiny; The Range Riders; Straight Shootin'; Shooting Straight; Western Courage. **1928** The Scarlet Arrow (serial); The Avenging Rider; Guardians of the Wild; Headin' for Danger; Terror; The Little Buckaroo; Tarzan—the Mighty (serial); Haunted Island (serial). **1929** Grit Wins; Hoofbeats of Vengeance; The Man from Nevada; Outlaw; The Saddle King; The Smiling Terror; The Vagabond Cub; Thundering Thompson; The Wagon Master; Wolves of the City; Tarzan—the Tiger (serial). **1930** The Lightning Express (serial); Near the Rainbow's End. **1931** Red Fork Range; Pueblo Terror; Two Gun Caballero; One Way Trail. **1932** The Lost Special (serial); Hurricane Express (serial). **1933** The Three Musketeers (serial); Pirate Treasure (serial); Tailspin Tommy (serial); The Vanishing Shadow (serial). **1934** Tailspin Tommy (serial); Pirate Treasure (serial); The Vanishing Shadow (serial). **1935** Desert Trail. **1936** Roamin' Wild; Flash Gordon (serial); Showboat. **1937** North of the Rio Grande; Rustler's Valley. **1942** Captain Midnight (serial); Reap the Wild Wind. **1944** Riders of the Santa Fe; Mrs. Parkington. **1945** Beyond the Pecos; Honeymoon Ahead; Road to Utopia; Salome, Where She Danced; Senorita from the West; Sudan. **1946** A Night in Paradise; Son of the Guardsman (serial). **1947** Brute Force; Wild Harvest. **1948** Johnny Belinda; Kiss the Blood Off My Hands; Blood on the Moon. **1949** Johnny Stool Pidgeon; Red, Hot and Blue; The Accused; Samson and Delilah. **1950** Francis; My Friend Irma Goes West. **1951** Along the Great Divide; A Place in the Sun; Vengeance Valley. **1952** Son of Paleface; Carrie. **1953** Forbidden. **1955** East of Eden. **1956** Perils of the Wilderness.

FERGUSON, CASSON M.
Born: 1894, Louisiana. Died: Feb. 12, 1929, Culver City, Calif. (pneumonia). Screen and stage actor. Married to actress Catherine Mallon (dec. 1939). Entered films with Selig.

Appeared in: **1919** Flame of the Desert. **1920** Madame X. **1921** At the End of the World; Bunty Pulls the Strings; The Unknown Wife; A Virginia Courtship; What's a Wife Worth? **1922** Manslaughter; Borderland; The Law and the Woman; Over the Border; The Truthful Liar. **1923** Grumpy; Drums of Fate; A Gentleman of Leisure; Her Reputation. **1925** Cobra; The Road to Yesterday; The Wedding Song. **1926** For Alimony Only; Forbidden Waters. **1927** King of Kings. **1928** Tenth Avenue.

FERGUSON, ELSIE
Born: Aug. 19, 1883, N.Y. Died: Nov. 15, 1961, New London, Conn. Screen and stage actress. Divorced from actor Frederick Worlock (dec. 1973).

Appeared in: **1917** Barbary Sheep (film debut); The Rise of Jennie

Cushing. **1918** Rose of the World; Song of Songs; The Lie; Heart of the Wilds; A Doll's House; The Danger Mark; Under the Greenwood Tree. **1919** The Counterfeit; A Society Exile; His Parisian Wife; The Marriage Price; Eyes of the Soul; The Witness for the Defense; The Avalanche. **1920** Lady Rose's Daughter; His House in Order. **1921** Forever; Sacred and Profane Love; Footlights. **1922** Outcast. **1924** Broadway After Dark. **1930** Scarlet Pages.

FERGUSON, FRANK
Born: Dec. 25, 1899 or 1908. Died: Sept. 12, 1978, Los Angeles, Calif. (cancer). Screen and television actor.

Appeared in: **1940** Father is a Prince; Gambling on the High Seas. **1942** This Gun is for Hire; Ten Gentlemen From West Point; Spy Ship; City of Silent Men; Boss of Big Town. **1943** Truck Busters; Mission to Moscow. **1946** Blonde for a Day; Secrets of a Sorority Girl; Swell Guy; Lady Chasers. **1947** The Beginning or the End; They Won't Believe Me; Killer at Large; Variety Girl. **1948** Abbott and Costello Meet Frankenstein; The Walls of Jericho; The Miracle of the Bells; The Vicious Circle; Rachel and the Stranger; Walk a Crooked Mile; The Wonderful Urge; The Hunted; The Inside Story. **1949** State Department File 649; Shockproof; Caught; Slightly French; Follow Me Quietly; Roseanna McCoy; Dynamite; Free for All; Dancing in the Dark. **1950** Under Mexicali Skies; The Good Humor Man; The Furies; He's a Cockeyed Wonder; The West Point Story; Tyrant of the Sea; Frenchie. **1951** Thunder in God's Country; Santa Fe; Warpath; The People Against O'Hara; The Barefoot Mailman; Elopement; On Dangerous Ground. **1952** Wagons West; Rancho Notorious; The Winning Team; Million Dollar Mermaid; Has Anybody Seen My Gal; It Grows on Trees; Oklahoma Annie; Rodeo; Models, Inc. **1953** The Marksman; The Beast From 20,000 Fathoms; Main Street to Broadway; The Star of Texas; Texas Bad Man; Wicked Woman. **1954** Johnny Guitar; Drum Beat; The Shanghai Story; The Outcast; Young at Heart. **1955** Moonfleet; Lawless Street; The McConnell Story; At Gun Point; Battle Cry; The Eternal Sea; New York Confidential. **1957** This Could be the Night; Gun Duel in Durango; The Iron Sheriff; The Lawless Eighties; The Phantom Stagecoach. **1958** The Light in the Forest; Andy Hardy Comes Home; Cole Younger, Gunfighter; Man of the West; Terror in a Texas Town. **1960** Sunrise at Campobello; Raymie; The Big Night. **1961** Pocketful of Miracles. **1964** Hush ... Hush, Sweet Charlotte; The Quick Gun. **1965** The Great Sioux Massacre.

FERGUSON, GEORGE S.
Born: 1884. Died: Apr. 24, 1944, Hollywood, Calif. Screen and stage actor. Appeared in silents.

FERGUSON, HELEN
Born: July 23, 1901, Decatur, Ill. Died: Mar. 14, 1977, Clearwater, Fla. Screen, stage actress, screenwriter, composer, writer and publicist. Married to actor William Russell (dec. 1929). Entered films with Essanay approximately 1914. Was a 1922 Wampas Baby Star.

Appeared in: **1917** Fools for Luck; The Small Town Guy; Gift O' Gab. **1919** The Gamblers. **1920** Going Some; Shod With Fire; Challenge of the Law; Just Pals; Straight From the Shoulder; Romance Promoters. **1921** The Call of the North; Desert Blossoms; The Freeze Out; Miss LuLu Bett; Making the Grade; The Right Way; To a Finish. **1922** Hungry Hearts; According to Hoyle; The Crusader; The Flaming Hour; Rough Shod. **1923** Brass; Double Dealing; Within the Law; The Unknown Purple; The Famous Mrs. Fair. **1924** Chalk Marks; Racing Luck; Never Say Die; The Valley of Hate; The Right of the Strongest. **1925** The Cloud Rider; The Isle of Hope; Thy Neighbor's Wife; The Scarlet West; Spook Ranch; None and Three-fifths Seconds; Wild West (serial). **1926** Casey of the Coast Guard (serial). **1927** Cheaters; Jaws of Steel; The Fire Fighters (serial). **1929** In Old California. **1930** Scarlet Pages.

FERGUSON, HILDA (Hildegarde Gibbons)
Born: 1903. Died: Sept. 3, 1933, N.Y. (heart desease). Screen actress and show girl. Appeared in Sennett films.

FERGUSON, LILE
Died: Nov. 21, 1921, Yuma, Ariz. Screen actor. Appeared in Thomas H. Ince films.

FERGUSON, MATTIE
Born: 1862. Died: Mar. 31, 1929, New York, N.Y. Screen and stage actress.

Appeared in: **1917** The Fatal Ring (serial).

FERGUSON, WILLIAM J.
Born: 1845. Died: May 4, 1930, Pikesville, Md. Screen and stage actor. He was last surviving member of cast that played in Our American Cousin the night President Lincoln was assassinated.

Appeared in: **1920** Passers By. **1921** Dream Street. **1922** John Smith; To Have and To Hold; Kindred of the Dust; Peacock Alley; The World's Champion; The Yosemite Trail.

FERN, FRITZIE
Born: Sept. 19, 1901, Akron, Ohio. Died: Sept. 10, 1932, Hollywood, Calif. Screen and stage actress.

Appeared in: **1929** It Can Be Done; Clear the Decks; The Charlatan.

FERNANDEL (Fernand Joseph Desire Contandin)
Born: May 8, 1903, Marseilles, France. Died: Feb. 26, 1971, Paris, France (lung cancer). Screen actor and singer.

Appeared in: **1930** Black and White (film debut). **1931** Le Rosier de Madame Husson. **1932** Angele (US 1934); Francois Her; Les Bois du Sport; Paris-Beguin. **1933** He. **1935** L'Ordonnance (The Orderly). **1936** Francois Premier; La Porteuse de Pain. **1937** Regain (aka Harvest—US 1939); Le Schountz; Un Carnet de Bal. **1939** Fric-Frac; Paris Honeymoon; Heartbeat. **1940** La Fille de Puisatier. **1946** The Well Digger's Daughter. **1947** Francis the First; Nais. **1950** Ignace; Hoboes in Paradise. **1951** L'Auberge Rouge (aka The Red Inn—US 1954). **1952** Little World of Don Camillo (US 1953, first of the Don Camillo series); Forbidden Fruit (US 1959); Three Sinners; Topaz; The Cupboard Was Bare. **1953** Ali Baba; L'Ennemi Public No. 1 (aka The Most Wanted Man in the World and The Most Wanted Man—US 1962). **1954** The French Touch. **1955** The Sheep Has Five Legs. **1956** The Return of Don Camillo; Around the World in 80 Days; The Wild Oat. **1957** Pantaloons; Fernandel the Dressmaker; Three Feet in a Bed. **1958** Paris Holiday; Senechal the Magnificent; The Man in the Raincoat. **1959** The Law Is the Law; The Virtuous Bigamist. **1959** La Vache et le Prisonnier (aka The Cow and I—US 1961). **1960** The Big Chief; The Easiest Profession; Croesus; Virgin Man. **1962** Le Diable et les dix Commands (The Devil and the Ten Commandments—US 1963); Le Voyage a Biarritz (The Trip to Biarritz). **1963** La Cuisine au Beurre (aka My Wife's Husband—US 1965). **1964** Cherchez L'Idole (Find the Idol). **1966** Your Money or My Life; Le Voyage du Pere. **1967** L'Homme a la Buick.

FERNANDES, BERTA LUISA
Born: 1935, Spain. Died: 1954, near Lisbon, Portugal (injuries from auto accident). Stage and screen actress. Appeared in Spanish and Portuguese films.

FERNANDES, NASCIMENTO
Born: c. 1880, Portugal. Died: Late 1955 or early 1956, Lisbon, Portugal. Screen, stage actor and film producer.

FERNANDEZ, BIJOU
Born: 1877. Died: Nov. 7, 1961, N.Y. Screen and stage actor.

Appeared in: **1925** New Toys. **1926** Just Suppose.

FERNANDEZ, RAMON S.
Born: 1922, Mexico. Died: Sept. 22, 1962, Mexico City, Mexico (heart attack). Screen actor. Appeared in approx. 200 Mexican films.

FERNANDEZ, ROY
Born: 1888. Died: June 22, 1927, Hollywood, Calif. Screen actor.

FERNANDEZ, SEVERO
Died: 1961, Argentina. Screen actor.

Appeared in: **1935** Noches de Buenos Aires (Buenos Aires Nights).

FERRAND, EULA PEARL
Died: July 17, 1970, Visalia, Calif. Screen actress.

FERREIRA, PROCOPIO
Born: 1899. Died: June 18, 1979, Rio de Janeiro, Brazil (cardiac/respiratory ailments). Screen, stage actor and playwright. Married to Aida Isquierdo (dec.) and actress Hamilta Rodrigues. Father of actress Bibi Procopio.

Appeared in: O Trevo de Quatro Folhas; Pureza; Berlin na Batucada (Berlin Afro-Brazilian); Quem Matou Anebela; Cronica da Cidade Amada.

FERRELL, JANE
Born: 1879. Died: June 4, 1952, Newark, N.J. Screen and stage actress.

FERRIS, DILLON J.
Born: 1914. Died: Apr. 25, 1951, Pittsburgh, Pa. Screen and stage actor.

FERRIZ, MIGUEL A.

Born: Mexico. Died: Jan. 1, 1967, Mexico City, Mexico (stroke). Screen and stage actor.

Appeared in: **1933** Mano A Mano (US 1938). **1939** El Beso Mortal (The Fatal Kiss). **1941** Night of the Mayas. **1943** Passion Island; Creo en Dios. **1945** Flor Sylvestre.

FETHERSTON, EDDIE (aka EDDIE FEATHERSTONE)

Died: June 12, 1965, Yucca Valley, Calif. (heart attack). Screen, stage, vaudeville and television actor.

Appeared in: **1925** The Flame Fighter (serial). **1926** Remember; Old Ironsides. **1930** True to the Navy; Worldly Goods. **1932** Movie Crazy; Taxi. **1933** Cheating Blondes. **1934** Here Comes the Navy; The St. Louis Kid. **1935** Gold Diggers of 1935; The Lone Wolf Returns; The Lost City (serial). **1936** Grand Slam Opera (short); Criminals of the Air; My Man Godfrey. **1937** The Game That Kills; Paid to Dance; The Man Who Cried Wolf; plus the following shorts: The Shadow; The Big Squirt; Gracie at Bat. **1938** The Lone Wolf in Paris; Women in Prison; Who Killed Gail Preston?; I Am the Law; Swing, Sister, Swing; There's Always a Woman; plus the following shorts: Time Out for Trouble; A Doggone Mixup; Violent is the Word for Curly. **1939** Homicide Bureau; The Amazing Mr. Williams; Hero for a Day. **1940** Danger on Wheels. **1941** Manpower; Unfinished Business; Bedtime Story; So You Won't Squawk (short). **1942** Lady in a Jam; Unseen Enemy. **1946** The Jolson Story; The Phantom Thief; Boston Blackie and the Law. **1947** Second Chance; Variety Girl. **1948** The Man from Colorado. **1951** Pecos River.

FEUSIER, NORMAN

Born: 1885. Died: Dec. 27, 1945, Hollywood, Calif. Screen and stage actor.

Appeared in: **1933** The Diamond Trail.

FEUSSNER, ALFRED

Born: 1936, Germany. Died: Aug. 25, 1969, Cologne, West Germany. Screen, stage actor and film director.

FIDLER, BEN

Born: 1867. Died: Oct. 19, 1932, Los Angeles, Calif. Screen actor.

FIELD, ALEXANDER

Born: June 6, 1892, London, England. Died: Aug., 1971, London, England. Screen and stage actor.

Appeared in: **1926** Screen Playlets series including: The Woman Juror. **1929** The Crooked Billet. **1930** The Call of the Sea; The Last Hour; Bedrock; Lord Richard in the Pantry; Beyond the Cities; The Cockney Spirit in the War series including: All Riot on the Western Front and the Cockney Spirit in the War Parts I and II. **1931** Third Time Lucky; Rodney Steps Out. **1932** The Crooked Lady; A Safe Proposition; Tin Gods; Ebb Tide; Men of Steel; When London Sleeps; Down Our Street. **1933** Head of the Family; Dick Turpin; F.P.1. **1934** The Double Event; Red Wagon (US 1935); The Wigan Express. **1935** Invitation to the Waltz; No Monkey Business. **1937** Don't Get Me Wrong. **1938** Secrets of F.P.1 (reissue of 1933 F.P.1); Make it Three. **1939** Dark Eyes of London (aka The Human Monster—US 1940); Tommy (reissue of 1930 Cockney Spirit in the War series); Traitor Spy (aka The Torso Murder Mystery—US 1940). **1942** The Next of Kin (US 1943). **1946** Loyal Heart. **1955** Secret Venture. **1957** There's Always a Thursday. **1959** The Woman Eater; Naked Fury (aka The Pleasure Lovers—US 1964).

FIELD, BETTY

Born: Feb. 8, 1918, Boston, Mass. Died: Sept. 13, 1973, Hyannis, Mass. (stroke). Screen, stage and television actress. Divorced from playwright Elmer Rice and from Edwin Lukas. Married to Raymond Olivere.

Appeared in: **1939** What a Life (film debut); Of Mice and Men. **1940** Seventeen; Victory. **1941** The Shepherd of the Hills; Blues in the Night; King's Row; The Little Foxes. **1942** Are Husbands Necessary?; Great Without Glory. **1943** Flesh and Fantasy. **1944** The Great Moment; Tomorrow the World. **1945** The Southerner. **1947** The Great Gatsby. **1955** Picnic. **1956** Bus Stop. **1957** Peyton Place. **1959** Hound-Dog Man; Middle of the Night. **1960** Butterfield 8. **1962** Birdman of Alcatraz. **1965** Never Too Late. **1966** Seven Women. **1968** How to Save a Marriage—And Ruin Your Life (aka Band of Gold); Coogan's Bluff; The Subject Was Roses.

FIELD, GEORGE

Born: 1878, San Francisco, Calif. Died: Mar. 9, 1925, Calif. (tuberculosis). Screen, stage and vaudeville actor.

Appeared in: **1912** The Sheriff's Round-Up; Young Wild West Leading a Raid; The Flower of the Forest; The Miner's Widow; Home and Mother. **1913** The Spartan Girl of the West. **1914** The Shriner's Daughter; The Hermit; Calamity Ann's Love Affair; Sheltering an Ingrate; Jim; Down by the Sea; The Dream Child; The Little House in the Valley; False Gods. **1915** The Derelict; The Truth of Fiction; Ancestry; His Mysterious Neighbor; The Greater Strength; The Reprisal; The Guiding Light; The Water Carrier of San Juan; Spider Barlow Cuts In; On Secret Service; It Was Like This; Out of the Ashes; Alice of Hudson Bay; Bonds of Deception; In the Shuffle; Justified; The Trail of the Thief. **1916** The Franchise; A Woman's Daring; The Profligate; Ruth Ridley's Return; The Key; Citizens All. **1918** Beware of Strangers; The Testing of Mildred Vane. **1919** A Trick of Fate; A Sage Brush Hamlet; End of the Game; A White Man's Chance; The Tiger's Trail (serial). **1920** The Moon Riders. **1921** Diamonds Adrift. **1922** Blood and Sand; The Crimson Challenge; You Never Know; North of the Rio Grande; The Young Rajah. **1923** Adam's Rib; Mr. Billings Spends His Dime; Stephen Steps Out; The Tiger's Claw. **1924** Trigger Finger.

FIELD, GLADYS (Gladys O'Brien)

Born: San Francisco, Calif. Died: Aug., 1920, Mount Vernon, N.Y. (childbirth). Screen actress. Married to film director John O'Brien. Appeared in early Essanay films.

FIELD, KATHLEEN (aka KATHLEEN KEMP)

Born: 1908. Died: Apr. 11, 1980, Oceanside, Calif. (cancer). Screen actress.

FIELD, NORMAN

Born: 1879. Died: Sept. 11, 1956, Hollywood, Calif. Screen and stage actor.

Appeared in: **1950** Destination Big House; Mister 880. **1951** Street Bandits. **1952** The Invitation; The Greatest Show on Earth. **1953** The Twonky; Crazylegs. **1954** Tobor the Great.

FIELD, ROBERT See ROUNESVILLE, ROBERT

FIELD, SID (Sidney Arthur Field)

Born: Apr. 1, 1904, Birmingham, England. Died: Feb. 3, 1950, Surrey, England (heart attack). Screen, stage and vaudeville actor.

Appeared in: **1940** That's the Ticket. **1946** London Town (aka My Heart Goes Crazy—US 1953). **1948** Cardboard Cavalier.

FIELD, WALTER

Born: 1875, On a boat between N.Y. and N.J. Died: June 5, 1976, Hollywood, Calif. Screen, television actor and circus performer.

Appeared in: **1935** Les Miserables; Barbary Coast. **1936** Born to Fight. **1938** Too Hot to Handle. **1939** Stagecoach; Gone With the Wind. **1941** Sea Wolf.

FIELDING, EDWARD

Born: 1879, N.Y. Died: Jan. 10, 1945, Beverly Hills, Calif. (heart attack). Screen and stage actor.

Appeared in: **1930** The following shorts: Grounds for Murder; Seeing Things; The Pest of Honor. **1939** Intermezzo, a Love Story. **1940** The House Across the Bay; The Invisible Man Returns; All This and Heaven Too; Down Argentine Way; South of Suez; Kitty Foyle; Rebecca. **1941** Suspicion; So Ends Our Night; In the Navy; Hold Back the Dawn; Badlands of Dakota; Scotland Yard; Parachute Battalion; Belle Starr. **1942** In This Our Life; Beyond the Blue Horizon; Star-Spangled Rhythm; Pride of the Yankees; The Major and the Minor; Pacific Rendezvous; Ten Gentlemen from West Point. **1943** Three Smart Guys (short); Mr. Lucky; What A Woman; Song of Bernadette. **1944** Mrs. Skeffington; Mrs. Parkington; The Story of Dr. Wassell; See Here, Private Hargrove; My Pal Wolf; The Man in Half Moon Street; Belle of the Yukon; Lady in the Dark; Dead Man's Eyes; Wilson. **1945** A Medal for Benny; The Beautiful Cheat; Guest Wife; Saratoga Trunk; Spellbound.

FIELDING, MARJORIE

Born: 1892, Gloucester, England. Died: Dec. 28, 1956. Screen and stage actress.

Appeared in: **1941** Quiet Wedding (stage and film versions); Jeannie (US 1943). **1943** Yellow Canary (US 1944); The Demi-Paradise (aka Adventure for Two—US 1945). **1946** Quiet Weekend (US 1948). **1947** Fame Is the Spur (US 1949). **1948** Easy Money (US 1949); Spring in

Park Lane (US 1949). **1949** Conspirator (US 1950); The Chiltern Hundreds (aka The Amazing Mr. Beecham—US). **1950** Portrait of Clare; Trio; The Mudlark. **1951** The Franchise Affair (US 1952); Circle of Danger; The Lavender Hill Mob; The Magic Box (US 1952). **1952** The Woman's Angle (US 1954); Mandy (aka Crash of Silence—US 1953). **1953** The Net (aka Project M7—US); Rob Roy the Highland Rogue.

FIELDING, MINNIE (Minnie Flynn)
Born: 1871. Died: July 22, 1936. Screen, stage and vaudeville actress. Appeared in early Biograph pictures.

FIELDING, ROMAINE
Born: 1882. Died: Dec. 16, 1927, Hollywood, Calif. (clot on brain due to infected tooth). Screen, stage actor, film director and film producer.

Appeared in: **1921** The Man Worth While; The Rich Slave. **1927** Gun Gospel; Rose of the Golden West; Ten Modern Commandments. **1928** The Noose; The Shepherd of the Hills.

FIELDS, BENNY (Benjamin Geisenfeld)
Born: 1894, Milwaukee, Wis. Died: Aug. 16, 1959, New York, N.Y. (heart attact). Screen, minstrel and vaudeville actor. Married to actress Blossom Seeley, his one time vaudeville partner (dec. 1974).

Appeared in: **1933** Mr. Broadway. **1936** The Big Broadcast of 1937. **1944** Minstrel Man.

FIELDS, DOROTHY
Born: 1904. Died: Mar. 28, 1974, New York, N.Y. (heart attack). Lyricist, screenwriter and screen actress. Daughter of actors Lew Fields (dec. 1941) and Rose Harris (dec.1948). Sister of actor Herbert Fields (dec. 1958).

Appeared in: **1943** Stagedoor Canteen.

FIELDS, GRACIE (Gracie Stansfield)
Born: Jan. 9, 1898, Rochdale, England. Died: Sept. 27, 1979, Capri, Italy (pneumonia). Screen, stage, vaudeville and television actress. Divorced from actor Archie Pitt (dec. 1940) and later married actor Monty Banks (dec. 1950) and Boris Alperovici. Was made Dame Commander of the Order of the British Empire in 1979.

Appeared in: **1931** Sally In Our Alley (film debut). **1932** Lookin on the Bright Side. **1933** This Week of Grace. **1934** Sing as We Go; Love, Life and Laughter. **1935** Look Up and Laugh. **1936** Queen of Hearts. **1937** The Show Goes On; It's Love I'm After. **1938** We're Going to be Rich; Keep Smiling (aka Smiling Along—US 1939). **1939** Shipyard Sally (US 1940). **1943** Stage Door Canteen; Holy Matrimony. **1945** Molly and Me; Paris Underground (aka Madame Pimpernel). **1949** Prejudice.

FIELDS, HERBERT
Born: July 26, 1898, New York, N.Y. Died: Mar. 24, 1958, New York, N.Y. (heart attack). Screen actor, playwright, scrrenwriter and composer. Son of actors Lew Fields (dec. 1941) and Rose Harris (dec. 1948). Brother of actress Dorothy Fields (dec. 1974).

FIELDS, JOHN
Born: 1876. Died: Nov. 8, 1938, Los Angeles, Calif. Screen and stage actor.

FIELDS, LEW (Lewis Maurice Fields)
Born: 1867, N.Y. Died: July 20, 1941, Beverly Hills, Calif. Screen, stage, vaudeville, burlesque and minstrel actor. Married to actress Rose Harris (dec. 1948). Father of actors Herbert (dec. 1958) and Dorothy Fields (dec. 1974). Was partner with Joe Weber (dec. 1962) in comedy team of "Weber and Fields." See Joe Weber for films they appeared in.

He appeared in the following without Weber: **1917** The Corner Grocer. **1930** 23 Skidoo (short); The Duel (short). **1936** an RKO short.

FIELDS, SHEP
Born: 1911, Brooklyn, N.Y. Died: Feb. 23, 1981, Los Angeles, Calif. (heart attack). Bandleader, screen, radio actor and film producer.

Appeared in: **1938** The Big Broadcast of 1938.

FIELDS, SID
Born: 1898, Milwaukee, Wis. Died: Sept. 28, 1975, Las Vegas, Nev. (lung cancer). Screen, stage, television, burlesque, vaudeville, radio actor, comedy writer and comedian. Appeared in vaudeville with Jack Greenman.

FIELDS, STANLEY (Walter L. Agnew)
Born: 1880, Allegheny, Pa. Died: Apr. 23, 1941, Los Angeles, Calif. (heart attack). Screen, stage and vaudeville actor.

Appeared in: **1930** See America Thirst; Hook, Line and Sinker; Mammy; The Border Legion; Ladies Love Brutes; The Street of Chance; Manslaughter; Cimarron; Little Caesar; City Streets; The Dove; Traveling Husbands; Her Man. **1931** A Holy Terror; Riders of the Purple Sage; Skyline; Cracked Nuts. **1932** Two Kinds of Women; Destry Rides Again; Girl of the Rio Grande; Painted Woman; Hell's Highway; Rackety Rax; The Mouthpiece; Sherlock Holmes; The Kid from Spain; Way Back Home; Girl Crazy. **1933** Constant Woman; Destination Unknown; Island of Lost Souls; Terror Abroad; He Couldn't Take It. **1934** Name the Woman; Rocky Rhodes; Palooka; Sing and Like It; Strictly Dynamite; Many Happy Returns; Kid Millions. **1935** Life Returns; Helldorado; Baby Face Harrington; Mutiny on the Bounty; The Daring Young Man. **1936** It Had to Happen; O'Malley of the Mounted; The Mine with the Iron Door; Showboat; The Gay Desperado; The Devil Is a Sissy; Ticket to Paradise. **1937** Way Out West; Maid of Salem; Souls at Sea; Wells Fargo; Three Legionnaires; The Hit Parade; The Sheik Steps Out; All Over Town; Counsel for Crime; The Toast of New York; Wife, Doctor and Nurse; Danger—Love at Work; Ali Baba Goes to Town; Midnight Court. **1938** Wide Open Faces; Panamint's Bad Man; The Adventures of Marco Polo; Algiers; Flirting With Fate; Painted Desert; Straight, Place and Show. **1939** Fugitive at Large; Pack Up Your Troubles; Exile Express; Chasing Danger; Hell's Kitchen; Blackwell's Island; The Kid from Kokomo. **1940** Viva Cisco Kid; Ski Patrol; The Great Plane Robbery; New Moon; King of the Lumberjacks. **1941** Where Did You Get That Girl?; I'll Sell My Life; The Lady from Cheyenne.

FIELDS, W. C. (Claude William Dukenfield)
Born: Feb. 20, 1879, Philadelphia, Pa. Died: Dec. 25, 1946, Pasadena, Calif. (dropsy and other ailments). Screen, stage, circus, vaudeville actor and screenwriter. Sometimes wrote under name of Otis Criblecoblis.

Appeared in: **1915** Pool Sharks (film debut). **1924** Janice Meredith. **1925** Sally of the Sawdust. **1926** So's Your Old Man; That Royle Girl; It's the Old Army Game. **1927** Two Flaming Youths; The Potters; Running Wild. **1928** Tillie's Punctured Romance; Fools for Luck. **1930** The Golf Specialist (short). **1931** Her Majesty Love. **1932** If I Had a Million; The Dentist (short); Million Dollar Legs. **1933** International House; Hollywood on Parade (short); Tillie and Gus; Alice in Wonderland; plus the following shorts: The Fatal Glass of Beer; The Pharmacist; Hip Action; The Barber Shop. **1934** Six of a Kind; You're Telling Me; Old-Fashioned Way; Mrs. Wiggs of the Cabbage Patch; It's a Gift. **1935** Mississippi; David Copperfield; The Man on the Flying Trapeze. **1936** Poppy. **1938** Big Broadcast of 1938. **1939** You Can't Cheat an Honest Man. **1940** My Little Chickadee; The Bank Dick. **1941** Never Give a Sucker an Even Break. **1942** Tales of Manhattan. **1944** Follow the Boys; Song of the Open Road; Sensations of 1945. **1964** Big Parade of Comedy (documentary). **1966** W. C. Fields Comedy Festival (documentary).

FIGMAN, MAX
Born: 1867. Died: Feb. 13, 1952, Queens, N.Y. Screen and stage actor. Brother of actor Oscar Figman (dec. 1930). Married to actress Lolita Robertson.

Appeared in: **1914** What's His Name; The Man on the Box. **1915** The Adventures of Wallingford; The Truth Wagon; The Hoosier Schoolmaster; Jack Chanty; The Master Stroke; Two Rings and a Goat; A Rheumatic Joint. **1925** The Old Home Week.

FIGMAN, OSCAR (Oscar Brimberton Figman)
Born: 1882. Died: July 18, 1930, Neponsit, N.Y. Screen and stage actor. Brother of actor Max Figman (dec. 1952).

Appeared in: **1924** Manhattan.

FILAURI, ANTONIO
Born: Mar. 9, 1889, Italy. Died: Jan. 18, 1964, San Gabriel, Calif. (emphysema). Screen actor.

Appeared in: **1934** Hi, Nellie! **1935** The Case of the Bride. **1936** Colleen. **1938** Three Blind Mice. **1939** Rio; Code of the Secret Service. **1940** They Knew What They Wanted. **1941** Affectionately Yours; Hold Back the Dawn; International Lady. **1942** Twin Beds; Road to Happiness. **1943** The Song of Bernadette. **1944** Wilson. **1946** The Mask of Dijon; Nocturne. **1947** Mother Wore Tights; King of the Bandits; Sport of Kings; Night Song; I Wonder Who's Kissing Her Now. **1948** Cry of the City. **1949** The Big Sombrero. **1950** Spy Hunt. **1951** The Great Caruso; Too Young to Kiss; On the Riviera. **1952** Five Fingers.

FILLMORE, CLYDE
Born: Oct. 25, 1874, McConnelsville, Ohio. Died: Dec. 19, 1946. Screen, stage and radio actor. Entered films in 1918.

Appeared in: **1919** Millionaire Pirate; Five Fingers; Sundown Trail. **1920** The Soul of Youth; The City Sparrow; The Devil's Pass Key; Nurse Marjorie. **1921** Sham; Moonlight Follies; The Outside Woman; The Sting of the Lash. **1923** The Real Adventure; The Midnight Guest. **1924** Alimony. **1941** The Shanghai Gesture; Unholy Partners. **1942** The Remarkable Andrew; Two Yanks in Trinidad; The Mystery of Marie Roget; The Talk of the Town; My Sister Eileen; When Johnny Comes Marching Home. **1943** Fall In; Margin for Error; Taxi, Mister?; The More the Merrier; Watch on the Rhine; City Without Men; What a Woman; Swing Fever. **1944** Bowery to Broadway; Laura; Three is a Family. **1945** I'll Remember April; Lady on a Train; Colonel Effingham's Raid; Strange Voyage; Hit the Hay.

FILLMORE, NELLIE
Born: 1864. Died: June 20, 1942, Winthrop, Mass. Screen, stage, vaudeville and radio actress.

FILSON, AL W.
Born: Jan. 27, 1857, Blufton, Ind. Died: Nov. 14, 1925. Screen, stage and vaudeville actor.

Appeared in: **1916** Twisted Trails. **1917** The Lad and the Lion; Mountain Dew. **1918** String Beans; Beware of Strangers; Who Shall Take My Life? **1919** Widow By Proxy. **1920** Homespun Folks; Treasure Island; Hairpins. **1921** Chickens; Made in Heaven; The Girl From God's Country. **1922** Watch Him Step; Monte Cristo.

FINA, JACK
Died: May 13, 1970, Los Angeles, Calif. (heart attack). Pianist, composer, conductor and screen actor.

Appeared in: **1946** It's Great to Be Young. **1951** Disc Jockey.

FINCH, FLORA
Born: 1869, England. Died: Jan. 4, 1940, Los Angeles, Calif. (streptococcus infection). Screen, stage, vaudeville actress and film producer. She made 260 shorts with actor John Bunny (dec. 1915) between 1910 and 1915. They appeared as Mr. and Mrs. Bunny and/or Mr. and Mrs. Brown and fans referred to these shorts as "Bunnygraphs," "Bunnyfinches," and "Bunnyfinchgraphs."

A few of these "Bunnygraphs," etc. shorts in which they appeared are as follows: **1910** The New Stenographer. **1911** The Subduing of Mrs. Nag; Her Crowning Glory; The Gossip; Selecting His Heiress; The Ventriloquist's Trunk; Two Overcoats; The Woes of a Wealthy Widow; Intrepid Davy; The Politician's Dream. **1912** A Cure for Pokeritis; Leap Year Proposals; Stenographer Wanted; Bunny and the Twins; Irene's Infatuation; The First Woman Jury in America; Pandora's Box; Her Old Sweetheart; The Awakening of Jones; Diamond Cut Diamond; Umbrellas to Mend; The Suit of Armor; How He Papered the Room; Thou Shalt Not Covet; Suing Susan; Martha's Rebellion; Red Ink Tragedy; Pseudo Sultan; A Persistent Lover; Bunny's Suicide; Doctor Bridget; Freckles. **1913** John Tobin's Sweetheart; There's Music in the Hair; And His Wife Came Back; Hubby Buys a Baby; His Honor, the Mayor; The Wonderful Statue; Bunny's Dilemma; He Answered the Ad; Cupid's Hired Man; Bunny's Birthday Surprise; Love's Quarantine; The Pickpocket; When the Press Speaks; Which Way Did He Go?; A Gentleman of Fashion; Those Troublesome Tresses; The Feudists; The Girl at the Lunch Counter; Mr. Bolter's Niece; The Three Black Bags; Stenographer Troubles; The Locket; Suspicious Henry; The Fortune; A Millinery Bomb; Hubby's Toothache; The Autocrat of Flapjack Junction; The Schemers. **1914** Bunny's Scheme; The Golf Game and the Bonnet; A Change in Baggage Checks; Bunny Buys a Harem; Bunco Bill's Visit; Love's Old Dream; Polishing Up; The Vases of Hymen; Tangled Tangoists; The Old Fire House and the New Fire Chief; The Old Maid's Baby; Bunny Buys a Hat for His Bride; Hearts and Diamonds; Such a Hunter; Father's Flirtation; Bunny's Swell Affair; Bunny in Disguise; Private Bunny; The Locked House; Bunny's Birthday; A Train of Incidents; Bunny Backslides; Bunny's Little Brother. **1915** How Cissy Made Good. Other films she appeared in: **1908** Mrs. Jones Entertains. **1909** Jones and the Lady Book Agent. **1912** The Church Across the Street; The First Violin. **1913** The Classmates Frolic; Love Laughs at Blacksmiths. **1914** Cutey's Vacation. **1915** The Starring of Flora Finchurch. **1916** Prudence the Pirate. **1917** War Prides. **1921** Lessons in Love; Orphans of the Storm. **1922** Man Wanted; Orphan Sally; When Knighthood Was in Flower. **1923** Luck. **1924** Monsieur Beaucaire; Roulette. **1925** The Adventurous Sex; The Early Bird; His Buddy's Wife; The Live Wire; Lover's Island; Men and Women; The Wrongdoers. **1926** The Brown Derby; Fifth Avenue; A Kiss for Cinderella; Oh, Baby. **1927** The Cat and the Canary; Captain

Salvation; Quality Street; Rose of the Golden West. **1928** The Wife's Relations; The Haunted House; Five and Ten-Cent Annie. **1929** The Faker; Come Across. **1930** Sweet Kitty Bellaire. **1931** I Take This Woman. **1934** The Scarlet Letter. **1936** Showboat; Way Out West; Postal Inspector. **1939** The Women.

FINCH, PETER (William Mitchell)
Born: Sept. 28, 1916, London, England. Died: Jan. 14, 1977, Beverly Hills, Calif. (heart attack). Screen, stage and television actor. Nominated for 1971 Academy Award for Best Actor in Sunday Bloody Sunday. Won 1976 Academy Award for Best Actor in Network.

Appeared in: **1937** Dad and Dave Came to Town; Red Sky at Morning. **1938** Mr. Chedworth Steps Out. **1945** The Power and the Glory. **1949** Eureka Stockade; Train of Events (US 1952). **1950** The Wooden Horse (US 1951); The Miniver Story. **1951** Massacre Hill; The Rats of Tobruk. **1952** The Story of Robin Hood and His Merrie Men. **1953** The Story of Gilbert and Sullivan (aka The Great Gilbert and Sullivan (US); The Heart of the Matter (US 1954). **1954** Father Brown (aka Detective—US); Make Me an Offer (US 1956); Elephant Walk; The Queen in Australia (narrator). **1955** Passage Home; The Dark Avenger (aka The Warriors—US); Simon and Laura (US 1956); Josephine and Men. **1956** A Town Like Alice (US 1957); The Battle of the River Plate (aka Pursuit of the Graf Spee—US 1957). **1957** The Shiralee; Robbery Under Arms (US 1958); Wisdom's Way (US 1958). **1958** A Far Cry (short-narrator). **1959** Operation Amsterdam (US 1960); The Nun's Story. **1960** The Trials of Oscar Wilde (aka The Man With the Green Carnation—US, aka The Green Carnation); Kidnapped. **1961** No Love for Johnnie; Sins of Rachel Cade; The Day (short). **1962** I Thank a Fool. **1963** In the Cool of the Day. **1964** Girl With Green Eyes; First Men in the Moon; The Pumpkin Eater. **1965** Flight of the Phoenix. **1966** Judith; 10:30 P.M. Summer. **1967** Far From the Madding Crowd. **1968** The Legend of Lylah Clare. **1971** The Red Tent; Sunday Bloody Sunday. **1973** England Made Me; A Bequest to the Nation (aka The Nelson Affair—US); Lost Horizon. **1974** The Abdication. **1976** Network; Something to Hide.

FINCK, WERNER
Born: 1902, Gorlitz, Germany. Died: Aug. 2, 1978, Germany? Screen, stage actor, screenwriter and cabaret artist.

Appeared in: **1932** Die Wasserteufel van Hieflau; Die Verliebte Firma; Ein Lied, ein Kuss, ein Maedel. **1933** Der Choral von Leuthen (aka Anthem of Leuthen); Die Fahrt ins Gruene; Keine Angst vor Liebe; Das Tankmaedel; Der Laufer von Marathon. **1934** Der Vetter aus Dingsda; Ferien vom Ich; Herr Kobin Geht auf Abenteur; Was bin ich ohne Dich; Jungfrau Gegen Moench; Die Freundin Eines Grossen Mannes; Das Blumenmaedchen vom Grand-Hotel; Die Liebe Siegt; Eine Frau, die Weiss was sie Will. **1935** Frischer Wind aus Kanada; April, April. **1937** Die Landstreicher; Die Unentschuldigte Stunde; Sherlock Holmes (aka Die graude Dame); Die Gluecklichste Ehe der Welt; La Habanera; Autobus S (aka Ein Mann kam Nicht Nach Hause). **1938** Der Maulkorb; Die Umwege des Schoenen Karl; Der Mann, der Nicht Nein Sagen Konnte; Das Maedchen von Gestern Nacht; Verklungene Melodie; The Gray Lady. **1948** Film ohne Titel (Film Without Title). **1949** Kleiner Wagen, Grosse Liebe. **1950** Tobias Knopp, Abenteuer Eines Junggesellen. **1951** Es Begann um Mitternacht; Es Geht Nicht ohne Gisela; Die Frauen des Herrn S. **1953** Wenn am Sonntagabend die Dorfmusik Spielt. **1955** Heldentum nach Ladenschluss; Hanussen; Lola Montes. **1956** Ich und Meine Schwiegersoehne; Lumpazivagabundus. **1957** Die Zuercher Verlobung (aka Engagement in Zurich und aka Affairs of Julie—US 1958); Tolle Nacht; Heiraten Verboten; Maya; Victor und Victoria; Die Liebe Familie; Die Zwillinge vom Zillertal; Der Muede Theodor. **1958** Heute Heiratet mein Mann. **1959** Und das am Montagmorgen; Labyrinth; Gangsterjagd in Lederhesen; Mein Schatz, Komm mit ans Blaue Meer; Rosen fuer den Statsanwalt (Roses for the Prosecutor—US 1961). **1960** Im Weissen Roessl. **1962** Liebe mit Zwanzig (Love at Twenty—US 1963). **1968** Klassenkeile; Der Partyphotograph.

FINDLAY, RUTH
Born: 1904, N.Y. Died: July 13, 1949, New York, N.Y. Screen and stage actress.

Appeared in: **1937** Heroes of the Alamo. **1939** The Women.

FINDLEY, THOMAS BRUCE
Born: 1874, Guelph, Ontario, Canada. Died: May 29, 1941, Aylmer, Quebec, Canada. Screen and stage actor.

Appeared in: **1920** Heliotrope. **1921** Buried Treasure. **1923** Little Old New York. **1924** Yolanda. **1925** Lucky Devil. **1926** Let's Get Married.

FINE, LARRY (Louis Fineburg)

Born: Oct. 5, 1911, Philadelphia, Pa. Died: Jan. 24, 1975, Woodland Hills, Calif. (stroke). Screen, stage and vaudeville actor. Married to actress Mabel Haney (dec. 1967) with whom he appeared in vaudeville. Appeared in vaudeville with Ted Healy in an act billed as "Ted Healy and His Stooges." Was member of the original Three Stooges comedy team which included Moe Howard (dec. 1975) and Jerome "Curly" Howard (dec. 1952).

Appeared in: **1930** Soup to Nuts (film debut). **1933** Myrt and Marge; Dancing Lady; Meet the Baron; Turn Back the Clock; plus the following shorts: Plane Nuts; Nertsery Rhymes; Hello Pop!; Hollywood on Parade; Screen Snapshots; Beer and Pretzels. **1934** Hollywood Party; Fugitive Lovers; The Captain Hates the Sea; Gift of Gab; plus the following shorts: The Big Idea; Woman Haters; Punch Drunks; Men in Black; Three Little Pigskins. **1935** The following shorts: Screen Snapshot #6; Horses' Collars; Restless Knights; Pop Goes the Easel; Uncivil Warriors; Pardon My Scotch; Hoi Polloi; Three Little Beers. **1936** The following shorts: Slippery Silks; Ants in the Pantry; Movie Maniacs; Half-Shot Shooters; Disorder in the Court; A Pain in the Pullman; False Alarms; Whoops I'm an Indian. **1937** Start Cheering; plus the following shorts: Grips, Grunts and Groans; Dizzy Doctors; Three Dumb Clucks; Back to the Woods; Goofs and Saddles; Cash and Carry; Playing the Ponies; The Sitter-Downers. **1938** The following shorts: Termites of 1938; Wee, Wee, Monsieur; Tassels in the Air; Flat Foot Stooges; Healthy, Wealthy and Dumb; Violent is the Word for Curly; Three Missing Links; Mutts to You; Three Little Sew and Sews; We Want our Mummy. **1939** The following shorts: A-Ducking They Did Go; Yes, We Have No Bonanza; Saved by the Belle; Calling All Curs; Oily to Bed, Oily to Rise; Three Sappy People. **1940** The following shorts: You Nazty Spy!; Rockin' Through the Rockies; A-Plumbing We Will Go; Nutty But Nice; How High is Up?; From Nurse to Worse; No Census, No Feeling; Cuckoo Cavaliers. **1941** Time Out for Rhythm; plus the following shorts: Boobs in Arms; So Long, Mr. Chumps; Dutiful But Dumb; All the World's a Stooge; I'll Never Heil Again; An Ache in Every Stake; In the Sweet Pie and Pie; Some More of Samoa; Loco Boy Makes Good. **1942** My Sister Eileen; plus the following shorts: Cactus Makes Perfect; What's the Matador?; Matri-Phony; Three Smart Saps; Even as I.O.U.; Sock-a-Bye Baby. **1943** The following shorts: They Stooge to Conga; Dizzy Detectives; Spook Louder; Back from the Front; Three Little Twerps; Higher Than a Kite; I Can Hardly Wait; Dizzy Pilots; Phony Express; A Gem of a Jam. **1944** The following shorts: Crash Goes the Hash; Busy Buddies; The Yoke's on Me; Idle Roomers; Gents Without Cents; No Dough, Boys. **1945** Rockin' in the Rockies; plus the following shorts: Three Pests in a Mess; Booby Dupes; Idiot's Deluxe; If a Body Meets a Body; Micro-Phonies. **1946** Swing Parade of 1946; plus the following shorts: Beer Barrel Polecats; A Bird in the Head; Uncivil War Birds; Three Troubledoers; Monkey Businessmen; Three Loan Wolves; G.I. Wanna Go Home; Rhythm and Weep; Three Little Pirates. **1947** The following shorts: Half-Wits Holiday; Fright Night; Out West; Hold That Lion; Brideless Groom; Sing a Song of Six Pants; All Gummed Up. **1948** The following shorts: Shivering Sherlocks; Pardon My Clutch; Squareheads of the Round Table; Fiddlers Three; Hot Scots; I'm a Monkey's Uncle; Mummy's Dummies; Crime on Their Hands. **1949** The following shorts: Heavenly Daze; The Ghost Talks; Who Done It?; Hocus Pocus; Feelin' Around; Malice in the Palace; Vagabond Loafers; Dunked in the Deep. **1950** The following shorts: Punchy Cowpunchers; Hugs and Mugs; Dopey Dicks; Love at First Bite; Self-Made Maids; Three Hams on Rye; Studio Stoops; Slap-Happy Sleuths; A Snitch in Time. **1951** Gold Raiders; plus the following shorts: Three Arabian Nuts; Baby Sitters' Jitters; Don't Throw That Knife; Scrambled Brains; Merry Mavericks; The Tooth Will Out; Hula La-La; The Pest Man Wins; A Missed Fortune. **1952** The following shorts: Listen, Judge; Corny Casanovas; He Cooked His Goose; Gents in a Jam; Three Dark Horses; Cuckoo on a Choo Choo. **1953** The following shorts: Up in Daisy's Penthouse; Booty and the Beast; Loose Loot; Tricky Dicks; Spooks; Pardon My Backfire; Rip, Sew and Stitch; Bubble Trouble; Goof on the Roof. **1954** The following shorts: Income Tax Sappy; Musty Musketeers; Pal and Gals; Knutzy Knights; Shot in the Frontier; Scotched in Scotland. **1955** The following shorts: Fling in the Ring; Of Cash and Hash; Gypped in the Penthouse; Bedlam in Paradise; Stone Age Romeos; Wham-Bam-Slam; Hot Ice; Blunder Boys. **1956** The following shorts: Husbands Beware; Creeps; Flagpole Jitters; For Crimin' Out Loud; Rumpus in the Harem; Hot Stuff; Scheming Schemers; Commotion on the Ocean. **1957** The following shorts: Hoofs and Goofs; Muscle Up a Little Closer; A Merry Mix-Up; Space Ship Sappy; Guns A-Poppin'; Horsing Around; Rusty Romeos; Outer Space Jitters. **1958** The following shorts: Quiz Whiz; Fifi Blows Her Top; Pies and Guys; Sweet and Hot; Flying Saucer Daffy; Oil's Well That Ends Well. **1959** Have Rocket Will Travel; Triple Crossed (short); Sappy Bullfighters (short). **1960** Three Stooges Scrapbook; Stop, Look and Laugh. **1961** Snow White and the Three Stooges. **1962** The Three Stooges Meet Hercules; The Three Stooges in Orbit. **1963** It's a Mad, Mad, Mad, Mad World; The Three Stooges Go Around the World in a Daze; Four for Texas. **1964** Big Parade of Comedy. **1965** The Outlaws IS Coming!

FINERON, DOROTHY (Dorothy Frances Fineron)

Born: 1902, Oswego, N.Y. Died: June 18, 1981, Los Angeles, Calif. (kidney failure and pneumonia). Screen, stage actor and reporter. Former Ziegfeld Girl.

FINK, EMMA

Born: 1910, Guanajuato, Mexico. Died: June 13, 1966, Mexico City, Mexico (cancer). Screen and stage actress.

FINLAY, PIERRE

Born: France. Died: Apr. 4, 1937, Paris, France. Screen and stage actor.

Appeared in: **1938** The Tender Enemy.

FINLAY, ROBERT "BOB" (Robert Finlay Bush)

Born: 1888, New Haven, Conn. Died: Apr. 2, 1929, Prescott, Ariz. Screen and vaudeville actor.

Appeared in: **1917** The Winning Punch.

FINLAYSON, JAMES (James Henderson Finlayson)

Born: Aug. 27, 1887, Falkirk, Scotland. Died: Oct. 9, 1953, Los Angeles, Calif. (heart attack). Screen, stage and television actor. Was in early Keystone Kop comedies.

Appeared in: **1921** Home Talent; A Small Town Idol. **1922** The Crossroads of New York. **1923** Hollywood. **1925** Welcome Home. **1927** No Man's Law; plus the following shorts: With Love and Hisses; Love 'Em and Weep; Do Detectives Think?; Flying Elephants; Sugar Daddies; The Call of the Cuckoo; The Second Hundred Years. **1928** Show Girl; Lady Be Good; Ladies Night in a Turkish Bath; Bachelor's Paradise. **1929** Two Weeks Off; Hard to Get; Wall Street; plus the following shorts: Liberty Big Business; Men O' War; The Hoose Gow. **1930** Young Eagles; Flight Commander; For the Defense; The Dawn Patrol; plus the following shorts: Dollar Dizzy; Night Owls; Another Fine Mess. **1931** Pardon Us; Stout Hearts and Willing Hands; Big Business; plus the following shorts: One of the Smiths; The Hasty Marriage; Our Wife; Chickens Come Home; One Good Turn; A Melon-Drama; Catch as Catch Can; Oh! Oh! Cleopatra. **1932** Thunder Below; Pack Up Your Troubles; plus the following shorts: Boy, Oh, Boy; The Chimp; The Iceman's Ball; The Millionaire Cat; Jitters the Butler. **1933** Fra Diavola (The Devil's Brother); The Girl In Possession; Dick Turpin; plus the following shorts: His Silent Racket; Me and My Pal; Hokus Focus; The Druggist's Dilemma; The Gay Nighties. **1935** Treasure Blues (photo only); Thicker Than Water; Bonnie Scotland; Manhattan Monkey Business (short). **1936** The Bohemian Girl; Our Relations; Way Out West; Life Hesitates at 40 (short). **1937** All Over Town; Pick a Star. **1938** Blockheads; False Roomers (short). **1939** The Great Victor Herbert; Hollywood Cavalcade; The Flying Deuces. **1940** A Chump at Oxford; Saps at Sea. **1942** To Be or Not to Be. **1943** Yanks Ahoy. **1947** Perils of Pauline; Thunder in the Valley (aka Bob, Son of Battle). **1948** Grand Canyon Trail. **1949** Down Memory Lane. **1951** Royal Wedding. **1960** When Comedy Was King (documentary). **1964** Big Parade of Comedy (documentary). **1965** Laurel and Hardy's Laughing 20's (documentary). **1968** The Further Perils of Laurel and Hardy (documentary).

FINLEY, NED

Died: Sept. 27, 1920, New York, N.Y. Screen actor and film director.

Appeared in: **1912** The Curio Hunters. **1913** A Heart of the Forest; A Game of Cards; Brother Bill; A Fighting Chance; The Leading Lady; Homespun Tragedy; Dr. Cathern's Experiment; Fortune's Turn. **1914** Children of the Feud; The Tattoo Mark; Steve O'Grady's Chance; The Reward of Thrift; Local Color; Good Gracious!; The Moonshine Maid and the Man. **1915** The Goddess (serial); O'Garry of the Royal Mounted; Breaking In; Lifting the Ban of Controversy; West Wind; A Man's Sacrifice; Hearts and the Highway; The Making Over of Geoffrey Manning; His Bunkie; From the Dregs. **1916** Britton of the Seventh; The Hunted Woman; Out of the Quagmire; The Kid; Myrtle the Manicurist; The Rookie; A Strange Case. **1917** Little Terror; The Bottom of the Well; The Secret Kingdom (serial). **1918** The Menace; The Raiders of Sunset Gap.

FINN, CATHERINE

Born: England. Died: 1980, England? Screen actress.

Appeared in: **1967** The Deadly Bees; Torture Garden (US 1968).

FINN, SAM

Born: 1893. Died: Dec. 14, 1958, Hollywood, Calif. (undergoing brain surgery). Screen actor and extra for 30 years.

Appeared in: **1935** Mary Burns, Fugitive. **1946** Our Hearts Were

Growing Up; The Hoodlum Saint. **1948** Hollow Triumphs. **1949** A Letter to Three Wives; Oh, You Beautiful Doll! **1951** The People Against O'Hara. **1952** Here Come the Marines. **1955** You're Never Too Young. **1957** Jeanne Eagels.

FINNEGAN, WALTER
Born: 1873. Died: May 30, 1943, Hollywood, Calif. Screen actor.

FINNERTY, LOUIS
Born: 1883, N.J. Died: Aug. 4, 1937, Los Angeles, Calif. (intestinal obstruction). Screen and vaudeville actor.

Appeared in: **1937** Saratoga.

FINNERTY, WARREN
Born: 1934. Died: Dec. 22, 1974, New York, N.Y. (heart attack). Screen, stage and television actor.

Appeared in: **1960** Murder, Inc. **1962** The Connection (stage and film versions). **1965** The Pawnbroker; The Brig; Andy. **1967** Cool Hand Luke. **1969** Easy Rider; Marlowe; Free Grass.

FIORENZA, ALFREDO
Born: 1868, Italy. Died: Feb. 24, 1931, Hollywood, Calif. Screen and stage actor. Entered films approx. 1924.

FIO RITO, TED (Ted Fiorito)
Born: Dec. 20, 1900, Newark, N.J. Died: July 22, 1971, Scottsdale, Ariz. (heart attack). Bandleader, screen, radio actor and songwriter.

Appeared in: **1934** Twenty Million Sweethearts (with his orchestra). **1943** Silver Skates.

FIRTH, THOMAS PRESTON
Born: 1883. Died: Jan. 9, 1945, North Hollywood, Calif. Screen actor. Entered films approx. 1918.

FISCHER, DAVID G.
Born: 1891. Died: Apr. 21, 1939, Hartford, Conn. Screen, stage actor and film director.

Appeared in: **1912** The Fall of Black Hawk.

FISCHER, MARGARITA (aka MARGARITE FISHER)
Born: Feb. 11, 1886, Missouri Valley, Iowa. Died: Mar. 11, 1975, Encinitas, Calif. (cerebral thrombosis). Screen and stage actress. Married to actor Harry Pollard (dec. 1934).

Appeared in: **1911** A Lesson to Husbands. **1912** The Trinity; The Worth of a Man; Call of the Drum; Better Than Gold; Winning the Latonia Derby; The Dove and the Serpent; On the Shore; Melodrama of Yesterday; Jim's Atonement; Love, War and a Bonnet; The Parson and the Medicine Man; Exchanging Labels; The Tribal Law; The Rights of a Savage. **1913** Uncle Tom's Cabin; His Old-Fashioned Dad; The Great Ganton Mystery; The Wayward Sister; The Shadow; The Stolen Idol; The Turn of the Tide; The Fight Against Evil; Slavery Days; The Wrong Road; The Power of Heredity; Sally Scraggs—Housemaid; The Diamond Makers; Shon the Piper; Like Darby and Joan; The Boob's Dream Girl. **1914** A Tale of a Lonely Coast; Bess the Outcast; The Wife; Nancy's Husband; The Professor's Awakening; Caught in a Tight Pinch; Closed at Ten; Jane—the Justice; A Joke on Jane; Susanna's New Suit; The Other Train; A Suspended Ceremony; The Silence of John Gordon; A Modern Othello; Susie's New Shoes; The Primeval Test. **1915** The Peacock Feather Fan; The Lonesome Heart; The Miracle of Life; The Dragon. **1916** Susie's New Shoes; Pearl of Paradise; The Quest; Miss Jackie of the Navy; Miss Jackie of the Army; The Devil's Assistant. **1918** Molly Go Get 'Em; Jilted Janet; Impossible Susan; A Square Deal; Ann's Finish; The Girl Who Couldn't Grow Up; Primitive Woman. **1919** Mantle of Charity; Tiger Lily; Money Isn't Everything; Trixie from Broadway; Fair Enough; Folly of the Follies; Charge It to Me; Put Up Your Hands! **1920** The Week-end; Dangerous Talent; The Thirtieth Piece of Silver; The Hellion. **1921** The Gamester; Payment Guaranteed; The Butterfly Girl; Their Mutual Child; Beach of Dreams. **1924** K—The Unknown. **1925** Any Woman. **1927** Uncle Tom's Cabin (and 1913 version).

FISCHMAN, DAVID
Born: 1910. Died: Jan. 24, 1958, Los Angeles, Calif. Screen actor.

FISHER, ALFRED
Born: 1849, England. Died: Aug. 26, 1933, Glendale, Calif. Screen, stage actor and stage director. Entered films in 1918.

Appeared in: **1919** Third Degree. **1923** Burning Words; Railroaded. **1924** The Breathless Moment; The Fighting American; The Storm Daughter. **1925** The Home Maker. **1926** Atta Boy; The Country Beyond. **1927** Broadway Madness; Driven from Home. **1928** Fangs of Fate; A Million for Love; Romance of a Rogue.

FISHER, FREDDIE "SCHNICKELFRITZ"
Born: 1904. Died: Mar. 28, 1967. Bandleader and screen actor.

Appeared in: **1930** The Song Writers Revue (short). **1938** Gold Diggers in Paris. **1943** The Sultan's Daughter. **1944** Seven Days Ashore; Jamboree; That's My Baby. **1949** Make Mine Laughs.

FISHER, GEORGE B.
Born: 1894, Republic, Mich. Died: Aug. 13, 1960, Los Angeles, Calif. Screen and stage actor.

Appeared in: **1913** The Man Who Went Out. **1915** His Affianced Wife; Her Easter Hat; Hearts and Swords; The Artist's Model. **1916** Civilization. **1917** Environment; Conscience; Annie-for-Spite. **1921** Bare Knuckles; Beach of Dreams; Colorado Pluck; Hearts of Youth; Moonlight Follies; A Parisian Scandal; Sure Fire. **1922** Domestic Relations; Don't Shoot; The Trail of the Axe. **1923** Divorce. **1924** The Bowery Bishop; Excitement. **1925** After Marriage; Justice of the Far North. **1929** Apartment Hunting (short). **1947** The Last Round-Up. **1949** Joe Palooka in the Big Fight. **1950** Champagne for Caesar. **1951** Hard, Fast and Beautiful.

FISHER, HARRY
Born: Sept. 13, 1885, New York, N.Y. Died: May 21, 1917, Los Angeles, Calif. (auto accident). Screen actor.

Appeared in: **1913** Gold is Not All. **1914** The Orange Bandit; The Man on the Box. **1915** Bertie's Stratagem; The Missing Clue; The Fire Escape; Getting Rid of Aunt Kate; Alone in the City of Sighs and Tears; Mr. Jarr and Gertrude's Beaux; The Morning After; Kidding the Goats; Fits and Chills; Itsky the Inventor; Hughey of the Circus; The Faith of Sonny Jim; The Pest Vamooser; The Patent Food Conveyor. **1916** The Cold Feet Getaway; The Wrong Mr. Wright; Myrtle the Manicurist; Love's Getaway; Poisoned Lips; The Rummy.

FISHER, MAGGIE (Maggie Holoway Fisher)
Born: 1854, England. Died: Nov. 3, 1938, Glendale, Calif. Screen and stage actress.

FISHER, MARGARITE See FISCHER, MARGARITA

FISHER, MAX
Born: 1909, Austria. Died: Oct. 11, 1974, New York, N.Y. Screen, stage, television actor, film and stage director and drama coach.

Appeared in: **1938** Grande Illusion.

FISHER, SALLY
Born: 1881. Died: June 8, 1950, Twenty-Nine Palms, Calif. (heart attack). Screen, stage and vaudeville actress.

FISHER, WILLIAM
Born: 1868. Died: July 4, 1933, Hollywood, Calif. (heart attack). Screen actor and acrobat.

Appeared in: **1922** The Broken Silence. **1925** The Keeper of the Bees.

FISHER, WILLIAM G.
Born: 1883. Died: Oct. 4, 1949, Hollywood, Calif. Screen actor.

FISHMAN, DUKE M.
Born: 1906. Died: Dec. 22, 1977, Palm Springs, Calif. (heart attack). Screen and television actor.

FISKE, MINNIE (Maria Augusta Davey, aka MRS. FISKE)
Born: Dec. 19, 1865, New Orleans, La. Died: Feb. 15, 1932, Hollis, N.Y. (heart failure). Screen, stage actress and stage director. Married to writer Harrison Grey Fiske.

Appeared in: **1913** Tess of the D'Urbervilles (stage and film versions). **1915** Vanity Fair.

FISKE, RICHARD (Thomas Richard Potts)
Born: Nov. 20, 1915, Shelton, Wash. Died: Aug., 1944 (killed in action). Screen actor.

Appeared in: **1938** The Little Adventuress; Blondie; The Spider's Web (serial). **1939** Overland With Kit Carson (serial); Homicide Bureau; Blondie Meets the Boss; Behind Prison Gates; Man From Sundown; Parents on Trial; The Stranger from Texas; plus the following shorts: Pest from the West; Rattling Romeo; Skinny the Moocher; Teacher's Pest; Andy Clyde Gets Spring Chicken; Oily to Bed, Oily to Rise; Three Sappy People. **1940** Pioneers of the Frontier; Konga—the Wild Stallion; Men Without Souls; The Man from Tumbleweed; Prairie Schooner; plus the following shorts: The Heckler; His Bridal Fright; Fireman—Save My Choo Choo; Boobs in Arms; Nothing But Pleasure; Pardon My Berth Marks; The Taming of the Snood. **1941** The Lone Wolf Takes a Chance; Outlaws of the Panhandle; The Devil

Commands; The Medico of Painted Springs; North from the Lone Star; Across the Sierras; The Officer and the Lady; The Son of Davy Crockett; All the World's a Stooge (short). **1942** Perils of the Royal Mounted (serial); The Major and the Minor; Valley of the Sun. **1943** Dizzy Pilots (short).

FISKE, ROBERT L.
Born: Oct. 20, 1889, Griggsville, Mo. Died: Sept. 12, 1944, Sunland, Calif. (congestive heart failure). Screen actor.

Appeared in: **1936** The Sky Parade. **1937** Old Louisiana; Battle Greed; Drums of Destiny. **1938** The Purple Vigilantes; Cassidy of Bar 20; Religious Racketeers; Numbered Woman; Flight into Nowhere; South of Arizona; Colorado Trail; Sunset Trail; Adventure in Sahara; I Am a Criminal. **1939** Flying G-Men (serial); West of Santa Fe; Racketeers of the Range; Mystic Circle Murder; Fools Who Made History (short). **1940** Deadwood Dick (serial); The Green Archer (serial); The Shadow (serial); East Side Kids; Passport to Alcatraz; Carolina Moon; Before I Hang; Texas Terrors; Law and Order. **1941** The Big Boss; Along the Rio Grande; Dick Tracy vs Crime, Inc. (serial); The Apache Kid; Borrowed Hero. **1942** Valley of the Sun; Black Dragons; Today I Hang. **1943** Batman (serial). **1944** Cyclone Prairie Rangers.

FITZ-ALLEN, ADELAIDE
Born: 1856. Died: Feb. 26, 1935, New York, N.Y. (bronchial pneumonia). Screen, stage and radio actress.

FITZGERALD, BARRY (William Joseph Shields)
Born: Mar. 10, 1888, Dublin, Ireland. Died: Jan. 4, 1961, Dublin, Ireland. Stage and screen actor. Won 1944 Academy Award for Best Supporting Actor in Going My Way, and was nominated as Best Actor for same film. Brother of actor Arthur Shields (dec. 1970).

Appeared in: **1929** Juno and the Paycock (US 1930). **1937** Ebb Tide; Plough and the Stars. **1938** Bringing Up Baby; Dawn Patrol; Four Men and a Prayer; Marie Antoinette. **1939** Pacific Liner; The Saint Strikes Back; Full Confessions. **1940** The Long Voyage Home. **1941** The Sea Wolf; San Francisco Docks; Tarzan's Secret Treasure; How Green Was My Valley. **1943** Amazing Mrs. Halliday; Corvette K-225; Two Tickets to London. **1944** None But the Lonely Heart; I Love a Soldier; Going My Way. **1945** Stork Club; Duffy's Tavern; Incendiary Blonde; And Then There Were None; Forever Yours; The Bells of St. Mary's. **1946** California; Two Years Before the Mast. **1947** Welcome Stranger; Easy Come, Easy Go; Variety Girl. **1948** Naked City; The Sainted Sisters; Miss Tatlock's Millions. **1949** Top O' the Morning; Story of Seabiscuit. **1950** Union Station. **1951** Silver City. **1952** The Quiet Man. **1954** Happy Ever After (aka Tonight's the Night—US). **1956** The Catered Affair. **1958** Rooney. **1959** Broth of a Boy.

FITZGERALD, CISSY
Born: 1874, England. Died: May 5, 1941, Ovingdean, England. Stage and screen actress. Entered films in a 50-foot film taken at the studio where Edison was attempting to perfect a motion picture camera.

Appeared in: **1914** The Accomplished Mrs. Thompson; The Win(k)some Widow. **1915** Curing Cissy; Cissy's Innocent Wink; The Widow Wins; The Dust of Egypt; A Corner in Cats; Zablitsky's Waterloo. **1916** Leave It to Cissy. **1924** Babbitt; Cornered; Daring Love; Flowing Gold; Lilies of the Field; Vanity's Price; A Woman Who Sinned. **1925** If Marriage Fails; I'll Show You the Town; Steppin' Out. **1926** The Crown of Lies; The Danger Girl; Flames; Her Big Night; The High Flyer; The Love Thief; Redheads Preferred. **1927** The Arizona Wildcat; Beauty Shoppers; Fire and Steel; Matinee Ladies; McFadden's Flats; Two Flaming Youths; Women Love Diamonds; Women's Wares. **1928** The Swim Princess (short); No Babies Wanted; Ladies of the Night Club; Laugh, Clown, Laugh. **1929** Seven Footprints to Satan; The Diplomat (short); His Lucky Day; Social Sinners (short). **1920** The Painted Angel. **1931** Transgression. **1933** The Masquerade; Only Yesterday. **1935** Strictly Legal.

FITZGERALD, EDWARD P.
Born: 1883. Died: May 1, 1942, Buffalo, N.Y. Screen and vaudeville actor. In vaudeville he was part of an act known as "Fitzgerald and Quigley" and later as "Fitzgerald and Madison." Appeared in Mack Sennett comedies during 1920's.

FITZGERALD, FLORENCE IRENE
Born: 1890. Died: Jan. 31, 1962, Hartford, Conn. Screen actress.

FITZGERALD, JAMES M.
Born: 1897. Died: Jan. 21, 1919, Los Angeles, Calif. (influenza). Screen actor.

FITZGERALD, LILLIAN
Born: New York. Died: July 9, 1947, New York, N.Y. Screen, stage, vaudeville actress and singer. Daughter of vaudeville performers Patrick and Catherine Fitzgerald.

Appeared in: **1939** Some Like it Hot.

FITZGERALD, WALTER (Walter Bond)
Born: May 18, 1896, Keyham, England. Died: Dec. 20, 1976, London, England. Screen, stage and television actor.

Appeared in: **1932** Murder at Covent Garden (film debut). **1941** This England (aka Our Heritage). **1942** In Which We Serve; Squadron Leader X. **1943** San Demetrio-London. **1945** Strawberry Roan (US 1948); Great Day (US 1946). **1947** Mine Own Executioner (US 1949). **1948** Blanche Fury; This Was a Woman (US 1949); The Fallen Idol (US 1949); The Winslow Boy (US 1950). **1949** Edward My Son; The Small Back Room (US 1952). **1950** Treasure Island. **1951** Lost Illusion. **1952** The Pickwick Papers (US 1953); The Ringer. **1953** Personal Affair (US 1954); Appointment in London (US 1955); The Cruel Sea; The Net (aka Project M7—US). **1954** Lease of Life (US 1955); Our Girl Friday (aka The Adventures of Sadie—US 1955); Front Page Story (US 1955). **1955** Cockleshell Heroes (US 1956). **1957** The Man in the Sky (aka Decision Against Time—US); The Birthday Present; Something of Value. **1958** The Camp on Blood Island. **1959** Darby O'Gill and the Little People; Third Man on the Mountain. **1962** We Joined the Navy; HMS Defiant (aka Damn the Defiant—US).

FITZHAMON, LEWIN
Born: June 5, 1869, Aldingham, England. Died: 1961, England? Screen actor, film producer and screenwriter. Married to actress Constance Somers-Clarke (aka Connie Somers).

Appeared in: **1900** Briton vs. Boer. **1904** The Slavey's Dream; Lady Plumpton's Motor; A Race for a Kiss. **1905** Lost, Stolen or Strayed; The Villian's Wooing. **1906** The Rivals; A Tragedy of the Sawmills; The Peasant Girl's Revenge; Dick Turpin's Ride to New York; The Squatter's Daughter; The Fatal Leap; Black Beauty; The Pirate Ship. **1907** A Sailor's Lass. **1908** The Gentleman Gypsy (aka The Trials of a Gypsy Gentleman); For the Little Lady's Sake. **1909** The Race for the Farmer's Cup; Invisibility. **1910** Black Beauty (and 1906 version); The Detective in Peril. **1911** A Horse and Mrs. Grundy; Tiger the 'Tec. **1912** The Blind Man's Dog. **1913** The Girl Next Door; The First Steeplechase; He Was So Fond of Animals.

FITZHARRIS, EDWARD "FITZ"
Born: 1890, England. Died: Oct. 12, 1974, Woodland Hills, Calif. (pneumonia). Screen actor and costumer.

FITZMAURICE, GEORGE
Born: Feb. 13, 1895, Paris, France. Died: June 13, 1940, Los Angeles, Calif. (streptococcus). Screen actor, film director, and screenwriter.

Appeared in: **1919** The Avalanche.

FITZMAURICE, MICHAEL T. (Michael Fitzmaurice-Kelly)
Born: Apr. 28, 1908, Chicago, Ill. Died: Aug. 31, 1967, New York, N.Y. Screen, stage, radio and television actor.

Appeared in: **1936** The House of a Thousand Candles; The Plough and the Stars. **1937** A Girl With Ideas; Reported Missing. **1951** Fourteen Hours.

FITZPATRICK, JAMES A.
Born: Feb. 26, 1902, Shelton, Conn. Died: June 12, 1980, Cathedral City, Calif. (stroke). Screen actor, film director, film producer and screenwriter. Originator, producer and narrator of Fitzpatrick Traveltalks.

FITZROY, EMILY
Born: 1861, London, England. Died: Mar. 3, 1954, Gardena, Calif. (stroke). Screen and stage actress.

Appeared in: **1916** East Lynne. **1919** The Climbers. **1920** Deadline at Eleven; Way Down East. **1921** Straight Is the Way; Jane Eyre; Out of the Chorus; Wife Against Wife. **1922** The Splendid Lie; Fascination; Find the Woman; No Trespassing. **1923** Fury; Driven; Strangers of the Night; The Purple Highway. **1924** Jealous Husbands; His Hour; Secrets; The Whispered Name; Girl of the Limberlost; Her Night of Romance; Love's Wilderness; The Red Lily; The Man Who Came Back; Untamed Youth. **1925** Are Parents People?; Lazybones; Bobbee Hair; Outwitted; Zander the Great; Thunder Mountain; The Denial; The Lady; Learning to Love; The Winding Stair; Never the Twain Shall Meet; The Spaniard. **1926** The Bat; Bardley's, the Magnificent; Marriage License?; What Happened to Jones; Hard Boiled; Don Juan; High Steppers. **1927** Love; The Cheerful Fraud; Orchids and Ermine;

Married Alive; Mockery; The Sea Tigers; Once and Forever; One Increasing Purpose. **1928** The Trail of '98; Foreign Devils; Gentlemen Prefer Blondes; Love Me and the World Is Mine; No Babies Wanted. **1929** The Bridge of San Luis Rey; The Case of Lena Smith; Show Boat; Flirting Widow; Man from Blankley's; She's My Weakness; Song O' My Heart; New Moon. **1931** Misbehaving Ladies; Aren't We All; The Green Spot Mystery; It's a Wise Child; Unfaithful. **1932** Detective Lloyd (serial); High Society; Lucky Ladies. **1933** Timbuctoo; Her Imaginary Lover; Dick Turpin. **1934** Don Quixote; Man With Two Faces; Two Heads on a Pillow; The Captain Hates the Sea. **1935** China Seas. **1936** The Beloved Rogue; The Bold Caballero. **1938** The Frontiersman. **1940** Vigil in the Night. **1941** The Flame of New Orleans; Two Faced Women. **1943** Forever and a Day.

FITZROY, LOUIS
Born: Nov. 24, 1870, Sault Sainte Marie, Mich. Died: Jan. 26, 1947. Screen and stage actor.

Appeared in: **1918** A Bird of Prey. **1919** The Four Flusher. **1920** A Beggar in Purple. **1924** Barbara Frietchie; Silk Stocking Sal. **1925** Galloping Jinx; On the Go.

FITZSIMMONS, BOB (Robert L. Fitzsimmons)
Born: June 4, 1862, Helston, Cornwall, England. Died: Nov. 22, 1917, Chicago, Ill (pneumonia). Blacksmith, prizefighter, screen and vaudeville actor. Do not confuse with actor of same name, not deceased.

Appeared in: **1968** The Legendary Champions (documentary).

FIX, RESS (Ressie Mae Fix)
Born: June 19, 1893, Indiana. Died: Jan. 5, 1975, Hollywood, Calif. (heart attack). Screen and television actress. Mother of actor Jay Stewart.

FLAGG, JAMES MONTGOMERY
Born: June 18, 1977, Pelham Manor, N.Y. Died: May 27, 1960, New York, N.Y. Illustrator, artist, screenwriter and screen actor.

Appeared in: **1913** Saved by Parcel Post. **1918** The Good Sport; Perfectly Fiendish Flanagan; The Spoiled Girl; Tell That to the Marines. **1919** One Every Minute; Beresford and the Baboons.

FLAGSTAD, KIRSTEN
Born: 1895. Died: Dec. 9, 1962, Oslo, Norway. Screen actress and opera performer.

Appeared in: **1938** The Big Broadcast of 1938.

FLAHERTY, PAT J., SR.
Born: Mar. 8, 1903, Washington, D.C. Died: Dec. 2, 1970, N.Y. (heart attack). Screen actor, film technician and professional baseball player.

Appeared in: **1934** Come on Marines; The Mighty Barnum; Twentieth Century; Baby, Take a Bow; Brand of Hate. **1935** Secret of the Chateau; Chinatown Squad; One Way Ticket; G-Men; China Seas. **1936** Love Before Breakfast; Mutiny on the Bounty; My Man Godfrey; Hearts in Bondage; Pigskin Parade; Flying Hostess. **1937** Woman Wise; Navy Blue and Gold; On Again, Off Again; A Day at the Races; A Star is Born; Hold 'Em Navy; A Girl With Ideas. **1938** Hollywood Stadium Mystery; Always in Trouble; She Loved a Fireman; Telephone Operator; The Main Event. **1939** Legion of Lost Flyers; Only Angels Have Wings; Newsboys' Home; Dodge City; Code of the Streets. **1940** City for Conquest; The Man from Montreal; A Miracle on Main Street; My Son, My Son; Midnight Limited; Black Diamonds; Fight Command. **1941** Sergeant York; Meet John Doe; Affectionately Yours; Highway West; Rise and Shine; Ball of Fire; The Strawberry Blonde. **1942** The Saboteur; Captains of the Clouds; Gentleman Jim; Who is Hope Schuyler?; It Happened in Flatbush; Yankee Doodle Dandy. **1943** Hit the Ice. **1946** It Shouldn't Happen to a Dog; Home Sweet Homicide; The Best Years of Our Lives. **1947** The Bachelor and the Bobby-Soxer; The Red House; The Long Night. **1948** Key Largo; Give My Regards to Broadway; All My Sons; The Noose Hangs High; The Babe Ruth Story; The Cobra Strikes. **1949** It's a Great Feeling; The Stratton Story. **1950** The Petty Girl; Harvey; The Asphalt Jungle; The Jackie Robinson Story; The Good Humor Man; Blondie's Hero. **1951** Meet Danny Wilson; Detective Story; The Racket; Angels in the Outfield. **1952** Hoodlum Empire; The Winning Team; Blackbeard the Pirate. **1954** Bowery Boys Meet the Monsters. **1955** The Desperate Hours.

FLANAGAN, BUD (Robert Winthrop)
Born: 1896, England. Died: Oct. 19, 1968, London, England. Screen, music hall, stage actor and songwriter. Married to comedienne/dancer Ann "Curley" Flanagan (dec. 1975) and father of actor Buddy

Flanagan. Appeared with Chesney Allen (dec. 1982) as part of comedy team "Flanagan and Allen." The team appeared in "Crazy Gang" films and stage presentations with Jimmy Nervo (dec. 1975), Teddy Knox (dec. 1974), Charlie Naughton (dec. 1976) and Jimmy Gold (dec. 1967).

The "Crazy Gang" films include: **1937** Okay for Sound. **1938** Alf's Button Afloat. **1939** The Frozen Limits. **1940** Gasbags. **1958** Life Is a Circus (US 1962). "Flanagan and Allen" appeared in: **1932** The Balliffs (short). **1933** They're Off (short); The Dreamers (short). **1934** Wild Boy. **1935** A Fire Has Been Arranged. **1937** Underneath the Arches. **1942** We'll Smile Again. **1943** Theatre Royal. **1944** Dreaming. **1945** Here Comes the Sun. **1952** Judgement Deferred (Flanagan only). **1958** Dunkirk. **1963** The Wild Affair (US 1966—Flanagan only).

FLANAGAN, EDWARD J.
Born: 1880, St. Louis, Mo. Died: Aug. 18, 1925, Los Angeles, Calif. (peritonitis). Screen, stage and vaudeville actor. Was on screen and in vaudeville as "Flanagan and Edwards" and also worked separately.

Appeared in: **1921** Don't Call Me Little Girl; Hunch.

FLANAGAN, HUGH
Died: Dec. 26, 1925, New York, N.Y. (pneumonia). Screen actor. Appeared in Famous Players Company Films.

FLANAGAN, REBECCA
Born: 1876. Died: Jan. 30, 1938, Hollywood, Calif. Screen and stage actress. Entered films approx. 1928. Married to actor D. J. Flanagan.

FLANDERS, MICHAEL (Michael Henry Flanders)
Born: Mar. 1, 1922, London, England. Died: Apr. 14, 1975, Wales. Screen, stage, radio, television actor, humorist and lyricist. Partner with Donald Swann in two-man show entitled "At the Drop of a Hat."

Appeared in: **1963** Doctor in Distress (US 1964). **1970** The Raging Moon.

FLATEAU, GEORGES
Born: 1882, France. Died: Feb. 13, 1953, Paris, France. Screen, stage, radio and television actor.

Appeared in: **1939** Katia. **1951** Adventures of Captain Fabian.

FLATT, LESTER
Born: 1915, Overton County, Tenn. Died: May 11, 1979, Nashville, Tenn. (heart attack). Bluegrass guitarist, singer and screen actor.

Appeared in: **1964** Country Music on Broadway.

FLAVIN, JAMES
Born: May 14, 1906, Portland, Maine. Died: Apr. 23, 1976, Los Angeles, Calif. (ruptured aorta). Screen, stage and television actor. Married to actress Lucille Browne (dec. 1976). Entered films in 1931.

Appeared in: **1932** McKenna of the Mounted; Back Street; Air Mail Mystery (serial); The All-American; Okay America. **1933** King Kong; Riot Squad; Mayfair; Ship of Wanted Men. **1934** Gift O' Gab; Baby Takes a Bow; Affairs of Cellini; After Office Hours; Beloved; Brand of Hate; The Crosby Case; Bright Eyes; White Gold; Society Doctor. **1935** G-Men; West Point of the Air; Death Flies East; Secret of the Chateau; One Way Ticket; People Will Talk; Man Proposes; Chinatown Squad. **1936** My Man Godfrey; Two in a Crowd. **1937** Mysterious Crossing; I Promise to Pay; Girls Can Play; The League of Frightened Men. **1938** The Buccaneer; Ride a Crooked Mile; Duke of West Point; Thanks for Everything; Lightening Carson Rides Again; Wives Under Suspicion. **1939** Mickey the Kid; Mr. Wong in Chinatown; The Gracie Allen Murder Case; Calling All Marines. **1940** The Devil's Pipeline; Grapes of Wrath; Knute Rockney, All American; The Great Profile; Cisco Kid and the Lady; South of Pago-Pago. **1941** Belle Starr; Buck Privates; Night of January 16th; We Go Fast; Kathleen; Affectionately Yours; Great Guns; Mr. and Mrs. North. **1942** Life Begins at 8:30; Gentleman Jim; Fingers at the Window; Juke Box Jenny; Ten Gentlemen from West Point; Thru Different Eyes; Iceland; Ride 'Em Cowboy; Treat 'Em Rough. **1943** Air Force; Corvette K-225; Riding High; Mission to Moscow; So Proudly We Hail; Murder on the Waterfront; It Ain't Hay. **1944** Uncertain Glory; Bermuda Mystery; Aboard With Two Yanks; Laura; Hollywood Canteen. **1945** Don Juan Quilligan; Within These Walls; Anchors Aweigh; The Spider; Shanghai Cobra; Conflict. **1946** Sentimental Journey; The Strange Love of Martha Ivers; Easy to Wed; It Shouldn't Happen to a Dog; Cloak and Dagger; The Missing Lady; Angel on My Shoulder; Nobody Lives Forever; Big Sleep; Tars and Spars; Spellbound. **1947** The Fabulous Dorseys; Joe Palooka in the Knockout; Nora Prentiss; Desert Fury; Nighmare Alley; Robin Hood of Texas. **1948** Secret Service Investigator; The Velvet Touch; Bungalow 13; The

Plunderers; One Touch of Venus; The Noose Hangs High. **1949** Homicide; Mighty Joe Young; Abbott and Costello Meet the Killer Boris Karloff; Mississippi Rhythm; Blondie Hits the Jackpot; The Devil's Henchman; Prison Warden. **1950** When Willie Comes Marching Home; Dakota Lil; South Sea Sinner; Destination Murder; Armed Car Robbery; The Savage Horde. **1951** Fighting Coast Guard; Oh Susanna; According to Mrs. Hoyle. **1952** My Pal Gus; Million Dollar Mermaid; Here Comes the Marines. **1953** Hot News; Fighter Attack; Massacre Canyon. **1955** Mister Roberts; The Naked Street; Apache Ambush. **1956** Francis in the Haunted House. **1957** The Restless Breed; Night Passage; Up in Smoke; Wild is the Wind. **1958** In the Money; The Last Hurrah; Johnny Rocco. **1963** It's a Mad, Mad, Mad, Mad World. **1964** Cheyenne Autumn. **1967** In Cold Blood; Good Times; Bullwhip Griffin. **1971** Barefoot Executive.

FLEISCHER, DAVE
Born: July 14, 1894, New York, N.Y. Died: June 25, 1979, Woodland Hills, Calif. (stroke). Animation pioneer, screen actor and film producer.

Appeared in: **1944** Trocadero.

FLEISCHMANN, HARRY
Born: 1899. Died: Nov. 28, 1943, Bakersfield, Calif. (heart attack). Screen actor.

Appeared in: **1937** She Asked For It. **1939** Ambush. **1942** Crossroads. **1943** Stand by for Action.

FLEMING, ALICE
Born: 1882. Died: Dec. 6, 1952, New York, N.Y. Screen, stage, and radio actress.

Appeared in: **1921** The Conquest of Canaan; His Greatest Sacrifice. **1941** Playmates. **1942** Who Done It? **1943** Moonlight in Vermont. **1944** Storm Over Lisbon; Phantom Lady; Vigilantes of Dodge City; Marshal of Reno; In Society; Reckless Age; Sunday Dinner for a Soldier. **1945** Lone Texas Ranger; A Medal for Benny; State Fair; Affairs of Susan; It's a Pleasure; Saratoga Trunk. **1946** California Gold Rush; Conquest of Cheyenne; The Dark Corner; Dead of Night; Queen of Burlesque; Sheriff of Redwood Valley. **1947** Smash-Up, The Story of a Woman.

FLEMING, BOB (Robert Fleming)
Born: 1878, Ontario, Canada. Died: Oct. 4, 1933. Screen and vaudeville actor.

Appeared in: **1914** The Man from Home; Rose of the Rancho; The Virginian. **1916** To Have and To Hold; The Love Mask; The Selfish Woman; The House with the Golden Windows. **1919** Nugget Nell. **1922** The Fighting Streak; Daring Danger. **1924** Riff Bang Buddy; The Fighting Sap. **1925** Hurricane Horseman; Saddle Horseman. **1926** Davy Crockett at the Fall of the Alamo; Riding for Life; Trumpin' Trouble. **1927** The Love of Paguita; Gun Gospel; The Mojave Kid. **1928** King Cowboy; The Avenging Rider; The Bantam Cowboy; The Fighting Redhead; The Riding Renegde; Vanishing Pioneer. **1930** The Dawn Trail; The Lone Star Ranger. **1931** Desert Vengeance. **1932** Texas Gun-Fighter.

FLEMING, BRYANT See YOUNG, GIG

FLEMING, CLAUDE
Born: Feb. 22, 1884, Sydney, Australia. Died: Mar. 24, 1952, Sydney, Australia. Screen, stage actor, film director, film producer and writer.

Appeared in: **1929** The Unholy Night. **1930** Mamba; Captain of the Guard; Bride of the Regiment; One Night at Susie's.

FLEMING, ERIC
Born: 1926, Santa Paula, Calif. Died: Sept. 28, 1966, Tingo Maria area, Peru (drowned). Screen, stage and television actor.

Appeared in: **1955** Conquest of Space. **1957** Fright. **1958** Queen of Outer Space. **1959** Curse of the Undead. **1966** The Glass Bottom Boat.

FLEMING, IAN
Born: Sept. 10, 1888, Melbourne, Australia. Died: Jan. 1, 1969, London, England. Screen, stage and television actor. Do not confuse with deceased writer. Was Dr. Watson in English version of Sherlock Holmes series of films in 1930s with Arthur Wonter as Holmes.

Appeared in: **1926** Second to None. **1928** The Ware Case (US 1929). **1929** The Devil's Maze. **1930** The School for Scandal. **1931** The Sleeping Cardinal (aka Sherlock Holmes' Fatal Hour—US). **1932** The Missing Rembrandt; Lucky Girl; After Dark. **1933** Called Back. **1934** The Third Clue. **1935** The Triumph of Sherlock Holmes; The Riverside

Murder; School for Stars; The Crouching Beast; Sexton Blake and the Mademoiselle. **1936** Prison Breaker. **1937** Jump for Glory (aka When Thief Meets Thief—US); Silver Blaze (aka Murder at the Baskervilles—US 1941); Racing Romance; Darby and Joan. **1938** If I Were Boss; Dial 999; The Reverse Be My Lot; Quiet Please; Double or Quits; Almost a Honeymoon; Ghost Tales Retold (series). **1939** The Nursemaid Who Disappeared; Men Without Honour; Shadowed Eyes. **1943** The Butler's Dilemma; Up With the Lark. **1945** I Didn't Do It. **1946** George in Civvy Street; Appointment With Crime (US 1950). **1947** Captain Boycott. **1948** Quartet. **1949** A Matter of Murder. **1950** The Woman in Question (aka Five Angles on Murder—US 1953). **1952** The Voice of Merrill (aka Murder Will Out—1953). **1953** Recoil; It's a Grand Life; Park Plaza (aka Norman Conquest). **1954** The Seekers (aka Land of Fury—US 1955). **1957** High Flight (US 1958). **1958** A Woman Possessed. **1959** Innocent Meeting; Web of Suspicion; Crash Dive; Man Accused. **1960** Bluebeard's Ten Honeymoons; Your Money or Your Wife (US 1965); The Trials of Oscar Wilde (aka The Man With the Green Carnation—US and The Green Carnation); Too Hot to Handle (aka Playgirl After Dark—US 1962). **1961** No, My Darling Daughter (US 1964). **1962** The Lamp in Assassin Mews; What Every Woman Wants; Return of a Stranger. **1963** The Boys; Tamahine (US 1964). **1964** Seventy Deadly Pills. **1965** The Return of Mr. Moto.

FLEMING, MARC
Born: 1931, England. Died: Mar. 19, 1979, London, England. Screen, stage actor and female impersonator.

Appeared in: **1969** Night of Bloody Horror.

FLENN, KARL
Born: 1931. Died: Apr. 9, 1978, Puerto Rico. Screen, stage and television actor.

FLETCHER, LAWRENCE M.
Born: 1902. Died: Feb. 11, 1970, Bridgeport, Conn. Screen, stage and television actor.

Appeared in: **1956** The Search for Bridey Murphy.

FLEU, DORRIS BELL
Born: 1922. Died: Sept. 12, 1955, Bryn Mawr, Pa. Screen actress and singer with bands of Bunny Berrigan, Harry James and Woody Herman.

FLICK, PAT C.
Born: 1899. Died: Nov. 1, 1955, Hollywood, Calif. (cancer). Screen, stage, radio actor and screenwriter.

Appeared in: **1935** Stars Over Broadway. **1937** The Black Legion. **1938** Little Tough Guy; The Missing Guest. **1943** Follies Girl.

FLICKENSCHILD, ELISABETH
Born: 1905, Hamburg, Germany. Died: Oct., 1977, Stade, West Germany (heart attack). Screen, stage actress, stage director, stage producer and playwright.

Appeared in: **1935** Grossreinemachen. **1936** Du Kannst Nicht Treu Sein; Der Ahnungslose Engel. **1937** Streit um den Knaben Jo; Der Zerbochene Krug (The Broken Jug); Tango Notturno; Starke Herzen; Heiratsschwindler. **1938** Der Maulkorb; Jugend; Ein Maedchen Geht an Land. **1939** Der Schritt vom Wege; Robert Koch; Die Barmherzige Luge; Die Uheimlichen Wunsche. **1940** Der Fuchs von Glenarvon; Trenck, der Pandur. **1941** Ohm Kruger. **1942** Der Grosse Koenig; Zwischen Himmel und Erde; Rembrandt. **1943** Altes Herz wird Wieder Jung; Liebesgeschichten; Romanze in Moll; Die Beiden Schwestern. **1944** Philharmoniker; Familie Buchholz; Neigungsehe (Part II of Family Buchholz); Seinerzeit zu Meiner Zeit. **1945** Meine Herren Sohne; Der Mann dem man den Namen Stahl; Ein Toller Tag; Shiva und die Galgenblume. **1949** Eine Grosse Liebe; Madonna in Ketten. **1951** Pikanterie. **1952** Toxi; Der Tag vor der Hochzeit. **1953** Hokuspokus; Die Nacht ohne Moral. **1954** Hochzeitsglocken; Das Ideale Brautpaar; Rittmeister Wronski. **1955** Die Spanische Fliege; Sohn ohne Heimat. **1957** Robinson Soll Nicht Sterben (The Girl and the Legend—US 1966); Herrscher ohne Krone (Ruler Without a Crown, aka King in Shadow—US 1961). **1958** Stefanie (US 1959); Auferstehung; Wir Wunderkinder (Aren't We Wonderful?—US 1959); Das Maedchen Scampolo (The Girl Scampolo, aka Scampolo—US 1959). **1959** Labyrinth. **1960** Agatha, Lass das Morden Sein; Die Bande des Schreckens (The Terrible People); Brucke des Schicksals Faust (US 1963). **1962** Faust; Eheinstitut Aurora; Frauenarzt Dr. Sibelius; Das Gasthaus an der Themse; Das Schwarz-Weiss-Rote Himmelbett. **1963** Das Grosse Liebesspiel (The Big Love Game, aka And So to Bed—US 1965); Ferien vom Ich; Das Indische Tuch. **1964** Einer Frisst den Anderen (Dog Eat Dog—US 1966); DM-Killer; Lausbubengeschichten; Das Phantom von Soho (The Phantom of

Soho—US 1967). **1965** Diamantenbillard; Tante Frieda—Neue Lausbubengeschichten. **1966** Onkel Filser—Allerneueste Lausbubengeschichten. **1967** Der Lugner und die Nonne; Wenn Ludwig ins Manover Zieht. **1969** Dr. Fabian—Lachen ist die Beste Medizin.

FLIEGEL, MRS. ERNIE
Born: Minneapolis, Minn. Died: June 25, 1966, Minneapolis, Minn. Screen and vaudeville actress. In vaudeville appeared as part of the "Albee Sisters" act.

Appeared in: **1937** Turn Off the Moon.

FLINT, HAZEL
Born: 1893. Died: Aug. 18, 1959, Hollywood, Calif. Screen and stage actress.

Appeared in: **1922** The Bootleggers. **1927** Modern Daughters.

FLINT, HELEN
Born: 1898. Died: Sept. 9, 1967, Washington, D.C. (auto injuries). Screen and stage actress.

Appeared in: **1920** Uncle Sam of Freedom Ridge. **1930** Married (short). **1934** The Ninth Guest; Broadway Bill; Midnight; Manhattan Love Song; Handy Andy. **1935** Devil Dogs of the Air; While the Patient Slept; Doubting Thomas; Ah, Wilderness. **1936** Fury; Riff Raff; Give Me Your Heart; Early to Bed; Little Lord Fauntleroy. **1937** Step Lively, Jeeves!; Married Before Breakfast; Blonde Trouble; Sea Devils; The Black Legion. **1942** Time to Kill.

FLINT, JOSEPH W.
Born: 1893. Died: May 5, 1933, Los Angeles, Calif. (suicide—gunshot wounds). Screen actor.

FLINT, SAM
Born: 1882. Died: Oct. 24, 1980, Woodland Hills, Calif. Screen actor.

Appeared in: **1933** Broken Dreams. **1934** Murder in the Museum; Mrs. Wiggs of the Cabbage Patch. **1935** People Can Talk; New Frontier. **1936** The Lawless Nineties; Winds of the Wasteland; The Accusing Finger; The Lonely Trail; Red River Valley; Florida Special. **1937** Windjammer; Red Lights Ahead; Two Minutes to Play. **1938** State Police; Fighting Devil Dogs (serial). **1940** I Take This Oath. **1941** Double Date; Under Fiesta Stars; Tuxedo Junction; Helping Hands (short). **1942** Road to Happiness; South of Santa Fe; Mountain Rhythm; Spy Smasher (serial). **1943** Crime Doctor's Strangest Case; Dead Men Walk; Swing Your Partner; The Stranger from Pecos; Thundering Trails; False Colors. **1944** The Monster Maker; The Chinese Cat; The Contender; Boss of Boomtown; Goin' to Town; Lights of Old Santa Fe; Silver City Kid. **1945** Swing Out, Sister; The Man from Oklahoma; Shadow of Terror; Along the Navajo Trail; Captain Tugboat Annie; Micro-Phonies (short); Who's Guilty? (serial). **1946** Junior Prom; Somewhere in the Night; My Pal Trigger; Sioux City Sue; Singing of the Trail; Lone Star Moonlight; The Crimson Ghost (serial). **1947** Swing the Western Way; The Wild Frontier; The Black Widow (serial). **1948** The Strawberry Roan; Four Faces West; Phantom Valley; Adventures of Frank and Jesse James (serial). **1949** Home in San Antone; The Gay Amigo. **1950** The Blazing Hills (aka The Blazing Sun); Timber Fury; The Return of Jesse James; Country Fair; Cherokee Uprising; Rock Island Trail; The Foreball. **1951** Snake River Desperadoes; Fort Savage Raiders; A Wonderful Life; Leave it to the Marines; Sky High; Northwest Territory. **1952** The Hawk of Wild River; Road Agent; Sea Tiger Yukon Gold; Ruby Gentry; The Steel Trap. **1953** Cow Country; The Moonlighter; The Vanquished. **1955** Abbott and Costello Meet the Keystone Kops; The Big Tip-Off; Night Freight. **1961** Snow White and the Three Stooges; I'll Give My Life. **1963** Soldier in the Rain.

FLIPPEN, JAY C.
Born: 1898, Little Rock, Ark. Died: Feb. 3, 1971, Hollywood, Calif. (aneurysm). Screen, stage, minstrel, vaudeville, radio and television actor. Married to screenwriter Ruth Brooks Flippen (dec. 1981).

Appeared in: **1928** The Ham What Am (short). **1934** Marie Galante; Million Dollar Ransom. **1947** Brute Force; Intrigue. **1948** They Live By Night (aka The Twisted Road and aka Your Red Wagon). **1949** A Woman's Secret; Down to the Sea in Ships; Oh, You Beautiful Doll. **1950** Buccaneer's Girl; The Yellow Cab Man; Love That Brute; Winchester "73"; Two Flags West. **1951** The Lemon Drop Kid; Flying Leathernecks; The People Against O'Hara; The Lady from Texas; The Model and the Marriage Broker. **1952** The Las Vegas Story; Bend of the River; Woman of the North Country. **1953** Thunder Bay; Devil's Canyon; East of Sumatra. **1954** The Wild One; Carnival Story. **1955** Six Bridges to Cross; The Far Country; Man Without a Star; It's

Always Fair Weather; Kismet; Oklahoma!; Strategic Air Command. **1956** The Killing; The Seventh Cavalry; The King and Four Queens. **1957** The Restless Breed; The Halliday Brand; Hot Summer Night; Public Pigeon No. 1; Night Passage; Run of the Arrow; The Midnight Story; Jet Pilot; The Deerslayer; Lure of the Swamp. **1958** Escape from Red Rock; From Hell to Texas (aka Manhunt). **1960** Wild River; Studs Lonigan; The Plunderers. **1962** Six-Gun Law; How the West Was Won. **1964** Looking for Love. **1965** Cat Ballou. **1967** The Spirit Is Willing. **1968** Firecreek; The Hellfighters. **1969** Hello, Dolly!

FLIPPER (Mitzi, the Dolphin)
Died: June 25, 1971, Grassy Key, Fla. (heart attack). Approx. 22 years old. Screen and television dolphin.

Appeared in: **1963** Flipper.

FLORATH, ALBERT
Born: 1888, Bielefeld, Germany. Died: Mar. 10, 1957, Gailsdorf-Nordwuertemberg, West Germany. Screen, stage actor, film director and producer. Entered films in 1920.

Appeared in: **1926** Die Letzte Droschke von Berlin. **1927** Gehetzte Frauen; Schinderhannes; Zwei Unterm Himmelszelt. **1929** Napoleon auf St. Helena. **1931** Man Braucht Kein Geld; Berlin-Alexanderplatz (US 1933). **1932** Goethe Lebt ...!; Die Herren vom Maxim. **1933** Das Meer Ruft; Reifende Jugend. **1934** Ein Kind, Ein Hund, Ein Vagabund (aka Vielleicht War's nur ein Traum); Der Schwarze Walfisch; Herz ist Trumpf; Liebe, Tod und Teufel. **1935** Kirschen aus Nachbars Garten; Das Maedchen Johanna; Der Gefangene des Koenigs; Glueckskinder. **1936** Donogoo Tonka; Eine Frau ohne Bedeutung; Die Grosse und die Kleine Welt; Dahinten auf der Heide; Boccaccio; Donner, Blitz und Sonnenschein; Weisse Sklavin (aka Panzerkreuzer Sewastopol). **1937** Unter Ausschluss der Oeffentlichkeit; Capriolen; Fremdenheim Filoda; Die Austernlilli; Der Schimmelkrieg in der Holedau; Brillanten; Ein Volksfeind; Der Biberpelz (The Beaver Coat—US 1939). **1938** Spiel im Sommerwind (Play in the Summer Breezes—US 1939); Fortsetzung Folgt; Eine Nacht im Mai; Eine Frau Kommt in die Tropen; Die Umwege des Schoenen Karl; Steputat & Co.; Skandal um den Hahn; Fuenf Millionen Suchen Einen Erben; Frauen Fuer Golden Hill; Yvette (aka Die Tochter Einer Kurtisane). **1939** Irrtum des Herzens; Im Namen des Volkes; Hurra! Ich bin Papa! (Hurrah! I'm a Papa—US 1940); Eine Frau wie Du; Alarm auf Station III; Die Stimme aus dem Aether; Drunter und Drueber; Ein Ganzer Kerl; Der Gouverneur; Schneider Wibbel; Das Paradies der Junggesellen; Roman Eines Arztes; Wer Kuesst Madeleine?; Die Reise Nach Tilsit. **1940** Die Unvollkommene Liebe; Die Rothschilds; Der Fuchs von Glenarvon; Angelika; Der Dunkle Punkt; Zwischen Hamburg und Haiti; Lauter Liebe; Jud Suess; Wunschkonzert; Friedrich Schiller (aka Der Triumph Eines Genies). **1941** Maennerwirtschaft; Jakko; Der Weg ins Freie; Friedemann Bach; Ich Klage An; Clarissa; Am Abend auf der Heide. **1942** Der Seniorchef; Das Grosse Spiel; Diesel; Himmelhunde; So ein Fruechtchen; Symphonie Eines Lebens; Weisse Waesche; Die Erbin vom Rosenhof; Stimme des Herzens. **1943** Immensee; Die Beiden Schwestern; Ein Walzer mit Dir; Um 9 Kommt Harald; Wenn die Sonne Wieder Scheint (aka Der Flachsacker). **1944** Nora; Junge Adler; Seinerzeit zu Meiner Zeit; Junge Herzen; Moselfahrt mit Monika; Am Abend nach der Oper; Die Feuerzangenbowle; Zwischen Nacht und Morgen (aka Augen der Liebe); Via Mala (aka Die Strasse des Boesen). **1945** Sag' die Wahrheit; Shiva und die Galgenblume; Das Kleine Hofkonzert; Die Schenke zur Ewigen Liebe; Dr. Phil. Doederlein; Der Puppenspieler (aka Pole Poppenspaeler). **1948** Die Kupferne Hochzeit; Der Herr vom Andern Stern. **1949** Schuld Allein ist der Wein; Verfuehrte Haende; Diese Nacht Vergess ich Nie; Nichts als Zufuelle; Die Freunde Meiner Frau; Derby; Der Bagnostraefling; Zukunft aus Zweiter Hand; Kaetchen Fuer Alles; Gefaehrliche Gaeste. **1950** Frauenarzt Dr. Praetorius; Schatten der Nacht; Absender Unbekannt; Dieser Mann Gehoert Mir; Gabriela; Die Wunderschoene Galathee; Export in Blond; Das Maedchen aus der Suedsee; Hochzeitsnacht im Paradies; Insel ohne Moral; Tobias Knopp, Abenteuer Einer Junggesellen (speaker). **1951** Das Gestohlene Jahr; Professor Nachtfalter; Das Haus in Montevideo; Was das Herz Befiehlt (aka Veronika, die Magd). **1952** Der Eingebildete Kranke; Toxi; Einmal am Rhein; Oh, du Lieber Fridolin; Heimatglocken; Rosen Bluehen auf dem Heidegrab; Wenn Abends die Heide Traeumt. **1953** Keine Angst vor Grossen Tieren; Suedlicke Naechte; Die Muehle im Schwarzwaeldertal; Moselfahrt aus Liebeskummer; Wenn der Weisse Flieder Wieder Blueht; Dein Herz ist Meine Heimat. **1954** Hochzeitsglocken; Sanatorium Total Verrueckt; Aennchen von Tharau; Columbus Entdeckt Kraehwinkel; Die Schoene Muellerin; Der Schweigende Engel. **1955** Die Spanische Fliege; Der Dunkle Stern; Zwei Blaue Augen; Das Forsthaus im Tirol; Die Herrin vom Soelderhof; Unternehmen Schlafsack. **1956** Das Erbe vom Puggerhof; Kirschen in Nachbars Garten; Drei Birken auf der Heide; Ein Herz Kehrt Heim; Wenn wir Alle Engel Waeren; Maedchen mit Schwachem Gedaechtnis.

"FLORELLE" (Odette Rousseau)
Born: 1901, France. Died: Oct. 1, 1974, La Roche-Sur-Yon, France. Screen, stage actress and singer.

Appeared in: **1931** Beggar's Opera. **1933** La Femme Nue; L'Opera de Quat'Sous; La Dame de Chez Maxim (The Woman at Mixim's). **1935** Liliom. **1936** Les Miserables. **1937** Amphytryon. **1957** Gervaise.

FLORESCO, MICHEL
Born: Italy. Died: Nov., 1925, Venice, Italy. Screen actor.

FLOREY, ROBERT
Born: Sept. 14, 1900, Paris, France. Died: May 16, 1979, Santa Monica, Calif. Screen actor, film director and television director.

FLOWERS, THEO (Theodore Flowers)
Born: Aug. 5, 1895, Camille, Ga. Died: Nov. 16, 1927, New York, N.Y. (following surgery). Boxer and screen actor. Father of actor Tiger Flowers, Jr.

Appeared in: **1926** The Fighting Deacon (aka Life of Tiger Flowers-documentary).

FLOWERTON, CONSUELO
Born: 1900. Died: Dec. 21, 1965, New York, N.Y. Screen, stage, television actress and singer. Mother of actress Nina Foch.

Appeared in: **1921** Camille. **1924** The Sixth Commandment.

FLUCKER, MACK A.
Born: 1904. Died: Apr. 28, 1929, Los Angeles, Calif. (plane accident). Screen and stage actor.

Appeared in: **1928** Win That Girl.

FLUGRATH, EDNA
Born: Brooklyn, N.Y. Died: 1928. Screen, stage, vaudeville actress and ballet dancer. Sister of screen actress Viola Dana and Shirley Mason (dec. 1979). Married to actor Harold Shaw (dec. 1926).

Appeared in: **1912** The Dam Builder; Hearts and Diamonds; Uncle Mun and the Minister; Like Knights of Old; The Third Thanksgiving; On Donovan's Division; Ann's Crawl Upstairs; A Proposal Under Difficulties. **1913** Between Orton Junction and Fallonville; Mother's Lazy Boy; Perilous Cargo; A Race to New York; The Photograph and the Blotter; His Undesirable Relatives. **1914** The Ring and the Rajah; Duty; Child O' My Heart; England's Menace; Nan Good-For-Nothing; His Reformation; Turtle Doves; Bootle's Baby; The King's Minister; Two Little Britons; A Christmas Carol; The Two Columbines; V.C. (aka The Victorian Cross—US); The Incomparable Bellairs (aka The Incomparable Mistress—US); Lil O' London; Liberty Hall. **1915** The Ashes of Revenge; The Heart of a Child (US 1916); A Garret in Bohemia; The Derby Winner; The Third Generation; Mr. Lyndon at Liberty; The Firm of Girdlestone; The Heart of Sister Ann; The Two Roads; The Victoria Cross. **1916** You; Me and Me Moke (aka Me and M' Pal—US 1917); The Man Without a Soul (aka I Believe—US 1917). **1920** The Pursuit of Pamela; London Pride; True Tilda; The Land of Mystery; The Land of Mystery. **1921** Kipps; The Adventures of Sherlock Holmes series including: A Case of Identity; A Dear Fool. **1922** False Evidence. **1923** The Social Code. **1924** Winning a Continent.

FLUGRATH, LEONIE *See* MASON, SHIRLEY

FLYNN, ELINOR (Elinor Golden Flynn)
Born: Mar. 17, 1910, Chicago, Ill. Died: July 4, 1938, near Glen Falls, N.Y. (auto accident). Screen, stage and radio actress. Entered films in 1927.

Appeared in: **1929** The Royal Pair (short). **1930** Ladies in Love; Let Us Be Gay. **1931** She Wolf; Mother's Millions.

FLYNN, ERROL
Born: June 20, 1909, Hobart, Tasmania. Died: Oct. 14, 1959, Vancouver, B.C., Canada (heart attack). Screen, stage, television actor, screenwriter and author. Married to screen actress Patrice Wymore. Divorced from actresses Lili Damita and Nora Eddington. Father of actor and correspondent Sean Flynn (dec.).

Appeared in: **1933** In the Wake of the Bounty (documentary). **1935** Murder at Monte Carlo; The Case of the Curious Bride; Don't Bet on Blondes; Captain Blood; I Found Stella Parish. **1936** Charge of the Light Brigade; Private Party on Catalina (short). **1937** Green Light; Prince and the Pauper; Another Dawn; The Perfect Specimen. **1938** Four's a Crowd; The Sisters; Dawn Patrol; Adventures of Robin Hood. **1939** Dodge City; The Private Lives of Elizabeth and Essex. **1940**

Santa Fe Trail; The Sea Hawk; Virginia City. **1941** They Died With Their Boots On; Dive Bomber; Footsteps in the Dark. **1942** Desperate Journey; Gentleman Jim. **1943** Edge of Darkness; Northern Pursuit; Thank Your Lucky Stars. **1944** Uncertain Glory. **1945** Objective, Burma!; San Antonio. **1946** Never Say Goodbye. **1947** Cry Wolf; Escape Me Never. **1948** Silver River; The Adventures of Don Juan. **1949** It's a Great Feeling; That Forsythe Woman. **1950** Rocky Mountain; Montana; Hello, God (US 1958); Kim. **1951** The Adventures of Captain Fabian. **1952** Against All Flags; Mara Maru. **1953** The Master of Ballantrae. **1954** Crossed Swords; Lilacs in the Spring (aka Let's Make Up—US 1956). **1955** The Dark Avenger (aka The Warriors—US); King's Rhapsody. **1957** Istanbul; The Sun Also Rises; The Big Boodle. **1958** Too Much, Too Soon; Roots of Heaven. **1959** Cuban Rebel Girls.

FLYNN, HAZEL E.
Born: Mar. 31, 1899, Chicago, Ill. Died: May 15, 1964, Santa Monica, Calif. (heart ailment). Screen extra actress, drama editor and newspaper film columnist. Appeared in early Essanay films.

FLYNN, JOE
Born: Nov. 8, 1924, Youngstown, Ohio. Died: July 19, 1974, Beverly Hills, Calif. (accidental drowning). Screen, stage and television actor.

Appeared in: **1948** The Babe Ruth Story (film debut). **1954** The Big Chase. **1955** The Seven Little Foys. **1956** The Ten Commandments; The Boss. **1957** Portland Expose; Panama Sal. **1958** This Happy Feeling. **1959** Thirty. **1961** Cry for Happy; Police Dog Story; The Last Time I Saw Archie; Lover Come Back. **1964** McHale's Navy. **1965** McHale's Navy Joins the Air Force. **1967** Divorce American Style. **1968** Did You Hear the One About the Traveling Saleslady?; The Love Bug. **1970** The Computer Wore Tennis Shoes. **1971** Million Dollar Duck. **1974** Superdad.

FLYNN, MAURICE B. "LEFTY"
Born: 1893. Died: Mar. 4, 1959. Screen actor. Divorced from actress Viola Dana.

Appeared in: **1920** The Silver Horde; Going Some; The Great Accident; Officer 666. **1921** Children of the Night; Dangerous Curve Ahead; Bucking the Line; Just Out of College; The Last Trail; The Night Rose; The Old Nest; Roads of Destiny. **1922** Omar the Tentmaker; Oath-bound; Rough Shod; Smiles Are Trumps; The Woman Who Walked Alone. **1923** Salomy Jane; The Snow Bride; Drums of Fate; Hell's Hole. **1924** Open All Night; The Breed of the Border; The Millionaire Cowboy; The No-Gun Man; Code of the Sea; The Uninvited Guest. **1925** O.U. West; Speed Wild; Heads Up; High and Handsome; Smilin' at Trouble. **1926** The College Boob; Glenister of the Mounted; Mulhall's Great Catch; The Traffic Cop; Sir Lumberjack. **1927** The Golden Stallion (serial).

FLYNN, SEAN
Died: Missing in Cambodia in 1970 (dec?). Screen actor and foreign correspondent. Son of actor Errol Flynn (dec. 1959) and actress Lily Damita.

Appeared in: **1962** El Hijo del Captain Blood (The Son of Captain Blood—US 1964). **1963** Delay in Marienborn. **1964** Le Train de Berlin est Arrete (aka Stop Train 349—US); Voir Venise et Crever (See Venice and Die). **1967** Cinq Gars pour Singapour (Singapore, Singapore—US 1969).

FOGEL, VLADIMIR
Born: Russia. Died: June 8, 1929, Russia? Screen actor.

Appeared in: **1928** The Yellow Ticket.

FOGG, ORIAN
Born: 1849. Died: May 24, 1923, New York, N.Y. Screen and stage actor. Appeared in Famous Players Company Films.

FOLEY, BILL
Born: 1914, Ireland. Died: Nov. 23, 1981, Dublin, Ireland. Screen, stage actor, stage director, drama coach and teacher.

Appeared in: **1957** Professor Tim (US 1959). **1959** Broth of a Boy. **1960** The Siege of Sidney Street (US 1961). **1961** The Mark. **1963** Never Put it in Writing (US 1964). **1965** Young Cassidy. **1969** Paddy (aka Goodbye to the Hill—US 1970).

FOLEY, JOSEPH F.
Born: 1910, Alpena, Mich. Died: July 22, 1955, Holyoke, Mass. (heart attack). Screen, stage and television actor.

Appeared in: **1951** The Whistle at Eaton Falls.

FOLEY, RED
Born: 1910, Bluelick, Ky. Died: Sept. 19, 1968, Fort Wayne, Ind. (acute pulmonary edema). Singer, screen, television, and radio actor.

Appeared in: **1966** Sing a Song, for Heaven's Sake.

FOLKERSON, BOB
Born: 1919. Died: Mar. 23, 1976, Los Angeles, Calif. (cancer). Screen, television actor and stuntman.

Appeared in: **1955** Run for Cover.

FOLWELL, DENIS
Born: 1905, England. Died: Apr. 26, 1971, England. Screen and stage actor.

FONSS, OLAF
Born: 1882, Denmark. Died: Nov. 4, 1949, Copenhagen, Denmark (heart ailment). Stage and screen actor. Appeared in German and Danish films from 1911 to 1929.

Appeared in: Ich Lebe fur Dichich (I Live for You).

FONTAINE, FRANK
Born: 1920. Died: Aug. 4, 1978, Spokane, Wash. (heart attack). Screen, stage, vaudeville, radio and television actor. Son of circus strong man Ray Fontaine and trapeze artist Anna McCarthy.

Appeared in: **1950** Nancy Goes to Rio; Stella; Hit Parade of 1951. **1951** The Model and the Marriage Broker; Call Me Mister.

FONTAINE, LILIAN
Born: 1886, Reading, England. Died: Feb. 20, 1975, Santa Barbara, Calif. Screen actress and stage director. Mother of actresses Olivia DeHavilland and Joan Fontaine.

Appeared in: **1945** The Lost Weekend. **1947** Time Out of Mind; Suddenly It's Spring; The Locket; Ivy; The Imperfect Lady. **1953** The Bigamist.

FONTAINE, TONY
Born: 1927. Died: June 30, 1974, Canoga Park, Calif. (cancer). Screen actor and singer.

FONTAN, GABRIELLE
Born: France. Died: 1959, France? Screen actress.

Appeared in: **1945** Ces Dames aux Chapeaux Verts (The Ladies in the Green Hats). **1950** The Miracle (aka The Ways of Love—US 1951); Sylvia and the Phantom; Francois Villon. **1956** Trapeze. **1957** Deadlier Than the Male. **1958** Gates of Paris; Premier Mai (The First of May); Crime et Chatinaut (Crime and Punishment, aka The Most Dangerous Sin—US). **1959** Julie la Rousse (Julie the Redhead—US 1963).

FOO, LEE TUNG
Died: May 1, 1966. Screen actor.

Appeared in: **1936** The General Died at Dawn. **1938** Mister Wong—Detective. **1939** Mister Wong in Chinatown. **1940** They Knew What They Wanted. **1941** Secrets of the Wastelands. **1942** Across the Pacific; Invisible Agent; Somewhere I'll Find You. **1943** Behind the Rising Sun; Mission to Moscow. **1944** Dragon Seed; Mrs. Parkington; Laura. **1945** They Were Expendable. **1946** It Shouldn't Happen to a Dog. **1947** Chinese Ring; The Red Hornet. **1948** Strange Gamble. **1949** Criss Cross; The Stratton Story; There's a Girl in My Heart. **1950** Annie Get Your Gun; The Cariboo Trail; Short Grass. **1952** Macao. **1955** Love Is a Many Splendored Thing. **1956** Meet Me in Las Vegas. **1957** Badlands of Montana.

FOO, WING
Born: 1910. Died: Dec. 9, 1953, Los Angeles, Calif. (heart attack). Screen and television actor.

Appeared in: **1941** Out of the Fog. **1944** The Purple Heart. **1945** Hotel Berlin; God Is My Co-Pilot; Blood on the Sun; Wonder Man.

FOOK, MONTE (Yuk Mong)
Born: 1908. Died: Mar. 27, 1933, Los Angeles, Calif. (gunshot wound). Screen actor.

FOOTE, COURTENEY
Born: Harregate, Yorkshire, England. Died: Mar. 4, 1925, Italy. Screen and stage actor.

Appeared in: **1912** Captain Barnacle—Reformer; Reincarnation of Komar. **1913** When Society Calls. **1915** Captain Courtesy; Cross Currents. **1916** An International Marriage. **1918** Love's Law. **1919** The Two Brides; His Parisian Wife. **1920** The Star Rover. **1921** The Passion Flower; The Bronze Bell. **1922** Fascination. **1923** Little Old New York; Ashes of Vengeance. **1924** Tess of the D'Urbervilles; Madonna of the Streets; Dorothy Vernon of Haddon Hall.

FORAN, ARTHUR F.
Born: 1912. Died: Jan. 30, 1967, Queens, N.Y. Screen and stage actor.

FORAN, DICK (John Nicholas Foran)
Born: June 18, 1910, Flemington, N.J. Died: Aug. 10, 1979, Panorama City, Calif. Screen and stage actor. Nominated for 1936 Academy Award as Best Supporting Actor in the Petrified Forest.

Appeared in: **1934** Stand Up and Cheer (film debut); Gentlemen Are Born. **1935** Moonlight on the Prairie; One More Spring; Lottery Lover; It's a Small World; Ladies Love Danger; Accent on Youth; Shipmates Forever; Dangerous. **1936** The Petrified Forest; Song of the Saddle; The Golden Arrow; Treachery Rides the Range; The Big Noise; Earthworm Tractors; Public Enemy's Wife; Trailin' West; The Black Legion. **1937** Guns of the Pecos; The Perfect Specimen; Land Beyond the Law; Cherokee Strip. **1938** Four Daughters; She Loved a Fireman; Love, Honor and Behave; Over the Wall; The Cowboy from Brooklyn, Boy Meets Girl; The Sisters; Secrets of a Nurse; Heart of the North; Forbidden Valley. **1939** Daughters Courageous; I Stole a Million; Four Wives; Hero for a Day; Inside Information. **1940** My Little Chickadee; The Fighting 69th; The Mummy's Hand; The House of Seven Gables; Rangers of Fortune; Winners of the West (serial). **1941** Four Mothers; Horror Island; In the Navy; Unfinished Business; Mob Town; Keep 'Em Flying; The Kid from Kansas; Road Agent; Riders of Death Valley (serial). **1942** Ride 'em Cowboy; Butch Minds the Baby; Private Buckaroo; The Mummy's Tomb; Behind the Eight Ball. **1943** He's My Guy; Hi Buddy. **1945** Guest Wife. **1947** Easy Come, Easy Go. **1948** Fort Apache. **1949** Deputy Marshall; El Paso. **1951** Al Jennings of Oklahoma. **1955** Treasure of Ruby Hills. **1956** Please Murder Me;. **1957** Sierra Stranger; Chicago Confidential. **1958** The Fearmakers; Hell's Highway; Thundering Jets; Violent Road. **1959** The Atomic Submarine. **1960** The Big Night; Studs Lonigan. **1963** Donovan's Reef. **1964** Taggart. **1967** Brighty of the Grand Canyon.

FORAN, MARY
Born: 1920. Died: Apr. 10, 1981, Los Angeles, Calif. Screen and television actress.

Appeared in: **1952** The Merry Widow. **1953** The Clown. **1954** Seven Brides for Seven Brothers. **1957** April Love; Will Success Spoil Rock Hunter. **1958** Rock-a-bye Baby; Rally Round the Flag, Boys. **1960** The Hypnotic Eye. **1961** Dondi. **1962** Sweet Bird of Youth.

FORBES, MARY
Born: Jan. 1, 1880, Hornsey, England. Died: July 22, 1974, Beaumont, Calif. Stage and screen actress. Divorced from actor Charles Quartermaine (dec. 1958). Mother of actor Ralph (dec. 1951) and actress Brenda Forbes.

Appeared in: **1916** Ultus and the Secret of the Night (aka Ultus—5 The Secret of the Night—US). **1919** Women Who Win; The Lady Clare. **1920** Nance; Inheritance. **1929** The Thirteenth Chair; Sunny Side Up; Her Private Life; The Trespasser. **1930** Abraham Lincoln; Holiday; East Is West; So This Is London; Strictly Unconventional; The Devil to Pay. **1931** The Man Who Came Back; Born to Love; The Brat; Working Girls; Chances. **1932** Silent Witness; Vanity Fair; Stepping Sisters; A Farewell to Arms. **1933** Bombshell; Cavalcade. **1934** Now I'll Tell; You Can't Buy Everything; Most Precious Thing in Life; Shock; Blind Date; We Live Again; Happiness Ahead; Two Heads on a Pillow; British Agent. **1935** Roberta; McFadden's Flats; Dizzy Dames; Les Miserables; Anna Karenina; Stranded; The Perfect Gentleman; Captain Blood; The Widow from Monte Carlo; Laddie. **1937** One Hundred Men and a Girl; Women of Glamour; Wee Willie Winkie; Stage Door; The Awful Truth; Another Dawn. **1938** Everybody Sing; Outside of Paradise; Always Goodbye; You Can't Take It With You; Three Loves of Nancy; Just Around the Corner. **1939** You Can't Cheat an Honest Man; Fast and Loose; Risky Business; The Sun Never Sets; The Adventures of Sherlock Holmes; Hollywood Cavalcade; Should Husbands Work?; Ninotchka. **1940** Private Affairs; South of Suez. **1941** Paris Calling; Nothing but the Truth. **1942** Twin Beds; We Were Dancing; Klondike Fury; The Great Impersonation; Almost Married; This Above All. **1943** Flesh and Fantasy; Tender Comrade; What a Woman; Two Tickets to London; Women in Bondage; Dangerous Blondes; Hitler's Women. **1944** Jane Eyre; Guest Wife. **1945** Earl Carroll Vanities; A Guy, a Gal and a Pal; I'll Remember April; Lady on a Train; The Picture of Dorian Gray. **1946** Down to Earth; Terror by Night. **1947** The Secret Life of Walter Mitty; Song of Love; It Had to Be You; Ivy; The Other Love; The Exile; Love Story; Indian Summer; Black Arrow. **1948** You Gotta Stay Happy. **1950** The Vanishing Lady. **1952** Les Miserables. **1958** Houseboat.

FORBES, MARY ELIZABETH
Born: 1880, Rochester, N.Y. Died: Aug. 20, 1964, Los Angeles, Calif. (heart attack). Stage and screen actress. She was one of the original models for artists Charles Dana Gibson and Harrison Fisher. Do not confuse with British born actress, Mary Forbes (dec. 1974).

Appeared in: **1913** Prisoner of Zenda. **1914** Zudora—The Twenty Million Dollar Mystery (serial). **1917** Cy Whittaker's Ward. **1921** The Child Thou Gavest Me. **1956** The Ten Commandments.

FORBES, RALPH (Ralph Taylor)
Born: Sept. 30, 1896, London, England. Died: Mar. 31, 1951, New York, N.Y. Stage and screen actor. Married to actress Dora Sayers and divorced from actresses Ruth Chatterton (dec. 1961) and Heather Angel. Son of actress Mary Forbes (dec. 1974) and brother of actress Brenda Forbes.

Appeared in: **1921** The Fifth Form at St Dominic's. **1922** A Lowland Cinderella. **1923** Comin' Thro' The Rye. **1924** Owd Bob; Reveille. **1926** Beau Geste. **1927** The Enemy; Mr. Wu. **1928** The Actress; Dog of War; The Masks of the Devil; The Latest from Paris; The Trail of '98; Under the Black Eagle; The Whip. **1929** Restless Youth; The High Road. **1930** The Lady of Scandal; Mamba; The Green Goddess; Inside the Lines; Her Wedding Night; The Devil's Battalion; Lilies of the Field. **1931** Beau Ideal; Bachelor Father. **1932** Thunder Below; Christopher Strong; Smilin' Through. **1933** False Front; Pleasure Cruise; Phantom Broadcast; The Avenger; The Solitaire Man. **1934** The Barretts of Wimpole Street; Shock; Bombay Mail; Outcast Lady; The Mystery of Mr. X; Riptide; Twentieth Century; The Fountain. **1935** Strange Wives; Enchanted April; Rescue Squad; Age of Indiscretion; Streamline Express; The Goose and the Gander; The Three Musketeers. **1936** Romeo and Juliet; Piccadilly Jim; Mary of Scotland; Daniel Boone; Love Letters of a Star. **1937** The Last of Mrs. Cheyney; The Thirteenth Chair; Make a Wish; Stage Door. **1938** Women Are Like That; Annabel Takes a Tour; Kidnapped; If I Were King; Women Against the World; Convicts at Large. **1939** The Hound of the Baskervilles; The Magnificent Fraud; Private Lives of Elizabeth and Essex; Tower of London. **1940** Calling Philo Vance; Curtain Call. **1944** Frenchman's Creek; Adventure in Diamonds.

FORBES, RICHARD
Born: 1936. Died: Sept. 12, 1979, Los Angeles, Calif. Screen, television actor and drama coach.

FORBES-ROBERTSON, ERIC (aka JOHN KELT)
Died: Mar. 10, 1935, London, England (consequence of a street accident). Screen, stage actor and stage director. For family info see Sir Johnston Forbes-Robertson listing.

Appeared in: **1914** The Murdock Trial. **1934** The Tell-Tale Heart (aka Bucket of Blood).

FORBES-ROBERTSON, FRANK
Born: Aug. 1, 1885, England. Died: Mar. 15, 1947, London, England. Screen and stage actor. Son of actor Norman Forbes-Robertson (dec. 1932). Divorced from stage actress Honoria Helen McDermott and later married to stage actress Sydney Thornton.

Appeared in: **1934** Danny Boy.

FORBES-ROBERTSON, JEAN
Born: Mar. 16, 1905, London, England. Died: Dec. 24, 1962, London, England. Screen, stage actress and stage director. Daughter of actor Sir Johnston Forbes-Robertson (dec. 1937) and actress Gertrude Elliott (dec. 1950). Divorced from James Hamilton and later married to actor-producer Andre Van Gyseghem (dec. 1979).

FORBES-ROBERTSON, SIR JOHNSTON
Born: 1853, London, England. Died: Nov. 6, 1937, St. Margaret's Bay, England. Screen and stage actor. Brother of stage actors Ian Robertson (dec. 1936) and Frances Forbes-Robertson (dec.) and actors Norman (dec. 1932) and Eric Forbes-Robertson (dec. 1935). Married to actress Gertrude Elliott (dec. 1950). Father of actress Jean Forbes-Robertson (dec. 1962).

Appeared in: **1913** Hamlet (US 1915). **1917** The Passing of the Third Floor Back.

FORBES-ROBERTSON, NORMAN (Norman Forbes)
Born: Sept. 24, 1858, London, England. Died: Sept. 29, 1932, London, England (results of auto accident). Screen and stage actor. Father of actor Frank Forbes-Robertson (dec. 1947). For family info see Sir Johnston Forbes-Robertson listing.

Appeared in: **1916** The Real Thing at Last; The Second Mrs. Tanqueray.

FORCE, FLOYD CHARLES
Born: 1876. Died: June 9, 1947, Hollywood, Calif. Screen actor. Was one of the original Keystone Kops.

Appeared in: **1921** Cupid's Brand. **1922** The Infidel; The Game Chicken; The Lone Rider. **1923** The Love Pirate. **1924** Turned Up; Surging Seas. **1926** Hearts and Spangles. **1927** The Heart of Maryland.

FORD, CECIL
Born: 1911, Dublin, Ireland. Died: Mar. 27, 1980, Reading, England (following surgery). Screen, stage actor, film producer and stage director.

Appeared in: **1938** Men of Ireland.

FORD, DAISY
Born: 1906. Died: Dec. 14, 1959, Hollywood, Calif. Screen, stage and vaudeville actress.

FORD, FENTON
Born: 1878. Died: May 1, 1938, Hollywood, Calif. Screen actor and playwright. Appeared in Hal Roach silent film comedies.

FORD, FRANCIS (Francis O'Fearna)
Born: Aug. 15, 1882, Portland, Maine. Died: Sept. 5, 1953, Los Angeles, Calif. Screen, stage actor, screenwriter, film director and producer. Father of actor and director Philip Ford (dec. 1976); brother of film director John Ford (Sean O'Fearna, dec. 1973). Entered films as an actor with Edison and then went to Vitagraph and directed and acted.

Appeared in: **1912** The Deserter; The Indian Massacre; The Invaders; Custer's Last Fight. **1913** The Favorite Son. **1914** Be Neutral; Bride of Mystery; In the Fall of '64; Lady Raffles; Lucille Love; Girl of Mystery (serial); The Madcap Queen of Gretzhoffen; The Mystery of the White Car; The Mysterious Leopard Lady; The Phantom of the Violin; Washington at Valley Forge. **1915** And They Called Him Hero; The Broken Coin (serial); The Campbells Are Coming; The Doorway of Destruction; The Hidden City; The Lumber Yard Gang; Nabbed; One Kind of a Friend; 3 Bad Men and a Girl; The Heart of Lincoln; A Study in Scarlet. **1916** The Bandit's Wager; Behind the Mask; Brennon O' the Moor; Chicken Hearted Jim; The Cry of Erin; The Dumb Bandit; The Elusive Enemy; Her Sister's Sin; The Heroine of San Juan; His Majesty Dick Turpin; Lady Raffles Returns; The Mad Hermit; The Madcap Queen of Crona; Phantom Island; The Adventures of Peg O' the Ring (serial); Poisoned Lips; The Powder Trail; The Princely Bandit; The Purple Mask (serial); The Sham Reality; The Strong Arm Squad; Mr. Vampire; Orders is Orders; The Unexpected. **1917** The Puzzle Woman; In Treason's Grasp; True to Their Colors; Unmasked; To Berlin Via America; The Little Rebel's Sacrifice; The Dazzling Miss Davison (aka Who Is She?); Motherhood; The Greater Woman; The Mirror. **1918** The Silent Mystery (serial); The Craving; The Mystery Ship (serial); Crimson Shoals (serial); Delirium. **1919** The Woman of Mystery (serial). **1920** The Mystery of 13. **1921** The Great Reward (serial); Action; The Lady from Longacre; The Stampede. **1922** The Heart of Lincoln (and 1915 version); Another Man's Boots; The Boss of Camp 4; So This is Arizona; Storm Girl; They're Off; The Village Blacksmith; Thundering Hoofs. **1923** Mine to Keep; Haunted Valley (serial); Three Jumps Ahead. **1924** Western Feuds; Lash of the Whip; The Measure of a Man; Rodeo Mixup; Hearts of Oak; In the Days of the Covered Wagon; The Diamond Bandit. **1925** "Scar" Hanan; The Fighting Heart; The Red Rider; The Four from Nowhere; Ridin' Thunder; The Taming of the West; Soft Shoes; The Sign of the Cactus; A Roaring Adventure. **1926** Speed Cop. **1927** The Devil's Saddle; Upstream; The Wreck of the Hesperus; The Cruise of the Hellion; The Heart of Maryland; Men of Daring; One Glorious Scrap; Uncle Tom's Cabin. **1928** The Branded Sombrero; Sisters of Eve; The Chinatown Mystery (serial); Four-Footed Ranger. **1929** The Black Watch; The Drake Case; The Lariat Kid. **1930** Mounted Stranger; Kathleen Mavourneen; Song of the Caballero; Sons of the Saddle; The Indians Are Coming (serial silent and sound versions); The Jade Box (serial silent and sound versions). **1931** Battling with Buffalo Bill (serial); Frankenstein; The Sea Beneath. **1932** Heroes of the West (serial); The Lost Special (serial); The Last Ride; Tangled Fortunes; Airmail. **1933** Clancy of the Mounted (serial); Gordon of Ghost City (serial); Pilgrimage; Charlie Chan's Greatest Case; Life in the Raw; Man from Monterey; Gun Justice. **1934** Cheaters; Charlis Chan's Courage; Murder in Trinidad; Judge Priest. **1935** Goin' to Town; This Is the Life; The Informer; The Arizonian; Steamboat 'Round the Bend; Paddy O'Day. **1936** Charlie Chan's Secret; The Prisoner of Shark Island; Gentle Julia; Charlie Chan at the Circus; Sins of Man; Educating Father. **1937** The Prisoner of Zenda; A Star Is Born; Slave Ship; Checkers. **1938** In Old Chicago; Kentucky Moonshine; The Texans. **1939** Stagecoach; Young Mr. Lincoln; Drums

Along the Mohawk; Bad Lands; Geronimo. **1940** Viva Cisco Kid; Lucky Cisco Kid; South of Pago Pago; Diamond Frontier. **1941** Tobacco Road; Last of the Duanes. **1942** King of the Mounted (serial); The Vanishing Virginian; The Loves of Edgar Allan Poe; Outlaws of Pine Ridge; The Man Who Wouldn't Die. **1943** Girls in Chains; The Ox-Bow Incident; Jitterbugs. **1944** The Climax; The Big Noise; Bowery Champs. **1945** Incendiary Blonde; San Antonio; Gilda; A Stolen Life; Gallant Journey; Hangover Square. **1946** Renegades; Accomplice; My Darling Clementine; California; Wake Up and Dream. **1947** Unconquered; Bandits of Dark Canyon; Driftwood; High Tide. **1948** The Timber Trail; Eyes of Texas; The Plunderers. **1949** The Far Frontier; Frontier Investigator; San Antone Ambush. **1950** Father Makes Good; Wagonmaster. **1952** The Quiet Man; Toughest Man in Arizona. **1953** The Sun Shines Bright; The Marshal's Daughter; It Happens Every Thursday.

FORD, HARRISON
Born: Mar. 16, 1894, Kansas City, Mo. Died: Dec. 2, 1957, Woodland Hill, Calif. Screen and stage actor.

Appeared in: **1916** The Mysterious Mrs. M. **1918** The Cruise of the Make-Believe; A Pair of Silk Stockings; Such a Little Pirate. **1919** The Lottery Man; The Veiled Adventure; Hawthorne of the U.S.A.; The Third Kiss. **1921** The Passion Flower; Wedding Bells; A Heart to Let; Love's Redemption; Wonderful Thing. **1922** Smilin' Through; Find the Woman; The Primitive Lover; When Love Comes; The Old Homestead; Foolish Wives; Her Gilded Cage; Shadows. **1923** Little Old New York; Vanity Fair; Bright Lights of Broadway; Maytime. **1924** Janice Meredith; The Average Woman; A Fool's Awakening; The Price of a Party; Three Miles Out. **1925** Proud Flesh; The Wheel; Lovers in Quarantine; The Mad Marriage; The Marriage Whirl; Zander the Great. **1926** Up in Mabel's Room; That Royal Girl; Almost a Lady; The Song and Dance Man; Hell's 400; Sandy; The Nervous Wreck. **1927** The Rejuvenation of Aunt Mary; No Control; The Girl in the Pullman; The Night Bride; Rubber Tires. **1928** Let 'Er Go Gallagher; A Woman Against the World; Golf Widows; Just Married; The Rush Hour; Three Week Ends. **1929** Her Husband's Women; The Flattering Word (short). **1932** Love in High Gear. Prior to **1933** Advice to Husbands (short).

FORD, JOHN (Sean O'Fearna)
Born: Feb. 1, 1895, Portland, Maine. Died: Aug. 31, 1973, Palm Desert, Calif. (cancer). Screen director, producer, screenwriter, cinematographer, stand-in and screen actor. Brother of actor Francis Ford (dec. 1953). Won 1935 Academy Award for Best Director for "The Informer," in 1940 for "The Grapes of Wrath," in 1941 for "How Green Was My Valley," and in 1952 for "The Quiet Man."

Appeared in: **1915** The Broken Coin (serial). **1917** The Tornado; Trail of Hate; The Scrapper. **1929** Big Time.

FORD, LETTIE
Born: 1847. Died: Sept. 26, 1936, New York, N.Y. Screen and stage actress.

FORD, MARTY
Born: 1900. Died: Nov. 12, 1954, Hollywood, Calif. Screen and stage actor.

FORD, MARY (Colleen Summers)
Born: 1924, El Monte, Calif. Died: Sept. 30, 1977, Arcadia, Calif. (complication of diabetes-pneumonia). Screen, radio, television actress and singer. Divorced from Les Paul with whom she sang as part of "Les Paul-Mary Ford" team. Later married Donald Hatfield.

Appeared in: **1958** Queen of Outer Space; Missile to the Moon.

FORD, PAUL (Paul Ford Weaver)
Born: Nov. 2, 1901, Baltimore, Md. Died: Apr. 12, 1976, Moneola, N.Y. Screen, stage, radio and television actor.

Appeared in: **1945** The House on 92nd Street. **1948** Naked City. **1949** Lust for Gold; All The King's Men. **1950** Perfect Strangers; The Kid from Texas. **1956** Teahouse of the August Moon (stage and screen versions). **1958** Missouri Traveler; The Matchmaker. **1962** Advise and Consent; The Music Man; Who's Got the Action. **1963** It's A Mad, Mad, Mad, Mad World. **1965** Never Too Late (stage and film versions). **1966** The Russians Are Coming, the Russians Are Coming; Big Hand for a Little Lady; The Spy With a Cold Nose. **1967** The Comedians. **1974** Journey Back to Oz.

FORD, PHILIP
Born: Oct. 16, 1902, Portland, Maine. Died: Jan. 12, 1976, Woodland Hills, Calif. Screen actor, film director and television director. Father of actor Francis Ford (dec. 1953).

Appeared in: **1917** Mystery Ship (serial). **1918** The Silent Mystery. **1919** The Mystery of 13 (serial). **1921** Cyclone Bliss; Shadows of the West. **1922** According to Hoyle; Heroes of the Street; Storm Girl; They're Off; Thundering Hoofs. **1924** Pride of Sunshine Alley. **1925** The Four From Nowhere. **1926** The Blue Eagle; Officer 444 (serial).

FORD, WALLACE
Born: Feb. 12, 1898, England. Died: June 11, 1966, Woodland Hills, Calif. (heart ailment). Screen and stage actor.

Appeared in: **1930** Swellhead; Absent Minded (short); Fore (short). **1931** Possessed; X Marks the Spot. **1932** Wet Parade; Hypnotized; Freaks; City Sentinel; Are you Listening?; Skyscraper Souls; Prosperity; Central Park; Beast of the City. **1933** Employees' Entrance; The Big Cage; She Had to Say Yes; Goodbye Again; Headline Shooter; Night of Terror; My Woman; East of Fifth Avenue; Three-Cornered Moon. **1934** A Woman's Man; Money Means Nothing; The Lost Patrol; Men in White; I Hate Women. **1935** The Nut Farm; The Informer; Another Face; Swell Head and 1930 version); The Whole Town's Talking; In Spite of Danger; Men of the Hour; She Couldn't Take It; The Mysterious Mr. Wong; One Frightened Night; Mary Burns, Fugitive; The Man Who Reclaimed His Head; Sanders of the River; Get That Man. **1936** Two in the Dark; Absolute Quiet; A Son Comes Home; The Rogues' Tavern; O.H.M.S. (You're in the Army Now—US 1937). **1937** Mad About Money (aka Stardust and aka He Loved an Actress—US 1938); Jericho (aka Dark Sands—US 1938); Swing It, Sailor; Exiled to Shanghai. **1939** Back Door to Heaven. **1940** The Mummy's Hand; Scatterbrain; Two Girls on Broadway; Isle of Destiny; Love, Honor and Oh Baby!; Give Us Wings. **1941** A Man Betrayed; The Roar of the Press; Murder by Invitation; Blues in the Night. **1942** All Through the Night; Inside the Law; Scattergood Survives a Murder; Seven Days' Leave; The Mummy's Tomb. **1943** The Ape Man; Shadow of a Doubt; The Marines Come Through; The Cross of Lorraine. **1944** Secret Command; Machine Gun Mama. **1945** On Stage Everybody; Spellbound; Blood on the Sun; They Were Expendable; The Great John L. **1946** Lover Come Back; Crack-Up; Black Angel; Rendezvous With Annie; A Guy Could Change; The Green Years. **1947** Magic Town; T-Men; Dead Reckoning. **1948** Coroner Creek; The Man from Texas; Shed No Tears; Embraceable You; Belle Starr's Daughter. **1949** Red Stallion in the Rockies; The Set-Up. **1950** The Furies; Dakota Lil; The Breaking Point; Harvey. **1951** Warpath; Painting the Clouds With Sunshine; He Ran All the Way. **1952** Flesh and Fury; Rodeo. **1953** The Great Jesse James Raid; The Nebraskan. **1954** Destry; She Couldn't Say No; The Boy from Oklahoma; Three Ring Circus. **1955** The Man from Laramie; The Spoilers; Lucy Gallant; Wichita; A Lawless Street. **1956** The Maverick Queen; Johnny Concho; Thunder Over Arizona; Stagecoach to Fury; The First Texan; The Rainmaker. **1958** The Last Hurrah; Twilight for the Gods; The Matchmaker. **1959** Warlock. **1961** Tess of the Storm Country. **1965** A Patch of Blue.

FORDE, EUGENIE
Born: New York, N.Y. Died: Sept. 5, 1940, Van Nuys, Calif. Screen and stage actress. Mother of actress Victoria Forde (dec. 1964).

Appeared in: **1912** A Pair of Jacks. **1913** Sheridan's Ride; Jim's Atonement. **1915** Pardoned; The Doughnut Vendor; An Eye for an Eye; Across the Desert; Polishing Up Polly; Mother's Birthday; The Great Question; The Diamond from the Sky; Curly. **1916** The White Rosette; Lying Lips; So Shall Ye Reap; The Undertow; The Girl Detective; The Courtesan; Purity; Out of the Shadows; Power of the Cross; Hedge of Heart's Desire. **1917** The Gentle Intruder; Annie-for-Spite; Conscience. **1918** Fair Enough. **1919** Strictly Confidential; Sis Hopkins; The Man Who Turned White. **1920** The Road to Divorce; The Virgin of Stamboul. **1923** Blow Your Own Horn. **1926** Memory Lane; That's My Baby. **1927** Captain Salvation; Wilful Youth.

FORDE, HAL
Born: 1877, Ireland. Died: Dec. 4, 1955, Philadelphia, Pa. Screen and stage actor.

Appeared in: **1912** Mayblossom. **1915** Maker of Dreams. **1924** The Great White Way. **1927** On Guard (serial).

FORDE, STANLEY H.
Born: 1881. Died: Jan. 28, 1929, New York, N.Y. Screen and stage actor.

Appeared in: **1924** The Great White Way.

FORDE, VICTORIA
Born: 1897, New York, N.Y. Died: July 24, 1964, Beverly Hills, Calif. Screen actress. Daughter of actress Eugenie Forde (dec. 1940). Divorced from actor Tom Mix (dec. 1940).

Appeared in: **1912** Lottery Ticket No. 13; Young Wild West Leading a Raid; Uncle Bill; A Pair of Jacks; Settled Out of Court; The Everlasting Judy; At Rolling Forks; Her Indian Hero; The Love Trail; The Renegade. **1913** Sheridan's Ride; The Yaqui Cur; The Stars and Stripes Forever. **1914** Those Persistent Old Maids; Cupid Pulls a Tooth; He Never Said a Word; Could You Blame Her?; The Troublesome Wink; The Way of Life; His Strenuous Honeymoon; She Was a Working Girl; Such a Villain; Her Moonshine Lover; When the Girls Joined the Force; A Lucky Deception; Captain Bill's Warm Reception; What a Baby Did; Sophie of the Films; When Eddie Went to the Front. **1915** Her Rustic Hero; When the Spirit Moved; Lizzie's Dizzy Career; When the Mummy Cried for Help; All Aboard; How Doctor Cupid Won; When He Proposed; The Mixup at Maxim's; In a Jackpot; Eddie's Awful Predicament; Two Hearts and a Ship; The Range Girl and the Cowboy; The Foreman's Choice; On the Eagle Trail; The Race for a Gold Mine; The Downfall of Potts; A Peach and a Pair; Athletic Ambitions; Never Again; When Her Idol Fell; When They Were Co-eds; Lost—Three Teeth; Tony the Wop; Lizzie and the Beauty Contest; When Lizzie Went to Sea; His Egyptian Affinity; When Cupid Caught a Thief; Jed's Little Elopement; Lizzie Breaks into the Harem. **1916** An Angelic Attitude; A Western Masquerade; A Bear of a Story; The Girl of Gold Gulch; Crooked Trails; Going West to Make Good; Taking a Chance; Making Good; Trilby's Love Disaster; Along the Border; The Man Within; Roping a Sweetheart; Tom's Strategy; The Desert Calls Its Own; A Corner in Water; After the Battle; Canby Hill Outlaws; An Eventful Evening; The Country That God Forgot; A Mistake in Rustlers; A Close Call; Tom's Sacrifice; When Cupid Slipped; The Sheriff's Blunder; Mistakes Will Happen; The Golden Thought. **1917** Starring Western Stuff; Hearts and Saddles; Please Be My Wife.

FORDRED, DORICE
Born: Nov. 25, 1902, Port Elizabeth, South Africa. Died: Aug. 4, 1980, London, England. Screen, stage, radio and television actress.

Appeared in: **1933** Day Dreams. **1936** As You Like It. **1937** Knight Without Armor. **1939** Stolen Life.

FOREST, FRANK (Frank Hayek aka FRANCO FORESTO)
Born: 1896, St. Paul, Minn. Died: Dec. 23, 1976, Santa Monica, Calif. Opera singer, radio and screen actor.

Appeared in: **1926** The Count of Luxembourg. **1936** The Big Broadcast of 1937. **1937** I'll Take Romance; Champagne Waltz. **1944** Take It Big.

FORESTO, FRANCO See FOREST, FRANK

FORMAN, TOM
Born: Feb. 22, 1893, Mitchell County, Texas. Died: Nov. 7, 1926, Venice, Calif. (suicide—gun). Screen, stage actor and film director.

Appeared in: **1915** Chimmie Fadden; Kindling; Chimmie Fadden Out West; The Wild Goose Chase. **1916** Sweet Kitty Bellairs. **1917** The Evil Eye; Those Without Sin; The Tides of Barngate; Jaguar's Claws; Her Strange Wedding; The American Consul; Forbidden Paths; A Kiss for Susie; Hashamura Togo; The Trouble Buster. **1919** Told in the Hills; The Tree of Knowledge; For Better, For Worse; Louisiana; The Heart of Youth. **1920** Round-Up; The Sea Wolf; The Ladder of Lies; Sins of Rosanne. **1922** White Shoulders. **1926** Devil's Dice; Kosher Kitty Kelly.

FORMBY, GEORGE, JR. (aka GEORGE HOY)
Born: May 26, 1904, Wigan, Lancashire, England. Died: Mar. 6, 1961, Preston, Lancashire, England. Screen, vaudeville, television actor, screenwriter and song writer. Son of British Music Hall star George Forby (dec.); brother of actress Beryl Formby. Voted among first ten money making stars in British productions in Motion Picture Herald-Fame Poll, 1942 and 1945.

Appeared in: **1914** No Fool Like an Old Fool. **1915** By the Shortest of Heads. **1934** Boots! Boots! **1935** Off the Dole; No Limit. **1936** Keep Your Seats, Please. **1937** Feather Your Nest; Keep Fit. **1938** I See Ice; It's In the Air (aka George Takes the Air—US 1940). **1939** Trouble Brewing; Come on George. **1940** Let George Do It; Spare a Copper. **1941** Turned Out Nice Again; South American George. **1942** Much Too Shy. **1943** Get Cracking; Bell-Bottom George. **1944** He Stoops to Conquer. **1945** I Didn't Do It. **1946** George in Civvy Street.

FORMES, CARL JR. (aka KARL FORMES)
Born: July 3, 1841, London, England. Died: Nov. 18, 1939, Los Angeles, Calif. (arteriosclerosis). Screen and stage actor.

Appeared in: **1915** Old Heidelberg. **1916** MacBeth. **1918** Up the Road with Sallie. **1919** A Rogue's Romance. **1920** The Red Lane; Felix O'Day; Flame of Youth; The Struggle. **1921** A Conneticut Yankee at King Arthur's Court. **1922** Trooper O'Neill.

FORREST, ALAN (Allan Forest Fisher)
Born: Sept. 1, 1889, Brooklyn, N.Y. Died: July 25, 1941, Detroit, Mich. Screen and stage actor.

Appeared in: **1916-18** American Film Mfg. Co. films. **1919** Rosemary Climbs the Heights. **1921** Cheated Love; Forgotten Woman; The Hole in the Wall; The Invisible Fear; The Man from Lost River; They Shall Pay; What Women Will Do. **1922** The Heart Specialist; Lights of the Desert; The New Teacher; Seeing's Believing; Tillie; Very Truly Yours. **1923** Long Live the King; Crinoline and Romance; Her Fatal Millions; The Man Between; A Noise in Newboro; Wandering Daughters. **1924** Don't Doubt Your Husband; In Love with Love; The Siren of Seville; Captain Blood; Dorothy Vernon of Haddon Hall. **1925** The Dressmaker from Paris; The Great Divide; Old Clothes; Pampered Youth; Rose of the World. **1926** The Carnival Girl; Fifth Avenue; Partners Again; The Phantom Bullet; The Prince of Polsen; Summer Bachelors; Two Can Play. **1927** Ankles Preferred; The Lovelorn. **1928** Black Feather; The Desert Bride; Riding for Fame; Sally of the Scandals; The Wild West Show. **1929** The Winged Horseman. **1930** Dangerous Nan McGrew.

FORREST, ARTHUR
Born: 1859, Bayreuth, Germany. Died: May 14, 1933, New York, N.Y. Screen and stage actor.

Appeared in: **1922** When Knighthood Was in Flower.

FORREST, BELFORD (Fenton Ford)
Born: 1878. Died: May 1, 1938, Hollywood, Calif. Screen actor and playwright. One of the first comics signed by Hal Roach in silent bathing beauty days.

FORREST, MABEL
Born: 1895. Died: July 5, 1967, Los Angeles, Calif? Screen actress. Married to actor Bryant Washburn, Sr. (dec. 1963). Mother of actor Bryant Washburn, Jr. (dec. 1960).

Appeared in: **1923** The Love Trap; Mint to Keep; Other Men's Daughters; The Satin Girl. **1924** In Love With Love. **1930** Scrappily Married; Holiday. **1933** Tied for Life (short). **1935** The Big Broadcast of 1936. **1936** Hollywood Boulevard. **1943** A Maid Made Mad (short). **1944** His Tale Is Told (short).

FORST, WILLI (Wilhelm Frohs)
Born: 1903, Vienna, Austria. Died: Aug. 12, 1980, Vienna, Austria (following surgery). Screen, stage actor, film director, film producer, screenwriter and author.

Appeared in: **1920** Der Wegweiser. **1922** Oh, du Lieber Augustin. **1924** Strandgut. **1927** Drei Niemandskinder; Die Elf Teufel; Cafe Electric (aka Wenn ein Weib den Weg Verliert, and aka Die Liebesboerse). **1928** Amor Aug Ski; Ein Besserer, Herr; Die Blaue Maus; Liebfraumilch; Die Listigen Vagabunden; Unfug der Liebe. **1929** Fraulein Faehnrich; Die Frau, die Jeder Liebt, Bist Du!; Katherina Knie; Gefahren der Brautzeit; Der Straefling aus Stambul; Die Weissen Rosen von Ravensburg; Atlantik. **1930** Zwei Hertzen in Drei-Viertel Takt (Two Hearts in Waltz Time); Ein Tango fuer Dich; Der Herr auf Bestellung; Das Lied ist Aus (US 1932); Ein Burschenlied aus Heidelberg (US 1931). **1931** Sein Liebeslied; Die Lustigen Weiber von Wien; Der Raub der Mona Lisa (Theft of the Mona Lisa). **1932** Peter Voss, der Millionendieb; So ein Maedel Vergisst Man Nicht (US 1935); Der Prinz von Arkadien; Ein Blonder Traum (Blonde Dream). **1933** Der Liebling von Wien; Ihre Durchlaucht, die Verkaueferin; Brennendes Geheimnis. **1934** So Endete Eine Liebe; Ich Kenn' Dich Nicht und Liebe Dich (I Don't Know You, But I Love You—US 1935). **1935** Koenigswalzer (The Royal Waltz—US 1936). **1939** Ich Bin Sebastain Otto; Bel Ami. **1940** Jud Suess; Operette (US 1949). **1942** Wiener Blut. **1945** Wiener Maedeln. **1951** Wonderful Times (narrator); Die Suenderin (The Sinner); Es Geschehen Noch Wunder. **1954** Bei Die war es Immer so Schoen; Weg in die Vergangenheit. **1955** Ein Mann Vergisst die Liebe.

FORSTER, JAMIE
Died: Sept. 7, 1970. Screen actor.

Appeared in: **1958** Attack of the Puppet People.

FORSTER, RUDOLF (aka RUDOLPH FORSTER)
Born: 1884, Groebming, Germany. Died: Oct. 25, 1968, Attersee, Germany. Screen, stage actor and film director.

Appeared in: **1919** Fahrt ins Blaue. **1920** Das Geheimnis der Gladiatorenwerke; Die Jagd Nach der Wahrheit; Kurfuerstendamn; Manolescus Memoiren; Der Schaedel der Pharaonentochter; Zehn Milliarden Volt; Der Abenteuer; Glanz und Elend der Kurtisanen (aka Moral, der Meister des Verbrechens). **1921** Die Rote Hexe. **1922** Frau

Suende; Das Licht um Mitternacht; Die Mausefalle; Die Schuhe Einer Schoenen Frau; Der Staerkste Trieb. **1923** Adam und Eva; Das Erbe; Die Marionetten der Fuerstin; S.O.S. Die Insel der Traenen; Tragoedie der Liebe (Love Tragedy); Auferstehung (aka Katjuscha Maslova); Erdgeist (Earth Spirit). **1924** Ssasin; Horrido. **1925** Zur Chronik von Grieshuus. **1926** Sein Grosser Fall. **1927** At the Grey House; Die Hose; Pique Dame. **1931** Ariane; Yorck (US 1932); Die Dreigroschenoper (The Threepenny Opera, aka The Beggar's Opera). **1932** Die Graefin von Monte Christo (The Countess of Monte Cristo); Der Traeumende Mund (Dreaming Mouth—US 1934). **1933** Morgenrot (Dawn, Red Dawn). **1934** Hohe Schule (College—US 1939 aka Das Geheimnis des Carlo Cavelli (The Secrets of Cavelli)). **1935** ...nur ein Komoediant. **1937** Die Ganz Grossen Torheiten. **1939** Island of Lost Men. **1942** Wien 1910. **1944** Der Gebieterische Ruf; Ein Blick Zurueck (aka Am Vorabend). **1945** Fahrt ins Glueck. **1950** Der Mann, der Zweimal Leban Wollte. **1951** Unvergaengliches Licht; Liebestraum (aka Die Toedlichen Traeume). **1952** Im Weissen Roessl. **1954** Viktoria und ihr Husar; Rittmeister Wronski. **1955** Eine Frau Genuegt Nicht?; Spionage. **1956** Regine; Waldwinter; Kaiserjaeger; Liane, das Maedchen aus dem Urwald (Liane, Girl of the Jungle, aka Liane, Jungle Goddess—US 1958). **1957** The White Horse Inn (US 1959); Und Fuehre uns Nicht in Versuchung; Skandal in Ischl; Spielbankaffaere; Die Unentschuldigte Stunde. **1958** Man Muesste Nochmal Zwanzig Sein. **1959** Die Halbzarte; Lass Mich am Sonntag Nicht Allein; Der Rest ist Schweigen (The Rest Is Silence—US 1960); Morgen Wirst Du um Mich Weinene. **1960** Die Dreigroschenoper (The Threepenny Opera, aka The Beggar's Opera, and 1931 version); Die Schachnovelle (Brainwashed—US 1961, aka The Royal); Das Glas Wasser (A Glass of Water—US 1962); Der Liebe Augustin. **1961** Im Stahlnetz des Dr. Mabuse (The Return of Dr. Mabuse—US 1966); Das Riesenrad; Der Teufel Spielte Balalaika (Until Hell is Frozen). **1962** Lulu (aka No Orchids for Lulu; Er Kann's Nicht Lassen). **1963** The Cardinal; Der Henker von London (aka The Mad Executioners—US 1965). **1964** Tonio Kroger (US 1968); Die Gruft mit dem Raetselschloss; Waelsungenblut. **1968** Der Turm der Verbotenen Liebe.

FORSYTH, ROBERT
Born: 1876. Died: Feb. 9, 1922. Screen actor.

Appeared in: **1917** Betsy Ross.

FORSYTHE, MIMI (Marie G. Armstrong)
Born: 1922. Died: Aug. 17, 1952, Hollywood, Calif. Screen actress.

Appeared in: **1944** Sensations of 1945; Three Russian Girls.

FORTE, JOE (Josef Forte)
Born: 1896. Died: Feb. 22, 1967, Hollywood, Calif. (heart attack). Screen, radio and television actor.

Appeared in: **1938** Pals of the Saddle. **1939** Dick Tracy's G Men (serial). **1941** King of the Texas Rangers (serial); A Panic in the Parlor (short). **1946** Magnificent Doll; The Crimson Ghost (serial). **1949** The Judge; Slattery's Hurricane; Task Force; Riders in the Sky. **1950** County Fair. **1951** Rodeo King and the Senorita. **1952** Scarlet Angel; Assignment Paris. **1953** Three Sailors and a Girl. **1955** Cell 2455, Death Row. **1956** Fury at Gunsight Pass; He Laughed Last; The Buster Keaton Story. **1957** Loving You; Gunfight at the O.K. Corral; Short Cut to Hell. **1958** Return to Warbow. **1961** Homicidal. **1963** The Nutty Professor. **1964** Roustabout; Law of the Lawless. **1965** Black Spurs.

FORTIER, HERBERT
Born: 1867, Toronto, Canada. Died: Feb. 16, 1949, Philadelphia, Pa. Screen and stage actor.

Appeared in: **1914** By Whose Hand. **1915** The Sacrifice. **1921** Beyond; Children of the Night; A Connecticut Yankee in King Arthur's Court; Garments of Truth; The Shark Master; Whatever She Wants. **1922** The Black Bag; Dusk to Dawn; Little Wildcat; Midnight. **1923** Clean-Up; Legally Dead; Railroaded; Slander the Woman. **1924** Ridgeway of Montana; The Western Wallop; The Whispered Name.

FORTUNE, EDMUND
Born: 1863, Monmouthshire, England. Died: Sept. 21, 1939. Screen and stage actor. Entered films in 1919.

Appeared in: **1925** Lost Lady; Never the Twain Shall Meet. **1927** Sorrell and Son. **1938** Blue Danube.

FORTUNE, WALLACE
Born: 1884. Died: Jan. 12, 1926, New York, N.Y. (typhoid, pneumonia). Screen actor and stage director.

FOSHAY, HAROLD A.
Born: 1884. Died: Feb. 23, 1953, Charleston, S.C. Screen actor, film producer and film director.

Appeared in: **1915** The Reward; The Lesson of the Narrow Street. **1916** Kennedy Square; Myrtle the Manicurist; The Tarantula; Winifred the Shop Girl. **1921** The Devil's Confession; The Shadow. **1922** Why Not Marry? **1923** The Fair Cheat. **1924** Youth for Sale. **1926** The Brown Derby. **1936** To Mary With Love.

FOSS, KENELM
Born: 1885, England. Died: Nov. 28, 1963, London, England. Screen, stage actor, film director, film producer, stage producer, screenwriter, playwright and set designer.

Appeared in: **1915** Fine Feather; Love in a Wood. **1916** Arsen Lupin; Odd Charges; The Skipper of the Osprey; The Persecution of Bob Pretty; A Marked Man; The Manxman. **1918** The Man and the Moment; The Top Dog; The Wages of Sin; Once Upon a Time. **1919** Whosoever Shall Offend; Not Guilty; Damages for Breach; Till our Ship Comes In (series); The Double Life of Mr. Alfred Burton. **1920** The Joyous Adventures of Aristide. **1922** Dicky Monteith.

FOSTER, DONALD
Born: 1889. Died: Dec. 22, 1969, Hollywood, Calif. Screen, stage and television actor.

Appeared in: **1959** The Al Capone Story; Horse Soldiers. **1960** Please Don't Eat the Daisies. **1961** All in a Night's Work. **1966** Lord Love a Duck.

FOSTER, DUDLEY
Born: 1925, England. Died: Jan. 8, 1973, London, England. Screen, stage and television actor. Married to actress Eileen Kenally.

Appeared in: **1959** The Two Headed Spy. **1962** Term of Trial (US 1963). **1963** Ricochet (US 1966). **1965** Study in Terror (US 1966); The Little Ones. **1969** Moon Zero Two (US 1970); Where's Jack? **1970** Wuthering Heights.

FOSTER, J. MORRIS
Born: 1882, Foxbert, Pa. Died: Apr. 24, 1966. Screen and stage actor. Married to actress Mignon Anderson.

Appeared in: **1914** Jean of the Wilderness; The Guiding Hand; His Reward. **1915** The Game; The Maker of Guns; The Final Reckoning; The Cycle of Hatred; The Adventures of Florence; The Bridal Banquet; Bianca Forgets; The Vagabonds; Monsieur Nikole Dupree; God's Witness; The Light of the Reef; Ambition; In the Hands of the Enemy; Out of the Sea; The Bowl Bearer; Beating Back; Her Menacing Past. **1917** It Makes a Difference; An Eight Cylinder Romance; The Storm Woman; Beloved Jim; The Secret Man. **1918** The Voice of Destiny; Winning Grandma; The Fighting Grin. **1919** Blind Man's Eyes; You Never Saw Such a Girl. **1920** Overland Red; What Happened to Jones; Sundown Slim.

FOSTER, MAY (aka May Campbell)
Born: Mar. 27, 1893, Ill. Died: Jan. 6, 1951, Los Angeles, Calif. (heart disease). Screen and stage actress.

Appeared in: **1920** Forty-Five Minutes from Broadway; Milestones. **1921** A Knight of the West. **1922** Shadows. **1923** The Silent Partner; The Midnight Alarm. **1925** A Woman of the World. **1926** Crown of Lies; Yellow Fingers. **1927** The Frontiersman. **1928** The Docks of New York. **1934** Scarlet Empress.

FOSTER, NORMAN (Norman Hoeffer)
Born: 1900, Richmond, Ind. Died: July 7, 1976, Santa Monica, Calif. (cancer). Screen, stage, television actor, film director, film producer, television director, screenwriter and playwright. Divorced from actress Claudette Colbert. Later married to actress Sally Blane.

Appeared in: **1929** Gentlemen of the Press (film debut). **1930** Young Man of Manhattan; Love at First Sight. **1931** Reckless Living; The Dove; Alias the Doctor; It Pays to Advertise; No Limit; Men Call It Love; Confessions of a Coed; Up Pops the Devil. **1932** Girl of the Rio; Under Eighteen; Skyscraper Souls; Strange Justice; Prosperity; Play Girl; Smilin' Through; Weekend Marriage; Steady Company; The Cohens and the Kellys in Hollywood. **1933** The Giant Swing; Professional Sweetheart; Ronny; Walls of Gold; State Fair; Pilgrimage. **1934** Rafter Romance; Orient Express; Strictly Dynamite. **1935** Elinor Norton; Behind the Evidence; Ladies Crave Excitement; Superspeed; The Firetrap; Escape from Devil's Island; Hoosier Schoolmaster; The Bishop Misbehaves; Behind the Green Lights. **1936** The Leavenworth Case; Everybody's Old Man; High Tension; Fatal Lady; I Cover Chinatown. **1965** Die Lustigen Weiber von Windsor (the Merry Wives of Windsor—US 1966).

FOSTER, PRESTON

Born: Aug. 24, 1900, Ocean City, N.J. Died: July 14, 1970, La Jolla, Calif. Screen, stage, opera and television actor. Divorced from Gertrude Warren. Married to actress Rebecca Heffner (aka Sheila D'Arcy).

Appeared in: **1929** Nothing But the Truth. **1930** Follow the Leader; Heads Up. **1931** His Woman. **1932** The Last Mile; Life Begins; Doctor X; Two Seconds; I Am a Fugitive from a Chain Gang; The All-American; You Said a Mouthful. **1933** Elmer the Great; Danger Crossroads; Corruption; The Man Who Dared; Hoopla; Devil's Mate; Ladies They Talk About; Sensation Hunters. **1934** Wharf Angel; Sleepers East; Heat Lightning; The Band Plays On. **1935** A Night at the Biltmore Bowl (short); People's Enemy; The Arizonian; Strangers All; Annie Oakley; The Last Days of Pompeii; The Informer. **1936** Muss 'Em Up; We Who Are About to Die; Love Before Breakfast; We're Only Human; The Plough and the Stars. **1937** Sea Devils; The Outcasts of Poker Flat; You Can't Beat Love ; The Westland Case; First Lady. **1938** Everybody's Doing It; Double Danger; Submarine Patrol; Up the River; The Lady in the Morgue; The Storm; The Last Warning; Army Girl; White Banners. **1939** Geronimo; Street of Missing Men; Chasing Danger; 20,000 Men a Year; Society Smugglers; News Is Made at Night; Missing Evidence. **1940** Moon Over Burma; Cafe Hostess; North West Mounted Police. **1941** The Roundup; Unfinished Business. **1942** Secret Agent of Japan; Night in New Orleans; Little Tokyo, U.S.A; American Empire; A Gentleman After Dark; Thunder Birds. **1943** Guadalcanal Diary; My Friend Flicka. **1944** The Bermuda Mystery; Roger Touhy, Gangster. **1945** Valley of Decision; The Last Gangster; Twice Blessed; Thunderhead, Son of Flicka; Abbott and Costello in Hollywood. **1946** The Harvey Girls; Tangiers; Inside Job; Strange Triangle; Blonde from Brooklyn. **1947** Ramrod; King of Wild Horses. **1948** Green Grass of Wyoming; The Hunted; Thunderhoof. **1949** I Shot Jesse James; The Big Cat. **1950** The Tougher They Come. **1951** The Big Gusher; Three Desperate Men (aka Three Outlaws); Tomahawk; The Big Night. **1952** Face to Face; Montana Territory; Kansas City Confidential. **1953** I, the Jury; Law and Order. **1957** Destination 60,000. **1964** The Man from Galveston; The Time Travelers; Advance to the Rear. **1967** You've Got to Be Smart. **1968** Chubasco.

FOUCE, FRANK (Francisco Fouce, Sr.)

Born: 1899. Died: Jan. 11, 1962, Hollywood, Calif. Screen actor and film producer. Appeared in Spanish language films during the 1920's.

FOUGERS, PIERRE

Born: France. Died: Nov. 28, 1922, Paris, France (accidentally shot himself). Screen actor.

FOUGEZ, ANNA

Born: 1895, Italy. Died: Sept., 1966, Santa Marinella, Italy. Screen, stage actress and singer. Entered films in 1920.

FOULGER, BYRON K.

Born: 1900. Died: Apr. 4, 1970, Hollywood, Calif. (heart condition). Screen and television actor.

Appeared in: **1937** Make Way for Tomorrow; The Prisoner of Zenda; The Awful Truth; Larceny on the Air; The Duke Comes Back; A Day at the Races. **1938** Born to Be Wild; Tenth Avenue Kid; Tarnished Angel; I Am a Criminal; It's All in Your Mind. **1939** At the Circus; Exile Express; The Man They Could Not Hang; Mutiny on the Blackhawk; Television Spy; The Girl from Rio; Fools of Desire; In Name Only; Union Pacific; Andy Hardy Gets Spring Fever; The Secret of Dr. Kildare. **1940** Flash Gordon Conquers the Universe (serial); Good Bad Boys (short); Edison, the Man; Heroes of the Saddle; The Saint's Double Trouble; Dr. Kildare's Crisis; The Man With Nine Lives; Ellery Queen, Master Detective; Arizona; Sky Murder. **1941** Sullivan's Travels; Man-Made Monster; The Gay Vagabond; Ridin' on a Rainbow; Sweetheart of the Campus; Mystery Ship; Dude Cowboy; Meet Boston Blackie. **1942** The Forest Rangers; Reap the Wild Wind; The Panther's Claw; The Tuttles of Tahiti; Harvard, Here I Come; Quiet Please, Murder; Stand By For Action; Man from Headquarters. **1943** The Human Comedy; The Falcon Strikes Back; So Proudly We Hail!; Sweet Rosie O'Grady; The Adventures of a Rookie; In Old Oklahoma; Hi Diddle Diddle; Hoppy Serves a Writ; Hangmen Also Die; Enemy of Women; The Power of God; Dixie Dugan; Coney Island; Silver Spurs; Black Raven; What a Woman!; Margin for Error. **1944** Casanova Brown; The Miracle of Morgan's Creek; Maisie Goes to Reno; He Forgot to Remember (short); Since You Went Away; Summer Storm; The Whistler; Roger Touhy, Gangster; Dark Mountain; Henry Aldrich's Little Secret; Ministry of Fear; Marriage Is a Private Affair; Swing in the Saddle; Beautiful But Broke. **1945** The Master Key (serial); The Hidden Eye; Let's Go Steady; Purity Squad (short); Circumstantial Evidence; The Adventures of Kitty O'Day;

Brewster's Millions; Arson Squad; The Blonde from Brooklyn; It's in the Bag; Nob Hill; Adventure. **1946** Blonde Alibi; House of Horrors; The Magnificent Doll; The Postman Always Rings Twice; The Mysterious Mr. M (serial); Snafu; Sensation Hunters; Sentimental Journey; The French Key; Dick Tracy vs. Cueball; 'Til the Clouds Roll By; The Plainsman and the Lady. **1947** The Michigan Kid; Lady Be Good; Hard-Boiled Mahoney; Adventures of Don Coyote; The Bells of San Fernando; Too Many Winners; The Red Hornet; The Chinese Ring; Stallion Road; Unconquered; Easy Come, Easy Go; Second Chance. **1948** Arch of Triumph; The Hunted; They Live By Night (aka The Twisted Road and Your Red Wagon); Return of October; Out of the Storm; I Surrender Dear. **1949** Arson, Inc.; Dancing in the Dark; I Shot Jesse James; The Inspector General; The Dalton Gang; Red Desert; Satan's Cradle. **1950** Champagne for Caesar; The Girl from San Lorenzo; The Return of Jesse James; Experiment Alcatraz; Salt Lake Raiders. **1951** Footlight Varieties; A Millionaire for Christy; FBI Girl; Gasoline Alley; The Sea Hornet; Lightning Strikes Twice; Home Town Story. **1952** Hold That Line; Cripple Creek; My Six Convicts; Apache Country; The Steel Fist. **1953** A Perilous Journey; The Magnetic Monster; Bandits of the West; Experiment; Confidentially Connie; Paris Model. **1954** Silver Lode. **1955** The Spoilers. **1956** You Can't Run Away from It. **1957** The River's Edge; Dino; Sierra Stranger; Gun Battle at Monterey; Up in Smoke; The Buckskin Lady; New Day at Sundown. **1958** In the Money; The Long, Hot Summer; Going Steady. **1959** King of the Wild Stallions. **1960** Ma Barker's Killer Brood; Twelve Hours to Kill. **1962** The Devil's Partner. **1963** Son of Flubber. **1967** The Gnome-Mobile. **1969** There Was a Crooked Man.

FOWLER, ALAMEDA

Born: Florence, Ala. Died: Sept. 8, 1964. Screen, stage and vaudeville actress.

Appeared in: **1930** Party Girl; A Notorious Affair. **1932** Alum and Eve (shorts); False Madonna. **1934** Carolina; Fifteen Wives. **1937** Damaged Lives; Hotel Haywire.

FOWLER, ART

Born: 1902. Died: Apr. 4, 1953, Suffern, N.Y. Screen, radio, and television actor.

Appeared in: **1943** Arizona Trail; Frontier Law.

FOWLER, BRENDA

Born: 1883, Los Angeles, Calif. Died: Oct. 27, 1942, Los Angeles, Calif. Screen, stage actress and playwright. Entered films with Kalem and Rex productions.

Appeared in: **1923** Money! Money! Money! **1934** The Mighty Barnum; The World Moves On; Judge Priest. **1935** Bride of Frankenstein; Carnival; Ruggles of Red Gap. **1936** The Story of Louis Pasteur; The Case Against Mrs. Ames; Second Wife. **1938** The Cowboy and the Lady. **1939** Stage Coach; Dust Be My Destiny. **1940** Comin' 'Round the Mountain; All This and Heaven Too; Untamed; They Drive By Night. **1941** Manpower; So Ends Our Night.

FOWLER, EDWIN BABBIT

Born: 1910. Died: Dec. 31, 1977. Screen, stage actor and opera singer.

Appeared in: **1948** Letter from an Unknown Woman.

FOWLER, ISABEL See KEITH, ISABEL

FOWLER, JOHN C. (John Crawford Fowler)

Born: July 25, 1869, New York, N.Y. Died: June 27, 1952, Los Angeles, Calif. (arteriosclerosis). Screen and stage actor.

Appeared in: **1924** Flapper Wives. **1925** Reckless Courage; S.O.S. Perils of the Sea. **1926** One Punch O'Day. **1927** Burning Gold; Wolf's Clothing. **1929** Campus Knights; The Peacock Fan. **1930** Fighting Legion. **1933** Midnight Patrol. **1934** Are We Civilized? **1945** The Dolly Sisters. **1946** Tomorrow Is Forever.

FOWLER, ROBERT G.

Born: Aug. 10, 1883, Kentucky. Died: June 15, 1966, San Jose, Calif. (cerebral hemorrhage). Screen actor and aviator. Appeared in Champion Company films in 1912.

FOX, FRANKLYN

Born: 1894, England. Died: Nov. 2, 1967, Wantagh, N.Y. (heart attack). Screen, stage, radio and television actor.

Appeared in: **1957** High Tide at Noon. **1959** First Man into Space.

FOX, FRED (Frederick Strachan Fox)
Born: Jan. 22, 1884, London, England. Died: Dec. 1, 1949, Los Angeles, Calif. (heart attack). Screen, stage, radio actor and assistant film director.

Appeared in: **1944** Government Girl; Our Hearts Were Young and Gay; Heavenly Days; Mrs. Parkington. **1947** Forever Amber; Killer Dill. **1948** Wake of the Red Witch; Kiss the Blood Off My Hands.

FOX, HARRY (Arthur Carringford)
Born: 1882, Pomona, Calif. Died: July 20, 1959, Woodland Hills, Calif. Screen, stage and vaudeville actor. Married to actress Evelyn Brent (dec. 1975). Divorced from actresses Yancsi (Jenny) Dolly, of the famed "Dolly Sisters" (dec. 1941) and Beatrice Curtis (dec. 1936). He appeared in vaudeville with his wife at the time, Beatrice Curtis, and together they made two film shorts.

Appeared in: **1916** Beatrice Fairfax (serial). **1928** The Lemon (short). **1929** Harry Fox and His Six American Beauties (short); The Fox and the Bee (short with Beatrice Curtis). **1930** The Play Boy (short with Beatrice Curtis); The Lucky Break. **1931** Fifty Million Frenchmen. **1934** Love Time; 365 Nights in Hollywood.

FOX, JOSEPHINE
Born: 1877. Died: Aug. 2, 1953, Englewood, N.J. Stage, screen, vaudeville and radio actress. Sister of stage actresses Elizabeth Malone and Grace Fox (dec. 1946). Appeared in early Edison Co. films.

FOX, ROSE
Born: 1899. Died: Feb. 2, 1966. Screen actress.

FOX, SIDNEY (aka SYDNEY FOX)
Born: Dec. 10, 1910, New York, N.Y. Died: Nov. 14, 1942, Beverly Hills, Calif. Stage and screen actress. Entered films in 1931 as a Wampas Baby.

Appeared in: **1931** Strictly Dishonorable; Bad Sister; Six Cylinder Love. **1932** Afraid to Talk; The Cohens and the Kellys in Hollywood; Mouthpiece; Once in a Lifetime; Nice Women; Murders in the Rue Morgue. **1933** Don Quixote. **1934** Down to Their Last Yacht; Midnight; School for Girls.

FOXE, EARLE A.
Born: Dec. 25, 1888 or 1891, Oxford, Ohio. Died: Dec. 10, 1973, Los Angeles, Calif. Screen, stage actor and educator.

Appeared in: **1914** The Escape. **1916** The Trail of the Lonesome Pine; The Dream Girl; The Love Mask; Public Opinion; Ashes of Embers; Alien Souls. **1917** Blind Man's Luck; The Honeymoon; Outwitted; Panthea; The Fatal Ring (serial). **1918** From Two to Six; Peck's Bad Girl. **1921** The Black Panther's Club. **1922** The Prodigal Judge; The Man She Brought Back. **1923** Vanity Fair; Lady of Quality; Innocence. **1924** Fashion Row; The Last Man on Earth; Oh, You Tony! **1927** Slaves of Beauty; Ladies Must Dress. **1928** None But the Brave; Four Sons; Sailor's Wives; Hangman's House; The News Parade; The River Pirate; Blindfold. **1929** Fugitives; The Ghost Talks; Through Different Eyes; Black Magic; New Years Eve. **1930** Good Intentions. **1931** Dance, Fools, Dance; Transatlantic; The Spider. **1932** Ladies of the Big House; Union Depot; The Expert; Strangers in Love; So Big; The Midnight Patrol; They Never Came Back; A Passport to Hell; Scarlet Dawn; Those We Love; Destry Rides Again; The All-American. **1933** Blondie Johnson; The Mind Reader; A Bedtime Story; Arizona to Broadway; Men are Such Fools. **1934** Counsel on de Fence (short); Little Man, What Now?; Bedside; Love Time. **1935** St. Louis Woman. **1936** The Golden Arrow; Mary of Scotland; Crack-Up. **1937** We're on the Jury; Dangerously Yours; Murder Goes to College. **1940** Military Academy.

FOY, BRYAN (Bryan Fitzgerald)
Born: Dec. 8, 1896, Chicago, Ill. Died: Apr. 20, 1977, Los Angeles, Calif. (heart failure). Screen, stage, vaudeville actor, film director, film producer, screenwriter and songwriter. Son of actor Eddie Foy, Sr. (dec. 1928). Member of vaudeville's "Seven Little Foys." For Family info see Eddie Foy, Sr. listing. Entered films in 1918.

Appeared in: **1932** Stout Hearts and Willing Hands (short).

FOY, EDDIE, SR. (Edward Fitzgerald)
Born: 1854. Died: Feb. 16, 1928, Kansas City, Mo. Screen, stage and vaudeville actor. Head of vaudeville team "Seven Foys." Married to stage actress Rose Howland (dec. of the Howland Sisters), Lola Sefton, Madeline Morondo (dec. 1918), and Maria Combs. Madeline was the mother of Bryan (dec. 1977), Eddie, Jr., Charlie, Mary, Richard (dec. 1947), Madeline and Irving Foy, who appeared in vaudeville as "The Seven Foys."

Appeared in: **1912** A Solax Celebration. **1915** A Favorite Fool. **1928** Foys for Joys (short).

FOYER, EDDIE
Born: 1883. Died: June 15, 1934, Los Angeles, Calif. Screen and vaudeville actor.

Appeared in: **1930** Big House.

FRALICK, FREDDIE
Born: June 4, 1888, Detroit, Mich. Died: May 13, 1958, Hollywood, Calif. Screen, stage and vaudeville actor. Entered films with Biograph in 1912 and remained in films until 1917.

FRANCE, CHARLES V.
Born: June 30, 1868, Bradford, England. Died: Apr. 13, 1949, Gerrards Cross, England. Screen and stage actor.

Appeared in: **1930** The Skin Game (film debut). **1931** These Charming People; Black Coffee; A Night Like This. **1934** Chu Chin Chow; Lord Edgware Dies. **1935** Scrooge; Tudor Rose. **1936** Secret Agent; Broken Blossoms; Crime Over London. **1937** Victoria the Great. **1938** A Yank at Oxford; Strange Borders; If I Were King; The Ware Case. **1939** Ten Days in Paris. **1940** Night Train to Munich. **1941** Missing Ten Days; Breach of Promise. **1942** Went the Day Well? **1943** Queen Victoria; The Yellow Canary. **1944** The Half-Way House; 48 Hours.

FRANCEN, VICTOR
Born: 1888, France. Died: Dec., 1977, Aix-en-Provence, France. Screen and stage actor. Divorced from actress Mary Marquet (dec. 1979).

Appeared in: **1921** Crepuscule d'Epouvante (Twilight of Horror-film debut). **1931** Apres L'Amour. **1934** End of the World. **1936** Nuits de Feu; Le Roi (The King—US 1941). **1938** J'Accuse (I Accuse); Sacrifice d'Honneur. **1939** La Fin du Jour (The End of the Day); Entente Cordiale; La Viege Folle; Double Crime in the Maginot Line; They May Live. **1940** The Living Corpse; The Open Road. **1941** Hold Back the Dawn. **1942** Ten Gentlemen from West Point; The Great Temptation; The Tuttles of Tahiti; Tales of Manhattan. **1943** Desert Song; Mission to Moscow; Madame Curie. **1944** Passage to Marseille; Mask of Dimitrios; The Conspirators; Hollywood Canteen; In Our Time. **1945** Confidential Agent; San Antonio. **1946** The Beast with Five Fingers; Night and Day. **1947** The Beginning of the End. **1948** To the Victor; Forbidden Love. **1949** La Nuit S'Acheve. **1951** Adventures of Captain Fabian; Stolen Affection. **1954** Hell and High Water. **1955** Bedevilled. **1957** A Farewell to Arms. **1961** Fanny. **1966** Top-Crash.

FRANCES, ROSE (Rose Francis Langdon)
Born: 1881, Milwaukee, Wis. Died: Jan. 27, 1962, Hollywood, Calif. Screen, stage and vaudeville actress. Divorced from actor Harry Langdon (dec. 1944) with whom she appeared in vaudeville.

Appeared in: **1926** The Road to Mandalay.

FRANCIS, ALEC B.
Born: Suffolk, England. Died: July 6, 1934, Hollywood, Calif. (following an emergency operation). Screen and stage actor. Entered films in 1911.

Appeared in: **1911** Their Charming Mama; The Military Air-Scout; Vanity Fair. **1912** Robin Hood; The Transgression of Deacon Jones; Their Children's Approval; Dick's Wife; Silent Jim. **1913** When Pierrot Met Pierrette; A Son's Devotion; When Light Came Back; A Tammany Boarder; For Better or Worse; The Witch; The Beaten Path; The Spectre Bridegroom. **1914** The Drug Traffic; Duty; The Man of the Hour; The Greatest of These. **1915** Lola. **1919** Flame of the Desert; Heartsease; Lord and Lady Algy. **1920** The Street Called Straight; The Man Who Had Everything; The Paliser Case. **1921** What's A Wife Worth?; Godless Men; A Voice in the Dark; The Great Moment; A Virginia Courtship; Courage. **1922** Smilin' Through; The Man Who Saw Tomorrow; Beyond the Rocks; North of the Rio Grande; The Forgotten Law. **1923** Three Wise Fools; Hollywood; Little Church Around the Corner; Children of Jazz; Is Divorce a Failure?; The Last Hour; The Eternal Three; The Spider and the Rose; The Drivin' Fool; Lucretia Lombard; Mary of the Movies; A Gentleman of Leisure; The Gold Diggers; His Last Race. **1924** A Fool's Awakening; Do It Now; Soiled; Listen Lester; The Tenth Woman; The Human Terror; Half-a-Dollar Bill; Beau Brummell. **1925** The Bridge of Sighs; Charley's Aunt; Thank You; The Coast of Folly; Champion of Lost Causes; A Thief in Paradise; The Mad Whirl; Thunder Mountain; The Circle; Rose of the World; Capital Punishment; The Reckless Sex; Waking up the Town; Wandering Footsteps; Where the Worst Begins; Man and Maid; Outwitted. **1926** Tramp, Tramp, Tramp; The Return of Peter Grimm; Forever After; Pals First; Three Bad Men; High Steppers; Faithful Wives; The Yankee Senor; Transcontinental Limited. **1927** The Music Master; Camille; Sally in Our Alley; The Tender Hour. **1928** The Lion and the Mouse; The Terror; The Little Snob; Companionate Marriage;

Broadway Daddies; Life's Mockery; The Shepherd of the Hills. **1929** Evidence; The Sacred Flame; Evangeline; Murder Will Out; The Mississippi Gambler. **1930** The Bishop Murder Case; Feet First; The Case of Sgt. Grischa; Captain Apple Jack; Outward Bound. **1931** Stout Hearts and Willing Hands (short); Arrowsmith; Oh! Oh! Cleopatra (short). **1932** .45 Calibre Echo; No Greater Love; The Last Man; The Last Mile; Alias Mary Smith; Mata Hari. **1933** Oliver Twist; Looking Forward; His Private Secretary; Alice in Wonderland. **1934** Mystery of Mr. X; I'll Tell the World; Outcast Lady.

FRANCIS, COLEMAN
Born: Jan. 24, 1919, Oklahoma. Died: Jan. 15, 1973, Hollywood, Calif. (arteriosclerosis). Screen actor, screenwriter and film director.

Appeared in: **1937** Uncivilized. **1940** The Howards of Virginia. **1942** The Black Swan. **1947** Blondie's Night Out. **1952** The Girl in White; Scarlet Angel; Leadville Gunslinger. **1957** The Phantom Stagecoach. **1958** Stakeout on Dope Street. **1960** Cimarron; From the Terrace; Spring Affair. **1965** Motor Psycho. **1966** The Lemon Grove Kids Meet the Grasshopper and the Vampire Lady from Outer Space (short); Night Train to Mundo Fine. **1970** Beyond the Valley of the Dolls.

FRANCIS, EVE
Born: 1896, Brussels, Belgium. Died: Dec. 6, 1980, Neuilly, France. Screen, stage actress and author. Married to film director Louis Delluc (dec. 1924).

Appeared in: **1919** Fumee Noire; Le Silence. **1920** Le Chemin d'Ernoa. **1922** Fievre; El Dorado. **1924** La Femme de Nulle Part; L'Inodation. **1937** Forfaiture; Club de Femmes. **1940** La Comedie du Bonheur.

FRANCIS, KAY (Katherine Edwina Gibbs)
Born: Jan. 13, 1903, Oklahoma City, Okla. Died: Aug. 26, 1968, New York, N.Y. (cancer). Screen, stage actress and film producer. Divorced from James Francis, actor William Gaston, and Kenneth MacKenna.

Appeared in: **1929** Dangerous Curves; Honest Finder; The Marriage Playground; The Illusion; Gentlemen of the Press; The Cocoanuts. **1930** Behind the Makeup; The Children; Paramount on Parade; A Notorious Affair; Raffles; Let's Go Native; For the Defense; The Virtuous Sin; Passion Flower; The Street of Chance. **1931** The Vice Squad; Transgression; Guilty Hands; Scandal Sheet; Ladies' Man; Girls About Town; 24 Hours. **1932** The False Madonna; House of Scandal; Strangers in Love; Man Wanted; Jewel Robbery; Street of Women; One Way Passage; Trouble in Paradise; Cynara. **1933** The Keyhole; The House of 56th Street; Mary Stevens, M.D.; Storm at Daybreak; I Loved a Woman. **1934** Mandalay; Wonder Bar; Dr. Monica; British Agent. **1935** Living on Velvet; The Goose and the Gander; Stranded; I Found Stella Parish. **1936** The White Angel; Give Me Your Heart; Stolen Holiday; One Hour of Romance. **1937** Another Dawn; Confession; First Lady; Unlawful. **1938** Secrets of an Actress; My Bill; Women Are Like That; Comet Over Broadway. **1939** In Name Only; King of the Underworld; Women in the Wind. **1940** It's a Date; Little Men; When the Daltons Rode. **1941** The Man Who Lost Himself; Charley's Aunt; The Feminine Touch; Play Girl. **1942** Always in My Heart; Between Us Girls. **1944** Four Jills in a Jeep; Hours Between. **1945** Divorce; Allotment Wives, Inc. **1946** Wife Wanted.

FRANCIS, NICKY
Born: 1920, Kirksville, Mo. Died: Sept. 28, 1960, St. Petersburg, Fla. (heart attack). Circus clown, screen and television actor.

Appeared in: **1960** Trapeze.

FRANCIS, NOEL
Born: 1911, Temple, Tex. Died: Oct. 30, 1959, Los Angeles, Calif? Screen and stage actor.

Appeared in: **1929** Turkey for Two. **1930** Up the River; Rough Romance; The New Movietone Follies of 1930; Her Hired Husband. **1931** Bachelor Apartment; Smart Money; Smart Woman; Blonde Crazy; Larceny Lane; Husband's Holiday; Old Man Minick. **1932** Ladies of the Big House; The Expert; The Mouthpiece; Night Court; Man About Town; Guilty as Hell; My Pal, the King; I am a Fugitive from a Chain Gang; Under-Cover Man. **1933** Frisco Jenny; Hold Me Tight; Bureau of Missing Persons; Only Yesterday; Manhattan Tower; Flames; Reform Girl; Her Resale Value; Important Witness; Son of a Sailor. **1934** What's Your Racket?; Good Dame; The Line-Up; Loud Speaker; Fifteen Wives. **1935** White Cockatoo; Stone of Silver Creek; Mutiny Ahead. **1938** Sudden Bill Dorn.

FRANCIS, OLIN
Born: Sept. 13, 1892, Mooreville, Miss. Died: June 30, 1952, Hollywood, Calif. Screen and stage actor.

Appeared in: **1921** A Knight of the West. **1922** Fighting Devil; The Jungle Goddess (serial). **1924** Rarin' to Go; Walloping Wallace. **1925** Let's Go Gallagher. **1926** Call of the Klondike; Sea Beast. **1927** Win That Girl; The Kid Brother; Cross Breed; Flying U Ranch. **1928** The Devil's Trademark; Stormy Waters; Free Lips. **1930** Kismet. **1931** Adios; Homicide Squad; Lariats and Sixshooters; Suicide Fleet. **1932** Tex Takes a Holiday; A Woman Commands; .45 Calibre Echo; The Drifter. **1935** Hard Rock Harrigan. **1936** Swing Time; I Conquer the Sea; O'Malley of the Mounted. **1938** Red River Range; Two-Gun Justice; Overland Stage Raiders. **1939** Overland With Kit Carson (serial); Captain Fury. **1940** Kit Carson.

FRANCIS, ROBERT (Robert Charles Francis)
Born: Feb. 26, 1930, Glendale, Calif. Died: July 31, 1955, Burbank, Calif. (plane crash). Screen actor.

Appeared in: **1954** The Caine Mutiny (film debut); They Rode West. **1955** The Long Gray Line; The Bamboo Prison.

FRANCIS, SANDRA (Sandra Francis Dian Bawdin aka SANDRA DONAT)
Born: 1934. Died: Oct. 3, 1981, Santa Monica, Calif. (results of a motorcycle accident). Screen, stage, television actress and ballerina. Divorced from actor Curt Conway (dec. 1974).

Appeared in: **1957** Time Lock (US 1959). **1958** Bachelor of Hearts (US 1962); Tread Softly, Stranger (US 1959); A Spy in the Sky. **1959** The Nun's Story.

FRANCISCO, BETTY
Born: 1900, Little Rock, Ark. Died: Nov. 25, 1950, El Cerito, Calif. (heart attack). Screen and stage actress.

Appeared in: **1920** The Furnace. **1921** Greater Than Love; A Guilty Conscience; Riding with Death; Straight from Paris. **1922** Across the Continent; Her Night of Nights. **1923** Ashes of Vengeance; Crinoline and Romance; The Darling of New York; Double Dealing; Flaming Youth; The Love Piker; Maytime; Noise in Newboro; The Old Fool; Poor Men's Wives. **1924** Big Timber; East of Broadway; Gambling Wives; How to Educate a Wife; On Probation. **1925** Faint Perfume; Fair Play; Fifth Avenue Models; Jimmie's Millions; Private Affairs; Seven Keys to Baldpate; Wasted Lives. **1926** Don Juan's Three Nights; The Lily; Man Bait; The Phantom of the Forest. **1927** The Gingham Girl; A Boy of the Streets; The Gay Retreat; Uneasy Payments; Too Many Crooks. **1928** Broadway Daddies; You Can't Beat the Law; Queen of the Chorus. **1929** Smiling Irish Eyes; Broadway; The Spirit of Youth. **1930** The Lotus Lady; Street of Chance; Madam Satan; The Widow from Chicago. **1931** Charlie Chan Carries On; Good Sport. **1932** Mystery Ranch; Stowaway.

FRANCK, JOHN L.
Born: 1850, Louisville, Ky. Died: Nov., 1920, Los Angeles, Calif. (burns while filming). Screen and stage actor.

Appeared in: **1919** Eyes of Youth; Flame of the Desert. **1920** Virgin of Stamboul; Pollyanna.

FRANCK, WALTER
Born: 1896, Germany. Died: Aug. 10, 1961, Bavaria. Screen and stage actor.

Appeared in: **1934** Der Herr Der Welt (US 1935). **1937** For Her Country's Sake. **1939** Der Gouverneur.

FRANEY, WILLIAM "BILLY"
Born: 1885, Chicago, Ill. Died: Dec. 9, 1940, Hollywood, Calif. (influenza). Screen actor and film producer. Entered films in 1915.

Appeared in: **1915** Hubby's Cure. **1917** One Damp Day. **1918** An Honest Man. **1921** A Knight of the West. **1922** Quincy Adams Sawyer; A Western Demon. **1923** The Town Scandal; Tea with a Kick. **1924** Mile-a-Minute Morgan; North of Alaska; Border Women. **1925** Manhattan Madness; S.O.S. Perils of the Sea; The Great Sensation; The Fear Fighter; Kit Carson Over The Great Divide. **1926** Senor Daredevil; King of the Saddle; The King of the Turf; A Desperate Moment; Code of the Northwest; Danger Quest; Moran of the Mounted; The Deadline; The Dangerous Dude. **1927** Aflame in the Sky; The Royal American; The Racing Fool; She's a Sheik; King of the Herd; Out All Night; The Lost Limited; Red Signals. **1928** Five and Ten-Cent Annie; Under the Tonto Rim; The Glorious Trail; Romance of a Rogue; The Canyon of Adventure. **1929** The Broadway Hoofer; Annie Against the World; The Royal Rider; Cheyenne. **1930** The

Heroic Lover. **1932** The Millionaire Cat (short); The Iceman's Ball (short). **1933** Somewhere in Sonora; Kickin' the Crown Around (short); Luncheon at Twelve (short). **1934** Bandits and Ballads (short); No More Women. **1935** Restless Knights (short); Old Sawbones (short). **1936** Wholesaling Along (short). **1937** Quick Money; The Marriage Business; Maid's Night Out; Joy of Living; Having a Wonderful Time; plus the following shorts: Locks and Bonds; Dumb's the Word; Tramp Trouble; Morning, Judge; Edgar and Goliath. **1938** The following shorts: Ears of Experience; False Roomers; Kennedy's Castle; Fool Coverage; Beaux and Errors; A Clean Sweep; Dummy Owner. **1939** The following shorts: Maid to Order; Clock Wise; Baby Daze; Feathered Pests; Act Your Age; Kennedy the Great. **1940** The following shorts: Slightly at Sea; Mutiny in the County; 'Taint Legal; Sunk by the Census; Trailer Tragedy; Drafted in the Depot. **1941** Mad About Moonshine (short); It Happened All Night (short).

FRANK, ALLAN
Born: 1915, New York, N.Y. Died: Aug. 9, 1979, New York, N.Y. Screen, stage, television actor and stage producer.

Appeared in: **1952** Never Wave at a WAC. **1954** On the Waterfront. **1956** The Eddy Duchin Story. **1957** The Wrong Man. **1961** The Sin of Mona Kent.

FRANK, BARBARA
Born: 1912. Died: July 4, 1976, Hollywood, Calif. (cancer). Screen actress. Married to talent agent George Frank (dec.).

Appeared in: **1930** Animal Crackers.

FRANK, CARL
Born: 1909. Died: Sept. 23, 1972, St. John, Virgin Islands. Screen, stage, radio and television actor.

Appeared in: **1948** Lady from Shanghai.

FRANK, CHRISTIAN J. (Christian Julius Frank)
Born: Mar. 13, 1890, New York. Died: Dec. 10, 1967, Los Angeles, Calif. (cancer). Screen actor.

Appeared in: **1920** Thunderbolt Jack (serial). **1922** The Guttersnipe; Out of the Silent North; Wild Honey. **1923** The Ragged Edge. **1924** The Love Bandit. **1925** The Ancient Highway; Black Cyclone; Manhattan Madness. **1926** Forlorn River; The Lady of the Harem. **1927** Nevada; Arizona Bound. **1928** The Cavalier; Chicago After Midnight; Easy Come, Easy Go. **1929** Sunset Pass. **1930** Under Montana Skies. **1931** Hard Hombre. **1932** My Pal the King. **1933** The Sunset Pass (and 1929 version). **1934** Embarrassing Moments.

FRANK, J. HERBERT
Born: May 12, 1885, New York, N.Y. Died: Mar. 11, 1926, Los Angeles, Calif. (chloroform poisoning). Screen and stage actor.

Appeared in: **1915** Mortmain; Destruction. **1916** Ashes of Embers; The Crucial Test; The Social Secretary. **1917** Brand of Satan; Fringe of Society; In Darkest Russia; the Iron Ring; Scandal; Secret of the Storm Country. **1918** Tempered Steel; For Freedom; Dodging a Million. **1920** Empty Arms. **1921** Idle Hands; Nobody; The Silver Lining; Wise Husbands. **1922** Up and At 'Em. **1923** Jazzmania; Your Friend and Mine.

FRANK, WILLIAM
Born: 1880. Died: Dec. 23, 1925, Hollywood, Calif. (Bright's disease). Screen and stage actor. Was in early Roach comedies.

Appeared in: **1925** The Last Edition.

FRANKAU, RONALD
Born: Feb. 22, 1894, London, England. Died: Sept. 11, 1951. Screen, stage and radio actor. Married to actress Cynthia Robins. Divorced from Hilda Priest and Renee Roberts.

Appeared in: **1931** The Skin Game; Potiphar's Wife (aka Her Strange Desire—US 1932); Let's Love and Laugh (aka Bridegroom for Two—US 1932); The Calendar (aka Bachelor's Folly—US 1932); The Other Mrs. Phipps. **1934** Radio Parade of 1935 (US 1935). **1936** Talking Hands; International Revue. **1939** His Brother's Keeper. **1947** The Ghosts of Berkeley Square.

FRANKEL, FRANCHON
Born: 1874. Died: Aug. 12, 1937, Hollywood, Calif. Screen and stage actress.

Appeared in: **1927** Jake the Plumber; Sensation Seekers. **1928** Desperate Courage. **1930** Pick 'Em Young (short).

FRANKEL, HARRY
Died: June 12, 1948. Screen and radio actor. Known on radio as "Singing Sam."

FRANKEN, EDGAR
Died: June 14, 1971. Screen actor.

Appeared in: **1970** Husbands.

FRANKEUR, PAUL
Born: 1905, France. Died: 1974, France? Screen actor.

Appeared in: **1947** Les Enfants du Paradis. **1948** Le Pere Tranquille (aka Mr. Orchid). **1949** Devil's Daughter; Counter Investigation. **1951** Nana (US 1957). **1952** Jour de Fete (The Big Day); Under the Paris Sky. **1957** We Are All Murderers; Every Second Counts; The Winner's Circle. **1958** Le Desordre et la Nuit (Disorder and Night aka Night Affair–US 1961). **1959** Touchez Pas au Grisbi (Don't Touch the Loot aka Grisbi—US); Oeil pour Oeil (An Eye for an Eye); Le Rouge est Mis (The Red Light Is On aka Speaking of Murder—US). **1960** Voulez-Vous Danser avec Moi (Come Dance with Me!); Rue de Paris; Marie Octobre. **1962** Archimede le Clochard (Archimede the Tramp aka The Magnificent Tramp—US); La Viaccia; Un Singe en Hiver (Monkey in Winter—US 1963). **1969** La Voie Lactee (The Milky Way).

FRANKLIN, ALBERTA
Born: 1897, San Francisco, Calif. Died: Mar. 14, 1976, Mountain View, Calif. Screen actress.

Appeared in: **1915** Birth of a Nation. **1919** The Devil's Trail.

FRANKLIN, IRENE
Born: 1876 or 1884, St. Louis, Mo. Died: June 16, 1941, Englewood, N.J. (cerebral hemorrhage). Screen, stage, radio, vaudeville actress and singer.

Appeared in: **1929** The American Comedienne (short); Those Were the Days (short). **1934** The President Vanishes; Finishing School; Change of Heart; A Very Honorable Guy; Registered Nurse; The Woman in His Life; Lazy River; Strictly Dynamite; Down to Their Last Yacht. **1935** Ladies Crave Excitement; Affairs of Susan; Death Flies East. **1936** The Garden of Allah; Whipsaw; The Song and Dance Man; Timothy's Quest; Fatal Lady; Wanted: Jane Turner; Along Came Love. **1937** Midnight Madonna; Married Before Breakfast; Blazing Barriers; Saratoga. **1938** Rebellious Daughters; Flirting with Fate. **1939** Fixer Dugan.

FRANKLIN, MARTHA
Born: 1876. Died: Apr. 19, 1929. Screen actress.

Appeared in: **1922** Little Miss Smiles. **1923** Other Men's Daughters; Trilby. **1924** Racing Luck. **1925** Don Q, Son of Zorro; Keep Smiling. **1926** The Duchess of Buffalo. **1927** The Beloved Rogue; Perch of the Devil; The Climbers; Serenade; Uncle Tom's Cabin. **1928** Love and Learn; Wheel of Chance; The Woman from Moscow. **1929** Points West; The Younger Generation.

FRANKLIN, RUPERT
Born: 1862. Died: Jan. 14, 1939, Los Angeles, Calif. Screen actor.

Appeared in: **1925** The Prairie Wife.

FRANKLIN, SIDNEY
Born: 1870. Died: Mar. 18, 1931, Hollywood, Calif. Screen and stage actor.

Appeared in: **1921** Playing with Fire; The Three Musketeers. **1922** Welcome Children; The Vermillion Pencil; The Guttersnipe; Call of Home; Dusk to Dawn. **1923** The Love Trap; Fashion Row. **1924** A Boy of Flanders; In Hollywood with Potash and Perlmutter. **1925** One of the Bravest; The Texas Trail; His People. **1926** Block Signal; Rose of the Tenements; Somebody's Mother. **1927** Fighting Failure; King of Kings; Colleen. **1928** Wheel of Chance. **1930** Lummox; Puttin' on the Ritz. **1932** The Kid from Spain.

FRANKLYN, IRWIN R.
Born: Jan. 8, 1904, New York, N.Y. Died: Sept. 7, 1966, Hollywood, Calif. (heart attack). Screen, stage actor, screenwriter, film producer and publicist. Married to actress Katherine Green.

FRANKLYN, LEO
Born: Apr. 7, 1897, London, England. Died: Sept. 17, 1975, London, England (heart attack). Screen, stage and television actor. Father of actor William Franklyn.

Appeared in: **1959** The Night We Dropped a Clanger (aka Make Mine a Double—US 1961).

FRANKS, DENNIS
Born: 1902. Died: Oct. 14, 1967, Dublin, Ireland (heart attack). Screen and stage actor.

Appeared in: **1965** Ballad in Blue (aka Blues for Lovers—US 1966).

FRANTZ, DALIES E.
Born: 1908, Colorado. Died: Dec. 1, 1965, Dallas, Tex. (heart attack). Screen actor, concert pianist and artist.

Appeared in: **1938** Sweethearts. **1939** Balalaika. **1940** I Take This Woman.

FRANZ, JOSEPH J.
Born: Oct. 12, 1883, Utica, N.Y. Died: Sept. 9, 1970. Screen, stage actor, film director and stage director.

Appeared in: **1928** Easy Come, Easy Go. **1934** Good Dame.

FRASER, CONSTANCE
Born: 1910, England. Died: May, 1973, Worthing, England. Screen and television actress.

Appeared in: **1956** The Feminine Touch (aka The Gentle Touch—US 1957).

FRASER, HARRY
Born: 1889. Died: Apr. 8, 1974, Pomona, Calif. Screen actor, film producer, director and screenwriter.

Appeared in: **1916** The Iron Claw (serial). **1917** The Mystery of the Double Cross (serial). **1921** Burn 'Em Up Barnes; Oh Mary Be Careful. **1923** Luck. **1924** Westbound.

FRASER, JAMES
Born: July 31, 1873, Dundee Scotland. Died: Oct. 19, 1943, Los Angeles, Calif. Screen, stage, radio actor and artist.

FRASER, RICHARD
Born: Mar. 15, 1913, Edinburgh, Scotland. Died: 1971. Screen actor.

Appeared in: **1941** A Yank in the RAF; How Green Was My Valley. **1942** Joan of Paris; Busses Roar; Desperate Journey; Eagle Squadron; The Gorilla Man. **1943** Truck Busters; Edge of Darkness; Holy Matrimony; Thumbs Up. **1944** Ladies Courageous. **1945** Scotland Yard Investigator; The Picture of Dorian Gray; White Pongo; Shadow of Terror. **1946** Bedlam; The Tiger Woman; The Undercover Woman; Blonde for a Day. **1947** The Private Affairs of Bel Ami; The Lone Wolf of London; Blackmail. **1948** Rouge's Regiment; The Cobra Strikes. **1949** Alaska Patrol.

FRAWLEY, T. DANIEL
Born: Nov. 8, 1876, Washington, D.C. Died: Apr. 26, 1936, Richmond, Va. (complication of diseases). Screen, stage and radio actor.

FRAWLEY, WILLIAM
Born: Feb. 26, 1887, Burlington, Iowa. Died: Mar. 3, 1966, Los Angeles, Calif. (heart attack). Screen, stage, vaudeville, and television actor. Divorced from Louise Frawley with whom he appeared in vaudeville.

Appeared in: **1916** Lord Loveland Discovers America. **1929** Turkey for Two (short); Fancy That (short). **1931** Surrender. **1933** Hell and High Water; Moonlight and Pretzels. **1934** Bolero; The Witching Hour; Shoot the Works; Here Is My Heart; The Lemon Drop Kid; The Crime Doctor; Miss Fane's Baby Is Stolen. **1935** Ship Cafe; Alibi Ike; Welcome Home; Harmony Lane; Car 99; Hold 'Em Yale; College Scandal. **1936** Strike Me Pink; Desire; The Princess Comes Along; F Man; Rose Bowl; Three Cheers for Love; Three Married Men; The General Died at Dawn. **1937** Blossoms on Broadway; Something to Sing About; High, Wide and Handsome; Double or Nothing. **1938** Mad about Music; Professor Beware; Sons of the Legion; Touchdown Army; Crime Takes a Holiday. **1939** Persons in Hiding; St. Louis Blues; Ambush; Huckleberry Finn; Rose of Washington Square; Ex-Champ; Grand Jury Secrets; Stop, Look and Love; Night Work. **1940** The Farmer's Daughter; Opened by Mistake; Those Were the Days; Untamed; Golden Gloves; Rhythm on the River; The Quarterback; Sandy Gets Her Man; One Night in the Tropics. **1941** The Bride Came C.O.D.; Public Enemies; Six Lessons from Madame La Zonga; Dancing on a Dime; Footsteps in the Dark; Cracked Nuts; Blondie in Society. **1942** Treat 'Em Rough; Roxie Hart; It Happened in Flatbush; Give Out, Sisters; Moonlight in Havana; Wildcat; Gentleman Jim. **1943** Larceny with Music; We've Never Been Licked; Whistling in Brooklyn. **1944** The Fighting Seabees; Going My Way; Minstrel Man; Lake Placid Serenade. **1945** Flame of Barbary Coast; Lady on a Train; Hitchhike to Happiness. **1946** The Ziegfeld Follies; Rendezvous with Annie; The Inner Circle; The Crime Doctor's Manhunt; The Virginian. **1947** Mother Wore Tights; Miracle of 34th Street; My Wild Irish Rose; I Wonder Who's Kissing Her Now; Monsieur Verdoux; Down to Earth; The Hit Parade of 1947; Blondie's Anniversary. **1948** The Babe Ruth Story; Good Sam; Texas, Brooklyn and Heaven; Joe Palooka in Winner Take All; Chicken Every Sunday; The Girl from Manhattan.

1949 Home in San Antone; The Lady Takes a Sailor; East Side, West Side; The Lone Wolf and His Lady. **1950** Kiss Tomorrow Goodbye; Pretty Baby; Blondie's Hero; Kill the Umpire. **1951** The Lemon Drop Kid (and 1934 version); Abbott and Costello Meet the Invisible Man; Rhubarb. **1952** Rancho Notorious. **1962** Safe at Home!

FRAZER, ALEX (Alex Fraser)
Born: 1900. Died: July 30, 1958, Hollywood, Calif. (heart attack). Screen, stage and radio actor.

Appeared in: **1947** Moss Rose; Brute Force. **1948** Shaggy; If Winter Comes. **1949** The Blonde Bandit; The Cowboy and the Indians; Secret of St. Ives. **1950** Fancy Pants; Three Came Home. **1951** Kind Lady; Royal Wedding. **1952** Les Miserables. **1953** Gentlemen Prefer Blondes; Loose in London; War of the Worlds. **1955** Interrupted Melody. **1956** Bigger Than Life; The Boss.

FRAZER, NITRA
Born: 1888. Died: May 2, 1979, Englewood, N.J. Screen actor. Married to actor Wally Van. Entered films with Vitagraph.

Appeared in: **1915** Love, Snow and Ice.

FRAZER, ROBERT W.
Born: June 29, 1891, Worchester, Mass. Died: Aug. 17, 1944, Los Angeles, Calif. Screen and stage actor.

Appeared in: **1912** Robin Hood. **1916** The Feast of Life. **1919** The Bramble Bush. **1921** Love, Hate and a Woman; Without Limit. **1922** The Faithless Sex; Fascination; How Women Love; My Friend the Devil; Partners of the Sunset; When the Desert Calls. **1923** As a Man Lives; A Chapter in Her Life; Jazzmania; The Love Piker. **1924** Women Who Give; Men; After the Ball; Bread; Broken Barriers; The Foolish Virgin; When a Man's a Man; The Mine with the Iron Door; Traffic in Hearts. **1925** Splendid Road; Keeper of the Bees; The Charmer; The Scarlet West; The Golden Strain; The Love Gamble; Miss Bluebeard; The Other Woman's Story; Why Women Love (aka Sea Woman and Barriers Aflame); The White Desert. **1926** The City; Dame Chance; Desert Gold; The Isle of Retribution; Secret Orders; Sin Cargo; The Speeding Venus. **1927** Back to God's Country; One Hour to Love; The Silent Hero; Wanted a Coward. **1928** Out of the Ruins; The Little Snob; The Scarlet Dove; Burning Up Broadway; City of Purple Dreams; Black Butterflies. **1929** The Woman I Love; Frozen Justice; Sioux Blood; Careers; The Drake Case. **1930** Beyond the Law. **1931** Ten Nights in a Barroom; Mystery Trooper (serial); Two-Gun Caballero. **1932** Two Lips and Juleps or Southern Love and Northern Exposure (short); Rainbow Trail; Saddle Buster; Discarded Lovers; Arm of the Law; King Murder; White Zombie; The Crooked Circle. **1933** The Three Musketeers (serial); Vampire Bat; Justice Takes a Holiday; Notorious But Nice; The Fighting Parson; Found Alive. **1934** Guilty Parents; Monte Carlo Nights; Fifteen Wives; Love Past Thirty; The Trail Beyond; Counsel for the Defense; Fight Trooper; One in a Million. **1935** The Miracle Rider (serial); The Fighting Pilot; Death from a Distance; Ladies Crave Excitement; Never Too Late; The World Accuses; Circumstantial Evidence; Public Opinion. **1936** The Black Coin (serial); Silver Spurs; The Clutching Hand (serial); Garden of Allah; Murder at Glen Athol; Below the Deadline; Gambling Souls; The Rest Cure; It Couldn't Have Happened; Easy Money. **1937** Black Aces; Left Handed Law. **1938** On the Great White Trail; Religious Racketeer; Cipher Bureau. **1939** Navy Secrets; Six-Gun Rhythm; Juarez and Maximilian; Mystic Circle Murder; Danger of the Tong; Crashing Thru. **1940** One Man's Law. **1941** Pals of the Pecos; Law of the Wilds; Roar of the Press; Gangs of Sonora; Gunman from Bodie. **1942** Black Dragons; Riders of the West; Dawn of the Great Divide; A Night for Crime. **1943** Daredevils of the West (serial); The Stranger from Pecos; Wagon Tracks West. **1944** Lawmen; Partners of the Trail; Forty Thieves.

FRAZIER, H. C.
Born: 1894. Died: Aug. 2, 1949, Hollywood, Calif. Screen actor and stand-in.

FRAZIN, GLADYS
Born: 1901. Died: Mar. 9, 1939, New York, N.Y. (suicide—jumped from apartment window). Screen and stage actress. Divorced from actor Monte Banks (dec. 1950).

Appeared in: **1924** Let Not Man Put Asunder. **1927** The Winning Oar. **1928** Inspiration; Spangles; Blue Peter. **1929** Power Over Men; The Return of the Rat. **1930** The Compulsory Husband; Kiss Me Sergeant. **1931** The Other Woman.

FRECHETTE, MARK
Born: Dec. 4, 1947. Died: Sept. 27, 1975, Norfolk, Mass. (accident while an inmate in prison). Screen actor.

Appeared in: **1970** Zabriskie Point.

FREDERICI, BLANCHE (Blanche Friderici Campbell aka BLANCHE FRIDERICI)
Born: 1878, Brooklyn, N.Y. Died: Dec. 24, 1933, Visalia, Calif. (heart attack). Screen and stage actress. Entered films in 1920.

Appeared in: **1922** No Trespassing. **1928** Fleetwing; Gentlemen Prefer Blondes; Sadie Thompson (stage and film versions). **1929** Stolen Love; Wonder of Women; The Trespasser; Jazz Heaven; The Awful Truth. **1930** Soldiers and Women; Courage; The Office Wife; Personality; Last of the Duanes; Kismet; The Bad One; Billy the Kid; The Cat Creeps; Numbered Men. **1931** Ten Cents a Dance; Woman Hungry; A Dangerous Affair; Wicked; Night Nurse; Murder by the Clock; The Woman Between; Friends and Lovers; Honor of the Family. **1932** Mata Hari; Thirteen Women; A Farewell to Arms; Lady with a Past; Love Starved; The Hatchet Man; So Big; Miss Pinkerton; Love Me Tonight; The Night Club; Young Bride. **1933** The Barbarian; Adorable; Hold Your Man; Aggie Appleby—Maker of Men; The Way to Love; Alimony Madness; Secrets; Behind Jury Doors; Man of the Forest; Flying Down to Rio. **1934** Thundering Herd; All of Me; It Happened One Night.

FREDERICK, PAULINE (Pauline Libbey)
Born: Aug. 12, 1884, Boston, Mass. Died: Sept. 19, 1938, Los Angeles, Calif. (asthma). Screen and stage actress. Divorced from actor Willard Mack (dec. 1934).

Appeared in: **1915** The Eternal City (film debut); Bella Donna; Zaza; Sold; Lydia Gilmore. **1916** The Moment Before; The Woman in the Case; Her Honor, the Governor; Audrey; The Spider; The World's Great Snare; Ashes of Embers; Nanette of the Wilds. **1917** Sapho; Her Better Self; The Love That Lives; Double-Crossed; The Hungry Heart; The Slave Island; Sleeping Fires. **1918** Her Final Reckoning; Fedora; La Tosca; Resurrection; Mrs. Dane's Defense; Madame Jealousy; A Daughter of the Old South. **1919** The Woman on the Index; The Fear Woman; Out of the Shadow; One Week of Life; The Peace of the Roaring River; Bonds of Love; Paid in Full. **1920** The Loves of Letty; The Woman in Room 13; Paliser Case; Madame X. **1921** Slave of Vanity; Roads of Destiny; Mistress of Shenstone; Salvage; The Sting of the Lash; The Lure of Jade. **1922** Two Kinds of Women; The Woman Breed; The Glory of Clementine. **1924** Three Women; Fast Set; Smouldering Fires; Let Not Man Put Asunder; Married Flirts. **1925** The Lady. **1926** Devil's Island; Her Honor, the Governor (and 1916 version); Josselyn's Wife. **1927** Mumsie; The Nest. **1928** Woman from Moscow; On Trial. **1929** The Sacred Flame; Evidence. **1931** This Modern Age. **1932** Wayward; The Phantom of Crestwood. **1933** Self-Defense. **1934** Social Register. **1935** My Marriage. **1936** Ramona. **1937** Thank You, Mr. Moto. **1938** The Buccaneer.

FREDERICK, WILLIAM
Born: 1861. Died: Mar. 2, 1931, Astoria, N.Y. Screen actor.

Appeared in: **1915** The Prince and the Pauper.

FREDERICKS, CHARLES
Born: 1920. Died: May 14, 1970, Sherman Oaks, Calif. (heart attack). Screen, stage, radio and television actor.

Appeared in: **1954** Thunder Pass; Port of Hell. **1955** Night Freight; Las Vegas Shakedown; Treasure of Ruby Hills; Tarzan's Hidden Jungle. **1957** Hell Canyon. **1961** Lad: A Dog. **1962** Hemingway's Adventures of a Young Man; Tender Is the Night; The Cabinet of Caligari. **1963** To Kill a Mockingbird. **1964** A House Is Not a Home; My Fair Lady. **1965** The Great Race.

FREEAR, LOUIE
Born: Nov. 26, 1871, London, England. Died: Mar. 23, 1939, London, England. Screen, stage and radio actress.

Appeared in: **1916** The Slavey's Legacy (aka The Lady Slavey). **1922** Eliza'a Romeo (US 1924); Auntie's Wedding Present.

FREED, ALAN
Born: Oct. 15, 1922. Died: Jan. 20, 1965, Palm Springs, Calif. (uremia). Radio disc jockey and screen actor.

Appeared in: **1956** Don't Knock the Rock; Rock Around the Clock. **1957** Mister Rock 'N Roll. **1959** Go Johnny Go.

FREED, LAZAR
Died: Date Unknown. Screen and stage actor. Divorced from actress Celia Adler (dec. 1979).

Appeared in: **1925** Salome of the Tenements. **1929** Ad Musae (The Eternal Prayer). **1936** Liebe Und Liegemshaft (Love and Sacrifice). **1940** Eli Eli; Overture to Glory.

FREEDLEY, VINTON
Born: 1892. Died: June 5, 1969, New York, N.Y. Stage producer and screen actor.

Appeared in: **1943** Stagedoor Canteen.

FREEMAN, AL
Born: 1884. Died: Mar. 22, 1956, Los Angeles, Calif. Screen actor. Father of screen actor Al Frereman, Jr.

FREEMAN, HOWARD
Born: Dec. 9, 1899, Helena, Mont. Died: Dec. 11, 1967, New York, N.Y. Screen, stage and television actor.

Appeared in: **1943** Pilot No. 5; Margin for Error; Girl Crazy; Whistling in Brooklyn; Lost Angel; Air Raid Wardens; Slightly Dangerous; Hitler's Hangman. **1944** Carolina Blues; Dancing in Manhattan; Meet Miss Bobby-Socks; Meet the People; Once Upon a Time; Rationing; Secret Command; The Unwritten Code. **1945** I'll Tell the World; Mexicana; This Love of Ours; That Night With You; You Came Along; Where Do We Go from Here?; A Song to Remember. **1946** The Killers; House of Horrors; Inside Job; Night and Day; So Goes My Love; Abilene Town; Susie Steps Out; Sweet Guy; Monsieur Beaucaire; The Blue Dahlia. **1947** Easy Come, Easy Go; California; Cigarette Girl; Cross My Heart; My Brother Talks to Horses; That Way with Women; Cass Timberland; Magic Town; Long Night; Perfect Marriage. **1948** Summer Holiday; The Time of Your Life; Cry of the City; Arthur Takes Over; Give My Regards to Broadway; Letter from an Unknown Woman; Up in Central Park; Girl from Manhattan; The Snake Pit; If You Knew Suzie. **1949** Take One False Step. **1950** Perfect Strangers. **1951** Double Dynamite. **1952** Scaramouche; The Turning Point; Million Dollar Mermaid. **1953** No Time for Sergeants; Remains to Be Seen; Raiders of the Seven Seas. **1965** Dear Brigitte. Foreign films: We Are All Gamblers; Carriage Trade; Monsieur Et Madame.

FREEMAN, MAURICE
Born: 1872. Died: Mar. 26, 1953, Bayshore, N.Y. Screen, stage and vaudeville actor. Was in vaudeville with his wife, Nadine Winston, in an act billed as "Tony and the Stork." Entered films in 1915.

Appeared in: **1923** Stephen Steps Out. **1937** Strangers on a Honeymoon.

FREEMAN, RAOUL (Reuel Silvan Freeman)
Born: Apr. 24, 1894, Georgia. Died: Feb. 17, 1971, Redondo Beach, Calif. (heart disease). Screen and stage actor.

Appeared in: **1947** Down to Earth. **1954** Executive Suite. **1955** The Long Gray Line. **1956** Around the World in 80 Days.

FREEMAN, STELLA
Born: Apr. 26, 1910, South Norwood, England. Died: May 13, 1936, London, England. Screen and stage actress. Married to actor Godfrey Tearle (dec. 1953).

Appeared in: **1930** The House of the Arrow.

FREEMAN, WILLIAM B.
Died: June 8, 1932, Brockton, Mass. Screen and stage actor.

Appeared in: **1918** Mirandy Smiles.

FREEMAN-MITFORD, RUPERT
Born: 1895. Died: Aug. 7, 1939, London, England. Screen actor.

Appeared in: **1939** Goodbye, Mr. Chips.

FREIL, DICK (Raymond A. Freil)
Born: 1894. Died: May 24, 1939, Yonkers, N.Y. (heart attack). Screen actor, film director, screenwriter and cartoonist. Appeared in Mack Sennett comedies.

FREIL, EDWARD
Born: 1878. Died: July 30, 1938, Los Angeles, Calif. Screen, vaudeville, circus actor and film stuntman.

FRENCH, CHARLES K. (Charles E. Krauss)
Born: 1860, Columbus, Ohio. Died: Aug. 2, 1952, Hollywood, Calif. (heart attack). Screen, stage, minstrel actor and film director. Married to actress Helen French (dec. 1917). Entered films in 1908.

Appeared in: **1909** A True Indian's Heart. **1915** The Coward. **1920** Stronger Than Death. **1921** Bare Knuckles; Hands Off; The Last Trail; The Night Horsemen; The Road Demon; Beyond. **1922** The Bearcat; Her Own Money; If You Believe It, It's So; Mixed Faces; The Unfoldment; West of Chicago; The Woman He Loved; The Yosemite

Trail; Moran of the Lady Letty; Smudge; The Truthful Liar; White Shoulders. **1923** The Extra Girl; The Abysmal Brute; Grumpy; The Lonely Road; A Woman of Paris; Alias the Night Wind; Blinky; Gentle Julia; Hell's Hole; Man's Size; The Ramblin' Kid. **1924** Abraham Lincoln; The Torrent; Free and Equal (reissue and retitle of The Coward—1915); Oh, You Tony; Pride of Sunshine Alley; The Sawdust Trail; Being Respectable. **1925** The Girl of Gold; The Saddle Hawk; Let 'Er Buck; Speed Mad; The Texas Trail; Too Much Youth; The Way of a Girl. **1926** War Paint; The Flaming Frontier; Frenzied Flames; Hands Up!; The Hollywood Reporter; The Rainmaker; Oh, What a Night; The Runaway Express; Under Western Skies; The Winning Wallop. **1927** Good as Gold; The Adventurous Soul; Cross Breed; The Cruise of the Hellion; The Down Grade; Fast and Furious; Man, Woman and Sin; The Meddlin' Stranger; One Chance in a Million; Ride 'Em High. **1928** Big Hop; The Charge of the Gauchos; The Cowboy Cavalier; The Flying Buckaroo; Riding for Fame. **1929** King of the Rodeo; The Last Warning. **1930** Fast Work (short); Overland Bound. **1931** Chickens Come Home (short). **1932** Boy, Oh, Boy (short). **1933** Design for Living; Man of Action; Big Squeal (short); Crossfire. **1934** The Red Rider (serial). **1935** The Rustlers of Red Dog (serial); When a Man Sees Red; The Crimson Trail; The Phantom Empire (serial). **1937** Courage of the West; The Prisoner of Zenda. **1939** Rovin' Tumbleweeds. **1941** Meet John Doe. **1944** Bowery to Broadway.

FRENCH, GEORGE B.
Born: Apr. 14, 1883, Storm Lake, Iowa. Died: June 9, 1961, Hollywood, Calif. (heart attack). Screen and stage actor.

Appeared in: **1917** Black Hands and Soap Suds; Her Friend the Chauffeur; Small Change; Twice in the Same Place; Love and the Ice Man; His Last Pill; Those Wedding Bells; Father's Bright Idea; Father Was Right; The Milky Way; With the Mummie's Help. **1918** Tarzan of the Apes; Wanted—A Leading Lady. **1921** His Pajama Girl. **1924** Reckless Romance; Wandering Husbands. **1925** Bashful Buccaneer; Flying Thru; The Snob Buster. **1926** Cupid's Knockout. **1927** Grinning Guns; Horse Shoes; The Lost Limited; One Glorious Scrap. **1928** Sawdust Paradise; Won in the Clouds; The Black Pear. Prior to 1929 "Christie" comedies. **1930** Street of Chance. **1935** Hoi Polloi (short). **1936** Silver Spurs. **1937** True Confession.

FRENCH, HELEN (Helen Krauss)
Born: Feb. 13, 1863, Ohio. Died: Mar. 12, 1917, Los Angeles, Calif. (endocarditis). Screen and stage actress. Married to actor Charles K. French (dec. 1952).

FRENCH, HUGH
Born: 1910, England. Died: Nov. 2, 1976, Los Angeles, Calif. (heart attack). Screen, stage actor and agent. Divorced from actress Eva Lester. Later married to France Debrignac.

Appeared in: **1947** A Woman's Vengeance; If Winter Comes. **1948** Mr. Peabody and the Mermaid. **1949** Sword in the Desert. **1950** Fancy Pants. **1951** Lucky Nick Cain. **1953** Rogue's March. **1955** Shadow of the Eagle.

FRENCH, TED
Died: July 3, 1978. Screen actor.

Appeared in: **1944** Saddle Leather Law. **1946** West of the Alamo. **1947** Law of the Lash; Range Beyond the Blue; Ridin' Down the Trail. **1948** The Hawk of Powder River. **1949** Bad Men of Tombstone; Roaring Westward (aka Boom Town Badmen). **1963** The Quick and the Dead.

FRESNAY, PIERRE (Pierre-Jules Laudenbach)
Born: Apr. 2, 1897, Paris, France. Died: Jan. 9, 1975, Neuilly-sur-Seine, France (respiratory ailment). Screen and stage actor. Divorced from actress Rachel Berendt (dec. 1957) and Berthe Hovy. Later married to actress Yvonne Printemps (dec. 1977).

Appeared in: **1915** France D'Abord. **1922** Les Mysteres de Paris. **1924** Rocanbole. **1929** La Vierge Folle. **1931** Marius. **1932** Fanny. **1934** Caesar; The Man Who Knew Too Much. **1935** Le Roman d'un Jeune Homme Pauvre; Koenigsmark; LaDame aux Camelias. **1936** Sous Les Yeux D'Occident; Mademoiselle Docteur. **1937** La Grande Illusion (The Grand Illusion—US 1938); Razumov; Alibi. **1938** Adrienne Lecouvreur. **1939** Three Waltzes; LaCharrette Fantome (The Phantom Chariotte aka The Phantom Wagon); Le Puritain (The Puritan). **1940** S.O.S. Mediterranean. **1941** Le Dernier des Six. **1943** L'Assassin Habite au 21 (The Murderer Lives at Number 21—US 1947); Le Voyageur Sans Barage; Le Corbeau (The Raven—US 1948). **1947** Le Visiteur; Carnival of Sinners. **1948** Barry; Les Condamnes; Vient de Paraitre; Street of Shadows. **1949** Monsieur Vincent; Devil's Daughter; Strangers in the House; La Valse de Paris. **1950** Tainted; The Paris Waltz; Dieu a Besoin des Hommes (God Needs Men—US 1951).

1951 Un Grand Patrol; Au Grand Balcon. **1952** Le Voyage en Amerique (Voyage to America); Il est Minuit Docteur Schweitzer; The Perfectionist; The Amazing Monsieur Fabre. **1953** La Rome Napoleon; La Defroque. **1944** Les Aristocrates; Les Evades. **1956** L'Homme aux Clefs D'Or. **1957** Les Oeufs de L'Autruche; Les Fanatiques (The Fanatics aka A Bomb for a Dictator—US 1963). **1958** Et ta Soeur; Tant D'Amour Perdu. **1959** Les Affreux. **1960** La Milliente Fenetre; Les Vieux de La Vielle; The Ostrich has Two Eggs.

FREY, ARNO
Born: Oct. 11, 1900, Munich, Germany. Died: June 26, 1961, Los Angeles, Calif. (heart attack). Screen, stage and radio actor.

Appeared in: **1933** Best of Enemies. **1934** Hell in the Heavens. **1935** Mystery Woman. **1936** Human Cargo. **1939** Midnight. **1940** The Fighting 69th; The Man I Married. **1941** Man Hunt. **1942** The Wife Takes a Flyer; Girl Trouble; The Valley of Vanishing Men (serial); Jungle Siren; Valley of Hunted Men. **1943** Appointment in Berlin; Chetniks; They Came to Blow Up America; Hangmen Also Die; Tiger Fangs; Northern Pursuit. **1944** None Shall Escape; Wilson; Tampico; U-Boat Prisoner. **1945** The Adventures of Rusty; Secret Agent X-9 (serial); Weekend at the Waldorf; Paris Underground; Where Do We Go From Here?; Counter-Attack. **1946** Rendezvous 24. **1947** The Beginning or the End. **1950** For Heaven's Sake. **1953** The Desert Rats.

FREY, NATHANIEL
Born: 1913, N.Y. Died: Nov. 7, 1970, New York, N.Y. (cancer). Screen, stage and television actor.

Appeared in: **1957** Kiss Them for Me. **1958** Damn Yankees (stage and film versions). **1968** What's So Bad about Feeling Good?

FRIC, MARTIN "MAC"
Born: Mar. 2, 1902, Prague, Czechoslovakia. Died: 1968, Czechoslovakia. Screen actor, film director and screenwriter.

Appeared in: **1928** Father Vojtech.

FRIEBUS, THEODORE
Born: 1879, Washington, D.C. Died: Dec. 26, 1917, New York, N.Y. (heart disease). Screen and stage actor. Married to stage actress Beatrice M. Friebus (dec.1980).

Appeared in: **1916** Pearl of the Navy (serial). **1917** Pearl of the Army (serial); The Warfare of the Flesh; The Mystery of the Double Cross (serial); Transgressors.

FRIEDBERGER, LOUIS
Born: Germany. Died: Feb. 16, 1924, Los Angeles, Calif. (cerebral hemorrhage). Screen actor. Appeared in Universal Film Company films.

FRIEDGEN, RAYMOND (John Raymond Friedgen)
Born: 1893, New York, N.Y. Died: Mar. 1, 1966, Los Angeles, Calif. Screen, stage actor, film director and film producer. Entered films as an actor with Vitagraph, Biograph.

FRIEDKIN, JOEL
Born: May 15, 1885, Russia. Died: Sept. 19, 1954, Burbank, Calif. Screen actor.

Appeared in: **1940** The Last Alarm; Who Killed Aunt Maggie? **1941** Borrowed Hero; Outlaws of the Cherokee Trail; Richest Man in Town. **1942** Bad Men of the Hills; The Cyclone Kid; The Sombrero Kid. **1943** Frontier Fury. **1944** Experiment Perilous; Uncertain Glory; Sundown Valley; Wyoming Hurricane; Sagebrush Heroes. **1945** God Is My Co-Pilot; Don Juan Quilligan; Murder, He Says; The Great John L. **1946** California Goldrush; Unexpected Guest; The Postman Always Rings Twice; Angel on my Shoulder; Easy to Wed; Chick Carter, Detective (serial). **1947** The Secret Life of Walter Mitty; Saddle Pals. **1948** Feudin', Fussin' and A-Fightin'; Phantom Valley; Money Madness; False Paradise; Strange Gamble. **1949** The Clay Pigeon; Impact. **1950** Lightning Guns. **1951** Bedtime for Bonzo; Fury of the Congo.

FRIEDMANN, SHRAGA
Born: 1923, Warsaw, Poland. Died: July, 1970, Tel Aviv, Israel (heart attack). Israeli screen and stage actor. Married to actress Shoshannah Ravid.

Appeared in: **1965** Sallah. **1966** Judith.

FRIEND, LOUISE
Died: Aug. 11, 1976. Screen actress.

FRIGANZA, TRIXIE (Delia O'Callahan)
Born: Nov. 29, 1870, Grenola, Kans. Died: Feb. 27, 1955, Flintridge, Calif. (arthritis). Screen, stage and vaudeville actress. Sister of actress Therese Thompson (dec. 1936).

Appeared in: **1923** Mind Over Motor. **1925** The Charmer; The Road to Yesterday; Proud Flesh; Borrowed Finery; The Coming of Amos. **1926** Almost a Lady; Monte Carlo; The Whole Town's Talking. **1927** A Racing Romeo. **1928** Thanks for the Buggy Ride; Gentlemen Prefer Blondes. **1929** My Bag O'Trix (short). **1930** Free and Easy; Strong and Willing (short). Other shorts prior to 1933: Motor Maniac; The March of Time. **1933** Myrt and Marge. **1935** Wanderer of the Wasteland. **1937** A Star Is Born. **1940** If I Had My Way.

FRINTON, FREDDIE (Freddie Hargate)
Born: 1912, England. Died: Oct. 16, 1968, Poole, England. Screen, vaudeville, television actor and comedian.

Appeared in: **1960** Make Mine Mink.

FRIS, MARIA
Died: May 27, 1961. Screen actress and ballet dancer.

Appeared in: **1953** Das Tanzende Herz (The Dancing Heart—US 1958).

FRISCH, LORE
Born: 1925, Germany. Died: July, 1962, East Berlin, Germany (suicide). Screen and television actress.

Appeared in: Csar and Carpenter; My Wife Makes Music.

FRISCO, JOE (Lewis Joseph)
Born: 1890, Rock Island, Ill. Died: Feb. 16, 1958, Hollywood, Calif. Screen, stage and vaudeville actor.

Appeared in: **1930** The following shorts: The Benefit; The Song Plugger; The Happy Hottentots; The Border Patrol. **1931** The Gorilla. **1933** Mr. Broadway. **1938** Western Jamboree. **1940** Ride, Tenderfoot, Ride. **1944** Atlantic City. **1945** Shady Lady. **1947** That's My Man. **1950** Riding High. **1957** Sweet Smell of Success.

FRITH, J. LESLIE *See* FRITH, JOHN

FRITH, JOHN (aka J. LESLIE FRITH)
Born: Sept. 28, 1884 or 1889, London, England. Died: Feb. 1, 1961, London, England. Screen, stage, television actor and playwright.

Appeared in: **1931** Dreyfus (aka The Dreyfus Case—US). **1935** Maria Marten, or, The Murder in the Red Barn (US 1936).

FRITSCH, WILLY
Born: Jan. 27, 1901, Kattowitz, Germany. Died: July 13, 1973, Hamburg, Germany (heart attack). Screen and stage actor. Entered films in 1921. Married to dancer Dinah Grace (dec. 1963). Father of actor Thomas Fritsch.

Appeared in: **1921** Razzia. **1923** Die Fahrt ins Gluck; Seine Frau, die Unbekannte. **1924** Guillotine; Mutter und Kind. **1925** Blittzug der Liebe; Der Farmer aus Texas; Das Madchen mit der Protektion; Der Tanzer meiner Frau; Ein Walzertraum. **1926** Die Doxerbraut; Die Fahrt ins Abenteuer; Die Keusche Susanne; Der Prinz und die Tanzerin. **1927** Die Frau im Schrank; Der Letzte Walzer (The Last Waltz); Schuldig (Guilty); Die Selige Excellenz (His Late Excellency); Die Sieben Tochter der Frau Guyrkovics; Die Carmen von St. Pauli; Ihr Dunkler Punkt. **1928** Spione (Spies); Der Tanzstudent; Ungarische Rhapsodie (Hungarian Rhapsody). **1929** Die Frau im Mond; Melodie des Herzens (Melody of the Heart). **1930** Die Drei von der Tankstelle (Three from the Gasoline Station—US 1931); Liebeswalzer (Love Waltzes); Einbrecher; Hokuspokus (aka The Temporary Widow). **1931** Ronny; Im Geheimdienst (In the Employ of the Secret Service); Ihre Hoheit Befiehlt (Her Highness Commands); Der Kongress Tanzt (The Congress Dances—US 1932); By Rocket to the Moon. **1932** Ich Bei Tag und du Bei Nacht; Ein Blonder Traum (A Blonde Dream); Der Frechdachs; Ein Toller Einfall (A Mad Idea). **1933** Saison in Kairo; Des Jungen Dessauers Grosse Liebe; Walzerkrieg. **1934** Prinzessin Tourandot; Die Tochter Ihrer Excellenz; Die Insel. **1935** Schwarze Rosen (aka Did I Betray?—US 1936); Amphitryon. **1936** Boccaccio; Gluckskinder. **1937** Streit um den Knaben Jo (Strife over the Boy Jo); Menschen ohne Vaterland; Gewitterflug zu Claudia; Sieben Ohrfeigen (Seven Slaps). **1938** Preussische Liebesgeschichte; Am Seidenen Faden; Zwischen den Eltern (Between the Parents); Das Madchen von Gestern Nacht (The Girl of Last Night). **1939** Frau am Steuer; Die Geliebte. **1940** Die Keusche Geliebte; Die Unvollkommene Liebe; Das Leichte Madchen. **1941** Leichte Muse; Dreimal Hochzeit; Frauen sind doch Bessere Diplomaten. **1942** Wiener Blut; Anschlag auf Baku; Geliebte Welt.

1943 Die Gattin; Der Kleine Grenzverkehr; Liebesgeschichten. **1944** Jung Adler. **1945** Die Tolle Susanne; Die Fledermaus (The Bat). **1948** Finale; Film Ohne Titel (Film without a Name—US 1950). **1949** Hallo—Sie Haben Ihre Frau Vergessen; Derby; Katchen fur Alles; Zwolf Herzen fur Charly. **1950** Konig fur Eine Nacht; Die Wunderschone Galathee; Herrliche Zeiten; Schatten der Nacht; Madchen mit Beziehungen. **1951** Schon muss man Sein; Die Verschleierte Maja; Grun ist die Heide; Die Dubarry; Mikosch Ruckt Ein. **1952** Von Liebe Reden wir Sparter; Damenwahl; Wenn der Weisse Flieder Wieder Bluht; Ungarische Rhapsodie (remake of 1928 version). **1953** Weg in die Vergangenheit; Maxie. **1954** Stern von Rio; Drei Tage Mittelarrest; Der Frohliche Wanderer; Liebe ist ja Nur Ein Marchen; Die Drei von der Tankstelle (and 1930 version). **1956** Solange Noch die Rosen Bluhn; Das Donkosakenlied; Schwarzwaldmelodie; Wo die Alten Walder Rauschen. **1957** Der Schrage Otto; Die Bein von Dolores. **1958** Zwei Herzen im Mai; Schwarzwalder Kirsch; Mit Eva fing die Sunde An (aka The Playgirls and the Bellboy—US 1962) Hubertusjagd. **1959** Liebling der Gotter. **1961** Was Macht Papa denn in Italien?. **1964** Das Hab ich von Papa Gelernt (I Learned That from Pop); Verliebt in Heidelberg. Other German films include: Die Carmen von T. Pauli; Ferien vom Ich; Am Brunnen vor dem Tore.

FRITZ
Died: Newhall, Calif. Horse screen performer used by actor William S. Hart. Entered films in 1914.

Appeared in: **1917** The Narrow Trail. **1919** Sand. **1920** The Toll Gate. **1921** Travelin' On. **1924** Pinto Ben; Singer Jim McKee.

FRIZZELL, LOU
Born: 1920. Died: June 17, 1979, Los Angeles, Calif. Screen, stage, television actor and musical director.

Appeared in: **1968** The Stalking Moon. **1969** Tell Them Willie Boy is Here; The Reivers. **1970** Halls of Anger. **1971** Summer of '42. **1972** The Other. **1974** The Front Page; The Crazy World of Julius Vrooder; The Nickel Ride. **1978** Capricorn One.

FROES, WALTER J. (aka WALLY DOUGLAS)
Born: 1922. Died: May 10, 1958, Los Angeles, Calif. Screen and radio actor. Known on radio as "Froggie Froes." Worked with Fred Waring and appeared in numerous film shorts.

Appeared in: **1940** Spies of the Air. **1941** Break the News; Chinese Den.

FROHMAN, BERT
Born: 1900. Died: June 23, 1974, New York, N.Y. Screen and vaudeville actor.

Appeared in: **1939** Back Door to Heaven.

FROMAN, JANE
Born: 1908, St. Louis, Mo. Died: Apr. 22, 1980, Columbia, Mo. (natural causes). Screen, stage, radio, television actress and singer. Divorced from actor/composer Don Ross, John Curtis Burns. Later married to Roland H. Smith.

Appeared in: **1935** Stars Over Broadway. **1938** Radio City Revels.

FRYE, DWIGHT
Born: Feb. 22, 1899, Salina, Kans. Died: Nov. 9, 1943, Los Angeles, Calif. (heart attack). Screen and stage actor.

Appeared in: **1927** The Night Bird. **1930** The Doorway to Hell. **1931** Man to Man; The Maltese Falcon; Dracula; The Black Camel; Frankenstein. **1932** By Whose Hand?; Attorney for the Defense. **1933** The Invisible Man; Strange Adventure; Western Code; The Vampire Bat; The Circus Queen Murder. **1935** King Solomon of Broadway; The Crime of Dr. Crespi; The Great Impersonation; Atlantic Adventure; Bride of Frankenstein. **1936** Florida Special; Alibi for Murder. **1937** The Man Who Found Himself; Something to Sing About; Beware of Ladies; The Shadow; The Great Guy; Sea Devils; Renfrew of the Royal Mounted. **1938** Think It Over (short); The Invisible Enemy; The Night Hawk; Fast Company; Adventure in the Sahara; Who Killed Gail Preston?; Sinners in Paradise. **1939** Conspiracy; Son of Frankenstein; The Man in the Iron Mask; The Cat and the Canary; I Take This Woman. **1940** Gangs of Chicago; Phantom Raiders; Drums of Fu Manchu (serial); Sky Bandits. **1941** Mystery Ship; Son of Monte Cristo; The People vs. Dr. Kildare; The Blonde from Singapore; The Devil Pays Off. **1942** Prisoner of Japan; The Ghost of Frankenstein; Sleepytime Gal; Danger in the Pacific. **1943** Frankenstein Meets the Wolf Man; Dead Men Walk; Drums of Fu Manchu; Submarine Alert; Hangmen Also Die; Dangerous Blondes.

FUEHRER, BENI
Died: Feb. 19, 1935, Pontresina, Switzerland (avalanche while filming). Screen actor.

FULLER, BOBBY (Robert Gaston Fuller)
Born: Oct. 22, 1942, Texas. Died: July 18, 1966, Hollywood, Calif. Screen actor and singer.

Appeared in: **1966** The Ghost in the Invisible Bikini.

FULLER, CLEM
Born: 1909. Died: May 24, 1961, Hollywood, Calif. (cancer). Screen, television actor and stuntman. Entered films approx. 1931.

Appeared in: **1941** Twilight on the Trail. **1949** Gun Runner; Shadows of the West. **1950** The Sundowners; High Lonesome. **1951** The Cave of the Outlaws. **1953** Gunsmoke; The Great Sioux Uprising. **1954** Riding Shotgun. **1959** They Came to Cordura.

FULLER, EDWARD "EDDIE"
Born: 1911, Newburg, Mo. Died: Jan. 22, 1979, New York, N.Y. (hit by bus). Screen, stage, radio and television actor.

Appeared in: **1946** Beyond Endurance (narrator).

FULLER, FRANCES
Born: Mar. 16, 1907, Charleston, S.C. Died: Dec. 18, 1980, New York, N.Y. Screen, stage, radio and television actress. Married to stage director Worthinton Minor.

Appeared in: **1933** One Sunday Afternoon. **1934** Elmer and Elsie. **1955** The Girl in the Red Velvet Swing. **1971** They Might Be Giants. **1974** Homebodies.

FULLER, IRENE "RENE" *See* LYGO, MARY. Do not confuse with actress listed below.

FULLER, IRENE
Born: 1898. Died: Mar. 20, 1945, Hollywood, Calif. Screen actress. Appeared in silent films.

FULLER, JESSE "LONE CAT"
Born: 1897. Died: Jan. 29, 1976, Oakland, Calif. Screen actor, folk-blues musician and one-man band.

FULLER, LESLIE
Born: 1889, Margate, England. Died: Apr. 24, 1948, Margate, England. Screen, stage and radio actress and screenwriter.

Appeared in: **1930** Not So Quiet on the Western Front; Kiss Me Sergeant; Why Sailors Leave Home. **1931** Old Soldiers Never Die; Poor Old Bill; What a Night!. **1932** The Last Coupon; Old Spanish Customers; Tonight's the Night. **1933** Hawleys of High Street; The Pride of the Force. **1934** A Political Party; The Outcast; Lost in the Legion; Doctor's Orders. **1935** Strictly Illegal; Captain Bill; The Stoker. **1936** One Good Turn. **1937** Boys Will Be Girls. **1939** The Middle Watch. **1940** Here Comes a Policeman (reissue of Strictly Illegal—1935); Two Smart Men. **1941** My Wife's Family. **1942** Front Line Kids. **1945** What Do We Do Now?

FULLER, LEW H.
Born: 1887. Died: Nov. 13, 1939, Chicago, Ill. Screen and stage actor.

FULLER, MARGARET
Born: 1905. Died: Jan. 6, 1952, Whittier, Calif. Screen, stage and radio actress. Married to actor Robert Griffin.

FULTON, MAUDE
Born: May 14, 1881, Eldorado, Kans. Died: Nov. 9, 1950, Los Angeles, Calif. Screen, stage, vaudeville actress, playwright, screenwriter and author.

Appeared in: **1927** The Gingham Girl; Silk Legs. **1928** Bare Knees. **1929** Nix on Dames. **1933** The Cohens and the Kellys in Trouble.

FUNG, WILLIE
Born: Mar. 3, 1896, Canton, China. Died: Apr. 16, 1945, Los Angeles, Calif. (coronary occlusion). Screen actor.

Appeared in: **1926** The Two-Gun Man; The Yellow Back. **1929** The Far Call; The Blackbook (serial). **1930** Dangerous Paradise; The Sea God. **1931** Gun Smoke. **1932** The Mask of Fu Manchu; Shanghai Express; One Way Passage; West of Broadway; Hatchet Man; Red Dust. **1933** The Cocktail Hour; Narrow Corner. **1934** The Gay Bride; Crime Doctor; A Lost Lady; Sequoia. **1935** Ruggles of Red Gap; Rocky Mountain Mystery; Red Morning; Oil for the Lamps of China; Shanghai; Hop-along Cassidy (aka Hopalong Cassidy Enters); One Way Ticket; China Seas. **1936** Call of the Prairie; Small Town Girl; We Who Are About to Die; Happy Go Lucky; White Hunter; Secret Valley; Pan Handlers; The General Died at Dawn; Stowaway. **1937** Lost Horizon; Git Along, Little Dogies; Come On Cowboys!; Wells Fargo; Wee Willie Winkie; The Trigger Trio; Jungle Menace (serial). **1938** Border Wolves; Sinners in Paradise; Too Hot to Handle; Pride of the West. **1939** Honolulu; The Gracie Allen Murder Case; Maisie; 6,000 Enemies; Hollywood Cavalcade; Barricade. **1940** Seven Sinners; The Great Profile; The Letter. **1941** Badlands of Dakota; Burma Convoy; The Gay Falcon; Public Enemies. **1942** Seven Days' Leave; North to the Klondike; Destination Unknown; The Black Swan. **1943** Halfway to Shanghai. **1944** The Adventures of Mark Twain.

FUQUA, CHARLES
Born: 1911. Died: Dec. 21, 1971, New Haven, Conn. Black screen actor and singer. A member of the original "Ink Spots" quartet.

FURBISH, RALPH E.
Born: 1914. Died: Oct. 8, 1974, Wilmington, Del. (heart attack). Screen, television actor and harmonica player. Was member of the "Harmonica Rascals" and once had his own band, The "Harmonica Ramblers."

FUREY, BARNEY
Born: Sept. 7, 1888, Boise, Idaho. Died: Jan. 18, 1938, Los Angeles, Calif. (liver ailment). Screen actor.

Appeared in: **1914** Algie's Sister. **1915** The Canceled Mortgage; The Queen of Hearts; The Fair God of Sun Island; Her Prey; The Shadows Fall; In Search of a Wife; The Gambler's IOU. **1916** The Family Secret; The Dupe; The Millionaire Plunger; Darcy of the Northwest Mounted; The Master Swindlers; Sauce for the Gander; The Fangs of the Tatler; A Stranger from Somewhere; The Golden Thought. **1917** Feet of Clay; A Branded Soul. **1918** True Blue. **1921** Experience; Headin' North; The Man Trackers; Terror Trail (serial). **1922** Four Hearts. **1923** The Sunshine Trail. **1924** The Loser's End; Riding Double. **1925** Ranchers and Rascals; The Trouble Buster; Winds of Chance. **1926** The Mile-a-Minute Man; Out of the West; Red Hot Hoofs; Stick to Your Story. **1927** The Sonora Kid; The Flying U Ranch; Splitting the Breeze; Tom's Gang. **1928** King Cowboy; Lightning Speed; Captain Careless; Red Riders of Canada; Tyrant of Red Gulch; When the Law Rides. **1929** Outlaw; The Pride of Pawnee; The Trail of the Horse Thieves; The Big Diamond Robbery; The Drifter; Gun Law; Idaho Red; 'Neath Western Skies; Night Parade. **1930** Beau Bandit. **1933** When a Man Rides Alone; The Penal Code. **1934** Meanest Gal in Town. **1935** Powdersmoke Range. **1936** Nevada. **1937** Don't Tell the Wife.

FURNISS, HARRY
Born: 1854, Wexford, Ireland. Died: Jan. 15, 1925, Hastings, England. Caricaturist and screen actor.

Appeared in: **1912** The Artist and the Brain Specialist; The Foundling; The Shadow on the Blind; Master and Pupil; The Artist's Joke; The Sketch with the Thumb Print.

FUSIER-GIR, JEANNE
Born: 1886, France. Died: 1974, France? Screen actress.

Appeared in: **1932** La Couturiere de Luneville. **1934** Crainquebille. **1940** Parole Fixer; Pop Always Pays; Claudine. **1943** Fire in the Straw. **1948** The Honorable Catherine; Le Corbeau (The Raven). **1951** Miquette. **1952** A Simple Case of Money. **1955** Il Mantello Rosso (The Red Cloak—US 1961). **1956** Fruits of Summer. **1958** Witches of Salem. **1960** Crazy for Love; Marie Octobre.

FYFFE, WILL
Born: 1911, Dundee, Scotland. Died: Dec. 14, 1947, St. Andrews, Scotland (fall from hotel window). Screen, stage and vaudeville actor.

Appeared in: **1930** Elstree Calling. **1934** Happy. **1935** Rolling Home. **1936** King of Hearts; Debt of Honour; Love in Exile; Men of Yesterday; Annie Laurie. **1937** Well Done, Henry; Spring Handicap; Cotton Queen; Said O'Reilly to McNab (aka Sez O'Reilly to McNab—US). **1938** Owd Bob (aka To the Victor—US). **1939** Rulers of the Sea; The Mind of Mr. Reeder (aka The Mysterious Mr. Reeder—US 1940); The Missing People (US 1940). **1940** They Came By Night; For Freedom; Neutral Port. **1941** The Prime Minister. **1944** Heaven Is Round the Corner; Give Me the Stars. **1947** The Brothers (US—1948).

FYODOROVA, ZOYA
Born: 1912, Russia. Died: Dec. 11, 1981, Moscow, Russia (heart attack). Screen and stage actor.

Appeared in: **1941** A Musical Story; Girl from Leningrad. **1945** Marriage. **1961** Vzroslyye deti (Grown-Up Children US—1963). **1980** Moscow Doesn't Believe in Tears.

GABIN, JEAN (Jean-Alexis Moncurge)
Born: May 17, 1904, Villette, France. Died: Nov. 15, 1976, Neuilly, France (heart attack). Screen, stage, television actor and music hall performer.

Appeared in: **1931** Chacun Sa Chance (Everybody Gets One Break, aka La Chute Dans le Bonheur—film debut); Paris-Beguin; Mephisto; Tout Ca Ne Vaut Pas L'Amour. **1932** Coeur de Lilas; La Belle Mariniere; Les Gaietes de L'Escadron. **1933** La Foule Hurle; L'Etoile de Valencia; Adieu les Beaux Jours (US 1934); Tunnel; Du Haunt en Bas; Au Bout du Monde. **1934** ZouZou; Maria Chapdelaine. **1935** Passage Interdit; Varietes; Golgotha. **1936** La Bandera; La Belle Equipe; Les Bas-Fonds (The Lower Depths—US 1937). **1937** La Grande; Illusion; Gueule D'Amour (US 1938); Le Messager; Pepe le Moko (US 1941). **1938** Quai des Brumes (Port of Shadows—US 1939); La Bete Humaine (The Human Beast—US 1940); They Were Five. **1939** Le Recif de Corail; Le Jour se Leve (Daybreak—US 1940). **1941** Remorques. **1942** Moontide. **1946** Martin Roumagnac. **1947** Miroir; Deadlier Than the Male. **1949** Au-dela des Grilles; The Walls of Malapaga (US 1950). **1950** La Marie du Port; E Diu Facile Che un Cammello. **1951** Victor; La Nuit est Mon Royaume (The Night is My Kingdom—US 1953); Le Plaisir (aka House of Pleasure—US 1953). **1952** La Verite sur Bebe Donge; La Minute de Verite (The Moment of Truth—US 1965). **1953** Bufere; La Viergr du Rhin; Leur Derniere Nuit. **1954** Le Port de Desir (Port of Desire, aka The House on the Waterfront—US 1958); Touchez Pas au Grisbi (Don't Touch the Loot, aka Grisbi—US 1959); L'Air de Paris. **1955** Napoleon; French Can-Can (aka Only the French Can—US 1957); Razzia dur la Chnouf (aka Razzia—US 1957); Chiens Perdus sans Collier; Gas-Oil. **1956** Des Gens Sans Importance; Voici les Temps des Assassins; Le Sang a la Tete; La Traversee de Paris. **1957** Four Bags Full; Le Cas du Docteur Laurent (The Case of Dr. Laurent—US 1958); Le Rouge est Mis (The Red Light Is On, aka Speaking of Murder—US 1959). **1958** Crime et Chatinaut (Crime and Punishment; aka The Most Dangerous Sin—US); Inspector Maigret; Le Desordre et la Nuit (Disorder and Night; aka The Night Affair—US 1961); Maigret Tend un Piege; Les Miserables; En Cas de Malheur. **1959** The Possessors; Archimede le Clochard (Archimede the Tramp; aka The Magnificent Tramp—US 1962); Les Grandes Familles; Maigret et L'Affaire Saint-Fiacre; Rue des Prairies. **1960** Le Baron D'Ecluse; Les Vieux de la Vieille; Le President. **1961** Le Cave se Rebiffe (aka Money, Money, Money; aka The Counterfeiters of Paris—US 1962). **1962** Un Singe en Hiver (A Monkey in Winter); Love Is My Profession; Le Gentleman D'Epsom (Gentleman from Epsom). **1963** Melodie en Sous-Sol (aka Any Number Can Win—US; aka The Big Snatch); Un Roi Sans Divertissement; Maigret Voit Rouge. **1964** Monsieur. **1966** Du Rififi a Paname (aka The Upper Hand—US 1967); Le Jardinier d'Argenteui. **1967** Le Soleil des Voyous (aka Action Man—US 1969). **1968** Le Tatoue. **1969** Le Clan des Siciliens (The Sicilian Clan—US 1950); Fin de Journee. **1975** Jury of One (aka Verdict); Le Chat.

GABLE, CLARK (Clark William Gable)
Born: Feb. 1, 1901, Cadiz, Ohio. Died: Nov. 16, 1960, Los Angeles, Calif. (heart attack). Stage and screen actor. Divorced from actress Josephine Dillon (dec. 1971), Rhea Langham and Sylvia Hawkes Ashley (dec. 1977). Married to actress Carole Lombard (dec. 1942) and later married to actress Kay (Williams) Spreckels. Won 1934 Academy Award for Best Actor in It Happened One Night. Nominated for 1935 Academy Award as Best Actor in Mutiny on the Bounty and in 1939 for Gone With the Wind.

Appeared in: **1924** White Man; Forbidden Paradise. **1925** The Merry Widow; Declassee; The Plastic Age; North Star. **1930** The Painted Desert. **1931** Night Nurse; The Easiest Way; The Secret Six; The Finger Points; Laughing Sinners; A Free Soul; Sporting Blood; Dance, Fools, Dance; Possessed; Hell Divers; Susan Lennox; Her Rise and Fall. **1932** Jackie Coopers Christmas Party (short); Polly of the Circus; Strange Interlude; Red Dust; No Man of Her Own. **1933** The White Sister; Hold Your Man; Night Flight; Dancing Lady. **1934** It Happened One Night; Men in White; Manhattan Melodrama; Chained; Forsaking All Others; Hollywood on Parade (short). **1935** After Office Hours; Call of the Wild; China Seas; Mutiny on the Bounty; Riffraff. **1936** Wife vs. Secretary; San Francisco; Cain and Mabel; Love on the Run. **1937** Parnell; Saratoga. **1938** Test Pilot; Too Hot to Handle. **1939** Idiot's Delight; Gone With the Wind. **1940** Strange Cargo; Boom Town; Comrade X. **1941** They Met in Bombay; Honky Tonk. **1942** Somewhere I'll Find You. **1943** Aerial Gunner; Wings Up (narr.); Hollywood in Uniform (short). **1944** Combat America (documentary). **1945** Adventure. **1947** The Hucksters. **1948** Command Decision; Homecoming. **1949** Any Number Can Play. **1950** Key to the City; To Please a Lady; Pygmy Island. **1951** Across the Wide Missouri; Callaway Went Thataway. **1952** Lone Star. **1953** Never Let Me Go; Mogambo. **1954** Betrayed. **1955** Soldier of Fortune; The Tall Men. **1957** Band of Angels; The King and Four Queens. **1958** Run Silent, Run Deep; Teacher's Pet. **1959** But Not for Me. **1960** It Started in Naples. **1961** The Misfits. **1964** The Big Parade of Comedy (documentary). **1974** That's Entertainment (film clips).

GABRIELL, JEAN (aka JEAN G. CITARELLA)
Born: 1898. Died: Oct. 9, 1977, Newark, N.J. Screen, stage actor, film director, film producer, stage director, stage producer, radio director and television director.

Appeared in: **1922** Between Two Husbands; The Wages of Sin.

GABRIELSON, FRANK
Born: 1911. Died: Jan. 24, 1980, Woodland Hills, Calif. Screen, stage actor, screenwriter, television writer and stage manager.

GABRIO, GABRIEL
Born: 1888, Champagne, France. Died: 1946, France? Screen and stage actor.

Appeared in: **1927** Les Miserables. **1930** La Lettre (The Letter). **1934** La Frochard et les Deux Orphelines. **1937** Razumov; Lucrezia Borgia. **1939** Harvest. **1941** Pepe le Moko. **1947** The Devil's Own Envoy.

GABY, FRANK
Born: 1896. Died: Feb. 12, 1945, St. Louis, Mo. (suicide—hanging). Screen, stage and vaudeville actor.

Appeared in: **1927** The Tout (short). **1941** Mr. Dynamite.

GAGE, BEN
Born: 1915. Died: Apr. 28, 1978, Los Angeles, Calif. Screen, radio, television actor and singer. Divorced from actress Esther Williams and later married to Anne Martin.

Appeared in: **1959** The Big Operator. **1978** Coma.

GAGE, ERFORD
Born: 1913. Died: Mar. 17, 1945. Screen actor.

Appeared in: **1942** Seven Miles from Alcatraz. **1943** Hitler's Children; The Falcon Strikes Back; Mr. Lucky; The Falcon in Danger; The Seventh Victim; The Adventures of a Rookie; Gangway for Tomorrow; Rookies in Burma. **1944** Days of Glory; The Curse of the Cat People.

GAGE, WALTER See INGE, WILLIAM

GAHAGAN, HELEN
Born: Nov. 25, 1901, Boonton, N.J. Died: Jan. 28, 1980, New York, N.Y. (cancer). Screen, stage actress, opera singer, congresswoman and drama coach. Married to actor Melvin Douglas (dec. 1981).

Appeared in: **1935** She.

GAIGE, RUSSELL
Died: 1974. Screen and stage actor.

Appeared in: **1944** Phantom Lady; Wilson. **1952** Something for the Birds. **1953** Sangaree; The Vanquished; Forever Female. **1954** Them. **1955** To Catch a Thief. **1956** The Court Jester.

GAILING, GRETCHEN
Born: 1918. Died: June 17, 1961, Hollywood, Calif. Screen actress.

GAINES, RICHARD H.
Born: July 23, 1904, Oklahoma City, Okla. Died: July 20, 1975, North Hollywood, Calif. (heart attack). Screen actor.

Appeared in: **1940** The Howards of Virginia. **1943** A Night to Remember; Tender Comrade; The More the Merrier. **1944** Double Indemnity; Mr. Winkle Goes to War; Double Exposure. **1945** A Gun in His Hand (short); Don Juan Quilligan; The Enchanted Cottage; Twice Blessed. **1946** The Bride Wore Boots; So Goes My Love; Do You Love Me?; White Tie and Tails; Humoresque; Nobody Lives Forever. **1947** Brute Force; The Invisible Wall; Cass Timberlane; Ride a Pink Horse; The Hucksters; Unconquered; Dangerous Years. **1948** Every Girl Should Be Married; That Wonderful Urge. **1949** The Lucky Stiff; Strange Bargain; A Kiss for Corliss. **1951** Flight to Mars; Ace in the Hole. **1953** Marry Me Again. **1954** Drum Beat. **1955** Trial; Love Me or Leave Me. **1956** Ransom; Francis and the Haunted House. **1957** Five Steps to Danger; Jeanne Eagels.

GALE, ALICE
Born: 1859 or 1868, Philadelphia, Pa. Died: Mar. 27, 1941, New York, N.Y. Screen, stage actress and opera singer.

Appeared in: **1916** Romeo and Juliet. **1917** The Darling of Paris; The New York Peacock; Camille; Magda. **1919** L'Apache.

GALE, GLADYS
Born: 1893. Died: 1948, Hollywood, Calif. Screen and stage actress.

Appeared in: **1931** Smart Woman. **1934** Soup and Fish (short). **1935** Thicker Than Water (short); Circus Shadows. **1936** Klondike Annie; Dancing Feet; Navy Born. **1938** Violent is the Word for Curly (short). **1945** An Angel Comes to Brooklyn.

GALE, LILLIAN R.
Died: Apr. 2, 1972, Englewood, N.J. Screen actress.

Appeared in: **1923** The Way of Man. **1924** The Fortieth Door (serial); Ten Scars Make a Man (serial); Way of a Man (serial); Walloping Wallace. **1925** Idaho (serial).

GALE, MARGUERITE H.
Born: 1885. Died: Aug. 20, 1948, Amsterdam, N.Y. Screen and stage actress. Entered films in 1914.

Appeared in: **1915** The Missing Link; How Molly Made Good. **1916** The Yellow Menace (serial).

GALEEN, HENRIK
Born: 1882, Holland. Died: July 30, 1949, Rochester, Va. Screen actor, film director and screenwriter. Entered films as an actor in 1910.

Appeared in: **1914** Der Golem. **1915** Peter Schlemihl.

GALENTO, TONY "TWOTON"
Born: Mar. 10, 1910, Orange, N.J. Died: July 22, 1979, Livingston, N.J. (heart attack). Screen actor and boxer.

Appeared in: **1954** On the Waterfront. **1955** Guys and Dolls. **1956** The Best Things in Life Are Free. **1958** Wind Across the Everglades.

GALINDO, NACHO
Born: Mexico? Died: June 23, 1973. Screen actor.

Appeared in: **1945** Who's Guilty (serial). **1946** The Gay Cavalier; Perilous Holiday; Rose of Santa Rosa. **1947** Tycoon; Fiesta; Twilight on the Rio Grande. **1949** The Big Steal; South of St. Louis; Holiday in Havana. **1950** Broken Arrow; Borderline; Surrender; Belle of Old Mexico; Killer Shark; Montana; The Showdown. **1951** Lightning Strikes Twice; Flaming Feather; Havana Rose; Yellow Fin. **1952** Macao; Lone Star. **1953** The Woman They Almost Lynched; The Hitch-Hiker. **1954** Border River; Jubilee Trail; Both Sides of the Law; Green Fire; Broken Lance; Gypsy Colt; The Outcast. **1955** Headline Hunters; Hell's Island. **1956** Wetbacks; Jaguar; Thunder Over Arizona. **1958** Buchanan Rides Again. **1959** Born Reckless. **1961** One-Eyed Jacks. **1968** The Pink Jungle.

GALLA, TITO (Pedro B. Galla)
Born: 1936, Denver, Colo. Died: Aug., 1979, Wilmington, Del. Screen actor. Brother of actress Gloria Romero.

Appeared in Phillipine films: Uhaw; Hayok; Nympho; Kamunduhan; Reflection.

GALLAGHER, GLEN B.
Born: 1909. Died: Mar. 31, 1960, Hollywood, Calif. (heart attack). Screen actor and cameraman.

Appeared in: **1946** Fool's Gold.

GALLAGHER, RAYMOND "RAY"
Born: Apr. 17, 1885, Calif. Died: Mar. 6, 1953, Camarillo, Calif. (heart attack). Screen and stage actor.

Appeared in: **1916** Crooked Trails. **1919** His Divorced Wife. **1920** The Phantom Melody. **1925** The People vs. Nancy Preston. **1928** Half a Bride. **1929** The Argyle Case. **1930** Sinner's Holiday. **1932** Border Devils. **1935** Judgement Book.

GALLAGHER, "SKEETS" (Richard Gallagher)
Born: July 28, 1890, Terre Haute, Ind. Died: May 22, 1955, Santa Monica, Calif. (heart attack). Screen, stage and vaudeville actor.

Appeared in: **1923** The Daring Years. **1927** The Potters; For the Love of Mike; New York. **1928** The Racket; Three Ring Marriage; Alex the Great; Stocks and Blondes. **1929** Close Harmony; Fast Company; Dance of Life; Pointed Heels. **1930** Paramount on Parade; Honey; The Social Lion; Let's Go Native; Her Wedding Night; Love Among Millionaires. **1931** It Pays to Advertise; Possessed; Up Pops the Devil; Road to Reno. **1932** The Night Club Lady; The Unwritten Law; Merrily We Go to Hell; Trial of Vivienne Ware; Bird of Paradise; The Phantom of Crestwood; The Conquerors; The Sport Parade; Universal shorts; Hollywood on Parade (short). **1933** Easy Millions; The Past of

Mary Holmes; Too Much Harmony; Reform Girl; Alice in Wonderland; Universal shorts. **1934** Riptide; The Meanest Girl in Town; Bachelor Bait; In the Money; Women Unafraid; The Crosby Case. **1935** Lightning Strikes Twice; The Perfect Clue. **1936** Polo Joe; Yours for the Asking; The Man I Marry; Hats Off. **1937** Espionage. **1938** Mr. Satan; Danger in the Air. **1939** Idiot's Delight. **1941** Zis Boom Bah; Citadel of Crime. **1942** Brother Orchid. **1949** The Duke of Chicago. **1952** Three for Bedroom C.

GALLARDO, LUIS ROJAS
Born: Chile. Died: Mar. 5, 1957, Santiago, Chile. Screen, stage, radio actor and writer.

GALLATIN, ALBERTA
Born: 1861. Died: Aug. 25, 1948, New York, N.Y. Screen and stage actress. Appeared in Vitagraph films.

GALLIAN, KETTI
Born: Dec. 25, ?, Nice, France. Died: Dec., 1972. Screen actress.

Appeared in: **1934** Marie Galante. **1935** Under the Pampas Moon. **1937** Espionage; Shall We Dance?

GALVANI, DINO (aka DINO GALVANONI)
Born: Oct. 27, 1890, Milan, Italy. Died: Sept. 14, 1960, London, England. Screen, stage, radio and television actor.

Appeared in: **1927** Blighty (aka Apres La Guerre). **1928** Adam's Apple (aka Honeymoon Ahead—US); Paradise; Adventurous Youth. **1929** Atlantic; Life's a Stage; The Vagabond Queen; The Flying Scotsman; Those Who Love. **1930** The Dizzy Limit; The Price of Things. **1931** The Chance of a Night Time; Black Coffee; Chin Chin Chinaman (aka Boat From Shanghai—US 1932). **1932** The Missing Rembrandt; In a Monastery Garden; Once Bitten; The Silver Greyhound. **1934** Princess Charming (US 1935); The Broken Rosary. **1936** Don't Rush Me; Ball at Savoy; Cafe Colette (aka Danger in Paris—US). **1937** Midnight Menace (aka Bombs Over London—US 1939). **1938** Mr. Satan; The Viper; The Last Barricade; Special Edition; George Bizet, Composer of Carmen. **1943** It's That Man Again. **1948** The Clouded Crystal; Sleeping Car to Trieste (US 1949). **1950** Paul Temple's Triumph (US 1951). **1951** Fugitive Lady; Three Steps North. **1953** Always a Bride (US 1954). **1954** Father Brown (aka The Detective—US). **1955** The Lyons in Paris. **1956** Fun at St. Fanny's; Checkpoint (US 1957). **1957** Second Fiddle. **1959** Breakout (US 1960—aka Danger Within). **1960** Bluebeard's Ten Honeymoons.

GAMBLE, FRED (Frederick Alvin Gambold)
Born: Oct. 26, 1868. Died: Feb. 17, 1939, Hollywood, Calif. Screen, stage and vaudeville actor. Billed in vaudeville as part of "Queen City Four" team. Entered films in 1906.

Appeared in: **1912-13** American Film Mfg. Co. films. **1915** Oh, Daddy. **1920** The Screaming Shadow (serial). **1921** Love Never Dies; Passing Thru. **1922** Boy Crazy; The Firebrand. **1923** The Virginian. **1924** The Torando; Black Oxen. **1925** Tumbleweeds. **1926** Chasing Trouble; Born to Battle. **1927** Laddie Be Good; The Red Mill. **1928** Painted Post.

GAMBLE, RALPH
Born: 1902. Died: Mar. 11, 1966, Hollywood, Calif. Screen and vaudeville actor.

Appeared in: **1953** Mister Scoutmaster. **1955** Sudden Danger. **1956** The Eddy Duchin Story. **1958** In the Money; Unwed Mother.

GAMBLE, WARBURTON
Born: 1883. Died: Aug. 27, 1945. Screen and stage actor.

Appeared in: **1919** The Silver King; A Society Exile; The Invisible Bond; Two Brides; Thirty a Week; As a Man Thinks; La Belle Russe. **1920** The Cost; The Palliser Case; Law of the Yukon. **1921** Poor Dear Margaret Kirby; Fine Feathers. **1922** The Outcast. **1931** Tonight or Never. **1932** As You Desire Me; Fast Life. **1933** Tonight is Ours; Child of Manhattan; A Study in Scarlet. **1934** By Candlelight.

GAMILIN, LIONEL
Born: 1903, England? Died: Oct. 16, 1967, London, England. Screen and stage actor.

Appeared in: **1960** Man in the Moon (US 1961). **1964** Seance on a Wet Afternoon. **1966** The Wrong Box.

GAN, CHESTER
Born: 1909. Died: June 30, 1959, San Francisco, Calif. Screen and television actor.

Appeared in: **1935** Stormy; China Seas. **1936** Ace Drummond (serial); San Francisco; Klondike Annie; Drift Fence; Sea Spoilers. **1937** West of Shanghai; The Good Earth. **1938** Shadows of Shanghai. **1939** Barricade; Mystery of Mr. Wong; Blackwell's Island; King of Chinatown. **1940** My Little Chickadee; 'Til We Meet Again; Victory. **1941** The Maltese Falcon; Man Made Monster; The Get-Away; Burma Convoy. **1942** Flying Tigers; Moontide; China Girl; Across the Pacific. **1943** Crash Dive. **1955** Blood Alley.

GANCE, ABEL
Born: 1889, Paris, France. Died: Nov. 10, 1981, Paris, France. Screen actor, film director, film producer, television producer, screenwriter and playwright.

Appeared in: **1934** The End of the World.

GANE, NOLAN
Died: Feb. 12, 1915. Screen actor, film director and screenwriter. Entered films with Thanhouser.

Appeared in: **1914** Politeness Pays; The Varsity Race. **1915** Shep the Sentinel; The Master's Model.

GANNON, JOHN "JACK"
Born: 1903. Died: Nov. 8, 1969, Hollywood, Calif. (respiratory failure). Screen actor and stuntman.

GANTVOORT, CARL
Born: 1883, Bowling Green, Ky. Died: Sept. 28, 1935, Los Angeles, Calif. (injuries from fall). Screen, stage actor and opera singer.

Appeared in: **1921** Lure of Egypt; A Certain Rich Man; The Mysterious Rider; Man of the Forest. **1922** The Gray Dawn; Heart's Haven; When Romance Rides; Golden Dreams. **1923** The Crusader.

GANTVOORT, HERMAN L.
Born: 1887. Died: Sept. 17, 1937, N.Y. Screen, stage actor and screenwriter.

GANZHORN, JOHN W. (aka JACK GANSHORN)
Born: 1881. Died: Sept. 19, 1956, Hollywood, Calif. Screen actor.

Appeared in: **1922** Thorobred. **1924** The Iron Horse. **1925** Fightin' Odds. **1927** Hawk of the Hills (serial). **1928** The Apache Raider; The Valley of Hunted Men. **1929** Hawk of the Hills (feature of 1927 serial).

GARASA, ANGEL
Born: 1905, Spain. Died: Aug. 27, 1976, Mexico City, Mexico. Screen, stage and television actor. Entered films in 1939.

Appeared in: **1944** Romeo and Juliet. **1977** The Minister and Me.

GARAT, HENRI
Born: Apr. 3, 1902, Paris, France. Died: Aug. 13, 1959, Toulon, France. Screen and stage actor.

Appeared in: **1932** Congress Dances; Il est Charmant (He Is Coming); La Fille et le Garcon (The Girl and the Boy); Le Roi des Resquilleurs. **1933** Adorable. **1935** Soir de Revillon. **1937** Amphytryon. **1938** Advocate D'Amour. Other French films; The Fair Dream; The Charm School; Her Highness' Command.

GARBER, JAN
Born: 1895, Indianapolis, Ind. Died: Oct. 5, 1977, Shreveport, La. Screen, radio actor and bandleader.

Appeared in: **1943** So's Your Uncle; Here Comes Elmer. **1944** Sweethearts of the U.S.; Jam Session. **1949** Make Believe Ballroom.

GARBO, SVEN (Sven Gustafsson)
Died: 1967, Santa Fe, N.M. Screen actor. Brother of actress Greta Garbo.

Appeared in: **1929** The Hole in the Wall (Swedish version). **1931** Nar Rosorna Slaut.

GARBUTT, FRANK A.
Born: 1869. Died: Nov. 19, 1947, Los Angeles, Calif. (heart attack). Screen actor, film director, film producer, sports promoter and business executive. Appeared as a bit actor during the late teens.

GARCES, ISABEL
Born: 1901, Spain. Died: Feb. 1, 1981, Madrid, Spain. Screen and stage actress.

GARCIA, ALLEN
Born: 1887. Died: Sept. 4, 1938, Los Angeles, Calif. Screen actor and screenwriter.

Appeared in: **1915** The Unafraid. **1921** Reputation. **1922** The Three Buckaroos. **1928** The Circus. **1929** Morgan's Last Raid. **1931** City Lights; The Deceiver. **1933** Under the Tonto Rim; California Trail. **1936** Modern Times; The Gay Desperado. **1937** I'll Take Romance. **1938** Blockade; In Old Mexico.

GARCIA, ANGEL
Died: 1948 (results of a fall while filming). Screen actor and stuntman.

Appeared in: **1948** Tarzan and the Mermaids.

GARCIA, CEFERINO
Born: 1912, Philippines. Died: Jan. 1, 1981, San Diego, Calif. Professional boxer and screen actor.

Appeared in: **1947** Joe Palooka, Champ.

GARCIA, HENRY
Born: 1904. Died: Nov. 3, 1970, San Antonio, Tex. Screen, stage actor, musician, screenwriter and film technician.

Appeared in: **1964** No Man's Land.

GARCIA, HUMBERTO RODRIGUEZ
Born: 1915, Mexico. Died: June 21, 1960, Mexico City, Mexico. Screen and stage actor.

GARCIA, SARA
Born: 1895. Died: Nov. 21, 1980, Mexico City, Mexico (heart attack). Screen, stage and radio actress. Known as the "Grandmother of Mexican Cinema."

Appeared in: **1936** Malditas Sean las Mujeres; Asi es la Mujer. **1937** No te Enganes, Corazon (Don't Fool Thyself, Heart). **1938** No Basta ser Madre (Motherhood Isn't Enough); El Traidor; Los Dos Cadetes. **1939** Perjura; Su Gran Aventura (His Great Adventure); Por Mis Pistolas (By My Pistols); Soy Chato, pero las Huelo (I am snub-nosed but I Can Smell); El Capitan Aventurero (The Adventurous Captain); Papacito Lindo (Sugar Daddy). **1940** En un Burro Tres Baturros (Three Rustics on One Donkey); Mi Madrecita (My Little Mother). **1943** Alla en el Tropico (Down in the Tropics). **1957** The Living Idol.

GARDEL, CARLOS (Charles Romuald Gardes)
Born: Dec. 11, 1887 or 1890?, Toulouse, France. Died: June 24, 1935, Colombia, South America (plane crash). Screen, stage actor and singer. Appeared in a series of pictures made by Paramount for Spanish Market.

Appeared in: **1931** Luces De Buenos Aires. **1932** La Casa es Seria. **1933** Esperame; Melodia de Arrabal. **1934** Cuesta Abajo; El Tango en Broadway. **1935** Tango-Bar; El Dia que me Quieras (The Day You Love Me); Cazadores de Estrellas (aka Big Broadcast of 1936).

GARDELLA, TESS
Born: 1898. Died: Jan. 3, 1950, New York, N.Y. Screen and stage actress.

Appeared in: **1934** Stand Up and Cheer.

GARDEN, MARY
Born: Feb. 20, 1874, Aberdeen, Scotland. Died: Jan. 3, 1967, Aberdeen, Scotland. Screen actress and opera performer.

Appeared in: **1918** The Splendid Sinner; Thais.

GARDIN, VLADIMIR
Born: 1877, Russia. Died: June 1, 1965, Moscow, Russia. Screen actor and film director. Entered films in 1913.

Appeared in: **1932** Vstrechnyi (Counterplan). **1934** Dom Zhadnosti; Miracles. **1935** Pesnya o Stchasti; Peasants. **1936** Dubrovsky. **1937** Beethoven Concerto; Young Pushkin. **1938** Pugachev. **1939** The Conquest of Peter the Great. **1942** Spring Song. **1947** Russian Ballerina. **1950** Sekretnaya Missiya (Secret Mission).

GARDINER, PATRICK
Born: 1926. Died: Sept. 30, 1970, Dublin, Ireland (heart attack). Screen, stage and radio actor.

Appeared in: **1967** The Viking Queen. **1970** Country Dance (aka Brotherly Love—US).

GARDINER, REGINALD (William Reginald Gardiner)
Born: Feb. 27, 1903, Wimbledon Surry, England. Died: July 7, 1980, Westwood, Calif. (heart attack). Screen, stage and television actor. Divorced from actress Wyn Richmond. Later married to model Nadia Petrova.

Appeared in: **1928** The Lodger (film debut). **1931** Bull Rushes. **1932** The Lovelorn Lady; Josser on the River. **1933** Just Smith; Leave it to Smith. **1934** How's Chances. **1936** Born to Dance. **1937** A Damsel in Distress. **1938** Everybody Sing; Marie Antoinette; Sweethearts. **1939** The Girl Downstairs; The Flying Deuces; The Night of Nights. **1940** Dulcy; The Doctor Takes a Wife; The Great Dictator. **1941** The Man Who Came to Dinner; My Life With Caroline; A Yank in the R.A.F.; Sundown. **1942** Captains of the Clouds. **1943** Claudia; The Immortal Sergeant; Forever and a Day; Sweet Rosie O'Grady. **1945** Molly and Me; The Horn Blows at Midnight; Christmas in Connecticut; The Dolly Sisters. **1946** Cluny Brown; Do You Love Me?; One More Tomorrow. **1947** I Wonder Who's Kissing Her Now? **1948** That Wonderful Urge; Fury at Furnace Creek; That Lady in Ermine. **1950** Wabash Avenue; The Halls of Montezuma. **1951** Elopement. **1953** Androcles and the Lion. **1954** The Barefoot Contessa; Black Widow. **1955** Ain't Misbehavin'. **1956** Around the World in 80 Days; The Birds and the Bees. **1957** The Story of Mankind. **1958** Rock-a-bye Baby. **1961** Back Street. **1962** Mr. Hobbs Takes a Vacation. **1964** What a Way to Go! **1965** Sergeant Deadhead; Do Not Disturb.

GARDNER, CYRIL
Born: May 30, 1898, Paris, France. Died: Dec. 30, 1942, Hollywood, Calif. (heart attack). Screen actor, film director and film editor. Appeared in films at the age of 13.

GARDNER, DON (aka DON GARNER)
Born: 1932. Died: Sept. 21, 1958, Malibu, Calif. (auto accident). Screen actor.

Appeared in: **1946** My Darling Clementine. **1950** A Lady Without Passport.

GARDNER, ED
Born: 1901, Astoria, N.Y. Died: Aug. 17, 1963, Los Angeles, Calif. (liver ailment). Screen, stage, radio actor, stage director, stage producer, film producer and writer for radio. Divorced from actress Shirley Booth.

Appeared in: **1945** Duffy's Tavern, a film take-off of his famous radio program of the same name.

GARDNER, GEORGE
Born: 1868. Died: May 12, 1929, East Islip, N.Y. Screen and stage actor.

GARDNER, HELEN LOUISE
Died: Nov. 20, 1968, Orlando, Fla. Screen actress and film producer. She was the first film star to form her own film company, Helen Gardner Picture Corporation (1912).

Appeared in: **1911** Vanity Fair; Ups and Downs; The Girl and the Sheriff; Regeneration; Madge of the Mountains; Arbutus. **1912** Cleopatra; A Princess of Bagdad; Where the Money Went; A Problem in Reduction; An Innocent Theft; The Heart of Esmeralda; The Party Dress; The Miracle. **1913** Alixe (aka The Test of Friendship); A Sister to Carmen; Eureka; A Vampire of the Desert; The Wife of Cain. **1922** Devil's Angel. **1925** Sandra. **1930** Monte Carlo.

GARDNER, HUNTER
Born: 1899. Died: Jan. 16, 1952, Hollywood, Calif. (suicide—slashed wrists). Screen and stage actor.

Appeared in: **1934** Gambling.

GARDNER, JACK
Born: 1900. Died: Feb. 13, 1977, Houston, Tex. Screen actor. Do not confuse with other actors with the same name.

GARDNER, JACK
Born: 1876. Died: Dec. 29, 1929, Glendale, Calif. (heart disease). Screen, stage and vaudeville actor. In vaudeville he had several partners: Jeanette Lowery, Al Lloyd, Marie Hartman and Edna Leedom.

GARDNER, JACK
Born: 1915. Died: Oct. 20, 1955, near Camarillo, Calif. Screen, television, radio actor and newscaster.

GARDNER, PETER
Born: 1898. Died: Nov. 13, 1953, Studio City, Calif. Screen and stage actor. Entered films approx. 1918.

GARDNER, SHAYLE
Born: Aug. 22, 1890, Auckland, New Zealand. Died: May 17, 1945. Screen and stage actor.

Appeared in: **1929** Three Live Ghosts; Disraeli; Three Passions; Tommy Atkins. **1930** The New Adventures of Dr. Fu Manchu; The Return of Dr. Fu Manchu. **1932** The Lodger (aka The Phantom Fiend—US 1935); Detective Lloyd (serial).

GARFIELD, JOHN (Jules Garfinkle)
Born: Mar. 4, 1913, New York, N.Y. Died: May 21, 1952, New York, N.Y. (heart attack). Screen and stage actor. Father of actor John Garfield, Jr. Nominated for 1938 Academy Award for Best Supporting Actor in Four Daughters and in 1947 for Best Actor in Body and Soul.

Appeared in: **1938** Four Daughters. **1939** Blackwell's Island; They Made Me a Criminal; Dust Be My Destiny; Daughters Courageous; Juarez; Four Wives. **1940** Saturday's Children; Castle on the Hudson; East of the River; Flowing Gold. **1941** The Sea Wolf; Out of the Fog; Dangerously They Live. **1942** Tortilla Flat. **1943** Show Business at War (short); The Fallen Sparrow; Air Force; Thank Your Lucky Stars. **1944** Between Two Worlds; Destination Tokyo; Hollywood Canteen. **1945** Pride of the Marines. **1946** Nobody Lives Forever; Humoresque; The Postman Always Rings Twice. **1947** Body and Soul; Gentleman's Agreement. **1948** Force of Evil. **1949** We Were Strangers. **1950** The Breaking Point; Under My Skin; Difficult Years (narr.). **1952** He Ran All the Way.

GARGAN, EDWARD
Born: 1902. Died: Feb. 19, 1964, New York, N.Y. Screen and stage actor. Brother of actor William Gargan.

Appeared in: **1933** The Girl in 419; Gambling Ship; Three-Cornered Moon. **1934** Good Dame; The Irish in Us; Behold My Wife; Registered Nurse; Belle of the Nineties; The Lemon Drop Kid; Wild Gold; David Harum; Twentieth Century. **1935** Barbary Coast; Port of Lost Dreams; Hold 'Em Yale; The Gilded Lily; Here Comes Cookie; Hands Across the Table; The Bride Comes Home; Behind the Green Lights; We're in the Money; False Pretenses. **1936** Anything Goes; Roaming Lady; Ceiling Zero; Stage Struck; Dangerous Waters; My Man Godfrey; Nobody's Fool; Two in a Crowd; Hearts in Bondage; Grand Jury; Wives Never Know; Great Guy. **1937** You Can't Buy Luck; We're on the Jury; High, Wide and Handsome; Jim Hanvey, Detective; Wake Up and Live; The Go-Getter; A Girl With Ideas; Danger Patrol. **1938** The Amazing Dr. Clitterhouse; That's My Story; Bringing Up Baby; The Devil's Party; The Texans; While New York Sleeps; Straight, Place and Show; Up the River; Thanks for the Memory; Annabel Takes a Tour; Crime School. **1939** Another Thin Man; Newsboys' Home; Honolulu; The Saint Strikes Back; Blondie Meets the Boss; Yes, My Darling Daughter; For Love or Money; Lucky Night; Fixer Dugan; Night Work; They All Come Out; Pack Up Your Troubles; 20,000 Men a Year. **1940** Northwest Passage; Charlie Chan in Panama; Johnny Apollo; City for Conquest; Three Cheers for the Irish; Road to Singapore; Wolf of New York; Brother Rat and a Baby; Spring Parade; Girl from God's Country; Queen of the Mob; Street of Memories; We're in the Army Now; Go West. **1941** Affectionately Yours; Meet the Chump; San Francisco Docks; The Lone Wolf Keeps a Date; Bowery Boys; Tight Shoes; Tillie the Toiler; Here Comes Happiness; Thieves Fall Out; A Date With the Falcon; Dr. Kildare's Victory; Niagara Falls. **1942** Fly By Night; Blondie for Victory; The Falcon's Brother; Over My Dead Body; The Falcon Takes Over; Meet the Stewarts; They All Kissed the Bride; A-Haunting We Will Go; Miss Annie Rooney; Between Us Girls. **1943** The Falcon Strikes Back; The Falcon in Danger; The Falcon and the Co-eds; Prairie Chickens; Princess O'Rourke; My Kingdom for a Cook; Taxi, Mister; Hit the Ice. **1944** The Falcon Out West; Detective Kitty Kelly; San Fernando Valley. **1945** Follow That Woman; Her Highness and the Bellboy; Sporting Chance; The Bullfighters; Diamond Horseshoe; High Powered; Wonder Man; The Beautiful Cheat; Earl Carroll Vanities; Sing Your Way Home; See My Lawyer; The Naughty Nineties. **1946** Blonde Alibi; Gallant Bess; Life With Blondie; Behind the Mask; Cinderella Jones; The Dark Horse; The Inner Circle; Gay Blades; Little Giant. **1947** Linda Be Good; That's My Girl; Saddle Pals; Web of Danger; Little Miss Broadway; Exposed. **1948** You Gotta Stay Happy; Scudda Hoo! Scudda Hay!; The Dude Goes West; Strike It Rich; Campus Honeymoon; Miss Annie Rooney (reissue of 1942 film); Argyle Secrets; Waterfront at Midnight. **1949** Hold That Baby; Red Light; Dynamite; Love Happy. **1950** Father of the Bride; Belle of Old Mexico; Spooky Wooky (short); Triple Trouble; Square Dance Katy; Hit Parade of 1951. **1951** Bedtime for Bonzo; Abbott and Costello Meet the Invisible Man; Cuban Fireball.

GARGAN, WILLIAM
Born: July 17, 1905, Brooklyn, N.Y. Died: Feb. 17, 1979, San Diego, Calif. (heart attack). Screen, stage, radio and television actor. Married to musical comedy dancer Mary Elizabeth Patrick Kenney. Nominated for 1940 Academy Award as best supporting actor in They Knew What They Wanted.

Appeared in: **1932** The Misleading Lady (film debut); Rain; The Animal Kingdom; The Sport Parade. **1933** Lucky Devils; Sweepings; Story of Temple Drake; Emergency Call; Night Flight; Headline Shooters; Aggie Appleby, Maker of Men. **1934** Four Frightened People; The Lineup; Strictly Dynamite; British Agent. **1935** Traveling Saleslady; Night at the Ritz; Black Fury; Broadway Gondolier; Don't Bet on Blondes; Bright Lights. **1936** Man Hunt; The Milky Way; The Sky Parade; Navy Born; Blackmailer; Alibi for Murder; Flying Hostess. **1937** You Only Live Once; Breezing Home; Fury and the Woman; Wings Over Honolulu; Reported Missing; She Asked For It; Some Blondes are Dangerous; Behind the Mike; You're a Sweetheart. **1938** The Crime of Dr. Hallet; The Devil's Party; The Crowd Roars; Personal Secretary. **1939** Within the Law; Broadway Serenade; Women in the Wind; Three Sons; The Housekeeper's Daughter; The House of Fear; Joe and Ethel Turp Call on the President. **1940** Double Alibi; Isle of Destiny; Star Dust; Sporting Blood; Turnabout; They Knew What They Wanted. **1941** Flying Cadets; Cheers for Miss Bishop; Keep 'Em Flying; Hot Spot; I Wake Up Screaming. **1942** Bombay Clipper; Miss Annie Rooney; The Mayor of Forty-Fourth Street; Destination Unknown; Who Done It?; Enemy Agents Meet Ellery Queen. **1943** Harrigan's Kid; Swing Fever. **1944** The Canterville Ghost. **1945** The Bells of St. Mary's; One Exciting Night; She Gets Her Man; Midnight Manhunt; Song of the Sarong; Follow That Woman. **1946** Hot Cargo; Swell Guy; Rendezvous 24; Behind Green Lights; Night Editor; Murder In the Music Hall; Till the End of Time; Strange Impersonation. **1948** Waterfront at Midnight; The Argyle Secrets. **1949** Dynamite. **1956** The Rawhide Years; Miracle in the Rain.

GARIBAY, EMILIO
Born: 1927, Mexico? Died: Aug. 31, 1965, Mexico City, Mexico. Screen actor.

Appeared in: **1953** Adventures of Robinson Crusoe.

GARLAND, EDWARD B. "MONTUDIE"
Born: Jan. 9, 1885, New Orleans, La. Died: Jan. 22, 1980, Los Angeles, Calif. Black jazz musician and screen actor.

Appeared in: **1934** Imitation of Life.

GARLAND, JUDY (Frances Gumm)
Born: June 10, 1922, Grand Rapids, Minn. Died: June 22, 1969, London, England (accidental overdose of drugs). Screen, stage, vaudeville and television actress. She and her sisters appeared in vaudeville in an act billed as the "Gumm Sisters." Won Academy's "Special" Award in 1939 for The Wizard of Oz. Nominated for 1954 Academy Award for Best Actress in A Star Is Born and in 1961 for Best Supporting Actress in Judgment at Nuremberg. Divorced from composer David Rose, film director Vincent Minnelli, producer Sid Luft. Married to Mickey Deans. Mother of Joseph Luft, actress-singer Liza Minnelli and singer Lorna Luft.

Appeared in: **1935** Every Sunday (short). **1936** Pigskin Parade. **1937** Thoroughbreds Don't Cry; Broadway Melody of 1938. **1938** Everybody Sing; Listen, Darling; Love Finds Andy Hardy. **1939** Babes in Arms; The Wizard of Oz. **1940** Strike Up the Band; Little Nellie Kelly; Andy Hardy Meets Debutante. **1941** Life Begins for Andy Hardy; Ziegfeld Girl; Babes on Broadway. **1942** For Me and My Gal. **1943** Girl Crazy; Presenting Lily Mars; Thousands Cheer. **1944** Meet Me in St. Louis. **1945** The Clock. **1946** Ziegfeld Follies; The Harvey Girls; Till the Clouds Roll By. **1948** The Pirate; Words and Music; Easter Parade. **1949** In the Good Old Summertime. **1950** Summer Stock. **1954** A Star Is Born. **1960** Pepe (voice only). **1961** Judgment at Nuremberg. **1962** Gay Purr-ee (voice only). **1963** A Child Is Waiting; I Could Go on Singing. **1974** That's Entertainment (film clips).

GARLAND, RICHARD
Died: May 24, 1969. Screen actor. Divorced from actress Beverly Garland.

Appeared in: **1951** The Cimarron Kid. **1952** The Battle of Apache Pass; Red Ball Express; Untamed Frontier; The Lawless Breed. **1953** Vicki; Column South; Torpedo Alley. **1954** Jesse James vs. The Daltons; Dawn at Socorro; Forever Female. **1955** The Man From Bitter Ridge. **1957** Attack of the Crab Monster; My Gun Is Quick; The Undead. **1960** 13 Fighting Men. **1962** Panic in Year Zero. **1965** Mutiny in Outer Space.

GARLY, EDWARD H.
Died: Nov. 25, 1938, Hollywood, Calif. Screen, vaudeville and minstrel actor.

GARNETT, TAY (William Taylor Garnett)
Born: June 13, 1893, Los Angeles, Calif. Died: Oct. 3, 1977, Los Angeles, Calif. (leukemia). Screen actor, film director, film producer, screenwriter, radio writer, television writer and author. Divorced from actresses Helga Moray and Patsy Ruth Miller. Later married to actress Mari Aldon.

Appeared in: **1922** Hurricane's Gal.

GARON, NORM
Born: 1934, Apr. 13, 1975. Died: New York, N.Y. (auto accident). Screen, stage and television actor.

GARON, PAULINE (Marie Pauline Garon)
Born: Sept. 9, 1901, Montreal, Canada. Died: Aug. 27, 1965. Stage and screen actress. Divorced from actor Lowell Sherman (dec. 1934). Was a 1923 Wampas Baby.

Appeared in: **1921** The Power Within. **1922** Sonny; Reported Missing. **1923** Adam's Rib; The Marriage Market; The Man from Glengary; You Can't Fool Your Wife; Children of Dust; Forgive and Forget. **1924** The Average Woman; The Turmoil; What the Butler Saw; Wine of Youth; Pal O'Mine; The Painted Flapper; The Spitfire. **1925** Satan in Sables; Compromise; Fighting Youth; Flaming Waters; The Love Gamble; Speed; The Great Sensation; Passionate Youth; Rose of the World; Where Was I?; The Splendid Road. **1926** Christine of the Big Tops. **1927** The Princess on Broadway; The College Hero; Eager Lips; Temptations of a Shop Girl; Love of Sunya; Naughty; Driven from Home; Ladies at Ease. **1928** The Candy Kid; Girl He Didn't Buy; The Heart of Broadway; The Devil's Cage; Dugan of the Dugouts; Riley of the Rainbow Division. **1929** The Gamblers; Must We Marry?; In the Headlines; Show of Shows. **1930** The Thoroughbred; Le Spectre Vert; plus the following shorts: Lovers Delight; Jack White Talking Pictures; Letters. **1931** Echec Au Roi; Le Fils de L'Autre. **1933** One Year Later; Phantom Broadcast; By Appointment Only; Lost in the Stratosphere. **1934** La Veuve Joyeuse (French version of The Merry Widow); Wonder Bar. **1935** Dangerous; The White Cockatoo; Becky Sharp. **1936** Colleen. **1937** Her Husband's Secretary. **1938** Bluebeard's Eighth Wife.

GARR, EDDIE
Born: 1900. Died: Sept. 3, 1956, Burbank, Calif. (heart ailment). Screen and stage actor.

Appeared in: **1933** Obey the Law; a Universal short. **1937** That's My Story. **1949** Ladies of the Chorus. **1951** Varieties on Parade.

GARRALAGA, MARTIN (Martin Gorralaag)
Born: 1895. Died: June 12, 1981, Woodland Hills, Calif. Screen actor and singer. Entered films in 1929.

Appeared in: **1932** The Gay Caballero. **1935** Lawless Border. **1936** A Message to Garcia; Song of the Gringo. **1937** Another Dawn. **1938** Rose of the Rio Grande; Outlaw Express; Starlight Over Texas. **1939** Law of the Pampas; The Fighting Gringo; Juarez; Di que me Quieres (Say That You Love Me); Papa Soltero (Bachelor Father). **1940** Rhythm of the Rio Grande; Stage to Chino. **1942** Undercover Man. **1943** For Whom the Bell Tolls; Adventure In Iraq. **1944** Black Arrow (serial); Voice in the Wind; The Laramie Trail; The Purple Heart; Tampico. **1945** South of the Rio Grande; The Cisco Kid Returns; The Cisco Kid in New Mexico; West of the Pecos; Strange Voyage. **1946** Beauty and the Bandit; Perilous Holiday; The Gay Cavalier; The Virginian; South of Monterey; Personality Kid; Don Ricardo Returns. **1947** Twilight on the Rio Grande; Riding the California Trail; Ride the Pink Horse; Tycoon; The Outlaw. **1948** Carnival in Costa Rica; Four Faces West; Port Said; Rogue's Regiment. **1949** The Big Sombrero; The Last Bandit; The Bribe; Shep Comes Home; Streets of San Francisco; Susanna Pass; Holiday in Havana; Joe Palooka in the Counterpunch. **1950** Bandit Queen; The Kid from Texas; The Outriders; Fortunes of Captain Blood; Branded; There's a Girl in My Heart. **1951** Havana Rose. **1952** The Fabulous Senorita; The Fighter (aka The First Time); The Ring; Woman in the Dark; Tropical Heat Wave; African Treasure. **1953** San Antone; The Hitch-hiker; Second Chance. **1954** Jubilee Trail; Secret of the Incas. **1955** A Man Alone. **1956** Blackjack Ketchum, Desperado. **1957** Gunsight Ridge; Man in the Shadow; Branded. **1958** The Left Handed Gun. **1962** Lonely are the Brave. **1964** Island of the Blue Dolphins. **1969** What Ever Happened to Aunt Alice?

GARRICK, RICHARD T.
Born: 1879. Died: Aug. 21, 1962, Hollywood, Calif. Screen actor.

Appeared in: **1947** Boomerang. **1948** Green Grass of Wyoming. **1951** A Streetcar Named Desire. **1952** Viva Zapata; Dream Boat; O. Henry's Full House; Something for the Birds; Stars and Stripes Forever. **1953** Call Me Madam; Law and Order. **1954** Desiree; Riding Shotgun. **1955** High Society; A Man Called Peter; Violent Saturday. **1956** Hilda Crane; The Mountain.

GARRISON, MICHAEL
Born: 1923. Died: Aug. 17, 1966, Bel Air, Calif. (skull fracture—fall). Screen, stage actor, film producer and television executive producer.

Appeared in: **1946** Dragonwyck. **1968** Girl in Gold Boots.

GARRITY, HARRY
Born: Nov. 15, 1872, N.J. Died: Dec. 12, 1928, Los Angeles, Calif. Screen and stage actor.

Appeared in: **1920** Unseen Forces.

GARRY, JOSEPH R.
Born: 1877, Marietta, Ohio. Died: June 7, 1954, Marietta, Ohio. Screen and stage actor. Appeared in early Crystal and Metro films.

Appeared in: **1939** Back Door to Heaven.

GARSIDE, JOHN
Born: Apr. 21, 1887, Salford, Manchester, England. Died: Apr. 18, 1958, England? Screen, stage, television actor and stage designer.

GARTH, OTIS
Born: 1901. Died: Dec. 21, 1955, Hollywood, Calif. Screen and television actor.

Appeared in: **1953** Mister Scoutmaster.

GARVIE, ED (Edward Garvie aka ED GARVEY)
Born: 1865. Died: Feb. 17, 1939, New York, N.Y. Screen and stage actor.

Appeared in: **1926** Love 'Em and Leave 'Em. **1927** East Side, West Side. **1932** Smiling Faces. **1934** Social Register. **1936** Soak the Rich. **1937** An educational short.

GARWOOD, WILLIAM
Born: Apr. 28, 1884, Mississippi. Died: Dec. 28, 1950, Los Angeles, Calif. (coronary occlusion). Screen actor.

Appeared in: **1911** Pasha's Daughter; Cally's Comet; For Her Sake; Baseball in Bloomers; Adrift; Checkmate; The Honeymooners; Courting Across the Court. **1912** Under Two Flags; Vengeance is Mine; Lucille; Put Yourself in His Place; The Thunderbolt. **1913** Carmen; Rick's Redemption; A Caged Bird; Beautiful Bismark; Dora; The Heart of a Fool; The Shoemaker and the Doll; The Van Warden Rubies; Through the Sluice Gates; The Oats of Tsuru San. **1914** Their Worldly Goods; The Hunchback; The Trap; The Taming of Sunnybrook Nell; His Faith in Humanity; The Lost Sermon; The Painted Lady's Child; A Ticket to Red Horse Gulch. **1915** Uncle's New Blazer; The Alibi; Larry O'Neill—Gentleman; Getting His Goat; A Man's Way; Lord John's Journal (series); The Wolf of Debt; The Legend Beautiful; On Dangerous Ground; The Supreme Impulse; Wild Blood. **1916** His Picture; Billy's War Brides; Broken Fetters; Two Seats at the Opera; The Gentle Art of Burglary; A Society Sherlock; He Wrote a Book; The Decoy; Arthur's Desperate Resolve; A Soul at Stake. **1917** The Little Brother; A Magdalene of the Hills. **1918** Her Moment.

GARY, SID
Born: 1901. Died: Apr. 3, 1973, New York, N.Y. Screen, vaudeville, radio actor and singer. Appeared in vaudeville with George Burns and later teamed with Freddy Bernard. Brother of actor Harold Gary.

Appeared in: **1937** A Columbia short.

GARZA, EVA
Born: 1917, Mexico. Died: Nov. 1, 1966, Tucson, Ariz. (pneumonia). Screen actress and singer.

GASKELL, CHARLES L. (Charles Lenoir Gaskill)
Born: Jan. 29, 1870, Newbern, N.C. Died: Dec. 9, 1943, Los Angeles, Calif. (heart attack). Screen actor, film director, film producer and screenwriter. Appeared in early Vitagraph films.

Appeared in: **1925** The Danger Zone.

GASPRAY, GASTON
Born: 1885. Died: Dec. 12, 1976, Brussels, Belgium. Screen and stage actor.

Appeared in: **1929** Atlantis. Plus the following films: House of Arrow; Hai-Tang; My Heart and My Million; Serments; Night Service; Azais; A Whim of the Pompadour; A Bride Has Been Lost; Eve's Father; Don't be Jealous; The Belle of Montparnasse; The Cheat.

GASTROCK, PHILIP "PHIL"
Born: 1877. Died: Apr. 10, 1956, Woodland Hills, Calif. Screen actor.

Appeared in: **1916** The Fall of a Nation. **1921** The Ranger and the Law. **1922** Blue Blazes; The Masked Avenger. **1928** The Perfect Crime.

GATES, BERT
Born: 1883. Died: Dec. 18, 1952, Aberdeen, Scotland. Screen actor. He gave "talking films" to audiences, standing behind the screen with his wife and speaking the various parts.

GATESON, MARJORIE
Born: Jan. 17, 1891, Brooklyn, N.Y. Died: Apr. 17, 1977, New York, N.Y. (pneumonia). Screen, stage, vaudeville and television actress.

Appeared in: **1931** Beloved Bachelor (film debut). **1932** Husband's Holiday; False Madonna; Street of Women; Society Girl; Silver Dollar; Okay America. **1933** Lilly Turner; Bureau of Missing Persons; Lady Killer; The King's Vacation; Employee's Entrance; Cocktail Hour; Melody Cruise; Walls of Gold; The World Changes; Blind Adventure. **1934** Coming Out Party; Let's Fall in Love; Side Streets; Chained; Happiness Ahead; Big-Hearted Herbert; Million Dollar Ransom; Down to Their Last Yacht; Gentlemen are Born; Fog; Hi, Nellie!; Operator 13. **1935** Goin' to Town; His Family Tree; Your Uncle Dudley. **1936** The Milky Way; Big Brown Eyes; The First Baby; Private Number; Three Married Men; The Gentlemen from Louisiana; The Man I Marry. **1937** We Have Our Moments; Arizona Mahoney; Turn Off the Moon; Vogues of 1938; First Lady. **1938** The House of Mystery; No Time to Marry; Making the Headlines; Gateway; The Duke of West Point; Spring Madness; Stablemates. **1939** My Wife's Relatives; Geronimo; Too Busy to Work. **1940** Parole Fixer; In Old Missouri; Pop Always Pays; I'm Nobody's Sweetheart Now; Til We Meet Again. **1941** Submarine Zone (aka Escape to Glory); Here Comes Happiness; Passage From Hong Kong; International Lady; Moonlight in Hawaii; You'll Never Get Rich; One More Tomorrow; Obliging Young Lady; Back Street. **1942** Rings on Her Fingers; Juke Box Jenny; Dues are Pretty People; Meet the Stewarts. **1943** Rhythm of the Islands; The Younger Profession; The Sky's the Limit; I Dood It; No Time for Love. **1944** Casanova in Burlesque; Hi, Good Lookin'; Seven Days Ashore; Ever Since Venus. **1946** One More Tomorrow. **1953** The Caddy.

GAUGE, ALEXANDER
Born: 1914, England. Died: Aug. 29, 1960, Woking, Surrey, England. Screen, stage and television actor.

Appeared in: **1949** The Interrupted Journey (film debut—US 1951). **1952** Murder in the Cathedral; The Pickwick Papers (US 1953); Penny Princess (US 1953). **1953** Counterspy (aka Undercover Agent—US); House of Blackmail; Will Any Gentleman? (US 1955); The Square Ring; Martin Luther; The Great Game. **1954** The Blazing Caravan; Double Exposure; The Golden Link; Mystery on Bird Island; Fast and Loose; Dance Little Lady (US 1955). **1955** Before I Wake (aka Shadow of Fear—US); Tiger By the Tail (aka Crossup—US 1958); The Reluctant Bride (aka Two Grooms For a Bride—US 1957); The Hornet's Nest. **1956** The Iron Petticoat; Port of Escape; Breakaway. **1957** The Passionate Stranger (aka A Novel Affair—US). **1961** Nothing Barred. **1963** Les Canailles (The Ruffians).

GAUGUIN, LORRAINE
Born: 1924. Died: Dec. 22, 1974, Los Angeles, Calif. (fire). Screen actress, author and columnist.

Appeared in: **1940** One Million B.C.

GAULT, MILDRED
Born: 1905. Died: Sept. 15, 1938, Los Angeles, Calif. Screen actress and film dancer.

GAUNTIER, GENE (Genevieve Gauntier Liggett)
Born: c. 1880. Died: Dec. 18, 1966, Cuernavaca, Mexico. Screen actress, screenwriter and film producer.

Appeared in: **1906** The Paymaster; The Skyscraper. **1908** Days of 61 (aka The Blue and the Gray). **1910** The Kalem Girl; The Little Spreewald Maiden. **1911** The Romance of a Dixie Belle; The Colleen Bawn. **1912** From the Manger to the Cross. **1913** In the Power of a

Hypnotist; The Wives of Jamestown; Lady Peggy's Escape; A Daughter of the Confederacy; When Men Hate; In the Clutches of the Ku Klux Klan. **1914** Come Back to Erin; Rory O'More; His Brother's Wife.

GAWTHORNE, PETER
Born: Sept. 1, 1884, Queen's County, Ireland. Died: Mar. 17, 1962, London, England. Screen, stage actor, stage producer and playwright.

Appeared in: **1929** Behind That Curtain; Sunny Side Up; His Glorious Night. **1930** One Hysterical Night; Those Three French Girls; Temple Tower. **1931** Charlie Chan Carries On; The Man Who Came Back. **1932** The Flag Lieutenant; Jack's the Boy (aka Night and Day—US 1933); The Lodger (aka The Phantom Fiend—US 1935); C.O.D.; His Lordship. **1933** Perfect Understanding; The Blarney Stone (aka The Blarney Kiss—US); Prince of Arcadia; Just Smith; The House of Trent. **1934** Two Hearts in Waltztime; Grand Prix; Something Always Happens; Money Mad; My Old Dutch; The Camels Are Coming; Dirty Work; Girls, Please! **1935** The Iron Duke; Murder at Monte Carlo; Who's Your Father?; Me and Marlborough; Crime Unlimited; The Crouching Beast; Man of the Moment; No Limit; Stormy Weather (US 1936). **1936** Wolf's Clothing; The Man Behind the Mask; Potluck; A Woman Alone (aka Two Who Dared—US 1937); Everybody Dance. **1937** Good Morning, Boys (aka Where There's a Will—US); Mr. Stringfellow Says No; Brief Ecstasy; Gangway; Under a Cloud; The Ticket of Leave Man; The Last Adventurers; Riding High (aka Remember When); Father Steps Out. **1938** Easy Riches; George Bizet, Composer of Carmen; Convict 99; Scruffy; Alf's Button Afloat; Hey! Hey! U.S.A. **1939** Dead Men Are Dangerous; Home from Home; Ask a Policeman; Sword of Honour; Secret Journey (aka Among Human Wolves—US 1940); Where's the Fire?; What Would You Do Chums?; Traitor Spy (aka The Torso Murder Mystery—US 1940); Flying Fifty-Five. **1940** Laugh It Off; Band Wagon; Two For Danger; Three Silent Men; Gasbags; They Came By Night. **1941** Inspector Hornleigh Goes to It (aka Mail Train—US); Old Mother Riley's Ghosts; Pimpernel Smith (aka Mister V—US 1942); Love on the Dole. **1942** Let the People Sing; Much Too Shy. **1943** The Hundred Pound Window; Bell-Bottom George. **1946** This Man Is Mine. **1948** Nothing Venture; Accidental Spy (reissue of Mr. Stringfellow Says No—1937). **1949** The Case of Charles Peace; High Jinks in Society. **1950** Soho Conspiracy. **1951** Death Is a Number. **1952** Paul Temple Returns. **1954** Five Days (aka Paid to Kill—US).

GAXTON, WILLIAM (Arturo Gaxiola)
Born: Dec. 2, 1893, San Francisco, Calif. Died: Feb. 2, 1963, New York, N.Y. Screen, stage and vaudeville actor.

Appeared in: **1926** Stepping Along; It's the Old Army Game. **1931** Fifty Million Frenchmen. **1932** Silent Partners (short). **1934** Their Big Moment. **1942** Something to Shout About. **1943** The Heat's On; Best Foot Forward. **1944** Tropicana. **1945** Diamond Horseshoe.

GAY, CHARLES
Born: 1887, France. Died: Feb. 23, 1950, Newport Beach, Calif. (heart attack). Screen actor and lion tamer.

Appeared in: **1921** The Adventures of Tarzan (serial).

GAY, FRED
Born: 1882. Died: June 11, 1955, Long Beach, Calif. Screen actor.

GAY, INEZ
Died: Oct. 3, 1975. Screen actress.

Appeared in: **1940** Meet John Doe. **1941** She Couldn't Say No.

GAY, MAISIE
Born: 1883, England. Died: Sept. 14, 1945, London, England. Screen and stage actress.

GAY, RAMON (Ramon Gaytan)
Born: 1917. Died: June, 1960, Mexico City, Mexico. Screen and stage actor.

Appeared in: **1953** Eugenia Grandet. **1956** Yambao (aka Young and Evil—US 1962). **1959** La Maldicion de la Momia Azteca (The Curse of the Aztec Mummy—US 1965); El Robot Humano (aka La Momia Azteca Contra el Robot Humano—The Robot vs. The Aztec Mummy—US 1965). **1960** Munecos Infernales (aka The Curse of the Doll People—US 1968); La Estrella Vacia (The Empty Star—US 1962).

GAY, WALTER
Born: 1863, England. Died: Jan. 8, 1936, England? Screen and stage actor.

Appeared in: **1914** Clancarty; Luncheon for Three.

GAYE, ALBIE
Died: Nov. 26, 1965, Chicago, Ill. Screen, stage, television actress and singer.

Appeared in: **1953** The Miami Story. **1956** The Vagabond King.

GAYE, HOWARD
Born: Hitchin, Hertfordshire, England. Died: Dec. 26, 1955, London, England. Screen actor and film director.

Appeared in: **1915** The Birth of a Nation. **1916** Intolerance. **1919** Uplifters. **1921** My Lady's Latchkey; What's a Wife Worth?; Sacred and Profane Love. **1922** A Prince of Lovers (aka Life of Lord Byron—US 1927). **1923** Scaramouche. **1924** Dante's Inferno.

GAYER, ECHLIN
Born: 1878. Died: Feb. 14, 1926, New York, N.Y. (pneumonia). Screen and stage actor.

Appeared in: **1924** Her Love Story. **1925** The Mad Dancer.

GAYNOR, RUTH
Died: May 28, 1919, Seattle, Wash. (auto accident). Screen actress.

GEAR, LUELLA
Born: 1900, New York. Died: Apr. 3, 1980, New York, N.Y. Screen and stage actress.

Appeared in: **1923** Adam and Eva. **1933** Poor Fish (short). **1938** Carefree. **1946** The Perfect Marriage. **1949** Jigsaw. **1954** Phffft.

GEARY, BUD (S. Maine Geary)
Born: 1899. Died: Feb. 22, 1946, Hollywood, Calif. (injuries sustained in motor crash). Screen actor.

Appeared in: **1921** Everyman's Price. **1922** Four Hearts; Robin Hood. **1931** Reaching for the Moon. **1932** High Flyers. **1935** Dante's Inferno. **1936** The Prisoner of Shark Island; Great Guy; The Trail of the Lonesome Pine. **1938** The Big Broadcast of 1938. **1939** Flying G-Men (serial). **1940** Mysterious Dr. Satan (serial); North West Mounted Police; No, No Nanette; Murder Over New York; Saps at Sea; Adventures of Red Ryder (serial). **1941** Great Guns; King of the Texas Rangers; Jungle Girl (serial). **1942** Alias Boston Blackie; The Talk of the Town; Life Begins at 8:30; Cowboy Serenade; Home in Wyomin'; A-Haunting We Will Go. **1943** Thundering Trails; Destroyer; Bataan; Let's Face It. **1944** Sheriff of Las Vegas; Haunted Harbor (serial); Song of the Open Road. **1945** The Purple Monster Strikes (serial). **1946** King of the Forest Rangers (serial); California; Smoky.

GEBHARDT, FRANK
Died: May 23, 1951. Screen actor. Appeared in early Biograph films.

GEBHARDT, GEORGE M.
Born: 1879, Basle, Switzerland. Died: May 2, 1919 (tuberculosis). Screen and stage actor. Married to stage actress Mrs. George Gebhardt (dec.).

Appeared in: **1908** Balked at the Alter; A Calamitous Elopement. **1911** Getting His Man; The Sheriff and His Brother. The Everlasting Judy; At Rolling Forks; The Fighting Chance; A Pair of Jacks; Across the Sierras; The Love Trail; Two Men and the Law; Her Indian Hero; The Renegade; The Miner's Claim; The Gambler; The Penalty Paid; A Race for Liberty; A Redman's Loyalty; A Redskin's Appeal; The Cactus County Lawyer; Misleading Evidence. **1913** The Frame Up; Her Faithful Yuma Servant; The Blind Gypsy; The Bear Hunter; The Poisoned Stream; The Pioneer's Recompense; A Faithful Servitor; An Accidental Shot; Lillian's Nightmare; The Thwarted Plot; A Bear Escape. **1914** By the Two Oak Trees; Against Heavy Odds; The Dishonored Medal. **1915** The Fighting Hope; The Cost; The Voice in the Fog; Ready for Reno; Blackbirds. **1916** A Modern Knight; The Power of Mind; The Dyspeptic; Professor Jeremy's Experiment; The Penalty of Treason; The Sign of the Spade. **1917** Eternal Love; Jerry in Yodel Land. **1918** Madame Spy.

GEBHART, ALBERT
Born: 1887. Died: Jan. 4, 1950, East Orange, N.J. Screen and stage actor.

GEBUEHR, OTTO
Born: 1877, Kettwig, Germany. Died: Mar. 13, 1954, Wiesbaden, West Germany. Screen and stage actor who greatly resembled Frederick the Great. Entered films in 1920.

Appeared in: **1920** Abend ... Nacht ... Morgen; Drei Naechte; Der Golem, wie er in die Welt Kam. **1921** Das Floss der Toten; Maedchen aus der Ackerstrasse; Die Taenzerin Barberina. **1922** Flammende

Voelker; Till Eulenspiegel; Sterbende Voelker (aka Populi Morituri). **1923** Fridericus Rex (aka Ein Koenigsschicksal); Der Goldteufel, Gobsek; Die Vergeltung; Wilhelm Tell; Mutter, Dein Kind Ruft (aka Das Brennende Geheimnis). **1924** Ich Hatt' Einen Kameraden; Neuland (aka Das Glueckhaft Schiff); Die Peruecke (The Wig). **1925** Die Eiserne Braut; Leidenschaft; ... und es Lockt ein Ruf aus Suendiger Welt; Die Gesunkenen (The Sunken). **1926** In Treue Stark; Die Muehle von Sanssauci; Die Sporckschen Jaeger. **1927** Der Alte Fritz; Die Heilige Luege. **1928** Waterloo (US 1929); Die Keusche Kokotte. **1930** Der Detektiv des Kaisers; Scapa Flow; Das Floetenkonzert von Sauaaouci (The Flute Concert at San Souci—US 1931). **1931** Der Erlkoenig. **1932** Barberina; Die Taenzerin von Sanssouci. **1933** Der Choral von Leuthen (The Anthem of Leuthen—US 1935). **1936** Fridericus (US 1939). **1937** Das Schoene Fraulein Schragg (Pretty Miss Schragg). **1938** Nanon. **1939** Die Barmherzige Luege. **1940** Leidenschaft (Passion); Bismarck; Casanova Heiratet. **1941** Kopf Hoch, Johannes. **1942** Viel Laerm um Nixi; Der Grosse Koenig. **1943** Immensee; Die Goldene Spinne; Nacht ohne Abschied; Wenn der Junge Wein Blueht; Fritze Bollmann Wollte Angeln (aka Wer Zuletzt Lacht). **1944** Der Erbfoerster. **1947** Und Ueber uns der Himmel. **1949** Anonyme Briefe; Der Bagnostraefling. **1950** City of Torment; Die Luege; Tobias Knopp, Abenteuer Eines Junggesellen (speaker); Melodie des Schicksals; Komplott auf Erlenhof. **1951** Unsterbliche Geliebte; Dr. Holl; Das Ewige Spiel; Stips; Sensation in San Remo; Gruen ist die Heide; Torreani; Wenn die Abendglocken Laeuten. **1952** The Devil Makes Three; Mein Herz Darfst Du Nicht Fragen; Tausend Rote Rosen Bluehn; Fritz und Friederike; Oh, du Lieber Fridolin. **1953** Hab' Sonne im Herzen; Die Blaue Stunde; Strassenserenade; Vati Macht Dummheiten. **1954** Angelika; Meines Vaters Pferde (ii); Die Gefangene des Maharadscha; Sauerbruch—das War Mein Leben; Rosen-Resli; Der Mann Meines Lebens. **1956** Circus Girl. **1962** Die Blonde Frau des Maharadscha.

GEE, GEORGE
Born: 1895, England. Died: Oct. 17, 1959, Coventry, England. Screen and stage actor.

Appeared in: **1928** Weekend Wives (US 1929). **1931** Let's Love and Laugh (aka Bridegroom for Two—US 1922). **1933** Leave It To Me; Cleaning Up; Strike It Rich.

GEE, GEORGE D.
Died: Dec., 1917, Brooklyn, N.Y. Screen actor.

Appeared in: **1917** Queen X.

GEER, WILL
Born: Mar. 9, 1902, Frankfort, Ind. Died: Apr. 22, 1978, Los Angeles, Calif. (respiratory arrest). Screen, stage, radio and television actor. Married to actress Herta Ware. Father of seven children including actors Kate Linville, Ellen and Raleigh Geer.

Appeared in: **1932** Misleading Lady. **1940** The Fight for Life. **1948** Deep Waters. **1949** Johnny Allegro; Anna Lucasta; Lust for Gold; Intruder in the Dust. **1950** The Kid from Texas; Comanche Territory; Broken Arrow; Winchester 73; To Please a Lady; Convicted; Double Crossbones. **1951** Bright Victory; The Tall Target; Barefoot Mailman. **1962** Advise and Consent. **1964** Black Like Me. **1965** Salt of the Earth. **1966** Seconds. **1967** In Cold Blood; The President's Analyst. **1968** Bandolero! **1969** The Reivers. **1970** The Moonshine War; Pieces of Dreams. **1971** Brother John. **1972** Napoleon and Samantha; Jeremiah Johnson. **1973** Executive Action. **1974** Silence; Memory of Us. **1975** Dear Dead Delilah; The Manchu Eagle Murder Mystery. **1976** Moving Violation; The Blue Bird.

GEHRIG, LOU (Henry Louis Gehrig)
Born: June 19, 1903, New York, N.Y. Died: June 2, 1941, New York (spinal paralysis). Professional baseball player and screen actor.

Appeared in: **1938** Rawhide. **1942** The Ninth Inning.

GEHRMAN, MRS. LUCY
Died: May 8, 1954, New York, N.Y. Yiddish screen and stage actress.

Appeared in: **1950** God, Man and Devil.

GEHRUNG, GENE
Born: 1882. Died: Oct. 19, 1938, Jacksonville, Fla. Screen and stage actor.

GEIGER, HERMANN
Born: 1913. Died: Aug. 25, 1966, near Sitten, West Germany (plane crash). Screen actor and pilot.

GELDERT, CLARENCE
Born: June 9, 1867, St. John, B.C., Canada. Died: May 13, 1935, Calabasas, Calif. (heart attack). Screen, stage actor and film director. Entered films with D. W. Griffith in 1915.

Appeared in: **1917** Joan the Woman. **1921** All Souls Eve; The Great Moment; The Hell Diggers; The House That Jazz Built; The Lost Romance; The Witching Hour. **1922** Rent Free. **1923** A Woman of Paris; Adam's Rib; Richard the Lion-Hearted; Wasted Lives. **1924** Behind the Curtain; The Fighting American; Love's Whirlpool; North of 36; The Whipping Boss; Oh, Doctor. **1925** The Bandit's Baby; My Neighbor's Wife. **1926** The Flaming Forest; Boy Friend; Hands Across the Border; Racing Blood; Young April. **1927** Dress Parade; One Man Game. **1929** Overland Telegraph; Square Shoulders; Sioux Blood; The Ghost Talks; Unholy Night; Thirteenth Chair. **1930** The Bishop Murder Case. **1931** Guilty Hands; Cuban Love Song; Daddy Long Legs. **1932** The Stoker; White Eagle; Emma. **1933** Jungle Bride; Lucky Dog; Telephone Trail; Revenge at Monte Carlo; Dance Hall Hostess; Rusty Rides Alone; Marriage on Approval; Lone Adventure. **1934** Twentieth Century; In Love With Life; Man Trailer. **1935** Mississippi. **1936** Go Get-'Em Haines.

GEMIER, FIRMIN
Born: 1886, France. Died: Nov. 26, 1933, Paris, France (heart failure). Screen, stage actor, stage director and screenwriter.

Appeared in: **1926** The Magician. **1937** Grandeur et Decadence.

GEMORA, CHARLIE
Born: 1903, Philippine Islands. Died: Aug. 19, 1961, Hollywood, Calif. (heart attack). Screen actor.

Appeared in: **1928** The Circus Kid. **1933** King Kong (was the gorilla). **1934** Bum Voyage (short). **1938** Swiss Miss. **1939** At the Circus; The Gorilla. **1941** Road to Zanzibar. **1945** Road to Utopia. **1948** Beauty and the Beast. **1953** War of the Worlds; White Witch Doctor. **1961** One-Eyed Jacks.

GENARO, FRANKIE (Frank DeGenero or DiGennara)
Born: 1901. Died: Dec. 12, 1966, Staten Island, N.Y. Professional boxer and screen actor.

Appeared in: **1926** The Prince of Broadway.

GENDRON, PIERRE
Born: Mar. 4, 1896, Toledo, Ohio. Died: Nov. 27, 1956, Hollywood, Calif. Screen, stage actor and screenwriter.

Appeared in: **1921** The Bashful Suitor. **1922** The Man Who Played God; The Young Painter. **1923** Broadway Broke; Does It Pay?; Outlaws of the Sea. **1924** Blue Water; The Dangerous Flirt; The City That Never Sleeps; Just Off Broadway; The Lover of Camille; Three Women. **1925** The Scarlet Honeymoon. **1927** The Enchanted Island. **1928** What Price Beauty.

GENIAT, MARCELE (Eugenie Martin)
Born: 1879, Petrograd, Russia. Died: Sept. 28, 1959, Paris, France. Screen and stage actress.

Appeared in: **1937** Les Mysteres de Paris; Grandeur et Decadence. **1938** They Were Five. **1940** The Man of the Hour. **1958** Sophie et le Crime (Sophie and the Crime, aka The Girl on the Third Floor—US). **1959** Proces au Vatican (Trial at the Vatican, aka Miracle of Saint Therese—US).

GENN, LEO
Born: Aug. 9, 1905, London, England. Died: Jan. 26, 1978, London, England. Screen, stage, radio and television actor. Won 1952 Nomination for Best Supporting Actor in Quo Vadis.

Appeared in: **1935** Immortal Gentlemen. **1936** The Dream Doctor. **1937** Jump for Glory (aka When Thief Meets Thief—US); The Cavalier of the Streets; The Rat. **1938** Kate Plus Ten; Governor Bradford (aka Governor William Bradford—US); The Drum; Dangerous Medicine. **1939** Ten Days in Paris (aka Missing Ten Days—US). **1940** Law and Disorder; Contraband (aka Blackout—US). **1944** The Way Ahead (US 1945); Tunisian Victory (documentary-voice). **1945** Julius Caesar (short); Henry V (US 1946). **1946** Caesar and Cleopatra; Green for Danger (US 1947). **1947** Mourning Becomes Electra. **1948** The Snake Pit; The Velvet Touch. **1950** No Place for Jennifer (US 1951); The Wooden Horse (US 1951); The Miniver Story; The Undefeated (US 1951 narration). **1951** The Magic Box (US 1952); Quo Vadis. **1952** 24 Hours of a Woman's Life (aka Affair in Monte Carlo—US 1953); Plymouth Adventure. **1953** The Red Beret (aka Paratrooper—US 1954); Personal Affair (US 1954); The Girls of Pleasure Island. **1954** The Green Scarf (US 1955). **1956** Beyond

Mombasa (US 1957); Moby Dick. **1957** The Steel Bayonet (US 1958). **1958** No Time to Die (aka Tank Force—US); I Accuse! **1959** Chantage (Blackmail, aka The Lowest Crime—US);Lady Chatterley's Lover; Invitation to Monte Carlo (US 1961). **1960** Too Hot to Handle (aka Playgirl after Dark—US 1962). **1962** The Longest Day. **1963** 55 Days at Peking. **1965** Ten Little Indians. **1966** Circus of Fear (aka Psycho-Circus—US 1967); Khartoum (voice). **1969** Connecting Rooms. **1970** Die Screaming, Marianne. **1971** Endless Nights. **1973** The Macintosh Man. **1974** Escape to Nowhere. **1975** Frightmare. **1976** The Martyr.

GENTLE, ALICE
Born: 1889, Chatsworth, Ill. Died: Feb. 28, 1958, Oakland, Calif. Screen, stage actress and opera performer. Mother of actor Bruce MacFarland (dec. 1967).

Appeared in: **1930** The Golden Dawn (film debut); Song of the Flame; A Scene from Carmen (short). **1933** Flying Down to Rio.

GEORGE, A. E.
Born: July 22, 1869, Lincoln, England. Died: Nov. 10, 1920, England? Screen and stage actor.

GEORGE, DAN *See* CHIEF DAN GEORGE

Appeared in: **1916** The Vicar of Wakefield (US 1917).

GEORGE, GEORGE M.
Born: 1889, St. Louis, Mo. Died: Jan., 1961. Screen and stage actor.

Appeared in: **1915** Jerry's Revenge; Jerry to the Rescue.

GEORGE, GLADYS (Gladys Clare)
Born: Sept. 13, 1900, Hatton, Maine. Died: Dec. 8, 1954, Los Angeles, Calif. (brain hemorrhage). Stage and screen actress. Daughter of actor Sir Arthur Clair. Divorced from actors Arthur Erway (dec. 1981), Leonard Penn (dec. 1975), Edward Fowler and Kenneth Bradley. Nominated for 1936 Academy Award for Best Actress in Valiant is the Word for Carrie.

Appeared in: **1920** Red Hot Dollars; Home Spun Folks. **1921** The Easy Road; Chickens; The House That Jazz Built. **1934** Straight Is the Way. **1936** Valiant Is the Word for Carrie. **1937** They Gave Him a Gun; Madame X. **1938** Love Is a Headache; Marie Antoinette. **1939** The Roaring Twenties; Here I Am a Stranger; I'm from Missouri. **1940** A Child Is Born; The Way of All Flesh; The House Across the Bay. **1941** The Lady from Cheyenne; The Maltese Falcon; Hit the Road. **1942** The Hard Way. **1943** Nobody's Darling; The Crystal Ball. **1944** Minstrel Man; Christmas Holiday. **1945** Steppin' in Society. **1946** The Best Years of Our Lives. **1947** Millie's Daughter. **1948** Alias a Gentleman. **1949** Flamingo Road. **1950** The Undercover Girl; Bright Leaf. **1951** Detective Story; He Ran All the Way; Lullaby of Broadway; Silver City. **1953** It Happens Every Thursday.

GEORGE, GRACE
Born: Dec. 25, 1879, New York, N.Y. Died: May 19, 1961, New York, N.Y. Screen, stage actress and stage director.

Appeared in one film only: **1943** Johnny Come Lately.

GEORGE, HEINRICH (Heinz Georg Schulz)
Born: 1893, Steltin, Germany. Died: Sept. 27, 1946, Russia (Soviet internment camp). Screen, stage actor and film director.

Appeared in: **1913** Der Andere. **1921** Kean; Der Roman der Christine von Herre. **1922** Das Fraenkische Lied; Der Graf im Pfluge; Lukrezia Borgia. **1923** Der Mensch am Wege; Quarantaene; Steuerlos; Erdgeist (Earth Spirit). **1924** Soll und Haben. **1925** Metropolis (US 1927). **1926** Mirakel der Liebe; Ueberfluessige Menschen; Die Versunkene Flotte; Das Panzergewoelbe (The Armoured Vault—US 1928). **1927** Bigamie; Die Leibeigenen; Das Meer; Orientexpress. **1928** Bondage; Kinder der Strasse; Das Letzte Fort; Das Letzte Souper; Der Mann mit dem Laubfrosch; Rutschbahn; Song; Die Dame mit der Maske (The Lady With the Mask). **1929** The Whirl of Life; The Wrath of the Seas; Wasted Love; Theatre; Manolescu; Sprengbagger 1010; Der Straefling aus Stambul. **1930** Der Andere ((US 1932) and 1913 version); Dreyfus. **1931** Der Mann der den Mord Beging (The Man Who Committed the Murder); Berlin-Alexanderplatz (US 1933); 1914, die Letzten Tage vor dem Weltbrand (1914: The Last Days Before the War—US 1932). **1932** Goethe Lebt ... **1933** Das Meer Ruft; Schleppzug M 17; Reifende Jugend (US 1936). **1934** Unsere Fahne Flattert uns Voran. **1935** Hermine und die Sieben Aufrechten; Das Maedchen Johanna; Hilterjunge Quex; Nacht der Verwandlung (aka Demaskierung); Stuetzen der Gesellschaft (US 1936). **1936** Wenn der Hahn Kraeht; Die Grosse und die Kleine Welt; Stjenka Rasin (aka Wolga-Wolga). **1937** Promise Me Nothing; Ein Volksfeind; Versprich mir Nichts; Ball im Metropol (US 1938); Der Biberpelz (The Beaver Coat—US 1939). **1938** Unternehmen Michale (The Private's Job); Frau Sylvester (US 1939); Heimat. **1939** Das Unsterbliche Herz; Sensationsprozess Casilla. **1940** Jud Suess; Der Postmeister (aka Her Crime Was Love); Friedrich Schiller (aka Der Triumph Eines Genies). **1941** Pedro Soll Haengen. **1942** Andreas Schlueter; Der Grosse Schatten; Wien 1910; Schicksal; Hochzeit auf Baerenhof. **1944** Der Verteidiger hat das Wort; Die Degenhardts; Kolberg. **1945** Dr. Phil. Doederlein; Das Leben Geht Weiter; Frau Ueber Bord (aka Kabine 27).

GEORGE, JOHN
Born: Jan. 21, 1898, Syria. Died: Aug. 25, 1968, Los Angeles, Calif. (emphysema). Screen actor.

Appeared in: **1921** Miracles of the Jungle (serial). **1922** Trifling Women. **1923** Where the Pavement Ends; Scaramouche. **1924** When a Girl Loves. **1926** The Road to Mandalay; Don Juan. **1927** The Night of Love; The Unknown. **1928** The Big City. **1930** Outside the Law. **1931** Smart Money. **1932** Island of Lost Souls. **1933** Trick for Trick. **1934** Babes in Toyland. **1935** The Man Who Broke the Bank at Monte Carlo; Bride of Frankenstein. **1936** Two in a Crowd; The Jungle Princess. **1944** Secrets of Scotland Yard; Show Business; The Heavenly Body; Mr. Skeffington. **1945** A Song to Remember. **1946** The Devil's Playground. **1947** This Time for Keeps; It Happened on Fifth Avenue; Little Miss Broadway; The Trespasser. **1948** The Lady in Ermine. **1952** Son of Paleface. **1953** The Lost Planet (serial). **1955** East of Eden. **1956** The Conqueror; Around the World in 80 Days.

GEORGE, MURIEL
Born: Aug. 29, 1883, London, England. Died: Oct. 22, 1965, England. Screen, stage, vaudeville and television actress. Divorced from actor Ernest Butcher (dec. 1965).

Appeared in: **1932** His Lordship. **1933** Cleaning Up; Yes, Mr. Brown. **1934** Wedding Eve; Old Faithful; Key to Harmony. **1936** The Happy Family; Limelight (aka Backstage—US); Whom the Gods Love (aka Mozart—US 1940); Not So Dusty; Busman's Holiday; Merry Comes to Town. **1937** Overcoat Sam; 21 Days (aka The First and the Last; aka 21 Days Together—US 1940); Who's Your Lady Friend?; Song of the Road; Talking Feet; Dr. Syn; Lancashire Luck. **1938** Darts Are Trumps; A Sister to Assist 'Er; Crackerjack (aka The Man With a Hundred Faces—US). **1940** The Briggs Family; Pack Up Your Troubles; Food for Thought. **1941** Telefooters; Freedom Radio (aka A Voice in the Night—US); Quiet Wedding; Lady Be Kind (short); Rush Hour; Love on the Dole; Cottage to Let (aka Bombsight Stolen—US). **1942** They Flew Alone (aka Wings and the Woman—US); Unpublished Story; Alibi; Went the Day Well? (aka 48 Hours—US 1944). **1943** The Bells Go Down; Dear Octopus (aka The Randolph Family—US 1945). **1944** The Man from Scotland Yard; Kiss the Bride Goodbye. **1945** For You Alone; Perfect Strangers (aka Vacation from Marriage—US); I'll Be Your Sweetheart. **1946** The Years Between (US 1947). **1947** When the Bough Breaks. **1950** The Dancing Years; Last Holiday. **1955** Simon and Laura (US 1956).

GEORGE, VOYA (Voya George Djordjevich)
Born: 1895. Died: May 8, 1951, New York, N.Y. Screen actor.

Appeared in: **1928** The Legion of the Condemned.

GEORGES, KATERINE
Born: France. Died: June, 1973, Mexico City, Mexico. Screen and stage actress.

GERAERDS, ROB (Jacobus Gerardus de Hass)
Born: 1903, Holland. Died: Sept. 4, 1981, Brussels, Belgium (auto accident). Screen, stage actor and writer.

GERAGHTY, CARMELITA
Born: 1901, Rushville, Ind. Died: July, 1966, New York, N.Y. Screen actress.

Appeared in: **1923** Bag and Baggage. **1924** Jealous Husbands; Black Oxen; Discontented Husbands; Geared to Go; High Speed; Through the Dark. **1925** Passionate Youth; Brand of Cowardice; Cyclone Cavalier; The Mysterious Stranger; Under the Rouge. **1926** My Lady of Whims; The Great Gatsby; The Canyon of Light; Pleasure Garden; The Flying Mail; Josselyn's Wife; The Lily. **1927** The Last Trail; My Best Girl; The Slayer; The Small Bachelor; Venus of Venice; What Every Girl Should Know. **1928** The Campus Carmen (short); The Goodbye Kiss. **1929** Object Alimony; Paris Bound; South of Panama; The Mississippi Gambler; This Thing Called Love. **1930** After the Fog; What Men Want; Men Without Law; Rogue of the Rio Grande; Fighting Through. **1931** Fifty Million Frenchmen; The Devil Plays; Millie; Texas Ranger; Night Life in Reno. **1932** The Jungle Mystery (serial); Prestige; Forgotten Women; Escapade. **1933** Malay Nights; Flaming Signal. **1935** Manhattan Butterfly.

GERALD, ARA
Born: 1894, Sydney, Australia. Died: Apr. 2, 1957, Ft. Lauderdale, Fla. Screen actress and opera singer.

Appeared in: **1933** Enlighten Thy Daughter. **1936** The White Angel.

GERALD, JIM (Jacques Guenod)
Born: 1889, France. Died: 1958. Screen and stage actor. Entered films approx. 1911.

Appeared in: **1927** An Italian Straw Hat. **1931** La Chant au Marin; La Nuit est a Nous (The Night Is Ours); The Horse Ate the Hat. **1934** The Constant Nymph. **1936** The Robber Symphony. **1937** Bulldog Drummond at Bay. **1939** French Without Tears. **1943** The Last Will of Dr. Mabuse. **1945** Boule de Suif. **1951** The Lady from Boston; Pardon My French; Adventures of Captain Fabian. **1952** L'Ile aux Femmes Nues (aka Naked in the Wind—US 1962); The Crimson Curtain. **1953** Moulin Rouge. **1954** Father Brown (aka The Detective); The Barefoot Contessa; The Moment of Truth. **1956** Foreign Intrigue. **1957** Eric Frac en Dentelles. **1959** Le Vente se Leve (The Wind Rises aka Time Bomb—US 1961).

GERARD, JOSEPH SMITH
Born: 1871. Died: Aug. 20, 1949, Woodland Hills, Calif. Screen actor.

GERARD, TEDDIE (Teresa Cabre)
Born: 1890, Buenos Aires, Argentina. Died: Aug. 31, 1942, London, England. Screen, stage actress and dancer. Married to stage actor Joe Raymond (dec. 1922).

Appeared in: **1915** Billy's Spanish Love Spasm. **1922** Cave Girl; Seventh Day.

GERAY, STEVEN
Born: Nov. 10, 1898, Uzhored, Czechoslovakia. Died: Dec. 26, 1973. Screen and stage actor.

Appeared in: **1935** Dance Band; The Student's Romance. **1936** A Star Fell from Heaven. **1937** Let's Make a Night of It (US 1938). **1939** Inspector Hornleigh. **1941** Man at Large; Blue, White and Perfect. **1942** Secret Agent of Japan; A Gentleman at Heart; Castle in the Desert; The Moon and Sixpence; Eyes in the Night. **1943** Pilot No. 5; Hostages; Night Plane from Chungking; Henry Aldrich Swings It; Appointment in Berlin; The Phantom of the Opera; Whistling in Brooklyn; To My Unborn Son. **1944** Meet the People; The Mask of Dimitrios; The Seventh Cross; In Society; The Conspirators; Easy Life. **1945** Tarzan and the Amazons; Hotel Berlin; Crimson Canary; Spellbound; Cornered; Mexicana. **1946** Gilda; Deadline at Dawn; So Dark the Night; Blondie Knows Best; The Return of Monte Cristo. **1947** Mr. District Attorney; Blind Spot; The Unfaithful; Gunfighters; When a Girl's Beautiful; The Crime Doctor's Gamble. **1948** I Love Trouble; Port Said. **1949** The Dark Past; El Paso; Ladies of the Chorus; Sky Liner; Once More My Darling; The Lone Wolf and His Lady; Holiday in Havana. **1950** Woman on the Run; The Harbor of Missing Men; Under My Skin; In a Lonely Place; A Lady Without a Passport; All About Eve; Pygmy Island. **1951** Target Unknown; I Can Get It For You Wholesale; The Second Woman; House on Telegraph Hill; Savage Drums; Little Egypt. **1952** Lady Possessed; Bal Tabarin; The Big Sky; Night Without Sleep; Affair in Trinidad; O'Henry's Full House. **1953** Tonight We Sing; Gentlemen Prefer Blondes; The Royal African Rifles; The Great Diamond Robbery; The Golden Blade; Call Me Madam; The Story of Three Loves. **1954** Knock on Wood; The French Line; Tobor, The Great; Paris Playboys. **1955** To Catch a Thief; New York Confidential; A Bullet for Joey; Daddy Long Legs; Artists and Models. **1956** Attack!; Stagecoach to Fury; The Birds and the Bees. **1958** A Certain Smile. **1959** Verboten!; Count Your Blessings. **1963** Dame With a Halo. **1964** The Evil of Frankenstein; Wild and Wonderful. **1965** Ship of Fools. **1966** The Swinger; Jesse James Meets Frankenstein's Daughter.

GERBOV, ALEXI
Born: 1902, Russia. Died: Nov., 1977, Russia? Screen and stage actor.

GERHARDT, KARL
Born: Apr. 14, 1891, Sweden. Died: Apr. 22, 1964, Stockholm, Sweden. Screen actor and songwriter.

Appeared in: **1931** The Immortal Vagabond. **1932** Der Unsterblinche Lump.

GERMI, PIETRO
Born: Sept. 14, 1904, Genoa, Italy. Died: Dec. 5, 1974, Rome, Italy (hepatitis). Screen actor, film director, producer, screenwriter and author.

Appeared in: **1949** Flight into France. **1957** L'Uomo di Paglia. **1959** Un Maledetto Imbroglio (aka The Facts of Murder—US 1965). **1961** La Viaccia (US 1962 and aka The Love Makers). **1965** Il Ferroviere (Man of Iron aka The Railroad Man—US).

GEROLD, HERMANN
Born: 1862, Austria. Died: Nov. 19, 1920, New York, N.Y. Screen and stage actor. Appeared in early Equitable, Famous Players and Metro films.

GERRARD, DOUGLAS (Douglas Gerrard McMurrogh-Kavanagh aka DOUGLAS GERARD)
Born: Aug. 12, 1888, Dublin, Ireland. Died: June 5, 1950, Hollywood, Calif. Screen, stage actor and film director. Entered films in 1913.

Appeared in: **1913** A Bear Escape. **1914** The Potter and the Clay; The Merchant of Venice. **1916** The Human Cactus; The Fur Trimmed Coat; Naked Hearts; Bettina Loved a Soldier; The Penalty of Treason; The Price of Victory; Under the Spell; The Evil Women Do; Through Baby's Voice; In the Dead O'Night; Her Wedding Day; The False Genius. **1919** Lord and Lady Algy. **1921** The Lady from Longacre. **1922** The Golden Gallows; Impulse; Omar the Tentmaker; A Tailor Made Man. **1924** On Time; In Fast Company; The Lighthouse by the Sea. **1925** My Neighbor's Wife; Wings of Youth. **1926** Doubling With Danger; Private Izzy Murphy; Footloose Widows. **1927** The College Widow; Dearie; The First Auto; The Desired Woman; Ginsberg the Great; Wolf's Clothing; A Million Bid. **1928** Five and Ten Cent Annie; Ladies of the Night Club. **1929** The Hottentot; The Glad Rag Doll; The Argyle Case; The Madonna of Avenue A; Painted Angel. **1930** General Crack; Sweet Kitty Bellairs; Lilies of the Field. **1931** Road to Singapore. **1932** The Tenderfoot; One Way Passage; Manhattan Parade. **1933** King's Vacation. **1934** Bombay Mail; Bulldog Drummond Strikes Back. **1935** The Ghost Walks. **1936** Under Two Flags; Ants in the Pantry. **1948** Unfaithfully Yours. **1951** The Dumb Girl on Portici.

GERRARD, GENE (Eugene O'Sullivan)
Born: Aug. 31, 1892, Clapham, London, England. Died: June, 1971, Sidmouth, Devon, England. Screen, stage actor, film director and playwright. Entered films with Hepworth Co. in 1912.

Appeared in: **1930** Let's Love and Laugh. **1932** Out of the Blue; My Wife's Family; Lucky Girl; Bridegroom for Two; Her Radio Romeo. **1933** Leave It to Me; Let Me Explain, Dear. **1935** No Monkey Business; It's a Bet. **1936** Mister Hobo. **1937** Wake Up Famous.

GERRON, KURT (Kurt Gerson)
Born: Berlin, Germany. Died: 1944, Auschwitz, Germany (executed). Screen and stage actor and film director.

Appeared in: **1922** Frau Suende. **1925** Halbseide; O Alte Burschenherrlichkeit; Vorderhause und Hinterhaus; Variete (Variety). **1926** Annemarie und ihr Ulan; Der Liebe Lust und Leid; Die Drei Mannequins; Der Goldene Schmetterling; Die Kleine und ihr Kavalier; Maedchenhandel; Der Soldat der Marie; Eine Tolle Nacht; Die Tragoedie Eines Verlorenen; Wien-Berlin. **1927** Benno Stehkragen; Die Dame mit dem Tigerfell; Dr. Bessels Verwandlung; Einbruch; Feme; Das Frauenhaus von Rio; Gefaehrdete Maedchen; Gehetzte Frauen; Glanz und Elend der Kurtisanen; Der Grosse Unbekannte; Manege (US 1928); Die Pflicht zu Schweigen; Die Schoensten Beine von Berlin; Ein Schwerer Fall; Sein Groesster Bluff; Ein Tag der Rosen im August ... da hat die Garde Fortgemusst; Das Tanzende Wien; Ueb' Immer Treu und Redlichkeit; Die Weisse Spinne; Wer Wirft den Ersten Stein; Ramper, der Tiermensch (aka The Strange Case of Captain Ramper—US 1928). **1928** Der Ueberfall (short, aka Polizeibericht Ueberfall); Casanovas Erbe; Heut Tanzt Mariett; Die Jacht der Sieben Suenden; Liebe und Diebe; Die Regimentstochter; Unmoral; Vom Taeter Fehlt Jede Spur. **1929** Berlin After Dark; Aufruhr im Junggesellenheim; Die Flucht vor der Liebe; Nachtgestalten; Wir Halten Fest und Treu Zusammen; Tagebuch Einer Verlorenen (Diary of a Lost Girl). **1930** Der Blaue Engel (The Blue Angel); Survival; Liebe im Ring; Einbrecher; Die vom Rummelplatz; Die Drei von der Tankstelle (US 1931); Die Marquise von Pompadour (US 1936); Dolly Macht Karriere (Dolly's Career—US 1931). **1931** Man Braucht Kein Geld (You Don't Need Any Money—US 1932); Vater Geht auf Reisen; Salto Mortale; Der Weg Nach Rio; Ihre Majestaet die Liebe (US 1933); Eine Nacht im Grandhotel; Bomben auf Monte Carlo (Monte Carlo Madness). **1932** Trapeze; Zwei in Einem Auto.

GERSON, EVA
Born: 1903. Died: Sept. 5, 1959, New York, N.Y. Screen, stage and television actress.

Appeared in: **1957** Street of Sinners. **1959** North by Northwest; Middle of the Night; The Last Angry Man.

GERSON, PAUL
Born: 1871. Died: June 5, 1957, Hollywood, Calif. Screen, stage actor and film director.

Appeared in: **1923** The Cricket on the Hearth.

GERSTAD, JOHN (John Leif Gjerstad)
Born: Sept. 3, 1924, Boston, Mass. Died: Dec. 1, 1981, New York, N.Y. (heart attack). Screen, stage actor, film director, stage director, stage producer, television director and author.
Appeared in: **1949** Lost Boundaries. **1958** Cop Hater. **1968** The Swimmer.

GERSTEN, BERTA
Born: 1894, Poland. Died: Sept. 10, 1972, New York. Yiddish screen, stage and television actress.
Appeared in: **1939** Mirele Efros. **1950** God, Man and Devil. **1955** The Benny Goodman Story.

GERSTLE, FRANK "FRANKIE" (Frank Morris Gerstle)
Born: Sept. 27, 1915, New York, N.Y. Died: Feb. 23, 1970, Santa Monica, Calif. (cancer). Screen and television actor.
Appeared in: **1951** I Was a Communist for the FBI; Blue Veil; You Never Can Tell; Strictly Dishonorable. **1953** Above and Beyond; Call Me Madam; The Glory Brigade; Killers from Space; The Magnetic Monster; Vicki. **1954** The Long, Long Trailer. **1955** I Cover the Underworld; Slightly Scarlet; Tight Spot. **1956** Autumn Leaves; Between Heaven and Hell; The Proud Ones. **1957** Top Secret Affair; The River's Edge; Under Fire. **1958** Ambush at Cimarron Pass. **1959** Vice Raid; The Wasp Woman; The Four Skulls of Jonathan Drake; Inside the Mafia; I, Mobster; Submarine Seahawk. **1962** 13 West Street. **1963** Shock Corridor. **1964** The Atomic Brain (aka Monstrosity); The Quick Gun. **1965** Young Dillinger. **1966** The Wild Angels; The Silencers. **1967** Hell on Wheels.

GERT, VALESKA
Born: Jan. 11, 1896, Berlin, Germany. Died: Mar. 18, 1978, Germany? Screen, stage actress, dancer and cabaret entertainer.
Appeared in: **1924** Ein Sommernachtstraum (The Street of Sorrow—US 1925); So ist das Leben (Such is Life). **1925** Die Freudlose Gasse (The Joyless Street). **1926** Nana (US 1929). **1927** Alraune (Unholy Love). **1929** Tagebuch einer Verlorenen (Diary of a Lost Girl). **1931** Die Dreigroschenoper (The Three Penny Opera, aka The Beggar's Opera). **1960** Die Dreigroschenoper (The Three Penny Opera—1931 version). **1965** Juliet of the Spirits.

GEST, INNA
Born: 1922. Died: Jan. 1, 1965, San Francisco, Calif. (hepatitis). Screen actress.
Appeared in: **1940** The Ghost Creeps; Boys of the City; Gun Code; The Golden Trail. **1943** The North Star. **1944** Pin-Up Girl; Up in Arms; Ladies of Washington. **1945** Bring On the Girls.

GETTINGER, WILLIAM *See* STEELE, WILLIAM "BILL"

GHIO, NINO
Born: 1887. Died: Jan. 15, 1956, Culver City, Calif. Screen actor and opera singer.

GHIONE, EMILIO
Born: 1880, Italy. Died: Jan., 1930, Turin, Italy. Screen actor.

GIACHETTI, FOSCO
Born: 1904, Italy. Died: Dec. 22, 1974, Rome, Italy (heart ailment). Screen and stage actor.
Appeared in: **1936** Luci Sommerse; Scipione L'Africano (Scipio Africanus—US 1939); Tredici Uomini e Un Cannone (Thirteen Men and a Cannon). **1937** Sentinelli di Bronzo (Bronze Sentinels); L'Ultima Nemica (The Last Enemy—US 1940); Il Ponto di Vetro (The Glass Bridge). **1938** Alba di Domani (Tomorrow at Dawn). **1939** Lo Squadrone Bianco (The White Squadron). **1940** Napoli che non Muore (Naples That Never Dies); Life of Giuseppe Verdi. **1941** The Dream of Butterfly. **1947** La Vita Ricomincia (Life Begins Anew). **1948** Les Maudits (The Damned). **1949** Fear No Evil. **1956** House of Ricordi. **1959** The Virtuous Bigamist. **1960** Il Mattatore (aka Love and Larceny—US 1963). **1961** El Relitto (The Wastrel aka To Be a Man—US 1963).

GIACOMINO (Giuseppe Cireni)
Born: 1884. Died: 1956, Milan, Italy. Screen actor and circus clown. Was a stand-in for Charles Chaplin in several films.

GIBBONS, ROBERT
Died: Feb. 21, 1977, Hollywood, Calif. Screen, stage and television actor.
Appeared in: **1967** Doctor, You've Got to Be Kidding. **1968** Sweet November.

GIBBONS, ROSE
Born: 1886. Died: Aug. 13, 1964, Oakland, Calif. Screen and stage actress.

GIBBS, FREDERIC (Frederick Joseph Gibbs)
Born: Apr. 5, 1884, England. Died: Apr. 13, 1921, New York, N.Y. (heart disease). Screen, stage and vaudeville actor.

GIBBS, ROBERT PATON
Born: 1860, Scranton, Pa. Died: Feb. 22, 1941, Clifton, N.Y. Screen and stage actor.
Appeared in: **1917** The Beloved Adventuress; Robinson Crusoe. **1919** Man Who Stayed at Home; Lure of Ambition. **1921** The Passion Flower.

GIBSON, CHARLES DANA
Born: Sept. 14, 1867, Roxbury, Mass. Died: Dec. 23, 1944, New York, N.Y. (heart failure). Artist, illustrator and screen actor. Creator of "The Gibson Girl."
Appeared in: **1913** Saved by Parcel Post.

GIBSON, EDWARD "HOOT" (Edward Richard Gibson)
Born: Aug. 6, 1892, Tememah, Nebr. Died: Aug. 23, 1962, Woodland Hills, Calif. (cancer). Screen, vaudeville actor and circus, rodeo performer. Married to singer Dorothy Dunstan and divorced from actresses Helen Johnson and Sally Eilers (dec. 1978).
Appeared in: **1910** The Two Brothers. **1911** The New Superintendent. **1912** His Only Son. **1914** The Hazards of Helen (serial); The Man from the East; Shotgun Jones. **1915** The Ring of Destiny; The Man from Texas; Judge Not, or The Woman of Mona Diggings. **1916** The Night Riders; A Knight of the Range; The Passing of Hell's Crown. **1917** A Woman in the Web; A Marked Man; The Voice on the Wire; A 44-Caliber Mystery; The Golden Bullet; The Wrong Man; Cheyenne's Pal; The Soul Herder; The Texas Sphinx; The Secret Man. **1918** Play Straight or Fight; The Midnight Flyer; The Branded Man; Danger Go Slow; Headin' South. **1919** The Fighting Brothers; By Indian Post; Gun Law; The Rustlers; Ace High; The Gun Packer; Kingdom Come; The Four-bit Man; The Jack of Hearts; The Fighting Heart; The Jay Bird; The Double Hold-Up; The Crow; The Tell Tale Wire; The Face in the Watch; The Lone Hand; The Trail of the Holdup Man. **1920** Roarin' Dan; The Sheriff's Oath; Hair Trigger Stuff; Runnin' Straight; Held Up for the Makin's; The Rattler's Hiss; The Texas Kid; Wolf Tracks; Masked; Thieves' Clothes; The Broncho Kid; The Fightin' Terror; The Shootin' Kid; The Smilin' Kid; The Champion Liar; The Big Catch; A Gamblin' Fool; Some Shooter; One Law for All; The Grinning Granger; In Wrong Wright; Cinders; Double Danger; The Two-Fisted Lover; Tipped Off; Superstition; Fight It Out; The Man With the Punch; The Trail of the Hound; The Saddle King; Marryin' Marion; A Pair of Twins; Harmony Ranch; Winning a Home; The Stranger; Ransom; The Teacher's Pet; The Shootin' Fool; A Nose in the Book. **1921** The Cactus Kid; Action; Red Courage; The Fire Eater; Sure Fire. **1922** Step On It; Headin' West; Trimmed; Ridin' Wild; The Galloping Kid; The Loaded Door; The Lone Hand; The Bearcat. **1923** Dead Game; Double Dealing; The Gentleman from America; Out of Luck; Kindled Courage; The Ramblin' Kid; Shootin' for Love; Single Handed; The Thrill Chaser; Blinky. **1924** The City of Stars (short); Hit and Run; Ride for Your Life; The Sawdust Trail; Hook and Ladder; Broadway or Bust; Forty Horse Hawkins; The Ridin' Kid from Powder River. **1925** Roads to Hollywood (short); Taming the West; Spook Ranch; The Saddle Hawk; The Hurricane Kid; Let 'Er Buck; The Calgary Stampede; Arizona Sweepstake. **1926** The Shoot 'Em Up Kid (short); The Buckaroo Kid; Chip of the Flying U; The Flaming Frontier; The Man in the Saddle; The Ohantom Bullet; The Texas Streak. **1927** The Denver Dude; Rawhide Kid; Galloping Fury; Straight Shootin'; A Hero on Horseback; Hey, Hey, Cowboy; Painted Ponies; The Prairie King; The Hawaiian Serenaders (short); The Silent Rider. **1928** Clearing The Trail; The Danger Rider; The Flying Cowboy; Ridin' for Fame; A Trick of Heart; The Wild West Show. **1929** Smilin' Guns; King of the Rodeo; The Lariat Kid; Burning the Wind; Winged Horseman; Courtin' Wildcats; Points West; The Long, Long Trail. **1930** Roaring Ranch; Spurs; Trigger Tricks; Trailin' Trouble; The Mounted Stranger; The Concentratin' Kid. **1931** Clearing the Range; Wild Horse; Hard Hombre. **1932** The Boiling Point; Spirit of the West; Gay Buckaroo; Local Bad Man; A Man's Land. **1933** Cowboy Counsellor; The Dude Bandit; The Fighting Parson; Boots of Destiny. **1935** Sunset Range; Powdersmoke Range; Rainbow's End. **1936** Lucky Terror (short); The Last Outlaw; The Riding Avenger; Swifty; Frontier Justice; Feud of the West; Cavalcade of the West. **1937** The Painted Stallion (serial). **1940** The Trail Blazers. **1943** The Law Rides Again; Death Valley Rangers; Blazing Guns; Wild Horse Stampede. **1944** Marked Trails; The Outlaw Trail; Sonora Stagecoach; Trigger Law; Arizona Whirlwind; The Utah Kid; Westward Bound. **1947** Screen Snapshots (short). **1948** Flight to Nowhere. **1953** The Marshal's Daughter. **1956** Hollywood Bronc Busters (short). **1959** The Horse Soldiers. **1961** Ocean's Eleven.

GIBSON, HELEN (Rose August Wenger aka ROSE GIBSON)
Born: Aug. 27, 1892, Cleveland, Ohio. Died: Oct. 10, 1977, Roseburg, Ore. (stroke and heart attack). Screen, vaudeville, radio actress, film producer, stuntwoman and rodeo performer. Married to Clifton Johnson, naval engineer and screen extra. Do not confuse with Helen Johnson who was married to Hoot Gibson. Entered films in 1911.

Appeared in: **1915** Man of God; The Hazards of Helen (serial). **1917** The Dynamite Special; The End of the Run; The Perilous Leap; Saving the Fast Mail. **1919** Fighting Mad. **1921** No Man's Woman; The Wolverine. **1922** Nine Points of the Law; Thoroughbred. **1928** The Vanishing West (serial). **1932** Human Targets. **1933** Law and Lawless. **1950** Fast on the Draw; Crooked River. **1951** The Hollywood Story. **1962** The Man Who Shot Liberty Valance.

GIBSON, JAMES
Born: 1866. Died: Oct. 13, 1938, Los Angeles, Calif. Screen and vaudeville actor.

Appeared in: **1924** The Right of the Strongest. **1925** Greed. **1926** Glenister of the Mounted. **1930** The Social Lion; Arizona Kid.

GIBSON, KENNETH
Born: Jan. 17, 1899, Sandusky, Ohio. Died: Nov. 26, 1972. Screen and stage actor.

Appeared in: **1921** Big Town Ideas. **1922** The Masqueraders; Broad Daylight. **1923** Ashes of Vengeance; Daytime Wives. **1924** The Turmoil; Passion's Pathway. **1928** The Loves of Ricardo. **1929** The Idle Rich; Words and Music. **1930** Madam Satan; Their Own Desire.

GIBSON, MARGARET See PALMER, PATRICIA

GIBSON, NORMAN
Born: 1950. Died: Sept. 29, 1976, Chicago, Ill. (shot by gunman). Screen actor.

Appeared in: **1975** Cooley High.

GIBSON, ROSE See GIBSON, HELEN

GIDE, ANDRE
Born: 1870, Paris, France. Died: Feb. 19, 1951, Paris, France (pneumonia). Screen actor, film producer and author.

Appeared in: **1952** Life Begins Tomorrow.

GIDEON, MELVILLE (Melville Joseph Gideon)
Born: May 21, 1884, New York, N.Y. Died: Nov. 11, 1933, London, England (following operation). Screen, vaudeville actor, composer and pianist.

Appeared in: **1930** The Co-optimists (stage and screen versions).

GIEHSE, THERESE
Born: 1899, U.S. Died: Mar. 3, 1975, Munich, West Germany. Screen and stage actress. Married to writer John Hampson.

Appeared in: **1931** Acht Tage Glueck. **1934** Der Meisterdetektiv. **1945** The Last Chance. **1948** Anna Karenina. **1958** Madchen in Uniform (Maedchen in Uniform—US 1965).

GIELGUD, VAL
Born: Apr. 28, 1900, London, England. Died: Nov. 30, 1981, London, England. Screen actor, stage producer, playwright and author. Brother of actor Sir John Gielgud.

Appeared in: **1936** Men are Not Gods (US 1937).

GIFFORD, ROSS
Born: 1928, Grosse Pointe, Mich. Died: Nov. 5, 1977, New York, N.Y. (murdered). Screen, stage actor and singer.

GIGLI, BENIAMINO
Born: 1890, Italy. Died: Nov. 30, 1957, Rome, Italy. Opera singer and screen actor. Was in US and Italian films.

Appeared in: **1927** The following shorts: Scenes from "Cavalleria Rusticana"; Quartet from "Rigoletto"; Bergere Legere; Scenes from "Lucia Di Lammermoor"; Scenes from "La Gioconda". **1928** The Pearl Fishers (short). **1937** Forever Yours; Ave Maria. **1938** Solo per Te (Only for You). **1939** Dein Gehort Mein Herz (My Heart Belongs to Thee). **1940** Du Bist mein Gluck (Thou Art My Joy); Legittima Difesa (Self Defense). **1942** Pagliacci. **1950** Night Taxi. **1951** Soho Conspiracy. **1953** Singing Taxi Driver.

GIGNORET, GABRIEL
Born: 1879, France. Died: Mar. 16, 1937, Paris, France. Screen and stage actor.

GILBERT, BILLY (William V. Campbell)
Born: 1891. Died: Apr. 29, 1961, Hollywood, Calif. Screen, stage and vaudeville actor. Do not confuse with "sneezing" comedian Billy Gilbert (dec. 1971). Entered films in 1928.

GILBERT, BILLY
Born: Sept. 12, 1894, Louisville, Ky. Died: Sept. 23, 1971, North Hollywood, Calif. (stroke). Screen, stage, vaudeville, minstrel, television actor and stage producer. Married to actress Lolly McKenzie.

Appeared in: **1916** Bubbles of Trouble. **1929** Noisy Neighbors; The Woman Tamer (short). **1930** The Beauties (short); The Doctor's Wife (short). **1931** Chinatown After Dark; plus the following shorts: Shiver My Timbers; Dogs Is Dogs; The Panic Is On; The Hasty Marriage; One Good Turn; A Melon-Drama; Catch As Catch Can; The Pajama Party. **1932** Pack Up Your Troubles; Million Dollar Legs; "The Taxi Boys" series, including: What Price Taxi, Strange Innertube and Wreckety Wreck; plus the following shorts: Free Eats; Spanky; The Tabasco Kid; The Nickel Nurser; In Walked Charley; First in War; You're Telling Me; County Hospital; Their First Mistake; The Music Box; The Chimp; Strictly Unreliable; Seal Skins; On the Loose; Red Noses; Sneak Easily; Towed in a Hole; Call Her Sausage; Young Ironsides. **1933** This Day and Age; plus the following shorts: Fallen Arches; Luncheon at Twelve; Asleep In the Fleet; Maids a la Mode; The Bargain of the Century; One Track Minds. **1934** Happy Landing; Peck's Bad Boy; Sons of the Desert (voice); Cockeyed Cavalier; plus the following shorts: The Cracked Iceman; Another Wild Idea (voice); Them Thar Hills; Men in Black; Soup and Fish; Apples to You. **1935** A Night at the Opera; plus the following shorts: Nurse to You; His Bridal Sweet; Pardon My Scotch; Just Another Murder; Hail Brother. **1936** Dangerous Waters; Sutter's Gold; Three of a Kind; The Bride Walks Out; Grand Jury; The Big Game; Night Waitress; Early to Bed; Kelly the Second; The Brain Busters (short). **1937** We're on the Jury; Sea Devils; The Man Who Found Himself; The Outcasts of Poker Flat; China Passage; Music for Madame; The Toast of New York; The Life of the Party; On the Avenue; Espionage; Broadway Melody of 1938; Rosalie; One Hundred Men and a Girl; Captains Courageous; The Firefly; Maytime; Fight for Your Lady. **1938** She's Got Everything; My Lucky Star; The Girl Downstairs; Maid's Night Out; The Joy of Living; Breaking the Ice; Mr. Doodle Kicks Off; Peck's Bad Boy With the Circus; Army Girl; Block Heads; Snow White and the Seven Dwarfs (voice of Sneezy); Angels With Dirty Faces; Happy Landing. **1939** Forged Passport; The Under-Pup; Rio; Destry Rides Again; The Star Maker. **1940** His Girl Friday; Women in War; Scatterbrain; Sing, Dance, Plenty Hot; Safari; A Night at Earl Carroll's; Sandy Is a Lady; A Little Bit of Heaven; Seven Sinners; Queen of the Mob; Cross Country Romance; The Villian Still Pursued Her; No, No, Nanette; The Great Dictator; Tin Pan Alley. **1941** Reaching for the Sun; One Night in Lisbon; Angels With Broken Wings; Model Wife; New Wine; Week-End in Havana; Our City. **1942** Sleepytime Gal; Arabian Nights; Valley of the Sun; Song of the Islands; Mr. Wise Guy. **1943** Shantytown; Crazy House; Spotlight Scandals; Stage Door Canteen; Always a Bride's Maid. **1944** Three of a Kind; Crazy Knights; Ghost Crazy; Three's a Family; Ever Since Venus. **1945** Anchors Aweigh; Trouble Chasers. **1947** Fun and Fancy Free (voice). **1948** The Kissing Bandit. **1949** Bride of Vengeance; Mickey and the Giant Killer (voice). **1953** Down Among the Sheltering Palms. **1962** Paradise Valley; Five Weeks in a Balloon. **1963** The Sound of Laughter (documentary).

GILBERT, BOBBY
Born: 1898. Died: Sept. 19, 1973, Hollywood, Calif. (hepatitis). Screen and vaudeville actor.

Appeared in: **1931** Never the Twain Shall Meet. **1937** A Vitaphone short.

GILBERT, JODY
Born: Fort Worth, Texas. Died: Feb. 3, 1979, Sherman Oaks, Calif. (complications suffered in an auto accident). Screen, stage, radio and television actress.

Appeared in: **1935** Ninotchka (film debut). **1939** Everything Happens at Night. **1940** Little Old New York; Seventeen; Star Dust; Flowing Gold; Hudson's Bay. **1941** Wild Geese Calling; Remember the Day; Never Give a Sucker an Even Break. **1942** Ride 'Em Cowboy; Tuttles of Tahiti; The Hard Way. **1945** Christmas in Connecticut. **1946** Deadline For Murder; Texas Panhandle; Decoy; Singing on the Trail. **1947** Blondie's Holiday. **1948** Albuquerque; Are You With It?; Bungalow 13; My Dear Secretary. **1949** Hellfire; The Loveable Cheat; One Last Fling. **1950** House by the River; The Blonde Bandit. **1951** Gene Autry and the Mounties. **1959** The Big Fisherman. **1969** Butch Cassidy and the Sundance Kid; Hello Dolly. **1971** Willard.

GILBERT, JOE
Born: 1903. Died: May 26, 1959, Hollywood, Calif. Screen actor. Entered films in 1923.

Appeared in: **1951** Jim Thorpe—All American; Hurricane Island; The Magic Carpet. **1954** The French Line.

GILBERT, JOHN (John Pringle)
Born: July 10, 1897, Logan, Utah. Died: Jan. 9, 1936, Los Angeles, Calif. (heart attack). Screen, stage actor, screenwriter, film producer and film director. Son of actor and extra John Pringle (dec. 1929). Divorced from actresses Olivia Burwell, Leatrice Joy, Ina Claire and Virginia Bruce (dec. 1982).

Appeared in: **1915** The Mother Instinct. **1916** Hell's Hinges. **1917** Princess of the Dark; The Devil Dodger; Apostle of Vengeance; Golden Rule Kate. **1919** Heart of the Hills; Should a Woman Tell; Busher; Widow by Proxy. **1920** White Circle; The Great Redeemer. **1921** Ladies in Love; Ladies Must Live; The Servant in the House; The Bait; Love's Penalty; Shame. **1922** The Love Gambler; Arabian Love; The Yellow Stain; Gleam O'Dawn; The Count of Monte Cristo; Calvert's Valley; Honor First. **1923** Madness of Youth; California Romance; Truxton King; Cameo Kirby; The Exiles; St. Elmo; While Paris Sleeps. **1924** Romance Ranch; The Wolf Man; Just Off Broadway; The Lone Chance; His Hour; Married Flirts; A Man's Mate; He Who Gets Slapped. **1925** The Big Parade; The Merry Widow; The Wife of the Centaur. **1926** La Boheme; Bardely's, The Magnificent. **1927** Flesh and the Devil; Twelve Miles Out; Love; The Show; Man, Woman and Sin. **1928** The Cossacks; Show People; Four Walls; Masks of the Devil. **1929** A Woman of Affairs; Desert Nights; His Glorious Night; Hollywood Revue of 1929. **1930** Redemption; Way for a Sailor. **1931** Phantom of Paris; Gentleman's Fate. **1932** Big Parade; West of Broadway; Downstairs. **1933** Queen Christina; Fast Workers. **1934** The Captain Hates the Sea. **1964** Big Parade of Comedy (documentary). **1967** Show People (reissue of 1928 film).

GILBERT, LOU
Born: 1909, Cleveland, Ohio? Died: Nov. 6, 1978, Reseda Calif. (heart attack). Screen, stage and television actor.

Appeared in: **1952** Viva Zapata. **1957** Street of Sinners. **1959** Middle of the Night. **1962** Requiem for a Heavyweight. **1965** Giulietta degli Spiriti (Juliet of the Spirits); Across the River. **1967** Frank's Greatest Adventure (aka Fearless Frank—US 1969). **1968** Petulia. **1970** The Great White Hope (stage and film versions). **1976** The Marathon Man.

GILBERT, MAE (Mae Burke Edwards)
Born: 1871. Died: Aug. 18, 1947, Los Angeles, Calif. Silent film actress.

GILBERT, MAUDE
Died: July 7, 1953, Laguna Beach, Calif. Screen and stage actress.

GILBERT, OLIVE
Born: 1900, Carmarthen, Wales. Died: Feb. 19, 1981, Hove, Sussex, England. Screen, stage actress and opera singer.

Appeared in: **1950** The Dancing Years.

GILBERT, PAUL (Paul MacMahon)
Born: 1917. Died: Feb. 12, 1976, Hollywood, Calif. Screen, vaudeville, television actor, circus performer, dancer and comic. Father of television actress Melissa Gilbert and actor Jonathan Gilbert.

Appeared in: **1954** So This is Paris. **1955** The Second Greatest Sex. **1956** You Can't Run Away From It. **1964** Three Nuts in Search of a Bolt. **19654** Sylvia; Cat Ballou. **1966** Women of the Prehistoric Planet.

GILBERT, WALTER
Born: 1887. Died: Jan. 12, 1947, Brooklyn, N.Y. (heart attack). Screen and stage actor.

Appeared in: **1925** The Pearl of Love. **1930** She's My Weakness. **1934** Gambling. **1938** Dynamite Delaney.

GILES, ANNA
Born: 1874. Died: Feb. 2, 1973, Los Angeles, Calif. Screen actress.

GILFETHER, DANIEL
Born: 1854, Boston, Mass. Died: May 3, 1919, Long Beach, Calif. (kidney disease). Screen and stage actor. Entered films in 1913.

Appeared in: **1914** The Higher Law. **1915** Who Pays? (serial); The Fruit of Folly; The Red Circle (serial). **1916** Mismates; The Homebreakers; Shadows and Sunshine; The Broken Promise; An Old Man's Folly; Pay Dirt; The Better Instinct; From the Deep. **1917** Twin

Kiddies; Told at the Twilight; Zollenstein; The Girl Angle; The Checkmate; The Wildcat; Brand's Daughter; His Old Fashioned Dad. **1918** No Children Wanted; The Locked Heart; Marylee Mixes In; Little Miss Grown-Up; Wanted—A Brother.

GILL, BASIL
Born: 1877, Birkenhead, England. Died: Apr. 23, 1955, Hove, England. Screen and stage actor.

Appeared in: **1911** Henry VIII (film debut). **1916** Chains of Bondage; On the Banks; of Allan Water. **1917** The Adventures of Dick Dolan (short); The Ragged Messenger. **1918** The Admirable Crichton; Missing the Tide; Spinner O'Dreams; Film Tags series including What's the Use of Grumbling (short). **1919** God's Good Man; The Home Maker; The Irresistible Flapper; Keeper of the Door; The Rocks of Valpre; A Soul's Crucifixion (aka Crucifixion or The Soul of Gilda Lois). **1920** The Worldlings. **1926** Julius Caesar (short); Santa Claus. **1929** High Treason. **1930** Should a Doctor Tell? (US 1931); The School for Scandal. **1931** Glamour. **1933** The Wandering Jew (US 1935); Mrs. Dane's Defence. **1935** The Immortal Gentleman; The Divine Spark; Royal Cavalcade (aka Regal Cavalcade—US). **1936** Rembrandt; His Lordship (aka Man of Affaires—US 1937); Gaol Break; The Crimson Circle. **1937** Knight Without Armour. **1938** St. Martin's Lane (aka Sidewalks of London—US 1940); The Citadel; Dangerous Medicine.

GILL, FLORENCE
Born: July 27, 1877, London, England. Died: Feb. 19, 1965, Woodland Hills, Calif. (arteriosclerosis). Screen and stage actress. Was the voice of numerous Disney characters.

Appeared in: **1933** Dora's Dunkin' Donuts. **1935** Every Night at Eight. **1937** Ever Since Eve; Larceny in the Air. **1941** The Reluctant Dragon (voice); Obliging Young Lady. **1942** I Married a Witch.

GILL, TOM
Born: July 26, 1916, Newcastle-on-Tyne, England. Died: July 22, 1971, England? Screen, stage and television actor. Entered films in 1937.

Appeared in: **1938** This Man is News (US 1939). **1948** The First Gentleman (aka The Affairs of a Rogue—US 1949). **1951** Hotel Sahara; Mister Drake's Duke. **1952** The Happy Family (aka Mr. Lord Says No—US). **1953** The Limping Man. **1955** The Reluctant Bride (aka Two Grooms for a Bride—US 1957). **1956** Wicked As They Come (US 1957). **1957** Carry on Admiral (aka The Ship Was Loaded—US 1959); The Good Companions (US 1958). **1958** Up the Creek. **1961** Double Bunk. **1962** The Iron Maiden (aka The Swingin' Maiden—US 1963). **1964** The Yellow Rolls-Royce (US 1965). **1965** The Night Caller (aka Night Caller from Space; aka Blood Beast from Outer Space—US 1966). **1967** Smashing Time; I Like Birds (aka Hot Girls for Men Only—US 1968; aka Girls for Men Only and For Men Only). **1969** A Nice Girl Like Me.

GILLESPIE, EDWARD C.
Born: 1874. Died: July 23, 1918, New York, N.Y. Silent film actor.

GILLESPIE, WILLIAM
Born: Jan. 23, 1894, Aberdeen, Scotland. Died: May 19, 1980. Screen, stage and vaudeville actor.

Appeared in: **1915** The Immigrant. **1917** Easy Street. **1921** Now or Never. **1922** Grandma's Boy. **1926** Exit Smiling; Stop, Look and Listen; The Valley of Bravery. **1927** High and Dizzy. **1928** Horse Shy. **1930** Pups is Pups (short); Fast Work (short). **1931** Helping Grandma (short). **1941** Blues in the Night.

GILLETT, ELMA
Born: 1874. Died: July 23, 1941, Hollywood, Calif. Screen and stage actress.

GILLETTE, BOBBY (Robert F. Gillette)
Born: July 28, 1903, Chicago, Ill. Died: Sept. 24, 1972, Dallas, Tex. Screen, vaudeville actor, banjoist and night club performer. Married to actress Shirley Richards with whom he appeared in vaudeville in an act billed as "Gillette and Richards."

Appeared in: **1929** Syncopated Breezes (short). **1961** Flight of the Lost Balloon.

GILLETTE, HARRY
Born: 1901. Died: Feb. 12, 1977. Screen actor and extra.

GILLETTE, WILLIAM
Born: 1856, Hartford, Conn. Died: Apr. 29, 1937, Hartford, Conn. (pulmonary hemorrhage). Stage, screen actor and playwright.

Appeared in: **1916** Sherlock Holmes.

GILLIAM, JIM (James William "Junior" Gilliam)
Born: Oct. 17, 1928, Nashville, Tenn. Died: Oct. 8, 1978, Inglewood, Calif. (brain hemorrhage). Professional baseball player, coach and screen actor.

Appeared in: **1958** Geisha Boy.

GILLIE, JEAN
Born: 1915, Kensington, London, England. Died: Feb. 19, 1949, London, England. Screen, stage actress and dancer. Divorced from film producer/writer Jack Bernhard.

Appeared in: **1935** His Majesty and Co.; Smith's Wives; Brewster's Millions; School for Stars; It Happened in Paris; While Parents Sleep. **1936** This'll Make You Whistle (screen and stage versions—US 1938). **1937** The Girl in the Taxi; The Live Wire. **1938** Sweet Devil. **1939** The Middle Watch; What Would You Do Chums?; The Spider. **1940** A Call to Arms (short); Tilly of Bloomsbury; Sailors Don't Cry. **1941** The Saint Meets the Tiger (US 1943). **1943** The Gentle Sex. **1944** Tawny Pipit (US 1947). **1945** Flight from Folly. **1947** The Macomber Affair; Decoy.

GILLILAND, HELEN
Born: Jan. 31, 1897, Belfast, Ireland. Died: Nov. 24, 1942, England? Screen, stage actress and singer.

Appeared in: **1938** The Storm.

GILLINGWATER, CLAUDE
Born: Aug. 2, 1870, Lauseanna, Mo. Died: Oct. 31, 1939, Beverly Hills, Calif. (suicide—gunshot). Screen and stage actor.

Appeared in: **1921** Little Lord Fauntleroy (film debut). **1922** My Boy; The Dust Flower; Fools First; Remembrance; The Stranger's Banquet. **1923** Alice Adams; Three Wise Fools; Dulcy; A Chapter in Her Life; The Christian; Crinoline and Romance; Souls for Sale; Tiger Rose. **1924** Daddies; How to Educate a Wife; Idle Tongues; Madonna of the Streets. **1925** Cheaper to Marry; Seven Sinners; A Thief in Paradise; Wages for Wives; We Moderns; Winds of Chance. **1926** For Wives Only; Into Her Kingdom; That's My Baby. **1927** Barbed Wire; Fast and Furious; The Gorilla; Naughty But Nice. **1928** Little Shepherd of Kingdom Come; Husbands for Rent; Oh, Kay; Women They Talk About; Remember. **1929** Stark Mad; Stolen Kisses; A Dangerous Woman; Smiling Irish Eyes; Glad Rag Doll. **1930** How I Play Golf—The Brassie (short); The Flirting Widow; The Great Divide; Toast of the Legion; Dumbbells in Ermine; So Long Letty. **1931** Illicit; The Conquering Horde; Kiss Me Again; Gold Dust Gertie; Daddy Long Legs; Compromised; Oh! Oh! Cleopatra (short). **1932** Wide Open Spaces (short); Tess of the Storm Country. **1933** Skyway; Ace of Aces; Ann Carver's Profession; Before Midnight; The Avenger. **1934** In Love With Life; Back Page; Green Eyes; Broadway Bill; The Captain Hates the Sea; You Can't Buy Everything; The Show-Off; The Unknown Blonde; City Limits. **1935** Strange Wives; Mississippi; Baby Face Harrington; Calm Yourself; A Tale of Two Cities; The Woman in Red. **1936** Florida Special; Counterfeit; The Prisoner of Shark Island; The Poor Little Rich Girl; Can This Be Dixie?; Ticket to Paradise; Wives Never Know. **1937** Top of the Town; Conquest. **1938** Little Miss Broadway; Just Around the Corner; There Goes My Heart; A Yank at Oxford. **1939** Cafe Society.

GILLIS, WILLIAM S.
Died: Apr. 24, 1946, Los Angeles, Calif. Screen actor. Entered films approx. 1906.

Appeared in: **1920** Ruth of the Rockies (serial).

GILLMORE, FRANK
Born: May 14, 1867, New York, N.Y. Died: Mar. 29, 1943, New York, N.Y. (cancer). Screen and stage actor. Father of actress Margalo Gillmore.

Appeared in: **1917** The Lifted Veil.

GILMAN, ADA
Born: 1854. Died: Dec. 18, 1921, Holmesburg, Pa. Screen and stage actress.

Appeared in: **1917** In Again, Out Again.

GILMORE, BARNEY
Died: Apr. 18, 1949, Hollywood, Calif. Screen and stage actor. Appeared in Solax Film Company films.

Appeared in: **1912** Dublin Dan. **1913** Kelly from the Emerald Isle. **1921** The Man Worth While. **1926** Almost a Lady; The Galloping Cowboy. **1927** Heroes in Blue; The Bandit's Son. **1928** South Sea Love. **1929** Smiling Irish Eyes.

GILMORE, DOUGLAS
Born: June 25, 1903, Boston, Mass. Died: July 26, 1950, New York, N.Y. Screen and stage actor.

Appeared in: **1925** Sally, Irene and Mary; His Buddy's Wife. **1926** Dance Madness; Paris; Love's Blindness. **1927** The Taxi Dancer; A Kiss in a Taxi; Rough House Rosie. **1929** The One Woman Idea; Pleasure Crazed; Married in Hollywood; A Song of Kentucky; Spirit of Youth; Object Alimony. **1930** Cameo Kirby; Hell's Angels; The Big Party. **1931** Unfaithful; The Naughty Flirt; The Girl Habit; Desert Vengeance.

GILMORE, HELEN
Born: 1901. Died: Apr. 11, 1936, New York, N.Y. (natural causes). Screen and stage actress. Do not confuse with actress Helen Gilmore (dec. 1947) nor Helen Gilmore (dec. Nov. 11, 1936).

GILMORE, HELEN (Antoinette Field)
Born: Jan. 4, 1862, Washington, D.C. Died: Nov. 16, 1936, Los Angeles, Calif. Screen and stage actress. Do not confuse with actress Helen Gilmore (dec. 1947) nor Helen Gilmore (dec. Apr. 11, 1936).

Appeared in: **1915** The Eagle's Nest; The Earle of Pawtucket. **1921** The Blazing Trail; Dangerous Paths. **1922** Too Much Business; Good Men and True Impulse. **1923** Safety Last. **1927** Sensation Seekers.

GILMORE, HELEN
Born: 1900, Chicago, Ill. Died: Oct. 8, 1947, New York, N.Y. (leukemia). Screen, stage actress and magazine editor. Do not confuse with stage actress Helen Gilmore (dec. 1936), and others with identical names.

GILMORE, LOWELL
Died: Feb. 1, 1960, Hollywood, Calif. Screen actor.

Appeared in: **1944** Days of Glory. **1945** Johnny Angel; The Picture of Dorian Gray. **1946** Step By Step; Strange Conquest. **1947** The Arnelo Affair; Calcutta. **1948** The Prince of Thieves; Black Arrow; Walk a Crooked Mile; Dream Girl. **1949** The Secret Garden; Sword in the Desert. **1950** Fortunes of Captain Blood; Tripoli; King Solomon's Mines; Rogues of Sherwood Forest. **1951** Roadblock; Hong Kong; Darling, How Could You?; The Highwayman. **1952** The Plymouth Adventure; Androcles and the Lion; Lone Star. **1953** Francis Covers the Big Town. **1954** Day of Triumph; Saskatchewan. **1955** The Sea Chase; Ma and Pa Kettle at Waikiki. **1956** Comanche.

GILMOUR, JOHN H. (aka JOHN H. GILMORE)
Born: 1857, Ottawa, Canada. Died: Nov. 24, 1922, New York, N.Y. Screen and stage actor.

Appeared in: **1919** Witness for the Defense; Impossible Catherine. **1920** Democracy; The Vision Restored. **1921** The Wakefield Case; The Magic Cup; School Days; The Kentuckians; Such a Little Queen. **1922** The Soul of Man.

GILPIN, CHARLES S.
Born: 1879, Richmond, Va. Died: May 6, 1930, Eldredge Park, N.J. Black screen, stage actor and playwright.

Appeared in: **1926** Ten Nights in a Barroom.

GILSON, TOM (Thomas Peter Gilson)
Born: Jan. 6, 1934, New York, N.Y. Died: Oct. 6, 1962; Van Nuys, Calif. (shot). Screen and television actor.

Appeared in: **1958** Young and Wild; Rally Round the Flag, Boys! **1959** Home from the Hill. **1960** This Rebel Breed; The Threat; The Crowded Sky. **1962** Convicts Four.

GIM, H. W. (Hom Wing Gim)
Born: Jan. 22, 1908, China. Died: Mar. 15, 1973, Los Angeles, Calif. Screen and television actor.

Appeared in: **1951** Peking Express. **1962** Gypsy. **1963** McLintock! **1966** Seven Women. **1969** True Grit; Paint Your Wagon.

GINIVA, JOHN "ALASKA JACK"
Born: 1868. Died: Feb. 22, 1936, Hollywood, Calif. Screen and vaudeville actor.

GINN, HAYWARD J.
Born: Sept. 8, 1878, Virginia City, Nev. Died: Feb. 14, 1926, Los Angeles, Calif. (suicide—gas inhalation). Screen actor.

Appeared in: **1915** The Sign of the Rose.

GINN, WELLS WATSON
Born: 1891, Bellefontaine, Ohio. Died: Apr. 15, 1959, Cincinnati, Ohio. Screen, stage, radio, vaudeville actor, and film director.

Appeared in and directed early Cosmopolitan Co. films in New York

GIOI, VIVI
Born: 1917, Italy? Died: July 12, 1975, Fregene, Italy (heart attack). Screen and stage actress.

Appeared in: **1956** La Risaia (aka Rice Girl—US 1963).

GIORDA, MARCELLO
Born: Italy. Died: Apr. 22, 1960, Italy? Screen actor.

Appeared in: **1938** L'Albero di Adamo (Adam's Tree). **1939** Scipio Africanus. **1949** Rigoletto. **1959** La Grande Guerra (aka The Great War—US 1961). **1960** Where the Hot Wind Blows (aka Le Leggo—The Law).

GIRADOT, ETIENNE
Born: 1856, London, England. Died: Nov. 10, 1939, Hollywood, Calif. Screen and stage actor. Entered films with Vitagraph Co. in 1912.

Appeared in: **1912** The Violin of Monsieur. **1933** The Kennel Murder Case; Blood Money; Advice to the Lovelorn. **1934** Twentieth Century (stage and film versions); Fashions of 1934; Mandalay; Return of the Terror; Little Man, What Now?; The Dragon Murder Case; The Fire Brand. **1935** Grand Old Girl; The Whole Town's Talking; Clive of India; Chasing Yesterday; Hooray for Love; In Old Kentucky; Curly Top; The Bishop Misbehaves; I Live My Life; Metropolitan. **1936** The Garden Murder Case; The Devil Is a Sissy; The Longest Night; Go West, Young Man; College Holiday; The Music Goes 'Round; Half Angel; Hearts Divided. **1937** Wake Up and Live; Danger—Love at Work; The Road Back; The Great Garrick; Breakfast for Two. **1938** Port of Seven Seas; Arizona Wildcat; Professor Beware; There Goes My Heart. **1939** Little Accident; The Hunchback of Notre Dame; The Story of Vernon and Irene Castle; Fast and Loose; Exile Express; For Love or Money; Hawaiian Nights. **1940** Isle of Destiny.

GIRARD, JOE (Joseph W. Girard)
Born: Apr. 2, 1871, Williamsport, Pa. Died: Aug. 12, 1949. Screen and stage actor.

Appeared in: **1911** Back to the Primitive. **1914** Shotgun Jones; Sheep's Clothing; The Birth of the Star Spangled Banner. **1915** The Trail of the Upper Yukon; The Last Act; The Parson of Pine Mountain; The Meddler. **1916** 20,000 Leagues Under the Sea; Aschenbroedel; The Laugh of Scorn; The Broken Spur; The Narrow Path; The Sheriff of Pine Mountain. **1917** The Voice on the Wire (serial); Treason; Hell Morgan's Girl; The Storm Woman; Fear Not. **1918** The Beast of Berlin; The Bride's Awakening; Danger, Go Slow; The Risky Road; Her Body in Bond; The Marriage Life; The Two-Soul Woman; The Brass Bullet (serial). **1919** What Am I Bid?; Bare Fists; Two Soiled Women; Kaiser—the Beast of Berlin; Loot; Paid in Advance; The Midnight Man (serial); Sign of the Rat. **1920** The Figurehead; The Branded Mystery; The Branded H (serial); The Screaming Shadow (serial); The Fatal Sign (serial); The Branded Four (serial). **1921** Dangerous Paths; Dead or Alive; Red Courage; The Sheriff of Hope Eternal; Her Social Value; A Yankee Go-Getter; The Blue Fox (serial). **1922** Step On It!; Chain Lightning; The Man Who Married His Own Wife; The Price of Youth; One Wonderful Night; Nan of the North (serial). **1923** Three Jumps Ahead; The Wild Party; The Devil's Dooryard; The Law Rustlers; Soft Boiled; Legally Dead; Lovebound; Where Is This West?; The Sting of the Scorpion. **1924** After a Million; Gambling Wives; Jack O'Clubs; The Night Hawk; Reckless Speed; In Hollywood With Potash and Perlmutter; Laughing at Danger; Leave It to Gerry; The Night Message; Wolves of the North (serial); Stolen Secrets; The Western Wallop. **1925** The Gambling Fool; Romance and Rustlers; Three Keys; The Fugitive; Ten Days; Speed Madness; The Pride of the Force; Vic Dyson Pays; Youth and Adventure. **1926** The Dangerous Dub; Doubling With Danger; Driftin' Thru; Forlorn River; The High Flyer; Lightning Reporter; Modern Youth; Tentacles of the North; The Warning Signal; Flying High; The Flying Mail; The Night Owl; Ladies of Leisure; Out of the Storm; Speed Crazed; We're in the Navy Now. **1927** The Final Extra; Fireman—Save My Child; In the First Degree; The Ladybird; The Silent Hero; The Shield of Honor; When Seconds Count; Whispering Sage. **1928** The Fleet's In; Hello Cheyenne; The Bullet Mark; Marlie the Miller; Partners in Crime; Stop That Man; The Terror; Heart Trouble. **1929** Broken Barriers; Courtin' Wildcats; From Headquarters; The Girl from Havana; The Leatherneck; Redskin; The One Woman Idea; King of the Rodeo. **1930** The Girl of the Golden West; Just Imagine; Back from Shanghai; Sons of the Saddle; Troopers Three; Third Alarm. **1931** Strictly Dishonorable; Gang Busters; Defenders of the Law; Mystery Train;

Sky Spider; Is There Justice? **1932** Scareheads; Radio Patrol; The Crusader; The Texas Bad Man; The Hurricane Express (serial). **1933** Officer 13; Racetrack; Renegades of the West; The World Gone Mad; The Whirlwind; Silent Men; Fiddlin' Buckaroo. **1934** Murder in the Museum; Woman Who Dared; Fighting Trouper. **1935** Kentucky Blue Streak; His Fighting Blood; Outlawed Guns; Ivory-Handled Gun; Outlaw Deputy. **1936** Frontier Justice; The Dragnet; The Oregon Trail; Ride 'Em Cowboy; The Clutching Hand (serial); Aces and Eights. **1937** Mystery of the Hooded Horseman. **1938** Unashamed; Held for Ransom. **1939** Ride 'Em Cowgirl; Tough Kid; Crashing Thru. **1940** The Green Archer (serial). **1941** The Spider Returns (serial). **1942** Captain Midnight (serial).

GIROUX, ANTOINETTE
Born: 1903, Canada. Died: July 8, 1978, Canada? Screen, stage and television actress.

GIROUX, LEE
Born: 1911. Died: Jan. 26, 1973, North Hollywood, Calif. (natural causes). Television newscaster, author and screen actor.

Appeared in: **1961** X-15. **1963** Son of Flubber.

GISH, DOROTHY (Dorothy de Guiche)
Born: Mar. 11, 1898, Dayton, Ohio. Died: June 4, 1968, Rapallo, Italy (bronchial pneumonia). Stage and screen actress. Daughter of actress Mary Gish (dec. 1948). Sister of actress Lillian Gish. Entered films in 1912. Divorced from actor James Rennie (dec. 1965).

Appeared in: **1912** An Unseen Enemy; The New York Hat; The Burglar's Dilemma; The Musketeers of Pig Alley; Gold and Glitter; The Informer; My Hero; A Cry for Help. **1913** The Perfidy of Mary; Her Mother's Oath; Oil and Water; The Lady and the Mouse; Just Gold; Almost a Wild Man; Pa Says; The Vengeance of Galora; Those Little Flowers; The Widow's Kids; The Adopted Brother; The Lady in Black; The House of Discord. **1914** Her Old Teacher; Judith of Bethulia; Her Father's Silent Partner; The Mysterious Shot; The Floor Above; The Old Man; Liberty Belles; The Mountain Rat; Silent Sandy; The Never Woman; Their First Acquaintance; Arms and the Gringo; The Suffragette's Battle in Nuttyville; The City Beautiful; The Painted Lady; Home Sweet Home; The Tavern of Tragedy; Her Mother's Necklace; A Lesson in Mechanics; Granny; A Fair Rebel; Down the Road to Creditville; The Wife; Sands of Fate; The Warning; Back to the Kitchen; The Availing Prayer; The Saving Grace; The Sisters; The Better Way. **1915** Out of Bondage; Jordan Is a Hard Road; In Old Heidelberg; An Old Fashioned Girl; How Hazel Got Even; The Lost Lord Lowell; Minerva's Mission; Her Grandparents; Her Mother's Daughter; The Mountain Girl; The Little Catamount; Victorine; Bred in the Bone. **1916** Little Meena's Romance; Betty of Graystone; Susan Rocks the Boat; The Little School Ma'rm; Gretchen, the Greenhorn; Atta Boy's Last Race; Children of the Feud. **1917** The Little Yank; Stage Struck; Her Official Fathers. **1918** Battling Jane; The Hun Within; Hearts of the World. **1919** Out of Luck; The Hope Chest; Boots; Peppy Polly; Nobody Home; Turning the Tables; I'll Get Him Yet; Nugget Nell. **1920** Remodeling Her Husband; Mary Ellen Comes to Town; Little Miss Rebellion; Flying Pat. **1921** The Ghost in the Garret; Oh, Jo! **1922** The Country Flapper; Orphans of the Storm. **1923** Fury; The Bright Shawl. **1924** Romola. **1925** Night Life in New York; Clothes Make the Pirate; The Beautiful City. **1926** Nell Gwyn. **1927** London; Madame Pompadour; Tip Toes. **1930** Wolves. **1936** Wanted Men. **1944** Our Hearts Were Young and Gay. **1946** Centennial Summer. **1951** The Whistle at Eaton Falls; Mornings at Seven. **1964** The Cardinal; The Chalk Garden.

GISH, MARY (Mary Robinson McConnell aka MAE BARNARD)
Died: Sept. 16, 1948, New York, N.Y. Screen and stage actress. Mother of actresses Dorothy (dec. 1968) and Lillian Gish.

Appeared in: **1918** Hearts of the World.

GIVNEY, KATHRYN
Born: 1897. Died: Mar. 16, 1978, Hollywood, Calif. Screen and stage actress.

Appeared in: **1930** Follow Thru. **1931** Lover Come Back. **1948** Isn't It Romantic? **1949** My Friend Irma. **1950** Ma and Pa Kettle Go to Town; Double Crossbones. **1951** Operation Pacific; Lightening Strikes Twice; A Place in the Sun; Too Young to Kiss; Little Egypt. **1953** Let's Do It Again. **1954** Three Coins in the Fountain. **1955** Daddy Long Legs; Guys and Dolls; Count Three and Pray. **1956** Congo Crossing. **1957** The Wayward Bus. **1958** A Certain Smile. **1959** The Man in the Net. **1960** From the Terrace. **1962** The Four Horsemen of the Apocalypse. **1969** Once You Kiss a Stranger.

GLADMAN, ANNABELLE
Born: 1899. Died: Jan. 15, 1948, Hollywood, Calif. Screen actress.

GLAGOLIN, BORIS S.
Born: 1878, Russia. Died: Dec. 12, 1948, Hollywood, Calif. Screen, stage actor and stage director.

GLASER, LULU
Born: June 2, 1874, Allegheny, Pa. Died: Sept. 5, 1958, Weston, Conn. Screen, stage, vaudeville actress and burlesque entertainer.

Appeared in: **1915** How Molly Made Good.

GLASER, VAUGHAN
Born: 1872. Died: Nov. 23, 1958, Van Nuys, Calif. Screen and stage actor.

Appeared in: **1939** What A Life; Rulers of the Sea. **1940** Those Were the Days. **1941** Adventure in Washington; Henry Aldrich for President. **1942** Henry Aldrich, Editor; Saboteur; Henry and Dizzy; My Favorite Spy. **1943** Henry Aldrich Gets Glamour; Henry Aldrich Swings It; Henry Aldrich Haunts a House. **1944** Arsenic and Old Lace; Henry Aldrich Plays Cupid.

GLASS, EVERETT
Born: 1891. Died: Mar. 22, 1966, Los Angeles, Calif. Screen actor.

Appeared in: **1948** The Girl from Manhattan. **1949** Pinky; The Undercover Man; Easy Living. **1950** Young Man With a Horn; Mother Didn't Tell Me; Father Makes Good; Two Flags West; The Petty Girl; Counter Spy Meets Scotland Yard. **1951** My Forbidden Post; The Magnificent Yankee. **1952** Macao; The Greatest Show on Earth; Deadline U.S.A.; Dreamboat. **1953** Inferno; Three Sailors and a Girl. **1954** Demetrius and the Gladiators; Day of Triumph. **1955** The Purple Mask; They Came from Another World. **1956** World Without End; Friendly Persuasion; Invasion of the Body Snatchers. **1957** Pal Joey; The Quiet Gun. **1958** Gunman's Walk. **1959** A Summer Place. **1960** Elmer Gantry; The Marriage-Go-Round.

GLASS, GASTON
Born: Dec. 31, 1898, Paris, France. Died: Nov. 11, 1965, Santa Monica, Calif. Screen, stage actor, assistant film director and television production manager. Married to actress "Bo-Peep" Karlin (dec. 1969).

Appeared in: **1919** Open Your Eyes. **1920** Humoresque; The World and His Wife. **1921** God's Crucible; Her Winning Way; The Lost Battalion; There Are No Villains. **1922** I Am the Law; Glass Houses; The Kingdom Within; Little Miss Smiles; Monte Cristo; Rich Men's Wives; The Song of Life. **1923** The Hero; Gimme; The Spider and the Rose; Mothers-in-Law; Daughters of the Rich. **1924** I Am the Man; After the Ball. **1925** The Bad Lands; The Danger Signal; Fair Play; Flying Fool; The Mad Marriage; Parisian Nights; The Prince of Success; Pursued; The Scarlet West; Three Keys; The Verdict. **1926** Broken Homes; The Call of the Klondike; Exclusive Rights; Her Sacrifice; The Jazz Girl; Midnight Limited; The Road to Broadway; The Romance of a Million Dollars; Subway Sadie; Sweet Sadie; Sweet Daddies; Tentacles of the North; Wives at Auction. **1927** Better Days; Compassion; False Morals; The Gorilla; The Love Wager; The Show Girl; Sinews of Steel. **1928** The Red Mark; Name the Woman; A Gentleman Preferred; Innocent Love; My Home Town; Obey Your Husband; The Wife's Relations. **1929** Broken Barriers; Untamed Justice; Behind Closed Doors; Geraldine; The Faker; Tiger Rose. **1930** Just Like Heaven; She Got What She Wanted; The South Sea Pearl (short). **1931** The Bad Man; The Big Trail (both French versions). **1934** LeGong (narr.). **1935** Sylvia Scarlett. **1936** The Clutching Hand (serial); Under Two Flags; Desire; The Man Who Broke the Bank at Monte Carlo; The Princess Comes Across; Gambling With Souls; Sutter's Gold; Mary of Scotland. **1937** Death in the Air; Espionage.

GLASSMIRE, AUGUSTIN J. "GUS"
Born: 1879. Died: July 23, 1946, Hollywood, Calif. Screen and stage actor. Entered films in 1932.

Appeared in: **1939** Our Leading Citizen. **1940** The Mortal Storm. **1941** Tom, Dick and Harry. **1942** My Gal Sal; Saboteur; The Big Shot; Syncopation. **1943** Sweet Rosie O'Grady; Batman (serial). **1944** Wilson. **1945** Fallen Angel; Scarlet Street; Enchanted Cottage; Col. Effingham's Raid; The Bullfighters.

GLAUM, LOUISE
Born: 1900, Baltimore, Md. Died: Nov. 25, 1970, Los Angeles, Calif. (pneumonia). Stage and screen actress. Appeared in Mack Sennett comedies.

Appeared in: **1915** The Lure of Woman; The Iron Strain. **1916** The Aryan; Honor Thy Name; Return of Draw Egan; Home; Hell's Hinges. **1919** The Poppy Girl's Husband; Sahara; The Lone Wolf's Daughter. **1920** Sex. **1921** I Am Guilty; The Leopard Woman; Love; Greater Than Love. **1925** Fifty-Fifty.

GLAZER, EVE F.
Born: 1903. Died: June 29, 1960, Hollywood, Calif. (cancer). Screen actress.

GLEASON, ADDA
Born: Dec. 19, 1888, Chicago, Ill. Died: Feb. 6, 1971, Woodland Hills, Calif. (pneumonia). Screen and stage actress.

Appeared in: **1913** The Rosary. **1914** Garrison's Finish. **1915** The Voice in the Fog. **1916** Ramona. **1917** Shackles of Truth; Fanatics. **1925** How Baxter Buttered In. **1926** The Old Soak. **1927** Man Bait. **1929** The College Coquette. **1946** The Spider Woman Strikes Back.

GLEASON, FRED
Born: 1854. Died: June 9, 1933, New York, N.Y. Screen and stage actor.

GLEASON, JAMES "JIMMY"
Born: May 23, 1886, New York, N.Y. Died: Apr. 12, 1959, Woodland Hills, Calif. (asthma). Screen, stage actor and screenwriter. Son of stage actress Mina Crolius Gleason (dec. 1931). Married to actress Lucille Gleason (dec. 1947). Father of actor Russell Gleason (dec. 1945). Nominated for 1941 Academy Award for Best Supporting Actor in Here Comes Mr. Jordan.

Appeared in: **1922** Polly of the Follies. **1928** The Count of Ten. **1929** Garden of Eatin'; Fairways and Foul; The Shannons of Broadway; The Broadway Melody; The Flying Fool; High Voltage; His First Command. **1930** Oh, Yeah!; Free Soul; Puttin' on the Ritz; Dumbbells in Ermine; The Matrimonial Bed; Big Money; Don't Believe It; No Brakes; The Swellhead; What a Widow!; Her Man. **1931** The Big Gamble; Sweepstakes; It's a Wise Child; Beyond Victory; Suicide Fleet. **1932** Rule 'Em and Weep (short); Information Kid; Blondie of the Follies; Lady and Gent; The Crooked Circle; The Penguin Pool Murder; The All American; The Devil Is Driving; Fast Companions. **1933** Hoopla; Billion Dollar Scandal; Clear All Wires. **1934** Pie for Two; Murder on the Blackboard; The Meanest Gal in Town; Search for Beauty; Orders Is Orders. **1935** Murder on a Honeymoon; Hot Tip; West Point of the Air; Helldorado. **1936** Murder on the Bridle Path; The Ex-Mrs. Bradford; Don't Turn 'Em Loose; The Big Game; The Plot Thickens; Yours for the Asking; We're Only Human. **1937** Forty Naughty Girls; Manhattan Merry-Go-Round. **1938** Army Girl; The Higgins Family; Dawn Over Ireland; Goodbye Broadway. **1939** On Your Toes; My Wife's Relatives; Should Husbands Work?; The Covered Trailer. **1940** Money to Burn; Grandpa Goes to Town; Earl of Paddlestone. **1941** Meet John Doe; Here Comes Mr. Jordan; Tanks a Million; Nine Lives Are Not Enough; Affectionately Yours; A Date with the Falcon; Babes on Broadway. **1942** Tramp, Tramp, Tramp; Hay Foot; My Gal Sal; The Falcon Takes Over; Footlight Serenade; Tales of Manhattan; Manila Calling; All Through the Night. **1943** A Guy Named Joe; Crash Dive. **1944** Keys of the Kingdom; Arsenic and Old Lace; Once Upon a Time; This Man's Navy. **1945** A Tree Grows in Brooklyn; Captain Eddie; The Clock. **1946** Lady Luck; Home Sweet Homicide; The Well-Groomed Bride; The Hoodlum Saint. **1947** Down to Earth; Tycoon; The Homestretch; The Tenderfoot; The Bishop's Wife. **1948** When My Baby Smiles at Me; The Return of October; Smart Woman; The Dude Goes West. **1949** The Life of Riley; Bad Boy; Take One False Step; Miss Grant Takes Richmond. **1950** The Jackpot; Joe Palooka in the Squared Circle; Key to the City; Riding High; Two Flags West; The Yellow Cab Man. **1951** Two Gals and a Guy; Come Fill the Cup; Joe Palooka in the Triple Cross; I'll See You in My Dreams. **1952** The Story of Will Rogers; What Price Glory; We're Not Married. **1953** Forever Female. **1954** Hollywood Thrillmakers; Suddenly. **1955** The Night of the Hunter; The Girl Rush. **1956** Star in the Dust. **1957** Spring Reunion; The Female Animal; Loving You; Money, Women and Guns; Man in the Shadow. **1958** Once Upon a Horse; Man or Gun; Rock-a-Bye Baby; The Last Hurrah.

GLEASON, LUCILLE (Lucille Webster)
Born: Feb. 6, 1888, Pasadena, Calif. Died: May 18, 1947, Brentwood, Calif. (heart attack). Stage and screen actress. Ran for California Assembly in 1944 but was defeated. Wife of actor James Gleason (dec. 1959) and mother of actor Russell Gleason (dec. 1945).

Appeared in: **1929** Garden of Eatin'; Fairways and Foul; The Shannons of Broadway; Pathe "Golden Rooster" comedies. **1930** Don't Believe It. **1931** Pagan Lady; Girls About Town. **1932** A Hockey Hick (short); Girl of the Rio; Nice Women. **1933** Don't Bet on Love; The Solitaire Man; Love, Honor and Oh, Baby! **1934** Woman Afraid; Successful Failure; Beloved; I Like It That Way. **1936** Klondike Annie; Rhythm on the Range; The Ex-Mrs. Bradford. **1937** Red Light Ahead; Navy Blues; First Lady. **1938** The Beloved Brat; The Nurse from Brooklyn; The Higgins Family. **1939** My Wife's Relatives; Should Husbands Work?; The Covered Trailer. **1940** Money to Burn; Grandpa Goes to Town; Earl of Puddlestone; Lucky Parners. **1941** The Gay Falcon. **1943** Stage Door Canteen. **1944** Take it Big. **1945** The Clock; Don't Fence Me In.

GLEASON, MINA (Mina Crolius)

Born: 1858, Boston, Mass. Died: June 27, 1931, Beverly Hills, Calif. (heart attack). Screen, stage and vaudeville actress. Mother of actor James Gleason (dec. 1959).

GLEASON, RUSSELL

Born: Feb. 6, 1908, Portland, Ore. Died: Dec. 26, 1945, New York, N.Y. (fall from hotel window). Screen actor. Son of actor James Gleason (dec. 1959) and actress Lucille Gleason (dec. 1947).

Appeared in: **1929** The Flying Fool; The Shady Lady; The Sophomore; Strange Cargo; Seven Faces. **1930** Officer O'Brien; All Quiet on the Western Front; Sisters. **1931** Beyond Victory; Laugh and Get Rich; Homicide Squad. **1932** Always Kickin' (sports short); The Strange Case of Clara Deane; Nice Women; Off His Base (sports short); A Hockey Hick (sports short). **1933** Private Jones. **1934** I Can't Escape. **1935** Hot Tip. **1936** Hitchhike to Heaven. **1937** Off to the Races; Big Business; Hot Water; Borrowing Trouble. **1938** Fury Below; The Higgins Family; Down on the Farm; Love on a Budget; A Trip to Paris; Safety in Numbers. **1939** My Wife's Relatives; News Is Made at Night; Should Husbands Work?; The Covered Trailer; Here I Am a Stranger. **1940** Money to Burn; Young as You Feel; Grandpa Goes to Town; Earl of Puddlestone; Yesterday's Heroes. **1941** Unexpected Uncle. **1942** Dudes Are Pretty People; Fingers at the Window. **1943** Salute to the Marines. **1944** Adventures of Mark Twain.

GLECKLER, ROBERT P.

Born: Jan. 11, 1890, Pierre, S.D. Died: Feb. 26, 1939, Los Angeles, Calif. (uremic poisoning). Screen and stage actor. Entered films in 1928.

Appeared in: **1928** The Dove. **1929** Mother's Boy. **1930** The Sea God; Big Money. **1931** Night Nurse; Defenders of the Law; She Went for a Tramp; Finger Points. **1933** Take a Chance. **1934** Now I'll Tell; The Defense Rests; Million Dollar Ransom; The Personality Kid. **1935** Great Hotel Murder; The Perfect Clue; The Daring Young Man; The Farmer Takes a Wife; Dante's Inferno; Mr. Dynamite; It Happened in New York; The Case of the Curious Bride; The Glass Key; Headline Woman; Here Comes the Band; Whipsaw; Show Them No Mercy. **1936** Absolute Quiet; Sworn Enemy; Love Begins at Twenty; Forgotten Faces; Yours for the Asking; I'd Give My Life; The Girl on the Front Page; North of Nome; Great Guy. **1937** Wings Over Honolulu; Pick a Star; King of Gamblers; Bulldog Drummond's Revenge; Hot Water; The Man Who Cried Wolf. **1938** Rascals; Alexander's Ragtime Band; Gangs of New York; Gun Law; Little Miss Broadway. **1939** They Made Me a Criminal; Stand Up and Fight.

GLENDINNING, ERNEST

Born: 1884, Ulverston, England. Died: May 17, 1936, South Coventry, Conn. Stage and screen actor.

Appeared in: **1922** When Knighthood Was in Flower. **1930** Grounds for Murder (short).

GLENDON, JONATHAN FRANK

Born: 1887. Died: Mar. 17, 1937, Hollywood, Calif. Screen and stage actor.

Appeared in: **1917** The Third Judgement. **1918** The Wooing of Princess Pat; A Woman in the Web (serial). **1920** Mid-Channel. **1921** Forgotten Woman; Hush; A Tale of Two Worlds; What Do Men Want? **1922** Belle of Alaska; Kissed; More to Be Pitied Than Scorned; Night Life in Hollywood; Yankee Doodle, Jr. **1923** Just Like a Woman; Rip Tide; Shattered Faith; South Sea Love. **1925** Lights of Old Broadway; Private Affairs; Tricks. **1926** Upstage. **1927** Cross Breed; Compassion. **1930** Border Romance. **1932** The Lost Special (serial); I Am a Fugitive from a Chain Gang. **1933** Sucker Money; Strange People; Gun Law; Her Splendid Folly. **1935** The Phantom Empire (serial); The Sagebrush Troubadour. **1936** King of the Pecos; Border Caballero; Aces and Eights; The Lion's Den.

GLENN, DONALD E.

Born: 1911. Died: Mar. 11, 1958, New Haven, Conn. (cancer). Screen, stage actor and press agent.

GLENN, FORREST

Born: 1900, Marissa, Ill. Died: Aug. 24, 1954, Saranac Lake, N.Y. Screen actor. Appeared in Mack Sennett Comedies.

GLENN, RAYMOND See CUSTER, BOB

GLENN, ROY E., SR.

Born: 1915, Pittsburg, Kans. Died: Mar. 12, 1971, Los Angeles, Calif. (heart attack). Black screen, stage and television actor.

Appeared in: **1952** Bomba and the Jungle Girl; Affair in Trinidad; Lydia Bailey; Chicago Calling. **1953** Jungle Drums of Africa (serial). **1954** Carmen Jones; The Golden Idol; Killer Leopard. **1955** A Man Called Peter; Panther Girl of the Congo (serial). **1956** The Man in the Gray Flannel Suit. **1958** Tarzan's Fight for Life. **1959** Porgy and Bess. **1961** A Raisin in the Sun. **1962** Sweet Bird of Youth. **1966** Dead Heat On a Merry-Go-Round; A Man Called Adam. **1967** Guess Who's Coming to Dinner; The Way West. **1968** Finian's Rainbow; Hang 'Em High; I Love You, Alice B. Toklas! **1970** The Great White Hope; Tick ... Tick ... Tick ... **1971** Escape From the Planet of the Apes; Support Your Local Gunfighter.

GLICK, JOSEPH

Born: 1906. Died: Sept. 5, 1978, Woodland Hills, Calif. Professional boxer and screen actor.

GLOECKNER-KRAMER, PEPI

Born: 1874, Austria. Died: Feb., 1954, Vienna, Austria. Screen and stage actress.

Appeared in: **1939** Verliebte Herzen (Hearts in Love).

GLORI, ANN

Died: Mar. 28, 1977. Screen actress.

GLORI, ENRICO

Born: 1901, Naples, Italy. Died: Apr. 22, 1966, Rome, Italy. Stage and screen actor.

Appeared in: **1936** Il Fu Mattia Pascal. **1937** Les Perles de la Couronne (Pearls of the Crown). **1948** Man of the Sea; The Spirit and the Flesh. **1949** Lost in the Dark. **1953** Stranger on the Prowl. **1960** La Giornata Balorda (aka A Crazy Day; Love Is a Day's Work; Pickup in Rome; From a Roman Balcony—US 1961); Les Nuits de Raspoutine (The Night They Killed Rasputin—US 1962). **1961** La Dolce Vita; Barabba (aka Barabbas—US 1962); Costantino il Grande (Constantine and the Cross—US 1962); Romolo e Remo (Romulus and Remus aka Duel of the Titans—US 1963); Il Mattatore (aka L'Homme aux Cent Visages—Love and Larceny—US 1963). **1962** Il Tiranno di Siracusa (aka Damone e Pitias—Damon and Pythias—US).

GLOSSOP-HARRIS, FLORENCE

Born: Oct. 8, 1883, London, England. Died: Oct. 26, 1931, London, England. Screen and stage actress. Divorced from actor Frank Cellier (dec. 1948). Daughter of stage actor Sir Augustus Harris (dec. 1896).

GLOSZ, MARIE

Born: 1880, United States. Died: Apr. 14, 1963, Rome, Italy. Screen actress and opera singer.

Appeared in: **1934** One Night of Love.

GLOVER, EDMUND

Born: June 17, 1914, Vancouver, British Columbia. Died: Nov. 24, 1978, New York, N.Y. Screen actor. Married to actress Prudence Glover. Father of actress Helen Yuill.

Appeared in: **1940** The Courageous Dr. Christian. **1942** Eagle Squadron. **1943** The Ghost Ship. **1944** A Night of Adventure; Marine Raiders; Mademoiselle Fifi. **1945** Two O'Clock Courage; Nevada; Dick Tracy. **1949** Shadows of the West. **1961** The Impersonator (US 1962).

GLUCKMAN, LEON

Born: Dec. 21, 1922, Johannesburg, South Africa. Died: Mar. 7, 1978, London, England (cancer). Screen, stage, television actor, stage director and stage producer. Divorced from actress Pamela Reed.

GLYN, ELINOR

Born: Oct. 17, 1864, Jersey, England. Died: Sept. 23, 1943, London, England. Novelist, journalist, screen actress and screenwriter.

Appeared in: **1927** It. **1928** Show People.

GLYN, NEVA CARR

Born: Australia. Died: Aug. 10, 1975, Mona Vale, Australia. Screen, stage, radio and television actress. Divorced from actor John Tate (dec. 1979) and mother of actor Nick Tate.

Appeared in: **1974** Ride a Wild Pony.

GLYNNE, MARY

Born: Jan. 25, 1898, Penarth, Wales. Died: Sept. 22, 1954, London, England. Screen, stage and television actress. Married to actor Dennis Neilsen-Terry (dec. 1932).

Appeared in: 1919 The Cry for Justice; His Last Defence. 1920 The Hundredth Chance; Unmarried; The Call of Youth (US 1921). 1921 Appearances; The Mystery Road; Dangerous Lies; The Princess of New York; Beside the Bonnie Briar Bush (aka The Bonnie Briar Bush—US); Candytuft, I Mean Veronica. 1931 Inquest. 1933 The Good Companions; The Lost Chord. 1934 The Outcast; Flat No. 3. 1935 Emil and the Detectives (aka Emil—US 1938); Royal Cavalcade (aka Regal Cavalcade—US); Scrooge. 1936 The Heirloom Mystery; Grand Finale. 1937 The Angelus. 1938 Cavalcade of the Stars.

GNASS, FRIEDRICH (aka FRITZ GNASS)

Born: 1892, Bochum, Germany. Died: 1958, Berlin, Germany. Screen and stage actor.

Appeared in: 1929 Jenseits der Strasse (Harbour Drift); Mutter Krausens Fahrt ins Gluck (Mother Krausen's Journey to Happiness). 1931 Fra Diavolo; M (aka Morder unter Uns); Luise, Konigin von Preussen (Luise, Queen of Prussia). 1939 Aufruhr in Damaskus (Tumult in Damascus). Other German films include: Troika; Danton, F.P.; 1 Antwortet Nicht; Rasputin; Ich bei Tag und Du bei Nacht; Razzia in St. Puali; Morgenrot; Fluchtlinge; Stern von Valancia; Achtung!; Wer kennt Diese Frau; Abenteuer eines Jungen Herrn in Polen; Hundert Tage; Blutsbruder; Pour le Merite; Nordlicht; Cappriccio; Kautschuk; Sergeant Barry; Geheimzeichen LB 17; Fahrendes Volk; Legion Condor; Wozzek; Der Biberpelz; Die Buntkarierten; Unser Taglich Brot; Familie Benthin; Der Untertan; Roman einer Jungen Ehe; Das Verurteile Dorf; Schatten uber den Inseln; Frauenschicksale; Die Geschichte vom Kleinen Muck; Anna Susanna; Leuchtfeuer; Einmal ist Keinmal; Wer Seine Frau Lieb Hat; Tinko; Gejagt bis sum Morgen; Madeleine und der Legionair.

GOBBLE, HARRY A. "HANK"

Born: 1923. Died: May 19, 1961, Hollywood, Calif. Screen actor and stuntman.

Appeared in: 1961 The Deadly Companions.

GODDARD, ALF

Born: Nov. 28, 1897, London, England. Died: Feb. 25, 1981, England? Screen actor.

Appeared in: 1925 Gainsborough Burlesques series including: So This is Jollygood. 1926 White Hot; Mademoiselle from Armentieres; Second to None; Every Mother's Son. 1927 Hindle Wakes (aka Fanny Hawthorne—US 1929); Remembrance'; Downhill (aka When Boys Leave Home—US 1928); Carry On!; The Flight Commander; A Sister to Assist 'Er. 1928 Sailors Don't Care; What Money Can Buy; Mademoiselle Parley-Voo; Smashing Through; You Know What Sailors Are; Balaclava (aka Jaws of Hell—US 1931). 1929 The Last Post; Down Channel; High Treason. 1930 Alf's Button; The Brat (aka The Nipper); The Cockney Spirit in the War (series); Bed and Breakfast. 1931 Old Soldiers Never Die; The Happy Ending; Splinters in the Navy; East Lynne on the Western Front. 1932 The Third String. 1933 Too Many Wives; The Pride of Force; Enemy of the Police. 1934 Lost in the Legion. 1935 It's a Bet; Strictly Illegal; No Limit. 1936 Song of Freedom. 1937 King Soloman's Mines; Farewell Again (aka Troopship—US 1938). 1938 The Squeaker (aka Murder on Diamond Row—US); Owd Bob (aka To the Victor—US); Convict 99; The Drum; St. Martin's Lane (aka Sidewalks of London—US 1940); Luck of the Navy (aka North Sea Patrol—US 1940); Night Journey. 1939 Tommy Atkins series (reissue of the Cockney Spirit in the War—1930); Murder in Soho (aka Murder in the Night—US 1940); Let's Be Famous; A Window in London (aka Lady in Distress—US 1942). 1940 Here Comes A Policeman (reissue of Strictly Illegal-1935); Spy for a Day. 1941 South American George; The Saint Meets the Tiger (US 1943). 1942 The Young Mr. Pitt. 1944 The Way Ahead (US 1945). 1945 The Way to the Stars (aka Johnny in the Clouds—US); I'll Be Your Sweetheart; Perfect Strangers (aka Vacation from Marriage); They Knew Mr. Knight. 1953 Innocents in Paris (US 1955).

GODDEN, JIMMY

Born: Aug. 11, 1879, Maidstone, England. Died: Mar. 5, 1955, England? Screen and stage actor. Entered films in 1931.

Appeared in: 1931 My Wife's Family. 1932 For the Love of Mike; The Last Coupon; His Wife's Mother; Money Talks. 1933 Meet My Sister; Their Night Out; Hawleys of High Street. 1934 Happy; Those Were the Days; Give Her a Ring; Sometimes Good; The Great Defender; My Song Goes Round the World; Radio Parade of 1935 (US 1935). 1935 It's a Bet; Dandy Dick; Royal Cavalcade (aka Regal Cavalcade—US). 1936 King of the Castle; Living Dangerously; Someone at the Door.

GODDERIS, ALBERT

Born: 1882, Belgium. Died: Feb. 2, 1971, Hollywood, Calif. Screen actor.

Appeared in: 1958 Me and the Colonel.

GODFREY, FREDA

Born: 1889, London, England. Died: Sept 5, 1980, Durban, South Africa. Screen and stage actress.

GODFREY, PETER

Born: Oct. 16, 1899, London, England. Died: Mar. 4, 1970, Hollywood, Calif. Screen, stage, vaudeville actor, screen, stage director and playwright. Married to actress Renee Haal (dec. 1966) with whom he appeared briefly in vaudeville.

Appeared in: 1938 Blockade. 1940 Raffles; The Earl of Chicago; Edison the Man. 1941 Dr. Jekyll and Mr. Hyde. 1947 The Two Mrs. Carrolls.

GODFREY, RENEE HAAL

Born: 1920. Died: May 2, 1964, (cancer). Screen and vaudeville actress. Married to actor and director Peter Godfrey (dec. 1970) with whom she appeared briefly in vaudeville. She was "Miss New York" in the 1937 Miss America contest. Entered films in 1941.

Appeared in: 1941 Unexpected Uncle; Hurry, Charlie, Hurry. 1942 Highways by Night; Wedded Blitz (short). 1944 The Hairy Ape; Since You Went Away. 1945 Bedside Manner. 1946 Terror by Night. 1960 Inherit the Wind; Can-Can. 1962 Tender Is the Night. 1965 Those Calloways.

GODFREY, SAMUEL T.

Born: Oct. 5, 1891, Brooklyn, N.Y. Died: Apr. 18, 1935, Los Angeles, Calif. (brain tumor). Screen, stage actor, playwright, dialog screenwriter and stage director.

Appeared in: 1932 Washington Merry-Go-Round. 1933 Frisco Jenny; I Loved a Woman; Parole Girl; After Tonight; Blondie Johnson. 1934 Beggars in Ermine; The Mighty Barnum; The Love Captive. 1935 Love in Bloom; Private Worlds; Straight from the Heart.

GODOWSKY, DAGMAR

Born: 1897. Died: Feb. 13, 1975, New York, N.Y. Screen, television actress and author. Divorced (annulled) from actor Frank Mayo (dec. 1963).

Appeared in: 1920 The Forged Bride; The Path She Chose; Hitchin' Posts; The Marriage Pit; Honor Bound. 1922 The Altar Stairs; The Stranger's Banquet; The Trap. 1923 The Common Law; Red Lights; Souls for Sale. 1924 Greater Than Marriage; Meddling Women; Playthings of Desire; The Price of a Party; Roulette; A Sainted Devil; The Story Without a Name; Virtuous Liars. 1925 The Lost Chord; Camille of the Barbary Coast. 1926 In Borrowed Plumes.

GOETZ, PAUL P. "POP"

Born: 1865. Died: Sept. 26, 1929. Screen actor.

GOETZKE, BERNHARD

Born: 1884, Danzig, Germany. Died: 1964, Berlin, Germany. Screen and stage actor.

Appeared in: 1918 Veritas Vincit. 1919 Madame Dubarry. 1920 Das Geheimnis von Bombay; Opfer der Keuschheit; Der Schaedel der Pharaoentochter; Die Toteninsel; Tschetschensen-Rache; Die Bruder Karamasoff (The Brothers Karamazov); Mord ohne Taeter (aka Herztrumpf). 1921 Aus dem Schwarzbuch Eines Polizeikommissars; Die Jagd Nach dem Tode; Das Indische Grabmal; Das Weib des Pharao (aka The Loves of Pharaoh—US 1922, and aka Pharaoh's Wife); Der Muede Tod (aka Between Worlds—US 1924, and aka Destiny). 1922 Vanina Oder die Galgenhochzeit; Dr. Mabuse der Spieler (Dr. Mabuse, the Gambler—US 1927); Peter der Grosse (Peter the Great—US 1923). 1924 Die Nibelungen (aka Kriemhild's Revenge—US 1928); Dekameron-Naechte (Decameron Nights—US 1928). 1925 Briefe, die ihn Nicht Erreichten; Die Prinzessin und der Geiger; Zapfenstreich; Zwei und die Dame; Die Verrufenen (aka Funfte Stand, and aka Slums of Berlin—uS 1927); Blackguard. 1926 Die Unehelichen; Die Versunkene Flotte; Der Bergadler (aka The Mountain Eagle; and aka Fear O'God). 1927 Feme; Das Gefaehrliche Alter; Der Gefangene von Shanghai; Die Sache mit Schorrsiegel; Schuldig (US 1928). 1928 Der Staatsanwalt Klagt An; Die Tragoedie im Zirkus Royal; Der Schoepfer (aka Zwischen Liebe und Pflicht); Children of No Importance; Guilty. 1929 Die Todesfahrt im Weltrekord; Fruehlings Erwachen (aka The Awakening of Spring); The Wrath of the Seas. 1930 Sturmisch die Nacht; Dreyfus (US 1931); Alraune (US 1934). 1931 Nachtkolonne; Die Koffer der Herrn O.F.

(The Luggage of Mr. O. F.); 1914, die Letzten Tage vor dem Weltbrand (1914: The Last Days Before the War—US 1932); Zwischen Nacht und Morgen (aka Dirnentragoedie); Cities and Years; Schachmatt; Luise, Koenigin von Preussen (Luisse, Queen of Prussia); Arme, Kleine Eva. **1932** Bauhaus Goldener Engel; Geheimnis des Blauen Zimmers; Theodor Koerner; Die elf Schillschen Offiziere; Teilnehmer Antwortet Nicht; Einmal Moecht ich Keine Sorgen Haben; Die Tanzerin von Sanssouci; Der Tolle Bomberg; Der Verliebte Blasekopf; Der Schwarze Husar (The Black Hussar); Rasputin (aka Der Daemon der Frauen); Kampf um die Frau (aka Die Tundra). **1933** Schuesse an der Grenze; Moral und Liebe; K 1 Greift Ein! **1934** Das Alte Recht; Abenteuer Eines Jungen Herrn in Polen; Polizeiakte 909 (aka Der Fall Tokeramo, and aka Taifun). **1935** Viktoria. **1936** Friedericus; Der Kurier des Zaren (aka The Tsar's Courier); Eskapade (aka Seine Offizielle Frau). **1939** Robert Koch, der Bekaempfer des Todes; Salonwagen E 417. **1940** Jud Suess; Die Gute Sieben; Die 3 Codonas; Zwischen Hamburg und Hatti; Der Fuchs von Glenarvon; Bismarck. **1941** Ich Klage An; Tanz mit dem Kaiser; Die Schwedische Nachtigall. **1942** Der Grosse Koenig (The Great King). **1943** Paracelsus; Muenchhausen. **1944** Der Majoratsherr; Das War Mein Leben. **1950** Das Kalte Herz.

GOFF, NORRIS
Born: 1906, Cove, Ark. Died: June 7, 1978, Palm Desert, Calif. (stroke). Screen, vaudeville, radio actor and writer for radio. Partner with Chester Lauck (Lum) in Lum and Abner radio/television team.

Appeared in: **1940** Dreaming Out Loud. **1942** The Bashful Bachelor. **1943** Two Weeks to Live; So This is Washington. **1944** Going to Town. **1946** Partners in Lime.

GOINES, BETTY
Born: 1904. Died: Jan., 1929. Screen and stage actress.

GOING, FREDERICA
Born: 1895. Died: Apr. 11, 1959, New York, N.Y. Stage, screen and television actress. Daughter of stage performers Frederick Going and Iola Munro Going. Appeared in early films for Edison Co., Pathe and Biograph.

GOLD, JIMMY
Born: 1886, Glasgow, Scotland. Died: Oct. 7, 1967, London, England. Screen, music hall and stage actor. Appeared with Charlie Naughton (dec. 1976) as part of comedy team "Naughton and Gold." The team appeared in "Crazy Gang" films and stage presentations with Jimmy Nervo (dec. 1975), Teddy Knox (dec. 1974), Bud Flannagan (dec. 1968) and Chesney Allen (dec. 1982).

The "Crazy Gang" films include: **1937** Okay for Sound. **1938** Alf's Button Afloat. **1939** The Frozen Limits. **1940** Gasbags. **1958** Life Is a Circus (US 1962). "Naughton and Gold" appeared in: **1933** Sign Please (short); My Lucky Star. **1935** Cock O'the North. **1936** Highland Fling. **1937** Wise Guys. **1943** Down Melody Lane.

GOLDBERG, RUBE (Reuben Lucius Goldberg)
Born: July 4, 1883, San Francisco, Calif. Died: Dec. 7, 1970, New York, N.Y. Cartoonist, artist, writer and screen actor.

Appeared in: **1914** He Danced Himself to Death.

GOLDEN, BOB
Born: 1925. Died: Nov. 5, 1979, Calabasas, Calif. (cancer). Screen and television actor.

Appeared in: **1974** Chinatown. **1975** Report to the Commissioner.

GOLDEN, RUTH (Ruth Fuller)
Born: 1901, New York, N.Y. Died: Aug. 15, 1931, Los Angeles, Calif. Screen actress. Sister of actress Olive Fuller Golden.

Appeared in: **1919** Over the Garden Wall; Cupid Forecloses. **1920** Pegeen; Human Stuff; Blue Streak McCoy.

GOLDENBERG, SAMUEL
Born: 1886. Died: Oct. 31, 1945, Brooklyn, N.Y. (heart attack). Screen and stage actor.

Appeared in: **1935** Shir Hashirim. **1943** Mission to Moscow; Fallen Sparrow.

GOLDIN, PAT (aka PAT GOLDEN)
Born: Dec. 5, 1902, Russia. Died: Apr. 24, 1971, Los Angeles, Calif. (heart attack). Screen actor.

Appeared in: **1946** Bringing Up Father. **1947** It Happened on Fifth Avenue; Sweet Genevieve; Sarge Goes to College; Kilroy Was Here; King of the Bandits. **1948** Jiggs and Maggie in Society; Jiggs and Maggie in Court. **1949** Jiggs and Maggie in Jackpot Jitters; Master Minds. **1950** Jiggs and Maggie Out West. **1952** Glory Alley. **1953** Fast Company. **1955** Hold Back Tomorrow. **1956** The Kettles in the Ozarks; Edge of Hell. **1957** Lizzie; Hit and Run. **1959** Born to Be Loved. **1962** Paradise Alley (aka Stars in the Backyard).

GOLDIN, SIDNEY M.
Born: 1880. Died: Sept. 19, 1937. Screen actor, film director and film producer.

Appeared in: **1913** Little Buster. **1927** Better Days; The Fightin' Comeback.

GOLDINA, MARIAM
Born: Russia. Died: Nov. 14, 1979, New York, N.Y. Screen, stage, television actress, stage director and writer.

Appeared in: **1932** Ladies of the Big House. **1958** Cop Hater. **1960** Flaming Star.

GOLDNER, CHARLES
Born: 1900, Austria. Died: Apr. 15, 1955, London, England. Stage and screen actor.

Appeared in: **1940** Room For Two (US 1944). **1946** The Laughing Lady (US 1950). **1947** Brighton Rock. **1948** One Night With You; Bond Street (US 1950); No Orchids for Miss Blandish (US 1951); Bonnie Prince Charlie (US 1952). **1949** Dear Mr. Prohack (US 1950); Give Us This Day (aka Salt to the Devil—US); The Rocking Horse Winner (US 1950); Third Time Lucky (US 1950); Black Magic. **1950** Shadow of the Eagle (US 1955). **1951** I'll Get You For This (aka Lucky Nick Cain—US); Encore (US 1952). **1952** Secret People; Top Secret (aka Mr. Potts Goes to Moscow—US 1954); South of Algiers (aka The Golden Mask—US 1954). **1953** The Captain's Paradise; The Master of Ballantrae; Always a Bride (US 1954). **1954** Duel in the Jungle; Flame and the Flesh. **1955** The End of the Affair; The Racers.

GOLDSTEIN, BECKY
Born: 1887. Died: May, 1971, London, England. Screen and stage actress.

GOLDSTEIN, JENNIE
Born: 1897, New York, N.Y. Died: Feb. 9, 1960, New York, N.Y. Screen and stage actress.

Appeared in: **1938** Two Sisters.

GOLDSTEIN, SHMULIK (Shmuel Goldstein)
Born: 1908, Lody, Poland. Died: Nov. 23, 1978, New York, N.Y. (heart attack). Screen and stage actor. Father of Stanley Goldstein and actor Harry Gold.

GOLDSWORTHY, JOHN HEATH
Born: Apr. 28, 1884. Died: July 10, 1958. Screen and stage actor.

Appeared in: **1915** The Yellow Streak. **1916** Corner in Cotton; The Red Window. **1918** Debt of Honor. **1919** The Divorcee; The Career of Katherine Bush. **1920** The Sporting Duchess. **1922** Notoriety. **1923** Marriage Morals. **1945** Hangover Square. **1946** The Dark Corner. **1948** The Emperor Waltz; The Luck of the Irish. **1949** Everybody Does It. **1951** The Desert Fox.

GOLLNER, NANA
Born: Tex. Died: Aug. 30, 1980, Antwerp, Belgium. Ballet dancer and screen actress. Married to ballet dancer/actor Paul Petroff (dec. 1981).

GOLM, ERNEST
Born: 1886. Died: May 29, 1962. Screen actor.

Appeared in: **1943** Mission to Moscow. **1944** Wilson; Address Unknown; The Hilter Gang. **1945** Rhapsody in Blue.

GOLM, LISA (aka LIZA GOLM)
Died: Jan. 6, 1964. Screen actress.

Appeared in: **1940** Escape. **1941** Underground. **1942** Journey for Margaret. **1943** They Came to Blow Up America; Mission to Moscow; Madame Curie; Calling Dr. Death; Above Suspicion. **1944** The Seventh Cross; The Hitler Gang. **1946** Night and Day; Shadow of a Woman; Without Reservations. **1947** Cry Wolf; Possessed. **1948** Homecoming; A Foreign Affair; Letter from an Unknown Woman. **1949** The Great Sinner; Anna Lucasta; The Doctor and the Girl; East Side, West Side. **1951** Payment on Demand; The Hoodlum; A Place in the Sun; The Blue Veil. **1952** The Invitation; Come Back, Little Sheba; My Pal Gus. **1956** Ride the High Iron. **1957** Monkey on My Back.

GOLUBEFF, GREGORY
Died: Feb. 11, 1958, Hollywood, Calif. Screen actor and musician.

Appeared in: **1934** Bolero. **1942** Journey into Fear. **1943** Mission to Moscow. **1945** The Seesaw and the Shoes (short); Rhapsody in Blue.

GOLZ, ROSEMARY (aka MARIE GLOSZ)
Born: 1880. Died: Apr. 14, 1963, Rome, Italy. Screen actress and opera performer.

Appeared in: **1934** One Night of Love. **1937** Wake Up and Live.

GOMBELL, MINNA
Born: 1892, Baltimore, Md. Died: Apr. 14, 1973, Santa Monica, Calif. Screen and stage actress.

Appeared in: **1929** Great Power. **1931** Good Sport; Skyline; Doctors' Wives; Bad Girl; Sob Sister. **1932** Stepping Sisters; The Rainbow Trail; Bachelors' Affairs; The First Year; Dance Team; Careless Lady; Walking Down Broadway (aka Hello Sister); After Tomorrow; Wild Girl. **1933** What Price Innocence?; The Big Brain; Wild Boys of the Road; The Way to Love; Hoopla; Pleasure Cruise. **1934** Marrying Widows; Cross Country Cruise; No More Women; Strictly Dynamite; The Hell Cat; The Merry Widow; Keep 'Em Rolling; Registered Nurse; The Lemon Drop Kid; Babbitt; The Thin Man; Cheating Cheaters. **1935** The White Cockatoo; Two Sinners; Women Must Dress; Miss Pacific Fleet. **1936** Champagne Charlie; Banjo on My Knee. **1937** Slave Ship; Wife, Doctor and Nurse; Make Way for Tomorrow. **1938** Block-Heads; Comet over Broadway; The Great Waltz; Going Places. **1939** Second Fiddle; Stop, Look and Love; The Hunchback of Notre Dame. **1940** Boom Town. **1941** High Sierra; Doomed Caravan; Thieves Fall Out. **1942** Mexican Spitfire Sees a Ghost; Cadets on Parade. **1943** Salute for Three. **1944** A Chip Off the Old Block; Johnny Doesn't Live Here Anymore; The Town Went Wild; Destiny. **1945** Night Club Girl; Man Alive; Swingin' on a Rainbow; Penthouse Rhythm; Sunbonnet Sue. **1946** Perilous Holiday; The Best Years of Our Lives. **1947** Wyoming. **1948** The Snake Pit; Mr. Reckless; Return of the Bad Men. **1949** The Last Bandit. **1950** Pagan Love Song. **1951** Here Comes the Groom; I'll See You in My Dreams.

GOMES, ELIEZER
Born: 1920, Brazil. Died: Feb. 12, 1979, Rio de Janeiro, Brazil (cerebral hemorrhage). Screen actor.

Appeared in: **1962** Assalto ao Frem Pagador (Robbery of the Train Paymaster, aka Train Robbery Confidential—US 1965).

GOMEZ, AUGUSTINE "AUGIE" WHITECLOUD
Born: 1891. Died: Jan. 1, 1966, Hollywood, Calif. Screen, stage and vaudeville actor.

Appeared in: **1939** Blue Mountain Skies. **1948** Old Los Angeles.

GOMEZ, RALPH
Born: 1897. Died: Apr. 18, 1954, Hollywood, Calif. (cancer). Screen actor and stuntman. Entered films approx. 1924.

Appeared in: **1947** Road to Rio.

GOMEZ, THOMAS
Born: July 10, 1905, Long Island, N.Y. Died: June 18, 1971, Santa Monica, Calif. Screen, stage and television actor. Nominated for 1947 Academy Award for Best Supporting Actor in Ride the Pink Horse.

Appeared in: **1942** Sherlock Holmes and the Voice of Terror (film debut); Arabian Nights; Pittsburgh; Who Done It? **1943** White Savage; Corvette K-225; Frontier Badman; Crazy House. **1944** The Climax; Phantom Lady; Dead Man's Eyes; Follow the Boys; In Society; Bowery to Broadway; Can't Help Singing. **1945** Patrick the Great; I'll Tell the World; That Daltons Ride Again; Frisco Sal. **1946** A Night in Paradise; Swell Guy; The Dark Mirror. **1947** Singapore; Ride the Pink Horse; Captain from Castile; Johnny O'Clock. **1948** Casbah; Angel in Exile; Key Largo; Force of Evil. **1949** Come to the Stable; Sorrowful Jones; That Midnight Kiss; I Married a Communist. **1950** Kim; The Woman on Pier 13; Toast of New Orleans; The Eagle and the Hawk; The Furies; Dynamite Pass. **1951** Anne of the Indies; The Harlem Globetrotters; The Sellout. **1952** The Merry Widow; Pony Soldier; Macao. **1953** Sombrero. **1954** The Gambler from Natchez; The Adventures of Haji Baba. **1955** The Looters; The Magnificent Matador; Las Vegas Shakedown; Night Freight. **1956** Trapeze; The Conqueror. **1959** John Paul Jones; But Not for Me. **1961** Summer and Smoke. **1968** Stay Away, Joe! **1970** Beneath the Planet of the Apes.

GONDI, HARRY
Born: 1900, Germany. Died: Nov., 1968, Hamburg, Germany. Screen, stage and radio actor.

GONZALES, ARTURO See ZAPATA, SPEEDY

GONZALEZ, GILBERTO
Born: 1906, Mexico. Died: Mar. 21, 1954, Palenque, Chiapas, Mexico (heart attack). Screen actor.

Appeared in: **1933** Viva Villa. **1940** Amor con Amor (Love for Love). **1948** The Pearl. **1948** Captain from Castile. **1952** Stronghold. **1955** The Littlest Outlaw.

GONZALEZ, MARIO TECERO
Born: 1919, Mexico. Died: Aug. 28, 1957, Mexico City, Mexico. Screen and stage actor.

GONZALEZ, MYRTLE
Born: Sept. 28, 1891, Los Angeles, Calif. Died: Oct. 22, 1918, Los Angeles, Calif. (heart disease and pneumonia). Screen and stage actress.

Appeared in: **1913** The Spell; The White Feather. **1914** Tony the Greaser; Anne of the Mines; Her Husband's Friend; The Masked Dancer; Millions for Defense; Ward's Claim. **1915** The Man from the Desert; A Natural Man; The Legend of the Lone Tree; The Chalice of Courage; Through Troubled Waters; The Repentance of Dr. Blimm; The Ebony Casket; The Quarrel; The Offending Kiss; The Bride of the Nancy Lee; The Terrible Truth; Her Last Flirtation; Does It End Right?; Inside Facts; His Golden Grain. **1916** Missy; Her Dream Man; The Gambler; The Wise Man and the Fool; The Secret Foe; Bill's Wife; Miss Blossom; The Windward Anchor; Her Great Part; It Happened in Honolulu; The Secret of the Swamp; The Pinnacle; The Girl of the Lost Lake; The End of the Rainbow; A Romance of Billy Goat Hill. **1917** Captain Alverez; God's Crucible; Mutiny; Southern Justice.

GONZALO, MARIA EDUARDA
Born: 1929, Portugal. Died: Jan. 24, 1955, Lisbon, Portugal (tuberculosis). Screen and stage actress.

GOOD, FRANK B. (Frank Bucher Good)
Born: Oct. 3, 1884, Columbus, Ohio. Died: June 1, 1939, Hollywood, Calif. (heart attack). Cameraman and screen actor. Played in 1911 Biograph auto racing pictures (shorts).

Appeared in: **1912** Love and Vengeance.

GOOD, KIP
Born: 1919. Died: May 1, 1964, Gadsden, Ala. Screen, stage actor and stage director.

Appeared in: **1943** Stage Door Canteen.

GOODALL, GRACE
Born: June 12, 1889, San Francisco, Calif. Died: Sept. 27, 1940. Screen and stage actress.

Appeared in: **1921** Affairs of Anatol; The Easy Road; Moonlight and Honeysuckle; Hearts of Youth. **1922** His Wife's Husband. **1927** The Opening Night. **1934** Lemon Drop Kid; Handy Andy. **1935** The Singing Vagabond; the following shorts: Top Flatt; Thicker Than Water; Pardon My Scotch; Hoi Polloi; Okay Toots!; The Four-Star Border; I'm a Father. **1936** Make Way for a Lady; Pan Handlers (short). **1937** California Straight Ahead. **1938** City Streets; Ankles Away (short).

GOODE, JACK (Irwin Thomas Whittridge)
Born: 1908, Columbus, Ohio. Died: June 24, 1971, New York, N.Y. (acute infectious hepatitis). Screen, stage and television actor. Married to stage dancer and actress Renalda Green.

Appeared in: **1933** Flying Down to Rio. **1935** Top Hat. **1936** Swing Time. **1948** Ruthless.

GOODLIFFE, MICHAEL
Born: 1914, Bebington, England. Died: Mar. 22, 1976, London, England (heart attack). Screen, stage and television actor.

Appeared in: **1949** The Small Back Room (US 1952) (film debut). **1950** The Wooden Horse (US 1951). **1952** Cry, The Beloved Country (aka African Fury—US); The Hour of 13. **1953** Sea Devils; Rob Roy, The Highland Rouge. **1954** Front Page Story (US 1955). **1955** The End of the Affair; Dial 999 (aka The Way Out—US 1956). **1956** The Adventures of Quentin Durward; Wicked As They Come (US 1957); The Battle of the River Plate (aka Pursuit of the Graf Spee—US 1957). **1957** The One That Got Away (US 1958); Fortune is a Woman (aka She Played With Fire—US 1958); Up the Creek. **1958** A Night to Remember (US 1959); The Camp on Blood Island. **1959** The 39 Steps (US 1960). **1960** Conspiracy of Hearts; The Trial of Oscar Wilde (aka The Man With the Green Carnation—US, aka The Green Carnation); Peeping Tom (US 1962); Sink the Bismarck!; Le Testament d'Orphee

(Testament of Orpheus—US 1962, narrator). **1961** The Day The Earth Caught Fire (US 1962); No Love for Johnnie. **1962** Jigsaw (US 1965). **1963** 80,000 Suspects; Man in the Middle (US 1964 aka The Winston Affair); The F20,000 Kiss (US 1964). **1964** Seventh Dawn; 633 Squadron; Woman of Straw; The Gorgon (US 1965). **1965** Von Ryan's Express. **1966** The Jokers (US 1967); The Night of the Generals (US 1967). **1968** The Fixer. **1970** Cromwell. **1927** Hitler, The Last Ten Days. **1974** The Man with the Golden Gun. **1976** To the Devil ... A Daughter.

GOODRICH, AMY (Amy Florench Goodrich)
Born: 1889. Died: July, 1939, Hollywood, Calif. (heart attack). Screen actress. Married to actor Hal Price (dec. 1964).

GOODRICH, CHARLES W.
Born: 1861. Died: Mar. 20, 1931, Norwalk, Conn. Screen and stage actor.

Appeared in: **1926** Show Off (stage and film versions).

GOODRICH, EDNA
Born: Dec. 22, 1883, Logansport, Ind. Died: May 26, 1971, New York, N.Y. Screen actress.

Appeared in: **1915** Armstrong's Wife. **1917** Her Second Husband; Queen X; A Daughter of Maryland; American Maid. **1918** Treason; Who Loved Him Best?; Her Husband's Honor.

GOODRICH, LOUIS (L. G. Abbott Anderson)
Born: 1865, Sandhurst, England. Died: Jan. 31, 1945, London, England. Screen, stage actor and playwright.

Appeared in: **1931** The Sleeping Cardinal (aka Sherlock Holmes' Fatal Hour—US). **1932** The Flag Lieutenant. **1933** The Thirteenth Candle. **1934** The Crimson Candle. **1935** Mr. What's His Name. **1936** Fair Exchange; The Captain's Table.

GOODWIN, BILL
Born: July 28, 1910, San Francisco, Calif. Died: May 9, 1958, Palm Springs, Calif. (heart attack). Screen, radio and television actor. Married to actress Phillippa Hilber.

Appeared in: **1940** Let's Make Music. **1941** Blondie in Society. **1942** Wake Island. **1943** Riding High; So Proudly We Hail; Henry Aldrich Gets Glamour; No Time for Love. **1944** Bathing Beauty. **1945** River Gang; Incendiary Blonde; Spellbound; The Stork Club. **1946** House of Horrors; Earl Carroll Sketchbook; To Each His Own; The Jolson Story. **1947** Hit Parade of 1947; Heaven Only Knows. **1948** Mickey; So This Is New York. **1949** It's a Great Feeling; The Life of Riley. **1950** Tea for Two; Jolson Sings Again. **1952** The First Time. **1954** The Atomic Kid; Lucky Me. **1956** The Opposite Sex; Bundle of Joy. **1958** The Big Beat; Going Steady.

GOODWIN, NAT C.
Born: 1857, Boston, Mass. Died: Jan. 31, 1919, New York, N.Y. Screen actor.

Appeared in: **1912** Oliver Twist; Nathan Hale. **1915** The Master Hand; Business Is Business. **1916** Wall Street Tragedy; The Marriage Bond.

GOODWIN, RUBY BERKLEY
Died: May 31, 1961, Hollywood, Calif. Screen, television actress and author.

Appeared in: **1955** The View from Pompey's Head. **1956** Strange Intruder. **1959** The Alligator People. **1961** Wild in the Country.

GOODWINS, LESLIE
Born: Sept. 17, 1899, London, England. Died: Jan. 8, 1969, Hollywood, Calif. (pneumonia). Screen actor, film director and screenwriter. Appeared in early Christie comedies.

Appeared in: **1934** Derby Decade (short).

GOOLDEN, RICHARD
Born: Feb. 23, 1891, London, England. Died: June 18, 1981, London, England. Screen and stage actor.

Appeared in: **1936** Whom The Gods Love (aka Mozart—US 1940). **1938** Meet Mr. Penny. **1939** Mistaken Identity. **1953** Heights of Danger (US 1962). **1961** In the Doghouse (US 1964). **1963** It's All Happening (aka The Dream Maker—US 1964). **1965** The Amorous Adventures of Moll Flanders. **1966** It! (US 1967). **1970** One More Time.

GORCEY, BERNARD
Born: 1888, Switzerland. Died: Sept. 11, 1955, Hollywood, Calif. (auto accident). Screen and stage actor. Father of actors Leo (dec. 1969) and David Gorcey.

Appeared in: **1928** Abie's Irish Rose. **1940** The Great Dictator. **1941** Out of the Fog. **1942** Joan of Paris. **1943** The Unknown Guest. **1944** Block Busters. **1946** Mr. Hex; In High Gear; Spook Busters; Scareheads; Bowery Bombshell; The French Key; In Fast Company. **1947** Bowery Buckaroos; Hard Boiled Mahoney; News Hounds. **1948** Angels' Alley; No Minor Vices; Jinx Money; Trouble Makers. **1949** Fighting Fools; Angels in Disguise; Hold That Baby; Master Minds. **1950** Blonde Dynamite; Lucky Losers; Blues Busters; Triple Trouble. **1951** Ghost Chasers; Crazy Over Horses; Bowery Battalion; Let's Go Navy; Pickup; Win, Place and Show. **1952** Here Come the Marines; Feudin' Fools; No Holds Barred; Hold That Line; Tell It to the Marines. **1953** Jalopy; Loose in London; Clipped Wings; Private Eyes. **1954** Paris Playboys; Jungle Gents; The Bowery Boys Meet the Monsters. **1955** Bowery to Bagdad; High Society; Jail Busters; Spy Chasers. **1956** Dig That Uranium.

GORCEY, LEO B.
Born: June 3, 1915, New York, N.Y. Died: June 2, 1969, Oakland, Calif. Screen and stage actor. Son of actor Bernard Gorcey (dec. 1955) and brother of actor David Gorcey. One of the original "Dead End Kids."

Appeared in: **1937** Dead End (stage and film versions); Mannequin; Portia on Trial. **1938** Crime School; Angels With Dirty Faces. **1939** Hell's Kitchen; Angels Wash Their Faces; Battle of City Hall; They Made Me a Criminal; The Dead End Kids on Dress Parade (aka Dress Parade). **1940** That Gang of Mine; Boys of the City; Gallant Sons; Junior G-Men (serial); Angels With Broken Wings; Invisible Stripes. **1941** Flying Wild; Pride of the Bowery; Road to Zanzibar; Out of the Fog; Spooks Run Wild; Bowery Blitzkrieg; Down in San Diego; Sea Raiders (serial). **1942** Mr. Wise Guy; Sunday Punch; Let's Get Tough; Smart Alecks; 'Neath Brooklyn Bridge; Maisie Gets Her Man; Born to Sing; Jr. G-Men of the Air (serial). **1943** Clancy Street Boys; Destroyer; Mr. Muggs Steps Out. **1944** Block Busters; Follow the Leader; Million Dollar Kid; Bowery Champs. **1945** One Exciting Night; Docks of New York; Mr. Muggs Rides Again; Come Out Fighting; Midnight Manhunt. **1946** In Fast Company; Mr. Hex; Bowery Bombshell; Spook Busters; Live Wires. **1947** Hard-Boiled Mahoney; News Hounds; Pride of Broadway; Bowery Buckaroos. **1948** So This Is New York; Jinx Money; Trouble Makers; Angel's Alley; Smugglers Cove. **1949** Hold That Baby; Angels in Disguise; Master Minds; Fighting Fools. **1950** Blonde Dynamite; Blues Busters; Triple Trouble; Lucky Losers. **1951** Win, Place and Show; Ghost Chasers; Bowery Battalion; Crazy Over Horses; Let's Go Navy. **1952** Hold That Line; Here Come the Marines; Feudin' Fools; No Holds Barred; Tell It to the Marines. **1953** Jalopy; Loose in London; Clipped Wings; Private Eyes. **1954** The Bowery Boys Meet the Monsters; Paris Playboys; Jungle Gents. **1955** Bowery to Bagdad; High Society; Spy Chasers; Jail Busters. **1956** Crashing Las Vegas; Dig That Uranium. **1957** Spook Chasers; Hold That Hypnotist; Looking for Danger; Up in Smoke. **1958** In the Money. **1963** It's a Mad, Mad, Mad, Mad World. **1965** Second Fiddle to a String Guitar. **1969** The Phynx.

GORDON, A. GEORGE
Born: 1882. Died: Dec. 27, 1953, Chicago, Ill. (heart ailment). Screen, stage actor and stage producer. Appeared in silents with Selig Poliscop Corp.

GORDON, BERT (aka THE MAD RUSSIAN)
Born: 1898, New York, N.Y. Died: Nov. 30, 1974, Duarte, Calif. (cancer). Screen, stage, vaudeville and radio actor. Appeared with his brother Harry Gordon in an act billed as "Stage Struck Kids" and later in an act billed as "Bert and Harry Gordon."

Appeared in: **1935** She Gets Her Man. **1937** New Faces of 1937. **1938** Outside of Paradise. **1939** Laugh Your Blues Away; Let's Have Fun. **1941** Sing for Your Supper. **1945** How Do You Do?

GORDON, BOBBY
Born: 1904. Died: Feb. 17, 1973, New York. Screen, vaudeville actor, comedian and comedy writer. Appeared in vaudeville as part of "Gordon, Reed and King" team. Do not confuse with other Gordons with similar first names.

GORDON, C. HENRY (Henry Racke)
Born: June 17, 1883, New York, N.Y. Died: Dec. 3, 1940, Los Angeles, Calif. (result of leg amputation). Screen and stage actor. Entered films in 1911.

Appeared in: **1930** A Devil With Women; Renegades. **1931** The Black

Camel; Honor of the Family; Young As You Feel; Woman of Experience; Charlie Chan Carries On; Once a Sinner; Hush Money. **1932** State's Attorney; The Strange Love of Molly Louvain; Washington Masquerade; Miss Pinkerton; Jewel Robbery; Roar of the Dragon; Kongo; Hell's Highway; Thirteen Women; Scarlet Dawn; Rasputin and the Empress; Doomed Battalion; Scarface; Mata Hari; Gay Caballero; The Crooked Circle. **1933** Whistling in the Dark; Secret of Madame Blanche; Clear All Wires; Made on Broadway; Gabriel Over the White House; Storm at Daybreak; Night Flight; Turn Back the Clock; Penthouse; Stage Mother; The Chief; The Devil's in Love; Broadway Thru a Keyhole; Advice to the Lovelorn; The Women in His Life. **1934** Straight Is the Way; Fugitive Lovers; This Side of Heaven; Hide-Out; Stamboul Quest; Death on a Diamond; Men in White; Lazy River. **1935** Lives of a Bengal Lancer; The Great Hotel Murder; Pursuit; The Crusades; The Big Broadcast of 1936. **1936** Professional Soldier; Under Two Flags; Hollywood Boulevard; The Big Game; Love Letters of a Star; Charge of the Light Brigade. **1937** Charlie Chan at the Olympics; Trouble in Morocco; The River of Missing Men; Trapped by G-Men; Sophie Lang Goes West; Stand-In; Conquest. **1938** Yellow Jack; Tarzan's Revenge; The Black Doll; Sharpshooters; The Long Shot; Adventure in Sahara; Invisible Enemy. **1939** Heritage of the Desert; Man of Conquest; Charlie Chan in City in Darkness; The Return of the Cisco Kid; Trapped in the Sky. **1940** Passport to Alcatraz; Kit Carson; Charlie Chan at the Wax Museum; Women in Hiding (short); You the People (short).

GORDON, COLIN
Born: Apr. 27, 1911, Ceylon. Died: Oct. 4, 1972, Haslemere, England. Screen, stage, radio and television actor.

Appeared in: **1948** Bond Street (US 1950); The Winslow Boy (US 1950). **1949** Traveller's Joy (US 1951); Edward My Son. **1950** The Happiest Days of Your Life. **1951** The Man in the White Suit (US 1952); Circle of Danger; The Third Visitor; Green Grow the Rushes. **1952** Folly to Be Wise; The Hour of 13. **1953** The Heart of the Matter (US 1954); Grand National Night (aka Wicked Wife—US 1955); Innocents in Paris (US 1955). **1955** Escapade (US 1957); Little Red Monkey (aka The Case of the Red Monkey—US). **1956** The Green Man (US 1957). **1957** The Key. **1958** Virgin Island (US 1960); The One That Got Away; Twelve Desperate Hours; The Safecracker. **1959** Alive and Kicking (US 1964); Please Turn Over (US 1960); Bobbikins (US 1960); The Mouse That Roared; The Doctor's Dilemma. **1960** The Day They Robbed the Bank of England. **1961** Don't Bother to Knock (aka Why Bother to Knock—US 1964); Very Important Person (aka A Coming Out Party—US 1962); In the Doghouse (US 1964); Three on a Spree. **1962** The Boys (US 1963); Night of the Eagle (aka Burn, Witch, Burn—US); Crooks Anonymous (US 1963); Strongroom. **1963** Bitter Harvest; The Running Man. **1964** Alley France! (aka The Counterfeit Constable—US 1966); The Pink Panther. **1965** The Liquidator (US 1966). **1966** The Great St. Trinian's Train Robbery (US 1967); The Family Way (US 1967); The Psychopath. **1967** Trygon Factor (US 1969); Casino Royale. **1968** Don't Raise the Bridge, Lower the River; Subterfuge. **1970** Body Beneath.

GORDON, CONSTANCE "KITTY"
Born: 1888, England. Died: May 26, 1974, Brentwood, N.Y. Screen, stage, vaudeville and television actress.

Appeared in: **1917** No Man's Land; Her Own; Diamonds and Pearls. **1918** The Divine Sacrifice; The Interloper; Merely Players; Stolen Orders; The Purple Lily; Tinsel. **1919** Playthings of Passion; The Scar; Adele; The Unveiling Hand.

GORDON, EDWARD R.
Born: 1886. Died: Nov. 10, 1938, Hollywood, Calif. Screen actor and film director.

Appeared in: **1927** Gun-Hand Garrison; Ridin' Luck; Wild Born.

GORDON, G. SWAYNE
Born: 1880. Died: June 23, 1949, New York, N.Y. Screen, stage, radio and vaudeville actor. Appeared in vaudeville with his wife, Spain Thorne.

Appeared in: **1943** Follies Girl.

GORDON, GAVIN
Born: Nov. 24, 1901, Ayr, Scotland. Died: Nov. 18, 1970, Londong, England (coronary thrombosis). Screen, stage actor, vocalist and composer. Do not confuse with U.S. actor with same name.

GORDON, GLEN
Born: 1916. Died: Sept., 1977, Hollywood, Calif. (cancer). Screen, stage and television actor.

Appeared in: **1955** Cell 2455, Death Row; Finger Man.

GORDON, GLORIA
Born: c. 1881. Died: Nov. 23, 1962, Hollywood, Calif. Screen and television actress. Mother of actor Gale Gordon.

Appeared in: **1926** Dancing Days; Exclusive Rights. **1949** My Friend Irma. **1953** Beneath the 12 Mile Reef; Titanic; Niagara. **1955** A Man Called Peter.

GORDON, GRANT
Died: July 7, 1972. Screen actor.

Appeared in: **1968** The Subject Was Roses.

GORDON, HAL
Born: Apr. 18, 1894, London, England. Died: 1946, England?. Screen and stage actor.

Appeared in: **1928** Adam's Apple (aka Honeymoon Ahead—US). **1929** When Knights Were Bold. **1930** The Windjammer. **1931** Old Soldiers Never Die; Poor Old Bill; Out of the Blue; Up For the Cup; Bill and Coo. **1932** Money for Nothing; Tonight's the Night; Partner's Please; Help Yourself; The Bad Companions; Indiscretions of Eve; Brother Alfred; Strip, Strip, Horray!; Lucky Girl; Insult; Old Spanish Customers; The Last Coupon; His Wife's Mother; Josser in the Army; Money Talks; For the Love of Mike; Lord Camber's Ladies; Let Me Explain Dear; The New Hotel; The Strangler; Sleepless Nights. **1933** Their Night Out; Crime on the Hill; The Pride of the Force; Facing the Music (US 1934); Hawleys of High Street; A Southern Maid. **1934** My Song Goes Round the World; Wishes; Lost in the Legion; Sometimes Good; The Outcast; Master and Man; A Political Party; Happy. **1935** The Deputy Drummer; Captain Bill; Dance Band; Invitation to the Waltz; Lend Me Your Wife; Play Up the Band; 18 Minutes; Dandy Dick. **1936** Southern Roses; Queen of Hearts; The Man Behind the Mask; One Good Turn; The Amazing Quest of Ernest Bliss (aka Romance and Riches—US 1937); It's in the Bag; Keep Your Seats Please; No Escape; Dusty Ermine (aka Hideout in the Alps—US 1938). **1937** Keep Fit. **1938** Father O'Nine; Dead Men Tell No Tales (US 1939); It's in the Air (aka George Takes the Air—US 1940); We're Going to be Rich. **1939** Come on George. **1940** Let George Do it; Spare a Copper.

GORDON, HAROLD
Born: 1919. Died: Jan. 19, 1959, New York, N.Y. Screen, stage, opera and television actor.

Appeared in: **1952** Viva Zapata; The Jazz Singer; The Iron Mistress. **1954** Bengal Brigade. **1955** East of Eden; Yellowneck.

GORDON, HARRIS
Born: July 4, 1884, Glenside, Pa. Died: Mar. 31, 1947, Burbank, Calif. (heart attack). Screen and stage actor.

Appeared in: **1921** Live and Let Live. **1922** Burning Sands; Out of the Silent North; The Woman Who Walked Alone; A Wonderful Wife. **1923** Hollywood. **1924** The Dawn of a Tomorrow. **1925** Easy Going Gordon; Let Women Alone; Romance and Rustlers; Too Much Youth. **1934** Our Daily Bread.

GORDON, HARRY
Born: 1894, Aberdeen, Scotland. Died: Jan. 21, 1957, Glasgow, Scotland (thrombosis). Screen and stage actor. Married to actress/dancer Jessie Dudgeon. Do not confuse with actor (dec. 1948).

GORDON, HARRY G.
Born: 1884, Buffalo, N.Y. Died: Nov. 20, 1948. Screen, stage and vaudeville actor. Do not confuse with Scottish actor (dec. 1957).

GORDON, HUNTLY
Born: 1897, Montreal, Quebec, Canada. Died: Dec. 7, 1956, Hollywood, Calif. (heart attack). Screen and radio actor.

Appeared in: **1918** The Common Cause; Our Mrs. McChesney. **1921** Chilvalrous Charley; Enchantment; The Girl From Nowhere; Society Snobs; Tropical Love; At the Stage Door. **1922** Beyond the Rainbow; His Wife's Husband; Man Wanted; Reckless Youth; What Fools Men Are; What's Wrong With the Women?; When the Desert Calls; Why Announce Your Marriage?. **1923** Bluebeard's Eighth Wife; The Famous Mrs. Fair; Chastity; Cordelia the Magnificent; Male Wanted; Pleasure Mad; The Wanters; Her Fatal Millions; The Social Code; Your Friend and Mine. **1924** The Enemy Sex; Shadows of Paris; True as Steel; Wine; Darling Love; Married Flirts. **1925** Golden Cocoon; The Love Hour; The Great Divide; Never the Twain Shall Meet; My Wife and I; The Wife Who Wasn't Wanted. **1926** Gilded Butterfly; Her Second Chance; Silken Shackles; Lost at Sea; Other Women's Husbands; The Golden Web. **1927** The Sensation Seekers; The Truthful Sex; One Increasing Purpose; Don't Tell the Wife. **1928**

Outcast; Sinners in Love; A Certain Young Man; Name the Women; Their Hour; Our Dancing Daughters; Sally's Shoulder; Gypsy of the North. **1929** The Marriage Playground; Melody Lane; Scandal. **1930** How I Play Golf—The Niblick (short); Anybody's Woman; Fox Movietone Follies of 1930. **1932** Phantom Express; Night World; From Broadway to Cheyenne; The King Murder; Red Haired Alibi; Speed Madness; The All American; Race Track; Sally of the Subway. **1933** Midnight Warning; Sailor Be Good; Secrets; Justice Takes a Holiday; The World Gone Mad; Corruption; Only Yesterday. **1934** The Dancing Man; Their Big Moment; Embarrassing Moments; Bombay Mail. **1935** The Irish in Us; The Spanish Cape Mystery; It Happened in New York; Front Page Woman; Circumstantial Evidence. **1936** Klondike Annie; Daniel Boone; Yours for the Asking. **1937** China Passage; Stage Door; Idol of the Crowds; Portia on Trial. **1938** Gangster's Boy. **1939** Mr. Wong in Chinatown. **1940** Phantom of Chinatown; The Lady With Red Hair.

GORDON, JACK

Born: Jan. 15, 1903, Ft. Worth, Tex. Died: Aug. 31, 1974. Screen actor.

Appeared in: **1930** Sagebrush Politics. **1945** Crime Incorporated. **1949** Mr. Soft Touch.

GORDON, JAMES

Born: 1881, Pittsburgh, Pa. Died: May 12, 1941, Hollywood, Calif. (operation complications). Screen and stage actor. Married to actress Mabel Van Buren (dec. 1947).

Appeared in: **1921** The Bait; The Man From Lost River; The Old Swimmin' Hole; Sunset Jones; Trailin'. **1922** Man's Size; The Game Chicken; The Love Gambler; Nancy From Nowhere; On the High Seas; Self-Made Man. **1923** Defying Destiny; Grail. **1924** The Courageous Coward; Hearts of Oak; The Iron Horse; The Man Who Came Back; Wanderer of the Wasteland; The White Sin. **1925** Beauty and the Bad Man; Tumbleweeds. **1926** The Buckaroo Kid; Devil's Dice; Flying High; The Ice Flood; Miss Nobody; Rose of the Tenements; The Social Highwayman. **1927** Babe Comes Home; Publicity Madness; Tongues of Scandal; The War Horse; The Wolf's Fangs; Cancelled Debts; Wanted—a Coward. **1928** The Escape. **1929** Masked Emotions. **1931** The Bachelor Father; The Front Page.

GORDON, JULIA SWAYNE

Born: 1879, Hollywood, Calif. Died: May 28, 1933, Los Angeles, Calif. Stage and screen actress.

Appeared in: **1910** Twelfth Night. **1911** The Missing Will; Lady Godiva; Tale of Two Cities. **1912** The Troublesome Stepdaughters; Cardinal Wolsey; Stenographers Wanted; Coronets and Hearts; The Woman Haters; The Gamblers; Two Women and Two Men. **1913** The Vengeance of Durand (aka The Two Portraits); Red and White Roses; The Tiger Lily; Beau Brummel. **1914** Two Women; The Battle of the Weak; The Sins of the Mothers; The Hidden Letters; The Painted World; Four Thirteen; A Million Bid; He Never Knew; The Shadow of the Past; Uncle Bill. **1915** The Juggernaut. **1916** My Lady's Slipper; The Suspect; The Daring of Diana. **1917** The Hawk; The Soul Master; The Maelstrom (aka Millionaire Hallet's Adventure); Clover's Rebellion; The Message of the Mouse; Her Right to Live; A Son of the Hills. **1918** Love Watches. **1919** The Girl Problem; The Bramble Bush. **1921** Behind the Masks; Burn 'Em Up Barnes; Handcuffs or Kisses; Love, Hate and a Woman; The Passionate Pilgrim; Shams of Society; The Silver Lining; Why Girls Leave Home. **1922** The Darling of the Rich; How Women Love; My Old Kentucky Home; The Road to Arcady; Till We Meet Again; What's Wrong With the Women?; When Desert Calls; Wildness of Youth; Women Men Marry. **1923** Scaramouche; Dark Secrets; The Tie That Binds; You Can't Fool Your Wife. **1925** Lights of Old Broadway; Not So Long Ago; The Wheel. **1926** Bride of the Storm; Diplomacy; Early to Wed; The Far Cry. **1927** Children of Divorce; Heaven on Earth; Wings; It; King of Kings. **1928** Hearts of Men; Road House; The Scarlet Dove; The Smart Set; 13 Washington Square; Three Week Ends. **1929** The Eternal Woman; The Younger Generation; The Divine Lady; The Girl in the Glass Cage; The Viking; Is Everybody Happy?; Gold Diggers of Broadway; Scandal. **1930** The Dude Wrangler; Today; Dumbbells in Ermine; For the Love O' Lil. **1931** Misbehaving Ladies; Primrose Path; Drums of Jeopardy; Captain Applejack. **1932** Secrets of the French Police; The Golden West; Broken Lullaby; False Madonna. **1933** Hello, Everybody!

GORDON, KELLY

Born: 1933. Died: Aug. 1, 1981, Los Angeles, Calif. (cancer). Screen actor, musician and composer.

Appeared in: **1955** Daddy Long Legs. **1959** Dadd-O. **1976** Once Upon a Girl.

GORDON, LEON

Born: Jan. 12, 1894, Brighton, England. Died: Jan. 4, 1960, Hollywood, Calif. (heart ailment). Screen, stage actor, film director, film producer, stage director, stage producer, screenwriter, playwright and author.

Appeared in: **1916** Then I'll Come Back to You. **1923** Adam and Eva. **1924** Sandra. **1930** White Cargo (stage and film versions).

GORDON, MACK (Morris Gittler)

Born: 1905, Warsaw, Poland. Died: Feb. 28, 1959, New York, N.Y. Screen, vaudeville actor, film producer and composer.

Appeared in: **1933** Sitting Pretty. **1936** Collegiate. **1949** You're My Everything.

GORDON, MARY

Born: 1882, Scotland. Died: Aug. 23, 1963, Pasadena, Calif. Screen and radio actress. Played housekeeper for Sherlock Holmes in films and radio, 1939-1946.

Appeared in: **1917** The Secret Life of Walter Mitty. **1925** The People vs. Nancy Preston; Tessie, The Home Maker. **1926** Black Paradise. **1927** Clancy's Kosher Wedding; Naughty Nanette. **1928** The Old Code. **1929** Dynamite; The Saturday Night Kid. **1930** When the Wind Blows (short); Dance With Me. **1931** Subway Express; The Black Camel. **1932** Dancing in the Dark; The Texas Cyclone; Almost Married; Pack Up Your Troubles. **1933** Nature in the Wrong (short); Design for Living. **1934** Beloved; The Little Minister. **1935** The Whole Town's Talking; I'm a Father (short); Mutiny On the Bounty; Vanessa, Her Love Story; Bonnie Scotland; The Bride of Frankenstein; The Irish in Us; Waterfront Lady. **1936** After the Thin Man; Share the Wealth (short); Yellowstone; Way Out West; Laughing Irish Eyes; Forgotten Faces; Mary of Scotland; Stage Struck; Great Guy. **1937** You Can't Have Everything; The Great O'Malley; The Plough and the Stars; Meet the Boy Friend; Double Wedding; Pick a Star; A Damsel in Distress. **1938** Angels With Dirty Faces; City Streets; Lady Behave; Kidnapped. **1939** Daytime Wife; Off the Record; Tell No Tales; Wings of the Navy; Code of the Streets; Tail Spin; She Married a Cop; Parents on Trial; Rulers of the Sea; The Hound of the Baskervilles; Captain Fury; The Adventures of Sherlock Holmes. **1940** The Doctor Takes a Wife; Tear Gas Squad; Joe and Ethel Turp Call on the President; The Last Alarm; I Take This Oath; Queen of the Mob; When the Daltons Rode; No, No, Nanette; Nobody's Children; My Son, My Son; Marshal of Mesa City. **1941** Sealed Lips; Unexpected Uncle; Pot O'Gold; Flight from Destiny; Appointment for Love; Riot Squad; The Invisible Woman; Borrowed Hero. **1942** Gentleman Jim; The Mummy's Tomb; Sherlock Holmes and the Voice of Terror; Sherlock Holmes and the Secret Weapon; Bombay Clipper; Meet the Stewarts; Dr. Broadway; Fly by Night; It Happened in Flatbush; Boss of Big Town. **1943** You're a Lucky Fellow, Mr. Smith; Forever and a Day; Half Way to Shanghai; Sarong Girl; Sherlock Holmes Faces Death; Keep 'Em Sluggin'; Two Tickets to London; Here Comes Kelly. **1944** Sherlock Holmes and the Spider Woman; Follow the Leader; Hat Check Honey; Hollywood Canteen; Whispering Footsteps; The Racket Man; Smart Guy; The Hour Before the Dawn; The Pearl of Death; The Last Ride. **1945** Divorce; See My Lawyer; Captain Eddie; The Woman in Green; Strange Confession; The Body Snatchers; Kitty. **1946** Dressed to Kill; Shadows Over Chinatown; The Dark Horse; In Fast Company; Sing While You Dance; The Hoodlum Saint; Little Giant; Sentimental Journey. **1947** Exposed; The Invisible Wall. **1948** Fort Apache; Highway 13; The Strange Mrs. Crane; Angel's Alley. **1949** Deputy Marshal; Shamrock Hill; Haunted Trails. **1950** West of Wyoming.

GORDON, MAUD TURNER

Born: May 10, 1868, Franklin, Ind. Died: Jan. 12, 1940, Los Angeles, Calif. (pneumonia). Stage and screen actress.

Appeared in: **1915** Kreutzer Sonata. **1917** Her Better Self. **1918** Mrs. Dane's Defense. **1921** Beyond Price; Enchantment; The Price of Possession. **1922** Back Home and Broke; Women Men Marry; Broadway Rose. **1923** Homeward Bound. **1924** Born Rich. **1925** The Early Bird; The Little French Girl. **1926** Mismates; The Palm Beach Girl. **1927** Home Made; Cheating Cheaters; The Wizard. **1928** Just Married; Hot News; The Naughty Duchess; Sporting Goods. **1929** The Glad Rag Doll; Illusion; The Hottentot; The Last of Mrs. Cheyney; Sally; The Marriage Playground; Kid Gloves. **1930** Lawful Larceny; The Florodora Girl. **1931** Ladies' Man; High Stakes. **1932** Careless Lady; Shopworn; Sinners in the Sun; Mata Hari; Back Street. **1934** She Loves Me Not; Flirtation Walk; Man With Two Faces. **1935** Alias Mary Dow; Living on Velvet; Black Sheep; Personal Maid's Secret. **1936** After the Thin Man. **1937** The Emperor's Candlesticks; Wings Over Honolulu. **1938** Sweethearts.

GORDON, NORA
Born: 1894, England. Died: May 11, 1970, London, England. Screen and television actress. Married to actor Leonard Sharp (dec. 1958).

Appeared in: **1948** The Fallen Idol (US 1949). **1950** Woman in Question (aka Five Angles on Murder—US 1953). **1951** Blackmailed; Night Was Our Friend. **1952** A Woman's Angle (US 1954). **1955** The Glass Cage (aka The Glass Tomb—US). **1959** Horrors of the Black Museum. **1964** Carry on Spying. **1965** The Nanny.

GORDON, PAUL (Thomas Achelis)
Born: 1886, Brooklyn, N.Y. Died: May 3, 1929, Florence, Italy. Screen actor. Married to actress Ann Mason (dec. 1948).

GORDON, PETER
Born: 1888. Died: May 25, 1943, Los Angeles, Calif. Screen, vaudeville actor and acrobat. Entered films in 1916. Appeared in Vitagraph shorts with Larry Lemon.

Appeared in: **1934** The Live Ghost (short). **1935** Tit for Tat (short).

GORDON, RICHARD H. (Richard H. Towey)
Born: 1893, Philadelphia, Pa. Died: Sept. 20, 1956, Hollywood, Calif. (after opertion). Screen and television actor. Entered films in 1918. Was president of Screen Extras Guild from 1948 to 1956.

Appeared in: **1925** Romance Road; The Flame Fighter (serial). **1929** Synthetic Sin; Words and Music. **1944** Charlie Chan in Black Magic. **1945** The Cisco Kid in Old New Mexico. **1946** The Best Years of Our Lives. **1947** The Senator Was Indiscreet; Repeat Performance; 13 Rue Madeleine. **1951** St. Benny the Dip. **1952** Somebody Loves Me. **1956** The Birds and the Bees.

GORDON, ROBERT (Robert Gordon Duncan)
Born: 1895, Kans. Died: Oct. 26, 1971, Victorville, Calif. Screen actor. Entered films in 1917.

Appeared in: **1917** Tom Sawyer. **1918** Huck and Tom; Missing. **1921** If Women Only Knew. **1922** The Super Sex; The Rosary. **1923** The Greatest Menace; The Mysterious Witness; Main Street. **1924** The Night Message; The Wildcat; Borrowed Husbands. **1925** Danger Signal; Night Ship; On the Threshold; Shattered Lives. **1926** Hearts and Spangles; King of the Pack.

GORDON, ROY
Born: 1896. Died: Oct. 12, 1978, Los Angeles, Calif. (cancer). Screen, stage actor and drama coach. Do not confuse with actor of same name (dec. 1972).

GORDON, ROY (Roy Wells Gordon)
Born: Oct. 18, 1884, Ohio. Died: July 23, 1972, Sherman Oaks, Calif. Screen and television actor. Do not confuse with actor of same name (dec. 1978).

GORDON, VERA
Born: June 11, 1886, Russia. Died: May 8, 1948, Beverly Hills, Calif. Screen, stage and vaudeville actress. Entered films in 1919.

Appeared in: **1920** Humoresque; North Wind's Malice. **1921** The Greatest Love. **1922** The Good Provider; Your Best Friend. **1923** Potash and Perlmutter. **1924** In Hollywood with Potash and Perlmutter. **1926** Cohens and Kellys; Millionaires; Sweet Daddies; Private Izzy Murphy; Kosher Kitty Kelly. **1928** The Cohens and the Kellys in Paris; Four Walls. **1929** The Cohens and the Kellys in Atlantic City. **1930** Madam Satan; The Cohens and Kellys in Scotland; The Cohens and the Kellys in Africa. **1931** Fifty Million Frenchmen. **1934** When Strangers Meet. **1937** Michael O'Halloran. **1938** You and Me. **1942** The Living Ghost; The Big Street. **1946** Abie's Irish Rose.

GORDONI, ARTHUR (Arthur Gordon, aka ARTHUR GORDINI)
Born: 1893. Died: Aug. 11, 1966, Beverly Hills, Calif. Screen, stage actor, singer and pianist. Married to stage actress Nora Bayes (dec. 1928).

Appeared in: **1921** Beyond Price; Why Girls Leave Home. **1923** The Net.

GORE, ROSA
Born: 1867. Died: Feb. 4, 1941, Hollywood, Calif. Screen, stage and vaudeville actress. Appeared in vaudeville with her husband, Alexander Lyon, in an act billed as "Crimmins and Gore." Entered films with Pathe in 1912.

Appeared in: **1921** Colorado; The Mistress of Shenstone. **1922** A Dangerous Game. **1923** The Town Scandal; Vanity Fair. **1924** Half-A-Dollar Bill; Hold Your Breath; Madonna of the Streets. **1925**

The Million Dollar Handicap; Seven Days. **1926** The Adorable Deceiver; Three Weeks in Paris; Lovey Mary. **1927** The Man from Hardpan; Play Safe; The Prairie King; The Royal American; Stranded. **1928** Anybody Here Seen Kelly?; The Head Man; That's My Daddy. **1929** Blue Skies; Shrimps for a Day (short).

GORGEOUS GEORGE (George Raymond Wagner)
Born: 1915. Died: Dec. 25, 1963, Los Angeles, Calif. (heart attack). Professional wrestler and televison, screen actor.

Appeared in: **1949** Alias the Champ.

GORMAN, CHARLES
Born: 1865. Died: Jan. 25, 1928. Screen actor.

Appeared in: **1921** Bare Knuckles; The Primal Law; The Devil Within. **1927** The Gay Retreat. **1929** The Far Call.

GORMAN, ERIC
Born: 1886. Died: Nov. 24, 1971, Dublin, Ireland. Screen, stage and television actor.

Appeared in: **1949** Saints and Sinners. **1952** The Quiet Man. **1957** The Rising Moon (aka The Majesty of the Law).

GORMAN, STEPHANIE
Born: June 11, 1949. Died: Aug. 5, 1965, Los Angeles, Calif. (murdered). Screen actress and dancer.

Appeared in: **1963** Bye Bye Birdie.

GORMAN, TOM
Born: 1908. Died: Oct. 2, 1971, Flushing, N.Y. (pulmonary embolism). Screen, stage, televison actor and gag writer. Married to actress Madeleine Hooley (dec. 1977).

Appeared in: **1957** Edge of the City; 12 Angry Men. **1968** The Detective; Pretty Poison.

GORSS, SAUL M.
Born: 1908. Died: Sept. 10, 1966, Los Angeles, Calif. (heart attack). Screen actor and stuntman. Entered films in 1933.

Appeared in: **1936** Bullets or Ballots; Sons O' Guns; God's Country and the Woman. **1940** Brother Orchid; The Fighting 69th; They Drive By Night; Til We Meet Again; Flowing Gold. **1941** Dive Bomber; The Bride Came C.O.D. **1943** Air Force. **1944** The Thin Man Goes Home. **1946** Angel on My Shoulder; The Razor's Edge. **1947** They Won't Believe Me. **1948** The Three Musketeers. **1949** Take Me Out to the Ball Game. **1951** His Kind of Woman. **1952** Blackbeard the Pirate. **1954** The Bounty Hunter. **1955** Unchained. **1956** Tea and Sympathy; Yaqui Drums. **1957** Baby Face Nelson. **1958** Legion of the Doomed; Bullwhip. **1959** Warlock. **1960** Spartacus. **1966** Murderer's Row. **1967** Red Tomahawk.

GOSFIELD, MAURICE
Born: 1913. Died: Oct. 19, 1964, Saranac Lake, N.Y. Screen, stage, television and radio actor.

Appeared in: **1947** Kiss of Death. **1948** The Naked City. **1961** Teenage Millionaire. **1963** The Thrill of It All.

GOSFORD, ALICE PECKHAM
Born: 1886. Died: Jan. 23, 1919, New York, N.Y. Screen actress.

GOSNELL, EVELYN
Born: 1896, Ill. Died: Nov. 11, 1947, New York, N.Y. (injuries from a fall). Stage and screen actress.

Appeared in: **1923** Under the Red Robe.

GOSTANIAN, JOSEPH A. (Joseph Ara Gostanian)
Born: 1940, San Francisco, Calif.? Died: July 9, 1981, San Francisco, Calif. (lung cancer). Screen actor, stage director, screenwriter and playwright.

Appeared in: **1973** Magnum Force.

GOTT, BARBARA
Born: Stirling, Scotland. Died: Nov. 18, 1944, England? Screen and stage actress.

Appeared in: **1927** Easy Virtue (US 1928); Downhill (aka When Boys Leave Home—US 1928). **1928** Not Quite a Lady; Glorious Youth (aka Eileen of the Trees). **1929** That Brute Simmons; Paradise. **1929** Mr. Smith Wakes Up; Ringing the Changes (aka The Crooked Suitcase); Lily of Killarney. **1930** Compromising Daphne (aka Compromised!—US

1931); Lord Richard in the Pantry; Bedrock; At the Villa Rose (aka Mystery at the Villa Rose—US); The Night Porter; The House of the Arrow. **1931** The Sport of Kings; The Professional Guest; The Flying Fool; Sally in Our Alley. **1932** The Water Gypsies; A Safe Proposition; Born Lucky. **1933** The Crime at Blossoms; The Good Companions; Great Stuff; Cleaning Up. **1934** Song at Eventide; The Medium. **1935** The Ghost Walks; Children of the Fog. **1936** The Beloved Vagabond.

GOTTLER, ARCHIE
Born: May 14, 1896, New York, N.Y. Died: June 24, 1959, Hollywood, Calif. Screen actor, film director, stage director and songwriter.

Appeared in: **1928** His Songs are Sung in a Million Homes (short). **1929** Fox Movietone Follies of 1929.

GOTTSCHALK, FERDINAND
Born: 1869, London, England. Died: Nov. 17, 1944, London, England. Screen, stage actor and author.

Appeared in: **1923** Zaza. **1930** Many Happy Returns (short). **1931** Tonight or Never. **1932** Without Honor; Land of the Wanted Men; Doomed Battalion; The Sign of the Cross; Grand Hotel. **1933** Parole Girl; Ex-Lady; Ann Vickers; Gold Diggers of 1933; Berkeley Square; Grand Slam; Goodbye Again; Girl Missing; Warrior's Husband; She Had to Say Yes; Female; Midnight Club. **1934** Cleopatra; Madame Du Barry; The Notorious Sophie Lang; King Kelly of the U.S.A.; I Sell Anything; One Exciting Adventure; Nana; Bombay Mail; Horse Play; The Witching Hours; Long Lost Father; Gambling Lady; Upper World; Sing Sing Nights. **1935** Secret of the Chateau; I Am a Thief; The Man Who Reclaimed His Head; Folies Bergere; Night Life of the Gods; Clive of India; Les Miserables; Break of Hearts; Vagabond Lady; Here Comes the Band; The Gay Deception; The Man Who Broke the Bank at Monte Carlo; The Melody Lingers On; Peter Ibbetson. **1936** Bunker Bean; The White Legion; The Garden of Allah; The Man I Marry; That Girl from Paris; Along Came Love. **1937** The Crime Nobody Saw; Cafe Metropole; Ali Baba Goes to Town; I'll Take Romance. **1938** The Adventures of Marco Polo; Romance in the Dark; Stolen Heaven; Josette. **1944** The Sign of the Cross (revised version of 1932 film).

GOTTSCHALK, JOACHIM
Born: 1904, Calau/Niederlausitz, Germany. Died: 1941, Berlin, Germany. Screen and stage actor.

Appeared in: **1938** Du und Ich. **1939** Flucht ins Dunkel; Aufruhr in Damaskus (Tumult in Damascus); Eine Frau wie Du. **1940** Das Maedchen von Fano; Ein Leben Lang. **1941** Die Schwedische Nachtigall (The Swedish Nightingale).

GOUGH, JOHN
Born: Sept. 22, 1897, Boston, Mass. Died: June 30, 1968, Hollywood, Calif. (cancer). Screen and stage actor. Entered films in 1916.

Appeared in: **1916** A Studio Satire; In the Land of the Tortilla; The Dreamer; A Dream or Two Ago. **1918** Ann's Finish. **1921** The Girl in the Taxi. **1922** Gleam O'Dawn; Up and at 'Em. **1924** Silk Stocking Sal. **1925** Alias Mary Flynn; Border Justice; High and Handsome; Three Wise Crooks; Midnight Molly; When Love Grows Cold; Broadway Lady; Smooth as Satin. **1926** Secret Orders; A Poor Girl's Romance; Flaming Waters. **1927** The Gorilla; Ain't Love Funny?; Hook and Ladder No. 9; Judgement of the Hills. **1928** The Street of Sin; The Circus Kid; The Haunted House; Air Legion. **1930** Sarah and Son. **1935** Two for Tonight.

GOULD, ALAN
Born: 1948. Died: Jan. 30, 1980, New York, N.Y. (influenza). Screen and stage actor.

Appeared in: **1979** Time of the Eagle.

GOULD, BILLY (William Gould)
Born: 1869, New York, N.Y. Died: Feb. 1, 1950, New York, N.Y. (cancer). Screen, stage, minstrel and vaudeville actor. Appeared in vaudeville with Valeska Suratt. Do not confuse with actor William Gould (dec. 1960).

Appeared in: **1924** The Great White Way.

GOULD, HAROLD WINTHROP
Born: 1873. Died: July 17, 1951, New York, N.Y. Screen and stage actor. Do not confuse with actor Harold Gould.

GOULD, JACK LEE
Born: 1949. Died: Dec. 6, 1977, Hollywood, Calif. (suicide—jumped from building). Screen actor.

GOULD, MYRTLE
Born: 1880. Died: Feb. 25, 1941, Los Angeles, Calif. Screen and stage actress. Appeared in silents until 1918.

GOULD, VIOLET
Born: 1884. Died: Mar. 29, 1962, England. Screen and television actress.

GOULD, WILLIAM A.
Born: 1915. Died: Mar. 20, 1960, Long Beach, Calif. (fire). Screen actor. Do not confuse with actor Billy Gould (dec. 1950).

Appeared in: **1934** Gun Justice; Smoking Guns; The Trail Drive; Wheels of Destiny. **1935** The Man Who Reclaimed His Head; Hard Rock Harrigan. **1937** Breezing Home; Prescription for Romance. **1938** Red Barry (serial); Mr. Wong, Detective. **1939** Women in the Wind; Buck Rogers (serial); Newsboys' Home; The Lone Ranger Rides Again (serial). **1940** Riders of Pecos Basin; Dr. Christian Meets the Women. **1942** Murder in the Big House; The Strange Case of Dr. Rx. **1943** Keep 'Em Sluffing. **1944** Adventures of Mark Twain. **1945** Texas Panhandle. **1947** The Devil Thumbs a Ride; Smash-Up, The Story of a Woman. **1948** The Winner's Circle.

GOULDING, ALFRED "ALF"
Born: 1896, Melbourne, Australia. Died: Apr. 25, 1972, Hollywood, Calif. (pneumonia). Screen, vaudeville, stage actor, film director and screenwriter. Married to actress Suzanne Raphael.

Appeared in: **1925** The Lady; Learning to Love.

GOULDING, EDMUND
Born: Mar. 20, 1891, London, England. Died: Dec. 24, 1959, Hollywood, Calif. Screen, stage, vaudeville actor, screenwriter, playwright, film, stage director, producer and composer.

Appeared in: **1911** Henry VIII. **1914** The Life of a London Shopgirl. **1922** Three Live Ghosts.

GOULDING, IVIS *See* PROCTER, IVIS GOULDING

GOURLEY, MERYL
Born: 1932, England. Died: Nov. 10, 1981, Dublin, Ireland. Screen and stage actress. Married to playwright/actor Conor Farrington.

Appeared in: **1967** Ulysses.

GOVE, OTIS M.
Born: 1852. Died: Jan. 23, 1931, Hollywood, Calif. Screen actor and cameraman.

Appeared in: **1912** Why Tightwad Tips.

GOVI, GILBERTO
Born: 1885, Italy. Died: 1966, Genoa, Italy (following pneumonia). Screen, stage and television actor.

GOWERS, SULKY
Died: Mar., 1970, London, England. Screen, television and cabaret actor.

GOWLAND, GIBSON
Born: Jan. 4, 1872, Spennymoor, England. Died: Sept. 9, 1951, London, England. Screen actor.

Appeared in: **1915** Birth of a Nation. **1919** Blind Husbands; The Fighting Shepherdess. **1921** Ladies Must Live. **1922** With Father's Help. **1923** Hutch Stirs 'Em Up (aka The Hawk); The Harbour Lights; Shifting Sands. **1924** Greed; The Border Legion; Love and Glory; The Red Lily. **1925** The Phantom of the Opera; The Prairie Wife. **1926** College Days; Don Juan; The Outsider. **1927** The Broken Gate; The Land Beyond the Law; The First Auto; Topsy and Eva; Isle of Forgotten Women; The Night of Love; The Tired Business Man. **1928** Rose Marie. **1929** The Mysterious Island. **1930** The Sea Bat; Hell Harbor; Phantom of the Opera (and 1925 version). **1932** Land of the Wanted Men; Without Honor; Doomed Battalion. **1933** S.O.S. Iceberg. **1934** The Private Life of Don Juan; The Secret of the Loch. **1935** The Mystery of the Mary Celeste (aka Phantom Ships—US 1937); The Stoken. **1936** Highland Fling. **1937** Cotton Queen; Wife of General Ling (US 1938); Ships Concert. **1938** Ten Leaves in the Wind. **1940** Northwest Passage. **1946** Kitty.

GOWMAN, MILTON J.
Born: 1907. Died: Aug. 17, 1952, Los Angeles, Calif. Screen actor.

GOZIER, BERNIE (Bernard Kikume Gozier)
Died: Oct. 2, 1979. Screen actor.

Appeared in: **1947** Green Dolphin Street. **1952** Viva Zapata! **1953** City Beneath the Sea. **1954** The Naked Jungle; Creature from the Black Lagoon; The Cowboy. **1955** Kiss of Fire. **1958** The Flame Barrier.

GRABLE, BETTY (Ruth Elizabeth Grable)
Born: Dec. 18, 1916, St. Louis, Mo. Died: July 2, 1973, Santa Monica, Calif. (cancer). Screen, stage, radio, television actress, dancer and singer. Divorced from actor Jackie Coogan and bandleader Harry James.

Appeared in: **1929** Happy Days (film debut). **1930** Whoopee; New Movietone Follies of 1930; Let's Go Places. **1931** Kiki; Palmy Days; Crashing Hollywood (short); Ex-Sweeties (short). **1932** Hold 'Em Jail; The Greeks Had a Word for Them; The Kid from Spain; Probation; plus the following shorts: The Flirty Sleepwalker; Hollywood Luck; Lady Please!; Hollywood Lights. **1933** Child of Manhattan; Melody Cruise; Sweetheart of Sigma Chi; What Price Innocence?; Cavalcade. **1934** Student Tour; The Gay Divorcee; Love Detectives (short). **1935** A Quiet Fourth (short); Old Man Rhythm; A Night at the Hollywood Bowl (short); The Nitwits. **1936** Collegiate; Don't Turn 'Em Loose; Pigskin Parade; Follow the Fleet. **1937** Thrill of a Lifetime; This Way, Please. **1938** Give Me a Sailor; Campus Confessions; College Swing. **1939** Man About Town; The Day the Bookies Wept; Million Dollar Legs. **1940** Tin Pan Alley; Down Argentine Way. **1941** A Yank in the RAF; Moon Over Miami; I Wake Up Screaming (aka Hot Spot). **1942** Song of the Islands; Footlight Serenade; Springtime in the Rockies. **1943** Show Business at War (short); Coney Island; Sweet Rosie O'Grady. **1944** Pin Up Girl; Four Jills in a Jeep. **1945** Billy Rose's Diamond Horseshoe; All-Star Band Rally (short); The Dolly Sisters. **1946** Do You Love Me? (cameo appearance). **1947** Hollywood Bound (short); The Shocking Miss Pilgrim; Mother Wore Tights. **1948** That Lady in Ermine; When My Baby Smiles at Me. **1949** The Beautiful Blonde from Bashful Bend. **1950** My Blue Heaven; Wabash Avenue. **1951** Call Me Mister; Meet Me After the Show. **1953** The Farmer Takes a Wife; How to Marry a Millionaire. **1955** Three for the Show; How to be Very, Very Popular. **1965** The Love Goddesses. **1970** Myra Breckinridge (film clip).

GRABLEY, URSULA
Born: 1899, Germany. Died: Apr. 11, 1977, Germany? Screen actress.

Appeared in: **1931** Und das ist die Hauptsache (That's All That Matters). **1932** Der Storch Streikt; Der Schwartze Husar. **1933** Einmal Moecht' ich Keine Sorgen Haben. **1934** ja, Treu die Soldatenliebe; Im Heidekrug. **1935** Der Schuechterne Felix. **1936** Zu Strassburg auf der Schanz (aka At the Strassburg); Die Frauen vom Tannjof; Annette in Paradise; Heisses Blut; Ist Mein Mann Nicht Fabelhaft. **1939** 1A in Oberbayern (1A in Upper Bavaria); Der Arme Millionar (The Poor Millionaire). **1940** Hurra! Ich bin Papa (Hurrah! I'm a Papa!).

GRACE, CHARITY
Born: 1879. Died: Nov. 28, 1965, St. Louis, Mo. (cancer). Screen, stage, opera and television actress.

GRACE, DICK
Born: 1915. Died: June 24, 1965, (cancer). Screen actor, stuntman, flier and author.

Appeared in: **1925** Flying Fool. **1927** Wide Open. **1928** Lilac Time. **1929** Wings; Hell's Angels. **1932** The Lost Squadron.

GRACE, DINAH (Ilse Schmidt)
Born: Germany. Died: May 12, 1963, Hamburg, Germany (cancer). Screen actress and dancer. Married to actor Willy Fritsch (dec. 1973).

GRAETZ, PAUL
Born: 1890. Died: Feb. 17, 1937, Hollywood, Calif. Screen actor.

Appeared in: **1923** Monna Vanna. **1931** Wien Du Stadt der Lieder (Vienna City of Song). **1934** Jew Suess; Blossom Time. **1935** Alias Bulldog Drummond; Mimi; Car of Dreams; 18 Minutes; Bulldog Jack. **1936** Mr. Cohen Takes a Walk; Red Wagon; Hot Money; Bengal Tiger; Isle of Fury. **1937** Heart's Desire; April Romance. **1939** The Fight for Matterhorn.

GRAF, PETER
Born: 1872. Died: Oct. 20, 1951, New York, N.Y. Screen, stage and radio actor. Appeared in Yiddish films.

GRAF, ROBERT
Born: 1923, Witten, Germany. Died: 1966, Munich, Germany. Screen, stage, radio and television actor.

Appeared in: **1957** Bekenntnisse des Hochstaplers Felix Krull; El Hakim; Jonas (US 1959). **1958** Wir Wunderkinder (Aren't We Wonderful?—US 1959). **1959** Buddenbrooks (US 1962); Das Schoene Abenteuer; ... und das am Montagmorgen. **1960** Lampenfieber; Eine Frau am Dunklen Fenster; Gauner in Uniform; Liebling der Goetter; Mein Schulfreund. **1961** Der Faelscher von London; Moerderspiel.

1962 Die Gluecklichen Jahre der Thorwalds; Wenn Beide Schuldig Werden. **1963** The Great Escape; Zwei Whisky und ein Sofa. **1964** Fruehstueck mit dem Tod; Verdammt zur Suende; Vorsicht, Mister Dodd; 2 mal 2 im Himmelbett. **1965** Young Cassidy.

GRAFF, WILTON
Born: 1903. Died: Jan. 13, 1969, Pacific Palisades, Calif. Screen and stage actor.

Appeared in: **1945** Pillow of Death; Strange Confession; An Angel Comes to Brooklyn; Earl Carroll Vanities; Gangs of the Waterfront; A Royal Scandal. **1946** Avalanche; Just Before Dawn; The Unknown; The Phantom Thief; Traffic in Crime; Valley of the Zombies. **1947** They Won't Believe Me; High Conquest; Shadowed; The Corpse Came C.O.D.; Bulldog Drummond Strikes Back; A Double Life; Gentleman's Agreement; Key Witness; The Web. **1948** Family Honeymoon; The Wreck of the Hesperus; Return of the Whistler; Gallant Blade; Another Part of the Forest. **1949** Take Me Out to the Ball Game; Once More, My Darling; Caught; Blondie's Big Deal; And Baby Makes Three; Reign of Terror; The Dark Past. **1950** Rogues of Sherwood Forest; Fortunes of Captain Blood; The West Point Story; Mother Didn't Tell Me; Girls' School. **1951** Mark of the Avenger; My True Story. **1952** Fearless Fagan; Springfield Rifle; Operation Secret; Million Dollar Mermaid; Something for the Birds; Young Man with Ideas. **1953** Lili; The I Don't Care Girl; Scandal at Scourie; Miss Sadie Thompson; So This Is Love. **1954** King Richard and the Crusaders; A Star Is Born. **1955** The Sea Chase; The Benny Goodman Story. **1956** Lust for Life. **1959** Compulsion. **1961** Return to Peyton Place; Sail a Crooked Ship; Bloodlust. **1963** Lonnie.

GRAHAM, BEN
Born: 1851. Died: Mar. 25, 1924, New Brighton, N.Y. Screen and stage actor.

Appeared in: **1915** The Better Woman.

GRAHAM, CHARLIE
Born: 1897. Died: Oct. 9, 1943, Los Angeles, Calif. Screen actor.

Appeared in: **1919** The Master Mystery (serial). **1921** The Mountain Woman; On the High Card. **1922** Cardigan; Dawn of Revenge; The Headless Horseman; The Love Nest; White Hell. **1925** The Making of O'Malley. **1926** The Untamed Lady. **1929** Frozen Justice.

GRAHAM, FRANK
Born: 1915. Died: Sept. 2, 1950, Hollywood, Calif. (possible suicide). Radio announcer and narrator of many films. Known as "the man with a thousand voices."

Appeared in: **1945** The Three Caballeros.

GRAHAM, FRED
Born: 1918. Died: Oct. 10, 1979, Scottsdale, Ariz. Screen actor, film producer, stunt coordinator and stuntman.

Appeared in: **1935** Mutiny on the Bounty. **1944** Marshall of Reno; Stagecoach to Monterey; Haunted Harbor (serial). **1945** Within These Walls; Great Stagecoach Robbery. **1946** Passkey to Danger; The Inner Circle; Out California Way; The Crimson Ghost (serial); Daughter of Don Q (serial). **1947** On the Old Spanish Trail; Brick Bradford (serial); Son of Zorro (serial). **1948** The Bold Frontiersman; The Timber Trail; Son of God's Country; Congo Bill (serial). **1949** The Fighting Kentuckian; I Married a Communist; She Wore a Yellow Ribbon. **1950** The Woman on Pier 13; Where the Sidewalk Ends; No Way Out; The Fuller Brush Girl. **1951** Overland Telegraph; Heart of the Rockies; Angels in the Outfield. **1952** Colorado Sundown; Old Oklahoma Plains; The San Francisco Story. **1953** Code Two; The Farmer Takes a Wife. **1954** Trader Tom of the China Seas (serial?); Demetrius and the Gladiators; Rear Window; Twenty Thousand Leagues Under the Sea. **1956** The Conqueror; The Last Hunt; Seven Men From Now. **1958** Badman's Country. **1959** The Giant Gila Monster; Woman Obsessed. **1960** Seven Ways From Sundown; North to Alaska. **1965** Arizona Raiders.

GRAHAM, JULIA ANN
Born: 1915. Died: July 15, 1935, Los Angeles, Calif. (suicide—gunshot). Screen actress.

Appeared in: **1935** Love in Bloom.

GRAHAM, MORLAND (aka MORELAND GRAHAM)
Born: Aug. 8, 1891, Glasgow, Scotland. Died: Apr. 8, 1949, London, England (heart attack). Screen and stage actor.

Appeared in: **1934** What Happened to Harkness? **1935** The Scarlet Pimpernel; Moscow Nights (aka I Stand Condemned—US 1936); Get

Off My Feet. **1936** Fair Exchange; Twelve Good Men; Where's Sally? **1939** Jamaica Inn; Full Speed Ahead. **1940** Night Train to Munich (aka Gestapo and Night Train—US); Old Bill and Son. **1941** Freedom Radio (aka A Voice in the Night—US); The Ghost Train; This England (aka Our Heritage—US); Ships With Wings (US 1942); The Tower of Terror (US 1942). **1942** The Big Blockade. **1943** The Shipbuilders. **1944** Medal for the General. **1945** Henry V (US 1946). **1946** Gaiety George (aka Showtime—US 1948). **1947** The Brothers (US 1948); The Upturned Glass. **1948** Bonnie Prince Charlie (US 1952). **1949** Whiskey Galore! (aka Mad Little Island and Tight Little Island—US).

GRAHAM, RONALD
Born: 1912, Hamilton, Scotland. Died: July 4, 1950, New York, N.Y. Screen, stage, radio and television actor.

Appeared in: **1935** Old Man Rhythm. **1944** Ladies of Washington.

GRAHAM, VIOLET
Born: Nov. 9, 1890, England. Died: 1967, England? Screen and stage actress.

Appeared in: **1919** The Lackey and the Lady. **1920** A Man's Shadow.

GRAHAME, BERT (R. A. S. Stanford)
Born: 1892. Died: Mar. 23, 1971, England. Screen, stage and vaudeville actor. Appeared in silents.

GRAHAME, GLORIA (Gloria Grahame Hallward)
Born: Nov. 28, 1929, Los Angeles, Calif. Died: Oct. 5, 1981, New York, N.Y. (cancer). Screen and stage actress. Daughter of actress Jean Grahame (aka Jean Hallward). Divorced from actor Stanley Clements (dec. 1981), actor/director Nicholas Ray (dec. 1979), writer Cy Howard and Anthony Ray. Nominated for 1947 Academy Award as Best Supporting Actress in Crossfire. Won 1952 Academy Award as Best Supporting Actress in The Bad and the Beautiful.

Appeared in: **1944** Blonde Fever (film debut). **1945** Without Love. **1946** It's a Wonderful Life. **1947** Merton of the Movies; Crossfire; Song of the Thin Man; It Happened in Brooklyn. **1949** Roughshod; A Woman's Secret. **1950** In a Lonely Place. **1952** The Greatest Show on Earth; The Bad and the Beautiful; Sudden Fear; Macao. **1953** The Big Heat; Man on a Tightrope; Prisoners of the Casbah; The Glass Wall. **1954** Human Desire; Naked Alibi; The Good Die Young (US 1955). **1955** The Cobweb; Not as a Stranger; Oklahoma! **1956** The Man Who Never Was. **1957** Ride Out for Revenge. **1959** Odds Against Tomorrow. **1966** Ride Beyond Vengeance. **1974** Mama's Dirty Girls. **1976** Mansion of the Doomed. **1979** Head Over Heels. **1980** Melvin and Howard.

GRAMATICA, EMMA
Born: 1875, Fidenza, Parma, Italy. Died: Nov. 8, 1965, Ostia, Italy. Screen, stage and television actress. Entered films in 1931.

Appeared in: **1932** La Vecchia Signora. **1935** Il Delitto di Mastrovanni. **1936** La Damigela di Bard; Il Fu Mattia Pascal. **1937** Marcella; Napoli d'Altri Tempi. **1938** Jeanne d'Ore; Il Destino; Quella (That One); La Vedova (The Widow). **1951** Miracle in Milan. Other Italian films: La Fortuna Di Zanze.

GRAN, ALBERT
Born: 1862. Died: Dec. 16, 1932, Los Angeles, Calif. (auto accident injuries). Screen actor.

Appeared in: **1916** Out of the Drifts. **1924** Her Night of Romance; Tarnish. **1925** Graustark. **1926** Beverly of Graustark; Early to Wed; Honesty—the Best Policy; More Pay—Less Work. **1927** Seventh Heaven; Breakfast at Sunrise; Children of Divorce; Hula; Love Makes 'Em Wild; Soft Cushions. **1928** We Americans; The Blue Danube; Dry Martini; Four Sons; Mother Knows Best; The Whip. **1929** The Gold Diggers of Broadway; Geraldine; The Glad Rag Doll; Our Modern Maidens; Show of Shows; Tanned Legs. **1930** Little Accident; Follow Thru; The Kibitzer; The Man from Blankley's; Sweethearts and Wives. **1931** Kiss Me Again; The Brat. **1932** Fast Life. **1933** Employees' Entrance.

GRANACH, ALEXANDER
Born: Apr. 18, 1890, Werbowitz, Poland. Died: Mar. 14, 1945, New York, N.Y. Screen and stage actor.

Appeared in: **1922** Lukrezia Borgia; Nosferatu—eine Symphonie des Grauens. **1923** I.N.R.I.; Der Mensch am Wege; Paganini; Erdgeist (Earth Spirit); Schatten (aka Warning Shadows—US 1928); Ein Weib, ein Tier, ein Diamant (aka Fuenf Kapitel aus Einem Alten Buch). **1924** Die Radio-Heirat; Ein Sommernachtstraum. **1925** Lazybones; Qualen der Nacht. **1927** Die Beruehmte Frau; Ich Hatte Einst ein Schoenes Vaterland; Svengali. **1928** Das Letzte Fort. **1929** Nosferatu the

Vampire; Flucht in die Fremdenlegion; Grosstadtschmetterling; Kampf ums Leben. **1930** Die Letzte Kompanie (The Last Company). **1931** Danton; Kameradschaft (Comradship—US 1934); Der Raub der Mona Lisa (US 1932); 1914, die Letzten Taege vor dem Weltbrand (1914: The Last Days Before the War—US 1934). **1935** Kaempfer. **1936** Gypsies; Der Kampf. **1939** So Ends Our Night; A Man Betrayed. **1942** Joan of Paris; Wrecking Crew; Half Way to Shanghai. **1943** For Whom the Bell Tolls; Hangmen Also Die; Three Russian Girls. **1944** The Hitler Gang; Seventh Cross. **1945** Voice in the Wind.

GRANBY, JOSEPH
Born: 1885. Died: Sept. 22, 1965, Hollywood, Calif. (cerebral hemorrhage). Screen, stage, radio and television actor.

Appeared in: **1916** Jealousy; The Haunted Bell; The Capital Prize; The Man From Nowhere; The Crystal's Warning; Temptation and the Man; Aschen Broedel; The Lie Sublime; Ashes; It Didn't Work Out Right. **1917** The Awakening. **1918** Peck's Bad Girl. **1920** The Imp. **1944** Kismet. **1945** The Great Flamarion; The Phantom Speaks. **1946** Her Adventurous Night; It's a Wonderful Life (voice). **1947** Magic Town. **1948** The Lady from Shanghai; Siren of Atlantis. **1949** The Berkleys of Broadway; Amazon Quest. **1950** Redwood Forest Trail; Where the Sidewalk Ends. **1951** Belle Le Grande; His Kind of Woman. **1952** Viva Zapata. **1956** Written on the Wind. **1957** The Tattered Dress.

GRANDAIS, SUSANNE
Born: France. Died: Aug., 1920 (auto accident). French screen actress. Was called the "Mary Pickford of France."

GRANDIN, ELMER
Born: 1861. Died: May 19, 1933, Patchogue, N.Y. Screen and stage actor.

Appeared in: **1919** Getting Mary Married. **1929** House of Secrets.

GRANDON, FRANCIS J.
Born: 1879, Chicago, Ill. Died: July 11, 1929, Los Angeles, Calif. (stroke). Screen actor and film director.

Appeared in: **1910** Ramona; The Englishman and the Girl.

GRANGER, ELSA G.
Born: 1904, Australia. Died: Feb. 8, 1955, New York, N.Y. Screen and stage actress. Appeared in Australian silent films; later appeared in US films.

GRANGER, MAUDE
Born: 1851. Died: Aug. 17, 1928, New York, N.Y. Screen and stage actress.

Appeared in: **1915** ZaZa.

GRANGER, MICHAEL
Born: 1923, Kansas City, Mo. Died: Oct. 22, 1981, New York, N.Y. (heart attack). Screen, stage and television actor.

Appeared in: **1952** Hiawatha. **1953** Salome; Fort Vengeance; The Big Heat; White Witch Doctor; Tarzan and the She-Devil. **1954** Battle of Rogue River; The Egyptian. **1955** New Orleans Uncensored; Jungle Moon Men; Creature With the Atom Brain. **1956** Mohawk; Miami Expose; Rumble on the Docks. **1957** Calypso Heat Wave; Looking For Danger. **1958** Gunman's Walk; Murder by Contract. **1959** Pier 5, Havana.

GRANGER, WILLIAM F.
Born: 1854. Died: Dec. 23, 1938, Hollywood, Calif. Screen and stage actor.

Appeared in: **1930** The Other Tomorrow. **1933** Footlight Parade. **1934** Six-Day Bike Ride.

GRANT, EARL
Born: 1931. Died: June 10, 1970, near Lordsburg, N.Mex. (auto accident). Black screen, television actor and musician.

Appeared in: **1959** Imitation of Life; Juke Box Rhythm. **1962** Tender Is the Night.

GRANT, JACK (John Sennett)
Born: 1895. Died: July 6, 1977, Woodland Hills, Calif. Screen actor and casting director. Do not confuse with Jack Grant, film writer.

Appeared in: **1933** The Penal Code.

GRANT, LARRY
Born: 1908. Died: Dec. 23, 1979, Honolulu, Hawaii. Screen and radio actor. Do not confuse with screen actor Lawrence Grant (dec. 1952).

Appeared in: **1958** Man or Gun.

GRANT, LAWRENCE
Born: 1870, England. Died: Feb. 19, 1952, Santa Barbara, Calif. Screen and stage actor.

Appeared in: **1918** To Hell with the Kaiser (film debut). **1921** Extravagance; The Great Impersonation. **1924** His Hour; Abraham Lincoln; Happiness. **1926** The Duchess of Buffalo; The Grand Duchess and the Waiter. **1927** A Gentleman of Paris; Sevice for Ladies; Serenade. **1928** Doomsday; Hold 'Em Yale; Red Hair; The Woman from Moscow; Something Always Happens. **1929** The Canary Murder Case; The Case of Lena Smith; The Rainbow; The Exalted Flapper; Is Everybody Happy?; Bulldog Drummond. **1930** Safety in Numbers; Boudoir Diplomat; The Cat Creeps; Oh, Sailor, Behave! **1931** Daughter of the Dragon; Command Performance; The Squaw Man; Their Mad Moment; The Unholy Garden. **1932** Man About Town; Speak Easily; Divorce in the Family; Jewel Robbery; Faithless; The Mask of Fu Manchu; Grand Hotel; Shanghai Express. **1933** Clear All Wires; Queen Christina; Looking Forward. **1934** The Count of Monte Cristo; By Candlelight; Nana; I'll Tell the World. **1935** The Man Who Reclaimed His Head; Werewolf of London; A Feather in Her Hat; Vanessa, Her Love Story; The Devil Is a Woman; The Dark Angel; Three Kids and a Queen; A Tale of Two Cities. **1936** Klondike Annie; Little Lord Fauntleroy; The House of a Thousand Candles; Mary of Scotland. **1937** S.O.S. Coast Guard (serial); Under the Red Robe; The Prisoner of Zenda. **1938** Marie Antoinette; Service de Luxe; Bluebeard's Eighth Wife; The Young in Heart. **1939** Son of Frankenstein; Wife, Husband and Friend; Rulers of the Sea. **1940** A Dispatch from Reuters; The Son of Monte Cristo; Women in War. **1941** Dr. Jekyll and Mr. Hyde. **1942** S.O.S. Coast Guard; The Ghost of Frankenstein; The Living Ghost. **1945** Confidential Agent.

GRANT, SYDNEY
Born: 1873. Died: July 12, 1953, Santa Monica, Calif. Screen and stage actor. Divorced from actress Zay Holland (dec. 1941).

Appeared in: **1915** Jane.

GRANT, VALENTINE
Born: 1894, Indiana. Died: Mar. 12, 1948, Hollywood, Calif. Screen actress. Married to actor, director Sidney Olcott (dec. 1949).

Appeared in: **1915** The Melting Pot; The Brute.

GRANVILLE, AUDREY
Born: 1910. Died: Oct. 20, 1972, Encino, Calif. (cancer). Screen, television actress and music editor. Child screen actress.

GRANVILLE, CHARLOTTE
Born: May 9, 1863, England. Died: July 8, 1942. Screen and stage actress.

Appeared in: **1931** Just a Gigolo; 24 Hours. **1934** Now and Forever. **1935** Behold My Wife; Werewolf of London. **1936** Rose of the Rancho.

GRANVILLE, LOUISE
Born: 1896. Died: Dec. 22, 1969, Hollywood, Calif. (Hong Kong flu). Screen actress.

Appeared in: **1915** The Scrapper. **1918** Vitagraph shorts.

GRANVILLE, SYDNEY
Born: 1880, Bolton, England. Died: Dec. 27, 1959, Stockport, England. Screen, stage actor and vocalist.

Appeared in: **1939** The Mikado.

GRAPEWIN, CHARLES "CHARLIE"
Born: Dec. 20, 1875, Xenia, Ohio. Died: Feb. 2, 1956, Corona, Calif. Screen, stage, vaudeville actor, playwright, composer and author. Married to actress Anna Chance (dec. 1943).

Appeared in: **1902** Above the Limit. **1929** The Shannons of Broadway; Starred in comedy series for Christie which included the following shorts: Jed's Vacation, Ladies' Choice, That Red Headed Hussy. **1930** Only Saps Work. **1931** Millionaire; Gold Dust Gertie. **1932** Hell's House; Big Timer; Disorderly Conduct; The Woman in Room 13; Lady and Gent; Wild Horse Mesa; The Night of June 13th. **1933** Hello, Everybody!; Kiss Before the Mirror; Lady of the Night; Heroes for Sale; Wild Boys of the Road; Midnight Mary; Beauty for Sale; Pilgrimage; Don't Bet on Love; Torch Singer; Hell and High Water.

1934 Return of the Terror; Caravan; Two Alone; Anne of Green Gables; Judge Priest; She Made Her Bed; The President Vanishes; The Quitter; The Loud Speaker. **1935** Superspeed; One Frightened Night; In Spite of Danger; Party Wire; Shanghai; Alice Adams; King Solomon of Broadway; Rendezvous; Ah, Wilderness; Eight Bells. **1936** The Petrified Forest; The Voice of Bugle Ann; Small Town Girl; Libeled Lady; Sinner Take All; Without Orders. **1937** The Good Earth; A Family Affair; Captains Courageous; Between Two Women; Bad Guy; Big City; Broadway Melody of 1938. **1938** Bad Man of Brimstone; Of Human Hearts; Girl of the Golden West; Three Comrades; Three Loves Has Nancy; Listen, Darling; Artists and Models Abroad. **1939** Sudden Money; I Am Not Afraid; The Man Who Dared; Hero for a Day; Sabotage; Dust Be My Destiny; Stand Up and Fight; Burn 'Em Up O'Connor; The Wizard of Oz. **1940** The Grapes of Wrath; Johnny Apollo; Earthbound; Rhythm on the River; Ellery Queen, Master Detective. **1941** Ellery Queen's Penthouse Mystery; Ellery Queen and the Perfect Crime; Ellery Queen and the Murder Ring; Texas Rangers Ride Again; Tobacco Road. **1942** Enemy Agents Meet Ellery Queen; They Died With Their Boots On. **1943** Crash Dive. **1944** Follow the Boys; The Impatient Years; Atlantic City. **1947** The Gunfighter. **1948** The Enchanted Valley. **1949** Sand. **1951** When I Grow Up.

GRASSBY, BERTRAM
Born: Dec. 23, 1880, Lincolnshire, England. Died: Dec. 7, 1953, Scottsdale, Ariz. Screen and stage actor.

Appeared in: **1916** Liberty—A Daughter of the U.S.A. (serial). **1918** Battling Jane. **1919** Romance of Happy Valley; The Lone Wolf's Daughter; The Hope Chest. **1920** For the Soul of Rafael; The Fighting Chance; The Week End. **1921** Fifty Candles; Her Social Value; Hush; A Parisian Scandal; Hold Your Horses; Serenade; Straight From Paris. **1922** Borderland; Golden Dreams; For the Defense; The Sleepwalker; Shattered Dreams; The Young Rajah. **1923** Drums of Fate; The Dancer of the Nile; The Man from Brodney's; Pioneer Trials; The Tiger's Claw; The Prisoner. **1924** The Shadow of the East; One Law for the Woman; The Midnight Express; His Hour; The Heart Bandit; The Girl on the Stairs; Captain Blood; Fools in the Dark. **1925** Havoc; She Wolves. **1926** The Beautiful Cheat; The Taxi Mystery; Made for Love. **1927** The Beloved Rogue; When a Man Loves.

GRASSBY, MRS. GERARD A.
Born: 1877. Died: Apr. 6, 1962, Hollywood, Calif. Screen actress.

GRATTAN, LAWRENCE
Born: 1870. Died: Dec. 9, 1941, New York, N.Y. Screen, stage, vaudeville actor and playwright. Married to vaudeville actress Eva Taylor.

Appeared in: **1915** Greater Love Hath No Man; Her Great Match.

GRAUER, BEN (Benjamin Franklin Grauer)
Born: June 2, 1908, Stanton Island, N.Y. Died: May 31, 1977, New York, N.Y. (heart attack). Screen, stage, vaudeville, radio actor, announcer, newsman and commentator.

Appeared in: **1920** The Town That Forgot God.

GRAUMAN, SID
Born: Mar. 17, 1879, Indianapolis, Ind. Died: Mar. 5, 1950, Hollywood, Calif. (heart attack). Managing director of Grauman's Chinese Theatre and screen actor.

Appeared in: **1938** Mad About Music. **1949** Dancing in the Dark.

GRAVERS, STEVE
Born: 1922. Died: Aug. 26, 1978, Studio City, Calif. (lung cancer). Screen, stage and television actor.

Appeared in: **1960** Hell Bent for Leather. **1961** Operation Eichmann. **1962** 40 Pound of Trouble.

GRAVES, GEORGE
Born: 1876, England. Died: Apr. 2, 1949, London, England. Screen and stage actor. Divorced from actress Madge Compton (dec. 1970).

Appeared in: **1936** The Robber Symphony (US 1937); The Tenth Man (US 1937).

GRAVES, KATHRYN
Born: 1898. Died: Feb. 26, 1977, San Diego, Calif. Screen actress. Appeared in films from 1925-1930.

GRAVES, RALPH
Born: Jan. 23, 1900, Cleveland, Ohio. Died: Feb. 18, 1977, Santa Barbara, Calif. (heart attack). Screen, stage actor, film director, film producer and screenwriter. Married to actress Marjorie Seaman (dec.

1923). Later married and divorced Virginia Goodwin. Married to actress Betty Flournoy. Entered films with Essanay Studios in 1917.

Appeared in: **1918** Sporting Life; Tinsel. **1919** The Home Town Girl; The White Heather; I'll Get Him Yet; Out of Luck; Scarlet Days. **1920** Polly With a Past; Little Miss Rebellion; The Greatest Question. **1921** Dream Street. **1922** Come on Over; The Jilt; Kindred of the Dust; The Lone Chance. **1923** The Extra Girl; The Ghost Patrol; Mind Over Motor; Just Like a Woman; Prodigal Daughters. **1924** Daughter of Today; Yolanda. **1926** Blarney; Womanpower; The Country Beyond. **1927** The Swell-Head; A Reno Divorce. **1928** Rich Man's Sons; Alias the Deacon; Bachelor's Paradise; Bitter Sweets; The Cheerleader; Submarine; The Sideshow; That Certain Thing. **1929** The Eternal Woman; Flight; The Flying Fleet; The Glad Rag Doll; The Song of Love; The Fatal Warning (serial). **1930** Hell's Island; Ladies of Leisure. **1931** Dirigible; Salvation Nell; A Dangerous Affair. **1932** Huddle; When a Feller Needs a Friend; War Correspondent. **1934** Ticket to a Crime. **1935** Counselitis (short). **1936** The Black Coin (serial). **1939** Street of Missing Men; Eternally Yours; Three Texas Steers. **1949** Amazon Quest; Alimony; Joe Palooka in the Counterpunch; Batman and Robin (serial).

GRAVET, FERNAND (Fernand Mertens aka FERNAND GRAVEY)
Born: Dec. 25, 1904, Belgium. Died: Nov. 2, 1970, Paris, France. Screen and stage actor. Son of actor Georges Mertens and actress Fernande Depernay.

Appeared in: **1913** Monsieur Beulemeester, Garde Civique; Ans Ou La Vie D'un Joueur; La Fille De Delft. **1930** L'Amour Chante; Cherie. **1931** Marions-Nous; Un Homme en Habit; Tu Seras Duchesse (US 1932); Coiffeur Pour Dames (US 1932). **1932** Passionnement; Le Fils Improvise; A Moi le Jour, A Toi la Nuit. **1933** Early to Bed; Le Pere Premature; La Guerre des Valses (The Court Waltzes); Bitter Sweet. **1934** The Queen's Affair (aka Runaway Queen—US 1935); C'Etait un Musicien; Si J'etais le Patron; Nuit de Mai. **1935** Antonio, Romance Hongroise; Monsieur Sans-Gene; Fanfare D'Amour; Varietes; Touche a Tout. **1936** Sept Hommes, Une Femme (aka Sept Hommes); Mister Flow (aka Compliments of Mr. Flow—US 1941); Le Grand Refrain. **1937** Le Mensonge de Nina Petrovna (aka Nina Petrovna and The Life of Nina Petrovna—US 1938); The King and the Chorus Girl (aka Romance is Sacred). **1938** Fools for Scandal; The Great Waltz. **1939** Paradis Perdu; Le Dernier Tournant. **1941** Histoire de Rire. **1942** Romance a Trois; La Nuit Fantastique (Fantastic Night); Le Capitaine Fracasse. **1943** Domino; La Rabouilleuse. **1944** Pamela. **1946** Il Suffit D'une Fois. **1947** Le Capitaine Blomet. **1949** Du Guesclin. **1950** Le Traque (Gunman in the Streets aka Time Running Out); La Ronde. **1951** Mademoiselle Josette Ma Femme; Ma Femme est Formidable. **1952** Le Plus Heureux des Hommes; Mon Mari est Merveilleux (My Husband Is Marvelous). **1953** L'Eta del' Amore (Age of Indiscretion aka Too Young For Love—US 1955); Si Versailles M'etait Conte (aka Versailles). **1956** Treize a Table; Courte Tete (Short Head); Mitsou (US 1958); La Garconne. **1958** Le Temps des Oeufs Durs (Time Running Out—US 1959); L'Ecole des Cocottes; Toto a Parigi. **1961** Les Croulants se Portent Bien; Les Petits Matins (Girl on the Road). **1965** La Dama de Beirut. **1966** How To Steal A Million. **1967** La Bataille de San Sebastian (The Guns for San Sebastian—US 1968). **1969** The Madwoman of Chaillot; Les Caprices de Marie (aka Give Her the Moon—US). **1970** La Promesse de L'aube (Promise at Dawn). **1971** L'Explosion (aka Sex Explosion).

GRAVINA, CESARE
Born: Jan. 23, 1858, Naples, Italy. Died: 1954, Italy. Screen and stage actor.

Appeared in: **1916** Less Than the Dust; Poor Little Pepina; Diplomacy. **1917** The Fatal Ring (serial). **1920** Scratch My Back; Madame X. **1921** God's Country and the Law; Beach of Dreams. **1922** Foolish Wives. **1923** Daddy; Merry-Go-Round; The Hunchback of Notre Dame; Circus Days. **1924** The Family Secret; The Humming Bird; Butterfly; The Rose of Paris; Those Who Dare; Greed. **1925** The Charmer; The Circus Cyclone; Contraband; Don Dare Devil; Flower of Night; Fifth Avenue Models; The Man in Blud; The Phantom of the Opera; A Woman's Faith. **1926** The Blonde Saint; Monte Carlo; The Midnight Sun. **1927** The Road to Romance; The Magic Garden; Cheating Cheaters. **1928** The Man Who Laughs; The Trail of '98; The Wedding March; The Divine Woman; How to Handle Women. **1929** Burning the Wind. **1930** Phantom of the Opera (1929 Version).

GRAY, BETTY (Lily Pederson aka BEATA GRAY)
Born: Pasaic, N.J. Died: June, 1919, New York, N.Y. (influenza). Screen, stage and vaudeville actress.

Appeared in: **1912** The Lass of Gloucester; His Little Indian Model; The Country Boy. **1913** The Beach Combers; The Cheapest Way; The Parting Eternal; $1,000 Reward. **1914** The Cricket on the Hearth. **1915** The Timid Mr. Troodles; The Girl Who Might Have Been; The Mystery of Mary (aka Mystery Mary); Blood Heritage; Who Killed Joe Merrion?; The Park Honeymooners. **1916** Pique; Sunlight and Shadow; His Wife's Mistake; Madeleine Morel; Scorched Wings; The Power of the Press; The Light That Failed.

GRAY, BILLY JOE
Born: Feb. 19, 1941, New Mexico. Died: Mar. 3, 1966, Canoga Park, Calif. (murdered—shot). Screen stuntman and horse trainer. Do not confuse with actor Billy Gray.

GRAY, DON (Leo Don Gray)
Born: 1901. Died: July 24, 1966, Woodland Hills, Calif. (cancer). Screen actor. Do not confuse with English actor Donald Gray (dec. 1978).

GRAY, DONALD (Eldred Tidbury)
Born: 1914, England. Died: Apr. 7, 1978, England? Screen, radio and television actor. Do not confuse with US actor (dec. 1966).

Appeared in: **1937** Strange Experiment. **1939** The Four Feathers. **1948** Idol of Paris. **1952** Saturday Island (aka Island of Desire—US). **1955** Timeslip (aka The Atomic Man—US). **1956** Satellite in the Sky. **1961** Out of the Shadow (aka Murder on the Campus—US 1963).

GRAY, DOROTHY
Born: Oct. 23, 1922, Hollywood, Calif. Died: May 9, 1976, Los Angeles, Calif. Screen, stage, radio actress and stage producer. Daughter of actress Jean Riley. Entered films at age two.

Appeared in: **1925** The Scarlet Letter. **1928** Forbidden Trails; Avalanche. **1929** Vagabond Lover. **1931** Cimarron; Beau Ideal. **1932** Symphony of Six Million. **1933** The Great Jasper; One Man's Journey; Little Women; Today We Live; The Wrecker; Daddy Long Legs. **1934** Bedside; Beloved; As the Earth Turns; Men in White; The Winning Ticket; Straight From the Heart. **1935** Black Fury; Princess O'Hara. **1943** Three Russian Girls.

GRAY, EDDIE
Born: 1898, England. Died: Sept. 15, 1969, England. Screen and stage actor.

Appeared in: **1935** First a Girl. **1938** Keep Smiling (aka Smiling Along—US 1939). **1958** Life is a Circus (US 1962). **1962** The Fast Lady (US 1965).

GRAY, GENE
Born: 1899. Died: Feb. 10, 1950, Hollywood, Calif. Screen actor. Known as "Silver King of the Cowboys" because of the rich silver trappings on his horse.

GRAY, GEORGE G.
Born: 1894. Died: Sept., 1967, Asheville, N.C. (stroke). Screen actor, stuntman and film director. Appeared in early Sennett films and was a Keystone Kop.

Appeared in: **1934** Woman Haters (short). **1935** Old Sawbones (short); Uncivil Warriors (short). **1937** Goofs and Saddles (short).

GRAY, GILDA
Born: Oct. 24, c. 1896, Krakow, Poland. Died: Dec. 22, 1959, Hollywood, Calif. (heart attack). Screen, stage and vaudeville actress.

Appeared in: **1923** Lawful Larceny. **1926** Aloma of the South Seas. **1927** The Devil Dancer; Cabaret. **1929** Piccadilly. **1936** Rose Marie.

GRAY, GLEN
Born: 1900, Roanoke, Ill. Died: Aug. 23, 1963, Plymouth, Mass. Orchestra leader, musician and screen actor. Leader of the "Casa Loma Orchestra."

Appeared in: **1941** Time Out for Rhythm. **1943** Gals, Inc. **1944** Jam Session.

GRAY, GLORIA
Born: 1900. Died: Apr. 4, 1918. Screen actress. Do not confuse with actress of same name (dec. 1957).

GRAY, GLORIA
Born: 1882. Died: Apr. 17, 1957, Stamford, Conn. Screen and stage actress. Do not confuse with actress of same name (dec. 1918).

Appeared in: **1932** Big Town. **1933** Hotel Variety. **1950** Western Pacific Agent; Holiday Rhythm.

GRAY, JACK
Born: 1880. Died: Apr. 13, 1956, Woodland Hills, Calif. Screen actor.

Appeared in: **1933** Fugitive Lovers.

GRAY, JEAN
Born: 1902. Died: Sept. 23, 1953, Beverly Hills, Calif. Screen actress.

Appeared in: **1935** Follies Bergere; Follow the Fleet; Uncivil Warriors (short). **1938** Three Loves Has Nancy. **1939** When Tomorrow Comes.

GRAY, JENNIFER (Jennifer Skinner)
Born: Nov. 5, 1916, Hankow, China. Died: Feb. 3, 1962, England? Screen, stage and television actress. Married to Robert Langford-Jones. Entered films in 1940. Do not confuse with US actress of similar name.

GRAY, JOE
Died: Mar. 15, 1971, Mexico. Screen actor and stuntman.

Appeared in: **1938** You and Me. **1942** The Miracle Kid. **1946** Mr. Hex. **1952** Flesh and Fury. **1964** Robin and the 7 Hoods. **1971** Something Big.

GRAY, LAWRENCE
Born: July 27, 1898, San Francisco, Calif. Died: Feb. 2, 1970, Mexico City, Mexico. Screen and stage actor.

Appeared in: **1925** Are Parents People?; Coast of Folly; The Dressmaker From Paris; Stage Struck. **1926** The American Venus; Everybody's Acting; Kid Boots; Love 'Em and Leave 'Em; The Palm Beach Girl; The Untamed Lady. **1927** After Midnight; Ankles Preferred; The Callahans and the Murphys; Convoy; Ladies Must Dress; Pajamas; The Telephone Girl. **1928** Diamond Handcuffs; Domestic Meddlers; Love Hungry; Marriage by Contract; Oh, Kay; The Patsy; Shadows of the Night. **1929** It's a Great Life; Marianne; The Rainbow; The Sin Sister; Trent's Last Case. **1930** Children of Pleasure; The Floradora Girl; Spring Is Here; Sunny; Temptation. **1931** Going Wild; Man of the World; Mother's Millions. **1933** Golden Harvest. **1934** Here Comes the Groom. **1935** Dizzy Dames Danger Ahead; The Old Homestead. **1936** Timber War; In Paris A.W.O.L.

GRAY, MACK
Died: Jan. 17, 1981, Los Angeles, Calif.? Screen actor.

Appeared in: **1935** Car 99. **1936** Florida Special. **1937** Night Club Scandal. **1940** The House Across the Bay. **1942** Broadway. **1945** Johnny Angel. **1946** Nocturne. **1948** Race Street. **1951** Exclusive. **1962** Who's Got the Action.

GRAY, NICHOLAS (Nicholas Stuart Gray)
Born: Oct. 23, 1919, Scotland. Died: Mar. 17, 1981, London, England. Screen, stage, television actor, stage director, playwright and author.

GRAY, ROGER
Born: May 26, 1887, Omaha, Nebr. Died: Jan. 20, 1959. Screen, stage actor and writer.

Appeared in: **1930** Hit the Deck. **1934** George White's Scandals; Come on Marines. **1935** Barbary Coast; Lightning Strikes Twice. **1936** Rebellion; Fury; Everyman's Law. **1937** Woman Chases Man; History is Made at Night. **1938** Barefoot Boy; You and Me. **1940** The Westerner; The Pinto Kid; Out West With the Peppers; Road to Singapore. **1943** Pardon My Gun. **1958** Gang War.

GRAYBILL, JOSEPH
Born: 1887, Milwaukee, Wis. Died: Aug. 3, 1913, New York, N.Y. (spinal meningitis). Screen actor.

Appeared in: **1909** The Light That Came. **1910** A Victim of Jealousy; The Face at the Window; The Marked Time-Table; The Purgation; Turning the Tables; The Lesson; White Roses. **1911** The Last Drop of Water; A Decree of Destiny; The Italian Barber; How She Triumphed; Priscilla and the Umbrella; A Romany Tragedy; Bobby the Coward; The Baron; Italian Blood; Saved From Himself; Love in the Hills; The Voice of the Child; The Diving Girl. **1912** The Painted Lady; On Probation. **1913** Love in an Apartment Hotel; The Wizard of The Jungle.

GREAZA, WALTER
Born: Jan. 1, 1897, St. Paul, Minn. Died: June 1, 1973, New York. Screen, stage, radio and television actor.

Appeared in: **1946** 13 Rue Madeleine. **1947** Boomerang. **1948** Call Northside 777; Larceny; The Street With No Name. **1949** The Great Gatsby. **1951** New Mexico. **1959** It Happened to Jane (aka Twinkle and Shine).

GREEN, ABEL
Born: June 3, 1900. Died: May 10, 1973, New York. Newspaperman (editor of *Variety*), author and screen actor.

Appeared in: **1947** Copacabana.

GREEN, DENIS
Born: Apr. 11, 1905, London, England. Died: Nov. 6, 1954, New York, N.Y. (heart ailment). Screen, stage actor, screenwriter, television and radio writer.

Appeared in: **1939** The Witness Vanishes; The Hound of the Baskervilles. **1940** Northwest Passage; Men Against the Sky. **1941** They Met in Bombay; Yank in the RAF; Scotland Yard; Dr. Jekyll and Mr. Hyde. **1942** This Above All. **1944** Frenchman's Creek. **1947** Lone Wolf in London. **1949** Mighty Joe Young.

GREEN, DOROTHY
Born: June 30, 1886, Hertfordshire, England. Died: Jan. 14, 1961, London, England. Screen and stage actress. Do not confuse with actress Dorothy Green (dec. 1963) and actress Dorothy Green, living.

Appeared in: **1929** The Informer.

GREEN, DOROTHY
Born: 1892. Died: Nov. 16, 1963, New York, N.Y. Screen actress. Do not confuse with British actress (dec. 1961) nor US actress.

Appeared in: **1916** A Parisian Romance. **1917** Patria (serial). **1918** The Grouch. **1919** The American Way; Forest Rivals; Her Mother's Secret; The Dark Star. **1920** The Good Bad Wife.

GREEN, EMILY
Born: 1889, Philadelphia, Pa. Died: Mar. 26, 1980, Willow Grove, Pa. Screen, stage and vaudeville actress. Married to actor William W. Long (dec.). Appeared in early Arthur Lubin films.

GREEN, FRED E.
Born: 1890. Died: Aug., 1940, near San Mateo, Calif. (auto accident injuries). Screen actor.

Appeared in: **1927** Topsy and Eva.

GREEN, HARRY (Harry Blitzer)
Born: Apr. 1, 1892, New York, N.Y. Died: May 31, 1958, London, England. Screen, stage, vaudeville, television actor and magician.

Appeared in: **1929** Close Harmony; Why Bring That Up?; The Man I Love. **1930** The Kibitzer; Paramount on Parade; Be Yourself; Honey; True to the Navy; Light of Western Stars; The Spoilers; Sea Legs; No Limit. **1932** Marry Me. **1933** This Day and Age; Too Much Harmony; Hollywood on Parade (short). **1934** Coming Out Party; Wild Gold; Love Time; Bottoms Up; She Learned About Sailors; A Woman's Man; Born to Be Bad. **1940** The Cisco Kid and the Lady; Star Dust. **1955** Joe Macbeth (US 1956). **1957** A King in New York (US 1973). **1958** Next to No Time (US 1960).

GREEN, KENNETH
Born: 1908. Died: Feb. 24, 1969, Hollywood, Calif. (heart attack). Screen actor. Appeared in "Our Gang" series.

Appeared in: **1922** Penrod.

GREEN, MARTYN (William Martyn Green)
Born: Apr. 22, 1899, London, England. Died: Feb. 8, 1975, Hollywood, Calif. (blood infection). Screen, stage actor, stage director, author and screenwriter. Married to opera singer Yvonne Chaveau.

Appeared in: **1939** The Mikado (stage and film versions). **1953** The Story of Gilbert and Sullivan (aka The Great Gilbert and Sullivan—US). **1968** A Lovely Way to Die. **1973** The Iceman Cometh.

GREEN, MITZI
Born: Oct. 22, 1920, New York, N.Y. Died: May 24, 1969, Huntington Harbour, Calif. (cancer). Screen and stage actress.

Appeared in: **1929** Marriage Playground. **1930** Honey; Paramount on Parade; Love Among the Millionaires; Santa Fe Trail; Tom Sawyer. **1931** Finn and Hattie; Skippy; Dude Ranch; Forbidden Adventure; Newly Rich; Huckleberry Finn. **1932** Girl Crazy; Little Orphan Annie; The Slippery Pearls (short). **1934** Transatlantic Merry-Go-Round. **1940** Walk With Music. **1952** Lost in Alaska; Bloodhounds of Broadway.

GREEN, NIGEL
Born: 1924, Pretoria, South Africa. Died: May 15, 1972, Brighton, England. Screen, stage and television actor.

Appeared in: **1954** The Sea Shall Not Have Them (US 1955). **1955** As Long as They're Happy (US 1957). **1956** Reach for the Sky (US 1957). **1957** Bitter Victory (US 1958). **1958** Corridors of Blood (US 1963); The Gypsy and the Gentleman. **1960** The Criminal (aka The Concrete Jungle—US 1962); Sword of Sherwood Forest (US 1961); Mysterious

Island. **1961** The Queen's Guards (US 1963). **1962** The Man Who Finally Died (US 1967); The Durant Affair; Wild for Kicks. **1963** Jason and the Argonauts; Zulu (US 1964); Mystery Submarine. **1964** The Masque of the Red Death; Saturday Night Out. **1965** The Skull; The Face of Fu Manchu; The Ipcress File. **1966** Khartoum; Deadlier Than the Male (US 1967); Let's Kill Uncle. **1967** Tobruk; Africa—Texas Style. **1968** Play Dirty (US 1969); The Pink Jungle. **1969** The Kremlin Letter (US 1970); The Wrecking Crew (aka House of 7 Joys); Fraulein Doktor (aka The Betrayal). **1970** Countess Dracula. **1971** The Ruling Class (US 1972).

GREEN, ROBERT
Born: 1940. Died: July 11, 1965, Oroville, Calif. (killed when parachute failed to open during filming). Screen actor and stuntman.

GREEN, SUE
Born: 1902. Died: Aug. 12, 1939, Hollywood, Calif. Screen actress.

Appeared in: **1931-1939** Hal Roach shorts.

GREEN, VICTOR HUGO
Born: Feb. 26, 1895, Georgia. Died: Aug. 9, 1971, Los Angeles, Calif. Black screen, stage and radio actor.

Appeared in: **1954** Human Desire.

GREEN, WILLIAM B.
Born: 1852. Died: Apr. 10, 1926, Utica, N.Y. Stage actor, lecturer and newspaperman. Do not confuse with actor William E. Green.

GREEN, WILLIAM E.
Born: 1894, Hoboken, N.J. Died: Jan. 3, 1962, Los Angeles, Calif. (heart attack). Screen, stage and television actor. Do not confuse with actor William B. Green.

Appeared in: **1949** Life of Riley; It Happens Every Spring. **1950** Beware of Blondie; The Last Continent; Yes Sir, Mr. Bones.

GREENE, ANGELA
Born: 1923, Ireland. Died: Feb. 9, 1978, Los Angeles, Calif. (stroke). Screen, stage, television actress and model.

Appeared in: **1942** Hollywood Canteen. **1945** Too Young to Know. **1946** The Time, the Place and the Girl. **1947** Love and Learn; King of the Bandits; Stallion Road. **1948** Wallflower. **1950** At War With the Army. **1952** Jungle Jim in the Forbidden Land. **1953** A Perilous Journey; The Lady Wants a Mink; The Royal African Rifles; Loose in London; Savage Mutiny. **1955** Shotgun. **1957** Spoilers of the Forest; Affair in Reno. **1958** Night of the Blood Beast. **1959** The Cosmic Man. **1965** Tickle Me. **1967** The Graduate. **1969** The Good Guys and the Bad Guys. **1971** Marriage of a Young Stockbroker. **1975** The Day of the Locust. **1976** Futureworld.

GREENE, BILLY M.
Born: Jan. 6, 1897. Died: Aug. 24, 1973, Los Angeles, Calif. (heart attack). Screen, vaudeville, radio and television actor. Do not confuse with actor William Green (dec. 1970).

Appeared in: **1930** His Birthday Suit (short). **1945** Frisco Sal; Shady Lady; Sunbonnet Sue. **1946** Tangier. **1947** Mother Wore Tights; My Wild Irish Rose; Violence. **1951** Yes Sir, Mr. Bones. **1955** The Shrike. **1957** Slaughter on Tenth Avenue. **1959** The Cape Canaveral Monsters; The Legend of Tom Dooley; Never Steal Anything Small. **1962** That Touch of Mink. **1968** Single Room—Furnished. **1973** Papillion.

GREENE, CLAY M.
Born: 1850, San Francisco, Calif. Died: Sept 5, 1933, San Francisco, Calif. Screen, stage actor and playwright.

Appeared in: **1914** Through Fire to Fortune or The Sunken Village.

GREENE, HARRISON
Born: 1884. Died: Sept. 28, 1945, Hollywood, Calif. Screen, stage and television actor.

Appeared in: **1933** International House; The Vampire Bat; Riot Squad; Murder on the Campus. **1934** Manhattan Love Song; Attention Suckers (short); Kentucky Kernels. **1935** Alibi Baby (short); She Couldn't Take It. **1936** The Big Broadcast of 1937; Ants in the Pantry (short); The Singing Cowboy; Will Power (short); Guns and Guitars; Ticket to Paradise; The Gentleman from Louisiana; The Sea Spoilers. **1937** Grips, Grunts and Groans (short); Midnight Court; Range Defenders; A Bride for Henry; Mr. Boggs Steps Out; The Go-Getter; Saratoga. **1938** Passport Husband; Born to Be Wild. **1939** Career; Dust Be My Destiny; New Frontier; The Honeymoon's Over; Little Accident; 20,000 Men a Year. **1941** Johnny Eager; Arkansas Judge.

1942 Tennessee Johnson; Blondie for Victory; Blondie Goes to College; Ice-Capades Revue. **1943** The More the Merrier; Unlucky Dog (short). **1944** Between Two Women; Prunes and Politics (short); Sailor's Holiday; She's a Soldier Too. **1945** Nob Hill. **1946** Studio Visit (short).

GREENE, STANLEY
Born: 1911. Died: July 4, 1981, New York, N.Y. (after long illness). Screen, television actor, film director and film producer.

Appeared in: **1964** Nothing But a Man. **1965** The Playground. **1968** For Love of Ivory. **1970** The Landlord. **1974** Death Wish. **1975** Lord Shango. **1978** The Wiz. **1980** Just Tell Me What You Want; Black Face—White Face (documentary).

GREENE, WILLIAM E.
Born: 1927, Ga. Died: Mar. 12, 1970, Cleveland Heights, Ohio (heart attack). Screen, stage, television actor, and stage director.

Appeared in: **1949** The Life of Riley; It Happens Every Spring. **1950** Beware of Blondie. **1952** The Bad and the Beautiful. **1958** Orders to Kill. **1962** Lolita.

GREENLEAF, MACE
Born: Maine. Died: Mar. 24, 1912, Philadelphia, Pa. (typhoid/pneumonia). Screen actor.

Appeared in: **1911** Grandfather. **1912** God Disposes; Falling Leaves; The Child of the Tenements; Blighted Lives.

GREENLEAF, RAYMOND
Born: 1892. Died: Oct. 29, 1963. Screen actor.

Appeared in: **1948** The Naked City; Deep Waters; For the Love of Mary. **1949** Pinky; Slattery's Hurricane; A Kiss in the Dark; East Side, West Side; All the King's Men. **1950** A Ticket to Tomahawk; David Harding, Counterspy; Harriet Craig; On the Isle of Samoa; Storm Warning; No Sad Songs for Me. **1951** As Young as You Feel; The Family Secret; FBI Girl; Pier 23; Al Jennings of Oklahoma; Secret of Convict Lake; A Millionaire for Christy; Ten Tall Men. **1952** Paula; She's Working Her Way Through College; Deadline U.S.A.; Washington Story. **1953** Powder River; The Last Posse; Three Sailors and a Girl; The Bandits of Corsica; South Sea Woman; Angel Face. **1954** Living It Up. **1955** Violent Saturday; Son of Sinbad; Headline Hunters; Texas Lady. **1956** When Gangland Strikes; Never Say Goodbye; Over-Exposed; You Can't Run Away From It; Three Violent People. **1957** Monkey on My Back; The Vampire; The Night the World Exploded. **1958** The Buccaneer. **1959** The Story of Page One. **1960** From the Terrace. **1961** Wild in the Country. **1962** Bird Man of Alcatraz.

GREENSTREET, SYDNEY
Born: Dec. 27, 1879, Sandwich, Kent, England. Died: Jan. 19, 1954, Los Angeles, Calif. (natural causes). Screen and stage actor. Nominated for 1941 Academy Award for Best Supporting Actor in The Maltese Falcon.

Appeared in: **1941** The Maltese Falcon (film debut); They Died With Their Boots On. **1942** Across the Pacific; Casablanca. **1943** Background to Danger. **1944** Hollywood Canteen; Passage to Marseille; Between Two Worlds; The Conspirators; The Mask of Dimitrios; One Man's Secret. **1945** Conflict; Christmas in Connecticut; Pillow to Post. **1946** Devotion; The Verdict; Three Strangers. **1947** That Way with Women; The Hucksters. **1948** Ruthless; The Velvet Touch; The Woman in White. **1949** Flamingo Road; East of the Rising Sun; It's a Great Feeling. **1950** Malaya.

GREENWAY, ANN
Born: Aug. 15, 1902, Alexandria, Egypt. Died: June 27, 1977, Van Nuys, Calif. (cardiac arrest). Screen, stage, vaudeville actress and singer.

Appeared in: **1929** Half Marriage; Night Parade. **1930** And Now! (short).

GREENWOOD, CHARLOTTE (Frances Charlotte Greenwood)
Born: June 25, 1893, Philadelphia, Pa. Died: Jan. 18, 1978, Beverly Hills, Calif. Screen, stage, vaudeville, radio actress and dancer.

Appeared in: **1918** Jane. **1928** Baby Mine. **1929** So Long Letty; So This is College. **1931** Girls Will be Boys (short); Parlor, Bedroom and Bath; The Man in Possession; Flying High; Palmy Days; Stepping Out. **1932** Cheaters at Play. **1933** Orders is Orders (US 1934). **1940** Down Argentine Way; Star Dust; Young People. **1941** The Perfect Snob; Moon Over Miami; Tall, Dark and Handsome. **1942** Springtime in the Rockies. **1943** Dixie Dugan; The Gang's All Here. **1944** Up in Mabel's

Room; Home in Indiana. **1946** Wake Up and Dream. **1947** Driftwood. **1949** The Great Dan Patch; Oh, You Beautiful Doll. **1950** Peggy. **1953** Dangerous When Wet. **1955** Oklahoma! **1956** Glory; The Opposite Sex. **1963** The Sound of Laughter.

GREENWOOD, ETHEL
Born: 1898. Died: Dec. 8, 1970, Hollywood, Calif. (heart attack). Screen and television actress.

GREENWOOD, WINIFRED L.
Born: 1892, Oswego, N.Y. Died: Nov. 23, 1961, Los Angeles, Calif. Screen, stage and vaudeville actress. Entered films in 1911 with Selig.

Appeared in: **1911** Two Orphans; A Tennessee Love Story; His Better Self. **1912** Where the Road Forks; The Slip; Murray the Masher; Under Suspicion; Hypnotized; The Adopted Son; The Last Dance; The Other Woman; An International Romance; Tempted by Necessity; A Detective's Strategy; A Citizen in the Making. **1913** A Divorce Scandal; The Spartan Girl of the West; A False Order; The Lesson; A Husband Won by Election; Pauline Cushman—the Federal Spy; The End of Black Bart; The Understudy; Dixieland; Love—the Winner; Belle Boyd—a Confederate Spy; The Post-Impressionists; Put to the Test. **1914** Like Father Like Son; The Shriner's Daughter; The Hermit; The Ruin of Manley; False Gods; The Little House in the Valley; Her Fighting Chance; The Dream Child; Down by the Sea; A Modern Free-Lance; Daylight; Sheltering an Ingrate; The Tin Can Shack; When a Woman Waits. **1915** The High Cost of Flirting; The Profligate; His Mysterious Neighbor; The Crucifixion of Al Brady; Justified; The Derelict; The Truth of Fiction; His Brother's Debt; Captain Courtesy; The Problem; The Water Carrier of San Juan; Imitations; Spider Barlow Cuts In; It Was Like This; Out of the Ashes; Alice of Hudson Bay; The Silver Lining; The Key to the Past; On Secret Service; The Clean-Up; The Sting of It; The Jilt; Comrades Three; Mixed Wires; The Greater Strength; His Obligation; Detective Blinn; The Reprisal; The Word; The Broken Window; The Resolve; The Guiding Light. **1916** A Woman's Daring; The Voice of Love; The Franchise; The Reclamation; Lying Lips; A Modern Sphinx; The Suppressed Order; The Happy Masquerader; Bonds of Deception; The Shuffle; Dust; The Trail of the Thief. **1917** The Crystal Gazer. **1918** Danger Within; M'Liss; Believe Me—Xantippe; The Deciding Kiss. **1919** Maggie Pepper; Men, Women and Money; Come Again Smith; The Lottery Man. **1920** The Life of the Party; An Adventure in Hearts; Sick-a-Bed. **1921** The Faith Healer; The Dollar-a-Year Man; Don't Call Me Little Girl; Love Never Dies; Sacred and Profane Love. **1923** To the Last Man. **1926** The Flame of the Yukon. **1927** King of Kings.

GREER, DAVID
Born: 1912. Died: Nov. 17, 1977, Los Angeles, Calif. Screen and television actor.

GREER, JULIAN
Born: 1871, London, England. Died: Apr. 15, 1928, N.Y. Screen, stage and vaudeville actor.

Appeared in: **1921** The Passion Flower. **1922** Sunshine Harbor.

GREET, CLARE
Born: June 14, 1871, England. Died: Feb. 14, 1939, London, England. Screen and stage actress.

Appeared in: **1921** Love at the Wheel; The Rotters. **1922** Three Live Ghosts. **1927** The Ring. **1928** The Rising Generation. **1929** The Manxman. **1930** Should A Doctor Tell? (US 1931). **1931** Third Time Lucky. **1932** The Sign of the Four; White Face; Lord Camber's Ladies; Lord Babs. **1933** Mrs. Dane's Defence; The Pointing Finger. **1934** Little Friend. **1935** Emil and the Detectives (aka Emil—US 1938); Maria Marten or, The Murder in the Red Barn. **1936** Sabotage (aka A Woman Alone—US 1937). **1938** St. Martin's Lane (aka Sidewalks of London—US 1940). **1939** Jamaica Inn.

GREGG, EVERLY
Died: June 9, 1959, Beaconfield, England. Screen, stage and television actress.

Appeared in: **1933** The Private Life of Henry VIII (film debut). **1936** The Ghost Goes West. **1937** Thunder in the City. **1938** Blondes for Danger; Pygmalion. **1939** Spies of the Air (US 1940). **1941** Major Barbara. **1942** Uncensored (US 1944); In Which We Serve; The First of the Few (aka Spitfire—US 1943). **1943** The Gentle Sex; The Demi-Paradise (aka Adventure for Two—US 1945). **1944** The Two Fathers; This Happy Breed (US 1947). **1945** Brief Encounter (US 1946). **1946** Gaiety George (aka Showtime—US 1948); Great Expectations (US 1947); Piccadilly Incident. **1950** Stage Freight; The Astonished Heart; The Woman in Question (aka Five Angles on Murder—US 1953). **1951** Worm's Eye View; The Franchise Affair (US 1952). **1952** Stolen

Face. **1954** The Night of the Full Moon; Father Brown (aka The Detective—US). **1956** Lost (aka Tears for Simon—US 1957); The Man Who Never Was. **1957** Brothers in Law; Carry on Admiral (aka The Ship Was Loaded—US 1959). **1959** Room at the Top; Deadly Record.

GREGOR, NORA
Born: Gorizia, Italy. Died: Jan. 20, 1949, Santiago, Chile. Screen and stage actress.

Appeared in: **1930** Olympia. **1931** Und das ist die Hauptsache (That's All That Matters). **1932** But the Flesh Is Weak. **1933** Was Frauen Traeumen (What Women Dream). **1950** The Rules of the Game.

GREGORY, BOBBY
Born: 1900. Died: May 13, 1971, Nashville, Tenn. Screen actor, bandleader, song writer and rodeo performer. His band was called "The Cactus Cowboys."

GREGORY, DORA
Born: 1873, England. Died: Mar. 5, 1954, London, England. Screen, stage, radio and vaudeville actress.

Appeared in: **1931** The Skin Game. **1937** The Dominant Sex. **1938** Star of the Circus (aka Hidden Menace—US 1940). **1942** In Which We Serve.

GREGORY, EDNA (Edna Steinberg)
Born: Jan. 25, 1905, Winnipeg, Canada. Died: July 3, 1965, Los Angeles, Calif. Screen and stage actress. Appeared in early educational comedies and in Cristie films.

Appeared in: **1921** Short Skirts. **1922** Defying the Law. **1923** Devil's Door Yard; In the Palace of the King; The Law Rustlers; Prepared to Die. **1924** The Folly of Vanity. **1925** The Calgary Stampede; Cold Nerve; Sporting Life; The Desert Flower. **1926** The Better Man; Doubling with Danger; One Man Trail; Red Hot Leather. **1927** Blazing Days; Down the Stretch; Grinning Guns; Men of Daring; Romantic Rogue; The Rose of Kildare; Rough and Ready; The Western Rover. **1929** The Great Garbo. **1937** Live, Love and Learn.

GREGORY, WILLIAM H.
Died: Dec. 24, 1926, Los Angeles, Calif. Screen and stage actor.

Appeared in: **1927** Sensation Seekers.

GREGSON, JOHN
Born: Mar. 15, 1919, Liverpool, England. Died: Jan. 8, 1975, Porlock Weir, England (heart attack). Screen, stage and television actor. Entered films in 1948.

Appeared in: **1948** Saraband for Dead Lovers; Scott of Antarctic. **1949** Train of Events (US 1952); Whiskey Galore (aka Tight Little Island and Mad Little Island—US). **1950** Treasure Island; Cairo Road. **1951** The Lavender Hill Mob. **1952** The Holly and the Ivy (US 1953); Angels One Five (US 1954); The Venetian Bird (aka The Assassin—US 1953); The Brave Don't Cry. **1953** The Titfield Thunderbolt; The Assassin; Genevieve (US 1954). **1954** To Dorothy, A Son (aka Cash on Delivery—US 1956); Conflict of Wings; The Crowded Day; The Weak and the Wicked. **1955** Three Cases of Murder (aka You Killed Elizabeth); Above Us the Waves (US 1956); Value for Money (US 1957). **1956** Jacqueline; Battle of the River Plate (aka Pursuit of the Graf Spee—US 1957); Cash on Delivery. **1957** True As a Turtle; Miracle in Soho. **1958** Rooney; Sea of Sand. **1959** The Captain's Table (US 1960); S.O.S. Pacific (US 1960). **1960** Faces in the Dark (US 1964); Hand in Hand (US 1961). **1961** The Frightened City (US 1962); The Treasure of Monte Cristo (aka The Secret of Monte Cristo—US). **1962** Live Now, Pay Later; Tomorrow at Ten (US 1964); The Longest Day; Desert Patrol. **1966** The Night of the Generals (US 1967). **1971** Fright.

GREIG, ROBERT
Born: Dec. 27, 1880, Melbourne, Australia. Died: June 27, 1958, Hollywood, Calif. Screen and stage actor.

Appeared in: **1930** Animal Crackers; Paramount on Parade. **1931** Tonight or Never. **1932** Trouble in Paradise; Jitters the Butler (short); Stepping Sisters; Beauty and the Boss; Man Wanted; The Cohens and the Kellys in Hollywood; The Tenderfoot; Merrily We Go to Hell; Jewel Robbery; Horse Feathers; Love Me Tonight. **1933** Pleasure Cruise; It's Great to Be Alive; Peg O' My Heart; They Just Had to Get Married; Dangerously Yours; Men Must Fight; The Mind Reader. **1934** Easy to Love; Upperworld; One More River; The Love Captive; Cockeyed Cavaliers. **1935** Clive of India; Follies Bergere; Woman Wanted; The Bishop Misbehaves; The Gay Deception; I Live for Love. **1936** Three Live Ghosts; Rose Marie; The Unguarded Hour; Small Town Girl; Trouble for Two; The Devil Doll; Witch of Timbuctu;

Suicide Club; Right in Your Lap; Theodora Goes Wild; Lloyds of London; Stowaway; Easy to Take; Michael O'Halloran. **1937** Easy Living; My Dear Miss Aldrich. **1938** Lady Behave; Midnight Intruder; The Adventures of Marco Polo; Algiers. **1939** Little Accident; Drums Along the Mohawk; It Could Happen to You; Way Down South. **1940** Hudson Bay; No Time for Comedy. **1941** The Lady Eve; Moon Over Miami; Sullivan's Travels. **1942** The Moon and Sixpence; I Married a Witch; Palm Beach Story. **1944** The Great Moment; Summer Storm. **1945** Hollywood and Vine; The Cheaters; Earl Carroll Vanities; Nob Hill; The Picture of Dorian Gray; Love, Honor and Goodbye. **1947** Forever Amber. **1948** Unfaithfully Yours. **1949** Bride of Vengeance.

GRENFELL, JOYCE (Joyce Irene Phipps)
Born: Feb. 10, 1910, London, England. Died: Nov. 30, 1979, London, England. Screen, stage, radio, television actress, writer and playwright. She was named an Officer of the Order of the British Empire in 1946.

Appeared in: **1943** The Demi-Paradise (aka Adventure for Two—US 1945); The Lamp Still Burns. **1947** While the Sun Shines (US 1950). **1949** A Run for Your Money (US 1950); Poet's Pub. **1950** The Happiest Days of Your Life; Stage Fright. **1951** Laughter in Paradise; The Galloping Major; The Magic Box (US 1952). **1952** Pickwick Papers. **1953** Genevieve (US 1954). **1954** Forbidden Cargo (US 1956); The Million Pound Note (aka The Man With a Million—US); The Belles of St. Trinian's (US 1955). **1957** Blue Murder at St. Trinian's (US 1958); The Good Companions (US 1958). **1958** Happy Is the Bride (US 1959). **1960** The Pure Hell of St. Trinian's (US 1961). **1963** The Old Dark House. **1964** The Yellow Rolls-Royce (US 1965); The Americanization of Emily.

GRETLER, HEINRICH
Born: 1897, Zurich, Switzerland. Died: Sept. 30, 1977, Zurich, Switzerland. Screen, stage actor and opera singer. Married to actress Marion Wuensche.

Appeared in: **1923** William Tell (US 1925). **1930** Die Letzte Kompanie (The Last Company). **1945** Marie-Louise. **1952** The Devil Makes Three. **1953** The White Hell of Pitz Palu; Heidi (aka Heidi and Peter—US 1955). **1955** Der Fischer von Heilingensee (The Fisherman from Heiligensee, aka The Big Barrier—US 1958). **1956** Kleines Zelt und Grosse Liebe (aka Two in a Sleeping Bag—US 1964); Robinson sol Nicht Sterben (aka The Girl and the Legend—US 1966). **1960** It Happened in Broad Daylight. **1961** Le Cave se Rebiffe (The Sucker Strikes Back, aka The Counterfeiters of Paris and aka Money, Money, Money—US 1962).

GREVILLE, EDMOND T.
Born: 1906, Nice, France. Died: 1966, France? Screen actor, film producer, director and screenwriter.

Appeared in: **1930** Sous les Toits de Paris (Under the Roofs of Paris).

GREW, MARY
Born: Aug. 21, 1902, London, England. Died: Mar. 20, 1971, England. Screen, stage actress and writer. Married to stage actor Victor Sheridan.

GREY, GLORIA
Born: 1909. Died: Nov. 22, 1947, Hollywood, Calif. Screen, stage and vaudeville actress. Was a 1924 Wampas Baby Star.

Appeared in: **1922** The Great Alone (film debut). **1923** Bag and Baggage; The Supreme Test. **1924** Girl of the Limberlost; Dante's Inferno; The House of Youth; Little Robinson Crusoe; The Millionaire Cowboy; No Gun Man; The Spirit of the U.S.A. **1925** Heartless Husbands; The Snob Buster. **1926** The Boaster; The Ghetto Shamrock; The Hidden Way; The Night Watch; Officer Jim; Thrilling Youth; Unknown Dangers. **1927** The Broncho Buster; Range Courage; Blake of Scotland Yard (serial). **1928** The Thrill Seekers; The Cloud Dodger; The Hound of Silver Creek; Put 'Em Up. **1929** Married in Hollywood.

GREY, JANE
Born: 1883, Middleburg, Vt. Died: Nov. 9, 1944, N.Y. Screen and stage actress. Entered films with Triangle in 1914.

Appeared in: **1914** The Little Gray Lady. **1923** The Governor's Lady. **1927** The Love Wager.

GREY, JERRY (Gerald J. Grey)
Born: 1910. Died: June 7, 1954, San Antonio, Tex. (heart attack). Screen, stage and television dancer.

GREY, KATHERINE
Born: 1873, San Francisco, Calif. Died: Mar. 21, 1950, Orleans, Mass. Screen and stage actress. Married to stage actor Paul Arthor (dec.) and later married to stage actor John Mason. She appeared in early Kulee Co. films.

GREY, LEONARD
Died: Aug. 4, 1918, New York, N.Y. Screen actor.

GREY, LYNDA
Born: 1913. Died: Sept. 4, 1963. Screen actress.

Appeared in: **1938** Shadows Over Shanghai. **1941** Louisiana Purchase. **1942** Holiday Inn; The Major and the Minor; Star-Spangled Rhythm. **1943** The Crystal Ball; For Whom the Bell Tolls; Salute for Three; Happy Go Lucky. **1944** The Uninvited; Lady in the Dark.

GREY, MADELINE
Born: 1887. Died: Aug. 16, 1950, Los Angeles, Calif. Screen and stage actress.

Appeared in: **1929** Nothing But the Truth. **1937** Artists and Models.

GREY, OLGA (Anna Zachak)
Born: 1897, Budapest, Hungary. Died: Apr. 25, 1973, Los Angeles, Calif. Screen actress.

Appeared in: **1915** Birth of a Nation; His Lesson; A Day That Is Dead; The Forged Testament; The Absentee; The Failure; A Bold Impersonation; A Woman of Nerve; Double Trouble; A Breath of Summer; Father Love. **1916** The Law of Success; A Wild Girl of the Sierras; Pillars of Society; Intolerance; The Little Liar. **1917** The Woman God Forgot; Jim Bludso; The Girl at Home; Fanatics; The Ghost House. **1918** When a Man Rides Alone. **1919** Trixie from Broadway; The Mayor of Filbert; Modern Husbands.

GREY, ROBERT HENRY (Henry Virtue Goerner)
Born: July 17, 1891, Oakland, Calif. Died: Apr. 26, 1934, Los Angeles, Calif. (accidental fall). Screen and stage actor.

Appeared in: **1912** The Regeneration of Worthless Dan. **1913** Single-Handed Jim. **1914** Brandon's Last Ride. **1916** Boots and Saddles; Twin Souls. **1917** Twin Kiddies. **1920** Cleaning Up; Speed. **1921** Harem Skarem; Nobody's Fool; R.S.V.P. **1922** West vs. East; Gas, Oil and Water; Big Stakes. **1923** The Silent Partner. **1930** Officer O'Brien.

GRIBBLE, HARRY WAGSTAFF
Born: Mar. 27, 1896, Sevenoaks, Kent, England. Died: Jan. 28, 1981, New York, N.Y. Screen, stage actor, film director, stage director, screenwriter and playwright.

GRIBBON, EDWARD T. "EDDIE"
Born: Jan. 3, 1890, New York, N.Y. Died: Sept. 29, 1965, North Hollywood, Calif. Screen, stage and vaudeville actor. Brother of actor Harry Gribbon (dec. 1961). Entered films with Mack Sennett in 1916.

Appeared in: **1921** Home Talent; Molly O; Playing with Fire; A Small Town Idol. **1922** Alias Julius Caesar; The Crossroads of New York; Tailor-Made Man; The Village Blacksmith; Captain Fly-by-Night. **1923** The Victor; Crossed Wires; Double Dealing; The Fourth Musketeer. **1924** Hoodman Blind; After the Ball; East of Broadway; Jack O'Clubs; The Border Legion. **1925** Seven Days; Code of the West; Just a Woman; Limited Mail; Mansion of Aching Hearts. **1926** Bachelor Brides; The Bat; Desert Gold; The Flaming Frontier; The Flying Mail; Man Bait; There You Are; Under Western Skies. **1927** Tell It to the Marines; The Callahans and the Murphys; Cheating Cheaters; Convoy; Night Life; Streets of Shanghai. **1928** United States Smith; Bachelor's Paradise; Buck Privates; Gang War; Nameless Men; Stop That Man. **1929** Two Weeks Off; Twin Beds; Honeymoon; Two Men and a Maid; Fancy Baggage; From Headquarters. **1930** Good Intentions; Lottery Bride; They Learned About Women; Born Reckless; Dames Ahoy; Song of the West. **1931** Mr. Lemon of Orange; Not Exactly Gentlemen. **1933** Hidden Gold. **1934** Search for Beauty; I Can't Escape; Everything's Ducky (short). **1935** The Cyclone Ranger; Rip Roaring Riley; Flying Down to Zero (short). **1936** The Phantom Rider (serial); Love on a Bet; The Millionaire Kid; I Cover Chinatown. **1937** The Big Shot; You Can't Buy Luck; Gangway. **1938** The Spy Ring; Anesthesia (short); Maid's Night Out. **1939** Moving Vanities (short). **1940** The Great Dictator; The Leather Pushers. **1943** Radio Runaround (short). **1944** To Heir is Human (short). **1946** Joe Palooka, Champ; Mr. Hex; Gentlemen Joe Palooka. **1947** Joe Palooka in the Knockout. **1948** Smugglers Cove; Fighting Mad; Winner Take All. **1949** Joe Palooka in the Big Fight; Fighting Fools; Joe Palooka in the Counterpunch. **1950** Joe Palooka Meets Humphrey; Joe Palooka in Humphrey Takes a Chance; Triple Trouble; Joe Palooka in Triple Cross; Joe Palooka in the Squared Circle.

GRIBBON, HARRY
Born: 1886, New York, N.Y. Died: July 28, 1961, Los Angeles, Calif. Screen, stage and vaudeville actor. Brother of actor Eddie Gribbon (dec. 1965). Entered films with Sennett.

Appeared in: **1915** Colored Villainy; Mabel, Fatty and the Law; Ye Olden Grafter; Ambrose's Sour Grapes; A Janitor's Wife's Temptation; The Idle Rich; Does Flirting Pay? **1916** The Worst of Enemies; Perils of the Park; Love Will Conquer; His Auto Ruination; A Dash of Courage; His Wild Oats; A Lover's Might (working title The Fire Chief); The Great Pearl Tangle. **1917** Stars and Bars; Pinched in the Finish; Two Crooks (working title A Noble Crook). **1918** A Pullman Blunder. **1922** Self-Made Man. **1923** The Extra Girl. **1924** The Tomboy. **1927** Knockout Reilly. **1928** The Cameraman; Shakedown; Rose Marie; Smart Set; Show People; Chinatown. **1929** Tide of Empire; Honeymoon; On With the Show; The Mysterious Island; Midnight Daddies; plus the following shorts: The Bride's Relations; Whirls and Girls; The Bee's Buzz; The Big Palooka; The Constable; The Golfers; The Lunkhead; A Hollywood Star; Clancy at the Bat; The New Halfback; Uppercut O'Brien. **1930** So Long Letty; Song of the West; Swell People; Big Hearted; The Lottery Bride; Sugar Plum Papa (short). **1931** The Gorilla; plus the following shorts: Just A Bear; In Conference; The Cow-Catcher's Daughter; Ghost Parade; All-American Kickback. **1932** Ride Him, Cowboy; You Said a Mouthful; Ladies They Talk About. **1932-33** "Whoopee" comedies and Mack Sennett "Featurettes." **1933** Baby Face; Snug in the Jug (short). **1936** Sleepless Hollow (short). **1944** Arsenic and Old Lace (stage and film versions). **1963** The Sound of Laughter (documentary).

GRIBOV, ALEXEI (Alexei Nikolaevich Gribov)
Born: Jan. 31, 1902, Moscow, Russia. Died: 1977, Russia. Screen, stage and television actor.

Appeared in: **1935** Red Army Days. **1939** Concentration Camp. **1945** Marriage; Military Secret. **1954** The Inspector General; True Friends. **1955** The Safety Match. **1961** Slepoy Muzykant (Sound of Life—US 1962); Vzroslyye Det (Grown-Up Children—US 1963).

GRIDOUX, LUCAS
Born: 1890, France. Died: 1952, France? Screen actor.

Appeared in: **1936** The Mystic Mountain. **1937** The Life and Loves of Beethoven. **1939** The Citadel of Silence. **1941** Pepe le Moko. **1947** Panic.

GRIER, JIMMY
Born: 1902, Pittsburgh, Pa. Died: June 4, 1959. Orchestra leader and screen actor.

Appeared in: **1934** Transatlantic Merry-Go-Round. **1937** Nobody's Baby.

GRIEVES, JACK
Born: 1901. Died: Jan. 10, 1935, Burbank, Calif. Screen actor and dancer.

GRIFFELL, JOSE MARTINEZ
Born: 1905, Mexico. Died: Nov. 14, 1955, Mexico City, Mexico. Screen and stage actor.

GRIFFIES, ETHEL (Ethel Woods)
Born: Apr. 26, 1878, England. Died: Sept. 9, 1975, London, England (stroke). Screen, stage and television actress. Daughter of actor-manager Samuel Rupert Woods and actress Lillie Roberts Woods. Married to stage actor Walter Beaumont (dec. 1910) and later married to actor Edward Cooper (dec. 1956).

Appeared in: **1930** Old English. **1931** Chances; Waterloo Bridge; The Road to Singapore; Once a Lady; Millionaire; Stepdaughters. **1932** Manhattan Parade; The Impatient Maiden; Westward Passage; Love Me Tonight; Are You Listening?; Union Depot; Lovers Courageous; Devil's Lottery; Payment Deferred. **1933** Tonight is Ours; A Lady's Profession; Alice in Wonderland; Midnight Club; Torch Singer; White Woman; Good Companions; Doctor Bull; Bombshell; Looking Forward. **1934** Bulldog Drummond Strikes Back; The House of Rothschild; We Live Again; Of Human Bondage; Jane Eyre; Olsen's Big Moment; Fog; Four Frightened People; Sadie McGee; Call It Luck; Painted Veil. **1935** Enchanted April; The Mystery of Edwin Drood; Vanessa—Her Love Story; Hold 'Em Yale; Anna Karenina; Werewolf of London; The Return of Peter Grimm. **1936** Twice Branded; Guilty Melody; Not so Dusty. **1937** Kathleen Mavourneen (aka Kathleen—US 1938). **1938** Crackerjack (aka The Man With 100 Faces—US). **1939** I'm from Missouri; We Are Not Alone; The Star Maker. **1940** Over the Moon; Vigil the Night; Irene; Anne of Windy Poplars; Stranger on the Third Floor; Waterloo Bridge. **1941** Dead Men Tell; A Yank in the RAF; Great Guns; How Green Was My Valley; Billy the Kid; Remember the Day; Man at Large. **1942** Mrs. Wiggs of the Cabbage Patch; Between Us Girls; Time to Kill; Castle in the Desert; Right to the Heart; Son of Fury; The Postman Didn't Ring. **1943** Holy Matrimony; Forever and a Day; First Comes Courage. **1944** The Canterville Ghost; Jane Eyre; Music for Millions; Pardon My Rhythm; White Cliff of Dover. **1945** The Horn Blows at Midnight; Thrill of a Romance; Molly and Me; Saratoga Trunk; Keys of the Kingdom; The Strange Affair of Uncle Harry. **1946** Devotion; Sing While You Dance. **1947** The Homestretch; Millie's Daughter; Forever Amber; Brasher Doubloon. **1963** Billy Liar (stage and film versions); The Birds. **1965** Bus Riley's Back in Town.

GRIFFIN, CARLTON ELLIOTT
Born: 1893. Died: July 23, 1940, Hollywood, Calif. (heart attack). Screen and vaudeville actor. Appeared in vaudeville with Grace Gordon in an act billed as "Magic Glasses." Divorced from actress Pauline Saxon. Entered films with Lubin Co.

Appeared in: **1921** At The Stage Door. **1922** Shackles of Gold. **1924** Girl Shy; The Painted Flapper. **1925** The Great Jewel Robbery. **1926** Her Big Adventure; The Imposter; Tramp, Tramp, Tramp. **1930** Shivering Shakespeare (short); High C's (short). **1931** The Pip From Pittsburgh (short); Rough Seas (short). **1932** First in War (short). **1933** Nature in the Wrong (short); Arabian Tights (short). **1934** Maid in Hollywood (short); Another Wild Idea (short). **1935** The following shorts: Southern Exposure; Nurse to You; Slightly Static. **1937** A Star Is Born.

GRIFFIN, CHARLES
Born: 1888. Died: Aug. 17, 1956, Hollywood, Calif. Screen actor.

GRIFFIN, FRANK L.
Born: 1889. Died: Mar. 17, 1953, Hollywood, Calif. (heart attack). Screen actor, screenwriter, film director, and film producer. Entered films as an actor with Lubin Co. in 1906.

GRIFFIN, GERALD
Born: 1892. Died: Jan. 11, 1962, Rhinebeck, N.Y. (complications after surgery). Vaudeville, stage and screen actor.

GRIFFIN, GERALD
Born: 1854, Pittsburgh, Pa. Died: Mar. 16, 1919, Venice, Calif. Screen actor. Do not confuse with vaudeville actor Gerald Griffin (dec. 1962).

Appeared in: **1916** The Yellow Menace (serial); Feathertop; The Sunbeam. **1918** A Pair of Cupids.

GRIFFIN, PHYLLIS
Died: Feb. 20, 1959, London, England. Screen actress. Mother of actress Bebe Daniels (dec. 1971).

GRIFFITH, CORINNE (aka CORA MARSHALL)
Born: Nov. 24, 1894, Texarkana, Ark. Died: July 13, 1979, Santa Monica, Calif. (cardiac arrest). Screen, stage actress, author and dancer. Divorced from actor Webster Campbell (dec. 1972); film producer Walter Morosco (dec. 1948); George Marshall and actor Danny Scholl. Entered films as an extra.

Appeared in: **1916** The Last Man (film debut?); A Fool and His Friend; Miss Adventure; The Yellow Girl; The Rich Idler; La Paloma; Through the Wall; The Cost of High Living; The Waters of Lethe; Bittersweet. **1917** Transgression; Ashes; Sin's Penalty; I Will Repay; Who Goes There? **1918** The Menace; The Mystery of Lake Lethe; Love Watches; The Love Doctor; Clutch of Circumstance; The Girl of Today; Miss Ambition; The Stolen Treaty. **1919** The Adventure Shop; The Girl Problem; The Unknown Quantity; Thin Ice; A Girl at Bay; The Bramble Bush; The Climbers. **1920** Tower of Jewels; The Whisper Market; The Garter Girl; Human Collateral; Deadline at Eleven; Bab's Candidate; The Broadway Bubble. **1921** It Isn't Being Done This Season; The Single Track; Moral Fibre; What's Your Reputation Worth? **1922** Divorce Coupons; Received Payment; Island Wives; A Virgin's Sacrifice (aka A Woman's Sacrifice). **1923** The Common Law; Six Days. **1924** Black Oxen; Lilies of the Field; Love's Wilderness; Single Wives. **1925** Classified; Infatuation; Declassee; The Marriage Whirl. **1926** Into Her Kingdom; Mademoiselle Modiste; Syncopating Sue. **1927** The Lady in Ermine; Three Hours. **1928** Outcast; The Garden of Eden. **1929** The Divine Lady; Saturday's Children; Prisoners. **1930** Lilies of the Field (and 1924 version); Back Pay. **1923** Lily Christine. **1962** Paradise Alley.

GRIFFITH, DAVID WARK
Born: Jan. 22, 1875, La Grange, Ky. Died: July 23, 1948, Los Angeles, Calif. (stroke). Screen, stage actor, screenwriter, playwright and film director. Divorced from actress Evelyn Marjorie Baldwin and Linda Arvidson (dec. 1948).

Appeared in: **1907** Rescued from an Eagle's Nest. **1908** At the Crossroads of Life. **1922** When Knighthood Was in Flower.

GRIFFITH, GORDON
Born: July 4, 1907, Chicago, Ill. Died: Oct. 12, 1958, Hollywood, Calif. (heart attack). Entered films as a child in 1913 and later became a film director and producer. Son of actors Harry Griffith (dec. 1926) and Katherine Griffith (dec.1921). Brother of actor Graham Griffith (dec.).

Appeared in: **1914** Chicken Chaser; Caught in a Cabaret (reissued as The Jazz Waiter). **1918** Tarzan of the Apes. **1920** Huckleberry Finn; The Son of Tarzan (serial). **1921** That Something. **1922** Catch My Smoke; More to Be Pitied Than Scorned; Penrod; The Village Blacksmith. **1923** Jungle Trail of the Son of Tarzan (reduced version of 1920 serial Son of Tarzan); Main Street. **1924** The Street of Tears. **1925** Little Annie Rooney. **1926** The Cat's Pajamas. **1928** The Branded Man. **1935** The Crusades.

GRIFFITH, GRAHAM
Died: prior to 1958. Screen actor. Son of actors Harry (dec. 1926) and Katherine Griffith (dec. 1921). Brother of actor Gordon Griffith (dec. 1958).

GRIFFITH, HARRY (Harry Sutherland Griffith)
Born: July 19, 1866, Ind. Died: May 4, 1926, Pasadena, Calif. (coronary). Screen actor. Father of actors Gordon (dec. 1958) and Graham (dec.). Married to actress Katherine Griffith (dec. 1921). Do not confuse with actor of the same name who appeared in films during 1930's.

GRIFFITH, HUGH
Born: May 30, 1912, Anglesey, North Wales. Died: May 14, 1980, London, England. Screen, stage, television actor and author. Won 1959 Academy Award for Best Supporting Actor in Ben Hur.

Appeared in: **1939** Neutral Port (film debut). **1948** London Belongs to Me (aka Dulcimer Street—US); The Three Wierd Sisters; The First Gentlemen (aka The Affairs of a Rogue—US 1949); So Evil My Love. **1949** Dr. Morelle—The Case of the Missing Heiress; Last Days of Dolwyn (aka The Woman of Dolwyn—US); A Run for Your Money (US 1950); Kind Hearts and Coronets (US 1950). **1950** Gone to Earth (aka The Wild Heart—US 1952). **1951** Laughter in Paradise; The Galloping Major. **1953** The Titfield Thunderbolt; The Beggar's Opera (US 1954). **1954** The Sleeping Tiger. **1957** Lucky Jim; The Good Companions (US 1958). **1959** Ben Hur; The Hound of the Baskervilles; The Story on Page One. **1960** Exodus; The Day They Robbed the Bank of England. **1962** The Inspector (aka Lisa—US); The Counterfeit Traitor; Mutiny on the Bounty; Term of Trial (US 1963). **1963** Tom Jones; Hide and Seek (US 1964). **1964** The Bargee. **1965** The Amorous Adventures of Moll Flanders. **1966** How to Steal a Million; The Poppy Is Also a Flower. **1967** Oh Dad, Poor Dad; The Sailor From Gibralter. **1968** Oliver!; The Fixer; La Centura di Castita (aka On My Way to the Crusades I Met a Girl Who ...—US 1969). **1970** The Abominable Dr. Phibes. **1972** Dr. Phibes Rides Again!. **1973** What? **1974** Luther; Canterbury Tales; Craze; Last Days of Man on Earth. **1976** Loving Cousins. **1977** The Last Remake of Beau Geste; The Passover Plot. **1979** Some Like it Cool; A Nightengale Sang in Berkeley Square. **1980** The Hound of the Baskervilles; The Canterbury Tales.

GRIFFITH, KATHERINE (Katherine Kierman)
Born: Sept. 30, 1976, San Francisco, Calif. Died: Oct. 17, 1921, Los Angeles, Calif. (cerebral hemorrhage). Screen, stage and vaudeville actress. Married to actor Harry Griffith (dec. 1926). Mother of actors Gordon (dec. 1958) and Graham Griffith (dec.).

Appeared in: **1917** Snow White. **1918** Face Value. **1919** Vicky Van; The Woman Thou Gavest Me. **1920** Huckleberry Finn; Pollyanna; Mothers of Men; Mid-Channel. **1921** They Shall Pay.

GRIFFITH, RAYMOND
Born: Jan. 23, 1890, Boston, Mass. Died: Nov. 25, 1957, Hollywood, Calif. Screen actor, film director, producer, and screenwriter. Married to actress Bertha Mann (dec. 1967). Entered films with Vitagraph in 1914.

Appeared in: **1917** The Surf Girl; The Scoundrel's Tale; A Royal Rogue. **1922** Crossroads of New York; Minnie; Fools First. **1923** Eternal Three; The Day of Faith; Going Up; Red Lights; Souls for Sale;

White Tiger. **1924** Poisoned Paradise; Changing Husbands; The Dawn of a Tomorrow; Lily of the Dust; Nellie, the Beautiful Cloak Model; Never Say Die; Open All Night; The Yankee Consul. **1925** The Night Club; Forty Winks; Paths to Paradise; A Regular Fellow; Fine Clothes; Miss Bluebeard; When Winter Went. **1926** Hands Up; Wet Paint; You'd Be Surprised. **1927** Wedding Bill$; Time to Love. **1929** Trent's Last Case; The Sleeping Porch. **1930** All Quiet on the Western Front.

GRIFFITH, WILLIAM M.
Born: 1897. Died: July 21, 1960, Hollywood, Calif. (heart attack). Stage and screen actor.

Appeared in: **1937** Time Out for Romance. **1949** Everybody Does It; Range Land. **1955** Devil Goddess.

GRIFFITHS, JANE
Born: Oct. 16, 1929, Peacehaven, Sussex, England. Died: June, 1975, England. Screen, stage and television actress.

Appeared in: **1950** Double Confession (US 1953). **1952** The Gambler and the Lady. **1954** The Million Pound Note (aka Man With a Million—US); The Green Scarf (US 1955). **1957** The Traitor (aka The Accursed—US 1958); Three Sundays to Live. **1958** Tread Softly Stranger (US 1959). **1961** The Impersonator. **1962** Dead Man's Evidence. **1963** The Double (US 1967).

GRIGGS, JOHN
Born: 1909. Died: Feb. 25, 1967, Englewood, N.J. Screen, stage and radio actor.

Appeared in: **1937** Annapolis Salute.

GRIMES, THOMAS
Born: 1887. Died: Aug. 19, 1934, Tujunga, Calif. Screen actor and stuntman.

Appeared in: **1918** Headin' South. **1923** The Secret of the Pueblo.

GRIMWOOD, HERBERT
Born: Mar. 7, 1875, Walthamstow, England. Died: Dec. 1, 1929, England? Screen and stage actor.

Appeared in: **1920** When the Clouds Roll By; Simple Souls; The Hope. **1924** Romola. **1926** The Amateur Gentleman.

GRISEL, LOUIS R.
Born: 1848, New Castle, Del. Died: Nov. 19, 1928, Fort Lee, N.J. Screen and stage actor.

Appeared in: **1921** The Black Panther's Club; Jane Eyre.

GRISWOLD, GRACE (Grace Hall)
Born: 1872, Ashtabula, Ohio. Died: June 13, 1927, New York, N.Y. Screen, stage actress and playwright.

Appeared in: **1921** Disraeli. **1922** One Exciting Night; Anna Ascends; Smilin' Through. **1923** The Ragged Edge.

GRISWOLD, JAMES
Born: Apr. 30, 1882, New Britain, Conn. Died: Oct. 4, 1935. Screen actor.

Appeared in: **1914** The Rose of the Rancho. **1915** Carmen. **1916** Tennessee's Partner.

GROAT, CARLTON
Born: 1896. Died: Aug. 29, 1940, Portland, Ore. Screen actor.

GROCK (Adrien Wettach)
Born: 1880, Switzerland? Died: July 14, 1959, Imperia, Italy. Screen, vaudeville actor, and clown. Appeared in British and German films.

GROENEVELD, BEN
Born: 1899, Netherlands. Died: Feb. 14, 1962, Amsterdam, Netherlands. Screen and stage actor.

Appeared in: **1949** Man to Men.

GRONBERG, AKE
Born: 1914, Stockholm, Sweden. Died: 1969, Sweden? Screen actor.

Appeared in: **1943** Sonja. **1954** Sir Arne's Treasure. **1956** Sawdust and Tinsel (aka The Naked Night). **1960** Private 91 Karlsson is Demobbed or So He Thinks. **1964** 491 (US 1967). Other Swedish films: Toward New Times; The Melody from the Old Town; We from Sunny Glade; Brave Boys in Uniform; The Merry-Go-Round in Full Swing; Everybody at His Station; Our Boys in Uniform; Boys from the South of Stockholm; Our Gang; A Sailor in a Dresscoat; Tomorrow's Melody; The Yellow Ward; A Singing Girl; People of Roslagen; Take Care of Ulla; Nothing Will be Forgotten; Woman Takes Command; Lack of Evidence; The Halta Lotta Tavern; Captivated By a Voice; Anna Lans; Young Blood; Watch Out for Spies!; Count the Happy Moments Only; Marie in the Windmill; Girls in the Harbour; In the Beautiful Province of Roslagen; The Girls from Smaland; The Six Karlssons; Brita in the Wholesaler's House; Between Brothers; A Woman on Board; Handsome Augusta; The Song About Stockholm; Woman Without a Face; Navvies; The Night Watchman's Wife; Each Goes His Own Way; Life Begins Now; Dangerous Spring; The Intimate Restaurant; The Kiss on the Cruise; The Beef and the Banana; Ingenious Johansson; Skipper in Storm Weather; She Came Like a Wind; Summer with Monika; People on Manoeuvres; Barabbas; We Three Are Making Our Debut; Merry Boys of the Navy; Seven Black Brassieres; Never With My Jemmy; A Storm Over Tjuro; A Lesson in Love; Simon the Sinner; Dolls and Balls; Beat It; Dangerous Freedom; The Merry-Go-Round in the Mountains; Paradise; Rasmus and the Tramp; The Matrimonial Advertisement; The Tough Game; Encounters and Dusk; Dlarar Bananen Biffen?; Line Six; Pirates on Lake Malar; Adam and Eve; My Love is a Rose; Loving Couples; Sailors and Sextants; A Summer Adventure.

GROONEY, ERNEST G.

Died: Jan. 20, 1946, Hollywood, Calif. Screen actor and film music director.

GROSS, WILLIAM J.

Born: 1837. Died: Apr. 12, 1924, Brooklyn, N.Y. Screen, stage, and vaudeville actor.

Appeared in: **1918** Prunelia. **1921** Rainbow; Ashamed of Parents.

GROSSKURTH, KURT

Born: 1909, Rhineland, Germany. Died: May 29, 1975, Bad Aibling, Germany (auto accident). Screen, television actor and singer.

Appeared in: **1956** Magic Fire. **1967** Liebesspiele Im Schnee (aka Ski Fever—US 1969). **1971** Willy Wonka and the Chocolate Factory.

GROSSMITH, ENA

Born: Aug. 14, 1896, London, England. Died: Mar. 20, 1944, London, England. Screen and stage actress. Daughter of actor George Grossmith (dec. 1935).

Appeared in: **1919** The Castle of Dreams. **1921** Candytuff—I Mean Veronica. **1927** A Daughter in Revolt. **1928** Virginia's Husband. .

GROSSMITH, GEORGE, JR.

Born: May 11, 1875, London, England. Died: June 6, 1935, London, England. Screen, stage actor, stage producer and playwright. Son of stage actor George Grossmith, Sr. (dec.) and brother of actor Lawrence Grossmith (dec. 1944). Father of actress Ena Grossmith (dec. 1944).

Appeared in: **1909** A Gaiety Duet. **1910** Winning a Widow. **1913** The Argentine Tango and Other Dances. **1930** Women Everywhere; Are You There?; Those Three French Girls. **1932** Wedding Rehearsal; Service for Ladies (aka Reserved for Ladies—US); The Girl from Maxim's (US 1936). **1933** L'Homme a l'Hispano (The Man in the Hispano-Suiza). **1934** Princess Charming (US 1935). **1940** Les Amoureux.

GROSSMITH, LAWRENCE

Born: Mar. 29, 1877, London, England. Died: Feb. 21, 1944, Woodland Hills, Calif. Stage and screen actor. Son of stage actor George Grossmith, Sr. (dec.) and brother of actor George Grossmith, Jr. (dec. 1935).

Appeared in: **1914** The Brass Bottle. **1918** The Common Cause. **1933** Counsel's Opinion; Cash (aka For Love or Money—US 1934); Tiger Bay. **1934** Rolling in Money; The Luck Of a Sailor; The Private Life of Don Juan; Sing As We Go. **1935** It Happened in Paris. **1936** Everything in Life; Men Are Not Gods (US 1937). **1937** Song of the Forge; Make Up; Silver Blaze (aka Murder at the Baskervilles—US 1941); The Girl in the Taxi; Smash and Grab. **1939** Captain Fury; I'm From Missouri. **1941** Larceny.

GROSSMITH, WEEDON (Walter Weedon Grossmith)

Born: 1852, London, England. Died: June 14, 1919, England?. Screen, stage actor and playwright. Married to actress May Palfrey (dec. 1929).

Appeared in: **1917** Masks and Faces.

GROSSO, PAUL "KANSAS"

Born: 1897. Died: July 5, 1979, Ft. Bragg, Calif. (stroke). Screen actor and stuntman. Entered films as a stuntman in the 1920's.

GROVES, CHARLES, JR.

Born: Nov. 22, 1875, Manchester, England. Died: May 23, 1955, England? Screen and stage actor. Son of stage actor Charles Groves, Sr. (dec. 1909) and Elizabeth Reynolds.

Appeared in: **1932** The Face in the Window; Once Bitten; Doubling Dealing.

GROVES, FREDERICK "FRED"

Born: Aug. 8, 1880, London, England. Died: June 4, 1955, England? Screen and stage actor. Son of stage actor Charles Groves (dec. 1909) and Lillian Gifford. Entered films in 1912.

Appeared in: **1913** Maria Marten; Or, The Murder in the Red Barn; Popsy Wopsy (short); Bridegrooms Beware (short). **1914** In the Days of Trafalgar (aka Black-Eyed Susan, aka The Battling British—US); The Cup Final Mystery; The Suicide; The Loss of the Birkenhead; Inquisitive Ike (short); Beautiful Jim (aka The Price of Justice—US); Her Luck in London; The Idol of Paris. **1915** The Firm of Girdlestone (US 1916); The Two Roads; Charity Ann; A Will of Her Own; Mr. Lyndon at Liberty; Fine Feathers; Yvonne; A Honeymoon for Three; There's Good in Everyone; Midshipman Easy; Gilbert Dying to Die (short); Gilbert Gets Tiger-Itis (short); The World's Desire (aka The Lord Gave); London's Yellow Peril; Florence Nightingale; From Shopgirl to Duchess; Her Nameless (?) Child; Another Man's Wife; Grip; Home. **1916** Driven (aka Desperation—US); Meg the Lady; Esther; Motherlove; The Maxman. **1917** Smith; Drink; The Labour Leader. **1919** Castle of Dreams. **1920** Garryowen; Judge Not; London Pride. **1921** The Mayor of Casterbridge. **1922** A Master of Craft; The Crimson Circle. **1923** Squibs' Honeymoon; Squibs; MP; Rogues of the Turf. **1925** Memories (short). **1930** Escape; Suspense. **1931** Out of the Blue. **1932** The World, The Flesh and the Devil. **1934** The Old Curiosity Shop (US 1935); A Glimpse of Paradise. **1935** Royal Cavalcade (aka Regal Cavalcade—US); Dance Band. **1936** Beloved Imposter; Royal Eagle; Second Bureau. **1937** 21 Days (aka The First and the Last, aka 21 Days Together—US 1940). **1938** The Challenge (US 1939); Vessel of Wrath (aka The Beachcomber—US); The Viper; No Parking. **1948** An Ideal Husband; Night Beat; My Brother's Keeper (US 1949). **1950** The Girl Who Couldn't Quit; Up the Cup; Old Mother Riley, Headmistress (US 1951).

GROWER, RUSSELL GORDON

Died: Feb. 21, 1958, Ontario, Calif. (shot by bandit). Screen actor.

GRUBER, JANE

Born: 1948, Czechoslovakia. Died: Dec. 4, 1968, Munich, West Germany. Screen actress.

GRUENDGENS, GUSTAF (aka GUSTAF GRUNDGENS)

Born: 1900, Dusseldorf, Germany. Died: Oct. 7, 1963, Manila, Philippine Islands (internal hemorrhage). Screen, stage actor and film director.

Appeared in: **1930** Va Banque; Hokuspokus (Hocuspocus); Ich Glaub' nie Mehr an Eine Frau; Brand in der Oper (Fire in the Opera House—US 1932, aka Barcarole). **1931** Danton; Yorck (US 1932); Der Raub der Mona Lisa (US 1932); M (aka Moerder Unter Uns—US 1933); Luise, Koenigin von Preussen (US 1932). **1932** Teilnehmer Antwortrt Nicht; Die Graefin von Monte Christo (The Countess of Monte Cristo). **1933** La Voce del Sangue; Liebelei (US 1936); Die Schoenen Tage van Aranjuez; Der Tunnel. **1934** Schwarzer Jaeger Johanna; Terra; So Endete Eine Liebe; Das Erbe von Pretoria (US 1936). **1935** Das Maedchen Johanna; Pygmalion; Hundert Tage (Hundred Days). **1936** Eine Frau ohne Bedeutung (US 1938). **1937** Capriolen. **1938** Liebe im Gleitflug (Love in Stunt Flying); Tanz auf dem Vulkan. **1941** Friedemann Bach; Ohm Krueger. **1960** Das Glas Wasser (A Glass of Water—US 1962); Faust (US 1963).

GRUND, LEO

Born: 1901, Germany. Died: Mar. 8, 1978, New York, N.Y. (heart attack). Screen, stage actor and talent agent. Entered films in Germany.

GRUNING, ILKA

Died: Nov. 11, 1964. Screen actress.

Appeared in: **1932** Drunter und Drueber. **1941** King's Row; Underground. **1942** Friendly Enemies; Desperate Journey; Iceland; Casablanca; Dangerously They Live. **1943** This Is the Army; Bomber's Moon. **1946** Murder in the Music Hall; Rendezvous 24; Temptation. **1947** Desperate; Repeat Performance. **1848** Words and Music. **1949** Captain China. **1950** Convicted. **1951** Passage West.

GUARD, KIT (Christen Klitgaard)

Born: May 5, 1894, Hals, Denmark. Died: July 18, 1961, Hollywood, Calif. Screen and stage actor. Entered films in 1922.

Appeared in: **1925** The "Go-Getters" series of shorts including: The Sleeping Cutie; Ain't Love Grand; The Way of a Maid. The "Pacemaker" series of shorts including: Welcome Granger; He Who Gets Rapped; Merton of the Goofies; The Great Decide; The Fast Male; The Covered Flagon; Madame Sans Gin; Three Bases East; The Merry Kiddo; What Price Gloria?; Don CooCoo; Miss Me Again. **1926** One Minute of Play; plus the "Bill Grimm's Progress" series of shorts including: The Lady of Lyons, N.Y.; The Fight That Failed; Where There's a Bill; The Last of His Face; When a Man's a Fan; The Midnight Son; Bruisers and Losers; Little Miss Bluffit; Ladies Prefer Brunettes; Assorted Nuts; Blisters Under the Skin; The Knight Before Christmas. **1927** Her Father Said No; In a Moment of Temptation; plus the "Beauty Parlor" series of shorts including: Beloved Rouge; Boys Will be Girls; Chin He Lived to Lift; Fresh Hair Fiends; Helene of Troy, N.Y.; New Faces for Old; Last Nose of Summers; Peter's Pan; She Troupes to Conquer; Toupay or Not Toupay. **1928** Lingerie; Legionnaires in Paris; Beau Broadway; Dead Man's Curve; Shamrock Alley (short). **1930** Big Money; Night Work; The Racketeer. **1931** Defenders of the Law; The Unholy Garden; Sky Raiders. **1932** The Thirteenth Guest; Two-Fisted Justice; County Fair; Flames; The Last Man; The Fighting Champ; Tom Brown of Culver; The Racing Strain. **1933** Carnival Lady; Corruption; One Year Later; Riot Squad; Sucker Money. **1934** It Happened One Night; Lady by Choice; The Mighty Barnum. **1935** Barbary Coast; Kid Courageous; Reckless Roads; Rip Roaring Riley. **1937** Shadow of the Orient. **1938** Code of the Rangers; You and Me; Frontier Scout; Heroes of the Hills; Prison Train. **1939** Homicide Bureau; Six-Gun Rhythm; El Diablo Rides; The Flying Deuces. **1940** The Green Archer (serial). **1941** Honolulu Lu. **1943** Blitz on the Fritz (short); It Ain't Hay. **1945** She Gets Her Man; Frontier Gal. **1947** Trail Street; Johnny O'Clock; The Perils of Pauline. **1948** So You Want to be a Detective (short). **1949** Master Minds. **1951** Fort Defiance; Abbott and Costello Meet the Invisible Man. **1952** Carrie. **1956** Around the World in 80 Days.

GUARD, SULLY

Died: Mar. 21, 1916, Jacksonville, Fla. (auto accident). Screen actor.

Appeared in: **1915** The Necklace of Pearls.

GUDGEON, BERTRAND C.

Died: Oct. 22, 1948, North Bergen, N.J. Screen actor and stuntman. Entered films in 1908.

Appeared in: **1914** The Exploits of Elaine (serial); The Perils of Pauline (serial). **1916** The Iron Claw (serial).

GUELSTORFF, MAX

Born: 1882, Germany. Died: Feb. 9, 1947, Berlin, Germany. Screen and stage actor.

Appeared in: **1929** His Late Excellency; Meistersingers. **1930** Hurrah I'm Alive. **1931** Der Grosse Tenor. **1932** Der Raub der Mona Lisa; Ich Geh aus und Du Bleibst Da. **1933** Der Hauptmann von Koepenick. **1934** Liebe Muss Verstanden Sein. **1935** Die Sonne Geht auf; Ich Sing Mich in Dein Herz Hinein; Frischer Wind aus Kanada; So ein Maedel Vergisst Man Nicht; Ich Kenn Dich Nicht und Liebe Dich (I Don't Know You, but I Love You). **1936** Das Schloss Im Sueden; Annette in Paradise; Heisses Blut. **1937** Der Raub der Sabinerinnen; Ein Falscher Fuffziger; Kirschen in Nachbars Garten; Schabernack; Susanne im Bade (Susanna in the Bath). **1938** Der Zerbroechene Krug (The Broken Jug); Herzensdieb (Heart Thief). **1939** Der Schritt vom Wege (The False Step).

GUENSTEQ, F. F.

Born: 1862. Died: Mar. 28, 1936, Glendale, Calif. Screen and stage actor. Entered films approx. 1916.

GUENTHER, RUTH (aka RUTH JEW BABY)

Born: 1910. Died: June 25, 1974, Culver City, Calif. (lung cancer). Screen actress and psychic. Married to actor Irwin Guenther.

GUEVREMONT, PAUL

Born: 1903, Canada? Died: May 9, 1979, Europe (plane crash). Screen actor.

Appeared in: **1951** The Thirteenth Letter; Quebec. **1964** The Luck of Ginger Coffey. **1967** Waiting for Caroline (US 1969).

GUHL, GEORGE

Died: June 27, 1943, Los Angeles, Calif. Screen, vaudeville, and burlesque actor. Was in vaudeville in an act billed as "The Guhl Bros." and later, with another partner, in an act billed as "Adams and Guhl."

Appeared in: **1935** Goin' to Town; The Case of the Curious Bride. **1936** After the Thin Man; The Case Against Mrs. Ames; Arbor Day (short); Sing Me a Love Song. **1937** Double Wedding; The Adventurous Blonde; Fly-Away Baby; Night Club Scandal. **1938** Young Fugitives; Torchy Gets Her Man; Blondes at Work; Torchy Blane in Panama; Gold Mine in the Sky. **1939** St. Louis Blues; Dodge City; Good Girls Go to Paris; Torchy Runs for Mayor; I Am Not Afraid; What a Life; Torchy Blane in Chinatown; Dust Be My Destiny; Nancy Drew and the Hidden Staircase. **1940** Virginia City; Buck Benny Rides Again; She Couldn't Say No. **1941** The Wagons Roll at Night; Love Crazy; The Great Train Robbery; Glamour Boy; Murder by Invitation. **1942** Woman of the Year; Reap the Wild Wind; Hidden Hand; Scattergood Survives a Murder. **1944** Crime by Night.

GUILBERT, YVETTE

Born: 1868, Paris, France. Died: Feb. 3, 1944, France. Screen, stage actress and singer.

Appeared in: **1926** Faust. **1929** L'Argent. **1934** La Frochard et les Deux Orphelienes. **1935** Pecheurs D'Islande.

GUILFOYLE, JAMES (James Ancel Guilfoyle)

Born: Apr. 18, 1892, Michigan. Died: Nov. 13, 1964, Woodland Hills, Calif. (heart disease). Screen actor.

Appeared in: **1929** Speakeasy. **1930** She Went for a Tramp; The Criminal Code; Dirigible; Officer O'Brien. **1931** Daybreak; Inspiration; A Free Soul; Graft. **1932** Get That Girl. **1949** Alimony.

GUILFOYLE, PAUL

Born: July 14, 1902, Jersey City, N.J. Died: 1961. Screen and stage actor.

Appeared in: **1935** The Crime of Dr. Crespi; Special Agent. **1936** Roaming Lady; Two-Fisted Gentleman; Wanted; Jane Turner; Winterset. **1937** Behind the Headlines; Danger Patrol; Fight for Your Lady; Flight from Glory; Hideaway; Soldier and the Lady; Super Sleuth; You Can't Buy Luck; The Woman I Love; You Can't Beat Love. **1938** Crashing Hollywood; Stage Fright (short); The Mad Miss Manton; Law of the Underworld; Double Danger; Blind Alibi; Fugitives for a Night; I'm from the City; The Law West of Tombstone; The Marriage Business; Quick Money; The Saint in New York; Sky Giant; Tarnished Angel. **1939** Heritage of the Desert; Money to Loan (short); The Story of Alfred Nobel (short); News Is Made at Night; Pacific Liner; Boy Slaves; One Hour to Live; Our Leading Citizen; Sabotage; Society Lawyer. **1940** Remember the Night; The Saint Takes Over; Brother Orchid; Millionaires in Prison; One Crowded Night; Thou Shalt Not Kill; East of the River; Wildcat Bus; Grapes of Wrath. **1941** The Saint in Palm Springs. **1942** The Man Who Returned to Life; Time to Kill; The Incredible Stranger (short); Madero of Mexico (short); Who is Hope Schuyler? **1943** Petticoat Larceny; The North Star; Three Russian Girls; White Savage; It Happened Tomorrow; Mark of the Whistler; The Seventh Cross. **1944** The Master Race; Dark Shadows (short). **1945** The Missing Corpse; Why Girls Leave Home. **1946** Sweetheart of Sigma Chi; The Virginian. **1947** Second Chance; The Millerson Case; Roses are Red. **1948** The Hunted. **1949** There's A Girl in My Heart; Trouble Preferred; Follow Me Quietly; Mighty Joe Young; The Judge; I Married A Communist; Miss Mink of 1949; White Heat. **1950** Bomba and the Hidden City; Davy Crockett, Indian Scout; The Woman on Pier 13; Messenger of Peace. **1951** When I Grow Up. **1952** Actors and Sin; Confidence Girl; Japanese War Bride. **1953** Julius Caesar; Torch Song. **1954** Apache; Golden Idol. **1955** Chief Crazy Horse; Valley of Fury; A Life at Stake. **1960** The Boy and the Pirates.

GUINAN, TEXAS (Mary Louise Cecelle Guinan)

Died: Nov. 5, 1933, Vancouver, B.C., Canada (infection of intestines). Screen, stage, vaudeville actress and club hostess.

Appeared in: **1917** Fuel of Life. **1918** The Gun Woman; The Love Broker. **1919** Little Miss Deputy; The Girl of Hell's Agony. **1921** I Am the Woman; The Stampede. **1929** Queen of the Night Clubs; Glorifying the American Girl. **1933** Broadway Thru a Keyhole.

GUIRON, CARLOS N.

Born: 1921, Mexico. Died: Feb. 12, 1969, Mexico City, Mexico. Screen actor.

GUITRY, SACHA
Born: Feb. 21, 1885, St. Petersburg, Russia. Died: July 24, 1957, Paris, France. Screen, stage actor, playwright, film producer, director and screenwriter. Divorced from actress Yvonne Printemps (dec. 1977).

Appeared in: **1915** Ceux de Chez Nous. **1932** Les Deux Couverts. **1936** Pasteur. **1937** Les Perles de la Couronne (Pearls of the Crown). **1938** Quadrille; The Story of a Cheat. **1939** Champs Elysees; Indiscretions. **1942** Nine Bachelors. **1943** Donne-Moi tes Yeux. **1948** En Scene (Private Life of an Actor); Mlle Desire. **1949** Le Comedien. **1951** Deburau. **1954** Versailles (aka Royal Affairs in Versailles—US 1957).

GUITTY, MADELEINE
Born: 1871. Died: Apr. 12, 1936, Paris, France. Screen, stage actress and songwriter.

Appeared in: **1925** Madame Sans-Gene. **1931** Il est Charmant. **1934** Le Roi des Champs Elysees. **1935** Les As Du Turf; Avec l'Assurance; Cette Veille Canaille; Sans Famille. **1936** La Porteuse de Pain; Ciboulette. Other French film: Barcarolle.

GULLAN, CAMPBELL
Born: Glasgow, Scotland. Died: Dec. 1, 1939, England? Screen, stage actor and film director.

Appeared in: **1915** A Welsh Singer; Far From the Madding Crowd; The Great Adventure. **1916** A Place in the Sun. **1919** A Member of Tattersall's; The Right Element. **1920** Her Story (US 1922); The Honeypot; At the Mercy of Tiberius (aka The Price of Silence—US 1921); Love in the Wilderness. **1921** Love Maggy; Tilly of Bloomsbury; One Week to Live; Mr. Pim Passes By. **1922** Castles in the Air (aka Let's Pretend); The Game of Life; If Four Walls Told. **1923** The Hotel Mouse; Strangling Threads; The Right to Strike; L'Pagliacci; Lily of the Alley. **1928** S.O.S. **1929** Pleasure Crazed. **1931** Inquest. **1932** The Flying Squad. **1934** Jew Suess (aka Power—US). **1935** The Iron Duke. **1936** The End of the Road. **1937** The Black Tulip.

GUNN, CHARLES E.
Born: July 31, 1883, Wis. Died: Dec. 6, 1918, Los Angeles, Calif. (Spanish influenza). Screen actor.

Appeared in: **1916** The Cry of Conscience; The Eye of God; The Eagle's Wings; They Wouldn't Take Him; Tillie The Little Swede; Priscilla's Prisoner; Along the Malibu; Weapons of Love; The Girl in Lower 9; The Eternal Way; Song of the Woods; Three of Many. **1917** Chicken Casey; Sweetheart of the Doomed; The Snarl; Love or Justice; A Phantom Husband; The Firefly of Tough Luck; Framing Framers. **1918** Betty Takes a Hand; Unfaithful; Captain of His Soul; Patriotism. **1919** The Midnight Stage.

GUNN, EARL
Born: 1902. Died: Apr. 14, 1963, San Francisco, Calif. Screen actor.

Appeared in: **1926** We Are from Kronstdt. **1937** The Missing Witness. **1939** Romance of the Redwoods; The Great Commandment; Devil's Island. **1940** Island of Doomed Men. **1941** Swamp Woman; Secret of the Wastelands; Billy the Kid.

GURIE, SIGRID (Sigrid Gurie Haukelid)
Born: 1911, Brooklyn, N.Y. Died: Aug. 14, 1969, Mexico City, Mexico (embolism). Screen actress.

Appeared in: **1938** The Adventures of Marco Polo (film debut); Algiers. **1939** Forgotten Woman. **1940** Rio; Three Faces West; The Refugee; Dark Streets of Cairo. **1943** The Private Life of Dr. Joseph Goebbels (apparently never released). **1944** Enemy of Women; A Voice in the Wind. **1946** Singing Under the Occupation (documentary). **1948** Sofia; Sword of the Avenger.

GURIN, ELLEN
Born: 1948, New York, N.Y. Died: June 5, 1972, New York, N.Y. (suicide). Screen and stage actress. Married to actor Richard Dow.

Appeared in: **1971** Who Killed Mary What's-Er-Name?

GURNEY, EDMUND
Born: 1852. Died: Jan. 14, 1925, N.Y. Screen and stage actor.

Appeared in: **1921** Tol'able David.

GUSTAFSSON, ALVA
Born: 1904. Died: 1926, Stockholm, Sweden. Screen actress. Sister of actress Greta Gara.

GUSTINE, PAUL (Paul Valentine Gustine)
Born: Dec. 8, 1893, Michigan. Died: July 16, 1974, Los Angeles, Calif. (cancer). Screen actor and aviator.

Appeared in: **1937** Hills of Old Wyoming. **1946** The Blue Dahlia. **1956** Around the World in 80 Days.

GUTHRIE, CHARLES W.
Born: 1871. Died: June 30, 1939, Washington, D.C. Screen and stage actor.

GUTHRIE, SIR TYRONE
Born: July 2, 1900, Tunbridge Wells, England. Died: May 15, 1971, Dublin, Ireland. Screen, stage actor, film director, film producer, stage director and playwright.

Appeared in: **1938** The Beachcomber. **1940** Sidewalks of London.

GUTIERREZ, ALICIA
Born: 1928, Mexico. Died: Jan. 17, 1967, Mexico. Screen actress.

GUY, EULA
Born: Corapolis, Pa. Died: Dec. 19, 1960. Screen and stage actress.

Appeared in: **1931** Over the Hill. **1932** The Rich are Always With Us; Rebecca of Sunnybrook Farm. **1934** Housewife; Jimmy the Gent. **1937** Expensive Husbands. **1941** The Great American Broadcast; Two-Faced Woman; Moon Over Her Shoulder. **1943** The Song of Bernadette; The Woman of the Town. **1944** Once Upon a Time; Storm Over Lisbon. **1946** The Bride Wore Boots; Gallant Journey; Undercurrent; The Spider Woman Strikes Back; The Glass Alibi. **1947** Blaze of Noon; Yankee Fakir; The Pretender. **1948** The Sainted Sisters; A Date With Judy; The Saxon Charm; Yellow Sky; The Boy With Green Hair. **1949** That Wonderful Urge; Call of the Forest. **1950** My Blue Heaven. **1952** Paula.

GWENN, EDMUND
Born: Sept. 26, 1875, Glamorgan, Wales. Died: Sept. 6, 1959, Woodland Hills, Calif. Screen and stage actor. Won 1947 Academy Award for Best Supporting Actor in The Miracle on 34th Street and nominated in 1950 for Mister 880.

Appeared in: **1916** The Real Thing at Last. **1920** Unmarried; The Skin Game. **1931** How He Lied to Her Husband; Hindle Wakes; The Skin Game (and 1920 verison). **1932** Money for Nothing; Frail Women; Condemned to Death; Tell Me Tonight (aka Be Mine Tonight—US 1933); Love on Wheels; The Good Companions; Cash (aka For Love or Money—US 1934); I Was a Spy (US 1934); Channel Crossing (US 1934); Marooned; Friday the Thirteenth (US 1934); Early to Bed. **1934** Passing Shadows; Warn London; Waltzes From Vienna (aka Strauss's Great Waltz—US 1935); Father and Son; Spring in the Air; The Admiral's Secret; Java Head (US 1935). **1935** Sylvia Scarlet; The Bishop Misbehaves. **1936** Laburnum Grove (stage and film versions—US 1931); The Walking Dead; Anthony Adverse; Country Bumpkin (aka All American Chump); Mad Holiday. **1937** Parnell. **1938** A Yank at Oxford; Penny Paradise; South Riding. **1939** Cheer Boys Cheer; An Englishman's Home (aka Mad Men of Europe—US 1940). **1940** The Earl of Chicago; The Doctor Takes a Wife; Pride and Prejudice; Foreign Correspondent. **1941** Scotland Yard; Cheers for Miss Bishop; The Devil and Miss Jones; Charley's Aunt; One Night in Lisbon. **1942** A Yank at Eton. **1943** The Meanest Man in the World; Forever and a Day; Lassie Come Home. **1944** Between Two Worlds. **1945** Keys to the Kingdom; Bewitched; Dangerous Partners; She Went to the Races. **1946** Of Human Bondage; Undercurrent. **1947** The Miracle on 34th Street; Thunder in the Valley; Life With Father; Green Dolphin Street. **1948** Apartment for Peggy; Hills of Home. **1949** Challenge to Lassie. **1950** A Woman of Distinction; Louisa; Pretty Baby; Mister 880; For Heaven's Sake. **1951** Peking Express. **1952** Sally and St. Anne; Bonzo Goes to College; Les Miserables; Something for the Birds. **1953** Mr. Scoutmaster; The Bigamist. **1954** Them; The Student Prince. **1955** The Trouble With Harry; It's a Dog's Life. **1958** Calabuch.

GWYNN, MICHAEL
Born: Nov. 30, 1916, Bath, England. Died: Jan. 29, 1976, London, England (heart attack). Screen and stage actor.

Appeared in: **1957** The Secret Place (US 1958). **1958** The Camp on Blood Island; Dunkirk; The Revenge of Frankenstein. **1959** The Doctor's Dilemma. **1960** Village of the Damned; Never Take Sweets From a Stranger (aka Never Take Candy From a Stranger—US 1961). **1961** Question 7; What a Carve Up! (aka No Place Like Homicide—US 1962); Barabbas (US 1962). **1962** Some People (US 1964). **1963** Jason and the Argonauts; Cleopatra. **1964** The Fall of the Roman Empire. **1965** Catch Us If You Can (aka Having a Wild Weekend—US). **1967** The Deadly Bees. **1969** The Virgin Soldiers (US 1970). **1970** The Scars of Dracula. **1974** The Terminal Man. **1976** Special Delivery.

GWYNNE, HAROLD W.
Died: Aug., 1927. Screen actor.

Appeared in: **1919** Virtuous Wives.

GYPSY GOULD See VAUGHN, VIVIAN

HAADE, WILLIAM
Born: Mar. 2, 1903, New York, N.Y. Died: Nov. 15, 1966. Screen actor.

Appeared in: **1937** Kid Galahad; Without Warning; The Missing Witness; He Couldn't Say No. **1938** Sing You Sinners; The Invisible Menace; Stadium Murders; The Texans; If I Were King; Shadows Over Shanghai. **1939** Union Pacific; Full Confession; Kid Nightingale; Reno; Forty Invisible Stripes; Geronimo; The Man from Dakota; One Crowded Night; Cherokee Strip. **1940** Johnny Apollo; Lillian Russell; Norht West Mounted Police; The Grapes of Wrath. **1941** Sergeant York; The Roundup; The Penalty; Dance Hall; Rise and Shine; You're in the Army Now; Pirates on Horseback. **1942** Torpedo Boat; The Spoilers; You're Telling Me; A Gentleman After Dark; Reap the Wild Wind; Juke Girl; The Jackass Mail; Just Off Broadway; Star Spangled Rhythm; Heart of the Rio Grande. **1943** You're a Lucky Fellow, Mr. Smith; Pittsburgh; The Dancing Masters (short); Daredevils of the West (serial). **1944** Sing a Jingle; Sheriff of Las Vegas. **1945** I'll Tell the World; Nob Hill; Dakota; Fallen Angel; Phantom of the Plains. **1947** Unconquered; Deep Valley; Down to Earth; Buck Privates Come Home. **1948** Last of the Wild Horses; Tap Roots; Shaggy; Lulu Belle. **1949** The Gal Who Took the West; Prairie Pirates (short); Flamingo Road; The Scene of the Crime; The Wyoming Bandit. **1950** Trial Without Jury; Outcast of Black Mesa; The Old Frontier; Buckaroo Sheriff of Texas; Joe Palooka in the Squared Circle. **1951** Santa Fe; Leave It to the Marines; Oh! Susanna; Rawhide; The Sea Hornet; Stop That Cab; Three Desperate Men (aka Three Outlaws); A Yank in Korea. **1952** Rancho Notorious; Here Come the Nelsons; Come Back, Little Sheba; Carson City. **1953** Red River Shore. **1954** Jubilee Trail; Silver Lode; Untamed Heiress. **1955** Abbott and Costello Meet the Keystone Kops.

HAAGEN, AL H.
Born: 1871. Died: Mar. 8, 1953, Los Angeles, Calif. Screen, stage, vaudeville and minstrel actor.

HAAL, RENEE See GODFREY, RENEE HAAL

HAAS, HUGO
Born: Feb. 19, 1903, Brno, Czechoslovakia. Died: Dec. 1, 1968, Vienna, Austria. Screen actor, stage and film director, film producer and screenwriter. Brother of composer Paul Haas (dec.). Divorced from actress Maria Bibikoff.

Appeared in: **1925** Ceskych Mylnu (From Czech Mills). **1930** Kdyz Struny Lkaji (When Strings Resound). **1931** Muzi V Offsidu (Men Out of Character); Kariera Pavla Camrdy (Career of Paul Camrdy); Obraceni Ferdyse Pistory (Conversion of Ferdys Pistora); Dobry Vojak Svejk (The Good Soldier Schweik); Naceradec Kral Kibicu (Naceradec, King of Kibitzers). **1932** Sestra Angelika (Sister Angelika); Zapadli Vlastenci (The Neglected Patriot). **1933** Okenko (The Small Window); Zivot Je Pes (A Dog's Life); Madla S Cimelny (Madia from the Brick Works); Dum Na Predmesti (The House in the Suburbs); Jeji Lekar (Her Doctor). **1934** Mazlicek (Mother's Boy); Posledni Muz (The Last Man); At Zije Neboztik (Hurrah for the Good Life). **1935** Jedenacte Prikazani (The Eleventh Commandment). **1936** Tri Muzi Ve Snehu (Three Men in the Snow); Ulicka V Raji (The Road to Paradise); Svadlenka (The Little Seamstress); Velbloud Uchem Jehly (The Camel Through the Needle's Eye); Mravnost Nade Vse (Morality Above All). **1937** Devcata, Nedejte Se! (Girl, Defend Yourself); Kvocna (The Clucking Hen); Bila Nemoc (The White Plague). **1938** Svet, Kde Se Zebra (The World in Which One Begs); Co Se Septa (What is Whispered); Andula Vyhrala (Andula Has Conquered); Our Combat; Shelton on Horseback. **1944** Summer Storm; Days of Glory; Mrs. Parkington; The Princess and the Pirate; Strange Affair. **1945** Jealousy; A Bell for Adano; Dakota; What Next, Corporal Hargrove?. **1946** Holiday in Mexico; Two Smart People. **1947** Northwest Outpost; The Foxes of Harrow; Fiesta; The Private Affairs of Bel Ami; Merton of the Movies. **1948** My Girl Tisa; Casbah; For the Love of Mary. **1949** The Fighting Kentuckian. **1950** King Solomon's Mines; Vendetta. **1951** Pickup; Girl on the Bridge. **1953** One Girl's Confession; Thy Neighbor's Wife; (90 Minut—? Prekvapeni (aka 90 Minut Smichu) (90 Minutes of Surprises or 90 Minutes of Laughs)). **1954** Bait; The Other Woman. **1955** Hold Back Tomorrow; Tender Trap. **1956** Edge of Hell. **1957** Hit and Run; Lizzie. **1959** Night of the Quarter Moon; Born to Be Loved. **1962** Paradise Alley.

HABERFIELD, GRAHAM
Born: 1941. Died: Oct. 17, 1975, Knutsford, Cheshire, England. Screen, stage and television actor.

HACK, HERMAN
Born: 1899. Died: Oct. 19, 1967, Hollywood, Calif. (heart attack). Screen actor.

Appeared in: **1940** Melody Ranch. **1941** The Singing Hill; Stick to Your Guns. **1950** Cow Town; Beyond the Purple Hills. **1953** Pack Train. **1956** Around the World in 80 Days.

HACK, SIGNE
Born: 1899. Died: Jan. 6, 1973, Hollywood, Calif. (leukemia). Screen actress and film extra. Mother of actress Dorothy Hack.

HACKATHORNE, GEORGE
Born: Feb. 13, 1896, Pendleton, Ore. Died: June 25, 1940, Los Angeles, Calif. Screen, stage and vaudeville actor.

Appeared in: **1916** Oliver Twist. **1918** The Heart of Humanity. **1920** To Please One Woman; The Last of the Mohicans. **1921** What Do Men Want?; The Little Minister; The Light in the Clearing; High Heels; The Sin of Martha Queed. **1922** Human Hearts; The Village Blacksmith; The Gray Dawn; Notoriety; The Worldly Madonna. **1923** Merry-Go-Round; The Human Wreckage. **1924** The Turmoil; When a Man's a Man; Judgment of the Storm; Surging Seas. **1925** Night Life in New York; Capital Punishment; Wandering Fires; The Lady; His Master's Voice. **1926** The Sea Urchin; The Highbinders. **1927** Cheaters; The Cabaret Kid; Paying the Price. **1928** Shepherd of the Hills; Sally Shoulders. **1929** Tip Off; The Squall. **1930** Lonesome Trail; Beyond the Law; Hideout. **1933** Self Defense; Flaming Guns. **1935** Strange Wives. **1936** I Cover Chinatown; Showboat; The Magnificent Obsession. **1939** Gone With the Wind.

HACKER, MARIA
Born: 1904, Germany. Died: Feb. 20, 1963, Sherman Oaks, Calif. Screen actress. Wife of actor/tenor Lauritz Melchior (dec. 1973).

HACKETT, CHARLES
Born: 1888, Worcester, Mass. Died: Jan. 1, 1942, Jamaica, N.Y. (appendicitis). Screen actor and opera singer.

Appeared in: **1927** Rigoletto (short); The Song of the Nile (short). **1928** Who is Sylvia? (short); I Looked into Your Garden (short). **1929** Il Mio Tesoro Intanto (short); Faust (short).

HACKETT, FLORENCE
Born: 1882. Died: Aug. 21, 1954, New York, N.Y. Screen and stage actress. Mother of actors Raymond (dec. 1958) and Albert Hackett. Married to actor Arthur Johnson (dec. 1916).

Appeared in: **1914** The Beloved Adventurer (serial). **1915** Siren of Corsica.

HACKETT, HAL
Born: 1923. Died: Dec. 4, 1967, New York, N.Y. Screen, stage, radio and television actor.

Appeared in: **1946** The Show Off; Love Laughs at Andy Hardy. **1948** Campus Honeymoon; Summer Holiday.

HACKETT, JAMES K.
Born: Sept. 6, 1869, Wolf Island, Ontario, Canada. Died: Nov. 8, 1926, Paris, France (cirrhosis of the liver). Screen and stage actor. Entered films with Famous Players in 1912.

Appeared in: **1913** The Prisoner of Zenda.

HACKETT, JEANETTE
Born: 1898. Died: Aug. 16, 1979, New York, N.Y. Screen, vaudeville actress, dancer, composer, lyricist and costumer. Married to singer John Steel (dec.).

Appeared in: **1914** The Beloved Adventurer (serial).

HACKETT, KARL
Born: 1893. Died: Oct. 24, 1948, Los Angeles, Calif. Screen actor.

Appeared in: **1935** Frisco Kid. **1936** Down to the Sea; The Public Pays (short); Happy Go Lucky. **1937** The Gold Racket; Sing, Cowboy, Sing; Tex Rides With the Boy Scouts; Texas Trail; Colorado Kid. **1938** Paroled to Die; Phantom Ranger; Down in "Arkansaw"; The Rangers Roundup; Starlight Over Texas; Where the Buffalo Roam; Frontier Town. **1940** The Man from Montreal; Yukon Flight; Take Me Back to Oklahoma; Chip of the Flying U. **1941** Boss of Bullion City; Man from Montana; Outlaws of the Rio Grande. **1942** Sons of the Pioneers; Pirates of the Prairie; Jesse James, Jr.; Billy the Kid's Smoking Guns; Phantom Killer; Outlaws of Boulder Pass. **1943** The Avenging Rider; Fugitive of the Plains; Bordertown Gunfighters; Thundering Trails; The Renegade; Lost Canyon. **1944** Tucson Raiders; Wolves of the Range; Sonora Stagecoach; Westward Bound; Mojave Firebrand; Arizona Whirlwind; Oath of Vengeance; Thundering Gunslinger; The Pinto Bandit; Brand of the Devil. **1945** Lightning Raiders; His Brother's Ghost; Rustlers of the Badlands; Prairie Rustlers. **1946** Lawless Breed; Ghost of Hidden Valley; Gentlemen With Guns; Terrors on Horseback; Outlaw of the Plains; Gunman's Code. **1947** The Michigan Kid; Frontier Fighters; Raiders of Red Rock; Code of the Plains.

HACKETT, LILLIAN
Born: Oct. 11, 1899, Chicago, Ill. Died: Feb. 28, 1973, Hollywood, Calif. Screen and stage actress.

Appeared in: **1920** Don't Tickle. **1921** Once a Plumber; Blue Sunday. **1922** Hired and Fired. **1923** Danger. **1924** In Hollywood with Potash and Perlmutter. **1927** Ladies at Ease.

HACKETT, RAYMOND
Born: July 15, 1902, New York, N.Y. Died: July 7, 1958, Hollywood, Calif. Stage and screen actor. Divorced from actress Myra Hampton (dec. 1945). Married to actress Blanche Sweet. Son of actress Florence Hackett (dec. 1954) and brother of actor Albert Hackett.

Appeared in: **1912** A Matter of Business; A Child's Devotion. **1913** Longing for a Mother. **1914** The Price of a Ruby; The Shadow of Tragedy. **1918** The Cruise of the Make-Believe. **1922** The Country Flapper. **1927** The Love of Sunya. **1928** Faithless Lover. **1929** Girl in the Show; The Trial of Mary Dugan; Madame X; Footlights and Fools. **1930** Let Us Be Gay; Our Blushing Brides; The Sea Wolf; Numbered Men; On Your Back; The Cat Creeps; Not So Dumb. **1931** Seed.

HADDON, PETER (Peter Tildsley)
Born: 1898, England. Died: Sept. 7, 1962, England. Screen, stage actor and author. Married to stage actress Rosaline Courtneidge (dec. 1926).

Appeared in: **1934** Death at Broadcasting House. **1935** Who's Your Father?; The Silent Passenger; No Monkey Business. **1936** Don't Rush Me!; Public Nuisance No. 1; The Beloved Vagabond; The House of the Spaniard; The Secret of Stamboul. **1937** Over the Moon (US 1940). **1938** Kate Plus Ten. **1949** Helter Skelter. **1952** The Second Mrs. Tangueray (US 1954).

HADEN, SARA (Sara Hadden)
Born: 1899, Galveston, Tex. Died: Sept. 15, 1981, Woodland Hills, Calif. Screen actress. Daughter of actress Charlotte Walker (dec. 1958). Divorced from actor Richard Abbott (aka Simon Vandenberg).

Appeared in: **1934** Spitfire (film debut); Music in the Air; Finishing School; Hat, Coat and Glove; The Fountain; The Life of Vergie Winters; The White Parade; Affairs of a Gentleman; Anne of Green Gables. **1935** O'Shaughnessy's Boy; Black Fury; Mad Love; Way Down East; Magnificent Obsession. **1936** Captain January; The Poor Little Rich Girl; The Crime of Dr. Forbes; Everybody's Old Man; Little Miss Nobody; Half Angel; Can This Be Dixie?; Reunion. **1937** First Lady; The Barrier; Laughing at Trouble; Under Cover of Night; The Family Affair; The Last of Mrs. Cheyney. **1938** You're Only Young Once; Out West With the Hardys. **1939** Four Girls in White; The Hardys Ride High; Tell No Tales; Remember?; The Secret of Dr. Kildare; Andy Hardy Gets Spring Fever; Judge Hardy and Son; Think First (short); Angel of Mercy (short). **1940** The Shop Around the Corner; Boom Town; Andy Hardy Meets Debutante; Hullabaloo. **1941** Come Back, Miss Pipps (short); Washington Melodrama; Barnacle Bill; The Trail of Mary Dugan; Love Crazy; H. M. Pulham, Esq.; Andy Hardy's Private Secretary; Life Begins for Andy Hardy. **1942** Woman of the Year; The Courtship of Andy Hardy; Andy Hardy's Double Life; Flag of Mercy (short); Once Upon a Thursday (aka The Affairs of Martha). **1943** The Youngest Profession; Above Suspicion; Best Foot Forward; Lost Angel; Thousands Cheer. **1944** Andy Hardy's Blonde Trouble. **1945** Our Vines Have Tender Grapes. **1946** She-Wolf of London; Bad Bascomb; She Wouldn't Say Yes; Our Hearts Were Growing Up; Mr. Ace; So Goes My Love; Love Laughs at Andy Hardy. **1947** The Bishop's Wife. **1948** Rachel and the Stranger. **1949** The Big Cat; Roughshod. **1950** The Great Rupert; A Life of Her Own. **1952** Rodeo. **1953** A Lion is in the Streets; Two Gun Marshal. **1954** The Outlaw's Daughter. **1955** Betrayed Woman. **1958** Andy Hardy Comes Home.

HADLEY, HAP (Alvan Cordell Hadley)
Born: Mar. 16, 1895, Findlay, Ill. Died: Aug. 4, 1976, New York, N.Y. (Parkinsons's disease). Screen, stage actor, cartoonist, commercial artist, film publicist and art critic.

Appeared in: **1924** Floodgates.

HADLEY, REED (Reed Herring)
Born: 1911, Petrolia, Tex. Died: Dec. 11, 1974, Los Angeles, Calif. (heart attack). Screen, stage, radio and television actor.

Appeared in: **1938** The Great Adventures of Wild Bill Hickock (serial); Hollywood Stadium Mystery; Female Fugitive; Orphans of the Street. **1939** Calling Dr. Kildare; Zorro's Fighting Legion (serial). **1940** Meet the Wildcat; I Take This Woman; Ski Patrol; The Bank Dick; Jack Pot (short); The Man from Montreal. **1941** Sea Raiders (serial); Sky Raiders (serial); The Flame of New Orleans; I'll Wait for You; Whistling in the Dark; Adventures of Captain Marvel (serial); Road

Agent. **1942** Lady in a Jam; I Married a Witch; Jail House Blues; Juke Box Jenny; Arizona Terrors; Mystery of Marie Roget. **1943** Guadalcanal Diary. **1944** The Eve of St. Mark; In the Meantime, Darling; Roger Touhy, Gangster; Wing and a Prayer; Rainbow Island. **1945** The House on 92nd Street; Circumstantial Evidence; Caribbean Mystery; Doll Face; Diamond Horseshoe; A Bell for Adano; Leave Her to Heaven. **1946** 13 Rue Madeleine (narr.); It Shouldn't Happen to a Dog; The Dark Corner; If I'm Lucky; Shock. **1947** Captain from Castile; The Fabulous Texan. **1948** The Iron Curtain; Walk a Crooked Mile; A Southern Yankee; Panhandle; The Man from Texas; The Return of Wildfire (serial); Last of the Wild Horses. **1949** I Shot Jesse James; Grand Canyon; Riders of the Range; Rimfire. **1950** Dallas; The Baron of Arizona; A Modern Marriage; Motor Patrol. **1951** The Wild Blue Yonder; Little Big Horn; Rhythm Inn; Insurance Investigator. **1952** The Half-Breed. **1953** Woman They Almost Lynched; Kansas Pacific. **1954** Highway Dragnet. **1955** Big House, USA. **1962** Frigid Marriage (rerelease of A Modern Marriage—1950). **1964** Moro Witch Doctor (aka Amok). **1965** Young Dillinger. **1967** The St. Valentines Day Massacre. **1969** The Fabulous Bastard from Chicago (aka The Fabulous Kid from Chicago; The Chicago Kid and The Bastard Wench from Chicago). **1971** Brain of Blood (aka The Creature's Revenge).

HAEFELI, CHARLES "JOCKEY"
Born: 1889. Died: Feb. 12, 1955, Hollywood, Calif. Screen actor.

Appeared in: **1921** Four Horsemen of the Apocalypse. **1923** The Hunchback of Notre Dame. **1935** Les Miserables.

HAFTER, ROBERT (Robert Mark Hafter)
Born: Jan. 7, 1897, London, England. Died: Aug. 9, 1955, North Hollywood, Calif. (heart attack). Screen, television actor and television director.

HAGEMAN, RICHARD
Born: July 9, 1882, Leeuwarden, Holland. Died: Mar. 6, 1966, Beverly Hills, Calif. Screen actor, musician and composer.

Appeared in: **1941** There's Magic in Music; The Hard-Boiled Canary. **1943** Hi Diddle Diddle. **1944** Sensations of 1945. **1946** The Bachelor's Daughter. **1947** New Orleans; Fun on a Week-End. **1950** The Toast of New Orleans. **1951** The Great Caruso; Grounds for Marriage. **1954** Rhapsody.

HAGEN, CHARLES F.
Born: 1872. Died: June 13, 1958, Hollywood, Calif. Screen and stage actor. Entered films with Griffith.

Appeared in: **1950** All About Eve.

HAGEN, JEAN (Jean Shirley Ver Hagen)
Born: 1923, Chicago, Ill. Died: Aug. 29, 1977, Woodland Hills, Calif. (cancer). Screen, stage, radio and television actress. Nominated for 1952 Academy Award for Best Supporting Actress in Singin' in the Rain.

Appeared in: **1949** Side Street (film debut); Adam's Rib; Ambush. **1950** The Asphalt Jungle; A Life of Her Own. **1951** Night into Morning; No Questions Asked; Shadow in the Sky. **1952** Carbine Williams; Singin' in the Rain. **1953** Arena; Half a Hero; Latin Lovers. **1955** The Big Knife. **1957** Spring Reunion. **1959** The Shaggy Dog. **1960** Sunrise at Campobello. **1962** Panic in Year Zero. **1964** Dead Ringer.

HAGEN, MARGARETHE
Born: 1890, Germany. Died: Dec. 14, 1966, Gruenwald, Germany. Stage and screen actress.

Appeared in: Uncle Filsner; Kohlhiesel's Daughter; In Those Days; Beloved Liar; Fireworks; Her 106th Birthday.

HAGEN, WALTER (Walter Charles Hagen)
Born: Dec. 21, 1892, Rochester, N.Y. Died: Oct. 5, 1969, Traverse City, Mich. Golfer and screen actor.

Appeared in: **1928** Green Grass Widows. **1930** Match Play.

HAGER, CLYDE
Born: 1887. Died: May 21, 1944, Harrisburg, Pa. (heart attack). Screen, stage, vaudeville actor and song writer.

Appeared in: **1930** Railroad Follies (short). **1936** Strike Me Pink.

HAGGARD, STEPHEN
Born: 1912, England. Died: Feb., 1943, Middle East (during war). Screen, stage actor and author.

Appeared in: **1939** Jamaica Inn. **1940** Fear and Peter Brown. **1942** The Young Mr. Pitt.

HAGNEY, FRANK S. (aka FRANK HAGNY)
Born: 1884, Sydney, Australia. Died: June 25, 1973, Los Angeles, Calif. Screen, stage, vaudeville, television actor and stuntman.

Appeared in: **1920** Gauntlet. **1921** Anne of Little Smoky; The Ghost in the Garret. **1923** The Backbone. **1924** The Martyr Sex; Poison; The Silent Stranger; Roaring Rails; The Breed of the Border; The Dangerous Coward; The Fighting Sap; Lightning Romance; Galloping Gallagher; The Mask of Lopez. **1925** New Champion; Wild Justice; Fighting Youth; Braveheart; Hogan's Alley; The Wild Bull's Lair. **1926** Fangs of Justice; The Ice Flood; The Fighting Marine (serial); The Sea Beast; Lone Hand Saunders; The Winning Wallop; The Two-Gun Man. **1927** All Aboard; One-Round Hogan; The Frontiersman; The Last Trail. **1928** On Your Toes; The Fight Pest (short); The Glorious Trail; Through the Breakers; Free Lips; The Rawhide Kid; Midnight Madness; Burning Daylight; The Charge of the Gauchos; Go Get 'Em Hutch (serial); Vultures of the Sea (serial). **1929** Broken Barriers; Masked Emotions; Captain Lash; Oh, Dear! **1931** The Phantom of the West (serial); Fighting Caravans; Sit Tight; The Squaw Man; I Like Your Nerve; No Limit; Reckless Living; City Sentinel; The Champ. **1932** The Airmail Mystery; A House Divided; You Said a Mouthful; The All American; Ride Him Cowboy!; The Golden West. **1933** Dancing Lady; Terror Aboard. **1934** Honor of the Range. **1935** Western Frontier. **1936** Modern Times; Wildcat Trooper; Heroes of the Range; The Plough and the Stars; Secret Valley; Conflict; Here Comes Trouble. **1937** Hollywood Cowboy; Ghost Town Gold; Riders of the Dawn; Windjammer; Valley of the Lawless; Night Key; Missing Men. **1938** The Mysterious Mr. Moto. **1939** Captain Fury. **1940** Northwest Passage; Misbehaving Husbands. **1941** Billy the Kid; The Lone Rider Ambushed; The Lone Rider in Ghost Town; The Lone Rider Fights Back; Mr. Celebrity; Blazing Frontier. **1942** Gentleman Jim; The Glass Key; Tomorrow We Live; The Broadway Big Shot. **1943** The Renegade. **1944** Lost in a Harem; Louisiana Hayride. **1945** Bring on the Girls; Senorita from the West; Saratoga Trunk; Abbott and Costello in Hollywood; Spook to Me (short). **1946** Easy to Wed; Girl on the Spot; A Night in Paradise; It's a Wonderful Life. **1947** Wild Harvest; Road to Rio; The Wistful Widow of Wagon Gap; Code of the Plains. **1948** Kiss the Blood Off My Hands; River Lady; Johnny Belinda; The Three Musketeers; Unconquered; Where the North Begins; The Paleface. **1949** On the Town; The Big Steal; Grand Canyon. **1951** Santa Fe; Man in the Saddle. **1952** Hangman's Knot; The San Francisco Story. **1953** A Perilous Journey; The Stranger Wore a Gun. **1954** Riot in Cell Block 11; Demetrius and the Gladiators. **1955** A Man Alone; Abbott and Costello Meet the Keystone Kops; A Bullet for Joey; A Lawless Street; Lucy Gallant; They Came from Another World. **1957** Gunfight at the O.K. Corral; The Kettles on Old McDonald's Farm; Zombies of Mora-Tau. **1958** The Buccaneer. **1963** McLintock!; Come Blow Your Horn.

HAHN, SALLY
Born: 1908. Died: June 2, 1933, Los Angeles, Calif. Screen actress.

HAID, GRIT
Born: Germany. Died: Date unknown, Germany. Screen actress. Sister of actress Liana Haid.

Appeared in: **1934** Die Mutter der Kompagnie. **1935** Drei Kaiserjaeger. **1937** Fuerst Sepp'l.

HAIG, RAYMOND V.
Born: 1917. Died: Sept. 17, 1963, Chicago, Ill. (auto accident). Screen and vaudeville actor. Appered in vaudeville in an act billed as "Haig and Haig" and the team made Paramount shorts.

HAINE, HORACE J.
Born: 1868, Detroit, Mich. Died: Sept. 26, 1940, New York, N.Y. Screen, stage actor, opera performer and stage producer.

Appeared in: **1916** The Other Man; The Moonshiners. **1924** The Fifth Horseman.

HAINES, DONALD
Died: c. 1942. Screen actor.

Appeared in: **1930** The following shorts: Shivering Shakespeare; The First Seven Years; Teacher's Pet; School's Out; Helping Grandma. **1931** Skippy; plus the following shorts: Readin' and Writin'; Little Daddy; Bargain Days; Love Business. **1932** When a Feller Needs a Friend; plus the following shorts: Spanky; Hook and Ladder; Free Eats; Choo Choo; Birthday Blues; A Lad an' a Lamp. **1933** Fish Hooky (short). **1934** Now I'll Tell; No Greater Glory; Little Man, What Now? **1935** A Tale of Two Cities; Straight from the Heart. **1936** Little Miss Nobody; Woman Trap; The Invisible Ray. **1938** Boys Town; Three Comrades; Kidnapped. **1939** Sergeant Madden. **1940** Prison Camp; The Ghost Creeps; East Side Kids; Seventeen; That Gang of Mine; Fugitive From a Prison Camp. **1941** Pride of the Bowery; Flying Wild; Spooks Run Wild; Bowery Blitzkrieg.

HAINES, RHEA
Born: 1895. Died: Mar. 12, 1964, Los Angeles, Calif. Screen actress.

Appeared in: **1916** The Chalice of Sorrow. **1917** The Man from Painted Post; Nina the Flower Girl; Hands Up. **1919** Scarlet Days. **1920** Mary Ellen Comes to Town; Always Audacious; Master Stroke; Girls Don't Gamble. **1921** Smiling All the Way; Uncharted Seas.

HAINES, ROBERT T.
Born: 1870, Muncie, Ind. Died: May 6, 1943, N.Y. Screen, stage, vaudeville, radio actor, stage producer, director, and playwright.

Appeared in: **1912** The Capitol. **1921** The Victim; God's Crucible. **1923** Does It Pay?; The Governor's Lady. **1924** The Lone Wolf. **1926** Lew Tyler's Wives. **1928** How to Handle Women; The First Kiss; Ladies of the Mob; The Noose; Ten Minutes (short). **1929** Careers; Dynamite; The Girl in the Glass Cage; The Shannons of Broadway. **1930** Guilty? **1934** These Thirty Years. **1935** Gigolette.

HAINES, WILLIAM
Born: Jan. 1, 1900, Staunton, Va. Died: Dec. 26, 1973, Santa Monica, Calif. (cancer). Screen actor and interior decorator.

Appeared in: **1922** Brothers Under the Skin (film debut). **1923** Three Wise Fools; Souls for Sale; Lost and Found. **1924** The Desert Outlaw; The Gaiety Girl Circe the Enchantress (aka Circe); Three Weeks; Wine of Youth; The Midnight Express; True as Steel; Wife of the Centaur. **1925** The Denial; Fighting the Flames; The Tower of Lies; Who Cares; A Fool and His Money; Little Annie Rooney; Sally, Irene and Mary; A Slave of Fashion. **1926** Brown of Harvard; Mike; Lovey Mary; Memory Lane; The Thrill Hunter. **1927** Spring Fever; Slide, Kelly, Slide; West Point; A Little Journey; Tell It to the Marines. **1928** Alias Jimmy Valentine; Excess Baggage; The Smart Set; Show People; Telling the World. **1929** A Man's Man; Speedway; The Duke Steps Out; The Hollywood Revue of 1929. **1930** The Girl Said No; Free and Easy; Remote Control; Way Out West; Navy Blues. **1931** A Tailor Made Man; Just a Gigolo; Get-Rich-Quick Wallingford (aka New Adventure of Get-Rich-Quick Wallingford). **1932** Are You Listening?; The Fast Life; The Slippery Pearls (short). **1934** Young and Beautiful; Marines are Coming.

HAINS, LOUIS
Died: July 25, 1929, New York, N.Y. Screen and stage actor.

Appeared in: **1921** Beyond Price.

HALE, ALAN, SR. (Rufas Alan McKanan)
Born: Feb. 10, 1892, Washington, D.C. Died: Jan. 22, 1950, Hollywood, Calif. (liver ailment—virus infection). Screen, stage actor, film director, writer and singer. Father of actor Alan Jr., actress Karen and Jeanne Hale. Married to actress Gretchen Hartman (dec. 1979).

Appeared in: **1911** The Cowboy and the Lady (film debut). **1914** Cricket on the Hearth. **1915** Jane Eyre; Under Two Flags; Dora; an untitled short. **1916** Pudd'n Head Wilson. **1917** The Price She Paid. **1921** A Voice in the Dark; A Wise Fool; The Four Horsemen of the Apocalypse; Shirley of the Circus; The Barbarian; The Fox; The Great Impersonation; Over the Wire. **1922** One Glorious Day; Robin Hood; A Doll's House; Dictator; The Trap. **1923** The Covered Wagon; Hollywood; Cameo Kirby; The Eleventh Hour; Long Live the King; Main Street; Quicksands. **1924** Troubles of a Bride; Black Oxen; Code of the Wilderness; For Another Woman; Girls Men Forget; One Night in Rome. **1925** Rolling Stones; Braveheart; The Crimson Runner; Dick Turpin; Flattery; The Scarlet Honeymoon; The Wedding Song. **1926** Forbidden Waters; Hearts and Fists; Risky Business; The Sporting Lover. **1927** Rubber Tires; Vanity; The Wreck of the Hesperus. **1928** The Leopard Lady; Skyscraper; The Cop; Power; Oh, Kay! **1929** Sal of Singapore; The Spieler; The Leatherneck; A Bachelor's Secret; Red Hot Rhythm; The Sap; Sailor's Holiday. **1930** She Got What She Wanted. **1931** Up and At 'Em; Aloha; The Night Angel; Susan Lennox, Her Rise and Fall; Sea Ghost; The Sin of Madelon Claudet; Rebound; So Big; Union Depot; Rebecca of Sunnybrook Farm; Gentlemen for a Day. **1932** The Match King. **1933** Picture Brides; What Price Decency?; Eleventh Commandment; Destination Unknown. **1934** It Happened One Night; Imitation of Life; Of Human Bondage; Little Man, What Now?; Great Expectations; The Lost Patrol; Miss Fane's Baby is Stolen; The Little Minister; Fog Over Frisco; The Scarlet Letter; Babbitt; There's Always Tomorrow; Broadway Bill. **1935** Grand Old Girl; Last Days of Pompeii; Another Face; The Good Fairy; The Crusades. **1936** Two in the Dark; A Message to Garcia; The Country Beyond; Parole!; Yellowstone; Our Relations; God's Country and the Woman. **1937** Jump for Glory (aka When Thief Meets Thief—US); High, Wide and Handsome; Thin Ice; Music for Madame; The Prince and the Pauper; Stella Dallas. **1938** Valley of the Giants; The Adventures of Marco Polo; The Adventures of Robin Hood; Algiers; Four Men and a Prayer; Listen, Darling; The Sisters. **1939** Pacific Liner; Dust Be My Destiny; On Your Toes; The Private Lives of Elizabeth and Essex; Dodge City; Man in the Iron Mask. **1940** The Sea Hawk; Three Cheers for the Irish; Green Hell; Virginia City; The Fighting 69th; They Drive by Night; Santa Fe Trail; Tugboat Annie Sails Again. **1941** The Great Mr. Nobody; Strawberry Blonde; Manpower; The Smiling Ghost; Thieves Fall Out; Footsteps in the Dark. **1942** Desperate Journey; Captains of the Clouds; Juke Girl; Gentleman Jim. **1943** Action in the North Atlantic; This Is the Army; Thank Your Lucky Stars; Destination Tokyo. **1944** The Adventures of Mark Twain; Make Your Own Bed; Janie; Hollywood Canteen; Strangers in Our Midst. **1945** Roughly Speaking; Hotel Berlin; God Is My Co-Pilot; Escape in the Desert. **1946** Perilous Holiday; The Time, the Place and the Girl; The Man I Love; Night and Day. **1947** My Wild Irish Rose; Cheyenne; That Way with Women; Pursued. **1948** The Adventures of Don Juan; My Girl Tisa; Whiplash. **1949** South of St. Louis; The Younger Brothers; The House Across the Street; Always Leave Them Laughing; The Inspector General. **1950** Rogues of Sherwood Forest; Stars in My Crown; Colt .45.

HALE, BARNABY
Born: 1927. Died: Nov. 5, 1964, Los Angeles, Calif. (following surgery). Screen, stage and television actor.

HALE, CREIGHTON (Patrick Fitzgerald)
Born: May, 1882, Cork, Ireland. Died: Aug. 9, 1965, South Pasadena, Calif. Screen actor.

Appeared in: **1915** The New Exploits of Elaine (serial); The Romance of Elaine (serial). **1916** The Iron Claw (serial). **1917** The Seven Pearls (serial). **1919** The Thirteenth Chair. **1920** The Idol Dancer; Way Down East. **1921** Forbidden Love. **1922** Orphans of the Storm; Fascination; Her Majesty. **1923** Broken Hearts of Broadway; Mary of the Movies; Tea With a Kick; Three Wise Fools; Trilby. **1924** How to Educate a Wife; The Mine with the Iron Door; Name the Man; Riders Up; This Woman; Wine of Youth; The Marriage Circle. **1925** The Bridge of Sighs; The Circle; Exchange of Wives; Seven Days; The Shadow on the Wall; Time, the Comedian; Wages for Wives. **1926** Beverly of Graustark; The Midnight Message; Oh, Baby; A Poor Girl's Romance; Speeding Through. **1927** Annie Laurie; The Cat and The Canary; Thumbs Down. **1928** The House of Shame; Sisters of Eve; Rose Marie. **1929** Seven Footprints to Satan; Reilly of the Rainbow Division. **1930** Holiday; School's Out (short); The Great Divide. **1931** Grief Street; Big Ears (short). **1932** Prestige; Shop Angel; Free Wheeling (short); Stage Whispers. **1933** The Masquerader. **1934** Sensation Hunters; What's Your Racket? **1935** Death from a Distance. **1936** Custer's Last Stand (serial); After the Thin Man; The Princess Comes Across; Born to Dance; The Millionaire Kid; Hollywood Boulevard. **1937** Charlie Chan on Broadway. **1939** Nancy Drew and the Hidden Staircase; Return of Dr. X; The Roaring Twenties. **1940** Calling Philo Vance; All This, and Heaven Too; The Fighting 69th; The Lady With Red Hair; Santa Fe Trail; One Million B.C.; Brother Orchid. **1941** The Bride Came C.O.D.; The Strawberry Blonde; She Couldn't Say No; Knockout (aka Right to the Heart); Footsteps in the Dark; Dive Bomber. **1942** Bullet Scars; Casablanca; Larceny, Inc.; Yankee Doodle Dandy; Murder in the Big House; Gorilla Man. **1943** Watch on the Rhine; The Mysterious Doctor; Action in the North Atlantic; Thank Your Lucky Stars; Old Acquaintance. **1944** Mr. Skeffington; Uncertain Glory; The Adventures of Mark Twain; Crime By Night. **1946** Night and Day. **1947** Life With Father; Nora Prentiss; Possessed; Cry Wolf; Always Together; That Way With Women; The Two Mrs. Carrolls; Perils of Pauline. **1948** Johnny Belinda; The Woman in White. **1949** The Story of Seabiscuit; Beyond the Forest. **1950** Montana; Perfect Strangers. **1951** On Moonlight Bay. **1952** Million Dollar Mermaid; Scarlet Angel. **1956** Serenade. **1959** Westbound.

HALE, DOROTHY
Born: 1905, Pittsburgh, Pa. Died: Oct. 21, 1938, New York, N.Y. Screen and stage actress.

Appeared in: **1934** Catherine the Great.

HALE, JONATHAN
Born: 1891. Died: Feb. 28, 1966, Woodland Hills, Calif. (suicide—gun). Screen actor.

Appeared in: **1934** Lightning Strikes Twice (film debut). **1935** G-Men; Navy Wife; Alice Adams; The Voice of Bugle Ann; Hit and Run Driver (short); A Night at the Opera. **1936** Charlie Chan's Secret; Fury; The Devil Is a Sissy; Too Many Parents; The Case Against Mrs. Ames; Educating Father; Charlie Chan at the Race Track; 36 Hours to Kill; Flying Hostess; Happy Go Lucky; Three Live Ghosts. **1937** Wings Over Honolulu; A Star Is Born; She's Dangerous; Charlie Chan at the Olympics; League of the Frightened Men; Big Time Girl; You Only

Live Once; Man of the People; Saratoga; Midnight Madonna; Outcast; John Meade's Woman; Madame X; This Is My Affair; Mysterious Crossing; Racketeers in Exile; Danger—Love at Work; Exiled to Shanghai. **1938** Blondie; The First Hundred Years; Bringing Up Baby; Arsene Lupin Returns; Judge Hardy's Children; Yellow Jack; Boys Town; Road Demon; There's That Woman Again; Her Jungle Love; Duke of West Point; Wives Under Suspicion; A Letter of Introduction; Over the Wall; The Saint in New York; Fugitives for a Night; Breaking the Ice; Tarnished Angel; Gangs of New York; Scandal Sheet. **1939** Thunder Afloat; The Saint Strikes Back; In Name Only; One Against the World (short); Blondie Meets the Boss; Fugitive at Large; Blondie Brings Up Baby; The Amazing Mr. Williams; The Story of Alexander Graham Bell; Barricade; In Old Monterey; Stand Up and Fight; Wings of the Navy; Tail Spin. **1940** The Big Guy; The Saint's Double Trouble; The Saint Takes Over; Private Affairs; We Who Are Young; Blondie Has Servant Trouble; Dulcy; Melody and Moonlight; Blondie Plays Cupid; Johnny Apollo. **1941** Blondie Goes Latin; Flight from Destiny; Ringside Maisie; The Pittsburgh Kid; Blondie in Society; The Saint in Palm Springs; The Great Swindle; Strange Alibi; The Bugle Sounds. **1942** Joe Smith, American; Blondie Goes to College; Lone Star Ranger; Miss Annie Rooney; Calling Dr. Gillespie; Flight Lieutenant; Blondie's Blessed Event; Blondie for Victory. **1943** What a Woman!; Hangmen Also Die; It's a Great Life; Footlight Glamour; Jack London; Mission 36; The Amazing Mrs. Holliday; Sweet Rosie O'Grady. **1944** She's a Soldier Too; This Is the Life; The Black Parachute; Since You Went Away; Hollywood Canteen; Dead Man's Eyes; My Buddy; And Now Tomorrow; The End of the Road. **1945** Leave It to Blondie; The Phantom Speaks; Dakota; Man Alive; G.I. Honeymoon; Allotment Wives. **1946** Angel on My Shoulder; Life With Blondie; Blondie Knows Best; Blondie's Lucky Day; The Cat Creeps; Easy to Wed; Riverboat Rhythm; The Walls Came Tumbling Down; The Strange Mr. Gregory; Gay Blades; Wife Wanted. **1947** The Beginning or the End; The Ghost Goes Wild; Rolling Home; The Vigilantes Return; Her Husband's Affair; High Wall. **1948** Michael O'Halloran; King of the Gamblers; Silver River; Johnny Belinda; Call Northside 777; Rocky. **1949** Rose of the Yukon; Stampede; The Judge; State Department File 649. **1950** Federal Agent at Large; Three Husbands; Short Grass; Triple Trouble. **1951** Insurance Investigator; On the Sunny Side of the Street; Strangers on a Train; Let's Go Navy!; Rodeo King and the Senorita; Rhythm Inn. **1952** Steel Trap; My Pal Gus; Son of Paleface; Scandal Sheet. **1953** A Blueprint for Murder; Kansas Pacific; Taxi. **1954** She Couldn't Say No; Duffy of San Quentin; Riot in Cell Block 11. **1955** The Night Holds Terror; A Man Called Peter. **1956** Jaguar; The Opposite Sex. **1957** The Way to the Gold.

HALE, LOUISE CLOSSER
Born: Oct. 13, 1872, Chicago, Ill. Died: July 26, 1933, Los Angeles, Calif. (following an accident). Screen, stage actress and playwright.

Appeared in: **1929** The Hole in the Wall; Paris. **1930** Dangerous Nan McGrew; Big Boy; The Princess and the Plumber. **1931** Captain Applejack; Born to Love; Rebound; Devotion; Daddy Long Legs; Platinum Blonde. **1932** Sky Bride; Faithless; No More Orchids; The Son-Daughter; Rebecca of Sunnybrook Farm; Movie Crazy; Rasputin and the Empress; The Shanghai Express; The Man Who Played God; New Morals for Old; Letty Lynton. **1933** The White Sister; Today We Live; The Barbarian; Storm at Daybreak; Another Language; Dinner at Eight.

HALE, RICHARD
Born: 1893. Died: May 18, 1981, Northridge, Calif. (natural causes). Screen, stage, television actor and opera singer.

Appeared in: **1944** None Shall Escape; Girl in the Case; Knickerbocker Holiday. **1945** Counter Attack; A Thousand and One Nights. **1946** Abilene Town; Badman's Territory; Man Who Dared. **1947** The Other Love. **1948** Port Said. **1949** All the King's Men; The Beautiful Blonde from Bashful Bend. **1950** Kim. **1951** Inside Straight; Soldiers Three; The Man With a Cloak. **1952** Scaramouche; The Miracle of Our Lady of Fatima; Springfield Rifle. **1953** San Antone; The Diamond Queen; Sea of Lost Ships; Rogue's March; Julius Caesar. **1954** Red Garters; Passion. **1955** Canyon Crossroads; Moonfleet. **1956** Pillars of the Sky; Friendly Persuasion. **1957** Short Cut to Hell. **1958** Voice in the Mirror. **1959** Ben Hur. **1962** To Kill a Mockingbird; Sergeants Three. **1971** Scandalous John. **1975** Rafferty and the Gold Dust Twins.

HALE, ROBERT
Born: Mar. 25, 1874, Devonshire, England. Died: Apr. 18, 1940, Maidenhead, Berkshire, England. Screen and stage actor. Father of music hall actress Binnie and actor Sonnie Hale (dec. 1959).

Appeared in: **1934** What Happened to Harkness?; Waltzes from Vienna (aka Strauss' Great Waltz—US 1935). **1935** Royal Cavalcade (aka Regal Cavalcade—US). **1936** It's Love Again. **1937** Storm in a Teacup.

HALE, ROBERTSON
Born: 1891, England. Died: 1967. Screen and stage actor.

HALE, SONNIE (John Robert Hale-Monro)
Born: May 1, 1902, London, England. Died: June 9, 1959, London, England. Screen, stage actor, film director and playwright. Wrote under name of Robert Monro. Son of actor Robert Hale (dec. 1940) and brother of actress Binnie Hale. Divorced from actresses Evelyn Laye and Jessie Matthews (dec. 1981), and later married to Mary Kelsey.

Appeared in: **1927** The Book of Psalms series including The Parting of the Ways—Psalm 57; On With the Dance series. **1932** Happy Ever After; Tell Me Tonight (aka Be Mine Tonight—US 1933). **1933** Early to Bed; Friday the Thirteenth (US 1934). **1934** Evergreen (US 1935); Wild Boy; Are You a Mason?; My Song for You; My Heart is Calling (US 1935). **1935** Marry the Girl; First a Girl. **1936** It's Love Again. **1938** The Gaunt Stranger (aka The Phantom Strikes—US 1939). **1939** Let's Be Famous. **1944** Fiddlers Three. **1946** London Town (aka My Heart Goes Crazy—US 1953).

HALEY, BILL (William John Clifton Haley, Jr.)
Born: July 6, 1925, Highland Park, Mich. Died: Feb. 9, 1981, Harlingen, Tex. (natural causes). Singer, guitarist, band leader and screen actor. Leader of Bill Haley and the Comets.

Appeared in: **1956** Rock Around the Clock; Don't Knock the Rock. **1981** Blue Suede Shoes.

HALEY, JACK (John Joseph Haley)
Born: Aug. 10, 1898, Boston, Mass. Died: June 6, 1979, Los Angeles, Calif. (heart attack). Screen, stage vaudeville, radio actor and singer. Married to actress Florence McFadden. Father of film/TV producer Jack Haley, Jr.

Appeared in: **1927** Broadway Madness. **1930** Follow Thru. **1933** Sitting Pretty. **1934** Here Comes the Groom. **1935** Coronado; The Girl Friend; Redheads on Parade. **1936** Pigskin Parade; Poor Little Rich Girl; F-Man; Mister Cinderella. **1937** She Had to Eat; Danger—Love at Work; Pick a Star; Wake Up and Live. **1938** Rebecca of Sunnybrook Farm; Alexander's Ragtime Band; Hold That Co-ed; Thanks for Everything. **1939** The Wizard of Oz. **1941** Moon Over Miami; Navy Blues. **1942** Beyond the Blue Horizon. **1943** Higher and Higher. **1944** One Body Too Many; Take It Big. **1945** Sing Your Way Home; George White's Scandals; Scared Stiff. **1946** People are Funny; Vacation in Reno. **1949** Make Mine Laughs. **1970** Norwood.

HALFI, AVRAHAM
Born: 1904, Lodz, Poland. Died: June 8, 1980, Tel Aviv, Israel. Screen, stage actor, poet and author.

HALL, ALEXANDER
Born: 1894, Boston, Mass. Died: July 30, 1968, San Francisco, Calif. (stroke). Screen, stage actor and film director.

Appeared in: **1927** Million Dollar Mystery (serial—film debut). **1936** Come and Get It. **1937** Woman Chases Man.

HALL, ALFRED HENRY
Born: 1880. Died: Apr. 21, 1943, Hollywood, Calif. (heart attack). Screen and stage actor.

Appeared in: **1942** Scattergood Survives a Murder; The Old Homestead; Pretty Dolly (short).

HALL, ARCH, SR. "ARCHIE"
Born: 1909. Died: Apr. 28, 1978, Los Angeles, Calif. (heart attack). Screen, stage, radio actor, film producer, screenwriter and newscaster. Married to writer Addelyn Hall. Father of actor Arch Hall, Jr.

Appeared in: **1938** Rhythm of the Saddle; Overland Stage Rider. **1941** Two-Gun Sheriff; The Lone Rider in Ghost Town. **1945** Border Badmen.

HALL, CHARLES D. "CHARLIE"
Born: Aug. 18, 1899, Birmingham, England. Died: Dec. 7, 1959, North Hollywood, Calif. Screen, stage actor and film art director. Entered films as an actor in 1923.

Appeared in: **1927** Battle of the Century; Love 'Em and Weep (short). **1928** Must We Marry?; Crooks Can't Win; plus the following shorts: You're Darn Tootin'; Two Tars; Leave 'Em Laughing. **1929** Why Bring That Up?; plus the following shorts: Boxing Gloves; The Hoose Gow; Skirt Shy; They Go Boom; Wrong Again; That's My Wife; Double Whoopee; Berth Marks; Men O'War; Bacon Grabbers; Angora Love. **1930** The following shorts: Bear Shooters; Pups Is Pups; The

Real McCoy; Fifty Million Husbands; Dollar Dizzy; The Fighting Parson; Below Zero. **1931** Pardon Us; plus the following shorts: Be Big; Bear Hunks; The Pip From Pittsburgh; Rough Seas!; The Panic Is On; What a Bozo!; Air Tight; The Kickoff; Mama Loves Papa; Let's Do Things; The Pajama Party; Laughing Gravy; Scratch As Catch Can; Come Clean; War Mamas. **1932** The following shorts: Young Ironsides; Mr. Bride; Too Many Women; Seal Skins; Sneak Easily; Any Old Port; The Music Box; Strictly Unreliable; Show Business; The Soilers; Bon Voyage. **1933** The following shorts: The Midnight Patrol; Fallen Arches; His Silent Racket; Luncheon at Twelve; Hold Your Temper; Maids A La Mode; One Tract Minds; Beauty and the Bus; Backs to Nature; Air Tight; Twice Two; Me and My Pal; Busy Bodies; Kickin' The Crown Around; Fits in a Fiddle; What Fur. **1934** Cockeyed Cavaliers; Sons of the Desert; Kentucky Kernels; plus the following shorts: Mike Fright; Hi Neighbor; I'll Take Vanilla; It Happened One Day; Something Simple; The Chases of Pimple Street; Them Thar Hills; The Live Ghost; Babes in the Goods; Soup and Fish; One Horse Farmers; Opened by Mistake; Maid in Hollywood. **1935** The following shorts: Beginner's Luck; Teacher's Beau; Okay Toots!; Poker at Eight; Southern Exposure; Treasure Blues; Sing, Sister, Sing; Twin Triplets; Hot Money; Tit for Tat; Thicker Than Water. **1936** Swing Time; Pick a Star; plus the following shorts: Pinch Singer; All-American Toothache; Neighborhood House. **1940** One Night in the Tropics; A Chump at Oxford; Saps at Sea; You Can't Fool Your Wife; Slightly at Sea (short); Trailer Tragedy (short). **1941** Top Sergeant Mulligan; plus the following shorts: An Apple in His Eye; I'll Fix That; A Quiet Fourth; A Polo Phony. **1942** The following shorts: Two For the Money; Rough on Rents; Framing Father. **1943** His Butler's Sister; Gem Jams (short). **1944** The Lodger; The Canterville Ghost; In Society; Radio Rampage (short); Girls, Girls, Girls (short). **1945** On Stage Everybody; Hangover Square; Mama Loves Papa. **1946** Wall Street Blues (short). **1947** Forever Amber; Singapore. **1948** How to Clean House (short); Home Canning (short); The Big Clock. **1950** Spooky Wooky (short). **1951** The Vicious Years. **1956** So You Want to Play the Piano (short). **1958** The Further Perils of Laurel and Hardy (documentary).

HALL, CHARLES R.
Born: Aug. 19, 1899, England. Died: Apr. 13, 1959, St. Petersburg, Fla. Screen actor, assistant film director and stuntman. Do not confuse with vaudeville actor "Charlie" Hall (dec. 1972) nor art director Charles D. Hall.

HALL, DONALD
Born: Aug. 14, 1878, Murree, East India. Died: July 25, 1948, Hollywood, Calif. Screen, stage actor and singer.

Appeared in: **1914** The Christian; Mr. Barnes of New York; The Crucible of Fate. **1915** Mortmain; Anselo Lee. **1916** The Law Decides; The Man Who Went Sane; The Scarlet Runner (serial). **1917** The On-the-Square Girl; The Awakening of Ruth; Alias Mrs. Jessop; The Raggedy Queen. **1919** The Broken Melody; The Carter Case (Craig Kennedy serial). **1920** A Woman's Business; The Greatest Love. **1922** A Woman's Woman. **1923** The Last Moment. **1924** Her Love Story; Unguarded Women. **1929** The Spirit of Youth; The Younger Generation. **1930** Oh, For a Man!

HALL, DOROTHY
Born: 1906. Died: Feb. 3, 1953, New York, N.Y. Screen and stage actress.

Appeared in: **1927** Back to Liberty; The Broadway Drifter; The Winning Oar. **1929** Nothing But the Truth; The Laughing Lady. **1930** Home Made (short).

HALL, ELLA (Ella Augusta Hall)
Born: Mar. 17, 1896, N.J. Died: Sept. 3, 1981, Canoga Park, Calif. Screen actress. Daughter of stage actress May Hall (dec.). Divorced from actor Emory Johnson. Entered films in 1912.

Appeared in: **1914** The Symphony of Souls. **1915** The Master Key (serial); Heritage; Jewel; The Little Blonde in Black; The Silent Command; Shattered Memories. **1916** The Bugler of Algiers. **1917** Her Soul's Inspiration; A Jewel in Pawn; The Charmer; The Gates of Doom; The Little Orphan; The Spotted Lily; My Little Boy. **1918** New Love for Old; Beauty in Chains; Which Woman; Heart of Rachael. **1919** Under the Top. **1921** The Great Reward (serial). **1922** In the Name of the Law; The Heart of Lincoln. **1923** The Third Alarm; The Flying Dutchman; The Westbound Limited. **1930** Madam Satan. **1933** The Bitter Tea of General Yen.

HALL, ETHEL
Died: June 30, 1927, Merced, Calif. (swept from a boat on Merced River during filming). Screen actress.

HALL, GABRIELLE
Died: Jan. 1, 1967, El Cajon, Calif. Screen and television actress. Entered films during silents.

HALL, GEORGE M.
Born: 1890, Sweden. Died: Apr. 24, 1930, Saranac Lake, N.Y. Screen and stage actor.

Appeared in: **1926** West of Broadway.

HALL, GERALDINE
Born: 1905. Died: Sept. 18, 1970, Woodland Hills, Calif. Screen and stage actress. Married to actor Porter Hall (dec. 1953).

Appeared in: **1936** More Than a Secretary. **1938** I Met My Love Again; Bringing Up Baby. **1951** The Big Carnival. **1952** The Captive City. **1954** Secret of the Incas. **1955** Five Against the House. **1956** Over-Exposed; The Proud and the Profane.

HALL, HENRY LEONARD
Died: Dec. 11, 1954, Woodland Hills, Calif. Screen and stage actor.

Appeared in: **1933** Story of Temple Drake (film debut); Sagebrush Trail. **1934** Our Daily Bread; The Dude Ranger. **1935** The Phantom Empire (serial); Mary Burns, Fugitive; G-Men. **1936** The Clutching Hand (serial); The Vigilantes Are Coming (serial); Jailbreak. **1937** County Fair; Yodelin' Kid from Pine Ridge. **1938** Blockheads. **1940** Blazing Six Shooter; Prairie Law; The Haunted House; The Ape; Chip of the Flying U. **1941** Pirates on Horseback; Stick to Your Guns; The Lone Star Vigilantes. **1942** Murder in the Big House; Stagecoach Buckaroo; Boss of Hangtown Mesa; The Old Homestead; Butch Minds the Baby; Queen of Broadway. **1943** Johnny Come Lately; Girls in Chains. **1944** Story of Dr. Wassell; Heavenly Days. **1945** San Antonio; Jade Mask. **1946** Flying Serpent. **1947** The Beginning of the End; I Wonder Who's Kissing Her Now; Wild Country; Pioneer Justice. **1948** Command Decision; Panhandle. **1949** Cover Up.

HALL, HOWARD
Born: May 30, 1867. Died: July 25, 1921, Long Beach, Calif. Screen, stage actor and author.

Appeared in: **1916** According to Law. **1917** The Barrier; Alias Mrs. Jessup; Weavers of Life; The Natural Law. **1919** The Gold Cure. **1922** Sunshine Harbor.

HALL, J. ALBERT
Born: Calcutta, India. Died: Apr. 18, 1920. Screen and stage actor.

Appeared in: **1915** Salamander; Children of the Ghetto. **1916** The Big Sister; The Ransom; The Yellow Menace (serial).

HALL, JAMES (James Brown)
Born: Oct. 22, 1900, Dallas, Tex. Died: June 7, 1940, Jersey City, N.J. (liver ailment). Screen and stage actor.

Appeared in: **1923** The Man Alone. **1926** The Campus Flirt; Stranded in Paris. **1927** Hotel Imperial; Love's Greatest Mistake; Ritzy; Swim, Girl, Swim; Senorita; Silk Legs; Rolled Stockings. **1928** Just Married; The Fifty-Fifty Girl; The Fleet's In; Four Sons. **1929** The Saturday Night Kid; The Canary Murder Case; Smiling Irish Eyes; The Case of Lena Smith; This Is Heaven. **1930** Hell's Angels; Dangerous Nan McGrew; Maybe It's Love; Let's Go Native; Paramount on Parade; The Third Alarm. **1931** Mother's Millions; Sporting Chance; Millie; Man to Man; Lightning Flyer; The Good Bad Girl; Divorce Among Friends. **1932** Manhattan Tower.

HALL, JANE
Born: 1880, Winona, Minn. Died: Oct. 13, 1975, St. Paul, Minn. Screen and stage actress.

Appeared in: **1915** Madame Butterfly. **1916** Less Than Dust.

HALL, JOHN (Michael Braughal)
Born: 1878. Died: Apr. 25, 1936, Los Angeles, Calif. Screen actor.

Appeared in: **1927** Men of Daring. **1928** The Wild West Show.

HALL, JON (Charles Lochner aka LLOYD CRANE)
Born: 1915, Fresno, Calif. Died: Dec. 13, 1979, Sherman Oaks, Calif. (suicide—shot). Screen, stage, television actor, film director, film producer and screenwriter. Divorced from actresses Frances Langford and Raquel Torres Ames.

Appeared in: **1935** Charlie Chan in Shanghai (film debut); Women Must Dress. **1936** Mind Your Own Business; The Lion Man; The Mysterious Avenger; The Clutching Hand (serial). **1937** The Hurricane; The Girl from Scotland Yard. **1940** South of Pago Pago; Sailor's Lady; Kit Carson. **1941** Aloma of the South Sea Islands. **1942** The Tuttles of Tahiti; Eagle Squadron; The Invisible Agent; Arabian Nights. **1943** White Savage. **1944** Ali Baba and the Forty Thieves; The Invisible Man's Revenge; San Diego, I Love You; Lady in the Dark;

Cobra Woman; Gypsy Wildcat; 1945 Sudan; Men in Her Diary. **1947** The Michigan Kid; Last of the Redmen; The Vigilante's Return. **1948** The Prince of Thieves. **1949** Deputy Marshall; The Mutineers; Zamba. **1950** On the Isle of Samoa. **1951** China Corsair; When the Redskins Rode; Hurricane Island. **1952** Brave Warrior; Last Train from Bombay. **1953** White Goddess; Eyes of the Jungle. **1955** Phantom of the Jungle; Thunder Over Sangoland. **1957** Hell Ship Mutiny. **1959** Forbidden Island. **1965** Beach Girls and the Monster.

HALL, JUANITA
Born: 1902. Died: Feb. 28, 1968, Keyport, N.J. (diabetes). Screen and stage actress.

Appeared in: **1949** Miracle in Harlem. **1958** South Pacific. **1961** Flower Drum Song.

HALL, LOUIS LEON
Born: 1879, Oneida, N.Y. Died: Apr. 17, 1930, Houghton, Maine. Screen, stage actor, screenwriter and playwright. Married to stage actress Ethel Robertson (dec.).

HALL, MAUD
Born: 1881, New Orleans, La. Died: May 1, 1938, Liberty, N.Y. Screen and stage actress. Married to actor Carlton Macy (dec. 1946).

Appeared in: **1914** A Mother's Heart.

HALL, NELSON L.
Born: 1881. Died: July 28, 1944, Philadelphia, Pa. Screen actor and acrobat stuntman.

Appeared in: **1915** The Man's Making.

HALL, PAULINE
Born: 1891. Died: Oct. 6, 1974, Reseda, Calif. (cancer). Screen actress. Married to assistant director Ralph Slosser (dec. 1971).

HALL, PORTER
Born: 1888, Cincinnati, Ohio. Died: Oct. 6, 1953, Los Angeles, Calif. (heart attack). Screen and stage actor. Won 1936 Screen Actors Guild Award for Best Supporting Actor in The Plainsman. Married to actress Geraldine Hall (dec. 1970).

Appeared in: **1934** The Thin Man (film debut); Murder in the Private Car. **1935** The Case of the Lucky Legs. **1936** The Story of Louis Pasteur; The Petrified Forest; The General Died at Dawn; Satan Met a Lady; Too Many Parents; Princess Comes Across; And Sudden Death; Snowed Under; The Plainsman. **1937** Let's Make a Million; Bulldog Drummond Escapes; Souls at Sea; Wells Fargo; Wild Money; Hotel Haywire; Make Way for Tomorrow; King of Gamblers; This Way, Please; True Confession. **1938** Scandal Street; Stolen Heaven; Dangerous to Know; Prison Farm; King of Alcatraz; The Arkansas Traveler; Men With Wings; Tom Sawyer, Detective; Bulldog Drummond's Peril. **1939** Grand Jury Secrets; They Shall Have Music; Mr. Smith Goes to Washington. **1940** Arizona; The Dark Command; Trail of the Vigilantes; His Girl Friday. **1941** The Parson of Panamint; Sullivan's Travels; Mr. and Mrs. North. **1942** The Remarkable Andrew; Tennessee Johnson; Butch Minds the Baby. **1943** A Stranger in Town; The Desperadoes; Woman of the Town. **1944** Standing Room Only; Double Indemnity; The Miracle of Morgan's Creek; Mark of the Whistler; Going My Way; The Great Moment. **1945** Murder, He Says; Kiss and Tell; Blood on the Sun; Weekend at the Waldorf; Bring on the Girls. **1947** Singapore; Miracle on 34th Street; Mad Wednesday. **1948** Unconquered; That Wonderful Urge. **1949** You Gotta Stay Happy; Beautiful Blonde From Bashful Bend; Chicken Every Sunday; Intruder in the Dust. **1951** The Big Carnival. **1952** The Half Breed; Carbine Williams; Holiday for Sinners. **1953** Pony Express; Vice Squad. **1954** Return of Treasure Island.

HALL, THURSTON
Born: 1883, Boston, Mass. Died: Feb. 20, 1958, Beverly Hills, Calif. (heart attack). Screen, stage, television, vaudeville actor and stage producer. Entered films in 1915.

Appeared in: **1917** Cleopatra. **1918** We Can't Have Everything; The Kaiser's Shadow; Brazen Beauty. **1921** Idle Hands; The Iron Trail; Mother Eternal. **1922** Fair Lady; Wildness of Youth. **1923** The Royal Oak. **1924** The Great Well (aka Neglected Women—US). **1930** Absent Minded (short). **1935** Hooray for Love; Metropolitan; Guard That Girl; Crime and Punishment; The Girl Friend; Too Tough to Live; Black Room; After the Dance; Love Me Forever; Public Menace; One Way Ticket; Case of the Missing Man; A Feather in Her Hat. **1936** Pride of the Marines; Roaming Lady; Two-Fisted Gentleman; Lady from Nowhere; The Lone Wolf Returns; Don't Gamble With Love; The Man Who Lived Twice; Killer at Large; Theodora Goes Wild;

Devil's Squadron; The King Steps Out; Trapped By Television; Shakedown; Three Wise Guys. **1937** I Promise to Pay; Women of Glamour; Parole Racket; It Can't Last Forever; Counsel for Crime; Murder in Greenwich Village; We Have Our Moments; Oh, Doctor; Don't Tell the Wife. **1938** No Time to Marry; There's Always a Woman; Little Miss Roughneck; Campus Confessions; The Affairs of Annabel; Professor Beware; Women Are Like That; The Amazing Dr. Clitterhouse; Hard to Get; Fast Company; Going Places; Extortion; Squadron of Honor; Main Event. **1939** You Can't Cheat an Honest Man; First Love; Stagecoach; Ex-Champ; Our Neighbors, the Carters; Mutiny on the Blackhawk; Hawaiian Nights; Million Dollar Legs; The Star Maker; Each Dawn I Die; Jeepers Creepers; Money to Burn; The Day the Bookies Wept; Dancing Co-ed. **1940** The Great McGinty; Sued for Libel; The Blue Bird; Kiddie Cure (short); Blondie on a Budget; In Old Missouri; Alias the Deacon; Millionaires in Prison; The Lone Wolf Meets a Lady; City for Conquest; Friendly Neighbors; The Golden Fleecing. **1941** The Great Lie; Life With Henry; The Lone Wolf Takes a Chance; Repent at Leisure; Tuxedo Junction; The Invisible Woman; Flight from Destiny; The Lone Wolf Keeps a Date; Where Did You Get That Girl?; Washington Melodrama; She Knew All the Answers; Accent on Love; Design for Scandal; Midnight Angel; Remember That Day; In the Navy; Hold That Ghost. **1942** The Night Before the Divorce; Sleepytime Gal; Rings on Her Fingers; The Great Man's Lady; Shepherd of the Ozarks; Call of the Canyon; Hello, Annapolis; Counter Espionage; The Hard Way; The Great Gildersleeve; Pacific Blackout. **1943** Sherlock Holmes in Washington; Hoosier Holiday; Footlight Glamour; Here Comes Elmer; He Hired the Boss; The Youngest Profession; This Land Is Mine; I Dood It. **1944** Adventures of Mark Twain; Good Night, Sweetheart; Something for the Boys; Song of Nevada; Wilson; Cover Girl; The Great Moment; In Society; Ever Since Venus. **1945** Brewster's Millions; Bring on the Girls; The Blonde from Brooklyn; Don Juan Quilligan; Col. Effingham's Raid; Saratoga Trunk; Lady on a Train; The Gay Senorita; Thrill of a Romance; Song of the Prairie; West of the Pecos. **1946** Dangerous Business; One More Tomorrow; She Wrote the Book; Three Little Girls in Blue; Two Sisters from Boston; Without Reservations. **1947** The Secret Life of Walter Mitty; Black Gold; The Unfinished Dance; It Had to Be You; The Farmer's Daughter; Welcome Stranger; Mourning Becomes Electra; Son of Rusty. **1948** King of Gamblers; Up in Central Park; Miraculous Journey. **1949** Stagecoach Kid; Manhattan Angel; Rim of the Canyon; Rusty Saves a Life; Square Dance Jubilee; Tell It to the Judge; Blondie's Secret. **1950** Bright Leaf; Bandit Queen; Belle of Old Mexico; Chain Gang; Federal Agent at Large; Girls' School; One Too Many. **1951** Belle Le Grand; Texas Carnival; Whirlwind. **1952** Carson City; One Big Affair; Night Stage to Galveston; Skirts Ahoy!; The Wac from Walla Walla. **1957** Affair in Reno.

HALL, WILLARD LEE
Born: 1863, Altoma, Pa. Died: Oct. 30, 1936, San Francisco, Calif. Screen actor.

Appeared in: **1921** The Conquering Power. **1923** Scaramouche.

HALL, WINTER
Born: June 21, 1878, New Zealand. Died: Feb. 10, 1947. Screen and stage actor. Entered films in 1916 at Lasky Studio.

Appeared in: **1919** The Turn in the Road; The Money Corporal; Why Smith Left Home. **1920** The Forbidden Woman; Behold My Wife. **1921** The Affairs of Anatol; The Breaking Point; Cheated Hearts; The Child Thou Gavest Me; Her Social Value; The Great Impersonation; The Little Clown; What Every Woman Knows; The Witching Hour. **1922** East Is West; On the High Seas; Burning Sands; Saturday Night; Skin Deep. **1923** Thundering Dawn; The Voice from the Minaret; Wasted Lives; Ashes of Vengeance; The Day of Faith; Little Church Around the Corner; Her Reputation. **1924** Husbands and Lovers; The Only Woman; Name the Man; The Right of the Strongest; The Turmoil; Secrets. **1925** Ben Hur; Free to Love; The Boomerang; Compromise; The Girl Who Wouldn't Work; The Pleasure Buyers; Graustark; Raffles—the Amateur Cracksman. **1928** Paradise; Balaclara (aka Jaws of Hell—US 1931); The Forger; The Wrecker (US 1929). **1929** The Lost Zeppelin; The Racketeer; The Love Parade; Kitty; After the Verdict (US 1930); Woman to Woman. **1930** Passion Flower; Road to Paradise. **1931** Girls Demand Excitement; Confessions of a Co-ed. **1932** Tomorrow and Tomorrow. **1933** Cavalcade. **1934** The Barretts of Wimpole Street; The Pursuit of Happiness. **1935** The Crusades. **1936** Lloyds of London; Two in a Crowd; The Invisible Ray. **1937** Slave Ship. **1938** Four Men and a Prayer; If I Were King.

HALLAM, HENRY
Born: 1867, London, England. Died: Nov. 9, 1921, United States. Screen and stage actor.

Appeared in: **1912** The Darling of C.S.A. **1915** The Haunting Fear. **1916** The Moment Before; Gloria's Romance. **1917** Aladdin's Other Lamp; Lady Barnacle; The Girl Wihout a Soul. **1919** The Lion and the Mouse; The Climbers; Help, Help, Police; Never Say Quit; Kathleen Mavourneen. **1920** The Prey; The Gauntlet; The Fatal Hour. **1921** Cousin Kate; The Conquest of Canaan; The Heart of Maryland; Tol'able David.

HALLARD, C. M.
Born: 1866, England. Died: Mar. 21, 1942, Surrey, England. Screen and stage actor. Entered films in 1917.

Appeared in: **1918** The Man Who Won; The Elder Mrs. Blossom (aka Wanted—a Wife—US). **1919** Convict 99; The Bridal Chair; In Bondage (aka Faith); Edge O'Beyond; Gamblers All; Mrs. Thompson. **1920** The Husband Hunter; Her Story (US 1922); The Case of Lady Camber; Love in the Wilderness; In the Night. **1922** The Pauper Millionaire. **1927** Carry On! **1928** A Light Woman. **1930** Knowing Men; The "W" Plan (US 1931); Two Worlds; Almost a Honeymoon (US 1931); Compromising Daphne (aka Compromised—US 1931). **1931** The Woman Between (aka The Woman Decides—US 1932); Tell England (aka The Battle of Gallipoli—US); The Rasp. **1932** Strictly Business; The Chinese Puzzle. **1933** On Secret Service (aka Secret Agent—US 1935). **1934** The Third Clue; Rolling in Money. **1935** Royal Cavalcade (aka Regal Cavalcade—US); Moscow Nights (aka I Stand Condemned—US 1936); Night Mail. **1936** King of the Damned; Jack of All Trades (aka The Two of Us—US 1937). **1937** The Sky's the Limit; The Live Wire.

HALLATT, HENRY
Born: Feb. 1, 1888, Whitehaven, England. Died: July 24, 1952, England? Screen and stage actor. Son of stage actor W. H. Hallett (dec. 1927). Entered films in 1908.

Appeared in: **1920** Foul Play. **1931** The Hound of the Baskervilles. **1937** Gangway; Victoria the Great. **1938** Sixty Glorious Years (aka Queen of Destiny—US).

HALL-DAVIS, LILIAN
Born: 1901, Hampstead, England. Died: Oct. 25, 1933, London, England (suicide—gas). Screen actress.

Appeared in: **1918** The Admirable Crichton; The Better 'Ole (aka The Romance of Old Bill and Carry On—US). **1920** The Honeypot; Ernest Maltravers. **1921** Love Maggie. **1922** Stable Companions; The Wonderful Story; Brown Sugar; The Faithful Heart; The Game of Life; If Four Walls Told; Castles in the Air (aka Let's Pretend). **1923** The Right to Strike; Afterglow; Should a Doctor Tell?; The Hotel Mouse; I Pagliacci; Maisie's Marriage (aka Married Love and Life); The Knockout; A Royal Divorce. **1924** The Unwanted; The Eleventh Commandment; The Passionate Adventure. **1926** If Youth But Knew; Boadicea. **1927** Blighty (aka Apres la Guerre); The Ring; Roses of Picardy; Lost One (aka As We Lie). **1928** The White Sheik (aka King's Mate); The Farmer's Wife (US 1930); Tommy Atkins. **1930** Just for a Song. **1931** Her Reputation; Many Waters. **1933** Volga Volga.

HALLE, CLIFF
Born: 1919, Benkelman, Nebr. Died: Apr. 3, 1976, North Hollywood, Calif. Screen, stage, radio and television actor.

Appeared in: **1944** Winged Victory.

HALLET, AGNES
Born: 1880. Died: Nov. 19, 1954, Hollywood, Calif. Screen actress.

HALLETT, ALBERT
Born: 1870. Died: Apr. 3, 1935, Hollywood, Calif. Screen and stage actor.

Appeared in: **1924** The Passing of Wolf McLean. **1925** The Gold Hunters. **1926** The Haunted Range; Midnight Faces.

HALLIDAY, GARDNER
Born: 1910. Died: Sept. 6, 1966, Hollywood, Calif. (suicide due to cancer). Stage and screen actor. Entered films in 1946.

HALLIDAY, JOHN
Born: Sept. 4, 1880, Brooklyn, N.Y. Died: Oct. 17, 1947, Honolulu, Hawaii (heart ailment). Screen and stage actor.

Appeared in: **1920** The Woman Gives. **1929** East Side Sadie. **1930** How I Play Golf—Chip Shots (short); Father's Sons; Recaptured Love;

Scarlet Pages. **1931** Smart Woman; Consolation Marriage; The Ruling Voice; Millie; Once a Sinner; Captain Applejack; Fifty Million Frenchmen; The Spy; Transatlantic. **1932** Men of Chance; Man Called Back; The Impatient Maiden; The Age of Consent; Weekends Only; Bird of Paradise. **1933** Perfect Understanding; Terror Aboard; Bed of Roses; The House on 56th Street; The Woman Accused. **1934** Return of the Terror; Housewife; A Woman's Man; Happiness Ahead; Registered Nurse; The Witching Hour; Desirable; Finishing School. **1935** Mystery Woman; The Dark Angel; The Melody Lingers On; Peter Ibbetson. **1936** Desire; Fatal Lady; Three Cheers for Love; Hollywood Boulevard. **1938** Arsene Lupin Returns; Blockade; That Certain Age. **1939** The Light That Failed; Hotel for Women; Intermezzo; A Love Story. **1940** The Philadelphia Story. **1941** Lydia; Escape to Glory.

HALLIDAY, LENA
Born: London, England. Died: Dec. 19, 1937, England? Screen and stage actress.

Appeared in: **1916** When Knights Were Bold. **1919** The Usurper. **1928** Adam's Apple (aka Honeymoon Ahead—US); The Bells of St. Mary's. **1929** When Knights Were Bold; Honeymoon Abroad.

HALLIGAN, THOMAS J. "TOM"
Born: May 17, 1914, New York. Died: July 19, 1970, Los Angeles, Calif. (heart disease). Screen and stage actor.

Appeared in: **1970** Beyond the Valley of the Dolls. **1972** Glass House.

HALLIGAN, WILLIAM
Born: Mar. 29, 1884. Died: Jan. 28, 1957, Woodland Hills, Calif. Screen, stage actor and screen writer.

Appeared in: **1919** The Wonder Man (film debut). **1929** Somewhere in Jersey (short). **1930** Follow the Leader; At Your Service (short); The Darling Brute (short). **1931** The Public Defender. **1932** Dancers in the Dark; Lady and Gent; The Crooner; Blessed Event; Babykins (short). **1940** You Can't Fool Your Wife; Hired Wife; 'Til We Meet Again; Boom Town; Third Finger, Left Hand. **1941** Gangs Incorporated. **1942** Life Begins at Eight-Thirty; Moontide; Lucky Jordan; The Powers Girl. **1943** He's My Guy; Rider of the Deadline; Coney Island; Dixie; The Leopard Man; Mission to Moscow. **1944** Show Business; Minstrel Man; Great Mike; The Hairy Ape. **1945** Within These Walls; The Spider; Dick Tracy. **1946** The Postman Always Rings Twice; If I'm Lucky; 'Til The Clouds Roll By. **1947** The Shocking Miss Pilgrim.

HALLOR, EDITH
Born: 1896, Washington, D.C. Died: May 21, 1971, Newport Beach, Calif. Stage and screen actress. Married to actor and film director John Francis Dillon (dec. 1934) and sister of actor Ray Hallor (dec. 1944) and actress Ethel Hallor.

Appeared in: **1915** Dr. Rameau. **1917** Seven Deadly Sins. **1920** The Blue Pearl; Children of Destiny. **1921** The Inside of the Cup; Just Outside the Door. **1922** Human Hearts. **1937** Maid of Salem. **1944** Wilson. **1945** A Tree Grows in Brooklyn.

HALLOR, RAY
Born: Jan. 14, 1900, Washington, D.C. Died: Apr. 16, 1944, near Palm Springs, Calif. (auto crash). Screen and stage actor. Brother of actresses Edith (dec. 1971) and Ethel Hallor.

Appeared in: **1917** An Amateur Orphan; Kidnapped. **1921** Dream Street. **1923** The Courtship of Miles Standish; The Dangerous Maid. **1924** The Circus Cowboy; Inez from Hollywood. **1925** The Last Edition; Learning to Love; Sally; The Storm Breaker. **1926** The High Flyer; It Must Be Love; Red Dice. **1927** Driven from Home; Quarantined Rivals; Tongues of Scandal. **1928** Man Crazy; The Haunted Ship; The Avenging Shadow; The Trail of '98; Black Butterflies; The Black Pearl; Green Grass Widows; Manhattan Knights; Nameless Men; Tropical Nights. **1929** Thundergod; Circumstantial Evidence; Fast Life; In Old California; Noisy Neighbors. **1930** The Truth About Youth.

HALLS, ETHEL MAY
Born: 1882. Died: Sept. 16, 1967, Hollywood, Calif. Screen, stage and television actress. Entered films with Biograph.

Appeared in: **1939** Our Leading Citizen; Island of Lost Men. **1940** Heroes of the Saddle; Thou Shalt Not Kill. **1944** Standing Room Only. **1945** Love Letters; Easy to Look At. **1946** The Dark Horse; Cross My Heart. **1949** Take One False Step. **1951** Katie Did It.

HALOP, BILLY (aka WILLIAM HALOP)
Born: Feb. 11, 1920, New York, N.Y. Died: Nov. 9, 1976, Brentwood, Calif. Screen, stage, radio and television actor. Brother of actress Florence Halop. Member of the original Dead End Kids.

Appeared in: **1937** Dead End (film debut and stage versions). **1938** Angels With Dirty Faces; Little Tough Guy; Crime School. **1939** Hell's Kitchen; Dust Be My Destiny; Angels Wash Their Faces; The Dead End Kids on Dress Parade (aka On Dress Parade); You Can't Get Away With Murder; Call a Messenger; They Made Me a Criminal. **1940** Sea Raider (serial); Junior G-Men (serial); Tom Brown's School Days; Sky Raiders (serial); Give Us Wings; You're Not So Tough. **1941** Mob Town; Blues in the Night; Hit the Road. **1942** Tough as They Come; Junior Army; Junior G-Men of the Air (serial). **1943** Mug Town. **1947** Dangerous Years. **1949** Challenge of the Range. **1955** Air Strike. **1963** For Love or Money; Move Over, Darling. **1964** A Global Affair. **1966** Mister Buddwing (aka On Dress Parade). **1967** Fitzwilly.

HALPERN, GERTRUDE (aka TRUDY LAWRENCE)
Born: 1927, New York, N.Y. Died: Sept. 23, 1978, Los Angeles, Calif. (heart attack). Screen, stage actress, singer and comedienne. Mother of dancer Phillip Halpern, pianist Jan Halpern and magician Richard Halpern.

Appeared in: **1969** Midnight Cowboy. **1974** Lenny.

HALTINER, FRED
Born: 1936, Switzerland. Died: Dec. 7, 1973, Zurich, Switzerland (suicide). Screen, stage and television actor.

Appeared in: **1969** Hannibal Brooks.

HALTON, CHARLES
Born: 1876. Died: Apr. 16, 1959, Los Angeles, Calif. (hepatitis). Screen and stage actor.

Appeared in: **1931** The Strange Case (short). **1936** Sing Me a Love Song; Dodsworth; Golddiggers of 1937; Stolen Holiday; Come and Get It; More Than a Secretary. **1937** The Road Back; The Black Legion; Penrod and Sam; Ready, Willing and Able; Talent Scout; Pick a Star; The Prisoner of Zenda; Woman Chases Man; Dead End; Blossoms on Broadway; Partners in Crime. **1938** Gold Is Where You Find It; Trouble at Midnight; Penitentiary; Bluebeard's Eighth Wife; Penrod and His Twin Brother; Penrod's Double Trouble; Stolen Heaven; The Saint in New York; Room Service; I'll Give a Million; I Am the Law; A Man to Remember. **1939** News is Made at Night; Swanee River; Nancy Drew—Reporter; They Made Her a Spy; Reno; Indianapolis Speedway; Charlie Chan at Treasure Island; I'm From Missouri; Juarez; Ex-Champ; They Asked For It; Young Mr. Lincoln; Dodge City; Jesse James; Federal Manhunt. **1940** Virginia City; They Drive By Night; The Shop Across the Corner; The Story of Dr. Ehrlich's Magic Bullet; Gangs of Chicago; Young People; Stranger on the Third Floor; The Doctor Takes a Wife; Tugboat Annie Sails Again; Calling All Husbands; Behind the News; Dr. Cyclops; 20 Mule Team; Lillian Russell; The Westerner. **1941** One Foot in Heaven; Mr. District Attorney; Mr. and Mrs. Smith; Meet the Chump; A Very Young Lady; Million Dollar Baby; I Was a Prisoner on Devil's Island; Dance Hall; The Smiling Ghost; Three Sons O'Guns; Look Who's Laughing; Unholy Partners; H. M. Pulham, Esq; Tobacco Road; The Body Disappears. **1942** There's One Born Every Minute; The Saboteur; The Lady is Willing; To Be or Not To Be; Juke Box Jenny; Whispering Ghosts; Priorities on Parade; Across the Pacific; You Can't Escape Forever; Henry Aldrich, Editor; That Other Woman; The Spoilers; In Old California; My Sister Eileen; Captains of the Clouds. **1943** Government Girl; Flesh and Fantasy; My Kingdom for a Cook; Jitterbugs; Lady Bodyguard; The Private Life of Dr. Paul Joseph Goebbels. **1944** It Happened Tomorrow; Rationing; Address Unknown; Enemy of Women; The Town Went Wild; Shadows in the Night; Wilson; Up in Arms. **1945** One Exciting Night; She Went to the Races; A Tree Grows in Brooklyn; The Fighting Guardsman; Rhapsody in Blue; Midnight Manhunt; Mama Loves Papa. **1946** It's a Wonderful Life; Sister Kenny; Singin' in the Corn; Because of Him; Three Little Girls in Blue; The Best Years of Our Lives. **1947** Merton of the Movies; The Bachelor and the Bobby Soxer; The Ghost Goes Wild. **1948** Three Godfathers. **1949** The Sickle or the Cross; The Daring Caballero; Hideout. **1950** Stells; Traveling Saleswoman; When Willie Comes Marching Home; Sabotage. **1951** Gasoline Alley. **1952** Carrie. **1953** The Moonlighter; A Slight Case of Larceny. **1956** Friendly Persuasion.

HAM, HARRY (aka HARRY HAMM)
Born: 1891, Napanee, Ontario, Canada. Died: July 27, 1943. Screen actor.

Appeared in: **1916** A Seminary Scandal. **1917** Tramp, Tramp, Tramp;

A Gay Deceiver; His Wedded Wife; Kidding Sister; He Fell on the Beach; Down by the Sea; Crazy by Proxy; The Honeymooners; Skirts. **1921** His Pajama Girl; Blood Money; The Broken Road; The Four Feathers. **1922** A Spanish Jade.

HAMER, FRED B.
Born: 1873. Died: Dec. 30, 1953, Los Angeles, Calif. Screen, stage actor and film director. Appeared in silents approx. 1910.

HAMER, GERALD
Born: 1886, South Wales. Died: July 6, 1972, Hollywood, Calif. (heart attack). Stage and screen actor.

Appeared in: **1936** Swing Time. **1937** Angel. **1938** Sweethearts; Blond Cheat. **1939** Bulldog Drummond's Bride. **1942** Pretty Dolly (short). **1943** Sherlock Holmes Faces Death. **1944** The Lodger; White Cliffs of Dover; The Scarlet Claw; Enter Arsene Lupin. **1945** Pursuit to Algiers. **1946** Terror By Night. **1947** Ivy. **1948** The Sign of the Ram.

HAMID, SWEENEY
Born: c. 1898, Morocco. Died: Mar. 25, 1968, Baltimore, Md. (lung cancer). Screen, vaudeville actor, circus performer and acrobat.

HAMILL, LUCILLE (Lucille Budd Hamill)
Born: 1902, Carthage, N.Y. Died: June 17, 1939, New York, N.Y. Screen and stage actress.

Appeared in: **1914** The Reward of Thrift. **1915** The Closing of the Circuit; The Battle Cry of Peace.

HAMILTON, BETTY
Born: 1914. Died: Apr. 10, 1935, New York, N.Y. Screen actress.

Appeared in: **1933** Victims of Persecution.

HAMILTON, FRED
Born: 1917. Died: Sept. 9, 1980, West Los Angeles, Calif. Screen actor, film producer, agent and television director.

Appeared in: **1935** Dante's Inferno. **1937** Dick Tracy (serial).

HAMILTON, GEORGE W. "SPIKE"
Born: 1901. Died: Mar. 31, 1957, New York, N.Y. Orchestra leader, songwriter and screen actor.

HAMILTON, GORDON GEORGE
Born: Coytesville, N.J. Died: Jan. 16, 1939, Fort Lee, N.J. (heart attack). Screen and stage actor.

Appeared in: **1914** The Perils of Pauline (serial).

HAMILTON, HALE
Born: Feb. 28, 1880, Ft. Madison, Iowa. Died: May 19, 1942, Los Angeles, Calif. (cerebral hemorrhage). Screen and stage actor. Married to actress Grace LaRue (dec. 1956) and later to stage actress Myrtle Tannahill (dec. 1977).

Appeared in: **1915** Her Painted Hero. **1918** The Winning of Beatrice. **1919** That's Good. **1923** His Children's Children. **1925** The Manicure Girl. **1926** The Great Gatsby; The Greater Glory; Summer Bachelors; Tin Gods. **1927** Girl in the Rain; The Telephone Girl. **1929** Listen, Lady. **1930** Common Clay; Good Intentions. **1931** Never the Twain Shall Meet; A Tailor-Made Man; Beau Ideal; Dance, Fools, Dance; Drums of Jeopardy; Rebound; The Great Lover; Strangers May Kiss; New Adventures of Get-Rich-Quick Wallingford; Cuban Love Song; The Champ; Paid; Susan Lennox; Her Rise and Fall; Murder at Midnight; Oh! Oh! Cleopatra (short). **1932** I Am a Fugitive from a Chain Gang; A Fool's Advice; Love Affair; Life Begins; Two Against the World; Those We Love; Call Her Savage; Most Dangerous Game; Three on a Match; Manhattan Tower; Grand Hotel; The Woman in Room 13; A Successful Calamity. **1933** Employees' Entrance; Billion Dollar Scandal; Reform Girl; Parole Girl; Black Beauty; Strange People; One Man's Journey; Sitting Pretty. **1934** City Park; Big-Hearted Herbert; When Strangers Meet; The Marines Are Coming; Curtain at Eight; The Quitter; Twin Husbands; Heartburn (short); Doctor Monica; The Girl from Missouri. **1935** I Live My Life; After Office Hours; Grand Old Girl; The Nitwits; Hold 'Em Yale; The Woman in Red; Let 'Em Have It; Calm Yourself; Three Kids and a Queen. **1938** The Adventures of Marco Polo; Meet the Mayor.

HAMILTON, JACK "SHORTY" (John H. Hamilton)
Born: Nov. 9, 1879 or 1888?, Chicago, Ill. Died: Mar. 7, 1925, Hollywood, Calif. (auto accident). Screen actor.

Appeared in: **1915** Shorty in the Clutches of the Cannibals; Shorty's Troubled Sleep; Shorty Turns Actor. **1916** Bucking Society; Gypsy Joe; She Loved a Sailor; His Busted Trust. **1917** Adventures of Shorty Hamilton. **1918** Denny from Ireland.

HAMILTON, JOHN
Born: 1887. Died: Oct. 15, 1958, Hollywood, Calif. (heart condition). Screen, stage, vaudeville and televison actor.

Appeared in: **1926** Rainbow Riley. **1930** White Cargo; Dangerous Nan McGrew; Heads Up. **1931** S. S. Van Dine series. **1936** Follow the Fleet; Two in a Crowd; The Legion of Terror; A Man Betrayed. **1937** Breezing Home; The Man Who Cried Wolf; One Hundred Men and a Girl; Two Wise Maids; Seventh Heaven; This is My Affair; Night Club Scandal; Bad Guy; Criminals of the Air. **1938** Boys Town; Angels With Dirty Faces; Stand Accused; Mr. Moto's Gamble; Over the Wall; Dr. Rhythm; Mr. Wong, Detective. **1939** The Roaring Twenties; Angels Wash Their Faces; Rose of Washington Square. **1940** The Lady With Red Hair; Dr. Ehrlich's Magic Bullet; The Shadow (serial); Flash Gordon Conquers the Universe; Oh Johnny How You Can Love; Johnny Apollo; Pound Foolish (short); The Great Plane Robbery. **1941** The Maltese Falcon; It Started With Eve; Hold Back the Dawn. **1942** Enemy Agents Meet Ellery Queen; Captain Midnight (serial); Yankee Doodle Dandy; Always in My Heart; To the Shores of Tripoli; In This Our Life; The Big Shot. **1943** Daredevils of the West (serial). **1944** Lake Placid Serenade; Captain America (serial); Zorro's Black Whip (serial); Allergic to Love; The Doughgirls; Wilson; Black Arrow (serial); The Girl Who Dared; Sheriff of Las Vegas; Meet Miss Bobby Socks; I'm From Arkansas; Crazy Knights. **1945** I'll Tell the World; The Naughty Nineties; On Stage Everybody; The Great Flamarion; Army Wives; Circumstantial Evidence. **1946** The Phantom Rider (serial); Girl on the Spot; Badmen's Territory; Wife Wanted; Johnny Comes Flying Home; The Brute Man; Home on the Range; Dangerous Business. **1947** The Foxes of Harrow; Blondie in the Dough; The Secret Life of Walter Mitty; Violence; Scareheads; The Beginning of the End. **1948** Return of the Bad Men; Song of My Heart. **1949** Fighting Man of the Plains; Law of the Golden West; The Wyoming Bandit; Sheriff of Wichita; Alias the Champ; Bandit King of Texas; Canadian Pacific; The Judge; Pioneer Marshall. **1950** Her Wonderful Lie; Davy Crockett, Indian Scout; Bells of Coronado; The Missourians; The James Brothers of Missouri (serial); Annie Get Your Gun. **1951** Belle Le Grand; Sugarfoot; Million Dollar Pursuit. **1952** The Pace That Thrills. **1953** Iron Mountain Trail; Donovan's Brain; Marshall of Cedar Rock. **1954** On the Waterfront; Sitting Bull. **1957** Chicago Confidential. **1958** Outcasts of the City.

HAMILTON, JOHN F.
Born: 1894. Died: July 11, 1967, Paramus, N.J. Screen, stage, vaudeville and television actor.

Appeared in: **1927** The Masked Menace (serial). **1939** Allegheny Uprising. **1940** The Saint's Double Trouble; Gold Rush Maisie. **1949** The Undercover Man; Prison Warden. **1950** Body Hold; Military Academy.

HAMILTON, JOSEPH H. "JOE"
Born: 1898. Died: Feb. 20, 1965. Screen actor.

Appeared in: **1956** The Solid Gold Cadillac. **1957** The Abductors. **1958** Jet Attack; Teenage Caveman; Cole Younger, Gunfighter. **1960** Cage of Evil; The Plunderers. **1961** The Hoodlum Priest. **1964** One Man's Way. **1965** Cat Ballou; Git.

HAMILTON, KAREN SUE
Born: 1946. Died: Sept. 3, 1969, Hollywood, Calif. (suicide). Screen and television actress.

HAMILTON, KIPP
Died: Jan. 29, 1981. Screen actor.

Appeared in: **1955** Good Morning, Miss Dove. **1956** Bigger Than Life. **1959** Never So Few. **1960** The Unforgiven. **1965** Harlow. **1966** Furankenshutain no Kaiju—Sanda tai Gailah (aka The War of the Gargantuas—US 1970).

HAMILTON, LAUREL L.
Died: Dec. 15, 1955, Hollywood, Calif. Screen, stage and vaudeville actress. Appeared in Sennett comedies.

HAMILTON, LLOYD
Born: Aug. 19, 1891, Oakland, Calif. Died: Jan. 19, 1935, Hollywood, Calif. (following surgery for stomach disorder). Screen, stage actor, screenwriter and film director. Was "Ham" in "Ham and Bud" comedy series (1914-1917) with Bud Duncan (dec. 1960). Appeared in "Sunshine" comedies (1918) and in "Mermaid" comedies (1921-1922). Divorced from actresses Ethel Floyd and Irene Dalton (dec. 1934). Entered films with Lubin Co. in 1914.

Appeared in: **1914** Ham at the Garbageman's Ball. **1915** Ham in the Harem; Ham and the Jitney Bus; Ham at the Fair; Ham's Easy Eats;

Ham the Detective; Ham in the Nut Factory; Ham's Harrowing Duel; Ham Among the Redskins; Ham at the Beach. **1916** Ham Takes a Chance; Ham the Diver; Ham Agrees With Sherman; Ham and the Hermit's Daughter; Ham and Preparedness; Ham's Waterloo; Ham's Busy Day; Ham the Explorer; Ham and the Masked Marvel; Ham's Whirlwind Finish; Ham's Strategy; Ham in the Drugstore; Ham the Fortune Teller; Patented by Ham. **1923** Hollywood. **1924** His Darker Self; A Self-Made Failure. **1925** The following shorts: Hooked; Half a Hero; King Cotton; Waiting; The Movies; Framed. **1929** The Show of Shows; Tanned Legs; Black Waters. **1931** Are You There? **1932-33** Universal shorts. **1934** An Old Gypsy Custom (short).

HAMILTON, MAHLON
Born: 1883. Died: June 20, 1960, Woodland Hills, Calif. (cancer). Screen and stage actor.

Appeared in: **1916** Molly Make-Believe; The Eternal Question; The Black Butterfly; Extravagance. **1917** Exile; Bridges Burned; The Red Woman; The Hidden Hand (serial); The Waiting Soul; More Truth Than Poetry; The Undying Flame; The Silence Sellers; The Soul of a Magdalen. **1918** The Danger Mark; The Death Dance. **1919** Adele; Daddy Long Legs; Her Kingdom of Dreams. **1920** The Third Generation; Earthbound; In Old Kentucky; The Deadlier Sex; Half a Chance. **1921** The Truant Husband; Under the Lash; I Am Guilty; Greater Than Love; Ladies Must Live; That Girl Montana. **1922** The Green Temptation; A Fool There Was; The Lane That Had No Turning; Paid Back; Peg O' My Heart; Under Oath. **1923** The Christian; The Heart Raider; Little Old New York; Her Children's Children; The Midnight Guest. **1924** The Recoil; Playthings of Desire. **1925** The Wheel; Enemies of Youth; The Other Woman's Story; The Winding Star; Idaho (serial). **1926** Morganson's Finish. **1927** Her Indiscretions; What Price Love. **1928** Life's Crossroads; White Flame. **1929** Honky Tonk; The Single Standard. **1930** Rich People; Code of Honor. **1931** Sporting Chance. **1932** Strangers of the Evening; Western Limited; Back Street. **1935** High School Girl; Mississippi. **1936** Boss Rider of Gun Creek; The Clutching Hand (serial). **1949** The Barkleys of Broadway.

HAMLER, JOHN E.
Born: 1891. Died: Dec. 2, 1969, N.Y. Screen actor and song and dance man.

HAMLIN, WILLIAM H.
Born: 1885. Died: Sept. 27, 1951, Los Angeles, Calif. Screen actor and stage director. Appeared in silents with Vitagraph.

HAMMER, FRED (Frederick William Hammer)
Born: Jan. 26, 1889, New York, N.Y. Died: Mar. 8, 1939, Hollywood, Calif. Screen actor.

HAMMER, INA
Died: Aug. 9, 1953, Brattleboro, Vt. Screen and stage actress. Married to stage producer Ira Hards (dec.).

Appeared in: **1915** The House of Fear.

HAMMERSTEIN, ELAINE
Born: 1897, Philadelphia, Pa. Died: Aug. 13, 1948, near Tijuana, Mexico (auto crash). Screen and stage actress. Daughter of producer Arthur Hammerstein.

Appeared in: **1917** The Argyle Case; The Mad Lover. **1920** Greater Than Fame. **1921** The Daughter Pays; The Miracle of Manhattan; Pleasure Seekers; Poor, Dear Margaret Kirby; The Girl from Nowhere; Remorseless Love; Way of a Maid; Handcuffs and Kisses. **1922** Evidence; Reckless Youth; Why Announce Your Marriage?; Under Oath; One Week of Love. **1923** Souls for Sale; Broadway Gold; Rupert of Hentzau. **1924** Daring Love; The Drums of Jeopardy; The Foolish Virgin; The Midnight Express; One Glorious Night. **1925** The Unwritten Law; After Business Hours; Every Man's Wife; Paint and Powder; Parisian Nights; S.O.S.; Perils of the Sea. **1926** The Checkered Flag; Ladies of Leisure.

HAMMERSTEIN, OSCAR, II
Born: July 12, 1895, New York, N.Y. Died: Aug. 23, 1960, Doylestown, Pa. (cancer). Composer, screenwriter and screen actor. Married to actress Dorothy Blanchard.

Appeared in: **1953** Main Street to Broadway.

HAMMOND, C. NORMAN (Charles Norman Hammond)
Born: 1878, San Jose, Calif. Died: June 5, 1941, New York, N.Y. Screen and stage actor.

Appeared in: **1914** Manon Lescaut. **1921** The Bronze Bell; The Smart

Sex; The Man Tamer; Through the Back Door. **1922** Smiles are Trumps; Dr. Jack; The Wise Kid; Received Payment; Women Men Marry. **1923** Big Brother. **1925** Irish Luck; Lucky Devil; Sally of the Sawdust.

HAMMOND, DOROTHY (Dorothy Plaskitt)
Died: Nov. 23, 1950, London, England. Screen and stage actress. Married to actor Sir Guy Standing (dec. 1937). Mother of actress Kay Hammond (dec. 1980).

Appeared in: **1935** Jubilee Window. **1936** Nothing Like Publicity.

HAMMOND, KAY (Dorothy Standing)
Born: Feb. 18, 1909, London, England. Died: May 4, 1980, Brighton, England. Screen and stage actress. Daughter of actor Sir Guy Standing, Sr. (dec. 1937). Married to actor/director Sir John Clements. For further family information see Sir Guy Standing, Sr. listing.

Appeared in: **1929** Her Private Affair. **1930** The Trespasser; Abraham Lincoln; Children of Chance. **1931** A Night in Montmartre; Almost a Divorce; Carnival (aka Venetian Nights—US); Fascination; Out of the Blue; The Chance of a Night Time. **1932** Money Means Nothing (US 1934); Sally Bishop; The Third String; Nine Till Six; A Night Like This. **1933** Double Harness; Racetrack; Yes, Madame; Sleeping Car; Britannia of Billingsgate; The Umbrella; Bitter Sweet. **1934** Eight Girls in a Boat; By-Pass to Happiness. **1936** Two on a Doorstep. **1941** Jeannie (US 1943). **1945** Blithe Spirit (film and stage versions). **1948** Call of the Blood. **1955** The Girl in the Red Velvet Swing.

HAMMOND, VIRGINIA
Born: 1894, Virginia. Died: Apr. 6, 1972, Washington, D.C. Stage and screen actress. Entered films with Essanay in 1916.

Appeared in: **1916** The Discard. **1919** The Hand Invisible; Miss Crusoe; The World to Live In. **1920** A Manhattan Knight. **1930** Anybody's Woman; A Lady Surrenders. **1931** Newly Rich. **1932** The Crash; The Rich Are Always With Us; No One Man; Cabin in the Cotton; Chandu the Magician; Rockabye. **1933** Eagle and the Hawk; Torch Singer; Chance at Heaven. **1934** Behold My Wife; Charlie Chan's Courage; Search for Beauty; Come on Marines; Doctor Monica; Desirable; Great Expectations. **1935** Rumba; The Virginia Judge; Lady Tubbs. **1936** Romeo and Juliet; The Great Impersonation; Goin' to Town; Straight from the Heart.

HAMPDEN, WALTER (Walter Hempden Daugherty)
Born: June 30, 1879, Brooklyn, N.Y. Died: June 11, 1955, Hollywood, Calif. (stroke). Screen, stage and television actor.

Appeared in: **1915** The Dragon's Claw. **1940** Northwest Mounted Police; The Hunchback of Notre Dame; All This, and Heaven Too. **1941** They Died With Their Boots On. **1942** Reap the Wild Wind. **1944** The Adventures of Mark Twain. **1950** All About Eve. **1951** The First Legion. **1952** Five Fingers. **1953** Treasure of the Golden Condor; Sombrero. **1954** The Silver Chalice; Sabrina. **1955** The Prodigal; Strange Lady in Town. **1956** The Vagabond King.

HAMPER, GENEVIEVE
Born: 1889. Died: Feb. 13, 1971, N.Y. Stage and screen actress. Married to actor John Alexander and widow of stage actor Robert Mantell.

Appeared in: **1916** A Wife's Sacrifice. **1923** Under the Red Robe.

HAMPTON, CRYSTAL
Died: June 17, 1922, New York, N.Y. Screen actress and film producer.

HAMPTON, FAITH
Born: 1909. Died: Apr. 1, 1949, Hollywood, Calif. (suffocation due to fire). Screen actress. Entered films during silents.

HAMPTON, GRAYCE (aka GRACE HAMPTON)
Born: 1876, England. Died: Dec. 20, 1963, Woodland Hills, Calif. Screen and stage actress.

Appeared in: **1916** The Pursuing Vengeance. **1931** The Bat Whispers; Broadminded; Ex-Bad Boy. **1932** Unexpected Father; Almost Married. **1935** Gigolette. **1936** Piccadilly Jim. **1941** Shanghai Gesture. **1943** Heaven Can Wait. **1944** Standing Room Only; Ministry of Fear; The Bridge of San Luis Rey; Nothing But Trouble. **1945** Her Highness and the Bell Boy; Hold That Blonde. **1946** Lady Luck; Without Reservations; Johnny Comes Flying Home. **1947** The Exile; Down to Earth; Love and Learn; Fun on a Weekend. **1948** Silver River; Sitting Pretty; The Snake Pit. **1949** Anna Lucasta; Bride for Sale; A Kiss in the Dark. **1950** Harvey; Love That Brute. **1951** The Mating Season. **1954** Forever Female.

HAMPTON, LOUISE
Born: 1881, Stockport, England. Died: Feb. 11, 1954, London, England (bronchial trouble). Screen and stage actress. Married to actor Edward Thane (dec. 1954).

Appeared in: **1932** Nine Till Six (film debut). **1939** Goodbye, Mr. Chips; Hell's Cargo (aka Dangerous Cargo—US 1940); The Middle Watch. **1940** The House of the Arrow (aka Castle of Crimes—US 1945); Busman's Honeymoon (aka Haunted Honeymoon—US). **1941** The Saint Meets the Tiger. **1946** Bedelia (US 1947). **1952** The Story of Robin Hood and His Merrie Men. **1953** The Oracle (aka The Horse's Mouth—US); Background (aka Edge of Divorce).

HAMPTON, MYRA
Born: 1901. Died: July 19, 1945, New York, N.Y. Screen, stage actress, author and stage casting director. Divorced from actor Raymond Hackett (dec. 1958).

Appeared in: **1929** The Trial of Mary Dugan. **1931** Once a Sinner.

HAMRICK, BURWELL F.
Born: 1906. Died: Sept. 21, 1970, Hollywood, Calif. Screen actor and film set designer.

Appeared in: **1916** The Pursuing Vengeance. **1917** The Devil Stone; John Ermine of the Yellowstone. **1918** A Law Unto Herself. **1922** The Face Between; Through A Glass Window. **1923** Rouged Lips.

HANCOCK, TONY (Anthony Hancock)
Born: May 12, 1924, Birmingham, England. Died: June 25, 1968, Sydney, Australia (overdose of sleeping tablets). Screen actor, author and screenwriter.

Appeared in: Orders Are Orders. **1961** The Rebel. **1962** The Punch and Judy Man (US 1963). **1965** Those Magnificent Men in Their Flying Machines or, How I Flew from London to Paris in 25 Hours and 11 Minutes. **1966** The Wrong Box.

HANDFORTH, RUTH
Born: July 11, 1882, Springfield, Mass. Died: Sept. 10, 1965. Screen and stage actress.

Appeared in: **1916** Intolerance. **1920** What Women Love; Slave of Vanity. **1923** Long Live the King. **1926** The Boy Friend. **1927** The Cruel Truth; Closed Gates.

HANDLEY, TOMMY
Born: 1902, England. Died: Jan. 9, 1949, London, England (cerebral hemorrhage). Screen, radio and vaudeville actor.

Appeared in: **1930** Elstree Calling. **1938** Two Men in a Box. **1943** It's That Man Again. **1944** Time Flies. **1946** Tom Tom Topia (short).

HANDWORTH, HARRY
Died: Mar. 22, 1916, Brooklyn, N.Y. Screen actor, film producer and director. Married to actress Octavia Handworth (dec. 1978).

Appeared in: **1915** Gone to the Dogs.

HANDWORTH, OCTAVIA (Octavia Boas)
Born: Dec. 24, 1887, New York, N.Y. Died: Oct. 3, 1978, Hemet, Calif. Screen actress. Married to actor/director Harry Handworth (dec. 1916). Later married to actor Gordon DeMain (dec. 1954).

Appeared in: **1912** The Compact; The Simple Maid. **1913** Unmasked. **1914** The Path Forbidden; When Fate Leads Trumps. **1915** The Great Ruby.

HANDYSIDES, CLARENCE
Born: 1854, Montreal, Canada. Died: Dec. 20, 1931, Philadelphia, Pa. Screen and stage actor.

Appeared in: **1914** One of Our Girls. **1916** Mice and Men; Silks and Satins. **1918** Turn of the Wheel.

HANEY, CAROL
Born: 1934. Died: May 10, 1964, Saddle River, N.J. (pneumonia—diabetes). Screen, television actress and dancer/choreographer. Divorced from actor Larry Blyden (dec. 1975).

Appeared in: **1945** Wonder Man. **1949** On the Town. **1950** Summer Stock. **1953** Kiss Me, Kate. **1956** Invitation to the Dance. **1957** Pajama Game (stage and film versions).

HANFORD, CHARLES B.
Born: May 5, 1859, Sutter Creek, Calif. Died: Oct. 16, 1926, Washington. Screen and stage actor.

HANLEY, JIMMY
Born: Oct. 22, 1918, Norwich, Norfolk, England. Died: Jan. 13, 1970, England. Screen, circus, radio, television actor and writer. Divorced from actress Dinah Sheridan.

Appeared in: **1934** Red Wagon (film debut—US 1935); Those Were the Days; Little Friend. **1935** Royal Cavalcade (aka Regal Cavalcade—US); Forever England (aka Brown on Resolution and Born For Glory—US 1935); Boys Will Be Boys; The Tunnel (aka Transatlantic Tunnel—US). **1937** Landslide; Cotton Queen; Night Ride. **1938** Housemaster (US 1939); Coming of Age. **1939** Beyond Our Horizon; There Ain't No Justice. **1940** Gaslight (aka Angel Street—US 1952). **1942** Salute John Citizen. **1943** The Gentle Sex. **1944** The Way Ahead (US 1945); Kiss the Bride Goodbye. **1945** For You Alone; Henry V (US 1946); 29 Acacia Avenue (aka The Facts of Love—US 1949); Murder in Reverse (US 1946). **1946** The Captive Heart (US 1947). **1947** Holiday Camp (US 1948); Master of Bankdam (US 1949); It Always Rains on Sunday (US 1949). **1948** Here Come the Huggetts (US 1950); It's Hard To Be Good (US 1950). **1949** The Huggetts Abroad; Don't Ever Leave Me; Boys in Brown. **1950** The Blue Lamp; Room to Let. **1951** The Galloping Major. **1954** Radio Car Murder; The Black Rider. **1955** The Deep Blue Sea. **1956** Satellite in the Sky. **1968** The Lost Continent.

HANLEY, MICHAEL E.
Born: 1858. Died: June 18, 1942, Fort Wayne, Ind. (suicide—gun). Screen actor, film director and film producer.

HANLEY, WILLIAM B., JR.
Born: 1900. Died: Oct. 2, 1959, Hollywood, Calif. (heart attack). Stage and screen actor. Married to actress Madge Kennedy.

HANLON, BERT
Born: Aug. 19, 1895, New York, N.Y. Died: Jan. 1, 1972, New York, N.Y. Screen, stage, vaudeville actor, film director, author, songwriter and screenwriter. Married to actress Doris Canfield.

Appeared in: **1931** City Streets; Surrender. **1932** The Trial of Vivienne Ware; Society Girl; Me and My Gal; The Golden West. **1935** Mary Burns, Fugitive; Wings in the Dark. **1936** Straight from the Shoulder. **1937** Park Avenue Logger; Double or Nothing. **1938** A Slight Case of Murder; The Amazing Dr. Clitterhouse; Boy Meets Girl. **1939** The Roaring Twenties; Sweepstakes Winner. **1942** The Big Street. **1943** Coney Island; Lady of Burlesque. **1948** Decision of Christopher Blake. **1949** Fighting Fools.

HANLON, TOM (Thomas Anthony Hanlon)
Born: Nov. 7, 1907, Kansas. Died: Sept. 29, 1970, Northridge, Calif. Screen actor and radio announcer.

Appeared in: **1934** Gift of Gab; Night Alarm. **1935** The Big Broadcast of 1936. **1938** Kentucky Moonshine. **1941** Harmon of Michigan. **1942** Home in Wyomin'. **1945** It's a Pleasure. **1949** Father Was a Fullback. **1950** Right Cross; I'll Get By. **1951** The Guy Who Came Back. **1952** Hold That Line; The Pride of St. Louis. **1953** Jalopy; White Lightning.

HANNA, FRANKLYN
Born: 1875. Died: Jan. 19, 1931. Screen, stage and vaudeville actor.

Appeared in: **1917** The Message of the Mouse; Kidnappesd; Richard the Brazen; One Hour. **1919** The Gold Cure; The Great Romance; The American Way. **1920** The Web of Deceit; The Fortune Hunter; Democracy, The Vision Restored. **1922** The Soul of Man. **1923** For You My Boy.

HANNAH, JAMES
Died: Sept. 11, 1978, Fresno, Calif. Screen and stage actor.

Appeared in: **1928** The Swim Princess; Lilac Time; Run, Girl, Run. **1929** Sea Fury. **1930** Hell's Angels.

HANNEFORD, EDWIN POODLES
Born: 1892, Barnsby, Yorkshire, England. Died: Dec. 9, 1967, Kattskill Bay, N.Y. Screen, circus and television actor, and trick horseback rider. Member of circus family known as "The Hannefords."

Appeared in: **1928** The Circus Kid. **1935** Our Little Girl; educational short. **1945** San Antonio. **1949** The Red Pony. **1951** The Golden Horde; When I Grow Up. **1952** Springfield Rifle. **1962** Jumbo.

HANNEMAN, FREDERICK
Born: 1914. Died: Oct. 3, 1980, Santa Barbara, Calif. Screen, vaudeville actor and stage manager.

HANNEN, NICHOLAS (Nicholas James Hannen)
Born: May 1, 1881, London, England. Died: July, 1972, London, England. Screen, stage actor and film director.

Appeared in: **1931** The Man They Couldn't Arrest (US 1933). **1933** F.P.1. **1934** Murder at the Inn. **1935** The Love Affair of the Dictator (aka The Dictator and The Loves of a Dictator—US). **1936** Hail and Farewell; Who Killed Doc Savage? **1938** Marigold; Secrets of F.P.1. (reissue of 1933 film). **1940** Spy for a Day; Fear and Peter Brown. **1941** The Prime Minister. **1945** Henry V (US 1946). **1948** The Winslow Boy (US 1950). **1951** Quo Vadis; Hell Is Sold Out. **1953** Three Steps in the Dark. **1955** Richard III (US 1956). **1956** The Adventures of Quentin Durward. **1957** Seawife. **1958** Dunkirk; Family Doctor (aka Rx Murder—US and Prescription for Murder). **1961** Francis of Assisi. **1962** Term of Trial (US 1963).

HANOFER, FRANK
Born: 1897, Hungary. Died: Dec. 16, 1955, Newhall, Calif. Screen actor and stuntman.

HANRAY, LAWRENCE
Born: May 16, 1874, London, England. Died: Nov. 28, 1947, England? Screen and stage actor.

Appeared in: **1923** The Pipes of Pan. **1930** Beyond the Cities. **1931** Her Reputation. **1932** Love on Wheels; Leap Year; The Faithful Heart (aka Faithful Hearts—US 1933); There Goes the Bride (US 1933). **1933** The Man From Toronto; The Private Life of Henry VIII; The Good Companions; His Grace Gives Notice; Loyalties. **1934** Chu Chin Chow; Easy Money; What Happened Then?; Catherine the Great; Those Were the Days; The Great Defender; Adventure Limited. **1935** Murder at Monte Carlo; Lorna Doone; Escape Me Never; The Scarlet Pimpernel; Mimi; Expert's Opinion; Brewster's Millions; Street Song. **1936** As You Like It; The Man Who Could Work Miracles (US 1937); Rembrandt; Whom the Gods Love (aka Mozart—US 1940); Beloved Imposter; Someone at the Door; The Lonely Road (aka Scotland Yard Commands—US 1937). **1937** Midnight Menace (aka Bombs Over London—US 1939); Moonlight Sonata (US 1938); Knight Without Armour; 21 Days (aka The First and the Last, aka 21 Days Together—US 1940); Smash and Grab; The Last Chance; The Girl in the Taxi; It's Never Too Late to Mend. **1938** A Royal Divorce. **1941** Hatter's Castle (US 1948). **1943** The Charmer (reissue of Moonlight Sonata 1937). **1944** On Approval (US 1945). **1947** Nicholas Nickleby; Mine Own Executiner (US 1949).

HANSEN, HANS
Born: 1886, Germany. Died: June 18, 1962, New York, N.Y. Screen and stage actor.

Appeared in: **1945** The House on 92nd Street.

HANSEN, JUANITA
Born: 1897, Des Moines, Iowa. Died: Sept. 26, 1961, Hollywood, Calif. (heart attack). Screen and stage actress. Was a Mack Sennett bathing beauty.

Appeared in: **1915** The Failure; Betty in Search of a Thrill; The Love Root; The Martyrs of the Alamo. **1916** His Pride and Shame; Secret of the Submarine (serial). **1917** Glory; A Royal Rogue; Dangers of a Bride; Whose Baby?; A Clever Dummy. **1918** The Brass Bullet (serial); The Risky Road; Broadway Love; The Rough Lover; Fast Company. **1919** A Midnight Romance. **1920** The Lost City (serial); The Phantom Foe (serial). **1921** The Yellow Arm (serial). **1922** The Broadway Madonna. **1923** Girl From the West; The Jungle Princess.

HANSEN, MAX
Born: Germany. Died: Nov. 13, 1961, Germany. Screen actor.

Appeared in: **1929** His Late Excellency. **1930** Der Hampelmann (The Jumping Jack—US 1931); Das Kabinett des Dr. Larifari (US 1931). **1931** Wer Nimmt die Liebe Ernst? (Who Takes Love Seriously?—US 1936); Die Privatsekretarin (Private Secretary—US 1936). **1932** Einmal Moecht ich Keine Sorgen Haben (US 1933); Die-oder Keine (US 1934). **1933** Glueckliche Reise (US 1936). **1937** Csardas, Ihre Tollste Nacht.

HANSEN, WILLIAM
Born: 1911. Died: June 23, 1975, Woodland Hills, Calif. Screen, stage and television actor.

Appeared in: **1949** Pinky. **1952** A Member of the Wedding. **1960** The Bramble Bush. **1961** The Young Doctors. **1962** Bird Man of Alcatraz. **1964** Fail Safe. **1969** The Arrangement. **1971** Willard. **1974** The Terminal Man.

HANSON, EINER (aka EINER HANSEN)
Born: June 15, 1899, Stockholm, Sweden. Died: June 3, 1927, Santa Monica, Calif. (auto accident). Screen actor.

Appeared in: **1926** Her Big Night; Into Her Kingdom. **1927** The Lady in Ermine; The Masked Woman; Barbed Wire; Children of Divorce; Fashions for Women; Woman on Trial.

HANSON, FRANK "SPOOK"
Born: Brooklyn, N.Y. Died: June 16, 1924, New York, N.Y. Screen, stage actor and clown.

HANSON, GLADYS
Born: 1884, Atlanta, Ga. Died: Feb. 24, 1973, Atlanta, Ga. Screen and stage actress.

Appeared in: **1914** The Straight Road. **1915** The Climbers; The Primrose Path. **1916** The Havoc.

HANSON, LARS
Born: 1887, Sweden. Died: Apr. 8, 1965, Stockholm, Sweden. Screen and stage actor who appeared in U.S. and Swedish films.

Appeared in: **1913** Ingeborg Holm. **1916** Dolken. **1919** Erotikon. **1924** The Atonement of Gosta Berling. **1926** The Scarlet Letter. **1927** The Flesh and the Devil; Captain Salvation; Buttons. **1928** The Divine Woman; The Wind; The Legend of Gosta Berling. **1929** The Informer; In Dalarna and Jerusalem; Homecoming. **1936** Paa Solsidan. **1964** One Minute to Hell (aka Gates of Hell). **1967** 491.

HANSON, PAUL
Born: 1894. Died: Oct. 4, 1940. Screen actor.

Appeared in: **1934** The Lost Patrol.

HARBAUGH, CARL
Born: 1886. Died: Feb. 26, 1960, Hollywood, Calif. Screen actor, screenwriter and film director.

Appeared in: **1912** What the Milk Did. **1915** The Regeneration; Carmen. **1916** The Serpent. **1923** Jazzmania; Lost and Found on a South Sea Island; The Silent Command. **1927** College. **1933** The Devil's Brother. **1938** The Texans; If I Were King. **1939** St. Louis Blues. **1941** High Sierra; The Strawberry Blonde; Manpower. **1942** Eagle Squadron. **1946** Dressed to Kill. **1947** Pursued. **1951** Along the Great Divide. **1952** Blackbeard the Pirate. **1955** The Far Country; Battle Cry; The Tall Men. **1956** The Revolt of Mamie Stover. **1957** Band of Angels.

HARBEN, HUBERT
Born: July 12, 1878, London, England. Died: Aug. 24, 1941, London, England. Screen and stage actor. Married to actress Mary Jerrold. Father of actress Joan Harben (dec. 1953).

Appeared in: **1915** The Great Adventure. **1916** Milestones. **1921** Mr. Pim Passes By. **1926** Every Mother's Son. **1931** Tell England (aka The Battle of Gallipoli—US); Uneasy Virtue; The Shadow Between. **1932** Fires of Fate (US 1933). **1933** Timbuctoo. **1934** The Secret of the Loch; Lady in Danger; Lilies of the Field. **1935** Fighting Stock; The City of Beautiful Nonsense. **1936** Whom the Gods Love (aka Mozart—US 1940); Dishonour Bright. **1937** For Valour; Sunset in Vienna (aka Suicide Legion—US 1940); Victoria the Great.

HARBEN, JOAN
Born: Feb. 22, 1909, London, England. Died: Oct. 19, 1953, London, England. Screen, stage and television actress. Daughter of actor Hubert Harben (dec. 1941) and actress Mary Jerrold. Married to actor Clive Morton (dec. 1975).

Appeared in: **1951** Encore (US 1952).

HARBORD, ISOBEL See ELSOM, ISOBEL

HARBOROUGH, WILLIAM
Born: 1899, Oct., 1924. Died: Oct., 1924, Yuma, Ariz. (drowned during filming of a Western movie). Screen actor and stuntman.

HARCOURT, GERALD
Born: 1886. Died: June 1, 1924, Sydney, Australia. Screen and stage actor.

Appeared in: **1914** The Sword of Damocles.

HARCOURT, JAMES
Born: Apr. 20, 1873, Headingly, Leeds, Yorkshire, England. Died: Feb. 18, 1951, England? Screen and stage actor.

Appeared in: **1931** Obson's Choice. **1933** Paris Plane; Song of the Plough. **1934** The Old Curiosity Shop (US 1935). **1935** All at Sea. **1936** Seven Sinners (aka Doomed Cargo—US); The Avenging Hand; Men Are Not Gods (US 1937); Wings Over Africa; Laburnum Grove (US 1941). **1937** Return of a Stranger (aka The Face Behind the Scar—US 1940). **1938** You're the Doctor; Kate Plus Ten; Penny Paradise; Follow Your Star. **1939** I Met a Murderer. **1940** Night Train to Munich (aka Gestapo, aka Night Train—US); The House of the Arrow (aka Castle of Crime—US 1945). **1941** Penn of Pennsylvania (aka The Courageous Mr. Penn—US 1944); Atlantic Ferry (aka Sons of the Sea—US); This England (aka Our Heritage). **1942** This Was Paris; Hard Steel. **1944** He Snoops to Conquer. **1946** The Captive Heart (US 1947); The Magic Bow (US 1947); I See a Dark Stranger (aka The Adventuress—US 1947). **1947** Meet Me at Dawn (US 1948); The End of the River—US 1948). **1949** Obsession (aka The Hidden Room—US 1950).

HARCOURT, PEGGIE
Died: Aug. 2, 1916, Hewletts, N.Y. (auto accident). Screen actress.

HARDIE, RUSSELL
Born: 1904, Buffalo, N.Y. Died: July 21, 1973, Clarence, N.Y. Screen, stage and television actor.

Appeared in: **1930** The Costello Case; The No-Account (short). **1933** Broadway to Hollywood; Stage Mother; Her Sweetheart—Christopher Bean. **1934** As the Earth Turns; Men in White; Opertor 13; Hell in the Heavens; The Band Plays On; Murder in the Private Car; Sequoia; Pursued. **1935** West Point of the Air; In Old Kentucky; Speed Devils. **1936** The Harvester; Meet Nero Wolfe; Down to the Sea; Killer at Large; Camille. **1951** The Frogmen; The Whistle at Eaton Falls. **1958** Cop Hater. **1964** Fail Safe. **1966** The Group.

HARDING, ALMA
Died: Oct. 17, 1961, Woodstock, N.Y. Screen, stage and vaudeville actress. Married to vaudeville actor Earl Dean (dec.). Appeared in silent films.

HARDING, ANN (Dorothy Walton Gatley)
Born: Aug. 7, 1902, San Antonio, Tex. Died: Sept. 1, 1981, Sherman Oaks, Calif. Screen, stage and television actress. Divorced from actor Harry Bannister (dec. 1961) and symphony conductor Werner Janssen.

Appeared in: **1929** Paris Bound (film debut); Condemned; Her Private Affair. **1930** Holiday; The Girl of the Golden West. **1931** East Lynne; Devotion. **1932** The Animal Kingdom; Prestige; Westward Passage; The Conquerors. **1933** Double Harness; When Ladies Meet; The Right to Romance; Gallant Lady. **1934** The Fountain; The Life of Vergie Winters. **1935** Biography of a Bachelor Girl; Peter Ibbetson; The Flame Within; Enchanted April. **1936** The Witness Chair; The Lady Consents. **1937** Love From a Stranger. **1942** Eyes in the Night. **1943** Mission to Moscow; The North Star. **1944** Janie; Nine Girls. **1945** Those Endearing Young Charms. **1946** Cinderella Jones; Janie Gets Married. **1947** It Happened on Fifth Avenue; Christmas Eve. **1950** The Magnificent Yankee; Two Weeks With Love. **1951** The Unknown Man; It's a Big Country. **1956** Strange Intruder; The Man in the Gray Flannel Suit; I've Lived Before.

HARDING, GILBERT
Born: June 5, 1907, Hereford, England. Died: Nov. 16, 1960, London, England. Screen and television actor.

Appeared in: **1955** Simon and Laura (US 1956); An Alligator Named Daisy (US 1957); As Long as They're Happy (US 1957). **1959** Expresso Bongo (US 1960).

HARDING, J. RUDGE
Born: 1862, Elvetham, Hants, England. Died: Apr. 24, 1932, England? Screen and stage actor.

Appeared in: **1914** The Brass Bottle.

HARDING, LYN (David Llewellyn Harding)
Born: Oct. 12, 1867, Newport, Wales. Died: Dec. 26, 1952, London, England. Screen and stage actor.

Appeared in: **1920** A Bachelor Husband; The Barton Mystery. **1922** When Knighthood Was in Flower; Tense Moments With Great Authors series including Les Miserables. **1924** Yolanda. **1927** Further Adventures of the Flag Lieutenant; Land of Hope and Glory. **1930** Sleeping Partners. **1931** The Speckled Band. **1932** The Barton Mystery (and 1920 version). **1933** The Constant Nymph. **1934** The Man Who

Changed His Name; Wild Boy; The Lash. **1935** The Triumph of Sherlock Holmes; Escape Me Never. **1936** The Invader (aka An Old Spanish Custom—US); The Man Who Changed His Mind (aka The Man Who Lived Again—US); Spy of Napoleon (US 1939). **1937** Fire Over England; Underneath the Arches; Knight Without Armour; Silver Blaze (aka Murder at the Baskervilles—US 1941); The Mutiny of the Elsinore (US 1939); Les Perles de la Couronne (Pearls of the Crown); Please Teacher. **1939** The Missing People (US 1940); Goodbye Mr. Chips. **1941** The Prime Minister.

HARDING, MURIEL See PETROVA, OLGA

HARDS, IRA A.
Born: June 24, 1872, Geneva, Ill. Died: May 2, 1938, West Norwalk, Conn. Screen, stage actor, film director, stage director and stage producer.

HARDTMUTH, PAUL
Born: 1889, Germany. Died: Feb. 5, 1962, London, England (fall from apartment building). Screen and television actor.

Appeared in: **1949** The Lost People; The Third Man (US 1950). **1950** Highly Dangerous (US 1951). **1951** The Wonder Kid. **1953** Desperate Moment; Street of Shadows (aka Shadow Man—US). **1954** The Diamond (aka The Diamond Wizard—US). **1955** Timeslip (aka The Atomic Man—US); All for Mary. **1956** The Gamma People; Assignment Readhead (aka Million Dollar Manhunt—US 1962). **1957** The Curse of Frankenstein. **1961** Doctor Blood's Coffin (aka Face of Evil); Guns of Navarone.

HARDWICKE, SIR CEDRIC (Cecil Webster Hardwicke)
Born: Feb. 19, 1893, Stourbridge, England. Died: Aug. 6, 1964, New York, N.Y. (lung ailment). Screen, stage, television actor, film director and producer. Father of actor Edward Hardwicke. Divorced from actress Helena Pickard and Mary Scott.

Appeared in: **1913** Riches and Rogues. **1926** Nelson. **1931** Dreyfus (aka The Dreyfus Case—US). **1932** Rome Express. **1933** Orders Is Orders (US 1934); The Ghoul. **1934** The Lady Is Willing; Nell Gwyn; Jew Suess (aka Power—US); The King of Paris; Bella Donna (US 1935). **1935** Les Miserables; Becky Sharp; Peg of Old Drury (US 1936). **1936** Things to Come; Tudor Rose (aka Nine Days a Queen—US); Laburnum Grove (US 1941); Calling the Truth. **1937** The Green Light; King Solomon's Mines. **1939** On Borrowed Time; Stanley and Livingstone; The Hunchback of Notre Dame. **1940** The Invisible Man Returns; Tom Brown's School Days; The Howards of Virginia; Victory. **1941** Suspicion; Sundown. **1942** Valley of the Sun; The Ghost of Frankenstein; Invisible Agent; Commandos Strike at Dawn. **1943** The Moon Is Down; Forever and a Day; The Cross of Lorraine. **1944** The Lodger; Wilson; The Keys of the Kingdom; Wing and a Prayer. **1945** The Picture of Dorian Gray (narration). **1946** Beware of Pity (US 1947); Sentimental Journey. **1947** Song of My Heart (aka Tragic Symphony); The Imperfect Lady; Ivy; Lured; Nicholas Nickleby; Tycoon; A Woman's Vengeance. **1948** The Winslow Boy (US 1950); I Remember Mama; Rope. **1949** Now Barabbas Was a Robber; A Connecticut Yankee in King Arthur's Court. **1950** The White Tower. **1951** Mr. Imperium; The Desert Fox. **1952** The Green Glove; Caribbean. **1953** Salome; Botany Bay; The War of the Worlds (narration). **1954** Bait (prologue). **1955** Richard III (US 1956); Diane; Helen of Troy. **1956** The Vagabond King; The Power and the Prize; The Ten Commandments; Around the World in 80 Days; Gaby. **1957** The Story of Mankind; Baby Face Nelson. **1962** Five Weeks in a Balloon. **1964** The Pumpkin Eater; The Magic Fountain.

HARDY, LOO
Born: 1898, Berlin, Germany. Died: 1934, London, England. Screen actress.

Appeared in: **1915** The Yellow Star.

HARDY, OLIVER (Oliver Norvell Hardy)
Born: Jan. 18, 1892, Atlanta, Ga. Died: Aug. 7, 1957, North Hollywood, Calif. (paralytic stroke). Screen, stage, minstrel actor and film director. Was partner in comedy team of "Laurel and Hardy" with Stan Laurel (dec. 1965). See Stan Laurel for films they appeared in together.

Appeared in the following films without Laurel: **1913** Outwitting Dad (film debut). **1914** The Rise of the Johnsons; Back to the Farm. **1914-1915** "Pokes and Jabbs" series; "Harry Meyers and Rosemary Theby" series. **1915** The Twin Sister; Who Stole the Doggies?; A Lucky Strike; Matilda's Legacy; Babe's School Days; Ethel's Romeos; The Paperhanger's Helper; "Kate Price" series including: Spaghetti a la Mode; Charley's Aunt; Artists and Models; The Tramps; Mother's

Child. **1916** What's Sauce for the Goose; The Brave Ones; Edison Bugg's Invention; The Water Cure; A Terrible Tragedy; Never Again; Thirty Days; Hungry Hearts; It Happened in Pikesville; Their Honeymoon; The Candy Trail; The Heroes; Life Savers; Stranded; An Aerial Joyride; Love and Duty; Royal Blood; Better Halves; Spaghetti; A Day at School; The Precious Parcel; Dreamy Knights; A Maid to Order; Pipe Dreams, "Billy West" series including: Back Stage; The Hero; The Millionaire; Dough Nuts; The Scholar; "Pokes and Jabbs" series including: The Try Out; Ups and Downs; This Way Out; Chickens; Frenzied Finance; Busted Hearts. **1916-1918** "Plump and Runt" series. **1917** The Slave; The Prospector; He Winked and Won; "Jimmy Aubrey" series. **1918** Hello Trouble; Lucky Dog; "Billy West" comedies; "King Bee Studios" series including: The Villian; The Artist; King Solomon; The Chief Cook. **1919-1921** "Jimmy Aubrey" comedy series. **1921-1925** "Larry Semon" series including: The Fly Cop; The Sawmill; Scars and Stripes; The Wizard of Oz; The Girl in the Limousine and Kid Speed. **1922** Fortune's Mask; Little Wildcat. **1923** The Three Ages; Be Your Age; One Stolen Night. **1926** Stop, Look and Listen; The Gentle Cyclone. **1927** No Man's Law. **1939** Zenobia; Elephants Never Forget. **1949** The Fighting Kentuckian; Riding High.

HARDY, SAM
Born: 1883, New Haven, Conn. Died: Oct. 16, 1935, Los Angeles, Calif. (intestinal problems). Screen, stage actor, and screenwriter. Entered films in 1917.

Appeared in: **1917** The Savage. **1918** A Woman's Experience. **1921** Get-Rich-Quick Wallingford. **1923** Little Old New York; Mighty Lak a Rose. **1925** The Half-Way Girl; When Love Grows Cold. **1926** Bluebeard's Seven Wives; The Great Deception; The Prince of Tempters; The Savage. **1927** High Hat; The Perfect Sap; Orchids and Ermine; Broadway Nights; The Life of Riley; A Texas Steer. **1928** Burning Up Broadway; Turn Back the Hours; The Big Noise; Diamond Handcuffs; The Butter and Egg Man; The Night Bird; Outcast; Give and Take. **1929** The Rainbow Man; On With the Show; Big News; Acquitted; Mexicali Rose; A Man's Man; Fast Company. **1930** Burning Up; True to the Navy; Reno; Song of the West; The Floradora Girl; Borrowed Wives. **1931** The Millionaire; June Moon; Annabelle's Affairs; The Magnificent Lie; The Miracle Woman; Peach O'Reno. **1932** Rule 'Em and Weep (short); The Dark Horse; Make Me a Star; The Phantom of Crestwood. **1933** Face in the Sky; King Kong; Goldie Gets Along; Three-Cornered Moon; The Big Brain; One Sunday Afternoon; Ann Vickers. **1934** Curtain at Eight; Little Miss Marker; I Give My Love; The Gay Bride; Transatlantic Merry-Go-Round; Night Alarm; Along Came Sally. **1935** Hooray for Love; Break of Hearts; Powdersmoke Range.

HARDY, SAM (Samuel Stewart Hayes)
Born: 1905, Cookesville, Ill. Died: July 28, 1958, San Diego, Calif. (heart attack). Screen actor and radio announcer. Do not confuse with actor Sam Hardy (dec. 1935).

Appeared in: **1938** Rebecca of Sunnybrook Farm. **1953** The Hitch-Hiker.

HARE, ERNIE
Born: 1883. Died: Mar. 9, 1939. Screen actor.

Appeared in: **1933** Rambling 'Round Radio Row.

HARE, F. LUMSDEN
Born: Oct. 17, 1874, Cashel, Ireland. Died: Aug. 28, 1964, Hollywood, Calif. Screen, stage actor and stage director. Entered films in 1916.

Appeared in: **1919** The Avalanche. **1921** The Education of Elizabeth. **1922** Sherlock Holmes. **1923** On the Banks of the Wabash. **1924** Second Youth. **1925** One Way Street. **1929** Fugitives; Masquerade; The Black Watch; Girls Gone Wild; Salute; The Sky Hawk. **1930** Crazy That Way; So This Is London; Scotland Yard. **1931** Under Suspicion; Always Goodbye; Svengali; Charlie Chan Carries On; The Road to Singapore; Arrowsmith. **1932** The Silent Witness; The Crusader. **1933** International House; College Humor. **1934** The World Moves On; Outcast Lady; His Double Life; Man of Two Worlds; The Little Minister; The House of Rothschild; Black Moon. **1935** Lady Tubbs; The Great Impersonation; Professional Soldier; Clive of India; Folies Bergere; Lives of a Bengal Lancer; The Crusades; Cardinal Richelieu; She; Freckles; The Three Musketeers; The Bishop Misbehaves. **1936** The Charge of the Light Brigade; Under Two Flags; Lloyds of London; The Princess Comes Across; The Last of the Mohicans. **1937** The Last of Mrs. Cheyney; The Life of Emile Zola; Life Begins With Love. **1939** The Giant of Norway (short). **1940** Northwest Passage; Rebecca; A Dispatch from Reuters. **1941** Shadows on the Stairs; Dr. Jekyll and Mr. Hyde; More Trifles of Importance (short); Confirm or Deny; The Blonde from Singapore; Suspicion; Passage from Hong Kong; Hudson's Bay. **1942** London Blackout Murders; The Gorilla Man.

1943 Mission to Moscow; Holy Matrimony; Jack London; Forever and a Day. **1944** Passport to Destiny; The Canterville Ghost; The Lodger. **1945** Captain Kidd; The Keys of the Kingdom; Love Letters; Valley of Decision. **1946** The Green Years; Sister Kenny; Three Strangers. **1947** Private Affairs of Bel Ami; The Swordsman; The Exile; Green Dolphin Street; The Secret Life of Walter Mitty. **1948** The Paradine Case; Mr. Peabody and the Mermaid; Hills of Home. **1949** That Forsythe Woman; Fighting O'Flynn; Challange to Lassie. **1950** Fortunes of Captain Blood. **1951** David and Bathsheba; The Lady and the Bandit; The Desert Fox. **1952** And Now Tomorrow; Diplomatic Courier; My Cousin Rachel. **1953** Julius Caesar; Young Bess. **1955** Battle Cry. **1957** Johnny Tremain. **1959** Count Your Blessings; The Oregon Trail; The Four Skulls of Jonathan Drake.

HARE, J. ROBERTSON
Born: Dec. 17, 1891, London, England. Died: Jan. 25, 1979, London, England. Screen, stage and television actor. Entered films in 1929.

Appeared in: **1930** Rookery Nook (aka One Embarassing Night—US); On Approval. **1931** Plunder; Tons of Money. **1932** Thark; A Night Like This. **1933** Just My Luck; It's a Boy!; Friday the Thirteenth (US 1934); A Cuckoo in the Nest. **1934** A Cup of Kindness; Are You a Mason?; Dirty Work. **1935** Fighting Stock; Oh Daddy; Stormy Weather (US 1936); Car of Dreams; Foreign Arraires. **1936** Jack of All Trades (The Two of Us—US 1937); You Must Get Married; Pot Luck. **1937** Aren't Men Beasts! **1938** A Spot of Bother. **1939** So This Is London (US 1940). **1940** Yesterday Is Over Your Shoulder (short). **1941** Banana Ridge. **1942** Women Aren't Angels. **1948** Things Happen at Night. **1951** The Magic Box (US 1952); One Wild Oat. **1954** Our Girl Friday (aka The Adventures of Sadie—US 1955). **1956** Three Men in a Boat (US 1958); My Wife's Family. **1960** The Night We Got the Bird. **1961** Out of the Shadow (aka Murder on the Campus—US 1963); The Young Ones (aka Wonderful to be Young—US 1963). **1962** Seven Keys; Crooks Anonymous (US 1963). **1966** Hotel Paradiso. **1968** Salt and Pepper. **1971** Raising the Roof.

HARE, SIR JOHN (John Fairs)
Born: 1844, Giggleswick, Yorkshire, England. Died: Dec. 28, 1921, London, England. Stage and screen actor.

Appeared in: **1916** A Pair of Spectacles; The Vicar of Wakefield (US 1917).

HARE, MARILYN
Born: 1924. Died: Oct. 9, 1981, Encino, Calif. (cancer). Screen, stage, television actress and singer.

Appeared in: **1941** Angels With Broken Wings; Lady for a Night. **1942** Sheperd of the Ozarks; Yokel Boy; Hi, Neighbor; Ice-Capades Revue. **1944** Since You Went Away. **1947** Shootin' Irons.

HARFORD, HARRY
Born: 1841, Boston, Mass. Died: Sept. 20, 1925, Bearnardsville, N.J. Screen, stage and vaudeville actor.

HARKER, GORDON
Born: Aug. 7, 1885, London, England. Died: Mar. 2, 1967, London, England. Screen, stage and radio actor.

Appeared in: **1927** The Ring (film debut). **1928** The Farmer's Wife (US 1930); Champagne; The Wrecker (US 1929). **1929** The Crooked Billet; Taxi for Two; The Return of the Rat. **1930** The W Plan (US 1931); The Squeaker; Escape; Elstree Calling; The Cockney Spirit in War series including All Riot on the Western Front. **1931** Third Time Lucky; The Sport of Kings; The Stronger Sex; The Ringer (US 1932); The Calendar (aka Bachelor's Folly—US 1932); The Professional Guest; The Man They Could Not Arrest (US 1933); Shadows. **1932** Condemned to Death; The Frightened Lady (aka Criminal at Large—US 1933); White Face; Love on Wheels; Rome Express. **1933** The Lucky Number; Britannia of Billingsgate; This Is the Life (US 1935); Friday the Thirteenth (US 1934). **1934** My Old Dutch; Road House; Dirty Work. **1935** The Phantom Light; The Lad; Admirals All; Squibs; Boys Will Be Boys; Hyde Park Corner. **1936** The Amateur Gentleman; Wolf's Clothing; Two's Company; Millions; The Story of Papworth (short). **1937** Beauty and the Barge; The Frog (US 1939). **1938** Blondes for Danger; No Parking; Lightning Conductor; The Return of the Frog. **1939** Inspector Hornleigh; Inspector Hornleigh on Holiday. **1940** Saloon Bar (US 1944); Chanel Incident (short). **1941** Inspector Hornleigh Goes to It (aka Mail Train—US); Once a Crook. **1943** Warn That Man. **1945** 29 Acacia Avenue (aka The Facts of Life—US 1949). **1948** Things Happen at Night. **1950** Her Favorite Husband (aka The Taming of Dorothy—US). **1951** The Second Mate. **1952** Derby Day (aka Four Against Fate—US 1955). **1954** Bang! You're Dead (aka Game of Danger—US 1955). **1955** Out of the Clouds (US 1957). **1956** A Touch of the Sun. **1957** Small Hotel. **1959** Left, Right and Center (US 1961).

HARKINS, DIXIE
Born: 1906. Died: Sept. 1, 1963, Jacksonville, Fla. Screen actress.

Appeared in: **1925** Sally, Irene and Mary. **1926** The Temptress. **1927** Resurrection.

HARKINS, JIM
Born: 1888. Died: Oct. 25, 1970, Media, Pa. Screen, stage and vaudeville actor. Married to vaudeville actress Marion Harkins (dec.) who appeared with him in an act billed as Jim and Marion Harkins.

Appeared in: **1929** Love at First Sight.

HARLAM, MACEY
Born: New York, N.Y. Died: June 17, 1923, Saranac Lake, N.Y. Screen and stage actor.

Appeared in: **1916** Nanette of the Wilds; Manhattan Madness; The Habit of Happiness. **1920** The Woman and the Puppet. **1921** The Conquest of Canaan; The Plaything of Broadway; Shams of Society; You Find It Everywhere. **1922** Always the Woman; Beyond the Rainbow; The Face in the Fog; Fair Lady; When Knighthood Was in Flower; Without Fear. **1923** Broadway Broke; The Tents of Allah; Bella Donna.

HARLAN, KENNETH
Born: July 26, 1895, Boston, Mass. Died: Mar. 6, 1967, Sacramento, Calif. (aneurysm). Screen, stage and vaudeville actor.

Appeared in: **1915** A Black Sheep. **1917** Betsy's Burglar; The Flame of the Yukon; The Lash of Power; Cheerful Givers. **1918** Midnight Madness; The Marriage Life; The Model's Confession. **1919** The Hoodlum. **1920** The Penalty; Dangerous Business. **1921** The Barricade; Dawn of the East; Finders Keepers; Mama's Affair; Lessons in Love; Nobody; Woman's Place. **1922** The Toll of the Sea; I Am the Law; Polly of the Follies; The Married Flapper; Received Payment; The Primitive Lover; Thorns and Orange Blossoms. **1923** The Virginian; The Beautiful and Damned; The Broken Wing; The World's a Stage; April Showers; East Side, West Side; The Girl Who Came Back; Little Church Around the Corner; A Man's Man; Temporary Marriage. **1924** Butterfly; For Another Woman; White Man; Soiled; Two Shall Be Born; The Virgin; The Man Without a Heart; On the Stroke of Three; Poisoned Paradise. **1925** Bobbed Hair; The Marriage Whirl; Learning to Love; The Crowded Hour; Drusilla With a Million; The Golden Strain; Ranger of the Big Pines; Re-Creation of Brian Kent. **1926** The Sap; King of the Turf; The Ice Flood; The Fighting Edge; Twinkletoes. **1927** Easy Pickings; Cheating Cheaters; Streets of Shanghai. **1928** Stage Kisses; Willful Youth; United States Smith; Midnight Rose; Code of the Air; Man, Woman and Wife. **1930** Under Montana Skies; Paradise Island. **1931** Air Police; Danger Island (serial); Finger Prints (serial); Women Men Marry. **1932** The Shadow of the Eagle (serial); Something to Sing About; Widow in Scarlet. **1935** Cappy Ricks Returns; Wanderer of the Wasteland. **1936** Man Hunt; The Walking Dead; Song of the Saddle; The Case of the Velvet Claws; Public Enemy's Wife; China Clipper; Movie Maniacs (short); San Francisco; They Met in a Taxi; Trail Dust; Flying Hostess. **1937** Hideaway Girl; Marked Woman; Wine, Women and Horses; The Shadow Strikes; Renfrew of the Royal Mounted; Paradise Isle; The Mysterious Pilot (serial); Penrod and Sam; Gunsmoke Ranch; Something to Shout About. **1938** Duke of West Point; The Saleslady; Under Western Stars; Blondes at Work; The Little Adventuress; Accidents Will Happen; Pride of the West; Law of the Texan; Sunset Trail; The Headleys at Home; Held for Ransom. **1939** Dick Tracy's G-Men (serial); Range War; On Trial; Port of Hate. **1940** The House Across the Bay; Slightly Honorable; Santa Fe Marshal; Murder in the Air; A Little Bit of Heaven; Prairie Schooners. **1941** Dick Tracy vs. Crime, Inc. (serial); Pride of the Bowery; Sky Raiders (serial); Paper Bullets; Dangerous Lady; Secret Evidence; Desperate Cargo; Wide Open Town. **1942** Black Dragon; Fighting Bill Fargo; Klondike Fury; Foreign Agent; The Corpse Vanishes; The Phantom Killer; Deep in the Heart of Texas. **1943** You Can't Beat the Law; Hitler—Dead or Alive; Wild Horse Stampede; The Law Rides Again; Melody Parade; The Underdog; Daredevils of the West (serial); The Masked Marvel (serial).

HARLAN, OTIS
Born: Dec. 29, 1864, Zanesville, Ohio. Died: Jan. 20, 1940, Martinsville, Ind. (stroke). Screen, stage and vaudeville actor.

Appeared in: **1920** The Romance Promoters. **1921** Diamonds Adrift; The Foolish Age; Keeping Up With Lizzie. **1922** The Girl in the Taxi; The Eternal Flame; Gay and Devilish; Is Matrimony a Failure?; The Ladder Jinx; Right That Failed; Two Kinds of Women; The Understudy; Up and at 'Em; Without Compromise; The World's a Stage. **1923** The Barefoot Boy; The Brass Bottle; Main Street; The

Near Lady; Pioneer Trails; The Spider and the Rose; Truxton King; The Victor. **1924** Abraham Lincoln; Captain Blood; The Clean Heart; The Code of the Wilderness; George Washington, Jr.; The Lullaby; Mademoiselle Midnight; One Law for the Woman; Welcome Stranger; The White Sin; Oh, Doctor! **1925** The Redeeming Sin; Lightin'; What Happened to Jones?; The Dixie Handicap; Dollar Down; Fine Clothes; How Baxter Butted In; The Limited Mail; 9 3/5 Seconds; The Perfect Clown; Thunder Mountain; Where Was I? **1926** The Cheerful Fraud; The Midnight Message; The Prince of Pilsen; Three Bad Men; The Unknown Cavalier; Winning the Futurity; The Whole Town's Talking. **1927** Don't Tell the Wife; Down the Stretch; Galloping Fury; The Silent Rider; Silk Stockings; The Student Prince. **1928** Shepherd of the Hills; The Speed Classic; Grip of the Yukon; Good Morning Judge. **1929** Silks and Saddles; Show Boat; Clear the Decks; Broadway; Girl Overboard; His Lucky Day; Barnum Was Right; The Mississippi Gambler. **1930** Take the Heir; Parade of the West; Captain of the Guard; The King of Jazz; Loose Ankles; Dames Ahoy; Embarrassing Moments; Mountain Justice; Parade of the West. **1931** Man to Man; Millie; The Grand Parade; Ex-Rooster; Air Eagles. **1932** Racing Youth; The Big Shot; No Living Witness; Ride Him, Cowboy; That's My Boy; Rider of Death Valley; Pardners; The Hawk. **1933** Women Won't Tell; Telegraph Trail; Laughing at Life; The Sin of Nora Morgan; Marriage on Approval. **1934** I Can't Escape; King Kelly of the U.S.A.; The Old-Fashioned Way; Let's Talk It Over; Married in Haste. **1935** Dr. Socrates; Life Returns; Chinatown Squad; Western Frontier; Hitchhike Lady; Diamond Jim; A Midsummer Night's Dream; The Hoosier Schoolmaster. **1936** Can This Be Dixie? **1937** Western Gold; Snow White and the Seven Dwarfs (voice of "Happy"). **1938** Mr. Boggs Steps Out; Outlaws of Sonora; The Texans.

HARLAN, RUSSELL B.
Born: Sept. 16, 1903. Died: Feb. 28, 1974, Newport Beach, Calif. Screen actor, stuntman and cinematographer. Entered films as a stuntman.

Appeared in: **1937** Hopalong Rides Again; North of the Rio Grande; Rustler's Valley; Texas Trail; Partners of the Plains. **1938** Cassidy of Bar 20. **1940** Stagecoach War. **1943** The Kansan. **1945** Walk in the Sun. **1948** Red River. **1952** The Big Sky. **1954** Riot in Cell Block 11. **1955** The Blackboard Jungle. **1957** This Could Be the Night; Witness for the Prosecution. **1958** Run Silent, Run Deep; King Creole. **1962** The Spiral Road; Hatari!; To Kill a Mockingbird. **1963** A Gathering of Eagles. **1964** Quick Before It Melts; Dear Heart; Man's Favorite Sport? **1965** The Great Race. **1966** Hawaii; Tobruk. **1967** Thoroughly Modern Millie. **1970** Darling Lili.

HARLAN, VEIT
Born: 1899, Berlin, Germany. Died: Apr. 13, 1964, Capri, Italy (cancer). Screen, stage actor, screenwriter, film director, writer and sculptor. Married to Hilde Korber (dec. 1969) and later married to actress Kristina Soderbaum.

Appeared in: **1927** Eins Plus Eins Gleich Drei; Das Maedchen mit den Fuenf Nullen; Die Hose (aka Royal Scandal); Der Meister von Nuernberg (The Master of Nuremberg). **1929** Es Fluestert die Nacht...; Somnambul; Revolte im Erziehungshaus (Revolt in the Reformatory); Meistersingers. **1930** Hungarian Nights. **1931** Hilfe! Ueberfall!; Yorck; Gefahren der Liebe. **1932** Die Unsichtbare Front; Friederike; Die Elf Schill'schen Offiziere. **1933** Fluechtlinge (Refugees); Der Choral von Leuthen (The Anthem of Leuthen). **1934** Nur Nicht Weich Werden; Der Fall Benken (aka Uberfall im Hotel); Susanne!; Polizeiakte 909 (aka Der Fall Tokeramo, and aka Taifun). **1935** Das Maedchen Johanna; Mein Leben Maria Isabell; Der Rote Reiter; Stradivari; Ein Kleines Maedchen mit Prokura.

HARLEIN, LILLIAN
Died: Apr. 13, 1971, New York, N.Y. Screen, stage and television actress.

HARLEY, EDWIN
Born: 1848, Philadelphia, Pa. Died: Oct. 29, 1933, Milwaukee, Wis. Screen, stage and vaudeville actor.

Appeared in: **1916** Martha's Vindication; Susan Rocks the Boat.

HARLOW, JEAN (Harlean Carpenter)
Born: Mar. 3, 1911, Kansas City, Mo. Died: June 7, 1937, Los Angeles, Calif. (uremic poisoning). Screen actress. Divorced from producer/actor Paul Bern (dec. 1932), Charles McGrew and cinematographer Hal Rosson.

Appeared in: **1928** Moran of the Marines; a Hal Roach short. **1929** The Saturday Night Kid; The Love Parade; Close Harmony; Double Whoopee (short); Bacon Grabbers (short); Liberty (short); The Unkissed Man (short); Weak but Willing (short). **1930** Hell's Angels;

New York Night. **1931** The Secret Six; The Iron Man; The Public Enemy; Goldie; Platinum Blonde; City Lights. **1932** Screen Snapshots (short); Three Wise Girls; The Beast of the City; Red Headed Woman; City Sentinel; Red Dust. **1933** Hold Your Man; Dinner at Eight; Bombshell. **1934** The Girl from Missouri; Reckless. **1935** China Seas; Riffraff. **1936** Wife vs. Secretary; Libeled Lady; The Man in Possession; Suzy. **1937** Personal Property; Saratoga. **1964** Big Parade of Comedy (documentary). **1968** The Further Perils of Laurel and Hardy (documentary); The Queen (documentary). **1974** That's Entertainment (film clips).

HARMER, LILLIAN
Born: 1886. Died: May 15, 1946, Hollywood, Calif. Screen and stage actress.

Appeared in: **1931** She-Wolf; Huckleberry Finn; Smart Woman. **1932** New Morals for Old; Guilty as Hell; No Man of Her Own. **1933** Alice in Wonderland; Jennie Gerhardt; A Shriek in the Night. **1934** Kansas City Princess; Mandalay; Forsaking All Others; Lady by Choice. **1935** Three Kids and a Queen; Romance in Manhattan; Public Hero No. 1; Riffraff. **1936** Don't Get Personal; Little Miss Nobody; Dancing Feet; Fugitive in the Sky; The Great O'Malley; Rainbow on the River. **1937** Internes Can't Take Money.

HARMON, PAT
Born: 1888. Died: Nov. 26, 1958, Riverside, Calif. Screen actor and double for actor Wallace Beery.

Appeared in: **1922** The Firebrand; The Kentucky Derby. **1923** Ruth of the Range (serial); The Eternal Struggle; The Midnight Guest. **1924** American Manners; The Back Trail; The Battling Fool; Behind the Curtain; The Martyr Sex; The Midnight Express; Ridgeway of Montana; The Sawdust Trail; Surging Seas. **1925** Barriers Burned Away; A Fight to the Finish; Fighting Youth; The Freshman; The Lure of the Wild; S.O.S. Perils of the Sea. **1926** The Barrier; Breed of the Sea; College Days; The Cowboy Cop; The Dixie Flyer; The Fighting Edge; Josselyn's Wife; The Phantom Bullet; Sin Cargo; The Unknown Cavalier; Winning the Futurity. **1927** The Bachelor's Baby; The Haunted Ship; Hazardous Valley; Lightning; Snowbound; The Warning. **1928** The Broken Mask; Court-Martial; Waterfront. **1929** Small Talk (short); Dark Streets; Sal of Singapore; Homesick; The Sideshow; Sunset Pass; Berth Marks (short). **1930** Fast Work (short); Hell's Angels. **1931** The Gang Buster. **1933** Fallen Arches (short). **1934** Another Wild Idea (short). **1944** Teen Age. **1947** Mad Wednesday.

HAROLDE, RALF (Ralf H. Wiggger)
Born: 1899, Pa. Died: Nov. 1, 1974, Santa Monica, Calif. Screen and stage actor.

Appeared in: **1922** Sunshine Harbor. **1927** Babe Comes Home. **1930** Dixiana; Officer O'Brien; Check and Double Check; Framed; Young Desire; Hook, Line and Sinker. **1931** Night Nurse; Smart Money; Alexander Hamilton; The Tip Off; Safe in Hell; The Secret Witness; Terror by Night; Are These Our Children? **1932** The Expert; Winner Take All; Hollywood Speaks. **1933** Her Resale Value; The Billion Dollar Scandal; Picture Snatcher; The Deluge; Cheating Blondes; Night Flight; I'm No Angel. **1934** Fifteen Wives; Jimmy the Gent; He Was Her Man; The Witching Hour; She Loves Me Not; Once to Every Bachelor; Baby, Take a Bow. **1935** Great God Gold; Stolen Harmony; Silk Hat Kid; My Marriage; A Tale of Two Cities; The Perfect Clue; Million Dollar Baby; If You Could Only Cook; This Is the Life; Forced Landing. **1936** Our Relations; Song and Dance Man; Human Cargo; 15 Maiden Lane; The Accusing Finger; Little Red School House. **1937** A Man Betrayed; Her Husband Lies; One Mile from Heaven; Conquest. **1939** The Rookie Cop. **1941** Horror Island; Ridin' on a Rainbow; Rags to Riches; The Sea Wolf; No Greater Sin; Lucky Devils; Bad Man of Deadwood; The Stork Pays Off; I Killed That Man. **1942** Baby Face Morgan; Broadway; Sin Town; Gang Busters (serial). **1943** Farewell, My Lovely (aka Murder My Sweet); Secret Service in Darkest Africa (serial). **1945** The Phantom Speaks. **1947** Jewels of Brandenburg. **1948** Assigned to Danger; Behind Locked Doors. **1949** Alaska Patrol. **1950** Killer Shark. **1965** The Greatest Story Ever Told.

HAROUT, YEGHISHE
Born: Armenia. Died: June 7, 1974, Hollywood, Calif. Screen, stage, television actor and restauranteur. Father of actress Magda Harout.

Appeared in: **1954** The Egyptian.

HARPER, JAMES See TIROFF, JAMES "JIM"

HARPSTER, HOWARD
Born: May 14, 1907, Akron, Ohio. Died: 1980, Pittsburgh, Pa. Football player, coach and screen actor.

Appeared in: **1930** Maybe It's Love.

HARR, SILVER
Born: 1893. Died: Sept. 19, 1968. Screen actor.

Appeared in: **1927** Flying Luck. **1931** Cylcone Kid. **1946** Ghost of Hidden Valley.

HARRIGAN, WILLIAM
Born: Mar. 27, 1894, New York, N.Y. Died: Feb. 1, 1966, New York, N.Y. (following surgery). Stage and screen actor. Son of playwright Edward Harrigan (dec.). Divorced from actress Louise Groody and later married to Grace Culbert.

Appeared in: **1927** Cabaret. **1929** Nix on Dames. **1930** On the Level; Born Reckless. **1933** Pick Up; The Girl on 419; Disgraced; The Invisible Man. **1935** G-Men; Stranded; Silk Hat Kid; His Family Tree; The Melody Lingers On; Whipsaw. **1936** Frankie and Johnnie. **1937** Over the Goal; Federal Bullets; Exiled to Shanghai. **1938** Hawaii Calls. **1939** Back Door to Heaven. **1947** The Farmer's Daughter; Desert Fury. **1948** Citizen Saint. **1951** Flying Leathernecks. **1952** Steel Town. **1953** Francis Covers the Big Town. **1954** Roogie's Bump. **1957** Street of Sinners.

HARRIMAN, MOSES H.
Born: 1861. Died: Sept. 16, 1928, East Islip, N.Y. Screen and stage actor.

HARRINGTON, BUCK
Died: Feb. 2, 1971. Screen actor.

Appeared in: **1944** Shake Hands With Murder.

HARRINGTON, KATE
Born: 1903, Boise, Idaho. Died: Nov. 23, 1978, New York, N.Y. Screen, stage and television actress.

Appeared in: **1941** Riding the Wind; Come on Danger; Scattergood Brains (serial). **1945** Rhapsody in Blue. **1968** Rachel, Rachel. **1970** Love Story. **1971** Hospital.

HARRIS, ALAN L.
Born: 1902. Died: June 15, 1980, Los Angeles, Calif. Screen and television actor.

Appeared in: **1939** Tevya. **1950** Holiday Rhythm.

HARRIS, ARLENE
Born: 1899, Toronto, Canada. Died: June 12, 1976, Woodland Hills, Calif. Screen, radio and television actress.

Appeared in: **1943** Here Comes Elmer. **1946** One Exciting Week. **1948** The Main Street Kid. **1955** Hold Back Tomorrow.

HARRIS, ASA "ACE"
Born: 1910. Died: June 11, 1964, Chicago, Ill. Black singer and screen actor. Was member of the original "Inkspots" singing group.

Appeared in: **1941** The Great American Broadcast. **1942** Pardon My Sarong.

HARRIS, AVERELL
Died: Sept. 25, 1966, New York, N.Y. Screen and stage actor.

Appeared in: **1929** Her New Chauffeur (short). **1931** Secrets of a Secretary; His Woman.

HARRIS, CAROLINE
Born: 1867. Died: Apr. 23, 1937, New York, N.Y. Screen and stage actress. Mother of actor Richard Barthelmess (dec. 1963).

Appeared in: **1909** The Necklace. **1916** Honor of Mary Blake.

HARRIS, ELMER
Born: 1878. Died: Sept. 6, 1966, Washington. Screen, stage actor, screenwriter, playwright and author.

Appeared in: **1923** Garrison's Finish.

HARRIS, ELSIE
Born: 1892. Died: May 17, 1953, Hollywood, Calif. Screen actress.

HARRIS, FLORENCE GLOSSOP See GLOSSOP-HARRIS, FLORENCE

HARRIS, JOSEPH
Born: 1870. Died: June 11, 1953, Hollywood, Calif. Screen and stage actor.

Appeared in: **1915** Oh, Daddy. **1921** Freeze-Out; Red Courage; Sure Fire; The Wallop. **1922** The Bearcat; For Big Stakes; Pardon My Nerve; The Loaded Door. **1923** Canyon of the Fools; Crashin' Thru.

HARRIS, JUDY
Died: Oct. 25, 1976. Screen actress.

Appeared in: **1960** Wild River.

HARRIS, KATHERINE
Born: 1893. Died: May 2, 1927, New York, N.Y. Screen actress. Divorced from actor John Barrymore (dec. 1942).

Appeared in: **1916** The Lost Bridegroom.

HARRIS, KAY
Born: 1920, Elkhorn, Wis. Died: Oct. 23, 1971, Calif. Screen, stage and radio actress.

Appeared in: **1941** Tillie the Toiler. **1942** Sabotage Squad; Parachute Nurse; The Spirit of Stanford; Smith of Minnesota. **1943** Fighting Buckaroo; Robin Hood of the Range; Lucky Legs.

HARRIS, LEONORE
Born: 1879, New York, N.Y. Died: Sept. 27, 1953, New York, N.Y. Screen actress.

Appeared in: **1916** Betty of Graystone. **1917** Today. **1922** The Faithless Sex.

HARRIS, MARCENE
Died: July 22, 1976. Screen actress.

HARRIS, MARION
Born: 1906, Henderson, Ky. Died: Apr. 23, 1944, New York, N.Y (burns). Screen, stage actress, cabaret entertainer and singer. Mother of screen actress Marion Harris, Jr.

Appeared in: **1929** Devil May Care. **1930** Not So Dumb.

HARRIS, MILDRED
Born: Nov. 29, 1901, Cheyenne, Wyo. Died: July 20, 1944, Los Angeles, Calif. (pneumonia after surgery). Screen, stage, burlesque and vaudeville actress. Entered films at the age of nine. Divorced from actor Charles Chaplin (dec. 1977).

Appeared in: **1915** The Warrens of Virginia. **1916** Intolerance. **1917** Price of Good Time; Bad Boy; An Old Fashioned Young Man. **1918** For Husbands Only; Borrowed Clothes. **1921** Old Dad; Habit; A Prince There Was; Fool's Paradise. **1922** The First Woman. **1923** The Fog; The Daring Years. **1924** One Law for the Women; Unmarried Wives; By Divine Right; The Desert Hawk; In Fast Company; The Shadow of the East; Soiled; Stepping Lively; Traffic in Hearts. **1925** Flaming Love; My Neighbor's Wife; Beyond the Border; The Dressmaker from Paris; Easy Money; Super Speed; The Unknown Lover; The Fighting Cub; Frivolous Sal; Iron Man; A Man of Iron; Private Affairs. **1926** The Cruise of the Jasper B; Dangerous Traffic; The Isle of Retribution; The Mystery Club; The Self Starter; The Wolf Hunters. **1927** The Adventurous Soul; Burning Gold; The Girl from Rio; Husband Hunters; One Hour of Love; Out of the Past; Rose of the Bowery; She's My Baby; The Show Girl; The Swell-Head; Wandering Girls; Wolves of the Air. **1928** Lingerie; Melody of Love; Heart of a Follies Girl; Power of the Press; Hearts of Men; Last Lap; The Speed Classic. **1929** Side Street; Sea Fury. **1930** No, No, Nanette; Ranch House Blues; The Melody Man. **1931** Night Nurse. **1935** Lady Tubbs; Never Too Late. **1936** Movie Maniacs (short). **1944** Here Come the Waves.

HARRIS, MITCHELL
Born: 1883, New York. Died: Nov. 16, 1948, New York, N.Y. Screen and stage actor. Son of stage actor William Harris (dec.).

Appeared in: **1930** The Sea Wolf; Fair Warning. **1931** A Connecticut Yankee; Peach O'Reno; Freighters of Destiny. **1932** Ghost Valley; Scandal for Sale. **1933** Hypnotized; Victims of Persecution. **1936** A Connecticut Yankee in King Arthur's Court. **1937** The Awful Truth. **1942** Reap the Wild Wind. **1944** The Story of Dr. Wassell; Hail the Conquering Hero.

HARRIS, MORRIS (Morris Oliver Harris)
Born: 1915. Died: Oct. 16, 1974, Syracuse, N.Y. Black screen actor and singer. One of the original members of the Ink Spots.

HARRIS, ROBERT H. (Robert H. Hurwitz)
Born: 1909. Died: Nov. 30, 1981, Los Angeles, Calif. Screen, stage, television actor and television director. Married to actress Viola Harris. Do not confuse with British actor with the same name.

Appeared in: **1954** Laughing Anne. **1955** That Lady. **1956** Bundle of Joy. **1957** The Big Caper; The Fuzzy Pink Nightgown; No Down Payment; The Invisible Boy; Peyton Place. **1958** How to Make a Monster. **1960** Oscar Wilde. **1961** The George Raft Story; Operation Eichmann; Twenty Plus Two. **1962** Convicts Four. **1963** America America. **1965** Mirage. **1967** Valley of the Dolls. **1972** The Great Northfield Minnesota Raid. **1973** Massacre in Rome. **1975** The Terrorists; The Man in the Glass Booth.

HARRIS, ROSE
Died: Feb. 17, 1948, New York, N.Y. Screen and stage actress. Married to actor Lew Fields (dec. 1941). Mother of actors Herbert (dec. 1958) and Dorothy Fields (dec.1974).

HARRIS, STACY B.
Born: 1918, Big Timber, Quebec, Canada. Died: Mar. 13, 1973, Los Angeles, Calif. (heart attack). Screen, stage, radio, television actor, journalist and cartoonist.

Appeared in: **1951** Appointment with Danger; His Kind of Woman. **1952** The Redhead from Wyoming. **1953** The Great Sioux Uprising. **1954** Dragnet. **1955** New Orleans Uncensored. **1956** The Brass Legend; Comanche; The Mountain. **1958** The Hunters; New Orleans After Dark; Good Day for a Hanging. **1959** Cast a Long Shadow. **1962** Four for the Morgue. **1965** Brainstorm; The Great Sioux Massacre. **1966** An American Dream. **1967** A Covenant with Death; First to Fight. **1968** Countdown (aka Moon Shot). **1970** Bloody Mama; The Swappers.

HARRIS, SYBIL
Born: July 22, 1883, Twickenham, England. Died: May 20, 1940, United States. Screen and stage actress.

Appeared in: **1936** Bunker Hill. **1937** Mountain Justice; They Wouldn't Forget. **1938** Crime School. **1939** Federal Man-Hunt; Angels Wash Their Faces. **1940** Untamed; My Son, My Son; All This and Heaven Too.

HARRIS, VAL
Died: Mar. 17, 1961, Van Nuys, Calif. Screen, stage and vaudeville actor. Appeared in vaudeville with Vera Griffin in an act billed as Harris and Griffin and with Anne Howe in an act billed as Val Harris and Anne Howe.

Appeared in: **1928** Fair Days (short); The Wild Westerner (short). **1935** Old Sawbones (short).

HARRIS, WADSWORTH
Born: Oct. 9, 1864, Boston, Mass. Died: Nov. 1, 1942, Los Angeles, Calif. (pneumonia). Screen and stage actor.

Appeared in: **1920** The Dragon's Net (serial). **1921** Rich Girl, Poor Girl. **1922** The Call of Home.

HARRISON, CAREY (Capt. Carey Harrison Reppeteau)
Born: 1890. Died: Mar. 25, 1957, Los Angeles, Calif. Screen actor.

Appeared in: **1929** Married in Hollywood. **1936** Pepper. **1938** The Buccaneer. **1942** Call of the Canyon. **1945** House of Dracula; On Stage Everybody; Secret Agent X-9 (serial); Senorita from the West. **1946** Girl on the Spot. **1948** Casbah.

HARRISON, CHARLES
Born: Boston, Mass. Died: Oct. 19, 1945, Brooklyn, N.Y. Screen and stage actor.

Appeared in: **1938** We're Going to be Rich.

HARRISON, JAMES "JIMMY"
Born: 1908, Milwaukee, Wis. Died: Nov. 9, 1977, Woodland Hills, Calif. Screen, stage and vaudeville actor. Married to actress Juanita Harrison.

Appeared in: **1925** Charley's Aunt; Stop Flirting. **1928** The Wife's Relations. **1929** Handcuffed; Hot Lemonade (short). **1931** Too Many Husbands (short). **1936** The Lawless Nineties. **1948** Borrowed Trouble; Silent Conflict; Panhandle. **1949** Stampede. **1951** Vengeance Valley; The Tall Target.

HARRISON, JUNE
Born: 1926. Died: Mar. 10, 1974, Hollywood, Calif. (cirrhosis of liver). Screen and radio actress. Entered films in 1937. Do not confuse with silent film actress June Harrison.

Appeared in: **1938** Girl of the Golden West. **1941** Sun Valley Serenade. **1945** The Affairs of Susan; Out of This World. **1947** Land of the Lawless. **1948** Bringing Up Father; Citizen Saint; Jiggs and Maggie in Society; Jiggs and Maggie in Court. **1949** Jiggs and Maggie in Jackpot Jitters. **1950** Jiggs and Maggie Out West.

HARRISON, MONA K.
Born: Edinburgh, Scotland. Died: Jan. 2, 1957, England? Screen and stage actress.

Appeared in: **1915** Light. **1917** Derelicts.

HARRISON, SAUL E.
Born: 1888, Brenham, Tex. Died: Oct. 13, 1944, New York, N.Y. Screen, stage actor and film director.

Appeared in: **1914** The Midnight Ride of Paul Revere. **1915** Their Happy Little Home.

HARRON, BOBBY (Robert Harron)
Born: Apr. 24, 1893. Died: Sept. 6, 1920, New York, N.Y. (gunshot—accident). Screen actor. Brother of actress Tessie Harron (dec. 1918) and actor John Harron (dec. 1939).

Appeared in: **1907** Dr. Skinum. **1908** At the Crossroads of Life; Bobby's Kodak; The Valet's Wife; The Test of Friendship; The Helping Hand. **1909** The Girls and Daddy; The Hindoo Dagger; A Burglar's Mistake; A Sound Sleeper; One Busy Hour; Jones and the Lady Book Agent; Two Memories; The Message; Pranks; The Little Darling; In a Hempen Bag; The Lonely Villa; The Drive for Life; Sweet Revenge. **1910** Ramona; In the Season of Buds; A Child's Impulse; An Old Story With a New Ending; Wilful Peggy; A Summer Idyll; Examination Day at School; The Banker's Daughters. **1911** The Battle; Fighting Blood; Enoch Arden, Part I; The White Rose of the Wilds; The Last Drop of Water; Bobby, the Coward; The Unveiling; Billy's Strategem. **1912** Man's Lust for Gold; Fate's Interception; A Pueblo Legend; The Sands of Dee; An Unseen Enemy; Home Folks; Friends; So Near, Yet So Far; The Musketeers of Pig Alley; The New York Hat; Brutality; My Hero; Oil and Water; The Burglar's Dilemma; A Cry for Help; The Tender Hearted Boy; Man's Genesis; The Mender of Nets; The Girl and Her Trust; A Temporary Truce; Brute Force; The Informer; Those Hicksville Boys. **1913** Love in an Apartment Hotel; Broken Ways; The Sheriff's Baby; A Misunderstood Boy; The Little Tease; His Mother's Son; The Yaqui Cur; A Timely Interception; Death's Marathon; Her Mother's Oath; In Prehistoric Days; The Lady and the Mouse; Brothers; Near to Earth; Fate; The Coming of Angelo; The Reformers (aka The Lost Art of Minding One's Own Business); Adopted Brother; Primitive Man (aka Wars of the Primal Tribes); The Escape. **1914** The Massacre; The Battle of Elderbush Gulch; The Odalisque; The Newer Woman; Their First Acquaintance; Down by the Sounding Sea; Moonshine Molly; The Weaker Strain; His Mother's Trust; The Pseudo Prodigal; Judith of Bethulia; The Battle of the Sexes; The Great Leap; The Avenging Conscience; The Rebellion of Kitty Belle; The Outcast; The Victim; A Lesson in Mechanics; Her Shattered Idol; Paid With Interest; Home Sweet Home. **1915** Birth of a Nation; The Escape; Big James' Heart. **1916** Hoodoo Ann; The Missing Links; The Little Liar; A Child of the Paris Streets; The Wild Girl of the Sierras; The Wharf Rat; Intolerance; The Marriage of Molly O. **1917** An Old Fashioned Young Man; Sunshine Alley; The Bad Boy. **1918** Hearts of the World; The Great Love; The Greatest Thing in Life; A Romance of Happy Valley. **1919** The Greatest Question; The Mother and the Law; The Girl Who Stayed at Home; True Heart Susie. **1920** Everybody's Sweetheart. **1921** Coincidence; Darling Mine; The Rebel of Kitty Beale.

HARRON, JOHN
Born: Mar. 31, 1903, N.Y. Died: Nov. 24, 1939, Seattle, Wash. Screen actor. Married to actress Betty Egan. Brother of actor Bobby Harron (dec. 1920) and actress Tessie Harron (dec. 1918).

Appeared in: **1918** Hearts of the World. **1921** Through the Back Door (film debut); The Grim Comedian; The Fox. **1922** The Five Dollar Baby; Love in the Dark; Penrod; The Ragged Heiress. **1923** Dulcy; The Gold Diggers; The Supreme Test; The Westbound Limited. **1924** Behind the Curtain; The Fire Patrol; The Painted Flapper; What Shall I Do? **1925** Learning to Love; Old Shoes; Below the Line; My Wife and I; Satan in Sables; The Wife Who Wasn't Wanted; The Woman Hater. **1926** Bride of the Storm; The Boy Friend; The False Alarm; The Gilded Highway; Hell-Bent for Heaven; The Little Irish Girl; The Night Cry; Rose of the Tenements. **1927** Once and Forever; Silk Stockings; Closed Gates; Love Makes 'Em Wild; Naughty; Night Life. **1928** Finders Keepers; Green Grass Widows; Their Hour. **1929** Man in Hobbles; Street Girl; Big Boy. **1931** The Czar of Broadway; Laugh and Get Rich; The Last of the Tongs. **1932** The Crowd Roars; White Zombie; Beauty Parlor. **1933** Sister to Judas; Midnight Warning. **1934** Stolen Sweets; City Park; Murder in the Private Car. **1935** Symphony of Living. **1937** That Girl from Paris; Without Warning; The Missing Witness; Talent Scout. **1938** Boy Meets Girl; Torchy Gets Her Man; Penrod's Double Trouble; A Slight Case of Murder; Torchy Blane in Panama; The Invisible Menace. **1939** The Oklahoma Kid; Each Dawn I Die; Women in the Wind; Secret Service of the Air; The Cowboy Quarterback; Indianapolis Speedway; Nancy Drew—Trouble Shooter; Torchy Runs for Mayor; Torchy Plays With Dynamite; Angels Wash Their Faces. **1940** The Fighting 69th.

HARRON, TESSIE (Anna Theresa Harron)
Born: Feb. 16, 1896, N.Y. Died: Nov. 9, 1918, Los Angeles, Calif. (Spanish influenza). Screen actress. Sister of actors Bobby (dec. 1920) and John Harron (dec. 1939).

HART, ALBERT
Born: 1874, Liverpool, England. Died: Jan. 10, 1940, Hollywood, Calif. Stage and screen actor.

Appeared in: **1921** Cotton and Cattle; A Cowboy Ace; Diane of Star Hollow; Flowing Gold; Out of the Clouds; Doubling for Romeo; The Range Pirate; Rustlers of the Night; The Trail to Red Dog; The White Masks. **1922** Angel Citizens; Cross Roads; The Girl Who Ran Wild; Gold Grabbers; So This Is Arizona; Trail's End; The Hidden Woman. **1923** Can a Woman Love Twice; Spawn of the Desert; Crooked Alley; Kindled Courage; Shadows of the North; The Sunshine Trail. **1924** The Breathless Moment; Excitement. **1925** The Pony Express; The Man Without a Country. **1926** Blind Trail; Forlorn River; The Outlaw Express. **1927** The Fire Fighters (serial); The Ridin' Rowdy; The Devil's Twin; Blake of Scotland Yard (serial); The Long Loop of the Pecos; The Man from Hardpan; The Mysterious Rider. **1928** The Ballyhoo Buster; The Boss of Rustler's Roost; Mother Knows Best; Honor Bound. **1929** Making the Grade; .45 Calibre War; The Diamond Master (serial). **1931** An American Tragedy. **1933** Big Executive. **1934** Home on the Range. **1938** Tom Sawyer, Detective.

HART, ANNIE
Born: 1860. Died: June 13, 1947, Fair Haven, N.J. Screen, stage, vaudeville actress and burlesque performer. Married to vaudeville actor Billy Lester (dec. 1889).

Appeared in: **1933** Universal shorts.

HART, BILLY (William Lenhart)
Born: 1864. Died: June 18, 1942, Los Angeles, Calif. Screen, stage, burlesque and vaudeville actor. Appeared in vaudeville as part of "Billy and Marie Hart" team.

HART, FLORENCE
Died: Mar. 30, 1960, Germantown, Pa. Screen, stage actress and dancer.

Appeared in: **1920** A Tokio Siren; The Prince Chap. **1921** The Son of Wallingford; It Can Be Done.

HART, JACK "INDIAN JACK"
Born: 1872. Died: Sept. 23, 1974, Las Vegas, Nev. Screen actor and rodeo performer.

Appeared in: **1968** Born to Buck.

HART, JAMES T.
Born: 1868. Died: Aug. 12, 1926, Los Angeles, Calif. (stroke). Screen actor.

HART, LEWIS O.
Born: 1847. Died: Jan. 9, 1920, Staten Island, N.Y. Screen and stage actor.

HART, LUCIA "SUNSHINE"
Born: July 5, 1886, Indianapolis, Ind. Died: Jan. 3, 1930, Los Angeles, Calif. Screen, stage and vaudeville actress. Entered films in 1914.

Appeared in: **1915** The Tiger Cub. **1920** The Master Mind; White Moll. **1926** Syncopating Sue; Lovey Mary. **1927** The Red Mill; The Student Prince; My Best Girl. **1928** Five and Ten Cent Annie. **1929** The Man in Hobbles; The Brides Relations (short); Sound Your A.

HART, MABEL
Born: Apr. 29, 1886, Illinois. Died: June 9, 1960, Los Angeles, Calif. (heart attack). Screen actress.

Appeared in: **1938** Over the Wall. **1948** Isn't It Romantic?

HART, MAURICE
Born: 1909. Died: June 10, 1978, Los Angeles, Calif. Screen, radio, television actor, radio writer and lyricist.

Appeared in: **1951** Disc Jockey. **1957** The Joker is Wild.

HART, NEAL (Cornelius A. Hart, Jr.)
Born: 1879, Richmond, N.Y. Died: Apr. 2, 1949, Woodland Hills, Calif. Screen actor and film director. Entered films in 1914.

Appeared in: **1916** Liberty, a Daughter of the USA (serial); The Committee on Credentials; For the Love of a Girl; Love's Lariat. **1917** The Raid; The Man from Montana; The Ninth Day; Roped In; Bill Brennan's Claim; Casey's Border Raid; Swede-Hearts. **1918** Beating the Limited; Roped and Tied; When Pan's Green Saw Red. **1919** The Wolf and His Mate (serial). **1921** South of Northern Lights; Danger Valley; Tangled Trails; Black Sheep; God's Gold. **1922**

The Kingfisher's Roost; Rangeland; Lure of Gold; The Heart of a Texan; Butterfly Range; Table Top Ranch; West of the Pecos. **1923** The Secret of the Pueblo; Below the Rio Grande; The Devil's Bowl; Salty Saunders; The Fighting Strain; The Forbidden Range. **1924** The Left Hand Brand; Tucker's Top Hand; Branded a Thief; Lawless Men; Safe Guarded; The Valley of Vanishing Men. **1925** The Verdict of the Desert. **1927** Scarlet Brand (serial). **1930** Trigger Tricks. **1931** Wild Horse. **1932** Law and Order. **1939** The Renegade Ranger. **1947** Saddle Pals.

HART, RICHARD
Born: 1916, Providence, R.I. Died: Jan. 2, 1951, New York, N.Y. (heart attack). Screen, stage and television actor.

Appeared in: **1947** Desire Me; Green Dolphin Street. **1948** B. F.'s Daughter. **1949** The Black Book; Reign of Terror.

HART, TEDDY
Born: 1897. Died: Feb. 17, 1971, Los Angeles, Calif. Screen, stage and television actor. Brother of lyricist Lorenz Hart (dec.). Won 1936 Screen Actors Guild Award for Best Supporting Actor for Three Men on a Horse.

Appeared in: **1932** Million Dollar Legs. **1933** Diplomaniacs. **1936** Three Men on a Horse (stage and film versions); After the Thin Man. **1937** Ready, Willing and Able; That Man's Here Again; Hotel Haywire; Marry the Girl; Talent Scout; The Footloose Heiress. **1941** You're the One. **1942** My Favorite Spy. **1946** Lady Luck. **1951** Ma and Pa Kettle Back on the Farm; The Fat Man. **1952** Ma and Pa Kettle at the Fair; A Girl in Every Port. **1953** Ma and Pa Kettle on Vacation. **1955** Ma and Pa Kettle at Waikiki. **1965** Mickey One.

HART, WILLIAM S. (William Surrey Hart, Sr.)
Born: Dec. 6, 1862, Newburgh, N.Y. Died: June 23, 1946, Los Angeles, Calif. (stroke). Screen, stage actor, writer and film director. Divorced from actress Winifred Westover (dec. 1978). Father of actor William S. Hart, Jr.

Appeared in: **1913** The Fugitive. **1914** His Hour of Manhood; The Bargain; Jim Cameron's Wife; The Passing of Two-Gun Hicks; The Scourge of the Desert. **1915** On the Night Stage; Pinto Ben; The Grudge; In the Sagebrush Country; The Man from Nowhere; Bad Buck of Santa Ynez; The Sheriff's Streak of Yellow; Mr. Silent Haskins; The Taking of Luke McVane; The Ruse; Cash Parrish's Pal; The Converison of Frosty Blake; The Rough Neck; Keno Bates; Liar; The Disciple; The Darkening Trail; A Knight of the Trail; The Tool of Providence; Grit; The Golden Claw; Between Men. **1916** The Last Act; Hell's Hinges; The Primal Lure; The Aryan; The Sheriff; The Captive God; The Apostle of Vengeance; The Patriot; The Dawn Maker; The Return of Draw Egan; The Devil's Double; Truthful Tolliver. **1917** The Gun Fighter; Square Deal Man; The Desert Man; Wolf Diary; The Cold Deck; The Narrow Trail; The Silent Man; The Last Ace. **1918** Wolves of the Trail; Blue Blazes Rawden; Tiger Man; Shark Monroe; Riddle Gawne; The Border Wireless; Branding Broadway; The Toll Gate; Selfish Yates; War Relief; John Petticoats. **1919** Breed of Men; The Poppy Girl's Husband; The Money Corral; Square Deal Sanderson; Wagon Tracks. **1920** Sand!; The Toll Gate; The Cradle of Courage; The Testing Block. **1921** O'Malley of the Mounted; The Whistle; Three Word Brand; White Oak. **1922** The Covered Wagon; Travelin' On. **1923** Wild Bill Hickock; Hollywood; The Spoilers. **1924** Singer Jim McKee; Grit (and 1915 version). **1925** Tumbleweeds. **1928** Show People. **1939** Tumbleweeds (also appeared in 1925 version and did the prologue for the 1939 version). **1943** One Foot in Heaven; The Silent Man (1917 footage). **1963** The Great Chase (documentary); That's Entertainment (film clips).

HART, WILLIAM V. "POP"
Born: 1867. Died: Oct. 14, 1925, New York, N.Y. Screen and vaudeville actor.

HARTE, BETTY (Daisy Mae Light)
Born: 1883, Philadelphia, Pa. Died: Jan. 3, 1965, Sunland, Calif. Screen actress.

Appeared in: **1908** The Roman. **1911** The Blacksmith's Son; In the Days of Gold; The Heart of John Barlow; Making a Man of Him; The Little Widow; The Profligate; Through Fire and Smoke; The Coquette. **1912** The Vow of Ysobel; Her Education; The Girl of the Lighthouse; The Pirate's Daughter; How the Cause Was Won; The Shrinking Rawhide; The Substitute Mode; The Junior Officer; An Assisted Elopement; Getting Atmosphere; The Ace of Spades; The Epidemic in Paradise Gulch; Making a Man of Her; Kings of the Forest. **1913** The Good in the Worst of Us; An Innocent Informer. **1914** The Pride of Jennico. **1915** The Buzzard's Shadow. **1916** The Bait. **1922** Eternal Peace.

HARTER, ROBERT L.
Died: Mar. 16, 1970. Screen actor.

Appeared in: **1966** The Daydreamer.

HARTFORD, DAVID
Born: Jan. 11, 1876, Ontonian, Mich. Died: Oct. 29, 1932, Hollywood, Calif. (heart attack). Screen and stage actor, film and stage director, stage and film producer.

Appeared in: **1926** Dame Chance. **1930** Rough Romance.

HARTIGAN, PAT (Patrick C. Hartigan)
Born: Dec. 21, 1881, New York, N.Y. Died: May 8, 1951, Los Angeles, Calif. (coronary). Screen actor and film director.

Appeared in: **1917** The Planter. **1921** Conceit. **1922** Channing of the Northwest; Down to the Sea in Ships; My Old Kentucky Home. **1923** Fury; Dark Streets; The Darling of New York; Where the North Begins. **1924** Welcome Stranger; Western Luck; Abraham Lincoln (aka The Dramatic Life of Abraham Lincoln); Find Your Man; The King of Wild Horses. **1925** Code of the West; Paint the Powder; The Thundering Herd; Below the Line; Bobbed Hair; Clash of the Wolves. **1926** Oh! What a Nurse!; Ransom's Folly; The Fighting Edge. **1927** The Enchanted Island; A Bowery Cinderella; Heaven on Earth; Too Many Crooks; Johnny Get Your Hair Cut. **1928** The Midnight Taxi; The Devil's Skipper; A Race for Life; Tenderloin; State Street Sadie. **1929** In Old Arizona; The Far Call; From Headquarters. **1930** The Man Hunter. **1931** Other Men's Women; Criminal Code; Big Brother; Corsair. **1932** Handle With Care.

HARTLEY, CHARLES
Born: 1852. Died: Oct. 13, 1930, Fort Lee, N.J. (complication of diseases). Screen and stage actor.

Appeared in: **1919** Prunella. **1921** The Conquest of Canaan.

HARTLEY, HELEN
Born: 1892. Died: Oct. 30, 1954, Denison, Tex. Circus performer and screen actress. Appeared in silent films.

HARTMAN, AGNES A.
Born: 1860, Sweden. Died: Dec. 22, 1932, Los Angeles, Calif. Screen actress. Mother of actress Gretchen Hartman.

HARTMAN, GRACE (Grace Barrett)
Born: 1907. Died: Aug. 8, 1955, Van Nuys, Calif. (cancer). Screen, stage and television actress. Divorced from actor Paul Hartman (dec. 1973) with whom she appeared in vaudeville as part of "The Dancing Hartmans."

Appeared in: **1937** 45 Fathers. **1941** Sunny. **1943** Higher and Higher.

HARTMAN, GRETCHEN (aka GRETA HARTMAN)
Born: Aug. 28, 1897, Chicago, Ill. Died: Jan. 27, 1979, Los Angeles, Calif. Screen and stage actress. Married to actor Alan Hale, Sr. (dec. 1950). Mother of actor Alan Hale, Jr.

Appeared in: **1917** The Painted Madonna; Mary Jane's Pa. **1918** Fantine; Les Miserables. **1919** The House Without Children; The Bandbox. **1920** Bride 13 (serial). **1921** His Brother's Keeper. **1922** Do and Dare; While Justice Waits. **1929** The College Coquette; She Goes to War; The Time, the Place, and the Girl.

HARTMAN, JONATHAN WILLIAM "POP"
Born: 1872, Louisville, Ky. Died: Oct. 19, 1965, Tampa, Fla. Screen, stage and vaudeville actor.

HARTMAN, PAUL
Born: 1904. Died: Oct. 2, 1973, Los Angeles, Calif. (heart attack). Screen, stage, vaudeville, television actor and dancer. Son of stage actor and producer Ferris Hartman (dec.). Married to actress Grace Hartman (dec. 1955) with whom he appeared in vaudeville as part of "The Dancing Hartmans." He later married actress Francis Miggins. Do not confuse with German actor Paul Hartmann.

Appeared in: **1937** 45 Fathers (film debut). **1941** Sunny. **1943** Higher and Higher. **1953** Man on a Tightrope. **1960** Inherit the Wind. **1963** Soldier in the Rain; The Thrill of It All. **1964** Those Calloways. **1965** Inside Daisy Clover. **1967** Luv; How to Succeed in Business Without Really Trying; The Reluctant Astronaut.

HARTMAN, RUTH
Died: July 9, 1956, Los Angeles, Calif. Screen actress. Married to actor Carlyle Blackwell (dec. 1955).

HARTMANN, SADAKICHI
Born: c. 1864, Japan. Died: Nov. 21, 1944, St. Petersburg, Fla. Author, dancer and screen actor.

Appeared in: **1924** The Thief of Baghdad.

HARTNELL, WILLIAM "BILLY"

Born: Jan. 8, 1908, Devon, England. Died: Apr. 24, 1975, London, England. Screen, stage and television actor. Married to actress and playwright Heather McIntyre.

Appeared in: **1933** I'm an Explosive; Follow the Lady; The Lure. **1934** Seeing Is Believing; The Perfect Flaw. **1935** Swinging the Lead; While Parents Sleep. **1936** Nothing Like Publicity; Midnight at Madame Tussaud's (aka Midnight at the Wax Museum—US). **1937** Farewell Again (aka Troopship—US 1938). **1938** They Drive By Night. **1939** Murder Will Out; Too Dangerous to Live. **1940** They Came By Night. **1942** Flying Fortress; Sabotage at Sea; Suspected Person; The Peterville Diamond. **1943** Bells Go Down; The Dark Tower; Headline. **1944** Way Ahead (US 1945). **1945** Strawberry Roan (US 1948); The Agitator; Murder in Reverse (US 1946). **1946** Appointment With Crime (US 1950). **1947** Odd Man Out; Temptation Harbour (US 1949); Brighton Rock (aka Young Scarface). **1948** Escape. **1949** Now Barrabas; The Lost People. **1950** Double Confession (US 1953). **1951** The Dark Man; The Magic Box (US 1952). **1952** Pickwick Papers (US 1953); The Ringer (US 1953); The Holly and the Ivy (US 1953). **1953** Will Any Gentleman? (US 1955). **1955** Footsteps in the Fog; Josephine and the Men. **1956** Doublecross; Private's Progress; Tons of Trouble. **1957** Yangtse Incident (aka Battle Hell—US); The Hypnotist (aka Scotland Yard Dragnet—US 1958); Hell Drivers (US 1958). **1958** On the Run; Carry on Sergeant (US 1959); Date With Disaster. **1959** Shake Hands With the Devil; The Mouse That Roared; The Night We Dropped a Clanger (aka Make Mine a Double—US 1961); The Desperate Man. **1960** And the Same to You; Jackpot; Piccadilly Third Stop (US 1968). **1962** Tomorrow at Ten (US 1964). **1963** This Sporting Life; The World Ten Times Over (aka Pussycat Alley—US 1965); Heavens Above.

HARVEY, BOB

Born: 1914. Died: Jan. 10, 1978. Screen, radio actor and orchestra leader.

Appeared in: **1963** Beach Party. **1964** Pajama Party. **1965** Beach Blanket Bingo; How to Stuff a Wild Bikini; Sergeant Deadhead. **1966** The Ghost in the Invisible Bikini.

HARVEY, CLARENCE

Born: 1865. Died: May 3, 1945, New York, N.Y. Screen and stage actor.

Appeared in: **1939** Gone With the Wind; Zaza.

HARVEY, DON C. (Don Carlos Harvey)

Born: Dec. 12, 1911, Kansas. Died: Apr. 24, 1963, Studio City, Calif. (heart attack). Screen, stage, radio and television actor. Married to actress Jean Harvey (dec. 1966).

Appeared in: **1949** Angels in Disguise; The Mutineers; Rimfire; Son of a Badman; Adventures of Sir Galahad (serial); Batman and Robin (serial). **1950** Atom Man vs. Superman (serial); Chain Gang; Forbidden Jungle; The Fighting Stallion; Trail of the Rustlers; The Girl from San Lorenzo; Gunmen of Abilene; Hoedown; Joe Palooka in The Triple Cross; The Lost Volcano. **1951** Night Riders of Montana; Teams Never Cry; Fort Worth; Northwest Territory; According to Mrs. Hoyle; Hurricane Island; Captain Video (serial). **1952** Blackhawk (serial); The Old West; Prince of Pirates; A Yank in Indo-China. **1954** Golden Idol; Pushover; Violent Men; Gunfighters of the Northwest (serial). **1955** The Far Country; Apache Ambush; Picnic; Wyoming Renegades; Creature With the Atom Brain; Women's Prison. **1956** Flagpole Sitters (short); Blackjack Kethcum, Desperado; Blazing the Overland Trail (serial); Jubal; The Werewolf; Perils of the Wilderness (serial; Dig That Uranium. **1957** Beginning of the End; No Time to Be Young; Dino. **1958** Buchanan Rides Alone. **1959** Gunmen from Laredo. **1962** The Wild Westerners. **1963** It's a Mad, Mad, Mad, Mad World.

HARVEY, DONALD (James Harvey Brundage)

Born: 1863, Brooklyn, N.Y. Died: Feb. 1, 1931, Hollywood, Calif. Screen actor.

HARVEY, EDWARD

Born: 1893. Died: Aug. 5, 1975, Ventor, Isle of Wight, England (heart attack). Screen, stage and television actor.

Appeared in: **1960** The Unstoppable Man (US 1961). **1962** The Damned (aka These Are the Damned—US 1964). **1965** The Spy Who Came In From The Cold.

HARVEY, FLETCHER

Born: 1865. Died: Sept. 8, 1931, Bayshore, N.Y. (complication of diseases). Screen and stage actor.

Appeared in: **1915** The Melting Pot.

HARVEY, FORRESTER

Born: 1880, County Cork, Ireland. Died: Dec. 14, 1945, Laguna Beach, Calif. (stroke). Screen and stage actor.

Appeared in: **1922** The Lilac Sunbonnet. **1923** The Man Who Liked Lemons. **1925** Somebody's Darling. **1926** Nell Gwynne; If Youth But Knew; The Flag Lieutenant; Street Playlets series including Cash on Delivery. **1927** The Ring. **1928** The White Sheik (aka King's Mate); Toni; Glorious Youth (aka Eileen of the Trees); Spangles; That Brute Simmons. **1929** Ringing the Changes (aka The Crooked Staircase). **1931** Devotion; A Tailor-Made Man; The Man in Possession; Guilty Hands. **1932** Smilin' Through; Red Dust; Kongo; Young Onion (short); Tarzan the Ape Man; Shanghai Express; Sky Devils; But the Flesh Is Weak; The Wet Parade; Mystery Ranch. **1933** Destination Unknown; The Eagle and the Hawk; Midnight Club; The Invisible Man. **1934** The Painted Veil; Menace; Limelight Blues; Great Expectations; Forsaking All Others; The Mystery of Mr. X; Tarzan and His Mate; Man of Two Worlds; Broadway Bill. **1935** China Seas; The Best Man Wins; The Woman In Red; Captain Blood; Vagabond Lady; The Perfect Gentleman; Jalna; Gilded Lily; Right to Live; Mystery of Edwin Drood. **1936** Love Before Breakfast; Petticoat Fever; Lloyds of London; White Hunter. **1937** Personal Property; Thoroughbreds Don't Cry; The Prince and the Pauper; The Man Who Cried Wolf. **1938** Bulldog Drummond in Africa; The Mysterious Mr. Moto. **1939** Bulldog Drummond's Secret Police; The Lady's from Kentucky; The Witness Vanishes. **1940** Rebecca; The Invisible Man Returns; A Chump at Oxford; Tom Brown's School Days. **1941** Free and Easy; The Wolf Man; Dr. Jekyll and Mr. Hyde. **1942** Random Harvest; Mrs. Miniver; This Above All. **1944** The Lodger; None But the Lonely Heart; Secrets of Scotland Yard. **1945** Scotland Yard Investigator; Devotion (and 1931 version).

HARVEY, GEORGETTE

Born: 1883. Died: Feb. 17, 1952, New York, N.Y. Black screen, stage actress, minstrel and singer.

Appeared in: **1934** Social Register. **1939** Back Door to Heaven.

HARVEY, GEORGIA

Born: 1875, Nova Scotia. Died: May 17, 1960, New York, N.Y. Screen and stage actress.

Appeared in: **1915** All For a Girl.

HARVEY, HANK (Herman Heacker)

Died: Dec. 4, 1929, Culver City, Calif. Screen actor.

HARVEY, JEAN (Jean Guy)

Born: Nov. 17, 1900, Ohio. Died: Dec. 14, 1966, Studio City, Calif. (arteriosclerosis). Screen actress. Married to actor Don C. Harvey (dec. 1963).

Appeared in: **1951** Chicago Calling. **1956** The Solid Gold Cadillac; The Werewolf. **1957** Guns Don't Argue. **1959** City of Fear. **1961** Circle of Deception. **1963** It's All Happening (aka The Dream Maker—US 1964).

HARVEY, JOHN

Born: June 28, 1917, New Rockford, N.Dak. Died: Dec. 25, 1970. Screen actor. Married to actress Judith Parrish. Do not confuse with British actor John Harvey nor U.S. actor (dec. 1954).

HARVEY, JOHN "JACK"

Born: 1881. Died: Nov. 10, 1954, Hollywood, Calif. (natural causes). Screen cowboy actor.

HARVEY, SIR JOHN MARTIN See MARTIN-HARVEY, SIR JOHN

HARVEY, KENNETH

Born: 1919. Died: June 6, 1979, Norwalk, Conn. (cancer). Screen, stage, radio, television actor, television director and television writer. Married to actress Rita Morley.

Appeared in: **1947** Smoky River Serenade.

HARVEY, LAURENCE (Larushka Mischa Skikne)

Born: Oct. 1, 1928, Yomishkis, Lithuania. Died: Nov. 25, 1973, London, England (cancer). Screen, stage and television actor, film producer and director. Married to model Paulene Stone. Divorced from actresses Margaret Leighton (dec. 1976) and Joan Cohn. Nominated for 1959 Academy Award for Best Actor in Room at the Top.

Appeared in: **1948** House of Darkness; The Man from Yesterday. **1949** Man on the Run (US 1951); Landfall. **1950** Cairo Road; The Black Rose; A Killer Walks. **1951** There Is Another Sun (aka Wall of Death—US 1952); Scarlet Thread. **1952** Women of Twilight (aka Twilight Women—US 1953); A Killer Walks; I Believe in You (US

1953). **1953** Ali Baba Nights; Innocents in Paris (US 1955). **1954** Dial M for Murder; The Good Die Young (US 1955); King Richard and the Crusaders; Romeo and Juliet. **1955** I Am a Camera; None But the Brave; Storm Over the Nile (US 1956). **1956** Three Men in a Boat (US 1958). **1957** After the Ball. **1958** The Truth About Women; The Silent Enemy. **1959** Room at the Top; Power Among Men (narrator); Expresso Bongo (US 1950). **1960** Butterfield 8; The Alamo. **1961** Two Loves; Summer and Smoke; The Spinster; The Long and the Short and the Tall. **1962** Jungle Fighters; The Wonderful World of the Brothers Grimm; A Walk on the Wild Side; A Girl Named Tamiko; The Manchurian Candidate. **1963** The Running Man; The Ceremony. **1964** The Outrage; Of Human Bondage. **1965** Darling; Life at the Top. **1966** The Spy with a Cold Nose. **1967** Ice Station Zebra. **1968** The Winter's Tale; A Dandy in Aspic; H-Bomb Beach Party; A Flea in Her Ear. **1969** He and She; Fight for Rome; Charge of the Light Brigade. **1970** Hall of Mirrors; WUSA; L'Absolute Naturale; The Magic Christian. **1973** Night Watch. **1974** Welcome to Arrow Beach (aka Tender Flesh).

HARVEY, LEE F.
Born: 1895. Died: Apr. 19, 1950, Philadelphia, Pa. Screen and stage actor. Appeared in Lubin Film Company films.

HARVEY, LILIAN (Lilian Muriel Helen Harvey)
Born: Jan. 19, 1907, Horsey, England. Died: July 27, 1968, Antibes, France. Screen actress. Entered films in Germany c. 1920.

Appeared in: **1925** Die Liebschaften der Hella von Gilsa (The Love Story from the Hella von Gilsa aka Leidenschaft); Der Fluch; Liebe und Trompetenblasen; Die Kleine von Bummel. **1926** Prinzessin Trulala (Princess Trulala); Die Keusche Susanne; Vater Werden ist Nicht Schwer (It's Easy to Become a Father—US 1929). **1927** Die Tolle Lola; Eheferien. **1928** Du Solst Nicht Stehlen (You Should Not Steal); The Love Commandment. **1929** A Knight in London; Adieu Mascotte; Ihr Dunkler Punkt. **1930** Wenn du Einmal Dein Herz Verschenkst; Liebeswalzer (The Love Waltz); Hokuspokus (aka The Temporary Widow); Die Drei von der Tankstelle (Three from the Gasoline Station); Einbrecher; Murder for Sale. **1931** Nie Wieder Liebe (No More Love); Ihre Holeit Befiehlt; Der Kongress Tanzt (Congress Dance—US 1932). **1932** Zwei Herzen und ein Schlag (Two Hearts Beat as One); Quick; Ein Blonder Traum (A Blonde Dream); Happy Ever After. **1933** Ich und Die Kaiserin (The Only Girl aka Heart Song—US 1934); My Weakness; My Lips Betray; Koenig der Clows. **1934** I am Suzanne. **1935** Let's Live Tonight; Schwarze Rosen (aka Did I Betray?—US 1936); Invitation to the Waltz; Mein ist die Rache. **1936** Gluechskinder (Lucky Children). **1937** Sieben Ohrfeigen (Seven Slaps); Fanny Elssler; Untitled Dance. **1938** Capriccio; Black Roses (reissue of Schwarze Rosen, 1935). **1939** Castelli in Aria; Frau am Steuer. **1940** Serenade; Miquette. **1950** Herrliche Zeiten (Wonderful Times). **1951** Miquette and Her Mother. **1958** Das Gag's Nur Einmal (It Only Happened Once). **1960** Das Kommt Nicht Wieder (It Won't Happen Again).

HARVEY, LOTTIE
Born: 1890. Died: Aug. 2, 1948, Hollywood, Calif. Screen actress.

HARVEY, MARILYN
Born: 1929. Died: Mar. 29, 1973, Hollywood, Calif. Screen, stage and television actress. Married to film director Gene Narum.

Appeared in: **1958** The Astounding She-Monster. **1963** A Child Is Waiting. **1968** Rosemary's Baby.

HARVEY, MORRIS
Born: Sept. 25, 1877, London, England. Died: Aug. 24, 1944, England? Screen, stage and vaudeville actor. Married to actress Mai Bacon.

Appeared in: **1930** The Man From Chicago (US 1931). **1931** Sunshine Susie (aka The Office Girl—US 1932). **1932** Down Our Street. **1933** Cash (aka For Love of Money—US 1934); Facing the Music (US 1934); A Southern Maid. **1934** Sing As We Go. **1935** The Love Test; Hello Sweetheart (aka The Butter and Egg Man—US); Squibs; Look Up and Laugh; Scrooge; D'ye Ken John Peel? (aka Captain Moonlight—US). **1936** In the Soup; Dreams Come True; The Mysterious Mr. Davis (aka My Partner, Mr. Davis); Crown V Stevens; Tropical Trouble. **1937** 21 Days (aka The First and the Last, aka 21 Days Together—US 1940); The Sky's the Limit; The Lilac Domino. **1940** Crook's Tour. **1942** The Great Mr. Handel (US 1943); Rose of Tralee.

HARVEY, PAUL
Born: 1884, Ill. Died: Dec. 14, 1955, Hollywood, Calif. (coronary thrombosis). Screen and stage actor. Entered films with Selig Film Co. in 1917.

Appeared in: **1929** The Awful Truth. **1930** Strong Arm (short). **1932** The Wiser Sex. **1933** Advice to the Lovelorn. **1934** Hat, Coat and Glove; Handy Andy; Kid Millions; She Was a Lady; A Wicked Woman; The President Vanishes; Looking for Trouble; The House of Rothschild; The Affairs of Cellini; Born to Be Bad; Broadway Bill; Charlie Chan's Courage. **1935** Broadway Melody of 1936; Alibi Ike; Thanks a Million; The Whole Town's Talking; I'll Love You Always; Four Hours to Kill; Goin' to Town. **1936** August Week-End; Postal Inspector; Rose of the Rancho; The Return of Sophie Lang; The Plainsman; Mind Your Own Business; The Petrified Forest; The Walking Dead; Three Men on a Horse; The Witness Chair; Private Number; Yellowstone. **1937** The Black Legion; Michael Strogoff; On Again—Off Again; High Flyers; The Devil Is Driving; Big City; My Dear Miss Aldrich; 23 1/2 Hours' Leave; The Soldier and the Lady. **1938** A Slight Case of Murder; If I Were King; Love on a Budget; Rebecca of Sunnybrook Farm; I'll Give a Million; Charlie Chan in Honolulu; There's That Woman Again; Algiers; The Higgins Family; The Sisters. **1939** Never Say Die; The Gorilla; News Is Made at Night; Stanley and Livingstone; Mr. Moto in Danger Island; High School; The Forgotten Woman; They Shall Have Music; Meet Dr. Christian. **1940** Brother Rat and a Baby; The Marines Fly High; Typhoon; Manhattan Heartbeat; Maryland; Behind the News; Arizona. **1941** Ride on, Vaquero; Out of the Fog; Puddin' Head; Law of the Tropics; Great Guns; You Belong to Me; Three Girls About Town; Remember the Night; Mr. District Attorney in the Carter Case; High Sierra; You're in the Army Now. **1942** A Tragedy at Midnight; The Man Who Wouldn't Die; Moonlight Masquerade; Heart of the Golden West; You Can't Escape Forever. **1943** The Man from Music Mountain; Mystery Broadcast. **1944** Four Jills in a Jeep; Henry Aldrich Plays Cupid; The Thoroughbreds; Jamboree; In the Meantime, Darling. **1945** Don't Fence Me In; Spellbound; Mama Loves Papa; The Chicago Kid; The Horn Blows at Midnight; Swingin' in a Rainbow; The Southerner; Swingin' on Broadway; State Fair; Pillow to Post. **1946** Gay Blades; They Made Me a Killer; Up Goes Maisie; In Fast Company; Blondie's Lucky Day; I've Always Loved You; The Bamboo Blonde; Helldorado; Early to Wed. **1947** The Beginning of the End; Out of the Blue; High Barbaree; Danger Street; When a Girl's Beautiful; The Late George Apley; Wyoming. **1948** Waterfront at Midnight; Lightnin' in the Forest; Give My Regards to Broadway; Blondie's Reward; Family Honeymoon; Smuggler's Cove; Speed to Spare; Call Northside 777. **1949** Take One False Step; The Fountainhead; The Girl from Jones Beach; Down to the Sea in Ships; The Duke of Chicago; Family Honeymoon; John Loves Mary; Make Believe Ballroom; Mr. Belvedere Goes to College. **1950** The Lawless; Father of the Bride; The Milkman; Side Street; The Skipper Surprised His Wife; Three Little Words; A Ticket to Tomahawk; Unmasked; Riding High; The Yellow Cab Man; Stella. **1951** The Tall Target; Let's Go, Navy!; Father's Little Dividend; Excuse My Dust; The Flying Missile; Thunder in God's Country; Up Front. **1952** The First Time; Has Anybody Seen My Gal?; Dreamboat; April in Paris; Here Come the Nelsons. **1953** Calamity Jane; Remains to Be Seen. **1954** Sabrina. **1955** Three for the Show; High Society. **1956** The Ten Commandments.

HARVEY, RUPERT
Born: Jan. 1, 1887, Iron Bridge, Shropshire, England. Died: July 7, 1954, England? Screen, stage actor and film producer.

Appeared in: **1914** The World, the Flesh and the Devil.

HASCALL, LON (Laurens Hascall, aka LON HASKELL)
Born: 1872. Died: Dec. 13, 1932, Fairhaven, N.J. Screen, stage actor and burlesque performer.

Appeared in: **1931** His Woman.

HASHIM, EDMUND "ED"
Born: 1932. Died: July 2, 1974, New York, N.Y. Screen and television actor.

Appeared in: **1955** Ghost Town. **1956** Quincannon—Frontier Scout. **1961** The Outsider. **1966** ... and Now Miguel. **1968** Hellfighters. **1971** Shaft.

HASKELL, AL
Died: Jan. 6, 1969. Screen actor.

Appeared in: **1939** Mexicali Rose. **1941** Border Vigilants. **1945** Masquerade in Mexico. **1953** The Stranger Wore a Gun. **1954** Silver Lode. **1956** Around the World in 80 Days.

HASKIN, CHARLES W.
Born: 1868. Died: June 10, 1927, New York, N.Y. Screen, stage actor and stage manager.

HASKINS, DOUGLAS (Douglas Neville Haskins)
Born: 1928, Canada. Died: June 8, 1973, Vancouver, B.C., Canada (cancer). Screen and radio actor, film director, television writer, producer, director and screenwriter.

HASSALL, IMOGEN

Born: 1942, England. Died: Nov. 16, 1980, London, England. Screen, stage and television actress. Divorced from director Kenneth Ives. Later married actor Andrew Knox.

Appeared in: **1967** The Long Duel. **1968** Bedtime. **1969** Take a Girl Like You (US 1970). **1970** El Condor; Mumsy, Nanny, Sonny and Girly (aka Girly); When Dinosaurs Ruled the Earth; The Virgin and the Gypsy.

HASSE, O. E. (Otto Eduard Hasse)

Born: 1903. Died: Sept. 12, 1978, West Berlin, Germany. Screen and stage actor.

Appeared in: **1932** Peter Voss, der Millionendieb; Muss man Sich Gleich Scheiden Lassen?; Kreuzer Emden. **1933** Fraulein Hoffmanns Erzahlungen. **1934** Die Vertauschte Braut; Peer Gynt. **1936** Ein Ganzer Kerl; Die Gefangene des Konigs; Der Schuchterne Casanova; Diener Lassen Bitten; Der Ahnungslose Engel; Die Grosse und die Kleine Welt. **1937** Wo Weit Geht die Liebe Nicht. **1939** Drei Wunderschone Tage. **1941** Illusion; Stukas; Alles für Gloria. **1942** Dr. Crippen an Bord; Die Entlassung; Rembrandt. **1943** Gefahrtin Meines Sommers; Geliebter Schatz; Der Ewige Klang. **1944** Philharmoniker; Aufruhr der Herzen; Der Grosse Preis; Komm zu mir Zuruck. **1948** Berliner Ballade (Ballad of Berlin). **1949** Anonyme Briefe. **1950** Epilog; The Big Lift. **1952** Der Grosse Zapfenstreich; Decision Before Dawn. **1953** Der Letzte Walzer (The Last Waltz—US 1958); Wenn am Sonntagabend die Dorfmusik Spielt; I Confess. **1954** Canaris (aka Deadly Decision—US 1958); Betrayed. **1955** Above Us the Waves (US 1956); 08/15 II; Alibi; 08/15 in der Heimat; The Sergeant's Daughter. **1956** Kitty und die Grosse Welt. **1957** Der Glaserne Turm (The Glass Tower—US 1959). **1958** Der Arzt von Stalingrad; Der Maulkorb; Solange das Her Schlagt (As Long as the Heart Beats); Sait-on-Jamais (One Never Knows, aka No Sun in Venice—US). **1960** Frau Warrens Gewerbe. **1961** Die Ehe des Herrn Mississippi. **1962** Le Caporal Epingle (The Hard Luck Corporal, aka The Elusive Corporal—US 1963); Das Leben Beginnt um Acht; Lulu; Affaire Nabob. **1963** Le Vice et la Vertu (Vice and Virtue—US 1965). **1964** Die Todesstrahlen des Dr. Mabuse. **1973** State of Siege.

HASSELL, GEORGE

Born: May 4, 1881, Birmingham, England. Died: Feb. 17, 1937, Chatsworth, Calif. (heart attack). Screen and stage actor.

Appeared in: **1915** Old Dutch. **1926** La Boheme. **1930** Where There's A Will (short). **1935** Night Life of the Gods; The Flame Within; Becky Sharp; Dressed to Thrill; Captain Blood. **1936** Petticoat Fever; The King Steps Out; Girl's Dormitory; White Hunter. **1937** Woman Wise; Think Fast, Mr. Moto.

HASTINGS, VICTORIA

Died: May 24, 1934, Hollywood, Calif. (heart ailment). Screen actress. Married to actor Trevor Bland-Addinsell.

HASWELL, PERCY

Born: 1871. Died: June 14, 1945, Nantucket, Mass. Screen and stage actress. She appeared as Mrs. George Fawcett and as Percy Haswell. Married to actor George Fawcett (dec. 1939).

Appeared in: **1929** Innocents of Paris; River of Romance.

HATCH, IKE (Isaac Flower Hatch)

Born: 1892, England. Died: Dec. 26, 1961, London, England. Screen and stage actor.

Appeared in: **1937** Jericho (aka Dark Sands—US 1938).

HATCH, RILEY (William Riley Hatch)

Born: Sept. 2, 1865, Cleveland, Ohio. Died: Sept. 6, 1925, Bayshore, N.Y. Screen, stage actor and opera singer.

Appeared in: **1916** Hazel Kirke. **1919** Teeth of the Tiger. **1920** The Inner Voice; Little Miss Rebellion. **1921** Something Different; The Matrimonial Web; The Conquest of Canaan; The Idol of the North; Sheltered Daughters; Nobody; What Women Will Do; You Find It Everywhere. **1922** Missing Millions. **1923** If Winter Comes; You Are Guilty; Zaza; Little Old New York. **1924** America; Trouping with Ellen; West of the Water Tower. **1925** The Street of Forgotten Men; Night Life of New York.

HATHAWAY, JEAN

Born: 1876. Died: Aug. 23, 1938, Los Angeles, Calif. Screen actress.

Appeared in: **1914** The Master Key (serial). **1916** The Purple Mask (serial). **1921** Short Skirts. **1922** Boy Crazy.

HATHAWAY, JIMMIE (Joan Hathaway)

Died: Feb. 6, 1981, Los Angeles, Calif. Screen, stage, vaudeville actress, dialog coach and stage director. Appeared in Thomas Ince and Robert Brunton films.

HATHAWAY, LILIAN

Born: 1876, Liverpool, England. Died: Jan. 12, 1954, Englewood Cliffs, N.J. Stage and screen actress.

HATHAWAY, RHODY

Born: 1869. Died: Feb. 18, 1944, Hollywood, Calif. Screen actor.

Appeared in: **1908** American Film Co. films. **1924** Not a Drum Was Heard. **1925** A Daughter of the Sioux. **1926** Bigger Than Barnum's; The Phantom of the Forest. **1928** Into the Night; The Old Code.

HATTON, BRADFORD

Born: 1906. Died: Aug. 11, 1969, Denver, Colo. Screen and stage actor.

Appeared in: **1932** Smiling Faces. **1952** Walk East on Beacon. **1954** Top Banana.

HATTON, FRANCES

Born: 1888. Died: Oct. 16, 1971, Palmdale, Calif. Screen and stage actress. Married to actor Raymond Hatton (dec. Oct., 1971).

Appeared in: **1921** The Mother Heart; Straight from the Shoulder; The Rowdy. **1922** At the Sign of the Jack O'Lantern. **1923** Java Head; The Grail; The Day of Faith. **1925** Confessions of a Queen.

HATTON, RAYMOND (Raymond William Hatton)

Born: July 7, 1892, Red Oak, Iowa. Died: Oct. 21, 1971, Palmdale, Calif. (heart attack). Screen, stage and television actor. Entered films with Kalem in 1911. Married to actress Frances Hatton (dec. Oct., 1971).

Appeared in: **1914** The Making of Bobby Burnit; The Circus Man. **1915** The Woman; The Unknown; The Immigrant; The Arab; Chimmis Fadden Out West; The Girl of the Golden West; The Unafraid; Chimmis Fadden; The Wild Goose Chase; Kindling; The Golden Chance; Temptation. **1916** Oliver Twist; The Sowers. **1917** Woman God Forgot; Joan the Woman; The Little American; The American Consul; What Money Can't Buy; Nan of Music Mountain. **1918** Arizona; The Whispering Chorus; We Can't Have Everything; Sandy; The Source. **1919** The Poor Boob; For Better for Worse; Secret Service; You're Fired; The Love Burglar; Male and Female; Everywoman. **1920** The Dancin' Fool; Jes' Call Me Jim. **1921** The Ace of Hearts; The Affairs of Anatol; Bunty Pulls the Strings; The Concert; Peck's Bad Boy; Salvage; All's Fair in Love; Pilgrims of the Night; Doubling for Romeo. **1922** Ebb Tide; Head Over Heels; Pink Gods; To Have and to Hold; Manslaughter; The Hottentot; His Back Against the Wall; At Bay. **1923** The Barefoot Boy; Java Head; The Virginian; Trimmed in Scarlet; The Tie That Binds; Three Wise Fools; A Man of Action; Big Brother; Enemies of Children; The Hunchback of Notre Dame. **1924** True As Steel; Triumph; The Mine with the Iron Door; Cornered; The Fighting American; Half-a-Dollar Bill. **1925** Adventure; Contraband; In the Name of Love; The Devil's Cargo; A Son of His Father; The Thundering Herd; The Top of the World; Tomorrow's Love; Lord Jim. **1926** Behind the Front; Born to the West; Silence; Forlorn River; We're in the Navy Now. **1927** Fashions for Women; Fireman Save My Child; Now We're in the Air. **1928** The Big Killing; Wife Savers; Partners in Crime. **1929** The Office Scandal; Trent's Last Case; When Caesar Ran a Newspaper (short); Dear Vivien; Christie talking plays; Hell's Heroes; Christie shorts. **1930** The Silver Horde; Rogue of the Rio Grande; Murder on the Roof; Her Unborn Child; Midnight Mystery; The Road to Paradise; Pineapples; The Mighty. **1931** The Squaw Man; Honeymoon Lane; The Lion and the Lamb; Arrowsmith; The Challenge; Woman Hungry. **1932** Law and Order; Polly of the Circus; The Fourth Horseman; Uptown New York; Exposed; The Crooked Circle; Vanity Street; Malay Nights; Stranger in Town; Drifting Souls; Vanishing Frontier; Alias Mary Smith; Long Loop Laramie; Divorce a la Mode (short). **1933** The Three Musketeers (serial); State Trooper; Under the Tonto Rim; Alice in Wonderland; Lady Killer; Penthouse; Day of Reckoning; Tom's in Town; Terror Trail; Cornered; Hidden Gold; The Big Cage. **1934** The Defense Rests; Women in His Life; Lazy River; Once to Every Bachelor; Fifteen Wives; The Thundering Herd; Straight Is the Way; Wagon Wheels. **1935** Times Square Lady; Desert Death (short); Murder in the Fleet; Calm Yourself; Rustlers of Red Dog (serial); Nevada; Wanderer of the Wasteland; Red Morning; G-Men; The Daring Young Man; Steamboat 'Round the Bend; Stormy. **1936** Undersea Kingdom (serial); Exclusive Story; Women Are Trouble; Mad Holiday; Laughing Irish Eyes; Desert Gold; Timothy's Quest; The Vigilantes Are Coming (serial); The Arizona Raiders; Yellowstone; Jungle Jim (serial). **1937** Marked

Woman; Fly-Away Baby; The Adventurous Blonde; Love Is on the Air; The Missing Witness; Roaring Timber; Public Wedding; Over the Goal. **1938** He Couldn't Say No; Come Rangers; Love Finds Andy Hardy; The Texans; Touchdown Army; Tom Sawyer, Detective; Over the Wall. **1939** I'm from Missouri; Ambush; Undercover Doctor; Rough Riders' Roundup; Frontier Pony Express; Paris Honeymoon; New Frontier; Wyoming Outlaw; Wall Street Cowboy; The Kansas Terrors; The Cowboys from Texas; Six Thousand Enemies; Career. **1940** Heroes of the Saddle; Pioneers of the West; Covered Wagon Days; Rocky Mountain Rangers; Oklahoma Renegades; Queen of the Mob; Kit Carson. **1941** White Eagle (serial); Arizona Bound; Gunman from Bodie; Forbidden Trails. **1942** Ghost Town Law; Cadets on Parade; Girl from Alaska; Down Texas Way; Riders of the West; Dawn on the Great Divide; Below the Border; West of the Law. **1943** The Texas Kid; Outlaws of Stampede Pass; Six-Gun Gospel; Stranger from Pecos; The Ghost Rider. **1944** Raiders of the Border; Rough Riders; Partners of the Trail; West of the Rio Grande; Land of the Outlaws; Tall in the Saddle; Ranger Law; Ghost Guns; The Law Men. **1945** Law of the Valley; Flame of the West; Sunbonnet Sue; Frontier Feud; Gun Smoke; The Lost Trail; Northwest Trail; Rhythm Roundup; Stranger from Santa Fe. **1946** Fool's Gold; Drifting Along; Under Arizona Skies; The Haunted Mine; Border Bandits; Shadows on the Range; Raiders of the South; The Gentleman from Texas; Silver Range; Trigger Fingers. **1947** Trailing Danger; Land of the Lawless; Rolling Home; Valley of Fear; Black Gold; The Law Comes to Gunsight; Code of the Saddle; Prairie Express; Gun Talk; Unconquered. **1948** Crossed Trails; Triggerman; Overland Trails; Frontier Agent; Back Trail. **1949** Sheriff of Medicine Bow; Gunning for Trouble; Hidden Danger; The Fighting Ranger. **1950** Operation Haylift; County Fair; West of the Brazos; Marshal of Heldorado; Crooked River; Colorado Ranger; Fast on the Draw; Hostile Country. **1951** Skipalong Rosenbloom; Kentucky Jubilee. **1952** The Golden Hawk. **1953** Cow Country. **1954** Thunder Pass. **1955** The Twinkle in God's Eye; Treasure of Ruby Hills. **1956** Dig That Uranium; Shake, Rattle and Rock; Flesh and the Spur; Girls in Prison. **1957** Pawnee; Invasion of the Saucer Men; Motorcycle Gang. **1959** Alaska Passage. **1964** The Quick Gun. **1965** Requiem for a Gunfighter. **1967** In Cold Blood.

HATTON, RICHARD "DICK"
Born: 1891. Died: July 9, 1931, Los Angeles, Calif. (traffic accident). Screen actor and film director.

Appeared in: **1922** Four Hearts; Fearless Dick; Hellhounds of the West. **1923** In the West; The Seventh Sheriff; Unblazed Trail; Blood Test; The Golden Flame; Playing Double; Ridin' Thru. **1924** Come on, Cowboys; Western Fate; The Whirlwind Ranger; Rip Snorter; Horse Sense; Sagebrush Gospel; Trouble Trail; Two-Fisted Justice. **1925** Sell 'Em Cowboy; "Scar" Hanan; The Cactus Cure; My Pal; Range Justice; Ridin' Easy; The Secret of Black Canyon; Warrior Gap; A Western Engagement; Where Romance Rides. **1926** He-Man's Country; In Broncho Land; Roaring Bill Atwood; Temporary Sheriff. **1927** The Action Graver; Saddle Jumpers; Speeding Hoofs; Western Courage. **1928** The Boss of Rustler's Roost. **1930** Romance of the Week. **1931** The Vanishing Legion (serial).

HATTON, RONDO
Born: Apr. 29, 1894, Hagerstown, Md. Died: Feb. 2, 1946, Beverly Hills, Calif. (heart attack). Screen actor.

Appeared in: **1930** Hell Harbor. **1938** In Old Chicago; Alexander's Ragtime Band. **1939** The Hunchback of Notre Dame; Captain's Fury. **1940** Chad Hanna; Moon Over Burma; The Big Guy. **1942** The Cyclone Kid; The Moon and Sixpence. **1943** The Sleepy Lagoon; The Ox-Bow Incident. **1944** The Pearl of Death; Raiders of Ghost City (serial); The Princess and the Pirate; Johnny Doesn't Live Here Anymore. **1945** The Royal Mounted Rides Again (serial); Jungle Captive. **1946** Spider Woman Strikes Back; House of Horrors (aka Joan Medford Is Missing); The Brute Man.

HAUBENSTOCK, HARALD *See* MEYEN, HARRY

HAUBER, WYNDHAM
Died: July 17, 1929, near Los Angeles, Calif. (plane crash). Stuntman and screen actor.

HAUGHT, AL (Albert B. Haught)
Born: Apr. 30, 1899, Dallas, Tex. Died: Oct. 29, 1936, Hollywood, Calif. Screen actor. Appeared in westerns.

HAUPT, ULLRICH
Born: Aug. 8, 1887, Prussia. Died: Aug. 5, 1931, near Santa Maria, Calif. (hunting accident). Screen, stage actor, stage director, stage producer and screenwriter. Entered films with Essanay Studios in Chicago.

Appeared in: **1917** The Fable of Prince Fortunatus, Who Moved Away from Easy Street and Silas, the Saver, Who Moved In; The Killjoy. **1928** Captain Swagger; The Tempest. **1929** Wonder of Women; The Far Call; Frozen Justice; The Iron Mask; Madame X; The Greene Murder Case. **1930** A Royal Romance; The Bad One; DuBarry, Woman of Passion; Morocco; The Rogue Song. **1931** The Man Who Came Back; The Unholy Garden.

HAVEL, JOE
Born: 1869. Died: Jan. 27, 1932, Los Angeles, Calif. Screen and vaudeville actor. Entered films in 1920.

HAVEN, CHARNA (Charna E. Kichaven)
Born: 1925. Died: Feb. 16, 1971, Hollywood, Calif. Screen actress, cellist and pianist. Entered films in 1941.

Appeared in: **1944** Song of the Open Road; Minstrel Man.

HAVER, PHYLLIS
Born: Jan 16, 1899, Douglas, Kans. Died: Nov. 19, 1960, Falls Village, Conn. (suicide). Screen actress. Was a Mack Sennett bathing beauty and appeared in many Keystone comedies.

Appeared in: **1917** The Sultan's Wife; A Bedroom Blunder; The Pullman Bride; That Night. **1918** Ladies First; His Wife's Friend; Whose Little Wife Are You?; The Village Chestnut. **1919** Never Too Old; The Foolish Age; When Love is Blind; Hearts and Flowers; Trying to Get Along; Among Those Present; Yankee Doodle in Berlin; Why Beaches are Popular; A Lady's Tailor; Up in Alf's Place; Salome vs. Shenandoah; His Last False Step; The Speakeasy. **1920** Ten Dollars or Ten Days (short); Married Life; Love, Honor and Behave. **1921** A Small Town Idol; Home Talent; plus the following shorts: On a Summer's Day; An Unhappy Finish; She Sighed by the Seaside. **1922** The following shorts: Bright Eyes; Step Forward; Home-Made Movies. **1923** The Temple of Venus; The Bolted Door; The Christian; The Common Law. **1924** The Hollywood Kid (short); The Perfect Flapper; The Breath of Scandal; The Fighting Coward; The Foolish Virgin; Lilies of the Field; The Midnight Express; One Glorious Night; Singer Jim McKee; Single Wives; The Snob. **1925** So Big; After Business Hours; A Fight to the Finish; The Golden Princess; Her Husband's Secret; I Want My Man; New Brooms; Rugged Water. **1926** What Price Glory; Up in Mabel's Room; The Nervous Wreck; The Caveman; Don Juan; Fig Leaves; Hard Boiled; Other Women's Husbands; Three Bad Men. **1927** The Way of All Flesh; No Control; The Little Adventuress; The Rejuvenation of Aunt Mary; The Wise Wife; The Fighting Eagle; Your Wife and Mine; Nobody's Widow. **1928** Chicago; Tenth Avenue; The Battle of the Sexes. **1929** Sal of Singapore; The Shady Lady; The Office Scandal; Thunder; Hell's Kitchen. **1963** 30 Years of Fun (documentary).

HAVEZ, JEAN C.
Born: 1870, Baltimore, Md. Died: Feb. 11, 1925, Beverly Hills, Calif. (heart attack). Screen actress, screenwriter and songwriter. Divorced from vaudeville and stage actor Cecil Cunningham (dec.).

Appeared in: **1925** Seven Chances.

HAVIER, JOSE ALEX
Born: 1909. Died: Dec. 18, 1945, Hollywood, Calif. (suicide—gun). Screen actor.

Appeared in: **1943** China; Bataan. **1944** Dragon Seed; Rainbow Island; Two-Man Submarine. **1945** Back to Bataan; They Were Expendable.

HAVILAND, RENA
Born: 1878. Died: Feb. 20, 1954, Woodland Hills, Calif. Screen, stage and vaudeville actress. Entered films in 1911.

HAWKE, ROHN OLIN
Born: 1924. Died: Feb. 15, 1967, Albuquerque, N.Mex. (suicide—gun). Screen actor, disc jocky and writer. Appeared in films during late 1940s.

HAWKINS, COLEMAN "BEAN"
Born: Nov. 21, 1904, St. Joseph, Mo. Died: May 19, 1969, New York, N.Y. (liver ailment). Jazz musician and screen actor.

Appeared in: **1945** The Crimson Canary.

HAWKINS, ETTA
Died: July 13, 1945, Beverly Hills, Calif. Screen and stage actress. Mother of Chester Morris (dec. 1970).

HAWKINS, JACK
Born: Sept. 14, 1910, London, England. Died: July 18, 1973, London, England (cancer). Screen, stage, television actor, screenwriter and film producer. Married to actress Doreen Lawrence and divorced from actress Jessica Tandy.

Appeared in: **1930** Birds of Prey (aka The Perfect Alibi—US 1931). **1932** The Lodger (aka The Phantom Fiend—US 1935). **1933** The Good Companions; The Lost Chord; I Lived With You; The Jewel; A Shot in the Dark (US 1935). **1934** Autumn Crocus; Death at Broadcasting House. **1935** Peg of Old Drury (US 1936). **1937** The Frog (US 1939); Beauty and the Barge. **1938** Who Goes Next?; A Royal Divorce (US 1939). **1939** Beau Geste; Murder Will Out. **1940** The Flying Squad. **1942** Next of Kin (US 1943). **1948** Bonnie Prince Charlie (US 1952); The Fallen Idol (US 1949). **1949** Caught; The Small Back Room (US 1952). **1950** The Elusive Pimpernel; The Black Rose; State Secret (aka The Great Manhunt—US 1951). **1951** No Highway (aka No Highway in the Sky—US); The Adventurers (aka The Great Adventure—US). **1952** Home at Seven (aka Murder on Monday—US 1953); Mandy (aka Crash of Silence—US 1953); The Planter's Wife (aka Outpost in Malaya—US); Angels One Five (US 1954). **1953** The Cruel Sea; Twice Upon a Time; Malta Story (US 1954); The Intruder (US 1955). **1954** The Fighting Pimpernel; The Seekers (aka Land of Fury—US 1955); Front Page Story (US 1955). **1955** Land of the Pharaohs; The Prisoner; Touch and Go (aka The Light Touch—US 1956). **1956** The Long Arm (aka The Third Key—US 1957). **1957** The Man in the Sky (aka Decision Against Time—US); The Bridge on the River Kwai; Fortune Is a Woman (aka She Played With Fire—US 1958); The Battle for Britain (short). **1958** The Two-Headed Spy (US 1959); Gideon's Day (aka Gideon of Scotland Yard—US 1959). **1959** Ben Hur. **1960** The League of Gentlemen (US 1961). **1961** Two Loves. **1962** Five Finger Exercise; Lawrence of Arabia. **1963** Lafayette; Rampage; Zulu (US 1964). **1964** The Third Secret; Guns at Batasi; Masquerade (US 1965). **1965** Lord Jim. **1966** Judith; The Poppy Is Also a Flower (aka Danger Grows Wild). **1967** The Great Catherine (US 1968). **1968** Shalako. **1969** Monte Carlo or Bust; Oh, What a Lovely War!; Twinky (aka Lola—US); Those Daring Young Men in Their Jaunty Jalopies. **1970** Jane Eyre; The Adventures of Gerard. **1971** Waterloo; Kidnapped; Nicholas and Alexandra; Beloved (aka Sin); The Last Lion. **1972** Young Winston; Escape to the Sun. **1973** Theatre of Blood; Tales That Witness Madness.

HAWKINS, "PUNY"
Died: Mar. 30, 1947, Wichita, Kans. (heart attack). Screen, stage and radio actor. Appeared in silent films.

HAWKS, CHARLES MONROE
Born: 1874. Died: Dec. 15, 1951, Los Angeles, Calif. Screen actor. Appeared in silents.

HAWLEY, ALLEN BURTON
Born: 1895. Died: Sept., 1925, Troy, N.Y. Screen actor. Entered films approx. 1915. Divorced from screen actress Wanda Hawley.

HAWLEY, DUDLEY
Born: 1879, England. Died: Mar. 29, 1941, New York, N.Y. (coronary thrombosis). Screen and stage actor.

Appeared in: **1917** An American Widow. **1930** Young Man of Manhattan.

HAWLEY, ORMI
Born: 1890. Died: June 3, 1942, Rome, N.Y. Screen actor.

Appeared in: **1912** The Price of a Silver Fox; The Social Secretary; The Reformation of Kid Hogan; A New Beginning; Honor and the Sword; The Puppet's Hour; Fire and Straw; The Choir at Densmere; Together; The Crooked Path; Satin and Gingham; The Good-for-Nothing; 'Twixt Love and Ambition; The Players; His Life; When Love Leads; The Shepherd's Flute; The Montebank's Daughter. **1913** A Mircle of Love; A Mother's Strategy; Literature and Love; The House in the Woods; Her Only Son; The Soul of a Rose; Dolores' Decision; Women of the Desert; Tamandra, the Gypsy; A Moonshiner's Wife; The Call of the Heart; Into the Light; Fashion's Toy. **1914** The Two Roses; Through Fire to Fortune; Codes of Honor; The Price; Strength of Family Ties; The Ragged Earl; His Brother's Blood; A Love of '64. **1915** The Insurrection; The Path of the Rainbow; Destiny's Skein; The Intriguers; The Friendship of Lamond; The Shanghaied Baby; The Rainy Day; The Thief in the Night; Such Things Really Happen; Just Retribution; The Phantom Happiness; The Telegrapher's Peril; The Last Rebel; The Man of God; The Second Shot; A Heart Awakened. **1916** The Last Shot; Temptation; The Social Highwayman; The Weakness of Strength. **1917** The Antics of Anne; Runaway Romany. **1918** The Splendid Romance; Mrs. Dane's Defense. **1919** The Road Called Straight; The Unwritten Code.

HAWLEY, WANDA (aka WANDA PETIT)
Born: July 30, 1895, Scranton, Pa. Died: Mar. 18, 1963, Los Angeles, Calif. Screen and stage actress.

Appeared in: **1917** The Derelict; This is the Life. **1918** Cupid's Roundup; Old Wives for New; We Can't Have Everything. **1919** You're Fired; Secret Service; For Better, For Worse; The Lottery Man; Every Woman; The Way of a Man With a Maid; Greased Lightning. **1920** Double Speed; The Tree of Knowledge; The Six Best Cellars; Mrs. Temple's Telegram; Held by the Enemy; Food for Scandal; Miss Hobbs. **1921** Her Sturdy Oak; Her Face Value; The Love Charm; The Snob; Her First Elopement; Her Beloved Villain; The Affairs of Anatol; The House That Jazz Built; A Kiss in Time; The Outside Woman. **1922** Too Much Wife; Bobbed Hair; The Truthful Liar; The Woman Who Walked Alone; Burning Sands; The Young Rajah; Thirty Days. **1923** Nobody's Money; Brass Commandments; The Man From Brodney's; Mary of the Movies; Masters of Men. **1924** Bread; Barriers Burned Away; Smouldering Fires; The Desert Sheik; The Man Who Played Square; Reckless Romance. **1925** Stop Flirting; Let Women Alone; The Unnamed Woman; Flying Fool; American Pluck; Graustark; Who Cares. **1926** The Combat; A Desperate Moment; Hearts and Spangles; The Last Alarm; Men of the Night; The Midnight Message; Midnight Limited; The Smoke-Eaters; Whom Shall I Marry. **1927** Eyes of the Totem; Pirates of the Sky. **1931** Trails of the Golden West; Pueblo Terror.

HAWLEY, WILLIAM E.
Born: 1910, Chicago, Ill. Died: Aug. 22, 1976, Long Beach, N.Y. (cardiac failure). Screen, stage and television actor.

Appeared in: **1947** Escape Me Never. **1972** The Possession of Joel Delaney.

HAWN, JOHN "HAPPY JACK"
Born: 1883. Died: Feb. 12, 1964, Fresno, Calif. Screen actor and stuntman.

HAWTHORNE, DAVID
Born: 1888, Kettering, England. Died: June 18, 1942. England? Screen and stage actor.

Appeared in: **1920** Testimony. **1921** The Autumn of Pride; Glass and No Class; The Fortune of Christina M'Nab (US 1923); In His Grip; Roses in the Dust; The Sword of Fate. **1922** A Soul's Awakening; Silent Evidence; Rob Roy; A Prince of Lovers (aka Life of Lord Byron); Open Country. **1923** The Last Adventures of Sherlock Holmes series including: The Disappearance of Lady Frances Carfax. **1924** The Great Prince Shan; The Mating of Marcus; The Conspirators; Thrilling Stories from the Strand Magazine series including: Fighting Snub Reilly. **1925** The Presumption of Stanley Hayes, M.P. **1928** His House in Order. **1930** The Barnes Murder Case (reissue of The Conspirators—1927); Bed and Breakfast; Birds of Prey (aka The Perfect Alibi—US 1931). **1931** The Woman Between (aka The Woman Decides—US 1932); Creeping Shadows (aka The Limping Man—US 1932); The Other Woman; Glamour. **1932** Mr. Bill the Conqueror (aka The Man Who Won—US 1933). **1936** Laburnum Grove (US 1941).

HAWTREY, ANTHONY
Born: Jan. 22, 1909, Claygate, Surrey, England. Died: Oct. 18, 1954, London, England (heart attack). Stage and screen actor. Son of actor Sir Charles Hawtrey (dec. 1923).

Appeared in: **1943** Warn That Man; Headline. **1945** The World Owes Me a Living; The Hundred Pound Window; Latin Quarter. **1948** The First Gentleman (aka Affairs of a Rogue—US 1949).

HAWTREY, SIR CHARLES
Born: 1858, England. Died: July 30, 1923, London, England. Screen, stage actor and stage producer. Married to stage actress Lady Hawtrey (The Honorable Miss Elsie Petie—dec. 1930). Father of actor Anthony Hawtrey (dec. 1954). Do not confuse with British actor Charles Hawtrey born in 1914.

Appeared in: **1913** A Message from Mars. **1915** A Honeymoon for Three. **1917** Masks and Faces.

HAY, MARY
Born: Aug. 22, 1901, Fort Bliss, Tex. Died: June 4, 1957, Inverness, Calif. Stage and screen actress. Former Ziegfeld Follies star. Divorced from actor Richard Barthelmess (dec. 1963).

Appeared in: **1920** Way Down East. **1925** New Toys.

HAY, RON See HAYDOCK, RONALD "RON"

HAY, WILLIAM "WILL"
Born: 1888, Stockton-on-Tees, England. Died: Apr. 18, 1949, London, England. Screen, stage, vaudeville, radio actor, screenwriter, screen director and author. Father of actor Will Hay, Jr.

Appeared in: **1933** Know Your Apples (short). **1934** Those Were the Days; Radio Parade of 1935 (US 1935). **1935** Dandy Dick; Boys Will Be Boys. **1936** Windbag the Sailor; Where There's a Will. **1937** Good Morning, Boys (aka Where There's a Will—US); Oh, Mr. Porter! **1938** Convict 99; Hey! Hey! USA; Old Bones of the River. **1939** Ask a Policeman; Where's That Fire? **1941** The Ghost of St. Michael's; The Black Sheep of Whitehall. **1942** The Big Blockade; The Goose Steps Out; Go to Blazes! (short). **1943** My Learned Friend.

HAYAKAWA, SESSUE (Kintaro Hayakawa)
Born: June 10, 1889, Chiba, Japan. Died: Nov. 23, 1973, Tokyo, Japan (cerebral thrombosis complicated by pneumonia). Screen, stage actor, film producer and author. Married to actress Tsuru Aoki (dec. 1961). Father of actress Yoskiko and dancer Fujiko Hayakawa. Nominated for 1957 Academy Award for Best Supporting Actor in Bridge on the River Kwai.

Appeared in: **1914** The Typhoon (film debut); The Last of the Line (aka Pride of Race); The Wrath of the Gods (aka The Destruction of Sakura Jima); The Ambassador's Envoy; The Vigil. **1915** The Secret Sin; After Five; The Clue; The Cheat. **1916** Naked Hearts; Alien Souls; Temptation; The Honorable Friend; The Soul of Kura-San. **1917** The Jaguar's Claw; Forbidden Paths; Each to His Kind; The Debt; The Victoria Cross (aka Honour Redeemed); The Bottle Imp; Hashimura Togo; The Call of the East; The Secret Game. **1918** The Temple of Dusk; Hidden Pearls; The Honor of His House; The City of Dim Faces; The White Man's Law; The Bravest Way; His Birth Right. **1919** The Illustrious Prince; The Tong Man; The Dragon Painter; Bonds of Honor; Heart in Pawn; Courageous Coward; Gray Horizon (aka A Dead Line); Man Beneath; The Rajah's Amulet (reissue of Each to His Kind—1917); His Debt (aka The Debt). **1920** The Beggar Prince; The Brand of Lopez; The Devil's Claim; Liting Lang; An Arabian Knight. **1921** Black Roses; The First Born; The Swamp; Where Lights Are Low. **1922** Five Days to Live; The Vermillion Pencil. **1923** La Bataille (aka The Danger Line—US 1924). **1924** The Great Prince Shan; J'ai Tue!; Sen Yan's Devotion. **1929** Sessue Hayakawa in The Man Who Laughed Last (short). **1931** Daughter of the Dragon. **1933** Tohjin Okichi. **1937** Die Tochter Des Samurai (aka La Fille du Samourai); Yoshiwara; Fofaiture. **1938** Tempete sur L'Asie. **1939** Macao; L'Enfer du Jeu (Gambling Hall). **1941** Patrouille Blanche. **1943** Die Liebe of Mitzer (reissue of 1937 Die Tochter Des Samurai). **1946** Le Cabaret du Grand. **1947** Quartier Chinois. **1949** Tokyo Joe. **1950** Three Came Home; Les Miserables. **1953** Higego No Shogun Yamashita Yasubumi (The Tragic General, Yamashita Yasubumi). **1955** House of Bamboo. **1957** The Bridge on the River Kwai. **1958** The Geisha Boy. **1959** Green Mansions. **1960** Hell to Eternity; The Swiss Family Robinson. **1962** The Big Wave. **1966** The Daydreamer.

HAYDEL, RICHARD (aka RICKY JORDAN)
Born: May 31, 1927, Helena, Ark. Died: Sept., 1949, St. Louis, Mo. Screen actor.

Appeared in: **1944** Henry Aldrich, Boy Scout.

HAYDEN, HARRY
Born: 1882. Died: July 24, 1955, Los Angeles, Calif. Screen, stage and television actor. Married to actress Lela Bliss (dec. 1980).

Appeared in: **1936** I Married a Doctor; Fool Proof (short); Two Against the World; Public Enemy's Wife; The Case of the Black Cat; God's Country and the Woman; The Man I Marry; Killer at Large; College Holiday; Fury; The Princess Comes Across. **1937** The Black Legion; Melody for Two; John Meade's Woman; Ever Since Eve; Love is on the Air. **1938** Angels With Dirty Faces; Little Tough Guy; Double Danger; Saleslady; Four Men and a Prayer; I'll Give a Million; Hold That Co-ed; Kentucky. **1939** The House of Fear; Society Smugglers; Mr. Smith Goes to Washington; Wife, Husband and Friend; Rose of Washington Square; Frontier Marshal; The Rains Came; Here I Am a Stranger; The Honeymoon's Over; Barricade; Swanee River; Hidden Power; Flight at Midnight; At the Circus. **1940** The Cisco Kid and the Lady; He Married His Wife; Lillian Russell; Yesterday's Heroes; You're Not So Tough; Christmas in July; Saps at Sea. **1941** The Last of the Duanes; Weekend in Havana; Footsteps in the Dark; High Sierra; Sleepers West; Hold That Ghost; A Man Betrayed; The Parson of Panamint; The Night of January 16th; Remember the Day. **1942** You're Telling Me; Sullivan's Travels; Rings on Her Fingers; Whispering Ghost; Mississippi Gambler; Tales of Manhattan; Yankee Doodle Dandy; The Palm Beach Story; War Against Mrs. Hadley; Joan of Ozark; Springtime in the Rockies; Get Hep to Love. **1943** You're a Lucky Fellow, Mr. Smith; Henry Aldrich Gets Glamour;

Hello, Frisco, Hello; Meanest Man in the World; Submarine Alert. **1944** Since You Went Away; Henry Aldrich Plays Cupid; Barbary Coast Gent; Hail the Conquering Hero; The Big Noise; Weird Woman; Up in Mabel's Room; The Great Moment. **1945** A Medal for Benny; Colonel Effingham's Raid; Boston Blackie's Rendezvous; Where Do We Go from Here?; Guest Wife. **1946** Without Reservations; The Hoodlum Saint; California; The Bride Wore Boots; Til the End of Time; The Blue Dahlia; Maid Trouble (short); The Virginian; If I'm Lucky; Two Sisters from Boston; The Killers; Til the Clouds Roll By. **1947** Perils of Pauline; Variety Girl; Easy Come, Easy Go; The Strange Love of Martha Ivers; Out of the Past; The Unfinished Dance; Key Witness; My Brother Talks to Horses; Merton of the Movies. **1948** Family Honeymoon; The Velvet Touch; Silver River; Docks of New Orleans; Every Girl Should Be Married; Good Sam. **1949** The Judge Steps Out; Beautiful Blonde from Bashful Bend; Bad Men of Tombstone; Deadly Is the Female; Joe Palooka in the Big Fight; Mr. Whitney Had a Notion; The Lone Wolf and His Lady; Prison Warden; Abbott and Costello Meet the Killer, Boris Karloff. **1950** Intruder in the Dust; Traveling Saleswoman; Union Station. **1951** Double Dynamite; Pier 23; Street Bandits; Deal Me In (short); Angels in the Outfield. **1952** Army Bound; Carrie; O'Henry's Full House; When in Rome. **1953** The Last Posse; Money From Home.

HAYDEN, J. CHARLES
Born: 1876, Frederick, Md. Died: Oct., 1943, Baltimore, Md. Screen, stage actor and film director.

HAYDEN, LELA
Born: 1896. Died: May 15, 1980, Woodland Hills, Calif. Screen and television actress. Mother of actor Donald Hayden.

HAYDEN, MARGARET See RORKE, MARGARET

HAYDEN, RUSSELL "LUCKY" (Pate Lucid)
Born: June 12, 1912, Chico, Calif. Died: June 10, 1981, Palm Springs, Calif. (pneumonia). Screen and television actor. Married to actress Lillian (Mousy) Porter.

Appeared in: **1937** The Hills of Old Wyoming (film debut); North of the Rio Grande; Rustler's Valley; Hopalong Rides Again; Texas Trail; Partners of the Plains. **1938** Heart of Arizona; Bar 20 Justice; Pride of the West; In Old Mexico; Sunset Trail; The Frontiersman; Cassidy of Bar 20; Mysterious Riders. **1939** Heritage of the Desert; Ranger War; Law of the Pampas; Silver on the Sage; The Renegade Trail. **1940** Santa Fe Marshall; The Showdown; Three Men From Texas; Hidden Gold; Stagecoach War; The Light of Western Stars; Knights of the Range. **1941** Two in a Taxi; Doomed Caravan; Pirates on Horseback; Wide Open Town; In Old Colorado; Border Vigilantes. **1942** Overland to Deadwood; West of Tombstone; Lawless Plainsmen; Down Rio Grande Way; Riders of the Northland; Bad Men of the Hills. **1943** Silver City Raider; Minesweeper. **1944** Gambler's Choice; The Vigilantes Ride; The Last Horseman; Wyoming Hurricane; Marshal of Gunsmoke. **1946** Lost City of the Jungle (serial). **1947** Seven Were Saved. **1948** Albuquerque; Sons of Adventure; 'Neath Canadian Skies. **1949** Apache Chief; Deputy Marshal. **1950** Fast on the Draw; Hostile Country; West of the Brazos; Marshal of Heldorado; Colorado Ranger; Crooked River; Fast on the Draw. **1951** Texans Never Cry; Valley of Fire.

HAYDOCK, JOHN
Died: Jan. 19, 1918, New York, N.Y. Screen actor.

HAYDOCK, RONALD "RON" (aka VIN SAXON aka LONNIE LORD aka RON HAY)
Born: 1940. Died: Aug. 14, 1977, near Monterey, Calif. (auto accident). Screen actor and screenwriter.

Appeared in: **1966** Rat Pfink and the Boo Boo. **1975** Mackintosh and T. J.

HAYE, HELEN
Born: Aug. 28, 1874, Assam, India. Died: Sept. 1, 1957, London, England. Screen and stage actress.

Appeared in: **1916** Honour in Pawn. **1917** Masks and Faces. **1918** Not Negotiable. **1919** His Last Defense. **1920** Bleak House; The Skin Game. **1921** Tilly of Bloomsbury. **1929** Atlantic. **1930** Knowing Men; Beyond the Cities; The Brat (aka The Nipper); The Officer's Mess. **1931** The Skin Game (and 1920 version); Brown Sugar; Der Kongress Tanzt (Congress Dance—US 1932). **1932** Monte Carlo Madness; Her First Affair. **1933** It's a Boy! (US 1934); This Week of Grace. **1934** Crazy People; Money Mad. **1935** The Love Affair of the Dictator (aka The Dictator and The Loves of a Dictator—US); Drake of England (aka Drake the Pirate—US); The 39 Steps. **1936** The Interrupted Honeymoon; Everybody Dance; Wolf's Clothing. **1937** Wings of the Morning; The Girl in the Taxi; Remember When; Cotton Queen. **1938**

St. Martin's Lane (aka Sidewalks of London—US 1940). **1939** The Spy in Black (aka U-Boat 29—US); A Girl Must Live (US 1941). **1940** The Case of the Frightened Lady (aka The Frightened Lady—US 1941). **1941** Kipps (aka The Remarkable Mr. Kipps—US 1942). **1943** The Man in Grey; Dear Octopus (aka The Randolph Family—US 1945). **1944** Fanny by Gaslight (aka Man of Evil—US 1948). **1945** A Place of One's Own (US 1949). **1947** Mine Own Executioner; Mrs. Fitzherbert (US 1950). **1948** Anna Karenina. **1949** Third Time Lucky (US 1950); Conspirator (US 1950). **1954** Front Page Story (US 1955); Hobson's Choice; Lilacs in the Spring (aka Let's Make Up—US). **1955** Richard III (US 1956). **1956** My Teenage Daughter (aka Teenage Bad Girl—US 1957). **1957** Action of the Tiger. **1958** The Gypsy and the Gentleman.

HAYES, ALLISON (Mary Jane Hayes)
Born: Mar. 6, 1930, Charleston, West Virginia. Died: Feb. 27, 1977, La Jolla, Calif. (blood poisoning). Screen and television actress.

Appeared in: **1954** Francis Joins the WACs; Sign of the Pagan; So This is Paris. **1955** The Purple Mask; Chicago Syndicate; Double Jeopardy; Count Three and Pray. **1956** Mohawk; The Gunslinger; The Steel Jungle. **1957** The Zombies of Mora Tau; Chicago Confidential; The Unearthly; The Disembodied; The Undead. **1958** Attack of the Fifty Foot Woman; Wolf Dog; Hong Kong Confidential. **1959** Counterplot; Pier 5—Havana. **1960** The Hypnotic Eye; The High Powered Rifle; Lust to Kill. **1963** The Crawling Hand; Who's Been Sleeping in My Bed? **1965** Tickle Me.

HAYES, CARRIE
Born: 1878. Died: Dec. 22, 1954, Philadelphia, Pa. Screen and stage actress. Appeared in silent films.

HAYES, CATHERINE
Born: 1886. Died: Jan. 4, 1941, Los Angeles, Calif. Screen, stage and vaudeville actress.

Appeared in: **1933** Zoo in Budapest; Warrior's Husband.

HAYES, EDGAR
Born: 1902. Died: June 28, 1979, San Bernardino, Calif. Screen actor, pianist and bandleader.

Appeared in: **1946** Wife Wanted.

HAYES, FRANK
Born: 1875. Died: Dec. 28, 1923, Hollywood, Calif. (pneumonia). Screen, stage and vaudeville actor.

Appeared in: **1915** Colored Villainy; Mabel, Fatty and the Law (reissue of Fatty's Spooning Day); Stolen Magic. **1916** Fatty and Mabel Adrift; Fido's Fate; A Bath House Blunder; Her Marble Heart; Madcap Ambrose. **1917** His Uncle Dudley. **1918** A Hoosier Romance. **1921** The Killer; The Lure of Egypt; The Man of the Forest; Mysterious Rider. **1922** Golden Dreams; Heart's Haven; The Old Homestead; When Romance Rides. **1923** Double Dealing; Souls in Bondage; Vanity Fair. **1924** Greed.

HAYES, GEORGE
Born: Nov. 13, 1888, London, England. Died: July 13, 1967, England? Stage and screen actor. Do not confuse with American actor George "Gabby" Hayes (dec. 1969).

Appeared in: **1935** Inside the Room; Old Roses; Emil and the Detectives (aka Emil—US 1938); The Guv'nor (aka Mister Hobo—US 1936). **1936** Land Without Music (aka Forbidden Music—US 1938); Wolf's Clothing; Everything Is Thunder. **1937** Death Croons the Blues. **1938** Break the News (US 1941); No Parking; The Return of the Frog. **1939** The Mind of Mr. Reeder (aka The Mysterious Mr. Reeder—US 1940); Secret Journey (aka Among Human Wolves—US 1940); Come on George. **1940** Spy for a Day. **1941** East of Piccadilly (aka The Strangler—US 1942). **1946** Great Expectations (US 1947). **1948** Esther Waters.

HAYES, GEORGE "GABBY"
Born: May 7, 1885, Wellesville, N.Y. Died: Feb. 9, 1969, Burbank, Calif. (heart ailment). Screen, stage and television actor. Married to actress Dorothy Earle (dec. 1958). Appeared in both Hopalong Cassidy film series and Roy Rogers film series.

Appeared in: **1929** The Rainbow Man (film debut); Smiling Irish Eyes. **1930** For the Defense. **1931** Rose of the Rio Grande; God's Country and the Man; Cavalier of the West; Nevada Buckaroo; Big Business Girl. **1932** Dragnet Patrol; Border Devils; Night Rider; Riders of the Desert; The Man from Hell's Edges; From Broadway to Cheyenne; Klondike; Texas Buddies; The Boiling Point; The Fighting Champ; Without Honor; Love Me Tonight; The Slippery Pearls (short). **1933**

Wild Horse Mesa; Sagebrush Trail; Self Defense; Trailing North; Return of Casey Jones; Skyway; Gallant Fool; The Ranger's Code; Galloping Romeo; The Fugitive; The Phantom Broadcast; The Sphinx; Crashing Broadway; Breed of the Border; Fighting Texans; Devil's Mate; Riders of Destiny. **1934** In Old Santa Fe; Brand of Hate; Monte Carlo Nights; The Man from Utah; The Star Packer; West of the Divide; The Lucky Texan; Beggars in Ermine; Mystery Liner; Blue Steel; Randy Rides Alone; City Limits; The Lost Jungle (serial); 'Neath Arizona Skies. **1935** Justice of the Range; The Throwback; $1,000 a Minute; Tumbling Tumbleweeds; Texas Terror; Lawless Frontier; Death Flies East; Rainbow Valley; The Hoosier School-Master; Honeymoon Limited; Headline Woman; Ladies Crave Excitement; Thunder Mountain; Hopalong Cassidy; The Eagle's Brood; Bar 20 Rides Again; Mister Hobo; Hitch Hike Lady; The Lost City (serial); Welcome Home. **1936** Silver Spurs; Call of the Prairie; Three on a Trail; The Lawless Nineties; Glory Parade; Hearts in Bondage; I Married a Doctor; Mr. Deeds Goes to Town; Heart of the West; Swiftly; The Texas Rangers; Valiant Is the Word for Carrie; Hopalong Cassidy Returns; The Plainsman; Trail Dust. **1937** Borderland; Hills of Old Wyoming; Mountain Music; North of the Rio Grande; Rustler's Valley; Hopalong Rides Again; Texas Trail. **1938** Forbidden Music; Gold Is Where You Find It; Heart of Arizona; Bar 20 Justice; Pride of the West; In Old Mexico; Sunset Trail; The Frontiersman; Emil. **1939** Man of Conquest; Let Freedom Ring; Southward Ho!; In Old Caliente; In Old Monterey; Wall Street Cowboy; The Arizona Kid; Saga of Death Valley; Silver on the Sage; Days of Jesse James; The Renegade Trail; Fighting Thoroughbreds. **1940** Wagons Westward; The Dark Command; Young Buffalo Bill; The Carson City Kid; The Ranger and the Lady; Colorado; Young Bill Hickok; Melody Ranch; The Border Legion. **1941** Robin Hood of the Pecos; In Old Cheyenne; Sheriff of Tombstone; Nevada City; Jesse James at Bay; Bad Man of Deadwood; Red River Valley; The Voice in the Night; Frightened Lady. **1942** South of Santa Fe; Sunset on the Desert; Romance of the Range; Man of Cheyenne; Sons of the Pioneers; Sunset Serenade; Heart of the Golden West; Ridin' Down the Canyon. **1943** Calling Wild Bill Elliott; Bordertown Gunfighters; Wagon Tracks West; The Man from Thunder River; Death Valley Manhunt; In Old Oklahoma. **1944** Tucson Raiders; Leave It to the Irish; Mojave Firebrand; Tall in the Saddle; Lights of Old Santa Fe; Hidden Valley Outlaws; Marshal of Reno. **1945** Utah; The Big Bonanza; The Man from Oklahoma; Sunset in Eldorado; Don't Fence Me In; Out California Way; Bells of Rosarita; Along the Navajo Trail. **1946** My Pal Trigger; Home in Oklahoma; Badman's Territory; Song of Arizona; Rainbow Over Texas; Roll on Texas Moon; Under Nevada Skies. **1947** Helldorado; Trail Street; Bells on San Angelo; Wyoming; The Trespasser; Great Expectations. **1948** Albuquerque; Slippy McGee; The Untamed Breed; Return of the Bad Men. **1949** Susanna Pass; Golden Stallion; Bells of Coronado; Trigger, Jr.; El Paso. **1950** The Cariboo Trail; Twilight in the Sierras. **1951** Pals of the Golden West.

HAYES, LAURENCE C.
Born: 1903. Died: Nov. 17, 1974, New York, N.Y. (heart complications). Screen, stage and television actor. Married to actress Anita Webb.

HAYES, MARGARET "MAGGIE" (Lorette Ottenheimer)
Born: Dec. 5, 1915 or 1916, Baltimore, Md. Died: Jan. 26, 1977, Miami Beach, Fla. (cancer). Screen, stage, television actress, model and fashion editor. Divorced from actor Leif Erickson and director Herbert B. Swope, Jr. Mother of actress Tracy Brooks Swope and Herbert Swope III.

Appeared in: **1940** City for Conquest. **1941** Skylark; New York Town; The Night of January 16th; Louisiana Purchase; Sullivan's Travels; In Old Colorado. **1942** Take a Letter, Darling; The Lady Has Plans; The Glass Key; The Saboteur. **1943** They Got Me Covered. **1955** Violent Saturday; The Blackboard Jungle. **1956** The Bottom of the Bottle. **1957** Omar Khayyam. **1958** Damn Citizen; Girl in the Woods; Fraulein; The Case Against Brooklyn. **1959** Good Day for Hanging; Girl's Town; The Beat Generation. **1962** House of Women; 13 West Street.

HAYES, SAM (Samuel Stewart Hayes)
Born: 1905, Cookesville, Ill. Died: July 28, 1958, San Diego, Calif. (heart attack). Screen actor and radio announcer.

Appeared in: **1932** The Crowd Roars. **1934** Kid Millions; Ali Baba Goes to Town. **1936** Fury; Pigskin Parade; The Ex Mrs. Bradford. **1937** Music for Madame; A Girl With Ideas. **1938** Letter of Introduction; Rebecca of Sunnybrook Farm. **1939** They Made Me a Criminal; Tail Spin. **1941** The Man Who Came to Dinner; The Bride Came C.O.D.; High Sierra. **1946** Joe Palooka—Champ. **1947** Joe Palooka in the Knockout; The Checkered Coat. **1949** It Happens Every Spring; Fighting Fools; Maggie and Jiggs in Jackpot Jitters; Joe Palooka in the Counterpunch.

HAYES, SIDNEY
Born: 1865. Died: May 2, 1940, Beverly Hills, Calif. Screen, stage and vaudeville actor. Appeared in vaudeville in an act billed as "Hayes and Hayes."

HAYES, WILLIAM
Born: 1887. Died: July 13, 1937, Hollywood, Calif. (heart attack). Screen actor.

Appeared in: **1921** Get-Rich-Quick Wallingford. **1924** Flashing Spurs. **1925** A Gentleman Roughneck; Lena Rivers. **1926** Ace of Action; Cupid's Knockout; Hollywood Reporter. **1931** Seasons Greetings (short).

HAYLE, GRACE
Born: 1889. Died: Mar. 20, 1963, Los Angeles, Calif. Screen actress.

Appeared in: **1932** Back Street. **1933** Gold Diggers of 1933; Design for Living; Hard to Handle. **1934** Wonder Bar; Twenty Million Sweethearts; Now and Forever; Chained. **1935** The Whole Town's Talking; Mary Burns; Fugitive; She Married Her Boss; Roberta. **1936** Ticket to Paradise; Winterset; Theodora Goes Wild; The Harvester; Under Two Flags. **1937** Music for Madame; Tovarich. **1938** The Shining Hour; Man-Proof; Three Loves Has Nancy; Sweethearts. **1939** Death of a Champion; Forgotten Women; Mr. Moto in Danger Island; The Starmaker; Lady of the Tropics. **1940** Our Neighbors, the Carters; The Great Dictator; Ma, He's Making Eyes at Me; 'Til We Meet Again; Third Finger—Left Hand; Road to Singapore; The Ghost Breakers. **1941** Unfinished Business; Knockout; The Wagons Roll at Night; Two-Faced Woman. **1942** Madame Spy; Just Off Broadway; Crossroads; I Married an Angel. **1943** Footlight Glamour; Let's Face It; She's for Me; Slightly Dangerous. **1944** Beautiful But Broke; Cover Girl. **1952** Flesh and Fury; Don't Bother to Knock. **1953** Houdini; Money From Home. **1954** Dangerous Mission. **1955** Foxfire. **1957** Loving You.

HAYMAN, ADAM CHARLES
Born: 1880, New York, N.Y. Died: July 11, 1945, Niagara Falls, N.Y. Screen actor and photographer.

Appeared in: **1903** The Great Train Robbery.

HAYMES, DICK
Born: 1919, Buenos Aires, Argentina. Died: Mar. 28, 1980, Los Angeles, Calif. (lung cancer). Screen, radio, television actor and vocalist. Divorced from Edith Harper, actresses Joanne Dru, Nora Eddington Flynn, Rita Hayworth, Fran Makris, Fran Jeffries and Wendy Smith. Brother of singer Bob Stanton (aka Bob Haymes—dec.).

Appeared in: **1944** Irish Eyes are Smiling (film debut); Four Jills in a Jeep. **1945** Billy Rose's; Diamond Horseshoe; State Fair. **1946** Do You Love Me? **1947** The Shocking Miss Pilgrim; Carnival in Costa Rica. **1948** One Touch of Venus; Up in Central Park. **1951** St. Benny the Dip. **1952** Hollywood Fun Festival (narrator). **1953** All Ashore; Cruisin' Down the River.

HAYNES, ARTHUR
Born: 1914. Died: Nov. 19, 1966, London, England (heart attack). Screen, vaudeville, radio and television actor.

Appeared in: **1964** Strange Bedfellows. **1965** Doctor in Clover (aka Carnaby, M.D.—US 1967).

HAYNES, DANIEL L.
Died: July 28, 1954, Kingston, N.Y. Black screen and stage actor and clergyman.

Appeared in: **1929** Hallelujah (first all Black film). **1932** The Last Mile. **1935** Mary Burns, Fugitive; So Red the Rose; Escape from Devil's Island. **1936** The Invisible Ray.

HAYNES, DICK
Born: 1911, Beaumont, Tex. Died: Nov. 25, 1980, Woodland Hills, Calif. (cancer). Screen, radio and television actor. "Haynes at the Reins" on radio.

Appeared in: **1957** The Fuzzy Pink Nightgown. **1961** The Phantom Planet. **1963** The Silent Witness. **1968** A Time to Sing. **1969** Support Your Local Sheriff. **1979** Real Life.

HAYNES, H. MANNING
Born: Lyminster, England. Died: 1957, England? Screen, stage actor, film director, film producer and screenwriter. Entered films in 1914.

Appeared in: **1917** The Lost Chord; Home Sweet Home. **1918** Ave Maria; Lead, Kindly Light. **1919** Sam, Jack and Pete. **1920** Lady Audley's Secret; Three Men in a Boat. **1921** Four Men in a Van; Monty Works the Wires.

HAYWARD, JAMES "JIM"
Died: July 12, 1981. Screen actor.

Appeared in: **1951** Vengeance Valley; Excuse My Dust; Rhubarb; Let's Make It Legal. **1952** Pony Soldier. **1953** Arena. **1954** Alaska Seas; Bitter Creek. **1956** Hilda Crane; The Kettles in the Ozarks; The Mountain; The Naked Hills. **1957** No Down Payment. **1962** Terror at Black Falls.

HAYWARD, RICHARD
Born: 1892, Ireland? Died: Oct. 13, 1964, Belfast, North Ireland (auto accident). Screen actor, film producer and poet.

Appeared in: **1935** The Luck of the Irish (US 1937). **1936** Irish and Proud of It (US 1938). **1958** Night to Remember.

HAYWARD, SUSAN (Edythe Marrener)
Born: June 30, 1918, Brooklyn, N.Y. Died: Mar. 14, 1975, Beverly Hills, Calif. (brain tumor). Screen and television actress. Divorced from actor Jess Barker. Married to Floyd Chalkley (dec. 1966). Won 1958 Academy Award as Best Actress in I Want to Live. Nominated for 1947 Academy Award as Best Actress in Smash Up; in 1949 for My Foolish Heart; in 1952 for With a Song in My Heart; and in 1955 for I'll Cry Tomorrow.

Appeared in: **1937** Hollywood Hotel. **1938** I Am the Law; Comet Over Broadway; The Sisters; Girls on Probation. **1939** Beau Geste; $1,000 a Touchdown; Our Leading Citizen. **1941** Among the Living; Sis Hopkins; Adam Had Four Sons. **1942** Reap the Wild Wind; The Forest Rangers; Star Spangled Rhythm; I Married a Witch. **1943** Young and Willing; Hit Parade of 1943; Jack London. **1944** And Now Tomorrow; The Fighting Seabees; The Hairy Ape. **1945** Murder—He Says. **1946** Canyon Passage; Deadline at Dawn. **1947** The Lost Moment; They Won't Believe Me; Smash-Up—The Story of a Woman (aka A Woman Destroyed). **1948** The Saxon Charm; Tap Roots. **1949** Change of Heart (reissue of Hit Parade of 1943); House of Strangers; Tulsa; My Foolish Heart. **1951** I Can Get It for You Wholesale; I'd Climb the Highest Mountain; Rawhide; David and Bathsheba. **1952** The Lusty Men; The Snows of Kilimanjaro; With a Song in My Heart. **1953** The President's Lady; White Witch Doctor. **1954** Garden of Evil; Demetrius and the Gladiators. **1955** Untamed; Soldier of Fortune; I'll Cry Tomorrow. **1956** The Conqueror. **1957** Top Secret Affair. **1958** I Want to Live. **1959** Thunder in the Sun; Woman Obsessed. **1960** The Marriage-Go-Round. **1961** Back Street; Ada. **1962** I Thank a Fool. **1963** Stolen Hours. **1964** Where Love Has Gone. **1967** The Honey Pot; Valley of the Dolls. **1972** The Revengers.

HAYWOOD, BILLIE
Born: 1904. Died: July 8, 1979, Hollywood, Calif. (natural causes). Blues singer, comedienne, screen, stage and television actress.

Appeared in: **1945** An Angel Comes to Brooklyn.

HAYWORTH, VINTON J.
Born: 1906. Died: May 21, 1970, Van Nuys, Calif. (heart attack). Screen, stage, radio and television actor. Married to actress Jean Owens.

Appeared in: **1956** The Girl He Left Behind; The Great Man. **1960** Spartacus. **1961** Police Dog Story. **1966** Chamber of Horrors.

HAZEL, HY (Hyacinth Hazel O'Higgins)
Born: 1920. Died: May 10, 1970, London, England. Screen and stage actress.

Appeared in: **1946** Meet Me at Dawn (US 1948). **1947** Just Williams' Luck (US 1948). **1949** Paper Orchid; Celia. **1950** The Body Said No; The Lady Craved Excitement; The Gay Duellist (reissue of Meet Me at Dawn—1947). **1951** Franchise Affair (US 1952). **1952** The Yellow Balloon (US 1954); The Night Won't Talk. **1953** Forces' Sweetheart. **1955** Stolen Assignment. **1956** Up in the World; Anastasia. **1957** The Mail Van Murder; Light Fingers; The Key Man. **1958** The Whole Truth. **1960** Trouble with Eve (aka In Trouble with Eve—US 1964). **1961** Five Golden Hours. **1962** What Every Woman Wants.

HAZELTON, JOSEPH
Born: 1853. Died: Oct. 8, 1936, Hollywood, Calif. Screen and stage actor.

Appeared in: **1921** False Kisses; "If Only" Jim; The Little Minister. **1922** Oliver Twist. **1937** Mountain Justice.

HAZLETT, WILLIAM See CHIEF MANY TREATIES

HEAD, EDITH
Born: Oct. 28, 1898, Los Angeles, Calif. Died: Oct. 24, 1981, Los Angeles, Calif. Costume designer, screen, radio and television actress. Married to art director Wiard Ihnen (dec. 1979).

Appeared in: **1955** Lucy Gallant. **1966** The Oscar.

HEALY, DAN

Born: 1889. Died: Sept. 1, 1969, Jackson Heights, N.Y. Stage and screen actor, song and dance man. Married to singer and actress Helen Kane (dec. 1966).

Appeared in: **1929** The Laughing Lady; Glorifying the American Girl. **1931** The Unfair Sex (short).

HEALY, TED (Charles Earnest Lee Nash)

Born: Oct. 1, 1896, Houston, Tex. Died: Dec. 21, 1937, Los Angeles, Calif. (heart attack). Screen, stage, radio and vaudeville actor. Billed in vaudeville as "Ted Healy and His Racketeers" and "Ted Healy and His Stooges (Larry, Moe and Shemp and later Larry, Moe and Curley)." Divorced from actress Betty Brown and later married to Betty Hickman.

Appeared with the Three Stooges in: **1930** Soup to Nuts (with Larry, Moe and Shemp—film debut). **1933** Turn Back the Clock; Meet the Baron; Dancing Lady; Myrte and Marge; plus the following shorts: Hollywood on Parade; Screen Snapshots; Nertsery Rhymes; Beer and Pretzels. **1934** The Big Idea (short); Appeared without Stooges in: **1934** Fugitive Lovers; Hollywood Party; Death on the Diamond; The Band Plays On; Lazy River; Operation 13; Paris Interlude (short). **1935** The Winning Ticket; The Casino Murder Case; La Fiesta de Santa Barbara (short); Reckless; Murder in the Fleet; Mad Love; Here Comes the Band; It's in the Air. **1936** Speed; San Francisco; The Longest Night; Mad Holiday; Sing, Baby, Sing. **1937** Man of the People; Varsity Show; Hollywood Hotel; Good Old Soak. **1938** Love Is a Headache. **1964** Big Parade of Comedy (documentary).

HEARN, EDWARD "EDDIE" (Guy Edward Hearn)

Born: Sept. 6, 1888, Dayton, Wash. Died: Apr. 15, 1963. Screen and stage actor.

Appeared in: **1915** The White Scar. **1916** The Lost Lode; Should She Have Told?; Idle Wives; Her Bitter Cup; The Seekers. **1917** Patsy; The Lost Express (serial); The Trapping of Two-Bit Tuttle; The American Girl series; Sage Brush Law. **1918** Lure of Luxury. **1919** The Undercurrent; The Last of His People. **1920** The Coast of Opportunity; Down Home. **1921** The Avenging Arrow (serial); All Dolled Up; Face of the World; Keeping Up with Lizzie; Things Men Do. **1922** The Fire Bride; Colleen of the Pines; The Flirt; The Glory of Clementina; Her Night of Nights; A Question of Honor; The Truthful Liar. **1923** The Love Letter; Mind over Motor; The Town Scandal; Daytime Wives; The Miracle Baby. **1924** When a Man's a Man; The Dangerous Blonde; Daughters of Today; Excitement; The Turmoil; Winner Take All. **1925** Lawful Cheaters; The Man Without a Country; One of the Bravest; Daring Days; The Outlaw's Daughter. **1926** Peril of the Rail; The Sign of the Claw; The Still Alarm. **1927** The Harvester; The Heart of the Yukon; Hero on Horseback; Hook and Ladder No. 9; Pals in Peril; Spuds; Winners of the Wilderness; The Desert Pirate. **1928** The Big Hop; Dog Justice; The Fightin' Redhead; The Yellow Cameo (serial). **1929** The One Man Dog; The Bachelor Girl; The Donovan Affair; The Drake Case; Ned McCobb's Daughter; Dare Devil Jack. **1930** Hide-Out; Reno; The Spoilers. **1931** Smart Money; The Vanishing Legion (serial); Ladies' Man; The Galloping Ghost (serial); The Avenger; Ex-Bad Boy; Son of the Plains. **1932** The Shadow of the Eagle (serial); Cheyenne Cyclone; Rainbow Trail; Local Bad Man. **1933** I'm no Angel; Fighting With Kit Carson. **1934** Belle of the Nineties; Burn 'Em Up Barnes (serial and feature film); Texas Tornado; Fighting Hero; Young and Beautiful; Fighting Through; In Old Santa Fe; Mystery Mountain (serial). **1935** Naughty Marietta; Behind the Green Lights; Tumbling Tumbleweeds; Hot Off the Press; The Miracle Rider (serial); Confidential; Headline Woman. **1936** King of the Pecos; Boss Rider of Gun Creek; Red River Valley. **1937** Paid to Dance; The Shadow; Something to Sing About; Anything for a Thrill; Springtime in the Rockies; Trouble at Midnight. **1938** Young Fugitives. **1939** St. Louis Blues; West of Santa Fe. **1940** Remedy for Riches; My Little Chickadee; I Love You Again. **1941** Caught in the Draft; Holt of the Secret Service (serial). **1942** Sullivan's Travels. **1943** Air Raid Wardens. **1951** Pistol Harvest; Storm Warning; Sugarfoot; Strangers on a Train. **1952** The Man Behind the Gun. **1953** Port Sinister; Conquest of Cochise.

HEARN, JULIA (Julia Knox)

Born: 1884, England. Died: May 1, 1976, New York, N.Y. Screen, stage and vaudeville actress. Sister of actor Teddy Knox (dec. 1974).

HEARN, SAM

Born: 1889, New York, N.Y. Died: Oct. 28, 1964, Los Angeles, Calif. (heart attack). Screen, stage, radio and television actor. Best known for his role of "Schlepperman" on Jack Benny's radio and television programs.

Appeared in: **1936** Florida Special; The Big Broadcast for 1937. **1942** The Man in the Trunk. **1949** Inspector General; Pat and Mike. **1953** The I Don't Care Girl. **1958** Once Upon a Horse.

HEARNE, RICHARD

Born: Jan. 30, 1909, Norwich, England. Died: Aug. 25, 1979, Bearstead, Kent, England. Screen, stage, television actor, circus performer, dancer, acrobat and screenwriter.

Appeared in: **1934** Give Her a Ring. **1935** No Monkey Business; Dance Band. **1936** Millions. **1937** Splinters in the Air. **1943** The Butler's Dilemma; Miss London. **1948** One Night With You; Woman Hater (US 1949). **1949** Helter Skelter. **1950** Something in the City; Method and Madness (aka Mr. Pastry Does the Laundry). **1951** Madame Louise; Captain Horatio Hornblower RN. **1952** What a Husband! (short); Miss Robin Hood. **1955** The Time of His Life. **1956** Tons of Trouble. **1963** The King's Breakfast.

HEATH, ARCH B.

Born: 1890, Brooklyn, N.Y. Died: Jan. 6, 1945. Screen actor and film director.

HEATH, TED

Born: 1902, Wadsworth, London, England. Died: Nov. 18, 1969, Virginia Water, England. Band leader, screen and radio actor.

Appeared in: **1956** It's a Wonderful World (US 1961). **1960** Jazz Boat. **1961** Ted Heath and His Music (short).

HEATHERLEY, CLIFFORD (Clifford Lamb)

Born: Oct. 8, 1888, Preston, Lancashire, England. Died: Sept. 15, 1937, London, England. Screen and stage actor.

Appeared in: **1911** Henry VIII. **1920** Bleak House; The Tavern Knight. **1921** The Autumn of Pride; The Mystery of Mr. Bernard Brown. **1922** The Adventures of Sherlock Holmes (series). **1926** The Sea Urchin; The Steve Donoghue series including: Beating the Book; Mademoiselle from Armentieres; Boadicea. **1927** The King's Highway; Roses of Picardy; The Rolling Road. **1928** The Constant Nymph; The Passing of Mr. Quin; Tesha; Champagne. **1929** High Treason. **1930** The Compulsory Husband; The "W" Plan (US 1931); Symphony in Two Flats. **1931** The Love Habit; Glamour; Who Killed Doc Robin?; My Old China. **1932** Goodnight Vienna (aka Magic Night—US); Help Yourself; Brother Alfred; Indiscretions of Eve; Fires of Fate (US 1933); Happy Ever After; After the Ball; A Letter of Warning. **1933** Discord; The Little Damozel; Forging Ahead; Cash (aka For Love or Money—US 1934); Bitter Sweet; Yes, Mr. Brown; Beware of Women; I Adore You. **1934** Trouble in the Store; Catherine the Great; The Church Mouse (US 1935); Get Your Man; The Private Life of Don Juan; Adventure Limited; The Queen's Affair (aka Runaway Queen—US 1935). **1935** Abdul the Damned; A Little Bit of Bluff; No Monkey Business; Our Husband. **1936** Cafe Mascot; The Invader (aka An Old Spanish Custom—US); Show Flat; Reasonable Doubt; If I Were Rich. **1937** Feather Your Nest; It's Not Cricket; Don't Get Me Wrong; There Was a Young Man.

HEATTER, GABRIEL

Born: 1890, New York, N.Y. Died: Mar. 30, 1972, Miami Beach, Fla. (pneumonia). Radio newscaster, journalist, television producer and screen actor.

Appeared in: **1950** Champagne for Caesar. **1951** The Day the Earth Stood Still.

HEAZLIT, EVA See MC KENZIE, EVA

HEBERT, HENRY J. (aka HENRY J. HERBERT)

Born: Nov. 12, 1879, Providence, R.I. Died: Jan. 18, 1956, Calif.? Screen and stage actor. Married to Helen Herbert (dec. 1946). Do not confuse with actor Henry Herbert (dec. 1947).

HECHT, BEN

Born: Feb., 1894, New York, N.Y. Died: Apr. 18, 1964, New York, N.Y. (heart attack). Newspaperman, novelist, screenwriter, screen director, producer and screen actor. Father of actress Jenny Hecht (dec. 1971).

Appeared in: **1935** The Scoundrel.

HECHT, JENNY

Born: July 30, 1943, New York, N.Y. Died: Mar. 25, 1971, North Hollywood, Calif. Stage and screen actress. Daughter of screenwriter Ben Hecht (dec. 1964).

Appeared in: **1952** Actors and Sin (aka Woman of Sin). **1962** Katy's Lot (short). **1971** The Jesus Trip.

HECHT, TED (Theodore Hekt)

Born: 1908, New York, N.Y. Died: June 24, 1969, Los Angeles, Calif. Screen, stage and television actor.

Appeared in: **1942** Time to Kill (film debut); Manila Calling. **1943** So

Proudly We Hail; Corregidor; Rookies in Burma. **1944** Dragon Seed; End of the Road. **1945** Secret Agent X-9 (serial); Three's a Crowd; Counterattack; The Lost Weekend. **1946** Danger Woman; Boston Blackie and the Law; Anna and the King of Siam; Lost City of the Jungle (serial); The Fighting Guardsman; Just Before Dawn. **1947** Tarzan and the Huntress; Spoilers of the North; The Gangster; Riding the California Trail. **1948** Man Eater of Kumaon. **1949** Apache Chief; Bad Men of Tombstone; Song of India; Tarzan's Magic Fountain. **1950** Tall Timber; Blue Grass of Kentucky; Killer Shark; Sideshow; Abbott and Costello in the Foreign Legion. **1953** Desert Legion. **1955** Abbott and Costello Meet the Mummy.

HECK, STANTON P.
Born: Jan. 8, 1877, Wilmington, Del. Died: Dec. 16, 1929, Los Angeles, Calif. (pneumonia). Screen and stage actor.

Appeared in: **1914** The Man From Mexico. **1920** Forbidden Trails; The Hawk's Trail (serial); Firebrand Trevision; Rose of Nome; Pink Tights; The Money Changers; A Beggar in Purple. **1921** A Perfect Crime; Scrap Iron. **1922** A Tailor Made Man; Ashes; The Gray Dawn; I Can Explain; The Power of a Lie. **1923** Man's Size; The Lone Star Ranger; The Bad Man; The Courtship of Miles Standish; Hearts Aflame. **1924** The Woman on the Jury; White Man; One Law for the Woman. **1925** Soft Shoes; Silent Sanderson; The Mystic; Old Clothes; The Fighting Demon; The Verdict. **1926** Her Honor the Governor; Driftin' Thru; The Gentle Cyclone; Is That Nice?; Rustler's Ranch. **1927** The Yankee Clipper; The Breed of Courage; The King of Kings. **1928** The Branded Sombrero.

HEDLUND, GUY E.
Born: Aug. 21, 1884, Connecticut. Died: Dec. 29, 1964, Culver City, Calif. (injuries from being hit by auto). Screen actor.

Appeared in: **1909** Pippa Passes. **1910** Wilful Peggy; The Broken Doll; The Modern Prodigal. **1911** The Squaw's Love; The Revenue Man and the Girl; Bobby the Coward; A Country Cupid; The Ruling Passion; The Rose of Kentucky; The Sorrowful Example; Swords and Hearts; The Stuff Heroes Are Made Of; The Old Confectioner's Mistake; The Eternal Mother; Dan the Dandy.

HEDQUIST, IVAN
Born: 1880, Sweden. Died: 1935. Screen actor and film director. Entered films as an actor in 1910.

Appeared in: **1927** Youth. **1932** Vaermlaenningavna.

HEFLIN, VAN (Emmet Evan Heflin)
Born: Dec. 13, 1910, Walters, Okla. Died: July 23, 1971, Hollywood, Calif. (heart attack). Screen, stage and television actor. Divorced from actress Frances Neal. Won 1942 Academy Award for Best Supporting Actor in Johnny Eager.

Appeared in: **1936** A Woman Rebels (film debut). **1937** The Outcasts of Poker Flat; Flight from Glory; Annapolis Salute; Saturday's Heroes; Salute to Romance. **1939** Back Door to Heaven. **1940** Santa Fe Trail. **1941** The Feminine Touch; H. M. Pulham, Esq.; Johnny Eager. **1942** Kid Glove Killer; Grand Central Murder; Seven Sweethearts; Tennessee Johnson. **1946** Presenting Lily Mars. **1946** The Strange Love of Martha Ivers; 'Til the Clouds Roll By. **1947** Green Dolphin Street; Possessed. **1948** B. F.'s Daughter; Act of Violence; The Three Musketeers; Tap Roots; Secret Land (narr.). **1949** East Side, West Side; Madame Bovary. **1951** The Prowler; Weekend with Father; Tomahawk. **1952** South of Algiers (aka The Golden Mask—US 1954); My Son, John. **1953** Shane; Wings of the Hawk. **1954** Tanganyika; The Raid; Woman's World; Black Widow. **1955** Battle Cry; Count Three and Pray. **1956** Patterns. **1957** 3:10 to Yuma; Gunman's Walk. **1959** Tempest; They Came to Cordura. **1960** Five Branded Women; Under Ten Flags. **1961** Il Relitto (The Wastrel, aka To Be a Man—US 1963). **1963** Cry of Battle. **1965** The Greatest Story Ever Told; Once a Thief. **1966** Stagecoach. **1968** The Man Outside; Das Gold von Sam Cooper (Sam Cooper's Gold aka Each Man for Himself and the Ruthless Four—US 1969). **1969** The Trackers; The Big Bounce. **1970** Airport. **1972** Revengers.

HEGGIE, O. P.
Born: Sept. 17, 1876, Angaston, South Australia. Died: Feb. 7, 1936, Los Angeles, Calif. (pneumonia). Screen and stage actor.

Appeared in: **1928** The Actress. **1929** The Letter; The Mysterious Dr. Fu Manchu; The Wheel of Life. **1930** Broken Dishes; Playboy of Paris; Sunny; The Mighty; The Vagabond King; The Return of Dr. Fu Manchu; The Bad Man; One Romantic Night. **1931** The Women Between; Too Young to Marry; Devotion; East Lynne. **1932** Smilin' Through. **1933** The King's Vacation; Zoo in Budapest. **1934** Anne of Green Gables; Count of Monte Cristo; Peck's Bad Boy; Midnight. **1935** Chasing Yesterday; Dog of Flanders; Return of Frankenstein; Ginger; Bride of Frankenstein. **1936** Prisoner of Shark Island.

HEGIRA, ANNE
Died: c. 1971. Screen actress. Divorced from actor and director Elia Kazan.

Appeared in: **1954** On the Waterfront. **1963** Love With the Proper Stranger. **1969** The Arrangement.

HEIDEMANN, PAUL "PAULCHEN"
Born: 1886, Cologne, Germany. Died: June 20, 1968, Berlin, Germany. Screen and stage actor.

Appeared in: **1931** Der Hampelmann (The Jumping Jack); Ihre Hoheit Befiehlt. **1932** Kyritz-Pyritz; Schoen Ist die Manoeverzeit; Pension Schoeller; Wenn die Soldaten. **1934** Die Mutter der Kompagnie; Ja, Treu Ist die Soldatenliebel; Wie Man Maenner Fesselt; Abel Mit der Mundharmonika; Liebe in Uniform. **1935** Drie von der Kavallerie; Der Schuechterne Felix; Der Tolle Bomberg. **1936** Der Vetter aus Dingsda; Die Ganze Welt Dreht Sich um Liebe; Ist Mein Mann Nich Fabelhaft; Der Junge Graf. **1937** Freuhling im Wien; Hilde Petersen; Postlagernd; Der Unwiderst Ehliche (The Irresistable Man). **1938** Der Lachdoktor (The Laugh Doctor). **1940** Peter, Paul and Nanette.

HEIKNERT, CARL-AXEL
Born: 1924, Sweden. Died: 1981, Stockholm, Sweden. Screen, stage and television actor.

Appeared in: **1977** Man on the Roof. **1978** The Score; Bomsalva (Misfire).

HEINE, ALBERT
Born: 1868, Germany. Died: Apr. 13, 1949, Germany? Screen actor.

Appeared in: **1933** Die Tochter des Regiments (US 1934).

HEINZ, GERARD
Born: Jan. 2, 1904, Hamburg, Germany. Died: 1972, Germany or England. Screen, stage and television actor. Entered films in 1928.

Appeared in: **1946** Caravan (US 1947). **1948** Portrait From Life (aka The Girl in the Painting—US 1949); The Fallen Idol (US 1949); Broken Journey (US 1949). **1949** Traveller's Joy (US 1951); That Dangerous Age (aka If This Be Sin—US 1950); The Lost People. **1950** The Clouded Yellow (US 1952). **1951** White Corridors (US 1952). **1952** His Excellency (US 1956). **1953** The Cruel Sea; Desperate Moment. **1955** The Prisoner. **1957** Accused (aka Mark of the Hawk—US 1958); You Pay Your Money. **1958** The Man Inside. **1959** The House of the Seven Hawks. **1960** I Aim at the Stars. **1961** Offbeat (US 1964). **1962** Operation Snatch. **1963** Mystery Submarine. **1964** Devils of Darkness (US 1965). **1965** The Heroes of Telemark (US 1966). **1966** Where the Bullets Fly; The Projected Man (US 1967).

HEISEY, MART E.
Born: 1865. Died: Apr. 21, 1925, Chicago, Ill. Screen and stage actor.

Appeared in: **1913** The Man of Him. **1914** The Wolf.

HEISLER, CHARLES JAMES
Born: 1912. Died: Sept. 22, 1933, Pasadena, Calif. (auto accident). Screen actor and race car driver.

HELD, ANNA
Born: Mar. 8, 1873, Paris, France. Died: Aug. 12, 1918, New York, N.Y. (pneumonia, pernicious anemia). Screen and stage actress. Married to stage producer Florenz Ziegfeld (dec. 1932).

Appeared in: **1902** Anna Held. **1916** Madame La Presidente.

HELLER, FRITZ
Born: 1893, Austria? Died: Dec. 30, 1966, Vienna, Austria. Screen and stage actor.

HELLINGER, MARK
Born: Mar. 21, 1903, New York, N.Y. Died: Dec. 21, 1947, Hollywood, Calif. (heart attack). Journalist, playwright, film producer and screen actor. Married to actress Gladys Glad.

Appeared in: **1943** Thank Your Lucky Stars. **1948** The Naked City (narration).

HELLUM, BARNEY
Born: Jan. 1, 1895, Seavyanv, Norway. Died: Dec. 22, 1935. Screen actor.

HELM, CHRISTA
Died: Feb. 12, 1977. Screen actress.

Appeared in: **1951** Go for Broke.

HELMS, RUTH
Died: Oct. 27, 1960. Screen actress. Divorced from actor Conrad Nagel (dec. 1970) and film director Sidney Franklyn.

HELTON, PERCY

Born: 1894, N.Y. Died: Sept. 11, 1971, Hollywood, Calif. Screen, stage and television actor.

Appeared in: **1916** The Flower of Faith. **1922** Silver Wings. **1947** Miracle on 34th Street. **1948** Hazard; Call Northside 777; Let's Live Again; Chicken Every Sunday; That Wonderful Urge; Larceny, Inc. **1949** Thieves' Highway; The Crooked Way; Criss Cross; The Set-Up; My Friend Irma; Abbott and Costello Meet the Killer, Boris Karloff. **1950** Riding High; Harbor of Missing Men; Copper Canyon; Wabash Avenue; The Sun Sets at Dawn; Cyrano de Bergerac; Under Mexicali Skies; Fancy Pants; Tyrant of the Sea. **1951** Chain of Circumstance; The Barefoot Mailman. **1952** A Girl in Every Port; The Belle of New York; I Dream of Jeanie. **1953** Down Laredo Way; Call Me Madam; The Robe; How to Marry a Millionaire; Wicked Woman; The Stooge; Scared Stiff; Ambush at Tomahawk Gap. **1954** 20,000 Leagues Under the Sea; A Star Is Born; About Mrs. Leslie; White Christmas. **1955** Kiss Me Deadly; Crashout; No Man's Woman; Jail Busters. **1956** Fury at Gunsight Pass; Terror at Midnight; Shake, Rattle and Rock. **1957** Jailhouse Rock; The Phantom Stagecoach; Spook Chasers; Looking for Danger. **1958** Rally 'Round the Flag, Boys! **1962** The Music Man; Ride the High Country. **1963** Four for Texas; The Wheeler Dealers. **1965** Hush, Hush, Sweet Charlotte; Zebra in the Kitchen; The Sons of Katie Elder. **1966** A Big Hand for the Little Lady; Don't Worry, We'll Think of a Title. **1968** Head; Funny Girl. **1969** Butch Cassidy and the Sundance Kid.

HEMING, VIOLET (Violet Hemming)

Born: Jan. 27, 1895, Leeds, England. Died: July 4, 1981, New York, N.Y. Screen, stage and television actress. Daughter of actor Alfred Heming (dec. 1942). Divorced from actor Grant Mills (dec. 1973). Later married to Judge Bennett Champ Clark (dec.). Entered films in 1912.

Appeared in: **1917** The Danger Trail; The Judgment House. **1918** Turn of the Wheel. **1919** Everywoman. **1920** The Cost. **1922** When the Desert Calls. **1932** Almost Married; The Man Who Played God.

HEMINGER, LOUIS

Died: June 3, 1966, Hollywood, Calif. Screen actor.

Appeared in: **1952** Pony Soldier. **1953** Treasure of the Golden Condor.

HEMINGWAY, MARIE

Born: 1893, Yorkshire, England. Died: June 11, 1939, England? Screen and stage actress. Divorced from actor Claude Rains (dec. 1967).

Appeared in: **1916** The Second Mrs. Tanqueray. **1917** A Master of Man.

HEMINGWAY, RICHARD C.

Died: Date unknown. Screen actor. Divorced from actress Irene Bentley (dec. 1965).

Appeared in: **1934** Woman Condemned; Hell Cat. **1935** Society Fever.

HEMMING, ALFRED

Born: 1851, London, England. Died: Dec. 17, 1942, New York, N.Y. Screen and stage actor. Father of actress Violet Heming (dec. 1981).

HEMSLEY, ESTELLE

Born: May 5, 1887, Boston, Mass. Died: Nov. 4, 1968, Los Angeles, Calif. Screen, stage, radio and television actress.

Appeared in: **1950** Harvey (stage and film versions). **1957** Edge of the City. **1959** Green Mansions. **1960** Take a Giant Step; The Leech Woman. **1963** America, America. **1965** Baby, The Rain Must Fall.

HENABERY, JOSEPH

Born: Jan. 15, 1887, Omaha, Nebr. Died: Feb. 18, 1976, Woodland Hills, Calif. Screen, stage actor, film director, film producer and opera singer. Entered films in 1913 as a bit player.

Appeared in: **1915** Birth of a Nation (as Lincoln). **1916** Intolerance; Children of the Feud. **1917** Man from Painted Post.

HENCKLES, PAUL

Born: 1885, Huerth, Germany. Died: 1967, Castle Hugenpoet, near Kettwich, Dusseldorf, Germany. Screen and stage actor.

Appeared in: **1923** Das Geheimnis von Brinkenhof. **1925** Das Haus der Luege. **1926** Staatsanwalt Jordan; Wenn das Herz der Jugend Spricht. **1927** Am Ruedesheimer Schloss Steht Eine Linde; Feme; Fruehere Verhaeltnisse; Der Kampf des Donald Westhof. **1928** Ariadne in Hoppegarten; Der Ladenprinz; Liebfraumilch; Polnische Wirtschaft; Revolutionshochzeit; Die Seltsame Nacht der Helgs Wangen; Der Unueberwindliche; Geschlecht in Fesseln (Sex in Fetters); Du Sollst Nicht Ehebrechen! (aka Therese Raquin); Der Biberpelz (The Beaver Coat); Shadows of Fear. **1929** Durchs Brandenburger Tor; Die Frau ohne Nerven; Fruchtbarkeit; Die Lieb der Brueder Rott; Meineid; Morgenroete; Das Naerrische Glueck; Napoleon auf St. Helena; Sprengbagger 1010; Tagebuch Einer Kokotte; Blutschande 173 St. G.B. (aka Strafbare Ehe); Fruehlings Erwachen (The Awakening of Spring); Mutterliebe (Motherlove—US 1931). **1930** Last Company; Hungarian Nights; Flachsmann als Erzieher; Dreyfus; Einbrecher; Skandal um Eva (The Eva Scandal—US 1931); Cyankali; Die Zaertlichen Verwandten; Die Lindenwirtin; Die Letzte Kompanie (The Last Company); Das Gestohlene Gesicht; Die Grosse Sehnsucht; Der Unsterbliche Lump; Dolly Macht Karriere (Dolly's Career). **1931** Der Wahre Jakob (aka Das Maedchen vom Variete); Das Ekel; Der Stolz der 3. Kompagnie; Taeter Gesucht; Ihre Majestaet die Liebe; Er und Seine Diener; Der Ungetreue Eckehart (US 1932); Mein Leopold; Gloria; Schneider Wibbel; Man Braucht Kein Geld (US 1932); Kadetten (aka Hinter den Roten Mauern von Lichterfelde). **1932** Unheinliche Geschichten; Mieter Schulze Gegen Alle; Der Hexer; Die—Oder Keine (US 1934); Eine Stadt Steht Kopf; Geheimnis des Blauen Zimmers; Der Tolle Bomberg (US 1935); Rasputin (aka Der Daemon der Frauen); Das Testament des Cornelius Gulden (aka Eine Erbschaft mit Hindernissen); Es Wird Schon Wieder Besser (Things Will Be Better Again). **1933** Der Jaeger aus Kurpfalz; Heideschulmeister Uwe Karsten; Der Traum vom Rhein; Reifende Jugend; Maedels von Heute; Die Schoenen Tage von Aranjuez; Glueckliche Reise (US 1936); Kleiner Mann—was Nun?; Die Nacht im Forsthaus (aka Der Fall Roberts); Das Testament des Dr. Mabuse (The Testament of Dr. Mabuse); Das Lustige Kleeblatt (aka Gasthaus zur Treuen Liebe). **1934** Zwischen Zwei Herzen (Between Two Hearts—US 1936); Charleys Tante (Charley's Aunt); Ein Maedchen mit Prokura; Die Grosse Chance; Das Erbe von Pretoria (US 1936); Der Herr Senator (aka Die Fliegende Ahnfrau); Die Finanzen des Grossherzogs (The Grand Duke's Finances—US 1935); Ferien vom Ich; Liebe Dumme Mama; Jede Frau hat ein Geheimnis; Ich Sachen Timpe; Der Verlorene Sohn; Der Meisterboxer (aka Pantoffelhelden—US 1935); Polizeiakte 99 (aka Der Fall Tokeramo, and aka Taifun); Peter, Paul und Nanette (Peter, Paul and Nanette—US 1940). **1935** Hermine und die Sieben Aufrechten; Ein Idealer Gatte (US 1937); Alle Tage ist Kein Sonntag (US 1936); Das Einmaleins der Liebe (US 1937); Verlieb' Dich Nicht am Bodensee; Liebestraeume; Der Alte und der Junge Koenig (The Young and the Old King); Eine Seefahrt, die ist Lustig (aka Die Fahrt ins Blaue, and aka A Merry Sea Trip—US 1938). **1936** Alte Kameraden; Der Wackere Schustermeister; Schabernack (US 1937); Der Dschungel Ruft; Paul und Pauline; Maedchenjahre Einer Koenigin; Eine Frau ohne Bedeutung; Der Lustige Witwenball; Die Grosse und die Kleine Welt; Ein Lied Klagt An; Die Unmoegliche Frau; Die Nacht mit dem Kaiser; Drei Tolle Tage; Ave Maria; Das Hermaennchen (aka Nee, Nee was es Nich' Alles Gibt). **1937** Karussell; Capriolen; Zwei mal Zwei im Himmelbett; Die Glaeserne Kugel (The Glass Ball—US 1939); Fremdenheim Filoda. **1938** Der Maulkorb; Skandal um den Hahn; Diskretion—Ehrensache; Napoleon ist an Allem Schuld. **1939** Der Florentiner Hut (The Leghorn Hat); Ein Ganzer Kerl; 12 Minuten Nach 12; Das Unsterbliche Herz. **1940** Herz Modern Moebliert; Weisser Flieder; Was Wird Hier Gespielt?; Ihr Privatsekretaer; Friedrich Schiller (aka Der Triumph Eines Genies). **1941** Frau Luna; Maennerwirtschaft; Immer nur Du. **1942** So ein Fruechtchen; Der Strom; Der Grosse Koenig; Rembrandt; Hab' Mich Lieb; Die Nacht in Venedig; Zwischen Himmel und Erde; Wiener Blut; Zwei in Einer Grossen Stadt. **1943** Herr Sanders Lebt Gefaehrlich; Grosstadtmelodie; Das Bad auf der Tenne; Altes Herz Wird Wieder Jung; Liebesgeschichten. **1944** Die Feuerzangenbowle; Die Zaubergeige; Traeumerei; Junge Adler; Das Leben Ruft; Kolberg. **1945** Das Kleine Hofkonzert; Das Leben Geht Weiter; Das Seltsamen Fraeulein Sylvia; Fruehlingsmelodie; Der Mann, dem man den Namen Stahl; Dr. Phil. Doederlein; Eine Alltaegliche Geschichte; Eine Reizende Familie (aka Danke, es Geht mir Gut). **1947** Wozzeck. **1948** Die Seltsamen Abenteuer des Herrn Fridolin B. **1949** Palace Scandal; Diese Nacht Vergess ich Nie; Hafenmelodie; Gesucht Wird Majora. **1950** Insel ohne Moral. **1951** Rausch Einer Nacht; Glueck aus Ohio. **1952** Herz der Welt; Drei Tage Angst; Klettermaze; Glueck am Rhein; Einmal am Rhein; Ferien vom Ich; Der Froehliche Weinberg. **1953** Hollandmaedel; Fraeulein Casanova; Die Staerkere; Fanfare der Ehe; Koenigliche Hoheit; Das Tanzende Herz (The Dancing Heart—US 1958). **1954** Cliva; Der Zarewitsch; Columbus Entdeckt Kraehwinkel; Ball der Nationen; Staatsanwaeltin Corda; Maxie. **1955** Die Spanische Fliege; Griff Nach den Sternen (Reaching for the Stars—US 1958); Die Maedels vom Immenhof; Du Darfst Nicht Laenger Schweigen; Mamitschka; Drei Maedels vom Rhein. **1956** Ich und Meine Schwiegersoehne; Kirschen in Nachbars Garten; Kuess Mich Noch Einmal; Tausend Melodien; Drei Birken auf der Heide;

Der Fremdenfueher von Lissabon; Hochzeit auf Immenhof. **1957** Bekenntnisse des Hochstaplers Felix Krull (aka The Confessions of Felix Krull—US 1958); Tolle Nacht; Der Tolle Bomberg; Egon, der Frauenheld; Ferien auf Immenhof; Heute Blau und Morgen Blau; Ein Stueck vom Himmel. **1958** Liebe Kann Wie Gift Sein (Love Can be Like Poison—US 1960, and aka Magdalena—US). **1959** Das Unsterbliche Herz (The Immortal Heart); Hier bin ich, Hier Bleib' Ich; Immer die Maedchen. **1960** Frau Irene Besser.

HENDEE, HAROLD F.
Born: 1879. Died: June 24, 1966, New York, N.Y. Screen and stage actor. Appeared in films during the 1920s.

HENDERSON, BETTY
Born: 1908, Scotland. Died: Sept., 1979, Airdrie, Scotland. Screen, stage, radio and television actress.

Appeared in: **1954** The Maggie (aka Highland Dry—US). **1959** The 39 Steps (US 1960).

HENDERSON, DEL (George Delbert Henderson)
Born: July 5, 1883, St. Thomas, Ontario, Canada. Died: Dec. 2, 1956, Hollywood, Calif. Screen, stage actor and film director. Entered films as a director with D. W. Griffith in 1909 and later turned to acting. Also directed several Mack Sennett films. Married to actress Florence Lee (dec. 1962).

Appeared in: **1909** Lines of White on a Sullen Sea. **1910** The Purgation; That Chink at Golden Gulch; When a Man Loves. **1911** Teaching Dad to Like Her; The Two Sides; The Poor Sick Men; Conscience; The Crooked Road; In the Days of '49; The Last Drop of Water; The Jealous Husband; The Ghost; The Baron; The Making of a Man; A Victim of Circumstances; A String of Pearls; Comrades. **1912** Who Got the Reward?; The Fatal Chocolate; A Message From the Moon. **1913** The Battle of Elderberry Gulch. **1916** Intolerance. **1926** The Clinging Vine. **1927** Getting Gertie's Garter. **1928** Wrong Again (short); Riley the Cop; The Patsy; The Crowd; Power of the Press; Three-Ring Marriage; Show People. **1930** The Richest Man in the World; Hit the Deck; Sins of the Children; plus the following shorts: Whispering Whoopee; All Teed Up; Fast Work; Looser Than Loose; Bigger and Better; The Laurel and Hardy Murder Case. **1931** The Easiest Way; The Champ; Playthings of Hollywood; Newly Rich; plus the following shorts: Helping Grandma; Thundering Tenors; Skip the Maloo! **1932** The following shorts: Choo Choo; In Walked Charley; Mr. Bride. **1933** Too Much Harmony; I Have Lived; From Hell to Heaven; The Big Brain; Rainbow Over Broadway. **1934** Lone Cowboy; The Notorious Sophie Lang; The Lemon Drop Kid; The Marines Are Coming; Mrs. Wiggs of the Cabbage Patch; It's A Gift; Search for Beauty; You're Telling Me; The Old Fashioned Way; Bottoms Up; Something Simple (short); Men in Black (short). **1935** Ruggles of Red Gap; Slightly Static (short); Here Comes Cookie; Diamond Jim; The Mystery Man; Fighting Youth; Hot Tip; Hitch Hike Lady; The Daring Young Man; Black Sheep; This Is the Life; Steamboat 'Round the Bend. **1936** Our Relations; Poppy. **1937** Artists and Models; Make Way for Tomorrow; Love in a Bungalow; High, Wide and Handsome. **1938** Rebellious Daughters; Goodbye Broadway. **1939** Love Affair; Frontier Marshal. **1940** Little Orvie; You Can't Fool Your Wife; If I Had My Way. **1941** Look Who's Laughing. **1942** The Major and the Minor. **1943** DuBarry Was a Lady; Dixie. **1944** Nothing But Trouble. **1945** Wilson; Abbott and Costello in Hollywood. **1948** State of the Union. **1949** Neptune's Daughter. **1965** Laurel and Hardy's Laughing 20s (documentary).

HENDERSON, DOUGLAS "DOUG"
Born: 1919. Died: Apr. 5, 1978, Studio City, Calif. (suicide—carbon monoxide). Screen and television actor.

Appeared in: **1951** Flying Leathernecks. **1953** Eight Iron Men; From Here to Eternity. **1955** King Dinosaur. **1957** The Dalton Girls; Invasion of the Saucer Man. **1958** No Place to Land. **1960** Cage of Evil. **1961** Sniper's Ridge. **1962** The Manchurian Candidate. **1963** Black Zoo; Johnny Cool. **1964** The Americanization of Emily. **1965** The Sandpiper. **1966** Fireball 500. **1967** Don't Make Waves. **1968** Stay Away, Joe. **1969** Pendulum. **1970** Zigzag.

HENDERSON, GEORGE A.
Born: New York, N.Y. Died: Nov. 28, 1923, San Francisco, Calif. (stroke). Screen, stage and vaudeville actor.

Appeared in: **1923** The Fog.

HENDERSON, GRACE
Born: 1860, Ann Arbor, Mich. Died: Oct. 30, 1944, New York, N.Y. Screen, stage actress and screenwriter.

Appeared in: **1909** Lucky Jim; A Corner in Wheat. **1910** The Marker Time-Table; The Purgation; A Midnight Cupid; The Usurer; His Trust Fulfilled. **1911** The Barren; The Diving Girl; A Convenient Burglar; The Old Confectioner's Mistake; Sunshine Through the Dark; A String of Pearls; Enoch Arden Part I; Her Sacrifice; The Unveiling. **1912** An Unseen Enemy.

HENDERSON, IVO
Born: England. Died: Apr. 12, 1968. Screen and stage actor.

Appeared in: **1936** Rogue's Tavern. **1937** Bulldog Drummond Comes Back. **1938** Adventures of Robin Hood. **1944** Mrs. Parkington.

HENDERSON, JACK
Born: 1878, Syracuse, N.Y. Died: Jan. 1, 1957, New York, N.Y. Screen and stage actor.

Appeared in: **1916** Bucking Society; Bubbles of Trouble. **1917** A Dog Catcher's Love. **1924** The Foolish Virgin. **1925** The Mystery Box (serial). **1926** Lightning Bill; A Captain's Courage. **1927** Thunderbolt's Tracks. **1928** Tracked. **1929** Taking a Chance. **1930** Headin' North. **1931** Ridin' Fool. **1933** Roaming Romeo (short). **1935** Here Comes Cookie. **1948** Strange Victor.

HENDERSON, JANE
Born: England. Died: Apr. 4, 1960, London, England. Screen actress.

Appeared in: **1954** The Belles of St. Trinian's (US 1955); The Green Scarf (US 1955).

HENDERSON, LUCIUS
Born: 1848. Died: Feb. 18, 1947, N.Y. Screen, stage, vaudeville actor, film director and film producer.

Appeared in: **1923** Toilers of the Sea. **1925** A Man Must Live; The New Commandment. **1926** The Great Deception; White Mice.

HENDERSON, STEFFI (Stephanie Le Beau)
Died: June 5, 1967, New York. Screen and television actress. Married to composer and arranger Luther Henderson.

Appeared in: **1966** Picture Mommy Dead.

HENDERSON, TED (Theodore Henderson)
Born: 1888. Died: July 20, 1962, Santa Paula, Calif. Screen actor and film producer.

Appeared in: **1924** Beyond All Odds. **1927** The Mojave Kid.

HENDERSON, V. TALBOT
Born: 1879. Died: May 24, 1946, Los Angeles, Calif. Screen and stage actor.

Appeared in: **1929** The Bachelors' Club.

HENDERSON-BLAND, ROBERT
Born: England. Died: Aug. 18, 1941, London, England. Screen and stage actor.

Appeared in:From Manger to Cross.

HENDRIAN, DUTCH (Oscar G. Hendrian)
Born: 1896. Died: Dec. 13, 1953. Screen actor.

Appeared in: **1932** Vanity Street; That's My Boy. **1933** Air Hostess. **1934** Most Precious Thing in Life; Three Little Pigskins (short). **1935** Restless Knights (short). **1936** Nevada. **1939** Bulldog Drummond's Secret Police. **1940** Little Old New York.

HENDRICKS, BEN, JR.
Born: Nov. 2, 1893, New York, N.Y. Died: Aug. 15, 1938, Los Angeles, Calif. Screen actor. Son of actor Ben Hendricks, Sr. (dec. 1930). Entered films in 1911.

Appeared in: **1921** The Land of Hope; Room and Board. **1922** The Headless Horseman; Free Air. **1923** The Broad Road; The Old Fool; Marriage Morals. **1924** Cyclone Rider; Just Off Broadway; Against All Odds; The Man Who Played Square. **1926** Take It from Me; The Fighting Buckaroo; One Minute to Play; Rolling Home; Skinner's Dress Suit; What Happened to Jones? **1927** Barbed Wire; Birds of Prey; A Racing Romeo. **1928** My Friend from India; Waterfront. **1929** Footlights and Fools; The Great Divide; Twin Beds; Synthetic Sin; The Wild Party. **1930** Men without Women; The Furies; The Girl of the Golden West; Ladies Love Brutes; Road to Paradise; Sunny. **1931** The

Public Enemy. **1932** Rain; Pack up Your Troubles; Fireman Save My Child; The Kid from Spain; Fast Life; The Woman from Monte Carlo. **1933** Out All Night; The Important Witness; After Tonight. **1934** The Big Shakedown; We're Not Dressing; Blind Date; Jimmy the Gent; The St. Louis Kid. **1935** Dr. Socrates; Don't Bet on Blondes; Front Page Woman; The Man Who Reclaimed His Head; Northern Frontier; O'Shaughnessy's Boy. **1936** Draegerman Courage; North of Nome; Great Guy; Theodora Goes Wild. **1937** The Go-Getter; Slim; Roaring Timber. **1938** Three Blind Men; A Slight Case of Murder; Sergeant Murphy; Born to be Wild.

HENDRICKS, BEN, SR.
Born: 1862, Buffalo, N.Y. Died: Apr. 30, 1930, Hollywood, Calif. Screen, stage and vaudeville actor. Father of actor Ben Hendricks, Jr. (dec. 1938).

Appeared in: **1923** Big Dan. **1924** The City That Never Sleeps. **1925** Greater Than a Crown; Tides of Passion; Welcome Home. **1926** Satan Town. **1930** Black Waters.

HENDRICKS, DUDLEY C.
Born: Aug. 3, 1870, La Grange, Ky. Died: Feb. 3, 1942, Pasadena, Calif. Screen actor.

Appeared in: **1920** The Kentucky Colonel; Honest Hutch; The Little Shepherd of Kingdom Come. **1921** His Back Against the Wall. **1926** The Scrappin' Kid; The Terror. **1927** Flying U Ranch; Grinning Guns.

HENDRICKS, LOUIS
Born: Buffalo, N.Y. Died: Dec. 18, 1923 (long illness). Screen and stage actor.

Appeared in: **1921** The Conquest of Canaan; The Sign on the Door. **1923** The Custard Cup.

HENDRIE, ERNEST
Born: June 10, 1859, England. Died: Mar. 11, 1929, England? Screen, stage actor and author.

Appeared in: **1922** The Skipper's Wooing; A Will and a Way.

HENDRIKSON, ANDERS
Born: 1896, Stockholm, Sweden. Died: 1965, Sweden. Screen actor, film director and writer.

Appeared in: **1921** Sir Arne's Treasure. **1934** The Song of the Scarlet Flower. **1937** Oh What a Night. **1938** John Ericsson—The Victor at Hampton Roads; Frun Tillhanda (Servant Girls). **1939** They Staked Their Lives. **1940** Everybody at His Station; Hennes Lilla Majestat (Her Little Majesty). **1941** Life Goes On. **1942** Youth in Chains. **1943** Mr. Collin's Adventures. **1944** I Am Fire and Air; Henlaspelet. **1945** Tired Teodor. **1946** Asa-Hanna. **1947** The Key and the Ring. **1949** Fangelse (aka The Devil's Wanton—US 1962). **1950** Blood and Fire. **1952** Miss Julie. **1956** The Girl in the Dress-Coat; Giftas (Married Life aka Of Love and Lust—US 1959). **1962** Pojken I Tradet (The Boy in the Tree). **1965** Morianerna (aka I, the Body aka Morianna—US 1967). Other Swedish films: It Pays to Advertise; The Great Love; Only a Trumpeter; A Crime; Only a Woman; Dangerous Roads; The Ingegerd Bremssen Case; Train 56; Nothing But Old Nobility; Blood and Fire; The Most Beautiful Thing on Earth; Alfred Loved by the Girls; Walpurgis Night; 33.333; Intermezzo; Conflict; A Cold in the Head; Let's Have Success; With the People for the Country; Mr. Karlsson Mate and His Sweethearts; A Woman's Face; Rejoice While You are Young; At the Lady's Service; Home from Babylon; The Road to Heaven; I Killed; Defiance; Love; The Journey to You; The Road to Klockrike; Barabbas; The Clergyman of Uddarbo.

HENDRIX, JIMI
Born: 1947. Died: Sept. 18, 1970, London, England (drug overdose). Guitarist, screen actor and singer.

Appeared in: **1969** Monterey Pop; Popcorn—An Audio/Visual Rock Thing. **1970** Woodstock. **1972** Superstars in Film Concert. **1973** Free; Jimi Plays Berkeley; Keep on Rockin' Jimi Hendrix; Rainbow Bridge.

HENDRIX, N. E. "SHORTY"
Died: Mar. 4, 1973. Screen actor.

Appeared in: **1924** Walloping Wallace; Battling Buddy; Cyclone Buddy; Galloping Gallagher. **1925** Double Action Daniels; Reckless Courage. **1926** Double Daring. **1930** Oklahoma Cyclone.

HENDRIX, WANDA (Dixie Wanda Hendrix)
Born: Nov. 3, 1928, Jacksonville, Fla. Died: Feb. 1, 1981, Burbank, Calif. (pneumonia). Screen, radio and television actress. Divorced from actor Audie Murphy (dec. 1971), James Stack and Steve LaMonte.

Appeared in: **1945** Confidential Agent. **1947** Welcome Stranger; Ride the Pink Horse; Nora Prentiss; Variety Girl. **1948** Miss Tatlock's Millions; My Own True Love. **1949** Prince of Foxes; Song of Surrender. **1950** Saddle Tramp; Captain Carey, U.S.A.; The Admiral Was a Lady; Sierra. **1951** The Highwayman; My Brother, the Outlaw (aka My Outlaw Brother). **1952** Montana Territory; South of Algiers (aka The Golden Mask—US 1954). **1953** The Last Posse; Sea of Lost Ships. **1954** Highway Dragnet; The Black Dakotas. **1961** Boy Who Caught a Crook. **1963** Johnny Cool. **1964** Stage to Thunder Rock.

HENDRY, ANITA
Born: 1868. Died: Apr. 15, 1940, Brooklyn, N.Y. Screen actress and screenwriter. Married to actor David Miles (dec. 1915). Appeared in early Biograph films.

HENDRY, LEN
Died: Feb. 18, 1981. Screen actor.

Appeared in: **1944** Hail the Conquering Hero. **1953** Pony Express. **1954** Rear Window. **1955** The Girl Rush. **1958** Hot Spell. **1967** The Fastest Guitar Alive.

HENIE, SONJA
Born: Apr. 8, 1912, Oslo, Norway. Died: Oct. 12, 1969, in air near Oslo (leukemia). Screen, television actress and Olympic skating star.

Appeared in: **1936** One in a Million (film debut). **1937** Thin Ice. **1938** Happy Landing; My Lucky Star. **1939** Second Fiddle; Everything Happens at Night. **1941** Sun Valley Serenade. **1942** Iceland. **1943** Wintertime. **1945** It's a Pleasure. **1948** The Countess of Monte Cristo. **1958** Hello, London.

HENLEY, HOBART
Born: Nov. 23, 1891, Louisville, Ky. Died: May 22, 1964, Los Angeles, Calif. Screen, stage actor, film director and producer. Appeared in one-reelers produced in New York during early days of film.

Appeared in: **1914** Forgetting; When There's A Will, There's A Way; His Land Chance. **1915** Graft; The House of Fear; The Black Pearl; The Bombay Buddha; Court Martialed; Agnes Kempler's Sacrifice; The Eagle; A Little Brother of the Rich; The Silent Battle; The Phantom Fortune; The Measure of Leon Dubray; The Man in the Chair; The Terror. **1916** The Rogue With a Heart; A Dead Yesterday; The Crystal's Warning; Somewhere on the Battlefield; Temptation and the Man; A Child of Mystery; Partners; A Knight of the Night; The Sign of the Poppy; The Evil Women Do. **1917** A Woman of Clay. **1918** Parentage.

HENNEBERGER, BARBARA-MARIE "BARBI"
Born: 1941. Died: Apr. 12, 1964, St. Moritz, Switzerland (avalanche). West German ski champion and screen actress. Killed while making a sports documentary.

HENNECKE, CLARENCE R.
Born: Sept. 16, 1894, Omaha, Nebr. Died: Aug. 28, 1969, Santa Monica, Calif. Screen, vaudeville, television actor, film director and screenwriter. Entered films as a stuntman with Vitagraph. Appeared in Keystone Kop comedies.

Appeared in: **1949** Neptune's Daughter. **1950** Joe Palooka in Humphrey Takes a Chance.

HENNESSEY, DAVID
Born: 1852. Died: Mar. 24, 1926, Chicago, Ill. Screen and stage actor.

HENNESSEY, JOHN A.
Born: 1853. Died: May 16, 1920. Screen and stage actor. Married to stage actress Amy Ames (dec.).

HENNESSY, MICHAEL (Michael O'Haonghusa)
Born: 1925, Cork, Ireland. Died: Jan. 20, 1981, Dublin, Ireland (liver ailment). Screen and stage actor.

Appeared in: **1959** Home Is the Hero (US 1961). **1964** Girl With Green Eyes.

HENNING, PAT
Born: 1911. Died: Apr. 28, 1973, Miami, Fla. Screen, vaudeville, television actor, and circus performer.

Appeared in: **1938** Shine on Harvest Moon. **1953** Man on a Tightrope. **1954** On the Waterfront. **1958** Wind Across the Everglades. **1963** The Cardinal. **1969** Hello Down There.

HENNINGS, JOHN
Died: Nov. 8, 1933, St. Joseph, Mo. (suicide—gun shot). Screen and stage actor.

Appeared in: **1930** The Poor Millionaire.

HENRY, CHARLOTTE (Charlotte Virginia Henry)
Born: Mar. 3, 1915, Brooklyn, N.Y. Died: Apr. 11, 1980, La Jolla, Calif. (cancer). Screen and stage actress.

Appeared in: **1928** Stand and Deliver. **1930** Harmony at Home; On Your Back; Courage. **1931** Huckleberry Finn; Arrowsmith. **1932** Lena Rivers; Rebecca of Sunnybrook Farm; Forbidden. **1933** Manhunt; Alice in Wonderland. **1934** Babes in Toyland; The Last Gentleman; The Human Side. **1935** The Hoosier Schoolmaster; Three Kids and a Queen; Laddie. **1936** The Gentleman from Louisiana; Charlie Chan at the Opera; Hearts in Bondage; Forbidden Heaven. **1937** Jungle Menace (serial). **1941** Bowery Blitzkreig. **1942** She's in the Army.

HENRY, EMMALINE
Died: Oct. 8, 1979. Screen actress.

Appeared in: **1954** Top Banana. **1967** Divorce American Style. **1968** Rosemary's Baby. **1974** Harrad Jummer.

HENRY, FRANK THOMAS PATRICK
Born: 1894. Died: Oct. 3, 1963, Hollywood, Calif. Screen and vaudeville actor.

Appeared in: **1947** Happy's Holiday. **1948** Hazard.

HENRY, GALE
Born: Apr. 15, 1893, Bear Valley, Calif. Died: June 17, 1972, Palmdale, Calif. (pneumonia). Screen, stage actress and film producer.

HENRY, HANK (Henry Rosenthal)
Born: 1907, New York, N.Y. Died: Mar. 31, 1981, Las Vegas, Nev. (cancer). Screen, stage, vaudeville, television actor and burlesque performer.

Appeared in: **1946** Junior Prom. **1957** Pal Joey; The Joker Is Wild. **1960** Pepe; Oceans Eleven. **1962** Sergeants Three. **1963** Johnny Cool. **1964** Robin and the Seven Hoods. **1970** The Only Game in Town.

HENRY, JAY
Born: July 14, 1910, New York, N.Y. Died: Dec. 23, 1951, White Plains, N.Y. Screen actor.

Appeared in: **1934** We're Not Dressing.

HENRY, JOHN
Born: 1882. Died: Aug. 12, 1958, Winthrop, Mass. Screen and vaudeville actor.

Appeared in: **1924** Poison; Those Who Judge; Yankee Speed.

HENRY, JOHN, JR.
Died: May 2, 1974. Screen actor.

HENRY, ROBERT "BUZZ"
Born: Sept. 4, 1931, Colorado. Died: Sept. 30, 1971, Los Angeles, Calif. (motorcycle accident). Screen actor, stuntman and rodeo performer.

Appeared in: **1936** The Unknown Ranger. **1940** Buzzy Rides the Range. **1941** Phantom Pinto (aka Buzzy and the Phantom Pinto); Mr. Celebrity. **1944** Trigger Trail; Three of a Kind; The Great Mike; Trail to Gunsight. **1945** The Virginian. **1946** Dragonwyck; Hop Harrigan (serial); Danny Boy; Wild Beauty; Son of the Guardsman (serial); Wild West. **1947** Last of the Redmen; Law of the Canyon; King of the Wild Horses. **1948** Tex Granger (serial); Moonrise; Prairie Outlaws. **1950** Blue Grass of Kentucky; Rocky Mountain. **1951** Heart of the Rockies. **1952** Against All Flags. **1953** The Homesteaders; Last of the Pony Riders. **1954** Jubilee Trail; The Outcast; Bamboo Prison; Hell's Outpost; Man With the Steel Whip. **1955** The Indian Fighters; The Road to Denver. **1956** Jubal; Duel at Apache Wells; 54 Washington Street. **1957** The Lawless Eighties; 3:10 to Yuma. **1958** Cowboy; The Sheepman; Tonka; Imitation General. **1959** Face of a Fugitive. **1960** The Rise and Fall of Legs Diamond. **1962** The Manchurian Candidate. **1963** Captain Newman, MD; Spencer's Mountain. **1964** Seven Days in May. **1965** Shenandoah; The Rounders; Von Ryan's Express. **1966** Major Dundee; Our Man Flint; Texas Across the River. **1967** Tony Rome; In Like Flint; Waterhole #3. **1969** The Wild Bunch; Mackenna's Gold. **1970** Scullduggery; Macho Callahan.

HENRY, THOMAS "TOM" BROWNE
Died: June 30, 1980, Calif. Screen, stage, radio and television actor.

Appeared in: **1948** Behind Locked Doors; Joan of Arc. **1949** Johnny Allegro; House of Strangers; Post Office Investigator. **1950** It's a Small World; My Blue Heaven; Double Deal. **1951** Mr. Belvedere Goes to College. **1952** O. Henry's Full House; The Winning Team; Stars and Stripes Forever; Operation Secret; Deadline U.S.A. **1953** The Lady Wants a Mink; The Robe; Julius Caesar. **1954** Sitting Bull. **1955** The Violent Men (aka Rough Company); A Man Alone; Toughest Man Alive. **1956** D-Day the Sixth of June; The Leather Saint; Earth vs. the Flying Saucers; A Strange Adventure; The Power and the Prize; Fighting Trouble; Calling Homicide. **1957** My Man Godfrey; Beginning of the End; 20 Million Miles to Earth; Chicago Confidential; Blood of Dracula. **1958** Space Master X-7; Showdown at Boot Hill; The Case Against Brooklyn; Wink of an Eye; How to Make a Monster; Quantrill's Raiders. **1959** Say One for Me. **1960** I Passed for White. **1963** Gunfight at Comanche Creek.

HENSON, LESLIE
Born: Aug. 3, 1891, London, England. Died: Dec. 2, 1957, England. Screen and stage actor.

Appeared in: **1916** The Lifeguardsman; Wanted a Widow; The Real Thing. **1920** Broken Bottles; Alf's Button. **1924** Tons of Money. **1927** On With the Dance series. **1930** A Warm Corner. **1931** The Sport of Kings. **1933** It's a Boy! (US 1934); The Girl from Maxim's. **1935** Oh Daddy! **1943** The Demi-Paradise (aka Adventure for Two—US 1945). **1956** Home and Away.

HEPBURN, BARTON
Born: Feb. 28, 1906, Minneapolis, Minn. Died: Oct. 10, 1955, Hollywood, Calif. Stage and screen actor. Entered films in 1928.

Appeared in: **1929** Dynamite. **1930** Painted Faces. **1943** Hi Diddle Diddle. **1944** The Bridge of San Luis Rey. **1945** A Song for Miss Julie.

HEPWORTH, CECIL M.
Born: 1874, England. Died: Feb. 9, 1953, Greenford, Middlesex, England. Film producer, director, actor and screen writer. Married to actress Mrs. Cecil Hepworth.

Appeared in: **1898** An Interrupted Picnic; Exchanges is no Robbery; The Immature Punter; The Quarrelsome Anglers (aka The Stolen Drink); Two Fools in a Canoe (aka Two Cockneys in a Canoe). **1900** Wiping Something Off the Slate; The Conjurer and the Boer; The Punter's Mishap; The Gunpowder Plat; The Explosion of a Motor Car (aka The Delights of Automobiling—US); The Egg-Laying Man; Clown and Policeman; How It Feels to be Run Over; The Bathers; Topsy-Turvy Villa. **1901** Interior of a Railway Carriage—Bank Holiday. **1902** The Call to Arms; How to Stop a Motor Car; Peace with Honour. **1903** Alice in Wonderland; The Tragical Tale of a Belated Letter; The Unclean World—The Suburban Bunkum Microbe-Guyoscope. **1904** The Joke that Failed; The Great Servant Question; The Honeymoon—First, Second and Third Class. **1905** Rescued by Rover; Bathers Will be Prosecuted.

HERBERT, HANS
Born: 1875. Died: June 21, 1957, Hollywood, Calif. Screen, stage and television actor.

Appeared in: **1941** Hold that Ghost. **1943** The Phantom of the Opera. **1944** Mr. Skeffington; Ali Baba and the Forty Thieves; The Seventh Cross; Lake Placid Serenade. **1945** House of Frankenstein; Sudan. **1946** A Night in Paradise. **1950** Under My Skin. **1956** The First Traveling Saleslady.

HERBERT, HELEN
Born: 1873. Died: Oct. 27, 1946, Hollywood, Calif. Screen and stage actress. Married to actor Henry J. Hebert (dec. 1956 aka Henry J. Herbert). Entered films approx. 1924.

HERBERT, HENRY
Born: 1879, England. Died: Feb. 20, 1947, Flushing, N.Y. Screen and stage actor. Married to Gladys Herbert. Do not confuse with actor Henry J. Hebert (dec. 1956 aka Henry J. Herbert).

HERBERT, HENRY J. *See* HEBERT, HENRY J.

HERBERT, HOLMES E. (Edward Sanger)
Born: July 3, 1882, Mansfield Notts, England. Died: Dec. 26, 1956, Hollywood, Calif. Screen, stage, circus and minstrel actor.

Appeared in: **1918** The Doll's House. **1919** The White Heather. **1920** Black Is White; His House in Order; My Lady's Garter; The Right to Love; Lady Rose's Daughter. **1921** The Inner Chamber; The Family Closet; The Wild Goose; Heedless Moths; Her Lord and Master. **1922** Any Wife; A Woman's Woman; Divorce Coupons; Evidence; A Stage Romance; Moonshine Valley. **1923** I Will Repay (aka Swords and the Woman—US 1924); Toilers of the Sea. **1924** Love's Wilderness; The Enchanted Cottage; Another Scandal; Sinners in Heaven; Her Own Free Will. **1925** Daddy's Gone A'Hunting; A Woman of the World; Wreckage; Up the Ladder; Wildfire. **1926** The Honeymoon Express; The Wanderer; The Passionate Quest; Josselyn's Wife. **1927** The Fire Brigade; East Side, West Side; Lovers?; Mr. Wu; The Heart of Salome;

One Increasing Purpose; The Silver Slave; When a Man Loves; Slaves of Beauty; The Gay Retreat; The Nest. **1928** The Terror; On Trial; Gentlemen Perfer Blondes; The Sporting Age; Their Hour; Through the Breakers. **1929** Madame X; The Charlatan; Careers; The Careless Age; Her Private Life; The Kiss; The Thirteenth Chair; Untamed; Say It with Songs. **1930** The Ship from Shanghai. **1931** Chances; Broadminded; Daughter of Fu Manchu; The Hot Heiress; The Single Sin; Daughter of the Dragon. **1932** Dr. Jekyll and Mr. Hyde; Shop Angel; Central Park; Miss Pinkerton. **1933** Mystery of the Wax Museum; Sister of Judas; The Invisible Man. **1934** Beloved; The House of Rothschild; Count of Monte Cristo; The Curtain Falls; One in a Million; Pursuit of Happiness. **1935** Captain Blood; Cardinal Richelieu; Mark of the Vampire; Sons of Steel; Accent on Youth. **1936** The Charge of the Light Brigade; The Country Beyond; 15 Maiden Lane; Lloyds of London; Brilliant Marriage; The Gentleman from Louisiana. **1937** The Life of Emile Zola; Slave Ship; The Girl Said No; Here's Flash Casey; The Prince and the Pauper; Love Under Fire; Lancer Spy; The Thirteenth Chair (and 1929 version); House of Secrets. **1938** The Adventures of Robin Hood; The Bucaneer; Mystery of Mr. Wong; Say It in French; The Black Doll. **1939** Juarez; Trapped in the Sky; Mr. Moto's Last Warning; The Little Princess; Hidden Power; Stanley and Livingstone; The Adventures of Sherlock Holmes; Everything Happens at Night; We Are not Alone; Wolf Call; Bad Boy. **1940** The Letter; South of Suez; Foreign Correspondent; British Intelligence. **1941** Kitty Foyle; Man Hunt; International Squadron. **1942** Lady in a Jam; This Above All; Invisible Agent; The Undying Monster; The Ghost of Frankenstein; Sherlock Holmes and the Secret Weapon. **1943** Coevette K-225; Two Tickets to London; Sherlock Holmes in Washington. **1944** The Uninvited; Our Hearts Were Young and Gay; The Pearl of Death; The Bermuda Mystery; Enter Arsene Lupin; The Mummy's Curse; Calling Dr. Death. **1945** Jealousy; The House of Fear; Confidential Agent. **1946** The Bandit of Sherwood Forest; Three Strangers; The Verdict; Sherlock Holmes and the Secret Code (aka Dressed to Kill). **1947** Ivy; This Time for Keeps; Over the Santa Fe Trail; Singapore; Bulldog Drummond Strikes Back; Bulldog Drummond at Bay; The Swordsman. **1948** Family Honeymoon; Johnny Belinda; Sorry, Wrong Number; Command Decision; Wreck of the Hesperus; Jungle Jim. **1949** The Stratton Story; Barbary Pirate; Post Office Investigator. **1950** The Iroquois Trail. **1951** David and Bathsheba; Anne of the Indies; Law and the Lady. **1952** At Sword's Point; The Brigand.

HERBERT, HUGH

Born: Aug. 10, 1887, Binghamton, N.Y. Died: Mar. 13, 1952, North Hollywood, Calif. (heart attack). Screen, stage, vaudeville, television actor, playwright and screenwriter. Brother of actor Thomas Herbert (dec. 1946). Married to actress Anita Pam (dec. 1974).

Appeared in: **1927** Realization (short); Solomon's Children (short). **1928** The Lemon (short); On the Air (short); The Prediction (short); Husbands for Rent; Caught in the Fog. **1930** Danger Lights; Hook, Line and Sinker; Mind Your Own Business; Sin Ship. **1931** Laugh and Get Rich; Traveling Husbands; Friends and Lovers. **1932** Shampoo the Magician (short); The Lost Squadron; Faithless; Million Dollar Legs. **1933** Strictly Personal; Diplomaniacs; Goodbye Again; Bureau of Missing Persons; Footlight Parade; College Coach; From Headquarters; She Had to Say Yes; Convention City; Goldie Gets Along. **1934** Fashions of 1934; Easy to Love; Dames; Kansas City Princess; Wonder Bar; Harold Teen; Merry Wives of Reno; Fog over Frisco; The Merry Frinks. **1935** The Traveling Saleslady; Gold Diggers of 1935; A Trip Through a Hollywood Studio (short); A Midsummer Night's Dream; We're in the Money; Miss Pacific Fleet; To Beat the Band; Sweet Adeline. **1936** Colleen; Love Begins at 20; Sing Me a Love Song; One Rainy Afternoon; We Went to College. **1937** That Man's Here Again; The Singing Marine; Marry the Girl; The Perfect Specimen; Sh! The Octopus; Hollywood Hotel; Top of the Town. **1938** Men Are Such Fools; Gold Diggers in Paris; Four's a Crowd; The Great Waltz. **1939** Eternally Yours; Dad for a Day (short); The Little Accident; The Family Next Door; The Lady's from Kentucky. **1940** La Conga Nights; Private Affairs; Slightly Tempted; A Little Bit of Heaven; The Villain Still Pursued Her; The Hit Parade of 1941. **1941** Hellzapoppin!; Cracked Nuts; Meet the Chump; The Black Cat; Hello Sucker; Badlands of Dakota; Nobody's Fool. **1942** Mrs. Wiggs of the Cabbage Patch; There's One Born Every Minute; Don't Get Personal; You're Killing Me. **1943** It's a Great Life; Stage Door Canteen. **1944** Kismet; Beauty for Sale; Ever since Venus; Music for Millions. **1946** One Way to Love; Carnegie Hall; The Mayor's Husband (short); When the Wife's Away (short). **1947** Tall Dark and Gruesome (short); Blondie in the Dough. **1948** A Pinch in Time (short); A Miracle Can Happen; So This is New York; A Song Is Born; Girl from Manhattan; On Our Merry Way. **1949** Beautiful Blonde from Bashful Bend. **1951** Havana Rose.

HERBERT, LEW

Born: 1903. Died: July 30, 1968, Pittsburgh, Pa. Screen, stage and television actor.

Appeared in: **1950** Young Man with a Horn. **1963** Love with a Proper Stranger.

HERBERT, SIDNEY

Died: Dec. 24, 1927. Screen actor.

Appeared in: **1920** The Thief; The Branded Woman. **1921** The Single Track. **1922** Orphans of the Storm; Missing Millions. **1923** If Winter Comes; Under the Red Robe. **1924** Her Love Story.

HERBERT, THOMAS F.

Born: Nov. 25, 1888, New York, N.Y. Died: Apr. 3, 1946, Los Angeles, Calif. Screen, stage and vaudeville actor. Brother of actor Hugh Herbert (dec. 1952).

Appeared in: **1931** Traveling Husbands. **1933** Bed of Roses. **1934** Belle of the Nineties. **1935** The Man Who Broke the Bank at Monte Carlo. **1937** Topper; Banjo On My Knee; Think Fast; Mr. Moto; Stars Over Arizona. **1938** Professor Beware. **1940** Remedy for Riches. **1941** Two-Faced Woman. **1942** Tennessee Johnson. **1943** Dixie.

HERBST, ROGER

Born: 1945, Germany. Died: Aug. 15, 1980, near Frankfurt, West Germany (auto accident). Screen and television actor.

HERFORD, WILLIAM B.

Born: May 5, 1853, Yorkshire, England. Died: Dec. 27, 1934, England? Screen actor.

HERIAT, PHILIPPE

Born: 1898, France. Died: Oct., 1971, France. Screen actor, author and screenwriter.

Appeared in: **1925** Les Miracles des Loups (The Miracle of the Wolves). **1929** Sea-Fever. **1938** Rothschild.

HERLEIN, LILLIAN

Born: c. 1895. Died: Apr. 13, 1971, New York, N.Y. Screen, stage, vaudeville, radio and television actress.

Appeared in: **1922** Solomon in Society.

HERMAN, AL

Born: 1886. Died: July 2, 1967, Los Angeles, Calif. Screen actor.

Appeared in: **1924** Captain Blood. **1926** Beyond the Trail. **1928** The Assassin of Grief (short). **1931** Bad Company. **1935** Harmony Lane. **1936** Fury. **1937** Hollywood Cowboy; Talent Scout; Paid to Dance; Torchy Blane, the Adventurous Blonde; Manhattan-Merry-Go-Round; Headin' East. **1939** Conspiracy; Swanee River. **1940** Oklahoma Renegades. **1941** Manpower; The Wagons Roll at Night. **1942** Boston Blackie Goes Hollywood. **1952** Dream Boat.

HERMAN, JACK

Died: Aug. 27, 1971. Screen actor.

Appeared in: **1960** Beyond the Time Barrier.

HERMAN, JILL KRAFT

Born: 1931, N.Y. Died: June 25, 1970, Chicago, Ill. (cancer). Screen, stage and television actress.

Appeared in: **1951** Goodbye, My Fancy.

HERMAN, MILTON C.

Born: 1896. Died: Jan. 21, 1951, Astoria, N.Y. (coronary thrombosis). Screen, radio and television actor.

HERMAN, TOM

Born: 1909. Died: Mar. 26, 1972, Hollywood, Calif. Screen actor and professional prizefighter.

Appeared in: **1956** The Harder They Fall.

HERMINE, HILDA

Died: June 15, 1975. Screen actress.

HERNANDEZ, ALBERT

Born: 1899, Mexico. Died: Jan. 2, 1948, Los Angeles, Calif. (after a fall). Screen actor. Appeared in silent films.

HERNANDEZ, ANNA (Anna Dodge)
Born: Oct. 19, 1867, River Falls, Wis. Died: May 4, 1945, Los Angeles, Calif. (pneumonia). Stage and screen actress. Married to actor George Hernandez (dec. 1922).

Appeared in: **1915** The Rosary; The Heritage. **1918** Battling Jane. **1919** Hearts Asleep; Leave it to Susan. **1920** The Gift Supreme; The Jack Knife; Darling Mine; Burglar Proof; An Amteur Devil (aka Wanted—A Blemish). **1924** Molly O'; The Rowdy. **1922** The Kentucky Derby. **1923** The Town Scandal; The Extra Girl. **1924** Name the Man; The Law Forbids. **1931** Fainting Lover (short); The Cannonball (short). **1932** Speed in the Gay Nineties.

HERNANDEZ, GEORGE F.
Born: June 6, 1863, Placerville, Calif. Died: Dec., 1922, Los Angeles, Calif. Screen and stage actor. Married to actress Anna Hernandez (dec. 1945).

Appeared in: **1912** When Helen was Elected; How the Cause Was Won; The Great Drought; Her Education; The Count of Monte Cristo. **1914** Footprints; Who Killed George Graves?; One Traveler Returns. **1915** The Lady of Cyclamen. **1917** The Greater Law; Broadway Arizona. **1918** Betty Takes a Hand. **1919** Mary Regan; The Silver Girl; Be a Little Sport; Courageous Coward. **1920** Village Sleuth; Seeds of Vengeance. **1921** After Your Own Heart; First Love; Just Out of College; The Innocent Cheat; The Lure of Egypt; The Road Demon. **1922** Arabia; Billy Jim; Bluebird, Jr.; The Man Under Cover; Flaming Hearts.

HERNANDEZ, JOE
Died: Feb. 2, 1972. Screen actor.

Appeared in: **1938** Long Shot. **1947** That's My Man; Black Gold. **1949** Maggie and Jiggs in Jackpot Jitters.

HERNANDEZ, JUAN G. "JUANO"
Born: 1896, San Juan, Puerto Rico. Died: July 17, 1970, San Juan, Puerto Rico (cerebral hemorrhage). Black screen, stage and circus actor.

Appeared in: **1932** Girl from Chicago. **1940** Lying Lips. **1949** Intruder in the Dust; The Accused. **1950** Stars in My Crown; The Breaking Point; Young Man with a Horn. **1955** Kiss Me Deadly; The Trial. **1956** Ransom. **1957** Something of Value. **1958** The Roots; St. Louis Blues; Machete; The Mark of the Hawk. **1960** Sergeant Rutledge. **1961** The Sins of Rachel Cade; Two Loves. **1962** Hemingway's Adventures of a Young Man. **1965** The Pawnbroker. **1969** The Reivers; The Extraordinary Seaman. **1970** They Call Me Mr. Tibbs.

HERON, JOYCE
Born: Nov. 6, 1916, Port Said, Egypt. Died: 1980, England? Screen and stage actress.

Appeared in: **1942** Women Aren't Angels (film debut). **1945** The Agitator (US 1949). **1950** She Shall Have Murder. **1959** Beyond This Place (aka Web of Evidence—US 1960).

HERRAND, MARCEL
Born: 1898, France. Died: June 11, 1953, France? Screen actor.

Appeared in: **1947** Les Enfants du Paradis; Etoile Sams Lumieve (Star Without Light); The Devils Own Envoy. **1948** The Room Upstairs; Ruy Blas. **1952** Fanfan the Tulip (US 1953). **1957** Respectful Prostitute.

HERREROS, ENRIQUE, SR.
Born: 1904, Spain. Died: Sept. 17, 1977, Santander, Spain (result of auto accident). Humorist, screen actor, film director, screenwriter and talent agent.

HERRICK, JACK
Born: 1891. Died: June 18, 1952. Screen actor.

Appeared in: **1923** The Abysmal Brute; Big Dan. **1924** In Fast Company. **1925** Dick Turpin; The Fear Fighter; The Happy Warrior; The Way of a Girl. **1926** Broadway Billy; One Punch O'Day; Walloping Kid. **1927** Is Zat So?; The Wheel of Destiny. **1928** Beau Broadway. **1930** The Arizona Kid. **1931** The Tip Off.

HERRING, AGGIE
Born: Feb. 4, 1876, San Francisco, Calif. Died: Oct. 28, 1939. Screen, stage and vaudeville actress.

Appeared in: **1916** Female of the Species. **1917** The Snarl; Mad Cap Madge. **1918** Within the Cup. **1919** Cupid Forecloses; A Yankee Princess; A Man's Fight; The Hoodlum. **1920** Hairpins; The Lord Loves the Irish; The Sagebusher; The Dream Cheater; The Dwelling Place of Light; Down Home; Big Happiness; Little Shepherd of Kingdom Come. **1921** The Rookies Return; Lure of Egypt; Mysterious Rider; Queenie. **1922** A Blind Bargain; Heart's Haven; Heroes of the Street; Nine Points of the Law; The Ninety and Nine; Oliver Twist; The Ragged Heiress. **1923** The Isle of Lost Ships; The Age of Desire; The Brass Bottle; Let's Go; Pioneer Trails; What a Wife Learned. **1924** The Silent Watcher. **1925** Any Woman; Pampered Youth; Peacock Feathers; Sally, Irene and Mary. **1926** Kosher Kitty Kelly; The Frontier Trail; Laddie; Sweet Daddies; Watch Your Wife. **1927** The Gorilla; Finnegan's Ball; Loco Luck; McFadden's Flats; The Princess From Hoboken. **1928** Do Your Duty; Lady Be Good; The Head of the Family; That Certain Thing. **1929** Children of the Ritz; Dark Streets; Smiling Irish Eyes. **1930** In the Next Room; Clancy in Wall Street; Billy the Kid; Kathleen Mavourneen; Fat Wives for Thin (short). **1931** Millie. **1933** She Done Him Wrong; Sin of Nora Moran. **1934** Green Eyes; The Quitter; Stolen Sweets; Curtain Falls. **1936** Daniel Boone; The Dark Hour. **1937** The Man in Blue; Don't Tell the Wife. **1938** Island in the Sky.

HERRMAN, ROBERT
Died: Jan. 3, 1978. Screen actor.

HERRNFELD, ANTON
Born: 1865. Died: Oct., 1929, Berlin, Germany. Yiddish screen and stage actor.

HERSHFIELD, HARRY (Abe Kabible)
Born: 1885. Died: Dec. 15, 1974, New York, N.Y. Cartoonist, journalist, humorist and screen actor.

Appeared in: **1942** The Great White Way.

HERSHOLT, JEAN
Born: July 12, 1886, Copenhagen, Denmark. Died: June 2, 1956, Beverly Hills, Calif. (cancer). Screen, stage and radio actor. Won 1939 Special Academy Award for his work for the Motion Picture Relief Fund and won 1949 Special Award for Dancing in the Dark.

Appeared in: **1915** Don Quixote. **1916** Princess Virtue. **1921** The Four Horsemen of the Apocalypse; A Certain Rich Man; The Man of the Forest; The Servant in the House. **1922** Tess of Storm Country; Golden Dreams; The Gray Dawn; Heart's Haven; When Romance Rides. **1923** Jazzmania; Quicksands; The Stranger's Banquet; Red Lights. **1924** Cheap Kisses; The Goldfish; Her Night of Romance; Sinners in Silk; Torment; The Woman on the Jury; Greed. **1925** Dangerous Innocence; Don Q; Fifth Avenue Models; So Big; If Marriage Fails; Stella Dallas; A Woman's Faith. **1926** Flames; The Greater Glory; It Must Be Love; My Old Dutch; The Old Soak. **1927** The Student Prince in Old Heidelberg; The Wrong Mr. Wright. **1928** Alias the Deacon; The Battle of the Sexes; Give and Take; Jazz Mad; The Secret Hour; 13 Washington Square; Abie's Irish Rose. **1929** The Girl on the Barge; Modern Love; The Younger Generation; You Can't Buy Love. **1930** The Case of Sergeant Grischa; The Cat Creeps; The Climax; Hell Harbor; Mamba; The Third Alarm; Viennese Nights; The Rise of Helga. **1931** Transatlantic; Susan Lennox, Her Rise and Fall; Sin of Madelon Claudet; Daybreak; Soldier's Plaything; Phantom of Paris; Private Lives; Lullaby. **1932** Emma; Grand Hotel; Hearts of Humanity; The Mask of Fu Manchu; Beast of the City; Are You Listening?; Night Court; New Morals for Old; Skyscraper Souls; Unashamed; Justice for Sale; Flesh. **1933** The Crime of the Century; Song of the Eagle; Dinner at Eight; Christopher Bean. **1934** Men in White; The Painted Veil; The Cat and the Fiddle; The Fountain. **1935** Mark of the Vampire; Murder in the Fleet; Break of Hearts. **1936** Tough Guy; His Brother's Wife; The Country Doctor; Sins of Man; Reunion; One in a Million; The Old Soak. **1937** Seventh Heaven; Heidi. **1938** Happy Landing; Alexander's Ragtime Band; I'll Give a Million; Five of a Kind. **1939** Mr. Moto in Danger Island; Meet Dr. Christian. **1940** The Courageous Dr. Christian; Dr. Christian Meets the Women; Remedy for Riches. **1941** They Meet Again; Melody for Three. **1943** Stage Door Canteen. **1949** Dancing in the Dark. **1955** Run for Cover.

HERTEL, ADOLPH R.
Born: 1878. Died: Mar. 16, 1958, Hollywood, Calif. Screen actor and film director.

HERTZINGER, CHARLES W.
Born: Aug. 10, 1864, Nevada City, Calif. Died: Feb. 18, 1953, Los Angeles, Calif. (cerebral hemorrhage). Screen and stage actor.

Appeared in: **1920** Honor Bound. **1921** Rich Girl, Poor Girl. **1926** The Bat; The Winning of Barbara Worth. **1927** Riders of the West; Snowbound. **1932** Tangled Fortunes. **1941** All That Money Can Buy. **1952** The Devil and Daniel Webster (reissue and retitle of All That Money Can Buy—1941).

HERVEY, GRIZELDA
Born: 1901, Plomesgate, Suffolk, England. Died: Dec. 17, 1980, England? Screen, stage and radio actress.

Appeared in: **1935** The Informer. **1938** Girl in the Street. **1948** Kiss the Blood Off My Hands. **1956** My Teenage Daughter (aka Teenage Bad Girl—US 1957). **1958** Gideon's Day (aka Gideon of Scotland Yard—US 1959).

HERZ, RALPH C.
Born: Mar. 25, 1878, Paris, France. Died: July 12, 1921, Atlantic City, N.J. (diabetes). Screen, stage and vaudeville actor. Divorced from actress Lucy Glaser. Married to Frances Logan.

Appeared in: **1917** Winning a Heiress; Married, But Single; The Mystery of No. 47.

HERZOG, FRED
Born: 1869. Died: May 2, 1928. Screen actor.

Appeared in: **1920** Forbidden Trails; King Spruce. **1921** The Big Adventure. **1926** The Scarlet Letter.

HESLEWOOD, TOM
Born: Apr. 8, 1868, Hessle, Yorks, England. Died: Apr. 28, 1959, England? Screen, stage actor and costume designer.

Appeared in: **1922** The Glorious Adventure.

HESLOP, CHARLES
Born: June 8, 1883, Thames Ditton, Surrey, England. Died: Apr. 13, 1966, London, England. Screen, stage and vaudeville actor.

Appeared in: **1920** Hobson's Choice. **1931** Sunshine Susie (aka The Office Girl—US 1932). **1933** This Is the Life (US 1935). **1934** Waltzes from Vienna (aka Strauss's Great Waltz—US 1935). **1935** Charing Cross Road. **1938** Crackerjack (aka The Man With a Hundred Faces—US). **1939** The Lambeth Walk (aka Me and My Girl—US 1940). **1942** Flying Fortress; The Peterville Diamond. **1950** Don't Say Die (aka Never Say Die). **1951** The Second Mate; The Late Edwina Black (aka Obsessed—US). **1959** Follow a Star (US 1961). **1962** A Pair of Briefs (US 1963).

HESSE, BARON WILLIAM
Born: 1885, Russia. Died: Apr. 4, 1936, West Coast, U.S. (following amputation of leg; also diabetes). Screen actor.

Appeared in: **1929** Prisoners. **1934** The Pursuit of Happiness. **1935** The Story of Louis Pasteur.

HESSEL, EDITH (Edith Bell)
Born: 1923, Seattle, Wash. Died: Dec. 16, 1981, Tarrytown, N.Y. (after long illness and due to exposure). Screen, stage actress, film producer and singer. Married to film producer Leigh Hessel.

HESTER, HARVEY
Born: 1897. Died: Mar. 28, 1967. Screen actor.

Appeared in: **1956** The Great Locomotive Chase.

HESTERBERG, TRUDE
Born: 1897, Berlin, Germany. Died: 1967, Munich, Germany. Screen and stage actress.

Appeared in: **1921** Der Roman Eines Dienstmaedchens. **1923** Fridericus Rex (aka Ein Koenigsschicksal). **1925** Die Frau mit dem Etwas; Vorderhaus und Hinterhaus. **1926** Manon Lescaut; Der Dumme August des Zirkus Romanelli; Der Juxbaron; Liebeshandel; Madame Wuenscht Keine Kinder (Madame Wants No Children—US 1927); Maedchenhandel; Wie Einst im Mai. **1927** Flucht vor Blond; Das Gefaehrliche Alter; Laster der Menschheit; Die Letzte Nacht; Die Lorelei; Zwei Unterm Himmelzelt. **1928** Die Grosse Abenteurerin; Heut' Spielt der Strauss; Die Kleine Sklavin; Wenn die Mutter und die Tochter ...; Zwei Rote Rosen. **1929** Strauss—The Waltz King; Forbidden Love; Aufruhr im Junggesellenheim; Der Straefling aus Stambul. **1930** In Wien hab' ich Einmal ein Maedel Geliebt (US 1934). **1931** Die Maenner um Lucie; Arme wie Eine Kirchenmaus; Die Nackte Wahrheit; Stuerme der Leidenschaft (US 1932); Die Nacht der Entscheidung (aka The Virtuous Sin). **1932** Mieter Schulze Gegen Alle; Ein Blonder Traum (Blonde Dream). **1933** Ich Will Dich Liebe Lehren; Ist Mein Mann Nicht Fabelhaft? (US 1936); Der Page vom Dalmasse-Hotel (US 1935). **1934** Mein Herz Ruft Nach Dir; Die Grosse Chance (US 1935); Der Fall Benken (aka Ueberfall im Hotel). **1935** Alles Weg'n dem Hund (US 1936, aka Das Verrueckte Testament); Der Gruene Domino. **1936** Drei Tolle Tage; Paul und Pauline; Befehl ist Befehl; Der Raub der Sabinerinnen;

Maedchenraeuber. **1937** Sein Bester Freund; Der Unwiderstehliche (The Irresistable Man). **1940** Golowin Geht Durch die Stadt; Tip auf Amalia. **1941** Jakko. **1942** Der Hochtourist. **1943** Am Ende der Welt (At the Edge of the World). **1949** Das Geheimnis der Roten Katze; Der Blaue Strohhut; Um Eine Nasenlaenge. **1950** Inkognito im Paradies; Die Nacht ohne Suende. **1951** Corinna Schmidt; Schatten Ueber Neapel (aka Camorra). **1952** Alraune. **1953** Die Geschiedene Frau; Brieftraeger Mueller; Jonny Rettet Nebrador; Unter den Sternen von Capri; Die Geschichte vom Kleinen Muck (aka Little Mook); Abenteuer aus 1001 Nacht. **1954** Der Zigeunerbaron. **1955** Oh—Diese "Lieben" Verwandten; Der Froehliche Wanderer; Parole Heimat; Sonnenschein und Wolkenbruch. **1956** Weil du arm Bist Musst Du Frueher Sterben; Das Alte Foersterhaus; Holiday am Woerthersee. **1957** Nachts im Gruenen Kakadu; Frauenarzt Dr. Bertram; Es Wird Alles Wieder Gut. **1959** Skandal um Dodo.

HEWITT, HENRY
Born: Dec. 28, 1885, London, England. Died: Aug., 1968, Newbury, England. Screen and stage actor.

Appeared in: **1931** Stamboul. **1932** Betrayal; The First Mrs. Fraser. **1934** Jew Suess (aka Power—US). **1935** Department Store (aka Bargain Basement). **1936** Rembrandt. **1937** The High Command. **1938** Just Like a Woman; Black Limelight (US 1939); Old Iron. **1940** Sailors Three (aka Three Cockeyed Sailors—US 1941). **1941** The Black Sheep of Whitehall. **1942** The Young Mr. Pitt; The Day Will Dawn (aka The Avengers—US). **1944** Give Us the Moon. **1951** Happy-Go-Lovely. **1952** Emergency Call (aka The Hundred Hour Hunt—US 1953); Top Secret (aka Mr. Potts Goes to Moscow—US 1954); Where's Charley? **1957** The Naked Truth (aka Your Past Is Showing—US 1958).

HEWSTON, ALFRED H. (aka ALFRED HEUSTON)
Born: Sept. 12, 1880, San Francisco, Calif. Died: Sept. 6, 1947. Screen and stage actor. Son of stage actress Lillian O'Dell and actor Clarence King (dec.). Entered films in 1911.

Appeared in: **1915** Just Jim. **1920** The following shorts: Prince of Daffydill; Rocked to Sleep; Hay Fever; Henpecked and Pecked Hens; Sweet Dynamite. **1922** Blind Circumstances; The Hate Trail; Diamond Carlisle. **1923** The Web of the Law. **1924** Cyclone Buddy; Horse Fly Wiggins; Trail Dust. **1925** Let's Go Gallagher; The Wyoming Wildcat; Fightin' Odds; On the Go; Flashing Steeds; Tearin' Loose; Warrior Gap. **1926** Beyond All Odds; Masquerade Bandit; The Arizona Streak; Out of the West; Lure of the West. **1927** Splitting the Breeze. **1928** The Sky Rider. **1929** 'Neath Western Skies; The Cowboy and the Outlaw; Silent Sentinel; The Man from Nevada; West of the Rockies. **1930** Breezy Bill; Near the Rainbow's End; Firebrand Jordan. **1931** Rainbow Trail.

HEYBURN, WELDON
Born: Sept. 19, 1904, Selma, Ala. Died: May 18, 1951, Los Angeles, Calif. Screen and stage actor. His film career was hampered due to his resemblance to actor Clark Gable. Divorced from actress Greta Nissen.

Appeared in: **1932** Careless Lady; Chandu the Magician; Call Her Savage; The Gay Caballero; The Silent Witness. **1933** West of Singapore. **1934** Hired Wife. **1935** Convention Girl. **1936** Speed. **1937** Git Along Little Dogies; Sea Racketeers; Atlantic Flight; The Thirteenth Man. **1938** Saleslady; Crime School; The Mysterious Rider; Dynamite Delaney. **1939** Fugitive at Large; Panama Patrol; Should a Girl Marry? **1940** North West Mounted Police; The Trail Blazers. **1941** Caught in the Draft; Flight from Destiny; Redhead; Criminals Within; In Old Chicago; Stick to Your Guns; Jungle Man. **1942** Code of the Outlaw; Rock River Renegades; Murder in the Fun House. **1943** Death Valley Manhunt; Bordertown Trails; Code of the Prairie; Westward Bound; Yellow Rose of Texas. **1944** The Princess and the Pirate; The Chinese Cat. **1945** Incendiary Blonde. **1946** Frontier Gun Law.

HEYDT, LOUIS JEAN
Born: Apr. 17, 1905, Montclair, N.J. Died: Jan. 29, 1960, Boston, Mass. Screen, stage and television actor. Entered films in 1937.

Appeared in: **1937** Make Way for Tomorrow. **1938** They're Always Caught (short); Test Pilot; I Am the Law. **1939** Charlie Chan at Treasure Island; Dad for a Day (short); Let Freedom Ring; They Made Her a Spy; Reno; Gone With the Wind; They Made Me a Criminal; Each Dawn I Die. **1940** Santa Fe Trail; Johnny Apollo; A Child is Born; The Man Who Talked Too Much; Pier 13; Let's Make Music; Abe Lincoln in Illinois; Dr. Ehrlich's Magic Bullet; All About Hash (short); The Hidden Master (short); The Great McGinty; Joe and Ethel Turp Call on the President. **1941** How Green Was My Valley; High Sierra; Sleepers West; Dive Bomber; Power Dive; Midnight Angel. **1942** Ten Gentlemen from West Point; Manilla Calling; Tortilla

Flat; Triumph Over Pain; Commandos Strike at Dawn; Pacific Blackout; Captains of the Clouds. **1943** Mission to Moscow; Stage Door Canteen; Gung Ho; One Dangerous Night; The Iron Major. **1944** The Story of Dr. Wassell; The Great Moment; See Here, Private Hargrove; Her Primitive Man; Thirty Seconds Over Tokyo. **1945** Betrayal from the East; Our Vines Have Tender Grapes; Zombies on Broadway; They Were Expendable. **1946** The Big Sleep; The Hoodlum Saint; Gentleman Joe Palooka. **1947** I Cover Big Town; Spoilers of the North. **1948** California's Golden Beginning; Bad Men of Tombstone. **1949** Make Believe Ballroom; Come to the Stable; The Kid from Cleveland. **1950** The Great Missouri Raid; The Furies; Paid in Full. **1951** Al Jennings of Oklahoma; Raton Pass; Rawhide; Criminal Lawyer; Roadblock; Drums in the Deep South; Warpath; Two of a Kind; Sailor Beware. **1952** Mutiny; The Old West; Models, Inc. **1953** The Vanquished; Island in the Sky. **1954** A Star Is Born; Boy From Oklahoma. **1955** The Eternal Sea; Ten Wanted Men; No Man's Woman. **1956** Stranger at My Door; Wetbacks. **1957** Badge of Marshal Brennan; Raiders of Old California; The Wings of Eagles. **1958** The Man Who Died Twice. **1959** Inside the Mafia.

HEYES, HERBERT
Born: Aug. 3, 1889, Vaner, Wash. Died: May 30, 1958, North Hollywood, Calif. Screen and stage actor.

Appeared in: **1915** A Man Afraid; The Whirlpool. **1916** Under Two Flags; The Vixen; The Final Curtain; Wild Oats; Straight Way. **1917** The Darling of Paris; The Outsider; The Tiger Woman; The Slave. **1918** The Heart of the Sunset; Salome; The Lesson; The Fallen Angel; Her Inspiration?; Gambling in Souls. **1919** The Adventures of Ruth (serial). **1920** Ruth of the Rockies (serial). **1921** The Queen of Sheba; The Blushing Bride; The Dangerous Moment; Dr. Jim; Wolves of the North; Ever Since Eve. **1922** Shattered Dreams. **1923** One Stolen Night. **1924** It Is the Law. **1942** Destination Unknown; Tennessee Johnson. **1943** Calling Wild Bill Elliott; Campus Rhythm; Death Valley Manhunt; Mission to Moscow; It Ain't Hay. **1944** Standing Room Only; The Fighting Seabees; It Happened Tomorrow; Detective Kitty O'Day; Outlaws of Santa Fe; Million Dollar Kid; Mr. Winkle Goes to War. **1945** Wilson. **1947** Miracle on 34th Street. **1948** T-Men; The Cobra Strikes; Behind Locked Doors. **1950** Kiss Tomorrow Goodbye; Tripoli; Union Station. **1951** Bedtime for Bonzo; A Place in the Sun; Three Guys Named Mike. **1952** Park Row; Carbine Williams; Ruby Gentry; Something to Live For. **1953** Man of Conflict; Let's Do It Again. **1955** The Court-Martial of Billy Mitchell; The Far Horizons; Love Is a Many Splendored Thing; New York Confidential; The Seven Little Foys; Sincerely Yours. **1956** The Ten Commandments.

HEYWOOD, HERBERT
Born: Feb. 1, 1881, Illinois. Died: Sept. 15, 1964, Van Nuys, Calif. (coronary thrombosis). Screen and stage actor.

Appeared in: **1934** Music in the Air; Gentlemen are Born; Marie Galante; Caravan. **1935** The Irish in Us; Black Fury; Go Into Your Dance; Moonlight on the Prairie; Escape from Devil's Island; Ladies Crave Excitement. **1936** The Story of Louis Pasteur; Road Gang; Draegerman Courage; King of the Pecos. **1937** The Life of Emile Zola; Slave Ship. **1938** Born to be Wild; Three Blind Mice; Swing, Sister, Swing; King of the Lumberjacks; Blockade. **1940** The Grapes of Wrath; No Time for Comedy; Legion of the Lawless; Little Old New York. **1941** They Died With Their Boots On; One Foot in Heaven; Strawberry Blonde; Blues in the Night; The Great American Broadcast. **1942** Almost Married. **1943** Northern Pursuit; Swingtime Johnny. **1944** None But the Lonely Heart; The Merry Monahans. **1945** Billy Rose's Diamond Horseshoe. **1946** Scarlet Street; Idea Girl; Smoky. **1947** The Egg and I; Brute Force. **1948** Feudin', Fussin', and A-Fightin'; Family Honeymoon; Green Grass of Wyoming; Scudda Hoo! Scudda Hay! **1949** Take One False Step. **1950** The Petty Girl; Ticket to Tomahawk (aka The Sheriff's Daughter).

HIBBARD, EDNA
Born: 1895, Calif. Died: Dec. 26, 1942, New York, N.Y. Screen, stage and vaudeville actress.

Appeared in: **1922** Island Wives. **1930** An Ill Wind (short).

HIBBERT, GEOFFREY
Born: June 2, 1922, Hull, Yorkshire, England. Died: Feb. 3, 1969, Epsom, England (heart attack). Screen, stage and television actor.

Appeared in: **1941** Love on the Dole (stage and film versions); The Common Touch. **1942** The Next of Kin (US 1943); In Which We Serve. **1943** The Shipbuilders. **1952** Secret People; Emergency Call (aka The Hundred Hour Hunt—US 1953). **1953** Albert RN (aka Break to Freedom—US 1955). **1954** For Better, For Worse (aka Cocktails in the Kitchen—US 1955). **1957** The End of the Line. **1958** Orders to Kill. **1959** The Great Van Robbery (US 1963); Crash Dive. **1962** Live Now—Pay Later. **1963** Heavens Above!

HIBY, CHARLES
Born: Dec. 27, 1880, Hamilton, Ontario, Canada. Died: Feb. 16, 1947, Los Angeles, Calif. Screen and stage actor.

HICKEY, HOWARD L.
Born: 1897. Died: Mar. 25, 1942, San Fernando, Calif. Screen actor and horse trainer.

HICKMAN, ALFRED D.
Born: Feb. 25, 1873, England. Died: Apr. 9, 1931, Hollywood, Calif. (cerebral hemorrhage). Screen and stage actor.

Appeared in: **1914** The Master Key (serial). **1917** Fall of The Romanoffs. **1919** The Mad Woman; Here Comes the Bride. **1924** The Enchanted Cottage. **1929** The Rescue. **1930** The Last of the Lone Wolf. **1931** Phantom of Paris; A Woman of Experience.

HICKMAN, HERMAN (Herman M. Hickman, Jr.)
Born: Oct. 1, 1911, Johnson City, Tex. Died: Apr. 25, 1958. Football player, coach, wrestler, screen and television actor.

Appeared in: **1953** The All-American.

HICKMAN, HOWARD C.
Born: Feb. 9, 1880, Columbia, Mo. Died: Dec. 31, 1949, Los Angeles, Calif. (heart attack). Screen, stage actor and film director. Married to actress Bessie Barriscale (dec. 1965).

Appeared in: **1913** Rancho (film debut). **1916** Matrimony; Civilization. **1928** Alias Jimmy Valentine. **1930** Hello Sister; Brothers; The Broadway Hoofer; His First Command. **1931** Civilization (reissue of 1916 version). **1933** The Right to Romance. **1934** Baby Take a Bow; George White's Scandals; Hi, Nellie!; The Man With Two Faces; Jimmy the Gent; Madame DuBarry; Mystery Liner; Sisters Under the Skin; Here Comes the Navy. **1935** Straight from the Heart; Bright Lights; Rendezvous; It's in the Air. **1936** Swing Time; Love Letters of a Star; Libeled Lady; Fury; Too Many Parents; Hell-Ship Morgan; We Who Are About to Die; Wild Brian Kent; Career Woman; Happy Go Lucky; Two Against the World; Crack-Up; August Weekend; Fifteen Maiden Lane. **1937** The Man Who Cried Wolf; Charlie Chan at the Olympics; Give Till It Hurts (short); Artists and Models; The Lady Escapes; One Mile from Heaven; Western Gold; Borrowing Trouble; Join the Marines; Jim Hanvey, Detective; The Crime Nobody Saw; One Hundred Men and a Girl. **1938** Holiday; Start Cheering; Flight into Nowhere; Juvenile Court; Rascals; Everybody's Baby; Numbered Woman; Come On, Leathernecks; I Stand Accused; Young Dr. Kildare. **1939** When Tomorrow Comes; Convicts Code; Angels Wash Their Faces; Wife, Husband and Friend; The Kansas Terrors; Good Girls Go to Paris; Espionage Agent; Little Accident; Gone With the Wind; The Return of Dr. X; Kid from Texas. **1940** City for Conquest; Virginia City; The Man from Dakota; Strike Up the Band; Gangs of Chicago; Girls of the Road; The Secret Seven; Slightly Honorable; It All Came True; Bullet Code. **1941** Paris Calling; Dive Bomber; Dick Tracy vs. Crime, Inc. (serial); Cheers for Miss Bishop; Washington Melodrama; Sign of the Wolf; Scattergood Pulls the Strings; Hurricane Smith; Nine Lives Are Not Enough; Belle Starr; Doctor's Don't Tell; Tuxedo Junction; Bowery Boy; Golden Hoofs; Robbers of the Range; Blossoms in the Dust; Hold That Ghost. **1942** The Vanishing Virginian; Andy Hardy's Double Life; I Was Framed; Bells of Capistrano; Tarzan's New York Adventure. **1943** The Masked Marvel (serial); Watch on the Rhine; Three Hearts for Julie. **1944** Follow the Boys; Bowery to Broadway; Mrs. Parkington.

HICKOK, RODNEY
Born: 1892. Died: Mar. 9, 1942, Los Angeles, Calif. Screen and stage actor.

Appeared in: **1921** Father Tom. **1924** The Bandolero. **1928** The Rawhide Kid.

HICKS, BERT
Born: 1920. Died: Jan. 8, 1965, Pacoima, Calif. Screen actor. Father of actress Dolores Hart.

Appeared in: **1943** Sweet Rosie O'Grady. **1946** Sentimental Journey. **1949** Move Over My Darling. **1952** O'Henry's Full House.

HICKS, ELEANOR
Born: 1886. Died: July 11, 1936, near Aurora, Ill. (auto accident). Screen and stage actress. Married to actor Chester Clute (dec. 1956). Mother of actor Doren Parnell.

HICKS, LEONARD M.
Born: 1918. Died: Aug. 8, 1971, New York, N.Y. (cancer). Screen and stage actor.

Appeared in: **1961** Guns of the Trees. **1964** Santa Claus Conquers the Martians.

HICKS, RUSSELL (Edward Russell Hicks)
Born: June 4, 1895, Baltimore, Md. Died: June 1, 1957, Hollywood, Calif. (heart attack). Screen, stage, television actor and film director.

Appeared in: 1928 Happiness Ahead. 1933 Enlighten Thy Daughter; Before Morning. 1934 Happiness Ahead (and 1928 version); The Firebird; The St. Louis Kid; Murder in the Clouds; Gentlemen Are Born; The Case of the Howling Dog; Babbitt. 1935 Sweet Music; While the Patient Slept; Living on Velvet; The Woman in Red; Lady Tubbs; Thunder in the Night; $1,000 a Minute; Devil Dogs of the Air; Cardinal Richelieu; Honeymoon Limited; Charlie Chan in Shanghai; Ladies Love Danger. 1936 Two in the Dark; Follow the Fleet; Special Investigator; Grand Jury; We Who Are About to Die; Ticket to Paradise; Bunker Bean; Woman Trap; Laughing Irish Eyes; Hearts in Bondage; 15 Maiden Lane; The Sea Spoilers. 1937 The Wildcatter; Secret Valley; Midnight Taxi; Espionage; Pick a Star; 23 1/2 Hours' Leave; Girl Overboard; The Westland Case; On Again, Off Again; The Toast of New York; The Big Shot; Fit for a King; Criminals of the Air. 1938 That Certain Age; In Old Chicago; Kidnapped; Little Miss Broadway; Gateway; Hold That Co-Ed; Kentucky; Fugitives for a Night; Big Broadcast of 1938. 1939 Union Pacific; The Real Glory; Hollywood Cavalcade; Our Leading Citizen; Hotel for Women; Boy Trouble; The Three Musketeers; The Story of Alexander Graham Bell; The Honeymoon's Over; Swanee River; Stanley and Livingstone; I Was a Convict; Joe and Ethel Turp Call on the President; Honolulu; East Side of Heaven. 1940 The Lady With Red Hair; Junior G-Men (serial); The Mortal Storm; Earthbound; The Big Guy; The Blue Bird; Virginia City; Johnny Apollo; Enemy Agent; Sporting Blood; The Return of Frank James; East of the River; Seven Sinners; A Night at Earl Carroll's; The Bank Dick; No, No, Nanette; Love Thy Neighbor. 1941 The Strawberry Blonde; Sealed Lips; The Big Store; Western Union; The Great Lie; The Arkansas Judge; A Man Betrayed; Man-Made Monster; Ellery Queen's Penthouse Mystery; Here Comes Happiness; Blood and Sand; The Parson of Panamint; Buy Me That Town; Hold That Ghost; The Little Foxes; Doctors Don't Tell; Public Enemies; Midnight Angle; Dangerous Game; Great Guns. 1942 King of the Mounties (serial); We Were Dancing; To the Shores of Tripoli; Butch Minds the Baby; Joe Smith, American; Fingers at the Window; Tarzan's New York Adventure; Tennessee Johnson; Pacific Rendezvous; Blondie for Victory; Wings for the Eagle; Ride 'Em Cowboy. 1943 Follow the Band; Strictly in the Groove; Harrigan's Kid; King of the Cowboys; Air Raid Wardens; The Woman of the Town; His Butler's Sister; Hitler—Dead or Alive. 1944 Captain America (serial); Lady in a Jam; Hat Check Honey; Janie; Louisiana Hayride; Port of Forty Thieves; Blind Fools. 1945 The Master Key (serial); Apology for Murder; The Valley of Decision; Flame of the Barbary Coast; A Game of Death; A Guy, a Gal and a Pal; The Hidden Eye; Scarlet Street; She Gets Her Man. 1946 Swing Parade of 1946; The Bandit of Sherwood Forest; Gay Blades; A Close Call for Boston Blackie; Dark Alibi; GI War Brides; The Plainsman and the Lady; The Bachelor's Daughters. 1947 Variety Girl; The Pilgrim Lady; Exposed; Fun on a Weekend; Sea of Grass; Louisiana; Web of Danger; Buck Privates Come Home. 1948 Silver River; The Hunted; Assigned to Danger; The Black Arrow; The Gallant Legion; Race Street; The Velvet Touch; The Shanghai Chest; My Dear Secretary; The Plunders; The Return of October; Maggie and Jiggs in Court; The Noose Hangs High. 1949 Samson and Delilah; I Cheated the Law; Shocking Affair (short); Barbary Pirate; Manhattan Angel. 1950 The Petty Girl; Blue Grass of Kentucky; The Flying Saucer; Unmasked; Square Dance Katy; Halls of Montezuma; The Big Hangover. 1951 Belle Le Grand; Fourteen Hours; Bowery Battalion; As You Were; Overland Telegraph; Kentucky Jubilee; All That I Have. 1952 The Maverick; Old Oklahoma Plains; Mr. Walkie Talkie. 1953 Man of Conflict. 1956 Seventh Cavalry.

HICKS, SIR SEYMOUR
Born: Jan. 30, 1871, St. Heliers, Jersey, England. Died: Apr. 6, 1949, Hampshire, England. Screen, stage actor, playwright, stage manager, film producer, screenwriter and film director. Married to actress Ellaline Terriss (Lady Hicks) (dec. 1971).

Appeared in: 1907 Seymour Hicks Edits "The Tatler." 1913 David Garrick; Seymour Hicks and Ellaline Terriss (short); Scrooge. 1914 Always Tell Your Wife. 1915 A Prehistoric Love Story. 1923 Always Tell Your Wife (and 1914 version). 1927 Blighty (aka Apres la Guerre). 1930 Sleeping Partners; Tell Tales (short). 1931 The Love Habit; Glamour. 1932 Money for Nothing. 1934 The Secret of the Loch. 1935 Royal Cavalcade (aka Regal Cavalcade); Mr. What's His Name; Vintage Wine; Scrooge (and 1913 version). 1936 Eliza Comes to Stay; It's You I Want. 1937 Change for a Sovereign. 1939 The Lambeth Walk (US 1940 and aka Me and My Girl); Young Man's Fancy (US 1943). 1940 Pastor Hall; Busman's Honeymoon (aka Haunted Honeymoon—US). 1947 Fame Is the Spur (US 1949). 1949 Silent Dust.

HIERS, WALTER
Born: July 18, 1893, Cordele, Ga. Died: Feb. 27, 1933, Los Angeles, Calif. (pneumonia). Screen and stage actor. Entered films as an extra in 1915 with Griffith at Biograph. Married to actress Gloria Williams.

Appeared in: 1915 Jimmy. 1919 It Pays to Advertise; Leave It to Susan; Why Smith Left Home. 1920 Hunting Trouble. 1921 Sham; A Kiss in Time; Her Sturdy Oak; The Speed Girl; The Snob; Two Weeks with Pay. 1922 The Ghost Breaker; Bought and Paid For; Her Gilded Cage; Is Matrimony a Failure? 1923 Mr. Billing Spends His Dime; Sixty Cents an Hour; Hollywood. 1924 Fair Week; Along Came Ruth; Christine of the Hungry Heart; The Triflers; Hold Your Breath; The Virgin; Flaming Barriers; plus educational shorts. 1925 Excuse Me; plus the following shorts: Good Spirits; A Rarin' Romeo; Tender Feet; Oh, Bridget; Off His Beat; Hot Doggies. 1926 Hold That Lion. 1927 Beware of Widows; A Racing Romeo; Naughty; Hot Lemonade (short); Blondes by Choice; The Girl from Gay Paree; The Wrong Mr. Wright; The First Night; Husband Hunters; Night Life. 1928 A Woman Against the World. 1931 Private Scandal; Oh! Oh! Cleopatra (short). 1932 Dancers in the Dark; 70,000 Witnesses.

HIGBY, WILBUR
Born: 1866. Died: Dec. 1, 1934, Hollywood, Calif. (heart attack). Screen and stage actor. Entered films in 1913. Married to stage actress Carolyn Higby.

Appeared in: 1916 Reggie Mixes In; Flirting With Fate; The Matrimaniac. 1919 Nugget Nell. 1921 Miracles of the Jungle (serial); Desert Blossoms; Live Wires; Play Square; Girls Don't Gamble. 1922 Do and Dare; My Dad; The Ladder Jinx. 1923 The Love Trap; Richard the Lion-Hearted. 1924 The Flaming Forties. 1925 Lights of Old Broadway; Confessions of a Queen. 1926 The Border Whirlwind. 1927 God's Great Wilderness. 1934 Hat, Coat and Glove; The Mighty Barnum.

HIGGINS, ANN
Died: May 2, 1978. Screen actress.

HIGGINS, DAVID
Born: 1858. Died: June 30, 1936, Brooklyn, N.Y. Screen, stage actor and playwright.

Appeared in: 1924 The Confidence Man.

HIGGS, RICHARD
Born: 1930. Died: Oct. 15, 1977. Screen and television actor.

Appeared in: 1964 Lilith. 1976 Taxi Driver.

HIGNETT, H. R.
Born: Jan. 29, 1870, Ringway, Cheshire, England. Died: Dec. 17, 1959, England? Screen and stage actor. Married to actress Frances Wetherall (dec. 1923).

Appeared in: 1919 Forgive Us Our Trespasses. 1920 The Dawn of Truth. 1922 A Prince of Lovers (aka Life of Lord Byron—US 1927); Silent Evidence. 1923 Light O'London. 1946 Caravan (US 1947). 1948 Spring in Park Lane (US 1949). 1952 Derby Day (aka Four Against Fate—US 1955).

HILDEBRAND, HILDE (Emma Minna Hildebrand)
Born: 1897, Hanover, Germany. Died: Apr. 28, 1976, Germany? Screen and stage actress.

Appeared in: 1925 Der Trodler von Amsterdam. 1927 Sechs Mädchen suchen Nachtquartier. 1928 Der Fesche Husar; Rasputins Liebesabenteuer. 1930 Zweierlei Moral. 1931 Arme Kleine Eva; Panik in Chikago; Mein Leopold; Bobby geht Los; Madame hat Ausgang; Der unbekannte Gast (The Unknown Guest—US 1935); Der Kleine Seitensprung (US 1932); Das Schicksal der Renate Langen (US 1933). 1932 Strafsache van Geldern; Uumogliche Liebe; Mode Macht (US 1933); Drei von der Kavallerie (US 1935); Ballhaus Goldener Engel; Das schone Abenteuer; Lieb; Scherz und Ernst; Der Frauendiplomat; Drei von der Kavallerie; Eink 1 Greif. 1933 Liebe Muss Verstanden (US 1934); Viktor und Viktoria (US 1935); Gruss und Kuss Veronika (US 1936); Keine Angst vor Liebe; Los Gretel zieht dos Grosse (US 1935); Ehe Wege zur Guten; Manolescu; Der Furst der Diebe; Sprung in den Abgrund; Moral und Liebe. 1934 Pipin der Kurze; Little Dorrit (US 1935); Polenblut (Polish Blood—US 1935); Peter, Paul und Nanette (US 1940); Die Englische Heirat; Mein Herz ruft Nach. 1935 Ein Falscher Fuffziger (US 1937); Artisten; Der Gefengene des Konigs; Barcarole; Amphytrion; Liselotte von der Pfalz; Ich war Jack Mortimer; Die Letzte Fahrt der Santa Margareta; Die Selige Exzellenz (US 1936). 1936 Maria, Die Magd (US 1937); Alles Für Veronika (US 1939); The Private Life of Louis XIV; Der Kurier des Zaren; Allotria. 1937 Mutterlied. 1938 Das Mädchen von

Gestern Nacht (The Girl of Last Night); Der Tag Nach der Scheidung (The Day After the Divorce—US 1940); Solo per To (Only for Thee); Tanz auf dem Vulkan; Der Tag nach der Scheidung. **1939** Bel Ami; Parkstrasse 13; Silvesternacht am Alexanderplatz; Das Gluck wohnt Nebenan; Ehn in Dosen. **1940** Frau nach Mass; Der Kleinstadtpoet; Meine Tochter tut dad Nicht. **1941** Alarm; Jenny und der Herr im Frack. **1943** Die Schwache Stunde; Reise in die Vergangenheit. **1944** Grosse Freiheit Nr. 7; Ich Bitte um Vollmacht; Spiel; Schuss um Mitternacht; Spuk im Schloss. **1945** Shiva und die Galgenblume; Das Gesetz der Liebe; Verlobte Leute; Ruf an das Gewissen. **1948** Der Herr vom Andern Stern. **1949** Katchen für Alles; Kleiner Wagen—Grosse Liebe. **1950** Epilog. **1951** Unvergangliches Licht; Der Tiger Akabar. **1954** Sie. **1955** Die Drei von der Tankstelle. **1959** Bezaubernde Arabella. **1960** Die Fastnachtsbeichte. **1963** Die Dreigroschenoper (The Three Penny Opera—US 1964).

HILDEBRAND, RODNEY W.
Born: 1893. Died: Feb. 22, 1962. Screen actor.

Appeared in: **1926** Early to Wed; Hell's 400. **1927** The Bush Leaguer. **1928** Mother Machree. **1933** The Three Musketeers (serial). **1934** Bright Eyes.

HILDERBRAND, LO
Born: 1894. Died: Sept. 11, 1936, Los Angeles, Calif. (heart attack). Screen actor. Appeared in westerns.

HILFORDE, MARY (Mary Griggs)
Born: 1853, Carbondale, Pa. Died: Dec. 12, 1927, Amityville, N.Y. Stage and screen actress.

HILL, AL
Born: July 14, 1892, New York, N.Y. Died: July 14, 1954. Screen, stage actor and author. Do not confuse with stage actor of same name.

Appeared in: **1927** The Drop Kick. **1928** Her Wild Oat; Dressed to Kill; The Escape; Me, Gangster; Sinner's Parade; Roadhouse; Stool Pigeon. **1929** Half Way to Heaven; Side Street; Alibi. **1930** Racketeer; Top Speed. **1931** Maid to Order; Ten Cents a Dance. **1932** Night After Night; The Last Mile; A Fool's Advice. **1933** Quiet, Please (short); The Death Kiss; Private Jones; Pick Up; One Year Later. **1934** Bedlam of Beards (short); Punch Drinks (short); Personality Kid; Wharf Angel; All of Me; Against the Law; Picture Brides; Name the Woman; Take the Stand; Lemon Drop Kid. **1935** Air Hawks; The Pay-Off; Buried Loot (short); The Virginia Judge; Riffraff. **1936** Three on the Trail; Border Patrolman; Crash Donovan; Call of the Prairie; The Big Noise. **1937** Parole Racket; Motor Madness; Hollywood Cowboy; San Quentin; The Big Shot; Partners of the Plains. **1938** The Lady in the Morgue; The Buccaneer; Gambling Ship. **1940** Good Bad Guys (short); The Bank Dick; The Man From Tumbleweeds. **1941** The Big Store. **1942** Tramp, Tramp, Tramp. **1943** Blitz on the Fritz (short). **1944** Lost in a Harem. **1946** Perilous Holiday. **1951** Sealed Cargo; Smuggler's Gold; The Girl on the Bridge. **1953** Money From Home; Vicki. **1954** Living It Up; Three Ring Circus.

HILL, ARTHUR
Born: 1875. Died: Apr. 9, 1932, Hollywood, Calif. (heart attack). Stage and screen actor.

HILL, ARTHUR R.
Born: 1890. Died: Apr. 17, 1941, Los Angeles, Calif. Screen and stage actor. Do not confuse with actor Arthur Hill who appeared in films during 1960s—1980s.

HILL, BEN A.
Born: 1894. Died: Nov. 30, 1969, Dallas, Tex. Screen actor.

Appeared in: **1921** On the High Card; The Border Raiders.

HILL, DUDLEY S.
Born: 1881. Died: Jan. 7, 1960, Wilkesboro, N.C. Screen and stage actor. Entered films in 1913.

HILL, (CAPTAIN) GEORGE
Born: 1872. Died: Mar. 2, 1945, Hollywood, Calif. Screen actor and stand-in for Nigel Bruce and Harry Lauder.

HILL, GRAHAM (Norman Graham Hill)
Born: Feb. 15, 1929, Hampstead, England. Died: Nov. 29, 1975, near London, England (plane crash). Race car driver and screen actor

Appeared in: **1962** The Fast Lady (US 1965). **1966** Grand Prix.

HILL, HALLENE (Hallene Christian Hill)
Born: Sept. 12, 1876, Missouri. Died: Jan. 6, 1966, Los Angeles, Calif. (cerebral thrombosis—arteriosclerosis). Screen actress.

Appeared in: **1935** One Hour Late. **1940** Remedy for Riches. **1942** The Wife Takes a Flyer; Tramp, Tramp, Tramp; Wedded Blitz (short). **1943** This Land Is Mine; The Gang's All Here. **1944** The Seventh Cross. **1946** Colonel Effingham's Raid. **1949** Beyond the Forest; The Lady Takes a Sailor. **1952** Ma and Pa Kettle at the Fair. **1956** The Search for Bridey Murphy. **1957** The Kettle's on Old MacDonald's Farm; The Great Man; The Vampire. **1960** Spartacus. **1963** Forty Pounds of Trouble. **1965** Cat Ballou.

HILL, HOWARD
Born: 1899. Died: Feb. 4, 1975, Birmingham, Ala. Screen actor and professional archer.

Appeared in: **1929** Sal of Singapore. **1935** The Last Wilderness (short). **1938** The Adventures of Robin Hood; Follow the Arrow (short). **1945** San Antonio. **1952** Cruise of Zaca (short).

HILL, JACK See KEEFE, CORNELIUS

HILL, JACK Y.
Born: Sept. 12, 1891, Va. Died: Nov. 22, 1963, Hollywood, Calif. Screen actor. Do not confuse with other Jack Hill.

HILL, KATHRYN See CARVER, KATHRYN

HILL, RAMSEY See RAMSEY-HILL, C.S.

HILL, RAYMOND
Born: 1891. Died: Apr. 16, 1941, Hollywood, Calif. Screen and radio actor.

HILL, THELMA (Thelma Hillerman)
Born: Dec. 12, 1906, Emporia, Kans. Died: May 11, 1938, Culver City, Calif. Screen actress. Entered films with Sennett in 1927 and was a Mack Sennett bathing beauty.

Appeared in: **1927** The Fair Co-Ed. **1928** The Chorus Kid; Hearts of Men; Crooks Can't Win; The Play Girl. **1929** The following shorts: The Old Barn; The Bee's Buzz; The Big Palooka; Girl Crazy; The Barber's Daughter; The Constable; The Bride's Relations; The Lunkhead; The Golfers. **1930** Two Plus Fours (short). **1931** The Miracle Woman. **1932** Sunkissed Sweeties (short).

HILL, VIRGINIA
Born: 1917. Died: Mar. 22, 1966, Koppl, Austria. Screen, vaudeville, television actress and dancer.

Appeared in: **1941** Ball of Fire.

HILLIARD, ERNEST
Born: Feb. 1, 1890, New York, N.Y. Died: Sept. 3, 1947, Santa Monica, Calif. (heart attack). Screen and stage actor. Entered films in 1912.

Appeared in: **1921** Annabel Lee; Tropical Love; The Matrimonial Web. **1922** Evidence; The Ruling Passion; Married People; Who Are My Parents?; Silver Wings. **1923** Love's Old Sweet Song; Man and Wife; Modern Marriage. **1924** Galloping Hoofs (serial); The Recoil; Trouping with Ellen. **1925** Broadway Lady. **1926** Forest Havoc; White Mice; The Frontier Trail; The High Flyer. **1927** Broadway After Midnight; The Wheel of Destiny; Wide Open; The Fighting Failure; A Bowery Cinderella; Let It Rain; Compassion; The Scorcher; The Racing Fool; The Silent Hero; Smile, Brother, Smile; The Midnight Watch; Modern Daughters. **1928** Divine Sinners; The Matinee Idol; Dugan of the Dugouts; Lady Raffles; Out with the Tide; The Big Hop; A Midnight Adventure; Burning Up Broadway; Devil Dogs; The Noose; Sinners in Love. **1929** Red Wine; When Dreams Come True; The Big Diamond Robbery; Red Hot Rhythm; Dynamite; Say It With Songs; Weary River; Wall Street; Awful Truth. **1930** Broadway Hoofer. **1931** Second Honeymoon; Drums of Jeopardy; Mother and Son; Good Sport; Millie. **1934** The Witching Hour; Flirting with Danger. **1935** Smart Girl; Racing Luck. **1936** Showboat; Boss Rider of Gun Creek; The Sea Spoilers. **1937** Life of the Party. **1942** The Magnificent Dope; Random Harvest. **1944** The Soul of a Monster. **1945** On Stage Everybody; Masquerade in Mexico. **1946** Deadline for Murder. **1947** Christmas Eve.

HILLIARD, HARRY S.
Died: Apr. 21, 1966, St. Petersburg, Fla. (complications after fall). Screen and stage actor.

Appeared in: **1916** Romeo and Juliet; The Little Fraud. **1917** The New York Peacock. **1918** A Successful Adventure. **1919** The Little White Savage; The Little Rowdy; The Sneak.

HILLIARD, MRS. MACK (Hazel Clayton)
Born: 1886. Died: Mar. 8, 1963, Forest Hills, N.Y. Screen and stage actress. Entered films during silents with original Fox Films Co. in Fort Lee, N.J. Appeared professionally as Mrs. Mack Hilliard.

HILLIAS, MARGARET "PEG"
Died: Mar. 18, 1960, Kansas City, Mo. Screen, stage, television and radio actress.

Appeared in: **1951** A Streetcar Named Desire. **1957** Peyton Place; The Wayward Girl.

HILLIS, HOUSTON
Died: Feb. 12, 1928, near Bakersfield, Calif. (auto accident). Screen actor.

HILO HATTIE (Clara Haili)
Born: 1901, Honolulu, Hawaii. Died: Dec. 12, 1979, Honolulu, Hawaii (cancer). Hula performer, screen, television actress, teacher and singer. Married to musician Carlyle Nelson.

Appeared in: **1942** Song of the Islands (film debut). **1948** Miss Tatlock's Millions. **1953** City Beneath the Sea. **1955** Ma and Pa Kettle at Waikiki. **1958** Suicide Battalion. **1961** Blue Hawaii.

HILPERT, HEINZ
Born: 1890, Germany. Died: Nov. 25, 1967, Goetingen, Germany. Screen, stage actor, film director and stage director. Married to actress Ursula Mueller.

Appeared in: **1936** The Golden Plaque.

HILTON, FRANK
Born: 1871. Died: Feb. 17, 1932, New York, N.Y. Screen and stage actor.

Appeared in: **1903** The Great Train Robbery.

HILTON, VIOLET AND DAISY
Born: Feb. 5, 1908, Brighton, England. Died: Jan. 4, 1969, Charlotte, N.C. (complications after flu). Siamese twins and vaudeville screen actresses. Violet was married to dancer James Moore (later annulled) and Daisy was married to actor Harold Estep (aka Buddy Sawyer).

Appeared in: **1932** Freaks. Chained for Life (date unknown).

HINCKLEY, WILLIAM
Born: 1894. Died: May, 1918, New York, N.Y. Screen and stage actor.

Appeared in: **1915** Out of Bondage; The Primitive Spirit; The Light in the Window; Bred in the Bone; The Wolf Man; The Feud; The Lily and the Rose; The Stab; The Wayward Son. **1916** Martha's Vindication; The Children in the House. **1917** Bab's Burglar; The Amazons; Reputation; The Secret of Eve.

HINDS, NINA
Born: 1904, Eureka, Calif. Died: May 24, 1961, Reno, Nev. (cancer). Screen and vaudeville actress.

Appeared in: **1927** The College Boy and California Melody Girls (short).

HINDS, SAMUEL S.
Born: Apr. 4, 1875, Brooklyn, N.Y. Died: Oct. 13, 1948, Pasadena, Calif. Screen, stage actor and attorney.

Appeared in: **1932** If I Had a Million. **1933** The World Changes; The House on 56th Street; Convention City; Women in His Life; The Crime of the Century; Gabriel Over the White House; The Nuisance; Day of Reckoning; Lady for a Day; Bed of Roses; Berkeley Square; The Deluge; Little Women; One Man's Journey; Penthouse; Hold the Press; This Day and Age; Son of a Sailor. **1934** The Big Shakedown; Manhattan Melodrama; Operator 13; A Wicked Woman; Most Precious Thing in Life; Evelyn Prentice; He Was Her Man; Massacre; Crime Doctor; Straightaway; The Defense Rests; Have a Heart; A Lost Lady; Men in White; The Ninth Guest; No Greater Glory; West of the Pecos; Sisters Under the Skin; Hat, Coat and Glove; Fog. **1935** Bordertown; Devil Dogs of the Air; Black Fury; Wings in the Dark; Sequoia; Strangers All; She; In Person; Mills of the Gods; Behind the Evidence; Dr. Socrates; Rhumba; Private Worlds; College Scandal; Accent on Youth; Annapolis Farewell; The Big Broadcast of 1936; Two Fisted; Millions in the Air; Shadow of Doubt; Rendezvous; The Raven; Living on Velvet. **1936** I Loved a Soldier; The Longest Night; Timothy's Quest; Woman Trap; The Trail of the Lonesome Pine; Border Flight; Fatal Lady; Rhythm on the Range; Sworn Enemy; His Brother's Wife; Love Letters of a Star. **1937** She's Dangerous; The

Black Legion; Top of the Town; The Mighty Treve; Night Key; Wings Over Honolulu; The Road Back; A Girl with Ideas; Prescription for Romance; Double or Nothing; Navy Blue and Gold; Stage Door. **1938** Forbidden Valley; Young Dr. Kildare; Personal Secretary; The Jury's Secret; The Devil's Party; Wives Under Suspicion; The Rage of Paris; The Road to Reno; The Storm; Swing That Cheer; Secrets of a Nurse; Test Pilot; You Can't Take It With You; Double Danger. **1939** Calling Dr. Kildare; Ex-Champ; Hawaiian Night; The Under-Pup; Newsboys' Home; Within the Law; Charlie McCarthy, Detective; Career; Tropic Fury; Rio; First Love; Hero for a Day; You're a Sweetheart; Pirates of the Skies; Destry Rides Again; No Greater Glory; One Hour to Live; The Secret of Dr. Kildare. **1940** It's a Date; Dr. Kildare's Strangest Case; Ski Patrol; Boys from Syracuse; I'm Nobody's Sweetheart Now; Dr. Kildare Goes Home; Spring Parade; Seven Sinners; Trail of the Vigilantes; Zanzibar. **1941** Man-Made Monster; Buck Privates; Tight Shoes; Dr. Kildare's Wedding Day; Unfinished Business; Badlands of Dakota; Mob Town; Road Agent; Back Street; The Lady from Cheyenne; Adventure in Washington; The Shepherd of the Hills; Blossoms in the Dust. **1942** Frisco Lil; Ride 'Em Cowboy; Jail House Blues; Pittsburgh; Don Winslow of the Navy (serial); The Strange Case of Dr. Rx; The Spoilers; Kid Glove Killer; Grand Central Murder; Lady in a Jam; Pardon My Sarong. **1943** Mr. Big; Top Man; Fired Wife; Larceny with Music; Weird Woman; Murder in the Blue Room; Son of Dracula; Strangers in Our Midst; It Ain't Hay; Good Morning Judge; Follow the Band; Hi, Buddy; We've Never Been Licked; Hers to Hold; Keep 'Em Slugging; He's My Guy. **1944** The Great Alaskan Mystery (serial); Sing a Jingle; Follow the Boys; Ladies Courageous; South of Dixie; The Singing Sheriff; Cobra Woman; A Chip Off the Old Block; Jungle Woman. **1945** Frisco Sal; Swing Out, Sister; I'll Remember April; Secret Agent X-9 (serial); Men in Her Diary; Lady on a Train; The Strange Affair of Uncle Harry; Weekend at the Waldorf; Scarlet Street; Escape in the Desert. **1946** It's a Wonderful Life; White Tie and Tails; Blonde Alibi; Strange Conquest; Little Miss Big; Danger Woman; Inside Job; Notorious Gentlemen; The Runaround. **1947** The Egg and I; Time Out of Mind; In Self Defense; Slave Girl. **1948** Perilous Waters; The Return of October; Call Northside 777; The Boy with the Green Hair. **1949** The Bribe.

HINES, ADRIAN R.
Born: 1903. Died: Mar. 6, 1946, San Antonio, Tex. Screen actor, extra and circus animal trainer.

HINES, ALTONELL
Born: 1905, Norfolk, Va. Died: Aug. 6, 1977, New York, N.Y. Black screen, stage, radio actress and singer. Married to stage actor Edward Matthews (dec.).

HINES, HARRY
Born: 1889. Died: May 3, 1967, Hollywood, Calif. (emphysema). Screen, burlesque and vaudeville actor.

Appeared in: **1950** Harvey; The Jackpot; One Too Many. **1951** The Unknown Man; Father's Little Dividend; Strangers on a Train; Mr. Belvedere Rings the Bell. **1952** Carrie; Boots Malone; Talk About a Stranger. **1953** Last of the Pony Riders; City of Bad Men; Houdini. **1954** Riding Shotgun; The Raid. **1956** The Catered Affair; The Kettles in the Ozarks. **1957** This Could Be The Night. **1958** The Brothers Karamazov. **1962** All Fall Down. **1965** The Cincinnati Kid. **1966** Texas Across the River.

HINES, JANEAR
Born: 1951. Died: Mar. 2, 1981, San Francisco, Calif. (Bright's disease). Screen and television actress. Daughter of jazz pianist Earl Hines.

Appeared in: **1974** Dirty Mary Crazy Larry.

HINES, JOHNNY
Born: July 25, 1897, Golden, Colo. Died: Oct. 24, 1970, Los Angeles, Calif. (heart attack). Screen and stage actor. Entered films in 1915. Brother of actor Samuel E. Hines (dec. 1939).

Appeared in: **1920** "Torchy" series of shorts. **1921** Burn 'Em Up Barnes. **1922** Sure-Fire Flint. **1923** Little Johnny Jones; Luck. **1924** The Speed Spook; Conductor 1492. **1925** The Crackerjack; The Early Bird; The Live Wire. **1926** The Brown Derby; Stepping Along; Rainbow Riley. **1927** All Aboard; Home Made; White Plains Willie. **1928** Chinatown Charlie; The Wright Idea. **1929** Alias Jimmy Valentine. **1930** Johnny's Week End (short). **1931** Runaround. **1932** Whistling in the Dark. **1933** The Girl in 419; Her Bodyguard. **1935** Society Doctor. **1938** Too Hot to Handle. **1940** The Domineering Male (short). **1946** The Magnificent Doll.

HINES, SAMUEL E.
Born: 1881. Died: Nov. 17, 1939, Los Angeles, Calif. Screen and stage actor. Brother of actor Johnny Hines (dec. 1970).

Appeared in: **1925** The Last Chord; Shore Leave. **1933** The Road Is Open (short). **1934** He Was Her Man.

HINNANT, BILL
Born: 1936. Died: Feb. 17, 1978, Dominican Republic (drowned). Screen, stage and television actor.

Appeared in: **1969** A Nice Girl Like Me.

HINTON, ED
Born: 1928. Died: Oct. 12, 1958, Catalina Island, Calif. (airplane accident). Screen actor. Father of actor Darby Hinton.

Appeared in: **1948** Harpoon. **1949** Samson and Delilah. **1951** The Red Badge of Courage. **1952** Flesh and Fury; At Sword's Point; The Lion and the Horse; Hellgate; Leadville Slinger. **1953** The Farmer Takes a Wife; Three Sailors and a Girl. **1954** Alaska Seas; River of No Return. **1955** Tight Spot; Devil Goddess; Jungle Moon Men; Seminole Uprising. **1956** Julie; The Ten Commandments; Walk the Proud Land. **1957** Shoot-Out at Medicine Bend; The 27th Day; Under Fire; The Dalton Girls. **1958** Cry Terror; The Decks Ran Red; Escape from Red Rock; Fort Bowie. **1959** Gidget.

HIPPE, LEW
Born: 1880. Died: July 19, 1952, Hollywood, Calif. (following operation for lung ailment). Screen actor. Appeared in Mack Sennett films.

Appeared in: **1920** The Mollycoddle.

HIROSE, GEORGE
Born: 1899. Died: Aug. 9, 1974, New York, N.Y. Screen, stage, radio, television actor and singer. Married to actress Naoe Kondo.

Appeared in: **1965** Daikaiju Gamera (Gammera, the Invincible—US 1966).

HIRST, ALAN
Born: 1931. Died: Jan. 16, 1937, Hollywood, Calif. Six-year-old screen actor.

HITCHCOCK, ALFRED
Born: Aug. 13, 1899, London, England. Died: Apr. 29, 1980, Los Angeles, Calif. (heart attack). Screen actor, film director, film producer and author. Married to screenwriter Alma Reville (dec. 1982). Father of actress Patricia Hitchcock. He made a cameo appearance in each of his movies, beginning with "The Lodger" in 1926 (aka The Case of Jonathan Drew—US 1928). Made Commander of the Order of the British Empire in 1979.

HITCHCOCK, KEITH *See* KENNETH, KEITH

HITCHCOCK, RAYMOND
Born: Oct. 22, 1865, Auburn, N.Y. Died: Nov. 24, 1929, Beverly Hills, Calif. (heart trouble). Screen, stage and vaudeville actor. Married to actress Flora Zabelle (dec. 1968).

Appeared in: **1915** My Valet; Stolen Magic; The Village Scandal. **1922** The Beauty Shop. **1924** Broadway After Dark. **1926** Redheads Preferred; Everybody's Acting. **1927** The Money Talks; Upstream; The Tired Business Man. **1929** An Evening at Home with Hitchy (short).

HITCHCOCK, REX *See* INGRAM, REX

HITCHCOCK, WALTER
Died: June 23, 1917, New York, N.Y. (heart failure). Screen actor.

Appeared in: **1912** Billy and the Butler. **1915** The Idler; The House of Tears; The Great Ruby Mystery. **1916** The Blindness of Love; The Snowbird. **1917** The Moral Code.

HIVELY, GEORGENIA
Born: 1891. Died: May 21, 1977, North Hollywood, Calif. Screen actress and stuntwoman. Mother of director Jack Hively.

Appeared in: **1917** Bucking Broadway.

HIX, DON (Don T. Hicks)
Died: Dec. 31, 1964, Hollywood, Calif. Screen, stage and radio actor. Entered films with Universal in 1914.

Appeared in: **1959** Diary of a High School Bride.

HOAGLAND, HARLAND
Born: 1896. Died: Jan. 9, 1971, Hollywood, Calif, (cancer). Screen and stage actor. Entered films in 1921.

Appeared in: **1949** The Gal Who Took the West.

HOBAN, STELLA
Born: 1890. Died: Jan. 24, 1962, Muskegon, Mich. Screen actress and singer.

Appeared in: **1915** The Luring Lights.

HOBBES, HALLIWELL
Born: Nov. 16, 1877, Stratford-on-Avon, England. Died: Feb. 20, 1962, Santa Monica, Calif. (heart attack). Screen and stage actor.

Appeared in: **1929** Lucky in Love; Jealousy. **1930** Grumpy; Charley's Aunt; Scotland Yard. **1931** The Right of Way; The Bachelor Father; Five and Ten; Platinum Blonde; The Sins of Madelon Claudet; The Woman Between. **1932** The Menace; The Devil's Lottery; Man About Town; Week Ends Only; Love Affair; Six Hours to Live; Dr. Jekyll and Mr. Hyde; Lovers Courageous; Forbidden; Payment Deferred. **1933** Lady of the Night; Looking Forward; Midnight Mary; Should Ladies Behave?; A Study in Scarlet; Captured; Lady for a Day; The Masquerader. **1934** I Am Suzanne; All Men Are Enemies; Mandalay; The Key; Riptide; Double Door; Bulldog Drummond Strikes Back; Madame DuBarry; British Agent. **1935** Captain Blood; Follies Bergere; Cardinal Richelieu; The Right to Live; Millions in the Air; Jalna; Charlie Chan in Shanghai; Father Brown, Detective. **1936** The Story of Louis Pasteur; Here Comes Trouble; Dracula's Daughter; Love Letters of a Star; The White Angel; Hearts Divided; Give Me Your Heart; Spendthrift; Whipsaw. **1937** Maid of Salem; The Prince and the Pauper; Varsity Show; Fit for a King. **1938** You Can't Take It With You; The Jury's Secret; Service DeLuxe; Bulldog Drummond's Peril; Storm Over Bengal; Kidnapped. **1939** The Light That Failed; Pacific Liner; The Hardy's Ride High; Naughty But Nice; Nurse Edith Cavell; Tell No Tales; Remember? **1940** The Lady With Red Hair; The Sea Hawk; The Earl of Chicago; Third Finger, Left Hand. **1941** That Hamilton Woman; Here Comes Mr. Jordan. **1942** To Be or Not to Be; The War Against Mrs. Hadley; Journey for Margaret; The Undying Monster; Son of Fury. **1943** Sherlock Holmes Faces Death; Forever and a Day. **1944** The Invisible Man's Revenge; Gaslight; Mr. Skeffington; Casanova Brown. **1946** Canyon Passage. **1947** If Winter Comes. **1948** You Gotta Stay Happy; Black Arrow. **1949** That Forsyte Woman. **1956** Miracle in the Rain.

HOBBS, CARLETON
Born: June 18, 1898, Farnborough, Hants, England. Died: Aug. 2, 1978, London, England. Screen, stage and radio actor. Married to actress Gladys Ponsonby. Entered films in 1932.

Appeared in: **1932** Where Is This Lady? **1935** The Clairvoyant. **1965** A King's Story (US 1967). **1974** Dark Places. **1970** Perfect Friday.

HOBBS, JACK
Born: Sept. 28, 1893, London, England. Died: June 4, 1968, Brighton, England. Screen and stage actor.

Appeared in: **1915** Love's Legacy (aka The Yoke). **1919** The Lady Clare. **1920** The Face at the Window; Inheritance (aka Bred in the Bone; The Call of Youth (US 1921); The Shuttle of Life; The Skin Game. **1922** The Lonely Lady of Grosvenor Square; The Crimson Circle; The Naval Treaty (short). **1923** The Last Adventures of Sherlock Holmes series including The Crooked Man. **1924** The Eleventh Commandment. **1925** The Happy Ending. **1931** Never Trouble Trouble; Love Lies; Dr. Josser KC; Mischief; The Love Race. **1932** Josser Joins the Navy; The Last Coupon; His Wife's Mother; Josser in the Army; A Honeymoon in Devon. **1933** Double Wedding; Too Many Wives; Beware of Women. **1934** Trouble in Store; Oh No Doctor! **1935** Handle With Care; Car of Dreams; No Limit. **1936** Millions; The Interrupted Honeymoon; All That Glitters. **1937** Why Pick on Me?; The Show Goes On; Leave It to Me; Intimate Relations; Fine Feathers; When the Devil Was Well. **1938** Make It Three; It's in the Air (aka George Takes the Air—US 1940); Miracles Do Happen.

HOCH, EMIL H.
Born: Oct. 27, 1866, Pforzheim, Germany. Died: Oct. 13, 1944, Hollywood, Calif. (heart attack). Screen actor.

Appeared in: **1919** The Dark Star. **1921** The Girl with a Jazz Heart. **1924** America. **1925** Stage Struck.

HOCK, RICHARD
Born: 1933. Died: July 13, 1961, Santa Monica, Calif. (burned in auto accident). Screen actor and stuntman. Married to stunt woman Margo Hock.

HOCTER, HARRIET
Born: 1903, Hoosick Falls, N.Y. Died: June 9, 1977, Arlington, Va. Screen, stage, vaudeville actress, choreographer and ballet dancer.

Appeared in: **1936** The Great Ziegfeld. **1937** Shall We Dance?

HODD, JOSEPH B., SR.
Born: 1896. Died: June 26, 1965, Philadelphia, Pa. Screen actor and stuntman. Entered films in 1927.

HODGE, AL "CAPTAIN VIDEO"
Born: 1913. Died: Mar., 1979, New York, N.Y. Screen and television actor.

HODGEMAN, THOMAS
Born: 1875. Died: Apr. 24, 1931, Los Angeles, Calif. Screen, stage actor and stage manager.

HODGES, GIL (Gilbert Raymond Hodges)
Born: Apr. 4, 1924, Princeton, Ind. Died: Apr. 2, 1972, West Palm Beach, Fla. Professional baseball player, manager and screen actor.

Appeared in: **1958** Geisha Boy.

HODGES, HORACE
Born: Dec. 19, 1865, England. Died: July 6, 1951, England? Screen, stage actor and playwright.

Appeared in: **1930** Escape. **1932** After Dark. **1936** The Three Maxims (aka The Show Goes On—US 1938). **1937** London Melody (aka Girls in the Street—US 1938); The Show Goes On. **1938** Follow Your Star. **1939** Jamaica Inn.

HODGES, WILLIAM CULLEN
Born: 1876, Newbury Township, Ohio. Died: July 28, 1961, Chardon, Ohio. Screen and stage actor.

HODGINS, EARL
Born: 1899. Died: Apr. 14, 1964, Hollywood, Calif. (heart attack). Screen, stage and television actor.

Appeared in: **1934** The Circus Clown. **1935** The Cyclone Ranger; The Texas Rambler; Paradise Canyon; Harmony Lane. **1936** The Singing Cowboy; Guns and Guitars; Ticket to Paradise; Oh, Susannah!; Border Caballero; Aces and Eights. **1937** Law for Tombstone; Borderland; Hills of Old Wyoming; Partners of the Plains; I Cover the War; Range Defenders; All Over Town; A Law Man Is Born; Round-up Time in Texas; Heroes of the Alamo; Headin' East; Nation Aflame. **1938** The Old Barn Dance; The Purple Vigilantes; Call the Mesquiteers; The Rangers Roundup; Long Shot; Pride of the West; Lawless Valley; Barefoot Boy. **1939** Dodge City; Home on the Prairie; Almost a Gentleman; Panama Lady; The Day the Bookies Wept. **1940** My Favorite Wife; Santa Fe Marshal; Men Against the Sky; The Range Busters; Under Texas Skies; Law and Order; The Bad Man from Red Butte. **1941** Sing for Your Supper; Scattergood Pulls the Strings; Riding the Wind; Sierra Sue; Keep 'Em Flying. **1942** The Bashful Bachelor; Call of the Canyon; Undercover Man; Deep in the Heart of Texas; Scattergood Survives a Murder; The Power of God; Inside the Law. **1943** Riders of the Deadline; False Colors; Tenting Tonight on the Old Camp Ground; The Old Chisholm Trail; The Avenging Rider; Hi! Ya, Chum; Colt Comrades; Bar 20; Lone Star Trail; Hoppy Serves a Writ. **1944** Hidden Valley Outlaws; Firebrands of Arizona; San Antonio Kid; Sensations of 1945. **1945** Practically Yours; The Southerner; Bedside Manner; GI Honeymoon; The Topeka Terror; Under Western Skies. **1946** Gun Town; The Bachelor's Daughters; Crime of the Century; The Devil's Playground; The Best Years of Our Lives; Live Wires; Fool's Gold; Unexpected Guest; Accomplice; Valley of the Zombies. **1947** Desire Me; The Marauders; Oregon Trail Scouts; Vigilantes of Boomtown; Rustler's Rounup; The Return of Rin-Tin-Tin. **1948** Hazard; Return of the Bad Men; The Main Street Kid; Silent Conflict; Borrowed Trouble; Old Los Angeles; Let's Live Again. **1949** Henry, the Rainmaker; Sheriff of Wichita; Jiggs and Maggie in Jackpot Jitters; Slightly French. **1950** Copper Canyon; The Petty Girl; The Savage Horde; Square Dance Katy. **1951** Show Boat. **1953** City of Bad Men; Thunder Over the Plains; The Great Jesse James Raid. **1954** Bitter Creek; The Forty-Niners. **1955** East of Eden; Guys and Dolls. **1956** Friendly Persuasion; The Fastest Gun Alive. **1957** The Oklahoman; The D.I.; Up in Smoke. **1958** In the Money; Mardi Gras; The Missouri Traveler. **1962** Saintly Sinners; The Man Who Shot Liberty Valance.

HODGINS, LESLIE
Born: 1885. Died: Sept., 1927, St. Louis, Mo. Screen actor and singer.

HODGSON, LAURA
Born: 1892. Died: June, 1980, Hollywood, Calif. Screen actress.

Appeared in: **1977** Bound for Glory. **1979** Butch and Sundance: The Early Days.

HODGSON, LELAND (aka LEYLAND HODGSON)
Born: England. Died: Mar. 16, 1949, Hollywood, Calif. (heart attack). Screen and stage actor.

Appeared in: **1930** The Case of Sergeant Grisha. **1932** Under Cover Man; Ladies of the Jury. **1933** The Eagle and the Hawk. **1935** Perfect Gentleman; Feather in Her Hat. **1936** Beloved Enemy; Trouble for Two. **1937** The Prince and the Pauper; The Adventurous Blonde. **1938** The Adventures of Robin Hood; The Buccaneer. **1939** Irving Berlin's Second Fiddle; We Are Not Alone; The Rains Came; The Witness Vanishes; Susannah of the Mounties; Eternally Yours; Mr. Moto's Last Warning. **1940** The Sea Hawk; He Married His Wife; My Son, My Son; Murder Over New York. **1941** The Adventures of Captain Marvel (serial); The Wolf Man; The Case of the Black Parrot; Scotland Yard; International Lady. **1942** Journey for Margaret; To Be or Not to Be; The Ghost of Frankenstein; Secret Agent of Japan; The Strange Case of Dr. Rx; Escape from Hong Kong; Sherlock Holmes and the Voice of Terror; Just Off Broadway. **1943** The Gang's All Here; Happy Go Lucky. **1944** Frenchman's Creek; Follow the Boys; The Invisible Man's Revenge; Enter Arsene Lupin. **1945** Hangover Square; The Frozen Ghost; Molly and Me. **1946** Three Strangers; Terror by Night; Rendezvous 24; Black Beauty; Bedlam. **1947** Forever Amber; Green Dolphin Street; Thunder in the Valley. **1948** Kiss the Blood Off My Hands; A Woman's Vengeance. **1949** That Forsyte Woman.

HODIAK, JOHN
Born: Apr. 16, 1914, Pittsburgh, Pa. Died: Oct. 19, 1955, Tarzana, Calif. (coronary thrombosis). Screen, stage, radio and television actor. Divorced from actress-writer Anne Baxter.

Appeared in: **1943** A Stranger in Town (film debut); I Dood It; Song of Russia; Swing Shift Maisie. **1944** Lifeboat; Marriage Is a Private Affair; Maisie Goes to Reno; Sunday Dinner for a Soldier; You Can't Do That to Me. **1945** A Bell for Adano. **1956** Ziegfeld Follies; The Harvey Girls; Somewhere in the Night; Two Smart People. **1947** The Arnelo Affair; Love from a Stranger; Desert Fury. **1948** Homecoming; Command Decision. **1949** Ambush; The Bribe. **1950** A Lady Without a Passport; Malaya; Battleground; The Miniver Story. **1951** Night into Morning; People against O'Hara; Across the Wide Missouri. **1952** Battle Zone; The Sellout. **1953** Conquest of Cochise; Ambush at Tomahawk; Mission Over Korea. **1954** Dragonfly Squadron. **1955** Trial. **1956** On the Threshold of Space.

HOEFLICH, LUCIE (Helene Lucie von Holwede)
Born: 1883, Hanover, Germany. Died: Oct. 9, 1956, Berlin, Germany (heart attack). Screen and stage actress. Married to actor Emil Jannings (dec. 1950).

Appeared in: **1919** Freie Liebe; Maria Magdalena. **1920** Der Langsame Tod. **1921** Die Bestie im Menschen; Die Erbin von Toris; Die Ratten. **1922** Ein Puppenheim. **1923** Nora; Der Verlorene Schuhn; Die Strasse (The Street); Das Spiel der Koenigin (aka Ein Glas Wasser). **1924** Der Geheime Agent; Kaddisch (aka Totengebet). **1925** Goetz von Berlichengen Zubenannt mit der Eisernen Hand; Das Haus der Luege; Tartueff; Ein Walzertraum (Waltz Dream). **1926** Nur Eine Taenzerin. **1927** Das Gefaehrliche Alter; Manege. **1928** Der Biberpelz (The Beaver Coat). **1931** Zum Goldenen Anker; 1914, die Letzten Tage vor dem Weltbrand (1914: The Last Days Before the War—US 1932). **1932** Kampf; Strafsache van Geldern; Der Weisse Daemon (aka Rauschgift). **1933** Brennedes Geheimnis. **1934** Peer Gynt (US 1939). **1936** Der Raub der Sabinerinnen (US 1937); Fridericus; Familienparade; Schatten der Vergangenheit; Der Kurier des Zaren (The Tsar's Courier). **1937** Der Berg Ruft; Manege (and 1927 version); Starke Herzen. **1938** Die Warschauer Zitadelle; War es der im 3. Stock?; Um Freiheit und Liebe (For Freedom and Love). **1939** Wir Tanzen um die Welt; Robert Koch, der Bekaempfer des Todes. **1940** Der Fuchs von Glenarvon. **1941** Ohm Krueger. **1942** Weiss Waesche; Das Grosse Spiel. **1943** Altes Herz Wird Wieder Jung; Lache Bajazzo. **1955** Himmel ohne Sterne. **1956** Anastasia, die Letzte Zarentochter (aka Is Anna Anderson Anastasia?); Weil Du Arm Bist, Musst Du Frueher Sterben. **1959** Sky Without Warning.

HOERBIGER, PAUL
Born: 1894, Germany. Died: Mar., 1981, Vienna, Austria. Screen and stage actor. Brother of actor Attila Hoerbiger. Father of actor Thomas Hoerbiger.

Appeared in: **1928** Die Dame mit der Maske (The Lady With the Mask); Der Fesche Husar; Die Grosse Abenteurerin; G'schichten aus dem Wienerwald; Heut' Spielt der Strauss; Das Letzte Souper; Die Raueberbande (The Robber Band); Sechs Maedchen Suchen Nachquartier; Song; Spione (The Spy); Die Tolle Komptesse; Die Wochenendbraut; Asphalt. **1929** Die Drei um Edith; Die Frau, die Jeder Liebt, bist Du!; Frauen am Abgrund; Das Gruene Monokel; Ein Kleiner Vorschuss auf die Seligkeit; Moebelierte Zimmer; Der

Straefling aus Stambul; Wer Wird den Weinen, Wenn man Auseinandergeht. **1930** Wie Werde ich Reich und Gluecklich?; Der Unsterbliche Lump; Ich Glaub' nie Mehr an Eine Frau (US 1933); Nur Du; Delikatesse; Das Alte Lied (aka Zu Jedem Kommt Einmal die Liebe); Der Herr auf Bestellung; Zwei Herzen im Drei-Viertel Takt; Drei Tage Mittelarrest (Three Days in the Guardhouse—US 1933); Das Lockende Ziel; Why Cry at Parting. **1931** Der Kongress Tanzt; Die Lustigen Weiber von Wien; Die Foersterchristl; Der Zinker; Arme wie Eine Kirchenmaus; Der Ungetreue Eckehart (US 1932); Reserve hat Ruh (US 1932); Walzerparadies (US 1933); Der Verjuengte Adolar; Luegen auf Ruegen (US 1934); Grock; Mein Herz Sehnt Sich Nach Liebe (aka Der Hellseher—US 1933); Sein Scheidungsgrund (US 1932); Ihre Hoheit Befielt; Kyritz-Pyritz (US 1932). **1932** Zwei Gluesckliche Tage; So ein Maedel Vergisst man Nicht (US 1935); Quick, Koenig der Clowns (US 1933); Annemarie, die Braut der Kompanie (US 1934); Das Geheimnis um Johann Orth (aka Ein Liebesroman im Hause Habsburg); Es War Einmal ein Walzer; Trenck (US 1934); Scampolo, ein Kind der Strasse; Peter Voss, der Millionendieb; Der Grosse Bluff (The Big Bluff—US 1937, aka Schuesse in der Nacht); Die Unsichtbare Front; Ein Toller Einfall; Ein Steinreicher Mann; Friederike (US 1933); Johann Strauss, K. und K. Hofballmusikdirektor (aka Kaiserwalzer—US 1934); Drei von der Kavallerie (US 1935). **1933** Zwei Gute Kameraden; Ein Lied fuer Dich; Skandal in Budapest; Liebelei (US 1936); Des Jungen Dessauers Grosse Liebe; Keinen Tag ohne Dich (aka Wovon soll der Schornstein Rauchen); Heimkehr ins Glueck; Gruss und Kuss, Veronika! (US 1936); Ein Maedel der Strasse; Wiener Blut. **1934** Speil mit dem Feuer; Besuch am Abend (US 1937); Der Herr ohne Wohnung; Die Csardasfuerstin (US 1935); Rosen aus dem Sueden (Roses From the South—US 1935); Petersburger Naechte (aka Walzer an der Newa); Fraulein Frau (US 1937); ... Heute Abend bei Mir; Mein Herz Ruft Nach Dir; Herz ist Trumpf; Ich Heirate Meine Frau; Eines Prinzen Junge Liebe; Pesti Szerelem; Wie Man Maenner Fesselt; Waltz Time in Vienna. **1935** Wenn die Musik Micht Waer'; Das Einmaleins der Liebe (US 1937); Fruehjahrsparade; Frischer Wind an Kanada; Liebeslied; Koenigswalzer; Endstation (US 1937); Seine Tochter ist der Peter (His Daughter is Peter—US 1938); The Czardas Duchess. **1936** Kinderarzt Dr. Engal (Dr. Engel, Child Specialist—US 1937); Schabernack (US 1937); Das Fiakerlied (aka The Cabbie's Song—US 1937); Die Puppenfee; Drei Maederl um Schubert (US 1937, aka Dreimaederlhaus); The Royal Waltz; Koenigin der Liebe; Ein Liebesroman im Hause Habsburg. **1937** Peter im Schnee; Der Scheidungsgrund; Florentine (aka Wir Fahren Gegen den Wind); Die Landstreicher (The Hoboes—US 1938); Lumpazivagabundus; Einmal Werd' ich Dir Gefallen. **1938** Immer, Wenn ich Gluecklich Bin; Prinzessin Sissy; Der Blaufuchs; Heiraten—Aber Wen?; Liebelei und Liebe; Heimat (aka O Scharzwald, O Heimat, Oh Black Forest, Oh Home—US 1939); Magda. **1939** Hochzeitsreise zu Dritt; Drunter und Drueber; Unsterblicher Walzer (Immortal Waltz); Ich bin Sebastian Ott; Maenner Muessen so Sein (Men Are That Way); Opernball; Kitty und die Weltkonferenz; Salonwagen E 417; Mutterliebe; Maria Ilona (US 1940). **1940** Wunschkonzert; Wiener G'schichten; Der Liebe Augustin; Operette (Operetta—US 1949); Falstaff in Wein; Herzensfreud—Herzensleid. **1941** Oh Diese Maenner; Wir Bitten zum Tanz. **1942** Die Grosse Liebe; So ein Fruechtchen; Wen die Goetter Lieben; Bruederlein Fein; Die Heimliche Graefin. **1943** Schwarz auf Weiss; Lache Bajazzo. **1944** Schrammeln; Die Azubergeige; Romantische Brautfahrt. **1947** Der Hofrat Geiger. **1948** Der Engel mit der Posaume; Kleine Melodie aus Wien; Laugh Pagliacci. **1949** Die Seltsame Geschichte des Brandner Kaspar; Der Bahnostraefling; The Third Man (US 1950). **1950** Der Seelenbraue; Eine Nacht im Separee; Epilog; Schwarzwaldmaedel; Tanze Mit Mir in dem Morgen (Dance With Me Into the Morning—and 1962 version). **1951** Daemonische Liebe; Der Alte Suender; Die Frauen des Herrn S.; Verklungenes Wien; Wenn Die Abendglocken Laueten; Der Fidele Bauer; Was das Herz Befiehlt. **1952** Fruehlingsstimmen; Hallo Dienstmann; Ich Heisse Niki; Mein Herz Darfst Du Nicht Kragen; Mikosch Rueckt ein; Ich Hab' Mein Herz in Heidelberg Verloren; Man Lebt nur Einmal; Das Land des Laechelns; Hannerl (aka Ich Tanze mit Dir in den Himmel Hinein). **1953** Glueck Muss Man Haben; Die Fiakermili; Von der Liebe Reden wir Spaeter; Die Rose von Stambul; Junges Herz Voll Liebe; Das Tanzende Herz (The Dancing Heart—US 1959); Mit Diebzehn Beginnt das Leben; Die Privatsekretaerin (Private Secretary); Der Feldherrenhuegel. **1954** Der Raub der Sabinerinnen; Der Treue Husar; Meine Shwester und ich; Der Zigeunerbaron (The Gypsy Baron—US 1959); Die Schoen Muellerin; Schuetzenliesel; Begegnung in Rom; Maedchenjahre einer Koenigin. **1955** Die Stadt ist Voller Geheimnisse; Eine Frau Genuegt Nicht?; Banditen der Autobahn; Der Froehliche Wanderer; Ein Herz Bleibt Allein; Du Mein Stiller Tal; Die Foersterbuben; Ja, Ja die Liebe in Tirol; An der Schoenen Blauen Donau; Die Deutschmeister; Ehesanatorium. **1956** Hilfe—sie Liebt Mich!; Die Christel von der Post; Das Donkosakenlied; Manoeverball;

Was doe Schwalbe Sang; Ihr Korporal (aka Husarenmanoever); Charleys Tante (Charley's Aunt); Bademeister Spargel; ... und wer Kuesst Mich? (aka Ein Herz und eine Seele); Lumpazivagabundus; Luegen Haben Huebsche Beine. **1957** Der Schraege Otto; Heimweh ... dort wo die Blumen Blueh'n; Ober, Zahlen!; Der Schoenste Tag Meines Lebens; Wien, Du Stadt Meiner Trauerne; Die Winzerin von Langenlois (aka Und Sowas Will Erwachsen Sein); Hoch Droben auf dem Berg; Lemkessel. Witwe; ... und die Liebe Lacht Dazu. **1958** Hallo Taxi; Heiratskandidaten; Hock Klingt der Radetzkymarsch; Sebastian Kneipp. **1959** Heimat—Diene Lieder. **1960** Sabine und die 100 Maenner. **1961** Kauf die einen Bunten Luftballon; Der Orgelbaurer von St. Marien; ... und Du, Mein Schatz, Bleibst Hier. **1962** Drei Liebesbriefe aus Tirol; Tanze mit mir in den Morgen (Dance With Me Into the Morning—and 1951 version); ... und Ewig Knallen die Raueber. **1963** Ferien vom Ich; Im Singenden Roessl am Koenigssee; Die Lustigen Vagabunden (aka Das Haben die Maedchen Gern); Sing, Aber Spiel Nicht Mit Mir; Unsere Tollen Nichten; City of Secrets. **1964** Das Hab' och von Papa Gelernt; Die Ganze Welt ist Himmelblau (aka Rote Lippen Sol man Kuessen); Die Grosse Kuer; Happy-end am Woerthesee (aka Happy-end am Attersee). **1965** Der Alpenkoenig und der Menschfeind; Das ist Mein Wien (aka ... ewiges Wienerlied). **1974** Liebelei.

HOEY, DENNIS (Samuel David Hyams)
Born: Mar. 30, 1893, England. Died: July 25, 1960, Palm Beach, Fla. Screen and stage actor. Played character of "Inspector Lestrade" in Basil Rathbone's Sherlock Holmes series from 1939 to 1945.

Appeared in: **1927** Tiptoes. **1930** The Man from Chicago (US 1931). **1931** Tell England (aka The Battle of Gallipoli—US); Never Trouble Trouble; Love Lies. **1932** Life Goes On (aka Sorry You've Been Troubled); The Maid of the Mountains; Baroud (aka Love in Morocco—US 1933). **1933** The Good Companions; Facing the Music (US 1934); Maid Happy; Oh What a Duchess! (aka My Old Duchess); I Spy; The Wandering Jew (US 1935). **1934** Lily of Killarney (aka Bride of the Lake—US); Jew Suess (aka Power—US); Chu Chin Chow. **1935** Brewster's Millions; Immortal Gentleman; Maria Marten, or, The Murder in the Red Barn; Honeymoon for Three; The Mystery of the Mary Celeste (aka Phantom Ship—US 1937). **1936** Faust; Did I Betray? **1937** Uncivilized. **1941** Confirm or Deny; A Yank in the R.A. F.; How Green Was My Valley. **1942** We Were Dancing; Son of Fury; This above All; Cairo; Sherlock Holmes and the Street Weapon. **1943** Frankenstein Meets the Wolf Man; They Came to Blow Up America; Forever and a Day; Sherlock Holmes Faces Death; Bomber's Moon. **1944** National Velvet; Keys of the Kingdoom; Uncertain Glory; The Pearl of Death; Sherlock Holmes and the Spider Woman. **1945** House of Fear; A Thousand and One Nights. **1946** Roll on Texas Moon; She-Wolf of London; Tarzan and the Leopard Woman; The Strange Woman; Kitty; Terror by Night; Anna and the King of Siam. **1947** The Crimson Key; Second Chance; Golden Earrings; The Foxes of Harrow; Christmas Eve; Where There's Life; If Winter Comes. **1948** Ruthless; Badmen of Tombstone; Wake of the Red Witch. **1949** The Secret Garden. **1950** Joan of Arc; The Kid from Texas. **1951** David and Bathsheba. **1952** Caribbean. **1953** Ali Baba Nights.

HOEY, GEORGE J.
Born: 1885. Died: Feb. 17, 1955, Hollywood, Calif. Screen actor.

HOEY, HERBERT (William Herbert Hoey)
Born: 1894, Atlanta, Ga. Died: Dec. 7, 1970, Miami Shores, Fla. Screen, stage, vaudeville actor and dancer. Appeared in early Pathe, Vitagraph and Kalem films.

HOEY, IRIS
Born: July 17, 1885, London, England. Died: May 13, 1979, London, England. Screen and stage actress. Divorced from actor Cyril Raymond (dec. 1973) and Max Leeds.

Appeared in: **1934** Those Were the Days. **1936** The Tenth Man (US 1937); Living Dangerously; The Limping Man. **1937** Let's Make a Night of It (US 1938); The Perfect Crime. **1938** The Terror; Jane Steps Out (US 1940); Pygmalion.

HOEY, JOHN "JOHNNY"
Born: 1919. Died: Aug. 11, 1978, Greystones, Ireland. Screen, stage and television actor. Married to actress Moira Deady.

Appeared in: **1957** Professor Tim (US 1959). **1959** Home is the Hero (US 1961). **1960** The Poacher's Daughter; Sword of Sherwood Forest (US 1961). **1970** Quackser Fortune Has a Cousin in the Bronx.

HOFER, CHRIS (Martin Christopher Hofer)
Born: 1920, N.Y. Died: Feb. 11, 1964, Rome, Italy (auto accident). Screen, stage and television actor.

Appeared in: **1959** Londra Chiama Polo Nord (London Calling North Pole aka The House of Intrigue).

HOFFE, MONCKTON
Born: Dec. 26, 1880, Connemara, Ireland. Died: Nov. 4, 1951, London, England. Screen, stage actor, playwright and screenwriter.

Appeared in: **1951** Lady with a Lamp.

HOFFMAN, BERN (Bernard Hoffman)
Born: 1913. Died: Dec. 15, 1979, Sherman Oaks, Calif. Screen, stage and television actor.

Appeared in: **1946** Nocturne. **1949** On the Town. **1959** Li'l Abner; The Man Who Understood Women. **1960** The Bramble Bush. **1962** The Scarface Mob. **1964** Kiss Me Stupid. **1968** Don't Just Stand There! **1974** The Outfit.

HOFFMAN, CLARENCE
Born: 1919. Died: Mar. 26, 1981, Las Vegas, Nev. (heart seizure). Screen, stage actor, singer and ringmaster at Circus Circus.

HOFFMAN, DAVID
Born: Feb. 2, 1904, Russia. Died: June 19, 1961, Seattle, Wash. Screen, stage and radio actor.

Appeared in: **1940** Underground (film debut). **1943** Mission to Moscow; Flesh and Fantasy. **1944** Dead Man's Eyes; The Mask of Dimitrios; The Conspirators. **1946** A Night in Casablanca; Beast With Five Fingers. **1947** Desire Me. **1948** Inner Sanctum. **1949** Rope of Sand; Backfire (aka Somewhere in the City); Trouble Makers. **1953** Titanic. **1954** Woman's World. **1955** Daddy Long Legs. **1958** A Certain Smile. **1959** The Best of Everything.

HOFFMAN, EBERHARD
Born: 1883. Died: June 16, 1957, Denville, N.Y. Screen actor. Appeared in silents.

HOFFMAN, GERTRUDE (Gertrude Anderson)
Born: 1898, Montreal, Canada. Died: June 3, 1955, Washington, D.C. Stage and screen actress.

HOFFMAN, GERTRUDE W.
Born: May 17, 1871, Heidelberg, Germany. Died: Oct. 21, 1966, Hollywood, Calif. (heart attack). Screen, vaudeville actress and dancer. Mother of actor Max Hoffman, Jr. (dec. 1945).

Appeared in: **1933** Hell and High Water; Before Dawn. **1935** Les Miserables. **1936** A Son Comes Home; The Gentleman from Louisiana. **1938** Cassidy of Bar 20. **1939** Laugh It Off. **1940** The Ape; Untamed; Foreign Correspondent. **1941** Suspicion; Lydia. **1942** I Married an Angel; Tish; North of the Rockies; Commandos Strike at Dawn; A Wife Takes a Flier. **1943** The Moon is Down; A Guy Named Joe; The Heavenly Body; What a Woman. **1946** The Bride Wore Boots. **1947** California; Welcome Stranger. **1949** Thelma Jordan (aka File on Thelma Jordan). **1951** Close to My Heart. **1953** The War of the Worlds.

HOFFMAN, HERMINE H.
Born: 1921. Died: Dec. 7, 1971, Broomall, Pa. Screen, stage and circus actress.

Appeared in: **1945** See My Lawyer.

HOFFMAN, HOWARD R. (Howard Ralph Hoffman)
Born: Nov. 4, 1893, Ohio. Died: June 27, 1969, Hollywood, Calif. (heart attack). Screen, stage, vaudeville, radio and television actor.

Appeared in: **1958** Macabre; The Littlest Hobo. **1959** House on Haunted Hill; A Summer Place.

HOFFMAN, JOHN IVAN
Born: 1905, Hungary. Died: Jan. 6, 1980, Los Angeles, Calif.? Special effects man, screenwriter, film editor and screen actor.

HOFFMAN, MAX, JR.
Born: Dec. 13, 1902, Norfolk, Va. Died: Mar. 31, 1945, New York, N.Y. Screen, stage and vaudeville actor. Son of dancer and actress Gertrude W. Hoffman (dec. 1966). Divorced from actress Helen Kane (dec. 1966).

Appeared in: **1931** Old Lace (short). **1936** Draegerman's Courage;

King of Hockey. **1937** The Game That Kills; Radio Patrol (serial); Secret Agent X-9 (serial); The Go-Getter; Kid Galahad; Counterfeit Lady; Rootin' Tootin' Rhythm; Swing It, Sailor; Sergeant Murphy; San Quentin. **1938** Sky Giant; Accidents Will Happen; The Great Waltz; Kidnapped; Little Orphan Annie. **1939** Wings of the Navy; Ambush; Wings of Victory; Topper Takes a Trip; Hell's Kitchen; Confessions of a Nazi Spy; Kid Nightingale; Dust Be My Destiny. **1940** Brother Orchid; Lady from Hell; Virginia City; It All Came True; Castle on the Hudson. **1941** They Died With Their Boots On; The Strawberry Blonde. **1942** The Wife Takes a Flyer; Man from Headquarters; Black Dragons.

HOFFMAN, OTTO (Otto Frederick Hoffman)
Born: May 2, 1879, New York, N.Y. Died: June 23, 1944, Woodland Hills, Calif. (lung cancer). Screen actor. Entered films in 1917 with Thomas Ince.

Appeared in: **1916** Behind Closed Doors. **1918** String Beans; Nine O'Clock. **1919** The Sheriff's Son; The Busher; The City of Comrades; The Egg Crate Wallop; 23 1/2 Hours' Leave; Paris Green. **1920** The Great Accident; It's a Great Life; The Jail Bird; Homer Comes Home. **1921** The Bronze Bell; Just Out of College; Bunty Pulls the Strings; The Devil Within; Passing Thru; Whatever She Wants; Who Am I?. **1922** The Bootlegger's Daughter; Boy Crazy; Confidence; A Dangerous Game; The Five Dollar Baby; Gas, Oil and Water; The Glorious Fool; Mr. Barnes of New York; The New Teacher; Pardon My Nerve!; Ridin' Wild; The Sin Flood; Trimmed; Very Truly Yours. **1923** One Stolen Night; Strangers of the Night; Double Dealing; Human Wreckage; Lucretia Lombard. **1924** Broadway After Dark; Daddies; The Gaiety Girl; High Speed; The Price She Paid; This Woman. **1925** The Circle; Satan in Sables; Secrets of the Night; Bobbed Hair; Confessions of a Queen; The Dixie Handicap; The Eagle. **1926** The Boy Friend; Millionaires; More Pay—Less Work. **1927** Beware of Widows; Painted Ponies; The Siren; The Stolen Bride. **1928** The Fourflusher; The Grain of Dust; Noah's Ark; The Terror; Rinty of the Desert. **1929** Acquitted; The Desert Song; The Hottentot; Hardboiled Rose; Is Everybody Happy?; The Madonna of Avenue A; On with the Show. **1930** Moby Dick; Kismet; Abraham Lincoln; The Other Tomorrow; Sinner's Holiday. **1931** The Criminal Code; Captain Applejack; Cimarron; Son of India; Side Show; The Avenger. **1932** Two Seconds; Downstairs; County Fair; Hello Trouble. **1933** The Iron Master; Haunted Gold; Cheyenne Kid; Man of Sentiment. **1934** Beloved; Death Takes a Holiday; Murder at the Vanities; Kid Millions. **1935** The Story of Louis Pasteur; Barbary Coast; Behold My Wife; Captain Hurricane; Flying Shadows; Smart Girl. **1936** The Case Against Mrs. Ames; Career Woman. **1937** Living on Love; Hideaway; Girl Loves Boy; All Over Town. **1938** Romance in the Dark; Mr. Boggs Steps Out. **1939** When Tomorrow Comes; Our Leading Citizen. **1940** My Little Chickadee; Lucky Partners; Lucky Cisco Kid; Stranger on the Third Floor. **1941** Ball of Fire; How Green Was My Valley. **1944** This is the Life.

HOGAN, DAN
Born: 1924, Stigler, Okla. Died: June 22, 1978, New York, N.Y. Screen, stage and television actor.

HOGAN, EARL "HAP" (Earl Richard Traynor)
Died: Oct. 14, 1944, Los Angeles, Calif. Screen actor.

Appeared in: **1928** The Haunted Ship.

HOGAN, JAMES P.
Born: 1891. Died: Nov. 4, 1943, North Hollywood, Calif. (heart attack). Screen actor, film director, film producer and screenwriter.

Appeared in: **1924** Black Lightning.

HOGAN, PAT
Born: 1931. Died: Nov. 22, 1966, Hollywood, Calif. (cancer). Screen actor.

Appeared in: **1951** Fixed Bayonets. **1952** Luke of the Wilderness; Return of Gilbert and Sullivan. **1953** The Nebraskan; Arrowhead; Back to God's Country; Gun Fury; Overland Pacific; Pony Express. **1954** Man with the Steel Whip (serial); Sign of the Pagan. **1955** Davy Crockett, King of the Wild Frontier; Kiss of Fire; Smoke Signal. **1956** The Last Frontier; Pillars of the Sky; Secret of Treasure Mountain; 7th Cavalry. **1962** Hemingway's Adventures of a Young Man. **1963** Savage Sam. **1965** Indian Paint.

HOGAN, "SOCIETY KID" (Salvatore de Lorenzo)
Born: 1899. Died: Apr. 10, 1962, Chicago, Ill. Screen actor.

Appeared in: **1951** Lemon Drop Kid. **1953** Money from Home.

HOGG, JACK "CURLY"
Born: 1917. Died: Sept., 1974, San Diego, Calif. (heart attack). Screen, television actor and musician. Was one of the orginal "Sons of the Pioneers" and was often called "King of the Banjoes."

HOGUE, ROLAND (John Roland Hogue)
Born: 1882. Died: Oct. 7, 1958, Morristown, N.J. Screen and stage actor.

Appeared in: **1933** His Double Life.

HOHL, ARTHUR
Born: May 21, 1889, Pittsburgh, Pa. Died: Mar. 10, 1964, Calif. Screen and stage actor.

Appeared in: **1924** It Is the Law. **1931** The Cheat. **1932** The Sign of the Cross. **1933** Island of Lost Souls; Captured; Baby Face; Silk Express; The Life of Jimmy Dolan; Private Detective 62; The Narrow Corner; Footlight Parade; The Kennel Murder Case; College Coach; Infernal Machine; Wild Boys of the Road; The World Changes; Brief Moment; A Man's Castle; Jealousy. **1934** The Defense Rests; Cleopatra; Lady by Choice; A Modern Hero; As the Earth Turns; Jimmy the Gents; Romance in Manhattan; Bulldog Drummond Strikes Back. **1935** Case of the Missing Man; The Whole Town's Talking; Eight Bells; In Spite of Danger; The Unknown Woman; I'll Love You Always; Guard That Girl; Village Tale; One Frightened Night. **1936** We're Only Human; It Had to Happen; Lloyds of London; Superspeed; The Lone Wolf Returns; Forgotten Faces; Showboat; The Devil Doll. **1937** Slave Ship; Hot Water; The Road Back; The River of Missing Men; Trapped by G-Men; Mountain Music. **1938** The Bad Man of Brimstone; Penitentiary; Kidnapped; Crime Takes a Holiday; Stablemates. **1939** Boy Slaves; You Can't Cheat an Honest Man; They Shall Have Music; Blackmail; Fugitive at Large; The Adventures of Sherlock Holmes; The Hunchback of Notre Dame. **1940** 20 Mule Team; Blondie Has Servant Trouble. **1941** Men of Boys Town; Ride On, Vaquero; We Go Fast. **1942** Son of Fury; Whispering Ghosts; Moontide. **1943** Idaho; The Woman of the Town. **1944** The Song of Bernadette; Mystery of the River Boat (serial); Sherlock Holmes and the Spider Woman; The Eve of St. Mark; The Scarlet Claw; Crime Doctor. **1945** Our Vines Have Tender Grapes; Salome Where She Danced; The Frozen Ghost; Love Letters. **1947** It Happened on 5th Avenue; Monsieur Verdoux; The Vigilantes Return; The Yearling. **1949** Down to the Sea in Ships.

HOLBROOK, JACK (John Knight Holbrook)
Born: Ripley, Tenn. Died: Nov. 17, 1934, Los Angeles, Calif. Screen actor and stuntman.

Appeared in: **1915** Exploits of Elaine (serial). **1916** Mysteries of Myra (serial).

HOLCOMB, GRANT
Born: 1917, San Bernardino, Calif. Died: Dec. 16, 1977, Los Angeles, Calif. (cancer). Screen, radio, television actor and newsman.

Appeared in: **1961** X-15.

HOLCOMBE, HERBERT
Died: Oct. 15, 1970. Screen actor.

Appeared in: **1938** Phantom Ranger. **1949** Project X.

HOLDEN, FAY (Dorothy Hammerton aka GABY FAY)
Born: Sept. 26, 1895, Birmingham, England. Died: June 23, 1973, Woodland Hills, Calif. (cancer). Screen and stage actress. Married to actor David Clyde (dec. 1945). Appeared as Andy Hardy's mother in the "Andy Hardy" films.

Appeared in: **1936** Polo Joe (film debut); I Married a Doctor; Wives Never Know; The White Angel. **1937** Guns of the Pecos; A Family Affair; Souls at Sea; Exclusive; Double or Nothing; Bulldog Drummond Escapes; Internes Can't Take Money; King of Gamblers; Nothing Sacred. **1938** Test Pilot; You're Only Young Once; Love Is a Headache; Judge Hardy's Children; Hold that Kiss; Love Finds Andy Hardy; Out West with the Hardys; Sweethearts; The Battle of Broadway. **1939** Sergeant Madden; The Hardys Ride High; Andy Hardy Gets Spring Fever; Judge Hardy and Son. **1940** Andy Hardy Meets a Debutante; Bitter Sweet. **1941** Andy Hardy's Private Secretary; Ziegfeld Girl; Washington Melodrama; I'll Wait for You; Blossoms in the Dust; Life Begins for Andy Hardy; H. M. Pulham, Esq. **1942** The Courtship of Andy Hardy; Andy Hardy's Double Life. **1944** Andy Hardy's Blonde Trouble. **1946** Canyon Passage; The Baxter Millions; Little Miss Big; Love Laughs at Andy Hardy. **1948** Whispering Smith. **1949** Samson and Delilah. **1950** The Big Hangover. **1958** Andy Hardy Comes Home.

HOLDEN, HARRY MOORE
Born: 1868. Died: Feb. 4, 1944, Woodland Hills, Calif. Screen and stage actor.

Appeared in: **1927** The Gay Defender; The Yankee Clipper; Winds of the Pampas; Show Boat. **1930** Code of Honor. **1938** What Price Glory? (short).

HOLDEN, VIOLA (Viola Martinelli)
Died: Aug. 23, 1967, Saratoga, N.Y. (heart attack). Screen and stage actress.

Appeared in: **1948** Mexican Hayride. **1952** Sailor Beware.

HOLDEN, WILLIAM (William Franklin Beedle, Jr.)
Born: Apr. 17, 1918, O'Fallon, Ill. Died: Nov. 16, 1981, Santa Monica, Calif. (results of a fall). Screen, stage, radio and television actor. Divorced from actress Brenda Marshall. Won 1953 Academy Award as Best Actor in Stalag 17. Nominated for 1950 Academy Award as Best Actor in Sunset Boulevard and in 1976 as Best Actor in Network.

Appeared in: **1939** Million Dollar Legs (film debut); Golden Boy. **1940** Invisible Stripes; Those Were the Days; Arizona; Our Town. **1941** I Wanted Wings; Texas. **1942** The Fleet's In; The Remarkable Andrew; Meet the Stewarts. **1943** Young and Willing. **1947** Dear Ruth; Variety Girl; Blaze of Noon. **1948** The Man From Colorado; Apartment for Peggy; Rachael and the Stranger. **1949** The Dark Past; Streets of Laredo; Miss Grant Takes Richmond; Dear Wife. **1950** Sunset Boulevard; Union Station; Father Is a Bachelor; Born Yesterday. **1951** Force of Arms; Submarine Command. **1952** Boots Malone; The Turning Point. **1953** Stalag 17; The Moon Is Blue; Forever Female; Escape From Fort Bravo. **1954** The Country Girl; The Bridges at Toko-Ri; Sabrina; Executive Suite. **1955** Love Is a Many Splendored Thing; Picnic; Samurai (narrator). **1956** The Proud and the Profane; Toward the Unknown. **1957** The Bridge of the River Kwai. **1958** The Key. **1959** The Horse Soldiers. **1960** The World of Susie Wong. **1962** Satan Never Sleeps; The Counterfeit Traitor; The Lion. **1964** Paris When It Sizzles; The 7th Dawn. **1966** Alvarez Kelly. **1967** Casino Royale. **1968** The Devils Brigade. **1969** The Revengers; The Wild Bunch; The Christmas Tree. **1971** The Wild Rovers. **1973** Breezy. **1974** Open Season; The Towering Inferno. **1976** Network; 21 Hours at Munich. **1978** Damien Omena II. **1979** Ashanti; Escape to Athena; Fedora; Golden Raiders (cameo roll). **1980** The Earthling; When Time Ran Out. **1981** S.O.B.

HOLDEN, WILLIAM
Born: May 22, 1872, Rochester, N.Y. Died: Mar. 2, 1932, Hollywood, Calif. (heart attack). Stage and screen actor. Do not confuse with actor born in 1918 (dec. 1981).

Appeared in: **1920** The Fortune Hunter; Bab's Candidate. **1928** Roadhouse; The First Kiss; Three Week Ends. **1929** Weary River; The Trespasser; Dynamite; His Captive Woman; Fast Life. **1930** Not So Dumb; Numbered Men; Framed; Holiday; What a Widow; Three Faces East. **1931** The Man Who Came Back; Charlie Chan Carries On; Six Cylinder Love; Dance, Fool, Dance; The Cheat. **1932** Night of June 13; Sign of the Cross; Island of Lost Souls.

HOLDING, THOMAS
Born: Jan. 25, 1880, Blackheath, Kent, England. Died: May 4, 1929, New York, N.Y. (heart disease). Screen, stage actor and film director.

Appeared in: **1915** The Eternal City; The White Pearl; The Moment Before. **1917** Redeeming Love; Magda. **1918** Daughter of Destiny; Vanity Pool. **1919** The Peace of Roaring River; The Lone Wolf's Daughter; The Danger Zone; The Lady of Red Butte; Tangled Threads; Beckoning Roads. **1920** The Honey Bee; In Folly's Trail; Woman in His House. **1921** The Lure of Jade; The Three Musketeers; Sacred and Profane Love; Without the Benefit of Clergy. **1922** Rose O' the Sea; The Trouper. **1923** Stranger's Banquet; The Courtship of Miles Standish; Ruggles of Red Gap. **1925** The Necessary Evil; One Way Street; The White Monkey; The Pace that Thrills.

HOLDREN, JUDD (Judd Clifton Holdren)
Born: Oct. 16, 1915, Iowa. Died: Mar. 11, 1974, West Los Angeles, Calif. (suicide—gun). Screen actor.

Appeared in: **1949** All the King's Men. **1951** Purple Heart Diary; Captain Video (serial). **1952** Zombies of the Stratosphere (serial); Lady in the Iron Mask; Gold Fever. **1953** The Lost Planet (serial). **1954** This Is My Love. **1957** The Amazing Colossal Man. **1958** Satan's Satellites; The Buccaneer.

HOLLAND, BERT C.
Born: 1923. Died: Mar. 8, 1980, Los Angeles, Calif. (cancer). Screen, stage, radio, television actor and drama instructor.

Appeared in: **1958** The Lineup.

HOLLAND, C. MAURICE
Died: Nov. 14, 1974, Greenwich, Conn. Stage, vaudeville, screen actor, television director and producer. Married to actress Frances Seaton.

Appeared in: **1929** Day of a Man of Affairs.

HOLLAND, CECIL C.
Born: 1887, Gravensend, Kent, England. Died: June 29, 1973, Los Angeles, Calif. Screen and stage actor.

Appeared in: **1916** The Crisis. **1917** His Sweetheart; Garden of Allah. **1918** The Still Alarm. **1921** The Great Impersonations; A Wise Fool. **1922** Moran of Lady Letty; The Woman Who Walked Alone; Burning Sands; Penrod. **1923** The Bishop of the Ozarks; The Girl of the Golden West; The Rendezvous. **1924** Name the Man.

HOLLAND, FRANK
Born: 1862, Hope, R.I. Died: Nov. 6, 1924, New York, N.Y. (heart failure). Screen, stage and vaudeville actor.

Appeared in: **1914** Lola; My Official Wife. **1917** Tides of Fate; The Wild Cat. **1921** The Traveling Salesman; The Blazing Trail.

HOLLAND, MILDRED
Born: Apr. 9, 1869, Chicago, Ill. Died: Jan. 27, 1944, New York, N.Y. Screen actress. Appeared in silents.

HOLLAND, MIRIAM
Born: 1917. Died: Sept. 24, 1948, Hollywood, Calif. Screen actress.

HOLLAND, PEANUTS (Herbert Lee Holland)
Born: 1910, Norfolk, Va. Died: Feb. 7, 1979, Stockholm, Sweden. Black musician (trumpeter), singer and screen actor.

HOLLAND, RALPH
Born: 1888. Died: Dec. 7, 1939, Los Angeles, Calif. Screen and stage actor. Entered films approx. 1927.

HOLLAND, ZAY
Born: 1878. Died: Nov. 7, 1941, Yonkers, N.Y. Screen, stage and vaudeville actress. Divorced from actor Sydney Grant (dec. 1953).

HOLLANDER, MILDRED
Born: 1900. Died: July 19, 1937, Middleton, Conn. Screen and stage actress.

HOLLES, ANTONY (aka ANTHONY HOLLES)
Born: Jan. 17, 1901, London, England. Died: Mar. 5, 1950. Screen and stage actor.

Appeared in: **1921** The Will. **1931** The Star Reporter. **1932** Hotel Splendide; Reunion; The Missing Rembrandt; Once Bitten; Life Goes On (aka Sorry You've Been Troubled); The Lodger (aka The Phantom Fiend—US 1935); Watch Beverly; The Midshipmaid. **1933** She Was Only a Village Maiden; Forging Ahead; Cash (aka For Love or Money—US 1934); Britannia of Billingsgate; That's a Good Girl. **1934** Borrowed Clothes; The Green Pack. **1935** Brewster's Millions; Gentleman's Agreement. **1936** Limelight (aka Backstage—US); Public Nuisance No. 1; Things to Come; Seven Sinners (aka Doomed Cargo—US); The Tenth Man (US 1937); Millions; This'll Make You Whistle (US 1938); The Gay Adventure. **1937** Glamorous Night; Smash and Grab; Paradise for Two (aka The Gaiety Girls—US 1938); The Sky's the Limit; Mademoiselle Docteur; Let's Make a Night of It (US 1938); Action for Slander (US 1938). **1938** Romance a la Carte; His Lordship Regrets; Dangerous Medicine; They Drive by Night; Miracles Do Happen; Weddings Are Wonderful. **1939** Down Our Alley; Ten Days in Paris (aka Missing Ten Days—US); The Spider; Blind Folly; The Missing People (US 1940). **1940** Neutral Port. **1942** Front Line Kids; Talk about Jacqueline; Lady from Lisbon; Tomorrow We Live (aka At Dawn We Die—US 1943). **1943** Warn that Man; Up with the Lark; It's in the Bag; Battle for Music; Old Mother Riley Overseas. **1944** A Canterbury Tale; Give Me the Stars. **1946** Caesar and Cleopatra; The Magic Bow (US 1947); Carnival; Gaiety George (aka Showtime—US 1948). **1947** Fortune Lane. **1948** The Dark Road. **1949** The Rocking Horse Winner (US 1950).

HOLLIDAY, BILLIE (Eleanor Gough McKay)
Born: Apr. 7, 1915, Baltimore, Md. Died: July 17, 1959, New York, N.Y. Black singer and screen actress.

Appeared in: **1935** Symphony in Black (short). **1947** New Orleans.

HOLLIDAY, FRANK, JR.
Born: 1913. Died: Aug. 3, 1948, Hollywood, Calif. (suicide—hanging). Screen and radio actor.

Appeared in: **1935** Alias Mary Dow.

HOLLIDAY, JUDY (Judith Turin)
Born: June 21, 1923, New York, N.Y. Died: June 7, 1965, New York, N.Y. (cancer). Stage and screen actress. Divorced from musician David Oppenheim. Won 1950 Academy Award for Best Actress in Born Yesterday.

Appeared in: **1944** Greenwich Village; Something for the Boys; Winged Victory. **1949** Adam's Rib. **1951** Born Yesterday. **1952** The Marrying Kind. **1954** Phffft; It Should Happen to You. **1956** The Solid Gold Cadillac; Full of Life. **1960** Bells Are Ringing.

HOLLIDAY, MARJORIE (Marjorie St. Angel)
Born: 1920. Died: June 16, 1969, Hollywood, Calif. (brain hemorrhage). Screen actress.

Appeared in: **1950** The Jackpot. **1952** Dreamboat; Monkey Business; O'Henry's Full House. **1954** She Couldn't Say No.

HOLLINGSHEAD, GORDON
Born: Jan. 8, 1892, Garfield, N.J. Died: July 8, 1952, Balboa, Calif. Screen actor and film director. Entered films as an actor in 1914.

HOLLINGSWORTH, ALFRED
Born: 1874, Nebraska. Died: June 20, 1926, Glendale, Calif. Screen and stage actor.

Appeared in: **1915** American Film Mfg. Co. films. **1916** Hell's Hinges; The Sable Blessing; The Stampede; Purity; The Right Direction. **1917** The Girl and the Crisis; The Sudden Gentleman. **1919** Leave It to Susan. **1921** The Infamous Miss Revell. **1922** The Bearcat; Trimmed. **1924** Marry in Haste. **1925** The Mystery Box (serial).

HOLLINGSWORTH, HARRY
Born: Sept. 3, 1888, Los Angeles, Calif. Died: Nov. 5, 1947, Los Angeles, Calif. Screen, stage, vaudeville and radio actor. Married to Nan Crawford (dec. 1975) with whom he appeared in vaudeville in act billed as "Hollingsworth and Crawford."

Appeared in: **1916** The Tarantula. **1929** Bedtime (short with "Hollingsworth and Crawford). **1933** Operator 13. **1936** Sing Me a Love Song. **1942** My Favorite Blonde.

HOLLIS, HYLDA
Born: July 10, 1889 or 1891, Philadelphia, Pa. Died: Dec. 9, 1961, Woodland Hills, Calif. Screen, stage and vaudeville actress. Married to director Edward Sloman.

Appeared in: **1915** The Jewel; The Little Brother of the Rich. **1916** The Secret of the Submarine (serial).

HOLLISTER, ALICE
Born: Sept., 1886, Worcester, Mass. Died: Feb. 24, 1973, Costa Mesa, Calif. Screen actress.

Appeared in: **1911** The Colleen Bawn. **1912** An Arab Tragedy; Tragedy of the Desert; Ireland the Oppressed; The Kerry Gow. **1913** Shenandoah; The Bribe; A Saw Mill Hazard; The Prosecuting Attorney; The Peril of the Dance Hall; A War-Time Siren; The Scimitar of the Prophet; The Alien; A Victim of Heredity; The Terror of Conscience; A Virginia Feud; The Lost Diamond; The Blind Basket Weaver; Primitive Man; The Smuggler; The Vampire. **1914** The Brand. **1915** The Destroyer; The Haunting Fear; The Stolen Ruby; The Siren's Religion; A Sister's Burden; The Net of Deceit; The Man in Hiding; The Siren's Reign (aka The Reign of the Siren); The Sign of the Broken Shackles; The Mysterious Case of Meredith Stanhope; The Money Gulf. **1917** Her Better Self. **1918** The Knife. **1920** From the Manger to the Cross or Jesus of Nazareth; Milestones; The Great Lover. **1921** A Voice in the Dark; A Wise Fool. **1922** The Forgotten Law. **1924** Married Flirts. **1925** The Dancers.

HOLLY, MARY
Born: 1887. Died: May 17, 1976, Palm Springs, Calif. Screen actress. Married to screenwriter William H. Clifford (dec.).

HOLLYWOOD, JIMMY
Died: July 2, 1955. Screen and radio actor.

Appeared in: **1935** Every Night at Eight. **1943** Spotlight Scandals.

HOLM, JOHN CECIL
Born: 1905. Died: Oct. 24, 1981, Westerly, R.I. Screen, stage actor, screenwriter, playwright and author.

Appeared in: **1959** It Happened to Jane.

HOLM, SONIA
Born: Feb. 24, 1922, England? Died: July 2, 1974, England. Stage and screen actress.

Appeared in: **1948** Miranda (US 1949); Broken Journey (US 1949). **1949** Warning to Wantons; The Bad Lord Byron (US 1952).

HOLMAN, HARRY
Born: 1874. Died: May 2, 1947, Hollywood, Calif. (heart attack). Screen, stage and vaudeville actor.

Appeared in: **1929** Hard Boiled Hampton (short). **1930** Give Me Action (short); The Big Deal (short). **1932** So Big. **1933** Hard to Handle; Lady Killer; State Fair; Lucky Dog; Devil's Mate; One Year Later; My Woman; East of Fifth Avenue; Circus Queen Murder; Roman Scandals. **1934** The Lost Jungle (serial); Jimmy the Gent; It Happened One Night. **1935** Dante's Inferno; Folies Bergere; Barbary Coast; Calling All Cars; Traveling Saleslady; In Caliente; Welcome Home; Cheers of the Crowd; Here Comes Cookie. **1936** Gentle Julia; The Count Takes the Count (short); The Criminal Within; Hitch Hike to Heaven. **1937** Nation Aflame. **1938** Western Jamboree. **1939** Jesse James; I Was a Convict. **1940** Slightly Tempted. **1941** Mexican Spitfire at Sea; The Bride Came C.O.D.; Manpower; Meet John Doe. **1942** The Spoilers; Inside the Law; Tennessee Johnson; Mexican Spitfire; Seven Days' Leave. **1943** Higher and Higher; Keep 'Em Slugging; Shadows on the Sage. **1944** Swing Hostess; Allergic to Love. **1946** Without Reservations; Badmen's Territory; It's a Wonderful Life.

HOLMAN, LIBBY (Elizabeth Holzman)
Born: 1906, Cincinnati, Ohio. Died: June 18, 1971, North Stamford, Conn. Screen, stage actress and singer. Married to Zachary Reynolds (dec. 1932), actor Ralph Holmes (dec. 1945) and painter-sculptor Louis Schanker.

Appeared in: **1943** The Russian Story (narrator).

HOLMAN, RICHARD
Born: 1900. Died: Aug., 1955, San Francisco, Calif. Screen actor.

HOLME, THEA (Thea Johnston)
Born: Dec. 27, 1907, London, England. Died: Dec., 1980, Northwood, England. Screen, stage, radio, television actress and author.

HOLMES, BEN
Born: 1890, Richmond, Va. Died: Dec. 2, 1943, Hollywood, Calif. Screen, stage actor, stage and film director.

Appeared in: **1932** The Expert.

HOLMES, BURTON
Born: Jan. 8, 1870, Chicago, Ill. Died: July 22, 1958, Hollywood, Calif. Screen actor and film producer. Pioneer of travel films and shorts. Made first travel films in Italy (1897) and first travel films in Hawaii (1898).

Appeared in: **1922** Around the World with Burton Holmes. **1924** Glorious Switzerland. **1925** Teak Logging with Elephants; Tyrolean Perspectives; Under Cuban Skies; The Salt of Amping; A Cabaret of Old Japan; The Garden of the East. **1926** So This Is Florida. **1927** Closeups of China. **1928** Happy Hawaii. **1929** Motoring Thru Spain; Siam, the Land of Chang. **1930** France; Germany; London; Mediterranean Cruise; Venice.

HOLMES, EDWARD
Born: 1911, Canada. Died: July 12, 1977, New York, N.Y. Screen, stage and television actor.

Appeared in: **1958** Wolf Dog. **1959** The Last Gunfighter (US 1961). **1966** The Group.

HOLMES, GERDA
Died: Date unknown. Screen and stage actress. Married to actor Rapley Holmes (dec. 1928).

Appeared in: **1914** Fingerprints; The Elder Brother.

HOLMES, GILBERT "PEE WEE"
Born: 1894. Died: Aug. 17, 1936, Hollywood, Calif. Screen actor.

Appeared in: **1921** The Big Town Round-up. **1923** The Buster; The Man Who Won. **1924** The Tenth Woman; Ladies to Board; The Mask of Lopez. **1926** The Phantom Bullet; Chip of the Flying U; The Border Sheriff. **1927** The Border Cavalier; One Glorious Scrap; Galloping Fury; The Denver Dude. **1928** The Cloud Dodger; Quick Triggers; Arizona Cyclone; The Fearless Rider; Put 'Em Up; A Made-to-Order Hero; Trail Riders; Thunder Riders. **1929** Sunset Pass; The Sky Skideer; Burning the Wind. **1930** Spurs; Mountain Justice; Sagebrush Politics. **1932** Man From Hell's Edges. **1933** Robber's Roost; Flaming Guns; Rustler's Roundup.

HOLMES, HELEN
Born: 1892, Chicago, Ill. Died: July 8, 1950, Burbank, Calif. (heart attack). Screen actress. Entered films with Sennett in 1912.

Appeared in: **1914** The Hazards of Helen (serial). **1915** The Girl and the Game (serial). **1916** A Lass of Lumberlands (serial). **1917** The Lost Express (serial); The Railroad Raiders (serial). **1919** The Fatal Fortune (serial). **1920** The Tiger Band (serial). **1921** A Crook's Romance. **1922** Ghost City; Hills of Missing Men; The Lone Hand. **1923** Stormy Seas; One Million in Jewels. **1924** Battling Brewster (serial); The Riddle Rider (serial); Fighting Fury; Forty Horse Hawkins. **1925** Blood and Steel; Barriers of the Cactus; The Sign of the Cactus; Webs of Steel; Duped; Outwitted; The Train Wreckers. **1926** Mistaken Orders; Crossed Signals; Peril of the Rail; The Lost Express; The Open Switch. **1936** Poppy. **1937** The Californian. **1941** Dude Cowboy. **1943** The More the Merrier.

HOLMES, J. MERRILL (Jack Merrill Holmes)
Born: July 21, 1889, Pennsylvania. Died: Feb. 27, 1950, Los Angeles, Calif. (heart failure). Screen actor.

Appeared in: **1934** The Last Round-Up; Thirty-Day Princess. **1941** The Bandit Trail; Land of the Open Range.

HOLMES, PHILLIPS
Born: July 22, 1909, Grand Rapids, Mich. Died: Aug. 12, 1942, near Armstrong, Ontario, Canada (air collision of two RCAF planes). Stage and screen actor. Son of actor Taylor Holmes (dec. 1959) and actress Edna Phillips (dec. 1952). Brother of actor Ralph Holmes (dec. 1945).

Appeared in: **1928** Varsity (film debut); His Private Life; The Return of Sherlock Holmes. **1929** The Wild Party; Stairs of Sand; Pointed Heels. **1930** The Dancers; Grumpy; Her Man; The Devil's Holiday; Only the Brave; Paramount on Parade. **1931** An American Tragedy; Stolen Heaven; Man to Man; Confessions of a Co-ed; The Criminal Code. **1932** Make Me a Star; Rockabye; Broken Lullaby (aka The Man I Killed); Two Kinds of Women; 70,000 Witnesses; Night Court (aka Justice for All). **1933** Dinner at Eight; Penthouse; Storm at Daybreak; Beauty for Sale; The Secret of Madame Blanche; Men Must Fight; Looking Forward; Stage Mother; The Big Brain; State Fair. **1934** Great Expectations; Nana; Million Dollar Ransom; Caravan; Private Scandal. **1935** No Ransom; Ten Minute Alibi; The Divine Spark. **1936** The House of a Thousand Candles; Chatterbox; General Spanky. **1937** The Dominant Sex. **1938** Housemaster (US 1939).

HOLMES, RALPH
Born: May 20, 1889, Detroit, Mich. Died: Nov., 1945, New York, N.Y. (natural causes). Screen, stage actor and editor. Son of actor Taylor Holmes (dec. 1959) and actress Edna Phillips (dec. 1952). Married to actress Libby Holman (dec. 1971). Brother of actor Phillips Holmes (dec. 1952).

Appeared in: **1914** The Mystery of Room 643; Fingerprints; His Stolen Fortune; The Masked Wrestler. **1936** Undersea Kingdom (serial).

HOLMES, RAPLEY
Born: 1868, Canada. Died: Jan. 11, 1928, Strathrey, Ontario, Canada. Screen actor. Married to actress Gerda Holmes (dec.).

Appeared in: **1914** In the Moon's Ray; Seeds of Chaos; One Wonderful Night; Night Hawks; Through Eyes of Love. **1915** The Creed of the Clan; The Fable of the Cold Gray Dawn of the Morning After; The Victory of Virtue. **1916** Gloria's Romance.

HOLMES, STUART
Born: Mar. 10, 1887, Chicago, Ill. Died: Dec. 29, 1971, Hollywood, Calif. (ruptured abdominal aortic aneurism). Screen, stage and vaudeville actor.

Appeared in: **1914** Life's Shop Window. **1916** Under Two Flags; A Daughter of the Gods. **1917** The Scarlet Letter. **1918** The Poor Rich Man. **1919** The New Moon; The Other Man's Wife. **1920** The Evil Eye (serial); Trailed by Three (serial). **1921** The Four Horsemen of the Apocalypse; No Woman Knows; All's Fair in Love; Passion Fruit. **1922** The Prisoner of Zenda; Her Husband's Trademark; Paid Back; Under Two Flags. **1923** Daughters of the Rich; The Stranger's Banquet; The Rip-Tide; Tea with a Kick; Hollywood; The Scarlet Lily; Tipped Off; Temporary Marriage; The Unknown Purple. **1924** Tess of the D'Urbervilles; The Age of Innocence; Between Friends; Vanity's Price; The Beloved Brute; Three Weeks; In Every Woman's Life; On Time; The Siren of Seville. **1925** Fighting Cub; Three Keys; Friendly Enemies; Heir-Loons; The Primrose Path; The Salvation Hunters; Steele of the Royal Mounted; A Fool and His Money; Paint and Powder. **1926** North Star; Devil's Island; Good and Naughty; The Hurricane; The Midnight Message; Broken Hearts of Hollywood; Beyond the Trail; The Shadow of the Law; Everybody's Acting; My

Official Wife. **1927** When a Man Loves; Your Wife and Mine; Polly of the Movies. **1928** The Man Who Laughs; Beware of Married Men; Burning Daylight; Danger Trail; Devil Dogs; The Cavalier; The Hawk's Nest. **1930** The Heroic Lover; Captain of the Guard. **1931** War Mamas (short). **1932** My Pal the King; The Millionaire Cat (short); Jitters the Butler (short). **1933** Sitting Pretty. **1934** Are We Civilized?; Belle of the Nineties. **1936** Murder by an Aristocrat; Earthworm Tractors; The Case of the Velvet Claws; Trailin' West. **1937** Her Husband's Secretary. **1938** The Sisters. **1939** The Oklahoma Kid; Each Dawn I Die; Dark Victory; On Trial. **1940** A Dispatch from Reuters; British Intelligence; Devil's Island. **1944** The Climax; Last Ride; The Adventures of Mark Twain. **1945** Shady Lady. **1946** Smooth as Silk. **1947** The Ghost and Mrs. Muir; Moss Rose. **1948** Night Has a Thousand Eyes; A Letter to Three Wives. **1949** A Kiss in the Dark. **1950** Copper Canyon. **1951** Rhubarb. **1952** The Bad and the Beautiful; Carrie; Singin' in the Rain. **1953** Remains To Be Seen. **1955** The Girl in the Red Velvet Swing; The Cobweb. **1956** The Kettles in the Ozarks; The Birds and the Bees. **1962** The Man Who Shot Liberty Valance.

HOLMES, TAYLOR

Born: May 16, 1872, Newark, N.J. Died: Sept. 30, 1959, Hollywood, Calif. Screen, stage, vaudeville and television actor. Married to actress Edna Phillips (dec. 1952). Father of actors Phillips (dec. 1942) and Ralph Holmes (dec. 1945).

Appeared in: **1917** Efficiency Edgar's Courtship; Fools for Luck; Two-Bit Seats; Small Town Guy; Uneasy Money. **1918** Ruggles of Red Gap. **1919** It's a Bear; A Regular Fellow; Taxi; Upside Down. **1920** Nothing But the Truth. **1924** Twenty Dollars a Week. **1925** The Crimson Runner; The Verdict; Borrowed Finery; Her Market Value. **1927** One Hour of Love. **1929** The following shorts: He Did His Best; He Loved the Ladies. **1930** Dad Knows Best (short). **1931** An American Tragedy. **1933** Git Along Little Wifie (short); Before Morning; Dinner at Eight. **1934** Nana. **1936** The Crime of Dr. Forbes; The First Baby; Make Way for a Lady. **1947** Kiss of Death; Nightmare Alley; The Egg and I; Time Out of Mind; In Self Defense; Boomerang; Great Expectations. **1948** Hazard; Smart Woman; Let's Love Again; The Plunderers; Act of Violence; That Wonderful Urge; Joan of Arc. **1949** Woman in Hiding; Joe Palooka in the Big Fight; Mr. Belvedere Goes to College; Once More My Darling. **1950** Bright Leaf; Caged; Copper Canyon; Double Deal; Father of the Bride; Quicksand. **1951** Drums in the Deep South; The First Legion; Rhubarb; Two Tickets to Broadway. **1952** Woman in the North Country; Beware My Lovely; Hold that Line; Hoodlum Empire; Ride the Man Down. **1953** Gentlemen Prefer Blondes. **1954** The Outcast; Tobor the Great; Untamed Heiress. **1955** The Fighting Chance; Hell's Outpost. **1956** The Maverick Queen; The Peace Maker. **1958** Wink of an Eye.

HOLMES, WENDELL

Born: 1915. Died: Apr. 26, 1962, Paris, France. Screen, stage and television actor.

Appeared in: **1949** Lost Boundaries. **1958** Young and Wild. **1959** Compulsion; Edge of Eternity; Good Day for a Hanging. **1960** Because They're Young; Elmer Gantry. **1961** The Absent-Minded Professor.

HOLMES, WILLIAM J.

Born: 1877. Died: Dec. 1, 1946, Hollywood, Calif. Screen, stage, vaudeville actor, playwright and stage producer.

Appeared in: **1930** Once a Gentleman. **1935** Frisco Kid.

HOLMES-GORE, ARTHUR

Born: 1871, England. Died: Aug., 1915, Dardanelles (killed in action). Screen, stage actor and stage producer. Father of actress Dorothy Holmes-Gore (dec. 1977).

Appeared in: **1914** The King's Minister; Her Children; The Ring and the Rajah; Branscombe's Pal; England's Menace. **1915** The Prisoner of Zenda.

HOLMES-GORE, DOROTHY

Born: May 26, 1896, London, England. Died: Oct. 14, 1977, London, England. Screen and stage actress. Daughter of actor Arthur Holmes-Gore (dec. 1915). Married to stage actor Evan John (dec. 1953).

Appeared in: **1915** The Third Generation. **1920** The Mirage.

HOLT, HELEN

Born: 1890. Died: Jan. 17, 1927, Vancouver, British Columbia (pneumonia). Screen actress.

HOLT, JACK (Charles John Holt)

Born: May 31, 1888, New York, N.Y. Died: Jan. 18, 1951, Los Angeles, Calif. (heart attack). Screen actor and Army officer. Father of actor Tim Holt (dec. 1973) and actress Jennifer Holt. Entered films in 1914 as a stuntman.

Appeared in: **1914** Salomy Jane. **1915** The Broken Coin (serial); A Cigarette—That's All; The Master Key (serial); Mother Ashton; The Power of Fascination; The Campbells Are Coming; The Lumber Yard Gang. **1916** The Better Man; The Black Sheep of the Family; Born of the People; Brennon O' the Moor; The Chalice of Sorrow; The Desperado; The Dumb Girl of Portici; The False Part; Her Better Self; His Majesty Dick Turpin; Liberty (serial); The Madcap Queen of Crona; Naked Hearts; The Princely Bandit; The Strong Arm Squad. **1917** The Call of the East; The Cost of Hatred; Giving Becky a Chance; The Inner Shrine; The Little American; Sacrifice; The Secret Game. **1918** The Claw; A Desert Wooing; Green Eyes; Headin' South; Love Me; The Marriage Ring; One More American; The Road Through the Dark; The White Man's Law; The Squaw Man. **1919** Cheating Cheaters; For Better, For Worse; The Life Line; A Midnight Romance; A Sporting Chance; Victory; The Woman Thou Gavest Me. **1920** The Best of Luck; Crooked Streets; Held by the Enemy; Kitty Kelly, M.D.; Midsummer's Madness; The Sins of Rosanne. **1921** After the Show; All Soul's Eve; The Call of the North; Ducks and Drakes; The Grim Comedian; The Lost Romance; The Mask. **1922** Bought and Paid for; Making a Man; The Man Unconquerable; North of the Rio Grande; On the High Seas; While Satan Sleeps. **1923** The Cheat; A Gentleman of Leisure; Hollywood; The Marriage Maker; Nobody's Money; The Tiger's Claw. **1924** Don't Call It Love; Empty Hands; The Lone Wolf; North of 36; Wanderer of the Wasteland. **1925** The Ancient Highway; Eve's Secret; The Light of the Western Stars; The Thundering Herd; Wild Horse Mesa. **1926** The Blind Goddess; Born to the West; The Enchanted Hill; Forlorn River; Man of the Forest; Sea Horses. **1927** The Mysterious Rider; The Tigress; The Warning. **1928** Avalanche; Court-Martial; The Smart Set; Sumbarine; The Vanishing Pioneer; The Water Hole. **1929** The Donovan Affair; Father and Son; Flight; Sunset Pass. **1930** The Border Legion; Hell's Island; The Squealer; Vengeance. **1931** A Dangerous Affair; Dirigible; Fifty Fathoms Deep; The Last Parade; Maker of Men; Subway Express; White Shoulders. **1932** Behind the Mask; Man Against Woman; This Sporting Age; War Correspondent. **1933** Master of Men; When Strangers Marry; The Whirlpool (aka The Forgotten Man); The Woman I Stole; The Wrecker. **1934** Black Moon; The Defense Rests; I'll Fix It. **1935** The Awakening of Jim Burke; The Best Man Wins; The Littlest Rebel; Storm Over the Andes; Unwelcome Stranger. **1936** Crash Donovan; Dangerous Waters; End of the Trail; North of Nome; San Francisco. **1937** Outlaws of the Orient; Roaring Timber; Trapped by G-Men; Trouble in Morocco; Under Suspicion. **1938** Crime Takes a Holiday; Flight into Nowhere; Making the Headlines; Outside the Law; Reformatory. **1939** Fugitive at Large; Hidden Power; Trapped in the Sky; Whispering Enemies. **1940** The Great Plane Robbery; Outside the Three Mile Limit; Passport to Alcatraz; Prison Camp. **1941** The Great Swindle; Holt of the Secret Service (serial). **1942** The Cat People; Northwest Rangers; Thunder Birds. **1943** Customs of the Service (Army training film). **1944** The Articles of War (Army training film). **1945** They Were Expendable. **1946** The Chase; My Pal Trigger; Renegade Girl. **1947** The Wild Frontier. **1948** Arizona Rangers; The Gallant Legion; Strawberry Roan; The Treasure of Sierra Madre. **1949** Brimstone; The Last Bandit; Loaded Pistols; Red Desert; Task Force. **1950** Return of the Frontiersman; Trail of Robin Hood; King of the Bullwhip; The Dalton's Women. **1951** Across the Wide Missouri.

HOLT, NICK

Born: 1933. Died: Oct. 1, 1979, Los Angeles, Calif. (injuries from motorcycle accident). Screen, stage, television actor and ordained minister.

HOLT, TIM (John Charles Holt, III)

Born: Feb. 5, 1919, Beverly Hills, Calif. Died: Feb. 15, 1973, Shawnee, Okla. (cancer). Film, stage and television actor. Son of actor Jack Holt (dec. 1951), brother of actress Jennifer Holt. Divorced from Virginia Ashcroft and Alice Harrison. Married to Birdie Stephens Holt.

Appeared in: **1928** The Vanishing Pioneer (film debut). **1937** Stella Dallas; History Is Made at Night. **1938** I Met My Love Again; Gold Is Where You Find It; Sons of the Legion; The Law West of Tombstone. **1939** The Renegade Ranger; Stagecoach; Spirit of Culver; The Girl and the Gambler; Fifth Avenue Girl; The Rookie Cop. **1940** Swiss Family Robinson; Laddie; The Fargo Kid; Wagon Train. **1941** Back Street; Dude Cowboy; Along the Rio Grande; Robbers of the Range; Riding the Wind; Six-Gun Gold; Cyclone on Horseback; Land of the Open Range; Come On, Danger!; Thundering Hoofs; The Bandit Trail. **1942** The Magnificent Ambersons; Pirates of the Prairie; Bandit Ranger. **1943** Hitler's Children; The Avenging Rider; Red River Robin

Hood; Sagebrush Law; Fighting Frontier. **1946** My Darling Clementine. **1947** Thunder Mountain; Wild Horse Mesa; Under the Tonto Rim; The Treasure of Sierra Madre. **1948** His Kind of Woman; The Arizona Ranger; Guns of Hate; Western Heritage; Indian Agent; Gun Smugglers. **1949** The Mysterious Desperado; Rustlers; The Stagecoach Kid; Brothers in the Saddle; Masked Raiders; Riders of the Range. **1950** Border Treasure; Rider from Tucson; Rio Grande Patrol; Storm Over Wyoming; Dynamite Pass; Law of the Badlands. **1951** His Kind of Woman; Saddle Legion; Gunplay; Pistol Harvest; Overland Telegraph; Hot Lead. **1952** Trail Guide; Target; Road Agent; Desert Passage. **1957** The Monster That Challenged the World.

HOLTZ, LOU
Born: 1893, San Francisco, Calif. Died: Sept. 22, 1980, Los Angeles, Calif. Screen, stage, radio, television and vaudeville actor. Married to actress Rita Boland with whom he appeared in vaudeville. Later married to Gloria Holtz.

Appeared in: **1930** Idle Chatter (short); Follow the Leader. **1943** Screen Snapshots #8 (short).

HOLTZ, TENEN
Born: Russia. Died: July 1, 1971. Screen actor.

Appeared in: **1926** Upstage; Exit Smiling. **1927** Frisco Sally Levy. **1928** The Latest From Paris; Bringing Up Father; The Trail of '98; The Cardboard Lover; Show People; Detectives; The Law of the Range. **1929** House of Terror; The Duke Steps Out; Three Live Ghosts; The Kibitzer. **1930** Whispering Whoopee (short); All Teed Up (short); Melody Man; The Woman Racket; Lilies of the Field. **1931** Gentleman's Fate. **1933** Whistling in the Dark; Big Executive. **1934** British Agent; Hollywood Hoodlum. **1938** International Crime; Cipher Bureau.

HOLTZMAN, GLENN
Born: 1931, Kilgore, Tex. Died: May 6, 1980, Reno, Nev. (heart attack). Professional football player, screen, stage, television actor, stage director and playwright.

Appeared in: **1980** Urban Cowboy.

HOLUBAR, ALLEN
Born: Aug. 3, 1889, Calif. Died: Nov. 20, 1923, Los Angeles, Calif. (pneumonia). Screen, stage actor, playwright, film director, producer and screenwriter.

Appeared in: **1913** A Wolf Among Lambs; The Prophecy. **1915** The White Terror. **1916** Twenty Thousand Leagues Under the Sea; Any Youth; The Phone Message; The Shadow; The Taint of Fear; Stronger than Steel; The Prodigal Daughter. **1917** Heart Strings; The Old Toymaker; The War Waif; Where the Glory Waits; Treason; The Double Topped Trunk; The Grip of Love.

HOLZWORTH, FRED
Died: Feb. 1, 1970, Cleveland, Ohio. Stage and screen actor.

HOMAN, GERTRUDE
Born: 1880. Died: May 29, 1951, Glen Grove, N.Y. Screen and stage actress. Married to producer Edwin Thauhouser.

Appeared in: **1911** Cinderella.

HOMANS, ROBERT E.
Born: 1875, Malden, Mass. Died: July 28, 1947, Los Angeles, Calif. (heart attack). Screen and stage actor.

Appeared in: **1923** Legally Dead. **1924** The Breathless Moment; Dark Stairways. **1925** Border Justice. **1926** Fighting with Buffalo Bill (serial); The Silent Power; College Days. **1927** The Fightin' Comeback; The Bandit Buster (serial); Ride 'em High; Fast and Furious; Range Courage; The Galloping Gobs; The Princess from Hoboken; Heroes of the Night; Mountains of Manhattan; The Silent Avenger. **1928** The Masked Angel; Pals in Peril; Obey Your Husband; Blindfold. **1929** Burning the Wind; The Isle of Lost Ships; Smiling Irish Eyes; Fury of the Wild. **1930** The Widow from Chicago; Abraham Lincoln; The Concentratin' Kid; Son of the Gods; Spurs; Trigger Tricks; The Thoroughbred. **1931** The Public Enemy; City Streets; The Black Camel; Silence. **1932** Pack Up Your Troubles; Young America; Madame Racketeer. **1933** Lady Killer; From Headquarters; She Done Him Wrong. **1934** Jimmy the Gent; Thirty Day Princess. **1935** The Whole Town's Talking; Stormy; Steamboat 'Round the Bend. **1936** Rhythm on the Range; Black Legion; The Prisoner of Shark Island; Ride, Ranger, Ride; Here Comes Trouble; Laughing Irish Eyes; The President's Mystery; Easy Money; It Couldn't Have Happened; Bridge of Sighs; Below the Deadline. **1937** Breezing Home; The Plough

and the Stars; Easy Living; Penrod and Sam; Don't Pull Your Punches; Dance, Charlie, Dance; Forlorn River; Jim Hanvey, Detective. **1938** Angels With Dirty Faces; The Sisters; The Kid Comes Back; Little Tough Guy; Penrod and His Twin Brother; Over the Wall; Little Miss Thoroughbred; The Amazing Dr. Clitterhouse; Heart of the North; Tom Sawyer, Detective; Gold Is Where You Find It; Hollywood Stadium Mystery; Gold Mine in the Sky; The Night Hawk; Hunted Men. **1939** The Oklahoma Kid; Each Dawn I Die; Dodge City; Stagecoach; Hell's Kitchen; Young Mr. Lincoln; Inside Information; Smuggled Cargo; The Old Maid; Ruler of the Sea; Five Came Back; King of the Turf. **1940** Enemy Agent; Son of Roaring Dan; Goin' Fishin' (short); West of Carson City; East of the River; The Grapes of Wrath; Lillian Russell. **1941** Whistling in the Dark; Rise and Shine; It Started With Eve; Wild Bill Hickok Rides; Glamour Boy; Sierra Sue; Out of the Fog. **1942** The Spoilers; The Forest Rangers; Fingers at the Window; For Me and My Gal; It Happened in Flatbush; Lady in a Jam; The Sombrero Kid; X Marks the Spot; Night Monster. **1943** G-Men vs. the Black Dragon (serial); Sweet Rosie O'Grady; Happy Go Lucky; You Can't Beat the Law; Shantytown; Frontier Badmen; It Ain't Hay. **1944** Sensations of 1945; Bowery to Broadway; Christmas Holiday; Haunted Harbor; Pin Up Girl; It Happened Tomorrow; Say Uncle (short); Nothing But Trouble; Jack London; The Whistler; The Merry Monahans; Cover Girl. **1945** The Clock; They Were Expendable; Rogues' Gallery; River Gang; Beyond the Pecos; A Medal for Benny; Come Out Fighting; Captain Eddie; The Scarlet Clue. **1946** The Strange Love of Martha Ivers; Girl on the Spot; Earl Carroll Sketchbook.

HOMOLKA, OSCAR
Born: Aug. 12, 1898, Vienna, Austria. Died: Jan. 27, 1978, Sussex, England. Screen, stage and television actor. Divorced from Grete Mosheim and Florence Meyer. Married to Baroness Vally Hatvany (dec.) and later to actress Joan Tetzel (dec. 1977). Nominated for 1948 Academy Award as Best Supporting Actor in I Remember Mama.

Appeared in: **1926** Die Abenteuer eines Zehnmarksheines (Adventures of a Ten Mark Note); Brennende Grenze. **1927** Dirnentragodie (Tragedy of the Street); Furst Order Clown; Die Heilige Luge; Der Kampf des Donald Westhof (The Trial of Donald Westhof—US 1928); Die Liebeigenen; Petronella; Regine, die Tragodie einer Frau; Schinderhannes; Die Rothausgasse. **1929** Masken; Revolte im Erziehungshaus (Revolt in the Reformatory). **1930** Dreyfus (aka Dreyfus Case—US 1940); Hokuspokus (Hocuspocus). **1931** Nachtkolonne; Zwischen Nacht und Morgen; 14, die Letzten Tage vor dem Weltbrand (1914: The Last Days Before the War—US 1932) ; Der Weg nach Rio; Im Geheimdienst (In the Employ of the Secret Service). **1932** Die Nachte von Port Said. **1933** Unsichtbare Gegner; Spione am Werk; Der Schweigende Mund. **1936** Rhodes of Africa (aka Rhodes—US); Sabotage (aka The Woman Alone—US 1937); Everything is Thunder. **1937** The Woman Alone; Ebb Tide; Hidden Power. **1940** Seven Sinners; Comrade X. **1941** Ball of Fire; Rage in Heaven; The Invisible Woman. **1943** Hostages; Mission to Moscow. **1947** The Shop at Sly Corner (aka The Code of Scotland Yard—US 1948). **1948** I Remember Mama (stage and film version). **1949** Anna Lucasta. **1950** The White Tower. **1952** Top Secret (aka Mr. Potts Goes to Moscow—US 1954). **1953** The House of the Arrow. **1954** Prisoner of War. **1955** The Seven-Year Itch (stage and film versions). **1956** War and Peace. **1957** A Farewell to Arms. **1958** The Key; The Tempest. **1961** Mr. Sardonicus. **1962** The Wonderful World of the Brothers Grimm; Boy's Night Out. **1964** The Long Ships. **1965** Joy in the Morning. **1966** Funeral in Berlin. **1967** The Happening; The Billion Dollar Brain. **1969** The Madwoman of Chaillot; Assignment to Kill. **1970** The Song of Norway; The Executioner. **1974** The Tamarind Seed.

HONDA, FRANK
Born: 1884, Japan. Died: Feb. 3, 1924, N.Y. Screen actor.

Appeared in: **1921** Dawn of the East; Wedding Bells. **1923** Lawful Larceny.

HONN, ELDON
Born: 1890. Died: Aug. 11, 1927, San Diego, Calif. (died in parachute fall). Screen actor and motorcycle stuntman.

HONTABAT, MARCELLE
Born: 1897. Died: Nov. 18, 1936, New York, N.Y. Screen and stage actress. Married to actor, producer and playwright Earl Carroll (dec. 1948).

HOOD, DARLA (Darla Jean Hood)
Born: Nov. 4, 1931, Leedey, Okla. Died: June 13, 1979, North Hollywood, Calif. Screen, television actress and nightclub singer.

Married to music publisher/agent Jose Granson. Appeared as Darla in Our Gang Comedies from 1935 to 1943.

Appeared in: **1935** Our Gang Follies of 1936 (short). **1936** The Bohemian Girl; the following shorts: Neighborhood House; Pinch Singer; Divot Diggers; Second Childhood; Arbor Day; Pay as You Exit; Bored of Education. **1937** The following shorts: Reunion in Rhythm; Three Smart Boys; Hearts Are Trumps; Roamin' Holiday; Night 'n' Gales; Fishy Tales; Framing Youth; Pigskin Palooka; Mail and Female; Our Gang Follies of 1938. **1938** The following shorts: Bear Facts; Three Men in a Tub; Came the Brawn; Feed 'Em and Weep; Hide and Shriek; The Little Ranger; Party Fever; Aladdin's Lantern; Men in Fright; Football Romeo; Practical Jokers. **1939** The following shorts: Tiny Troules; Duel Personalities; Clown Princess; Cousin Wilbur; Dog Daze; Auto Antics; Captain Spanky's Show Boat; Time Out for Lessons. **1940** The following shorts: Alfalfa's Double; The Big Premiere; All About Hash; The New Pupil; Bubbling Trouble; Kiddie Cure; Waldo's Last Stand. **1941** The following shorts: Ye Old Minstrels; Robot Wrecks; Helping Hands; Come Back, Miss Pipps; Wedding Worries. **1943** Happy Land. **1957** The Calypso Heat Wave; The Helen Morgan Story. **1959** The Bat.

HOOD, JOSEPH B., SR.
Born: 1896. Died: June 26, 1965, Philadelphia, Pa. Screen actor and stuntman. Enterd films in 1927.

HOOD, TOM
Born: 1919. Died: Dec. 8, 1950, Hollywood, Calif. (murdered). Screen actor.

HOOD, WALLY (Wallace James Hood, Sr.)
Born: Feb. 9, 1895, Whittier, Calif. Died: May 2, 1965, Hollywood, Calif. Baseball player and screen actor. Father of baseball player Wally Hood, Jr.

Appeared in: **1928** Warming Up.

HOOKER, SON
Died: Oct. 14, 1974. Screen actor.

Appeared in: **1965** The Incredibly Strange Creatures Who Stopped Living and Became Crazy Mixed-Up Zombies. **1972** J. W. Coop.

HOOLEY, MADELEINE
Born: 1916. Died: June 10, 1977. Screen actress. Married to actor Tom Gorman (dec. 1971).

HOOPE, AAF BOUBER-TEN
Died: May 23, 1974. Dutch screen actor.

HOOPII, SOL (Sol Hoopii Kaaiai)
Born: 1905, Hawaii. Died: Nov. 16, 1953, Seattle, Wash. Screen actor and musician.

HOOPS, ARTHUR
Born: 1870. Died: Sept. 17, 1916. Screen actor.

Appeared in: **1914** The Better Man; The Straight Road; Such a Little Queen. **1915** Gretna Green; A Woman's Resurrection; Should a Mother Tell?; The Song of Hate; Mistress Nell; Esmeralda; The Mummy and the Humming Bird; The Danger Signal. **1916** The Lure of Heart's Desire; The Devil's Prayer Book; The Final Curtain; The Soul Market; The Scarlet Woman; The Eternal Question; Extravagance. **1917** Bridges Burned; The Secret of Eve.

HOOSMAN, AL
Born: 1918, U.S. Died: Oct. 26, 1968, Munich, Germany. American professional boxer turned screen actor.

Appeared in: **1962** Toller Hecht auf Krummer Tour (aka The Phoney American—US 1964). **1967** Jack of Diamonds.

HOOVER, J. EDGAR (John Edgar Hoover)
Born: Jan. 1, 1895, Washington, D.C. Died: May 2, 1972, Washington, D.C. (heart disease). Director of F.B.I., author and screen performer.

Appeared in: **1943** Next of Kin. **1959** The FBI Story.

HOPE, DIANA
Born: 1872, England. Died: Nov. 20, 1942, Hollywood, Calif. (heart attack). Screen, stage and vaudeville actress.

Appeared in: **1930** The Man from Blankley's.

HOPE, EVELYN
Born: London, England. Died: Dec. 23, 1966, England? Screen and stage actress.

Appeared in: **1913** Ivanhoe.

HOPE, FRANCIS J.
Born: 1891, Wales. Died: July 27, 1975, Hollywood, Calif. Screen and radio actor. Brother of actor Bob Hope.

HOPE, MAIDIE
Born: Feb. 15, 1881, London, England. Died: Apr. 20, 1937, London, England (following a fall). Screen, stage actress and singer.

Appeared in: **1920** The Honeypot; All the Winners. **1921** Love Maggy.

HOPE, VIDA
Born: Dec. 16, 1918, Liverpool, England. Died: Dec. 23, 1963, Chelmsford, England (auto accident). Screen, stage actress and stage director. Married to film director Derek Twist.

Appeared in: **1944** English Without Tears (aka Her Man Gilbey—US 1949). **1945** The Way to the Stars (aka Johnny in the Clouds—US). **1947** While the Sun Shines (US 1950); Nicholas Nickleby; It Always Rains on Sunday (US 1949); They Made Me a Fugitive (aka I Became a Criminal—US 1948). **1949** For Them That Trespass (US 1950); Paper Orchid; The Interrupted Journey (US 1951). **1950** Double Confession (US 1953); The Woman in Question (aka Five Angles on Murder—US 1953). **1951** The Man in the White Suit (US 1952); Cheer the Brave; Green Grow the Rushes. **1952** Angels One Five (US 1954); Emergency Call (aka The Hundred Hour Hunt—US 1953); Women of Twilight (aka Twilight Women—US 1953). **1953** The Broken Horseshoe; The Long Memory; Marilyn (aka Roadhouse Girl—US 1955). **1954** Fast and Loose; Lease of Life (US 1955). **1958** Family Doctor (aka Prescription for Murder and Rx Murder—US). **1961** In the Doghouse (US 1964).

HOPKINS, BOB
Born: 1918. Died: Oct. 5, 1962, Hollywood, Calif (acute leukemia). Screen, stage and television actor.

Appeared in: **1945** On Stage Everybody. **1949** The Lucky Stiff. **1953** The Kid from Left Field. **1956** Autumn Leaves; Flight to Hong Kong. **1962** The Errand Boy; Saintly Sinners. **1963** Papa's Delicate Condition.

HOPKINS, MIRIAM (Ellen Miriam Hopkins)
Born: Oct. 18, 1902, Bainbridge, Ga. Died: Oct. 9, 1972, New York, N.Y (heart attack). Stage and screen actress. Divorced from actor Brandon Peters; playwright Austin Parker; film producer Anatol Litvak (dec. 1974) and newspaperman Raymond Block. Nominated for 1935 Academy Award for Best Actress in Becky Sharp.

Appeared in: **1930** Holiday; Fast and Loose. **1931** Honest Finder; 24 Hours; The Smiling Lieutenant; Hours Between. **1932** The Best People; Dancers in the Dark; Two Kinds of Women; The World and the Flesh; Trouble in Paradise; Dr. Jekyll and Mr. Hyde. **1933** Strangers Return; Design for Living; The Story of Temple Drake. **1934** All of Me; She Loves Me Not; The Richest Girl in the World. **1935** Becky Sharp; Barbary Coast; Splendor. **1936** These Three. **1937** Men Are Not Gods; The Woman I Love; Wise Girl; Woman Chases Man. **1939** The Old Maid. **1940** Lady With Red Hair; Virginia City. **1942** A Gentleman After Dark. **1943** Old Acquaintance. **1949** The Heiress. **1951** The Mating Season. **1952** Carrie; The Outcasts of Poker Flat. **1962** The Children's Hour. **1965** Fanny Hill; Memoirs of a Woman of Pleasure. **1966** The Chase.

HOPPER, DE WOLF (William DeWolf Hopper)
Born: Mar. 30, 1858, New York, N.Y. Died: Sept. 23, 1935, Kansas City, Mo. Stage and screen actor. Married to stage actress Lillian Glaser (dec. 1969) and divorced from actresses Edna Wallace (dec. 1959) and Elda Furry (known professionally as Hedda Hopper) (dec. 1966) and father of actor William Hopper (decc. 1970).

Appeared in: **1914** The Newsboy's Friend. **1915** Don Quixote. **1916** Casey at the Bat; Macbeth; A Rough Knight; Wings and Wheels; The Girl and the Mummy; Puppets; Sunshine Dad. **1930** For Two Cents (short); At the Round Table (short). **1935** The Return of Dr. X.

HOPPER, EDNA WALLACE
Born: Jan. 17, 1864, San Francisco, Calif. Died: Dec. 14, 1959, N.Y. Stage and screen actress. Filmed her own face-lifting operation. Divorced from actor DeWolf Hopper (dec. 1935).

HOPPER, HAL (Harold Stevens Hopper)
Born: Nov. 11, 1912, Oklahoma. Died: Nov. 2, 1970, Sylmar, Calif. (emphysema). Screen actor, composer and screenwriter.

Appeared in: **1964** Kitten with a Whip; Lorna. **1966** Beau Geste. **1969** Mud Honey (aka Rope of Flesh).

HOPPER, HEDDA (Elda Furry)

Born: June 2, 1890, Hallisdaysburg, Pa. Died: Feb. 1, 1966, Los Angeles, Calif. (pneumonia). Screen, stage, radio, television actress and columnist. Divorced from actor DeWolf Hopper (dec. 1935) and mother of actor William Hopper (dec. 1970).

Appeared in: **1916** Battle of Hearts (film debut). **1917** Seven Keys to Baldpate; Her Excellency, the Governor; The Food Gamblers; Nearly Married. **1918** By Right of Purchase. **1919** Virtuous Wives. **1920** The New York Idea; The Man Who Lost Himself. **1921** Heedless Moths; Conceit. **1922** Women Men Marry; What's Wrong With Women?; Sherlock Holmes. **1923** Has the World Gone Mad?; Reno. **1924** Happiness; Free Love; Miami; Another Scandal; Gambling Wives; The Snob; Sinners in Silk; Why Men Leave Home. **1925** Declassee; Raffles, the Amateur Cracksman; Zander the Great; Borrowed Finery; Dangerous Innocence; Her Market Value; The Teaser. **1926** Mona Lisa (short); Don Juan; The Caveman; Obey the Law; The Silver Treasure; Pleasures of the Rich; Dance Madness; Fools of Fashion; Lew Tyler's Wives; Skinner's Dress Suit. **1927** Wings; Children of Divorce; Adam and Evil; Black Tears; One Woman to Another; Matinee Ladies; The Cruel Truth; Orchids and Ermine; Venus of Venice; The Drop Kick; A Reno Divorce. **1928** Diamond Handcuffs; Companionate Marriage; The Chorus Kid; The Whip Woman; Giving In (short); Runaway Girls; Green Grass Widows; Harold Teen; The Port of Missing Girls; Undressed; Love and Learn. **1929** The Racketeer; Girls Gone Wild; Hurricane; His Glorious Night; The Last of Mrs. Cheyney; Half Marriage; A Song of Kentucky. **1930** Our Blushing Brides; High Society Blues; Divorcee; Such Men Are Dangerous; Holiday; War Nurse; Let Us Be Gay; Murder Will Out. **1931** Shipmates; The Easiest Way; Up for Murder; The Prodigal; Men Call It Love; Strangers May Kiss; A Tailor-Made Man; Rebound; Mystery Train; Flying High; Good Sport; Common Law. **1932** West of Broadway; Happy Landing; Night World; Speak Easily; Skyscraper Souls; The Unwritten Law; Downstairs; As You Desire Me; The Man Who Played God; The Slippery Pearls (short). **1933** The Barbarian; Pilgrimage; Beauty for Sale; Men Must Fight. **1934** Bombay Mail; Let's Be Ritzy; Little Man, What Now?; No Ransom. **1935** I Live My Life; Society Fever; One Frightened Night; Lady Tubbs; Three Kids and a Queen; Alice Adams. **1936** Dracula's Daughter; Doughnuts and Society; Bunker Bean; Dark Hour. **1937** You Can't Buy Luck; Topper; Dangerous Holiday; Artists and Models; Nothing Sacred; Vogues of 1938. **1938** Tarzan's Revenge; Dangerous to Know; Thanks for the Memory; Maid's Night Out. **1939** The Women; What a Life; Laugh It Off; Midnight; That's Right—You're Wrong. **1940** Queen of the Mob; Cross Country Romance. **1941** Life With Henry; I Wanted Wings. **1942** Reap the Wild Wind. **1946** Breakfast in Hollywood. **1950** Sunset Boulevard. **1960** Pepe. **1964** The Patsy. **1966** The Oscar.

HOPPER, WILLIAM (William DeWolf Hopper, Jr.)

Born: Jan. 26, 1915, New York, N.Y. Died: Mar. 6, 1970, Palm Springs, Calif. Screen, stage and television actor. Entered films in 1937. Son of actress Hedda Hopper (dec. 1966) and actor DeWolf Hopper (dec. 1935).

Appeared in: **1936** Sissy (film debut); The Big Broadcast of 1937. **1937** Back in Circulation; The Adventurous Blonde; Footloose Heiress; Over the Goal; Love Is on the Air; Public Wedding; Women Are Like That. **1938** Mystery House; Daredevil Drivers. **1939** Stagecoach; The Return of Dr. X; Angels Wash Their Faces; The Old Maid; Pride of the Bluegrass; Nancy Drew and the Hidden Staircase; The Cowboy Quarterback. **1940** Santa Fe Trail; Lady With Red Hair; 'Til We Meet Again; The Man Who Talked Too Much; Calling Philo Vance; Brother Orchid; Virginia City; Knute Rockne—All American; The Fighting 69th; Tear Gas Squad; Flight Angels; Ladies Must Live. **1941** Affectionately Yours; Manpower; Footsteps in the Dark; Dive Bomber; Knockout; High Sierra; The Maltese Falcon; The Bride Came C.O.D.; Flight from Destiny; Bullets for O'Hara; They Died With Their Boots On; Here Comes Happiness. **1942** Desperate Journey; Gentleman Jim; Larceny, Inc.; The Male Animal; Yankee Doodle Dandy; Lady Gangster. **1943** Air Force; The Mysterious Doctor; Murder on the Waterfront.

HOPTON, RUSSELL "RUSS"

Born: Feb. 18, 1900, New York, N.Y. Died: Apr. 7, 1945, North Hollywood, Calif. Screen, stage actor and film director.

Appeared in: **1926** Ella Cinders. **1930** College Lovers; The Pay Off (short); Call of the Flesh; Min and Bill; Remote Control. **1931** Dance, Fools, Dance; Street Scene; Miracle Woman; Reckless Living; Arrowsmith; Twenty Grand; Blond Crazy; Dance Team; The Criminal Code; Star Witness; Falling Star; Law and Order. **1932** Man Who Played God; The Drifter; Discarded Lovers; Big Timber; Night World; The Famous Ferguson Case; Radio Patrol; Back Street; Fast Companions; Air Mail; Tom Brown of Culver; Once in a Life Time.

1933 The Moonshiner's Daughter or Aboard in Old Kentucky (short); Successful Failure; I Sell Anything; Take the Stand; Destination Unknown; Desirable; Elmer the Great; The Little Giant; Lady Killer; One Year Later; Secret of the Blue Room; I'm No Angel. **1934** Good Dame; Men in White; Curtain at Eight; Half a Sinner; He Was Her Man; Born to Be Bad; School for Girls. **1935** Circus Shadows; Valley of Wanted Men; Time Square Lady; Northern Frontier; G-Men; Wings in the Dark; The World Accuses; Death from a Distance; False Pretenses; Star of Midnight; Headline Woman; Cheers of the Crowd; Frisco Waterfront; Car 99. **1936** The Last Outlaw; We Who Are About to Die; Below the Deadline; Rose of the Rancho. **1937** High, Wide and Handsome; Beware of Ladies; Angel's Holiday; One Mile from Heaven; Idol of the Crowds. **1938** Crime Takes a Holiday. **1939** Made for Each Other; The Saint Strikes Back; Torture Ship; Mutiny in the Big House; The Renegade Trail. **1944** A Night of Adventure; plus the following shorts: Love Your Landlord; Radio Rampage; Girls! Girls! Girls! **1945** Birthday Blues (short); Zombies on Broadway; West of the Pecos.

HORAN, CHARLES T.

Born: 1882, New York, N.Y. Died: Jan. 11, 1928, Hollywood, Calif. (heart attack). Screen, stage actor, film director, screenwriter and opera singer.

Appeared in: **1916** The Quitter. **1917** Polly of the Circus.

HORAN, JAMES W.

Born: 1908. Died: May 4, 1967, Hollywood, Calif. (cancer). Screen and television actor.

Appeared in: **1955** The Far Country. **1964** The Unsinkable Molly Brown; My Fair Lady.

HORNBROOK, CHARLES "GUS"

Born: 1874. Died: May 8, 1937, Los Angeles, Calif. (pneumonia). Screen and vaudeville actor.

HORNE, DAVID

Born: July 14, 1898, Blacome, Sussex, England. Died: Mar. 15, 1970, London, England. Screen, stage actor and playwright.

Appeared in: **1933** General John Regan; Lord of the Manor. **1934** Badger's Queen; The Case for the Crown. **1935** Late Extra; That's My Uncle; The Village Squire; Gentleman's Agreement. **1936** Under Proof; Seven Sinners (aka Doomed Cargo—US); It's Love Again; The Interrupted Honeymoon; The House of the Spaniard; Debt of Honour; A Touch of the Moon. **1937** The Mill on the Floss (US 1939); Farewell Again (aka Troopship—US 1938); Four Dark Hours; 21 Days (aka The First and the Last, aka 21 Days Together—US 1940). **1939** Blind Folly. **1940** The Door with Seven Locks (aka Chamber of Horrors—US 1940); Crimes at the Dark House. **1941** Inspector Hornleigh Goes to It (aka Mail Train—US); Breach of Promise (aka Adventure in Blackmail—US 1943). **1942** The First of the Few (aka Spitfire—US 1943); The Day Will Dawn (aka The Avengers—US); They Flew Alone (aka Wings and the Woman—US). **1943** San Demetrio—London; Yellow Canary (US 1944). **1945** They Were Sisters (US 1946); The Seventh Veil (US 1946); The Rake's Progress (aka Notorious Gentleman—US 1946); The Man from Morocco; The Wicked Lady (US 1946). **1946** Gaiety George (aka Showtime—US 1948); Caravan (US 1947); Spring Song (aka Springtime—US); The Magic Bow (US 1947); Men of Two Worlds (aka Kisenga, Man of Africa—US 1952). **1947** The Green Cockatoo (rerelease of Four Dark Hours—1937); The Man Within (aka The Smugglers—US 1948). **1948** Saraband for Dead Lovers (aka Saraband—US 1949); It's Hard to Be Good (US 1950). **1949** Once Upon a Dream; History of Mr. Polly (US 1951). **1950** Madeleine. **1951** Appointment with Venus (aka Island Rescue—US 1952). **1953** Spaceways; Street Corner. **1954** Beau Brummel. **1955** Three Cases of Murder. **1956** The Last Man to Hang; Lust for Life. **1957** The Prince and the Showgirl. **1958** The Safecracker; The Sheriff of Fractured Jaw. **1959** The Devil's Disciple. **1961** The Clue at New Pin; Goodbye Again; Dentist on the Job (aka Get On With It!—US 1963). **1963** Nurse on Wheels (US 1964). **1968** A Flea in Her Ear; Diamonds for Breakfast.

HORNE, EDNA (aka FRANKIE ASHLEY)

Born: 1886. Died: July 17, 1945, Culver City, Calif. Screen and stage actress. Appeared in silent films.

HORNE, JAMES W.

Born: Dec. 14, 1881, San Francisco, Calif. Died: June 29, 1942, Los Angeles, Calif. (cerebral hemorrhage). Screen, stage actor and film director. Married to actress Cleo Ridgely (dec. 1962). Entered films in 1911.

Appeared in: **1915** The False Clue; The Pitfall; The Mysteries of the Grand Hotel.

HORNE, WILLIAM T.
Born: June 4, 1869, Batavia, Ill. Died: Dec. 15, 1942. Screen and stage actor.

Appeared in: **1915** Graft (serial). **1917** Who Was the Other Man? **1919** The Enchanted Barn. **1921** Western Firebrands; Bare Knuckles; Boys Will Be Boys. **1922** The Star Reporter; Putting It Over. **1923** Purple Dawn.

HORNICK, HARRY
Born: Charleston, S.C. Died: Feb. 7, 1975. Screen actor.

Appeared in: **1921** Princess Jones. **1922** Orphans of the Storm. **1923** Enemies of Women.

HORNING, BENJAMIN
Born: 1853. Died: Jan. 18, 1936, Los Angeles, Calif. Screen and stage actor.

Appeared in: **1915** The Bond of Friendship; Fate's Vengeance; With Stolen Money. **1917** A Dark Room Secret.

HORSLEY, DAVID
Born: 1874. Died: Feb. 23, 1933, Sunland, Calif. Screen actor and film producer.

Appeared in: **1914** The Great Universal Mystery.

HORTON, BENJAMIN
Born: 1872. Died: Aug. 9, 1952, Hollywood, Calif. Screen actor.

HORTON, CLARA (Clara Marie Horton)
Born: July 29, 1904, Brooklyn, N.Y. Died: Dec. 4, 1976, Whittier, Calif. (heart disease). Screen actress.

Appeared in: **1917** The Plow Woman; Tom Sawyer. **1918** Huck and Tom. **1919** Everywoman; The Girl from the Outside; In Wrong; Golden One. **1920** Blind Youth; Nineteen and Phyllis; The Servant in the House; Little Shepherd of Kingdom Come; It's a Great Life. **1921** Action; Prisoners of Love; The Light in the Clearing. **1922** Penrod. **1923** Mind Over Motor. **1924** Wrongs Righted. **1925** The Wheel; All Around Frying Pan; Makers of Men; Speed Madness. **1926** The Broadway Gallant; Beyond the Trail; Winning the Futurity. **1927** The Fighting Comeback; Sailor Izzy Murphy. **1928** The Fortune Hunter.

HORTON, EDWARD EVERETT
Born: Mar. 18, 1886, Brooklyn, N.Y. Died: Sept. 29, 1970, Encino, Calif. (cancer). Screen, stage, vaudeville, radio, television actor, stage producer and stage director.

Appeared in: **1922** A Front Page Story; The Lady Jinx; Two Much Business. **1923** Ruggles of Red Gap; To the Ladies. **1924** Try and Get It; Flapper Wives; Helen's Babies; The Man Who Fights Alone. **1925** Marry Me; Beggar on Horseback; The Nut-Cracker (aka You Can't Fool Your Wife). **1926** The Whole Town's Talking; The Business of Love; La Boheme; Poker Faces; plus six Harold Lloyd shorts. **1927** Taxi! Taxi!; Edward Everett Horton Comedy (short). **1928** The Terror; plus the following shorts: Miss Information; Behind the Counter; Scrambled Weddings; Vacation Waves and Dad's Choice. **1929** Sonny Boy; The Hottentot; The Sap; The Aviator; plus the following shorts: Ask Dad; Trusting Wives; Prince Gabby; The Eligible Mr. Bangs; Good Medicine; The Right Bed. **1930** Take the Heir; Wide Open; Holiday; Once a Gentleman. **1931** Kiss Me Again (aka The Toast of the Legion); Reaching for the Moon; Lonely Wives; Smart Woman; Six Cylinder Love; The Front Page; The Age for Love. **1932** But the Flesh Is Weak; Roar of the Dragon; Trouble in Paradise. **1933** Soldiers of the King (aka The Woman in Command—US 1934); The Way to Love; Design for Living; Alice in Wonderland; It's a Boy (US 1934); A Bedtime Story. **1934** Easy to Live; Sing and Like It; Uncertain Lady; Success at Any Price; The Merry Widow; Kiss and Make Up; Ladies Should Listen; The Poor Rich; The Gay Divorcee (aka The Gay Divorce); Smarty (aka Hit Me Again). **1935** Biography of a Bachelor Girl; The Night Is Young; All the King's Horses; The Devil Is a Woman (aka Caprice Espagnol); In Caliente (aka Mr. Faintheart); Going Highbrow; Little Big Shot; Top Hat; The Private Secretary; His Night Out; Your Uncle Dudley. **1936** The Man in the Mirror (US 1937); Her Master's Voice; The Singing Kid; Hearts Divided (aka Glorious Betsy); Nobody's Fool (aka Unconscious). **1937** Lost Horizon; Let's Make a Million; Angel; Wild Money; The King and the Chorus Girl; The Perfect Specimen; The Great Garrick; Oh, Doctor; Shall We Dance?; Hitting a New High; Danger—Love at Work. **1938** Bluebeard's Eighth Wife; College Swing (aka Swing, Teacher, Swing); Holiday (aka Free to Live); Little Tough Guys in Society. **1939** Paris Honeymoon; The Gang's All Here (aka The Amazing Mr. Forrest); That's Right—You're Wrong. **1941** You're the One; Ziegfeld Girl; Sunny; Bachelor Daddy (aka Sandy Steps Out);

Here Comes Mr. Jordan; Weekend for Three; The Body Disappears. **1942** I Married an Angel; The Magnificent Dope; Springtime in the Rockies. **1943** Forever and a Day; Thank Your Lucky Stars; The Gang's All Here (aka The Girls He Left Behind). **1944** Her Primitive Man; Summer Storm; San Diego I Love You; Arsenic and Old Lace; Brazil; The Town Went Wild. **1945** Steppin' in Society; Lady on a Train. **1946** Cinderella Jones; Faithful in My Fashion; Earl Carroll Sketchbook (aka Hats Off to Rhythm). **1947** The Ghost Goes Wild; Down to Earth; Her Husband's Affairs. **1952** Elstree Story (doc. with films clips of 1939 movie The Gangs All Here). **1957** The Story of Mankind. **1961** Pocketful of Miracles. **1963** It's a Mad, Mad, Mad, Mad World. **1964** Sex and the Single Girl. **1967** The Perils of Pauline. **1969** 2,000 Years Later. **1970** Cold Turkey.

HORVATH, CHARLES (Charles Frank Horvath)
Born: 1921. Died: July 23, 1978, Woodland Hills, Calif. Screen actor and stuntman. Married to former dancer Margot Horvath.

Appeared in: **1951** Bonanza Town; The Cave of the Outlaws; The Strange Door; Snake River Desperadoes. **1952** Aladdin and His Lamp; Voodoo Tiger. **1953** Money From Home; His Majesty O'Keefe. **1954** Border River; Charge of the Lancers; Vera Cruz; Rails Into Laramie; Sign of the Pagan. **1956** Dakota Incident; Pillars in the Sky; Around the World in 80 Days; Francis in the Haunted House. **1957** Damn Citizen; Duranago; The Girl in the Kremlin; Guns of Fort Petticoat; Man in the Shadow; Pawnee. **1958** Twilight of the Gods; The Thing That Couldn't Die. **1959** Gunmen from Laredo. **1960** The Story of Ruth. **1961** Posse From Hell. **1962** The Wild Westerners. **1963** California; Showdown. **1965** Cat Ballou; War Party. **1966** Johnny Reno. **1969** Kenner. **1974** A Woman Under the Influence.

HORWITZ, JOSEPH
Born: 1858. Died: Oct. 26, 1922, Mt. Clemens, Mich. (uremic poisoning). Screen actor.

HOSKINS, ALLEN "FARINA" (Alan Clay Hoskins, Jr.)
Born: Aug. 9, 1920, Boston, Mass. Died: July 26, 1980, Oakland, Calif. (cancer). Black screen, vaudeville actor, cinematographer and radio writer. Brother of actress Jannie Hoskins. Appeared as "Farina" in Our Gang Comedies.

Appeared in: **1922** The following shorts: Firefighters; Young Sherlocks; One Terrible Day. **1923** The following shorts: The Big Show; The Cobbler; The Champeen; Boys to Board; A Pleasant Journey; Giants vs. Yanks; Back Stage; Dogs of War; Lodge Night; Stage Freight; July Days; Sunday Calm; No Noise; Derby Day. **1924** The following shorts: Fast Company; The Trouble; Big Business; The Buccaneers; Seein' Things; It's a Bear; Cradle Robbers; Jubilo, Jr.; High Society; The Sun Down Limited; Every Man for Himself. **1925** The following shorts: The Big Town; Circus Fever; Dog Days; Ask Grandma; Shootin' Injuns; Official Officers; Boys Will Be Joys; Your Own Back Yard. **1926** The following shorts: Good Cheer; Burried Treasure; Monkey Business; Baby Clothes; Uncle Tom's Uncle; Thundering Fleas; Shivering Spooks; The Fourth Alarm; War Feathers. **1927** The following shorts: Seeing the World; Telling Whoppers; Bring Home the Turkey; Ten Years Old; Love My Dog; Tired Business Men; Baby Brother; Chicken Feed; Olympic Games; The Glorious Fourth; Yale vs. Harvard; The Old Wallop; Heebee Jeebees; Dog Heaven. **1928** The following shorts: Playin' Hookey; The Smile Wins; Spook Spoofing; Rainy Days; Edison, Marconi & Co; Barnum & Ringling, Inc.; Fair and Muddy; Crazy House; Growing Pains; Old Gray Hoss; School Begins; The Spanking Age. **1929** The following shorts: Election Day; Noisy Noises; The Holy Terror; Wiggle Your Ears; Fast Freight; Little Mother; Cat, Dog & Co; Saturday's Lesson; Small Talk; Railroadin'; Lazy Days; Boxing Gloves; Bouncing Babies; Moan & Groan, Inc. **1930** The following shorts: The First Seven Years; Shivering Shakespeare; When the Wind Blows; Bear Shooters; A Tough Winter; Pups is Pups; Teacher's Pet; School's Out. **1931** The following shorts: The Stolen Jools; Helping Grandma; Love Business; Little Daddy; Bargain Day; Fly My Kite. **1932** You Said a Mouthful. **1933** The Mayor of Hell; The Life of Jimmy Dolan; Fish Hookey (short). **1935** Reckless. **1936** After the Thin Man.

HOSSENFELDT, VERA (Vera Krupp)
Born: 1910, Germany. Died: Oct. 16, 1967, Los Angeles, Calif. Screen actress.

HOSTETTER, ROY
Born: 1885. Died: Sept. 22, 1951, near Carlsbad, Calif. (auto accident). Screen actor.

HOTALING, ARTHUR D. (Arthur Douglas Hotaling)
Born: 1872. Died: July 13, 1938, enroute to San Pedro from Palm Springs, Calif. (heart attack). Screen actor and film director. Married to actress Mae Hotely (dec. 1954).

Appeared in: **1925** Kit Carson Over the Great Divide. **1927** Better Days; King of the Herd. **1928** The Little Wild Girl; Old Age Handicap.

HOTALING, FRANK (John Francis Hotaling)
Born: 1900. Died: Apr. 13, 1977, Woodland Hills, Calif. Screen actor and art director. Entered films in 1923.

HOTELY, MAE
Born: Oct. 7, 1872, Maryland. Died: Apr. 6, 1954, Coronado, Calif. Screen actress. Married to actor Arthur D. Hotaling (dec. 1938).

Appeared in: **1911** A Question of Modesty; The Wise Detective; A Stage Door Flirtation; Business and Love. **1912** The New Constable; Nora—the Cook. **1913** The Gay Time series; Fixing Aunty Up; A Masked Mix-Up; Kate, the Cop; Building a Trust; The Widow's Wiles; Her Wooden Leg; The Engaging Kid; The Actress and Her Jewels; Giving Bill a Rest; An Interrupted Courtship; She Must Elope; The Missing Jewels; Training a Tightwad; The Fake Soldiers; His Widow; Minnie the Widow. **1915** The Twin Sister; A Lucky Strike; An Artful Artist; The Telegrapher's Peril; Price of Pies; Think of the Money; The Golden Oysters; The Cellar Spy; Playing Horse; His Bodyguard; His Suicide; Clothes Count; Si and Sue—Acrobats; The New Butler. **1929** Girls Who Dare.

HOUDINI, HARRY (Erik aka Ehrich Weisz and Henry Weiss)
Born: Mar. 24, 1874, Hungary. (Numerous publications indicate date of birth as Feb. 29, 1876, however, correct date explained as follows: "Perhaps to give Ehrich the security of American citizenship, she (his mother) told him that he, like his younger brother Theo, had been born in Appleton. The date she said was Apr. 6, 1874. That became his 'adopted birthday.'")*. Died: Oct. 31, 1926, Detroit, Mich. (following appendectomy). Magician, screen, stage, vaudeville actor and film producer. Entered films in 1918. Married to vaudeville performer Bess Rahner (dec. 1943).

Appeared in: **1918** The Master Mystery (serial). **1919** The Grim Game. **1920** Terror Island. **1921** The Soul of Bronze. **1922** The Man from Beyond. **1923** Haldane of the Secret Service. **1961** Days of Thrills and Laughter (documentary).

HOUGHTON, ALICE
Born: 1888. Died: May 12, 1944, Los Angeles, Calif. Screen actress.

HOUSE, BILLY
Born: 1890. Died: Sept. 23, 1961, Hollywood, Calif. (heart attack). Screen, stage and vaudeville actor.

Appeared in: **1930** Resolution (short). **1931** The Reckless Hour; A Tale of Two Cities; Smart Money; God's Gift to Women. **1932-33** Paramount shorts. **1937** Merry-Go-Round of 1938. **1945** Thrill of a Romance. **1946** Bedlam; The Strangers. **1947** The Egg and I; Trail Street. **1950** Rogues of Sherwood Forest; Where Danger Lives. **1951** Silver City; People Will Talk; Santa Fe. **1952** Aladdin and His Lamp; Outlaw Women. **1955** Imitation of Life.

HOUSE, JACK
Born: 1887. Died: Nov. 20, 1963, Hollywood, Calif. Screen actor and stuntman. Doubled for Rudolf Valentino and Fred Thomas.

Appeared in: **1924** The Smoking Trail. **1925** Fightin' Odds.

HOUSEMAN, ARTHUR (aka ARTHUR HOUSMAN)
Born: 1890, New York, N.Y. Died: Apr. 7, 1942, Los Angeles, Calif. (pneumonia). Screen and stage actor.

Appeared in: **1917** Red, White and Blue Blood. **1921** The Fighter; The Way of a Maid; Clay Dollars; Room and Board; Worlds Apart; Is Life Worth Living? **1922** The Snitching Hour; Man Wanted; Destiny's Isle; Love's Masquerade; Shadows of the Sea; Why Announce Your Marriage?; The Prophet's Paradise. **1923** Male Wanted; Under the Red Robe; Wife in Name Only. **1924** Manhandled; Nellie, the Beautiful Cloak Model. **1925** A Man Must Live; The Necessary Evil; Thunder Mountain; The Coast of Folly; The Desert's Price; Night Life of New York. **1926** The Bat; Braveheart; Early to Wed; Whispering Wires; The Midnight Kiss. **1927** Bertha, the Sewing Machine Girl; Publicity Madness; The Spotlight; Sunrise; Rough House Rosie; Love Makes 'Em Wild. **1928** The Singing Fool; Partners in Crime; Fools For Luck. **1929** Sins of the Fathers; Side Street; Queen of the Night Clubs; Fast Company; Times Square; Broadway; The Song of Love. **1930** Girl of the Golden West; The Squealer; Officer O'Brien; Feet First. **1931** Bachelor Girl; Five and Ten; Night Life in Reno; Anybody's Blonde; Caught Plastered. **1932** Movie Crazy; No More Orchids; Afraid to Talk; plus the following shorts: Parlor, Bedroom and Wrath; Scram!; Any Old Port. **1933** She Done Him Wrong; The Intruder; Her Bodyguard; The Way to Love; Sing, Sinner, Sing; Good Housewrecking (short). **1934** Mrs. Wiggs of the Cabbage Patch; Here

*From *Houdini: The Untold Story* by Milbourne Christopher, c 1969 by Milbourne Christopher. With permission of the publisher, Thomas Y. Crowe.

Is My Heart; plus the following shorts: Something Simple; The Chases of Pimple Street; The Live Ghost; Babes in the Goods; Done in Oil; Punch Drunks. **1935** Hold 'Em Yale; Riffraff; Paris in the Spring; Here Comes Cookie; Diamond Jim; The Fire Trap; plus the following shorts: It Always Happens; The Fixer-Uppers; Treasure Blues; Sing, Sister, Sing. **1936** Showboat; Our Relations; Wives Never Know; Racing Blood; With Love and Kisses; Am I Having Fun (short). **1937** Step Lively, Jeeves! **1939** Navy Secrets. **1940** Go West. **1941** Billy the Kid.

HOUSTON, BILLIE
Born: Scotland. Died: 1955, London, England. Screen and vaudeville actress. See Renee Houston for family information.

Appeared in: **1926** The Houston Sisters (short). **1932** Musical Medley (reissue of 1926 The Houston Sisters). **1933** Radio Parade. **1935** Variety. **1936** Happy Days Are Here Again; **1938** Happy Days Revue (reissue of 1936 Happy Days are Here Again). **1943** Down Melody Lane.

HOUSTON, CISCO
Born: 1919. Died: Apr. 23, 1961, San Bernardino, Calif. Screen actor, folk singer and song writer. Appeared in western films.

HOUSTON, GEORGE
Born: 1900, Hampton, N.J. Died: Nov. 12, 1944, Los Angeles, Calif. (heart ailment). Screen, stage actor and opera performer.

Appeared in: **1935** The Melody Lingers On (film debut). **1936** Let's Sing Again; Captain Calamity. **1937** Hurricane; Conquest; Wallaby Jim of the Islands. **1938** Marie Antoinette; Frontier Scout; The Great Waltz. **1940** Laughing at Danger; The Howards of Virginia. **1941** The Lone Rider in Ghost Town; The Lone Rider Ambushed; The Lone Rider Fights Back. **1942** The Lone Rider in Border Roundup; The Lone Rider in Cheyenne.

HOUSTON, JEAN
Died: Jan., 1965, Paisley, Scotland. Screen, stage, radio actress and singer.

HOUSTON, JOSEPHINE
Died: Date unknown. Screen actress.

Appeared in: **1929** On With the Show.

HOUSTON, MATTHEW "FATS"
Born: 1911, New Orleans, La. Died: Feb. 25, 1981, New Orleans, La. Black jazz musician and screen actor.

Appeared in: **1965** The Cincinnati Kid. **1973** Live and Let Die.

HOUSTON, RENEE (Katherine Houston Gribbin)
Born: July 24, 1902, Johnstone, Scotland. Died: Feb. 9, 1980, London, England. Screen, stage, vaudeville, radio actress and author. Daughter of vaudeville actors James Gribbon (dec.) and Elizabeth Houston (dec.). Sister of actress Billie Houston Gribbin (dec.) with whom she appeared in vaudeville in an act billed as "The Houston Sisters." Divorced from actor Patrick Aherne (dec. 1970). Later married to actor Donald Stewart (dec. 1966).

Appeared in: **1926** The Houston Sisters (short). **1932** Musical Medley (reissue of 1926 The Houston Sisters); Come Into My Parlour. **1933** Radio Parade; Their Night Out. **1934** Mr. Cinders; Lost in the Legion. **1935** Variety; No Monkey Business. **1936** Happy Days Are Here Again. **1937** Fine Feathers. **1938** Happy Days Revue (reissue of 1936 Happy Days Are Here Again). **1939** A Girl Must Live (US 1941). **1940** Old Bill and Son. **1943** Down Melody Lane. **1944** 2,000 Women. **1951** Lady Godiva Rides Again (US 1954). **1954** The Bells of St. Trinian's (US 1955). **1955** Track the Man Down (US 1956). **1956** A Town Like Alice (US 1957); The Big Money. **1957** Time Without Pity. **1958** Them Nice Americans. **1959** The Horse's Mouth. **1960** And the Same to You; The Flesh and the Fiends (aka Mania—US 1961). **1961** No, My Darling Daughter (US 1964); Watch It Sailor!; Three on a Spree. **1962** Tomorrow at Ten (US 1964); Twice Round the Daffodils; The Phantom of the Opera; Out of the Fog. **1963** Nurse on Wheels (US 1964); Carry on Cabby (aka Call Me A Cab—US 1967); The Resuce Squad. **1964** Carry on Spying. **1965** Repulsion. **1966** Cul-de-sac; The Idol; Secrets of a Windmill Girl; The Spy With a Cold Nose. **1967** River Rivals. **1974** Legend of the Werewolf.

HOVEN, ADRAIN
Born: 1924, Austria. Died: Apr. 28, 1981, West Germany (heart attack). Screen, television actor, film director and film producer.

Appeared in: **1949** Where's the One I Love. **1952** I Can't Marry Anyone; Tromba, the Tiger Man. **1953** Stars Over Columbo; The Story of Vickie. **1954** Canaris (aka Deadly Decision—US 1958); Angelika;

The Maharajah's Prisoner. **1955** Die Stadt ist Voller Geheimnisse (aka City of Secrets—US 1963, aka Secrets of the City). **1956** Liane, Jungle Goddess; Pulversee Nach Uebersee, Circus Girl. **1960** I Aim at the Stars; Foxhole in Cairo (US 1961). **1961** Liane die Weisse Sklavin (Liane, the White Slave, aka Nature Girl and the Slaver—US); Insel du Amazonen (Amazon Island, aka Seven Darling Girls—US 1962). **1964** Der Fluch der Grunen Augen (Cave of the Living Dead—US 1966). **1968** Necronomicon—Getraumte Sunden (aka Succubus—US 1969). **1975** Kiss Me Monster. **1976** Inside Out; Fox and His Friends.

HOVICK, ROSE LOUISE *See* LEE, GYPSY ROSE

HOWARD, ART
Born: 1892. Died: May 28, 1963, Hollywood, Calif. (coronary thrombosis). Screen and stage actor.

Appeared in: **1950** Peggy; Stage Fright.

HOWARD, BERT
Born: 1873. Died: Oct. 27, 1958, Hollywood, Calif. Stage and screen actor.

HOWARD, BOOTH (Boothe Howard)
Born: 1889. Died: Oct. 4, 1936, Los Angeles, Calif. (hit by auto). Screen and stage actor.

Appeared in: **1933** My Woman; Hot Pepper; Trick for Treat; The Avenger. **1934** The Gay Bride; Mystery Liner; Midnight Alibi. **1935** Smart Girl; Every Night at Eight; Mary Burns, Fugitive; Show Them No Mercy. **1936** The Robin Hood of El Dorado; Charlie Chan at the Circus; Undersea Kingdom (serial); Red River Valley; Oh, Susannah!

HOWARD, CHARLES (Charles Ray Howard)
Born: 1882, San Diego, Calif. Died: June 28, 1947, New York, N.Y. (heart attack). Screen, stage, burlesque and vaudeville actor.

Appeared in: **1917** Eternal Sin. **1918** Every Mother's Son; Neighbors. **1927** Home Struck. **1930** All Stuck Up (short). **1931** The Night Angel.

HOWARD, DAVID H.
Born: 1860, N.Y. Died: Dec. 9, 1944, Woodland Hills, Calif. Stage and screen actor.

HOWARD, EDDY
Born: 1909, Ill. Died: May 23, 1963, Palm Desert, Calif. (cerebral hemorrhage). Bandleader, song writer and screen actor.

HOWARD, ELSTON (Elston Gene Howard)
Born: Feb. 23, 1929, St. Louis, Mo. Died: Dec. 14, 1980, New York, N.Y. (cardiac arrest). Professinal baseball player, coach and screen actor.

Appeared in: **1980** It's My Turn.

HOWARD, ERNEST (Ernest Ladd)
Born: 1875. Died: Nov. 8, 1940, Brooklyn, N.Y. Screen and stage actor.

Appeared in: **1915** Beneath the Coat of a Butler. **1917** Her Beloved Enemy; Fires of Youth; The Man Without a Country.

HOWARD, ESTHER
Born: 1893. Died: Mar. 8, 1965, Hollywood, Calif. (heart attack). Screen and stage actress. Married to actor Arthur Albertson (dec. 1926).

Appeared in: **1930** The following shorts: Twixt Love and Duty; Ship Ahoy; The Woman Tamer; Who's the Boss; The Victim. **1931** Wicked; The Vice Squad. **1932** Ladies of the Big House; The Cohens and the Kellys in Hollywood; Merrily We Go to Hell; Winner Take All; Rackety Rax. **1933** Below the Sea; Second Hand Wife; The Iron Master. **1935** Mary Burns, Fugitive; The Farmer Takes a Wife; Straight from the Heart; Ready for Love; The Misses Stooge (short); It Always Happens (short). **1936** Klondike Annie; M'Liss; Love Comes to Moneyville (short); Foolproof (short). **1937** Swing High, Swing Low; Dead End; Rhythm in the Clouds; Stuck in the Sticks (short). **1938** Marie Antoinette; The Texans; Scandal Street; Swing, Sister, Swing. **1939** Broadway Serenade. **1940** The Great McGinty; plus the following shorts: Boobs in the Woods; Fireman, Save My Choo Choo; A Bundle of Bliss. **1941** The Lady from Cheyenne; Sullivan's Travels; Lovable Trouble (short). **1942** My Favorite Blonde; The Palm Beach Story; Sappy Birthday (short). **1943** True to Life. **1944** Murder My Sweet; Hail the Conquering Hero; The Big Noise; The Miracle of Morgan's Creek. **1945** Adventure; The Great Flamarion; Detour; A Letter for Evie; The Falcon in San Francisco. **1946** Without Reservations; The Falcon's Alibi; Dick Tracy vs. Cueball. **1947** Born to Kill; The Trouble With Women. **1948** June Bride; The Velvet Touch. **1949** Look for the Silver Lining; Champion; The Lady Gambles; The Beautiful Blonde from Bashful Bend; Hellfire; Homicide. **1950** Caged. **1951** All That I Have. **1952** A Blissful Blunder (short—stock footage).

HOWARD, EUGENE (Eugene Levkowitz)
Born: Nov. 7, 1881, Nevstadt, Germany. Died: Aug. 1, 1965, New York, N.Y. Screen, stage, vaudeville and radio actor. Brother of screen actor Willie Howard (dec. 1949); together they appeared in vaudeville as "Eugene and Willie Howard."

The team appeared in: **1927** The following shorts: A Theatrical Manager's Office; Between the Acts of the Opera; Pal. **1929** The Music Makers (short); My People (short).

HOWARD, FLORENCE
Born: 1888. Died: Aug. 11, 1954, Hollywood, Calif. (heart attack). Stage and screen actress.

HOWARD, FRANCES (Frances McLaughlin)
Born: 1903, Kansas City, Kans. Died: July 2, 1976, Beverly Hills, Calif. Screen, stage actress, model and film producer. Married to film producer Samuel Goldwyn (dec. 1974).

Appeared in: **1925** The Swan; Too Many Kisses; The Shock Punch.

HOWARD, FRANKIE
Born: 1895, Ireland. Died: Dec. 17, 1981, Dublin, Ireland. Screen and stage actor. Do not confuse with British entertainer of the same name.

HOWARD, GEORGE W.
Born: 1875, Philadelphia, Pa. Died: Aug. 25, 1928, N.Y. (septic poisoning). Screen and stage actor.

Appeared in: **1916** The Blue Envelope Mystery. **1920** The Thief; The Whisper Market; Piccadilly Jim. **1921** What's Your Reputation Worth? **1922** Ashes. **1925** I Want My Man.

HOWARD, GERTRUDE
Born: Oct. 13, 1892, Hot Springs, Ark. Died: Sept. 30, 1934, Los Angeles, Calif. Black screen and stage actress. Entered films in 1914.

Appeared in: **1925** The Circus Cyclone. **1927** River of Romance; Easy Pickings; South Sea Love; Uncle Tom's Cabin. **1928** On Your Toes. **1929** Hearts in Dixie; His Captive Woman; Synthetic Sin; Mississippi Gambler; Show Boat. **1930** Guilty; Conspiracy. **1931** Father's Son; The Prodigal. **1932** Strangers in Love; The Wet Parade. **1933** I'm No Angel. **1934** Peck's Bad Boy. **1959** Uncle Tom's Cabin (rerelease of 1927 film).

HOWARD, HELEN
Born: May 2, 1903, Colorado Springs, Colo. Died: Mar. 14, 1927, Hollywood, Calif. (accidental fall). Screen actress. Do not confuse with Helen Howard (dec. 1975).

Appeared in: **1919** Brass Buttons. **1922** Deserted at the Altar; My Wild Irish Rose; When Romance Rides. **1924** Captain Blood.

HOWARD, HELEN
Born: 1899. Died: Oct. 31, 1975, West Los Angeles, Calif. (cancer). Screen actress. Married to actor Moe Howard (dec. 1975).

HOWARD, JEROME "CURLY" (Jerome Lester Horwitz)
Born: 1906, Brooklyn, N.Y. Died: Jan. 19, 1952, San Gabriel, Calif. Screen, stage and vaudeville actor. One of the original "Three Stooges" of stage and screen. Brother of actors Samuel "Shemp" (dec. 1955) and Moe Howard (dec. 1975).

Appeared in: **1933** Turn Back the Clock; Myrt and Marge; Meet the Baron; Dancing Lady; plus the following shorts: Beer and Pretzels; Hello Pop; Plane Nuts. **1934** Fugitive Lovers; Hollywood Party; Gift of Gab; The Captain Hates the Sea; plus the following shorts: Nertsery Rhymes; Screen Snapshots; Woman Haters; Men in Black; Punch Drunks; Three Little Pigskins. **1935** The following shorts: Horses Collars; Restless Knights; Pop Goes the Easel; Uncivil Warriors; Pardon My Scotch; Hoi Polloi; Three Little Beers; Screen Snapshot #6. **1936** The following shorts: Ants in the Pantry; Movie Maniacs; Half-Shot Shooters; Disorder in the Court; A Pain in the Pullman; False Alarms; Whoops I'm an Indian; Slippery Silks. **1937** The following shorts: Grips, Grunts and Groans; Dizzy Doctors; Three Dumb Clucks; Goofs and Saddles; Back to the Woods; Cash and Carry; Playing the Ponies; The Sitter-Downers. **1938** Start Cheering; plus the following shorts: Termites of 1938; Wee Wee Monsieur; Tassels in the Air; Healthy, Wealthy and Dumb; Three Missing Links; Violent Is the Word for Curly; Mutts to You; Flat Foot Stooges. **1939** The following shorts: Three Little Sew and Sews; We Want Our Mummy; A-Ducking They Did Go; Yes, We Have No Bonanza; Saved by the Belle; Calling All Curs; Oily to Bed and Oily to Rise; Three Sappy People. **1940** The following shorts: You Natzy Spy!; Rockin' Through the Rockies; A-Plumbing We Will Go; From Nurse to Worse; Nutty But Nice; How High Is Up?; No Census No Feeling; Cuckoo Cavaliers; Boobs in Arms.

1941 Time Out for Rhythm; plus the following shorts: So Long, Mr. Chumps; Dutiful But Dumb; All the World's a Stooge; I'll Never Heil Again; An Ache in Every Stake; In the Sweet Pie and Pie; Some More of Samoa. **1942** My Sister Eileen; plus the following shorts: Loco Boy Makes Good; Cactus Makes Perfect; What's the Matador?; Matri-Phony; Three Smart Saps; Even as I.O.U.; Sock-a-Bye Baby. **1943** The following shorts: They Stooge to Conga; Dizzy Detectives; Spook Louder; Back from the Front; Three Little Twerps; Higher Than a Kite; I Can Hardly Wait; Dizzy Pilots; Phony Express; A Gem of a Jam. **1944** Ghost Crazy; plus the following shorts: Crash Goes the Hash; Busy Buddies; The Yoke's on Me; Idle Roomers; Gents Without Cents; No Dough, Boys. **1945** Rockin' in the Rockies; plus the following shorts: Three Pests in a Mess; Booby Dupes; Idiots Deluxe; If a Body Meets a Body; Micro Phonies. **1946** The following shorts: Beer Barrel Polecats; A Bird in the Head; Uncivil Warbirds; Three Troubledoers; Monkey Businessmen; Three Loan Wolves; G.I. Wanna Go Home; Rhythm and Weep; Three Little Pirates. **1947** The following shorts: Hold That Lion; Half-Wits Holiday.

HOWARD, KATHLEEN
Born: July 17, 1880, Niagara Falls, Canada. Died: Apr. 15, 1956, Hollywood, Calif. Screen actress, opera performer and magazine editor.

Appeared in: **1934** Once to Every Bachelor; Death Takes a Holiday; It's a Gift; You're Telling Me; One More River. **1935** The Man on the Flying Trapeze. **1936** Stolen Holiday. **1938** Letter of Introduction. **1939** Little Accident; First Love. **1940** Young People; Mystery Sea Raider; One Night in the Tropics; Five Little Peppers in Trouble. **1941** Miss Polly; Blossoms in the Dust; A Girl, a Guy and a Gob; Sweetheart of the Campus; Ball of Fire. **1942** The Mad Marindales; You Were Never Lovelier; Lady in a Jam. **1943** The Human Comedy; Crash Dive; My Kingdom for a Cook; Swing Out the Blues. **1944** Laura; Reckless Age. **1945** Sadie Was a Lady; Shady Lady; Snafu. **1946** Cross My Heart; Centennial Summer; Miss Susie Slagle's; Dangerous Woman; The Mysterious Intruder. **1947** The Late George Apley; Take a Letter, Darling; Cynthia; Curley. **1948** The Bride Goes Wild; Cry of the City. **1950** Born to Be Bad; Petty Girl.

HOWARD, LESLIE (Leslie Howard Stainer)
Born: Apr. 3, 1893, London, England. Died: June 2, 1943, Bay of Biscay (air crash). Screen, stage actor, film director and film producer. Nominated for 1932/33 Academy Award for Best Actor in Berkeley Square and in 1938 for Pygmalion. Father of actor Ronald Howard.

Appeared in: **1914** The Heroine of Mons. **1917** The Happy Warrior. **1919** The Lackey and the Lady. **1920** Bookworms (short); Five Pounds Reward (short). **1930** Outward Bound. **1931** Devotion; Five and Ten (aka A Daughter of Luxury); Never the Twain Shall Meet; A Free Soul. **1932** Service for Ladies (aka Reserved for Ladies—US); Smilin' Through; The Animal Kingdom (aka Woman in the House). **1933** Secrets; Berkeley Square; Captured. **1934** British Agent; The Lady is Willing; Of Human Bondage; Hollywood on Parade (short). **1935** The Scarlet Pimpernel. **1936** The Petrified Forest; Romeo and Juliet. **1937** It's Love I'm After; Stand-In. **1938** Pygmalion. **1939** Intermezzo (aka Escape to Happiness); Gone With the Wind. **1941** Pimpernel Smith (aka Mister V—US 1942); 49th Parallel (aka The Invaders—US 1942); From the Four Corners (short). **1942** The First of the Few (aka Spitfire—US 1943).

HOWARD, LEWIS
Born: Jan. 16, 1919, New York, N.Y. Died: Sept. 29, 1951. Screen actor.

Appeared in: **1939** First Love. **1940** It's a Date; I'm Nobody's Sweetheart Now. **1941** Hellzapoppin; Horror Island; Meet the Chump; Hello Sucker; San Francisco Docks. **1942** Seven Sweethearts. **1946** Up Goes Maisie; I've Always Loved You. **1948** Song of My Heart. **1950** In a Lonely Place.

HOWARD, LISA K.
Born: Apr. 24, 1930. Died: July 4, 1965, East Hampton, N.Y. Screen actress and newscaster. Married to film producer Felix Feist (dec. 1965).

Appeared in: **1950** The Man Who Cheated Himself. **1953** Donovan's Brain; The Hindu (aka Sabaka—US 1955).

HOWARD, MAY
Born: 1870. Died: Feb. 1, 1935, Hollywood, Calif. (heart attack). Screen, stage, burlesque and vaudeville actress.

HOWARD, MOE (Moses Horwitz)
Born: June 19, 1897, Brooklyn, N.Y. Died: May 4, 1975, Hollywood, Calif. (cancer). Screen, stage, television and vaudeville actor. Married to actress Helen Howard (dec. 1975). Brother of actors Jerome "Curly" (dec. 1952) and Samuel "Shemp" Howard (dec. 1955). Appeared in vaudeville with Ted Healy in an act billed as "Ted Healy and His Stooges" and that same act (also referred to as "Ted Healy and His Racketeers").

Appeared in: **1930** Soup to Nuts (film debut). **1933** Meet the Baron; Myrt and Marge; Dancing Lady; Fugitive Lovers; Turn Back the Clock; plus the following shorts: Nertsery Rhymes; Hello Pop!; Hollywood on Parade; Beer and Pretzels; Plane Nuts. **1934** The Captain Hates the Sea; Fugitive Lovers; Hollywood Party; Gift of Gab; plus the following shorts: Woman Haters; The Big Idea; Punch Drunks; Men in Black; Three Little Pigskins. **1935** The following shorts: Horses Collars; Pop Goes the Easel; Uncivil Warriors; Pardon My Scotch; Hoi Polloi; Restless Knight; Three Little Beers; Screen Snapshot #6. **1936** The following shorts: Ants in the Pantry; Movie Maniacs; Half-Shot Shooters; Disorder in the Court; A Pain in the Pullman; False Alarms; Whoops I'm an Indian; Slippery Silks. **1937** Start Cheering; plus the following shorts: Grips, Grunts and Groans; Dizzy Doctors; Three Dumb Clucks; Back to the Woods; Goofs and Saddles; Cash and Carry; Playing the Ponies; The Sitter-Downers. **1938** The following shorts: Termites of 1938; Wee Wee Monsieur; Tassels in the Air; Healthy, Wealthy and Dumb; Three Missing Links; Violent Is the Word for Curly; Mutts to You; Flat Foot Stooges; Three Little Sew and Sews; We Want Our Mummy. **1939** The following shorts: Yes, We Have No Bonanza; A-Ducking They Did Go; Saved by the Belle; Calling All Curs; Oily to Bed and Oily to Rise; Three Sappy People. **1940** The following shorts: You Natzy Spy!; Rockin' Through the Rockies; A-Plumbing We Will Go; Nutty But Nice; How High Is Up?; From Nurse to Worse; No Census, No Feeling; Cuckoo Cavaliers. **1941** Time Out for Rhythm; plus the following shorts: Boobs in Arms; So Long, Mr. Chumps; Dutiful But Dumb; All the World's a Stooge; I'll Never Heil Again; An Ache in Every Stake; In the Sweet Pie and Pie; Some More of Samoa; Loco Boy Makes Good. **1942** My Sister Eileen; plus the following shorts: Cactus Makes Perfect; What's the Matador?; Matri-Phony; Three Smart Saps; Even as I.O.U.; Sock-a-Bye Baby. **1943** The following shorts: They Stooge to Conga; Dizzy Detectives; Back from the Front; Three Little Twerps; Higher Than a Kite; Spook Louder; I Can Hardly Wait; Dizzy Pilots; Phony Express; A Gem of a Jam. **1944** The following shorts: Crash Goes the Hash; Busy Buddies; The Yoke's on Me; Idle Roomers; Gents Without Cents; No Dough, Boys. **1945** Rockin' in the Rockies; plus the following shorts: Three Pests in a Mess; Booby Dupes; Idiots Deluxe; If a Body Meets a Body; Micro-Phonies. **1946** Swing Parade of 1946; plus the following shorts: Beer Barrel Polecats; A Bird in the Head; Uncivil Warbirds; Three Troubledoers; Monkey Businessmen; Three Loan Wolves; G.I. Wanna Go Home; Rhythm and Weep; Three Little Pirates. **1947** The following shorts: Half-Wits Holiday; Fright Night; Out West; Hold That Lion; Brideless Groom; Sing a Song of Six Pants; All Gummed Up. **1948** The following shorts: Shivering Sherlocks; Pardon My Clutch; Squareheads of the Round Table; Fiddlers Three; Hot Scots; I'm a Monkey's Uncle; Mummy's Dummies; Crime on Their Hands. **1949** The following shorts: The Ghost Talks; Who Done It?; Hocus Pocus; Feulin' Around; Heavenly Daze; Malice in the Palace; Vagabond Loafers; Dunked in the Deep. **1950** The following shorts: Punchy Cowpunchers; Dopey Dicks; Self-Made Maids; Hugs and Mugs; Love at First Bite; Three Hams on Rye; Studio Stoops; Slap Happy Sleuths; A Snitch in Time. **1951** Gold Raiders; plus the following shorts: Three Arabian Nuts; Baby Sitters' Jitters; Don't Throw That Knife; Scrambled Brains; Merry Mavericks; The Tooth Will Out; Hula La La; The Pest Man Wins; A Missed Fortune. **1952** The following shorts: Listen Judge; Corny Casanovas; He Cooked His Goose; Gents in a Jam; Three Dark Horses; Cuckoo on a Choo Choo. **1953** The following shorts: Booty and the Beast; Up in Daisy's Penthouse; Loose Loot; Tricky Dicks; Spooks; Pardon My Backfire; Rip, Sew and Stitch; Bubble Trouble; Goof on the Roof. **1954** The following shorts: Income Tax Sappy; Musty Musketeers; Pals and Gals; Knutzy Knights; Shot in the Frontier; Scotched in Scotland. **1955** The following shorts: Fling in the Ring; Of Cash and Hash; Gypped in the Penthouse; Bedlam in Paradise; Stone Age Romeos; Wham Bam Slam; Hot Ice; Blunder Boys. **1956** The following shorts: Husbands Beware; Creeps; Flagpole Jitters; For Crimin' Out Loud; Rumpus in the Harem; Hot Stuff; Scheming Schemers; Commotion on the Ocean. **1957** The following shorts: Hoofs and Goofs; Muscle Up a Little Closer; A Merry Mix-Up; Space Ship Sappy; Guns A-Poppin; Horsing Around; Rusty Romeos; Outer Space Jitters. **1958** Space Master X-7; plus the following shorts: Quiz Whiz; Fifi Blows Her Top; Flying Saucer Daffy; Pies and Guys; Sweet and Hot; Oil's Well That Ends Well. **1959** Have Rocket, Will Travel; plus the following shorts: Triple Crossing; Sappy Bull Fighters. **1960** Stop, Look and Laugh; Three

Stooges Scrapbook. **1961** Snow White and the Three Stooges. **1962** The Three Stooges Meet Hercules; The Three Stooges in Orbit. **1963** The Three Stooges Go Around the World in a Daze; It's a Mad, Mad, Mad, Mad, Mad World. **1964** Four for Texas; Big Parade of Comedy. **1965** The Outlaws is Coming! **1966** Don't Worry, We'll Think of a Title.

HOWARD, NORAH
Born: Dec. 12, 1901, England. Died: Apr., 1968, England? Screen, stage and radio actress.

Appeared in: **1932** Condemned to Death. **1935** Car of Dreams. **1937** Last Adventures. **1938** A Yank at Oxford; Star of the Circus (aka Hidden Menace—US 1940); I've Got a Horse. **1939** Lambeth Walk (aka Me and My Girl—US 1940); The Saint in London; An Englishman's Home (aka Madmen of Europe—US). **1961** Two Loves.

HOWARD, PETER
Born: Dec. 20, 1908, Maidenhead, England. Died: Mar. 25, 1965, Lima, Peru (heart failure). Playwright, screenwriter, author and screen actor. Do not confuse with actor Peter Howard (dec. 1968).

Appeared in: **1940** Man of the Hour.

HOWARD, PETER
Born: 1934. Died: Sept. 12, 1968. Screen actor. Do not confuse with actor Peter Howard (dec. 1965).

HOWARD, PETER "PETE THE HERMIT"
Born: June 26, 1878, Knocklong, Ireland. Died: Mar. 14, 1969, Los Angeles, Calif. (brain hemorrhage). Screen actor.

Appeared in: **1923** Souls in Bondage.

HOWARD, RUTH
Born: 1894. Died: Dec. 28, 1944, Los Angeles, Calif. Screen and vaudeville actress. Member of the "Ross and Howard" vaudeville team.

Appeared in: **1933** My Woman.

HOWARD, SAMUEL "SHEMP"
Born: Mar. 17, 1900, New York, N.Y. Died: Nov. 22, 1955, Hollywood, Calif. (coronary occlusion). Screen, stage and vaudeville actor. Brother of screen actors Jerome "Curly" (dec. 1952) and Moe Howard (dec. 1975). Appeared in vaudeville with Ted Healy in an act billed as "Ted Healy and His Stooges" and that same act (also referred to as "Ted Healy and His Racketeers"). He became a member of the "Three Stooges" team of screen fame upon the retirement of his brother "Curly" in 1947.

Appeared in: **1930** Soup to Nuts (film debut). **1934-36** Numerous Vitaphone shorts. **1937** Hollywood Round-Up; Headin' East. **1938** Home on the Range (short). **1939** Another Thin Man. **1940** Millionaires in Prison; The Leather Pushers; Give Us Wings; The Bank Dick; Money Squawks (short); Boobs in the Woods (short). **1941** Flame of New Orleans; Meet the Chump; Buck Privates; The Invisible Woman; Six Lessons from Madame La Zonga; Mr. Dynamite; In the Navy; Tight Shoes; San Antonio Rose; Hold That Ghost; Hit the Road; Too Many Blondes; Hellzapoppin. **1942** The Strange Case of Dr. Rx; Butch Minds the Baby; Mississippi Gambler; Private Buckaroo; Pittsburgh; Arabian Nights. **1943** It Ain't Hay; Keep 'Em Slugging; How's About It?; Strictly in the Groove; Crazy House; Farmer for a Day (short). **1944** Three of a Kind; Moonlight and Cactus; Strange Affair. **1945** Rockin' in the Rockies. **1946** Blondie Knows Best; Dangerous Business; The Gentleman Misbehaves; One Exciting Week; Swing Parade of 1946; plus the following shorts: Beer Barrel Polecats; A Bird in the Head; Uncivil Warbirds; Monkey Businessmen; The Three Troubledoers; Three Loan Wolves; G.I. Wanna Go Home; Rhythm and Weep; Three Little Pirates. **1947** The following shorts: Half-Wits Holiday; Fright Night; Out West; Hold That Lion; Brideless Groom; Sing a Song of Six Pants; All Gummed Up. **1948** The following shorts: Shivering Sherlocks; Pardon My Clutch; Squareheads of the Round Table; Fiddlers Three; Heavenly Daze; Hot Scots; I'm a Monkey's Uncle; Mummy's Dummies; Crime on Their Hands. **1949** Africa Screams; plus the following shorts: The Ghost Talks; Who Done It?; Hocus Pocus; Fuelin' Around; Malice in the Palace; Vagabond Loafers; Dunked in the Deep. **1950** Punchy Cowpunchers; Hugs and Mugs; Dopey Dicks; Love at First Bite; Self-Made Maids; Three Hams on Rye; Studio Stoops; Slap Happy Sleuths; A Snitch in Time. **1951** Gold Raiders; plus the following shorts: Three Arabian Nuts; Baby Sitters' Jitters; Don't Throw That Knife; Scrambled Brains; Merry Mavericks; The Tooth Will Out; Hula La La; The Pest Man Wins. **1952** The following shorts: A Missed Fortune; Listen Judge; Corny Casanovas; He Cooked His Goose; Gents in a Jam; Three Dark Horses; Cuckoo on a Choo Choo. **1953** The following shorts: Loose Loot; Spooks; Up in Daisy's Penthouse; Booty and the Beast; Tricky Dicks; Pardon My Backfire; Rip, Sew and Stitch; Goof on the Roof; Bubble Trouble. **1954** The following shorts: Income Tax Sappy; Musty Musketeers; Pals and Gals; Knutzy Knights; Shot in the Frontier; Scotched in Scotland. **1955** The following shorts: Fling in the Ring; Of Cash and Hash; Gypped in the Penthouse; Bedlam in Paradise; Stone Age Romeos; Wham Bam Slam; Hot Ice; Blunder Boys. **1956** The following shorts: Husbands Beware; Creeps; Flagpole Jitters; For Crimin' Out Loud; Rumpus in the Harem; Hot Stuff; Scheming Schemers; Commotion on the Ocean.

HOWARD, SYDNEY
Born: Aug. 7, 1885, Yeadon, England. Died: June 12, 1946, London, England. Screen and stage actor.

Appeared in: **1929** Splinters (film debut). **1930** French Leave. **1931** Tilly of Bloomsbury; Almost a Divorce; Up for the Cup; Splinters in the Navy. **1932** The Mayor's Nest; It's a King. **1933** Up for the Derby; Night of the Garter; Trouble. **1934** It's a Cop; Girls Please! **1935** The Hope of His Side (aka Where's George?). **1936** Fame; Chick. **1937** Splinters in the Air; What a Man! **1939** Shipyard Sally. **1940** Tilly of Bloomsbury (and 1931 version). **1941** Once a Crook; Mr. Proudfoot Shows a Light (short). **1943** When We Are Married. **1945** Flight from Folly.

HOWARD, TOM
Born: 1886, County Tyrone, Ireland. Died: Feb. 27, 1955, Long Branch, N.J. Screen, stage, vaudeville, burlesque, radio and television actor.

Appeared in: **1930** Rain or Shine. **1932** The following shorts: The Mouse Trapper; The Acid Test; The Vest With a Tale; plus several Paramount shorts. **1933** The following shorts: A Drug on the Market; The Great Hokum Mystery; plus several Paramount shorts. **1934** The following shorts: Static; The Big Meow; A Good Scout. **1935** The following shorts: Easy Money; An Ear for Music; Grooms in Gloom; Time Out; The Magic Word; Stylish Stouts; He's a Prince. **1936** Where Is Wall Street?

HOWARD, VINCENTE
Died: Nov. 2, 1946. Screen actor.

Appeared in: **1917** Vengeance and the Woman (serial). **1921** Breaking Through (serial); The Purple Riders (serial). **1922** Flower of the North.

HOWARD, WARDA
Born: 1881, San Francisco, Calif. Died: Mar. 17, 1943, New York, N.Y. Screen and stage actress. Married to actor Leo Kennedy (dec. 1939).

Appeared in: **1915** The Raven; The Inner Brute; The Great Deceit. **1916** That Sort; The Higher Destiny.

HOWARD, WENDY (Wendy Black)
Born: 1925. Died: Feb. 21, 1972, North Hollywood, Calif. Screen actress.

Appeared in: **1955** That Lady. **1970** Airport.

HOWARD, WILLIAM
Born: 1884. Died: Jan. 23, 1944, Hollywood, Calif. Screen and stage actor.

Appeared in: **1935** Diamond Jim. **1936** Come and Get It.

HOWARD, WILLIE (William Levkowitz)
Born: 1887, Germany. Died: Jan. 14, 1949, New York, N.Y. Screen, stage, vaudeville and radio actor. Brother of actor Eugene Howard (dec. 1965) and together they appeared in vaudeville as "Eugene and Willie Howard" and in 1927-29 they made shorts as a team. He later appeared in vaudeville with Al Kelly.

Appeared in: **1927** The following shorts: A Theatrical Manager's Office; Between the Acts of the Opera; Pals. **1929** The following shorts: The Music Makers; My People. **1930** The Thirteenth Prisoner (aka The Thirteenth Hour). **1935** Millions in the Air. **1936** Rose of the Rancho. **1937** Broadway Melody of 1938. **1937-38** Starred in a series of Educational shorts.

HOWDY, CLYDE
Born: 1920. Died: Oct. 3, 1969, Calif. Screen actor and stuntman.

Appeared in: **1959** Yellowstone Kelly. **1963** PT 109.

HOWELL, ALICE

Born: May 5, 1888, New York, N.Y. Died: Apr. 12, 1961, Los Angeles, Calif. Screen, stage and vaudeville actress.

Appeared in: **1914** Mabel's Married Life (aka The Square Head); Shot in the Excitement (aka The Doughnut Designers); The Mother-in-Law; The Honor of the Sawdust; Neptune's Naughty Daughter; Alice of the Sawdust; Her Horseshoe Obligation; Caught in the Cabaret; The Knock-Out (aka The Pugilist); Laughing Gas; His Musical Career. **1917** Balloonatics. **1922** Love Is an Awful Thing. **1923** Wandering Daughters.

HOWERTON, CLARENCY "MAJOR MITE"

Born: 1913. Died: Nov. 18, 1975, Salem, Ore. Screen actor and circus performer.

Appeared in: **1939** The Wizard of Oz; various "Our Gang" comedies.

HOWES, BOBBY

Born: Aug. 4, 1895, Chelsea, London, England. Died: Apr. 27, 1972, London, England. Screen, stage, radio and vaudeville actor. Father of actress Sally Ann Howes and actor Peter Howes.

Appeared in: **1927** On with the Dance series. **1928** The Guns of Loos. **1931** Third Time Lucky. **1932** Lord Babs; For the Love of Mike. **1934** Over the Garden Wall. **1937** Please Teacher. **1938** Sweet Devil; Yes, Madam? **1946** The Trojan Brothers. **1951** Happy Go Lovely. **1957** The Good Companions (US 1958). **1961** Watch It Sailor!

HOWES, REED (Herman Reed Howes)

Born: July 5, 1900, Washington, D.C. Died: Aug. 6, 1964, Woodland Hills, Calif. Screen and stage actor.

Appeared in: **1923** High Speed Lee; The Broken Violin. **1924** Geared to Go; Lightning Romance. **1925** Courageous Fool; The Cyclone Rider; Bobbed Hair; Crack O'Dawn; Youth's Gamble; The Snob Buster; Cyclone Cavalier; Bashful Buccaneer; Super Speed. **1926** The Night Owl; The High Flyer; The Gentle Cyclone; The Self-Starter; Wings of the Storm; Kentucky Handicap; Danger Quest; The Dangerous Dude; Moran of the Mounted; Racing Romance. **1927** Rough House Rosie; The Lost Limited; The Racing Fool; The Royal American; The Scorcher; Romantic Rogue; Catch as Catch Can. **1928** Ladies' Night in a Turkish Bath; Hellship Bronson; Fashion Madness; Sawdust Paradise; A Million for Love; Russ Farrell, Aviator (series). **1929** The Singing Fool; Stolen Kisses; Come Across. **1930** Clancy in Wall Street; Terry of the Times (serial). **1931** Catch as Catch Can (short); Sheer Luck; Hell Divers; Anybody's Blond. **1932** Devil on Deck; 70,000 Witnesses; Gorilla Ship. **1935** Paradise Canyon; Confidential; The Dawn Rider; Queen of the Jungle. **1936** The Last Assignment; Custer's Last Stand (serial); Feud of the West; The Clutching Hand (serial). **1937** Sweetheart of the Navy; Death in Air; Zorro Rides Again (serial). **1938** Flight to Fame; Fighting Devil Dogs (serial); Dick Tracy Returns (serial); The Lone Ranger (serial); Flash Gordon's Trip to Mars (serial); The Secret of Treasure Island (serial). **1939** The Phantom Stage; Honor of the West; Dick Tracy's G-Men (serial); Zorro's Fighting Legion (serial); South of the Border; Texas Wildcats; Fighting Renegade; Flaming Lead; Six-Gun Rhythm; Roll, Wagons, Roll; Buck Rogers (serial); Daredevil of the Red Circle (serial). **1940** Virginia City; Flash Gordon Conquers the Universe (serial); Adventures of Red Ryder (serial); Westbound Stage; Riders of the Sage; Heroes of the Saddle; Straight Shooter; Texas Terrors; Mystery Sea Raider; Covered Wagon Days. **1941** Fugitive Valley; The Lone Rider in Ghost Town. **1943** Lone Star Trail; Wild Horse Stampede; Thundering Trails. **1944** Outlaw Roundup; Law of the Saddle; Brand of the Devil; Saddle Leather Law. **1945** The Stork Club. **1946** Til the Clouds Roll By; Under Arizona Skies. **1947** The Spirit of West Point. **1948** Black Bart; The Untamed Breed; Mexican Hayride. **1949** Loaded Pistols; The Walking Hills; Task Force; The Doolins of Oklahoma; Range Land. **1950** Stage to Tucson; Captain China; Gunslingers; The Savage Horde; Ambush; Santa Fe; Silver Raiders; Fortunes of Captain Blood. **1951** Man in the Saddle; Rich, Young and Pretty; Saddle Legion; Indian Uprising. **1952** The Iron Mistress; Hangman's Knot. **1953** The Stranger Wore a Gun; Calamity Jane; The Last Posse; The Man Behind the Gun. **1954** The Boy from Oklahoma; Three Hours to Kill; Violent Men. **1955** Ten Wanted Men; A Lawless Street. **1957** Decision at Sundown; The Guns of Fort Petticoat; Runaway Daughters. **1958** Sierra Baron; Seven Guns to Mesa; Screaming Mimi. **1959** Arson for Hire; Zorro Rides Again. **1960** Gunfighters of Abilene. **1961** The Sinister Urge (aka The Young and Immoral).

HOWLAND, JOBYNA

Born: Mar. 31, 1880, Indianapolis, Ind. Died: June 7, 1936, Los Angeles, Calif. (heart attack). Stage and screen actress. Sister of actor Olin Howlin (Howland) (dec. 1959).

Appeared in: **1919** The Way of a Woman. **1924** Second Youth. **1930** A Lady's Morals; Soul Kiss; Honey; Dixiana; Hook, Line and Sinker; The Cuckoos; The Virtuous Sin. **1932** Big City Blues; Silver Dollar; Once in a Lifetime; Rockabye; Stepping Sisters. **1933** Topaze; Story of Temple Drake; Cohens and Kellys in Trouble. **1935** Ye Old Saw Mill (short).

HOWLIN, OLIN (aka OLIN HOWLAND)

Born: Feb. 10, 1896, Denver, Colo. Died: Sept. 20, 1959, Hollywood, Calif. Screen, stage and vaudeville actor. Brother of actress Jobyna Howland (dec. 1936).

Appeared in: **1918** Independence B'Gosh. **1924** The Great White Way; Janice Meredith. **1925** Zander the Great. **1931** Over the Hill. **1932** Cheaters at Play; So Big. **1933** Blondie Johnson. **1934** Treasure Island; Wagon Wheels. **1935** Dr. Socrates; Behold My Wife; The Case of the Curious Bride; The Case of the Lucky Legs; Follies Bergere. **1936** The Widow from Monte Carlo; Man Hunt; Satan Met a Lady; Road Gang; I Married a Doctor; Boulder Dam; The Big Noise; The Case of the Velvet Claws; Earthworm Tractors; Country Gentlemen; Love Letters of a Star; The Longest Night; Gold Diggers of 1937. **1937** A Star Is Born; Mountain Music; Marry the Girl; Wife, Doctor and Nurse; Nothing Sacred; Men in Exile. **1938** Mad Miss Manton; Swing Your Lady; The Adventures of Tom Sawyer; The Old Raid Mule (short); Girl of the Golden West; Sweethearts; Kentucky Moonshine; Little Tough Guy; Brother Rat. **1939** Nancy Drew—Detective; Blondie Brings Up Baby; Return of Dr. X; Days of Jesse James; Zenobia; Gone With the Wind; Disbarred; Boy Slaves; Made for Each Other; One Hour to Live. **1940** Lucky Partners; Comin' 'Round the Mountain; Young People; Chad Hanna. **1941** You're in the Army Now; Shepherd of the Hills; Buy Me That Town; One Foot in Heaven; Ellery Queen and the Murder Ring; The Great Lie; Belle Starr. **1942** Almost Married; Henry and Dizzy; Sappy Birthday (short); Dr. Broadway; When Johnny Comes Marching Home; The Man Who Wouldn't Die; Home in Wyomin'; This Gun for Hire; Blondie's Blessed Event; You Can't Escape Forever; Orchestra Wives. **1943** Lady Bodyguard; Young and Willing; Secrets of the Underground; A Stranger in Town; The Good Fellows; Jack London; The Falcon and the Co-eds. **1944** Alergic to Love; Since You Went Away; A Strange Lady in Town; Sing, Neighbor, Sing; Bermuda Mystery; Can't Help Singing; I'll Be Seeing You; The Man from Frisco; The Town Went Wild; Twilight on the Prairie; Goodnight, Sweetheart; Bermuda; In the Meantime, Darling; Nothing But Trouble. **1945** She Gets Her Man; Sheriff of Cimarron Gap; Captain Eddie; Her Lucky Night; Colonel Effingham's Raid; Dakota; Fallen Angel; Senorita from the West; Santa Fe Saddlemates. **1946** The Strange Love of Martha Ivers; Home Sweet Homicide; Crime Doctor's Man Hunt; Secrets of the Underworld. **1947** Wyoming; Easy Come, Easy Go; The Angel and the Badman; The Wistful Widow of Wagon Gap; Apache Rose; For the Love of Rusty; The Tenderfoot. **1948** Isn't It Romantic?; The Dude Goes West; Return of the Whistler; My Dog Rusty; The Paleface; The Last of the Wild Horses; Station West; Bad Men of Tombstone. **1949** Anna Lucosta; Massacre River; Grand Canyon; Leave It to Henry; Little Women. **1950** The Nevadan; Father Makes Good; Rock Island Trail; A Ticket to Tomahawk; Stage to Tucson. **1951** Fighting Coast Guard; Santa Fe. **1952** The Fabulous Senorita; Gobs and Gals. **1954** A Star Is Born; Them. **1957** The Spirit of St. Louis. **1958** The Blob.

"HOWLIN' WOLF" (Chester Arthur Burnett)

Born: June 20, 1910, West Point, Miss. Died: Jan. 10, 1976, Chicago, Ill. (kidney disease). Black blues singer, guitarist, harmonica player and screen actor.

Appeared in: **1967** Festival.

HOWSON, ALBERT (Albert Sydney Howson)

Born: Feb. 3, 1881, Brooklyn, N.Y. Died: Aug. 2, 1960, Forest Hills, N.Y. Screen, stage actor and author.

Appeared in: **1915** My Madonna. **1927** Matinee Ladies. **1929** The Greyhound Limited.

HOXIE, JACK

Born: Jan. 24, 1890, Okla. Died: Mar. 28, 1965, Keyes, Okla. Screen actor. Brother of actor Al Hoxie (dec. 1982). Entered films in 1918.

Appeared in: **1919** Lightning Bryce (serial). **1920** Thunderbolt Jack (serial). **1921** The Broken Spur; Sparks of Flint; Hills of Hate; Cupid's Brand; Dead or Alive; Cyclone Bliss; Devil Dog Dawson; The Sheriff of Hope Eternal; Man from Nowhere. **1922** The Marshal of Moneymind; Two Fisted Jefferson; Barb-Wire; The Crow's Nest; Back Fire; The Desert's Crucible; Riders of the Law; A Desert Bridegroom. **1923** The Double O; Desert Rider; The Forbidden Trail; Don Quickshot of the Rio Grande; Wolf's Tracks; Men in the Raw; Where Is the West?; Galloping Thru; The Red Warning. **1924** Ridgeway of

Montana; Fighting Fury; The Western Wallop; The Back Trail; Daring Chances; The Man from Wyoming; The Phantom Horseman; The Galloping Ace. **1925** The White Outlaw; A Roaring Adventure; Bustin' Thru; Don Daredevil; The Sign of the Cactus; Flying Hoofs; Hidden Loot; Two Fisted Jones; The Red Rider; Ridin' Thunder. **1926** The Last Frontier; The Border Sheriff; The Fighting Peacemaker; Red Hot Leather; The Wild Horse Stampede; The Demon; Looking for Trouble; Six Shootin' Romance. **1927** Men of Daring; The Fighting Three; Rough and Ready; The Western Whirlwind; Grinning Guns; The Rambling Ranger; Heroes of the Wild (serial). **1932** Gold. **1933** Law and Lawless; Via Pony Express; Gun Law; Trouble Buster; Outlaw Justice.

HOY, GEORGE *See* FORMBY, GEORGE, JR.

HOYOS, RUDOLFO, SR.
Born: 1896, Mexico City, Mexico. Died: May 24, 1980, Los Angeles, Calif. (results of a fall). Screen, radio, television actor, opera singer and vocal coach. Father of actor Rudolfo Hoyos, Jr.

Appeared in: **1935** A Night at the Opera. **1951** Raton Pass. **1954** Secret of the Incas. **1956** The First Texan; Secret of Treasure Mountain; Stagecoach to Fury; The Three Outlaws. **1957** The Brave One. **1958** Ten Days to Tulara; Toughest Guy in Tombstone; Crash Landing; Villa. **1959** The Little Savage. **1961** Operation Eichman. **1963** California; The Gun Hawk. **1964** Seven Days in May. **1969** Change of Habit.

HOYT, ARTHUR
Born: 1874, Georgetown, Colo. Died: Jan. 4, 1953, Woodland Hills, Calif. Screen, stage actor and stage director. Entered films in 1916.

Appeared in: **1920** Nurse Marjorie. **1921** The Foolish Age; The Four Horsemen of the Apocalypse; Camille; Don't Neglect Your Wife; Red Courage. **1922** Restless Souls; The Top of New York; Is Matrimony a Failure?; Kissed; Love Is an Awful Thing; The Understudy; Little Wildcat; Too Much Wife. **1923** The Love Piker; The Stranger's Banquet; An Old Sweetheart of Mine; To the Ladies; The White Flower; Souls for Sale. **1924** Bluff; Do It Now; Sundown; When a Man's a Man; Her Marriage Vow; The Dangerous Blonde; Daring Youth. **1925** The Lost World; Any Woman; Eve's Lover; The Sporting Venus; The Coming of Amos; Head Winds; Private Affairs. **1926** For Wives Only; The Crown of Lies; The Danger Girl; Monte Carlo; Eve's Leaves; Dangerous Friends; Up in Mabel's Room; Footloose Widows; The Gilded Butterfly; The Midnight Sun. **1927** An Affair of the Follies; The Rejuvenation of Aunt Mary; A Texas Steer; The Love Thrill; The Mysterious Rider; Shanghai Bound; Ten Modern Commandments; Tillie the Toiler. **1928** Just Married; My Man; Husband for Rent; Home James. **1929** The Wheel of Life; Stolen Kisses; Protection; Her Private Affair. **1930** Peacock Alley; Extravagance; The Life of the Party; Dumbbells in Ermine; Night Work; On Your Back; Going Wild; The Boss's Orders; Seven Days' Leave. **1931** The Criminal Code; Inspiration; The Flood; Gold Dust Gertie; Young Sinners; Side Show; Palmy Days; Peach O'Reno; Bought. **1932** Impatient Maiden; Love in High Gear; American Madness; The Devil and the Deep; Dynamite Ranch; Madame Racketeer; Make Me a Star; The Crusader; Washington Merry-Go-Round; Red Haired Alibi; Vanity Street; Call Her Savage; All American. **1933** Dangerously Yours; The Eleventh Commandment; Hold Your Temper (short); Shriek in the Night; Pleasure Cruise; Shanghai Madness; Darling Daughters; Cohens and Kellys in Trouble; Only Yesterday; Laughing at Life; Goldie Gets Along; Emergency Call; His Private Secretary; Sing, Sinner, Sing; 20,000 Years in Sing Sing. **1934** Super Snooper (short); The Meanest Girl in Town; In the Money; The Notorious Sophie Lang; Kansas City Princess; Wake Up and Dream; When Strangers Meet; Babbitt; It Happened One Night; The Crosby Case; Uncertain Lady; Springtime for Henry; Unknown Blonde; Let's Try Again. **1935** Men of Action; No Ransom; A Night at the Ritz; Chinatown Squad; The Raven; Welcome Home; $1,000 a Minute; One Hour Late; Murder on a Honeymoon. **1936** Fury; Great Guy; Lady Luck; Magnificent Obsession; Mr. Deeds Goes to Town; The Poor Little Rich Girl; M'Liss; Walking on Air; Early to Bed. **1937** Love in a Bungalow; Four Days' Wonder; Easy Living; Join the Marines; Paradise Express; The Westland Case; The Wrong Road; A Star Is Born; It's All Yours; Ever Since Eve; Love Takes Flight; She's No Lady. **1938** The Black Doll; The Devil's Party; Start Cheering; The Cowboy and the Lady; The Sisters; You and Me; Girls on Probation. **1939** It Could Happen to You; Should Husbands Work?; Made for Each Other; East Side of Heaven. **1940** I Take This Oath; Goin' Fishin' (short); The Great McGinty. **1941** 1-2-3 Go! (short). **1942** Sullivan's Travels. **1943** Keep 'Em Slugging. **1944** Hail the Conquering Hero. **1947** Mad Wednesday; My Favorite Brunette; Brute Force.

HOYT, CLEGG
Born: 1911. Died: Oct. 6, 1967, Hollywood, Calif. (complications following stroke). Screen and television actor.

Appeared in: **1956** Fighting Trouble; Santiago. **1957** Damn Citizen; The Restless Breed; The True Story of Jesse James. **1958** Gun Fever. **1961** The Young Savages. **1962** Incident in an Alley; Pressure Point; 13 West Street; Paradise Alley. **1964** Seven Days in May. **1965** The Great Race. **1967** In the Heat of the Night.

HOYT, JULIA
Born: 1897. Died: Oct. 31, 1955, New York, N.Y. Screen and stage actress. Entered films in 1921.

Appeared in: **1921** The Wonderful Thing. **1925** The Man Who Found Himself.

HOYT, LEO
Died: Jan. 3, 1937. Screen and stage actor.

Appeared in: **1930** Everything Happens to Me (short).

HUBBARD, TOM (Thomas G. Hubbard)
Born: 1919. Died: June 4, 1974, Rochester, Mich. (cancer). Screen actor and screenwriter.

Appeared in: **1946** Without Reservations. **1951** The Hoodlum; Two Lost Worlds. **1952** Buffalo Bill in Tomahawk Territory. **1953** Murder Without Tears. **1954** Highway Dragnet; Thunder Pass; Port of Hell. **1956** Hidden Guns; Secret of Treasure Mountain. **1957** Hell Canyon (aka Hell Canyon Outlaws); Raiders of Old California. **1958** Legion of the Doomed. **1959** Arson for Hire. **1960** Lust to Kill.

HUBER, HAROLD
Born: 1910. Died: Sept. 29, 1959, New York, N.Y. Screen, stage, radio, television actor and radio and television writer.

Appeared in: **1932** Central Park; The Match King. **1933** Central Airport; Girl Missing; Mary Stevens, M.D.; Mayor of Hell; Midnight Mary; The Silk Express; The Life of Jimmy Dolan; The Bowery; Police Car; Frisco Jenny; 20,000 Years in Sing Sing; Parachute Jumper; Ladies They Talk About. **1934** Cheating Cheaters; Hi, Nellie; He Was Her Man; The Merry Frinks; No More Women; A Very Honorable Guy; The Crosby Case; The Line-Up; The Thin Man; The Defense Rests; Hide-Out. **1935** Naughty Marietta; Mad Love; Pursuit; G-Men. **1936** We're Only Human; The Gay Desperado; Muss 'Em Up; Klondike Annie; Women Are Trouble; San Francisco; The Devil Is a Sissy; Kelly the Second. **1937** The Good Earth; Trouble in Morocco; Midnight Taxi; Angel's Holiday; Charlie Chan on Broadway; Love Under Fire; Charlie Chan at Monte Carlo; You Can't Beat Love; Outlaws of the Orient. **1938** International Settlement; Mr. Moto's Gamble; A Trip to Paris; The Mysterious Mr. Moto; Passport Husband; While New York Sleeps; The Adventures of Marco Polo; A Slight Case of Murder; Going Places; Gangs of New York; Little Tough Guys in Society. **1939** Charlie Chan in City in Darkness; King of the Turf; Chasing Danger; Main Street Lawyer; You Can't Get Away with Murder; Charlie McCarthy, Detective; Beau Geste; 6,000 Enemies; The Lady and the Mob. **1940** The Ghost Comes Home; Kit Carson; Dance, Girls, Dance. **1941** A Man Betrayed; Country Fair; Down Mexico Way; Charlie Chan in Rio. **1942** Pardon My Stripes; Sleepytime Gal; A Gentleman After Dark; Little Tokyo, U.S.A.; Lady from Chungking; Manila Calling. **1943** Crime Doctor. **1950** My Friend Irma Goes West; Let's Dance. **1957** The Joker Is Wild.

HUBER, MRS. JUANITA "BILLIE"
Born: 1905. Died: May 22, 1965, Camden, N.J. Screen actress and dancer. Entered films in early 1930s.

Appeared in: **1935** Dante's Inferno.

HUBER, PAUL
Born: 1896. Died: Mar. 14, 1981, New York, N.Y. Screen, stage and radio actor.

HUBERT, GEORGE
Born: 1881. Died: May 8, 1963, Hollywood, Calif. Screen, stage and vaudeville actor. Entered films in 1917.

Appeared in: **1956** Foreign Intrigue.

HUBERT, HAROLD
Born: 1858. Died: Mar. 31, 1916, auto accident. Screen actor. Appeared in Vitagraph Comedies.

HUDD, WALTER
Born: Feb. 20, 1898, London, England. Died: Jan. 20, 1963, London, England. Screen, stage, television actor and playwright.

Appeared in: **1935** Moscow Nights (aka I Stand Condemned—US 1936) (film debut). **1936** Rembrandt. **1937** Elephant Boy. **1938** Housemaster (US 1939); Black Limelight (US 1939). **1939** Two Minutes (aka The Silence—US); Dead Man's Shoes; The Outsider (US 1940). **1940** Dr. O'Dowd. **1941** Major Barbara. **1942** Uncensored (US 1944). **1944** Love Story (aka A Lady Surrenders—US 1947). **1945** I Live in Grosvenor Square (aka A Yank in London—US 1946); I Know Where I'm Going (US 1947). **1948** Escape. **1949** Paper Orchid; Landfall. **1952** The Importance of Being Earnest. **1953** Cosh Boy (aka The Slasher—US); All Hallow'en. **1954** The Good Die Young (US 1955). **1955** Cast a Dark Shadow (US 1957). **1956** Reach for the Sky (US 1957); The Last Man to Hang?; Satellite in the Sky; Loser Takes All (US 1957). **1958** The Man Upstairs (US 1959); Further Up the Creek; The Two-Headed Spy (US 1959). **1959** Look Back in Anger. **1960** Two-Way Stretch (US 1961); Sink the Bismarck! **1962** Life for Ruth (aka Walk in the Shadow—US 1966); The Punch and Judy Man. **1963** It's All Happening (aka The Dream Maker—US 1964).

HUDMAN, WESLEY
Born: 1916. Died: Feb. 29, 1964, Williams, Ariz. (murdered). Screen and television actor.

Appeared in: **1949** Satan's Cradle. **1950** Indian Territory; Battle of Rogue River; The Girl from San Lorenzo. **1951** Fort Defiance. **1952** Leadville Gunslinger; Barbed Wire; Black Hills Ambush. **1953** Pack Train. **1954** Masterson of Kansas. **1956** The Lonely Man; Blackjack Ketchum, Desperado. **1958** The Sheepman.

HUDSON, ETHEL
Born: 1888. Died: Jan. 18, 1962, Hollywood, Calif. (heart attack). Screen actress and singer.

Appeared in: **1940** The Ramparts We Watch.

HUDSON, LARRY
Born: 1920. Died: Jan. 8, 1961, Hollywood, Calif. (suicide). Screen and television actor.

Appeared in: **1952** Smoky Canyon. **1953** The Redhead from Wyoming. **1956** Jubal; Solid Gold Cadillac; The Creature Walks Among Us. **1959** Tank Commandos.

HUDSON, ROCHELLE
Born: Mar. 6, 1914, Claremore, Okla. Died: Jan. 17, 1972, Palm Desert, Calif. Screen, stage and television actress. Divorced from film editor Hal Thompson, sportswriter Dick Hyland and Robert L. Mindell. Entered films in 1930. Was a 1931 Wampas Baby Star.

Appeared in: **1930** Laugh and Get Rich; Are These Our Children? **1931** Fanny Foley Herself; Beyond the Rockies; Liberty Road; Hell's Highway; Top of the Bill; Mysteries of the French Police; The Penguin Pool Murder. **1933** Love is Like That; She Done Him Wrong; Wild Boys of the Road; Walls of Gold; Doctor Bull; Notorious but Nice; Mr. Skitch; Love is Dangerous; The Savage Girl. **1934** Harold Teen; Judge Priest; Imitation of Life; The Mighty Barnum; Bachelor Bait; Such Women Are Dangerous. **1935** I've Been Around; Show Them No Mercy; Life Begins at Forty; Les Miserables; Curly Top; Way Down East. **1936** Everybody's Old Man; The Music Goes Round; The Country Beyond; Poppy; Reunion. **1937** That I May Live; Born Reckless; Woman Wise; She Had to Eat. **1938** Mr. Moto Takes a Chance; Rascals; Storm Over Bengal. **1939** Pride of the Navy; Smuggled Cargo; A Woman is the Judge; Missing Daughters; Pirates of the Skies. **1940** Babies for Sale; Convicted Woman; Girls Under Twenty-One; Men Without Souls; Island of Doomed Men; Konga, the Wild Stallion. **1941** Meet Boston Blackie; The Stork Pays Off; The Officer and the Lady. **1942** Queen of Broadway; Rubber Racketeers. **1947** Bush Pilot. **1948** The Devil's Cargo. **1949** Sky Liner. **1955** Rebel Without a Cause. **1964** Strait-Jacket; The Night Walker. **1965** Broken Sabre. **1967** Dr. Terror's Gallery of Horrors (aka Return from the Past).

HUDSON, WILLIAM (William Woodson Hudson, Jr.)
Born: Jan. 24, 1925, Calif. Died: Apr. 5, 1974, Woodland Hills, Calif. (Laennec's cirrhosis). Screen and stage actor. Brother of actor John Hudson.

Appeared in: **1943** Destination Tokyo (film debut). **1945** Over 21; Objective Burma. **1946** Lover Come Back. **1949** Task Force. **1950** Father Makes Good. **1951** Starlift; Hard, Fast and Beautiful. **1955** Mister Roberts; Strategic Air Command. **1956** Battle Hymn. **1957** Band of Angels; The Man Who Turned to Stone; The Amazing Colossal Man; My Man Godfrey. **1958** Attack of the 50 Foot Woman. **1962** Moon Pilot. **1970** Airport.

HUEBLER-KAHLA, J. A.
Born: Germany. Died: Apr., 1965, Berlin, Germany (heart attack). Screen actor and film director.

HUESTIS, RUSSELL
Born: 1894. Died: Dec. 1, 1964, Seattle, Wash. (heart attack). Screen actor.

Appeared in: **1942** Beyond the Blue Horizon.

HUFF, FORREST
Born: 1876. Died: Aug. 21, 1947, New York, N.Y. Screen, stage actor and opera performer.

Appeared in: **1927** The Love of Sunya.

HUFF, JACK See KIRK, JACK "PAPPY"

HUFF, LOUISE
Born: 1896, Columbus, Ga. Died: Aug. 22, 1973, New York. Screen and stage actress.

Appeared in: **1916** The Reward of Patience; Seventeen; Great Expectations. **1917** What Money Can't Buy; Tom Sawyer; Freckles; The Varmint; The Ghost House; Jack and Jill. **1918** T'Other Dear Charmer; Sea Waif. **1919** Oh, You Woman; Crook of Dreams. **1920** What Women Want; Dangerous Paradise. **1922** The Seventh Day.

HUGH, EDWIN CHARLES
Born: 1919. Died: Dec. 3, 1979, Longwood, Fla. Screen and stage actor.

HUGHES, C. ANTHONY (Charles Anthony Hughes)
Born: Mar. 21, 1890, Augusta, Ga. Died: 1968. Screen actor.

Appeared in: **1930** Heads Up. **1934** Crime Without Passion. **1938** Touchdown Army; The Frontiersman. **1939** Women in the Wind. **1949** Call of the Forest. **1951** The People Against O'Hara. **1952** Buffalo Bill in Tomahawk Territory. **1955** Daddy Long Legs.

HUGHES, CHARISSA
Died: June 13, 1963, Hollywood, Calif. Screen actress.

HUGHES, DAVID (David Hughes Blees)
Born: 1924. Died: June 8, 1945, Hollywood, Calif. (heart attack). Screen and radio actor. Do not confuse with actor David Hillary Hughes (dec. 1974).

HUGHES, DAVID HILLARY
Died: Feb. 5, 1974. Screen actor.

Appeared in: **1952** The Quiet Man. **1954** Shield for Murder. **1958** The Brain Eaters.

HUGHES, GARETH
Born: Aug. 23, 1894, Llanelly, Wales. Died: Oct. 1, 1965, Woodland Hills, Calif. Stage and screen actor. Entered films in 1919.

Appeared in: **1919** Mrs. Wiggs and the Cabbage Patch; Eyes of Youth. **1921** Sentimental Tommy; The Hunch; Garments of Truth; Indiscretion; Life's Darn Funny; The Lure of Youth. **1922** Don't Write Letters; Little Eva Ascends; Forget-Me-Not. **1923** The Christian; The Spanish Dancer; The Enemies of Women; Kick In; Penrod and Sam. **1924** The Sunset Trail; Shadows of Paris. **1925** The Midnight Girl. **1926** Men of the Night. **1927** The Whirlwind of Youth; The Auctioneer; Broadway After Midnight; Heroes in Blue; Better Days; Eyes of the Totem; In the First Degree. **1928** The Sky Rider; Old Age Handicap; Better Days; Comrades; Top Sergeant Mulligan. **1929** Silent Sentinel; Mister Antonio; Broken Hearted. **1931** Scareheads.

HUGHES, JOSEPH ANTHONY
Born: May 2, 1904, New York, N.Y. Died: Feb. 11, 1970, Pasadena, Calif. (undetermined—suicide or accident—acute alcohol and barbituate mixture). Screen actor.

Appeared in: **1935** Murder in the Fleet. **1936** Whipsaw; The Country Doctor; Educating Father. **1937** Armored Car. **1938** Wives Under Suspicion; In Old Chicago; Just Around the Corner. **1939** Hollywood Cavalcade; The Lone Wolf Spy Hunt; Tail Spin. **1940** The Fighting 69th; Two Girls on Broadway; The Howards of Virginia; The Cisco Kid and the Lady; Beyond Tomorrow; Diamond Frontier. **1941** The Bride Came C.O.D.; You'll Never Get Rich; The Last of the Duanes. **1942** Captains of the Clouds; Men of San Quentin. **1944** Destination Tokyo; Keys of the Kingdom; Follow the Boys. **1949** Fighting Man of the Plains. **1950** The Caribou Trail. **1951** The Guy Who Came Back; The People Against O'Hara. **1953** The Mississippi Gambler. **1954** Highway Dragnet. **1955** Daddy Long Legs. **1956** Tribute to a Bad Man; Miracle in the Rain. **1959** Warlock.

HUGHES, LLOYD

Born: Oct. 21, 1897, Bisbee, Ariz. Died: June 6, 1958, Los Angeles, Calif. Screen actor.

Appeared in: **1915** Turn of a Road. **1918** Out of the Night. **1919** The Haunted Bedroom; The Virtuous Thief; The Heart of Humanity; Satan, Jr. **1920** The False Road; Below the Surface; Dangerous Hours; Home Spun Folks. **1921** Love Never Dies; Beau Revel; Mother O'Mine. **1922** Hail the Woman; Tess of the Storm Country. **1923** Scars of Jealousy; The Old Fool; Are You a Failure?; Her Reputation; Children of Dust; The Huntress. **1924** The Sea Hawk; The Heritage of the Desert; Untamed Youth; Judgment of the Storm; Welcome Stranger; In Every Woman's Life; The Whipping Boss. **1925** Declassee; The Dixie Handicap; The Desert Flower; The Half-Way Girl; If I Marry Again; The Lost World; Sally; Scarlet Saint. **1926** Pals First; Valencia; Ella Cinders; Irene; Loose Angles; Forever After; High Steppers; Ladies at Play. **1927** No Place to Go; American Beauty; The Stolen Bride; An Affair of the Follies; Too Many Crooks. **1928** Heart to Heart; Sailors' Wives; Three-Ring Marriage. **1929** Where East Is East; Acquitted; The Mysterious Island. **1930** Big Boy; The Runaway Bride; Sweethearts on Parade; Love Comes Along; Hello Sister; Moby Dick; Extravagance. **1931** Hell Bound; Ships of Hate; Drums of Jeopardy; Sky Raiders; Unwanted; Air Eagles; The Deceiver; Private Scandal. **1932** The Miracle Man; Heart Punch. **1935** The Man Who Reclaimed His Head; Reckless Roads; Midnight Phantom; Skybound; Society Fever; Rip Roaring Riley; Honeymoon Limited; Harmony Lane; Ticket or Leave It (short). **1936** Night Cargo; Little Red School House; Kelly of the Secret Service. **1937** Blake of Scotland Yard (serial); A Man Betrayed. **1938** Numbered Woman; Clipped Wings; I Demand Payment. **1939** Romance of the Redwoods. **1940** Vengeance of the Deep.

HUGHES, ROY

Died: Jan. 12, 1928. Screen actor. Entered films in 1915.

Appeared in: **1926** Officer Jim.

HUGHES, RUPERT

Born: Jan. 31, 1872, Lancaster, Mo. Died: Sept. 9, 1956, Los Angeles, Calif. (heart failure). Author, historian, composer, poet, film director, screenwriter and screen actor. Married to actress Patterson Dial (dec. 1945).

Appeared in: **1913** Saved by Parcel Post.

HUGHES, RUSH (Russell Sheldon Hughes)

Born: Jan. 15, 1910, Ohio. Died: Apr. 16, 1958, Studio City, Calif. (heart attack). Screen actor, television writer and screenwriter.

Appeared in: **1922** The Wall Flower. **1923** Ashes of Vengeance; Reno; Souls for Sale. **1928** Beware of Married Men. **1938** Love and Hisses.

HUGHES, THOMAS ARTHUR

Born: 1887. Died: Nov. 25, 1953, Los Angeles, Calif. Screen actor. Resemblance to Sir Winston Churchill brought historical roles. Also played in many westerns.

Appeared in: **1945** The Woman in Green.

HUGHES, YVONNE EVELYN

Born: 1900. Died: Dec. 26, 1950, New York, N.Y. (murdered—strangled). Screen and stage actress.

Appeared in: **1923** Zaza; Big Brother; Lawful Larceny. **1924** A Society Scandal; Monsieur Beaucaire.

HUGO, MAURITZ

Born: 1909. Died: June 16, 1974, Woodland Hills, Calif. (heart ailment). Screen, stage and radio actor.

Appeared in: **1938** Wanted by the Police. **1943** Mission to Moscow; Revenge of the Zombies. **1944** The Utah Kid; Marked Trails; Whirlpool. **1945** Secret Agent X-9 (serial); Jealousy. **1946** The Dark Horse; The Bandit of Sherwood Forest; The Mask of Dijon; Secrets of a Sorority Girl; Blonde for a Day; Rustler's Round-Up. **1947** Gentleman's Agreement; Homesteaders of Paradise Valley. **1948** The Saxon Charm; When My Baby Smiles at Me; Renegades of Sonora; The Iron Curtain. **1949** Search for Danger; Death Valley Gunfighter. **1950** Frisco Tornado; Love That Brute; Ticket to Tomahawk (aka The Sheriff's Daughter). **1951** Government Agent vs. Phantom Legion (serial); Saddle Legion; The Dakota Kid; Gun Play; No Questions Asked; Pistol Harvest. **1952** Blue Canadian Rockies; The Kid from Broken Gun; Yukon Gold; Road Agent; Captive of Billy the Kid. **1954** Man With the Steel Whip (serial); Dragnet. **1955** Love Me or Leave Me; King of the Carnival (serial). **1956** The First Traveling Saleslady; Crime Against Joe. **1957** Gun Battle at Monterey; The Vampire; War Drums. **1958** The Old Man and the Sea; Seven Guns to Mesa. **1959** The Gunfighter at Dodge City. **1960** The Purple Gang; Thirteen Fighting Men. **1962** Stagecoach to Dancer's Rock. **1966** Alvarez Kelly. **1969** Marooned.

HULBERT, CLAUDE (Claude Noel Hulbert)

Born: Dec. 25, 1900, London, England. Died: Jan. 22, 1964, Sydney, Australia. Screen, stage, radio actor, screenwriter and composer. Brother of actor Jack Hulbert (dec. 1978).

Appeared in: **1928** Champagne. **1930** Naughty Husbands. **1932** A Night Like This; The Mayor's Nest; Thark; The Face at the Window; Let Me Explain Dear. **1933** Their Night Out; Radio Parade; Heads We Go (aka The Charming Deceiver—US); The Song You Gave Me (US 1934). **1934** A Cup of Kindness; Love at Second Sight (aka The Girl Thief—US 1938); Lilies of the Field; Big Business. **1935** Bulldog Jack (aka Alias Bulldog Drummond—US); Hello Sweetheart; Man of the Moment. **1936** Wolf's Clothing; Where's Sally?; The Interrupted Honeymoon; Hail and Farewell; Honeymoon Merry-Go-Round (aka Olympic Honeymoon). **1937** Take a Chance; The Vulture; It's Not Cricket; Ship's Concert; You Live and Learn. **1938** Simply Terrific; The Viper; It's in the Blood; His Lordship Regrets; Many Tanks Mr. Atkins. **1940** Sailors Three (aka Three Cockeyed Sailors—US 1941). **1941** The Ghost of St. Michael's. **1943** The Dummy Talks; My Learned Friend. **1946** London Town (aka My Heart Goes Crazy—US 1953). **1947** The Ghosts of Berkeley Square. **1948** Under the Frozen Falls. **1949** Cardboard Cavalier. **1956** Fun at St. Fanny's. **1960** Not a Hope in Hell.

HULBERT, JACK

Born: Apr. 24, 1892, Ely, Cambs, England. Died: Mar. 25, 1978, London, England. Screen, stage, vaudeville actor, film director, stage producer, screenwriter and author. Brother of actor Claude Hulbert (dec. 1964). Married to actress Cicely Courtneidge (dec. 1980). Entered films in 1921.

Appeared in: **1921** Told in a Two-Seater. **1930** Elstree Calling. **1931** Sunshine Susie (aka The Office Girl—US 1932); The Ghost Train (US 1933). **1932** Love on Wheels; Jack's the Boy (aka Night and Day—US 1933); Happy Ever After. **1933** Falling For You. **1934** The Camels Are Coming; Jack Ahoy! **1935** Bulldog Jack (aka Alias Bulldog Drummond—US). **1936** Jack of All Trades (aka The Two of Us—US 1937). **1937** Take My Trip; Paradise for Two (aka The Gaiety Girls—US 1938). **1938** Kate Plus Ten. **1940** Under Your Hat. **1941** Queen of Crime. **1951** Into the Blue (aka The Man in the Dinghy—US); The Magic Box (US 1952). **1955** Miss Tulip Stays the Night. **1960** The Spider's Web. **1972** Not Now Darling; The Cherry Picker.

HULBURD, H. L. "BUD"

Died: Feb. 10, 1973, Burbank, Calif. Screen actor, stuntman and special effects technician.

Appeared in: **1915** Birth of a Nation.

HULEY, PETE (aka KLONDIKE PETE)

Born: 1893, Austria. Died: Feb. 6, 1973, Vancouver, B.C., Canada. Screen actor and gold prospector.

HULL, ARTHUR STUART

Born: May 8, 1878, Pa. Died: Feb. 28, 1951, Los Angeles, Calif. Screen actor.

Appeared in: **1921** The Great Moment; The New Disciple; A Prince There Was; What's Worth While?; Good Women. **1922** The Impossible Mrs. Bellow; Midnight; Paid Back; A Question of Honor; The Song of Life; The Great Temptation; Thorns and Orange Blossoms. **1923** A Man of Action; Within the Law; Going Up; The Love Brand; Fools and Riches; Bag and Baggage; Broken Hearts of Broadway; Java Head; A Wife's Romance. **1924** The Woman on the Jury; The Yankee Consul; Stolen Secrets; Good Bad Boy. **1925** Secrets of the Night. **1931** Bought. **1932** Racing Youth; The All American. **1934** Sisters Under the Skin; The Human Side. **1935** Hold 'Em Yale.

HULL, HENRY

Born: Oct. 3, 1890, Louisville, Ky. Died: Mar. 8, 1977, Cornwall, England. Screen and stage actor. Brother of actor Shelley Hull (dec. 1919).

Appeared in: **1917** The Volunteer. **1922** One Exciting Night. **1923** A Bride for a Knight; The Last Moment. **1924** For Woman's Favor; Roulette; The Hoosier Schoolmaster. **1925** The Wrongdoers; Wasted Lives. **1934** Midnight; Great Expectations. **1935** Transient Lady; The Werewolf of London. **1938** Paradise for Three; Yellow Jack; Three Comrades; Boys' Town; The Great Waltz. **1939** Babes in Arms; Return of the Cisco Kid; Judge Hardy and Son; Spirit of Culver; Bad Little Angel; Miracles for Sale; Nick Carter—Master Detective; Jesse James; Stanley and Livingstone. **1940** My Son, My Son; The Return of Frank James. **1941** High Sierra. **1943** The Woman of the Town. **1944** Voodoo Man; Lifeboat; Goodnight, Sweetheart. **1945** Objective Burma. **1947**

High Barbaree; Deep Valley; Mourning Becomes Electra. **1948** Scudda Hoo! Scudda Hay!; The Walls of Jericho; Belle Starr's Daughter; Portrait of Jenny; Fighter Squadron. **1949** Rimfire; El Paso; The Great Gatsby; Colorado Territory; The Fountainhead; The Great Dan Patch; Song of Surrender. **1950** Return of Jesse James. **1951** The Hollywood Story. **1952** The Treasure of Lost Canyon; Inferno; Thunder Over the Plains. **1953** The Last Posse. **1955** Man With the Gun. **1956** Kentucky Rifle. **1957** The Buckskin Lady. **1958** The Proud Rebel; Sheriff of Fractured Jaw; The Buccaneer. **1959** The Oregon Trail. **1961** Master of the World. **1965** The Fool Killer. **1966** The Chase. **1967** Covenant With Death.

HULL, JOSEPHINE (Josephine Sherwood)
Born: Jan. 3, 1886, Newton, Mass. Died: Mar. 12, 1957, New York, N.Y. (cerebral hemorrhage). Screen, stage, radio, television actress and stage director. Married to actor Shelly Hull (dec. 1919). Won 1950 Academy Award for Best Supporting Actress in Harvey.

Appeared in: **1929** The Bishop's Candlestick (short). **1932** After Tomorrow; Careless Lady. **1944** Arsenic and Old Lace (stage and film versions). **1950** Harvey (stage and film versions). **1951** The Lady from Texas.

HULL, SHELLY (aka SHELLEY HULL)
Born: 1885, Louisville, Ky. Died: Jan. 14, 1919, New York, N.Y. (pneumonia). Screen and stage actor. Brother of actor Henry Hull (dec. 1977). Married to actress Josephine Hull (dec. 1957).

Appeared in: **1913** Sapho.

HULL, WARREN (John Warren Hull)
Born: Jan 17, 1903, Gasport, N.Y. Died: Sept. 14, 1974, Waterbury, Conn. (heart failure). Screen, stage, radio, television actor and singer.

Appeared in: **1935** Personal Maid's Secret (film debut); Miss Pacific Fleet; an Educational short. **1936** The Law in Her Hands; Love Begins at Twenty; The Big Noise; Bengal Tiger; Freshman Love; The Walking Dead. **1937** Fugitive in the Sky; Her Husband's Secretary; Big Business; Night Key; Michael O'Halloran; Rhythm in the Clouds; Paradise Isle; A Bride for Henry. **1938** Hawaii Calls; The Spider's Web (serial). **1939** Star Reporter; Mandrake the Magician (serial); Smashing the Spy Ring; Should a Girl Marry?; The Girl from Rio; Crashing Thru. **1940** The Green Hornet Strikes Again (serial); The Lone Wolf Meets a Lady; Wagons Westward; Remedy for Riches; The Last Alarm; Ride, Tenderfoot, Ride; Yukon Flight; Marked Men. **1941** Bowery Blitzkrieg; The Spider Returns (serial).

HULMAN, TONY (Anton M. Hulman)
Born: 1901?, Terre Haute, Ind. Died: Oct. 27, 1977, Indianapolis, Ind. (heart failure). Screen actor and owner of Indianapolis Motor Speedway.

Appeared in: **1969** Winning.

HUMBERGER, WILLIAM See MURDOCK, WILLIAM

HUMBERT, GEORGE
Born: 1881. Died: May 8, 1963, Hollywood, Calif. Screen actor.

Appeared in: **1921** Stardust. **1923** The Bright Shawl. **1924** The Greatest Love of All. **1931** Street Scene. **1932** Ladies of the Jury; A Farewell to Arms; The Night Club Lady; Hearts of Humanity. **1933** I Cover the Waterfront; California Trail; Officers 13; Laughing at Life. **1934** When the Gods Destroy; Hi Nellie; Redhead; Fugitive Road; Name the Woman; Fashions of 1934. **1935** In Caliente; Hard Rock Harrigan; Case of the Curious Bride. **1936** Winterset; In Paris A.W.O.L.; Pepper; Banjo On My Knee; The Public Pays; Sea Spoilers. **1937** You Can't Have Everything; Dead End; The Go Getter; Love Under Fire; Heidi; Love is News; Nancy Steele is Missing; A Girl With Ideas; Expensive Husbands. **1938** No Time to Marry; Island in the Sky; Professor Beware; City Streets; Trouble at Midnight; Flirting With Fate. **1939** Fisherman's Wharf; Daughters Courageous; Full Confession; Mr. Moto's Last Warning; Song of Steel; Topper Takes a Trip. **1940** Music Is My Heart; The Ghost Creeps; Hired Wife; A Miracle on Main Street; Boys of the City; Girl from Avenue A. **1941** Moon Over Miami. **1942** Fiesta. **1943** Trunk Busters; It Ain't Hay. **1944** The Adventures of Mark Twain; Sensations of 1945; Winged Victory. **1950** My Friend Irma Goes West. **1955** The Rose Tattoo.

HUME, BENITA
Born: Oct. 14, 1906, London, England. Died: Nov. 1, 1967, Egerton, England. Screen, stage, radio and television actress. Married to actor Ronald Coleman (dec. 1958) and later married to actor George Sanders (dec. 1972).

Appeared in: **1925** Milestone Melodies series including: They Wouldn't Believe Me; Her Golden Hair Was Hanging Down Her Back. **1926** Second to None. **1927** Easy Virtue (US 1928). **1928** The Constant Nymph; A South Sea Bubble; A Light Woman; The Lady of the Lake (US 1930); The Wrecker (US 1929); Balaclava (aka Jaws of Hell—US 1931). **1929** The Clue of the New Pin; High Treason. **1930** The House of the Arrow; Symphony in Two Flats. **1931** The Flying Fool; A Honeymoon Adventure (aka Footsteps in the Night—US 1933); The Happy Ending. **1932** Service for Ladies (aka Reserved for Ladies—US); Women Who Play; Men of Steel; Diamond Cut Diamond (aka Blame the Woman—US); Sally Bishop; Lord Camber's Ladies; Help Yourself. **1933** Discord; The Little Damozel; Gambling Ship; Worst Woman in Paris?; Only Yesterday; Looking Forward; Clear All Wires. **1934** The Private Life of Don Juan; Jew Suess (aka Power—US). **1935** The Divine Spark; 18 Minutes; The Gay Deception. **1936** The Garden Murder Case; Moonlight Murder; Suzy; Tarzan Escapes; Rainbow on the River. **1937** The Last of Mrs. Cheyney. **1939** Peck's Bad Boy With the Circus.

HUME, ILEAN
Born: 1898, Toronto, Canada. Died: Nov. 20, 1978, Studio City, Calif. Screen and stage actress.

Appeared in: **1915** Stronger Than Love. **1916** Where Love Lands; The Turmoil; The Kiss of Hate. **1917** Duchess of Doubt; The Lifted Veil; His Father's Son; Miss Nobody.

HUMES, HELEN
Born: June 23, 1913, Louisville, Ky. Died: Sept. 9, 1981, Santa Monica, Calif. (cancer). Black screen actress and jazz singer.

HUMMELL, MARY ROCKWELL
Born: 1889. Died: Feb. 16, 1946, Hollywood, Calif. Screen actress. Entered films approx. 1916.

HUMPHREY, BESSIE
Born: Boston, Mass. Died: Mar. 8, 1933, Hollywood, Calif. Stage and screen actress.

HUMPHREY, WILLIAM (William Jonathan Humphrey)
Born: Jan. 2, 1874, Chicopee Falls, Mass. Died: Oct. 4, 1942, Woodland Hills, Calif. (coronary thrombosis). Screen, stage actor, film director and screenwriter.

Appeared in: **1911** An Aeroplane Elopment; The Heart of the King's Jester; Forgotten. **1912** The Bogus Napoleon; The King's Jester. **1913** The Chains of an Oath; My Lady of Idleness; Red and White Roses; Hearts of the First Empire; His Life for His Emperor; The Line-Up; The Flirt; The Penalties of Reputation; My Land Idleness; An Unwritten Chapter; Mixed Identities. **1914** The Man Who Knew; The Barnes of New York; The Awakening of Barbara Dare; The Upper Hand; His Wedded Wife; Fine Feathers Make Fine Birds; His Dominant Passion; Uncle Bill; The Spirit of Christmas; Hearts of Women. **1915** Heredity. **1916** From Out of the Past; Father of Men. **1917** In and Out (aka In Again Out Again). **1921** The Sky Pilot. **1922** Foolish Monte Carlo; The Stranger's Banquet. **1923** Vanity Fair; Haldane of the Secret Service; The Man Life Passed By; The Social Code; Rouged Lips; Scaramouche. **1924** Beau Brummell; Abraham Lincoln; The Arizona Express; One Night in Rome. **1925** Dangerous Innocence; The Gold Hunters; Lady Robin Hood; Three Wise Crooks; Drusilla With a Million; The Unholy Three; Stella Dallas; Phantom of the Opera. **1925** Midnight Limited; The Silent Lover; The Danger Girl; The Volga Boatman. **1927** The Dice Woman; Aflame in the Sky; Yours to Command; Temptations of a Shop Girl. **1928** The Actress; Life's Crossroads. **1929** Devil May-Care; The Godless Girl. **1930** Not so Dumb. **1931** Subway Express; Murder at Midnight. **1932** Tangled Destinies; Manhattan Parade. **1933** One Year Later; Cheating Blondes; Secret Sinners; Strange Adventure; Cowboy Councellor; Vampire Bat; Sing, Sinner, Sing. **1934** Are We Civilized? **1935** False Pretenses.

HUMPHREYS, CECIL
Born: July 21, 1883, Cheltenham, England. Died: Nov. 6, 1947, New York, N.Y. Screen and stage actor. Entered films in 1916.

Appeared in: **1916** The Lifeguardsman; The Pleydell Mystery. **1917** The Sorrows of Satan; The Veiled Woman; The Profligate. **1919** The Romance of Lady Hamilton; The Swindler; The Elusive Pimpernel. **1920** The Pride of the North; The Hour of Trial; The House on the Marsh; The Amateur Gentleman; The Tavern Knight; The Winding Road. **1921** The White Hen; Greatheart; The Four Just Men; Shadow of Evil; The Adventures of Sherlock Holmes series including The Dying Detective. **1922** The Glorious Adventure; Dick Turpin's Ride to York; False Evidence. **1924** The Gayest of the Gay (aka Her Redemption). **1925** Irish Luck. **1929** The Woman in White; The Broken Melody. **1931** 77 Park Lane; The Old Man. **1932** It's a King. **1933** Strictly in Confidence; Dick Turpin. **1934** The Silver Spoon; Oh, No, Doctor!; The Unfinished Symphony (US 1935); Adventure Limited; Guest of Honour. **1935** Knoenigsmark. **1936** Fair Exchange; Accused; Chick; Reasonable Doubt. **1939** Wuthering Heights. **1946** The Razor's Edge. **1947** Desire Me. **1948** A Woman's Vengeance.

HUMPHREYS, DICK
Born: 1929. Died: Dec. 27, 1977, Los Angeles, Calif. (heart attack). Screen, stage, television actor and choreographer.

Appeared in: **1948** If You Knew Susie.

HUN, HADI
Born: 1900, Turkey. Died: Dec., 1969, Istanbul, Turkey (heart attack). Screen and stage actor.

HUNGERFORD, MONA
Born: 1900, England. Died: July 17, 1942, New York, N.Y. Screen, stage and radio actress.

Appeared in: **1914** The Stranger at Hicory Nut Gap.

HUNNICUTT, ARTHUR
Born: Feb. 17, 1911, Gravelly, Ark. Died: Sept. 27, 1979, Woodland Hills, Calif. (cancer). Screen, stage and television actor. Nominated for 1952 Academy Award as Best Supporting Actor in The Big Sky.

Appeared in: **1942** Wildcat (film debut). **1943** Hail to the Rangers; Robin Hood of the Range; Frontier Fury; Law of the Northwest; Pardon My Gun; Riding Through Nevada; Fall In; Johnny Come Lately; Fighting Buckaroo. **1944** Abroad With Two Yanks; Riding West. **1949** Lust for Gold; Pinky; Border Incident; The Great Dan Patch. **1950** A Ticket to Tomahawk; Broken Arrow; Stars in My Crown; Two Flags West. **1951** Passage West; The Red Badge of Courage; Sugarfoot; Distant Drums. **1952** The Big Sky; The Lusty Men. **1953** Split Second; Devil's Canyon. **1954** She Couldn't Say No; The French Line. **1955** The Last Command. **1956** The Kettles in the Ozarks. **1957** The Tall T. **1959** Born Reckless. **1963** The Cardinal. **1964** A Tiger Walks. **1965** Cat Ballou. **1966** Apache Uprising. **1967** The Adventures of Bullwhip Griffin; El Dorado. **1974** The Spikes Gang; Harry and Tonto; Moonrunners. **1975** Winter Hawk.

HUNT, ELEANOR
Died: Sept., 1981. Screen actress.

Appeared in: **1930** Whoopee! **1931** Goldie; Good Sport. **1932** Tess of the Storm Country. **1933** On Ice (short). **1934** Trimmed in Furs (short); Circus Hoodoo (short); Blue Steel; I Hate Women. **1935** Northern Frontier. **1936** Yellow Cargo; Go Get 'Em Haines. **1937** Navy Spy; The Gold Racket; Bank Alarm. **1941** Stolen Paradise.

HUNT, GOVERNOR W. P. (George Wylie Paul Hunt)
Born: Nov. 1, 1859, Huntsville, Mo. Died: Dec. 24, 1934. Former governor of Arizona and screen performer.

Appeared in: **1915** A Western Governor's Humanity.

HUNT, JAY
Born: 1857, Pa. Died: Nov. 18, 1932, Los Angeles, Calif. Screen and stage actor.

Appeared in: **1923** Hunchback of Notre Dame. **1924** After a Million; Yankee Speed. **1925** Counsel for the Defense; Lightnin'. **1926** A Man Four-Square; Three Bad Men; The Gentle Cyclone; The Golden Web; Men of the Night; My Own Pal; Out of the Storm; One Minute to Play. **1927** The Harvester; The Overland Stage; Captain Salvation; Better Days. **1930** The Poor Millionaire. **1931** The Sky Spider.

HUNT, MADGE
Born: 1875, New York, N.Y. Died: Aug. 2, 1935. Screen, stage and vaudeville actress. Married to stage actor and director William Hunt (dec.). Entered films with Reliance approximately 1915.

Appeared in: **1921** False Kisses; The Lamplighter; The Blazing Trail; Reputation. **1923** Can a Woman Love Twice?; Lorna Doone. **1924** Abraham Lincoln. **1926** The Runaway Express; Fiddlesticks. **1927** The Heart of Maryland; The Texas Steer. **1928** Heart Trouble; Sins of the Fathers. **1929** Show Boat.

HUNT, MARTITA
Born: 1900, Argentina. Died: June 13, 1969, London, England. Screen and stage actress.

Appeared in: **1932** Service For Ladies (aka Reserved for Ladies—US); Love on Wheels. **1933** I Was a Spy (US 1934); Friday the Thirteenth. **1934** Too Many Millions. **1935** Mr. What's-His-Name; The Case of Gabriel Perry; First a Girl. **1936** When Knights Were Bold (US 1942); Pot Luck; Tudor Rose (aka Nine Days a Queen—US); The Interrupted Honeymoon. **1937** The Mill on the Floss (US 1939); Good Morning, Boys (aka Where There's a Will—US); Farewell Again (aka Troopship—US 1938). **1938** Second Best Bed; Strange Boarders; Prison Without Bars (US 1939). **1939** Trouble Brewing; A Girl Must

Live (US 1941); The Good Old Days; Young Man's Fancy (US 1943); At the Villa Rose (aka House of Mystery—US 1941); Old Mother Riley Joins Up; The Middle Watch; The Nursemaid Who Disappeared. **1940** Tilly of Bloomsbury; Miss Grant Goes to the Door. **1941** East of Piccadilly (aka The Strangler—US 1942); Freedom Radio (aka A Voice in the Night—US); Quiet Wedding; The Seventh Survivor. **1942** They Flew Alone (aka Wings and the Woman—US); Sabotage at Sea; Lady from Lisbon. **1943** The Man in Grey (US 1945). **1944** Welcome Mr. Washington. **1945** The Wicked Lady (US 1946). **1946** Great Expectations (US 1947). **1947** The Little Ballerina (US 1951); The Ghosts of Berkeley Square. **1948** So Evil My Love; Anna Karenina; My Sister and I. **1952** Treasure Hunt; Folly to be Wise; The Story of Robin Hood and His Merrie Men; It Started in Paradise (US 1953); Meet Me Tonight. **1953** Melba; Tonight at 8:30. **1955** King's Rhapsody (US 1956). **1956** Anastasia; Three Men in a Boat (US 1958). **1957** The Admirable Crichton (aka Paradise Lagoon—US); Dangerous Exile (US 1958). **1958** Bonjour Tristesse; Me and the Colonel. **1960** Bottoms Up; The Brides of Dracula; Song Without End. **1961** Mr. Topaze (aka I Like Money—US 1962). **1962** The Wonderful World of the Brothers Grimm. **1964** Becket; The Unsinkable Molly Brown. **1965** Bunny Lake is Missing. **1968** The Long Day's Dying. **1969** The Best House in London.

HUNT, PAULA *See* DEAN, PAULA

HUNT, REA M.
Born: 1893. Died: June 21, 1961. Screen actor. Was one of the original Keystone Kops.

HUNTER, EDNA
Born: 1876, Toledo, Ohio. Died: Feb. 5, 1920, New York, N.Y. Screen and stage actress.

Appeared in: **1915** The Soul of Broadway; The Two Orphans. **1916** Half a Rogue; Marble Heart; Prince in a Pawn Shop; Circular Room; Man Across the Street; The Common Law. **1917** Two Little Imps; Jimmie Dale, Alias the Grey Seal (serial). **1918** Deluxe Annie.

HUNTER, GLENN
Born: 1897, Highland Hills, N.Y. Died: Dec. 30, 1945, New York, N.Y. Screen, stage and vaudeville actor.

Appeared in: **1921** The Case of Becky. **1922** The Country Flapper; The Cradle Buster; Smilin' Through. **1923** Puritan Passions; Second Fiddle; Youthful Cheaters; The Scarecrow. **1924** Grit; The Silent Watcher; Merton of the Movies; West of the Water Tower. **1925** The Little Giant; His Buddy's Wife. **1926** The Pinch Hitter; The Broadway Boob; The Romance of a Million Dollars; The Little Giant.

HUNTER, HARRISON
Died: Jan. 2, 1923, Boston, Mass. (complications after surgery). Screen and stage actor.

Appeared in: **1920** The Strongest.

HUNTER, IAN
Born: June 13, 1900, Cape Town, S.Africa. Died: Sept. 24, 1975, England. Screen, stage, television actor and screenwriter.

Appeared in: **1922** Mr. Oddy. **1924** Not for Sale. **1925** Confessions; A Girl of London. **1927** Downhill (aka When Boys Leave Home—US 1928); Easy Virtue (US 1928); The Ring. **1928** His House in Order; The Physician (US 1929); The Thoroughbred; The Valley of the Ghosts. **1929** Syncopation. **1930** Escape. **1931** Cape Forlorn (aka The Love Storm—US); Sally in Our Alley. **1932** The Water Gypsies; The Sign of Four; Marry Me. **1933** The Man from Toronto; Orders is Orders (US 1934); Skipper of the Osprey (short). **1934** Something Always Happens; The Silver Spoon; The Night of the Party; The Church Mouse (US 1935); No Escape; Death at Broadcasting House. **1935** The Phantom Light; Lazybones; Lazybones; The Morals of Marcus (US 1936); The Girl from Tenth Avenue; Jalna; A Midsummer Night's Dream; I Found Stella Parrish; Dinky. **1936** The White Angel; To Mary—With Love; The Devil is a Sissy; Stolen Holiday. **1937** Call It a Day; Another Dawn; That Certain Woman; Confession; 52nd Street. **1938** Comet Over Broadway; The Sisters; The Adventures of Robin Hood; Always Goodbye; Secrets of an Actress. **1939** Tower of London; Tarzan Finds a Son; Yes, My Darling Daughter; The Little Princess; Broadway Serenade; Maisie; Bad Little Angel. **1940** Strange Cargo; Bitter Sweet; Broadway Melody of 1940; Dulcy; The Long Voyage Home; Gallant Sons. **1941** Billy the Kid; Dr. Jekyll and Mr. Hyde; Andy Hardy's Private Secretary; Come Live with Me; Ziegfeld Girl; Smilin' Through. **1942** A Yank at Eton. **1943** Forever and a Day; It Comes Up Love. **1946** Bedelia (US 1947). **1947** White Cradle Inn (aka High Fury—US 1948); The White Unicorn (aka Bad Sisters—US 1948). **1949** Edward, My Son. **1952** It Started in Paradise (US 1953).

1953 Appointment in London (US 1955). **1954** Eight O'Clock Walk (US 1955); Don't Blame the Stork. **1956** The Battle of the River Plate (aka Pursuit of the Graf Spee—US 1957); The Door in the Wall (short). **1957** Fortune is a Woman (aka She Played With Fire—US 1958). **1958** Rockets Galore (aka Mad Little Island—US). **1959** Northwest Frontier (aka Flame Over India—US 1960). **1960** The Bulldog Breed. **1961** The Queen's Guards (US 1963); Dr. Blood's Coffin (aka Face of Evil); The Treasure of Monte Cristo (aka The Secret of Monte Cristo—US). **1962** Guns of Darkness (aka Act of Mercy).

HUNTER, JACKIE
Born: 1901, Canada. Died: Nov. 21, 1951, London, England. Screen, stage, vaudeville and radio actor.

HUNTER, JEFFREY (Henry Herman McKinnies)
Born: Nov. 23, 1926, New Orleans, La. Died: May 27, 1969, Van Nuys, Calif. (injuries from fall). Screen, stage, radio and television actor. Married to actress Emily McLaughlin and divorced from actress Barbara Rush, and Dusty Bartlett.

Appeared in: **1951** Call Me Mister; The Frogman; Take Care of My Little Girl; Fourteen Hours. **1952** Red Skies of Montana (aka Smoke Jumpers); Belles on Their Toes; Lure of the Wilderness; Dreamboat. **1953** Single Handed (aka Sailor of the King—US). **1954** Three Young Texans; Princess of the Nile. **1955** Seven Angry Men; White Feather; Seven Cities of Gold. **1956** The Proud Ones; A Kiss Before Dying; The Great Locomotive Chase; Four Girls in Town; The Searchers. **1957** The True Story of Jesse James; The Way to the Gold; No Down Payment; Gun for a Coward. **1958** The Last Hurrah; In Love and War; Count Five and Die; Mardi Gras. **1960** Key Witness; Hell to Eternity; Sergeant Rutledge. **1961** Man-Trap; King of Kings. **1962** The Longest Day; No Man Is An Island. **1964** The Man form Galveston; Gold for the Caesars. **1965** Vendetta; Brainstorm; The Woman Who Wouldn't Die. **1966** Dimension 5. **1967** A Witch Without a Broom; The Christmas Kid; A Guide for the Married Man. **1968** The Private Navy of Sgt. O'Farrell; Custer of the West; Sexy Susan at the King's Court; Joe, Find a Place to Die. **1969** The Hostess Also Has a County.

HUNTER, RICHARD
Born: 1875. Died: Dec. 22, 1962, Santa Monica, Calif. Cowboy screen actor.

HUNTLEY, CHET (Chester Robert Huntley)
Born: 1912, Cardwell, Mont. Died: Mar. 20, 1974, Bozeman, Mont. (lung cancer). Television, radio news commentator and screen actor.

Appeared in: **1943** Gung Ho (narrator). **1949** I Cheated the Law; Arctic Manhunt. **1952** The Pride of St. Louis. **1954** Executive Suite (voice). **1955** Mau Mau (narrator). **1958** Cry Terror. **1959** Behind the Great Wall (narrator).

HUNTLEY, FRED (aka FRED HUNTLY)
Born: 1862. Died: Nov. 1, 1931, Hollywood, Calif. (heart attack). Screen and stage actor.

Appeared in: **1918** Heart of Wetona. **1919** Heart o' the Hills; Everywoman. **1921** Brewster's Millions; Bronze Bell; Face of the World; Gasoline Gus; A Prince There Was; A Wise Fool; Little Minister; What Every Woman Knows. **1922** Crimson Challenge; Man With Two Mothers; Borderland; North of the Rio Grande; To Have and to Hold; While the City Sleeps. **1923** Peg O' My Heart; Law of the Lawless; Where the North Begins; To the Last Man; Call of the Canyon; Go Getter. **1924** The Age of Innocence; Thundering Hoofs. **1927** King of Kings.

HUNTRESS, MARY
Born: Richmond, Va. Died: Dec. 11, 1933, Manila, P.I. Screen and stage actress.

Appeared in: **1921** Romance Promoters; It Can Be Done; The Millionaire. **1922** Elope If You Must.

HURLEY, JOHN
Born: 1920. Died: Apr. 9, 1978, Los Angeles, Calif.? (cancer). Screen, stage actor and film extra.

HURLEY, JULIA
Born: 1847, New York, N.Y. Died: June 4, 1927, New York, N.Y. Screen and stage actress.

Appeared in: **1913** Blood and Water; A Child's Intuition. **1914** The Jungle. **1915** The Price He Paid. **1916** Gold and the Woman. **1918** Love's Conquest. **1919** Little Women; Poison Pen. **1920** Easy to Get; The Cost; Guilty of Love; New York Idea. **1921** The Bride's Play; Jane Eyre. **1924** Argentine Love. **1925** The Little French Girl; The Making of O'Malley. **1926** Married?

HURN, DOUGLAS
Born: 1925, England. Died: Oct. 22, 1974, London, England. Screen, stage actor and television producer.

HURST, BRANDON
Born: Nov. 30, 1866, London, England. Died: July 15, 1947, Burbank, Calif. (arteriosclerosis). Stage and screen actor.

Appeared in: **1923** The Hunchback of Notre Dame; World's Applause; Legally Dead. **1924** He Who Gets Slapped; Thief of Bagdad; Silent Watcher; Cytherea; Lover of Camille; One Night in Rome. **1925** Lightnin' Lady. **1926** Amateur Gentleman; Grand Duchess and the Waiter; Secret Orders; Lady of the Harem; Volcano; Enchanted Hill; Made for Love; Paris at Midnight; Rainmaker; Shamrock Handicap. **1927** Seventh Heaven; High School Hero; Love; King of Kings; Annie Laurie. **1928** Man Who Laughs; Interference; News Parade. **1929** Voice of the Storm; Her Private Life; Greene Murder Case; Wolf of Wall Street. **1930** High Society Blues; Eyes of the World. **1931** A Connecticut Yankee; Right of Way; Young as You Feel; Murder at Midnight. **1932** Down to Earth; White Zombies; Sherlock Holmes; Murders in the Rue Morgue; Scarface; Midnight Lady. **1933** Cavalcade. **1934** Sequoia; Bombay Mail; Lost Patrol; Little Minister; House of Rothschild. **1935** The Great Impersonation; While the Patient Slept; Bright Eyes; Red Morning; Bonnie Scotland; Woman in Red. **1936** The Charge of the Light Brigade; Gasoloons (short); The Plough and the Stars; The Moon's Our Home; Mary of Scotland. **1937** The Firefly; Maid of Salem; Wee Willie Winkle. **1938** If I Were King; Four Men and a Prayer; Suez. **1939** The Adventures of Sherlock Holmes; Stanley and Livingstone. **1940** The Blue Bird; If I Had My Way; Rhythm on the River. **1941** Charley's Aunt; Sign of the Wolf. **1942** Mad Martindales; The Remarkabel Andrew; Tennessee Johnson; The Ghost of Frankenstein, The Pied Piper; Road to Happiness. **1943** Dixie; Frankenstein Meets the Wolfman. **1944** The Princess and the Pirate; The Man in Half Moon Street. **1945** Road to Utopia; The Corn is Green; House of Frankenstein. **1946** Monsieur Beaucaire. **1947** Road to Rio; My Favorite Brunette; My Wild Irish Rose.

HURST, PAUL C.
Born: 1888, Tulare County, Calif. Died: Feb. 27, 1953, Hollywood, Calif. (suicide). Screen, stage actor, film director and screenwriter.

Appeared in: **1912** The Stolen Invention; When Youth Meets Youth; Red Wing and the Paleface; Driver of the Deadwood Coach; The Mayor's Crusade. **1913** The Big Horn Massacre; Daughter of the Underworld; The Struggle; On the Brink of Ruin; The Last Blockhouse; The Redemption. **1914** The Barrister of Ignorance; The Rajah's Vow; The Smugglers of Lone Isle. **1915** The Pitfall. **1916** The Social Pirates; The Missing Millionaire; Whispering Smith; Medicine Bend; Judith of the Cumberlands; The Manager of the B & A; The Moth and the Star; A Voice in the Wilderness; The Taking of Stingaree; To the Vile Dust; The Black Hole of Glenranald; The Millionaire Plunger. **1917** A Race for a Fortune (serial); The Railroad Raiders (serial); The Further Adventures of Stingaree (series) including: The Jackaroo and The Tracking of Stingaree. **1918** Smashing Through. **1926** The High Hand; The Outlaw Express. **1927** Buttons; The Valley of Giants; The Red Raiders; The Devil's Saddle; The Man from Hardpan; The Overland Stage. **1928** The Cossacks. **1929** Tide of Empire; The California Mail; The Lawless Legion; The Rainbow; Sailor's Holiday. **1930** The Swellhead; Mountain Justice; The Runaway Bride; Hot Curves; Shadow of the Law; Paradise Island; Borrowed Wives; The Third Alarm; Oh, Yeah?; The Racketeer; His First Command; Officer O'Brien; Lucky Larkin. **1931** The Single Sin; The Secret Six; The Kick In; The Public Defender; Sweepstakes; Bad Company; Terror by Night; The Secret Witness. **1932** Panama Flow; The 13th Guest; Hold 'Em Jail; The Big Stampede; My Pal the King. **1933** Island of Lost Souls; Men Are Such Fools; Hold Your Man; Saturday's Millions; Women in His Life; Scarlet River; Terror Abroad; The Sphinx; Tugboat Annie; Day of Reckoning. **1934** The Big Race; Among the Missing; Take the Stand; Sequoia; The Line-Up; Midnight Alibi; There Ain't No Justice (short). **1935** Tomorrow's Youth; Star of Midnight; The Case of the Curious Bride; Mississippi; Shadow of Doubt; Public Hero No. 1; Calm Yourself; Wilderness Mail; The Gay Deception; Riffraff. **1936** Mr. Deeds Goes to Washington; The Blackmailer; It Had to Happen; To Mary With Love; I'd Give My Life; The Gay Desperado; We Who Are About to Die; North of Nome; Robin Hood of El Dorado. **1937** Trouble in Morocco; You Can't Beat Love; Super Sleuth; Fifty Roads to Town; Wake Up and Live; Angel's Holiday; This is My Affair; Slave Ship; Wife, Doctor and Nurse; Danger—Love at Work; Ali Baba Goes to Town; Second Honeymoon; Small Town Boy; She's No Lady; The Lady; The Lady Fights Back. **1938** In Old Chicago; Rebecca of Sunnybrook Farm; Island in the Sky; Alexander's Ragtime Band; Josette; My Lucky Star; Hold That Co-ed; Thanks for Everything; No Time to Marry; Prison Break; The Last Express; Secrets of a Nurse. **1939** The Glove Slingers (short); Broadway Serenade; Cafe Society;

Topper Takes a Trip; It Could Happen to You; Each Dawn I Die; Remember?; The Kid from Kokomo; Quick Millions; Bad Lands; On Your Toes; Gone With the Wind. **1940** Edison the Man; Torrid Zone; Goin' Fishing (short); They Drive by Night; South of Karango; The Westerner; Heaven With a Barbed Wire Fence; Tugboat Annie Sails Again; Star Dust; Men Against the Sky. **1941** The Parson of Panamint; This Woman is Mine; Tall, Dark and Handsome; The Great Mr. Nobody; Ellery Queen and the Murder Ring; Bowery Boy; Petticoat Politics; Virginia; Caught in a Draft. **1942** Pardon My Stripes; Sundown Jim; Night in New Orleans; Dudes Are Pretty People. **1943** The Ox-Bow Incident; Hi'Ya, Chum; Young and Willing; Jack London; The Sky's the Limit; Coney Island; Calaboose. **1944** The Ghost That Walks Alone; Greenwich Village; Barbary Coast Gent; Something for the Boys; Girl Rush; Summer Storm. **1945** One Exciting Night; Nob Hill; The Big Show-Off; Dakota; The Dollly Sisters; Penthouse Rhythm; Midnight Manhunt; Scared Stiff; Steppin' in Society. **1946** In Old Sacramento; The Virginian; The Plainsman and the Lady; Murder in the Music Hall. **1947** The Angel and the Badman; Death Valley; Under Colorado Skies. **1948** The Arizona Ranger; California Firebrand; Heart of Virginia; Son of God's Country; Gun Smugglers; Yellow Sky; A Miracle Can Happen; Old Los Angeles; Madonna of the Desert. **1949** Law of the Golden West; Outcasts of the Trail; Prince of the Plains; Ranger of Cherokee Strip; San Antone Ambush; South of Rio. **1950** The Missourians; The Old Frontier; Pioneer Marshal; The Vanishing Westerner. **1951** Million Dollar Pursuit. **1952** Big Jim McLain; Toughest Man in Arizona. **1953** The Sun Shines Bright; Pine Bluff.

HURT, MARY
Born: 1889. Died: Oct. 6, 1976, Woodland Hills, Calif. Screen actress and film extra. Entered films in 1926.

HUSING, TED (Edward Husing)
Born: Nov. 27, 1901, Bronx, N.Y. Died: Aug. 10, 1962, Pasadena, Calif. (brain tumor). Screen actor, radio announcer, screenwriter and sportswriter.

Appeared in: **1932-33** Sport Thrills series. **1933** Mr. Broadway. **1934-37** Grantland Rice Sportlights (narrator). **1935-37** Broadway Highlights. **1936-37** Hollywood Star Reporter. **1937-38** Paramount shorts. **1940** Broadway Highlights (narrator). **1948** The Olympic Games (narrator). **1950** To Please a Lady.

HUSSENOT, OLIVIER
Born: 1913. Died: Sept., 1978, Paris, France. Screen, stage and television actor.

Appeared in: **1952** The Amazing Monsieur Fabre; Fanfan the Tulip (US 1953); Voyage to America. **1954** Paris Incident. **1955** Bedeviled. **1956** The Grand Maneuver. **1958** Inspector Maigret; Lovers of Paris (aka Pot Bouille); The Roots of Heaven. **1965** Sfida a Rio Bravo (Gunmen of the Rio Grande). **1968** A Flea in Her Ear.

HUSSY, JIMMY (aka JIMMY HUSSEY)
Born: Jan. 19, 1891, Chicago, Ill. Died: Nov. 20, 1930, Woodcliff, N.Y. (stomach trouble and tuberculosis). Screen, stage and vaudeville actor. Appeared in early Vitaphone shorts.

HUSTING, LUCILLE
Born: c. 1900. Died: June 30, 1972, Hollywood, Calif. (stroke). Screen, radio and television actress. Married to actor Leo Curley (dec. 1960).

HUSTON, PHILIP
Born: 1908. Died: July 25, 1980, New York, N.Y. Screen and stage actor. Father of actress Dulcie Huston.

Appeared in: **1936** The Big Game. **1937** We're On the Jury; The Man Who Found Himself; Behind the Headlines. **1948** Close-Up.

HUSTON, WALTER
Born: Apr. 6, 1884, Toronto, Canada. Died: Apr. 7, 1950, Beverly Hills, Calif. (aneurism). Screen, stage and vaudeville actor. Divorced from Bayonne Whipple. Married to actress Nan Sutherland (dec. 1973). Father of film director John Huston. Won 1948 Academy Award for Best Supporting Actor in Treasure of Sierra Madre; Nominated for 1936 Academy Award for Best Actor in Dodsworth and in 1941 for All That Money Can Buy; and in 1942 as Best Supporting Actor in Yankee Doodle Dandy.

Appeared in: **1929** Gentlemen of the Press (film debut); The Lady Lies; The Bishop's Candlesticks (short); The Carnival Man (short); Two Americans (short); The Virginian. **1930** How I Play Golf—The Spoon (short); The Bad Man; Abraham Lincoln; The Virtuous Sin. **1931** The Criminal Code; The Star Witness; The Ruling Voice; Upper Underworld. **1932** A Woman from Monte Carlo; A House Divided; Law and Order; The Beast of the City; The Wet Parade; American Madness; Rain; Night Court; Kongo. **1933** The Prizefighter and the Lady; Hell Below; Gabriel Over the White House; Ann Vickers; Storm at Daybreak. **1934** Keep 'Em Rolling. **1935** The Tunnel (aka Transatlantic Tunnel). **1936** Rhodes of Africa (aka Rhodes—US); Dodsworth. **1938** Of Human Hearts. **1939** The Light That Failed. **1941** All That Money Can Buy; Swamp Water; Maltese Falcon; The Shanghai Gesture. **1942** Our Russian Front (narr. Russian war relief documentary); Always in My Heart; Yankee Doodle Dandy; Prelude to War (narr. U.S. War Dept. documentary); In This Our Life. **1943** Armored Attack (documentary); Edge of Darkness; The Outlaw (released nationally 1950); Mission to Moscow; The North Star; Safeguarding Military Information (Army training film documentary). **1944** Dragon Seed. **1945** And Then There Were None. **1946** Dragonwyck; Duel in the Sun. **1947** Let There Be Light (Signal Corps film). **1948** Summer Holiday; The Treasure of the Sierra Madre. **1949** The Great Sinner. **1950** The Furies. **1952** The Devil and Daniel Webster (reissue and retitle of All That Money Can Buy, 1941).

HUTCHINS, RICHARD
Born: 1876. Died: Sept. 5, 1950, New York, N.Y. Silent screen actor.

HUTCHINSON, CANON CHARLES
Born: 1887, England. Died: Apr. 22, 1969, Brighton, England. Actor Canon Charles Hutchinson is not to be confused with American actor and director "Lightning Hutch" (Charles Hutchinson). Canon Charles Hutchinson was former president of the Actors Church Union.

HUTCHINSON, HARRY
Born: 1893, Dublin, Ireland. Died: Mar. 16, 1980, Milan, Italy. Screen, stage and television actor.

Appeared in: **1957** The Story of Esther Costello. **1958** Alive and Kicking (US 1964); She Didn't Say No! (US 1962). **1967** Up the Junction (US 1968); Salt and Pepper.

HUTCHINSON, MURIEL
Born: 1915, New York. Died: Mar. 24, 1975, New York, N.Y. (cancer). Stage and screen actress.

Appeared in: **1939** The Women; Another Thin Man; One Third of a Nation.

HUTCHINSON, WILLIAM
Born: May 16, 1869, Edinburgh, Scotland. Died: Sept. 7, 1918, Los Angeles, Calif. Stage and screen actor.

Appeared in: **1912** Her Education; The Count of Monte Cristo. **1913** The Governor's Daughter; The Three Wise Men; Yankee Doodle Dixie; The Old Clerk; An Old Actor; The Beaded Buckskin Bag; The Flight of the Crow. **1914** The Rummage Sale. **1915** Landing the Hose Reel; Sho Fly; The Comeback of Percy; A Thing or Two in Movies; The Run on Percy; The Chronicles of Bloom Center; The Manicure Girl; Perkin's Pep Producer. **1916** Diamonds are Trumps; Apple Butter; No Sir-ee Bob; Small Town Stuff; Regeneration of Jim Halsey. **1917** The Happiness of Three Women; Everybody was Satisfied; Baseball at Mudville; The Fair Barbarian. **1918** Captain Kidd, Jr.

HUTH, HAROLD
Born: 1892, Huddersfield, Yorkshire, England. Died: Oct. 26, 1967, London, England. Screen, stage actor, film director, film producer and screenwriter.

Appeared in: **1927** One of the Best. **1928** A South Sea Bubble; The Triumph of the Scarlet Pimpernel (aka The Scarlet Daredevil—US 1929); Balaclava (aka Jaws of Hell—US 1931); Sir or Madam. **1929** When Knights Were Bold; The Silver King; City of Play; Downstream. **1930** Hours of Loneliness (aka An Obvious Situation); Leave it to Me. **1931** Guilt; Bracelets; The Outsider; Down River; A Honeymoon Adventure (aka Footsteps in the Night—US 1933). **1932** Aren't We All?; The First Mrs. Fraser; Sally Bishop; Rome Express; The Flying Squad; The World, The Flesh and the Devil. **1933** My Lucky Star; The Ghoul; Discord. **1934** The Camels Are Coming. **1937** Take My Tip. **1942** This was Paris. **1951** Blackmailed.

HUTTON, JIM (James Hutton)
Born: 1934, Binghamton, N.Y. Died: June 2, 1979, Los Angeles, Calif. (cancer). Screen, stage and television actor. Father of Rebecca, Heidi and actor Tim Hutton.

Appeared in: **1958** A Time to Love, and a Time to Die. **1959** Ten Seconds to Hell. **1960** The Subterraneans; Where the Boys Are. **1961** The Honeymoon Machine; Bachelor in Paradise. **1962** Period of Adjustment; The Horizontal Lieutenant. **1964** Looking for Love. **1965** Major Dundee; The Hallelujah Trail; Never Too Late. **1966** Walk, Don't Run; The Trouble With Angels. **1967** Who's Minding the Mint. **1968** The Green Berets; Hellfighters. **1975** Psychic Killer.

HUTTON, LEONA
Born: 1892. Died: Apr. 1, 1949, Toledo, Ohio (overdose of sleeping pills). Screen and stage actress. Appeared in films from 1913 to 1924.

Appeared in: **1924** The Painted Lady.

HUXHAM, KENDRICK
Born: 1892. Died: July 24, 1967, Hollywood, Calif. (heart attack). Screen and stage actor.

Appeared in: **1961** Pirates of Tortuga. **1967** Games.

HYAMS, JOHN
Born: 1877, Syracuse, N.Y. Died: Dec. 9, 1940, Hollywood, Calif. Screen, stage, vaudeville and minstrel actor. Appeared in vaudeville with his wife actress Leila McIntyre (dec. 1953). Father of actress Leila Hyams.

Appeared in: **1927** Life of an Actres; All in Fun (short). **1929** Broadway Scandals. **1930** Cameo Kirby; Swell People; Mind Your Business; Give Me Action; Some Babies. **1934** The Mighty Barnum. **1935** Murder in the Fleet; In Caliente; The Virginia Judge. **1936** And Sudden Death. **1937** Pick a Star; A Day at the Races. **1939** The Housekeeper's Daughter.

HYAMS, LEILA
Born: May 1, 1905, New York, N.Y. Died: Dec. 4, 1977, Bel-Air, Calif. Screen, stage and vaudeville actress. Daughter of vaudeville actor John Hyams (dec. 1940) and actress Leila McIntyre (dec. 1953). Entered films in 1924.

Appeared in: **1924** Sandra. **1926** The Kick-Off; Summer Bachelors. **1927** The Brute; The Bush Leaguer; One-Round Hogan; White Pants Willie; The Wizard. **1928** The Crimson City; The Branded Sombrero; A Girl in Every Port; Land of the Silver Fox; Honor Bound. **1929** The Idle Rich; Masquerade; Spite Marriage; Wonder of Women; The Thirteenth Chair; Alias Jimmy Valentine; The Far Call; Hurricane. **1930** The Big House; The Bishop Murder Case; The Girl Said No; The Flirting Widow; Part Time Wife; Sweethearts and Wives; Sins of the Children; Way Out West; Way for a Sailor; Richest Man in the World. **1931** Jackie Cooper's Christmas Party (short); Men Call It Love; Stepping Out; Gentlemen's Fate; Phantom of Paris; New Adventures of Get Rich Quick Wallingford; Surrender. **1932** Freaks; Red Headed Woman; The Big Broadcast. **1933** Island of Lost Souls; Constant Woman; Sing Sinner Sing; Saturday's Millions. **1934** The Poor Rich; Affairs of a Gentleman. **1935** Ruggles of Red Gap; No Ransom; People Will Talk; $1,000 a Minute. **1936** Yellow Dust. **1940** First Aid (short).

HYATT, CLAYTON
Died: July, 1932, Windsor, Ontario, Canada (suicide—hanging). Screen actor.

HYATT, HERMAN
Born: 1906, Russia. Died: Jan. 24, 1968, Baltimore, Md. Screen and burlesque actor.

HYLAN, DONALD
Born: 1899. Died: June 20, 1968, New York, N.Y. (heart attack). Screen, stage and television actor. Appeared in silent films.

HYLAND, AUGUSTIN ALLEN
Born: 1905. Died: Feb. 8, 1963, Hollywood, Calif. Screen actor and stand-in for James Cagney.

HYLAND, DIANA (Diana Gentner)
Born: 1936, Cleveland Heights, Ohio. Died: Mar. 27, 1977, Westwood, Calif. (cancer). Screen, stage and television actress.

Appeared in: **1964** One Man's Way (film debut). **1966** The Chase; Smoky. **1968** Jigsaw.

HYLTON, JANE (Gwen Clark)
Born: July 16, 1927, London, England. Died: Feb. 28, 1979, Glasgow, Scotland (heart attack). Screen, stage and television actress.

Appeared in: **1946** Day Break (US 1949—film debut); The Years Between (US 1947); A Girl in a Million (US 1950). **1947** The Upturned Glass; Dear Murderer; When the Bough Breaks; It Always Rains on Sunday (US 1949); Holiday Camp (US 1948). **1948** My Brother's Keeper (US 1949); My Sister and I; Here Come the Huggetts (US 1950). **1949** Passport to Pimlico. **1950** Dance Hall. **1951** Out of True; The Quiet Woman. **1952** Tall Headlines (aka The Frightened Bride—US 1953); It Started in Paradise (US 1953). **1954** Burnt Evidence; The Weak and the Wicked. **1955** Secret Venture. **1957** You Pay Your Money. **1959** Deadly Record; Violent Moment (US 1966); Devil's Bait. **1960** Night Train for Inverness; Circus of Horrors. **1961** House of Mystery. **1962** The Monster. **1963** Bitter Harvest.

HYLTON, RICHARD
Born: 1921. Died: May 12, 1962, San Francisco, Calif. (heart attack). Screen, stage and television actor.

Appeared in: **1949** Lost Boundaries. **1950** Halls of Montezuma. **1951** Secret of Convict Lake; Fixed Bayonets! **1952** The Pride of St. Louis.

HYMACK, MR. *See* MC PHERSON, QUINTON

HYMAN, ROBERT
Born: 1885. Died: Mar. 30, 1934. Screen actor.

HYMER, JOHN B.
Born: 1876. Died: June 16, 1953, Los Angeles, Calif. Screen, stage, vaudeville actor, screenwriter playwright and author. Married to vaudeville actress Elinor Kent (aka Elsie Kent). Father of actor Warren Hymer (dec. 1948).

Appeared in: **1914** The Pah Forbidden.

HYMER, WARREN
Born: Feb. 25, 1906, New York, N.Y. Died: Mar. 25, 1948, Los Angeles, Calif. Stage and screen actor. Son of actor John B. Hymer (dec. 1953) and actress Elsie Kent (dec. 1957). Divorced from actress Virginia Meyer.

Appeared in: **1929** The Cock-Eyed World; The Far Call; The Girl from Havana; Speak-easy; Frozen Justice; Fox Movietone Follies of 1929. **1930** Born Reckless; Lone Star Ranger; Oh, For a Man!; Men Without Women; Sinner's Holiday; Up the River; Men on Call. **1931** The Spider; Seas Beneath; Goldie; The Unholy Garden; Charlie Chan Carries On. **1932** Hold 'Em Jail; One Way Passage; The Night Mayor; Madison Square Garden; Love is a Racket. **1933** 20,000 Years in Sing Sing; I Love That Man; Midnight Mary; Her First Mate; King for a Night; My Woman; In the Money; The Billion Dollar Scandal; Mysterious Rider; A Lady's Profession. **1934** The Gold Ghost (short); George White's Scandals; The Crosby Case; Belle of the Nineties; Little Miss Marker; The Cat's Paw; She Loves Me Not; Young and Beautiful; One is Guilty; Woman Unafraid; Kid Millions. **1935** Hold 'Em Yale; The Gilded Lily; The Case of the Curious Bride; The Daring Young Man; Silk Hat Kid; She Gets Her Man; Confidential; Show Them No Mercy; Navy Wife; Hitch Hike Lady; Straight from the Heart; Our Little Girl; Beauty's Daughter; Hong Kong Nights. **1936** Tango; Desert Justice; The Widow from Monte Carlo; The Leavenworth Case; Laughing Irish Eyes; Everybody's Old Man; 36 Hours to Kill; Mr. Deeds Goes to Town; San Francisco; Rhythm on the Range; Nobody's Fool; Love Letters of a Star. **1937** You Only Live Once; Join the Marines; Navy Blues; Meet the Boy Friend; Sea Racketeers; We Have Our Moments; Wake Up and Live; Ali Baba Goes to Town; Married before Breakfast; Bad Guy; Tainted Money; She's Dangerous. **1938** Lady Behave; Arson Gang Busters; Joy of Living; Gateway; Submarine Patrol; Thanks for Everything; Bluebeard's Eighth Wife; You and Me. **1939** The Lady and the Mob; Coast Guard; Destry Rides Again; Boy Friend; Calling All Marines; Charlie McCarthy, Detective; Mr. Moto in Danger Island. **1940** I Can't Give You Anything But Love, Baby; Love, Honor and Oh-Baby! **1941** Meet John Doe; Buy Me That Town; Birth of the Blues; Skylark. **1942** Mr. Wise Guy; So's Your Aunt Emma; Henry and Dizzy; Dr. Broadway; Girl's Town; Baby Face Morgan; She's in the Army; One Thrilling Night; Phantom Killer; Police Bullets; Jail House Blues; Meet the Mob; Lure of the Islands. **1943** Danger! Women at Work; Hitler—Dead or Alive; Gangway for Tomorrow. **1944** Since You Went Away; Three is a Family. **1946** Gentleman Joe Palooka; Joe Palooka, Champ.

HYNES, JOHN E.
Born: 1853. Died: Apr. 12, 1931, Long Island, N.Y. Stage and screen actor.

HYTTEN, OLAF
Born: 1888, Scotland. Died: Mar. 11, 1955, Los Angeles, Calif. (heart attack). Screen actor.

Appeared in: **1921** The Knave of Diamonds; Demos (aka Why Men Forget—US); Money; Sonia (aka The Woman Who Came Back—US 1922); The Leaves From My Life series including The Girl Who Came Back. **1922** The Knight Errant; Trapped by the Mormons; The Wonderful Story; Tense Moments from Opera series including The Bride of Lammermoor; The Crimson Circle; The Missioner; His Wife's Husband; "Famous Poems by George" series including Sir Rupert's Wife; The Further Adventure of Sherlock Holmes including The Stockbrokers Cousin. **1923** Out to Win; The Little Door into the World (aka The Evil That Men Do); Chu Chin Chow (US 1925); A Gamble with Hearts; The Reverse of the Medal; The Cause of all the Trouble. **1924** The White Shadow (aka White Shadows—US); It Is the Law.

1925 The Salvation Hunters. **1928** Old Age Handicap. **1929** Kitty; Master and Man; City of Play. **1930** Grumpy; Playboy of Paris. **1931** Daughter of the Dragon. **1933** Lost in Limehouse or Lady Esmerelda's Predicament (short); Lady Killer; Berkeley Square. **1934** Jimmy the Gent; Mystery Liner; Jane Eyre; Money Means Nothing; Glamour. **1935** Clive of India; Strange Wives; Anna Karenina; The Spanish Cape Mystery; Becky Sharp; The Dark Angel; Two Sinners; The Last Outpost; Les Miserables; Bonnie Scotland. **1936** Sylvia Scarlett; Lloyds of London; Camille; The House of a Thousand Candles; The Last of the Mohicans; White Hunter. **1937** Angel; We Have Our Moments; Easy Living; The Good Earth; California Straight Ahead; I Cover the War; Dangerous Holiday; First Lady. **1938** Marie Antoinette; The Lone Wolf in Paris; Adventures of Robin Hood; Blonde Cheat; Youth Takes a Fling. **1939** We Are Not Alone; Little Accident; Andy Hardy Gets Spring Fever; Rulers of the Sea; Allegheny Uprising; Our Leading Citizen. **1940** Drums of Fu Manchu (serial); Captain Caution; Arise, My Love; Our Neighbors, The Carters; Gaucho Serenade. **1941** Footsteps in the Dark; Washington Melodrama; All the World's a Stooge (short); That Hamilton Woman. **1942** This Above All; Son of Fury; The Black Swan; Sherlock Holmes; Spy Ship; The Ghost of Frankenstein; Sherlock Holmes and the Voice of Terror; To Be or Not To Be; Bedtime Story; Destination Unknown; The Great Commandment. **1943** Hit Parade of 1943; Happy Go Lucky; Sherlock Holmes Faces Death. **1944** National Velvet; Our Hearts Were Young and Gay; The Lodger; The Return of the Vampire. **1945** Hold That Blonde; The Woman in Green; My Name is Julia Ross; The Brighton Strangler; Christmas in Connecticut; House of Frankenstein. **1946** Magnificent Doll; The Notorious Lone Wolf; Three Strangers; Black Beauty. **1947** If Winter Comes; The Private Affairs of Bel Ami; Bells of San Angelo; That Way With Women. **1948** Unconquered; Shanghai Chest. **1950** Kim; Fancy Pants; Rogues of Sherwood Forest. **1952** Les Miserables (and 1935 version); Against All Flags. **1953** Perils of the Jungle.

IHNAT, STEVE
Born: 1935, Hungary or Czechoslovakia? Died: May 12, 1972, Cannes, France (heart attack). Screen, television actor, film director and screenwriter. Married to actress Sally Carter.

Appeared in: **1958** Dragstrip Riot (film debut). **1962** Passion Street (aka Bourbon Street). **1966** The Chase. **1967** Hour of the Gun; In Like Flint. **1968** Madigan; Kona Coast; Countdown (aka Moon Shot). **1970** Zig Zag. **1972** Fuzz.

ILLING, PETER
Born: 1899, Vienna, Austria. Died: Oct. 29, 1966, London, England. Screen, stage, television and radio actor. Was the voice of Winston Churchill on BBC European radio programs.

Appeared in: **1947** The End of the River. **1948** Against the Wind (US 1949). **1949** Eureka Stockade; Floodtide; Madness of the Heart (US 1950); Children of Chance; Traveller's Joy (US 1951). **1950** State Secret (aka The Great Manhunt—US 1951); My Daughter Joy (aka Operation X—US 1951). **1951** I'll Get You for This (aka Lucky Nick Cain—US); Outcast of the Islands. **1952** The Woman's Angle (US 1954); 24 Hours of a Woman's Life (aka Affair in Monte Carlo—US 1953). **1953** Never Let Me Go; Innocents in Paris (US 1955). **1954** Flame and the Flesh; The House Across the Lake (aka Heatwave—US); West of Zanzibar; The Young Lovers (aka Chance Meeting—US 1955); Mask of Dust (aka Race for Life—US); Svengali. **1955** That Lady; As Long as They're Happy (US 1957). **1956** Bhowani Junction; Loser Takes All; The Battle of the River Plate (aka Pursuit of the Graf Spee—US 1957); Passport to Treason. **1957** Zarak; Interpol (aka Pickup Alley—US); Fire Down Below; A Farwell to Arms; Manuela (aka Stowaway Girl—US); Miracle in Soho; Campbell's Kingdom; Man in the Shadow. **1958** I Accuse!; Escapement (aka The Electric Monster—US 1960). **1959** Whirlpool; The Angry Hills; The Wreck of the Mary Deare; Jet Storm (US 1961); Friends and Neighbors (US 1963). **1960** Moment of Danger (aka Malaga—US 1962); Bluebeard's Ten Honeymoons; Sands of the Desert. **1961** The Secret Partner; The Happy Thieves; Das Geheimnis der Gelben Narzissen (aka Daffodil Killer and The Devil's Daffodil—US 1967). **1962** Village of Daughters; The Middle Course. **1963** Nine Hours to Rama; The V.I.P.'s Echo of Diana. **1964** The Secret Door (aka Now It Can Be Told). **1965** Devils of Darkness. **1966** A Man Could Get Killed.

ILLINGTON, MARGARET
Born: July 23, 1881, Bloomington, Ill. Died: Mar. 11, 1934, Miami Beach, Fla. Stage and screen actress. Married to radio and screen actor Major Bowes (dec. 1946).

Appeared in: **1917** The Inner Shrine (film debut); Sacrifice.

IMBODEN, DAVID C.
Born: Mar. 6, 1887, Kansas City, Mo. Died: Mar. 19, 1974, Kansas City, Mo. Screen actor, stage director and muralist. Married to actress Hazel Bourne (dec. 1956).

Appeared in: **1923** Gimme; Souls for Sale. **1927** King of Kings.

IMBODEN, HAZEL (Hazel Bourne)
Born: Washburn, Ill. Died: Oct. 8, 1956, Kansas City, Mo. Stage and screen actress. Married to actor David Imboden (dec. 1974). Entered films in 1914.

IMHOF, MARCELLE See COREEN, MARCELLE

IMHOF, ROGER
Born: Apr. 15, 1875, Rock Island, Ill. Died: Apr. 15, 1958, Hollywood, Calif. Screen, stage, circus and vaudeville actor. Married to actress Marcelle Coreine (dec. 1977) with whom he appeared in vaudeville. Appeared in most of Will Rogers' pictures.

Appeared in: **1930** Rural Hospital (short). **1933** Paddy, The Next Best Thing; Charlie Chan's Greatest Case; Hoopla. **1934** David Harum; Wild Gold; Judge Priest; Handy Andy; Ever Since Eve; Grand Canary; Music in the Air; Under Pressure. **1935** One More Spring; Life Begins at Forty; The Farmer Takes a Wife; George White's 1935 Scandals; Steamboat 'Round the Bend. **1936** Riff Raff; Three Godfathers; San Francisco; A Son Comes Home; In His Steps; North of Nome. **1937** High, Wide and Handsome; There Goes the Groom; Every Day's a Holiday. **1939** Young Mr. Lincoln; Nancy Drew—Trouble Shooter; They Shall Have Music; Everything Happens at Night; Drums along the Mohawk. **1940** Abe Lincoln in Illinois; The Grapes of Wrath; Little Old New York; The Way of All Flesh; I Was an Adventuress. **1941** Mystery Ship; Man Hunt. **1942** It Happened in Flatbush; Tennessee Johnson; This Gun for Hire. **1944** Casanova in Burlesque; Home in Indiana; Adventures of Mark Twain. **1945** Wilson.

IMPERIO, PASTORA (Pastora Rojas Monge)
Born: 1889, Seville, Spain. Died: Sept., 1979, Madrid, Spain. Flamenco dancer and screen actress.

Appeared in: **1914** La Danza Fatal. **1936** Mario de la O. **1940** La Marquesona. **1843** Canelita en Rama. **1949** El Amor Brujo. **1959** Duelo en la Canada.

IMPOLITO, JOHN
Born: 1887. Died: May 1, 1962, Los Angeles, Calif. Screen actor.

Appeared in: **1935** G-Men; Top Hat. **1956** Around the World in 80 Days.

INAGAKI, HIROSHI
Born: 1906, Japan. Died: May 21, 1980, Tokyo, Japan. Screen actor, film director, screenwriter and author. Entered films as an actor in 1923.

INCE, ETHEL See KENT, ETHEL

INCE, JOHN E. (John Edward Ince)
Born: 1877, New York, N.Y. Died: Apr. 10, 1947, Hollywood, Calif. (pneumonia). Screen, stage actor, film director and film producer. Brother of actors Thomas (dec. 1924) and Ralph Ince (dec. 1937). Entered films in 1913 in various capacities.

Appeared in: **1918** Madame Sphinx. **1921** The Hole in the Wall. **1922** Hate. **1927** The Hour of Reckoning. **1930** Alias French Gertie; Hot Curves; Little Caesar; Moby Dick. **1931** Children of Dreams. **1932** The Thirteenth Guest; Human Targets; Passport to Paradise; No Living Witness; Afraid to Talk. **1933** Picture Snatcher; The Penal Code; One Year Later; Thrill Hunter. **1935** Star of Midnight; Folies Bergere; The Man Who Reclaimed His Head; China Seas; Circle of Death; Circus Shadows; Men of Action; Behind the Green Lights; In Old Kentucky. **1936** Peppery Salt (short); Comin' Round the Mountain; Grand Slam Opera (short); Three on a Limb (short); Night Cargo; Way Out West; The Speed Reporter; Don't Turn 'Em Loose. **1939** Hollywood Cavalcade; Mr. Smith Goes to Washington. **1940** The Heckler (short). **1941** Here Comes Mr. Jordan; Mr. Celebrity. **1942** Code of the Outlaw; The Miracle Kid; The Panther's Claw; Tennessee Johnson; Prison Girls; Broadway Big Shot; Pride of the Yankees. **1943** Man of Courage; What a Man! **1944** Heavenly Days; Wilson. **1945** The Lost Trail. **1946** The Best Years of Our Lives. **1947** Welcome Stranger; The Last Frontier Uprising. **1948** The Paradine Case.

INCE, RALPH WALDO
Born: 1887, Boston, Mass. Died: Apr. 10, 1937, London, England (auto accident). Screen, stage actor, film director and screenwriter. Brother of actors Thomas (dec. 1924) and John Ince (dec. 1947). Entered films in 1905 as a director. Married to Helen Triggers and divorced from actresses Lucille Stewart and Lucille Mendez.

Appeared in: **1906** "Historical" series on Lincoln for Vitagraph. **1911** One Flag at Last. **1912** The Lady of the Lake. **1920** Land of

Opportunity. **1921** The Highest Law; Wet Gold. **1926** The Sea Wolf; Yellow Fingers. **1927** Not for Publication; Shanghaied. **1928** Chicago After Midnight; The Singapore Mutiny. **1929** Wall Street. **1930** Numbered Men; The Big Fight; Little Caesar. **1931** A Gentleman's Fate; Hell Bound; The Star Witness; Big Gamble; Law and Order; The Dove; Exposed. **1932** The Lost Squadron; Men of Chance; Girl of the Rio; The Mouthpiece; State's Attorney; The Tenderfoot; Guilty as Hell; The Pride of the Legion; Law of the Sea; Gorilla Ship; Maylay Nights; Men of America; Lucky Devils; The Hatchet Man; County Fair. **1933** Havana Widows; No Escape; The Big Payoff. **1934** Love at Second Sight (aka The Girl Thief—US 1938). **1935** Blue Smoke; Rolling Home; So You Won't Talk? **1936** Gaol Break. **1937** The Perfect Crime.

INCE, RICHARD
Born: 1915. Died: Nov. 27, 1938, Oakland, Calif. Film stunt rider. Son of actress Elenor Kershaw (dec. 1971) and producer/actor Thomas H. Ince (dec. 1924).

INCE, THOMAS H.
Born: 1882. Died: Nov. 20, 1924, Beverly Hills, Calif. (heart failure). Screen, stage actor, film director, producer and screenwriter. Entered films in 1911. Brother of actors John (dec. 1947) and Ralph Ince (dec. 1937). Married to actress Elinor Kershaw (dec. 1971). Father of actor Richard (dec. 1938), writer Thomas, Jr. and William Ince.

Appeared in: **1910** His New Lid.

INCLAN, MIGUEL
Born: 1900, Mexico. Died: July 25, 1956, Tijuana, Mexico. Screen actor.

Appeared in: **1943** Creo en Dios. **1947** The Fugitive. **1948** Fort Apache. **1952** Indian Uprising; The Young and the Damned. **1955** Seven Cities of Gold. **1956** Bandido.

INDRISANO, JOHN "JOHNNY"
Born: 1906, Boston, Mass. Died: July 9, 1968, San Fernando Valley, Calif. (apparent suicide—hanging). Screen actor and boxer.

Appeared in: **1935** The Winning Ticket; She Gets Her Man; Two Fisted. **1936** Go West, Young Man; Laughing Irish Eyes. **1937** Every Day's a Holiday. **1941** Ringside Maisie. **1942** The Big Street. **1944** Lost in a Harem. **1945** Live Wires; Johnny Angel; Duffy's Tavern; The Naughty Nineties. **1946** Our Hearts Were Growing Up; The Kid From Brooklyn; Criminal Court; Crack-Up. **1947** Body and Soul; Killer McCoy; Christmas Eve; A Palooka Named Joe. **1948** In This Corner; Lulu Belle; Trouble Makers; The Numbers Racket; Knock on Any Door; The Accused; Bodyguard; Fighting Fools. **1949** Joe Palooka in the Big Fight; Bride for Sale; Tension; Shadow on the Wall; Joe Palooka in the Counterpunch; The Lady Gambles. **1950** The Yellow Cab Man. **1951** Meet Danny Wilson; Pier 23; Callaway Went Thataway. **1952** Something to Live For; Glory Alley; No Holds Barred. **1953** Island in the Sky; Shane. **1955** Guys and Dolls. **1956** The Cruel Tower. **1957** Chicago Confidential. **1958** Hot Spell. **1959** Some Like It Hot; Career. **1960** The Purple Gang; Ocean's Eleven. **1961** Blueprint for Robbery. **1962** Who's Got the Action? **1963** Come Blow Your Horn; For Love or Money; Hud; Four for Texas; Under the Yum Yum Tree. **1964** Where Love Has Gone; The Best Man; A House Is Not a Home. **1965** The Human Duplicator. **1967** The Ambushers; Barefoot in the Park. **1968** The Legend of Lylah Clare.

INESCORT, FRIEDA (Frieda Wightman)
Born: June 28, 1901, Edinburgh, Scotland. Died: Feb. 21, 1976, Woodland Hills, Calif. (multiple sclerosis). Screen and stage actress.

Appeared in: **1935** The Dark Angel; If You Could Only Cook. **1936** Hollywood Boulevard; Mary of Scotland; Give Me Your Heart; The King Steps Out; The Garden Murder Case. **1937** Portia on Trial; Call it a Day; The Great O'Malley; Another Dawn. **1939** Woman Doctor; Beauty for the Asking; A Woman is the Judge; Zero Hour; Trazan Takes a Son. **1940** Pride and Prejudice; The Letter; Convicted Woman. **1941** Father's Son; Shadows on the Stairs; You'll Never Get Rich; The Trial of Mary Dugan; Remember the Day; Sunny. **1942** The Sweater Girl; Street of Chance; The Courtship of Andy Hardy. **1943** The Amazing Mrs. Holliday; It Comes Up Love; Mission to Moscow. **1944** The Return of the Vampire; Heavenly Days. **1949** The Judge Steps Out. **1950** The Underworld Story. **1951** A Place in the Sun. **1952** Never Wave at a WAC. **1954** Casanova's Big Night. **1955** Foxfire; Flame of the Islands. **1956** The Eddy Duchin Story; The She-Creature. **1958** Darby's Rangers; Senior Prom. **1959** Juke Box Rhythm; The Alligator People. **1960** The Crowded Sky.

INFANTE, PEDRO
Born: 1918, Mexico. Died: Apr. 15, 1957, Merida, Yucatan (airplane crash). Mexican screen, radio actor and singer.

INGE, WILLIAM (aka WALTER GAGE)
Born: 1913, Independence, Kans. Died: June 10, 1973, Hollywood, Calif. (suicide). Playwright, screenwriter and screen actor.

Appeared in: **1961** Splendor in the Grass.

INGERSOLL, WILLIAM
Born: 1860. Died: May 7, 1936, Los Angeles, Calif. (acute indigestion). Screen and stage actor. Married to actress Mab Ingersoll.

Appeared in: **1920** Partners of the Night. **1931** The Cheat. **1935** Mary Burns, Fugitive; Whipsaw. **1936** Half Angel.

INGLE, RED
Born: 1907. Died: Sept. 7, 1965, Santa Barbara, Calif. Screen actor and musician.

INGRAHAM, LLOYD
Born: Rochelle, Ill. Died: Apr. 4, 1956, Woodland Hills, Calif. (pneumonia). Screen, stage actor and stage and film director. Entered films in 1912.

Appeared in: **1914** A Law Unto Himself; Aurora of the North. **1922** A Front Page Story. **1923** Sacramouche. **1924** The Chorus Lady. **1929** Untamed; Night Parade; The Rainbow Man. **1930** So Long Letty; Montana Moon; The Spoilers; Last of the Duanes; A Lady to Love; Wide Open. **1931** The Lady Who Dared. **1932** Texas Gun Fighter; The Crusader; Get That Girl; Sinister Hands; The Widow in Scarlet. **1933** I Love That Man; The World Gone Mad; Midnight Warning; Officer 13; Cornered; Revenge at Monte Carlo; Silent Men. **1934** The Lost Jungle (serial); Sixteen Fathoms Deep; In Love With Life; The Dude Rancher; The Curtain Falls; The Gold Ghost (short). **1935** The World Accuses; Northern Frontier; Rainbow Valley; Circumstantial Evidence; The Cowboy Millionaire; Headline Woman; Sons of Steel; On Probation; Rider of the Law; Between Men. **1936** The Vigilantes Are Coming (serial); Modern Times; Ghost Patrol; Empty Saddles; The Lonely Trail; Timber Way; Frontier Justice; Captain Calamity; Rogue of the Range; Burning Gold; Hearts in Bondage; Too Much Beef; Everyman's Law; Go Get 'Em Haines!; Conflict; Stormy Trails; Red River Valley. **1937** Oh, Doctor!; Park Avenue Logger; Battle of Greed; Riders of the Dawn; Tramp Trouble (short). **1938** Vivacious Lady; Swing, Sister, Swing; Painted Desert; Man From Music Mountain; Reformatory; Gun Packer. **1939** Destry Rides Again; Oklahoma Frontier; In Name Only; Love Affair; Home Boner (short); Truth Aches (short). **1940** Enemy Agent; Pony Post; Adventures of Red Ryder (serial); Melody Ranch; Marshal of Mesa City; 20 Mule Team; Bad Man from Red Butte; Colorado; My Little Chicadee. **1941** Dude Cowboy; Never Give a Sucker an Even Break. **1942** Tennessee Johnson; Stagecoach Buckaroo; Boss of Big Town. **1943** The Seventh Victim; Strictly in the Groove; Blazing Guns; The Mystery of the 13th Guest. **1944** Partners of the Trail; Range Law; West of the Rio Grande; The Merry Monahans; Love Your Landlord (short). **1945** Sudan; Frontier Gal; Frontier Feud; Lawless Empire; The Man Who Walked Alone; Springtime in Texas. **1946** Sister Kenny; Lover Come Back; The Caravan Trail. **1947** Slave Girl. **1950** The Savage Horde.

INGRAM, JACK
Born: 1903. Died: Feb. 20, 1969, Canoga Park, Calif. (heart attack). Screen actor.

Appeared in: **1936** Rebellion; The Lonely Trail; With Love and Kisses. **1937** Public Cowboy No. 1; Zorro Rides Again (serial); Headline Crasher; Yodelin' Kid From Pine Ridge; Wild Horse Rodeo. **1938** Code of the Rangers; Outlaws of Sonora; Riders of the Black Hills; Dick Tracy Returns (serial); Frontier Scout; Western Jamboree. **1939** The Night Riders; Home on the Prairie; Blue Montana Skies; Wyoming Outlaw; Colorado Sunset; New Frontier; Wall Street Cowboy; Sage of Death Valley; Rovin' Tumbleweeds; Down the Wyoming Trail; Mexicali Rose; Mountain Rhythm. **1940** Boom Town; Deadwood Dick (serial); The Shadow (serial); Terry and the Pirates (serial); Ghost Valley Raiders; Under Texas Skies; Young Bill Hickock; The Green Archer (serial); Melody Ranch. **1941** White Eagle (serial); South of Panama; King of the Texas Rangers (serial); Sheriff of Tombstone; Nevada City; The Gang's All Here; Prairie Pioneers; Law of the Wolf; The Lone Rider Ambushed. **1942** Perils of the Royal Mounted (serial); The Valley of Vanishing Men (serial); The Man from Cheyenne; Tomorrow We Live; Billy the Kid Trapped. **1943** Raiders of San Joaquin; The Mysterious Rider; Fugitive of the Plains; Lone Star Trail; Border Buckaroos; Riders of the Rio Grande; Silver Raiders; Santa Fe Scouts. **1944** Boss of Boomtown; Range Law. **1945** Federal Agent 99 (serial); Jungle Raiders (serial); Manhunt of Mystery Island (serial); The Monster and the Ape (serial); Who's Guilty? (serial); Brenda Starr, Reporter (serial); Bandits of the Badlands; Devil Riders; Enemy of the Law; Flame of the West; The Jade Mask; Out of Vengeance; Outlaw Roundup; Saddle Serenade; Sheriff of Cimarron; Stranger from Santa Fe; Frontier Gal. **1946** Canyon Passage; The Magnificent Doll; Chick Carter, Detective; The Mysterious Mr. M (serial); The

Scarlet Horseman (serial); Frontier Fugitives; Moon Over Montana; West of the Alamo. **1947** Brick Bradford (serial; Jack Armstrong (serial); The Sea Hound (serial); The Vigilante (serial); Pioneer Justice; Slave Girl; South of the Chisholm Trail; Ghost Town Renegades. **1948** Congo Bill (serial); Superman (serial); Tex Granger (serial); Bruce Gentry—Daredevil of the Skies (serial); The Strawberry Roan; Whirlwind Raiders; Racing Luck. **1949** Calamity Jane and Sam Bass; The Gal Who Took the West; Son of a Badman; Law of the West; Roaring Westward; Desert Vigilante. **1950** Atom Man vs. Superman (serial); Cody of the Pony Express (serial); The Texan Meets Calamity Jane; Short Grass; Bandit Queen; Sierra; Sideshow; Streets of Ghost Town. **1951** The Cave of the Outlaws; Captain Video (serial); Roar of the Iron Horse (serial); Fort Dodge Stampede. **1952** King of the Congo (serial); The Battle of Apache Pass; Fargo. **1953** Cow Country; Son of the Renegade. **1954** Riding With Buffalo Bill (serial). **1955** Man Without a Star; Five Guns West. **1957** Utah Blaine. **1959** Zorro Rides Again.

INGRAM, REX (Reginald Ingram Montgomery Hitchcock aka REX HITCHCOCK)
Born: Jan. 15, 1893, Dublin, Ireland. Died: July 21, 1950, North Hollywood, Calif. (cerebral hemorrhage). Screen, stage actor, film director, producer and screenwriter. Do not confuse with black actor who died Sept. 19, 1969. Divorced from actress Doris Pawn. Married to actress Alice Terry.

Appeared in: **1914** The Necklace of Rameses; The Spirit and the Clay; Her Biggest Scoop; Eve's Daughter (aka Artist's Madonna); The Crime of Cain; The Evil Men Do; The Circus and the Boy; His Wedded Wife; The Upper Hand; Fine Feathers Make Fine Birds; The Moonshine Maid and the Man; Snatched from Burning Death. **1923** Mary of the Movies. **1932** Baroud (aka Love in Morocco—US 1933); Passion in the Desert and Les Hommes Blus).

INGRAM, REX
Born: Oct. 20, 1895, Cairo, Ill. Died: Sept. 19, 1969, Los Angeles, Calif. (heart attack). Black screen, stage and television actor.
Appeared in: **1915** Snatched from a Burning Death. **1918** Tarzan of the Apes; Salome. **1923** Sacramouche; The Ten Commandments. **1926** The Big Parade. **1927** King of Kings. **1929** Hearts in Dixie; The Four Feathers. **1932** Sign of the Cross. **1933** King Kong; The Emperor Jones; Love in Morocco. **1934** Harlem after Midnight. **1935** Captain Blood. **1936** Green Pastures. **1938** Let My People Live. **1939** Adventures of Huckleberry Finn. **1940** The Thief of Bagdad. **1942** The Talk of the Town. **1943** Fired Wife; Sahara; Cabin in the Sky. **1944** Dark Waters. **1945** A Thousand and One Nights. **1948** Moonrise. **1950** King Solomon's Mines. **1955** Tarzan's Hidden Jungle; Desire in the Dust. **1956** The Ten Commandments (and 1923 version); Congo Crossing. **1957** Hell on Devil's Island. **1958** God's Little Acre; Anna Lucasta. **1959** Escort West; Watusi. **1960** Elmer Gantry. **1964** Your Cheatin' Heart. **1967** Hurry Sundown; Journey to Shiloh; How to Succeed in Business Without Really Trying.

INGRAM, WILLIAM D.
Born: 1857. Died: Feb. 2, 1926, New York, N.Y. Screen and stage actor.

INNES, EDWARD "EDDIE" (Edward Gordon Innes)
Born: 1907, Quebec, Canada. Died: Dec. 29, 1980, Las Vegas, Nev. (heart attack). Screen, stage actor and burlesque entertainer.
Appeared in: **1959** The Angry Red Planet.

INNESS, JEAN
Died: Dec. 27, 1978, Santa Monica, Calif. (cancer). Screen, television actress and stage director. Married to actor Victor Jory (dec. 1982). Mother of producer, director and playwright Jon Jory and actress Jean Jory Anderson.
Appeared in: **1950** Mrs. Mike; The Gunfighter; Edge of Doom. **1951** I'd Climb the Highest Mountain. **1957** The Green-Eyed Blonde; the Night Runner. **1958** Gun Fever. **1960** The Story of Ruth.

INSTONE, ANNA
Born: 1923, England. Died: Apr. 2, 1978, England? Screen and radio actress.

IRELAND, ANTHONY
Born: Feb. 5, 1902, Peru. Died: Dec. 4, 1957, London, England. Screen, stage and television actor.
Appeared in: **1931** These Charming People. **1932** The Water Gypsies. **1933** Called Back. **1936** The Three Maxims; Juggernaut. **1937** When Thief Meets Thief; Twin Faces; Sweet Devil; Sweet Racket. **1942** The Prime Minister. **1952** Gambler and the Lady. **1953** Spaceways. **1958** I Accuse!

IRENE (Irene Lentz)
Born: Dec. 8, 1907, Mont. Died: Nov. 15, 1962, Hollywood, Calif.

(suicide). Screen actress and costume designer. Married to screenwriter Elliot Gibbons.
Appeared in: **1922** A Tailor Made Man.

IRGAT, CAHIT
Born: 1916, Luleburgaz, Turkey. Died: June, 1971, Sisli, Turkey (lung cancer). Screen, stage actor, poet and writer.
Appeared in: Yil maz Ali (film debut).

IRVIN, LESLIE
Born: 1895. Died: Oct. 9, 1966. Screen actor and stuntman.

IRVINE, ROBIN
Born: Dec. 2, 1901, London, England. Died: Apr. 28, 1933, England? Screen and stage actor. Married to actress Ursula Jeans (dec. 1973).
Appeared in: **1925** The Secret Kingdom. **1927** Land of Hope and Glory; Confetti; Downhill (aka When Boys Leave Home—US 1928); Easy Virtue (US 1928). **1928** Palais de Danse; The Rising Generation. **1929** A Knight in London; Beyond the Veil (reissue of 1925 The Secret Kingdom); The Isle of Lost Ships; Young Woodley (US 1930). **1930** Leave it to Me. **1931** Keepers of Youth.

IRVING, CHARLES
Born: 1913. Died: Feb., 1981, Minneapolis, Minn. Screen, radio, television actor, radio producer and television producer.
Appeared in: **1957** A Face in the Crowd. **1964** Fate is the Hunter; Three Nuts in Search of a Bolt. **1968** Countdown; Head; Project X.

IRVING, ETHEL "BIRDIE"
Born: Sept. 5, 1869, England. Died: May 3, 1963, Bexhill, England. Screen and stage actress. Daughter of stage actor Joseph Irving (dec. 1870). Married to stage actor Gilbert Porteous (dec. 1928).
Appeared in: **1917** The Three Daughters.

IRVING, GEORGE
Born: 1874, New York. Died: Sept. 11, 1961, Hollywood, Calif. (heart attack). Screen, stage actor and film director. Entered films in 1913.
Appeared in: **1924** Wanderer of the Wasteland; The Man Who Fights Alone; North of 36; For Sale; Madonna of the Streets. **1925** The Goose Hangs High; The Air Mail; The Golden Princess; Wild Horse Mesa; Her Market Value. **1926** Desert Gold; The City; His Jazz Bride; The Midnight Kiss; The Eagle of the Sea; Fangs of Justice; Three Bad Men; Risky Business; The King of the Turf. **1927** The Broncho Twister; Home Struck; Two Flaming Youths; Man Power; Drums of the Desert; One Increasing Purpose; Shanghai Bound; Wings. **1928** The Lady of Victories (short); Modern Mothers; The Port of Missing Girls; Craig's Wife; Feel My Pulse; Honor Bound; Partners in Crime; The Wright Idea; Runaway Girls. **1929** The Godless Girl; The Dance of Life; Thunderbolt; Paris Bound; Coquette; The Last Performance. **1930** Son of the Gods; The Divorcee; Puttin' on the Ritz; Shadow of the Law; The Poor Millionaires; Conspiracy; Maybe It's Love; Only Saps Work; Free Love; Young Eagles; Young Desire. **1931** Dishonored; Hush Money; The Naughty Flirt; Cisco Kid; Hot Heiress; Five and Ten; A Free Soul; Resurrection; Graft; Confessions of a Co-ed; The Runaround; Shipmates; Girls Demand Excitement; The Star Witness; Touchdown; Wicked. **1932** Merrily We Go to Hell; Vanishing Frontier; Thrill of Youth; Guilty or Not Guilty; All-American; Broken Lullaby; Lady with a Past; Ladies of the Big House. **1933** Island of Lost Souls; The Worst Woman in Paris; Humanity; One Year Later; Son of a Sailor. **1934** The World Moves On; Bright Eyes; Wonder Bar; Here Comes the Navy; George White's Scandals; Manhattan Love Song; Once to Every Bachelor; You're Telling Me. **1935** Charlie Chan in Egypt; Buried Loot (short); Beauty's Daughter; Society Fever; Dangerous; Death Flies East; Age of Indiscretion; A Vance; Knute Rockne—All American; A Child is Born; Florian; Johnny Apollo; New Moon; Yesterday's Heroes. **1941** Bullets for O'Hara; Golden Hoofs; She Couldn't Say No; Out of the Fog; The Vanishing Virginian. **1942** King of the Mounties (serial); The Great Notorious Gentleman; Navy Wife; Under the Pampas Moon; A Night at the Opera. **1936** Captain January; Charlie Chan at the Race Track; Hearts Divided; Hearts in Bondage; Hats Off; It Had to Happen; Nobody's Fool; Private Number; Sutter's Gold; The Sea Spoilers; Navy Born. **1937** Border Cafe; China Passage; Morning Judge (short); The Mandarin Mystery; Don't Tell the Wife; The Big Shot; High Flyers; The Life of the Party; The Man Who Found Himself; Meet the Missus; Saturday's Heroes; She's Got Everything; There Goes the Groom; The Toast of New York; Too Many Wives; We're on the Jury; You Can't Buy Luck. **1938** Blind Alibi; Condemned Women; Crashing Hollywood; Crime Ring; Bringing up Baby; Go Chase Yourself; The Law of Tombstone; Maid's Night Out; Mother Carey's Chickens; Mr. Doodle Kicks Off; Smashing the Rackets; This Marriage Business. **1939** Wife, Husband and Friend; The Hardy's Ride High; Dust Be My Destiny; Hotel for Women; Streets of New York. **1940** Calling Philo

Man's Lady; Spy Ship. **1943** Dr. Gillespie's Criminal Case; Hangmen Also Die; Son of Dracula. **1944** The Imposter; Christmas Holiday; Lady in the Death House. **1947** Magic Town.

IRVING, H. B. (Henry Broadribb Irving)
Born: Aug. 5, 1870, London, England. Died: Oct. 17, 1919, London, England. Stage and screen actor. Son of stage actor Henry Irving (dec. 1905). Married to actress Dorothea Baird. Father of actress Elizabeth Irving.

Appeared in: **1911** Princess Clementina. **1916** The Lyons Mail. **1917** Masks and Faces.

IRVING, JULES
Born: Apr. 13, 1925, Bronx, N.Y. Died: July 28, 1979, Reno, Nev. (heart attack). Screen, stage actor, film producer, stage director, television director and television producer. Married to actress Priscilla Pointer. Father of actress Amy, producer David and Kate Irving.

Appeared in: **1955** It Came From Beneath the Sea.

IRVING, PAUL
Born: 1877, Boston, Mass. Died: May 8, 1959, Hollywood, Calif. Screen and stage actor.

Appeared in: **1932** Bill of Divorcement. **1933** The Silver Cord. **1934** Count of Monte Cristo. **1936** The Great Ziegfeld; Gold Diggers of 1937. **1937** The Life of Emile Zola; On the Avenue; Hollywood Hotel. **1938** Battle of Broadway; Gold Diggers of 1939. **1939** Balalaika; Rose of Washington Square. **1940** A Dispatch from Reuters.

IRVING, WILLIAM J.
Born: 1893. Died: Dec. 25, 1943, Los Angeles, Calif. Screen and vaudeville actor.

Appeared in: **1923** Gentle Julia; The Love Trap. **1924** Love Letters. **1925** Pampered Youth. **1927** She's My Baby; Ham and Eggs at the Front. **1928** Coney Island; Beautiful but Dumb; The Singapore Mutiny; Nothing to Wear; Red Hair. **1929** From Headquarters; Hearts in Exile. **1930** All Quiet on the Western Front; Song of the Caballero; On the Border; Rough Waters; plus the following shorts: The Body Slam; Won to Lose; Surprise; Ginsberg of Newberg; Skin Game. **1931** Her Majesty, Love; Manhattan Parade. **1933** Diplomaniacs; plus the following shorts: The Hitch Hiker; Tired Feet; Hooks and Jabs; On Ice. **1934** Orient Express; Melody in Spring; plus the following shorts: Mike Fright; Washee Ironee; It's the Cat's; One Too Many; Punch Drunks; Three Little Pigskins. **1935** Air Hawks; The Big Broadcast of 1936. **1936** The following shorts: Caught in the Act; Restless Knights; Hoi Polloi. **1937** The Shadow; plus the following shorts: Calling All Doctors; Gracie at the Bat; Grips, Grunts, and Groans; Playing the Ponies. **1938** Convicted. **1939** Ninotchka. **1940** The Mortal Storm. **1941** Wedding Worries (short).

IRWIN, BOBBY
Born: 1913. Died: Jan. 11, 1956, Los Angeles, Calif. Film stunt pilot and screen actor.

IRWIN, BOYD
Born: Mar. 12, 1880, Brighton, England. Died: Jan. 22, 1957, Woodland Hills, Calif. Screen and stage actor.

Appeared in: **1921** The Three Musketeers. **1922** The Long Chance. **1923** Ashes of Vengeance; Enemies of Children. **1924** Captain Blood. **1930** The Lone Defender (serial). **1932** The Man from Yesterday. **1934** What Every Woman Knows; Pursuit of Happiness. **1935** The Man Who Reclaimed His Head; Cardinal Richelieu; The Crusades; The Werewolf of London. **1936** The Charge of the Light Brigade; Dangerous Intrigue; The Blackmailer; Killer at Large; Devil's Squadron; Meet Nero Wolfe. **1937** Lost Horizon; Prisoner of Zenda. **1939** We Are Not Alone; The Witness Vanishes; Man in the Iron Mask; Sky Patrol. **1940** The Invisible Killer; Drums of the Desert. **1941** Unfinished Business; Mr. and Mrs. North; Secret Evidence; City of Missing Girls; The Great Swindle; Passage from Hong Kong. **1942** North of the Rockies; The Black Swan; Joe Smith, American; True to the Army; The Major and the Minor; Random Harvest; Foreign Agent. **1943** Thank Your Lucky Stars; Chatterbox. **1944** Frenchman's Creek; The Lodger; Double Indemnity; Our Hearts Were Young and Gay; The Story of Dr. Wassell. **1945** Molly and Me. **1946** Girl on the Spot; Magnificent Doll; Scarlet Street; Rendezvous 29; Dragonwyck; Tomorrow is Forever; Devotion; The Time of Their Lives. **1947** Down to Earth; Ivy; A Double Life; Forever Amber; King of the Bandits. **1948** Unconquered; The Paradine Case; I, Jane Doe; Docks of New Orleans; Campus Honeymoon.

IRWIN, BUD
Died: Sept. 30, 1977. Screen actor.

Appeared in: **1964** Bunny Yeager's Nude Las Vegas. **1970** Room 11.

IRWIN, CHARLES W.
Born: 1888, Ireland. Died: Jan. 12, 1969, Woodland Hills, Calif. (cancer). Screen, stage actor and screenwriter.

Appeared in: **1928** The Debonair Humorist (short). **1930** The King of Jazz; Blind Adventure. **1933** Looking Forward; Racket Cheers (short); Hell Below; Kickin' the Crown Around (short). **1934** Bulldog Drummond Strikes Back; The Mystery of Mr. X. **1935** Mutiny on the Bounty; China Seas; The Gilded Lily; Whipsaw. **1936** Go West, Young Man; The White Angel. **1937** Wings Over Honolulu; Another Dawn; The League of Frightened Men. **1938** Kidnapped; Lord Jeff. **1939** Little Accident; We Are Not Alone; Susannah of the Mounties; The Light That Failed; Man About Town. **1940** The Letter; The Man I Married. **1941** San Antonio Rose; International Squadron. **1942** Eagle Squadron; Son of Fury; To Be or Not To Be; Desperate Journey; Great Impersonation; Mrs. Miniver; Yankee Doodle Dandy; The Black Swan. **1943** Lassie Come Home; Johnny Come Lately; Thank Your Lucky Stars; Wintertime; No Time for Love; The Gorilla Man. **1944** National Velvet; Jane Eyre; The White Cliffs of Dover; Frenchman's Creek; Sing, Neighbor, Sing; Nothing but Trouble. **1945** Kitty; Practically Yours; Hangover Square. **1947** The Foxes of Harrow; Thunder in the Valley; My Wild Irish Rose. **1948** The Luck of the Irish. **1949** Bomba on Panther Island; Challenge to Lassie. **1950** Montana. **1951** Mystery Junction. **1952** Captain Pirate; A Tale of Five Women. **1953** Charge of the Lancers; Fort Vengeance; The Caddy; Son of the Renegade. **1954** The Iron Glove. **1956** The King and I; The Court Jester. **1959** The Sheriff of Fractured Jaw. **1964** He Rides Tall.

IRWIN, MAY
Born: June 27, 1862, Whitby, Ontario, Canada. Died: Oct. 22, 1958, New York, N.Y. Screen and stage actress.

Appeared in: **1896** The Kiss (Edison—One of the most famous of the early films showing the kissing scene from the stage play, The Widow Jones). **1914** Mrs. Black is Back.

IRWIN, WALLACE
Born: Mar. 15, 1875, Oneida, N.Y. Died: Feb. 14, 1959, Southern Pines, N.C. Humorist, screenwriter and screen actor. Brother of journalist and actor Will Irwin (dec. 1948).

Appeared in: **1913** Saved by Parcel Post.

IRWIN, WILL (William Henry Irwin)
Born: 1874, Oneida, N.Y. Died: Feb. 24, 1948, New York, N.Y. (cerebral occlusion). Journalist, playwright, novelist and screen actor. Brother of humorist and actor Wallace Irwin (dec. 1959).

Appeared in: **1913** Saved by Parcel Post. **1914** Our Mutual Girl No. 33.

ISAACS, ISADORE "IKE"
Born: 1901. Died: Mar. 18, 1957, Culver City, Calif. Screen actor and stand-in. Entered films approx. 1932.

ISBERT, JOSE
Born: 1884, Spain. Died: Nov. 28, 1966, Madrid, Spain (heart ailment). Stage and screen actor.

Appeared in Spanish films: Ramon and Dalila; Broken Lives; The Whole Truth; The Dancer and the Laborer; Welcome, Mr. Marshall; Manolo the Policeman; Calabuch; An Afternoon of Bulls; El Verdugo. **1961** An Angel Paso Sobre Brooklyn (The Man Who Wagged His Tail). **1963** The Executioner (aka El Ver and aka Not on Your Life—US 1965). **1967** Operacion Dalila (Operation Delilah).

ISHAM, SIR GYLES
Born: Oct. 31, 1903, Lamport, Northampton, England. Died: Jan. 29, 1976, England? Screen and stage actor. Entered films in 1933.

Appeared in: **1935** The Iron Duke; Anna Karenina.

ISHII, KAN
Born: 1901, Japan. Died: Apr. 29, 1972, Tokyo, Japan (cancer). Screen, stage, television actor and composer. Entered films in 1922 with Shochiku Motion Picture Co.

ISIK, AYHAN
Born: 1929, Turkey. Died: July, 1979, Istanbul, Turkey (cerebral hemorrhage). Screen actor. Entered films in 1951.

ITO, MICHIO
Born: 1894, Japan. Died: Nov. 6, 1961, Tokyo, Japan. Screen, stage actor, dancer and dance director.

Appeared in: **1922** Dawn of the East. **1938** Spawn of the North.

ITURBI, AMPARO
Born: 1899, Spain. Died: Apr. 21, 1969, Beverly Hills, Calif. Screen actress and pianist. Sister of actor and pianist Jose Iturbi (dec. 1980).

Appeared in: **1946** Holiday in Mexico. **1949** That Midnight Kiss.

ITURBI, JOSE Q
Born: 1896, Valencia, Spain. Died: June 28, 1980, Los Angeles, Calif. (heart attack). Screen actor and concert pianist. Brother of actress Amparo Iturbi (dec. 1969).

Appeared in: **1942** That Midnight Kiss (film debut). **1943** Thousands Cheer. **1944** Music for Millions; Two Girls and a Sailor; Adventure in Music. **1945** Anchors Aweigh; A Song to Remember. **1946** Holiday in Mexico. **1948** Three Darling Daughters. **1956** The Birds and the Bees.

IVAN, ROSALIND
Born: 1884, England. Died: Apr. 6, 1959, New York, N.Y. Screen and stage actress. Entered films in 1936.

Appeared in: **1936** The Garden Murder Case. **1941** Paris Calling. **1944** None but the Lonely Heart; The Suspect. **1945** The Corn is Green; Scarlet Street; Pillow of Death; Pursuit to Algiers. **1946** The Verdict; Three Strangers; That Brennan Girl; Alias Mr. Twilight. **1947** Ivy. **1948** Johnny Belinda. **1953** The Robe. **1954** Elephant Walk.

IVANS, ELAINE
Born: 1900, New York, N.Y. Died: Apr. 5, 1975, New York, N.Y. Screen, stage and vaudeville actress.

Appeared in: **1914** The Bomb Boy; The Floor Above. **1915** John Glayde's Honor; New Adam and Eve. **1916** The Struggle. **1917** A Son of the Hills.

IVES, ANNE (Anne Florinda Ives)
Born: 1887, Providence, R.I. Died: May 15, 1979, New York, N.Y. (natural causes). Screen, stage and television actress.

Appeared in: **1968** The Producers. **1975** The Reincarnation of Peter Proud.

IVES, DOUGLAS
Died: Mar. 6, 1969, London, England. Screen and stage actor.

Appeared in: **1953** Innocents in Paris (US 1955). **1954** Doctor in the House (US 1955). **1955** Room in the House. **1957** Miracle in Soho; The Big Chance; Man in the Shadow. **1961** Raising the Wind (aka Roommates—US 1962). **1962** The Iron Maiden (aka The Swingin' Maiden—US 1963). **1963** Live It Up (aka Sing and Swing—US 1964); Just for Fun.

IVINS, PERRY (Carrell Perry Ivins)
Born: Nov. 21, 1895, Trenton, N.J. Died: Aug. 22, 1963, Los Angeles, Calif. (arteriosclerosis). Screen actor, assistant film director and dialogue director.

Appeared in: **1930** The Benson Murder Case. **1931** Reckless Living. **1932** Trouble in Paradise. **1934** The Merry Widow; Stamboul Quest; Charlie Chan in London; Orient Express; Notorious Sophie Lang. **1935** Folies Bergere; G-Men; Charlie Chan in Paris; Les Miserables; Hooray for Love; Lady Tubbs; Smart Girl. **1938** Arsene Lupin Returns; Red River Range; Fighting Devil Dogs (serial). **1939** Son of Frankenstein; Made for Each Other. **1948** That Wonderful Urge. **1949** Samson and Delilah; Streets of Laredo. **1950** The Sun Sets at Dawn; The Missourians; The Redhead and the Cowboy. **1951** Belle Le Grand. **1959** The Big Fisherman.

IZVITZKAYA, ISOLDA
Born: 1933, Russia. Died: 1971, Russia. Screen actress.

Appeared in: **1957** The Forty-First. **1960** Fathers and Sons. **1961** Mir Vkhodyashchemu (aka Peace to Him and aka Peace to Him that Enters—US 1963).

JACHIM, ANTHONY See JOCHIM, ANTHONY "TONY"

JACK, T. C.
Born: 1882. Died: Oct. 4, 1954, Hollywood, Calif. (heart attack). Screen actor. Entered films approx. 1914.

Appeared in: **1925** Daring Days.

JACKIE, WILLIAM "BILL"
Born: 1890. Died: Sept. 19, 1954, San Francisco, Calif. (heart attack). Screen actor. Entered films during silents.

Appeared in: **1937** Don't Tell the Wife.

JACKSON, ANDREW, IV
Born: 1887. Died: May 23, 1953, Los Angeles, Calif. Screen actor. Great grandson of President Andrew Jackson.

Appeared in: **1953** The President's Lady.

JACKSON, COLLETTE
Died: May 15, 1969. Screen and television actress.

Appeared in: **1957** Teenage Doll. **1958** Unwed Mother; The Beast of Budapest. **1962** House of Women; All Fall Down. **1964** Seven Days in May.

JACKSON, DALE
Born: 1896. Died: Aug. 9, 1961, Pittsburgh, Pa. Screen, radio, vaudeville actor, screenwriter and radio writer.

Appeared in: **1932** Shanghai Express.

JACKSON, EDDIE
Born: 1896, Brooklyn, N.Y. Died: July 15 or 16, 1980, Van Nuys, Calif. (massive stroke). Screen, stage, vaudeville actor, burlesque entertainer and singer. Partners with Jimmy Durante (dec. 1980) and Lou Clayton (dec. 1950) in an act billed as "Clayton, Jackson and Durante."

Appeared in: **1930** Roadhouse Nights.

JACKSON, ETHEL See KENT, ETHEL

JACKSON, ETHEL SHANNON See SHANNON, ETHEL

JACKSON, HENRY (Henry Conrad Jackson)
Born: 1927. Died: July 30, 1973, New York, N.Y. Screen, stage, television actor and film producer.

Appeared in: **1957** The Night Runner; Panama Sal; The Monolith Monsters. **1958** The True Story of Lynn Stuart. **1960** Strangers When We Meet. **1962** Bird Man of Alcatraz.

JACKSON, JENIE
Born: 1922. Died: Mar. 14, 1976, Hollywood, Calif. Screen, stage actress and singer.

Appeared in: **1962** Ride the High Country. **1968** How Sweet It Is! **1970** Imago.

JACKSON, JOE
Born: 1880 or 1881. Died: May 14, 1942, New York, N.Y. (heart attack). Screen, stage and vaudeville actor. Do not confuse with screenwriter of same name.

Appeared in: **1915** Fatty and the Broadway Stars. **1916** Gypsy Joe; A Modern Enoch Arden. **1917** The Lion and the Girl.

JACKSON, MAHALIA
Born: Oct. 25, 1911, New Orleans, La. Died: Jan. 27, 1972, Evergreen Park, Ill. (heart disease). Black gospel singer and screen actress.

Appeared in: **1958** St. Louis Blues. **1959** Imitation of Life. **1960** Jazz on a Summer's Day. **1964** The Best Man.

JACKSON, SELMER (Selmer Adolph Jackson)
Born: May 7, 1888, Iowa. Died: Mar. 30, 1971, Burbank, Calif. (heart disease). Screen actor.

Appeared in: **1921** The Supreme Passion. **1929** Thru Different Eyes; Why Bring That Up? **1930** Lovin' the Ladies. **1931** Subway Express; Dirigible; Secret Call; Left Over Ladies. **1932** Big City Blues; Winner Take All; You Said a Mouthful. **1933** Little Giant; Picture Snatcher; Forgotten; Hell and High Water. **1934** I've Got Your Number; Let's Fall in Love; Sisters Under the Skin; The Witching Hour; Defense Rests; I'll Fix It. **1935** Don't Bet on Blondes; Devil Dogs of the Air; Black Fury; Traveling Saleslady; Public Hero Number One; Front Page Woman; This is the Life; Grand Exit; A Night at the Opera. **1936** Next Time We Love; Showboat; Bridge of Sighs; Public Enemy's Wife; Ace Drummond (serial); My Man Godfrey; Parole; Easy Money; The Magnificent Brute; Robinson Crusoe of Clipper Island (serial). **1937** Breezing Home; Charlie Chan at the Olympics; Two Wise Maids; A Family Affair; The Case of the Stuttering Bishop; The Man in Blue; The Thirteenth Man; Meet the Boy Friend; The Westland Case; The Wrong Road; Federal Bullets; Manhattan Merry-Go-Round; Hot Water; The Duke Comes Back; West of Shanghai; Jungle Jim (serial). **1938** Little Tough Guy; You're Only Young Once; Prison Nurse; Midnight Intruder; Arson Gang Busters; Alexander's Ragtime Band; The Missing Guest; Gambling Ship; Flight to Fame; Gangster's Boy; Personal Secretary; Rhythm of the Saddle; Secrets of an Actress; Down in "Arkansaw." **1939** The Forgotten Woman; Another Thin Man; Sorority House; Each Dawn I Die; Confessions of a Nazi Spy; Off the Record; Stand Up and Fight; Inside Information; The Star Maker; On Dress Parade; Calling All Marines; South of the Border. **1940** Scandal Sheet; The Grapes of Wrath; Son of the Navy; Johnny Apollo; Wagons

Westward; Millionaires in Prison; Babies for Sale; Sailor's Lady; Men Against the Sky; Hired Wife; City for Conquest; Brigham Young; Public Deb No. 1; The Ape; Lady With Red Hair. **1941** Meet John Doe; Here Comes Mr. Jordan; Love Crazy; Bowery Boy; International Squadron; The Man Who Lost Himself; Tight Shoes; Paper Bullets; Parachute Battalion; Navy Blues; Remember the Day; Buck Privates; Play Girl; They Died With Their Boots On. **1942** Sing Your Worries Away; Road to Happiness; Secret Agent of Japan; Ten Gentlemen from West Point; Miss Annie Rooney; Through Different Eyes; The Falcon Takes Over. **1943** It Ain't Hay; Adventures of the Flying Cadets (serial); You Can't Beat the Law; Harrigan's Kid; Margin for Error; Guadalcanal Diary. **1944** The Sullivans; Roger Touhy—Gangster; Hey, Rookie; Stars on Parade; The Big Noise. **1945** Out of This World; They Shall Have Faith; Circumstantial Evidence; The Caribbean Mystery; A Sporting Chance; Dakota; This Love of Ours; The Royal Mounted Rides Again (serial); Allotment Wives; Black Market Babies. **1946** Girl on the Spot; The Glass Alibi; Johnny Comes Flying Home; The French Key; Child of Divorce; Wife Wanted; Boston Blackie and the Law; Dangerous Money; The Time of Their Lives; Shock. **1947** Cass Timberlane; Magic Town; Sarge Goes to College; Stepchild; Her Husband's Affair; The Pretender; Key Witness. **1948** Dream Girl; Every Girl Should be Married; King of the Gamblers; The Fuller Brush Man; Pitfall; The Girl from Manhattan; Stage Struck. **1949** Sorrowful Jones; Alaska Patrol; Forgotten Women; Renegades of the Sage; The Crime Doctor's Diary. **1950** Gunmen of Abilene; Mark of the Gorilla; Buckaroo Sheriff of Texas; Lucky Losers. **1951** Elopement; That's My Boy; Bowery Battalion; Purple Heart Diary. **1952** We're Not Married; Deadline USA. **1953** The President's Lady; Sky Commando; Rebel City; Jack McCall; Desperado. **1954** Demetrius and the Gladiators. **1955** Devil Goddess. **1956** Autumn Leaves. **1957** Hellcats of the Navy. **1958** The Lost Missile. **1959** The Atomic Submarine. **1960** The Gallant Hours.

JACKSON, THOMAS (Thomas E. Jackson)
Born: 1886, New York, N.Y. Died: Sept. 8, 1967, Hollywood, Calif. (heart attack). Screen, stage and television actor.

Appeared in: **1929** Broadway (stage and film versions). **1930** Little Caesar; Good News; The Fall Guy; Double Cross Roads; For the Defense. **1931** Lawless Woman; Sweepstakes; Twenty-four Hours; Women Go on Forever; Reckless Living. **1932** Afraid to Talk; Big City Blues; Escapade; Unashamed; Doctor X; Strange Justice. **1933** Terror Abroad; The Avenger; Parachute Jumper; The Mystery of the Wax Museum; From Hell to Heaven; Strictly Personal. **1934** Myrt and Marge; Manhattan Melodrama; The Personality Kid; Melody in Spring. **1935** Carnival; Call of the Wild; Gold Diggers of 1935; The Case of the Curious Bride; The Irish in Us; George White's 1935 Scandals. **1936** Preview Murder Mystery; A Son Comes Home; Hollywood Boulevard; It Had to Happen; Little Miss Nobody; Grand Jury; A Man Betrayed; The Magnificent Brute. **1937** Beware of Ladies; Dangerous Holiday; Outcast; The Westland Case; Fugitive in the Sky; She's No Lady. **1938** The Amazing Dr. Clitterhouse; Blondes at Work; International Crime; I Stand Accused; Crime Takes a Holiday; The Lady in the Morgue; Torchy Gets Her Man. **1939** Nancy Drew—Reporter. **1940** Oh Johnny, How You Can Love; Love, Honor and Oh Baby!; Free, Blonde and 21; A Fugitive from Justice; Millionaires in Prison; Golden Gloves; Girl from God's Country. **1941** Law of the Tropics. **1942** Yankee Doodle Dandy; Crime Doctor's Strangest Case. **1944** Woman in the Window; "Thin Man" series. **1945** Circumstantial Evidence; Why Girls Leave Home; How Do You Do; Shady Lady; The Hidden Eye. **1946** Scarlet Street; Valley of the Zombies; The Face of Marble; Just Before Dawn; The Big Sleep. **1947** The Guilty; Dead Reckoning; The Guilt of Janet Ames. **1948** Here Comes Trouble. **1949** The Great John L. **1952** Stars and Stripes Forever; Phone Call from a Stranger. **1953** Meet Me at the Fair. **1958** Attack of the 50 Foot Woman. **1965** Synanon.

JACKSON, WARREN
Born: 1893. Died: May 10, 1950, Hollywood, Calif. (auto accident). Screen and television actor.

Appeared in: **1937** Hollywood Round-Up. **1938** Call the Mesquiteers. **1940** Drafted in the Depot (short). **1941** A Polo Phony (short). **1943** Dixie. **1945** Her Lucky Night; On Stage Everybody; Under Western Skies. **1946** The Brute Man. **1947** Trail Street; The Secret Life of Walter Mitty. **1948** Return of the Bad Men; Coroner Creek. **1949** Oh, You Beautiful Doll. **1950** Montana; Square Dance Katy.

JACOBINI, MARIA
Born: Feb. 17, 1890, Rome, Italy. Died: 1944, Italy? Screen actress.

Appeared in: **1910** Lucrezia Borgia; Beatrice Cenci. **1912** La Fugitiva; Vampe di Gelosia. **1913** Giovanna d' Arco. **1915** La Corsara. **1917** Resurrezione. **1918** La Signora Arlecchino; Addio Giovinezza. **1919** La Vergine Folle. **1921** Il Viaggio.

JACOBS, ANGELA
Born: 1893, Sioux City, Iowa. Died: Feb. 7, 1951, Detroit, Mich. (heart attack). Screen, stage and vaudeville actress.

Appeared in: **1933** Counsellor-at-Law (stage and film versions).

JACOBS, THOMAS
Born: 1903. Died: Mar. 3, 1976, Nice, Calif. Screen actor. Stand-in for actor/brother Danny Thomas.

JACOBSON, IRVING
Born: 1898, Cincinnati, Ohio. Died: Dec. 17, 1978, New York, N.Y. Screen, stage actor, stage director and stage producer. Married to actress Mae Schonfield (dec. 1978).

Appeared in: **1965** The Art of Love.

JACQUES, HATTIE (Josephine Edwina Jacques)
Born: Feb. 7, 1924, Kent, England. Died: Oct. 6, 1980, London, England (heart attack). Screen, stage, radio and television actress. Entered films in 1946.

Appeared in: **1947** Nicholas Nickleby. **1948** Oliver Twist (US 1951). **1949** Trottie True (aka Gay Lady—US 1950). **1950** Chance of a Lifetime (US 1951). **1952** The Pickwick Papers (US 1953). **1954** Our Girl Friday (aka The Adventures of Sadie—US 1955); The Love Lottery. **1955** As Song as They're Happy (US 1957). **1958** Carry on Sergeant (US 1959). **1959** Carry on Teacher (US 1962); Carry on Nurse (US 1960); Follow a Star (US 1961); The Night we Dropped a Clanger (aka Make Mine a Double—US 1961); Left, Right and Centre (US 1961). **1960** Make Mine Mink; Carry on Constable (US 1961); Watch Your Stern (US 1961). **1961** Carry on Regardless (US 1963); In the Doghouse (US 1964). **1962** She'll Have to Go (aka Maid for Murder—US 1963). **1963** Carry on Cabby (aka Call Me a Cab—US 1967). **1967** Carry on Doctor; The Bobo. **1969** Crooks and Coronets (aka Sophie's Place—US 1970); Monte Carlo or Bust (aka Those Daring Young Men in Their Jaunty Jalopies); Carry on Again, Doctor; The Magic Christian (US 1970).

JAFFE, CARL
Born: 1902, Germany. Died: Apr. 12, 1974, London, England. Screen, stage actor and stage producer.

Appeared in: **1937** Over the Moon (US 1940). **1938** Second Best Bed. **1939** An Englishman's Home (aka Madmen of Europe—US); The Silent Battle (aka Continental Express—US 1942); The Lion Has Wings (US 1940); The Saint in London. **1940** All Hands; Law and Disorder; Gasbags. **1942** Uncensored (US 1944). **1943** The Night Invader; The Life and Death of Colonel Blimp (aka Colonel Blimp—US 1945); Warn that Man. **1944** 2,000 Women. **1945** I Didn't Do It. **1946** Gaiety George (aka Showtime—US 1948). **1948** The Blind Goddess (US 1949); Counterblast. **1950** The Black Rose; Lilli Marlene (US 1951); State Secret (aka The Great Manhunt—US 1951). **1951** A Tale of Five Cities (aka A Tale of Five Women—US 1952). **1952** Ivanhoe. **1953** Appointment in London (US 1955); Park Plaza (aka Norman Conquest—US); Desperate Moment. **1954** Child's Play. **1955** Cross Channel; Timeslip (aka The Atomic Man—US). **1956** Satelite in the Sky; House of Secrets (aka Triple Deception—US 1957); The Hostage. **1957** The Traitors (aka The Accursed—US 1958). **1959** Subway in the Sky; First Man into Space. **1958** Battle of the VI (aka Unseen Heroes—US); I Accuse; Escapement (aka The Electric Monster—US 1960); Rockets Galore (aka Mad Little Island—US). **1961** The Roman Spring of Mrs. Stone. **1965** Operation Crossbow (aka The Great Spy Mission). **1967** The Double Man (US 1968); Battle Beneath the Earth.

JAHAR, ROY
Born: 1919, India. Died: Aug. 11, 1977, Calcutta, India. Screen and stage actor.

JAHR, ADOLF
Born: 1894. Died: Apr. 19, 1964, Stockholm, Sweden. Screen, stage actor and opera performer. Known as the "Sweedish Douglas Fairbanks."

Appeared in: **1924** Den Gamia Herrgarden (The Old Manor). **1934** Petterson and Bendel. **1937** Adolf Armstrong. **1940** Kryss med Albertin (Cruise in the Albertina). **1944** Homsoborna.

JAIDEV See AANDY, K

JAMES, ALF P. (Alfred Peter James)
Born: 1865, Australia. Died: Oct. 9, 1946, Hollywood, Calif. Screen, stage and vaudeville actor. Was in vaudeville with his wife in an act billed as "James and Pryor."

Appeared in: **1931** Everything's Rosie; Heaven on Earth. **1933** Thrill Hunter; Hokus Focus (short). **1934** Rocky Rhodes; Six of a Kind; Wonder Bar; Most Precious Things in Life; Elmer and Elsie; Cockeyed Cavaliers. **1935** Dr. Socrates. **1936** The Great Ziegfeld; Next Time We Love; The Singing Cowboy.

JAMES, BEN (James B. Solomon)
Born: 1921. Died: Mar. 29, 1966, Hollywood, Calif. (natural causes). Screen and television actor.

JAMES, EDDIE
Born: 1880. Died: Dec. 22, 1944, New York. Screen, stage actor and assistant film director.

Appeared in: **1925** Lucky Devil. **1926** Wild Oaks Lane.

JAMES, GARDNER
Born: 1901, New York, N.Y. Died: June 23, 1953, United States. Screen and stage actor.

Appeared in: **1924** The Love Bandit. **1925** Silent Sanderson; The Happy Warrior; Unrestrained Youth. **1926** The Night Patrol; Hell-Bent for Heaven; The Amateur Gentleman; The Flaming Forest; The Gilded Highway; The Passionate Quest. **1927** Ladies at Ease; Eager Lips. **1928** Kentucky Courage; The Big Killing; Soul's Aflame; The Mating Call; the Little Shepherd of Kingdom Come; The Singapore Mutiny. **1929** The Flying Fleet; The Studio Murder Mystery. **1930** The Dawn Patrol. **1935** Captain Blood. **1936** Crash Donovan. **1940** Adventures of Red Ryder (serial).

JAMES, GLADDEN
Born: 1892, Zanesville, Ohio. Died: Aug. 28, 1948, Hollywood, Calif. (leukemia). Screen and stage actor.

Appeared in: **1917** The Mystery of the Double Cross (serial). **1919** The Heart of the Wetona. **1920** Yes or No. **1921** His Brother's Keeper; Bucking the Tiger; Wise Husbands; The Silver Lining; Footfalls. **1922** Channing of the Northwest; The Faithless Sex. **1923** The Broken Violin; The Woman with Four Faces; A Clouded Name. **1924** Marry in Haste. **1925** Alias Mary Flynn; The Wedding Song. **1926** Tex. **1927** The Temptations of a Shop Girl. **1928** Sweet Sixteen; Adorable Cheat; Driftin' Sands; The Hound of Silver Creek; The Look Out Girl; The Girl He Didn't Buy. **1929** The Peacock Fan; His Captive Woman; The Girl from Woolworth's; Weary River. **1930** Paradise Island. **1931** Bad Company. **1933** Lucky Devils. **1935** Magnificent Obsession. **1936** Three Smart Girls; The Case Against Mrs. Ames; The Princess Comes Across. **1937** Captains Courageous. **1938** Boys Town. **1939** Another Thin Man; Pirates of the Skies. **1941** I Wanted Wings; Mr. and Mrs. North. **1942** Joe Smith, American; True to the Army; For Me and My Gal; The Postman Didn't Ring; Tennessee Johnson. **1944** Casanova Brown; Henry Aldrich Plays Cupid. **1945** Wilson.

JAMES, HORACE D.
Born: 1853, Baltimore, Md. Died: Oct. 16, 1925, Orange, N.J. Screen and stage actor.

Appeared in: **1921** Get-Rich Quick Wallingford (stage and film versions). **1922** A Woman's Woman. **1923** Adam and Eve.

JAMES, JOHN
Died: May 20, 1960, New York. Screen and stage actor.

Appeared in: **1942** Spy Smasher (serial); Westward Ho; Flying Tigers. **1943** Thundering Trails; Santa Fe Scouts; Gung Ho! **1944** Ladies Courageous; Since You Went Away; Story of Dr. Wassell; Practically Yours; Sign of the Cross. **1945** Renegades of the Rio Grande; Anchors Aweigh; Bedside Manner; This Man's Navy; Saddle Pals. **1946** Our Hearts Were Growing Up. **1948** The Countess of Monte Cristo; Tap Roots; Command Decision. **1949** The Gal Who Took the West; Gun Law Justice; The Valiant Hombre. **1953** Topeka.

JAMES, RUTH
Died: May 11, 1970. Screen actress.

JAMES, SIDNEY
Born: May 8, 1913, Johannesburg, South Africa. Died: Apr. 26, 1976, Sunderland, England. Screen, stage, radio, television actor and burlesque entertainer.

Appeared in: **1947** Black Memory. **1948** Once a Jolly Swagman (aka Maniacs on Wheels—US 1951); Night Beat. **1949** Give Us This Day (aka Salt to the Devil—US); Paper Orchid; The Small Back Room (US 1952). **1950** Last Holiday; The Man in Black; The Lady Craved Excitement. **1951** The Lavender Hill Mob; The Galloping Major; Talk of a Million (aka You Can't Beat the Irish—US); Lady Godiva Rides Again (US 1954). **1952** Father's Doing Fine; Venetian Bird (aka The

Assassin—US 1953); Miss Robin Hood; The Gift Horse (aka Glory at Sea—US 1953); I Believe in You (US 1953); Emergency Call (aka The Hundred Hour Hunt—US 1953); Time Gentlemen Please!; Tall Headlines (aka The Frightened Bride—US 1953); The Yellow Balloon (US 1954). **1953** The Flanagan Boy (aka Bad Blonde—US); The Square Ring (US 1955); The Titfield Thunderbolt; Park Plaza (aka Norman Conquest—US); Will Any Gentleman? (US 1955); Cosh Boy (aka The Slasher—US); The Wedding of Lilli Marlene; Is Your Honeymoon Really Necessary?; Malta Story (US 1954). **1954** For Better, For Worse (aka Cocktails in the Kitchen—US 1955); Orders are Orders; Seagulls Over Sorrento (aka Crest of the Wave—US); The House Across the Lake (aka Heat Wave—US); Father Brown (aka The Detective—US); The Belles of St. Trinian's (US 1955); Escape by Night; The Crowded Day; Aunt Clara; The Rainbow Jacket. **1955** John and Julie (US 1957); The Deep Blue Sea; The Glass Cage (aka The Glass Tomb—US); Joe Macbeth (US 1956); Out of the Clouds (US 1957); A Kid For Two Farthings (US 1956); A Yank in Ermine. **1956** The Iron Petticoat; It Was a Great Day; Trapeze; Wicked as They Come (US 1957); The Extra Day; Ramsbottom Rides Again; Dry Rot. **1957** A King in New York (US 1973); Campbell's Kingdom (US 1958); Quatermass II (aka Enemy from Space—US); Interpol (aka Pickup Alley—US); The Shiralee; Hell Drivers (US 1958); The Story of Esther Costello; The Smallest Show on Earth. **1958** Twelve Desperate Hours; Another Time, Another Place; I Was Monty's Double (aka Hell, Heaven or Hoboken); The Sheriff of Fractured Jaw; The Silent Enemy; The Man Inside; Next to No Time (US 1960). **1959** Too Many Crooks; Upstairs and Downstairs (US 1961); The 39 Steps (US 1960); Tommy the Toreador; Make Mine a Million (US 1965); Idol on Parade; Desert Mice. **1960** The Pure Hell of St. Trinian's (US 1961); Carry on Constable (US 1961); Watch Your Stern (US 1961); And the Same to You. **1961** Double Bunk; The Green Helmet; What a Carve Up! (aka No Place Like Homicide—US 1962); A Weekend With Lulu; What a Whopper!; Raising the Wind (aka Roommates—US 1962); Carry on Regardless (US 1963). **1962** Carry on Cruising; We Joined the Navy. **1963** Carry on Cabby (aka Call Me a Cab—US 1967). **1964** Carry on Cleo (US 1965); The Beauty Jungle (aka Contest Girl—US 1966). **1965** The Big Job; Carry on Cowboy. **1966** Where the Bullets Fly; Don't Lose Your Head; Arabesque; Three Hats for Lisa. **1967** Carry on Doctor. **1969** Carry on Camping. **1970** Carry on Up the Jungle; Carry on Loving; Carry on Henry. **1971** Carry on at Your Own Convenience. **1972** Bless This House; Carry on Matron; Carry on Abroad. **1973** Carry on Girls. **1974** Carry on Dick.

JAMES, WALTER
Born: 1886, Tenn. Died: June 27, 1946, Gardena, Calif. (heart attack). Screen and stage actor.

Appeared in: **1922** Fair Lady; The Secrets of Paris. **1924** Two Shall Be Born. **1925** Little Annie Rooney; The Everlasting Whisper; The Monster. **1926** The Seventh Bandit; Battling Butler; Glenister of the Mounted. **1927** The Blood Ship; Patent Leather Kid; The Irresistible Lover; The Kid Brother. **1928** The Wright Idea; The Big Killing; Me, Gangster. **1930** Shadow of the Law. **1931** Street Scene. **1936** Modern Times.

JAMESON, HOUSE
Born: 1903. Died: Apr. 23, 1971, Danbury, Conn. Screen, stage, radio and television actor. Noted for his radio and television portrayals as the father in "The Aldrich Family" series.

Appeared in: **1948** The Naked City. **1961** Parrish. **1965** Mirage. **1968** The Swimmer.

JAMIN, GEORGES
Born: 1907. Died: Feb. 23, 1971, Hemptinne, Belgium. Screen, stage and television actor.

Appeared in: **1931** Occupe-toi d'Amelia (film debut). **1939** Bouquets from Nicholas.

JAMIS, BILL (William John Gameos)
Born: 1925. Died: July 10, 1977, New York, N.Y. Screen, stage actor, dancer and choreographer.

JAMISON, ANNE
Born: 1910. Died: Apr. 16, 1961, Hollywood, Calif. Screen actress and radio opera performer.

Appeared in: **1938** Hollywood Hotel.

JAMISON, WILLIAM "BUD"
Born: 1894, Vallejo, Calif. Died: Sept. 30, 1944, Hollywood, Calif. Screen, stage and vaudeville actor.

Appeared in: **1917** Lonesome Luke. **1924** Troubles of a Bride; Dante's

Inferno; Darwin Was Right; The Cyclone Rider. **1927** Jake the Plumber; Closed Gates; Ladies Beware; His First Flame; Play Safe; Texas Steer; Wolves of the Air. **1928** Buck Privates; The Chaser; Heart Trouble. **1930** The Grand Parade; Traffic; plus the following shorts: Sugar Plum Papa; Bulls and Bears; Match Play; The Chumps. **1931** Taxi Troubles (short); Folly Comedies: second series of shorts including: Help Wanted Female; Gossipy Plumber; Parents Wanted; No, No, Lady. **1932** Hurry Call; Make Me a Star; plus the following shorts: The Dentist; Strictly Unreliable; All-American Toothache; Heavens! My Husband; The Giddy Age; In the Devil's Doghouse; In a Pigs Eye. **1933** The following shorts: California Weather; Loose Relations; Big Squeal; Dora's Dunkin' Donuts; His Weak Moment; Good Housewrecking; Quiet, Please; Hold Your Temper. **1934** The following shorts: Wrong Direction; One Too Many; Woman Haters; Men in Black; Devil's Doghouse; Three Little Pigskins. **1935** The following shorts: Old Sawbones; Alimony Aches; It Always Happens; Home Work; Honeymoon Bridge; Flying Down to Zero; Alibi Bye Bye; Uncivil Warriors; Hoi Polloi; Three Little Beers. **1936** Come and Get It; Ticket to Paradise; plus the following shorts: Aladdin from Manhattan; Caught in the Act; Disorder in the Court; Grand Slam Opera; Movie Maniacs; On the Wrong Trek; A Pain in the Pullman; Ants in the Pantry; Whoops I'm an Indian. **1937** Melody of the Plains; plus the following shorts: The Grand Hooter; The Wrong Miss Wright; The Big Squirt; Man Bites Lovebug; Gracie at the Bat; Morning, Judge; Jail Bait; Love Nest on Wheels; Back to the Woods; Dizzy Doctors. **1938** The following shorts: Time Out For Trouble; A Doggone Mixup; Sue My Lawyer; The Old Raid Mule; Jump, Chump, Jump; Soul of a Heel; Kennedy's Castle; Stage Fright; Termites of 1938; Wee Wee, Monsieur; Tassels in the Air; Healthy, Wealthy and Dumb; Violent Is the Word for Curly; Mutts to You. **1939** Topper Takes a Trip; plus the following shorts: The Sap Takes a Wrap; Rattling Romeo; Teacher's Pest; The Awful Good; Crime Rave; Moving Vanities; Ring Madness; Pest from the West; Mooching Through Georgia; Three Little Sew and Sews; A-Ducking They Did Go; We Want Our Mummy; Three Sappy People. **1940** Li'l Abner; Slightly Honorable; Captain Caution; plus the following shorts: The Heckler; His Bridal Fright; Cold Turkey; Boobs in the Woods; Nothing But Pleasure; A-Plumbing We Will Go. **1941** Model Wife; Wild Bill Hickcock Rides; plus the following shorts: A Polo Phony; So You Won't Squawk; She's Oil Mine; General Nuisance; I'll Never Heil Again; Dutiful But Dumb; All the World's a Stooge; An Ache in Every Stake. **1942** You Can't Escape Forever; Her Cardboard Lover; plus the following shorts: Stardust on the Sage; What Makes Lizzy Dizzy?; Tireman, Spare My Tires; All Work and No Pay; Rough on Rents; Dear! Deer!; Three Smart Saps; Sock-a-Bye Baby; Loco Boy Makes Good; Even as I.O.U. **1943** Coney Island; True to Life; plus the following shorts: Farmer for a Day; Hot Foot; Double Up; Seeing Nellie Home; Dizzy Detectives; Back from the Front; Three Little Twerps; I Can Hardly Wait; Phony Express; A Gem of a Jam; Blitz on the Fritz. **1944** It Happened Tomorrow; Mrs. Parkington; Lost in a Harem; plus the following shorts: His Tale Is Told; Gold Is Where You Lose It; Love Your Landlord; Say Uncle; Crash Goes the Hash. **1945** Nob Hill; See My Lawyer; Billy Rose's Diamond Horseshoe.

JAMOIS, MARGUERITE
Born: 1901, France. Died: Nov. 20, 1964, Paris, France (cancer). Screen, stage actress and stage director.

Appeared in: **1951** The Secret of Mayerling.

JANIS, ELSIE (Elsie Bierbower)
Born: Mar. 16, 1889, Ohio. Died: Feb. 26, 1956, Beverly Hills, Calif. Screen, stage, vaudeville actor, composer, author and screenwriter. Married to actor Gilbert Wilson.

Appeared in: **1915** The Caprices of Kitty; Betty in Search of a Thrill; Nearly a Lady. **1919** A Regular Girl. **1920** Everybody's Sweetheart. **1927** Behind the Lines (short). **1940** Women in War; also several short subjects.

JANNEY, LEON (Leon Ramon)
Born: Apr. 1, 1917, Ogden, Utah. Died: Oct. 28, 1980, Chapala, Jalisco, Guadalajara, Mexico (cancer). Screen, stage, vaudeville, radio and television actor.

Appeared in: **1928** Abie's Irish Rose; The Wind. **1930** Bear Shooters (short); Father's Son; The Doorway to Hell; Old English; Courage. **1931** Penrod and Sam; Their Mad Moment. **1932** Police Court; Fame Street. **1933** Terror Abroad; Should Ladies Behave? **1935** Laddie. **1936** The Return of Jimmie Valentine. **1941** Stolen Paradise. **1959** The Last Mile. **1968** Charly.

JANNINGS, EMIL (Theodor Friedrich Janenz)
Born: July 26, 1886, Brooklyn, N.Y. Died: Jan. 3, 1950, Stroblhof/Wolfgangsee, Austria (cancer). Screen and stage actor. Entered films in 1915. Married to actress Lucie Hoeflich (dec. 1956). Won 1927/28 Academy Award for Best Actor for his two roles in The Way of All Flesh and The Last Command. Was the first actor ever to receive an Academy Award.

Appeared in: **1914** Arme Eva; Im Banne der Leidenschaften; Passionels Tagebuch. **1915** Stein Unter Steinen. **1916** Die Ehe der Luise Rohrbach; Nacht des Grauens. **1917** Passion; Ein Fideles Gefaengnis; Lulu; Klingendes Leben; Die Seeschlacht. **1918** Der Mann der Tat. **1919** Rose Bernd; Madame DuBarry (aka Passion—US 1920 and 1917 version). **1920** Algol; Das Grosse Licht; Kohlhiesels Toechter; Der Schaedel der Pharaonentochter; Anna Boleyn (aka Deception—US 1921); Die Brueder Karamasoff (The Brothers Karamazov). **1921** Vendetta; Die Berghatze; Die Ratten; Der Stier von Olivera; Danton (aka All for a Woman); Das Weib des Pharao (The Loves of Pharaoh—US 1922, and aka Pharaoh's Wife). **1922** August der Starke; Fuhrmann Henschel; Die Graefin von Paris (The Countess of Paris); Othello (US 1923); Peter der Grosse (Peter the Great—US 1923). **1923** Alles fuer Geld (All for Money); Tragoedie der Liebe (Love Tragedy); Liebe Macht Blind (Love Makes One Blind). **1924** Der Letzte Mann (The Last Laugh—US 1925); Nju (aka Eine Unverstandene Frau, and aka Husbands and Lovers—US 1927); Das Wachsfigurenkabinett (Waxworks). **1925** Quo Vadis (US 1929); Tartuff (US 1927); Variete (Variety—US 1925). **1926** Faust; The Three Way Works. **1927** The Way of All Flesh. **1928** The Street of Sin; The Patriot; Fortune's Fool; The Last Command; Power; Sins of the Fathers. **1929** Betrayal; Fighting the White Slave Traffic. **1930** Der Blaue Engel (The Blue Angel); Liebling der Gotter (Darling of the Gods). **1931** Stuerme der Leidenschaft (Storms of Passion—US 1932). **1932** The Tempest. **1933** Der Grosse Tenor (The Great Tenor); Die Abenteuer des Koenigs Pausole (aka Koenig Pausole). **1934** Der Schwarze Walfisch. **1935** Der Alte und der Junge Koenig (The Young and the Old King). **1936** Traumulus. **1937** The Ruler; Der Herrscher; Der Zerbrochene Krug (The Broken Jug—US 1928). **1939** Robert Koch, der Bekaempfer des Todes. **1941** Ohm Kruger (German propaganda film). **1942** Die Entlassung. **1943** Altes Herz Wird Wieder Jung. **1945** Wo ist Herr Belling?

JANOV, ELLEN
Born: 1954. Died: Jan. 7, 1976 (result of fire). Screen and television actress.
Appeared in: **1968** The Horse in the Gray Flannel Suit.

JANS, HARRY
Born: 1900. Died: Feb. 4, 1962, Hollywood, Calif. (heart attack). Screen, stage and vaudeville actor. Was in vaudeville team of "Jans and Whalen."

Appeared in: **1929** Two Good Boys Gone Wrong (short). **1936** Special Investigator; Two in Revolt; The Last Outlaw; Grand Jury; Don't Turn 'Em Loose; Smartest Girl in Town; Racing Lady; Charlie Chan at the Race Track; Murder on a Bridal Path. **1937** Don't Tell the Wife; That Girl from Paris.

JANSEN, HARRY A. *See* DANTE

JANSON, VICTOR
Born: 1885, Germany. Died: July, 1960, Berlin. Screen actor and film director.

Appeared in: **1929** At the Edge of the World. **1932** 1914: The Last Days Before the War. **1939** Nanu; Sie Kennen Korff noch Nicht (So You Don't Know Korff Yet?). **1950** Marriage of Figaro. **1952** Prince of Pappenheim. **1953** Hit Parade. **1954** Anne of Tharau.

JANSSEN, DAVID (David Harold Meyer)
Born: Mar. 27, 1931, Naponee, Nebr. Died: Feb. 13, 1980, Malibu, Calif. (heart attack). Screen and television actor. Divorced from Ellie Graham. Later married to Dani Greco.

Appeared in: **1945** It's a Pleasure (film debut). **1946** Swamp Fire. **1952** Bonzo Goes to College; Yankee Buccaneer. **1955** The Private War of Major Benson; Chief Crazy Horse; The Square Jungle; Francis in the Navy; To Hell and Back; Cult of the Cobra. **1956** Toy Tiger; The Girl He Left Behind; Away All Boats; Never Say Goodbye; Francis in the Haunted House; Showdown at Abilene. **1958** Lafayette Escadrille. **1960** Hell to Eternity. **1961** The Big Bankroll; Twenty Plus Two; Dondi; Ring of Fire; King of the Roaring Twenties; Man Trap; The Story of Arnold Rothstein. **1962** Belle Sommers. **1963** My Six Loves. **1967** Warning Shot. **1968** The Green Berets; The Shoes of the Fisherman. **1969** Where It's At; Generation (aka A Time for Giving); Marooned. **1970** Macho Callahan. **1975** Once is Not Enough. **1976** Two-Minute Warning. **1977** Warhead; The Swiss Conspiracy. **1980** Covert Action.

JAQUET, FRANT (Frank Garnier Jaquet)
Born: Mar. 16, 1885, Wis. Died: May 11, 1958, Los Angeles, Calif. (heart attack). Screen actor.

Appeared in: **1934** War is a Racket. **1938** Strange Faces; Crime School; When Were You Born?; My Lucky Star; Shine on Harvest Moon; Hold That Co-Ed; Party Fever. **1939** Mr. Smith Goes to Washington; Stanley and Livingstone; Dust be My Destiny; Eternally Yours. **1941** No Greater Sin. **1942** Tales of Manhattan; Ice-Capades Revue; Call of the Canyon; Raiders of the Range. **1944** The Thin Man Goes Home; None Shall Escape; Beneath Western Skies; Black Magic; Call of the South Seas; Call of the Rockies; Bowery Champs; Silver City Kid. **1945** Trail to Vengeance; Federal Operator 99 (serial); The Vampire's Ghost; Grissly's Millions; A Bell for Adano; Mr. Muggs Rides Again; The Cisco Kid in Old New Mexico.

JARDINE, BETTY (Elizabeth Kittrick Jardine)
Born: Heaton Moor, Manchester, England. Died: Feb. 28, 1945, England? Screen and stage actress. Entered films in 1937.

Appeared in: **1938** Almost a Honeymoon. **1940** The Girl in the News (US 1941). **1944** A Canterbury Tale.

JARRETT, ARTHUR L. "ART"
Born: Feb. 5, 1888, Marysville, Calif. Died: June 12, 1960, New York, N.Y. Screen, stage, television actor and songwriter. Father of Art Jarrett, singer and orchestra leader and brother of actor Dan Jarrett (dec. 1938).

Appeared in: **1932-33** Universal "Radio Star Reels." **1933** Ace of Aces; Dancing Lady; Sitting Pretty; Let's Fall in Love. **1934** Riptide; Hollywood Party. **1936** Blue Blazes (short). **1937** An Educational short. **1938** My Lucky Star. **1939** Trigger Pals. **1950** The Tattooed Stranger.

JARRETT, DAN
Born: 1894. Died: Mar. 13, 1938, Hollywood, Calif. (heart ailment). Screen, stage actor, screenwriter and playwright. Brother of actor Arthur Jarrett (dec. 1960).

Appeared in: **1922** Sunshine Harbor. **1935** The Cowboy Millionaire.

JARRETT, DANIEL
Born: Wales. Died: Sept. 23, 1917, Brooklyn, N.Y. (pneumonia). Screen and stage actor. Do not confuse with actor of same name (dec.).

Appeared in: **1917** The Slacker.

JARVIS, AL
Born: 1910, Winnipeg, Canada. Died: May 6, 1970, Newport Beach, Calif. (heart attack). Screen, radio and television actor.

Appeared in: **1953** The Twonky. **1962** The Phantom Planet.

JARVIS, JEAN
Born: 1903. Died: Mar. 16, 1933, Hollywood, Calif. Screen actress and showgirl.

Appeared in: **1925** Fear Bound. **1926** The Little Giant.

JARVIS, LAURA E.
Born: 1866. Died: Mar. 9, 1933, near Downey, Calif. (injuries received from hit and run driver). Screen actress.

JARVIS, ROBERT C.
Born: 1892. Died: Nov. 13, 1971, Bloomsbury, N.J. Screen, stage actor and stage director.

Appeared in: **1930** Putting It On (short). **1933** Gold Diggers of 1933. **1938** Torchy Gets Her Man. **1939** Torchy Blane Runs for Mayor; Torchy Blane in Chinatown.

JARVIS, SYDNEY (aka SIDNEY JARVIS)
Born: 1881, New York, N.Y. Died: June 6, 1939, Hollywood, Calif. Screen, stage and vaudeville actor. Entered films in 1914.

Appeared in: **1927** Casey at the Bat; The Prairie King. **1928** Circus Rookies; The Upland Rider; The Wagon Show. **1929** The Unholy Night; Footlights and Fools. **1930** Kismet. **1932** Movie Crazy. **1934** The Count of Monte Cristo; The Mighty Barnum; Hey Nanny Nanny (short).

JAUDENES, JOSE ALVARES "LEPE"
Born: 1891, Spain. Died: July, 1967, Madrid, Spain. Screen actor. Entered films in 1935.

Appeared in: Nine Letters to Bertha.

JAVOR, PAL (Paul Javor)
Born: Jan. 31, 1902, Arad, Hungary. Died: Aug. 14, 1959, Budapest, Hungary. Screen and stage actor.

Appeared in: **1933** A Key Balvany. **1934** Iza Neni (Aunt Isa); My Wife; The Miss; Rakoczi Indulo. **1935** Huszarszerelem; Koeszoenoem Hogy Elgazolt; Igloi Diakok; Elnoek Kisasszony; A Csunya Lany. **1936** The New Squire; Nem Elhetek Muzsikaszo Nelkuel; Az uj Foeldersur. **1937** Salary, 200 a Month; Naszut Felaron; Fizessen Nagysag; Viki; A Ferfi Mind Oeruelt (All Men Are Crazy); Toprini Nasz (Wedding in Toprin). **1938** Pusztai Szel (Beauty of the Pusta); Torockoi Menyasszony (Torockoi Bride); Ill-es Szobaban (In Room 111); Mother Love; Noszty Flue Este Toth Marival; Maga Lesz a Ferjem (You Will Be My Husband); Marika; Ket Fogoly (Two Prisoners). **1939** Fekete Gyemantok (Black Diamonds). **1940** Uz Bence. **1949** Carmela. **1951** The Great Caruso; Assignment—Paris.

JAY, DOROTHY
Born: 1908. Died: July 28, 1936, Los Angeles, Calif. Screen actress.

Appeared in: **1927** Is Your Daughter Safe?

JAY, ERNEST
Born: Sept. 18, 1893, London, England. Died: 1957. Screen and stage actor.

Appeared in: **1933** Tiger Bay. **1935** The Iron Duke. **1936** Broken Blossoms (US 1937). **1937** O.H.M.S. (aka You're in the Army Now—US). **1938** I See Ice. **1944** Don't Take it to Heart (US 1949). **1946** School for Secrets. **1948** Vice Versa; Death in the Hand; Blanche Fury. **1949** The History of Mr. Polly (US 1951); Edward My Son; Golden Arrow (aka Three Men and a Girl). **1951** The Franchise Affair (US 1952). **1952** I Believe in You (US 1953); Top Secret (aka Mr. Potts Goes to Moscow—US 1954). **1953** The Sword and the Rose. **1955** The Reluctant Bride (aka Two Grooms for a Bride—US 1957). **1956** Who Done It? **1957** The Curse of Frankenstein; Doctor at Large.

JEAN
Died: 1916. The Vitagraph Dog.

JEANS, URSULA (Ursula McMinn)
Born: May 5, 1906, Simla, India. Died: Apr. 21, 1973, near London, England. Screen and stage actress. Married to actor Robin Irvine (dec. 1933) and later married to actor Roger Livesey (dec. 1976).

Appeared in: **1922** A Gypsy Cavalier (film debut). **1923** The Virgin Queen. **1924** My Lady April (rerelease of A Gypsy Cavalier—1922). **1926** Silence. **1927** Quinneys; The Fake; False Colours. **1928** The Passing of Mr. Quin; S.O.S. **1931** The Love Habit; The Flying Fool. **1932** The Crooked Lady; Once Bitten; The Barton Mystery. **1933** Cavalcade; I Lived With You; Friday, the Thirteenth (US 1934); On Thin Ice. **1936** The Man in the Mirror (US 1937). **1937** Dark Journey; Over the Moon (US 1940); Storm in a Teacup. **1943** The Life and Death of Colonel Blimp (aka Colonel Blimp—US 1945). **1944** Mr. Emmanuel (US 1945). **1946** Gaiety George (aka Showtime—US 1948). **1947** The Woman in the Hall (US 1949). **1948** The Weaker Sex (US 1949). **1955** The Night My Number Came Up; The Dam Busters. **1959** Northwest Frontier (aka Flame Over India—US 1960). **1961** The Green Helmet; The Queen's Guards (US 1963). **1964** Boy With a Flute. **1965** The Battle of the Villa Fiorita.

JEAYES, ALLAN
Born: Jan. 19, 1885, London, England. Died: Sept. 20, 1963, London, England (heart attack). Screen, stage actor, playwright and author.

Appeared in: **1918** Nelson; A Gentleman of France; The Hound of the Baskervilles. **1921** The Adventures of Sherlock Holmes series including The Solitary Cyclist. **1922** The Missioner. **1925** Bulldog Drummond's Third Round (aka The Third Round). **1929** The Hate Ship. **1931** The Ghost Train (US 1933); Stranglehold. **1932** Above Rubies; The Impassive Footman (aka Woman in Bondage—US). **1933** Anne One Hundred; Purse Strings; Little Napoleon; Paris Plane; Song of the Plough; Eves of Fate; Ask Beccles. **1934** Colonel Blood; Catherine the Great; Red Ensign (aka Strike!—US); The Camels Are Coming. **1935** Koenigsmark; Drake of England (aka Drake the Pirate—US); The Scarlet Pimpernel; Sanders of the River. **1936** King of the Damned; Things to Come; Crown V Stevens; Forget-Me-Not (aka Forever Yours—US 1937); Seven Sinners (aka Doomed Cargo—US); The House of the Spaniard; Rembrandt; His Lordship (aka Man of Affaires—US 1937). **1937** The High Command; Elephant Boy; The Squeaker (aka Murder on Diamond Row—US); The Return of the Scarlet Pimpernel (US 1938); The Green Cockatoo (aka Four Dark Hours). **1938** Dangerous Medicine; 13 Men and a Gun; They Drive By Night; A Royal Divorce. **1939** The Good Old Days; The Four Feathers; The Stars Look Down (US 1941); The Spider. **1940**

You Will Remember; The Proud Valley; Spy For a Day; Convoy (US 1941); The Thief of Bagdad; Sailors Three (aka Three Cockeyed Sailors—US 1941). **1941** Pimpernel Smith (aka Mister V—US 1942). **1942** Tomorrow We Live (aka At Dawn We Die—US 1943); Talk About Jacqueline. **1943** The Shipbuilders. **1945** Perfect Stangers (aka Vacation from Marriage—US). **1946** Lisbon Story. **1947** The Man Within (aka The Smugglers—US 1948). **1948** An Ideal Husband; Blanche Fury; Saraband for Dead Lovers (aka Saraband—US 1949). **1949** Obsession (aka The Hidden Room—US 1950). **1950** Waterfront (aka Waterfront Women—US 1952); The Reluctant Widow (US 1951). **1962** Reach For Glory (US 1963).

JEFFERIES, DOUGLAS
Born: Apr. 21, 1884, Hamstead, England. Died: Dec., 1959, England? Screen and stage actor.

Appeared in: **1934** Channel Crossing. **1947** Frieda.

JEFFERS, JOHN S.
Born: 1874. Died: Jan. 3, 1939, Long Beach, N.Y. Screen and stage actor. Entered films with Bison Company.

JEFFERS, WILLIAM L.
Born: 1898. Died: Apr. 18, 1959, Hollywood, Calif. Screen and stage actor. Appeared in silents.

JEFFERSON, DAISY
Born: 1889. Died: June 3, 1967, Calif. Screen actress. Appeared in silents.

JEFFERSON, HILTON W.
Born: 1902. Died: Nov. 14, 1968, Sydenham, N.Y. Black screen actor and musician.

Appeared in: **1943** Stormy Weather.

JEFFERSON, JOSEPH, III
Born: Feb. 20, 1829, Philadelphia, Pa. Died: Apr. 23, 1905, West Palm Beach, Fla. (pneumonia). Screen and stage actor. Joseph Jefferson was a fourth generation member of the Jefferson theatrical family. He was the father of stage actor Charles Burke (dec.?) and William Winter (dec. 1946) and Thomas Jefferson (dec. 1932). Married to stage actress Margaret Clements Lockyer (dec.) and later married to Sarah Warren.

Appeared in: **1903** Rip Van Winkle (stage and film versions).

JEFFERSON, TED
Born: 1893, Australia. Died: Dec. 17, 1933, Santa Monica, Calif. (reaction after tooth extraction). Screen and stage actor. Brother of actor Stan Laurel (dec. 1965).

JEFFERSON, THOMAS
Born: 1859. Died: Apr. 2, 1932, Hollywood, Calif. Screen and stage actor. Entered films with D. W. Griffith in 1909. Regarding family, see Joseph Jefferson III.

Appeared in: **1913** Judith of Bethulia. **1915** Sable Lorcha; The Fortune Hunter; The Old Chemist; The Fencing Master; The Old Clothes Shop. **1916** The Beloved Liar; Corporal Billy's Comeback; The Attic Princess; The Sea Lily; Betty's Hobo; A Child of Mystery; The Grip of Crime; Little Eve Edgarton; Under the Gaslight; Classmates; Through Solid Walls. **1918** The Romance of Tarzan; A Hoosier Romance; Tarzan of the Apes. **1919** Sis Hopkins; The Spenders. **1921** Rip Van Winkle; The Idle Rich; My Lady's Latchkey; Straight from Paris. **1922** Beauty's Worth; A Tailor Made Man; The Son of the Wolf; Good Men and True; Vermillion Pencil. **1925** Thoroughbred. **1927** Paid to Love. **1928** The Fortune Hunter (and 1915 version); Soft Living. **1929** On With the Show. **1930** Double Cross Roads; Just Like Heaven; Lightnin'. **1931** Ten Nights in a Bar Room. **1932** Forbidden.

JEFFERSON, WILLIAM WINTER
Born: 1876, London, England. Died: Feb. 10, 1946, Honolulu, Hawaii. Stage and screen actor. Divorced from stage actress Christie MacDonald (dec. 1962) and married to stage actress Vivian Martin. Regarding family, see Joseph Jefferson III.

Appeared in: **1913** The Rivals. **1915** Marrying Money. **1917** Her Own People.

JEFFREY, HUGH S.
Born: 1880, Belfast, Ireland. Died: Jan. 18, 1927, Hollywood, Calif. (asphixiated). Screen, stage actor and casting director.

Appeared in: **1914** The Governor's Ghost. **1915** The Grey Mask. **1916** The Price of Malice; The Wager. **1917** The End of the Tour. **1919** Virtuous Men; Out of the Fog.

JEFFREY, MICHAEL
Born: 1895. Died: Sept. 30, 1960, Hollywood, Calif. (heart attack). Screen, stage and television actor.

Appeared in: **1937** Dangerous Holiday; Mr. Boggs Steps Out. **1956** Man in the Gray Flannel Suit.

JEFFREYS, ELLIS
Born: May 17, 1877, Ceylon. Died: Jan. 21, 1943, Surrey, England. Stage and screen actress.

Appeared in: **1930** Birds of Prey (aka The Perfect Alibi—US 1931). **1934** Lilies of the Field. **1935** While Parents Sleep; Limelight (aka Backstage—US). **1936** Eliza Comes to Stay.

JEFFRIES, JAMES J. (James Jackson Jeffries)
Born: Apr. 15, 1875, Carroll, Iowa. Died: Mar. 3, 1953, Burbank, Calif. (stroke). Screen actor and professional boxer.

Appeared in: **1915** Pennington's Choice. **1924** Jeffries, Jr. (short); Kid Speed (short). **1926** Prince of Broadway. **1927** One Round Hogan. **1928** Beau Broadway. **1932** Midnight Patrol; They Never Come Back; The Fighting Gentleman. **1937** Big City. **1940** Barnyard Follies. **1941** Mr. Celebrity. **1968** The Legendary Champions (documentary).

JENKINS, ALLEN (Alfred McGonegal)
Born: Apr. 9, 1890 or 1900?, New York, N.Y. Died: July 20, 1974, Santa Monica, Calif. (complications following surgery). Screen, stage and television actor.

Appeared in: **1930** Straight and Narrow (short). **1931** The Girl Habit. **1932** Blessed Event; Three on a Match; I Am a Fugitive from a Chain Gang; Lawyer Man. **1933** The Mind Reader; Silk Express; Hard to Handle; Bureau of Missing Persons; The Keyhole; The Mayor of Hell; Tomorrow at Seven; Professional Sweetheart; Havana Widows; 42nd Street; Blondie Johnson; Employees' Entrance; Ladies They Talk About; A Vitaphone short. **1934** I've Got Your Number; Jimmy the Gent; The Merry Frinks; Twenty Million Sweethearts; Happiness Ahead; Beside; Whirlpool; St. Louis Kid; The Big Shakedown; The Case of the Howling Dog. **1935** Sweet Music; While the Patient Slept; A Night at the Ritz; I Live for Love; Miss Pacific Fleet; Case of the Curious Bride; Page Miss Glory; The Irish in Us; The Case of the Lucky Legs; Broadway Hostess. **1936** The Singing Kid; Three Men on a Horse; Sins of Man; Cain and Mabel; Sing Me a Love Song. **1937** Ever Since Eve; The Perfect Specimen; Dead End; Ready, Willing and Able; Marked Woman; Dance, Charlie, Dance; There Goes My Girl; The Singing Marine; Marry the Girl; Sh! The Octopus. **1938** Swing Your Lady; Going Places; A Slight Case of Murder; The Amazing Dr. Clitterhouse; Golddiggers in Paris; Racket Busters; Hard to Get; Fools for Scandal; Heart of the North. **1939** Five Came Back; Destry Rides Again; Torchy Plays with Dynamite; Naughty But Nice; Sweepstakes Winner. **1940** Tin Pan Alley; Brother Orchid; Meet the Wildcat; Oh Johnny—How You Can Love; Margie. **1941** Go West, Young Lady; Footsteps in the Dark; Ball of Fire; A Date with the Falcon; The Gay Falcon; Time Out for Rhythm; Dive Bomber. **1942** Maisie Gets Her Man; The Falcon Takes Over; Tortilla Flat; Eyes in the Night; They All Kissed the Bride. **1943** Stage Door Canteen. **1945** Wonder Man; Lady on a Train. **1946** Meet Me on Broadway; The Dark Horse; Singin' in the Corn. **1947** Wild Harvest; The Hat Box Mystery; The Senator Was Indiscreet; Fun on a Weekend; Easy Come, Easy Go. **1948** The Inside Story. **1949** The Big Wheel. **1950** Bodyhold. **1951** Behave Yourself; Let's Go Navy; Win, Place and Show; Crazy Over Horses. **1952** Oklahoma Annie; Wac from Walla Walla. **1959** Pillow Talk. **1963** It's a Mad, Mad, Mad, Mad World. **1964** Robin and the 7 Hoods; I'd Rather be Rich; For Those Who Think Young. **1967** Doctor—You've Got to be Kidding! **1974** Front Page.

JENKINS, ELIZABETH
Born: 1879. Died: Jan. 18, 1965, Caldwell, N.Y. Screen and stage actress. Appeared in silent films.

JENKS, FRANK
Born: 1902, Des Moines, Iowa. Died: May 13, 1962, Hollywood, Calif. (cancer). Screen and television actor.

Appeared in: **1933** College Humor. **1936** Swing Time; Farmer in the Dell; The Smartest Girl in Town; Follow the Fleet; The Witness Chair; The Last Outlaw; Walking on Air; Don't Turn 'Em Loose; We Who Are About to Die; That Girl from Paris; The Big Broadcast of 1937. **1937** When's Your Birthday?; There Goes My Girl; Saturday's Heroes; Angel's Holiday; One Hundred Men and a Girl; The Westland Case; You're a Sweetheart; Prescription for Romance. **1938** Love is a Headache; Goodbye Broadway; Reckless Living; The Lady in the Morgue; The Devil's Party; A Letter of Introduction; Youth Takes a Fling; The Storm; Strange Faces; The Last Warning. **1939** Society

Smugglers; Big Town Czar; S.O.S.; Tidal Wave; First Love; You Can't Cheat an Honest Man; The Under-Pup. **1940** Melody and Moonlight; Three Cheers for the Irish; A Little Bit of Heaven; His Girl Friday. **1941** Tall, Dark and Handsome; Dancing on a Dime; Scattergood Meets Broadway; Back Street; Flame of New Orleans. **1942** Maisie Gets Her Man; The Navy Comes Through; Manhattan Maisie; Syncopation; Two Yanks in Trinidad; Seven Miles from Alcatraz. **1943** Hi Ya, Sailor; Shantytown; Corregidor; Thousands Cheer; His Butler's Sister; Gildersleeve's Bad Day; So's Your Uncle. **1944** Take It or Leave It; Dixie Jamboree; This Is the Life; Shake Hands with Murder; Ladies Courageous; Rosie the Riveter; Follow the Boys; Two Girls and a Sailor; Three Little Sisters; The Falcon in Hollywood; The Impatient Years; Strange Affair; Rogue's Gallery; Roger Touhy—Gangster. **1945** The Kid Sister; The Missing Corpse; Zombies on Broadway; The Phantom of 42nd Street; Christmas in Conneticut; Bedside Manner; G.I. Honeymoon; Steppin' in Society. **1946** Blondie's Lucky Day; That Brennan Girl; White Tie and Tails; One Way to Love. **1947** Joe Palooka in Winner Take All; Philo Vance's Gamble; That's My Girl; Kilroy Was Here; Philo Vance's Secret Mission. **1948** You Gotta Stay Happy; Blonde Savage; Family Honeymoon; Mary Lou; Winner Take All; Blondie's Reward. **1949** Shep Comes Home. **1950** Lucky Losers; Motor Patrol; Blondie's Hero; To Please a Lady; Woman on the Run; The Petty Girl; The Dungeon; Mother Didn't Tell Me; Joe Palooka in the Squared Circle. **1951** Silver City Bonanza; The Scarf; Let's Go Navy; Bowery Battalion; Utah Wagon Train; Pecos River. **1952** Mr. Walkie-Talkie. **1953** White Lightning. **1954** Highway Dragnet. **1955** Artists and Models; Sudden Danger. **1956** Dig That Uranium; The She-Creature; The Houston Story; Shake, Rattle and Rock. **1957** The Amazing Colossal Man.

JENKS, LULU BURNS

Born: 1870. Died: Apr. 15, 1939, Los Angeles, Calif. Screen actress.

JENKS, SI (Howard Jenkins)

Born: Sept. 23, 1876, Pa. Died: Jan. 6, 1970, Woodland Hills, Calif. (heart disease). Screen, stage, vaudeville actor and circus performer. Entered films in 1920.

Appeared in: **1931** Man from Death Valley; Oklahoma Jim. **1932** Galloping Through. **1933** Self Defense; Dr. Bull and Mr. Skitch. **1934** Stand Up and Cheer; Charlie Chan's Courage; Sixteen Fathoms Deep. **1935** Music is Magic; Steamboat 'Round the Bend; Law Beyond the Range; Fighting Shadows; Rider of the Law; Outlaw Deputy; Another Face; plus the following shorts: Old Sawbones; Uncivil Warriors; The E-Flat Man. **1936** Fury; Pigskin Parade; Captain January; Special Investigator; Follow Your Heart; The President's Mystery; All American Toothache (short). **1937** The Lady Fights Back; Saratoga; Thrill of a Lifetime; You Can't Have Everything; The Outcasts of Poker Flat; Don't Tell the Wife; Topper; Hillbilly Goat (short); Pick a Star; A Day at the Races. **1938** Rawhide; Kentucky Moonshine; Tom Sawyer—Detective. **1939** Stagecoach; Gone With the Wind; Drums Along the Mohawk; Frontier Marshal; Union Pacific. **1940** The Ranger and the Lady; Girl from God's Country; Ride, Tenderfoot, Ride; The Trail Blazers; The Old Swimmin' Hole; Chad Hanna. **1941** Sergeant York; Bad Men of Missouri; The Great Train Robbery; Buy Me That Town. **1942** Ice-Capades Revue; Cowboy Serenade. **1943** It's a Great Life; Wild Horse Stampede. **1944** Zorro's Black Whip (serial). **1945** The Man from Oklahoma. **1946** Duel in the Sun; The Dark Horse. **1947** Son of Zorro (serial); Trail Street; Unconquered. **1948** The Dude Goes West. **1951** Kentucky Jubilee. **1952** Oklahoma Annie.

JENNER, GEORGE

Born: Dec. 19, 1875, Kent, England. Died: Dec. 16, 1946, Hollywood, Calif. (heart attack). Screen actor.

JENNINGS, AL

Born: 1864, Va. Died: Dec 26, 1961, Tarzana, Calif. Screen actor and author. Onetime real "badman" of the Old West—convicted train robber, cattle thief and gunman.

Appeared in: **1908** The Bank Robbery. **1915** When Outlaws Meet; Beating Back; The Lady of the Dugout. **1916** The Dalton Boys. **1918** The Captain of the Gray Horse Troop; Beyond the Law; The Fighting Trail (serial). **1924** Fighting Fury; The Sea Hawk. **1926** The Demon; The Ridin' Rascal. **1927** Loco Luck. **1930** The Land of Missing Men.

JENNINGS, CLAUDIA (Mimi Chesterton)

Born: 1950, Evanston, Ill. Died: Oct. 3, 1979, Malibu, Calif. (auto accident). Screen, stage, television actress and model.

Appeared in: **1972** The Unholy Rollers. **1974** Truck Stop Woman; The Single Girls; Gator Bait. **1975** Willie and Scratch. **1977** The Great Texas Dynamite Chase; Moonshine County Express; Sisters of Death. **1978** Deathsport. **1979** Fast Company.

JENNINGS, DE WITT

Born: June 21, 1879, Cameron, Mo. Died: Mar. 1, 1937, Hollywood, Calif. Screen and stage actor. Entered films in 1920.

Appeared in: **1921** Lady Fingers; The Invisible Power; Alias Lady Fingers; Beating the Game; There Are No Villains; Three Sevens; The Poverty of Riches; The Greater Claim; The Golden Snare; From the Ground Up. **1922** The Face Between; Mixed Faces; Flesh and Blood; Sherlock Brown; The Right That Failed. **1923** Circus Days; Out of Luck; Within the Law; Blinky. **1924** Name the Man; Hit and Run; Along Came Ruth; By Divine Right; The Silent Watcher; The Heart Bandit; The Deadwood Coach; The Desert Outlaw; The Enemy Sex; The Gaiety Girl; Merton of the Movies. **1925** Go Straight; Don't; The Mystic; The Splendid Road; The Re-Creation of Brian Kent. **1926** Chip of the Flying U; The Passionate Quest; The Ice Flood; Exit Smiling; While London Sleeps; The Fire Brigade. **1927** McFadden's Flats; The Great Mail Robbery; Home Made; Two Arabian Knights. **1928** The Night Flyer; Marry the Girl; The Air Mail Pilot; The Crash. **1929** Thru Different Eyes; Fox Movietown Follies of 1929; Seven Keys to Baldpate; Alibi; The Trial of Mary Dugan; The Valiant; Seven Footprints to Satan; Red Hot Speed. **1930** The New Racket (short); The Big House; Scarlet Pages; Outside the Law; The Bat Whispers; Min and Bill; In the Next Room; Captain of the Guard; Those Who Dance; Night Ride; The Big Trail. **1931** The Criminal Code; Primrose Path; Secret Six; The Squaw Man; Full of Notions; Salvation Nell; Caught Plastered; A Dangerous Affair; The Deceiver; Arrowsmith. **1932** The Bride's Bereavement or Snake in the Grass (short); Dancers in the Dark; Midnight Morals; Movie Crazy; Tess of the Storm Country; Central Park; The Match King; Silver Dollar. **1933** Mystery of the Wax Museum; Strictly Personal; Ladies They Talk About; A Lady's Profession; Reform Girl; One Year Later; Police Car 17. **1934** Death on the Diamond; The Fighting Rookie; Charlie Chan's Courage; A Man's Game; Take the Stand; A Wicked Woman; The President Vanishes; Massacre; Little Man, What Now? **1935** Secret of the Chateau; The Daring Young Man; A Dog of Flanders; Murder on a Honeymoon; The Village Tale; Mary Jane's Pa; Mutiny on the Bounty. **1936** Sins of Man; The Crime of Dr. Forbes; Kelly the Second; We Who Are About to Die; The Accusing Finger. **1937** That I May Live; Nancy Steele Is Missing; This Is My Affair; Slave Ship; Fifty Roads to Town.

JENSEN, EULALIE

Born: Dec. 24, 1884, St. Louis, Mo. Died: Oct. 7, 1852, Los Angeles, Calif. Screen, stage and vaudeville actress.

Appeared in: **1914** A Song of the Ghetto. **1916** Salvation Joan; The Strength of the Weak; The Tarantula; For a Woman's Fair Name; the Kid. **1917** Mary Jane's Pa; Clover's Rebellion. **1918** Beating the Odds; The Cinema Murder; The Girl Problem; A Tempermental Wife. **1920** Respect by Proxy; Man and His Woman; The House of the Tolling Bell; The Whisper Market. **1921** The Passion Flower. **1922** Any Wife; Rags to Riches; Deserted at the Alter; When Husbands Deceive. **1923** Slave of Desire; The Hunchback of Notre Dame; The Woman With Four Faces. **1924** The Yankee Consul; Being Respectable; Wine of Youth; With This Ring; The Scarlet Honeymoon; Havoc; The Happy Warrior. **1925** Charley's Aunt; The Ranger of the Big Trees; The Circle; Flower of the Night; Thundering Herd. **1926** Forever After; Bachelor Brides; Fig Leaves; Laddie; The Sap; Volcano. **1927** A Kiss in a Taxi; The Heart Thief; Uncle Tom's Cabin; The King of Kings. **1928** God of Mankind; Freckles; Mother Machree; Kentucky Courage; Little Shepherd of Kingdom Come; Figures Don't Lie. **1929** Strong Boy; She Goes to War. **1930** Eyes of the World. **1931** Arrowsmith; Up Pops the Devil; Never the Twain Shall Meet; Confessions of a Co-ed. **1932** Two Against the World; The Hatchet Man; Union Depot; So Big; Miss Pinkerton; Hat Check Girl.

JEPSON, KATE

Born: 1860, Clinton, N.J. Died: Sept 27, 1923, Philadelphia, Pa. Screen and stage actress.

Appeared in: **1914** The Education of Mr. Pipp.

JEROME, EDWIN

Born: 1884. Died: Sept. 10, 1959, Pasadena, Calif. (following surgery). Screen, stage, radio and television actor.

Appeared in: **1930** Grounds for Murder (short). **1945** The House on Ninety-Second Street. **1948** The Naked City. **1957** The Three Faces of Eve; Peyton Place; The Tattered Dress. **1958** Gigi. **1959** The Man Who Understood Women.

JEROME, ELMER

Born: 1872. Died: Aug. 10, 1947. Screen actor.

Appeared in: **1937** True Confession. **1942** The Magnificent Ambersons; Ice-Capades Revue; Youth on Parade. **1943** This Land Is Mine; False Colors; Heavenly Music (short). **1944** Heavenly Days. **1947** Merton of the Movies.

JEROME, PETER
Born: 1893. Died: July 9, 1967, Tucson, Ariz. Screen, stage, television actor, playwright and novelist.

JERROLD, MARY (Mary Allen)
Born: Dec. 4, 1877. Died: Mar. 3, 1955, London, England. Screen, stage and television actress. Mother of actor Philip Harben.

Appeared in: **1916** Disraeli. **1919** A Sinless Sinner (aka Midnight Gambols—US 1920). **1921** "Candytuft, I Mean Veronica." **1925** Twisted Tales series including Parted. **1930** The "W" Plan (US 1931). **1931** Alibi; The Sport of Kings; THe Shadow Between. **1932** The Last Coupon; Blind Spot. **1933** Perfect Understanding; Friday the Thirteenth (US 1934). **1934** The Lash; The Great Defender; Doctor's Orders; Spring in the Air. **1935** The Price of Wisdom; Fighting Stock; The Tunnel (aka Transatlantic Tunnel—US). **1936** Jack of all Trades (aka The Two of Us—US 1937). **1937** Saturday Night Revue. **1941** The Man at the Gate (aka Men of the Sea—US). **1943** The Gentle Sex; The Flemish Farm. **1944** The Way Ahead (US 1945). **1946** The Magic Bow (US 1947). **1947** The Ghosts of Berkeley Square. **1948** Bond Street (US 1950); Mr. Perrin and Mr. Traill; Woman Hater (US 1949); Colonel Bogey. **1949** Marry Me (US 1951); The Queen of Spades. **1950** She Shall Have Murder. **1952** Meet Me Tonight. **1953** Top of the Form; Tonight at 8:30.

JESKE, GEORGE
Born: 1891. Died: Oct. 28, 1951, Hollywood, Calif. Screen actor and film director. One of the original seven Keystone Kops.

Appeared in: **1927** Heart of the Yukon.

JESSEL, GEORGE
Born: Apr. 3, 1898, New York, N.Y. Died: May 23, 1981, Los Angeles, Calif. (heart attack). Screen, stage, vaudeville, radio, television actor, film director, film producer, composer and screenwriter. "Toastmaster General of the USA." Divorced from actresses Florence Courtney; Norma Talmadge (dec. 1957) and Lois Andrews (dec. 1968). He was married and divorced twice from Florence Courtney.

Appeared in: **1919** The Other Man's Wife. **1926** Private Izzy Murphy; At Peace With the World (short). **1927** A Few Minutes with George Jessel (short); Sailor Izzy Murphy; A Theatrical Booking Office (short). **1928** George Washington Cohen; Ginsburgh the Great. **1929** Lucky Boy; Love, Live and Laugh. **1930** Happy Days. **1931** George Jessel and His Russian Art Choir (short). **1943** Stage Door Canteen; Screen Snapshots #5 (short). **1944** Four Jills in a Jeep. **1953** Yesterday and Today (narrator); The I Don't Care Girl. **1957** Beau James. **1959** Juke Box Rhythm. **1967** Valley of the Dolls; The Busy Body. **1969** Can Heironymus Merkin Ever Forget Mercy Humppe and Find True Happiness? **1970** The Phynx. **1981** Reds.

JESSEL, PATRICIA
Born: Oct. 15, 1920, Hong Kong, British Crown Colony. Died: June 10, 1968, London, England (heart attack). Screen, stage and television actress.

Appeared in: **1951** Quo Vadis. **1957** The Flesh Is Weak. **1958** The Man Upstairs (US 1959). **1959** Model for Murder. **1960** No Kidding (aka Beware of Children—US 1961); The City of the Dead (aka Horror Hotel—US 1962). **1963** A Jolly Bad Fellow (aka They All Died Laughing—US 1964). **1966** A Funny Thing Happened on the Way to the Forum.

JESSUP, STANLEY
Born: 1878. Died: Oct. 26, 1945, Bronx, N.Y. Screen and stage actor.

Appeared in: **1930** Heads Up.

JETT, SHELDON
Born: 1901. Died: Feb. 1, 1960, New York. Screen and television actor.

Appeared in: **1935** Goin' to Town; Crime and Punishment. **1942** The Palm Beach Story; The Pride of the Yankees. **1944** Heavenly Days; Hollywood Canteen. **1945** Yolanda and the Thief. **1947** Body and Soul. **1951** The Lady and Bandit. **1952** Macao. **1953** The Robe. **1961** King of Kings.

JEW BABY, RUTH See GUENTHER, RUTH

JEWELL, ISABEL
Born: July 19, 1910, Shoshoni, Wyo. Died: Apr. 5, 1972, Hollywood, Calif. (natural causes). Screen, stage and television actress. Divorced from actor Paul Marion.

Appeared in: **1933** Bondage; Beauty for Sale; Bombshell; Day of Reckoning; Counsellor at Law; Design for Living; Advice to the Lovelorn; The Women in His Life. **1934** Manhattan Melodrama; Evelyn Prentice; Here Comes the Groom; Let's Be Ritzy; She Had to Choose. **1935** Times Square Lady; The Casino Murder Case; Shadow of Doubt; Mad Love; A Tale of Two Cities; I've Been Around; Ceiling Zero. **1936** The Leathernecks Have Landed; Dancing Feet; Small Town Girl; Big Brown Eyes; Valiant Is the Word for Carrie; Go West, Young Man; Career Woman; The Man Who Lived Twice; Thirty-Six Hours to Kill. **1937** Lost Horizon; Marked Woman; Swing It, Sailor. **1938** Love on Toast; The Crowd Roars. **1939** Gone With the Wind; They Asked for It; Missing Daughters. **1940** Northwest Passage; Babies for Sale; Little Men; Scatterbrain; Oh, Johnny—How You Can Love; Irene; Marked Men. **1941** High Sierra; For Beauty's Sake. **1943** Danger—Women at Work!; The Falcon and the Co-eds; The Leopard Man; The Seventh Victim; Calling Doctor Death. **1944** The Merry Monahans. **1945** Steppin' in Society. **1946** Sensation Hunters; Badman's Territory. **1947** Born to Kill; The Bishop's Wife. **1948** Michael O'Halloran; Belle Starr's Daughter; The Snake Pit; Unfaithfully Yours. **1949** The Story of Molly X. **1954** Drum Beat; The Man in the Attic. **1957** Bernadine.

JEWETT, BOBBY (Robert Jewett)
Born: 1886. Died: Nov. 10, 1970, Woodland Hills, Calif. Screen, stage and television actor.

"JIGGS"
Died: June, 1932 (paralytic stroke). Screen animal performer—Boston Bulldog.

Appeared in: **1922** The Leather Pushers series (film debut). **1931** Skippy.

JIMINEZ, SOLEDAD
Born: Feb. 28, 1874, Santander, Spain. Died: Oct. 17, 1966, Hollywood, Calif. (stroke). Screen actress.

Appeared in: **1915** Carmen. **1929** In Old Arizona; The Cock-Eyed World; Romance of the Rio Grande. **1930** The Texan; Billy the Kid; A Devil With Women; The Arizona Kid. **1931** Captain Thunder. **1932** Broken Wing; Spanish versions of films prior to 1933: Resurrection; Cat and the Canary; Ten Cents a Dance. **1935** Bordertown; Rumba; The Cyclone Ranger; Under the Pampas Moon; In Caliente. **1936** Robin Hood of El Dorado; The Traitor. **1937** Live, Love and Learn; When You're in Love; Man of the People; Kid Galahad. **1938** Forbidden Valley; California Frontier. **1939** The Oklahoma Kid; The Real Glory; The Return of the Cisco Kid; The Kid from Rio. **1940** Northwest Mounted Police. **1941** Hold Back the Dawn. **1943** For Whom the Bell Tolls. **1945** Bad Men of the Border; South of the Rio Grande. **1946** Holiday in Mexico. **1947** Christmas Eve; Carnival in Costa Rica. **1948** Black Bart. **1949** Red Light. **1950** Crisis. **1953** Seminole.

JINGU, MIYOSHI
Born: 1894. Died: Jan. 19, 1969, Los Angeles, Calif. Screen actress.

Appeared in: **1962** The Machurian Candidate. **1966** Walk Don't Run. **1970** Dreams of Glass.

JOBES, MARIGRAY
Born: 1953. Died: Mar. 3, 1976, Chicago, Ill. Screen and stage actress.

JOBSON, EDWARD
Born: 1864, Philadelphia, Pa. Died: Feb. 7, 1925, San Jose, Calif. Screen and stage actor.

Appeared in: **1917** A Bit of Kindling; Twin Kiddies. **1919** The Mints of Hell; The Merry-Go-Round; The Egg Crate Wallop; Cheating Herself. **1920** Mrs. Temple's Telegram; Burning Daylight; Someone in the House; The City of Masks; The Married Virgin. **1921** Offshore Pirate; The Saphead; First Love; the Match Breaker. **1922** A Chorus Girl's Romance; A Dangerous Game; Extra! Extra!; Kisses; The Scrapper; The Young Rajah. **1923** The Brass Bottle; Brass; Stepping Fast; Tea—With a Kick.

JOBY, HANS
Born: 1884. Died: Apr. 30, 1943, Los Angeles, Calif. Screen, stage actor and opera performer.

Appeared in: **1929** The Prince of Hearts. **1930** Hell's Angels. **1931** Suicide Fleet. **1936** Sons O' Guns. **1937** I Met Him in Paris. **1939** Thunder Afloat; Beasts of Berlin.

JOCHIM, ANTHONY "TONY" (aka ANTHONY JACHIM)
Born: Jan., 1892, Jersey City, N.J. Died: Apr. 10, 1978, Waynesville, N.C. Screen, stage, radio and television actor.

Appeared in: **1950** David Harding Counterspy; Western Pacific Agent. **1951** Three Desperate Men (ala Three Outlaws); Girl on the Bridge (aka The Bridge). **1952** Strange Fascination. **1953** City of Bad Men;

Dangerous Crossing; One Girl's Confession; Problem Girls; The Robe. **1955** Thy Neighbor's Daughter. **1956** Edge of Hell. **1957** Joe Dakota; Drango. **1858** Hot Spell. **1959** Born to Be Loved; The Big Fisherman; The Legend of Tom Dooley. **1960** The Story of Ruth. **1969** A Dream of Kings.

JOHANNSEN, CARY
Born: 1939. Died: Aug. 28, 1966, San Quentin Prison, Calif. (suicide). Screen, stage actor and writer. Appeared in a documentary film dealing with the Farm Labor Program for the Department of Corrections while in prison.

JOHN, ALICE
Born: 1881, Llanelly, Wales. Died: Aug. 9, 1956, Binghamton, N.Y. Screen and stage actress.

Appeared in: **1934** These Thirty Years.

JOHNS, BERTRAM "BERTIE"
Born: 1874, Plymouth, England. Died: May 9, 1934, Los Angeles, Calif. (heart attack). Screen and stage actor.

Appeared in: **1920** The Prince Chap; Conrad in Quest of His Youth. **1921** The Blushing Bride; Colorado Pluck; Forbidden Fruit; A Kiss in Time; The Great Impersonation. **1922** Too Much Wife. **1923** Clarence; Grumpy; Stephen Steps Out; The Marriage Maker; What a Wife Learned. **1924** Cornered. **1925** Declassee. **1926** Take it From Me. **1927** The Claw. **1929** Hired and Fired (short); Thirteenth Chair. **1930** Seven Days Leave.

JOHNSON, A. EMORY
Born: 1894. Died: Apr. 18, 1960, San Mateo, Calif. (burns from fire). Screen actor, film director, producer and screenwriter.

Appeared in: **1914** The Calling of Jim Barton. **1916** Her Husband's Honor; Heartaches; Two Mothers; Her Soul's Song; The Way of the World; No. 16 Martin Place; A Yoke of Gold; The Unattainable; The Devil's Bondwoman; The Human Gamble; Barriers of Society; The Right to Be Happy. **1917** The Gray Ghost (serial); A Kentucky Cinderella; The Gift Girl; My Little Boy; The Circus of Life. **1918** The Ghost Flower; New Love for Old; Beauty in Chains; A Mother's Secret. **1919** Put Up Your Hands; Trixie from Broadway; Alias Mike Moran; Charge It to Me; The Girl Next Door. **1920** Prisoners of Love; The Walk-Offs. **1921** The Sea Lion. **1922** Don't Doubt Your Wife; In the Name of the Law; Always the Woman.

JOHNSON, A. MARTYN
Born: 1883. Died: Jan. 22, 1934, Los Angeles, Calif. Screen, stage actor and writer. Do not confuse with actor Martin Johnson.

JOHNSON, ARTHUR V.
Born: Feb. 2, 1876, Cincinnati, Ohio. Died: Jan. 17, 1916, Philadelphia, Pa. Screen, stage actor, film director and producer. Married to actress Florence Hackett (dec. 1954).

Appeared in: **1908** The Bandit's Waterloo; The Adventures of Dollie; The Fight for Freedom; Balked at the Altar; After Many Years; The Planter's Wife; Concealing a Burglar; Where Bankers Roar; The Vaquero's Vow; The Taming of the Shrew; The Valet's Wife; The Test of Friendship; The Helping Hand. **1909** The Song of the Shirt; Resurrection; The Gibson Goddess; The Light That Came; The Little Teacher; Pippa Passes; A Drunkard's Reformation; The Way of a Man; The Girls and Daddy; A Sound Sleeper; Two Memories; Pranks; Confidence; The Little Darling; At the Altar; The Politician's Love Story; The Converts; The Mills of the Gods; The Mountaineers' Honor; The Trick That Failed; A Corner in Wheat; To Save Her Soul. **1910** All on Account of the Milk; The Cloister's Touch; Taming a Husband; The Final Settlement; The Newlyweds; The Thread of Destiny; Faithful; Unexpected Help; Rose O' Salem-Town; In Old California; The Unchanging Sea; A Rich Revenge; The Day After; A Romance of the Western Hills; Her Two Sons. **1911** Her Awakening; The Lily of the Tenants; Through Jealous Eyes; A Rebellious Blossom; The Maniac; The Slave's Affinity; The Life Saver; The Match Maker; The Actress and the Singer; His Chorus Girl Wife; A Girlish Impulse; Higgins vs. Judsons; One on Reno; A Head for Business; A Rural Conqueror. **1912** An Antique Ring; A Cure for Jealousy; A Matter of Business; My Princess; The Physician's Honor; The Preacher and the Gossips; A College Girl; A Leap Year Lottery Prize; In After Years; The Violin's Message; Her Gift; The Wooden Bowl; The New Physician; The Spoiled Child; The Stolen Ring; A Child's Devotion; A Little Family Affair; An Amateur Iceman; The Substitute Heiress; The Sporting Editor; The Heavenly Voice; The Country School Teacher; The Samaritan of Coogan's Tenement. **1913** Two Boys; John Arthur's Trust; The Artist's Romance; The Insurance Agent; A Timely Rescue; Annie Rowley's Fortune; A Counterfeit Courtship; Dr.

Maxwell's Experiment; When John Brought Home His Wife; Friend John; The Gift of the Storm; The Burden Bearer; The Pawned Bracelet; The Power of the Cross; The District Attorney's Conscience; His Niece from Ireland; Her Husband's Wife; The School Principal; His Better Self; The Stolen Melody; A Jealous Husband; The Benefactor; The Sea Eternal; Just Cissy's Little Way; The Road to the Dawn. **1914** The Parasite; The Blinded Heart; The Question and Answer Man; Lord Algy; An American Heiress; The Beloved Adventurer (series); The Holdup; The Girl from the West; A Partner to Providence; A Man's Faith; The Untarnished Shield; The Shadow of Tragedy. **1915** An Hour of Freedom; Country Blood; Comrade Kitty; When Father Interfered; Socially Ambitious; Her Martyrdom; Poet and Peasant; Winning Winsome Winnie; Who Violates the Law; On the Road to Reno; The Cornet; The Last Rose.

JOHNSON, BILL
Died: Mar. 16, 1957. Stage and screen actor.

Appeared in: **1945** It's a Pleasure; Keep Your Powder Dry.

JOHNSON, BRAD
Born: 1925. Died: Apr. 4, 1981, Burbank, Calif. Screen and television actor.

Appeared in: **1951** Bedtime for Bonzo. **1952** Outlaw Woman. **1953** The Lady Wants Mink. **1958** The Buccaneer.

JOHNSON, BURGES
Born: 1878. Died: Feb. 23, 1963, Schenectady, N.Y. Author, humorist and screen actor.

Appeared in: **1913** Saved by Parcel Post.

JOHNSON, CHIC (Harold Ogden Johnson)
Born: Mar. 5, 1891 or 1895, Chicago, Ill. Died: Feb. 25, 1962, Las Vegas, Nev. (kidney ailment). Screen, stage, vaudeville and television actor. Married to actress Catherine Creed (dec. 1978). Was partner in comedy team of "Olsen and Johnson" with Ole Olsen (dec. 1963). For films they appeared in, see Ole Olsen.

JOHNSON, CHUBBY (Charles Randolph Johnson)
Born: 1903, Terre Haute, Ind. Died: Oct. 31, 1974, Hollywood, Calif. Screen, radio, television actor and columnist.

Appeared in: **1950** Rocky Mountain. **1951** Fort Worth; The Scarf; Fort Dodge Stampede; Night Riders of Montana; Wells Fargo Gunmaster; The Raging Tide. **1952** Bend of the River; Here Come the Nelsons (aka Meet the Nelsons); Last of the Comanches; The Treasure of Lost Canyon. **1953** Calamity Jane; Gunsmoke; Back to God's Country. **1954** The Human Jungle; Overland Pacific; Cattle Queen of Montana. **1955** The Far Country; Tennessee's Partner; Headline Hunters. **1956** Tribute to a Bad Man; The Rawhide Years; The First Texan; The Fastest Gun Alive; The Young Guns. **1957** The True Story of Jesse James; The River's Edge; Drango. **1958** Gunfire at Indian Gap. **1962** The Firebrand. **1964** Seven Faces of Dr. Lao. **1966** Cyborg 2087. **1969** Sam Whiskey.

JOHNSON, EDITH
Born: Aug. 10, 1894, Rochester, N.Y. Died: Sept. 6, 1969, Los Angeles, Calif. (injuries from fall). Screen actress. Married to actor William Duncan (dec. 1961).

Appeared in: **1918** A Fight for Millions (serial). **1919** Man of Might (serial); Smashing Barriers (serial). **1920** The Silent Avenger (serial). **1921** No Defense; Where Men Are Men; Steelheart; Fighting Fate (serial). **1922** The Fighting Guide; When Danger Smiles; The Silent Vow. **1923** The Steel Trail (serial); Smashing Barriers (rerelease of 1919 serial as a feature film); Playing It Wild. **1924** The Fast Express (serial); Wolves of the North (serial).

JOHNSON, EDWARD
Born: 1862. Died: Feb. 7, 1925, San Jose, Calif. Screen actor.

Appeared in: **1919** The Egg Crate Wallop. **1923** The Hunchback of Notre Dame.

JOHNSON, FOSTER
Born: 1915. Died: Oct. 30, 1981, Los Angeles, Calif. Black screen and stage actor.

JOHNSON, FRANCES
Born: 1912. Died: Jan. 1, 1933. Screen actor and film extra.

JOHNSON, HALL
Born: 1888, Athens, Ga. Died: Apr. 30, 1970, New York, N.Y. (apartment fire). Black screen actor, musician and playwright. Founder of the Hall Johnson Choir.

Appeared in: **1936** Hearts Divided; The Green Pastures. **1939** Swanee River; St. Louis Blues; Zenobia; Way Down South. **1941** Lady for a Night; Meet John Doe. **1942** Syncopation; Tales of Manhattan; Heart of the Golden West. **1943** Cabin in the Sky.

JOHNSON, HUGH A. "HACKBERRY"
Born: 1888. Died: Dec. 3, 1979, Austin, Tex. (heart attack). Screen actor and rodeo promoter.

Appeared in: **1967** Motel Confidential. **1980** Honeysuckle Rose.

JOHNSON, JACK
Born: Mar. 31, 1878, Galveston, Tex. Died: June 10, 1946, Raleigh, N.C. Black professional boxer and screen actor.

Appeared in: **1919** Strength. **1921** As the World Rolls On. **1922** The Black Thunderbolt; For His Mother's Sake. **1935** Steamboat 'Round the Bend. **1970** Jack Johnson (documentary).

JOHNSON, JASON
Died: Nov. 24, 1977, Burbank, Calif. (stroke). Screen and television actor.

Appeared in: **1957** The Persuader; The Abductors; Invasion of the Saucer Men. **1959** Arson for Hire; The Legend of Tom Dooley. **1964** Strange Compulsion. **1968** If He Hollers, Let Him Go!

JOHNSON, JAY
Born: 1928. Died: June 13, 1954, San Fernando Valley, Calif. (motorcycle accident). Screen actor and vocalist with Stan Kenton orchestra.

Appeared in: **1936** Born to Dance. **1955** A Star Is Born.

JOHNSON, KATIE (Katherine Johnson)
Born: 1878, England. Died: May 4, 1957, Elham, England. Stage and screen actress. Voted the best British actress in 1955 for her performance in The Lady Killers.

Appeared in: **1936** Dusty Ermine (aka Hideout in the Alps—US 1938); Laburnum Grove (US 1941). **1937** Farewell Again (aka Troopship—US 1938); Sunset in Vienna (aka Suicide Legion—US 1940); The Last Adventure; The Rat. **1941** Jeannie; Hellzapoppin. **1942** Talk About Jacqueline. **1946** The Years Between (US 1947). **1947** Meet Me at Dawn (US 1948). **1952** I Believe in You (US 1953). **1953** The Gay Duelist (reissue of Meet Me at Dawn—1947). **1957** The Lady Killers (US 1956); How to Murder a Rich Uncle.

JOHNSON, KAY
Born: Nov. 29, 1905, Mt. Vernon, N.Y. Died: Nov. 17, 1975, Waterford, Conn. Screen and stage actress. Divorced from director/producer John Cromwell (dec. 1980). Mother of actor James Oliver Cromwell and Jonathan Cromwell.

Appeared in: **1929** Dynamite. **1930** The Ship From Shanghai; This Mad World; Madam Satan; Billy the Kid; The Spoilers; Passion Flower. **1931** The Single Sin; The Spy. **1932** American Madness; Thirteen Women. **1934** This Man is Mine; Eight Girls in a Boat; Of Human Bondage; Their Big Moment. **1935** Jalna; Village Tale. **1938** White Banners. **1939** The Real Glory. **1942** Son of Fury. **1943** Mr. Lucky. **1944** The Adventures of Mark Twain.

JOHNSON, KENNETH
Born: 1912. Died: 1974. Screen actor.

JOHNSON, LORIMER GEORGE
Born: 1859. Died: Feb. 20, 1941, Hollywood, Calif. Screen, stage actor and film director.

Appeared in: **1922** The Stranger's Banquet. **1923** Scaramouche; The Cricket on the Hearth; Ruth of the Range (serial). **1924** A Fool's Awakening; The Shadow of the East; Dante's Inferno. **1925** Enticement; The Top of the World; Never Too Late. **1926** Modern Youth. **1928** Midnight Rose; Tarzan, The Mighty (serial). **1930** Madam Satan; Ex-Flame. **1935** Crime and Punishment. **1939** Son of Frankenstein.

JOHNSON, M. MCELROY
Born: 1880. Died: July 10, 1960. Screen and stage actor.

JOHNSON, MARILYN
Born: 1923. Died: July 19, 1960, Beverly Hills, Calif. Screen actress and dancer.

Appeared in: **1944** She's a Soldier Too. **1945** Tonight and Every Night. **1946** Uncivil Warbirds (short); Secrets of a Sorority Girl.

JOHNSON, MARTIN
Born: Oct. 9, 1884, Rockford, Ill. Died: Jan. 13, 1937, Los Angeles, Calif. (plane crash). Explorer, writer, film producer, director and screen actor. Married to actress Osa Johnson (dec. 1953) with whom he produced and appeared in numerous travelogues, etc.

Appeared in: **1912** Cannibals of the South Seas. **1921** Jungle Adventure. **1922** Head Hunters of the South Seas. **1923** Trailing African Wild Animals. **1928** Simba, the King of Beasts—a Saga of the African Veldt. **1930** Across the World with Mr. and Mrs. Johnson. **1932** Congorilla.

JOHNSON, MURIEL
Born: 1893. Died: Feb. 28, 1974, Hollywood, Calif. Extra and film double.

Appeared in: **1936** As You Like It.

JOHNSON, ORRIN
Born: 1865, Louisville, Ky. Died: Nov. 24, 1943, Neenah, Wis. Stage and screen actor. Appeared in films for Triangle.

JOHNSON, OSA (Osa Leighty)
Born: Mar. 14, 1894, Chanute, Kans. Died: Jan. 7, 1953, New York, N.Y. (heart attack). Explorer, writer, film producer and screen actress. Married to explorer and actor Martin Johnson (dec. 1937) with whom she produced and appeared in numerous travelogues, etc. See Martin Johnson for the films they made together.

JOHNSON, PAULINE
Born: 1900, England. Died: 1947, England. Screen and stage actress. Married to actor/director Walter Forde.

Appeared in: **1920** The Great Gay Road; Bookworms (short). **1921** Class and No Class; The Imperfect Lover; Love at the Wheel. **1922** A Sailor Tramp. **1824** Pett Ridge Stories series including, Wanted, A Boy. **1925** An Inconvenient Infant (short). **1927** One of the Best; My Lord the Chauffeur; Mr. Nobody; Cameo Opera series including, The Bohemian Girl. **1929** The Flying Scotsman; Little Miss London; Would You Believe It? (US 1930). **1949** Maytime in Mayfair (US 1952).

JOHNSON, RAY
Died: Jan. 25, 1976. Screen actor.

Appeared in: **1936** Born to Dance.

JOHNSON, RITA
Born: Aug. 13, 1913, Worcester, Mass. Died: Oct. 31, 1965, Los Angeles, Calif. (brain hemorrhage). Screen actress.

Appeared in: **1931** The Spy. **1937** London by Night; My Dear Miss Aldrich. **1938** Man Proof; A Letter of Introduction; Rich Man, Poor Girl; Smashing the Rackets. **1939** Stronger Than Desire; Honolulu; Within the Law; 6,000 Enemies; They All Come Out; Nick Carter, Master Detective; The Girl Downstairs; Broadway Serenade. **1940** Congo Maisie; The Golden Fleecing; Forty Little Mothers; Edison the Man. **1941** Here Comes Mr. Jordan; Appointment for Love. **1942** The Major and the Minor. **1943** My Friend Flicka. **1944** Thunderhead, Son of Flicka. **1945** The Affairs of Susan; The Naughty Nineties. **1946** The Perfect Marriage; Pardon My Past. **1947** They Won't Believe Me; The Michigan Kid. **1948** Sleep My Love; The Big Clock; The Innocent Affair; Family Honeymoon. **1950** The Second Face. **1954** Susan Slept Here. **1956** Emergency Hospital. **1957** The Day They Gave Babies Away; All Mine to Give.

JOHNSON, S. KENNETH 2ND
Born: 1912. Died: Nov. 1, 1974, Los Angeles, Calif. Screen actor. Was one of the early "Our Gang" members.

JOHNSON, SHORTY
Died: Mar. 13, 1978. Screen actor.

JOHNSON, TEFFT
Born: Sept. 23, 1887, Washington. Died: Oct., 1956. Screen actor.

Appeared in: **1911** Vanity Fair; Foraging. **1912** Cardinal Wolsey; The Light of St. Bernard; The Cave Man; Old Love Letters; As You Like It; The Mills of the Gods; The Lady of the Lake; Yellow Bird; The Light That Failed; Fate's Awful Jest; The Miracle; An Official Apartment; Wild Pat; A Leap Year Proposal. **1915** The Knight Before Christmas. **1926** The New Klondike; Striving for Fortune.

JOHNSON, TOR (Tor Johansson)
Born: Oct. 19, 1903, Sweden. Died: May 12, 1971, San Fernando, Calif. (heart condition). Screen actor and wrestler.

Appeared in: **1935** The Man on the Flying Trapeze. **1943** Swing Out the Blues. **1944** The Canterville Ghost; Lost in a Harem; The Ghost Catchers. **1945** Sudan. **1947** Road to Rio. **1948** State of the Union; Behind Locked Doors. **1949** Alias the Champ. **1950** Abbott and Costello in the Foreign Legion; The Reformer and the Redhead. **1951** Dear Brat; The Lemon Drop Kid. **1952** The San Francisco Story; The Lady in the Iron Mask. **1953** Houdini. **1956** Carousel; The Black Sleep; Bride of the Monster. **1957** The Unearthly; Journey to Freedom. **1959** Plan 9 from Outer Space; Night of the Ghouls (aka Revenge of the Dead). **1961** The Beast of Yucca Flats.

JOHNSON, WILLIAM
Born: 1916. Died: Mar. 6, 1957, Flemington, N.J. (heart attack). Screen, stage, television actor and singer.

Appeared in: **1945** Keep Your Powder Dry; It's a Pleasure.

JOHNSTON, CAROLINE (Caroline Cook)
Born: 1876. Died: July 15, 1962, Los Angeles, Calif. Screen and stage actress.

JOHNSTON, JOHN W.
Born: 1876, Kilkee, Ireland. Died: Aug. 1, 1946, Hollywood, Calif. Screen and stage actor.

Appeared in: **1914** The Man from Home; Rose of the Rancho; The Virginian; Where the Trail Divides. **1915** Runaway June (serial). **1917** Adopted Son. **1921** The Kentuckians; Mother Eternal. **1922** The Ruling Passion; The Valley of Silent Men; Channing of the Northwest; Partners of the Sunset. **1923** Backbone; Unseeing Eyes. **1925** The Greatest Love of All; Winds of Chance. **1926** Desert Valley; The New Klondike. **1927** Flying Luck; The Black Diamond Express. **1928** Driftwood; Take Me Home; The Sawdust Paradise.

JOHNSTON, JOHNNY
Born: 1869. Died: Jan. 4, 1931, Hollywood, Calif. (heart disease). Screen and vaudeville actor. Was partner in vaudeville team of "Hardy and Johnston."

JOHNSTON, MAC
Born: 1906, Doniphan, Mo. Died: Mar. 22, 1977, Mt. Vernon, Mo. Screen, vaudeville actor, dancer, tent show producer and director. Father of actor/director Jerry-Mac Johnston. Appeared in vaudeville as part of "Hamel and Johnston" team.

JOHNSTON, MOFFAT
Born: Aug. 18, 1886, Edinburgh, Scotland. Died: Nov. 3, 1935, Norwalk, Conn. (following appendectomy). Stage and screen actor. Father of actor Peter Johnston.

Appeared in: **1934** Midnight.

JOHNSTON, OLIVER
Born: 1888. Died: Dec. 22, 1966, London, England. Screen, stage and television actor.

Appeared in: **1955** Room in the House. **1957** The Hypnotist (aka Scotland Yard Dragnet—US 1958); A King in New York (US 1973). **1958** Indiscreet. **1959** Beyond This Place (aka Web of Evidence—US); A Touch of Larceny; The Night We Dropped a Clanger (aka Make Mine a Double—US 1961). **1960** Kidnapped. **1961** Francis of Assisi; Raising the Wind (aka Roommates—US 1962). **1962** Dr. Crippin (US 1964); The Fast Lady (US 1965); Backfire. **1963** Cleopatra; The Three Lives of Thomasina; Island of Love (aka Not on Your Life). **1964** The Tomb of Ligeia. **1965** You Must Be Joking. **1966** It (US 1967—aka The Curse of the Golem). **1967** A Countess from Hong Kong.

JOHNSTONE, LAMAR
Born: 1886, Fairfax, Va. Died: May 21, 1919, Palm Springs, Calif. Screen actor.

Appeared in: **1912** Robin Hood; Because of Bobby; Filial Love; Caprices of Fortune; Silent Jim; Their Children's Approval; Foiling a Fortune Hunter; Dick's Wife. **1913** His Sister; Grease Paint Indians; A Trade Secret; A Perilous Ride. **1914** One Traveler Returns; Fate and Ryan; Mollie and the Old King; Helen's Stratagem; The Tie that Binds; The Portrait of Anita; The Reformed Candidate. **1915** The Face in the Mirror; Jimmy; The Unfinished Portrait; The Lady or the Tiger; The Face at the Window; The Blood Yoke; Willie Goes to Sea; The Van Thornton Diamonds. **1916** The Return of James Jerome; The Secret of the Submarine (serial); The Tongues of Man. **1918** That Devil—Bateese. **1919** A Man in the Open; The Sheriff's Son; Diane of the Green Van.

JOINER, PATRICIA
Born: 1929. Died: Oct. 30, 1978, Santa Monica, Calif. (leukemia). Screen actress.

Appeared in: **1950** The Men. **1951** The Enforcer; Missing Women.

JOLLEY, I. STANFORD
Born: 1900. Died: Dec. 7, 1978, Woodland Hills, Calif. Screen, stage, vaudeville, radio and television actor. Father of director Stan Jolley and Sandra Carson.

Appeared in: **1937** The Big Show. **1940** Midnight Limited; Chasing Trouble; The Fatal Hour. **1941** The Trail of the Silver Spur; Rolling Home to Texas; A Gentleman From Dixie; Arizona Bound; Emergency Landing; Desperate Cargo. **1942** Black Dragons; The Sombrero Kid. **1943** Corregidor; Frontier Fury; What a Man!; The Rangers Take Over. **1944** Trail of Terror; The Chinese Cat; Call of the Jungle; Return of the Rangers; Wolves of the Range; Shake Hands With Murder; Oklahoma Raiders; Brand of the Devil; Outlaw Roundup; Gangsters of the Frontier; The Whispering Skull; Cyclone Prairie Rangers; The Desert Hawk (serial). **1945** Lightning Raiders; The Scarlet Clue; Jungle Raiders (serial). **1946** The Crimson Ghost (serial); Daughter of Don Q (serial); Son of the Guardsman (serial); Silver Range; Six Gun Man; Ambush Trail; Terrors on Horseback. **1947** The Black Widow (serial); West of Dodge City; Wild Country; Land of the Lawless; Prairie Express; Thundergap Outlaws. **1948** Adventures of Frank and Jesse James (serial); Congo Bill (serial); Dangers of the Canadian Mounted (serial); Tex Granger (serial); Feudin' Fussin' and A Fightin'; Gunning for Justice; Oklahoma Blues; Check Your Guns; The Prince of Thieves; The Fighting Ranger. **1949** Roll Thunder Roll!; King of the Rocket Men (serial); Bandit King of Texas; Stampede; Gun Law Justice; Haunted Trails; Rimfire. **1950** Trigger, Jr.; Sierra; Hostile Country; Desperadoes of the West (serial); Pirates of the High Seas (serial); The Baron of Arizona; Curtain Call at Cactus Creek; Colorado Ranger; Fast on the Draw. **1951** Nevada Badmen; Whistling Hills; Texans Never Cry; Stage from Blue River; Don Daredevil Rides Again (serial); Captain Video (serial); Canyon Raiders; Texas Lawmen; Lawless Cowboys. **1952** Waco; Rodeo; Rancho Notorious; The Man from Black Hills; Leadville Gunslinger; Dead Man's Trail; Fort Osage; Gunman; Hired Gun; Kansas Territory; Wyoming Roundup; Wagons West; Wild Stallion; Yukon Gold. **1953** The Lost Planet (serial); The Marksman; Rebel City; Son of Belle Starr; Topeka; Tumbleweed; Vigilante Terror. **1954** Man With the Steel Whip (serial); The Desperado; The Rebel Set; Two Guns and a Badge; White Christmas; The Forty-Niners. **1956** The Wild Dakotas; The Young Guns. **1957** Gun Battle at Monterey; New Day at Sundown; Gunsight Ridge; The Iron Sheriff. **1958** The Long Hot Summer; The Lone Texan. **1959** Here Come the Jets; The Miracle of the Hills. **1960** Thirteen Fighting Men. **1961** Valley of the Dragons; The Little Shepherd of Kingdom Come. **1962** Terror at Black Falls; The Firebrand. **1963** The Haunted Palace. **1965** The Bounty Killer; The Restless Ones.

JOLSON, AL (Asa Yoelson)
Born: May 26, 1886, St. Petersburg, Russia. Died: Oct. 23, 1950, San Francisco, Calif. (heart attack). Screen, stage, vaudeville, radio actor and singer. Brother of stage actor Harry Jolson (dec. 1953). Married to actress Erle Galbraith. Divorced from Henrietta Keller, actresses Ruby Keeler and Alma Osborne (aka Ethel Delmar).

Appeared in: **1926** Vitaphone short. **1927** The Jazz Singer. **1928** The Singing Fool. **1929** Say It With Songs; New York Nights; Sonny Boy; Lucky Boy. **1930** Mammy; Big Boy. **1933** Hallelujah, I'm a Bum. **1934** Wonder Bar. **1935** Go Into Your Dance. **1936** The Singing Kid; Sons O' Guns; The New Yorker. **1938** Alexander's Ragtime Band. **1939** Rose of Washington Square; Swanee River; Hollywood Cavalcade. **1945** Rhapsody in Blue; Burlesque. **1946** The Jolson Story (voice). **1949** Jolson Sings Again (voice). **1950** The Golden Twenties (documentary).

JONAY, ROBERTA
Born: 1920. Died: Apr. 19, 1976, Tarzana, Calif. Screen and stage actress. Married to actor Judson D. Pratt.

Appeared in: **1947** Ladies' Man; Suddenly It's Spring. **1948** The Emperor Waltz.

JONES, ANISSA
Born: 1958. Died: Aug. 29, 1976, Oceanside, Calif. (barbituate overdose). Screen and television actress.

Appeared in: **1969** The Trouble With Girls.

JONES, BOBBY (Robert Tyre Jones, Jr.)
Born: Mar. 17, 1902, Atlanta, Ga. Died: Dec. 18, 1971, Atlanta, Ga. Screen actor and professional golfer.

Appeared in: Series of instructional golf shorts including: **1930** Bobby Jones' Golf Strokes; How I play golf series including: The Putter; Chip Shots; The Niblick; The Mashie Niblick; The Medium Irons; The Big Irons; The Spoon; The Brassie; The Driver; Trouble Shots; Practice Shots; A Round of Golf. **1933** How to Break 90 series including: Down Swing; Fine Points; Grip; Hip Action; Impact; Position and Back Swing.

JONES, BRIAN
Born: 1943, England? Died: July 3, 1969, London, England (drowned). Musician and screen actor. Member of the Rolling Stones rock group.

Appeared in: **1964** Rolling Stones Gather Moss (short). **1967** The T.A.M.I. Show (Teenage Awards Music International). **1968** Tonight Let's All Make Love in London; Sympathy for the Devil (US 1969).

JONES, BUCK (Charles Frederick Gebhart)
Born: Dec. 4, 1889, Vincennes, Ind. Died: Nov. 30, 1942, Boston, Mass. (burned in fire). Screen actor, film director and circus performer.

Appeared in: **1917** Blood Will Tell. **1918** Western Blood; True Blue; Riders of the Purple Sage; The Rainbow Trail; Pitfalls of a Big City. **1919** Speed Maniac. **1920** Brother Bill; Uphill Climb; Desert Rat; The Two Doyles; The Last Straw; Forbidden Trails; Square Shooter; Firebrand Trevision; Sunset Sprague; Just Pals; Two Moons. **1921** The Big Punch; One Man Trail; Get Your Man; Straight from the Shoulder; To a Finish; Riding with Death. **1922** Pardon My Nerve; Western Speed; Trooper O'Neil; West of Chicago; Fast Mail; Bells of San Juan; The Boss of Camp Four; Bar Nothin'. **1923** Footlight Ranger; The Eleventh Hour; Hell's Hole; Second Hand Love; Skid Proof; Snowdrift; Big Dan; Cupid's Fireman. **1924** Western Luck; Against All Odds; The Vagabond Trail; Not a Drum Was Heard; The Circus Cowboy; The Desert Outlaw; Winner Take All. **1925** Arizona Romeo; Gold and the Girl; The Trail Rider; Hearts and Spurs; The Man Who Played Square; The Timber Wolf; Lazybones; Durand of the Bad Lands; The Desert's Price; Good as Gold. **1926** The Fighting Buckaroo; 30 Below Zero; The Cowboy and the Countess; The Gentle Cyclone; A Man Four Square. **1927** The Flying Horseman; War Horse; Hills of Peril; Chain Lightning; Whispering Sage. **1928** The Branded Sombrero; The Big Hop; Blood Will Tell (and 1917 version). **1930** Stranger from Arizona; The Lone Rider; Shadow Ranch; Men Without Law. **1931** Border Law; Branded; Range Feud; Ridin' for Justice; Desert Vengeance; The Avenger; The Texas Ranger; Fugitive Sheriff; South of the Rio Grande; Sundown Trail. **1932** Deadline; Born to Trouble; High Speed; One Man Law; Hello Trouble; McKenna of the Mounted; White Eagle; Riders of Death Valley; Reckless Romance. **1933** California Trail; Unknown Valley; Treason; The Forbidden Trail; Thrill Hunter; Gordon of Ghost City (serial); The Sundown Rider; Child of Manhattan; Fighting Sheriff. **1934** Dawn Trail; The Fighting Code; The Fighting Rangers; The Man Trailer; Rocky Rhodes; When a Man Sees Red; The Red Rider (serial); Texas Ranger. **1935** The Crimson Trail; Stone of Silver Creek; The Roaring West (serial); Border Brigands; Outlawed Guns; The Throwback; The Ivory-Handled Gun; Square Shooter. **1936** The Boss of Gun Creek; The Phantom Rider (serial); Sunset of Power; Silver Spurs; For the Service; The Cowboy and the Kid; Empty Saddles; Ride 'em Cowboy! **1937** Sandflow; Law for Tombstone; The Left-Handed Law; Smoke Tree Range; Black Aces; Hollywood Round-Up; Headin' East; Boss of Lonely Valley; Pony Express. **1938** The Overland Express; Sudden Bill Dorn; California Frontier; Law of the Texan; Stranger from Arizona. **1939** Unmarried. **1940** Wagons Westward. **1941** Riders of Death Valley (serial); White Eagle (serial); Arizona Bound; The Gunman from Bodie; Forbidden Trails. **1942** Ghost Town Law; Down Texas Way; Riders of the West; West of the Law; Below the Border; Down on the Great Divide.

JONES, CHESTER
Died: June 27, 1975. Screen actor.

Appeared in: **1949** You're My Everything. **1954** The Country Girl. **1958** The Buccaneer. **1965** Clarence the Cross-Eyed Lion. **1966** Dark Intruder; The Bubble.

JONES, CURTIS ASHY "CURT"
Born: 1873. Died: Dec., 1956, Winchester, Ill. Screen, vaudeville actor and stuntman.

JONES, ELIZABETH "TINY"
Died: Mar. 22, 1952, Hollywood, Calif. Screen actress. Entered films during silents.

Appeared in: **1930** The Man from Blankey's. **1934** Lady by Choice. **1935** Dante's Inferno. **1939** Drums Along the Mohawk. **1943** The Seventh Victim. **1947** Nora Prentiss. **1948** You Gotta Stay Happy; The Lady from Shangahi.

JONES, EMRYS
Born: Sept. 22, 1915, Manchester, England. Died: July 10, 1972, Johannesburg, South Africa (heart attack). Screen, stage and television actor.

Appeared in: **1942** One of Our Aircraft is Missing (film debut). **1944** Give Me the Stars. **1945** The Wicked Lady (US 1946); The Rake's Progress (aka Notorious Gentleman—US 1946). **1947** Holiday Camp (US 1948); Nicholas Nickleby. **1948** This Was a Woman (US 1949). **1949** The Small Back Room (US 1952); Blue Scar. **1953** Deadly Nightshade. **1955** Three Cases of Murder. **1960** The Trials of Oscar Wilde (aka The Green Carnation and The Man with the Green Carnation—US). **1961** Ticket to Paradise. **1963** On the Run (US 1967).

JONES, FREDA M.
Born: 1897. Died: Oct. 24, 1976, Hollywood, Calif. (cancer). Screen actress. Mother of Macon, Margaret, and actors Marvin and Marcia Mae Jones.

JONES, FUZZY Q. See ST. JOHN, AL "FUZZY"

JONES, GORDON
Born: Apr. 5, 1911, Alden, Iowa. Died: June 20, 1963, Tarzana, Calif. (heart attack). Screen and television actor.

Appeared in: **1930** Beau Bandit. **1935** Let 'Em Have It; Red Salute. **1936** Strike Me Pink; The Devil's Squadron; Walking on Air; Don't Turn 'Em Loose; We Who Are About to Die; Night Waitress. **1937** They Wanted to Marry; Sea Devils; China Passage; There Goes My Girl; The Big Shot; Fight for Your Lady. **1938** Quick Money; Long Shot; Night Spot; Rich Man, Poor Girl; I Stand Accused; Out West with the Hardys. **1939** When Tomorrow Comes; Disputed Passage; Pride of the Navy; Big Town Czar. **1940** The Green Hornet (serial); I Take This Oath; The Doctor Takes a Wife; Girl from Havana. **1941** Up in the Air; Among the Living; The Blonde from Singapore; You Belong to Me; The Feminine Touch. **1942** To the Shores of Tripoli; True to the Army; They All Kissed the Bride; My Sister Eileen; Flying Tigers; Highways by Night. **1947** The Secret Life of Walter Mitty; The Wistful Widow of Wagon Gap. **1948** A Foreign Affair; The Untamed Breed; The Black Eagle; Sons of Adventure. **1949** Easy Living; Dear Wife; Mr. Soft Touch; Black Midnight; Tokyo Joe. **1950** Belle of Old Mexico; Sunset in the West; Trigger, Jr.; Bodyhold; The Palomino; North of the Great Divide; Arizona Cowboy. **1951** Spoilers of the Plains; Corky of Gasoline Alley; Heart of the Rockies; Yellow Fin. **1952** Sound Off; The Winning Team; Wagon Team; Gobs and Gals. **1953** Island in the Sky; The Woman They Almost Lynched. **1954** The Outlaw Stallion. **1955** Treasure of Ruby Hills; Smoke Signals. **1957** The Monster That Challenged the World; Spring Reunion; Shoot-Out at Medicine Bend. **1958** Live Fast, Die Young; The Perfect Furlough. **1959** Battle of the Coral Sea; Battle Flame. **1960** The Rise and Fall of Legs Diamond. **1961** Everything's Ducky. **1963** McLintock!; Son of Flubber.

JONES, HAZEL
Born: Oct. 17, 1896, Swarraton, England. Died: Nov. 13, 1974, New York, N.Y. Stage and screen actress.

Appeared in: **1916** The Merchant of Venice. **1927** Is Your Daughter Safe? **1930** Mamba. **1933** Strictly Personal.

JONES, HOWARD H.
Born: Aug. 23, 1885, Excello, Ohio. Died: July 26, 1941, Toluea Lake, Calif. Football coach and screen actor.

Appeared in: **1930** Maybe It's Love. **1933** College Humor.

JONES, J. PARKS (James Park Jones)
Born: Aug. 22, 1890, Cincinnati, Ohio. Died: Jan. 11, 1950, Los Angeles, Calif. Screen actor.

Appeared in: **1915** The Arab. **1916** The Ragamuffin. **1917** The Evil Eye. **1918** Old Wives for New; The Whispering Chorus. **1920** Little Shepherd of Kingdom Com; Faith. **1921** The Old Nest. **1924** What Three Men Wanted. **1926** Sunshine of Paradise Alley. **1927** Salvation Jane; Hawk of the Hills (serial). **1929** Hawk of the Hills (feature of 1927 serial).

JONES, JAMES
Born: 1922, Robinson, Ill. Died: May 9, 1977, Southhampton, N.Y. Screen actor, novelist and screenwriter.

JONES, JANE

Born: 1888, Sharon, Pa. Died: Jan., 1968, Los Angeles, Calif. Screen, stage, vaudeville actress and singer.

Appeared in: **1935** Hayseed Romance (short). **1937** Slave Ship. **1938** The Port of Missing Girls; Alexander's Ragtime Band. **1939** East Side of Heaven. **1944** Going My Way. **1945** Nob Hill. **1947** Night Song.

JONES, JOAN GRANVILLE

Died: Jan. 3, 1974, Hollywood, Calif. (cancer). Screen and television actress.

Appeared in: **1959** The Young Captives.

JONES, JOHNNY (Charles Edward Peil, Jr.)

Born: 1908. Died: Nov. 7, 1962, San Andreas, Calif. Screen actor. Appeared as a child actor during silents as Johnny Jones and later as Edward Peil, Jr. See Edward Peil, Jr. for later films.

Appeared in: **1920** Edgar and the Teacher's Pet; Edgar's Little Saw. **1921** The Old Nest. **1922** Night Life in Hollywood.

JONES, JONATHAN

Died: Mar. 30, 1978. Screen actor.

JONES, MARK

Born: 1890. Died: Apr., 1965, Hollywood, Calif. Screen actor. Appeared in silents and early Hal Roach shorts.

JONES, MORGAN

Born: 1879. Died: Sept. 21, 1951, New York, N.Y. Screen actor.

Appeared in: **1903** The Great Train Robbery. **1928** Mark of the Frog (serial).

JONES, NORMAN

Born: 1928. Died: Mar. 26, 1963, London, England. Screen and television actor.

JONES, PARRY

Born: 1891, England. Died: Dec. 26, 1963, London, England. Screen actor and opera singer.

Appeared in: **1933** Waltz Time. **1934** My Heart Is Calling (US 1935).

JONES, PAUL MEREDITH

Born: 1897, Bristol, Tenn. Died: Dec. 30, 1966, North Hollywood, Calif. (heart attack). Screen actor, extra, film producer and screenwriter.

Appeared in: **1916** Intolerance. **1958** Some Came Running.

JONES, R. D.

Died: Jan. 13, 1925 (drowned while shooting rapids in canoe for the film Ancient Highway). Screen actor and stuntman.

JONES, ROZENE K.

Born: 1890. Died: July 8, 1964, Hollywood, Calif. (heart attack). Stage and screen actor. Entered films approximately 1940.

JONES, SAM (Samuel Major Jones)

Born: 1863, Birkenhead, England. Died: Aug. 25, 1952, England? Screen, stage actor and stage manager.

Appeared in: **1912** Lt. Daring and the Ship's Mascot.

JONES, SPIKE (Lindley Armstrong Jones)

Born: Dec. 14, 1911, Long Beach, Calif. Died: May 1, 1965, Beverly Hills, Calif. (emphysema). Screen, radio actor and bandleader.

Appeared in: **1943** Thank Your Lucky Stars. **1944** Meet the People. **1945** Bring on the Girls. **1946** Breakfast in Hollywood. **1947** Variety Girl; Ladies' Man. **1954** Fireman Save My Child.

JONES, STANLEY "STAN D."

Born: 1914. Died: Dec. 13, 1963, Los Angeles, Calif. Screen, television actor and songwriter.

Appeared in: **1950** Rio Grande. **1951** Whirlwind. **1952** The Last Musketeer. **1956** The Great Locomotive Chase; The Rainmaker. **1959** The Horse Soldiers. **1960** Ten Who Dared. **1964** Invitation to a Gunfighter.

JONES, T. C. (Thomas Craig Jones)

Born: 1921. Died: Sept. 25, 1971, Duarte, Calif. (cancer). Femme impersonator, screen, stage, television and nightclub actor.

Appeared in: **1963** Promises, Promises. **1964** Three Nuts in Search of a Bolt. **1966** Movie Star American Style or: LSD, I Hate You. **1967** The President's Analyst. **1968** Head; The Name of the Game Is Kill!

JONES, WALLACE

Born: 1883, London, England. Died: Oct. 7, 1936, Los Angeles, Calif. Screen actor.

Appeared in: **1925** Red Love.

JOPLIN, JANIS

Born: 1943, Port Arthur, Tex. Died: Oct. 4, 1970, Hollywood, Calif. (drug overdose). Singer and screen actress.

Appeared in: **1968** Petulia; Big Brother. **1969** Monterey Pop. **1970** Woodstock (documentary).

JORDAN, MARIAN (Marian Driscoll)

Born: Apr. 15, 1897, Peoria, Ill. Died: Apr. 7, 1961, Encino, Calif. (cancer). Screen, stage, radio and vaudeville actress. Married to Jim Jordan and the two of them teamed as "Fibber McGee and Molly"—famous radio program.

They appeared in the following films: **1938** This Way, Please (their film debut). **1941** Look Who's Laughing. **1942** Here We Go Again. **1944** Heavenly Days.

JORDAN, RHODA

Died: Feb. 8, 1962. Screen actress.

Appeared in: **1948** The Snake Pit. **1949** Thelma Jordan (aka The File on Thelma Jordan).

JORDAN, RICKY See HAYDEL, RICHARD

JORDAN, ROBERT "BOBBY"

Born: 1923, Harrison, N.Y. Died: Sept. 10, 1965, Los Angeles, Calif. (liver ailment). Screen and stage actor.

Appeared in: **1933** A Universal short. **1937** Dead End (stage and film versions). **1938** A Slight Case of Murder; My Bill; Crime School; Angels with Dirty Faces; Reformatory. **1939** Dust Be My Destiny; The Dead End Kids on Dress Parade (aka Dress Parade); They Made Me a Criminal; Off the Record; Hell's Kitchen; Angels Wash Their Faces. **1940** Young Tom Edison; Boys of the City; That Gang of Mine; You're Not So Tough; Give Us Wings; Military Academy. **1941** Bride of the Bowery; Flying Wild; Bowery Blitzkrieg; Spooks Run Wild. **1942** Mr. Wise Guy; Let's Get Tough; Smart Alecks; 'Neath Brooklyn Bridge. **1943** Clancy Street Boys; Keep 'Em Slugging; Adventures of the Flying Cadets (serial); Kid Dynamite; Ghosts on the Loose. **1944** Bowery Champs. **1946** Bowery Bombshell; In Fast Company; Mr. Hex; Spook Busters; Live Wires. **1947** Scareheads; Hard-Boiled Mahoney; News Hounds; Bowery Buckaroos. **1949** Treasure of Monte Cristo. **1956** The Man Is Armed.

JORDON, HARRY (Harry Jordon Joseph)

Born: 1902. Died: June, 1945, Hollywood, Calif. Screen actor and double.

JORDON, JULES

Born: 1871, Birmingham, England. Died: July 22, 1925, Toledo, Ohio (cancer). Screen, stage and vaudeville actor.

Appeared in: **1925** New Toys.

JORDON, LOUIS

Born: July 8, 1908, Brinkley, Ariz. Died: Feb. 4, 1975, Los Angeles, Calif. Screen actor and bandleader.

Appeared in: **1944** Follow the Boys. **1945** Caldonia. **1946** Beware; Toot That Trumpet; Swing Parade of 1946. **1947** Reat, Petite and Gone. **1948** Look Out Sister.

JORDON, OSCAR

Died: Feb. 12, 1977. Screen actor.

JORGE, PAUL

Born: 1849, France. Died: Dec. 31, 1928, France. Screen actor.

Appeared in: **1926** Les Miserables. **1929** La Passion de Jeanne d'Arc.

JOSE, EDWARD

Born: Antwerp, Belgium. Died: Dec. 18, 1930, Nice, France. Screen, stage actor, film director and stage director.

Appeared in: **1914** The Perils of Pauline (serial). **1915** A Fool There Was.

JOSEPH, LARRY (Lawrence A. Joseph)

Born: Oct. 13, 1911, New York, N.Y. Died: Mar. 12, 1974, Los Angeles, Calif. (heart attack). Screen actor.

JOSHI, PRAVIN

Born: 1933, India. Died: Jan. 19, 1979, Bombay, India (fall from balcony). Screen, stage actor, playwright and broadcaster.

JOSLIN, HOWARD
Born: 1908. Died: Aug. 1, 1975, Woodland Hills, Calif. (heart attack). Screen actor and assistant film director.

Appeared in: **1951** Detective Story; Here Comes the Groom; The Racket; Quebec. **1952** Somebody Loves Me. **1953** The Vanquished; Pony Express. **1954** The Country Girl. **1955** Run for Cover. **1958** The Space Children. **1965** Black Spurs.

JOSLIN, MARGARET
Born: Aug. 6, 1881, Cleveland, Ohio. Died: Oct. 14, 1956, Glendale, Calif. Screen and stage actress. Married to actor Harry Todd (dec. 1935).

Appeared in: **1912** Love on Tough Luck Ranch; Alkali Ike Stung; Alkali Ike's Motorcycle. **1913** Alkali Ike's Auto; Alkali Ike's Gas; Alkali Ike's Misfortunes; Alkali Ike's Mother-In-Law; A Snakeville Courtship. **1914** Snakeville's Fire Brigade; Snakeville's Most Popular Lady. **1915** Snakeville's Weak Woman; Snakeville's Twins; Snakeville's Hen Medic; Snakeville's Eugenic Marriage; Snakeville's Champion; Snakeville's Beauty Parlor. **1917** Pete's Pants. **1921** Girls Don't Gamble. **1922** The Danger Point. **1923** Three Jumps Ahead.

JOSLYN, ALLYN
Born: July 21, 1905, Milford, Pa. Died: Jan. 21, 1981, Woodland Hills, Calif. (cardiac failure). Screen, stage, radio, television actor and writer. Married to stage actress Dorothy Yockel (dec. 1978).

Appeared in: **1937** They Won't Forget (film debut); Hollywood Hotel; Expensive Husbands. **1938** Sweethearts; The Shining Hour. **1939** Fast and Furious; Cafe Society; Only Angels Have Wings. **1940** No Time for Comedy; The Great McGinty; If I Had My Way; Spring Parade. **1941** This Thing Called Love; Hot Spot; Bedtime Story. **1942** My Sister Eileen; The Wife Takes a Flyer; Once Upon a Thursday; I Wake Up Screaming. **1943** The Immortal Sergeant; Heaven Can Wait; Young Ideas. **1944** Bride By Mistake; Sweet and Lowdown; Strange Affair; The Imposter. **1945** The Horn Blows at Midnight; Junior Miss; Colonel Effingham's Raid. **1946** The Thrill of Brazil; It Shouldn't Happen to a Dog. **1947** The Shocking Miss Pilgrim. **1948** If You Knew Susie; Moonrise. **1949** The Lady Takes a Sailor. **1950** Harriet Craig. **1951** As Young as You Feel. **1953** The Jazz Singer; I Love Melvin; Island in the Sky; Titanic. **1956** The Fastest Gun Alive; You Can't Run Away From It. **1957** Public Pigeon No. 1. **1964** Nightmare in the Sun. **1972** Brother O'Toole.

JOSOL, SANTY
Born: 1940. Died: Jan. 25, 1980, Los Angeles, Calif. Screen, stage and television actor.

Appeared in: **1964** The Assassin. **1970** Too Late the Hero.

JOSTYN, JAY
Died: July 24, 1976. Screen and radio actor.

Appeared in: **1947** Kiss of Death. **1956** Hilda Crane. **1958** Live Fast, Die Fast. **1960** Wake Me When It's Over.

JOUVET, LOUIS
Born: 1888, Brittany, France. Died: Aug. 16, 1951, Paris, France (heart attack). Screen, stage actor, film and stage producer.

Appeared in: **1932** Topaze. **1933** Dr. Knock. **1936** Carnival in Flanders; La Kermesse Heroique. **1937** Un Carpet de Bal; The Lower Depths; Mademoiselle Docteur; Life Dances On. **1938** Hotel de Nord; La Fin du Jour; L'Alibi. **1939** Bizarre, Bizarre; The Curtain Rises; The End of a Day; Marseillaise. **1940** La Charrette Fantome; Schubert's Serenade. **1941** Compliments of Mr. Iflow. **1943** The Heart of a Nation. **1945** De Drame Shanghai (The Shanghai Drama); The Barge-Keeper's Daughter. **1946** Sirocco; Le Revenant (A Lover's Return). **1947** Quai des Orfeures; Volpone. **1948** Jenny Lamour; Return to Life; Confessions of a Rogue; Street of Shadows. **1949** Retour a la Vie. **1950** Between Eleven and Midnight; Dr. Knock (and 1933 version). **1951** Miquette; Lady Paname; Un Histoire d'Amour. **1952** Ramuntcho.

JOY, ERNEST C.
Born: 1880, Minneapolis, Minn. Died: Feb. 12, 1924, Los Angeles, Calif. Screen and stage actor. Married to actress Mabel Van Buren (dec. 1947).

Appeared in: **1915** Chimmie Fadden; Maria Rosa; Chimmie Fadden Out West. **1916** The Golden Chance; The Heart of Nora Flynn; The Sowers; The Victoria Cross; Public Opinion. **1917** The Call of the East; The Silent Partner; Pride of the Clan; Freckles; Little Miss Optimist; The Squaw Man's Son; Hashimura Toga; The American Consul; Forbidden Paths. **1918** We Can't Have Everything; The Squaw Man; The White Man's Law; One More American. **1919** Johnny Get Your Gun. **1920** The Dancin' Fool; What's Your Hurry?

JOY, NICHOLAS
Born: 1884, Paris, France. Died: Mar. 16, 1964, Philadelphia, Pa. Screen, stage and television actor.

Appeared in: **1947** Daisy Kenyon; Dishonored Lady; A Gentleman's Agreement; If Winter Comes. **1948** The Fuller Brush Man; Joan of Arc; Larceny; The Iron Curtain. **1949** The Great Gatsby; Bride of Vengeance; The Sun Comes Up; Abbott and Costello Met the Killer, Boris Karloff; Song of Surrender. **1950** Surrender; And Baby Makes Three. **1951** Native Son; Here Comes the Groom; The Man with a Cloak. **1953** Affair with a Stranger. **1957** Desk Set.

JOYCE, ALICE
Born: Oct. 1, 1890, Kansas City, Mo. Died: Oct. 9, 1955, Hollywood, Calif. (heart ailment). Screen actress. Divorced from actor Tom Moore (dec. 1955). Entered films with Kalem in 1909.

Appeared in: **1910** The Engineer's Sweetheart. **1911** When California Was Won; For Her Brother's Sake; Don Ramon's Daughter; Reckless Reddy Reforms; Too Much Realism; The Indian Maiden's Sacrifice; The Trail of the Pomos Charm; The Lost Ribbon; Slim Jim's Last Chance; Slabsides; The Loyalty of Don Luis Verdugo; The Carrier Pigeon; The Love of Summer Morn; Over the Garden Wall; The Wasp; Peggy, the Moonshiner's Daughter; The Branded Shoulder; The Alpine Lease; The Peril of the Plains; The Engineer's Daughter; The Temptation of Rodney Vane. **1912** A Bell of Penance; Mrs. Simms Serves on the Jury; Jean of the Jail; The Russian Peasant; A Princess of the Hills; Between Father and Son; An American Invasion; The Alcade's Conspiracy; The Spanish Revolt of 1836; The Adventures of American Joe; The Mexican Revolutionist; The Stolen Invention; The Outlaw; The Organ Grinder; Saved by Telephone; The Badge of Courage; The Suffragette Sheriff; Fantasca the Gypsy; Freed from Suspicion; Rube Marquand Wins; The Mystery of Grandfather's Clock; The Street Singer; The Country Fair; The Strange Story of Elsie Mason; The Young Millionaire; A Battle of Wits; A Daughter's Sacrifice; A Race With Time; The Finger of Suspicion; A Business Buccaneer. **1913** Nina of the Theatre; The Flag of Freedom; The Nurse at Mulberry Bend; The Cub Reporter's Temptation; The Senator's Dishonor; The Power of Blacklegs; The $20,000 Carat; The American Princess; The Exposure of the Land Swindlers; In the Grip of a Charlatan; A Streak of Yellow; The Sneak; The Heart of an Actress; The Adventure of an Heiress; The Artist's Sacrifice; When Fate Decrees; The Pawnbroker's Daughter; The Attorney for the Defense; The Cloak of Guilt; A Victim of Deceit; A Thief in the Night; A Bolt from the Sky; For Her Sister's Sake; The Christian; A Midnight Message; The Riddle of the Tin Soldier; Our New Minister; The Hunchback; An Unseen Terror. **1914** The Brand; The Dance of Death; Fate's Midnight Hour; The Cabaret Dancer; A Celebrated Case; The Green Rose; The Old Army Coat; The Beast; The Vampire's Trail; The School for Scandal; The Mystery of the Sleeping Death; The Hand Print Mystery; The Shadow; The Show Girl's Glove; The Weakling; In Wolf's Clothing; The Girl and the Stowaway; The Viper; The Lynbrook Tragedy; The Riddle of the Green Umbrella; The Theft of the Crown Jewels; The Price of Silence; The Mayor's Secretary. **1915** Battle Cry of Peace; Cast Up by the Sea; The Leech; The Swindler; Her Supreme Sacrifice; The White Goddess; Unfaithful to His Trust; The Girl of the Music Hall; The Face of the Madonna. **1916** Whom the Gods Destroy. **1917** Within the Law; The Courage of Silence; Womanhood; The Glory of the Nation; Her Secret; The Question; Richard the Brazen; An Alabaster Box; The Fettered Woman. **1918** A Woman Between Friends; Captain's Captain; The Song of the Soul; The Business of Life; The Triumph of the Week; Find the Woman; To the Highest Bidder; Everybody's Girl. **1919** The Cambric Mask; The Third Degree; The Lion and the Mouse; The Spark Divine; The Winchester Woman; The Vengeance of Durand (aka The Two Portraits). **1920** The Sporting Duchess; Slaves of Pride; Dollars and the Woman; The Prey; Vice of Fools. **1921** The Scarab Ring; Cousin Kate; Her Lord and Master; The Inner Chamber. **1923** The Green Goddess. **1924** Passionate Adventurer; White Man. **1925** Stella Dallas; The Little French Girl; Headlines; Daddy's Gone A-Hunting; The Home Maker. **1926** Beau Geste; So's Your Old Man; Dancing Mothers; The Ace of Cads; Mannequin. **1927** Sorrell and Son. **1928** 13 Washington Square; The Rising Generation; The Noose. **1929** The Squall. **1930** The Green Goddess (and 1923 version); Song O' My Heart; He Knew Women; The Midnight Mystery. **1931-32** Paramount Screen Songs (shorts).

JOYCE, JAMES CAMPBELL
Born: 1921, Toledo, Ohio. Died: May 17, 1974, Santa Monica, Calif. Screen actor, singer, arranger and production manager. Married to choral director Betty Joyce. Father of singer/actor Randolph Joyce (dec. 1977).

Appeared in: **1962** Too Late Blues.

JOYCE, JIMMY
Born: 1923. Died: Jan. 5, 1979, Summit, N.J. (heart attack). Screen, stage, television actor and comedian.

Appeared in: **1962** Too Late Blues. **1964** The Killers. **1968** The Swimmer.

JOYCE, MARTIN
Born: 1915. Died: Jan. 2, 1937, Los Angeles, Calif. (injuries received in auto accident). Screen actor.

JOYCE, PEGGY HOPKINS (Margaret Upton)
Born: 1893, Norfolk, Va. Died: June 12, 1957, New York, N.Y. Stage and screen actress.

Appeared in: **1926** Skyrocket. **1933** International House.

JOYCE, RANDOLPH (Randolph Perkins Joyce)
Born: 1952. Died: Nov. 11, 1977, Argyle, Tex. (leukemia). Screen, radio, television actor, singer, composer and guitarist. Son of choral arranger James Joyce (dec. 1974) and choral director Betty Joyce.

Appeared in: **1965** The Sound of Music.

JOYCE, YOOTHA
Born: 1927, England. Died: Aug. 24, 1980, London, England (hepatitis). Screen, stage and television actress. Divorced from actor Glynn Edwards.

Appeared in: **1963** Sparrows Can't Sing. **1964** The Pumpkin Eater. **1965** Fanatic (aka Die, Die My Darling—US); Catch Us If You Can (aka Having a Wild Weekend—US). **1966** Kaleidoscope; A Man for all Seasons. **1967** Stranger in the House (aka Cop-Out—US 1968); Our Mother's House; Charlie Bubbles (US 1968). **1968** The Bank Breaker (rerelease of Kaleidoscope 1966).

JOYER, RAY
Born: 1925. Died: Mar. 17, 1975, Los Angeles, Calif. (heart attack). Stuntman and stand-in.

JUDEL, CHARLES
Born: Aug. 17, 1882, Amsterdam, Netherlands. Died: Feb. 14, 1969. Screen, stage actor, stage and film director.

Appeared in: **1915** The Commuter; Old Dutch. **1923** Little Old New York; Under the Red Robe. **1928** The Air Circus; Mother Knows Best. **1929** Frozen Justice; Hot for Paris. **1930** The Big Party; Cheer Up and Smile; College Lovers; The Doorway to Hell; Let's Go Places; The Life of the Party. **1931** Captain Thunder; Fifty Million Frenchmen; Gold Dust Gertie; War Mamas (short); Oh, Sailor, Behave!; God's Gift to Women; Women of All Nations. **1932** One Hour with You; Hurry Call; High Pressure. **1934** The Good Bad Man. **1935** The Night Is Young; Enchanted April; Florentine Dagger; Symphony of Living. **1936** Love on the Run; The Great Ziegfeld; San Francisco; Suzie; I'd Give My Life; Along Came Love; Give Us This Night; The Plainsman. **1937** It Can't Last Forever; The Big Show; Maytime; Swing High, Swing Low; When's Your Birthday?; Song of the City; Rhythm in the Clouds; Life of the Party; Wife, Doctor and Nurse; Marry the Girl; Ebb Tide; Fight for Your Life; Live, Love and Learn; High Flyers; Love and Hisses. **1938** Swing Miss; Reckless Living; You're Only Young Once; Mad About Music; Stolen Heaven; Flirting with Fate. **1939** Ninotchka. **1940** Pinnochio (voice only); Florian; Viva Cisco Kid; It All Came True; On Their Own; Gold Rush Mazie; Down Argentine Way; Public Deb No. 1; Bitter Sweet. **1941** Broadway Rhythm; Cheers for Miss Bishop; Sweetheart of the Campus; Law of the Tropics; The Chocolate Soldier; Kathleen; This Woman is Mine. **1942** Close Call for Ellery Queen; Baby Face Morgan; The Hard Way. **1943** Something to Shout About; I Dood It; Kid Dynamite; Swing Your Partner; Career Girl. **1944** Knickerbocker Holiday; Kismet. **1945** A Bell for Adano; Sunbonnet Sue; Two Local Yokels (short). **1946** Whistle Stop; Tangier; In Old Sacramento; Her Adventurous Night; Plainsman and the Lady; The Mighty McGurk. **1947** I Wonder Who's Kissing Her Now. **1949** Samson and Delilah.

JUDGE, ARLENE
Born: Feb., 1912, Bridgeport, Conn. Died: Feb. 7, 1974, West Hollywood, Calif. (natural causes). Screen, stage and television actress. Divorced from actor-director Wesley Ruggles (dec. 1972); Dan Topping; Capt. James R. Addams; Vincent Morgan Ryan; Henry J. (Bob) Topping; George Ross, Jr.; and Edward Cooper Heard. Entered films in 1931.

Appeared in: **1931** Everything's Rosie; Bachelor Apartment; An American Tragedy; Are These Our Children? **1932** Love Starved; Girl Crazy; The Roadhouse Murder; Roar of the Dragon; The Age of Consent; Young Bride; Is My Face Red? **1933** Flying Devils. **1934** The

Party's Over; Party's Over; Sensation Hunters; Bachelor of Arts; When Strangers Meet; Looking for Trouble; Shoot the Works; Name the Woman. **1935** College Scandal; The Mysterious Mr. Wong; One Hour Late; George White's 1935 Scandals; Million Dollar Baby; Ship Cafe; Welcome Home; King of Burlesque. **1936** Here Comes Trouble; Pigskin Parade; Valiant is the Word for Carrie; It Had to Happen; One in a Million; Star for a Night. **1942** The Lady is Willing; Wildcat; Harvard—Here I Come; Smith of Minnesota; Law of the Jungle. **1943** Girls in Chains; Song of Texas. **1944** Take It Big; The Contender. **1945** G.I. Honeymoon. **1946** From this Day Forward. **1947** Mad Wednesday (aka Sin of Harold Diddlebock). **1963** A Swingin' Affair. **1964** The Crawling Hand.

JULIAN, ALEXANDER
Born: 1893. Died: May 18, 1945, Hollywood, Calif. Screen actor.

JULIAN, RUPERT
Born: Jan. 25, 1889, Auckland, New Zealand. Died: Dec. 27, 1943, Hollywood, Calif. (stroke). Screen, stage actor, film director and screenwriter. Married to actress Elsie Jane Wilson (dec. 1965).

Appeared in: **1914** The Merchant of Venice. **1915** The Dumb Girl of Portici. **1916** The Bugler of Algiers. **1917** A Kentucky Cinderella. **1918** Kaiser, The Beast of Berlin.

JUNE, MILDRED
Born: 1906. Died: June 19, 1940, Hollywood, Calif. Screen actress. Entered films in 1920.

Appeared in: **1922** Ma and Pa; The Crossroads of New York; The Rosary; Rich Men's Wives. **1923** Crinoline and Romance; Fashionable Fakers; The Greatest Menace. **1924** Troubles of a Bride; Hook and Ladder. **1927** The Snarl of Hate; When Seconds Count.

JUNKERMANN, HANS
Born: 1872 or 1876?, Stuttgart, Germany. Died: 1943, Berlin, Germany. Screen and stage actor. Son of stage actor August Junkermann (dec.). Entered films in 1912.

Appeared in: **1913** Wo ist Coletti? **1915** Geloeste Ketten. **1919** Marie D'amour und Ihre Liebhaber. **1920** Hamlet; Lachte Man Gerne. **1922** Die Dame und ihr Friseur; Dr. Mabuse der Spieler; Der Film ohne Namen; Maciste und die Tochter des Silberkoenigs; Das Maedel mit der Maske; Sodoms Ende; Der Taugenichts; Wem nie Durch Liebe Leid Geschah; C.d.E. (Club der Entgleisten). **1923** Die Fledermaus; Der Mann ohne Herz; Das Milliardensouper; Nanon. **1924** Colibri; Die Grosse Unbekannte; Koenigsliebchen; Die Radio-Heirat; Ein Traum vom Glueck; Der Gestohlene Professor (aka Vitus Thavons Generalcoup). **1925** Das Alte Ballhaus; Der Farmer aus Texas; Herrn Filip Collins Abenteuer; Die Kleine vom Bummel; Liebe und Trompetenblasen Luxusweibchen; Das Maedchen mit der Protektion; Der Taenzer Meiner Frau; Die Unberuehrte Frau; Der Tanzende Tod (aka Rex Mundi); Die Kleine aus der Konfektion (aka Grosstadtkavaliere); Blitzzug der Liebe (Express Train of Love). **1926** An der Schoenen Blauen Donau; Annemarie und ihr Ulan Durchlaucht Radieschen; Der Feldherrenhuegel; Die Fuerstin der Riviera; Die Keusche Suzanne; Menschen Untereinander; Prinzessin Trulala. **1927** Der Bettelstudent; Es Zogen Drei Burschen; Der Fuerst von Pappenheim; Die Geliebte; Das Heiratsnest; Der Orlow; Das Schicksal Einer Nacht; Der Sprung ins Glueck; Die Tolle Lola; Die Selige Exzellenz (His Late Excellency—US 1929). **1928** Die Beiden Seehunde; Dragonerliebchen; Der Faschingsprinz; Die Geliebte Seiner Hoheit; Heiratsfieber; Liebe im Mai; Liebeskarneval; Das Maedchen von der Strasse; Majestaet Schneidet Bubikoepfe; Der Mann mit dem Laubfrosch; Mikosch Rueckt Ein; Die Zirkusprinzessin; Serenissimus und die Letzte Jungfrau. **1929** Beautiful Blue Danube; Meine Schwester und Ich; Das Naerrische Glueck; Der Schwarze Domino; Suendig und Suess; Das Verschwundene Testament. **1930** Liebeswalzer (The Love Waltz—US 1931); Anna Christie (US 1931); Delikatessen; Aschermittwoch; Der Detektiv des Kaisers; Er Oder Ich; Zapfenstreich am Rhein; Der Korvettenkapitaen (aka Blaue Jungs von der Marine); In Wein Hab' ich Einmal ein Maedel Geliebt (US 1934); Olympia (aka His Glorious Night). **1931** Der Storch Streikt (US 1932); Die Schlacht von Bademuende; Das Geheimnis der Roten Katz; Man Braucht Kein Geld (US 1932); Die Fledermaus (and 1923 version); Solang Noch ein Walzer von Strauss Erklingt; Mamsell Nitouche; Schatten der Unterwelt; Liebe auf Befehl (aka Boudoir Diplomat). **1932** Ein Walzer vom Strauss; Ein Prinz Verliebt Sich; Barberina; Die Taenzerin von Sanssouci; Die Vier vom Bob 13; Durchlaucht Amuesiert Sich; Traum von Schoenbrunn (US 1933); Die Graefin von Monte Cristo (The Countess of Monte Cristo); Glueck Ueber Nacht; Liebe in Uniform (Love in Uniform—US 1934). **1933** Zapfenstreich am Rhein; Volldampf Voraus; Ist Mein Mann Nicht Fabelhaft? (US 1936); Hochzeit am Wolfgangsee (US 1934); Heimat am Rhein (US

1934); Ein Leid fuer Dich; Die Kleine Schwindlerin; Der Page vom Dalmasse-Hotel (US 1935); Die Blume von Hawaii. **1934** Regine; Rosen aus dem Sueden (Roses from the South—US 1935); Musik im Blut; Der Letzte Walzer; Der Meisterboxer (aka Pantoffelhelden—US 1935); Eine Frau, die Weiss, Was sie Will; Die Czazdasfuerstin; Peter, Paul and Nanette (Peter, Paul und Nanette—US 1940); Pipin der Kurze. **1935** Aschermittwoch (Ash Wednesday); Artisten; Der Aussenseiter; Der Junge Graf (US 1936); Koenigstiger; Der Gefangene des Koenigs; Mein Leben fuer Maria Isabell; Laerm um Weidemann. **1936** Der Verkannte Lebemann; Der Lustige Witwenball (The Merry Widows' Ball—US 1939); Ein Hochzeitstraum; Eine Frau ohne Bedeutung; Drei Maederl um Schubert (aka Dreimaederlhaus); Ein Kleiner Goldener Berg (aka Hummel-Hummel—US 1939); Maedchen in Weiss (aka Ich bin auf der Welt, um Glueclich zu Sein). **1937** Serenade; Der Mann, der Sherlock Holmes War; Die Goettliche Jette. **1938** Ziel in den Wolken; Verliebtes Abenteuer; Der Unmoegliche Herr Pitt; Fortsetzung Folgt; Schuesse in Kabine 7; Unsere Kleine Frau. **1939** Ueber Alles die Treue; Das Ekel (The Grouch); Verdacht auf Ursula; Frau am Steuer; Salonwagen E 417. **1940** Der Herr im Haus; Das Herz Einer Koenigin; Leidenschaft (Passion); Der Kleinstadtpoet; Liebesschule. **1943** Akrobat Schoe-oe-oen; Altes Herz Wird Wieder Jung; Muenchhausen.

JUSTICE, JAMES ROBERTSON
Born: 1905, Scotland. Died: July 2, 1975, Winchester, Hampshire, England. Screen actor, journalist and naturalist. Married to actress Baroness Irena von Myerndoff.

Appeared in: **1944** Fiddlers Three (film debut). **1948** Scott of the Antarctic (US 1949); Vice Versa; My Brother Jonathan (US 1949); Against the Wind (US 1949); The Facts of Life. **1949** Poets Pub; Christopher Columbus; Whiskey Galore! (aka Tight Little Island and Mad Little Island); Stop Press Girl; Private Angelo. **1950** The Black Rose; My Daughter Joy (aka Operation X—US 1951); Prelude to Fame. **1951** Blackmailed; Pool of London; Captain Horatio Hornblower; David and Bathsheba; Anne of the Indies; The Lady Says No. **1952** The Story of Robin Hood and His Merrie Men; The Voice of Merrill (aka Murder Will Out—US 1953); Miss Robin Hood; Les Miserables. **1953** The Sword and the Rose; Rob Roy the Highland Rogue. **1954** Doctor in the House (US 1955). **1955** Out of the Clouds (US 1957); Above Us the Waves (US 1956); An Alligator Named Daisy (US 1957); Storm Over the Nile (US 1956); Doctor at Sea (US 1956); Land of the Pharaohs. **1956** Checkpoint (US 1957); The Iron Petticoat; Moby Dick. **1957** Campbell's Kingdom (US 1958); Seven Thunders (aka The Beasts of Marseilles—US 1959); Doctor at Large. **1958** Orders to Kill. **1959** Upstairs and Downstairs (US 1961). **1960** Doctor in Love (US 1962); Foxhole in Cairo (US 1961); A French Mistress. **1961** Very Important Person (aka A Coming Out Party—US 1962); Raising the Wind (aka Roommates—US 1962); Murder She Said (US 1962); The Guns of Navarone. **1962** A Pair of Briefs (US 1963); Crooks Anonymous (US 1963); Dr. Crippen (US 1964); The Fast Lady (US 1965); Guns of Darkness. **1963** Doctor in Distress (US 1964); Le Repos du Guerrier (Love on a Pillow and aka Warrior's Rest); Father Came Too (US 1966 and aka We Want to Live Alone); Mystery Submarine. **1965** Doctor in Clover (aka Carnaby, M.D.—US 1967); The Face of Fu Manchu; You Must be Joking; Up from the Beach; Those Magnificent Men in Their Flying Machine. **1967** The Trygon Factor (US 1969); Two Weeks in September; Hell is Empty. **1968** Mayerling (US 1969); Histories Extraordinaires (aka Spirits of the Dead—US 1969); Chitty Chitty Bang Bang. **1970** Some Will—Some Won't; Doctor in Trouble.

JUSTIN, MORGAN (Claude Olin Wurman)
Born: 1927, Wichita Falls, Tex. Died: July 7, 1974, Tarzana, Calif. (cancer). Screen and television actor.

Appeared in: **1953** The Kid from Left Field (film debut). **1956** The Court Jester. **1970** Dirty Dingus Magee.

JUUL, RALPH
Born: 1888. Died: Nov. 5, 1955, Chicago, Ill. Screen, stage and radio actor.

KAART, HANS
Born: 1924. Died: June, 1963, Amsterdam, Holland (following ear surgery). Screen actor and operatic singer. Appeared in German and Dutch films.

KAART, JOHAN
Born: 1898, Holland. Died: Feb. 2, 1976, Holland? Screen and stage actor.

Appeared in: **1955** Ciske, ein Kind Braucht Liebe (aka Ciske—US 1963).

KACHALOV, VASSILI IVANOVICH
Born: 1875, Russia. Died: Oct., 1948, Russia. Screen and stage actor.

Appeared in: **1929** Lash of the Czar. **1947** The Lower Depths.

KADEMOVA, LITKA
Born: 1908, Bulgaria. Died: Nov. 15, 1979, Marina, Calif. Screen, stage, vaudeville actress, singer, dancer, acrobat and comedienne.

KAHANAMOKU, DUKE P.
Born: Aug. 24, 1890, Honolulu, Hawaii. Died: Jan. 22, 1968, Honolulu, Hawaii (heart attack). Screen actor and Olympic swimming champion.

Appeared in: **1925** Adventure; Lord Jim. **1926** Old Ironsides. **1927** Isle of Sunken Gold. **1928** Woman Wise. **1929** The Rescue. **1930** Girl of the Port; Isle of Escape. **1948** Wake of the Red Witch. **1955** Mr. Roberts. **1969** I Sailed to Tahiti With an All Girl Crew.

KAHN, FLORENCE (aka LADY BEERBOHM)
Born: Mar. 3, 1878, Memphis, Tenn. Died: Jan. 13, 1951, Rapallo, Italy. Screen and stage actress. Married to author Max Beerbohm.

Appeared in: **1936** Secret Agent.

KAHN, RICHARD C.
Born: 1897. Died: Jan. 28, 1960, Hollywood, Calif. (heart attack). Screen actor, film director and film producer. Entered films as an actor in silents.

KAHN, WILLIAM "SMITTY"
Born: 1882. Died: May 14, 1959, Hollywood, Calif. Screen and television actor.

Appeared in: **1951** Girl on the Bridge. **1956** Edge of Hell.

KALICH, BERTHA
Born: May 17, 1874, Lemberg, Poland. Died: Apr. 18, 1939, New York, N.Y. Stage and screen actress.

Appeared in: **1914** Marta of the Lowlands. **1916** Slander; Ambition.

KALICH, JACOB
Born: 1892, Rymanov, Poland. Died: Mar. 16, 1975, Lake Mahopac, N.Y. (cancer). Yiddish screen, stage, television actor, stage director and playwright. Married to actress Molly Picon.

Appeared in: **1924** Mazel Tov. **1971** Fiddler on the Roof.

KALIONZES, JANET (Janet Manson)
Born: 1922. Died: Aug. 10, 1961, New York, N.Y. Screen and television actress.

Appeared in: **1948** A Double Life.

KALIZ, ARMAND
Born: Oct. 23, 1892, Paris, France. Died: Feb. 1, 1941, Beverly Hills, Calif. (heart attack). Screen, stage, vaudeville actor and screenwriter.

Appeared in: **1919** A Temperamental Wife. **1926** Josselyn's Wife; The Temptress; Yellow Fingers; The Belle of Broadway; The Better Way. **1927** The Stolen Bride; Fast and Furious; Say It with Diamonds; Temptations of a Shop Girl; Wandering Girls. **1928** The Love Mart; The Devil's Cage; Lingerie; That's My Daddy; The Wife's Relations; A Woman's Way. **1929** The Marriage Playground; Twin Beds; The Aviator; Gold Diggers of Broadway; Noah's Ark. **1930** L'Enigmatique Monsieur Parkes (The Mysterious Mr. Parkes); Little Caesar; The Eternal Triangle (short). **1931** Honeymoon Lane. **1932** Three Wise Girls. **1933** Secret Sinners; Design for Living; Flying Down to Rio. **1934** Caravan; George White's Scandals. **1935** Diamond Jim; Ruggles of Red Gap; Here's to Romance. **1936** Desire. **1937** Cafe Metropole; The King and the Chorus Girl. **1938** Algiers; A Trip to Paris; Josette; I'll Give a Million; Gold Diggers in Paris; Vacation from Love. **1939** For Love or Money; Ninotchka; Off the Record; Topper Takes a Trip; Midnight. **1940** Down Argentine Way. **1941** Skylark.

KALKHURST, ERIC
Born: 1902. Died: Oct. 13, 1957, Washington, D.C. Screen and stage actor. Entered films in 1922.

Appeared in: **1930** The Virtuous Sin. **1931** Unfaithful.

KALLMAN, DICK (Richard Killman)
Born: 1934. Died: Feb., 1980, New York, N.Y. (shot—murdered). Screen, stage, television actor, songwriter and clothing designer.

Appeared in: **1957** Hell Canyon (aka Hell Canyon Outlaws). **1959** Born to be Loved; Verboten! **1961** Back Street. **1963** It's All Happening (aka The Dream Maker—US 1964). **1967** Doctor, You've Got to be Kidding.

KALLOS, NELLIE (aka NELLIE KNIGHT)
Born: 1897, England. Died: Oct. 10, 1977, Sepulveda, Calif. Screen and stage actress.

KALSER, ERWIN
Born: 1883, Germany. Died: Mar. 26, 1958, Germany. Screen and stage actor.

Appeared in: **1930** Rasputin: The Holy Devil. **1931** The Last Company; Thirteen Men and a Girl. **1933** Hertha's Erwachen. **1941** Kings Row; Escape to Glory (aka Submarine Zone); Dressed to Kill. **1942** Berlin Correspondent. **1943** Watch on the Rhine; Underground. **1944** The Purple Heart; Address Unknown; America's Children; Strange Affair; U-Boat Prisoner. **1945** Hotel Berlin. **1952** The Girl in White. **1953** Stalag 17.

KALTHOUM, UM
Born: 1898, Tamay al-Zahirah, Egypt. Died: Feb. 3, 1975, Cairo, Egypt (cerebral hemorrhage). Screen, radio actress and singer. Known as "Daughter of the Nile."

KAMARYT, JOSEPH
Died: June 14, 1977. Screen actor.

Appeared in: **1943** Mission to Moscow.

KAMEN, MILT
Born: c. 1922, Hurleyville, N.Y. Died: Feb. 25, 1977, Beverly Hills, Calif. (heart attack). Screen, stage, television actor, screenwriter and satirist.

Appeared in: **1969** Me, Natalie. **1970** The Out-of-Towners. **1976** W. C. Fields and Me; Mother, Jugs and Speed.

KAMENZKY, ELIEZER
Born: 1889, Russia. Died: 1957, Lisbon, Portugal. Screen and stage actor.

KAMIYAMA, SOJIN *See* SOJIN

KAMINSKA, IDA
Born: 1899, Odessa, Russia. Died: May 21, 1980, New York, N.Y. (heart ailment). Yiddish screen, stage, television actress, stage director, stage producer and author. Daughter of Yiddish stage producer Avram Izhak Kaminska (dec.) and stage actress Ester Rachel Halpern (dec.). Divorced from producer Zygmunt Turkow. Later married to producer Marion Melman. Nominated for 1966 Academy Award as Best Supporting Actress in The Shop on Main Street.

Appeared in: **1939** Without a Home. **1949** A Vilna Legend. **1957** Jews in Poland. **1965** The Shop on High Street (aka The Shop on Main Street—US 1966). **1970** The Angel Levine.

KAMMER, KLAUS
Born: 1929, Hannover, Germany. Died: May 9, 1964, Berlin, Germany (suicide—carbon monoxide). Screen, stage and television actor.

Appeared in: **1959** Kriegsgericht (Court Martial—US 1962).

KAMPERS, FRITZ
Born: 1891, Garmisch-Partenkirchen, Germany. Died: 1950, Garmisch-Partenkirchen, Germany. Screen and stage actor and film director.

Appeared in: **1920** Flametti. **1921** Die Apotheke des Teufels; Das Offen Grab; Soehne der Hoelle. **1922** Der Grosse Preis; Jeanette Bussier; Monna Vanna; Passagier in der Zwangsjacke; Schamlose Seelen; Der Todesreigen. **1923** Lord Reginalds Derbyritt; Der Mensch am Wege; Nachtsyerme; Nanon; Schlagende Wetter; Wilhelm Tell; Der Steinerne Reiter (The Stone Rider); Der Weg zu Gott (aka Das Schicksal des Thomas Balt). **1924** Arabella; Aufstieg der Kleinen Lilian; Komoedianten; Die Liebesbriefe Einer Verlassenen; Die Stimme des Herzens; Ein Traum vom Glueck; In den Krallen der Schuld (aka Muttersorgen). **1925** Die vom Niederrhein; Goetz von Berlichingen Zubenannt mit der Eisernen Hand; Gruesse mir das Blonde Kind am Rhein; Halbseide; Heiratsannoncen; Menschen am Meer; Reveille, das Grosse Wecken; Unser Taeglich Brot; Wallenstein; Zapfenstreich. **1926** Die Flucht in den Zirkus; Fuenfuhrtee in der Ackerstrasse; Der Hauptmann von Koepenick; Ich Hatt' Einen Kameraden; In der Heimat, da Gibt's ein Wiedersehn!; Der Jaeger von Fall; Der Juxbaron; Die Kleine und ihr Kavalier; Kubinke, der Barbier, und die Drei Dienstmaedchen; Der Mann ohne Schlaf; Nanette Macht Alles; Der Pfarrer von Kirchfeld; Die Piraten der Ostseebaeder; Der Prinz und die Taenzerin; Der Provinzonkel; Das Rosa Pantoeffelchen; Ueberfluessige Menschen; Wir Sind vom K. und K. Infanterie-Regiment; Die Perle des Regiments (aka Der Stolz der Kompagnie). **1927** Almenrausch und Edelweiss; Der Bettler vom Koelner Dom; Da Haelt die Welt den Atem An; Es Zogen Drei Burschen; Der Fluch der

Vererbung; Fruehere Verhaeltnisse; Funkazuber; Gustav Mond ..., Du Gehst so Stille; Ich Habe im Mai von der Liebe Getraeumt; Leichte Kavallerie; Ein Maedel aus dem Volke; Der Meister der Welt; Petronella; Schwere Jungens—Leichte Maedchen; Ein Schwerer Fall; Verbotene Liebe; Wenn Nenschen Reif zur Liebe Werden; Die Selige Exzelleng (His Late Excellency—US 1929); Wochenendzauber; Deutsche Frauen—Deutsche Treue. **1928** Ein Besserer Herr; Die Dame und ihr Chauffeur; Die Dame mit der Maske (The Lady With the Mask); Dragonerliebchen; Fraeulein Chauffeur; Das Haus ohne Maenner; Heiratsfieber; Herbstzeit am Rhein; Lamkes sel. Witwe; Mary Lou; Ossi hat die Hosen An; Der Piccolo vom Goldenen Loewen; Robert und Bertram; Der Staatsanwalt Klagt An; Vom Taeter Fehlt Jede Spur; Der Weiberkrieg; Die Zirkusprinzessin. **1929** Berlin After Dark; Autobus Nr. 2; Drei Tage auf Leben und Tod; Durchs Brandenburger Tor; Ehe in Not; Die Fidele Herrenpartie; Fraeulein Faehnrich; Die Frau, die Jeder Liebt, Bist Du!; Die Herrin und ihr Knecht; Jugendtragoedie; Katharina Knie; Das Recht des Ungeborenen; Das Donkosakenlied; Somnambul; Tempo! Tempo! Wem Gehoert Meine Frau?; Wenn Du Noch Eine Heimat Hast. **1930** O Maedchen, Mein Maedchen, wie Lieb' ich Dich!; Der Witwenball; Lumpenball (US 1931); Pension Schoeller (US 1932); Die Drei von der Tankstelle (US 1931); Kohlhiesels Toechter (Kohlhiesel's Daughters, aka Gretel and Liesel—US 1931); Tingel-Tangel; Westfront 1918 (aka Vier von der Infanterie, and aka Comrades of 1918—US 1931); Zwei Welten (Two Worlds); Der Korvettenkapitaen (US 1933, aka Blaue Jungs von der Marine); Dreyfus (aka The Dreyfus Case—US 1940); Die Lustigen Musikanten (US 1933, and aka Laubenkolonie). **1931** Strohwitwer; Schuetzenfest in Schilda; Gloria (US 1932); Reserve hat Ruh (US 1932); Der Stolz der 3. Kompanie (US 1932); Kameradschaft (US 1932); Die Braeutigamswitwe (Bridegroom for Two). **1932** Balhaus Goldener Engel; Eine Stadt Steht Kopf; Drei von der Stempelstelle; Drei von der Kavallerie (US 1935); Das Blaue vom Himmel (US 1934); Strich Durch die Rechnung (US 1934); Frau Lehmanns Toechter (Mrs. Lehmann's Daughters—US 1933); Liebe in Uniform (Love in Uniform—US 1934); Strafsache van Geldern; Skandal in der Parkstrasse; Gruen ist die Heide (US 1935); Der Rebell (The Rebel). **1933** Zwei Gute Kameraden; Die vom Niederrhein (aka Lower Rhine Folks—US 1935); Die Fahrt ins Gruene (US 1936); Der Jaeger aus Kurpfalz; Der Meisterdetektiv (US 1934); Schuesse an der Grenze; Drei Blaue Jungs—ein Blondes Maedel (US 1936); Drei Kaiserjaeger (US 1935); Ein Lied Geht um die Welt (US 1936); Eine Frau wie Du (US 1934); Manolescu, der Fuerst der Diebe; Kleiner Mann—was Nun?; Ganovenehre; Grosstadtnacht; Der Judas von Tirol (US 1935, aka Der Ewige Verrat); Schoen ist Jeder Tag, den Du mir Schenkst, Marie Louise (aka Die Sonne Geht Auf—US 1935). **1934** Kaiserwalzer; La Paloma (US 1936); Der Doppelbraeutigam; Die Vier Musketiere (The Four Musketeers—US 1935); Die Liebe und die Erste Eisenbahn (Love and the First Railroad—US 1935); Die Herr Senator (aka Die Fliegende Ahnfrau). **1935** Zigeunerbaron; Leichte Kavallerie (US 1936); Die Drei um Christine (The Three After Christine—US 1940); Das Veilchen vom Potsdamer Platz (Violet of Potsdam Square—US 1939); Martha (aka Letzte Rose—US 1936). **1936** Der Bettelstudent; Stadt Anatol; Weisse Sklaven (US 1937, aka Panzerkreuzer Sewastopol).**1937** Drama on the Threshing Floor; Urlaub auf Ehrenwort (Furlough on Word of Honor—US 1938); Spiel auf der Tenne; Meiseken (aka Gelegenheit Macht Diebe). **1938** Pour le Merite (US 1939); Konzert in Tirol (US 1939); Nordlicht; Spassvoegel. **1939** Das Ekel (The Grouch); Im Namen des Volkes; Die Goldene Maske; Verdacht auf Ursula; Robert und Bertram (and 1928 version); Legion Condor. **1940** Weltrekord im Seitensprung; Stern von Rio; Das Fraeulein von Barnhelm; Links der Isar—Rechts der Spree; Der Feuerteufel; Bal Pare (aka Muenchner G'schichten). **1941** Ueber Alles in der Welt; Der Laufende Berg; Immer nur Du. **1942** Anschlag auf Baku; Der Ochsenkrieg; Die Entlassung. **1943** Kollege Kommt Gleich; Gabriele Dambrone; Der Zweite Schuss; Akrobat Schoe-oe-oen; Kohlhiesels Toechter (Kolhiesel's Daughters, and 1930 version). **1944** Freitag, der 13.; Das Konzert; Die Zaubergeige; In Flagranti; Neigungsehe; Jugendliebe; Der Meisterdetektiv (and 1933 version, aka Eine Reizende Familie). **1945** Wir Beiden Liebten Katharina; Der Scheiterhaufen; Die Kreuzlschreiben; Peter Voss, der Millionendieb. **1948** Morgen ist Alles Besser. **1949** Nichts als Zufaelle; Ich Mach' Dich Gluecklich. **1950** Des Lebens Ueberfluss; Schwarzwaldmaedel; Sensation im Savoy; Die Sterne Luegen Nicht; Die Nacht ohne Suende; Das Geheimnis des Hohen Falken (aka Die Steinerne Goettin). **1951** The Joseph Schmidt Story.

KANE, BLANCHE
Born: 1889. Died: Aug. 24, 1937, Hollywood, Calif. Screen and stage actress.

KANE, EDDIE

Born: Aug. 12, 1889, Missouri. Died: Apr. 30, 1969, Hollywood, Calif. (heart attack). Screen, stage, vaudeville and television actor. Was part of "Kane and Herman" vaudeville team.

Appeared in: **1928** Lights of New York. **1929** Why Bring That Up?; The Broadway Melody; Street Girl; Times Square; Illusion. **1930** The Cohens and the Kellys in Africa; The Doorway to Hell; The Squealer; Puttin' On the Ritz; Framed; The Kibitzer. **1931** My Past; Stolen Jools (short); Dirigible; Public Enemy; Smart Money; Goldie; Son of Rajah; Ex Bad Boy; Bought; Susan Lennox, Her Rise and Fall; Forbidden; Peach O' Reno; Forgotten Women. **1932** Rule 'Em and Weep (short); Stepping Sisters; Once In a Lifetime; Love Is a Racket; The Slippery Pearls (short); The Mummy. **1933** Dangerous Crossroads; Thrill Hunter. **1934** Autobuyography (short); Fixing a Stew (short); Wonder Bar. **1935** Hunger Pains (short); Million Dollar Baby; Hooray for Love; Hit and Run (short); Counselitis (short). **1936** Two in a Crowd; RKO short. **1937** A Star is Born; Something to Sing About; Melody For Two; All Over Town; Manhattan Merry-Go-Round; Hollywood Round-up; Mr. Boggs Steps Out; Small Town Boy; Pick a Star. **1938** Swiss Miss; The Gladiator; You Can't Take It With You; Give Me a Sailor; Dummy Owner (short). **1939** Some Like It Hot; Missing Daughters; Crime Rave (short); Home Boner (short); Rovin' Tumbleweeds. **1940** Music In My Heart. **1941** The Great American Broadcast. **1942** Yankee Doodle Dandy; Inferior Decorator (short); Tarzan's New York Adventure. **1943** Mission to Moscow. **1944** Lake Placid Serenade; Jam Session; Two Girls and a Sailor; Up In Arms; Minstrel Man; The Hairy Ape; Dark Mountains. **1945** Swing Out, Sister; Man from Oklahoma; You Drive Me Crazy (short); The Big Beef (short). **1947** My Wild Irish Rose; Ladies' Man; Wife Tames Wolf (short). **1948** Mexican Hayride. **1949** Jiggs and Maggie in Jackpot Jitters. **1956** The Ten Commandments.

KANE, GAIL (Abigail Kane)

Born: 1885. Died: Feb. 17, 1966, Augusta, Maine. Screen and stage actress.

Appeared in: **1916** Paying the Price. **1917** Southern Pride; A Game of Wits; Souls in Pawn. **1918** Love's Law. **1921** A Good Woman; Idle Hands; Wise Husbands. **1923** The White Sisters. **1927** Convoy.

KANE, HELEN

Born: Aug. 4, 1908, New York, N.Y. Died: Sept. 26, 1966, Jackson Heights, N.Y. (chest cancer). Screen, stage, vaudeville and television actress. Divorced from businessman Joseph Kane; actor Max Hoffman, Jr. (dec. 1945) and later married to emcee and singer Dan Healey.

Appeared in: **1929** Nothing But the Truth; Sweetie; Pointed Hills. **1930** Dangerous Nan McGrew; Paramount on Parade; Heads Up. **1931** Billboard Girl (short). **1932** The Spot on the Rug (short). **1934** Counsel on the Fence. **1950** Three Little Words (voice only).

KANE, JOHN J. "JOHNNY"

Died: Mar. 15, 1969, N.Y. Screen, stage, radio and television actor.

Appeared in: **1951** Man With My Face. **1959** The FBI Story. **1964** Fail Safe.

KANE, LIDA

Died: Oct. 7, 1955, New York, N.Y. Screen, stage, radio and television actress.

Appeared in: **1930** Follow the Leader. **1931** Secrets of a Secretary.

KANE, SARA (Sara Reed)

Born: 1938. Died: Dec. 11, 1977, Los Angeles, Calif. (cancer). Screen and stage actress. Married to actor Robert Pickering.

KANE, WHITFORD

Born: Jan. 30, 1881, Larne, Ireland. Died: Dec. 17, 1956, New York, N.Y. Stage and screen actor.

Appeared in: **1934** Hideout. **1944** The Adventures of Mark Twain. **1947** The Ghost and Mrs. Muir. **1948** The Walls of Jericho. **1949** The Judge Steps Out.

KANN, LILLY

Born: 1898, Peitz, Spreewald, Germany. Died: 1978, Germany? Screen, stage and television actress.

Appeared in: **1943** The Flemish Farm. **1945** Latin Quarter. **1946** Frenzy. **1947** The Woman in the Hall (US 1949); Mrs. Fitzherbert (US 1950). **1950** The Clouded Yellow (US 1952). **1951** A Tale of Five Cities (US 1952). **1953** Edge of Divorce. **1954** Betrayed; Eight O'Clock Walk (US 1955). **1955** A Kid for Two Farthings (US 1956). **1959** No Trees in the Street (aka No Tree in the Street—US 1964).

KANNON, JACKIE

Born: 1919, Windsor, Ontario, Canada. Died: Feb. 1, 1974, New York, N.Y. (heart attack). Nightclub comedian, television and screen actor.

Appeared in: **1964** Diary of a Bachelor.

KANTOR, MACKINLAY

Born: 1904. Died: Oct. 11, 1977. Historian, novelist, screenwriter and screen actor.

Appeared in: **1958** Wind Across the Everglades.

KAPOOR, PRITHVI RAJ

Born: 1906, India. Died: May 29, 1972, Bombay, India. Screen, stage actor, film producer, director and member of the Upper House of the Indian Parliament. Father of actors Raj Kapoor, Shammi Kapoor and Shasi Kapoor. In 1972 he received the Dadasaheb Phalke film award.

Appeared in: Alam Ara (first Indian film). **1956** The Vagabond. **1958** Boot Polish. **1960** Khozhdenie Za Tri Morya (Journey Beyond Three Seas).

KAPPELER, ALFRED

Born: 1877, Zurich, Switzerland. Died: Oct. 30, 1945, New York, N.Y. Screen and stage actor. Appeared in early Vitagraph Co. films.

Appeared in: **1921** Sentimental Tommy.

KARELS, HARVEY

Died: Nov. 17, 1975. Screen actor.

Appeared in: **1925** The Merry Widow.

KARLIN, BO-PEEP

Died: Feb. 25, 1969, Hollywood, Calif. Screen and television actress. Married to actor Gaston Glass (dec. 1965).

Appeared in: **1929** Happy Days. **1930** Just Imagine. **1933** Bye Bye Birdie.

KARLOFF, BORIS (William Henry Pratt)

Born: Nov. 23, 1887, London, England. Died: Feb. 2, 1969, London, England (respiratory ailment). Screen, stage, radio and television actor.

Appeared in: **1919** His Majesty the American; Prince and Betty. **1920** The Deadlier Sex; The Courage of Marge O'Doone; The Last of the Mohicans. **1921** Without Benefit of Clergy; The Hope Diamond Mystery; Cheated Hearts; The Cave Girl. **1922** The Man from Downing Street; The Infidel; The Altar Stairs; Omar the Tentmaker. **1923** Woman Conquers; The Prisoner. **1924** Dynamite Dan. **1925** Parisian Nights; Forbidden Cargo; The Prairie Wife; Lady Robinhood; Never the Twain Shall Meet. **1926** The Bells; The Greater Glory; Her Honor, the Governor; The Nicklehoppper; Eagle of the Sea; Old Ironsides; Flames; The Golden Web; Flaming Fury; Man in the Saddle. **1927** The Meddlin' Stranger; The Phantom Buster; Tarzan and the Golden Lion; Soft Cushions; Two Arabian Knights; Let It Rain; The Princess from Hoboken. **1928** The Love Mart; Vultures of the Sea (serial). **1929** The Fatal Warning (serial); Little Wild Girl; The Phantom of the North; Two Sisters; Devil's Chaplain; King of the Kongo (serial); The Unholy Night; Behind That Curtain; Burning the Wind. **1930** The Sea Bat; The Bad One; The Utah Kid; Mother's Cry; The Scar on the Nation; Assorted Nuts (short). **1931** King of the Wild (serial); The Criminal Code; Cracked Nuts (short); Smart Money; The Public Defender; I Like Your Nerve; Five Star Final; The Mad Genius; Frankenstein; Young Donovan's Kid; The Guilty Generation; The Yellow Ticket; Graft; Tonight or Never. **1932** Business and Pleasure; Behind the Mask; The Cohens and the Kellys in Hollywood; The Mummy; Night World; The Old Dark House; The Mask of Fu Manchu; Alias The Doctor; The Miracle Man; Scarface. **1933** The Man Who Dared; The Ghoul. **1934** Screen Snapshots #11 (short); The House of Rothschild; The Lost Patrol; The Black Cat; Gift of Gab. **1935** The Raven; The Black Room; Mysterious Mr. Wong; The Bride of Frankenstein. **1936** Juggernaut (US 1937); The Walking Dead; The Invisible Ray; Charlie Chan at the Opera; The Man Who Changed His Mind (aka The Man Who Lived Again—US). **1937** Night Key; Without Warning; West of Shanghai; War Lord. **1938** Mr. Wong, Detective; The Invisible Menace. **1939** The Man They Could Not Hang; Mr. Wong in Chinatown; Son of Frankenstein; Tower of London; The Mystery of Mr. Wong. **1940** British Intelligence; The Man With Nine Lives; Devil's Island; Doomed to Die; The Ape; You'll Find Out; Before I Hang; The Fatal Hour; Black Friday. **1941** Behind the Door; The Devil Commands. **1942** The Boogie Man Will Get You. **1944** The Climax. **1945** House of Dracula; House of Frankenstein; Isle of the Dead; The Body Snatchers. **1946** Bedlam. **1947** The Secret Life of Walter Mitty; Lured; Dick Tracy Meets Gruesome; Unconquered. **1948** Tap Roots. **1949** Abbott and Costello

Meet the Killer, Boris Karloff. **1951** The Strange Door; Emperor's Nightingale (narr.). **1952** The Black Castle. **1953** Abbott and Costello Meet Dr. Jekyll and Mr. Hyde; The Monster of the Island; The Hindu (aka Sabaka—US 1955). **1957** Voodoo Island; The Juggler of Our Lady. **1958** Corridor of Blood (US 1963); Grip of the Strangler (aka The Haunted Strangler-US); Frankenstein—1970. **1961** Days of Thrills and Laughter (documentary). **1963** The Raven (and 1935 version); The Terror. **1964** A Comedy of Terrors; Black Sabbath; Bikini Beach; Today's Teen (short—narr.); Scarlet Friday. **1965** Die, Monster, Die!. **1966** The Daydreamer (narr.); Ghost in the Invisible Bikini; The Venetian Affair; Monster of Terror; The House at the End of the World. **1967** The Corpse Collector; Mondo Balordo (narr.); The Sorcerers. **1968** The Curse of the Crimson Altar (aka The Crimson Cult—US 1970); Targets. **1969** Mad Monster Party (narr.).

KARLSTADT, LIESL

Born: 1893, Germany. Died: Aug. 1, 1960, Garmisch-Partenkirchen, Germany (stroke). Screen, stage actress, singer and dancer.

Appeared in: **1934** Mit dir Durch Dick und Duenn. **1937** Kirschen in Nachbars Garten. **1956** Die Trapp Familie (The Trapp Family—US 1961). **1958** Wir Wunderkinder (We Amazing Children, aka Aren't We Wonderful—US 1959). Other German film: Feuerwerk.

KARLWEISS, OSCAR

Born: 1895, Vienna, Austria. Died: Jan. 24, 1956, New York, N.Y. (heart attack). Stage and screen actor.

Appeared in: **1930** Zwei Hertzen in Drei-Viertel Takt. **1931** Die Foresterchristl; Die Drei von ver Tankstelle; Dolly Macht Karriere; Sein Liebeslied. **1933** Der Tanzhusar. **1951** St. Benny the Dip. **1952** Anthing Can Happen; Five Fingers. **1953** The Juggler; Tonight We Sing. **1956** Meet Me in Las Vegas.

KARNES, ROBERT

Born: 1917, Ky. Died: Dec. 4, 1979, Sherman Oaks, Calif. (heart failure). Screen, stage, radio and television actor.

Appeared in: **1947** Gentleman's Agreement; Daisy Kenyon; Captain from Castile. **1948** Road House; The Street With No Name; Scudda-Hoo, Scudda-Hay. **1949** Trapped. **1950** Hills of Oklahoma; Kiss Tomorrow Goodbye; Three Husbands. **1951** Utah Wagon Train; According to Mrs. Hoyle; Casa Manana. **1952** Rodeo; Storm Over Tibet; Lure of the Wilderness. **1953** From Here to Eternity; Project Moonbase. **1954** Riders to the Stars. **1955** Jujin Yukiotoko (Half Human). **1956** Stagecoach to Fury. **1961** Fear no More; Five Guns to Tombstone. **1964** Apache Rifles. **1969** Charro!

KARNO, FRED (John Westcott)

Born: Mar. 26, 1866, Exeter, England. Died: Sept. 18, 1941, Dorsetshire, England. Screen, stage, vaudeville actor, stage producer and writer.

Appeared in: **1923** Early Birds.

KARNS, ROSCOE

Born: Sept. 7, 1893, San Bernardino, Calif. Died: Feb. 6, 1970, Los Angeles, Calif. Screen, stage and television actor.

Appeared in:A Western Governor's Humanity. **1921** The Man Turner; Too Much Married. **1922** Afraid to Fight; Conquering the Woman; Her Own Money; The Trouper. **1923** Other Man's Daughters. **1924** Bluff; The Foolish Virgin; The Midnight Express. **1925** Headlines; The Overland Limited; Dollar Down. **1927** The Jazz Singer; Ritzy; Ten Modern Commandments. **1928** Win That Girl; Warming Up; The Desert Bride; Object—Alimony; Moran of the Marines; Beggars of Life; Something Always Happens; Jazz Mad; Beau Sabreau. **1929** This Thing Called Love; New York Nights. **1930** Safety in Numbers; Troopers Three; New York Lights; Man Trouble; The Costello Case; Little Accident. **1931** The Gorilla; Dirigible; Laughing Sinners; Leftover Ladies; Many a Slip. **1932** Ladies of the Big House; Lawyer Man; Night After Night Roadhouse Murder; Week-End Marriage; Two Against the World; The Crooked Circle; I Am a Fugitive from a Chain Gang; One Way Passage; If I Had a Million; Under Cover Man; The Stowaway; Pleasure; Rockabye. **1933** Gambling Ship; One Sunday Afternoon; Alice in Wonderland; Today We Live; A Lady's Profession; 20,000 Years in Sing Sing. **1934** Twentieth Century; Search for Beauty; The Women in His Life; Shoot the Works; Come on Marines; Elmer and Elsie; It Happened One Night; I Sell Anything. **1935** Red Hot Tires; Stolen Harmony; Four Hours to Kill; Wings in the Dark; Two-Fisted; Alibi Ike; Front Page Woman. **1936** Woman Trap; Border Flight; Three Cheers for Love; Three Married Men; Cain and Mabel. **1937** Murder Goes to College; A Night of Mystery; On Such a Night; Clarence; Partners in Crime. **1938** Scandal Sheet; Dangerous to Know; Tip-Off Girls; You and Me; Thanks for the Memory. **1939**

King of Chinatown; Everything's on Ice; That's Right—You're Wrong; Dancing Co-ed. **1940** Double Alibi; His Girl Friday; Saturday's Children; They Drive By Night; Ladies Must Live; Meet the Missus. **1941** Petticoat Politics; Footsteps in the Dark; The Gay Vagabond. **1942** The Road to Happiness; A Tragedy at Midnight; Yokel Boy; You Can't Escape Forever; Woman of the Year. **1943** Stage Door Canteen; My Son, the Hero; His Butler's Sister; Old Acquaintance. **1944** The Navy Way; Hi, Good Lookin'; Minstrel Man. **1946** I Ring Doorbells; One Way to Love; The Kid from Brooklyn; Avalanche; It's a Wonderful Life; Down Missouri Way. **1947** That's My Man; Vigilantes of Boomtown; Will Tomorrow Ever Come? **1948** The Devil's Cargo; The Inside Story; Speed to Spare; Texas, Brooklyn and Heaven. **1958** Onionhead. **1964** Man's Favorite Sport?

KARR, DARWIN

Born: July 25, 1875, Almond, N.Y. Died: Dec. 31, 1945, Calif. Screen and stage actor. Married to actress Florence Bindley. Entered films in 1911 with Edison Co.

Appeared in: **1911** That Winsome Winnie Smile; Eugene Wraygrun; The Girl and the Motor Boat; A Modern Cinderella; Willie Wise and His Motor Boat; The Ghost's Warning; The Story of the Indian Ledge. **1912** Falling Leaves; The Boarding House Heiress; The Detective Dog; Billy's Shoes; The Child of the Tenements; The Fugitive; The Idol Worshipper; Saved by a Cat; Phantom Paradise; Father and the Boys; Canned Harmony; The Equine Spy; The Wooing of Alice; Souls in the Shadow; Mickey's Pal; For the Love of the Flag; Auto Suggestion. **1913** Love's Sunset. **1914** Her Husband; The Mischief Maker; The Tangle. **1915** His Bunky. **1921** Our Mutual Friend. **1922** The Sin Flood; Mr. Barnes of New York.

KARRINGTON, FRANK

Born: Mar. 9, 1858. Died: Mar. 5, 1936, Cornwall, N.Y. Stage and screen actor.

KASHEY, ABE

Born: Nov. 28, 1903, Syria. Died: Sept. 24, 1965, Lynwood, Calif. (congestive heart failure). Screen actor and professional wrestler.

Appeared in: **1943** That Nazty Nuisance. **1945** Crime Doctor's Courage. **1947** Tarzan and the Leopard Woman.

KASTNER, BRUNO

Born: Germany. Died: Prior to 1958. Screen actor. Married to actress Ida Wuest (dec. 1958).

Appeared in: **1929** Thou Shalt Not Steal; Carnival of Crime; Luther.

KASZNAR, KURT (Kurt Serwicher)

Born: Aug. 12, 1913, Vienna, Austria. Died: Aug. 6, 1979, Santa Monica, Calif. (cancer). Screen, stage and television actor. Married to Cornelia Whooly (dec. 1948). Later married and divorced from actress Leora Dana.

Appeared in: **1920** Max, King of the Circus (film debut). **1951** The Light Touch. **1952** The Happy Time (stage and film versions); Lovely to Look At; Glory Alley; Talk About a Stranger; Anything Can Happen. **1953** Kiss Me, Kate; All the Brothers Were Valiant; Ride, Vaquero!; Sombrero; Give a Girl a Break; The Great Diamond Robbery; Lili. **1954** The Last Time I Saw Paris; Valley of the Kings. **1955** My Sister Eileen; Flame of the Islands; Jump into Hell. **1956** Anything Goes. **1957** Legend of the Lost; A Farewell to Arms. **1959** For the First Time; The Journey; Helden (aka Arms and the Man—US 1962). **1963** 55 Days at Peking. **1967** The Ambushers; Casino Royale; The King's Pirate; The Perils of Pauline.

KATCH, KURT (Isser Kac)

Born: Jan. 28, 1896, Grodno, Poland. Died: Aug. 14, 1958, Los Angeles, Calif. (during cancer surgery). Screen and stage actor.

Appeared in: **1938** Tkies Khaf (The Vow). **1941** Men at Large. **1942** The Wife Takes a Flyer; Berlin Correspondent; Counter Espionage; They Came to Blow Up America; Edge of Darkness; Quiet Please, Murder; Secret Agent of Japan. **1943** Secret Service in Darkest Africa (serial); Background to Danger; Mission to Moscow; Watch on the Rhine. **1944** Ali Baba and the Forty Thieves; The Purple Heart; The Mask of Dimitrios; Make Your Own Bed; The Conspirators; The Seventh Cross. **1945** The Mummy's Curse; Salome; Where She Danced. **1946** Angel On My Shoulder; Rendezvous 24. **1947** Song of Love; Strange Journey. **1954** The Secret of the Incas; The Adventures of Hajji Baba. **1955** Abbott and Costello Meet the Mummy. **1956** Hot Cars. **1957** The Girl in the Kremlin; The Pharaoh's Curse. **1958** The Young Lions; The Beast of Budapest.

KAUFMAN, JOSEPH
Born: 1882, Washington, D.C. Died: Feb. 1, 1918, New York, N.Y. (pneumonia). Screen actor, film producer and director.

Appeared in: **1914** Madam Cigarette; A Daughter of Eve. **1915** When the Light Came In; Money! Money! Money!; His Soul Mate; The Little Detective; The Millinery Man; A Woman Went Forth; The Blessed Miracle; Monkey Business; The Stroke of Fate; Just Look at Jake; The Darkness Before Dawn; In the Dark; The Silent Accuser.

KAUFMAN, WILLIAM "WILLY"
Died: 1967. Screen actor.

Appeared in: **1939** Confessions of a Nazi Spy; Beast of Berlin; Nurse Edith Cavell. **1940** The Man I Married; Mystery Sea Raider; British Intelligence. **1944** Storm Over Lisbon; The Seventh Cross. **1947** Escape Me Never. **1948** Arch of Truimph. **1960** G.I. Blues. **1962** Hitler (aka Women of Nazi Germany).

KAUTNER, HELMUT
Born: 1908, Dusseldorf, Germany. Died: Apr. 20, 1980, Castellina, Italy. Screen, stage actor, film director, film producer, screenwriter, playwright and author.

Appeared in: **1932** Kreuzer Emden. **1943** Romanze in Moll. **1944** Grosse Freiheit Nr. 7 (aka La Paloma). **1948** Der Apfel ist Ab. **1950** Epilog; Koenigskinder; The Original Sin.

KAY, CLAUDEL See KEITH, ISABEL

KAY, HENRY
Born: 1911. Died: Dec. 9, 1968, London, England. Screen and television actor.

Appeared in: **1962** The Dock Brief (aka Trial and Error—US). **1968** Oliver.

KAY, MARJORIE
Died: June 25, 1949, Hartford, Conn. Screen, stage actress and singer.

Appeared in: **1916** Sherlock Holmes.

KAYE, PHIL
Born: 1912. Died: Nov. 28, 1959, New York, N.Y. Screen, stage, vaudeville actor and singer.

Appeared in: **1934** Romance in the Rain. **1950** The Asphalt Jungle. **1951** The Red Badge of Courage.

KAYE, SPARKY (Philip Kaplan)
Born: 1906, New York, N.Y. Died: Aug. 23, 1971, Las Vegas, Nev. (heart attack). Screen, stage, burlesque and nightclub actor.

Appeared in: **1937** Firefly. **1960** Ocean's 11.

KAYSSLER, CHRISTIAN
Born: 1898, Germany. Died: 1944, Germany? Screen and stage actor. Son of actor Friedrich Kayssler (dec. 1945). Married to actress Mila Kopp (dec. 1973).

Appeared in: **1940** Die Neue Deutsche Luftwaffe Greift An (The New German Airforce Attacks).

KAYSSLER, FRIEDRICH
Born: 1874, Neurode-Grafschaft Glatz, Germany. Died: 1945, Leinmachnow, Germany. Screen and stage actor. Father of actor Christian Kayssler (dec. 1944).

Appeared in: Die Liebe Einer Koenigin. **1924** Graefin Donelli; Schicksal; Mutter und Kind (Mother and Child); Tragoedie im Hause Habsburg (aka Das Drama von Mayerling). **1925** Ein Lebenskuenstler. **1926** Eine Dubarry von Heute (A Modern DuBarry—US 1928). **1927** Feme. **1929** Das Brennende Herz (The Burning Heart—US 1930). **1930** Zwei Menschen; Stuerme Ueber dem Montblanc (aka Avalanche—US 1932); Zwei Welten (Two Worlds); Das Floetenkonzert von Sanssouci (The Flute Concert at Sans Souci—US 1931). **1931** Der Hauptmann von Koepenick (US 1933); Yorck (US 1932); 24 Stunden im Leben Einer Frau; Im Geheimdienst; Taeter Gesucht; Kadetten (aka Hinter den Roten Mauern von Lichterfelde); Luise, Koenigin von Preussen (Luise, Queen of Prussia—US 1932); Der Mann, der den Mord Beging (The Man Who Murdered, aka Naechte am Bosporus). **1932** Marschall Vorwaerts; Strafsache von Geldern; Goethe Lebt ...!; Unter Falscher Flagge; Die Elf Schill-schen Offiziere; Das Schiff ohne Hafen (aka Das Gespensterschiff). **1934** Gold; Peer Gynt; Der Ewige Traum (aka Der Koenig des Mont-Blanc). **1935** Der Hoehere Befehl; Das Maedchen vom Moorhof; Mazurka; Friesennot (US 1936); Der Alte und der Junge Koenig (The Young and

the Old King). **1936** Der Hund von Baskerville; Eine Frau ohne Bedeutung. **1937** Der Zerbrochene Krug (The Broken Jug—US 1938). **1938** Winter Stuerme (Winter Storms); Dreizehn Mann und Eine Kanone; Anna Favetti; Verwehte Spuren Covered Tracks—US 1939); Zwischen den Eltern (Between the Parents). **1939** Der Singende Tor. **1940** Der Fuchs von Glenarvon; Angelika; Bismarck; Friedrich Schiller (aka Der Triumph Eines Genies). **1942** Der Strom. **1944** Traeumrei. **1945** Das Leben Geht Weiter.

KEAN, RICHARD
Born: 1892. Died: Dec. 30, 1959, Laguna Beach, Calif. (heart attack). Screen and stage actor.

Appeared in: **1942** Somewhere I'll Find You. **1949** The Beautiful Blonde from Bashful Bend. **1950** Storm Over Wyoming. **1952** The Story of Will Rogers. **1956** The Court Jester; The Ten Commandments.

KEANE, CONSTANCE See LAKE, VERONICA

KEANE, DORIS
Born: Dec. 12, 1881, Mich. Died: Nov. 25, 1945, New York, N.Y. Stage and screen actress. Divorced from actor Basil Sydney (dec. 1968).

Appeared in: **1920** Romance (stage and film versions); Kismit.

KEANE, EDWARD
Born: May 28, 1884, New York, N.Y. Died: Oct. 12, 1959. Screen actor.

Appeared in: **1921** The Supreme Passion. **1931** Stolen Heaven; His Woman. **1933** Ann Carver's Profession; I Have Lived. **1934** The Count of Monte Cristo; I Am Suzanne; Man of Iron; Green Eyes; One Exciting Adventure; Girl in Danger. **1935** Dangerous; G-Men; The Irish in Us; Frisco Kid; Mills of the Gods; Circumstantial Evidence; Public Opinion; Whispering Smith Speaks; Hard Rock Harrigan; Behind the Evidence; Border Brigands; Manhattan Butterfly; A Night at the Opera. **1936** The Singing Kid; Princess Comes Across; The Dragnet; Parole; Down the Stretch; Gambling With Souls; Mummy's Boy; an RKO Radio short. **1937** High, Wide and Handsome; Charlie Chan at the Olympics; The Firefly; I Promise to Pay; Seventh Heaven; The Californian; Hollywood Round-Up. **1938** Alexander's Ragtime Band; Alcatraz Island; Shadows Over Shanghai; Nancy Drew—Detective; I Demand Payment; Slander House; Torchy Gets Her Man; Border G-Men. **1939** Confessions of a Nazi Spy; Frontier Pony Express; Heroes in Blue; The Roaring Twenties; My Wife's Relatives. **1940** Virginia City; Winners of the West (serial); Charlie Chan in Panama; Midnight Limited; Devil's Island; City for Conquest; Money and the Woman; The Son of Monte Cristo; A Fugitive from Justice. **1941** They Died With Their Boots On; Sergeant York; Sea Raiders (serial); Ride, Kelly, Ride; Riders of the Timberline. **1942** Yankee Doodle Dandy; The Man With Two Lies; Wildcat; The Traitor Within; Who Done It?; Who is Hope Schulyer? **1943** Let's Have Fun; Truck Busters; The Good Fellows; Mission to Moscow; I Escaped from the Gestapo. **1944** When Strangers Marry; Haunted Harbor (serial); Captain America (serial); Bermuda Mystery; Nothing But Trouble. **1945** Rogue's Gallery; Fashion Model. **1946** Angel On My Shoulder; Scarlet Street; Night Editor; Roll on Texas Moon; Out California Way. **1947** The Unfinished Dance; Desire Me; Trail to San Antone; The Invisible Wall; Roses are Red; Saddle Pals. **1948** Chicken Every Sunday. **1949** Henry, the Rainmaker; It Happens Every Spring. **1950** A Modern Marriage; Twilight in the Sierras; The Baron of Arizona. **1951** Show Boat; Belle Le Grande. **1952** Deadline, U.S.A.

KEANE, RAYMOND (Raymond Kortz)
Born: 1900, Denver, Colo. Died: Aug. 24, 1973, Los Angeles, Calif. Screen actor and radio producer.

Appeared in: **1926** The Midnight Sun; April Fool. **1927** The Lone Eagle; The Magic Garden. **1928** How to Handle Women; Marriage by Contract; Marriage of Tomorrow; Patievce; Tomorrow; The Power of Silence. **1929** My Lady's Past. **1930** Loose Ankles; Hello Sisters.

KEANE, ROBERT EMMETT
Born: 1885. Died: July 2, 1981, Hollywood, Calif. Screen and vaudeville actor. Married to actress Claire Whitney (dec. 1969).

Appeared in: **1929** Gossip (short); Room 909 (short). **1931** Captain Thunder; Men Call It Love; Laugh and Get Rich. **1933** Enlighten Thy Daughter. **1936** Grand Jury; Panic on the Air; The Big Noise; Jailbreak; Down the Stretch; Hot Money. **1937** The Captain's Kid; Beware of Ladies; Jim Hanvey, Detective; Under Suspicion; Man of the People. **1938** Boys' Town; The Chaser; The Last Express; Billy the Kid Returns; Fool Coverage (short); Think It Over (short). **1939** Pack Up Your Troubles; Confessions of a Nazi Spy; Cafe Society; Hawaiian

Nights; The Spellbinder; One Hour to Live; Fifth Avenue Girl. **1940** The Saint Takes Over; Tin Pan Alley; Michael Shane, Private Detective; Slightly Tempted; Double Alibi; The Border Legion; Lillian Russell; The Lone Wolf Meets a Lady. **1941** The Devil and Miss Jones; Wild Geese Calling; Hello Sucker; In the Navy; Men of Boys' Town; The Cowboy and the Blonde; Midnight Angel; All That Money Can Buy. **1942** A-Haunting We Will Go; Sabotage Squad; The Man Who Wouldn't Die; Remember Pearl Harbor. **1943** Jitterbugs; The Dancing Masters; Crazy House; He Hired the Boss. **1944** The Whistler; Sweet and Lowdown; Hi, Good Lookin'; Kansas City; South of Dixie; The Impatient Years. **1945** Why Girls Leave Home; The Red Dragon; Sacred Stiff; Her Lucky Night. **1946** Fool's Gold; Live Wires; The Strange Mr. Gregory; The Shadow Returns; Rainbow Over Texas; Night Editor. **1947** Millie's Daughter; New Hounds; Jungle Flight; I Wonder Who's Kissing Her Now?; Fear in the Night; The Beginning of the End. **1948** When My Baby Smiles at Me; The Timber Trail; Angel's Alley; Out of the Storm; Incident; The Return of the Whistler; I Surrender Dear. **1949** You're My Everything; Susanna Pass; Henry, the Rainmaker; Crime Doctor's Diary; Jolson Sings Again; Navajo Trail Raiders; Frontier Investigator; Everybody Does It. **1950** Blondie's Hero; Father Makes Good; Mary Ryan, Detective; Hills of Oklahoma. **1952** The Devil and Daniel Webster (reissue of All That Money Can Buy—1941). **1954** The Atomic Kid. **1956** When Gangland Strikes.

KEANREY, JOHN L.
Born: 1871, New York, N.Y. Died: Aug. 3, 1945, New York, N.Y. Screen, stage actor and circus performer.

Appeared in: **1927** East Side, West Side. **1931** Honor Among Lovers.

KEARNS, ALLEN B.
Born: 1895, Canada. Died: Apr. 20, 1956, Albany, N.Y. Screen, stage and television actor.

Appeared in: **1929** Tanned Legs; The Very Idea. **1930** Lovin' the Ladies; Purely an Accident (short).

KEARNS, JOSEPH
Born: 1907, Salt Lake City, Utah. Died: Feb. 17, 1962, Los Angeles, Calif. Screen, television and radio actor. Played Mr. Wilson on "Dennis the Menace" television show.

Appeared in: **1951** Hard, Fast and Beautiful. **1955** Daddy Long Legs. **1956** Our Miss Brooks; Storm Center. **1958** The Gift of Love. **1959** Anatomy of Murder.

KEATAN, A. HARRY
Born: 1896. Died: June 18, 1966, Hollywood, Calif. (heart attack). Screen actor, film producer, director and screenwriter. A comic in two-reelers during silents.

KEATING, FRED
Born: Mar. 27, 1902, New York, N.Y. Died: June 29, 1961, N.Y. (heart attack). Screen, stage, vaudeville actor, circus performer and writer.

Appeared in: **1929** Illusions (short). **1934** The Captain Hates the Sea. **1935** The Nitwit; To Beat the Band; Shanghai; I Live My Life. **1936** 13 Hours by Air; The Devil on Horseback. **1937** Melody for Two; When's Your Birthday? **1938** Dr. Rhythm; Prison Train. **1939** Eternally Yours; Society Smugglers. **1940** Tin Pan Alley.

KEATING, KATHERINE *See* SAGE, FRANCES

KEATING, LARRY
Born: 1896, St. Paul, Minn. Died: Aug. 26, 1963, Hollywood, Calif. (leukemia). Screen, radio and television actor.

Appeared in: **1945** Song of the Sarong. **1949** Whirlpool. **1950** Mister 880; Right Cross; I Was a Shoplifter; My Blue Heaven; Three Secrets; Mother Didn't Tell Me; Stella. **1951** The Mating Season; Francis Goes to the Races; Follow the Sun; Bright Victory; Too Young to Kiss; Bannerline; The Light Touch; Come Fill the Cup; When Worlds Collide. **1952** Carson City; About Face; Monkey Business; Something for the Birds; Above and Beyond. **1953** Inferno; She's Back on Broadway; Give a Girl a Break; A Lion Is in the Streets. **1954** Gypsy Colt. **1955** Daddy Long Legs. **1956** The Eddie Duchin Story; The Best Things in Life Are Free. **1957** The Wayward Bus; The Buster Keaton Story; Stopover Tokyo. **1960** Who Was That Lady? **1962** Boys' Night Out; Be Careful How You Wish (aka The Incredible Mr. Limpet—US 1964).

KEATON, BUSTER, JR. (Joseph Keaton, Jr.)
Born: Oct. 4, 1895, Piqua, Kans. Died: Feb. 1, 1966, Woodland Hills, Calif. (lung cancer). Screen, stage, vaudeville, television actor, screenwriter and film director. Son of actor Joseph Keaton, Sr. (dec. 1946) and actress Myra Keaton (dec. 1955). Divorced from actress Natalie Talmadge (dec. 1969) and Mae Scribbens. Later married to Eleanor Norris. Father of actor Robert Talmadge. After his divorce from Miss Talmadge, she had their son's name legally changed from Keaton to Talmadge. See Joseph Keaton, Sr. for family information.

Appeared in: **1917** The Butcher Boy (film debut); The Rough House; His Wedding Night; Fatty at Coney Island; Oh, Doctor!; A Country Hero; A Reckless Romeo. **1918** The Bell Boy; Goodnight Nurse; Moonshine; The Cook; Out West. **1919** A Desert Hero; The Hayseed; Back Stage. **1920** The Saphead; plus the following shorts: The Garage, One Week; Convict 13; The Scarecrow; Neighbors. **1921** The following shorts: The Haunted House; Hard Luck; The Goat; The Electric House (incomplete first version, destroyed); The Playhouse; The Boat; The Paleface; The High Sign. **1922** The following shorts: Cops; My Wife's Relations; The Blacksmith; The Frozen North; Daydreams; The Electric House (second version). **1923** The Three Ages; Our Hospitality; plus the following shorts: Balloonics; The Love Nest. **1924** Sherlock, Jr.; Navigator. **1925** Seven Chances; Go West. **1926** Battling Bulter; The General. **1927** College. **1928** Steamboat Bill, Jr.; The Cameraman. **1929** Spite Marriage; Hollywood Review of 1929. **1930** Free and Easy; The Big Shot; Dough Boys. **1931** Sidewalks of New York. **1932** Speak Easily; Parlor, Bedroom and Bath; The Passionate Plumber; The Slippery Pearls (short). **1933** What, No Beer? **1934** Le Rio Des Champs-Elysees (The Champs of the Champs Elysees); The Gold Ghost (short); Allez Ooop (short). **1935** The following shorts: La Fiesta de Santa Barbara; Palooka from Paducah; Tars and Stripes; Hayseed Romance; The E-Flat Man; The Timid Young Man; One Run Elmer. **1936** Three Men on a Horse; The Invader (aka An Old Spanish Custom—US); plus the following shorts: The Chemist; Three on a Limb; Grand Slam Opera; Blue Blazes; Mixed Magic. **1937** The following shorts: Ditto; Jail Bait; Love Nest on Wheels. **1938** Hollywood Handicap; Streamlined Swing; Life in Sometown U.S.A. **1939** Hollywood Cavalcade; The Jones Family in Hollywood; The Jones Family in Quick Millions; Mooching Through Georgia (short); The Pest from the West (short). **1940** L'il Abner; The Villain Still Pursued Her; plus the following shorts: Nothing But Pleasure; His Ex Marks the Spot; Pardon My Berth Marks; The Spook Speaks; The Taming of the Snood. **1941** The following shorts: So You Won't Squawk; She's Oil Mine; General Nuisance. **1943** Forever and a Day. **1944** San Diego, I Love You; Two Girls and a Sailor; Bathing Beauty. **1945** That's the Spirit; That Night With You. **1946** El Moderno Barba Azul; God's Country. **1948** Un Duel a Mort. **1949** A Southern Yankee; You're My Everything; In the Good Old Summertime; The Cheat; Neptune's Daughter. **1950** Sunset Boulevard. **1952** Limelight. **1953** The Awakening; Paradise for Buster (never released commercially). **1956** Around the World in 80 Days. **1960** The Adventures of Huckleberry Finn; When Comedy Was King (documentary). **1962** Ten Girls Ago. **1963** Pajama Party; It's a Mad, Mad, Mad, Mad World; The Triumph of Lester Snapwell; The Great Chase (documentary); 30 Years of Fun (documentary); The Sound of Laughter (documentary). **1965** Sergeant Deadhead; Beach Blanket Bingo; The Railrodder; How to Stuff a Wild Bikini; Marines e un General. **1966** A Funny Thing Happened on the Way to the Forum; The Scribee. **1967** War Italian Style. **1974** That's Entertainment (film clips).

KEATON, JOSEPH, SR.
Born: 1867. Died: Jan. 13, 1946, Hollywood, Calif. Screen, vaudeville and burlesque actor. Appeared in vaudeville as "The Three Keatons" and also with magician Harry Houdini. Married to actress Myra Keaton (dec. 1955) with whom he appeared in vaudeville along with son Buster in an act billed as "The Three Keatons." Father of actors Buster (dec. 1966), Louise (dec. 1981) and Harry Keaton.

Appeared in: **1918** Out West; The Bell Boy. **1920** Convict 13. **1921** The Electric House (incomplete first version, destroyed). **1922** The Electric House (second version). **1923** Our Hospitality. **1924** Sherlock, Jr. **1927** The General. **1935** Palooka from Paducah (short).

KEATON, LOUISE
Born: 1902. Died: Feb. 18, 1981, Van Nuys, Calif, (cancer). Screen, stage and vaudeville actress. For family information see Joseph Keaton, Sr. listing.

Appeared in: **1920** Convict 13 (short). **1934** Trimmed in Furs (short). **1935** Palooka from Paducah (short). **1937** Love Nest on Wheels (short).

KEATON, MYRA

Died: July 21, 1955. Hollywood screen and vaudeville actress. Married to screen actor Joseph Keaton, Sr. (dec. 1946). See Joseph Keaton, Sr. for family information.

Appeared in: **1920** Convict 13. **1921** The Electric House (incomplete first version, destroyed). **1922** The Electric House (second version). **1935** Way Up Thar (short); Palooka from Paducah (short). **1937** Love on Wheels (short).

KECKLEY, JANE

Born: Sept. 10, 1876, Charleston, S.C. Died: Aug. 14, 1963, South Pasadena, Calif. Screen and stage actress. Entered films in 1910.

Appeared in: **1920** Sweet Lavender. **1921** Sacred and Profane Love; Everything for Sale. **1922** A Virginia Courtship; Rags to Riches. **1923** Are You a Failure?; Just Like a Woman; Only 38. **1924** The Deadwood Coach; Fair Week; The Hill Billy. **1926** The Mile-a-Minute Man. **1927** Country Doctor; Angel on Broadway; The King of Kings; The Lady in Ermine; Aflame in the Sky. **1928** Harold Teen; Craig's Wife; Walking Back; Masked Angel; On to Reno; Road House. **1929** Noisy Neighbors; Dynamite; Object-Alimony; The Godless Girl; Detectives Wanted (short). **1930** Hide-Out; Conspiracy; Broken Dishes. **1933** Strange People; Notorious But Nice; One Year Later; Dance Hall Hostess. **1934** The Quitter; City Limits; Stolen Sweets; The Curtain Falls. **1935** The World Accuses; A Shot in the Dark; False Pretenses. **1936** Girl of the Ozarks. **1937** Gunsmoke Range. **1939** In Old Montana. **1941** Buy Me That Town.

KEDRAKAS, NASSOS

Born: 1918, Tricala, Greece. Died: Aug. 25, 1981, Athens, Greece (heart attack). Screen and television actor.

Appeared in: **1968** Les Patres du Desordre (aka Thanos and Despina—US 1970). **1978** The Greek Tycoon.

KEDROV, MIKHAIL N.

Born: 1894, Russia. Died: Mar. 22, 1972, Moscow, Russia. Stage actor, director, drama coach and screen actor.

Appeared in: **1932** Sibirsky Patrul.

KEEFE, CORNELIUS (aka JACK HILL)

Born: July 13, 1900, Boston, Mass. Died: Dec. 11, 1972, Los Angeles, Calif. (heart attack). Screen and stage actor. Do not confuse with actor-comedian Jack Hill or film producer-director Jack Hill.

Appeared in: **1924** The Fifth Horseman; The Law and the Lady; A Society Scandal; Those Who Judge. **1925** The Fighting Demon; The Unguarded Hour. **1927** Come to My House; Hook and Ladder No. 9; In a Moment of Temptation; A Light in the Window; The Poor Nut (stage and film versions); Three's a Crowd. **1928** Thanksgiving Day (short); Hearts of Men; The Adorable Cheat; Man from Headquarters; Satan and the Woman; Thundergod; You Can't Beat the Law. **1929** Brothers; Circumstantial Evidence; The Cohens and Kellys in Atlantic City; Devil's Chaplin. **1930** Ex-Flame; Those Who Dance; Hearts and Hoofs (short). **1932** A Lady with a Past; Disorderly Conduct; The Silver Lining. **1933** Tomorrow at Seven; Charlie Chan's Greatest Case; Man of Sentiment; Grand Slam. **1934** Mystery Liner; Three on a Honeymoon; The Chases of Pimple Street (short). **1935** Kentucky Blue Streak; Thunder in the Night; Death from a Distance; Tumbling Tumbleweeds; Hong Kong Nights; Harmony Lane. **1937** The Old Corral; The Trigger Trio. **1938** Telephone Operator; My Old Kentucky Home. **1939** Fifth Avenue Girl; Stagecoach; Mooching Through Georgia (short). **1941** Saddlemates. **1951** Gunplay. **1953** The Vanquished. **1956** Female Jungle. **1958** The Brain Eaters.

KEEFE, ZENA (Zena Virginia Keefe)

Born: June 26, 1896, San Francisco, Calif. Died: Nov. 16, 1977, Danvers, Mass. Screen, stage and vaudeville actress.

Appeared in: **1916** The Hero of Submarine D-2; La Boheme; Perils of Our Girl Reporters (serial); The Scarlet Runner (serial). **1917** One Hour; Enlighten Thy Daughter. **1918** Shame. **1919** The Challenge Accepted; Oh Boy!; The Woman That God Sent. **1920** Piccadilly Jim; His Wife's Money; Marooned Hearts; Out of the Snow. **1921** Red Foam; After Midnight; Proxies. **1922** The Broken Silence; Prejudice; When Love is Young. **1923** None So Blind; The Broken Violin. **1924** Another Man's Wife; The Lure of Love; Who's Cheating?; Trouping With Ellen.

KEEGAN, ARTHUR

Died: 1967. Screen actor.

Appeared in: **1953** From Here to Eternity. **1954** On the Waterfront.

KEELER, ANNA MAY

Born: 1916. Died: Mar. 31, 1935, Hollywood, Calif. Screen actress. Sister of actress Ruby Keller.

KEELER, SUGAR WILLIE

Born: 1891. Died: Jan. 17, 1964, Los Angeles, Calif. Screen actor.

KEEN, MALCOLM

Born: Aug. 8, 1887, Bristol, England. Died: Jan. 30, 1970, England. Screen and stage actor.

Appeared in: **1916** Jimmy. **1917** A Master of Men; The Lost Chord. **1920** The Skin Game. **1922** A Bill for Divorcement. **1925** Settled Out of Court (aka Evidence Enclosed). **1926** The Lodger (aka The Case of Jonathan Drew—US 1928); The Mountain Eagle (aka Fear O' God—US); Julius Caesar (short). **1927** Packing Up. **1929** The Manxman. **1930** Wolves (aka Wanted Men—US 1936). **1931** 77 Park Lane; Jealousy; The House of Unrest. **1934** The Night of the Party; Whispering Tongues; Dangerous Ground. **1936** The Lonely Road (aka Scotland Yard Commands—US 1937). **1938** Sixty Glorious Years (aka Queen of Destiny—US); Mr. Reeder in Room 13 (aka Mystery of Room 13—US 1941). **1942** The Great Mr. Handel (US 1943). **1951** The Lady and the Bandit; Lorna Doone; The Mating Season; 14 Hours; Queen for a Day. **1953** Rob Roy the Highland Rogue. **1957** Fortune is a Woman (aka She Played with Fire—US 1958); The Birthday Present. **1959** Operation Amsterdam (US 1960). **1961** Macbeth (US 1963); Francis of Assisi. **1962** Life for Ruth (aka Walk in the Shadow—US 1966); Two and Two Make Six (aka A Change of Heart and The Girl Swappers).

KEENAN, FRANCES

Born: 1886, Boston, Mass. Died: Feb. 28, 1950, Los Angeles, Calif. Screen actress. Daughter of actor Frank Keenan (dec. 1929).

KEENAN, FRANK

Born: Apr. 8, 1858, Dubuque, Iowa. Died: Feb. 24, 1929, Hollywood, Calif. (pneumonia). Screen, stage and vaudeville actor. Father of actress Frances Keenan (dec. 1950).

Appeared in: **1915** The Coward. **1916** Honor Thy Name; The Thoroughbred. **1918** More Trouble; The Bells. **1922** Hearts Aflame; Lorna Doone. **1923** Brass; Scars of Jealousy. **1924** Women Who Give. **1925** The Dixie Handicap; My Lady's Lips; When the Door Opened; East Lynne. **1926** The Gilded Butterfly.

KEENAN, HILDA

Died: Aug. 20, 1940, New York, N.Y. Screen, stage and vaudeville actress. Daughter of vaudeville actor Frank Keenan (dec.). Divorced from actor Ed Wynn (dec. 1966). Mother of actor Keenan Wynn.

KEENE, ELSIE

Died: Dec. 29, 1973, Ft. Lauderdale, Fla. Stage and screen actress.

KEENE, MATTIE

Born: 1862. Died: Sept. 1, 1944, New York, N.Y. Screen, stage actress and writer.

KEENE, PATRICIA

Born: 1947. Died: Dec. 9, 1981, Los Angeles, Calif. Screen, stage and television actress.

Appeared in: **1980** Xanadu.

KEENE, RICHARD

Born: Sept. 16, 1890, Philadelphia, Pa. Died: Mar. 11, 1971. Screen, stage and vaudeville actor. Entered films in 1929.

Appeared in: **1929** Why Leave Home?; Words and Music. **1930** Happy Days; The Big Party; The Golden Calf; Up the River; Wild Company; The Middle Watch. **1933** Moonlight and Pretzels. **1939** The Mutiny of the Elsinore; She Married a Cop. **1940** Charlie Chan's Murder Cruise. **1941** Road to Zanzibar. **1943** They Got Me Covered. **1946** Murder Is My Business. **1947** Variety Girl; My Favorite Brunette. **1948** Isn't It Romantic? **1952** Road to Bali. **1954** White Christmas; The Country Girl. **1956** That Certain Feeling.

KEENE, TOM (George Duryea aka RICHARD POWERS)

Born: Dec. 20, 1898, Rochester, N.Y. Died: Aug. 4, 1963, Woodland Hills, Calif. Screen, stage actor and cowboy.

Appeared in: **1928** Marked Money. **1929** The Godless Girl; Honky Tonk; Thunder; Tide of Empire; In Old California. **1930** Night Work; Radio Kisses (short); The Dude Wrangler; Tol'able David; Beau Bandit; Pardon My Gun. **1931** Freighters of Destiny; Sundown Trail. **1932** Partners; Ghost Valley; Saddle Buster; Beyond the Rockies. **1933** Renegades of the West; Come on Danger; Scarlet River; Cheyenne Kid; Strictly Business; Crossfire; Son of the Border; Sunset Pass. **1934** Our Daily Bread. **1935** Hong Kong Nights. **1936** Timothy's Quest; Drift Fence; Desert Gold; The Glory Trail; Rebellion. **1937** The Law

Commands; Where Trails Divide; Battle of Greed; Old Louisiana; Drums of Destiny. **1938** Under Strange Flags; The Painted Trail. **1941** Wanderers of the West; Riding the Sunset Trail; The Driftin' Kid; Dynamite Cargo. **1942** Arizona Roundup; Where the Trail Ends. **1944** Up in Arms. **1945** The Enchanted Cottage; Girls of the Big House. **1946** San Quentin. **1947** Crossfire. **1948** Blood on the Moon; If You Knew Susie. **1950** Desperadoes of the West (serial); Trail of Robin Hood. **1951** Texans Never Cry. **1952** Red Planet Mars. **1955** Dig That Uranium. **1958** Once Upon a Horse. **1959** Plan 9 from Outer Space.

KEENER, HAZEL
Born: Oct. 22, 1904, Fairbury, Ill. Died: Aug. 7, 1979, Ventura, Calif. (heart attack). Screen actress. Wampas Baby Star of 1924.

Appeared in: **1922** The Married Flapper. **1923** The Brass Bottle; Tea—With a Kick. **1924** The Dangerous Coward; Empty Hands; The Fighting Sap; Galloping Gallagher; Hard Hittin' Hamilton; The Mask of Lopez; His Forgotten Wife; The Silent Stranger; North of Nevada. **1925** Ports of Call; Parisian Love; The Freshman; Ten Days. **1926** Vanishing Hoofs. **1927** College Widow; The First Night; One Hour of Love; The Gingham Girl; Whispering Sage. **1928** The Scarlet Arrow (serial). **1940** That Gang of Mine. **1941** Murder By Invitation.

KEFAUVER, ESTES (Carey Estes Kefauver)
Born: July 26, 1903, near Madisonville, Tenn. Died: Aug. 10, 1963, Bethesda, Md. (heart attack). Former United States Senator, author and screen performer.

Appeared in: **1952** The Captive City.

KEIGHTLEY, CYRIL
Born: Nov. 10, 1875, Wellington, New South Wales, Australia. Died: Aug. 14, 1929, New York, N.Y. Screen and stage actor.

Appeared to: **1915** The Spendthrift.

KEIM, BUSTER C.
Born: 1906. Died: July 23, 1974, Hollywood, Calif. (cardiac condition). Screen, vaudeville actor and choreographer. Married to actress Dorothy Keim.

KEINZ, BARBARA LEONA
Born: 1888. Died: Nov. 4, 1939, Oklahoma City, Okla. Screen and stage actress.

KEITH, EUGINE
Born: 1879. Died: Feb. 6, 1955, New York, N.Y. Screen, stage and vaudeville actor.

Appeared in: **1920** Uncle Sam of Freedom Ridge. **1921** Get-Rich-Quick Wallingford.

KEITH, IAN (Keith Ross)
Born: Feb. 27, 1899, Boston, Mass. Died: Mar. 26, 1960, New York, N.Y. Screen and stage actor. Married to actress Ethel Clayton (dec. 1966) and divorced from actress Blanche Yurka (dec. 1974).

Appeared in: **1924** Christine of the Hungry Heart; Love's Wilderness; Manhandled; Her Love Story. **1925** Enticement; My Son; The Tower of Lies; The Talker. **1926** The Lily; The Prince of Tempters; The Truthful Sex; Greater Glory. **1927** Convoy; Two Arabian Knights; A Man's Past; The Love of Sunya; What Every Girl Should Know. **1928** The Street of Illusion; Look-Out Girl. **1929** Prisoners; Light Fingers; The Divine Lady. **1930** Abraham Lincoln; The Great Divide; The Big Trail; Prince of Diamonds; The Boudoir Diplomat. **1931** A Tailor Made Man; The Phantom of Paris; The Deceiver; Sin Ship; Susan Lennox, Her Rise and Fall. **1932** The Sign of the Cross. **1933** Queen Christina. **1934** Dangerous Corner; Cleopatra. **1935** The Crusades; The Three Musketeers. **1936** Preview Murder Mystery; Don't Gamble with Love; Mary of Scotland; The Wife Legion. **1938** The Buccaneer; Comet Over Broadway. **1940** All This and Heaven Too; The Sea Hawk. **1942** Remember Pearl Harbor; The Pay-Off. **1943** Five Graves to Cairo; The Sundown Kid; Wild Horse Stampede; That Nazty Nuisance; Bordertown Gun Fighters; Corregidor; I Escaped from the Gestapo; Here Comes Kelly. **1944** Casanova in Burlesque; Arizona Whirlwind; The Cowboy from Lonesome River; The Chinese Cat; Bowery Champs; The Sign of the Cross (revised version of 1932 film). **1945** The Spanish Main; Identity Unknown; Under Western Skies; Phantom of the Plains; Captain Kidd; China's Little Devils. **1946** Fog Island; Northwest Trail; She Gets Her Man; Song of Old Wyoming; Valley of the Zombies; Mr. Hex; Dick Tracy vs. Cueball. **1947** Dick Tracy's Dilemma; Border Feud; Nightmare Alley; The Strange Woman. **1948** The Three Musketeers (and 1935 version). **1954** The Black Shield of Falworth. **1955** Prince of Players; New York Confidential; It Came From Beneath the Sea; Duel on the Mississippi. **1956** The Ten Commandments.

KEITH, ISABEL (aka CLAUDEL KAY aka ISABEL FOWLER)
Born: 1898, Omaha, Nebr. or New York, N.Y.? Died: July 20, 1979, Mill Valley, Calif. Screen, stage actress and singer. Was one of the original Mack Sennett Bathing Beauties. Entered films in 1918.

Appeared in: **1921** The Four Horsemen of the Apocalypse. **1925** The Desert Flower. **1926** The Greater Glory. **1927** The King of Kings; Very Confidential. **1929** Anne Against the World; Barnum was Right; Perfect Day (short); Keeping Love (short). **1931** Be Big (short).

KEITH, JAMES
Born: 1902. Died: Dec. 27, 1970, Pasadena, Calif. (heart attack). Stage and screen actor.

KEITH, RICHARD
Died: Sept. 16, 1976. Screen and stage actor.

Appeared in: **1957** Zero Hour! **1958** Crash Landing.

KEITH, ROBERT
Born: Feb. 10, 1898, Fowler, Ind. Died: Dec. 22, 1966, Los Angeles, Calif. Screen, stage and television actor. Father of actor Brian Keith.

Appeared in: **1924** The Other Kind of Love. **1930** Just Imagine. **1931** Bad Company. **1939** Destry Rides Again; Spirit of Culver. **1947** Boomerang; Kiss of Death. **1949** My Foolish Heart. **1950** Branded; Woman on the Run; The Reformer and the Redhead; Edge of Doom. **1951** Fourteen Hours; Here Comes the Groom; I Want You. **1952** Just Across the Street; Somebody Loves Me. **1953** Small Town Girl; Battle Circus; Devil's Canyon. **1954** The Wild One; Drum Beat; Young at Heart. **1955** Underwater!; Guys and Dolls; Love Me or Leave Me. **1956** Ransom; Written on the Wind; Between Heaven and Hell. **1957** Men in War; My Man Godfrey. **1958** The Lineup; The Tempest. **1959** They Came to Cordura; Orazi et Curiazzi (Duel of Champions—US 1964). **1960** Cimarron. **1961** Posse from Hell.

KEITH, SHERWOOD (Sherwood Keith LaCount)
Born: 1912. Died: Feb. 21, 1972, Hollywood, Calif. (cancer). Screen, stage and television actor. Married to radio actress Louise Winter.

Appeared in: **1961** The Case of Patty Smith (aka The Shame of Patty Smith); The Silent Call. **1963** Terrified. **1964** The Best Man. **1965** Dear Brigitte. **1968** Funny Girl. **1969** Pendulum.

KELCEY, HERBERT
Born: Oct. 10, 1856, England. Died: July 10, 1917, Bayport, N.Y. Stage and screen actor.

Appeared in: **1914** After the Ball. **1916** The Sphinx.

KELLARD, RALPH
Born: June 16, 1882, New York, N.Y. Died: Feb. 5, 1955. Screen and stage actor.

Appeared in: **1915** Her Mother's Secret. **1916** The Precious Racket; Pearl of the Army (serial); The Shielding Shadow (serial). **1918** The Hillcrest Mystery. **1919** Scream in the Night. **1920** The Cost; The Restless Sex; The Master Mind. **1921** Love, Hate and a Woman. **1924** Virtuous Liars. **1930** Women Everywhere. **1931** Upper Underworld; The Ruling Voice.

KELLAWAY, CECIL
Born: Aug. 22, 1893, Capetown, S.Africa. Died: Feb. 28, 1973, West Los Angeles, Calif. Screen, stage, radio, television actor, film director, stage producer and screenwriter. Father of actor Bryan Kellaway. Nominated for 1948 Academy Award for Best Supporting Actor in The Luck of the Irish and in 1967 for Guess Who's Coming to Dinner.

Appeared in: **1937** It Isn't Done. **1938** Double Danger; Everybody's Doing It; Law of the Underworld; Tarnished Angel; This Marriage Business; Maid's Night Out; Night Spot; Wise Girl; Blonde Cheat. **1939** Wuthering Heights; Intermezzo—A Love Story; We Are Not Alone; Mexican Spitfire; The Sun Never Sets; The Under-Pup. **1940** The Invisible Man Returns; The House of the Seven Gables; Brother Orchid; Phantom Raiders; The Mummy's Hand; Diamond Frontier; Mexican Spitfire Out West; The Letter; Lady With Red Hair; South of Suez. **1941** West Point Widow; Burma Convoy; Appointment for Love; New York Town; The Night of January 16th; A Very Young Lady; Small Town Deb; Bahama Passage. **1942** The Lady Has Plans; Take a Letter Darling; Are Husbands Necessary?; I Married a Witch; My Heart Belongs to Daddy; Night in New Orleans; Star-Spangled Rhythm. **1943** The Crystal Ball; It Ain't Hay; The Good Fellows; Forever and a Day; Practically Yours. **1944** Frenchman's Creek; Mrs. Parkington; And Now Tomorrow; Practically Yours. **1945** Love Letters; Bring on the Girls; Kitty. **1946** The Postman Always Rings Twice; Easy to Wed; Monsieur Beaucaire; The Cockeyed Miracle. **1947** Unconquered;

Always Together; Variety Girl. **1948** The Luck of the Irish; Joan of Arc; The Decision of Christopher Blake; Portrait of Jennie. **1949** Down to the Sea in Ships. **1950** Kim; The Reformer and the Redhead; Harvey. **1951** Half Angel; Francis Goes to the Races; Katie Did It; The Highwayman. **1952** Just Across the Street; My Wife's Best Friend. **1953** Thunder in the East; Young Bess; The Beast from 20,000 Fathoms; Crusin' Down the River; Paris Model; Hurricane at Pilgrim Hill. **1955** Interrupted Melody; The Prodigal; The Female on the Beach. **1956** Toy Tiger. **1957** Johnny Trouble. **1958** The Proud Rebel. **1959** The Shaggy Dog. **1960** The Private Lives of Adam and Eve; The Cage of Evil; The Walking Target. **1961** Tammy Tell Me True; Francis of Assisi. **1962** Zotz! **1963** The Cardinal. **1965** Hush ... Hush, Sweet Charlotte. **1966** Spinout. **1967** Guess Who's Coming to Dinner; Fitzwilly; The Adventures of Bullwhip Griffin; A Garden of Cucumbers. **1970** Getting Straight.

KELLER, GERTRUDE
Born: 1881. Died: July 12, 1951, Hollywood, Calif. Screen and stage actress.

Appeared in: **1915** The Unafraid; The Clue. **1934** Flirtation Walk.

KELLER, GRETA
Born: c. 1904, Vienna, Austria. Died: Nov. 4, 1977, Vienna, Austria. Screen, stage, radio actress and cabaret singer. Divorced from singer John Sargent, and later married to actor David Bacon (dec. 1943).

Appeared in: **1942** Reunion in France.

KELLER, HELEN
Born: June 27, 1881, near Tuscumbia, Ala. Died: June 1, 1968, Westport, Conn. Author and lecturer with one screen performance.

Appeared in: **1919** Deliverance.

KELLER, NAN
Died: Dec. 10, 1975, Oklahoma City, Okla. Vaudeville, radio and screen actress. Appeared in vaudeville with her sister and brother in an act billed as "Keller Sisters and Lynch."

Appeared in: **1930** Metro Movietone Act #88.

KELLER, NELL CLARK
Born: 1876. Died: Sept. 2, 1965, Tacoma, Wash. Screen and stage actress.

Appeared in: **1922** Ten Nights in a Bar Room. **1924** The Virgin. **1925** Lightnin'.

KELLERMAN, ANNETTE
Born: July 6, 1887, Sydney, New South Wales, Australia. Died: Nov. 5, 1975, Southport, Australia. Screen, stage, vaudeville actress, champion swimmer and dancer. Known as Australia's "Million Dollar Mermaid."

Appeared in: **1909** "Miss Annette Kellerman." **1914** Neptune's Daughter. **1916** A Daughter of the Gods. **1917** The Honor System. **1918** Queen of the Sea. **1920** What Women Love; The Art of Diving. **1924** Venus of the South Seas.

KELLEY, BOB
Born: 1917. Died: Sept. 9, 1966. Screen, radio and television actor.

Appeared in: **1957** The Fuzzy Pink Nightgown.

KELLINO, ROY
Born: Apr. 22, 1912, London, England. Died: Nov. 18, 1956, England. Screen actor, film director and screenwriter. Son of film director W. P. Kellino (dec. 1958). Entered films in 1915 as a child actor.

Appeared in: **1922** Rob Roy.

KELLOGG, CONELIA
Born: 1877. Died: Feb. 21, 1934, Los Angeles, Calif. Screen actress and fashion model.

Appeared in: **1928** Lingerie.

KELLY, DERMOT
Born: England. Died: 1980, England? Screen actor.

Appeared in: **1959** Broth of a Boy; Home is the Hero (US 1961). **1960** Cover Girl Killer; The Poacher's Daughter. **1962** The Quare Fellow; The Wrong Arm of the Law (US 1963). **1963** Panic (US 1966). **1964** The Yellow Rolls-Royce (US 1965). **1968** Mrs. Brown, You've Got a Lovely Daughter; Subterfuge. **1969** Staircase.

KELLY, DON (Donald Patrick Kelly aka DON O'KELLY)
Born: Mar. 17, 1924, New York, N.Y. Died: Oct. 2, 1966, Culver City, Calif. (pneumonia, etc.). Screen, stage and television actor.

Appeared in: **1957** The Big Land; Bombers B-52; The Crooked Circle. **1958** The Notorious Mr. Monks; Suicide Battalion; Tank Battalion. **1961** Frontier Uprising. **1962** Shoot Out at Big Sag. **1966** The Hostage.

KELLY, DOROTHY "DOT"
Born: Feb. 12, 1894, Philadelphia, Pa. Died: May 31, 1966, Minneapolis, Minn. (cerebral hemorrhage). Screen actress. Do not confuse with actress Dorothy H. Kelly (dec. 1969).

Appeared in: **1912** All for a Girl; Rip Van Winkle; Suing Susan; O'Hare—Squatter and Philosopher; Popular Betty; The Counts; None But the Brave Deserve the Fair. **1913** The Penalties of Reputation; Playing the Pipers; M's Apron Strings; O'Hara's Godchild; Bunny's Honeymoon; Disciplining Daisy; Tricks of the Trade; The Flirt; A Modern Psyche; The Glove; An Unwritten Chapter; My Lady Idleness; The Tables Turned. **1914** The Wheat and the Tares; Two Stepchildren; The Toll; The Love of Pierre LaRosse; The First Indorsement; In the Old Attic; The Vanity Case; Regan's Daughter; A Double Error; The Greater Motive. **1915** Four Grains of Rice; The Kidnapped Stockbroker; In the Days of Famine; The Wheels of Justice; From Out of the Big Snows; The Sultan of Zulon; Pawns of Mars; Stage Money; The Law Decides; A Wireless Rescue; The Man, the Mission and the Maid; Mother's Roses; A Madcap Adventure. **1917** The Money Mill; The Awakening; The Secret Kingdom (serial).

KELLY, DOROTHY HELEN
Born: 1918. Died: Nov. 28, 1969, La Jolla, Calif. (burned to death). Screen actress. Entered films during the 1940s.

Appeared in: **1942** Yankee Doodle Dandy. **1943** The Sky's the Limit. **1944** Lady in the Dark.

KELLY, EMMETT
Born: Dec. 9, 1898, Sedan, Kans. Died: Mar. 28, 1979, Sarasota, Fla (heart attack). Clown, screen actor and nightclub entertainer.

Appeared in: **1940** Keep Off the Grass. **1951** The Fat Man. **1952** The Greatest Show on Earth. **1958** Wind Across the Everglades. **1968** The Clown and the Kids.

KELLY, (MRS.) FANNIE
Born: 1876. Died: Jan. 27, 1925, Hollywood, Calif. Screen and vaudeville actress. Appeared in vaudeville with her husband Pat Kelly (dec. 1938) in an act billed as "Pat and Fannie Kelly." Entered films with Sennett approx. 1922.

KELLY, GREGORY
Born: 1891. Died: July 9, 1927, New York, N.Y. (heart attack). Screen, stage and vaudeville actor. Married to screen actress Ruth Gordon.

Appeared in: **1924** Manhattan. **1926** The Show-Off.

KELLY, HARRY
Born: 1873, New York. Died: Mar. 19, 1936, New York, N.Y. Screen and stage actor.

Appeared in: **1922** Thundering Hoofs.

KELLY, JAMES T.
Born: July 10, 1854, Castlebar, County Mayo, Ireland. Died: Nov. 12, 1933, United States. Screen, stage and vaudeville actor.

Appeared in: **1915** A Night in the Show. **1916** Police; The Floorwalker; The Fireman; The Vagabond; The Count; The Pawnshop Behind the Screen; The Rink. **1917** Easy Street; The Cure; The Immigrant. **1918** A Dog's Life. **1921** Cyclone Bliss. **1924** Rarin' to Go. **1925** The Business of Love. **1926** Man Rustlin'. **1927** Men of Daring.

KELLY, JAMES "TINY"
Born: 1915. Died: May 5, 1964, Hollywood, Calif. (heart ailment). Screen and vaudeville actor. Known in vaudeville as "Tiny" (340 lbs).

Appeared in: **1947** I Wonder Who's Kissing Her Now. **1948** If You Knew Susie. **1952** Million Dollar Mermaid; Pat and Mike.

KELLY, JOE
Died: May 26, 1959. Screen and radio actor.

Appeared in: **1944** National Barn Dance.

KELLY, JOHN (John Gerard Kelly)
Born: 1904, Ireland. Died: May 19, 1977, Monkstown, Dublin, Ireland. Screen, stage and television actor. Do not confuse with US actor with same name (dec. 1947).

KELLY, JOHN

Born: June 29, 1901, Boston, Mass. Died: Dec. 9, 1947. Screen actor.

Appeared in: **1927** After Midnight. **1928** Blindfold; Dressed to Kill. **1929** From Headquarters. **1930** The Man Hunter. **1931** Hell Divers; Subway Express. **1932** Winner Take All; Two Seconds; The Devil Is Driving; Hold 'Em Jail. **1933** Little Giant; Three-Cornered Moon; The Bowery. **1934** Goodbye Love; Little Miss Marker; Many Happy Returns; Fifteen Wives; Old Fashioned Way; Kid Millions. **1935** Navy Wife; Men in the Night; Police Hero Number One; Motive for Revenge; Doctor Socrates. **1936** Born to Dance; Timothy's Quest; In Paris—AWOL; Bridge of Sighs; Poor Little Rich Girl; Easy Money; The Gentleman from Louisiana; Polo Joe; Lady Luck; After the Thin Man. **1937** Wings Over Honolulu; The Last Gangster; Fugitive in the Sky; 23 1/2 Hours Leave; Angel's Holiday; You Can't Buy Luck; Armored Car; The Big Shot; Portia on Trial. **1938** Bringing Up Baby; Female Fugitive; Convicts at Large; Exposed. **1939** Sergeant Madden; Wolf Call; Meet Dr. Christian. **1940** My Little Chickadee; Young Tom Edison; Road to Singapore; Black Friday; The Green Hornet (serial). **1941** Shadow of the Thin Man; Bowery Boy; The Pittsburgh Kid; Three Sons' O' Guns. **1942** Larceny, Inc.; Tales of Manhattan; Jailhouse Blues; My Gal Sal; Moontide; Dr. Broadway; Girl Trouble. **1943** Sweet Rosie O'Grady; No Time for Love; Jack London. **1944** See Here, Private Hargrove; Summer Storm; Wing and a Prayer. **1945** Trail to Vengeance; Blonde from Brooklyn. **1946** Cross My Heart; Blue Skies; Joe Palooka—Champ; The Tiger Woman. **1948** Sofia.

KELLY, JOHN T.

Born: 1852, South Boston, Mass. Died: Jan. 16, 1922, New York, N.Y. (Bright's disease). Screen, stage, vaudeville actor, song and dance man and songwriter. Divorced from actress Florence Moore Eques with whom he appeared in a vaudeville sketch billed as "A Game of Con." He also appeared in vaudeville with Thomas J. Ryan in an act billed as "Kelly and Ryan" and later appeared with Dan Mason in an act billed as "Kelly and Mason."

KELLY, KITTY

Born: 1902, New York, N.Y. Died: June 29, 1968, Hollywood, Calif. (cancer). Screen and stage actress.

Appeared in: **1925** A Kiss in the Dark. **1930** The Head Man (short). **1931** Behind Office Doors; White Shoulders; Bachelor Apartment; La Nuit est a Nous (The Night Is Ours). **1932** Men of Chance; Ladies of the Jury; Girl Crazy. **1933** The Girl in 419; Too Much Harmony. **1934** All of Me; A Woman's Man; The Lemon Drop Kid. **1935** Beginner's Luck (short); The Farmer Takes a Wife. **1937** Blossoms on Broadway; Heart's Desire. **1938** Men With Wings. **1939** Grand Jury Secrets; All Women Have Secrets; The Mutiny of the Elsinore; Geronimo. **1940** Women Without Names; Road to Singapore. **1941** Hold Back the Dawn; The Mad Doctor. **1942** Holiday Inn; Lucky Jordan; The Lady is Willing. **1943** They All Kissed the Bride; So Proudly We Hail. **1945** Practically Yours. **1958** The Lost Missile.

KELLY, LEW

Born: 1879, St. Louis, Mo. Died: June 10, 1944, Los Angeles, Calif. Screen, stage, vaudeville and burlesque actor.

Appeared in: **1929** Barnum Was Right. **1930** The Woman Racket; The Chumps (short). **1931** I Take This Woman; Heaven on Earth. **1932** I Am a Fugitive from a Chain Gang; Scandal for Sale; The Miracle Man; Pack Up Your Troubles. **1933** Hard to Handle; Man of the Forest; State Trooper; Strange People; Laughter in Hell. **1934** What's Your Racket?; Six of a Kind; Old Fashioned Way; Something Simple (short); Fixing a Stew (short). **1935** Goin' to Town; In Person; The Nitwits; Diamond Jim; The Man on the Flying Trapeze; Circumstantial Evidence; Death from a Distance; Public Opinion; Hit and Rum (short); Salesmanship Ahoy (short). **1936** Winds of the Wasteland; The Lone Wolf Returns; It Had to Happen; Three of a Kind; Wild Brian Kent; Rainbow on the River; The Man I Marry. **1937** Breezing Home; High, Wide and Handsome; Paradise Express; All Over Town; Forlorn River; Western Gold; Some Blondes are Dangerous. **1938** Born to Be Wild; Man from Music Mountain; The Overland Express; Lawless Valley; Flirting With Fate; Painted Desert; Gold Mine in the Sky. **1939** Tough Kid; Home Boner (short); Three Texas Steers. **1940** The Westerner; Shooting High. **1941** Lucky Devils; Road Agent; The Last of the Duanes; It Started With Eve; The Little Foxes. **1942** The Magnificent Ambersons; Cooks and Crooks (short). **1943** Keep 'Em Slugging; So's Your Uncle; Lady of Burlesque; Taxi, Mister. **1944** To Heir Is Human (short).

KELLY, MARY "BUBBLES"

Born: 1895, Chicago, Ill. Died: June 7, 1941, Hollywood, Calif. Screen, stage, radio and vaudeville actress.

Appeared in: **1937** Universal short. **1940** Margie; Love Thy Neighbor. **1941** Model Wife.

KELLY, MAURICE

Born: Mar. 6, 1928, Maidstone, England. Died: Aug. 28, 1974, Hollywood, Calif. (heart attack). Screen, stage, vaudeville actor and dancer.

Appeared in: **1940** You Will Remember; Old Mother Riley in Business. **1942** Went the Day Well? (aka 48 Hours—US 1944). **1943** My Learned Friend; It's That Man Again. **1946** 'Till the Clouds Roll By. **1948** You Were Meant for Me. **1957** The Guy Most Likely. **1965** The Family Jewels.

KELLY, NAN

Born: 1895. Died: Oct. 26, 1978, Camarillo, Calif. (heart attack). Screen actress and model. Mother of actors Jack, Nancy, and Carol Kelly. Appeared in silent films.

KELLY, NELL

Born: 1910, Memphis, Tenn. Died: Dec. 16, 1939, New York, N.Y. (diabetes). Screen, stage and vaudeville actress.

Appeared in: **1928** College Swing. **1935** The following shorts: Rhythm of Paree; Sorority Blues; Perfect Thirty-Sixes. **1936** Thanks, Mr. Cupid (short).

KELLY, PAT (Patrick J. Kelly)

Born: July 18, 1891, Philadelphia, Pa. Died: Mar. 19, 1938. Screen and vaudeville actor. Married to actress Fannie Kelly (dec. 1925) with whom he appeared in vaudeville in an act billed as "Pat and Fannie Kelly."

Appeared in: **1916** Love Under Cover; Heart Strategy; A Mail Governess; Done in Oil!; His Hereafter. **1917** His Rise and Tumble; Her Birthday Knight; Skirt Strategy; His Marriage Failure; His Perfect Day; A Warm Reception; Half and Half. **1938** Hawk of the Wilderness (serial); The Missing Guest; The Secret of Treasure Island (serial).

KELLY, PATSY (Sarah Veronica Rose Kelly)

Born: Jan. 12, 1910, Brooklyn, N.Y. Died: Sept. 24, 1981, Woodland Hills, Calif. Screen, stage, vaudeville and television actress. Appeared as part·of the film, comedy team of "Todd and Kelly" with Thelma Todd (dec. 1935).

Appeared in: **1933** Going Hollywood (film debut); plus the following shorts: Beauty and the Bus; Back to Nature; Air Fright. **1934** Countess of Monte Cristo; The Party's Over; Girl from Missouri; plus the following shorts: Babes in the Goods; Soup and Fish; Maid in Hollywood; I'll Be Suing You; Three Chumps Ahead; One Horse Farmers; Opened by Mistake; Done in Oil; Bum Voyage. **1935** Every Night at Eight; Go Into Your Dance; Page Miss Glory; Thanks a Million; plus the following shorts: Treasure Blues; Sing, Sister, Sing; The Tin Man; The Misses Stooge; Slightly Static; Twin Triplets; Hot Money; Top Flat; All American Toothache. **1936** Private Number; Sing, Baby, Sing; Pigskin Parade; Kelly the Second; plus the following shorts: Pan Handlers; At Sea Ashore; Ill Tillies. **1937** Pick a Star; Nobody's Baby; Wake Up and Live; Ever Since Eve. **1938** Merrily We Live; The Cowboy and the Lady; There Goes My Heart. **1939** The Gorilla. **1940** Hit Parade of 1941. **1941** Road Show; Broadway Limited; Playmates; Topper Returns. **1942** In Old California; Sing Your Worries Away. **1943** My Son, the Hero; Ladies' Day; Danger! Women at Work. **1944** The Naked Kiss. **1960** Please Don't Eat the Daisies; The Crowded Sky. **1966** The Ghost in the Invisible Bikini. **1967** C'mon Let's Live a Little. **1968** Rosemary's Baby. **1970** The Phynx. **1977** Freaky Friday. **1979** The North Avenue Irregulars.

KELLY, PAUL (Paul Michael Kelly)

Born: Aug. 9, 1899, Brooklyn, N.Y. Died: Nov. 6, 1956, Los Angeles, Calif. (heart attack). Screen, stage and television actor. Married to actress Dorothy MacKaye (dec. 1940) and later married to actress Claire Owen (Zona Mardell). Served two years for manslaughter of Miss MacKaye's first husband, stage actor Ray Raymond.

Appeared in: **1911** Captain Barnacle, Diplomat; How Milly Became an Actress. **1912** A Juvenile Love Affair; An Expensive Shine; Captain Barnacle's Waif. **1913** The Mouse and the Lion; Counselor Bobby. **1914** Buddy's First Call; Buddy's Downfall; Lillian's Dilemma; Heartease. **1915** The Marr Family Discovers Harlem; The Shabbies; A Family Picnic. **1916** Myrtle the Manicurist; Claudia. **1918** Fit to Fight (U.S. government information film). **1919** Ann of Green Gables. **1920** Uncle Sam of Freedom Ridge. **1921** The Old Oaken Bucket; The Great Adventure. **1926** The New Klondike. **1927** Special Delivery; Slide, Kelly, Slide. **1932** Girl from Calgary. **1933** Broadway Thru a Keyhole. **1934** The Love Captive; The President Vanishes; Blind Date; Death on the Diamond; Side Streets; School for Girls. **1935** When a Man's a Man; Star of Midnight; Public Hero No. 1; Silk Hat Kid; My Marriage; Speed Devils. **1936** Here Comes Trouble; Song and Dance Man; The

Country Beyond; Women Are Trouble; Murder With Pictures; The Accusing Finger; It's a Great Life. **1937** Join the Marines; Fit for a King; Parole Racket; Navy Blue and Gold; The Frame Up; It Happened Out West. **1938** Island in the Sky; Nurse from Brooklyn; The Devil's Party; The Missing Guest; Torchy Blane in Panama; Juvenile Court; Adventure in Sahara. **1939** Forged Passport; The Flying Irishman; 6,000 Enemies; Within the Law; The Roaring Twenties. **1940** Girls Under 21; Invisible Stripes; Queen of the Mob; The Howards of Virignia; Flight Command; Wyoming. **1941** Ziegfeld Girl; I'll Wait for You; Parachute Battalion; Mystery Ship; Mr. and Mrs. North. **1942** Call Out the Marines; Tarzan's New York Adventure; Tough As They Come; Not a Ladies' Man; Flying Tigers; The Secret Code (serial); Gang Busters (serial). **1943** The Man from Music Mountain. **1944** The Story of Dr. Wassell; That's My Baby; Dead Man's Eyes; Faces in the Fog. **1945** Grissly's Millions; China's Little Devils; San Antonio; Allotment Wives. **1946** The Cat Creeps; Strange Impersonation; Strange Journey; Deadline for Murder; The Glass Alibi. **1947** Adventure Island; Fear in the Night; Wyoming; Adventures of the North; Crossfire. **1949** Thelma Jordan (aka File on Thelma Jordan); Guilty of Treason. **1950** Side Street; There's a Girl in My Heart; The Secret Fury; Frenchie; Treason. **1951** The Painted Hills. **1952** Springfield Rifle. **1953** Split Second; Gunsmoke. **1954** Duffy of San Quentin; The High and the Mighty; Johnny Dark; Steel Cage. **1955** Narcotic Squad; The Square Jungle. **1956** Storm Center. **1957** Bailout at 43,000.

KELLY, RENEE
Born: June 4, 1888, London, England. Died: Aug. 28, 1965, London, England. Screen, stage and vaudeville actress.

Appeared in: **1919** Westward Ho! **1920** Foul Play. **1921** All Sorts and Conditions of Men; The Likeness of the Night. **1951** The Scarlet Thread.

KELLY, SCOTCH (James Steele)
Born: 1889, England. Died: Feb. 19, 1967, Isle of Man. Screen, stage and vaudeville actor.

Appeared in: **1929** The Return of the Rat.

KELLY, WALTER C.
Born: Oct. 29, 1873, Mineville, N.Y. Died: Jan. 6, 1939, Philadelphia, Pa. (result of head injury). Screen, stage, vaudeville actor and screenwriter.

Appeared in: **1931** Seas Beneath. **1935** McFadden's Flats; The Virginia Judge. **1936** Laughing Irish Eyes.

KELLY, WILLIAM J.
Born: c. 1875, Boston, Mass. Died: May 17, 1949, New York, N.Y. (heart attack). Stage and screen actor.

Appeared in: **1924** Lily of the Dust. **1925** Parisian Nights; Proud Flesh. **1926** Her Second Chance. **1933** Below the Sea; The Woman Accused. **1934** Six of a Kind. **1943** Spook Louder (short).

KELSALL, MOULTRIE R.
Born: 1902. Died: Feb. 12, 1980, Blair Logie, Scotland. Screen, stage, television actor, radio director, radio producer, radio and television writer. Married to musician Ruby Dun.

Appeared in: **1950** Last Holiday. **1951** The Captain Horatio Hornblower RN; The Franchise Affair (US 1952); The Lavender Hill Mob. **1952** The Hour of Thirteen. **1953** The Master of Ballantrae; Albert RN (aka Break to Freedom—US 1955). **1954** The Maggie (aka High and Dry—US); The Sea Shall Not Have Them (US 1955). **1955** The Dark Avenger (aka The Warriors—US). **1956** The Adventures of Quentin Durward; The Man Who Never Was. **1957** Seven Waves Away (aka Abandon Ship—US); The Barretts of Wimple Street; The Naked Truth (aka Your Past is Showing—US 1858). **1958** The Inn of the Sixth Happiness. **1959** The Battle of the Sexes (US 1960); Left, Right and Centre (US 1961); Beyond This Place (aka Web of Evidence—US). **1961** Greyfriars Bobby; Light in the Piazza (US 1962). **1970** One More Time; The Birthday Party.

KELSEY, FRED A.
Born: Aug. 20, 1884, Sandusky, Ohio. Died: Sept. 2, 1961, Hollywood, Calif. Screen actor. Entered films in 1909.

Appeared in: **1921** Four Horsemen of the Apocalypse (played four roles); The Match Breaker; There Are No Villains; Puppets of Fate. **1922** The Song of Life; Captain Fly-By-Night; Manslaughter; One Clear Call; South of Suva; Deserted at the Altar; Don't Shoot. **1923** The Eleventh Hour; Lovebound; Bag and Baggage; The Bishop of the Ozarks; Souls for Sale; Lights Out. **1924** Stepping Lively; The Yankee Consul; Madonna On the Street. **1925** Excuse Me; Seven Sinners;

Smooth As Satin; Seven Keys to Baldpate; Paths to Paradise; Friendly Enemies; Youth and Adventure. **1926** Atta Boy; The Social Highwayman; That's My Baby; Doubling with Danger. **1927** The Third Degree; Held by the Law; Thirteenth Juror; Thirteenth Hour; The Gorilla; Soft Cushions. **1928** Ladies Night in a Turkisk Bath; Harold Teen; A Midnight Adventure; Tenderloin; The Wright Idea; On Trial. **1929** The Donovan Affair; The Faker; The Fall of Eve; The Last Warning; Naughty Baby; Smiling Irish Eyes. **1930** Murder on the Roof; She Got What She Wanted; Men Without Law; The Laurel and Hardy Murder Case (short); Only Saps Work; The Big Jewel Case; Going Wild; Wide Open; Scarlet Pages. **1931** The Falling Star; Subway Express; Young Donovan's Kid. **1932** Discarded Lovers; Love in High Gear; Guilty As Hell; Red Haired Alibi; The Iceman's Ball (short); Shopping with Wifie (short). **1933** Footlight Parade; Girl Missing; School for Girls; Quiet; Please (short); Grin and Bear It (short). **1934** Young and Beautiful; Shadows of Sing Sing; Beloved; The Crime Doctor; I'll Be Suing You (short). **1935** One Frightened Night; Danger Ahead; Public Menace; Hot Off the Press; The Sagebrush Troubadour; Carnival; Death Flies East; Diamond Jim; Lightning Strikes Twice; plus the following shorts: Nurse to You; Horses Collar; Hot Money. **1936** At Sea Ashore (short). **1937** Second Honeymoon; All Over Town; Super Sleuth; That I May Live; Time Out for Romance; A Damsel in Distress. **1938** Many Sappy Returns (short); Berth Quakes (short); Mr. Moto's Gamble. **1939** Rough Riders' Round-Up; Too Busy to Work; plus the following shorts: Tiny Troubles; Clock Wise; Moving Vanities. **1940** A Little Bit of Heaven; The Green Archer (serial); The Lone Wolf Meets a Lady; The Lone Wolf Keeps a Date; A Bundle of Bliss (short); Mutiny in the County (short). **1941** One Foot in Heaven; The Lone Wolf Takes a Chance; Secrets of the Lone Wolf. **1942** Counter Espionage; Yankee Doodle Dandy; Gentleman Jim; Murder in the Big House; X Marks the Spot; Dear! Dear! **1943** Thank Your Lucky Stars; Northern Pursuit; Murder on the Waterfront; True to Life; One Dangerous Night. **1944** Adventures of Mark Twain; Crime by Night; The Great Mystic; Busy Buddies (short). **1945** Incendiary Blonde; Christmas in Connecticut; Come Out Fighting; How Do You Do?; plus the following shorts: Snooper Service; Microphonies; If a Body Meets a Body. **1946** My Reputation; Bringing Up Father; Strange Mr. Gregory; Monkey Busines (short); So You Want to Play the Horses (short). **1947** Nora Prentiss. **1948** Silver River; Jiggs and Maggie in Court; The Noose Hangs High. **1951** So You Want to Buy a Used Car (short); So You Want to Be a Bachelor (short). **1952** Hans Christian Andersen; O. Henry's Full House; A Blissful Blunder (short). **1953** Murder Without Tears; plus the following short: Pardon My Backfire; So You Want to Be a Musician; So You Want a Television Set; So You Think You Can't Sleep. **1954** Racing Blood; plus the following shorts: So You Want to Be Your Own Boss; So You Want to Be a Banker; So You're Taking in a Roomer. **1955** So You Don't Trust Your Wife (short).

KELSO, MAYME
Born: Feb. 28, 1867, Dayton, Ohio. Died: June 5, 1946, South Pasadena, Calif. (heart attack). Screen, stage and vaudeville actress.

Appeared in: **1912** Human Hearts. **1915** The Bigger Man; One Million Dollars; The Warning; The Little Singer; Man and His Angel. **1917** Castles for Two; The Cost of Hatred; The Silver Partner; The Secret Game. **1918** The Widow's Might; The Thing We Love; The White Man's Law; The Honor of His House; Old Wives for New; His Birthright; The Cruise of the Make-Believers; Mirandy Smiles. **1919** In for Thirty Day; You Never Saw Such a Girl; Johnny Get Your Gun; Experimental Marriage; Men, Women and Money; Daughter of the Wolf; Male and Female; Peg O' My Heart; Don't Change Your Husband; Cheating Cheaters; Wy Smith Left Home. **1920** Jack Straw; The Week-End; Simple Souls; The Hope; Never Get Married; Help Wanted—Male; The Furnace; Why Change Your Wife?; Conrad in Quest of His Youth; The Brand of Lopez. **1921** Ducks and Drakes; Her Sturdy Oak; The Lost Romance; The March Hare; One Wild Week. **1922** For the Defense; Glass Houses; Kick In; The Woman Who Walked Alone; Clarence; Penrod. **1923** Hollywood; The Love Piker; The Marriage Market; Modern Matrimony; Slander the Woman; The World's Applause. **1924** Girls Men Forget; Nellie—The Beautiful Cloak Model. **1925** The Danger Signal; Flaming Waters; The Unchastened Woman; Dollar Down; Seven Keys to Baldpate. **1926** Lightning Reporter; Whispering Wires. **1927** Vanity; The Drop Kick.

KELT, JOHN *See* FORBES-ROBERTSON, ERIC

KELTON, DORRIT
Died: Aug. 19, 1971. Screen actress.

Appeared in: **1955** The Rose Tattoo.

KELTON, PERT
Born: 1907, Great Falls, Mont. Died: Oct. 30, 1968, Westwood, N.Y. (stroke). Screen, stage, vaudeville, television and radio actress. Mother of actor Brian Bell (dec. 1982). Married to actor Ralph Bell.

Appeared in: **1929** Sally. **1930** Hot Curves. **1933** Wine, Women and Song; Bed of Roses; The Bowery. **1934** Pursued; The Meanest Gal in Town; Sing and Like It; Bachelor Bait. **1935** Lightning Strikes Twice; Hooray for Love; Annie Oakley; Mary Burns, Fugitive. **1936** Sitting on the Moon; Kelly the Second; Cain and Mabel; Pan Handlers (short). **1937** Women of Glamour; The Hit Parade; Meet the Boy Friend; Laughing at Trouble. **1938** You Can't Take It With You; Slander House; Whispering Enemies; Rhythm of the Saddle. **1962** The Music Man (stage and film versions). **1965** Love and Kisses. **1969** The Comic (aka Billy Bright).

KELTON, RICHARD
Born: 1943, Lincoln, Nebr. Died: Nov. 27, 1978, Denver, Colo. Screen, stage and television actor.

Appeared in: **1974** McQ; Silence. **1976** The Ultimate Warrior.

KEMBLE-COOPER, LILLIAN
Born: 1892, England. Died: May 4, 1977, Los Angeles, Calif. Screen and stage actress. Married to Louis Bernheimer (dec.) and actor Guy Bates Post (dec. 1968). For family information see Violet Kemble-Cooper listing.

Appeared in: **1921** Ten Nights in a Bar Room. **1923** Shattered Faith. **1936** A Woman Rebels. **1937** Ready, Willing and Able. **1939** Gone With the Wind; We Are Not Alone. **1941** A Woman's Face; Rage in Heaven. **1955** Moonfleet. **1964** My Fair Lady.

KEMBLE-COOPER, VIOLET
Born: 1886, London, England. Died: Aug. 17, 1961, Hollywood, Calif. (Parkinson's disease—stroke). Stage and screen actress. Daughter of stage actor Frank Kemble-Cooper (dec. 1918). Sister of stage actress Greta (dec.) and actors Anthony and Lillian Kemble-Cooper (dec. 1977).

Appeared in: **1933** Our Betters. **1934** The Fountain. **1935** David Copperfield; Vanessa, Her Love Story; Cardinal Richelieu. **1936** Romeo and Juliet; The Invisible Ray.

KEMP, EVERETT
Born: 1874, Shelbyville, Ill. Died: Oct. 1, 1958, Kansas City, Mo. (heart attack). Screen, stage, radio and television actor. Appeared in shorts with Mr. and Mrs. Sidney Drew (1915-1919).

KEMP, HAL
Born: 1904. Died: Dec. 21, 1940, Madera, Calif. (pneumonia after auto injuries). Orchestra leader and screen actor.

Appeared in: **1938** Radio City Revels.

KEMP, KATHLEEN See FIELD, KATHLEEN

KEMP, PAUL
Born: May 20, 1899, Bad Godesburg, Germany. Died: Aug. 13, 1953, Bad Godesberg, West Germany. Screen and stage actor.

Appeared in: **1930** Cyankali; Seitensprunge; Dann Schon Lieber Lebertran; Die Grosse Sehnsucht (US 1931); Die Blonde Nachtigall (US 1931); Der Schuss im Tonfilmatelier; Der Koenig von Paris; Lumpenball (US 1931); Dolly Macht Karriere (Dolly's Career—US 1931). **1931** Die Schwebende Jungfrau; Um Eine Nasenlaenge; Meine Cousine aus Warschau; Der Raub der Mona Lisa; Ein Auto und Kein Geld; M (aka Moerder Unter Uns); Die Dreigroschenoper (The Threepenny Opera, aka The Beggar's Opera). **1932** Gitta Entdeckt ihr Herz; Sehnsucht 202 (Longing 202); Zigeuner der Nacht; Die Verkaufte Braut (US 1934); Drei von der Stempelstelle; Ein Mann mit Herz; Mieter Schulze Gegen Alle. **1933** Unsichtbare Gegner; Das Schloss im Sueden (US 1936); Ihre Durchlaucht, die Verkaeuferin; Roman Einer Nacht (US 1934); Ein Lied fuer Dich (A Song for You); Das Lied vom Glueck (The Song of Happiness—US 1935, and aka Es Gibt nur Eine Melodie). **1934** Mein Herz Ruft Nach Dir; Der Fluchtling aus Chikago (US 1936); Mit dir Durch Dick und Duenn; Die Czardasfuerstin (The Czardes Duchess—US 1935); Charleys Tante (Charlie's Aunt, stage and film versions); Prinzessin Turandot. **1935** Les Dieuxs' Amusent; Der Gefangene des Koenigs; Der Mutige Seefahrer (US 1936); Glueckskinder (US 1937); Amphitryon (aka Aus den Wolken Kommt das Glueck (Luck Comes from the Clouds—US 1938). **1936** Der Schuechterne Casanova; Blumen aus Nizza (Flowers from Nice—US 1939); Heisses Blut; Boccaccio. **1937** Die Verschwundene Frau; Musik fuer Dich; Ihr Leibhusar (US 1938); Zauber der Boheme (The Charm of La Boheme—US 1938). **1938**

Capriccio; Unsere Kleine Frau; Dir Gehoert Mein Herz (My Heart Belongs to Thee—US 1939). **1939** Solo per Danne; Premiere per Butterfly; Kornblumenblau; Das Abenteuer Geht Weiter (aka Jede Frau hat ein Suesses Geheimnis). **1940** Das Leichte Maedchen; Der Kleinstadtpoet; Was Wird Hier Gespielt? **1941** Immer nur Du; Frau Luna; Jenny und der Herr im Frack. **1942** Ein Windstoss; Die Grosse Nummer. **1943** Das Lied der Nachtigall; Fahrt ins Abenteuer (US 1944). **1944** Glueck Unterwegs; Dir Zuliebe; Sieben Briefe; Frech und Verliebt; Spuk im Schloss. **1945** Liebe Nach Noten; Leuchtende Schatten. **1947** Triumph der Liebe. **1948** Das Singende Haus; Der Himmlische Walzer; Lysistrata. **1949** Lambert Fuhlt Sich Bedroht; Gefaehrliche Gaeste. **1950** Der Mann, der Sich Selber Sucht; Maedchen mit Beztehunger; Die Nacht ohne Suende; Die Dritte von Rechts; Kein Engel ist so Rein; Absender Unbekannt. **1951** Die Mitternachtsvenus; Engel im Abendlkleid; ... Mutter sein Dagegen Sehr; Fraulein Bimbi (aka Das Unmoegliche Maedchen). **1952** In Muechen Steht ein Hofbraeuhaus; Die Diebin von Bagdad; Koenigin der Arena. **1953** Glueck Muss Man Haben (aka Drei von Denen Man Spricht); Salto Mortale; Liebeskrieg Nach Noten.

KEMPER, CHARLES
Born: 1900. Died: May 12, 1950, Burbank, Calif. (auto crash injuries). Screen, stage, minstrel, vaudeville and radio actor.

Appeared in: **1929** Beach Babies; Haunted; His Operation; Wednesday at the Ritz. **1945** The Southerner. **1946** Gallant Journey; Scarlet Street; Sister Kenny. **1947** The Shocking Miss Pilgrim; Gunfighters; That Hagen Girl. **1948** Fighting Father Dunne; Fury at Furnace Creek; Yellow Sky. **1949** Adventure in Baltimore; The Doolins of Oklahoma; Belle Starr's Daughter; Intruder in the Dust. **1950** A Ticket to Tomahawk; Mr. Music; Stars in My Crown; Mad with Much Heart; California Passage; The Nevadan; Wagonmaster; Where Danger Lives. **1951** On Dangerous Ground.

KEMPER, JOE
Born: 1883. Died: Aug. 3, 1948, Long Beach, Calif. Screen and stage actor.

KEMPER, ROZENE
Born: 1890. Died: July 8, 1964, Hollywood, Calif. Screen actress.

Appeared in: **1954** Passion.

KENDALL, CY (Cyrus W. Kendall)
Born: Mar. 10, 1898, St. Louis, Mo. Died: July 22, 1953, Woodland Hills, Calif. Screen, stage and radio actor.

Appeared in: **1936** San Francisco; Man Hunt; Hot Money; Dancing Feet; The Public Pays (short); King of the Pecos; Bulldog Edition; The Lonely Trail; Women Are Trouble; Sworn Enemy; Sea Spoilers; Dancing Pirate. **1937** Once a Doctor; White Bondage; They Won't Forget; Without Warning; Angel's Holiday; Borrowing Trouble; Meet the Boy Friend; The Shadow Strikes. **1938** Rawhide; Crime School; Valley of the Giants; The Night Hawks; Hollywood Hotel; The Invisible Menace; Hawaii Calls. **1939** Stand Up and Fight; Twelve Crowded Hours; Fugitive at Large; Angels Wash Their Faces; Calling All Marines; Pacific Liner. **1940** My Favorite Wife; The Green Hornet (serial); Junior G-Men (serial); The House Across the Bay; The Saint Takes Over; Prairie Law; The Fargo Kid; Men Without Souls; Andy Hardy Meets Debutante; Youth Will Be Served; 'Til We Meet Again. **1941** Honky Tonk; Billy the Kid; Midnight Angel; Johnny Eager; Coffins on Wheels (short); Robin Hood of the Pecos; Ride, Kelly, Ride; Mystery Ship. **1942** Alias Boston Blackie; Fly by Night; Road to Morocco; Tarzan's New York Adventure; The Wife Takes a Flyer; Silver Queen. **1943** A Lady Takes a Chance; After Midnight With Boston Blackie. **1944** Kismet; The Chinese Cat; Laura; Outlaw Trail; Roger Touhy, Gangster; A Wave, a Wac and a Marine; Whispering Footsteps; Crime by Night; Girl Rush; The Last Ride; Dancing in Manhattan; Lady in the Death House; The Whistler. **1945** Secret Agent X-9 (serial); Jungle Queen (serial); Scarlet Street; She Gets Her Man; Docks of New York; The Cisco Kid Returns; Wilson; Tahiti Nights; The Tiger Woman; Shadow of Terror; Power of the Whistler; A Thousand and One Nights. **1946** The Scarlet Horseman (serial); Without Reservations; Blonde for a Day; The Glass Alibi; The Invisible Informer. **1947** The Farmer's Daughter; Sinbad the Sailor; In Self Defense. **1948** Call Northside 777; In This Corner; Fighting Mad; Sword of the Avenger; Perilous Waters.

KENDALL, HENRY
Born: May 28, 1898, London, England. Died: June 9, 1962, France (heart attack). Screen, stage actor, stage producer, screenwriter and songwriter.

Appeared in: **1921** Mr. Pim Passes By; Tilly of Bloomsbury. **1930** French Leave. **1931** The House Opposite; The Flying Fool; Rich and

Strange (aka East of Shanghai—US 1932). **1932** The Innocents of Chicago (aka Why Saps Leave Home—US); Watch Beverly; Mr. Bill the Conqueror (aka The Man Who Won—US 1933). **1933** The Shadow (US 1936); The Iron Stair; Counsel's Opinion; Timbuctoo; King of the Ritz; The Man Outside; Great Stuff; The Stickpin; This Week of Grace; The Ghost Camera; The Flaw. **1934** The Girl in Possession; Guest of Honour; Without You; The Man I Want; Sometimes Good; Leave It to Blanche; Death at Broadcasting House; Crazy People. **1935** Death on the Set (aka Murder on the Set—US 1936); Three Witnesses; Lend Me Your Wife. **1936** A Wife or Two; Twelve Good Men; The Amazing Quest of Ernest Bliss (aka Romance and Riches—US 1937); The Mysterious Mr. Davis (aka My Partner Mr. Davis). **1937** Take a Chance; The Compulsory Wife; Side Street Angel; It's Not Cricket; Ship's Concert; School for Husbands (US 1939). **1943** The Butler's Dilemma. **1945** 29 Acacia Avenue (aka The Facts of Love—US 1949); Dumb Dora Discovers Tobacco. **1947** Fag End (reissue of Dumb Dora Discovers Tobacco—1945). **1949** Helter Skelter. **1952** The Voice of Merrill (aka Murder Will Out—US). **1955** An Alligator Named Daisy (US 1957). **1961** The Shadow of the Cat.

KENDALL, KAY (Justine McCarthy)
Born: 1926, Hull, Yorkshire, England. Died: Sept. 6, 1959, London, England (leukemia). Stage and screen actress. Married to actor Rex Harrison.

Appeared in: **1945** Waltz Time. **1946** Caesar and Cleoptra; London Town (aka My Heart Goes Crazy—US 1953). **1950** Dance Hall. **1951** Happy-Go-Lovely; Lady Godiva Rides Again (US 1954). **1952** Wings of Danger (aka Dead on Course—US); Curtain Up (US 1953); It Started in Pradise (US 1953). **1953** Street of Shadows (aka Shadow Man-US); Man Trap (aka Woman in Hiding—US); Genevieve (US 1954); The Square Ring (US 1955); Meet Mr. Lucifer. **1954** Doctor in the House (US 1955); Fast and Loose. **1955** The Constant Husband; Simon and Laura (US 1956). **1956** The Adventures of Quentin Durward; Abdullah's Harem. **1957** Les Girls. **1958** The Reluctant Debutant. **1960** Once More, With Feeling.

KENDRICK, BRIAN
Born: 1930. Died: Mar. 11, 1970, Ruislip, England (heart attack). Screen, television and radio actor.

KENNEDY, CHARLES RANN
Born: Feb. 11, 1871, Derby, England. Died: Feb. 16, 1950, Westwood, Calif. Screen, stage actor and playwright. Married to actress Edith Wynne Matthison (dec. 1955).

Appeared in: **1923** Little Old New York. **1934** Crime Without Passion. **1941** The Bride Came C.O.D.

KENNEDY, DOUGLAS (Douglas Richards Kennedy aka KEITH DOUGLAS)
Born: Sept. 14, 1915, New York, N.Y. Died: Aug. 10, 1973, Kailua, Hawaii (cancer). Screen and television actor.

Appeared in: **1940** Opened by Mistake (film debut); The Way of All Flesh; Northwest Mounted Police; Women Without Names. **1941** The Roundup; The Great Mr. Nobody. **1947** Life With Father; Possesed; The Unfaithful; Dark Passage; That Hagen Girl; Always Together; Deep Valley; Nora Prentiss. **1948** To the Victor; The Decision of Christopher Blake; Adventures of Don Juan; Whiplash; Embraceable You; Johnny Belinda. **1949** South of St. Louis; Look for the Silver Lining; One Last Fling; Fighting Man of the Plains; East Side, West Side; Ranger of Cherokee Strip; The Strawberry Blonde; Flaxy Martin; South of Rio; Whirlpool. **1950** Montana; The Caribou Trail; Convicted; Chain Gang. **1951** Oh Susanna; I Was an American Spy; The Texas Rangers; Callaway Went Thataway; The Lion Hunters; China Corsair. **1952** The Next Voice You Hear; For Men Only; Ride the Man Down; Fort Osage; Indian Uprising; Last Train from Bombay. **1953** War Paint; Gun Belt; Torpedo Alley; Safari Drums; San Antone; Sea of Lot Ships; Mexican Manhunt; Jack McCall—Desperado. **1954** Massacre Canyon; Sitting Bull; The Big Chase; Lone Gun; Ketchikan; Cry Vengeance. **1955** The Eternal Sea; Wyoming Renegades; Strange Lady in Town. **1956** The Last Wagon; Wiretappers; Strange Intruder. **1957** Chicago Confidential; Rockabilly Baby; The Land Unknown; Last of the Badmen; Hell's Crossroads. **1958** The Lone Ranger and the Lost City of Gold; The Bonnie Parker Story. **1959** The Lone Texan; The Alligator People. **1961** Flight of the Lost Balloon. **1967** The Fastest Guitar Alive; Valley of Mystery. **1968** The Destructors.

KENNEDY, EDGAR
Born: Apr. 26, 1890, Monterey, Calif. Died: Nov. 9, 1948, Woodland Hills, Calif. (throat cancer). Screen, stage and vaudeville actor.

Married to actress Patricia Allwyn, with whom he appeared in vaudeville. Was one of the original Keystone Kops. Was star of "Mr. Average Man" series from 1929 to 1934.

Appeared in: **1912** Hoffmeyer's Legacy. **1914** The Star Boarder; Twenty Minutes of Love; Caught in a Cabaret (reissued as The Jazz Waiter); The Knockout (reissued as The Pugilist); Our Country Cousin; The Noise of Bombs; Getting Acquainted; Tillie's Punctured Romance. **1915** Fatty's Tin Type Tangle; A Game Old Knight; The Great Vacuum Robbery. **1916** His Hereafter (working title Murry' Mix-up); His Bitter Pill; Madcap Ambrose; Bombs; The Scoundrel's Tale; Ambrose's Cup of Woe; Bucking Society. **1917** Her Fame and Shame; Oriental Love; Her Torpedoed Love. **1918** She Loved Him Plenty. **1922** The Leather Pushers. **1924** The Night Message. **1925** Golden Princess; His People; Proud Heart. **1926** Better 'Ole; My Old Dutch; Oh! What a Nurse! **1927** Wedding Bill$; The Wrong Mr. Wright. **1928** The Chinese Parrot; plus the following shorts: The Finishing Touch; Leave 'Em Laughing; Should Married Men Go Home?; Two Tars. **1929** The Gay Old Bird; Going Crooked; They Had to See Paris; Trent's Last Case; plus the following short: Moan and Groan, Inc; Great Gobs; Hotter Than Hot; Bacon Grabbers; Unaccustomed as We Are; Hurdy-Gurdy; Dad's Day; Perfect Day; Angora Love. **1930** The following shorts: Night Owls; Shivering Shakespeare; The First Seven Years; When the Wind Blows; The Real McCoy; All Teed Up; Fifty Million Husbands; Girl Shock; Dollar Dizzy; Looser Than Loose; The Head Guy; The Big Kick; Doctor's Orders; Bigger and Better; Ladies Last. **1931** Midnight Patrol; Bad Company; High Gear (short); Love Fever (short); "Mr. Average Man" series including: Rough House Rhythm; Lemon Meringue; Thanks Again; Camping Out. **1932** Carnival Boat; The Penguin Pool Murder; Little Orphan Annie; "Mr. Average Man" serie including: Bon Voyage; Mother-In-Law's Day; Giggle Water; The Gold Chump; Parlor, Bedroom and Wrath; Fish Feathers. **1933** Scarlet River; Crossfire; Professional Sweetheart; Son of the Border; Duck Soup; Tillie and Gus; Kickin' the Crown Around (short—seen in stock footage); "Mr. Average Man" series including: Art in the Raw; The Merchant of Menace; Good Housewrecking; Quiet, Please; What Fur; Grin and Bear It. **1934** Flirting With Danger; All of Me; Lightning; Murder on the Blackboard; The Silver Streak; We're Rich Again; Kid Millions; Twentieth Century; Money Means Nothing; Gridiron Flash; King Kelly of the USA; The Marines Are Coming; "Mr. Average Man" series including: Love on a Ladder; Wrong Direction; In-Laws Are Out; A Blasted Event; Poisoned Ivory. **1935** Living on Velvet; Woman Wanted; The Cowboy Millionaire; Little Big Shot; In Person; A Thousand Dollars a Minute; The Bride Comes Home; Rendezvous at Midnight; A Night at the Biltmore Bowl (short); "Mr. Average Man" series including: Bric-A-Brac; South Seasickness; Sock Me to Sleep; Edgar Hamlet; In Love at 40; Happy Tho Married; Gobs of Trouble (short). **1936** San Francisco; The Return of Jimmy Valentine; Small Town Girl; Mad Holiday; Fatal Lady; Yours for the Asking; Three Men on a Horse; Robin Hood of El Dorado; "Mr. Average Man" series including: Gasoloons; Will Power; High Beer Pressure; Dummy Ache; Vocalizing. **1937** When's Your Birthday?; Super Sleuth; A Star Is Born; Double Wedding; True Confession; Hollywood Hotel; "Mr. Average Man" series including: Hillbilly Goat; Bad Housekeeping; Locks and Bonds; Dumb's the Word; Tramp Trouble; Morning, Judge; Edgar and Goliath. **1938** The Black Doll; Scandal Street; Hey! Hey! U.S.A; Peck's Bad Boy with the Circus; "Mr. Average Man" series including: Ears of Experience; False Roomers; Kennedy's Castle; Fool Coverage; Beaux and Error; A Clean Sweep. **1939** It's a Wonderful World; Little Accident; Everything's on Ice; Charlie McCarthy, Detective; Laugh It Off; "Mr. Average Man" series including: Maid to Order; Clock Wise; Baby Daze; Feathered Pests; Act Your Age; Kennedy the Great. **1940** Sandy Is a Lady; Dr. Christian Meets the Women; The Quarterback; Margie; Who Killed Aunt Maggie?; Remedy for Riches; Sandy Gets Her Man; Li'l Abner; "Mr. Average Man" series including: Slightly at Sea; Mutiny in the County; 'Taint Legal; Sunk by the Census; Trailer Tragedy; Drafted in the Depot. **1941** The Bride Wore Crutches; Public Enemies; Blondie in Society; "Mr. Average Man" series including: Mad about Moonshine; It Happened All Night; An Apple in His Eye; Westward Ho-Hum; I'll Fix That; A Quiet Fourth. **1942** Snuffy Smith, Yard Bird; Pardon My Stripes; In Old California; Hillbilly Blitzkrieg; "Mr. Average man" series including: Heart Burn; Inferior Decorator; Cooks and Crooks; Two for the Money; Rough on Rents; Duck Soup. **1943** The Falcon Strikes Back; Cosmo Jones—Crime Smasher; Air Raid Wardens; Hitler's Madman; The Girl from Monterey; Crazy House; "Mr. Average Man" series including: Hold Your Temper; Indian Signs; Hot Foot; Not on My Account; Unlucky Dog. **1944** It Happened Tomorrow; The Great Alaskan Mystery (serial); "Mr. Average Man" series including; Prunes and Politics; Love Your Landlord; Radio Rampage; The Kitchen Cynic; Feather Your Nest. **1945** Anchors Aweigh; Captain Tugboat

Annie; "Mr. Average Man" series including: Alibi Baby; Sleepless Tuesday; What, No Cigarettes?; It's Your Move; You Drive Me Crazy; The Big Beef; Mother-In-Law's Day (and 1932 version). **1946** "Mr. Average Man" series including: Trouble or Nothing; Wall Street Blues; Motor Maniacs; Noisy Neighbors; I'll Build It Myself; Social Terrors. **1947** Heaven Only Knows; Sin of Harold Diddlebock (aka Mad Wednesday—US 1951); "Mr. Average Man" series including: Do or Diet; Heading for Trouble; Host of a Ghost; Television Turmoil; Mind Over Mouse. **1948** Variety Time; Unfaithfully Yours; "Mr. Average Man" series including: Brother Knows Best; No More Relatives; How to Clean House; Dig That Gold; Home Canning; Contest Crazy. **1949** My Dream Is Yours. **1960** When Comedy Was King (documentary). **1963** The Sound of Laughter (documentary). **1965** Laurel and Hardy's Laughing '20s (documentary). **1968** The Further Perils of Laurel and Hardy (documentary).

KENNEDY, FREDERICK O.
Born: 1910. Died: Dec. 5, 1958, Natchitoches, La. (killed while filming The Horse Soldiers). Screen actor and stuntman.

Appeared in: **1949** She Wore a Yellow Ribbon. **1950** Rio Grande. **1953** The Charge at Feather River. **1959** The Horse Soldiers.

KENNEDY, HELEN
Died: Oct. 21, 1973, Hollywood, Calif. Screen and vaudeville actress. Mother of actor George Kennedy. Appeared in vaudeville as star of "Le Ballet Classique."

KENNEDY, JOHN F.
Died: Nov. 6, 1960, Hollywood, Calif. Screen actor. Appeared in "Keystone Kop" comedies.

Appeared in: **1935** She Gets Her Man. **1936** Parole; San Francisco.

KENNEDY, JOSEPH C.
Born: 1890, Canada. Died: May 4, 1949, Halifax, Canada. Stage and screen actor. Appeared in Canadian Bioscope Co. films.

KENNEDY, JOYCE
Born: July 1, 1898, London, England. Died: Mar. 12, 1943, London, England (pneumonia). Screen and stage actress.

Appeared in: **1930** The Man from Chicago (US 1931). **1931** Bracelets. **1932** Say It With Music. **1934** Dangerous Ground; The Return of Bulldog Drummond. **1935** Black Mask. **1936** Debt of Honour; Twelve Good Men; Hail and Farewell; Seven Sinners (aka Doomed Cargo—US). **1937** Big Fella.

KENNEDY, KING
Born: Dec. 1, 1903, Kokomo, Ind. Died: Nov. 11, 1974, Los Angeles, Calif. (heart attack). Screen, stage actor, playwright, journalist and public relations executive. Divorced from film producer Harriet Parsons.

Appeared in: **1935** On Probation. **1942** Seven Days' Leave. **1943** Higher and Higher.

KENNEDY, LEO A.
Born: 1883 or 1886, Wilmington, Del. Died: Dec. 11, 1939, New York, N.Y. Screen and stage actor. Married to actress Warda Howard (dec. 1943).

Appeared in: **1916** Little Miss Hapiness.

KENNEDY, MERNA (Maude Kahler)
Born: Sept. 7, 1908, Kankakee, Ill. Died: Dec. 20, 1944, Los Angeles, Calif. (heart attack). Screen and stage actress. Divorced from dance director Busby Berkeley (dec. 1976).

Appeared in: **1928** The Circus. **1929** Broadway; Barnum Was Right; Skinner Steps Out. **1930** The Rampant Age; Worldly Good; Midnight Special; Embarassing Moments; The King of Jazz. **1931** Stepping Out. **1932** The Gay Buckaroo; Ghost Valley; The All American; Laughter in Hell; Red Haired Alibi; Reputation; Lady With a Past. **1933** Come On Tarzan; Big Chance; Easy Millions; Emergency Call; Don't Bet on Love; Arizona to Broadway; Police Call; Son of a Sailor. **1934** Wonder Bar; I Like It That Way; Jimmy the Gent.

KENNEDY, TOM
Born: 1884, New York, N.Y. Died: Oct. 6, 1965, Woodland Hills, Calif. (bone cancer). Screen and television actor. Entered films in 1915. (Do not confuse with television host Tom Kennedy).

Appeared in: **1916** The Village Blacksmith; Hearts and Sparks; Ambrose's Rapid Rise. **1917** Nick of Time Baby. **1921** Serenade; Skirts. **1922** The Flirt; If You Believe It, It's So; Afraid to Fight; The

Flaming Hour; Our Leading Citizen. **1923** Scaramouche; With Naked Fists. **1924** Loving Lies; Madonna of the Streets. **1925** The Knockout; As Man Desires; The Best Bad Man; High and Handsome; The Fearless Lover. **1926** Behind the Front; Mantrap; Better 'Ole; Sir Lumberjack; We're in the Navy Now; The Yankee Senor; Born to the West; Man of the Forest. **1927** Fireman Save My Child; Silver Valley; The Mysterious Rider; One Round Hogan; Alias the Deacon. **1928** Hold 'Em Yale; The Cop; Tillie's Punctured Romance; Love Over Night; Marked Money; None But the Brave; Wife Savers. **1929** The Glad Rag Doll; Post Mortems; Big News; The Cohens and the Kellys in Atlantic City; The Shannons of Broadway; Liberty (short). **1930** See America Thirst; The Big House; Fall Guy. **1931** It Pays to Advertise; Caught; The Gang Busters; Monkey Business. **1932** Pack Up Your Troubles; The Devil Is Driving; The Boudoir Butler (short); Fish Feathers (short). **1933** Blondie Johnson; Man of the Forest; She Done Him Wrong (short). **1934** Hollywood Party; Strictly Dynamite; Down to Their Last Yacht; plus the following shorts: Derby Decade; Circus Hoodoo; In the Devil's Doghouse; Odor in the Court. **1935** The Bride Comes Home; Bright Lights; Alibi Bye Bye (short); Sock Me to Sleep (short). **1936** Poppy; Hollywood Boulevard; Smart Blonde (short); Free Rent (short). **1937** Fly-Away Baby; Marry the Girl; The Adventurous Blonde; He Couldn't Say No; Behind the Headlines; The Big Shot; Forty Naughty Girls; Living on Love; Married Before Breakfast; Armored Car; Swing It, Sailor; She Had to Eat; The Case of the Stuttering Blonde (short). **1938** Making the Headlines; Torchy Blane in Panama; Pardon Our Nerve; Long Shot; Crime Ring; Go Chase Yourself; Wise Girl; Crashing Hollywood; House of Mytery; Blondes at Work; Torchy Gets Her Man; A Criminal Is Born (short). **1939** Torchy Blane in Chinatown; Torchy Runs for Mayor; Covered Trailer; Society Lawyer; Torchy Plays with Dynamite; The Day the Bookies Wept; Mexican Spitfire. **1940** Flowing Gold; Remember the Night; Millionaire Playboy; Curtain Call; Pop Always Pays; Mexican Spitfire Out West; An Angel from Texas; Sporting Blood. **1941** The Great Swindle; Angels with Broken Wings; The Officer and the Lady; Sailors On Leave; Yankee Doodle Andy (short); Man I Cured (short); Mexican Spitfire's Baby. **1942** Pardon My Stripes; Wildcat; plus the following shorts: Home Work; Hold 'Em Jail; Pretty Dolly. **1943** Ladies' Day; Dixie; Here Comes Elmer; My Darling Clementine; Petticoat Larceny; Hit Parade of 1943; Stage Door Canteen; Cutie on Duty (short); Wedtime Stories (short). **1944** Rosie the Riveter; Princess and the Pirate; And the Angels Sing; Moonlight and Cactus; plus the following shorts: Love Your Landlord; Radio Rampage; Girls, Girls, Girls. **1945** Blonde Alibi; The Man Who Walked Alone; It Shouldn't Happen to a Dog (short). **1946** The Kid from Brooklyn; Voice of the Whistler; Bringing Up Father; Motor Maniacs (short). **1947** The Burning Cross; The Case of the Baby Sister; The Pretender. **1948** They Live by Night (aka The Twisted Road and Your Red Wagon); The Devil's Cargo; Jinx Money; The Paleface; Thunder in the Pines. **1949** Fighting Fools; Jackpot Jitters; Square Dance Jubilee; The Mutineers. **1950** Border Rangers. **1951** Havana Rose; Let's Go Navy. **1952** Invasion U.S.A.; Gold Fever. **1953** Loose Loot (short); Spooks (short). **1959** Some Like It Hot. **1963** It's a Mad, Mad, Mad, Mad World. **1968** The Further Perils of Laurel and Hardy (documentary).

KENNETH, HARRY D.
Born: 1854. Died: Jan. 18, 1929, Newark, N.J. (brain hemorrhage). Screen, stage and vaudeviile actor. Appeared in early Essanay films.

KENNETH, KEITH (aka KEITH HITCHCOCK)
Born: 1887, England. Died: Apr. 11, 1966, California. Screen, stage, television actor and author. Married to actress/talent agent Betty Fairfax (dec. 1962).

Appeared in: **1934** Limehouse Blues. **1935** Anna Karenina; Clive of India; Cardinal Richelieu; Uncivil Warriors (short). **1936** Daniel Boone. **1937** I Cover the War. **1938** Paris Honeymoon. **1939** We Are Not Alone; The Little Princess; Adventures of Sherlock Holmes; Kennedy the Great (short). **1940** Little Old New York; Hudson's Bay; Raffles; The Blue Bird. **1941** Man Hunt; A Polo Phony (short). **1942** Bombay Clipper; Son of Fury; The Black Swan; London Blackout Murders; Interior Decorator (short). **1944** The White Cliffs of Dover; Jane Eyre; Frenchman's Creek. **1945** Tonight and Every Night; Captain Kidd. **1946** The Locket; Three Stangers; Dragonwyck. **1947** The Exile; Lured; Love from a Stranger; The Homestretch. **1948** Kiss the Blood Off My Hands. **1951** Belle Le Grande.

KENNEY, DOUGLAS
Born: c. 1947. Died: Aug., 1980, Hanapepe Valley Lookout, Kauai, Hawaii (fall while hiking). Satirist, screenwriter, screen actor and film producer.

Appeared in: **1977** Between the Lines. **1978** National Lampoon's Animal House.

KENNEY, JACK
Born: 1888. Died: May 26, 1964, Hollywood, Calif. Screen actor.

Appeared in: **1929** Not Quite Decent; Beauty and Bullets. **1935** I'm a Father (short). **1936** Movie Maniacs (short). **1937** Breezing Home. **1938** Reckless Living. **1939** Laugh It Off. **1940** Strike Up the Band. **1941** Blues in the Night. **1942** Larceny, Inc. **1944** Atlantic City. **1952** Cattle Town. **1953** South Sea Woman; Up in Daisy's Penthouse (short). **1954** Riding Shotgun; The Country Girl. **1956** These Wilder Years. **1957** The Tin Star; Chicago Confidential. **1958** Hong Kong Confidential; Toughest Gun in Tombstone. **1959** Inside the Mafia; Invisible Invaders. **1960** Vice Raid; When the Clock Strikes; Cage of Evil; Three Came to Kill; Walking Target. **1961** The Gambler Wore a Gun; Gun Fight.

KENNY, BILL
Born: 1915. Died: Mar. 23, 1978, New Westminister, British Columbia, Canada (respiratory illness). Black singer and screen actor. One of the original members of the "Ink Spots" singing group. Do not confuse with art director with same name.

KENNY, COLIN
Born: Dublin, Ireland. Died: Dec. 2, 1968. Screen and stage actor.

Appeared in: **1917** Price of a Good Time. **1918** Unexpected Places; Tarzan of the Apes. **1919** Girl from Outside; Toby's Bow. **1920** Return of Tarzan; Blind Youth; The Triflers; 813. **1921** Black Beauty; The Fighting Lover; Heart of Youth; Little Lord Fauntleroy. **1922** The Ladder Jinx; Seeing's Believing; They Like 'Em Rough; Watch Him Step. **1924** Dorothy Vernon of Haddon Hall. **1925** Silent Pal. **1928** Adam's Apple (aka Honeymoon Abroad—US). **1930** Grumpy. **1933** Alice in Wonderland. **1934** Manhattan Melodrama; Limehouse Blues. **1935** The Man Who Reclaimed His Head; Captain Blood; Bonnie Scotland; The Four-Star Boarder (short). **1936** Thank You, Jeeves; The Charge of the Light Brigade; 'Till We Meet Again. **1938** Adventures of Robin Hood; Booloo. **1939** Raffles; The Oregon Trail (serial); We Are Not Alone. **1940** My Son, My Son. **1941** Rage in Heaven. **1943** Two Tickets to London. **1944** The Princess and the Pirate. **1945** Kitty. **1946** Night and Day; The Locket; Three Strangers. **1947** Mourning Becomes Electra. **1948** Kiss the Blood Off My Hands; Johnny Belinda. **1949** Johnny Stool Pidgeon. **1951** Kind Lady. **1953** The Story of Three Loves. **1954** Desiree. **1964** My Fair Lady.

KENNY, LEOLA (aka LEE KENNY)
Born: 1892. Died: Oct. 17, 1956, Hollywood, Calif. Screen and stage actress.

Appeared in: **1930** Just Imagine.

KENNY, NICK
Born: 1895. Died: Dec. 1, 1975, Sarasota, Fla. Songwriter, sports columnist, professional football player, author and screen actor.

Appeared in: **1933** Universal shorts. **1934** Radio Star series of shorts.

KENT, ARNOLD (Lido Manetti)
Born: Jan. 21, 1899, Florence, Italy. Died: Sept. 29, 1928, Los Angeles, Calif. (auto accident). Screen actor.

Appeared in: **1927** The Woman on Trial; Hula; The World at Her Feet. **1928** Beau Sabreur; Easy Come, Easy Go; The Woman Disputed; The Showdown.

KENT, CHARLES
Born: 1852, London, England. Died: May 21, 1923, Brooklyn, N.Y. Stage and screen actor. Entered films with Vitagraph in 1905.

Appeared in: **1910** Uncle Tom's Cabin; Twelfth Night. **1911** The Death of Edward III; Vanity Fair; The Ninety and Nine; Suffer Little Children; Madge of the Mountains. **1912** The Party Dress; The Bond of Music; The Woman Haters; The Awakening of Bianca; She Never Knew; The Unknown Violinist; The Days of Terror. **1913** Daniel; Lily; The Last Millionaire; The Tiger; A Window on Washington Park; The Diamond Mystery; The Treasure of Desert Isle; The Carpenter; The Only Veteran in Town. **1914** The Christian; His Last Call; Mrs. Maloney's Fortune; In the Old Attic; The First Indorsement; The Barnes of New York. **1915** A Price for Folly; Hearts and the Highway; Heights of Hazard. **1916** The Enemy; Kennedy Square; The Supreme Temptation; The Blue Envelope Mystery; The Tarantula; Carew and Son; The Chattel; The Scarlet Runner; Whom the Gods Destroy. **1917** The Marriage Speculation; The Money Mill; Soldiers of Chance; Duplicity of Hargraves. **1919** Miss Dulcie from Dixie; The Gamblers. **1920** The Dream; Body and Soul; Forbidden Valley. **1921** Rainbow; The Single Track; The Charming Deceiver. **1922** The Prodigal Judge. **1923** The Ragged Edge; The Leopardess; The Purple Highway.

KENT, CRAUFORD
Born: 1881, London, England. Died: May 14, 1953, Los Angeles, Calif. Screen actor. Entered films in 1915.

Appeared in: **1917** Thais. **1918** The Song of Songs. **1919** Good Gracious Annabelle. **1920** Other Men's Shoes. **1921** Silas Marner; Jane Eyre; The Plaything of Broadway. **1922** Shadows of the Sea; The Hidden Woman; Shirley of the Circus; Other Women's Clothes. **1923** The Eagle's Feather; Mothers-in-Law; Self Made Wife; The Abysmal Brute. **1924** Daddies; Flowing Gold; Lover's Lane; Virtue's Revolt; The Painted Flapper; The Guilty One; Lilies of the Field; Turned Up. **1925** Easy Money; The Pride of the Force; The Midshipman; Seven Keys to Baldpate; Man and Maid. **1926** Fifth Avenue; Out of the Storm; College Days; Morganson's Finish; The Outsider; The Winning Wallop; That Model from Paris. **1927** The Missing Link; Pirates of the Sky; His Dog; Little Mickey Grogan; See You in Jail; Mother. **1928** The Foreign Legion; Blindfold; Man, Woman and Wife; Into No Man's Land; Bitter Sweets; Manhattan Knights; Out with the Tide; Wallflowers; The Olympic Hero; Queen of the Chorus; Show Folks. **1929** The Charlatan; Seven Keys to Baldpate (and 1925 version); The Wolf of Wall Street; Come Across; The Ace of Scotland Yard (serial); Careers. **1930** Ladies Love Brutes; In the Next Room; Sweethearts and Wives; The Second Floor Mystery; The Devil to Pay; Three Faces East; The Unholy Three. **1931** Grief Street; Body and Soul; Transatlantic; Delicious; The Feathered Serpent; Women Men Marry; His Last Performance; Goldberg; Oh! Oh! Cleopatra (short). **1932** Sinister Hands; The 13th Guest; File 113; The Menace; Murder at Dawn; The Fighting Gentleman; Western Limited; Sally of the Subway; The Purchase Price. **1933** Sailor Be Good; The Eagle and the Hawk; Only Yesterday; Humanity. **1934** The Lost Jungle; The House of Rothschild; Little Miss Marker. **1935** The Man Who Reclaimed His Head; Vanessa, Her Love Story; Mutiny on the Bounty. **1936** The Charge of the Light Brigade; Hitchhike to Heaven; Down the Streets; Magnificent Obsession; Daniel Boone; O'Malley of the Mounted; It Couldn't Have Happened. **1937** Navy Spy. **1938** Letter of Introduction; The Buccaneer; The Adventures of Robin Hood; Love, Honor and Behave; Service de Luxe. **1939** I Was a Convict; Rovin' Tumbleweeds; We Are Not Alone. **1940** Foreign Correspondent; South of Suez. **1941** Shining Victory; International Squadron. **1942** Keeper of the Flame. **1943** The Constant Nymph; Mysterious Doctor. **1944** The Black Parachute. **1945** The Dolly Sisters; The Fatal Witness. **1946** Kitty. **1948** The Woman in White. **1949** Samson and Delilah. **1950** Tea for Two. **1952** Pat and Mike.

KENT, DON A.
Died: June 27, 1978. Screen actor.

KENT, DOUGLAS See MONTGOMERY, DOUGLAS

KENT, ELINOR (Elsie Kent)
Died: Sept. 15, 1957, Hollywood, Calif. Screen actress. Mother of actor Warren Hymer (dec. 1948). Married to actor and playwright John B. Hymer (dec. 1953).

KENT, ETHEL (Ethel Jackson aka ETHEL INCE)
Born: 1884, New York, N.Y. Died: July 27, 1952, Hollywood, Calif. (cerebral hemorrhage). Screen actress. Entered films in 1911. Divorced from actor Robert Armstrong (dec. 1973). Married to actor and director John Ince (dec. 1947).

Appeared in: **1950** Buccaneer's Girl.

KENT, GERALD (Gerald MacIntosh Johnston)
Born: Canada. Died: Nov. 5, 1944, Germany (German prison camp). Stage and screen actor.

Appeared in British film: Four Corners.

KENT, KATE
Born: 1864. Died: Dec., 1934, Hollywood, Calif. (hit by auto). Screen actress.

KENT, KENETH
Born: Apr. 20, 1892, Liverpool, England. Died: Nov. 17, 1963, London, England. Screen, stage, opera, television actor and playwright.

Appeared in: **1940** Night Train to Munich (aka Gestapo and Night Train—US). **1941** Dangerous Moonlight (aka Suicide Squadron—US 1942).

KENT, LARRY
Born: Sept. 15, 1900, England. Died: Nov. 7, 1967, Los Angeles, Calif. (pneumonia). Screen, television actor, film director and film producer.

Appeared in: **1926** Eyes Right!; Obey the Law. **1927** The Whirlwind of Youth; Women's Wares; The Lovelorn; The Masked Menace (serial); The Sea Tiger; McFadden's Flat. **1928** The Head Man; Her Wild Oat; The Heart of a Follies Girl; The Mad Hour; Hangman's House; The Haunted House. **1929** The Devil's Apple Tree; Midstream; Spirit of Youth. **1930** Around the Corner. **1931** Seas Beneath. **1932** Women Won't Tell. **1936** Man Hunt. **1955** A Man Called Peter; Daddy Long Legs. **1964** What a Way to Go. **1966** More Milk Evette (aka Lana Turner).

KENT, MARSHA (Marjorie Kent)
Born: 1919. Died: Mar., 1971, Huntington, N.Y. Screen actress and ballerina.

Appeared in: **1936** The Great Ziefeld. **1937** Prisoner of Zenda; The Bride Wore Red. **1938** The Great Waltz. **1939** The Wizard of Oz; Gone With the Wind.

KENT, RAY
Born: 1886. Died: Nov. 1, 1948, New York, N.Y. Screen actor. Entered films during the silents.

KENT, ROBERT (Douglas Blackley)
Born: Dec. 3, 1908, Hartford, Conn. Died: May 4, 1955. Screen and stage actor. Divorced from actress Astrid Allwyn.

Appeared in: **1934** One Hour Late. **1935** Car 99; Two for Tonight; Love in Bloom. **1936** The Country Beyond; The Crime of Dr. Forbes; King of the Royal Mounted; Dimples; Reunion; Love Before Breakfast. **1937** That I May Live; Nancy Steele Is Missing; Angel's Holiday; Born Reckless; Charlie Chan at Monte Carlo; Step Lively, Jeeves! **1938** The Gladiator; Mr. Moto Takes a Chance; Wanted by the Police; Little Orphan Annie; Gang Bullets. **1939** The Phantom Creeps (serial); East Side of Heaven; For Love or Money; Andy Hardy Gets Spring Fever; Calling All Marines; Secret of Dr. Kildare; Almost a Gentleman. **1941** Sunset in Wyoming; Twilight on the Trail; The Blonde Comet. **1942** The Forest Rangers; Stagecoach Express. **1943** Northern Pursuit; Gung Ho!; Yanks Ahoy; Find the Blackmailer; What a Man! **1944** Hot Rhythm. **1945** Who's Guilty? (serial); What Next, Corporal Hargrove?. **1946** Blonde Alibi; Joe Palooka—Champ; The Phantom Rider (serial). **1947** Shoot to Kill; Jungle Flight; Dragnet; Big Town After Dark. **1948** The Counterfeiters. **1950** Federal Agent at Large; Radar Secret Service; For Heaven's Sake. **1951** The Wild Blue Yonder. **1953** Rebel City. **1954** The Country Girl.

KENT, STAPLETON
Born: 1884. Died: Apr. 3, 1962. Screen actor.

Appeared in: **1950** Shakedown. **1951** The Lady and the Bandit. **1952** Invitation. **1953** Donovan's Brain. **1955** Guys and Dolls.

KENT, WILLARD
Born: 1883. Died: Sept. 5, 1968, Woodland Hills, Calif. Screen actor. Entered films during the silents.

Appeared in: **1936** Prison Shadows. **1937** Death in the Air.

KENT, WILLIAM T.
Born: 1886. Died: Oct. 5, 1945, N.Y. Screen, stage, vaudeville, burlesque actor and circus performer.

Appeared in: **1922** When Knighthood Was in Flower. **1930** The King of Jazz. **1933** Saturday's Millions. **1934** The Scarlet Letter.

KENTON, ERLE (Erle Cawthorn Kenton)
Born: Aug. 1, 1896, Norbonne, Mo. Died: Jan. 28, 1980, Glendale, Calif, (Parkinson's disease). Screen actor, film and television director.

Appeared in: **1915** Peer Gynt. **1936** End of the Trail.

KENTON, JAMES B. "POP"
Born: 1867. Died: Feb. 11, 1952. Screen actor.

Appeared in: **1933** Big Executive. **1934** Search for Beauty; You're Telling Me; Wagon Wheels. **1935** Law Beyond the Range.

KENTON, STAN (Stanley Newcombe Kenton)
Born: 1912, Wichita, Kans. Died: Aug. 25, 1979, Hollywood, Calif (stroke). Screen, radio actor, bandleader and composer.

Appeared in: **1946** Talk About a Lady.

KENTUCK, JOE
Died: Feb. 7, 1923, Lapqai, Idaho. Screen actor.

Appeared in: **1919** Told in the Hills.

KENYON, DORIS
Born: Sept. 12, 1897, Syracuse, N.Y. Died: Sept. 1, 1979, Beverly Hills, Calif. Screen, stage and television actress. Married to actor Milton Sills (dec. 1930). Later married and divorced Arthur Hopkins, Albert D. Lasker, and Bronislaw Mlynarski.

Appeared in: **1915** The Rack. **1916** The Pawn of Fate. **1917** A Girl's Folly; The Hidden Hand (serial); On Trial; The Traveling Salesman. **1918** The Secret of Seven Stars; Strictly Business. **1919** The Band Box; The Inn of the Blue Moon; Twilight; Wild Honey. **1921** The Conquest of Canaan; Get-Rich-Quick Wallingford. **1922** Shadows of the Sea; The Ruling Passion; Sure-Fire Flint. **1923** Bright Lights of Broadway; You Are Guilty; The Last Moment. **1924** Born Rich; Idle Tongues; Lend Me Your Husband; Monsieur Beaucaire; The Love Bandit; The New School Teacher; Restless Wives. **1925** The Half-Way Girl; The Unguarded Hour; If I Marry Again; I Want My Man; A Thief in Paradise. **1926** The Blonde Saint; Ladies at Play; Men of Steel; Mismates. **1927** The Valley of the Giants. **1928** The Hawk's Nest; Burning Daylight; The Home Towners. **1929** Interference. **1930** Beau Bandit. **1931** Upper Underworld; Alexander Hamilton; Road to Singapore; The Bargain; Ruling Voice. **1932** Young America; Man Called Back. **1933** Voltaire; No Marriage Ties; Counsellor at Law. **1934** Whom the Gods Destroy; The Human Side. **1936** Along Came Love. **1938** Girl's School. **1939** The Man in the Iron Mask.

KENYON, NEIL (Neil McKinnon)
Born: 1873, Greenock, Scotland. Died: June 1, 1946, London, England. Screen, stage and vaudeville actor.

Appeared in: **1930** The Great Game; The Loves of Robert Burns.

KENYON, ROBERT
Born: 1889. Died: Dec. 19, 1928. Screen and stage actor.

Appeared in: **1919** The Love Nest. **1921** Silas Marner; The Power Within.

KEPPENS, EMILE (aka EMILE KOPPENS)
Born: France. Died: Oct., 1926, France. Screen actor.

KERBY, MARION
Born: 1877. Died: Dec. 18, 1956, Hollywood, Calif. Screen, stage actress and singer.

Appeared in: **1912** Two Daughters of Eve.

KERN, CECIL
Born: 1892, Portland, Ore. Died: June, 1928, New York, N.Y. (natural causes). Screen and stage actor.

Appeared in: **1919** Gray Towers Mystery. **1920** The Prey; The House of Mystery. **1921** Rainbow; The Eternal Mother.

KERN, JAMES V.
Born: Sept. 22, 1909, New York, N.Y. Died: Nov. 9, 1966, Encino, Calif. (pneumonia). Screen actor, film and television director, screenwriter, composer and member of "Yacht Club Boys" singers on stage, radio and screen.

KERNY
Born: France. Died: Mar. 8, 1933, Prague, Czechoslavakia. Screen actor.

KERR, DONALD "DON"
Born: Eagle Grove, Iowa. Died: Jan. 25, 1977. Screen and stage actor.

Appeared in: **1933** Carnival Lady; From Hell to Heaven; Picture Snatcher. **1934** Murder in the Museum. **1935** Hot Tip; George White's 1935 Scandals; Spanish Cape Mystery. **1936** The Dragnet. **1937** Circus Girl; Don't Tell the Wife; Forty Naughty Girls. **1938** Dummy Owner (short); Room Service; The Lady in the Morgue; Mars Attacks the World; Four Daughters; Sky Giant; Gang Bullets; Flash Gordon's Trip to Mars (serial). **1939** King of the Turf. **1940** The Saint's Double Trouble; Chasing Trouble; Mad Youth. **1941** It Happened All Night (short); Man I Cured (short); Rolling Home to Texas; Devil Bat; Birth of the Blues; Riot Squad. **1943** Happy Go Lucky; True to Life. **1944** And the Angels Sing; Atlantic City. **1945** There Goes Kelly; The Man Who Walked Alone; The Naughty Nineties; Here Come the Co-eds. **1946** Murder Is My Business. **1947** Buck Privates Come Home; The Spook Speaks (short). **1948** So You Want to Build a House (short); So You Want to Be a Detective (short). **1949** Shadows of the West; Oh, You Beautiful Doll. **1950** Sideshow; Square Dance Katy. **1951** Abbott and Costello Meet the Invisible Man; Pride of Maryland; The Flaming Feather. **1952** Lost in Alaska; Carrie. **1953** Abbott and Costello Meet Dr. Jekyll and Mr. Hyde. **1954** Three Ring Circus. **1955** Abbott and Costello Meet the Keystone Kops; Abbott and Costello Meet the Mummy. **1956** Yaqui Drums.

KERR, FREDERICK (Frederick Keen)
Born: Oct. 11, 1858, London, England. Died: May 3, 1933, London, England. Stage and screen actor.

Appeared in: **1916** The Lifeguardsman. **1927** The Honour of the Family (US 1931). **1929** Raffles. **1930** The Devil to Pay; The Lady of Scandal. **1931** Born to Love; Frankenstein; Waterloo Bridge; Always Good-Bye. **1932** The Midshipmaid; Lovers Courageous; Beauty and the Boss; But the Flesh Is Weak. **1933** The Man from Toronto.

KERR, JANE
Born: 1871 or 1891. Died: Nov. 19, 1954, Compton, Calif. Screen, stage, vaudeville and television actress.

Appeared in: **1934** The Painted Veil; Broadway Bill. **1935** She Gets Her Man; Les Miserables. **1936** The Garden of Allah.

KERR, LORENCE "LARRY"
Died: 1968. Screen actor.

Appeared in: **1956** The Best Things in Life Are Free. **1958** The Lost Missile.

KERR, ROBERT "BOB"
Born: 1895, Burlington, Conn. Died: Sept. 5, 1960, Porterville, Calif. (heart attack). Screen actor, film director and writer. Father of actress Ardell Kerr.

Appeared in: **1929** They Had to See Paris. **1932** Island of Lost Souls.

KERRICK, THOMAS
Born: 1895. Died: Apr. 27, 1927. Screen actor.

Appeared in: **1923** Men in the Raw.

KERRIGAN, J. WARREN (George Warren Kerrigan)
Born: July 25, 1889, Louisville, Ky. Died: June 9, 1947, Balboa, Calif. (bronchial pneumonia). Screen, stage actor and film producer. Brother of actress Kathleen Kerrigan (dec. 1957).

Appeared in: **1909** Hand of Uncle Sam. **1910-11** American Film Mfg. Co. films. **1912** Strangers at Coyote; For the Flag. **1913** The Wishing Seat. **1914** Samson. **1915** The Adventures of Terrence O'Rourke. **1916** Landon's Legacy. **1918** A Man's Man. **1919** A White Man's Chance. **1920** Thirty Thousand Dollars. **1921** Coast of Opportunity; House of Whispers. **1923** The Man from Brodney's; The Girl of the Golden West; Hollywood; Mary of the Movies; Thundering Dawn; The Covered Wagon. **1924** Captain Blood.

KERRIGAN, JOSEPH M.
Born: Dec. 16, 1887, Dublin, Ireland. Died: Apr. 29, 1964, Hollywood, Calif. Screen, stage actor and film director.

Appeared in: **1916** The Food of Love; The Miser's Gift; An Unfair Love Affair; Woman's Wit; A Romance of Puck Fair; O'Neil of Glen. **1923** Little Old New York. **1924** Captain Blood. **1929** Lucky in Love. **1930** Song O' My Heart; New Movietone Follies of 1930; Under Suspicion; Lightnin'. **1931** Don't Bet on Women; Merely Mary Ann; The Black Camel. **1932** The Rainbow Trail; Careless Lady; Rockabye. **1933** Air Hostess; Lone Cowboy; A Study in Scarlet; Paddy, the Next Best Thing. **1934** The Fountain; Happiness Ahead; The Lost Patrol; A Modern Hero; The Key; Gentlemen Are Born; Treasure Island. **1935** The Farmer Takes a Wife; A Feather in Her Hat; Mystery of Edwin Drood; Werewolf of London; The Informer; Hot Tip; Barbary Coast. **1936** Timothy's Quest; Spendthrift; The General Died at Dawn; Colleen; The Prisoner of Shark Island; Lloyds of London; Laughing Irish Eyes; Hearts in Bondage; Special Investigator. **1937** The Plough and the Stars; Lets Make a Million; The Barrier; London by Night. **1938** Vacation from Love; Ride a Crooked Mile; Little Orphan Annie; The Great Man Votes; Boy Slaves. **1939** The Flying Irishman; Sorority House; The Kid from Texas; Two Thoroughbreds; Two Bright Boys; 6,000 Enemies; Gone With the Wind; The Zero Hour; Sabotage; Union Pacific; The Witness Vanishes. **1940** Congo Maisie; Young Tom Edison; The Long Voyage Home; Three Cheers for the Irish; The Sea Hawk; No Time for Comedy; Curtain Call; One Crowded Night; Untamed. **1941** Adventure in Washington; Appointment for Love; The Wolf Man. **1942** Captains of the Clouds; The Vanishing Virginian. **1943** None But the Lonely Heart; Mr. Lucky; Action in the North Atlantic; The American Romance. **1944** The Fighting Seabees; Wilson. **1945** The Great John L; Big Bonanza; Tarzan and the Amazons; The Crime Doctor's Warning; The Spanish Main. **1946** Abie's Irish Rose; Black Beauty; She Went to the Races. **1948** Call Northside 777; The Luck of the Irish. **1949** Mrs. Mike; Fighting O'Flynn. **1951** Sealed Cargo; Two of a Kind. **1952** The Wild North; Park Row; My Cousin Rachel. **1953** The Silver Whip. **1954** 20,000 Leagues Under the Sea. **1955** It's a Dog's Life. **1956** The Fastest Gun Alive.

KERRIGAN, KATHLEEN
Born: 1869. Died: Feb., 1957. Screen actress. Sister of actor J. Warren Kerrigan (dec. 1947).

Appeared in: **1914** Samson. **1919** The Uplifters. **1920** The Walk-Off. **1923** None So Blind. **1927** The Music Master. **1929** Sinner Steps Out. **1931** Wicked.

KERRY, NORMAN (Arnold Kaiser)
Born: June 16, 1889, Rochester, N.Y. Died: Jan. 12, 1956, Hollywood, Calif. Screen and stage actor.

Appeared in: **1916** Manhattan Madness (film debut); The Black Butterfly. **1918** The Rose of Paradise. **1919** The Dark Star; Soldiers of Fortune. **1921** Get-Rich-Quick Wallingford; Buried Treasure; The Wild Goose; Little Italy; Proxies. **1922** Brothers Under the Skin; Three Live Ghosts; Find the Woman; The Man from Home; 'Til We Meet Again. **1923** Merry-Go-Round; The Hunchback of Notre Dame; The Spoilers; The Acquittal; Is Money Everything?; The Satin Girl; The Thrill Chaser. **1924** Cytherea; Butterfly; Between Friends; Daring Youth; The Shadow of the East; True As Steel; Tarnish. **1925** Fifth Avenue Models; The Price of Pleasure; Lorraine of the Lions; The Phantom of the Opera. **1926** The Love Thief; Mlle. Modiste; The Barrier; Under Western Skies. **1927** The Unknown; Annie Laurie; Body and Soul; The Claw; The Irresistible Lover. **1928** Man, Woman and Wife; The Foreign Legion; Love Me and the World Is Mine; The Woman from Moscow; Affairs of Hannerl. **1929** The Bondman; Trial Marriage; The Prince of Hearts; The Woman I Love. **1930** Phantom of the Opera (and 1925 version). **1931** Ex-Flame; Bachelor Apartments; Air Eagles. **1941** Tanks a Million.

KERSHAW, ELINOR
Born: 1885. Died: Sept. 12, 1971, Hollywood, Calif. Screen actress and dancer. Married to film director/producer/actor Thomas H. Ince (dec. 1924). Mother of actor Richard (dec. 1938), writer Thomas, Jr. (dec.), and William Ince.

Appeared in: **1910** The Course of True Love.

KERSHAW, WILLETTE
Born: 1882. Died: May 6, 1960. Screen actress.

Appeared in: **1918** Men; Cecilia of the Pink Rose; Sporting Life. **1928** The Vortex.

KERWOOD, DICK
Died: Oct. 16, 1924, Pico Canyon, Calif. (fall from plane while doing a film stunt). Screen stuntman. Appeared in Franklyn Farnum Film Company films.

KESSEL, ADAM
Born: 1866. Died: Sept. 21, 1946, Keeseville, N.Y. Screen actor and film producer.

Appeared in: **1909** Disinherited Son's Loyalty.

KETCHUM, ROBYNA NEILSON
Died: Nov. 9, 1972, Greenwich, Conn. Screen, stage and radio actress.

KEY, KATHLEEN
Born: 1906, Buffalo, N.Y. Died: Dec. 22, 1954, Woodland Hills, Calif. Screen actress.

Appeared in: **1921** The Four Horsemen of the Apocalypse; The Rookie's Return. **1922** Bells of San Juan; Where Is My Wandering Boy Tonight?; West of Chicago. **1923** Beautiful and Damned; Hell's Hole; The Rendezvous; Reno; The Man from Brodney's; North of Hudson Bay. **1924** The Sea Hawk; The Trouble Shooter; Revelation. **1925** A Lover's Oath; The Midshipman. **1926** Ben Hur; College Days; Money Talks; The Desert's Toll; Under Western Skies; The Flaming Frontier. **1927** Hey! Hey! Cowboy; Irish Hearts. **1928** Golf Widows. **1929** The Phantom of the North. **1931** Ben Hur (sound version). **1936** Klondike Annie.

KEYES, JOHN
Born: 1892. Died: Aug. 28, 1966. Screen actor.

Appeared in: Rackety Rax.

KEYS, NELSON
Born: 1887. Died: Apr. 26, 1939, London, England (heart attack). Screen and stage actor.

Appeared in: **1910** Drowsy Dick Dreams He's a Burglar; Drowsy Dick's Dream. **1914** Alone I Did It. **1916** Judged by Appearances; The Real Thing at Last. **1918** Once Upon a Time. **1922** Castles in the Air (aka Let's Pretend). **1927** Tip Toes; Mumsie; Madame Pompadour. **1928** The Triumph of the Scarlet Pimpernel (aka The Scarlet Daredevil—US 1929). **1929** When Knights Were Bold; Splinters. **1931** Almost a Divorce. **1933** Send 'Em Back Half Dead. **1935** We've Got to Have Love; The Last Journey (US 1936). **1936** Eliza Comes to Stay; In the Soup; Dreams Come True. **1937** Knights for a Day; Wake Up Famous.

KHAN, MAZHAR

Born: India. Died: Sept. 24, 1950, India? Screen actor, film producer and director.

KHMELYOV, NIKOLAI (aka N. P. KHMELOF)

Born: 1901, Russia. Died: Nov., 1945, Russia. Screen, stage actor and stage director.

Appeared in: **1932** House of Death. **1936** Revolutionists.

KHOURY, EDITH LESLIE

Died: Apr. 9, 1973, Los Angeles, Calif. (cancer). Screen and stage actress.

Appeared in: **1969** Hello Dolly. **1971** Bedknobs and Broomsticks.

KIBBEE, GUY (Guy Bridges Kibbee)

Born: Mar. 6, 1886, El Paso, Tex. Died: May 24, 1956, East Islip, N.Y. (Parkinson's disease). Screen and stage actor. Married to stage actress Lois Kibbee. Brother of actor Milton Kibbee (dec. 1970).

Appeared in: **1930** How I Play Golf—The Big Irons (short). **1931** Man of the World; Stolen Heaven; Laughing Sinners; Happy Landing; Side Show; New Adventures of Get-Rich-Quick Wallingford; Flying High; Blonde Crazy; Larceny Lane; City Streets. **1932** Crooner; Scarlet Dawn; Taxi; Fireman Save My Child; Mouthpiece; Weekend Marriage; Union Depot; High Pressure; Play Girl; Central Park; The Conquerors; The Crowd Roars; Rain; Gentleman for a Day; Two Seconds; Big City Blues; Man Wanted; The Dark Horse; Strange Love of Molly Louvain; So Big; Winner Take All. **1933** They Just Had to Get Married; 42nd Street; Lilly Turner; The Silk Express; Girl Missing; The Life of Jimmy Dolan; Gold Diggers of 1933; Footlight Parade; Lady for a Day; The World Changes; Havana Widows; Convention City. **1934** Easy to Love; Dames; Harold Teen; Big Hearted Herbert; Merry Wives of Reno; The Merry Frinks; Wonder Bar; Babbitt. **1935** While the Patient Slept; Mary Jane's Pa; Don't Bet on Blondes; Crashing Society; Going Highbrow; I Live for Love; Captain Blood. **1936** Three Men on a Horse; Little Lord Fauntleroy; Captain January; I Married a Doctor; The Big Noise; Earthworm Tractors; M'Liss; The Captain's Kid. **1937** Mamma Steps Out; Don't Tell the Wife; Riding on Air; The Big Shot; Jim Hanvey, Detective; Mountain Justice. **1938** Bad Man of Brimstone; Of Human Hearts; Three Comrades; Rich Man, Poor Girl; Three Loves Has Nancy; Joy of Living. **1939** It's a Wonderful World; Bad Little Angel; Let Freedom Ring; Mr. Smith Goes to Washington; Babes in Arms. **1940** Our Town; Henry Goes Arizona; Street of Memories; Chad Hanna. **1941** Scattergood Baines; Scattergood Pulls the Strings; Scattergood Meets Broadway; It Started with Eve; Design for Scandal. **1942** Scattergood Rides High; This Time for Keeps; Sunday Punch; Miss Annie Rooney; Tish; Whistling in Dixie; Scattergood Survives a Murder. **1943** Cinderella Swings It; Girl Crazy; White Savage; The Power of the Press. **1944** Dixie Jamboree. **1945** The Horn Blows at Midnight; White Pongo. **1946** Singing on the Trail; Cowboy Blues; Gentleman Joe Palooka; Lone Star Moonlight. **1947** Over the Santa Fe Trail; The Red Stallion; The Romance of Rosy Ridge. **1948** Fort Apache; Three Godfathers. **1974** That's Entertainment (film clips).

KIBBEE, MILTON

Born: 1896. Died: Apr. 17, 1970, Simi Valley, Calif. Screen actor. Brother of actor Guy Kibbee (dec. 1956).

Appeared in: **1933** Picture Snatcher. **1934** The Man With Two Faces; Jimmy the Gent; Hi, Nellie!; The St. Louis Kid; Registered Nurse. **1935** Dr. Socrates; Frisco Kid; Black Fury; The Case of the Curious Bride; Don't Bet on Blondes; Dangerous; Mary Jane's Pa; Bright Lights. **1936** Black Legion; Bullets or Ballots; Man Hunt; The Law in Her Hands; Treachery Rides the Range; Murder By An Aristocrat; Love Begins at Twenty; The Case of the Black Cat; Polo Joe; Trailin' West. **1937** Kid Galahad; Green Light; White Bondage; Guns of the Pecos. **1939** The Roaring Twenties; Blondie Takes a Vacation; Another Thin Man; Women in the Wind; The Cat and the Canary. **1940** That Gang of Mine; Strike Up the Band. **1941** Design for Scandal; One Foot in Heaven; Unholy Partners; Kansas Cyclone; Two-Gun Sheriff; Across the Sierras. **1942** Gentleman Jim; My Gal Sal; The Major and the Minor; Billy the Kid—Trapped; Billy the Kid's Smoking Guns; Jungle Siren; In Old California; My Heart Belongs to Daddy; The Mad Doctor of Market Street; Heart of the Rio Grande; Queen of

Broadway. **1943** Hit Parade of 1943; Northern Pursuit; Air Raid Wardens; Dixie Dugan; Happy Land. **1944** Bowery to Broadway; Casanova Brown; The Eve of St. Mark; The Contender; When Strangers Marry; Three Little Sisters; In the Meantime, Darling; Rogues' Gallery. **1945** Billy Rose's Diamond Horseshoe; Out of This World; The Affairs of Susan; Wilson; Anchors Aweigh; Scarlet Street; Who's Guilty? (serial); The Scarlet Clue; Muggs Rides Again; Come Out Fighting; Strange Holiday; White Pongo. **1946** Undercurrent; Easy to Wed; The Blue Dahlia; Miss Susie Slagle's; Cross My Heart; The Bride Wore Boots; Junior Prom; The Flying Serpent; Larceny in Her Heart; Freddie Steps Out; High School Hero; Homesteaders of Paradise Valley; Conquests of Cheyenne; Strange Holiday. **1947** The Arnelo Affair; Desert Fury; Body and Soul; The Sea Hound (serial); Vacation Days; Little Miss Broadway; Frontier Fighters; Luckiest Guy in the World (short). **1948** River Lady; An Old-fashioned Girl. **1949** State Department File 649; Daughter of the West. **1950** County Fair. **1951** Blue Blood; Three Desperate Men (aka Three Outlaws); When the Redskins Rode. **1952** The Las Vegas Story; Here Come the Nelsons; Rodeo.

KIDD, JIM

Born: 1846, Texas. Died: Dec. 9, 1916, Los Angeles, Calif. Screen cowboy actor. Appeared in Kay-Bee films.

KIDD, KATHLEEN

Born: 1899, England. Died: Feb. 23, 1961, Toronto, Canada. Screen, stage, radio and television actress.

Appeared in: **1926** What Price Glory?

KIDDER, HUGH

Born: 1880. Died: June 3, 1952, Hollywood, Calif. Screen, stage and radio actor.

Appeared in: **1933** His Private Secretary.

KIEPURA, JAN

Born: May 16, 1902, Sosnowice, Poland. Died: Aug. 15, 1966, Harrison, N.Y. (heart ailment). Screen, opera and stage actor.

Appeared in: **1930** Die Singende Stadt (US 1935). **1932** Das Lied Einer Nacht (Tell Me Tonight). **1933** Ein Lied fuer Dich (A Song for You); Farewell to Love; Be Mine Tonight. **1934** Mein Herz Ruft Nach Dir; My Song Goes Round the World. **1935** Ich Liebe Alle Frauen; My Heart is Calling. **1936** Give Us This Night; Im Sonnenscheine (aka Opernring). **1937** Zauber der Boheme (The Charm of La Boheme—US 1938); Thank You Madame. **1949** La Vie de Boheme. **1950** Her Wonderful Lie. **1952** Das Land des Laechelns.

KIERAN, JOHN

Born: 1892. Died: Dec. 9, 1981, Rockport, Mass. Screen, radio, television actor and author.

Appeared in: **1944** The Uninvited.

KIERNAN, JAMES

Born: 1939. Died: July 24, 1975, Palms, Calif. (murdered—shot). Stage and screen actor.

KIKUME, AL

Born: 1894, Hawaii? Died: Mar. 27, 1972, Hollywood, Calif. (heart ailment). Screen actor. Father of actor Bernie Gozier.

Appeared in: **1936** The Jungle Princess. **1937** Wings Over Honolulu; The Hurricane. **1938** Air Devils; Mr. Moto Takes a Chance. **1939** Mandrake the Magician (serial). **1940** Typhoon. **1941** South of Tahiti; Jungle Girl (serial). **1942** The Mad Doctor of Market Street. **1945** Song of the Sarong; She Gets Her Man. **1947** Dream Girl; High Barbaree; Green Dolphin Street. **1948** The Wake of the Red Witch. **1949** Daughter of the Jungle. **1950** On the Isle of Samoa. **1951** Operation Pacific. **1952** Road to Bali; Hurricane Smith. **1953** Fair Wind to Java; Miss Sadie Thompson.

KILBRIDE, PERCY

Born: July 16, 1888, San Francisco, Calif. Died: Dec. 11, 1964, Los Angeles, Calif. (brain injury due to auto accident). Screen and stage actor.

Appeared in: **1933** White Woman. **1936** Soak the Rich. **1942** Keeper of the Flame. **1943** George Washington Slept Here; Crazy House; The Woman of the Town. **1944** The Adventures of Mark Twain; Guest in the House; Knickerbocker Holiday. **1945** She Wouldn't Say Yes; State Fair; Fallen Angel. **1946** The Well-Groomed Bride. **1947** The Egg and I; Riffraff; Welcome Stranger. **1948** Black Bart; Feudin', Fussin' and A-Fightin'; You Were Meant for Me; You Gotta Stay Happy. **1949** Mr. Soft Touch; The Sun Comes Up; Free for All; Ma and Pa Kettle.

1950 Ma and Pa Kettle Go To Town. 1951 Ma and Pa Kettle Back on the Farm. 1952 Ma and Pa Kettle at the Fair. 1953 Ma and Pa Kettle on Vacation; Ma and Pa Kettle Hit the Road. 1954 Ma and Pa Kettle at Home. 1955 Ma and Pa Kettle at Waikiki.

KILBRIDE, RICHARD D.
Born: 1919. Died: June 20, 1967, Cambridge, Mass. Screen, stage and television actor.

Appeared in: **1965** The Playground.

KILDUFF, HELEN See ALLERTON, LITTLE HELEN

KILGALLEN, DOROTHY
Born: July 3, 1913, Chicago, Ill. Died: Nov. 8, 1965, N.Y. Radio, television, screen actress and columnist. Married to actor Richard Kollman (dec. 1971).

Appeared in: **1936** Sinner Take All. **1964** Pajama Party.

KILGOUR, JOSEPH
Born: 1864, Ayr, Ontario, Canada. Died: Apr. 21, 1933, Bay Shore, N.Y. Screen and stage actor. Entered films in 1915.

Appeared in: **1915** The Battle Cry for Peach; My Lady's Slipper. **1917** The Easiest Way; The Secret Kingdom (serial). **1919** The Divorcee. **1920** Thou Art the Man; Hearts are Trumps; The Leopard Woman; Love. **1921** At the End of the World; I Am Guilty; Lying Lips; Mother O' Mine. **1923** Within the Law; The Woman With Four Faces; Ponjola; The Midnight Alarm. **1924** Try and Get It; Janice Meredith; On Probation; Torment; The Torrent. **1925** Percy; Capital Punishment; The Top of the World; One Year to Live; The King on Main Street. **1926** Let's Get Married.

KILIAN, VICTOR
Born: Mar. 6, 1898, Jersey City, N.J. Died: Mar. 11, 1979, Hollywood, Calif (murdered-bludgeoned). Screen, stage, vaudeville and television actor.

Appeared in: **1932** Wiser Sex. **1935** Air Hawks; The Girl Friend; After the Dance; Bad Boy; Public Menace; Riffraff. **1936** The Music Goes 'Round; The Road to Glory; Shakedown; Ramona; Adventure in Manhattan; Banjo on My Knee; Lady from Nowhere. **1937** Seventh Heaven; Fair Warning; The League of Frightened Men; Tovarich; It Happened in Hollywood. **1938** It's All Yours; Boys' Town; Miracle Money (short); The Adventures of Tom Sawyer; Gold Diggers in Paris; Prison Break; Orphans of the Street. **1939** Only Angels Have Wings; The Story That Couldn't be Printed; The Return of the Cisco Kid; Paris Honeymoon; St. Louis Blues; Huckleberry Finn; Dust Be My Destiny; Fighting Thoroughbreds. **1940** Chad Hanna; Barnyard Follies; Out West With the Peppers; Little Old New York; Gold Rush Maisie; Tugboat Annie Sails Again; Dr. Cyclops; 'Till We Meet Again; Torrid Zone; The Return of Frank James; Young Tom Edison; They Knew What They Wanted; Virginia City; King of the Lumberjacks; All This and Heaven Too. **1941** Blood and Sand; A Date With the Falcon; Western Union; I Was a Prisoner on Devil's Island; Mob Town. **1942** Reap the Wild Wind; Atlantic Convoy; This Gun for Hire. **1943** Bomber's Moon; Hitler's Madman (aka Hitler's Hangman); Johnny Come Lately; The Ox-Bow Incident. **1944** Uncertain Glory; Barbary Coast Gent; The Adventures of Mark Twain. **1945** Belle of the Yukon; The Fighting Guardsman; The Spanish Main; Spellbound; Dangerous Passage; Behind City Lights. **1946** Little Giant; Smoky. **1947** Gentlemen's Agreement. **1948** Northwest Stampede; Yellow Sky. **1949** Colorado Territory; I Shot Jesse James; Rimfire; The Wyoming Bandit. **1950** Bandit Queen; The Flame and the Arrow; No Way Out; The Return of Jesse James; The Showdown; The Old Frontier; One Too Many. **1951** The Tall Target; Unknown World.

KILNER, OLIVE
Born: 1903, England. Died: Sept., 1964, Bolton, England. Screen and stage actress.

KILPACK, BENNETT
Born: 1883, England. Died: Aug. 17, 1962, Santa Monica, Calif. Screen, stage and radio actor. Star of radio's Mr. Keen, Tracer of Lost Persons.

Appeared in: **1932** Way Back Home.

KIMBALL, DOUGLAS
Died: Jan. 28, 1974. Screen actor.

Appeared in: **1969** Medium Cool.

KIMBALL, EDWARD M.
Born: June 26, 1859, Keokuk, Iowa. Died: Jan. 4, 1938, Hollywood, Calif. Screen and stage actor. Father of actress Clara Kimball Young (dec. 1960). Entered films with Solax Studio in 1910.

Appeared in: **1911-14** Vitagraph films. **1914-16** World films. **1915** Lola. **1917** Magda; The Marionettes. **1920** Mid-Channel. **1921** An Unwilling Hero; Charge It; Boys Will Be Boys. **1922** The Masquerader; Yankee Doodle, Jr.; Omar the Tentmaker. **1923** The Woman of Bronze; The Cheat; Trilby; The Remittance Woman. **1924** Passion's Pathway. **1925** I'll Show You the Town. **1936** Modern Times.

KIMBALL, PAULINE (Pauline Garrett)
Born: Mar. 15, 1860, Chicago, Ill. Died: Dec. 11, 1919. Screen, stage actress and opera performer. Mother of actress Clara Kimball Young (dec. 1960).

Appeared in: **1913** Memories that Haunt. **1916** The Feast of Life; The Deep Purple.

KIMBROUGH, BETTY
Born: 1902. Died: Nov. 8, 1979, Woodland Hills, Calif. Screen actress and extra.

KIMMINS, ANTHONY
Born: Nov. 10, 1901, Harrow-on-the-Hill, Middlesex, England. Died: May 19, 1964, England? Screen, stage actor, film director, film producer, screenwriter and author.

Appeared in: **1933** The Golden Cage. **1934** White Ensign.

KIMURA, MASSA KICHI
Born: 1890. Died: Nov. 21, 1918, New York, N.Y. (Spanish influenza). Screen actor.

KINCH, MYRA
Born: 1904, Los Angeles, Calif. Died: Nov. 20, 1981, Bonita Springs, Fla. Screen actress, film director, dancer and choreographer.

Appeared in: **1929** Redskin. **1935** Lives of a Bengal Lancer.

KING, ADA
Born: 1862, England. Died: June 8, 1940, England? Screen, stage and vaudeville actress.

Appeared in: **1920** Hobson's Choice.

KING, ALLYN
Born: 1901. Died: Mar. 30, 1930, New York, N.Y. (suicide—leap from building). Stage and screen actress.

Appeared in: **1923** The Fighting Blade.

KING, ANITA
Born: 1889. Died: June 10, 1963, Hollywood, Calif. (heart attack). Stage and screen actress.

Appeared in: **1914** The Man from Home; The Virginian. **1915** Snobs; The Girl of the Golden West; Chimmie Fadden; Carmen.

KING, BOYD
Born: 1906. Died: Feb. 19, 1940, Los Angeles, Calif. (cerebral hemorrhage). Screen actor.

KING, BURTON
Born: Aug. 5, 1887, Cincinnati, Ohio. Died: May 4, 1944, Los Angeles, Calif. Screen, stage actor, film director, film producer and stage director. Married to actress Adele Lane (dec. 1957). Entered films as an actor with Lubin Co.

KING, CHARLES
Born: Oct. 31, 1889, New York, N.Y. Died: Jan. 11, 1944, London, England (pneumonia). Screen, stage and vaudeville actor. Brother of actresses Mollie (dec. 1981) and Nellie King.

Appeared in: **1929** Broadway Melody (film debut); Road Show; Hollywood Revue of 1929; Orange Blossom Time; Climbing the Golden Stairs. **1930** The Girl in the Show; Chasing Rainbows; Remote Control. **1934** Perfectly Mismated (short); Men in Black (short). **1935** The Miracle Rider (serial); The Singing Vagabond; Tumbling Tumbleweeds. **1936** The Lawless Nineties; Guns and Guitars; Red River Valley. **1937** Rootin' Tootin' Rhythm; The Trusted Outlaw; A Lawman Is Born; Ridin' the Lone Trail. **1938** Thunder in the Desert; Gold Mine in the Sky. **1939** South of the Border. **1943** Riders of the Rio Grande.

KING, CHARLES L., SR.
Born: 1899. Died: May 7, 1957, Hollywood, Calif. Screen actor. Father of actor Charles L. King, Jr.

Appeared in: **1921** A Motion to Adjourn; Singing River. **1922** The Black Bag; Price of Youth. **1923** Merry-Go-Round. **1925** Hearts of the West; Triple Action. **1926** What Happened to Jane (serial). **1927** Range Courage. **1928** You Can't Beat the Law; Sisters of Eve. **1929** Slim Fingers. **1930** Dawn Trail; Fighting Through; Oklahoma Cyclone; Beyond the Law. **1931** Oh, Sailor, Behave!; Branded Men; Range Law. **1932** The Hurricane Express (serial); Gay Buckaroo; A Man's Land; The Fighting Champ; Ghost City; Honor of the Mounted. **1933** The Fighting Parson; Crashing Broadway; Son of the Border; The Lone Avenger; Strawberry Roan; Young Blood; Outlaw Justice. **1934** Mystery Ranch; Men in Black. **1935** Northern Frontier; Outlawed Guns; The Ivory-Handled Gun; His Fighting Blood; Mississippi; Red Blood of Courage. **1936** Just My Luck; O'Malley of the Mounted; Headin' for the Rio Grande; Sunset of Power; Desert Phantom; Sundown Saunders; Men of the Plains; Last of the Warrens; Idaho Kid. **1937** The Painted Stallion (serial); Trouble in Texas; Sing, Cowboy, Sing; Tex Rides with the Boy Scouts; Headline Crasher; Island Captives; Black Aces; Riders of the Rockies; The Red Rope; The Mystery of the Hooded Horesemen; Hittin' the Trail. **1938** Starlight Over Texas; Where the Buffalo Roam; Gun Packer; Frontier Town; Song and Bullets; Phantom Ranger; Man's Country. **1939** Wild Horse Canyon; Song of the Buckaroo; Zorro's Fighting Legion (serial); Rollin' Westward; Mutiny in the Big House; Down the Wyoming Trail; Oklahoma Frontier. **1940** Pony Post; Deadwood Dick (serial); Son of the Navy; West of Carson City; Wild Horse Range. **1941** The Iron Claw (serial); White Eagle (serial); Billy the Kid's Fighting Pals; Outlaws of the Rio Grande; The Roar of the Press; The Lone Ranger in Ghost Town; Texas Marshal; Gunman from Bodie; Borrowed Hero; Billy the Kid Wanted; Billy the Kid's Roundup; The Lone Ranger Fights Back. **1942** Below the Border; Ghost Town Law; Riders of the West; Law and Order; Pirates of the Prairie. **1943** Ghost Rider; Two-Fisted Justice; The Rangers Take Over; The Stranger from Pecos; Border Buckaroos; Riders of the Rio Grande. **1945** Jungle Raiders (serial); Who's Guilty? (serial). **1946** Chick Carter, Detective (serial); The Caravan Trail. **1947** Brick Bradford (serial); The Wistful Widow of Wagon Gap. **1948** Congo Bill (serial); Superman (serial). **1949** Adventures of Sir Galahad (serial); Bruce Gentry (serial).

KING, CLAUDE (Claude Ewart King)
Born: Jan. 15, 1879, Northhampton, England. Died: Sept. 18, 1941, Los Angeles, Calif. Screen, stage actor and stage director.

Appeared in: **1920** Judy of Rogue's Harbor. **1921** The Scarab Ring; Why Girls Leave Home. **1923** Bella Donna; Six Days. **1925** The Making of O'Malley; Irish Luck; The Unguarded Hour; The Knockout. **1926** Paradise; The Silent Lover. **1927** Mr. Wu; Becky; Singed; London After Midnight. **1928** Red Hair; A Night of Mystery; Love and Learn; Outcast; Oh, Kay!; Warming Up; Sporting Goods. **1929** Strange Cargo; Nobody's Children; Madame X; Behind That Curtain; The Black Watch; Blue Skies; The Mysterious Dr. Fu Manchu. **1930** Son of the Gods; In Gay Madrid; Second Floor Mystery; Love Among the Millionaires; Prince of Diamonds; One Night at Susie's; Follow Thru. **1931** Rango; The Reckless Hour; Women Love Once; Transatlantic; Devotion; Once a Lady; Heartbreak; Arrowsmith; Born to Love. **1932** Behind the Mask; He Learned About Women; Sherlock Holmes; Shanghai Express. **1933** Cavalcade; The Big Brain; Charlie Chan's Greatest Case; White Woman. **1934** Charlie Chan in London; The Moonstone; Stolen Sweets; The World Moves On; Two Heads on a Pillow; Long Lost Father; Murder in Trinidad. **1935** The Great Impersonation; The Right to Live; The Gilded Lily; Smart Girl; The Last Outpost; Circumstantial Evidence; A Thousand Dollars a Minute; Bonnie Scotland. **1936** The Country Doctor; The Leathernecks Have Landed; Shanghai Gesture; Three on the Trail; The Last of the Mohicans; Beloved Enemy; It Couldn't Have Happened; Happy Go Lucky. **1937** A Star is Born; Lover Under Fire; Lancer Spy. **1938** Marie Antoinette; If I Were King; Four Men and a Prayer; Booloo. **1939** Within the Law. **1940** The Philadelphia Story; New Moon.

KING, DENNIS (aka DENNY PRATT aka DENNIS PRATT)
Born: Nov. 2, 1897, Warwickshire, Coventry, England. Died: May 21, 1971, New York, N.Y. (heart condition). Screen and stage actor. Married to stage actress Edith Wright (dec. 1963).

Appeared in: **1919** Monsieur Beaucaire (film debut). **1930** The Vagabond King; Paramount on Parade. **1931** Fra Diavolo (The Devil's Brother). **1937** Between Two Worlds. **1959** The Miracle. **1969** The One With the Fuzz; Some Kind of Nut.

KING, EMMETT C.
Born: 1866, Griffin, Ga. Died: Apr. 21, 1953, Woodland Hills, Calif. Screen, stage and radio actor.

Appeared in: **1921** Fightin' Mad; Flower of the North; Lying Lips; Three Sevens; Eden and Return; The Mistress of Shenstone; Little Lord Fauntleroy; The Silver Car. **1922** The Adventures of Robinson Crusoe (serial); The Beautiful and Damned; The Call of Home; The Kentucky Derby; Human Hearts; Manslaughter. **1923** Don Quickshot of the Rio Grande; The Flame of Life; The Acquittal; Trifling With Honor; The Near Lady; The Day of Faith. **1924** Barbara Fritchie; Captain January; T.N.T.; The Air Hawk; Dark Stairways; The Fighting American. **1925** The Man Without a Country; The Devil's Cargo; Counsel for the Defense; Peacock Feathers; Pampered Youth; The Overland Limited. **1926** The Arizona Sweepstakes; The Man in the Saddle. **1928** Laugh, Clown, Laugh; God of Mankind; Midnight Madness. **1929** When Dreams Come True; On Trial; Noisy Neighbors; Shopworn Angel. **1930** Reno; Africa Speaks; The Right of Way. **1931** Three Who Loved; Public Defender. **1932** Mata Hari; Westward Passage. **1937** The Prisoner of Zenda.

KING, EUGENE W.
Born: 1884. Died: Nov. 26, 1950, Hollywood, Calif. Screen actor.

Appeared in: **1936** Camille. **1937** Bill Cracks Down. **1951** The Great Caruso.

KING, JACK
Born: 1883. Died: Oct. 8, 1943, New York, N.Y. (stroke). Screen, vaudeville actor and songwriter. Married to actress Rhea King who appeared with him in vaudeville in a song-dance-patter act.

Appeared in: **1930** Madam Satan; Harmonizing Songs (short). **1936** Love Before Breakfast. **1938** Charlie Chan in Honolulu. **1939** The Hardy's Ride. **1941** Billy the Kid.

KING, JOE (Joseph King)
Born: Feb. 9, 1883, Austin, Tex. Died: Apr. 11, 1951, Woodland Hills, Calif. Screen and stage actor. Entered films in 1913.

Appeared in: **1913** The Missionary and the Actress; Mounted Officer Flynn; The Mysterious Way; The Battle of Gettysburg. **1914** Suspended Sentence. **1915** The Face in the Mirror; The Dancer; A Girl of the Pines; The Faith of Her Father; Haunted Hearts; The Mother Instinct. **1917** The Rose of Blood. **1919** Love's Prisoner. **1920** Humoresque; Children Not Wanted; The North Wind's Malice; The Broadway Bubble. **1921** Salvation Nell; Anne of Little Smoky; The Girl With a Jazz Heart; The Idol of the North; Man and Woman; Moral Fibre; The Scarab Ring. **1922** The Face in the Fog; Sisters; The Valley of Silent Men. **1923** Big Brother; The Daring Years; Counterfeit Love; Twenty-One. **1924** The Masked Dancer; Unguarded Women. **1926** Tin Gods. **1929** The Laughing Lady. **1930** Roadhouse Nights; Battle of Paris. **1934** Woman in the Dark. **1935** Front Page Woman; Alibi Ike; Special Agent; Moonlight on the Prairie; Frisco Kid; Shipmates Forever; Man of Iron; Broadway Hostess; Let 'Em Have It. **1936** Anthony Adverse; The Case of the Velvet Claw; Polo Joe; Bengal Tiger; Road Gang; The Walking Dead; The Singing Kid; Jail Break; Sons O' Guns; Bullets or Ballots; Public Enemy's Wife; China Clipper; God's Country and the Woman. **1937** Once a Doctor; Slim; That Man's Here Again; Armored Car; San Quentin; White Bondage; Fly Away Baby; Hot Water. **1938** Strange Faces; In Old Chicago; City Streets; Alexander's Ragtime Band; Heart of the North. **1939** My Son is a Criminal; Off the Record; You Can't Get Away With Murder; Code of the Secret Service; Smashing the Money Ring; Destry Rides Again. **1940** Danger on Wheels; Three Cheers for the Irish; Black Friday; It's a Date; You're Not So Tough; Charlie Chan at the Wax Museum; Always a Bride. **1941** Blondie Goes Latin; Bullets for O'Hara; Strange Alibi. **1942** The Big Shot; The Glass Key; Butch Minds the Baby; Gentleman Jim; The Iron Major. **1943** Keep 'Em Slugging.

KING, JOHN REED
Born: Oct. 25, 1914, Wilmington, Del. Died: July 8, 1979, Woodstown, N.J. (heart attack). Screen, radio, television actor, radio producer, television producer and newscaster. Voice of Paramount newsreels.

KING, LESLIE
Born: 1876, Baltimore, Md. Died: Oct. 10, 1947, Amityville, N.Y. Stage and screen actor.

Appeared in: **1916** Temperance Town; Milk White Flag. **1919** The Fatal Fortune (serial). **1921** Experience; Orphans of the Storm. **1922** The Bond Boy; The Streets of New York. **1923** If Winter Comes; Broadway Broke. **1924** The New School Teacher. **1931** Alice in Wonderland.

KING, MATTY
Born: 1906. Died: Aug. 19, 1978, Fla. Screen, vaudeville actor, film director, dancer and choreographer. Appeared in vaudeville act with his brothers, known as "King, King & King."

Appeared in: **1950** Blues Busters.

KING, MOLLIE
Born: April 16, 1898, New York, N.Y. Died: Dec. 28, 1981, Ft. Lauderdale, Fla. (stroke). Screen, stage and vaudeville actress. Sister of actor Charles King (dec. 1944) and actress Nellie King.

Appeared in: **1916** A Woman's Power; The Summer Girl. **1917** The Mystery of the Double Cross (serial); Kick In; The Seven Pearls (serial); On-The-Square Girl; Blind Man's Luck. **1919** Human Clay; Suspense. **1920** Greater Than Love; Women Men Forgot. **1921** Suspicious Wives. **1922** Her Majesty.

KING, PHILIP
Born: 1905, Harrogate, Yorkshire, England. Died: Feb. 9, 1979, Brighton, England. Screen, stage actor, screenwriter, playwright and author.

Appeared in: **1954** Eight O'Clock Walk (US 1955).

KING, STANLEY E.
Born: London, England. Died: Dec. 3, 1975, Calif. (coronary). Screen, stage, vaudeville, radio and television actor.

Appeared in: **1937** It Could Happen to You.

KING, WILL
Born: 1886. Died: Jan. 22, 1958, San Francisco, Calif. Screen, stage, vaudeville actor, playwright and stage producer. Married to actress Claire Starr who appeared in vaudeville with him.

Appeared in: **1929** The Fatal Forceps; Weak but Willing.

KINGDON, DOROTHY
Born: 1894. Died: Mar. 31, 1939, Los Angeles, Calif. Screen and stage actress.

Appeared in: **1925** The Iron Man; A Man of Iron; The Lost Chord.

KINGDON, FRANK
Born: 1865, Providence, R.I. Died: Apr. 9, 1937, Englewood, N.J. (pneumonia). Screen and stage actor.

Appeared in: **1920** Remodeling Her Husband; Partners of the Night.

KINGSFORD, ALISON
Born: 1899. Died: June 10, 1950, North Hollywood, Calif. Screen actress. Married to actor Walter Kingsford (dec. 1958).

KINGSFORD, WALTER
Born: Sept. 20, 1882, Redhill, England. Died: Feb. 7, 1958, North Hollywood, Calif. (heart attack). Stage and screen actor. Married to actress Alison Kingsford (dec. 1950).

Appeared in: **1934** Pursuit of Happiness; The President Vanishes. **1935** The Mystery of Edwin Drood; The White Cockatoo; Naughty Marietta; Shanghai; I Found Stella Parish; The Melody Lingers On; Frankie and Johnnie. **1936** The Story of Louis Pasteur; Hearts Divided; Stolen Holiday; Professional Soldier; The Invisible Ray; Little Lord Fauntleroy; Trouble for Two; Mad Holiday; Meet Nero Wolfe; The Music Goes 'Round. **1937** Maytime; Behind the Criminal (short); Captains Courageous; My Dear Miss Aldrich; Bulldog Drummond Escapes; Double or Nothing; The Life of Emile Zola; The League of Frightened Men; The Devil Is Driving; I'll Take Romance; It Could Happen to You. **1938** The Young in Heart; Paradise for Three; A Yank at Oxford; The Toy Wife; Lord Jeff; There's Always a Woman; Algiers; Carefree; If I Were King; Say It in French; The Lone Wolf in Paris; Young Dr. Kildare. **1939** Juarez; Smashing the Spy Ring; Calling Dr. Kildare; Man in the Iron Mask; Miracles for Sale; The Witness Vanishes; The Secret of Dr. Kildare; Dancing Co-ed. **1940** Star Dust; Lucky Partners; A Dispatch from Reuters; Kitty Foyle; Dr. Kildare Goes Home; Dr. Kildare's Crisis; Adventure in Diamonds; Dr. Kildare's Strangest Case. **1941** The Devil and Miss Jones; The Lone Wolf Takes a Chance; The People vs. Dr. Kildare; Hit the Road; Ellery Queen and the Perfect Crime; Dr. Kildare's Wedding Day; Unholy Partners; Dr. Kildare's Victory; The Corsican Brothers. **1942** Fly by Night; Fingers at the Window; My Favorite Blonde; Calling Dr. Gillespie; Dr. Gillespie's New Assistant; The Loves of Edgar Allan Poe. **1943** Flight for Freedom; Forever and a Day; Bomber's Moon; Dr. Gillespie's Criminal Case; Hi Diddle Diddle; Mr. Lucky. **1944** Secrets of Scotland Yard; Three Men in White; The Hitler Gang; Mr.

Skeffington; Ghost Catchers; Between Two Women. **1948** The Black Arrow; The Velvet Touch. **1949** Slattery's Hurricane. **1950** Experiment Alcatraz. **1951** My Forbidden Past; The Desert Fox; Tarzan's Peril; Two Dollar Bettor. **1952** The Brigand; Confidence Girl. **1953** Loose in London; Walking My Baby Back Home; The Pathfinder. **1956** The Search for Bridey Murphy; Around the World in 80 Days. **1958** Merry Andrew.

KINGSLEY, FLORIDA
Born: 1879, Jacksonville, Fla. Died: Mar. 19, 1937, Bay Shore, N.Y. Screen and stage actress.

Appeared in: **1916** The Turmoil. **1917** The Boy-Girl; The Iron Heart. **1918** Mrs. Slacker. **1919** Woman Under Oath; Sealed Hearts; Thou Shalt Not. **1920** Love; Greater Than Fame; Youthful Folly; Dangerous Business. **1921** Anabel Lee; Is Life Worth Living?; Clay Dollars. **1923** The Little Red Schoolhouse.

KINGSTON, HAROLD "HARRY" (Harold Berman)
Born: 1914. Died: July 4, 1951, Hollywood, Calif. Screen, stage and television actor.

Appeared in: **1952** Viva Zapata.

KINGSTON, THOMAS
Born: 1902. Died: Jan. 27, 1959, Hollywood, Calif. (heart attack). Screen and television stand-in.

KINGSTON, WINIFRED
Born: 1895. Died: Feb. 3, 1967, La Jolla, Calif. Screen actress. Married to actor Dustin Farnum (dec. 1929).

Appeared in: **1913** The Squaw Man. **1914** The Call of the North; The Virginian; Son of Erin; Where the Trail Divides. **1915** The Light of the Reef. **1916** David Garrick. **1917** The Scarlet Pimpernel. **1919** The Corsican Brothers. **1921** Beyond. **1922** The Trail of the Axe. **1929** The Virginian.

KINLOCK, LOUISE See COLT, ETHEL BARRYMORE

KINNELL, MURRAY
Born: 1889, London, England. Died: Aug. 11, 1954, Santa Barbara, Calif. Screen and stage actor.

Appeared in: **1930** Old English (film debut); The Princess and the Plumber. **1931** Reckless Living; The Secret Six; The Public Enemy; The Black Camel; The Guilty Generation; Honor of the Family; The Deceiver. **1932** A Successful Calamity; Grande Hotel; Under Eighteen; The Beast of the City; The Man Who Played God; The Menace; The Mouthpiece; The Purchase Price; The Painted Woman; Secrets of the French Police. **1933** Zoo in Budapest; Voltaire; From Headquarters; I Loved a Woman; Ann Vickers; The Avenger. **1934** I Am Suzanne; Such Women Are Dangerous; The House of Rothschild; Affairs of a Gentleman; Hat, Coat and Glove; Murder in Trinidad; Charlie Chan's Courage; Charlie Chan in London; Anne of Green Gables. **1935** Captain Blood; Charlie Chan in Paris; Cardinal Richelieu; Mad Love; Kind Lady; The Silver Streak; The Great Impersonation; The Last Days of Pompeii; The Three Musketeers; Fighting Youth. **1936** The Witness Chair; Mary of Scotland; The Big Game; Make Way for a Lady; One Rainy Afternoon; Lloyds of London; Fifteen Maiden Lane. **1937** Four Days' Wonder; Outcast; Think Fast, Mr. Moto; Damaged Lives; The Prince and the Pauper; Captains Courageous.

KINSELLA, KATHLEEN (Kathleen Freeland)
Born: 1878, Liverpool, England. Died: Mar. 25, 1961, Washington. Stage and screen actress. Appeared in silents for Biograph.

KINSELLA, WALTER A.
Born: Aug. 16, 1900, New York, N.Y. Died: May 11, 1975, Englewood, N.J. Screen, stage, television, radio actor and amateur track star.

Appeared in: **1950** The Tattooed Stranger.

KINSOLVING, LEE (Arthur Lee Kinsolving, Jr.)
Born: 1938. Died: Dec. 4, 1974, Palm Beach, Fla. Screen, stage and television actor.

Appeared in: **1960** All the Young Men; Khovanschina; The Dark at the Top of the Stairs. **1961** The Explosive Generation.

KIPLING, RICHARD
Born: 1880. Died: Mar. 11, 1965. Screen actor.

Appeared in: **1940** Calling Philo Vance. **1943** Miss V from Moscow. **1944** The Adventures of Mark Twain. **1946** Danny Boy. **1952** Voodoo Tiger. **1954** Alaska Seas. **1955** The Girl Rush.

KIPPEN, MANART
Born: 1892. Died: Oct. 12, 1947, Claremore, Okla. (auto accident injuries). Screen, stage and radio actor.

Appeared in: **1941** Flight from Destiny. **1942** The Wife Takes a Flyer; Jungle Siren. **1943** Mission to Moscow; The Song of Bernadette. **1944** Three Russian Girls. **1945** Mildred Pierce; Roughly Speaking; Flame of Barbary Coast.

KIRBY, DAVID D.
Born: 1880. Died: Apr. 4, 1954, Hollywood, Calif. Screen actor.

Appeared in: **1921** The Ranger and the Law. **1923** Danger Ahead; The Mailman; In the Palace of the King. **1924** Darwin Was Right; Spirit of the U.S.A.; The Man Who Came Back; Nellie, the Beautiful Cloak Model; The Dangerous Coward; Life's Greatest Game; The Man Who Played Square; Lightning Romance; The Mask of Lopez. **1925** Easy Money; Ridin' the Wind; Youth's Gamble; The Last Edition; Lawful Cheaters; The Snob Buster. **1926** Danger Quest; The King of the Turf; The Fighting Edge; The Dangerous Dude; The Night Owl. **1927** The Royal American; The Shield of Honor; The Sunset Derby; The Silent Avenger. **1928** Burning Bridges; The Upland Rider.

KIRBY, GEORGE T.
Born: 1879, London, England. Died: Dec. 2, 1953, Van Nuys, Calif. Screen and stage actor.

Appeared in: **1934** The Human Side.

KIRBY, JOHN
Born: 1932, Australia. Died: July 3, 1973, Madrid, Spain (apparent heart attack). Screen, stage and television actor.

Appeared in: **1944** Zorro's Black Whip (serial). **1947** Sepia Cinderella. **1955** An Annapolis Story; Air Strike.

KIRBY, OLLIE
Born: Sept. 26, 1886, Philadelphia, Pa. Died: Oct. 7, 1965, Glendale, Calif. (pneumonia). Screen, stage and vaudeville actress. Married to actor George Larkin (dec. 1946).

Appeared in: **1916** The Social Pirates. **1923** The Apache Dancer; Tango Cavalier; Mysterious Goods; Gentleman Unafraid. **1924** Yankee Madness; Midnight Secrets. **1925** Never Too Late.

KIRBY, WILLIAM WARNER
Born: Apr. 4, 1876, Germany. Died: Apr. 17, 1914, Los Angeles, Calif. (blood poisoning following lacerations inflicted by lion during filming). Screen actor.

KIRK, FAY B. (Fay Baker)
Born: 1894. Died: Nov. 13, 1954, New York, N.Y. (heart attack). Screen, stage and vaudeville actress.

Appeared in: **1946** Notorious. **1950** Chain Lightning. **1951** The House on Telegraph Hill.

KIRK, JACK "PAPPY" (aka JOHN KIRKHUFF aka JACK HUFF)
Born: 1895. Died: Sept. 3, 1948, Alaska. Screen actor. Was one of the first singing cowboys.

Appeared in: **1925** Sackcloth and Scarlet; Limited Mail; Zander the Great. **1926** The Stolen Ranch. **1934** In Old Santa Fe. **1936** The Singing Cowboy; Guns and Guitars; The Lonely Trail. **1937** Hit the Saddle; Git Along, Little Dogies; Yodelin' Kid from Pine Ridge; Springtime in the Rockies. **1938** Guilty Trails; Outlaw Express; Prairie Justice; Gold Mine in the Sky; Pals of the Saddle; Rhythm of the Saddle; The Last Stand. **1939** Honor of the West; Rovin' Tumbleweeds; Rough Riders' Round-Up. **1940** Gaucho Serenade; Melody Ranch; Lone Star Raiders; Rocky Mountain Rangers; The Tulsa Kid. **1941** Under Fiesta Stars; Sierra Sue; Prairie Pioneers; In Old Cheyenne; Bad Man of Deadwood; Jesse James at Bay; Death Valley Outlaws; Prairie Schooners; The Shining Hill; Kansas Cyclone. **1942** Home in Wyomin'; Westward Ho; The Phantom Plainsmen; West of Tombstone; Jesse James, Jr.; South of Santa Fe; Sunset Serenade. **1943** Hail to the Rangers; Carson City Cyclone; Death Valley Manhunt. **1944** Storm Over Lisbon; The Cowboy and the Senorita; Beneath Western Skies; The Vigilantes Ride; Call of the Rockies; The San Antonio Kid; Pride of the Plains; Mojave Firebrand; Silver City Kid; Stagecoach to Monterey; Sheriff of Sundown; Firebrands of Arizona; Cheyenne Wildcat; Code of the Prairie; Bordertown Trail; Zorro's Black Whip (serial). **1945** Sheriff of Cimarron; Trail of Kit Carson. **1946** Her Adventurous Night; King of the Forest Rangers (serial); Home on the Range; Gunning for Vengeance; California Gold Rush; Texas Panhandle; Desert Horseman; Conquest of Cheyenne; The Phanton Rider (serial). **1947** Oregon Trail Scouts; Law of the Canyon; Son of Zorro (serial). **1948** Adventures of Frank and Jesse James (serial). **1949** Oklahoma Badlands; The Bold Frontiersman.

KIRKE, DONALD (William H. F. Kirk)
Born: May 17, 1902, Jersey City, N.J. Died: May 18, 1971. Screen actor.

Appeared in: **1930** Follow the Leader. **1933** Women Won't Tell; Blondie Johnson; Hidden Gold. **1935** Let 'Em Have It; The Ghost Walks. **1936** Country Gentlemen; Border Flight; In His Steps; Sunset of Power; Ride 'Em Cowboy; Oh, Susanna! **1937** Venus Makes Trouble; The Shadow; The Emperor's Candlesticks; Midnight Madonna; Take the Heir; The Big Shot; Paradise Express. **1938** Hawaii Calls; I Demand Payment. **1940** The Showdown. **1942** A Night for Crime; Outlaws of Pine Ridge. **1943** G-Men vs. the Black Dragon (serial). **1947** Hoppy's Holiday. **1956** Scandal, Inc.

KIRKHUFF, JOHN See KIRK, JACK "PAPPY"

KIRKLAND, DAVID
Born: 1878, San Francisco, Calif. Died: Oct. 27, 1964. Screen, stage actor, film director, producer, stage director and screenwriter. Entered films as an extra in 1911 with Melies Company.

Appeared in: **1914-15** Snakeville Comedies.

KIRKLAND, HARDEE
Born: c. 1864, England. Died: Feb. 20, 1929, Calif. Screen, stage and vaudeville actor.

Appeared in: **1918** Sporting Life. **1919** The Peace of Roaring River. **1921** The Ace of Hearts; Ladies Must Live; From the Ground Up; A Perfect Crime; Roads of Destiny; The Lure of Jade. **1922** Sherlock Brown; Honor First; Youth to Youth; Without Compromise; They Like 'Em Rough; The Face Between; Very Truly Yours. **1923** Woman-Proof; Are You a Failure?; The Mailman; Quicksands; Hell's Hole; While Paris Sleeps. **1924** The Great Diamond Mystery. **1925** The Shadow on the Wall; Private Affairs; The Arizona Romeo.

KIRKLAND, MURIEL
Born: Aug. 19, 1903, Yonkers, N.Y. Died: Sept. 25, 1971, New York, N.Y. (emphysema and complications). Screen, stage, radio and television actress. Married to actor Staats Cotsworth (dec. 1979).

Appeared in: **1933** Fast Workers; Hold Your Man; Cocktail Hour; To the Last Man; Secret of the Blue Room. **1934** Nana; Little Man, What Now?; The White Parade.

KIRKPATRICK, JESSE
Born: 1898. Died: Aug. 9, 1976, La Jolla, Calif. (heart attack). Screen, radio actor and singer.

Appeared in: **1949** The Judge. **1950** D.O.A. **1951** Stop That Cab; The Well. **1952** The Captive City. **1956** On the Threshold of Space. **1958** The Long Hot Summer; Ten North Frederick; Space Master X-7. **1959** These Thousand Hills; Alaska Passage. **1961** The Tomboy and the Champ. **1962** Incident in an Alley.

KIRKWOOD, JACK
Born: 1895, Scotland. Died: Aug. 2, 1964, Las Vegas, Nev. (heart attack). Screen, stage, vaudeville, burlesque, radio and television actor.

Appeared in: **1949** Chicken Every Sunday. **1950** Father Makes Good; Joe Palooka in Humphrey Takes a Chance; Never a Dull Moment; Fancy Pants. **1951** One Wild Night (short).

KIRKWOOD, JAMES
Born: Feb. 22, 1883, Grand Rapids, Mich. Died: Aug. 21, 1963, Woodland Hills, Calif. Screen and stage actor. Divorced from actresses Gertrude Robinson (dec. 1962), Beatrice Power and Lila Lee (dec. 1973).

Appeared in: **1909** The Road to the Heart; The Message; Was Justice Served?; The Renunciation; The Seventh Day; A Convict's Sacrifice; The Indian Runner's Romance; The Better Way; Pippa Passes; The Death Disc; 1776, or The Hessian Renegades; Through the Breakers; A Corner in Wheat; The Redman's View; The Rocky Road; The Honor of His Family; The Last Deal; The Renovations; The Mended Lute; Comato the Sioux. **1910** The Final Settlement; A Victim of Jealousy; The Modern Prodigal; Winning Back His Love. **1914** The Eagle's Mate; Home Sweet Home. **1920** Luck of the Irish; Heart of a Fool; Man, Woman and Marriage; The Branding Iron. **1921** The Sin Flood; The Great Impersonation; Bob Hampton of Placer; A Wise Fool. **1922** The Man from Home; Ebb Tide; Pink Gods; Under Two Flags. **1923** The Eagle's Feather; Ponjola; Human Wreckage; You Are Guilty. **1924** Wandering Husbands; Another Man's Wife; Broken Barriers; Circe, the Enchantress; The Painted Flapper; Discontented Husbands; Gerald Cranston's Lady; Love's Whirlpool. **1925** Lover's Island; Secrets of the Night; The Top of the World; The Police Patrol. **1926**

That Royle Girl; Butterflies in the Rain; The Reckless Lady; The Wise Guy. **1927** Million Dollar Mystery. **1928** Someone to Love. **1929** Hearts in Exile; Black Waters; The Time, the Place and the Girl. **1930** Devil's Holiday; Worldly Goods; The Spoilers. **1931** A Holy Terror; Over the Hill; Young Sinners. **1932** Cheaters at Play; Charlie Chan's Chance; Lena Rivers; Careless Lady; She Wanted a Millionaire; The Rainbow Trail; My Pal, the King. **1934** Hired Wife. **1941** The Lady from Cheyenne; No Hands on the Clock. **1943** Government Girl. **1947** Driftwood. **1948** The Untamed Breed. **1949** The Doolins of Oklahoma; Red Stallion in the Rockies. **1950** The Nevadan; Fancy Pants; Stage to Tucson. **1951** Belle Le Grande; Santa Fe; Man in the Saddle. **1952** I Deam of Jeanie. **1953** Winning of the West; The Last Posse. **1954** Passion. **1956** The Search for Bridey Murphy. **1963** The Ugly American.

KIRKWOOD-HACKETT, EVA
Born: 1877, England. Died: Feb. 8, 1968, Dublin, Ireland. Screen actress and singer.

KISSEN, MURRAY
Born: 1889. Died: Feb. 17, 1958, Pompano Beach, Fla. Screen, vaudeville and radio actor.

KITZMILLER, JOHN
Born: 1913, Battlecreek, Mich. Died: Feb. 23, 1965, Rome, Italy (cirrhosis of the liver). Black screen actor. Received Cannes Film Festival Best Acting Award in 1957 for Dolina Mira.

Appeared in: **1946** Paisa; To Live in Peace. **1948** Senza Pieta (Without Pity—US 1950). **1951** Lieutenant Craig-Missing; Luci del Varieta (Variety Lights—US 1965). **1956** Dolina Mira (aka Sergeant Jim—US 1962 and Mr. Jim—American). **1957** The Naked Earth. **1958** Vite Perdute (Lost Souls—US 1961). **1960** The Island Sinner. **1962** La Rivolta dei Mercenari (Revolt of the Mercenaries—US 1964); El Hijo del Capitan Blood (The Son of Captain Blood—US 1964). **1963** Dr. No; La Tigre dei Sette Mari (Tiger of the Seven Seas—US 1964). **1964** Der Fluch der Grunen Augen (Cave of the Living Dead—US 1966). **1965** Onkel Toms Hutte (Uncle Tom's Cabin—US 1969).

KLEIN, AL
Born: 1885, New York, N.Y. Died: Sept. 5, 1951, Los Angeles, Calif. (cancer). Screen, stage and vaudeville actor. Part of vaudeville team of "The Klein Bros."

Appeared in: **1928** Jest Moments (short). **1932** Opportunity Night (short); Gold Digging Gentlemen (short). **1933** Broadway Bad; One Year Later. **1934** That's Gratitude; Million Dollar Ransom; 365 Nights in Hollywood. **1949** Oh, You Beautiful Doll.

KLEIN, JULIUS
Born: 1886, Hungary. Died: July 16, 1966, Hollywood, Calif. Screen actor, screenwriter and musician.

Appeared in: **1929** City of Temptation. **1958** The Brothers Karamazov.

KLEIN, ROBERT "BOB"
Born: 1880, Paris, France. Died: Dec. 21, 1960. Screen and stage actor.

Appeared in: **1915** Lure of the Mask; Secretary of Frivolous Affairs; Souls in Pawn. **1917** The Bride's Silence; Charity Castle; Southern Pride; Annie for Spite. **1919** Married in Haste. **1920** Challenge of the Law. **1921** The Blushing Bride; Live Wires. **1922** The Lady from Longacre; Do and Dare; The Man from Hell's River. **1923** Good-by Girls!; The Temple of Venus; Alias the Night Wind. **1924** Dante's Inferno; The Desert Outlaw; The Folly of Vanity. **1925** The Ancient Mariner; Greater Than a Crown. **1932** Thirteenth Guest.

KLEINAU, WILLY A.
Born: Germany. Died: Oct. 23, 1957, Berlin-Nuernberg Hwy., Germany (auto accident). Screen and stage actor.

Appeared in: **1958** Der Hauptmann von Koepenick (The Captain from Koepenick); Wie Ein Sturmwind (Tempestuous Love). Other German film: Mein Bruder Josua.

KLEIN-ROGGE, RUDOLF
Born: 1889, Cologne, Germany. Died: 1955, Graz, Austria. Screen actor.

Appeared in: **1919** Morphium. **1920** Das Wandernde Bild. **1921** Perlen Bedeuten Traenen; Zirkus des Lebens; Der Muede Tod (Between Worlds—US 1924, aka Destiny); Kaempfende Herzen (aka Vier um die Frau). **1922** Dr. Mabuse, de Spieler (Dr. Mabuse, the Gambler—US 1937). **1923** Die Prinzessin Suwarin; Der Steinerne Reiter (The Stone Rider). **1924** Pietro, der Korsar; Die Nibelungen (aka Kriemhilds Rache (Kriemhild's Revenge—US 1928)). **1925** Der

Mann Seiner Frau; Der Rosa Diamant. **1926** Der Herr der Nacht; Die Lachende Grille; Maedchenhandel; Metropolis. **1927** Peter the Pirate; Die Letzte Nacht; Das Maedchen aus Frisco; Die Raffinierteste Frau Berlins; Die Sandgraefin; Tingel-Tangel; Der Zingeunerbaron. **1928** Spione (The Spy); Maedchenschicksale; Die Schoenste Frau von Paris; Wolga-Wolga. **1929** Meineid; Loves of Casanova; Forbidden Love. **1931** Der Weisse Gott. **1933** Das Testament des Dr. Mabuse (The Testament of Dr. Mabuse); Der Judas von Tirol (aka Der Ewige Verrat); Elisabeth und ihr Narr (aka Elisabeth, die Weisse Schwester von St. Veith). **1934** Zwischen Himmel und Erde (Between Heaven and Earth—US 1935); Hanneles Himmelfahrt; Die Welt ohne Maske; Grenzfeuer (US 1936); Die Frauen vom Tannhof (US 1936); Der Fall Benken (aka Ueberfall im Hotel); Gern hab' ich die Frau'n Gekuesst (aka Paganini). **1935** Das Einmaleins der Liebe; Der Kosak und die Nachtigall; Der Ammenkoenig (aka Das Tal des Lebens); Der Alte und der Junge Koenig (The Young and the Old King). **1936** Ein Seltsamer Gast; Moral; Truxa (US 1937); Das Hofkonzert; Der Kaiser von Kalifornien; Intermezzo; Die Un-erhoerte Frau (aka Ich Kenne Dich Nicht Mehr). **1937** Madame Bovary; Die Goettlilhe Jette; Der Herrscher; Die Gelbe Flagge; Streit um den Knaben Jo; Der Katzensteg. **1938** Zwei Frauen; Ab Mitternacht. **1939** Kennwort Machin; Robert Koch, der Bekaemfer des Todes; Schneider Wibbel; Rheinische Brautfahrt; Menschen vom Variete; Parkstrasse 13 (aka Verhoer um Mitternacht); Abenteuer in Marokko (aka Die Frau und der Tod). **1940** Die Unvollkommene Liebe; Das Herz Einer Koenigin. **1942** Hochzeit auf Baerenhof.

KLERCKER, GEORG A. F.
Born: 1877, Kristianstad, Sweden. Died: 1951, Sweden?. Screen actor, film director and screenwriter.

Appeared in: **1913** For Your Country. **1916** Love Will Conquer. Other Swedish films; This is Too Much for Me; The Power of Music; Arms in Your Hands; The Scandal; Tied to One's Memories; The First Prize; In the Spring of Life; When Love Kills; The Virago of the Osterman Brothers; The Secret of the Paradise Hotel; South of the Main Road.

KLOEPFER, EUGEN
Born: 1886, Thalheim, Germany. Died: 1950, Wiesbaden, Germany. Screen and stage actor. Entered films in 1918.

Appeared in: **1919** Cagliostros Totenhemd; Maria Magdalena. **1920** Brandherr; Die Lebende Fackel; Die Letzten Menschen; Um der Liebe Willen; Torgus (aka Totendlaus); Sehnsucht (aka Bajazzo); Jugend (Youth). **1921** Die Ratten. **1922** Der Falsche Dimitri; Das Geld auf der Strasse; Der Graf von Charolais; Der Graf von Essex; Macbeth; Menschenopfer; Der Brennende Acker (Burning Soil). **1923** Der Puppenmacher von Kiang-Ning; Schlagende Wetter; Die Austreibung (aka Driven from Home); Die Strasse (The Street—US 1927); Sylvester (aka New Year's Eve). **1924** Carlos und Elisabeth; Komoedianten. **1925** Elebantes Pack; Der Erste Stand; Goetz von Berlichingen Zubenannt mit der Eisernen Hand; O Alte Burschenherrlichkeit; Der Tanzende Tod (aka Rex Mundi). **1926** Die Lachende Grille; Ueberfluessige Menschen. **1927** Luther (US 1929); Die Vorbestraften; Explosion. **1929** Katherina Knie. **1931** Die Pranke; 1914, die Letzren Tage vor dem Weltbrand (1914: The Last Day Before the War—US 1932); Der Herzog von Reichstadt. **1932** Unheimliche Geschichten; Gehetzte Menschen (aka Steckbrief Z 48—US 1934). **1933** Fluechtlinge (Refugees—US 1934). **1934** Wilhelm Tell. **1935** Pygmalion; Ich War Jack Mortimer; Anschlag auf Schweda; Liselotte von der Pfalz (aka Frauen um den Sonnenkoenig). **1936** Liebeserwachen; The Private Life of Louis XIV. **1938** Jugend (Youth—US 1939); Der Spieler (aka Roman Eines Spielers). **1939** Umwege zum Glueck; Die Fremde Frau; Der Ewige Quell. **1940** The Living Dead; Jud Suess; Friedrich Schiller (aka Der Triumph Eines Genies). **1941** Mein Leben fuer Irland; Friedemann Bach. **1942** Stimme des Herzens; Die Goldene Stadt. **1943** Der Unendliche Weg; Gabriele Dambrone. **1944** Der Erbfoerster; Philharmoniker; Die Zaubergeige; Solistin Anna Alt (aka Wenn die Musik Nicht Waer). **1945** Shiva und die Galgenblume; Die Brueder Noltenius; Der Puppenspieler (aka Pole Poppenspaeler).

KNABB, HARRY G.
Born: 1891. Died: Dec. 17, 1955, Cincinnati, Ohio (heart attack). Stage and screen actor. Appeared in silent films.

KNAGGS, SKELTON (Skelton Barnaby Knaggs)
Born: June 27, 1911, England. Died: Apr. 30, 1955, Los Angeles, Calif. (cirrhosis of the liver). Screen actor.

Appeared in: **1943** The Ghost Ship. **1944** The Lodger. **1945** None But the Lonely Heart; Island of the Dead; House of Dracula. **1946** Terror by Night; A Scandal in Paris; Dick Tracy vs. Cueball. **1947** Forever Amber; Dick Tracy and Gruesome. **1948** The Paleface. **1949** Master Minds. **1951** Captain Video (serial). **1952** Blackbeard the Pirate. **1953** Rogues' March. **1954** Casanova's Big Night. **1955** Moonfleet.

KNAPP, EVELYN
Born: June 17, 1908, Kansas City, Mo. Died: June 10, 1981, West Hollywood, Calif. Screen and stage actress.

Appeared in: **1929** The following shorts: Gentlemen of the Evening; Hard Boiled Hampton; Big Time Charlie; Love, Honor and Oh Baby; The Smooth Guy; Beach Babies; Haunted; Wednesday at the Ritz. **1930** Mother's Cry; Sinner's Holiday; plus the following shorts: Chills and Fever; Keeping Company; The Tight Squeeze; All Stuck Up. **1931** Smart Money; The Millionaire; Fifty Million Frenchmen; River's End; The Bargain; Side Show. **1932** The Night Mayor; This Sporting Age; High Pressure; Fireman Save My Child; Bachelor Mother; The Vanishing Frontier; The Strange Love of Molly Louvain; Successful Calamity; Slightly Married; Big City Blues; Madame Racketeer. **1933** State Trooper; Air Hostess; Hollywood on Parade; Corruption; His Private Secretary; Police Car 17; Dance, Girl, Dance. **1934** Perils of Pauline (serial); In Old Santa Fe; Speed Wings; A Man's Game. **1935** One Frightened Night; The Firetrap; Confidential; Ladies Crave Excitement. **1936** Laughing Irish Eyes; Three of a Kind; Bulldog Edition. **1938** Hawaiian Buckaroo; Rawhide; Wanted by the Police. **1941** The Lone Wolf Takes a Chance; The Roar of the Press. **1943** Two Weeks to Live.

KNAPP, MAX
Born: 1899, Zurich, Switzerland. Died: Dec. 16, 1979, Basle, Switzerland. Screen, stage actor and opera singer.

Appeared in: **1976** Confrontation.

KNIGHT, CHARLOTT
Born: 1894. Died: May 16, 1977, Woodland Hills, Calif. Screen, stage, television actress, screenwriter and dramatic coach.

Appeared in: **1955** Sincerely Yours. **1958** Desire Under the Elms.

KNIGHT, FUZZY (John Forrest Knight)
Born: May 9, 1901, Fairmont, W.Va. Died: Feb. 23, 1976, Hollywood, Calif. Screen, vaudeville actor, composer and musical revue performer.

Appeared in: **1932** Hell's Highway. **1933** She Done Him Wrong; Sunset Pass; Her Bodyguard; Speed Demon; Under the Tonto Rim; This Day and Age; To the Last Man. **1934** The Last Round-Up; Music in the Air; I Hate Women; Moulin Rouge; Operator 13; Night Alarm; Come On Marines; Belle of the Nineties; She Had to Choose. **1935** Behold My Wife; Home on the Range; George White's Scandals; Dizzy Dames; Danger Ahead; The Old Homestead; Hot Off the Press; Trails of the Wild; The Murder Man; Mary Burns, Fugitive; Wanderer of the Wasteland; Top Flat (short). **1936** With Love and Kisses; The Plainsman; Song of the Gringo; The Sea Spoilers; Song of the Trail; Kelly of the Secret Service; Rio Grande Romance; Wildcat Trooper; Put on the Spot; And Sudden Death; Trail of the Lonesome Pine; Singing Outlaw. **1937** County Fair; The Gold Racket; Mountain Justice; Mountain Music; Courage of the West. **1938** Silks and Saddles; Quick Money; Flying Fists; Border Wolves; The Last Stand; The Cowboy and the Lady; Spawn of the North. **1939** Union Pacific; The Oregon Trail (serial); Desperate Trails; Oklahoma Frontier. **1940** Chip of the Flying U; West of Carson City; Riders of Pasco Basin; The Bad Man of Red Butte; Son of Roaring Dan; Brigham Young; Ragtime Cowboy Joe; Law and Order; Pony Post; My Little Chickadee; Johnny Apollo. **1941** Horror Island; The Cowboy and the Blonde; The Shepherd of the Hills; Law of the Range; New York Town; Badlands of Dakota; The Masked Rider; Man from Montana. **1942** Arizona Cyclone; Fighting Bill Fargo; Apache Trail; Stagecoach Buckaroo; The Silver Bullet; The Boss of Hangtown Mesa; Deep in the Heart of Texas; Little Joe, the Wrangler; Butch Minds the Baby, Juke Girl. **1943** Corvette K-225; He's My Guy; Tenting Tonight on the Old Camp Ground; The Old Chisholm Trail; Cheyenne Roundup; Lone Star Trail. **1944** The Great Alaskan Mystery (serial); Hi, Good Lookin'; The Cowboy and the Senorita; Arizona Trail; Take It Big; The Singing Sheriff; Allergic to Love; Oklahoma Raiders; Marshal of Gunsmoke; Boss of Boomtown; Trail to Gunsight; Trigger Trail; Riders of the Sante Fe; The Old Texas Trail. **1945** Swing Out, Sister; Song of the Sarong; Senorita from the West; Frontier Gal; Frisco Sal. **1946** Girl on the Spot; Gun Town; Her Adventurous Night; Rustler's Round-Up; Gunman's Code. **1947** The Egg and I. **1948** Adventures of Gallant Bess. **1949** Rimfire; Feudin' Rhythm; Down to the Sea in Ships; Apache Ambush. **1950** Hostile Country; Hills of Oklahoma; West of the Brazos; Marshal of Helldorado; Colorado Ranger; Crooked River; Fast on the Draw. **1951** Canyon Raiders; Nevada Badmen; Lawless Cowboys; Stage from Blue River; Honeychile; Gold Raiders. **1952** Rodeo; Oklahoma Annie; Kansas Territory; Fargo; The Gunman; Night Raiders; Feudin' Fools. **1953** Topeka; Vigilante Terror. **1956** The Naked Hills. **1958** The Nortorious Mr. Monks. **1959** These Thousand Hills. **1965** The Bounty Killer. **1966** Waco. **1967** Hostile Guns.

KNIGHT, HENRY K.
Born: 1847. Died: Apr. 24, 1930, Los Angeles, Calif. Screen actor.

KNIGHT, JAMES
Born: May 4, 1891, Canterbury, England. Died: Date unknown. Screen and stage actor.

Appeared in: **1917** The Happy Warrior. **1918** The Splendid Coward; A Romany Lass (US 1919); Big Money; Deception; Nature's Gentleman. **1919** The Silver Greyhound; The Power of Right; The Man Who Forgot; Gates of Duty (aka Tower of Strength). **1920** Brenda of the Barge. **1921** The Education of Nicky; Love in the Welsh Hills. **1922** No. 7, Brick Row; Crushing the Drug Traffic; Famous Poems by George R. Sims series including: Ticket o' Leave; The Old Actor's Story, and The Lights o' London; The Sporting Twelve series including: Rowing to Win, Playing the Game; Pluck V Plot and the Last Hundred Yards. **1923** The Lady Owner; Beautiful Kitty; What Price Loving Cup?; Hornet's Nest. **1924** The Great Turf Mystery; Claude Duval; Pett Ridge Stories series including The Happy Prisoner. **1925** Thrilling Stories from the Strand Magazine series including A Dear Liar; Famous Music Melodies series including: Songs of England, Songs of Ireland, Songs of Scotland, and Songs of the British Isles; Trainer and Temptress; The Impatient Patient (short). **1926** The Steve Donoghue series including: The Legend of Tichborne Dole and Woodcroft Castle; The Ball of Fortune; Romances of the Prize Ring series including When Giants Fought; The Happy Rascals series. **1927** Motherland; Mr. Nobody; Rilka, or, The Gypsy (re-release of A Romany Lass—1919). **1928** Maria Marten; When We Were Very Young series including Bad Sir Brian Botany; Houp-La; Spangles. **1929** Cupid in Clover; Power Over Men; Dick Turpin series including The Snare. **1930** Kissing Cup's Race. **1931** A Safe Affair. **1932** The Third String; That Night in London (aka Overnight—US 1934). **1933** Commissionaire. **1934** Lost in the Legion. **1935** Sexton Blake and the Bearded Doctor. **1943** The Life and Death of Colonel Blimp (aka Colonel Blimp—US 1945); San Demetrio-London. **1944** Medal for the General. **1946** Loyal Heart; A Girl in a Million (US 1950). **1948** My Sister and I.

KNIGHT, LILLIAN
Born: 1881. Died: May 16, 1946, Pomona, Calif. Screen actress.

Appeared in: **1927** Stage Madness.

KNIGHT, NELLIE *See* KALLOS, NELLIE

KNIGHT, PERCIVAL
Born: c. 1873. Died: Nov. 27, 1923, Switzerland (tuberculosis). Stage and screen actor.

Appeared in: **1922** Sherlock Holmes.

KNOTT, ADELBERT (Adelbert del Knott)
Born: 1859. Died: May 3, 1933, Los Angeles, Calif. (injuries from fall). Screen and stage actor.

Appeared in: **1920** Flame of Youth. **1921** Serenade; The Lamplighter; Straight from the Shoulder. **1924** Dynamite Smith. **1925** Percy.

KNOTT, CLARA
Born: 1882. Died: Nov. 11, 1926, Hollywood, Calif. Screen and stage actress.

Appeared in: **1920** Old Lady 31.

KNOTT, ELSE
Born: 1912, Germany. Died: Aug. 10, 1975, Frankfurt-Main, West Germany (cancer). Screen, stage and television actress.

Appeared in: **1932** Morgenrot.

KNOTT, LYDIA
Born: Oct. 1, 1866, Tyner, Ind. Died: Mar. 30, 1955, Woodland Hills, Calif. Screen, stage and vaudeville actress.

Appeared in: **1917** Sudden Jim; The Clodhopper; Crime and Punishment. **1918** His Mother's Boy. **1919** Home; The Pointing Finger; Heart of Youth; What Every Woman Learns; In Wrong; Should a Woman Tell. **1920** Blackmail; Dwelling Place of Light; Homespun Folks; Peaceful Valley. **1921** Beating the Game; The Breaking Point; A Certain Rich Man; The Infamous Miss Revell; The Lure of Youth; Playing With Fire; Scrap Iron. **1922** Across the Dead Line; Afraid to Fight; The Broadway Madonna; The Dangerous Little Demon; Dusk to Dawn; The Flirt; The Isle of Love; The Super Sex; Turn to the Right; The Unfoldment. **1923** Dollar Devils; Garrison's Finish; Held to Answer; The Man Life Passed By; St. Elmo; A Woman of Paris. **1924** Chalk Marks; Dynamite Smith; Gerald Cranston's Lady; The Perfect Flapper; Racing for Life; Those Who Dance; The Whipping Boss; Women First. **1925** East Lynne; The Fearless Lover; High and Handsome; The Primrose Path; Rose of the World. **1926** Going

Crooked; Kentucky Handicap. **1927** The King of Kings; Pretty Clothes; Life of an Actress. **1928** The House of Scandal; Two Lovers; Our Dancing Daughters; Guilty. **1930** Overland Bound; Men Without Law. **1931** The Conquering Horde; Skippy. **1932** Valley of Lawless Men; Final Edition. **1933** If I Had a Million; Hit the Deck. **1934** I'll Fix It; Rocky Rhodes. **1937** Fair Warning.

KNOWLAND, ALICE
Born: Oct 6, 1879 or 1885, Ft. Fairfield, Maine. Died: May 27, 1930, Los Angeles, Calif. Screen and stage actress.

Appeared in: **1915** The Secret Sin. **1917** Giving Becky a Chance. **1918** The Demon. **1919** Delicious Little Devil; Satan, Jr.; Rustling a Bride. **1920** The Six Best Cellars. **1921** Partners of the Tide; Parish Priest; All Soul's Eve; The Heart Line; Girls Don't Gamble. **1922** On the High Seas. **1925** Coming Through. **1927** The King of Kings; Simple Sis. **1928** Dugan of the Dugouts; Adorable Cheat.

KNOWLES, R.G. (Richard George Knowles)
Born: 1858, Canada. Died: Jan. 1, 1919, London, England. Screen and stage actor.

KNOX, HUGH (Hugh B. Koch)
Died: Sept. 9, 1926, Seattle, Wash. Screen, stage actor, film and stage director.

KNOX, TEDDY
Born: 1896, England. Died: Dec. 1, 1974, England. Screen, stage actor and music hall performer. Brother of actress Julia Hearn (dec. 1976). Appeared with Jimmy Nervo (dec. 1975) as part of comedy team "Nervo and Knox." The team appeared in "Crazy Gang" films and stage presentations with Bud Flanagan (dec. 1968), Chesney Allen (dec. 1982), Charlie Naughton (dec. 1976) and Jimmy Gold (dec. 1967).

The "Crazy Gang" films include: **1937** Okay for Sound. **1938** Alf's Button Afloat. **1939** The Frozen Limits. **1940** Gasbags. **1958** Life is a Circus (US 1962). "Nervo and Knox" appeared in: **1926** Phonofilm (short). **1928** The Rising Generation. **1930** Alf's Button. **1932** Camera Cocktails (re-issue of 1926 short). **1936** It's in the Bag; Skylarks. **1938** Cavalcade of the Stars.

KNUDSEN, PEGGY
Born: 1923, Duluth, Minn. Died: July 11, 1980, Encino, Calif. (cancer). Screen, stage, radio and television actress.

Appeared in: **1946** Humoresque; The Big Sleep; A Stolen Life; Shadow of a Woman; Never Say Goodbye. **1947** Stallion Road; The Unfaithful; In Self Defense; Roses are Red. **1948** Perilous Waters; Trouble Preferred; Half Past Midnight. **1950** Copper Canyon. **1955** Unchained; Good Morning, Miss Dove; Betrayed Women. **1956** The Bottom of the Bottle; Hilda Crane. **1957** Istanbul.

KOBS, ALFRED
Born: 1881. Died: Oct. 20, 1929, Los Angeles, Calif. (tuberculosis). Screen actor.

KOERBER, HILDE
Born: 1906, Vienna, Austria. Died: June 1, 1969, Berlin, Germany. Screen and stage actress. Married to actor/producer Veit Harlan (dec. 1964).

Appeared in: **1936** Maria Die Magd (Maria, the Maiden); Fridericus. **1937** Der Herrscher; Patrioten; Mein Sohn, der Herr Minister; Die Kreutzersonate; Brillanten; Heiratsschwindler (aka Die Rote Muetze). **1938** Maja Zwischen Zwei Ehen; Eine Frau Kommt in die Tropen; Grossalarm; Der Spieler (aka Roman Eines Spielers). **1939** Fasching; Der Singende Tor; Salonwagen E 417; Robert Koch, der Bekaempfer des Todes. **1940** Leidenschaft; Der Suendenbock; Der Guchs von Glenarvon. **1941** Ohm Krueger; Jakko. **1942** Der Grosse Koenig. **1943** Damals. **1944** Ein Blick Zurueck (aka Am Vorabend); Via Mala (aka Die Strasse des Boesen). **1945** Das Leben Geht Weiter; Wie Sagen wir es Unseren Kindern? **1948** Morituri. **1950** Verfuehrte Jungend (aka Das Suendige Haus, and aka Die Treppe). **1951** Wenn die Abendglocken Laueten. **1952** Das Letzte Rezept; Mein Herz Darfst Du Nicht Fragen; Rosen Bluehen auf dem Heidegrab. **1953** Ave Maria; Mit Siebzehn Beginnt das Leben. **1954** Sauerbruch—Das war Mein Leben; Rittmeister Wronski; Das Bekenntnis der Ina Kahr (aka Afraid to Love). **1955** Die Toteninsel. **1956** Mein Vater, der Schauspieler; Teufel in Seide; Heisse Ernte; Hot Harvest. **1957** Anders als Du und Ich (aka Das Dritte Geschlecht). **1958** Das Maedchen vom Moorhof (The Girl of the Moors—US 1961); Ich Werde Dich auf Haenden Tragen. **1959** The Third Sex.

KOHLER, FRED, SR.
Born: Apr. 20, 1889, Kansas City, Mo. Died: Oct. 28, 1938, Los Angeles, Calif. (heart attack). Screen, stage and vaudeville actor. Father of actor Fred Kohler, Jr.

Appeared in: **1911** Code of Honor (film debut). **1919** The Tiger's Trail (serial); Soldiers of Fortune. **1921** Cyclone Bliss; The Stampede; Thunder Island; A Daughter of the Law; Partners of the Tide. **1922** The Son of the Wolf; His Back Against the Wall; Trimmed; The Scrapper; Without Compromise; Yellow Men and Gold. **1923** Anna Christie; Three Who Paid; The Eleventh Hour; The Flame of Life; Through the Flames; Hell's Hole; The Red Warning; Shadows of the North. **1924** North of Hudson Bay; The Iron Horse; Abraham Lincoln; Fighting Fury. **1925** Dick Trupin; Winds of Chance; The Prairie Pirate; The Thundering Herd; Riders of the Purple Sage. **1926** The Country Beyond; The Ice Flood; Old Ironsides; Danger Quest. **1927** Shootin' Irons; The Way of All Flesh; The City Gone Wild; Underworld; The Blood Ship; The Gay Defender; Open Range; Loves of Carmen; The Devil's Masterpiece; The Rough Riders. **1928** The Spieler; Chinatown Charlie; The Vanishing Pioneer; The Dragnet; The Showdown; Forgotten Faces. **1929** Tide of Empire; Sal of Singapore; Say It With Songs; The Leatherneck; The Quitter; Broadway Babies; The Case of Lena Smith; The Dummy; River of Romance; Stairs of Sand; Thunderbolt. **1930** The Light of Western Stars; Nuits de Chicago (French release of Underworld—1927); Roadhouse Nights; Hell's Heroes; Under a Texas Moon; The Steel Highway. **1931** The Lash; Fighting Caravans; Right of Way; Woman Hungry; Other Men's Women; Soldiers' Plaything; Corsair; X Marks the Spot. **1932** Carnival Boat; Call Her Savage; Wild Horse Mesa; Rider of Death Valley; The Texas Bad Man. **1933** The Wolf Dog (serial); Constant Woman; The Fiddlin' Buckaroo; Under the Tonto Rim; The Deluge; Ship of Wanted Men; The Fourth Horseman. **1934** The Man from Hell; Last Round Up; Honor of the Range; Little Man; What Now? **1935** The Frisco Kid; The Pecos Kid; Outlawed Guns; Border Brigand; Men of Action; The Trail's End; Toll of the Desert; Mississippi; Times Square Lady; West of the Pecos; Wilderness Mail; Goin' to Town; Hard Rock Harrigan; Stormy; Horses Collars (short). **1936** The Vigilantes Are Coming (serial); Dangerous Intrigue; I Loved a Soldier; For the Service; Heart of the West; The Accusing Finger; Texas Ranger; The Plainsman. **1937** Arizona Mahoney; Daughter of Shanghai. **1938** Forbidden Valley; Gangs of New York; Painted Desert; Billy the Kid Returns; The Buccaneer; Blockade; Pure in Mind; Lawless Valley.

KOHLER, WALTER
Died: 1967. Screen actor.

Appeared in: **1952** Affair in Trinidad. **1956** The Wrong Man. **1962** Hitler.

KOHLMAR, LEE
Born: 1878, Nuremberg, Germany. Died: May 15, 1946, Hollywood, Calif. (heart attack). Stage and screen actor.

Appeared in: **1920** The Flaming Disc (serial). **1921** High Heels; Orphans of the Storm. **1922** Breaking Home Ties. **1923** Potash and Perlmutter. **1930** Caught Short; Children of Pleasure; The Thirteenth Prisoner (short); The Richest Man in the World; Sins of the Children; The Kibitzer; The Melody Man; Personality. **1932** Jewel Robbery; Scarlet Dawn; The Strange Case of Clara Deane; The Tenderfoot; Silver Dollar. **1933** She Done Him Wrong; I Love That Man; Forgotten; Roman Scandals; Son of Kong. **1934** When Strangers Meet; The House of Rothschild; Twentieth Century; Shoot the Works. **1935** One More Spring; Ruggles of Red Gap; The Girl Friend; McFadden's Flats; Love in Bloom; Four Hours to Kill; Here Comes Cookie; Break of Hearts; Death From a Distance. **1936** A Son Comes Home. **1941** The Big Store.

KOKO
Born: 1940, Mexico, Mo. Died: 1968, Calif. Screen animal performer. Rex Allen's movie horse.

Appeared in: **1950** Under Mexicali Stars; Redwood Forest Trail; Hills of Oklahoma. **1951** Silver City Bonanza; Thunder in God's Country; Rodeo King and the Senorita; Utah Wagon Trail. **1952** The Last Musketeer; Colorado Sundown; Border Saddlemates; Old Oklahoma Plains. **1953** Old Overland Trail; Iron Mountain Trail; Down Laredo Way; Shadows of Tombstone. **1954** Red River Shore; Phantom Stallion.

KOLB, CLARENCE
Born: 1875. Died: Nov. 25, 1964, Los Angeles, Calif. (stroke). Screen, vaudeville and television actor. Partner with Max Dill (dec. 1949) in vaudeville team billed as "Kolb and Dill." The team appeared in film comedies 1916-1917.

Appeared in: **1917** Beloved Rogue; Mutual Star; Glory (Kolb and Dill). **1936** Fury; After the Thin Man. **1937** The Toast of New York; Portia on Trial; Wells Fargo. **1938** Gold Is Where You Find It; Merrily We Live; Give Me a Sailor; Carefree; The Law West of Tombstone. **1939** The Great Man Votes; It Could Happen to You; Honolulu; Society Lawyer; Five Little Peppers; I Was a Convict; Good Girls Go to Paris; Beware, Spooks!; Amazing Mr. Williams; Our Leading Citizen. **1940** The Five Little Peppers at Home; His Girl Friday; The Man Who Talked Too Much; No Time for Comedy; Tugboat Annie Sails Again; Michael Shayne, Private Detective. **1941** You're in the Army Now; Caught in the Draft; Nothing But the Truth; Bedtime Story; Night of January 16th; Hellzapoppin; Blossoms in the Dust. **1942** True to Life; The Ship's the Limit. **1943** The Falcon in Danger. **1944** Standing Room Only; Irish Eyes Are Smiling; Something for the Boys; Three Is a Family. **1945** Road to Alcatraz; What a Blonde. **1946** The Kid from Brooklyn; White Tie and Tails. **1947** The Pilgrim Lady; Fun on a Weekend; Christmas Eve; The Lost Honeymoon; The Fabulous Joe; Shadowed; The High Cost of Living; Blondie in the Dough. **1949** Impact; Adam's Rib. **1952** The Rose Bowl Story. **1956** Glory; Shake, Rattle and Rock. **1957** Man of a Thousand Faces.

KOLB, THERESE
Born: 1856, Alsace, France. Died: Aug. 19, 1935, Levallois-Perret, France. Stage and screen actress.

Appeared in: **1929** Appasionata.

KOLKER, HENRY
Born: 1874, Germany. Died: July 15, 1947, Los Angeles, Calif. (injured in fall). Screen, stage actor, stage, film director and writer.

Appeared in: **1915** How Molly Made Good. **1916** Gloria's Romance. **1921** Disraeli; Bucking the Tiger; The Fighter; Who Am I? **1923** The Leopardess; The Snow Bride; The Purple Highway. **1925** Any Woman; Sally, Irene and Mary. **1926** Hell's 400; The Palace of Pleasure; Winning the Futurity; Wet Paint. **1927** Kiss in a Taxi; Rough House Rosie. **1928** Don't Marry; The Charge of the Gauchos; Midnight Rose; Soft Living. **1929** The Valiant; Pleasure Crazed; Coquette; Love, Live and Laugh. **1930** Abraham Lincoln; The Bad One; East is West; Way of All Men; Good Intentions; Dubarry, Woman of Passion. **1931** Don't Bet on Women; The Spy; Indiscreet; I Like Your Nerve. **1932** Rasputin and the Empress; Washington Masquerade; The Devil and the Deep; The First Year; The Crash; Faithless; Jewel Robbery; Invincible. **1933** Gigolettes of Paris; Baby Face; The Keyhole; The Narrow Corner; Bureau of Missing Persons; A Bedtime Story; Golden Harvest; The Power and the Glory; Blood Money; I Loved a Woman; Meet the Baron; Notorious but Nice; Love, Honor and Oh, Baby! **1934** Name the Woman; Madame DuBarry; Blind Date; Imitation of Life; Exciting Adventure; The Band Plays On; A Lost Lady; Love Time; Million Dollar Ransom; Lady by Choice; Sing Sing Nights; Massacre; Wonder Bar; Sisters Under the Skin; The Hell Cat; Whom the Gods Destroy; Journal of a Crime; Success at Any Price; She Loves Me Not; The Girl from Missouri; Now and Forever. **1935** One New York Night; Only Eight Hours; The Black Room Mystery; Ladies Love Danger; Times Square Lady; Red Hot Tires; The Case of the Curious Bride; Shipmates Forever; Charlie Chan in Paris; Diamond Jim; Three Kids and a Queen; Society Doctor; Mad Love; Here Comes the Band; Red Salute; The Mystery Man; Honeymoon Limited; My Marriage; The Ghost Walks; The Florentine Dagger; Last Days of Pompeii; Frisco Waterfront. **1936** Collegiate; Bullets or Ballots; Romeo and Juliet; Sitting on the Moon; In His Steps; Great Guy; The Man Who Lived Twice; Theodora Goes Wild. **1937** They Wanted to Marry; Under Cover of Night; Conquest; Thoroughbreds Don't Cry; Green Light; Once a Doctor; Without Warning; Maid of Salem; Let Them Live; The Devil Is Driving. **1938** The Invisible Menace; The Adventures of Marco Polo; The Cowboy and the Lady; Holiday; Safety in Numbers; Too Hot to Handle. **1939** Let Us Live; Hidden Power; Parents on Trial; Should Husbands Work?; Main Street Lawyer; The Real Glory; Here I Am a Stranger; Union Pacific. **1940** Grand Ole Opry; Money and the Woman. **1941** The Parson of Panamint; The Man Who Lost Himself; The Great Swindle; A Woman's Face; Sing for Your Supper; Las Vegas Nights. **1942** Reunion. **1943** Sarong Girl. **1944** Bluebeard. **1947** Monsieur Verdoux; The Secret Life of Walter Mitty.

KOLLER, HERMINE
Born: Germany. Died: 1920, Geneva, Switzerland. Screen actress.

KOLLMAR, RICHARD SR.
Born: Dec. 31, 1910, Ridgewood, N.J. Died: Jan. 8, 1971, New York, N.Y. (heart attack). Screen, stage, radio actor and stage producer. Married to columnist Dorothy Kilgallen (dec. 1965), and later married to Ann Fogarty. Father of actor Richard Killmar, Jr.

Appeared in: **1948** Close-Up.

KOLOSSY, ERIKA
Born: Hungary. Died: Aug. 14, 1963, New York, N.Y. (leukemia). Screen actress, opera performer and singer.

KOMAI, TETSU (Tetsuo Komai)
Born: Apr. 23, 1894, Kumamoto, Japan. Died: Aug. 10, 1970, Gardena, Calif. (congestive heart failure). Screen actor. Entered films in 1923.

Appeared in: **1926** Old Ironsides. **1927** Shanghai Bound; Streets of Shanghai. **1928** Detectives; Moran of the Marines; The Woman from Moscow. **1929** Bulldog Drummond; Chinatown Nights (aka Tong War). **1930** East is West; The Return of Dr. Fu Manchu. **1931** Daughters of the Dragon. **1932** She Wanted a Millionaire; War Correspondent. **1933** Island of Lost Souls; Secrets of Wu Sin; A Study in Scarlet. **1934** Four Frightened People; Now and Forever. **1935** Oil for the Lamps of China; Without Regret. **1936** Klondike Annie; Roaming Lady; Princess Comes Across; Isle of Fury. **1937** China Passage; That Man's Here Again; West of Shanghai. **1939** The Real Glory. **1940** The Letter. **1941** Sundown; Adventures of Captain Marvel (serial). **1949** Task Force; Green Dolphin Street; Tokyo Joe. **1952** Japanese War Bride. **1958** Tank Battalion. **1964** The Night Walker.

KOMISSAROV, ALEKSANDR
Born: 1904, Russia. Died: Aug. 4, 1975, Moscow, Russia. Stage and screen actor.

Appeared in: **1968** War and Peace.

KONSTAM, PHYLLIS (Phyllis Kohnstamm)
Born: Apr. 14, 1907, London, England. Died: Aug. 20, 1976, Stoke St. Gregory, Somerset County, England (heart attack). Screen, stage, radio, television actress, stage producer, playwright and author.

Appeared in: **1928** Champagne (film debut). **1929** Blackmail. **1930** Escape; Murder; Comprising Daphne (aka Compromise—US 1931). **1931** A Gentleman of Paris; Tilly of Bloomsbury; The Skin Game. **1932** Murder on the Second Floor. **1952** The Forgotten Factor; Gotham Valley. **1959** The Crowning Experience. **1960** Voice of the Hurricane.

KONSTANTIN, LEOPOLDINE
Born: c. 1890. Died: 1950s, Vienna, Austria? Screen and stage actress.

Appeared in: **1933** Saison in Kairo. **1935** Prinzessin, Turandot; Liebe Dumme Mama (Stupid Mamma); Frischer Wind aus Kanada; Der Alte und der Junge Koenig. **1946** Notorious.

KOOY, PETE
Died: Apr. 20, 1963, Hollywood, Calif. Screen actor.

Appeared in: **1945** Objective, Burma! **1946** The Big Sleep. **1957** Death in Small Doses; Dino.

KOPKE, WOLFGANG HANS GUNTHER
Born: 1946, West Germany. Died: Aug. 26, 1980, San Francisco, Calif. (accident in jump attempt). Stuntman and screen actor.

KOPP, MILA
Born: 1905, Vienna, Austria. Died: Jan. 15, 1973, Stuttgart, Germany (circulatory ailment). Screen, stage and television actress. Married to actor Christian Kayssler (dec. 1944).

KOPPENS, EMILE See KEPPENS, EMILE

KORAYIM, MOHAMED
Born: 1898, Egypt. Died: May 28, 1972, Cairo, Egypt. Screen actor, film producer and director. Appeared in films during the silents.

KORFF, ARNOLD
Born: 1871. Died: June 2, 1944, New York, N.Y. (heart ailment). Screen, stage and radio actor.

Appeared in: **1923** Tragodie der Liebe (Love Tragedy). **1929** Dancing Vienna. **1930** Doughboys; Monsieur Le Fox; The Royal Family of Broadway; Men of the North; Olympia; The Jazz King. **1931** An American Tragedy; Ambassador Bill; The Unholy Garden. **1932** Scarlet Dawn; Evenings for Sale; Secrets of the French Police. **1934** Black Moon. **1935** Alias Mary Dow; Shanghai; All the Kings Horses; Wings in the Dark; Paris in Spring. **1936** Magnificent Obsession.

KORJUS, MILIZA
Born: 1907, Warsaw, Poland. Died: Aug. 26, 1980, Culver City, Calif. (heart attack). Screen, stage, radio actress and singer. Nominated for 1939 Academy Award for Best Supporting Actress in The Great Waltz.

Appeared in: **1938** The Great Waltz; Caballeria del Imperio (Imperial Calvary).

KORNMAN, MARY

Born: 1917, Idaho Falls, Idaho. Died: June 1, 1973, Glendale, Calif. (cancer). Screen and vaudeville actress. Sister of actress Mildred Kornman. Divorced from cameraman Leo Tovar and later married to screen extra and animal trainer Ralph McCutcheon (dec. 1975). Was first leading lady in the "Our Gang" comedies.

Appeared in: **1923** The following shorts: The Big Show; The Cobbler; The Champeen; A Pleasant Journey; Dogs of War; Lodge Night; Stage Fright; No Noise; Derby Day. **1924** The following shorts: Tire Trouble; Big Business; The Buccaneer; Seein' Things; Commencement Day; It's a Bear; Cradle Robbers; Jubilo, Jr.; High Society; The Sun Down Limited; Every Man for Himself. **1925** The following shorts: The Big Town; Circus Fever; Dog Days; The Love Bug; Ask Grandma; Official Officers; Mary, Queen of Tots; Boys Will Be Joys; Betted Movies; Your Own Back Yard; One Wild Ride. **1926** The following shorts: Good Cheer; Buried Treasure; Monkey Business; Baby Clothes; Uncle Tom's Uncle; Thundering Fleas; Shivering Spooks; The Fourth Alarm. **1930** The following shorts: Doctor's Orders; Bigger and Better; Ladies Last. **1931** Are These Our Children?; plus the following shorts: Blood and Thunder; High Gear; Love Fever; Air Tight; Call a Cop; Mama Loves Papa; The Kickoff. **1932** The following shorts: Love Pains; The Knockout; You're Telling Me; Too Many Women; Wild Babies. **1933** Flying Down to Rio; Bondage (aka The House of Refuge); Neighbors' Wives; College Humor; Fish Hooky (short); Please (short). **1934** The Quitter; Strictly Dynamite; Picture Brides; Just an Echo (short). **1935** Roaring Roads; Desert Trail; Adventurous Knights; Smoky Smith. **1936** The Calling of Dan Matthews. **1937** Youth on Parole; Swing It, Professor; Reunion in Rhythm (short). **1938** King of the Newsboys; I Am a Criminal; Outside of Paradise. **1940** On the Spot.

KORTMAN, ROBERT F.

Born: Dec. 24, 1887, Philadelphia, Pa. Died: Mar. 13, 1967, Long Beach, Calif. (cancer). Screen actor.

Appeared in: **1916** Lieut. Denny, U.S.A.; Ambrose's Rapid Rise; Safety First Ambrose; The Waifs; The No-Good Guy; Capative God. **1917** Cactus Nell; His Naughty Thought. **1918** The Narrow Trail. **1919** The Great Radium Mystery; Square Deal Sanderson. **1921** Godless Men; Montana Bill. **1922** Another Man's Boots; Arabian Love; Gun Shy; The Lone Hand; Travelin' On; Wolf Pack. **1923** Fleetwing; All the Brothers Were Valiant. **1924** The White Sheep. **1926** The Devil Horse. **1927** Blood Will Tell; Hills of Peril; Sunrise—A Song of Two Humans. **1928** The Big Killing. **1930** The Lone Defender (serial); Bear Shooters (short); The Big Kick (short). **1931** City Streets; Cimarron; The Lightning Warrior (serial); The Vanishing Legion (serial); Pardon Us; Beau Hunks (short); The Conquering Horde; 24 Hours; Branded. **1932** The World and the Flesh; Fighting Fool; Night Rider; White Eagle; Gold; Forty Niners. **1933** Rainbow Ranch; Whispering Shadows (serial); The Midnight Patrol (short); Phantom Thunderbolt; Terror Trail; Island of Lost Souls; Come on Danger; Sunset Pass; The Fugitive; King of the Arena. **1934** Sixteen Fathoms Deep; Fighting Code; Smoking Guns; A Man's Game; Burn 'Em Up Barnes (serial and feature); Mystery Mountain (serial); The Trail Drive. **1935** When a Man Sees Red; The Miracle Rider (serial); Crimson Trail; The Ivory-Handled Gun; Wild Mustang. **1936** Swifty; Heroes of the Ranger; Feud of the West; Winds of the Wasteland; Romance Rides the Range; The Lonely Trail; Robinson Crusoe of Clipper Island (serial); The Vigilantes Are Coming (serial); On the Wrong Trek (short); Trail of the Lonesome Pine; Ghost Town Gold. **1937** Secret Agent X-9 (serial); Sandflow; Black Aces; Texas Trail; Zorro Rides Again (serial); Wild West Days (serial). **1938** Law of the Texan. **1939** The Oklahoma Kid; The Renegade Trail; The Renegade Ranger; Oklahoma Frontier. **1940** Law and Order; Adventures of Red Ryder (serial). **1941** Fugitive Valley. **1942** The Forest Rangers. **1943** Avenging Rider; The Sundown Kid; The Black Hills Express. **1944** Forty Thieves; Wyoming Hurricane; The Vigilantes Ride; Call of the Rockies; The Pinto Bandit; Guns of the Law; The Whispering Skull; Saddle Leather Law. **1945** Along Came Jones. **1946** Frontier Gun Law; Gunning for Vengeance; Landrush; Wild Harvest. **1947** Unconquered. **1948** The Paleface; Whispering Smith. **1949** Sorrowful Jones; Copper Canyon. **1950** Branded; Fancy Pants. **1951** The Mating Season; Ace in the Hole (aka The Big Carnival); Flaming Feather.

KORTNER, FRITZ

Born: May 12, 1892, Vienna, Austria. Died: July 22, 1970, Munich, Germany (leukemia). Screen actor, stage director and writer.

Appeared in: **1916** Police 1111; Das Zweite Leben. **1917** Der Brief Eine Toten. **1918** Das Andere Ich; Frauenehre; Sonnwendhof; Der Staerkere; Maerthyrer Seines Herzens (aka Beethovens Lebensroman). **1919** Das Auge des Buddha; Else von Erlenhof; Gerechtigkeit; Ohne Zeugen; Prinz Kuckuck; Satanas. **1920** Das Haus zum Mond; Die Jagd Nach der Wahrheit; Katherina die Grosse; Die Lieblingsfrau des Maharadscha; Die Nacht der Koenigin Isabeau; Das Haus der Qualen; Der Schaedel der Pharaonentochter; Va Banque; Die Vershwoerung zu Genua; Weltbrand; Die Brueder Karamasoff (The Brothers Karamazov). **1921** Am Roten Kliff; Christian Wahnschaffe; Der Eisenbahnkoenig; Die Hintertreppe (Backstairs—US 1926); Danton (aka All for a Woman). **1922** Die Finsternis ist ihr Eigentum; Flammende Voelker; Der Graf von Essex; Landstrasse und Grosstadt; Die Mausefalle; Peter des Grosse; Ein Puppenheim; Ruf des Schicksals; Der Staerkste Trieb; Arme Suenderin; Sterbende Voelker (aka Populi Morituri); Luise Millerin (aka Kabale und Liebe). **1923** Nora; Schatten (aka Warning Shadows—US 1927); Ein Weib, ein Tier, ein Diamant (aka Fuenf Kapitel Aus Eine Alten Buch). **1924** Dr. Wislizenus; Moderne Ehen; Armes Kleine Maedchen (aka Das Maedchen mit den Schwefelhoelzchen). **1925** Orleans Haende. **1926** Duerfen wir Schweigen? **1927** Beethoven (aka The Life of Beethoven—US 1929); Alpentragoedie; Die Ausgestossenen; Die Gelibte des Gouverneurs; Maria Stuart (US 1928); Mata Hari (US 1928); Mein Leben Fuer das Deine; Primanerliebe (US 1928); Frau Sorge. **1928** Dame Care; The Hands of Orlac; The Red Dancer; Revolutionschochzeit; Marquis d'Eon, der Spion der Pompadour (aka The Spy of Madame de Pompadour—US 1929). **1929** Die Beuchse der Pandora (Pandora's Box); Die Frau im Talar; Die Frau Nach der man Sich Sehnt; Giftgas; Die Staerkere Macht; Das Schiff der Verlorenen Menschen; Somnambul; Atlantik; A Scandal in Paris; Three Loves. **1930** Caught in Berlin's Underworld; The Last Night; Die Grosse Sehnsucht; Dreyfus (US 1931); Der Andere (US 1932); Menschen im Kaefig (aka Cape Fear, and aka Love Storm). **1931** Moerder Dimitri Karamasoff (Murderer Dimitri Karamasoff); The Dreyfus Case; Danton (and 1921 version). **1934** Chu Chin Chow; Evensong. **1935** Abdul the Damned. **1936** The Crouching Beast. **1940** The Dreyfus Case (and 1931 version). **1943** The Strange Case of Adolf Hitler. **1945** The Hitler Gang. **1946** Somewhere in the Night; The Wife of Monte Cristo. **1947** The Brasher Doubloon; The High Window; The Razor's Edge. **1948** The Vicious Circle; Berlin Express. **1949** Der Ruf. **1951** The Last Illusion. **1953** Ali Baba Nights. **1955** Die Stadt ist Voller Geheinnisse (aka City of Secrets—US 1963).

KOSHETZ, NINA

Born: 1892, Russia. Died: May 14, 1965, Santa Ana, Calif. Screen actress and singer. Mother of actress Marina Koshetz.

Appeared in: **1938** Algiers. **1944** Our Hearts Were Young and Gay. **1946** The Chase. **1950** It's a Small World. **1952** Captain Pirate. **1956** Hot Blood.

KOSHIJI, FUBUKI

Born: 1924, Japan. Died: Nov. 9, 1980, Japan? Screen and stage actor.

Appeared in: **1966** Daiboken (aka Don't Call Me a Con Man—US).

KOSLOFF, THEODORE

Born: Russia. Died: Nov. 22, 1956, Los Angeles, Calif. Screen actor and ballet dancer.

Appeared in: **1917** The Woman God Forgot. **1920** Why Change Your Wife?; The City of Masks. **1921** The Affairs of Anatol; Fool's Paradise; Forbidden Fruit. **1922** The Green Temptation; Manslaughter; To Have and to Hold; The Dictator; The Lane That Had No Turning; The Law of the Lawless. **1923** Adam's Rib; Children of Jazz; Hollywood. **1924** Triumph; Don't Call It Love; Feet of Clay. **1925** Beggar on Horseback; The Golden Bed; New Lives for Old. **1926** The Volga Boatman. **1927** King of Kings; The Little Adventuress. **1928** Woman Wise. **1930** Sunny; Madam Satan.

KOSTELANETZ, ANDRE

Born: 1901, St. Petersburg, Russia. Died: Jan. 13, 1980, Haiti (complications from pneumonia). Musical conductor and screen actor. Divorced from actress/singer Lily Pons (dec. 1976), and Sara Gene Orcutt.

Appeared in: **1940** Music in My Heart.

KOTSONAROS, GEORGE

Born: Nauplie, Greece. Died: July 13, 1933. Screen actor.

Appeared in: **1926** Cupid's Knockout; While London Sleeps. **1927** Catch As Catch Can; The Private Life of Helen of Troy; The Wizard; The Tender Hour; King of the Jungle (serial). **1928** Beggars of Life; The Fifty-Fifty Girl; The Street of Sin. **1929** The Shakedown; The Body Punch. **1930** Dangerous Paradise. **1931** Honeymoon Lane.

KOUTAIE, ARI

Born: 1900. Died: Sept. 30, 1980, Israel. Screen and stage actor.

KOVACS, ERNIE
Born: Jan. 23, 1919, Trenton, N.J. Died: Jan. 12, 1962, Beverly Hills, Calif. (auto accident). Screen, stage and television actor. Son of actress Mary Kovacs (dec. 1981). Married to actress Edie Adams.

Appeared in: **1957** Operation Mad Ball (film debut). **1958** Bell, Book and Candle; Showdown at Ulcer Gulch (a commercial short for Saturday Evening Post). **1959** It Happened to Jane. **1960** Our Man in Havana; Strangers When We Meet; Wake Me When It's Over; North to Alaska; Pepe. **1961** Sail a Crooked Ship; Five Golden Hours.

KOVACS, MARY
Born: 1901. Died: Aug. 24, 1981, West Hollywood, Calif. (heart attack). Screen actress. Mother of actor Ernie Kovacs (dec. 1962).

KOWAL, MITCHELL
Born: 1916. Died: May 2, 1971, near Fuernitz, Austria (train wreck). Screen actor. Appeared in U.S., Italian and Polish films.

Appeared in: **1944** Marriage is a Private Affair. **1953** Violated. **1954** River of No Return; Francis Joins the WACS. **1955** The Big Bluff; Abbott and Costello Meet the Mummy. **1959** John Paul Jones. **1962** Jada Goscie Jada (Guests Are Coming-US 1965). **1963** 55 Days at Peking. **1969** Francesco Bertazzoli; Investigator.

KOZINTSEV, GRIGORY
Born: 1905, Russia. Died: May 11, 1973, Leningrad, Russia. Screen actor, film director, producer, screenwriter and author. Entered film as an actor and then turned director.

KRAH, MARC (Max Krahmalkov)
Born: Jan. 24, 1906. Died: Sept. 25, 1973 (nephrosclerosis). Screen actor.

Appeared in: **1947** Riff-raff; Devilship; Intrigue. **1948** Alias a Gentleman. **1949** Sorrowful Jones; Criss Cross. **1950** Black Hand; Call of the Klondike. **1951** Sky High. **1952** Macao; Strange Fascination. **1953** Beneath the 12 Mile Reef. **1955** Love Is a Many Splendored Thing.

KRAHLY, HANNS (aka HANS KRALY)
Born: 1885. Died: 1950, Los Angeles, Calif. Screen actor, film director and screenwriter.

Appeared in: **1910?** Der fesche Tiroler. **1912** Die Kinder des Generals; Das Madchen ohne Vaterland. **1913** Engelein (aka Lille Engels); Engeleins Hochzeit; Die Filmprimadonna. **1914** Aschenbrodel; Elena Fontana; Die Ewige Nacht; Das Feuer; Das Kind ruft; Standrechtlich erschossen; Weisse Rosen. **1916** Schuhpalast Pinkus. **1918** Die Augen der Mumie Ma; Carmen; Fuhrmann Henschel; Der gelbe Schein; Meine Frau; die Filmschauspielerin. **1919** Komptesse Doddy (Comptesse Doddy); Die Austernprizessin (The Oyster Princess); Fahrt ins Blaue; Madame DuBarry (aka Passion); Monika Vogelsang; Die Puppe (The Doll); Rausch; Die verlorenen Tochter (Lost Daughters). **1920** Anna Boleyn; Arme Violetta; Kohlhiesels Tochter (Kohlhiesel's Daughters); Medea; Romeo und Julia im Schnee; Sumurun (aka One Arabian Night). **1921** Die Bergkatze (The Mountain Cat); Das Weib des Pharao (Pharaoh's Wife, aka The Loves of Pharaoh). **1922** Die Flamme/Montmatre. **1923** Alles fur Geld (All for Money); Boheme; Das Paradies im Schnee. **1924** Komodianten des Lebens.

KRAMER, IDA
Born: 1878. Died: Oct. 15, 1930, Brooklyn, N.Y. (heart attack). Stage and screen actress.

Appeared in: **1928** Abie's Irish Rose (stage and film versions).

KRAMER, JONATHAN
Born: 1946. Died: May 6, 1976. Screen and stage actor.

Appeared in: **1969** Midnight Cowboy.

KRAMER, PHIL
Born: 1900. Died: Mar. 31, 1972, North Hudson, N.J. (heart attack). Screen, radio and television actor.

Appeared in: **1935** Hands Across the Table. **1942** Suicide Squadron.

KRAMER, WRIGHT
Born: 1870. Died: Nov. 14, 1941, Hollywood, Calif. Screen, stage and vaudeville actor.

Appeared in: **1938** The Gladiator; Professor Beware. **1939** Mr. Smith Goes to Washington; Good Girls Go to Paris; It Could Happen to You. **1940** Anne of Windy Poplars; Before I Hang; Dark Streets of Cairo; The Showdown.

KRANZ, ALFRED
Born: 1869, Brooklyn, N.Y. Died: Dec. 2, 1937, Providence, R.I. Screen and stage actor. Appeared in silent films.

KRAUS, CHARLES
Born: 1866, Budapest, Hungary. Died: July 12, 1931, New York, N.Y. Screen and stage actor. Married to stage actress Camilla Dalberg(dec.). Do not confuse with French actor Charles Krauss (dec. 1926).

Appeared in: **1914** One of Our Girls. **1915** Love and Money.

KRAUSS, CHARLES
Born: France. Died: Oct., 1926. Screen actor and film producer.

KRAUSS, WERNER
Born: June 23, 1884, Gestungshausen, Germany. Died: Oct. 20, 1959, Vienna, Austria. Screen and stage actor. Married to actress Maria Bard (dec. 1944).

Appeared in: **1914** Die Pagode. **1916** Hoffmanns Erzahlungen; Nacht des Grauens; Zirkusblut. **1917** Die Rache der Toten; Die Seeschlacht; Wenn Frauen Lieben und hassen. **1917-18** Es werde Licht (Let There Be Light). **1918** Opium. **1919** Das Kabinett des Dr. Caligari (The Cabinet of Dr. Caligari); Rose Bernd; Totentanz. **1919-20** Johannes Goth. **1920** Die Beichte einer Toten; Die Bruder Karamasoff (The Brothers Karamozov); Der Bucklige und die Tanzerin; Das lachende Grauen; Der Mann ohne Namen (Man Without a Name); Das Medium. **1920?** Holle und Verfall (or Hohe und Verfall). **1921** Danton/All for a Woman; Christian Wahnschaffe; Die Beute der Erinnyen; Der Roman der Christine von Herre; Die Frau ohne Seele; Scherben (Shattered); Grausige Nachte; Der Tanz um Liebe und Gluck; Sappho; Zirkus des Lebens. **1922** Der brennende Acker (Burning Soil); Der Graf von Essex; Josef und seine Bruder (Joseph and His Brothers); Luise Millerin/Kabale und Liebe; Lady Hamilton; Die Marquise von Pompadour; Die Nacht der Medici; Nathan der Weise; Othello (US 1923); Tragikomodie. **1923** Adam und Eva; Das alte Gesetz; Alt-Heidelberg (aka The Student Prince); Fraulein Raffke; Fridericus Rex/Ein Konigsschicksal; I.N.R.I.; Der Kaufmann von Venedig; Der Menschenfeind; Der Puppenmacher von Kiang-Ning; Der Schatz (The Treasure—US 1929); Das unbekannte Morgen; Zwischen Abend und Morgen; Das Wachsfigurenkabinett (The Waxworks—US 1924). **1924** Dekameron—Nachte (Decameron Nights—US 1928); Ein Sommernachtstraum. **1925** Die Dame aus Berlin; Eifersucht (Jealousy—US 1928); Die freundlose Gasse (The Joyless Street) (aka Streets of Sorrow—US 1927); Das Haus der Luge; Die Moral der Gasse; Reveille, das grosse Wecken; Das Tartuff (Tartuffe—US 1927); Der Trodler von Amsterdam; Geheimnisse einer Seele (Secrets of a Soul). **1926** Das graue Haus; Kreuzzug des Wibes (aka Unwelcome Children—US 1928); Man spielt nicht mit der Liebe (Don't Play with Love); Nana (US 1929); Der Student von Prag (The Student of Prague); Uberflussige Menschen. **1927** Der fidele Bauer (The Jolly Peasant—US 1929); Funkzauber; Die Holle der Jungfrauen; Die Hose (aka Royal Scandal—US 1929). **1926-27** Laster der Menschheit (Lusts of Mankind); Unter Ausschluss der Offentlichkeit; Da halt die Welt den Atem an. **1928** Looping the Loop (US 1929). **1929** Napoleon auf St. Helena. **1931** Yorck (US 1932). **1932** Mensch ohne Namen (Man Without a Name and 1920 version). **1935** Hundert Tage. **1936** Burgtheater (aka Vienna Burgtheater—US 1937). **1939** Robert Koch, der Bekampfer des Todes. **1940** Jud Suss (Jew Suss—German propaganda version). **1941** Annelie/Die Geschichte eines Lebens. **1942** Die Entlassung; Zwischen Himmel und Erde. **1943** Paracelsus. **1950** Pramien auf den Tod; Der fallende Stern. **1955** Sohn ohne Heimat.

KRECH, WARREN
Died: Sept. 24, 1948. Screen actor.

Appeared in: **1920** Tne Town That Forgot God. **1923** Plunder (serial).

KRIEGER, LEE
Born: 1919. Died: Dec. 22, 1967, Van Nuys, Calif. Screen, stage and television actor.

Appeared in: **1961** Bachelor in Paradise. **1962** Period of Adjustment; Convicts Four; The Horizontal Lieutenant. **1967** The Reluctant Astronaut.

KROELL, ADRIENNE
Born: 1892. Died: Oct. 2, 1949, Evanston, Ill. (arthritis). Screen actress.

Appeared in: **1911** Two Orphans; Strategy. **1912** The Law of the North; An Unexpected Fortune; Into the Genuine; The Fire-Fighter's Love; The Miller of Burgundy; Her Bitter Lesson; The Adopted Son; Under Suspicion; Murray the Masher. **1913** Nobody's Boy; Don't Let Mother Know or, The Bliss of Ignorance; Tommy's Atonement; A Change of Administration; The Water Rat; The Ex-Convict's Plunge; The Pink Opera Cloak.

KROHNER, SARAH
Born: 1883. Died: June 9, 1959, Brooklyn, N.Y. Screen, stage and radio actress. Appeared in Yiddish films.

Appeared in: **1939** Molly. **1951** Mirele Efros.

KRUEGER, BUM (Willy Krueger)
Born: 1906, Germany. Died: Mar. 15, 1971, West Berlin, Germany (heart attack). Screen, stage and television actor.

Appeared in: **1956** Du Bist Musik (US 1962). **1959** The Eighth Day of the Week; Verbrechen nach Schulschluss (The Young Go Wild—US 1962). Other German films: Film Without Title; The Gentleman from the Other Star; The Devil's General.

KRUGER, ALMA
Born: 1868, Pittsburgh, Pa. Died: Apr. 5, 1960, Seattle, Wash. Screen, stage and radio actress. Her best known role was as Mollie Bird, head nurse, in "Dr. Kildare" film series.

Appeared in: **1936** These Three; Craig's Wife; Love Letters of a Star. **1937** Breezing Home; The Mighty Treve; The Man in Blue; One Hundred Men and a Girl; Vogues of 1938. **1938** The Toy Wife; Marie Antoinette; The Great Waltz; Mother Carey's Chickens; Tarnished Angel; Four's a Crowd. **1939** The Secret of Dr. Kildare; Made for Each Other; Balalaika; Calling Dr. Kildare. **1940** His Girl Friday; Dr. Kildare's Strangest Case; Dr. Kildare's Crisis; Dr. Kildare Goes Home; Anne of Windy Poplars; You'll Find Out. **1941** Blonde Inspiration; Trial of Mary Dugan; Puddin' Head; The People vs. Dr. Kildare; Dr. Kildare's Wedding Day; Dr. Kildare's Victory. **1942** Saboteur; Calling Dr. Gillespie; Dr. Gillespie's New Assistant; That Other Woman. **1943** Dr. Gillespie's Criminal Case. **1944** Mrs. Parkington; Three Men in White; Our Hearts Were Young and Gay; Babes on Swing Street; Between Two Women. **1945** The Crime Doctor's Warning; A Royal Scandal. **1946** Colonel Effingham's Raid; Do You Love Me? **1947** Forever Amber; Dark Delusion; Fun On a Weekend.

KRUGER, FRED H.
Born: 1913. Died: Dec. 5, 1961, Hollywood, Calif. (cerebral hemorrhage). Screen and television actor.

Appeared in: **1958** Girls on the Loose.

KRUGER, HAROLD "STUBBY"
Born: 1897, Honolulu, Hawaii. Died: Oct. 7, 1965, Hollywood, Calif. (heart attack). Screen stuntman and swimmer. Doubled for Douglas Fairbanks in the Black Pirate (1926) and Spencer Tracy in The Old Man and the Sea (1958).

Appeared in: Paramount shorts; Grantland Rice Sportlight for Pathe. **1926** Black Pirate; Beloved Rogue. **1941** Hellzapoppin'. **1942** Reap the Wild Wind. **1945** They Were Expendable. **1955** Mister Roberts. **1958** The Old Man and the Sea. **1960** Spartacus.

KRUGER, OTTO
Born: Sept. 6, 1885, Toledo, Ohio. Died: Sept. 6, 1974, Woodland Hills, Calif. (stroke and cerebral vascular complications). Screen, stage, radio, vaudeville and television actor. Married to stage actress Sue MacManamy (dec. 1976).

Appeared in: **1915** When the Call Came. **1923** Under the Red Robe. **1929** Mr. Intruder (short). **1933** Turn Back the Clock; Beauty for Sale; Ever in My Heart; Gallant Lady; The Prizefighter and the Lady; The Women in His Life. **1934** The Crime Doctor; Men in White; Springtime for Henry; Paris Interlude; Chained; Treasure Island. **1935** Vanessa—Her Love Story; Two Sinners. **1936** Lady of Secrets; Dracula's Daughter; Living Dangerously. **1937** They Won't Forget; Glamorous Nights; Counsel for Crime; The Barrier. **1938** Thanks for the Memory; I Am the Law; The Housemaster (US 1939); Exposed; Star of the Circus (aka Hidden Menace—US 1940). **1939** Disbarred; Another Thin Man; Zero Hour; A Woman Is the Judge; The Gang's All Here (aka The Amazing Mr. Forrest—US); Black Eyes. **1940** Seventeen; Scandal Sheet; The Story of Dr. Ehrlich's Magic Bullet (aka Dr. Ehrlich's Magic Bullet); A Dispatch from Reuters; The Man I Married. **1941** The Big Boss; The Men in Her Life; Mercy Island. **1942** Saboteur; Friendly Enemies; Secrets of a Co-ed. **1943** Corregidor; Night Plane from Chungking; Stage Door Canteen; Tarzan's Desert Mystery; Hitler's Children. **1944** Cover Girl; Knickerbocker Holiday; Storm Over Lisbon; Farewell, My Lovely (aka Murder My Sweet); They Live in Fear; American's Children; The Amazing Mr. Forrest. **1945** Wonder Man; The Chicago Kid; Earl Carroll's Vanities; The Great John L; Jungle Captive; On Stage Everybody; The Woman Who Came Back; Allotment Wives; Escape in the Fog. **1946** Duel in the Sun; The Fabulous Suzanne. **1947** Love and Learn. **1948** Smart Woman; Lulu Belle. **1950** 711 Ocean Drive. **1951** Payment on Demand (aka Story of Divorce); Valentino. **1952** High Noon. **1954**

Magnificent Obsession; Black Widow. **1955** The Last Command. **1958** The Colossus of New York. **1959** The Young Philadelphians; Cash McCall. **1962** The Wonderful World of the Brothers Grimm. **1964** Sex and the Single Girl.

KRUMSCHMIDT, EBERHARD
Born: 1905. Died: June 3, 1956, New York, N.Y. Screen, stage, radio, television actor and stage director.

Appeared in: **1946** Notorious.

KRUPA, GENE
Born: Jan. 15, 1909, Chicago, Ill. Died: Oct. 16, 1973, Yonkers, N.Y. (leukemia). Musician, drummer, band leader and screen actor.

Appeared in: **1939** Some Like It Hot. **1942** Ball of Fire. **1945** George White's Scandals. **1947** Beat the Band. **1948** Glamour Girl. **1949** Make Believe Ballroom. **1954** The Glenn Miller Story. **1955** The Benny Goodman Story.

KRUPP, VERA (Vera Hosenfeldt)
Born: 1910, Germany. Died: Oct. 16, 1967, Los Angeles, Calif. Screen actress.

KUEHNE, EDNA
Died: Aug., 1922, Los Angeles, Calif. (auto accident). Screen actress. Appeared in Vitagraph Co. films.

KUHN, EVELYN
Born: 1893. Died: June 29, 1976. Screen actress.

KULKAVICH, BOMBER See KULKY, HENRY "HANK"

KULKY, HENRY "HANK" (aka BOMBER KULKAVICH)
Born: Aug. 11, 1911, Hastings-on-the-Hudson, N.Y. Died: Feb. 12, 1965, Oceanside, Calif. (heart attack). Screen, television actor and professional wrestler known as "Bomber Kulkavich."

Appeared in: **1947** A Likely Story. **1948** A Foreign Affair; Alias a Gentleman; Call Northside 777. **1949** Alias the Champ; The Red Danube; Tarzan's Magic Fountain; Bandits of El Dorado. **1950** Wabash Avenue; South Sea Sinner; Bodyhold; Jiggs and Maggie Out West. **1951** You Never Can Tell; The Guy Who Came Back; The Love Nest; Chinatown Chump (short); The Kid from Amarillo; Fixed Bayonets. **1952** The World in His Arms; Gobs and Gals; No Holds Barred; Target Hong Kong; My Wife's Best Friend; Red Skies of Montana; What Price Glory? **1953** Powder River; The Robe; 5,000 Fingers of Dr. T.; Down Among the Sheltering Palms; The Glory Brigade; The Charge at Feather River. **1954** A Star Is Born; Fireman Save My Child; Yukon Vengeance; Hell and High Water; Tobor the Great; The Steel Cage. **1955** To Hell and Back; Jail Busters; Love Me or Leave Me; The Girl in the Red Velvet Swing; Prince of Players; New York Confidential; Abbott and Costello Meet the Keystone Kops; Illegal. **1957** Sierra Stranger. **1959** Compulsion; Up Periscope; The Gunfight at Dodge City. **1960** Guns of the Timberland. **1964** A Global Affair.

KUMARI, MEENA (Mehzabeenara Begum)
Born: 1932, India. Died: Mar. 31, 1972, Bombay, India (liver ailment). Screen actress and screenwriter.

Appeared in: Baiju Bawra; Parineeta; Bandish; Sahib Bibi Aur Ghulam; Ek Hi Bhool.

KUN, MAGDA
Born: Feb. 7, 1912, Pagan, Hungary. Died: Nov. 7, 1945, London, England. Screen and stage actress.

Appeared in: **1933** Filleres Gyoers. **1934** Und Es Leuchtet die Puszta. **1935** Dance Band. **1938** Busuini Men Jo (Don't Worry); Majd a Zsuzsi.

KUNDE, AL
Born: 1888. Died: Aug. 10, 1952, Los Angeles, Calif. (cancer). Screen actor and professional boxer known as "Al Krieger."

Appeared in: **1943** Gangway for Tomorrow; Mission to Moscow. **1947** Pursued. **1951** Santa Fe. **1952** Something to Live For.

KUNDE, ANNE
Born: 1896. Died: June 14, 1960, Hollywood, Calif. Screen actress.

Appeared in: **1943** Gangway for Tomorrow. **1949** Madame Bovary. **1950** Father of the Bride. **1952** Something to Live For. **1956** The First Traveling Saleslady. **1959** Li'l Abner. **1961** One-Eye Jacks.

KUNKEL, GEORGE
Born: 1867. Died: Nov. 8, 1937, Hollywood, Calif. (heart attack). Screen actor.

Appeared in: **1919** Leave It to Susan. **1921** An Unwilling Hero; Where Men Are Men.

KUPCINET, KARYN
Born: Mar. 6, 1941. Died: Nov. 28, 1963, West Los Angeles, Calif. (murdered). Screen, stage and television actress.

Appeared in: **1961** The Ladies' Man.

KURENKO, MADAME MARIA
Born: 1891, Russia. Died: May 17, 1980, New York, N.Y. Screen actress, opera and concert singer.

KUWA, GEORGE K.
Born: Apr. 7, 1885, Japan. Died: Oct. 13, 1931. Screen and stage actor.

Appeared in: **1919** Toby's Bow. **1921** Invisible Fear; Nobody's Fool. **1922** The Beautiful and Damned; Bought and Paid For; Enter Madame; Five Days to Live; The Half Breed; Moran of the Lady Letty; Sherlock Brown. **1923** Daddy; The Eternal Struggle; The World's Applause. **1924** Broken Barriers; Curlytop; The Storm Daughter; The Man from Wyoming. **1925** Head Winds; Oh, Doctor!; The Wife Who Wasn't Wanted; A Son of His Father. **1926** A Trip to Chinatown; The Enchanted Hill; That Model from Paris; The Nut-Cracker; Money Talks; The Silver Treasure; The House Without a Key (serial). **1927** The Chineses Parrot; The Dice Woman; Perch of the Devil; The Night Bride; White Pants Willie; The Warning; Melting Millions (serial). **1928** After the Storm; Chinatown Charlie; The Showdown; The Secret Hour.

KUZNETZOFF, ADIA
Born: 1890, Russia. Died: Aug. 10, 1954, Port Washington, N.Y. Screen, television actor and gypsy singer.

Appeared in: **1930** A Russian Rhapsody. **1935** A Universal short. **1937** I'll Take Romance; Maytime; Easy Living; Madame X. **1938** Pacific Liner; Spawn of the North; The Mysterious Mr. Moto; Swiss Miss. **1939** Tropic Fury; Devil's Island. **1941** Second Chorus; The Wolf Man. **1942** Arabian Nights; My Sister Eileen. **1943** The Seventh Victim; Frankenstein Meets the Wolf Man; For Whom the Bell Tolls; Hello, Frisco, Hello. **1944** Lost in a Harem; Rainbow Island; Song of Russia; The Princess and the Pirate.

KYLE, AUSTIN C.
Born: 1893. Died: Nov. 10, 1916, France (killed in action). Screen actor.

KYLE, HOWARD
Born: 1861. Died: Dec. 1, 1950, New York. Screen and stage actor.

Appeared in: **1912** A Star Reborn.

KYVELI (Kyveli Adrianou)
Born: 1887, Greece. Died: May 25, 1978, Athens, Greece. Screen and stage actress.

Appeared in: **1960** Madame X.

LABADIE, FLORENCE
Born: 1893, Canada. Died: Oct. 13, 1917, Ossining, N.Y. (auto accident). Screen actress and model.

Appeared in: **1911** The Broken Cross; Enoch Arden; How She Triumphed; Cinderella; Blind Princess and the Poet; The Primal Call. **1912** The Merchant of Venice; Lucile; Undine; Star of Bethlehem; East Lynne; Aurora Floyd; Flying to Fortune; My Baby's Voice; A Love of Long Ago; Rejuvenation; The Saleslady; Jess; Under Two Flags; The Ring of a Spanish Grandee; Dottie's New Doll; The Troublemaker; Arab's Bride; Whom God Hath Joined; Extravagance; Dr. Jekyll and Mr. Hyde; The Case of the Lady Anne; The Baseball Bug; A Star Reborn; Miss Robinson Crusoe; When Mercy Tempers Justice; Through the Flames; Mme. Rex; The Thief and the Girl; As It Was in the Beginning; Blossom Time. **1913** Little Brother; The Junior Partner; A Poor Relation; The Marble Heart; A Twentieth Century Farmer; Some Fools There Were; Louie the Life Saver; Life's Pathway; The Snare of Fate; Cymbeline; When the Worm Turned; Oh! Such a Beautiful Ocean; The Ward of the King; Tannhauser; Curfew Shall Not Ring Tonight; A Peaceful Victory. **1914** The Million Dollar Mystery (serial); Under False Colors; The Somnambulist; The Success of Selfishness; A Mohammedan Conspiracy. **1915** The Country Girl; Crossed Wires; God's Witness; The Cycle of Hatred; Bianca Forgets; The Final Reckoning; Graft Versus Love; The Adventures of Florence; A

Smuggled Diamond; Monsieur Nikola Dupree; When the Fleet Sailed In; The Price of Her Silence; The Price of Her Silence; A Freight Car Honeymoon; A Disciple of Nietzsche; Mr. Meeson's Will; All Aboard; Her Confession. **1916** Master Shakespeare; Her Sacrifice; Divorce and the Daughter; The Five Faults of Flo. **1917** Her Life and His; When Love Was Blind.

LA BISSONIER, ERIN
Born: Aug. 5, 1901, Red Lake Falls, Minn.? Died: Sept. 22, 1976. Screen actress.

Appeared in: **1925** The Wheel. **1926** The Still Alarm. **1927** The Heart of a Salome; Light in the Window; Million Dollar Mystery; Eager Lips. **1928** The Branded Man; Gypsy of the North; The Stronger Will. **1929** Knights Out (short). **1930** Playboy of Paris; The Storm. **1932** Widow in Scarlet; Guilty or Not Guilty. **1934** Good Dame; Woman Unafraid; In the Money.

LABRAKE, HARRISON
Born: 1891. Died: Dec. 2, 1936, Malone, N.Y. Circus performer and screen actor. Appeared in silent films.

LACEY, ADELE
Born: 1914. Died: July 3, 1953, Mexico City, Mexico. Screen actress and dancer. Married to film producer Walter A. Futter.

Appeared in: **1933** When a Man Rides Alone.

LACEY, CATHERINE
Born: May 6, 1904, London, England. Died: Sept. 23, 1979, London, England. Screen, stage and television actress. Divorced from Geoffrey Howard Clark. Later married to actor Roy Emerton (dec. 1944), and Anthony Wright.

Appeared in: **1938** The Lady Vanishes (film debut). **1939** All Living Things; Poison Pen (US 1941). **1941** Cottage to Let (aka Bombsight Stolen—US). **1945** Pink String and Sealing Wax (US 1950); I Know Where I'm Going (US 1947). **1946** Carnival. **1947** The White Unicorn (aka Bad Sister—US 1948); The October Man (US 1948). **1949** Whisky Galore (aka Mad Little Island and aka Tight Little Island—US). **1957** The Man in the Sky (aka Decision Against Time—US). **1958** Rockets Galore (aka Mad Little Island—US). **1961** The Shadow of the Cat. **1963** The Servant. **1967** The Mummy's Shroud; The Sorcerors (US 1968). **1970** The Private Life of Sherlock Holmes. **1975** Abduction.

LACK, SIMON (Simon MacAlpine)
Born: Dec. 19, 1917, Cleland, Scotland. Died: Aug. 8, 1980, London, England. Screen, stage and television actor.

Appeared in: **1940** The Proud Valley (US 1941). **1960** Clue of the Twisted Candle (US 1968); Cone of Silence (aka Trouble in the Sky—US 1961). **1961** Macbeth (US 1963); On the Fiddle (aka Operation Snafu—US 1965, and aka War Head, and Operation Warhead). **1970** The Bushbaby; Trog.

LACKAYE, HELEN
Died: Oct. 19, 1940, Jersey City, N.J. Screen and stage actress. Sister of actors Wilton (dec. 1932) and James Lackaye (dec. 1919).

Appeared in: **1915** Neal of the Navy.

LACKAYE, JAMES
Born: 1867, Washington, D.C. Died: June 8, 1919, New York, N.Y. (pneumonia). Stage and screen actor. For family information see Wilton Lackaye, Sr.

Appeared in: **1913** That Suit at Ten; If Dreams Came True; Bingles Mends the Clock; Counselor Bobby; Three to One; Two Hearts That Beat As One; Two's Company—Three's a Crowd; The Forgotten Latch Key; The Coming of Gretchen; Bingles and the Cabaret; Troublesome Daughters; An Old Man's Love Story. **1914** Good Gracious; Mr. Bingle's Melodrama. **1915** The Battle Cry of Peace; York State Folks. **1916** The Upstart.

LACKAYE, RICHARD
Born: May 9, 1873, Mich. Died: Mar. 5, 1951, Hollywood, Calif. (heart attack). Screen and stage actor.

LACKAYE, WILTON, SR.
Born: Sept. 30, 1862, Loudoun County, Va. Died: Aug. 22, 1932, New York, N.Y. (heart attack). Stage and screen actor. Brother of actors James (dec. 1919) and Helen Lackaye (dec. 1940). Father of stage actor/writer Wilton Lackaye, Jr. (dec. 1977).

Appeared in: **1915** "World" productions. **1921** God's Crucible. **1922** What's Wrong With Women? **1924** For Woman's Favor; The Lone Wolf. **1925** The Sky Raider.

LACKTEEN, FRANK
Born: Aug. 29, 1894, Kubber-Ilias, Asia Minor. Died: July 8, 1968, Woodland Hills, Calif. (cerebral and respiratory illness). Screen actor.

Appeared in: **1916** Less Than Dust; The Yellow Menace (serial). **1921** The Avenging Arrow (serial). **1922** White Eagle (serial). **1924** The Virgin; The Fortieth Door (serial). **1925** The Pony Express; plus the following serials: The Green Archer; Idaho; Sunken Silver. **1926** Desert Gold; The Last Frontier; The Unknown Cavlier; House Without a Key (serial). **1927** Melting Millions (serial); Hawk of the Hills (serial). **1928** The Warning; Court Martial; Prowlers of the Sea; Mark of the Frog (serial). **1929** The Black Book (serial); The Fire Detective (serial); Hawk of the Hills (feature of 1927 serial). **1931** Law of the Tong (serial); Hell's Valley; Cracked Nuts. **1932** Heroes of the West (serial); Texas Pioneer; Jungle Mystery (serial). **1933** Nagana; Rustler's Roundup; Tarzan the Fearless (serial and feature film). **1934** The Perils of Pauline (serial); Escape from Devil's Island. **1936** Anthony Adverse; Under Two Flags; Mummy's Boys; Isle of Fury; Comin' Round the Mountain. **1937** I Cover the War; Radio Patrol (serial); The Mysterious Pilot (serial); Man Bites Lovebug (short). **1938** Red Barry (serial). **1939** The Girl and the Gambler; Juarez; The Kansas Terrors. **1940** Stagecoach War; The Girl from Havana; Moon Over Burma; The Mummy's Hand. **1941** The Sea Wolf; South of Tahiti; Jungle Girl (serial). **1942** Don Winslow of the Navy (serial); Bombs Over Burma; All Work and No Pay (short). **1943** Chetniks; Frontier Badmen. **1944** The Desert Hawk (serial); Moonlight and Cactus. **1945** Frontier Gal; Under Western Skies. **1946** A Bird in the Head (short). **1947** Oregon Trail Scouts; Singin' in the Corn. **1948** Man-Eater of Kumoan. **1949** The Cowboy and the Indians; Amazon Quest; Daughter of the Jungle; Son of the Badman; The Mysterious Desperado; Malice in the Palace (short). **1950** Indian Territory. **1951** Flaming Feather. **1953** King of the Khyber Rifles; Northern Patrol. **1955** Devil Goddess; Of Cash and Hash (short). **1956** Flesh and the Spur; The Ten Commandments. **1959** The Atomic Submarine. **1960** Three Came to Kill. **1962** The Underwater City. **1965** Requiem for a Gunfighter; The Bounty Killer.

LADD, ALAN
Born: Sept. 3, 1913, Hot Springs, Ark. Died: Jan. 29, 1964, Palm Springs, Calif. (accidental death). Screen, television and radio actor. Divorced from Marjorie June Harrold (dec. 1957). Married to actress Sue Carol (dec. 1982) and father of actor David, Alma and producer Alan Ladd, Jr.

Appeared in: **1932** Once in a Lifetime. **1936** Pigskin Parade. **1937** Last Train from Madrid; Souls at Sea; Hold 'Em Navy. **1938** Born to the West; The Goldwyn Follies; Freshman Year; Come on Leathernecks. **1939** Green Hornet; Rulers of the Sea; Beasts of Berlin. **1940** Light of Western Stars; In Old Missouri; Meet the Missus; Captain Caution; Her First Romance; Gangs of Chicago; Howards of Virginia; Those Were the Days; Wildcat Bus. **1941** The Reluctant Dragon; Paper Bullets; Citizen Kane; Great Guns; Cadet Girl; Petticoat Politics; The Black Cat. **1942** This Gun for Hire; Joan of Paris; The Glass Key; Star Spangled Rhythm; Lucky Jordan. **1943** China; Hollywood Uniform (short). **1944** And Now Tomorrow; Skirmish on the Home Front (short); Salty O'Rourke. **1945** Duffy's Tavern; Hollywood Victory; Caravan. **1946** Two Years Before the Mast; Blue Dahlia; O.S.S. **1947** Wild Harvest; Variety Girl; Calcutta; My Favorite Brunette. **1948** Saigon; Beyond Glory; Whispering Smith. **1949** Great Gatsby; Chicago Deadline; Eyes of Hollywood (short); Variety Club Hospital (trailer). **1950** Captain Carey, U.S.A.; Branded; Quantrell's Raiders. **1951** Appointment With Danger; Red Mountain. **1952** The Iron Mistress. **1953** Shane; Thunder in the East; Botany Bay; Desert Legion; The Red Beret (aka Paratrooper—US 1954). **1954** Hell Below Zero; Saskatchewan; The Black Knight; Drum Beat. **1955** The McConnell Story; The Long Gray Line; Hell on Frisco Bay. **1956** Santiago. **1957** The Big Land; Boy on a Dolphin. **1958** The Deep Six; The Proud Rebel; The Badlanders. **1959** The Man in the Net. **1960** Guns of the Timberland; One Foot in Hell; All the Young Men. **1961** Orazio Orazi E Curiazi (aka Duel of Champions—US 1964). **1963** 13 West Street. **1964** The Carpetbaggers. **1982** Dead Men Don't Wear Plaid (film clips).

LADD, WALTER S. (Walter Schuyler Ladd)
Born: 1877. Died: Apr. 14, 1961, Alhambra, Calif. Screen and stage actor. Appeared in early Metro films.

Appeared in: **1921** Land of Hope.

LA DEAUX, EVELYN
Born: 1905. Died: Mar., 1944, Philadelphia, Pa. (coronary thrombosis). Screen actress.

LADMIRAL, NICOLE
Born: 1931, France. Died: Apr., 1958, Paris, France (fell or jumped under subway train?). Stage and screen actress.

Appeared in: **1954** The Diary of a Country Priest.

LADY BEERBOHM See KAHN, FLORENCE

LADY MENDL See DE WOLFE, ELSIE

LADY PLAYFAIR See MARTYN, MAY

LAEMMLE, CARL, SR.
Born: Jan. 17, 1867, Laupheim, Wurtemburg, Germany. Died: Sept. 24, 1939, Beverly Hills, Calif. (heart attack). Film producer and screen actor.

Appeared in: **1914** Love and Vengeance. **1915** The Broken Coin; Cy Perkins in the City of Delusions. **1929** Show Boat (gave a short speech in an 18-minute prologue).

LAFAYETTE, RUBY
Born: July 22, 1844. Died: Apr. 3, 1935, Bell, Calif. Screen and stage actress. Married to stage actor John Curran (dec. 1918). Entered films approx. 1917.

Appeared in: **1918** My Mother. **1919** The Miracle Man; Toby's Bow. **1922** Borderland; Catch My Smoke; The Power of a Lie. **1923** The Day of Faith; Hollywood. **1924** Idle Tongues; The Phantom Horseman. **1925** The Coming of Amos; The Wedding Song; Tomorrow's Love. **1926** Butterflies in the Rain. **1928** Mother O' Mine; Marriage By Contract. **1930** Not So Dumb.

LA FLEUR, JOY
Born: 1914, Canada. Died: Nov. 6, 1957, Los Angeles, Calif. Screen, stage, radio and television actress.

Appeared in: **1948** Whispering City. **1956** D-Day the Sixth of June.

LA GARDE, JOCELYN
Born: 1924, Tahiti. Died: Sept. 12, 1979, Papeete, Tahiti. Screen actress.

Appeared in: **1966** Hawaii.

LAGRANCE, MAURICE
Born: France. Died: 1955, France? Screen actor.

Appeared in: **1949** Devil in the Flesh.

LAGRANGE, LOUISE
Born: France. Died: Mar., 1979, France? Screen actress.

Appeared in: **1924** The Side Show of Life; A Sainted Devil. **1929** La Marche Nuptiale.

LAHR, BERT (Irving Lahrheim)
Born: Aug. 13, 1895, New York, N.Y. Died: Dec. 4, 1967, New York, N.Y. (internal hemorrhage). Screen, stage, television, vaudeville and burlesque actor. Married to actress Mercedes Lahr (dec. 1965).

Appeared in: **1929** Faint Heart (short). **1931** Flying High. **1933** Mr. Broadway. **1934** Hizzoner (short). **1936** Gold Bricks (short). **1937** Merry-Go-Round of 1938; Love and Hisses. **1938** Josette; Just Around the Corner. **1939** Wizard of Oz; Zaza. **1940** DuBarry Was a Lady. **1942** Sing Your Worries Away; Ship Ahoy. **1944** Meet the People. **1949** Always Leave Them Laughing. **1951** Mr. Universe. **1954** Rose Marie. **1955** The Second Greatest Sex. **1962** Ten Girls Ago. **1963** The Sound of Laughter (documentary). **1964** Big Parade of Comedy (documentary). **1965** The Fantasticks. **1968** The Night They Raided Minskey's. **1974** That's Entertainment (film clips).

LAHR, MERCEDES
Born: 1898. Died: May 12, 1965, Tucson, Ariz. Screen and vaudeville actress. Married to actor Bert Lahr (dec. 1967).

LAHTINEN, WARNER H. "DUKE"
Born: 1910. Died: Dec. 12, 1968, Minneapolis, Minn. Screen and stage actor.

LAIDLAW, ETHAN
Born: Nov. 25, 1899, Butte, Mont. Died: May 25, 1963. Screen actor. Entered films in 1923.

Appeared in: **1925** The Wyoming Wildcat; No Man's Law; Crack O'Dawn; Makers of Men. **1926** Born to Battle; Is That Nice?; Racing Romance; Out of the West; Dangerous Traffic; The Masquerade Bandit; Wild to Go. **1927** The Sonora Kid; Wolf's Clothing; When Danger Calls; Breed of Courage; The Silent Rider; Thunderbolt's Tracks. **1928** The Big Killing; Bitter Sweets; Rough Ridin' Red; Danger Patrol; The Riding Renegade. **1929** Big Diamond Robbery; Laughing at Death; The Little Savage; Outlawed; Bride of the Desert.

1930 Pardon My Gun. 1931 A Melon Drama (short); Monkey Business. 1933 Gordon of Ghost City (serial). 1934 Pirate Treasure (serial); The Mighty Barnum. 1935 Powdersmoke Range. 1936 Silly Billies; Yellow Dust; Special Investigator; Two in Revolt; The Sea Spoilers; Mummy's Boys. 1937 Goofs and Saddles (short). 1938 Rhythm of the Saddle; I'm From the City; Border G-Man. 1939 Home on the Prairie; The Night Riders; Cowboys from Texas; Western Caravans; Three Texas Steers. 1940 The Marines Fly High; Son of Roaring Dan; The Tulsa Kid; Wagon Train; Stage to Chino; Law and Order. 1941 Westward Ho-Hum (short); Law of the Range; The Lone Star Vigilantes. 1942 Stagecoach Express; Cowboy Serenade. 1943 Riding Through Nevada; Border Buckaroos; The Desperados; Fugitive from Sonora. 1944 Marshal of Gunsmoke; Oklahoma Raiders. 1945 Lawless Empire; Blazing the Western Trail. 1946 Three Troubledoers (short). 1947 Rustler's Round-Up; Singin' in the Corn. 1948 Six-Gun Law; Buckaroo from Powder River; Joan of Arc. 1950 The Great Missouri Raid; Traveling Saleswoman. 1951 Flaming Feather. 1952 Against All Flags; Montana Territory. 1953 Powder River. 1956 The Ten Commandments.

LAIDLAW, ROY
Born: Mar. 25, 1883, Comber, Ontario, Canada. Died: Feb. 2, 1936, Hollywood, Calif. (heart attack). Screen, stage actor and make-up artist.

Appeared in: 1916 Female of the Species; The Patriot. 1917 The Gun Fighter. 1918 Honor's Cross; With Hoops of Steel; His Robe of Honor. 1919 Back to God's Country. 1920 The Great Accident; Live Sparks; The Weaker Sex. 1921 The Cowpuncher; The Ace of Hearts; The Poverty of Riches. 1923 Fools and Riches; Hunchback of Notre Dame. 1924 The Snob; The Gaiety Girl. 1925 Never Too Late; The Ridin' Streak; When the Door Opened; The Splendid Road; When Romance Rides; The White Desert. 1926 Beyond the Rockies; Bred in Old Kentucky; Is That Nice?; The Devil's Gulch; Modern Youth. 1927 Cactus Trails; Not for Publication; God's Great Wilderness. 1928 The Wild West Show.

LAING, CAPTAIN ALFRED BENSON
Born: 1890? Died: Aug. 3, 1976, Hollywood, Calif. (emphysema). Screen actor and writer. Entered films during the silents.

LAIR, GRACE (Grace Gaylor)
Died: Jan. 5, 1955, Cleveland, Ohio. Screen, stage actress and singer. Was the original "Coca-Cola Girl" in Coca Cola's advertising.

LAIRD, KENNETH
Born: 1921, England. Died: May 20, 1980, Sydney, Australia. Screen, stage actor and publisher.

LAIRE, JUDSON
Born: 1903, New York, N.Y. Died: July 5, 1979, Rhinebeck, N.Y. Screen, stage and television actor.

Appeared in: 1963 The Ugly American. 1964 Shock Treatment.

LAIT, JACK (Jacquin Leonard Lait)
Born: Mar. 13, 1883, New York, N.Y. Died: Apr. 1, 1954, Beverly Hills, Calif. (ciculatory ailment). Newspaperman, screenwriter, author and screen actor.

Appeared in: 1932 Madison Square Garden.

LAITE, CHARLES
Born: 1886. Died: Feb. 17, 1937, Cleveland, Ohio (heart attack). Screen and stage actor.

Appeared in: 1915 An Affair of Three Nations; The Menace of the Mute.

LA JANA (Henriette Margarethe Hiebel)
Born: 1905, Berlin, Germany. Died: 1940, Berlin, Germany. Screen actress and dancer. Married to actor Michael Bohnen (dec. 1965).

Appeared in: 1926 Die Weisse Geisha. 1927 Gaunerliebchen. 1928 Der Biberpelz (The Beaver Coat); Der Herzensphotograph; Der Ladenprinz; Ritter der Nacht; Zwei Rote Rosen; Du Sollst Nicht Ehebrechen! (aka Therese Raquin); Shadows of Fear. 1929 Der Lustige Witwer; Meineid. 1931 Der Schlemihl (US 1934). 1936 Truxa (US 1937). 1938 Die Warschauer Zitadelle; Es Leuchten die Sterne; Das Indische Grabmal (The Indian Tomb, including Der Tiger von Eschnapur). 1939 Menschen vom Variete. 1940 Stern von Rio.

LAKE, ALICE
Born: Brooklyn, N.Y. Died: Nov. 15, 1967, Paradise, Calif. (heart attack). Screen actress.

Appeared in: 1912 Her Picture Idol. 1915 The Boarding House Feud. 1916 The Moonshiners; The Waiter's Ball; A Creampuff Romance (sometimes referred to as His Alibi). 1917 Her Nature Dance; The Butcher Boy; His Wedding Night; Oh, Doctor; Come Through. 1918 Out West; Coney Island; Goodnight Nurse; Moonshine; The Cook. 1919 Cupid's Day Off; A Desert Hero; Backstage; A Country Hero; The Garage. 1920 Shore Acres; Should a Woman Talk? 1921 Broken Hearts of Broadway; Body and Soul; The Greater Claim; Uncharted Seas; A Hole in the Wall; Over the Wire; The Infamous Miss Revell. 1922 The Golden Gift; Hate; Kisses; Environment; I Am the Law; More to Be Pitied Than Scorned. 1923 The Spider and the Rose; Red Lights; The Unknown Purple; The Marriage Market; Modern Matrimony; Souls for Sale; Nobody's Bride. 1924 The Dancing Cheat; The Law and the Lady; The Virgin. 1925 Broken Homes; The Hurricane; The Wives of the Prophet. 1927 The Angel of Broadway; Roaring Fires; The Haunted Ship; Spider Webs. 1928 Obey Your Husband; Women Men Like; Runaway Girls. 1929 Untamed Justice; Circumstantial Evidence; Twin Beds; Frozen Justice. 1930 Dining Out (short); I'll Fix It (short); Young Desire. 1931 Wicked. 1933 Skyward. 1934 Wharf Angel; Glamour; The Mighty Barnum; Broadway Bill.

LAKE, FLORENCE
Born: 1905, Charleston, S.C. Died: Apr. 11, 1980, Woodland Hills, Calif. Screen, radio actress and screenwriter. Sister of actor Arthur Lake.

Appeared in: 1929 Thru Different Eyes; New Year's Eve; Waltzing Around (short). 1930 The Rogue Song; Romance. 1931 Drums of Jeopardy; Secret Service; plus the following shorts: Rough House Rhythm; Lemon Meringue; Thanks Again; Camping Out. 1932 Night World; Ladies of the Jury; plus the following shorts: Bon Voyage; Mother-in-Law's Day; Parlor, Bedroom, and Wrath; Giggle Water; The Golf Chump; Fish Feathers. 1933 Sweetheart of Sigma Chi; Midshipman Jack; plus the following shorts: Art in the Raw; The Merchant of Menace; Good Housewrecking; Quiet, Please; What Fur; Grin and Bear It. 1934 The following shorts: Love on a Ladder; Wrong Direction; In-Law's Are Out; A Blasted Event; Poisoned Ivory; Shivers. 1935 Two Fisted; plus the following shorts: Bric-A-Brac; South Seasickness; Sock Me to Sleep; Edgar Hamlet; In Love at 40; Happy Tho Married. 1936 To Mary—With Love; plus the following shorts: Gasoloons; Will Power; High Beer Pressure; Dummy Ache. 1937 Quality Street; Love in a Bungalow; Edgar and Goliath (short). 1938 I Met My Love Again; Convicts at Large; Condemned Women; Ears of Experience (short). 1939 Stage Coach. 1942 Scattergood Survives a Murder; plus the following shorts: Two for the Money; Rough on Rents; Duck Soup. 1943 Crash Dive. 1944 San Diego, I Love You; Goin' to Town; Hi, Beautiful; plus the following shorts: Love Your Landlord; Radio Rampage; The Kitchen Cynic; Feather Your Nest. 1945 The following shorts: Alibi Baby; Sleepless Tuesday; What, No Cigarettes?; It's Your Move; You Drive Me Crazy; The Big Beef; Mother-in-Law's Day. 1946 Little Giant; plus the following shorts: Trouble or Nothing; Wall Street Blues; Motor Maniacs; Noisy Neighbors; I'll Build It Myself; Social Terrors. 1947 The following shorts: Do or Diet; Heading for Trouble; Host to a Ghost; Television Turmoil; Mind Over Mouse; All Gummed Up. 1948 Variety Time; plus the following shorts: Brother Knows Best; No More Relatives; Home Canning; Contest Crazy; How to Clean a House; Dig That Gold. 1952 Fargo; Man from the Black Hills; The Maverick. 1953 Fresh Painter (short). 1954 Bitter Creek; The Desperado. 1975 The Day of the Locust.

LAKE, FRANK
Born: 1849. Died: Apr. 19, 1936, Los Angeles, Calif. Screen actor.

Appeared in: 1930 The Rogue Song.

LAKE, HARRY
Born: 1885. Died: Mar. 4, 1947, Chicago, Ill. Screen actor.

LAKE, JOHN (John W. Laycock)
Born: 1904, Leesburg, Va. Died: June 28, 1960, Saranac Lake, N.Y. (tuberculosis). Screen and radio actor.

LAKE, LEW
Born: 1874, England. Died: Nov. 5, 1939, London, England. Screen and stage actor.

Appeared in: 1929 Splinters. 1931 Splinters in the Navy. 1937 Splinters in the Air.

LAKE, VERONICA (Constance Ockelman aka CONSTANCE KEANE)
Born: Nov. 15, 1921, Brooklyn, N.Y. Died: July 7, 1973, Burlington, Vt. (acute hepatitis). Screen, stage actress and author. Divorced from film director Andre De Toth, art film director John Detlie, music publisher Joseph A. McCarthy and Robert Carleton Munro.

Appeared in: **1939** All Women Have Secrets; Wrong Room (short); Sorority House. **1940** Young as You Feel; Forty Little Mothers. **1941** I Wanted Wings; Sullivan's Travels; Hold Back the Dawn. **1942** This Gun for Hire; I Married a Witch; The Glass Key; Star Spangled Rhythm. **1943** So Proudly We Hail. **1944** The Hour Before the Dawn. **1945** Bring on the Girls; Leave It to Blondie; Hold That Blonde; Duffy's Tavern; Out of This World; Miss Susie Slagle's. **1946** The Blue Dahlia. **1947** Ramrod; Variety Girl. **1948** Saigon; The Sainted Sisters; Isn't It Romantic. **1949** Slattery's Hurricane. **1952** Stronghold. **1966** Footsteps in the Snow. **1970** Flesh Feast. **1982** Dead Men Don't Wear Plaid (film clips).

LALOR, FRANK
Born: Aug. 20, 1869, Washington, D.C. Died: Oct. 15, 1932, New York, N.Y. (acute indigestion). Screen, stage and vaudeville actor.

Appeared in: **1917** In Again—Out Again. **1922** Red Hot Romance; Polly of the Follies.

LAMAIRE, WILLIAM
Born: 1892. Died: Nov. 11, 1933, Hollywood, Calif. Screen actor.

LAMARR, BARBARA (Reatha Watson aka FOLLY LYTELL)
Born: July 28, 1896, North Yakima, Wash. Died: Jan. 30, 1926, Altadena, Calif. (overdieting). Screen, stage actress, screenwriter and cabaret artist. Married to Cowboy Jack Lytell (dec. 1914), lawyer Larence Converse (dec. 1914), dancer Ben Deely (dec. 1923) and actor Jack Dougherty (dec. 1938). Divorced from performer Phil Ainsworth.

Appeared in: **1920** Harriet and the Piper. **1921** Desperate Trails; The Nut; Cinderella of the Hills; The Three Musketeers. **1922** Poor Men's Wives; Trifling Women; The Prisoner of Zenda; Quincy Adams Sawyer; Arabian Love; Domestic Relations. **1923** The Eternal Struggle; Strangers of the Night; The Eternal City; The Brass Bottle; The Hero; St. Elmo; Mary of the Movies. **1924** The Name Is Woman; The White Moth; The Shooting of Dan McGrew; My Husband's Wives; The White Monkey; Sandra. **1925** The Heart of a Siren; The Girl from Montmartre.

LA MARR, LAURENCE F.
Died: Oct. 28, 1973. Screen actor.

Appeared in: **1931** Lawyer's Secret. **1941** Sundown. **1963** Living Between Two Worlds.

LAMARR, RICHARD
Died: Apr. 24, 1975. Screen actor, stuntman and stand-in.

LAMB, FLORENCE
Born: 1884. Died: May 9, 1966. Screen actress.

LAMBERT, ALBERT
Born: France. Died: Aug., 1918, Paris, France. Screen and stage actor.

Appeared in: **1908** Assassination of the Duc de Guise.

LAMBERT, CLARA
Died: 1921. Screen actress. Married to actor James L. Daly (dec. 1933).

LAMBERT, GLEN (Lucian Glen Lambert)
Born: Jan. 28, 1894 or 1896, Richmond, Va. Died: Dec. 9, 1973, Jacksonville Beach, Fla. Screen, stage, vaudeville actor, film director, film producer and writer. Appeared in early Crystal, Solax and Biograph films.

LAMBERT, JANE
Died: July 6, 1980. Screen actress.

Appeared in: **1974** The Harrad Summer. **1978** The Fury.

LAMBERTI, PROFESSOR (Michael Lamberti)
Died: Mar. 13, 1950, Hollywood, Calif. Screen, stage and vaudeville actor.

Appeared in: **1945** Tonight and Every Night. **1946** The Gay Intruders. **1947** Linda Be Good.

LA MONT, HARRY (Alfred Gilbert)
Born: June 17, 1887, New York, N.Y. Died: May 8, 1957, Venice, Calif. Screen, stage, vaudeville and radio actor.

Appeared in: **1915** A Tale of Two Cities (film debut). **1920** Fazil. **1922** Blood and Sand; Peaceful Peters. **1923** Robin Hood, Jr. **1928** Two Lovers; Romance in the Dark. **1938** Artists and Models Abroad; Romance in the Dark. **1942** The Black Swan; China Girl. **1945** House of Dracula. **1947** San Antonio; Slave Girl; Pursued.

LAMONT, JACK (Jack Capitola)
Born: 1893. Died: Feb. 28, 1956, Cleveland, Ohio (heart attack). Screen, stage and burlesque actor. Appeared in silents and was in several "Keystone Kop" comedies.

LAMOURET, ROBERT
Died: Mar. 16, 1959. Screen actor and ventriloquist.

Appeared in: **1949** Make Mine Laughs.

LAMPTON, DEE
Born: 1898, Ft. Worth, Tex. Died: Sept. 2, 1919, New York, N.Y. (appendicitis). Screen and stage actress.

Appeared in: **1915** A Night in a Show. **1917** Them Were the Happy Days; Lonesome Luke series.

LAMY, DOUGLAS N. *See* MITCHELL, JOHN

LANCASTER, ANN
Born: 1920. Died: Oct. 31, 1970, London, England. Screen, stage, television and radio actress.

Appeared in: **1952** Angels One Five (US 1954). **1965** The Secret of My Success. **1967** Fathom; Three Bites of the Apple. **1968** Hot Millions; Inadmissible Evidence; Decline and Fall ... of a Birdwatcher! (US 1969). **1969** A Nice Girl Like Me.

LANCASTER, JOHN
Born: 1857, Richmond, Va. Died: Oct. 11, 1935, Washington, D.C. Screen actor and circus performer.

Appeared in: **1912** The Katzenjammer Kids. **1913** Sweeney and the Million; Alas! Poor Yorick.

LANDAU, DAVID
Born: 1878. Died: Sept. 20, 1935, Hollywood, Calif. Screen and stage actor.

Appeared in: **1931** Street Scene; Arrowsmith. **1932** I Am a Fugitive from a Chain Gang; Union Depot; Taxi; This Reckless Age; 70,000 Witnesses; Under Cover Man; Polly of the Circus; It's Tough to Be Famous; Amateur Daddy; Roadhouse Murder; The Purchase Price; Horse Feathers; Air Mail; False Faces; Lawyer Man. **1933** Heritage of the Desert; She Done Him Wrong; The Crime of the Century; One Man's Journey; Gabriel Over the White House; The Nuisance; No Marriage Ties; They Just Had to Get Married. **1934** As the Earth Turns; Judge Priest; Bedside; Wharf Angel; The Man With Two Faces; Death on the Diamond.

LANDERS, MURIEL
Born: 1921. Died: Feb. 19, 1977, Woodland Hills, Calif. (illness following stroke). Screen, television actress and nightclub entertainer. Sister of actress Janis Davies.

Appeared in: **1952** Pony Soldier. **1958** Sweet and Hot (short). **1959** Pillow Talk. **1967** Dr. Dolittle.

LANDI, ELISSA (Elizabeth Marie Zanardi-Landi)
Born: Dec. 6, 1904, Venice, Italy. Died: Oct. 21, 1948, Kingston, N.Y. (cancer). Screen, stage, radio actress and novelist.

Appeared in: **1926** London. **1928** Bolibar (aka The Marquis of Bolibar); Underground. **1929** The Inseperables; The Betrayal. **1930** Knowing Men; The Price of Things; Children of Chance. **1931** Body and Soul; Sin; Always Goodbye; Wicked; The Yellow Ticket; She Parisian. **1932** Devil's Lottery; Woman in Room 13; A Passport to Hell; Sign of the Cross. **1933** The Masquerader; The Warrior's Husband; I Loved You Wednesday. **1934** Man of Two Worlds; By Candlelight; The Count of Monte Cristo; The Great Flirtation; Sisters Under the Skin. **1935** Koenigsmark; Enter Madame; Without Regrets. **1936** The Amateur Gentleman; Mad Holiday; After the Thin Man. **1937** The Thirteenth Chair. **1943** Corregidor. **1944** The Sign of the Cross (revised version of 1932 film).

LANDICK, OLIN
Born: 1895. Died: Mar. 26, 1972, New York, N.Y. Screen, radio and television actor.

Appeared in: **1930** All Stuck Up (short).

LANDIN, HOPE
Born: 1893, Minneapolis, Minn. Died: Feb. 28, 1973, Hollywood, Calif. Screen and stage actress.

Appeared in: **1941** Where Did You Get That Girl? **1942** Reap the Wild Wind. **1943** Gangway for Tomorrow; Dixie. **1944** Sweet and Lowdown; Three Men in White; Bridge of San Luis Rey. **1945** Where Do We Go from Here?; Weekend at the Waldorf; George White's Scandals; The Great John L. **1946** The Mask of Dijon; The Dark Corner; Gas House Kids. **1947** Unconquered. **1948** I Remember Mama (stage and film versions); The Walls of Jericho. **1949** The Sun Comes Up. **1951** Sugarfoot. **1952** Scaramouche. **1953** How to Marry a Millionaire. **1954** She Couldn't Say No (aka She Had to Say Yes). **1955** New York Confidential. **1965** The Greatest Story Ever Told.

LANDIS, CAROLE (Frances Ridste)
Born: Jan. 1, 1919, Fairchild, Wis. Died: July 5, 1948, Brentwood Heights, Calif. (suicide). Stage and screen actress. The screen's original "Sweater Girl."

Appeared in: **1937** A Day at the Races; The Emperor's Candlesticks; Broadway Melody of 1938; Varsity Show; Adventurous Blonde; Hollywood Hotel; A Star Is Born. **1938** Girls on Probation; Golddiggers in Paris; Four's A Crowd; Blondes at Work; Boy Meets Girl; Men Are Such Fools; Over the Wall; When Were You Born? **1939** Daredevils of the Red Circle (serial); Three Texas Steers; Cowboys from Texas. **1940** Mystery Sea Raider; One Million, B.C.; Turnabout. **1941** I Wake Up Screaming (aka Hot Spot); Topper Returns; Dance Hall; Cadet Girl; Road Show; Moon Over Miami. **1942** A Gentleman at Heart; The Power's Girl; My Gal Sal; Orchestra Wives; It Happened in Flatbush; Manila Calling. **1943** Screen Snapshot #2 (short); Wintertime. **1944** Secret Command; Four Jills in a Jeep. **1945** Having a Wonderful Crime; Behind Green Lights. **1946** It Shouldn't Happen to a Dog; A Scandal in Paris. **1947** Out of the Blue. **1948** The Brass Monkey (aka The Lucky Mascot—US 1951); Noose (aka The Silk Noose—US 1950).

LANDIS, CULLEN
Born: July 19, 1898, Nashville, Tenn. Died: Aug. 26, 1975, Bloomfield Hills, Mich. Screen, stage actor, film director and later became director-producer of industrial films and war documentaries. Divorced from actress Minon LeBrun (dec. 1941).

Appeared in: **1916** Joy and the Dragon. **1917** The Checkmate; Who Is Number One (serial). **1918** What Will Father Say?; Her Friend—the Enemy; All Kinds of a Girl; Beware of Blondes. **1919** The Outcasts of Poker Flat; The Girl from Outside; Almost a Husband; Where the West Begins; Upstairs; Jinx. **1920** It's A Great Life; Pinto; Going Some. **1921** Bunty Pulls the Strings; Snowblind; The Infamous Miss Revell; The Night Rose; The Old Nest. **1922** Remembrance; Watch Your Step; Where Is My Wandering Boy Tonight?; Forsaking All Others; Gay and Devilish; Love in the Dark; The Man With Two Mothers; Youth to Youth. **1923** The Famous Mrs. Fair; Masters of Men; Pioneer Trails; Soul of the Beast; Dollar Devils; Crashin' Thru; The Fog; The Man Life Passed By; The Midnight Alarm. **1924** The Fighting Coward; Born Rich; Cheap Kisses; A Girl of the Limberlost; One Law for the Woman. **1925** A Broadway Butterfly; Easy Money; The Mansion of Aching Hearts; The Midnight Flyer; Pampered Youth; Peacock Feathers; Wasted Lives; Sealed Lips. **1926** Buffalo Bill on the U.P. Trail; Christine of the Big Tops; Davy Crockett at the Fall of the Alamo; The Dixie Flyer; Frenzied Flames; Jack O'Hearts; My Old Dutch; Perils of the Coast Guard; The Smoke Eaters; Sweet Rosie O'Grady; Then Came the Woman; Winning the Futurity. **1927** The Fighting Failure; Broadway After Midnight; Finnegan's Ball; Heroes of the Night; We're All Gamblers; The Crimson Flash (serial); On Guard (serial). **1928** The Broken Mask; Lights of New York; The Devil's Skipper; The Little Wild Girl; A Midnight Adventure; On to Reno; Out with the Tide. **1930** The Convict's Code.

LANDIS, JESSIE ROYCE (Jessie Royce Medbury)
Born: Nov. 25, 1904, Chicago, Ill. Died: Feb. 2, 1972, Danbury, Conn. (cancer). Screen, stage and television actress.

Appeared in: **1930** Derelict. **1937** Oh, Doctor! **1939** First Love. **1949** It Happens Every Spring; Mr. Belvedere Goes to College; My Foolish Heart. **1950** Mother Didn't Tell Me. **1952** Meet Me Tonight. **1953** Tonight at Eight-Thirty. **1954** She Couldn't Say No. **1955** To Catch a Thief. **1956** The Girl He Left Behind; The Swan. **1957** My Man Godfrey. **1958** I Married a Woman. **1959** A Private Affair; North By Northwest. **1961** Goodbye Again. **1962** Boys' Night Out; Bon Voyage! **1963** Critic's Choice; Gidget Goes to Rome. **1970** Airport.

LANDONE, AVICE
Born: Sept. 1, 1910, India. Died: June, 1976, London, England. Screen and stage actress. Married to actor Bruno Barnabe.

Appeared in: **1948** My Brother Jonathan (US 1949). **1951** The Franchise Affair (US 1952). **1955** An Alligator Named Daisy (US 1957). **1956** My Teenage Daughter (aka Teenage Bad Girl—US 1957); Reach for the Sky (US 1957). **1957** True as a Turtle. **1958** Carve Her Name With Pride; A Cry From the Streets (US 1959); Family Doctor (aka Prescription for Murder, and aka RX Murder—US); The Wind Cannot Read (US 1960). **1960** Operation Cupid. **1961** Five Golden Hours. **1963** The Leather Boys (US 1965); Nothing But the Best (US 1964); This is My Street (US 1964). **1969** Two Gentlemen Sharing.

LANDRETH, GERTRUDE GRIFFITH
Born: 1897, New York, N.Y. Died: Nov. 25, 1969, Palo Alto, Calif. Screen and vaudeville actress. Appeared in silent films and was in several "Keystone" comedies. She founded the Hollywood Studio Club, a home for aspiring actresses.

LANE, ADELE
Born: July 17, 1877, N.J. Died: Oct. 23, 1957, Los Angeles, Calif. Screen actress. Married to actor/director Burton King (dec. 1944). Do not confuse with British actress Adile Lane (dec. 1962).

Appeared in: The Family Secret (aka Editha's Burglar).

LANE, ALLAN "ROCKY" (Harry Albershart)
Born: c. 1901 or 1904?, Mishawaka, Ind. Died: Oct. 27, 1973, Woodland Hills, Calif. (bone marrow disorder). Screen, stage, television actor and professional football player. Was the voice of "Mr. Ed" in the television series of same name.

Appeared in: **1929** Not Quite Decent; The Forward Pass; Knights Out (short); Detectives Wanted (short). **1930** Madam Satan; Love in the Rough. **1931** Night Nurse; Honor of the Family; Expensive Women; War Mamas (short). **1932** Winner Take All; Miss Pinkerton; The Tenderfoot; Heavens! My Husband (short). **1936** Stowaway. **1937** Charlie Chan at the Olympics; Big Business; Fifty Roads to Town; Sing and Be Happy; Laughing at Trouble; The Duke Comes Back. **1938** Crime Ring; Fugitives for a Night; The Law West of Tombstone; Night Spot; Maid's Night Out; This Marriage Business; Having a Wonderful Time. **1939** Pacific Liner; Twelve Crowded Hours; They Made Her a Spy; Conspiracy; The Spellbinder; Panama Lady. **1940** Grande Ole Opry; King of the Royal Mounted (serial). **1941** All-American Coed. **1942** King of the Mounties (serial); Yukon Patrol. **1943** Daredevils of the West (serial); The Dancing Masters. **1944** Tiger Woman (serial); Call of the South Seas; Stagecoach to Monterey; Sheriff of Sundown; The Silver City Kid. **1945** Bells of Rosarita; Corpus Christi Bandits; The Topeka Terror; Trail of Kit Carson. **1946** Gay Blades; A Guy Could Change; Night Train to Memphis; Out California Way; Santa Fe Uprising; Stagecoach to Denver. **1947** Homesteaders of Paradise Valley; Vigilantes of Boomtown; Oregon Trail Scouts; Marshal of Cripple Creek; Rustlers of Devil's Canyon; Bandits of Dark Canyon; The Wild Frontier. **1948** Bold Frontiersman; Oklahoma Badlands; Carson City Raiders; Desperadoes of Dodge City; Marshal of Amarillo; The Denver Kid; Sundown at Santa Fe; Renegades of Sonora. **1949** Bandit King of Texas; Death Valley Gunfighter; Frontier Investigator; Navajo Trail Raiders; Powder River Rustlers; Sheriff of Wichita; The Wyoming Bandit. **1950** Covered Wagon Raiders; Frisco Tornado; Gunmen of Abilene; Rustlers on Horseback; Salt Lake Raiders; Vigilante Hideout; Trail of Robin Hood; Code of the Silver Sage. **1951** Desert of Lost Men; Fort Dodge Stampede; Night Raiders of Montana; Night Riders of Durango; Wells Fargo Gunmaster. **1952** Black Hills Ambush; Desperadoes' Outpost; Leadville Gunslinger; Thundering Caravans; Captive of Billy the Kid. **1953** Savage Frontier; Marshal of Cedar Rock; Bandits of the West; El Paso Stampede. **1958** The Saga of Hemp Brown. **1960** Hell Bent for Leather. **1961** Posse from Hell.

LANE, CHARLES (Charles Willis Lane)
Born: Jan. 25, 1869, Madison, Ill. Died: Oct. 17, 1945, Van Nuys, Calif. (cancer). Stage and screen actor. Do not confuse with actor Charles Lane who was born approximately 1905.

Appeared in: **1921** If Women Only Knew; Without Limit; Love's Penalty. **1922** Fascination; How Women Love; Broadway Rose. **1923** The Tents of Allah; The White Sister. **1924** Second Youth. **1925** The Dark Angel; I Want My Man; The Marriage Whirl; Romola; The Pearl of Love. **1926** Padlocked; The Winning of Barbara Worth; The Blind Goddess; The Outsider; Marriage License?; The Mystery Club. **1927** Barbed Wire; Married Alive; Service for Ladies; The Whirlwind of Youth; The Music Master. **1928** Sadie Thompson. **1929** Saturday's Children; The Canary Murder Case.

LANE, DOROTHY
Born: 1905. Died: Oct. 7, 1923, New York, N.Y. (heart disease). Screen actress and dancer.

LANE, GRACE
Born: Jan. 13, 1876, England. Died: Jan. 14, 1956, Hove, England. Screen, stage actress and stage producer. Married to stage actor Kenneth Douglas (dec. 1923).

Appeared in: **1929** Taxi for Two; The Feather.

LANE, HARRY
Born: 1910. Died: July, 1960, London, England. Screen, stage and television actor.

Appeared in: **1946** Appointment With Crime (US 1950). **1950** My Daughter Jay (aka Operation X—US 1951). **1951** Old Mother Riley's Jungle Treasure. **1953** Watch Out! **1954** Malaga (aka Fire Over Africa—US). **1959** The Night We Dropped a Clanger (aka Make Mine a Double—US 1961). **1960** Too Hot to Handle (aka Playgirl After Dark—US 1962).

LANE, LOLA (Dorothy Mulligan)
Born: May 21, 1906, Macy, Ind. Died: June 22, 1981, Santa Barbara, Calif. (inflamation of the arteries). Screen, stage and vaudeville actress. Sister of Martha Mulligan (dec.), singer Leota (dec. 1963), and actresses Rosemary (dec. 1974) and Pricilla Lane. Divorced from actor Lew Ayres, directors Alexander Hall and Henry Dunham, and Roland West. Later married to businessman Robert Hanlon.

Appeared in: **1929** Speakeasy (film debut); Fox Movietone Follies of 1929; The Girl from Havana; The Case of Lena Smith. **1930** The Big Fight; Good News; Let's Go Places; The Costello Case. **1931** Hell Bound; Ex-Bad Boy. **1934** Ticket to a Crime; Public Stenographer; Burn 'Em Up Barnes (serial); Woman Condemned; Woman Who Dared. **1935** Death From a Distance; Murder on a Honeymoon; Port of Lost Dreams; Alias Mary Dow; The Costello Case. Burn 'Em Up Barnes (feature of 1934 serial). **1936** In Paris A.W.O.L. **1937** Marked Woman; The Sheik Steps Out; Hollywood Hotel. **1938** Torchy Blane in Panama; Four Daughters; When Were Your Born?; Mr. Chump. **1939** Daughters Courageous; Four Wives. **1940** Zanzibar; Convicted Woman; Girls of the Road; Gangs of Chicago. **1941** Four Mothers; Mystery Ship. **1943** Miss V from Moscow; Buckskin Frontier; Lost Canyon. **1945** Why Girls Leave Home; Steppin' in Society; Identity Unknown. **1946** Deadline at Dawn; They Made Me a Killer.

LANE, LUPINO "NIPPER" (Henry George Lupino)
Born: June 16, 1892, London, England. Died: Nov. 10, 1959, London, England. Screen, stage actor, playwright and director. Brother of actor Wallace Lupino (dec. 1961).

Appeared in: **1915** The Man in Possession; Nipper and the Curate; His Cooling Courtship; Nipper's Busy Holiday. **1916** The Dummy; Nipper's Busy Bee Time; A Wife in a Hurry. **1917** The Missing Link; Splash Me Nicely; Hullo! Who's Your Lady Friend? **1918** "Kinekature Comedies" series including: The Blunders of Mr. Butterbun; Unexpected Treasure; Trips and Tribunals; His Busy Day; His Salad Days; Love and Lobster. **1919** Clarence, Crooks and Chivalry; A Dreamland Frolic. **1920** A Night Out and a Day In; A Lot About Lottery. **1922** The Broker; The Reporter. **1923** A Friendly Husband. **1924** Isn't Life Wonderful? **1925** The Fighting Dude (short). **1927** Monty of the Mounted. **1929** Show of Shows; The Love Parade; "Educational—Lupino Lane" comedies including: Ship Mates; Buying a Gun; Fireproof; Purely Circumstantial; Only Me; Evolution of the Dance. **1930** Bride of the Regiment; Golden Dawn; Yellow Mask. **1931** Never Trouble Trouble; No Lady. **1933** A Southern Maid. **1935** The Deputy Drummer; Who's Your Father?; Trust the Navy. **1936** Hot News. **1939** Me and My Gal (aka The Lambeth Walk—US 1940).

LANE, PAT (Patrick Daniel Lane aka PATRICK DANIEL LEANE)
Born: 1900. Died: July 4, 1953, Beverly Hills, Calif. (heart attack). Screen and vaudeville actor.

Appeared in: **1942** The Wife Takes a Flyer; My Sister Eileen. **1945** Christmas in Connecticut. **1946** She Wrote the Book; The Jolson Story. **1947** Wild Harvest; The Guilt of Janet Ames. **1948** Appointment With Murder. **1949** Sorrowful Jones. **1950** Branded. **1954** Demetrius and the Gladiators.

LANE, ROSEMARY (Rosemary Mullican)
Born: Apr. 4, 1914, Indianola, Iowa. Died: Nov. 25, 1974, Woodland Hills, Calif. (diabetes and pulmonary obstruction). Screen, stage, radio actress and singer. Sister of Martha Mulligan (dec.), actresses Priscilla and Lola Lane (dec. 1981) and singer Leota Lane (dec. 1960). Divorced from makeup artist Bud Westmore.

Appeared in: **1937** Hollywood Hotel; Varsity Show. **1938** Four Daughters; Gold Diggers in Paris. **1939** Blackwell's Island; Daughters Courageous; Four Wives; The Oklahoma Kid; The Return of Dr. X. **1940** The Boys from Syracuse; Ladies Must Live; An Angel from Texas; Always a Bride. **1941** Time Out for Rhythm; Four Mothers. **1943** Chatterbox; Harvest Melody; All By Myself. **1944** Trocadero. **1945** Sing Me a Song of Texas; Fortune Hunter (aka The Outcast).

LANE, WALLACE See LUPINO, WALLACE

LANG, FRITZ
Born: Dec. 5, 1890, Vienna, Austria. Died: Aug. 2, 1976, Beverly Hills, Calif. Screen actor, film director, screenwriter and writer. Divorced from writer Thea von Harbou.

Appeared in: **1963** Le Meprie (Contempt—US 1964).

LANG, GERTRUDE
Born: 1898. Died: July 14, 1971, Marathon, Fla. Screen, stage actress and opera singer.

LANG, HAROLD
Born: 1923, England. Died: Nov. 16, 1970, Cairo, Egypt. Screen, stage and television actor.

Appeared in: **1949** Floodtide; The Spider and the Fly (US 1952). **1950** Cairo Road. **1951** The Franchise Affair (US 1952); Cloudburst (US 1952); Calling Bullldog Drummond. **1952** It Started in Paradise (US 1953); Wings of Danger (aka Dead on Course—US); So Little Time. **1953** The Long Memory; Laughing Anne (US 1954); The Saint's Return (aka The Saint's Girl Friday—US). **1954** Dance Little Lady (US 1955); The Passing Stranger; Thirty-Six Hours (aka Terror Street—US); Star of My Night; Men of Sherwood Forest. **1955** Murder By Proxy (aka Blackout—US); The Quatermass Experiment (aka The Creeping Unknown—US 1956). **1956** It's a Wonderful World. **1957** The Flesh Is Weak. **1958** The Betrayal; Carve Her Name With Pride; Man With a Gun; Chain of Events. **1963** West 11; Paranoiac. **1964** Dr. Terror's House of Horrors (US 1965). **1965** The Nanny. **1966** The Psychopath. **1969** Two Gentlemen Sharing.

LANG, HARRY
Born: 1895. Died: Aug. 3, 1953, Hollywood, Calif. (heart attack). Screen, radio, television and vaudeville actor. Part of vaudeville teams "Lang and Haley" and "Lang and O'Neill."

Appeared in: **1929** Who's Who (short). **1951** Soldiers Three.

LANG, HOWARD
Born: 1876. Died: Jan. 26, 1941, Hollywood, Calif. Screen and stage actor.

Appeared in: **1922** Peacock Alley. **1933** This Day and Age; Cradle Song. **1934** The Witching Hour; Born to Be Bad. **1935** Bar 20 Rides Again; Mystery Woman. **1936** Call of the Prairie. **1937** Navy Spy; Here's Flash Casey; The Prisoner of Zenda. **1940** The Mortal Storm.

LANG, LOUISE
Born: 1907. Died: Feb. 2, 1977, Los Angeles, Calif. (cancer). Screen actress. Mother of actors Darryl and Dwayne Hickman.

LANG, MATHESON
Born: May 5, 1879, Montreal, Canada. Died: Apr. 11, 1948, Bridgeton, Barbados. Screen, stage actor and playwright. Entered films in 1916. Married to actress Hutin "Nellie" Britton (dec. 1965).

Appeared in: **1916** The Merchant of Venice. **1917** Everybody's Business; The House Opposite; Masks and Faces; The Ware Case. **1918** Victory and Peace. **1919** Mr. Wu. **1921** The Carnival. **1922** Dick Turpin's Ride to York; A Romance of Old Baghdad. **1923** The Wandering Jew; Guy Fawkes. **1924** White Slippers; Henry, King of Navarre; Slaves of Destiny (aka Miranda of the Balcony). **1925** The Qualified Adventurer; The Secret Kingdom. **1926** The Chinese Bungalow; Island of Despair. **1927** The King's Highway. **1928** The Triumph of the Scarlet Pimpernel (aka The Scarlet Daredevil—US 1929); The Blue Peter. **1929** Beyond the Veil (rerelease of The Secret Kingdom—1925). **1930** The Chinese Bungalow (and 1926 version). **1931** Carnival (aka Venetian Nights—US and 1921 version). **1933** Channel Crossing (US 1934). **1934** Little Friend; The Great Defender. **1935** Royal Cavalcade (aka Regal Cavalcade—US); Drake of England (aka Drake The Pirate—US). **1936** The Cardinal.

LANG, PETER
Born: 1867. Died: Aug. 20, 1932, New York (heart attack). Stage and screen actor.

Appeared in: **1913** Peter's Pledge (serial). **1924** Dangerous Money.

LANG, WALTER
Born: Aug. 10, 1898, Memphis, Tenn. Died: Feb. 7, 1972, Palm Springs, Calif. (kidney failure). Film director, screenwriter, screen and stage actor.

Appeared in: **1935** Lady Tubbs.

LANGDON, HARRY

Born: June 15, 1884, Council Bluffs, Iowa. Died: Dec. 22, 1944, Los Angeles, Calif. (cerebral hemorrhage). Screen, stage, vaudeville actor, film director, producer and screenwriter. Divorced from actress Rose Frances (dec. 1962).

Appeared in: **1918** The Mastery Mystery. **1924** Picking Peaches; plus the following shorts: The Luck O' the Foolish; Smile Please; Feet of Mud; All Night Long; Shanghaied Lovers; Flickering Youth; The Cat's Meow; His New Mama; The First Hundred Years; The Hanson Cabman. **1925** The following shorts: The Sea Squawk; Boobs in the Woods; His Marriage Vow; Plain Clothes; Remember When?; Lucky Stars; Horace Greeley, Jr.; There He Goes; The White Wing's Bride. **1926** Ella Cinders; The Strong Man; Tramp Tramp Tramp; plus the following shorts: Saturday Afternoon; Fiddlesticks; The Soldier Man. **1927** Long Pants; Three's a Crowd; His First Flame. **1928** The Chaser; Heart Trouble; There He Goes. **1929** The following shorts: Hotter Than Hot; The Fighting Parson; Sky Boy; Skirt Shy. **1930** See America Thirst; plus the following shorts: The Head Guy; The Shrimp; The King; The Big Kick. **1931** Soldier's Plaything. **1932** The Big Flash (short). **1933** My Weekness; Hallelujah, I'm A Bum; plus the following shorts: Tired Feet; The Hitch Hiker; Knight Duty; Tied for Life; Hooks and Jabs; Marriage Humor; The Stage Hand; Leave It to Dad; On Ice; Pop's Pal; A Roaming Romeo. **1934** No Sleep on the Deep; plus the following shorts: Trimmed in Furs; Circus Hoodoo; Petting Preferred; Counsel on de Fence; Shivers. **1935** Atlantic Adventure; plus the following shorts: His Bridal Sweet; The Leather Necker; His Marriage Mixup; I Don't Remember. **1937** Mad About Money (aka Stardust, aka He Loved an Actress—US 1938). **1938** Block Heads; There Goes My Heart; A Doggone Mixup (short); Sue My Lawyer (short). **1939** Zenobia; Elephants Never Forget. **1940** A Chump at Oxford; Saps at Sea; Misbehaving Husbands; Goodness, a Ghost (short); Cold Turkey (short). **1941** Road Show; All-American Coed; Double Trouble. **1942** House of Errors; plus the following shorts: What Makes Lizzy Dizzy?; Tireman, Spare My Tires; Carry Harry; Piano Mooner. **1943** Spotlight Scandals; plus the following shorts: Blitz on the Fritz; Here Comes Mr. Zerk; Blonde and Groom. **1944** The following shorts: Hot Rhythm; To Heir Is Human; Defective Detectives; Block Busters Mopey Dope. **1945** Swingin' On a Rainbow; Snooper Service (short); Pistol Packin' Nitwits (short). **1961** Days of Thrills and Laughter (documentary). **1963** Thirty Years of Fun (documentary); The Sound of Laughter (documentary).

LANGDON, LILLIAN

Born: New Jersey. Died: Feb. 8, 1943, Santa Monica, Calif. Screen and stage actress.

Appeared in: **1915** Kindling; Double Trouble; The Lamb. **1916** Intolerance; Flirting With Fate; The Americano. **1919** His Majesty, the American. **1921** The Swamp; What's a Wife Worth?; The Mother Heart. **1922** Another Man's Shoes; Kissed; Lights of the Desert; The Glorious Fool; The Stranger's Banquet; Fools of Fortune; Too Much Wife. **1923** The Prisoner; Going Up; Nobody's Bride; Crossed Wires; Footlight Ranger; The Wanters. **1924** Daring Youth; Circe the Enchantress. **1925** Cobra; Raffles, The Amateur Cracksman; After Business Hours; The Wall Street Whiz; The Thoroughbred; Joanna; Enticement. **1926** The Millionaire Policeman; The Blonde Saint; Pleasures of the Rich; Fifth Avenue. **1927** What Every Girl Should Know; Compassion. **1928** The Cheer Leader.

LANGE, MARY

Born: 1913. Died: Apr. 20, 1973, Coral Gables, Fla. Screen and stage actress. Entered films in 1933.

Appeared in: **1933** Roman Scandals; Moonlight and Pretzels. **1934** Bottoms Up. **1936** The Great Ziegfeld. **1951** Here Comes the Groom.

LANGFORD, MARTHA

Died: Apr. 21, 1935, Syracuse, N.Y. Stage and screen actress.

LANGFORD, WILLIAM

Born: 1920, Montreal, Canada. Died: July 20, 1955, New York, N.Y. Screen, stage and television actor.

Appeared in Swedish film: The True and the False.

LANGLEY, FAITH

Born: 1929. Died: 1972, New York, N.Y. Stage and screen actress.

Appeared in: **1953** Donovan's Brain.

LANGLEY, HERBERT

Born: 1888. Died: Oct., 1967. Screen actor and opera baritone.

Appeared in: **1922** The Wonderful Story; Flames of Passion. **1923** Chu Chin Chow (US 1925). **1924** Southern Love (aka Spanish Passion). **1927** Cameo series including: The Bohemian Girl, Maritana, Rigoletto, Faust and Carmen.

LANGTON, PAUL

Born: Apr. 17, 1913, Salt Lake City, Utah. Died: Apr. 15, 1980, Burbank, Calif. (heart attack). Screen, stage, radio and television actor.

Appeared in: **1924** The Thin Man. **1943** Destination Tokyo. **1944** Thirty Seconds Over Tokyo; Gentle Annie. **1945** The Hidden Eye; What Next, Corporal Hargrove?; They Were Expendable. **1946** My Brother Talks to Horses; Till the Clouds Roll By. **1947** The Romance of Rosy Ridge; For You I Die. **1948** A Song is Born; Trouble Preferred; Fighting Back. **1953** The Big Leaguer; Jack Slade. **1954** Return from the Sea; The Snow Creature. **1955** Murder is My Beat; To Hell and Back; The Big Knife. **1957** Peyton Place; The Incredible Shrinking Man; Utah Blaine; Chicago Confidential; Calypso Heat Wave. **1958** Girl in the Woods; It! The Terror From Beyond Space. **1959** The Cosmic Man; Invisible Invaders. **1960** The Big Night; Three Came to Kill. **1963** Four for Texas; Dime With a Halo. **1964** Man's Favorite Sport?; Shock Treatment.

LANGTRY, LILLIE (Emilie Charlotte Le Breton)

Born: Oct. 13, 1853, Isle of Jersey, Great Britain. Died: Feb. 12, 1929, Monaco (heart attack). Screen, stage actress and author. Entered films with Famous Players in 1913.

Appeared in: **1913** His Neighbor's Wife.

LANI, MARIA

Born: 1906, Warsaw, Poland. Died: Mar. 11, 1954, Paris, France. Screen, stage actress and writer. Appeared in French silents.

LANNING, EDWARD

Died: Sept. 19, 1918, Los Angeles, Calif. Screen actor.

LANNING, FRANK L.

Born: Aug. 14, 1872 or 1899, Marion, Iowa. Died: June 17, 1945. Screen and stage actor.

Appeared in: **1916** Three Godfathers; The Victoria Cross; John Needham's Double. **1917** The Black Wolf; A Tale of Two Cities; North of Fifty-Three; A Little Patriot. **1918** Bull's Eye (serial); The Lion's Claw (serial). **1920** Daredevil Jack (serial); Huckleberry Finn. **1921** That Girl Montana. **1922** The Storm; Step on It!; Out of the Silent North; East is West; Another Man's Boots; Hellhounds of the West. **1923** The Remittance Woman; The Bad Man; Drifting. **1925** Fighting Ranger (serial). **1927** The Kid Brother; Black Jack; The Unknown. **1928** Stand and Deliver; Love Mart. **1929** Ships of the Night; Unknown Rider. **1930** Temple Tower; Rough Romance; The Lone Defender (serial). **1931** The Phantom of the West (serial); The Lightning Warrior (serial).

LANPHIER, FAYE

Born: 1906. Died: June 21, 1959, Oakland, Calif. (pneumonia). Screen actress. She was "Miss America" of 1925.

Appeared in: **1926** The American Venus.

LANPHIER, JAMES F.

Born: 1921. Died: Feb. 11, 1969, Los Angeles, Calif. (stroke). Screen, stage and television actor.

Appeared in: **1957** Operation Mad Ball. **1958** Bell, Book and Candle; The Perfect Furlough. **1961** Flight of the Lost Balloon; Breakfast at Tiffany's. **1962** Experiment in Terror; Days of Wine and Roses. **1964** The Pink Panther. **1966** What Did You Do in the War, Daddy? **1968** The Party; The Legend Of Lylah Clare. **1970** Darling Lili.

LANSING, JOI (Joi Wasmansdorff)

Born: April 6, 1930, Salt Lake City, Utah. Died: Aug. 7, 1972, Santa Monica, Calif. (cancer). Screen, stage, television actress and singer.

Appeared in: **1948** The Counterfeiters; Easter Parade; Julia Misbehaves. **1949** Take Me Out to the Ball Game; Neptune's Daughter; Super Cue Men (short). **1950** Holiday Rhythm. **1951** F.B.I. Girl; Two Tickets to Broadway; Pier 23; On the Riviera. **1952** Singin' in the Rain. **1954** The French Line; So You Want to Go to a Nightclub (short); So You've Taken in a Roomer (short). **1955** So You Want to Be a V.P. (short); So You Want to Be a Policeman (short); The Kentuckian; Son of Sinbad. **1956** So You Think the Grass Is Greener (short); The Brave One; Hot Cars; Hot Shots; The Fountain of Youth (short). **1958** Touch of Evil. **1959** It Started With a Kiss; But Not for Me; Hole in the Head; The Atomic Submarine. **1960** Who Was That Lady?; CinderFella. **1965** Marriage on the Rocks. **1967** Hillbillys in a Haunted House. **1970** Bigfoot.

LANSING, RUTH DOUGLAS

Born: 1881. Died: Aug. 19, 1931, Hollywood, Calif. (toxic poisoning). Stage and screen actress.

LANZA, MARIO (Alfred Arnold Cocozza)
Born: Jan. 31, 1921 or 1925, Philadelphia, Pa. Died: Oct. 7, 1959, Rome, Italy (heart attack). Screen, television actor and opera performer.

Appeared in: **1944** Winged Victory (appeared as an extra while in the service). **1949** That Midnight Kiss. **1950** Toast of New Orleans. **1951** The Great Caruso. **1952** Because You're Mine. **1954** The Student Prince (voice). **1956** Serenade. **1958** Seven Hills of Rome. **1959** For the First Time. **1974** That's Entertainment (film clips).

LAPAURI, ALEKSANDR
Born: 1926, Russia. Died: Aug. 5, 1975, Russia (auto accident). Screen actor and ballet dancer. Married to dancer Raissa Struchkova.

Appeared in: **1956** The Ballet of Romeo and Juliet. **1961** Khrustalnyy Bashmachok (aka Cinderella—US).

LAPID, JESS
Born: Philippines. Died: July 13, 1968, Manila, Philippines (murdered—shot). Screen actor.

LA PLANCHE, ROSEMARY
Born: 1925, Calif. Died: May 6, 1979, Glendale, Calif. Screen, radio and television actress. Married to producer Harry Koplan. Miss America of 1941.

Appeared in: **1938** Mad About Music. **1943** Two Weeks to Live; Swing Your Partner; Prairie Chickens; The Falcon in Danger. **1946** Devil Bat's Daughter; Strangler of the Swamp. **1947** Betty Co-Ed; Jack Armstrong (serial). **1948** Angel's Alley; An Old-Fashioned Girl. **1949** Federal Agents vs. Underworld, Inc. (serial).

LA RENO, RICHARD "DICK"
Born: Oct. 31, 1873, County Limerick, Ireland. Died: July 26, 1945, Hollywood, Calif. Screen and stage actor.

Appeared in: **1913** The Squaw Man. **1914** The Virginian; The Man from Home; Rose of the Rancho. **1915** Cameo Kirby; The Warrens of Virginia. **1917** The Gray Ghost (serial). **1921** A Daughter of the Law. **1922** One-Eighth Apache; Out of the Silent North; Trimmed. **1923** Playing It Wild; Times Have Changed; Single Handed. **1924** Oh, You Tony!; Crashin' Through; Ridin' Mad; Waterfront Wolves; Three Days to Live. **1925** Flashing Steeds; Drug Store Cowboy. **1926** The High Hand; Buffalo Bill on the U.P. Trail; Sea Horses. **1927** The Long Loop on the Pecos; The Border Cavalier; Gold from Weepah; The Silent Rider. **1928** The Apache Raider.

LARGAY, RAYMOND J. "RAY"
Born: 1886. Died: Sept. 28, 1974, Woodland Hills, Calif. (stroke). Screen, stage, vaudeville and radio actor. Married to vaudeville actress Sue Snee.

Appeared in: **1930** Soldiers and Women; Lilies of the Field. **1931** Grief Street; Rebound. **1938** Holiday. **1945** The Hidden Eye. **1946** The Dark Horse; She Wrote the Book. **1947** Repeat Performance; Variety Girl; Louisiana; The Shocking Miss Pilgrim; Gentleman's Agreement. **1948** Are You With It?; Four Faces West; Force of Evil; Slippy McGee; The Girl from Manhattan. **1949** Rusty's Birthday; The Lawton Story (aka Prince of Peace). **1950** The Petty Girl; Johnny One-Eye; Experiment Alcatraz. **1951** The Second Woman; Katie Did It. **1952** April in Paris. **1954** Jesse James vs. the Daltons.

LARGE, WILFRED H. (Wilfred Howard Large)
Born: 1890, Canada. Died: Apr. 2, 1979, Regina, Saskatchewan, Canada. Screen, stage and radio actor.

LARIMORE, EARLE
Born: 1899, Portland, Ore. Died: Oct. 22, 1947, New York, N.Y. Screen, stage and radio actor.

Appeared in: **1922** Inspection. **1926** The Kickoff.

LARKIN, GEORGE
Born: Nov. 11, 1888, New York, N.Y. Died: Mar. 27, 1946. Screen, stage, vaudeville actor and circus performer. Married to actress Ollie Kirkby (dec. 1965).

Appeared in: **1912** The Return of Lady Linda; The Transgression of Deacon Jones; The Letter With the Black Seals; Robin Hood; A Choice By Accident; Making Uncle Jealous. **1913** While Father Telephoned. **1916** Unto Those Who Sin. **1918** Zongar; Hands Up (serial); Border Raiders. **1919** The Tiger's Trail (serial); The Terror of the Ranger (serial); The Lurking Peril (serial). **1920** The Unfortunate Sex. **1921** The Man Trackers; Terror Trail (serial). **1922** Boomerang Justice; Saved by the Radio; Barriers of Folly; Bulldog Courage. **1923** The

Apache Dancer; Flames of Passion; The Flash; Gentleman Unafraid; Mysterious Goods; Her Reputation; Tango Cavalier; The Way of the Transgressor. **1924** Deeds of Daring; Stop at Nothing; Midnight Secrets; The Pell Street Mystery; Yankee Madness. **1925** Getting 'Em Right; Quick Change; The Right Man; Rough Stuff. **1926** Silver Fingers. **1928** Midnight Rose. **1931** Alexander Hamilton.

LARKIN, JOHN
Born: 1874. Died: Mar. 19, 1936, Los Angeles, Calif. (pneumonia). Black screen actor.

Appeared in: **1931** Smart Money; Man to Man; The Prodigal; Sporting Blood. **1932** Wet Parade; The Tenderfoot; Stranger in Town. **1933** Black Beauty; Day of Reckoning; The Great Jasper. **1934** Southern Style (short); The Witching Hour. **1935** Mississippi; A Notorious Gentleman. **1936** Frankie and Johnny; Hearts Divided; Green Pastures; Trail of the Lonesome Pine.

LARKIN, JOHN
Born: 1912, Oakland, Calif. Died: Jan. 29, 1965, Studio City, Calif. (heart attack). Screen, radio and television actor. Do not confuse with John Larkin, black actor (dec. 1936) nor stage actor (dec. 1929).

Appeared in: **1949** Saints and Sinners. **1950** Farewell to Yesterday; Twelve O'Clock High. **1964** Seven Days in May; Those Calloways. **1965** The Satan Bug.

LA ROCHE, EDWARD (aka EDOUARD LA ROCHE)
Born: 1879, France. Died: Dec. 26, 1935, N.Y. Screen, stage and vaudeville actor.

Appeared in: **1925** Soul Fire.

LA ROCQUE, ROD (Roderique La Rocque La Tour)
Born: Nov. 29, 1898, Chicago, Ill. Died: Oct. 15, 1969, Beverly Hills, Calif. Screen, stage actor and radio producer. Married to actress Vilma Banky.

Appeared in: **1914** The Snow Man. **1916** The Lightbearer. **1917** Would You Believe It?; A Corner in Smiths; Vernon the Bountiful; The Long Green Trail; The Fable of the Wandering Boy and the Wayward Parent; The Fable of the 12-Cylinder Speed of the Leisure Class; The Fable of All That Triangle Stuff is Sized Up by the Meal Ticket; The Fable of the Film Fed Family; Uneasy Money; Efficiency Edgar's Courtship; Much Obliged; Sundaying in Fairview; Filling His Own Shoes; The Girl Who Took Notes and Got Wise and Then Fell Down; The Rainbow Box; The Fable of the Back Trackers from the Hot Sidewalks; The Fable of the Speedy Sprite; The Fable of What Transpires After the Wind-Up; The Fable of the Uplifter and His Dandy Little Opus; The Dream Doll; Sadie Goes to Heaven. **1918** The Venus Model; Ruggles of Red Gap; Let's Get a Divorce; Money Mad; A Perfect 36; Hidden Fires; A Perfect Lady. **1919** The Trap; Miss Crusoe; Love and the Woman. **1920** Stolen Kiss; Thimble Thimble; Easy to Get; A Philistine in Bohemia; The Garter Girl; The Discarded Woman; Life. **1921** For Your Daughter's Sake (reissue of 1920 film The Discarded Woman); Paying the Piper; Suspicious Wives. **1922** What's Wrong With the Women?; Notoriety; The Challenge; Slim Shoulders; A Woman's Woman. **1923** The Ten Commandments; Zaza; Jazzmania; The French Doll; Don't Call It Love. **1924** Triumph; Feet of Clay; Forbidden Paradise; A Society Scandal; Code of the Sea; Phantom Justice. **1925** The Coming of Amos; Braveheart; The Golden Bed; Night Life in New York; Wild, Wild, Susan. **1926** Red Dice; Bachelor's Brides; Gigolo; The Cruise of the Jasper B. **1927** The Fighting Eagle; Resurrection. **1928** Stand and Deliver; Hold 'Em Yale; Love Over Night; Captain Swagger. **1929** The Man and the Moment; The One Woman Idea; Our Modern Maidens; The Locked Door; Our Dancing Daughter; The Delightful Rogue; Forbidden Paradise. **1930** One Romantic Night; Let Us Be Gay; Beau Bandit. **1931** The Yellow Ticket. **1933** S.O.S. Iceberg. **1935** Taming of the Wild; Mystery Woman; Frisco Waterfront. **1936** The Preview Murder Mystery; 'Til We Meet Again; Hi, Gaucho!; The Dragnet. **1937** The Shadow Strikes; Clothes and the Woman. **1938** International Crime. **1939** The Hunchback of Notre Dame. **1940** Beyond Tomorrow; Dr. Christian Meets the Women; Dark Streets of Cairo. **1941** Meet John Doe.

LA ROUZ, CARMEN (Carmen Le Roux)
Born: Sept. 4, 1909, Durango, Mexico. Died: Aug. 24, 1942, Mexico? Screen actress.

Appeared in: **1931** Cavalier of the West; Two Gun Caballero. **1932** Son of Oklahoma. **1933** California Trail. **1934** Demon for Trouble. **1937** Island Captives. **1938** Starlight Over Texas.

LARQUEY, PIERRE
Born: 1884, France. Died: Apr. 17, 1962, Paris, France. Screen actor.

Appeared in: **1935** Topaze. **1936** Second Bureau. **1937** Dr. Knock. **1939** A Man and His Wife; Mademoiselle ma Mere; The Citadel of Silence. **1940** The Mayor's Dilemma; Two Women. **1944** Moulin Rouge. **1945** Des Dames aux Chapeaux Verts (The Ladies in the Great Hats). **1946** Jericho. **1947** The Murderer Lives at Number 21; The Blue Veil. **1948** Le Corbeau (The Raven); Jenny Lamour; Portrait of Innocence. **1950** Sylvie and the Phantom. **1951** Face to the Wind. **1952** A Simple Case of Money; Topaze (and 1935 version). **1955** Diabolique. **1958** Witches of Salem.

LARRIMORE, FRANCINE
Born: 1898, France. Died: Mar. 7, 1975, New York, N.Y. (pneumonia). Screen and stage actress.

Appeared in: **1915** The Devil's Darling. **1916** The Princess from the Poorhouse. **1917** Max Wants a Divorce; Somewhere in America; Royal Pauper. **1918** Resurrection. **1937** John Meade's Woman.

LARRY, MIKE, SR.
Born: 1882. Died: Dec. 22, 1967, Hollywood, Calif. Prizefighter and screen actor. Father of Thomas and actors Mike, Jr. and Timothy Larry.

LARSON, LORLEE
Born: 1935. Died: Oct. 4, 1954, Los Angeles, Calif. Screen and radio actress.

LARSON, VIGGO
Born: Aug. 14, 1880, Denmark? Died: Jan. 6, 1957, Germany. Screen actor and film director.

LA RUE, FRANK H. (Frank Herman La Rue)
Born: Dec. 5, 1878, Ohio. Died: Sept. 26, 1960, Woodland Hills, Calif. Screen, stage and vaudeville actor.

Appeared in: **1931** Sidewalks of New York. **1932** Once in a Lifetime. **1933** Strange People; Flying Devils; Thrill Hunter. **1934** Here Comes the Navy; When a Man Sees Red; Mike Fright (short); The Fighting Ranger. **1935** The Throwback; Motive for Revenge; The Girl Who Came Back; The Singing Vagabond; Red River Valley. **1936** The Phantom Rider (serial). **1937** Bar-Z Bad Men; Gun Lords of Stirrup Basin; A Lawman Is Born; It Happened Out West; Boothill Brigade; Public Cowboy No. 1; Colorado Kid. **1938** West of Rainbow's End; Song and Bullets; Lightning Carson Rides Again; I Demand Payment; Outlaws of Sonora; Overland Stage Raiders; Knight of the Plains; Frontier Scout. **1939** In Old Montana; Down the Wyoming Trail; Port of Hate; Roll Wagons Roll; Code of the Fearless; Song of the Buckaroo; Trigger Pals. **1940** Riders of Black Mountain; Brigham Young; Frontier Crusader; The Durango Kid; Arizona Frontier; Westbound Stage; Land of the Six Guns; The Range Busters; Riders of Pasco Basin; Return of Wild Bill; Fugitive From a Prison Camp; The Courageous Dr. Christian; The Shadow (serial). **1941** Beyond the Sacramento; Gunman from Bodie; Robbers of the Range; Prairie Stranger; Hands Across the Rockies; A Missouri Outlaw. **1942** Frontier Law; Stardust on the Sage. **1943** The More the Merrier; Robin Hood of the Range; Saddles and Sagebrush. **1944** Ghost Guns; The Last Horseman; Saddle Leather Law; West of the Rio Grande; Laura; Follow the Boys. **1945** Blazing the Western Trail; Devil Riders; Frontier Feud; The Lost Trail. **1946** Border Bandits; The Fighting Frontiersman; Frontier Gun Law; The Gentleman from Texas; Gunning for Vengeance; The Haunted Mine; Silver Range; Under Arizona Skies. **1947** Prairie Raiders; South of Chisholm Trail; Cheyenne Takes Over; Gun Talk. **1948** Song of the Drifter; Frontier Agent. **1949** Sheriff of Medicine Bow.

LA RUE, GRACE
Born: 1881. Died: Mar. 12, 1956, Burlingame, Calif. Screen, stage and vaudeville actress. Married to actor Hale Hamilton (dec. 1942).

Appeared in: **1919** That's Good (she used the name of Stella Gray and received no billing for that film). **1929** The International Star of Songs (short). **1933** She Done Him Wrong. **1940** If I Had My Way.

LA RUE, JEAN (Eugene Marcus Bailey)
Born: 1901. Died: June, 1956, San Antonio, Tex. Screen actor.

Appeared in: **1923** Where the Pavement Ends. **1928** Tracy, the Outlaw.

LASCOE, HENRY
Born: 1914. Died: Sept. 1, 1964, Hollywood, Calif. (heart attack). Screen, stage and television actor.

Appeared in: **1951** The Man With My Face.

LASSIE
Born: 1941. Died: 1959. Screen animal performer (collie).

Appeared in: **1943** Lassie Come Home. **1945** Son of Lassie. **1946** Courage of Lassie.

LATELL, LYLE (Lyle Zeiem)
Born: Apr. 9, 1905, Elma, Iowa. Died: Oct. 24, 1967, Hollywood, Calif. (heart attack). Screen and television actor. Married to actress Mary Foy (one of the Seven Little Foys). Appeared in the "Boston Blackie" series during the 1940s.

Appeared in: **1941** Texas; Great Guns; In the Navy; Sky Raiders (serial). **1942** The Wife Takes a Flyer; The Night Before the Divorce. **1943** Happy Go Lucky. **1944** One Mysterious Night. **1945** Hold That Blonde; Dick Tracy vs. Cueball. **1947** Dick Tracy's Dilemma; Dick Tracy and Gruesome; Buck Privates Come Home. **1948** The Noose Hangs High. **1949** Sky Dragon. **1951** A Street Car Named Desire; Deal Me In (short). **1953** Pardon My Wrench (short). **1955** The Girl Rush.

LATHROP, DONALD
Born: 1888, England. Died: July 15, 1940, London, England (heart ailment). Stage and screen actor.

LATIMER, HENRY
Born: 1876, England? Died: Jan. 25, 1963, London, England. Screen and stage actor.

Appeared in: **1927** The King's Highway.

LATINOVITS, ZOLTAN
Born: 1932, Hungary. Died: June, 1976, near Lake Balaton, Hungary (suicide—threw himself in front of a railroad train). Screen, stage, radio, television actor, stage director and author. Married to actress Eva Ruttkay.

Appeared in: **1964** Oldas es Kotes (aka Cantata). **1966** Szegenylegenyek (aka The Round-Up, and aka The Hopeless Ones—US 1969). **1975** Sinbad.

LAUCK, CHESTER H.
Born: 1901, Ark. Died: Feb. 21, 1980, Hot Springs, Ark. Screen, radio actor and radio writer. Appeared with Norris Goff (dec. 1978) as radio and films "Lum N' Abner."

Appeared in: **1940** Dreaming Out Loud. **1942** The Bashful Bachelor. **1943** Two Weeks to Live; So This Is Washington. **1944** Goin' to Town. **1946** Partners in Time.

LAUDER, SIR HARRY
Born: Aug. 4, 1870, Portobello, Scotland. Died: Feb. 25, 1950, Lenarkshire, Scotland (kidney ailment). Screen and stage actor.

Appeared in: **1927** Huntingtower. **1929** Happy Days; Auld Lang Syne. **1936** The End of the Road. **1940** Song of the Road.

LAUGHLIN, ANNA
Born: 1885, Sacramento, Calif. Died: Mar. 6, 1937, New York, N.Y. (suicide). Screen, stage and vaudeville actress.

Appeared in: **1915** Crooky Scruggs.

LAUGHLIN, BILLY (William Laughlin)
Born: July 5, 1932, San Gabriel, Calif. Died: Aug. 31, 1948, Covina, Calif. (motor scooter—truck accident). Screen actor. Was the "Froggy" character in the Our Gang Comedies.

Appeared in: **1940** The following shorts: The New Pupil; Waldo's Last Stand; Kiddie Cure. **1941** The following shorts: Fightin' Fools; Baby Blues; Ye Olde Minstrels; 1-2-3 Go!; Robot Wrecks; Helping Hands; Come Back, Miss Pipps; Wedding Worries. **1942** The following shorts: Melodies Old and New; Going to Press; Don't Lie; Surprised Parties; Doin' Their Bit; Rover's Big Chance; Mighty Lak a Goat; Unexpected Riches. **1943** The following shorts: Benjamin Franklin, Jr.; Family Troubles; Calling All Kids; Farm Hands; Election Daze; Little Miss Pinkerton; Three Smart Guys. **1944** The following shorts: Radio Bugs; Tale of a Dog; Dancing Romeo.

LAUGHTON, CHARLES
Born: July, 1, 1899, Scarborough, England. Died: Dec. 15, 1962, Los Angeles, Calif. (cancer). Screen, stage actor, film and stage director. Married to actress Elsa Lanchester. Won 1932/33 Academy Award for Best Actor for Private Life of Henry VIII. Nominated for 1935 Academy Award for Best Actor in Mutiny on the Bounty and in 1957 for Witness for the Prosecution.

Appeared in: **1928** H. G. Wells Comedic series including: Bluebottles;

Daydreams. **1929** Piccadilly. **1930** Wolves (aka Wanted Men—US 1936); Comets. **1931** Down River. **1932** Devil and the Deep; Payment Deferred (stage and film versions); The Old Dark House; The Sign of the Cross; If I Had a Million. **1933** Island of Lost Souls; White Woman; The Private Life of Henry VIII. **1934** The Barretts of Wimpole Street. **1935** Les Miserables; Ruggles of Red Gap; Mutiny on the Bounty; Frankie and Johnny (short). **1936** I Claudius (never released); Rembrandt. **1938** Vessel of Wrath (aka The Beachcomber—US); St. Martin's Lane. **1939** A Miracle Can Happen; Jamaica Inn; The Hunchback of Notre Dame. **1940** They Knew What They Wanted. **1941** It Started With Eve. **1942** The Tuttles of Tahiti; Tales of Manhattan; Stand By for Action. **1943** Forever and a Day; This Land Is Mine; The Man from Down Under. **1944** The Canterville Ghost; The Suspect; The Sign of the Cross (revised version of 1932 film). **1945** Captain Kidd. **1946** Because of Him. **1947** The Queen's Necklace. **1948** The Paradine Case; Arch of Triumph; Girl from Manhattan; The Big Clock; On Our Merry Way (aka A Miracle Can Happen). **1949** The Bribe; Man on the Eiffel Tower. **1951** The Strange Door; The Blue Veil. **1952** O'Henry's Full House; Abbott and Costello Meet Captain Kidd; "News of the Day" (newsreel). **1953** Young Bess; Salome. **1954** Hobson's Choice. **1957** Witness for the Prosecution. **1960** Spartacus; Under Ten Flags. **1962** Advise and Consent. **1968** Head (film clips). **1982** Dead Men Don't Wear Plaid (film clips).

LAUGHTON, EDWARD "EDDIE"

Born: 1903, Sheffield, England. Died: Mar. 21, 1952, Hollywood, Calif. (pneumonia). Screen and vaudeville actor.

Appeared in: **1939** The Lone Wolf Spy Hunt; My Son Is a Criminal; Flying G-Men (serial); North of Shanghai; Romance of the Redwood; Scandal Sheet; Outside These Walls; Mandrake the Magician; Beware Spooks; Those High Grey Walls; The Amazing Mr. Williams; Cafe Hostell; Bullets for Rustlers; Oily to Bed, Oily to Rise (short); Pest from the West (short). **1940** Blondie Has Servant Trouble; Blazing Six Shooters; Texas Stagecoach; Men Without Souls; The Doctor Takes a Wife; Girls of the Road; Cold Turkey (short); A-Plumbing We Will Go (short). **1941** The Lone Wolf Keeps a Date; Confessions of Boston Blackie; Meet Boston Blackie; Outlaws of the Panhandle; I Was a Prisoner on Devil's Island; Mystery Ship; In the Sweet Pie and Pie (short); She's Oil Mine (short). **1942** Canal Zone; Lawless Plainsmen; Submarine Raider; Honolulu Lu; Sabotage Squad; The Boogie Man Will Get You; Atlantic Convoy; All Work and No Pay (short); What's the Matador? (short); One Dangerous Night (short). **1944** The Girl in the Case; Defective Detectives (short). **1945** Masquerade in Mexico; The Lost Weekend; Idiot's Deluxe (short). **1947** The Shocking Miss Pilgrim. **1949** Chicken Every Sunday.

LAUHER, BOB

Born: 1931. Died: Aug. 22, 1973, Tarzana, Calif. Screen, television, radio actor, radio and television writer.

Appeared in: **1970** Which Way to the Front?

LAUNDERS, PERC

Born: 1905. Died: Oct. 2, 1952, Hollywood, Calif. Screen actor and studio musician.

Appeared in: **1941** Sing for Your Supper. **1944** The Falcon in Hollywood; And the Angels Sing; The Falcon Out West; Ali Baba and the Forty Thieves; Weekend Pass; Experiment Perilous. **1945** Under Western Skies; The Stork Club; Her Lucky Night; Secret Agent X-9 (serial); Masquerade in Mexico. **1946** The Killers; Lover Come Back; The Brute Man. **1947** They Won't Believe Me; Suddenly It's Spring; Easy Come, Easy Go; The Exile. **1948** The Sainted Sisters; River Lady; You Were Meant for Me. **1949** Abandoned. **1950** For Heaven's Sake. **1951** Crazy Over Horses. **1952** The Rose Bowl Story; It Grows on Trees.

LAUREL, KAY

Born: 1890, Newcastle, Pa. Died: Jan. 31, 1927, London, England (pneumonia). Stage and screen actress.

Appeared in: **1919** The Brand. **1921** Lonely Heart.

LAUREL, STAN (Arthur Stanley Jefferson)

Born: June 16, 1890, Ulverston, England. Died: Feb. 23, 1965, Santa Monica, Calif. (heart attack). Screen, stage, vaudeville actor, film producer, director and screenwriter. Was partner in comedy team of "Laurel and Hardy" with Oliver Hardy (dec. 1957). The pair won an Academy Award in 1933 for Best Short Subject for The Music Box. Brother of actor Ted Jefferson (dec. 1933). Married to singer Ida Kitaeva (dec. 1980). Divorced from Lois Nielson, Mae Charlotte Dahlberg (dec. 1969) and Virginia Ruth.

Appeared in: **1917** Nuts in May; The Evolution of Fashion. **1918** Hoot Mon; Hickory Hiram; Whose Zoo; Huns and Hyphens; Just Rambling Along; No Place Like Jail; Bears and Bad Men; Frauds and Frenzies; Do You Love Your Wife?; Lucky Dog. **1919** Mixed Nuts; Scars and Stripes; When Knights Were Cold. **1920** The following shorts: Under Two Jags; Wild Bill Hiccup; Rupert of Hee-Haw (aka Coleslaw); The Spilers; Oranges and Lemons. **1921** The Rent Collector (short). **1922** The following shorts: The Pest; The Egg; Mud and Sand. **1923** The following shorts: The Noon Whistle; White Wings; Pick and Shovel; Kill and Cure; Gas and Air; Mud and Sand; The Handy Man; Short Orders; A Man About Town; The Whole Truth; Scorching Sands; Save the Ship; Roughest Africa; Frozen Hearts; Mother's Joy. **1924** The following shorts: Smithy; Zeb vs. Paprika; Postage Due; Near Dublin; Brothers Under the Chin; Short Kilts; Monsieur Don't Care; West of Hot Dog. **1925** The following shorts: Somewhere in Wrong; Dr. Pycle and Mr. Pryde; Pie-Eyed; Mandarin Mix-Up; The Snow Hawk; Navy Blues Days; Twins; The Sleuth; Half a Man; Cowboys Cry for It. **1926** The following shorts: Atta Boy; Slipping Wives (with Oliver Hardy); On the Front Page; Get 'Em Young. The following film listings include both Laurel and Hardy. **1927** The following shorts: With Love and Hisses; Sailors Beware; Forty-Five Minutes from Hollywood; Do Detectives Think?; Flying Elephants; Sugar Daddies; Call of the Cuckoo; The Rap; Duck Soup; Eve's Love Letters; Love 'Em and Weep; Why Girls Love Sailors; Should Tall Men Marry?; Hats Off; The Battle of the Century; The Second Hundred Years; Let George Do It; Putting Pants on Philip (the first "Laurel and Hardy" film). **1928** The following shorts: Leave 'Em Laughing; From Soup to Nuts; You're Darn Tootin'; Their Purple Moment; Should Married Men Go Home?; Habeas Corpus; Two Tars; We Faw Down; The Finishing Touch; Early to Bed. **1929** Hollywood Revue of 1929; plus the following shorts: Liberty; Unaccustomed As We Are; Double Whoopee; Big Business; Men O'War; A Perfect Day; Angora Love; Bacon Grabbers; They Go Boom; The Hoose Gow; Berth Marks; Wrong Again; That's My Wife. **1930** The Rogue Song; plus the following shorts: Night Owls; Blotto; Hay Wire; Brats; Below Zero; The Laurel and Hardy Murder Case; Another Fine Mess; Hog Wild (aka Aerial Antics). **1931** Pardon Us; plus the following shorts: Chickens Come Home; Our Wife; Laughing Gravy; Come Clean; One Good Turn; Beau Hunks (aka Beau Chumps); Slippery Pearls; Be Big; On the Loose (short). **1932** Pack Up Your Troubles; plus the following shorts: Any Old Port; The Music Box; The Chimp; County Hospital; Scram; Their First Mistake; Helpmates; Towed in a Hole. **1933** Fra Diavolo (The Devil's Brother); plus the following shorts: Busy Bodies; Twice Two; Me and My Pal; The Midnight Patrol; Wild Poses; Dirty Work. **1934** Sons of the Desert; Babes in Toyland; Hollywood Party of 1934; plus the following shorts: Going Bye-Bye; Oliver the Eighth; Them Thar Hills; The Live Ghost. **1935** Bonnie Scotland; plus the following shorts: Tit for Tat; The Fixer-Uppers; Thicker Than Water. **1936** The Bohemian Girl; Our Relations; On the Wrong Trek (short). **1937** Way Out West; Pick a Star. **1938** Swiss Miss; Blockheads. **1939** The Flying Deuces. **1940** A Chump at Oxford; Saps at Sea. **1941** Great Guns. **1942** A-Haunting We Will Go. **1943** Air Raid Wardens; Jitterbugs; The Dancing Masters; Tree in a Test Tube (Government short). **1944** The Big Noise; Nothing But Trouble. **1945** The Bullfighters. **1951** Atoll K (aka Escapade—England 1952, aka Utopia 1954, aka Robincrusoeland—France 1952). **1957** Big Parade of Comedy (documentary). **1960** When Comedy Was King (documentary). **1961** Days of Thrills and Laughter (documentary). **1963** 30 Years of Fun (documentary). **1964** Big Parade of Comedy (documentary). **1967** The Crazy World of Laurel and Hardy (documentary); Further Perils of Laurel and Hardy (documentary).

LAURENZ, JOHN

Born: 1909. Died: Nov. 7, 1958, Brooklyn, N.Y. Screen actor and singer.

Appeared in: **1946** The Razor's Edge; A Walk in the Sun. **1947** Apache Rose. **1948** Captain from Castile; Tarzan and the Mermaids. **1950** Border Outlaws; Federal Agent at Large.

LAURIE, JOE, JR.

Born: 1892, New York, N.Y. Died: Apr. 29, 1954, New York, N.Y. Screen, stage actor, author and columnist. Married to Aleen Bronson (dec.), and stage actress June Tempest (dec. 1956).

LAURIE, JOHN

Born: Mar. 25, 1897, Dumfries, Scotland. Died: June 23, 1980, Chalfont St. Peter, England. Screen, stage and television actor.

Appeared in: **1929** Juno and the Paycock (US 1930). **1934** Red Ensign (aka Strike—US). **1935** The 39 Steps. **1936** East Meets West; Tudor Rose (aka Nine Days a Queen—US); As You Like It. **1937** Farewell Again (aka Troopship—US 1938); Jericho (aka Dark Sands—US 1938); The Edge of the World (US 1938). **1938** The Ware Case (US 1939). **1939** Four Feathers. **1940** Convoy (US 1941); Sailors Three (aka Three Cockeyed Sailors—US 1941). **1941** Dangerous Moonlight (aka Suicide Squadron—US 1942). **1943** The Life and Death of Colonel Blimp (aka Colonel Blimp—US 1945). **1944** A Medal for the' General; The Way Ahead (US 1945); Fanny by Gaslight (aka Man of Evil—US 1948). **1945** The Agitator (US 1949); Henry V (US 1946); I Know Where I'm Going (US 1947). **1946** Caesar and Cleopatra; School for Secrets; The Gay Intruders; Gaiety George (aka Showtime—US 1948). **1947** Uncle Silas (aka The Inheritance—US 1951); The Brothers (US 1948); Jassy (US 1948); Mine Own Executioner (US 1949); Bonnie Prince Charlie (US 1952). **1948** Hamlet. **1949** Floodtide. **1950** Trio; Madeleine; Treasure Island; No Trace. **1951** Happy-Go-Lovely; Laughter in Paradise; Pandora and the Flying Dutchman; Encore (US 1952). **1952** Saturday Island (aka Island of Desire—US); Secret Flight. **1953** The Fake. **1954** Hobson's Choice; The Black Knight; Devil Girl from Mars. **1955** Richard III (US 1956). **1957** Murder Reported (US 1960); Campbell's Kingdom (US 1958). **1958** Next to No Time (US 1960); Rockets Galore (aka Mad Little Island—US). **1960** Kidnapped. **1961** Don't Bother to Knock (aka Why Bother to Knock—US 1964). **1963** Ladies Who Do; The Siege of the Saxons. **1965** The Reptile (US 1966). **1967** Mister Ten Percent. **1980** The Prisoner of Zenda.

LAURIER, JAY (Jay Chapman)
Born: May 31, 1879, Birmingham, England. Died: Apr., 1969, Durban, South Africa. Screen, stage and vaudeville actor.

Appeared in: **1931** Hobson's Choice. **1932** Pajamas Preferred. **1933** Waltz Time; I'll Stick to You. **1937** Black Tulip.

LAVELLE, KAY
Born: 1889. Died: Nov. 18, 1965, Tujunga, Calif. Screen actress.

Appeared in: **1928** Don't Handle the Goods (short). **1934** Cross Country Cruise. **1951** People Will Talk.

LAVERNE, DOROTHY
Born: 1910. Died: Dec. 29, 1940, Los Angeles, Calif. Screen actress.

LA VERNE, LUCILLE
Born: Nov. 8, 1872, Nashville, Tenn. Died: Mar. 4, 1945, Culver City, Calif. Screen and stage actress. Her voice was that of the Queen and the Wicked Witch in Walt Disney's Snow White (1937). Entered films in 1914.

Appeared in: **1917** Polly of the Circus. **1922** Orphans of the Storm. **1923** The White Rose; Zaza. **1924** America; His Darker Self. **1925** Sun Up. **1928** The Last Moment. **1930** Abraham Lincoln; Sinner's Holiday; Little Caesar. **1931** The Great Meadow; Union Depot; An American Tragedy; Twenty-four Hours; The Unholy Garden. **1932** Hearts of Humanity; Breach of Promise; Alias the Doctor; She Wanted a Millionaire; When Paris Sleeps. **1933** Wild Horse Mesa; The Last Trail; Strange Adventure; Pilgrimage. **1934** Kentucky Kernels; The Mighty Barnum; Beloved; School for Girls. **1935** A Tale of Two Cities. **1937** Snow White (voice).

LA VERNIE, LAURA (Laura Anderson)
Born: Mar. 2, 1853, Jefferson City, Mo. Died: Sept. 18, 1939, Los Angeles, Calif. Screen and stage actress. Entered films in 1909.

Appeared in: **1916** Sweet Kitty Bellairs. **1925** Who's Your Friend? **1930** Devil's Holiday; Lummox. **1931** Kiki.

LAW, BETTY (Betty Valentine)
Born: Mar. 2, 1882, N.Y. Died: Feb. 3, 1955, Woodland Hills, Calif. Screen and stage actress.

LAW, BURTON
Born: 1880. Died: Nov. 2, 1963. Screen, stage, burlesque actor and screenwriter.

Appeared in: **1915** Broken Coin; Graft. **1916** The Sea Lily; A Mountain Tragedy. **1917** Treason; Like Wildfire. **1921** Winners of the West (serial). **1922** They Like 'Em Rough; Under Two Flags. **1923** The Oregon Trail (serial).

LAW, DONALD
Born: 1920, Tampa, Fla. Died: Feb. 26, 1959, Meadville, Pa. Screen actor.

Appeared in: "Our Gang" comedies.

LAW, RODMAN
Born: 1885, Massachusetts. Died: Oct. 14, 1919, Greenville, S.C. (tuberculosis). Aviator, parachute jumper and screen actor.

Appeared in: **1913** Death's Short Cut.

LAW, WALTER
Born: 1876. Died: Aug. 8, 1940, Hollywood, Calif. Screen, stage and vaudeville actor.

Appeared in: **1916** Her Double Life; Romeo and Juliet. **1917** The Darling of Paris; Heart and Soul; Camille. **1918** The Forbidden Path; A Perfect Lady. **1920** If I Were King. **1922** Forgotten Law; Great Alone. **1923** Flying Dutchman. **1924** Janice Meredith. **1925** Clothes Make the Pirate. **1930** Whoopee. **1936** The Adventures of Frank Merriwell (serial).

LAWES, LEWIS E.
Born: 1884. Died: Apr. 23, 1947, Garrison, N.Y. (cerebral hemorrhage). Film, radio actor and writer. Had been warden of Sing Sing Prison for 20 years.

Appeared in: **1946** Prologue of San Quentin.

LAWFORD, BETTY
Born: 1910, England. Died: Nov. 20, 1960, N.Y. Screen, stage and television actress. Daughter of actor Ernest Lawford (dec. 1940) and actress Janet Seeter Lawford.

Appeared in: **1925** The Night Club. **1928** Return of Sherlock Holmes. **1929** Gentlemen of the Press; Lucky in Love. **1930** Old English. **1931** Secrets of a Secretary. **1933** Berkeley Square; Gallant Lady. **1934** Let's Be Ritzy; The Human Side. **1936** Love Before Breakfast; Stolen Holiday. **1937** Criminal Lawyer. **1943** Stage Door Canteen. **1947** The Devil Thumbs a Ride.

LAWFORD, ERNEST
Born: 1871, England. Died: Dec. 27, 1940, New York, N.Y. Screen and stage actor. Divorced from actress Janet Seeter. Father of Edward and actress Betty Lawford (dec. 1960).

Appeared in: **1921** The Fighter. **1925** Irish Luck. **1931** Personal Maid.

LAWFORD, LADY MAY (May Somerville)
Born: England. Died: Jan. 23, 1972, Monterey Park, Calif. Screen actress and author. Married to Lt. Gen. Sir Sydney Lawford (dec. 1953). Mother of actor Peter Lawford.

Appeared in: **1948** Mr. Peabody and the Mermaid. **1952** Hong Kong.

LAWFORD, LT. GEN. SIR SYDNEY
Born: 1866, England. Died: Feb. 15, 1953, Hollywood, Calif. British army officer and screen actor. Married to actress Lady May Lawford (dec. 1972). Father of actor Peter Lawford.

LAWLER, ANDERSON
Born: Virginia. Died: 1959. Screen, stage actor and film producer.

Appeared in: **1929** The River of Romance; Half Marriage. **1930** Only Saps Work; A Lady to Love. **1932** Girls About Town. **1932** Hollywood Speaks. **1933** Cheyenne Kid; Ace of Aces. **1934** Beloved; Let's Talk It Over. **1937** Fly-Away Baby; The Adventurous Blonde; Confession. **1938** Alcatraz Island; The Invisible Menace; Accidents Will Happen; Mystery House; Heart of the North. **1939** Torchy Blane in Chinatown.

LAWRENCE, CHARLIE *See* LORENZON, LIVIO

LAWRENCE, ED (Edwin Agustus Austin)
Born: Aug. 27, 1866, Paris, Idaho. Died: Feb. 2, 1937, Los Angeles, Calif. (arteriosclerosis). Screen and stage actor. Do not confuse with actor Eddy or Edward Lawrence.

LAWRENCE, EDDY
Born: San Francisco, Calif. Died: Dec. 5, 1931, San Diego, Calif. (suicide—gas). Stage and screen actor.

Appeared in: **1925** The Knockout.

LAWRENCE, FLORENCE
Born: 1888. Died: Dec. 27, 1938, Beverly Hills, Calif. (suicide—ant paste). Screen actress. Was known as the "Biograph Girl" and the "Imp Girl." Entered films with Vitagraph in 1907.

Appeared in: **1908** A Calamitous Elopement; The Girl and the Outlaw; Betrayed By a Hand Print; Behind the Scenes; Where the Breakers Roar; The Heart of Oyama; A Smoked Husband; The Devil; The Barbarian; Ingomar; The Vaquero's Vow; The Planter's Wife; The Zulu's Heart; Romance of a Jewess; The Call of the Wild; Mr. Jones at the Ball; Concealing a Burglar; Taming of the Shrew; The Ingrate; A Woman's Way; The Song of the Shirt; Mr. Jones Entertains; An Awful Moment; The Christmas Burglars; Mr. Jones Has a Card Party; The Salvation Army Lass; Romeo and Juliet. **1909** Redemption;

"Jonesy Picture" series: Mrs. Jones Entertains; The Mended Lute; The Slave; The Brahma Diamond; Resurrection; The Jones Have Amateur Theatricals; His Wife's Mother; The Deception; The Lure of the Gown; Lady Helen's Escapade; Jones and His New Neighbor; The Winning Coat; The Road to the Heart; Confidence; The Note in the Shoe; Eloping With Auntie; Her First Biscuits; The Peach Basket Hat; The Necklace; Mrs. Jones' Lover; The Cardinal's Conspiracy; Mr. Jones' Burglar. **1910** The Angel of the Studio. **1911** Flo's Discipline; Her Two Sons; A Good Turn; Through Jealous Eyes; A Rebellious Blossom; The Slave's Affinity; The Wife Saver; The Match Maker; One on Reno; The Professor's Ward; A Rural Conqueror; His Chorus Girl Wife; A Girlish Impulse. **1912** In Swift Waters. **1914** A Singular Cynic. **1922** The Unfoldment. **1923** Satin Girl. **1924** Gambling Wives.

LAWRENCE, GERALD
Born: Mar. 23, 1873, London, England. Died: May 16, 1957, England. Screen and stage actor. Married to actresses Fay Davis (dec. 1945), and Lilian Braithwaite (dec. 1948). Do not confuse with U.S. actor with same name.

Appeared in: **1911** Henry VIII. **1912** David Garrick. **1914** Enoch Arden; Harbour Lights. **1915** The Romany Rye. **1916** A Bunch of Violets; The Grand Babylon Hotel. **1917** Carrots. **1920** The Fall of a Saint. **1922** The Glorious Adventure; The Romance of British History series including An Affair of Honour. **1935** The Iron Duke. **1936** As You Like It.

LAWRENCE, GERTRUDE (Gertrude Klasen and Alexandre Dagmar Lawrence Klasen)
Born: July 4, 1898 or 1902, London, England. Died: Sept. 6, 1952, New York, N.Y. (cancer of the liver). Screen, stage actress and dancer.

Appeared in: **1929** The Battle of Paris (film debut). **1932** Aren't We All; Lord Camber's Ladies. **1933** No Funny Business. **1935** Mimi. **1936** Rembrandt; Men Are Not Gods (US 1937). **1938** Cavalcade of Stars. **1950** The Glass Menagerie.

LAWRENCE, HUGH
Died: July 13, 1969. Screen actor.

Appeared in: **1957** Short Cut to Hell. **1958** Flood Tide; Juvenile Jungle.

LAWRENCE, JEANNE
Born: 1901. Died: July 12, 1945, Hollywood, Calif. Screen actress.

LAWRENCE, JOHN (John Darms Lawrence)
Born: July, 1910, Utah. Died: June 26, 1974, Los Angeles, Calif. (heart attack). Screen actor; film producer and screenwriter.

Appeared in: **1939** Of Mice and Men. **1951** Where No Vultures Fly (aka The Ivory Hunters—US 1952). **1954** Riding Shotgun. **1955** A Lawless Street. **1958** The Goddess. **1962** The Manchurian Candidate. **1964** The Great American Can Swindle. **1965** The Family Jewels; Tales of a Salesman. **1966** Seconds; Out of Sight; Nevada Smith. **1967** The Glory Stompers. **1968** The Destructors. **1969** Free Grass. **1971** The Seven Minutes. **1974** Busting.

LAWRENCE, LILLIAN
Born: 1870, Alexander, W.Va. Died: May 7, 1926, Beverly Hills, Calif. Screen and stage actress.

Appeared in: **1921** Making the Grade; A Parisian Scandal. **1922** A Girl's Desire; The Eternal Flame; East Is West; White Shoulders. **1923** The Common Law; Fashionable Fakers; Three Ages; Crinoline and Romance; The Voice from the Minaret. **1924** Christine of the Hungry Heart. **1925** Graustark. **1926** Stella Maris. **1927** Sensation Seekers.

LAWRENCE, MARJORIE
Born: Feb. 17, 1907, Melbourne, Australia. Died: Jan. 13, 1979, Little Rock, Ark. (cardiac arrest). Opera singer, concert performer and screen actress.

LAWRENCE, RAYMOND
Born: Dec. 8, 1888, London, England. Died: May 28, 1976, United States. Screen actor.

Appeared in: **1928** Interference. **1929** The Careless Age. **1935** Secrets of Chinatown. **1936** Alibi for Murder. **1954** Drums of Tahiti.

LAWRENCE, TRUDY *See* HALPERN, GERTRUDE

LAWRENCE, WALTER
Born: 1902. Died: Jan., 1961. Screen actor.

LAWRENCE, WILLIAM E. "BABE"
Born: 1896, Los Angeles, Calif. Died: Nov. 28, 1947, Hollywood, Calif. Screen and stage actor.

Appeared in: **1915** Birth of a Nation. **1920** Bride 13 (serial). **1921** Get Your Man; The Kiss; The Snob; Fightin' Mad; Morals; Ducks and Drakes. **1922** They Like 'Em Rough; Blood and Sand; Forget-Me-Not; A Front Page Story; The Love Gambler. **1923** Blinky; Cameo Kirby; The Thrill Chaser. **1924** The Law Forbids; The Reckless Age; The Whispered Name. **1926** A Man Four-Square; Hard Boiled. **1930** The Costello Case. **1931** Hell Bound. **1936** Ride 'Em Cowboy; Silver Spurs. **1938** Sudden Bill Dorn.

LAWSON, ELEANOR (Eleanor Smith)
Born: Dec. 23, 1875, Illinois. Died: Mar. 22, 1966, Pasadena, Calif. (heart attack). Screen actress.

Appeared in: **1918** A Mother's Sin. **1923** Hollywood. **1924** Merton of the Movies. **1925** Lights of Broadway. **1927** It. **1933** Pick Up. **1942** The Man With Two Lives. **1944** Ladies Courageous. **1951** Take Care of My Little Girl.

LAWSON, JOHN
Born: Jan. 9, 1865, Hollingwood, England. Died: Nov. 25, 1920, England? Screen and stage actor.

Appeared in: **1913** Humanity, or, Only a Jew. **1915** The Monkey's Paw.

LAWSON, KATE (aka KATE DRAIN)
Born: 1894. Died: Nov. 14, 1977, Woodland Hills, Calif. Screen actress and costume designer.

Appeared in: **1932** Little Orphan Annie. **1940** Girl from God's Country. **1943** It Ain't Hay. **1947** Song of My Heart. **1949** Bride of Vengeance; Thelma Jordon (aka File on Thelma Jordon). **1950** The Nevadan; Rock Island Trail. **1952** The Steel Fist. **1956** First Traveling Saleslady.

LAWSON, LOUISE
Died: Feb. 8, 1924, New York, N.Y. Screen actress.

LAWSON, MARY
Born: Aug. 30, 1910, Darlington, England. Died: May 4, 1941, Liverpool, England (air raid attack). Screen and stage actress. Entered films in 1933.

Appeared in: **1934** Falling in Love (aka Trouble Ahead—US 1936). **1935** Scrooge; Can You Hear Me Mother?; A Fire Has Been Arranged. **1936** House Broken; To Catch a Thief; Toilers of the Sea. **1937** Cotton Queen. **1938** Oh Boy!

LAWSON, PRISCILLA
Born: Mar. 8, 1915, Indianapolis, Ind. Died: 1960. Screen actress.

Appeared in: **1935** His Night Out. **1936** Flash Fordon (serial); Rose Bowl; The Big Broadcast of 1937; College Holiday. **1937** Double Wedding. **1938** The Girl of the Golden West; Test Pilot; Heroes of the Hills.

LAWSON, STAN
Born: 1909. Died: July 17, 1977, Hollywood, Calif. Screen and vaudeville actor. Appeared with Dewey Barton in a vaudeville act billed as "Barton and Lawson." Appeared in early Mack Sennett comedies.

LAWSON, WILFRID (Wilfred Worsnop)
Born: Jan. 14, 1900, Bradford, Yorkshire, England. Died: Oct. 10, 1966, London, England (heart attack). Screen, stage and television actor.

Appeared in: **1931** East Lynne; On the Western Front. **1933** Strike It Rich. **1935** Turn of the Tide. **1936** Ladies in Love; White Hunter. **1937** The Man Who Made Diamonds. **1938** Bank Holiday (aka Three on a Weekend—US); Yellow Sands; The Terror; Pygmalion; The Gaunt Stranger (aka The Phantom Strikes—US 1939). **1939** Stolen Life; Allegheny Uprising; Dead Man's Shoes. **1940** Pastor Hall; Gentleman of Venture (aka It Happened to One Man—US 1946); The Long Voyage Home. **1941** The Farmer's Wife; Danny Boy (US 1941); The Tower of Terror (US 1942); Jeannie (US 1943); The Man at the Gate (aka Men of the Sea—US). **1942** Hard Steel; The Night Has Eyes (aka Terror House—US 1943); The Great Mr. Handel (US 1943). **1943** Thursday's Child. **1944** Fanny By Gaslight (aka Man of Evil—US 1948). **1945** Macbeth (short). **1947** The Turners of Prospect Road. **1954** Make Me An Offer (US 1956). **1955** The Prisoner; An Alligator Named Daisy (US 1957). **1956** War and Peace. **1957** Miracle in Soho;

Hell Drivers (US 1958). **1958** Tread Softly Stranger (US 1959). **1959** Room at the top; Expresso Bongo (US 1960). **1961** The Naked Edge; Nothing Barred; Over the Odds. **1962** Postman's Knock; Go to Blazes. **1963** Tom Jones. **1964** Becket. **1966** The Wrong Box. **1967** Viking Queen.

LAWTON, FRANK

Born: Sept. 30, 1904, London, England. Died: June 10, 1969, London, England. Stage and screen actor. Married to actress Evelyn Laye, son of actor Frank Mokeley and actress Daisy May Collier.

Appeared in: **1930** Young Woodley (stage and film versions); Birds of Prey (aka The Perfect Alibi—US 1931). **1931** The Skin Game; The Outsider; Michael and Mary (US 1953). **1932** After Office Hours. **1933** Heads We Go (aka The Charming Deceiver—US); Friday the Thirteenth; Cavalcade. **1934** One More River. **1935** David Copperfield; Bar-20 Rides Again. **1936** The Invisible Ray; Devil Doll. **1937** The Mill on the Floss (US 1939). **1939** The Four Just Men (aka The Secret Four—US 1940). **1942** Went the Day Well? (aka 48 Hours—US 1944). **1948** The Winslow Boy (US 1950). **1953** Rough Shot (aka Shoot First—US). **1956** Doublecross. **1957** The Rising of the Moon. **1958** Gideon's Day (aka Gideon of Scotland Yard—US 1959); A Night to Remember. **1961** The Queen's Guards (US 1963).

LAWTON, THAIS

Born: 1881, Louisville, Ky. Died: Dec. 18, 1956, N.Y. Stage and screen actress.

Appeared in: **1915** The Battle Cry for Peace.

LAX, FRANCES

Born: Oct. 5, 1895, New York, N.Y. Died: May 6, 1975, Santa Monica, Calif. (heart disease). Screen and television actress.

Appeared in: **1960** The Apartment. **1961** The Errand Boy. **1965** The Family Jewels.

LAY, IRVING T.

Died: Mar., 1932, Seneca Falls, N.Y. (suicide—gas poisoning). Screen actor.

LAYDEN, ELMER

Born: 1903, Davenport, Iowa. Died: June 30, 1973, Chicago, Ill. Football player, coach, NFL commissioner and screen actor.

Appeared in: **1931** The Spirit of Notre Dame.

LAYMON, GENE

Born: July 25, 1889, Michigan City, Ind. Died: June 6, 1946, Los Angeles, Calif. Screen actor.

LAZOWSKI, YUREK

Born: 1914, Warsaw, Poland. Died: July 6, 1980, Studio City, Calif. (heart attack). Screen actor, ballet dancer and instructor.

Appeared in: **1973** First Position.

LAZZERI, TONY (Anthony Michael Lazzeri)

Born: Dec. 6, 1903, San Francisco, Calif. Died: Aug. 6, 1946, San Francisco, Calif. Baseball player and screen actor.

Appeared in: **1927** Slide, Kelly, Slide.

LEACH, SUSANNE

Born: Aug. 17, 1865, Ontario, Canada. Died: Aug. 16, 1945. Screen actress.

LEAHY, EUGENE

Born: Mar. 14, 1883, Newcastle West Co., Limerick, Ireland. Died: Mar., 1967, London, England. Stage and screen actor.

Appeared in: **1922** A Prince of Lovers (US 1927 and aka Life of Lord Byron). **1937** Love from a Stranger. **1957** The Curse of Frankenstein.

LEAHY, MARGARET

Born: Aug. 17, 1902, London, England. Died: Feb. 17, 1967, Los Angeles, Calif. (possible suicide). Screen actress.

Appeared in: **1923** The Three Ages.

LEAL, MILAGROS

Born: 1902. Died: Mar. 1, 1975, Madrid, Spain (cancer). Screen and stage actress. Married to actor Salvador Soler Marti. Mother of actress Amparo Soler Leal.

Appeared in: **1949** The Nail.

LEANDER, ZARAH (Zarah Stina Hedberg)

Born: Mar. 15, 1907, Karlstad, Sweden. Died: June 23, 1981, near Stockholm, Sweden. Screen, stage actress, singer and pianist. Married to stage actor Nils Leander (dec.). Divorced from Vidar Forsell, and later married to jazz pianist Arne Hulpher (dec. 1978). Entered films in 1936.

Appeared in: **1937** La Habanera; Premiere; Zu Neuen Ufern (To New Shores—US 1938). **1938** Heimat; Der Blaufuchs (The Blue Fox—US 1939); Die Heimt Ruft (Home is Calling); Magda. **1939** Es War eine Rauschende de Ballnacht (One Enchanted Evening); Das Lied der Wueste (The Desert Song—US 1940). **1940** Das Herz Einer Koenigin (The Heart of a Queen). **1941** Der Weg ins Freie. **1942** Die Grosse Liebe (The Grand Love). **1943** Damals. **1950** Gabriela. **1952** Cuba Cabana. **1953** Ave Marie. **1954** Bei dir War es Immer so Schoen. **1959** Der Blaue Nachtfalter (The Blue Nightreveller).

LEANE, PATRICK DANIEL See LANE, PAT

LEARY, GILDA

Born: 1896, England. Died: Apr. 17, 1927, New York, N.Y. (Addison's disease). Screen and stage actress.

Appeared in: **1915** The Seventh Noon.

LEASE, REX

Born: Feb. 11, 1901, Central City, W.Va. Died: Jan. 3, 1966, Hollywood, Calif. Screen actor. Entered films as an extra.

Appeared in: **1924** A Woman Who Sinned; Chalk Marks. **1925** Before Midnight; The Last Edition; Easy Money. **1926** The Timid Terror; Mystery Pilot (serial); The Last Alarm; Race Wild; Somebody's Mother. **1927** Clancy's Kosher Wedding; Moulders of Men; Heroes of the Night; The Cancelled Debt; The College Hero; Not for Publication; The Outlaw Dog. **1928** The Law of the Range; Last Lap; Riders of the Dark; Broadway Daddies; The Candy Kid; Red Riders of Canada; The Speed Classic; Phantom of the Turf; Making the Varsity; Queen of the Chorus. **1929** Stolen Love; The Younger Generation; Two Sisters; When Dreams Come True; Girls Who Dare. **1930** Borrowed Wives; The Utah Kid; Wings of Adventure; Troopers 3; Sunny Skies; Hot Curves; So This Is Mexico. **1931** In Old Cheyenne; Why Marry; Chinatown After Dark; Monster Walks; Is There Justice; Sign of the Wolf (serial). **1932** The Lone Trail; Midnight Morals; Cannonball Express. **1934** Inside Information. **1935** Fighting Caballero; The Ghost Rider; The Man from Guntown; Cowboy and the Bandit; Pals of the Range; Rough Riding Ranger; Cyclone of the Saddle. **1936** Custer's Last Stand (serial); Fast Bullets; Lightnin' Bill Carson; Roarin' Guns; Cavalcade of the West; Aces and Eight; The Clutching Hand (serial); Gentleman Jim McGee. **1937** The Silver Trail; Heroes of the Alamo; The Freedom; Swing It Sailor; The Mysterious Pilot (serial). **1938** Fury Below; Code of the Rangers; Desert Patrol; A Criminal Is Born (short). **1939** South of the Border; In Old Monterey; The Lone Ranger Rides Again (serial). **1940** The Grapes of Wrath; Rancho Grande; Under Texas Skies; Lone Star Raiders; A Chump at Oxford; The Trail Blazers. **1941** Outlaws of the Rio Grande; The Phantom Cowboy; Death Valley Outlaws; Pals of the Range; Sierra Sue; Outlaws of the Cherokee Trail. **1942** Arizona Terrors; The Silver Bullet; The Cyclone Kid; Tomorrow We Live; The Boss of Hangtown Mesa; Home in Wyomin'; Stardust on the Sage; Lady in a Jam; Eagle Squadron; The Saboteur. **1943** He's My Guy; So's Your Uncle; Daredevils of the West (serial); Haunted Ranch; Tenting on the Old Camp Ground; Dead Man's Gulch. **1944** Firebrands of Arizona; Bordertown Trail; The Cowboy and the Senorita; Yellow Rose of Texas; Sensations of 1945; The Singing Sheriff. **1945** On Stage Everybody; The Great John L.; Earl Carroll Vanities; Dakota; Texas Rangers; The Naughty Nineties; Santa Fe Saddlemates; Frontier Gal; Flame of Barbary Coast. **1946** Days of Buffalo Bill; Sun Valley Cyclone; The Time of Their Lives; Rustler's Roundup; The Phantom Rider (serial); Canyon Passage; The Plainsman and the Lady; The Crimson Ghost (serial). **1947** Brute Force; Wyoming; The Perils of Pauline; Easy Come, Easy Go; California; Helldorado; Slave Girl; The Wistful Widow of Wagon Gap; Buck Privates Come Home. **1948** Out of the Storm; A Foreign Affair; Letter from an Unknown Woman. **1949** The Lady Gambles; Ma and Pa Kettle. **1950** Singing Guns; Bells of Coronado; Code of the Silver Sage; Curtain Call at Cactus Creek; Covered Wagon Raiders; Hills of Oklahoma; Frisco Tornado. **1952** The Wild North (aka The Big North); The Man Behind the Gun; Ma and Pa Kettle at the Fair; Lone Star; Abbott and Costello Meet Captain Kidd; Montana Belle. **1953** Ride, Vaquero!; Money From Home; Abbott and Costello Go to Mars. **1955** The Prodigal. **1956** Back From Eternity; Perils of the Wilderness (serial); The Rawhide Years. **1957** A Hatful of Rain.

LEAVITT, DOUGLAS "ABE"
Born: 1883. Died: Mar. 3, 1960, Levittown, Pa. Screen, burlesque and vaudeville actor. Was part of vaudeville team of "Leavitt and Lockwood."

Appeared in: **1942** You Were Never Lovelier; Smith of Minnesota. **1943** Reveille With Beverly; Murder in Times Square; Two Senoritas from Chicago; Blitz on the Fritz (short); Farmer for a Day (short); It's a Great Life.

LE BEAU, LUCILLE
Born: 1873, Minn. Died: Jan. 31, 1980, Columbia, S.C. Screen and stage and vaudeville actress.

LE BEAU, STEPHANIE
Died: June 5, 1967, New York, N.Y. Screen, stage and television actress.

LEBEDEFF, IVAN
Born: June 18, 1899, Uspoliai, Lithuania. Died: Mar. 31, 1953, Hollywood, Calif. (heart attack). Screen actor, screenwriter and author. Appeared in French, German, U.S. films, etc. Married to actress Vera Engels.

Appeared in: **1922** King Frederick (German film debut). **1924** The Lucky Death; The Soul of an Artist; 600,000 Francs Per Month; The Charming Prince. **1925** Burned Fingers. **1926** The Sorrows of Satan. **1927** The Loves of Sunya; The Angel of Broadway; The Forbidden Woman. **1928** Let 'Er Go Gallagher; Walking Back. **1929** Sin Town; The Veiled Woman; The Cuckoos; The Midnight Mystery; The Conspiracy; Half-Shot at Sunrise. **1931** The Bachelor Apartment; The Lady Refuses; Deceit; Woman Pursued; The Gay Diplomat. **1932** Unholy Love; Hollywood Handicap (short); Hollywood on Parade (short). **1933** Bombshell; Made on Broadway; Laughing at Life; Sweepings. **1934** Strange Wives; Kansas City Princess; Merry Widow; The Merry Frinks; Moulin Rouge. **1935** China Seas; Sweepstakes Annie; Goin' to Town. **1936** Pepper; The Golden Arrow; Love on the Run. **1937** Maytime; Fair Warning; History Is Made at Night; Atlantic Flight; Mama Steps Out; Conquest; Angel. **1938** Straight, Place and Show; Wise Girl. **1939** Trapped in the Sky; The Mystery of Mr. Wong; Hotel for Women; You Can't Cheat an Honest Man. **1940** Passport to Alcatraz; Public Deb No. 1. **1941** The Shanghai Gesture; Blue, White and Perfect. **1942** Lure of the Islands; Foreign Agent. **1943** Mission to Moscow; Around the World. **1944** Oh, What a Night!; Are These Our Parents? **1945** Rhapsody in Blue; They Are Guilty. **1952** The Snows of Kilimanjaro; California Conquest.

LEBERFELD, ALFRED
Died: Aug. 28, 1973. Screen actor.

Appeared in: **1959** Middle of the Night.

LEBLANC, GEORGETTE
Born: 1875, Rouen, France. Died: Oct. 26, 1941, France? Screen actress.

LE BRANDT, GERTRUDE N.
Born: 1863. Died: Aug. 28, 1955, Hollywood, Calif. Screen and stage actress.

Appeared in: **1921** Mama's Affair.

LE BRUN, MINON
Born: 1888. Died: Sept. 20, 1941, Los Angeles, Calif. Screen actress. Divorced from actor Cullen Landis (dec. 1975).

LECLERCY, REGINA
Born: Brazil. Died: 1973, France (plane crash). Screen actress.

LEDERER, GRETCHEN
Born: 1891. Died: Dec. 20, 1955, Anaheim, Calif. Screen actress. Divorced from actor Otto Lederer (dec. 1965). Entered films in 1910.

Appeared in: **1914** An Eleventh Hour Reformation. **1917** A Kentucky Cinderella; The Spotted Lily; Polly Redhead; Bondage; The Double Topped Trunk; The Cricket; My Little Boy; The Pointed Finger; The Townsend Divorce Case; Bartered Youth. **1918** Beauty in Chains; Hungry Eyes; The Red, Red Heart; Riddle Gawne. **1919** Wife or Country.

LEDERER, OTTO
Born: Apr. 17, 1886, Prague, Czech. Died: Sept. 3, 1965. Screen actor. Divorced from actress Gretchen Lederer (dec. 1955). Entered films with Vitagraph.

Appeared in: **1913** Why Tightwad Tips. **1914** The Love of Tokiwa; The

Face of Fear. **1915** The Legend of the Lone Tree; The Chalice of Courage; What Did He Whisper?; Ghosts and Flypaper; The Offending Kiss; The Quarrel; Cal Marvin's Wife; Her Last Flirtation; His Golden Grain; Willie Stayed Single. **1916** La Paloma; Pansy's Poppas; Sin's Penalty; When It Rains It Pours; A Squared Account; The Waters of Lethe; Some Chicken; Curfew at Simpton Center; Miss Adventure; A Race for Life. **1917** The Captain of the Gray Horse Troop; The Fighting Trail (serial); Dead Shot Baker; When Men Are Tempted; The Flaming Omen. **1918** The Woman in the Web; The Wild Strain; Cavanaugh of the Forest Rangers; The Changing Woman; By the World Forgot. **1919** Cupid Forecloses. **1920** The Dragon's Net (serial). **1921** Making the Grade; The Struggle; Without Benefit of Clergy; The Spenders; The Avenging Arrow (serial). **1922** Forget-Me-Not; Hungry Hearts; White Eagle (serial). **1923** Souls in Bondage; Vanity Fair; Your Friend and Mine. **1924** Behind Two Guns; A Fighting Heart; Black Oxen; Poison; The Sword of Valor; What Three Men Wanted; Worldly Goods; Turned Up. **1925** Bowery Finery. **1926** Sweet Rosie O'Grady; That Model from Paris; The Cruise of the Jasper B. **1927** Chicago; The Jazz Singer; King of Kings; Sailor Izzy Murphy; The Shamrock and the Rose; The Trunk Mystery; Music Master. **1928** A Bit of Heaven; Celebrity; The Prediction (short); You're Darn Tootin! (short). **1929** From Headquarters; Smiling Irish Eyes; One Stolen Night. **1933** Forgotten.

LEDERER, PEPI (Josephine Rose Lederer)
Born: Mar. 18, 1910, Chicago, Ill. Died: June 11, 1935, Los Angeles, Calif. Screen actress.

Appeared in: **1928** The Cardboard Lover.

LEDERMAN, D. ROSS
Born: Dec. 11, 1895, Lancaster, Pa. Died: Aug. 24, 1972, Hollywood, Calif. (heart condition). Screen actor, prop man, film director and screenwriter. Entered films as an extra in 1913 in Mack Sennett Comedies.

LEDNER, DAVID
Born: 1900. Died: Dec. 17, 1957, Hollywood, Calif. (heart attack). Screen actor and stand-in. Entered films in 1941.

Appeared in: **1958** The Buccaneer (stand-in).

LEDUC, CLAUDINE (Sadi Lindsay)
Born: Paris, France. Died: Feb. 15, 1969, New York, N.Y. Screen, stage, television, radio actress and writer.

Appeared in: **1943** Once Upon a Honeymoon; The Song of Bernadette.

LEE, ALLEN
Born: 1875. Died: Feb. 5, 1951, New York, N.Y. Screen and stage actor.

LEE, AURIOL
Born: London, England. Died: July 2, 1941, Hutchison, Kans. (auto accident). Screen, stage actress, stage producer and stage director.

Appeared in: **1938** A Royal Divorce. **1941** Suspicion.

LEE, BELINDA
Born: June 15, 1935, Devon, England. Died: Mar. 13, 1961, San Bernardino, Calif. (auto accident). Screen, stage and television actress.

Appeared in: **1954** The Runaway Bus; Life With the Lyons (aka Family Affair—US); Meet Mr. Gallaghan; The Belles of St. Trinian's (US—1955). **1955** Murder By Proxy (aka Blackout—US); Footsteps in the Fog; Man of the Moment; No Smoking. **1956** Who Done It?; The Feminine Touch (aka The Gentle Touch—US 1957); Eyewitness; The Big Money. **1957** The Secret Place (US—1958); Miracle in Soho; Dangerous Exile (US 1958). **1958** Nor the Moon By Night (aka Elephant Gun—US 1959); Big Money (US 1962). **1960** Giuseppe Venduto dai Fratelli (The Story of Joseph and His Brethren—US 1962); Femine de Lusso (Love the Italian Way—US 1964); Goddess of Love; Le Notti De Lucrezia Borgia (The Nights of Lucretia Borgia); The Chasers (aka Les Dragueurs—The Dredgers). **1961** She Walks By Night; Aphrodite; Die Warheit Uber Rosemarie (The Truth About Rosemarie); Constantino il Grande (Constantine and the Cross—US 1962). **1962** Messalina. **1963** Long Night at 43 (aka It Happened in '43); The Devil's Choice. Other foreign films: Marie des Iles; Visa Pour Caracas; Ce Corps Tant Desire; I Magliari; Katja.

LEE, BERNARD
Born: Jan. 10, 1908, London, England. Died: Jan. 16, 1981, London, England (cancer). Screen, stage and television actor.

Appeared in: **1934** The Double Event. **1935** The River House Mystery. **1936** Rhodes of Africa (aka Rhodes—US). **1937** The Black Tulip. **1938**

The Terror. **1939** The Frozen Limits; Murder in Soho (aka Murder in the Night—US 1940). **1940** Spare a Copper; Let George Do It. **1941** Once a Crook. **1946** This Man is Mine. **1947** Dusty Bates; The Courtneys of Curzon Street (aka The Courtney Affair—US). **1948** Quartet (US 1949); The Fallen Idol (US 1949). **1949** The Third Man (US 1950); Elizabeth of Ladymead. **1950** Odette; Morning Departure (aka Operation Disaster—US 1951); Last Holiday; Cage of Gold (US 1951); The Blue Lamp. **1951** Appointment With Venus (aka Island Rescue—US 1952); The Adventurers (aka The Great Adventure—US); Mr. Denning Drives North (US 1953); Calling Bulldog Drummond; White Corridors (US 1952). **1952** The Yellow Balloon (US 1954); The Gift Horse (aka Glory at Sea—US 1953). **1953** Beat the Devil (US 1954); Single-Handed (aka Sailor of the King—US). **1954** Seagulls Over Sorrento (aka Crest of the Wave—US); The Rainbow Jacket; Father Brown (aka The Detective—US); The Purple Plain (US 1955). **1955** Out of the Clouds (US 1957); The Ship That Died of Shame (US 1956). **1956** The Battle of the River Plate (aka Pursuit of the Graf Spee—US 1957); The Spanish Gardener (US 1957). **1957** Fire Down Below; High Flight (US 1958); Across the Bridge. **1958** The Key; The Man Upstairs (US 1959); Dunkirk; Nowhere to Go (US 1959). **1959** Danger Within (aka Breakout—US 1960); Beyond This Place (aka Web of Evidence—US). **1960** The Clue of the Twisted Candle (US 1968); The Angry Silence; Kidnapped; Cone of Silence (aka Trouble in the Sky—US 1961). **1961** The Secret Partner; Whistle Down the Wind (US 1962); Partners in Crime; Clue of the Silver Key; Fury at Smugglers Bay (US 1963). **1962** The L-Shaped Room (US 1963); The Share Out (US 1966); Vengeance (aka The Brain—US 1964); Dr. No (US 1963). **1963** From Russia With Love (US 1964); Two Left Feet; Ring of Spies (aka Ring of Treason—US 1964); A Place to Go. **1964** Dr. Terror's House of Horrors (US 1965); Saturday Night Out; Who Was Maddox?; Goldfinger. **1965** The Amorous Adventures of Moll Flanders; Thunderball; The Legend of Young Dick Turpin; The Spy Who Came In From The Cold. **1967** You Only Live Twice; O.K. Connery (aka Operation Kid Brother—US). **1969** On Her Majesty's Secret Service; Crossplot. **1970** 10 Rillington Place; The Raging Moon. **1971** Dulcima; Diamonds Are Forever; Danger Point. **1973** Live and Let Die; Frankenstein and the Monster from Hell. **1974** The Man With The Golden Gun. **1977** The Spy Who Loved Me. **1978** It's Not the Size That Counts. **1979** Moonraker.

LEE, BESSIE
Born: Sept. 8, 1903, Utah. Died: Nov. 9, 1931, Hollywood, Calif. (cerebral hemorrhage). Screen actress. Do not confuse with actress deceased 1972.

LEE, BESSIE
Born: 1906. Died: June 28, 1972, Pittsburgh, Pa. Screen and stage actress.

Appeared in: **1928** The Night Bird. **1939** Mr. Wong in Chinatown.

LEE, BRUCE (Lee Yuen Kam aka LEE SIU LOONG)
Born: Nov. 27, 1940, San Francisco, Calif. Died: July 19, 1973, Hong Kong (acute cerebral edema). Screen and television actor and martial arts expert. Son of a Cantonese opera and vaudeville performer. Made 20 films as a child actor in Hong Kong under the name, Lee Siu Loong (The Little Dragon).

Appeared in: **1969** Marlowe. **1973** Fists of Fury (aka The Chinese Connection—US and aka The Big Boss); Five Fingers of Death; Way of the Dragon (aka Return of the Dragon—US); Enter the Dragon.

LEE, CANADA
Born: 1907. Died: May 9, 1952, New York, N.Y. (heart attack). Black screen, stage, radio, television actor and orchestra leader.

Appeared in: **1939** Keep Punching. **1944** Lifeboat. **1947** Body and Soul; The Roosevelt Story (narr.). **1949** Lost Boundaries. **1952** Cry, the Beloved Country. **1955** Othello.

LEE, CHARLES T.
Born: 1882. Died: Mar. 14, 1927, Los Angeles, Calif. (heart trouble). Screen actor.

LEE, CHINGWAH (Ching Wah Lee)
Born: 1902. Died: Jan. 2, 1980, San Francisco, Calif. Screen actor and technical advisor.

Appeared in: **1937** The Good Earth (film debut); Daughter of Shanghai. **1943** China. **1944** Thirty Seconds Over Tokyo. **1946** Little Mr. Jim. **1961** Flower Drum Song.

LEE, COSETTE
Born: 1910, Canada. Died: Sept. 19, 1976. Screen actress.

Appeared in: **1969** Change of Mind; The First Time; My Side of the Mountain. **1974** Deranged.

LEE, DIXIE (Wilma Wyatt)
Born: Nov. 4, 1911, Harriman, Tenn. Died: Nov. 1, 1952, Holmby Hills, Calif. (cancer). Stage and screen actress. Married to singer Bing Crosby (dec. 1977). Mother of actors Gary, Phillip, Dennis and Lindsay Crosby.

Appeared in: **1924** Not for Sale. **1929** Fox Movietone Follies of 1929; Knights Out (short); Why Leave Home? **1930** Happy Days; Cheer Up and Smile; The Big Party; Let's Go Places; Harmony at Home. **1931** No Limit; Night Life in Reno. **1934** Manhattan Love Song. **1935** Love in Bloom; Redheads on Parade.

LEE, DUKE R.
Born: 1881, Va. Died: Apr. 1, 1959, Los Angles, Calif. Screen, stage and vaudeville actor. Entered films in 1918.

Appeared in: **1918** Lure of the Circus. **1921** Trailin'; "If Only" Jim. **1922** In the Days of Buffalo Bill (serial); Don't Shoot; Just Tony; Tracked to Earth. **1923** Mile-a-Minute Romeo; In the Days of Daniel Boone (serial). **1924** The Gaiety Girl; Fighting Fury; The Western Wallop. **1925** The Red Rider; Don Daredevil; Flying Hoofs; The Call of Courage; The White Outlaw. **1926** Tony Runs Wild; The Canyon of Light; Sky High Corral; The Man in the Saddle; Man of the Forest; Rustler's Ranch. **1927** Galloping Fury; The Terror of Bar X; The Circus Ace; Lands of the Lawless; Outlaws of Red River. **1928** Crashing Through; Clearing the Trail; Son of the Golden West; The Big Hop; The Heart of Broadway. **1929** .45 Calibre War. **1930** The Concentratin' Kid. **1933** Man of the Forest. **1936** The Prisoner of Shark Island. **1939** Stagecoach. **1948** Fort Apache.

LEE, EARL
Born: 1886. Died: June 2, 1955, Redwood City, Calif. Screen and stage actor.

Appeared in: **1951** Five. **1952** Assignment—Paris; The Story of Will Rogers; Tropical Heat Wave. **1954** Geraldine.

LEE, ETTA
Born: 1906. Died: Oct. 27, 1956, Eureka, Calif. Screen actress.

Appeared in: **1921** The Sheik; A Tale of Two Worlds. **1922** The Toll of the Sea. **1923** The Untameable; The Remittance Woman. **1924** The Thief of Bagdad. **1925** A Thief in Paradise; The Trouble With Wives; Recompense. **1927** Camille; The Chinese Parrot. **1928** Out with the Tide. **1933** International House.

LEE, FLORENCE
Born: 1888. Died: Sept. 1, 1962, Hollywood, Calif. Screen and stage actress. Married to actor Del Henderson (dec. 1956).

Appeared in: **1922** The Top O' the Morning; The Trouper. **1923** Blood Test; Mary of the Movies. **1924** Jack O' Clubs; Virtue's Revolt; Way of a Man (serial and feature). **1925** Luck and Sand; Across the Deadline; Speed Mad. **1926** The High Hand; Man Rustlin'. **1928** The Bronc Stomper; The Little Buckaroo. **1929** Illusion of Love. **1931** City Lights.

LEE, GWEN (Gwendolyn LePinski)
Born: Nov. 12, 1904, Hastings, Nebr. Died: Aug. 20, 1961. Screen and stage actress.

Appeared in: **1924** His Hour. **1925** The Plastic Age; His Secretary; Pretty Ladies. **1926** The Boy Friend; There You Are!; The Lone Wolf Returns; Upstage. **1927** Adam and Evil; After Midnight; Heaven on Earth; Her Wild Oats; Twelve Miles Out; Orchids and Ermine; Women Love Diamonds. **1928** The Actress; A Thief in the Dark; The Baby Cyclone; Diamond Handcuffs; A Lady of Chance; Laugh, Clown, Laugh; Sharp Shooters; Show Girl. **1929** Lucky Boy; Fast Company; The Hollywood Revue of 1929; Untamed; The Man and the Moment; The Duke Steps Out; The Road Show. **1930** Caught Short; Chasing Rainbows; Extravagance; Free and Easy; Lord Byron of Broadway; Paid; Our Blushing Brides. **1931** The Galloping Ghost (serial); Inspiration; The Lawless Woman; Pagan Lady; Traveling Husbands. **1932** Alias Mary Smith; Midnight Morals; West of Broadway; From Broadway to Cheyenne; Boy, Oh, Boy (short). **1933** The Intruder; Corruption. **1934** City Park; One in a Million. **1937** Double Wedding; Candid Cameramaniacs (short); A Night at the Movies (short). **1938** Paroled from the Big House; Penny's Party (short); Mannequin.

LEE, GYPSY ROSE (Rose Louise Hovick)
Born: Jan. 9, 1914, Seattle, Wash. Died: Apr. 26, 1970, Los Angeles, Calif. (cancer). Screen, stage, burlesque, radio, vaudeville actress and author. Divorced from actor Julio de Diego (dec. 1979). Sister of actress June Havoc.

Appeared in: **1936** The Ziegfeld Follies of 1936. **1937** You Can't Have

Everything; Ali Baba Goes to Town. **1938** Sally, Irene and Mary; The Battle of Broadway. **1939** My Lucky Star. **1943** Stage Door Canteen. **1944** Belle of the Yukon. **1945** Doll Face. **1952** Babes in Bagdad. **1958** Wind Across the Everglades; The Screaming Mimi. **1963** The Stripper. **1966** The Trouble With Angels.

LEE, HARRY (William Henry Lee)
Born: June 1, 1872, Richmond, Va. Died: Dec. 8, 1932, Hollywood, Calif. (suicide—jump). Stage and screen actor.

Appeared in: **1921** Bucking the Tiger. **1922** Channing of the Northwest; Boomerang Bill; The Man She Brought Back. **1924** Monsieur Beaucaire. **1925** The Wrongdoers. **1926** Men of Steel. **1929** Gentlemen of the Press; Sunny Skies.

LEE, JANE
Born: 1912. Died: Mar. 17, 1957, New York, N.Y. Screen and vaudeville actress. Sister of actress Katherine Lee and actor Davey Lee. Was member of vaudeville team "Katherine and Jane Lee."

Appeared in: **1914** Neptune's Daughter; Two Little Imps. **1915** The Galley Slave; Soul of Broadway; His Prior Claim. **1916** Her Double Life; Daredevil Kate; Love and Hate; The Unwelcome Mother. **1917** Trouublemakers. **1918** American Buds; We Should Marry?; Swat the Spy; Doing Their Bit. **1919** Smiles. **1927** Jane and Katherine Lee (short).

LEE, JENNIE
Born: 1850. Died: Aug. 4, 1925, Hollywood, Calif. Screen, stage and vaudeville actress. Do not confuse with stage actress Jennie Lee (dec. 1930).

Appeared in: **1913** His Mother's Son; Her Mother's Oath. **1915** Birth of a Nation. **1921** The Big Punch; One Man in a Million. **1923** North of Hudson Bay. **1924** Young Ideas; Hearts of Oak.

LEE, JOHNNY (John Dotson Lee, Jr.)
Born: July 4, 1898, Missouri. Died: Dec. 12, 1965, Los Angeles, Calif. (heart attack). Black screen, television and radio actor. Played "Calhoun" in both the radio and television"Amos 'n Andy" shows. Do not confuse with British actor John Lee.

Appeared in: **1927** St. Louis Blues. **1932** Rufus Jones for President. **1943** Stormy Weather. **1946** Come On Cowboy. **1947** Mantan Runs for Mayor. **1948** Return of Mandy's Husband; She's Too Mean to Me; Boarding House Blues. **1951** My Forbidden Past. **1956** The Bottom of the Bottle. **1957** The Cat Girl; The Spirit of St. Louis. **1958** Hot Spell. **1960** The Rat Race; North to Alaska.

LEE, LEONA
Died: Aug., 1975, Los Angeles, Calif. Screen actress.

LEE, LILA (Augusta Appel)
Born: July 25, 1902, Union Hill, N.J. Died: Nov. 13, 1973, Saranac Lake, N.Y. (stroke). Screen, stage and vaudeville actress. Divorced from actor Jack Kirkwood (dec. 1963), Jack R. Paine and John E. Murphy. Mother of playwright James Kirkwood. Entered films at age 13 with Jesse Lasky.

Appeared in: **1918** The Cruise of the Makebelieve; Such a Little Pirate. **1919** Puppy Love; Secret Garden; Rustling a Bride; Rose of the River; Heart of Youth; Male and Female; Hawthorne of the U.S.A.; Daughter of the Wolf; Lottery Man. **1920** Terror Island; The Prince Chap; The Soul of Youth; Midsummer Madness. **1921** After the Show; The Charm School; Crazy to Marry; The Dollar-a-Year Man; The Easy Road; Gasoline Gus; If Women Only Knew. **1922** Back Home and Broke; Blood and Sand; The Dictator; Ebb Tide; The Ghost Breaker; Is Matrimony a Failure?; One Glorious Day; Rent Free; The Road to Arcady. **1923** Hollywood; Homeward Bound; The Ne'er-Do-Well; Woman Proof. **1924** Another Man's Wife; Love's Whirlpool; Wandering Husbands. **1925** Coming Through; The Midnight Girl; Old Home Week; The Unholy Three. **1926** Broken Hearts; Fascinating Youth; The New Klondike. **1927** Million Dollar Mystery; One Increasing Purpose. **1928** The Adorable Cheat; A Bit of Heaven; Black Butterflies; The Black Pearl; Just Married; The Little Wild Girl; The Man in Hobbies; Thundergod; Top Sergeant Mulligan; United States Smith; You Can't Beat the Law. **1929** The Argyle Case; Dark Streets; Drag; Fight; Honky Tonk; Love, Live and Laugh; Queen of the Night Clubs; The Sacred Flame; The Show of Shows. **1930** Double Cross Roads; The Gorilla; Murder Will Out; Second Wife; Those Who Dance; The Unholy Three (and in 1925 version). **1931** Misbehaving Ladies; Woman Hungry. **1932** War Correspondent; Radio Patrol; Exposure; Unholy Love; Night of June 13; False Faces. **1933** Officer 13; Face in the Sky; Iron Master; The Intruder; Lone Cowboy. **1934** Whirlpool; In Love With Life; I Can't Escape. **1935** Champagne for Breakfast; Marriage Bargain; People's Enemy. **1936** The Ex-Mrs. Bradford; Country Gentleman. **1937** Two Wise Maids; Nation Aflame.

LEE, LILA DEAN
Born: 1890. Died: Nov. 3, 1959, West Covina, Calif. Screen actress. Do not confuse with actress Lila Lee (dec. 1973).

LEE, MARGO
Died: Oct. 8, 1951, Los Angeles, Calif. Screen, radio and television actress.

Appeared in: **1950** So Young, So Bad.

LEE, NORMA
Born: 1899, Newport, Ky. Died: Dec. 12, 1980, New York, N.Y. Screen and stage actress. Married to actor/playwright Elliott Nugent (dec. 1980).

Appeared in: **1923** Counterfeit Love. **1929** Wise Girls.

LEE, RAYMOND
Born: 1910. Died: June 26, 1974, Canoga Park, Calif. (cancer). Screen actor and author.

Appeared in: **1921** No Woman Knows. **1923** Long Live the King; The Pilgrim. **1924** Abraham Lincoln; Bread.

LEE, ROSE *See* MC QUOID, ROSE LEE

LEE, ROWLAND
Born: 1891, Findlay, Ohio. Died: Dec. 21, 1975, Palm Desert, Calif. (heart attack). Screen actor, screenwriter and film director. Son of stage actress Marie (dec.) and stage actor C. W. Lee (dec.).

Appeared in: **1917** The Stainless Barrier; The Maternal Spark; Wild Winship's Widow. **1920** Woman in the Staircase; Water, Water, Everywhere; Her Husband's Friend. **1921** His Own Law.

LEE, RUTH (Ruth Rhodes)
Born: 1896. Died: Aug. 3, 1975, Woodland Hills, Calif. Screen actress. Married to actor Grandon Rhodes.

Appeared in: **1932** The Rich Are Always With Us. **1939** How to Eat (short). **1940** The Trouble with Husbands (short). **1941** Crime Control (short); The Forgotten Man (short). **1942** The Witness (short); The Man's Angle (short); Get Hep to Love; Behind the Eight Ball. **1943** Hers to Hold; Moonlight in Vermont; Mexican Spitfire's Blessed Event; Silver Skates; The Adventures of a Rookie; My Tomato (short). **1944** Tucson Raiders; Sensations of 1945; Goin' to Town; The Town Went Wild; Important Business (short); Why, Daddy? (short); Hi, Beautiful. **1945** I'll Tell the World; Weekend at the Waldorf; On Stage Everybody; The Man Who Walked Alone; Honeymoon; Divorce; Mama Loves Papa; The Daltons Ride Again; The Naughty Nineties; Here Come the Co-eds. **1946** Partners in Time; Ding Dong Williams; The Dark Horse; The Magnificent Rogue; The Magnificent Doll; The Razor's Edge; Idea Girl. **1948** Larceny. **1949** It Happens Every Spring; Cover Up; Henry, the Rainmaker; Whirlpool; Annie Was a Wonder (short); The Lady Takes a Sailor. **1950** Eye Witness. **1951** When I Grow Up; Insurance Investigator; As You Were; On Dangerous Ground; Payment on Demand. **1954** The Long Long Trailer. **1955** Hell's Outpost. **1956** These Wilder Years; High Society. **1957** Wild Is the Wind. **1961** Three on a Spree.

LEE, SAMMY
Born: 1890, New York, N.Y. Died: Mar. 20, 1968, Woodland Hills, Calif. Screen, stage actor and dance director. Do not confuse with vaudeville actor Sam Lee (dec. 1980).

Appeared in: **1933** I Loved You Wednesday. **1938** The Last Express. **1939** The Gracie Allen Murder Case.

LEE, SYLVAN
Born: 1906. Died: Oct. 30, 1962, New York, N.Y. Screen and stage actor.

Appeared in: The Cocoanuts.

LEE, WENDIE
Born: 1923. Died: Aug. 23, 1968, Los Angeles, Calif. Television model and screen actress.

Appeared in: **1950** Everybody's Dancing.

LEE, WILLIAM
Born: 1916. Died: Nov. 15, 1980, Los Angeles, Calif. (brain tumor). Screen, radio actor, singer, musician and choral director. Member of the Mellomen Quartet.

Appeared in: **1949** The Lone Wolf and His Lady. **1951** St. Benny the Dip. **1953** Little Fugitive. **1955** Lady and the Tramp (voice). **1965** The Sound of Music (voice).

LEEDS, MARIAN
Died: June 26, 1961. Screen actress.

Appeared in: **1948** Naked City.

LE FABER, ELEANOR
Died: Mar. 18, 1978. Screen actress.

Appeared in: **1960** House of Usher.

LEFAUR, ANDRE (Andre Lefaurichon)
Born: 1879, France. Died: Dec. 4, 1952, Paris, France. Screen and stage actor.

Appeared in: **1932** Le Bal. **1939** Ils Etaient Neufs Celibataires (Nine Bachelors—US 1942); With a Smile. **1941** The King. **1944** 32 Rue de Montmartre.

LEFEUVRE, GUY (Guy Anstruther-Mainguy)
Born: Oct 17, 1883, Ottawa, Canada. Died: Feb. 15, 1950, England. Screen, stage actor, vocalist and composer.

Appeared in: **1942** Thunder Rock (film debut—US 1944). **1948** Bonnie Prince Charlie (US 1952). **1949** Christopher Columbus.

LE FEUVRE, PHILIP
Born: 1871. Died: Aug. 23, 1939, Arcadia, Calif. Screen and stage actor.

LEFEVRE, NED (Roy Ned LeFevre)
Born: Mar. 9, 1912, Indiana. Died: June 10, 1966, Sun Valley, Calif. (cancer). Radio announcer, screen and television actor.

Appeared in: **1954** Creature from the Black Lagoon. **1957** The Joker Is Wild.

LEFTWICH, ALEXANDER
Born: 1884, Philadelphia, Pa. Died: Jan. 13, 1947, Los Angeles, Calif. (heart attack). Screen, radio actor, stage director-producer and television director-producer. Father of actress Patricia Ellis (dec. 1970).

Appeared in: **1937** Swing It Sailor; The Life of Emile Zola; Waikiki Wedding. **1938** Prison Train; Midnight Intruder; Reckless Living. **1939** Dark Victory; Juarez; Zaza. **1941** Melody for Three.

LEGAL, ERNEST
Born: 1881, Germany. Died: June 29, 1955, Berlin, Germany. Screen, stage actor, playwright and stage director.

Appeared in: **1938** Kater Lampe. **1939** Das Unsterbliche Herz (The Immortal Heart). **1950** Marriage of Figaro. Other German film: Heaven Is Never Brought Out.

LEGARE, OVILA
Born: 1902, Canada. Died: Feb. 9, 1978. Screen actress.

Appeared in: **1951** 13th Letter. **1953** I Confess. **1954** Operation Manhunt. **1964** The Luck of Ginger Coffey.

LEGNEUR, CHARLES
Born: 1892. Died: Feb. 14, 1956, Hollywood, Calif. (heart attack). Screen actor.

LEGUERE, GEORGE
Born: 1871. Died: Nov. 21, 1947, New York, N.Y. Screen and stage actor.

Appeared in: **1918** Cecilia of the Pink Roses. **1919** The Way of a Woman; The Hand Invisible. **1921** Mama's Affair. **1922** Missing Millions. **1930** Men Without Women. **1933** Three-Cornered Moon.

LEHMANN, BEATRIX
Born: July 1, 1903, Bourne End, Bucks, England. Died: Aug. 1, 1979, London, England. Screen, stage, radio, television actress and author. Entered films in 1935.

Appeared in: **1935** The Passing of the Third Floor Back (US 1936). **1936** Strangers on a Honeymoon (US 1937). **1937** The Rat. **1958** The Key. **1961** On the Fiddle (aka War Head, aka Operation Warhead, and aka Operation Snafu—US 1965). **1963** Psyche 59 (US 1964). **1965** The Spy Who Came In From The Cold. **1966** A Funny Thing Happened on the Way to the Forum. **1969** Staircase.

LEHMANN, LOTTE
Born: Feb. 27, 1888, Perleberg, Germany. Died: Aug. 26, 1976, Santa Barbara, Calif. Opera singer, screen actress and author.

Appeared in: **1948** The Big City.

LEHR, LEW
Born: May 14, 1895, Philadelphia, Pa. Died: Mar. 6, 1950, Brookline, Mass. Screen, stage, vaudeville, radio actor, screenwriter and film producer. Married to actress Anna Leonhardt, professionally known as Nancy Belle, with whom he toured in vaudeville. Well known for his comedy newsreel commentary, "Monkeys is the Craziest People.".

Appeared in prior to **1936** Looking Back (voice); Tintypes (comm.); Adventures of a Newsreel Cameraman (comm.); Magic Carpet; Newsettes; Lew Lehr's Unnatural History. **1937** Borneo (narr.).

LEHRER, GEORGE J.
Born: 1889. Died: Aug. 25, 1966, Cleveland, Ohio. Screen, stage actor and stage director. Known for his Abraham Lincoln impersonations.

LEHRMAN, HENRY
Born: Mar. 30, 1886, Vienna, Austria. Died: Nov. 7, 1946, Hollywood, Calif. (heart attack). Screen actor, film producer, film director and screenwriter. Entered films with Griffith in 1910. Founded L-KO productions ("Lehrman-Knockout" comedies) in 1914.

Appeared in: **1910** As the Bells Rang Out; The Iconoclast; Her Sacrifice. **1912** A Beast at Bay. **1914** Making a Living (later reissued as A Bustled Johnny); Kid Auto Races at Venice.

LEIBER, FRITZ
Born: Jan. 31, 1882, Chicago, Ill. Died: Oct. 14, 1949, Pacific Palisades, Calif. (heart attack). Stage and screen actor.

Appeared in: **1917** Cleopatra. **1920** If I Were King. **1921** Queen of Sheba. **1935** A Tale of Two Cities. **1936** Sins of Man; Under Two Flags; Down to the Sea; Camille; The Story of Louis Pasteur; Anthony Adverse; Hearts in Bondage. **1937** Champagne Waltz; The Prince and the Pauper; The Great Garrick. **1938** The Jury's Secret; Flight into Nowhere; Gateway; If I Were King (and 1920 version). **1939** Nurse Edith Cavell; They Made Her a Spy; Pack Up Your Troubles; The Hunchback of Notre Dame. **1940** The Mortal Storm; Lady With Red Hair; The Way of All Flesh; All This and Heaven Too; The Sea Hawk. **1941** Aloma of the South Seas. **1942** Crossroads. **1943** The Song of Bernadette; The Desert Song; First Comes Courage; Phantom of the Opera. **1944** The Imposter; Cry of the Werewolf; Bride of the Vampire. **1945** The Cisco Kid Returns; This Love of Ours; The Spanish Main; Son of Lassie. **1946** Scarlet Street; A Scandal in Paris; Strange Journey; Humoresque; Angel On My Shoulder. **1947** High Conquest; Bells of San Angelo; The Web; Monsieur Verdoux; Dangerous Venture. **1948** Adventures of Casanova; To the Ends of the Earth; Inner Sanctum; Another Part of the Forest. **1949** Bagdad; Bride of Vengeance; Samson and Delilah; Song of India; Devil's Doorway.

LEICESTER, WILLIAM (William Francis Leichester)
Born: 1915. Died: Jan. 9, 1969, Van Nuys, Calif. Screen actor and television writer.

Appeared in: **1948** Command Decision; Strange Gamble. **1949** Battleground. **1952** Operation Secret. **1955** Finger Man. **1956** Beyond a Reasonable Doubt.

LEIGH, ANDREW GEORGE
Born: Nov. 30, 1887, Brighton, England. Died: Apr. 21, 1957, Brighton, England. Screen, stage, radio actor and stage producer.

Appeared in: **1949** A Run for Your Money (US 1950). **1950** Double Confession (US 1953). **1957** The Curse of Frankenstein.

LEIGH, FRANK
Born: London, England. Died: May 9, 1948, Hollywood, Calif. Screen and stage actor. Entered films in England in 1912.

Appeared in: **1918** Fedora. **1919** Lord and Lady Algy. **1920** Nurse Marjorie; Cup of Fury; Dangerous Days; One Hour Before Dawn. **1921** Bob Hampton of Placer; The Light in the Clearing; Pilgrims of the Night. **1922** Golden Dreams; Domestic Relations; Out of the Silent North. **1923** Ashes of Vengeance; Truxton King; The Gentleman from America; North of Hudson Bay; Rosita; The Lonely Road. **1924** Hill Billy; The Breath of Scandal; The Reckless Age; Flames of Desire; Hutch of the U.S.A.; Honor Among Men. **1925** Contraband; The Winding Stair; His Majesty Bunker Bean; American Pluck; As Man Desires. **1926** The Adorable Deceiver; Flame of the Argentine; The Flaming Forest; The Lady of the Harem; The Imposter; Secret Orders. **1927** Soft Cushions; The Tigress; Somewhere in Sonora. **1928** A Night of Mystery; King Cowboy; Prowlers of the Sea. **1929** Below the Deadline; Love in the Desert; Montmartre Rose; Thirteenth Chair; Captain's Wife. **1930** The Lotus Lady. **1931** The Woman from Monte Carlo; Ten Nights in a Barroom. **1936** The Clutching Hand (serial).

LEIGH, LISLE
Born: 1879, Salt Lake City, Utah. Died: May 19, 1927, New York, N.Y. (heart trouble). Screen, stage and vaudeville actress.

Appeared in: **1916** Caprice of the Mountains; Slander.

LEIGH, NELSON
Born: 1914. Died: 1967. Screen actor.

Appeared in: **1944** The Return of the Vampire; Texas Masquerade; U-Boat Prisoner; Louisiana Hayride. **1945** Identity Unknown. **1947** Brick Bradford (serial). **1948** Congo Bill (serial); Angel's Alley; Racing Luck. **1949** Barbary Pirate; Adventures of Sir Galahad (serial); The Lost Tribe. **1950** Captive Girl. **1951** Home Town Story; Hurricane Island; Yukon Manhunt. **1952** Thief of Damascus. **1953** Texas Bad Man; Savage Mutiny; Valley of the Headhunters; Jack Slade; Prisoners of the Casbah. **1954** The Outlaw's Daughter; Jesse James vs. the Daltons; The Saracen Blade. **1955** Creature With the Atom Brain. **1956** World Without End; The First Texan; Hold Back the Night. **1957** Gunfight at the OK Corral; Bombers B-52; God Is My Partner. **1958** In Love and War. **1959** These Thousand Hills. **1960** The Gallant Hours; Ma Barker's Killer Brood. **1961** A Fever in the Blood; The Little Shepherd of Kingdom Come. **1962** Incident in an Alley. **1963** A Gathering of Eagles.

LEIGH, PHILIP
Born: 1880. Died: June 19, 1935. Screen and stage actor.

Appeared in: **1919** The Virtuous Wives.

LEIGH, VIVIEN (Vivian Mary Hartley)
Born: Nov. 5, 1913, Darjeeling, India. Died: July 8, 1967, London, England (natural causes). Screen and stage actress. Divorced from actor Sir Laurence Olivier and from Herbert Leigh Holman. Won 1939 Academy Award for Best Actress in Gone With the Wind and in 1951 for A Streetcar Named Desire.

Appeared in: **1934** Things Are Looking Up (film debut). **1935** Village Squire; Gentleman's Agreement; Look Up and Laugh. **1937** Fire Over England; Dark Journey; Storm in a Teacup; 21 Days (aka 21 Days Together—US 1940, aka The First and the Last). **1938** St. Martin's Lane (aka Sidewalks of London—US 1940); A Yank at Oxford. **1939** Gone With the Wind. **1940** Waterloo Bridge. **1941** That Hamilton Woman. **1946** Caesar and Cleopatra. **1948** Anna Karenina. **1951** A Streetcar Named Desire. **1955** The Deep Blue Sea. **1961** The Roman Spring of Mrs. Stone. **1965** Ship of Fools. **1974** That's Entertainment (film clips).

LEIGHTON, DANIEL
Born: 1880. Died: June 20, 1917, Los Angeles, Calif. Screen actor.

Appeared in: **1915** A Question of Right or Wrong; The Patent Food Conveyor. **1916** The Crown Prince's Double; The Supreme Temptation; Oh! Oh! Oh! Henry!; A Man's Sin; When She Played Broadway; The Answer. **1917** The Girl Who Lost; The Startling Climax; Chubby Takes a Hand; The Phantom's Secret; The Thief Maker; A Blissful Calamity.

LEIGHTON, FRANK (Frank Athelston Leighton)
Born: July 16, 1908, Sydney, Australia. Died: Oct. 17, 1962, England? Screen and stage actor. Entered films in 1932 in Australia.

Appeared in: **1938** It's in the Air (US 1940). **1955** The Stateless Man.

LEIGHTON, LILLIAN (aka LYLLIAN BROWN LEIGHTON)
Born: 1874, Auroville, Wis. Died: Mar. 19, 1956, Woodland Hills, Calif. Screen, stage and vaudeville actress.

Appeared in: **1911** The Two Orphans; Cinderella. **1912** Katzenjammer Kids; My Wife's Bonnet; The Three Valises; Bread Upon the Waters; The Other Woman. **1913** Sweeney and the Million; Turn Him Out; The Fugitive; Sweeney and the Fairy; Sweeney's Other Dream; Two Artists and One Suit of Clothes; Henrietta's Hair; The College Chaperone; The Clue. **1914** King Baby's Birthday; Castles in the Air. **1915** Shoo-Fly; Apple Butter. **1916** Small Town Stuff; The Plow Girl. **1917** The Tides of Barnegat; Joan the Woman; The American Consul; The Little American; The Devil Stone; Bill and the Bearded Lady; Everybody Was Satisfied; Betty to the Rescue; Castles for Two; Romance and Roses; Freckles; The Ghost House. **1918** Old Wives for New; A Lady's Name; Till I Come Back to You. **1919** Male and Female; Men, Women and Money. **1920** All-of-a-Sudden Peggy; A Girl Named Mary. **1924** Crazy to Marry; The Lost Romance; Peck's Bad Boy; The Barbarian; The Girl from God's Country; Under the Lash. **1922** Is Matrimony a Failure?; The Lane That Had No Turning; Rent Free; Red Hot Romance; Saturday Night; Tillie. **1923** The Call of the Canyon; Hollywood; Only 38; Crinoline and Romance; Ruggles of Red Gap; Wasted Lives; The Eternal Three. **1924** The Bedroom Window; $50,000 Reward; Code of the Sea; Phantom Justice. **1925** Code of the West; Go Straight; In the Name of Love; Parisian Love; Tumbleweeds; The Thundering Herd; Contraband. **1926** The False Alarm; Sandy; The Torrent. **1927** California; The Fair Co-Ed; The Frontiersman; By Whose Hand?; The Golden Yukon; Lovers? **1930**

Feet First; The Grand Parade; The Last Dance. **1931** Subway Express; Sweepstakes. **1932** The Sign of the Cross. **1933** The Sphinx. **1935** Whipsaw; College Scandal; Millions in the Air. **1941** Where Did You Get That Girl?

LEIGHTON, MARGARET
Born: Feb. 26, 1922, Barnt Green, Worcestershire, England. Died: Jan. 13, 1976, Chichester, England (multiple sclerosis). Screen, stage and television actress. Divorced from publisher Max Reinhardt and actor Laurence Harvey (dec. 1973). Married to actor Michael Wilding (dec. 1979). Nominated for 1971 Academy Award for Best Supporting Actress in The Go-Between.

Appeared in: **1948** The Winslow Boy (film debut—US 1950); Bonnie Prince Charlie (US 1952). **1949** Under Capricorn. **1950** The Astonished Heart; The Elusive Pimpernel. **1951** Calling Bulldog Drummond. **1952** Home at Seven (aka Murder on Monday—US 1953); The Holly and the Ivy (US 1953). **1954** The Teckman Mystery (US 1955); Carrington VC (aka Court-Martial—US 1955). **1955** The Constant Husband. **1957** The Passionate Stranger (aka A Novel Affair—US). **1959** The Sound and the Fury. **1962** Waltz of the Toreadors. **1964** The Best Man. **1965** The Loved One. **1966** Seven Women. **1969** The Madwoman of Chaillot. **1970** The Go-Between (US 1971). **1971** Zee & Co. **1972** Lady Caroline Lamb (US 1973). **1973** A Bequest to the Nation (aka The Nelson Affair—US); From Beyond the Grave (US 1975). **1974** Galileo (US 1975). **1976** Dirty Knights' Work.

LEISEN, J. MITCHELL
Born: Oct., 1898, Menomie, Mich. Died: Oct. 27, 1972, Woodland Hills, Calif. (coronary complications). Film producer, director and screen actor. Divorced from actress and singer Sandra Gahle.

Appeared in: **1941** Hold Back the Dawn. **1947** Variety Girl. **1948** Miss Tatlock's Millions.

LELAND, BILLY
Died: July 15, 1976. Screen actor.

LE MAIRE, GEORGE
Born: 1884, Fort Worth, Tex. Died: Jan. 20, 1930, New York, N.Y. (heart attack). Screen, stage, vaudeville actor and film producer. Appeared in vaudeville with his brother William and later as partner in "Conroy and Le Maire" vaudeville team. Brother of screen actor William Le Maire (dec. 1933).

Appeared in: **1928** The Circus Kid. **1929** Seventeen "George Le Maire" shorts.

LE MAIRE, WILLIAM
Born: Dec. 21, 1892, Fort Worth, Tex. Died: Nov. 11, 1933, Los Angeles, Calif. (heart ailment). Screen, vaudeville and radio actor. Brother of actor George Le Maire (dec. 1930). Appeared in vaudeville with his brother George and later with Ed Gallagher. Entered films in 1928.

Appeared in: **1928** The Circus Kid. **1930** The Light of Western Stars; Only the Brave; Whoopee; Common Clay. **1931** The Painted Desert. **1932** Cabin in the Cotton; I Am a Fugitive from a Chain Gang. **1933** 20,000 Years in Sing Sing; Captured.

LE MANS, MARCEL
Born: 1897, Antwerp, Belgium. Died: Jan. 9, 1946, Lyons, N.J. Stage and screen actor. Flying ace of Lafayette Escadrille in W.W. I. Entered films with Pathe in 1924.

LEMESHEV, SERGEI Y.
Born: 1902, Russia. Died: June, 1977, Moscow, Russia. Opera singer and screen actor.

Appeared in: **1946** Moscow Music Hall. **1967** Requiem for Mozart.

LE MOYNE, CHARLES (Charles J. Lemon)
Born: 1880. Died: Sept. 13, 1956, Hollywood, Calif. Screen and stage actor.

Appeared in: **1921** Colorado; The Fox; The Freeze Out; The Wallop. **1922** Headin' West; The Kick Back; Rough Shod; Good Men and True; Man to Man. **1923** Canyon of the Fools; Desert Driven; Brass Commandments; Crashin' Thru. **1925** Riders of the Purple Sage. **1936** The Cowboy and the Kid; Empty Saddles; The Phantom Rider (serial); Ride 'Em Cowboy. **1937** Black Aces. **1938** Sudden Bill Dorn.

LEMUELS, WILLIAM E.
Born: 1891. Died: Feb. 21, 1953, Los Angeles, Calif. Screen, stage and vaudeville actor. Appeared in vaudeville with James Barton and they made several short subjects.

Appeared in: **1935** His Family Tree.

LEMUS, RON ELROY
Died: Sept. 24, 1976. Screen actor.

LENGLEN, SUZANNE
Born: 1899, France. Died: July 4, 1938, Paris, France (pernicious anemia). Screen actress and tennis champion. Appeared in film shorts.

LENI, PAUL
Born: July 8, 1885, Stuttgart, Germany. Died: Sept. 2, 1929, Hollywood, Calif. Screen, stage actor and film director.

LENIHAN, WINIFRED
Born: 1899, Brooklyn, N.Y. Died: July 27, 1964, Sea Cliff, N.Y. Screen, stage, radio actress and radio director.

Appeared in: **1949** Jigsaw.

LENNARD, ARTHUR
Born: Mar. 8, 1867, Woolwich, England. Died: Jan. 14, 1954, Shoreham-by-Sea, England. Screen, stage, vaudeville actor and vocalist.

Appeared in: **1919** Sweet and Twenty. **1920** A Man's Shadow; Black Sheep; By Berwyn Banks; The Children of Gibeon. **1922** Fires of Innocence; The Lilac Sunbonnet.

LENNON, JOHN
Born: Oct. 9, 1940, Liverpool, England. Died: Dec. 8, 1980, New York, N.Y. (murdered—shot). Screen, television actor, composer and musician. Member of "The Beatles" rock group. Divorced from Cynthia Powell and later married to singer/musician Yoko Ono.

Appeared in: **1964** A Hard Day's Night. **1965** Help! **1967** How I Won the War. **1968** Yellow Submarine (voice). **1969** Diaries, Notes and Sketches (documentary). **1970** Let It Be (documentary); What's Happening (documentary); Woodstock (documentary). **1973** Imagine. **1978** Matilda.

LENOIR, PASS
Born: 1874. Died: June 12, 1946, Hollywood, Calif. (heart attack). Screen, stage actor, circus and minstrel gymnast. Married to actress Florence Morrison (dec. 1942).

Appeared in: **1936** Mixed Magic (short).

LENROW, BERNARD "BERNIE"
Born: 1903. Died: Oct. 9, 1963, Englewood, N.J. Screen, stage, television and radio actor.

Appeared in: **1957** The Violators.

LENTZ, IRENE See IRENE

LENYA, LOTTE (Karoline Blamauer)
Born: Oct. 18, 1898, Penzing, Austria. Died: Nov. 27, 1981, New York, N.Y. Screen, stage actress, singer and circus performer. Married to composer Kurt Weill (dec. 1950), editor George Davis (dec. 1957), and painter Russel Detwiler (dec. 1969).

Appeared in: **1931** Die Dreigroschenoper (The Threepenny Opera, aka The Beggar's Opera—stage and film versions). **1961** The Roman Spring of Mrs. Stone. **1963** From Russia With Love (US 1964). **1968** The Appointment (US 1970). **1973** What? **1977** Semi-Tough.

LEON, CONNIE
Born: 1880. Died: May 10, 1955, Hollywood, Calif. Screen actress.

Appeared in: **1935** A Feather in Her Hat; Clive of India. **1937** The Great Garrick. **1938** The Light That Failed; The Adventures of Robin Hood. **1939** The Rains Came; The Little Princess. **1940** The Westerner. **1941** Where Did You Get That Girl?; Singapore Woman. **1942** Bombs Over Burma; Mrs. Miniver; This Above All; Thunder Birds; Tales of Manhattan; Bombay Clipper; Cat People. **1944** And Now Tomorrow; Going My Way; The Lodger. **1945** Love Letters; Hangover Square. **1946** Anna and the King of Siam; That Brennan Girl; Of Human Bondage; Three Strangers; The Locket. **1947** Smash-Up, the Story of a Woman. **1948** The Woman in White.

LEON, PEDRO
Born: 1876, Tucson, Ariz. Died: July 14, 1931. Screen actor.

Appeared in: **1916** Liberty (serial); The Knight of the Range. **1917** Casey's Border Raid. **1920** Vanishing Trails (serial).

LEON, VALERIANO
Born: 1892, Spain. Died: Dec., 1955 or Jan., 1956, Madrid, Spain. Stage and screen actor.

LEONARD, ARCHIE
Born: 1917. Died: Feb. 7, 1959, Des Moines, Iowa (heart attack). Screen, stage, radio actor, television director and writer.

Appeared in: **1949** Mrs. Mike; The Set-Up.

LEONARD, DAVID A.
Born: 1892. Died: Apr. 2, 1967, Encino, Calif. Screen, stage, radio, television actor and screenwriter.

Appeared in: **1933** Victims of Persecution. **1947** Philo Vance's Secret Mission; Desire Me; The Unsuspected. **1948** The Bishop's Wife; Arch of Triumph; Adventures of Don Juan; Song of My Heart; Sword of the Avenger. **1949** The Daring Caballero. **1950** Captain Carey, U.S.A. **1951** Payment on Demand. **1953** Fighter Attack; The Robe; Salome. **1954** Desiree; Forever Female. **1955** The Prodigal; Trial. **1956** Somebody Up There Likes Me; Lust for Life. **1959** Say One for Me.

LEONARD, EDDIE
Born: 1870, Richmond, Va. Died: July 29, 1941, New York, N.Y. Minstrel and screen actor.

Appeared in: **1929** Melody Lane. **1940** If I Had My Way.

LEONARD, GUS (Gustav Lerond)
Born: 1856, Marseilles, France. Died: Mar. 27, 1939, Los Angeles, Calif. Screen, stage and vaudeville actor. Married to actress Minnie Leonard (dec. 1940). Entered films in 1915.

Appeared in: **1917** The Lonesome Luke. **1921** Two Minutes to Go. **1922** The Deuce of Spades; The Barnstormer; Watch Your Step. **1923** The Girl I Loved; Second Hand Love; Her Reputation; Times Have Changed. **1928** Coney Island. **1932** Babes in Toyland; When a Feller Needs a Friend. **1933** Mush and Milk (short). **1934** The Mighty Barnum. **1935** Teacher's Beau (short). **1936** The Petrified Forest; The Lucky Corner (short); Life Hesitates at 40 (short). **1937** Maytime. **1950** Revenge Is Sweet (reissue of 1932 version of Babes in Toyland).

LEONARD, JACK
Born: England. Died: Oct., 1921, Los Angeles, Calif. Screen actor. Appeared in Selig films.

LEONARD, JACK E. (Leonard Lebitsky)
Born: Apr. 24, 1911, Chicago, Ill. Died: May 9, 1973, New York, N.Y. (diabetic complications). Screen, vaudeville, television actor and nightclub performer.

Appeared in: **1964** The Disorderly Orderly. **1965** The World of Abbott and Costello. **1966** The Fat Spy.

LEONARD, JAMES
Born: 1868. Died: July 4, 1930, Glendale, Calif. Screen, vaudeville and burlesque actor. Was partner in vaudeville team of "Jim and Sadie Leonard."

Appeared in: **1927** All Aboard. **1928** The Cheer Leader.

LEONARD, MARION
Born: 1880. Died: Jan. 9, 1956, Woodland Hills, Calif. Screen actress.

Appeared in: **1908** At the Crossroads of Life; The Test of Friendship; An Awful Moment; Father Gets in the Game; The Fatal Hour; The Christmas Burglars; A Calamitous Elopement; A Wreath in Time; The Welcome Burglar; The Criminal Hypnotist. **1909** Comato the Sioux; The Gibson Goddess; The Maniac Cook; A Burglar's Mistake; The Hindu Dagger; Pranks; The Cord of Life; Shadows of Doubt; Two Memories; The Roue's Heart; The Lovely Villa; At the Altar; Fools of Fate; The Convert; The Voice of the Violin; A Rude Hostess; The Eavesdropper; The Jilt; With Her Card; The Mills of the Gods; His Lost Love; Nursing a Viper; The Sealed Room; The Expiation; The Restoration; Through the Breakers; In Little Italy; A Trap for Santa Claus; Pippa Passes. **1910** On the Reef; Gold Is Not All; Love Among the Roses; In Old California; The Two Brothers; Over Silent Paths; The Day After; His Wife's Sweethearts; A Salutory Lesson; The Sorrows of the Unfaithful; The Two Paths. **1912** The Voice of the Million; The Defender of the Name; So Speaks the Heart; Taming Mrs. Shrew; Under Her Wing; The End of the Circle; The Final Pardon; Through Flaming Gates; Songs of Childhood Days; Eyes That See Not; In Payment Full; What Avails the Crown; The Tears O'Peggy; Through Memory Blank; Thus Many Souls; The Leader of the Band; In Honor Bound; Lost—A Husband; What's in an Aim? **1913** Carmen; As In a Looking Glass; The Dead Secret; A Leaf in the Storm; In the Watches of the Night. **1914** A Sight Unseen. **1915** Dragon's Claw.

LEONARD, MINNIE
Born: 1873. Died: Jan. 2, 1940, Los Angeles, Calif. Screen actress. Married to actor Gus Leonard (dec. 1939).

LEONARD, MURRAY

Born: 1898. Died: Nov. 6, 1970, Sherman Oaks, Calif. (heart attack). Screen, stage, burlesque and vaudeville actor.

Appeared in: **1944** Lost in a Harem; In Society. **1945** Thousand and One Nights. **1947** The Wistful Widow of Wagon Gap. **1955** Bring Your Smile Along.

LEONARD, ROBERT

Born: 1889, Poland. Died: Jan. 5, 1948, Brooklyn, N.Y. (heart ailment). Screen, stage and vaudeville actor. Do not confuse with actor Robert Z. Leonard (dec. 1968).

Appeared in: **1916** The Tailor of Bend Street. **1917** Just Deception.

LEONARD, ROBERT Z.

Born: Oct. 7, 1889, Chicago, Ill. Died: Aug. 27, 1968, Beverly Hills, Calif. (aneurysm). Screen, stage actor, opera performer, film producer, film director and screenwriter. Married to actress Gertrude Olmstead (dec. 1975). Divorced from actress Mae Murray (dec. 1965). Entered films as an actor with Selig in 1907.

Appeared in: **1910** The Courtship of Miles Standish; The Roman. **1913** Robinson Crusoe; His Old Fashioned Dad; Shon the Piper; The Turn of the Tide; The Stolen Idol; The Power of Heredity; Sally Scraggs, Housemaid; Like Darby and Joan; The Boob's Dream Girl; The Wayward Sister; The Shadow; The Diamond Makers; By Fate's Decree. **1914** The Primeval Test; The Master Key (serial); The Mistress of Deadwood Basin; The Senator's Bill; The Boob Incognito; The House Discordant; The Fox; The Boob Detective; The Boob's Legacy; For the Secret Service; Little Sister; Olaf Erickson, Boss; At the Foot of the Stairs; Aurora of the North; The Boob's Nemesis; The Little Blond Lady; Out of the Darkness; An Awkward Cinderella. **1937** The Firefly. **1945** Abbott and Costello in Hollywood.

LEONARD-BOYNE, EVA

Born: 1883, England. Died: Apr. 12, 1960, New York, N.Y. Screen and stage actress. Daughter of stage actor Leonard Boyne (dec. 1920).

Appeared in: **1944** None But the Lonely Heart.

LEONARDO, HARRY (H. L. Gottsacker)

Born: 1903. Died: Nov. 23, 1964, New York, N.Y. (heart ailment). Screen and vaudeville actor. Was partner in vaudeville team of "Ward Hall and Leonardo."

LEONE, HENRY

Born: Mar. 30, 1958, Vienna, Austria. Died: June 9, 1922, Mount Vernon, N.Y. (apoplexy). Screen, stage actor, film director and screenwriter. Entered films in 1909.

Appeared in: **1915** Sin. **1918** My Cousin. **1921** His Greatest Sacrifice; Such a Little Queen. **1922** Fair Lady.

LEONETTI, TOMMY (Nicola Tomaso Leonetti)

Born: 1929. Died: Sept. 15, 1979, Houston, Tex. (cancer). Screen, television actor and singer. Brother of singers Etta, Kay, Sandy and Jackie Leonetti.

Appeared in: **1965** The Human Duplicators.

LEONING, JOHN

Born: 1927, Hawaii. Died: Mar. 23, 1977, North Hollywood, Calif. (heart attack). Screen and television actor.

Appeared in: **1976** Pipe Dreams. **1977** Kentucky Fried Movie.

LE PAUL, PAUL (Paul Braden)

Born: 1901. Died: June 8, 1958, St. Louis, Mo. Screen, stage actor, magician and author.

Appeared in: **1939** Eternally Yours.

LEPEARL, HARRY

Born: 1885, Danville, Ill. Died: Jan. 13, 1946, Hollywood, Calif. Circus clown and screen actor.

Appeared in: **1915** Still Waters; Once Is Enough; Bunks Bunked; Where's Oliver?; The Trouble Maker.

LE ROY, VICTOR

Born: 1884. Died: Apr. 20, 1920, Bergenfield, N.Y. (bronchial asthma). Screen and stage actor.

Appeared in: **1915** Dad's Awful Crime.

LE SAINT, EDWARD J.

Born: 1871. Died: Sept. 10, 1940, Hollywood, Calif. Screen, stage actor, film director and screenwriter. Entered films in 1912. Married to actress Stella Razetto (dec. 1948).

Appeared in: **1923** Mary of the Movies. **1929** The Talk of Hollywood. **1930** The Dawn Trail; For the Defense. **1931** City Streets; Fighting Marshal; The Last Parade. **1932** The Night of June 13th; The Last Man; Central Park; The Cohens and the Kellys in Trouble; Tomorrow at Seven; The Wrecker; Horse Feathers; Boy, Oh, Boy (short); Virtue; I Am a Fugitive from a Chain Gang. **1933** No More Orchids; Thrill Hunter; Torch Singer; Broken Dreams; Feeling Rosy (short). **1934** George White's Scandals; The Lemon Drop Kid; The Frontier Marshal; Once to Every Woman; The Old Fashioned Way; Half-Baked Relations (short); She Learned About Sailors. **1935** Frisco Kid; The Lost Jungle (serial); In Old Kentucky; In Spite of Danger; Fighting Shadows; Public Opinion; Thunder Mountain; Ruggles of Red Gap. **1936** The Trail of the Lonesome Pine; The Witness Chair; We Who Are About to Die; The Case Against Mrs. Ames; The Cowboy Star; The Gallant Defender; The Legion of Terror; End of the Trail; Bulldog Edition; College Holiday; Disorder in the Court (short); Too Many Parents; Modern Times; Rhythm on the Range; The Big Broadcast of 1937; Fury. **1937** Paid to Dance; Oh, Doctor!; Counterfeit Lady; The Gold Racket; A Day at the Races. **1938** The Buccaneer; College Swing; My Lucky Star. **1939** Jesse James; Arizona Legion; The Stranger from Texas; Union Pacific; Honolulu; The Oregon Trail (serial).

LE SAINT, STELLA See RAZETTO, STELLA

LESLEY, CAROLE (Maureen Rippingale)

Born: 1935, Chelmsford, England. Died: Feb. 28, 1974, New Barnet, England. Screen, television actress and dancer.

Appeared in: **1957** Good Companions (US 1958); Those Dangerous Years (aka Dangerous Youth—US 1958); Woman in a Dressing Gown. **1959** No Trees in the Street (US 1964); Operation Bullshine (US 1963). **1960** Doctor in Love (US 1962). **1961** What a Whopper (US 1962); Three on a Spree. **1962** The Pot Carriers.

LESLIE, ADAM

Born: 1916, Salisbury, South Rhodesia. Died: Apr. 25, 1979, Johannesburg, South Africa (cancer). Screen actor, film director, stage director, playwright, revue artist and lyricist.

Appeared in: **1934** Thursday's Child; The Night Invader; Adventures of Tartu (aka Tartu—US). **1944** Fiddlers Three; Champagne Charlie (US 1948).

LESLIE, ARTHUR

Born: 1902, England. Died: June 30, 1970, Cardigan, Wales. Screen, stage and television actor.

LESLIE, EDITH

Died: Apr. 9, 1973. Screen, stage and television actress.

Appeared in: **1947** Green Dolphin Street. **1948** Jiggs and Maggie in Society. **1949** The Blue Veil; Red, Hot and Blue. **1953** Private Eye. **1954** She Couldn't Say No; Casanova's Big Night. **1957** Just for You; Will Success Spoil Rock Hunter? **1965** The Greatest Story Ever Told. **1969** Hello Dolly.

LESLIE, ELEANOR

Born: 1874, London, England. Died: June 14, 1929, Glendale, Calif. Screen and stage actress.

Appeared in: **1929** Dream Melody; Clear the Decks.

LESLIE, FRED

Born: 1884. Died: Aug. 1, 1945. Screen actor.

LESLIE, GENE (Leslie Eugene Halverson)

Born: 1904. Died: Feb. 20, 1953, Los Angeles, Calif. Screen actor, dancer and ice skater.

Appeared in: **1945** The Bells of St. Mary's; The Spanish Main; Ten Cents a Dance; Twice Blessed. **1946** The Gay Senorita; Holiday in Mexico; People Are Funny. **1948** Duel in the Sun.

LESLIE, GLADYS

Born: Mar. 5, 1899, New York, N.Y. Died: Oct. 2, 1976, Boynton Beach, Fla. Screen actress.

Appeared in: **1915** The Mating. **1917** The Vicar of Wakefield. **1918** His Own People; Little Miss No Account; The Soap Girl; Wild Primrose; The Wooing of Princess Pat. **1919** The Beloved Imposter; Fortune's Child; The Girl Woman; Miss Dulcie of Dixie; Nymph of the Woods;

A Stitch in Time; Too Many Crooks. **1920** A Child for Sale; Golden Shower; The Midnight Bride; The Mystery of Gray Towers. **1921** Elsie in New York; Jim the Penman; Straight Is the Way. **1922** The Girl from Porcupine; God's Country and the Law; The Snitching Hour; Timothy's Quest. **1923** Haldene of the Secret Service; The Darling of the Rich. **1924** If Winter Comes. **1925** Enemies of Youth; The Pearl of Youth.

LESLIE, JOHN MITCHELL
Born: 1875. Died: Apr. 25, 1945, Miami, Fla. Screen actor.

Appeared in: **1943** The Moon Is Down; Coney Island.

LESLIE, LAWRENCE
Born: 1908. Died: July 15, 1930, New York, N.Y. Screen and stage actor.

Appeared in: **1929** Gentlemen of the Press; Why Bring That Up?

LESLIE, LILIE "LILA"
Born: 1892, Scotland. Died: Sept. 8, 1940, Los Angeles, Calif. Screen and stage actress.

Appeared in: **1918** The Silent Woman. **1919** The Man Who Stayed at Home; Johnny on the Spot; Satan Junior; Little Brother of the Rich. **1920** The Butterfly Man; Blue Streak McCoy; Best of Luck; Would You Forgive?; Number 99; Molly and I; Love's Harvest. **1921** I Am Guilty; The Son of Wallingford; Keeping Up With Lizzie. **1922** A Guilty Conscience; A Front Page Story; Any Night; Bluebeard, Jr.; Gay and Devilish; The Hottentot; The Men of Zanzibar. **1923** The Huntress; What Wives Want. **1924** Why Men Leave Home; Being Respectable; A Fat Chance (short). **1925** The Last Edition; Skinner's Dress Suit. **1926** Forever After. **1927** Getting Gertie's Garter; The Secret Studio; The Trunk Mystery; The First Night; Kid Tricks (short). **1928** The following shorts: Navy Beans; No Fare; Angel Eyes. **1930** Grandma's Girl (short).

LESLIE, MARGUERITE
Born: Apr. 3, 1884, Sweden. Died: 1958, United States? Screen and stage actress.

Appeared in: **1915** Jim the Penman. **1917** The Question.

LESLIE, NOEL
Born: 1889, England. Died: Mar. 10, 1974, New York, N.Y. Screen, stage and television actor.

Appeared in: **1956** The Search for Bridey Murphy.

LESNEVITCH, GUS
Born: 1915. Died: Feb. 28, 1964, Cliffside Park, N.J. (heart attack). Professional boxer and screen actor.

Appeared in: **1962** Requiem for a Heavyweight.

LESSEY, GEORGE A.
Born: Amherst, Mass. Died: June 3, 1947, Westbrook, Conn. Screen, stage actor and film director. Married to actress May Abbey (dec. 1952).

Appeared in: **1911** Romeo and Juliet. **1912** A Romance of the Rails; The Governor; The Corsican Brothers; Mother and Daughter; A Fresh Air Romance; The Little Artist from the Market; The Dam Builder; The Harbinger of Peace; The Boss of Lumber Camp No. 4; Rowdy and His New Pal; Their Hero; The Man Who Made Good. **1913** The Governess; The Ambassador's Daughter; Sally's Romance; Leonie. **1914** The Witness to the Will. **1915** The Parson's Horse Race. **1918** To Him That Hath. **1919** Twilight. **1920** The $1,000,000 Reward. **1921** A Divorce of Convenience; Handcuffs or Kisses; Is Life Worth Living?; Rainbow; School Days; Why Girls Leave Home. **1922** The Snitching Hour. **1923** The Silent Command. **1924** It Is the Law. **1925** Durand of the Bad Lands; The Fool; Scar Hanan; White Thunder. **1940** Edison the Man; Sporting Blood; Boom Town; Strike Up the Band; The Golden Fleecing; Sky Murder; Gallant Sons; Go West; Dr. Kildare's Strangest Case; Andy Hardy Meets Debutante; Good Bad Guys (short); Soak the Old (short). **1941** Blonde Inspiration; The Big Boss; Moon Over Miami; Blossoms in the Dust; Sweetheart of the Campus; We Go Fast; Men of Boys Town. **1942** Now Voyager; Rings on Her Fingers; The Gay Sisters; The Pride of the Yankees; Girl Trouble. **1943** Dixie Dugan; Old Acquaintance; Pistol Packin' Mama. **1944** None Shall Escape; Buffalo Bill; Henry Aldrich, Boy Scout; Charlie Chan in the Secret Service; The Adventures of Mark Twain; Roger Touhy—Gangster; Sweet and Lowdown. **1945** Wilson.

L'ESTELLE, ELEANOR (Eleanor Scott)
Born: 1880. Died: Apr. 25, 1962, Los Angeles, Calif. Screen actress.

LESTER, KATE
Born: Thorpe, England. Died: Oct. 12, 1924 (burns suffered in fire). Screen and stage actress.

Appeared in: **1916** A Coney Island Princess. **1918** Little Women; The Unbeliever. **1919** A Man and His Money; Bonds of Love. **1920** The Woman in Room 13; The Paliser Case; Cup of Fury; Scratch My Back; Earthbound; Simple Souls. **1921** The Beautiful Liar; Dangerous Curve Ahead; The Hole in the Wall; Don't Neglect Your Wife; Made in Heaven. **1922** The Eternal Flame; The Fourteenth Lover; The Glorious Fool; One Week of Love; Rose O' the Sea; Remembrance; Quincy Adams Sawyer; A Tailor Made Man. **1923** Can a Woman Love Twice?; Gimmie; The Fourth Musketeer; Her Accidental Husband; The Love Trap; The Hunchback of Notre Dame; The Marriage Market; The Rendezvous; Modern Matrimony; The Satin Girl; The Wild Party. **1924** The Goldfish; Beau Brummell; The Beautiful Sinner; Black Oxen; Leave It to Gerry; Wife of the Centaur. **1925** The Meddler; Raffles, the Amateur Cracksman; The Price of Pleasure.

LESTER, LOUISE
Born: 1867. Died: Nov. 18, 1952, Hollywood, Calif. Screen and stage actress. Married to actor and director Frank Beal (dec. 1934) and mother of actress Dolly and actor Scott Beal (dec. 1973). Entered films in 1910 with the Flying A Co. in Santa Barbara.

Appeared in: "Calamity Ann" series beginning in 1912. **1923** Her Reputation. **1924** The Desert Hawk. **1925** Galloping On. **1935** Straight from the Heart.

L'ESTRANGE, DICK (Gunther von Strensch)
Born: Dec. 27, 1889, Asheville, N.C. Died: Nov. 19, 1963, Burbank, Calif. Screen, vaudeville actor, opera performer and film director. Appeared in early Sennett films and was one of the original Keystone Kops.

Appeared in: **1913** The Squaw Man. **1927** Blazing Days; The Border Cavalier; The Silent Rider; Desert Dust; One Glorious Scrap. **1928** Arizona Cyclone; Made-to-Order Hero; Thunder Riders; Quick Triggers.

L'ESTRANGE, JULIAN
Born: 1880, England. Died: Oct. 22, 1918, New York, N.Y. (Spanish influenza). Stage and screen actor. Married to actress Constance Collier (dec. 1955).

Appeared in: **1915** Sold; Bella Donna; Zaza. **1916** The Girl With the Green Eyes; The Quest of Life. **1918** Daybreak.

LE STRANGE, NORMAN
Born: France. Died: June 5, 1936, London, England. Screen actor.

Appeared in: **1928** The Black Ace. **1929** Taxi for Two.

LE SUEUR, HAL
Born: 1904. Died: May 3, 1963, Los Angeles, Calif. (ruptured appendix). Screen actor. Brother of actress Joan Crawford (dec. 1977).

Appeared in: **1935** Mutiny on the Bounty. **1957** Jeanne Eagles.

LETONDAL, HENRI
Born: 1902, France. Died: Feb. 14, 1955, Burbank, Calif. (heart attack). Screen actor.

Appeared in: **1946** The Magnificent Doll; The Razor's Edge. **1947** Crime Doctor's Gamble; The Foxes of Harrow. **1948** The Big Clock; Apartment for Peggy. **1949** Come to the Stable; Madame Bovary; Mother Is a Freshman. **1950** Please Believe Me. **1951** Across the Wide Missouri; Kind Lady; On the Riviera; Royal Wedding; Ten Tall Men. **1952** The Big Sky; Monkey Business; What Price Glory?; The Wild North (aka The Big North). **1953** Dangerous When Wet; Desert Legion; South Sea Woman; Gentlemen Prefer Blondes; Little Boy Lost. **1954** The Gambler From Natchez; Deep in My Heart. **1955** A Bullet for Joey.

LETTIERI, ALFREDO "AL"
Born: Feb. 24, 1928, New York, N.Y. Died: Oct. 18, 1975, New York, N.Y. Screen, stage actor and screenwriter.

Appeared in: **1957** The Bobo. **1969** The Night of the Following Day. **1972** The Godfather; The Getaway. **1973** The Don Is Dead; Deadly Trackers. **1974** Mr. Majestyk; McQ.

LEUBAS, LOUIS
Born: 1870, France. Died: Aug. 29, 1932, Digne, France. Screen and stage actor.

LEVANCE, CAL (Charles Waite)
Died: Sept. 6, 1951, Toronto, Canada. Screen, stage and vaudeville actor.

LEVANT, OSCAR
Born: Dec. 27, 1906, Pittsburgh, Pa. Died: Aug. 14, 1972, Beverly Hills, Calif. (heart attack). Screen, radio, television actor, composer, author, pianist and screenwriter. Divorced from dancer Barbara Smith. Married to actress June Gale.

Appeared in: **1929** The Dance of Life. **1939** Five Information Please shorts. **1940** Rhythm on the River; plus thirteen Information Please shorts. **1941** Kiss the Boys Good-bye; plus eleven Information Please shorts. **1942** Fellow Americans (short); plus nine Information Please shorts. **1945** Rhapsody in Blue. **1946** Humoresque. **1948** Romance on the High Seas; You Were Meant for Me. **1949** The Barkleys of Broadway. **1951** An American in Paris. **1952** O Henry's Full House. **1953** The Band Wagon; The I Don't Care Girl. **1955** The Cobweb.

LEVELLE, ESTELLE
Born: 1896. Died: Jan. 6, 1960, Chicago, Ill. Screen, stage actress, dancer and singer.

LEVENE, SAM (Samuel Levine)
Born: Aug. 28, 1905 or 1907, New York, N.Y. or Russia? Died: Dec. 1980, New York, N.Y. (heart attack). Screen, stage, television actor and stage director.

Appeared in: **1936** Three Men on a Horse (film debut); After the Thin Man. **1938** Yellow Jack; The Shopworn Angel; The Mad Miss Manton; Golden Boy. **1941** Married Bachelor; Shadow of the Thin Man. **1942** Sing Your Worries Away; Sunday Punch; Grand Central Murder; The Big Street; Destination Unknown. **1943** Action in the North Atlantic; I Dood It; Gung Ho!; Whistling in Brooklyn. **1944** The Purple Heart. **1946** The Killers. **1947** Boomerang; A Likely Story; Brute Force; Crossfire; Killer McCoy. **1948** The Babe Ruth Story. **1950** Guilty Bystander; Dial 1119; With These Hands. **1953** Three Sailors and a Girl. **1956** The Opposite Sex. **1957** Sweet Smell of Success; Slaughter on Tenth Avenue; A Farewell to Arms; Designing Woman; 1958 Kathy O'. **1963** Act One. **1969** A Dream of Kings. **1976** The Money; God Told Me To. **1977** Demon. **1979** The Champ; Last Embrace; ... And Justice for All.

LEVESQUE, MARCEL
Born: 1877, France. Died: 1962, France? Screen actor.

Appeared in: **1915** The Vampires. **1936** Le Crime de Monsieur Lange (The Crime of Monsieur Lange).

LEVEY, ETHEL
Born: Nov. 22, 1881, San Francisco, Calif. Died: Feb. 27, 1955, New York, N.Y. (heart attack). Screen and stage actress. Divorced from actor George M. Cohan (dec. 1942), and Claude Grahame-White.

Appeared in: **1931** High Stakes. **1933** Call Me Mame. **1940** Tattle Television (short).

LEVIN, LUCY
Born: 1907, Russia. Died: Sept. 4, 1939, New York, N.Y. Screen and stage actor. Appeared in Yiddish films.

LE VINESS, CARL
Born: 1885. Died: Oct. 15, 1964, Hollywood, Calif. (pneumonia). Screen actor and film director.

Appeared in: **1915** A Bag of Diamonds; Terror. **1929** Twin Beds. **1935** Slightly Static (short). **1946** The Kid from Brooklyn. **1956** Around the World in 80 Days. **1958** In Love and War.

LEVRINO, CLAUDIO
Born: 1945. Died: Jan. 19, 1980, Mar del Plata (accidental shooting). Screen and television actor. Married to actress Christina del Valle.

LEVY, SYLVAN
Born: 1906. Died: Oct. 30, 1962, New York. Screen, stage and vaudeville actor.

Appeared in: **1929** The Cocoanuts.

LEWIN, IKE
Born: July 5, 1889, Chicago, Ill. Died: June 9, 1941, Hollywood, Calif. (suicide—gunshot). Screen actor and stuntman.

LEWIS, BARBARA (Barbara Burns)
Died: Sept. 14, 1981, Studio City, Calif. Screen and television actress.

LEWIS, CATHY
Born: 1918. Died: Nov. 20, 1968, Hollywood Hills, Calif. (cancer). Screen, stage, television, radio actress and singer.

Appeared in: **1941** Dr. Kildare's Wedding Day; Play Girl; Model Wife; Double Trouble. **1942** The Kid Glove Killer. **1943** Slightly Dangerous. **1949** My Friend Irma; The Story of Molly X. **1950** My Friend Irma Goes West. **1958** Party Crashers. **1961** The Devil at 4 O'Clock.

LEWIS, DOROTHY W.
Born: 1871. Died: June 16, 1952, Hollywood, Calif. Screen actress.

Appeared in: **1941** Ice Capades.

LEWIS, ED "STRANGLER" (Robert H. Friedrich)
Born: 1890. Died: Aug. 7, 1966, Muskogee, Okla. Professional wrestler and screen actor.

Appeared in: **1943** The Nazty Nuisance. **1950** Bodyhold.

LEWIS, EDGAR
Born: June 22, 1872, Holden, Missouri. Died: May 21, 1938, Los Angeles, Calif. Screen, stage actor, film producer, director and screenwriter.

Appeared in: **1911** The Violin Maker of Nuremberg. **1912** Magnon. **1915** The Plunderer. **1921** The Sage Hen. **1932** Human Targets; Texas Gunfighter.

LEWIS, ELLIOTT See REMLEY, FRANK

LEWIS, ERIC (Fred Eric Lewis Tuffley)
Born: Oct. 23, 1855, Northampton, England. Died: Apr. 1, 1935, England? Screen, stage actor and playwright.

Appeared in: **1925** Happy Ending.

LEWIS, EVA
Born: 1881. Died: May 6, 1939, Los Angeles, Calif. Screen and stage actress. Entered films in 1916.

Appeared in: **1923** The Hunchback of Notre Dame.

LEWIS, FLO
Born: 1898. Died: June 11, 1938. Screen actress.

Appeared in: **1929** Give Us a Lift (short).

LEWIS, FORREST
Born: 1900. Died: June 2, 1977, Burbank, Calif. (heart attack). Screen, radio and television actor.

Appeared in: **1952** Has Anybody Seen My Gal?; It Grows on Trees; Lawless Breed. **1953** Gun Fury; Take Me to Town; Stand at Apache River. **1955** Apache Ambush; The Spoilers. **1957** Man in the Shadow. **1958** The Thing That Couldn't Die. **1959** Shaggy Dog. **1961** Posse from Hell; The Absent-Minded Professor. **1963** Son of Flubber; Tammy and the Doctor. **1964** Man's Favorite Sport. **1966** Out of Sight. **1967** Riot on Sunset Strip.

LEWIS, FRED (Fred Till)
Born: Dec. 23, 1860, Kingston-on-Thames, England. Died: Dec. 25, 1927, England. Screen and stage actor. Do not confuse with other actors with same name.

Appeared in: **1920** Once Aboard the Lugger. **1921** Tilly of Bloomsbury. **1922** Thhe Game of Life.

LEWIS, FREDERICK G.
Born: 1874, Oswego, N.Y. Died: Mar. 19, 1947, Amityville, N.Y. Stage and screen actor.

Appeared in: **1924** The Moral Sinner.

LEWIS, GENE
Born: 1888, Philadelphia, Pa. Died: Mar. 27, 1979, Woodland Hills, Calif. (heart failure). Screen, stage actor, film producer, screenwriter and dialog director.

Appeared in: **1931** Honeymoon Lane. **1951** Flaming Feather.

LEWIS, GORDON
Died: Mar. 17, 1933, Tucson, Ariz (suicide—gun). Screen actor.

LEWIS, HARRY

Born: 1886. Died: Nov. 18, 1950, Hollywood, Calif. Screen and stage actor.

Appeared in: **1926** God Gave Me Twenty Cents. **1941** Dive Bomber. **1942** The Hard Way; Always in My Heart; Busses Roar. **1944** The Last Ride; Winged Victory. **1946** Her Kind of Man. **1947** The Unsuspected. **1948** Key Largo. **1949** Bomba on Panther Island; Deadly Is the Female; Joe Palooka in the Counterpunch. **1950** Blonde Dynamite; Gun Crazy. **1951** The Fat Man.

LEWIS, IDA

Born: 1871, New York. Died: Apr. 21, 1935, Hollywood, Calif. Screen, stage and vaudeville actress. Entered films with Horsley Co.

Appeared in: **1918** The Bells. **1923** A Man's Man. **1925** Some Pun'kins. **1926** Sweet Adeline. **1928** Law of Fear. **1932** Sinners in the Sun.

LEWIS, JAMES H. "DADDY"

Died: Nov. 3, 1928, Pawtucket, R.I. Stage and screen actor.

Appeared in: **1923** The Broken Violin.

LEWIS, JEFFREYS

Born: 1857, London, England. Died: Apr. 29, 1926, New York, N.Y. Screen and stage actress. Married to stage actor Harry Marshall (dec. 1902).

Appeared in: **1919** A Regular Girl.

LEWIS, JOE

Born: 1898. Died: Oct. 9, 1938, Corning, Calif. Screen actor and stunt flyer. Do not confuse with world champion prize-fighter Joe Louis (dec. 1981).

LEWIS, JOE E.

Born: 1902, New York, N.Y. Died: June 4, 1971, New York, N.Y. (liver and kidney ailments). Screen actor, burlesque and vaudeville comedian. Divorced from singer Martha Stewart.

Appeared in: **1931** Too Many Husbands. **1942** Private Buckaroo. **1969** Lady in Cement.

LEWIS, MARTIN

Born: Sept. 8, 1888, Blackheath, England. Died: Apr., 1970, Farnborough, Kent, England. Screen, stage and radio actor.

Appeared in: **1916** The Vicar of Wakefield.

LEWIS, MARY (Mary Kidd)

Born: 1900, Hot Springs, Ark. Died: Dec. 31, 1941, New York. Screen, stage actress and opera performer. Entered films in 1920 and appeared in early Christie comedies.

Appeared in: **1927** Way Down South (short).

LEWIS, MEADE LUX

Born: 1906. Died: June 6, 1964, Minneapolis, Minn. (auto accident). Screen actor and jazz pianist.

Appeared in: **1947** New Orleans.

LEWIS, MICHAEL

Born: 1931. Died: Mar. 6, 1975, Summit, N.J. Stage and screen actor. Son of author Sinclair Lewis and journalist Dorothy Thompson (dec.).

Appeared in: **1961** The Curse of the Werewolf. **1969** Baby Love.

LEWIS, MITCHELL J.

Born: June 26, 1880, Syracuse, N.Y. Died: Aug. 24, 1956, Woodland Hills, Calif. Stage and screen actor. Entered films in 1914 with Thanhouser.

Appeared in: **1914** The Million Dollar Mystery (serial). **1917** The Barrier; The Bar Sinister. **1918** The Sign Invisible; Safe for Democracy. **1921** At the End of the World. **1922** The Siren Call; Salome; The Marriage Chance; On the High Seas; The Woman Conquers. **1923** The Destroying Angel; The Little Girl Next Door; The Miracle Makers; The Spoilers; Gold Madness; Her Accidental Husband; A Prince of a King; Rupert of Hentzau. **1924** The Mine With the Iron Door; Half-a-Dollar Bill; The Red Lily; Three Weeks. **1925** Frivolous Sal; The Crimson Runner; The Mystic; Tracked in the Snow Country; Flaming Love. **1926** The Eagle of the Sea; Ben Hur; The Last Frontier; Miss Nobody; Old Ironsides; The Sea Wolf; Tell It to the Marines; Wild Oats Lane; Typhoon Love. **1927** Hard Boiled Hagerty; Back to God's Country. **1928** Tenderloin; The Way of the Strong; Beau Sabreur; The Docks of New York; The Hawk's Nest; Out With the Tide; The Speed Classic; The Death Ship (short). **1929** The Bridge of San Luis Rey; Madame X; The Leatherneck; Linda; The Black Watch; One Stolen Night. **1930** The Cuckoos; Beau Bandit; See America Thirst; The Bad One; Girl of the Port; Mammy. **1931** Never the Twain Shall Meet; The Squaw Man; Oh! Oh! Cleopatra (short); Song of India; Ben Hur (sound of 1926 version). **1932** World and the Flesh; New Morals for Old; McKenna of the Mounted; Kongo. **1933** Secret of Madame Blanche; Ann Vickers. **1934** Count of Monte Cristo. **1935** The Farmer Takes a Wife; Red Morning; The Best Man Wins; A Tale of Two Cities. **1936** Sutter's Gold; The Dancing Pirate; Mummy's Boys; The Bohemian Girl. **1937** Mama Steps Out; Espionage; Waikiki Wedding. **1938** Three Comrades; The Mysterious Mr. Moto; Anesthesia (short); What Price Safety? (short). **1940** Go West; Strange Cargo. **1941** Meet John Doe; The Big Store; I'll Wait for You; Billy the Kid. **1942** Cairo; Rio Rita. **1944** Lost in a Harem; The Seventh Cross. **1946** Courage of Lassie; The Green Years; The Harvey Girls. **1947** Desire Me. **1948** Julia Misbehaves. **1949** The Stratton Story; Mr. Whitney Had a Notion (short). **1950** Kim. **1951** Man With a Cloak. **1952** Talk About a Stranger. **1953** All the Brothers Were Valiant; The Sun Shines Bright; Torch Song; Lili. **1955** Trial.

LEWIS, RALPH

Born: 1872, Englewood, Ill. Died: Dec., 1937, Los Angeles, Calif. Screen and stage actor. Entered films with Reliance-Majestic in 1912.

Appeared in: **1915** Birth of a Nation. **1919** Eyes of Youth. **1921** The Conquering Power; Man-Woman-Marriage; A Private Scandal; Salvage; Outside the Law; Prisoners of Love; Sowing the Wind. **1922** Broad Daylight; Environment; The Five-Dollar Baby; Flesh and Blood; The Third Alarm; In the Name of the Law; The Sin Flood. **1923** Blow Your Own Horn; Desire; The Fog; Manhattan; Vengeance of the Deep; The Westbound Limited; Tea With a Kick. **1924** Dante's Inferno; East of Broadway; The Man Who Came Back; In Every Woman's Life; Untamed Youth. **1925** Heir-Loons; The Last Edition; The Million Dollar Handicap; The Bridge of Sighs; Who Cares; The Recreation of Brian Kent; The Overland Limited; One of the Bravest. **1926** Bigger Than Barnum's; The Lady from Hell; The Silent Power; The Block Signal; The False Alarm; Fascinating Youth; The Shadow of the Law. **1927** Casey Jones; Held By the Law; Outcast Souls. **1929** The Girl in the Glass Cage. **1930** Abraham Lincoln; The Bad One; The Fourth Alarm. **1933** Sucker Money; Riot Squad. **1934** Mystery Liner. **1935** Behind the Green Light.

LEWIS, RICHARD

Born: 1869. Died: Apr. 30, 1935, Los Angeles, Calif. Screen actor.

Appeared in: **1924** Yankee Speed. **1926** Stick to Your Story.

LEWIS, ROBERT

Died: Apr. 11, 1977. Screen actor. Do not confuse with actor Robert Q. Lewis, or film editor Robert Lewis.

Appeared in: **1943** Tonight We Raid Calais; Bomber's Moon; Paris After Dark. **1944** Dragon Seed. **1945** Son of Lassie; The Last Installment (short). **1946** Ziegfeld Follies. **1947** Monsieur Verdoux. **1950** The Lost Volcano.

LEWIS, SAM

Born: 1878. Died: Apr. 28, 1963, Hollywood, Calif. (heart ailment). Screen actor and extra.

LEWIS, SHELDON

Born: 1869, Philadelphia, Pa. Died: May 7, 1958, San Gabriel, Calif. Stage and screen actor. Married to actress Virginia Pearson (dec. 1958).

Appeared in: **1914** The Exploits of Elaine (serial). **1916** The Iron Claw (serial); Dr. Jekyll and Mr. Hyde. **1917** The Hidden Hand (serial). **1918** Wolves of Kultur (serial). **1919** The Bishop's Emeralds. **1922** Orphans of the Storm; When the Desert Calls. **1923** The Darling of New York; The Little Red Schoolhouse; Jacqueline of Blazing Barriers. **1924** The Enemy Sex; Honor Among Men; In Fast Company; Missing Daughters; Those Who Dare; The Dangerous Flirt. **1925** Top of the World; Bashful Buccaneer; Fighting the Flames; Kit Carson Over the Great Divide; Super Speed; Lure of the Track; Accused; Defend Yourself; The Mysterious Stranger; New Lives for Old; Silent Sanderson; The Sporting Chance. **1926** Bride of the Storm; Lightning Hutch (serial); Vanishing Millions (serial); Beyond the Trail; Buffalo Bill on the U.P. Trail; Exclusive Rights; A Desperate Moment; The Sky Pirate; Senor Daredevil; The Self Starter; The Gilded Highway; Moran of the Mounted; Don Juan; The Two-Gun Man; The Red Kimono. **1927** Burning Gold; Hazardous Valley; Life of an Actress; The Cruise of the Hellion; Driven from Home; The Ladybird; The Love Wager; The Overland Stage. **1928** The Sky Rider; The Chorus Kid; The Code of the Scarlet; Marlie the Killer; The Little Wild Girl; The River Woman; Turn Back the Hours; Top Sergeant Mulligan. **1929** Untamed Justice; Seven Footprints to Satan; Black Magic. **1930** Firebrand Jordan; Terry of the Times (serial released in two versions, silent and sound); Danger Man. **1932** The Monster Walks; Tex Takes a Holiday. **1933** Tombstone Canyon. **1934** Gun Justice. **1936** The Cattle Thief.

LEWIS, TED (Theodore Leopold Friedman)
Born: June 6, 1891, Circleville, Ohio. Died: Aug. 25, 1971, New York, N.Y. (heart attack). Screen, stage, vaudeville actor and bandleader. Married to dancer Adah Lewis (dec. 1981). Entered films in 1929.

Appeared in: **1929** Is Everybody Happy?; Show of Shows. **1935** Here Comes the Band. **1937** Manhattan Merry-Go-Round. **1941** Hold That Ghost. **1943** Follow the Boys; Is Everybody Happy? (and 1929 version).

LEWIS, TED "KID" (Gershon Mendeloff)
Born: Oct. 24, 1894, St. George's-in-the-East, London, England. Died: Oct. 14, 1970, London, England. Boxer, boxing instructor and screen actor. Do not confuse with bandleader/actor Ted Lewis (dec. 1971).

Appeared in: **1925** Sporting Life.

LEWIS, TOM
Born: 1864, St. John, New Brunswick, Canada. Died: Oct. 19, 1927, New York (cancer). Screen, stage, minstrel actor and circus performer.

Appeared in: **1920** Passers By. **1921** Enchantment. **1923** Adam and Eva; The Go-Getter; Marriage Morals. **1924** The Great White Way. **1927** The Callahans and the Murphys. **1928** Steamboat Bill, Jr.

LEWIS, VERA
Born: New York, N.Y. Died: Feb. 8, 1956, Los Angeles, Calif. Stage and screen actress. Entered films in 1914.

Appeared in: **1916** Intolerance. **1919** The Mother and the Law. **1920** Nurse Marjorie. **1922** The Glorious Fool; Nancy from Nowhere. **1923** Peg O' My Heart; Long Live the King; Brass; Desire; The Marriage Market. **1924** Broadway After Dark; The Dark Swan; How to Educate a Wife; Cornered; In Every Woman's Life. **1925** Enticement; Eve's Secret; Stella Dallas; The Only Thing; Who Cares. **1926** Ella Cinders; The Gilded Butterfly; King of the Pack; Take It from Me; The Lily; The Passionate Quest. **1927** Thumbs Down; Resurrection; The Broken Gate; The Small Bachelor; What Happened to Father. **1928** The Home Towners; Ramona; Satan and the Woman. **1929** The Iron Mask. **1930** Wide Open. **1931** Command Performance; Night Nurse. **1933** Hold Your Man. **1935** Alias Mary Dow; Never Too Late; The Man on the Flying Trapeze; Way Down East; Paddy O'Day. **1936** Missing Girls; Dancing Pirate; Don't Get Personal. **1937** Maid of Salem; Nothing Sacred. **1938** In Old Chicago; The Amazing Dr. Clitterhouse; The Sisters; Hard to Get; Boy Meets Girl; Angels With Dirty Faces; Four Daughters; Nancy Drew, Detective; Comet Over Broadway. **1939** Naughty But Nice; Sweepstakes Winner; Nancy Drew and the Hidden Staircase; Mr. Smith Goes to Washington; Women in the Wind; On Trial; Hell's Kitchen; The Roaring Twenties; Four Wives; Return of Dr. X; Dodge City; Each Dawn I Die. **1940** Women in War; The Man Who Talked Too Much; They Drive By Night; Granny Get Your Gun; A Night At Earl Carroll's; The Courageous Dr. Christian. **1941** Nine Lives Are Not Enough; She Couldn't Say No; Four Mothers; Here Comes Happiness; They Died With Their Boots On; Three Girls About Town; The Man Who Came to Dinner; Remember the Day; Knockout; One Foot in Heaven; Miss Polly; Captain Koepenick. **1942** Larceny, Inc.; Lady Gangster; Busses Roar; Moon Tide; The Hard Way; Yankee Doodle Dandy. **1943** Edge of Darkness; Princess O'Rourke. **1944** Mr. Skeffington. **1945** Hollywood and Vine; Rhythm on the Range; The Suspect. **1946** The Cat Creeps; Spook Busters; The Time, the Place and the Girl; The Killers; Cinderella Jones. **1947** It Had to Be You; Stallion Road; It Happened on Fifth Avenue; It's a Joke, Son; Wife to Spare (short).

LEWIS, WALTER "FURRY"
Born: 1893, Miss. Died: Sept. 14, 1981, Memphis, Tenn. (heart attack). Black screen, television actor, singer and musician.

Appeared in: **1975** W.W. and the Dixie Dance Kings.

LEWIS, WALTER P.
Born: June, 1871, Albany, N.Y. Died: Jan. 30, 1932. Screen, stage and vaudeville actor.

Appeared in: **1912** My Hero; Gold and Glitter; The God Within; Musketeers of Pig Alley. **1914** Cinderella. **1915** Gambler of the West. **1916** Big Jim Garrity. **1921** The Family Closet; The Ghost in the Garret; Tol'able David. **1922** Lonesome Corners. **1923** The Steadfast Heart. **1924** Three Miles Out. **1925** Down Upon the Swannee River. **1927** The Crimson Flash (serial). **1928** The Little Shepherd of Kingdom Come; Beware of Blondes. **1930** The Arizona Kid; A Royal Romance.

LEWISOHN, VICTOR M. (Victor Max Lewisohn)
Born: Apr. 21, 1897, London, England. Died: Nov. 13, 1934, England? Screen and stage actor.

Appeared in: **1932** The River House Ghost.

LEWMAN, HIRAM "HIGHE" (Hiram Wallingford Lewman)
Born: 1902. Died: Aug. 27, 1976, Canoga Park, Calif. (internal bleeding and kidney failure). Screen actor, songwriter and boxer.

LEXA, JAKE
Died: Jan. 21, 1973. Screen actor.

Appeared in: **1972** Fuzz.

LEYSSAC, PAUL
Born: Denmark. Died: Aug. 20, 1946, Copenhagen, Denmark. Screen, stage and radio actor.

Appeared in: **1937** Victoria the Great; Head Over Heels. **1941** Paris Calling.

LEYTON, GEORGE
Born: Apr. 28, 1864, New Orleans, La. Died: June 5, 1948, London, England. Screen, stage actor and vocalist.

Appeared in: **1916** The Boys of the Old Brigade. **1917** It's Never Too Late to Mend (US 1918).

LIBBEY, J. ALDRICH
Born: 1872. Died: Apr. 29, 1925, San Francisco, Calif. (heart failure). Screen and stage actor.

Appeared in: **1924** Greed.

LIBBY, AL (Alfred A. Liberatore)
Born: 1905. Died: Apr. 15, 1978, Boston, Mass. (heart attack). Screen and vaudeville actor.

LICHINE, DAVID (David Lichtenstein)
Born: 1910, Russia? Died: June 28, 1972, Los Angeles, Calif. (kidney failure). Screen actor, choreographer and ballet dancer.

Appeared in: **1943** The Heat's On. **1944** Sensations of 1945.

LICHO, EDGAR ADOLPH
Born: 1876, Russia. Died: Oct. 11, 1944, Hollywood, Calif. Screen and stage actor.

Appeared in: **1930** Menschen Hinter Gettern. **1941** Man Hunt. **1942** Once Upon a Honeymoon; To Be or Not to Be. **1943** Mission to Moscow. **1944** White Cliffs of Dover; Seventh Cross; Days of Glory.

LIDELL, ALVAR
Born: 1909, London, England. Died: Jan. 7, 1981, Northwood, England (cancer). Screen and radio actor.

Appeared in: **1964** It Happened Here (US 1966).

LIEB, HERMAN
Born: 1873, Chicago, Ill. Died: Mar. 9, 1966, Tucson, Ariz. Screen, stage and vaudeville actor.

Appeared in: **1918** Daybreak. **1936** The Chemist (short).

LIEBERMAN, JACOB
Born: 1879. Died: Feb. 16, 1956, Philadelphia, Pa. Screen and stage actor. Married to actress Elsie Freed.

LIEBMANN, HANS H.
Born: 1895. Died: Jan. 24, 1960, Hannacroix, N.Y. Screen, vaudeville, television actor and dancer. With his wife Lois, was known in vaudeville as the team of "Harold and Lola."

Appeared in: **1945** Pan-Americana. **1948** Variety Time.

LIEDTKE, HARRY
Born: 1881, Konigsberg, Germany. Died: 1945, Bad Saarow-Pieskow, Germany. Screen and stage actor.

Appeared in: **1911** Zu Spaet. **1912** Eva. **1913** Schuldig. **1916** Die Leere Wasserflasche. **1917** Das Bild der Ahnfrau; Ein Fideles Gefaengnis; Die Hochzeit im Excentricclub; Die Kameliendame; Komptesse Doddy; Lulu; Das Raetsel von Bangalore. **1918** Die Augen der Mumie Ma; Die Blaue Mauritius; Der Gelbe Schein; Das Maedel vom Ballett; Der Rodelkavalier; Carmen (aka Gypsy Love). **1919** Das Karussell des Lebens; Kreuziget Sie; Tropenblut; Madame DuBarry (aka Passion); Die Austernprinzessin (The Oyster Princess). **1920** Medea; Sumurun (aka One Arabian Night); Der Mann ohne Namen (The Man Without a Name). **1921** Vendetta; Indische Rache; Die Taenzerin Barberina; Das Weib des Pharao (aka The Loves of Pharaoh—US 1922, aka Pharoah's Wife); Gypsy Blood. **1922** Peter Voss, der Millionendieb; So Sind die Maenner. **1923** Die Fledermaus; Der Kaufmann von Venedig; Die Liebe Einer Koenigin; Der Seeteufel; Nanon; Die Finanzen des Grossherzogs (The Grand Duke's Finances). **1924** Die Hermannsschlacht; Die Puppenkoenigin; Ein Traum vom Glueck; Orient (aka Die Tochter der Wueste); Paragraph 144 (aka Muss die Frau Mutter Werden?). **1925** Die Frau fuer 24 Stunden; Graefin Mariza; Die Insel der Traeume; Liebe und Trompetenblasen; Um Recht und Ehre. **1926** Der Feldherrenhuegel; An der Schoenen Blauen Donau; Die Foersterchristl; Kreuzzug des Weibes; Die Lachende Grille; Madame Wuenscht Keine Kinder (Madame Wants No Children—US 1927); Das Maedchen auf der Schaukel; Der Mann ohne Schlaf; Nixchen; Der Soldat der Marie; Eine Tolle Nacht; Der Veilchenfresser; Die Welt Will Belogen Sein; Die Wiskottens. **1927** The Queen Was in the Parlor; Der Bettelstudent; Faschingzauber; Das Fuerstenkind; Die Geliebte; Das Heiratsnest; Die Letzte Nacht; Ein Maedel aus dem Volke; Mein Freund Harry; Regine, die Tragoedie Einer Frau; Die Rollende Kugel; Das Schicksal Einer Nacht; Die Spielerin; Wochenendzauber. **1928** Love is a Lie; Dragonerliebchen; Der Faschingsprinz; Grosstadtjugend; Amor auf Ski; Der Herzensphotograph; Der Moderne Casanova; Robert und Bertram; Das Spiel mit der Liebe; Die Zirkusprinzessin. **1929** Bohemian Dancer; Beautiful Blue Danube; Forbidden Love; Der Erzieher Meiner Tochter; Der Held Aller Maedchentraueme; Die Konkurrenz Platzt; Der Lustige Witwer; Der Schwarze Domino; Vater und Sohn; Donauwaltzer; O Maedchen, Mein Maedchen, wie Leib' ich Dich!; Ich Kuesse Ihre Hand, Madame (I Kiss Your Hand, Madame—US 1932). **1930** Die Grosse Sehnsucht; Delikatessen; Der Keusche Joseph; Der Korvettenkapitaen (US 1933 aka Blaue Jungs von der Marine). **1931** Nie Wieder Liebe (No More Love); ... und das ist die Hauptsache; Der Liebesarzt. **1932** Liebe in Uniform (Love in Uniform—US 1934). **1933** Eine Liebesnacht; Wenn am Sonntagabend die Dorfmusik Spielt (US 1935); Der Page vom Dalmasse-Hotel (US 1935). **1934** Zwischen Zwei Herzen (Between Two Hearts—US 1936). **1935** Liebesleute (US 1936, aka Hermann und Dorothea von Heute). **1936** Stadt Anatol. **1937** Gefaehrliches Spiel. **1938** Preussische Liebesgeschichte (aka Liebeslegende). **1941** Quax, der Bruchpilot. **1943** Sophienlund. **1944** Das Konzert; Der Majoratsherr.

LIEVEN, ALBERT
Born: June 23, 1906, Hohenstein, Prussia. Died: Dec. 22, 1971, near London, England. Screen, stage, television actor and opera performer. Divorced from actresses Tatiana Lieven (dec. 1978), Petra Peters, Valerie White and Susan Shaw (dec. 1978).

Appeared in: **1935** Krach um Iolanthe; Die vom Niederrhein (Lower Rhine Folks); Fraulein Liselott; Hermine und Die Sieben Aufrechten. **1936** Reifende Jugend; Glueckspilze. **1938** Ein Frau Ohne Bedeutung; Kater Lampe. **1940** Jeannie; Night Train to Munich. **1941** Convoy. **1942** The Young Mr. Pitt; Big Blockade (war documentary). **1943** The Yellow Canary. **1944** English Without Tears (aka Her Man Gilbey—US 1949). **1945** The Life and Death of Colonel Blimp. **1946** The Seventh Veil; Beware of Pity. **1947** Frieda. **1949** Sleeping Car to Trieste. **1951** Hotel Sahara. **1953** Desperate Moment. **1955** Der Fischer Von Heilingenesee (The Fisherman from Heilingenesee aka The Big Barrier—US 1958). **1956** Dei Halbstarken (Wolf Pack); Loser Takes All (US 1957). **1957** Des Teufels General (The Devil's General). **1959** Subway in the Sky; The House of Intrigue; Londra Chiama Polo Nord (London Calling North Pole). **1960** Conspiracy of Hearts. **1961** Foxhole in Cairo; The Guns of Navarone; Brainwashed. **1963** The Victors; Mystery Submarine. **1965** City of Terror; Coast of Skeletons. **1966** Traitor's Gate. Other German films: Yellow Daffodils; Secret City; Ride the High Wind.

LIEVEN, TATIANA
Born: 1910, Leningrad, Russia. Died: Nov. 30, 1978, London, England. Screen, stage actress, television director and author. Divorced from Albert Lieven (dec. 1971), and later married to actor Miles Malleson (dec. 1969).

LIGERO, MIGUEL
Born: 1898, Spain. Died: Feb. 20, 1968, Madrid, Spain. Screen, stage and television actor.

Appeared in: **1927** Frivolina (film debut). **1938** Nobleza Baturra (Rustic Chivalry); La Verbena de la Paloma; Morena Clara; Hamelin. **1939** La Vida Bohemia. **1940** Rumbo al Cairo (Bound for Cairo).

LIGETY, LOUIS
Born: 1881, Hungary. Died: Nov. 27, 1928, Los Angeles, Calif. (results of auto accident). Screen actor.

LIGHTNER, WINNIE
Born: Sept. 17, 1901, Greenport, N.Y. Died: Mar. 5, 1971, Sherman Oaks, Calif. (heart attack). Screen, stage and vaudeville actress. Married to film director/screenwriter Roy Del Ruth (dec. 1961).

Appeared in: **1928** The Song-a-Minute Girl (short); Broadway Favorite (short). **1929** Show of Shows; Gold Diggers of Broadway. **1930** She Couldn't Say No; Hold Everything; Life of the Party. **1931** Sit Tight; Why Changer Your Husband?; Side Show; Gold Dust Gertie. **1932** Play Girl; Eight to Five; Manhattan Parade; The Slippery Pearls (short). **1933** She Had to Say Yes; Dancing Lady. **1934** I'll Fix It.

LIGON, GROVER (aka GROVER LIGGON)
Born: 1885. Died: Mar. 4, 1965, Hollywood, Calif. Screen actor and stuntman. Entered films with Biograph.

Appeared in: **1913** Sennett films and was one of the first Keystone Kops. **1917** A Maiden's Trust. **1929** The Million Dollar Collar. **1931** Father's Son. **1934** The St. Louis Kid.

LILLARD, CHARLOTTE
Born: 1844. Died: Mar. 4, 1946, Hollywood, Calif. Screen and stage actress. Entered films with Edison and Vitagraph Companies.

Appeared in: **1935** Mary Burns, Fugitive; The Great Impersonation. **1936** The Garden of Allah. **1938** Kentucky; Marie Antoinette.

LILLFORD, HARRY
Died: Jan. 9, 1931, New York, N.Y. Screen and stage actor.

Appeared in: **1914** The $5,000,000 Counterfeiting Plot.

LILLIE, MAJOR GORDON W. "PAWNEE BILL"
Born: Feb. 14, 1860, Bloomington, Ill. Died: Feb. 3, 1942, Pawnee, Okla. Screen actor and circus performer. Married to circus performer May Little (dec. 1936).

Appeared in: **1911** Buffalo Bill Wild West and Pawnee Bill Far East. **1915** Pawnee Bill. **1935** Two Hearts in Harmony.

LINCOLN, E. K. (Edward Kline Lincoln)
Born: Johnstown, Pa. Died: Jan. 9, 1958, Los Angeles, Calif. Stage and screen actor. Do not confuse with Elmo Lincoln (dec. 1952).

Appeared in: **1912** The Wood Violet. **1913** Two's Company, Three's a Crowd; A Regiment of Two; The Prince of Evil; The Lost Millionaire; The Treasure of Desert Island; The Wreck; The Swan Girl; His Second Wife; The Carpenter; The Call. **1914** The Littlest Rebel; Diana's Dress Reform; The Right and the Wrong of It; Lincoln the Lover; A Million Bid; Back to Broadway; The Painted World. **1916** Heart's Tribute; Expiation; World Against Him. **1917** Jimmy Dale Alias the Grey Seal (serial); For the Freedom of the World. **1921** Devotion; The Woman God Changed. **1922** The Light in the Dark; Man of Courage; Women Men Marry. **1923** The Little Red Schoolhouse; The Woman in Chains. **1924** The Right of the Strongest. **1925** My Neighbor's Wife.

LINCOLN, ELMO (Otto Elmo Linkenhelt)
Born: 1889. Died: June 27, 1952, Hollywood, Calif. (heart attack). Screen actor and circus performer. He was the original "Tarzan" of silent films.

Appeared in: **1915** Birth of a Nation. **1916** Intolerance. **1918** Tarzan of the Apes; The Romance of Tarzan. **1919** Elmo the Mighty (serial); The Greatest Thing in Life; Lafayette, We Come. **1920** Elmo the Fearless (serial); The Flaming Disc (serial); Under Crimson Skies. **1921** The Adventures of Tarzan (serial—recut and rereleased with sound effects in 1928). **1922** Quincy Adams Sawyer. **1923** Fashion Row; Rupert of Hentzau; The Rendezvous. **1925** All Around Frying Pan. **1926** Whom Shall I Marry? **1934** The Hunchback of Notre Dame. **1939** Union Pacific; The Real Glory; Blue Montana Skies; Colorado Sunset; Wyoming Outlaw. **1942** Tarzan's New York Adventure. **1944** The Story of Dr. Wassell. **1946** Bad Man's Territory. **1948** Tap Roots. **1949** Tarzan's Magic Fountain. **1951** The Hollywood Story; The Iron Man. **1952** Carrie.

LINDEN, ROBERT
Born: 1914. Died: Nov. 1, 1980, West Hollywood, Calif. (heart attack). Screen actor, stage producer and stage casting director.

Appeared in: **1931** Subway Express.

LINDENBERG, KAETHE
Born: 1906, Germany. Died: Dec. 15, 1980, Stuttgart, West Germany. Screen and stage actress.

LINDENBURN, HENRY
Born: 1874. Died: Mar. 28, 1952, Cincinnati, Ohio. Riverboat captain and screen actor.

Appeared in: **1939** Gone With the Wind (piloted steamer in the film).

LINDER, ALFRED
Died: July 6, 1957, Hollywood, Calif. Screen, stage actor and stage director.

Appeared in: **1945** The House on 92nd Street. **1947** 13 Rue Madeline; The Brasher Doubloon. **1948** Canon City. **1949** I Was a Male War Bride. **1950** Guilty of Treason. **1952** Diplomatic Courier. **1957** The Invisible Boy; The Girl in the Kremlin.

LINDER, MAX (Gabriel Leviell)
Born: 1883, France. Died: Oct. 31, 1925, Paris, France. Screen, stage actor, screenwriter and film director.

Appeared in: **1917** Max Wants a Divorce; Max Comes Across. **1921** Be My Wife; Seven Years Bad Luck. **1922** The Three Must-Get-Theres; Au Secours! (never released).

LINDO, OLGA
Born: July 13, 1899, London, England. Died: May 7, 1968, London, England. Screen, stage and television actress.

Appeared in: **1931** The Shadow Between. **1935** The Case of Gabriel Perry; The Last Journey (US 1936); Dark World. **1939** The Stars Look Down (US 1941). **1943** When We Are Married. **1946** Bedelia (US 1947). **1949** Obsession (aka The Hidden Room—US 1950); Train of Events (US 1952). **1954** An Inspector Calls. **1955** Raising a Riot (US 1957). **1956** Yield to the Night (aka Blonde Sinner—US). **1957** Woman in a Dressing Gown. **1958** Twelve Desperate Hours. **1959** Sapphire. **1962** Dr. Crippen (US 1964).

LINDROTH, HELEN
Born: 1874. Died: Oct. 5, 1956, Boston, Mass. Screen and stage actress.

Appeared in: **1913** From the Manger to the Cross. **1916** Audrey; The Spider; Little Lady Eileen; Seventeen. **1918** The House of Gold. **1919** The Great Romance; Shadows of Suspicion; The Eternal Magdalene. **1920** Point of View. **1921** Poor, Dear Margaret Kirby; The Fighter; The Way of a Maid; Peggy Puts It Over; the Right Way; Worlds Apart; The Passionate Pilgrim. **1923** Unseeing Eyes; Java Head. **1924** The Humming Bird; The Confidence Man; Unguarded Women. **1925** The Swan; Unrestrained Youth. **1926** The Song and Dance Man.

LINDSAY, HOWARD
Born: Mar. 29, 1889, Waterford, N.Y. Died: Feb. 11, 1968, New York, N.Y. Screen, stage, vaudeville and burlesque actor, playwright, stage director and stage producer. Appeared in silent films.

LINDSAY, JAMES
Born: Feb. 26, 1869, Devonshire, England. Died: June 9, 1928, England? Screen and stage actor.

Appeared in: **1914** The Cry of the Captive; The Dead Heart; Through the Valley of Shadows. **1915** The Life of an Actress; The Dungeon of Death; Lost and Won (aka Odds Against); Alone in London. **1916** The Second Mrs. Tanqueray; The Girl Who Loved a Sailor; Dr. Wake's Patient; Her Greatest Performance; The Lyons Mail. **1918** The Admirable Crichton; Missing the Tide; A Fortune at Steak; The Snare; Tinker, Tailor, Soldier, Sailor. **1919** The Life of a London Actress; The Thundercloud; A Little Bit of Fluff; Gamblers All; Edge O' Beyond; A Member of Tattersall's; The Disappearance of the Judge; Mrs. Thompson; The City of Beautiful Nonsense; The Double Life of Mr. Alfred Burton; Damaged Goods. **1920** The Grip of Iron; The Honeypot; Nance; Aunt Rachel. **1921** Love Money; The Bachelor's Club; For Her Father's Sake; All Sorts and Conditions of Men. **1922** The Game of Life. **1923** The Temptation of Carlton Earlye; Rogues of the Turf; Lights of London; What Price Loving Cup?; Afterglow. **1924** Claude Duval; The World of Wonderful Reality; The Cost of Beauty. **1925** Forbidden Cargoes (aka Contraband); The Rat; Twisted Tales series including The Choice. **1926** The Steve Donoghue series including Beating the Book. **1927** One of the Best.

LINDSAY, KEVIN
Born: 1924, Australia. Died: May, 1975, London, England (heart attack). Screen, stage and television actor.

LINDSAY, LEX
Born: 1901. Died: Apr. 24, 1971, Pa. (stroke). Stage and screen actor.

Appeared in: **1931** Sob Sister.

LINDSAY, MARGARET (Margaret Kies)
Born: Sept. 19, 1910, Dubuque, Iowa. Died: May 9, 1981, Los Angeles, Calif. (emphysema). Screen, stage and television actress.

Appeared in: **1932** Okay America; The All American. **1933** Baby Fce; House on 56th Street; The Fourth Horseman; Calvacade; Lady Killer; West of Singapore; The World Changes; Voltaire; Private Detective 62; Captured; Paddy the Next Best Thing; From Headquarters. **1934** Fog Over Frisco; Merry Wives of Reno; Dragon Murder Case; Gentlemen are Born. **1935** Frisco Kid; Bordertown; The G-Men; The Case of the Curious Bride; Personal Maid's Secret; Dangerous; Devil Dogs of the Air; The Florentine Dagger. **1936** The Lady Consents; The Law in Her Hands; Public Enemy's Wife; Isle of Fury; Sinner Take All. **1937** Back in Circulation; The Green Light; Slim. **1938** Garden of the Moon; Broadway Musketeers; Jezebel; Gold Is Where You Find It; When Were You Born?; There's That Woman Again. **1939** Hell's Kitchen; On Trial; The Under-Pup; 20,000 Men a Year. **1940** The House of the Seven Gables; British Intelligence; Double Alibi; Honeymoon Deferred; Meet the Wildcat; Ellery Queen, Master Detective. **1941** There's Magic in Music (aka The Hard Boiled Canary); Ellery Queen's Penthouse Mystery; Ellery Queen and the Perfect Crime; Ellery Queen and the Murder Ring. **1942** A Close Call for Ellery Queen; The Spoilers; A Tragedy at Midnight; Enemy Agents Meet Ellery Queen. **1943** No Place for a Lady; Crime Doctor. **1944** Alaska. **1945** Scarlet Street; The Adventures of Rusty. **1946** Her Sister's Secret; Club Havana. **1947** Cass Timberlane; The Vigilantes Return; Louisiana; Seven Keys to Baldpate. **1948** B. F.'s Daughter. **1956** Emergency Hospital; The Bottom of the Bottle. **1958** The Restless Years; Jet Over the Atlantic (US 1960). **1960** Please Don't Eat the Daisies. **1963** Tammy and the Doctor.

LINDSAY, MARQUERITA
Born: 1883. Died: Dec. 26, 1955, Calif. (heart attack). Screen actress. Married to actor Noah Beery (dec. 1946) and mother of actor Noah Beery, Jr. She appeared in silent films.

LINDSEY, EMILY
Born: 1887. Died: Mar. 3, 1944, Los Angeles, Calif. Screen, stage, opera, vaudeville actress and singer.

LINDT, KARL (Carl Ludwig Lindt)
Died: Oct. 17, 1971. Screen actor.

Appeared in: **1953** Dangerous Crossing. **1955** This Island Earth. **1957** Five Steps to Danger. **1958** A Time to Love and a Time to Die. **1959** Buddenbrooks (US 1962). **1961** One, Two, Three.

LING, RITCHIE
Born: 1867, England. Died: Mar. 5, 1937, New York, N.Y. (heart attack). Screen and stage actor. Married to Lotta Faust (dec. 1909), and later married and divorced from stage actress Rose Winter.

Appeared in: **1915** The Green Clock; The Sentimental Lady; The Woman Next Door.

LINGEN, THEO (Franz Theodor Schmitz)
Born: 1903, Hanover, Germany. Died: 1978, Germany? Screen, stage actor, film director, stage director and writer.

Appeared in: **1930** Dolly Macht Karriere (Dolly's Career—US 1931); Das Flotenkonzert von Sanssouci (The Flute Concert at Sans Souci); Zwei Krawatten. **1931** Nie Wieder Liebe; M (US 1933); Zwei Himmelblaue Augen; Meine Frau, die Hochstaplerin. **1932** Der Grosse Bluff (The Big Bluff—US 1937); Eine Stadt Steht Kopf (US 1934); Friederike; Die Grafin von Monte Christo; Das Testament des Cornelius Gulden; Der Frauendiplomat; Der Diamant des Zaren; Ziegeuner der Nacht; So ein Maedel Vergisst Man Nicht; Moderne Mitgift; Marion, das Gehort Sich Nicht; Im Banne des Eulenspiegels; Flucht nach Nizza; Ein Toller Einfall. **1933** Gipfelsturmer; Ein Unsichtbarer Geht Durch die Stadt; Die Kleine Schwindlerin; Der Jager aus Kurpfalz; Das Lied vom Glueck (aka The Song of Happiness—US 1935); Das Testament des Dr. Mabuse; Zwei im Sonnenschein; Kleines Maedel—Grosses Glueck; Liebe Muss Verstanden Sein; Hollentempo; Ihre Durchlaucht die Verkauferin; Walzerkrieg; Und wer Kusst Mich?; Kleiner Mann—was Nun?; Keine Angst vor Liebe (US 1936); Schon ist es, verliebt zu Sein. **1934** Ihr Grosster Erfolg; Mein Herz Ruft Nach Dir; Petersburger Nachte; Kunjunkturritter (US 1935); Liebe Dumme Mama (Stupid Mama—US 1935); Das Blumenmaedchen vom Grand-Hotel; Die Finanzen des Grossherzogs; Der Doppelganger; Ich Sehne Mich Nach (US 1936); Ich Kenn' Dich Nicht und Liebe Dich; Ich Heirate Meine Frau; ... Heute Abend Bei Mir; Ein Maedel Wirbelt Durch die Welt; Ein Walzer fuer Dich; Fruchtchen; Gern hab ich die Frau'n Gekusst. **1935** Einmaleins der Liebe (US 1937); Winternachtstraum; Im Weissen Rossl; Der Ammenkonig; Der Himmel auf Erden; Der Schlafwagenkontrolleur; Ich Liebe alle Frauen; Held Einer Nacht; Fruhjahrsparade; Ein Falscher Fuffziger (US 1937). **1936** Der Verkannte Lebemann (aka The Unrecognized Man of the World—US 1939); Ungekusst Soll Man Nicht Schlafen Geh'n; Im Sonnenschein; Es Geht um Mein Leben; Ein Hochzeitstraum; Der Kurier des Zaren

(The Tsar's Courier); Die Leute mit Dem Sonnenstich; Alles fuer Veronika (US 1939); Die Entfuhrung (The Abduction—US 1938). **1937** Der Mann von dem man Spricht; Premier; Fremdenheim Filoda; Gefahrliches Spiel; Heiratsinstitut Ida & Co. Die Unentschuldigte Stunde; Die Austernlilli; Die Verschwundene Frau; Azuber der Bohene (The Charm of Boheme—US 1938). **1938** Der Optimist; Die Unruhigen Maedchen; Das Indische Grabmal (The Indian Tomb); Der Tiger von Eschnapur; Tanz auf dem Vulkan; Dir Gehort Mein Herz; Immer Wenn ich Gluecklich Bin; Diskretion—Ehrensache. **1939** Das Abenteuer Geht Weiter (Another Experience—US 1940); Opernball (Opera Ball—US 1940); Marquerite; Drunter und Drueber; Hochzietsreise zu Dritt. **1940** Was Wird Hier Gespielt?; Das Fraulein von Barnhelm; Rosen aus Tirol; 7 Jahre Pech; Ihr Privatsekretar; Der Ungetreue Eckehart; Rote Muehle; Herz Modern Mobliert. **1941** Dreimal Hochzeit; Sonntagskinder; Was Geschah in Dieser Nacht; Frau Luna. **1942** Wiener Blut; Liebeskomodie; Sieben Jahre Glueck. **1943** Das Lied der Nachtigall; Johann; Tolle Nacht. **1944** Schuss um Mitternacht; Es Fing so Harmlos An. **1945** Philine; Liebesheirat. **1949** Nichts als Zufalle; Um Eine Nasenlange. **1950** Der Theodor im Fussballtor; Jetzt Schlagt's 13; Hin und Her. **1951** Die Mitternachts-Venus; Hilfe, ich Bin Unsichtbar; Durch Dich und Dunn; Die Tochter der Kompanie. **1952** Man Lebt nur Einmal; Die Diebin von Bagdad; Wir Werden das Kind Schon Schaukeln. **1953** Heute Nacht Passiert's; Hurra—ein Junge!; Die Vertagte Hochzeitsnacht; Heimlich, Still und Leise; Heidi (aka Heidi and Peter—US 1955). **1955** Die Wirtin zur Goldenen Krone; Wenn die Alpenrosen Bluhen; Wie Werde ich Filmstar? **1956** Meine Tante, Deine Tante; Das Liebesleben des Schonen Franz; Ein Tolles Hotel; Wo die Lerche Singt; Der Mustergatte; ... und wer Kusst Mich? **1957** Vater Macht Karriere; August der Halbstarke; Familie Schimek; Die Unschuld vom Lande; Drei Mann auf Einem Pferd; Mit Rosen Fangt die Liebe An; Egon der Frauenheld; Almenrausch und Edelweiss; Die Beine von Dolores. **1958** Im Prater Bluh'n Wieder die Baume; Die Sklavenkarawane; Ein Lied Geht um die Welt. **1959** Die Nacht vor der Premiere; Der Lowe von Babylon; Die Gans von Sedan (US 1962). **1960** Pension Scholler; Eine Frau furs Ganze Leben. **1961** Bei Pichler Stimmt die Kasse Nicht. **1963** Der Musterknabe. **1964** Tonio Kroger (US 1968). **1965** Die Fromme Helene. **1967** Das Grosse Glueck; Die Heiden von Kummerov und Ihre Lustigen Streiche; Die Lummel von der Ersten Bank I. **1968** Die Lummel von der Ersten Bank II. **1969** Die Lummel von der Ersten Bank III, IV & V.

LINGHAM, THOMAS J.
Born: Apr. 7, 1874, Indianapolis, Ind. Died: Feb. 19, 1950, Woodland Hills, Calif. Screen and stage actor. Entered films in 1913.

Appeared in: **1916** Lass of the Lumberlands (serial). **1917** The Railroad Raiders (serial); The Lost Express (serial). **1918** The Lion's Claw (serial). **1919** The Adventures of Ruth (serial); The Red Glove (serial). **1920** Ruth of the Rockies (serial); The Vanishing Dagger (serial). **1921** My Lady Friends; The Fire Eater. **1922** The Crow's Nest. **1923** The Forbidden Trail; Desert Driven; Desert Rider; Eyes of the Forest; The Lone Star Ranger; Itching Palms. **1924** The Lightning Rider; Western Luck. **1925** Don Daredevil; Riders of Mystery; Where Was I?; Heartless Husbands; Across the Deadline. **1926** The Set-Up; The Border Sheriff; Sky High Corral; Davy Crockett at the Alamo. **1927** The Bandit's Son; Tom's Gang; Splitting the Breeze; The Desert Pirate; Daring Dude; Sitting Bull at the Spirit Lake Massacre. **1928** The Bandit Cowboy; Fangs of the Wild; Orphan of the Sage; The Trail of Courage; Young Whirlwind; The Rawhide Kid; The Bantam Cowboy; Into the Night; Man in the Rough; Son of the Golden West. **1929** The Cowboy and the Outlaw; The Fatal Warning; The Amazing Vagabond; The Freckles Rascal; Pals of the Prairie; Two Sisters; The Invaders.

LINK, ADOLF
Born: Sept. 15, 1881, Budapest, Hungary. Died: Sept. 23, 1933, New York, N.Y. Screen and stage actor.

Appeared in: **1924** The Hoosier Scoutmaster.

LINK, WILLIAM
Born: 1867. Died: Apr. 17, 1937, Hollywood, Calif. Screen and stage actor.

LINK, WILLIAM E.
Born: 1897. Died: Dec. 13, 1949, Hollywood, Calif. Screen and stage actor.

LINLEY, BETTY
Born: 1890, Malmesbury, England. Died: May 9, 1951, New York, N.Y. Stage and screen actress.

Appeared in: **1949** The Heiress (stage and film versions).

LINN, BUD (Grafton E. Linn)
Born: 1909. Died: Juiy 31, 1968, Conejo Valley, Calif. (heart attack). Screen, radio actor and singer. Founder of the "King's Men Quarter." Father of daughters Penelope, Kathy and Susan who sang as the "Linn Sisters."

Appeared in: **1942** Call Out the Marines. **1944** Heavenly Days.

LINN, MARGARET
Born: 1934, Richmond, Ind. Died: Sept. 12, 1973, Hollywood, Calif. (brain hemorrhage). Screen, stage and television actress.

Appeared in: **1970** Puzzle of a Downfall Child. **1971** Klute.

LINNANE, JOE
Born: 1910, Ireland. Died: Sept. 28, 1981, Dublin, Ireland. Screen, stage and radio actor.

Appeared in: **1950** Woman in Question (aka Five Angels on Murder—US 1953). **1954** The Angel Who Pawned Her Harp (US 1956).

LION, LEON M.
Born: 1879, England. Died: Mar. 28, 1947, Sussex, England. Screen, stage actor, stage producer and playwright.

Appeared in: **1915** Hard Times; Grip. **1917** The Woman Who Was Nothing. **1919** The Chinese Puzzle. **1931** The Chinese Puzzle (and 1919 version). **1932** Number Seventeen. **1934** Lady in Danger. **1936** The Amazing Quest of Ernest Bliss (aka Romance and Riches—US 1937). **1938** Strange Boarders; Crackerjack (aka The Man With a Hundred Faces—US).

LIPSON, MELBA
Born: 1901. Died: July 1, 1953, Hollywood, Calif. Screen actress.

LIPTON, LAWRENCE
Born: 1898. Died: July 9, 1975, San Francisco, Calif. Poet and screen actor.

Appeared in: **1960** The Hypnotic Eye. **1968** You Are What You Eat.

LISA, ANNA (Anna Lisa Andreasen)
Born: 1910. Died: May, 1977, Carmel, Calif. Screen, stage actress and dancer.

Appeared in: **1959** Have Rocket, Will Travel.

LISTER, FRANCIS
Born: Apr. 2, 1899, London, England. Died: Oct. 28, 1951, London, England. Screen and stage actor.

Appeared in: **1920** Branded. **1921** The Fortune of Christina McNab (US 1923). **1923** Should a Doctor Tell?; Boden's Boy; Comin' Through the Rye. **1924** The Unwanted; Chappy—That's All. **1929** Atlantic. **1930** At the Villa Rose (aka Mystery at the Villa Rose—US). **1931** Uneasy Virtue; Brown Sugar. **1932** Jack's the Boy (aka Night and Day—US 1933). **1933** Counsel's Opinion; Hawley's of High Street. **1935** Mutiny on the Bounty. **1936** Living Dangerously. **1937** Sensation; The Return of the Scarlet Pimpernel (US 1938). **1939** Murder in Soho (aka Murder in the Night—US 1940). **1944** Henry V (US 1946). **1945** The Wicked Lady (US 1946). **1949** Christopher Columbus. **1951** Home to Danger. **1958** Henry V (reissue of 1944 film).

LISTON, MILLIE
Born: 1859. Died: Feb. 20, 1920, New York, N.Y. (pneumonia). Screen and stage actress.

Appeared in: **1915** A Man's Shadow.

LISTON, SONNY (Charles Liston)
Born: May 8, 1932, near Little Rock, Ark. Died: Dec., 1970, Las Vegas. Black professional boxer and screen actor.

Appeared in: **1965** Harlow. **1968** Head.

LITEL, JOHN (John Beach Litel)
Born: Dec. 30, 1894, Albany, Wis. Died: Feb. 3, 1972, Woodland Hills, Calif. Screen, stage and television actor.

Appeared in: **1929** The Sleeping Porch (short). **1930** Don't Believe It; On the Border. **1932** Wayward. **1936** Black Legion. **1937** Fugitive in the Sky; The Life of Emile Zola; Marked Woman; Midnight Court; Slim; The Missing Witness; Back in Circulation. **1938** Alcatraz Island; Nancy Drew—Detective; Gold Is Where You Find It; A Slight Case of Murder; My Bill; Broadway Musketeers; Love, Honor and Behave;

Jezebel; Over the Wall; Little Miss Thoroughbred; The Amazing Dr. Clitterhouse; Valley of the Giants; Comet Over Broadway. **1939** Secret Service of the Air; On Trial; Dust Be My Destiny; Dodge City; Dead End Kids on Dress Parade (aka On Dress Parade); The Return of Dr. X; Nancy Drew, Trouble Shooter; Nancy Drew and the Hidden Staircase; One Hour to Live; Wings of the Navy; You Can't Get Away With Murder; Nancy Drew, Reporter. **1940** A Child is Born; The Fighting Sixty-Ninth; Castle on the Hudson; Flight Nurse; They Drive By Night; Knute Rockne—All American; Virginia City; It All Came True; An Angel from Texas; The Man Who Talked Too Much; Murder in the Air; Money and the Woman; Lady With Red Hair; Santa Fe Trail; Flight Angels; Men Without Souls; Father Is a Prince; Gambling on the High Seas. **1941** The Trial of Mary Dugan; Father's Son; Thieves Fall Out; The Big Boss; Henry Aldrich for President; Sealed Lips; The Great Mr. Nobody; They Died With Their Boots On. **1942** Kid Glove Killer; Henry and Dizzy; The Mystery of Marie Roget; Men of Texas; Mississippi Gambler; Invisible Agent; A Desperate Chance for Ellery Queen; Henry Aldrich, Editor; Boss of Big Town; Madame Spy; Don Winslow of the Navy (serial). **1943** Henry Aldrich Gets Glamour; Submarine Base; Dangerous Age; Murder in Times Square; Henry Aldrich Swings It; Henry Aldrich Haunts a House; Crime Doctor; Where Are Your Children? **1944** Henry Aldrich Plays Cupid; Henry Aldrich's Little Secret; Henry Aldrich, Boy Scout; Murder in the Blue Room; Faces in the Fog; Lake Placid Serenade; My Buddy. **1945** The Crime Doctor's Warning; Brewster's Millions; The Daltons Ride Again; Northwest Trail; The Enchanted Forest; Salome, Where She Danced; San Antonio; Crimson Canary. **1946** A Night in Paradise; The Return of Rusty; Sister Kenny; She Wrote the Book; Smooth as Silk; Swell Guy; Lighthouse; The Madonna's Secret; Notorious Gentleman. **1947** The Beginning of the End; Christmas Eve; The Guilty; Cass Timberlane; Heaven Only Knows; Easy Come, Easy Go. **1948** Rusty Leads the Way; My Dog Rusty; I, Jane Doe; Pitfall; The Valiant Hombre; Triple Threat; Smart Woman. **1949** Rusty Saves a Life; Rusty's Birthday; The Gal Who Took the West; Outpost in Morocco; Shamrock Hill; Woman in Hiding. **1950** Mary Ryan, Detective; The Sundowners; Fuller Brush Girl; Kiss Tomorrow Goodbye. **1951** Texas Rangers; The Groom Wore Spurs; Cuban Fireball; Little Egypt; Two Dollar Better; Flight to Mars; Take Care of My Little Girl. **1952** Jet Job; Montana Belle; Scaramouche. **1953** Jack Slade. **1954** Sitting Bull. **1955** Texas Lady; The Kentuckian; Double Jeopardy. **1956** The Wild Dakotas; Comanche. **1957** The Hired Gun; Decision at Sundown. **1958** Houseboat. **1961** A Pocketful of Miracles; Lover Come Back; Voyage to the Bottom of the Sea. **1963** The Gun Hawk. **1965** The Sons of Katie Elder. **1966** Nevada Smith.

LITTLE, JAMES F.
Born: 1907. Died: Oct. 12, 1969, Miami, Fla. (cancer). Screen, stage and television actor.

Appeared in: **1953** Taxi.

LITTLE, LADY *See* MAROLDO, MARIE J.

LITTLE, LITTLE JACK (John Leonard)
Born: 1901, England. Died: Apr. 9, 1956, Hollywood, Calif. (possible suicide). Screen, radio, vaudeville actor, bandleader, songwriter and singer.

Appeared in: **1932-33** Universal's "Radio Star Reels." **1934** A Vitaphone short; a Paramount short. **1936** A Vitaphone short.

LITTLE BILLY (Billy Rhodes)
Born: 1895. Died: July 24, 1967, Hollywood, Calif. (stroke). Midget screen and stage actor.

Appeared in: **1926** Oh Baby. **1929** The Flaming Youth (short); The Head of the Family (short); The Side Show. **1930** Swing High; No Questions Asked (short); prior to 1933: Some Babies (short); The Bigger They Are (short). **1934** Men in Black (short). **1938** The Terror of Tiny Town. **1939** The Wizard of Oz. **1961** Not Tonight, Henry. **1967** Mondo Hollywood.

LITTLE BOZO (John F. Pizzo)
Born: 1907. Died: May 9, 1952, Los Angeles, Calif. (heart ailment). Screen actor and circus performer.

Appeared in: **1927** White Pants Willie. **1932** Sign of the Cross; Freaks. **1939** At the Circus.

LITTLE CHAMP *See* CHAMPION # 3

LITTLEFIELD, EMMA
Died: June 25, 1934, N.Y. Screen, stage and vaudeville actress. Married to actor Victor Moore (dec. 1962).

LITTLEFIELD, LUCIEN
Born: Aug. 16, 1895, San Antonio, Tex. Died: June 4, 1960, Hollywood, Calif. Screen actor and screenwriter. Entered films in 1913.

Appeared in: **1915** The Wild Goose Chase. **1916** The Gutter Magdalene. **1921** The Little Clown; The Hell Diggers; The Sheik; Too Much Speed; Crazy to Marry. **1922** Her Husband's Trademark; Rent Free; Tillie; To Have and to Hold; Across the Continent; Our Leading Citizen; Manslaughter; The Siren Call. **1923** The French Doll; The Tiger's Claw; Three Wise Fools; In the Palace of the King; The Rendezvous; Mr. Billings Spends His Dime. **1924** Babbitt; The Deadwood Coach; Gold Heels; True as Steel; Gerald Cranston's Lady; Name the Man; The Painted Lady; Teeth; A Woman Who Sinned; Never Say Die. **1925** Tumbleweeds; Charley's Aunt; Gold and the Girl; The Rainbow Trail; Soul Mates. **1926** The Torrent; Bachelor Brides; Brooding Eyes; Take It from Me; Tony Runs Wild; Twinkletoes. **1927** The Small Bachelor; My Best Girl; The Cat and the Canary; Cheating Cheaters; Taxi!, Taxi!; Uncle Tom's Cabin; A Texas Steer. **1928** Heart to Heart; The Head Man; Do Your Duty; Mother Knows Best; Harold Teen; A Ship Comes In. **1929** Seven Keys to Baldpate; Drag; The Girl in the Glass Cage; Saturday's Children; Making the Grade; This is Heaven; Clear the Decks; The Man in Hobble's; Dark Streets. **1930** How I Play Golf—The Driver (short); Tom Sawyer; Clancy in Wall Street; She's My Weakness; No, No, Nanette; Captain of the Guard; The Great Divide; High Society Blues; also starred in "The Potter" series of shorts, including the following: Getting a Raise; At Home; Done in Oil; Pa Gets a Vacation; Big Money; Out for Game; His Big Ambition. **1931** Misbehaving Ladies; It Pays to Advertise; Reducing; Scandal Sheet; Young As You Feel. **1932** Rasputin and the Empress; High Pressure; Broken Lullaby; Strangers in Love; Shopworn; Strangers of the Evening; Miss Pinkerton; Downstairs; Speed Madness; Pride of the Legion; That's My Boy; Evenings for Sale; If I Had a Million; a Paramount short. **1933** The Bitter Tea of General Yen; Dirty Work (short); Sailor's Luck; Sweepings; Skyway; ; Rainbow Over Broadway; Alice in Wonderland; The Big Brain; Professional Sweetheart; Chance at Heaven; East of Fifth Avenue; a Paramount short. **1934** When Strangers Meet; Love Time; Sons of the Desert; Thirty Day Princess; Kiss and Make Up; Mandalay; Gridiron Flash. **1935** Ruggles of Red Gap; Sweepstake Annie; The Man on the Flying Trapeze; One Frightened Night; The Murder Man; She Gets Her Man; The Return of Peter Grimm; I Dream Too Much; Cappy Ricks Returns; Magnificent Obsession. **1936** Rose Marie; Early to Bed; The Moon's Our Home; Let's Sing Again. **1937** Hotel Haywire; Wild Money; Partners in Crime; High, Wide and Handsome; Souls at Sea; Bulldog Drummond's Revenge; Wells Fargo. **1938** Reckless Living; Wide Open Faces; Born to the West; Scandal Street; Hollywood Stadium Mystery; The Night Hawk; The Gladiator. **1939** Mystery Plane; Sky Pirate; Tumbleweeds; Unmarried; What a Life!; Sabotage; Jeepers Creepers. **1940** Money to Burn; Those Were the Days; The Great American Broadcast. **1941** Murder Among Friends; Henry Aldrich for President; Man at Large; The Little Foxes; Mr. and Mrs. North; Life With Henry. **1942** Hillbilly Blitzkrieg; Castle in the Desert; The Great Man's Lady; Bells of Capistrano; Whistling in Dixie. **1943** Henry Aldrich Haunts a House; Johnny Come Lately. **1944** Zorro's Black Whip (serial); Lady, Let's Dance; When the Lights Go On Again; Lights of Old Santa Fe; Casanova in Burlesque; Goodnight, Sweetheart; Cowboy and the Senorita; One Body Too Many. **1945** The Caribbean Mystery; Detour; Scared Stiff. **1946** Love Laughs at Andy Hardy; Rendezvous With Annie; That Brennan Girl. **1947** The Hal Roach Comedy; The Fabulous Joe; Sweet Genevieve. **1948** Lightnin' in the Forest; Jinx Money; Badmen of Tombstone. **1949** Susanna Pass. **1952** At Sword's Point. **1953** Roar of the Crowd. **1954** Casanova's Big Night. **1955** Sudden Danger. **1957** Bop Girl. **1958** Wink of an Eye.

LITVAK, ANATOLE (Michael Anatole Litvak)
Born: May 21, 1902, Kiev, Russia. Died: Dec. 15, 1974, Paris, France. Film director, producer, screenwriter, stage and screen actor. Divorced from actress Miriam Hopkins (dec. 1972). Married to fashion designer Sophie Steur Litvak.

LIVANOV, BORIS
Born: 1904, Russia. Died: Sept. 23, 1972, Moscow, Russia. Screen, stage actor and stage director.

Appeared in: **1934** Deserter. **1935** Peter Vinogradov. **1936** Dubrovsky. **1937** Baltic Deputy. **1938** Men of the Sea. **1947** The Great Glinka. **1949** The First Front. **1954** Admiral Ushakov. **1959** Poem of the Sea. **1961** Slepoy Muzykant (Sound of Life—US 1962).

LIVESEY, JACK

Born: 1901, England. Died: Oct. 12, 1961, Burbank, Calif. Screen, stage and television actor. Son of actor Sam Livesey (dec. 1936) and brother of actor Roger Livesey (dec. 1976).

Appeared in: **1933** The Wandering Jew (US 1935). **1935** The Passing of the Third Floor Back; Variety. **1936** The Howard Case. **1937** Behind Your Back; When the Poppies Bloom Again; It's Never Too Late to Mend; First Night. **1938** Murder Tomorrow; Penny Paradise; Old Bones of the River; Bedtime Story. **1940** Old Bill and Son. **1945** The World Owes Me a Living. **1948** The First Gentleman (aka Affairs of a Rogue—US 1949). **1949** Murder at the Windmill (aka Murder at the Burlesque—US). **1950** Paul Temple's Triumph (US 1951). **1962** The Notorious Landlady; That Touch of Mink.

LIVESEY, ROGER

Born: June 25, 1906, Barry, Wales. Died: Feb. 5, 1976, Watford, England. Screen, stage and television actor. Son of actor Sam Livesey (dec. 1936). Brother of actor Jack Livesey (dec. 1961). Married to actress Ursula Jeans (dec. 1973).

Appeared in: **1921** Four Feathers; Where the Rainbow Ends. **1923** Married Love (aka Married Life, retitled Maisie's Marriage). **1931** East Lynne on the Western Front. **1933** A Veteran of Waterloo; A Cuckoo in the Nest. **1934** Blind Justice. **1935** The Price of Wisdom; Midshipman Easy (aka Men of the Sea—US); Lorna Doone. **1936** Rembrandt. **1938** The Drum; Keep Smiling (aka Smiling Along—US). **1939** Spies of the Air (US 1940). **1940** The Girl in the News (US 1941). **1943** The Life and Death of Colonel Blimp (aka Colonel Blimp—US 1945). **1945** I Know Where I'm Going (US 1947). **1946** A Matter of Life and Death (aka Stairway to Heaven—US). **1948** Vice Versa. **1949** That Dangerous Age (aka If This Be Sin—US 1950). **1951** Green Grow the Rushes; Men of the Sea. **1953** The Master of Ballantrae. **1956** The Intimate Stranger (aka Finger of Guilt—US). **1960** The League of Gentlemen (US 1961); The Entertainer; It Happened in Broad Daylight. **1961** No, My Darling Daughter (US 1964). **1964** Of Human Bondage. **1965** The Amorous Adventures of Moll Flanders. **1967** Oedipus the King (US 1968). **1969** Hamlet. **1970** Futtock's End (short).

LIVESEY, SAM

Born: Oct. 14, 1873, Flintshire, England. Died: Nov. 7, 1936, London, England (following surgery). Screen and stage actor. Father of actors Jack (dec. 1961) and Roger Livesey (dec. 1976).

Appeared in: **1916** The Lifeguardsman. **1918** Spinner O' Dreams; Victory and Peace. **1919** A Chinese Puzzle; The Sins of Youth; A Sinless Sinner (aka Midnight Gambols—US 1920). **1920** All the Winners; The Black Spider; Burnt In. **1921** The Marriage Lines. **1923** Married Life (aka Married Love or Maisie's Marriage). **1928** Wait and See; The Forger; Zero. **1929** Young Woodley (US 1930); Blackmail (silent version). **1930** One Family; Raise the Roof. **1931** The Hound of the Baskervilles; Jealousy; Dreyfus (aka The Dreyfus Case—US); The Girl in the Night; Up for the Cup; The Wickham Mystery; Many Waters. **1932** Insult; The Flag Lieutenant; Mr. Bill the Conqueror (aka The Man Who Won—US 1933); The Wonderful Story. **1933** The Private Life of Henry VIII; The Shadow; Commissionaire. **1934** Tangled Evidence; Jew Suess (aka Power—US); The Great Defender. **1935** Royal Cavalcade (aka Regal Cavalcade—US); Turn of the Tide; Variety; Drake of England (aka Drake the Pirate—US); The Hope of His Side (aka Where's George?). **1936** Rembrandt; Men of Yesterday; Calling the Tune. **1937** Wings of the Morning; Dark Journey; The Mill on the Floss (US 1939).

LIVINGSTONE, FRANK H.

Born: 1870, San Francisco, Calif. Died: Nov. 26, 1932, Oakland, Calif. Screen, stage actor, film and stage director.

LLEWELLYN, FEWLASS

Born: Mar. 5, 1886, Hull, England. Died: June 16, 1941, England? Screen, stage, radio actor, stage producer and author.

Appeared in: **1918** Goodbye. **1919** The Lady Clare. **1922** A Bill for Divorcement. **1823** This Freedom. **1926** The Flag Lieutenant. **1927** Further Adventures of the Flag Lieutenant. **1931** Lloyd of the C.I.D. (aka Detective Lloyd, serial—US 1932). **1935** Stormy Weather (US 1936); The Phantom Light. **1936** Jack of All Trades (aka The Two of Us—US 1937); On Top of the World. **1937** Good Morning, Boys (aka Where There's a Will—US); It's a Grand Old World; Brief Ecstasy. **1938** Special Edition; A Spot of Bother; Crackerjack (aka The Man With a Hundred Faces—US).

LLOYD, AL (Albert Lloyd)

Born: 1884. Died: July 10, 1964, Hollywood, Calif. (heart attack). Screen and vaudeville actor. Appeared as partner in vaudeville team of "Aveling and Lloyd."

Appeared in: **1938** Penrod's Double Trouble.

LLOYD, ALICE

Born: 1885, England. Died: Jan. 31, 1981, Burbank, Calif. (complications during surgery). Screen actress and film extra. Sister of actress Mabel Lloyd. Do not confuse with actress Alice Lloyd (dec. 1949). Entered films in 1914.

LLOYD, ALICE

Born: 1873, England. Died: Nov. 17, 1949, Banstead, England. Screen, stage, vaudeville actress and singer. Sister of actress Marie (dec. 1922) and stage actress Grace Lloyd (dec.). Appeared in early Kinemacolor shorts.

LLOYD, CHARLES M.

Born: 1870. Died: Dec. 4, 1948, Hollywood, Calif. (heart attack). Screen, stage and vaudeville actor. Entered films with Mack Sennett.

LLOYD, DORIS

Born: 1900, Liverpool, England. Died: May 21, 1968, Santa Barbara, Calif. ("strained" heart). Screen and stage actress. Sister of actress Rosie Lloyd (dec. 1944).

Appeared in: **1920** The Shadow Between. **1925** The Lady; The Man from Red Gulch. **1926** The Black Bird; Exit Smiling; The Midnight Kiss; Black Paradise. **1927** Is Zat So?; The Auctioneer; Two Girls Wanted; Lonesome Ladies; The Bronco Twister; Rich But Honest. **1928** Come to My House; Trail of '98. **1929** The Careless Age; The Drake Case. **1930** Disraeli; Sarah and Son; Reno; Old English; Way for a Sailor; Charley's Aunt. **1931** The Bachelor Father; Once a Lady; Waterloo Bridge; Bought; Transgression; Devotion. **1932** Back Street; Tarzan the Ape Man. **1933** Oliver Twist; Always a Lady; Robbers' Roost; Looking Forward; Peg O' My Heart; A Study in Scarlet; Voltaire; Secrets. **1934** Glamour; Sisters Under the Skin; She Was a Lady; One Exciting Adventure; Tarzan and His Mate; Dangerous Corner; Kiss and Make Up; British Agent. **1935** Two for Tonight; Mutiny on the Bounty; Strange Wives; Clive of India; Straight from the Heart; Kind Lady; The Perfect Gentleman; The Woman in Red; Motive for Revenge; Chasing Yesterday; Becky Sharp; A Shot in the Dark; Peter Ibbetson; A Feather in Her Hat. **1936** Don't Get Personal; Too Many Parents; Mary of Scotland; Brilliant Marriage. **1937** The Plough and the Stars; Tovarich. **1938** The Black Doll; Alcatraz Island; Letter of Introduction. **1939** We Are Not Alone; I'm from Missouri; The Under-Pup; Barricade; First Love; The Private Lives of Elizabeth and Essex; The Old Maid; The Spellbinder. **1940** The Great Plane Robbery; 'Til We Meet Again; The Letter; Vigil in the Night; The Lady With Red Hair. **1941** Life Begins for Andy Hardy; Keep 'Em Flying; The Great Lie; Shining Victory; The Wolf Man; Life With Henry. **1942** Night Monster; This Above All; Journey for Margaret; The Ghost of Frankenstein. **1943** Mission to Moscow; Forever and a Day; The Constant Nymph; Eyes of the Underworld; What a Woman!; Frankenstein Meets the Wolf Man; Flesh and Fantasy. **1944** The White Cliffs of Dover; The Invisible Man's Revenge; Frenchman's Creek; Follow the Boys; The Conspirators; Phantom Lady; The Lodger. **1945** Allotment Wives; Molly and Me; Scotland Yard Investigates; My Name is Julia Ross; Incendiary Blonde. **1946** Devotion (and 1931 version); G.I. War Brides; Holiday in Mexico; Of Human Bondage; Tarzan and the Leopard Woman; To Each His Own; Three Strangers; Sister Kenny; Kitty; The Jolson Story. **1947** Escape Me Never; The Secret Life of Walter Mitty. **1948** Sign of the Ram. **1949** The Red Danube. **1950** Tyrant of the Sea. **1951** The Son of Dr. Jekyll; Kind Lady. **1953** Young Bess. **1955** A Man Called Peter. **1956** The Swan. **1957** Jeanne Eagels. **1960** Midnight Lace; The Time Machine. **1962** The Notorious Landlady. **1964** Mary Poppins. **1965** The Sound of Music. **1967** Rosie.

LLOYD, ETHEL

Born: Brooklyn, N.Y. Died: Jan. 12, 1923, Brooklyn, N.Y. Screen actress. Married to actor Howard Noble Johnson.

Appeared in: **1914** The Old Flute Player; The Locked Door; Love's Old Dream.

LLOYD, FRANK

Born: Feb. 2, 1886, Glasgow, Scotland. Died: Aug. 10, 1960, Santa Monica, Calif. Screen, stage actor, film director, producer and screenwriter. Married to stage actress Alma Heller (dec. 1952) and later married to writer Virginia Kellogg. Entered films as an actor in 1910 and then as a writer and director.

Appeared in: **1913** The Sea Wolf; Shadows of Life; Captain Kidd; The Madonna of the Slums; Under the Black Flag; The Buccaneers. **1914** Dangers of the Veldt; The Mexican's Last Raid; Won in the Clouds; By Radium's Ray; Captain Jenny; Unjustly Accused; The Law of His Kind; For the Freedom of Cuba; One of the Bravest; The Test; Stolen Glory; On the Verge of War; The Spy; The Woman in Black; The

Opened Shutters; The Chorus Girl's Thanksgiving; The Link That Binds; The Vagabond; Kid Regan's Hands; As the Wind Blows; A Prince of Bavaria; Through the Flames; Circle 17; The Sob Sister; Prowlers of the Wild; On the Rio Grande; Traffic in Babes; Damon and Pythias; A Page from Life. **1915** Pawns of Fate; Wolves of Society; The Temptation of Edwin Swayne; His Last Serenade; The Black Box (serial). **1916** The Stronger Love.

LLOYD, FREDERICK W.

Born: Jan. 15, 1880, London, England. Died: Nov. 24, 1949, Hove, England. Screen, stage and radio actor.

Appeared in: **1911** Princess Clementina. **1928** Balaclava (aka Jaws off Hell—US 1931). **1930** The "W" Plan (US 1931); The Temporary Widow. **1931** Tell England (aka The Battle of Gallipoli—US); The Perfect Lady; The Great Gay Road; The Hound of the Baskervilles; The Beggar Student; A Gentleman of Paris. **1932** Arms and the Man; Sleepless Nights. **1933** The Crime at Blossoms; Up for the Derby; The Song You Gave Me (US 1934); Mixed Doubles. **1934** Blossom Time (aka April Romance—US 1937). **1935** Radio Pirates; Royal Cavalcade (aka Regal Cavalcade—US); Lieutenant Daring, RN. **1936** Everything Is Thunder. **1937** Mademoiselle Docteur; 21 Days (aka The First and the Last, aka 21 Days Together—US 1940); Secret Lives (aka I Married a Spy—US 1938). **1938** Weddings Are Wonderful. **1948** Oliver Twist (US 1951).

LLOYD, GAYLORD E.

Born: 1888, Burchard, Nebr. Died: Sept. 1, 1943, Beverly Hills, Calif. (heart attack). Screen actor. Brother of actor Harold Lloyd (dec. 1971).

Appeared in: **1920** His Royal Slyness. **1923** Why Worry.

LLOYD, GLADYS

Born: 1896, Yonkers, N.Y. Died: June 6, 1971, Culver City, Calif. (stroke). Stage and screen actress. Divorced from actor Edward G. Robinson (dec. 1973). Mother of actor Edward G. Robinson, Jr. (dec. 1974). Played roles as an extra in many films with Robinson.

Appeared in: **1931** Smart Money; Five Star Final. **1932** The Hatchet Man; Two Seconds. **1935** Clive of India.

LLOYD, HAROLD (Harold Clayton Lloyd)

Born: Apr. 20, 1893, Burchard, Nebr. Died: Mar. 8, 1971, Beverly Hills, Calif. (cancer). Screen, stage actor, film producer, director and screenwriter. Brother of actor Gaylord E. Lloyd (dec. 1943). Married to actress Mildred Davis (dec. 1969). Father of actor Harold Lloyd, Jr. (dec. 1971). Appeared in "Lonesome Luke" series. In 1952 received Special Academy award as "Master Comedian and Good Citizen." Entered films in 1912.

Appeared in: **1914** From Italy's Shore; Curses! They Remarked. **1915** Once Every Ten Minutes; Spit Ball Sadie; Soaking the Clothes; Pressing the Suit; Terribly Stuck Up; A Mixup for Mazie; Some Baby; Fresh from the Farm; Giving Them Fits; Bughouse Bell Hops; Tinkering With Trouble; Great While It Lasted; Ragtime Snap Shots; A Fozzle at a Tea Party; Ruses, Rhymes, Roughnecks; Peculiar Patients Pranks; Social Gangster; Just Nuts; A One Night Stand; "Phunphilms" series. **1916** Luke Leans to the Literary; Luke Lugs Luggage; Luke Rolls in Luxury; Luke the Candy Cut-Up; Luke Foils the Villain; Luke and Rural Roughnecks; Luke Pipes the Pippins; Lonesome Luke; Circus King; Skylight Sleep; Luke's Double; Them Was the Happy Days; Trouble Enough; Luke and the Bomb Throwers; Reckless Wrestlers; Luke's Late Lunches; Ice; Luke Laughs Out; An Awful Romance; Luke's Fatal Fliver; Luke's Washful Waiting; Luke Rides Roughshod; Unfriendly Fruit; Luke, Crystal Gazer; A Matrimonial Mixup; Luke's Lost Lamb; Braver Than the Bravest; Luke Does the Midway; Caught in a Jam; Luke Joins the Navy; Busting the Beanery; Luke and the Mermaids; Jailed; Luke's Speedy Club Life; Luke and the Bang-Tails; Luke Laughs Last; Luke's Society; Mix-Up. **1916** Luke, the Chauffeur; Luke's Preparedness Preparation; Luke's Newsie Knockout; Luke, Gladiator; Luke, Patient Provider; Luke's Movie Muddle; Luke's Fireworks Fizzle; Luke Locates the Loot; Luke's Shattered Sleep; Marriage a la Carte. **1917** Luke's Last Liberty; Luke's Busy Days; Drama's Dreadful Deal; Luke's Trolley Trouble; Lonesome Luke, Lawyer; Luke Wins Ye Ladye Faire; Lonesome Luke's Lively Rifle; Lonesome Luke on Tin Can Alley; Lonesome Luke's Lively Life; Lonesome Luke's Honeymoon; Lonesome Luke, Plumber; Stop! Luke! Listen!; Lonesome Luke, Messenger; Lonesome Luke, Mechanic; Lonesome Luke's Wild Women; Over the Fence; Lonesome Luke Loses Patients; Pinched; By the Sad Sea Waves; Birds of a Feather; Bliss; Lonesome Luke from London to Laramie; Rainbow Island; Love, Laughs and Lather; The Flirt; Clubs Are Trump; All Aboard; We Never Sleep; Bashful; The Tip; Step Lively; Move On. **1918** The Big Idea; The Lamb; Hit Him Again; Beat It; A Gasoline Wedding; Look Pleasant Please; Here Comes the Girls; Let's Go; On

the Jump; Follow the Crowd; Pipe the Whiskers; It's a Wild Life; Hey There; Kicked Out; The Non-Stop Kid; Two-Gun Gussie; Fireman Save My Child; The City Slicker; Sic 'Em Towser; Somewhere in Turkey; Are Crooks Dishonest?; An Ozark Romance; Kicking the Germ Out of Germany; That's Him; Too Scrambled; Swing Your Partner; Why Pick on Me?; Nothing But Trouble; Hear 'Em Rave; Take a Chance; She Loses Me; Bride and Groom; Bees in His Bonnet; She Loves Me Not. **1919** Wanted—$5,000; Going! Going! Going!; Ask Father; On the Fire; I'm on My Way; Look Out Below; The Dutiful Dub; Next Aisle Over; A Sammy in Siberia; Just Dropped In; Crack Your Heels; Ring Up the Curtain; Young Mr. Jazz; Si, Senor; Before Breakfast; The Marathon; Back to the Woods; Pistols for Breakfast; The Rajah; Swat the Crook; Off the Trolley; Spring Fever; Billy Blazes, Esq.; Just Neighbors; A Jazzed Honeymoon; Count Your Change; Chop Suey and Co.; Heap Big Chief; Don't Shove; Be My Wife; He Leads, Others Follow; Soft Money; Count the Votes; Pay Your Dues; Bumping Into Broadway; Captain Kidd's Kids; From Hand to Mouth; His Royal Slyness. **1920** The following shorts: Haunted Spooks; An Eastern Westerner; High and Dizzy; Get Out and Get Under; Number, Please. **1921** Among Those Present; I Do; A Sailor-Made Man; plus the following shorts: Now or Never; Never Weaken. **1922** Grandma's Boy; Doctor Jack. **1923** Safety Last; Why Worry? **1924** Girl Shy; Hot Water. **1925** The Freshman. **1926** For Heaven's Sake. **1927** The Kid Brother. **1928** Speedy. **1929** Welcome Danger. **1930** Feet First. **1931** Stout Hearts and Willing Hands. **1932** Movie Crazy. **1934** The Cat's Paw. **1936** The Milky Way. **1938** Professor Beware. **1947** Mad Wednesday (aka The Sin of Harold Diddlebock). **1957** The Golden Age of Comedy (documentary). **1962** Harold Lloyd's World of Comedy (documentary). **1964** Funny Side of Life.

LLOYD, HAROLD, JR. "DUKE" (Harold Clayton Lloyd, Jr.)

Born: Jan. 25, 1931, Calif. Died: June 9, 1971, North Hollywood, Calif. Screen, television actor and singer. Son of actor Harold Lloyd, Sr. (dec. 1971) and actress Mildred Davis (dec. 1969).

Appeared in: **1949** Our Very Own (film debut). **1955** Yank in Ermine. **1958** Frankenstein's Daughter. **1959** Girls Town. **1960** Platinum High School. **1962** Married Too Young. **1965** Mutiny in Outer Space.

LLOYD, JACK

Born: 1923, Germany. Died: May 21, 1976, Hollywood, Calif. (heart attack). Screen, stage, radio, television actor, songwriter, radio and television writer. Do not confuse with actor with same name who was in films prior to 1940.

LLOYD, MARIE (Matilda Alice Victoria Lloyd)

Born: Feb. 12, 1870, London, England. Died: Oct. 7, 1922, London, England. Screen, stage actress and music hall performer. Sister of actress Alice (dec. 1949), and stage actress Grace Lloyd (dec.).

Appeared in: **1909** Marie Lloyd's Little Joke. **1913** Marie Lloyd at Home and Bunkered.

LLOYD, ROLLO

Born: Mar. 22, 1883, Akron, Ohio. Died: July 24, 1938, Los Angeles, Calif. Screen, stage actor, screenwriter, stage and film director.

Appeared in: **1932** Okay America; Laughter in Hell; Prestige. **1933** Destination Unknown; Today We Live; Carnival Lady; Strictly Personal; Out All Night. **1934** Private Scandal; Madame Spy; The Party's Over; Whom the Gods Destroy. **1935** The Bride of Frankenstein; Straight from the Heart; Lives of a Bengal Lancer; His Night Out; Mad Love; Barbary Coast; Hot Tip; The Mystery Man; Murder on a Honeymoon; The Man Who Reclaimed His Head. **1936** Desire; Come and Get It; Professional Soldier; Magnificent Obsession; Yellowstone; The Man I Marry; Love Letters of a Star; I Conquer the Sea; The White Legion; Hell-Ship Morgan; Anthony Adverse; The Devil Doll; Straight from the Shoulder. **1937** Four Days Wonder; Armored Car; The Westland Case; Seventh Heaven; Women Men Marry. **1938** Arsene Lupin Returns; The Lady in the Morgue; Goodbye Broadway; Spawn of the North.

LLOYD, ROSIE (Rose Wood)

Born: June 5, 1879, London, England. Died: Jan. 19, 1944, London, England. Screen, stage and vaudeville actress. Sister of actress Doris Lloyd (dec. 1968). Married to stage actor William Pulaski (dec.).

LOBACK, MARVIN (aka MARVIN LOBACH)

Born: 1898. Died: Aug. 18, 1938, Hollywood, Calif. Screen and stage actor.

Appeared in: **1921** Hands Off. **1932** Shopping with Wifie (short); Speed in the Gay 90's (short). **1935** Uncivil Warriors (short); Old Sawbones (short).

LOCHARY, DAVID
Born: 1946. Died: July 29, 1977, New York, N.Y. Screen and stage actor.

Appeared in: **1970** Mondo Trasho; Multiple Maniacs. **1974** Pink Flamingo. **1975** Female Trouble.

LOCHER, FELIX (Felix Maurice Locher)
Born: July 16, 1882, Switzerland. Died: Mar. 13, 1969, Sherman Oaks, Calif. Screen and television actor. Father of actor Jon Hall.

Appeared in: **1957** Hell Ship Mutiny; Don Mike. **1958** Curse of the Faceless Man; Desert Hell; Frankenstein's Daughter; Kings Go Forth. **1959** Thunder in the Sun; The Man Who Understood Women; Beloved Infidel. **1960** Walk Tall. **1962** The Firebrand. **1963** California; House of the Damned. **1965** The Greatest Story Ever Told.

LOCKE, WILLIAM JOHN
Born: Mar. 20, 1863, Barbados, British West Indies. Died: May 15, 1930, England? Screen actor, playwright and novelist.

Appeared in: **1920** A Tragedy of the East Side.

LOCKETT, CLAY
Died: Oct. 14, 1978. Screen actor.

LOCKHART, GENE (Eugene Lockhart)
Born: July 18, 1891, London, Ontario, Canada. Died: Apr. 1, 1957, Santa Monica, Calif. (coronary thrombosis). Screen, stage, television, radio actor, songwriter, stage director, stage producer and radio writer. Father of actress June Lockhart. Married to actress Kathleen Arthur (aka Kathleen Lockhart dec. 1978). Wrote the song "The World is Waiting for the Sunrise." Nominated for 1938 Academy Award for Best Supporting Actor in Algiers.

Appeared in: **1934** By Your Leave. **1935** I've Been Around; Captain Hurricane; Star of Midnight; Thunder in the Night; Storm Over the Andes; Crime and Punishment. **1936** Brides Are Like That; Times Square Playboy; Earthworm Tractors; The First Baby; Career Woman; The Garden Murder Case; The Gorgeous Hussy; The Devil Is a Sissy; Wedding Present; Mind Your Own Business; Come Closer, Folks! **1937** Mama Steps Out; Too Many Wives; The Sheik Steps Out; Something to Sing About; Make Way for Tomorrow. **1938** Of Human Hearts; Listen, Darling; A Christmas Carol; Sweethearts; Penrod's Double Trouble; Men Are Such Fools; Blondie; Sinners in Paradise; Algiers; Meet the Girls. **1939** Blackmail; I'm from Missouri; Hotel Imperial; Our Leading Citizen; Geronimo; Tell No Tales; Bridal Suite; The Story of Alexander Graham Bell. **1940** Edison the Man; Dr. Kildare Goes Home; We Who Are Young; South of Pago Pago; A Dispatch from Reuter's; His Girl Friday; Abe Lincoln in Illiois. **1941** Keeping Company; Meet John Doe; The Sea Wolf; Billy the Kid; All That Money Can Buy; One Foot in Heaven; They Died With Their Boots On; Steel Against the Sky; International Lady. **1942** Juke Girl; The Gay Sisters; You Can't Escape Forever. **1943** Forever and a Day; Hangmen Also Die; Mission to Moscow; The Desert Song; Madame Curie; Find the Blackmailer; Northern Pursuit. **1944** Going My Way; The White Cliffs of Dover; Action in Arabia; The Man from Frisco. **1945** The House on 92nd Street; That's the Spirit; Leave Her to Heaven. **1946** A Scandal in Paris; Meet Me on Broadway; She-Wolf of London; The Strange Woman. **1947** Miracle on 34th Street; The Shocking Miss Pilgrim; The Foxes of Harrow; Cynthia; Honeymoon; Her Husband's Affairs. **1948** Joan of Arc; Inside Story; That Wonderful Urge; Apartment for Peggy; I, Jane Doe. **1949** The Inspector General; Down to the Sea in Ships; Madame Bovary; Red Light. **1950** The Big Hangover; Riding High. **1951** Rhubarb; I'd Climb the Highest Mountain; Seeds of Destruction; The Lady from Texas. **1952** Face to Face; Hoodlum Empire; Bonzo Goes to College; Androcles and the Lion; Apache War Smoke; A Girl in Every Port; The Devil and Daniel Webster (reissue of All That Money Can Buy, 1941). **1953** Francis Covers the Big Town; Down Among the Sheltering Palms; Confidentially Connie; The Lady Wants Mink. **1954** World for Ransom. **1955** The Vanishing American. **1956** The Man in the Gray Flannel Suit; Carousel. **1957** Jeanne Eagles.

LOCKHART, KATHLEEN (Kathleen Arthur)
Born: 1894, England. Died: Feb. 18, 1978, Los Angeles, Calif. Screen and stage actress. Married to actor Gene Lockhart (dec. 1957). Mother of actress June Lockhart.

Appeared in: **1936** Broadway Playboy; Brides are Like That; Times Square Playboy; The Devil is a Sissy; Master Cinderella; Career Woman. **1937** Something to Sing About. **1938** A Christmas Carol; Men Are Such Fools; Penrod's Double Trouble; Blondie; Sweethearts; Give Me a Sailor. **1939** Men of Conquest; Our Leading Citizen; What a Life. **1941** Love Crazy. **1942** Are Husbands Necessary? **1943** Mission to

Moscow; The Good Fellows; Lost Angel. **1945** Roughly Speaking; Bewitched. **1946** Lady in the Lake; Two Years Before the Mast. **1947** Mother Wore Tights; Gentlemen's Agreement. **1951** I'd Climb the Highest Mountain. **1952** Plymouth Adventure. **1953** Walking My Baby Back Home; Confidentially Connie. **1954** The Glenn Miller Story. **1959** The Purple Gang.

LOCKHART, TIM
Born: 1930, Columbus, Ga. Died: Mar. 26, 1963, Louisville, Ky. (heart attack). Screen, stage, radio and television actor.

LOCKIN, DANIEL J.
Born: 1943. Died: Aug. 21, 1977, Anaheim, Calif. (stabbed to death). Screen and stage actor.

Appeared in: **1963** Gypsy. **1969** Hello Dolly (film and stage versions).

LOCKLEAR, OMAR
Born: Oct. 28, 1891, Fort Worth, Tex. Died: Aug. 2, 1920, Los Angeles, Calif. (airplane accident). Screen actor and stunt flyer in films. Died during filming of The Skywayman.

Appeared in: **1919** Cassidy of the Air Lanes. **1920** The Great Air Robbery; The Skywayman.

LOCKWOOD, HAROLD A.
Born: 1887, Brooklyn, N.Y. Died: Oct. 19, 1918, New York, N.Y. (Spanish influenza). Screen, stage and vaudeville actor.

Appeared in: **1908** Harbor Island. **1912** The Lost Address; The Torn Letter; Over a Cracked Bowl; The Bachelor and the Baby. **1913** Northern Hearts; A Mansion of Misery; The Spanish Parrot-Girl; Phantoms; The Burglar Who Robbed Death; The Lipton Cup; With Love's Eyes; Two Men and a Woman; Lieutenant Jones; A Little Child Shall Lead Them; The Stolen Melody; Her Only Son; Woman—Past and Present; Diverging Paths; Love Before Ten; The Tie of the Blood; Maragarita and the Mission Funds; Child of the Sea. **1914** The Unwelcome Mrs. Hatch; Wildflower; Tess of the Storm Country; Hearts Adrift; Through the Centuries; The Attic Above; The Country Chairman; Elizabeth's Prayer; A Message from Across the Sea; When Thieves Fall Out; Such a Little Queen; The Conspiracy. **1915** The Turn of the Road; Shopgirls; Secretary of Frivolous Affairs; The Lure of the Mask; Jim the Penman; The Great Question; The House of a Thousand Scandals; Pardoned; The Buzzard's Shadow; The Tragic Circle. **1916** The Secret Wire; Big Temaine; The River of Romance; Life's Blind Alley; The Other Side of the Door; The Gamble; The Man in the Sombrero; The Broken Cross; Lillo of the Sulu Seas; The Comeback; Pidgin Island; The Masked Rider. **1917** The Promise; The Haunted Pajamas; The Avenging Trail; The Hidden Children; The Square Deceiver; Paradise Garden. **1918** Broadway Bill; Under the Handicap; The Landloper; Lend Me Your Name. **1919** The Great Romance; Shadows of Suspicion; The Crucible; A Man of Honor; Yankee Doodle in Berlin; Pals First.

LOCKWOOD, HELEN
Died: Apr. 27, 1946, Philadelphia, Pa. Screen, stage and vaudeville actress. Married to actor Harry Burns (dec. 1948).

LOCKWOOD, KING
Born: 1898. Died: Feb. 23, 1971, Hollywood, Calif. (stroke). Screen and television actor.

Appeared in: **1956** The Man in the Gray Flannel Suit.

LODEN, BARBARA
Born: 1932, Marion, N.C. Died: Sept. 5, 1980, New York, N.Y. (cancer). Screen, stage, television actress, film director, film producer, stage director and screenwriter. Divorced from producer Larry Joachim. Later married to writer/director Elia Kazan.

Appeared in: **1960** Wild River. **1961** Splendor in the Grass. **1971** Wanda.

LODER, KATHRYN
Died: Oct. 18, 1978. Screen actress.

Appeared in: **1970** Night of the Witches. **1974** Foxy Brown.

LODGE, BEN
Died: Jan. 10, 1927, Long Island, N.Y. Screen, stage and vaudeville actor.

Appeared in: **1912** The Winner and the Spoils.

LOEB, LEO, JR.
Born: 1913, Charleston, W.Va. Died: Dec. 14, 1980, Atlantic City, N.J. Professional ice skater, screen actor, screenwriter and author.

LOEB, PHILIP
Born: 1894. Died: Sept. 1, 1955, New York, N.Y. Screen, stage and television actor.

Appeared in: **1938** Sweethearts; Room Service. **1948** A Double Life. **1951** Molly.

LOEDEL, ADI
Born: 1937, Germany. Died: June 2, 1955, Hamburg, Germany (suicide—hanging). Screen, stage, radio and television actor.

Appeared in: **1950** Lockende Gefahr. **1955** Kinder, Mutter und ein General.

LOEFFLER, EDWARD H.
Born: 1882. Died: Jan. 18, 1962, Staten Island, N.Y. (hit by automobile). Screen, stage and vaudeville actor.

LOEHR, DOLLY *See* LYNN, DIANA

LOESSER, FRANK
Born: June 29, 1910, New York, N.Y. Died: July 28, 1969, New York, N.Y. (lung cancer). Composer, screenwriter and screen actor.

Appeared in: **1949** Red, Hot and Blue.

LOFF, JEANETTE (Jeanette Lov)
Born: Oct. 9, 1906, Orofino, Idaho. Died: Aug. 4, 1942, Los Angeles, Calif. (ammonia poisoning). Screen and stage actress.

Appeared in: **1927** My Friend from India. **1928** The Black Ace; Man-Made Woman; Hold 'Em Yale; Love Over Night; Annapolis; Geraldine; The Man Without a Face (serial). **1929** The Racketeer; .45 Calibre War; The Sophomore. **1930** The Boudoir Diplomat; Fighting Through; Party Girl; The King of Jazz. **1934** Hide-Out. **1935** Million Dollar Baby; St. Louis Woman.

LOFGREN, MARIANNE
Born: 1910, Stockholm, Sweden. Died: 1957, Sweden. Screen actress.

Appeared in: **1934** The Song of the Scarlet Flower. **1942** En Enda Natt. **1943** Elvira Madigan. **1949** Incorrigible; Fangelse (The Devil's Wanton—US 1962). **1952** Affairs of a Model. **1956** Flamman (The Flame aka Girls Without Rooms—US 1963) Children of the Night. **1958** The Time for Desire. Other Swedish films: The Dangerous Game; What Do Men Know?; On the Sunny Side; A Lady Becomes a Maid; The Great Love; With the People for the Country; Mr. Karlsson Mate and His Sweethearts; The Old is Coming; One Single Night; Nothing But the Truth; The Little WRAC of the Veteran Reserves; Charmers at Sea; My Little Brother and I; Night in June; A Big Hug; The Little Shrew of the Veteran Reserves; The Gentleman Gangster; Fransson the Terrible; A Poor Millionaire; Only a Woman; Talk of the Town; A Singing Lesson; Scanian Guerilla; The Ingegerd Bremssen Case; Sailor in a Dresscoat; Nothing Will be Forgotten; Jacob's Ladder; Woman Takes Command; Women in Prison; As You Like Me; Mr. Collin's Adventures; King's Street; Life Is There to be Lived; Kajan Goes to Sea; I Killed; Darling I Surrender; The Halta Lotta Tavern; Little Napoleon; She Thought It Was Him; Dangerous Roads; The Awakening of Youth; A Girl for Me; His Official Fiancee; I Am Fire and Air; And All These Women; The Emperor of Portugal; The Holy Lie; Watch Out for Spies!; Stop! Think of Something Else; Wandering with the Moon; The Suffering and Happiness of Motherhood; Hunted; The New Affairs of Pettersson and Bendel; The Rose of Thistle Island; Good Morning Bill; Asa-Hanna; The Gay Party; It's My Model; Bad Eggs; A Lovely Young Lady; Crisis; When the Door Was Closed; The Balloon; Dynamite; A Father Wanted; The Most Beautiful Thing on Earth; The Sixth Commandment; The Women; Woman Without a Face; Life at Forsbyholm; On These Shoulders; A Swedish Tiger; Miss Sunbeam; Gentlemen of the Navy; Woman in White; The Street; Boman Gets Crazy; Girl With Hyacinths; Knockout at the "Breakfast Club"; The Quartet That Split Up; The Kiss on the Cruise; A Gentleman Maybe; My Name is Puck; Divorced; Bom the Customs Officer; A Fiancee for Hire; Defiance; Salka Valka; Simon the Sinner; Hoppsan!; The Merry Boys of the Fleet; Matrimonial Announcement; Love Chastised; Little Fridolf and I; Private Entrance.

LOFT, ARTHUR
Born: May 25, 1897, Colorado. Died: Jan. 1, 1947, Los Angeles, Calif. Screen and stage actor.

Appeared in: **1933** Behind Jury Doors; Alimony Madness. **1935** On Probation; What Price Crime?; Danger Ahead; Kid Courageous. **1936** M'Liss; Postal Inspector; King of the Royal Mounted; Without Orders; Legion of Terror; Night Waitress; The Prisoner of Shark Island; Ace Drummond (serial). **1937** Woman in Distress; Paradise Express; Motor Madness; The Game That Kills; It Happened in Hollywood; Public

Cowboy No. 1; The Shadow; Paid to Dance. **1938** Start Cheering; No Time to Marry; Women in Prison; All-American Sweetheart; Rawhide; Extortion; Who Killed Gale Preston?; City Streets; The Main Event; I Am the Law; Highway Patrol; Squadron of Honor; Down in Arkansaw; The Lady Objects; Gang Bullets; Rhythm of the Saddle. **1939** Risky Business; Hell's Kitchen; Street of Missing Men; Southward Ho; A Woman is the Judge; Pride of the Blue Grass; Smuggled Cargo; Days of Jesse James; Everybody's Baby; Help Wanted (short); The Roaring Twenties; The Ice Follies of 1939. **1940** The Green Hornet (serial); Cafe Hostess; The Crooked Road; Riders of Pasco Basin; The Carson City Kid; Colorado; Texas Terrors; Glamour for Sale. **1941** Back in the Saddle; Caught in the Draft; Hold Back the Dawn; North from the Lone Star; We Go Fast; Down Mexico Way; The Stork Pays Off; Blue, White and Perfect; Henry Aldrich for President; Life Begins for Andy Hardy; The Green Hornet Strikes Again (serial); They Died With Their Boots On. **1942** The Forest Rangers; Star Spangled Rhythm; Fly By Night; South of Santa Fe; The Lady Has Plans; The Magnificent Dope; Priorities on Parade; The Glass Key; The Man in the Trunk; Girl Trouble; Street of Chance; Dr. Broadway. **1943** My Friend Flicka; Hangmen Also Die; Happy Go Lucky; The Meanest Man in the World; Mission to Moscow; Let's Face It; Frontier Badmen; Wintertime; Jack London; Flesh and Fantasy; The Outlaw; Henry Aldrich Gets Glamour; Footlight Glamour; Dr. Gillespie's Criminal Case. **1944** And the Angels Sing; Standing Room Only; The Miracle of Morgan's Creek; Henry Aldrich Plays Cupid; Charlie Chan in the Secret Service; Rosie the Riveter; The Hitler Gang; Louisiana Hayride; Wilson; Leave It to the Irish; The Woman in the Window; Lights of Old Santa Fe. **1945** Beware of Redheads (short); Blood on the Sun; Nob Hill; Along Came Jones; The Shanghai Cobra; The Man from Oklahoma; Arson Squad; The Strange Affair of Uncle Harry; Men in Her Diary; Scarlet Street; The Naughty Nineties; Blonde from Brooklyn; Honeymoon Ahead; It's a Pleasure!; Incendiary Blonde; On Stage Everybody; Road to Utopia. **1946** The Jolson Story; To Each His Own; The Cat Creeps; Sheriff of Redwood Valley; One Exciting Week; Blondie Knows Best; Traffic in Crime; Lone Star Moonlight; The Searching Wind; The Blue Dahlia; Our Hearts Were Growing Up; Cross My Heart. **1947** Cigarette Girl.

LOFTUS, CECILIA "CISSIE"
Born: Oct. 22, 1876, Glasgow, Scotland. Died: July 12, 1943, New York, N.Y. (heart attack). Screen, stage and vaudeville actress.

Appeared in: **1913** Lady of Quality. **1917** Diana of Dobson's . **1929** Famous Impersonations (short). **1931** Doctor's Wives; Young Sinners; East Lynn. **1935** Once in a Blue Moon. **1939** The Old Maid; The Dead End Kids on Dress Parade (aka On Dress Parade). **1940** It's a Date; The Bluebird; Lucky Partners. **1941** The Black Cat.

LOFTUS, WILLIAM C.
Born: 1862. Died: Mar. 11, 1931, Hollywood, Calif. (hit by auto). Screen actor.

LOGAN, ELLA
Born: Mar. 6, 1913, Glasgow, Scotland. Died: May 1, 1969, San Mateo, Calif. Screen, stage, vaudeville actress and vocalist. Divorced from producer Fred Finklehoffe (dec. 1977).

Appeared in: **1936** Flying Hostess. **1937** Top of the Town; Woman Chasees Man; 52nd Street. **1938** The Goldwyn Follies.

LOGAN, JANET
Born: 1919. Died: Oct. 23, 1965, Glendale, Calif. Screen, radio and television actress.

LOGAN, JOHN
Born: 1924. Died: Dec. 7, 1972, San Pedro, Calif. (auto accident). Screen actor.

Appeared in: **1952** The Man Behind the Gun. **1955** Tall Man Riding. **1956** Behind the High Wall. **1970** Beyond the Valley of the Dolls.

LOGAN, STANLEY
Born: June 12, 1885, Earlsfield, England. Died: Jan. 30, 1953, New York. Screen, stage actor, stage producer, film producer, director and screenwriter.

Appeared in: **1918** What Would a Gentleman Do? **1919** As He Was Born. **1939** We Are Not Alone. **1940** Arise, My Love; My Son, My Son; Women in War; South of Suez. **1941** Submarine Zone (aka Escape to Glory); Singapore Woman; Wedding Worries (short). **1942** Counter Espionage; Nightmare; Unexpected Riches (short). **1943** Two Tickets to London. **1944** The Return of the Vampire. **1945** Wilson. **1946** Three Strangers; Home Sweet Homicide. **1949** Sword in the Desert. **1950** Double Crossbones; Young Daniel Boone. **1951** Pride of Maryland. **1952** The Prisoner of Zenda; Five Fingers; With a Song in My Heart.

LOGOTHETIDIS, BASIL
Born: 1898. Died: Feb. 20, 1960. Screen actor.

Appeared in: **1956** Mademoiselle—Age 39. **1958** Delistarro Kai Gios (Father and Son, aka Trouble for Father). **1959** Santa Chikita.

LOHMAN, ZALLA
Born: 1906, Yugoslavia. Died: July 17, 1967, Hollywood, Calif. Screen actress. Appeared in silent films.

LOHR, MARIE
Born: July 28, 1890, Sydney, Australia. Died: Jan. 21, 1975, London, England. Screen, stage and television actress.

Appeared in: **1932** Aren't We All? (film debut). **1934** My Heart is Calling You (US 1935); Road House. **1935** Oh Daddy! **1936** Whom the Gods Love (aka Mozard—US 1940); It's You I Want. **1938** South Riding; Pygmalion. **1940** George and Margaret. **1941** Major Barbara. **1942** Went the Day Well? (aka 48 Hours—US 1944). **1945** The Rake's Progress (aka Notorious Gentleman—US 1946). **1946** The Magic Bow (US 1947). **1947** The Ghosts of Berkeley Square. **1948** Counterblast; The Winslow Boy (US 1950); Anna Karenina. **1949** Silent Dust. **1952** Little Big Shot. **1953** Always a Bride (US 1954). **1955** Escapade (US 1957); Out of the Clouds (US 1957). **1956** A Town Like Alice (US 1957). **1957** Seven Waves Away (aka Abandon Ship—US); Small Hotel. **1959** Carlton-Browne of the F.O. (aka Man in a Cocked Hat—US 1960). **1967** Great Catherine (US 1968).

LOMAS, HERBERT
Born: 1887, Burnley, England. Died: Apr. 11, 1961, Devonshire, England. Screen, stage and television actor.

Appeared in: **1931** Hobson's Choice (film debut); Many Waters. **1932** The Missing Rembrandt; When London Sleeps; The Sign of the Four; Frail Women. **1933** Daughters of Today; The Man from Toronto. **1934** Java Head (US 1935). **1935** The Phantom; Black Mask; Fighting Stock; Lorna Doone. **1936** Rembrandt; The Ghost Goes West; Fame. **1937** Knight Without Armour. **1938** South Riding. **1939** Inquest; Jamaica Inn; Ask a Policeman; The Lion Has Wings (US 1940). **1940** Mr. Borland Thinks Again. **1941** The Ghost Train; South American George; Penn of Pennsylvania (aka The Courageous Mr. Penn—US 1944). **1943** They Met in the Dark (US 1945). **1945** I Know Where I'm Going (US 1947). **1947** The Man Within (aka The Smugglers—US 1948); Master of Bankdam (US 1949). **1948** The Guinea Pig (US 1949); Bonnie Prince Charlie (US 1952). **1951** The Magic box (US 1952). **1953** The Net (aka Project M7—US).

LOMAS, JACK M.
Born: 1911. Died: May 13, 1959, Hollywood, Calif. Screen actor.

Appeared in: **1940** The Story of Seabiscuit. **1950** The Daughter of Rosie O'Grady. **1952** April in Paris. **1953** The Glass Web. **1955** Seven Angry Men. **1956** There's Always Tomorrow; That Certain Feeling; Miracle in the Rain. **1957** An Affair to Remember; Copper Sky; The Night Runner; The Shadow on the Window. **1958** Cattle Empire. **1959** Last Train from Gun Hill; Compulsion.

LOMAX, LOUIS
Born: Aug. 16, 1922, Valdosta, Ga. Died: July 30, 1970, Santa Rosa, New Mexico (auto accident). Black television commmentator, screen actor and writer.

Appeared in: **1968** Wild in the Streets.

LOMBARD, CAROLE (Jane Peters)
Born: Oct. 6, 1909, Fort Wayne, Ind. Died: Jan. 16, 1942, near Las Vegas (air crash). Screen actress. Divorced from actor William Powell; Married to actor Clark Gable (dec. 1960). Nominated for 1936 Academy Award for Best Actress in My Man Godfrey.

Appeared in: **1921** The Perfect Crime. **1925** Marriage in Transit; Hearts and Spurs; Durand of the Bad Lands. **1927** The Girl from Everywhere (short). **1928** Power; Me, Gangster; Show Folks; Ned McCobb's Daughter; Divine Sinner; plus the following shorts: Run, Girl, Run; The Beach Club; The Best Man; The Swim Princess; The Bicycle Flirt; The Girl from Nowhere; The Campus Vamp; The Campus Carmen. **1929** Big News; The Racketeer; Dynamite; High Voltage; Parachute; Matchmaking Mamas (short). **1930** Fast and Loose; Safety in Numbers; The Arizona Kid; It Pays to Advertise. **1931** Man of the World. **1932** Ladies' Man; No Man of Her Own; Up Pops the Devil; I Take This Woman; Sinners in the Sun; No More Orchids; Virtue; No One Man. **1933** White Woman; The Match King; Supernatural; From Hell to Heaven; Brief Moment; Billion Dollar Scandal; The Eagle and the Hawk. **1934** Bolero; The Gay Bride; Now and Forever; 20th Century; We're Not Dressing; Lady by Choice. **1935** Hands Across the Table; Rumba. **1936** My Man Godfrey; Love

Before Breakfast; The Princess Comes Across. **1937** Swing High, Swing Low; Nothing Sacred; True Confession. **1938** Fools for Scandal. **1939** Made for Each Other; In Name Only; Vigil in the Night. **1940** They Knew What They Wanted. **1941** Mr. and Mrs. Smith; To Be or Not To Be. **1964** Big Parade of Comedy (documentary).

LOMBARDI, VINCE (Vincent Thomas Lombardi)
Born: June 11, 1913, Brooklyn, N.Y. Died: Sept. 3, 1970 (cancer). Football coach and screen actor.

Appeared in: **1968** Paper Lion.

LOMBARDO, CARMEN
Born: 1904. Died: Apr. 17, 1971, North Miami, Fla. (cancer). Musician (saxophonist), songwriter and screen actor. Brother of bandleader Guy Lombardo (dec. 1977).

Appeared in: **1934** Many Happy Returns.

LOMBARDO, GUY (Gaetano Albert Lombardo)
Born: June 19, 1902, London, Ontario, Canada. Died: Nov. 5, 1977, Houston, Tex. Orchestra leader, screen, radio and television actor. Brother of bandleader Carmen Lombardo (dec. 1971). For family information see Carmen Lombardo listing.

Appeared in: **1934** Many Happy Returns. **1946** No Leave, No Love. **1970** The Phynx.

LONDON, JACK
Born: 1924. Died: Nov. 13, 1981, New York, N.Y. (heart attack). Screen actor and magician.

LONDON, JACK
Born: 1905, British Guiana. Died: May 31, 1966, London, England. Screen actor and pianist.

LONDON, JEAN "BABE"
Born: 1901, Des Moines, Iowa. Died: Nov. 29, 1980, Woodland Hills, Calif. Screen actress and portraitist. Married to musical director Phil Boutelje.

Appeared in: **1916** Merely Mary Ann. **1919** A Day's Pleasure. **1920** When the Clouds Roll By. **1922** Golden Dreams; When Romance Rides. **1926** The Boob; Is That Nice? **1927** Ain't Love Funny?; All Aboard; The Princess from Hoboken. **1928** The Fortune Hunter; Tillie's Punctured Romance. **1931** Our Wife (short). **1950** Mother Didn't Tell Me. **1951** Scrambled Brains (short). **1960** Sex Kittens Go to College. **1968** Single Room Furnished. **1970** Dirty Dingus Magee.

LONDON, TOM (Leonard Clapham)
Born: Aug. 24, 1893, Louisville, Ky. Died: Dec. 5, 1963, North Hollywood, Calif. Screen and television actor.

Appeared in: **1903** The Great Train Robbery. **1917** Lone Larry. **1924** The Loser's End. **1925** The Demon Rider; Ranchers and Rascals; Three in Exile; Winds of Chance. **1926** Snowed In (serial); Chasing Trouble; Code of the Northwest; The Grey Devil; West of the Rainbow's End; Dangerous Traffic. **1927** Return of the Riddle Rider (serial); King of Kings; Border Blackbirds; The Devil's Twin; The Long Loop of the Pecos. **1928** The Mystery Rider (serial); The Yellow Cameo (serial); The Apache Raider; The Boss of Rustler's Roost; The Bronc Stomper; Put 'Em Up; Yellow Contraband; The Price of Fear. **1929** Lawless Region; The Devil's Twin; Hell's Heroes; The Harvest of Hate; Untamed Justice; The Border Wildcat. **1930** Troopers Three; The Third Alarm; Romance of the West; Firebrand Jordan; The Woman Racket; The Storm; All Quiet on the Western Front; Borrowed Wives. **1931** Under Texas Skies; Westbound; Air Police; Two Gun Man; Trails of the Golden West; Range Law; The Arizona Terror; Lightnin' Smith Returns; Secret Six; Hell Divers; River's End; East of Borneo; The Men in Her Life; Dishonored; Spell of the Circus (serial); The Galloping Ghost (serial). **1932** The Lost Special (serial); The Thirteenth Guest; Night Rider; Gold; Beyond the Rockies; The Boiling Point; Trailing the Killer; Without Honors; Freaks; Dr. Jekyll and Mr. Hyde. **1933** Iron Master; Outlaw Justice; The Fugitive; Sunset Pass; One Year Later; Whispering Shadows (serial); I'm No Angel; Clancy of the Mounted (serial). **1934** Burn 'Em Up Barnes (serial); Mystery Ranch; Outlaw's Highway; Fighting Hero; Mystery Mountains (serial). **1935** Tumbling Tumbleweedss; The Miracle Rider (serial); Toll of the Desert; Courage of the North; The Sagebrush Troubadour; Just My Luck; The Last of the Clintons; Hong Kong Nights; Skull and Crown; Gun Play; The Whole Town's Talking; Barbary Coast; Goin' to Town. **1936** The Lawless Nineties; Guns and Guitars; O'Malley of the Mounted; The Border Patrolman; Heroes of the Range. **1937** Bar-Z Bad Men; Law of the Range; Roaring Timber; Springtime in the Rockies; Western Gold; The Mysterious Pilot (serial); Zorro Rides

Again (serial). **1938** Prairie Moon; Pioneer Trail; Six Shootin' Sheriff; Phantom Ranger; Outlaws of Sonora; Riders of the Black Hills; Santa Fe Stampede; Sunset Trail; Fighting Devil Dogs (serial); The Lone Ranger (serial). **1939** Jesse James; Made for Each Other; Rollin' Westward; Mexicali Rose; The Renegade Ranger; Southward Ho!; The Night Riders; Mountain Rhythm; Roll, Wagons, Roll; Song of the Buckaroo. **1940** Westbound Stage; Gaucho Serenade; Shooting High; Ghost Valley Raiders; Hi-Yo Silver; Covered Wagon Days; Wild Horse Range; Stage to Chino; Trailing Double Trouble; Melody Ranch; The Kid from Santa Fe; Lone Star Raiders; Northwest Passage; Lillian Russell. **1941** Billy the Kid; The Last of the Duanes; Dude Cowboy; Robbers of the Range; Land of the Open Range; Romance of the Rio Grande; Pals of the Pecos; Twilight on the Trail; Ridin' on a Rainbow; Stick to Your Guns; Fugitive Valley. **1942** West of Tombstone; Stardust on the Sage; Down Texas Way; Arizona Terrors; Ghost Town Law; Cowboy Serenade; Sons of the Pioneers; American Empire; Spy Smasher (serial); The Valley of Vanishing Men (serial). **1943** Tenting Tonight on the Old Campground; The Renegade; Wild Horse Stampede; False Colors; Daredevils of the West; Hail to the Rangers; Shadows on the Sage; Wagon Tracks West; Fighting Frontier. **1944** Yellow Rose of Texas; Sheriff of Sundown; Code of the Prairie; The Cheyenne; Beneath Western Skies; The San Antonio Kid; Hidden Valley Outlaws; Vigilantes of Dodge City; Stagecoach to Monterey; Firebrands of Arizona; The Cheyenne Wildcat; Faces in the Fog; Three Little Sisters; Thoroughbreds; Zorro's Black Whip (serial). **1945** Federal Operator 99 (serial); Colorado Pioneers; Three's a Crowd; Don't Fence Me In; Sunset in Eldorado; Corpus Christi Bandits; Wagon Wheels Westward; Marshal of Laredo; The Cherokee Flash; Oregon Trail; Trail of Kit Carson; Rough Riders of Cheyenne; The Topeka Terror; Sheriff of Cimarron; Grissly's Millions; Earl Carroll Vanities; Behind City Lights. **1946** Sheriff of Redwood Valley; Days of Buffalo Bill; Crime of the Century; Out California Way; California Gold Rush; The Undercover Woman; Alias Billy the Kid; Roll on Texas Moon; Rio Grande Raiders; The Invisible Informer; Man From Rainbow Valley; Red River Renegades; Murder in the Music Hall; Passkey to Danger; The Phantom Rider (serial); King of the Forest Rangers (serial). **1947** Jesse James Rides Again (serial); Wyoming; Last Frontier Uprising; Homesteaders of Paradise Valley; Twilight on the Rio Grande; Santa Fe Uprising; Saddle Pals; Marshal of Cripple Creek; Rustlers of Devil's Canyon; Thunder Gap Outlaws; Along the Oregon Trail; The Wild Frontier; Shootin' Irons; Under Colorado Skies; Code of the Plains. **1948** Mark of the Lash; Marshal of Amarillo. **1949** Brand of Fear; Sand; Red Desert; Riders in the Sky; Frontier Investigator; South of Rio; San Antone Ambush. **1950** The Old Frontier; Cody of the Pony Express (serial); The Blazing Hills (aka The Blazing Sun). **1951** The Secret of Convict Lake; Hills of Utah; Rough Riders of Durango. **1952** The Old West; High Noon; Trail Guide; Blue Canadian Rockies; Apache Country. **1953** Pack Train; The Marshal's Daughter. **1956** Tribute to a Bad Man. **1957** The Storm Rider. **1958** The Lone Texan; The Saga of Hemp Brown. **1959** Friendly Persuasion. **1961** Underworld. **1962** 13 West Street.

LONERGAN, LESTER
Born: 1869. Died: Aug. 13, 1931, Lynn, Mass. Screen, stage actor, film director and stage producer. Father of actor Lester Lonergan, Jr. (dec. 1959). Entered films with Thanhauser Co.

Appeared in: **1929** Seven Faces.

LONERGAN, LESTER, JR.
Born: 1894. Died: Dec. 23, 1959, New York, N.Y. Screen, stage, vaudeville, television actor and stage director. Son of actor Lester Lonergan (dec. 1931).

Appeared in: **1947** Boomerang.

LONG, FREDERIC
Born: 1857. Died: Oct. 18, 1941, Hollywood, Calif. Screen, stage and vaudeville actor.

Appeared in: **1929** The Lost Patrol.

LONG, JACK
Died: Aug. 7, 1938, Los Angeles, Calif. (motorcycle accident). Screen actor and stuntman.

Appeared in: **1933** Police Car. **1934** Speed Wings. **1937** The Sitter-Downers (short).

LONG, JOHNNY
Born: 1916. Died: Oct. 31, 1972, Parkersburg, W.Va. (heart attack). Bandleader and screen actor. Do not confuse with other actors John and Johnny Long.

Appeared in: **1943** Hit the Ice.

LONG, LURAY (Luray Roble)
Born: Dec. 3, 1890, Wis. Died: Jan. 2, 1919, Los Angeles, Calif. (Spanish influenza). Screen actress. Married to actor Walter Long (dec. 1952).

LONG, MELVYN HARRY
Born: 1895. Died: Nov. 14, 1940, Los Angeles, Calif. (stroke). Screen, stage and vaudeville actor.

Appeared in: **1940** Queen of the Yukon. **1941** Meet John Doe.

LONG, NICK, JR.
Born: 1906, Greenlawn, N.Y. Died: Aug. 31, 1949, New York, N.Y. (results of an auto accident). Screen, stage and vaudeville actor. Son of actor Nick Long.

Appeared in: **1935** Broadway Melody of 1936. **1936** King of Burlesque.

LONG, RICHARD
Born: Dec. 17, 1927, Chicago, Ill. Died: Dec. 22, 1974, Los Angeles, Calif. (heart ailment). Screen and television actor. Married to actress Suzan Ball (dec. 1955) and later married to actress Mara Corday.

Appeared in: **1946** Tomorrow is Forever (film debut); The Stranger; The Dark Mirror. **1947** The Egg and I. **1948** Tap Roots. **1949** Ma and Pa Kettle; Criss Cross; The Life of Riley. **1950** Kansas Raiders; Ma and Pa Kettle Go to Town. **1951** Ma and Pa Kettle Back on the Farm; Air Cadet. **1952** Back at the Front. **1953** The All-American; All I Desire. **1954** Saskatchewan; Playgirl; Return to Treasure Island. **1955** Cult of the Cobra. **1956** Fury at Gunsight Pass; He Laughed Last. **1958** House on Haunted Hill. **1959** Tokyo After Dark. **1960** Home from the Hill. **1963** Follow the Boys. **1964** Tenderfoot. **1967** Make Like a Thief.

LONG, WALTER
Born: Mar. 5, 1879, Milford, N.H. Died: July 4, 1952, Los Angeles Calif. (heart attack). Black screen, stage actor and film director. Married to actress Luray Long (dec. 1919). Entered films in 1909.

Appeared in: **1915** The Birth of a Nation. **1916** Intolerance. **1917** Joan the Woman; The Evil Eye; The Little America. **1918** The Queen of the Sea. **1919** The Mother and the Law; Scarlet Days. **1920** A Giant of a Race; What Women Love; The Fighting Shepherdess; Go and Get It. **1921** The Fire Cat; The Sheik; Tiger True; A Giant of His Race; White and Unmarried. **1922** A Shot in the Night; Moran of the Lady Letty; The Dictator; Blood and Sand; Across the Continent; The Beautiful and the Damned; My American Wife; Omar the Tentmaker; To Have and to Hold; South of Suva; Shadows. **1923** The Devil's Match; Kick In; The Broken Wing; Desire; The Call of the Wild; His Great Chance; Little Church Around the Corner; The Isle of Lost Ships; Quicksands; The Shock; The Huntress; The Last Hour. **1924** Daring Love; The Ridin' Kid from Powder River; Yankee Madness; Wine; White Man; Missing Daughters. **1925** Soul-Fire; Raffles, the Amateur Cracksman; The Verdict; Bobbed Hair; The Lady; The Reckless Sex; The Road to Yesterday; The Shock Punch. **1926** Eve's Leaves; Red Dice; Steel Preferred; The High Binders; West of Broadway. **1927** White Pants Willie; Back to God's Country; The Yankee Clipper; Jewels of Desire; Jim the Conqueror. **1928** Gang War; Me, Gangster; Forbidden Grass; Thundergod. **1929** Black Cargoes of the South Seas; The Black Watch. **1930** Beau Bandit; Conspiracy; Moby Dick; The Steel Highway. **1931** Sea Devils; Taxi Troubles (short); The Maltese Falcon; Other Men's Women; Souls of the Slums; Pardon Us. **1932** I Am a Fugitive from a Chain Gang; Silver Dollar; Dragnet Patrol; Escapade; Any Old Port (short). **1933** Women Won't Tell. **1934** The Thin Man; Three Little Bigskin's (short); The Live Ghost (short); Going Bye Bye (short); Six of a Kind; Operator 13; Lightning Strikes Twice. **1935** Naughty Marietta; The Whole Town's Talking. **1936** Drift Fence; The Glory Trail; The Beloved Rogue; The Bold Caballero. **1937** Pick a Star; North of the Rio Grande. **1938** The Painted Trail; Bar 20 Justice; Six-Shootin' Sheriff; Man's Country. **1939** Union Pacific; Wild Horse Canyon. **1941** Silver Stallion; Ridin On a Rainbow; City of Missing Girls. **1948** No More Relatives (short). **1950** Wabash Avenue.

LONG, WILLIAM W.
Died: Date unknown. Screen, stage and vaudeville actor. Married to actress Emily Green (dec. 1980). Appeared in early Lubin films.

LONGDEN, JOHN
Born: Nov. 11, 1900, West Indies. Died: May 26, 1971, England? Screen, stage actor and screenwriter. Married to actress Jean Jay (Charlotte Frances Jay). Entered films in 1925.

Appeared in: **1926** The House of Marney; The Ball of Fortune. **1927** The Glad Eye; Quinneys; The Flight Commander; The Arcadians; Daily Jesters series including Bright Young Things. **1928** Mademoiselle Parley-Voo; Palais de Danse; What Money Can Buy.

1929 The Flying Squad; The Last Post; Blackmail; Memories; Atlantic; Juno and the Paycock (US 1930). **1930** The Flame of Love; Elstree Calling; Children of Chance; Two Worlds. **1931** The Wickham Mystery; The Skin Game; Rynox; The Ringer (US 1932). **1932** Murder on the Second Floor; Born Lucky; A Lucky Sweep. **1937** French Leave; Jenifer Hale; Little Miss Somebody; Young and Innocent (aka A Girl Was Young—US 1938). **1938** Dial 999; The Gaunt Stranger (aka The Phantom Strikes—US 1939); Bad Boy. **1939** Jamaica Inn; Q Planes (aka Clouds Over Europe—US); Goodbye Mr. Chips; The Lion Has Wings (US 1940). **1940** Branded (reissue of Bad Boy—1938); Contraband (aka Blackout—US). **1941** The Tower of Terror (US 1942); The Common Touch; Old Mother Riley's Circus. **1942** Rose of Tralee; Unpublished Story. **1943** The Silver Fleet (US 1945); Death by Design. **1947** Dusty Bates; The Ghosts of Berkeley Square. **1948** Anna Karenina; The Last Load; Bonnie Prince Charlie (US 1952). **1949** Trapped by the Terror. **1950** The Elusive Pimpernel; The Lady Craved Excitement. **1951** The Dark Light; Black Widow (US 1954); Pool of London; The Man With the Twisted Lip; The Magic Box (US 1952); Trek to Mashomba (short). **1952** The Wallet. **1954** Dangerous Cargo; Meet Mr. Callaghan. **1955** The Ship That Died of Shame (US 1956); Alias John Preston. **1956** Raiders of the River (serial). **1957** Quatermass II (aka Enemy from Space—US); Three Sundays to Live. **1960** An Honourable Murder. **1961** So Evil So Young. **1963** Lancelot and Guinevere (aka Sword of Lancelot—US). **1964** Der Fall X701 (aka Frozen Alive—US 1966).

LONGMAN, EDWARD G.

Born: 1881, Brooklyn, N.Y. Died: Apr. 14, 1969, Miami, Fla. (heart attack). Screen and stage actor.

Appeared in: **1915** All For a Girl. **1917** The Builder of Castles.

LONSDALE, HARRY G.

Born: Dec. 6, ?, Worcester, England. Died: June 12, 1923. Screen, stage and opera performer.

Appeared in: **1912** The Devil, the Servant and the Man; An Unexpected Fortune; When Women Rule. **1913** Master of the Garden. **1915** Ebbtide. **1916** The Ne'er-Do-Well; The Brand of Cain. **1917** Conscience; The Garden of Allah. **1918** Beware of Strangers. **1919** The Illustrious Prince; The Last of His People; Shepherd of the Hills. **1920** The Week-End. **1921** The Mask; The Night Horseman; Payment Guaranteed; Where Men Are Men. **1922** Thelma; The Call of Home; The Fighting Guide; A Fool There Was; The Great Night; Monte Cristo; The Rosary. **1924** The Last of the Duanes; The Vagabond Trail. **1925** Her Husband's Secret; Brand of Cowardice.

LONTOC, LEON

Born: 1909. Died: Jan. 22, 1974, Los Angeles, Calif. Screen and television actor.

Appeared in: **1943** Behind the Rising Sun. **1944** Rainbow Island. **1945** Secret Agent X-9 (serial). **1950** On the Isle of Samoa. **1951** I Was an American Spy; Peking Express. **1952** Mara Maru; Hurricane Smith. **1953** City Beneath the Sea. **1954** The Naked Jungle. **1955** Jump Into Hell; The Left Hand of God. **1956** The Revolt of Mamie Stover. **1958** The Hunters. **1959** Operation Petticoat. **1960** Gallant Hours. **1962** The Spiral Road. **1963** The Ugly American. **1966** One Spy Too Many. **1968** Panic in the City.

LOOMES, HARRY E.

Died: Mar. 17, 1946, Philadelphia, Pa. Screen actor. Appeared in D. W. Griffith films.

LOONG, LEE SIU See LEE, BRUCE

LOOP, PHIL

Died: June 11, 1975. Screen actor.

LOOS, ANITA

Born: Apr. 26, 1888, Sisson, Calif. Died: Aug. 18, 1981, Manhattan, N.Y. Screen, stage actress, film producer, screenwriter, playwright and novelist. Appeared in comedy one-reelers during the silents.

LOOS, THEODOR

Born: 1883, Zwingenburg, Germany. Died: June 27, 1954, Stuttgart, West Germany. Screen and stage actor.

Appeared in: **1912** Das Goldene Bett. **1914** Arme Eva; Das Haus ohne Fenster und Tueren. **1916** Friedrich Werders Sendung; Homunculus. **1917** Es Werde Licht (Let There Be Light). **1919** Nach dem Gesetz; Die Verbote Frucht. **1920** Geschwister Barelli; Im Banne der Suggestion; Der Reigen; Sehende Liebe; Die Spielerin; Steuermann Holk; Der Zeugende Tod. **1921** Christian Wahnschaffe. **1922** Das Blinde Glueck; Hanneles Himmelfahrt; Jugend; Der Kampf ums Ich;

Lady Hamilton; Malmaison; Schuld und Suehne. **1923** Friedrich Schiller. **1924** Aufsteig der Kleinen Lilian; Soll und Haben; Claire (aka Die Geschichte Eines Jungen Maedchens); Die Nibelungen (including Siegfried—US 1925 and Kriemhild's Rache (Kriemhild's Revenge—US 1928)). **1925** Goetz von Berlichingen Zubenannt mit der Eisernen Hand; Was Steine Erzaehlen; Wunder der Schoepfung (Miracles of Creation); Der Tanzende Tod (aka Rex Mundi); Der Erste Stand (aka Der Grosskapitaen, and aka Daemon Geld). **1926** Manon Lescaut; Frauen der Leidenschaft; Der Herr der Nacht; Das Lebenslied; Liebeshandel; Der Veilchenfresser; Zopf und Schwert; Metropolis (aka Mr. Metropolis—US 1927). **1927** Anastasia, die Falsche Zarentochter; Bigamie; Die Hochstaplerin; Luther; Petronella; Prinz Louis Ferdinand; Die Weber (The Weaver—US 1929); Koenigin Luise (Queen Luise). **1928** Die Sache mit Schorrsiegel; Sensationsprozess; Heimkehr (Homecoming). **1929** Blutschande § 173 St. G.B.; Diane; Ludwig der Zweite, Koenig von Bayern; Die Staerkere Macht; Napoleon auf St. Helena; Vertauschte Geshichter; Atlantik. **1930** Zwei Menschen; Die Grosse Sehnsucht (US 1931); Das Floetenkonzert von Saussouci (The Flute Concert at Sans Souci). **1931** Ich Geh' aus und Du Bleibst Da (US 1932); Die Andere Seite; M (aka Moerder Unter Uns—US 1933); Yorck (US 1932); 1914, die Letzen Tage vor dem Weltbrand (1914: The Last Days Before the War—US 1932); Ariane; Der Fall das Gernerlastabs-Oberts Redl (US 1932); Im Geheimdienst (aka In the Employ of the Secret Service). **1932** Unter Falscher Flagge; Tod Ueber Shanghai (US 1933) Die Elf Schill'schen Offiziere; Gruen ist die Heide; Holzapfel Weiss Alles (US 1933); 8 Maedels im Boot; Schuss im Morgengrauen; Trenck (US 1934); Ikarus (speaker—aka Gunther Plueschows Fliegerschicksal); Rasputin (aka Der Daemon der Frauen); Marschall Vorwaerts; Die Unsicktbare Front; An Heiligen Wasser (aka Sieg der Liebe); Geheimnis des Bauen Zimmers; Goethe—Filme der Ufa. **1933** Wege zur Guten Ehe; Spione am Werk; Was Wissen Denn Maenner; Hoellentempo; Die Blonde Christel (US 1934); Ein Gewisser Herr Gran; Stradivari; Gipfelstuermer; Elisabeth und ihr Narr (aka Elisabeth, die Weisse Schwester von St. Veith); Das Testament des Dr. Mabuse (The Testament of Dr. Mabuse); Der Judas von Tirol (Der Ewige Verrat). **1934** Wilhelm Tell; Die Freundin Eines Grossen Mannes; Ein Maedchen mit Prokura; Hanneles Himmelfahrt (and 1922 version); Die Speech'schen Jaeger. **1935** Das Maedchen Johanna; Viktoria; Der Hoehere Befehl; Das Gruene Domino; Der Alte und der Junge Koenig (The Young and the Old King); Das Maedchen vom Moorhof (The Girl of the Moors). **1936** Der Abenteurer von Paris; Verraeter; Schlussakkord; Die Stunde der Versuchung; Weisse Sklaven (aka Panzerkreuzer Sewastopol). **1937** Das Geheimnis um Betty Bonn; Der Herrscher; Die Glaeserne Kugel (US 1939); Monika (aka Eine Mutter Kaempft um ihr Kind). **1938** Kameraden auf See; Geheimzeichen LB 17; Der Maulkorb; Schatten Ueber St Pauli. **1939** Roman Eines Arztes; Parkstrasse 13 (aka Verhoer um Mitternacht); Robert Koch, der Bekaempfer des Todes. **1940** Falschmuenzer; Jus Suess; Kora Terry. **1941** Heimaterde; Alarm. **1942** Andreas Schlueter; Rembrandt; Die Entlassung; Die Sache mit Styx. **1943** Reise in die Vergangenheit; Titanic; Gabriele Dambrone. **1944** Philharmoniker. **1945** Shiva und die Galgenblume; Der Fall Molander; Geld ins Haus (aka Der Millionaer). **1949** Mordprozess Dr. Jordan. **1953** Sterne Ueber Colombo. **1954** Dei Gefangene des Maharadscha; Rosen aus dem Sueden. **1956** Circus Girl.

LOPER, DON

Born: 1906, Toledo, Ohio. Died: Nov. 22, 1972, Santa Monica, Calif. (complications following a lung puncture). Fashion designer, screen actor and dancer.

Appeared in: **1943** Thousands Cheer. **1944** Lady in the Dark. **1945** It's a Pleasure.

LOPEZ, CARLOS (Carlos Chaflan Lopez y Valles)

Born: Nov. 4, 1887, Durango, Mexico. Died: Feb. 13, 1942, Tapachula, Mexico (drowned). Stage and screen actor.

Appeared in: **1925** El Aguila y el Nopal. **1933** Sobre las Olas; Una Vida por Otra. **1934** El Compadre Mendoza; El Escandalo; Clemencia; La Sangre Manada; Quien mato a Eva. **1935** Hu Hijo; Chucho El Roto; Oro y Plata; Silencio Subline; Mujeres sin Alma; Martin Garatuza; Corazon Bandolero; Cruz Diablo; Juarez y Maximiliano; El Tesora de Pancho Villa; Monja u Casada; Virgen y Martir; Payada de la vida. **1936** Vamanos Con Pancho Villa; El Baul Macabro (The Big Trunk); Alla en el Rancho Grande (Three on the Big Ranch); Cielito Lindo. **1938** Ave sin Rumbo (Wandering Bird); Rancho Grande. **1939** El Inio.

LOPEZ, MANUEL

Died: Jan. 31, 1976. Screen actor.

Appeared in: **1943** Adventure in Iraq. **1955** Hell's Island. **1956** Cha-Cha-Boom. **1962** Deadly Duo.

LOPEZ, TONY

Born: 1902, Mexico. Died: Sept. 23, 1949, Hollywood, Calif. Screen actor.

LOPEZ, VINCENT (Vincent Joseph Lopez)
Born: Dec. 10, 1898, Brooklyn, N.Y. Died: Sept. 20, 1975, Miami Beach, Fla. (liver and pancreas failure). Orchestra leader, radio performer and screen actor.

Appeared in: **1932** The Big Broadcast. **1933** Universal, Warner Bros., Metro and Paramount shorts. **1940** Vitaphone shorts.

LORAINE, VIOLET
Born: July 23, 1886, London, England. Died: July 18, 1956, Newcastle, England. Screen and stage actress.

Appeared in: **1933** Britiannia of Billingsgate.

LORCH, THEODORE A.
Born: 1873, Springfield, Ill. Died: Nov. 12, 1947, Hollywood, Calif. Screen, stage and vaudeville actor.

Appeared in: **1921** Gasoline Gus. **1923** Shell Shocked Sammy. **1924** The Sea Hawk; Westbound. **1925** Heir-Loons; Once in a Lifetime; Where the Worst Begins; Manhattan Madness; The Man on the Box. **1926** Across the Pacific; Unknown Dangers; The Better 'Ole. **1927** Black Jack; King of Kings; Sailor Izzy Murphy; Tracked by the Police. **1928** Ginsberg the Great; The Canyon of Adventure; Grip of the Yukon. **1929** Show Boat; The Royal Rider; Wild Blood; Spite Marriage. **1930** The Runaway Bride; plus the following shorst: An Ill Wind; The Border Patrol; More Sinned Against Than Usual. **1931** The Galloping Ghost (serial); The Lightning Warrior (serial). **1933** Black Beauty; The Whirlwind. **1934** The Mighty Barnum; The Affairs of Cellini; Kid Millions. **1935** Rustler's Paradise; Uncivil Warriors (short); Hold 'Em Yale. **1936** Romance Rides the Range; Rebellion; Flash Gordon (serial); Showboat. **1937** Dick Tracy (serial); The Big Squirt (short); Goofs and Saddles (short). **1939** Stagecoach. **1945** If a Body Meets a Body (short). **1946** Uncivil Warbirds (short). **1947** Half-Wits Holiday (short). **1948** Hot Scots (short).

LORD, LONNIE See HAYDOCK, RONALD "RON"

LORD, MARION
Born: 1883. Died: May 25, 1942, Hollywood, Calif. Screen and stage actress.

Appeared in: **1929** Broadway. **1930** Queen of Scandal. **1931** One Heavenly Night. **1935** Salesmanship Ahoy (short); Straight from the Heart.

LORD, PAULINE
Born: 1890, Hanford, Calif. Died: Oct. 11, 1950, Alamogordo, N.Mex. (heart trouble). Screen and stage actress.

Appeared in: **1934** Mrs. Wiggs of the Cabbage Patch. **1935** A Feather in Her Hat.

LORD, PHILIP F. (Philip Francis Lord)
Born: 1879. Died: Nov. 25, 1968, Chicago, Ill. (heart ailment). Screen, stage, television and radio actor.

LORD, PHILLIPS H. (Phillips Haynes Lord aka SETH PARKER)
Born: July 13, 1902, Hartford, Vt. Died: Oct. 19, 1975, Ellsworth, Maine. Radio, television writer, radio actor, producer and screen actor.

Appeared in: **1929** Silver King. **1932** Way Back Home. **1935** Obeah.

LORDE, ATHENA
Born: 1915. Died: May 23, 1973, Van Nuys, Calif. (cancer). Screen, stage, radio and television actress. Married to actor Jim Boles (dec. 1977). Mother of actress Barbara and actor Eric Boles.

Appeared in: **1958** Marjorie Morningstar. **1965** Hush, Hush Sweet Charlotte. **1968** Firecreek. **1969** Angel in My Pocket; Fuzz. **1971** How to Frame a Figg. **1972** Fuzz. **1973** Dr. Death—Seeker of Souls.

LORENZ, JOHN A.
Born: 1887, Buffalo, N.Y. Died: Apr. 30, 1972, Paramus, N.J. Screen and stage actor. Entered films with Essanay.

Appeared in: **1916** When Justice Won; Money to Burn.

LORENZON, LIVIO (aka CHARLIE LAWRENCE)
Born: May 6, 1926, Trieste, Italy. Died: Dec. 23, 1971, Latisana, Italy. Screen actor.

Appeared in: **1953** Ombre Su Trieste. **1957** El Amamei; L'Inferno Trema. **1958** Captain Fuoco; Il Calaliere del Castello Maledetto; Il Filgio del Corsaro Rosso. **1959** L'Arcierre Nero; El Terrore della Maschera Rossa; Il Vedovo; Il Terrore dell' Oklahoma; Il Reali di Francia; La Sceriffa; La Grande Guerra (The Great War—US 1961).

1960 Cavalcata Selvaggia; Le Signore; Le Venere dei Pirati; La Furia dei Barbari (Fury of the Barbarians aka Fury of the Pagans—US 1963); Il Pirati della Costa. **1961** La Rivolta dei Mercenari; Una Spada Nell 'Ombra; I Masnadieri; Il Segreto dello Sparviero; La Vendetta di Ursus; Ponsio Pilato; Il Terrore del Mare (Terror of the Sea, aka Guns of the Black Witch—US); El Gladiatore Invincible (The Invincible Gladiator—US 1963). **1962** Zorro alla Corte di Spagna; Tharus Figlio di Attila; Un 'Ora per Vivere; I Sette Gladiatori; L'Ultimo Czar (The Last Czar aka The Night They Killed Rasputin). **1963** Maciste L'Eroe Piu 'Grande del Mondo (aka Goliath and the Sins of Babylon—US); Frenesia dell 'Estate; Zorro E I Tre Moschettiert. **1964** Ercole Contro I Trianni di Babilonia; Ercole Contro Roma; Il Figlio di Cleopatra; Jim El Primo; La Vendetta dei Gladiatori. **1965** Colorado Charlie; Ercole, Sonsome, Maciste e Ursus gli Invincibili; Il Gladiatore che Sfido L'Impero. **1966** The Secret Seven; Il Buono, Il Bruto, Il Cattivo (The Good, the Bad and the Ugly—US 1967). **1967** Colpo Maestro di Sua Maestra' Britannica; Texas Addio; Cjamango. **1969** Ace High.

LORING, VAL (Billy Eugene Williford)
Born: 1940. Died: Aug. 20, 1978, Calif. (heart attack). Screen, television actor and stuntman.

LORNE, CONSTANCE (Constance MacLaurin)
Born: Apr. 26, 1914, Peebles, Scotland. Died: Dec. 21, 1969, London, England. Screen and stage actress. Entered films in 1948.

Appeared in: **1951** One Wild Oat. **1952** Curtain Up (US 1953).

LORNE, MARION (M. L. MacDougal)
Born: 1888, Pa. Died: May 9, 1968, New York, N.Y. (heart attack). Screen, stage and television actress.

Appeared in: **1951** Strangers on a Train. **1955** The Girl Rush. **1967** The Graduate.

LORRAINE, BETTY
Born: June 30, 1908, Louisville, Ky. Died: Sept. 1, 1944. Screen and stage actress.

Appeared in: **1929** Red Wine; When Caesar Ran a Newspaper (short). **1933** A Bedtime Story. **1937** Souls at Sea.

LORRAINE, EMILY
Born: 1878, England. Died: July 6, 1944, New York, N.Y. Screen and stage actress.

Appeared in: **1912** The Heart of John Grimm. **1923** The Custard Cup.

LORRAINE, HARRY (Henry Herd)
Born: 1886, Brighton, England. Died: Date unknown, England? Screen actor and film director.

Appeared in: **1912** Lieutenant Rose and the Train Wreckers; Robin Hood Outlawed. **1913** Stock is as Good as Money; Tom Cringle in Jamaica; Signals in the Night; Through the Clouds; Lieutenant Daring and the Mystery of Room 41 (aka Lieutenant Daring and the International Jewel Thieves—US); In Fate's Grip; The Little Snow Waif; The Master Crook; The Favourite for the Jamaica Cup; A Tragedy in the Alps. **1914** Lieutenant Daring, Aerial Scout; Lieutenant Rose and the Sealed Orders; Detective Daring and the Thames Coiners; The Belle of Crystal Palace; Mary the Fishergirl; The Great Spy Raid; The World at War; Huns of the North Sea; London's Underworld; Queenie of the Circus. **1915** The Great Cheque Fraud; The Stolen Heirlooms; Wireless; The Counterfeiters; The Thornton Jewel Mystery. **1917** The Happy Warrior; If Thou Wert Blind. **1918** The Great Imposter. **1920** The Hawk's Trail (serial). **1921** A Certain Rich Man; Garments of Truth; The Hunch; The Man of the Forest; The Lure of Egypt. **1922** Don't Write Letters; Heart's Haven; I Can Explain; Golden Dreams; Little Eva Ascends; The Lavender Bath Lady. **1923** Tea—With a Kick; Slave of Desire. **1924** The Shooting of Dan McGrew. **1925** Steppin' Out; Siege. **1928** Sweeney Todd. **1929** Unto Each Other. **1930** Stranger Than Fiction.

LORRAINE, LEOTA
Born: 1893, Kansas City, Mo. Died: July 9, 1975. Screen actress.

Appeared in: **1915** Rule Sixty Three. **1917** Feet of Clay; The Promise. **1918** Playing the Game; The Kaiser's Shadow; A Daughter of the West; The Finger of Justice. **1919** The Pest; The Gay Lord Quex; Be a Little Sport; Luck in Pawn; The Girl Dodger. **1920** The Turning Point; Her Five Foot Highness; The Misfit Wife; The Loves of Letty. **1924** The Bowery Bishop. **1925** Infatuation. **1929** The Woman I Love. **1935** Ruggles of Red Gap; Sprucin' Up (short). **1938** His Pest Friend (short). **1942** Are Husbands Necessary?. **1943** The Youngest Profession. **1945** They Were Expendable. **1946** From This Day Forward; Notorious; Night and Day. **1947** Sea of Grass. **1956** The Bride and the Bees.

LORRAINE, LILLIAN (Eulallean de Jacques)
Born: Jan. 1, 1892, San Francisco, Calif. Died: Apr. 17, 1955, New York, N.Y. Screen and stage actress.

Appeared in: **1915** Should a Wife Forgive? **1916** Neal of the Navy (serial). **1918** Playing the Game; The Kaiser's Shadow. **1919** The Pest. **1920** The Flaming Disc. **1922** Lonesome Corners.

LORRAINE, LOUISE (Louise Escovar)
Born: Oct. 1, 1901, San Francisco, Calif. Died: Feb. 2, 1981, Sacramento, Calif. Screen actress. Divorced from actor Art Acord (dec. 1931), and later married to Chester Hubbard (dec. 1963). Was a 1922 Wampas Baby star and was the second actress to portray Jane in the Tarzan films.

Appeared in: **1920** The Flaming Disc (serial); Elmo, the Fearless (serial). **1921** The Adventures of Tarzan (serial); The Fire Eater. **1922** With Stanley in Africa (serial); The Radio King (serial); Headin' West; Up in the Air About Mary; The Altar Stairs. **1923** The Gentlemen from America; McGuire of the Mounted; The Oregon Trail (serial). **1925** Three in Exile; The Verdict; The Wild Girl; Pals; Borrowed Finery; The Great Circus Mystery (serial). **1926** The Blue Streak; The Silent Guardian; The Stolen Ranch; The Silent Flyer (serial); Exit Smiling. **1927** The Frontiersman; Hard Fists; Winners of the Wilderness; Rookies. **1928** Chinatown Charlie; Shadows of the Night; The Wright Idea; Legionnaires in Paris; Baby Mine; Circus Rookies. **1929** A Final Reckoning (serial); The Diamond Master (serial). **1930** Beyond the Law; The Mounted Stranger; Near the Rainbow's End; The Lightning Express (serial); The Jade Box (serial).

LORRAINE, OSCAR
Born: 1878. Died: May 10, 1955, Hollywood, Calif. Screen and vaudeville actor. Was partner in vaudeville team of "Lorraine and Starr."

LORRAINE, ROBERT
Born: Jan. 14, 1876, New Brighton, Cheshire, England. Died: Dec. 23, 1935, London, England. Screen and stage actor.

Appeared in: **1922** Bentley's Conscience. **1928** S.O.S. **1930** Birds of Prey (aka The Perfect Alibi—US 1931). **1934** Outcast Lady; Marie Galante; Limehouse Blues. **1935** Father Brown—Dectecive.

LORRE, PETER
Born: June 26, 1904, Rosenberg, Hungary. Died: Mar. 23, 1964, Hollywood, Calif. (stroke). Screen, stage, television actor, film director and screenwriter. Divorced from actresses Karen Verne (dec. 1967) and Celia Lovsky (dec. 1979) and later married to Anna Brenning. Father of actor Peter Lorre, Jr.

Appeared in: **1928** Pioniere in Inoplastadt; Springs Awakening. **1931** Die Koffer des Herrn O.F. (The Luggage of Mr. O.F., aka The Thirteen Trunks of Mr. O.F.—US); M (US 1933, aka Moerder Unter Ums); Bomben auf Monte Carlo (Monte Carlo Madness); De Haute a Bas. **1932** Schuss im Morgengrauen; Fuenf von der Jazzband; Der Weisse Daemon (The White Demon); F.P. 1 Antwortet Nicht (F.P. 1 Does Not Answer). **1933** Was Frauen Trauemen (What Women Dream); Unsichtbare Gegner. **1934** The Man Who Knew Too Much. **1935** Mad Love (aka The Hands of Orlac); Crime and Punishment. **1936** The Hidden Power; The Secret Agent; Crack-Up. **1937** Nancy Steele is Missing; Think Fast, Mr. Moto; Lancer Spy; Thank You, Mr. Moto. **1938** Mr. Moto Takes a Chance; Mr. Moto's Gamble; The Mysterious Mr. Moto; I'll Give a Million. **1939** Mr. Moto Takes a Vacation; Mr. Moto's Last Warning; Mr. Moto in Danger Island; Confessions of a Nazi Spy. **1940** Strange Cargo; I Was an Adventuress; Island of Doomed Men; The Stranger on the Third Floor; You'll Find Out. **1941** The Face Behind the Mask; Mr. District Attorney; They Met in Bombay; The Maltese Falcon. **1942** All Through the Night; Invisible Agent; The Boogie Man Will Get You; Casablanca; In This Our Life. **1943** Strictly in the Groove; The Constant Nymph; Background to Danger; The Cross of Lorraine. **1944** Passage to Marseilles; The Mask of Dimitrios; The Conspirators; Arsenic and Old Lace; Hollywood Canteen. **1945** Hotel Berlin; Confidential Agent. **1946** Three Strangers; The Verdict; The Black Angel; The Chase; The Beast With Five Fingers. **1947** My Favorite Brunette. **1948** Casbah. **1949** Rope of Sand. **1950** Quicksand; Double Confession (US 1953). **1951** Der Verlorene. **1954** Beat the Devil; 20,000 Leagues Under the Sea. **1956** Congo Crossing; Meet Me in Las Vegas; Around the World in 80 Days. **1957** The Buster Keaton Story; The Story of Mankind; The Sad Sack; Silk Stockings. **1958** Hell Ship Mutiny. **1959** The Big Circus. **1960** Scene of Mystery. **1961** Voyage to the Bottom of the Sea. **1962** Five Weeks in a Balloon; Tales of Terror. **1963** The Raven; The Comedy of Terrors. **1964** Muscle Beach Party; The Patsy.

LORYS, DENISE
Died: Nov. 19, 1930, Paris, France. Screen actress.

Appeared in: **1925** Madame Sans Gene.

LOSCH, TILLY (Ottilie Ethel Losch)
Born: Nov. 15, 1902, Vienna, Austria. Died: Dec. 24, 1975, New York, N.Y. (cancer). Screen, stage actress, dancer and painter.

Appeared in: **1936** The Garden of Allah. **1937** The Good Earth. **1946** Duel in the Sun.

LOSEE, FRANK
Born: 1856. Died: Nov. 14, 1937, Yonkers, N.Y. (pulmonary embolism). Screen and stage actor.

Appeared in: **1915** The Masqueraders; The Old Homestead. **1916** Ashes of Embers; Hulda from Holland. **1917** The Valentine Girl. **1918** La Tosca; Uncle Tom's Cabin; The Song of Songs; In Pursuit of Polly. **1919** His Parisian Wife; Here Comes the Bride. **1920** Lady Rose's Daughter. **1921** Dangerous Toys; Orphans of the Storm; Such a Little Queen; Disraeli. **1922** False Fronts; The Man She Brought Back; Man Wanted; The Seventh Day; Missing Millions. **1923** As a Man Lives. **1924** The Speed Spook; Unguarded Women. **1935** Four Hours to Kill; Annapolis Farewell.

LOTHAR, HANNS (Hanns Neutze)
Born: Hanover, Germany. Died: Mar. 11, 1967, Hamburg, Germany (heart attack). Screen, stage and television actor. Married to actress Ingrid Andree.

Appeared in: **1959** Menschen im Netz (aka Unwilling Agent—US 1968); Die Buddenbrooks (US 1962). **1960** Sturm im Wasserglas; Der Letzte Zeuge. **1961** Eine, Zwei, Drei (One, Two, Three); Bis Zum Ende Aller Tage (aka Girl from Hong Kong—US 1966). **1962** Wenn Beide Schuldig Werden. **1963** Piccadilly, Null Uhr Zwoelf; Schloss Gripsholm (The Gripsholm Castle—US 1964); Wochentags Immer. **1964** Seelenwanderung; Polizeirevier Davidswache (aka Seven Consenting Adults—US 1970). **1965** Vier Schluessel (The Four Keys). **1966** Lange Beine, Lange Finger.

LOTINGA, ERNEST (aka DAN ROY)
Born: 1876, Sunderland, England. Died: Oct. 28, 1951. Screen, stage, vaudevillle actor, screenwriter and stage producer.

Appeared in: **1928** The Raw Recruit (short); The Orderly Room (short); Nap (short); Joining Up (short). **1929** Josser, KC (short); Doing His Duty (short); Acci-dental Treatment (short); Spirits (short). **1931** P.C. Josser; Dr. Josser, K.C. **1932** Josser Joins the Navy; Josser on the River; Josser in the Army. **1934** Josser on the Farm. **1935** Smith's Wives. **1936** Love Up the Pole.

LOUDEN, THOMAS
Born: 1874. Died: Mar. 15, 1948, Hollywood, Calif. (stroke). Screen and stage actor.

Appeared in: **1938** Kidnapped; Prison Break. **1939** Our Leading Citizen. **1940** Safari. **1942** Mrs. Miniver; Are Husbands Necessary; The Pied Piper. **1943** The Masked Marvel (serial). **1944** The Hour Before the Dawn. **1945** The Corn Is Green; Dangerous Partners. **1946** Tomorrow Is Forever; The Dark Corner; The Strange Love of Martha Ivers. **1947** Till the Clouds Roll By.

LOUGHRAN, LEWIS
Born: 1950. Died: Feb. 24, 1975. Screen actor.

LOUIS, JOE (Joseph Louis Barrow)
Born: May 13, 1914, Lafayette, Ala. Died: Apr. 12, 1981, Las Vegas, Nev. (cardiac arrest). Black professional prize fighter and screen actor. Known as "The Brown Bomber."

Appeared in: **1937** The Holy Terror; Spirit of Youth. **1943** This is the Army. **1947** The Fight Never Ends. **1955** The Square Jungle. **1970** The Phynx; The Super Fight.

LOUIS, WILLARD
Born: 1886. Died: July 22, 1926, Glendale, Calif. (typhoid fever and pneumonia). Screen and stage actor.

Appeared in: **1920** Going Some; Madame X. **1921** Moonlight and Honeysuckle; Roads of Destiny. **1922** The Man Unconquerable; Robin Hood; Too Much Wife; Only a Shop Girl. **1923** Vanity Fair; McGuire of the Mounted; Daddies; The French Doll; The Marriage Market. **1924** Beau Brummell; Babbitt; The Lover of Camille; Three Women; Pal O' Mine; A Lady of Quality; The Age of Innocence; Broadway After Dark; Don't Doubt Your Husband; Her Marriage Vow. **1925** A Broadway Butterfly; Eve's Lover; Kiss Me Again; Three Weeks in Paris; The Man Without a Conscience; His Secretary; Hogan's Alley; The Limited Mail; The Love Hour. **1926** Mlle. Modiste; Don Juan; The Honeymoon Express; The Love Toy; The Shamrock Handicap; The Passionate Quest. **1928** A Certain Young Man.

LOUISE, ANITA (Anita Louise Fremault)
Born: Jan. 9, 1915, New York, N.Y. Died: Apr. 25, 1970, West Los Angeles, Calif. (massive stroke). Screen, stage and television actress. Married to producer Buddy Adler (dec.) and later to importer Henry Berger.

Appeared in: **1920** The Sixth Commandment (film debut at age 5). **1922** Down to the Sea in Ships. **1924** Lend Me Your Husband. **1927** The Music Master; The Life of Franz Schubert (short). **1928** Four Devils; A Woman of Affairs. **1929** Wonder of Women; Square Shoulders; The Marriage Playground. **1930** The Floradora Girl; What a Man!; Just Like Heaven; The Third Alarm. **1931** The Great Meadow; Heaven on Earth; Everything's Rosie; Millie; Madame Julie; Marriage Interlude; Fraternity House; Are These Our Children?; The Woman Between. **1932** Pack Up Your Troubles; Phantom of Crestwood; Duck Soup. **1933** Little Women; Our Betters. **1934** The Most Precious Thing in Life; Are We Civilized?; Madame Du Barry; The Firebrand; Cross Streets; Bachelor of Arts; I Give My Love; Judge Priest. **1935** Here's to Romance; Personal Maid's Secret; Midsummer Night's Dream; Lady Tubbs; The Story of Louis Pasteur. **1936** Anthony Adverse; Brides Are Like That. **1937** The Go Getter; That Certain Woman; Green Lights; Call It a Day; First Lady; Tovarich. **1938** Going Places; Marie Antoinette; My Bill; The Sisters. **1939** These Glamour Girls; Reno; The Little Princess; The Gorilla; Main Street Lawyer; Hero for a Day; The Personality Kid. **1940** Glamour for Sale; Wagons Westward; The Villain Still Pursued Her. **1941** Harmon of Michigan; Two in a Taxi; The Phantom Submarine. **1943** Dangerous Blondes. **1944** Nine Girls; Cassanova Brown. **1945** Love Letters; The Fighting Guardsman. **1946** The Bandit of Sherwood Forest; The Devil's Mask; The Swan Song; Shadowed; Personality Kid. **1947** Bulldog Drummond at Bay; Blondie's Holiday; Blondie's Big Moment. **1952** Retreat, Hell!.

LOVE, DOROTHY
Born: 1904. Died: Nov. 27, 1979, Los Angeles, Calif. (cancer). Screen, television actress, radio director, radio producer and drama coach.

Appeared in: **1974** Caged Heat. **1975** Aloha, Bobby and Rose. **1977** The Incredible Melting Man.

LOVE, LAURA
Died: Date unknown. Screen actress. Married to actor Henry Belmar (dec. 1931).

LOVE, MABEL
Born: Oct. 16, 1874, England. Died: May 15, 1953, Waybridge, England. Screen, stage and vaudeville actress.

LOVE, MONTAGU (aka MONTAGUE LOVE)
Born: 1877, Portsmouth, England. Died: May 17, 1943, Beverly Hills, Calif. Screen, stage and vaudeville actor.

Appeared in: **1914** The Suicide Club. **1916** A Woman's Way; Bought and Paid For. **1917** Rasputin; The Black Monk. **1919** The Gilded Cage. **1920** The World and His Wife. **1921** The Case of Becky; The Wrong Woman; Forever; Love's Redemption; Shams of Society. **1922** What's Wrong With the Woman?; The Beauty Shop; The Darling of the Rich; The Secrets of Paris. **1923** The Eternal City; The Leopardess. **1924** Restless Wives; Week End Husbands; Roulette; Who's Cheating?; Love of Women; A Son of the Sahara; Sinners in Heaven. **1925** The Mad Marriage; The Ancient Highway; The Desert's Price. **1926** Hands Up!; Don Juan; Brooding Eyes; The Son of the Sheik; The Social Highwayman; The Silent Lover; Out of the Storm. **1927** The Night of Love; Good Time Charley; The Haunted Ship; King of Kings; Jesse James; One Hour of Love; Rose of the Golden West; The Tender Hour. **1928** The Haunted House; The Devil's Skipper; The Hawk's Nest; The Wind; The Noose; Character Studies (short). **1929** The Divine Lady; Her Private Life; A Most Immoral Lady; Synthetic Sin; The Mysterious Island; Charming Sinners; Midstream; Bulldog Drummond; The Last Warning; Silks and Saddles; The Voice Within. **1930** Back Pay; A Notorious Affair; Double Cross Roads; Reno; Inside the Lines; Outward Bound; Love Comes Along; The Cat Creeps; Kismit; The Furies. **1931** Alexander Hamilton; Lion and the Lamb. **1932** The Bride's Bereavement or Snake in the Grass (short); Stowaway; The Fighting Tornado; Vanity Fair; The Silver Lining; Midnight Lady; The Broadway Tornado; Love Bond; Dream Mother; The Engineer's Daughter; Out of Singapore. **1933** His Double Life. **1934** The Menace; Limehouse Blues. **1935** Clive of India; The Crusades; The Man Who Broke the Bank at Monte Carlo. **1936** The Country Doctor; Sing, Baby, Sing; Reunion; Lloyds of London; One in a Million; Sutter's Gold; The White Angel; Hi Gaucho; Champagne Charlie. **1937** The Prince and the Pauper; The Life of Emile Zola; Tovarich; Parnell; London By Night; The Prisoner of Zenda; Adventure's End; A Damsel in Distress. **1938** Fighting Devil Dogs (serial); The Buccaneer; The Adventures of Robin Hood; Professor

Beware; If I Were King; Kidnapped. **1939** Gunga Din; Ruler of the Seas; Man in the Iron Mask; Juarez; We Are Not Alone. **1940** Son of Monte Cristo; Northwest Passage; A Dispatch from Reuter's; The Lone Wolf Strikes; Private Affairs; Hudson's Bay; Dr. Ehrlich's Magic Bullet; Northwest Mounted Police; All This and Heaven Too; The Mark of Zorro; The Sea Hawk. **1941** The Devil and Miss Jones; Shining Victory; Lady for a Night. **1942** Devotion; Tennessee Johnson; The Remarkable Andrew; Sherlock Holmes and the Voice of Terror. **1943** Forever and a Day; Constant Nymph; Holy Matrimony.

LOVE, ROBERT
Born: 1914. Died: July 8, 1948, Hollywood, Calif. (suicide—leap). Screen actor.

Appeared in: **1945** Counterattack; Blonde from Brooklyn.

LOVEJOY, FRANK
Born: Mar. 28, 1914, New York, N.Y. Died: Oct. 2, 1962, New York, N.Y. (heart attack). Screen, stage, radio and television actor. Married to actress Joan Banks.

Appeared in: **1948** Black Bart. **1949** Home of the Brave. **1950** Three Secrets; Breakthrough; South Sea Sinner; In a Lonely Place. **1951** Force of Arms; I Was a Communist for the FBI; Goodby, My Fancy; Starlift; I'll See You in My Dreams; Try and Get Me. **1952** Retreat, Hell!; The Winning Team. **1953** The Hitch Hiker; House of Wax; The System; She's Back on Broadway; The Charge at Feather River. **1954** Beachhead; Men of the Fighting Lady. **1955** The Americano; Strategic Air Command; Mad at the World; Top of the World; Finger Man; The Crooked Web; Shack Out on 101. **1956** Julie; Country Husband. **1957** Three Brave Men. **1958** Cole Younger, Gunfighter.

LOVELL, LEIGH
Born: 1872, England. Died: Aug. 3, 1935, England. Screen, stage and radio actor.

LOVELL, RAYMOND
Born: Apr. 13, 1900, Montreal, Canada. Died: Oct. 2, 1953, London, England. Screen, stage actor and stage director.

Appeared in: **1934** Love, Life and Laughter; The Third Clue; Warn London. **1935** The Case of Gabriel Perry; Some Day; Crime Unlimited; Sexton Blake annd the Mademoiselle. **1936** King of the Damned; Not So Dusty; Gypsy Melody; Fair Exchange; Gaol Break; Troubled Waters. **1937** Secret Lives (aka I Married a Spy—US 1938); Midnight Menace (aka Bombs Over London—US 1939); Glamorous Night; Mademoiselle Docteur; Behind Your Back. **1938** Murder Tomorrow. **1939** Q Planes (aka Clouds Over Europe—US). **1940** Contraband (aka Blackout—US). **1941** He Found a Star; The Common Touch; 49th Parallel (aka The Invaders—US 1942). **1942** Alibi; The Young Mr. Pitt; The Goose Steps Out; Uncensored (US 1944). **1943** Candlelight in Algeria (US 1944); Warn That Man; The Man in Grey (US 1945). **1944** The Way Ahead (US 1945); Hotel Reserve (US 1946). **1946** Caesar and Cleopatra; Night Boat to Dublin; Appointment With Crime (US 1950). **1947** End of the River (US 1948). **1948** Easy Money; Who Killed Van Loon?; The Three Weird Sisters; So Evil My Love; My Brother's Keeper (US 1949); The Blind Goddess (US 1949); Quartet; The Calendar; But Not in Vain. **1949** Once Upon a Dream; Fools Rush In; The Bad Lord Byron (US 1952); Madness of the Heart (US 1950); The Romantic Age (aka Naughty Arlette—US 1951). **1950** The Mudlark. **1952** Time Gentlemen Please!; The Pickwick Papers. **1953** The Steel Key.

LOVELY, LOUISE (Louise Corbasse)
Born: 1896, Sydney, Australia. Died: Mar. 18, 1980, Hobart, Australia. Screen, stage and vaudeville actress. Divorced from film director Wilton Welsh, and later married to theatre manager Bert Cowen.

Appeared in: **1917** The Field of Honor; The Reed Case; Sirens of the Sea; The Wolf and His Mate. **1919** Wings of the Morning; Wolves of the Night; The Last of the Duanes. **1920** The Skywayman; The Joyous Troublemaker; Twins of Sufferings Creek; The Orphan; The Third Woman; The Butterfly Man. **1921** The Poverty of Riches; Partners of Fate; While the Devil Laughs; The Old Nest; The Heart of the North. **1922** Shattered Idols; Life's Greatest Question.

LOVERIDGE, MARGUERITE See MARSH, MARGUERITE

LOVSKY, CELIA
Born: 1897, Vienna, Austria. Died: Oct. 12, 1979, Los Angeles, Calif. Screen, stage and television actress. Divorced from actor Peter Lorre (dec. 1964).

Appeared in: **1947** The Foxes of Harrow. **1948** The Snake Pit; Sealed Verdict; Letter From an Unknown Woman. **1949** Flaming Fury. **1950**

Captain Carey, U.S.A.; The Killer That Stalked New York. **1951** Night Into Morning; The Scarf. **1952** Because You're Mine. **1954** The Last Time I Saw Paris; Rhapsody; Three Coins in the Fountain. **1955** New York Confidential; Texas Lady; Foxfire; Duel on the Mississippi. **1956** Rumble of the Docks; Death of a Scoundrel; The Opposite Sex. **1957** Trooper Hook; The Garment Jungle; Man of a Thousand Faces. **1958** Crash Landing; Me and the Colonel; Twilight for the Gods; I, Mobster. **1959** The Gene Krupa Story. **1962** Hitler. **1965** Harlow; 36 Hours; The Greatest Story Ever Told. **1967** The St. Valentine's Day Massacre. **1968** The Power. **1975** Airport.

LOW, JACK
Born: 1898. Died: Feb. 21, 1958, Hollywood, Calif. Screen and television actor. Entered films approx. 1930.

Appeared in: **1956** The Proud Ones.

LOWE, BARBARA
Died: May 23, 1976. Screen actress.

Appeared in: **1964** Lilith.

LOWE, EDMUND
Born: Mar. 3, 1892, San Jose, Calif. Died: Apr. 21, 1971, Woodland Hills, Calif. (lung ailment). Screen, stage and television actor. Married to actress Lilyan Tashman (dec. 1934) and later married and divorced designer Rita Kaufman and actress Ester Miller.

Appeared in: **1915** The Wild Olive. **1917** The Spreading Dawn. **1918** Vive La France. **1919** Eyes of Youth. **1921** The Devil; My Lady's Latchkey. **1922** Living Lies; Peacock Alley. **1923** The Silent Command; The White Flower; In the Palace of the King; Wife in Name Only. **1924** Barbara Frietchie; Honor Among Men; The Brass Bowl; Nellie, the Beautiful Cloak Model. **1925** The Winding Stair; Soul Mates; The Kiss Barrier; Marriage in Transit; Greater Than a Crown; East Lynne; Ports of Call; The Fool; Champion of Lost Causes; East of Suez. **1926** What Price Glory?; Black Paradise; Soul Mates; The Palace of Pleasure; Siberia. **1927** Is Zat So?; Publicity Madness; Baloo; One Increasing Purpose; The Wizard. **1928** Happiness Ahead; Dressed to Kill; Outcast. **1929** Cock Eyed World; Making the Grade; In Old Arizona; This Thing Called Love; Thru Different Eyes. **1930** Good Intentions; Born Reckless; The Painted Angel; The Bad One; Happy Days; Men on Call; More Than a Kiss; Scotland Yard; Part Time Wife; The Squealer; The Shepper—Newfounder. **1931** Women of All Nations; The Spider; The Cisco Kid; Don't Bet on Women; Transatlantic. **1932** Attorney for the Defense; Guilty As Hell; The Misleading Lady; American Madness; Chandu, the Magician; The Devil Is Driving; The Slippery Pears (short). **1933** Hot Pepper; I Love That Man; Her Bodyguard; Dinner at Eight. **1934** Let's Fall in Love; No More Women; Bombay Mail; Gift of Gab. **1935** Under Pressure; La Fiesta de Santa Barbara (short); The Great Hotel Murder; Black Sheep; Mr. Dynamite; The Best Man Wins; Thunder in the Night; King Solomon of Broadway; The Great Impersonation. **1936** The Grand Exit; The Wrecker; The Garden Murder Case; Mad Holiday; Doomed Cargo; The Girl on the Front Page; Seven Sinners. **1937** Under Cover of Night; Espionage; The Squeakers (aka Murder on Diamond Row—US); Every Day's a Holiday. **1938** Secrets of a Nurse. **1939** The Witness Vanishes; Our Neighbors, the Carters; Newsboys' Home. **1940** The Crooked Road; Honeymoon Deferred; I Love You Again; Men Against the Sky; Wolf of New York. **1941** Double Date; Flying Cadets. **1942** Call Out the Marines; Klondike Fury. **1943** Dangerous Blonde; Oh, What a Night!; Murder in Times Square. **1944** The Girl in the Case. **1945** Dillinger; The Enchanted Forest; The Great Mystic. **1946** The Strange Mr. Gregory. **1948** Good Sam. **1956** Around the World in 80 Days. **1957** The Wings of Eagles. **1958** The Last Hurrah. **1959** Plunderers of Painted Flats. **1960** Heller in Pink Tights.

LOWE, JAMES B.
Born: 1880. Died: May 18, 1963, Hollywood, Calif. Screen and stage actor.

Appeared in: **1925** The Demon Rider. **1926** Blue Blazes. **1927** Uncle Tom's Cabin.

LOWE, K. ELMO
Born: 1900. Died: Jan. 26, 1971, Cleveland, Ohio (stroke). Screen, stage actor and stage director. Married to actress Dorothy Paxton.

Appeared in: **1949** The Kid from Cleveland. **1950** Trial Without Jury; Woman from Headquarters.

LOWELL, DOROTHY
Born: 1916. Died: July 1, 1944, New York. Screen and radio actress. Entered films approx. 1936.

LOWELL, HELEN (Helen Lowell Robb)
Born: June 2, 1866, New York, N.Y. Died: June 28, 1937, Hollywood, Calif. Screen and stage actress.

Appeared in: **1923** Love's Old Sweet Song. **1924** Three Days to Live; Isn't Life Wonderful? **1934** Midnight Alibi; Side Street; The Dragon Murder Case; Madame du Barry; The Merry Frinks; Big Hearted Herbert; The Case of the Howling Dog. **1935** Maybe It's Love; Transient Lady; Devil Dogs of the Air; Page Miss Glory; The Goose and the Gander; Dr. Socrates; Living on Velvet; Party Wire. **1936** Strike Me Pink; Snowed Under; I'd Give My Life; Valiant is the Word for Carrie; Wild Brian Kent. **1937** Four Days Wonder; Racketeers in Exile; The Party Getter; High, Wide and Handsome.

LOWELL, JOAN (aka HELEN TRASK)
Born: 1900. Died: Nov. 7, 1967, Brasilia, Brazil. Screen, stage actress and author.

Appeared in: **1924** Loving Lies. **1925** Cold Nerve. **1934** Adventure Girl.

LOWELL, JOHN (John L. Russell)
Died: Sept. 19, 1937, Los Angeles, Calif. Screen actor and film director.

Appeared in: **1922** Ten Nights in a Barroom. **1923** Lost in a Big City. **1924** Floodgates. **1925** Red Love. **1926** The Big Show. **1928** Silent Trail; Headin' Westward. **1929** Bad Men's Money; Captain Cowboy; Fighters of the Saddle.

LOWENADLER, HOLGER
Born: 1904, Sweden. Died: June 18, 1977, Sweden? Screen and stage actor.

Appeared in: **1944** Himlaspelet. **1949** Frustration. **1966** Har har du Ditt Liv (Here's Your Life—US 1968). **1967** Jag ar Nyfiken—Gul (I Am Curious (Yellow)—US 1969). **1974** Lacombe Lucien. **1976** Maitresse.

LOWERY, ROBERT (Robert Lowery Hanks)
Born: 1914, Kansas City, Mo. Died: Dec. 26, 1971, Hollywood, Calif. (heart attack). Screen, stage, television actor and singer. Divorced from actresses Vivian Wilcox, Rusty Farrell and Jean Parker.

Appeared in: **1936** Great Guy. **1937** Second Honeymoon; Wife, Doctor and Nurse; You Can't Have Everything; Wake Up and Live; Life Begins in College. **1938** Passport Husband; Submarine Patrol; Alexander's Ragtime Band; Four Men and a Prayer; Happy Landing. **1939** Daytime Wife; Irving Berlin's Second Fiddle; Wife, Husband and Friend; Young Mr. Lincoln; Charlie Chan in Reno; Hollywood Cavalcade; Drums Along the Mowhawk; Mr. Moto in Danger Island; Tail Spin. **1940** City of Chance; Free, Blonde and Twenty-One; Shooting High; Star Dust; Charlie Chan's Murder Cruise; Four Sons; Maryland; The Mark of Zorro; Murder Over New York. **1941** Private Nurse; Ride On, Vaquero!; Cadet Girls; Great Guns. **1942** Who Is Hope Schuyler?; She's in the Army; Criminal Investigator; Lure of the Islands; Rhythm Parade; Dawn on the Great Divide. **1943** The Immortal Sergeant; Tarzan's Desert Mystery; So's Your Uncle; The North Star; Campus Rhythm; Revenge of the Zombies. **1944** The Navy Way; Hot Rhythm; Dark Mountain; Dangerous Passage; The Mummy's Ghost; Mystery of the River Boat (serial); A Scream in the Dark. **1945** Thunderbolt; Homesick Angel; Road to Alcatraz; Fashion Model; High Powered; Prison Ship; The Monster and the Ape (serial). **1946** Sensation Hunters; They Made Me a Killer; House of Horrors; God's Country; Lady Chaser; The Gas House Kids. **1947** Big Town; Danger Street; I Cover Big Town; Killer at Large; Queen of the Amazons; Jungle Flight. **1948** Death Valley; Mary Lou; Heart of Virginia; Highway 13. **1949** Shep Comes Home; Arson, Inc.; The Dalton Gang; Batman and Robin (serial); New Adventures of Batman (serial); Call of the Forest. **1950** Gunfire; Border Rangers; Western Pacific Agent; Train to Tombstone; Everybody's Dancing. **1951** Crosswinds. **1953** Jalopy; Cow Country; The Homesteaders. **1955** Lay That Rifle Down. **1956** Two Gun Lady. **1957** The Parson and the Outlaw. **1960** The Rise and Fall of Legs Diamond. **1962** When the Girls Take Over; Deadly Duo; Young Guns of Texas. **1963** McClintock! **1964** Stage to Thunder Rock. **1965** A Zebra in the Kitchen. **1966** Johnny Reno; Waco; Pride of Virginia. **1967** The Adventures of Batman and Robin; The Undertaker and His Pals; The Ballad of Josie.

LOWERY, WILLIAM
Born: July 22, 1885, St. Louis, Mo. Died: Nov. 15, 1941, Calif. Screen and stage actor.

Appeared in: **1914** The Ten of Spades. **1915** The Lamb. **1916** The Toll of the Law. **1917** The Spy; The Man from the Painted Post. **1921** The

Nut; The Primal Law. **1922** Robin Hood; Pals of the West. **1923** Why Women Re-Marry; Dangerous Trails; Men in the Raw; McGuire of the Mounted. **1924** Battling Buddy; Thundering Hoofs. **1925** Makers of Men; A Daughter of the Sioux; Red Hot Tires; Tricks. **1926** Crossed Signals; The Call of the Klondike; Faithful Wives. **1928** The Haunted Ship.

LOWRY, JUDITH (Judith Ives)
Born: July 27, 1890, Ft. Still, Okla. or Morristown, N.J.?. Died: Nov. 29, 1976, New York, N.Y. (heart attack). Screen, stage and television actress. Married to actor Rudd Lowry (dec. 1965).

Appeared in: **1946** 13 Rue Madeleine. **1962** The Miracle Worker. **1963** Ladybug, Ladybug. **1965** Andy. **1966** The Trouble With Angels. **1967** The Tiger Makes Out; Valley of the Dolls. **1968** The Night They Raided Minsky's. **1969** Popi; Sweet Charity. **1970** Husbands; On a Clear Day You Can See Forever. **1971** The Anderson Tapes; Cold Turkey. **1973** The Effect of Gamma Rays on Man-in-the-Moon Marigolds. **1974** Superdad.

LOWRY, RUDD
Born: 1892. Died: Dec. 15, 1965, New York, N.Y. Screen, stage and television actor. Married to actress Judith Ives Lowry (dec. 1976).

LUAHINE, IOLANI
Born: 1915, Anpoopoo, Hawaii. Died: Dec. 11, 1978, Hawaii. Screen actress and dancer.

Appeared in: **1978** A documentary featuring Hawaiian hula dancing and chants.

LUBETTY, MADELINE
Died: Sept., 1968, Miami, Fla. Screen and stage actress.

Appeared in: **1922** Cardigan.

LUBITSCH, ERNST
Born: Jan. 28, 1892, Berlin, Germany. Died: Nov. 30, 1947, Los Angeles, Calif. (heart attack). Screen, stage actor, film producer, film director and screenwriter. Entered films in 1913.

Appeared in: **1913** Bedingung; Kein Anhang; Die Firma Heiratet; Meyer auf der Alm. **1914** Venezianische Nacht; Fraulein Piccolo; Die Ideale Gattin; Serenissimus Lernt Tango; Der Stolz der Firma; Blinde Kuh; Fraulein Seifenschaum; Meyer als Soldat. **1915** Auf Eis Gefuehrt; Robert und Bertram; Zucker und Zimt. **1916** Dr. Satansohn; Der Gemischte Frauenchor; Der Erste Patient; Der GmbH-Tenor; Leutnant auf Befehl; Schuhpalast Pinkus; Der Schwarze Moritz Wo ist Mein Schatz? **1917** Der Blusenkoenig; Hans Trutz im Schlaraffenland; Der Kraftmeyer; Ossis Tagebuch; Prinz Sami; Der Letzte Anzug; Venn Vier Dasselbe Tun. **1918** Der Fall Rosentopf; Der Rodelkavalier. **1919** Meyer aus Berlin. **1920** Kohlhiesels Toechter. **1923** Souls for Sale. **1933** Mr. Broadway.

LUBY, EDNA
Born: 1891, N.Y. Died: Oct. 1, 1928, New York, N.Y. Screen and stage actress.

Appeared in: **1913** Shadows; The Ganster; Just Nobody. **1916** Immortal Flame.

LUCAN, ARTHUR (Arthur Towle)
Born: 1887, England. Died: May 17, 1954, Hull, England. Screen, stage and vaudeville actor. Married to actress Kitty McShane (dec. 1964) with whom he appeared in vaudeville and films in an act billed as "Lucan and McShane." The two played in "Old Mother Riley" series of films, Lucan playing the mother and his wife playing the daughter.

They appeared in: **1936** Kathleen Mavourneen (aka Kathleen—US 1938; Stars on Parade. **1937** Old Mother Riley. **1938** Old Mother Riley in Paris. **1939** Old Mother Riley MP; Old Mother Riley Joins Up. **1940** Old Mother Riley in Business; Old Mother Riley in Society. **1941** Old Mother Riley's Circus; Old Mother Riley's Ghosts. **1942** Old Mother Riley Catches a Quisling (reissue of Old Mother Riley in Paris—1938). **1943** Old Mother Riley Overseas. **1945** Old Mother Riley at Home. **1949** Old Mother Riley's New Venture. **1950** Old Mother Riley, Headmistress (US 1951). **1951** Old Mother Riley's Jungle Treasure. **1952** Mother Riley Meets the Vampire (aka Vampire Over London—US, without McShane).

LUCAS, JIMMY
Born: 1888. Died: Feb. 21, 1949, Hollywood, Calif. (heart attack). Screen, vaudeville actor and song writer.

Appeared in: **1942** My Heart Belongs to Daddy; Call of the Canyon; Saboteur. **1943** Strictly in the Groove.

LUCAS, SAM
Born: 1841. Died: Jan. 10, 1916, New York, N.Y. Black screen actor.

Appeared in: **1914** Uncle Tom's Cabin.

LUCAS, WILFRED
Born: 1871, Ontario, Canada. Died: Dec. 13, 1940, Los Angeles, Calif. Screen, stage actor, film director and screenwriter. Entered films with Biograph Co. in 1907.

Appeared in: **1908** The Barbarian; Ingomar. **1909** 1776, or the Hession Renegades. **1910** Fisher Folks; The Lonedale Operator; Winning Back His Love; His Trust; His Trust Fulfilled; Heart Beats of Long Ago; The Diamond Star. **1911** Was He a Coward?; The Spanish Gypsy; His Mother's Scarf; The New Dress; Enoch Arden, Part I and Part II; The Primal Call; The White Rose of the Wild; The Indian Brother; The Thief and the Girl; The Rose of Kentucky; The Sorrowful Example; Swords and Hearts; The Old Confectioner's Mistake; Dan and Dandy; Italian Blood; A Woman Scorned; The Miser's Heart; The Failure; As in a Looking Glass; A Terrible Discovery; The Transformation of Mike; Billy's Stratagem. **1912** Under Burning Skies; Fate's Interception; Just Like a Woman; When Kings Were the Law; Man's Genesis; A Pueblo Legend; The Massacre; The Girl and Her Trust. **1913** Cohen's Outing. **1916** Acquitted; The Wild Girl of the Sierras; Hell-to-Pay Austin. **1919** The Westerners. **1921** The Beautiful Liar; The Breaking Point; The Fighting Breed; The Better Man; Through the Back Door; The Shadow of Lightning Ridge. **1922** The Kentucky Derby; Barriers of Folly; Flesh and Blood; Across the Dead-Line; Paid Back; The Barnstormer; Heroes of the Street. **1923** Can a Woman Love Twice?; Jazzmania; Trilby; The Girl of the Golden West; The Greatest Menace; Innocence; Why Women Remarry. **1924** The Fatal Mistake; Daughters of Pleasure; Racing for Life; Women First; Cornered; The Valley of Hate; The Price She Paid; Dorothy Vernon of Haddon Hall; A Fight for Honor; Lightning Romance; The Fighting Sap; Girls Men Forget; North of Nevada; Passion's Pathway; On Probation; The Mask of Lopez. **1925** Easy Money; How Baxter Butted In; The Snob Buster; The Bad Lands; Youth's Gamble; Cyclone Cavalier; A Broadway Butterfly; The Wife Who Wasn't Wanted; Was It Bigamy?; Riders of the Purple Sage; The Man Without a Country. **1926** Her Sacrifice. **1927** The Nest; Burnt Fingers. **1930** One Good Deed (short); Hello Sister; Madame Satan; Looser Than Loose (short); The Arizona Kid; Those Who Dance; Cock of the Walk; Just Imagine. **1931** Big Ears (short); The Age for Love; House of Mystery ("Shadow" detective series); The Phantom; Convicted; Homicide Squad; His Woman; Caught; Politics; Pardon Us; Le Petit Cafe; Dishonored; Young Donovan's Kid; Are These Our Children?; Thirty Days; Men Call It Love; Rich Man's Folly; Millie. **1932** Silver Dollar; Cross Examination; Midnight Patrol; The Tenderfoot; The Unwritten Law; plus the following shorts: Free Wheeling; The Tabasco Kid; Red Noses. **1933** Sister to Judas; Lucky Larrigan; The Intruder; Fra Diavolo (aka The Devil's Brother); Phantom Thunderbolt; The Big Cage; The Sphinx; Day of Reckoning; I Cover the Waterfront; Notorious but Nice; Breed of the Border; Racetrack; Strange People; The Major of Hell. **1934** Cleopatra; Count of Monte Cristo; Shrimps for a Day (short); The Chases of Pimple Street (short); The Moth; Sweden, Land of Vikings (narr.). **1935** Frisco Kid. **1936** The Story of Louis Pasteur; The Charge of the Light Brigade; Black Legion; The Country Doctor; Modern Times; Chatterbox; Mary of Scotland; We Who Are About to Die. **1937** Mile a Minute Love; Dizzy Doctors (short); Criminal Lawyer; The Perfect Specimen. **1938** Angels With Dirty Faces; Crime Afloat; The Baroness and the Butler; Each Dawn I Die; Dodge City; Zenobia. **1940** A Chump at Oxford; Ragtime Cowboy Joe; Triple Justice; Brother Orchid; The Fighting 69th; Virginia City; Santa Fe Trail; Raffles. **1941** The Sea Wolf. **1949** It's a Great Feeling.

LUCHAIRE, CORINNE
Born: 1921, France. Died: Jan. 22, 1950, Paris, France. Screen and stage actress.

Appeared in English and French versions of: **1939** Prison Without Bars; The Affair Lafont (Conflict). **1944** Three Hours.

LUCK, ROBERT "LUCKY"
Died: Feb. 11, 1977. Screen actor.

Appeared in: **1961** The Devil at 4 O'Clock. **1968** Kona Coast.

LUCY, ARNOLD
Born: 1865, Tottenham, England. Died: Dec. 15, 1945. Screen and stage actor. Entered films in 1915.

Appeared in: **1916** The Devil's Toy; Merely Mary Ann. **1917** In Again—Out Again. **1920** In Search of a Sinner; Love Expert. **1921** School Days; You Find It Everywhere. **1922** Fair Lady. **1923** Modern Marriage; Little Old New York. **1929** The Ghost Talks; Masquerade; The One Woman Idea. **1930** All Quiet on the Western Front; City Girl; Manslaughter; Scotland Yard; The Princess and the Plumber. **1931** Merely Mary Ann (and the 1916 version). **1932** Dr. Jekyll and Mr. Hyde; Lady With a Past; Alias the Doctor; Guilty as Hell; Sherlock Holmes. **1933** The Wandering Jew (US 1935). **1935** Midshipman Easy (aka Men of the Sea—US). **1937** Victoria the Great.

LUDDEN, ALLEN

Born: 1918, Mineral Point, Wis. Died: June 10, 1981, Los Angeles, Calif. (cancer). Screen, radio, television actor, radio director, radio producer and author. Married to actress Betty White.

Appeared in: **1976** Futureworld.

LUDDY, BARBARA

Born: 1908. Died: Apr. 1, 1979, Los Angeles, Calif. (lung cancer). Screen, stage, radio actress and singer. Known in radio as "Baby Barbara."

Appeared in: **1925** Rose of the World; Sealed Lips. **1927** Wilful Youth. **1928** See You Later. **1930** Headin' North. **1933** Her Secret. **1955** Lady and the Tramp (voice). **1961** One Hundred and One Dalmations (voice). **1963** Terrified! **1970** Lost Flight.

LUEDERS, GUENTHER

Born: 1905, Germany. Died: Mar. 1, 1975, Duesseldorf, Germany (cancer). Screen, stage, television actor and stage director.

Appeared in: **1935** Fraulein Liselott. **1938** Dell Etappenhase; Musketier Meir III. **1958** Das Wirthaus in Spessart (The Spessart Inn—US 1961). **1960** Eternal Love.

LUFKIN, HARLAN W.

Born: 1918. Died: Mar. 13, 1980, Los Angeles, Calif. (cancer). Screen, stage and television actor.

LUFKIN, SAM (Samuel William Lufkin)

Born: May 8, 1892, Utah. Died: Feb. 19, 1952, Los Angeles, Calif. (uremia). Screen and stage actor.

Appeared in: **1924** The Battling Orioles. **1926** The Fighting Boob. **1927** Sugar Daddies; Hats Off; The Battle of the Century. **1928** Leave 'Em Laughing; The Finishing Touch; From Soup to Nuts; Their Purple Moment; Should Married Men Go Home?; Two Tars. **1929** Confessions of a Wife; Liberty; Wrong Again; That's My Wife; Double Whoopee; They Go Boom; Bacon Grabbers; The Hoose-Gow (short). **1930** The Shepper-Newfounder; Part Time Wife; The Big Kick (short). **1931** Pardon Us; Beau Hunks; Call a Cop (short). **1932** The following shorts: Any Old Port; The Music Box; County Hospital; Scram. **1933** Sons of the Desert. **1934** Going Bye-Bye (short); Them Thar Hills; Babes in Toyland; The Live Ghost (short). **1935** Bonnie Scotland; It Always Happens (short); The Mystery Man. **1936** The Bohemian Girl; Our Relations; plus the following shorts: The Lucky Corner; Am I Having Fun; Life Hesitates at 40. **1937** Way Out West; Pick a Star; Grips, Grunts and Groans (short); Boots and Saddles (short). **1938** Swiss Miss; Blockheads. **1939** The Flying Deuces. **1940** A Chump at Oxford; Saps at Sea.

LUGG, WILLIAM

Born: June 4, 1852, Portsea, Portsmouth, England. Died: 1940, England? Screen and stage actor.

Appeared in: **1921** The Old Curiosity Shop. **1923** Becket.

LUGOSI, BELA (Bela Lugosi Blasko aka ARISZTID OLT)

Born: Oct. 20, 1882, Lugos, Hungary. Died: Aug. 16, 1956, Hollywood, Calif. (heart attack). Screen and stage actor. Entered films in Budapest in 1915.

Appeared in: **1917** Lulu; A Leopard; Az Elet Kiralya; Tavaszi; Alarcosbal; Az Ezredes. **1918** Casanova; Kuzdelem a Letert; 99. **1919** Nachenschnur des Tot (Necklace of Death); Der Tanz Auf Dem Vulken (Daughters of the Night); Sklaven Fremder Willens; Hamlet. **1920** Szineszno; Die Frau in Delphin; Der Januskopf (aka Dr. Jekyll and Mr. Hyde); Le Dernier des Mohicans (Last of the Mohicans); Hohan Hopkins der Dritte. **1923** Diadalmas; Elet; The Silent Command. **1924** The Rejected Woman; The Daughters Who Pay. **1925** The Midnight Girl; Prisoners. **1928** How to Handle Women; Wild Strawberries. **1929** The Thirteenth Chair; Veiled Woman; Prisoners (and 1925 version). **1930** Renegades; Wild Company; Such Men Are Dangerous; Oh, for a Man!; Viennese Nights. **1931** Fifty Million Frenchmen; Women of All Nations; Dracula; The Black Camel; Broadminded. **1932** Murders in the Rue Morgue; White Zombie; Chandu the Magician; The Phantom Creeps (serial); The Yellow Phantom (serial). **1933** Whispering Shadows (serial); Island of Lost Souls; The Death Kiss; International House; Night of Terror. **1934** Return of Chandu (serial); The Black Cat; The Gift of Gab. **1935** Best Man Wins; Mysterious Mr. Wong; The Mystery of the Mary Celeste (aka Phantom Ship—US 1937); Mandrake the Magician (serial). **1936** Screen Snapshots #11 (short); Shadow of Chinatown (serial); The Invisible Ray; Dracula's Daughter; Postal Inspector. **1937** SOS Coast Guard (serial); Blake of Scotland Yard (serial). **1938** Killer Rats. **1939** The Phantom Creeps (serial); Son of Frankenstein; Dark Eyes of

London (aka The Human Monster—US 1940); Ninotchka; The Gorilla. **1940** The Saint's Double Trouble; Black Friday; You'll Find Out; Fantasia (voice only). **1941** Devil Bat; The Wolf Man; The Invisible Ghost; Spooks Run Wild. **1942** Black Dragons; The Corpse Vanishes; Night Monster; The Ghost of Frankenstein; Bowery at Midnight; Phantom Killer. **1943** The Ape Man; Ghosts on the Loose; Eyes of the Underworld; Frankenstein Meets the Wolf Man. **1944** Return of the Vampire; Voodoo Man; Return of the Ape Man; One Body Too Many. **1945** Zombies on Broadway; The Body Snatcher. **1946** Genius at Work; My Son, the Vampire. **1947** Scared to Death. **1948** Abbott and Costello Meet Frankenstein. **1949** Master Minds. **1952** Bela Lugosi Meets the Brooklyn Gorilla; Mother Riley Meets the Vampire (aka Vampire Over London—US). **1956** He Lived to Kill; Bride of the Monster; The Black Sheep; The Shadow Creeps. **1959** Plan 9 from Outer Space. **1965** The World of Abbott and Costello (film clips).

LUKAS, PAUL (Paul Lukacs)

Born: May 26, 1895, Budapest, Hungary. Died: Aug. 15, 1971, Tangier, Morocco (heart attack). Screen, stage and television actor. Appeared in both stage and screen versions of Watch on the Rhine, receiving New York Drama League Award for stage role and the 1943 Academy Award for Best Actor in the film version.

Appeared in: **1915** Man of the Earth. **1917** Sphinx; Song of the Heart. **1920** The Yellow Shadow; Little Fox; The Castle Without a Name; The Milliner; The Actress. **1921** Telegram from New York; Love of the 18th Century. **1922** The Lady in Grey; Lady Violette; Samson and Delilah; Eine Versunkene Welten. **1923** The Glorious Life; A Girl's Way. **1928** Loves of an Actress; Three Sinners; The Woman from Moscow; Hot News; Two Lovers; Manhattan Cocktail; The Night Watch. **1929** Illusion; The Wolf of Wall Street; Half Way to Heaven; The Shopworn Angel. **1930** Behind the Make Up; The Benson Murder Case; The Devil's Holiday; Slightly Scarlet; Young Eagles; Grumpy; Anybody's Woman; The Right to Love. **1931** Beloved Bachelor; Women Love Once; Unfaithful; City Streets; Working Girls; Strictly Dishonorable; The Vice Squad. **1932** No One Man; Tomorrow and Tomorrow; Downstairs; Burnt Offering; Rockabye; A Passport to Hell; Thunder Below. **1933** Grand Slam; The Kiss Before the Mirror; Captured!; Sing, Sinner, Sing; The Secret of the Blue Room; Little Women. **1934** By Candlelight; Nagana; The Countess of Monte Cristo; Glamour; Affairs of a Gentleman; I Give My Love; Gift of Gab; The Fountain. **1935** The Casino Murder Case; Father Brown, Detective; The Three Musketeers; I Found Stella Parrish; Age of Indiscretion. **1936** Dodsworth; Ladies in Love. **1937** Brief Ecstasy; Espionage; Dinner at the Ritz; Mutiny on the Elsinore (US 1939). **1938** The Lady Vanishes; Dangerous Secrets; Rebellious Daughters. **1939** Confessions of a Nazi Spy; Captain Fury. **1940** The Ghost Breakers; Strange Cargo; A Window in London. **1941** The Monster and the Girl; The Chinese Den; They Dare Not Love. **1942** Lady in Distress. **1943** Watch on the Rhine; Hostage. **1944** Uncertain Glory; Address Unknown; One Man's Secret; Experiment Perilous. **1946** Deadline at Dawn; Temptation. **1947** Whispering City. **1948** Berlin Express. **1950** Kim. **1954** 20,000 Leagues Under the Sea. **1956** The Chinese Bungalow. **1957** Under Fire. **1958** The Roots of Heaven. **1960** Scent of Mystery. **1962** The Four Horsemen of the Apocalypse; Tender Is the Night. **1963** 55 Days At Peking; Fun in Acapulco. **1965** Lord Jim. **1968** Sol Madrid.

LULLI, FOLCO

Born: 1912, Italy. Died: May 24, 1970, Rome, Italy (heart attack). Screen actor.

Appeared in: **1948** Tragic Hunt. **1949** The Bandit; Flight Into France. **1950** Senza Pieta (Without Pity). **1951** No Peace Among the Olive Trees; Altri Tempi (Times Gone By—US 1953); Luci del Varieta (Variety Lights—US 1965). **1954** Carosello Napoletano (Neapolitan Carousel—US 1961). **1955** Maddalena. **1956** Wages of Fear; Air of Paris; La Risaia (aka La Fille de la Riziere and aka Rice Girl—US 1963). **1959** La Grande Guerra (The Great War—US 1961); Oeil Pour Oeil (An Eye for an Eye); Companions; Sign of the Gladiator; Londra Chiama Polo Nord (London Calling North Pole aka The House of Intrigue); La Grande Speranza (The Great Hope aka Torpedo Zone). **1960** Esther and the King; Under Ten Flags; Always Victorious; The Island Sinner. **1961** La Reine des Barbares (The Huns—US 1962); I Tartari (The Tartars—US 1962); Gli Invasori (Erik the Conqueror—US 1963 aka The Invaders). **1962** La Guerra Continua (Warriors 5—US and aka The War Continues); La Fayette (Lafayette—US 1963); Dulcinea. **1963** I Compagni (The Organizer—US 1964 aka The Strikers). **1964** Parias de Gloire (Pariahs of Glory). **1965** Oltraggio al Pudore (aka Cheating Italian Style and All the Other Girls Do—US 1966); La Fabuleuse Aventure de Marco Polo (Marco the Magnificent—US 1966). **1966** Operazione Goldman (Lightning Bolt—US 1967). **1967** Le Vicomte Regle ses Comptes (The Viscount).

LUNA, DONYALE (Peggy Anne Donyale Aragonea Pegeon Freeman)
Born: 1946, Detroit, Mich. Died: May 17, 1979, Rome, Italy. Black screen actress and model.

Appeared in: **1968** Skidoo; Tonight Let's All Make Love in London. **1969** Fellini-Satyricon (US 1970).

LUNCEFORD, JIMMY (James Melvin Lunceford)
Born: June 6, 1902, Fulton, Mo. Died: July 13, 1947, Seaside, Ore. Orchestra leader, musician, composer and screen actor.

Appeared in: **1941** Blues in the Night.

LUND, GUS A.
Born: 1896. Died: June 5, 1951, Los Angeles, Calif. Screen, stage and television actor.

LUND, RICHARD
Born: 1885, Goteborg, Sweden. Died: Sept. 17, 1960, Sweden. Screen and stage actor.

Appeared in: **1928** The Three Who Were Doomed. Other Swedish films: A Secret Marriage; Smiles and Tears; Lady Marion's Summer Flirtation; The Voice of Blood; On the Fateful Roads of Life; Ingeborg Holm; Life's Conflicts; The Modern Suffragette; The Clergyman Love Stronger than Hate; People of the Border; Because of Her Love; Do Not Judge; Stormy Petrel; A Good Girl Should Solve Her Own Problems; Hearts That Meet; The Strike; The Playmates; It Was in May; His Wife's Past; To Each His Calling; His Father's Crime; The Avenger; The Governor's Daughters; Sea Vultures; His Wedding Night; At the Moment of Trial; The Lucky Brooch; Love and Journalism; The Struggle for His Heart; The Ballet Primadonna; The Architect of One's Own Fortune; Who Fired?; The Jungle Queen's Jewel; The Living Mummy; Sir Arne's Treasure; The Monastery of Sendomir; The Executioner; Family Traditions; The Girls from Are; Carolina Rediviva; The Surrounded House; Life in the Country; A Million Dollars; Uncle Frans; False Svensson; Voice of the Heart; What Do Men Know?; Under False Colours; Walpurgis Night; Conscientious Adolf; Johan Ulfstjerna; He, She and the Money; The "Paradise" Boarding House; A Cold in the Head; Adolf Armstrong; A Rich Man's Son; With the People for the Country; Great Friends and Faithful Neighbours; Nothing But the Truth; Rejoice While You Are Young; The Little WRAC of the Veteran Reserves; Whalers; Steel; Night in June; Kiss Her; A Big Hug; We Are All Errand Boys; The Gentleman Gangster; A Schoolmistress on the Spree; Sextuplets; Life on a Perch; The Knockout Clergyman; Katrina; There Burned a Flame; Frenzy (aka Torment).

LUNDEQUIST, GERDA
Born: 1871. Died: Oct., 1959. Screen actress.

Appeared in: **1956** Giftas (aka Married Life, and aka Of Love and Lust—US 1959).

LUNDIGAN, WILLIAM "BILL"
Born: June 12, 1914, Syracuse, N.Y. Died: Dec. 20, 1975, Duarte, Calif. (lung and heart congestion). Screen, radio and television actor.

Appeared in: **1937** Armored Car (film debut); The Lady Fights Back. **1938** State Police; The Black Doll; Reckless Living; That's My Story; Wives Under Suspicion; Danger on the Air; The Missing Guest; Freshman Year. **1939** Dodge City; They Asked for It; Legion of the Lost Flyers; Three Smart Girls Grow Up; The Old Maid; Forgotten Woman. **1940** The Fighting 69th; Three Cheers for the Irish; The Man Who Talked Too Much; The Sea Hawk; East of the River; Santa Fe Trail; a Vitaphone short. **1941** The Case of the Black Parrot; A Shot in the Dark; The Great Mr. Nobody; Highway West; International Squadron; Sailors on Leave; The Bugle Sounds. **1942** Sunday Punch; The Courtship of Andy Hardy; Apache Trail; Andy Hardy's Double Life; Northwest Rangers. **1943** Dr. Gillespie's Criminal Case; Salute to the Marines; Headin' for God's Country. **1945** What Next, Corporal Hargrove? **1947** The Fabulous Dorseys; Dishonored Lady. **1948** Inside Story; Mystery in Mexico. **1949** Follow Me Quietly; State Department—File 649; Pinky. **1950** I'll Get By; Mother Didn't Tell Me. **1951** I'd Climb the Highest Mountain; Love Nest; House on Telegraph Hill; Elopement. **1953** Down Among the Sheltering Palms; Inferno; Serpent of the Nile. **1954** Riders to the Stars; The White Orchid; Terror Ship. **1962** The Underwater City. **1967** The Way West. **1968** Where Angels Go ... Trouble Follows!

LUNG, CHARLES "CHARLIE"
Died: June 22, 1974. Screen actor.

Appeared in: **1942** Destination Unknown. **1943** Flight for Freedom; Headin' for God's Country; Jack London. **1944** Dragon Seed. **1951** Secrets of Monte Carlo. **1953** Thunder in the East; Siren of Bagdad. **1954** Jivaro. **1955** Ma and Pa Kettle at Waikiki.

LUNT, ALFRED
Born: Aug. 19, 1892, Milwaukee, Wis. Died: Aug. 3, 1977, Chicago, Ill. (cancer). Screen, stage, vaudeville, television actor and stage director. Married to actress Lynn Fontanne. Nominated for 1931/32 Academy Award for Best Actor in The Guardsman.

Appeared in: **1923** The Ragged Edge; Backbone. **1924** Second Youth. **1925** Sally of the Sawdust; The Man Who Found Himself; Lovers in Quarantine. **1931** The Guardsman (stage and film versions). **1943** Stage Door Canteen.

LUPINO, BARRY
Born: Jan. 7, 1882, London, England. Died: Sept. 26, 1962, Brighton, England. Screen, stage actor and pantomime artist. Son of stage actor George Lupino (dec. 1932). Brother of actors Stanley (dec. 1942), and Mark Lupino (dec. 1930).

LUPINO, MARK
Born: 1894. Died: Apr. 4, 1930, London, England. Screen and stage actor. Brother of actors Stanley (dec. 1942) and Barry Lupino (dec. 1962).

Appeared in: **1927** The King's Highway.

LUPINO, STANLEY
Born: June 17, 1893, London, England. Died: June 10, 1942, London, England. Screen, stage actor, screenwriter, playwright, screen and stage producer. Married to stage actress Connie Emerald. Father of actress Ida Lupino and brother of actors Mark (dec. 1930) and Barry Lupino (dec. 1962). Entered films in 1931.

Appeared in: **1931** Love Lies; The Love Race. **1932** Sleepless Nights. **1933** King of the Ritz; Facing the Music (US 1934); You Made Me Love You. **1934** Happy. **1935** Honeymoon for Three. **1936** Cheer Up!; Sporting Love. **1937** Over She Goes (stage and film versions). **1938** Hold My Hand. **1939** Lucky to Me.

LUPINO, WALLACE (aka WALLACE LANE)
Born: Jan. 23, 1898, Edingburgh, Scotland. Died: Oct. 11, 1961, Ashford, England. Screen and stage actor. Brother of actor Lupino Lane (dec. 1959).

Appeared in: **1918** "Kinekature Comedies" series including: The Blunders of Mr. Butterbun; Unexpected Treasure. **1922-33** Educational shorts including Buying a Gun. **1930** The Yellow Mask; Children of Chance. **1931** The Love Race; Love Lies; Aroma of the South Seas; No Lady; Never Trouble Trouble; Bull Rushes. **1932** The Maid of the Mountains; Josser on the River; Old Spanish Customers; The Innocents of Chicago (aka Why Saps Leave Home—US); The Bad Companions. **1933** The Melody Maker; The Stolen Necklace; Forging Ahead; Song Birds. **1934** Master and Man; Bagged; Wishes; Lyde Park. **1935** The Student's Romance; The Deputy Drummer; Trust the Navy. **1936** The Man Who Could Work Miracles (US 1937); Hot News; Shipmates o'Mine; Love Up the Pole. **1937** The First and the Last (aka 21 Days—US 1940). **1939** Me and My Gal (aka The Lambeth Walk—US 1940). **1940** Waterloo Road (US 1949).

LUPO, GEORGE G.
Born: 1924. Died: Aug. 8, 1973, Long Beach, Calif. (massive stroke). Screen and television actor.

LUSK, FREEMAN
Born: 1906. Died: Aug. 25, 1970, Orange, Calif. Screen, radio and television actor.

Appeared in: **1951** Go for Broke; Little Egypt; Half Angel; The Day the Earth Stood Still. **1952** Phone Call from a Stranger; The Pride of St. Louis. **1953** The War of the Worlds; From Here to Eternity; The Caddy. **1955** The Girl Rush. **1966** To the Shores of Hell.

LUTHER, ANN (aka ANNA LUTHER)
Born: 1893, Newark, N.J. Died: Dec. 16, 1960, Hollywood, Calif. Screen actress. Married to actor Edward Gallagher.

Appeared in: **1915** I'm Glad My Boy Grew Up to Be a Soldier; The Manicure Girl; Crooked to the End. **1916** The Village Vampire. **1917** Her Father's Station; Neglected Wife (serial). **1918** Moral Suicide; Her Moment. **1919** The Great Gamble (serial); The Lurking Peril (serial). **1921** Soul and Body. **1922** The Woman Who Believed. **1923** The Governor's Lady; The Truth About Wives. **1924** The Fatal Plunge; Sinners in Silk. **1944** Casanova Brown.

LUTHER, FRANK
Born: 1900. Died: Nov. 16, 1980. Screen actor and singer. Appeared in Educational short subjects.

LUTHER, JOHNNY
Born: 1909. Died: July 31, 1960, San Pedro, Calif. (drowned in boating accident). Screen actor.

LUTHER, LESTER
Born: 1888. Died: Jan. 19, 1962, Hollywood, Calif. (stroke). Screen, stage and radio actor.

Appeared in: **1949** The Red Menace.

LUTTRINGER, ALFONSE "AL"
Born: 1879, San Francisco, Calif. Died: June 9, 1953, Hollywood, Calif. Screen and stage actor.

Appeared in: **1945** A Song to Remember.

LYEL, VIOLA
Born: Dec. 9, 1900, Hull, Yorkshire, England. Died: 1972, England? Screen and stage actress.

Appeared in: **1925** S.O.S. **1931** Hobson's Choice. **1932** After Office Hours; Let Me Explain, Dear. **1941** This Man is Dangerous (aka The Patient Vanishes—US 1947). **1948** Mr. Perrin and Mr. Traill. **1957** The Little Hut; Suspended Alibi.

LYELL, LOTTIE
Born: 1892, Australia. Died: Dec. 21, 1925, Sydney, Australia. Screen actress.

Appeared in: **1911** The Fatal Wedding; The Romance of Margaret Catchpole. **1917** The Church and the Woman. **1922** The Blue Mountain Mystery.

LYGO, MARY (Irene Goodall aka IRENE "RENE" FULLER)
Died: June 1, 1927, Los Angeles, Calif. (suicide—poison). Screen and vaudeville actress. Appeared professionally under both names.

LYLE, LYSTON (Edward Gibson)
Born: 1856, England. Died: Feb. 19, 1920, England? Screen and stage actor.

Appeared in: **1915** A Vagabond's Revenge. **1916** A Place in the Sun. **1917** The Woman Who Was Nothing; The Gay Lord Quex.

LYMAN, ABE
Born: 1897. Died: Oct. 23, 1957, Los Angeles, Calif. Screen, radio actor, bandleader and song writer.

Appeared in: **1933** A Vitaphone short; Mr. Broadway; Broadway; Thru a Keyhole.

LYMON, FRANKIE
Born: 1942. Died: Feb. 27, 1968, New York, N.Y. Screen actor and singer.

Appeared in: **1957** Mister Rock and Roll.

LYNCH, BRID (Brid Ni Loinsigh)
Born: 1913, County Kerry, Ireland. Died: Oct. 27, 1969, Dublin, Ireland (heart ailment). Stage and screen actress.

Appeared in: **1957** Professor Tim (US 1959). **1960** The Poacher's Daughter.

LYNCH, FRANK J.
Died: Dec. 4, 1932, Springfield, Mass. (air crash burns). Screen actor, stunt flyer and exhibitionist. Divorced from actress Roberta Arnold.

LYNCH, FRANK T.
Born: 1869. Died: Dec. 18, 1933, New York, N.Y. (heart attack). Screen, stage actor, professional baseball player and stage manager.

LYNCH, HELEN
Born: Apr. 6, 1900, Billings, Mont. Died: Mar. 2, 1965, Miami Beach, Fla. Screen and stage actress. Married to actor Carroll Nye (dec. 1974). She was a Wampas Baby Star of 1923.

Appeared in: **1917** Showdown. **1920** Honor Bound. **1921** The House That Jazz Built; My Lady Friends; Live and Let Live; What's a Wife Worth? **1922** The Dangerous Age; The Other Side; Midnight; Fools First; Glass Houses. **1923** Cause for Divorce; Thee Eternal Three; The Meanest Man in the World. **1924** The Village of Hate; On Probation; The Tomboy; American Manners; In High Gear. **1925** After Marriage; Bustin' Thru; Smilin' at Trouble; Fifth Avenue Models; Three Weeks in Paris; Smouldering Fires; Oh, Doctor! **1926** My Own Pal; The Arizona Sweepstakes; General Custer at Little Big Horn; Tom and His Pals; Speeding Through. **1927** Avenging Fangs; Cheaters; Husbands for Rent; Underworld. **1928** Ladies of the Mob; Love and Learn; Romance of the Underworld; The Singing Fool; The Showdown; Thundergod. **1929** Stolen Love; In Old Arizona; Speedeasy; Why Bring That Up? **1930** Behind the Make-Up; City Girl. **1934** Elmer and Elsie. **1940** Women Without Names.

LYNCH, JIM
Died: Apr. 20, 1916, Chicago, Ill. (pneumonia). Screen and stage actor.

LYNCH, RUTH SPROULE See SPROULE, RUTH

LYNDON, ALICE
Born: 1874. Died: July 9, 1949, Woodland Hills, Calif. Screen and vaudeville actress. Entered films with Sennett in 1914.

Appeared in: **1936** Bullets or Ballots. **1937** Mountain Justice.

LYNEN, ROBERT
Born: May 24, 1921, Paris, France. Died: 1944, France? Screen actor. Entered films as a child actor in the early 1930's.

Appeared in: **1932** Poil de Carotte. **1933** Le Petit Roi. **1934** Sans Famille. **1936** Man of the Hour; They Were Five. **1937** Un Garnet de Bal. **1938** Hatred; The Bargekeeper's Daughter. **1939** La Vie est Magnifique.

LYNN, DIANA (Dolores Loehr aka DOLLY LOEHR)
Born: Oct. 7, 1926, Los Angeles, Calif. Died: Dec. 18, 1971, Los Angeles, Calif. (brain hemorrhage). Screen, stage actress and pianist.

Appeared in: **1939** They Shall Have Music. **1941** There's Magic in Music. **1942** The Major and the Minor; Star-Spangled Rhythm. **1943** Henry Aldrich Gets Glamour. **1944** The Miracle of Morgan's Creek; Henry Aldrich Plays Cupid; And the Angels Sing; Our Hearts Were Young and Gay. **1945** Out of This World; Duffy's Tavern. **1946** Our Hearts Were Growing Up; The Bride Wore Boots. **1947** Variety Girl; Easy Come, Easy Go. **1948** Ruthless; Texas, Brooklyn and Heaven; Every Girl Should Be Married. **1949** My Friend Irma. **1950** Paid in Full; Rogues of Sherwood Forest; My Friend Irma Goes West; Peggy. **1951** Bedtime for Bonzo; Take Care of My Little Girl; The People Against O'Hara. **1952** Meet Me at the Fair. **1953** Plunder of the Sun. **1954** Track of the Cat. **1955** An Annapolis Story; You're Never Too Young; The Kentuckian. **1970** Company of Killers.

LYNN, EDDIE (Edward Lynn Meminger)
Born: 1905, Toledo, Ohio. Died: Apr. 18, 1975, New York, N.Y. Screen, stage actor and stage producer.

Appeared in: **1939** Reform School.

LYNN, EMMETT
Born: Feb. 14, 1897, Muscatine, Iowa. Died: Oct. 20, 1958, Hollywood, Calif. (heart attack). Screen, stage, vaudeville, radio and burlesque actor. Entered films with Biograph in 1913.

Appeared in: **1913** The Imp. **1940** Grandpa Goes to Town; Scatterbrain; Wagon Train; The Fargo Kid. **1941** Along the Rio Grande; Robbers of the Range; Thunder Over the Ozarks; Puddin' Head. **1942** Frisco Lil; Baby Face Morgan; Tireman, Spare My Tires (short); Stagecoach Express; In Old California; Road Agent; The Spoilers; City of Silent Men; Tomorrow We Live; Outlaws of Pine Ridge; Westward Ho!; Queen of Broadway. **1943** Carson City Cyclone; The Law Rides Again; Girls in Chains; Sundown Kid; Dead Man's Gulch. **1944** You Were Never Uglier (short); Gold Is Where You Lose It (short); Good Night, Sweetheart; Outlaws of Santa Fe; Frontier Outlaws; Return of the Rangers; Cowboy Canteen; When the Lights Go On Again; The Laramie Trail; Johnny Doesn't Live Here Any More; The Town Went Wild; Swing Hostess; Bluebeard. **1945** Song of Old Wyoming; Shadow of Terror; Hollywood and Vine; The Big Show-Off; The Cisco Kid Returns. **1946** The Caravan Trail; Romance of the West; Throw a Saddle on a Star; Man from Rainbow Valley; The Fighting Frontiersman; Stagecoach to Denver; Conquest of Cheyenne; Landrush; Sante Fe Uprising. **1947** Code of the West; Oregon Trail Scouts; Rustler's of Devil's Canyon. **1948** Relentless; West of Sonora; Grand Canyon Trail; Here Comes Trouble. **1949** Roll, Thunder, Roll; Cowboy and the Prizefighter; Ride, Ryder, Ride; The Fighting Redhead. **1950** The Dungeon. **1951** Badman's Gold; Best of the Badmen; The Scarf. **1952** Hooked and Rooked (short); Desert Pursuit; Lone Star; Monkey Business; Oklahoma Annie; Skirts Ahoy!; Apache War Smoke; Sky Full of Moon. **1953** Pickup on South Street; The Robe; The Homesteaders; Northern Patrol. **1954** Ring of Fear; Living It Up; Bait. **1955** A Man Called Peter. **1956** The Ten Commandments.

LYNN, GEORGE M.
Died: 1967. Screen actor.

Appeared in: **1936** Sinner Take All. **1937** Charlie Chan at Monte Carlo; The Duke Comes Back; City Girl. **1941** Adventures of Captain Marvel (serial). **1942** To Be or Not to Be; Grand Central Murder; A Haunting We Will Go. **1943** Crime Doctor's Strangest Case; Tonight We Raid Calais. **1944** Two-Man Submarine. **1945** Secret Agent X-9 (serial); The Master Key (serial); Sudan; House of Frankenstein. **1946** Tangier; The Last Installment (short); Under Nevada Skies. **1947** Killer at Large. **1948** Best Man Wins; Homicide for Three; Criss Cross.

1951 The Day the Earth Stood Still. 1952 The Atomic City; The Bushwackers. 1954 Magnificent Obsession. 1956 The Werewolf; The Boss. 1957 The Man Who Turned to Stone; I Was a Teenage Frankenstein. 1958 Girl in the Woods.

LYNN, HASTINGS
Born: 1879. Died: June 30, 1932, Elstree, England (liver ailment). Screen actor.

LYNN, NATALIE
Died: Dec. 3, 1964, Isleworth, England. Screen, stage, radio and television actress.

Appeared in: 1960 For Members Only (aka The Nudist Story).

LYNN, RALPH
Born: 1881, Manchester, England. Died: Aug. 8, 1962, London, England. Screen, stage actor and film director. Father of film director Robert Lynn.

Appeared in: 1929 Peace and Quiet (short). 1930 Rookery Nook (aka One Embarrassing Night—US). 1931 Plunder; Tons of Money; The Chance of a Night Time; Mischief. 1932 A Night Like This; Thark. 1933 Just My Luck; Summer Lightning; Up to the Neck; Turkey Time; A Cuckoo in the Nest. 1934 A Cup of Kindness; Dirty Work. 1935 Fighting Stock; Stormy Weather (US 1936); Foreign Affaires. 1936 In the Soup; All In. 1937 For Valour.

LYNN, ROBERT
Born: 1897. Died: Dec. 18, 1969, Los Angeles, Calif. Screen actor.

Appeared in: 1951 The Barefoot Mailman. 1958 The Return of Dracula; Good Morning Miss Dove.

LYNN, SHARON E. (D'Auvergne Sharon Lindsay)
Born: 1904, Weatherford, Tex. Died: May 26, 1963, Hollywood, Calif. Screen actress and songwriter. Entered films as an extra.

Appeared in: 1927 Aflame in the Sky; Clancy's Kosher Wedding; Jake the Plumber; The Cherokee Kid; Tom's Gang; The Coward. 1928 Red Wine; Give and Take; None But the Brave; Son of the Golden West. 1929 Fox Movietone Follies of 1929; Speakeasy; Sunny Side Up; Hollywood Night; The One Woman Idea; Trail of the Horse Thieves; Dad's Choice. 1930 Crazy That Way; Lightnin'; Up the River; Happy Days; Let's Go Places; Wild Company; Man Trouble. 1931 Men on Call; Too Many Cooks; Fallen Star. 1932 Discarded Lovers; The Big Broadcast. 1933 Big Executive. 1935 Enter Madame; Go into Your Dance. 1937 Way Out West. 1941 West Point Widow.

LYNN, WILLIAM H.
Born: 1889. Died: Jan. 5, 1952, New York, N.Y. Screen, stage, vaudeville, radio and television actor.

Appeared in: 1951 Mr. Belvedere Rings the Bell; Harvey; Katie Did It. 1952 Outcasts of Poker Flat. 1953 The Twonky.

LYON, BEN
Born: Feb. 6, 1889 or 1901, Atlanta, Ga. Died: Mar. 22, 1979, aboard a ship in the Pacific Ocean. Screen, stage radio actor and author. Married to actresses Bebe Daniels (dec. 1971), and Marian Nixon. Father of actors Richard and Barbara Lyons.

Appeared in: 1917 The Slacker. 1918 Morgan's Raiders; The Transgressor. 1919 Open Your Eyes. 1921 The Heart of Maryland. 1923 The Custard Cup; Flaming Youth; Potash and Perlmutter. 1924 Lily of the Dust; So Big; Pointed People; The White Moth; Wages of Virtue; Wine of Youth. 1925 The Necessary Evil; The New Commandment; One Way Street; The Pace That Thrills; Winds of Chance. 1926 The Savage; The Reckless Lady; Bluebeard's Seven Wives; The Great Deception; The Prince of Tempters. 1927 Dance Magic; For the Love of Mike; High Hat; The Perfect Sap; The Tender Hour. 1929 The Flying Marine; The Air Legion; The Quitter; Dancing Vienna. 1930 Alias French Gertie; Hell's Angels; Lummox; What Men Want. 1931 Aloha; My Past; The Hot Heiress; A Soldier's Plaything; Indiscreet; Night Nurse; Bought; Compromised; Her Majesty, Love. 1932 Lady With a Past; Week Ends Only; Hat Check Girl; Big Timer; By Whose Hand?; The Crooked Circle. 1933 Girl Missing; I Cover the Waterfront; The Women in His Life; The Morning After. 1934 Crimson Romance. 1935 Lightning Strikes Twice; Beauty's Daughter; Frisco Waterfront. 1936 Dancing Feet; Down to the Sea; Not Wanted on Voyage (aka Treachery on the High Seas—US 1939). 1938 He Loved an Actress. 1939 I Killed the Count (aka Who is Guilty?—US 1940). 1941 Hi Gang. 1954 Life With the Lyons (aka Family Affair—US).

LYON, FRANK
Born: 1901, Bridgeport, Conn. Died: Jan. 6, 1961, Gardner, Mass. Screen and stage actor.

Appeared in: 1930 The Big Pond. 1932 Lovers Courageous. 1936 After the Thin Man. 1937 Parnell; Night Must Fall; Conquest. 1938 I Met My Love Again; Dramatic School; Invisible Enemy; The Road to Reno. 1943 Paris After Dark.

LYON, PRICILLA
Born: 1928. Died: Mar. 7, 1980, Winston-Salem, N.C. (cancer). Screen actress.

Appeared in: 1938 Beloved Brat. 1946 Strange Holiday.

LYON, THERESE
Died: Apr. 15, 1975. Screen and stage actress.

Appeared in: 1945 Love, Honor and Goodbye; A Letter for Evie; Strangler of the Swamp. 1946 The Killers; The Green Years. 1947 The Late George Apley. 1948 All My Sons; Apartment for Peggy. 1951 Half Angel. 1962 The Music Man.

LYONS, CANDY
Born: 1945. Died: June 19, 1966, aboard an Atlantic liner. Screen actress.

Appeared in: 1963 Palm Springs Holiday.

LYONS, CLIFF "TEX" (Clifford William Lyons)
Born: 1902. Died: Jan. 6, 1974, Los Angeles, Calif. Screen actor, film director and stuntman.

Appeared in: 1926 West of the Law. 1928 Flashing Hoofs; Master of the Range; The Riddle Trail; Across the Plains; Headin' Westward; Manhattan Cowboy; The Old Code. 1929 The Arizona Kid; Captain Cowboy; The Cowboy and the Outlaw; Fighters of the Saddle; The Fighting Terror; The Last Roundup; West of the Rockies; The Sheriff's Lash; The Galloping Lover; Saddle King; Law of the Mounted. 1930 Code of the West; Crusaders of the West; Red Gold; Breezy Bill; Call of the Desert; Canyon Hawks; The Canyon of Missing Men; Firebrand Jordan; O'Malley Rides Alone; The Oklahoma Sheriff; Western Honor. 1931 Painted Desert; Red Fork Range. 1932 Night Rider. 1935 The Miracle Rider (serial); Tumbling Tumbleweeds; Outlawed Guns. 1936 The Lawless Nineties. 1943 Wagon Tracks West. 1944 The Tiger Woman (serial). 1949 She Wore a Yellow Ribbon. 1950 Wagonmaster. 1952 Bend of the River. 1957 The Abductors; Apache Warrior. 1959 Ben Hur; The Young Land. 1960 Sparatcus; The Alamo. 1961 Two Rode Together; The Comancheros. 1962 Taras Bulba. 1963 The Great Train Robbery; Donovan's Reef; McLintock! 1964 The Long Ships. 1965 Genghis Khan; Major Dundee. 1966 Marco the Magnificent. 1967 The War Wagon. 1968 The Green Berets. 1970 Chisum.

LYONS, EDDIE
Born: Nov. 25, 1886, Beardstown, Ill. Died: Aug. 30, 1926, Pasadena, Calif. Screen, stage actor and stage director. Married to actress Virginia Kirtley, and brother of actor Harry M. Lyons (dec. 1919).

Appeared in: 1912 The Dove and the Serpent; Melodrama of Yesterday; Making a Man of Her; Jim's Atonement; Henpecked Ike; Love, War and a Bonnet; The Parson and the Medicine Man; Big Sin; Almost a Suicide. 1913 Some Runner. 1914 She Was a Working Girl; What a Baby Did; Such a Villain; When Eddie Went to the Front. 1915 Love in a Hospital; Wanted—A Chaperone; Eddie's Awful Predicament; Mrs. Plumb's Pudding. 1917 The Rushin' Dancers; A Fire Escape Finish; A Hasty Hazing; His Wife's Relatives. 1918 There and Back. 1920 Fixed by George; Everything But the Truth; La, La, Lucille. 1921 Once a Plumber; Roman Romeos; A Shocking Night. 1925 Declasse. 1926 The Lodge in the Wilderness; The Shadow of the Law.

LYONS, FRANKIE
Died: Jan. 26, 1937 (auto accident). Screen stuntman.

Appeared in: 1937 Racing Luck.

LYONS, FRECKLES (Francis Lunakiaki Lyons)
Born: 1909. Died: Sept. 1, 1960, Honolulu, Hawaii. Screen, stage actor, musician and singer.

LYONS, FRED (Fred F. Leyva)
Died: Mar. 16, 1921 (auto accident). Screen actor.

LYONS, GENE
Born: 1921. Died: July 8, 1974, Hollywood, Calif. Screen and stage actor.

Appeared in: 1957 The Young Don't Cry. 1965 Sylvia. 1969 Daddy's Gone A-Hunting.

LYONS, HARRY M.
Born: Nov. 12, 1879, Ill. Died: Mar. 12, 1919, Los Angeles, Calif. (aneurism of aorta). Screen actor. Brother of actor Eddie Lyons (dec. 1926).

LYSES, CHARLOTTE
Born: 1878, France. Died: Apr. 7, 1956, Saint-Jean-Cap-Ferrat, France. Screen and stage actress. Divorced from actor Sacha Guitry (dec. 1957).

LYTELL, BERT
Born: Feb. 24, 1885, New York, N.Y. Died: Sept. 28, 1954, New York, N.Y. (following surgery). Screen, stage, radio, television, vaudeville actor and film director. Married to actress Grace Mencken (dec. 1978), divorced from actress Claire Windsor (dec. 1972); and brother of actor Wilfred Lytell (dec. 1954). Entered films in 1917.

Appeared in: 1917 The Lone Wolf. 1918 The Trail to Yesterday. 1919 Easy to Make Money. 1920 Alias Jimmy Valentine. 1921 A Message from Mars; Misleading Lady; Price of Redemption; The Man Who; A Trip to Paradise; The Idle Rich; Ladyfingers; Alias Ladyfingers. 1922 The Face Between; The Right That Failed; Sherlock Brown; To Have and to Hold. 1923 Kick In; Rupert of Hentzau; The Eternal City; The Meanest Man in the World. 1924 Born Rich; A Son of the Sahara. 1925 Sandra; Lady Windermere's Fan; Steele of the Royal Mounted; The Boomerang; Eve's Lover; Never the Twain Shall Meet; Ship of Souls; Sporting Life. 1926 That Model from Paris; The Lone Wolf Returns; The Gilded Butterfly; Obey the Law. 1927 Alias the Lone Wolf; The First Night; Women's Wares. 1928 On Trial. 1929 The Lone Wolf's Daughter. 1930 The Last of the Lone Wolf; Brothers (stage and film versions). 1931 The Single Sin; Stolen Jools (short). 1943 Stage Door Canteen.

LYTELL, FOLLY See LAMARR, BARBARA

LYTELL, WILFRED
Born: 1892. Died: Sept. 10, 1954, Salem, N.Y. Screen, stage, radio and television actor. Brother of actor Bert Lytell (dec. 1954).

Appeared in: 1916 The Combat. 1918 Our Mrs. McChesney. 1920 Heliotrope. 1921 Know Your Men; The Kentuckians. 1922 The Man Who Paid; The Wolf's Fangs. 1923 The Fair Cheat; The Leavenworth Case. 1924 Trail of the Law; The Wardens of Virginia. 1926 Bluebeard's Seven Wives.

LYTTON, HERBERT "HERB"
Died: June 26, 1981. Screen actor.

Appeared in: 1945 The Last Installment (short). 1951 Navy Bound. 1953 The Glass Web; Marshal of Cedar Rock. 1959 The Cosmic Man. 1960 The Gallant Hours.

LYTTON, L. ROGERS
Born: 1867, New Orleans, La. Died: Aug. 9, 1924. Screen actor.

Appeared in: 1912 Off the Road; Checkmated; The Final Justice; Papa Puts One Over. 1913 The Model for St. John; Three Girls and a Man. 1914 Heartease; Jerry's Uncle's Namesake; The Shadow of the Past; The Win(k)some Widow. 1915 Battle Cry of Peace. 1916 The Tarantula; The Scarlet Runner; My Official Wife; The Price of Fame. 1917 Panthea; The Vengeance of Durand (aka Two Portraits); Lest We Forget. 1918 Burden of Proof; The Forbidden City. 1919 A Regular Girl; The Third Degree. 1920 High Speed; Love or Money. 1921 His Brother's Keeper. 1922 The Road to Arcady; Silver Wings; Who Are My Parents? 1923 Zaza. 1924 A Sainted Devil.

MABLEY, JACKIE "MOMS" (Loretta Mary Aiken)
Born: 1897, Brevard, North Carolina. Died: May 23, 1975, White Plains, N.Y. Black screen, stage, vaudeville, radio and television actress.

Appeared in: 1933 Emperor Jones. 1947 Killer Diller; Big Timers. 1949 Boardinghouse Blues. 1970 It's Your Thing. 1974 Amazing Grace.

MAC, NILA
Born: 1891, Arkansas City, Kans. Died: Jan. 20, 1953, New York, N.Y. Screen, stage, vaudeville actress, radio director, producer and writer.

Appeared in: 1916 War Brides.

MC ALLISTER, PAUL
Born: 1875, New York, N.Y. Died: July 8, 1955. Screen and stage actor. Married to actress Margaret McKinney.

Appeared in: 1914 Scales of Justice. 1921 Forever; The Sign on the

Door. 1922 A Stage Romance; What's Wrong with the Women? 1923 Trilby; Columbus; Jamestown; You Can't Fool Your Wife. 1924 The Lone Wolf; For Woman's Favor; The Moral Sinner; Manhandled; Yolanda. 1926 Beau Geste; The Winning of Barbara Worth. 1927 She's a Sheik; Sorrell and Son. 1928 The Big Killing; Noah's Ark; The Yellow Ticket. 1929 Hearts in Exile; Evangeline. 1930 The Case of Sergeant Grischa. 1931 Beau Ideal; Inspiration. 1933 Pilgrimage. 1934 Judge Priest. 1936 Mary of Scotland. 1940 The Doctor Takes a Wife.

MC ALPINE, JANE
Born: 1896. Died: Oct. 19, 1947, Long Branch, N.J. Screen and stage actress. Member of the Ziegfeld Follies.

Appeared in: 1919 The Winning Stroke.

MACARIO, ERMINIO
Born: 1902, Italy. Died: Mar. 26, 1980, Turin, Italy. Screen, stage, burlesque and vaudeville actor.

Appeared in: 1957 Little Italy. 1959 The Promissory Note. Other Italian films: Country Air; The Kid of the West; Highway Hero; How to Discover America.

MAC ARTHUR, CHARLES
Born: Nov. 5, 1895, Scranton, Pa. Died: Apr. 21, 1956, New York, N.Y. (internal hemorrhage). Screenwriter, film director, film producer, playwright and screen actor. Married to actress Helen Hayes and father of actor James MacArthur.

Appeared in: 1934 Crime Without Passion. 1935 The Scoundrel.

MC ATEE, BEN
Born: 1903. Died: Dec. 3, 1961, Hollywood, Calif. Screen, stage, vaudeville, television and minstrel actor.

MC ATEE, CLYDE
Born: 1880. Died: Feb. 20, 1947, Woodland Hills, Calif. Screen actor.

Appeared in: 1925 Percy. 1926 Crossed Signals.

MACAULEY, JOSEPH
Born: 1891, San Francisco, Calif. Died: Oct. 6, 1967, New York, N.Y. Screen and stage actor.

Appeared in: 1930 The Lottery Bride.

MC AVOY, CHARLES "CHARLIE"
Born: 1885. Died: Apr. 20, 1953. Screen actor.

Appeared in: 1930 Those Who Dance; Night Owls (short). 1934 I'll Be Suing You (short); Murder at the Vanities; Shoot the Works. 1936 The Singing Cowboy; Strike Me Pink. 1939 King of the Turf. 1945 Strange Holiday.

MC AVOY, JOAN (Elsie M. Dugan aka JOAN CARLSON)
Born: 1912. Died: May 18, 1934, Los Angeles, Calif. (auto accident). Screen and stage actress.

MC BRIDE, CARL
Born: 1894, Sioux City, Iowa. Died: Dec. 17, 1937, Los Angeles, Calif. Screen, vaudeville actor and film director. Appeared in Charles B. Dillingham productions on screen.

MC BRIDE, DONALD (aka DONALD MACBRIDE)
Born: 1889, Brooklyn, N.Y. Died: June 21, 1957, Los Angeles, Calif. Screen, stage, television and vaudeville actor. Appeared in films at old Vitagraph studio in Brooklyn approx. 1913.

Appeared in: 1932 Misleading Lady. 1933 Get That Venus. 1936 The Chemist (short). 1938 Room Service (stage and film versions); Annabel Takes a Tour. 1939 The Great Man Votes; Twelve Crowded Hours; The Girl and the Gambler; The Flying Irishman; The Story of Vernon and Irene Castle; The Girl From Mexico; The Gracie Allen Murder Case; Blondie Takes a Vacation; The Amazing Mr. Williams; Charlie Chan at Treasure Island. 1940 The Saint's Double Trouble; Northwest Passage; Murder over New York; Michael Shayne, Private Detective; Curtain Call; My Favorite Wife; Hit Parade of 1941. 1941 The Invisible Woman; Footlight Fever; Topper Returns; High Sierra; Love Crazy; Here Comes Mr. Jordan; You'll Never Get Rich; Rise and Shine; You're in the Navy Now; Louisiana Purchase. 1942 Two Yanks in Trinidad; Juke Girl; The Mexican Spitfire Sees a Ghost; The Glass Key; My Sister Eileen. 1943 A Night to Remember; They Got Me Covered; Best Foot Forward; Lady Bodyguard; A Stranger in Town. 1944 The Doughgirls; The Thin Man Goes Home. 1945 Penthouse Rhythm; Hold That Blonde; Out of This World; Girl on the Spot; She Gets Her Man; Abbott and Costello in Hollywood; Doll Face. 1946

Blonde Alibi; Little Giant; The Killers; The Time of Their Lives; The Dark Horse; The Brute Man. **1947** Beat the Band; The Old Gray Mayor; Joe Palooka in the Knockout; Hal Roach Comedy Carnival; Good News; Buck Privates Come Home; The Egg and I; The Fabulous Joe. **1948** Campus Sleuth; Jinx Money; Smart Politics. **1949** The Story of Seabiscuit; Challenge to Lassie. **1950** Joe Palooka Meets Humphrey; Holiday Rhythm. **1951** Cuban Fireball; Bowery Batallion; Texas Carnival; Sailor Beware. **1952** Gobs and Gals. **1953** The Stooge. **1955** The Seven Year Itch.

MC BRIDE, EDITH (Edith Ethel McBride)
Died: Dec. 10, 1927, New York, N.Y. Screen and stage actress. Married to actor George Beban (dec. 1928). Mother of actor George Beban, Jr.

Appeared in: **1922** The Sign of the Rose.

MC BRIDE, OLIVIA
Born: 1896, Hemet, Calif. Died: Aug. 27, 1976, Anaheim, Calif. Screen actress.

MC BRIDE, THOMAS
Died: July 29, 1974. Screen actor.

MC CABE, GEORGE
Born: Chicago, Ill. Died: Dec. 17, 1917, Bellevue, N.Y. Screen actor.

MC CABE, HARRY
Born: 1881. Died: Feb. 11, 1925, Los Angeles, Calif. Screen actor.

Appeared in: **1916** American Film Mfg. Co. films. **1922** A Western Thoroughbred. **1924** The No-Gun Man.

MC CABE, MAY
Born: 1873. Died: June 22, 1949, New York, N.Y. Screen and stage actor. Married to stage actor Jack McCabe (dec. 1967) and mother of stage actor Clyde North. Appeared in silents.

MC CALL, LIZZIE
Born: July 14, 1857. Died: Apr. 18, 1942, New York, N.Y. Screen and stage actress.

Appeared in: **1915** The Other Girl.

MC CALL, WILLIAM
Born: May 19, 1879, Delavan, Ill. Died: Jan. 10, 1938, Hollywood, Calif. Screen, stage and television actor. Was billed in vaudeville as part of "McCall Trio."

Appeared in: **1919** Smashing Barriers (serial). **1921** Fighting Fate (serial); Flower of the North; Where Men Are Men; It Can Be Done. **1922** Across the Border; The Angel of Crooked Street; Fortune's Mask; The Fighting Guide; The Little Minister; Rounding up the Law; When Danger Smiles. **1923** Sell 'Em Cowboy; The Back Trail; Daring Chances; The Phantom Horseman. **1925** His Marriage Vow; The Red Rider; Ridin' Thunder. **1930** The Lonesome Trail; Under Texas Skies; Trailin' Trouble. **1937** Lodge Night (short).

MC CALLIN, CLEMENT
Born: Mar. 6, 1913, London, England. Died: 1977, London, England. Screen, stage and television actor. Married to Phillippa Anne Gurney, and actress Brenda Bruce.

Appeared in: **1939** Stolen Life. **1949** Edward My Son; Queen of Spades (US 1950). **1951** The Rossiter Case. **1952** Murder in the Cathedral; Folly to the Wise; Story of Robin Hood and His Merrie Men.

MC CALLUM, JOHN A.
Died: Feb., 1923, Hollywood, Calif. Screen and stage actor. Do not confuse with actor with same name.

Appeared in: **1922** A Tailor Made Man.

MC CALLUM, NEIL
Born: 1930, Canada. Died: Apr. 26, 1976, Reading, England (brain hemorrhage). Screen, television actor and director.

Appeared in: **1959** Jet Storm (US 1961); The Siege of Pinchgut (aka Four Desperate Men); The Devil's Disciple. **1960** Foxhole in Cairo (US 1961). **1962** The Longest Day; The Inspector (aka Lisa—US); The War Lover. **1963** Walk a Tightrope (US 1964). **1964** Witchcraft; Dr. Terror's House of Horrors (US 1965); Catacombs (aka The Woman Who Wouldn't Die—US 1965). **1966** Thunderbirds Are Go (voice—US 1968). **1968** The Lost Continent. **1969** Moon Zero Two (US 1970).

MC CANN, CHARLES ANDREW
Died: Sept., 1927, Paris, France. Screen actor and musician.

Appeared in: **1917** The Tiger Woman (film debut).

MC CANN, FRANCES
Born: 1922. Died: Mar. 14, 1963. Opera singer and screen actress.

Appeared in: **1962** The Creation of the Humanoids.

MC CARROLL, FRANK
Died: Mar. 9, 1954, Burbank, Calif. (accidental fall at home). Screen actor, stuntman and rodeo performer.

Appeared in: **1949** Brand of Fear; Lawless Code; Renegades of the Sage. **1950** Fence Riders; Gunslingers; Over the Border.

MC CARTHY, EARL
Born: 1906, Fort Wayne, Ind. Died: May 28, 1933, Hollywood, Calif. (heart attack). Screen actor.

Appeared in: **1927** The Magic Garden. **1928** Red Lips. **1929** Words and Music. **1932** The All American. **1933** Sucker Money; Cheating Blondes; Clancy of the Mounted (serial).

MC CARTHY, JOE
Born: Apr. 21, 1887. Died: Jan. 13, 1978, Buffalo, N.Y. Baseball manager and screen actor.

Appeared in: **1941** Safe at Home.

MC CARTHY, JOHN P.
Born: Mar. 17, 1885, San Francisco, Calif. Died: Sept. 4, 1962, Pasadena, Calif. (coronary thrombosis). Screen, stage actor, film director, film producer and screenwriter. Do not confuse with actor with same name.

Appeared in: **1916** Intolerance. **1935** His Fighting Blood.

MC CARTHY, MYLES (aka MILES MC CARTHY)
Born: Toronto, Canada. Died: Sept. 27, 1928, Hollywood, Calif. (heart attack). Screen, stage and vaudeville actor.

Appeared in: **1922** Smiles Are Trumps. **1923** Dollar Devils; The Day of Faith. **1924** Captain Blood; Abraham Lincoln; Oh, You Tony! **1925** Tricks; The Lady. **1926** The Heart of a Coward. **1927** The Racing Fool.

MC CARTHY, PAT (Patricia Cook)
Born: 1911. Died: Jan. 25, 1943, New York. Screen, stage actress and dancer.

MC CARTY, MARY
Born: 1923, Winfield, Kans. Died: Apr. 3, 1980, Los Angeles, Calif. (heart attack). Screen, stage and television actress. Entered films as a child actress.

Appeared in: **1938** Rebecca of Sunnybrook Farm; Keep Smiling. **1944** The Sulivans. **1954** The French Line. **1959** The Big Fisherman; Pillow Talk. **1961** Babes in Toyland. **1963** My Six Loves. **1978** Somebody Killed Her Husband. **1979** All That Jazz.

MC CAULEY, EDNA
Born: Detroit, Mich. Died: Jan. 28, 1919, Rome, Italy (typhoid fever). Screen actress. Appeared in Famous Players films.

MC CAULEY, JACK (John B. McCauley)
Born: 1901, N.Y. Died: June 13, 1980, Menlo Park, Calif. (natural causes). Screen and stage actor. Married to actress Amy Revere.

MACCHIA, JOHN
Born: 1932. Died: July 30, 1967, Los Angeles, Calif. (stroke). Screen actor.

Appeared in: **1963** Beach Party; The Nutty Professor. **1964** The Disorderly Orderly. **1965** Beach Blanket Bingo; Family Jewels; How to Stuff a Wild Bikini; Sergeant Deadhead. **1966** Three on a Couch; The Ghost in the Invisible Bikini.

MC CLAIN, BILLY (William C. McClain)
Born: 1857. Died: Jan. 28, 1950, near Los Angeles, Calif. (trailer fire). Black screen, and minstrel actor.

Appeared in: **1933** Nagana. **1934** The Mighty Barnum; Rhapsody in Black. **1935** The Virginia Judge. **1936** Dimples. **1937** Bargain with Bullets. **1938** Angels with Dirty Faces.

MC CLARTY, JAMES E. *See* MC LARTY, JAMES E.

MC CLAY, CLYDE
Born: 1895. Died: June 30, 1939, Hollywood, Calif. (accident on location filming In Old Monterey—crushed by army tank). Screen actor and extra.

Appeared in: **1939** In Old Monterey.

MC CLELLAN, HURD
Died: Apr. 20, 1933, Los Angeles, Calif. (accidental gunshot while filming). Screen actor and stuntman.

MC CLELLAN, ROBERT FRANCIS E.
Born: 1888. Died: Mar. 20, 1976. Screen and stage actor. Appeared in early Biograph, Reliance and Metro films.

MC CLELLAND, DONALD
Born: Sept. 29, 1903, New York, N.Y. Died: Nov. 15, 1955. Screen actor.

MC CLINTOCK, JAMES R. "POLEY"
Born: 1901. Died: Jan., 1980, East Stroudsburg, Pa. Screen, radio, television actor, drummer and comedian.

Appeared in: **1937** Varsity Show.

MC CLOSKEY, ELIZABETH H.
Born: 1870. Died: Jan. 8, 1942, Hollywood, Calif. Screen and stage actress. Entered films approx. 1920.

MAC CLOSKEY, YSABEL
Born: 1917. Died: Mar. 11, 1981, Burbank, Calif. Screen, stage and television actress.

Appeared in: **1967** Point Blank. **1968** Petulia; Star. **1971** Bedknobs and Broomsticks; Harold and Maude.

MC CLOSKY, FRANK
Born: 1913. Died: Nov. 8, 1979, Orlando, Fla. Screen actor and circus owner.

Appeared in: **1952** The Greatest Show on Earth.

MC CLUNG, BOBBY
Born: 1921. Died: Jan. 27, 1945, Columbia, S.C. (pneumonia). Screen, stage and vaudeville actor. Appeared in "Dead End Kids" series.

Appeared in: **1937** Two Wise Maids; Paradise Express; The Toast of New York.

MC CLURE, BUD
Born: 1886. Died: Nov. 2, 1942, North Hollywood, Calif. Screen actor and cowboy.

MC CLURE, FRANK
Born: 1895. Died: Jan. 23, 1960. Stage and screen actor.

MC CLURE, GLADYS
Born: 1915. Died: Dec., 1933, near San Francisco, Calif. (auto accident). Screen actress. Sister of actresses Adrienne Ames (dec. 1947), and Linda March (dec. 1933).

MC CLURE, IRENE
Died: Sept. 4, 1928, Bakersfield, Calif. (injuries from auto accident). Screen actress.

MAC COLL, JAMES A.
Born: 1912. Died: Apr. 18, 1956, New York, N.Y. Screen, stage, television actor and playwright.

Appeared in: **1954** This Is the Army (stage and film versions).

MC COLLUM, H. H.
Born: 1887, Wilkes-Barre, Pa. Died: Dec. 19, 1938, New York, N.Y. Screen and stage actor.

Appeared in: **1915** Mishaps of Musty Suffer (serial).

MC COMAS, CARROLL
Born: 1886, Albuquerque, N.Mex. Died: Nov. 9, 1962, New York. Screen, stage, vaudeville, television actress, singer and dancer.

Appeared in: **1916** When Love is King. **1953** Jamaica Run. **1955** Chicago Syndicate.

MC COMAS, GLENN
Born: 1900. Died: June 10, 1959, Los Angeles, Calif. Screen actor.

MC COMAS, LILA
Born: 1906. Died: June 13, 1936, Los Angeles, Calif. (auto accident). Screen actress.

MC COMAS, RALPH C.
Born: 1889. Died: July 14, 1924, San Luis Obispo, Calif. (heart failure). Screen actor.

Appeared in: **1915** How Callahan Cleaned Up Little Hell; The Strategist.

MC CONNELL, GLADYS
Born: Oct. 22, 1907, Oklahoma City, Okla. Died: Mar., 1979. Screen actress. Was a 1927 Wampas Baby Star.

Appeared in: **1926** The Flying Horseman; The Midnight Kiss; A Trip to Chinatown. **1927** Marriage; Three's a Crowd; Riding to Fame. **1928** The Chaser; The Bullet Mark; The Perfect Crime; The Tiger's Shadow (serial); The Code of the Scarlet; The Glorious Trail. **1929** Cheyenne. **1930** The Woman Who Was Forgotten; Parade of the West.

MC CONNELL, LULU
Born: 1882, Kansas City, Mo. Died: Oct. 9, 1962, Hollywood, Calif. (cancer). Screen, stage, vaudeville and radio actress. Married to actor Grant Simpson (dec. 1932).

Appeared in: **1936** Stage Struck.

MC CONNELL, MOLLY
Born: 1870, Chicago, Ill. Died: Dec. 10, 1920. Screen and stage actress. Married to stage manager William McConnell (dec.) and later married to stage actor Sherwood McDonald (dec.).

Appeared in: **1915** Who Pays? (serial). **1916** Joy and the Dragon. **1917** The Checkmate; The Wildcat; Bab the Fixer; The Best Man; The Girl Angle. **1921** Black Beauty; Hearts and Masks; The Home Stretch.

MC CORD, MRS. LEWIS
Born: Philadelphia, Pa. Died: Dec. 24, 1917, New York, N.Y. (pneumonia, diabetes). Screen, stage, opera and vaudeville actress. Married to stage actor Lewis McCord (dec. 1911).

Appeared in: **1914** The Virginian. **1915** The Marriage of Kitty; The Chorus Lady; Chimmie Fadden; Kindling; Chimmie Fadden Out West; The Wild Goose Chase; The Secret Orchard; The Warrens of Virginia. **1916** The Heart of Nora Flynn; The Dream Girl; Common Ground; The Race; Unprotected; The Ragamuffin. **1917** The Golden Fetter; The Ghost House.

MC CORD, VERA
Born: 1877. Died: Mar. 3, 1949, New York, N.Y. Screen and stage actress.

Appeared in: **1920** The Good-Bad Wife.

MC CORMACK, BILLIE (Blanche E. Burke)
Died: Feb. 1, 1935, Santa Monica, Calif. Screen actress.

MC CORMACK, FRANK
Born: 1876, Washington, D.C. Died: May 22, 1941, Conn. Screen, stage actor and stage director.

Appeared in: **1921** The Case of Becky; Experience. **1930** The Case of Sergeant Grischa; Brothers.

MAC CORMACK, FRANKLYN
Born: 1908. Died: June 12, 1971. Screen actor. Do not confuse with actor Frank McCormack (dec. 1941).

MC CORMACK, JOHN
Born: June 14, 1884, Athlone, Ireland. Died: Sept. 16, 1945, Dublin, Ireland. Screen actor, radio and opera tenor.

Appeared in: **1930** Song O' My Heart. **1937** Wings of the Morning.

MC CORMACK, WILLIAM M.
Born: 1891. Died: Aug. 19, 1953, Hollywood, Calif. (heart attack). Screen actor.

Appeared in: **1921** Red Courage; The Robe. **1922** Robin Hood. **1923** Danger; Good Men and Bad. **1924** Abraham Lincoln. **1925** Fangs of Fate; Reckless Courage; The Secret of Black Canyon; Flashing Steeds; Vic Dyson Pays. **1926** The Desperate Game. **1927** The Long Loop on the Pecos; Arizona Nights; Whispering Smith Rides (serial). **1928** The Apache Raider; A Son of the Desert. **1929** Romance of the Rio Grande; Born to the Saddle; Riders of the Rio Grande. **1936** Trail of the Lonesome Pine; Tundra. **1953** Salome; The Robe (and 1921 version).

MC CORMICK, ALYCE (aka JOY AUBURN)
Born: Jan. 13, 1904, Chicago, Ill. Died: Jan. 7, 1932, Hollywood, Calif. (pneumonia). Screen and stage actress.

Appeared in: **1928** Mother Knows Best. **1930** Reno. **1931** Spirit of Notre Dame; Frankenstein; Bad Girl. **1939** The Mysterious Mr. X.

MC CORMICK, F. J.
Born: 1891. Died: Apr. 24, 1947, Dublin, Ireland. Screen and stage actor. Married to actress Eileen Crowe (dec. 1978).

Appeared in: **1937** The Plough and the Stars. **1947** Odd Man Out; Hungry Hill.

MC CORMICK, MERRILL (William Merrill McCormick)
Born: Feb. 5, 1892, Denver, Colo. Died: Aug. 19, 1953, Hollywood, Calif. (heart attack). Screen and stage actor.

Appeared in: **1921** Red Courage. **1922** Robin Hood. **1923** Good Men and Bad. **1925** Fangs of Fate; Flashing Steeds; Reckless Courage; The Secret of Black Canyon; Vic Dyson Pays. **1926** The Desperate Game. **1927** The Long Loop on the Pecos. **1928** The Apache Raider; A Son of the Desert. **1929** Born to the Saddle; Riders of the Rio Grande; Romance of the Rio Grande. **1930** Near the Rainbow's End; The Spoilers. **1931** Fighting Caravans; Trails of the Golden West. **1932** Whistlin' Dan; A Man's Land Cornered; The Cowboy Counsellor; The Boiling Point; Tombstone Canyon. **1933** The Dude Bandit; Deadwood Pass; King of the Arena; Man of the Forest. **1934** Wheels of Destiny; West on Parade; The Fighting Trooper; The Westerner; Boss Cowboy; Lightning Range; Range Riders. **1935** The New Adventures of Tarzan (serial and feature); Gallant Defender; Law of the 45's; Lawless Borders. **1936** Winds of the Wasteland; Rebellion. **1937** The Old Corral; Cheyenne Rides Again; Phantom of Santa Fe; Guns in the Dark; Come On, Cowboys; Two-Fisted Sheriff; Range Defenders; The Fighting Texan; One Man Justice; Forlorn River; Empty Holsters; God's Country and the Man; Boots and Saddles; Danger Valley; Zorro Rides Again (serial). **1938** Tarzan and the Green Goddess; Cattle Raiders; Outlaws of Sonora; Prairie Moon; Ghost Town Riders. **1939** Water Rustlers; Ride 'Em, Cowgirl; Stagecoach; Lone Star Pioneers; Mexicali Rose; In Old Caliente; The Singing Cowgirl; Riders of the Frontier; The Adventures of the Masked Phantom; The Kansas Terrors; Overland Mail. **1940** Hidden Gold; Billy the Kid in Texas; Prairie Schooners; Melody Ranch. **1941** In Old Cheyenne; Desert Bandit; The Son of Davy Crockett; The Lone Rider Fights Back; Fighting Bill Fargo. **1942** Below the Border; South of Santa Fe; Boot Hill Bandits; Stardust of the Range; Texas Justice; In Old California; The Sombrero Kid; The Silver Bullet; Pirates of the Prairie. **1943** Border Patrol; Robin Hood of the Range; The Kansan; Lost Canyon; Raiders of Red Gap; Silver City Raiders. **1949** Arctic Fury. **1950** Beyond the Purple Hills. **1953** Eyes of the Jungle.

MC CORMICK, MYRON
Born: Feb. 8, 1908, Albany, N.Y. Died: July 30, 1962, New York, N.Y. (cancer). Screen, stage, radio and television actor.

Appeared in: **1937** Winterset. **1939** One Third of a Nation. **1940** The Fight for Life. **1943** China Girl. **1949** Jigsaw; Jolson Sings Again; Gun Moll. **1955** Three for the Show; Not As a Stranger. **1958** No Time for Sergeants. **1959** The Man Who Understood Women. **1961** The Hustler. **1962** The Haircut (short); A Public Affair.

MC CORMICK, PARKER
Died: July 22, 1980, New York, N.Y. (cancer). Screen, stage and television actress. Divorced from actor John Forsythe, Earl Wilken, and actors Peter Hobbs, and Moultrie Patton.

Appeared in: **1964** Dear Heart. **1970** The Magic Garden of Stanley Sweetheart. **1971** Going Home. **1980** The Fan.

MC COY, GERTRUDE (Gertrude Lyon)
Born: 1896, Rome, Ga. Died: July 17, 1967, Atlanta, Ga. Screen actress. Entered films as an extra and appeared in early Edison Co. films. Married to actor Duncan McRae (dec. 1931).

Appeared in: **1911** That Winsome Winnie Smile. **1912** Cynthia's Agreement; Every Rose Has its Stem; The Stranger and the Taxi Cab; The Userer's Grip; Under False Colors; A Baby's Shoe; The Sketch with the Thumb Print; A Dangerous Lesson; The Little Girl Next Door; Annie Crawls Upstairs; Kitty's Holdup; Her Face. **1913** The Mountaineers; The Manicure Girl; Peg O' the Movies; A Serenade by Proxy; How They Outwitted Father; Kathleen Mavourneen; The Road of Transgression; Aunt Elsa's Visit; His Enemy; A Letter to Uncle Sam. **1914** The Birth of the Star Spangled Banner; When the Cartridges Failed; The Man in the Street; A Real Help-Mate; The Mystery of the Silver Snare; The Shattered Tree; Sheep's Clothing; The Stuff that Dreams Are Made Of; The New Partner. **1918** The Blue Bird. **1919** Angle, Esquire; The Usurper. **1920** The Auction Mart; Burnt In; Tangled Hearts (aka The Wife Whom God Forgot). **1921** Christie Johnston; The Golden Dawn; Out of the Darkness. **1922** Tell Your Children; Was She Guilty? (aka Thou Shalt Not Kill). **1923** Heartstrings; A Royal Divorce; The Temptation of Carlton Earle; Always Tell Your Wife. **1924** Chappy—That's All; The Diamond Man; Nets of Destiny; Miriam Rozella. **1928** On the Stroke of 12. **1931** The Working Girl. **1932** The Silent Witness.

MC COY, HARRY
Born: 1894. Died: Sept. 1, 1937, Hollywood, Calif. (heart attack). Screen, radio actor, film director and song writer. Was a Keystone Kop and appeared in "Joker" comedies.

Appeared in: **1913** Mike and Jake at the Beach; The Cheese Special (short). **1914** Mabel's Strange Predicament; Caught in a Cabaret; Mabel at the Wheel; Mabel's Busy Day; Mabel's Married Life; The Masquerader; Getting Acquainted. **1915** One Night Stand; For Better—But Worse; A Human Hound's Triumph; Those Bitter Sweets; Merely a Married Man; Saved by Wireless; The Village Scandal. **1916** His Last Laugh; The Great Pear Tangle; Love Will Conquer; Perils of the Park; A Movie Star; Cinders of Love; His Auto Ruination; Bubbles of Trouble; She Loved a Sailor. **1921** Skirts; plus "Hallroom Boys" comedies. **1924** The Fatal Mistake. **1925** Dashing Thru; Heads Up; Heir-Loons. **1938** Hearts of Men.

MC COY, TIM "COLONEL T. J." (Timothy John Fitzgerald McCoy)
Born: Apr. 10, 1891, Saginaw, Mich. Died: Jan. 29, 1978, Ft. Huachuca, Ariz. Screen, television actor, film director, circus and wild west show performer. Do not confuse with film director with same name.

Appeared in: **1923** The Covered Wagon (film debut). **1925** The Thundering Herd. **1926** War Paint. **1927** California; Foreign Devils; The Frontiersman; Spoilers of the West; Winners of the Wilderness. **1928** Adventurer; Beyond the Sierras; The Bushranger; Riders of the Dark; The Law of the Range; Wyoming. **1929** The Overland Telegraph; The Desert Rider; Morgan's Last Raid; Sioux Blood. **1930** The Indians Are Coming (serial). **1931** One Way Trail; Shotgun Pass; Heroes of the Flames (serial). **1932** The Fighting Marshal; Fighting Fool; Two-Fisted Law; Texas Cyclone; Daring Danger; Riding Tornado. **1933** Cornered; Western Code; Man of Action; End of the Trail; Fighting for Justice; Police Car 17; The Whirlwind; Rusty Rides Alone; Silent Men; Hold the Press. **1934** Straightaway; Speed Wings; Voice in the Night; Hell Bent for Love; Beyond the Law; A Man's Game. **1935** The Westerner; Square Shooter; Revenge Rider; Law Beyond the Range; Justice of the Range; Fighting Shadows; Man from Guntown; Outlaw Deputy. **1936** The Lion's Den; Lightnin' Bill Carson; Border Caballero; Roarin' Guns; Ghost Patrol; The Prescott Kid; Aces and Eights; The Traitor. **1938** Code of the Rangers; Two-Gun Justice; Phantom Ranger; Lightning Carson Rides Again. **1940** Straight Shooter; Frontier Crusader; Gun Code. **1941** Outlaws of the Rio Grande; Texas Marshal; Arizona Bound; Gunman from Bodie; Forbidden Trails. **1942** Ghost Town Law; Down Texas Way; Riders of the West; West of the Law; Below the Border.

MC COY, VAN
Born: 1944. Died: July 6, 1979, Englewood, N.J. (heart attack). Black singer, composer, arranger and screen actor.

Appeared in: **1979** Sextet.

MC CRACKEN, JOAN
Born: 1923. Died: Nov. 1, 1961, New York, N.Y. (heart condition). Screen, stage actress and dancer.

Appeared in: **1944** Hollywood Canteen. **1947** Good News.

MC CULLOUGH, PAUL
Born: 1884, Springfield, Ohio. Died: Mar. 25, 1936, Boston, Mass. (suicide). Screen, stage, vaudeville, minstrel actor, and circus performer. Was partner with Bobby Clark (dec. 1960) in comedy team of "Clark and McCullough." For films he appeared in see Bobby Clark.

MC CULLOUGH, PHILO
Born: June 16, 1890, San Bernardino, Calif. Died: June 5, 1981, Burbank, Calif. Screen, stage actor and film director. Entered films in 1912.

Appeared in: **1913** The Brute. **1915** The Red Circle (serial); Neal of the Navy (serial); Blue Blood and Yellow Backs; Who Pays? (serial). **1916** The Neglected Wife (serial); Grip of Evil (serial). **1917** Tears and Smiles; Miss Captain Kiddo; The Martinache Marriage; The Secret of Black Mountain. **1918** The Legion of Death. **1919** Soldiers of Fortune. **1920** Splendid Hazard. **1921** The Blushing Bride; The Lamplighter; Partners of Fate; The Primal Law. **1922** Calvert's Valley; A Dangerous Adventure (serial and feature); The Married Flapper; More to Be Pitied Than Scorned; The Right That Failed; Seeing's Believing; Strange Idols; West of Chicago. **1923** Heroes of the Street; The Stranger's Banquet; The First Degree; Forgive and Forget; The Fourth Musketeer; The Man Between; Trilby; Trimmed in Scarlet; Yesterday's Wife. **1924** The Chorus Lady; The Dangerous Blonde; Daughters of Today; The Great Diamond Mystery; Hook and Ladder; Judgement of the Storm; Ladies to Board; Racing for Life; The Slanderers. **1925** Blue Blood; The Boomerang; The Calgary Stampede; Dick Turpin; Faint Perfume; Lorraine of the Lions; The Mansion of Aching Hearts; Winds of Chance; The Wife of the Centaur. **1926** The Arizona Sweepstakes; Chip of the Flying U; Everybody's Acting;

Ladies at Play; Mismates; The Savage. **1927** The Bar-C Mystery (serial); Easy Pickings; Fire and Steel; Silver Valley; Smile, Brother, Smile; We're All Gamblers; The Woman Who Did Not Care. **1928** Clearing the Trail; The Night Flyer; Painted Post; The Power of the Press; Warming Up; Lost in the Arctic. **1929** South of Panama; The Charlatan; The Million Dollar Collar; The Show of Shows; The Apache; Untamed Justice; The Leatherneck. **1930** Spurs; On the Border. **1931** The Phantom of the West (serial); The Vanishing Legion (serial); Swanee River; The Sky Spider; Branded; Sheer Luck; Defenders of the Law. **1932** Heroes of the West (serial); The Jungle Mystery (serial); Sunset Trail; Breach of Promise; South of the Rio Grande. **1933** Laughing at Life; Tarzan, the Fearless (serial). **1934** Mystery Mountain (serial); Riding Thru; I Hate Women; Wheels of Destiny; Inside Information; Thunder Over Texas; Outlaws' Highway. **1935** Captured in Chinatown. **1936** The Lawless Nineties. **1937** Texas Trail; On Such a Night. **1938** The Buccaneer. **1940** The Ape. **1947** That Way With Women. **1949** Stampede. **1965** The Great Race. **1969** They Shoot Horses, Don't They?

MC CULLUM, BARTLEY
Died: Mar. 25, 1916, Philadelphia, Pa. Screen actor.

Appeared in: **1913** The Village Blacksmith; The Old Oaken Bucket; The Heart Brokers; Granny; Home, Sweet Home. **1915** The Comedienne's Strategy; The Mirror; Think Mothers; Playing the Same Game; The Silent Accuser; Sorrows of Happiness. **1916** Dollars and the Woman.

MC CUTCHEON, GEORGE BARR
Born: July 26, 1866, Tippecanoe County, Ind. Died: Oct. 23, 1928, New York, N.Y. (heart disease). Novelist and screen actor.

Appeared in: **1913** Saved by Parcel Post.

MC CUTCHEON, RALPH
Born: 1899. Died: Apr. 16, 1975, North Hollywood, Calif. (pneumonia). Film extra and animal trainer. Married to actress Mary Kornman (dec. 1973).

MC CUTCHEON, WALLACE
Born: 1881. Died: Jan. 27, 1928, Los Angeles, Calif. (shot himself). Screen, stage actor and film director. Divorced from actress Pearl White (dec. 1938).

Appeared in: **1904** The Moonshiner. **1919** A Virtuous Vamp; The Black Street (serial). **1920** The Phantom Foe (serial).

MC DANIEL, ETTA
Born: Dec. 1, 1890, Wichita, Kans. Died: Jan. 13, 1946. Black screen, stage, vaudeville and radio actress. Sister of actor Sam (dec. 1962), actress Hattie (dec. 1952) and Otis McDaniel.

Appeared in: **1934** Smoking Guns. **1935** So Red the Rose; The Virginia Judge. **1936** The Invisible Ray; The Magnificent Brute; The Prisoner of Shark Island; The Lawless Nineties; The Lonely Trail; Palm Spring; The Glory Trail; The Devil Is a Sissy; Hearts in Bondage. **1937** Man Bites Lovebug; Living On Love; Mile a Minute Love; Sweetheart of the Navy; On Such a Night. **1938** Keep Smiling; Crime Afloat; Tom Sawyer—Detective. **1939** Sergeant Madden. **1940** The House Across the Bay; Carolina Moon; Charter Pilot. **1941** Thieves Fall Out; The Pittsburgh Kid; Life With Henry; The Big Store. **1942** The Great Man's Lady; Mokey; American Empire. **1943** They Came to Blow Up America; What a Man!; Son of Dracula. **1945** Incendiary Blonde.

MC DANIEL, GEORGE
Born: 1886. Died: Aug. 20, 1944, Hollywood, Calif. Screen and stage actor.

Appeared in: **1915** The Girl and the Game (serial). **1921** Silent Years. **1922** The Scrapper. **1923** The Barefoot Boy. **1926** Burning Words. **1927** The Iron Hearts.

MC DANIEL, HATTIE
Born: June 10, 1895, Wichita, Kans. Died: Oct. 26, 1952, San Fernando Valley, Calif. Black screen, radio, vaudeville and television actress and singer. Sister of actor Sam (dec. 1962), actress Etta (dec. 1946) and Otis McDaniel. Won 1939 Academy Award for Best Supporting Actress in Gone With the Wind.

Appeared in: **1932** The Golden West; Blonde Venus; Hypnotized; Washington Masquerade. **1933** I'm No Angel; The Story of Temple Drake. **1934** Operator 13; Little Men; Judge Priest; Fate's Fathead (short); Lost in the Stratosphere; The Chases of Pimple Street (short); Babbitt; Imitation of Life. **1935** Music Is Magic; China Seas; Another Face; Alice Adams; The Little Colonel; The Travelling Saleslady; plus the following shorts: Anniversary Trouble; Okay Toots!; and The Four-

Star Boarder. **1936** Gentle Julia; The First Baby; High Tension; Star for a Night; Can This Be Dixie?; Reunion; Showboat; Postal Inspector; Hearts Divided; The Bride Walks Out; Big Time Vaudeville Reels (shorts); Valiant Is the Word for Carrie; Next Time We Love; Libeled Lady; High Treason; Arbor Day (short); The Singing Kid. **1937** Don't Tell the Wife; Racing Lady; The Crime Nobody Saw; True Confession; Saratoga; Over the Goal; 45 Fathers; Nothing Sacred; Merry-Go-Round of 1938; The Wildcatter. **1938** Battle of Broadway; Everybody's Baby; Shopworn Angel; The Shining Hour; The Mad Miss Manton. **1939** Gone With the Wind; Zenobia. **1940** Maryland. **1941** Affectionately Yours; The Great Lie; They Died With Their Boots On. **1942** The Male Animal; In This Our Life; George Washington Slept Here; Reap the Wild Wind. **1943** Thank Your Lucky Stars; Johnny Come Lately. **1944** Since You Went Away; Janie; Three Is a Family. **1945** Hi, Beautiful. **1946** Margie; Never Say Goodbye; Janie Gets Married. **1947** Song of the South; The Flame. **1948** Mr. Blandings Builds His Dream House; Mickey. **1949** Family Honeymoon; The Big Wheel.

MC DANIEL, SAM "DEACON" (Samuel Rufus McDaniel)
Born: Jan. 28, 1886, Columbus, Kans. Died: Sept. 24, 1962, Woodland Hills, Calif (throat cancer). Black screen actor. Brother of Otis and actresses Hattie (dec. 1952) and Etta McDaniel (dec. 1946).

Appeared in: **1931** The Public Enemy. **1932** The Rich Are Always With Us; Once in a Lifetime. **1933** Footlight Parade; Lady Killer. **1934** Here Comes the Navy; Fashions of 1934; Manhattan Melodrama; Evelyn Prentice; Lemon Drop Kid. **1935** George White's 1935 Scandals; Unwelcome Stranger; Lady Tubbs; The Virginia Judge; Rendezvous; Stormy. **1936** The Gorgeous Hussy; Love Letters of a Star; Hearts Divided. **1937** Captains Courageous; Bargain with Bullets; Dark Manhattan; The Go-Getter; Git Along, Little Dogies. **1938** Jezebel; Three Loves Has Nancy; Sergeant Murphy; Gambling Ship; Stablemates. **1939** Pride of Blue Grass; Good Girls Go to Paris. **1940** Virginia City; Brother Orchid; The Man Who Talked Too Much; Too Many Husbands; Calling All Husbands; Am I Guilty? **1941** The Great Lie; South of Panama; Broadway Limited; New York Town; Bad Men of Missouri; Mr. and Mrs. North; Louisiana Purchase; The Great American Broadcast. **1942** In This Our Life; Silver Queen; All Through the Night; I Was Framed; Mokey; The Traitor Within; Johnny Doughboy. **1943** Dixie Dugan; The Ghost and the Guest; Gangway for Tomorrow. **1944** Three Men in White; Sweet and Low Down; The Adventures of Mark Twain; Home in Indiana; Three Little Sisters; Andy Hardy's Blonde Trouble; Double Indemnity; Experiment Perilous. **1945** She Wouldn't Say Yes; The Naughty Nineties; A Guy, a Gal and a Pal. **1946** Joe Palooka—Champ; Gentleman Joe Palooka; Never Say Goodbye; Centennial Summer; Without Reservations; My Reputation; Do You Love Me? **1947** The Foxes of Harrow. **1948** Pride of Virginia; Secret Service Investigator; Heavenly Daze (short). **1949** Flamingo Road. **1950** Girl's School; The File on Thelma Jordan. **1951** Too Many Wives (short). **1952** Something for the Birds. **1955** A Man Called Peter.

MC DERMOTT, HUGH
Born: Mar. 20, 1908, Edinburgh, Scotland. Died: Jan. 30, 1972, London, England. Screen, stage, television actor and author.

Appeared in: **1936** David Livingstone (film debut); The Captain's Table. **1937** Wife of General Ling (US 1938); Well Done, Henry. **1939** Where's That Fire? **1940** For Freedom; Neutral Port. **1941** Pimpernel Smith (aka Mister V—US 1942); Spring Meeting. **1942** Young Mr. Pitt. **1945** The Seventh Veil (US 1946). **1946** This Man is Mine. **1948** Good Time Girl (US 1950); No Orchids for Miss Blandish (US 1951). **1949** The Huggetts Aboard. **1950** Lilli Marlene (US 1951). **1951** Two on the Tiles; Four Days. **1952** Trent's Last Case (US 1953). **1953** The Wedding of Lilli Marlene. **1954** The Love Lottery; Johnny on the Spot; Night People; Malaga (aka Fire Over Africa); Devil Girl from Mars. **1955** As Long as They're Happy (US 1957). **1957** You Pay Your Money; A King in New York. **1958** The Man Who Wouldn't Talk (US 1960). **1960** Moment of Danger (aka Malaga—US 1962). **1964** First Men In The Moon. **1968** The File of the Gold Goose (US 1969). **1969** The Adding Machine; Guns in the Heather; The Games (US 1970). **1971** Captain Apache. **1972** Chato's Land.

MAC DERMOTT, JOHN W. "JACK"
Born: Sept. 9, 1892, Green River, Wyo. Died: July 22, 1946, Los Angeles, Calif. Screen, stage actor, screenwriter and film director. Entered films in 1913.

Appeared in: **1923** Mary of the Movies.

MC DERMOTT, MARC (aka MARC MAC DERMOTT)
Born: 1881, London, England. Died: Jan. 5, 1929, Glendale, Calif. (gall bladder surgery). Screen and stage actor.

Appeared in: **1911** Aida; Papa's Sweetheart; Eleanore Cuyler; Please Remit; Two Officers; The Declaration of Independence; At the Threshold of Life; The Girl and the Motor Boat; An Old Sweetheart of Mine; An Island Comedy; The Ghost's Warning; The Death of Nathan Hale; The Story of the Indian Ledge; The Heart of Nichette; How Sir Andrew Lost His Vote. **1912** A Letter to the Princess; The Foundling; A Suffragette in Spite of Herself; What Happened to Mary (serial); His Daughter; The Heir Apparent; Politics and Love; Her Face; The Maid of Honor; When She Was About Sixteen; The Little Girl Next Door; The Dumb Wooing; Billie; Their Hero; The Sunset Gun; The Little Wooden Show; The Convict's Parole; The Passer-By; The Angel and the Stranded Troupe; After Many Days; The Close of the American Revolution; An Unsullied Shield; A Dangerous Lesson; Nerves and the Man; Jack and the Beanstalk; The Little Organist; Lady Clare; Fog; An Old Appointment; The Corsican Brothers. **1913** An Old Appointment; The Lady Clare; The New Squire; The Coastguard's Sister; The Floodtide; The Stroke of Phoebus Eight; Fog; The Stolen Plans; While John Bolt Slept; A Clue to Her Parentage; Barry's Breaking In; The Gauntlets of Washington; Kathleen Mavourneen; With the Eyes of the Blind; The Dear Daughters; The Portrait; The Duke's Dilemma; The Heart of Valeska; A Splendid Scapegrace; A Daughter of Romany; A Concerto for the Violin; Flood Tide; Keepers of the Flock. **1914** The Foreman's Treachery; The Stolen Plans; The Antique Broach; The Man Who Disappeared (serial); With His Hands; Sophia's Imaginary Visitors; A Princess of the Desert; All for His Sake; When East Meets West in Boston; The Hunted Animal; The Living Dead; Comedy and Tragedy; The Man in the Street; A Question of Hats and Gowns; Face to Face; A Matter of Minutes; The Necklace of Rameses; By the Aid of a Film. **1915** Sallie Castleton, Southerner; The Man Who Could Not Sleep; Theft in the Dark. **1916** Ranson's Folly; The Price of Fame; Whom the Gods Destroy. **1917** The Blind Adventure; Intrigue; The Last Sentence; Mary Jane's Pa; The Sixteenth Wife. **1918** The Green God. **1919** Buchanan's Wife; New Moon. **1920** While New York Sleeps. **1921** Blind Wives; Amazing Lovers; Footlights. **1922** The Lights of New York; Spanish Jade. **1923** Hoodman Blind; Lucretia Lombard; The Satin Girl. **1924** Dorothy Vernon of Haddon Hall; In Every Woman's Life; The Sea Hawk; This Woman; Three Miles Out; He Who Gets Slapped. **1925** The Lady; The Goose Woman; Siege; Graustark. **1926** Flesh and the Devil; Kiki; The Temptress; The Love Thief; The Lucky Lady. **1927** California; Man, Woman and Sin; The Taxi Driver; The Road to Romance; Resurrection. **1928** The Whip; The Yellow Lily; Under the Black Eagle; Glorious Betsy.

MC DEVITT, RUTH (Ruth Thane Shoecraft)
Born: Sept. 13, 1895, Coldwater, Mich. Died: May 27, 1976, Hollywood, Calif. Screen, stage, radio and television actress.

Appeared in: **1951** The Guy Who Came Back. **1959** The Trap. **1961** The Parent Trap. **1962** Boys' Night Out. **1963** Love Is a Ball; The Birds. **1964** Dear Heart. **1968** The Shakiest Gun in the West. **1969** Change of Habit; An Angel in My Pocket; The Love God? **1970** The Out-of-Towners. **1974** Homebodies; Mixed Company.

MACDONA, CHARLES T.
Born: 1860, Dublin, Ireland. Died: Nov. 15, 1946, Brighton, England. Screen, stage actor and stage manager.

Appeared in: **1917** Daddy. **1918** Once Upon a Time.

MACDONALD, BLOSSOM See BLAKE, MARIE

MC DONALD, CHARLES
Born: 1876. Died: Aug. 7, 1953, Tucson, Ariz. Screen, stage actor, film producer, screenwriter and songwriter. Entered films with Essanay Film Co. Do not confuse with actor Charles McDonald (dec. 1964).

Appeared in: **1914** Michael Strogoff. **1921** Salvation Nell. **1925** Irish Luck.

MC DONALD, CHARLES B.
Born: May 26, 1886, Springfield, Mass. Died: Dec. 29, 1964, Hollywood, Fla. Screen, stage and vaudeville actor, journalist and film executive. Entered films with Essanay in early 1900s. Do not confuse with actor dec. 1953.

MAC DONALD, DONALD
Born: Mar. 13, 1898, Denison, Tex. Died: Dec. 9, 1959, New York, N.Y. Screen, stage, television and radio actor. Married to stage actress Ruth Hammond.

Appeared in: **1955** The Kentuckian. **1956** The Brass Legend; Great Day in the Morning.

MAC DONALD, EDMUND
Born: May 7, 1908. Died: Sept., 1951, Los Angeles, Calif. Screen and radio actor.

Appeared in: **1933** Enlighten Thy Daughter. **1938** Prison Break. **1939** I Stole a Million. **1940** Sailor's Lady; Black Friday; The Gay Caballero. **1941** Great Guns; The Bride Wore Crutches; Texas. **1942** Whispering Ghosts; To the Shores of Tripoli; Call of the Canyon; Castle in the Desert; The Strange Case of Dr. Rx; Flying Tigers; Heart of the Golden West; Madame Spy; Who Done It? **1943** Hangmen Also Die; Sherlock Holmes in Washington; Hi Ya Chum; Corvette K-225. **1944** Sailor's Holiday. **1945** The Lady Confesses; Detour; Hold That Blonde. **1946** The Mysterious Mr. M. (serial); They Made Me a Killer. **1947** Shoot to Kill; Blondie's Anniversary. **1948** That Lady in Ermine; Black Eagle. **1949** Red Canyon.

MC DONALD, FRANCIS J.
Born: Aug. 22, 1891, Bowling Green, Ky. Died: Sept. 18, 1968, Hollywood, Calif. Screen and stage actor.

Appeared in: **1918** The Gun Woman. **1920** Nomads of the North. **1921** The Call of the North; The Golden Snare; Puppets of Fate; Hearts and Masks. **1922** Captain Fly-by-Night; The Man Who Married His Own Wife; The Woman Conquers; Trooper O'Neil; Monte Cristo. **1923** Mary of the Movies; South Sea Love; Going Up; Trilby; The Buster; Look Your Best. **1924** The Arizona Express; East of Broadway; Racing Luck; So This Is Marriage. **1925** Anything Once; Bobbed Hair; Go Straight; The Hunted Woman; My Lady of Whims; Satin in Sables; Northern Code. **1926** Battling Butler; The Yankee Senor; The Desert's Toll; Puppets; The Temptress; The Palace of Pleasure. **1927** The Notorious Lady; The Valley of Hell; Outlaws of Red River; The Wreck. **1928** The Dragnet; Legion of the Condemned; A Girl in Every Port. **1929** The Carnation Kid; Girl Overboard. **1930** Brothers; Dangerous Paradise; Safety in Numbers; The Runaway Bride; Burning Up; Morocco. **1931** The Lawyer's Secret; In Line of Duty; The Gang Buster. **1932** Honor of the Mounted; Texas Buddies; The Devil Is Driving; Trailing the Killer; Woman from Monte Carlo. **1933** Broadway Bad; Terror Trail; Kickin' the Crown Around. **1934** Voice in the Night; Girl in Danger; Straightaway; No More Bridge (short); The Trumpet Blows; The Line-Up; Burn 'Em Up Barnes (feature film and serial). **1935** Ceiling Zero; Anna Karenina; Mississippi; Marriage Bargain; Star of Midnight; Red Morning; Ladies Crave Excitement. **1936** Robin Hood of El Dorado; The Prisoner of Shark Island; Under Two Flags; Big Brown Eyes; The Plainsman; Mummy's Boys. **1937** Wild West Days (serial); The Devil's Playground; Parole Racket; Born Reckless; Love Under Fire; Every Day's a Holiday. **1938** Gun Law; If I Were King. **1939** Range War; Union Pacific; The Bad Lands; The Light That Failed. **1940** One Night in the Tropics; The Carson City Kid; The Sea Hawk; Northwest Mounted Police; Green Hell; The Devil's Pipeline. **1941** Blood and Sand; The Sea Wolf; Men of Timberland; The Kid from Kansas. **1942** The Girl from Alaska. **1943** Buckskin Frontier; Bar 20; The Kansan. **1944** Mystery of the River Boat (serial); Texas Masquerade; Cheyenne Wildcat; Lumberjack; Mystery Man; Border Town; Zorro's Black Whip (serial). **1945** The Great Stagecoach Robbery; South of the Rio Grande; Strange Confessions; Corpus Christi Bandits. **1946** The Bandit of Sherwood Forest; Duel in the Sun; Bad Men of the Border; Canyon Passage; The Catman of Paris; The Devil's Playground; Invisible Informer; Tangier; My Pal Trigger; Roll on Texas Moon; Night Train to Memphis; The Magnificent Doll. **1947** Saddle Pals; Dangerous Venture; Spoilers of the North; The Perils of Pauline; Brute Force. **1948** Bold Frontiersman; The Paleface; The Dead Don't Dream; Panhandle; Desert Passage; Bandits of Corsica. **1949** Son of God's Country; Brothers in the Saddle; Daughter of the Jungle; Rose of the Yukon; Son of the Badman; Apache Chief; Samson and Delilah; Strange Gamble; Rim of the Canyon; Abandoned; Powder River Rustlers; The Lady Gambles. **1950** Kim; California Passage. **1951** Gene Autry and the Mounties. **1952** The Raiders; Rancho Notorious; Red Mountain; Fort Osage. **1954** Three Hours to Kill; The Bandits of Corsica. **1955** Ten Wanted Men. **1956** Thunder Over Arizona; The Ten Commandments. **1957** Last Stagecoach West; Duel at Apache Wells; Pawnee. **1958** Saga of Hemp Brown; Fort Massacre. **1959** The Big Fisherman. **1965** The Great Race.

MC DONALD, FRANK
Born: 1900, Baltimore, Md. Died: Mar. 8, 1980, Oxnard, Calif. Screen, stage actor, film director, televison director and author. Married to actress Goodee Montgomery (dec. 1978).

MC DONALD, HARRY (John Henry McDonald)
Born: 1870, Barbados, West Indies. Died: 1943, Hollywood, Calif. Screen and stage actor.

Appeared in: **1930** Hello Sister.

MAC DONALD, J. FARRELL
Born: June 6, 1875, Waterbury, Conn. Died: Aug. 2, 1952, Hollywood, Calif. Screen, stage actor, film director and opera performer.

Appeared in: **1911** Imp Productions films. **1915** The Heart of Maryland. **1921** Little Miss Hawkshaw; Bucking the Line; Riding With Death; Trailin'; Sky High; Action; Desperate Youth; The Freeze Out; The Wallop. **1922** The Ghost Breaker; The Bachelor Daddy; The Bonded Woman; Manslaughter; Tracks; Come On Over; The Young Rajah; Over the Border. **1923** Drifting; Quicksands; The Age of Desire; Fashionable Fakers; Racing Hearts; While Paris Sleeps. **1924** Western Luck; The Brass Bowl; The Iron Horse; Fair Week; Mademoiselle Midnight; The Signal Tower; The Storm Daughter. **1925** Gerald Cranston's Lady; The Scarlet Honeymoon; The Fighting Heart; Lightnin'; Thank You; The Lucky Horseshoe; Kentucky Pride; Let Women Alone. **1926** The First Year; A Trip to Chinatown; The Dixie Merchant; The Shamrock Handicap; The Family Upstairs; The Country Beyond; Three Bad Men. **1927** Bertha the Sewing Machine Girl; Love Makes 'Em Wild; Ankles Preferred; The Cradle Snatchers; Rich But Honest; Colleen; Paid to Love; Sunrise; East Side, West Side. **1928** The Cohens and the Kellys in Paris; Bringing Up Father; Abie's Irish Rose; Riley the Cop; None But the Brave. **1929** In Old Arizona; Masked Emotion; Masquerade; Strong Boy; Four Devils; South Sea Rose. **1930** Broken Dishes; The Truth About Youth; Song O' My Heart; Born Reckless; The Painted Angel; The Steel Highway; Men Without Women; Happy Days; The Girl of the Golden West. **1931** The Easiest Way; The Millionaire; Woman Hungry; The Maltese Falcon; Other Men's Women; The Squaw Man; Too Young to Marry; The Brat; Sporting Blood; The Spirit of Notre Dame; Touchdown; The Painted Desert; River's End. **1932** The Hurricane Express (serial); Under Eighteen; Discarded Lovers; Hotel Continental; Probation; The Phantom Express; Week-End Marriage; The 13th Guest; 70,000 Witnesses; The Vanishing Frontier; Hearts of Humanity; This Sporting Age; The Pride of the Legion; No Man of Her Own; Me and My Gal; Steady Company; The Racing Strain; Scandal for Sale. **1933** The Iron Master; Heritage of the Desert; Under Secret Orders; The Working Man; Peg O' My Heart; Laughing at Life; The Power and the Glory; I Loved a Woman; Murder on the Campus. **1934** Myrt and Marge; Man of Two Worlds; The Crime Doctor; Romance in Manhattan; Once to Every Woman; The Cat's Paw; The Crosby Case; Beggar's Holiday. **1935** Swell Head; Maybe It's Love; Danger Ahead; Square Shooter; The Whole Town's Talking; Northern Frontier; Star of Midnight; The Best Man Wins; The Healer; Let 'Em Have It; Our Little Girl; The Irish in Us; Front Page Woman; Stormy; Fighting Youth; Waterfront Lady. **1936** Hitchhike Lady; Florida Special; Riff Raff; Exclusive Story; Showboat. **1937** The Game That Kills; Courage of the West; Shadows of the Orient; Maid of Salem; Mysterious Crossing; The Silent Barrier; Roaring Timber; The Hit Parade; Slave Ship; County Fair; Slim; Topper; My Dear Miss Aldrich. **1938** My Old Kentucky Home; Numbered Woman; Gang Bullets; State Police; Little Orphan Annie; White Banners; Come on Rangers; The Crowd Roars; Submarine Patrol; Flying Fists; There Goes My Heart. **1939** The Lone Ranger Rides Again (serial); Susannah of the Mounties; Mickey the Kid; Conspiracy; The Gentleman from Arizona; Zenobia; Coast Guard; East Side of Heaven. **1940** Knights of the Range; The Dark Command; Light of the Western Stars; Prairie Law; I Take This Oath; The Last Alarm; Untamed; Stagecoach War; Friendly Neighbors. **1941** Meet John Doe; The Great Lie; In Old Cheyenne; Riders of the Timberline; Law of the Timber; Broadway Limited. **1942** One Thrilling Night; Phantom Killer; Bowery at Midnight; Little Tokyo, U.S.A.; Snuffy Smith, Yardbird; The Living Ghost; Captains of the Clouds. **1943** The Ape Man; Clancy Street Boys; True to Life; Tiger Fangs. **1944** Irish Eyes Are Smiling; The Miracle of Morgan's Creek; Texas Masquerade; The Great Moment; Follow the Boys; Shadow of Suspicion. **1945** The Dolly Sisters; The Woman Who Came Back; A Tree Grows in Brooklyn; Nob Hill; Johnny Angel; Pillow of Death. **1946** Smoky; My Darling Clementine; Joe Palooka; Champ. **1947** The Bachelor and the Bobby Soxer; Thunder in the Valley; Web of Danger; Keeper of the Bees. **1948** Whispering Smith; Panhandle; Fury at Furnace Creek; Walls of Jericho; Belle Starr's Daughter. **1949** She Comes Home; Streets of San Francisco; Beautiful Blonde from Bashful Bend; Fighting Man of the Plains; The Dalton Gang; Law of the Barbary Coast. **1950** Dakota Lil; Hostile Country; Woman on the Run. **1951** Elopement; Mr. Belvedere Rings the Bell; Here Comes the Groom.

MC DONALD, JAMES
Born: 1886. Died: Dec. 26, 1952, Los Angeles, Calif. Screen actor and trick rider.

MAC DONALD, JAMES W.
Born: 1899. Died: Aug. 31, 1962, Santa Cruz, Calif. Screen and stage actor.

Appeared in: **1949** Cinderella (voice only).

MAC DONALD, JEANETTE
Born: June 18, 1906, Philadelphia, Pa. Died: Jan. 14, 1965, Houston, Tex. (heart attack). Screen, stage, television, radio actress and opera performer. Married to actor Gene Raymond. Sister of actress Marie Blake (dec. 1978).

Appeared in: **1929** The Love Parade (film debut). **1930** The Vagabond King; The Lottery Bride; Let's Go Native; Monte Carlo; Oh, for a Man! **1931** Don't Bet on Women; Annabelle's Affairs (aka The Affairs of Annabelle). **1932** One Hour with You; Love Me Tonight. **1934** The Merry Widow (US and French version); The Cat and the Fiddle. **1935** Naughty Marietta. **1936** Rose Marie; San Francisco. **1937** Maytime; The Firefly. **1938** The Girl of the Golden West; Sweethearts. **1939** Broadway Serenade. **1940** New Moon; Bitter Sweet. **1941** Smilin' Through. **1942** I Married an Angel; Cairo. **1944** Follow the Boys. **1948** Three Daring Daughters; The Birds and the Bees. **1949** The Sun Comes Up. **1974** That's Entertainment (film clips).

MC DONALD, JOSEPH
Born: 1861. Died: Oct. 24, 1935, Redondo Beach, Calif. (drowned). Screen actor.

MAC DONALD, KATHERINE
Born: 1894. Died: June 4, 1956, Santa Barbara, Calif. Screen actress and film producer. Sister of actress Mary MacLaren. Do not confuse with stage actress Catherine Mac Donald (dec. 1929).

Appeared in: **1918** Headin' South; Riddle Gawne. **1919** The Woman Thou Gavest Me; The Squaw Man. **1920** Curtain; The Beauty Market. **1921** The Beautiful Liar; My Lady's Latchkey; Passion's Playground; Stranger Than Fiction; Trust Your Wife. **1922** Domestic Relations; Her Social Value; Heroes and Husbands; The Infidel; The Woman Conquers; The Woman's Side; White Shoulders. **1923** The Lonely Road; Money, Money, Money; Refuge; Chastity; The Scarlet Lily. **1925** The Unnamed Woman. **1926** Old Loves and New.

MC DONALD, MARIE (Marie Frye)
Born: 1923, Burgin, Ky. Died: Oct. 21, 1965, Hidden Hills, Calif. (accidental drug overdose). Screen, stage actress and singer. Known as "The Body." Entered films in 1941.

Appeared in: **1941** It Started with Eve; You're Telling Me. **1942** Pardon My Sarong; Lucky Jordan. **1943** Tornado; Riding High. **1944** I Love a Soldier; Standing Room Only; Guest in the House; A Scream in the Dark. **1945** It's a Pleasure; Getting Gertie's Garter. **1946** Swell Guy. **1947** Living in a Big Way. **1949** Tell It to the Judge. **1950** Once a Thief; Hit Parade of 1951. **1958** The Geisha Boy. **1963** Promises, Promises.

MAC DONALD, PAULINE
Born: 1911. Died: Jan. 29, 1976, Encino, Calif. Screen and radio actress. Married to cameraman Joe Mac Donald (dec.).

MC DONALD, RAY
Born: 1924, Boston, Mass. Died: Feb. 20, 1959, New York, N.Y. Screen, stage and vaudeville actor. Brother of actress Grace McDonald. Divorced from actress Elizabeth Fraser.

Appeared in: **1941** Down in San Diego; Life Begins for Andy Hardy; Babes on Broadway. **1942** Born to Sing. **1943** Presenting Lily Mars. **1946** Till the Clouds Roll By. **1947** Good News. **1949** Shamrock Hill. **1950** There's a Girl in My Heart. **1953** All Ashore.

MAC DONALD, WALLACE
Born: 1891, Mulgrave, Nova Scotia. Died: Oct. 30, 1978, Santa Barbara, Calif. Screen, stage actor, film director, film producer and story editor.

Appeared in: **1914** Mabel's Married Life. **1916** Youth's Endearing Charms; Purity. **1917** The Princess Necklace; The Princess of Park Row. **1919** Leave It to Susan. **1920** Trumpet Island. **1921** The Fire Cat; A Poor Relation; The Sage Hen; The Foolish Matrons; Breaking Through (serial). **1922** Caught Bluffing; Under Oath; The Understudy; Youth Must Have Love; A Fool There Was. **1923** The Day of Faith; Girl from the West; The Spoilers; Maytime. **1924** The Heart Bandit; Love and Glory; Curlytop; The Sea Hawk; Roaring Rails; Thy Name Is Woman. **1925** The Charmer; Heir-Looms; Learning to Love; Lightnin'; The Lady; New Lives for Old; Wandering Fires; The Primrose Path; Pampered Youth. **1926** The Bar-C Mystery (serial); Faithful Wives; The Checkered Flag; Hell's 400; Two Can Play; Fighting With Buffalo Bill (serial). **1927** Red Signals; His Foreign Wife; Drums of the Desert; Your Wife and Mine; Tumbling River; Whispering Smith Rides (serial). **1928** Blockade; Tropical Nights. **1929** Dark Skies (aka Darkened Skies); Darkened Rooms; Fancy Baggage; Sweetie. **1930** Fighting Through, or California in 1878; Hit the Deck;

Madam Satan; The Rogue Song. **1931** Fifty Fathoms Deep; Drums of Jeopardy; Range Feud; Pagan Lady; Branded. **1932** High Speed; Two-Fisted Law; Texas Cyclone; Daring Danger; Riding Tornado; Vanishing Frontier; Hello Trouble; Tex Takes a Holiday. **1933** Between Fighting Men; King of the Wild Horses. **1944** Sailor's Holiday. **1945** A Guy, a Gal and a Pal; My Name is Julie Ross. **1946** Out of the Depths. **1947** When a Girl's Beautiful. **1950** Counterspy Meets Scotland Yard. **1952** Harem Girl; Okinawa. **1953** El Alamein. **1954** Outlaw Stallion (aka The White Stallion). **1955** Apache Ambush. **1958** Return to Warbow.

MC DONOUGH, MICHAEL
Born: 1876. Died: Aug. 8, 1956, Hollywood, Calif. Screen actor.

MAC DOUGALL, ALLAN R.
Born: 1894, Scotland. Died: July 19, 1956, Paris, France. Screen, stage actor, author and editor.

Appeared in: **1936** Soak the Rich.

MAC DOUGALL, JAMES D.
Born: Glasgow, Scotland. Died: 1932, Los Angeles, Calif. Screen actor and publisher.

Appeared in: **1930** So This is London.

MC DOWELL, CLAIRE (aka CLAIRE MAC DOWELL)
Born: Nov. 2, 1877, New York, N.Y. Died: Oct. 23, 1966, Woodland Hills, Calif. Stage and screen actress. Entered films with American Biograph Co. in 1910. Married to actor Charles Hill Mailes (dec. 1937).

Appeared in: **1910** His Last Burglary; Wilful Peggy; A Mohawk's Way; The Golden Supper; His Trust Fulfilled; In the Days of '49; A Romany Tragedy; The Primal Call; The Sorrowful Example. **1911** Swords and Hearts; A Woman Scorned; As in a Looking Glass; A Blot on the 'Scutcheon; Billy's Strategem; The Sunbeam. **1912** A Temporary Truce; A Sailor's Heart; The God Within; The Female of the Species; Lena and the Geese; The Sands of Dee; The Daughters of Eve; In the Aisles of the Wild; The Unwelcome Guest. **1913** A Welcome Intruder; The Wanderer; The House of Darkness; Olaf—an Atom; The Ranchero's Revenge. **1914** The Massacre. **1918** The Return of Mary. **1919** Heart O' the Hills. **1920** Something to Think About; Midsummer Madness; The Woman in the Suitcase. **1921** Love Never Dies; Prisoners of Love; Wealth; Chickens; What Every Woman Knows; Mother O'Mine. **1922** The Gray Dawn; Heart's Haven; In the Name of the Law; The Lying Truth; Penrod; Quincy Adams Sawyer; Nice People; Rent Free; The Ragged Heiress. **1923** The Westbound Limited; Ponjola; Michael O'Halloran; Ashes of Vengeance; Enemies of Children; Human Wreckage; Circus Days. **1924** Black Oxen; A Fight for Honor; Judgement of the Storm; Leave It to Gerry; Secrets; Thy Name is Woman; Those Who Date. **1925** The Big Parade; One of the Bravest; The Reckless Sex; Waking Up the Town; The Town of Lies; Dollar Down; The Midnight Flyer. **1926** Ben Hur; The Show-Off; The Devil's Circus; The Dixie Merchant; The Flaming Forest; The Shamrock Handicap. **1927** Almost Human; The Auctioneer; The Black Diamond Express; The Taxi Dancer; Winds of the Pampas; Cheaters; A Little Journey; The Shield of Honor; Tillie the Toiler. **1928** The Viking; Don't Marry; Marriage by Contract; The Tragedy of Youth. **1929** Silks and Saddles; Whispering Winds; The Quitter; When Dreams Come True; Four Devils. **1930** The Big House; Mothers Cry; Redemption; Wild Company; Young Desire; The Second Floor Mystery; Brothers. **1931** An American Tragedy. **1932** Manhattan Parade; It's Tough to Be Famous; Strange Love of Molly Louvain; Phantom Express; Rebecca of Sunnybrook Farm. **1933** Cornered; Two Heads on a Pillow; Central Airport; The Working Man; Paddy, the Next Best Thing; Wild Boys of the Road; By Appointment Only. **1934** Imitation of Life. **1935** Black Fury. **1936** August Weekend. **1937** Two-Fisted Sheriff; High, Wide and Handsome. **1939** Honolulu; One Against the World (short); Three Comrades; Idiot's Delight. **1943** The Youngest Profession. **1944** Are These Our Parents?; Men on Her Mind; Teen Age. **1945** Adventure.

MAC DOWELL, MELBOURNE
Born: 1857, South River, N.J. Died: Feb. 18, 1941, Decoto, Calif. (blood clot on the brain). Stage and screen actor. Married to actress Fanny Davenport.

Appeared in: **1920** Nomads of the North. **1921** Diamonds Adrift; The March Hare; The Golden Snare; Outside the Law. **1922** Beyond the Crossroads; The Bootlegger's Daughter; Confidence; The Infidel; The Flaming Hour; Forsaking All Others. **1923** The Ghost Patrol; The Love Pirate; A Million to Burn; Richard the Lion-Hearted. **1924**

Virtue's Revolt; Geared to Go. **1925** Bandits of the Air; Savages of the Sea; Sky's the Limit; The Cloud Rider; Fighting Courage; Speed Mad. **1926** The Outlaw Express; Behind the Front; The Rainmaker; The Winning Wallop; Stick to Your Story; What Happened to Jones; The City. **1927** Code of the Cow Country; Driven from Home. **1928** Feel My Pulse; The Old Code.

MC DOWELL, NELSON
Born: Aug. 18, 1875, Greenville, Mo. Died: Nov. 3, 1947, Hollywood, Calif. (suicide—gun). Screen actor. Entered films with American Biograph in 1910.

Appeared in: **1916** Wheels of Destiny. **1921** The Silent Call; Home Stuff; Shadows of Conscience; The Last of the Mohicans. **1922** The Phantom Bullet; Whispering Smith; Blind Trail; Crossed Signals; Lightning Reporter; The Outlaw Express; The Frontier Trail; The Valley of Bravery. **1927** Uncle Tom's Cabin; The Claw; Code of the Range; Hands Off; Border Blackbirds; The Bugle Call; The Great Mail Robbery. **1928** Heart Trouble; The Vanishing Rider (serial); The Little Shepherd of Kingdom Come; Kit Carson; Kentucky Courage. **1929** Wild Blood; Born to the Saddle; Grit Wins. **1930** The Real McCoy (short); All Tied Up (short); Billy the Kid. **1932** The Airmail Mystery (serial). **1933** Oliver Twist. **1934** Wheels of Destiny (and 1916 version). **1935** Wilderness Mail. **1936** The Desert Phantom; Feud of the West; Girl of the Ozarks; Ride, Ranger, Ride. **1938** College Swing.

MC DUNNOUGH, WALTER S.
Died: July 1, 1942, Calif. Screen actor.

Appeared in: **1922** Afraid to Fight.

MACE, FRED
Born: 1879, Philadelphia, Pa. Died: Feb. 21, 1917, New York, N.Y. (apoplexy). Screen, stage actor, film producer and director.

Appeared in: **1911** The Village Hero; A Convenient Burglar; Too Many Burglars; Trailing the Counterfeiters; Through His Wife's Picture; A Victim of Circumstances; Dooley's Scheme; Why He Gave Up; Caught with the Goods; $500.00 Reward. **1912** Brave and Bold; A Near-Tragedy; A Spanish Dilemma; Their First Kidnapping Case; The Leading Man; One Round O'Brien; The Speed Demon; A Dash Through the Clouds; Cohen Collects a Debt; The Water Nymph; Riley and Schultz; Lie Not to Your Wife; The New Neighbor; Pedro's Dilemma; Stolen Glory; Ambitious Butler; A Desperate Lover; Mr. Fixer; The Deacon's Trouble; A Bear Escape; Hoffmeyer's Legacy. **1913** Mabel's Adventures; Mabel's Strategem; Drummer's Vacation; The Elite Ball; Just Brown's Luck; The Battle of Who Run; The Stolen Purse; His Nobs—The Plumber; Teddy Loosebelt from Africa; At Twelve O'Clock; A Widow's Wiles; The Turkish Bath; Her New Beau; Algy on the Force; The Tale of a Black Eye; Mimosa's Sweetheart; The Gangsters; One Round O'Brien Comes Back; Gaffney's Gladiator; A Horse on Fred; The Doctor's Ruse; A Would-Be Detective; The Speed Bear; Fred's Trained Nurse; The Rube Boss; Catchem and Killem; The Mexican Sleep Producer. **1914** Heinze's Resurrection; Mabel's Heroes; The Professor's Daughter; A Red Hot Romance; The Sleuth's Last Stand; The Rural Third Degree; Her New Beau; Love and Pain; The Man Next Door; A Deaf Burglar; The Sleuth at the Floral Parade; The Rube and the Baron; Jenny's Pearls; Cupid in a Dental Parlour; Black Hand Conspiracy; Rafferty's Raffle; Up in the Air over Sadie; The Bangville Police; The Darktown Belle; Village School Days; Some Bull's Daughter; The Firebugs; The Tale of a Shirt; Hubby's Job; The Foreman of the Jury; Dad's Terrible Match; The Battle of Chili and Beans; A Parcel's Post Auto; Apollo Fred Sees the Point; Up and Down; The Cheese of Police; Apollo Fred Becomes a Homeseeker; Very Much Alive. **1915** What Happened to Jones?; My Valet; A Janitor's Wife's Temptation; Crooked to the End. **1916** Love Will Conquer; The Village Vampire; Bath Tub Perils; A Lover's Might; An Old Scoundrel; His Last Scent.

MC ELROY, JACK
Born: 1914. Died: Mar. 2, 1959, Santa Monica, Calif. (lung cancer). Screen, radio and television actor.

Appeared in: **1956** Hollywood or Bust.

MC EVOY, DOROTHEA
Born: 1897. Died: Feb. 6, 1976, La Jolla, Calif. Screen and vaudeville actress. Entered films in 1915 with Universal.

MC EVOY, ERNEST SIMON
Born: 1894. Died: Apr. 14, 1953, Hollywood, Calif. Screen and stage actor.

MC EWAN, ISABELLE
Born: 1897, Scotland. Died: Feb. 19, 1963, Vancouver, B.C., Canada. Screen, stage and radio actress.

MAC FADDEN, BERNARR (Bernard A. MacFadden)
Born: Aug. 16, 1868, near Mill Springs, Mo. Died: Oct. 12, 1955, Jersey City, N.J. (jaundice). Health culturist, publisher and screen actor.

Appeared in: **1915-16** Building of the Health of a Nation series. **1925** The Wrongdoers.

MAC FADDEN, CHARLES I. *See* MC FADDEN, IVOR

MAC FADDEN, GERTRUDE "MICKEY"
Born: 1900. Died: June 3, 1967, Hollywood, Calif. Screen, stage and vaudeville actress. Appeared with her sister, Florence, in vaudeville and films as the "MacFadden Sisters."

MC FADDEN, IVOR (Charles Ivor McFadden aka CHARLES I. MAC FADDEN)
Born: Aug. 6, 1887, San Francisco, Calif. Died: Aug. 14, 1942, Los Angeles, Calif. (cerebral hemorrhage). Screen actor and film producer.

Appeared in: **1916** The Measure of a Man; Giant Powder. **1919** Elmo, the Mighty (serial); The Delicious Little Devil. **1921** The Heart Line; Three Word Brand; The Wolverine. **1924** Big Timer. **1925** Fangs of Fate; Tides of Passion. **1926** Two-Gun Man. **1935** Frisco Kid.

MC FARLAND, CARROLL A.
Born: 1885. Died: Mar. 4, 1935, Portland, Ore. Screen and stage actor. Appeared in Selig Film Co. films.

MAC FARLANE, BRUCE
Born: 1910. Died: Nov. 25, 1967, Hollywood, Calif. Screen, stage and television actor. Son of opera singer Alice Gentle (dec. 1958).

Appeared in: **1938** Come On, Leathernecks; Come On, Rangers. **1939** Torchy Plays with Dynamite.

MAC FARLANE, GEORGE
Born: 1877. Died: Feb. 22, 1932, Hollywood, Calif. (auto accident). Screen, stage and vaudeville actor.

Appeared in: **1929** Frozen Justice; Nix on Dames; South Sea Rose; Wall Street; Happy Days. **1930** Cameo Kirby; Double Cross Roads; The Painted Angel; Half Shot at Sunrise; Up the River. **1931** Rich Man's Folly. **1932** Union Depot; Taxi; Fireman, Save My Child; The Heart of New York.

MC GARRY, GARRY
Born: Oct. 17, 1889, Franklin, Pa. Died: Nov. 15, 1927, New York, N.Y. (pneumonia). Screen, stage and vaudeville actor.

Appeared in: **1914** A Question of Clothes. **1915** A Daughter of Israel; The Capitulation of the Major; The Wrong Girl; The Tigress; The Esterbrook Case; Sis. **1916** Prince in a Pawnshop. **1919** False Faces. **1921** Plaything of Broadway.

MC GAUGH, WILBUR
Born: 1895. Died: Jan. 31, 1965, Hollywood, Calif. (heart attack). Screen actor and film director. Entered films in 1911.

Appeared in: **1921** The Broken Spur; Dead or Alive; Devil Dog Dawson; Cupid's Brand; The Sheriff of Hope Eternal. **1922** One Eighth Apache; Peaceful Peters. **1923** At Devil's Gorge; The Law Rustlers; The Devil's Dooryard. **1924** Days of '49 (serial); California in '49 (feature of Days of '49 serial); Bringin' Home the Bacon; Ridin' Mad; Cupid's Rustler. **1925** The Cactus Cure; Whistling Jim; The Fugitive. **1926** Bad Man's Bluff. **1929** The Sky Skidder.

MC GHEE, GLORIA (Gloria McGehee)
Born: 1922. Died: May 4, 1964, Meadville, Miss. (heart attack). Screen, stage and television actress.

Appeared in: **1956** The Boss. **1957** Sierra Stranger. **1963** A Child Is Waiting.

MAC GILL, MOYNA (Moyna McIldowie)
Born: Dec. 10, 1895, Belfast, Ireland. Died: Nov. 25, 1975, Santa Monica, Calif. Stage and screen actress. Mother of actress Angela Lansbury, film producers Edgar and Bruce Denham and Isolde Denham. Divorced from film director Reginald Denham and later married Edgar Lansbury (dec. 1935).

Appeared in: **1920** Garry Owen; Nothing Else Matters. **1924** Miriam Rozella. **1940** Gaslight (aka Angel Street—US 1944). **1943** Forever and a Day. **1944** National Velvet; Winged Victory; Frenchman's Greek. **1945** Uncle Harry; Picture of Dorian Gray. **1946** Black Beauty. **1947** Green Dolphin Street. **1948** Three Daring Daughters; Texas, Brooklyn and Heaven. **1951** Kind Lady. **1952** Les Miserables. **1964** My Fair Lady; The Unsinkable Molly Brown.

MC GINN, WALTER
Born: 1939, Providence, R.I. Died: Mar. 30, 1977, Los Angeles, Calif. (auto accident). Screen, stage and television actor. Married to actress Robyn Goodman.

Appeared in: **1974** The Parallax View. **1975** Farewell, My Lovely; Three Days of the Condor. **1977** Bobby Deerfield.

MC GIVENEY, OWEN
Born: 1884. Died: July 31, 1967, Woodland Hills, Calif. Screen, stage and vaudeville actor.

Appeared in: **1948** If Winter Comes. **1951** Show Boat. **1952** Scaramouche; Pat and Mike; Plymouth Adventure. **1953** The Maze. **1954** Brigadoon. **1955** The King's Thief. **1958** Hong Kong Confidential; In the Money. **1961** Snow White and the Three Stooges. **1964** My Fair Lady.

MC GIVER, JOHN (George Morris)
Born: Nov. 5, 1913. Died: Sept. 9, 1975, West Fulton, N.Y. (heart attack). Screen, stage and television actor. Married to designer Ruth Shmigelsky.

Appeared in: **1957** Love in the Afternoon. **1958** Once Upon a Horse; I Married a Woman; The Man in the Raincoat. **1959** The Gazebo. **1961** Love in a Goldfish Bowl; Bachelor in Paradise; Breakfast at Tiffany's. **1962** The Manchurian Candidate; Mr. Hobbs Takes a Vacation; Period of Adjustment; Who's Got the Action? **1963** Take Her, She's Mine; Who's Minding the Store?; Johnny Cool; Hot Horse (reissue of Once Upon a Horse—1958); My Six Loves. **1964** A Global Affair; Man's Favorite Sport. **1965** Marriage on the Rocks. **1966** The Glass Bottom Boat; Made in Paris. **1967** The Spirit Is Willing; Fitzwilly. **1969** Midnight Cowboy.

MC GLYNN, FRANK
Born: 1867, San Francisco, Calif. Died: May 17, 1951, Newburgh, N.Y. Screen and stage actor. Played Abraham Lincoln in many films. Appeared in Edison Stock Company films in 1907.

Appeared in: **1916** Gloria's Romance (serial). **1924** America. **1927** Judgement of the Hills. **1930** Min and Bill; Good News; Jazz Cinderella. **1931** The Secret Six; Huckleberry Finn; Riders of the Purple Sage. **1932** The Silent Partners (short); No Man of Her Own. **1933** The Moonshiner's Daughter or Aboard in Old Kentucky (short); Unknown Valley; Charlie Chan's Greatest Case; Frisco Jenny; Face in the Sky. **1934** Massacre; Little Miss Marker; The Mighty Barnum; Kentucky Kernels; Search for Beauty; Are We Civilized?; Lost in the Stratosphere. **1935** Dr. Socrates; Folies Bergere; It's a Small World; Roaring West (serial); Outlawed Guns; The Littlest Rebel; Custer's Last Stand (serial); Captain Blood; Hopalong Cassidy. **1936** The Prisoner of Shark Island; King of the Royal Mounted; Career Woman; Hearts in Bondage; Parole; The Last of the Mohicans; North of Nome; The Plainsman; For the Service; The Trail of the Lonesome Pine. **1937** Wild West Days (serial); Western Gold; Wells Fargo; Silent Barriers; Sing and Be Happy. **1938** The Lone Ranger (serial); Sudden Bill Dorn; Kentucky Moonshine. **1939** Love Affair; The Honeymoon's Over; Union Pacific; The Mad Empress. **1940** Hi-Yo Silver; Boom Town. **1941** A Girl, a Guy and a Gob; Marry the Boss's Daughter; Three Girls in Town. **1944** Delinquent Daughters. **1945** Rogues' Gallery. **1947** Hollywood Barn Dance.

MC GOWAN, JOHN P. (John Paterson McGowan)
Born: Feb. 24, 1880, Terowie, South Australia. Died: Mar. 26, 1952, Hollywood, Calif. Screen, stage actor, film director, film producer and screenwriter. Entered films as an actor with Kalem in 1909.

Appeared in: **1912** From the Manger to the Cross. **1915** Hazards of Helen (serial). **1917** The Railroad Raiders (serial). **1921** Do or Die (serial); Discontented Wives; Cold Steel; A Crook's Romance; The White Horseman (serial); King of the Circus (serial). **1922** Hills of Missing Men; Reckless Chances; The Ruse of the Rattler. **1923** The Whipping Boss; One Million in Jewels; Stormy Seas. **1924** Crossed Trails; A Two Fisted Tenderfoot. **1925** Barriers of the Law; Border Intrigue; Crack O'Dawn; Duped; The Fear Fighter; Makers of Men; Outwitted; Blood and Steel; The Fighting Sheriff. **1926** Danger Quest; Moran of the Mounted; The Patent Leather Kid; Red Blood; Senor Daredevil; The Ace of Clubs; The Lost Express. **1927** Arizona Nights; Gun Gospel; The Lost Limited; Red Signals; The Red Raiders; The Slaver; Whispering Smith Rides (serial); The Royal American; Tarzan and the Golden Lion. **1928** The Black Ace; Arizona Days; The Code of the Scarlet; Devil Dogs; Devil's Tower; Dugan of the Dugouts; Headin' Westward; Law of the Mounted; Lighting Shot; The Old Code; On the Divide; Ships of the Night; Silent Trail; Texas Tommy; The Two Outlaws; West of Santa Fe; Painted Trail; Chinatown Mystery (serial); Senor Americano. **1929** The Phantom Raider; The

Invaders; Fighting Terror; Arizona Days; Bad Man's Money; The Clean Up; Below the Deadline; The Lawless Legion; Captain Cowboy; On the Divide; The Silent Trail; The Last Roundup; West of Santa Fe; The Lone Horseman; Oklahoma Kid; The Golden Bridle; Ships of the Night; Plunging Hoofs; Riders of the Rio Grande; 'Neath Western Skies. **1930** Cowboy and the Outlaw; Pioneers of the West; Canyon of Missing Men; Covered Wagon Trails; O'Malley Rides Alone; Breezy Bill; Near the Rainbow's End. **1931** Riders of the North. **1932** Hurricane Express. **1933** Somewhere in Arizona; When a Man Rides Alone. **1934** The Red Rider (serial); No More Women; Wagon Wheels; Fighting Hero. **1935** Rustlers of Red Dog (serial); Mississippi; Border Brigands; Bar 20 Rides Again. **1936** Stampede; Guns and Guitars; The Three Mesquiteers; Secret Patrol; Ride 'Em Cowboy. **1937** Fury and the Woman; Hit the Saddle; Heart of the Rockies; Slave Ship. **1938** The Great Adventures of Wild Bill Hickok (serial); The Buccaneer; Kennedy's Castle (short); Hunted Men. **1939** In Old Montana; Code of the Fearless; Calling All Marines; Stagecoach.

MC GOWAN, JOHN P. "JACK"
Born: 1896. Died: May 28, 1977, New York, N.Y. Screen, stage, vaudeville actor, screenwriter, playwright, singer, composer, lyricist and burlesque entertainer. Do not confuse with actor/director John P. McGowan (dec. 1952).

MC GOWAN, OLIVER F.
Born: 1907. Died: Aug. 23, 1971, Hollywood, Calif. Screen, stage, radio and television actor.

Appeared in: **1958** Screaming Mimi. **1966** Stagecoach. **1967** Banning.

MAC GOWRAN, JACK
Born: Oct. 13, 1918, Dublin, Ireland. Died: Jan. 31, 1973, New York, N.Y. (London flu). Screen, stage and television actor.

Appeared in: **1951** No Resting Place (US 1952). **1952** The Quiet Man; The Gentle Gunman (US 1953). **1953** The Titfield Thunderbolt. **1954** The Young Lovers (aka Chance Meeting—US 1955). **1956** Jacqueline. **1957** The Rising of the Moon (aka The Majesty of the Law); Manuela (aka Stowaway Girl—US). **1958** Rooney; She Didn't Say No (US 1962). **1959** Darby O'Gill and the Little People; Behemoth the Sea Monster (aka The Giant Behemoth—US). **1962** Mix Me a Person; Captain Clegg (aka Night Creatures—US); Two and Two Make Six; Vengeance (aka The Brain—US 1964). **1963** Tom Jones; The Ceremony. **1965** Lord Jim; Young Cassidy; Doctor Zhivago. **1966** Cul-de-Sac. **1967** How I Won the War; Dance of the Vampires (aka The Fearless Vampire Killers or Pardon Me, but Your Teeth are in My Neck—US). **1968** Wonderwall. **1969** Age of Consent (US 1970). **1970** King Lear. **1973** The Exorcist.

MC GRAIL, WALTER B.
Born: 1899, Brooklyn, N.Y. Died: Mar. 19, 1970. Screen and stage actor.

Appeared in: **1916** The Scarlet Runner (serial). **1917** Within the Law. **1918** Miss Ambition. **1919** The Black Secret (serial); The Adventure Shop; The Girl Problem. **1921** Playthings of Destiny; The Invisible Fear; The Breaking Point; Her Mad Bargain; Pilgrims of the Night. **1922** The Cradle; The Kentucky Derby; Suzanna; The Top of New York; The Yosemite Trail. **1923** The Bad Man; The Eleventh Hour; Flaming Youth; Is Divorce a Failure?; Nobody's Money; Lights Out; Where the North Begins. **1924** A Son of the Sahara; Gerald Cranston's Lady; Is Love Everything?; Unguarded Women. **1925** Havoc; The Dancers; The Mad Marriage; Champion of Lost Causes; Adventure; A Son of His Father; When the Door Opened; The Teaser; Her Husband's Secret; The Scarlet West. **1926** Across the Pacific; The City; The Combat; Forbidden Waters; Marriage License?; Prisoners of the Storm. **1927** The Secret Studio; American Beauty. **1928** Man Crazy; The Play Girl; Stop That Man; Midnight Madness; Blockade; The Old Code. **1929** One Splendid Hour; Confessions of a Wife; Hey Rube!; The Veiled Woman; River of Romance. **1930** Soldiers and Women; The Lone Star Ranger; Men Without Women; Women Everywhere; Last of the Duanes; Anybody's War; The Pay-Off; Part Time Wife. **1931** River's End; The Seas Beneath; Murder by the Clock; Night Nurse. **1932** Night Beat; Under Eighteen; McKenna of the Mounted; Exposed. **1933** State Trooper; Robbers' Roost; Sing, Sinner, Sing!; Police Call. **1935** All the King's Horses; Sunset Range; Men of the Night. **1937** The Shadow Strikes. **1938** Held for Ransom. **1939** Stagecoach; Calling All Marines; The Sun Never Sets. **1940** Mysterious Dr. Satan (serial); The Green Hornet (serial); My Little Chickadee. **1942** Billy the Kid Trapped; Riders of the West.

MC GRANARY, AL (Aloysius Cornelius McGranary)
Born: Sept. 3, 1902, Pa. Died: May 15, 1971, Los Angeles, Calif. (uremia, arteriosclerosis). Screen actor.

Appeared in: **1959** Riot in Juvenile Prison. **1960** Sunrise at Campobello. **1962** Advise and Consent.

MC GRATH, DENNIS
Born: c. 1875. Died: 1955, New York, N.Y. Stage and screen actor. Appeared in silent films.

MC GRATH, FRANK
Born: 1903. Died: May 13, 1967, Beverly Hills, Calif. (heart attack). Screen and television actor. Entered films as a stuntman.

Appeared in: **1942** Sundown Jim. **1945** They Were Expendable. **1949** She Wore a Yellow Ribbon. **1953** Ride, Vaquero. **1957** Hell Bound; The Tin Star. **1965** The Sword of Ali Baba. **1967** The Last Challenge; Tammy and the Millionaire; Gunfight in Abilene; The War Wagon; The Reluctant Astronaut. **1968** The Shakiest Gun in the West.

MC GRATH, LARRY (Lawrence Joseph McGrath)
Born: Aug. 28, 1888, N.Y. Died: July 6, 1960, Los Angeles, Calif. (heart attack). Screen actor.

Appeared in: **1927** Knockout Reilly. **1930** The Arizona Kid; The Big Fight. **1934** Picture Brides. **1935** Dr. Socrates; Dangerous. **1936** The Milky Way. **1937** The Perfect Specimen. **1941** Moon Over Miami. **1942** The Miracle Kid. **1944** Wilson. **1950** Kansas Raiders; The Jackie Robinson Story. **1951** Flaming Feather.

MC GRATH, MICHAEL
Died: Jan. 16, 1976, New York, N.Y. (pneumonia). Screen and stage actor.

MC GRATH, PAUL
Born: 1904, Chicago, Ill. Died: Apr. 13, 1978, London, England. Screen, stage, radio and television actor. Married to actress Anne Sargent.

Appeared in: **1940** Parole Fixer; Wildcat Bus. **1941** This Thing Called Love; Dead Men Tell; We Go Fast; Marry the Boss's Daughter. **1943** No Time for Love. **1957** A Face in the Crowd. **1962** Advise and Consent. **1969** Pendulum.

MC GRATH, THOMAS
Born: 1867. Died: Apr. 22, 1937, Ft. Wayne, Ind. (complication of diseases). Screen and stage actor.

Appeared in: **1913** Our New Minister.

MC GRAW, CHARLES (Charles Butters)
Born: May 10, 1914, in the Orient. Died: July, 1980, Studio City, Calif. (result of a fall). Screen, stage, radio and television actor.

Appeared in: **1943** The Moon Is Down (film debut); They Came to Blow Up America; The Mad Ghoul. **1944** The Imposter. **1946** The Killers. **1947** The Big Fix; T-Men; The Long Night; The Gangster; On the Old Spanish Trail; Roses Are Red. **1948** Blood on the Moon; The Hunted; Hazard. **1949** The Black Book; Reign of Terror; Once More, My Darling; Border Incident; The Story of Molly X; The Threat; Side Street. **1950** Double Crossbones; The Armed Car Robbery; Ma and Pa Kettle Go to Town. **1951** His Kind of Woman. **1952** One Minute to Zero; The Narrow Margin. **1953** War Paint; Thunder Over the Plains. **1954** The Bridges at Toko-Ri; Loophole. **1956** Away All Boats; Toward the Unknown; The Cruel Tower. **1957** Slaughter on Tenth Avenue; Joe Butterfly; Joe Dakota. **1958** The Defiant Ones; Saddle the Wind; Twilight for the Gods. **1959** The Wonderful Country; The Man in the Net. **1960** Spartacus; Cimarron. **1962** The Horizontal Lieutenant. **1963** It's a Mad, Mad, Mad, Mad World; The Birds. **1967** In Cold Blood; The Busy Body. **1968** Hang 'Em High. **1969** Pendulum; Tell Them Willie Boy Is Here. **1975** A Boy and His Dog. **1976** The Killer Inside Me. **1977** Twilight's Last Gleaming.

MC GRAW, JOHN
Born: Apr. 7, 1873, Truxton, N.Y. Died: Feb. 25, 1934, New Rochelle, N.Y. Professional baseball player and screen actor.

Appeared in: **1914** The Universal Boy.

MAC GREGOR, HARMAN
Born: 1878, New York, N.Y. Died: Dec. 5, 1948, Marblehead, Mass. Stage and screen actor.

Appeared in: **1923** Cause for Divorce; Slave of Desire; Vengeance of the Deep. **1924** The Dancing Cheat.

MAC GREGOR, LEE (aka LEE MC GREGOR)
Died: June, 1961. Screen actor.

Appeared in: **1947** Gentleman's Agreement; Moss Rose; Mother Wore Tights. **1948** You Were Meant for Me; Sitting Pretty; The Luck of the Irish; Road House; Scudda Hoo! Scudda Hay!; When My Baby Smiles at Me. **1949** Mother is a Freshman; You're My Everything; Slattery's Hurricane; Mr. Belvedere Goes to College; It Happens Every Spring; Father was a Fullback; Twelve O'Clock High. **1950** Where the Sidewalk Ends; A Ticket to Tomahawk; Two Flags West; When Willie Comes Marching Home; My Blue Heaven; Three Came Home; Under My Skin. **1951** Sealed Cargo; Best of the Badmen; Hot Lead. **1952** The Half-Breed; Above and Beyond; Toughest Man in Arizona; What Price Glory?

MC GREGOR, MALCOLM (aka MALCOLM MAC GREGOR)
Born: Oct. 13, 1892, Newark, N.J. Died: Apr. 29, 1945, Los Angeles, Calif. (burns). Screen actor.

Appeared in: **1922** The Prisoner of Zenda; Broken Chains. **1923** The Untamable; All the Brothers Were Valiant; The Dancer of the Nile; Can a Woman Love Twice?; A Noise in Newboro; The Social Code; You Can't Get Away With It. **1924** Smouldering Fires; The House of Youth; The Bedroom Window; Idle Tongues. **1925** Headlines; Alias Mary Flynn; The Circle; The Happy Warrior; Flaming Waters; The Girl of Gold; Lady of the Night; The Overland Limited; The Vanishing American. **1926** Infatuation; The Silent Flyer (serial); Don Juan's Three Nights; It Must Be Love; The Gay Deceiver; Money to Burn. **1927** A Million Bid; The Girl from Gay Paree; The Kid Sister; The Ladybird; Matinee Ladies; The Wreck; The Price of Honor. **1928** Buck Privates; Freedom of the Press; Lingerie; The Port of Missing Girls; Tropical Nights; Stormy Waters. **1929** The Girl on the Barge; Whispering Winds. **1930** Murder Will Out. **1933** Whispering Shadows (serial). **1935** Happiness C.O.D.

MC GREGOR, PARKE (Parke Cushnie)
Born: 1907. Died: Dec. 5, 1962, Hollywood, Calif. (heart attack). Screen actor and singer.

MC GUINN, JOSEPH FORD "JOE"
Born: Jan. 21, 1904, Brooklyn, N.Y. Died: Sept. 22, 1971, Hollywood, Calif. (heart attack). Screen and stage actor.

Appeared in: **1939** Dick Tracy's G-Men (serial). **1940** Mysterious Dr. Satan (serial); Ride, Tenderfoot, Ride; Pioneers of the West. **1941** Jungle Girl (serial); Holt of the Secret Service (serial); Back in the Saddle. **1942** The Glass Key; Flight Lieutenant; Bells of Capistrano; In Old California; Two Yanks in Trinidad; The Cyclone Kid. **1945** Three's a Crowd. **1953** Prince of Pirates. **1957** Chicago Confidential; Three Brave Men. **1958** Ten North Frederick; Showdown at Boot Hill. **1959** The Story on Page One. **1961** The Gambler Wore a Gun. **1962** The Wild Westerners.

MC GUIRE, BENJAMIN
Born: 1875. Died: Apr. 10, 1925, New York, N.Y. (heart failure). Screen actor. Appeared in Famous Players' films.

MC GUIRE, BILLY
Born: 1947, Hendersonville, N.C. Died: July 14, 1979, Niagara Falls, Ontario, Canada (complications from a motorcycle accident). Screen actor, sideshow exhibitor and ukulele player. Known, with his brother Benny, as the "World's Largest Twins."

Appeared in: **1942** Thunder Birds.

MC GUIRE, HARP (Henry Herbert McGuire)
Born: Nov. 1, 1921, Tenn. Died: Oct. 21, 1966, Los Angeles, Calif. (coronary sclerosis). Screen actor.

Appeared in: **1959** On the Beach. **1960** The Cage of Evil; The Walking Target. **1962** Incident in an Alley.

MC GUIRE, JOHN J.
Died: Oct. 2, 1980, Los Angeles, Calif.? Screen actor.

Appeared in: **1935** Steamboat Round the Bend; Your Uncle Dudley; This Is the Life. **1936** The Prisoner of Shark Island; Charlie Chan at the Opera; Wanted: Jane Turner; End of the Trail; Human Cargo; Charlie Chan at the Circus. **1940** Women Without Names; Street of Memories; Stranger on the Third Floor. **1941** Sea Raiders (serial); The Invisible Ghost. **1947** Bells of San Angelo. **1948** The Strawberry Roan. **1949** Sands of Iwo Jima; Sky Liner. **1950** Military Academy (aka Military Academy With That 10th Avenue Gang); Federal Agent at Large; Where the Sidewalk Ends. **1951** The First Legion; The Tanks Are Coming; Call Me Mister.

MC GUIRE, KATHRYN
Born: Dec. 6, 1904, Peoria, Ill. Died: Oct. 10, 1978, Los Angeles, Calif. (cancer). Screen actress. Married to publicist George Landy (dec. 1955). Entered films with Mack Sennett.

Appeared in: **1921** Bucking the Line; Playing With Fire; Home Talent; The Silent Call. **1922** The Crossroads of New York. **1923** The Love Pirate; The Printer's Devil; The Flame of Life; The Woman of Bronze; The Sheik of Araby. **1924** The Navigator; Phantom Justice; Sherlock, Jr. **1925** Two-Fisted Justice; Tearing Through; Dashing Thru; Easy Going Gordon; The Gold Hunters. **1926** Davy Crockett at the Fall of the Alamo; Buffalo Bill on the U.P. Trail; Stacked Cards; Midnight Faces; Somebody's Mother; The Thrill Hunter; Mystery Pilot (serial). **1927** The Girl in the Pullman; Naughty But Nice. **1928** Lilac Time. **1929** The Big Diamond Robbery; The Border Wildcat; Children of the Ritz; The Long, Long Trail; Synthetic Sin; He Did His Best. **1930** The Lost Zeppelin.

MC GUIRE, TOM
Born: 1874. Died: May 6, 1954, Hollywood, Calif. Screen and stage actor.

Appeared in: **1921** The Girl in the Taxi; R.S.V.P.; See My Lawyer; Stranger Than Fiction. **1922** Afraid to Fight; The Five Dollar Baby; A Front Page Story; The Ladder Jinx; The Married Flapper. **1923** April Showers; A Million to Burn; The Scarlet Car; The Self-Made Wife; Single Handed; The Spoilers; The Victor. **1924** Captain Blood; Dark Stairways; Her Man; The Reckless Age. **1925** Fighting Fate; Red Hot Tires; We Moderns. **1926** The Better 'Ole; My Own Pal. **1927** Babe Comes Home; Colleen; The Missing Link; Pleasure Before Business; Shanghai Bound. **1928** Lights of New York; A Thief in the Dark; The Sawdust Paradise; Steamboat Bill, Jr. **1930** Voice of the City. **1931** Politics; Oh! Oh! Cleopatra (short). **1932** No Greater Love. **1933** She Done Him Wrong. **1936** Charlie Chan at the Opera.

MC GUIRK, HARRIET (Harriet Nawrot)
Born: 1903, Chicago, Ill. Died: Dec. 19, 1975, Wilmington, Del. Professional roller skater, screen, stage and television actress.

Appeared in: **1935** Transient Lady.

MC GURK, BOB
Born: 1907. Died: May 30, 1959, Los Angeles, Calif. Screen actor.

MC HALE, JAMES
Died: Feb. 4, 1973. Screen actor.

Appeared in: **1970** Kelly's Heroes.

MC HUGH, CATHERINE
Born: Mont. Died: Mar. 25, 1954, Los Angeles, Calif. Silent screen actress.

MC HUGH, CATHERINE
Born: 1869. Died: June 28, 1944, Hollywood, Calif. Screen actress. Mother of actors Matt (dec. 1971) and Frank McHugh.

MC HUGH, CHARLES PATRICK
Born: Philadelphia, Pa. Died: Oct. 22, 1931, Los Angeles, Calif. (heart attack). Screen and stage actor.

Appeared in: **1921** Be My Wife; A Shocking Night; Smiling All the Way. **1922** The Beautiful and Damned. **1923** Cupid's Fireman; The Eagle's Feather; The Girl of the Golden West. **1924** The Trouble Shooter. **1925** Brand of Cowardice; The Golden Cocoon; Lights of Old Broadway; Smilin' at Trouble. **1926** Her Honor the Governor; The Prince of Broadway; The Sporting Lover; The Waning Sex. **1927** Finnegan's Ball; The Princess from Hoboken. **1928** Phantom of the Range. **1929** Smiling Irish Eyes; The Quitter.

MC HUGH, EDWARD A.
Born: 1860. Died: Oct. 9, 1935, Los Angeles, Calif. (heart attack). Screen, stage and vaudeville actor. Father of Edward, Jr., Matt, Katherine, and actor Frank McHugh (dec. 1981).

MC HUGH, FRANK
Born: May 23, 1899, Homestead, Pa. Died: Sept. 11, 1981, Greenwich, Conn. Screen, stage, vaudeville and television actor. Son of actor Edward A. McHugh (dec. 1935). Married to actress Dorothy Spencer.

Appeared in: **1926** Mademoiselle Modiste. **1928** If Men Played Cards as Women Do. **1930** Top Speed; The Widow From Chicago; The Dawn Patrol; College Lovers. **1931** Traveling Husbands; Going Wild; Up for Murder; Bright Lights; The Front Page; Men of the Sky; Kiss Me Again; Corsair; Fires of Youth; Bad Company; Millie. **1932** Wide Open Spaces (short); Union Depot; One Way Passage; Life Begins; Blessed

Event; Dark Horse; The Strange Love of Molly Louvain; The Crowd Roars; High Pressure. **1933** The Mystery of the Wax Museum; Footlight Parade; Parachute Jumper; Havana Widows; Grand Slam; Private Jones; Telegraph Trail; Ex-Lady; Elmer the Great; Professional Sweetheart; Hold Me Tight; House on 56th Street; Lilly Turner; Convention City; Tomorrow at Seven; Son of a Sailor. **1934** Here Comes the Navy; Heat Lightning; Fashions of 1934; Smarty; Let's Be Ritzy; Merry Wives of Reno; Return of the Terror; Six Day Bike Rider; Happiness Ahead. **1935** Gold Diggers of 1935; Page Miss Glory; Maybe It's Love; Stars Over Broadway; Devil Dogs of the Air; The Irish in Us; A Midsummer Night's Dream. **1936** Three Men on a Horse; Stage Struck; Freshman Love; Moonlight Murder; Bullets or Ballots. **1937** Snowed Under; Ever Since Eve; Mr. Dodd Takes the Air; Marry the Girl; Submarine D-1. **1938** Boy Meets Girl; Valley of the Giants; Four Daughters; Swing Your Lady; He Couldn't Say No; Little Miss Thoroughbred. **1939** Indianapolis Speedway; Four Wives; On Your Toes; Dust Be My Destiny; Dodge City; The Roaring Twenties; Wings of the Navy; Daughters Courageous. **1940** The Fighting 69th; I Love You Again; Virginia City; City for Conquest; 'Til We Meet Again. **1941** Back Street; Manpower; Four Mothers. **1942** Her Cardboard Lover; All Through the Night. **1944** Going My Way; Bowery to Broadway; Marine Raiders. **1945** A Medal for Benny; State Fair. **1946** The Hoodlum Saint; Little Miss Big. **1947** Easy Come, Easy Go; Carnegie Hall. **1948** The Velvet Touch. **1949** Mighty Joe Young; Miss Grant Takes Richmond. **1950** Paid in Full; The Tougher They Come. **1952** The Pace That Thrills; My Son John. **1953** A Lion Is in the Streets; It Happens Every Thursday. **1954** There's No Business Like Show Business. **1958** The Last Hurrah. **1959** Say One for Me. **1964** A Tiger Walks. **1967** Easy Come, Easy Go (and 1947 version).

MC HUGH, GRACE
Born: 1898. Died: July 1, 1914, near Canon City, Colo. (drowned while filming). Screen actress.

Appeared in: **1914** Across the Border.

MC HUGH, JIMMY
Born: July 10, 1894, Boston, Mass. Died: May 23, 1969, Beverly Hills, Calif. (heart attack). Songwriter and screen actor.

Appeared in: **1957** The Helen Morgan Story.

MC HUGH, MATT (Mathew O. McHugh)
Born: 1894, Connellsville, Pa. Died: Feb. 22, 1971, Northridge, Calif. (heart attack). Screen, stage and vaudeville actor. Entered films with Mack Sennett. Brother of actor Frank McHugh. Son of actress Catherine McHugh (dec. 1944).

Appeared in: **1931** Street Scene (screen and stage versions); Reckless Living. **1932** Alaska Love (short); Freaks; The Wet Parade; Afraid to Talk. **1933** Paramount shorts; The Last Trail; The Man Who Dared; Jimmy and Sally; Devil's Brother; Night of Terror. **1934** She Loves Me Not; Sandy McKee; Judge Priest; Wake Up and Dream. **1935** Wings in the Dark; Lost in the Stratosphere; Murder on a Honeymoon; The Good Fairy; Enter Madame; Mr. Dynamite; Diamond Jim; The Glass Key; Ladies Crave Excitement; Barbary Coast. **1936** Two in a Crowd; The Big Broadcast of 1937. **1937** Navy Blue and Gold. **1938** No Time to Marry; Tropic Holiday. **1939** Federal Man Hunt; Jones Family in Hollywood; The Escape; At the Circus. **1940** His Ex Marks the Spot (short); You the People (short); Yesterday's Heroes. **1941** So You Won't Squawk (short). **1942** The Perfect Snob; Sappy Birthday (short); It Happened in Flatbush; The Man in the Trunk; Girl Trouble. **1943** Thank Your Lucky Stars; Henry Aldrich Swings It; Flight for Freedom; The West Side Kid. **1944** My Buddy; Home in Indiana. **1945** Salome, Where She Danced; The Bells of St. Mary's; How Do You Do? **1946** The Strange Love of Martha Ivers; Deadline for Murder; Dark Corner; Vacation in Reno. **1947** The Trouble with Women. **1948** Scudda Hoo! Scudda Hay!; Pardon My Clutch (short). **1949** Duke of Chicago. **1950** Kiss Tomorrow Goodbye; Bodyhold; Return of the Frontiersman. **1955** Wham-Bam-Slam (short).

MC ILLWAIN, WILLIAM A.
Born: 1863. Died: May 27, 1933, Los Angeles, Calif. (heart attack). Screen and stage actor.

Appeared in: **1924** Abraham Lincoln. **1925** Passionate Youth; Reckless Courage.

MC INTOSH, BURR
Born: Aug. 21, 1862, Wellsville, Ohio. Died: Apr. 28, 1942, Hollywood, Calif. (heart attack). Screen, stage, radio actor, screenwriter and writer for radio. Entered films in 1913.

Appeared in: **1915** Adventures of Wallingford. **1920** Way Down East.

1923 Driven; The Exciters; On the Banks of the Wabash. **1924** The Average Woman; Lend Me Your Husband; Reckless Wives; The Spitfire; Virtuous Liars. **1925** Camille of the Barbary Coast; Enemies of Youth; The Pearl of Love; The Green Archer (serial). **1926** The Buckaroo Kid; Dangerous Friends; Lightning Reporter; The Wilderness Woman. **1927** The Golden Stallion (serial); A Hero for the Night; Breakfast at Sunrise; Fire and Steel; Framed; Hazardous Valley; Naughty But Nice; Once and Forever; See You in Jail; Silk Stockings; Taxi! Taxi!; The Yankee Clipper; Non Support (short). **1928** Across the Atlantic; The Adorable Cheat; The Grip of the Yukon; Me, Gangster; The Racket; That Certain Thing; Lilac Time; The Four Flusher; Sailor's Wives. **1929** The Last Warning; Fancy Baggage; Skinner Steps Out. **1930** The Rogue Song. **1933** The Sweetheart of Sigma Chi. **1934** The Richest Girl in the World.

MAC INTOSH, LOUISE
Born: 1865. Died: Nov. 1, 1933, Beverly Hills, Calif. Screen and stage actress.

Appeared in: **1930** Up the River.

MC INTYRE, DUNCAN
Born: 1907, Scotland? Died: Dec., 1973, London, England. Screen, radio, stage and television actor.

Appeared in: **1954** The Maggie (aka High and Dry—US). **1962** Strongroom.

MC INTYRE, FRANK
Born: Feb. 25, 1878. Died: June 8, 1949, Ann Arbor, Mich. Screen, stage and radio actor.

Appeared in: **1917** The Traveling Salesman. **1918** Too Fat to Fight.

MC INTYRE, LEILA
Born: 1882. Died: Jan. 9, 1953, Los Angeles, Calif. Screen, stage and vaudeville actress. She appeared in vaudeville with her husband, actor John Hyams (dec. 1940), in an act called "Hyams and McIntyre." Mother of actress Leila Hyams. Her married name was Leila Hyams, but do not confuse her with her daughter by the same name (Leila Hyams) who was born 1905 and dec 1977.

Appeared in: **1927** All in Fun (Hyams and McIntyre short). **1929** Hurricane. **1930** On the Level; Swell People; All for Mabel. **1933** Marriage on Approval. **1935** Murder in the Fleet. **1936** The Plainsman; The Prisoner of Shark Island. **1937** Pick a Star; Live, Love and Learn; Topper. **1939** The Housekeeper's Daughter; Three Smart Girls Grow Up; The Women; Zenobia. **1940** Third Finger, Left Hand. **1942** Tennessee Johnson. **1943** Wintertime. **1945** Fallen Angel. **1946** The Hoodlum Saint.

MC INTYRE, MARION (Marion Gray)
Born: 1885. Died: Nov. 19, 1975, Woodland Hills, Calif. Screen, radio and television actress.

MC IVOR, MARY
Born: 1901. Died: Feb. 28, 1941, Hollywood, Calif. (heart attack). Screen and vaudeville actress. Married to actor William Desmond (dec. 1949).

Appeared in: **1925** The Burning Trail.

MACK, ANDREW
Born: 1863, Boston, Mass. Died: May 21, 1931, Bayside, N.Y. Screen, stage actor and singer.

Appeared in: **1914** The Ragged Earl. **1926** Bluebeard's Seven Wives.

MACK, ARTHUR
Born: 1877. Died: June 19, 1942, Jamaica Plain, Mass. (gas poisoning suffered in Flanders during W.W.I). Screen and stage actor.

Appeared in: **1928** The Return of Sherlock Holmes.

MACK, BILL "BILLY"
Died: Jan. 27, 1961, New York, N.Y. (stroke). Screen and vaudeville actor. Was part of vaudeville acts of "Reigel and Mack" and later as "Richard and Mack."

Appeared in: **1926** The Black Bird. **1944** A Wave, a Wac and a Marine.

MACK, CACTUS (Thomas McPheeters)
Born: Aug. 9, 1899, Weed, N.Mex. Died: Apr. 17, 1962, Hollywood, Calif. (heart attack). Screen actor.

Appeared in: **1939** Racketeers of the Range; The Fighting Gringo. **1941** The Singing Hill; West of Cimarron. **1946** Shadows of the Range;

Trigger Fingers; Raiders of the South; Silver Range. **1947** Trailing Danger; Land of the Lawless; Valley of Fear; Six Gun Serenade; Gun Talk. **1948** Range Renegades; The Rangers Ride. **1949** The Dalton Gang. **1951** Don Daredevil Rides Again (serial).

MACK, CHARLES (Charles McGaughey)
Born: 1878. Died: Nov. 29, 1956, Hollywood, Calif. Screen, stage actor, film producer and costumer. Entered films in 1919.

Appeared in: **1925** The Lost Chord; Silent Pal; The White Monkey. **1927** The Trunk Mystery.

MACK, CHARLES E. (Charles E. Sellers)
Born: Nov. 22, 1887, White Cloud, Kans. Died: Jan. 11, 1934, near Mesa, Ariz. (auto accident). Screen, stage, vaudeville, radio minstrel and actor. He was the Mack in "Moran and Mack" comedy team, usually referred to as the "Two Black Crows."

Films he appeared in as part of team are: **1927** Two Flaming Youths. **1929** Why Bring That Up. **1930** Anybody's War (previous title was Two Black Crows in the A.E.F.). **1932** Hypnotized. **1932-33** Appeared in "Moran and Mack" shorts for Educational: Two Black Crows in Africa; As The Crows Fly. A few other shorts were without George Moran who left the team after, Why Bring That Up, but returned to do Hypnotized and a few shorts.

MACK, CHARLES EMMETT
Born: 1900, Scranton, Pa. Died: Mar. 17, 1927, Riverside, Calif. (auto accident). Screen and vaudeville actor. Entered films as a property man with Griffith in 1917.

Appeared in: **1921** Dream Street. **1922** One Exciting Night. **1923** Driven; The Daring Years; The White Rose. **1924** America; The Sixth Commandment; Youth for Sale. **1925** Down Upon the Swanee River; Bad Company; A Woman of the World; The White Monkey. **1926** The Devil's Circus; The Unknown Soldier. **1927** The First Auto; The Rough Riders; Old San Francisco.

MACK, DICK
Born: 1854. Died: Feb. 4, 1920, San Francisco, Calif. Screen, stage and vaudeville actor.

MACK, FRANCES
Born: 1907. Died: Sept. 26, 1967, Hollywood, Calif. Screen and stage actress. Entered films approx. 1945. Married to screen actor and costumer Alexis Davidoff.

Appeared in: **1949** The Set-Up.

MACK, GEORGE E.
Born: 1866, Boston, Mass. Died: May 20, 1948, Cheyenne, Wyo. Screen and stage actor. Married to stage actress Mabel Strickland (dec. 1947).

Appeared in: **1915** Wildfire.

MACK, HAYWARD
Born: Albany, N.Y. Died: Dec. 24, 1921, Los Angeles, Calif. Screen, stage and vaudeville actor.

Appeared in: **1910** Little Nell's Tobacco. **1915** Graft (serial). **1916** The Isle of Life. **1917** The Spindle of Life (aka Gladsome); The Phantom's Secret; Flirting With Death; The Double Room Mystery; The Pullman Mystery. **1918** Impossible Susan. **1919** Put Up Your Hands; Some Liar; Fighting Through; Love Is Love; The Speed Maniac; Thieves. **1920** Girl in the Web. **1921** Why Trust Your Husband?; Burglar Proof; Live Wires; Oliver Twist, Jr.; Payment Guaranteed; Play Square.

MACK, HUGHIE (Hugh McGowan)
Born: Nov. 26, 1884, Brooklyn, N.Y. Died: Oct. 13, 1927, Santa Monica, Calif. (heart disease). Screen actor.

Appeared in: **1913** John Tobin's Sweatheart; Roughing the Cub. **1914** The Win(k)some Widow; The New Secretary. **1915** Count 'Em (aka The Counts). **1922** Trifling Women. **1923** Going Up; Reno. **1924** The Riddle Rider (serial); Greed. **1925** A Woman's Faith; The Merry Widow. **1926** Mare Nostrum. **1927** The Arizona Whirlwind; Where Trails Begin. **1928** Four Sons; The Wedding March.

MACK, JAMES "BUCK"
Died: Sept. 19, 1959, Los Angeles, Calif. Screen, stage and vaudeville actor. Do not confuse with actor James T. Mack. Was member of vaudeville dance team of "Miller and Mack."

Appeared in: **1934** One Hour Late. **1937** Something to Sing About. **1941** Billy the Kid.

MACK, JAMES T.
Born: 1871, Chicago, Ill. Died: Aug. 12, 1948, Hollywood, Calif. Screen and stage actor.

Appeared in: **1926** The Cruise of the Jasper B; Sin Cargo; Fools of Fashion. **1927** Wild Geese; The First Night; Husband Hunters; Women's Wares; Swim, Girl, Swim. **1928** The Home Towners. **1929** Ain't It the Truth (short); Queen of the Night Clubs. **1930** Anna Christie; Hello Sister. **1932** Arsene Lupin. **1933** One Year Later. **1934** I Hate Women; In Love with Life. **1935** Mary Burns, Fugitive; G-Men.

MACK, JOSEPH P. "JOE"
Born: May 4, 1878, Rome, Italy. Died: Apr. 8, 1946, Hollywood, Calif. Screen and vaudeville actor.

Appeared in: **1903** Great Train Robbery. **1918** Wild Honey. **1920** Wonder Man. **1927** Cross Breed. **1928** Finders Keepers; Man from Headquarters; Driftwood. **1936** A Woman Rebels.

MACK, LESTER
Born: 1906. Died: Oct. 11, 1972, New York, N.Y. Screen, stage and television actor.

Appeared in: **1968** Funny Girl; Star; The Night They Raided Minsky's; For Love of Ivy.

MACK, MAX
Born: 1885, Germany. Died: Mar., 1973, London, England. Film producer, director, author and screen actor.

Appeared in: **1934** You Belong to Me.

MACK, ROBERT
Born: 1877. Died: May 2, 1949, Jamaica, N.Y. Screen, stage, vaudeville actor and songwriter. Do not confuse with actor Bobby Mack.

Appeared in: **1922** Under Two Flags; The Cowboy and the Lady. **1923** Vanity Fair. **1925** Smouldering Fires; Timber Wolf.

MACK, ROSE
Born: 1866. Died: Oct. 9, 1927, New York, N.Y. Screen, stage and vaudeville actor.

MACK, WILBUR
Born: 1873, Binghamton, N.Y. Died: Mar. 13, 1964, Hollywood, Calif. Screen, stage, vaudeville actor and long time film extra. Married to actress Gertrude Prudy with whom he appeared in vaudeville in the team of "Mack and Purdy." Divorced from actress Nella Walker with whom he appeared in vaudeville in the team of "Mack and Walker."

Appeared in: **1925** Gold and Grit. **1926** The Hidden Way. **1927** The Love of Paquita; Shooting Straight; Straight Shootin'. **1928** The Avenging Shadow; Quick Triggers; The Crimson Canyon; The Body Punch. **1929** Honky Tonk; The Argyle Case; Slim Fingers; Beauty and Bullets; "Mack and Purdy" appeared in An Everyday Occurance (short). **1930** The Jade Box (serial); Remote Control; The Girl Said No; Up the River; Woman Racket; Sweethearts on Parade; The Czar of Broadway; Scarlet Pages; The Stand Up (short). **1931** Annabelle's Affairs. **1933** Gold Diggers of 1933. **1934** The Loud Speaker. **1935** Redheads on Parade; Million Dollar Baby; A Night at the Opera. **1936** The Crime Patrol. **1937** Larceny on the Air; Atlantic Flight; A Day at the Races. **1938** Law of the Texan; Angels With Dirty Faces. **1939** Tough Kid. **1940** Doomed to Die; That Gang of Mine; Half a Sinner. **1943** Dixie. **1944** Atlantic City. **1946** She Wrote the Book. **1947** Ladies' Man. **1948** Stage Struck. **1949** Trail of the Yukon. **1951** Rhubarb; According to Mrs. Hoyle. **1957** Up in Smoke. **1958** In the Money.

MACK, WILLARD
Born: Sept. 18, 1878, Morrisburg, Ontario, Canada. Died: Nov. 18, 1934, Los Angeles, Calif. Screen, stage actor, film director, screenwriter and playwright. Divorced from actresses Pauline Fredericks (dec. 1938) and Marjorie Rambeau (dec. 1970).

Appeared in: **1916** Aloha Oe. **1923** Your Friend and Mine. **1929** The Voice of the City. **1933** What Price Innocence; Broadway to Hollywood.

MACK, WILLIAM B.
Born: 1872. Died: Sept. 13, 1955, Islip, N.Y. Screen and stage actor.

Appeared in: **1920** Heliotrope. **1922** Missing Millions. **1923** Backbone; The Steadfast Heart. **1926** The Song and Dance Man; The American Venus.

MACKAY, CHARLES
Born: 1867. Died: Nov. 19, 1935, Englewood, N.J. Screen and stage actor. Entered films with Edison.

Appeared in: **1921** Diane of Star Hollow; Ten Nights in a Barroom; Peggy Puts It Over; The Matrimonial Web. **1922** The Inner Man; The Man She Brought Back; Without Fear. **1923** Lost in a Big City.

MACKAY, EDWARD J.
Born: 1874. Died: Dec. 26, 1948, Elizabeth, N.J. Screen, stage actor, film producer and film director. Appeared in early silents.

MACKAY, ELSIE *See* WYNDHAM, POPPY

MC KAY, GEORGE W. (George Reuben)
Born: 1880, Minsk, Russia. Died: Dec. 3, 1945, Hollywood, Calif. Screen, stage and vaudeville actor. Married to actress Ottie Ardine with whom he appeared in vaudeville; prior to that he teamed with Johnny Cantwell in vaudeville acts.

Appeared in: **1929** Back from Abroad (McKay and Ardine short). **1930** Sixteen Sweeties. **1935** The Case of the Missing Man. **1936** Don't Gamble With Love; You May Be Next; Superspeed; Shakedown; Killer at Large; End of the Trail; One Way Ticket; Crime and Punishment; Pride of the Marines; Counterfeit; The Final Hour; Two Fisted Gentleman; Come Closer, Folks. **1937** A Fight to the Finish; Frame-Up; Right Guy; Counterfeit Lady; Woman in Distress; The Devil's Playground; It's All Yours; Murder in Greenwich Village; Racketeers in Exile. **1938** There's Always a Woman; Highway Patrol; Convicted; Duke of West Point; Illegal Traffic. **1939** King of the Turf; Babes in Arms. **1940** The Big Guy. **1941** The Face Behind the Mask. **1942** Canal Zone; Sabotage Zone; The Boogie Man Will Get You. **1943** Murder in Times Square. **1944** Going My Way. **1945** Road to Utopia.

MC KAY, NORMAN
Born: 1906. Died: Apr. 24, 1968, New York, N.Y. Screen, stage, radio and television actor.

Appeared in: **1947** Untamed Fury; Kiss of Death. **1948** Call Northside 777. **1951** The Frogmen; USS Teakettle (aka You're in the Navy Now). **1953** Niagra. **1961** The Hoodlum Priest.

MACKAYE, DOROTHY
Born: 1898. Died: Jan. 5, 1940, San Fernando Valley, Calif. (injuries sustained in an auto accident). Stage and screen actress. Married to stage actor Ray Raymond (dec. 1927) and later married to actor Paul Kelly (dec. 1956).

Appeared in: **1917** Jack and the Beanstalk.

MC KECHNIE, JAMES
Born: 1911, Glasgow, Scotland. Died: May 7, 1964, London, England. Screen, stage and radio actor. Married to actress Mary Ross.

Appeared in: **1946** The Years Between (US 1947). **1948** Bond Street (US 1950); Scott of the Antarctic (US 1949). **1950** Madeleine.

MC KEE, BUCK
Born: 1865, Claremore, Okla. Died: Mar. 1, 1944, Roseville, Calif. Screen actor.

MC KEE, DONALD M.
Born: 1899. Died: June 27, 1968, Chebeague Island, Maine. Screen, stage and television actor.

Appeared in: **1951** The Whistle at Eaton Falls. **1958** The Goddess.

MC KEE, LAFE (Lafayette Stocking McKee)
Born: Jan. 23, 1872, Morrison, Ill. Died: Aug. 10, 1959, Temple City, Calif. (arteriosclerosis). Screen and stage actor. Entered films in 1912.

Appeared in: **1913** The Adventures of Kathlyn (serial). **1915** The Jaguar Trap; The Two Natures Within Him; How Callahan Cleaned Up Little Hell. **1922** Blazing Arrows. **1923** Blood Test; The Lone Wagon. **1924** Mile a Minute Morgan; Western Girl; Hard Hittin' Hamilton; Bringin' Home the Bacon; Rainbow Rangers; Thundering Romance; Battling Brewster (serial). **1925** Double Action Daniels; Triple Action; The Human Tornado; On the Go; Pursued; Saddle Cyclone; Warrior Gap; The Mystery Box (serial). **1926** Baited Trap; The Bandit Buster; The Bonanza Buckaroo; A Captain's Courage; Fort Frayne; Rawhide; Twin Triggers; West of the Law. **1927** Roarin' Broncs; Daring Deeds; The Ridin' Rowdy; Riding to Fame; The Fire Fighters (serial). **1928** The Ballyhoo Buster; Reilly of the Rainbow Division; The Upland Rider; Desperate Courage; Freckles; Manhattan Cowboy; On the Divide; Painted Trail; The Riding Renegade; Saddle Mates; Trail Riders; Trailin' Back. **1929** The California Mail; The Amazing

Vagabond. **1930** Code of Honor; The Lonesome Trail; The Utah Kid; The Lone Defender (serial); Under Montana Skies; The Rainbow's End. **1931** Red Fork Range; The Vanishing Legion (serial); The Lightning Warrior (serial); Two Gun Man; Alias—the Bad Man; Partners of the Trail; Grief Street; Hurricane Horseman; Range Law; Neck and Neck; Lariats and Six Shooters; Cyclone; Hell's Valley; The Cyclone Kid; The Pocatello Kid; Fighting Marshal. **1932** Ridin' for Justice; Dynamite Ranch; The Big Stampede; Young Blood; Battling Buckaroo; The Texan; End of the Trail; Fighting for Justice; Without Honors; Gay Buckaroo; Mark of the Spur; Spirit of the West; Hell Fire Austin; Riding Tornado; Man from New Mexico; Klondike; Gold; Hell Trouble; The Boiling Point; The Fighting Champ; Tombstone Canyon. **1933** Terror Trail; Fighting Texans; Self Defense; Young Blood; Mystery Squadron (serial); Deadwood Pass; Dude Bandit; Man from Monterey; Crossfire; Galloping Romeo; War of the Range; Whispering Shadows (serial); Riders of Destiny; Under Secret Orders; The Telegraph Trail; King of the Arena; Fighting With Kit Carson (serial); Jaws of Justice; Trail Drive; Gun Justice. **1934** Nevada Cyclone (short); Mystery Ranch; Honor of the Range; Blue Steel; Rawhide Mail; Ridin' Gents (short); The Saw of the Wild (serial); The Dude Ranger; The Fighting Trooper; The Westerner; The Border Menace; Boss Cowboy; Lightning Bill; Lightning Range; Rawhide Romance; Riding Speed; The Quitter; Mystery Mountain (serial); West of the Divide; Riding Thru; Straightaway; Tracy Rides; Hellbent for Love; Man from Utah; City Park; Demon for Trouble; Outlaws' Highway; Frontier Days. **1935** The Keeper of the Bees; Rustlers of Red Dog (serial); Port of Lost Dreams; What Price Crime?; Kid Courageous; The Hawk; Desert Trail; The Ivory-Handled Gun; Northern Frontier; Tracy Rides; Rainbow Valley; Range Warfare; The Revenge Rider; The Cowboy and the Bandit; The Silver Bullet; Gunsmoke of the Guadalupe; Trail of the Hawk; The Roaring West (serial); The Last of the Clintons; Ridin' Thru; Heir to Trouble; Big Boy Rides Again; Blazing Guns; Cheyenne Toronado; Coyote Trails; The Ghost Rider; The Miracle Rider (serial); Rio Rattler; Thunderbolt; Western Justice; Wolf Riders; Swifty. **1936** The Mysterious Avenger; The Kid Ranger; Lightnin' Bill Carson; The Phantom Rider (serial); Santa Fe Bound; The Fugitive Sheriff; Custers Last Stand (serial—stage and film versions); Frontier Justice; Roamin' Wild; Bridge of Sighs; The Cowboy and the Kid; The Last of the Warrens; Idaho Kid; Men of the Plains. **1937** The Mystery of the Hooded Horseman; North of the Rio Grande; Melody of the Plains; Law of the Ranger; Santa Fe Rides; The Feud of the Trail; Mystery Range; Reckless Ranger; Orphan of the Pecos; The Painted Stallion (serial); Brothers of the West; Wild West Days (serial); Lost Ranch; The Rangers Step In; The Fighting Deputy. **1938** The Singing Outlaw; Rolling Caravans; The Lone Ranger (serial); Six-Shootin' Sheriff; Stagecoach Days; South of Arizona; Rawhide; I'm from the City; Knight of the Plains. **1939** Arizona Legion; The Lone Ranger Rides Again (serial); The Oregon Trail (serial). **1940** Pioneer Days; Wild Horse Valley; Pioneers of the Frontier; Covered Wagon Trails; Riders of Pasco Basin; The Bad Man from Red Butte; Son of Roaring Dan. **1942** Inside the Law.

MC KEE, PAT
Born: 1897. Died: Jan. 9, 1950, El Monte, Calif. Screen actor.

Appeared in: **1938** Straight, Place and Show. **1943** Coney Island; Behind Prison Walls. **1944** Voodoo Man.

MC KEE, TOM
Born: 1917. Died: June 20, 1960, Burbank, Calif. (accidental fall). Screen, radio and television actor.

Appeared in: **1955** The Court Martial of Billy Mitchell. **1956** The Search for Bridey Murphy. **1957** Fury at Showdown; The River's Edge; Under Fire; Valerie. **1960** Three Came to Kill; Vice Raid.

MC KEEN, LAWRENCE D., JR. "SNOOKUMS"
Born: 1925. Died: Apr. 2, 1933, Los Angeles, Calif. (blood poisoning). Screen actor. Made his film debut as "Baby Snookums" at age of 18 months. By the time he was four he had his own series.

Appeared in: **1926** The Newlyweds and Their Baby (series).

MC KEEVER, MIKE
Born: Jan. 1, 1940. Died: Aug. 24, 1967, Hollywood, Calif. (brain injuries resulting from an auto accident). All-American football player and screen actor. Brother of actor and football player Marlin McKeever.

Appeared in: **1961** Love in a Goldfish Bowl. **1962** The Three Stooges Meet Hercules.

MC KELVIE, HAROLD
Born: 1910. Died: June 9, 1937, Los Angeles, Calif. Screen actor and stuntman.

MACKEN, WALTER
Born: 1915, Ireland. Died: Apr. 22, 1967, Galway, Ireland (heart attack). Playwright, novelist, screenwriter, stage and screen actor.

Appeared in: **1959** Home Is the Hero (US 1961). **1962** The Quare Fellow.

MC KENNA, HENRY T.
Born: 1894, Brooklyn, N.Y. Died: June 17, 1958, Hollywood, Calif. (heart attack). Screen actor.

MAC KENNA, KATE
Born: 1877. Died: June 14, 1957, Hollywood, Calif. (lung cancer). Screen and television actress.

Appeared in: **1935** The Bride Comes Home. **1941** So Ends Our Night. **1942** The Wife Takes a Flyer; Fly by Night. **1951** Lemon Drop Kid. **1956** Bus Stop.

MAC KENNA, KENNETH (Leo Mielziner)
Born: Aug. 19, 1899, Canterbury, N.H. Died: Jan. 15, 1962, Hollywood, Calif. (cancer). Screen, stage actor, film director, story editor, stage director and stage producer. Married to actress Mary Phillips (dec. 1975). Entered films with Paramount Astoria Studios in 1925.

Appeared in: **1925** A Kiss in the Dark; Miss Bluebeard. **1926** The American Venus. **1927** The Lunatic at Large. **1929** Pleasure Crazed; South Sea Rose. **1930** Crazy That Way; Men Without Women; Temple Tower; The Three Sisters; Man Trouble; Sin Takes a Holiday; Virtuous Sin. **1931** The Man Who Came Back. **1932** Those We Love. **1960** High Time. **1961** Judgment at Nuremberg. **1962** 13 West Street.

MAC KENZIE, ALEXANDER (aka ALEX MC KENZIE)
Born: 1886, Scotland. Died: Jan., 1966, Scotland. Screen and stage actor.

Appeared in: **1954** The Maggie (aka High and Dry—US). **1955** Geordie (aka Wee Geordie—US 1956). **1958** Rockets Galore (aka Mad Little Island—US). **1959** The Bridal Path; The Battle of the Sexes (US 1960). **1960** Kidnapped. **1961** Greyfriars' Bobby. **1963** The Three Lives of Thomasina.

MACKENZIE, COMPTON
Born: 1883. Died: Nov. 30, 1972, Edinburgh, Scotland. Screen actor, screenwriter and writer.

Appeared in: **1949** Whiskey Galore! (aka Tight Little Island—US, and aka Mad Little Island). **1950** Chance of a Lifetime (US 1951).

MAC KENZIE, DONALD (aka DONALD MC KENZIE)
Born: Apr. 17, 1879, Edinburgh, Scotland. Died: July 21, 1972, Jersey City, N.J. Screen actor and film producer.

Appeared in: **1914** Perils of Pauline (serial). **1929** The Studio Murder Mystery; The Mysterious Dr. Fu Manchu; True Heaven. **1930** Conspiracy; Scarlet Pages; Girl of the Port. **1931** Fighting Caravans; Unfaithful; Kick In.

MC KENZIE, EVA B. (Eva Heazlit)
Born: Nov. 5, 1889, Toledo, Ohio. Died: Sept. 15, 1967, Hollywood, Calif. Screen actress. Entered films in 1915. Married to actor Robert McKenzie (dec. 1949) and mother of actresses Ida Mae, Lally and Fay McKenzie.

Appeared in: **1915** Essaney films. **1921** A Knight of the West. **1931** Virtuous Husband. **1937** The following shorts: The Wrong Miss Wright; Stuck in the Sticks; Lodge Night. **1938** Juvenile Court; plus the following shorts: The Nightshirt Bandit; Soul of a Heel; Beaux and Errors; Stage Fright. **1939** Little Accident; The Amazing Mr. Williams; plus the following shorts: Andy Clyde Gets Spring Chicken; Oily to Bed, Oily to Rise; Feathered Pests. **1944** Gold Is Where You Lose It (short); Heavenly Days.

MAC KENZIE, GEORGE
Born: 1901, England. Died: Sept. 4, 1975, England? Screen actor and magician.

MACKENZIE, MARY
Born: May 3, 1922. Died: Sept. 20, 1966, London, England (auto accident). Screen, stage and television actress.

Appeared in: **1952** Stolen Face; Lady in the Fog (aka Scotland Yard Inspector—US). **1953** The Long Memory; The Man Who Watched Trains Go By. **1954** Duel in the Jungle; The Master Plan; Trouble in the Glen. **1955** Track the Man Down. **1956** Cloak Without Dagger (aka Operation Conspiracy—US 1957); Yield to the Night (aka Blonde Sinner—US). **1958** A Question of Adultery (US 1959).

MC KENZIE, ROBERT B.
Born: Sept. 22, 1883, Bellymania, Ireland. Died: July 8, 1949, R.I. (heart attack). Stage and screen actor. Entered films in 1915. Married to actress Eva McKenzie (dec. 1967) and father of actresses Ida Mae, Lally and Fay McKenzie.

Appeared in: **1921** A Knight of the West. **1922** Fightin' Devil; The Sheriff of Sun-Dog; A Western Demon. **1923** The Devil's Dooryard; Don Quickshort of the Rio Grande; The Gentleman from America; Single Handed; Where Is This West?; In the West. **1924** The Covered Trail; The Desert Hawk; The Whirlwind Ranger. **1925** Fifth Avenue Models. **1926** A Six Shootin' Romance; Bad Man's Bluff; The Fighting Peacemaker. **1927** One Glorious Scrap; Red Signals; Set Free. **1929** The White Outlaw. **1930** Shadow Ranch. **1931** Cimarron. **1933** Tillie and Gus; Beauty and the Bus (short). **1934** You're Telling Me; Opened by Mistake (short); Little Minister. **1935** Stone of Silver Creek; A Shot in the Dark; The Bride Comes Home; plus the following shorts: Beginner's Luck; Teacher's Beau; It Always Happens; Hoi Polloi. **1936** Love Before Breakfast; Comin' Round the Mountain; Rebellion; Heart of the West; Love Comes to Mooneyville (short). **1937** Something to Sing About; Sing, Cowboy, Sing; Hideaway; Stars Over Arizona; plus the following shorts; The Wrong Miss Wright; Stuck in the Sticks; He Done His Duty; The Sitter-Downers. **1938** The Old Raid Mule (short). **1939** They Asked For It; Blondie Takes a Vacation; Death of a Champion. **1940** Dreaming Out Loud; Buried Alive; Triple Justice. **1941** Citadel of Crime; Death Valley Outlaws; Sierra Sue. **1942** In Old California; The Sombrero Kid. **1943** Jive Junction. **1944** Texas Masquerade; Three of a Kind; Tall in the Saddle; The Yoke's on Me (short). **1946** Duel in the Sun; Romance of the West; Colorado Serenade.

MC KENZIE, TANDY
Born: 1892, Maui, Hawaii. Died: Nov. 9, 1963, Hollywood, Calif. (struck by auto). Opera singer and screen actor.

Appeared in: **1936** San Francisco.

MC KERRON, MABEL See BACON, MABEL

MACKEY, BERNARD
Born: 1910. Died: Mar. 5, 1980, Miami, Fla. (cancer). Black, screen, stage, radio actor, singer and guitarist. Member of the original "Ink Spots" singing quartet.

MC KIBBON, COLUMBIA
Born: 1896. Died: Oct. 4, 1948, Los Angeles, Calif. Screen and stage actress.

MACKIE, BERT (Robert James Mackie)
Born: 1893. Died: July 23, 1967, Hollywood, Calif. Screen actor.

MC KIM, ROBERT
Born: Aug. 26, 1887, San Francisco, Calif. Died: June 2, 1927, Hollywood, Calif. (cerebral hemorrhage). Screen and vaudeville actor.

Appeared in: **1915** The Edge of the Abyss; The Disciple. **1916** The Primal Lure; The Stepping Stone; The Return of Draw Egan. **1919** The Wolf; Wagon Tracks; Her Kingdom of Dreams. **1920** The Mark of Zorro; Riders of the Dawn; The Silver Horde. **1921** A Certain Rich Man; The Lure of Egypt; The Man of the Forest; Mysterious Rider; The Spenders. **1922** The Gray Dawn; Heart's Haven; Monte Cristo; White Hands; Without Compromise. **1923** All the Brothers Were Valiant; Dead Game; His Last Race; Hollywood; Human Wreckage; Maytime; Mr. Billings Spends His Dime; The Spider and the Rose; The Spoilers; Strangers of the Night; Thundergate. **1924** Flaming Barriers; The Galloping Ace; Mademoiselle Midnight; Ride for Your Life; The Torent; When a Girl Loves. **1925** North of Nome; The Police Patrol; Spook Ranch. **1926** The Bat; The Dead Line; Kentucky Handicap; The Pay Off; A Regular Scout; The Strong Man; Tex; The Tough Guy; The Wolf Hunters. **1927** A Flame in the Sky; The Denver Dude; The Show Girl; The Thrill Seekers.

MACKIN, CLARA
Died: Apr. 5, 1973, Santa Monica, Calif. Screen actress. Married to actor Eric Blore (dec. 1959).

Appeared in: **1938** Little Tough Guy; Swing, Sister, Swing. **1939** Little Accident; The Light That Failed.

MACKIN, WILLIAM
Born: 1883. Died: Sept. 9, 1928, Los Angeles, Calif. Screen actor.

MC KINNELL, NORMAN
Born: 1870, England. Died: Mar. 29, 1932, London, England (heart disease). Screen, stage actor and stage director. Married to actress Gertrude Scott (dec. 1951).

Appeared in: **1899** King John. **1915** The Shulamite. **1917** Everybody's Business; Dombey and Son; Mary Girl. **1918** Hindle Wakes. **1920** Pillars of Society; A Gamble in Lives. **1927** Hindle Wakes (aka Fanny Hawthorne—US 1929); Downhill (aka When Boys Leave Home—US 1928); The Fake. **1931** Potiphar's Wife (aka Her Strange Desire—US 1932); The Sleeping Cardinal (aka Sherlock Holmes' Fatal Hour—US); The Outsider; Hindle Wakes (also 1918 and 1927 versions). **1932** The Frightened Lady (aka Criminal at Large—US 1933); White Face.

MC KINNEY, FLORINE
Born: Dec. 13, 1912, Mart, Tex. Died: July 28, 1975. Screen actress. Married to screenwriter Barry Trivers (dec. 1981).

Appeared in: **1932** Cabin in the Cotton; The Miracle Man; Horse Feathers; Cynara; The Strange Case of Clara Deane. **1933** Beauty for Sale. **1934** Student Tour. **1935** David Copperfield; Night Life of the Gods; Dizzy Dames; Strangers All; Cappy Ricks Returns. **1936** Muss 'Em Up. **1937** Blazing Barriers. **1940** Oklahoma Renegades; A Night at Earl Carroll's. **1942** Brooklyn Orchid; Take a Letter, Darling; Little Joe, the Wrangler; Pardon My Sarong.

MC KINNEY, MIRA
Died: May 2, 1978. Screen actress.

Appeared in: **1938** Young Fugitives; The Road to Reno. **1939** Cafe Society. **1940** Alias the Deacon. **1941** A Dangerous Game; Bachelor; Double Trouble. **1943** Moonlight in Vermont. **1944** Till We Meet Again. **1945** Fallen Angel. **1946** Junior Prom; Talk About a Lady; Shadows Over Chinatown; Beat the Band. **1949** Prejudice. **1950** Harriet Craig; Trail of the Rustlers. **1951** Heart of the Rockies; The Groom Wore Spurs. **1952** Rainbow 'Round My Shoulder. **1953** The Last Posse. **1955** Women's Prison.

MC KINNEY, NINA MAE
Born: 1913, Lancaster, S.C. Died: May, 1967. Black screen and stage actress.

Appeared in: **1929** Hallelujah. **1930** Congo Road. **1931** Safe in Hell. **1932** Pie Pie Blackbirds. **1935** Sanders of the River; Reckless. **1938** Gang Smashers; St. Louis Gal. **1939** Pocomania; The Devil's Daughter; Straight to Heaven. **1944** Dark Waters; Together Again. **1946** Night Train to Memphis; Mantan Messes Up. **1947** Danger Street. **1949** Pinky.

MC KINTRY, ELIZABETH
Born: 1899. Died: Sept. 3, 1920, New York, N.Y. Screen actress.

MACKRIS, ORESTES
Born: 1900, Chalkis, Eubea. Died: Jan. 30, 1975, Athens, Greece. Stage and screen actor.

MC LAGLEN, CLIFFORD
Born: 1892, England. Died: Sept., 1978, Huddersfield, Yorkshire, England. Screen actor. Brother of actors Leopold, Arthur, Kenneth (dec. 1979), Victor (dec. 1959), and Cyril McLaglen.

Appeared in: **1925** Forbidden Cargoes (aka Contraband). **1926** Boadicea; The Chinese Bungalow. **1928** The White Sheik (US 1929, aka King's Mate); At the Villa Falconer; A Little Bit of Fluff (aka Skirts—US). **1929** The Three Kings; The Alley Cat. **1930** Bride of 68. **1936** The Marriage of Corbal (aka Prisoner of Corbal—US 1939).

MC LAGLEN, KENNETH
Born: 1901, England. Died: Jan. 20, 1979, England. Screen actor. Brother of actors Leopold, Arthur, Clifford (dec. 1978), Victor (dec. 1959), and Cyril McLaglen.

Appeared in: **1927** Land of Hope and Glory.

MC LAGLEN, VICTOR
Born: Dec. 11, 1886, Tunbridge Wells, Kent, England. Died: Nov. 7, 1959, Newport Beach, Calif. (heart attack). Screen, stage and vaudeville actor. Won 1935 Academy Award for Best Actor in The Informer. Nominated for 1952 Academy Award for Best Supporting Actor in The Quiet Man. Brother of actors Leopold, Arthur, Clifford (dec. 1978), Kenneth (dec. 1979) and Cyril McLaglen.

Appeared in: **1920** The Call of the Road. **1921** Corinthian Jack; The Prey of the Dragon; Carnival; The Sport of Kings. **1922** The Glorious Adventure; A Romance of Old Bagdad; Little Brother of God; A Sailor Tramp; The Crimson Circle. **1923** The Romany; Heartstrings; M'Lord of the White Road; In the Blood. **1924** The Beloved Brute; The Boatswain's Mate; Women and Diamonds (aka Conscripts of Misfortune or It Happened in Africa); The Gay Corinthian; The Passionate Adventure. **1925** The Haunted Woman; Percy; The Fighting Heart; The Unholy Three; Winds of Chance. **1926** Beau Geste; What Price Glory; Men of Steel; The Isle of Retribution. **1927** Loves of Carmen. **1928** Mother Machree; A Girl in Every Port; Hangman's House; The River Pirate. **1929** Captain Lash; Strong Boy; King of the Khyber Rifles; The Cock Eyed World; The Black Watch; Sez You—Sez Me; Hot for Paris. **1930** Happy Days; On the Level; A Devil With Women; Wings of Adventures. **1931** Not Exactly Gentlemen; Dishonored; Women of All Nations; Wicked; Annabelle's Affairs. **1932** Guilty as Hell; Devil's Lottery; While Paris Sleeps; The Slippery Pearls (short); The Gay Caballero; Rackety Rax. **1933** Hot Pepper; Laughing at Life; Dick Turpin. **1934** The Lost Patrol; No More Women; Wharf Angel; Murder at the Vanities; The Captain Hates the Sea. **1935** Under Pressure; Great Hotel Murder; The Informer; Professional Soldier. **1936** Under Two Flags; Klondike Annie; The Magnificent Brute. **1937** Sea Devils; Nancy Steele is Missing; Wee Willie Winkie; This Is My Affair. **1938** We're Going to Be Rich; The Devil's Party; Battle of Broadway. **1939** Gunga Din; Pacific Liner; Rio; Let Freedom Ring; Black Watch; Captain Fury; Ex-Champ; Full Confession. **1940** The Big Guy; Diamond Frontier; South of Pago Pago. **1941** Broadway Limited. **1942** Call Out the Marines; Powder Town; China Girl. **1943** Forever and a Day. **1944** Tampico; The Princess and the Pirate. **1945** Rough, Tough and Ready; Roger Touhy, Gangster; Love, Honor and Goodbye. **1946** Whistle Stop. **1947** Michigan Kid; Foxes of Harrow; Calendar Girl. **1948** Fort Apache. **1949** She Wore a Yellow Ribbon. **1950** Rio Grande. **1952** The Quiet Man. **1953** Fair Wind to Java. **1954** Prince Valiant; Trouble in the Glen. **1955** Many Rivers to Cross; Bengazi; Lady Godiva; City of Shadows. **1956** Around the World in 80 Days. **1957** The Abductors. **1959** Sea Fury (US 1959).

MAC LANE, BARTON
Born: Dec. 25, 1900, Columbia, S.C. Died: Jan. 1, 1969, Santa Monica, Calif. (double pneumonia). Screen, stage and television actor.

Appeared in: **1926** The Quarterback (film debut). **1929** The Cocoanuts. **1933** Men of the Forest; Big Executive; The Torch Singer; To the Last Man; Tillie and Gus; Hell and High Water; Let's Dance (short). **1934** The Last Round-Up; The Thundering Herd; Lone Cowboy. **1935** Black Fury; Go Into Your Dance; The G-Men; Case of the Curious Bride; Stranded; Page Miss Glory; Dr. Socrates; I Found Stella Parish; Frisco Kid; The Case of the Lucky Legs; Man of Iron; Ceiling Zero. **1936** The Walking Dead; Times Square Playboy; Jail Break; Bullets or Ballots; Bengal Tiger; Smart Blonde; God's Country and the Woman. **1937** Draegerman Courage; You Only Live Once; Don't Pull Your Punches; San Quentin; The Prince and the Pauper; Fly-Away Baby; Ever Since Eve; Wine, Woman and Horses; The Adventurous Blonde; Born Reckless. **1938** The Kid Comes Back; Blondes at Work; Torchy Gets Her Man; Gold Is Where You Find It; You and Me; Prison Break; The Storm. **1939** Big Town Czar; Torchy Blane in Chinatown; I Was a Convict; Stand Up and Fight; Torchy Runs for Mayor; Mutiny in the Big House. **1940** Men Without Souls; The Secret Seven; Gangs of Chicago; Melody Ranch. **1941** Manpower; Barnacle Bill; Wild Geese Calling; Hit the Road; Come Live with Me; Western Union; Dr. Jekyll and Mr. Hyde; The Maltese Falcon; High Sierra. **1942** The Big Street; Highways by Night; All Through the Night. **1943** The Underdog; The Crime Doctor's Strangest Case; Man of Courage; Bombardier; Song of Texas. **1944** The Cry of the Werewolf; The Mummy's Ghost; Nobonga; Marine Raiders; Secret Command; Gentle Annie. **1945** Treasure of Fear; The Spanish Main; Scared Stiff; Tarzan and the Amazons. **1946** Santa Fe Uprising; Mysterious Intruder; San Quentin. **1947** Tarzan and the Huntress; Jungle Flight; Cheyenne. **1948** Silver River; The Dude Goes West; The Walls of Jericho; Angel in Exile; Relentless; Unknown Island; The Treasure of Sierra Madre. **1949** Red Light. **1950** Kiss Tomorrow Goodbye; Rookie Fireman; The Bandit Queen; Let's Dance. **1951** Best of the Badmen; Drums in the Deep South. **1952** The Half Breed; Thunderbirds; Bugles in the Afternoon. **1953** Kansas Pacific; Cow Country; Jack Slade; Sea of Lost Ships; Captain Scarface. **1954** Rails into Laramie; Jubilee Trail; The Glenn Miller Story. **1955** The Last of the Desperadoes; Hell's Outpost; Treasure of Ruby Hills; The Silver Star; Foxfire; Jail Busters. **1956** The Man Is Armed; Three Violent People; The Naked Gun; Jaguar; Backlash; Wetbacks. **1957** Sierra Stranger; Naked in the Sun; The Storm Rider; Hell's Crossroads. **1958** Girl in the Woods; Frontier Gun; The Geisha Boy. **1960** Noose for a Gunman; Gunfighters of Abilene. **1961** Pocketful of Miracles. **1964** Law of the Lawless. **1965** The Rounders; Town Tamer. **1968** Arizona Bushwackers; Buckskin.

MAC LANE, MARY (aka MARY MC LANE)
Born: Butte, Mont. Died: Aug., 1929. Screen actress and novelist.

Appeared in: **1918** Men Who Have Made Love to Me. **1924** Which Shall It Be? **1925** The Night Ship. **1926** Sparrows.

MC LAREN, BRUCE
Born: Aug. 30, 1937, Auckland, New Zealand. Died: June 2, 1970, Goodwood, England (car crash). Race car driver and designer, and screen actor.

Appeared in: **1963** The Young Racers. **1966** Grand Prix.

MACLAREN, IVOR
Born: 1904, Wimbledon, England. Died: Oct. 30, 1962, London, England. Screen, television actor and film director.

Appeared in: **1933** Aunt Sally. **1934** Evergreen; Princess Charming; Friday the 13th; The Woman in Command; Along Came Sally. **1935** Radio Parade of 1935.

MAC LARNIE, THOMAS
Born: 1871. Died: Dec. 1, 1931, Brighton, Mass. Screen and stage actor.

Appeared in: **1915** The Blindness of Virtue.

MC LARTY, JAMES E. (aka JAMES E. MC CLARTY)
Born: 1931, Tex. Died: Apr. 16, 1979, Templeton, Calif. Screen, stage, television actor, stage director and screenwriter.

Appeared in: **1963** None But the Brave. **1968** The Pick-Up. **1969** The Babysitter. **1970** Weekend With the Babysitter. **1979** Meatballs.

MAC LEAN, DOUGLAS
Born: Jan. 14, 1890 or 1897?, Philadelphia, Pa. Died: July 9, 1967, Beverly Hills, Calif. (stroke). Screen, stage actor, film producer and screenwriter.

Appeared in: **1916** American Film Mfg. Co. films. **1917** Souls in Pawn. **1918** Johanna Enlists; The Hun Within; Fuss and Feathers; Mirandy Smiles. **1919** Captain Kidd, Jr.; As Ye Sow; The Home Breaker; Twenty-Three and a Half Hour's Leave. **1920** Let's Be Fashionalbe; Mark's Ankle; The Jailbird. **1921** Chickens; The Home Stretch; One a Minute; Passing Thru; The Rookie's Return. **1922** The Hottentot. **1923** The Sunshine Trail; Going Up; Bell Boy 13; A Man of Action; Mary of the Movies. **1924** Never Say Die; The Yankee Counsul. **1925** Introduce Me; Seven Keys to Baldpate. **1926** That's My Baby; Hold That Lion. **1927** Soft Cushions; Let It Rain. **1929** The Carnation Kid; Divorce Made Easy.

MAC LEAN, DUNCAN
Born: 1884, England. Died: Jan., 1981, London, England. Screen, stage and vaudeville actor.

MAC LEAN, R. D. (Rezin Donald MacLean)
Born: 1859, New Orleans, La. Died: June 27, 1948. Screen, stage actor and stage director.

Appeared in: **1920** The Silver Horde; Little Shepherd of Kingdom Come. **1921** Don't Neglect Your Wife. **1933** Cradle Song.

MC LENNAN, RODNEY "ROD"
Born: Australia. Died: Nov. 27, 1973, England? Screen and stage actor.

Appeared in: **1930** Charley's Aunt. **1932** The Man I Killed. **1964** Devils of Darkness (US 1965).

MC LEOD, BARBARA (Barbara Fielding)
Born: 1908. Died: May 26, 1940, Van Nuys, Calif. (suicide—gun). Screen actress.

MC LEOD, HELEN
Born: 1924. Died: Apr. 20, 1964, Bakersfield, Calif. (cancer). Screen actress.

MAC LEOD, KENNETH
Born: 1895. Died: Dec. 6, 1963, Hollywood, Calif. Screen actor.

MC LEOD, TEX (Alexander D'Avila McLeod)
Born: Nov. 11, 1896, Gonzales, Tex. Died: Feb. 12, 1973, Brighton, England (heart attack). Screen, stage, vaudeville actor, circus and rodeo performer.

Appeared in: **1915** Broncho Billy (serial). **1928** A Rope and a Story (short). **1933** Radio Parade.

MAC LIAMMOIR, MICHAEL (aka ALFRED WILLMORE)
Born: Oct. 25, 1899, Cork, Ireland. Died: Mar. 6, 1978, Dublin, Ireland. Screen, stage, television actor and playwright.

Appeared in: **1955** Othello. **1963** Tom Jones (narrator). **1968** 30 Is a Dangerous Age, Cynthia. **1970** The Kremlin Letter. **1971** What's the Matter With Helen?.

MC MAHON, DAVID
Born: 1909. Died: Jan. 27, 1972, Pasadena, Calif. (heart attack). Screen actor.

Appeared in: **1949** I Was a Male War Bride. **1950** Where the Sidewalk Ends; When Willie Comes Marching Home. **1951** The Scarf. **1952** Eight Iron Men; Glory Alley. **1955** Top of the World. **1956** The Peacemaker; Dance With Me, Henry; The Creature Walks Among Us. **1957** Operation Mad Ball. **1962** The Case of Patty Smith (aka The Shame of Patty Smith).

MC MAHON, HORACE (aka HORACE MAC MAHON)
Born: May 17, 1907, South Norwalk, Conn. Died: Aug. 17, 1971, Norwalk, Conn. (heart ailment). Screen, stage, vaudeville, radio and television actor. Married to actress Louise Campbell.

Appeared in: **1937** The Last Gangster; Navy Blues; The Wrong Road; Exclusive; A Girl With Ideas; They Gave Him a Gun; Double Wedding; Kid Galahad. **1938** I Am the Law; King of the Newsboys; When G-Men Step In; Fast Company; Ladies in Distress; Tenth Avenue Kid; Secrets of a Nurse; Broadway Musketeers; Pride of the Navy; Alexander's Ragtime Band; Gangs of New York. **1939** Sergeant Madden; The Gracie Allen Murder Case; Rose of Washington Square; I Was a Convict; Federal Man-Hunt; Laugh It Off; Big Town Czar; For Love or Money; She Married a Cop; Quick Millions; Sabotage. **1940** The Marines Fly High; Dr. Kildare's Strangest Case; Dr. Kildare Goes Home; I Can't Give You Anything But Love, Baby; Gangs of Chicago; Millionaires in Prison; Oh Johnny, How You Can Love!; We Who Are Young; The Leather Pushers; Melody Ranch; Dr. Kildare's Crisis. **1941** Come Live With Me; Rookies on Parade; The Bride Wore Crutches; Lady Scarface; Buy Me That Town; Birth of the Blues; The Stork Pays Off. **1942** Jail House Blues. **1944** Roger Rouhy, Gangster; Timber Queen. **1945** Lady Gangster. **1946** 13 Rue Madeleine. **1948** Smart Woman; Fighting Mad; Waterfront at Midnight; The Return of October. **1951** Detective Story (stage and film versions). **1953** Abbott and Costello Go to Mars; Man in the Dark; Fast Company; Champ for a Day. **1954** Duffy of San Quentin; Susan Slept Here. **1955** The Blackboard Jungle; My Sister Eileen; Texas Lady. **1957** The Delicate Delinquent; Beau James. **1959** Never Steal Anything Small. **1966** The Swinger. **1968** The Detective.

MC MAHON, JOHN G.
Died: Aug. 18, 1968. Screen actor.

MC MANUS, GEORGE
Died: Oct. 22, 1954. Cartoonist and screen actor. Creator of comic strip "Bringing Up Father."

Appeared in: **1924** The Great White Way. **1946** Bringing Up Father. **1948** Jiggs and Maggie In Court. **1949** Maggie and Jiggs in Jackpot Jitters. **1950** Jiggs and Maggie Out West.

MC MILLAN, RODDY
Born: Mar. 23, 1923, Glasgow, Scotland. Died: July 9, 1979, Glasgow, Scotland (heart attack). Screen, stage, television actor, playwright and folk singer.

Appeared in: **1950** Morning Departure (aka Operature Disaster—US 1951). **1953** Laxdale Hall (aka Scotch on the Rocks—US 1954). **1954** The Maggie (aka High and Dry—US). **1959** The Bridal Path; The Battle of the Sexes (US 1960). **1962** A Prize of Arms; The Amorous Pawn (aka The Playgirl and the War Minister—US 1963). **1963** The Mouse on the Moon. **1969** Ring of Bright Water.

MC MILLAN, WALTER KENNETH
Born: 1917. Died: Jan., 1945 (killed in action in Philippine invasion, W.W. II). Stage and screen actor. Was a member of Hal Roach's "Our Gang."

MAC MILLIAN, VIOLET
Born: Mar. 4, 1887. Died: Dec. 28, 1953, Grand Rapids, Mich. Screen and stage actress.

Appeared in: **1915** Mrs. Plumb's Pudding. **1920** The Mystery Mind (serial).

MC MURPHY, CHARLES
Born: July 31, 1894, Vernon, Ind. Died: Oct. 24, 1969. Screen and stage actor.

Appeared in: **1915** Going to the Dogs. **1929** The Greene Murder Case. **1930** The Benson Murder Case; The Silver Horde. **1933** Thundering Herd. **1935** Hold 'Em Yale. **1936** I Conquer the Sea; Song of the Trail. **1941** The Phantom Submarine. **1942** The Spoilers.

MC NAMARA, EDWARD C.
Born: 1884, Paterson, N.J. Died: Nov. 9, 1944, on train near Boston, Mass. (heart attack). Screen, stage actor and opera tenor.

Appeared in: **1929** Lucky in Love. **1932** I Am a Fugitive from a Chain Gang. **1933** 20,000 Years in Sing Sing. **1937** Great Guy; Girl Overboard; The League of Frightened Men. **1941** Strawberry Blonde; The Devil and Miss Jones. **1943** Johnny Come Lately; Margin of Error. **1944** Arsenic and Old Lace.

MC NAMARA, JAMES C.
Born: 1913. Died: May 18, 1980, Los Angeles, Calif.? (cancer). Screen, radio and television actor.

Appeared in: **1938** You and Me. **1942** Home in Wyoming.

MC NAMARA, JOHN
Died: Oct 27, 1968. Screen actor.

Appeared in: **1957** Slaughter on Tenth Avenue; From Hell It Came. **1958** Suicide Battalion; The Return of Dracula; War of the Colossal Beast; Crash Landing. **1960** Ma Barker's Killer Brood; Portrait in Black.

MC NAMARA, MAGGIE
Born: June 18, 1928, New York, N.Y. Died: Feb. 18, 1978, New York, N.Y. ("acute chemical poisoning"). Screen and stage actress. Nominated for 1953 Academy Award for Best Actress in The Moon Is Blue.

Appeared in: **1953** The Moon Is Blue (film debut). **1954** Three Coins in the Fountain. **1955** Prince of Players. **1963** The Cardinal.

MC NAMARA, TED
Born: Australia. Died: Feb. 3, 1928, Ventura, Calif. (pneumonia). Screen and vaudeville actor.

Appeared in: **1925** Shore Leave. **1926** What Price Glory? **1927** Chain Lightning; Colleen; The Gay Retreat; The Monkey Talks; Rich But Honest; Upstream. **1928** The Gateway of the Moon; Mother Machree; Why Sailors Go Wrong.

MC NAMARA, THOMAS J.
Died: May 21, 1953, Brooklyn, N.Y. Screen and vaudeville actor.

MC NAMEE, DONALD
Born: 1897. Died: July 17, 1940, Hollywood, Calif. (skull fracture). Screen and stage actor.

Appeared in: **1928** Fashion Madness. **1929** The Great Garbo.

MC NAMEE, GRAHAM
Born: July 10, 1888, Washington, D.C. Died: May 9, 1942, New York, N.Y. Screen, radio actor and sportscaster.

Appeared in: **1926** Oh Baby! **1934** Gift of Gab. **1935** Wings in the Dark.

MC NAUGHTON, CHARLES
Born: Apr. 24, 1878, Walthamstow, Essex, England. Died: Dec. 4, 1955, England? Screen and stage actor.

Appeared in: **1921** Wet Gold. **1929** Three Live Ghosts. **1930** The Bad One; Common Clay. **1931** The Single Sin. **1932** Charlie Chan's Chance. **1933** Big Brain; Midnight Club; Alice in Wonderland. **1934** Treasure Island; The Fountain. **1936** Lloyds of London. **1937** Bulldog Drummond Escapes. **1942** The Black Swan. **1947** Moss Rose.

MC NAUGHTON, FRED
Born: 1869, England. Died: Feb. 1920, London, England. Screen, stage and vaudeville actor. Brother of actor Tom McNaughton (dec. 1923), with whom he appeared in an act billed as "The McNaughtons." Married to stage actress Georgina Preston (dec.).

MC NAUGHTON, GUS (August Le Clerq)
Born: 1884, London, England. Died: Dec., 1969, Castor, England. Screen and stage actor.

Appeared in: **1930** Murder; Children of Chance. **1932** Lucky Girl; The Maid of the Mountains; The Last Coupon; His Wife's Mother; Money Talks. **1933** Radio Parade; Leave It to Me; Their Night Out; Heads We Go (aka The Charming Deceiver—US); The Love Nest; Song Birds; Crime on the Hill. **1934** Seeing Is Believing; Bagged; Spring in the Air; Happy; Wishes; Master and Man; The Luck of a Sailor; There Goes Susie (aka Scandals of Paris—US 1935). **1935** Barnacle Bill; Royal Cavalcade (aka Regal Cavalcade—US); The 39 Steps; Joy Ride; The Crouching Beast; Invitation to the Waltz; Music Hath Charms. **1936** No So Dusty; Southern Roses; Busman's Holiday; Keep Your Seats Please; The Heirloom Mystery; When We Get Married. **1937** The Strange Adventures of Mr. Smith; Action for Slander (US 1938); Storm in a Teacup; Keep Fit. **1938** You're the Doctor; South Riding; The Divorce of Lady X; Easy Riches; We're Going to Be Rich; St. Martin's Lane (aka Sidewalks of London—US 1940); Keep Smiling (aka Smiling Along US—1939). **1939** Q Planes (aka Clouds Over Europe—US); Trouble Brewing; I Killed the Count (aka Who is Guilty?—US 1940); There Ain't No Justice; Blind Folly; What Would You Do Chums?; All at Sea. **1940** That's the Ticket; Old Bill and Son; George and Margaret; Two for Danger. **1941** Facing the Music; Penn of Pennsylvania (aka The Courageous Mr. Penn—US 1944); Jeannie (US 1943); South American George. **1942** Let the People Sing; Much Too Shy; Rose of Tralee. **1943** The Shipbuilders. **1944** Demobbed. **1945** A Place of One's Own (US 1949); Here Comes the Sun. **1946** The Trojan Brothers. **1947** The Turners of Prospect Road.

MC NAUGHTON, HARRY
Born: 1897, England. Died: Feb. 26, 1967, Amityville, N.Y. Screen, stage and radio actor.

Appeared in: **1921** Wet Gold (short). **1930** The following shorts: All Stuck Up; Sixteen Sweeties; The Fight; Office Steps; Her Hired Husband; Seeing Off Service; Tom Thumbs Down. **1956** The Vagabond King.

MC NAUGHTON, TOM
Born: July 1, 1867, England. Died: Nov. 28, 1923, London, England. Screen, stage and vaudeville actor. Brother of actor Fred McNaughton (dec. 1920), with whom he appeared in an act billed as "The McNaughtons." Married to actress Alice Lloyd (dec. 1949).

Appeared in: **1915** Tillie's Tomato Surprise.

MAC NEAL, F. A. (Frank Ashby MacNeal)
Born: Nov. 18, 1867, Mo. Died: Feb. 27, 1918, Los Angeles, Calif. (coronary occlusion). Screen actor.

MC NEAR, HOWARD
Born: 1905. Died: Jan. 3, 1969, San Fernando Valley, Calif. Screen, radio and television actor. Played Doc Adams on radio's Gunsmoke.

Appeared in: **1954** Drums Across the River. **1956** You Can't Run Away From It; Bundle of Joy. **1957** Public Pigeon No. 1; Affair in Reno. **1958** Bell, Book and Candle; Good Day for a Hanging. **1959** Anatomy of a Murder; The Big Circus. **1961** Bachelor Flat; Blue Hawaii; Voyage to the Bottom of the Sea. **1962** Follow That Dream; The Errand Boy. **1963** Irma La Douce; The Wheeler Dealers. **1964** Kiss Me, Stupid! **1965** My Blood Runs Cold; Love and Kisses. **1966** The Fortune Cookie.

MC NISH, FRANK E.
Born: Dec. 14, 1853, Camden, N.J. Died: Dec. 27, 1924, Chicago, Ill. (stroke). Screen, stage, vaudeville actor and minstrel performer.

Appeared in: **1915** The Conductor's Classy Champion; The Postmaster of Pineapple Plains.

MC NULTY, HAROLD
Born: 1903. Died: June 6, 1978, Hollywood, Calif. (heart attack). Screen and television actor.

MACOLLUM, BARRY
Born: Apr. 6, 1889 or 1894?, Ireland. Died: Feb. 22, 1971, West Los Angeles, Calif. (peritonitis). Screen and stage actor.

Appeared in: **1923** Fury. **1929** The Hole in the Wall. **1937** Interns Can't Take Money; Parnell; Murder in Greenwich Village. **1938** If I Were King. **1939** Beau Geste; Rulers of the Sea. **1943** Hi Diddle Diddle. **1944** Jayne Eyre; Make Your Own Bed; Kismet; Marine Raiders; National Velvet. **1954** On the Waterfront. **1955** The Trouble With Harry.

MACOWAN, NORMAN
Born: Jan. 2, 1877, St. Andrews, Scotland. Died: Dec. 29, 1961. Screen actor.

Appeared in: **1951** Valley of the Eagles. **1953** Laxdale Hall. **1955** Footsteps in the Fog. **1956** X the Unknown. **1957** Action of the Tiger. **1958** Tread Softly Stranger (US 1959). **1959** The Boy and the Bridge; Battle of the Sexes (US 1960). **1960** Kidnapped. **1961** Horror Hotel (US 1963 aka City of the Dead).

MC PETERS, TAYLOR
Born: 1900. Died: Apr. 16, 1962, Hollywood, Calif. (heart attack). Screen actor.

Appeared in: **1963** The Ugly American.

MC PHAIL, DOUGLAS
Born: Apr. 16, 1910, Los Angeles, Calif. Died: Dec. 7, 1944, Los Angeles, Calif. (effects of poison). Screen, stage actor and singer. Divorced from actress Betty Jaynes.

Appeared in: **1936** Born to Dance. **1937** Maytime. **1938** Sweethearts; Toy Wife; Test Pilot. **1939** Babes in Arms; Honolulu. **1940** Little Nellie Kelly; Broadway Melody of 1940. **1942** Born to Sing.

MC PHATTER, CLYDE
Born: 1931. Died: June 13, 1972, Bronx, N.Y. (heart attack). Screen actor and singer.

Appeared in: **1957** Mister Rock and Roll.

MAC PHERSON, JEANIE
Born: Boston, Mass. Died: Aug. 26, 1946, Hollywood, Calif. Screen, stage actress, screenwriter and film director.

Appeared in: **1908** The Vaquero's Vow; Mr. Jones at the Ball; Mrs. Jones Entertains. **1909** The Death Disc; A Corner in Wheat. **1910** Winning Back His Love; Heart Beats of Long Ago; The Last Drop of Water; Enoch Arden, Part I; Fisher Folks. **1911** The Blind Princess and the Poet; Out From the Shadow; The Village Hero; A Man For All That; Home; The Two Flats. **1912** The Butler and the Maid; Partners For Life; A Man; The Wreckers. **1913** The Tarantula; The Violet Bride; The Awakening; The Sea Urchin; Carmen. **1914** Rose of the Rancho; The Undertow. **1915** The Girl of the Golden West; The Captive. **1923** Hollywood. **1939** Land of Liberty (narr.).

MC PHERSON, QUINTON (aka HYMACK, MR.)
Born: 1871, England. Died: Jan. 2, 1940, London, England. Screen, stage and vaudeville actor.

Appeared in: **1933** Mixed Doubles; Anne One Hundred. **1934** The Third Clue. **1935** Maria Marten, or The Murder in the Red Barn. **1936** The Ghost Goes West; If I Were Rich; Annie Laurie; The Beloved Vagabond; The Tenth Man (US 1937); Land Without Music (aka Forbidden Music—US 1938); Talk of the Devil (US 1937). **1937** Storm in a Teacup; 21 Days (aka The First and the Last and 21 Days Together—US 1940); Captain's Orders. **1938** Dangerous Medicine.

MC QUADE, JOHN
Born: 1916, Pittsburgh, Pa. Died: Sept. 21, 1979, New York, N.Y. Screen, stage and television actor.

MAC QUARRIE, ALBERT "AL" (aka ALBERT "AL" MC QUARRIE)
Born: Jan. 8, 1882, San Francisco, Calif. Died: Feb. 17, 1950. Screen and stage actor.

Appeared in: **1916** Eagle's Wings; High Speed. **1917** Melody of Death; The Almost Good Man; The Midnight Man. **1918** He Comes Up Smiling; Bound in Morocco; Arizona. **1919** The Knickerbocker Buckaroo; His Majesty, the American. **1920** When the Clouds Roll By; The Mollycoddle. **1921** Cheated Hearts. **1922** Bulldog Courage; The Flaming Hour; One Clear Call; The Super-Sex; The Scrapper; The Lavender Bath Lady. **1923** Crimson Gold; The Hunchback of Notre Dame. **1924** What Three Men Wanted. **1925** Don Q., Son of Zorro. **1928** The Gaucho; The Viking.

MAC QUARRIE, FRANK
Born: 1875, San Francisco, Calif. Died: Dec., 1950, Los Angeles, Calif. Screen and stage actor.

Appeared in: **1915** The Black Box (serial). **1916** The Pool of Flame; Secret of the Swamp. **1917** The Field of Honor; The Charmer; Flirting With Death; The Man Trap; Two Men of Sandy Bar. **1918** The Flash of Fate; Girl of My Dreams. **1919** Whitewashed Walls; Loot; Under Suspicion.

MAC QUARRIE, MURDOCK
Born: Aug. 26, 1878, San Francisco, Calif. Died: Aug. 22, 1942, Los Angeles, Calif. Screen, stage actor and film director. Entered films with Biograph in 1902.

Appeared in: **1913** The Embezzler; The Lamb, the Woman, the Wolf; The End of the Feud; Red Margaret—Moonshiner; The Lie. **1914** The Honor of the Mounted; Remember Mary Magdalen; Discord and Harmony; The Menace of Charlotte (aka Carlotta, the Bead Stringer); The Tragedy of Whispering Creek; The Unlawful Trade; The Forbidden Room; The Old Cobbler; A Ranch Romance; Her Grave Mistake; By the Sun's Ray; The Oubliette; A Miner's Romance; The Higher Law; Richelieu; The Wall of Flame; The Star Gazer; The Old Bellringer; Monsieur Bluebeard; The End of the Feud; The Hopes of Blind Alley. **1915** The Stranger Mind; The Trap. **1917** Bloodhounds of the North. **1921** Cheated Hearts; Sure Fire. **1922** If I Were Queen; The Unfoldment; The Hidden Woman. **1923** Ashes of Vengeance; Canyon of the Fools. **1924** The Only Woman. **1925** A Gentleman Roughneck. **1926** Going the Limit; Hair Trigger Baxter; The High Hand; The Jazz Girl. **1927** Black Jack; The Long Loop on the Pecos. **1928** The Man From Hardpan; The Apache Raider. **1929** A .45 Calibre War. **1930** Captain of the Guard. **1932** Wild Girls; Dr. Jekyll and Mr. Hyde. **1933** Cross Fire. **1934** Return of Chandu; The Mighty Barnum. **1935** The Dark Angel; Stone of Silver Creek. **1936** Great Guy. **1937** Git Along, Little Dogies. **1938** Tom Sawyer, Detective; Blockage; Guilty Trails. **1940** The Mummy's Hand. **1941** Man from Montana. **1942** Tennessee Johnson; Cat People.

MC QUARY, CHARLES S.
Born: 1908. Died: Feb. 9, 1970, Hollywood, Calif. (stroke). Screen, television actor, stand-in for Buddy Ebsen in television and double for Smiley Burnett in films.

MC QUEEN, STEVE (Terence Stephen McQueen)
Born: Mar. 24, 1930, Slater, Mo. or Indianapolis, Ind.? Died: Nov. 7, 1980, Juarez, Mexico (heart attack following surgery for cancer). Screen, stage and television actor. Divorced from actress Neile Adams and Ali McGraw. Later married to model Barbara Minty. Father of Chad and Teri McQueen. Nominated for 1966 Academy Award for Best Actor in The Sand Pebbles.

Appeared in: **1956** Somebody Up There Likes Me. **1958** Never Love a Stranger; The Blob. **1959** The Great St. Louis Bank Robbery; Never So Few. **1960** The Magnificent Seven. **1961** The Honeymoon Machine. **1962** Hell Is for Heroes; The War Lover. **1963** Love With the Proper Stranger; Soldier in the Rain; The Great Escape. **1965** Baby, the Rain Must Fall; The Cincinnati Kid. **1966** Nevada Smith; The Sand Pebbles. **1968** Bullitt; Thomas Crown and Company (aka The Thomas Crown Affair). **1969** The Reivers. **1970** Le Mans. **1971** On Any Sunday (documentary). **1972** Junior Bonner; The Getaway. **1973** Papillon. **1974** The Towering Inferno. **1979** Tom Horn. **1980** An Ememy of the People; The Hunter.

MC QUOID, ROSE LEE (aka LEE, ROSE)
Born: 1887. Died: May 4, 1962, Hollywood, Calif. Screen actress. Entered films approx. 1912.

Appeared in: **1930** Just Imagine.

MACRAE, ARTHUR (Arthur Schroepfer)
Born: Mar. 17, 1908, London, England. Died: Feb. 25, 1962, Brighton, England. Screen, stage actor, screenwriter and playwright.

Appeared in: **1937** Silver Blaze (aka Murder at the Baskervilles—US 1941). **1941** The Saint's Vacation. **1959** The Horse's Mouth.

MC RAE, BRUCE
Born: Jan. 18, 1867, India. Died: May 7, 1927, City Island, N.Y. (heart trouble). Stage and screen actor. Brother of actor Duncan McRae (dec. 1931).

Appeared in: **1916** Hazel Kirke. **1919** A Star Overnight. **1922** The World's a Stage.

MC RAE, DUNCAN
Born: 1881, London, England. Died: Feb. 4, 1931, London, England. Screen, stage actor, film and stage producer. Brother of actor Bruce McRae (dec. 1927). Married to actress Gertrude McCoy (dec. 1967). Entered films with Edison Film Company in 1913. Do not confuse with Scottish actor Duncan Macrae (dec. 1967).

Appeared in: **1914** The Impersonator. **1915** Greater Than Art. **1916** The Flower of No Man's Land. **1917** Red, White and Blue Blood.

MACRAE, DUNCAN (aka JOHN DUNCAN GRAHAM MACRAE)
Born: 1905, Glasgow, Scotland. Died: Mar. 23, 1967, Glasgow, Scotland. Screen, stage and television actor. Do not confuse with actor Duncan McRae (dec. 1931).

Appeared in: **1947** The Brothers (US 1948). **1949** Whisky Galore (aka Tight Little Island—US and Mad Little Island). **1950** The Woman in Question (aka Five Angels on Murder—US 1953). **1952** You're Only Young Twice! **1953** The Kidnappers (aka The Little Kidnapper—US 1954). **1955** Geordie (aka Wee Geordie—US 1956). **1958** Rockets Galore (aka Mad Little Island—US). **1959** The Bridal Path. **1960** Kidnapped; Our Man in Havana; Tunes of Glory. **1961** Greyfriar's Bobby. **1962** The Best of Enemies. **1963** Girl in the Headlines (aka The Model Murder Case—US 1964); A Jolly Bad Fellow (US 1964 aka They All Died Laughing). **1967** Casino Royale; 30 Is a Dangerous Age; Cynthia (US 1968).

MACREADY, GEORGE
Born: Aug. 29, 1909, Providence, R.I. Died: July 2, 1973, Los Angeles, Calif. (emphysema). Screen, stage and television actor. Divorced from actress Elizabeth Dana.

Appeared in: **1942** Commandos Strike at Dawn (film debut). **1944** Wilson; The Seventh Cross; Story of Dr. Wassell; The Conspirators; Follow the Boys; Soul of a Monster. **1945** Counter-Attack; Don Juan Quilligan; The Fighting Guardsman; My Name is Julia Ross; I Love a Mystery; A Song to Remember; The Missing Juror; The Monster and the Ape (serial). **1946** Gilda; The Bandit of Sherwood Forest; The Walls Came Tumbling Down; The Man Who Dared; The Return of Monte Cristo. **1947** Down to Earth; The Swordsman. **1948** The Big Clock; Beyond Glory; Gallant Blade; The Black Arrow; Coroner Creek. **1949** Knock on Any Door; Alias Nick Beal (aka The Contact Man); The Doolins of Oklahoma; Johnny Allegro. **1950** The Nevadan; A Lady Without Passport; The Desert Hawk; Fortunes of Captain Blood; Rogues of Sherwood Forest. **1951** The Desert Fox; Detective Story; The Golden Horde; Tarzan's Peril. **1952** The Green Glove. **1953** Treasure of the Golden Condor; The Stranger Wore a Gun; The Golden Blade; Julius Caesar. **1954** Duffy of San Quentin; Vera Cruz. **1956** Thunder Over Arizona; A Kiss Before Dying. **1957** Paths of Glory; The Abductors. **1958** Gunfire at Indian Gap; Jet Over the Atlantic (US 1960). **1959** Plunderers of Painted Flats; The Alligator People. **1962** Two Weeks in Another Town; Taras Bulba. **1964** Dead Ringer; Seven Days in May; Where Love Has Gone. **1965** The Great Race; The Human Duplicators. **1970** Count Yorga, Vampire (narrator); Tora! Tora! Tora! **1971** Return of Count Yorga.

MACRORIE, ALMA (Alma Ruth Macrorie)
Born: 1905, Davenport, Iowa. Died: June 28, 1970, Woodland Hills, Calif. Screen actress and film editor.

Appeared in: **1944** Frenchmen's Creek. **1946** To Each His Own. **1948** The Emperor Waltz. **1956** Anything Goes.

MAC SARIN, KENNETH (Max Kenneth Sarin)
Born: 1912. Died: Jan. 17, 1967, New York, N.Y. (cancer). Stage and screen actor.

MC SHANE, KITTY
Born: 1898. Died: Mar. 24, 1964, London, England. Screen, stage and vaudeville actress. Married to actor Arthur Lucan (dec. 1954), with whom she appeared in vaudeville films in an act billed as "Lucan and McShane." The two played in "Old Mother Riley" series of films, McShane playing the mother. For the films they appeared in, see Arthur Lucan.

MAC TAGGART, JAMES
Born: 1928. Died: May 29, 1974, London, England. Screen, stage actor, film producer, television director and screenwriter.

MC TAGGART, JAMES
Born: 1911. Died: May 29, 1949, Beverly Hills, Calif. (swimming pool accident). Screen actor.

MC TURK, JOE
Born: 1899. Died: July 19, 1961, Hollywood, Calif. (heart attack). Screen, stage and television actor.

Appeared in: **1950** Mister 880. **1953** Money From Home. **1955** Guys and Dolls. **1956** Man With the Golden Arm. **1958** Houseboat. **1961** Pocketful of Miracles.

MC VEY, LUCILLE *See* DREW, MRS. SIDNEY

MC VEY, PATRICK "PAT"
Born: 1910. Died: July 6, 1973, New York, N.Y. Screen, stage and television actor.

Appeared in: **1942** Pierre of the Plains; The Mummy's Tomb. **1946** Two Guys from Milwaukee; Swell Guy. **1957** The Big Caper. **1958** Party Girl. **1959** North By Northwest. **1968** The Detective. **1972** The Visitors.

MC VICKER, JULIUS
Born: 1876. Died: Mar. 11, 1940, Beverly Hills, Calif. Screen and stage actor.

Appeared in: **1932** The Phantom President.

MC WADE, EDWARD
Died: May 16, 1943, Hollywood, Calif. Screen actor. Married to actress Margaret McWade (dec. 1956).

Appeared in: **1921** Wing Toy. **1922** The Stranger's Banquet. **1923** The Town Scandal. **1925** The Monster. **1932** Big City Blues; The Big Shot; Two Seconds; Six Hours to Live; Lawyer Man. **1933** Murders in the Zoo. **1934** I'll Tell the World; Journal of a Crime; The Notorious Sophie Lang; A Lady Lost. **1935** Murder in the Clouds; Oil for the Lamps of China; Stranded; Frisco Kid; The Girl from Tenth Avenue; Red Salute; Dr. Socrates; Bordertown. **1936** Darkest Africa (serial); Satan Met a Lady; The Country Doctor; The Calling of Dan Matthews; The Big Noise; The Man I Marry; Reunion. **1937** Let's Get Married; They Won't Forget; The Women Men Marry. **1938** White Banners; Garden of the Moon; Comet Over Broadway; The Patient in Room 18; Jezebel. **1939** They Asked For It; Indianapolis Speedway; The Magnificent Fraud. **1940** Our Neighbors, the Carters; Hot Steel; The Return of Frank James; Chad Hanna; A Dispatch from Reuters. **1941** I Wake Up Screaming (aka Hot Spot); Meet John Doe; The Big Store. **1942** Woman of the Year; Keeper of the Flame; The Hard Way; You Can't Escape Forever; Yankee Doodle Dandy; Famous Boners (short); Lady in a Jam. **1943** Crash Dive. **1944** Arsenic and Old Lace.

MC WADE, MARGARET
Born: Sept. 3, 1872. Died: Apr. 1, 1956. Screen, stage and vaudeville actress. Married to actor Edward McWade (dec. 1943). Appeared in vaudeville with Margaret Seddon (dec. 1968) in an act billed as the "Pixilated Sisters."

Appeared in: **1914** A Foolish Agreement; The Blind Fiddler. **1915** Taming a Grouch. **1917** Blue Jeans. **1918** Flower of the Dusk. **1919** Why Germany Must Pay; Broken Commandments. **1920** Alias Miss Dodd; Shore Acres; Food for Scandal; Her Beloved Villain; When a Man Loves; Stronger Than Death. **1921** Blue Moon; The Blot; The Foolish Matrons; Her Mad Bargain; A Tale of Two Worlds; Garments of Truth. **1923** Alice Adams. **1924** Broken Barriers; The Cyclone Rider; Sundown; The Painted Lady. **1925** The Lost World; White Fang. **1926** High Steppers. **1928** Women Who Dare. **1936** Postal Inspector; Theodora Goes Wild; Mr. Deeds Goes to Town. **1937** Lost Horizon; Let's Make a Million; Wings Over Honolulu; Love in a Bungalow; Danger—Love at Work; We Have Our Moments. **1938** The Texans; Holiday; Forbidden Valley. **1939** When Tomorrow Comes. **1940** Remedy for Riches. **1942** Scattergood Survives a Murder; The Woman of the Year. **1943** The Meanest Man in the World. **1947** It's a Joke, Son; The Bishop's Wife. **1953** It Should Happen to You.

MC WADE, ROBERT, JR.
Born: 1882, Buffalo, N.Y. Died: Jan. 20, 1938, Culver City, Calif. (heart attack). Stage and screen actor. Son of actor Robert McWade, Sr. (dec. 1913).

Appeared in: **1924** Second Youth. **1925** New Brooms. **1928** The Home Towners. **1930** Night Work; Good Intentions; Feet First; The Pay Off; Sins of the Children. **1931** Cimarron; Too Many Cooks; Kept Husbands; Skyline; It's a Wise Child. **1932** I Am a Fugitive from a Chain Gang; Grand Hotel; The First Year; Ladies of the Jury; Madame Racketeer; Back Street; The Match King; Movie Crazy; The Phantom of Crestwood; Once in a Lifetime. **1933** I Loved a Woman; The Prize Fighter and the Lady; Journal of a Crime; Heroes for Sale; The Solitaire Man; Fog; The Kennel Murder Case; A Lost Lady; Employees' Entrance; Big City Blues; High Spot; Two Seconds; Hard to Handle; Ladies They Talk About; 42nd Street; Pick Up; The Big Cage. **1934** Countess of Monte Cristo; Let's Be Ritzy; No Ransom; Operator 13; Cross Country Cruise; Hold That Girl; Thirty-Day Princess; Midnight Alibi; The Dragon Murder Case; The Lemon Drop Kid; College Rhythm; The President Vanishes. **1935** The County Chairman; Society Doctor; Here Comes the Band; Straight from the Heart; Diamond Jim; His Night Out; Mary Jane's Pa; The Healer; Cappy Ricks Returns; Frisco Kid. **1936** Next Time We Love; The Big Noise; Anything Goes; Early to Bed; Moonlight Murder; Old Hutch; High Tension; 15

Maiden Lane; Bunker Bean. **1937** Benefits Forgot; We're on the Jury; California Straight Ahead; The Good Old Soak; This Is My Affair; Mountain Justice; On Such a Night; Under Cover of Night. **1938** Gold Is Where You Find It; Of Human Hearts; I Am the Law.

MC WADE, ROBERT, SR.
Born: 1835. Died: Mar. 5, 1913, Screen and stage actor. Screen and stage actor. Father of actor Robert McWade, Jr. (dec. 1938).

Appeared in: **1912** Rip Van Winkle; As You Like It; The Curio Hunters; Captain Barnacle—Reformer. **1913** The Joke Wasn't on Ben Bolt; Papa Puts One Over; There's Music in the Air.

MC WATTERS, ARTHUR J.
Born: 1871. Died: July 16, 1963, Freeport, N.Y. Screen, stage and vaudeville actor. Appeared in vaudeville with his wife, Grace Tyson, as "McWatters and Tyson." Appeared in early George Burns and Gracie Allen films.

MACY, CARLETON
Born: 1861. Died: Oct. 18, 1946, Bay Shore, N.Y. Screen, stage and vaudeville actor. Was in vaudeville with his wife, actress Maude Hall (dec. 1938), in an act billed as "Magpie and the Jay" and later was with Al Lydell in an act billed as "Two Old Cronies."

Appeared in: **1929** Seven Keys to Baldpate.

MACY, JACK
Born: 1886. Died: July 2, 1956, Wyo. (heart attack). Screen, stage and television actor.

Appeared in: **1955** Untamed.

MADDEN, PETER
Born: 1910, England. Died: Feb. 24, 1976, England? Screen and stage actor.

Appeared in: **1948** Counterblast. **1951** Tom Brown's Schooldays. **1958** Battle of the V.1 (aka Unseen Heroes—US); Floods of Fear (US 1959); Fiend Without a Face. **1960** Exodus; Hell Is a City; Saturday Night and Sunday Morning (US 1961). **1962** A Kind of Loving; The Road to Hong Kong; The Loneliness of the Long Distance Runner (aka Rebel With a Cause). **1963** The Very Edge; Nothing But the Best (US 1964); Stolen Hours; From Russia With Love (US 1964); The Kiss of the Vampire. **1964** Dr. Terror's House of Horrors (US 1965); Woman of Straw. **1965** Doctor Zhivago. **1967** Frankenstein Created Woman. **1968** He Who Rides a Tiger. **1970** The Private Life of Sherlock Holmes. **1977** Mohammad, Messenger of God.

MADEIRA, HUMBERTO
Born: 1921, Portugal. Died: July 15, 1971, Lisbon, Portugal (cancer). Stage and screen actor.

Appeared in: **1956** Lisbon.

MADISON, C. J.
Died: Jan. 20, 1975. Animal trainer and screen actor.

Appeared in: **1962** Jumbo.

MADISON, CLEO
Born: 1883. Died: Mar. 11, 1964, Burbank, Calif. (heart attack). Screen actress.

Appeared in: **1913** The Buccaneers; Captain Kidd; Shadows of Life; The Heart of a Cracksman. **1914** The Dead Line; The Mexican's Last Raid; Unjustly Accused; The Trey of Hearts (serial); The Pine's Revenge; The Fascination of the Fleur de Lis; Alas and Alack; A Mother's Atonement. **1915** Damon and Pythias; Liquid Dynamite; The Power of Fascination; The Ring of Destiny. **1916** Alias Jane Jones; The Chalice of Sorrow; Cross Purposes; Eleanor's Catch; The Girl in Lower 4; The Guilty One; Her Bitter Cup; Her Defiance; His Return; The Severed Hand; To Another Woman; Virginia; When the Wolf Howls; The Crimson Yoke; Priscilla's Prisoner; The Triumph of Truth. **1917** Black Orchids; The Daring Change. **1918** The Romance of Tarzan. **1919** The Great Radium Mystery (serial). **1920** The Girl From Nowhere. **1921** Ladies Must Live; The Lure of Youth. **1922** The Dangerous Age; A Woman's Woman. **1923** Gold Madness; Souls in Bondage. **1924** The Roughneck; The Lullaby; True as Steel; Discontented Husbands; Unseen Hands.

MADISON, HARRY
Born: 1877. Died: July 8, 1936, Los Angeles, Calif. (throat ailment). Screen, stage and vaudeville actor. Was part of vaudeville team of "Bailey and Madison" and later "Thurber and Madison."

Appeared in: **1920** King of the Circus (serial).

MADISON, NOEL N. (Noel Moscovitch)
Born: c. 1905, New York, N.Y. Died: Jan. 6, 1975, Fort Lauderdale, Fla. Screen, stage actor and stage director. Son of actor Maurice Moscovitch (dec. 1940).

Appeared in: **1930** The Doorway to Hell; Sinners Holiday; Little Caesar; The Honorable Mr. Wong. **1931** The Star Witness. **1932** Me and My Gal; Hat Check Girl; The Last Mile; The Trial of Vivienne Ware; Man About Town; The Hatchet Man; Play Girl; Symphony of Six Million. **1933** The Important Witness; West of Singapore; Laughter in Hell; Destination Unknown; Humanity. **1934** Manhattan Melodrama; I Like It That Way; Journal of a Crime; The House of Rothschild. **1935** Four Hours to Kill; The Morals of Marcus (US 1936); G-Men; Woman Wanted; The Girl Who Came Back; Three Kids and a Queen; My Marriage. **1936** Our Relations; Muss 'Em Up; The Criminal Within; Missing Girls; Easy Money; Straight from the Shoulder; Champagne Charlie; Murder at Glen Athol. **1937** Man of the People; Gangway; The Man Who Made Diamonds; Kate Plus Ten; Nation Aflame; House of Secrets. **1938** Climbing High (US 1939); Sailing Along; Anything to Declare?; Crackerjack (aka The Man With a Hundred Faces—US). **1939** Charlie Chan in City in Darkness; Missing Evidence. **1940** Know Your Money (short); The Great Plane Robbery. **1941** Sucker List; Queen of Crime; Ellery Queen's Penthouse Mystery; Footsteps in the Dark; Highway West; A Shot in the Dark. **1942** Secret Agent of Japan; Bombs Over Burma; Joe Smith—American. **1943** Miss V. from Moscow; Jitterbugs; Shantytown; Black Raven. **1949** Gentleman From Nowhere.

MADRIGUERA, ENRIC
Born: 1902. Died: Sept. 7, 1973. Screen actor, composer, musician and orchestra leader.

Appeared in: **1946** The Thrill of Brazil (with his orchestra).

MADSEN, HARALD
Born: Nov. 20, 1980, Silkeborg, Denmark. Died: 1949, Denmark? Screen and stage actor. Partner of Carl Schenstrom (dec. 1942) with whom he appeared in an act billed as "Fyrtaarnet and Bigoven."

MAEL, AARON
Born: 1891. Died: Mar. 26, 1948, Sheboggan Falls, Wis. (heart attack). Screen actor and make-up artist.

MAENO, MITSUYASU (Shimoichiro Maeno)
Born: 1947, Japan. Died: Mar. 23, 1976, Tokyo, Japan (suicide—kamikaze style). Screen and stage actor. Divorced from actress Noriko Kurosawa and Deborah Jean Hiller. Entered films in 1967.

Appeared in: **1976** Tokyo's Madame Emmanuelle.

MAERTENS, WILLY
Born: 1893, Brunswick, Germany. Died: Nov. 28, 1967, Hamburg, Germany. Screen, stage, television actor and stage director.

Appeared in: **1942** Anschlag auf Baku. **1947** In Jenen Tagen. **1948** Arche Nora. **1949** Der Apfel ist Ab. **1950** Absender Unbekannt; Die Schatten des Herrn Monitor; Nur Wine Nacht. **1951** Schon Muss Man Sein; Engel im Abendkleid. **1952** Unter den Tausend Laternen (aka Die Stimme des Andern); Toxi; Oh, du Lieber Fridolin; Ich Warte auf Dich. **1953** Keine Angst vor Grossen Tieren. **1954** Bei Dir war es Immer so Schon; Konsul Strotthoff; Gestandnis Unter Vier Augen; Drei vom Variete. **1955** Musik, Musik und nur Musik; Wie Werde ich Filmstar. **1956** Die ehe des Dr. Med. Danwitz; Der Haupmann von Kopenick; Madchen mit Schwachem Gedachtnis; Wenn wir Alle Engel Waren; Tierarzt Dr. Vlimmen. **1957** Nachts im Grunen Kakadu. **1958** Das Haut Einen Seemann Doch Night Um. **1959** Frau im Besten Mannesalter; Die Nacht vor der Premiere; Die Schone Lugnerin. **1960** Nacht Fiel Uber Gotenhafen. **1961** Das Wunder der Malachias.

MAGALLANES, NICHOLAS
Born: 1923. Died: May 2, 1977. Ballet dancer and screen actor.

Appeared in: **1967** A Midsummer Night's Dream.

MAGEE, HARRIETT
Born: 1878. Died: Apr. 19, 1954, Los Angeles, Calif. Screen actress. Appeared in silent films.

MAGGI, LUIGI
Born: Dec. 21, 1867, Italy. Died: 1946, Italy? Screen actor and film director. Entered films in 1906.

Appeared in: **1909** Luigi XI Re di Francia. **1911** Nozze d'Oro. **1918** Il Mistero dei Bauli Neri. **1920** La Danza Delle Ore; I Conquistatori.

MAGNANI, ANNA
Born: 1909, Alexandria, Egypt. Died: Sept. 26, 1973, Rome, Italy (cancer). Screen, stage, vaudeville, television actress and screenwriter. Married to film director Goffredo Alessandrini. Entered films in 1934. Won National Board of Review Award in 1946 as Best Foreign Actress for Open City; in 1947 won Venice Festival Award for Best International Actress and the Italian Silver Ribbon Award for Love; and won 1955 Academy Award for Best Actress in The Rose Tattoo. Nominated for 1957 Academy Award for Best Actress in Wild is the Wind.

Appeared in: **1934** The Blind Woman of Sorrento; Calvary; Down with Misery. **1936** Tempo Massimo; La Cieca di Sorrento. **1946** Woman Trouble (US 1949); Dreams in the Streets; Citta Aperta (Open City); The Bandit (US 1949); Unknown Men of San Marino. **1947** Before Him All Rome Trembled; Revenge; Love. **1948** Angelina. **1949** The Peddler and the Lady (US 1952); Peddlin' in Society (US 1950). **1950** The Miracle (aka The Ways of Love—US 1951). **1951** Doctor, Beware; Scarred. **1953** Volcano; Bellissima (US 1954); Anita Garibaldi. **1954** The Golden Coach; We Women. **1955** The Rose Tatoo. **1957** Wild is the Wind. **1958** The Awakening; Of Life and Love; Nella Citta L'Inferno (aka Hell in the City and The Wild Wild Women—US 1961). **1959** Woman Obsessed. **1960** The Fugitive Kind; Risate di Gioia (aka The Passionate Thief—US 1963). **1962** Hell in the City; Mamma Roma. **1963** Le Margot de Josefa. **1964** Volles Hera und Leere Taschen. **1965** Made in Italy (US 1967). **1969** The Secret of Santa Vittoria; Year of the Lord. **1972** 1870. **1980** I Am Anna Magnani (documentary).

MAGRI, COUNT PRIMO
Born: 1849. Died: Oct. 31, 1920, Middleboro, Mass. Circus midget and screen actor. Married to circus performer and actress Mrs. General Tom Thumb (dec. 1919).

Appeared in: **1915** The Lilliputian's Courtship.

MAGRILL, GEORGE
Born: Jan. 5, 1900, New York, N.Y. Died: May 31, 1952, Los Angeles, Calif. Screen, stage actor and stuntman. Entered films in 1921.

Appeared in: **1922** Rose of the Sea. **1924** Fast and Fearless; North of Nevada; The Mask of Lopez; Stolen Secrets. **1925** Lord Jim; Vanishing American; Wild Horse Mesa; Duped; The Fighting Smile. **1926** The Enchanted Hill. **1927** The Desert of the Lost; The Ballyhoo Buster; Roarin' Broncs; Hawk of the Hills (serial); Ride 'Em High; The Cyclone Cowboy. **1928** Blockage; Vultures of the Sea (serial); The Count of Ten. **1929** Hawk of the Hills (feature of 1927 serial). **1932** The Lost Special (serial). **1933** The Three Musketeers (serial). **1934** Charlie Chan's Courage. **1935** The Phantom Empire (serial). **1936** Too Many Parents. **1937** Outcast; Midnight Madonna. **1938** Born to Be Wild; Passport Husbands; Romance in the Dark; Give Me a Sailor. **1939** The Flying Irishman. **1941** Meet Boston Blackie. **1947** Pirates of Monterey; G-Men Never Forget (serial); Twilight on the Rio Grande. **1948** G-Men Never Forget (serial); So You Want to Be a Detective (short). **1950** When Willie Comes Marching Home. **1952** At Sword's Point.

MAGUIRE, CHARLES J.
Born: 1882. Died: July 22, 1939, North Hollywood, Calif. Screen, stage and circus actor. Married to actress Janet Sully.

MAGUIRE, EDWARD
Born: 1867. Died: Apr. 10, 1925, New York, N.Y. (heart disease). Screen extra.

MAGUIRE, TOM "LITTLE TOM MAGUIRE"
Born: Sept. 7, 1869, Milford, Conn. Died: June 21, 1934, North Hollywood, Calif. (blood clot on the heart). Stage and screen actor.

Appeared in: **1921** Star Dust. **1922** The Bond Boy. **1926** The Savage; Then Came the Woman. **1927** One Increasing Purpose; Shanghai Bound; Colleen. **1928** Cameraman; The Sawdust Paradise. **1930** City Girl.

MAGYARI, IMRE
Born: 1894, Hungary. Died: June, 1940. Hungarian screen, stage actor and gypsy band leader.

MAHALINGAN, T. R.
Born: 1924, India. Died: Apr. 20, 1978, Madurai, India. Screen actor and singer.

MAHAN, VIVIAN L.
Born: 1902. Died: Oct. 13, 1933, Los Angeles, Calif. (suicide). Screen actress and film extra. Married to actor Harry Bayfield.

MAHER, WALTER "WALLY"
Born: 1908. Died: Dec. 27, 1951, Los Angeles, Calif. Screen, radio and television actor.

Appeared in: **1935** Murder in the Fleet. **1937** 23 1/2 Hours' Leave; Submarine D-1; Hollywood Hotel. **1938** Miracle Money (short). **1940** Pound Foolish (short). **1945** Strange Holiday. **1949** Johnny Stool Pigeon. **1950** Mystery Street; The Reformer and the Redhead; Right Cross; The Story of Molly X.

MAHONEY, FRANCIS X.
Born: 1885. Died: Jan. 27, 1948. Screen actor.

Appeared in: **1936** Showboat.

MAHONEY, WILKIE
Born: 1897, San Miguel, Calif. Died: July 30, 1976, Los Gatos, Calif. Screen, stage, vaudeville actor and screenwriter.

Appeared in: **1926** Exit Smiling. **1927** Evening Clothes; Casey At the Bat. **1928** The Battle of the Century (short).

MAHONEY, WILL
Born: 1894, U.S. Died: Feb. 8, 1966 or 1967?, Melbourne, Australia. Screen actor.

Appeared in: **1928** Lost in the Arctic; Gang War. **1933** A Columbia short. **1937** Said O'Reilly to McNab (aka Sez O'Reilly to McNab—US 1938). **1939** Come Up Smiling (aka Ants in His Pants). **1963** The Sound of Laughter.

MAIGNE, CHARLES M.
Born: 1879, Va. Died: Nov. 23, 1929, San Francisco, Calif. (pneumonia). Screen actor, film director and screenwriter.

MAILES, CHARLES HILL
Born: May 25, 1870, Halifax, Nova Scotia, Canada. Died: Feb. 17, 1937, Los Angeles, Calif. Stage and screen actor. Married to actress Claire McDowell (dec. 1966).

Appeared in: **1909** At the Altar. **1911** A Woman Scorned; The Miser's Heart; A Terrible Discovery; A Tale of the Wilderness; A Blot on the 'Scutcheon. **1912** The Girl and Her Trust; Just Like a Woman; A Beast at Bay; Home Folks; Lena and the Geese; Man's Genesis; The Sands of Dee; The Narrow Road; Iola's Promise; A Change of Spirit; Friends; So Near, Yet So Far; The Painted Lady; The Unwelcome Guest; The New York Hat; An Adventure in the Autumn Woods. **1913** A Welcome Intruder; The Hero of Little Italy; A Misunderstood Boy; The House of Darkness; Olaf—an Atom; Her Mother's Oath; The Coming of Angelo; The Reformers; The Battle of Elderberry Gulch; Judith of Bethulia. **1918** The Brass Bullet (serial). **1919** Red Hot Dollars. **1920** The Mark of Zorro; Treasure Island; Go and Get It. **1921** Chickens; The Home Stretch; Courage; The Ten Dollar Raise; Uncharted Seas. **1922** The Bond Boy; The Man from Downing Street; The Lying Truth. **1923** Held to Answer; East Side—West Side; Soft Boiled; Crashin' Thru; The Town Scandal; Michael O'Halloran. **1924** Thundering Hoofs; Find Your Man; Name the Man; When a Man's a Man. **1925** The Lighthouse by the Sea; The Midnight Flyer; The Fighting Demon; The Crimson Runner; The Overland Limited; Free to Love; Playing With Souls. **1926** Old Ironsides; The Combat; The Blue Streak; The Social Highwayman; Exclusive Rights; The Man in the Saddle; The Frontier Trail; Hearts and Fists; The Better Man. **1927** Bitter Apples; Play Safe; Man Power; Ain't Love Funny?; The City Gone Wild; The College Widow; Somewhere in Sonora. **1928** What a Night!; Give and Take; The Charge of the Gauchos; Drums of Love; Queen of the Chorus. **1929** The Bellamy Trial; The Faker; The Carnation Kid; One Stolen Night; Phantom City. **1930** Mother's Cry; Lilies of the Field. **1931** The Unholy Garden. **1932** No More Orchids. **1933** Women Won't Tell.

MAIN, MARJORIE (Mary Tomlinson)
Born: Feb. 24, 1890, Acton, Ind. Died: Apr. 10, 1975, Los Angeles, Calif. (cancer). Screen, stage, vaudeville, radio and television actress. Married to psychologist-lecturer Dr. Stanley L. Krebs (dec. 1935). Nominated for 1947 Academy Award for Best Supporting Actress in The Egg and I.

Appeared in: **1932** A House Divided. **1933** Take a Chance. **1934** Music in the Air (stage and film versions); Crime Without Passion; New Deal Rhythm (short). **1935** Naughty Marietta. **1937** Love in a Bungalow; The Man Who Cried Wolf; The Wrong Road; The Shadow; Boy of the Streets; Stella Dallas; Dead End (stage and film versions). **1938** City Girl; Three Comrades; Penitentiary; Girl's School; Romance of the Limberlost; Under the Big Top; King of the Newsboys; Test Pilot; Too Hot To Handle; Prison Farm; Little Tough Guy; There Goes My Heart. **1939** Two Thoroughbreds; Another Thin Man; Angels Wash

Their Faces; Lucky Night; The Women; They Shall Have Music. **1940** Women Without Names; The Dark Command; Turnabout; Susan and God; The Captain Is a Lady; I Take This Woman; Wyoming; Bad Man of Wyoming. **1941** The Trial of Mary Dugan; The Wild Man of Borneo; Barnacle Bill; The Bugle Sounds; The Shepherd of the Hills; Honky Tonk; A Woman's Face. **1942** Jackass Mail; Once Upon a Thursday; Tish; Tennessee Johnson; The Affairs of Martha; We Were Dancing. **1943** Johnny Come Lately; Woman of the Town; Heaven Can Wait. **1944** Meet Me in St. Louis; Rationing. **1945** Gentle Annie; Murder, He Says. **1946** Undercurrent; Bad Bascomb; The Harvey Girls; The Show-Off. **1947** The Egg and I; The Wistful Widow of Wagon Gap. **1948** Feudin' and Fussin' and A-Fightin'. **1949** Ma and Pa Kettle; Big Jack. **1950** Mrs. O'Malley and Mr. Malone; Ma and Pa Kettle Go to Town; Summer Stock. **1951** Ma and Pa Kettle Back on the Farm; Mr. Imperium; The Law and the Lady; It's a Big Country. **1952** The Belle of New York; Ma and Pa Kettle at the Fair. **1953** Ma and Pa Kettle on Vacation; Fast Company. **1954** Ricochet Romance; The Long, Long Trailer; Rose Marie; Ma and Pa Kettle at Home. **1955** Ma and Pa Kettle at Waikiki. **1956** The Kettles in the Ozarks; Friendly Persuasion. **1957** The Kettles on Old MacDonald's Farm.

MAINES, DON
Born: 1869. Died: Jan. 2, 1934, Los Angeles, Calif. (heart trouble). Screen actor.

Appeared in: **1922** The Man Who Waited.

MAIRE, EDWARD (Edward John Maire)
Born: July 2, 1892, Hoboken, N.J. Died: Dec. 24, 1947, Long Beach, Calif. Screen actor.

MAISON, EDNA
Born: 1893. Died: Jan. 11, 1946, Hollywood, Calif. Screen actress and opera singer. Entered films in 1911.

MAITLAND, LAUDERDALE
Born: 1877, London, England. Died: Feb. 28, 1929, England? Screen and stage actor. Son of stage actor Bill (Maitland) Mansell (dec.). Married to actress Janet Alexander (dec. 1961).

Appeared in: **1913** Ivanhoe (aka Rebecca the Jewess—US). **1915** The Beggar Girl's Wedding. **1916** What's Bred ... Comes Out in the Flesh. **1919** Queen's Evidence. **1923** The Right to Strike; Gems of Literature series including The Taming of the Shrew.

MAITLAND, RUTH (Ruth Erskine)
Born: Feb. 3, 1880, London, England. Died: Mar. 12, 1961, Dorking, England. Screen and stage actress.

Appeared in: **1930** Bread and Breakfast. **1932** Tin Gods. **1933** The Only Girl (aka Heart Song—US 1934); Going Gay (aka Kiss Me Goodbye—US 1935). **1938** A Spot of Bother.

MAJERONI, GEORGE "GIORGIO"
Born: 1877. Died: Aug. 5, 1924. Screen actor.

Appeared in: **1919** A Marriage for Convience; Fighting Destiny; The Gamblers; In Honor's Web. **1921** What Women Will Do; Diana of Star Hollows. **1922** How Women Love.

MAJERONI, MARIO
Born: 1870. Died: Nov. 18, 1931, New York, N.Y. Screen and stage actor.

Appeared in: **1917** Heart's Desire; The Broadway Sport; A Sleeping Memory. **1920** Partners of the Night. **1921** The Face in the Fog; The Valley of Silent Men; Destiny's Isle. **1923** The Enemies of Women; The Snow Bride; The Steadfast Heart. **1924** Argentine Love; The Humming Bird; Her Love Story. **1925** Share and Share Alike; The Little French Girl; The Substitute Wife; The King on Main Street. **1927** Rubber Heels.

MAJOR, SAM COLLIER
Died: July 31, 1955, Houston, Tex. Screen, stage actor and stage director. Father of actress Colleen Moore.

MAKEHAM, ELIOT
Born: Dec. 22, 1882, London, England. Died: Feb. 8, 1956, London, England. Screen and stage actor.

Appeared in: **1932** Rome Express. **1933** The Lost Chord; I Lived With You; Orders Is Orders (US 1934); Little Napoleon; I Was A Spy (US 1934); Friday the Thirteenth; The Laughter of Fools; Home Sweet Home; The Roof; I'm An Explosive; Forging Ahead. **1934** The Unfinished Symphony (US 1935); By-Pass to Happiness; The Crimson Candle. **1935** Lorna Doone; The Clairvoyant; Peg of Old Drury (US

1936); The Last Journey (US 1936); Once in a Blue Moon; His Last Affaire; Two Hearts in Harmony. **1936** The Brown Wallet; A Star Fell From Heaven; To Catch A Thief; Born That Way; East Meets West; Calling the Tune; Tomorrow We Live. **1937** Head Over Heels (aka Head Over Heels in Love—US); The Mill On the Floss (US 1939); Dark Journey; Farewell Again (aka Troopship—US 1938); Storm In a Teacup; Racing Romance; East of Ludgate Hill; Take My Tip. **1938** Darts Are Trumps; Coming of Age; Bedtime Story; Vessel of Wrath (aka The Beachcomber—US); It's In the Air (aka George Takes the Air—US 1940); The Citadel; Merely Mr. Hawkins; You're the Doctor; Anything to Declare? **1939** The Nursemaid Who Disappeared; Me and My Pal; Inspector Hornleigh; The Four Just Men (aka The Secret Four—US 1940); What Men Live By. **1940** Spy For a Day; Pastor Hall; Night Train to Munich (aka Night Train—US and Gestapo); Busman's Honeymoon (aka Haunted Honeymoon—US); Food For Thought; John Smith Wakes Up; Spare a Copper; All Hands. **1941** The Common Touch; Facing the Music. **1942** They Flew Alone (aka Wings and the Woman—US); Suspected Person; Uncensored (US 1944). **1943** Bell-Bottom George. **1944** The Halfway House (US 1945); A Canterbury Tale; Candles at Nine; Give Us the Moon. **1945** I'll Be Your Sweetheart; Perfect Strangers (aka Vacation from Marriage—US). **1946** Daybreak (US 1949); The Magic Bow (US 1947). **1947** Frieda; The Little Ballerina (US 1951); Jassy (US 1948). **1948** Call of the Blood. **1949** Murder at the Windmill (aka Murder at the Burlesque—US); Children of Chance (US 1951); Forbidden. **1950** The Miniver Story; Trio. **1951** Green Grow the Rushes; Scarlet Thread; Scrooge. **1952** Decameron Nights; The Crimson Pirate; The Yellow Balloon. **1953** The Fake; Always a Bride (US 1954). **1954** The Million Pound Note (aka Man With a Million—US); Doctor in the House (US 1955). **1956** Sailor Beware! (aka Panic in the Parlour—US 1957).

MALA, RAY "MALA"
Born: 1906, near Candle, Alaska. Died: Sept. 23, 1952, Hollywood, Calif. (heart attack). Screen actor.

Appeared in: **1932** Igloo. **1933** Eskimo. **1935** The Last of the Pagans. **1936** Jungle Princess; Robinson Crusoe of Clipper Island (serial). **1938** Call of the Ykon; The Great Adventure of Wild Bill Hickok (serial); Hawk of the Wilderness (serial). **1939** Mutiny on the Blackhawk; Coast Guard; Desperate Trails. **1940** North West Mounted Police; Zanzibar; Green Hell; Girl from God's Country; The Devil's Pipeline. **1941** Hold Back the Dawn. **1942** Son of Fury; The Mad Doctor of Market Street; The Tuttles of Tahiti. **1952** Red Snow.

MALAN, WILLIAM
Born: 1868. Died: Feb. 13, 1941, Hollywood, Calif. Screen and stage actor. Appeared in early Sennett films.

Appeared in: **1923** Slow as Lightning. **1924** Flashing Spurs. **1926** The College Boob; Red Hot Leather; One Punch O'Day. **1927** The Broncho Buster; Men of Daring; The Fighting Three; A One Man Game; The Overland Stage; Three Miles Up. **1929** The Border Wildcat.

MALATESTA, FRED
Born: Apr. 18, 1889, Naples, Italy. Died: Apr. 8, 1952, Burbank, Calif. (following surgery). Screen actor and film director. Entered films in 1915.

Appeared in: **1919** The Terror of the Range (serial). **1921** The Mask; All Dolled Up; Little Lord Fauntleroy. **1922** White Shoulders; The Woman He Loved. **1923** The Girl Who Came Back; Refuge; The Man Between. **1924** The Lullaby; Broadway or Bust; Honor Among Men; The Reckless Age; Forbidden Paradise; The Night Hawk. **1925** Without Mercy. **1926** Bardely's the Magnificent. **1927** The Gate Crasher; The Wagon Show. **1929** The Peacock Fan. **1930** Wings of Adventure. **1932** A Farewell to Arms. **1933** Picture Brides; What's Your Racket? **1934** The Thin Man; Perfectly Mismated (short). **1935** The Crusades; A Night at the Opera; Bordertown; The Lone Wolf Returns. **1936** Love on the Run; Anthony Adverse. **1938** The Black Doll; Suez; Artists and Models Abroad. **1939** Juarez. **1940** Arise, My Love.

MALCOLM, REGINALD
Born: 1884, Nottingham, England. Died: Jan. 20, 1966, Ottawa, Canada. Screen, stage and radio actor.

MALEY, DENMAN
Born: 1877, Holyoke, Mass. Died: May 22, 1927, Collingswood, N.J. Screen and stage actor. Brother of Patrick H. Maley and stage actor Stephen Maley (dec.).

Appeared in: **1915** Finn and Haddie.

MALIPIERO, LUIGI
Born: 1901, Germany. Died: Feb. 24, 1975, Sommerhausen, W. Germany (heart attack). Screen, stage, television actor, playwright and screenwriter. Married to actress Ingelborg Matly.

MALLALIEU, AUBREY
Born: June 8, 1873, Liverpool, England. Died: May 28, 1948, England? Screen and stage actor.

Appeared in: **1935** Cross Currents; The Riverside Murder; Music Hath Charms. **1936** Such is Life; A Touch of the Moon; Nothing Like Publicity; Love at Sea; All That Glitters; Prison Breaker. **1937** Holiday's End; The Last Chance; East of Ludgate Hill; 21 Days (aka The First and the Last, and aka 21 Days Together—US 1940); The Black Tulip; Keep Fit; Change for a Sovereign; Patricia Gets Her Man; The Strange Adventures of Mr. Smith; Fifty-Shilling Boxer; When the Devil Was Well; Pearls Bring Tears. **1938** Easy Riches; Coming of Age; Simply Terrific; Almost a Honeymoon; The Reverse Be My Lot; Save a Little Sunshine; Paid in Error; The Return of Carol Deane; The Gables Mystery; Thank Evans; His Lordship Regrets; Dangerous Medicine; You're the Doctor; His Lordship Goes to Press; Miracles do Happen; The Return of the Frog; The Claydon Treasure Mystery. **1939** Dead Men are Dangerous; Me and My Pal; The Face at the Window (US 1940); All at Sea; I Killed the Count (aka Who Is Guilty?—US 1940); So This Is London (US 1940). **1940** Salvage With a Smile; Busman's Honeymoon (aka Haunted Honeymoon—US); Bulldog Sees It Through; The Briggs Family; The Door With Seven Locks (aka Chamber of Horrors—US 1941). **1941** Breach of Promise (aka Adventure in Blackmail—US 1943); Gert and Daisy's Weekend; Penn of Pennsylvania (aka The Courageous Mr. Penn—US 1944); The Fine Feathers. **1942** Unpublished Story; Asking for Trouble; The Goose Steps Out; Squadron Leader X; Let the People Sing; The Young Mr. Pitt; They Flew Alone (aka Wings and the Woman—US). **1943** My Learned Friend; The Demi-Paradise (aka Adventure for Two—US 1945); Adventures of Tartu (aka Tartu—US); Yellow Canary (US 1944). **1944** Kiss the Bride Goodbye; He Snoops to Conquer. **1945** Murder in Reverse (US 1946); I Live in Grosvenor Square (aka A Yank in London—US 1946); The Wicked Lady (US 1946); Acacia Avenue (aka The Facts of Love—US 1949). **1946** Under New Management; School for Secrets; A Girl in a Million (US 1950). **1947** Meet Me at Dawn (US 1948). **1948** Counterblast; Saraband for Dead Lovers (aka Saraband—US 1949). **1949** The Queen of Spades (US 1950). **1953** The Gay Duellist (reissue of Meet Me at Dawn—1947).

MALLESON, MILES
Born: May 25, 1888, Croydon, England. Died: Mar. 15, 1969, London, England. Screen, stage, television actor, playwright and screenwriter. Divorced from actress Colette O'Neil (dec. 1975). Married to actress Tatiana Lieven (dec. 1978).

Appeared in: **1921** The Headmaster. **1931** City of Song (aka Farewell to Love—US 1933). **1932** The Sign of Four; The Mayor's Nest; Love on Wheels; Money Means Nothing (US 1934); The Love Contract. **1933** Summer Lightning. **1934** The Queen's Affair (aka Runaway Queen—US 1935); Nell Gwyn. **1935** Lazybones; Vintage Wine. **1936** Tudor Rose (aka Nine Days a Queen—US). **1937** Knight Without Armour; Victoria the Great. **1940** The Thief of Bagdad. **1941** Major Barbara. **1942** Unpublished Story; They Flew Alone (aka Wings and the Woman—US). **1943** Thunder Tock (US 1944); This Was Paris; The Gentle Sex. **1945** Dead of Night. **1947** While the Sun Shines (US 1950). **1948** Saraband for Dead Lovers (aka Saraband—US 1949); One Night With You; Woman Hater (US 1949); The Mark of Cain; Idol of Paris. **1949** The Queen of Spades; The Perfect Woman (US 1950); Kind Hearts and Coronets (US 1950); Train of Events (US 1952); The History of Mr. Polly (US 1951); Cardboard Lover. **1950** Stage Fright; Golden Salamander. **1951** The Man in the White Suit (US 1952); The Magic Box (US 1952); Scrooge. **1952** The Happy Family (aka Mr. Lord Says No—US); Treasure Hunt; The Importance of Being Earnest (stage and film versions); Venetian Bird (aka The Assassin—US 1953); Trent's Last Case (US 1953); The Woman's Angle (US 1954); Folly to Be Wise. **1953** The Captain's Paradise. **1955** King's Rhapsody (US 1956); Geordie (aka Wee Geordie—US 1956). **1956** The Silken Affair (US 1957); The Man Who Never Was; Private's Progress; Three Men in a Boat (US 1958); Dry Rot. **1957** Brothers-in-Law; The Admirable Crichton (aka Paradise Lagoon); Barnacle Bill (aka All at Sea—US 1958); The Naked Truth (aka Your Past Is Showing—US 1958). **1958** Dracula (aka Horror of Dracula—US); Bachelor of Hearts (US 1962); Gideon's Day (aka Gideon of Scotland Yard—US 1959); Happy Is the Bride (US 1959); Behind the Mask. **1959** I'm All Right, Jack (US 1960); The Captain's Table (US 1960); Carlton-Browne of the F.O. (aka Man in a Cocked Hat—US 1960); The Hound of the Baskervilles. **1960** Kidnapped; Peeping Tom (US 1962); The Day They Robbed the Bank of England; The Brides of Dracula; And the Same to You. **1961** Double Bunk; The Hellfire Club (US 1963); Fury at Smugglers Bay (US

1963). **1962** Postman's Knock; Go to Blazes; The Phantom of the Opera; Vengeance (aka The Brain—US 1964). **1963** Heavens Above; A Jolly Bad Fellow (US 1964 aka They All Died Laughing). **1964** First Men in the Moon; Murder Ahoy; Circus World. **1965** You Must Be Joking.

MALLINSON, RORY
Died: Mar. 26, 1976. Screen actor.

Appeared in: **1945** Pride of the Marines. **1947** King of the Bandits; Nora Prentiss; Cry Wolf; Dark Passage; For You I Die. **1948** Panhandle; I Wouldn't Be in Your Shoes; Open Secret; Docks of New Orleans; Blonde Ice; Last of the Wild Horses; The Checkered Coat; The Denver Kid. **1949** Prince of the Plains; South of Rio; Task Force; Trapped; Angels in Disguise; Rim of the Canyon; Bad Men of Tombstone. **1950** Salt Lake Raiders; County Fair; Short Grass. **1951** Three Desperate Men; Fingertips Don't Lie; According to Mrs. Hoyle; Rodeo King and the Senorita; Fort Dodge Stampede; Purple Heart Diary; Abbott and Costello Meet the Invisible Man; Calvary Scout. **1952** Hellgate; Blackhawk (serial); A Yank in Indo-China; Brave Warrior; Laramie Mountains; Waco; Montana Belle. **1953** Cow Country; Killer Ape; The Great Jesse James Raid. **1954** Jesse James vs. the Daltons; Killer Leopard. **1955** A Bullet for Joey; Seminole Uprising; Shotgun. **1959** King of the Wild Stallions.

MALLON, CATHERINE
Died: Feb. 13, 1939, Hollywood, Calif. (pneumonia). Screen actress. Married to actor Casson Ferguson (dec. 1929).

MALLOR, JOHN J. *See* MALLOY, JOHN J.

MALLORY, PATRICIA "BOOTS"
Born: Oct. 22, 1913, New Orleans, La. Died: Dec. 1, 1958, Santa Monica, Calif. (chronic throat ailment). Screen and stage actress. Divorced from actor Charles Bennett (dec. 1943) and William Cagney. Married to actor Herbert Marshall (dec. 1966). Was a 1932 Wampas Baby star.

Appeared in: **1932** Handle With Care. **1933** The Wolf Dog (serial); Humanity; Walking Down Broadway (aka Hello Sister); Carnival Lady; Hollywood on Parade (short). **1935** Sing Sing Nights; Powdersmoke Range. **1937** Here's Flash Casey.

MALLOY, FRANCETTA
Born: 1907. Died: July 17, 1978, Los Angeles, Calif. Screen, stage and vaudeville actress. Married to actor Hank Ladd (dec. 1982).

Appeared in: **1941** Las Vegas Nights.

MALLOY, JOHN J. (aka JOHN J. MALLOR)
Born: 1898, Dover, Del. Died: Feb. 9, 1968, Los Angeles, Calif. (heart attack). Screen actor, singer and artist. Appeared in silents.

MALNECK, MATTY
Born: 1903, Newark, N.J. Died: Feb. 25, 1981, Los Angeles, Calif. Screen, radio actor, bandleader, composer, violinist and television musical director.

Appeared in: **1939** St. Louis Blues; East Side of Heaven. **1941** You're in the Army Now. **1943** Shantytown. **1944** Trocadero. **1957** Love in the Afternoon.

MALO, GINA (Janet Flynn)
Born: June 1, 1909, Cincinnati, Ohio. Died: Nov. 30, 1963, New York, N.Y. Stage and screen actress. Married to actor Romney Brent (dec. 1976).

Appeared in: **1932** In a Monastery Garden; Good-Night Vienna; One Magic Night; King of the Ritz. **1933** Waltz Time; Strike It Rich; Lily of Killarney. **1934** The Private Life of Don Juan. **1936** My Song for You; Where There's a Will; Jack of All Trades. **1937** The Gang Show. **1938** Over She Goes. **1939** The Gentle People. **1940** Door With Seven Locks. **1941** Chamber of Horrors.

MALONE, DUDLEY FIELD
Born: 1882. Died: Oct. 5, 1950, Culver City, Calif. (heart attack). Screen actor. He was Asst. Secretary of State for Woodrow Wilson.

Appeared in: **1943** Mission to Moscow (played role of Churchill, whom he resembled).

MALONE, FLORENCE
Died: Mar. 4, 1956, Lyons, N.Y. Screen, stage, radio and television actress.

Appeared in: **1916** The Yellow Menace (serial).

MALONE, MOLLY (Edith Roberts)
Born: Dec. 7, 1888, Wis. Died: Feb. 15, 1952, Hollywood, Calif. Screen, vaudeville and radio actress. Do not confuse with actress born in 1897 in Colorado.

MALONE, PAT
Died: Oct. 5, 1963, New York, N.Y. Screen, stage and television actor. Appeared in films prior to 1941.

MALONE, PICK
Died: Jan. 22, 1962. Screen and radio actor. Was "Pick" on radio's "Pick and Pat" program.

Appeared in: **1937** The Hit Parade.

MALONE, RAY
Died: Apr. 18, 1970. Screen actor.

Appeared in: **1943** Moonlight in Vermont. **1944** Slightly Terrific.

MALONEY, JAMES J. "JIM"
Born: 1915. Died: Aug. 19, 1978. Screen, stage, radio and television actor.

Appeared in: **1951** Detective Story. **1952** Wait 'Til the Sun Shines Nellie. **1955** Mister Roberts. **1957** Hell Canyon (aka Hell Canyon Outlaws). **1960** Lust to Kill. **1961** Two Little Bears. **1962** Third of a Man.

MALONEY, LEO D.
Born: 1888, San Jose, Calif. Died: Nov. 2, 1929, New York, N.Y. (heart disease). Screen actor, film director and producer.

Appeared in: **1914** Hazards of Helen (serial). **1915** The Girl and the Game. **1916** The Lumberlands (serial). **1920** The Fatal Sign (serial). **1921** No Man's Woman; The Wolverine. **1922** Ghost City; Nine Points of the Law; The Western Musketeer. **1923** King's Creek Law; The Rum Runners. **1924** Built for Running; Headin' Through; Payable on Demand; Riding Double; Huntin' Trouble; The Perfect Alibi; Not Built for Runnin'; The Loser's End. **1925** Across the Deadline; The Blood Bond; Flash O' Lightning; Ranchers and Rascals; Luck and Sand; The Shield of Silence; Win, Lose or Draw; The Trouble Buster. **1926** Blind Trail; The High Hand; The Outlaw Express; Without Orders. **1927** Border Blackbirds; The Devil's Twin; Don Desparado; The Long Loop on the Pecos; The Man from Hardpan; Two-Gun of the Tumbleweed. **1928** The Apache Raider; The Boss of Rustler's Roost; Yellow Contraband. **1929** 45 Calibre War. **1930** Overland Bound.

MALTBY, HENRY F.
Born: Nov. 25, 1880, Ceres, South Africa. Died: Oct. 25, 1963, London, England. Screen, stage actor, playwright, screenwriter and author.

Appeared in: **1933** I Spy. **1934** A Political Party; Those Were the Days; The Luck Of a Sailor; Freedom of the Seas; Lost in the Legion; Falling in Love (aka Trouble Ahead—US); Girls Will Be Boys (US 1935); Josser On the Farm. **1935** The Morals of Marcus (US 1936); A Little Bit of Bluff; The Right to Marry; Vanity. **1936** King of the Castle; Queen of Hearts; Jack of All Trades (aka The Two of Us—US 1937); Not So Dusty; Two's Company; To Catch A Thief; Where There's a Will; Fame; Calling the Tune; Everything Is Thunder; Head Office; Busman's Holiday; The Heirloom Mystery; Everything in Life; Reasonable Doubt. **1937** Wake Up Famous; Pearls Bring Tears; Okay for Sound; Take My Tip; Mr. Smith Carries On; The Live Wire; Paradise For Two (aka The Gaiety Girls—US 1938); Young and Innocent (aka A Girl Was Young-US 1938); What a Man!; The Sky's the Limit; Captain's Orders; Song of the Road. **1938** Owd Bob (aka To the Victor—US); Darts Are Trumps; A Yank at Oxford; His Lordship Goes to Press; Pygmalion; Everything Happens to Me. **1939** The Good Old Days; The Gang's All Here (aka The Amazing Mr. Forrest—US); Old Mother Riley Joins Up. **1940** Garrison Follies; Under Your Hat. **1941** Facing the Music. **1942** The Great Mr. Handel (US 1943). **1943** Old Mother Riley, Detective; Somewhere in Civvies. **1944** A Canterbury Tale; Medal For the General. **1945** Home Sweet Home. **1946** The Trojan Brothers; Caesar and Cleopatra.

MALYON, EILY (Eily Sophie Lees-Craston)
Born: Oct. 30, 1879, London, England. Died: Sept. 26, 1961, South Pasadena, Calif. Screen and stage actress. Daughter of actress Agnes Thomas and Harry Lees-Craston.

Appeared in: **1932** Lovers Courageous; Wet Parade; Night Court. **1933** Looking Forward; Today We Live. **1934** Forsaking All Others; Romance in Manhattan; The Little Minister; His Greatest Gamble; Great Expectations; Limehouse Blues. **1935** The Widow from Monte

Carlo; The Florentine Dagger; Stranded; Nina; Clive of India; Les Miserables; The Flame Within; A Tale of Two Cities; Kind Lady; The Melody Lingers On. **1936** Camille; Little Lord Fauntleroy; One Rainy Afternoon; Angel of Mercy; Anthony Adverse; Cain and Mabel; Three Men on a Horse; God's Country and the Woman; Dracula's Daughter; The White Angel; A Woman Rebels; Career Woman. **1937** Night Must Fall; Another Dawn. **1938** Rebecca of Sunnybrook Farm; Kidnapped; The Young in Heart. **1939** Confessions of a Nazi Spy; The Hound of the Baskervilles; The Little Princess; On Borrowed Time; We Are Not Alone; Barricade. **1940** Young Tom Edison; Untamed; Foreign Correspondent. **1941** Arkansas Judge; Man Hunt; Hit the Road. **1942** The Man in the Trunk; The Undying Monster; Scattergood Survives a Murder; I Married a Witch; You're Telling Me. **1943** Above Suspicion. **1944** Jane Eyre; Going My Way; The Seventh Cross. **1945** Roughly Speaking; Scared Stiff; Grissly's Millions; Paris Underground; Son of Lassie; She Wouldn't Say Yes. **1946** She Wolf of London; Devotion; The Secret Heart. **1948** The Challenger.

MANDEL, FRANCES WAKEFIELD
Born: 1891. Died: Mar. 26, 1943, Batavia, N.Y. Screen actress. Posed for a number of James Montgomery Flagg's W.W. I posters.

MANDELL, NATHAN *See* MARTELL, MARTY

MANDER, MILES (Lionel Mander aka LUTHER MANDER)
Born: Nov. 14, 1888, Wolverhampton, England. Died: Feb. 8, 1946, Hollywood, Calif. (heart attack). Screen actor, film director, film producer and screenwriter.

Appeared in: **1918** Once Upon a Time. **1920** The Children of Gideon; Testimony; The Old Arm Chair; A Rank Outsider. **1921** A Temporary Lady; The Road to London; The Place of Honour. **1922** Open Country; Half a Truth. **1924** Lovers in Araby; The Prude's Fall. **1925** The Art of Love series including: Red Lips (aka The Painted Lady) and Sables of Death (aka The Lady in Furs; Racing Dramas (shorts). **1926** The Steve Donoghue series including: Riding for a King; The Pleasure Garden; London Love; Castles in the Air (short). **1927** Lost One Wife (aka As We Lie); Tiptoes; The Fake. **1928** The Physician (US 1929); The First Born; Balaclava (aka Jaws of Hell—US 1931). **1929** The Crooked Billet. **1930** Loose Ends; Murder. **1932** Frail Women; The Missing Rembrandt; Lily Christine; That Night in London (aka Overnight—US 1934). **1933** Matinee Idol; Loyalties; Don Quixote (US 1934); Bitter Sweet; The Private Life of Henry VIII. **1934** Four Masked Men; The Queen's Affair (aka Runaway Queen—US 1935); The Battle (aka Thunder in the East); The Case for the Crown. **1935** Death Drives Through; Here's to Romance; The Three Musketeers. **1936** Lloyd's of London. **1937** Slave Ship; Wake up and Live; Youth on Parole. **1938** Kidnapped; Suez; The Mad Miss Manton. **1939** Daredevils of the Red Circle (serial); Stanley and Livingstone; Man in the Iron Mask; Little Princess; The Three Musketeers (and 1935 version); Wuthering Heights; Tower of London. **1940** Road to Singapore; Primrose Path; The House of Seven Gables; Babies for Sale; Captain Caution; Laddie; South of Suez. **1941** Shadows on the Stairs; Dr. Kildare's Wedding Day; That Hamilton Woman. **1942** Captains of the Clouds (voice); Fingers at the Window; Mrs. Miniver (voice); Fly By Night; A Tragedy at Midnight; To Be or Not To Be; Tarzan's New York Adventure; Journey for Margaret; The War Against Mrs. Hadley; Apache Trail; This Above All. **1943** Assignment in Britany; Secrets of the Underground; Guadalcanal Diary; Five Graves to Cairo; The Phantom of the Opera. **1944** Enter Arsene Lupin; Four Jills in a Jeep; The Pearl of Death; The Return of the Vampire; The Scarlet Claw. **1945** Confidential Agent; The Picture of Dorian Gray; Brighton Strangler; Weekend at the Waldorf; The Crime Doctor's Warnings. **1946** The Bandit of Sherwood Forest; The Walls Came Tumbling Down. **1947** The Imperfect Lady.

MANDVILLE, WILLIAM C.
Born: 1867, Louisville, Ky. Died: Apr. 19, 1917, New York, N.Y. (heart disease). Screen actor.

MANDY, JERRY
Born: 1893. Died: May 1, 1945, Hollywood, Calif. (heart attack). Screen, stage and vaudeville actor.

Appeared in: **1925** North Star. **1927** The Gay Defender; Underworld. **1928** Hold 'Em Yale!; Love and Learn. **1929** The Sap; Love, Live and Laugh. **1930** Girl Shock (short); Nuits de Chicago (French release of Underworld—1927); The Doorway to Hell. **1931** Girls Demand Excitement; plus the following shorts: Rough Seas; Skip the Maloo!; Let's Do Things. **1932** Bon Voyage (short). **1933** Strange People; Sailor's Luck. **1935** It's a Gift; The Bride Who Comes Home; McFadden's Flats. **1936** King of Burlesque; Spendthrift. **1938** Hawaii Calls. **1939** Naughty But Nice. **1940** The Ghost Creeps.

MANJEAN, TEDDY
Born: 1901. Died: Sept. 9, 1964, Hollywood, Calif. Screen actor and stuntman.

Appeared in: **1934** The Mighty Barnum.

MANLEY, CHARLES "DADDY"
Born: Sept. 25, 1830, Ireland. Died: Feb. 26, 1916, Los Angeles, Calif. (arteriosclerosis). Screen and stage actor. Married to actress Marie Manley.

Appeared in: **1913** The Calling of Louis Mona. **1915** The Master Key (serial); The Golden Wedding; Learning to Be a Father; His Last Thirty; The Last Word; The Fair God of Sun Island. **1916** The Cry of Erin; Brennan O' the Moor. **1917** Her Wayward Parents.

MANLEY, DAVE
Born: 1883. Died: May, 1943, Calif. Screen and vaudeville actor.

Appeared in: **1931** The Struggle.

MANN, BERTHA
Born: 1893, Atlanta, Ga. Died: Dec. 20, 1967. Screen and stage actress. Married to actor Raymond Griffith (dec. 1957).

Appeared in: **1930** All Quiet on the Western Front; Little Accident; Free Love. **1931** Father's Son; A Woman of Experience; Caught Cheating. **1932** The Final Edition; Behind the Mask.

MANN, BILLY (William B. Mann)
Died: Apr. 14, 1974, New York, N.Y. Screen actor and singer.

Appeared in: **1935** Thanks a Million; Hoi Polloi (short). **1936** Stage Struck; Pigskin Parade; The Singing Kid. **1937** Artists and Models; Thrill of a Lifetime.

MANN, GENE
Born: 1906. Died: Aug. 6, 1978, Los Angeles, Calif. Screen actor, stage producer, publicist and theatrical agent.

MANN, GEORGE KLINE
Born: 1905. Died: Nov. 23, 1977, Santa Monica, Calif. (cancer). Screen, vaudeville and television actor. Member of vaudeville team of "Bardo and Mann."

Appeared in: **1946** The Yearling. **1949** Neptune's Daughter.

MANN, HANK (David W. Lieberman)
Born: 1887, New York, N.Y. Died: Nov. 25, 1971, South Pasadena, Calif. Screen actor and film director. Entered films in 1912.

Appeared in: **1914** In the Clutches of a Gang; Tillie's Punctured Romance; Mabel's Strange Predicament; Caught in a Cabaret (reissued as The Jazz Waiter); The Knock-Out (reissued as the Pugilist); Mabel's Married Life (reissued as the Squarehead). **1915** L-KO comedies. **1916** Fox Film Co. productions; A Modern Enoch Arden; The Village Blacksmith; His Bread and Butter; Hearts and Sparks. **1920** Arrow Film shorts. **1922** Quincy Adams Sawyer. **1923** Hollywood; Lights Out; Tea With a Kick; Don't Marry for Money; The Near Lady; A Noise in Newboro; The Wanters. **1924** The Man Who Played Square; A Woman Who Sinned; Empty Hands; Rivers Up. **1925** The Arizona Romeo; The Sporting Venus. **1926-27** Tennek Film Corp. Shorts. **1926** Wings of the Storm; The Skyrocket; The Boob; The Flying Horseman. **1927** The Patent Leather Kid; Broadway After Midnight; When Danger Calls; Paid to Love; Smile, Brother, Smile; The Scorcher; Lady Bird. **1928** Fazil; The Garden of Eden. **1929** Morgan's Last Raid; The Donovan Affair; Fall of Eve; Spite Marriage. **1930** The Arizona Kid; Sinner's Holiday; The Dawn Trail. **1931** City Lights; Annabelle's Affairs; Stout Hearts and Willing Hands (short). **1932** Scarface; Shame of a Nation; Ridin' for Justice; Strange Love of Molly Louvain; Million Dollar Legs. **1933** The Big Chance; Smoky. **1934** Fugitive Road; Men in Black (short). **1935** A Vitaphone short; The Devil Is a Woman; The Big Broadcast of 1936. **1936** Call of the Prairie; Modern Times; Reunion; Preview Murder Mystery. **1937** Goofs and Saddles (short). **1938** Stranger from Arizona. **1939** Hollywood Cavalcade. **1940** Alfalfa's Double (short); Bubbling Trouble (short); The Great Dictator. **1941** King's Row; Bullets for O'Hara. **1942** The Hard Way; Larceny, Inc.; Yankee Doodle Dandy; Bullet Scars. **1943** The Mysterious Doctor; The Dancing Masters. **1944** Arsenic and Old Lace; Gold Is Where You Lose It (short); Crime by Night. **1947** The Perils of Pauline. **1949** Jackpot Jitters. **1950** Joe Palooka in Humphrey Takes a Chance. **1953** The Caddy. **1954** Brigadoon; Living It Up. **1955** Abbott and Costello Meet the Keystone Kops; Abbott and Costello Meet the Mummy. **1956** Pardners. **1957** Man of a Thousand Faces. **1958** Rock-a-Bye Baby. **1959** Daddy-O; Last Train from Gun Hill.

MANN, HELEN R.
Born: 1916, Fort Worth, Tex. Died: Apr. 20, 1947, Hollywood, Calif. Screen actress.

Appeared in: **1932** Speed in the Gay '90s (short); Central Park; Silver Dollar. **1933** Employee's Entrance; Ladies They Talk About; The Little Giant.

MANN, LOUIS
Born: Apr. 20, 1865, New York, N.Y. Died: Feb. 15, 1931, New York, N.Y. Screen, stage actor and playwright.

Appeared in: **1929** Father's Day. **1930** The March of Time; The Richest Man in the World; Sins of the Children.

MANN, MARGARET
Born: Apr. 4, 1868, Aberdeen, Scotland. Died: Feb. 4, 1941, Los Angeles, Calif. (cancer). Screen actress.

Appeared in: **1918** The Heart of Humanity. **1919** The Right to Happiness. **1921** Black Beauty; Desert Blossoms; Man-Woman-Marriage; The Millionaire; The Smart Sex; The New Disciple. **1922** The Call of Home; Don't Write Letters; Love in the Dark. **1925** Her Sister from Paris. **1928** Four Sons. **1929** The River; Disraeli. **1931** the following shorts: Helping Grandma; Fly My Kite; The Panic Is On. **1932** Bachelor Mother. **1934** The Man Who Reclaimed His Head; Charlie Chan in London; The Painted Veil; I Hate Women; Little Men; Beloved. **1935** Bonnie Scotland; Kentucky Blue Streak. **1936** The Bohemian. **1937** Conflict. **1939** Federal Man-Hunt.

MANN, NED H.
Born: 1893, Redkey, Ind. Died: July 1, 1967, La Jolla, Calif. Screen actor and special effects director. Entered films as an actor in 1920 and then became technical director, etc.

MANN, STANLEY
Born: 1884. Died: Aug. 10, 1953, Los Angeles, Calif. Screen actor. Entered films during silents.

Appeared in: **1938** If I Were King. **1942** Mrs. Miniver. **1953** The Robe.

MANNERING, LEWIN
Born: Jan. 19, 1876, Poland. Died: June 7, 1932, London, England. Screen and stage actor.

MANNES, FLORENCE V.
Born: 1896. Died: Oct. 30, 1964, Hollywood, Calif. (heart attack). Screen actress. Entered films as a bit player and extra approx. 1924. Married to actor Max Mannes.

MANNHEIN, LUCIE
Born: Apr. 30, 1895, near Berlin, Germany. Died: July 28, 1976, Braunlage, West Germany. Screen, stage and television actress. Married to actor Marius Goring (aka Charles Richardson).

Appeared in: **1923** Die Austreibung (Driven from Home); Die Prinzessin Suwarin; Der Puppenmacher von Kiang-Ning; Der Schatz; Der Steinerne Reiter (The Stone Rider). **1929** Atlantik. **1931** Der Ball; Danton. **1933** Madame Wuenscht Keine Kinder. **1935** The 39 Steps. **1936** East Meets West. **1937** The High Command. **1943** Yellow Canary (US 1944). **1944** Tawny Pipit (US 1947); Hotel Reserve (US 1946). **1952** So Little Time. **1953** Nachts auf den Strassen; Ich und Du. **1954** Das Ideale Brautpaar. **1955** Die Stadt ist Voller Geheimnisse (aka City of Secrets, and aka Secrets of the City—US 1963); Du Darfst Nicht Langer Schweigen. **1957** Frauenarzi Dr. Bertram. **1958** Gestehen Sie, Dr. Corda (Confess, Dr. Corda—US 1961); Ihr 106 Geburtstag; Der Eiserne Gustav. **1959** Arzt aus Leidenschaft. **1960** Der Letzte Zeuge; Beyond the Curtain. **1965** Bunny Lake Is Missing. **1969** Erste Liebe.

MANNI, ETTORE
Born: 1927, Italy. Died: July 27, 1979, Rome, Italy (accidental gun shot). Screen actor.

Appeared in: **1952** White Slavery (film debut). **1953** La Nave delle Donne Maledette (The Ship of Condemned Women—US 1963); Cavalleria (aka Fatal Desire—US 1963). **1954** Due Notti con Cleopatra (Two Nights With Cleopatra—US 1963); Lupa (She Wolf). **1955** Le Amiche (aka The Girl Friends—US 1962). **1958** Attila; Il Pirata Dello Sparviero Nero (aka The Pirate of the Hawk—US 1961); Belle ma Povere (Beautiful But Poor, aka Poor But Beautiful—US). **1959** La Rivolta del Gladiatri (The Revolt of the Gladiators, aka The Warrior and the Slave Girl—US 1960). **1960** Le Legioni di Cleopatra (The Legions of Cleopatra, aka Legions of the Nile—US). **1961** Ercole alla Conquista di Atlantide (aka Hercule a la Conquete de L'Atlantide, and aka Hercules and the Captive Women—US 1963); El Sepolcro del

Re (aka Cleopatra's Daughter—US 1963); Le Vergini di Roma (Amazons of Rome—US 1963); La Rivolta Degli Schlavi (The Revolt of the Slaves). **1962** The Valiant (aka L'Affondamento della Valiant); Lo Sceicco Rosso (The Red Sheik—US 1963). **1963** Oro per i Cesari (Gold for the Caesars—US 1964); Roma Contro Roma (aka The War of the Zombies—US 1965). **1964** La Pupa (The Doll); Voir Venise et Crever (See Venice and Die). **1965** The Battle of the Villa Fiorita. **1966** Mademoiselle; L'Archidiavolo (The Devil in Love—US 1968). **1968** Un Uomo, un Cavallo, una Pistola (aka The Stranger Returns—US). **1976** The Street People. **1979** The Divine Nymph.

MANNING, AILEEN
Born: 1886, Denver, Colo. Died: Mar. 25, 1946, Hollywood, Calif. Screen actress.

Appeared in: **1921** Home Stuff. **1922** The Power of Love; A Tailor Made Man; Rags to Riches; Mixed Faces; Beauty's Worth. **1923** Main Street; Nobody's Money. **1924** The House of Youth; Lovers' Lane; The Snob; Her Marriage Vow. **1925** The Bridge of Sighs; Enticement; Under the Rouge; Thank You. **1926** Stella Maris; The Whole Town's Talking; The Boy Friend. **1927** Uncle Tom's Cabin; Man, Woman and Sin. **1928** Heart to Heart; The Olympic Hero; Home James. **1929** "Great Events" series; Sweetie. **1930** Wedding Rings; The Third Alarm. **1931** Huckleberry Finn.

MANNING, AMBROSE
Born: 1861. Died: Mar. 22, 1940, Brixham, South Devon, England. Screen and stage actor. Son of stage actor John Manning (dec. 1890).

Appeared in: **1921** Squibs.

MANNING, JOSEPH
Died: July 31, 1946, Hollywood, Calif. (heart attack). Screen and stage actor.

Appeared in: **1920** The Screaming Shadow (serial).

MANNING, KNOX
Born: 1904. Died: Aug. 26, 1980, Woodland Hills, Calif. Screen and radio actor.

Appeared in: **1941** Meet John Doe; Cheers for Miss Bishop; Tanks a Million. **1942** A Yank on the Burma Road. **1946** The Kid from Brooklyn. **1947** Buck Privates Come Home; Hit Parade of 1947. **1948** The Babe Ruth Story.

MANNING, MARY LEE
Died: Dec. 7, 1937, Hollywood, Calif. Screen actress.

MANNING, TOM
Born: 1880. Died: Oct. 10, 1936, Hollywood, Calif. Screen and stage actor.

Appeared in: **1936** The Singing Kid.

MANNING, W. H. "SPEED"
Born: 1899. Died: Sept. 10, 1933, between South Bend, Ind. and Chicago, Ill. (plane crash). Screen actor, stuntman and parachute jumper.

MANSFIELD, ALICE
Born: 1858. Died: Feb. 17, 1938. Screen and stage actress.

Appeared in: **1913** Flood Tide.

MANSFIELD, DUNCAN
Born: 1897. Died: Sept. 15, 1971, Hollywood, Calif. Screen actor, film director, film producer, screenwriter and production editor.

Appeared in: **1923** The White Sister.

MANSFIELD, JAYNE (Jayne Palmer)
Born: Apr. 19, 1932, Bryn Mawr, Pa. Died: June 29, 1967, New Orleans, La. (auto accident). Screen, stage and television actress. Divorced from Paul Mansfield, actor and former Mr. Universe Mickey Hargitay, and actor/director Matteo Ottaviano aka Matt Cimber. Mother of Mickey, Zoltan, Mariska Hargitay, Antonio Cimber and actress Jayne Marie.

Appeared in: **1955** Underwater; Pete Kelly's Blues; Illegal. **1956** Hell on Frisco Bay (aka The Darkest Hour); Female Jungle (aka Hangover). **1957** The Girl Can't Help It; Will Success Spoil Rock Hunter? (aka Oh, For a Man); The Burglar; The Wayward Bus; Kiss Them for Me. **1958** The Sheriff of Fractured Jaw. **1960** The Challenger (aka It Takes a Thief—US 1962); Gil Amore di Ercole (The Loves of Hercules and aka The Life of Hercules); Playgirl After Dark (aka Spin of a Coin). **1961**

The George Raft Story. **1962** It Happened in Athens. **1963** Promises! Promises! **1964** Panic Button; Heimweh Nach St. Pauli (Homesick for St. Paul); L'amore Primitivo (Primitive Love—US 1966); Einer Frisst den Anderen (Dog Eat Dog—US 1966). **1966** The Fat Spy; Las Vegas Hillbillys (aka Country Music U.S.A.). **1967** A Guide for the Married Man; Spree (aka Las Vegas by Night). **1968** Single Room Furnished; The Wild, Wild World of Jayne Mansfield (doc).

MANSFIELD, JOHN
Born: 1919. Died: Sept. 18, 1956, Hollywood, Calif. (heart attack). Screen actor.

Appeared in: **1948** Man-Eater of Kumaon. **1951** F.B.I. Girl; Savage Drums; Silver City; Warpath. **1952** Denver and Rio Grande. **1953** Pony Express; Prisoners of the Casbah. **1954** The Naked Jungle. **1956** The Boss.

MANSFIELD, MARTHA (Martha Ehrlich)
Born: 1900, Mansfield, Ohio. Died: Nov. 30, 1923, San Antonio, Tex. (burns). Stage and screen actress. Died while filming The Warrens of Virginia, when her dress was accidentally ignited.

Appeared in: **1918** Broadway Bill. **1920** Civilian Clothes; Dr. Jekyll and Mr. Hyde. **1921** The Man of Stone; Gilded Lies; The Last Door; Women Men Love; His Brother's Keeper. **1922** Queen of the Moulin Rouge; 'Til We Meet Again. **1923** Youthful Cheaters; Fog Bound; Is Money Everything?; The Leavenworth Case; Potash and Perlmutter; The Little Red Schoolhouse; The Silent Command; The Woman in Chains. **1924** The Warrens of Virginia.

MANSFIELD, RANKIN
Died: Jan. 22, 1969. Screen actor.

Appeared in: **1953** How to Marry a Millionaire. **1954** The Human Jungle. **1955** Dial Red O. **1956** World Without End. **1957** Badlands of Montana. **1959** Face of a Fugitive.

MANSO, JUANITA
Born: 1873, Spain. Died: Feb. 25, 1957, Madrid, Spain. Stage and screen actress.

MANSON, ISABEL MERSON
Born: 1884. Died: May 19, 1952, New York, N.Y. Screen and stage actress.

MANTELL, ROBERT BRUCE, JR.
Born: 1909, Atlantic Highland, N.J., or New York, N.Y.? Died: Oct. 24, 1933, Hollywood, Calif. (suicide—gunshot). Screen and stage actor. Son of actor Robert Bruce Mantell, Sr. (dec. 1928).

Appeared in: **1915** When You and I Were Young.

MANTELL, ROBERT BRUCE, SR.
Born: 1854, Ayrshire, Scotland. Died: June 27, 1928, Atlantic Highlands, N.J. (effects of a breakdown). Stage and screen actor. Father of actor Robert Bruce Mantell, Jr. (dec. 1933).

Appeared in: **1915** The Blindness of Devotion. **1916** The Green Eyed Monster; A Wife's Sacrifice. **1923** Under the Red Robe.

MANTEQUILLA (Fernando Soto)
Born: 1920, Mexico. Died: May 11, 1980, Mexico? Screen actor.

MANTOVANI (Annunzio Paolo Mantovani)
Born: 1905, Venice, Italy. Died: Mar. 29, 1980, Tunbridge Wells, England. Orchestra conductor and screen actor. Son of concertmaster Benedetto Paolo (dec.). Brother of musician Enrico Mantovani.

Appeared in: **1958** Gitarren der Liebe (Guitars of Love).

MANTZ, PAUL (Albert Paul Mantz)
Born: 1904, Redwood City, Calif. Died: July 8, 1965, Buttercup Valley, Calif. (Ariz. border plane crash). Screen actor and aerial stuntman. Died in plane crash while filming The Flight of the Phoenix.

Appeared in: **1930** Airmail; Hell's Angels. **1935** Ceiling Zero. **1938** Men With Wings; Test Pilot. **1949** Twelve O'Clock High. **1951** Flying Leathernecks. **1957** The Spirit of St. Louis. **1963** A Gathering of Eagles; It's a Mad, Mad, Mad, Mad World. **1965** The Flight of the Phoenix.

MANX, KATE
Born: 1930. Died: Nov. 15, 1964, Torrance, Calif. (suicide—pills). Screen and television actress.

Appeared in: **1960** Private Property. **1962** Hero's Island.

MANZO, CARLO
Born: 1915. Died: June 21, 1955, Yonkers, N.Y. Screen and stage actor.

MAPLE, AUDREY
Born: 1899. Died: Apr. 18, 1971, N.Y. Screen, stage and vaudeville actress.

Appeared in: **1934** Enlighten Thy Daughter.

MARBLE, JOHN
Born: 1844. Died: June 23, 1919, New York, N.Y. Screen actor.

MARBURGH, BERTRAM
Born: May 17, 1875. Died: Aug. 22, 1956, Woodland Hills, Calif. Stage and screen actor.

Appeared in: **1919** Checkers; The Social Pirate; You Never Know Your Luck. **1920** Whispers. **1921** The Greatest Love. **1922** Timothy's Quest. **1925** His People; A Streak of Luck; Proud Heart. **1926** The Outsider; Unknown Treasures; Silken Shackles. **1927** An Affair of the Follies; King of Kings; The Woman on Trial. **1930** For the Defense; The Melody Man. **1933** They Just Had to Get Married. **1940** Before I Hang. **1942** Crossroads; A Gentleman at Heart. **1943** The Human Comedy; Two Weeks to Live.

MARCH, EVE
Died: Sept. 19, 1974, Hollywood, Calif. (cancer). Screen, stage and television actress.

Appeared in: **1941** How Green Was My Valley. **1943** Calling Wild Bill Elliott; Song of Texas. **1944** Curse of the Cat People. **1945** They Were Expendable. **1946** Danny Boy. **1947** The Guilt of Janet Ames; Killer McCoy. **1949** Adam's Rib; Streets of San Francisco. **1951** The Model and the Marriage Broker. **1953** The Sun Shines Bright.

MARCH, FREDRIC (Ernest Frederick McIntyre Bickel)
Born: Aug. 31, 1897, Racine, Wis. Died: Apr. 14, 1975, Los Angeles, Calif. (cancer). Screen, stage and television actor. Married to actress Florence Eldridge. Won 1931/32 Academy Award for Best Actor in Dr. Jekyll and Mr. Hyde and in 1946 for The Best Years of Our Lives. Nominated for 1930/31 Academy Award for Best Actor in The Royal Family of Broadway; in 1937 for A Star Is Born and in 1951 for Death of a Salesman. Entered films as an extra.

Appeared in: **1921** Paying the Piper (film debut). **1929** The Dummy; Footlights and Fools; Jealousy; The Marriage Playground; Paris Bound; The Studio Murder Mystery. **1930** Ladies Love Brutes; Laughter; Manslaughter; Paramount on Parade; Sarah and Son; True to the Navy; The Royal Family of Broadway. **1931** Honor Among Lovers; The Night Angel; My Sin. **1932** Strangers in Love; Merrily We Go to Hell; Make Me a Star; Smilin' Through; The Sign of the Cross; Dr. Jekyll and Mr. Hyde. **1933** Tonight is Ours; The Eagle and the Hawk; Design for Living. **1934** The Affairs of Cellini; We Live Again; All of Me; Good Dame; The Barretts of Wimpole Street; Death Takes a Holiday. **1935** Lives of a Bengal Lancer; The Dark Angel; Anna Karenina; Les Miserables. **1936** Mary of Scotland; The Road to Glory; Anthony Adverse. **1937** Nothing Sacred; A Star Is Born. **1938** There Goes My Heart; Trade Winds; The Buccaneer. **1940** Victory; Susan and God. **1941** So Ends Our Night; One Foot in Heaven; Bedtime Story. **1942** I Married a Witch. **1943** Seventh Victim. **1944** The Adventures of Mark Twain; Tomorrow the World. **1946** The Best Years of Our Lives. **1948** Live Today for Tomorrow; Another Part of the Forest; An Act of Murder. **1949** Christopher Columbus. **1950** The Titan—Story of Michelangelo. **1951** Death of a Salesman; It's a Big Country. **1953** Man on a Tightrope. **1954** Executive Suite; The Bridges at Toko-Ri. **1955** The Desperate Hours. **1956** The Man in the Gray Flannel Suit; Alexander the Great. **1957** Albert Schweitzer (narrator). **1959** Middle of the Night. **1960** Inherit the Wind. **1961** The Young Doctors. **1962** I Sequestrati di Altona (The Condemned of Altona—US 1963). **1964** Seven Days in May. **1967** Hombre. **1970** Tick ... Tick ... Tick ... **1973** The Iceman Cometh.

MARCH, HAL
Born: Apr. 22, 1920, San Francisco, Calif. Died: Jan. 19, 1970, Los Angeles, Calif. (pneumonia—lung cancer). Screen, stage, radio, television, burlesque and vaudeville actor.

Appeared in: **1939** The Gracie Allen Murder Case. **1950** Ma and Pa Kettle Go to Town; Outrage. **1953** Combat; The Eddie Cantor Story. **1954** Yankee Pasha; The Atomic Kid. **1955** It's Always Fair Weather; My Sister Eileen. **1957** Hear Me Good. **1964** Send Me No Flowers. **1967** A Guide for the Married Man.

MARCH, IRIS
Died: Feb. 23, 1966, Hollywood, Calif. (heart attack). Screen, stage actress and drama coach. Mother of puppeteer Marilyn March.

Appeared in: **1936** Coleen; Snowed Under.

MARCH, LINDA
Died: Nov. 25, 1933, near Burlingame, Calif. (auto accident). Screen and stage actress. Sister of actresses Adrienne Ames (dec. 1947), and Gladys McClure (dec. 1933).

MARCH, NADINE
Born: July 30, 1898, London, England. Died: Oct. 10, 1944, England? Screen and stage actress.

Appeared in: **1932** After Office Hours. **1937** The Rat; Dangerous Fingers (aka Wanted by Scotland Yard—US).

MARCH, PHILIPPE
Born: 1925, France. Died: July 12, 1980, Paris, France (brain tumor). Screen and stage actor.

Appeared in: **1969** Sirokko (aka Winter Wind—US 1970). **1973** Two People. **1977** Le Passe Simple (The Simple Past). **1978** Replay; Once in Paris.

MARCHAT, JEAN
Born: 1902, France. Died: Oct., 1966, Paris, France (following surgery). Screen, stage actor and stage director.

Appeared in: **1946** Stormy Waters. **1953** L'ennemi Public No. 1 (aka The Most Wanted Man—US 1962). **1960** Le Passage du Rhin (aka Tomorrow Is My Turn—US 1962). **1964** Les Dames du Bois de Boulogne. **1963** La Glaive et la Balance (aka Two Are Guilty—US 1964).

MARCIANO, ROCKY (Rocco Francis Marchegiano)
Born: Sept. 1, 1924, Brockton, Mass. Died: Aug. 31, 1969, near Des Moines, Iowa (plane crash). Professional fighter and screen actor.

Appeared in: **1957** The Delicate Delinquent. **1960** College Confidential. **1970** The Super Fight (documentary).

MARCONI, JEAN
Born: 1907, France. Died: Jan., 1972, France? Screen actor.

MARCUS, BERNIE
Died: Nov. 19, 1971. Screen actor.

Appeared in: **1950** Outrage.

MARCUS, JAMES A.
Born: Jan. 21, 1868, New York, N.Y. Died: Oct. 15, 1937, Hollywood, Calif. (heart attack). Stage and screen actor. Entered films in 1915.

Appeared in: **1921** Little Lord Fauntleroy; Serenade. **1922** Broken Chains; Oliver Twist; Come On Over; The Stranger's Banquet. **1923** Scaramouche; Vanity Fair; Quicksands. **1924** The Iron Horse; Beau Brummell. **1925** The Eagle; The Goose Hangs High; All Around Frying Pan; Lightnin'; Dick Turpin; The Fighting Heart; The Isle of Hope. **1926** The Lily; The Scarlet Letter; The Eagle of the Sea; Hell-Bent for Heaven; Siberia; The Traffic Cop; The Texas Streak. **1927** Captain Salvation; The Bachelor's Baby; The Meddlin' Stranger; Beauty Shoppers; King of Kings; Life of an Actress; Marriage. **1928** Revenge; Sadie Thompson; The Border Patrol; Isle of Lost Men; The Broken Mask; Buck Privates. **1929** Evangeline; In Old Arizona; Whispering Winds; In Holland (short). **1930** Back Pay; Captain of the Guard; Billy the Kid; Liliom; The Texan. **1931** Fighting Caravans; Arrowsmith. **1932** Hell's House. **1933** The Lone Avenger; Strawberry Roan. **1934** Wagon Wheels; Honor of the Range. **1936** The Lonely Trail.

MARCUSE, THEODORE "THEO"
Born: 1920. Died: Nov. 29, 1967, Los Angeles, Calif. (auto accident). Screen, stage and television actor.

Appeared in: **1961** Operation Eichmann; The Two Little Bears. **1962** Hitler. **1963** For Love or Money. **1964** A Tiger Walks. **1965** Mara of the Wilderness; Harem Skarum; The Cincinnati Kid. **1966** The Glass Bottom Boat; Sands of Beersheba; Last of the Secret Agents. **1967** Picasso Summer. **1968** The Wicked Dreams of Paula Schultz.

MARDEN, ADRIENNE
Born: 1909. Died: Nov. 9, 1978, Los Angeles, Calif. (heart attack). Screen, stage, television actress, stage director and producer. Divorced from actor Whit Bissell.

Appeared in: **1936** 13 Hours by Air; F-Man; Star for a Night. **1948** For the Love of Mary. **1953** Dangerous Crossing; Inferno. **1955** Count Three and Pray; One Desire; The Shrike. **1956** Man From Del Rio. **1962** Birdman of Alcatraz; Walk on the Wild Side. **1964** Kisses for My President.

MARETSKAYA, VERA PETROVANO
Born: 1906, Moscow, Russia. Died: Aug., 1978, Moscow, Russia. Screen and stage actress.

Appeared in: **1924** The Cutter from Torzhok. **1936** Revolutionists. **1937** Paris Commune. **1944** No Greater Love. **1945** Marriage. **1947** Selskaya Uchitelnitsa (Village Schoolteacher, aka Village Teacher—US 1948). **1956** 1905. **1962** Sredi Dobrykh Lyudey (Mother and Daughter—US 1965). **1965** Ukrainian Festival. Other Russian films: The Living Corpse; Simple Hearts; A Hundred and Twenty Thousand a Year; Shameful to Say.

MARFIELD, DWIGHT
Born: 1908. Died: Aug. 15, 1978, New York, N.Y. (heart attack). Screen, stage, television actor and artist.

Appeared in: **1955** The Trouble With Harry. **1975** One Flew Over the Cuckoo's Nest.

MARGETSON, ARTHUR
Born: Apr. 27, 1897, England. Died: Aug. 12, 1951, London, England. Screen and stage actor. Divorced from actress Vera Lennox and Shirley Grey. Married to actress Barbara Wood.

Appeared in: **1931** Other People's Sins. **1933** His Grace Gives Notice. **1934** The Great Defender; Little Friend. **1935** The Divine Spark; Music Hath Charms; I Give My Heart. **1936** Wanted Men. **1937** Broken Blossoms; Juggernaut; Pagliacci (aka A Clown Must Laugh); Action for Slander. **1938** The Loves of Madame DuBarry. **1940** Return to Yesterday. **1941** Larceny Street. **1942** Commandos Strike at Dawn. **1943** Random Harvest; Sherlock Holmes Faces Death.

MARGOLIS, CHARLES "DOC"
Born: 1874. Died: Sept. 22, 1926, Glendale, Calif. Screen actor.

Appeared in: **1925** The Merry Widow.

MARGULIES, VIRGINIA M.
Born: 1916. Died: Feb. 16, 1969, Hollywood, Calif. Screen actress. Daughter of actor Edward Peil (dec. 1958).

MARGULIS, CHARLES "CHARLIE"
Born: 1903, Minneapolis, Minn. Died: Apr. 24, 1967, Little Falls, Minn. Musician, screen and television actor.

Appeared in: **1930** King of Jazz.

MARIAN, FERDINAND
Born: 1902, Vienna, Austria. Died: 1946, near Durneck, Germany (auto accident). Stage and screen actor.

Appeared in: **1933** Der Tunnel. **1936** Ein Hochzeitstraum. **1937** Madame Bovary; La Habanera; Die Stimme des Herzens (aka Der Saenger Ihrer Hoheit). **1938** Die Heimat Ruft (Home is Calling); Nordlicht. **1939** Morgen Werde ich Verhaftet; Der Vierte Kommt Nicht; Dein Leben Gehoert Mir. **1940** Der Fuchs von Glenarvon; Aus Erster Ehe; Jud Suess. **1941** Ohm Krueger. **1942** Ein Zug Faehrt Ab. **1943** Die Reise in die Vergangenheit; Tonelli; Romanze in Moll; Muenchhausen. **1944** Freunde; In Flagranti. **1945** Das Gesetz der Liebe; Die Nacht der Zwoelf; Dreimal Konoedie (aka Liebeswirbel).

MARIANO, LUIS (Luis Gonzalez)
Born: 1920, Irun, Spain. Died: July 14, 1970, Paris, France (cerebral hemorrhage). Screen actor and singer.

Appeared in: **1954** Zarewitsch (US 1961). **1960** Candide, Ou L'Optimisme au XXe Siecle (aka Candide—US 1962).

MARINO, ART (Rudy Cotz)
Born: 1918. Died: June 1, 1979, Hollywood, Calif. (heart attack). Screen, stage and television actor.

MARINOFF, FANIA
Born: Mar. 20, 1890, Russia. Died: Nov. 17, 1971, Englewood, N.J. Stage and screen actress.

Appeared in: **1915** The Money Master; Nedra; McTeague. **1917** The Rise of Jennie Cushing.

MARIO (Mario Salvaneschi)
Born: 1912. Died: Apr. 26, 1977, Tucson, Ariz. (stroke). Screen actor and dancer.

MARION, EDNA (Edna Hannam)
Born: Dec. 12, 1908, Chicago, Ill. Died: Dec. 2, 1957, Hollywood, Calif. Screen, stage and vaudeville actress. Appeared in Charlie Chase and Edna Marion comedies.

Appeared in: **1925** The Desert's Price; plus the following shorts: Her Daily Dozen; My Baby Doll; Powdered Chickens; Putting on Airs; Puzzled by Crosswords; Dangerous Peach. **1926** The Call of the Wilderness; Readin' Ritin' Rithmetic; The Still Alarm. **1927** For Ladies Only; Flying Elephants (short); Sugar Daddies (short). **1928** From Soup to Nuts (short); Should Married Men Go Home? **1929** Skinner Steps Out. **1930** Romance of the West; Today.

MARION, FRANCES
Born: 1888, San Francisco, Calif. Died: May 12, 1973, Los Angeles, Calif. Screen actress, screenwriter, film director, author and commercial artist. Married to actor Fred Thomson (dec. 1928) and later married to film director George Hill (dec.). Do not confuse with actor Francis Marion.

Appeared in: **1915** A Girl of Yesterday; The Jest of Jealousy. **1921** Little Lord Fauntleroy. **1941** New York Town.

MARION, GEORGE F., SR.
Born: July 16, 1860, San Francisco, Calif. Died: Nov. 30, 1945, Carmel, Calif. (heart attack). Screen, stage actor and stage director. Father of screenwriter George F. Marion, Jr. Entered films in 1914.

Appeared in: **1921** Go Straight. **1922** Gun Shy. **1923** Anna Christie; The Girl I Loved; A Million to Burn. **1924** Bringin' Home the Bacon. **1925** On the Go; Cloths Make the Pirate; Straight Through; Tumbleweeds; The White Monkey. **1926** The Highbinders; Rolling Home; The Wise Guy. **1927** King of Kings; A Texas Steer; Loco Luck; Skedaddle Gold. **1929** Evangeline. **1930** Anna Christie (and 1923 version); The Bishop Murder Case; The Pay Off; The Sea Bat; A Lady's Morals; Hook, Line and Sinker; The Big House. **1931** Man to Man; Laughing Sinners; Safe in Hell. **1932** Six Hours to Live. **1933** Her First Mate. **1935** Port of Lost Dreams; Rocky Mountain Mystery; Death from a Distance; Metropolitan.

MARION, SID
Born: 1900. Died: June 29, 1965, Hollywood, Calif. (heart attack). Screen and stage actor.

Appeared in: **1934** The Mighty Barnum. **1936** Magnificent Obsession. **1937** An RKO-Radio short. **1943** Lady of Burlesque. **1949** Oh, You Beautiful Doll; Jiggs and Maggie in Jackpot Jitters. **1950** Love That Brute; Trial Without Jury; Woman from Headquarters. **1953** Call Me Madam. **1965** The Outlaws IS Coming.

MARION, WILLIAM
Born: 1878. Died: Jan. 3, 1957. Screen and stage actor.

Appeared in: **1915** The Boss; The Heart of Blue Ridge. **1917** The Streets of Illusion; One Hour. **1921** The Hope Diamond Mystery (serial). **1922** Across the Dead Line; One Clear Call; The Worldly Madonna. **1923** The Huntress. **1928** Sally's Shoulders.

MARISCHKA, HUBERT
Died: Dec., 1959. Screen actor, film director, screenwriter and author.

Appeared in: **1935** Graefin Mariza.

MARK, JULIA
Born: 1928, England. Died: Apr., 1977, London, England. Screen, stage and radio actress.

MARK, MICHAEL
Born: Mar. 15, 1889, Russia. Died: Feb. 3, 1975, Woodland Hills, Calif. Screen, stage, vaudeville actor, stage director and producer.

Appeared in: **1924** Four Sons. **1931** Frankenstein; Resurrection. **1934** The Black Cat. **1935** All the King's Horses. **1936** The Dark Hour; Sons O' Guns. **1937** Prescription for Romance; Missing Witness. **1938** Ride a Crooked Mile. **1940** Flash Gordon Conquers the Universe (serial); The Mummy's Hand. **1942** Casablanca; The Ghost of Frankenstein; Men of San Quentin. **1943** Mission to Moscow. **1945** House of Frankenstein; The Great Glamarion. **1946** Joe Palooka—Champ. **1947** The Trespasser; Joe Palooka in the Knockout. **1948** Appointment with Murder; Fighting Mad; The Vicious Circle. **1949** Search for Danger. **1950** Once a Thief. **1953** The Juggler. **1955** The Big Combo. **1956** Rock Around the Clock; Edge of Hell. **1957** Lizzie. **1958** The Brothers Karamazoo. **1959** Attack of the Puppet People; The Big Fisherman; The Return of the Fly.

MARKEY, ENID
Born: Feb. 22, 1896, Dillon, Colo. Died: Nov. 16, 1981, Bay Shore, N.Y. (natural causes). Screen, stage, vaudeville, radio and television actress. Portrayed the first "Jane" in the Tarzan films. Entered films in 1915.

Appeared in: **1916** Civilization; Jim Grimsby's Boy. **1917** The Yankee Way; The Curse of Eve. **1918** Tarzan of the Apes; The Romance of Tarzan. **1946** Snafu. **1948** The Naked City. **1968** The Boston Strangler.

MARKHAM, DEWEY "PIGMEAT"
Born: Apr. 18, 1906, Durham, N.C. Died: Dec. 13, 1981, New York, N.Y. Black screen, stage, vaudeville, radio actor and screenwriter.

Appeared in: **1939** Gang War. **1940** One Big Mistake; Mr. Smith Goes Ghost; Am I Guilty? **1944** That's My Baby! **1946** House Rent Party; Fight That Ghost. **1947** Pigmeat Markham's Laugh Hepcats.

MARKHAM, HARRY
Born: 1906, England. Died: Dec., 1981, Bolton, England. Screen, stage, radio and television actor.

Appeared in: **1962** A Kind of Loving. **1963** This Sporting Life. **1975** Mr. Quilp.

MARKS, JOE E.
Born: June 15, 1891. Died: June 14, 1973, New York, N.Y. (pneumonia). Screen, stage, burlesque and vaudeville actor. Appeared in vaudeville in an act billed as "Joe Marks and Co."

Appeared in: **1938** Outside of Paradise. **1941** So Ends Our Night. **1959** Li'l Abner (stage and film versions). **1968** The Night They Raided Minsky's. **1970** Diary of a Mad Housewife.

MARKS, SIDNEY
Born: 1923. Died: Apr. 3, 1974, Hollywood, Calif. Screen actor.

MARKS, WILLIS
Born: Aug. 20, 1865, Rochester, Minn. Died: Dec. 6, 1952, Los Angeles, Calif. Screen and stage actor. Entered films in 1915.

Appeared in: **1917** The Mysterious Mrs. M. **1919** Greased Lightning; The Wishing Ring Man; Over the Garden Wall; The Trembling Hour. **1920** The Dancin' Fool; The Little Gray Mouse; Everything But the Truth; Homespun Folks; Jack Knife Man; The Family Honor. **1921** The Greater Profit; Chickens; The Beautiful Gambler. **1922** The Man Under Cover; Travelin' On. **1923** Man from Funeral Range; Truxton King. **1924** The Dramatic Life of Abraham Lincoln; Which Shall It Be? (aka Not One to Spare); His Forgotten Wife. **1925** The Night Ship; On the Threshold; Private Affairs; Shattered Lives; The Shadow on the Wall; Silent Pal. **1926** The Unknown Soldier. **1932** Rebecca of Sunnybrook Farm.

MARLAUD, PHILIPPE
Born: 1959, France. Died: Aug. 18, 1981, Lyon, France (second degree burns). Screen and television actor.

Appeared in: **1978** Passe Ton Bac d'Abord (aka Get Your Diploma First—US 1979). **1980** The Aviator's Wife.

MARLE, ARNOLD (aka A. MARLE)
Born: 1888, England. Died: Feb. 21, 1970, London, England. Screen, stage and television actor. Married to actress Lilly Frued Marle.

Appeared in: **1942** One of Our Aircraft Is Missing. **1944** Mr. Emmanuel (US 1945). **1946** Men of Two Worlds (aka Kisenga, Man of Africa—US 1952). **1948** Portrait From Life (aka The Girl In the Painting—US 1949). **1949** The Glass Mountain. **1954** The Green Buddha (US 1955). **1955** Little Red Monkey (aka The Case of the Red Monkey—US); Cross Channel; The Glass Cage (aka The Glass Tomb—US); Break In the Circle (US 1957). **1957** The Abominable Snowman. **1959** The Man Who Could Cheat Death. **1961** The Snake Woman.

MARLEY, BOB
Born: Feb. 6, 1945, Rhoden Hall, St. Ann, Jamaica. Died: May 11, 1981, Miami, Fla. (cancer). Screen actor and musician.

Appeared in: **1980** Reggae Sunsplash.

MARLO, MARY
Born: 1898. Died: Feb. 25, 1960, Hollywood, Calif. (heart attack). Screen, stage, radio and television actress.

Appeared in: **1955** The Second Greatest Sex.

MARLOWE, ALAN
Born: 1935. Died: Jan. 5, 1975, near Seward, Nebr. (plane crash). Jazz musician, screen, stage and television actor.

Appeared in: **1970** Sweet Vengeance.

MARLOWE, ANTHONY
Born: 1910. Died: June 29, 1962, Detroit, Mich. Screen actor and opera tenor.

Appeared in: **1941** Flame of New Orleans. **1942** The Great Commandment. **1944** Mrs. Parkington. **1953** Saadia. **1954** Doctor in the House (US 1955). **1955** Room in the House.

MARLOWE, FRANK
Born: 1904. Died: Mar. 30, 1964, Hollywood, Calif. (heart attack). Screen and television actor.

Appeared in: **1934** Hi, Nellie!; Now I'll Tell. **1935** The Glass Key; G-Men; We're in the Money; The Informer. **1937** Wings Over Honolulu; Live, Love and Learn. **1938** Bringing Up Baby. **1941** Sergeant York; Caught in the Draft. **1942** Madame Spy. **1944** Irish Eyes are Smiling; Murder in the Blue Room. **1946** Sioux City Sue; Dark Alibi. **1947** Riding the California Trail. **1948** They Live By Night (aka The Twisted Road and Your Red Wagon). **1950** Barricade; Triple Trouble. **1952** The Winning Team; My Pal Gus. **1954** The Long Wait. **1955** The Square Jungle; Lucy Gallant; The Americano. **1956** Hot Shots; The Man with the Golden Arm. **1957** Rockabilly Baby; Chicago Confidential. **1958** Escape From Red Rock; The Lone Texan. **1959** North By Northwest.

MARLOWE, JAMES C.
Born: 1865. Died: Sept. 4, 1926, New York, N.Y. Screen and stage actor.

Appeared in: **1922** Back Home and Broke.

MARLOWE, MARILYN
Born: 1927. Died: Sept. 1, 1975, Hollywood, Calif. (heart attack). Screen actress and stand-in. Married to actor Rock Marlowe.

MARLOWE, NORA
Born: 1915, Worcester, Mass. Died: Dec. 7, 1977, Los Angeles, Calif. (heart ailment). Screen and television actress. Married to actor James McCallion.

Appeared in: **1957** An Affair to Remember. **1959** North by Northwest. **1964** The Brass Bottle; Kitten With a Whip. **1965** That Funny Feeling. **1966** The Hostage; Texas Across the River. **1968** The Thomas Crown Affair. **1969** Gaily, Gaily. **1973** Westworld.

MARLY, FLORENCE
Born: 1919, Moravia, Czechoslovakia. Died: Nov. 9, 1978, Glendale, Calif. (heart attack). Screen, stage, television actress and singer. Divorced from film director Pierre Chenal, and later married to Count Degenhard von Wurmbrand (dec.).

Appeared in: **1939** L'Alibi (film debut). **1946** Les Maudits. **1948** Sealed Verdict. **1949** Tokyo Joe. **1951** Tokyo File 212; Krakitt. **1952** Gobs and Gals. **1957** Undersea Girl. **1966** Queen of Blood (aka Planet of Blood). **1967** Games. **1970** The Damned. **1973** Doctor Death; Seeker of Souls. **1975** The Astrologer.

MARMER, LEA
Born: Aug. 16, 1918, Michigan. Died: May 11, 1974, Los Angeles, Calif. (brain tumor). Screen and stage actress.

Appeared in: **1961** Walk the Angry Beach. **1967** What Am I Bid? **1968** The War Between Men and Women. **1969** Easy Rider.

MARMONT, PERCY
Born: Nov. 25, 1883, Gunnersbury, London, England. Died: Mar. 3, 1977, Denville Hall, England. Screen, stage actor and film director. Father of actress Patricia Marmont. Entered films in 1913.

Appeared in: **1918** Turn of the Wheel. **1919** Vengeance of Durand; The Winchester Woman; The Climbers; Three Men and a Girl. **1920** Branded Woman; The Sporting Duchess; Dead Men Tell No Tales; The Price. **1921** Love's Penalty; Wife Against Wife; What's Your Reputation Worth? **1922** The First Woman; Married People. **1923** Broadway Broke; The Light That Failed; If Winter Comes; You Can't Get Away With It; The Midnight Alarm; The Man Life Passed By. **1924** Broken Laws; The Clean Heart; The Enemy Sex; K—the Unknown; The Marriage Cheat; The Shooting of Dan McGrew; The Legend of Hollywood; Winning a Continent; When a Girl Loves. **1925** Just a Woman; Infatuation; Daddy's Gone-a-Hunting; Fine Clothes; A Woman's Faith; The Street of Forgotten Men; Lord Jim; The Shining Adventure. **1926** Mantrap; The Miracle of Life; Fascinating Youth; Aloma of the South Seas. **1928** The Lady of the Lake (US 1930); Yellow Stockings; Sir or Madam; The Warning (short); The Stronger Will; San Francisco Nights. **1929** The Silver King. **1930** The Squeaker; Cross Roads. **1931** The Love of Ariane (aka Ariane—US 1939); The Written Law; Rich and Strange (aka East of Shanghai—US 1932).

1932 The Silver Greyhound; Blind Spot; Say It With Music. 1933 Her Imaginary Lover. 1935 Vanity; White Lilac. 1936 Secret Agent; David Livingstone; Conquest of the Air; Captain's Table. 1937 Action for Slander (US 1938); Young and Innocent (aka A Girl Was Young—US 1938). 1938 Les Perles de la Couronne (Pearls of the Crown). 1940 Bringing It Home (short). 1941 Penn of Pennsylvania (aka The Courageous Mr. Penn—US 1944). 1942 Those Kids From Town. 1943 I'll Walk Beside You. 1946 Loyal Heart. 1947 Swiss Honeymoon (short). 1948 No Orchids for Miss Blandish (US 1951). 1949 Dark Secret. 1952 The Gambler and the Lady. 1953 Four Sided Triangle. 1954 Knave of Hearts (aka Lover Boy, and aka Lovers, Happy Lovers—US). 1955 Footsteps in the Fog. 1956 Lisbon. 1968 Hostile Witness.

MAROLDO, MARIE J. (aka LADY LITTLE)
Born: 1902, France. Died: Mar. 20, 1979, San Diego, Calif. Screen actress, singer, dancer, carnival and circus performer. Married to performer Johnny Winters.

Appeared in: 1933 The Terror of Tiny Town. 1939 The Wizard of Oz.

MARQUARD, RUBE
Born: 1889, Cleveland, Ohio. Died: June 2, 1980, Baltimore, Md. (cancer). Baseball player, screen and vaudeville actor. Divorced from actress Blossom Seeley (dec. 1974).

Appeared in: 1913 Rube Marquard Wins.

MARQUET, MARY
Born: 1895, France. Died: Aug. 29, 1979, Paris, France (result of a fall). Screen, stage, television actress and cabaret performer. Divorced from actor Victor Francen (dec. 1977).

Appeared in: 1957 Maid in Paris; Royal Affairs in Versailles. 1963 Landru (aka Bluebeard—US). 1966 La Vie de Chateau (aka A Matter of Resistance—US 1967); La Grand Vadrouille (aka Don't Look Now—US 1969). 1968 Ce Sacre Grand-Pere (aka The Marriage Came Tumbling Down—US).

MARR, PAULA
Born: 1875. Died: Dec. 22, 1960, on a train en route from Los Angeles to San Francisco, Calif. (heart attack). Screen actress. Married to actor William Collier, Sr. (dec. 1944). Mother of actor William "Buster" Collier, Jr.

MARR, WILLIAM (William Dobie)
Born: 1897. Died: May 15, 1960, N.Y. Stage and screen actor.

Appeared in: 1926 Men of Steel.

MARRIOTT, CHARLES
Born: 1859, England. Died: Dec. 8, 1917, Los Angeles, Calif. (tuberculosis). Screen and stage actor.

Appeared in: 1915 Sunshine Molly; The Wild Olive; False Colors; It's No Laughing Matter. 1916 The Tongues of Men; Wanted—A Home. 1917 Betty and the Buccaneers.

MARRIOTT, JOHN
Born: 1894, Bolie, Okla. Died: Apr. 5, 1977, Jamaica, N.Y. Black screen, stage, radio and television actor.

Appeared in: 1941 The Little Foxes. 1953 The Joe Louis Story. 1964 The Cool World; Black Like Me. 1973 Badge #373. 1974 Willie Dynamite. 1975 Dear Dead Delilah; Dog Day Afternoon.

MARRIOTT, MICHAEL P.
Born: 1946. Died: Oct. 15, 1967, near Malibu, Calif. (motorcycle accident). Screen actor.

Appeared in: 1968 Ice Station Zebra.

MARRIOTT, MOORE (George Thomas Moore-Marriott)
Born: 1885, West Drayton, England. Died: Dec. 11, 1949. Screen and stage actor.

Appeared in: 1914 His Sister's Honour. 1915 By the Shortest of Heads. 1920 The Flying Scotsman; The Grip of Iron; Mary Latimer, Nun; The Winding Road. 1921 Four Men in a Van. 1922 The Head of the Family; The Skipper's Wooing. 1923 Monkey's Paw; An Odd Freak. 1924 The Mating of Marcus; Not For Sale; Lawyer Quince; Dixon's Return; The Clicking of Cuthbert series including: The Clicking of Cuthbert; The Long Hole; Ordeal by Golf; The Old Man in The Corner series including The Affair at the Novelty Theatre. 1925 King of the Castle; The Gold Cure; Afraid of Love; The Qualified Adventurer; There's Many a Slip; The Only Man (aka The Leading Man); Thrilling Stories

from the Strand Magazine series including A Madonna of the Cells. 1926 The Conspirators; Every Mother's Son; London Love; Second to None; The Happy Rascals series; Screen Playlet Series including: Cash on Delivery; The Greater War. 1927 Carry On; Huntingtower; Passion Island; The Silver Lining. 1928 Widecombe Fair; Sweeney Todd; Toni; Victory; The Burglar and the Girl; When We Were Very Young series including The King's Breakfast. 1929 Kitty; Mr. Smith Wakes Up. 1930 The Barnes Murder (rerelease of The Conspirators—1926); The Lady From the Sea (aka The Goodwin Sands); Kissing Cup's Race. 1931 Aroma of the South Seas; Up for the Cup; The Lyons Mail. 1932 Mr. Bill the Conqueror (aka The Man Who Won—US 1933); The Wonderful Story; Little Waitress; The Water Gypsies; Dance Pretty Lady; The Crooked Lady; Nine Till Six; Heroes of the Mine. 1933 A Moorland Tragedy; Money for Speed; Hawleys of High Street; Love's Old Sweet Song; The House of Trent; The Crime at Blossoms; Dora; Lucky Blaze. 1934 A Political Scoop; Not for Publication series including The Black Skull. 1935 His Apologies; Turn of the Tide; Gay Old Dog; Dandy Dick; Drake of England (aka Drake the Pirate—US); The Man Without a Face; The Half-Day Excursion. 1936 When Knights Were Bold (US 1942); Strange Cargo; Wednesday's Luck; Accused; Windbag the Sailor; What the Puppy Said; The Amazing Quest of Ernest Bliss (aka Romance and Riches—US 1937); Luck of the Turf; Talk of the Devil. 1937 O, Mr. Porter; The Fatal Hour; Feather Your Nest; Fifty-Shilling Boxer; Night Ride; Intimate Relations. 1938 Owd Bob (aka To the Victor—US); Old Bones of the River; Convict 99. 1939 Cheer Boys Cheer; Ask A Policeman; Where's That Fire?; A Girl Must Live (US 1941); The Frozen Limits. 1940 Gasbags; Band Wagon; Charley's (Big Hearted) Aunt. 1941 I Thank You; Hi Gang! 1942 Back Room Boy. 1943 Millions Like Us. 1944 Time Flies; Don't Take It to Heart (US 1949); It Happened One Sunday. 1945 A Place of One's Own (US 1949); The Agitator; I'll Be Your Sweetheart. 1946 Green For Danger (US 1947). 1947 Green Fingers; The Hills of Donegal; The Root of All Evil. 1949 The History of Mr. Polly (US 1951); High Jinks in Society.

MARRIOTT, SANDEE
Born: 1899. Died: June 7, 1962, Hollywood, Calif. (heart attack). Screen actor and stuntman. Entered films in 1927.

Appeared in: 1956 Hilda Crane; Around the World in 80 Days.

MARSH, CHARLES L. "CHARLIE"
Died: Mar. 7, 1953, Hollywood, Calif. Screen and vaudeville actor.

Appeared in: 1942 Gentleman Jim. 1944 Atlantic City. 1945 Christmas in Connecticut; Out of This World; Too Young to Know. 1947 My Wild Irish Rose.

MARSH, DELLA
Died: May 6, 1973, Ithaca, N.Y. Screen and vaudeville actress. Married to vaudeville actor Walter Fischter (dec.).

MARSH, GARRY (Leslie March Gerahty)
Born: May 21, 1902, St. Margaret's, Richmond, Surrey, England. Died: Mar., 1981, London, England (natural causes). Screen, stage and vaudeville actor. Divorced from Adele Lawson and actress Muriel Martin-Harvey.

Appeared in: 1930 Night Birds. 1931 Uneasy Virtue; The Eternal Feminine; P. C. Josser; Third Time Lucky; The Man They Could Not Arrest (US 1933); Keepers of Youth; Dreyfus (aka The Dreyfus Case—US); Stranglehold; Stamboul; The Star Reporter. 1932 Don't be a Dummy; The Maid of the Mountains; C.O.D.; Postal Orders (short); After Office Hours; Fires of Fate (US 1933); Number Seventeen. 1933 Taxi to Paradise; The Love Nest; Falling for You; The Lost Chord; Ask Beccles; Two Wives for Henry; That's a Good Girl. 1934 It's a Cop; The Silver Spoon; Rolling in Money; Warn London; Gay Love; Money Mad; The Green Pack; Josser on the Farm. 1935 Widow's Might; Death on the Set (aka Murder on the Set—US 1936); Three Witnesses; Inside the Room; Full Circle; Mr. What's-His-Name; Department Store (aka Bargain Basement); Night Mail; Scrooge; Charing Cross Road. 1936 A Wife or Two; When Knights Were Bold (US 1942); Debt of Honor; The Man in the Mirror (US 1937); The Amazing Quest of Ernest Bliss (aka Romance and Riches—US 1937); All In. 1937 It's a Grand Old World; Who Killed Fen Markham? (aka The Angelus); The Vicar of Bray; Leave It to Me; A Romance in Flanders (aka Lost on the Western Front—US 1940); Melody and Romance; Intimate Relations. 1938 The Dark Stairway; Bank Holiday (aka Three on a Weekend—US); The Claydon Treasure Mystery; I See Ice; Convict 99; This Man is News (US 1939); Break the News (US 1941); It's in the Air (aka George Takes the Air—US 1940). 1939 Trouble Brewing; Let's be Famous; The Four Just Men (aka The Secret Four—US 1940); This Man in Paris; Hoots Mon. 1940 Return to Yesterday; Let George Do It. 1945 Pink String and Sealing Wax (US 1950); The Rake's

Progress (aka Notorious Gentleman—US 1946); Dead of Night; I'll Be Your Sweetheart. **1946** I See a Dark Stranger (aka The Adventuress—US 1947); A Girl in a Million (US 1950). **1947** The Shop at Sly Corner (aka The Code of Scotland Yard—US); While the Sun Shines (US 1950); Freida; Dancing With Crime; Just William's Luck. **1948** Good Time Girl (US 1950); William Comes to Town; My Brother's Keeper (US 1949); Things Happen at Night. **1949** Badger's Green; Forbidden; Paper Orchid; Murder at the Windmill (aka Murder at the Burlesque—US). **1950** Miss Pilgrim's Progress; Something in the City; Someone at the Door. **1951** Worm's Eye View; Madame Louise; Old Mother Riley's Jungle Treasure. **1952** The Lost Hours (aka The Big Frame—US 1953). **1953** Those People Next Door. **1954** Double Exposure; Aunt Clara. **1955** Man of the Moment. **1956** Who Done It?; Johnny You're Wanted. **1960** Trouble With Eve (aka In Trouble With Eve—US 1964). **1963** Ring of Spies (aka Ring of Treason—US 1964). **1966** Where the Bullets Fly. **1967** Ouch!; Camelot.

MARSH, MAE (Mary Warne Marsh)
Born: Nov. 9, 1895, Madrid, N.Mex. Died: Feb. 13, 1968, Hermosa Beach, Calif. (heart attack). Screen actress. Mother of prominent La Jolla attorney Brewster Arms and sister of screen actress Marguerite Marsh (dec. 1925). She won the George Eastman Award in 1957 naming her one of five leading actresses of the silent era. Was known as Samuel Goldwyn's original "Goldwyn Girl."

Appeared in: **1912** the Spirit Awakened; Man's Genesis; The Lesser Evil; The New York Hats; One Is Business, The Other Crime; Lena and the Geese; The Sands of Dee; Brutality; An Adventure in the Autumn Woods. **1913** Judith of Bethulia; The Telephone Girl and the Lady; Love in an Apartment Hotel; The Perfidy of Mary; The Little Tease; The Wanderer; His Mother's Son; The Reformers; The Battle of Elderberry Gulch; In Prehistoric Days; Broken Ways; Two Men on the Desert. **1914** The Escape; Home Sweet Home; The Avenging Conscience. **1915** The Birth of a Nation. **1916** Intolerance; The Wild Girl; A Child of the Paris Streets; The Wharf Rat; Hoodoo Ann; The Marriage of Molly-O. **1917** Cinderella Man; Polly and the Circus; Brute Force. **1918** The Beloved Traitor; All Woman; The Face in the Dark; Money Mad; Hidden Fires. **1919** Spotlight Sadie; The Mother and the Law. **1921** Little 'Fraid Lady; Nobody's Kid. **1922** Flames of Passion; Till We Meet Again. **1923** The White Rose; Paddy-the-Next-Best-Thing. **1924** A Woman's Secret; Daddies. **1925** The Rat; Rides of Passion. **1928** Racing Through. **1931** Over the Hill. **1932** That's My Boy; Rebecca of Sunnybrook Farm. **1933** Alice in Wonderland. **1934** Little Man What Now?; Bachelor of Arts. **1935** Black Fury. **1936** Hollywood Boulevard. **1939** Drums Along the Mohawk. **1940** The Grapes of Wrath; The Man Who Wouldn't Talk; Young People. **1941** How Green Was My Valley; Remember the Day; Swamp Water; Great Guns; Blue, White and Perfect; Belle Starr; Tobacco Road. **1942** The Loves of Edgar Allan Poe; Son of Fury; Tales of Manhattan. **1943** Dixie Dugan; The Song of Bernadette. **1944** The Sullivans; In the Meantime, Darling; Jane Eyre. **1945** A Tree Grows in Brooklyn; The Dolly Sisters; Leave Her to Heaven. **1946** My Darling Clementine. **1947** The Late George Apley. **1948** Apartment for Peggy; Three Godfathers; Deep Waters; The Snakepit; Fort Apache. **1949** It Happens Every Spring; The Fighting Kentuckian; Impact; Everybody Does It. **1950** My Blue Heaven; When Willie Comes Marching Home; The Gunfighter. **1951** The Model and the Marriage Broker. **1952** The Quiet Man; Night Without Sleep; The Sun Shines Bright. **1953** The Robe; Blueprint for Murder; Titanic. **1954** A Star is Born. **1955** The Tall Men; Hell on Frisco Bay; Prince of Players; Good Morning, Miss Dove. **1956** Julie; While the City Sleeps. **1957** The Wings of Eagles. **1958** Cry Terror. **1960** Sergeant Rutledge; From the Terrace. **1961** Two Rode Together. **1963** Donovan's Reef. **1968** Arabella.

MARSH, MARGUERITE (Margaret Marsh aka MARGUERITE LOVERIDGE)
Born: 1892. Died: Dec. 8, 1925, New York, N.Y. (bronchial pneumonia). Screen actress. Sister of actress Mae Marsh (dec. 1968). Married to film production manager and assistant director George Bertholon (dec.).

Appeared in: **1912** The Mender of the Nets. **1913** Marguerite and the Mission Funds; Buck Richard's Bride; His Nobs, The Plumber; The Woodman's Daughter; Dora; A Trade Secret; Seeds of Silver. **1914** Blue Blood and Red. **1915** The Old High Chair; The Housemaid; The Turning Point; The Doll-House Mystery; The Queen of the Band; A Romance of the Alps. **1916** Intolerance; The Price of Power; Casey at the Bat; The Devil's Needle; Little Meena's Romance; Mr. Goode, the Samaritan. **1918** A Voice From the Deep; Our Little Wife; Conquered Hearts; Fields of Honor. **1919** Royal Democrat; Fair Enough; Eternal Magdalene; The Master Mystery (serial). **1920** Phantom Honeymoon; Wits vs. Wits. **1921** The Idol of the North; Oh Mary Be Careful; Women Men Love. **1922** Boomerang Bill; Face to Face; Iron to Gold; The Lion's Mouse.

MARSH, MYRA
Born: Oct. 29, 1894. Died: 1964. Screen actress.

Appeared in: **1935** Paddy O'Day. **1936** Anthony Adverse; Devil is a Sissy; Gentle Julia; Navy Born; More than a Secretary. **1937** Night of Mystery; Captains Courageous. **1938** Rascals. **1939** Invitation to Happiness; Boy Friend; The Kansas Terrors. **1940** Glamour for Sale. **1941** Father's Son; Private Nurse. **1942** Young America. **1943** Hitler—Dead or Alive. **1947** The Bachelor and the Bobby Soxer. **1952** Ruby Gentry. **1953** The Man from the Alamo; The Moonlighter. **1954** Down Three Dark Streets. **1955** The Cobweb.

MARSH, RISLEY HALSEY
Born: 1927. Died: Jan. 14, 1965, Newark, N.J. Screen and stage actor.

MARSHAL, ALAN
Born: Jan. 29, 1909, Sydney, Australia. Died: July 9, 1961, Chicago, Ill. Screen and stage actor.

Appeared in: **1936** After the Thin Man; The Garden of Allah. **1937** Conquest; Night Must Fall; Parnell; The Robbery Symphony. **1938** Dramatic School; I Met My Love Again; Invisible Enemy; The Road to Reno. **1939** The Adventures of Sherlock Holmes; Exile Express; Four Girls in White; The Hunchback of Notre Dame. **1940** He Stayed for Breakfast; The Howards of Virginia; Irene; Married and in Love. **1941** Lydia; Tom, Dick and Harry. **1944** Bride by Mistake; The White Cliffs of Dover. **1949** The Barkeleys of Broadway. **1956** The Opposite Sex. **1958** House on Haunted Hill. **1959** Day of the Outlaw.

MARSHALL, BOYD
Born: 1885, Ohio. Died: Nov. 9, 1950, Jackson Heights, N.Y. Screen and stage actor.

Appeared in: **1913** Bread Upon the Waters; Her Right to Happiness; His Imaginary Family. **1914** The Tangled Cat; The Keeper of the Light. **1915** A Call From the Dead; The Mill on the Floss; At the Patrician's Club; Hannah's Henpecked Husband; Their Last Performance; The Baby and the Boss. **1916** King Lear; Lucky Larry's Lady Love; The Optimistic Oriental Occults; The World and the Woman. **1917** A Modern Monte Cristo; When Love Was Blind.

MARSHALL, CHARLES E. "RED"
Born: 1899. Died: Apr. 15, 1975, Jersey City, N.J. (pneumonia). Screen, stage, burlesque and vaudeville actor.

Appeared in: **1944** A Wave, A Wac and A Marine. **1946** Specter of the Rose.

MARSHALL, CHET
Born: 1932. Died: June 22, 1974. Screen actor. Divorced from actress Karen Sharpe.

Appeared in: **1952** The Las Vegas Story. **1956** D-Day the Sixth of June.

MARSHALL, CORA See GRIFFITH, CORINNE

MARSHALL, GEORGE E.
Born: Dec. 29, 1891, Chicago, Ill. Died: Feb. 17, 1975, Los Angeles, Calif. Screen, television actor, film director and screenwriter. Entered films as an extra and stuntman in 1912.

Appeared in: **1914** Universal shorts. **1932** Pack Up Your Troubles; Their First Mistake (short); The Soilers (short). **1947** Variety Girl. **1974** The Crazy World of Julius Vrooder.

MARSHALL, HERBERT
Born: May 23, 1890, London, England. Died: Jan. 22, 1966, Beverly Hills, Calif. (heart attack). Screen, stage, radio, television actor and writer. Married to actress Boots Mallory (dec. 1958) and later married Dee Anne Kahmann. Divorced from model Lee Russell, actress Edna Best (dec. 1974), and model Molly Mailtland. Father of actress Sarah Best Marshall.

Appeared in: **1927** Mumsie. **1929** The Letter. **1930** Murder. **1931** Michael and Mary (US 1932); The Calendar (aka Bachelor's Folly—US 1932); Secrets of a Secretary. **1932** The Faithful Heart (aka Faithful Hearts—US 1933); Evenings for Sale; Blonde Venus; Trouble in Paris. **1933** I Was a Spy (US 1934); White Woman; Clear All Wires; The Solitaire Man. **1934** Four Frightened People; Outcast Lady; The Painted Veil; Riptide. **1935** If You Could Only Cook; The Good Fairy; The Flame Within; Accent on Youth; The Dark Angel. **1936** Crack-Up; The Lady Consents; A Woman Rebels; Make Way for a Lady; Till We Meet Again; Forgotten Faces; Girls' Dormitory. **1937** Fight for Your Lady; Angel; Breakfast for Two. **1938** Marie Antoinette; Mad About Music; Always Goodbye; Woman Against Woman. **1939** Zaza. **1940** A Bill of Divorcement; Foreign

Correspondent; The Letter (and 1929 version). **1941** The Little Foxes; Adventure in Washington; When Ladies Meet; Kathleen. **1942** The Moon and Sixpence; Portrait of a Rebel. **1943** Flight for Freedom; Forever and a Day; Young Ideas. **1944** Andy Hardy's Blonde Trouble. **1945** The Unseen; The Enchanted Cottage. **1946** The Razor's Edge; Duel in the Sun; Crack-Up. **1947** High Wall; Ivy. **1949** The Secret Garden. **1950** Underworld Story. **1951** Anne of the Indies. **1952** Captain Black Jack. **1952** Angel Face. **1954** Riders to the Stars; Gog; The Black Shield of Falworth. **1955** The Virgin Queen. **1956** Portrait in Smoke; Wicked As They Come (US 1957); The Weapon (US 1957). **1958** Stage Struck; The Fly. **1960** Midnight Lace; College Confidential. **1961** Fever in the Blood. **1962** Five Weeks in a Balloon. **1963** The List of Adrian Messenger; The Caretakers. **1965** The Third Day.

MARSHALL, MORT (Mortimer Haig Lichtenstein)
Born: Aug. 17, 1918, New York, N.Y. Died: Feb. 1, 1979, New York, N.Y. (coronary arrest). Screen, stage and television actor.

Appeared in: **1954** Go, Man, Go. **1955** The Silver Chalice; Target Earth; Kiss Me Deadly; Pete Kelly's Blues. **1966** Gammera the Invincible. **1970** Lovers and Other Strangers; Skullduggery. **1971** The Crissom Gang. **1974** The Longest Yard. **1979** Starting Over.

MARSHALL, OSWALD
Born: 1875, Newcastle-on-Tyne, England. Died: Apr. 19, 1954, New York, N.Y. Screen and stage actor.

MARSHALL, TULLY (William Phillips)
Born: Apr. 13, 1864, Nevada City, Calif. Died: Mar. 10, 1943, Encino, Calif. (heart and lung ailment). Screen and stage actor. Entered films in 1915.

Appeared in: **1916** Oliver Twist; Intolerance; Joan the Woman. **1917** Countess Charming. **1918** We Can't Have Everything; Too Many Millions. **1919** Cheating Cheaters; The Girl Who Stayed Home; The Crimson Gardenia; The Fall of Babylon; Her Kingdom of Dreams; The Life Line; The Lottery Man; Hawthorne of the U.S.A.; Everywoman. **1920** The Slim Princess; Double Speed; The Dancin' Fool. **1921** The Cup of Life; Hail the Woman; Silent Years; What Happened to Rosa? **1922** Any Night; Good Men and True; Is Matrimony a Failure?; The Super-Sex; Without Compromise; The Village Blacksmith; The Beautiful and Damned; Deserted at the Altar; Fools of Fortune; The Ladder Jinx; The Lying Truth; Only a Shop Girl; Penrod; The Marriage Chance; Too Much Business. **1923** The Hunchback of Notre Dame; Let's Go; The Barefoot Boy; Broken Hearts of Broadway; Temporary Marriage; Thundergate; The Covered Wagon; The Brass Bottle; The Dangerous Maid; Dangerous Trails; Defying Destiny; Fools and Riches; His Last Race; The Law and the Lawless; Ponjola; Richard, the Lion-Hearted; Her Temporary Husband. **1924** He Who Gets Slapped; Hold Your Breath; Pagan Passions; Passion's Pathway; Along Came Ruth; For Sale; The Stranger; The Right of the Strongest; The Ridin' Kid from Powder River; Reckless Romance. **1925** The Merry Widow; Clothes Make the Pirate; Anything Once; The Half-Way Girl; The Pace That Thrills; Smouldering Fires; The Talker. **1926** Her Big Night; Torrent; Twinkletoes; Old Loves and New. **1927** Beware of Widows; The Gorilla; The Cat and the Canary; Jim the Conqueror. **1928** Drums of Love; The Mad Hour; The Perfect Crime; Queen Kelly; Trail of '98; Alias Jimmy Valentine. **1929** Redskin; The Show of Shows; Thunderbolt; Tiger Rose; Conquest; The Bridge of San Luis Rey; The Mysterious Dr. Fu Manchu; Skin Deep. **1930** Murder Will Out; The Big Trail; Numbered Men; One Night at Susie's; Burning Up; Mammy; She Couldn't Say No; Under a Texas Moon; Common Clay; Redemption; Dancing Sweeties; Tom Sawyer. **1931** Fighting Caravans; The Unholy Garden; The Millionaire; The Virtuous Husband; Mr. Wong; City Sentinels. **1932** Broken Lullaby; The Beast of the City; Night Court; Scandal for Sale; Strangers of the Evening; Two-Fisted Law; Exposure; Klondike; Cabin in the Cotton; Afraid to Talk; Hurricane Express (serial); Arsene Lupin; The Hatchet Man; Scarface; Red Dust; Grand Hotel; The Man I Killed. **1933** Laughing at Life; Corruption; Night of Terror. **1934** Massacre; Murder on the Blackboard. **1935** Black Fury; A Tale of Two Cities; Diamond Jim. **1937** California Straight Ahead; Souls at Sea; She Asked for It; Hold 'Em Navy; Stand In; Behind Prison Bars. **1938** Mr. Boggs Steps Out; Making the Headlines; A Yank at Oxford; Arsene Lupin Returns; College Swing; Hold That Kiss; House of Mystery. **1939** Blue Montana Skies; The Kid from Texas. **1940** Invisible Stripes; Brigham Young, Frontiersman; Youth Will Be Served; Go West; Chad Hanna. **1941** Ball of Fire; For Beauty's Sake. **1942** This Gun for Hire; Moontide; Ten Gentlemen From West Point. **1943** Behind Prison Walls; Hitler's Madman.

MARSHALOV, BORIS
Born: 1902, Russia. Died: Oct. 16, 1967, New York, N.Y. Stage and screen actor.

Appeared in: **1964** Pie in the Sky (aka Terror in the City—1966).

MARSON, AILEEN (Aileen Pitt Marson)
Born: 1913, England. Died: May 5, 1939, London, England (childbirth). Screen and stage actress.

Appeared in: **1932** Watch Beverly. **1934** Lucky Loser; Way of Youth; My Song for You; Roadhouse; Passing Shadows; The Green Pack; Ten Minute Alibi. **1935** Honeymoon for Three; The Black Mask. **1936** Living Dangerously; The Tenth Man (US 1937); Someone at the Door. **1937** The Green Cockatoo (aka Four Dark Hours); Spring Handicap.

MARSTINI, ROSITA
Born: 1894. Died: Apr. 24, 1948, Hollywood, Calif. Screen actress.

Appeared in: **1917** Tale of Two Cities. **1918** Goodnight, Paul. **1919** The Veiled Adventure. **1921** The Outside Woman; The Primal Law; Serenade. **1922** Enter Madame. **1924** Shadows of Paris; The Lover of Camille. **1925** The Big Parade; The Redeeming Sin; Proud Flesh. **1926** Flame of the Argentine. **1928** We Americans; No Other Woman. **1929** Hot for Paris. **1932** The Fourth Horseman. **1933** I Cover the Water. **1934** In Love with Life. **1945** This Love of Ours. **1948** Casbah.

MARSTON, ANN
Born: 1939. Died: Mar. 6, 1971, Detroit, Mich. (stroke caused by vascular complications of diabetes). Screen actress (starlet at age 9). Was "Miss Michigan" of the 1960 Miss America Pageant.

MARSTON, JOHN
Born: 1890. Died: Sept. 2, 1962, New York, N.Y. Screen and stage actor.

Appeared in: **1932** Cabin in the Cotton; Three on a Match; Silver Dollar; Love Is a Racket; Skyscraper Souls; Scarlet Dawn. **1933** Son of a Sailor; Good Dame; All of Me; Hell and High Water; Heroes for Sale; Lady Killer; Mary Stevens, M.D.; Mayor of Hell; Son of Kong. **1934** The Pursuit of Happiness. **1937** History Is Made at Night. **1939** Union Pacific. **1950** Broken Arrow.

MARTEL, ALPHONSE
Born: Mar. 27, 1890, Strasbourg, France. Died: Mar. 18, 1976. Screen actor, film director and screenwriter.

Appeared in: **1924** After a Million; Hutch of the U.S.A.; A Fighting Heart. **1925** Sky's the Limit. **1926** Strings of Steel (serial); The Mystery Club; The Love Thief. **1927** Grinning Guns; Naughty Nanette; She's My Baby. **1928** The Night Bird; Dream of Love; The Divine Sinner; Scarlet Youth. **1929** Unguarded Girls. **1930** Sweethearts and Wives. **1934** The Count of Monte Cristo; Maid in Hollywood (short); Black Cat; Notorious Sophie Lang. **1935** Manhattan Butterfly. **1937** The Girl from Scotland Yard. **1938** Doctor Rhythm; The Jitters (short). **1939** Topper Takes a Trip. **1943** Swingtime Johnny. **1944** Enter Arsine Lupin. **1946** The Catman of Paris. **1948** French Leave. **1949** The Fan. **1950** Under My Skin. **1953** Gentlemen Prefer Blondes; Treasure of the Golden Condor. **1954** Paris Playboys. **1960** Seven Thieves.

MARTEL, JUNE
Born: Nov. 19, 1909, Chicago, Ill. Died: Nov. 23, 1978. Screen actress.

Appeared in: **1935** Front Page Woman; Going Highbrow; Fighting Youth. **1936** Sitting on the Moon. **1937** Arizona Mahoney; Forlorn River; Her Husband Lies. **1938** Wild Horse Rodeo; Santa Fe Stampede.

MARTELL, MARTY (aka NATHAN MANDELL)
Born: 1900. Died: May 7, 1979, Miami, Fla. (cancer). Screen, stage, radio actor, stage director and singer. Father of actress/singer/songwriter Joy Martell, and concert and theatre conductor Robert Mandell.

Appeared in: **1939** Sabotage; One Third of a Nation.

MARTIN, CHRIS-PIN
Born: 1894, Tucson, Ariz. Died: June 27, 1953, Montebello, Calif. (heart attack). Screen actor.

Appeared in: **1929** In Old Arizona. **1931** The Squaw Man; The Cisco Kid. **1932** Winner Take All; South of Santa Fe; Girl Crazy; The Stoker; The Painted Woman. **1933** Outlaw Justice; California Trail. **1934** Four Frightened People; Chained. **1935** Res Salute; Captain Blood; Bordertown; Under the Pampas Moon. **1936** The Gay Desperado; The Beloved Rogue; The Bold Caballero. **1937** Boots and Saddles. **1938** Flirting with Fate; Tropic Holiday; The Texans. **1939** Stagecoach; The Return of the Cisco Kid; The Girl and the Gambler; Fighting Gringo; Frontier Marshal; The Llano Kid. **1940** Down Argentine Way; The Cisco Kid and the Lady; Charlie Chan in Panama; Viva Cisco Kid; Lucky Cisco Kid; The Gay Caballero; The Mark of Zorro. **1941**

Romance of the Rio Grande; Ride On, Vaquero; The Bad Man; Weed-End in Havana. **1942** Undercover Man; Tombstone, the Town Too Tough to Die; American Empire. **1943** The Sultan's Daughter; The Ox-Bow Incident. **1944** Ali Baba and the Forty Thieves; Tampico. **1945** Along Came Jones; San Antonio. **1946** Suspense; Gallant Journey. **1947** The Captain from Castile; King of the Bandits; Robin Hood of Monterey; The Fugitive. **1948** Blood on the Moon; Belle Starr's Daughter; The Return of Wildfire; Mexican Hayride. **1949** Rimfire; The Beautiful Blonde from Bashful Bend. **1950** Arizona Cowboy. **1951** The Lady from Texas; A Millionaire for Christy. **1952** Ride the Man Down. **1953** Mesa of Lost Women.

MARTIN, CYE (Seymore Martin)
Born: 1914. Died: Mar. 28, 1972, New York, N.Y. (heart attack). Screen actor and theatrical clothier.

Appeared in: **1948** Naked City. **1961** The Hustler. **1966** A Man Called Adam.

MARTIN, EDIE
Born: 1880. Died: Feb. 23, 1964, London, England. Screen, stage and vaudeville actress. Entered films in 1932.

Appeared in: **1937** Farewell Again (aka Troopship—US 1938); Under the Red Robe. **1943** The Demi-Paradise (aka Adventure for Two—US 1945). **1945** A Place of One's Own. **1948** Oliver Twist (US 1951). **1949** The History of Mr. Polly (US 1951). **1951** The Lavender Hill Mob; The Man in the White Suit (US 1952). **1952** Time Gentlemen Please!. **1953** The Titfield Thunderbolt. **1954** The End of the Road (US 1957); Lease of Life (US 1955). **1955** As Long As They're Happy; The Lady Killers (US 1956). **1956** My Teenage Daughter (aka Teenage Bad Girl—US 1957). **1959** Too Many Crooks. **1961** A Weekend with Lulu. **1963** Sparrows Can't Sing.

MARTIN, FRANK WELLS
Born: 1880: Died: Aug. 9, 1941, Los Angeles, Calif. Screen actor and film director.

MARTIN, IRENE
Died: Dec. 12, 1973. Screen actress.

Appeared in: **1952** Actors and Sin.

MARTIN, JOHN E.
Born: 1865. Died: Nov. 22, 1933, New York. Screen and stage actor.

MARTIN, LEWIS H.
Died: Feb. 21, 1969, Los Angeles, Calif. (heart attack). Screen, stage and television actor.

Appeared in: **1950** Experiment Alcatraz. **1951** Criminal Lawyer; The Big Carnival; Drums in the Deep South; Operation Pacific; Three Guys Named Mike. **1952** Angel Face; Red Planet Mars; The Wild North. **1953** Arrowhead; The Caddy; Houdini; No Escape; Pony Express; The War of the Worlds. **1954** Cry Vengeance; Knock on Wood; Men of the Fighting Lady; Witness to Murder. **1955** Las Vegas Shakedown; Night Freight; Night Nurse. **1956** The Man Who Knew Too Much; The Court Jester; These Wilder Years. **1957** Last Stagecoach West; The Quiet Gun; Rockabilly Baby; Slander. **1958** Crash Landing. **1963** Diary of a Madman.

MARTIN, LOCK
Died: c. 1959. Screen actor.

Appeared in: **1951** The Day the Earth Stood Still.

MARTIN, MICKEY
Born: 1921. Died: July 25, 1973, Los Angeles, Calif. (heart attack). Screen actor.

Appeared in: **1954** The French Line. **1967** The Gnome-Mobile.

MARTIN, OWEN
Born: 1889. Died: May 4, 1960, Saranac Lake, N.Y. Screen and stage actor.

Appeared in: **1957** The Pajama Game.

MARTIN, PETE (Peter Halfpenny)
Born: 1899. Died: May, 1973, Glasgow, Scotland. Stage, vaudeville and screen actor. Married to vaudeville performer Edith Thomson. He appeared in vaudeville as part of "Martin and Holbein" team.

MARTIN, ROSS (Martin Rosenblatt)
Born: Mar. 22, 1920, Grodek, Poland. Died: July 3, 1981, Poway, Calif. (heart attack). Screen, stage and television actor.

Appeared in: **1955** Conquest of Space. **1958** Underwater Warrior; The Colossus of New York. **1962** Geronimo; Experiment in Terror. **1963** The Ceremony. **1964** The Great Race. **1965** The Man From Button Willow.

MARTIN, SILVER MOON (Michael James Martin)
Born: 1891. Died: Jan. 20, 1969, Comanche, Okla. Screen actor.

MARTIN, STROTHER
Born: Mar. 26, 1919, Kokomo, Ind. Died: Aug. 1, 1980, Thousand Oaks, Calif. (heart attack). Screen, stage and television actor. Entered films as an extra in the late 1940s.

Appeared in: **1950** The Asphalt Jungle (film debut); The Damned Don't Cry. **1951** Rhubarb; People Against O'Hara. **1952** Storm Over Tibet. **1953** South Sea Woman. **1954** A Star is Born. **1955** The Big Knife; Kiss Me Deadly; Strategic Air Command; Target Zero. **1956** Attack! **1957** The Black Whip; The Blackpatch; Copper Sky. **1958** Cowboy. **1959** The Horse Soldiers; The Shaggy Dog; The Wild and the Innocent. **1961** Sanctuary; The Deadly Companions. **1962** The Man Who Shot Liberty Valance. **1963** McLintock!; Showdown. **1964** Invitation to a Gunfighter. **1965** Brainstorm; The Sons of Katie Elder; Shenandoah. **1966** Harper; An Eye for an Eye; Nevada Smith. **1967** The Flim-Flam Man; Cool Hand Luke; True Grit; Butch Cassidy and the Sundance Kid; The Wild Bunch. **1970** The Ballad of Cable Hogue. **1971** Fools' Parade; The Brotherhood of Satan; Red Sky at Morning. **1972** Pocket Money; Hannie Caulder. **1973** Sssssss. **1975** Rooster Cogburn; Hard Times. **1976** The Great Scout and Cathouse Thursday. **1977** Slap Shot. **1978** Up in Smoke; The End; Steel Cowboy. **1979** Love and Bullets; The Champ; Nightwing; The Villain. **1980** Hotwire; The Secret Life of Nokola Tesla.

MARTIN, TONY
Died: Feb., 1932, N.Y. Screen actor. Do not confuse with singer and actor. Appeared in shorts as half of "Nick and Tony" comedy team.

MARTIN, TOWNSEND
Born: 1896, New York, N.Y. Died: Nov. 22, 1951, New York, N.Y. Screen actor, screenwriter, playwright and author.

Appeared in: **1922** The Cradle Buster. **1923** Second Fiddle. **1924** Grit.

MARTIN, VIRGINIA
Born: 1922. Died: Mar. 8, 1971, Los Angeles, Calif. Screen actress and singer.

MARTINDEL, EDWARD B.
Born: July 8, 1876, Hamilton, Ohio. Died: May 4, 1955, Woodland Hills, Calif. (heart attack). Screen, stage and vaudeville actor. Entered films in 1917.

Appeared in: **1921** The Call of the North; Ducks and Drakes; Greater Than Love; Short Skirts; Hail the Woman. **1922** The Dangerous Little Demon; Nice People; Clarence; Little Eva Ascends; The Ordeal; A Daughter of Luxury; The Glory of Clementina; Manslaughter; Midnight. **1923** The White Flower; Lovebound; The Day of Faith. **1924** Love's Whirlpool. **1925** The Dixie Handicap; The Sporting Venus; Compromise; Lady Windermere's Fan; Scandal Proof; The Man Without a Country. **1926** The Duchess of Buffalo; The Dixie; You'd Be Surprised; Everybody's Acting; Tony Runs Wild; Somebody's Mother. **1927** Lovers?; In Old Kentucky; Children of Divorce; Fashions for Women; Lonesome Ladies; Taxi! Taxi!; Venus of Venice. **1928** The Singing Fool; On Trial; Companionate Marriage; We Americans; The Desert Bride; The Garden of Eden. **1929** The Devil's Apple Tree; Footlights and Fools; Why Be Good?; The Desert Song; Modern Love; Hardboiled Rose; The Phantom of the Opera; The Aviator. **1930** Second Choice; Mamba; Song of the West; Golden Dawn; Rain or Shine; Check and Double Check; Song O' My Heart. **1931** Divorce among Friends; High Stakes; Woman Pursued; The Gay Diplomat. **1932** American Madness; False Faces; Afraid to Talk. **1933** By Appointment Only. **1934** Two Heads on a Pillow. **1935** Champagne for Breakfast; The Girl Who Came Back.

MARTINELLI, GIOVANNI
Born: Oct. 24, 1885, Montagana, Italy. Died: Feb. 2, 1969, New York, N.Y. Opera singer and screen actor.

Appeared in: **1927** The following shorts: Pagliacci; Aida; Carmen; La Juive. **1929** Martha (short). **1930** The following shorts: Il Trovatore; Celeste Aida; Faust; Aida (and 1927 version).

MARTINEZ, CONCHITA
Born: 1912, Mexico. Died: May, 1960, Mexico City, Mexico (heart attack). Screen, stage, radio actress and singer.

MARTINEZ, EDUARDO L.
Born: 1900, Mexico. Died: Oct. 31, 1968, San Antonio, Tex. Screen actor and orchestra leader.

MARTINEZ, PEDRO
Born: 1945, Monterey, Mexico. Died: Dec. 25, 1978, Hollywood, Calif. (auto accident). Screen, stage and television actor.

Appeared in: **1976** Lifeguard. **1979** Raices de Sangre (Roots of Blood).

MARTIN-HARVEY, SIR JOHN (John Martin Harvey)
Born: June 22, 1863, Wivenhoe, Essex, England. Died: May 14, 1944, London, England. Screen and stage actor. Father of actress Muriel Martin-Harvey.

Appeared in: **1913** A Cigarette Maker's Romance. **1920** The Breed of the Treshams. **1925** The Only Way. **1931** The Lyons Mail.

MARTINI, LOU
Died: Apr. 11, 1971. Screen actor.

Appeared in: **1961** The Hoodlum Priest.

MARTINI, NINO
Born: 1904, Verona, Italy. Died: Dec. 9, 1976, Verona, Italy (heart attack). Screen, stage, radio actor and opera singer.

Appeared in: **1930** Paramount on Parade. **1935** Here's to Romance. **1936** The Gay Desperado. **1937** Music for Madame. **1948** One Night With You. **1949** The Song of India.

MARTYN, MARTY
Died: Dec. 25, 1964, Beverly Hills, Calif. Screen, stage actor and dance director.

Appeared in: **1932** Night after Night.

MARTYN, MAY (aka LADY PLAYFAIR)
Born: 1877, England. Died: June 8, 1948, Sandwich, England (heart attack). Screen and stage actress. Married to actor Sir Nigel Playfair (dec. 1934).

MARTYN, PETER
Born: 1928, England. Died: Feb. 16, 1955, London, England. Screen, stage and television actor.

Appeared in: **1952** Folly to Be Wise. **1954** Orders Are Orders; You Know What Sailors Are.

MARUM, MARILYN (Marilyn Harvey)
Born: 1929. Died: Mar. 29, 1973, Hollywood, Calif. Screen, stage and television actress. Married to assistant director Gene Marum.

Appeared in: **1963** A Child Is Waiting. **1968** Rosemary's Baby.

MARVIN, JACK
Died: Oct. 17, 1956. Screen actor.

MARX, ALBERT A. (aka ALMAR THE CLOWN)
Born: 1892. Died: Feb. 18, 1960, Houston, Tex. Screen, radio actor and clown. Known professionally as "Almar the Clown." Appeared in film shorts.

MARX, CHICO (Leonard Marx)
Born: Mar. 22, 1891, New York, N.Y. Died: Oct. 11, 1961, Hollywood, Calif. (heart attack). Screen, stage, vaudeville and television actor. Son of actor Frenchie Marx (dec. 1932). Member of Marx Brothers Comedy Team including Groucho, Harpo, Chico and sometimes Zeppo. For family information see Frenchie Marx listing and for the films the Marx Brothers appeared in, see Groucho Marx listing.

Appeared in: **1933** Hollywood on Parade (Chico only—short).

MARX, GROUCHO (Julius Henry Marx)
Born: Oct. 2, 1890, New York, N.Y. Died: Aug. 19, 1977, West Hollywood, Calif. (pneumonia). Screen, stage and vaudeville actor. Son of actor Samuel "Frenchie" Marx (dec. 1933). Member of Marx Brothers Comedy Team (Groucho, Harpo, Chico and sometimes Zeppo). For family information see Samuel Marx listing.

The Marx Brothers appeared in: **1929** The Cocoanuts. **1930** Animal Crackers. **1931** Monkey Business. **1932** Horse Feathers; Hollywood on Parade (short). **1933** Duck Soup. **1935** A Night at the Opera. **1937** A Day at the Races. **1938** Room Service. **1939** At the Circus. **1940** Go West. **1941** The Big Store. **1943** Screen Snapshots #8 (short). **1946** A Night in Casablanca. **1949** Love Happy. **1957** The Story of Mankind. **1958** Showdown at Ulcer Gulch (short). **1964** Big Parade of Comedy

(documentary). **1976** That's Entertainment Part 2 (film clips). Groucho only appeared in: **1943** Screen Snapshots #2 (short). **1947** Copacabana. **1950** Mr. Music. **1951** Double Dynamite (aka It's Only Money). **1952** A Girl in Every Port. **1957** Will Success Spoil Rock Hunter? **1968** Skidoo. **1977** Salsa.

MARX, HARPO (Adolph—later changed to Arthur Marx)
Born: Nov. 23, 1893, New York, N.Y. Died: Sept. 28, 1964, Los Angeles, Calif. (heart surgery). Screen, stage, vaudeville, television actor and author. Son of actor Frenchie Marx (dec. 1932). Member of the Marx Brothers Comedy Team including Grocho, Harpo, Chico and sometimes Zeppo Marx. For family information see Frenchie Marx listing and for the films the Marx Brothers appeared in, see Grocho Marx listing.

Harpo only appeared in: **1925** Too Many Kisses. **1935** La Fiesta de Santa Barbara (short). **1944** Hollywood Canteen. **1945** All-Star Bond Rally (short).

MARX, MARVIN
Born: 1925. Died: Dec. 23, 1975, Miami Beach, Fla. (heart failure). Screen, stage actor, television writer and producer.

MARX, MAX
Died: 1925, Universal City, Calif. (killed when rope snapped during shooting of Strings of Steel). Screen actor and stuntman.

Appeared in: **1926** Strings of Steel (serial).

MARX, SAMUEL "FRENCHIE" (Simon Marx)
Born: 1861. Died: May 11, 1933, Hollywood, Calif (heart failure). Screen actor. Father of the Marx Brothers: Vaudeville actor Gummo (dec. 1977), and actors Groucho (dec. 1977), Harpo (dec. 1964), Chico (dec. 1961) and Zeppo (dec. 1979).

Appeared in: **1931** Monkey Business.

MARX, ZEPPO (Herbert Marx)
Born: 1901, New York, N.Y. Died: Nov. 30, 1979, Palm Springs, Calif. Screen, stage and vaudeville actor. Son of Samuel "Frenchie" Marx (dec. 1933). Member of the Marx Brothers Comedy Team until 1933. For family information see Samuel Marx listing.

Appeared in: **1929** The Cocoanuts. **1930** Animal Crackers. **1931** Monkey Business. **1932** Horse Feathers. **1933** Duck Soup. **1964** Big Parade of Comedy (documentary).

MARZOLA, JOE
Died: Dec. 31, 1976. Screen actor.

MASISTO (Bartholomeo Pagano)
Born: 1878, San Ilario, Italy. Died: 1947, Italy. Screen actor.

Appeared in: **1914** Cabiria. **1925** Maciste Contro lo Sceicco.

MASKELL, VIRGINIA
Born: Feb. 27, 1936, Shepherd's Bush, London, England. Died: Jan. 25, 1968, Stoke Mandeville, England (exposure and overdose of drugs). Screen, stage and television actress. Married to stage director Goeffrey Shakerley.

Appeared in: **1958** Virgin Island (film debut—US 1960); Happy Is the Bride (US 1959); The Man Upstairs (US 1959). **1959** Jet Storm (US 1961). **1960** Suspect (aka The Risk—US 1961); Doctor in Love (US 1962). **1962** Only Two Can Play; The Wild and the Willing (aka Young and Willing—US 1964). **1967** Interlude (US 1968).

MASLER, STUART See MICHLES, STEWART

MASON, ANN
Born: 1889. Died: Feb. 6, 1948, New York, N.Y. (burns sustained in fire). Stage and screen actress. Married to actor Paul Gordon (dec. 1929) and later married and divorced actor Philip Pepper.

Appeared in: **1919** Deliverance.

MASON, BERTHA N.
Born: 1877. Died: Nov. 9, 1950, Los Angeles, Calif. Screen actress.

MASON, BUDDY
Born: 1903. Died: Apr. 15, 1975, Woodland Hills, Calif. Screen stuntman and stand-in.

Appeared in: **1927** College. **1963** The Comedy of Terrors.

MASON, DAN (Dan Grassman)
Born: 1853. Died: July 6, 1929, Baersville, N.Y. Screen and stage actor. Created the role of Skipper in the "Toonerville Trolley" series. Entered films approximately 1912.

Appeared in: **1913** The Horrible Example; A Pair of Foils; Porgy's Bouquet; The Comedian's Downfall; The Awakening of a Man; How Did It Finish?; Professor William Nutt; As the Tooth Came Out; The Thrifty Janitor; The Janitor's Flirtation. **1914** Dinkelspiel's Baby; Lena; A Night Out; Tango in Tuckerville; A Tight Squeeze; The Janitor's Quiet Life. **1915** Joey and His Trombones; That Heavenly Cook; Where Can I Get a Wife? **1917** The Broadway Sport; Unknown 274. **1918** Over the Hill; Bonnie Annie Laurie; Brave and Bold; Jack Spurlock, Prodigal; Sherman Was Right; The Yellow Ticket. **1921** Why Girls Leave Home; "Toonerville Trolley" series of shorts including: Boos-Em-Friends; Skipper's Scheme; Skipper's Treasure Garden; Toonerville Tactics; Skipper Has His Fling. **1922** Iron to Gold; Is Matrimony a Failure? **1924** A Self-Made Failure; Conductor 1492; Darwin Was Right; The Plunderer; Idle Tongues. **1925** Sally; Seven Sinners; The Wall Street Whiz; American Pluck; Thunder Mountain; Wages for Wives. **1926** A Desperate Moment; The Fire Brigade; Stepping Along; Hearts and Fists; Forbidden Waters; Rainbow Riley; Hard Boiled. **1927** The Chinese Parrot; A Hero on Horseback; The Price of Honor; Out All Night.

MASON, ELLIOTT
Born: 1897. Died: June 20, 1949. Screen and stage actress.

Appeared in: **1936** The Ghost Goes West; Jailbreak; Born That Way; First and the Last; Owd Bob; Break the News. **1938** The Ware Case; Marigold; The Citadel. **1939** Black Limelight. **1940** 21 Days Together. **1941** The Ghost of St. Michael's; Turned Out Nice Again. **1943** The Gentler Sex. **1944** On Approval. **1945** Vacation from Marriage. **1946** The Captive Heart. **1949** The Agitator.

MASON, EVELYN M.
Born: 1892. Died: Oct. 29, 1926, Los Angeles, Calif. (following surgery for ptomaine poisoning). Black screen and stage actress.

MASON, GREGORY
Born: 1889. Died: Nov. 29, 1968, Greenwich, Conn. Journalist and screen actor.

Appeared in: **1914** Our Mutual Girl No. 33.

MASON, HADDON
Born: Feb. 21, 1898, London, England. Died: Apr. 30, 1966, London, England. Screen, stage actor and talent agent.

Appeared in: **1925** The Art of Love series including: Heel Taps (aka The Lady in High Heels). **1926** Every Mother's Son; Palaver. **1928** A Little Bit of Fluff (aka Skirts—US); Dawn; The Triumph of the Scarlet Pimpernel (aka The Scarlet Daredevil—US 1929); The Lady of the Lake (US 1930); God's Clay; Sacred Dramas series including: The Rosary. **1929** The Woman in White; A Peep Behind the Scenes. **1930** Painted Pictures; The Yellow Mask; London Melody; French Leave. **1931** Contraband; To Oblige a Lady; Birds of a Feather; The Shadow Between; Inquest. **1932** Castle Sinister. **1933** A Moorland Tragedy. **1935** The Village Squire. **1937** Under the Red Robe.

MASON, HAL
Born: 1905. Died: May 13, 1956, Bakersfield, Calif. Screen actor, film producer and stuntman.

MASON, HOMER
Born: 1877, Poughkeepsie, N.Y. Died: Sept. 27, 1959, Van Nuys, Calif. Screen and vaudeville actor. Married to actress Marguerite Keeler with whom he appeared in vaudeville in an act billed as "Mason and Keller."

Appeared in: **1930** Money, Money, Money (short).

MASON, JAMES
Born: 1890, Paris, France. Died: Nov. 7, 1959, Hollywood, Calif. (heart attack). Screen actor. Do not confuse with British actor James Mason.

Appeared in: **1914** The Squaw Man. **1918** Knickerbocker Buckaroo. **1921** The Silent Call; Godless Men; The Sage Hen; Two Weeks with Pay; Mysterious Rider. **1922** The Fast Mail; Lights of the Desert; The Old Homestead. **1923** Why Worry?; Scars of Jealousy; Mile-a-Minute Romeo; The Footlight Ranger. **1924** The Flaming Forties; The Heritage of the Desert; Wanderer of the Wasteland; The Plunderer. **1925** Beggar on Horseback; Rugged Water; Barriers Burned Away; Dashing Thru; Old Clothes; Under the Rouge. **1926** Bred in Old Kentucky; For Heaven's Sake; Ladies of Leisure; The Phantom of the Forest; Whispering Smith; Whispering Canyon; The Unknown

Cavalier; The Night Owl. **1927** King of Kings; Let It Rain; Alias the Lone Wolf; Back to God's Country; Dead Man's Curve. **1928** Chicago After Midnight; Race for Life; The Big Killing; Across to Singapore; A Thief in the Dark; The Singapore Mutiny; The Speed Classic. **1929** The Phantom City; The Long Long Trail. **1930** The Concentratin' Kid; The Shrimp (short); Last of the Duanes. **1931** The Painted Desert; Caught; Fly My Kite (short); Border Love. **1932** Texas Gun Fighter. **1933** Renegades of the West; Drum Taps; The Story of Temple Drake; Sunset Pass. **1934** The Dude Ranger; The Last Round-Up. **1935** Hopalong Cassidy. **1936** Call of the Prairie; The Plainsman. **1937** Public Cowboy No. 1. **1938** Rhythm of the Saddle. **1939** The Renegade Stranger; I Met a Murderer; In Old Monterey.

MASON, JOHN B.
Born: Oct. 28, 1858, Orange, N.J. Died: Jan. 12, 1919, Stamford, Conn. Stage and screen actor. Do not confuse with stage actor John Mason born c. 1875.

Appeared in: **1915** Jim the Penman; The Fatal Card. **1916** The Libertine. **1918** Moral Suicide.

MASON, LEROY
Born: 1903, Larimore, N.Dak. Died: Oct. 13, 1947, Los Angeles, Calif. (heart attack). Screen actor. Entered films with the old William Fox studios.

Appeared in: **1926** The Arizona Streak; Born to Battle; Flying High; Tom and His Pals. **1927** Closed Gates. **1928** The Law's Lash; Hit of the Show; Revenge; The Viking; The Avenging Shadow; Golden Shackles. **1929** Bride of the Desert. **1930** The Climax; See America Thirst; The Danger Man; The Woman Who Was Forgotten. **1932** The Last Frontier (serial). **1933** The Phantom of the Air (serial); Smoky. **1934** Redhead; Are We Civilized?; The Dude Ranger; When a Man Sees Red. **1935** The Mystery Man; Rainbow Valley. **1936** Comin' 'Round the Mountain; Ghost Town Gold; The Border Patrolman. **1937** California Straight Ahead; Yodelin' Kid from Pine Ridge; Round Up Time in Texas; Western Gold; The Painted Stallion (serial); It Happened Out West; Jungle Menace (serial). **1938** The Spy Ring; The Painted Trail; Gold Mine in the Sky; Heroes of the Hills; Rhythm of the Saddle; Santa Fe Stampede; Topa Topa. **1939** West of Santa Fe; Wyoming Outlaw; Mexicali Rose; New Frontier; Fighting Gringo; Sky Patrol; Saved by the Belle (short). **1940** Shooting High; Rocky Mountain Rangers; The Range Busters; Triple Justice; Ghost Valley Raiders; Killers of the Wild. **1941** Silver Stallion; Across the Sierras; Robbers of the Range; The Apache Kid; The Perfect Snob; Great Guns. **1942** Time to Kill; It Happened in Flatbush; Six-Gun Gold; Sundown Jim; The Man Who Wouldn't Die; The Silver Bullet. **1943** Chetniks; Blazing Guns; Hands Across the Border. **1944** The Tiger Woman (serial); Beneath Western Skies; Firebrands of Arizona; Hidden Valley Outlaws; The Rockies; Call of the South Seas; None Shall Escape; The Silver City Kid; Marshal of Reno; The Mojave Firebrand; Outlaws of Santa Fe; The San Antonio Kid; Song of Nevada; Stagecoach of Monterey; Tucson Raiders; Vigilantes of Dodge City. **1945** Federal Operator 99 (serial); Home on the Range. **1946** King of the Forest Rangers (serial); The Phantom Rider (serial); Heldorado; My Pal Trigger; Sioux City Sue; Daughter of Don Q. (serial); Night Train to Memphis; Red River Renegades; Under Nevada Skies; Valley of the Zombies; Murder in the Music Hall. **1947** The Black Widow (serial); Jesse James Rides Again (serial); Apache Rose; Along the Oregon Trail; Under Colorado Skies; Saddle Pals; Bandits of Dark Canyon. **1948** California Firebrand; The Gay Ranchero.

MASON, LOUIS
Born: 1888, Danville, Ky. Died: Nov. 12, 1959, Hollywood, Calif. Screen, stage and radio actor. Entered films in 1933.

Appeared in: **1934** Kentucky Kernals; Spitfire; This Man Is Mine; Judge Priest. **1935** Mary Jane's Pa; In Person; Steamboat 'Round the Bend. **1936** Girl of the Ozarks; M'Liss; Banjo On My Knee. **1937** Marry the Girl; Trouble at Midnight. **1939** Stagecoach; Young Mr. Lincoln. **1940** The Grapes of Wrath; Gold Rush Maisie; The Return of Frank James. **1941** The Sea Wolf. **1942** Tennessee Johnson; Yankee Doodle Dandy; Whistling in Dixie; Keeper of the Flame. **1943** Sweet Rosie O'Grady; What's Buzzin' Cousin? **1944** See Here, Private Hargrove; Broadway Rhythm. **1945** Grissly's Millions; Hit the Hay. **1946** Somewhere in the Night; Decoy. **1947** Sport of Kings; Desire Me. **1948** The Velvet Touch. **1949** Adam's Rib; All the King's Men; I Cheated the Law.

MASON, MARJORIE
Died: Nov. 21, 1968. Screen actress. Appeared in silent films.

MASON, MARY (Betty Ann Jenks)
Born: 1911, Pasadena, Calif. Died: Oct. 13, 1980, New York, N.Y. (cancer). Screen, stage, radio and television actress.

Appeared in: **1923** The Extra Girl. **1932** Penguin Pool Murder; The Age of Consent. **1933** Walls of Gold; The Mad Game; Cheyenne Kid.

MASON, REGINALD
Born: 1882, San Francisco, Calif. Died: July 10, 1962, Hermosa Beach, Calif. Stage and screen actor.

Appeared in: **1920** Two Weeks. **1921** The Highest Bidder. **1932** Life Begins. **1933** A Bedtime Story; Emergency Call; Topaze; Shanghai Madness; Brief Moment; The Big Brain; Baby Face; Mary Stevens, M. D.; Kiss Before the Mirror. **1934** Call It Luck; Charlie Chan's Courage; You Can't Buy Everything. **1936** Suzy.

MASON, RITA *See* CAREWE, RITA

MASON, SHIRLEY (aka LEONIE FLUGRATH)
Born: June 6, 1901, Brooklyn, N.Y. Died: July 27, 1979, Los Angeles, Calif. (cancer). Screen and stage actress. Sister of actresses Viola Dana and Edna Flugrath (dec. approximately 1928). Married to actor Bernard J. Durning (dec. 1923), and screenwriter Sidney Lanfield (dec. 1972).

Appeared in: **1910** A Christmas Carol. **1911** April Fool; Betty's Buttons; For the Queen; At the Threshold of Life; Uncle Hiram's List. **1912** Mary Had a Little Lamb; Children Who Labor; The Street Beautiful; The Little Girl Next Door; A Fresh Air Romance; The Third Thanksgiving. **1913** A Youthful Knight; The Risen Soul of Jim Grant; The Two Merchants; Her Royal Highness; The Dream Fairy; A Mistake in Judgment; Embarrassment of Riches. **1915** An Unwilling Thief; Vanity Fair. **1916** Blade O'Grass; The Littlest Magdalene; Celeste of the Ambulance Corps. **1917** The Seven Deadly Sins; The Law of the North; The Tell Tale Step; Light in Darkness; The Little Chevalier; The Lady of the Photograph; The Awakening of Ruth; The Apple-Tree Girl; Cy Whittaker's Ward. **1918** Come On In; Good-Bye Bill. **1919** The Winning Girl; The Rescuing Angel; The Final Closeup; The Unwritten Code. **1920** Her Elephant Man; Treasure Island; Molly and I; Love's Harvest; The Little Wanderer; Merely Mary Ann; Girl of My Heart; The Flame of Youth. **1921** Wing Toy; The Lamplighter; The Mother Heart; Lovetime; Ever Since Eve; Queenie; Jackie. **1922** Little Miss Smiles; The Ragged Heiress; Very Truly Yours; Lights of the Desert; The New Teacher; Youth Must Have Love; Shirley of the Circus; Pawn Ticket 210. **1923** The Eleventh Hour; Lovebound; South Sea Love. **1924** Love Letters; That French Lady; The Star Dust Trail; The Great Diamond Mystery; My Husband's Wives; Curlytop. **1925** The Scarlet Honeymoon; The Talker; Scandal Proof; What Fools Men; Lord Jim. **1926** Desert Gold; Don Juan's Three Nights; Sweet Rosie O'Grady; Sin Cargo; Rose of the Tenements; So This Is Paris. **1927** The Wreck; Let It Rain; Rich Men's Sons; Stranded; Sally in Our Alley. **1928** The Wife's Relations; So This Is Love; Vultures of the Sea; Runaway Girls. **1929** Anne Against the World; The Flying Marine; The Show of Shows; Dark Skies.

MASON, SIDNEY L.
Born: 1886, Paterson, N.J. Died: Mar. 1, 1923, New York, N.Y. Screen and stage actor.

Appeared in: **1916** The Blackmailer; The Daughter of MacGregor; The Honor of Mary Blake. **1917** The Little Terror; The Painted Madonna; The Promise. **1918** The Forbidden Path; Moral Suicide; Bonnie Annie Laurie. **1919** The Fallen Idol; The Trap. **1920** The Good Bad Wife; A Modern Salome.

MASON, SULLY P.
Born: 1906. Died: Nov. 27, 1970, Los Angeles, Calif. (cerebral hemorrhage). Screen, television actor, saxophonist and vocalist.

Appeared in: **1939** That's Right, You're Wrong. **1940** You'll Find Out. **1941** Playmates. **1943** Around the World.

MASON, SYDNEY
Born: 1905. Died: Apr. 11, 1976, Los Angeles, Calif. (heart attack). Screen, stage and radio actor. Do not confuse with actor Sidney L. Mason (dec. 1923).

Appeared in: **1951** Three Guys Named Mike. **1952** Apache Country; Paula. **1953** The Cowboy. **1954** Creature From the Black Lagoon. **1955** Teen-Age Crime Wave. **1956** A Day of Fury; Blackjack Ketchum, Desperado. **1959** Frontier Gun. **1962** Secret File: Hollywood.

MASON, WILLIAM C. "SMILING BILLY"
Born: 1888. Died: Jan. 24, 1941, Orange, N.J. Screen, stage and vaudeville actor. He aided Thomas Edison in early film experimentation.

Appeared in: **1912** Cupid's Quartet; Hearts of Men; A Corner in Whiskers; The Snare; Miss Simkins' Summer Boarder; The Stain; Almost a Man; A Money? **1913** Essanay films. **1916** Dizzy Heights and Daring Hearts; Cinders of Love; A Dash of Courage. **1919** The Wolf. **1922** A series of short comedies.

MASSEY, ILONA (Ilona Hajmassy)
Born: 1910, Budapest, Hungary. Died: Aug. 20, 1974, Bethesda, Md. Screen, stage, radio, television actress and opera performer. Divorced from actor Alan Curtis (dec. 1953), Nicholas Szarozd, and Charles Walker. Married to Air Force General Donald Dawson.

Appeared in: **1937** Rosalie. **1939** Balalaika; Honeymoon in Bali. **1941** International Lady; New Wine. **1942** Invisible Agent. **1943** Frankenstein Meets the Wolf Man. **1945** Tokyo Rose. **1946** The Gentleman Misbehaves; Holiday in Mexico. **1947** Northwest Outpost. **1948** The Plunderers. **1949** Love Happy. **1957** Sabu and the Magic Ring. **1958** Jet Over the Atlantic (US 1960).

MASSINE, LEONIDE (Leonid Fedorovitch Myassin)
Born: Aug. 9, 1896, Moscow, Russia. Died: Mar. 16, 1979, Cologne, West Germany. Screen actor, ballet dancer and choreographer. Divorced from dancers Vera Savina, Eugenia Delarova, and Tatiana Orlov. Father of dancers Leonide, Jr. and Tatiana Massine.

Appeared in: **1929** Versailles. **1948** The Red Shoes. **1951** Tales of Hoffmann. **1954** Carosello Napoletano (Neopolitan Carousel—US 1961).

MASSINGHAM, RICHARD
Born: 1898, England. Died: 1953. Screen actor, film director, producer, screenwriter and physician. He produced, directed, wrote and acted in numerous short subjects 1935-1953.

MASSON, TOM (Thomas L. Masson)
Born: July 21, 1866, Essex, Conn. Died: June 18, 1934, Glen Ridge, N.J. Humorist, magazine editor and screen actor.

Appeared in: **1913** Saved by Parcel Post.

MASTERS, DARYL
Born: 1913. Died: May 24, 1961, Toronto, Canada. Screen and television actor.

Appeared in: **1958** Wolf Dog; Flaming Frontier; 1 + 1 (Exploring the Kinsey Reports).

MASTERS, HARRY
Born: 1885. Died: May 12, 1974, Los Angeles, Calif. Screen and vaudeville actor.

Appeared in: **1930** The Beauties (short).

MASTERS, RUTH
Born: 1899. Died: Sept. 22, 1969, Stamford, Conn. Screen, stage and television actress.

Appeared in: **1961** Bridge to the Sun.

MASTERSON, BAT (William Barclay Masterson)
Born: Nov. 24, 1853, Iroquois County, Ill. Died: Oct. 25, 1921, New York, N.Y. (heart attack). Frontier peace officer, newspaperman and screen actor. Appeared in early film clips.

MASTREN, CARMEN (Carmen Mastandrea)
Born: 1913. Died: Mar. 31, 1981, Valley Stream, N.Y. Jazz guitarist and screen actor.

MATA, MIGUEL P.
Born: 1914, Spain. Died: Feb., 1956, Madrid, Spain (auto accident). Screen, stage and radio actor.

MATEOS, HECTOR
Born: 1901, Mexico. Died: Feb. 13, 1957, Mexico City, Mexico. Screen actor.

MATHER, AUBREY
Born: Dec. 17, 1885, Minchinhampton, England. Died: Jan. 16, 1958, London, England. Screen, stage, radio and television actor.

Appeared in: **1930** Young Woodley. **1932** The Impassive Footman (aka Woman in Bondage—US); Love on the Spot; Aren't We All?; Tell Me Tonight (aka Be Mine Tonight—US 1933). **1934** Red Wagon (US 1935); The Admiral's Secret; The Man Who Changed His Name; The Lash; Anything Might Happen. **1935** The Silent Passenger. **1936** Ball at Savoy; When Knights Were Bold (US 1942); As You Like It; Chick; The Man in the Mirror (US 1937); Sabotage (aka The Woman Alone—US 1937). **1937** Underneath the Arches; Night Must Fall; Life Begins with Love. **1939** Jamaica Inn; Just William. **1940** No, No, Nanette. **1941** Rage in Heaven. **1942** The Wife Takes a Flyer; Mrs. Miniver; Careful, Soft Shoulders; The Undying Monster; The Great Impersonation; Random Harvest; Ball of Fire. **1943** Hello, Frisco,

Hello; Forever and a Day; Heaven Can Wait. **1944** Jane Eyre; The Lodger; The Song of Bernadette. **1945** Wilson; National Velvet; Keys of the Kingdom; The House of Fear. **1947** The Mighty McGurk; Temptation; It Happened in Brooklyn; For the Love of Rusty; The Hucksters. **1948** Julia Misbehaves. **1949** That Forsyte Woman; Adventures of Don Juan; Everybody Does It; The Secret Garden; Secret of St. Ives. **1950** Joan of Arc. **1952** The Importance of Being Earnest; South of Algiers (aka The Golden Mask—US 1954). **1954** To Dorothy a Son (aka Cash on Delivery—US 1956); Fast and Loose.

MATHER, JACK
Born: 1908. Died: Aug. 15, 1966, Wauconda, Ill. (heart attack). Screen, radio and television actor.

Appeared in: **1952** Dream Boat. **1954** River of No Return; Broken Lance. **1955** How to Be Very, Very Popular; The View from Pompey's Head (aka Secret Interlude). **1956** The Man in the Gray Flannel Suit; The Revolt of Mamie Stover. **1957** My Man Godfrey. **1958** The Bravados. **1959** This Earth Is Mine.

MATHER, WALTER
Born: 1908. Died: Dec. 27, 1951, Los Angeles, Calif. Screen, radio and television actor.

MATHEWS, GEORGE H.
Born: 1877. Died: June 7, 1952, Woodland Hills, Calif. Screen and stage actor.

Appeared in: **1945** The Corn Is Green. **1953** Act of Love.

MATHEWSON, CHRISTY (Christopher Mathewson)
Born: Aug. 12, 1880, Factorville, Pa. Died: Oct. 7, 1925, Saranac Lake, N.Y. (tuberculosis). Professional baseball player and screen actor.

Appeared in: **1914** Love and Baseball.

MATHIESON, MUIR
Born: Jan. 24, 1911, Stirling, Scotland. Died: Aug. 2, 1975, Oxford, England. Screen actor, musical director and conductor.

Appeared in: **1936** Things to Come. **1941** Dangerous Moonlight (aka Suicide Squadron—US 1942). **1942** In Which We Serve. **1945** The Seventh Veil (US 1946); Brief Encounter (US 1946). **1951** The Magic Box (US 1952). **1952** Sound Barrier (aka Breaking the Sound Barrier—US). **1960** Swiss Family Robinson.

MATHISON, RICHARD R.
Born: 1920, Idaho. Died: Jan. 31, 1980, Los Angeles, Calif. (heart attack). Journalist, writer and screen actor.

Appeared in: **1974** The Godfather: Part Two.

MATHOT, LEON
Born: 1896, France. Died: Mar. 6, 1968, Paris, France. Screen actor and film director. Entered films in 1914.

Appeared in: **1928** A Daughter of Israel. **1929** Apassionata.

MATIESEN, OTTO
Born: Mar. 27, 1873, Copenhagen, Denmark. Died: Feb. 20, 1932, Safford, Ariz. Screen and stage actor.

Appeared in: **1922** Bells of San Juan; Money to Burn. **1923** Scaramouche; Alias the Night Wind; Boston Blackie; Vanity Fair; The Dangerous Maid. **1924** The Dawn of Tomorrow; Captain Blood; The Folly of Vanity; Revelation. **1925** The Happy Warrior; Morals for Men; Parisian Love; Sackcloth and Scarlet; The Salvation Hunters. **1926** Bride of the Storm; The Silver Treasure; Christine of the Big Tops; While London Sleeps; Whispering Wires; Yellow Fingers. **1927** The Beloved Rogue; The Road to Romance; Too Many Crooks; Surrender. **1928** The Lady of Victories (short); The Desert Bride; The Last Moment; The Woman from Moscow; The Scarlet Lady. **1929** Strange Cargo; Prisoners; General Crack; Behind Closed Doors; The Show of Shows; Golden Dawn; Last of the Lone Wolf; Conspiracy. **1931** Beau Ideal; Man of the Sky; Soldier's Plaything; The Maltese Falcon.

MATLOCK, JULIAN C. "MATTY"
Born: 1907, Kentucky. Died: June 14, 1978, Van Nuys, Calif. (arteriosclerosis). Screen, radio, television actor, jazz musician and composer.

Appeared in: **1955** Pete Kelly's Blues.

MATRAY, ERNST
Born: 1891, Budapest, Hungary. Died: Nov. 12, 1978, Los Angeles, Calif. (heart attack). Screen, stage actor, film director, film producer, screenwriter and choreographer. Divorced from actresses Greta Schroeder and Maria Solveg. Later married to Elizabeth McKinley.

Appeared in: **1912** Venezianische Nacht. **1913** Insel der Seligen (Elysian Island). **1915** Die Erbtante; Lumpehens Glueck (The Luck of the Vagabond); Zucker und Zimt (Sugar and Spice). **1916** Schloss Plantomas; The Phantom of the Opera.

MATSON, THOMAS
Born: 1888. Died: Feb. 2, 1978, Woodland Hills, Calif. Screen actor and studio security guard.

MATSUI, SUISEI
Born: 1900, Japan. Died: Aug. 1, 1973, Kamakura City, Japan (cancer). Screen, radio and vaudeville actor. Narrated films during the silents.

Appeared in: **1951** Tokyo File 212.

MATTERSTOCK, ALBERT
Born: 1912. Died: June 30, 1960, Hamburg, West Germany. Screen actor.

Appeared in: **1937** Stimme des Blutes (Blood Bond). **1939** Ziel den Wolken (Goal in the Clouds); Solo per Danne. **1940** Our Little Wife.

MATTESON, RUTH
Born: 1910. Died: Feb. 5, 1975, Westport, Conn. Screen, stage and radio actress. Divorced from actor and director Arthur Pierson (dec. 1975).

MATTHEWS, A. E. "MATTY" (Alfred Edward Matthews)
Born: Nov. 22, 1869, Bridlington, England. Died: July 25, 1960, Bushey Heath, England. Screen, stage and television actor.

Appeared in: **1914** A Highwayman's Honour. **1916** The Real Thing at Last; The Lifeguardsman; Wanted—a Widow. **1918** Once Upon a Time. **1919** The Lackey and the Lady; Castles of Dreams. **1935** The Iron Duke. **1936** Men Are Not Gods (US 1937). **1941** Quiet Wedding; Pimpernel Smith (aka Mister V—US 1942); Suprise Broadcast (short). **1942** The Great Mr. Handel (US 1943); Thunder Rock (US 1944). **1943** The Life and Death of Colonel Blimp (aka Colonel Blimp—US 1945); Escape to Danger; The Man in Grey (US 1945). **1944** The Way Ahead (US 1945); They Came to a City; Love Story (aka A Lady Surrenders—US 1947); Twilight Hour. **1945** Flight from Folly. **1946** Picadilly Incident. **1947** The Ghosts of Berkeley Square; Just William's Luck (US 1948). **1948** William Comes to Town; Britannia Mews (aka Forbidden Street—US 1949). **1949** The Chiltern Hundreds (stage and film versions—aka The Amazing Mr. Beecham—US); Landfall; Whiskey Galore (aka Tight Little Island—US and Mad Little Island). **1951** Mr. Drake's Duck; The Galloping Major; Laughter in Paradise; The Magic Box (US 1952). **1952** Castle in the Air; Something Money Can't Buy; Penny Princess (US 1953); Made in Heaven; Who Goes There! (aka The Passionate Sentry—US 1953). **1953** Skid Kids. **1954** The Million Pound Note (aka Man with a Million—US); The Weak and the Wicked; Happy Ever After (aka Tonight's the Night—US); Aunt Clara. **1955** Miss Tulip Stays the Night. **1956** Jumping for Joy; Loser Takes All (US 1957); Three Men in a Boat (aka Around the World in 80 Days. **1957** Doctor at Large; Carry on Admiral (aka The Ship Was Loaded—US 1959). **1960** Inn for Trouble.

MATTHEWS, BEATRICE
Born: 1890. Died: Nov. 10, 1942, Hollywood, Calif. Screen actress.

MATTHEWS, DOROTHY
Born: 1912, New York, N.Y. Died: May 18, 1977, Los Angeles, Calif. (stroke). Screen, stage actress, film and television producer. Married to playwright Donald Davis.

Appeared in: **1926** Love 'Em and Leave 'Em. **1928** A Girl in Every Port. **1930** Doorway to Hell; The Truth About Youth; Son of the Gods; The Widow from Chicago; The Way of All Men.

MATTHEWS, FORREST
Born: 1908. Died: Nov. 22, 1951, Dallas, Tex. (heart attack). Screen and television actor.

Appeared in: **1948** Docks of New Orleans; Triggerman; Joe Palooka in Winner Take All; Fighting Mustang; Sunset Carson Rides Again.

MATTHEWS, JESSIE
Born: Mar. 11, 1907, Soho, London, England. Died: Aug. 20, 1981, London, England (cancer). Screen, stage, vaudeville, radio, television actress and film director. Divorced from stage actor Henry Lytton, Jr.

(dec. 1965), actor Sonnie Hale (dec. 1959), and Lieutenant Brian Lewis.

Appeared in: **1923** The Beloved Vagabond (film debut). **1924** Straws in the Wind. **1931** Out of the Blue. **1932** There Goes the Bride; The Midshipmaid. **1933** The Man from Toronto; The Good Companions; Friday the Thirteenth (US 1934). **1934** Waltzes from Vienna (aka Strauss's Great Waltz—US 1935); Evergreen (US 1935). **1935** First a Girl. **1936** It's Love Again. **1937** Head Over Heels (aka Head Over Heels in Love—US); Gangway. **1938** Sailing Along; Climbing High (US 1939). **1943** Forever and a Day. **1944** Candles at Nine. **1947** Making the Grade (short). **1958** Tom Thumb. **1978** The Hound of the Baskervilles. **1980** Second Star on the Right.

MATTHEWS, JUNIUS
Born: 1892. Died: Jan. 18, 1978. Screen, stage, vaudeville and radio actor. Appeared in early Essanay and Famous Players films.

Appeared in: **1946** Black Angel. **1947** The Shocking Miss Pilgrim. **1948** Chicken Every Sunday. **1951** Half Angel. **1952** My Wife's Best Friend. **1955** Good Morning, Miss Dove. **1963** The Sword in the Stone (voice).

MATTHEWS, LESTER (aka LESTER MATHEWS)
Born: Dec. 3, 1900, Nottingham, England. Died: June 6, 1975. Screen, stage and television actor.

Appeared in: **1931** The Lame Duck; Creeping Shadows (aka The Limping Man—US 1932); The Man at Six (aka The Gables Mystery—US 1932); The Wickham Mystery; Gipsy Blood (aka Carmen—US 1932); The Old Man. **1932** Indiscretions of Eve; Fires of Fate (US 1933); Her Night Out. **1933** On Secret Service (aka Secret Agent—US 1935); The Stolen Necklace; Out of the Past; Called Back; She Was Only a Village Maiden; The Melody Maker; Facing the Music (US 1934); The Song You Gave Me (US 1934); House of Dreams. **1934** Borrowed Clothes; Boomerang; Song at Eventide; Blossom Time (aka April Romance—US 1937); Irish Hearts (aka Norah O'Neale—US); The Poisoned Diamond. **1935** The Werewolf of London; The Raven. **1936** Thank You, Jeeves; Professional Soldier; Song and Dance Man; Spy 77; Too Many Parents; Lloyd's of London; 15 Maiden Lane; Crack Up; Tugboat Princess. **1937** Prince and the Pauper; Lancer Spy. **1938** There's Always a Woman; The Adventures of Robin Hood; Three Loves Has Nancy; Mysterious Mr. Moto; I Am a Criminal; If I Were King; Time Out for Murder; Think It Over (short). **1939** The Three Musketeers; Susannah of the Mounties; Should a Girl Marry; Conspiracy; Rulers of the Sea; Everything Happens at Night. **1940** The Sea Hawk; Northwest Passage; British Intelligence; The Biscuit Eater; Women in War; Sing, Dance, Plenty Hot. **1941** The Lone Wolf Keeps a Date; Man Hunt; A Yank in the RAF. **1942** The Pied Piper; Desperate Journey; Across the Pacific; London Blackout Murders; Son of Fury; Manila Calling. **1943** Corvette K-225; Northern Pursuit; Mysterious Doctor; Tonight We Raid Calais. **1944** Nine Girls; The Invisible Man's Revenge; Gaslight; Wing and a Prayer; Four Jills in a Jeep; Between Two Worlds; The Story of Dr. Wassell; Ministry of Fear; Shadows in the Night. **1945** Objective, Burma!; I Love a Mystery; The Beautiful Cheat; Salty O'Rourke; Two O'Clock Courage. **1947** Dark Delusion; Bulldog Drummond at Bay; The Exile. **1948** Fighting Father Dunne. **1949** Free for All. **1950** Tyrant of the Sea; Montana; Rogues of Sherwood Forest; Her Wonderful Life. **1951** The Son of Dr. Jekyll; Lorna Doone; Corky of Gasoline Alley; Tales of Robin Hood; The Desert Fox. **1952** Against All Flags; Five Fingers; Lady in the Iron Mask; Les Miserables; Operation Secret; Stars and Stripes Forever; Jungle Jim and the Forbidden Land; Brigand; Captain Pirate. **1953** Niagara; Trouble Along the Way; Young Bess; Fort Ti; Bad for Each Other; Savage Mutiny; Jamaica Run; Sangaree. **1954** Charge of the Lancers; King Richard and the Crusaders; Desiree; Jungle Man-Eaters. **1955** The Seven Little Foys; Moonfleet; The Far Horizons; Ten Wanted Men. **1956** Flame of the Island. **1959** The Miracle. **1960** Song Without End. **1964** Mary Poppins. **1966** Assault on a Queen. **1968** Star!

MATTHISON, EDITH WYNNE
Born: Nov. 23, 1875, England. Died: Sept. 23, 1955, Los Angeles, Calif. Stage and screen actress. Married to actor Charles Rann Kennedy (dec. 1950). Entered films with Lasky Co. in 1915.

Appeared in: **1915** The Governor's Lady.

MATTIMORE, VAN See ARLEN, RICHARD

MATTIOLI, RAF
Born: 1936, Naples, Italy. Died: Oct. 12, 1960, Rome, Italy (heart attack). Screen actor.

Appeared in: **1958** Guendalina. **1959** Estate Violenta (Violent Summer); Vacanzie a Izchia (Holiday Island). **1960** Where the Hot Wind Blows (aka La Legge—The Law). **1961** Le Baccanti (US 1963); Other Italian films: First Love; Young Husbands; Tunisi Top Secret.

MATTO, SESTO (Sisto Mata)
Born: Aug. 6, 1894, Durango, Mexico. Died: Feb. 20, 1934, Los Angeles, Calif. (auto accident). Screen actor.

MATTOX, MARTHA
Born: 1879, Natchez, Miss. Died: May 2, 1933, Sidney, N.Y. (heart ailment). Screen and stage actress. Entered films in 1913.

Appeared in: **1920** Huckleberry Finn. **1921** The Conflict; The Son of Wallingford. **1922** Restless Souls; Rich Men's Wives; The Top O' the Morning; Beauty's Worth; The Angel of Crooked Street; The Game Chicken; The Hands of Nara; The Married Flapper. **1923** The Hero; Three Wise Fools; Bavu; Hearts Aflame; Look Your Best; Penrod and Sam; Maytime; Times Have Changed; Woman-Proof. **1924** The Family Secret. **1925** Dangerous Innocence; East Lynne; Heir-Loons; I'll Show You the Town; The Keeper of the Bees; The Home Maker; Oh, Doctor!; The Man in Blue; With This Ring. **1926** Lonely Mary; Torrent; Infatuation; Christine of the Big Tops; Forest Havoc; The Nut-Cracker; The Rainmaker; Shameful Behavior?; The Waning Sex; The Warning Signal; The Yankee Senor. **1927** The Cat and the Canary; The Devil Dancer; Finger Prints; Snowbound; The 13th Juror. **1928** Love Me and the World Is Mine; Her Wild Oat; A Bit of Heaven; Fools for Luck; The Little Shepherd of Kingdom Come; The Naughty Duchess; The Singapore Mutiny; Kentucky Courage. **1929** The Big Diamond Robbery; Montmartre Rose. **1930** Night Work; Extravagance; The Love Racket. **1931** Misbehaving Ladies; Born to Love; Dangerous Affair; Thirty Days; Murder by the Clock. **1932** Murder at Dawn; The Silver Lining; The Monster Walks; Careless Lady; So Big; No Greater Love; Heroes of the West (serial); Dynamite Ranch; Torchy Raises the Auntie (short). **1933** Haunted Gold; Bitter Tea of General Yen.

MATTRAW, SCOTT
Born: Oct. 19, 1885, Evans Mills, N.Y. Died: Nov. 9, 1946, Hollywood, Calif. Screen, stage and minstrel actor.

Appeared in: **1924** The Thief of Bagdad (film debut). **1927** The Return of the Riddle Rider (serial); One Glorious Scrap. **1928** Haunted Island (serial); A Made-to-Order Hero; Quick Triggers; Two Lovers. **1929** Captain Cowboy. **1934** Babes in Toyland. **1935** Okay Toots! (short). **1938** In Old Chicago. **1950** Revenge Is Sweet (reissue of 1934 version of Babes in Toyland).

MATURIN, ERIC
Born: May 30, 1883, India. Died: Oct. 17, 1957, England? Screen and stage actor.

Appeared in: **1935** Sanders of the River. **1943** The Life and Death of Colonel Blimp (aka Colonel Blimp—US 1945). **1950** Last Holiday.

MATZENAUER, MARGUERITE
Born: June 1, 1881, Temesvar, Hungary. Died: Mar. 19, 1963, Van Nuys, Calif. Opera singer and screen actress.

Appeared in: **1936** Mr. Deeds Goes to Town.

MAUDE, CHARLES RAYMOND
Born: 1882, England. Died: Nov. 14, 1943, England? Screen, stage actor, composer and author. Married to actress Nancy Price (dec. 1970). Father of actresses Elizabeth and Joan Maude.

Appeared in: **1913** House of Temperley.

MAUDE, CYRIL
Born: Apr. 24, 1862, London, England. Died: Feb. 20, 1951, Torquay, England. Screen and stage actor. Married to actress Winifred Emery (dec. 1924) and later married to Mrs. P. H. Trew. Father of actress Margery Maude (dec. 1979).

Appeared in: **1914** Beauty and the Barge. **1915** Peer Gynt. **1921** The Headmaster. **1930** Grumpy (stage and film versions). **1931** These Charming People. **1933** Counsel's Opinon; Orders Is Orders (US 1934). **1935** Heat Wave. **1947** While the Sun Shines (US 1950).

MAUDE, MARGERY
Born: 1889, England. Died: Aug. 7, 1979, Cleveland, Ohio. Screen and stage actress. Daughter of actor Cyril Maude (dec. 1951).

Appeared in: **1955** You're Never Too Young. **1956** The Birds and the Bees.

MAUGHAM, W. SOMERSET (William Somerset Maugham)
Born: Jan. 25, 1874, Paris, France. Died: Dec. 16, 1965, Nice, France. Playwright, author, screenwriter and screen actor.

Appeared in: **1950** Trio.

MAUPAIN, ERNEST
Born: 1881, Paris, France. Died: 1949, France. Screen and stage actor.

Appeared in: **1915** Graustark. **1930** Le Miracle des Loups.

MAURICE
Died: May 18, 1927, Lausanne, Switzerland (consumption). Screen, stage, vaudeville actor and ballroom dancer. Appeared in vaudeville as part of dance team "Valentino, Muris and Maurice," with Rudolph Valentino.

Appeared in: **1916** The Quest of Life.

MAURICE, BOBBY
Born: 1906. Died: Oct. 17, 1981, New York, N.Y. (heart attack). Screen, stage actor, radio producer, television producer and broadcaster.

Appeared in: **1936** Modern Times.

MAURICE, MARY "MOTHER" (Mary Birch)
Born: Nov. 15, 1844, Morristown, Ohio. Died: Apr. 30, 1918, Pa. Screen and stage actress. Entered films with Vitagraph in 1910.

Appeared in: **1911** One Touch of Nature; My Old Dutch; Wisteria. **1912** The Seventh Son; Saving an Audience; The Firing of the Patchwork Quilt; Her Choice; Her Boy; The Diamond Brooch; His Mother's Shroud; Mrs. Lirriper's Lodgers; Their Golden Anniversary; The Picture Idol; Martha's Rebellion; The Church Across the Way; Her Grandchild; Aunty's Romance; Captain Barnacle, Reformer; The Crossroads. **1913** The Carpenter; Her Sweetest Memory; The Only Way; The Wings of a Moth; In the Shadow; Troublesome Daughters; O'Hara Helps Cupid; The Locket; Luella's Love Story; O'Hara and the Youthful Prodigal; One Can't Always Tell; An Unwritten Chapter; O'Hara as Guardian Angel. **1914** The Portrait; The Memories That Haunt. **1915** The Sins of the Mothers; The Goddess (serial); The Battle Cry of Peace; Twice Rescued; A Keyboard Strategy; The Scar; The Return of Maurice Donnelly; The Barrier of Faith; The Man Who Couldn't Beat God; The Gods Redeem; The Lesson of the Narrow Street; On With the Dance; Rags and the Girl; Sam's Sweetheart; Is Christmas a Bore?; Dorothy. **1916** The Chattel; Rose of the South; The Man He Used to Be; The Supreme Temptation; Carew and Son; Phantom Fortunes; The Dollar and the Law; The Redemption of Dave Darcey; The Price of Fame; Whom the Gods Destroy. **1917** For France; I Will Repay (aka The Courage of Fidelity); Who Goes There?; Her Secret; Transgression. **1918** Over the Top; The Little Runaway.

MAURICE, NEWMAN
Born: England. Died: Sept. 11, 1920, England? Screen, stage actor and author.

Appeared in: **1916** The Female Swindler.

MAURUS, GERDA
Born: 1909, Germany. Died: Aug. 25, 1968, Dusseldorf, Germany. Screen and stage actress.

Appeared in: **1928** Spione (The Spy). **1929** Die Frau im Mond (The Girl in the Moon, aka The Woman on the Moon); Hochverrat (High Treason). **1930** Seitenspruenge; Der Schuss im Tonfilmatelier. **1931** Taeter Gesucht; Hilfe! Ueberfall!; Schachmatt; Die Fremde; Der Draufgaenger; By Rocket to the Moon. **1932** Der Weisse Daemon (The White Demon, aka Rauschgift); Tod Ueber Shanghai (US 1933). **1933** Unsichtbare Gegner. **1934** Der Doppelgaenger; Grenzfeuer; Ein Maedchen mit Prokura. **1935** Der Kosak und die Nachtigall. **1936** Der Dschungel Ruft; Arzt aus Leidenschaft. **1937** Daphne und der Diplomat. **1938** Prinzessin Sissy (US 1939). **1940** Die Gute Sieben. **1949** Schicksal aus Zweiter Hand; Die Freunde Meiner Frau. **1954** Die Kleine Stadt will Schlafen Gehen.

MAWDESLEY, ROBERT
Born: 1900, England. Died: Sept. 30, 1953, London, England. Screen, stage and radio actor.

Appeared in: **1933** Loyalties (US 1934).

MAWSON, EDWARD
Born: 1861. Died: May 20, 1917, New York, N.Y. Screen and stage actor.

Appeared in: **1916** Return of Eve.

MAX, EDWIN "ED"
Born: May 4, 1909, Ga. Died: Oct. 17, 1980, Los Angeles, Calif. Screen actor.

Appeared in: **1946** Strange Holiday; Stairway to Heaven. **1949** Everybody Does It; Come to the Stable; Ride, Ryder, Ride; The Set-Up; Follow Me Quietly; Thieve's Highway; Law of the Barbary Coast; Side Street; Abandoned. **1950** Love That Brute; Mister 880. **1951** Francis Goes to the Races; Half Angel; Meet Me After the Show; The Well. **1952** Here Come the Nelsons; Models, Inc.; Tropical Heat Wave; Bloodhounds of Broadway; Jumping Jacks. **1953** The Twonky.

MAX, JEAN
Born: 1897, France. Died: Jan., 1971, France. Screen and stage actor.

Appeared in: **1932** Paris Beguin. **1936** Pension Mimosas. **1938** Dark Eyes. **1939** That They May Live.

MAXAM, LOUELLA MODIE (aka LOUELLA MODIE)
Born: 1896. Died: Sept. 4, 1970, Burbank, Calif. Screen actress. Married to actor William Brunton (dec. 1965).

Appeared in: **1916** A Movie Star; An Oily Scoundrel; Bucking Society; His Bitter Pill; His Lying Heart; Ambrose's Rapid Rise.

MAXEY, PAUL
Born: 1908, Wheaton, Ill. Died: June 3, 1963, Pasadena, Calif. (heart attack). Screen, stage and television actor.

Appeared in: **1941** Father Steps Out; I'll Sell My Life; City Limits; Let's Go Collegiate. **1946** Social Terrors (short); Oil's Well That Ends Well (short); Till the Clouds Roll By; Below the Deadline; Personality Kid. **1947** Ride the Pink Horse; Borrowed Blonde (short); In Room 303 (short); Millie's Daughter. **1948** Contest Crazy (short); Winter Meeting; Brother Knows Best (short); The Noose Hangs High. **1949** Mississippi Rhythm; Bride for Sale; Sky Dragon; Fighting Fools; South of St. Louis; All the King's Men; Joe Palooka in the Big Fight. **1950** Father of the Bride; The Reformer and the Redhead; The Return of Jesse James. **1951** Casa Manana; Abbott and Costello Meet the Invisible Man; Too Many Wives (short); An American in Paris. **1952** The Narrow Margin; Kid Monk Baroni; Here Come the Marines; Singin' in the Rain; With a Song in My Heart; Stars and Stripes Forever; Dream Boat. **1953** So You Want to Be a Musician (short); The Stranger Wore a Gun; The Story of Three Loves. **1954** Black Tuesday. **1955** City of Shadows.

MAXIM, HUDSON
Born: Feb. 3, 1853, Orneville, Maine. Died: May 6, 1927, Hopatocong, N.J. Screen actor, screenwriter and author.

Appeared in: **1915** The Battle Cry of Peace. **1921** Love's Redemption.

MAXTED, STANLEY
Born: 1900, England. Died: May 10, 1963, London, England. Screen, stage, television and radio actor.

Appeared in: **1953** Never Let Me Go; The Final Test (US 1954). **1955** I Am a Camera. **1956** The Weapon (US 1957). **1957** Campbell's Kingdom (US 1958); Fiend Without a Face. **1958** Across the Bridge; The Strange Awakening (aka Female Friends—US 1960).

MAXWELL, EDWIN
Born: 1886, Dublin, Ireland. Died: Aug. 12, 1948, Falmouth, Mass. (cerebral hemorrhage). Screen, stage actor, stage director and associate film director.

Appeared in: **1929** The Taming of the Shrew. **1930** All Quiet on the Western Front; Top Speed; Du Barry, Woman of Passion. **1931** Kiki; Inspiration; Daybreak; The Gorilla; Daddy Long Legs; Men of the Sky; Yellow Ticket; Ambassador Bill. **1932** Two Kinds of Women; Shopworn; Scarface; American Madness; Those We Love; Six Hours to Live; You Said a Mouthful; The Girl from Calgary; Grand Hotel; The Cohens and the Kellys in Hollywood; Blessed Event. **1933** The Mystery of the Wax Museum; Tonight Is Ours; State Trooper; Fog; The Mayor of Hell; Heroes for Sale; Dinner at Eight; Gambling Ship; Duck Soup; Emergency Call; The Woman I Stole; Night of Terror; Police Car 17; Big Time or Bust. **1934** The Dancing Man; Cleopatra; Gift of Gab; Happiness C.O.D.; Miss Fane's Baby Is Stolen; The Ninth Guest; Mystery Liner; Burn 'Em Up Barnes (feature and serial); The Cat's Paw. **1935** Public Ghost No. 1 (short); Men of Action; The Devil Is a Woman; All the King's Horses; Great God Gold; Motive for Revenge; The Crusades; Thanks a Million; G-Men. **1936** The Plainsman; Dangerous Waters; Big Brown Eyes; Panic on the Air; Fury; Come and Get It. **1937** Love is News; Night Key; The Road Back; Slave Ship; Love Takes Flight; A Man Betrayed. **1938** Romance on the Run. **1939** Young Mr. Lincoln; Drums Along the Mohawk; Way Down South; Ninotchka. **1940** The Shop Around the Corner; Pound Foolish (short); The Blue Bird; New Moon; His Girl Friday; Know Your Money (short); Kit Carson; Brigham Young—Frontiersman. **1941** The Devil and Miss Jones; Ride On, Vaquero!; Midnight Angel. **1942** I Live on Danger; Ten Gentlemen from West Point. **1943** Holy Matrimony; Behind Prison Walls; Mr. Big; The Great Moment; Since You Went Away; Waterfront; Wilson. **1945** Mama Loves Papa. **1946** Swamp Fire; The Jolson Story. **1947** Second Chance; The Gangster. **1948** The Vicious Circle. **1949** Ride, Ryder, Ride!; The Set Up; Follow Me Quietly; Thieves' Highway; Law of the Barbary Coast; Side Street.

MAXWELL, ELSA
Born: May 24, 1883, Keokuk, Iowa. Died: Nov. 1, 1963, New York, N.Y. Columnist, songwriter, professional party giver and screen actress.

Appeared in: **1939** Hotel for Women. **1940** Public Deb. No. 1. **1943** Stagedoor Canteen.

MAXWELL, JANE
Born: 1851. Died: Aug., 1924, Wilmington, Calif. Screen actress.

MAXWELL, JENNY
Born: 1942. Died: June 10, 1981, Los Angeles, Calif. (shot—robbery attempt). Screen actress.

Appeared in: **1959** Blue Denim. **1961** Blue Hawaii. **1963** Take Her, She's Mine; The Shotgun Wedding.

MAXWELL, MARILYN (Marvel Marilyn Maxwell)
Born: Aug. 3, 1922, Clarinda, Iowa. Died: Mar. 20, 1972, Beverly Hilly, Calif. (high blood pressure and a pulmonary ailment). Screen, radio, television actress and singer. Divorced from actor John Conte, restauranteur Andy McIntyre and producer Andy Davis.

Appeared in: **1942** Cargo of Innocents (film debut); Stand By For Action. **1943** Swing Fever; Thousands Cheer; Presenting Lily Mars; DuBarry Was a Lady; Dr. Gillespie's Criminal Case; Salute to the Marines; Right About Face; Crazy to Kill; Pilot No. 5; Best Foot Forward. **1944** Lost in a Harem; Ziegfeld Follies; Music for Millions; Three Men in White; Between Two Women. **1946** The Show-Off. **1947** High Barbaree. **1948** Summer Holiday; Race Street. **1949** The Champion. **1950** Key to the City; Outside the Wall. **1951** The Lemon Drop Kid; New Mexico. **1953** Off Limits; East of Sumatra; Paris Model. **1955** New York Confidential. **1956** Forever Darling. **1958** Rock-A-Bye Baby. **1963** Critic's Choice. **1964** The Lively Set; Stage to Thunder Rock. **1968** Arizona Bushwhackers. **1969** From Nashville with Music. **1970** The Phynx.

MAXWELL-WILLSHIRE, GERARD
Born: 1893, England. Died: Apr. 3, 1947, London, England. Screen actor.

MAY, ADA (aka ADA MAY WEEKS)
Born: Mar. 8, 1898. Died: Apr. 25, 1978, New York, N.Y. Screen, stage, vaudeville and television actress. Sister of actress Marion Weeks (dec. 1968).

Appeared in: **1933** Dance, Girl, Dance.

MAY, ALYCE
Born: c. 1915, Los Angeles, Calif. Died: Dec. 31, 1980, Rosa Rito Beach, Baja, Mexico (heart attack). Screen and television actress. Entered films as a child actress.

Appeared in: **1921** The Passion Flower. **1922** The Curse of Drink; Missing Millions; My Friend, the Devil; A Wide Open Town. **1923** The Ragged Edge. **1924** The Fifth Horseman. **1925** The Phantom of the Opera. **1927** Twinkle Toes. **1938** Rich Man, Poor Girl.

MAY, EDNA
Born: Sept. 2, 1878, Syracuse, N.Y. Died: Jan. 1, 1948, Lausanne, Switzerland (heart attack). Stage and screen actress.

Appeared in: **1913** David Copperfield. **1916** Salvation Joan.

MAY, HAROLD R.
Born: 1903. Died: Sept. 16, 1973, Hollywood, Calif. Screen actor. Appeared in Mack Sennett comedies.

MAY, JAMES
Born: 1857, England. Died: Aug. 25, 1941, Los Angeles, Calif. Screen actor and double for W. C. Fields.

MAY, MARTY
Born: 1898, New York, N.Y. Died: Nov. 11, 1975, Las Vegas, Nev. (heart ailment). Stage, vaudeville, radio, television and screen actor. Appeared in vaudeville with Olsen and Johnson. Married to vaudeville actress June Johnson.

Appeared in: **1943** Salute for Three.

MAY, MIA
Born: 1884, Germany. Died: Nov. 28, 1980, Los Angeles, Calif. Screen actress. Mother of stage actress Eva May (dec.).

Appeared in: **1922** The Wife Trap; The Greatest Truth; The Dragon's Claw; The Mistress of the World. **1938** The Indian Tomb.

MAY, SAMUEL RODERICK
Born: 1910, Lamont, Iowa. Died: Aug. 9, 1963, Lebanon, Mo. Screen, stage and radio actor.

MAYALL, HERSHELL
Born: 1863. Died: June 10, 1941, Detroit, Mich. (cerebral hemorrhage). Screen, stage and radio actor.

Appeared in: **1917** Cleopatra. **1919** The Money Corporal. **1920** Daredevil Jack (serial). **1921** The Beautiful Gambler; The Blushing Bride; Three Word Brand; To a Finish; The Queen of Sheba; Straight from the Shoulder. **1922** Arabian Love; The Yellow Stain; Thirty Days; Smiles Are Trumps; Extra! Extra!; Calvert's Valley; Oathbound. **1923** The Isle of Lost Ships; Itching Palms; Money! Money! Money!; Wild Bill Hickok. **1924** Alimony. **1925** After Marriage. **1929** Great Power. **1930** Fast and Loose; The Royal Family of Broadway. **1931** His Women; plus the following shorts: The Antique Shop; Second Childhood; Revenge Is Sweet. **1934** War Is a Racket. **1936** The Adventures of Frank Merriwell (serial).

MAYDOCH, JOHN
Born: 1894, Jan., 1918. Died: New York, N.Y. Screen and stage actor.

MAYE, JIMSY
Born: 1893, Spokane, Wash. Died: Apr. 10, 1968, Jackson, Ore. Screen actress. Divorced from director Reeves Eason (dec. 1956). Married to Clarence Rowley.

Appeared in: **1915** Damaged Goods.

MAYER, LOUIS B.
Born: July 4, 1885, Europe. Died: Oct. 29, 1957, Los Angeles, Calif. (leukemia). Screen actor and founder of MGM.

Appeared in: **1931** Jackie Cooper's Christmas Party (short).

MAYER, PAUL M.
Born: 1914. Died: June, 1968, Tucson, Ariz. (traffic accident). Screen and television actor and commentator.

MAYER, RAY
Born: 1901. Died: Nov. 22, 1948, Salt Lake City, Utah (heart attack). Screen, stage, vaudeville actor, screenwriter and musician. Married to vaudeville actress Edith Evans (do not confuse with British actress Edith Evans, dec. 1976).

Appeared in: **1934** Call It Luck; Young and Beautiful; Jealousy. **1935** The Arizonian; Village Tale; His Family Tree; Powersmoke Range; To Beat the Band; Seven Keys to Baldpate. **1936** The Farmer in the Dell; Follow the Fleet; I Married a Doctor; Special Investigator; The Last Outlaw; We Who Are About to Die; M'Liss. **1937** Racing Lady; Top of the Town; Make Way for Tomorrow; Meet the Missus; Hideaway; Swing It—Sailor. **1938** Prison Nurse; Comet Over Broadway; Garden of the Moon. **1939** King of Chinatown. **1944** Sweet and Lowdown. **1946** Snafu; High Wall. **1949** Mr. Soft Touch.

MAYFIELD, CLEO
Born: 1897. Died: Nov. 8, 1954, New York, N.Y. Screen, stage and vaudeville actress.

Appeared in: **1930** MGM shorts.

MAYHEW, KATE
Born: Sept. 2, 1853. Died: June 16, 1944, New York, N.Y. Screen and stage actress.

Appeared in: **1916** Hazel Kirke. **1924** Tongues of Flame.

MAYNARD, CLAIRE (Marie McCarthy)
Born: 1912, Brooklyn, N.Y. Died: July 19, 1941, New York, N.Y. (suicide—gas). Stage and screen actress.

Appeared in: **1931** Over the Hill; Good Sport.

MAYNARD, HARRY
Born: 1898. Died: July 23, 1976, Saratoga, Calif. Screen actor and talent agent.

Appeared in: **1926** Speed Crazed.

MAYNARD, KEN
Born: July 21, 1895, Vevey, Ind. Died: Mar. 23, 1973, Woodland Hills, Calif. Screen actor, rodeo and circus performer. Brother of actor Kermit Maynard (dec. 1971).

Appeared in: **1923** The Man Who Won. **1924** Janice Meredith; $50,000 Reward. **1925** The Haunted Ranch; The Demon Rider; Fighting

Courage. **1926** North Star; Unknown Cavalier; Senor Daredevil. **1927** Overland Stage; Somewhere in Sonora; Land Beyond the Law; Devil's Saddle; The Red Raiders; Gun Gospel. **1928** The Canyon of Adventure; The Wagon Show; The Upland Rider; The Code of the Scarlet; The Glorious Trail. **1929** Senor Americano; The Phantom City; Cheyenne; The Lawless Legion; The California Mail; The Royal Rider; Wagon Master; The Voice of Hollywood (short). **1930** Parade of the West; The Fighting Legion; Lucky Larkin; Mountain Justice; Song of the Caballero; Sons of the Saddle; Fighting Thru (aka California in 1878). **1931** Two Gun Man; Alias—The Bad Man; Arizona Terror; Range Law; Branded Men; Pocatello Kid. **1932** Texas Gun-Fighter; Sunset Trail; Whistlin' Dan; Hell Fire Austin; Dynamite Ranch; Trail Blazers (serial). **1933** The Lone Avenger; Drum Taps; Phantom Thunderbolt; King of the Arena; Strawberry Roan; The Fiddlin' Buckaroo; Between Fighting Men; Tombstone Canyon; Come On Tarzan; Fargo Express. **1934** Gun Justice; Trail Drive; Wheels of Destiny; Smoking Guns; In Old Santa Fe; Mystery Mountain (serial); Honor of the Range; Doomed to Die. **1935** Western Frontier; Heir to Trouble; Lawless Riders; Northern Frontier. **1936** Heroes of the Range; Avenging Waters; The Cattle Thief; The Fugitive Sheriff. **1937** Boots of Destiny; Trailing Trouble. **1938** Whirlwind Horseman; Six Shootin' Trouble. **1943** Wild Horse Stampede; The Law Rides Again; Blazing Guns; Death Valley Rangers. **1944** Westward Bound; Arizona Whirlwind. **1945** Blazing Frontier. **1961** Frontier Uprising; Gun Fight; You Have to Run Fast. **1970** Bigfoot.

MAYNARD, KERMIT

Born: Sept. 20, 1902, Mission, Tex. or Vevey, Ind. Died: Jan. 16, 1971, Hollywood, Calif. (heart attack). Screen and circus actor. Once doubled for actors George O'Brien, Victor McLaglen, Warner Baxter and Edmund Lowe. Brother of actor Ken Maynard (dec. 1973) for whom he doubled in early films. Entered films in 1926 with F.B.O. Studio.

Appeared in: **1927** Gun-Hand Garrison; Prince of the Plains; Ridin' Luck; Wanderer of the West; Wild Born. **1928** The Drifting Kid. **1931** Lightning Warrior (serial); The Phantom of the West (serial). **1932** Dynamite Ranch. **1933** Drum Taps; Outlaw Justice. **1934** The Fighting Trooper; Sandy of the Mounted. **1935** Northern Frontier; Code of the Mounted; The Red Blood of Courage; Wilderness Mail; His Fighting Blood; Trails of the Wild. **1936** Timber War; Song of the Trail; Phantom Patrol; Wildcat Trooper; Wild Horse Roundup; Whistling Bullets. **1937** The Fighting Texan; Valley of Terror; Galloping Dynamite; Roaring Six-Guns. **1938** The Great Adventures of Wild Bill Hickok (serial); Western Jamboree; The Law West of Tombstone. **1939** Code of the Cactus; Chip of the Flying U; The Night Riders; Colorado Sunset. **1940** The Showdown; The Range Busters; Pony Post; Heroes of the Saddle; Riders of the Pasco Basin; West of Carson City; Ragtime Cowboy Joe; Northwest Mounted Police; Law and Order. **1941** Trail of the Silver Spurs; Wyoming Wildcat; Boss of Bullion City; Bury Me Not on the Lone Prairie; Badlands of Dakota; The Royal Mounted Patrol; Arizona Cyclone; A Missouri Outlaw; Fighting Bill Fargo; King of the Texas Rangers (serial); Billy the Kid; The Man from Montana; Sierra Sue; Stick to Your Guns; Blazing Frontier. **1942** Home in Wyomin'; Rock River Renegades; Stagecoach Buckaroo; Jesse James, Jr.; Down Rio Grande Way; Law and Order (and 1940 version); Riders of the West; The Omaha Trail; Prairie Pals; Along the Sundown Trail; The Lone Prairie; Riding Through Nevada; Sheriff of Sage Valley; Trail Riders; Arabian Nights; Perils of the Royal Mounted (serial). **1943** Two Fisted Justice; Santa Fe Scouts; Cheyenne Roundup; Death Rides the Plains; Western Cyclone; Border Buckaroo; The Stranger from Pecos; Silver Spurs; Raiders of Red Gap; The Texas Kid; The Blocked Trail; The Mysterious Rider; Fugitive of the Plains; Beyond the Last Frontier. **1944** The Drifter; Gunsmoke Mesa; Frontier Outlaws; Thundering Gunslingers; Brand of the Devil; Raiders of the Border. **1945** Marked for Murder; Gangster's Den; Flaming Bullets; Jungle Raiders (serial); They Were Expendable; Devil Riders; Enemy of the Law; Fighting Bill Carson; Gangsters; Stagecoach Outlaws; Wild Horse Phantom. **1946** Oath of Vengeance; Ambush Trail; Galloping Thunder; Prairie Badmen; Prairie Rustlers; Under Arizona Skies; Stars Over Texas; Terror on Horseback; Badman's Territory; Rustler's Roundup; Tumbleweed Trails; Duel in the Sun. **1947** The Law Comes to Gunsight; Along the Oregon Trail; Return of the Lash; Buckaroo from Powder River; Ridin' Down the Trail; Raiders of Red Rock; Frontier Fighters; Panhandle Trail. **1948** 'Neath Canadian Skies; Fury at Furnace Creek. **1949** Massacre River; Riders in the Sky; Range Land. **1950** Law of the Panhandle; Silver Raiders; The Savage Horde; Trail of Robin Hood; Short Grass. **1951** In Old Amarillo; Three Desperate Men (aka Three Outlaws); Fort Dodge Stampede; Golden Girl. **1952** The Black Lash. **1953** Pack Train. **1956** Flesh and the Spur. **1958** Once Upon a Horse. **1960** North to Alaska; Noose for a Gunman.

MAYNE, CLARICE

Born: 1890. Died: Jan. 17, 1966, London, England. Screen, stage and vaudeville actress. Divorced from actor James Tate. Married to actor Teddy Knox.

Appeared in: **1916** Nursie! Nursie!

MAYNE, ERIC

Born: 1866, Dublin, Ireland. Died: Feb. 10, 1947, Hollywood, Calif. Screen and stage actor.

Appeared in: **1921** Garments of Truth; Little Miss Hawkshaw; The Silver Car; The Conquering Power. **1922** Suzanne; Doctor Jack; My American Wife; Turn to the Right; Pawned; Shattered Dreams. **1923** The Last Hour; Prodigal Daughters; Refuge; A Prince of a King; Cameo Kirby; The Christian; Human Wreckage; Her Reputation; Drums of Jeopardy. **1924** Behind the Curtain; Black Oxen; His Forgotten Wife; The Goldfish; Gerald Cranston's Lady; Never Say Die; The Yankee Consul; The Extra Girl. **1926** The Black Bird; Money to Burn; Beyond the Trail; Hearts and Spangles; Midnight Limited; Transcontinental Limited; Barriers Burned Away. **1927** Married Alive; Driven from Home. **1928** The Canyon of Adventure; Hangman's House. **1931** The Easiest Way; East Lynne. **1932** Rackety Rax. **1933** Duck Soup. **1935** All the King's Horses. **1936** Ticket to Paradise; The Story of Louis Pasteur. **1938** There's That Woman Again. **1943** The Constant Nymph. **1946** Lady Luck; The Bamboo Blonde.

MAYO, ALBERT

Born: 1887. Died: May 20, 1933, Los Angeles, Calif. (heart attack). Stage and screen actor.

MAYO, ARCHIE

Born: 1898, New York, N.Y. Died: Dec. 4, 1968, Guadalajara, Mexico. Screen actor, film director and screenwriter. Entered films as an extra.

MAYO, EDNA

Born: 1893, Philadelphia, Pa. Died: May 5, 1970, San Francisco, Calif. Screen and stage actress.

Appeared in: **1914** The Key to Yesterday. **1915** Stars Their Courses Change; The Blindness of Virtue; Frauds; The Greater Courage; Means and Morals; The Little Deceiver; Vengeance; A Bit of Lace; The Edge of Things; The Woman Eater; The Little Straw Wife. **1916** The Misleading Lady; The Return of Eve; The Chaperone; The Strange Case of Mary Page (serial); The Prince of Graustork (aka Graustork).

MAYO, FRANK

Born: 1886, New York. Died: July 9, 1963, Laguna Beach, Calif. (heart attack). Screen, stage, vaudeville actor and film director. Married to actress Dagmar Godowsky (dec. 1975) annulled in 1928. Entered films with World Film Co. of New Jersey approx. 1913.

Appeared in: **1915** The Red Circle (serial). **1918** The Interloper. **1919** The Brute Breaker; Mary Regan. **1921** The Blazing Trail; Colorado; Honor Bound; Magnificent Brute; The Marriage Pit; Tiger True; Dr. Jim; Go Straight; The Fighting Lover; The Shark Master. **1922** Afraid to Fight; Across the Dead Line; Man Who Married His Own Wife; Out of the Silent North; Tracked to Earth; Wolf Law; The Flaming Hour; The Altar Stairs; Caught Bluffing. **1923** The Bolted Door; The First Degree; Souls for Sale; Six Days. **1924** Is Love Everything?; The Perfect Flapper; The Price She Paid; The Shadow of the East; The Plunderer; The Triflers; The Woman on Jury; Wild Oranges. **1925** If I Marry Again; Passionate Youth; Barriers Burned Away; The Necessary Evil; The Unknown Lover; Women and Gold. **1926** Lew Tyler's Wives; Then Came the Woman. **1930** Doughboys; Big Shot. **1931** Alias the Bad Man; Range Law; Chinatown after Dark. **1932** The Last Ride; Hell's Headquarters. **1934** The Mighty Barnum. **1935** One Hour Late. **1936** Hollywood Boulevard; Desert Gold; Burning Gold; Too Many Parents; Magnificent Obsession; The Story of Louis Pasteur. **1937** The Life of Emile Zola; The Perfect Specimen. **1939** The Oklahoma Kid; Confessions of a Nazi Spy; Nancy Drew and the Hidden Staircase. **1940** British Intelligence; Torrid Zone; Flowing Gold; The Fighting 69th; Santa Fe Trail. **1941** Knockout (aka Right at the Heart); The Strawberry Blonde; King's Row; The Bride Came C.O. D.; The Gorilla Man; She Couldn't Say No; The Wagons Roll at Night. **1942** Lady Gangster; The Male Animal; Yankee Doodle Dandy; Gentleman Jim. **1943** Murder on the Waterfront; Mysterious Doctor; Old Acquaintance. **1944** Adventures of Mark Twain; The Last Ride (and 1932 version). **1945** The Great Mystic. **1946** The Devil's Mask; The Strange Mr. Gregory. **1947** Her Husband's Affair; Buck Privates Come Home; Variety Girl. **1948** Easter Parade; The Emperor Waltz. **1949** Samson and Delilah.

MAYO, GEORGE

Born: 1891. Died: Dec. 21, 1950, Hollywood, Calif. (heart ailment). Screen, stage and vaudeville actor.

Appeared in: **1930** A Perfect Match (short). **1934** A Woman's Man.

MAYO, HARRY A. (Ray Sampson)

Born: Mar. 11, 1898, Helena, Mont. Died: Jan. 6, 1964, Woodland Hills, Calif. (heart illness). Screen actor.

Appeared in: **1912** A Juvenile Love Affair. **1915** The Birth of a Nation. **1916** His Lucky Day; Harold the Nurse Girl; A Lucky Tumble; Wrong Beds. **1956** Around the World in 80 Days.

MAYO, JOSEPH ANTHONY
Born: 1930. Died: Nov. 12, 1966, Hollywood, Calif. (heart attack). Stage and screen actor.

MAYO, MARGARET (Lillian Clatten)
Born: Nov. 19, 1882, Brownsville, Ill. Died: Feb. 25, 1951, Ossining, N.Y. Screen, stage actress, screenwriter, playwright and author. Divorced from actor/playwright Edgar Selwyn (dec. 1944).

Appeared in: **1915** The Arab.

MAYOR, AGUSTIN G.
Born: 1935. Died: Nov. 19, 1968, Woodside, N.Y. Screen, stage, television actor, dancer and at one time a matador in Spain.

Appeared in: **1962** Requiem for a Heavyweight. **1964** The Horror of Party Beach.

MAZZAROPI, AMACIO
Born: 1912, Brazil. Died: June 13, 1981, Sao Paulo, Brazil (cancer). Screen actor and film producer.

MEADE, BILL
Died: 1941 (fell from horse onto his sword during filming of They Died With Their Boots On). Screen actor.

MEADE, CLAIRE (Marguerite Fields)
Born: Apr. 2, 1883, N.J. Died: Jan. 14, 1968, Encino, Calif. (pneumonia). Screen actress.

Appeared in: **1945** Roughly Speaking. **1946** Daughter of Don Q (serial); Night and Day. **1947** The Unfaithful. **1949** Mother Is a Freshman; Miss Grant Takes Richmond; A Kiss in the Dark. **1950** Belle of Old Mexico. **1952** Ma and Pa Kettle at the Fair. **1953** Three Sisters and a Girl.

MEADER, GEORGE
Born: July 6, 1888, Minneapolis, Minn. Died: Dec., 1963. Screen actor. Entered films in 1940.

Appeared in: **1940** The Courageous Dr. Christian; Gambling on the High Seas. **1941** Life With Henry; Man-Mad Monster; Father Takes a Wife; The Smiling Ghost; The Monster and the Girl; Petticoat Politics; Dancing on a Dime; New York Town; Bachelor Daddy. **1942** The Glass Key. **1943** Madame Curie. **1945** Roughly Speaking; A Tree Grows in Brooklyn; Boston Blackie Booked on Suspicion; Spellbound. **1947** Crossfire; Life With Father; Smash-Up; The Story of a Woman; Betty Co-Ed; Too Many Winners; For the Love of Rusty; Keeper of the Bees. **1949** That Midnight Kiss; On the Town. **1950** Champagne for Caesar. **1951** The Groom Wore Spurs. **1952** She's Working Her Way Through College.

MEADER, WILLIAM "BILL"
Died: Apr. 15, 1979. Screen actor.

Appeared in: **1947** Wild Harvest. **1956** The Leather Saint. **1957** The Lonely Man.

MEAKIN, CHARLES
Born: 1880. Died: Jan. 17, 1961, Hollywood, Calif. Screen and stage actor. Married to actress Ruth Meakin (dec. 1939).

Appeared in: **1921** Maid of the West. **1922** Penrod. **1926** Lightning Bill; The Marriage Clause; Upstage. **1927** Ladies at Ease.

MEAKIN, RUTH (Ruth Eldredge)
Born: 1879. Died: Nov. 3, 1939, Los Angeles, Calif. Screen and stage actress. Married to actor Charles Meakin (dec. 1961).

MEARS, BENJAMIN S.
Born: 1872. Died: Jan. 27, 1952, Cliffside, N.J. Screen, stage and vaudeville actor.

MEARS, MARION
Born: 1899. Died: Jan. 26, 1970, Hollywood, Calif. Screen and stage actress. Stand-in for Margaret Lindsay, Hilary Brooks and Natalie Schaefer.

MEASOR, BERYL
Born: Apr. 22, 1908, Shanghai, China. Died: Feb. 8, 1965, England? Screen and stage actress. Married to actor Terence de Marney (dec. 1971). Entered films in 1938.

Appeared in: **1944** English Without Tears (aka Her Man Gilbey—US 1949). **1947** Odd Man Out.

MEDFORD, KAY (Ruth Fikus, Maggie O'Regan)
Born: Sept. 14, 1920, New York, N.Y. Died: Apr. 10, 1980, New York, N.Y. (cancer). Screen, stage and television actress. Nominated for 1968 Academy Award for Best Supporting Actress in Funny Girl.

Appeared in: **1942** The War Against Mrs. Hadley (film debut); Random Harvest. **1943** Swing Shift Maisie. **1944** Mrs. Parkington; Return From Nowhere (short). **1945** Adventure. **1949** The Undercover Man. **1950** Guilty Bystander. **1957** A Face in the Crowd; Jamboree. **1960** The Rat Race; Butterfield 8; Girl of the Night. **1962** Two Tickets to Paris. **1964** Ensign Pulver. **1966** A Fine Madness. **1967** The Busy Body. **1968** Angel in My Pocket; Funny Girl (stage and film versions). **1977** Fire Sale. **1980** Windows.

MEDLIN, VICTORIA
Died: Feb. 27, 1978. Screen and stage actress.

MEECH, EDWARD "MONTANA" (Edward Raymond Meech)
Died: Mar. 2, 1952, Findlay, Ohio. Screen, radio actor and circus performer. Appeared in silents riding horses and performed riding feats.

MEEHAN, DANNY (Daniel Joseph Meehan)
Born: 1931, White Plains, N.Y. Died: Mar. 29, 1978, New York, N.Y. (cancer). Screen, stage, television actor, singer and songwriter.

Appeared in: **1961** Blast of Silence. **1969** Don't Drink the Water.

MEEHAN, JOHN
Born: May 8, 1890, Lindsay, Ontario, Canada. Died: Nov. 12, 1954, Woodland Hills, Calif. Screen, stage actor, playwright, stage director, screenwriter and film director.

MEEHAN, LEW (aka LEW MEAHAN)
Born: 1891. Died: Aug. 10, 1951. Screen actor.

Appeared in: **1921** Crossing Trails. **1922** Blazing Arrows; Daring Danger. **1923** The Greatest Menace. **1924** Ace of the Law; Lightnin' Jack; Man From God's Country; Rainbow Rangers; Ridgeway of Montana; Thundering Romance; Travelin' Fast; Walloping Wallace. **1925** Kit Carson Over the Great Divide; Silent Sheldon; Thundering Through; White Thunder. **1926** Beyond All Odds; The Desert's Toll; The Desperate Game; Fighting Luck; Hair Trigger Baxter; Red Blood. **1927** Cactus Trails; The Code of the Range. **1928** King Cowboy; The Sky Rider. **1929** Gun Law; Idaho Red; The Pride of Pawnee; Silent Sentinel; The White Outlaw. **1930** Firebrand Jordan; Hunted Men; Pardon My Gun; South of Sonora; Those Who Dance; Trails of Peril. **1931** Pocatello Kid. **1934** The Lost Jungle (serial). **1935** The Unconquered Bandit. **1936** The Black Coin (serial); The Roarin' Guns. **1937** Melody of the Plains; Gun Lords of Stirrup Basin; The Red Robe; Arizona Gunfighter; Ridin' the Lone Trail. **1938** Thunder in the Desert.

MEEK, DONALD
Born: July 14, 1880, Glasgow, Scotland. Died: Nov. 18, 1946, Los Angeles, Calif. Screen and stage actor.

Appeared in: **1923** Six Cylinder Love. **1929** The Hole in the Wall. **1930** The Love Kiss. **1931** The Girl Habit; Personal Maid. **1932-33** "S.S. Van Dine" series. **1932** The Babbling Brook (short). **1933** Love, Honor and Oh, Baby!; College Coach. **1934** Hi, Nellie; Bedside; Mrs. Wiggs of the Cabbage Patch; Murder at the Vanities; The Merry Widow; The Last Gentleman; The Defense Rests; The Captain Hates the Sea; Romance in Manhattan. **1935** Biography of a Bachelor Girl; Peter Ibbetson; Happiness C.O.D.; The Whole Town's Talking; The Informer; Only Eight Hours; Village Tale; The Return of Peter Grimm; Old Man Rhythm; The Gilded Lily; Accent on Youth; The Bride Comes Home; Society Doctor; Mark of the Vampire; Baby Face Harrington; Kind Lady; Barbary Coast; She Couldn't Take It; Captain Blood; China Seas; Top Hat. **1936** Everybody's Old Man; And So They Were Married; Pennies From Heaven; One Rainy Afternoon; Three Wise Guys; Old Hutch; Love on the Run; Three Married Men; Two in a Crowd. **1937** Double Wedding; Maid of Salem; Artists and Models; Parnell; Three Legionnaires; Behind the Headlines; The Toast of New York; Make a Wish; Breakfast for Two; You're a Sweetheart. **1938** Double Danger; Having a Wonderful Time; The Adventures of Tom Sawyer; Goodbye Broadway; Little Miss Broadway; Hold That Co-ed; You Can't Take It With You. **1939** Hollywood Cavalcade; Jesse James; Young Mr. Lincoln; The Housekeeper's Daughter; Blondie Takes a Vacation; Nick Carter—Master Detective; Stagecoach. **1940** Hullabaloo; Oh Johnny, How You Can Love; Dr. Ehrlich's Magic Bullet; The Man from Dakota; Turnabout; Star Dust; Phantom Raiders; The Return of Frank James; Third Finger, Left Hand; Sky Murder; The Ghost Comes Home; My Little Chickadee. **1941** Blonde Inspiration; Come Live With Me; Rise and Shine; Babes on Broadway; A Woman's Face; Wild

Man of Borneo; Barnacle Bill; The Feminine Touch. 1942 Tortilla Flat; Maisie Gets Her Man; Seven Sweethearts; The Omaha Trail; Keeper of the Flame. 1943 Air Raid Wardens; They Got Me Covered; Du Barry Was a Lady; Lost Angel; The Honest Thief. 1944 Rationing; Two Girls and a Sailor; Bathing Beauty; Barbary Coast Gent; Maisie Goes to Reno; Thin Man Goes Home. 1945 Colonel Effingham's Raid; State Fair. 1946 Because of Him; Janie Gets Married; Affairs of Geraldine. 1947 The Hal Roach Comedy Carnival; The Fabulous Joe; Magic Town. 1974 That's Entertainment (film clips).

MEEK, KATE
Born: 1838. Died: Aug. 3, 1925, New York, N.Y. Screen and stage actress.

Appeared in: 1915 David Harum.

MEEKER, ALFRED
Born: 1901. Died: June 6, 1942, Los Angeles, Calif. (heart attack). Screen and stage actor.

MEGOWAN, DON (aka DAN MEGOWAN)
Born: 1922, Inglewood, Calif. Died: June 26, 1981, Panorama City, Calif. (throat cancer). Screen and television actor.

Appeared in: 1951 The Mob; Kid from Amarillo. 1954 Prince Valiant. 1955 To Catch a Thief; Davy Crockett, King of the Wild Frontier; A Lawless Street. 1956 Anything Goes; The Creature Walks Among Us; The Great Locomotive Chase; The Werewolf; Gun the Man Down. 1957 The Story of Mankind; The Delicate Delinquent; Hell Canyon Outlaws; Women, Money and Guns. 1958 Snowfire; The Man Who Died Twice. 1960 Lust to Kill. 1961 Il Terrore del Mare (Terror of the Sea, aka Guns of the Black Witch—US). 1962 The Creation of the Humanoids. 1963 For Love or Money. 1966 Tarzan and the Valley of Gold. 1968 The Devil's Brigade; If He Hollers, Let Him Go! 1974 Blazing Saddles; Truck Turner.

MEHAFFEY, BLANCHE
Born: July 28, 1907, Cincinnati, Ohio. Died: Mar. 31, 1968, Los Angeles, Calif. Screen and stage actress. Married to film producer Ralph M. Like. Was a Wampas Baby Star of 1924.

Appeared in: 1924 The Battling Orioles; The White Sheep. 1925 His People; Proud Heart; A Woman of the World. 1926 The Runaway Express; Take It From Me; The Texas Street. 1927 The Denver Dude; The Princess from Hoboken; The Silent Rider; The Tired Business Man. 1928 The Air Mail Pilot; Marlie the Killer; Finnegan's Ball; Silks and Saddles. 1929 Smilin' Guns. 1930 Medicine Man. 1931 Soul of the Slums; Sunrise Trail; Riders of the North; Dugan of the Bad Lands; Dancing Dynamite; The Sky Spider; Is There Justice?; Mounted Fury. 1932 Sally of the Subway; Alias Mary Smith; Dynamite Denny; Passport to Paradise. 1938 Held for Ransom.

MEHRMANN, HELEN ALICE
Died: Sept. 25, 1934, Oakland, Calif. Stage and screen actress.

Appeared in: 1929 The Shannons on Broadway.

MEIGHAM, MARGARET
Died: Sept. 29, 1961, Chatsworth, Calif. Screen actress. Entered films approx. 1930.

MEIGHAN, THOMAS
Born: Apr. 9, 1879, Pittsburgh, Pa. Died: July 8, 1936, Great Neck, N.Y. Screen and stage actor.

Appeared in: 1914 Dandy Donovan, The Gentleman Cracksman. 1915 The Secret Sin; Kindling; The Fighting Hope; Out of Darkness; Blackbirds; Armstrong's Wife; The Immigrant. 1916 Puddi'nhead Wilson; The Sowers; The Trail of the Lonesome Pine; The Clown; The Dupe; Common Ground; The Storm; The Heir to the Hoorah. 1917 The Land of Promise; The Mysterious Miss Terry; The Slave Market; Sapho; Sleeping Fires; The Silent Partner; Her Better Self; Arms and the Girl. 1918 M'Liss; Out of a Clear Sky; Heart of the Wilds; Her Moment; Madame Jealousy; Eve's Daughter; Missing; In Pursuit of Polly; The Forbidden City; The Heart of Wetona. 1919 The Miracle Man; The Probation Wife; Peg O' My Heart; The Thunderbolt; Male and Female (aka The Admirable Crichton). 1920 Conrad in Quest of His Youth; Why Change Your Wife?; Civilian Clothes; The Prince Chap. 1921 The Easy Road; City of Silent Men; The Frontier of the Stars; White and Unmarried; A Prince There Was; The Conquest of Canaan; Cappy Ricks. 1922 The Bachelor Daddy; Our Leading Citizen; Back Home and Broke; If You Believe It, It's So; The Man Who Saw Tomorrow; Manslaughter; Hollywood. 1923 The Ne'er-Do-Well; Homeward Bound; Woman Proof. 1924 Pied Piper Malone; Tongues of Flame; The Confidence Man; The Alaskan. 1925 Irish

Luck; The Man Who Found Himself; Old Home Week; Coming Through. 1926 Tin Gods; The New Klondike; The Canadian; Fascinating Youth. 1927 We're All Gamblers; The City Gone Wild; Blind Alleys. 1928 The Racket; The Mating Call. 1929 The Argyle Case. 1931 Young Sinners; Skyline. 1932 Madison Square Garden; Cheaters at Play. 1934 Peck's Bad Boy.

MEIKLEJOHN, CHARLOTTE
Born: Nov. 5, 1900. Died: Feb. 19, 1971. Screen actress.

MEINEL, ERNEST
Died: Feb. 22, 1977. Screen actor.

MEISTER, OTTO L.
Born: 1869. Died: July 10, 1944, Milwaukee, Wis. Screen, stage and medicine show actor.

Appeared in: 1914 Droppington's Family Tree.

MELACHRINO, GEORGE
Born: 1909. Died: June 18, 1965, London, England. Orchestra leader, screen and television actor.

MELCHIOR, LAURITZ
Born: Mar. 20, 1890, Copenhagen, Denmark. Died: Mar. 18, 1973, Santa Monica, Calif. (following gall bladder operation). Opera tenor, screen, stage, radio and television actor. Married to actress Maria Hacker (dec. 1963) and later married and divorced Mary Markham.

Appeared in: 1945 Thrill of a Romance. 1946 Two Sisters from Boston. 1947 This Time for Keeps. 1948 Luxury Liner. 1953 The Stars Are Singing.

MELESH, ALEX (Alexander Melesher)
Born: Oct. 21, 1890, Kiev, Russia. Died: Mar. 5, 1949, Hollywood, Calif. Screen and stage actor.

Appeared in: 1928 His Private Life; The Adventurer. 1929 Charming Sinners. 1932 The Big Broadcast. 1933 Girl Without a Room. 1938 Golden Boy; Artists and Models Abroad. 1939 Paris Honeymoon; On Your Toes. 1940 Beyond Tomorrow. 1942 Once Upon a Honeymoon. 1943 A Lady Takes a Chance. 1948 The Fuller Brush Man.

MELFORD, GEORGE
Born: Rochester, N.Y. Died: Apr. 25, 1961, Hollywood, Calif. (heart attack). Screen, stage actor and film director. Married to actress Diana Miller (dec. 1927) and later married to Louise Melford (dec. 1942).

Entered films as an actor with Kalem 1933 The Cowboy Counselor; Officer 13. 1939 Ambush; Rulers of the Sea. 1940 My Little Chickadee; Safari; Brigham Young—Frontiersman. 1941 Robbers of the Range; Flying Cadets. 1942 That Other Woman; Lone Star Ranger. 1943 Dixie Dugan. 1944 The Miracle of Morgan's Creek; Hail the Conquering Hero. 1945 Col. Effingham's Raid; Diamond Horseshoe; A Tree Grows in Brooklyn. 1946 Strange Triangle. 1948 Call Northside 777. 1953 A Blueprint for Murder; City of Bad Men; President's Lady; The Robe. 1954 The Egyptian; There's No Business Like Show Business; Woman's World. 1955 Prince of Players. 1956 The Ten Commandments. 1960 Bluebeard's Ten Honeymoons.

MELFORD, LOUISE
Born: 1880. Died: Nov. 15, 1942, North Hollywood, Calif. Screen and stage actress. Married to actor and film director George Melford (dec. 1961).

MELGAREJO, JESUS
Born: 1876, Mexico. Died: Dec. 29, 1941, Mexico City, Mexico. Screen and stage actor.

MELIES, GEORGES
Born: Dec. 8, 1861, Paris, France. Died: Jan. 21, 1938, Paris, France. Film director, producer and screen actor. Was one of the pioneers of the French cinema.

Appeared in: 1902 A Trip to the Moon. 1905 Rip's Dream.

MELL, JOSEPH "JOE"
Born: 1915. Died: Aug. 31, 1977, Los Angeles, Calif. (heart condition). Screen, stage and television actor.

Appeared in: 1952 Actors and Sin; Deadline USA; Monkey Business. 1953 Flame of Calcutta; 49th Man; The Lost Planet (serial). 1954 A Star Is Born; Magnificent Obsession. 1957 Jeanne Eagels; I Was a Teenage Werewolf; Hot Rod Rumble. 1958 Murder by Contract. 1959 City of Fear. 1961 Back Street. 1963 Black Zoo. 1965 36 Hours. 1966 Lord Love a Duck. 1967 Thoroughly Modern Millie. 1969 Sweet Charity.

MELLER, HARRO
Born: 1907. Died: Dec. 26, 1963, New York, N.Y. Screen actor and playwright.

Appeared in: **1945** The House on 92nd Street; Counter-Attack. **1946** A Night in Casablanca. **1947** Jewels of Brandenburg.

MELLER, RAQUEL
Born: 1888, Madrid, Spain. Died: July 26, 1962, Barcelona, Spain. Screen actress and singer. Appeared in U.S. films during the 1920s.

Appeared in: **1928** Carmen; La Veneosa; Violette Imperiale (The Imperial Violet). **1929** The Oppressed. **1935** La Viletera. Other foreign films: The Promised Land; The White Gypsy.

MELLINGER, MAX (Maxon Mellinger)
Born: Mar. 18, 1906, Oregon. Died: Feb. 25, 1968, Burbank, Calif. (lung cancer). Screen actor.

Appeared in: **1960** I Passed for White. **1961** When the Clock Strikes; You Have to Run Fast; Return to Peyton Place; Secret of Deep Harbor. **1962** Incident in an Alley; Saintly Sinners.

MELLISH, FULLER, JR.
Born: 1895. Died: Feb. 8, 1930, Forest Hills, N.Y. (cerebral hemorrhage). Screen and stage actor. Son of actor Fuller Mellish, Sr. (dec. 1936) and stage actress Mrs. Fuller Mellish, Sr. (dec. 1950). Married to stage actress Olive Reeves-Smith (dec. 1972).

Appeared in: **1921** Diane of Star Hollow; The Land of Hope; The Scarab Ring; The Single Track. **1923** Sinner or Saint. **1924** Two Shall Be Born. **1929** Applause. **1930** Sarah and Son.

MELLISH, FULLER, SR. (Mellish Fuller)
Born: Jan. 3, 1865, London, England. Died: Dec. 7, 1936, New York, N.Y. (heart attack). Screen and stage actor. Married to stage actress Mrs. Fuller Mellish (dec. 1950). Father of actors Fuller, Jr. (dec. 1930) and Vera Fuller Mellish.

Appeared in: **1915** The Royal Family. **1916** The Tortured Heart; A Fool's Revenge. **1917** The Unforseen.

MELNATI, UMBERTO
Born: 1901, Italy. Died: Mar. 30, 1979, Italy? Screen actor.

Appeared in: **1938** La Contessa di Parma. **1939** Un Matrimonio Ideale. **1955** Too Bad She's Bad. **1962** La Freccia D'Ora (The Golden Arrow—US 1964).

MELTON, FRANK
Born: Dec. 6, 1907, Pineapple, Ala. Died: Mar. 19, 1951, Hollywood, Calif. (heart attack). Screen actor.

Appeared in: **1933** Cavalcade; State Fair; Mr. Skitch; Ace of Aces. **1934** The White Parade; 365 Nights in Hollywood; Stand Up and Cheer; David Harum; Handy Andy; Judge Priest; The World Moves On. **1935** The County Chairman; $10 Raise; The Daring Young Man; Welcome Home. **1936** The Return of Jimmy Valentine; The Glory Trail; They Met in a Taxi. **1937** Outcast; Too Many Wives; The Affairs of Cappy Ricks; Damaged Goods; Wild and Wooly; Trouble at Midnight. **1938** Riders of the Black Hills; Freshman Year; Marriage Forbidden. **1939** Big Town Czar; Cat and the Canary. **1940** The Fighting 69th; Second Chorus. **1941** Pot O' Gold; They Meet Again; Tanks a Million. **1942** The Loves of Edgar Allan Poe; To the Shores of Tripoli; Wrecking Crew. **1945** It's a Pleasure. **1946** Do You Love Me?

MELTON, JAMES
Born: Jan. 2, 1905, Moultrie, Ga. Died: Apr. 21, 1961, New York, N.Y. (pneumonia). Screen, stage, radio actor and opera performer.

Appeared in: **1934** Song Hit Stories (short). **1935** Stars Over Broadway. **1936** Sing Me a Love Song. **1937** Melody for Two. **1946** Ziegfeld Follies.

MELVILLE, EMILIE
Born: 1852. Died: May 19, 1932, San Francisco, Calif. Screen and stage actress. Daughter of stage actress Julie Miles (dec.).

Appeared in: **1929** Illusion.

MELVILLE, ROSE
Born: Jan. 30, 1873, Terre Haute, Ind. Died: Oct. 8, 1946. Screen, stage and vaudeville actress. Married to actor Frank Minzey (dec. 1949). They appeared in early Biograph and Keystone films and later in shorts produced by Fox, Goldwyn, etc.

Appeared in: **1916** She Came, She Saw, She Conquered; Leap Year Wooing; A Flock of Skeletons; When Things Go Wrong; A Double Barreled Courtship; Almost a Heroine; Romance and Riot; A Lunch Room Legacy; An Innocent Vampire; A Baby Grand; The Dumb Heiress; Sis the Detective; Juggling Justice; Her Great Invention; A Lucky Mistake; Setting the Fashion; The Wishing Ring; The Psychic Phenomenon; A Double Elopement.

MENAHAN, JEAN
Died: 1963. Stage and screen actress. Mother of actress Eileen Brennan.

Appeared in: **1927** The Jazz Singer.

MENANT, PAUL
Born: 1892, France. Died: Apr. 27, 1934, Paris, France. Screen actor.

MENARD, MICHAEL M.
Born: 1898. Died: Apr. 27, 1949, Los Angeles, Calif. Screen actor.

MENDEL, JULES
Born: 1875. Died: Mar. 17, 1938, Los Angeles, Calif. Screen and stage actor.

MENDELSSOHN, ELEONORA
Born: 1900. Died: Jan. 24, 1951, New York, N.Y. (suicide—pills). Stage and screen actress.

Appeared in: **1950** The Black Hand.

MENDES, JOHN PRINCE
Born: 1919. Died: Sept. 30, 1955, New York, N.Y. Screen, stage, television actor and magician.

Appeared in: **1943** This Is Your Army (stage and film versions).

MENDES, LOTHAR
Born: May 19, 1894, Berlin, Germany. Died: Feb. 25, 1974, London, England. Film producer, director, author, stage and screen actor.

MENDEZ, RAFAEL G.
Born: Mar. 26, 1906, Jiquilpah, Mexico. Died: Sept. 15, 1981, Encino, Calif. (heart attack). Screen, radio, television actor, bandleader and trumpet player.

MENDOZA, HARRY
Born: 1905. Died: Feb. 15, 1970, Houston, Tex. (heart ailment). Screen actor and magician.

MENHART, ALFRED
Born: 1899, Germany. Died: Nov. 14, 1955, Munich, Germany (following surgery). Screen actor.

Appeared in: The Major and the Steers.

MENJOU, ADOLPHE (Adolphe Jean Menjou)
Born: Feb. 18, 1890, Pittsburgh, Pa. Died: Oct. 29, 1963, Beverly Hills, Calif. (chronic hepatitis). Screen, stage and television actor. Brother of actor Henre Menjou (dec. 1956). Divorced from Katharine Tinsley and actress Kathryn Carver (dec. 1947). Married to actress Veree Teasdale. Nominated for 1930/31 Academy Award for Best Actor in The Front Page.

Appeared in: **1916** The Habit of Happiness; Manhattan Madness; Blue Envelope. **1917** The Amazons; The Valentine Girl; The Moth. **1921** The Sheik; Courage; The Three Musketeers; Queenie; Through the Back Door; Kiss; The Faith Healer. **1922** Clarence; The Eternal Flame; The Fast Mail; Head Over Heels; Is Matrimony a Failure?; Pink Gods; Singed Wings. **1923** A Woman of Paris; Rupert of Hentzau; The World's Applause; The Spanish Dancer; Bella Donna. **1924** Broadway After Dark; Broken Barriers; The Fast Set; The Marriage Circle; For Sale; Forbidden Paradise; The Marriage Cheat; Open All Night; Shadows of Paris; Sinners in Silk. **1925** Are Parents People?; The King on Main Street; A Kiss in the Dark; Lost—A Wife; The Swan. **1926** The Grand Duchess and the Waiter; The Sorrows of Satan; A Social Celebrity; The Ace of Cads; Fascinating Youth. **1927** Blonde or Brunette; Service for Ladies; Serenade; A Gentleman of Paris; Evening Clothes. **1928** His Private Life; The Tiger Lady; A Night of Mystery. **1929** Marquis Preferred; Fashions in Love; Bachelor Girl; The Kiss (and 1921 version). **1930** Morocco; New Moon; Mon Gosse de Pere; L'Enigmatique Monsieur Parkes. **1931** Easiest Way; Men Call It Love; The Great Lover; The Front Page; Friends and Lovers; The Marriage Interlude; The Parisian. **1932** Prestige; The Man from Yesterday; Two White Arms (aka Wives Beware—US 1933); Diamond Cut Diamond (aka Blame the Woman—US); Bachelor's Affair; Forbidden; A

Farewell to Arms; The Night Club Lady. **1933** Convention City; Morning Glory; The Circus Queen Murder; The Worst Woman in Paris? **1934** The Trumpet Blows; Little Miss Marker; Journal of a Crime; Easy to Love; The Great Flirtation; The Human Side; The Mighty Barnum. **1935** Broadway Gondolier; Gold Diggers of 1935. **1936** The Milky Way; Wives Never Know; One in a Million; Sing, Baby, Sing! **1937** One Hundred Men and a Girl; A Star Is Born; Stage Door; Cafe Metropole. **1938** The Goldwyn Follies; Thanks for Everything; Letter of Introduction. **1939** Golden Boy; That's Right, You're Wrong; The Housekeeper's Daughter; King of the Turf. **1940** A Bill of Divorcement; Turnabout. **1941** Road Show; Father Takes a Wife. **1942** Roxie Hart; Syncopation; You Were Never Lovelier. **1943** Sweet Rosie O'Grady; Hi Diddle Diddle. **1944** Step Lively. **1945** Man Alive. **1946** The Bachelor's Daughter; Heartbeat. **1947** I'll Be Yours; Mr. District Attorney; The Hucksters. **1948** State of the Union. **1949** My Dream Is Yours; Dancing in the Dark. **1950** To Please a Lady. **1951** Across the Wide Missouri; The Tall Target. **1952** The Sniper. **1953** Man on a Tightrope. **1955** Timberjack. **1956** Bundle of Joy; Ambassador's Daughter. **1957** The Fuzzy Pink Nightgown; Paths of Glory. **1958** I Married a Woman. **1960** Pollyanna.

MENJOU, HENRI (Henry Arthur Menjou)
Born: June 2, 1891, Pittsburgh, Pa. Died: Jan. 27, 1956, West Los Angeles, Calif. Screen actor. Brother of actor Adolph Menjou (dec. 1963). Married to actress Fran Pallay (dec. 1981).

Appeared in: **1923** A Woman of Paris. **1926** The Ace of Cads. **1927** Blonde or Brunette; Pleasure Before Business.

MENKEN, GRACE
Born: 1892. Died: Aug. 14, 1978, New York, N.Y. Screen, stage and radio actress. Sister of actress Helen Menken (dec. 1966). Married to actor Bert Lytell (dec. 1954).

MENKEN, HELEN
Born: 1902, New York. Died: Mar. 27, 1966, New York, N.Y. (heart attack). Screen, stage and radio actress. Divorced from actor Humphrey Bogart (dec. 1957). Sister of actress Grace Menken (dec. 1978).

Appeared in: **1943** Stage Door Canteen.

MENKEN, MARIE
Born: 1909. Died: Dec., 1970, Brooklyn, N.Y. Screen actress.

Appeared in: **1965** The Life of Juanita Castro. **1966** The Chelsea Girls. **1969** Diaries, Notes and Sketches.

MERA, EDITH
Born: France. Died: Feb. 24, 1935, Paris, France (anthrax). Screen and stage actress. Had appeared in French and U.S. films.

Appeared in: **1931** Le Culte de Beaute; Un Soire de Ralfe. **1932** Miche. **1933** Les Trois Mousquetaires (The Three Musketeers). **1935** Criez-Le Sur les Toits (Shout It from the Housetops). **1937** Grandeur et Decadence.

MERANDE, DORO (Dora Matthews)
Born: c. 1970, Columbia, Kans. Died: Nov. 1, 1975, Miami, Fla. (massive stroke). Screen, stage and television actress.

Appeared in: **1931** Front Page (stage and film versions). **1935** State Fair. **1940** Our Town. **1949** Cover Up. **1951** The Whistle at Eaton Falls (stage and film versions). **1955** The Man With the Golden Arm; The Seven Year Itch. **1959** The Remarkable Mr. Pennypacker; The Gazebo. **1963** The Cardinal. **1964** Kiss Me Stupid. **1966** The Russians Are Coming, The Russians Are Coming. **1967** Hurry Sundown. **1968** Skidoo. **1969** Change of Habit. **1971** Making It.

MERCER, BERYL
Born: Aug. 13, 1882, Seville, Spain. Died: July 28, 1939, Santa Monica, Calif. Screen and stage actress.

Appeared in: **1916** The Final Curtain. **1922** Broken Chains. **1923** Christian. **1928** We Americans. **1929** Mother's Boy; Three Live Ghosts. **1930** In Gay Madrid; All Quiet on the Western Front; Dumbells in Ermine; Common Clay; The Matrimonial Bed; Outward Bound; Seven Days Leave. **1931** East Lynne; The Public Enemy; Inspiration; Always Goodbye; Merely Mary Ann; The Miracle Woman; The Man in Possession; Are These Our Children?; Sky Spider. **1932** The Devil's Lottery; Forgotten Women; Lovers Courageous; Lena Rivers; Young America; No Greater Love; Unholy Love; Smilin' Through; Six Hours to Live; Midnight Morals. **1933** Cavalcade; Berkeley Square; Her Splendid Folly; Her Broken Dreams; Blind Adventure; Supernatural. **1934** Change of Heart; The Little Minister; Jane Eyre; Richest Girl in the World. **1935** Age of Indiscretion; My

Marriage; Hitch Hike Lady; Magnificent Obsession; Three Live Ghosts (and 1929 version). **1936** Forbidden Heaven. **1937** Call It a Day; Night Must Fall. **1939** The Hound of the Baskervilles; The Little Princess; A Woman Is the Judge.

MERCER, JOHNNY
Born: Nov. 18, 1909, Savannah, Ga. Died: June 25, 1976, Bel Air, Calif. Composer, lyricist, singer, screen, stage and radio actor. Married to dancer Ginger Mehan.

Appeared in: **1935** Old Man Rhythm; To Beat the Band.

MERCER, TONY
Born: 1922. Died: July 14, 1973, London, England (heart complaint). Screen actor and singer.

Appeared in: **1956** Davy Crockett and the River Pirates. **1963** It's All Happening (aka The Dream Maker—US 1964).

MEREDITH, CHARLES
Born: 1894, Knoxville, Pa. Died: Nov. 28, 1964, Los Angeles, Calif. Screen, stage and television actor.

Appeared in: **1919** Luck in Pawn. **1920** Simple Souls. **1921** The Beautiful Liar; Beyond; The Cave Girl; The Foolish Matrons; Hail The Woman; That Something. **1922** The Cradle; Woman, Wake Up! **1924** In Hollywood with Potash and Perlmutter. **1947** Daisy Kenyon. **1948** The Boy with the Green Hair; They Live By Night (aka The Twisted Road and Your Red Wagon); All My Sons; A Foreign Affair; The Miracle of the Bells; For the Love of Mary. **1949** Tokyo Joe; Francis; The Lady Takes a Sailor. **1950** Perfect Strangers; The Sun Sets at Dawn; Counterspy Meets Scotland Yard. **1951** Al Jennings of Oklahoma; Along the Great Divide; Submarine Command. **1952** The Big Trees; Cattle Town. **1953** So This Is Love. **1956** The Lone Ranger; The Birds and the Bees. **1957** Chicago Confidential. **1958** The Buccaneer. **1960** Twelve Hours to Kill. **1962** Be Careful How You Wish (US 1964). **1964** The Incredible Mr. Limpet; The Quick Gun.

MEREDITH, CHEERIO
Born: 1890. Died: Dec. 25, 1964, Woodland Hills, Calif. Screen and television actress.

Appeared in: **1955** I'll Cry Tomorrow. **1958** The Case Against Brooklyn; I Married a Woman. **1959** The Legend of Tom Dooley. **1962** The Wonderful World of the Brothers Grimm; The Three Stooges in Orbit. **1964** Sex and the Single Girl.

MEREDITH, IRIS
Born: 1916. Died: Jan. 22, 1980, Los Angeles, Calif. Screen actress.

Appeared in: **1933** Roman Scandals. **1937** A Lawman Is Born; The Mystery of the Hooded Horsemen. **1938** The Spider's Web (serial); Outlaws of the Prairie; Cattle Raiders; Colorado Trail; West of Cheyenne; Law of the Plains; South of Arizona; Call of the Rockies. **1939** Outpost of the Mounties; Taming of the West; West of Santa Fe; Spoilers of the Range; Western Caravans; Riders of Black River; Man from Sundown; Those High Grey Walls; Overland With Kit Carson (serial). **1940** The Green Archer (serial); Convicted Woman; Two-Fisted Rangers; Blazing Six-Shooters; Texas Stagecoach; The Man From Tumbleweeds; The Return of Wild Bill; Thundering Frontier; His Bridal Fright (short). **1941** Caught in the Act; The Son of Davy Crockett; Louisiana Purchase. **1943** The Rangers Take Over.

MEREDITH, JANE
Born: 1885, San Francisco, Calif. Died: Feb. 15, 1945, New York, N.Y. Screen and stage actress.

Appeared in: **1934** The Love Captive. **1935** Behind the Green Lights; Alias Mary Dow.

MEREDYTH, BESS (Helen MacGlashan)
Born: Buffalo, N.Y. Died: July 13, 1969, Woodland Hills, Calif. Screen actress and screenwriter. Entered films as an extra with Biograph in 1911.

Appeared in: **1914** The Magnet; Bess the Detectress, or The Old Mill at Midnight; When Bess Got in Wrong; Her Twin Brother; The Little Auto-Go-Mobile; Father's Bride; Willie Walrus and the Awful Confession. **1916** A Sailor's Heart.

MERIVALE, PHILIP
Born: Nov. 2, 1880, Rehutia, Manickpur, India. Died: Mar. 12, 1946, Los Angeles, Calif. (heart ailment). Screen, stage actor and writer. Married to actress Viva Birkett (dec. 1934) and later married to actress Gladys Cooper (dec. 1971). Entered films during silents.

Appeared in: **1933** I Loved You Wednesday. **1935** The Passing of the Third Floor Back. **1936** Give Us This Night. **1941** Midnight Angel; Rage in Heaven; Mr. and Mrs. Smith; Lady for a Night. **1942** Crossroads; This Above All; Pacific Blackout. **1943** This Land Is Mine. **1944** Lost Angel; Nothing But Trouble; The Hour Before Dawn. **1945** Adventure; Tonight and Every Night. **1946** Sister Kenny; The Stranger.

MERKURYEV, VASILY
Born: 1904, Russia. Died: 1978, Russia? Screen and stage actor.

Appeared in: **1949** The First Front. **1956** Twelfth Night. **1960** The Cranes Are Flying; Seryozha (aka A Summer to Remember—US 1961). **1963** Cheryomushki (aka Song Over Moscow—US 1964).

MERKYL, WILMUTH
Born: Jan. 2, 1885, Iowa. Died: May 1, 1954, Los Angeles, Calif. (coronary occlusion). Screen actor.

Appeared in: **1915** Gretna Green; Wife for Wife; The Price; The Victory of Virtue; The Fortunate Youth; The Soul Maker. **1916** Her Surrender. **1918** Fedora; Let's Get a Divorce.

MERLO, ANTHONY "TONY"
Born: 1887, Italy. Died: Apr. 25, 1976, Woodland Hills, Calif. Screen actor.

Appeared in: **1916** The Black Butterfly; The Great Problem; Human Driftwood. **1917** The Eternal Sin; Maid of Belgium; The Awakening. **1918** Daughter of France; The Cross Bearer; The Sea Waif; Woman; Sporting Life. **1919** The Heart of Gold; Phil for Short; Mandarin's Gold; The Unveiling Hand. **1920** The Thief. **1923** Broken Hearts of Broadway. **1925** Greater Than a Crown. **1929** Shanghai Rose. **1932** The Mummy; Love Me Tonight. **1934** Shoot the Works; Enter Madame.

MERRALL, MARY (Mary Lloyd)
Born: Jan. 5, 1890, Liverpool, England. Died: 1973, England? Screen and stage actress. Divorced from J. B. Hissey, and actor Ion Swinley (dec. 1937). Later married to actor Franklin Dyall (dec. 1950).

Appeared in: **1945** Love on the Dole; Pink String and Sealing Wax (US 1950); Dead of Night. **1947** Nicholas Nickleby. **1949** For Them That Trespass (US 1950). **1951** The Late Edwina Black (aka The Obsessed—US); Encore (US 1952). **1952** The Pickwick Papers (US 1953). **1953** Tonight at 8:30. **1954** Duel in the Jungle; The Bells of St. Trinian's (US 1955); The Green Buddha (US 1955). **1956** It's Great to be Young (US 1958). **1957** Campbell's Kingdom (US 1958). **1958** The Camp on Blood Island; Family Doctor (aka Prescription for Murder, aka RX Murder—US). **1963** Bitter Harvest. **1965** The Amorous Adventures of Moll Flanders.

MERRIAM, HAROLD ALVORD
Born: 1876. Died: Dec. 21, 1937, Elmsford, N.Y. Screen and stage actor. Appeared in silent films.

MERRILL, FRANK
Born: 1894. Died: Feb. 12, 1966, Hollywood, Calif. Screen actor. Fifth actor to portray Tarzan in the Tarzan films.

Appeared in: **1921** The Adventures of Tarzan (serial). **1924** Battling Mason; A Fighting Heart; Reckless Speed. **1925** Dashing Thru; A Gentleman Roughneck; Savages of the Sea; Shackled Lightning; Speed Madness. **1926** Cupid's Knockout; The Fighting Doctor; The Hollywood Reporter; Unknown Dangers. **1927** Perils of the Jungle (serial). **1928** Tarzan the Mighty (serial); The Little Wild Girl. **1929** Below the Deadline; Tarzan the Tiger (serial).

MERRILL, LOUIS "LOU"
Born: 1911. Died: Apr. 7, 1963, Hollywood, Calif. Screen and television actor.

Appeared in: **1939** Tropic Fury. **1940** Kit Carson. **1948** The Lady from Shanghai. **1953** Charge of the Lancers; The Hindu (aka Sabaka—US 1955). **1955** The Crooked Web. **1957** The Giant Claw. **1961** The Devil at 4 O'Clock.

MERRITT, GEORGE
Born: Dec. 10, 1890, London, England. Died: Aug. 27, 1977, London, England. Screen, stage and television actor.

Appeared in: **1930** The "W" Plan (US 1931); Thread O'Scarlet. **1931** A Gentleman of Paris; Dreyfus (aka The Dreyfus Case—US); Bracelets. **1932** White Face; Blind Spot; Little Fella; The Lodger (aka The Phantom Fiend—US 1935). **1933** Crime on the Hill; Mr. Quincey of Monte Carlo; Going Straight; F. P. 1; I Was a Spy (US 1934); The Ghost Camera; The Fire Raisers; Double Bluff. **1934** No Escape; My Song for You; Jew Suess (aka Power—US); Nine Forty-Five; The Silver Spoon. **1935** Forever England (aka Brown on Resolution aka Born for Glory—US); Emil and the Detectives (aka Emil—US 1938); Ten Minute Alibi; Drake of England (aka Drake the Pirate—US); Me and Marlborough; Mr. Cohen Takes a Walk (US 1936); Line Engaged; Crime Unlimited. **1936** The Man Behind the Mask; Prison Breaker; Educated Evans; Everything is Thunder; Rembrandt; Love at Sea; Ticket of Leave. **1937** The Compulsory Wife; The Vulture; The Vicar of Bray; Dr. Syn; Young and Innocent (aka A Girl Was Young—US 1938); Dangerous Fingers (aka Wanted by Scotland Yard—US); The Return of the Scarlet Pimpernel (US 1938); The Rat. **1938** Secrets of F. P. 1 (reissue of 1933 version—F. P. 1); Mr. Reeder in Room 13 (aka Mystery of Room 13—US 1941); The Gaunt Stranger (aka The Phantom Strikes—US 1939). **1939** Q Planes (aka Clouds Over Europe—US); A Window in London (aka Lady in Distress—US 1942); Meet Maxwell Archer (aka Maxwell Archer, Detective—US 1942); The Four Just Men (aka The Secret Four—US 1940); All at Sea. **1940** The Proud Valley (US 1941); Spare the Copper; The Case of the Frightened Lady (aka The Frightened Lady—US 1941); Two for Danger; They Came by Night. **1941** He Found a Star; Hatter's Castle (US 1948); Breach of Promise (aka Adventure in Blackmail—US 1943). **1942** Alibi; Back Room Boy; They Flew Alone (aka Wings and the Woman—US). **1943** I'll Walk Beside You. **1944** Demobbed; A Canterbury Tale; Don't Take it to Heart (US 1949). **1945** For You Alone; Home Sweet Home; I'll Be Your Sweetheart; The Voice Within; Waterloo Road. **1946** I'll Turn to You; The Root of All Evil. **1947** The Man Within (aka The Smugglers—US 1948); Nicholas Nickleby. **1948** My Brother's Keeper; Love in Waiting. **1949** Dark Secret; Marry Me (US 1951). **1950** Something in the City. **1953** Small Town Story; Noose for a Lady. **1954** The Green Scarf (US 1955); The End of the Road (US 1957); The Night of the Full Moon. **1957** Quatermass II (aka Enemy From Space—US). **1958** Tred Softly Stranger (US 1959). **1961** The Full Treatment (aka Stop Me Before I Kill!—US). **1970** Cromwell.

MERSON, BILLY (William Henry Thompson)
Born: Mar. 29, 1881, Nottingham, England. Died: June 25, 1947, London, England. Screen, stage, vaudeville actor and music hall performer.

Appeared in: **1915** Billy's Spanish Love Spasm; The Man in Possession; The Only Man. **1916** The Terrible Tec; The Tale of a Shirt; Perils of Pork Pie; Billy's Stormy Courtship. **1917** Billy Strikes Oil; Billy the Truthful. **1920** Comets. **1931** Bill and Coo. **1936** The Three Maxims (aka The Show Goes On—US 1938). **1937** Riding High (aka Remember When). **1938** Chips; Scruffy.

MERTON, COLLETTE (Collette Helene Mazzoletti)
Born: Mar. 7, 1907, New Orleans, La. Died: July 24, 1968, Hollywood, Calif. Screen actress. Appeared in three of the "Collegians" series prior to 1929.

Appeared in: **1929** Clear the Decks; Walking Back; Why Be Good; King of the Campus; The Godless Girl.

MERTON, JOHN (John Merton La Varre)
Born: 1901. Died: Sept. 19, 1959, Los Angeles, Calif. (heart attack). Screen and stage actor. Father of actor Robert Lavarre and Lane Bradford (dec. 1973).

Appeared in: **1934** Sons of the Desert. **1935** The Eagle's Brood; Bar 20 Rides Again. **1936** The Vigilantes Are Coming (serial); Call of the Prairie; Aces and Eights; The Three Mesquiteers. **1937** Drums of Destiny; Range Defenders; Colorado Kid; Federal Bullets. **1938** The Lone Ranger (serial); Female Fugitive; Two Gun Justice; Where the Buffalo Roam; Gang Bullets; Knight of the Plains; Dick Tracy Returns (serial). **1939** Zorro's Fighting Legion (serial); The Renegade Trail; Code of the Fearless. **1940** Melody Ranch; Drums of Fu Manchu (serial); Hi-Yo Silver; Covered Wagon Days; The Trail Blazers; Lone Star Raiders; Frontier Crusader; Queen of the Yukon. **1941** White Eagle (serial); Under Fiesta Stars. **1942** Billy the Kid's Smoking Guns; Law and Order. **1943** Frontier Marshal in Prairie Pals; Mysterious Rider. **1944** Zorro's Black Whip (serial); Mystery Man; Texas Masquerade; Girl Rush. **1945** Brenda Starr, Reporter (serial). **1946** Hop Harrigan (serial); Son of the Guardsman (serial); The Gay Cavalier. **1947** Cheyenne Takes Over; Jack Armstrong (serial); Brick Bradford (serial). **1949** Adventures of Sir Galahad (serial); Riders of the Dusk; Thieves' Highway; Western Renegades. **1950** Radar Patrol vs. Spy King (serial); Marinated Mariner (short); Arizona Territory; Bandit Queen; Border Rangers; Fence Riders; West of Wyoming. **1951** Silver Canyon; Gold Raiders; Man from Sonora. **1952** The Old West; Blue Canadian Rockies. **1953** Up In Daisy's Penthouse (short); Saginaw Trail. **1956** The Ten Commandments.

MERVYN, WILLIAM (William Pickwoad)
Born: Jan. 3, 1912, Nairobi, Kenya. Died: Aug. 6, 1976, London, England. Screen, stage and television actor. Entered films in 1946.

Appeared in: **1949** That Dangerous Age (aka If This Be Sin—US 1950). **1950** The Blue Lamp. **1956** The Long Arm (aka The Third Key—US 1957). **1958** Carve Her Name With Pride. **1960** Circus of Horrors. **1961** Invasion Quartet. **1963** Hot Enough for June (aka Agent 8 3/4—US 1965); Tamahine (US 1964). **1964** Murder Ahoy. **1965** Operation Crossbow (aka The Great Spy Mission aka Code Name: Operation Crossbow). **1966** The Jokers (US 1967); Deadlier Than the Male (US 1967). **1967** Follow That Camel (US 1968). **1968** Salt and Pepper; Hammerhead; Hot Millions. **1969** The Best House in Town. **1970** The Railway Children (US 1971). **1972** The Ruling Class. **1976** The Bawdy Adventures of Tom Jones.

MESKILL, KATHERINE C.
Born: Sommerville, Mass. Died: Jan., 1979, New York, N.Y. Screen, stage and television actress.

Appeared in: **1951** The House on Telegraph Hill; Hollywood Story. **1970** Diary of a Mad Housewife.

MESKIN, AHARON
Born: 1897, Russia. Died: Nov. 11, 1974, Tel Aviv, Israel (heart attack). Stage and screen actor. Father of actor and director Amon Meskin.

Appeared in: **1934** Chalutzin. **1965** Shnei Kuni Lemel (The Flying Matchmaker—US 1970).

MESSENGER, BUDDY (Melvin Joe Messinger)
Born: Oct. 26, 1909, San Francisco, Calif. Died: Oct. 25, 1965, Hollywood, Calif. Stage and screen actor. Son of actress Josephine Messenger (dec. 1968) and brother of actress Gertrude Messenger.

Appeared in: **1917** Aladdin and His Wonderful Lamp; Treasure Island. **1919** The Hoodlum; Fighting Joe. **1921** The Old Nest. **1922** The Flirt; A Front Page Story; Shadows; When Love Comes. **1923** The Abysmal Brute; Penrod and Sam; Trifling with Honor. **1924** The Whispered Name; Young Ideas; Buddy Messenger Comedies (shorts) including: All for a Girl; Breaking into the Movies; The Homing Birds. **1928** Undressed. **1929** A Lady of Chance; Hot Stuff. **1930** Cheer Up and Smile. **1934** Most Precious Thing in Life. **1936** All American Toothache (short); College Holiday; Our Relations. **1937** Wings Over Honolulu. **1939** Idiot's Delight. **1941** Hold Back the Dawn; Mexican Spitfire's Baby. **1943** Henry Aldrich Gets Glamour.

MESSINGER, JOSEPHINE
Born: 1885. Died: Mar. 3, 1968, Calif. Screen actress. Mother of actress Gertrude and actor Buddy Messenger (dec. 1965). Appeared in silent films.

MESSITER, ERIC
Born: 1892. Died: Sept. 13, 1960, London, England (heart attack). Stage and screen actor.

Appeared in: **1949** Kind Hearts and Coronets (US 1950). **1951** The Mudlark.

MESSLEIN, JOHN
Born: 1899. Died: Aug., 1920, Weehawken, N.J. (auto accident). Screen actor.

MESTEL, JACOB
Born: 1884, Poland. Died: Aug. 5, 1958, New York, N.Y. Screen, stage, television actor, stage director and screenwriter.

Appeared in: **1933** The Wandering Jew. **1939** Mirele Efros. **1949** A Vilna Legend.

METAXA, GEORGES
Born: Sept. 11, 1899, Bucharest, Romania. Died: Dec. 8, 1950, Monroe, La. Screen and stage actor.

Appeared in: **1931** Secrets of a Secretary. **1936** Swing Time. **1940** Submarine Base; The Doctor Takes a Wife. **1942** Paris Calling. **1943** Hi Diddle Diddle. **1944** The Mask of Dimitrios. **1945** Scotland Yard Investigator.

METCALF, EARL
Born: 1889, Newport, Ky. Died: Jan. 27, 1928, Burbank, Calif. (flying accident—fell from plane). Screen and stage actor. Entered films with Vitagraph.

Appeared in: **1915** The Insurrection. **1916** Perils of Our Girl Reporters (serial). **1920** Deadline at Eleven. **1921** Eden and Return; Mother Eternal; What Women Will Do. **1922** White Eagle (serial); The New Teacher; While Justice Waits; Back to Yellow Jacket; The Great Night; Ignorance; The Power of a Lie. **1923** The Lone Wagon; Skid Proof; Look Your Best. **1924** The Courageous Coward; Fair Week; The Valley of Hate; The Silent Accuser; Silk Stocking Sal; Surging Seas. **1925** The Man Without a Country; Ship of Souls; Kit Carson Over the Great Divide. **1926** Atta Boy; Love's Blindness; The Midnight Message; The Midnight Sun; The Mystery Club; Partners Again; Buffalo Bill on the U.P. Trail; The Call of the Klondike; The High Flyer; Remember; Sin Cargo. **1927** King of Kings; Night Life; Daring Deeds; The Devil's Saddle; The Notorious Lady. **1928** The Air Mail Pilot; Eagle of the Night (serial).

METCALF, EDWARD
Born: 1867. Died: Apr. 2, 1951, Brentwood, N.Y. Screen, stage and vaudeville actor.

Appeared in: **1930** Animal Crackers (stage and film versions).

METCALFE, JAMES S.
Born: 1901. Died: Apr. 2, 1960, Northridge, Calif. (heart attack). Screen and stage actor.

Appeared in: **1941** The Iron Claw (serial). **1942** The Hard Way; Who Is Hope Schuyler?; A Gentleman at Heart.

METHOT, MAYO
Born: 1904, Portland, Ore. Died: June 9, 1951, Portland, Ore. Screen and stage actress. Divorced from actor Humphrey Bogart (dec. 1957).

Appeared in: **1930** Taxi Talks (short). **1931** Corsair; Squaring the Triangle (short). **1932** The Night Club Lady; Virtue; Vanity Street; Afraid to Talk. **1933** The Mind Reader; Lilly Turner; Counsellor-at-Law. **1934** Jimmy the Gent; Goodbye Love; Harold Teen; Side Streets; Registered Nurse. **1935** We're in the Money; Mills of the Gods; The Case of the Curious Bride; Dr. Socrates. **1936** Mr. Deeds Goes to Town; The Case Against Mrs. Ames. **1937** Marked Woman. **1938** Women in Prison; The Sisters; Numbered Woman. **1939** Unexpected Father; A Woman Is the Judge; Should a Girl Marry? **1940** Brother Rat and a Baby. **1944** Report from the Front (short).

METZ, ALBERT
Born: 1886. Died: Aug. 20, 1940, North Hollywood, Calif. Screen and stage actor.

METZ, OTTO
Born: 1891. Died: Feb. 1, 1949, Hollywood, Calif. Screen, vaudeville actor and stunt flyer.

METZETTI, VICTOR
Born: 1895. Died: Aug. 21, 1949, Los Angeles, Calif. (pneumonia). Screen actor, circus performer and stuntman.

Appeared in: **1922** Putting It Over. **1924** Stepping Lively. **1927** Bulldog Pluck. **1950** The Border Outlaws.

MEURISSE, PAUL
Born: 1912, Dunkirk, France. Died: Jan. 19, 1979, Paris, France (heart attack). Screen, stage and radio actor.

Appeared in: **1939** Bel Indifferent. **1941** Montemartre Sur Seine. **1945** Marie La Misere. **1948** Back Streets of Paris. **1950** The Red Angel. **1954** Diabolique (US 1955). **1958** La Tete Contre Les Nurs. **1959** Picnic in the Grass (aka Lunch on the Grass—US 1960). **1960** Marie Octobre; La Francaise Et L'Amour (Love and the Frenchwoman—US 1961); La Veriti (The Truth—US 1961). **1963** Mefiez-vous Mesdames (Be Careful Ladies); Du Mouron Pour Les Petits Oismeaux (Chicken Feed for Little Birds). **1976** Les Suspects.

MEUSEL, BOB (Robert William Meusel)
Born: July 19, 1896, San Jose, Calif. Died: Nov. 28, 1977, Downey, Calif. Baseball player and screen actor. Brother of baseball player/actor Irish Meusel (dec. 1963).

Appeared in: **1927** Slide, Kelly, Slide. **1942** The Pride of the Yankees. **1948** The Babe Ruth Story.

MEUSEL, IRISH (Emil Frederick Meusel)
Born: June 9, 1893, Oakland, Calif. Died: Mar. 1, 1963, Long Beach, Calif. Baseball player and screen actor. Brother of baseball player/actor Bob Meusel (dec. 1977).

Appeared in: **1927** Slide, Kelly, Slide. **1929** Fast Company.

MEYEN, HARRY (Harald Haubenstock)

Born: Germany. Died: 1979, Hamburg, Germany (suicide). Screen actor and film director. Divorced from actress Romy Schneider (dec. 1982).

Appeared in: **1955** The Sergeant's Daughter. **1957** Des Teufels General (The Devil's General). **1961** Lebensborn (aka Ordered to Love—US 1963). **1966** Is Paris Burning?; Triple Cross (US 1967).

MEYER, EVE *See* MILLER, EVE

MEYER, FREDERIC

Born: 1910. Died: Sept. 16, 1973, en route from Mt. Gretna, Pa. to New York, N.Y. (heart attack). Screen, stage, vaudeville actor and stage director. Married to actress Cathleen Claypool.

MEYER, GRETA

Born: 1883, Germany. Died: Oct. 8, 1965. Screen actress.

Appeared in: **1929** Royal Box. **1931** Tonight or Never. **1932** The Match King; Flesh. **1933** The Nuisance; Jennie Gerhardt. **1934** Let's Fall in Love; Servant's Entrance; Forsaking All Others; The Line Up. **1935** Biography of a Bachelor Girl; Naughty Marietta; Laddie; Mr. Dynamite; The Return of Peter Grimm; Twin Triplets (short); Smart Girl. **1936** Spendthrift; Suzy; Libeled Lady; The Gorgeous Hussy. **1937** When Love Is Young; Thin Ice; Bill Cracks Down; Damaged Goods. **1938** Torchy Gets Her Man; The Great Waltz. **1939** No Place to Go; When Tomorrow Comes. **1940** Four Sons; Bitter Sweet. **1941** Come Live With Me. **1942** Friendly Enemies.

MEYER, HYMAN "HY"

Born: 1875, San Francisco, Calif. Died: Oct. 7, 1945, Hollywood, Calif. Screen and vaudeville actor.

Appeared in: **1929** The Saturday Night Kid. **1934** Judge Priest.

MEYER, OTTO

Born: 1851. Died: Nov. 8, 1921, Jamaica, N.Y. Screen and stage actor.

Appeared in: **1915** With a Girl at Stake.

MEYER, TORBEN

Born: Dec. 1, 1884, Copenhagen, Denmark. Died: May 22, 1975, Hollywood, Calif. (bronchial pneumonia). Screen and stage actor.

Appeared in: **1927** The Man Who Laughs. **1928** Jazz Mad; The Viking. **1929** Behind Closed Doors; The Last Warning. **1930** Just Like Heaven; Lummox; Mamba. **1932** Big City Blues. **1933** The Crime of the Century. **1934** Pursued. **1935** Special Agent; Enter Madam; The Girl Who Came Back; Splendor; East of Java; Roberta; Black Room Mystery; The Man Who Broke the Bank at Monte Carlo. **1936** Till We Meet Again; Anything Goes. **1937** Thin Ice; The King and the Chorus Girl; The Prisoner of Zenda; Tovarich. **1938** Romance in the Dark; Bulldog Drummond's Peril; The First Hundred Years. **1939** Topper Takes a Trip. **1940** Four Sons; Christmas in July; No, No, Nanette; Dr. Ehrlich's Magic Bullet. **1941** The Lady Eve; Sunny. **1942** Sullivan's Travels; Berlin Correspondent; Palm Beach Story. **1943** Edge of Darkness; Jack London. **1944** The Purple Heart; Hail the Conquering Hero; The Miracle of Morgan's Creek; The Great Moment; Greenwich Village. **1945** Hotel Berlin. **1946** Mad Wednesday (aka Sin of Harold Diddlebock); The Mighty McGurk. **1947** Variety Girl; Alias Mr. Twilight. **1948** Unfaithfully Yours; Julia Misbehaves. **1949** The Beautiful Blonde from Bashful Bend. **1951** Come Fill the Cup. **1952** What Price Glory? **1953** Call Me Madam; The Story of Three Loves. **1954** Living It Up. **1955** We're No Angels. **1956** Anything Goes; The Conquerors. **1958** The Matchmaker; The Fly. **1960** G.I. Blues. **1961** Judgment at Nuremberg.

MEYN, ROBERT

Born: 1896, Germany? Died: Mar. 3, 1972, Hamburg, Germany. Screen and stage actor.

Appeared in: **1954** Sunderin. **1956** Teufel in Seide (Devil in Silk—US 1968). **1957** The Last Bridge. **1959** Kriegsgericht (Court Martial—US 1962). **1960** Der Rest Ist Schweigen (The Rest is Silence).

MICHAEL, GERTRUDE

Born: June 1, 1911, Talladega, Ala. Died: Dec. 31, 1964, Beverly Hills, Calif. Screen, stage and television actress. She was heroine of "Sophie Lang" series.

Appeared in: **1932** Wayward; Unashamed. **1933** A Bedtime Story; Night of Terror; Ann Vickers; Sailor Be Good; Cradle Song; I'm No Angel. **1934** She Was a Lady; Murder on the Blackboard; Notorious Sophie Lang; Murder at the Vanities; Menace; George White's Scandals; I Believed in You; Search for Beauty; Hold That Girl; Bolero;

Cleopatra; The Witching Hour. **1935** Father Brown, Detective; It Happened in New York; Four Hours to Kill; The Last Outpost; Protegees. **1936** Woman Trap; The Return of Sophie Lang; Make Way for a Lady; Second Wife; 'Til We Meet Again. **1937** Sins of the Fathers; Mr. Dodd Takes the Air; Sophie Lang Goes West. **1938** Just Like a Woman. **1939** Hidden Power. **1940** The Farmer's Daughter; The Hidden Menace; Pound Foolish (short); I Can't Give You Anything But Love, Baby; Parole Fixer; Slightly Tempted. **1942** Prisoner of Japan. **1943** Behind Prison Walls; Where Are Your Children?; Women in Bondage. **1944** Faces in the Fog. **1945** Three's a Crowd; Club Havana; Allotment Wives. **1948** That Wonderful Urge. **1949** Flamingo Road. **1950** Caged. **1951** Darling, How Could You?. **1952** Bugles in the Afternoon. **1953** No Escape. **1955** Women's Prison. **1961** The Outsider. **1962** Twist All Night.

MICHAEL, MICKIE

Born: 1943. Died: Nov. 18, 1973, Hollywood, Calif. (auto accident). Screen and stage actress. Married to cinematographer Jim Childs.

MICHAELS, SULLY

Born: 1917. Died: Jan. 4, 1966, New York, N.Y. Screen, stage and television actor.

Appeared in: **1959** The Last Mile.

MICHALESKO, MICHAEL (Michael Michalesco)

Born: 1885, Russia. Died: Apr. 28, 1957, New York, N.Y. Yiddish screen and stage actor.

Appeared in: **1938** Power of Life. **1950** God, Man and Devil; Catskill Honeymoon.

MICHEL, GASTON

Born: 1856, France? Died: Nov., 1921, Lisbon, Portugal. Screen actor.

Appeared in: **1922** L'Orpheline (The Orphan).

MICHELENA, BEATRICE (Beatriz Michelena)

Born: 1890. Died: Oct. 10, 1942, San Francisco, Calif. Stage and screen actress. Sister of actress Vera Michelena (dec. 1961). Entered films in 1913.

Appeared in: **1914** Salomy Jane; Mrs. Wiggs of the Cabbage Patch. **1915** Mignon; Salvation Nell; The Lily of Poverty Flat; The Rose of the Misty Pool; A Phyllis of the Sierras; The Unwritten Law. **1916** The Passion Flower; The Heart of Juanita; Just Squaw; Jaust; The Woman Who Dared. **1917** The Flame of Hellgate.

MICHELENA, VERA

Born: 1884. Died: Aug. 26, 1961, Bayside, N.Y. Screen, stage and vaudeville actress. Sister of actress Beatrice Michelena (dec. 1942).

MICHLES, STEWART (aka STUART MASLER)

Died: Apr. 28, 1978. Screen actor.

MIDDLEMASS, ROBERT M.

Born: Sept. 3, 1885, New Britain, Conn. Died: Sept. 10, 1949, Los Angeles, Calif. Screen, stage, vaudeville actor, playwright and author.

Appeared in: **1934** Hotel Anchovy (short). **1935** Air Hawks; Awakening of Jim Burke; After the Dance; Unknown Woman; Atlantic Adventure; Public Menace; Grand Exit; One Way Ticket; Superspeed; Too Tough to Kill; Air Fury. **1936** You May Be Next; F-Man; The Lone Wolf Returns; Muss 'Em Up; Nobody's Fool; Two Against the World; A Son Comes Home; The Case of the Velvet Claws; Cain and Mabel; General Spanky; Hats Off; Grand Jury. **1937** Hideaway Girl; Guns of the Pecos; A Day at the Races; Meet the Boyfriend; Navy, Blue and Gold. **1938** While New York Sleeps; Miracle Money (short); Blondes at Work; Highway Patrol; Spawn of the North; I Am the Law; Kentucky; I Stand Accused. **1939** Stanley and Livingstone; Indianapolis Speedway; Blondie Brings Up Baby; Stand Up and Fight; The Magnificent Fraud; Coast Guard. **1940** The Saint Takes Over; Little Old New York; Slightly Dishonorable; Pop Always Pays. **1941** No Hands on the Clock; Road to Zanzibar. **1943** Truck Busters. **1944** Lady in the Death House; Wilson. **1945** A Sporting Chance; The Dolly Sisters.

MIDDLETON, CHARLES B.

Born: Oct. 3, 1879, Elizabethtown, Ky. Died: Apr. 22, 1949, Los Angeles, Calif. Screen, stage, circus and vaudeville actor. Entered films in 1927. Best remembered as "Ming the Merciless" in the "Flash Gordon" serials. Married to actress Leora Spellman (dec. 1945) with whom he appeared in vaudeville as "Middleton and Spellmeyer."

Appeared in: **1928** A Man of Peace (short); The Farmer's Daughter. **1929** Bellamy Trail; The Far Call; Welcome Danger. **1930** Beau Bandit;

Way Out West; The Frame (short); Christmas Knight (short); East Is West; More Sinned Against Than Usual (short). **1931** An American Tragedy; Beau Hunks (short); Full of Notions; Ships of Hate; Caught Plastered; Miracle Woman; Palmy Days; Alexander Hamilton. **1932** I Am a Fugitive from a Chain Gang; The Sign of the Cross; High Pressure; The Hatchet Man; Manhattan Parade; Strange Love of Molly Louvain; Pack Up Your Troubles; Hell's Highway; Silver Dollar; Rockabye; Breach of Promise; Mystery Ranch; Kongo. **1933** Pickup; Destination Unknown; Tomorrow at Seven; Sunset Pass; Disgraced; This Day and Age; Big Executive; White Woman; Duck Soup. **1934** When Strangers Meet; Lone Cowboy; Last Round Up; Murder at the Vanities; Behold My Wife; Massacre; David Harum; Mrs. Wiggs of the Cabbage Patch. **1935** Frisco Kid; The Miracle Rider (serial); Special Agent; The Fixer-Uppers (short); Steamboat 'Round the Bend; County Chairman; Hopalong Cassidy; Square Shooter; In Spite of Danger; Red Morning; The Virginia Judge. **1936** Texas Rangers; Space Soldiers; Sunset of Power; Road Gang; The Trail of the Lonesome Pine; Flash Gordon (serial); Showboat; Empty Saddles; Song of the Saddle; Jail Break; A Son Comes Home; Career Woman. **1937** The Good Earth; Two-Gun Law; We're on the Jury; Hollywood Cowboy; Yodelin' Kid from Pine Ridge. **1938** Flash Gordon's Trip to Mars (serial aka Mars Attacks the World); Flaming Frontiers (serial); Dick Tracy Returns (serial); Outside the Law; Kentucky. **1939** Captain Fury; Blackmail; Daredevils of the Red Circle (serial); Wyoming Outlaw; Slave Ship; Cowboys from Texas; Juarez; Way Down South; $1,000 a Touchdown; One Against the World (short); Jesse James; The Flying Deuces; The Oklahoma Kid. **1940** Thou Shalt Not Kill; Charlie Chan's Murder Cruise; Virginia City; Flash Gordon Conquers the Universe (serial); Chad Hanna; Abe Linclon in Illinois; The Grapes of Wrath; Shooting High; Santa Fe; Island of Doomed Men. **1941** Western Union; Wild Geese Calling; Belle Starr; Wild Bill Hickok Rides; Jungle Man. **1942** Perils of Nyoka (serial); The Mystery of Marie Roget; Men of San Quentin. **1943** Batman (serial); The Black Raven; Two Weeks to Live. **1944** Black Arrow (serial); The Desert Hawk (serial); The Sign of the Cross (revised version of 1932 film); The Town Went Wild. **1945** Who's Guilty? (serial); Our Vines Have Tender Grapes; Hollywood and Vine; Captain Kidd; How Do You Do. **1946** The Killers; Spook Busters; Strangler of the Swamp. **1947** Jack Armstrong (serial); The Pretender. **1948** Station West; Jiggs and Maggie in Court; Mr. Blandings Builds His Dream House. **1949** The Last Bandit; The Black Arrow.

MIDDLETON, GUY
Born: Dec. 14, 1908, Hove, England. Died: July 30, 1973, near London, England. Screen, stage and television actor.

Appeared in: **1935** Jimmy Boy; Two Hearts in Harmony; Trust the Navy. **1936** Under Proof; A Woman Alone (aka Two Who Dared—US 1937); The Mysterious Mr. Davis (aka My Partner Mr. Davis); Gay Adventure; Fame. **1937** Keep Fit; Take a Chance. **1938** Break the News (US 1941). **1939** French Without Tears (US 1940); Goodbye, Mr. Chips. **1940** For Freedom. **1941** Dangerous Moonlight (aka Suicide Squadron—US 1942). **1942** Talk About Jacqueline. **1943** The Demi-Paradise (aka Adventure for Two—US 1945). **1944** Halfway House (US 1945); Champagne Charlie; English Without Tears (aka Her Man Gilbey—US 1949). **1945** The Rake's Progress (aka Notorious Gentleman—US 1946); 29 Acacia Avenue (aka The Facts of Love—US 1949). **1946** The Captive Heart (US 1947); Night Boat to Dublin. **1947** The White Unicorn (aka Bad Sister—US 1948); A Man About the House (US 1949). **1948** Snowbound (US 1949); One Night With You. **1949** Marry Me (US 1951); Once Upon a Dream. **1950** No Place for Jennifer (US 1951); The Happiest Days of Your Life. **1951** Laughter in Paradise; Young Wives' Tale (US 1954); The Third Visitor. **1952** Never Look Back. **1953** Albert, RN (aka Break to Freedom—US 1955); The Fake. **1954** The Belles of St. Trinian's (US 1955); Malaga (aka Fire Over Africa—US); Make Me an Offer (US 1956); The Sea Shall Not Have Them (US 1955); Front Page Story (US 1955); The Harassed Hero; Conflict of Wings. **1955** Gentlemen Marry Brunettes; Break in the Circle (US 1957); A Yank in Ermine. **1957** Alive on Saturday; Let's Be Happy; Doctor at Large; Light Fingers; Now and Forever. **1958** The Passionate Summer. **1960** Escort for Hire. **1962** The Waltz of the Toreadors; What the Woman Wants. **1969** Oh! What a Lovely War; The Magic Christian (US 1970).

MIDDLETON, JOSEPHINE
Born: 1883. Died: Apr. 8, 1971, England. Screen, stage and vaudeville actress.

Appeared in: **1944** Love Story (aka A Lady Surrenders—US 1947). **1950** The Woman in Question (aka Five Angles on Murder—US 1953). **1951** The Browning Version. **1955** Before I Wake (aka Shadow of Fear—US 1956).

MIDDLETON, JOSEPHINE See SPELLMAN, LEORA

MIDDLETON, ROBERT (Samuel G. Messer)
Born: May 13, 1911, Cincinnati, Ohio. Died: June 14, 1977, Burbank, Calif. (heart failure). Screen, stage, radio and television actor.

Appeared in: **1954** The Silver Chalice (film debut). **1955** The Desperate Hours; Trial; The Big Combo. **1956** Friendly Persuasion; Love Me Tender; The Court Jester; Red Sundown; The Proud Ones. **1957** The Lonely Man; The Tarnished Angels. **1958** Day of the Bad Man; The Law and Jake Wade; No Place to Land. **1959** Don't Give Up the Ship; Career. **1960** Hell Bent for Leather. **1961** Gold of the Seven Saints; The Great Imposter. **1963** Cattle King. **1964** For Those Who Think Young. **1966** A Big Hand for the Little Lady. **1970** The Cheyenne Social Club; Company of Killers; Which Way to the Front? **1977** The Lincoln Conspiracy.

MIDDLETON, WALLACE (Walter Franklin Outler)
Born: Oct. 15, 1902, Wash. Died: Nov. 7, 1960, Hollywood, Calif. (heart attack). Screen actor and dancer.

Appeared in: **1931** An American Tragedy.

MIDGELY, FANNIE
Born: Nov. 26, 1877, Cincinnati, Ohio. Died: Jan. 4, 1932. Screen and stage actress. Entered films with Biograph.

Appeared in: **1915** Aloha Oe. **1916** The Waifs; The Apostle of Vengeance; Civilization; The Man from Oregon; Somewhere in France; The Criminal; Jim Grimsby's Boy. **1919** The Lottery Man. **1921** All Soul's Eve; First Love; Don't Call Me Little Girl; Patsy. **1922** Blue Blazes; When Love Comes; Through a Glass Window; The Young Rajah. **1923** Wasted Lives; Stephen Steps Out. **1925** Three Wise Crooks; Greed; Marry Me; The Bridge of Sighs; Some Pun'kins. **1926** Hair Trigger Baxter; Ace of Action; The Fighting Cheat; The Dangerous Dub; Laddie. **1927** The Harvester. **1928** The Flying Buckaroo; The Cowboy Cavalier. **1929** Behing Closed Doors; Naughty Baby; Welcome Danger. **1930** The Poor Millionaire. **1931** An American Tragedy.

MIDGLEY, FLORENCE
Born: 1890. Died: Nov. 16, 1949, Hollywood, Calif. Screen and stage actress. Entered films in 1918.

Mother of actor Richard Midgley **1921** The Great Impersonation; Partners of the Tide. **1926** Memory Lane. **1928** Sadie Thompson; Burning Bridges. **1929** The Three Outcasts; Painted Faces.

MIDGLEY, RICHARD A.
Born: 1910. Died: Nov. 30, 1956, New York, N.Y. Screen and stage actor.

MIGNONE, CAROLINA See MILLY

MIHAIL, ALEXANDRA
Born: 1947, Belgium? Died: Dec. 17, 1975, Brussels, Belgium (asphyxiation). Stage and screen actress.

MIKHOELS, SALOMON M.
Born: 1890, Dvinsk, Russia. Died: 1948, Moscow, Russia. Screen actor.

Appeared in: **1923** The Return of Nathan Becker. **1939** The Oppenheim Family.

MILAM, PAULINE
Born: 1912. Died: May 2, 1965, Hollywood, Calif. Screen, vaudeville actress and dancer. Was a "Goldwyn Girl."

MILAN, FRANK
Born: 1906. Died: Apr. 8, 1977, New York, N.Y. (heart attack). Screen, stage and television actor.

Appeared in: **1937** Hollywood Cowboy; The Gold Racket; Slave Ship. **1938** Danger on the Air; Pals of the Saddle; Joy of Living. **1940** Kitty Foyle; And One Was Beautiful. **1941** Kings Row.

MILANI, JOSEPH See CHEF MILANI

MILASH, ROBERT E. (aka ROBERT E. MILASCH)
Born: Apr. 18, 1885, New York, N.Y. Died: Nov. 14, 1954, Woodland Hills, Calif. (uremic poisioning). Screen and stage actor. Entered films with Edison Co.

Appeared in: **1903** The Great Train Robbery. **1921** Black Beauty. **1922** Confidence; The Prodigal Judge; Catch My Smoke. **1924** Abraham Lincoln; The Right of the Strongest; Captain Blood. **1925** Thank You. **1927** Grinning Guns; Men of Daring; A Hero for a Night. **1928** The Little Shepherd of Kingdom Come; The Upland Rider. **1930** Dangerous Nan McGrew. **1936** Give Us This Night.

MILCREST, HOWARD
Born: 1892. Died: Nov. 23, 1920, Huachuca Mountains, Ariz. (fall from horse). Screen actor. Entered films with Griffith approx. 1910.

MILES, ARTHUR K.
Born: 1899. Died: Nov. 6, 1955, Hollywood, Calif. Screen actor.

Appeared in: **1939** The Gorilla. **1942** Perils of the Royal Mounted (serial); The Spoilers. **1944** Gentle Annie. **1945** Paris Underground. **1946** Night in Paradise.

MILES, DAVID
Born: Milford, Conn. Died: Oct. 28, 1915, New York, N.Y. (hemorrhage). Screen actor and film director. Married to actress Anita Hendrie (dec. 1940). Entered films with Biograph in 1909.

Appeared in: **1909** The Violin Maker of Cremona.

MILES, LOTTA (Florence Court)
Born: 1899. Died: July 25, 1937, Los Angeles, Calif. (heart ailment). Screen and stage actress.

Appeared in: **1935** Waterfront Lady.

MILES, GENERAL NELSON APPLETON
Born: Aug. 8, 1839, Westminster, Mass. Died: May 15, 1925, Washington, D.C. (heart disease). Professional soldier, author and screen actor. He fought in the Civil War, various Indian campaigns, etc.

Appeared in: **1914** The Indian Wars.

MILESTONE, LEWIS (Lewis Milstein)
Born: Sept. 1895, Chisinaw, Russia. Died: Sept. 25, 1980, Los Angeles, Calif. Screen actor, film producer, film director, film editor and screenwriter.

Appeared in: **1926** Fascinating Youth.

MILHAUD, DARIUS
Born: 1893, Aix-en-Provence, France. Died: June 22, 1974, Geneva, Switzerland. Composer, conductor, writer and screen actor.

Appeared in: **1924** Entracte.

MILJAN, JOHN
Born: Nov. 9, 1893, Lead City, S.D. Died: Jan. 24, 1960, Hollywood, Calif. Screen and stage actor.

Appeared in: **1923** Love Letters (film debut). **1924** The Painted Lady; Romance Ranch; The Lone Wolf; On the Stroke of Three; Empty Hearts; The Lone Chance. **1925** The Unnamed Woman; Silent Sanderson; Sackcloth and Scarlet; Morals for Men; The Overland Limited; The Phantom of the Opera; Sealed Lips; Wreckage; The Unchastened Woman. **1926** The Devil's Circus; Flaming Waters; Almost a Lady; Footloose Widows; My Official Wife; The Amateur Gentleman; Brooding Eyes; Devil's Island; Race Wild; Unknown Treasures. **1927** The Yankee Clipper; Old San Francisco; Wolf's Clothing; The Ladybird; What Happened to Father?; A Sailor's Sweetheart; The Desired Woman; Sailor Izzy Murphy; The Silver Slave; The Clown; Stranded; The Final Extra; Framed; Lovers?; Paying the Price; Quarantined Rivals; Rough House Rosie; The Satin Woman; The Slaver. **1928** Lady Be Good; Husbands for Rent; The Beast (short); The Crimson City; The Little Snob; Glorious Betsy; Tenderloin; Land of the Silver Fox; Women They Talk About; The Terror; The Home Towners; His Night Out (short); Devil May-Care. **1929** Untamed; The Desert Song; Hardboiled Rose; Hunted; Stark Mad; The Unholy Night; Queen of the Night Club; Speedway; Voice of the City; The Eternal Woman; Times Square; Fashions in Love; Innocents in Paris; Gossip (short). **1930** Lights and Shadows; Remote Control; Not So Dumb; Free and Easy; Our Blushing Brides; The Sea Bat; The Woman Racket; Showgirl in Hollywood; The Unholy Three. **1931** Inspiration; The Iron Man; The Secret Six; A Gentleman's Fate; Son of India; Rise of Helga; The Green Meadow; War Nurse; Politics; Hell Divers; Susan Lennox, Her Rise and Fall; Possessed; Paid. **1932** Emma; Sky Devils; West of Broadway; Beast of the City; Arsene Lupin; The Wet Parade; Are You Listening?; Justice for Sale; Grand Hotel; The Rich Are Always With Us; Unashamed; Flesh; Night Court; Prosperity; The Kid from Spain. **1933** What! No Beer?; Whistling in the Dark; The Sin of Nora Moran; The Nuisance; King for a Night; Blind Adventure; The Way to Love; The Mad Game. **1934** Young and Beautiful; The Poor Rich; Madame Spy; Whirlpool; The Line-Up; The Belle of the Nineties; Unknown Blonde; Irish Husbands. **1935** Tomorrow's Youth; Mississippi; Charlie Chan in Paris; Under the Pampas Moon; The Ghost Walks; Three Kids and a Queen. **1936** Murder at Glen Athol; Sutter's Gold; The Criminal Within; Private Number; The Gentleman from Louisiana; North of Nome; The Plainsman. **1937** Arizona Mahoney. **1938** Man-Proof; If I Were King; Pardon Our Nerve; Miracle Money (short); Border G-Man; Ride a Crooked Mile. **1939** Juarez; The Oklahoma Kid; Torchy Runs for Mayor; Fast and Furious.

1940 Emergency Squad; Women Without Names; Queen of the Mob; New Moon; Young Bill Hickok. **1941** Texas Rangers Ride Again; Forced Landing; The Cowboy and the Blonde; The Deadly Game; Riot Squad; Double Cross. **1942** The Big Street; True to the Army; Scattergood Survives a Murder; Boss of the Big Town; Criminal Investigator. **1943** Bombardier; Submarine Alert; The Fallen Sparrow. **1944** Bride by Mistake; I Accuse My Parents; The Merry Monahans. **1945** It's in the Bag. **1946** Lost City of the Jungle (serial); The Last Crooked Mile; The Killers; White Tie and Tails; Gallant Man. **1947** Unconquered; Sinbad, the Sailor; Queen of the Amazons; In Self Defense; The Flame; That's My Man; Quest of Willie Hunter. **1948** Perilous Waters. **1949** Adventure in Baltimore; Mrs. Mike; Stampede; Samson and Delilah. **1950** Mule Train. **1951** M. **1952** The Savage; Bonzo Goes to College. **1955** Pirates of Tripoli; Run for Cover. **1956** The Ten Commandments; The Wild Dakotas. **1957** Apache Warrior. **1958** The Lone Ranger and the Lost City of Gold.

MILLAR, ADELQUI
Born: Aug. 5, 1891, Concepcion, Chile. Died: Aug. 7, 1956, Santiago, Chile. Screen, stage actor and film director.

Appeared in: **1924** The Arab. **1927** Moon of Israel.

MILLAR, ADOLPH
Born: 1886, Germany. Died: May 25, 1950. Screen actor.

Appeared in: **1920** The Silent Barrier. **1921** Something Different; Road of Ambition; The Girl from Porcupine. **1922** My Friend, the Devil. **1923** Backbone; Fury. **1924** Love's Wilderness. **1925** Marriage in Transit. **1927** Back to God's Country; Uncle Tom's Cabin. **1928** The Michigan Kid; Gateway to the Moon; Devil's Skipper; Clothes Make the Woman. **1929** Bulldog Drummond. **1930** Der Tahz Geht Weiter; Isle of Escape; Rain or Shine; Medicine Man. **1931** Honeymoon Lane. **1933** The Savage Girl.

MILLAR, LEE, JR.
Born: 1925. Died: Sept. 21, 1980, Los Angeles, Calif. (cancer). Screen, radio and television actor. Son of actors Lee Millar, Sr. (dec. 1941), and Verna Felton (dec. 1966).

Appeared in: **1955** Lady and the Tramp (voice).

MILLAR, LEE, SR.
Born: 1888. Died: Dec. 24, 1941, Glendale, Calif. (heart attack). Screen, stage and radio actor. Voice of Pluto in Walt Disney cartoons. Married to actress Verna Felton (dec. 1966). Father of actor Lee Millar (dec. 1980).

MILLAR, MARJIE
Born: Tacoma, Wash. Died: 1966. Screen actress. Divorced from television director John Florea.

Appeared in: **1953** Money from Home. **1954** About Mrs. Leslie. **1956** When Gangland Strikes.

MILLARD, HARRY W. (Harry Millard Williams)
Born: 1928. Died: Sept. 2, 1969, New York, N.Y. (cancer). Screen, stage, television actor and film producer.

Appeared in: **1959** The Last Mile.

MILLARDE, HARRY
Born: Nov. 12, 1885. Died: Nov. 2, 1931, Queens, N.Y. (heart attack). Screen actor and film director. Married to actress June Caprice (dec. 1936).

Appeared in: **1913** The War Correspondent; The Woe of Battle; The Fire Fighting Zouaves; The Secret Marriage; The Mermaid. **1914** The Hand of Fate; The Vampire's Trail; The Storm at Sea; Into the Depths; The False Guardian; Seed and the Harvest. **1915** The Sign of the Broken Shackles; The Man in Hiding; The Money Gulf; The Mysterious Case of Meredith Stanhope; Don Caesar de Bazan. **1916** Elusive Isabel.

MILLEN, FRANK H.
Born: 1861. Died: Dec. 26, 1931, Albuquerque, N.Mex. Screen and stage actor. Appeared in silents.

MILLER, ALICE (Alice Duer)
Born: July 28, 1874, N.Y. Died: Aug. 22, 1942, New York, N.Y. Screen actress, screenwriter and novelist.

Appeared in: **1936** Soak the Rich.

MILLER, ASHLEY
Born: 1867. Died: Nov. 19, 1949, New York, N.Y. Screen, stage actor and stage director. Appeared in early films.

MILLER, ALICE MOORE See MOORE, ALICE

MILLER, CARL (Carlton Miller)
Born: Aug. 9, 1893, Wichita County, Tex. Died: Feb., 1979, Honolulu, Hawaii. Screen actor. Entered films in 1916.

Appeared in: **1919** Mary Regan. **1921** Cinderella of the Hills; The Kid; The Parish Priest; The Bride's Play. **1923** Condemned; Jealous Husbands; A Woman of Paris. **1924** The Dark Swan (aka The Black Swan); The Lover of Camille. **1925** The Redeeming Sin; We Moderns; The Wall Street Whiz; Trapped. **1926** The Red Kimono; The Canyon of Light; The Power of the Weak; The Great K & A Train Robbery. **1927** Good as Gold; Whispering Sage. **1928** Why Sailors Go Wrong; Haunted Island; Making the Varsity. **1931** Traveling Husbands; Honor of the Family. **1933** Renegades of the West; Phantom Broadcast. **1934** Embarrassing Moments. **1935** No Ransom.

MILLER, CHARLES B.
Born: 1891. Died: June 5, 1955, Hollywood, Calif. (shot). Screen actor.

Appeared in: **1939** The Night of Nights. **1940** Phantom of Chinatown. **1941** The Spiderman Returns (serial); Caught in the Act. **1942** South of Santa Fe; Raiders of the Range; The Phantom Plainsman; Joan of Ozark; They All Kissed the Bride. **1943** Daredevils of the West (serial); Days of Old Cheyenne. **1944** Black Hills Express. **1945** Wilson; House of Frankenstein; Honeymoon Ahead; The Caribbean Mystery. **1946** Rendezvous 24-F; Rustler's Round-Up; Gunman's Code. **1947** Persued; I'll Be Yours. **1948** Mexican Hayride.

MILLER, DAVID (David Prince Miller)
Born: Mar. 31, 1871, Glasgow, Scotland. Died: Jan. 1, 1933, England? Screen, stage actor, stage producer and manager.

Appeared in: **1931** Out of the Blue. **1932** The Verdict of the Sea; Sleepless Nights; Lord Camber's Ladies. **1940** The Face at the Window.

MILLER, DIANA (Diana Moreland)
Born: Mar. 18, 1902, Seattle, Wash. Died: Dec. 18, 1927, Monrovia, Calif. (tuberculosis). Screen actress. Married to actor/director George Melford (dec. 1961).

Appeared in: **1924** Honor Among Men; The Desert Outlaw. **1925** Curley Top; The Kiss Barrier. **1926** The Cowboy and the Countess.

MILLER, DONALD C. "DON"
Born: c. 1902, Defiance, Ohio. Died: July 28, 1979, Cleveland, Ohio (heart attack). Football player and coach, attorney, judge and screen actor.

Appeared in: **1931** The Spirit of Notre Dame.

MILLER, E. G. (Edward George Miller)
Born: 1883. Died: Dec. 1, 1948, Los Angeles, Calif. Screen actor. Entered films with Biograph.

Appeared in: **1921** Without Benefit of Clergy.

MILLER, EDDIE
Born: 1891. Died: Mar. 9, 1971, Amityville, N.Y. Screen actor and singer. Headed musical group known as "Eddie Miller and His Bob Cats."

Appeared in: **1941** Safe at Home. **1943** Mister Big. **1955** Pete Kelly's Blues.

MILLER, EVE (aka EVE TURNER aka EVE MEYER)
Born: 1933. Died: Mar. 27, 1977, Canary Islands (plane crash). Screen, stage actress and film producer. Married to film director Russ Meyer.

Appeared in: **1947** I Wonder Who's Kissing Her Now; Buckaroo from Powder River. **1948** Inner Sanctum. **1949** Arctic Fury. **1950** Never Fear; The Young Lovers. **1951** Pier 23. **1952** The Big Trees; The Winning Team; The Story of Will Rogers; April in Paris; She's Working Her Way Through College. **1953** Kansas Pacific. **1954** There's No Business Like Show Business. **1955** The Big Bluff; Artists and Models. **1959** Operation Dames. **1961** Eve and the Handyman.

MILLER, FLOURNOY E.
Born: 1889, Columbia, Tenn. Died: June 6, 1971, Hollywood, Calif. (coronary failure). Black screen, stage, vaudeville actor, script writer for television, playwright and stage producer. Partner in vaudeville team of "Miller and Lyles."

Appeared in: **1935** Lem Hawkins' Confession. **1938** The Bronze Buckaroo; Harlem on the Prairie. **1939** Double Deal; Harlem Rides the Range. **1940** Mr. Washington Goes to Town; Brigham Young—Frontiersman; Lady Luck; Mystery in Swing; Santa Fe Trail. **1941** Professor Creeps. **1943** Stormy Weather. **1946** Mantan Runs for Mayor. **1948** Return of Mandy's Husband; She's Too Mean to Me. **1951** Yes Sir, Mr. Bones.

MILLER, FRANK
Born: 1891, London, England. Died: c. 1950, England? Screen actor, film director and screenwriter. Do not confuse with other actors with same name.

Appeared in: **1906** Oh That Doctor's Boy. **1910** The Terror and the Terrier. **1919** Fancy Dress. **1936** Bed and Breakfast.

MILLER, FRANK
Died: Nov. 2, 1933, Glendale, Calif. Screen and stage actor. Do not confuse with other actors with same name.

MILLER, GLENN (Alton Glenn Miller)
Born: Mar. 1, 1904, Clarinda, Iowa. Died: Dec. 15, 1944, Europe (plane crash). Bandleader, composer and screen actor.

Appeared in: **1942** Orchestra Wives; Sun Valley Serenade.

MILLER, GORDON (Luke Aloysious Miller)
Born: May 18, 1882, Pa. Died: Apr. 9, 1962, Encino, Calif. (pneumonia). Screen and stage actor.

MILLER, HAROLD ATCHISON
Born: 1894, Redondo Beach, Calif. Died: July 18, 1972, Calif. Screen actor.

Appeared in: **1919** Upstairs and Down. **1920** Heart of a Fool. **1921** Desperate Youth; Playing With Fire; Short Skirts. **1922** Very Truly Yours; Kissed. **1923** Tipped Off. **1924** Leatherstocking (serial); Way of a Man (serial). **1927** Out of the Past; The Princess on Broadway; Woman's Law. **1953** Three Sailors and a Girl. **1956** The Best Things in Life Are Free; The Birds and the Bees.

MILLER, HENRY (Henry Valentine Miller)
Born: Dec. 26, 1891, New York, N.Y. Died: June 7, 1980, Pacific Palisades, Calif. (circulatory ailments). Screen actor and novelist.

Appeared in: **1970** Tropic of Cancer. **1980** Reds

MILLER, HUGH J.
Born: 1902. Died: May 11, 1956, Los Angeles, Calif. Screen actor. Father of actress Barbara Heller.

Appeared in: **1927** Blind Alleys. **1935** The Divine Spark; I Give My Heart. **1937** The Dominant Sex; Victoria the Great; Bulldog Drummond at Bay. **1938** The Rat; The Return of the Scarlet Pimpernel; The Loves of Madame Du Barry.

MILLER, IVAN
Born: 1889. Died: Sept. 27, 1967, Calif. Screen actor.

Appeared in: **1935** Dr. Socrates; Mary Burns—Fugitive; Calm Yourself. **1936** Charlie Chan's Secret; Nobody's Fool; Back to Nature; Bulldog Edition; Country Gentlemen. **1937** A Fight to the Finish; Let's Make a Million. **1938** Call of the Yukon; I Am the Law; Scouts to the Rescue (serial); The Old Barn Dance; Man from Music Mountain. **1939** Cowboys from Texas; Geronimo. **1940** The Man With Nine Lives; Frontier Vengeance; Shooting High. **1941** The Devil Pays Off; Lady for a Night; Man-Made Monster; Under Fiesta Stars; Jesse James at Bay. **1943** G-Men vs. the Black Dragon (serial).

MILLER, JACK
Born: 1888. Died: Sept. 25, 1928, San Diego, Calif. (intestinal trouble). Stage and screen actor.

Appeared in: **1930** Hell's Angels.

MILLER, JACK "SHORTY"
Born: 1895. Died: Feb. 28, 1941, Burbank, Calif. (heart attack). Screen cowboy actor.

MILLER, JUANITA
Born: 1880. Died: Apr., 1970, Oakland, Calif. Poet and screen actress. Appeared in films during early 1920s. Daughter of poet Joaquin Miller (dec. 1913). "Her second marriage in April, 1921, began with the bride in a corpse-like state in a funeral setting. The groom kissed her and she awoke. There followed a naturalistic ritual involving the sacrifice of a goat and a demonstration of Miss Miller's cooking prowess."

MILLER, KAY
Born: 1907. Died: June 17, 1933, Hollywood, Calif. Screen actress. Do not confuse with radio actress Kay Miller (dec. 1975).

MILLER, LORRAINE (aka LORRAINE YOUNG)
Born: 1928. Died: Feb. 6, 1978. Screen and stage actress. Married to actor Eddie Buzzell.

Appeared in: **1943** Happy Go Lucky; Riders of the Rio Grande (serial). **1944** Between Two Women. **1945** Men in Her Diary. **1946** Ambush Trail; Rendezvous. **1950** Rapture; It's a Small World.

MILLER, LOU (aka LU MILLER)
Born: 1906. Died: May 2, 1941, Hollywood, Calif. Screen actress. Married to actor William Ruhl.

Appeared in: **1937** Easy Living. **1938** Hunted Men.

MILLER, MARILYN (Marilyn or Mary Ellen Reynolds)
Born: Sept. 1, 1898, Evansville, Ind. Died: Apr. 7, 1936, New York, N.Y. (toxic poisoning). Stage and screen actress. Divorced from screen actor Jack Pickford (dec. 1933).

Appeared in: **1929** Sally. **1930** Sunny. **1931** Her Majesty, Love.

MILLER, MARTIN (Rudolph Muller)
Born: 1899, Czechoslovakia. Died: Aug. 26, 1969, Austria (heart attack). Screen, stage and television actor.

Appeared in: **1942** Squadron Leader X (US 1943). **1943** Adventures of Tartu (aka Tartu—US). **1944** English Without Tears (aka Her Man Gilbey—US 1949). **1948** Counterblast; Bonnie Prince Charlie (US 1952). **1949** The Huggets Abroad. **1951** Encore (US 1952). **1952** Where's Charley? **1954** Front Page Story (US 1955); You Know What Sailors Are; Mad About Men; To Dorothy a Son (aka Cash on Delivery—US 1956). **1955** An Alligator Named Daisy (US 1957). **1956** The Gamma People; The Baby and the Battleship. **1957** Seven Thunders (aka The Beasts of Marseilles—US 1959). **1959** Libel; Expresso Bongo (US 1960); Exodus; The Rough and the Smooth (aka Portrait of a Sinner—US 1961); Violent Moment (US 1966). **1960** Peeping Tom (US 1962). **1962** 55 Days at Peking; The Phantom of the Opera. **1963** The VIPs; Children of the Damned (US 1964); The Yellow Rolls Royce (US 1965); Incident at Midnight (US 1966). **1964** The Pink Panther. **1965** Up Jumped a Swagman.

MILLER, MAX (Thomas Sargent)
Born: 1895, England. Died: May, 7, 1963, Brighton, England. Screen, circus and vaudeville actor. Known as "The Cheeky Chappie."

Appeared in: **1933** The Good Companions; Channel Crossing (US 1934); Friday the 13th (US 1934). **1934** Princess Charming (US 1935). **1935** Things Are Looking Up; Get Off My Foot. **1936** Educated Evans. **1937** Don't Get Me Wrong; Take It from Me (aka Transatlantic Trouble). **1938** Thank Evans; Everything Happens to Me. **1939** The Good Old Days; Hoots Mon! **1942** Asking for Trouble.

MILLER, RANGER BILL
Born: 1878. Died: Nov. 12, 1939, Los Angeles, Calif. Screen actor. Adopted son of Buffalo Bill.

Appeared in: **1923** The Web of the Law. **1924** A Pair of Hellions. **1925** Heartbound.

MILLER, RUBY
Born: July 14, 1889, London, England. Died: Apr. 2, 1976, Chichester, England. Screen, stage, television actress, music hall entertainer, and author. Married to Lt. Philip Samson (dec. 1918), and composer Max Darewski (dec. 1929).

Appeared in: **1916** Frills. **1917** In Another Girl's Shoes; Little Women. **1919** The Edge O'Beyond; Gamblers All. **1921** The Mighty Road; The Mystery of Mr. Bernard Brown. **1924** Alimony. **1927** Land of Hope and Glory. **1928** The Infamous Lady. **1933** Sorrell and Son. **1935** The Love Affair of the Dictator (aka The Dictator, aka The Loves of a Dictator—US 1943); Gay Old Dog; The Right Age to Marry. **1936** Nothing Like Publicity; Talking Hands (short). **1937** Coming of Age; Double Exposure. **1939** Shadowed Eyes. **1940** Law and Disorder. **1941** Facing the Music. **1948** Anna Karenina.

MILLER, RUTH
Born: 1903. Died: June 13, 1981, Santa Monica, Calif. Screen and stage actress. Entered films in 1915 with Samuelson Studios in England. Appeared in Mack Sennett Comedies.

Appeared in: **1926** The Volga Boatman. **1927** The King of Kings.

MILLER, SETON I.
Born: May 3, 1902, Chehalis, Wash. Died: Mar. 29, 1974, Woodland Hills, Calif. (emphysema). Film, television producer, screenwriter, stage and screen actor. Married to stage actress Ann Evers. Entererd films in 1926 as an actor.

Appeared in: **1926** Brown of Harvard.

MILLER, THOMAS
Born: 1872. Died: Dec. 6, 1942, Los Angeles, Calif. Screen and stage actor.

Appeared in: **1934** The Old Fashioned Way.

MILLER, W. CHRISTY (William Christy Miller)
Born: 1843. Died: Sept. 23, 1922, Staten Island, N.Y. Screen and stage actor.

Appeared in: **1909** The Redman's View; The Day After. **1910** The Rocky Road; The Newlyweds; In Old California; The Thread of Destiny; The Way of the World; The Tenderfoot; Triumph; Her Father's Pride; The Lesson; Examination Day at School; The Two Brothers; A Plain Song. **1911** What Shall We Do With Our Old?; Dooley's Scheme; In the Days of '49; The Last Drop of Water; Swords and Hearts; The Old Bookkeeper. **1912** The Unwelcome Guest; An Indian Summer; The Chief's Blanket; Man's Genesis; The Sands of Dee; The Old Actor; The Informer; My Baby. **1913** The Battle at Elderberry Gulch; His Mother's Son; A Timely Interception; The Reformers.

MILLER, WALTER C. (Walter Corwin Miller)
Born: Mar. 9, 1892, Dayton, Ohio. Died: Mar. 30, 1940, Los Angeles, Calif. Screen, stage and vaudeville actor.

Appeared in: **1912** The Musketeers of Pig Alley; Oil and Water; Two Daughters of Eve; So Near, Yet So Far; A Feud in the Kentucky Hills; Brutality; An Adventure in the Autumn Woods; Bill Boggs' Windfall; A Change of Spirit; A Cry for Help; The Informer; An Unseen Enemy. **1913** A Girl's Stratagem; Near to Earth; Two Men of the Desert; The Yaqui Cur; A Modest Hero; Love in an Apartment Hotel; The Perfidy of Mary; His Mother's Son; Death's Marathon; The Wanderer; The Mothering Heart; The Coming of Angelo. **1914** A Beggar Prince of India; Enmeshed by Fate; The Fatal Wedding; The Girl and the Smuggler; Humanity in the Rough; The Road to Yesterday; Seven Days; The Wages of Sin; Through the Eyes of the Blind. **1915** The Family Stain; The Man Who Found Himself. **1916** The Marble Heart. **1917** Miss Robinson Crusoe; The Slacker. **1919** Thin Ice; A Girl at Bay. **1920** The Stealers. **1921** The Shadow; Luxury. **1922** Beyond the Rainbow; The Bootleggers; 'Till We Meet Again; The Woman Who Believed; Unconquered Woman. **1923** The Tie That Binds; Unseeing Eyes. **1924** Leatherstocking (serial); Men, Women and Money; Those Who Judge; Playthings of Desire. **1925** Sunken Silver (serial); Play Ball (serial); The Green Archer (serial); The Sky Raider. **1926** The House Without a Key (serial); The Fighting Marine (serial and feature film); Snowed In (serial); The Unfair Sex. **1927** Hawk of the Hills (serial); Melting Millions (serial). **1928** Police Reporter (serial); The Man Without a Face (serial); The Mysterious Airman (serial); The Terrible People (serial); Manhattan Knights. **1929** The Black Book (serial); King of the Kongo (serial released in silent and sound versions); Queen of the Northwoods (serial); Hawk of the Hills (feature of 1927 serial). **1930** Lone Defender (serial); On the Border; The Utah Kid; Rogue of the Rio Grande; King of the Wild; Rough Waters. **1931** The Galloping Ghost (serial); Swanee River; Street Scene; Hell's Valley; Sky Raiders; Hurricane Horseman; Danger Island (serial); King of the Wild (serial). **1932** The Shadow of the Eagle (serial); Three Wise Girls; Manhattan Parade; The Famous Ferguson Case; Ridin' for Justice; Ghost City; Face on the Barroom Floor; Heart Punch. **1933** Sin of a Sailor; Parachute Jumper; Maisie; Behind Jury Doors; Gordon of Ghost City (serial). **1934** Rocky Rhodes; Fighting Trooper; Gun Justice; Pirate Treasure (serial); The Vanishing Shadow (serial); The Red Rider (serial); Smoking Guns; Tailspin Tommy (serial). **1935** Call of the Savage (serial); Magnificent Obsession; Alias Mary Dow; Gun Valley; Valley of Wanted Men; Rustlers of Red Dog (serial); The Roaring West (serial); Stormy. **1936** Heart of the West; Desert Gold; The Fugitive Sheriff; Ghost Patrol; Without Orders; Night Waitress. **1937** Draegerman Courage; Boss of Lonely Valley; Midnight Court; Slim; Border Cafe; Flight from Glory; Saturday's Heroes; Danger Patrol; Wild West Days (serial); The Last Gangster. **1938** Wild Horse Rodeo; The Secret of Treasure Island (serial); Blind Alibi; Crime Ring; Lawless Valley; Come on Leathernecks; Down in "Arkansaw"; Smashing the Rackets. **1939** Dick Tracy's G-Men (serial); Home on the Prairie; Each Dawn I Die. **1940** Johnny Apollo; Virginia City; Bullet Code; Grandpa Goes to Town; Three Cheers for the Irish; Gaucho Serenade; The Saints' Double Trouble.

MILLICAN, JAMES
Born: 1910, Palisades, N.Y. Died: Nov. 24, 1955, Los Angeles, Calif. Screen actor.

Appeared in: **1932** The Sign of the Cross. **1933** Mills of the Gods. **1938** Who Killed Gail Preston? **1939** The Sap Takes a Wrap (short). **1942** The Remarkable Andrew; Star Spangled Rhythm. **1943** So Proudly We Hail! **1944** The Story of Dr. Wassell; The Sign of the Cross (revised version of 1932 film). **1945** Bring on the Girls; Tokyo Rose; The Affairs of Susan; Love Letters. **1946** The Tender Years; The Trouble With Women; Stepchild; Rendezvous With Annie. **1948** Mr. Reckless; Hazard; Let's Live Again; Disaster; Man from Colorado; Return of Wildfire; Last of the Wild Horses; Rogue's Regiment; In This Corner;

1949 Command Decision; The Dalton Gang; Fighting Man of the Plains; The Gal Who Took the West; Grand Canyon; Rimfire. **1950** Beyond the Purple Hills; The Devil's Doorway; Gunfighter; Military Academy With That 10th Ave. Gang; Mister 880; Winchester "73.". **1951** Al Jennings of Oklahoma; Calvary Scout; Fourteen Hours; The Great Missouri Raid; I Was a Communist for the FBI; Missing Women; Rawhide; Warpath. **1952** Bugles in the Afternoon; Carson City; Diplomatic Courier; High Noon; Scandal Sheet; Springfield Rifle; The Winning Team. **1953** Cow Country; Gun Belt; Silver Whip; Torpedo Alley; A Lion in the Streets. **1954** Crazylegs; Dawn at Socorro; Jubilee Trail; The Long Wait; The Outcast; Riding Shotgun. **1955** Las Vegas Shakedown; Top Gun; The Vanishing American; Strategic Air Command; The Man from Laramie; Big Tip Off; Chief Crazy Horse; I Died One Thousand Times. **1956** Red Sundown.

MILLIGAN, MARY "MIN"
Born: 1882, Ireland. Died: Mar. 10, 1966, Belfast, Ireland. Screen, stage and television actress.

MILLINGTON, MARY
Born: 1945, England. Died: Aug. 19, 1979, Banstead, Surrey, England. Screen actress.

Appeared in: **1968** Come Play With Me. **1974** End of August.

MILLMAN, WILLIAM (William L'Estrange Millman)
Born: 1883. Died: July 19, 1937, Hollywood, Calif. Screen and stage actor.

Appeared in: **1935** The Lost City (serial); Motive for Revenge. **1937** Silent Barriers.

MILLNER, MARIETTA
Died: June 26, 1927. Screen actress.

Appeared in: **1927** We're All Gamblers; Drums of the Desert; The City Gone Wild. **1928** The Magnificent Flirt.

MILLS, BOB
Born: 1898, Detroit, Mich. Died: Oct. 16, 1934, Colo. Screen actor.

MILLS, EDITH
Died: May 16, 1962. Screen actress.

Appeared in: **1939** Legion of Lost Flyers. **1950** Cherokee Uprising.

MILLS, EDWIN
Died: May 23, 1981, Los Angeles, Calif.? Screen actor.

Appeared in: **1924** Pied Piper Malone. **1943** Jitterbugs; Happy Land; The Unknown Guest. **1944** Bermuda Mystery. **1946** Sioux City Sue. **1947** Monsieur Verdoux. **1966** Stagecoach. **1976** Mother, Jugs and Speed.

MILLS, FRANK
Born: 1870. Died: June 11, 1921. Silent screen actor. Do not confuse with actor Frank Mills (dec. 1973).

MILLS, FRANK
Born: Jan. 26, 1891, Kalamazoo, Mich. Died: Aug. 18, 1973, Los Angeles, Calif. (arteriosclerosis). Screen and stage actor. Do not confuse with actor dec. 1921.

Appeared in: **1928** Chicago After Midnight; Hit of the Show; Danger Street. **1930** Those Who Dance. **1932** Make Me a Star. **1933** Gold Diggers of 1933. **1935** The Bride Comes Home; Another Face. **1936** Hi, Gaucho; Parole; Way Out West; Follow the Fleet; Great Guy. **1937** Dizzy Doctors (short). **1938** The Goldwyn Follies. **1940** Father Was a Fullback; Lucky Partners. **1942** Heart of the Rio Grande. **1943** Mr. Lucky. **1944** Gold Is Where You Lose It. **1949** Holiday Affair; Mr. Belvedere Goes to College. **1956** Around the World in 80 Days. **1957** The Joker Is Wild. **1970** The Golden Box.

MILLS, FREDDIE
Born: 1919. Died: July 22, 1965, London, England (suicide—shot). Former world's light heavyweight champion, restaurateur, screen and television actor.

Appeared in: **1952** Emergency Call (aka The Hundred Hour Hunt—US 1953). **1958** Kiss Me Tomorrow. **1960** Carry on Constable (US 1961). **1961** Carry on Regardless (US 1963). **1964** Saturday Night Out.

MILLS, GRANT
Died: Aug. 4, 1973, Skowhegan, Maine. Stage and screen actor. Divorced from actress Violet Heming (dec. 1981).

Appeared in: **1938** Professor Beware.

MILLS, GUY (Louis Miller)
Born: 1898. Died: Oct. 15, 1962, Chichester, England. Stage and screen actor. Appeared in films mostly doubling for stars in riding sequences.

MILLS, JAY
Born: 1899. Died: Mar. 6, 1951, West Palm Beach, Fla. Screen, vaudeville actor and composer.

MILLS, JIM
Born: 1920. Died: Apr. 24, 1980, Los Angeles, Calif. Screen, vaudeville, radio actor and minstrel performer.

Appeared in: **1977** Close Encounters of the Third Kind. **1978** The Swarm.

MILLS, JOHN, JR.
Born: 1910, Piqua, Ohio. Died: Jan. 23, 1936, Bellefontaine, Ohio (tuberculosis). Black singer, screen, radio and vaudeville actor. Brother of singers Herbert, Harry (dec. 1982) and Donald Mills with whom he appeared as a member of the "Mills Brothers Quartet." Son of singer John Mills, Sr. (dec. 1967).

Appeared in: **1932** The Big Broadcast; Paramount Screen Songs (shorts). **1934** 20 Million Sweethearts; Operator 13; Strictly Dynamite. **1935** Broadway Gondolier.

MILLS, JOHN, SR.
Born: Feb. 11, 1889, Bellefonte, Pa. Died: Dec. 8, 1967, Ohio. Black singer, screen, radio and vaudeville actor. Father of singers, Herbert, Harry (dec. 1982) and Donald Mills with whom he appeared as a member of the "Mills Brothers Quartet" and singer John Mills, Jr. (dec. 1936).

Appeared in: **1943** He's My Guy; Reveille with Beverly; Chatterbox.

MILLS, JOSEPH S. (Joseph Stapleton Mills)
Born: 1875. Died: Oct. 19, 1935, (heart attack). Screen and stage actor.

Appeared in: **1924** Abraham Lincoln; Love's Whirlpool. **1934** Men in Black (short).

MILLS, THOMAS R.
Born: 1878. Died: Nov. 29, 1953, Woodland Hills, Calif. Screen, stage and radio actor.

Appeared in: **1916** The Scarlet Runner (serial). **1924** The Guilty One; The Star Dust Trail; A Man's Mate; The Wolf Man. **1925** The Kiss Barrier; Tides of Passion; The Arizona Romeo. **1926** The Gilded Highway. **1934** Great Expectations. **1935** Les Miserables. **1937** It's Love I'm After. **1938** MGM short. **1939** We Are Not Alone.

MILLWARD, MIKE
Born: 1943, England. Died: Mar. 8, 1966, Bromoborough, England (throat cancer). Screen actor, singer and guitarist. Member of pop group "The Fourmost."

Appeared in: **1965** Go Go Mania.

MILLY (aka CAROLINA MIGNONE)
Born: 1905, Italy. Died: Oct., 1980, Nepi, Italy (heart attack). Screen, vaudeville actress and singer. Entered films during the early 1930's.

Appeared in: **1936** Tempo Massimo; Musica in Piazza; Amo te Sola. **1974** Le Petit Theatre de Jean Renoir (The Little Theatre of Jean Renoir).

MILNE, LENNOX
Born: 1910. Died: June, 1980, Edinburgh, Scotland. Screen, stage, radio and television actor.

Appeared in: **1970** Brotherly Love (aka Country Dance).

MILOS, MILOS (Milos Milosevic)
Born: July 1, 1941, Yugoslavia. Died: Jan. 31, 1966, Los Angeles, Calif. (suicide—gun). Screen actor.

Appeared in: **1961** Lion of Sparta. **1962** The 300 Spartans. **1965** Incubus. **1966** The Russians Are Coming, The Russians Are Coming.

MILTERN, JOHN
Born: 1870. Died: Jan. 15, 1937, Los Angeles, Calif. (hit by auto). Screen and stage actor.

Appeared in: **1920** On With the Dance. **1921** Experience; The Kentuckians. **1922** Manslaughter; The Hands of Nara; Kick In; Love's Boomerang; The Man Who Saw Tomorrow; Three Live Ghosts; The

Man from Home. **1923** The Ne'er-Do-Well. **1924** Tongues of Flame. **1925** Coming Through. **1926** Fine Manners. **1927** East Side, West Side; The Love of Sunya. **1935** Diamond Jim; The Dark Angel. **1936** Give Us This Night; Everybody's Old Man; Sins of Man; Ring Around the Moon; Murder on the Bridle Path; Parole. **1937** The Lost Horizon.

MILTON, ERNEST
Born: Jan. 10, 1890, San Francisco, Calif. Died: July 27, 1974, London, England. Screen, stage, television actor, playwright and author. Married to playwright Naomi Royde Smith (dec. 1964).

Appeared in: **1935** The Scarlet Pimpernel. **1936** It's Love Again. **1944** Fiddlers Three. **1951** Alice in Wonderland. **1957** The Cat Girl.

MILTON, GEORGES (Georges Michaud)
Born: 1888, France. Died: Oct. 16, 1970, Nice, France. Screen and stage actor.

Appeared in: **1932** Le Roi des Resquilleurs (King of the Gate Crashers). **1933** Nu Comme un Ver (Naked As a Worm). **1944** The Queen and the Cardinal.

MILTON, HARRY
Born: June 26, 1900, London, England. Died: Mar. 8, 1965, London, England. Screen, stage actor and assistant director. Divorced from actress Chili Bouchier.

Appeared in: **1933** The King's Cup; To Brighton With Gladys; King of the Ritz. **1934** Adventure Limited. **1936** Pagliacci (aka A Clown Must Laugh—US 1938).

MILTON, LOUETTE
Born: 1907. Died: Oct. 29, 1930, Wyo. Stage and screen actress.

Appeared in: **1930** Bride of the Regiment.

MILTON, MAUD
Born: Mar. 24, 1859, Gravesend, England. Died: Nov. 19, 1945, England? Screen and stage actress.

Appeared in: **1913** The Old Woodcarver. **1921** A Message From Mars.

MILWARD, DAWSON
Born: July 13, 1870, Woolwich, England. Died: May 15, 1926, England? Screen, stage actor and playwright.

Appeared in: **1920** General Post; The Skin Game. **1921** The Magistrate. **1922** The Recoil. **1924** The Eleventh Commandment. **1925** King of the Castle. **1926** One Colombo Night.

MIMS, LUKE
Born: 1901. Died: Aug. 26, 1933, Burbank, Calif. (airplane crash). Screen actor and stuntman.

MINCIOTTI, ESTHER
Born: 1888, Italy. Died: Apr. 15, 1962, New York, N.Y. Screen, stage and television actress. Married to actor Silvio Minciotti (dec. 1961).

Appeared in: **1949** House of Strangers; Shockproof; The Undercover Man. **1951** Strictly Dishonorable. **1955** Marty. **1956** Full of Life. **1957** The Wrong Man.

MINCIOTTI, SILVIO
Born: 1883, Italy. Died: May 2, 1961, Elmhurst, N.Y. Stage and screen actor. Married to actress Esther Minciotti (dec. 1962).

Appeared in: **1949** House of Strangers. **1950** Deported. **1951** Strictly Dishonorable; The Great Caruso; Up Front; Fourteen Hours. **1952** Clash by Night. **1953** Francis Covers the Big Town. **1955** Marty; Kiss Me Deadly. **1956** Serenade; Full of Life. **1957** The Wrong Man.

MINEO, SAL (Salvatore Mineo, Jr.)
Born: Jan. 10, 1939, New York, N.Y. Died: Feb. 12, 1976, West Hollywood, Calif. (murdered—stabbed). Screen, stage, television actor and stage director. Nominated for 1955 Academy Award for Best Supporting Actor in Rebel Without a Cause and in 1960 for Exodus.

Appeared in: **1955** Six Bridges to Cross (film debut); Rebel Without a Cause; The Private War of Major Benson. **1956** Crime in the Streets; Somebody Up There Likes Me; Giant; Rock, Pretty Baby. **1957** The Young Don't Cry; Dino. **1958** Tonka. **1959** The Gene Krupa Story; A Private's Affair. **1960** Exodus. **1962** Escape From Zahrain; The Longest Day. **1964** Cheyenne Autumn. **1965** The Greatest Story Ever Told; Who Killed Teddy Bear? **1969** Krakatoa, East of Java; 80 Steps to Jonah. **1971** Escape From the Planet of the Apes. **1976** James Dean—The First American Teenager (documentary).

MINER, DANIEL
Born: 1880. Died: June 24, 1938, Hollywood, Calif. Screen and stage actor. Entered films approx. 1914.

MINEVITCH, BORRAH
Born: c. 1904, Kiev, Russia. Died: June 25, 1955, Paris, France. Screen actor, television producer and musician.

Appeared in: **1934** Vitaphone short (with his "Harmonica Rascals"). **1936** One in a Million. **1937** Love Under Fire. **1938** Rascals. **1942** Always in My Heart. **1952** Jour de Fete.

MING, MOY LUKE
Born: 1863, Canton, China. Died: Aug. 16, 1964, Granada Hills, Calif. Screen actor.

Appeared in: **1933** The Bitter Tea of General Yen. **1937** Broken Blossoms; The Good Earth; China Passage. **1948** The Time of Your Life. **1955** The Left Hand of God.

MINGUS, CHARLES
Born: Apr. 22, 1922, Nogales, Ariz. Died: Jan. 5, 1979, Cuernavaca, Mexico (heart attack). Jazz musician, screen actor, composer and author.

Appeared in: **1963** All Night Long. **1968** Mingus (documentary).

MINNER, KATHRYN
Born: 1892. Died: May 26, 1969, Van Nuys, Calif. (heart attack). Screen, stage and television actress.

Appeared in: **1968** The Love Bug; Blackbeard's Ghost.

MINOR, ROY
Born: 1905. Died: Mar. 28, 1935, Los Angeles, Calif. (heart attack). Screen actor and stunt flyer.

Appeared in: **1930** Hell's Angels.

MINTER, WILLIAM F.
Born: 1892. Died: July 13, 1937, Los Angeles, Calif. (bullet wound). Screen actor. Entered films approx. 1922.

MINZEY, FRANK
Born: 1879. Died: Nov. 12, 1949, Lake George, N.Y. Screen, stage and vaudeville actor. Married to actress Rose Melville (dec. 1946). Appeared in early Biograph and Keystone films. Later in shorts produced by Fox, Goldwyn, etc.

Appeared in: **1916** Leap Year Wooing.

MIRANDA, CARMEN (Maria Da Carmo Miranda da Cunha)
Born: Feb. 9, 1904, Marco Canavezes, Portugal. Died: Aug. 5, 1955, Beverly Hills, Calif. (heart attack). Screen and television actress. Married to film producer David Sebastian.

Appeared in: **1934-38** Alo, Alo, Brazil; Estudiantes; Alo, Alo, Carnaval; Banana La Terra. **1940** Down Argentine Way. **1941** That Night in Rio; Weekend in Havana. **1942** Springtime in the Rockies. **1943** The Gang's All Here. **1944** Four Jills in a Jeep; Greenwich Village; Something for the Boys. **1945** Doll Face; Hollywood on Parade (short). **1946** If I'm Lucky; Come Back to Me. **1947** Copacabana. **1948** A Date With Judy. **1950** Nancy Goes to Rio. **1953** Scared Stiff. **1974** That's Entertainment (film clips).

"MIRANDY" See BAUERSFIELD, MARJORIE

MIROSLAVA (Miroslava Stern)
Born: Feb. 26, 1926, Prague, Czechoslovakia. Died: Mar. 10, 1955, Mexico City, Mexico (suicide—poison). Screen and stage actress.

Appeared in: **1946** Conco Nostras de Mujer (A Woman's Five Faces); Bodas de Sangre (Blood Wedding). **1947** Juan Charrasqueado; Nocturno de Amor (Nocturne of Love); A Volar Joven (Let's Fly, Guy). **1948** Secreto Entre Mujeres (Women's Secret); Adventures of Cassanova. **1949** La Liga de las Muchachas (The Girls' League); La Casa Chica (The Small House); La Posesion (The Possession). **1950** La Muerte Enamorada (Death is in Love). **1951** The Brave Bulls; El Puerto de los Siete Vicios (The Port of the Seven Sins); Trotacalles (The Street Walker); Ella y Yo; Carcel de Mujeres. **1952** Las Tres Perfectas Casadas (Three Happily Married Girls); The Bullfighter and the Lady; La Bestia Magnifica (The Magnificent Beast). **1953** Suenos de Gloria (Dreams of Glory); El Monstruo Resucitado (The Resuscitated Monster). **1954** Escuelade Vagabundos (School for Vagabonds); Mas Fuerte que el Amor (Stronger than Love); La Visita Queno Toco el Timbre. **1955** Stranger on Horseback; Ensayo de un Crimen (Rehearsal for a Murder).

MISENER, HELEN
Born: 1909. Died: Aug. 1, 1960, London, England. Screen actress. Entered films as a child actress.

Appeared in: **1958** A Night to Remember.

MISHIMA, MASAO
Born: 1906, Japan. Died: July 18, 1973, Tokyo, Japan (heart ailment). Screen, stage and television actor.

Appeared in: **1952** Saikaku Ichidai Onna (aka Life of Oharu—US 1964). **1959** Ningen No Joken (The Human Condition). **1961** Buta to Gunkan (The Flesh Is Hot—US 1963 aka The Dirty Girls). **1962** Seppuku (Harakiri—US 1963). **1965** Yotsuya Kaidan (aka Illusion of Blood—US 1966). **1967** Joi-Uchi (Rebellion). **1968** Fushin No Taki (The Time of Reckoning—US 1970). **1970** No Greater Love (reissue of Ningen No Joken—1959).

MISHIMA, YUKIO
Born: Japan. Died: Nov. 25, 1971, Tokyo, Japan (hara-kiri). Screen actor, film director, film producer, screenwriter and novelist. The film Yukoku (1966) was destroyed at his widow's request because the movie and novel which he wrote, starred in and directed featured a hero who committed hara-kiri also.

MISTER CATO (Cato Mann)
Born: 1887. Died: Dec. 14, 1977, Belleaire Bluffe, Fla. Screen, radio actor, bandleader and film promoter. Appeared in silent films.

MISTRAL, JORGE (aka GEORGE MISTRAL)
Born: 1923. Died: Apr. 20, 1972, Mexico City, Mexico (self-inflicted gunshot wound). Screen and television actor.

Appeared in: **1950** The Mad Queen. **1954** Mas Fuerte que el Amor (Stronger than Life). **1955** Cabo de Hornos (Cape Horn). **1957** Boy on a Dolphin. **1958** El Vaquero and the Girl. **1960** Le Schiave de Cartegene (The Slaves of Carthage aka The Sword and the Cross). **1962** The Devil Made a Woman. **1963** A Girl Against Napoleon; Abismos de Pasion (Depths of Passion); Sheherazada (Scheherazade—US 1965). **1964** Love on the Riviera. **1965** Gunfighters of Casa Grande.

MITCHEL, LES
Born: 1905. Died: Jan. 12, 1975, Sacramento, Calif. Screen actor, film, radio director and stage producer.

Appeared in: **1957** Outlaw's Son.

MITCHELL, BARBARA
Born: 1929, England. Died: Dec. 9, 1977, Richmond, Surrey, England (cancer). Screen and television actress

Appeared in: **1960** Inn for Trouble. **1963** Ladies Who Do.

MITCHELL, BELLE
Born: 1888. Died: Feb. 12, 1979, Woodland Hills, Calif. Screen and stage actress.

Appeared in: **1928** Flying Romeos. **1933** I Love That Man. **1936** The Leavenworth Case. **1937** The Firefly. **1938** Blockade. **1940** The Mark of Zorro; One Night in the Tropics. **1944** Ali Baba and the Forty Thieves. **1945** House of Frankenstein; That Night With You; Who's Guilty (serial). **1946** High School Hero; Son of the Guardsman (serial); Junior Prom; Freddie Steps Out. **1947** Vacation Days. **1948** The Vicious Circle; Sword of the Avenger; The Prince of Thieves; That Lady in Ermine. **1951** Ghost Chasers. **1952** Viva Zapata. **1954** Passion. **1958** The Lone Ranger and the Lost City of Gold. **1965** The War Lord.

MITCHELL, BRUCE (H. Bruce Mitchell)
Born: Nov. 16, 1883, Freeport, Ill. Died: Sept. 26, 1952, Hollywood, Calif. (anemia). Screen actor, film director and screenwriter. Entered films as a director in 1912.

Appeared in: **1932** The Airmail Mystery (serial). **1934** The St. Louis Kid; Burn 'Em Up Barnes (serial). **1935** The Phantom Empire (serial); G-Men; Four Hours to Kill; The Case of the Curious Bride. **1936** Great Guy; Half Angel. **1937** Paradise Express. **1938** Bar 20 Justice; Pride of the West. **1939** Silver on the Sage; Riders of the Frontier; Golden Boy. **1941** Sky Raiders (serial).

MITCHELL, CAROLYN (Barbara Ann Thomason)
Born: Jan. 25, 1937, Arizona. Died: Jan. 31, 1966, Los Angeles, Calif. (murdered—shot). Screen actress. Married to actor Mickey Rooney.

Appeared in: **1958** Dragstrip Riot; The Cry Baby Killer.

MITCHELL, CHARLES
Born: 1884. Died: Dec. 14, 1929, Hollywood, Calif. (suicide). Screen actor.

MITCHELL, DOBSON (aka DODSON MITCHELL)
Born: Jan. 23, 1868. Died: June 2, 1939, New York, N.Y. Screen, stage actor and playwright.

Appeared in: **1914** The Conspiracy. **1920** Deadline at Eleven. **1926** The Little Giant.

MITCHELL, DUKE
Born: 1926. Died: Dec. 2, 1981, Los Angeles, Calif. Screen actor and nightclub entertainer.

Appeared in: **1951** Sailor Beware. **1952** Bela Lugosi Meets a Brooklyn Gorilla. **1956** Crime in the Streets. **1957** Baby Face Nelson.

MITCHELL, GENEVA
Born: Feb. 3, 1907, Medarysville, Ind. Died: Mar. 10, 1949, Calif. Screen and stage actress.

Appeared in: **1930** Son of the Gods; Back Pay; Safety in Numbers; Her Wedding Night. **1931** Millie; The Single Sin; The Big Gamble; No Limit; Good Sport. **1932** Disorderly Conduct; Night World; False Faces; The Devil Is Driving; Get That Girl. **1933** The World Gone Mad; Morning Glory; He Learned About Women; Only Yesterday; Man of Sentiment; Above the Clouds. **1934** I Am Suzanne; Blind Date; Born to Be Bad; Springtime for Henry; The Captain Hates the Sea. **1935** Behind the Evidence; Night Life of the Gods; Air Hawks; plus the following shorts: Hoi Polloi; I Don't Remember; His Bridal Sweet; I'm a Father; It Always Happens; Honeymoon Bridge; Restless Knights. **1941** In the Sweet Pie and Pie (footage from Hoi Polloi—1935).

MITCHELL, GEORGE
Born: 1905. Died: Jan. 18, 1972, Washington, D.C. Screen and stage actor.

Appeared in: **1955** The Phenix City Story. **1957** 3:10 to Yuma. **1959** The Wild and the Innocent. **1962** Kid Galahad; Bird Man of Alcatraz; Fallguy; Third of a Man. **1963** Twilight of Honor. **1964** The Unsinkable Molly Brown. **1966** Nevada Smith. **1967** The Flim Flam Man. **1969** The Learning Tree. **1971** The Andromeda Strain.

MITCHELL, GRANT
Born: June 17, 1874, Columbus, Ohio. Died: May 1, 1957, Los Angeles, Calif. Screen and stage actor.

Appeared in: **1923** Radio Mania. **1931** Man to Man; The Star Witness; a DeForest Phonofilm short. **1932** M.A.R.S.; Three on a Match; Big City Blues; The Famous Ferguson Case; Week-End Marriage; No Man of Her Own; 20,000 Years in Sing Sing; A Successful Calamity. **1933** Central Airport; Lily Turner; Heroes for Sale; I Love That Man; Tomorrow at Seven; Dinner at Eight; Stranger's Return; Dancing Lady; Saturday's Millions; King for a Night; Wild Boys of the Road; Convention City; Our Betters. **1934** The Poor Rich; The Show-Off; We're Rich Again; The Gridiron Flash; Twenty Million Sweethearts; The Secret Bride; Shadows of Sing Sing; The Cat's Paw; The Case of the Howling Dog; 365 Nights in Hollywood; One Exciting Adventure. **1935** One More Spring; Traveling Saleslady; Gold Diggers of 1935; Straight from the Heart; Broadway Gondolier; Men Without Names; A Midsummer Night's Dream; In Person; Seven Keys to Baldpate; It's in the Air. **1936** Next Time We Love; The Garden Murder Case; Moonlight Murder; Picadilly Jim; The Devil Is a Sissy; Her Master's Voice; My American Wife; The Ex-Mrs. Bradford; Parole! **1937** The Life of Emile Zola; Hollywood Hotel; Music for Madame; The Last Gangster; First Lady; Lady Behave. **1938** The Headleys at Home; Women Are Like That; Peck's Bad Boy at the Circus; Reformatory; Youth Takes a Fling; That Certain Age. **1939** 6,000 Enemies; On Borrowed Time; Mr. Smith Goes to Washington; Juarez; The Secret of Dr. Kildare; Hell's Kitchen. **1940** It All Came True; The Grapes of Wrath; My Love Came Back; Edison the Man; New Moon; We Who Are Young; Father Is a Prince. **1941** Tobbacco Road; The Bride Wore Crutches; Nothing But the Truth; Skylark; One Foot in Heaven; Footsteps in the Dark; The Penalty; The Feminine Touch; The Man Who Came to Dinner; The Great Lie. **1942** Larceny, Inc.; Meet the Stewarts; My Sister Eileen; In Person; Cairo; Orchestra Wives. **1943** The Amazing Mrs. Holiday; The Gold Tower; Dixie; All By Myself. **1944** Laura; See Here, Private Hargrove; The Impatient Years; And Now Tomorrow; When the Lights Go On Again; Arsenic and Old Lace; Step Lively. **1945** Crime, Inc.; A Medal for Benny; Bring on the Girls; Colonel Effingham's Raid; Bedside Manner; Guest Wife; Leave Her to Heaven; Conflict. **1946** Cinderella Jones; Easy to Wed. **1947** The Corpse Came C.O.D.; It Happened on Fifth Avenue; Blondie's Anniversary; Blondie's Holiday; Honeymoon. **1948** Who Killed "Doc" Robbin?

MITCHELL, HELEN (Helen McRuer)
Died: June 25, 1945, Los Angeles, Calif. Screen, stage actress and playwright. Divorced from producer Oliver Morosco and married to actor Robert Sterling Lawson.

Appeared in: **1929** Unmasked.

MITCHELL, HOWARD
Born: 1888. Died: Oct. 9, 1958, Hollywood, Calif. Screen actor and film director.

Appeared in: **1914** The Beloved Adventurer (serial). **1915** The Road of Strife (serial). **1927** A Bowery Cinderella. **1936** Too Many Parents. **1938** Hunted Men; Tom Sawyer, Detective; Prison Farm. **1940** Queen of the Mob. **1941** The Mad Doctor. **1942** Gentleman Jim; Heart of the Rio Grande. **1949** Abandoned. **1950** The Invisible Monster (serial).

MITCHELL, JAMES IRVING
Born: 1891. Died: Aug. 3, 1969, Hollywood, Calif. (heart attack). Screen, stage and television actor. Do not confuse with actor Irving Mitchell born in 1920.

MITCHELL, JOHN (Douglas N. Lamy)
Born: 1919. Died: Jan. 19, 1951, New York, N.Y. (suicide—gun). Screen and radio actor. Known in films as John Mitchell and on radio as Douglas Drake.

Appeared in: **1944** Mr. Skeffington. **1945** Pillow to Post. **1952** Navajo.

MITCHELL, JULIEN
Born: Nov. 13, 1888, Glossop, Derbyshire, England. Died: Nov. 4, 1954. Screen and stage actor.

Appeared in: **1935** The Last Journey (film debut, US 1936). **1937** Double Exposures; The Frog (US 1939); Mr. Smith Carries On. **1938** Quiet Please; The Drum (aka The Drums—US); It's in the Air (aka George Takes the Air—US 1940). **1940** Vigil in the Night; The Sea Hawk. **1942** The Goose Steps Out. **1943** Rhythm Serenade. **1944** Hotel Reserve (US 1946). **1945** The Echo Murders. **1946** Belinda (US 1947). **1948** Bonnie Prince Charlie (US 1952). **1949** A Boy, a Girl and a Bike. **1950** Chance of a Lifetime (US 1951); The Magnet (US 1951). **1951** The Galloping Major. **1954** Hobson's Choice.

MITCHELL, LESLIE "LES" (Leslie Harold Mitchell)
Born: 1885, Brandon, Manitoba, Canada. Died: Oct. 25, 1965, Vancouver, B.C. Screen actor. Entered films in 1911 with Keystone and was an early Keystone Kop and retired in 1920. Do not confuse with screen and radio actor Les Mitchell (dec. 1975).

MITCHELL, MARY RUTH
Born: 1906. Died: May 21, 1941, Los Angeles, Calif. Screen actress.

MITCHELL, MILLARD
Born: 1900, Havana, Cuba. Died: Oct. 12, 1953, Santa Monica, Calif. (lung cancer). Screen and stage actor.

Appeared in: **1941** Mr. and Mrs. North (film debut). **1942** The Mayor of 44th Street; Grand Central Murder; Get Hep to Love; Little Tokyo; Big Street. **1943** Slightly Dangerous. **1946** Swell Guy. **1947** Kiss of Death. **1948** A Double Life; A Foreign Affair. **1949** Twelve O'Clock High; Everybody Does It; Thieves' Highway. **1950** The Gunfighter; Mr. 880, Winchester "73"; Convicted. **1951** The Day the Earth Stood Still (voice); Strictly Dishonorable; You're in the Navy Now (aka U.S.S. Teakettle). **1952** My Six Convicts; Singin' in the Rain. **1953** The Naked Spur; Here Come the Girls.

MITCHELL, NORMA
Born: Boston, Mass. Died: May 29, 1967, Essex, Conn. Screen, stage actress and playwright.

Appeared in: **1933** The Woman Accused. **1934** Melody in Spring. **1940** Susan and God.

MITCHELL, RHEA "GINGER"
Born: 1905. Died: Sept. 16, 1957, Los Angeles, Calif. (found strangled). Screen actress.

Appeared in: **1915** On the Night Stage. **1916** The Sequel to the Diamond from the Sky (serial); The Overcoat; The Release of Dan Forbes. **1918** Honor's Cross; The Blindness of Divorce; Social Ambition; Satan's Pawn; Boston Blackie's Little Pal. **1919** The Money Corporal; The Sleeping Lion. **1920** The Hawk's Trail; The Devil's Claim. **1934** One Hour Late. **1944** Mrs. Parkington. **1946** The Hoodlum Saint. **1947** Green Dolphin Street. **1948** State of the Union. **1951** It's a Big Country.

MITCHELL, THOMAS
Born: 1895, Elizabeth, N.J. Died: Dec. 17, 1962, Beverly Hills, Calif. (cancer). Screen, stage, television actor, stage producer, stage director, playwright and screenwriter. Won 1939 Academy Award for Best Supporting Actor in Stagecoach, and nominated in 1937 for Hurricane.

Appeared in: **1934** Cloudy with Showers. **1936** Craig's Wife; Theodora Goes Wild; Adventure in Manhattan. **1937** Man of the People; When You're in Love; Lost Horizon; I Promise to Pay; Make Way for Tomorrow; The Hurricane. **1938** Love, Honor and Behave; Trade Winds. **1939** Stagecoach; Only Angels Have Wings; Mr. Smith Goes to Washington; The Hunchback of Notre Dame; Gone With the Wind. **1940** Three Cheers for the Irish; Our Town; The Long Voyage Home; Angels Over Broadway; Swiss Family Robinson. **1941** Flight from Destiny; Out of the Fog. **1942** Joan of Paris; Song of the Islands; This Above All; Moontide; Tales of Manhattan; The Black Swan. **1943** The Outlaw; Bataan; Flesh and Fantasy; The Immortal Sergeant. **1944** The Sullivans; Wilson; Buffalo Bill; The Keys of the Kingdom; Dark Waters. **1945** Within These Walls; Captain Eddie; Adventure. **1946** It's a Wonderful Life; Three Wise Fools; The Dark Mirror. **1947** High Barbaree; The Romance of Rosy Ridge; Silver River. **1949** Alias Nick Beal; The Big Wheel. **1951** Journey Into Light. **1952** High Noon. **1953** Tumbleweed. **1954** Destry; Secret of the Incas. **1956** While the City Sleeps. **1958** Handle With Care. **1961** By Love Possessed; Pocketful of Miracles.

MITCHELL, YVONNE (Yvonne Joseph)
Born: 1925, London, England. Died: Mar. 24, 1979, London, England (cancer). Screen, stage, television actress, playwright and author. Married to writer/film critic Derek Monsey (dec. 1979). Entered films in 1947.

Appeared in: **1949** The Queen of Spades (film debut, US 1950); Children of Chance (US 1950). **1953** Turn the Key Softly (US 1954). **1954** The Divided Heart (US 1955). **1955** Escapade (US 1957). **1956** Yield to the Night (aka Blonde Sinner—US). **1957** Woman in a Dressing Gown. **1958** Passionate Summer. **1959** Sapphire; Tiger Bay. **1960** Conspiracy of Hearts; The Trials of Oscar Wilde (aka The Green Carnation, aka The Man With the Green Carnation—US). **1961** Johnny Nobody (US 1965). **1962** The Main Attraction. **1965** Genghis Khan. **1970** The Corpse. **1971** Demons of the Mind (US 1976). **1972** The Great Waltz. **1976** The Incredible Sarah.

MITTELL, LYN DONALDSON
Born: 1892. Died: Mar. 2, 1966, Los Angeles, Calif. Screen and radio actress.

MIX, RUTH
Born: 1907. Died: Sept. 21, 1977, Corpus Christi, Tex. Rodeo rider and screen actress. Daughter of actor Tom Mix (dec. 1940).

Appeared in: **1926** Tex; The Girl From Oklahoma. **1927** The Little Boss. **1928** Four Sons. **1931** Red Fork Range. **1935** Fighting Pioneers; Saddle Aces. **1936** The Riding Avenger; The Black Coin (serial); The Clutching Hand (serial).

MIX, TOM (Thomas Hezikiah Mix)
Born: Jan. 6, 1880, Mix Run, Pa. Died: Oct. 12, 1940, Florence, Ariz. (auto accident). Screen actor, producer, screenwriter, vaudeville, circus and rodeo performer. Father of actress Ruth Mix (dec. 1977). Marriage annulled from Grace Allin; divorced from Olive Stokes (dec. 1972), Kitty Jewel Perrine and actress Victoria Forde (dec. 1964). Married to circus aerialist Mabel Ward.

Appeared in: **1910** Ranch Life in the Great Southwest; Up San Juan Hill; Briton and Boer; The Millionaire Cowboy; The Range Rider; An Indian Wife's Devotion. **1911-12** Back to the Primitive; The Wagon Trail; Single Shot Parker; Days of Daring; The Sheriff's Girl; My Haywood Producer; Weary Goes Wooing; Sagebrush Tom. **1913** Child of the Prairie; Escape of Jim Dolan; Law and the Outlaw; The Stage Coach Driver and the Girl. **1914** The Wilderness Mail; Moving Picture Cowboy; In the Days of the Thundering Herd; The Man from the East; Ranger's Romance; Saved by a Watch; The Scapegoat; The Sheriff's Reward; The Telltale Knife; The Way of the Redman; Why the Sheriff is a Bachelor; The Defiance of the Law; The Rival Stage Lines; Chip of the Flying U; Cactus Jake, Heartbreaker; The Mexican; The Real Thing in Cowboys. **1915** An Arizona Wooing; On the Eagle Trail; Cactus Jim's Shop Girl; Foreman of the Bar Z; The Outlaw's Bride; The Parson Who Fled West; Saved by Her Horse; Getting a Start in Life; Athletic Ambitions; The Brave Deserve the Fair; Child of the Prairie (and 1913 version); Heart of the Sheriff; Lucky Deal; The Man from Texas; Ma's Girls; Mrs. Murphy Cooks; Never Again; Pals in Blue; The Range Girl and the Cowboy; Sage Brush Tom; Slim Higgins; Stagecoach Guard; The Auction Sale of a Run-Down Ranch; Bad Man Bobbs; The Girl in the Mail Bag; The Chef at Circle G; The Child, The Dog and the Villain; The Conversion of Smiling Tom; The Foreman's Choice; Forked Trails; The Gold Dust and the Squaw; The Grizzly Gulch Chariot Race; Her Slight Mistake; The Impersonation of Tom; The Legal Light; A Matrimonial Boomerang; The Race for a Gold Mine; Roping a Bride; The Taking of Mustang Pete; The Tenderfoot's Triumph. **1916** Making an Impression; A $5,000 Elopement; Along the

Border; A Bear of a Story; The Canby Hill Outlaws; A Close Call; Comer in Water; The Drifter; The Cowpuncher's Peril; Crooked Trails; Going West to Make Good; Legal Advice; Local Color; Making Good; Mistakes in Rustlers; Mix-up in Movies; The Passing of Pete; The Pony Express Rider; The Raiders; Roping a Sweetheart; The Sheriff's Blunder; The Sheriff's Duty; Shooting Up the Movies; Some Duel; Taking a Chance; The Taming of Grouchy Bill; Tom's Sacrifice; Tom's Strategy; Too Many Chefs; Trilby's Love Disaster; Western Masquerade; The Desert Circle Calls Its Own; An Eventful Evening; The Girl of Gold Gulch; The Golden Thought; The Man Within; Mistakes Will Happen; Starring In Western Stuff. **1917** Hearts and Saddles; Roman Cowboy; Six Cylinder Love; The Soft Tenderfoot; Tom and Jerry Mix; Twisted Trails; The Heart of Texas Ryan; Six Shooter Andy. **1918** Cupid's Roundup; Western Blood; Ace High; The Rainbow Trail; Durand of the Badlands. **1919** Fame and Fortune; The Wilderness Trail; Hell Roarin' Reform; Fighting for Gold; Coming of the Law. **1920** Desert Love; The Daredevil; The Cyclone; The Speed Maniac; The Terror; The Feud; Three Gold Coins; The Untamed; Mr. Logan, U.S.A.; Treat 'Em Rough; Rough Riding Romance. **1921** The Rough Diamond; Hands Off; Prairie Trails; The Queen of Sheba; A Ridin' Romeo; The Road Demon; The Texan; Big Town Round-Up; The Night Horsemen; After Your Own Heart; Trailin'! **1922** Up and Going; Sky High; For Big Stakes; The Fighting Streak; Chasing the Moon; Do and Dare; Just Tony; Tom Mix in Arabia; Arabia; Catch My Smoke. **1923** The Lone Star Ranger; Romance Land; Softboiled; Stepping Fast; Three Jumps Ahead; Mile-a Minute Romeo. **1924** Oh, You Tony; North of Hudson Bay; A Golden Thought; The Last of the Duanes; Ladies to Board; Teeth; Eyes of the Forest; The Trouble Shooter; The Heart Buster; The Foreman of Bar Z Ranch. **1925** Everlasting Whisper; The Lucky Horseshoe; Law and the Outlaw; The Best Bad Man; Riders of the Purple Sage; The Rainbow Trail; Dick Turpin; The Deadwood Coach; A Child of the Prairie. **1926** The Great K and a Train Robbery; The Yankee Senor; No Man's Gold; Hardboiled; The Canyon of Light; My Own Pal; Tony Runs Wild. **1927** Tumbling River; The Circus Ace; The Last Trail; Silver Valley; Outlaws of Red River; The Broncho Twister. **1928** Painted Post; King Cowboy; Hello Cheyene; A Horseman of the Plains; Arizona Wildcat; Son of the Golden West; Daredevil's Reward. **1929** Drifter; Outlawed; The Big Diamond Robbery. **1932** The Fourth Horseman; Destry Rides Again; My Pal, the King; Texas Bad Man; The Cohens and the Kellys in Hollywood; Rider of Death Valley. **1933** Flaming Guns; Hidden Gold; Terror Trail; Rustler's Roundup. **1935** The Miracle Rider (serial). **1943** Daredevils of the West (serial).

MIZOGHUCHI, KENJI
Born: 1898, Japan. Died: Aug. 24, 1956. Screen actor and film director. Entered films as an actor during early silents.

Appeared in: **1940** Naniwa Onna. **1944** Danjuro Sandai; Miyamoto Musashi. **1946** Josei No Shori; Utamaro O Meguru Gonin No Onna. **1947** Joyu Sumako No Koi. **1948** Yoru No Onna-Tachi. **1949** Waga Koi Wa Moenu. **1951** Oyu-Sama; Musachina Fijin. **1952** Saikaku Ichidai Onna. **1953** Ugetsu Monogatari. **1954** Sansho Dayu; Uwasa No Onna.

MOCHIZUKI, YUKO
Born: c. 1917, Japan. Died: Dec. 1 or 2, 1977, Japan? Screen actress.

Appeared in: **1952** Ochazuke no Aji (aka The Flavor of Green Tea Over Rice, aka Tea and Rice—US 1964). **1958** Narayama-bushi-ko (aka The Ballad of Narayama—US 1961). **1960** Carmen Comes Home. **1961** Kohayagawa-ke no Aki (aka Last of Summer, aka Early Autumn—US 1962). **1962** Futari no Musuko (aka Different Sons—US); Kusa-O Karu Musume (The Grass Cutters). **1969** Akage (aka Red Lion—US).

MOCK, ALICE
Died: Oct. 24, 1972. Screen actress.

Appeared in: **1945** Wonder Man.

MODEEN, THOR
Died: 1950. Screen actor.

Appeared in: **1934** Kaera Slackten. **1937** Klart till Drabbning (Cleared for Action). **1939** Kustens Glada Kavaljerer (The Coast's Happy Cavaliers).

MODIE, LOUELLA See MAXUM, MODIE LOUELLA

MODLEY, ALBERT
Born: 1892, England. Died: Feb. 23, 1979, Morecambe, England. Screen, radio, television actor and music hall comedian.

Appeared in: **1951** Take Me to Paris.

MODOT, GASTON
Born: 1887, Paris, France. Died: 1970, France? Screen actor and screenwriter. Appeared in the Onesime series beginning in 1908.

Appeared in: **1920** La Fete Espagnole; Fievre. **1925** Le Miracle des Loups (The Miracle of the Wolves). **1928** Carmen. **1930** Sous les Toits de Paris (Under the Roofs of Paris). **1931** Die Dreigroschenoper. **1932** Secrets of the Orient. **1934** Fantomas; Crainquebille. **1936** Pepe le Moko. **1938** Grand Illusion. **1939** Escape from Yesterday; The End of a Day; The Devil Is An Empress; La Regle du Jeu (Rules of the Game—US 1950). **1947** Les Enfants du Paradis. **1948** Antoine and Antoinette. **1951** Passion for Life. **1952** Casque d'Or; Beauty and the Devil. **1956** French Can Can (aka Only the French Can). **1959** The Lovers; Le Testament de Dr. Cordelier (aka Experiment in Evil). **1961** Les Menteurs (The Liars—US 1964). **1962** Le Diable et les Dix Commandments (The Devil and the Ten Commandments—US 1963). **1964** L'Age d'Or (The Golden Age—originally released in 1930).

MOEBUS, HANS
Died: Apr. 3, 1976. Screen actor.

Appeared in: **1931** Comrades of 1918. **1956** The Birds and the Bees.

MOEHRING, KANSAS
Born: July 9, 1897. Died: Oct. 2, 1968. Screen actor.

Appeared in: **1923** Out of Luck; Shootin' for Love. **1942** Down Texas Way. **1944** Land of the Outlaws. **1947** Trailing Danger. **1948** Frontier Agent. **1950** The Cariboo Trail.

MOFFAT, MARGARET
Born: 1892, England. Died: Feb. 19, 1942, Los Angeles, Calif. (pneumonia). Screen actress. Married to film producer Sewell Collins.

Appeared in: **1934** Just Smith. **1936** The End of the Road. **1937** Farewell Again. **1938** Troopship. **1939** U-Boat 29. **1940** Song of the Road. **1941** Ringside Maisie. **1942** My Gal Sal.

MOFFATT, GRAHAM
Born: 1919, London, England. Died: July 2, 1965, Bath, England. Screen and television actor. Do not confuse with stage actor-playwright Graham Moffatt (dec. 1951).

Appeared in: **1933** Till the Bells Ring. **1934** A Cup of Kindness. **1935** Stormy Weather (US 1936). **1936** Windbag the Sailor. **1937** Good Morning, Boys (aka Where There's a Will—US); Okay For Sound; Gangway; Dr. Syn; Oh, Mr.Porter! **1938** Owd Bob (aka To the Victor—US); Convict 99; Old Bones of the River. **1939** Ask a Policeman; Where's the Fire?; Cheer Boys Cheer. **1940** Charley's (Big Hearted) Aunt. **1941** Hi Gang!; I Thank You. **1942** Back Room Boys. **1943** Dear Octopus (aka The Randolph Family—US 1945). **1944** Time Flies; Welcome Mr. Washington. **1945** I Know Where I'm Going (US 1947). **1946** The Voyage of Peter Joe series. **1947** Stage Frights. **1948** Woman Hater (US 1949). **1949** Three Bags Full. **1950** The Dragon of Pendragon Castle. **1951** The Second Mate. **1952** Mother Riley Meets the Vampire (aka Vampire Over London—US). **1960** Inn for Trouble.

MOHAN, CHANDRA
Born: India. Died: Apr. 2, 1949, India?. Screen actor.

Appeared in: **1947** Shakuntala.

MOHAN, EARL
Died: Oct. 15, 1928, Los Angeles, Calif. Screen actor.

Appeared in: **1927** Love Makes 'Em Wild.

MOHR, GERALD
Born: June 11, 1914, New York, N.Y. Died: Nov. 10, 1968, Stockholm, Sweden. Screen, stage, radio and television actor. He was on the "Lone Wolf" series, both radio and screen, and was "Philip Marlowe, radio private eye."

Appeared in: **1941** We Go Fast; Jungle Girl (serial); The Monster and the Girl. **1942** The Lady Has Plans. **1943** Murder in Times Square; King of the Cowboys; Lady of Burlesque; One Dangerous Night; The Desert Song. **1946** The Notorious Lone Wolf; Gilda; A Guy Could Change; The Catman of Paris; Passkey to Danger; Invisible Informer; The Truth About Murder; Dangerous Business; The Magnificent Rogue. **1947** Lone Wolf in Mexico; Heaven Only Knows; The Lone Wolf in London. **1948** Two Guys from Texas. **1949** The Blonde Bandit. **1950** Undercover Girl; Hunt the Man Down. **1951** Sirocco; Ten Tall Men; Detective Story. **1952** The Sniper; The Ring; Son of Ali Baba; The Duel at Silver Creek; Invasion U.S.A. **1953** Raiders of the Seven Seas; Money From Home; The Eddie Cantor Story. **1954** Dragonfly Squadron. **1957** The Buckskin Lady. **1958** Terror in the Haunted House; Guns, Girls and Gangsters. **1959** A Date With Death. **1960** This Rebel Breed; The Angry Red Planet. **1968** Funny Girl.

MOISSI, ALEXANDER
Born: 1880, Trieste, Italy. Died: Mar. 22, 1935, Vienna, Austria (pneumonia). Stage and screen actor.

Appeared in: **1929** The Royal Box. **1936** Lorenzino de Medici.

MOJA, HELLA
Born: 1898, Germany. Died: Feb., 1937, Berlin, Germany. Screen actress and screenwriter. Entered films approx. 1916.

Appeared in: **1929** U-Boat 9.

MOJAVE, KING
Died: Mar. 23, 1973. Screen actor.

Appeared in: **1937** Public Cowboy No. 1.

MOJICA, JOSE
Born: Sept. 14, 1899, San Gabriel, Jalisco, Mexico. Died: Sept. 20, 1974, Lima, Peru (heart ailment). Screen, stage actor, opera performer, writer and later an ordained priest.

Appeared in: **1925** Dick Turpin. **1930** One Mad Kiss. **1933** El Rey de los Gitanos; La Ley Del Haren; El Precio de un Beso; Su Ultimo Amor; La Melodia Prohibida (Forbidden Melody); Quando el Amor Rie. **1934** La Cruz y la Espada; Las Fronteras del Amor. **1939** El Capitan (Adventureous Captain). **1940** La Cancion del Milagro (The Miracle Song).

MOLANDER, OLAF
Born: 1892, Helsinki, Finland. Died: 1966, Finland? Screen actor and film director.

Appeared in: **1917** Thomas Graal's Ward. **1940** A Big Hug. **1945** Wandering With the Moon.

MOLINA, JOE
Born: 1899. Died: Dec. 16, 1977, Woodland Hills, Calif. Screen actor. Entered films in 1919.

Appeared in: **1919** Ebb Tide. **1939** Zorro's Fighting Legion (serial). **1960** Comanche Station.

MOLNAR, FERENC
Born: Jan. 12, 1878, Budapest, Hungary. Died: Apr. 1, 1952, New York, N.Y. Screen actor, screenwriter, playwright and author. Married to actress Lili Darvis (dec. 1974).

Appeared in: **1930** Olympia.

MOLNAR, LILY
Died: Oct. 20, 1950. Screen actress.

Appeared in: **1951** No Orchids for Miss Blandish; The Long Dark Hall.

MOLONEY, JOHN
Born: 1911. Died: July 14, 1969, Los Angeles, Calif. Screen actor, emcee and singer.

Appeared in: **1955** Mister Roberts. **1962** Gypsy.

MOLYNEAUX, EILEEN
Born: Aug. 26, 1893, Pietermaritzburg, Natal, South Africa. Died: Apr. 13, 1962, Bryn Mawr, Pa. Screen, stage actress and music hall entertainer.

Appeared in: **1918** Eve Comedies. **1919** The Key of the World.

MOMO, ALESSANDRO
Born: Nov. 25, 1953, Italy. Died: Nov. 20, 1974, Rome, Italy (motorcycle accident). Screen and television actor.

Appeared in: **1974** Malizia. Other Italian films: Venial Sin; Honey and Darkness.

MONBERY, GEORGE
Born: Aug. 9, 1890, Ill. Died: Mar. 7, 1925. Screen actor.

MONCLOVA, FELIX
Born: 1935, Puerto Rico. Died: Apr. 15, 1977, Vega Banja, Puerto Rico (heart failure). Screen, stage and radio actor. Father of actors Felix Rene, Eugenio Luis, and Hector Ivan Monclova.

Appeared in: **1965** Heroina.

MONCRIES, EDWARD (aka EDWARD MONCRIEF)
Born: 1859. Died: Mar. 22, 1938, Hollywood, Calif. (heart attack). Screen, stage actor and stage manager. Was in many Charles Chaplin films.

Appeared in: **1921** Western Hearts. **1923** The Girl I Loved.

MONDOSE, ALEX (Alexandre Onsmonde)
Born: 1894, Liege, Belgium. Died: Feb. 8, 1972, Brussels, Belgium. Screen, stage actor and singer. Apparently appeared in only one film in 1955.

MONG, WILLIAM V.
Born: 1875, Clambersbury, Pa. Died: Dec. 10, 1940, Studio City, Calif. Screen, stage and vaudeville actor. Entered films in 1910.

Appeared in: **1910** The Connecticut Yankee. **1911** Lost in the Jungle. **1912** The Redemption of Greek Joe. **1915** Alias Holland Jimmy; The Word; Out of the Silence; Tainted Money. **1916** The Son of a Rebel Chief; To Another Woman; The Wrath of Cactus Moore; The Last of the Morgans; The Iron Hand; When the Wolf Howls; Shoes; Crimson Yoke; Husks of Love; A Son of Neptune; Tillie the Little Swede; The Girl in Lower 9; Along the Malibu; Two Men of Sandy Bar; The Good Woman; Her Bitter Cup; Fighting Joe; Birds of a Feather; The Severed Hand. **1917** An Old Soldier's Romance; Good-for-Nothing Gallagher; The Daring Chance; Bartered Youth; The Girl and the Crisis; The Grudge; Chubby Takes a Hand; Fanatics. **1918** The Hopper; The Painted Lily. **1919** Love's Prisoner; The Spender; Put Up Your Hands; The Follies Girl; After His Own Heart; The Amateur Adventurers; Fools and Their Money; The Master Man. **1921** Connecticut Yankee at King Arthur's Court; Sowing the Wind; Shame; The Ten Dollar Raise; The Winding Trail; Ladies Must Live; Pilgrims of the Night; Playthings of Destiny. **1922** Fool There Was; Shattered Idols; The Woman He Loved; Monte Cristo. **1923** All the Brothers Were Valiant; Drifting; In the Palace of the King; Lost and Found; Wandering Daughters; Penrod and Sam. **1924** Thy Name Is Woman; Flapper Wives; Why Men Leave Home; Welcome Stranger; What Shall I Do? **1925** Alias Mary Flynn; Excuse Me; Fine Clothes; Under the Rouge; The Unwritten Law; Barriers Burned Away; Off the Highway; Oh, Doctor!; The People vs. Nancy Preston; The Shadow on the Wall; Speed. **1926** The Old Soak; What Price Glory; Brooding Eyes; Fifth Avenue; The Shadow of the Law; The Silent Lover; Steel Preferred; The Strong Man. **1927** Alias the Lone Wolf; The Clown; The Magic Garden; Taxi! Taxi!; The Price of Honor; Too Many Crooks. **1928** The Broken Mask; The Haunted House; Code of the Air; The Devil's Trademark; No Babies Wanted; Ransom; Telling the World; White Flame. **1929** Should a Girl Marry?; Dark Skies; The House of Horror; Seven Footprints to Satan; Noah's Ark. **1930** The Girl Said No; In Gay Madrid; Murder on the Roof; Double Cross Roads; The Big Trail. **1931** The Flood; Gun Smoke; Bad Company; A Dangerous Affair. **1932** Cross Examination; By Whose Hands?; Fighting Fool; Widow in Scarlet; Dynamite Denny; The Sign of the Cross; No More Orchids. **1933** Footlight Parade; Women Won't Tell; Strange Adventure; The Vampire Bat; The 11th Commandment; Fighting for Justice; Silent Men; Her Forgotten Past; The Mayor of Hell; The Narrow Corner; I Loved a Woman. **1934** Dark Hazard; Massacre; Treasure Island. **1935** Rendezvous; The County Chairman; The Hoosier Schoolmaster; The Last Days of Pompeii; Whispering Smith Speaks. **1936** Dancing Pirate; The Last of the Mohicans; The Dark Hour. **1937** Stand-In. **1938** Painted Desert. **1944** The Sign of the Cross (revised version of 1932 film).

MONKMAN, PHYLLIS
Born: Jan. 8, 1892, London, England. Died: Dec. 2, 1976, London, England. Screen, stage, vaudeville actress and dancer. Married to actor Laddie Cliff (dec. 1937).

Appeared in: **1919** Her Heritage. **1927** On With the Dance (series). **1929** Blackmail; The Co-Optimists (US 1930). **1934** The King of Paris. **1942** Uncensored (US 1944).

MONROE, MARILYN (Norma Jeane Mortensen)
Born: June 1, 1926, Los Angeles, Calif. Died: Aug. 5, 1962, Brentwood, Calif. (suicide?). Screen actress. Divorced from merchant seaman James Dougherty, professional baseball player Joe DiMaggio and playwright Arthur Miller.

Appeared in: **1948** Scudda Hoo! Scudda Hay!; Dangerous Years. **1949** Love Happy; Ladies of the Chorus. **1950** A Ticket to Tomahawk; All About Eve; Asphalt Jungle; Right Cross; The Fire Ball. **1951** Let's Make It Legal; Love Nest; As Young as You Feel; Hometown Story. **1952** Don't Bother to Knock; We're Not Married; Clash by Night; Monkey Business; O. Henry's Full House. **1953** Gentlemen Prefer Blondes; How to Marry a Millionaire; Niagara. **1954** River of No Return; There's No Business Like Show Business. **1955** The Seven Year Itch. **1956** Bus Stop. **1957** The Prince and the Showgirl. **1959** Some Like It Hot. **1960** Let's Make Love. **1961** The Misfits. **1963** Marilyn (film clips documentary).

MONROE, VAUGHN
Born: Oct. 7, 1911, Akron, Ohio. Died: May 21, 1973, Stuart, Fla. Radio, television singer, bandleader, author and screen actor.

Appeared in: **1944** Meet the People. **1947** Carnegie Hall. **1950** Singing Guns. **1952** Toughest Man in Arizona.

MONTAGUE, EDNA *See* WOODRUFF, EDNA

MONTAGUE, FREDERICK
Born: 1864, London, England. Died: July 3, 1919, Los Angeles, Calif. (acute intestinal obstruction). Screen and stage actor. Married to actress Rita Montague (dec. 1962).

Appeared in: **1914** The Squaw Man; Where the Trail Divides; The Man on the Box; The Ghost Breaker; What's His Name; The Man from Home; The Circus Man; The Call of the North; Ready Money. **1915** Cameo Kirby. **1916** The Bait; The Hidden Law; The Leopard's Bride; Barriers of Society; Circumstantial Guilt; The Lawyer's Secret; The Lion Nemesis; The Haunted Symphony; For Her Good Name; Destiny's Boomerang; The Good for Nothing Brat; The Kaffir's Gratitude; Clouds in Sunshine Valley; The Star of India; A Siren of the Jungle. **1917** The Red Stain; God's Crucible; The Gift Girl; The Flame of Youth; A Prince for a Day; Little Marian's Triumph; The Winged Mystery; The Saintly Sinner; Good-for-Nothing Gallagher. **1918** Fast Company; The Fighting Grin; His Robe of Honor; The Rough Love. **1919** His Debt (aka The Debt); The Ghost Girl; The Best Man; All Wrong.

MONTAGUE, MONTE (Walter Montague)
Born: 1892, Somerset, Ky. Died: Apr. 6, 1959, Burbank, Calif. Screen, stage and vaudeville actor.

Appeared in: **1920** Under Crimson Skies; The Flaming Disc (serial); Elmo the Fearless (serial). **1922** Defying the Law; The Three Buckaroos; Peaceful Peters; A Western Demon. **1923** The Secret of the Pueblo. **1926** One Man Trail; The Mystery Club; The Wild Horse Stampede. **1927** Hey! Hey! Cowboy; The Rambling Ranger; Range Courage; Somewhere in Sonora; Rough and Ready; Spurs and Saddles; Blake of Scotland Yard (serial). **1928** The Body Punch; The Danger Rider; The Price of Fear; The Air Patrol; Clearing the Trail; The Gate Crasher; The Wild West Show. **1929** Slim Fingers; King of the Rodeo; The Tip Off; Wolves of the City; The Ace of Scotland Yard (serial); Courtin; Wild Cats; The Diamond Master (serial); Eyes of the Underworld. **1930** Trigger Tricks; Lonesome Trail. **1931** Quick Trigger Lee; Finger Prints (serial); Spell of the Circus (serial). **1932** The Impatient Maiden. **1934** Tailspin Tommy (serial). **1935** Rustlers of Red Dog (serial); Outlawed Guns. **1936** Song of the Saddle; The Adventures of Frank Merriwell (serial); Treachery Rides the Range. **1937** Radio Patrol (serial); Guns of the Pecos; The Californians; Git Along, Little Dogies. **1938** The Law West of Tombstone; Riders of the Black Hills. **1939** The Renegade Ranger; Racketeers of the Range; Allegheny Uprising. **1940** Legion of the Lawless; Young Bill Hickok; Wagon Train; Prairie Law. **1941** The Singing Hill; Along the Rio Grande; King of the Texas Rangers (serial); Cyclone on Horseback; The Apache Kid; Thundering Hoofs. **1942** The Cyclone Kid; The Phantom Plainsmen; Stardust on the Sage. **1943** Fighting Frontier. **1947** The Vigilantes Return. **1949** Brothers in the Saddle; Rustlers. **1952** The Last Musketeer.

MONTAGUE, RITA
Born: 1884. Died: May 5, 1962, Hollywood, Calif. Screen, stage actress and playwright. Married to actor Frederick Montague (dec. 1919).

MONTALVAN, CELIA
Born: 1899, Mexico. Died: Jan. 10, 1958, Mexico City, Mexico (heart attack). Stage and screen actress.
Appeared in: **1936** Les Amours de Toni.

MONTANA, BULL (Lugia Montagna)
Born: May 16, 1887, Vogliera, Italy. Died: Jan. 24, 1950, Los Angeles, Calif. (coronary thrombosis). Screen actor and professional wrestler. Entered films in 1918.

Appeared in: **1917** In Again-Out Again; Wild and Woolly; Down to Earth. **1918** He Comes Up Smiling. **1919** When the Clouds Roll By; Victory; Brass Buttons; The Unpardonable Sin. **1920** Treasure Island; Go and Get It. **1921** The Four Horsemen of the Apocalypse; Crazy to Marry; The Foolish Age; One Wild Week. **1922** Gay and Devilish; The Three Must-Get-There's; The Timber Queen (serial). **1923** Breaking Into Society; Hollywood; Held to Answer. **1924** Jealous Husbands; The Fire Patrol; Painted People. **1925** Bashful Buccaneer; Dick Turpin; The Gold Hunters; Manhattan Madness; Secrets of the Night; The Lost World. **1926** Vanishing Millions (serial); The Skyrocket; The Son of the Sheik; Stop, Look and Listen. **1928** How to Handle Women; Good Morning Judge. **1929** The Show of Shows; Tiger Rose. **1935** Palooka from Paducah (short). **1937** Big City. **1943** Good Morning Judge.

MONTANO, A.
Born: Barbados, West Indies. Died: Sept. 6, 1914, Long Island, N.Y. (heart failure after performing stunt in film). Screen actor and stuntman.

MONTEIRO, PILAR
Born: 1886, Portugal. Died: Dec., 1962, Lisbon, Portugal. Screen actress. Appeared in films during 1920s and 1930s.

MONTEREY, CARLOTTA (Hazel Neilson Taasinge)
Born: Dec. 28, 1888. Died: Nov. 18, 1970, Westwood, N.J. Screen and stage actress. Married to playwright Eugene O'Neill (dec. 1953).

Appeared in: **1925** The King on Main Street; Soul Fire.

MONTEZ, MARIA (Maria Antonia Garcia Van Dahl de Santo Silas)
Born: June 6, 1917 or 1920?, Barahona, Dominican Republic. Died: Sept. 7, 1951, France (heart failure or drowning?). Screen and stage actress. Married to actor Jean Pierre Aumont.

Appeared in: **1941** Lucky Devils; Boss of Bullion City; The Invisible Woman That Night in Rio; Raiders of the Desert; Moonlight in Hawaii; South of Tahiti. **1942** Bombay Clipper; The Mystery of Marie Roget; Arabian Nights. **1943** White Savage. **1944** Ali Baba and the Forty Thieves; Follow the Boys; Cobra Woman; Gypsy Wildcat; Bowery to Broadway. **1945** Sudan. **1946** Tangier. **1947** Pirates of Monterey; The Exile; Song of Scheherezade. **1949** The Siren of Atlantis; Hans Le Marin (The Wicked City—US 1951); Portrait d'un Assassin (Portrait of an Assassin). **1950** Il Ladro di Venezia (The Thief of Venice—US 1952). **1951** Amore E Sangue (City of Violence); La Vendetta del Corsaro.

MONTGOMERY, BETTY
Died: Jan. 1, 1922, San Francisco, Calif. Screen actress.

MONTGOMERY, DOUGLAS (Robert Douglass Montgomery aka KENT DOUGLAS)
Born: Oct. 29, 1908, Los Angeles, Calif. Died: July 23, 1966, Ridgefield, Conn. Screen, stage and television actor. Appeared in films as Douglass Montgomery and Kent Douglas.

Appeared in: **1931** Waterloo Bridge; Five and Ten; Paid; Daybreak. **1932** A House Divided. **1933** Little Women. **1934** Music in the Air; Little Man, What Now?; Eight Girls in a Boat. **1935** The Mystery of Edwin Drood; Lady Tubbs; Harmony Lane. **1936** Tropical Trouble; Everything Is Thunder. **1937** Life Begins With Love; Counsel for Crime. **1939** The Cat and the Canary. **1945** The Way to the Stars (aka Johnny in the Clouds—US). **1946** Woman to Woman. **1949** Forbidden. **1952** When in Rome.

MONTGOMERY, EARL (Earl Triplett Montgomery)
Born: 1893, Santa Cruz County, Calif. Died: Oct. 28, 1966. Stage and screen actor.

Appeared in: **1918** Bums and Boarders; Chumps and Cops; Farms and Fumbles. **1919** Love and Leather; Damsels and Dandies; Zip and Zest; Harems and Hokum; Caves and Croquetts; Vamps and Variety. **1923** Tea With a Kick. **1926** Stop, Look and Listen. **1936** Navy Born.

MONTGOMERY, FRANK
Born: 1870, Petrolia, Pa. Died: July 18, 1944, Hollywood, Calif. Screen, stage actor and film director. Married to actress Mary Darkfeather. Entered films in 1908.

Appeared in: **1922** Cardigan; The Man from Beyond; The Man Who Paid. **1924** Who's Cheating?; A Sainted Devil; Floodgates. **1925** The Mad Dancer; Children of the Whirlwind; Red Love. **1926** Aloma of the South Seas; So's Your Old Man.

MONTGOMERY, GOODEE
Born: 1906. Died: June 5, 1978, Hollywood, Calif. Screen actress. Married to actor/film director/television director Frank McDonald (dec. 1980).

Appeared in: **1930** Lightnin'; Up the River. **1931** Charlie Chan Carries On; Transatlantic. **1934** Stolen Sweets; Let's Talk It Over. **1935** Stolen Harmony. **1937** Beware of Ladies; Mountain Music.

MONTGOMERY, JACK
Born: 1892. Died: Jan. 21, 1962, Hollywood, Calif. (cancer). Screen actor and stuntman. Married to actress Marian Baxter (dec. 1977). Entered films during early silents. Father of "Baby Peggy," silent film moppet.

Appeared in: **1955** Run for Cover.

MONTGOMERY, MABEL
Born: Brooklyn, N.Y. Died: July 20, 1942, Honolulu, Hawaii. Screen and stage actress.

Appeared in: **1915** Mrs. Dane's Defense.

MONTGOMERY, MARIAN *See* BAXTER, MARIAN

MONTGOMERY, RALPH

Born: 1912. Died: May 10, 1980, Hollywood, Calif. (cancer). Screen, vaudeville, radio, television actor, singer, dancer and teacher. Married to actress/singer Mary Lee Montgomery. Father of actress Kim and actor/producer Phil Montgomery.

Appeared in: **1954** Living It Up; Johnny Dark. **1955** The Girl Rush. **1956** The Leather Saint. **1957** Fear Strikes Out; The Joker Is Wild. **1962** Don't Knock the Twist. **1970** Watermelon Man. **1977** Which Way Is Up?

MONTGOMERY, ROBERT (Henry Montgomery, Jr.)

Born: May 21, 1904, Fishkill Landing, Dutchess County, N.Y. Died: Sept. 27, 1981, New York, N.Y. (cancer). Screen, stage, radio, television actor, film director and producer, stage director and producer, television director and producer. Divorced from actress Elizabeth Bryan Allen, and later married to Elizabeth Grant Harkness. Father of Robert, Jr., and actress Elizabeth Montgomery. Nominated for 1937 Academy Award for Best Actor in Night Must Fall, and again in 1941 in Here Comes Mr. Jordan. Entered films in 1929.

Appeared in: **1929** So This Is College; Three Live Ghosts; The Single Standard; Untamed; Father's Day. **1930** War Nurse; Love in the Rough; Their Own Desire; Free and Easy; The Divorcee; The Big House; Sins of the Children (aka Richest Man in the World); Our Blushing Brides. **1931** The Easiest Way; Strangers May Kiss; Shipmates; Inspiration; Man in Possession; Private Lives. **1932** Lovers Courageous; Letty Lynton; But the Flesh Is Weak; Blondie of the Follies; Faithless. **1933** Hell Below; Made on Broadway; When Ladies Meet; Another Language; Night Flight; Tinfoil. **1934** Hideout; Fugitive Lovers; Riptide; Mystery of Mr. X; Forsaking All Others. **1935** Biography of a Bachelor Girl; Venessa, Her Love Story; No More Ladies. **1936** Petticoat Fever; Piccadilly Jim; Trouble for Two. **1937** Night Must Fall; The Last of Mrs. Cheyney; Ever Since Eve; Live, Love and Learn. **1938** The First Hundred Years; Yellowjack; Three Loves Has Nancy. **1939** Fast and Loose; The Cat and the Canary. **1940** The Earl of Chicago; Haunted Honeymoon. **1941** Rage in Heaven; Mr. and Mrs. Smith; Here Comes Mr. Jordan; Unfinished Business. **1945** They Were Expendable. **1946** Lady in the Lake. **1947** Ride the Pink Horse. **1948** The Saxon Charm; The Secret Land (narrator); June Bride. **1949** Once More, My Darling. **1950** Your Witness (aka Eye Witness—US). **1960** The Gallant Hours.

MONTIEL, NELLY

Born: Mexico. Died: Sept. 14, 1951, near Acapulco, Mexico (auto accident). Screen actress.

MONTOYA, ALEX P.

Born: Oct. 19, 1907, Texas. Died: Sept. 25, 1970, Los Angeles, Calif. (congestive heart failure). Screen and television actor. Brother of actress Julia Montoya.

Appeared in: **1946** Beauty and the Bandit; Trail to Mexico. **1947** Twilight on the Rio Grande; The Last Round-Up; Riding the California Trail; Robin Hood of Monterey. **1949** Square Dance Jubilee; Ghost of Zorro (serial); The Big Sombrero; Daughter of the Jungle. **1951** Hurricane Island. **1952** Macao; California Conquest; Wild Horse Ambush; The Golden Hawk; King of the Congo (serial); Voodoo Tiger. **1953** Son of Belle Starr; Conquest of Cochise. **1954** Passion; Three Young Texans. **1955** Hell's Island; Escape to Burma; Apache Ambush. **1956** Stagecoach to Fury. **1957** War Drums. **1958** The Toughest Gun in Tombstone. **1959** Ghost of Zorro (serial). **1962** Dangerous Charter. **1964** Island of the Blue Dolphins. **1965** The Flight of the Phoenix. **1966** The Appaloosa. **1967** King's Pirate. **1968** Daring Game.

MONTOYA, MARGARET (Margaret Peterson)

Born: 1910. Died: Sept. 23, 1935, National City, Calif. Screen and stage actress.

MONTROSE, BELLE

Born: 1886. Died: Oct. 25, 1964, Hollywood, Calif. (heart attack). Screen, vaudeville and television actress. Mother of actor Steve Allen. Appeared in vaudeville as part of team "Allen and Montrose."

Appeared in: **1961** The Absent-Minded Professor.

MONTT, CHRISTINA

Born: 1897, Chile. Died: Apr. 22, 1969, Hollywood, Calif. (coronary failure). Screen actress.

Appeared in: **1924** The Sea Hawk. **1927** The Rose of the Golden West. **1930** Alma de Gaucho.

MOODY, RALPH

Born: Nov. 5, 1887, St. Louis, Mo. Died: Sept. 16, 1971, Burbank, Calif. (heart attack). Screen, stage, radio, television actor and circus performer. Entered films in 1944.

Appeared in: **1948** Man-Eater of Kumaon. **1949** Square Dance Jubilee. **1951** Red Mountain. **1952** Affair in Trinidad; Road to Bali. **1953** The Juggler; Seminole; Column South; Tumbleweed. **1955** Many Rivers to Cross; Strange Lady in Town; Rage at Dawn; The Far Horizons; I Died a Thousand Times. **1956** The Last Hunt; The Steel Jungle; Toward the Unknown; Reprisal! **1957** The Monster That Challenged the World; Pawnee. **1958** Going Steady; The Lone Ranger and the Lost City of Gold. **1959** The Legend of Tom Dooley; The Big Fisherman. **1960** The Story of Ruth. **1961** Homicidal; The Outsider.

MOOERS, DE SACIA

Born: 1888, Allesandro, Mojave Desert, Calif. Died: Jan. 11, 1960, Hollywood, Calif. Screen and stage actress.

Appeared in: **1904** The Great Train Robbery. **1922** The Blonde Vampire; The Challenge. **1923** Potash and Perlmutter. **1924** The Average Woman; It Is the Law; Restless Wives. **1925** Any Woman. **1926** Forbidden Waters. **1927** Tongues of Scandal; Lonesome Ladies; By Whose Hand?; Back to Liberty. **1928** Broadway Daddies; Confessions of a Wife. **1929** Shanghai Rose; Just Off Broadway. **1930** The Arizona Kid.

MOON, DONNA

Died: Oct. 24, 1918, Helena, Montana (Spanish influenza). Screen actress. Married to actor Morse Moon (dec. 1918).

Appeared in: **1917** The Flame of Youth.

MOON, GEORGE

Born: 1886, Australia. Died: June 4, 1967, London, England. Screen and stage actor. Son of actor George Moon (dec.). Married to vaudeville actress Gertie McQueen.

Appeared in: **1938** Lightning Conductor. **1939** Me and My Pal. **1944** Time Flies. **1955** An Alligator Named Daisy (US 1957). **1957** Carry on Admiral (aka The Ship Was Loaded—US 1959); Davy. **1962** The Boys (US 1963). **1965** Monster of Terror (aka Die Monster Die—US). **1966** Promise Her Anything. **1967** Half a Sixpence (US 1968).

MOON, KEITH

Born: Aug. 23, 1947, London, England. Died: Sept. 7, 1978, London, England. Musician, drummer, screen actor. Member of the "Who" rock band.

Appeared in: **1974** That'll Be the Day. **1975** Tommy; Stardust.

MOON, MORSE

Died: Oct., 1918, Helena, Montana (Spanish influenza). Screen actor. Married to actress Donna Moon (dec. 1918).

MOONEY, THOMAS

Died: Apr. 5, 1978. Screen actor.

Appeared in: **1970** The Cross and the Switchblade.

MOORE, ALICE (Alice Moore Miller)

Born: 1916. Died: May 7, 1960, Washington, D.C. Screen actress. Daughter of actor Tom Moore (dec. 1955) and actress Alice Joyce (dec. 1955). Niece of actors Matt (dec. 1960), Joe (dec. 1926), Owen (dec. 1939) and actress Mary Moore (dec. 1919).

Appeared in: **1934** Babes in Toyland. **1950** Revenge Is Sweet (reissue of 1934 film Babes in Toyland).

MOORE, CARLYLE, JR.

Born: 1909. Died: Mar. 3, 1977, Sun Valley, Idaho. Screen actor. Son of actor Carlyle Moore, Sr. (dec. 1924).

Appeared in: **1935** Ceiling Zero; High School Girl. **1936** China Clipper; Road Gang; Treachery Rides the Range; Bengal Tiger; The Case of the Black Cat; Two Against the World; Trailin' West. **1937** Fugitive in the Sky; Slim; Midnight Court. **1938** The Overland Express; Outlaw Express. **1940** Knute Rockne—All American.

MOORE, CARLYLE, SR.

Born: 1875. Died: June 26, 1924. Screen and stage actor. Father of actor Carlyle Moore, Jr. (dec. 1977).

MOORE, CLARENCE J. "DUKE"

Born: 1913. Died: Nov. 16, 1976, Hollywood, Calif. (heart attack). Screen actor.

Appeared in: **1956** Bride of the Monster. **1959** Plan 9 From Outer Space.

MOORE, CLEO
Born: Oct. 31, 1928, Baton Rouge, La. Died: Oct. 25, 1973, Inglewood, Calif. Screen actress.

Appeared in: **1948** Congo Bill (serial). **1950** Bright Leaf; Rio Grande Patrol; This Side of the Law; Dynamite Pass; Hunt the Man Down; Gambling House. **1951** On Dangerous Ground. **1952** Strange Fascination; The Pace that Thrills. **1953** One Girl's Confession; Thy Neighbor's Daughter. **1954** The Other Woman; Bait. **1955** Women's Prison; Hold Back Tomorrow. **1956** Over Exposed. **1957** Hit and Run.

MOORE, CLEVE
Born: June 10, 1904, Port Huron, Mich. Died: Jan. 25, 1954, Miami, Fla. Screen and stage actor. Brother of actress Colleen Moore.

Appeared in: **1923** Cause for Divorce. **1925** We Moderns. **1926** It Must Be Love. **1927** The Stolen Bride; Her Summer Hero; The Prince of Headwaiters; Too Many Crooks. **1928** Lilac Time; The Air Circus. **1929** Footlights and Fools.

MOORE, DEL
Born: 1917. Died: Aug. 30, 1970, Encino, Calif. (heart attack). Screen, stage and television actor.

Appeared in: **1952** So You Want to Enjoy Life (short). **1954** So You Want to Go to a Nightclub (short). **1955** So You Want to Be a Gladiator (short); So You Want to Be a V.P. (short). **1956** So You Think the Grass Is Greener (short). **1961** The Last Time I Saw Archie. **1962** The Errand Boy; It's Only Money; Stagecoach to Dancer's Rock. **1963** The Nutty Professor. **1964** The Patsy; The Disorderly Orderly. **1966** Movie Star—American Style or: LSD I Hate You. **1967** The Big Mouth. **1968** The Catalina Caper.

MOORE, DENNIS
Born: 1914, Fort Worth, Tex. or New York, N.Y.? Died: Mar. 1, 1964. Screen actor.

Appeared in: **1935** Sylvia Scarlett; The Sagebrush Troubadour. **1936** Down the Stretch; China Clipper; Here Comes Carter; Meet Nero Wolfe; Sing Me a Love Song. **1937** The Perfect Speciman; Angel; Submarine D-1. **1938** Cowboy From Brooklyn; Mystery House; Boy Meets Girl; Four's a Crowd; Secrets of an Actress; Rebellious Daughters. **1939** Overland Mail; Danger Flight; Mutiny in the Big House; The Girl From Rio; I'm From Missouri; Eternally Yours; Bachelor Mother; Irish Luck; Wild Horse Canyon; No Place to Go; The Women. **1940** Rainbow Over the Range; East Side Kids; Fugitive From Prison Camp; Know Your Money (short); Saturday's Children; Women in War; Rocky Mountain Rangers. **1941** Flying Wild; Pals of the Pecos; The Roar of the Press; Law of the Wild; Pirates on Horseback; Arizona Bound; Cyclone on Horseback; Dive Bomber; Ellery Queen and the Murder Ring; Spooks Run Wild; The Lone Rider Fights Back. **1942** Dawn on the Great Divide; Bombs Over Burma; Raiders of the Range; Riders of the West. **1943** Cowboy Commandos; Black Market Rustlers; Tenting Tonight on the Old Camp Ground. **1944** The Imposter; Raiders of Ghost City (serial); Weekend Pass; Arizona Trail; Twilight on the Prairie; West of the Rio Grande; Oklahoma Raiders; Song of the Range. **1945** The Crime Doctor's Courage; The Mummy's Curse; The Master Key (serial); The Purple Monster Strikes (serial). **1946** The Mysterious Mr. M (serial); Rainbow Over the Rockies. **1948** The Gay Ranchero; The Tioga Kid; Frontier Agent; Range Renegades. **1949** Anna Lucasta; Navajo Trail Raiders; Across the Rio Grande; Haunted Trails; Boom Town Badmen (aka Roaring Westward); Riders in the Sky. **1950** Hostile Country; West of Wyoming; Arizona Territory; Gunslingers; West of the Brazos; Marshal of Heldorado; Colorado Ranger; Crooked River; Fast on the Draw; Silver Raiders; Hot Rod. **1951** Blazing Bullets; Abilene Trail; Man From Sonora; The Model and the Marriage Broker; Fort Defiance. **1952** And Now Tomorrow; Canyon Ambush; Guns Along the Border. **1956** Blazing the Overland Trail (serial); Perils of the Wilderness (serial). **1957** Chicago Confidential; Utah Blaine.

MOORE, EULABELLE
Born: 1903. Died: Nov. 30, 1964, New York, N.Y. Screen, stage and television actress.

Appeared in: **1964** The Horror of Party Beach.

MOORE, EVA
Born: Feb. 9, 1870, Brighton, Sussex, England. Died: Apr. 27, 1955. Screen and stage actress.

Appeared in: **1920** The Law Divine. **1922** The Crimson Circle; Flames of Passion. **1923** Chu Chin Chow (US 1925). **1924** The Great Well (aka Neglected Women—US). **1927** Motherland. **1931** Brown Sugar; The Other Woman; Almost a Divorce. **1932** The Old Dark House; The Flesh is Weak. **1933** I Was a Spy (US 1934); Just Smith; The Song You Gave Me; House of Dreams. **1934** Little Stranger; Blind Justice; Jew Suess (aka Power—US); A Cup of Kindness. **1935** Annie, Leave the Room; Vintage Wine. **1938** Old Iron. **1945** Scotland Yard Investigator. **1946** The Bandit of Sherwood Forest; Of Human Bondage.

MOORE, FLORENCE
Born: 1886, Philadelphia, Pa. Died: Mar. 23, 1935, Darby, Pa. (operation complications). Stage and screen actress. Sister of Frank F. Moore (dec. 1924).

Appeared in: **1924** Broadway After Dark. **1928** Broadway Comedienne (short); Soldier Composer (short).

MOORE, FRANK F.
Died: May 28, 1924, Los Angeles, Calif. Screen, stage and vaudeville actor. Brother of actress Florence Moore (dec. 1935).

MOORE, GERALD (Chester Beekman)
Born: 1899. Died: June 17, 1954, Brooklyn, N.Y. Screen and stage actor.

Appeared in: **1946** The Gay Intruders. **1950** The Blonde Bandit.

MOORE, GRACE
Born: Dec. 5, 1901, Jellico, Tenn. Died: Jan. 26, 1947, Copenhagen, Denmark (plane crash). Screen, stage actress and opera performer. Nominated for 1934 Academy Award for Best Actress in One Night of Love.

Appeared in: **1930** A Lady's Morals; New Moon. **1934** One Night of Love. **1935** Love Me Forever. **1936** The King Steps Out. **1937** When You're in Love; I'll Take Romance. **1940** Louise.

MOORE, HARRY R. "TIM"
Born: 1888, Rock Island, Ill. Died: Dec. 13, 1958, Los Angeles, Calif. Screen, radio and television actor. Was Kingfish of "Amos 'n Andy" radio series.

MOORE, HILDA
Born: England. Died: May 18, 1929, New York, N.Y. (throat infection). Stage and screen actress. Married to actor Austin Fairman (dec. 1964).

Appeared in: **1916** The Broken Melody; The Second Mrs. Tanqueray; Whoso is Without Sin. **1917** Justice. **1928** Palais de Danse. **1929** Jealousy.

MOORE, IDA
Born: 1883. Died: Sept., 1964. Screen actress.

Appeared in: **1925** The Merry Widow; Thank You. **1943** Cuty on Duty (short). **1944** Riders of the Santa Fe; The Ghost Walks Alone; Once Upon a Time; She's a Soldier, Too; Reckless Age. **1945** Easy to Look At; I'll Tell the World; She Wouldn't Say Yes; Rough, Tough and Ready; Her Lucky Night; Girls of the Big House. **1946** To Each His Own; Cross My Heart; The Bride Wore Boots. **1947** Host to a Ghost (short); The Egg and I; Easy Come, Easy Go; It's a Joke, Son. **1948** Good Sam; Johnny Belinda; Money Madness; Rusty Leads the Way; Return of the Bad Men. **1949** Rope of Sand; Manhattan Angel; Ma and Pa Kettle; Leave it to Henry; Hold That Baby; Paid in Full. **1950** Harvey; Backfire; Mr. Music; Mother Didn't Tell Me; Fancy Pants; Let's Dance. **1951** The Lemon Drop Kid; Comin' 'Round the Mountain; Leave It to the Marines; Honeychile. **1952** Scandal Sheet; Rainbow 'Round My Shoulders; Something to Live For. **1953** Scandal at Scourie. **1954** The Country Girl; The Long, Long Trailer. **1955** Ma and Pa Kettle at Waikiki. **1957** The Desk Set. **1958** Rock-a-bye Baby.

MOORE, JOE
Born: County Meath, Ireland. Died: Aug. 22, 1926, near Santa Monica, Calif. (heart attack). Screen actor. Married to actress Grace Cunard (dec. 1967). See Alice Moore for family information.

Appeared in: **1920** Love's Battle. **1921** Arrest Norma MacGregor. **1922** Judgement; False Brands; Wolf Pack; Up in the Air About Mary. **1924** Wages of Virtue. **1925** Goat Getter. **1926** The Golden Web.

MOORE, MARY
Born: July 3, 1861, London, England. Died: Apr. 6, 1931, France. Screen and stage actress. See Alice Moore for family information. Married to playwright James Albery (dec. 1889) and later married to actor/playwright Sir Charles Wyndham (dec. 1919).

Appeared in: **1913** David Garrick (screen and stage versions). **1915** Lola.

MOORE, MATT
Born: Jan., 1888, County Meath, Ireland. Died: Jan. 21, 1960, Hollywood, Calif. Screen actor. See Alice Moore for family information.

Appeared in: **1913** Traffic in Souls. **1914** A Singular Cynic. **1917** Pride of the Clan. **1919** The Unpardonable Sin; Sahara; A Regular Girl. **1920** Everybody's Sweetheart; Don't Ever Marry; Hairpins. **1921** A Man's Home; The Miracle of Manhattan; The Passionate Pilgrim; Straight Is the Way. **1922** Back Pay; Minnie; Sisters; The Storm; The Jilt. **1923** White Tiger; Strangers of the Night; Drifting. **1924** Fools in the Dark; Another Man's Wife; The Breaking Point; The Narrow Street; A Self-Made Failure; No More Women; The Wise Virgin. **1925** How Baxter Butted In; Grounds for Divorce; A Lost Lady; His Majesty, Bunker Bean; The Unholy Three; Where the Worst Begins; The Way of a Girl. **1926** His Jazz Bride; The First Year; Three Weeks in Paris; The Caveman; Early to Wed; The Mystery Club; Summer Bachelors; Diplomacy. **1927** Married Alive; Tillie the Toiler. **1928** Dry Martini; Beware of Blondes; Phyllis of the Follies. **1929** Coquette; Side Street. **1930** The Squealer; Call of the West. **1931** Stout Hearts and Willing Hands (short); Penrod and Sam; The Front Page; Married in Haste; Consolation Marriage. **1932** Rain; Cock of the Air. **1933** The Deluge. **1934** All Men Are Enemies; Such Women Are Dangerous. **1936** Anything Goes; Absolute Quiet. **1939** Bad Boy; Range War. **1941** My Life with Caroline. **1942** Mokey. **1943** Happy Land. **1944** Wilson. **1945** Spellbound. **1946** The Hoodlum Saint. **1948** Good Sam. **1949** Neptune's Daughter; That Forsyte Woman. **1950** The Big Hangover. **1952** Plymouth Adventure; Invitation. **1954** Executive Suite; Seven Brides for Seven Brothers. **1955** The King's Thief. **1956** These Wilder Years; The Birds and the Bees; Pardners. **1957** An Affair to Remember. **1958** I Bury the Living.

MOORE, MONETTE
Born: 1912. Died: Oct. 21, 1962, Anaheim, Calif. (heart attack). Screen and stage actress.

Appeared in: **1951** Yes Sir, Mr. Bones.

MOORE, OWEN
Born: Dec. 12, 1886, County Meath, Ireland. Died: June 9, 1939, Beverly Hills, Calif. Screen, stage actor and film producer. Divorced from actress Mary Pickford (dec. 1979). Married to actress Kathryn Perry. See Alice Moore for family information. Entered films in 1908 with Biograph.

Appeared in: **1908** In a Lonely Villa; In Old Kentucky; The Honor of Thieves; The Salvation Army Lass. **1909** The Cricket on the Hearth; The Winning Coat; A Baby's Shoe; The Violin Maker of Cremona; The Mended Lute; Pippa Passes; 1776, or the Hessian Renegades; Leather Stocking; A Change of Heart; His Lost Love; The Expiation; The Restoration; The Light That Came; The Open Gate; The Dancing Girl of Butte; Her Terrible Ordeal; The Last Deal; The Iconoclast. **1911** Flo's Discipline; The Courting of Mary. **1912** Swift Waters. **1913** Caprice. **1914** Battle of the Sexes. **1915** Mistress Nell; Pretty Mrs. Smith; Nearly a Lady; The Little Teacher (reissued as A Small Town Bully). **1916** A Coney Island Princess; Betty of Graystone; Little Meena's Romance; Under Cover. **1917** The Little Boy Scout; The Silent Partner; A Girl Like That. **1919** Crimson Gardenia. **1920** Piccadilly Jim; Poor Simp. **1921** A Divorce of Convenience; The Chicken in the Case. **1922** Oh, Mabel Behave; Reported Missing; Love Is an Awful Thing. **1923** Hollywood; Modern Matrimony; Her Temporary Husband; The Silent Partner. **1924** Thundergate; Torment; East of Broadway. **1925** The Parasite; Go Straight; Married?; Camille of the Barbary Coast; Code of the West. **1926** False Pride; The Skyrocket; The Black Bird; Money Talks; The Road to Mandalay. **1927** The Red Mill; The Taxi Dancer; Women Love Diamonds; Becky; Tea for Three. **1928** The Actress; Husbands for Rent. **1929** High Voltage; Stolen Love; Side Street. **1930** Outside the Law; What a Widow!; Extravagance. **1931** Stout Hearts and Willing Hands (short); Hush Money. **1932** Cannonball Express; As You Desire Me. **1933** She Done Him Wrong; Man of Sentiment. **1937** A Star Is Born.

MOORE, PATTI
Born: 1901. Died: Nov. 26, 1972, Los Angeles, Calif. (cancer). Screen, stage and vaudeville actress.

Appeared in: **1941** Shadow of the Thin Man. **1964** When the Boys Meet the Girls.

MOORE, PERCY
Born: 1878. Died: Apr. 8, 1945, New York, N.Y. Screen and stage actor.

Appeared in: **1925** The Shock Punch.

MOORE, REX
Born: Feb. 16, 1900. Died: Apr. 21, 1975. Screen actor.

MOORE, RUTH HART
Died: May 2, 1952, New York, N.Y. Screen, stage and vaudeville actress.

Appeared in: **1913** Judith of Bethulia. **1928** The Companionate Marriage.

MOORE, SCOTT
Born: 1889. Died: Dec. 18, 1967, Miami Beach, Fla. Screen actor.

Appeared in: **1931** The Struggle.

MOORE, SUE
Born: 1916. Died: Apr. 10, 1966, Calif. Screen and stage actress.

Appeared in: **1936** After the Thin Man. **1938** Gold is Where You Find It; Swing Your Lady. **1939** Tiny Troubles (short). **1940** The Mortal Storm. **1941** Cheers for Miss Bishop; Lady From Cheyenne. **1944** An American Romance; Ladies of Washington; Henry Aldrich Plays Cupid. **1945** Pillow to Post; Adventure. **1949** The Reckless Moment.

MOORE, TOM
Born: 1885, County Meath, Ireland. Died: Feb. 12, 1955, Santa Monica, Calif. (cancer). Screen, stage, vaudeville and television actor. Married to actress Eleanor Merry. Divorced from actresses Alice Joyce (dec. 1955) and Renee Adoree (dec. 1933). See Alice Moore for family information. Entered films with the Kalem Company.

Appeared in: **1912** The Strange Story of Elsie Mason; The Mystery of Grandfather's Clock; A Daughter's Sacrifice; A Business Buccaneer. **1913** The Flag of Freedom; The Nurse at Mulberry Bend; The Cub Reporter's Temptation; The Senator's Dishonor; In the Power of Blacklegs; The American Princess; In the Grip of a Charlatan; A Streak of Yellow; The Sneak; The Heart of an Actress; Nina of the Theatre; The Adventure of an Heiress; The Artist's Sacrifice; The Pawnbroker's Daughter; The Attorney for the Defense; The Cloak of Guild; For Her Sister's Sake; The Christian; A Midnight Message; Our New Minister; The Hunchback; An Unseen Terror. **1914** The Hand Print Mystery; The Shadow; The Cabaret Dancer; The Dance of Death; The Weakling; In Wolf's Clothing; The Beast; The Girl and the Stowaway; The Lynbrook Tragedy; The Brand; Vampire's Trail; The Mystery of the Sleeping Death. **1916** Who's Guilty. **1917** The Cinderella Man; The Primrose Ring. **1918** Thirty a Week; The Kingdom of Youth. **1919** Lord and Lady Algy; Toby's Bow; City of Comrades; Heartsease; Dub; A Man and His Money; One of the Finest. **1920** Great Accident; Officer 666; Stop Thief. **1921** Dangerous Money; Made in Heaven; Hold Your Horses; Beating the Game; From the Ground Up. **1922** Over the Border; Mr. Barnes of New York; The Cowboy and the Lady; Pawned. **1923** Rouged Lips; Big Brother; Marriage Morals; Harbor Lights; Mary of the Movies. **1924** One Night in Rome; Manhandled; The Isle of Vanishing Men; Dangerous Money. **1925** Adventure; The Trouble with Wives; On Thin Ice; Pretty Ladies; Under the Rough. **1926** Kiss for Cinderella; The Clinging Vine; Good and Naughty; Syncopating Sue; The Song and Dance Man. **1927** The Love Thrill; The Wise Wife; Cabaret; The Siren. **1928** Anybody Here Seen Kelly?. **1929** The Yellowback; His Last Haul; Side Street. **1930** The Costello Case; The Woman Racket. **1931** Stout Hearts and Willing Hands (short); The Last Parade. **1932** Cannonball Express; Vanishing Men. **1933** Men Are Such Fools; Neighbors' Wives; Mr. Broadway. **1934** Bombay Mail. **1936** Trouble for Two; Reunion. **1946** Behind Green Lights. **1947** Mother Wore Tights; Moss Rose; Forever Amber. **1948** The Walls of Jericho; Scudda Hoo! Scudda Hay! **1949** The Fighting O'Flynn. **1950** The Redhead and the Cowboy.

MOORE, VICTOR
Born: Feb. 24, 1876, Hammonton, N.J. Died: July 23, 1962, Long Island, N.Y. (heart attack). Screen, stage and vaudeville actor. Married to actress Emma Littlefield (dec. 1934) and later married to Shirley Page. Entered films in 1915.

Appeared in: **1915** Chimmie Fadden; Chimmie Fadden Out West; Snobs. **1916** The Clown; The Race; The Best Man. **1917** Invited Out; Oh! U-Boat; Faint Heart and Fair Lady; Bungalowing; Commuting; Moving; Flivering; Home Defense. **1925** The Man Who Found Himself; prior to 1930 appeared in 41 Lever Co. shorts. **1930** Heads Up; Dangerous Nan McGrew. **1932-33** Appeared in Vitaphone shorts. **1934** Romance in the Rain; Gift of Gab. **1936** Swing Time; Gold Diggers of 1937. **1937** We're on the Jury; Meet the Missus; The Life of the Party; She's Got Everything; Make Way for Tomorrow. **1938** Radio City Revels; This Marriage Business. **1941** Louisiana Purchase. **1942** Star Spangled Rhythm. **1943** True to Life; Riding High; The Heat's On. **1944** Carolina Blues. **1945** Duffy's Tavern; It's in the Bag. **1946** Ziegfeld Follies. **1947** It Happened on Fifth Avenue. **1948** A Miracle Can Happen. **1949** A Kiss in the Dark. **1952** We're Not Married. **1955** The Seven Year Itch.

MOORE, VIN
Born: 1878, Mayville, N.Y. Died: Dec. 5, 1949, Hollywood, Calif. Screen, stage actor, film director and screenwriter.

Appeared in: **1916** By Stork Delivery. **1926** Lazy Lightning; The Man from the West.

MOOREHEAD, AGNES (Agnes Robertson Moorehead)
Born: Dec. 6, 1906, Clinton, Mass. Died: Apr. 30, 1974, Rochester, Minn. (lung cancer). Screen, stage, vaudeville, radio and television actress. Divorced from actors Jack G. Lee and Robert Gist. Nominated for 1942 Academy Award as Best Supporting Actress in The Magnificent Ambersons, in 1944 for Mrs. Parkington, in 1948 for Johnny Belinda, and in 1964 for Hush, Hush, Sweet Charlotte.

Appeared in: **1941** Citizen Kane (film debut). **1942** The Magnificent Ambersons; The Big Street; Journey into Fear. **1943** The Youngest Profession; Government Girl. **1944** Mrs. Parkington; Since You Went Away; The Seventh Cross; Dragon Seed; Tomorrow the World. **1945** Her Highness and the Bell Boy; Keep Your Powder Dry; Our Vines Have Tender Grapes. **1947** Dark Passage; The Lost Moment. **1948** Johnny Belinda; Summer Holiday; The Woman in White; Station West. **1949** Without Honor; The Stratton Story; The Great Sinner. **1950** Caged. **1951** Adventures of Captain Fabian; Show Boat; Fourteen Hours; The Blue Veil. **1952** Captain Blackjack; The Blazing Forest. **1953** The Story of Three Loves (aka The Jealous Lover); Main Street to Broadway; Scandal at Scourie; Those Redheads from Seattle. **1954** Magnificent Obsession. **1955** The Left Hand of God; Untamed; All That Heaven Allows. **1956** Meet Me in Las Vegas; The Conqueror; The Revolt of Mamie Stover; The Swan; Pardners; The Opposite Sex. **1957** Raintree County; The True Story of Jesse James; Jeanne Eagels; The Story of Mankind. **1959** Night of the Quarter Moon; Tempest; The Bat. **1960** Pollyanna. **1961** Twenty Plus Two; Bachelor in Paradise. **1962** Jessica; How the West Was Won. **1963** Who's Minding the Store? **1964** Hush, Hush, Sweet Charlotte. **1965** The Singing Nun. **1971** What's the Matter with Helen?; Dear Dead Delilah; Charlotte's Web (voice).

MOOREY, STEFA
Born: 1934, London, England. Died: Feb. 3, 1972, Birmingham, England (suicide—drowned). Screen actress. Married to actor Frank Moorey.

MOORHOUSE, BERT
Born: 1895. Died: Jan. 26, 1954, Hollywood, Calif. (suicide—gun). Screen actor.

Appeared in: **1928** Rough Ridin' Red. **1929** Hey Rube!; The Woman I Love; The Delightful Rogue; The Girl from Woolworths. **1930** Conspiracy; Pay Off. **1934** Smarty. **1935** Broadway Melody of 1936. **1943** Government Girl. **1944** Kitchen Cynic (short). **1950** Sunset Boulevard; The Big Hangover; Duchess of Idaho. **1952** Ace in the Hole (aka The Big Carnival).

MORALES, ISHMAEL "ESY"
Born: 1917, Puerto Rico. Died: Nov. 2, 1950, New York, N.Y. (heart attack). Screen actor and orchestra leader.

Appeared in: **1945** Film Vodvil (short with his Copacabana Orchestra). **1949** Criss Cross.

MORAN, FRANK (Frank Charles Moran)
Born: Mar. 18, 1887, Ohio. Died: Dec. 14, 1967, Hollywood, Calif. (heart attack). Screen actor and professional heavyweight boxer.

Appeared in: **1928** Ships of the Night. **1933** Hooks and Jabs (short); Sailor's Luck; Gambling Ship. **1934** Three Chumps Ahead (short); No More Women; The World Moves On; By Your Leave. **1936** Mummy's Boys. **1937** Shall We Dance?. **1938** Battle of Broadway. **1939** Captain Fury. **1940** The Great McGinty. **1941** The Lady Eve; Federal Fugitives; A Date with the Falcon; Sullivan's Troubles. **1942** Butch Minds the Baby; Sullivan's Travels; The Corpse Vanishes. **1943** Ghosts on the Loose. **1944** The Great Moment; Return of the Ape Man; Hail the Conquering Hero; The Miracle of Morgan's Creek. **1945** Yolanda and the Thief. **1946** Pardon My Past. **1947** Mad Wednesday. **1948** A Miracle Can Happen. **1949** The Lady Gambles.

MORAN, GEORGE (George Searcy)
Born: 1882, Elwood, Kans. Died: Aug. 1, 1949, Oakland, Calif. (stroke). Screen, stage, vaudeville, minstrel and radio actor. He was the Moran in "Moran and Mack" comedy team, usually referred to as the "Two Black Crows"; however, he did not appear in several shorts and films as he was replaced by Bert Swor, but did return to the team for Hypnotized and later shorts.

Appeared in: **1927** Two Flaming Youths. **1929** Why Bring That Up. **1932** Hypnotized. **1932-33** "Moran and Mack" short comedies for Educational: Two Black Crows in Africa; As the Crows Fly. **1940** My Little Chickadee; The Bank Dick.

MORAN, LEE
Born: June 23, 1890, Chicago, Ill. Died: Apr. 24, 1961, Woodland Hills, Calif. (heart attack). Stage and screen actor. Part of comedy team of "Lyons and Moran" in Christie comedies from 1914 to 1920.

Appeared in: **1912** The Sheriff Outwitted; Making a Man of Her. **1913** Weighed in the Balance; Her Friend the Butler; Locked Out at Twelve. **1914** She Was a Working Girl; What a Baby Did; Such a Villain; Her Moonshine Lover; Captain Bill's Warm Reception; When the Girls Joined the Force; A Lucky Deception; Sophie of the Films; When Eddie Went to the Front; When Bess Gets in Wrong. **1915** When the Mummy Cried for Help; Wanted, a Leading Woman; Eddie's Little Love Affair; His Only Pants; He Fell in a Cabaret; When His Lordship Proposed; When Cupid Caught a Thief; When the Deacon Swore; How Doctor Cupid Won; Jed's Little Elopement; The Mix-Up at Maxim's; The Baby's Fault; When He Proposed; A Coat's a Coat; Eddie's Awful Predicament; When Her Idol Fell; Too Many Crooks; When They Were Co-Eds; The Downfall of Potts; A Peach and a Pair; When the Spirit Moved; The Tale of His Pants; The Rise and Fall of Officer 13; Little Egypt Malone; Tony the Wop; Kids and Corsets; Their Happy Honeymoon; Too Many Smiths; When Lizzie Went to Sea; Their Quiet Honeymoon; Love and a Savage; Some Chaperone; It Almost Happened; Some Fixer; Almost a Knockout. **1916** Jed's Trip to the Fair; When Aunt Matilda Fell; Mingling Spirits. **1917** War Bridegrooms; A Hasty Hazing; Down Wen the Key; A Million in Sight; A Bundle of Trouble; When the Cat's Away; Some Specimens; Shot in the West; Mixed Matrimony; The Home Wreckers; Under the Bed; Follow the Tracks; To Oblige a Vampire; The Lost Appetite; What a Clue Will Do; Moving Day; Tell Morgan's Girl; A Burgler by Request; Who's Looney Now?; Jilted in Jail; His Wife's Relations; Pete the Prowler; To Be or Not to Be Remarried; Hot Applications; A Fire Escape Finish; Why, Uncle!; The Other Stocking; One Thousand Miles an Hour; Treat 'Em Rough; A Macaroni Sleuth. **1918** Please Hit Me; The Extra Bridegroom; Hearts and Let'us; The Knockout; Almost Welcome; The Vamp Cure; Giver Her Gas; Damaged Goods; Housecleaning Horrors. **1919** The Wife Breakers; Skidding Thrones; Kitchen Police; How's Your Husband?; Three in a Closet; The Bullskeviki; Fun in a Flat; The Expert Eloper; Lay Off!; The Smell of the Yukon. **1920** Bungled Bungalows; Caught in the End. **1921** A Shocking Night; Fixed by George; Once a Plumber. **1924** The Fast Worker; Gambling Wives; Daring Youth; The Tomboy; Listen, Lester. **1925** After Business Hours; Fifth Avenue Models; Where Was I?; Tessie; My Lady of Whims; Jimmie's Millions. **1926** Her Big Night; Syncopating Sue; The Little Irish Girl; Take It from Me. **1927** Fast and Furious; The Rose of Kildare; The Irrestible Lover; Spring Fever; The Thrill Seekers; Wolf's Clothing. **1928** The Actress; Ladies of the Night Club; Outcast; Look-Out Girl; The Racket; Taxi 13; Thanks for the Buggy Ride; A Woman Against the World; Show Girl. **1929** On With the Show; The Aviator; Children of the Ritz; Dance Hall; Glad Rag Doll; Gold Diggers of Broadway; Madonna of Avenue A; No Defense; The Show of Shows; Hearts in Exile. **1930** Golden Dawn; Hide Out; Mammy; Pardon My Gun; Sweet Mama. **1931** Other Men's Women; A Soldier's Plaything; Caught Plastered. **1932** Stowaway; Exposure; Racetrack; The Fighting Gentleman; Uptown New York; The Death Kiss. **1933** Footlight Parade; Sister of Judas; Grand Slam; The 11th Commandment; Goldie Gets Along; High Gear; Sitting Pretty. **1934** Jimmy the Gent; Circus Clown. **1935** Circumstantial Evidence; Honeymoon Limited. **1936** The Calling of Dan Matthews.

MORAN, MANOLO
Born: 1904, Madrid, Spain. Died: Apr. 27, 1967, Alicante, Spain. Screen actor. Won the Spanish Oscar in 1958 for his role in Viva la Imposible (Long Live the Impossible).

Appeared in: **1949** Don Quixote de la Mancha. **1958** Viva la Imposible (Long Live the Impossible). **1966** Operation Delilah. **1967** Flame Over Viet Nam; Other Spanish films: Angels of the Wheel; Manolo, Guardia Urbana (Manolo, Traffic Cop).

MORAN, PAT
Born: 1901. Died: Aug. 9, 1965, Woodland Hills, Calif. Screen, stage actor and stuntman. Married to actress Patsy Moran (dec. 1968).

Appeared in: **1937** Something to Sing About; Artists and Models. **1947** Variety Girl. **1949** Trouble Makers. **1956** The Ten Commandments. **1958** Houseboat. **1963** Move Over Darling. **1964** The Unsinkable Molly Brown.

MORAN, PATSY
Born: 1905. Died: Dec. 10, 1968, Hollywood, Calif. Screen and stage actress. Married to actor and stuntman Pat Moran (dec. 1965).

Appeared in: **1938** Topa Topa; Blockheads. **1940** Cowboy from Sundown; The Golden Trail. **1942** 'Neath the Brooklyn Bridge; Foreign Agent. **1945** Come Out Fighting; Trouble Chasers. **1949** Billie Gets Her Man (short).

MORAN, PERCY

Born: Ireland. Died: 1958, England? Screen actor, film director, stuntman, circus performer and music hall entertainer.

Appeared in: **1911** Lieutenant Daring RN and the Secret Service Agents (aka Lieutenant Daring RN Saves HMS Medina). **1912** Lieutenant Daring Avenges an Insult to the Union Jack; Lieutenant Daring and the Ship's Mascot; The Belle of Bettws-Y-Coed (aka The Belle of North Wales—US); Lieutenant Daring Defeats the Middleweight Champion; The Great Anarchist Mystery; Lieutenant Daring Quells a Rebellion; The Bargee's Revenge; The Mountaineer's Romance; Lieutenant Daring and the Plans of the Minefields (aka The International Spies—US); Lily of Letchworth Lock; The First Chronicles of Don Q—The Dark Brothers of the Civil Guard; Don Q—How He Outwitted Don Luis; The Smuggler's Daughter of Anglesea; Lieutenant Daring and the Photographing Pigeon; The Adventures of Dick Turpin series including: The King of Highwaymen; The Gunpowder Plot; 200 Guineas Reward, Dead or Alive; A Deadly Foe, a Pack of Hounds, and Some Merry Monks. **1913** Bliggs on the Briny; A Flash of Lightning; The Favourite for the Jamaica Cup; Lieutenant Daring and the Labour Riots; The Old College Badge; Tom Cringle in Jamaica; A Creole's Love Story; Lieutenant Daring and the Dancing Girl; The Planter's Daughter; Dick Turpin's Ride to York; Heroes of the Mine (aka The Great Mine Disaster—US). **1914** The Live Wire; The Mystery of the Diamond Belt; The Houseboat Mystery; OHMS—Our Helpless Millions Saved; The Chase of Death; A Fishergirl's Folly. **1915** Britain's Naval Secret; Slavers of the Thames; London Nighthawks; At the Torrent's Mercy; How Men Love Women; Parted by the Sword; Nurse and Martyr. **1916** London's Enemies; It Is for England. **1919** Jack, Sam and Pete. **1922** The Field of Honour. **1924** Lieutenant Daring RN and the Water Rats.

MORAN, POLLY (Pauline Theresa Moran)

Born: June 28, 1883, Chicago, Ill. Died: Jan. 25, 1952, Los Angeles, Calif. (heart ailment). Screen, stage, vaudeville and radio actress. Entered films as a Mack Sennett bathing beauty in 1915.

Appeared in: **1915** Their Social Splash; Those College Girls (reissued as His Better Half); A Favorite Fool; Her Painted Hero; The Hunt. **1916** The Village Blacksmith; By Stork Alone; A Bath House Blunder; His Wild Oats; Madcap Ambrose; Pills of Peril; Vampire Ambrose; Love Will Conquer; Because He Loved Her. **1917** Her Fame and Shame; His Naughty Thought; Cactus Nell; She Needed a Doctor; His Uncle Dudley; Roping Her Romeo. **1921** The Affairs of Anatol; Two Weeks with Pay; Skirts. **1923** Luck. **1926** Scarlet Letter. **1927** The Callahans and the Murphys; London After Midnight; Buttons; The Thirteenth Hour. **1928** The Enemy; Rose Marie; The Divine Woman; Bringing Up Father; Telling the World; Show People; Beyond the Sierras; Shadows of the Night; While the City Sleeps; Movie Chatterbox (short). **1929** Unholy Night; Honeymoon; China Bound; Dangerous Females; Hollywood Revue of 1929; Hot for Paris; So This Is College; Speedway. **1930** Remote Control; Way for a Sailor; Way Out West; The Girl Said No; Chasing Rainbows; Caught Short; Paid. **1931** Guilty Hands; Reducing; Politics; It's a Wise Child. **1932** Jackie Cooper's Christmas Party (short); The Passionate Plumber; Prosperity; The Slippery Pearls (short). **1933** Alice in Wonderland. **1934** Hollywood Party; Down to Their Last Yacht. **1936** Columbia shorts. **1937** Two Wise Maids. **1938** Ladies in Distress. **1939** Ambush. **1940** Tom Brown's School Days; Meet the Missus. **1941** Petticoat Politics. **1949** Red Light; Adam's Rib. **1950** The Yellow Cab Man. **1964** Big Parade of Comedy (documentary).

MORANTE, JOSEPH

Born: 1853. Died: Apr. 13, 1940, Hollywood, Calif. Screen actor.

MORANTE, MILBURN (Milburn Charles Morante aka MILBURN MORANTI)

Born: Apr. 6, 1887, San Francisco, Calif. Died: Jan. 28, 1964, Pacoima, Calif. (heart disease). Screen, stage actor, film director and producer.

Appeared in: **1915** A Millionaire for a Minute; No Babies Allowed; Pete's Awful Crime; Mysterious Lady Baffles and Detective Duck in the Lost Roll; Lemonade Aids Cupid; The Ore Mystery; Freaks; The Way He Won the Widow. **1916** A Perfect Match; Wanted—A Piano Turner; Leap and Look Thereafter; The Tale of a Telegram; The Jitney Driver's Romance; His Highness the Janitor; Hubby Puts One Over; Muchly Married; Some Vampire; I've Got Yer Number; Kate's Affinities; She Wrote a Play and Played It; A Marriage for Revenge; Soup to Nuts; In Onion There Is Strength; The Elixir of Life; The Deacon Stops the Show; Father Gets in Wrong; Bears and Bullets; A Crooked Mix-Up; A Shadowed Shadow; In Love With a Fireman; Their First Arrest; A Janitor's Vendetta; Musical Madness; Scrappily Married; A Wife for a Ransom; A Dark Suspicion; Love Quarantined; Bashful Charley's Proposal; An All Around Cure; A Raffle for a

Husband; A Stage Villain; The Fall of Deacon Stillwaters; The Harem Scarem Deacon; The Tramp Chef; Their Dark Secret; Jags and Jealousy; Mines and Matrimony. **1917** Love in Suspense; Love Me—Love My Biscuits; His Coming-Out Party; Out for the Dough; Mule Mates; Rosie's Rancho; Passing the Grip; Wanta Make a Dollar; 'Art Aches; Whose Baby?; What the—?; A Boob for Luck; The Careless Cop; The Leak; Left in the Soup; The Man With the Package; The Last Scent; The Boss of the Family; Uneasy Money; One Damp Day; His Fatal Beauty; Her Naughty Choice; The Shame of the Bullcon; Water on the Brain. **1919** Mixed Wives. **1921** Hearts O' the Range. **1922** Diamond Carlisle; The Hate Trail. **1924** Battling Mason; A Fighting Heart; Rainbow Rangers. **1925** Don X; Flying Fool; The Range Terror; The Rip Snorter; Triple Action; Wolf Blood. **1926** Buffalo Bill on the U.P. Trail; The Desperate Game; Lawless Trails; Modern Youth; West of the Rainbow's End. **1927** The Grey Devil; Cactus Trails; Daring Deeds; The Swift Shadow; Perils of the Jungle (serial). **1928** The Fightin' Redhead; The Pinto Kid; The Little Buckaroo; Wizard of the Saddle. **1929** The Freckled Rascal; The Little Savage; The Vagabond Cub; Pals of the Prairie. **1935** The Lost City (serial); The Vanishing Riders; Wild Mustang. **1936** Blazing Justice; Sundown Saunders; plus the following serials: The Black Coin; The Clutching Hand; Custer's Last Stand. **1937** Public Cowboy No. l; The Old Corral; Bar Z Bad Men. **1938** Gold Spur; Gold Mine in the Sky. **1941** Buzzy and the Phantom Pinto; Trail of the Silver Spur. **1942** West of the Law. **1943** Ghost Rider. **1946** Drifting Along. **1947** Ridin' Down the Trail. **1948** Oklahoma Blues; Range Renegades; Hidden Danger; The Rangers Ride; Cowboy Cavalier; The Fighting Ranger. **1949** Western Renegades; West of El Dorado; Haunted Trails. **1950** Six Gun Mesa; Over the Border; Law of the Panhandle; Outlaw Gold; West of Wyoming. **1951** Abilene Trail; Blazing Bullets.

MORDANT, EDWIN

Born: 1868, Baltimore, Md. Died: Feb. 15, 1942, Hollywood, Calif. Screen and stage actor. Married to actress Grace Atwell.

Appeared in: **1915** Seven Sisters; The Prince and the Pauper; The Royal Family. **1916** Molly-Make-Believe; Poor Little Peppina. **1917** The Undying Flame. **1920** The Cost. **1934** I'll Tell the World. **1938** Shadows over Shanghai; Outlaws of Sonora.

MORDANT, GRACE (Grace Atwell)

Born: 1872. Died: Nov. 2, 1952, Hollywood, Calif. Screen and stage actress. Married to actor Edwin Mordant (dec. 1942).

MORE, UNITY

Born: July 27, 1894, Galway, Ireland. Died: Feb., 1981, London, England. Screen and stage actress.

Appeared in: **1918** Jo, the Crossing Sweeper; Women Who Win. **1919** Queen's Evidence.

MORELAND, MANTAN

Born: Sept. 4, 1901, Monroe, La. Died: Sept. 28, 1973, Hollywood, Calif. Black screen, stage, vaudeville, minstrel, television actor and circus performer. Appeared in the Charlie Chan films as "Birmingham Brown," Charlie's chauffeur.

Appeared in: **1936** Lucky Ghost. **1937** Spirit of Youth. **1938** Gang Smashers; Harlem on the Prairie; Frontier Scout; Next Time I Marry; There's That Woman Again. **1939** Two-Gun Man from Harlem; Irish Luck; One Dark Night; Tell No Tales; Riders of the Frontier. **1940** While Thousands Cheer; Lady Luck; Four Shall Die; Laughing at Danger; Millionaire Playboy; Pier 13; Chasing Trouble; On the Spot; The City of Chance; Drums of the Desert; Mr. Washington Goes to Town; The Man Who Wouldn't Talk; Star Dust; Maryland; Viva Cisco Kid. **1941** Up Jumped the Devil; Four Jacks and a Jill; Marry the Boss's Daughter; World Premiere; King of the Zombies; Ellery Queen's Penthouse Mystery; Up in the Air; The Gang's All Here; Hello Sucker; Dressed to Kill; You're Out of Luck; Sign of the Wolf; Let's Go Collegiate; Cracked Nuts; Footlight Fever; Sleepers West. **1942** Andy Hardy's Double Life; A-Haunting We Will Go; Professor Creeps; The Strange Case of Dr. Rx; Treat 'Em Rough; Mexican Spitfire Sees a Ghost; Footlight Serenade; Phantom Killer; Eyes in the Night; Girl Trouble; Tarzan's New York Adventure; The Palm Beach Story. **1943** Cabin in the Sky; The Crime Smasher; Sarong Girl; Revenge of the Zombies; Melody Parade; She's for Me; Hit the Ice; My Kingdom for a Cook; Slightly Dangerous; Swing Fever; You're a Lucky Fellow, Mr. Smith; We've Never Been Licked. **1944** Chip Off the Old Block; See Here, Private Hargrove; Charlie Chan in the Secret Service; The Chinese Cat; Moon Over Las Vegas; Pin-Up Girl; South of Dixie; Black Magic; Bowery to Broadway; This Is the Life; The Mystery of the River Boat (serial). **1945** The Scarlet Clue; The Jade Mask; The Shanghai Cobra; The Spider; Captain Tugboat; Annie; She Wouldn't Say Yes. **1946** Come on Cowboy; Tall, Tan and Terrific;

Dark Alibi; Shadows Over Chinatown; Mantan Messes Up; Mantan Runs for Mayor. **1947** Ebony Parade; What a Guy; Murder at Malibu Ranch; The Trap; Chinese Ring. **1948** The Dreamer; She's Too Mean to Mean; Return of Mandy's Husband; Docks of New Orleans; Shanghai Chest; The Feathered Serpent; The Mystery of the Golden Eye; The Best Man Wins. **1949** Sky Dragon. **1956** Rockin' the Blues. **1957** Rock n' Roll Revue. **1967** Enter Laughing. **1968** Spider Baby (aka Cannibal Orgy; The Maddest Story Ever Told; The Liver Eaters). **1970** Watermelon Man.

MORELL, ANDRE (Andre Mesritz)
Born: Aug. 20, 1909, London, England. Died: Nov. 29, 1978, London, England. Screen, stage and television actor. Married to actress Joan Greenwood.

Appeared in: **1938** 13 Men and a Gun (film debut). **1939** Ten Days in Paris (aka Missing Ten Days—US 1941). **1950** No Place for Jennifer (US 1951); Clouded Yellow (US 1952); Seven Days to Noon; Stage Fright; Trio; Madeleine; So Long at the Fair (US 1951). **1951** High Treason (US 1952). **1952** Tall Headlines (aka The Frightened Bride—US 1953); Stolen Face. **1954** His Majesty O'Keefe; The Black Knight. **1955** Summertime; Three Cases of Murder. **1956** The Baby and the Battleship; The Black Tent (US 1957); The Man Who Never Was. **1957** Bridge on the River Kwai; Interpol (aka Pickup Alley—US). **1958** The Camp on Blood Island; Diamond Safari; Paris Holiday. **1959** Behemoth the Sea Monster (aka The Giant Behemoth—US); The Hound of the Baskervilles; Ben Hur. **1960** Cone of Silence (aka Trouble in the Sky—US 1961). **1961** Cash on Demand (US 1963); Shadow of the Cat. **1964** Woman of Straw; The Moon-Spinners. **1965** She; The Plague of the Zombies (US 1966). **1966** The Wrong Box; Judith. **1967** The Mummy's Shroud. **1968** The Vengeance of She; The Mercenaries (aka Dark of the Sun—US). **1970** Julius Caesar; 10 Rillington Place. **1975** Barry Lyndon. **1976** The Slipper and the Rose. **1977** Mohammad, Messenger of God.

MORELLI, MICHAEL
Born: 1910. Died: Aug. 14, 1976, Burbank, Calif. (heart attack). Screen actor.

MORELLI, RINI
Born: 1909, Italy. Died: July 17, 1976, Rome, Italy (heart attack). Screen, stage and television actress. Daughter of stage actors Amilcare (dec.), and Narcisa Brillante (dec.).

Appeared in: **1940** Avventura di Salvator Rosa (Adventure of Salvator Rosa). **1948** The Loves of Don Juan. **1949** The Iron Crown. **1951** Altri Tempi (Times Gone By, aka The Idyll—US 1953). **1953** Strange Deception (aka The Forbidden Christ). **1961** La Viaccia (US 1962, aka The Love Makers). **1962** Bell' Antonio; Crime Does Not Pay. **1963** The Leopard. **1968** Senso.

MORENCY, ROBERT "BUSTER"
Born: 1932. Died: Mar. 30, 1937, Regina, Saskatchewan, Canada (leukemia). Child screen actor.

MORENO, ANTONIO
Born: Sept. 26, 1888, Madrid, Spain. Died: Feb. 15, 1967, Beverly Hills, Calif. Screen actor.

Appeared in: **1912** Two Daughters of Eve; So Near, Yet So Far; Voice of the Million. **1913** Judith of Bethulia. **1914** In the Latin Quarter. **1915** The Island of Regeneration. **1916** The Tarantula; Kennedy Square. **1917** The Magnificent Meddler; Aladdin from Broadway. **1918** The House of Hate (serial); The Iron Test (serial); The House of a Thousand Candles. **1919** Perils of Thunder Mountain (serial). **1920** The Invisible Hand (serial); The Veiled Mystery (serial). **1921** Three Sevens; The Secret of the Hills. **1922** Guilty Conscience. **1923** The Exciters; The Trail of the Lonesome Pine; The Spanish Dancer; My American Wife; Look Your Best; Lost and Found. **1924** The Story Without a Name; The Border Legion; Bluff; Flaming Barriers; Tiger Love. **1925** Learning to Love; Her Husband's Secret; One Year to Live. **1926** Mare Nostrum; The Temptress; Beverly of Graustark; Love's Blindness; The Flaming Forest. **1927** It; Venus of Venice; Madame Pompadour; Come to My House. **1928** The Midnight Taxi; Adoration; The Air Legion; The Whip Woman; Nameless Men. **1929** The Voice of Hollywood (short); Careers; Synthetic Sin; Romance of the Rio Grande. **1930** One Mad Kiss; Rough Romance; The Benson Murder Case; The Cat Creeps; Those Who Dance. **1932** Aguilas Frente al Sol (Eagles Across the Sun); Wide Open Spaces (short). **1933** Primavera en Otono; El Precio de un Beso. **1934** La Cuidad de Carton. **1935** Senora Casada Necesita Marido (My Second Wife); Storm Over the Andes; Rosa de Francia; Asegure a su Mujer (Insure Your Wife); He Trusted His Wife. **1936** The Bohemian Girl; Rose of the Rancho. **1938** Rose of the Rio Grande. **1939** Ambush. **1940** Seven Sinners. **1941** They Met in Argentina; Two Latins from Manhattan; The Kid from Kansas. **1942** Undercover Man; Valley of the Sun; Fiesta. **1944** Tampico. **1945** The Spanish Main. **1946** Notorious. **1947** Captain from Castile. **1949** Lust for Gold. **1950** Crisis; Dallas; Saddle Tramp. **1951** Mark of the Renegade. **1952** Untamed Frontier. **1953** Wings of the Hawk; Thunder Bay. **1954** Saskatchewan; Creature from the Black Lagoon. **1956** The Searchers. **1958** El Senore Faron y la Cleopatra (Mr. Pharoah and Cleopatra).

MORENO, DARIO
Born: Apr. 3, 1921, Smirne, Turkey. Died: Dec., 1968, Istanbul, Turkey. Screen, stage actor and singer.

Appeared in: **1951** Pas des Vacances pour Monsieur. **1952** Le Salire de la Peur; Rires de Paris; Deux de l'Escadrille; La Mome Vert-de-Gris. **1953** Les Femmes s'en Balancent; Quai des Blondes. **1954** Le Mouton a Cinq Pattes. **1956** Pardonnez-nous nos Offenses. **1957** Le feu aux Poudres. **1958** Incognito; Oh! Que Mambo. **1959** Oeil pour Oeil (Eye for an Eye); Wages of Fear; The Prisoner. **1960** Come Dance With Me; The Female (aka A Woman Like Satan); Toucher pas aux Blondes; Nathalie Agent Secrete. **1961** The Revolt of the Slaves. **1962** Candide. **1966** Hotel Paradiso. **1969** La Prisonniere.

MORENO, MARGUERITE
Born: 1871, France. Died: July 14, 1948, France. Screen and stage actress.

Appeared in: **1910** Un Marie Qui se Fait Attendre. **1922** Le Mauvais Garcon. **1923** Gonzague. **1930** Paramount en Parade (French version); Mi-Chemin du Ciel. **1931** Cherie; Marions-Nous. **1937** Amphytryon; Les Perles de la Couronne (Pearls of the Crown). **1939** Ils Etaient Neufs Celibataires (aka Nine Bachelors—US 1942). **1944** 32 Rue de Montmarte; La Dame de Pique. **1945** Ladies in Green Hats. **1946** Carmen; Les Miserables. **1948** A Lover's Return. **1949** Love Story; The Chips Are Down. **1953** Naughty Martine.

MORENO, PACO
Born: 1886. Died: Oct. 15, 1941, Beverly Hills, Calif. Screen and stage actor. Father of actress Rosita Moreno.

Appeared in: **1935** The Devil Is a Woman; Storm over the Andes. **1939** Papa Soltero (Bachelor Father).

MORENO, THOMAS "SKY BALL"
Born: 1895. Died: Oct. 25, 1938, West Los Angeles, Calif. Screen actor and stuntman.

MOREY, HARRY T.
Born: 1873, Mich. Died: Jan. 25, 1936, Brooklyn, N.Y. (abscessed lung). Screen, stage actor and opera performer. Entered films with Vitagraph.

Appeared in: **1911** The Deerslayer; The Thumb Print; The Missing Will. **1912** The Lady of the Lake; The Red Barrier. **1913** The Delayed Letter; Alixe; Playing With Fire; Hearts of the First Empire; His Life for the Emperor; The Line-Up. **1914** The Battle of the Weak; My Official Wife. **1916** Salvation Joan. **1917** Within the Law; The Courage of Silence. **1918** Forgotten Faces. **1921** A Man's Home. **1922** Beyond the Rainbow; Wildness of Youth; The Curse of Drink. **1923** The Green Goddess; The Empty Cradle; Marriage Morals; Where the Pavement Ends. **1924** Captain January; The Painted Lady; The Roughneck. **1925** Camille of the Barbary Coast; The Adventurous Sex; Heart of a Siren; Headlines; Barriers Burned Away. **1926** Aloma of the South Seas. **1927** Twin Flappers. **1928** Return of Sherlock Holmes; Under the Tonto Rim.

MOREY, HENRY A.
Born: 1848. Died: Jan. 8, 1929, Astoria, N.Y. (heart trouble). Stage and screen actor.

Appeared in: **1921** Inside of the Cup.

MORGAN, BUCK (Louis B. Chirco)
Died: Aug., 1981, Los Angeles, Calif. Screen actor and stuntman.

Appeared in: **1935** Texas Rambler; Vanishing Riders.

MORGAN, CLAUDIA
Born: Nov. 12, 1911, Brooklyn, N.Y. Died: Sept. 17, 1974, New York, N.Y. Screen, stage and radio actress. Daughter of actor Ralph Morgan (dec. 1956).

Appeared in: **1932** Vanity Street; Once in a Lifetime. **1938** That's My Story. **1939** Stand Up and Fight. **1952** Venus Observed.

MORGAN, DAN
Died: Mar. 4, 1975. Screen actor.

Appeared in: **1968** Charly; Pretty Poison.

MORGAN, FRANK (Francis Philip Wupperman)
Born: July 1, 1890, New York, N.Y. Died: Sept. 18, 1949, Beverly Hills, Calif. Screen, stage, vaudeville and radio actor. Brother of actor Ralph Morgan (dec. 1956). Nominated for 1934 Academy Award for Best Actor in Affairs of Cellini and in 1942 for Best Supporting Actor in Tortilla Flat.

Appeared in: **1916** The Daring of Diana; The Suspect. **1917** The Girl Philippa; Raffles the Amateur Cracksman; Modern Cinderella; Baby Mine. **1918** At the Mercy of Men. **1924** Born Rich; Manhandled. **1925** The Crowded Hour; The Man Who Found Himself; Scarlet Saint. **1927** Love's Greatest Mistake. **1930** Dangerous Nan McGrew; Queen High; Fast and Loose; Laughter. **1932** Secrets of the French Police; The Half-Naked Truth. **1933** Luxury Liner; Reunion in Vienna; The Nuisance; Bombshell; Best of Enemies; When Ladies Meet; Broadway to Hollywood; The Billion Dollar Scandal; Sailor's Luck; Kiss Before the Mirror; Hallelujah, I'm a Bum. **1934** The Cat and the Fiddle; Affairs of Cellini; There's Always Tomorrow; By Your Leave; Success at Any Price; The Mighty Barnum; Sisters Under the Skin; Lost Lady. **1935** Naughty Marietta; The Good Fairy; Escapade; I Live My Life; The Perfect Gentleman; Enchanted April. **1936** Dancing Pirate; Trouble for Two; Piccadilly Jim; Dimples; The Great Ziegfeld. **1937** The Last of Mrs. Cheyney; The Emperor's Candlesticks; Saratoga; Beg, Borrow or Steal; Rosalie. **1938** Paradise for Three; Port of Seven Seas; Sweethearts; The Crowd Roars. **1939** Broadway Serenade; The Wizard of Oz; Balalaika. **1940** The Shop Around the Corner; Henry Goes Arizona; Broadway Melody of 1940; The Ghost Comes Home; The Mortal Storm; Boom Town; Hullabaloo. **1941** Keeping Company; Washington Melodrama; Wild Man of Borneo; Honky Tonk; The Vanishing Virginian. **1942** Tortilla Flat; White Cargo; Night Monster. **1943** A Stranger in Town; The Human Comedy; Thousands Cheer. **1944** The White Cliffs of Dover; Casanova Brown; Dear Barbara; The Miracle of Morgan's Creek; Hail the Conquering Hero. **1945** Yolanda and the Thief. **1946** Courage of Lassie; The Great Morgan; Mr. Griggs Returns; Pardon My Past; Lady Luck; The Cockeyed Miracle. **1947** Green Dolphin Street. **1948** The Three Musketeers; Summer Holiday. **1949** Any Number Can Play; The Stratton Story; The Great Sinner. **1950** Key to the City. **1974** That's Entertainment (film clips).

MORGAN, GENE (Eugene Schwartzkopf)
Born: 1892, Montgomery, Ala. Died: Aug. 13, 1940, Santa Monica, Calif. (heart attack). Screen, stage, vaudeville actor and orchestra leader. Appeared in Pathe "Folly" comedies and in early Hal Roach silent films.

Appeared in: **1926** Kid Boots. **1930** The Boss; Rogue of the Rio Grande; Orders; Railroad (shorts). **1932** Night World; Blonde Venus. **1933** Railroad (shorts); Elmer the Great; Song of the Eagle; Jennie Gerhardt. **1935** Dr. Socrates; G-Men; Men of the Hour; Crime and Punishment; Bright Lights; If You Could Only Cook. **1936** Lady from Nowhere; Come Closer, Folks; The Music Goes 'Round; You May Be Next; Mr. Deeds Goes to Town; Devil's Squadron; Meet Nero Wolfe; Shakedown; Alibi for Murder; End of the Trail; Panic on the Air; Counterfeit. **1937** Counterfeit Lady; Woman in Distress; Speed to Spare; Parole Racket; Counsel for Crime; Murder in Greenwich Village; All American Sweetheart; Make Way for Tomorrow. **1938** Home on the Rage (short); Ankles Away (short); Start Cheering; There's Always a Woman; The Main Event; When G-Men Step In; Who Killed Gail Preston? **1939** Captain Fury; The Sap Takes a Wrap (short); Mr. Smith Goes to Washington; Federal Man-Hunt; Homicide Bureau; The Housekeeper's Daughter. **1940** Gaucho Serenade; Girl from God's Country; Saps at Sea. **1941** Meet John Doe.

MORGAN, HELEN
Born: 1922. Died: July 19, 1955, Burbank, Calif. (cancer). Screen actress and former Olympic diving champion. Do not confuse with actress and singer Helen Morgan (dec. 1941).

MORGAN, HELEN
Born: 1900, Danville, Ill. Died: Oct. 9, 1941, Chicago, Ill. (kidney and liver ailments). Screen, stage actress and club entertainer.

Appeared in: **1929** Applause (film debut); Glorifying the American Girl; Show Boat. **1930** Roadhouse Nights. **1932** Gigolo Racket (short). **1933** The Doctor (short); Manhattan Lullaby (short). **1934** Marie Galante; The Lemon Drop Kid; You Belong to Me. **1935** Go into Your Dance; Sweet Music; Frankie and Johnnie. **1936** Showboat (and 1939 version).

MORGAN, JANE
Born: 1881, England. Died: Jan. 1, 1972, Burbank, Calif. (heart attack). Screen, radio, vaudeville and television actress. Do not confuse with singer Jane Morgan.

Appeared in: **1965** Our Miss Brooks (and television series).

MORGAN, LEE (Raymond Lee Morgan)
Born: June 12, 1902, Texas. Died: Jan. 30, 1967, Los Angeles, Calif. (heart disease). Screen actor. Entered films during the silents.

Appeared in: **1947** Return of the Lash; Black Hills; Shadow Valley; Cheyenne Takes Over; Stage to Mesa City; The Fighting Vigilantes. **1948** Dangers of the Canadian Mounted (serial); The Westward Trail. **1949** Roll, Thunder, Roll!; Rio Grande. **1950** Raiders of Tomahawk Creek. **1951** Hills of Utah; Riding the Outlaw Trail. **1956** Blazing the Overland Trail (serial); Daniel Boone—Trailblazer. **1958** Sierra Baron; The Last of the Fast Guns; Villa. **1961** The Last Rebel. **1962** The Weird Ones. **1964** Dungeons of Terror; No Man's Land.

MORGAN, MARGARET
Died: Aug. 29, 1926, Glendale, Calif. Screen actress.

Appeared in: **1923** The Snow Bride.

MORGAN, MARGO (Margaret Rockwood)
Born: 1897. Died: May 16, 1962, Hollywood, Calif. Screen actress and singer.

MORGAN, PAUL
Born: Germany. Died: Jan., 1939 (congestion of the lungs). Screen and stage actor.

Appeared in: **1930** Why Cry at Parting?; Menschen Hinter Geitern; Zwei Hertzen in Drei-Viertel Takt. **1931** Wien Du Stadt der Lieder (Vienna City of Song); Das Kabinett des Dr. Larifari. **1932** Theaternaechte von Bath; Liebeskommando. **1933** Holzapfel Weiss Alles.

MORGAN, RALPH (Raphael Kuhner Wupperman)
Born: July 6, 1883, New York, N.Y. Died: June 11, 1956, N.Y. Screen and stage actor. Married to actress Grace Arnold (dec. 1948). Father of actress Claudia Morgan (dec. 1974) and brother of actor Frank Morgan (dec. 1949). One-time president of the Screen Actors Guild.

Appeared in: **1930** Excuse the Pardon (short). **1931** Honor Among Lovers. **1932** Charlie Chan's Chance; Dance Team; Rasputin and the Empress; Strange Interlude; Cheaters at Play; Disorderly Conduct; The Devil's Lottery; The Son-Daughter. **1933** The Power and the Glory; Shanghai Madness; Humanity; Trick for Trick; The Mad Game; Walls of Gold; Doctor Bull; The Kennel Murder Case. **1934** Transatlantic Merry-Go-Round; Their Big Moment; Hell in the Heavens; Orient Express; She Was a Lady; Stand Up and Cheer; No Greater Glory; Girl of the Limberlost; The Last Gentleman; Little Men; The Cat and the Fiddle. **1935** Condemned to Live; I've Been Around; Star of Midnight; Unwelcome Stranger; Calm Yourself. **1936** Anthony Adverse; Magnificent Obsession; Yellowstone; Muss 'Em Up; The Ex-Mrs. Bradford; Little Miss Nobody; Human Cargo; Speed; General Spanky; Crack-Up. **1937** The Man in Blue; The Life of Emile Zola; Exclusive; Wells Fargo; Behind Prison Bars. **1938** Love Is a Headache; Out West with the Hardys; Wives Under Suspicion; Army Girl; Orphans of the Street; Mother Carey's Chickens; Barefoot Boy; Shadows Over Shanghai; Mannequin; That's My Story. **1939** Off the Record; Fast and Loose; Man of Conquest; Smuggled Cargo; Way Down South; Trapped in the Sky; The Lone Spy Hunt; Geronimo. **1940** Forty Little Mothers; I'm Still Alive; Soak the Old (short); Wagons Westward. **1941** The Mad Doctor; Adventure in Washington; Dick Tracy vs. Crime, Inc. (serial). **1942** Close Call for Ellery Queen; Klondike Fury; Night Monster; The Traitor Within; Gang Busters (serial). **1943** Stage Door Canteen; Jack London; Hitler's Madman. **1944** Trocadero; Double Furlough; I'll Be Seeing You; The Monster Maker; Weird Woman; The Imposter; The Great Alaskan Mystery (serial); Enemy of Women. **1945** Black Market Babies; This Love of Ours; Hollywood and Vine; Monster and the Ape (serial). **1947** The Last Round-Up; Song of the Thin Man; Mr. District Attorney. **1948** Sleep My Love; The Sword of the Avenger; The Creeper. **1950** Blue Grass of Kentucky. **1951** Heart of the Rockies. **1952** Dick Tracy vs. The Phantom Empire (serial); Gold Fever.

MORGAN, RAY (Raymond Storrs Morgan)
Died: Jan. 5, 1975, Englewood, N.J. (cancer). Screen, radio, television actor and announcer. Appeared mainly in industrial, educational and army films.

Appeared in: **1950** Congolaise (narrator). **1951** Two Gals and a Guy. **1952** The Old West. **1960** Wild Rapture.

MORGAN, RUSS
Born: 1904, Scranton, Pa. Died: Aug. 7, 1969, Las Vegas, Nev. (cerebral hemorrhage). Bandleader, songwriter and screen actor. Wrote hit songs "You're Nobody Till Somebody Loves You," "Somebody New Is Taking My Place" and "Does Your Heart Beat for Me?"

Appeared in: **1951** Disc Jockey. **1956** The Great Man; Mister Cory. **1958** The Big Beat.

MORGAN, SYDNEY
Born: Oct. 21, 1885, Dublin, Ireland. Died: Dec. 5, 1931, London, England. Screen, stage and vaudeville actor.

Appeared in: **1929** Dark Red Roses; Juno and the Paycock (aka The Shame of Mary Boyle—US).

MORGAN, VICTOR J.
Born: 1906. Died: Apr. 18, 1933, New York, N.Y. Screen and stage actor.

MORIARTY, JOANNE
Born: 1939. Died: Mar. 2, 1964, Hollywood, Calif. (suicide—pills). Screen actress. Married to actor Michael Parks.

Appeared in: **1964** Bedtime Story.

MORIARTY, MARCUS
Died: June 21, 1916, New York, N.Y. Screen actor.

Appeared in: **1915** The Pretenders. **1916** The Flower of No Man's Land; The Little Fraud; Partners.

MORIYA, SHIZU
Born: 1911, Japan. Died: Mar. 12, 1961, N.Y. Screen, stage and television actress.

MORLAY, GABY (Blanche Fumoleau)
Born: 1897. Died: July 4, 1964, Nice, France. Screen and stage actress.

Appeared in: **1913** La Sandale Rouge. **1929** Les Nouveaux Messieurs (The New Gentlemen). **1934** Le Scandale. **1935** Jeanne. **1936** Le Bonheur. **1938** Derriere La Facade; The Kreutzer Sonata. **1939** Entente Cordiale. **1940** Life of Giuseppe Verdi; The Living Corpse. **1941** The King. **1942** La Voile Bleu (The Blue Veil—US 1947). **1944** 32 Rue de Montmartre. **1948** Gigi (US 1950); Le Reveant (A Lover's Return); Mlle. Desiree. **1951** Le Plaisir (House of Pleasure—US 1953); Anna. **1952** Father's Dilemma; A Simple Case of Money. **1954** The Mask. **1955** Mitsou (US 1958). **1957** Royal Affairs in Versailles; Les Collegiennes (aka The Twilight Girls—US 1961). **1958** Crime et Clatinaut (Crime and Punishment aka The Most Dangerous Sin—US); Ramuntcho. Other French Films: Accusee; Levez-Vous; Les Amants Terribles; Entente Cordiale; Sa Majeste M. Dupont; L' Amour d'Une Femme; Paris-New York.

MORLEY, ROBERT JAMES
Born: 1892. Died: Aug. 30, 1952, Hollywood, Calif. Screen actor.

MORNE, MARYLAND
Born: 1900. Died: July 28, 1935, Hollywood, Calif. Screen actress.

MORPHY, LEWIS H. (Lewis Harris Morphy)
Born: 1904. Died: Nov. 7, 1958, Hollywood, Calif. (suicide). Screen actor, stuntman and rodeo performer.

Appeared in: **1950** The Blazing Hills (aka The Blazing Sun).

MORRELL, GEORGE
Born: 1873. Died: Apr. 28, 1955, Hollywood, Calif. Screen and stage actor.

Appeared in: **1921** The Heart of the North. **1929** Silent Sentinel. **1936** Guns and Guitars. **1937** Yodelin' Kid from Pine Ridge; Git Along, Little Dogies; Hit the Saddle. **1938** Pride of the West. **1943** False Colors. **1944** Mystery Man; Texas Masquerade. **1950** Mule Train.

MORRIS, ? (married name: Mrs. Harold (Buddy) Kusell)
Born: 1903. Died: May 13, 1971, Buffalo, N.Y. Screen, stage, radio and vaudeville actress. See William Morris for family information.

MORRIS, ADRIAN
Born: 1903, Mt. Vernon, N.Y. Died: Nov. 30, 1941, Los Angeles, Calif. Screen, stage and vaudeville actor. See William Morris for family information.

Appeared in: **1929** Fast Life; The Jazz Age. **1931** The Age for Love. **1932** Me and My Gal. **1933** Little Giant; Mayor of Hell; Trick for Trick; Bureau of Missing Persons; Wild Boys on the Road. **1934** The Big Shakedown; Let's Be Ritzy; The Pursuit of Happiness. **1935** Age of Indiscretion; One Frightened Night; Powdersmoke Range; Fighting Marines (serial); G-Men; Dr. Socrates. **1936** The Petrified Forest; Poppy; My American Wife; Rose Bowl. **1937** Radio Patrol (serial); Her Husband Lies; The Woman I Love; There Goes the Groom; Every Day's a Holiday. **1938** You and Me; If I Were King; Angels with Dirty Faces. **1939** The Return of the Cisco Kid; 6,000 Enemies; Wall Street Cowboy; Gone With the Wind. **1940** Florian; The Grapes of Wrath Know Your Money (short). **1941** Blood and Sand.

MORRIS, BARBOURA (aka BARBOUR O'NEIL)
Born: Oct. 22, 1932. Died: Oct. 23, 1975, Santa Monica, Calif. Screen and stage actress.

Appeared in: **1954** The Helen Keller Story (aka The Unconquered). **1957** Rock All Night; Teenage Doll; Sorority Girl. **1959** The Wild and the Innocent; A Bucket of Blood. **1961** Atlas. **1963** The Haunted Palace. **1967** The Trip; St. Valentine's Day Massacre. **1970** The Dunwich Horror.

MORRIS, CHESTER (John Chester Brooks Morris)
Born: Feb. 16, 1901, New York, N.Y. Died: Sept. 11, 1970, New Hope, Pa. (overdose of barbiturates). Screen, stage, vaudeville, radio and television actor. Married to model Lillian Kenton Barker (the original "Chesterfield Girl") and divorced from actress Suzanne Kilbourne. Entered films at age 9 in 1910. Best known as film and television's "Boston Blackie." See William Morris for family information. Nominated for 1928-29 Academy Award for Best Actor in Alibi.

Appeared in: **1917** An Amateur Orphan. **1918** The Beloved Traitor. **1923** Loyal Lives. **1925** The Road to Yesterday. **1929** Alibi; Fast Life; Woman Trap; The Show of Shows. **1930** Playing Around; The Big House; The Divorcee; The Case of Sergeant Grischa; She Couldn't Say No; Second Choice. **1931** Bat Whispers; Corsair. **1932** Cock of the Air; The Miracle Man; Breach of Promise; Sinners in the Sun; Red Headed Woman. **1933** Blondie Johnson; The Infernal Machine; Kid Gloves; Tomorrow at Seven; Golden Harvest; King for a Night. **1934** The Hollywood Gad-About (short); The Gay Bride; Let's Talk It Over; Embarrassing Moments; Gift of Gab. **1935** Princess O'Hara; Public Hero No. 1; Society Doctor; Pursuit; I've Been Around; Frankie and Johnnie. **1936** Three Godfathers; Moonlight Murder; They Met in a Taxi; Counterfeit. **1937** I Promise to Pay; The Devil's Playground; Flight from Glory. **1938** Law of the Underworld; Sky Giant; Smashing the Rackets. **1939** Blind Alley; Pacific Liner; Five Came Back; Thunder Afloat. **1940** The Marines Fly High; Wagons Westward; The Girl from God's Country. **1941** Meet Boston Blackie; Confessions of Boston Blackie; No Hands on the Clock; The Phantom Thief. **1942** Alias Boston Blackie; Canal Zone; I Live on Danger; The Wrecking Crew; Boston Blackie Goes to Hollywood. **1943** High Explosive; Aerial Gunner; After Midnight with Boston Blackie; Tornado; Thunderbolt; The Chance of a Lifetime. **1944** Dark Mountain; One Mysterious Night; Gambler's Choice; Derelict Ship; Secret Command; The Awakening of Jim Burke; Double Exposure; Men of the Deep. **1945** The Blonde from Brooklyn; Rough, Tough and Ready; Boston Blackie Booked on Suspicion; Boston Blackie's Rendezvous. **1946** One Way to Love; Boston Blackie and the Law; A Close Call for Boston Blackie; Phantom Thief. **1947** Blind Spot. **1948** Trapped by Boston Blackie. **1949** Boston Blackie's Chinese Venture. **1955** Unchained. **1956** The She-Creature. **1964** Big Parade of Comedy (documentary). **1970** The Great White Hope.

MORRIS, CORBET (Louis McClanahan Thompson)
Born: Dec. 31, 1881, Colorado. Died: Mar. 10, 1951, Los Angeles, Calif. (broncho-pneumonia). Screen actor.

Appeared in: **1936** I'd Give My Life. **1937** The Firefly. **1938** Tarzan's Revenge; The House of Mystery; Making the Headlines. **1940** The Westerner. **1942** Now, Voyager.

MORRIS, DENIESE
Died: Feb. 20, 1969. Screen actress.

MORRIS, DIANA
Born: 1907. Died: Feb. 19, 1961, Hollywood, Calif. (throat cancer). Screen and stage actress.

MORRIS, GLENN
Born: 1911. Died: Jan. 1, 1974, Palo Alto, Calif. Professional football player, Olympic gold medal winner and screen actor.

Appeared in: **1937** Decathlon Champion (short). **1938** Tarzan's Revenge; Hold That Co-Ed.

MORRIS, GORDON
Born: 1899. Died: Apr. 7, 1940, Hollywood, Calif. Screen, stage actor and screenwriter. See William Morris for family information.

MORRIS, JOHNNIE (John Morris Erickson)
Born: 1886, New York, N.Y. Died: Oct. 7, 1969, Hollywood, Calif. Screen, stage, burlesque and vaudeville actor.

Appeared in: **1928** Beggars of Life; The Fifty-Fifty Girl; The Street of Sin; Love and Learn. **1929** Innocents of Paris; Square Shoulders. **1930** Big Money; Dance With Me. **1932** Once in a Lifetime; Checker Comedies (shorts). **1938** Barefoot Boy; Sons of the Legion; Thanks for the Memory. **1939** The Star Maker; The Gentleman from Arizona. **1940** Golden Gloves.

MORRIS, LEE
Born: June 23, 1863 or 1869, Mo. or Sioux City, Iowa? Died: Feb. 6, 1933, Calif. Screen actor.

Appeared in: **1914** The Adventures of Kathlynn (serial); The Golden Patch. **1916** Bath Tub Perils; Bucking Society; The Snow Cure; His First False Step. **1917** Her Father's Station; Durand of the Bad Lands.

MORRIS, LILY
Born: 1884, England. Died: Oct. 3, 1952, London, England. Screen, stage and vaudeville actress.

Appeared in: **1934** Radio Parade of 1935 (US 1935).

MORRIS, MARGARET
Born: Nov. 7, 1903, Minneapolis, Minn. Died: June 7, 1968. Screen and stage actress. Was a Wampas Baby Star of 1924. Do not confuse with choreographer Margaret Morris (dec. 1980).

Appeared in: **1921** Hickville to Broadway. **1923** The Town Scandal. **1924** The Galloping Ace; Horseshoe Luck. **1925** The Best People; Welcome Home; Wild Horse Mesa; Womanhandled; Youth's Gamble. **1926** Born to the West; That's My Baby. **1927** The Magic Garden; Moulders of Men. **1928** The Avenging Shadow; Mark of the Frog (serial). **1929** The Woman I Love. **1932** Single-Handed Sanders. **1934** Gambling Lady. **1936** Desert Guns; The Bride Walks Out.

MORRIS, MARY
Born: Jan. 24, 1895, Mass. Died: Jan. 16, 1970, N.Y. Screen and stage actress. Do not confuse with Mary Morris born in 1915.

Appeared in: **1934** Double Door. **1937** Victoria the Great.

MORRIS, PHILIP (Francis Charles Philip Morris)
Born: Jan. 20, 1893, Duluth, Minn. Died: Dec. 18, 1949, Los Angeles, Calif. Screen and stage actor.

Appeared in: **1934** Home on the Range. **1935** Seven Keys to Baldpate. **1936** Desert Gold. **1937** High, Wide and Handsome; Super Sleuth. **1938** Passport Husband. **1946** Cluny Brown; Home Sweet Homicide. **1947** Out of the Past; Crossfire; Buckaroo from Powder River. **1948** Whirlwind Raiders. **1949** The Flying Saucer; Holiday Affair.

MORRIS, REGGIE (James Reginald Morris)
Born: June 25, 1886, New Jersey. Died: Feb. 16, 1928, Los Angeles, Calif. (heart attack). Screen, stage actor, film producer, screenwriter and author.

Appeared in: **1916** A Male Governess; Madcap Ambrose; Haystacks and Steeples.

MORRIS, RICHARD (W. Richard Stuart Morris)
Born: 1861, Boston, Mass. Died: Oct. 11, 1924, Los Angeles, Calif. Screen, stage actor and opera performer. Entered films in 1909.

Appeared in: **1916** The Devil's Bondswoman; Morals of Hilda. **1921** The Sea Lion. **1922** In the Name of the Law. **1923** The Third Alarm; The Mailman; The Westbound Limited. **1924** The Spirit of the U.S.A.

MORRIS, STEPHEN *See* ANKRUM, MORRIS

MORRIS, WAYNE (Bert de Wayne Morris)
Born: Feb. 17, 1914, Los Angeles, Calif. Died: Sept. 14, 1959, Pacific Ocean, aboard aircraft carrier (heart attack). Screen, stage and television actor.

Appeared in: **1936** China Clipper (film debut); King of Hockey; Here Comes Carter; Polo Joe; Smart Blonde. **1937** Don't Pull Your Punches; Kid Galahad; Submarine D-1; Once a Doctor. **1938** Love, Honor and Behave; Men Are Such Fools; Valley of the Giants; The Kid Comes Back; Brother Rat. **1939** The Kid from Kokomo; Return of Dr. X. **1940** Brother Rat and a Baby; An Angel from Texas; Double Alibi; Ladies Must Live; The Quarterback; Gambling on the High Seas; Flight Angels. **1941** Three Sons O'Guns; I Wanted Wings; Bad Men of Missouri; The Smiling Ghost. **1947** Deep Valley; The Voice of the Turtle. **1948** The Big Punch; The Time of Your Life. **1949** A Kiss in the Dark; The Younger Brothers; John Loves Mary; The House across the Street; Task Force. **1950** Johnny One Eye; The Tougher They Come; Stage to Tucson. **1951** Sierra Passage; The Big Gusher; Yellow Fin. **1952** The Bushwhackers; Desert Pursuit; Arctic Flight. **1953** The Fighting Lawman; The Marksman; The Star of Texas. **1954** Riding Shotgun; The Desperado; The Green Buddha (US 1955); Two Guns and a Badge; Port of Hell. **1955** Lord of the Jungle; The Master Plan; Cross Channel; The Lonesome Trail. **1956** The Dynamiters. **1957** Plunder Road. **1958** Paths of Glory. **1958** The Crooked Sky.

MORRIS, WILLIAM
Born: 1861. Died: Jan. 11, 1936, Los Angeles, Calif. (heart attack). Screen and stage actor. Married to actress Etta Hawkins Morris (dec. 1945) and father of actors Chester (dec. 1970), Adrian (dec. 1941) and Gordon Morris (dec. 1940) and actress Mrs. Harold Kusell (Morris) (dec. 1971).

Appeared in: **1930** Brothers; The Convict's Code. **1931** The Gang Buster; Behind Office Doors. **1932** The Washington Masquerade.

MORRISON, ADRIENNE
Born: 1878, New York, N.Y. Died: Nov. 20, 1940, New York, N.Y. (heart attack). Screen and stage actress. Daughter of stage actors Lewis Morrison (dec.) and Rose Wood (dec.). Divorced from actor Richard Bennett (dec. 1944), and later married to stage actor Eric S. Pinker. Mother of actresses Constance (dec. 1965), Barbara (dec. 1958), and Joan Bennett.

Appeared in: **1915** Damaged Goods.

MORRISON, ANN
Born: 1916. Died: Apr. 18, 1978, Woodland Hills, Calif. Screen, stage, radio and television actress.

Appeared in: **1948** The Walls of Jericho. **1949** Thieves' Highway; Caught; House of Strangers. **1950** No Way Out. **1951** People Will Talk; Close to My Heart. **1952** My Pal Gus; The Girl in White. **1953** The President's Lady; Battle Circus. **1955** Violent Sunday. **1958** The Brothers Karamazov. **1975** Swiss Bank Account.

MORRISON, ANNA MARIE
Born: 1874. Died: July 5, 1972, Hollywood, Calif. Screen actress. Married to actor Chick Morrison (dec. 1924). Appeared in silent films.

MORRISON, ARTHUR
Born: 1880, St. Louis, Mo. Died: Feb. 20, 1950, Los Angeles, Calif. Screen, stage and vaudeville actor. Entered films with World Films in 1917.

Appeared in: **1921** The Light in the Clearing; The Sage Hen; Singing River; The Roof Tree. **1922** The Men of Zanzibar; Strength of the Pines. **1923** The Gunfighter; In the West; The Sting of the Scorpion. **1925** Cold Nerve; Riders of the Purple Sage. **1926** Lazy Lightning; Riding Romance; Tony Runs Wild; Silver Fingers. **1927** The Silent Rider; Grinning Guns; King of the Jungle (serial). **1928** Willful Youth. **1929** Slim Fingers. **1930** The Lone Defender (serial).

MORRISON, BRET
Born: 1912, Chicago, Ill. Died: Sept. 25, ·1978, Hollywood, Calif. Screen and radio actor. Known as "The Shadow" on radio.

Appeared in: **1955** Green Magic (narrator). **1964** Behind the Nudist Curtain (narrator, aka Nature Girls Unlimited, aka Nudist Curtain). **1970** Guess What We Learned in School Today? (voice, aka Guess What?, aka I Ain't No Buffalo).

MORRISON, C. P. "CHICK" aka "CHIT"
Born: 1878, Colorado. Died: June 20, 1924, Hollywood, Calif. (fall from horse). Screen actor and animal trainer. Brother of actor Pete Morrison (dec. 1973). Married to actress Anna Marie Morrison (dec. 1972).

Appeared in: **1910** Cowboy and the Squaw. **1916** The Half-Breed. **1921** The Duke of Chimeny Butte. **1922** Hair Trigger Casey.

MORRISON, CHESTER A.
Born: 1922. Died: Mar. 28, 1975, Portland, Ore. Screen actor. Appeared in Our Gang Comedies.

MORRISON, EFFIE
Born: 1917, Scotland. Died: Oct., 1974, Glasgow, Scotland. Screen, stage, radio and television actress.

MORRISON, FLORENCE
Born: 1887. Died: June, 1942, Denison, Tex. Screen, stage, radio actress and drama coach. Married to actor Pass Lenoir (dec. 1946). Do not confuse with actress Florence Morrison (dec. 1928).

MORRISON, FLORENCE
Died: May 8, 1928. Screen actress. Do not confuse with actress Florence Morrison (dec. 1942).

MORRISON, GEORGE "PETE"
Born: Aug. 8, 1891, Denver, Colo. Died: Feb. 5, 1973, Los Angeles, Calif. Screen actor. Brother of actor Chit Morrison (dec. 1924). Entered films in 1908.

Appeared in: **1918** His Buddy; By Indian Post; Even Money; Gun Law; Ace High; The Gun Packer. **1921** Headin' North; Crossing Trails. **1922** Duty First; Daring Danger; The Better Man Wins; West vs. East. **1923** Making Good; Smilin' On; Western Blood; Ghost City (serial). **1924** Black Gold; False Trails; Pioneer's Gold; Buckin' the West; Pot Luck Pards; Rainbow Rangers. **1925** One Shot Ranger; Range Buzzards; Always Ridin' to Win; Cowboy Grit; The Empty Saddle; The Ghost Rider; The Mystery of Lost Ranch; A Ropin' Ridin' Fool; Santa Fe Pete; Stampede Thunder; Triple Action; West of Arizona. **1926** Blue Blazes; Bucking the Truth; Chasing Trouble; The Desperate Game; The Escape. **1929** Chinatown Nights; Courtin' Wildcats; The Three Outcasts. **1930** The Big Trail; Beyond the Rio Grande; Phantom of the Desert; Spurs; Ridin' the Law; Trails of Peril; Trailin' Trouble; Westward Bound.

MORRISON, HOWARD PRIESTLY
Born: 1872, Baltimore, Md. Died: Jan. 26, 1938, Kew Gardens, N.Y. Screen, stage actor, film director and producer.

Appeared in: **1918** The Adventure Shop.

MORRISON, JAMES (James Woods Morrison)
Born: Nov. 15, 1888, Mattoon, Ill. Died: Nov. 15, 1974, New York, N.Y. Screen, stage actor, novelist and drama coach.

Appeared in: **1911** A Tale of Two Cities. **1912** The Seventh Son; Coronets and Hearts; As You Like It; Two Battles; The Foster Child; Saving an Audience; The Miracle; Willie's Sister; Dr. Lafleur's Theory; Beau Brummel; An Eventful Elopement. **1913** The Butler's Secret; The Glove; His Life for His Emperor; An Infernal Tangle; A Husband's Trick. **1914** The Vanity Case; A Double Error; The Love of Pierre Larosse; The Hero; He Never Knew; Regan's Daughter; The Greater Motive; The Toll; Fanny's Melodrama; The Portrait; The Honeymooners; The Wheat and the Tares; Two Stepchildren. **1915** From Out of the Big Snows; In the Days of Famine; Four Grains of Rice; The Wheels of Justice; The Battle Cry of Peace; A Wireless Rescue; The Man, the Mission and the Maid; Mother's Roses; A Madcap Adventure; The Ruling Power; For the Honor of the Crew; Pawns of Mars; Stage Money; A Fortune Hunter. **1916** The Hero of Submarine D2; The Redemption of Dave Darcey; The Enemy; Phantom Fortune; The Sex Lure. **1917** The Battle Hymn of the Republic; Babbling Tongues; Life Against Honor; One Law for Both; A Tale of Two Cities. **1918** Over the Top; Moral Suicide. **1919** Sacred Silence; Womanhood; Miss Dulcie from Dixie. **1920** Love Without Question; The Midnight Bride. **1921** Black Beauty; Danger Ahead; When We Were Twenty-One; A Yankee Go-Getter. **1922** The Little Minister; The Dangerous Age; Handle with Care; Shattered Idols; Only a Shop Girl. **1923** Held to Answer; The Little Girl Next Door; The Unknown Purple; The Nth Comandment; On the Banks of the Wabash. **1924** Captain Blood; Wine of Youth. **1925** Don't; Wreckage; The Pride of the Force. **1926** The Count of Luxembourg; The Imposter; The Seventh Bandit. **1927** Twin Flappers.

MORRISON, JIM
Born: 1944, France. Died: July 2, 1971, Paris, France (heart attack). Singer, lyricist and screen actor. Was leader of combo "The Doors."

Appeared in: **1970** Machine Gun McGain.

MORRISON, LOUIS "LOU"
Born: Feb. 8, 1866 or 1876, Portland, Maine. Died: Apr. 22, 1946, Calif. Screen and stage actor. Entered films in 1913.

Appeared in: **1915** The Beckoning Flame. **1916** Gypsy Joe; The Lion and the Girl; Madcap Ambrose; A Lover's Might. **1920** Village Sleuth. **1922** His Back Against the Wall. **1923** The Dangerous Maid; The Man Alone. **1924** The Sea Hawk. **1925** The Unholy Three; Peter Pan; Flattery. **1927** Sorrel and Son. **1929** The Rescue; Frozen Justice.

MORRISSEY, BETTY (aka BETTY MORRISEY)
Born: N.Y. Died: Apr. 20, 1944, New York, N.Y. Screen actress.

Appeared in: **1923** A Woman of Paris. **1924** What Shall I Do?; The Fast Worker; Virtue's Revolt; Traffic in Hearts; Turned Up. **1925** Lady of the Night; The Gold Rush; Skinner's Dress Suit; The Desert Demon. **1928** The Circus.

MORRISSEY, JOHN F.
Born: 1883. Died: Oct. 6, 1941, New York, N.Y. Screen and stage actor. Married to stage actress Phyllis Ray.

Appeared in: **1930** Girl in the Show.

MORRISSEY, WILL
Born: 1885. Died: Dec. 16, 1957, Santa Barbara, Calif. Screen, vaudeville actor, stage producer, song writer and playwright. Was in vaudeville with Midgie Miller in an act billed as "Morrissey and Miller."

Together they appeared in the following shorts: **1927** The Morrissey and Miller Vitaphone Revue. **1928** The Morrissey and Miller Night Club.

MORROW, DORETTA (Doretta Marano)
Born: 1927, Brooklyn, N.Y. Died: Feb. 28, 1968, London, England (cancer). Screen, stage, television actress and singer.

Appeared in: **1952** Because You're Mine.

MORROW, JANE See DREW, MRS. SIDNEY

MORSE, KARL
Born: 1888. Died: Jan. 22, 1936, Los Angeles, Calif. Screen actor.

Appeared in: **1927** Underworld.

MORSE, LEE
Born: 1904. Died: Dec. 16. 1954, Rochester, N.Y. Screen, vaudeville, radio actress, singer and composer.

Appeared in: **1930** The Music Racket (short).

MORSE, ROBIN
Born: 1915. Died: Dec. 11, 1958, Hollywood, Calif. (heart attack). Screen and television actor.

Appeared in: **1953** The Great Jesse James Raid. **1955** Marty; Abbott and Costello Meet the Mummy. **1956** The Boss; He Laughed Last. **1957** Pal Joey; Sabu and the Magic Ring.

MORTIMER, CHARLES
Born: 1885. Died: Apr. 1, 1964, London, England. Screen and stage actor.

Appeared in: **1933** You Made Me Love You. **1934** The Return of Bulldog Drummond. **1935** The Guv'nor (aka Mister Hobo—US 1936); The Small Man; The Price of a Song; Old Roses; The Triumph of Sherlock Holmes. **1936** Rhodes of Africa (aka Rhodes—US); Living Dangerously; Someone at the Door. **1937** Aren't Men Beasts! **1939** Poison Pen (US 1941). **1955** Dial 999 (aka The Way Out—US 1956). **1957** The Counterfeit Plan.

MORTIMER, DOROTHY
Born: 1898. Died: Feb. 15, 1950, New York, N.Y. Screen and stage actress.

Appeared in: **1912** The Old Chess Player. **1921** Just Out of College. **1922** Caught Bluffing.

MORTIMER, EDMUND
Born: 1875. Died: May 21, 1944, Hollywood, Calif. Screen actor, film director and screenwriter.

Appeared in: **1935** Bordertown. **1937** It's Love I'm After; The Awful Truth. **1938** The Amazing Dr. Clitterhouse.

MORTIMER, HENRY (John O. D. Rennie)
Born: 1875. Died: Aug. 20, 1952, Whitby, Ontario, Canada. Stage and screen actor. Entered films during silents.

Appeared in: **1930** La Grande Mare.

MORTON, CHARLES S.
Born: Jan. 28, 1907, Vallejo, Calif. Died: Oct. 26, 1966, North Hollywood, Calif. (heart disease). Screen, stage and vaudeville actor. Son of actor Frank Morton.

Appeared in: **1927** Colleen; Rich But Honest; Wolf Fangs. **1928** Dressed to Kill; Four Sons; None But the Brave. **1929** Christina; The Far Call; Four Devils; New Year's Eve. **1930** Cameo Kirby; Caught Short; The Dawn Trail; Check and Double Check. **1932** Last Ride. **1933** Goldie Gets Along. **1934** Dawn Trail. **1936** Hollywood Boulevard. **1939** Stunt Pilot. **1944** Lumberjack; Outlaws of Santa Fe; Trail to Gunsight.

MORTON, CLIVE
Born: Mar. 16, 1904, London, England. Died: Sept. 24, 1975, London, England. Screen, stage and television actor. Married to actress Joan Harben (dec. 1953) and later to Fanny Rowe.

Appeared in: **1932** Fires of Fate (US 1933). **1933** The Blarney Stone (aka The Blarney Kiss—US). **1934** The Great Defender; Evergreen. **1938** Dead Men Tell No Tales (US 1939). **1947** While the Sun Shines

(US 1950); Jassy (US 1948); Mine Own Executioner (US 1949). **1948** Scott of the Antarctic (US 1949); The Blind Goddess (US 1949). **1949** Kind Hearts and Coronets (US 1950); A Run for Your Money (US 1950). **1950** The Blue Lamp; Trio. **1951** Night Without Stars (US 1953); The Lavender Hill Mob. **1952** His Excellency (US 1956); Castles in the Air. **1953** Turn the Key Softly (US 1954). **1954** Carrington VC (aka Court-Martial—US 1955). **1955** Richard III (US 1956). **1957** Seven Waves Away (aka Abandon Ship!—US); Lucky Jim. **1958** The Safecracker. **1959** Make Mine a Million (US 1965); Shake Hands With the Devil. **1960** The Pure Hell of St. Trinian's (US 1961). **1961** A Matter of Who (US 1962). **1962** I Thank a Fool; Lawrence of Arabia. **1965** The Alphabet Murders (US 1966). **1967** Stranger in the House (aka Cop-Out—US 1968). **1969** Lock Up Your Daughters!; Goodbye Mr. Chips. **1970** Jane Eyre.

MORTON, DREW
Born: 1855. Died: Sept. 4, 1916, New York, N.Y. Screen actor and film director.

MORTON, HANK
Born: 1913. Died: Jan. 4, 1963. Screen actor.

MORTON, JAMES C.
Born: 1884, Helena, Mont. Died: Oct. 24, 1942, Reseda, Calif. Screen, stage and vaudeville actor.

Appeared in: **1930** Follow the Leader. **1932** Pack Up Your Troubles; plus the following shorts: A Lad an' a Lamp; Sneak Easily; Alum and Eve; The Spoilers. **1933** The Devil's Brother; plus the following shorts: Fallen Arches; His Silent Racket; Hold Your Temper; The Midnight Patrol; Me and My Sal; Hokus Focus; Snug in the Jug. **1934** The following shorts: Mike Fright; Washee Ironee; I'll Take Vanilla; Another Wild Idea; It Happened One Day; Something Simple; You Said a Hateful; Circus Hoodoo; One Horse Farmers; Maid in Hollywood. **1935** The following shorts: Beginner's Luck; Old Sawbones; Uncivil Warriors; Tit for Tat; The Fixer-Uppers; Pardon My Scotch; The Misses Stooge; Hoi Polloi; Poker at Eight. **1936** The Bohemian Girl; Our Relations; Way Out West, plus the following shorts: The Lucky Corner; Caught in the Act; Share the Wealth; Hill Tillies; Ants in the Pantry; Disorder in the Court; A Pain in the Pullman. **1937** Two Wise Maids; Rhythm in the Clouds; Public Cowboy #1; Mama Runs Wild, plus the following shorts: Calling All Doctors; Dizzy Doctors; The Sitter-Downers. **1938** Topper Takes a Trip, plus the following shorts: The Nightshirt Bandit; A Doggone Mixup; Soul of a Heel; Healthy, Wealthy and Dumb; Three Missing Links. **1939** The following shorts: Clock Wise; Moving Vanities; We Want Our Mummy; Three Little Sew and Sews. **1940** Earl of Puddlestone; My Little Chickadee; The Courageous Dr. Christian; Mutiny in the County (short). **1941** The Iron Claw (serial); Never Give a Sucker an Even Break; Dutiful but Dumb (short); Lady from Louisiana; Wild Geese Calling; A Polo Phony (short). **1942** Yokel Boy; The Boogie Man Will Get You. **1944** Gold is Where You Lose It (short).

MORTON, MAXINE See WEST, KATHERINE

MOSCONI, LOUIS
Born: 1895. Died: Aug. 1, 1969, Hollywood, Calif. Screen actor.

Appeared in: **1951** Operation Pacific.

MOSCOVITCH, MAURICE
Born: Nov. 23, 1871, Odessa, Russia. Died: June 18, 1940, Los Angeles, Calif. (following operation). Screen and stage actor.

Appeared in: **1936** Winterset. **1937** Lancer Spy; Make Way for Tomorrow. **1938** Gateway; Suez. **1939** Everything Happens at Night; Susanna of the Mountains; Love Affair; In Name Only; Rio. **1940** Dance, Girl, Dance; South to Karanga; The Great Dictator. **1942** The Great Commandment.

MOSCOWITZ, JENNIE
Died: July 26, 1953, Bronx, N.Y. Yiddish screen and stage actress. Married to stage producer/manager Max Moscowitz (dec. 1947).

Appeared in: **1929** Mother's Boy.

MOSER, HANS (Jean Juliet)
Born: 1880, Austria. Died: June 19, 1964, Vienna, Austria (cancer). Screen actor.

Appeared in: **1930** Liebling der Gotter (Darling of the Gods). **1931** Der Grosse Tenor. **1932** His Majesty; King Ballyhoo; Causa Kaiser (The Kaiser Case); Man Braucht Kein Geld. **1933** Madame Wuenscht Keine Kinder. **1935** Polenblut (Polish Blood); Der Himmel auf Erden; Winternachtstraum. **1936** Frasquite; Karneval und Liebe; Die Fahrt in Die Jugend. **1937** The World's in Love; Masquerade in Vienna; Endstation; Schabernack; Das Gaesschen zum Paradies; Vienna Burgtheater. **1938** Eva, das Fabriksmaedel; Solo per To (Only for Three); Die Gluecklichste Ehe von Wien (Happiest Married Couple in Vienna); Wir Sind von K u K Infantrie-Regiment. **1939** Alles Fuer Veronika; Kleines Bezirksgericht (Little Country Court); Fasching in Wien; Hohe Schule (College); Familie Schimek; Das Ekel (The Grouch). **1940** Walzerlange (Waltz Melodies); Wiener Geschichten (Vienna Tales); Opernball (Opera Ball). **1950** State Secret (aka The Great Manhunt—US 1951); Vienna Blood. **1953** Der Onkel aus Amerika (Uncle from America). **1955** Congress Dances. **1962** Der Flendermaus.

MOSICK, MARIAN
Born: 1906. Died: Feb. 2, 1973. Screen actress.

Appeared in: **1954** Jivaro.

MOSJOUKINE, IVAN
Born: 1889. Died: Jan. 18, 1939, Paris, France. Screen actor.

Appeared in: **1911** The Defense of Sevastopol. **1922** Satan Triumphant; Tempest. **1923** Shadows That Mass. **1926** Michael Strogoff. **1927** Surrender; The Living Dead Man; Edmund Kean; Prince among Lovers; The Loves of Casanova (US 1929); Surrender. **1929** The President; The White Devil (US 1931). **1936** Nitchevo; Other French film, Sergeant X.

MOSKVIN, IVAN M.
Born: 1874, Russia. Died: Feb. 16, 1946, Moscow, Russia. Screen and stage actor.

Appeared in: **1927** Polikushka. **1928** The Station Master. **1933** An Hour with Tchekhof; Other Russian film, Death of a Government Clerk.

MOSLEY, FRED (Frederick Charles Mosley)
Born: 1854. Died: Mar. 9, 1927, Staten Island, N.Y. Stage and screen actor.

MOSS, BASIL GEOFFREY
Born: 1909. Died: June 10, 1935. London, England. Screen and stage actor.

MOSS, GAYLIN
Born: 1959. Died: Apr. 13, 1979, Colorado River area (auto accident). Screen, television actress, singer and musician.

Appeared in: **1978** American Hot Wax; The Buddy Holly Story.

MOSTEL, ZERO (Samuel Joel Mostel)
Born: Feb. 28, 1915, Brooklyn, N.Y. Died: Sept. 8, 1977, Philadelphia, Pa (cardiac disorder). Screen, stage, television actor and nightclub entertainer. Married to dancer Kathryn Harkin.

Appeared in: **1943** DuBarry Was a Lady (film debut). **1950** Panic in the Streets. **1951** The Enforcer; Sirocco; The Guy Who Came Back; Mr. Belvedere Rings the Bell; The Model and the Marriage Broker. **1966** A Funny Thing Happened on the Way to the Forum (stage and film versions). **1967** The Producers. **1968** The Great Catherine. **1969** The Great Bank Robbery. **1970** The Angel Levine. **1972** The Hot Rock. **1974** Rhinoceros; Marco. **1975** Foreplay. **1976** The Front. **1977** Mastermind.

MOULAN, FRANK
Born: 1876. Died: May 13, 1939, New York, N.Y. Screen actor and opera performer.

Appeared in: **1927** Oh, How I Love My Little Bed (short). **1937** The Girl Said No.

MOULDER, WALTER C.
Born: 1933. Died: July 1, 1967, New York, N.Y. (heart attack). Screen, stage and television actor.

Appeared in: **1959** North by Northwest; That Kind of Woman.

MOUNTAIN, CHARLES
Died: Feb. 28, 1980. Screen actor.

Appeared in: **1978** Damien—Omen II.

MOURER, MARYSE See CAROL, MARTINE

MOVAR, DUNJA
Born: 1940, Germany. Died: Mar. 30, 1963, Goettingen, Germany (suicide-sleeping pills). Screen, stage and television actress. Received Federal Youth Film Award in 1959 for The Angel That Pawned a Harp.

Appeared in: **1959** The Angel That Pawned a Harp. **1968** Hamlet.

MOWBRAY, ALAN
Born: Aug. 18, 1896, London, England. Died: Mar. 25, 1969, Hollywood, Calif. (heart attack). Screen, stage, television actor and playwright.

Appeared in: **1931** Guilty Hands; Honor of the Family; God's Gift to Women; Alexander Hamilton; The Man in Possession; Leftover Ladies. **1932** The Bride's Bereavement or Snake in the Grass (short); Two Lips and Julips or Southern Love and Northern Exposure (short); The Silent Witness; Lovers Courageous; Man about Town; Winner Take All; Jewel Robbery; Two Against the World; The Man Called Back; Nice Women; Hotel Continental; The World and the Flesh; The Man from Yesterday; Sherlock Holmes. **1933** Our Betters; Her Secret; Peg O' My Heart; A Study in Scarlet; Voltaire; Berkeley Square; Midnight Club; The World Changes; Roman Scandals. **1934** One More River; Embarrassing Moments; Long Lost Father; Where Sinners Meet; The Girl from Missouri; Charlie Chan in London; The House of Rothschild; Cheaters; Little Man, What Now? **1935** Lady Tubbs; Night Life of the Gods; Becky Sharp; The Gay Deception; In Person; She Couldn't Take It. **1936** Rose Marie; Muss 'Em Up; Mary of Scotland; Rainbow on the River; Desire; Give Us This Night; The Case Against Mrs. Ames; Fatal Lady; My Man Godfrey; Ladies in Love. **1937** Four Days' Wonder; As Good As Married; Topper; Stand-In; On Such a Night; Music for Madame; On the Avenue; The King and the Chorus Girl; Marry the Girl; Hollywood Hotel; Vogues of 1938. **1938** Merrily We Live; There Goes My Heart. **1939** Never Say Die; Way Down South; The Llano Kid; Topper Takes a Trip. **1940** Music in My Heart; Curtain Call; The Villain Still Pursued Her; The Boys from Syracuse; Scatterbrain; The Quarterback. **1941** Ice-Capades; The Perfect Snob; That Hamilton Woman; That Uncertain Feeling; Footlight Fever; The Cowboy and the Blonde; I Woke up Screaming; Moon over Her Shoulder. **1942** Yokel Boy; So This Is Washington; Panama Hattie; The Mad Martindales; A Yank at Eton; Isle of Missing Men; The Devil with Hitler; We Were Dancing; The Powers Girl. **1943** Stage Door Canteen; His Butler's Sister; Holy Matrimony; Slightly Dangerous; Screen Snapshots No. 8 (short). **1944** Ever since Venus; The Dough Girls; My Gal Loves Music. **1945** Tell It to a Star; The Phantom of 42nd Street; Earl Carroll Vanities; Men in Her Diary; Where Do We Go from Here?; Sunbonnet Sue; Bring on the Girls. **1946** Terror by Night; My Darling Clementine; Idea Girl. **1947** Captain from Castile; Lured; Merton of the Movies; Pilgrim Lady. **1948** My Dear Secretary; An Innocent Affair; Every Girl Should Be Married; Main Street Kid; Prince of Thieves. **1949** Abbott and Costello Meet the Killer, Boris Karloff; The Lone Wolf and His Lady; You're My Everything; The Lovable Cheat. **1950** The Jackpot; Wagonmaster. **1951** Crosswinds; The Lady and the Bandit; Dick Turpin's Ride. **1952** Just across the Street; Blackbeard the Pirate. **1953** Androcles and the Lion. **1954** Ma and Pa Kettle at Home; The Steel Cage. **1955** The King's Thief. **1956** Around the World in 80 Days; The Man Who Knew Too Much; The King and I. **1962** A Majority of One.

MOWBRAY, HENRY (Harry E. Sweeney)
Born: Sept. 5, 1882, Australia. Died: July 9, 1960, Woodland Hills, Calif. (arteriosclerosis). Screen actor.

Appeared in: **1931** Fifty Fathoms Deep. **1934** Pursuit of Happiness. **1936** The Leathernecks Have Landed.

MOWER, JACK
Born: 1890, Honolulu, Hawaii. Died: Jan. 6, 1965, Hollywood, Calif. Screen, stage and vaudeville actor.

Appeared in: **1915** The Wanderers. **1916** A Race for Life; Miss Jackie of the Navy. **1917** The Devil's Assistant; Miss Jackie of the Army. **1918** Molly Go Get 'Em; Jilted Janet; A Square Deal; Impossible Susan; Ann's Finish; The Primitive Woman. **1919** The Island of Intrigue; Fair Enough; Molly of the Follies. **1920** The Third Eye (serial); The Tiger Band (serial). **1921** The Beautiful Gambler; Cotton and Cattle; Danger Ahead; Silent Years; The Trail to Red Dog; A Cowboy Ace; Flowing Gold; Out of the Clouds; The Range Pirate; Riding with Death; The Rowdy; Rustlers of the Night; Short Skirts. **1922** Manslaughter; The Crimson Challenge; The Golden Gallows; Saturday Night; When Husbands Deceive. **1923** The Last Hour; Pure Grit; The Shock; In the Days of Daniel Boone (serial). **1924** Robes of Sin; Ten Scars Make a Man (serial). **1925** Cyclone Cavalier; Kit Carson over the Great Divide; Perils of the Wind (serial); The Rattler. **1926** False Friends; Her Own Story; Officer 444 (serial); The Ghetto Shamrock; The Radio Detective (serial); Sky High Corral; Melodies; The Lost Express. **1927** Trail of the Tiger (serial); Uncle Tom's Cabin; Pretty Clothes; Face Value. **1928** The Water Hole; Sailor's Wives; The Air Patrol; Sinners' Parade. **1929** Anne Against the World; Ships of the Night. **1930** Ridin' Law; The Woman Who Was Forgotten. **1932** Midnight Patrol; Phantom Express; Lone Trail. **1933** Come on Tarzan; Law and the Lawless; King of the Arena; Fiddlin' Buckaroo. **1935**

Mary Burns, Fugitive; Red Salute; Revenge Rider. **1936** Next Time We Love; Hollywood Boulevard. **1937** White Bondage; Love is on the Air; Without Warning; The Missing Witness; That Certain Woman; It's Love I'm After. **1938** The Sisters; Penrod's Double Trouble; Penrod and His Twin Brother; Crime School; Hard to Get; Comet Over Broadway; Tarzan and the Green Goddess; The Invisible Menace. **1939** Code of the Secret Service; Smashing the Money Ring; Everybody's Hobby; Confessions of a Nazi Spy; The Return of Dr. X; Private Detectives; The Oklahoma Kid; The Kid from Kokomo; Dark Victory. **1940** My Love Came Back; Always a Bride; British Intelligence; King of the Lumberjacks; Torrid Zone; Tugboat Annie Sails Again. **1941** The Bride Came C.O.D.; Bullets for O'Hara; The Wagons Roll at Night; King's Row; The Man Who Came to Dinner; The Maltese Falcon. **1942** Gentleman Jim; Yankee Doodle Dandy; Murder in the Big House; Spy Ship. **1943** Mysterious Doctor; Thank Your Lucky Stars; Old Acquaintance; Princess O'Rourke. **1944** Destination Tokyo; Adventures of Mark Twain; The Last Ride. **1945** San Antonio; They Were Expendable; Christmas in Connecticut. **1946** Dangerous Business; A Stolen Life. **1947** Cry Wolf; That Way With Women; Shadows Over Chinatown. **1948** Fighting Mad. **1949** Angels in Disguise; A Kiss in the Dark. **1950** Montana; County Fair. **1952** So You Want to Get It Wholesale (short). **1953** House of Wax. **1955** The Long Gray Line.

MOYLES, DANIEL
Born: 1873. Died: Sept. 25, 1933, New York, N.Y. (heart attack). Screen and stage actor.

Appeared in: **1915** The Commuters.

MOZART, GEORGE
Born: Feb. 15, 1864, Yarmouth, England. Died: Dec. 10, 1947, London, England. Screen, stage actor and music hall singer.

Appeared in: **1913** Coney as Peacemaker; Coney Gets the Glad Eye; Coney—Ragtimer. **1932** Indiscretions of Eve. **1933** The Medicine Man. **1935** The Private Life of Henry the Ninth; Breakers Ahead; The Mystery of the Mary Celeste (aka Phantom Ship—US 1939). **1936** Cafe Mascot; Full Speed Ahead; The Bank Messenger Mystery; Two on a Doorstep; Strange Cargo (US 1940); Song of Freedom; Polly's Two Fathers. **1947** Overcoat Sam; Dr. Sin Fang. **1938** Pygmalion.

MOZHUKIN, IVAN
Born: 1890, Russia. Died: 1939, Russia. Screen actor and film director.

Appeared in: **1923** Kean, ou Desordre et Genie; Le Brasier Ardent.

MUDIE, LEONARD (Leonard Mudie Cheetham)
Born: Apr. 11, 1884, England. Died: Apr. 14, 1965, Hollywood, Calif. (heart ailment). Screen and stage actor.

Appeared in: **1921** A Message from Mars. **1922** Through the Storm. **1932** The Mummy. **1933** Voltaire. **1934** Jimmy the Gent; The Mystery of Mr. X; The House of Rothschild; Cleopatra. **1935** Clive of India; Cardinal Richelieu; Becky Sharp; Rendezvous; Captain Blood; The Great Impersonator; Les Miserables. **1936** The Story of Louis Pasteur; Magnificent Obsession; Anthony Adverse; Mary of Scotland; His Brother's Wife; Lloyds of London. **1937** The King and the Chorus Girl; They Won't Forget; The League of Frightened Men; London by Night; Lancer Spy; Lost Horizon; Another Dawn. **1938** The Mysterious Mr. Moto; The Jury's Secret; Adventures of Robin Hood; Kidnapped; Suez; When Were You Born? **1939** Tropic Fury; Arrest Bulldog Drummond; Dark Victory; Mutiny on the Black Hawk; Man About Town. **1940** Congo Maisie; Charlie Chan's Murder Cruise; South of Suez; Devil's Island; British Intelligence; The Letter; Foreign Correspondent; The Sea Hawk; Brother Orchid; A Dispatch from Reuters. **1941** Shining Victory; The Nurse's Secret. **1942** Berlin Correspondent; Random Harvest. **1943** Appointment in Berlin. **1944** Winged Victory; Dragon Seed. **1945** Divorce; My Name is Julia Ross; The Corn Is Green. **1946** The Locket; Don't Gamble with Strangers. **1947** Private Affairs of Bel Ami; Bulldog Drummond at Bay. **1948** The Checkered Coat; Song of My Heart. **1951** Bomba and the Elephant Stampede. **1952** Bomba and the Jungle Girl; African Treasure. **1953** Safari Drums; The Magnetic Monster; Perils of the Jungle. **1954** Killer Leopard; Golden Idol. **1955** Lord of the Jungle. **1956** Autumn Leaves. **1957** The Story of Mankind. **1959** Timbuktu; Rosen fur den Staatsanwalt (Roses for the Prosecutor—US 1961); The Big Fisherman. **1965** The Greatest Story Ever Told.

MUELLER, BARBARA
Born: 1909, Germany. Died: Jan. 3, 1967, Germany? Screen and stage actress.

MUELLER, GERDA
Born: 1895, Germany. Died: Apr. 26, 1951, Berlin, Germany (heart ailment). Screen and stage actress.

MUELLER, WOLFGANG (aka WOLFGANG MULLER)
Born: 1923, Berlin, Germany. Died: Apr. 26, 1960, Lostallo, Switzerland (plane crash). Screen and stage actor.

Appeared in: **1958** Wir Wunderkinder (narr.) (We Amazing Children aka Aren't We Wonderful—US 1959). **1958** Das Wirthaus im Spessart (Restaurant in the Spessart aka The Spessart Inn—US 1961).

MUIR, FLORABEL
Born: 1889, Laramie, Wyo. Died: Apr. 27, 1970, Los Angeles, Calif. (heart attack). Columnist, screenwriter, author, stage and screen actress. Married to newspaperman Dennis "Denny" Morrison (dec. 1966).

MUIR, GAVIN
Born: Sept. 8, 1907, Chicago, Ill. Died: May 24, 1972, Fort Lauderdale, Fla. Screen and stage actor.

Appeared in: **1936** Mary of Scotland; Lloyds of London; Charlie Chan at the Racetrack; Half Angel. **1937** Wee Willie Winkie; The Holy Terror; Fair Warning. **1939** Tarzan Finds a Son. **1942** Nightmare; Eagle Squadron. **1943** Hitler's Children; Sherlock Holmes in Washington; Passport to Suez; Sherlock Holmes Faces Death. **1944** The Master Race; Passport to Adventure; The Merry Monahans. **1945** The House of Fear; Salome—Where She Danced; Patrick the Great; Tonight and Every Night. **1946** O.S.S.; Temptation; California. **1947** Unconquered; Ivy; Calcutta. **1948** The Prince of Thieves. **1949** Chicago Deadline. **1950** Rogues of Sherwood Forest. **1951** The Son of Dr. Jekyll; Thunder on the Hill; Abbott and Costello Meet the Invisible Man. **1953** King of the Khyber Rifles. **1955** Sea Chase. **1957** Johnny Trouble; The Abductors. **1959** Island of Lost Women. **1963** Night Tide.

MUIR, HELEN
Born: 1864. Died: Dec. 2, 1934, Los Angeles, Calif. Screen and stage actress. Entered films with Griffith in 1915.

Appeared in: **1919** Strictly Confidential. **1921** Live and Let Live; The Mistress of Shenstone.

MUIRHEAD, OLYVE See O'DAY, MAGINNIS

MUKESH
Died: Aug. 27, 1976. Screen actor and singer. Dubbed voices in Indian films.

MULCASTER, GEORGE H.
Born: 1891, London, England. Died: Jan. 19, 1964, England. Screen and stage actor.

Appeared in: **1918** God Bless Our Red, White and Blue. **1920** Tangled Hearts (aka The Wife Whom God Forgot). **1921** Wild Heather. **1923** The Pipes of Pan; Mist in the Valley. **1925** The Squire of Long Hadley; The Wonderful Wooing; A Girl of London. **1928** Ghosts of Yesterdays series including: The Princess in the Tower; The Man in the Iron Mask. **1929** Sacrifice. **1930** A Romance of Riches (rerelease of The Squire of Long Hadley—1925); The Way of a Woman (rerelease of The Wonderful Wooing—1925). **1931** Inquest. **1933** Purse Strings. **1935** The River House Mystery. **1936** Second Bureau. **1937** The Five Pound Man; The Gap; Old Mother Riley. **1938** Lily of Laguna; Little Dolly Daydream. **1939** The Lion Has Wings (US 1940); All Living Things. **1940** Pack Up Your Troubles; Sailors Don't Care. **1941** The Patient Vanishes (US 1947 aka This Man is Dangerous). **1942** Let the People Sing; Asking for Trouble; The Owner Goes Aloft (short). **1943** The Dummy Talks; My Learned Friend. **1945** For You Alone. **1946** Under New Management. **1948** Spring in Park Lane (US 1949). **1949** That Dangerous Age (aka If This Be Sin—US 1950); Under Capricorn. **1951** The Naked Heart. **1955** Contraband Spain (US 1958). **1957** Lady of Vengeance.

MULCAY, JIMMY
Born: 1900. Died: Dec. 31, 1968. Screen actor.

Appeared in: **1945** Night Club Girl. **1947** Variety Girl. **1951** Varieties on Parade. **1966** The Girl from Tobacco Row.

MULGREW, THOMAS G.
Born: 1889. Died: Dec. 3, 1954, Providence, R.I. Screen, stage and vaudeville actor. Appeared in early films with Eastern Film Co.

MULHALL, JACK
Born: Oct. 7, 1891, Wappinger Falls, N.Y. Died: June 1, 1979, Woodland Hills, Calif (heart failure). Screen, stage, vaudeville, radio and television actor. Entered films in 1914.

Appeared in: **1917** Sirens of the Sea. **1918** Mickey; The Brass Bullet.

1920 All of a Sudden Peggy; Should a Woman Tell?; You Can Never Tell. **1921** The Off-Shore Pirate; Molly 'O; Two Weeks With Pay. **1922** Turn to the Right; Broad Daylight; Dusk to Dawn; Flesh and Blood; The Forgotten Law; The Fourteenth Lover; Heroes of the Street; Midnight; The Sleepwalker. **1923** Within the Law; The Bad Man; Dulcy; The Social Buccaneer; The Call of the Wild; The Drums of Jeopardy; The Marriage Market. **1924** The Goldfish; Into the Net; Breath of Scandal; T.N.T. (aka The Naked Truth). **1925** The Folly of Vanity; Friendly Enemies; The Mad Whirl; Classified; We Moderns; Joanna; She Wolves; Three Keys. **1926** Silence; Sweet Daddies; Subway Sadie; Girl From Coney Island (aka Just Another Blonde); The Dixie Merchant; The Far Cry; God Gave Me Twenty Cents; Pleasures of the Rich. **1927** Man Crazy; The Crystal Cup; Smile, Brother, Smile; Orchids and Ermine; The Poor Nut; See You in Jail. **1928** Lady Be Good; The Butter and Egg Man; Waterfront; Ladies' Night in a Turkish Bath. **1929** Naughty Baby; Children of the Ritz; Two Weeks Off; Twin Beds; Show of Shows; Dark Streets. **1930** The Fall Guy; For the Love O' Lil; Golden Calf; In the Next Room; Murder Will Out; Road to Paradise; Second Choice; Showgirl in Hollywood. **1931** Reaching for the Moon; Lover Come Back. **1932** Night Beat; Murder at Dawn; Sally of the Subway; Love Bound; Hell's Headquarters; Sinister Hands; Passport to Paradise. **1933** Mystery Squadron (serial); The Three Musketeers (serial); Secret Sinners. **1934** The Old-Fashioned Way; Burn 'Em Up Barnes (serial); Curtain at Eight; Notorious Sophie Lang; The Human Side. **1935** Sweet Adeline; The Big Broadcast of 1936; Love in Bloom; Mississippi; People Will Talk; Fighting Lady; Roaring Roads; Paris in Spring; What Price Crime?; Chinatown Squad; Headline Woman; His Night Out; Skull and Crown. **1936** Wedding Present; Kelly of the Secret Service; Rogue's Tavern; The Preview Murder Mystery; 13 Hours by Air; Beloved Enemy; The Big Broadcast of 1937; Hollywood Boulevard; The Clutching Hand (serial); Undersea Kingdom (serial); Caesar's Last Stand (serial); Secret Valley. **1937** 100 Men and a Girl; Dangerous Holiday; Framing Youth (short). **1938** Outlaws of Sonora; You and Me; The Spy Ring; Crime Ring; The Chaser; The Storm; Held for Ransom. **1939** First Love; Home on the Prairie; Buck Rogers (serial); Black Friday; The Son of Monte Cristo; Mysterious Dr. Satan (serial); That Inferior Feeling (short); The Heckler (voice, short). **1941** Cheers for Miss Bishop; The Invisible Ghost; Bowery Blitzkrieg; Dangerous Lady; Desperate Cargo; Hard Guy; Adventures of Captain Marvel (serial); I Killed That Man; Dick Tracy vs. Crime, Inc. (serial); Saddle Mountain Round-Up. **1942** Sin Town; Man From Headquarters; Mr. Wise Guy; Foreign Agent; Queen of Broadway; 'Neath the Brooklyn Bridge. **1943** Wedtime Stories (short); Kid Dynamite; The Ape Man; Ghosts on the Loose; The Falcon in Danger. **1944** South of Dixie; A Wave, a Wac, and a Marine. **1945** The Man Who Walked Alone; The Phantom of 42nd Street. **1949** Sky Liner. **1957** Up in Smoke. **1958** In the Money. **1959** The Atomic Submarine.

MULHAUSER, JAMES
Born: Oct. 31, 1890, Brooklyn, N.Y. Died: June 15, 1939, Beverly Hills, Calif. Screen, stage actor and screenwriter. Entered films in 1918.

Appeared in: **1928** The Head Man. **1929** China Bound. **1932** Slim Summerville Comedies.

MULLE, IDA
Born: c. 1864. Died: Aug. 9, 1934, New York, N.Y. (complications from fall). Stage and screen actress.

MULLEN, BARBARA
Born: June 9, 1914, Boston, Mass. Died: Mar. 9, 1979, London, England (heart attack). Screen, stage, television actress, dancer and writer. Married to film producer John Taylor.

Appeared in: **1941** Jeannie (film debut, US 1943). **1942** Thunder Rock (US 1944). **1944** Welcome Mr. Washington. **1945** A Place of One's Own (US 1949). **1946** The Trojan Brothers. **1948** My Sister and I; Corridor of Mirrors. **1951** Talk of a Million (aka You Can't Beat the Irish—US). **1952** So Little Time; The Gentle Gunman (US 1953). **1953** The Bosun's Mate (short). **1958** Innocent Sinners. **1959** The Siege of Pinchgut (aka Four Desperate Men). **1960** The Challenge (aka It Takes a Thief—US 1962). **1963** The Very Edge. **1966** Miss Mactaggart Won't Lie Down (short).

MULLENS, JOHNNIE
Born: 1884, Granbury, Tex. Died: Jan. 2, 1978, Eagle Rock, Calif. Rodeo performer and screen actor. Member of The Cowboy Hall of Fame.

Appeared in: **1972** Junior Bonner.

MULLER, RENATE (aka RENATE MUELLER)
Born: 1907, Germany. Died: Oct. 7, 1937, Berlin, Germany. Screen actor.

Appeared in: **1929** Peter, der Matrose; Drei Machen ihr Glueck; Revolte im Erziehungshaus (Revolt in the Reformatory). **1930** Liebe im Ring; Liebling der Goetter (Darling of the Gods); Der Sohn der Weissen Berge (US 1933, aka Das Geheimnis von Zermatt); Das Floetenkonzert von Saussouci (The Flute Concert at Sans Souci—US 1931). **1931** Der Grosse Tenor (The Great Tenor); Liebeslied; Der Kleine Seitensprung (US 1932); Die Privatsekretaerin (Private Secretary, aka Office Girl—US 1932); Die Blumenfrau von Lindenau (The Flower Lady of Lindenau—US 1932, aka Sturm im Wasserglas). **1932** Herzblut; Maedchen zum Heiraten; Wie Sag ich's Meinem Mann (US 1934); Wenn die Liebe Mode Macht (US 1933). **1933** Saison in Kairo; Viktor und Viktoris (US 1935); Walzerkrieg (War of the Waltzes). **1934** Walatz Time in Vienna; Die Englische Heirat. **1935** Liselotte von der Pfalz (aka Frauen um den Sonnenkoenig); Liebesleute (US 1936, aka Hermann und Dorothea von Heute). **1936** The Private Life of Louis XIV; Allotria; Eskapade (aka Seine Offizielle Frau). **1937** Togger; For Her Country's Sake.

MULOCK, AL
Born: England? Died: c. 1970, Rome, Italy. Screen actor.

Appeared in: **1955** Joe MacBeth (US 1956). **1957** Interpol (aka Pickup Alley—US); Kill Me tomorrow (US 1958). **1958** High Hell. **1959** Tarzan's Greatest Adventure. **1960** Jazzboat; Tarzan the Magnificent. **1961** The Hellions (US 1962). **1962** Play it Cool (US 1963). **1963** Call Me Bwana; The Small World of Sammy Lee. **1964** Dr. Terror's House of Horrors (US 1965). **1966** Lost Command; Il Buono, Il Brutto, Il Cattiro (The Good, the Bad and the Ugly—US 1967). **1967** A Witch Without a Broom; The Treasure of Makuba; The Hellbenders; Reflections in a Golden Eye; Battle Beneath the Earth (US 1968).

MUMBY, DIANA
Born: July 1, 1922, Detroit, Mich. Died: May 19, 1974, Westlake, Calif. Screen and stage actress.

Appeared in: **1940** A Night at Earl Carroll's (film debut). **1944** Up in Arms. **1946** The Kid from Brooklyn. **1947** Winter Wonderland. **1948** A Song is Born. **1951** G.I. Jane.

MUNDIN, HERBERT
Born: Aug. 21, 1898, England. Died: Mar. 4, 1939, Van Nuys, Calif. (auto accident). Screen and stage actor.

Appeared in: **1932** Life Begins; One Way Passage; The Silent Witness; Almost Married; The Devil's Lottery; The Trial of Vivienne Ware; Bachelor's Affairs; Chandu, the Magician; Sherlock Holmes; Love Me Tonight. **1933** Dangerously Yours; Cavalcade; Pleasure Cruise; Adorable; It's Great to Be Alive; Arizona to Broadway; The Devil's in Love; Shanghai Madness; Hoopla. **1934** Bottoms Up; Call It Luck; Such Women Are Dangerous; Orient Express; Springtime for Harry; All Men Are Enemies; Hell in Heavens; Love Time; Ever Since Eve. **1935** Mutiny on the Bounty; Black Sheep; The Perfect Gentlemen; The Widow from Monte Carlo; Ladies Love Danger; King of Burlesque; David Copperfield. **1936** Charlie Chan's Secret; A Message to Garcia; Under Two Flags; Tarzan Escapes; Champagne Charlie. **1937** Another Dawn; You Can't Beat Love; Angel. **1938** The Adventures of Robin Hood; Lord Jeff; Invisible Enemy; Exposed. **1939** Society Lawyer.

MUNDY, BOB
Born: 1928. Died: Apr. 8, 1978, Rockport, Maine (heart attack). Screen actor.

MUNDY, EDWARD "CAP" (Edward Landis Mundy)
Born: May 11, 1888, Ill. Died: Feb., 1962, Woodland Hills, Calif. Screen actor.

Appeared in: **1940** Chad Hanna. **1944** Wilson. **1950** Gunfighter. **1953** The Robe. **1955** Untamed. **1956** Carousel; The Proud Ones.

MUNI, PAUL (Muni Weisenfreund)
Born: Sept. 22, 1895, Austria or Poland. Died: Aug. 25, 1967, Montecito, Calif. (heart trouble). Screen, stage, vaudeville and burlesque actor. Son of stage actor Nathan Philip (dec.) and actress Sally Weisenfreund (dec.). Won 1936 Academy Award for Best Actor in The Story of Louis Pasteur. Nominated for 1928/29 Academy Award for Best Actor in The Valiant; in 1932/33 for I Am a Fugitive from a Chain Gang; in 1937 for The Life of Emile Zola; and in 1959 for The Last Angry Man.

Appeared in: **1929** The Valiant (film deubt); Seven Faces. **1932** I Am a Fugitive from a Chain Gang; Scarface. **1933** The World Changes. **1934** Hi, Nellie. **1935** Bordertown; Dr. Socrates; Black Fury. **1936** The Story of Louis Pasteur. **1937** The Good Earth; The Life of Emile Zola; The Woman I Love. **1938** Rasputin. **1939** Juarez; For Auld Lang Syne (short); We Are Not Alone. **1940** Hudson's Bay. **1942** The Commandos Strike at Dawn. **1943** Stage Door Canteen. **1945** A Song to Remember; Counter-Attack. **1946** Angel on My Shoulder. **1953** Stranger on the Prowl. **1959** The Last Angry Man.

MUNIER, FERDINAND
Born: Dec. 3, 1889, San Diego, Calif. or Boston, Mass? Died: May 27, 1945, Hollywood, Calif. (heart attack). Screen, stage, radio and vaudeville actor.

Appeared in: **1923** The Broken Wing. **1931** Ambassador Bill. **1932** Stepping Sister; Wild Girl; After Tomorrow. **1933** The Woman I Stole; Queen Christina; The Bowery; Kickin' the Crown Around (short). **1934** The Barretts of Wimpole Street; Love and Hisses (short); Babes in Toyland; The Merry Widow; Count of Monte Cristo. **1935** I'm a Father (short); Okay Toots! (short); Roberta; Clive of India; The Gilded Lily; China Seas; His Family Tree; Follies Bergere; Page Miss Glory; Hands Across the Table; Harmony Lane; Two Sinners; Top Flat (short). **1936** One Rainy Afternoon; The White Legion; Can This Be Dixie?; The Beloved Rogue; The Bold Caballero; The White Angel. **1937** Tovarich; Damaged Goods. **1938** Marriage Forbidden; The Great Waltz; Going Places. **1939** Midnight; Everything Happens at Night. **1941** Model Wife. **1942** Invisible Agent; Commandos Strike at Dawn; Tennessee Johnson. **1943** Claudia. **1945** Diamond Horseshoe. **1950** Revenge Is Sweet (reissue of Babes in Toyland, 1934 film).

MUNIZ, JUAN DE DIOS
Born: 1906. Died: Oct., 1951, Madrid, Spain. Screen and stage actor. Dubbed Spanish voice of Spencer Tracy.

MUNRO, DOUGLAS
Died: Feb., 1924, Birmingham, England (double pneumonia). Screen and stage actor.

Appeared in: **1914** On His Majesty's Service (aka 0-18 or a Message From the Sky—US); For the Empire (aka For Home and Country—US); Lil O' London; Liberty Hall. **1915** The Christian; The King's Outcast (aka His Vindication—US); Rupert of Hentzau (US 1916); The Heart of a Child (US 1916); Jelf's (aka A Man of His Word—US); The Two Roads. **1916** Arsene Lupin; When Knights Were Bold; The Princess of Happy Chance; Vice Versa; The Morals of Weybury (aka The Hypocrites); Me and Me Moke (aka Me and M' Pal—US); The Game of Liberty (aka Under Suspicion—US); You; The Persecution of Bob Pretty. **1917** Justice; The Woman Who Was Nothing; Quicksands (aka Broken Barrier); Flames; Dombey and Son. **1918** Goodbye; The Greatest Wish in the World; The Top Dog. **1919** The City of Beautiful Nonsense; Darby and Joan; The Garden of Resurrection. **1920** A Temporary Vagabond; The Lure of Crooning Water; London Pride; The Pursuit of Pamela; General Post; The Glad Eye; Duke's Son (aka Squandered Lives—US); The Amazing Quest of Mr. Ernest Bliss (serial); Testimony; True Tilda; The Mirage. **1921** The Bigamist; The Sport of Kings. **1922** Tense Moments With Great Authors series including: Vanity Fair; Beauty and the Beast (short); The Persistent Lovers; A Romance of Old Bagdad; Boy Woodburn; A Sporting Double; The Grass Orphan. **1923** Mist in the Valley; Fires of Fate. **1924** The Desert Sheik.

MUNRO, JANET
Born: 1934, Blackpool, England. Died: Dec. 6, 1972, London, England. Screen, stage and television actress. Divorced from actors Tony Wright and Ian Hendry.

Appeared in: **1957** Small Hotel. **1958** The Trollenberg Terror (aka The Crawling Eye—US); The Young and the Guilty. **1959** Third Man on the Mountain; Tommy the Toreador; Darby O'Gill and the Little People. **1961** Swiss Family Robinson; The Day the Earth Caught Fire (US 1962). **1962** The Horsemasters. **1962** Life for Ruth (aka Walk in the Shadow—US 1966). **1963** Bitter Harvest; Hide and Seek (US 1964); A Jolly Bad Fellow (US 1964 aka They All Died Laughing). **1964** Daylight Robbery. **1967** Sebastian (US 1968).

MUNSHIN, JULES
Born: 1915, New York, N.Y. Died: Feb. 19, 1970, N.Y. (heart attack). Stage and screen actor.

Appeared in: **1948** Easter Parade. **1949** On the Town; Take Me Out to the Ball Game; That Midnight Kiss. **1954** Monte Carlo Baby. **1957** Silk Stockings; Ten Thousand Bedrooms. **1964** Wild and Wonderful. **1967** Monkeys, Go Home! **1974** That's Entertainment (film clips).

MUNSON, ONA (Ona Wolcott)
Born: June 16, 1903, Portland, Ore. Died: Feb. 11, 1955, New York, N.Y. (suicide—sleeping pills). Screen, stage, vaudeville and radio actress.

Appeared in: **1928** Head of the Family. **1931** Going Wild; The Hot Heiress; The Collegiate Model (short); Broadminded; Five Star Final. **1938** Dramatic School; His Exciting Night. **1939** Gone With the Wind; Legion of Lost Flyers. **1940** The Big Guy; Wagons Westward; Scandal Sheet. **1941** Lady from Louisiana; Wild Geese Calling; The Shanghai Gesture. **1942** Drums of the Congo. **1943** Idaho. **1945** Dakota; The Cheaters. **1946** The Magnificent Rogue. **1947** The Red House.

MURA, CORRINE (Corinna Wall)
Born: 1910. Died: Aug. 1, 1965, Mexico City, Mexico (cancer). Screen, stage, radio actress and singer.

Appeared in: **1942** Call Out the Marines. **1943** Casablanca. **1944** Passage to Marseille. **1945** The Gay Senorita. **1947** Honeymoon.

MURAT, JEAN
Born: 1888, France. Died: Jan. 5, 1968, Aix-en-Provence, France (coronary thrombosis). Stage and screen actor. Divorced from actress Annabella. Entered films in 1922.

Appeared in: **1928** Carmen; The Legion of Honor; L'Eau du Nil. **1929** Venus; Escaped from Hell; The Soul of France; La Nuit est a Nous (The Night is Ours—US 1931—also a 1953 version). **1932** Paris-Mediterranee. **1936** Second Bureau; La Kermesse Heroique. **1938** Generals Without Buttons; L'Equipage (aka Flight into Darkness). **1948** L'Eternel Retour (The Eternal Return). **1949** The Wench. **1951** On the Riviera; Rich, Young and Pretty. **1955** Il Mantello Rosso (The Red Cloak—US 1961). **1958** Paris Holiday. **1959** Lady Chatterley's Lover; The Possessors; Le Vent se Leve (The Wind Rises aka Time Bomb—US 1961). **1962** It Happened in Athens; Les Sept Peches Capitaux (Seven Capital Sins—US 1963).

MURATORE, LUCIEN
Born: 1878, Marseilles, France. Died: July 16, 1954, Paris, France. Opera singer and screen actor.

Appeared in: **1914** Manon Lescaut.

MURDOCK, ANN (Irene Coleman)
Born: Nov. 10, 1890, Port Washington, N.Y. Died: Apr. 22, 1939, Lucerne, Switzerland. Screen and stage actress. Entered films in 1915.

Appeared in: **1916** Captain Jinks of the Horse Marines. **1917** Where Love Is; The Beautiful Adventure; My Wife; The Outcast; Please Help Emily; The Richest Girl; Seven Deadly Sins (aka Envy). **1918** The Imposter.

MURDOCK, KERMIT
Born: 1909. Died: Feb. 11, 1981, Tenafly, N.J. Screen, stage, radio and television actor.

Appeared in: **1950** Farewell to Yesterday (narrator). **1967** In the Heat of the Night. **1970** On a Clear Day You Can See Forever.

MURNANE, ALLAN L.
Born: 1882, Philadelphia, Pa. Died: Apr. 2, 1950, New Rochelle, N.Y. Screen, stage actor and stage director.

Appeared in: **1916** Mysteries of Myra (serial). **1917** Patria (serial).

MURO, HENRI
Born: July 13, 1884, France. Died: Dec. 12, 1967, Hollywood, Calif. (heart attack). Screen actor.

MURPHY, ADA
Born: 1888. Died: Aug. 25, 1961, Encino, Calif. Screen actress. Entered films in 1915.

MURPHY, ALMA
Born: 1889. Died: Dec. 16, 1978, Los Angeles, Calif. Screen, stage, television actress, playwright, poet and lyricist.

MURPHY, AUDIE
Born: June 20, 1924, Kingston, Tex. Died: May 28, 1971, near Roanoke, Va. (plane crash). Screen, television actor and author. Most decorated hero of W.W. II. Married to Pamela Archer. Divorced from actress Wanda Hendrix (dec. 1981).

Appeared in: **1948** Beyond Glory (film debut); Texas, Brooklyn and Heaven. **1949** Bad Boy. **1950** Sierra; The Kid from Texas; Kansas Raiders. **1951** The Cimarron Kid; The Red Badge of Courage. **1952**

Duel at Silver Creek. **1953** Gunsmoke; Column South; Tumbleweed. **1954** Ride Clear of Diablo; Drums Across the River; Destry. **1955** To Hell and Back. **1956** World in My Corner; Walk the Proud Land. **1957** Guns of Fort Petticoat; Joe Butterfly; Night Passage. **1958** Ride a Crooked Trail; The Gun Runner; The Quiet American. **1959** No Name on the Bullet; Cast a Long Shadow; The Wild and the Innocent. **1960** Hell Bent for Leather; The Unforgiven; Seven Ways from Sundown. **1961** Posse from Hell; The Battle at Bloody Beach. **1962** Six Black Horses. **1963** Showdown; Gunfight at Comanche Creek. **1964** The Quick Gun; Bullet for a Badman; Apache Rifles; War Is Hell (narr.). **1965** Arizona Raiders. **1966** Gunpoint; The Texican. **1967** Forty Guns to Apache Pass; Trunk to Cairo. **1969** A Time for Dying (cameo).

MURPHY, CHARLES B.
Born: 1884. Died: June 11, 1942, Bakersfield, Calif. (accident on location of Lost Canyon). Screen actor.

Appeared in: **1921** The Man of the Forest; The Rowdy; The Man Tamer. **1922** Golden Dreams; The Gray Dawn. **1923** Single Handed; Red Lights. **1931** Spell of the Circus (serial). **1937** County Fair. **1938** Zorro's Fighting Legion (serial); The Road to Reno. **1942** Lost Canyon.

MURPHY, EDNA (Elizabeth Edna Murphy)
Born: Nov. 17, 1904, New York, N.Y. Died: Aug. 3, 1974, Santa Monica, Calif. Screen actress. Divorced from film director Mervyn Le Roy. Entered films in 1919.

Appeared in: **1920** Over the Hill to the Poor House; The North Wind's Malice. **1921** Dynamite Allen; Live Wires; Play Square; What Love Will Do. **1922** Jolt; Extra! Extra!; Caught Bluffing; Don't Shoot; The Ordeal; The Galloping Kid; Paid Back; Ridin' Wild. **1923** Going Up; Her Dangerous Path (serial); Nobody's Bride; The Man Between. **1924** Daughters of Today; The White Moth; King of the Wild Horses; Into the Net (serial); Leatherstocking (serial); After the Ball. **1925** A Man Must Live; Wildfire; Lying Wives; Clothes Make the Pirate; Ermine and Rhinestones; His Buddy's Wife; Lena Rivers; The Police Patrol. **1926** College Days; The Little Giant; Obey the Law; Oh, What a Night!; Wives at Auction. **1927** All Aboard; Dearie; McFadden's Flats; Tarzan and the Golden Lion; The Black Diamond Express; Burnt Fingers; The Cruise of the Hellion; His Foreign Wife; Modern Daughters; Rose of the Bowery; The Silent Hero; Silver Comes Through; The Valley of Hell; Wilful Youth. **1928** The Sunset Legion; My Man; Across the Atlantic; A Midnight Adventure. **1929** Show of Shows; Stolen Kisses; The Bachelor's Club; Kid Gloves; Greyhound Limited; The Sap. **1930** Little Johnny Jones; Lummox; Second Choice; Dancing Sweeties; The Man from Blankley's; Wide Open. **1931** Finger Prints (serial); Behind Office Doors; Anybody's Blonde. **1932** Girl of the Rio; Forgotten Women. **1965** Laurel and Hardy's Laughing 20's (documentary). **1967** The Further Perils of Laurel and Hardy (documentary).

MURPHY, GEORGE
Born: 1899. Died: Aug. 15, 1941, Hollywood, Calif. (fall from horse). Screen actor. Do not confuse with actor/dancer/former U.S. Senator George Murphy.

MURPHY, JIMMY (James Anthony Murphy)
Born: 1894, San Francisco, Calif. Died: Sept. 15, 1924, Syracuse, N.Y. (auto racing accident). Auto racer, mechanic and screen actor. Do not confuse with actor Jim Murphy.

Appeared in: **1923** Racing Hearts.

MURPHY, JOHN DALY
Born: 1873, Ireland. Died: Nov. 20, 1934, New York, N.Y. (heart attack). Stage and screen actor.

Appeared in: **1918** Our Mrs. McChesney. **1921** Thunderclap. **1922** Polly of the Follies. **1923** The Truth About Wives; You Can't Fool Your Wife. **1924** Icebound.

MURPHY, JOSEPH J.
Born: 1877. Died: July 31, 1961, San Jose, Calif. Screen actor. One of the original Keystone Kops. Also portrayed "Andy Gump" on the screen.

MURPHY, MAURICE
Born: 1913. Died: Nov. 23, 1978, Los Angeles, Calif. Screen and television actor.

Appeared in: **1923** The Self-Made Wife. **1924** The Last Man on Earth. **1925** Thank You; Stella Dallas; The Home Maker. **1926** Beau Geste. **1928** The Michigan Kid; Shepherd of the Hills; Alias the Deacon; Call of the Heart. **1929** The College Coquette; The Spirit of Youth; The

Three Outcasts. **1931** All Quiet on the Western Front; Seas Beneath; Women Go on Forever. **1932** Divorce in the Family; Faithless. **1933** Found Alive; Pilgrimage. **1934** Tailspin Tommy (serial); There's Always Tomorrow. **1935** Curly Top; Private Worlds. **1936** Gentle Julia; Romeo and Juliet; Down to the Sea. **1937** The Road Back; Tovarich; Under Suspicion. **1938** Nurse From Brooklyn; My Bill. **1939** Forged Passport; Career; The Covered Trailer. **1940** Abe Lincoln in Illinois; Wolf of New York. **1941** The Reluctant Dragon. **1943** Destination Tokyo.

MURPHY, ROBERT "BOB" (Duke Foster Dunnell)
Born: 1889, Webster, N.Y. Died: Aug. 6, 1948, Santa Monica, Calif. (pneumonia). Screen and vaudeville actor.

Appeared in: **1935** Broadway Gondolier. **1936** The Case Against Mrs. Ames; Hideaway Girl; Two in a Crowd. **1937** Nancy Steele Is Missing; Portia on Trial; You're a Sweetheart. **1938** Girl of the Golden West; In Old Chicago. **1944** Shine on Harvest Moon.

MURRAY, BOBBY (Robert Hayes Murray)
Born: July 4, 1898, St. Albans, Vt. Died: Jan. 4, 1979, Nashua, N.H. Professional baseball player and screen actor.

Appeared in: **1928** Warming Up.

MURRAY, CHARLIE (Charles Murray)
Born: June 22, 1872, Laurel, Ind. Died: July 29, 1941, Hollywood, Calif. (pneumonia). Screen, stage and vaudeville actor. Entered films with Biograph Co. in 1912. He was Murray of the vaudeville team "Murray and Mack"; Mack was Oliver Trumbull (dec. 1934). In the Keystone comedies, Murray was the Hogan character, and in later years, he was the Kelly of "The Cohens and the Kellys" series.

Appeared in: **1914** The Passing of Izzy; A Fatal Flirtation; Her Friend the Bandit; Love and Bullets (reissued as The Trouble Mender); Soldiers of Misfortune; The Great Toe Mystery; She's a Cook (reissued as The Bungling Burglars); The Masquerader; The Anglers; Stout Heart But Weak Knees; Cursed by His Beauty; His Talented Wife; The Noise of Bombs; His Halted Career; The Plumber; Tillie's Punctured Romance; Hogan's Annual Spree; His Second Childhood; The Fatal Bumping; Mabel's Married Life; A Missing Bride; A Gambling Rube. **1915** Hogan's Wild Cats; Hogan's Mussy Job; Hogan the Porter; Hogan's Romance Upset; Hogan's Aristocratic Dream; Hogan Out West; From Patches to Plenty; The Beauty Bunglers; Their Social Splash; Those College Girls; A Game Old Knight; Her Painted Hero; The Great Vacuum Robbery; Only a Farmer's Daughter. **1916** His Hereafter; Fido's Fate; The Judge; A Love Riot; Her Marble Heart; Pills of Peril; The Feathered Nest (aka Girl Guardian); Maid Mad; Bombs. **1917** Maggie's First False Step; Her Fame and Shame; The Betrayal of Maggie; His Precious Life; A Bedroom Blunder. **1918** Watch Your Neighbor. **1921** A Small Town Idol; Home Talent. **1922** The Crossroads of New York. **1923** Luck; Bright Lights of Broadway. **1924** Empty Hearts; Lilies of the Field; The Girl in the Limousine; The Fire Patrol; The Mine with the Iron Door; Fool's Highway; Painted People; Sundown. **1925** My Son; Who Cares; Classified; Fighting the Flames; White Fang; Paint and Powder; Percy; Why Women Love (aka Sea Women and Barriers Aflame); The Wizard of Oz. **1926** The Cohens and the Kellys; Irene; The Boob; Mismates; Subway Sadie; Her Second Chance; Mike; Paradise; The Reckless Lady; Steel Preferred; The Silent Lover; Sweet Daddies. **1927** McFadden's Flats; The Gorilla; The Life of Riley; Lost at the Front; The Poor Nut; The Masked Woman. **1928** The Head Man; Flying Romeos; The Cohens and the Kellys in Paris; Do Your Duty; Vamping Venus. **1930** Clancy in Wall Street; Around the Corner; Cohens and the Kellys in Scotland; The King of Jazz; The Duke of Dublin; His Honor the Mayor; The Cohens and the Kellys in Africa; 10 Universal shorts. **1931** Caught Cheating. **1932** The Cohens and the Kellys in Hollywood; Hypnotized. **1933** The Cohens and the Kellys in Trouble. **1936** Dangerous Waters. **1937** Circus Girl. **1938** Breaking the Ice.

MURRAY, DAVID MITCHELL
Born: 1853. Died: Oct. 20, 1923, Long Island, N.Y. Stage and screen actor.

Appeared in: **1924** The Silent Watcher.

MURRAY, EDGAR
Born: 1865. Died: Oct. 31, 1932, Hollywood, Calif. (complication of diseases). Screen actor.

MURRAY, EDGAR
Born: 1892. Died: Oct. 16, 1959, Hollywood, Calif. (heart attack). Screen actor. Married to actress Nadia Popkova. Entered films with Vitagraph.

MURRAY, ELIZABETH M.
Born: 1871. Died: Mar. 27, 1946, Philadelphia, Pa. Screen, stage and vaudeville actress.

Appeared in: **1923** Little Old New York. **1929** Lucky in Love. **1931** The Bachelor Father.

MURRAY, J. HAROLD (Harry Roulon)
Born: Feb. 17, 1891, South Berwick, Maine. Died: Dec. 11, 1940, Killingworth, Conn. Screen, stage and vaudeville actor.

Appeared in: **1929** Married in Hollywood. **1930** Cameo Kirby; Happy Days; Women Everywhere. **1937** Universal and RKO shorts.

MURRAY, JACK (John W. B. Murray)
Died: May 1, 1941, Bronx, N.Y. Screen, stage, vaudeville, burlesque and radio actor.

MURRAY, JAMES
Born: Feb. 9, 1901, New York, N.Y. Died: July 11, 1936, New York, N.Y. (drowned in Hudson River). Screen and stage actor.

Appeared in: **1922** When Knighthood Was in Flower. **1923** The Pilgrims. **1927** In Old Kentucky; The Last Outlaw; The Lovelorn; Stark Love; Rough House Rosie. **1928** The Crowd; Rose Marie; The Big City. **1929** The Little Wildcat; The Shakedown; Thunder; Shanghai Lady. **1930** Hide-Out; The Rampant Age. **1931** Kick In; In Line of Duty; Bright Lights. **1932** The Reckoning; Alaska Love (short); Bachelor Mother. **1933** Air Hostess; Heroes for Sale; Frisco Jenny; High Gear; Central Airport; Baby Face; Peerless. **1935** $20 a Week; Skull and Crown; Ship Cafe.

MURRAY, JEAN
Born: Sydney, Nova Scotia, Canada. Died: Oct. 5, 1966, Winnipeg, Canada. Screen, stage and radio actress.

MURRAY, JOHN T.
Born: 1886, Australia. Died: Feb. 12, 1957, Woodland Hills, Calif. (stroke). Screen and vaudeville actor. Married to actress Vivian Oakland (dec. 1958) with whom he appeared in vaudeville as "John T. Murray and Vivian Oakland" and also made several shorts together during 1929-30.

Appeared in: **1924** Madonna of the Streets. **1925** Joanna; Sally; Stop Flirting; Winds of Chance. **1926** High Steppers; The Magnificent Bardely's. **1927** Finger Prints; The Gay Old Bird. **1928** Fazil. **1929** Sonny Boy; Honky Tonk; plus the following shorts billed as "John T. Murray and Vivian Oakland": Satires; The Hall of Injustice. **1930** How I Play Golf—The Mashie Niblick (short); Personality; Night Work; plus the following shorts with his wife: Who Pays; The Servant Problems. **1931** Charlie Chan Carries On; Young As You Feel; Alexander Hamilton. **1932** Man Called Back; Vanity Comedies shorts. **1933** Keyhole Katie (short). **1934** Air Maniacs (short); Love Birds. **1935** Great God Gold. **1936** Cain and Mabel; Here Comes Carter; Caught in the Act (short). **1937** The Lost Horizon; Ever Since Eve; True Confession; Girl Loves Boy; Sweetheart of the Navy; plus the following shorts: the Wrong Miss Wright; Calling All Doctors; Man Bites Lovebug. **1938** Gang Bullets; plus the following shorts: Violent Is the Word for Curley; The Mind Needer; Many Sappy Returns; Ankles Away. **1939** The Hardys Ride High; Andy Hardy Gets Spring Fever; The Sap Takes a Wrap (short); Skinny the Moocher (short). **1940** Mr. Clyde Goes to Broadway (short).

MURRAY, JULIAN "BUD"
Born: Nov. 21, 1888, New York, N.Y. Died: Nov. 1, 1952, West Los Angeles, Calif. (cerebral hemorrhage). Screen actor, stage and film dance director.

MURRAY, LOLA
Born: 1914. Died: Nov. 11, 1961, Shrewsbury, N.J. Screen actress.

MURRAY, MAE (Marie Adrienne Koenig)
Born: May 10, 1886 or 1889?, Portsmouth, Va. Died: Mar. 23, 1965, North Hollywood, Calif. (heart condition). Screen, stage actress and dancer. Divorced from actor and film director Robert Z. Leonard (dec. 1968).

Appeared in: **1916** To Have and To Hold (film debut); Honor Thy Name; Sweet Kitty Bellaire; The Dream Girl; The Big Sister; The Plow Girl. **1917** The Primrose Ring; The Morman Maid; On Record; First Sight; Princess Virtue. **1918** Modern Love; Her Body in Bond; Face Value; Danger—Go Slow; The Bride's Awakening. **1919** The Delicious Little Devil; Blind Husbands; The Scarlet Shadow; What Am I Bid (aka Girl for Sale); The Big Little Person; A.B.C. of Love; Twin Pawns (aka The Curse of Greed). **1920** On With the Dance; The Right to Love; Idols of Clay. **1921** The Gilded Lily. **1922** Fascination; Peacock Alley; Broadway Rose. **1923** The French Doll; Jazzmania; Fashion Row. **1924** Mademoiselle Midnight; Married Flirts; Circe, The Enchantress. **1925** The Masked Bride; The Merry Widow. **1927** Valencia; Altars of Desire. **1928** Show People. **1930** Peacock Alley (and 1922 version). **1931** Bachelor Apartment; High Stakes. **1951** Valentino.

MURRAY, MARION
Born: 1885. Died: Nov. 11, 1951, New York, N.Y. Screen actress. Entered films during silents. Married to actor Jed Prouty (dec. 1956).

Appeared in: **1942** Paris Calling. **1948** The Pirate.

MURRAY, ROY
Died: Sept. 24, 1973. Screen actor.

Appeared in: **1959** Wild Women of Wongo. **1966** The Wrong Box.

MURRAY, THOMAS
Born: 1902. Died: Nov. 20, 1961, Hollywood, Calif. (heart attack). Screen actor.

MURRAY, TOM
Born: 1875. Died: Aug. 27, 1935, Hollywood, Calif. Screen, vaudeville and radio actor.

Appeared in: **1922** French Hells; The Ladder Jinx; Too Much Business. **1923** The Pilgrim; The Meanest Man in the World. **1925** The Business of Love; The Gold Rush. **1926** Private Izzy Murphy; Tramp, Tramp, Tramp; Into Her Kingdom.

MURRAY, ZON
Died: Mar. 2, 1979. Screen actor.

Appeared in: **1946** Terror Trail; The Fighting Frontiersman; The El Paso Kid;; Ghost of Hidden Valley; Rainbow Over the Rockies. **1947** Song of the Sierras; West of Dodge City; West to Glory; Law of the Canyon; Code of the Saddle; The Law Comes to Gunsight; Gun Talk. **1948** Olkahoma Blues; Crossed Trails; Phantom Valley; Blood on the Moon; False Paradise. **1949** Gun Law Justice; Trail's End; Son of a Badman; Grand Canyon. **1950** The Kid from Texas; Dallas; Outlaws of Texas; Captain China. **1951** Night Riders of Montana; Fingerprints Don't Lie; Hurricane Island; Pecos River. **1952** Border Saddlemates; Cripple Creek; Desperadoe's Outpost; Laramie Mountains; The Longhorn; Barbed Wire. **1953** The President's Lady; Six Gun Decision; Vigilante Terror; Old Overland Trail; Down Laredo Way; On Top of Old Smoky; Phantom Stallion. **1954** Highway Dragnet; Bitter Creek; Passion. **1956** The Lone Ranger. **1957** The Lonely Man; Motorcycle Gang. **1958** Escape From Red Rock; Gunsmoke in Tucson. **1965** Requiem for a Gunfighter.

MURRAY-HILL, PETER
Born: Apr. 20, 1908, Bushy Heath, England. Died: 1957. Screen and stage actor. Married to actress Phyllis Calvert.

Appeared in: **1938** Mr. Reeder in Room 13 (film debut—aka Mystery of Room 13—US 1941); A Yank at Oxford; Jane Steps Out (US 1940). **1939** The Outsider (US 1940); At the Villa Rose (aka House of Mystery—US 1941). **1941** The Ghost Train. **1943** Rhythm Serenade; Bell-Bottom George. **1944** Madonna of the Seven Moons. **1945** They Were Sisters (US 1946).

MURROW, EDWARD R.
Born: Apr. 25, 1908, Greensboro, N.C. Died: Apr. 27, 1965, Pawling, N.Y. Radio, television commentator and screen actor.

Appeared in: **1943** Siege of Leningrad (narr.). **1956** Around the World in 80 Days. **1958** Satchmo the Great (narr.). **1960** Sink the Bismarck.

MURTH, FLORENCE
Born: 1902. Died: Mar. 29, 1934, Los Angeles, Calif. Screen actress. Appeared in early Sennett and Christie comedies.

Appeared in: **1922** Thundering Hoofs.

MUSE, CLARENCE
Born: Oct. 7, 1889, Baltimore, Md. Died: Oct. 13, 1979 , Perris, Calif. (cerebral hemorrhage). Black screen, stage, vaudeville actor, stage producer, screenwriter, songwriter and circus performer.

Appeared in: **1929** Hearts in Dixie. **1930** Rain or Shine; Royal Romance; Guilty? **1931** Huckleberry Finn; Dirigible; Secret Witness; Fighting Sheriff; The Last Parade; Safe in Hell; Terror by Night. **1932** Woman from Monte Carlo; Prestige; Winner Take All; Washington Merry-Go-Round; Cabin in the Cotton; The Wet Parade; Lena Rivers;

Attorney for the Defense; Night World; Is My Face Red?; White Zombie; Hell's Highway; Man Against Woman; Laughter in Hell. **1933** From Hell to Heaven; The Mind Reader; The Wrecker. **1934** Massacre; Black Moon; The Personality Kid; Fury of the Jungle; The Count of Monte Cristo; Broadway Bill. **1935** Alias Mary Dow; O'Shaughnessy's Boy; Harmony Lane; East of Java; So Red the Rose. **1936** Muss 'Em Up; Laughing Irish Eyes; Daniel Boone; Show Boat; Follow Your Heart. **1937** Mysterious Crossing. **1938** The Toy Wife; Secrets of a Nurse; Prison Train; The Spirit of Youth. **1939** Way Down South. **1940** Maryland; Sporting Blood; Zanzibar; Murder Over New York; That Gang of Mine; Broken Strings. **1941** The Invisible Ghost; Adam Had Four Sons; Love Crazy; Flame of New Orleans; The Gentleman From Dixie. **1942** Tales of Manhattan; The Black Swan. **1943** Shadow of a Doubt; Heaven Can Wait; Watch on the Rhine; Johnny Come Lately; Flesh and Fantasy. **1944** Jam Session; The Racket Man; In the Meantime, Darling; Follow the Boys. **1946** Night and Day; It's a Wonderful Life; Two Smart People. **1947** Joe Palooka in the Knockout; Unconquered; My Favorite Brunette; Welcome, Stranger. **1948** Live Today for Tomorrow; An Act of Murder. **1949** The Great Dan Patch. **1950** Riding High; County Fair. **1951** My Forbidden Past; Apache Drums. **1952** Caribbean; The Las Vegas Story. **1953** Jamaica Run. **1959** Porgy and Bess. **1976** Car Wash. **1979** The Black Stallion.

MUSIDORA (Jeanne Roques)
Born: 1889, France. Died: Dec., 1957, Paris, France. Screen, stage actress and film director. Became celebrated for her work in two 12-episode serials, Les Vampires and Judex.

Appeared in: **1914** Severo Torelli. **1915** Les Vampires (serial). **1916** Judex (serial). **1918** La Vagabonda. **1919** Johannes fils de Johannes. **1921** Pour Don Carlos; La Geole. **1924** La Tierra de los Toros. **1926** Le Berceau de Dieu.

MUSSELMAN, JOHNSON J.
Born: 1890. Died: Apr. 8, 1958, Louisville, Ky. Magician, screen and vaudeville actor. Known as "Aska the Magician."

MUSSEY, FRANCINE
Born: France. Died: Mar. 26, 1933, Paris, France (suicide—poison). Screen actress.

Appeared in: **1932** La ronde des Heures.

MUSSIERE, LUCIENE (Lucien Meurisse)
Born: 1890. Died: Dec. 23, 1972, Brussels, Belgium. Stage and screen actor.

Appeared in: **1956** Around the World in 80 Days.

MUSSILLI, BOOTS
Born: 1916. Died: Sept. 23, 1967, Norfolk, Mass. Jazz musician and screen actor. Appeared in silent films.

MUSSOLINI, BENITO
Born: July 29, 1883, Dovia di Predappio, Forli Province, Italy. Died: Apr. 28, 1945, Congo, Como Province, Italy (executed). Italian Fascist Premier and dictator. Appeared on screen.

Appeared in: **1923** The Eternal City.

MUSSON, BENNET
Born: 1866. Died: Feb. 17, 1946, Amityville, N.Y. Screen and stage actor.

Appeared in: **1921** White Oak.

MUSTIN, BURT
Born: Feb. 8, 1882, Pittsburgh, Pa. Died: Jan. 28, 1977, Glendale, Calif. Screen, stage, radio and television actor.

Appeared in: **1951** Detective Story; The Sellout. **1952** Just Across the Street; The Lusty Men. **1953** The Silver Whip; One Girl's Confession. **1955** The Desperate Hours. **1956** Storm Center; Bus Stop. **1958** Rally 'Round the Flag Boys!; The Big Country. **1960** The Adventures of Huckleberry Finn. **1963** Son of Flubber; The Thrill of It All. **1964** The Killers; What a Way to Go!. **1965** Sex and the Single Girl; Cat Ballou; The Cincinnati Kid. **1967** The Reluctant Astronaut. **1968** Speedway. **1969** Hail, Hero!; The Witchmaker. **1970** Tiger by the Tail. **1971** The Skin Game. **1975** Train Ride to Hollywood.

MUTHURAMAN, R.
Born: 1929, India. Died: Oct. 16, 1981, Ootacamund, India (heart attack). Screen and stage actor.

Appeared in: **1981** Ayiram Muthangal (A Thousand Kisses).

MUTION, RICARDO
Born: 1884, Mexico. Died: Apr. 2, 1957, Mexico City, Mex. (heart attack). Stage and screen actor.

Appeared in: **1939** Nobleza Ranchero (Rural Chivalry).

MUZQUIZ, CARLOS
Born: 1906, Mexico. Died: Feb., 1960, Mexico City, Mexico. Screen actor. Known as "Compadre Muzquiz."

Appeared in: **1950** Hidden River. **1951** My Outlaw Brother. **1955** A Life in the Balance. **1957** The Sun Also Rises; The Black Scorpion.

MYERS, CARMEL
Born: Apr., 1901, San Francisco, Calif. Died: Nov. 9, 1980, Los Angeles, Calif. (heart attack). Screen, stage, vaudeville, radio, television actress and singer. Mother of novelist Ralph Blum, actress Susan Adams Kennedy, and Mary Ufland.

Appeared in: **1916** Intolerance; The Matri-Maniac. **1917** Love Sublime; Sirens of the Sea; The Haunted Pajamas; My Unmarried Wife; Stage Struck. **1918** The Dream Lady; A Society Sensation; All Night. **1919** Who Will Marry Me?; The Little White Savage. **1920** In Folly's Trail. **1921** Breaking Through (serial); Cheated Love; The Dangerous Moment; The Kiss; A Daughter of the Law; The Mad Marriage. **1922** The Love Gambler; The Danger Point. **1923** Reno (aka Law Against Law); The Dancer of the Nile; The Famous Mrs. Fair; Good-by Girls!; The Little Girl Next Door; The Last Hour; Mary of the Movies; The Love Pirate; Slave of Desire (aka The Magic Skin). **1924** Beau Brummell; Babbitt; Broadway After Dark; Poisoned Paradise; The Forbidden Story of Monte Carlo. **1925** Ben Hur. **1926** The Gay Deceiver; Tell It to the Marines; The Devil's Circus. **1927** Sorrell and Son; Girl from Rio; The Demi-Bride; The Understanding Heart. **1928** A Certin Young Man; Four Walls; Prowlers of the Sea; Dream of Love. **1929** Broadway Scandals; The Careless Age; Careers; The Red Sword; The Ghost Talks; The Show of Shows; The Bath Between (short). **1930** Ship From Shanghai; A Lady Surrenders. **1931** Svengali; Ben Hur (and 1925 version); The Mad Genius; Lion and the Lamb; Chinatown After Dark. **1932** Nice Women; Pleasure; No Living Witness. **1934** Countess of Monte Cristo. **1941** Lady for a Night. **1942** Pretty Dolly (short). **1946** Whistle Stop.

MYERS, HARRY
Born: 1886, Philadelphia, Pa. or New Haven, Conn.? Died: Dec. 26, 1938, Los Angeles, Calif. (pneumonia). Screen and stage actor. Married to actress Rosemary Theby with whom he made a series of films as "Myers and Theby."

Appeared in: **1908** The Guerrilla. **1909** Her First Biscuits; The Jonesy Pictures. **1911** Her Two Sons. **1916** Housekeeping (first Myers and Theby film in series made from 1916 to April 1917). **1919** The Masked Rider (serial). **1920** Peaceful Valley. **1921** A Connecticut Yankee in King Arthur's Court; On the High Card; The March Hare; Nobody's Fool; Oh, Mary Be Careful; R.S.V.P. **1922** The Adventures of Robinson Crusoe (serial); Boy Crazy; Handle With Care; Kisses; Turn to the Right; Top O' the Morning; When the Lad Comes Home. **1923** The Bad Man; The Beautiful and Damned; Stephen Steps Out; Brass; Brass Bottle; Little Johnny Jones; The Printer's Devil; The Common Law; Main Street. **1924** Behold This Woman; Daddies; Listen, Lester; Reckless Romance; The Marriage Circle; Tarnish. **1925** Grounds for Divorce; She Wolves; Zander the Great. **1926** Exit Smiling; Up in Mabel's Room; The Beautiful Cheat; Monte Carlo; Nut Cracker. **1927** Getting Gertie's Garter; The Girl in the Pullman; The Bachelor's Baby; The First Night. **1928** The Dove; The Street of Illusion; Dream of Love. **1929** The Clean Up; Montmartre Rose; Wonder of Women. **1931** City Lights; Meet the Wife. **1932** The Savage Girl. **1933** Police Call; The Important Witness; Strange Adventure. **1935** Mississippi. **1936** Hollywood Boulevard. **1937** Dangerous Lives.

MYERS, LENORA
Born: 1904. Died: Feb. 10, 1950, Chicago, Ill. Screen and vaudeville actress. Married to vaudeville actor Robert Myers (dec.).

MYERS, PETER
Born: 1928. Died: Oct. 4, 1968. Screen actor and screenwriter.

Appeared in: **1958** The Reluctant Debutante; Bachelor of Hearts (US 1962). **1959** Expresso Bongo (US 1960). **1961** Very Important Person (aka A Coming-Out Party—US 1962). **1963** Mystery Submarine; The Punch and Judy Man. **1969** The Magic Christian (US 1970). **1970** Hello-Goodbye.

MYERS, ROBERT FRANCIS
Born: 1925. Died: July 18, 1962, Hollywood, Calif. (murdered—stabbed). Screen, stage actor and cab driver.

MYERS, SELDY
Born: 1866. Died: May 6, 1939, San Francisco, Calif. Screen, stage and radio actor.

MYLONG, JOHN
Born: 1893, Austria. Died: Sept. 8, 1975, Beverly Hills, Calif. Screen, stage and television actor. Appeared in Austrian and German films prior to going to Hollywood in 1937.

Appeared in: **1937** Conquest. **1940** Overture to Glory. **1942** Crossroads. **1943** The Moon is Down; For Whom the Bell Tolls; Hostages; The Strange Death of Adolph Hitler. **1944** Experiment Perilous. **1945** The Falcon in San Francisco; Hotel Berlin. **1946** Lost City of the Jungle (serial). **1949** Oh, You Beautiful Doll; Battleground. **1950** Annie Get Your Gun; Young Daniel Boone. **1951** Magnificent Obsession; His Kind of Woman. **1955** The Crooked Web. **1956** The Eddy Duchin Story. **1958** The Beast of Budapest; I, Mobster. **1962** The Mermaids of Tiburon.

MYRTIL, ODETTE
Born: 1898, France. Died: Nov. 19, 1978, Doylestown, Pa. (stroke). Screen, stage actress and singer.

Appeared in: **1936** Dodsworth. **1937** The Girl from Scotland Yard. **1940** Kitty Foyle. **1941** Out of the Fog. **1942** Yankee Doodle Dandy; The Pied Piper; Reunion. **1943** Assignment in Brittany; Forever and a Day. **1944** Uncertain Glory; Dark Waters. **1946** Devotion. **1949** The Fighting Kentuckian. **1951** Here Comes the Groom. **1952** A Lady Possessed.

NADAJAN
Died: Sept. 20, 1974, Hollywood, Calif. (heart attack). Screen actor. Known in clubs in an act billed as "Beauty and the Beast."

Appeared in: **1969** Justine.

NADI, ALDO
Born: 1899, Leghorn, Italy. Died: Nov. 10, 1965, Los Angeles, Calif. Screen actor, champion foil expert and author.

Appeared in: **1929** Le Tourmoi. **1943** Frenchman's Creek. **1945** To Have and Have Not.

NAGEL, ANNE (Ann Dolan)
Born: Sept. 30, 1912, Boston, Mass. Died: July 6, 1966, Los Angeles, Calif. (cancer). Screen and stage actress.

Appeared in: **1933** I Loved You Wednesday (film debut); College Humor. **1934** Stand up and Cheer. **1935** George White's 1935 Scandals. **1936** Hot Money; China Clipper; King of Hockey; Bullets or Ballots; Here Comes Carter; Love Begins at Twenty. **1937** Guns of the Pecos; The Case of the Stuttering Bishop; Footloose Heiress; Three Legionnaires; The Hoosier Schoolboy; A Bride for Henry; Escape by Night; The Adventurous Blonde; She Loved a Fireman. **1938** Saleslady; Under the Big Top; Gang Bullets; Mystery House. **1939** Convict's Code; Unexpected Father; Call a Messenger; Legion of Lost Flyers; Should a Girl Marry? **1940** Black Friday; Ma, He's Making Eyes at Me; Winners of the West (serial); Hot Steel; My Little Chicadee; Argentine Nights; Diamond Frontier; The Green Hornet (serial); The Green Hornet Strikes Again (serial). **1941** Road Agent; The Invisible Woman; Meet the Chump; Man-Made Monster; Mutiny in the Arctic; Sealed Lips; Never Give a Sucker an Even Break. **1942** Don Winslow of the Navy (serial); The Mad Doctor of Market St.; Dawn Express; Nazi Spy Ring; Stagecoach Buckaroo; The Secret Code (serial). **1943** Women in Bondage. **1946** Murder in the Music Hall; Traffic in Crime. **1947** Hucksters; Blondie's Holiday; The Trap; The Spirit of West Point. **1948** Don't Trust Your Husband. **1949** Prejudice; The Stratton Story; Every Gal Should be Married; Family Honeymoon; Homecoming.

NAGEL, BETH (Elizabeth Heckor)
Born: Apr. 9, 1877, Chicago, Ill. Died: Oct. 29, 1936, Beverly Hills, Calif. (kidney disease). Screen actress. Entered films during silents.

Appeared in: **1937** Mountain Justice.

NAGEL, CONRAD
Born: Mar. 16, 1897, Keokuk, Iowa. Died: Feb. 24, 1970, New York, N.Y. Screen, stage, radio, television actor and film director. Divorced from actress Ruth Helms (dec.), actress Lynn Merrick and Michel Coulson Smith. In 1940 he received a Special Academy Award for his work on the Motion Picture Relief Fund.

Appeared in: **1919** The Lion and the Mouse; Red Head; Little Women. **1920** Unseen Forces; The Fighting Chance; Midsummer Madness. **1921** What Every Woman Knows; The Lost Romance; A Fool's Paradise; Sacred and Profane Love. **1922** The Impossible Mrs. Bellew; Nice People; Hate; The Ordeal; Saturday Night; Singed Wings. **1923** The Rendezvous; Lawful Larceny; Bella Donna; Grumpy. **1924** Three Weeks; Tess of the D'Urbervilles; The Snob; Married Flirts; Name the

Man; The Rejected Woman; Sinners in Silk; So This Is Marriage. **1925** Sun-Up; The Only Thing; Cheaper to Marry; Pretty Ladies; Lights of Old Broadway; Excuse Me. **1926** The Waning Sex; Tin Hats; The Exquisite Sinner; Memory Lane; Dance Madness; There You Are. **1927** Quality Street; The Hypnotist; Slightly Used; The Jazz Singer; Heaven on Earth; The Girl from Chicago; London After Midnight. **1928** The Mysterious Lady; If I Were Single; Glorious Betsy; Caught in the Fog; The Terror; Tenderloin; Diamond Handcuffs; The Michigan Kid; State Street Sadie; The Divine Woman. **1929** Dynamite; Red Wine; The Idle Rich; Kid Gloves; The Kiss; Thirteenth Chair; The Sacred Flame; Hollywood Revue of 1929; The Redeeming Sin. **1930** Redemption; The Ship from Shanghai; Numbered Men; Second Wife; DuBarry; Woman of Passion; One Romantic Night; A Lady Surrenders; Free Love; The Divorcee; Today. **1931** The Right of Way; East Lynne; Bad Sister; The Reckless Hour; Son of India; Three Who Loved; Hell Divers; The Pagan Lady. **1932** The Man Called Back; Divorce in the Family; Kongo; Fast Life. **1933** The Constant Woman (aka Auction in Souls and Hell in a Circus); Ann Vickers. **1934** Dangerous Corner; Marines Are Coming. **1935** One Hour Late; Death Flies East; One New York Night. **1936** Ball at the Savoy; Wedding Present; Yellow Cargo; Girl from Mandalay. **1937** Bank Alarm; Love Takes Flight; Navy Spy; The Gold Racket. **1939** The Mad Express (aka Juarez and Maximilian). **1940** I Want a Divorce; One Million B.C. (narr.). **1944** They Shall Have Faith (aka Forever Yours); Dangerous Money (narr.). **1945** The Adventures of Rusty. **1947** The Vicious Circle. **1948** Stage Struck; The Woman in Brown. **1949** Dynamite. **1955** All That Heaven Allows. **1957** Hidden Fear. **1959** Stranger in My Arms; The Man Who Understood Women. **1974** That's Entertainment (film clips).

NAGIAH, V.
Born: 1903, India. Died: Dec. 30, 1973, Madras. Screen actor, film director and singer.

Appeared in: **1930** Gruhalakshmi (film debut).

NAGY, BILL
Born: Canada. Died: Jan. 19, 1973, London, England. Screen, stage, radio and television actor.

Appeared in: **1955** The Brain Machine (US 1956); Joe MacBeth (US 1956). **1956** Assignment Redhead (aka Million Dollar Manhunt-US 1962). **1957** High Tide at Noon; Accused (aka Mark of the Hawk—US 1958); Across the Bridge. **1959** First Man Into Space; I Was Monty's Double (aka Hell, Heaven or Hoboken). **1960** Surprise Package. **1961** Never Take Candy from a Stranger; The Boy Who Stole a Million. **1962** The Road to Hong Kong. **1963** The Girl Hunters. **1964** Goldfinger. **1965** Those Magnificent Men in Their Flying Machines; Where the Spies Are (US 1966). **1967** Battle Beneath the Earth (US 1968); The Man Outside; A Countess from Hong Kong. **1968** Subterfuge. **1969** The Adding Machine. **1970** The Revolutionary.

NAIDOO, BOBBY
Born: 1927, South Africa. Died: July 6, 1967, London, England. Black screen, stage and television actor.

Appeared in: **1960** The Criminal (aka The Concrete Jungle—US 1962). **1963** Nine Hours to Rama.

NAINBY, ROBERT
Born: Feb. 17, 1869, Dublin, Ireland. Died: Feb. 17, 1948, England? Screen and stage actor.

Appeared in: **1934** Radio Parade of 1935 (US 1935); My Old Dutch. **1935** Dandy Dick; The Student's Romance. **1936** When Knights Were Bold (US 1942); Public Nuisance No. 1; Land Without Music (aka Forbidden Music—US 1938); Chick; All In. **1937** Wise Guys. **1938** We're Going to Be Rich.

NAISH, J. CARROL (Joseph Patrick Carrol Naish)
Born: Jan. 21, 1900, New York, N.Y. Died: Jan. 24, 1973, La Jolla, Calif. Screen, stage, radio, vaudeville and television actor. Married to actress Gladys Heaney. Nominated for 1945 Academy Award for Best Supporting Actor in A Medal for Benny and in 1943 for Sahara.

Appeared in: **1930** Cheer Up and Smile; Good Intentions; Scotland Yard. **1931** Royal Bed; Gun Smoke; Kick In; Homicide Squad. **1932** The Hatchet Man; The Conquerors; Cabin in the Cotton; Famous Ferguson Case; Crooner; Tiger Shark; No Living Witness; The Kid from Spain; Two Seconds; It's Tough to be Famous; Beast of the City. **1933** Mystery Squadron (serial); Central Airport; World Gone Mad; The Past of Mary Holmes; The Avenger; Arizona to Broadway; The Devil's in Love; The Whirlwind; Captured; The Big Chance; Notorious But Nice; Last Trail; Mad Game; Silent Men; Elmer the Great; No Other Woman; Frisco Jenny; Infernal Machine. **1934** Defense Rests;

Sleepers East; What's Your Racket; Murder in Trinidad; One Is Guilty; Upper World; Hell Cat; Girl in Danger; Hell in the Heavens; Return of the Terror; The President Vanishes; Marie Galante. **1935** The Crusades; The Lives of a Bengal Lancer; Captain Blood; Special Agent; Behind the Green Lights; Black Fury; Under the Pampas Flood; Little Big Shot; Front Page Woman; Confidential. **1936** Two in the Dark; Anthony Adverse; Absolute Quiet; We Who Are About to Die; Robin Hood of El Dorado; The Charge of the Light Brigade; The Leathernecks Have Landed; Moonlight Murder; The Return of Jimmy Valentine; Exclusive Story; Charlie Chan at the Circus; Special Investigator; Ramona; Crack-Up. **1937** Song of the City; Think Fast Mr. Moto; Hideaway; Border Cafe; Bulldog Drummond Comes Back; Sea Racketeers; Thunder Trail; Night Club Scandal; Daughter of Shanghai. **1938** Her Jungle Love; Tip-Off Girls; Hunted Men; Prison Farm; Bulldog Drummond in Africa; Illegal Traffic; King of Alcatraz. **1939** King of Chinatown; Persons in Hiding; Hotel Imperial; Undercover Doctor; Beau Geste; Island of Lost Men. **1940** Typhoon; Queen of the Mob; Golden Gloves; Down Argentine Way; A Night at Earl Carroll's. **1941** The Corsican Brothers; Birth of the Blues; Blood and Sand; The Pied Piper; That Night in Rio; Mr. Dynamite; Forced Landing; Accent on Love. **1942** Dr. Renault's Secret; A Gentleman at Heart; Sunday Punch; Dr. Broadway; Jackass Mail; Tales of Manhattan; The Man in the Trunk; The Secret Code (serial). **1943** Harrigan's Kid; Good Morning Judge; Behind the Rising Sun; Calling Mr. Death; Sahara; Gung Ho!; Batman (serial). **1944** Voice in the Wind; The Monster Maker; Two-Man Submarine; Waterfront; Jungle Woman; Enter Arsene Lupin; Dragon Seed. **1945** A Medal for Benny; House of Frankenstein; The Southerner; Getting Gerte's Garter; Strange Confession. **1946** The Beast with Five Fingers; Bad Bascomb; Humoresque. **1947** Carnival in Costa Rica; The Fugitive. **1948** Joan of Arc; The Kissing Bandit. **1949** Canadian Pacific; The Midnight Kiss. **1950** Annie Get Your Gun; Black Hand; Please Believe Me; The Toast of New Orleans; Rio Grande. **1951** Across the Wide Missouri; Mark of the Renegade; Bannerline. **1952** The Denver and Rio Grande; Clash by Night; Woman of the North Country; Ride the Man Down. **1953** Beneath the 12 Mile Reef; Fighter Attack. **1954** Sitting Bull; Saskatchewan. **1955** Hit the Deck; Rage at Dawn; The Last Command; Desert Sands; Violent Saturday; New York Confidential. **1956** Rebel in Town; Yaqui Drums. **1957** The Young Don't Cry; This Could be the Night. **1961** Force of Impulse. **1964** The Hanged Man. **1965** An Evening with Batman and Robin. **1971** Dracula vs. Frankenstein.

NALDI, NITA (Anita Donna Dooley)
Born: Apr. 1, 1899, New York, N.Y. Died: Feb. 17, 1961, New York, N.Y. Screen, stage and television actress.

Appeared in: **1920** Dr. Jekyll and Mr. Hyde. **1921** Experience; A Divorce of Convenience; The Last Door. **1922** Blood and Sand; Anna Ascends; Channing of the Northwest; The Man from Beyond; The Snitching Hour; Reported Missing. **1923** The Glimpses of the Moon; Lawful Larceny; The Ten Commandments; You Can't Fool Your Wife; Hollywood. **1924** A Sainted Devil; The Breaking Point; Don't Call It Love. **1925** Clothes Make the Pirate; Cobra; The Lady Who Lied; The Marriage Whirl. **1926** The Unfair Sex; The Pleasure Garden; The Mountain Eagle (aka Fear-o-God—US); The Miracle of Life. **1928** What Price Beauty?; The Model from Montmarte.

NAMARA, MARGUERITE
Born: Nov. 19, 1893, Cleveland, Ohio. Died: Nov. 3, 1974, Spain. Screen, stage actress, opera singer, composer and pianist.

Appeared in: **1921** Stolen Moments. **1930** Gypsy Blood. **1932** Carmen. **1934** Thirty Day Princess. **1935** Peter Ibbetson.

NAMU
Died: July, 1966, Seattle, Wash. (drowned). Animal screen performer (whale). The first killer whale to become a film star.

Appeared in: **1966** Namu, the Killer Whale.

NANOOK
Born: Alaska. Died: Nov., 1925, Alaska? Screen actor.

Appeared in: **1925** Nanook of the North.

NANSEN, BETTY
Born: 1876. Died: Mar. 15, 1943, Copenhagen, Denmark (pneumonia). Stage and screen actress.

Appeared in: **1915** Man Without a Country; A Woman of Impulse. **1916** For Her Son.

NAPIER, RUSSELL
Born: 1910, Australia. Died: 1975, England. Screen and stage actor.

Appeared in: **1954** Conflict of Wings; The Stranger Came Home (aka The Unholy Four—US). **1955** The Brain Machine (US 1956); Little Red Monkey (aka The Case of the Red Monkey—US); The Blue Peter (aka Navy Heroes—US 1959). **1956** The Last Man in Tang?; The Man in the Road (US 1957). **1957** The Shiralee; Robbery Under Arms (US 1958). **1958** A Night to Remember; Tread Softly Stranger (US 1959). **1960** The Angry Silence; Hell Is a City. **1961** Francis of Assisi; The Mark. **1962** Mix Me a Person; H.M.S. Defiant (Damn the Defiant—US). **1963** Man in the Middle (US 1964—aka The Winston Affair). **1967** It. **1968** Nobody Runs Forever (aka The High Commissioner—US); Twisted Nerve (US 1969); The Blood Beast Terror (aka The Vampire Beast Craves Blood—US 1969).

NARCISO, GRAZIA
Died: Dec. 10, 1967. Screen actress.

Appeared in: **1948** The Time of Your Life; Madonna of the Desert; Music Man. **1950** Black Hand; Between Midnight and Dawn; September Affair. **1951** Up Front. **1954** Three Coins in the Fountain. **1957** Dragstrip Girl.

NARDELLI, GEORGE
Died: Sept. 15, 1973. Screen actor.

Appeared in: **1924** Galloping Hoofs (serial). **1933** Cocktail Hour. **1934** Another Wild Idea (short). **1956** Around the World in 80 Days. **1958** Lafayette Escadrille.

NARES, ANNA
Born: 1870. Died: Dec. 19, 1916, Flushing, N.Y. Screen actress. Appeared in Gaumont Film Co. films.

NARES, OWEN (Owen Ramsay)
Born: Aug. 11, 1888, Maiden Erlegh, England. Died: July 30, 1943, Brecon, Wales. Screen and stage actor. Entered films in 1913.

Appeared in: **1913** His Choice. **1914** Dandy Donovan, The Gentleman Cracksman. **1916** Just a Girl; Milestones; The Real Thing at Last. **1917** The Sorrows of Satan; The Labour Leader; One Summer's Day; Flames. **1918** God Bless Our Red, White and Blue; The Elder Miss Blossom (aka Wanted a Wife—US); Onward Christian Soldiers; The Man Who Won; Tinker, Tailor, Soldier, Sailor. **1919** Edge O'Beyond; Gamblers All. **1920** The Last Rose of Summer; All the Winners; A Temporary Gentleman. **1921** For Her Father's Sake. **1922** The Faithful Heart; Brown Sugar. **1923** The Indian Love Lyrics; Young Lochinvar. **1924** Miriam Rozella. **1927** This Marriage Business; His Great Moment (aka The Sentence of Death). **1930** Loose Ends; The Middle Watch. **1931** The Woman Between (aka The Woman Decides—US 1932); Sunshine Susie (aka The Office Girl—US 1932). **1932** Frail Women; Aren't We All?; The Impassive Footman (aka Woman in Bondage—US); The Love Contract; There Goes the Bride; Where Is This Lady? **1933** Discord; One Precious Night. **1934** The Private Life of Don Juan. **1935** Royal Cavalcade (aka Regal Cavalcade—US); I Give My Heart. **1936** Head Office. **1937** The Show Goes On. **1941** The Prime Minister.

NARVAEZ, SARA
Born: Nicaragua. Died: Dec., 1935, Mexico City, Mexico. Screen, stage, vaudeville and radio actress.

NASH, EUGENIA
Born: 1866. Died: Apr. 8, 1937, Culver City, Calif. Screen actress. Mother of Ted Healy (dec. 1937).

NASH, FLORENCE
Born: 1888, Troy, N.Y. Died: Apr. 2, 1950, Los Angeles, Calif. Screen, stage and vaudeville actress. Sister of actress Mary Nash (dec. 1976).

Appeared in: **1939** The Women.

NASH, GEORGE FREDERICK
Born: 1873. Died: Dec. 31, 1944, Amityville, N.Y. Screen and stage actor. Married to stage actress Julia Hay (dec. 1937).

Appeared in: **1922** The Face in the Fog; The Valley of Silent Men; When Knighthood Was in Flower. **1923** Under the Red Robe. **1924** The Confidence Man; Janice Meredith. **1925** A Man Must Live. **1926** The Gret Gatsby; The Song and Dance Man. **1933** Oliver Twist; Fighting Texans; Phantom Broadcast. **1943** Sixteen Fathoms Deep; Mystery Liner; Blue Steel; City Limits.

NASH, JUNE
Born: 1911. Died: Oct. 8, 1979, Hampton Bays, N.Y. Screen actress.

Appeared in: **1929** Daughters of Desire; Strange Cargo; Dynamite. **1930** Their Own Desire; Madam Satan. **1932** Two Kinds of Woman.

NASH, MARY (Mary Ryan)
Born: Aug. 15, 1885, Troy, N.Y. Died: Dec. 3, 1976, Brentwood, Calif. Screen and stage actress. Sister of actress Florence Nash (dec. 1950). Divorced from actor Jose Ruben (dec. 1969).

Appeared in: **1934** Uncertain Lady (film debut). **1935** College Scandal. **1936** Come and Get It. **1937** The King and the Chorus Girl; Easy Living; Wells Fargo; Heidi. **1939** The Little Princess; The Rains Came. **1940** Charlie Chan in Panama; Sailor's Lady; Gold Rush Maisie; The Philadelphia Story. **1941** Men of Boys Town. **1942** Calling Dr. Gillespie. **1943** The Human Comedy. **1944** Cobra Woman; The Lady and the Monster; In the Meantime, Darling. **1945** Yolanda and the Thief. **1946** Monsieur Beaucaire; Swell Guy; Till the Clouds Roll By.

NASH, MARY EVELYN
Died: June 28, 1965, Paramus, N.J. Stage and screen actress. Do not confuse with actress Mary Nash (dec. 1976).

NAT, LUCIEN
Born: 1895, France. Died: July, 1972, France? Screen, stage and television actor.

Appeared in: **1938** The Tender Enemy. **1943** The Heart of a Nation. **1950** The Paris Waltz. **1959** Die Gans von Sedan (US 1962). **1962** Therese Desqueyroux (aka Therese—US 1963). **1964** Les Amities Particulieres (aka This Special Friendship—US 1967).

NATHEAUX, LOUIS
Born: 1898, Pine Bluff, Ark. Died: Aug. 23, 1942, Los Angeles, Calif. Screen actor.

Appeared in: **1921** Passing Thru. **1922** The Super Sex. **1924** The Fast Set. **1926** Man Bait; Risky Business; Sunny Side Up. **1927** The Country Doctor; Dress Parade; Harp in Hock; Fighting Love; King of Kings; My Friend from India; Turkish Delight. **1928** Stand and Deliver; Midnight Madness; A Ship Comes In; Tenth Avenue; The Cop; Four Walls; Stool Pigeons; Ned McCobb's Daughter. **1929** Broadway Babies; Weary River; Why Be Good?; Girls Gone Wild; Mexicali Rose. **1930** Madame Satan; Big Money; The Big House; The Squealer; Lightnin'; This Mad World. **1931** Secret Six; Bad Girl; Transatlantic; Young as You Feel; Reckless Living; Street Scene. **1932** Behind the Mask. **1933** Gambling Ship. **1935** Freckles; Slightly Static (short); The Four-Star Boarder (voice only—short); Southern Exposure (short); Hot Money (short). **1936** Murder on the Roof; Modern Times; Captain Calamity; Yours for the Asking; Go Get 'Em Haines. **1937** Missing Witnesses.

NATRO, JIMMY
Born: 1908. Died: Jan. 31, 1946, Los Angeles, Calif. Screen actor.

NAUGHTON, CHARLIE
Born: 1887, Glasgow, Scotland. Died: Feb. 11, 1976, London, England. Screen, stage actor and music hall entertainer. Appeared with Jimmy Gold (dec. 1967) as part of comedy team of "Naughton and Gold." The team appeared in "Crazy Gang" films and stage presentations with Jimmy Nervo (dec. 1975), Teddy Knox (dec. 1974), Bud Glanagan (dec. 1968), and Chesney Allen. See Jimmy Gold listing re "Crazy Gang" films.

"Naughton and Gold" appeared in: **1933** Sign Please (short); My Lucky Star. **1935** Cock O' the North. **1936** Highland Fling. **1937** Wise Guys. **1943** Down Melody Lane.

NAVARRO, CARLOS
Born: Feb. 24, 1922, Mexico. Died: Feb. 13, 1969, Mexico City, Mexico. Screen and television actor.

Appeared in: **1956** The Brave One. **1962** La Estrella Vacia (The Empty Star); Other Mexican film, Dona Perfecta.

NAVARRO, JESUS GARCIA
Born: 1913, Mexico. Died: Sept., 1960, Mexico City, Mexico (heart attack). Stage and screen actor.

Appeared in: **1952** The Young and the Damned.

NAZARRO, CLIFF
Born: Jan. 31, 1904, New Haven, Conn. Died: Feb. 18, 1961. Screen, stage and vaudeville actor.

Appeared in: **1927** Cliff Nazarro and the Two Marjories (short). **1936** Romance Rides the Range. **1938** A Desperate Adventure; Outside of Paradise. **1939** King of the Turf; St. Louis Blues; Forged Passport. **1940** Arise, My Love. **1941** Mr. Dynamite; Rookies on Parade; World Premiere; Dive Bomber; You'll Never Get Rich; In Old Colorado; Artists and Models Abroad; Sailors on Leave; Night of January 16th;

Melody for Three; Blondie Goes to College. **1942** Pardon My Stripes; Call of the Canyon; Hillbilly Blitzkrieg; Rhythm Parade. **1943** Shantytown. **1944** Swing Hostess; I'm from Arkansas; Trocadero. **1946** Ding Dong Williams; Gentleman Joe Palooka.

NAZIMOVA, ALLA (Alla Lavendera)
Born: June 4, 1879, Yalta, Crimea, Russia. Died: July 13, 1945, Los Angeles, Calif. (coronary thrombosis). Screen, stage actress, film producer and screenwriter.

Appeared in: **1916** War Brides (film debut). **1918** Revelation; Eye for Eye; Toys of Fate. **1919** The Red Lantern; The Brat; Out of the Fog. **1920** Stronger Than Death; Billions; Heart of a Child. **1921** Madame Peacock; Camille. **1922** A Doll's House. **1923** Salome. **1924** The Madonna of the Streets. **1925** My Son; The Redeeming Sin. **1940** Escape. **1941** Blood and Sand. **1943** Song of Bernadette. **1944** Since You Went Away; In Our Time; The Bride of San Luis Rey.

NAZZARI, AMEDEO (Salvatore Amedeo Buffa)
Born: Dec. 10, 1907, Cagliari, Sardinia. Died: Nov., 1979, Rome, Italy (cardiac arrest). Screen, stage and television actor. Father of actress Evalina Nazzari.

Appeared in: **1932** Tormento (Torment). **1936** Cavalleria (Calvary). **1937** Luciano Serra, Pilota. **1938** Montevergine; Lancieri di Savoia. **1940** Il Cavaliere Senza Nome; La Grande Luce (The Great Light); Caravaggio. **1941** La Cena delle Beffe (The Jester's Supper); Scampolo. **1942** Bengasi. **1943** Donna della Montagna; Il Romanzo di un Giovane Povero (The Romance of a Poor Young Man). **1946** Il Bandito (The Bandit—US 1949); Un Giorno nella Vita. **1947** La Figlia del Capitano (The Captain's Daughters), Il Lupo della Sila (The Wolf of Sila—US 1950). **1951** The Brigand. **1952** Il Brigante di Tacca del Lupo; Sensualita (US 1954); Processo alla Citta; Brief Rapture; The Life of Donizetti. **1953** Un Marito per Anna Zaccheo (A Husband for Anna); Lure of the Sila; Of Love and Bandits; Times Gone By (aka The Vise). **1956** Le Notti di Cabiria (Nights of Cabiria—US 1957). **1957** We Are All Assassins (aka We Are All Murderers). **1958** Anna di Brooklyn; The Ten Commandments. **1959** The Naked Maja; Labyrinth; Carmen, la de Ronda (aka The Devil Made a Woman—US 1962). **1960** Fast and Sexy. **1961** I Fratelli Corsi; Antinea, L'amante della Citta Sepolta (aka Journey Beneath the Desert—US 1967); I due Nemici (aka The Best of Enemies—US 1962). **1962** Nefertite, Regina del Nilo (aka Queen of the Nile—US 1964); La Leggenda de Fra Diavolo. **1963** Le Monachine (The Little Nuns—US 1965). **1965** Juliet of the Spirits. **1966** The Poppy Is Also a Flower. **1969** Le Clan des Siciliens (The Sicilian Clan—US 1970). **1972** The Valachi Papers.

NEAL, FRANK
Born: 1917. Died: May 8, 1955, Astoria, N.Y. (auto accident). Black screen actor and dancer.

Appeared in: **1943** Stormy Weather. **1955** Three in the Round (short).

NEAL, TOM
Born: Jan. 28, 1914, Evanston, Ill. Died: Aug. 7, 1972, North Hollywood, Calif. (natural causes). Screen actor. Divorced from non-professional Patricia Neal (dec. 1958) and actress Vicki Lane. Later married to Gail Evatt whom he was convicted of slaying in 1965.

Appeared in: **1938** Out West with the Hardys; The Great Heart (short—aka Father Damien the Leper Priest). **1939** Four Girls in White; Within the Law; Burn 'Em Up O'Connor; Another Thin Man; 6000 Enemies; They All Come Out; Joe and Ethel Turp Call on the President; Honolulu; Stronger Than Desire; plus the following shorts: Prophet Without Honor (aka Matthew Fontaine); Money to Loan; Help Wanted. **1940** Andy Hardy Meets Debutante; Sky Murder; The Courageous Dr. Christian; Jack Pot (short). **1941** Under Age; To Sergeant Mulligan; Jungle Girl (serial). **1942** Top Sergeant Mulligan; Flying Tigers; Bowery at Midnight; The Miracle Kid; Ten Gentlemen from West Point; One Thrilling Night; Pride of the Yankees. **1943** Air Force; No Time for Love; Rear Gunner; China Girl; Behind the Rising Sun; Good Luck, Mr. Yates; Klondike Kate; There's Something About a Soldier; She Has What It Takes. **1944** Thoroughbreds; Unwritten Code; Two Man Submarine; The Racket Man. **1945** Crime, Inc.; First Yank Into Tokyo; Detour. **1946** The Unknown; Club Havana; The Brute Man; Blonde Alibi; My Dog Shep. **1947** The Case of the Babysitter; The Hat Box Mystery. **1948** Beyond Glory. **1949** Red Desert; Apache Chief; Amazon Quest; Bruce Gentry (serial). **1950** Radar Secret Service; Joe Palooka in Humphrey Takes a Chance; King of the Bullwhip; Train to Tombstone; Everybody's Dancing; Call of the Klondike; I Shot Billy the Kid. **1951** G.I. Jane; Let's Go Navy!; Danger Zone; Navy Bound; Stop That Cab; Fingerprints Don't Lie; Varieties on Parade. **1952** The Dalton's Women; The Dupont Story. **1953** The Great Jesse James Raid.

NEASON, HAZEL
Died: Jan. 24, 1920. Screen actress. Married to film producer and actor Albert E. Smith (dec. 1958).

Appeared in: **1911** A Friendly Marriage; By Way of Mr. Browning; Their Charming Mama; Aunt Hulda, the Matchmaker.

NEDD, JEROME
Born: 1922. Died: Jan. 26, 1976. Screen actor, film director, film producer and writer.

NEDD, STUART
Died: Mar. 5, 1971. Screen actor.

Appeared in: **1953** The Glory Brigade. **1955** Illegal.

NEDELL, BERNARD (Bernard Jay Nedell)
Born: Oct. 14, 1898, New York, N.Y. Died: Nov. 23, 1972, Hollywood, Calif. Screen and stage actor. Son of stage actors William Nedell (dec.) and Rose Speyer (dec. 1944). Married to actress Olive Blakeney (dec. 1957).

Appeared in: **1916** The Serpent (film debut). **1929** The Silver King; The Return of the Rat; A Knight in London. **1930** The Call of the Sea (US 1935); The Man from Chicago (US 1931). **1931** Shadows (US 1936). **1932** Innocents of Chicago (aka Why Saps Leave Home—US). **1933** Her Imaginary Lover. **1934** Girl in Possession. **1935** Lazybones; Heat Waves (US 1936). **1936** Terror on Tiptoe; Man Who Could Work Miracles (US 1937); First Offense. **1937** The Shadow Man; Plunder in the Air. **1938** Oh Boy!; Mr. Moto's Gamble; Exposed; Come Across (short). **1939** Lucky Night; They All Come Out; Secret Service of the Air; Some Like It Hot; Fast and Furious; Angels Wash Their Faces; Those High Grey Walls. **1940** Rangers of Fortune; Slightly Honorable; Strange Cargo; So You Won't Talk. **1941** Ziegfeld Girl. **1942** Ship Ahoy. **1943** The Desperadoes; Northern Pursuit. **1944** Lucky Cowboy (short); Maisie Goes to Reno; One Body Too Many. **1945** Allotment Wives. **1946** Crime Doctor's Man Hunt; Behind Green Lights. **1947** Monsieur Verdoux. **1948** Albuquerque; The Loves of Carmen. **1960** Heller in Pink Tights. **1972** Hickey and Boggs.

NEFF, RALPH
Died: Feb. 27, 1973. Screen actor.

Appeared in: **1955** The Man with the Golden Arm. **1956** The Man Who Knew Too Much. **1958** The Last of the Fast Guns. **1960** Cage of Evil. **1961** The Case of Patty Smith (aka The Shame of Patty Smith). **1963** For Love or Money.

NEGAS, CHRISTOS
Born: 1946, Zakynthos, Greece. Died: June 21, 1981, Cape Sounion, Anavissos, Greece (heart attack). Screen actor.

Appeared in: **1965** The Red Lanterns (film debut).

NEGIN, KOLIA
Born: 1886, Kiev, Russia. Died: Mar. 4, 1947, San Francisco, Calif. Screen actor and concert singer.

NEGRETE, JORGE
Born: 1911, Mexico. Died: Dec. 5, 1953, Los Angeles, Calif. (cirrhosis of liver). Mexican screen, stage actor and singer.

Appeared in: **1938** La Madrina del Diablo (The Devil's Godmother). **1939** Perjura; El Cemetario de las Aquilas (The Eagles' Cemetary); Juntos Pero No Revueltos (United But Not Mixed). **1943** Silk, Blood and Sun; Ay Jalisco No te Rajes; Asi Se Quiere En Jalisco. **1944** Tierra de Pasiones.

NEILAN, MARSHALL
Born: 1891, San Bernardino, Calif. Died: Oct. 26, 1958, Woodland Hills, Calif. (cancer). Screen actor, film director, film producer and screenwriter. Divorced from actress Blanche Sweet.

Appeared in: **1911** American Film Mfg. Co. films. **1912** The Reward of Valour; The Weaker Brother; The Stranger at Coyote. **1913** Judith of Bethulia; When Women are Police; The Rude and the Boob; The Tenderfoot's Luck; A Busy Day in the Jungle; Coupon Courtship; The Peace Offering; The Mission of a Bullet; A Mountain Tragedy; Fatty's Deception; Jones' Jonah Day; The Hash House Count; The Fired Cook; The Manicurist and the Mutt; Toothache. **1914** The Tattered Duke; The Deadly Battle at Hicksville; The Slavery of Foxicus; Only One Skirt. **1915** Rags; A Girl of Yesterday; Cupid Backs the Winners; Love, Oil and Grease; The Winning Whiskers; Madam Butterfly. **1916** Men and Women; The House of Discord; The Wedding Gown; Classmates; Calamity Anne; Guardian; The Crisis. **1919** Daddy Long Legs. **1923** Broadway Gold; Souls for Sale. **1957** A Face in the Crowd.

NEILDENDAM, SIGRID
Born: Denmark. Died: Jan. 26, 1955, Copenhagen, Denmark. Screen and stage actor.

Appeared in: **1948** Day of Wrath.

NEILL, JAMES
Born: Dec. 28, 1860, Savannah, Ga. Died: Mar. 16, 1931, Glendale, Calif. (heart trouble). Screen and stage actor. Married to actress Edythe Chapman (dec. 1948).

Appeared in: **1914** The Man from Home; Rose of the Rancho. **1915** The Cheat; The Warrens of Virginia. **1916** Maria Rose; The Dream Girl; Oliver Twist. **1917** The Bottle Imp; Joan the Woman. **1918** Sandy. **1919** Men, Women and Money; Everywoman. **1920** The Paliser Case. **1921** Bits of Life; Dangerous Curve Ahead; A Voice in the Dark. **1922** Dusk to Dawn; The Heart Specialist; Her Husband's Trademark; Our Leading Citizen; Saturday Night; Manslaughter. **1923** The Thrill Chaser; Ten Commandments; The Lonely Road; Nobody's Money; Salomy Jane; Scars of Jealousy; The World's Applause. **1924** A Man's Mate. **1925** Any Woman; The Crimson Runner; New Brooms; Thank You. **1926** A Desperate Moment. **1927** King of Kings. **1928** The Border Patrol; Love Hungry; Three-Ring Marriage. **1929** Idle Rich. **1930** Shooting Straight; Only the Brave. **1931** Man to Man.

NEILL, RICHARD R.
Born: 1876, Philadelphia, Pa. Died: Apr. 8, 1970, Woodland Hills, Calif. Stage and screen actor.

Appeared in: **1914** The Active Life of Dolly of the Dailies (serial). **1919** The Great Gamble (serial). **1920** The Whirlwind (serial). **1922** Go Get 'Em Hutch (serial); Jan of the Big Snows. **1923** A Clouded Name; Sinner or Saint. **1924** Trail of the Law; The Heritage of the Desert; Wanderer of the Wasteland; The Fighting Coward. **1925** Tumbleweeds; Peggy of the Secret Service; Percy. **1926** Born to the West; Whispering Smith; Satan Town. **1927** Bulldog Pluck; Galloping Thunder; Code of the Cow Country; The Fightin' Comeback; King of Kings; Somewhere in Sonora; The Trunk Mystery. **1928** Beyond the Sierras; The Law's Lash; The Desert of the Lost; The Bushranger.

NEILL, ROY WILLIAM (Roland de Gostrie)
Born: 1887, Queenstone Harbor, Ireland. Died: Dec. 14, 1946, London, England (heart attack). Screen, stage actor, film director and producer.

Appeared in: **1913** The Big Sister. **1915** The Mother Instinct. **1918** The Price Mark; Flare-Up Sal.

NEILSON-TERRY, DENNIS
Born: 1895. Died: July 12, 1932, Bulawayo, South Africa (double pneumonia). Screen, stage actor, stage producer and stage manager. Son of actor Fred Terry (dec. 1933) and stage actress Julia Neilson (dec. 1959). Brother of actress Phyllis Neilson-Terry (dec. 1977). Married to actress Mary Glynne (dec. 1954).

Appeared in: **1916** Her Greatest Performance. **1917** Masks and Faces. **1919** His Last Defence. **1920** The Hundredth Chance; The Magic Skin (aka Desire). **1922** The Romance of British History series including: The Flight of the King; A Story of Nell Gwynne. **1930** The House of the Arrow. **1931** 77 Park Lane. **1932** Murder at Covent Garden.

NEILSON-TERRY, JULIA
Born: June 12, 1868, London, England. Died: May 27, 1959, London, England. Screen, stage actress and stage producer. Married to stage actor Fred Terry (dec. 1933). Mother of actors Dennis Neilson-Terry (dec. 1932), and Phyllis Neilson-Terry (dec. 1977).

Appeared in: **1899** King John.

NEILSON-TERRY, PHYLLIS
Born: Oct. 15, 1892, London, England. Died: Sept. 25, 1977, London, England. Screen, stage, vaudeville and television actress. Daughter of stage actor Fred Terry (dec. 1933), and actress Julia Neilson-Terry (dec. 1959). Sister of actor Dennis Neilson-Terry (dec. 1932). Married to stage actor Cecil King (dec. 1958), and Heron Carvir.

Appeared in: **1920** Call of the Blood. **1926** Boadicea. **1930** One Family. **1958** Family Doctor (aka RX Murder—US, and aka Prescription for Murder). **1959** Look Back in Anger. **1960** Conspiracy of Hearts.

NELL, MRS. LOUISE M.
Born: 1884. Died: Nov. 1, 1944, Los Angeles, Calif. (killed—bus). Screen and stage actress.

NELSON, ANNE
Born: 1911. Died: July 6, 1948, Torrance, Calif. Screen actress.

NELSON, BILLY
Born: 1904. Died: June 12, 1979, Los Angeles, Calif. (heart attack). Screen, vaudeville actor and theatrical booker.

Appeared in: **1934** Maid in Hollywood (short); I'll be Suing You (short). **1942** I Live on Danger. **1949** Search for Danger. **1951** The Milkman. **1952** The Pride of St. Louis. **1953** Vicki; Mister Scoutmaster. **1957** Twelve Angry Men.

NELSON, DOLPH
Born: 1913. Died: Dec. 7, 1981, Los Angeles, Calif. (heart attack). Screen, radio actor, radio director and singer. Divorced from actress Sarajane Wells.

NELSON, EDDIE "SUNKIST"
Born: 1894. Died: Dec. 5, 1940, Hollywood, Calif. (heart attack). Screen and vaudeville actor.

Appeared in: **1928** Stop and Go (short).

NELSON, EVELYN
Born: 1900. Died: June 16, 1923, Los Angeles, Calif. Screen actress.

Appeared in: **1921** The Broken Spur; Cyclone Bliss; The Double O; Dead or Alive; The Recoil; A Motion to Adjourn. **1922** The Crow's Nest; A Desert Bridegroom; Two-Fisted Jefferson; Peaceful Peters. **1923** Forbidden Trail; Desert Rider.

NELSON, FRANK
Born: 1872. Died: Nov. 27, 1932, Calif. Screen actor. Do not confuse with other actors with same name.

NELSON, GORDON
Born: 1898. Died: Feb. 19, 1956, New York, N.Y. Screen and stage actor.

Appeared in: **1949** Knock on Any Door. **1950** Champagne for Caesar. **1951** The Groom Wore Spurs. **1952** My Pal Gus; The Iron Mistress; Something for the Birds. **1953** Mister Scoutmaster; The Farmer Takes a Wife; City of Bad Men.

NELSON, HAROLD
Died: Jan. 26, 1937, Los Angeles, Calif. (pneumonia). Screen actor.

Appeared in: **1928** Sisters of Eve. **1932** The Lost Special (serial).

NELSON, LOTTIE
Born: 1875. Died: May 8, 1966, Hollywood, Calif. (stroke). Screen actress. Appeared in silents.

NELSON, OZZIE (Oswald George Nelson)
Born: Mar. 20, 1906, Jersey City, N.J. Died: June 3, 1975, Hollywood, Calif. (cancer). Screen, stage, radio, television actor, film producer, director, bandleader, television producer, director and author. Married to actress Harriet Hilliard. Father of actors Rick and David Nelson.

Appeared in: **1940** A Vitaphone short. **1941** Sweetheart of the Campus. **1942** The Big Street. **1943** Strictly in the Groove; Honeymoon Lodge. **1944** Take It Big; Hi Good Lookin'. **1946** People Are Funny. **1952** Here Come the Nelsons. **1965** Love and Kisses. **1968** The Impossible Years.

NELSON, VIRGINIA (Virginia Tallent)
Born: 1911. Died: Sept. 26, 1968, Escondido, Calif. Screen actress. Daughter of actress Jane Tallent.

NERVO, JIMMY (James Nervo)
Born: 1890, England. Died: Dec. 5, 1975, London, England. Screen, music hall and stage actor. Married to dancer Minna Nervo. Appeared with Teddy Knox (dec. 1974) as part of comedy team "Nervo and Knox." The team appeared in "Crazy Gang" films and stage presentations with Charlie Naughton (dec. 1976), Jimmy Gold (dec. 1967), Bud Flanagan (dec. 1968) and Chesney Allen.

NESBIT, EVELYN See THAW, EVELYN NESBIT
The "Crazy Gang" films include: **1937** Okay for Sound. **1938** Alf's Button Afloat. **1939** The Frozen Limits. **1940** Gasbags. **1958** Life Is a Circus (US 1962). "Nervo and Knox" appeared in: **1926** Phonofilm (short). **1928** The Rising Generation. **1930** Alf's Button. **1932** Camera Cocktails (reissue of 1926 short). **1936** It's in the Bag; Skylarks. **1938** Cavalcade of the Stars.

NESBITT, JOHN
Born: Aug. 23, 1910, Victoria, B.C., Canada. Died: Aug. 10, 1960. Screen, radio actor, screenwriter and film producer.

NESBITT, MIRIAM
Born: Sept. 14, 1873, Chicago, Ill. Died: Aug. 11, 1954, Hollywood, Calif. Screen and stage actress.

Appeared in: **1911** The Three Musketeers; Mary's Masquerade; An Old Sweetheart of Mine; An Island Comedy; The Reform Candidate; The Story of Indian Ledge; Home; A Man for all That; Eleanor Cuyler; The Awakening of John Bond; The Ghost's Warning; The Girl and the Motor Boat; The Minute Man; Bob and Rowdy; The New Church Carpet; The Unfinished Letter; A Suffragette in Spite of Himself; Friday the Thirteenth; The Winds of Fate; Then You'll Remember Me; Captain Barnacle's Baby; Betty's Buttons; Her Face; The Declaration of Independence; Aida. **1912** The Lord and the Peasant; Jack and the Beanstalk; The Bank President's Son; Mother and Daughter; The Jewels; The Sunset Gun; The Artist and the Brain Specialist; Nerves and the Man; The Foundling; Helping John; A Letter to the Princess; Fog; Lady Clare. **1913** The Foreman's Treachery; A Youthful Knight; The Two Merchants; A Clue to Her Parentage; The Portrait; He Swore Off Smoking; The Princess and the Man; Leonie; The Ambassador's Daughter; The Heart of Valeska; A Daughter of Romany; Flood Tide; Keepers of the Flock; A Concerto for the Violin. **1914** Lena; The Living Dead; Sophia's Imaginary Visitor; A Question of Hats and Gowns; By the Aid of a Film; Face to Face; A Matter of Minutes; The Coward and the Man; Stanton's Last Flight; The Necklace of Rameses. **1915** The Glory of Clementina; A Theft in the Dark; The Portrait in the Attic; Killed Against Orders; Her Proper Place; A Woman's Revenge. **1917** The Last Sentence; Infidelity.

NESBITT, TOM (Thomas Nesbitt, Jr.)
Born: 1891, England? Died: Mar. 31, 1927, Johannesburg, South Africa (heart failure). Screen and stage actor. Brother of actress Cathleen Nesbitt (dec. 1982).

Appeared in: **1925** The Last Witness.

NESMITH, OTTOLA
Born: 1888. Died: Feb. 7, 1972, Hollywood, Calif. Screen, stage, radio and television actress.

Appeared in: **1915** Still Waters. **1921** Beyond Price; Wife Against Wife. **1928** The Girl-Shy Cowboy. **1935** Becky Sharp; Wings in the Dark; A Feather in Her Hat; She Gets Her Man. **1936** Three Men on a Horse. **1937** Nobody's Baby. **1938** Fool's for Scandal. **1939** The Star Maker; Television Spy. **1940** Lillian Russell; Her First Romance. **1941** The Invisible Ghost; The Deadly Game; There's Magic in Music. **1942** A Yank on the Burma Road; Mrs. Miniver; Reap the Wild Wind; Journey for Margaret. **1943** The Seventh Victim. **1944** The Return of the Vampire; The Story of Dr. Wassell; Casanova Brown; Our Hearts Were Young and Gay; Practically Yours. **1945** Love Letters; My Name is Julia Ross; Molly and Me. **1946** Cluny Brown. **1947** Buck Privates Come Home; The Late George Apley; Forever Amber; Down to Earth; Unconquered. **1949** Samson and Delilah. **1950** Sunset Boulevard. **1952** The Greatest Show on Earth; Scaramouche. **1953** The Story of Three Loves. **1954** Man Crazy. **1957** Witness for the Prosecution. **1960** From the Terrace. **1962** The Notorious Landlady. **1965** Inside Daisy Clover.

NESS, OLE M.
Born: 1888. Died: July 19, 1953, North Hollywood, Calif. Screen actor.

Appeared in: **1928** Chicago After Midnight; The Price of Fear; Skinner's Big Idea; Danger Street; Hit of the Show. **1929** Jazz Heaven; Hardboiled. **1931** The Sin of Madelon Claudet. **1933** Dawn to Dawn. **1935** The Last Days of Pompeii.

NESTELL, BILL
Born: 1895. Died: Oct. 18, 1966, Bishop, Calif. (stroke—heart attack). Screen actor.

Appeared in: **1926** Sir Lumberjack. **1928** Cheyenne Trails; Texas Flash; The Thrill Chaser; When the Law Rides. **1929** The Trail of the Horse Thieves. **1930** The Fighting Legion; The Man from Nowhere. **1932** The Shadow of the Eagle (serial). **1939** The Night Riders. **1942** Stardust on the Sage. **1947** Dangerous Venture.

NESTLE, JACK
Died: Aug. 30, 1978. Screen actor.

NEU, OSCAR F.
Born: June 22, 1886, Buffalo, N.Y. Died: Aug. 26, 1957, Crestwood, N.Y. Screen, vaudeville actor and film director. He toured in vaudeville with comedian Al Wilson. Appeared in films from 1911 to 1912.

NEUGEBAUER, ALFRED
Born: 1888, Austria? Died: Sept. 16, 1957, Vienna, Austria (stroke). Screen and stage actor.

Appeared in: **1932** Purpur und Waschblau. **1937** Thank You, Madame; The World's in Love. **1949** Operetta. **1952** Singing Angels. **1958** The Story of Vickie.

NEUMANN, KURT
Born: Apr. 5, 1908, Nuremburg, Germany. Died: Aug. 21, 1958, Hollywood, Calif. Screen actor and film director.

Appeared in: **1943** Above Suspicion; Action in the North Atlantic; Hostages; Hangmen Also Die. **1945** Counter-Attack.

NEUSSER, ERIC
Born: 1902. Died: Aug. 30, 1957, Vienna, Austria (heart attack). Screen actor and film producer. Appeared in German films.

NEVARO (Otto Willkomm)
Born: 1887. Died: Nov. 13, 1941, Milwaukee, Wis. Screen actor and acrobat. Was part of acrobatic act billed as "Mareena, Nevaro and Mareena."

NEVILLE, GEORGE
Born: Oct. 17, 1865. Died: Aug. 18, 1932, New York, N.Y. Screen, stage and vaudeville actor.

Appeared in: **1920** Way Down East (reissued in 1931). **1921** Dream Street. **1923** On the Banks of the Wabash. **1825** Scarlet Saint.

NEVILLE, HARRY
Born: 1868, Launceston, Tasmania. Died: Jan. 25, 1945, Rockville Center, N.Y. (heart attack). Screen, stage, radio actor and stage director.

Appeared in: **1916** Dimples. **1917** The Man Hater.

NEWALL, GUY
Born: 1885, England. Died: Feb. 25, 1937, London, England. Screen, stage actor, film director and screenwriter. Divorced from actress Ivy Duke with whom he appeared in films. Married to actress Dorothy Batley. Entered films with London Film Co. in 1912.

Appeared in: **1915** The Heart of Sister Ann. **1916** Trouble for Nothing; Money for Nothing; Motherlove; The Manxman; Driven (aka Desperation—US); Esther; Vice Versa. **1917** Smith. **1919** Comradeship (aka Comrades in Arms); Fancy Dress; I Will; The Garden of Resurrection. **1920** The Lure of Crooning Water; Duke's Son (aka Squandered Lives—US). **1921** The Bigamist. **1922** Beauty and the Beast (short); The Persistent Lovers; Boy Woodburn; Fox Farm; A Maid of the Silver Sea. **1923** The Starlit Garden. **1924** What the Butler Saw. **1927** The Ghost Train. **1928** Number Seventeen. **1930** The Road to Fortune. **1931** Potiphar's Wife (aka Her Strange Desire—US 1932); The Eternal Feminine. **1932** The Marriage Bond. **1936** Grand Finale. **1937** Merry Comes to Town.

NEWBERRY, HAZZARD P.
Born: 1907. Died: May 27, 1952, Chicago, Ill. Screen and stage actor. Entered films approx. 1935.

NEWBURG, FRANK
Born: 1886. Died: Nov. 11, 1969, Woodland Hills, Calif. Screen and vaudeville actor. Entered films approx. 1912.

Appeared in: **1916** The Windward Anchor; The Beloved Liar; The Iron Hand; The Grip of Crime; The Sea Lilly. **1917** Fuel of Life. **1924** Abraham Lincoln. **1925** The Sign of the Cactus; The Home Maker; Smouldering Fires; Lorraine of the Lions. **1927** Fire and Steel. **1928** The Singapore Mutiny.

NEWCOMB, MARY
Born: Aug. 2, 1897, North Adams, Mass. Died: Dec. 26, 1966, Dorchester, England. Screen and stage actress. Divorced from actor Robert Edeson (dec. 1931).

Appeared in: **1921** The Passionate Pilgrim. **1932** Frail Women; Women Who Play.

NEWCOMBE, CAROLINE
Born: 1872, Shreveport, La. Died: Dec. 17, 1941, New York, N.Y. Screen and stage actress. Appeared in early Kalem and Edison Co. films.

NEWCOMBE, JESSAMINE
Born: London, England. Died: Mar. 15, 1961, Hollywood, Calif. Screen, stage and radio actress.

NEWELL, DAVID

Born: Jan. 23, 1905, Carthage, Mo. Died: Jan. 25, 1980, Los Angeles, Calif. Screen, stage and vaudeville actor, film director and makeup artist.

Appeared in: **1929** The Hole in the Wall (film debut) Dngerous Curves; The Marriage Playground; Darkened Rooms; The Kibitzer. **1930** Murder on the Roof; Paramount on Parade; The Runaway Bride; Let's go Native; Just Like Heaven. **1931** The Flood; Woman Hungry; Ten Cents a Dance. **1932** New Morals for Old; A Woman Commands; Divorce in the Family. **1933** Hell Below; Made on Broadway. **1934** White Heat. **1935** Mutiny on the Bounty. **1936** Polo Joe; Educating Father. **1937** Artists and Models. **1938** Sergeant Murphy. **1939** Gone With the Wind; Blondie Meets the Boss.

NEWELL, WILLIAM "BILLY"

Born: 1894. Died: Feb. 21, 1967, Hollywood, Calif. Screen, stage, vaudeville and television actor.

Appeared in: **1935** Riffraff. **1936** Robinson Crusoe of Clipper Island (serial); The Voice of Bugle Ann; Libeled Lady; Navy Born; Bulldog Edition; Sitting on the Moon; The Mandarin Mystery; Happy Go Lucky; A Man Betrayed. **1937** Make Way for Tomorrow; Larceny on the Air; Beware of Ladies; Bill Cracks Down; Rhythm in the Clouds; Dangerous Holiday. **1938** Ride a Crooked Mile; Mr. Smith Goes to Washington. **1939** The Amazing Mr. Williams. **1940** City for Conquest; The Invisible Killer; Slightly Tempted; Mysterious Dr. Satan (serial); Fugitive From Justice; Hold That Woman. **1941** Caught in the Act; The Bride Came C.O.D.; Miss Polly; Three Girls About Town. **1942** Keeper of the Flame; A Tragedy at Midnight; Who is Hope Schuyler?; Get Hep to Love; Orchestra Wives; Priorities on Parade. **1944** Sing a Jingle; Kansas City Kitty. **1945** Without Love; Captain Eddie; Her Lucky Night; Out of the Depths; Stork Club; The Dolly Sisters; The Lost Weekend. **1946** Till the End of Time; The Kid from Brooklyn; The Best Years of Our Lives; Girl on the Spot. **1947** Key Witness; The Second Chance. **1948** Song of My Heart; The Fuller Brush Man. **1949** Tell It to the Judge; The Lone Wolf and His Lady. **1950** Traveling Saleswoman. **1951** Bright Victory. **1952** High Noon. **1955** Our Miss Brooks. **1957** Short Cut to Hell. **1958** Tank Force; The Missouri Traveler. **1959** High Flight; The Man Inside; Last Train from Gun Hill. **1960** Who Was That Lady?; The High-Powered Rifle.

NEWHALL, MAYO

Born: 1890. Died: Dec. 11, 1958, Burbank, Calif. Screen actor.

Appeared in: **1944** Meet Me in St. Louis. **1945** Yolanda and the Thief; Her Highness and the Bellboy. **1946** Of Human Bondage. **1948** That Lady in Ermine.

NEWILL, JAMES "JIM"

Born: Aug. 12, 1911, Pittsburgh, Pa. Died: July 31, 1975 (cancer). Screen actor and singer.

Appeared in: **1937** Something to Sing About; Renfrew of the Royal Mounted. **1939** Crashing Thru. **1940** Yukon Flight; Danger Ahead; Young People; Murder on the Yukon. **1941** The Great American Broadcast. **1942** The Falcon's Brother. **1943** The Rangers Take Over; Bombardier. **1944** Trail of Terror; Return of the Rangers; Boss of Rawhide; OutLaw Roundup; The Pinto Bandit; Spook Town; Brand of the Devil; Guns of the law. **1947** Shootin' Irons; Thundergap Outlaws.

NEWLAND, ANNA DEWEY

Born: 1881. Died: June 24, 1967, Hollywood, Calif. Screen actress, model and author.

NEWLAND, PAUL (Paul Emory Newland)

Born: June 29, 1903, Nebraska. Died: Nov. 23, 1973, Studio City, Calif. (congestive failure). Screen actor.

Appeared in: **1937** Wells Fargo. **1938** Cocoanut Grove; You and Me. **1941** The Gay Vagabond. **1942** Down Rio Grande Way. **1943** True to Life. **1944** The Adventures of Mark Twain; I'm from Arkansas; Lost in a Harem. **1945** The Man Who Walked Alone; Within These Walls. **1946** The Harvey Girls; Don Ricardo Returns. **1947** Bells of San Francisco; Dragnet. **1951** David and Bathsheba. **1952** Something to Live For; Captive City; Against All Flags. **1953** The Adventures of Captain Kidd (serial); Prisoners of the Casbah. **1954** River of No Return. **1955** Pirates of Tripoli. **1964** The Americanization of Emily. **1965** The Slender Thread. **1970** There Was a Crooked Man.

NEWMAN, ALFRED

Born: Mar. 17, 1901, New Haven, Conn. Died: Feb. 17, 1970, Los Angeles, Calif. (emphysema and complications). Composer, conductor and screen actor.

Appeared in: **1939** They Shall Have Music.

NEWMAN, ALLAN SCOTT (aka ALLEN SCOTT)

Born: 1950, New York, N.Y. Died: Nov. 20, 1978, Los Angeles, Calif. (accidental overdose of drugs and alcohol). Screen actor. Son of actor Paul Newman and Jackie Witt.

Appeared in: **1975** The Great Waldo Pepper. **1977** Fraternity Row.

NEWMAN, ANGELA

Born: 1930, Ireland. Died: Apr. 15, 1979, Dublin, Ireland. Screen, stage and radio actress. Married to actor Philip O'Flynn.

Appeared in: **1960** The Siege of Sidney Street (US 1961, aka The Siege of Hell Street).

NEWMAN, CANDY

Born: 1945. Died: June 19, 1966. Screen actress.

Appeared in: **1963** Palm Springs Weekend.

NEWMAN, HENRY "HANK"

Born: 1905. Died: July 25, 1978, Columbus, Ohio. Country western singer, screen and radio actor.

Appeared in: **1946** The Fighting Frontiersman. **1947** South of the Chisholm Trail.

NEWMAN, HORACE

Born: 1863. Died: Nov. 13, 1947, New York, N.Y. Screen and stage actor.

Appeared in: **1914** The Drama in Heyville; Three Knaves and the Heathen Chinee.

NEWMAN, JOHN K.

Born: 1864. Died: Mar. 2, 1927, New York, N.Y. Screen and stage actor.

Appeared in: **1924** Greatest Love of All.

NEWMAN, KAREN

Born: 1934. Died: Feb. 16, 1979, Burbank, Calif. (massive cerebral hemorrhage). Screen actress.

NEWMAN, LUR BARDEN

Died: Dec. 1, 1918. Screen actress. Appeared in Biograph films.

NEWMAN, NELL

Born: 1881. Died: Aug., 1931, Hollywood, Calif. (pneumonia). Screen actress.

NEWMARK, STEWART (Max Nathan)

Born: Jan. 23, 1916, California. Died: July 11, 1968, North Hollywood, Calif. (heart disease). Screen actor.

NEWSOME, CARMEN

Born: 1912. Died: July 18, 1974, Cleveland, Ohio. Black bandleader, radio and screen actor.

Appeared in: **1938** Swing; God's Stepchildren. **1939** Lying Lips; Birthright. **1940** The Notorious Elinor Lee.

NEWTON, CHARLES

Died: 1926. Screen and stage actor. Married to actress Dorrit Ashton (dec. 1936).

Appeared in: **1916-17** American Film Mfg. Co. films. **1920** The Moon Riders (serial). **1921** Red Courage; Sure Fire; Action; High Gear Jeffrey; Colorado. **1922** The Loaded Door; Western Speed. **1923** Danger; In the Palace of the King. **1924** The Iron Horse; $50,000 Reward; Vanity's Price. **1925** Riders of the Purple Sage. **1926** Yellow Fingers; Western Pluck.

NEWTON, IRVING "FIG"

Born: 1898. Died: June 13, 1980, Sherman Oaks, Calif. (heart failure). Screen and vaudeville actor.

NEWTON, RALPH

Born: 1901. Died: Mar. 14, 1977, Sawtelle, Calif. Screen actor.

NEWTON, ROBERT

Born: June 1, 1905, Shaftesbury, Dorset, England. Died: Mar. 25, 1956, Beverly Hills, Calif. (heart attack). Screen, stage and television actor. Voted one of top ten British moneymaking stars in Motion Picture Herald-Fame Poll, 1947-51.

Appeared in: **1932** Reunion. **1937** Fire Over England; Dark Journey; The Squeaker (aka Murder on Diamond Row—US); Farewell Again

(aka Troopship—US 1938); The Green Cockatoo (US 1947 aka Four Dark Hours); 21 Days (aka 21 Days Together—US 1940 and The First and the Last). **1938** Vessel of Wrath (aka The Beachcomber—US); Yellow Sands. **1939** Jamaica Inn; Dead Men Are Dangerous; Poison Pen (US 1941); Hell's Cargo (aka Dangerous Cargo—US 1940). **1940** Gaslight (aka Angel Street—US 1944); Bulldog Sees It Through; Cannel Incident (short); Busman's Honeymoon (aka Haunted Honeymoon—US). **1941** Major Barbara; Hatter's Castle. **1942** They Flew Alone (aka Wings and the Woman—US). **1944** The Happy Breed (US 1947). **1945** Henry V (US 1946). **1946** Night Boat to Dublin. **1947** Odd Man Out; Temptation Harbour (US 1949). **1948** Snowbound (US 1949); Oliver Twist (US 1951); Kiss the Blood Off My Hands. **1949** Obsession (aka The Hidden Room—US 1950). **1950** Treasure Island; Waterfront (aka Waterfront Women—US 1952). **1951** Tom Brown's School Days; Soldiers Three. **1952** Blackbeard the Pirate; Les Miserables. **1953** The Desert Rats; Androcles and the Lion. **1954** The Beachcomber (US 1955); The High and the Mighty. **1955** Long John Silver. **1956** Around the World in 80 Days.

NEWTON, THEODORE
Born: 1905, Lawrenceville, N.Y. Died: Feb. 23, 1963, Hollywood, Calif. (cancer). Screen, stage and television actor.

Appeared in: **1933** The House on 56th Street; The Working Man; Voltaire; From Headquarters; Ace of Aces; The World Changes; The Sphinx. **1934** Gambling; Blind Date; Heat Lightning; Upperworld; Now I'll Tell; A Modern Hero; Let's Try Again. **1935** Jalna. **1945** The Hidden Eyes; What Next, Corporal Hargrove? **1946** Two Years Before the Mast; Miss Susie Slagle's. **1956** The Come On; The Proud and the Profane; Friendly Persuasion; Somebody Up There Likes Me. **1959** The Story on Page One (US 1960). **1963** Dime With a Halo.

NEY, MARIE (Marie Fix)
Born: July 18, 1895, Chelsea, England. Died: Apr. 11, 1981, London, England. Screen, stage, radio and television actress. Entered films in 1930.

Appeared in: **1930** Escape. **1935** Scrooge. **1939** Jamaica Inn. **1949** Conspirator (US 1950); The Romantic Age (aka Naughty Arlette—US 1951). **1950** Seven Days to Noon. **1951** Night Was Our Friend. **1955** Simba. **1956** Yield to the Right (aka Blonde Sinner—US). **1957** The Surgeon's Knife. **1964** Witchcraft.

NIBLO, FRED, JR.
Born: Jan. 23, 1903, New York, N.Y. Died: Feb. 18, 1973, Encino, Calif. Screenwriter, author and screen actor. Son of film director and actor Fred Niblo, Sr. (dec. 1948).

Appeared in: **1930** Free and Easy. **1940** I'm Still Alive; Ellery Queen, Master Detective. **1941** Life With Henry.

NIBLO, FRED, SR. (Federico Nobile)
Born: Jan. 6, 1874, York, Nebr. Died: Nov. 11, 1948, New Orleans, La. (pneumonia). Screen, stage, vaudeville actor, film, stage director and stage producer. Father of screenwriter and actor Fred Niblo, Jr. (dec. 1973). Divorced from actress Josephine Cohan. Married to actress Enid Bennett (dec. 1969).

NICHOLLS, ANTHONY
Born: Oct. 16, 1907, Windsor, England. Died: Feb., 1977, London, England. Screen, stage and television actor.

Appeared in: **1946** The Laughing Lady (US 1950). **1948** The Guinea Pig (US 1949). **1949** The Hasty Heart. **1950** The Woman With No Name (aka Her Panelled Door—US 1951); The Dancing Years; No Place for Jennifer (US 1951); Portrait of Clare. **1951** The Franchise Affair (US 1952); High Treason (US 1952). **1952** The Woman's Angle (US 1954). **1953** Street Corner; The House of the Arrow. **1954** The Weak and the Wicked; Make Me an Offer (US 1956); Happy Ever After (aka Tonight's the Night—US); The Green Scarf (US 1955). **1958** Dunkirk; The Safecracker (US 1962). **1961** Victim (US 1962). **1962** Seven Keys; Night of the Eagle (aka Burn Witch Burn—US). **1964** The Pumpkin Eater. **1965** Othello. **1966** A Man for All Seasons. **1967** Our Mother's House; Mister Ten Percent. **1968** If (US 1969). **1969** Battle of Britain; A Walk With Love and Death. **1970** One More Time; The Walking Stick.

NICHOLS, ANNE
Born: Nov. 26, 1891, Dales Mill, Ga. Died: Sept. 15, 1966, Englewood Cliffs, N.J. Screen actress, screenwriter, playwright and author.

Appeared in: **1911** In the Hot Lands.

NICHOLS, BARBARA (Barbara Marie Nicheraeur)
Born: 1929, Mineola, N.Y. Died: Oct. 5, 1976, Hollywood, Calif. (liver ailment). Screen, stage, radio and television actress.

Appeared in: **1954** River of No Return. **1956** Miracle in the Rain; A King and Four Queens; Manfish; The Wild Party; Beyond a Reasonable Doubt. **1957** The Pajama Game; Sweet Smell of Success; Pal Joey. **1958** The Naked and The Dead; 10 North Frederick. **1959** Woman Obsessed; That Kind of Woman. **1960** Who Was That Lady?; Where the Boys Are. **1961** The George Raft Story. **1962** House of Women; The Scarface Mob. **1964** Looking for Love; Dear Heart; The Disorderly Orderly. **1965** The Human Duplicators. **1966** The Swinger. **1968** The Power. **1970** Criminal Symphony. **1973** Charley and the Angel. **1976** Won Ton Ton, the Dog That Saved Hollywood.

NICHOLS, BEATRICE
Born: 1892. Died: Sept. 26, 1970, New York, N.Y. Screen, stage and television actress.

NICHOLS, ERNEST LORING "RED"
Born: May 8, 1905, Ogden, Utah. Died: June 28, 1965, Las Vegas, Nev. (heart attack). Bandleader, screen, television and radio actor.

Appeared in: **1929** Red Nichols and His Five Pennies (short). **1935** Melody Masters (short). **1936** Red Nichols and His World Famous Pennies (short).

NICHOLS, GEORGE, JR.
Born: May 5, 1897, San Francisco, Calif. Died: Nov. 13, 1939, Los Angeles, Calif. (auto accident). Screen actor and film director. Son of actor and director George Nichols, Sr. (dec. 1927).

Appeared as a child actor in early Biograph films

NICHOLS, GEORGE, SR.
Born: 1865. Died: Sept. 20, 1927, Hollywood, Calif. Screen actor and film director. Father of actor and director George Nichols, Jr. (dec. 1939).

Appeared in: **1910** The Usurer. **1919** The Wolf; The Turn in the Road. **1920** The Greatest Question. **1921** The Fox; Live and Let Live; Shame; The Queen of Sheba; Molly O.; Oliver Twist, Jr. **1922** The Barnstormer; Don't Get Personal; Suzanna; The Pride of Palomar; The Flirt; One Glorious Day. **1923** Children of Dust; The Country Kid; Let's Go; The Miracle Makers; The Ghost Patrol; The Extra Girl; Don't Marry for Money. **1924** The Midnight Express; Secrets; The Beautiful Sinner; Daughters of Today; Geared to Go; The Red Lily; The Slanderers; East of Broadway; The Silent Strangers; The Silent Watcher. **1925** The Goose Woman; Capital Punishment; The Eagle; Proud Flesh; His Majesty, Bunker Bean; The Light of Western Stars. **1926** Bachelor Brides; Broken Hearts of Hollywood; The Timid Terror; Sea Horses; Senor Daredevil; Flames; Gigolo; Miss Nobody; Rolling Home. **1927** Ritzy; White Gold; White Flannels; Finger Prints. **1928** The Wedding March.

NICHOLS, MARGARET
Born: 1900. Died: Mar. 17, 1941, Los Angeles, Calif. (pneumonia). Screen actress. Married to film producer Hal Roach.

NICHOLS, MARJORIE J.
Died: Sept. 26, 1970, N.Y. Screen, stage and television actress.

Appeared in: **1959** North By Northwest. **1961** Splendor in the Grass.

NICHOLS, NELLIE V.
Born: 1885. Died: July 16, 1971, Los Angeles, Calif. Screen and vaudeville actress.

Appeared in: **1930** Playing Around (film debut). **1931** Women Go On Forever. **1934** Our Daily Bread. **1937** Manhattan Merry-Go-Round. **1939** Another Thin Man.

NICHOLS, PAUL "TINY"
Born: 1922. Died: Oct., 1980, Los Angeles, Calif. Screen, television actor, film and television director.

NICHOLSON, JOHN
Born: 1873, Charleston, Ill. Died: June 24, 1934, New York, N.Y. Screen and stage actor.

Appeared in: **1915** The Woman Next Door; The Danger Signal; The Politicians. **1917** Wrath; The Planter.

NICHOLSON, NORA
Born: Dec. 7, 1892, Leamington, Warwickshire, England. Died: Sept. 18, 1973, London, England. Screen, stage actress, novelist and playwright. Entered films in 1934.

Appeared in: **1949** The Blue Lagoon. **1952** Crow Hollow; Tread Softly. **1955** Raising a Riot (US 1957). **1956** A Town Like Alice (US 1957). **1957** Light Fingers; Seawife. **1958** Law and Disorder. **1959** The Captain's Table (US 1960); Upstairs and Downstairs (US 1961). **1963** The Devil Doll (US 1964); Three Lives of Thomasina. **1968** Diamonds for Breakfast.

NICHOLSON, PAUL
Born: 1877, Orange, N.J. Died: Feb. 2, 1935, Santa Monica, Calif. (influenza). Screen, stage and vaudeville actor. Appeared in vaudeville as part of the "Mimic Four" act. Entered films with American Motoscope and Biograph Co. in 1897.

Appeared in: **1921** The Woman God Changed. **1924** Married Flirts. **1925** As Man Desires; Chickie; I Want My Man; Joanna. **1926** Bachelor Brides; The Johnstown Flood; The Nervous Wreck; Up in Mabel's Room. **1927** The Broncho Twister; The Brute; Bertha the Sewing Machine Girl. **1928** The Smart Set; Port of Missing Girls. **1929** Not Quite Decent. **1930** Fox Movietone Follies of 1930. **1931** Oh! Oh! Cleopatra (short); Man to Man; Silence. **1932** Scandal for Sale. **1934** Two Alone.

NICKOLS, WALTER
Born: 1853. Died: Dec. 25, 1927, New York, N.Y. (heart trouble). Stage and screen actor.

NICOL, JOSEPH E.
Born: 1856. Died: June 1, 1926, Bernardsville, N.J. Screen, stage actor and musicial director.

NICOLETTI, LOUIS
Born: 1907. Died: Oct. 16, 1969, Hollywood, Calif. (lung illness). Screen actor and assistant film director.

Appeared in: **1951** Vengeance Valley; Across the Wide Missouri. **1953** Money From Home.

NIELSEN, ASTA (aka DIE ASTA)
Born: 1882, Copenhagen, Denmark. Died: May 24, 1972, Copenhagen, Denmark. Screen, stage actress and film producer.

Appeared in: **1910** The Abyss (film debut); Der Abgrund. **1913** Engelein. **1914** The Devil's Assistant; Lady Madcap's Way. **1921** Hamlet. **1923** Downfall; Erdgeist. **1924** Hedda Gabler. **1925** The Joyless Street. **1927** The Lusts of Mankind; Streets of Sorrow; The Tragedy of the Street. **1928** Pandora's Box; Women Without Men; Small Town Sinners; Vanina. **1934** Crown of Thorns. Other films include: The Little Angel; Miss Julie; The Black Dream; Gypsy Blood; Woman Without Country; Youthful Folly; Die Suffragette; Das Liebes A-B-C; Intoxication.

NIELSEN, HANS
Born: 1911, Hamburg, Germany. Died: 1967, Berlin, Germany. Screen and stage actor.

Appeared in: Tango Notturno; Das Geheimnis der Betty Bonn; Daphne und der Diplomat. **1938** Rote Orchideen (Red Orchids—US 1939); Heimat; Fracht von Baltimore; Kautschuk; Preussische Liebesgeschichte (Liebeslegende). **1939** Aufruhr in Damaskus (Tumult in Damascus); Dein Leben Gehoert Mir; Fasching; Alarm auf Station III. **1940** Falstaff in Wien; Trenck, der Pandur; Friedrich Schiller (Der Triumph Eines Genies). **1941** Ich Klage An. **1942** Die Nach in Venedig; Der Grosse Koenig (The Great King). **1943** Um 9 Kommt Harald; Ich Werde Dich auf Haenden Tragen; Titanic; Leichtes Blut; Der Engel mit dem Saitenspiel. **1944** Musik in Salzburg; Mein Mann darf es Nicht Wissen (aka Sabine und der Zufall). **1945** Das Kleine Hofkonzert; Der Scheiterhaufen; Dr. Phil. Doederlein. **1947** In Jenen Tagen; Herzkoenig (aka Ein Walzer ins Glueck). **1948** Die Kupferne Hochzeit; Chemie und Liebe; Unser Mittwoch Abend. **1949** Palace Scandal; Heimliches Rendezvous; Nachtwache. **1950** Kronjuwelen; Fuenf Unter Verdacht (aka Stadt im Nebel). **1951** Die Tat des Anderen; Das Spaete Maedchen. **1952** Die Spur Fuehrt Nach Berlin (Adventure in Berlin). **1953** Keepers of the Night; Die Blaue Stunde; Des Feuers Macht (speaker); Hokuspokus; Heimlich, Still und Leise; Die Geschiedene Frau; Aus Eigener Kraft (speaker). **1954** Der Erste Kuss; Geliebtes Frauelein Doktor (aka Liebesbriefe aus Mittenwald); Hochstaplerin der Liebe. **1955** Zwischenlandung in Paris; Die Heilige Luege; Meine Kinder und Ich; Roman Einer Siebzehnhaehrigen. **1956** Teufel in Seide (Devil in Silk—US 1968); Vor Sonnenuntergang (US 1961); Kleines Zelt und Grosse Liebe (Two in a Sleeping Bag—US

1964); Vergiss, Wenn Du Kannst; Hochzeit auf Immenhof; Ein Herz Kehrt Heim; Der Bauer vom Brucknerhof (aka Mein Bruder Josua). **1957** Made in Germany; Kein Auskommen mit dem Einkommen; Gluecksritter; Koenigin Luise (Queen Luise); Die Liebe Familie; Tolle Nacht; Von Allen Geliebt; Nachts im Gruenen Kakadu; Zwei Matrosen auf der Alm; Anders als Du und Ich (aka Das Dritte Geschlecht, aka The Third Sex, and aka Bewildered Youth—US 1959). **1958** Das Maedchen vom Moorhof (The Girl of the Moors—US 1961); International Counterfeiters; Zwei Herzen im Mai; Schmutziger Engel; Mann im Strom; Der Lachende Vagabund; Das Haut Einen Seemann Doch Nicht Um; Ich Werde Dich auf Haenden Tragen; Herz ohne Gnade; Gestehen Sie Dr. Corda! (Confess, Dr. Corda!—US 1961). **1959** Verbrechen Nach Schulschluss (aka The Young Go Wild—US 1962); Kriegspericht (Court Martial—US 1962); Die Feuerrote Baronesse; La Paloma; Bie der Blonden Kathrein; Das Blaue Meer und Du; Frau im Besten Mannesalter; Heimat—Deine Lieder; Bezaubernde Arabella; Die Wahrheit Ueber Rosemarie (The Truth About Rosemarie—US 1961, aka Love Now—Pay Later, and aka She Walks by Night—US). **1960** Der Jugendrichter (aka The Judge and the Sinner—US 1964); Herrin der Welt; Die Zornigen Jungen Maenner; Freddy und die Melodie der Nacht; Das Erbe von Bjoerndal; Mal Drunter—Mal Drueber; Ich Traueme von der Liebe; Gustav Adolfs Page; Gaunerserenade. **1961** Town Without Pity; Barbara. **1962** Liebling, ich Muss Dich Erschiessen; Sein Bester Freund; So Toll wie Anno Dazumal; Ein Toter Sucht Seinen Moerder; Die Tuer mit den Sieben Schloessern; Sherlock Holmes und das Halsband des Todes (Sherlock Holmes and the Deadly Necklace); Ich Kann Nicht Laenger Schweigen (aka The Tragedy of Silence); Vengeance (aka The Brain—US 1964); Ich Bin Auch nur Eine Frau (I, too, am Only a Woman—US 1966). **1963** Das Indische Tuch; Die Nacht am See; Scotland Yard Jagt Dr. Mabuse; Das Todesauge von Ceylon; Der Wuerger von Schloss Blackmoor. **1964** Das Ungerheur von London City (The Monster of London City—US 1967); Das Phantom von Soho (The Phantom of Soho—US 1967); Herrenpartie; Das Siebente Opfer. **1965** Die Holle von Manitoba (aka A Place Called Glory—US 1966); Hotel der Toten Gaeste; Die Pyramide des Sonnengottes; Der Schatz der Azteken.

NIEMEYER, JOSEPH H.
Born: 1887. Died: Sept. 27, 1965, Santa Monica, Calif. Screen, vaudeville actor and dancer.

NIESEN, GERTRUDE
Born: 1918, en route Europe to U.S. Died: Mar. 27, 1975, Hollywood, Calif. Screen, stage, vaudeville, radio actress and singer.

Appeared in: **1934** Keeps Rainin' All the Time (short). **1937** Top of the Town. **1938** Start Cheering. **1941** Rookies on Parade. **1943** He's My Guy; This Is the Army. **1948** The Babe Ruth Story.

NIGH, WILLIAM
Born: Oct. 12, 1881, Berlin, Wis. Died: Nov. 28, 1955, Burbank, Calif. Screen actor, film producer, director and screenwriter. Entered films in 1911 with Mack Sennett.

Appeared in: **1914** The Clerk; The Higher Law; A Yellow Streak; A Royal Family; Salome Jane. **1916** His Great Triumph; Life's Shadows. **1920** Democracy, the Vision Restored. **1925** Fear-Bound.

NIGHT, HARRY A. "HANK"
Born: 1847. Died: Apr. 24, 1930, Hollywood, Calif. Screen actor. Abraham Lincoln impersonator.

NILE, FLORIAN MARTINEZ
Born: 1936, Spain. Died: Jan. 8, 1959, Madrid, Spain. Screen actor.

NILE, GRACE DUNBAR
Died: Nov. 14, 1958, Lakewood, Colo? (cancer). Screen, stage and vaudeville actress.

Appeared in: **1912** Only a Miller's Daughter.

NILLSON, CARLOTTA
Born: 1878. Died: Dec. 31, 1951, New York, N.Y. Screen and stage actress.

Appeared in: **1913** Leah Kleschna.

NILSSON, ANNA Q. (Anna Querentia Nilsson)
Born: Mar. 30, 1888, Ystad, Sweden. Died: Feb. 11, 1974, Hemet, Calif. (natural causes). Screen and stage actress. Entered films in 1910.

Appeared in: **1911** Molly Pitcher. **1912** The Fraud at the Hope Mines; War's Havoc; "Fighting" Dan McCool; Under a Flag of Truce; The Siege of Petersburgh; The Prison Ship; Saved from Court Martial; The

Darling of the C.S.A.; The Grit of the Girl Telegrapher; The Confederate Ironclad; His Mother's Picture; The Farm Bully; Toll Gate Raiders. **1913** The Grim of War; Prisoners of War; The Battle of Bloody Ford; A Mississippi Tragedy; John Burns of Gettysburg; Shenandoah; Shipwrecked; The Fatal Legacy; Retribution; The Breath of Scandal; The Counterfeiter's Confederate; Uncle Tom's Cabin. **1914** A Shot in the Dark; Tell-Tale Stains; Perils of the White Lights; The Secret of the Will; A Diamond in the Rough; The Man with the Glove; The Ex-Convict; The Man in the Vault. **1915** In the Hands of the Jury; Barriers Swept Aside; The Night Operator at Buxton; The Siren's Reign; The Second Commandment; The Haunted House of Wild Isle; The Destroyer; A Sister's Burden; Rivals; The Haunting Fear; Hiding from the Law; The Regeneration; Voices in the Dark; The Night of the Embassy Ball; Barbara Frietchie. **1916** Who's Guilty? (serial); The Scarlet Road; Puppets of Fate (serial); Her Surrender. **1917** Infidelity; The Moral Code; The Inevitable; Seven Keys to Baldpate; Over There; The Silent Master. **1918** Venus in the East; Heart of the Sunset; The Trail to Yesterday; No Man's Land; In Judgement Of; Vanity Pool. **1919** Cheating Cheaters; The Way of the Strong; The Love Burglar; Her Kingdom of Dreams; Soldiers of Fortune; A Very Good Young Man. **1920** The Thirteenth Commandment; The Luck of the Irish; The Toll Gate; The Figurehead; One Hour Before Dawn; The Fighting Chance; In the Heart of a Fool; The Brute Master. **1921** What Women Will Do; Without Limit; The Oath; Why Girls Leave Home; Varmlanningarna; The Lotus Eater; Ten Nights in a Bar Room. **1922** A Trip to Paramountown (short); Three Live Ghosts; The Man from Home; Pink Gods; Hearts Aflame. **1923** Adam's Rib; The Isle of Lost Ships; Souls for Sale; The Rustle of Silk; The Spoilers; Hollywood; Ponjola; Thundering Dawn; Innocence; Enemies of Children; Judgement of the Storm. **1924** Half-a-Dollar Bill; Painted People; Flowing Gold; Between Friends; Broadway After Dark; The Side Show of Life; The Fire Patrol; Vanity's Price; Inez from Hollywood. **1925** The Top of the World; If I Marry Again; One Way Street; The Talker; Winds of Chance; The Splendid Road; The Breath of Scandal; The Viennese Medley. **1926** Too Much Money; Her Second Chance; The Greater Glory; Miss Nobody; Midnight Lovers. **1927** The Masked Woman; Easy Pickings; Babe Comes Home; Lonesome Ladies; Sorrell and Son; The Thirteenth Juror. **1928** Blockade; The Whip. **1933** The World Changes. **1934** School for Girls; The Little Minister. **1935** Wanderer of the Wasteland. **1937** Behind the Criminal (short). **1938** Prison Farm; Paradise for Three. **1941** They Died With Their Boots On; The Trial of Mary Dugan; Riders of the Timberline; The People vs. Dr. Kildare. **1942** Crossroads; Girl's Town; The Great Man's Lady; I Live on Danger. **1943** Headin' for God's Country; Cry Havoc. **1945** The Sailor Takes a Wife; The Valley of Decision. **1946** The Secret Heart. **1947** The Farmer's Daughter; Cynthia; It Had to Be You. **1948** Fighting Father Dunne; Every Girl Should be Married; The Boy with Green Hair; In the Good Old Summertime. **1949** Adam's Rib; Malaya. **1950** Sunset Boulevard; The Big Hangover; Grounds for Marriage. **1951** Show Boat; An American in Paris; The Law and the Lady; The Unknown Man. **1953** The Great Diamond Robbery. **1954** Seven Brides for Seven Brothers.

NINCHI, CARLO
Born: 1896, Italy. Died: May 1, 1974, Italy. Screen, stage and television actor.

Appeared in: **1931** Terra Madre. **1939** La Wally; Scipio Africanus. **1947** The King's Jester; Marco Visconti; Cavalleria Rusticana. **1948** The Spirit and the Flesh. **1949** Il Grido della Terra (The Earth Cries Out). **1950** Woman; Bullet for Stefano. **1952** The Island of Procida; Beauty and the Devil. **1953** L'Ennemi Public No. 1 (aka The Most Wanted Man—US 1962). **1954** Anita Garibaldi; Side Street Story; Sins of Rome. **1956** Queen of Babylon. **1960** La Ciociara (aka Two Women—US 1961). **1961** Constantino il Grande (aka Constantine and the Cross—US 1962). **1963** La Tigre dei Sette Mari (Tiger of the Seven Seas—US 1964).

NIXON, ARUNDEL
Born: 1907, England. Died: Apr. 4, 1949, Brisbane, Australia (cerebral hemorrhage). Screen actor.

NIXON, CLINT (Clinton James Hecht)
Born: 1906. Died: Oct. 22, 1937, Hollywood, Calif. Screen actor.

NOA, JULIAN
Born: 1879. Died: Nov. 26, 1958, New York, N.Y. Screen, stage, radio and television actor. Married to actress Jane Salisbury.

Appeared in: **1956** Pacific Destiny.

NOAKOVA, JANA
Born: 1948, Czechoslovakia. Died: Dec. 4, 1968, Prague, Czechoslovakia. Screen actress.

NOBLE, RAY
Born: 1907, Brighton, England. Died: Apr. 3, 1978, London, England (cancer). Screen, radio actor, orchestra leader and songwriter.

Appeared in: **1935** Big Broadcast of 1936. **1937** A Damsel in Distress. **1942** Here We Go Again; The Pride of the Yankees. **1944** Lake Placid Serenade. **1945** Out of the World.

NOBLES, DOLLY See WOOLVINES, DOLLY

NOBLES, MILTON
Born: 1844, Cincinnati, Ohio, or Almont, Mich.?. Died: June 14, 1924, Brooklyn, N.Y. (heart trouble). Screen, stage and vaudeville actor. Father of stage actor Milton Nobles, Jr. (dec. 1925). Married to actress Dollie Woolwine (dec. 1930) and together they appeared in vaudeville in an act billed as "Dolly and Milton Nobles."

Appeared in: **1924** America.

NOBRIGA, TED
Born: 1911, Hawaii. Died: June 5, 1981, Honolulu, Hawaii. Professional baseball player and screen actor.

Appeared in: **1966** Hawaii.

NOEL, ALAN
Died: May 5, 1977. Screen actor.

NOEL, BERNARD
Born: France. Died: Sept., 1970, France? Screen actor.

Appeared in: **1963** Le Feu Follet (The Fire Within—US 1964). **1964** La Ronde (aka Circle of Love—US 1965); La Femme Mariee (The Married Woman—US 1965).

NOEMI, LEA
Born: 1883. Died: Nov. 6, 1973, New York, N.Y. Yiddish screen and stage actress.

Appeared in: **1937** Green Fields. **1938** The Singing Blacksmith. **1939** Mirele Efros (stage and film versions).

NOHAIN, JEAN (Jean Franc-Nohain)
Born: 1900, France. Died: Jan. 25, 1981, Paris, France. Screen, radio, television actress and lyricist. Brother of actor Claude Dauphin (dec. 1978).

Appeared in: **1946** Portrait of a Woman.

NOLAN, BOB
Born: 1908, Canada. Died: June 16, 1980, Newport Beach, Calif. (heart attack). Screen, radio actor, singer and composer. Formed the "Pioneer Trio" which was changed to the "Sons of the Pioneers."

Appeared in: **1935** The Old Homestead. **1936** Revolt of the Zombies. **1938** The Law of the Plains; West of Cheyenne; Colorado Trail; South of Arizona. **1939** West of Santa Fe; Spoilers of the Range; Western Caravans; Riders of Black River; Man from Sundown; Outpost of the Mounties; Stranger from Texas. **1940** Two-Fisted Rangers; Blazing Six-Shooters; Bullets for Rustlers; Texas Stagecoach; West of Abilene; The Durango Kid; Thundering Frontier. **1941** Outlaws of the Panhandle; The Pinto Kid. **1942** Sunset Serenade; Heart of the Golden West. **1943** King of the Cowboys; Idaho; Song of Texas; Silver Spurs; The Man from Music Mountain; Hands Across the Border. **1944** The Cowboy and the Senorita; The Yellow Rose of Texas; Song of Nevada; San Fernando Valley; Lights of Old Santa Fe. **1945** Utah; Bells of Rosarita; The Man from Oklahoma; Sunset in Eldorado; Don't Fence Me In; Along the Navajo Trail. **1946** Song of Arizona; Ding Dong Williams; Home on the Range; Rainbow Over Texas; My Pal Trigger; Roll On Texas Moon; Under Nevada Skies; Home in Oklahoma; Bells of San Angelo. **1947** Apache Rose; Hit Parade of 1947; On the Old Spanish Trail. **1948** The Gay Ranchero; Under California Skies (aka Under California Stars); Melody Time; Race Street; Nighttime in Nevada.

NOLAN, MARY (Mary Imogene Robertson aka IMOGENE ROBERTSON aka MARY ROBERTSON aka IMOGENE "BUBBLES" WILSON)
Born: Dec. 18, 1905, Louisville, Ky. Died: Oct. 31, 1948, Los Angeles, Calif. Screen, stage actress and model. Sister of actress Mabel Robertson. She used numerous names: Imogene "Bubbles" Wilson while with Ziegfeld; Mary Robertson while film star in Germany; Imogene Robertson, also while in Germany; and Mary Nolan in American films.

Appeared in: **1925** Thoroughbreds; Die Feuertanzerin; Die Panzergewolbe (Armored Vault—US 1928). **1926** Die Unberugte Frau; Das Suesse Maedel. **1927** Taglich Brot; Die Madchen von Paris;

Topsy and Eva; Sorrell and Son. **1928** Silks and Saddles; The Foreign Legion; Uneasy Money; Good Morning Judge. **1929** Charming Sinners; Desert Nights; Eleven Who Were Loyal; Shanghai Lady; West of Zanzibar. **1930** Outside the Law; Undertow; Young Desire. **1931** Enemies of the Law; X Marks the Spot. **1932** The Big Shot; File 113; Docks of San Francisco; Midnight Patrol.

NOLL, KARL
Born: Czechoslovakia. Died: Mar., 1928, Prague, Czechoslovakia. Screen actor.

NOLL, LOUISE M.
Born: 1884. Died: Nov. 1, 1944, Los Angeles, Calif. Screen and stage actress.

NOMIS, LEO
Born: Iowa. Died: Feb. 5, 1932, Los Angeles, Calif. (plane crash while filming Sky Bride). Film stunt flyer.

Appeared in: **1926** California Straight Ahead. **1930** Hell's Angels. **1932** The Lost Squadron; The Crowd Roars; Sky Bride.

NOON, PAISLEY
Born: 1897, Los Angeles, Calif. Died: Mar. 27, 1932, Hollywood, Calif. (appendicitis). Stage and screen actor. Entered films approx. 1927.

Appeared in: **1932** Night World.

NOONAN, PATRICK
Born: Jan. 9, 1887, Dublin, Ireland. Died: May 19, 1962, Wokinham, England. Stage and screen actor.

Appeared in: **1915** Do Unto Others; Royal Love. **1932** Arms and the Man. **1934** Lily of Killarney (aka Bride of the Lake—US). **1936** Ourselves Alone (aka River of Unrest—US). **1937** Kathleen Mavoureen (aka Kathleen—US 1938); The Mutiny of the Elsinore (US 1939); Over the Moon (US 1940). **1938** Mountains O' Mourne. **1940** Dr. O'Down. **1947** Captain Boycott. **1948** Anna Karenina.

NOONAN, TOMMY (Tommy Noon)
Born: Apr. 29, 1922, Bellingham, Wash. Died: Apr. 24, 1968, Woodland Hills, Calif. (brain tumor). Screen, stage, burlesque actor, film producer and screenwriter. Part of film comedy team "Noonan and Marshall." Half-brother of actor John Ireland.

Appeared in: **1945** George White's Scandals (film debut); What No Cigarettes? (short); The Big Beef (short); Beware of Redheads (short). **1946** Ding Dong Williams; The Truth About Murder; The Bamboo Blonde. **1947** The Big Fix. **1948** Jungle Patrol; Open Secret. **1949** Trapped; I Shot Jesse James; I Cheated the Law. **1950** The Return of Jesse James; Holiday Rhythm. **1951** Starlift (with Marshall); F.B.I. Girl. **1953** Gentlemen Prefer Blondes. **1954** A Star Is Born. **1955** How to Be Very, Very Popular; Violent Saturday. **1956** The Ambassador's Daughter; Bundle of Joy; The Best Things in Life Are Free. **1957** The Girl Most Likely. **1959** The Rookie (with Marshall). **1961** Double Trouble. **1962** Swingin' Along (with Marshall). **1963** Promises! Promises!. **1964** Three Nuts in Search of a Bolt. **1967** Cotton Pickin' Chickenpickers.

NORCROSS, FRANK
Born: 1856. Died: Sept. 13, 1926, Glendale, Calif. Screen and stage actor.

Appeared in: **1921** All Dolled Up; Garments of Truth. **1922** The Challenge. **1924** The Flaming Forties. **1925** The Man from Red Gulch. **1926** The Escape; King of the Pack.

NORDEN, CLIFF
Born: 1923. Died: Sept. 23, 1949, Hollywood, Calif. (suicide—pills). Screen actor.

NORDSTROM, CLARENCE
Born: 1893. Died: Dec. 13, 1968, East Orange, N.J. Screen and stage actor.

Appeared in: **1922** The Lights of New York. **1930** Ship Ahoy (short). **1932** The Crooner. **1933** Gold Diggers of 1933; 42nd Street.

NORIEGA, MANOLO
Born: 1880, Mexico. Died: Aug., 1961, Mexico City, Mexico. Screen actor, film director and screenwriter.

Appeared in: **1935** Los Muertos Hablan (The Dead Speak). **1936** Malditas Sean las Mujeres; Asi es la Mujer. **1937** El Misterio del Rostro Palida; El Baul Macabro (The Macabre Trunk). **1938** Ave Sin Rumbo (Wandering Bird); El Traidor; Huapango; Rancho Grande. **1939** Ojos Tapatios; Estrellita (Starlet); Odio (Hate); Vivire Otra Vez (I Shall Live Again).

NORMAN, AMBER
Born: June 6, 1901, Utah. Died: Oct. 21, 1972. Screen actress.

Appeared in: **1926** Hell's 400; The Dude Cowboy; Many Scrappy Returns. **1927** Uneasy Payments. **1928** A Midnight Adventure; The Port of Missing Girls; Playful Papas. **1929** The Drake Case; Love and the Devil.

NORMAN, BRUCE (Norman L. Bean)
Born: 1903. Died: Jan. 11, 1976, New York, N.Y. Screen, stage, radio actor and opera singer. Do not confuse with actor Bruce G. Norman.

NORMAN, GERTRUDE
Born: 1848, London, England. Died: July 20, 1943, Hollywood, Calif. Screen and stage actress.

Appeared in: **1914** The Unwelcome Mrs. Hatch. **1917** Adopted Son. **1918** The Studio Girl. **1919** Widow by Proxy; Strictly Confidential. **1921** Partners of the Tide; Little Italy; A Voice in the Dark; Beach of Dreams. **1922** The Game Chicken. **1924** The Age of Innocence; The Right of the Strongest. **1927** King of Kings. **1929** The Greene Murder Case. **1932** The Sign of the Cross. **1933** Cradle Song. **1934** The Trumpet Blows.

NORMAN, JOSEPHINE (Josephine Arrich)
Born: Nov. 12, 1904, Vienna, Austria. Died: Jan. 24, 1951, Roslyn, N.Y. Screen actress. Married to actor Herbert Rawlins (dec. 1947).

Appeared in: **1924** Ramshackle House. **1925** The Road to Yesterday. **1926** Fifth Avenue; Prince of Pilsen. **1927** King of Kings; Wreck of the Hesperus; The Forbidden Woman. **1928** Chicago; Into No Man's Land.

NORMAN, NORMAN V.
Born: Oct. 24, 1964, Somerset, England. Died: Feb. 26, 1943, England? Screen, stage actor and stage producer.

NORMAND, MABEL
Born: Nov. 10, 1894, Boston, Mass. Died: Feb. 23, 1930, Monrovia, Calif. (tuberculosis). Screen, stage actress and film director. Married to actor Lew Cody (dec. 1934).

Appeared in: **1911** The Unveiling; The Eternal Mother; The Squaw's Love; Her Awakening; Saved from Herself; The Subduing of Mrs. Nag. **1912** Race for a Life; The Mender of the Nets; The Water Nymph; Pedro's Dilemma; Ambitious Butler; The Grocery Clerk's Romance; Mabel's Lovers; The Deacon's Trouble; A Temperamental Husband; A Desperate Lover; A Family Mixup; Mabel's Adventures; Mabel's Stragem; The New Neighbor; Stolen Glory; The Flirting Husband; Cohen at Coney Island; At It Again; The Rivals; Mr. Fix-It; Brown's Seance; A Midnight Elopement; The Duel. **1913** Teddy Telzlaff and Earl Cooper; Speed Kings; Love Sickness at Sea; Cohen Saves the Flag; Fatty's Flirtation; Zuzu, the Band Leader; The Cure That Failed; For Lizzie's Sake; The Battle of Who Run; Mabel's Heroes; A Tangled Affair; A Doctored Affair; The Rural Third Degree; Foiling Fickle Father; At Twelve O'Clock; Her New Beau; Hide and Seek; The Ragtime Band (reissued as The Jazz Band); Mabel's Awful Mistake (reissued as Her Deceitful Lover); The Foreman of the Jury; The Hansom Driver; The Waiter's Picnic; The Telltale Light; Love and Courage; A Muddy Romance (reissued as Muddled in Mud); The Gusher; Saving Mabel's Dad; The Champion; The Mistaken Masher; Just Brown's Luck; Heinze's Resurrection; The Professor's Daughter; A Red Hot Romance; The Sleuths at the Floral Parade; A Strong Revenge; The Rube and the Baron; The Chief's Predicament; Those Good Old Days; Father's Choice; A Little Hero; Hubby's Job; Barney Oldfield's Race for a Life; The Speed Queen; For the Love of Mabel; A Noise from the Deep; Professor Bean's Removal; The Riot; Mabel's New Hero; The Gypsy Queen; The Faithful Taxicab; Baby Day; Mabel's Dramatic Career (reissued as Her Dramatic Debut); The Bowling Match. **1914** A Misplaced Foot; Mabel's Stormy Love Affair; Mabel's Bare Escape; Love and Gasoline; Mabel at the Wheel; Mabel's Nerve; The Fatal Mallet; Mabel's Busy Day; Mabel's New Job; Those Country Kids; Mabel's Blunder; Hello, Mabel; Lovers Post Office; How Heroes Are Made; Fatty's Wine Party; Getting Acquainted; A Missing Bride; Between Showers; A Glimpse of Los Angeles; Won in a Closet; Mabel's Strange Predicament; Back at It Again; Caught in a Cabaret; The Alarm; Her Friend the Bandit; Mabel's Married Life (reissued as The Squarehead); Mabel's Latest Prank (reissued as Touch of Rheumatism); Gentlemen of Nerve (reissued as Some Nerve); His Trysting Place; Fatty's Jonah Day; The Sea Nymphs (reissued as His Diving Beauty); Tillie's Punctured Romance; A Gambling Rube. **1915** Rum and Wallpaper; Mabel and Fatty's Simple Life; Mabel, Fatty and the Law (reissued as Fatty's Spooning Day); That Little Band of Gold (reissued as For Better or Worse); Wished on Mabel; Mabel's Wilful Way; Mabel Lost and Won; My Valet; Stolen Magic; Mabel and

Fatty's Wash Day; Fatty and Mabel at the San Diego Exposition; Fatty's and Mabel's Married Life; His Luckless Love; Their Social Splash; Mabel and Fatty Viewing the World's Fair at San Francisco; The Little Teacher (reissued as A Small Town Bully). **1916** Fatty and Mabel Adrift; The Bright Lights (aka The Lure of Broadway); He Did and He Didn't (aka Love and Lobsters). **1918** Back to the Woods; The Venus Model; The Floor Below; Mickey; Peck's Bad Girl. **1919** Sis Hopkins; Sis; Upstairs. **1920** The Slim Princess. **1921** Mooly O'; What Happened to Rose?. **1922** Head Over Heels; Oh, Mabel, Behave. **1923** Suzanna; The Extra Girl. **1960** When Comedy Was King (documentary). **1961** Days of Thrills and Laughter (documentary).

NORRIS, ALEXANDER M. *See* NOSSECK, MAX

NORRIS, CLAUDE
Died: May 10, 1916. Screen actor.

NORRIS, WILLIAM
Born: 1872, New York, N.Y. Died: Mar. 20, 1929, West Bronxville, N.Y. Screen and stage actor.

Appeared in: **1922** When Knighthood Was in Flower. **1923** The Go Getter; The Love Piker; Maytime; Adam and Eve; The Eternal Three. **1924** My Man. **1925** Never the Twain Shall Meet. **1927** The Joy Girl.

NORTH, BOB (Harold Young)
Born: 1881. Died: Mar. 18, 1936, Hollywood, Calif. (suicide—gas inhalation). Screen actor.

NORTH, JOSEPH B.
Born: 1874, England. Died: Jan. 8, 1945, Woodland Hills, Calif. Screen and stage actor.

Appeared in: **1924** Stolen Secrets; The Whispered Name. **1930** Ex-Flame. **1934** Ladies Should Listen. **1935** Paris Spring; Without Regret.

NORTH, MARY
Born: 1897. Died: Sept. 9, 1976, Santa Monica, Calif. (stroke). Screen and stage actress.

NORTH, ROBERT "BOBBY"
Born: Feb. 2, 1884, New York, N.Y. Died: Aug. 13, 1976, Los Angeles, Calif. (heart attack). Screen, stage, vaudeville actor, burlesque performer, film and stage producer. Married to musical comedy dancer Stella Maury (dec.). Entered films as an actor in 1914.

NORTH, WILFRID
Born: 1853, London, England. Died: June 3, 1935, Hollywood, Calif. Screen actor and film director. Joined Vitagraph as a director in 1915.

Appeared in: **1921** A Millionaire for a Day; The Son of Wallingford. **1923** The Huntress; The Love Brand; The Drivin' Fool. **1924** The Beloved Brute; A Man's Mate; Captain Blood. **1925** The Happy Warrior; On Thin Ice. **1926** The Belle of Broadway; Hell Bent for Heaven; Peril of the Rail. **1927** Tongues of Scandal; The Bush Leaguer; Tracked by the Police. **1928** The Terrible People (serial); The Four-Flusher; Captain Careless. **1929** Girl Overboard; The Trial of Mary Dugan. **1930** The Dude Wrangler. **1932** Unashamed.

NORTHLANE, EDNA
Born: 1893. Died: Feb. 2, 1981, N.Y. Screen, stage and vaudeville actress. Mother of actresses Edna Ward Laing and Mary Ward Bates.

NORTHRUP, HARRY S.
Born: July 31, 1877, Paris, France. Died: July 2, 1936, Los Angeles, Calif. Screen and stage actor. Entered films in 1911.

Appeared in: **1911** Vanity Fair; The Star Reporter; The Cave Man; At the Eleventh Hour; Rock of Ages; The Indian Mutiny; His Lordship the Valet; The Mills of the Gods. **1912** The Lady of the Lake; Coronets and Hearts; The Dawning; Two Women and Two Men. **1913** Roughing the Cub; Alixe (aka The Test of Friendship); Playing with Fire; A Soul in Bondage; His Life for His Emperor. **1914** The Christian. **1915** Two Women. **1916** My Lady's Slippers. **1920** The Blue Moon; The White Circle; Sowing the Wind; Polly of the Storm Country. **1921** Flower of the North; The Four Horsemen of the Apocalypse; Wing Toy. **1922** Winning with Wits; Hate; Saved by Radio. **1923** The Christian; The Greatest Menace; Jazzmania; Human Wreckage; A Woman of Paris. **1924** A Fool's Awakening. **1925** The Gambling Fool; He Who Laughs Last; The Unchastened Woman. **1926** Devil's Island; Wanted—a Coward. **1927** Shield of Honor; The Heart of Maryland. **1928** Burning Daylight; The Cheer Leader; Divine Sinner. **1929** The Last Warning; Prisoners. **1930** Party Girl. **1931** Men Call it Love; Squaw Man; Arizona (aka Men Are Like That).

NORTON, BARRY (Alfredo Biraben)
Born: June 16, 1905, Buenos Aires, Argentina. Died: Aug. 24, 1956, Hollywood, Calif. (heart attack). Screen actor.

Appeared in: **1926** The Black Pirate; The Lily; What Price Glory; The Canyon of Light. **1927** The Wizard; The Heart of Salome; Ankles Preferred; Sunrise. **1928** Fleetwing; Mother Knows Best; Legion of the Condemned; Sins of the Fathers. **1929** The Exalted Flapper; Four Devils. **1930** The Benson Murder Case (Spanish version); Slightly Scarlet (French and Spanish versions). **1931** Dishonored. **1933** Cascarrabias; The Cocktail Hour; Only Yesterday; Lady for a Day. **1934** Imitation of Life; Nana; Unknown Blonde; Grand Canary; The World Moves On. **1935** Storm Over the Andes. **1936** Camille; The Criminal Within; Murder at Glen Athol; Captain Calamity; El Diablo Del Mar; Asi es la Mujer. **1937** History Is Made at Night; I'll Take Romance; Timberesque. **1938** The Buccaneer; El Trovador de la Radio (Radio Troubador); El Traidor; El Pasado Acusa (The Accusing Past). **1939** Should Husbands Work?; Papa Soltero (Bachelor Father). **1946** The Razor's Edge; Devil Monster. **1947** Twilight on the Rio Grande. **1952** What Price Glory? **1955** To Catch a Thief. **1956** Around the World in 80 Days.

NORTON, CECIL A.
Born: 1895. Died: Nov. 30, 1955, Hollywood, Calif. Screen, stage actor and television writer. Entered films approx. 1915.

NORTON, EDGAR
Born: Aug. 11, 1868, England. Died: Feb. 6, 1953, Woodland Hills, Calif. Screen actor.

Appeared in: **1922** The Light in the Dark; The High Road. **1923** Woman Proof. **1924** Men; Broadway After Dark; Tiger Love; The Fast Set; The Female; The Wolf Man. **1925** The Marriage Whirl; Learning to Love; Enticement; Lost-a-Wife; A Regular Fellow; The King of Main Street. **1926** The Boy Friend; Diplomacy; The Lady from Hell; Marriage License? **1927** Fast and Furious; Singed; The Student Prince in Old Heidelberg; My Friend from India. **1928** The Man Who Laughs; Oh, Kay. **1929** The Love Parade. **1930** The Lady of Scandal; Monte Carlo; A Lady Surrenders; East Is West; Ladies Love Brutes; The Runaway Bride; Sweet Kitty Bellaire; Du Barry, Woman of Passion; Charley's Aunt; One Romantic Night; The Man from Blankley's. **1931** The Bachelor Father; The Lady Refuses; The Squaw Man; Meet the Wife; I Like Your Nerve; Compromised. **1932** Love Me Tonight; Dr. Jekyll and Mr. Hyde. **1933** A Lady's Profession; Big Brain; Sing Sinner Sing. **1934** The Richest Girl in the World; Thirty Day Princess; Million Dollar Ransom; We Live Again. **1935** When a Man's a Man; Sons of Steel. **1937** You Can't Buy Luck. **1939** Son of Frankenstein; Juarez and Maximilian; Captain Fury. **1940** The House of the Seven Gables. **1942** Rings on Her Fingers. **1944** Are These Our Parents? **1947** Bob, Son of Battle; Thunder in the Valley.

NORTON, ELDA
Born: 1891. Died: Apr. 22, 1947, Hollywood, Calif. Screen and stage actress.

NORTON, FLETCHER
Born: 1877. Died: Oct. 3, 1941, Los Angeles, Calif. Screen and stage actress.

Appeared in: **1926** The Cowboy and the Countess; Davy Crockett at the Fall of the Almo; Exclusive Rights. **1928** Dream of Love. **1930** Sweethearts and Wives; The Big House; Let's Go Places; Men of the North. **1931** The Phantom of Paris; The Secret Six; The Star Witness. **1932** Is My Face Red. **1933** Sucker Money; The Bowery. **1934** Most Precious Thing in Life; The Private Scandal. **1935** Call of the Wild.

NORTON, HENRY FIELD
Born: 1899. Died: Aug. 10, 1945, Hollywood, Calif. (following operation). Screen actor and singer. One of the founders of the Screen Extras Guild.

NORTON, JACK (Mortimer J. Naughton)
Born: 1889, Brooklyn, N.Y. Died: Oct. 15, 1958, Saranac Lake, N.Y. (respiratory ailment). Screen, stage and vaudeville actor. Played the drunk in more that 200 films; in real life he never took a drink. Married to actress Lucille Norton (dec. 1959) with whom he appeared in vaudeville.

Appeared in: **1934** Now I'll Tell; Sweet Music; Cockeyed Cavaliers; plus the following shorts: Super Snooper; Fixing a Stew; One too Many; Counsel on De Fence; Woman Haters. **1935** Bordertown; Ship Cafe; Calling All Cars; Stolen Harmony; Don't Bet on Blondes; His Night Out; Ruggles of Red Gap; Dr. Socrates; Alibi Ike; Front Page Woman. **1936** Too Many Parents; Down the Ribber (short). **1937** Swing Fever (short); Marked Woman; Meet the Missus; Pick a Star;

A Day at the Races; The Great Garrick. **1938** Jezebel; The Awful Truth (short); Meet the Girls; Thanks for the Memory. **1939** Society Smugglers; Grand Jury Secrets; Joe and Ethel Turp Call on the President. **1940** The Farmer's Daughter; Opened by Mistake; A Night at Earl Carroll's; The Bank Dick; The Ghost Breakers. **1941** Louisiana Purchase; Road Show. **1942** The Fleet's In; The Spoilers; The Palm Beach Story; Moonlight Havana; Dr. Renault's Secret; Brooklyn Orchid; Tennessee Johnson. **1943** Taxi, Mister; Lady Bodyguard; Prairie Chicken; It Ain't Hay; The Falcon Strikes Back. **1944** The Miracle of Morgan's Creek; And the Angels Sing; Here Come the Waves; His Tale is Told (short); The Chinese Cat; Hail the Conquering Hero; The Big Noise; Ghost Catchers. **1945** Wonder Man; Fashion Model; Flame of the Barbary Coast; A Guy, A Gal, A Pal; Captain Tugboat Annie; Strange Confession; Man Alive; Hold That Blonde; Her Highness and the Bellboy; The Scarlet Clue; The Naughty Nineties; Double Honeymoon (short). **1946** The Hoodlum Saint; Blue Skies; No Leave, No Love; The Kid from Brooklyn; The Sin of Harold Diddlebock (aka Mad Wednesday); Shadows Over Chinatown; Corpus Delecti; The Strange Mr. Gregory; Bringing Up Father; Rendezvous 24; Rhythm and Weep (short). **1947** Down to Earth; Linda, Be Good; The Hired Husband (short). **1948** Variety Time.

NORTON, LUCILLE
Born: 1894. Died: June 17, 1959, Beverly Hills, Calif. Screen, stage and vaudeville actress. Was in vaudeville as one of the "Haley Sisters" and later teamed in vaudeville with husband, actor Jack Norton (dec. 1958).

NORWOOD, EILLE (Anthony Brett)
Born: Oct. 11, 1861, Yorkshire, England. Died: Dec. 24, 1948, England? Screen and stage actor.

Appeared in: **1911** Princess Clementina. **1916** The Charlatan; Frailty (aka Temptation's Hour). **1920** The Hundredth Chance; The Tavern Knight. **1921** A Gentleman of France; Gwyneth of the Welsh Hills; The Adventures of Sherlock Holmes series including: The Dying Detective; The Devil's Foot; A Case of Identity; Yellow Face; The Red-Headed League; The Resident Patient; A Scandal in Bohemia; The Man With the Twisted Lip; The Beryl Coronet; The Noble Bachelor; The Copper Beeches; The Empty House; The Tiger of San Pedro; The Priory School; The Solitary Cyclist. **1922** The Hound of the Baskervilles; The Recoil; The Crimson Circle; The Further Adventures of Sherlock Holmes series including: The Abbey Grange; Charles Augustus Milverton; The Norwood Builder; The Reigate Squires; The Naval Treaty; The Second Stain; The Red Circle; The Six Napoleons; Black Peter; The Bruce Partington Plans; The Stockbroker's Clerk; The Boscombe Valley Mystery; The Musgrave Ritual; The Golden Prince; The Greek Interpreter. **1923** The Sign of Four; The Last Adventures of Sherlock Holmes series including: Silver Blaze; The Speckled Band; The Gloria Scott; The Blue Carbuncle; The Engineer's Thumb; His Last Bow; The Cardboard Box; The Disappearance of Lady Frances Carfax; The Three Students; The Missing Three Quarter; The Mystery of Thor Bridge; The Stone of Mazarin; The Mystery of the Dancing Men; The Crooked Man; The Final Problem.

NORWORTH, JACK
Born: Jan. 5, 1879, Philadelphia, Pa. Died: Sept. 1, 1959, Laguna Beach, Calif. Screen, stage, vaudeville, minstrel, radio, television actor and songwriter. Married to stage actress Amy Swor (dec. 1974). Divorced from stage actress Nora Bayes (dec. 1965), actress Dorothy Norworth (with whom he appeared in "Nagger" film series) and Louise Dresser (dec. 1965). Entered films in 1928.

Appeared in: **1929** Queen of the Night Clubs; plus the following shorts: Song and Things; Odds and Ends. The following "Nagger" series shorts:. **1930** The Naggers; The Naggers at Breakfast; The Naggers Go South. **1931** The Naggers' Day of Rest; The Naggers Go Rooting; The Naggers Go Camping; The Naggers at the Dentist's; The Naggers in the Subway. **1932** The Naggers at the Ringside; The Naggers Go Shopping; The Naggers at the Races; The Naggers' Housewarming. **1942** Shine on Harvest Moon. **1945** The Southerner.

NORWORTH, NED
Born: 1889. Died: Feb. 12, 1940, New York, N.Y. (after fall and brain operation). Screen and vaudeville actor. Appeared in vaudeville with his first wife, actress Josephine Bennett, in an act billed as "Ned Norworth and Co." Married to performer Wanda Nash.

NOSSECK, MARTIN
Born: 1903. Died: Nov. 29, 1981, Los Angeles, Calif. Screen extra. Father of actor Don and director Noel Martin.

NOSSECK, MAX (aka ALEXANDER M. NORRIS)
Born: Sept. 19, 1902, Nakel, Poland. Died: Sept. 29, 1972, Bad Wiesse, Germany. Screen, stage actor, film director, producer and screenwriter. Entered films as an actor.

Appeared in: **1927** Around the World Without Money.

NOTARI, GUIDO
Born: 1894, Italy. Died: Jan. 21, 1957, Rome, Italy. Screen and radio actor.

Appeared in: **1947** Before Him All Rome Trembled. **1955** Helen of Troy.

NOVACK, SHELLY
Born: 1945. Died: May 27, 1978, Los Angeles, Calif. Screen and television actor. Married to actress/model Belle Novack.

NOVARRO, RAMON (Ramon Samaniegoes)
Born: Feb. 6, 1899, Durango, Mexico. Died: Oct. 31, 1968, Hollywood, Calif. (murdered). Screen, television actor, screenwriter and film director.

Appeared in: **1917** The Little American; Joan the Woman. **1919** The Goat (film debut). **1921** A Small Town Idol. **1922** The Prisoner of Zenda; Trifling Women; Mr. Barnes of New York. **1923** Scaramouche; Where the Pavement Ends. **1924** The Arab; The Red Lily; Thy Name Is Woman. **1925** The Midshipman; A Lover's Oath. **1926** Ben Hur. **1927** The Student Prince; The Road to Romance; Lovers? **1928** A Certain Young Man; Forbidden Hours; Across to Singapore. **1929** The Flying Fleet; The Pagan; Devil May Care. **1930** La Sevillana (aka Sevilla de Mis Amores—Spanish language version of Call of the Wild); In Gay Madrid; The Singer of Seville; Call of the Flesh. **1931** Son of India; Ben Hur (rerelease of 1926 version in sound); Daybreak. **1932** Mata Hari; Son-Daughter; Huddle. **1933** The Barbarian. **1934** The Cat and the Fiddle; Laughing Boy. **1935** The Night Is Young. **1937** The Sheik Steps Out. **1938** La Comedie de Bonheur; A Desperate Adventure; As You Are. **1942** La Virgen Que Forjo una Patria. **1949** We Were Strangers; The Big Steal. **1950** The Outriders; Crisis. **1960** Heller in Pink Tights.

NOVELLI, ANTONY See NOVELLI, ERMETI

NOVELLI, ERMETI (aka ANTONY NOVELLI)
Born: May 5, 1851, Lucca, Italy. Died: Jan. 30, 1919, Rome, Italy. Screen and stage actor.

Appeared in: **1914** Julius Caesar (US 1922).

NOVELLO, IVOR (Ivor Novello Davies)
Born: Jan. 15, 1893, Cardiff, Wales. Died: Mar. 6, 1951, London, England (coronary thrombosis). Screen, stage actor, screenwriter, playwright and composer. Wrote song, "Keep the Home Fires Burning."

Appeared in: **1921** Carnival. **1922** The Bohemian Girl. **1923** The White Rose; Bonnie Prince Charlie; The Man without Desire. **1925** The Rat. **1926** The Triumph of the Rat; The Lodger (aka The Case of Jonathan Drew—US 1928). **1927** Downhill (aka When Boys Leave Home—US 1928); The Vortex (US 1928). **1928** A South Sea Bubble; The Constant Nymph. **1929** The Return of the Rat. **1930** Symphony in Two Flats. **1931** Once a Lady. **1932** The Lodge (aka The Phantom Fiend—US 1935). **1933** I Lived with You; Sleeping Car. **1934** Autumn Crocus.

NOVIKOFF, RASHEL
Died: Mar. 28, 1980. Screen actress.

Appeared in: **1974** Lenny. **1975** The Sunshine Boys. **1976** Next Stop, Greenwich Village. **1977** Annie Hall.

NOVINSKY, ALEXANDER "ALEX"
Born: July 2, 1878, St. Petersburg, Russia. Died: June 30, 1960. Screen actor.

Appeared in: **1928** Abie's Irish Rose; Red Dance; Night Watch. **1929** Leatherneck. **1930** The Princess and the Plumber. **1931** Transatlantic; Ambassador Bill. **1932** Union Depot; Love Me Tonight; Six Hours to Live. **1933** Cavalcade; Night of Terror. **1936** Give Us This Night; Suzy. **1937** Nothing Sacred; Second Honeymoon. **1938** Happy Landing. **1945** Thrill of a Romance.

NOVIS, DONALD
Born: Mar. 3, 1907, Hastings, England. Died: July 23, 1966, Norwalk, Calif. Screen, stage, radio actor and singer.

Appeared in: **1929** New York Nights; Irish Fantasy (short). **1930** Monte Carlo. **1931** The Pajama Party (short). **1932** The Singing Plumber (short); One Hour With You; The Big Broadcast; "Mack Sennett Star" series. **1933** The Singing Boxer (short); a Vitaphonne short. **1934** An RKO short. **1935** Paramount shorts. **1944** Slightly Terrific. **1951** Mr. Universe.

NOWELL, WEDGEWOOD
Born: 1878, Portsmouth, N.H. Died: June 17, 1957, Philadelphia, Pa. Screen, stage actor and stage producer. Entered films in 1915.

Appeared in: **1916** The Deserter. **1921** 813; Devotion; The Match-Breaker. **1922** The Eternal Flame; Enter Madame; Ashes; A Doll's House; The Song of Life; Thelma. **1923** The Westbound Limited; A Wife's Romance; Heroes of the Street; Adam's Rib; Don't Marry for Money. **1924** Jealous Husbands. **1936** To Mary, With Love; Stolen Holiday. **1937** Dick Tracy (serial); The Big Show. **1940** Calling Philo Vance.

NOWLIN, HERMAN (Herman Franklin Nowlin)
Born: Jan. 16, 1892, Ill. Died: Sept. 2, 1951, Los Angeles, Calif. Screen actor.

Appeared in: **1951** Flaming Feather.

NOX, ANDRE
Born: 1889, France. Died: 1946, France? Screen actor.

Appeared in: **1929** The Jolly Peasant. **1939** That They May Live.

NOYES, JOSEPH
Born: 1869. Died: Apr. 17, 1936, Los Angeles, Calif. (hit by auto). Screen actor.

NUATJIM, CHAMROON
Born: 1914, Thailand. Died: May 9, 1979, Bangkok, Thailand (heart attack). Screen, stage and television actor. Married to actress Aroonsri Noithip. Father of actress Pranij Koomdej.

NUEMANN, CHARLES
Born: 1873. Died: July 16, 1927, Glendale, Calif. Screen actor.

NUGENT, ELLIOT
Born: Sept. 20, 1899, Dover, Ohio. Died: Aug. 9, 1980, New York, N.Y. Screen, stage, vaudeville actor, film director, stage producer, screenwriter, playwright and author. Son of vaudeville actors J. C. Nugent (dec.), and Grace Mary Fertig (dec.). Married to actress Norma Lee (dec. 1980).

Appeared in: **1925** Headlines. **1929** So This Is College; Father's Day; The Single Standard. **1930** Wise Girls; Not So Dumb; The Unholy Three; The Richest Man in the World; Sins of the Children; Romance; For the Love O' Lil. **1931** Virtuous Husband; The Last Flight. **1943** Stage Door Canteen. **1951** My Outlaw Brother.

NUGENT, J. C.
Born: Apr. 6, 1875, Niles, Ohio. Died: Apr. 21, 1947, New York, N.Y. (coronary thrombosis). Screen, stage actor, playwright, screenwriter and film director. Father of actor Elliot Nugent.

Appeared in: **1929** Wise Girls; Navy Blues. **1930** They Learned About Women; Love in the Rough; Remote Control; The Big House. **1931** The Millionaire; Many a Slip; Virtuous Husbands. **1935** Love in Bloom; Men Without Names. **1937** A Star Is Born; Stand-In; This Is My Affair; Life Begins in College. **1938** It's All Yours; Midnight Intruder; Give Me a Sailor.

NUGENT, MOYA
Born: 1901, England. Died: Jan. 26, 1954, London, England. Screen and stage actress.

Appeared in: **1913** The Old Curiosity Shop.

NUNEZ, JUAN MANUEL
Born: Cuba. Died: Jan. 24, 1966, Havana, Cuba. Screen actor.

NUNN, WAYNE (Shephard Wayne Nunn)
Born: 1881, Ind. Died: Dec. 17, 1947, New York, N.Y. Screen and stage actor. Divorced from actress Grace Valentine (dec. 1964). Married to actress Zoe Barnett.

Appeared in: **1939** One Third of a Nation.

NUSSER, JAMES "JIM"
Born: 1905. Died: June 8, 1979, Hollywood, Calif. Screen and television actor.

Appeared in: **1953** One Girl's Confession. **1957** Hell Canyon (aka Hell Canyon Outlaws). **1969** Hail, Hero!

NYE, CARROLL
Born: Oct. 4, 1901, Canton, Ohio. Died: Mar. 17, 1974, North Hollywood, Calif. (heart attack and kidney failure). Screen, stage actor, radio commentator and columnist. Married to actress Helen Lynch (dec. 1965) and later married to Dorothy Nye.

Appeared in: **1925** Classified; Three Wise Crooks. **1926** The Earth Woman; The Imposter; Kosher Kitty Kelly; Her Honor the Governor. **1927** The Black Diamond Express; Death Valley; The Silver Slave; The Brute; The Girl from Chicago; The Heart of Maryland; Little Mickey Grogan; The Rose of Kildare; What Every Girl Should Know. **1928** The Perfect Crime; Powder My Back; A Race for Life; Rinty of the Desert; The Sporting Age; While the City Sleeps; Craig's Wife; Jazzland; Land of the Silver Fox. **1929** Madame X; The Squall; The Flying Fleet; Light Fingers; The Girl in the Glass Cage. **1930** The Bishop Murder Case; The Lottery Bride; Sons of the Saddle. **1931** King of the Wild (serial); The Lawless Woman; Hell Bent for Frisco; Neck and Neck; One Way Trail. **1935** Traveling Saleslady. **1938** Rebecca of Sunnybrook Farm; Kentucky Moonshine. **1939** Gone With the Wind. **1940** The Trail Blazers. **1944** Dark Mountain.

OAKES, ROBERT CHANDLER See CHANDLER, LANE R.

OAKIE, JACK (Lewis Delaney Offield)
Born: Nov. 12, 1903, Sedalia, Mo. Died: Jan. 23, 1978, Northridge, Calif. (aortic aneurysm). Screen, stage, vaudeville, radio, television actor and writer. Son of actress Evelyn Offield (dec. 1939). Divorced from actress Venita Varden (dec. 1948) and later married to actress Victoria Horne. Nominated for 1940 Academy Award for Best Supporting Actor in The Great Dictator.

Appeared in: **1928** Finders Keepers (film debut); The Fleet's In; Road House; Someone to Love. **1929** Chinatown Nights; The Dummy; Close Harmony; Fast Company; Hard to Get; Sin Town; Street Girl; The Man I Love; The Wild Party; Sweetie. **1930** The Social Lion; Hit the Deck; Let's Go Native; Paramount on Parade; Sea Legs; The Sap from Syracuse. **1931** Gang Buster; June Moon; Dude Ranch; Touchdown. **1932** Slippery Pearls (short); Dancers in the Dark; Sky Bride; Million Dollar Legs; Madison Square Garden; If I Had a Million; Once in a Lifetime; Uptown New York; Make Me a Star. **1933** From Hell to Heaven; Sailor Be Good; Eagle and the Hawk; College Humor; Too Much Harmony; Sitting Pretty; Alice in Wonderland. **1934** Looking for Trouble; Murder in the Vanities; Shoot the Works; College Rhythm; Hip Hip Horray. **1935** Call of the Wild; Big Broadcast of 1936; King of Burlesque. **1936** Collegiate; Colleen; Florida Special; The Texas Rangers; That Girl from Paris. **1937** Champagne Waltz; Super Sleuth; The Toast of New York; Flight for Your Life; Hitting a New High. **1938** Radio City Revels; Annabella Takes a Tour; Thanks for Everything; The Affairs of Annabel. **1940** Young People; The Great Dictator; Tin Pan Alley; Little Men. **1941** The Great American Broadcast; Navy Blues; Rise and Shine. **1942** Song of the Islands; Iceland; Footlight Serenade. **1943** Hello, Frisco, Hello; Wintertime; Something to Shout About. **1944** It Happened Tomorrow; The Merry Monahans; Sweet and Low Down; Bowery to Broadway. **1945** That's the Spirit; On Stage Everybody. **1946** She Wrote the Book. **1948** Northwest Stampede; When My Baby Smiles at Me. **1949** Thieves' Highway. **1950** The Last of the Buccaneers. **1951** Tomahawk. **1956** Around the World in 80 Days. **1959** The Wonderful Country. **1960** The Rat Race. **1961** Lover Come Back.

OAKLAND, VIVIEN (Vivian Anderson)
Born: 1895. Died: Aug. 1, 1958, Hollywood, Calif. Screen, stage and vaudeville actress. Married to actor John T. Murray (dec. 1957). They appeared in vaudeville as "John T. Murray and Vivian Oakland," and also made several shorts together during 1929-30.

Appeared in: **1924** Madonna of the Streets. **1925** The Teaser; The Rainbow Trail. **1926** Tony Runs Wild; Redheads Preferred; Tell 'Em Nothing (short). **1927** Love 'Em and Weep (short); Wedding Bills; Uncle Tom's Cabin. **1929** The Man in Hobbles; The Time, the Place and the Girl; The Crazy Nut; In the Headlines, "Educational Mermaid" shorts; plus the following shorts billed as "John T. Murray and Vivian Oakland": Satires; The Hall of Injustice. **1930** How I Play Golf—The Niblick (short); The Floradora Girl; Personality; Back Pay; A Lady Surrenders; The Matrimonial Bed; plus the following shorts: Oh, Sailor, Behave!; Below Zero; Big Hearted; Let Me Explain; Vanity; A Mother of Ethics; and the following two with her husband: Who Pays; The Servant Problem. **1931** Many a Slip; The Age for Love; Gold Dust Gertie. **1932** A House Divided; Cock of the Air; The Tenderfoot; Scram! (short). **1933** They Just Had to Get Married; Neighbors' Wives; Only Yesterday. **1934** The Defense Rests; Money Means Nothing; plus the following shorts: In the Doghouse; Perfectly Mismated; One Too Many. **1935** Atlantic Adventure; Rendezvous at Midnight; Star of Midnight; Alimony Aches (short). **1936** The Bride

Walks Out; Lady Luck; One Live Ghost (short). **1937** Way Out West; Mile a Minute Love; plus the following shorts: Knee Action; Bad Housekeeping; Dumb's the Word; Tramp Trouble; Wrong Romance; Should Wives Work?. **1938** Double Danger; Crime Afloat; Slander House; Rebellious Daughters; plus the following shorts: Fool Coverage; Beaux and Errors; A Clean Sweep; The Pest Friend; Berth Quakes. **1939** Island of Lost Men; plus the following shorts: Boom Goes the Groom; Maid to Order; Clock Wise; Baby Daze; Feathered Pests; Act Your Age; Kennedy the Great. **1940** On Their Own; plus the following shorts: Mr. Clyde Goes to Broadway; Slightly at Sea; Mutiny in the County; 'Taint Legal; Sunk by the Census; Trailer Tragedy; Drafted in the Depot. **1941** The following shorts: Ring and the Belle; Mad About Moonshine; It Happened All Night; An Apple in His Eye. **1942** The Man in the Trunk; Sappy Pappy (short). **1943** Laugh Your Blues Away. **1944** The Girl Who Dared. **1945** Utah; The Man Who Walked Alone. **1946** The Locket; Social Terrors (short). **1947** Smash Up, the Story of a Woman; Borrowed Blonde (short). **1948** Home Canning (short). **1950** The Secret Fury; Bunco Squad. **1951** Punchy Pancho (short). **1965** Laurel and Hardy's Laughing 20's (documentary).

OAKLAND, WILL
Born: 1883. Died: May 15, 1956, Bloomfield, N.J. Screen, radio, vaudeville, minstrel actor and singer.

Appeared in: **1927** While We Danced Till Dawn; Dreamy Melody (both shorts).

OAKLEY, ANNIE (Phoebe Anne Oakley Mozee)
Born: Aug. 13, 1860, Patterson Township, Darke County, Ohio. Died: Nov. 3, 1926, Greenville, Ohio. Rodeo, vaudeville, circus performer and screen actress. Married to marksman Frank E. Butler. Appeared in a pre-1900 film.

OAKLEY, FLORENCE
Born: 1891. Died: Sept. 25, 1956, Hollywood, Calif. Screen actress. Divorced from actor Lewis Stone (dec. 1953).

Appeared in: **1929** A Most Immoral Lady.

OAKLEY, LAURA
Born: July 10, 1879, Oakland, Calif. Died: Jan, 30, 1957, Altadena, Calif. (heart ailment). Screen actress.

Appeared in: **1915** Star of the Sea; Changed Lives; The Black Box (serial). **1920** The Vanishing Dagger (serial).

OAKLEY, ROBERT
Died: Mar. 4, 1975. Screen actor.

Appeared in: **1966** Hawaii.

OAKMAN, WHEELER
Born: 1890, Va. Died: Mar. 19, 1949, Van Nuys, Calif. Screen and stage actor.

Appeared in: **1913** The Long Ago. **1914** The Spoilers. **1916** The Ne'er-Do-Well. **1920** The Virgin of Stamboul. **1921** Peck's Bad Boy; Outside the Law; Penny of Top Hill Trail. **1922** The Half Breed; The Son of the Wolf. **1923** Slippery McGee; The Love Trap; Mine to Keep; Other Men's Daughters. **1925** Lilies of the Street; The Pace That Thrills. **1926** In Borrowed Plumes; Fangs of Justice; Outside the Law (revised version of 1921 film). **1927** Out All Night; Hey! Hey! Cowboy; Heroes of the Night. **1928** Top Sergeant Mulligan; Lights of New York; The Broken Mask; Masked Angel; The Power of the Press; What a Night; While the City Sleeps; Black Feather; Danger Patrol; The Good-Bye Kiss; The Heart of Broadway. **1929** The Show of Shows; The Hurricane; The Girl from Woolworth's; On With the Show; Devil's Chaplain; Handcuffed; Morgan's Last Raid; The Donovan Affair; Father and Son; Shanghai Lady; The Shakedown. **1930** Little Johnny Jones; On Your Back; The Big Fight; The Costello Case; Roaring Ranch. **1931** The Good Bad Girl; The Lawless Woman; First Aid; Sky Raiders. **1932** The Air Mail Mystery (serial); Texas Cyclone; Two-Fisted Law; Riding Tornado; Gorilla Ship; Beauty Parlor; The Heart Punch; The Boiling Point; Guilty or Not Guilty; Devil on Deck. **1933** Revenge at Monte Carlo; Sundown Rider; Rusty Rides Alone; Silent Men; Hold the Press; Man of Action; Western Code; Speed Demon; End of the Trail; Soldiers of the Storm. **1934** Lost Jungle (serial); Frontier Days; In Old Santa Fe; Murder in the Clouds; One is Guilty; Palooka. **1935** G-Men; The Phantom Empire (serial); Code of the Mounted; Death From a Distance; Annapolis Farewell; Trails of the Wild; The Man from Guntown; Square Shooter; Motive for Revenge; Headline Woman; The Case of the Curious Bride. **1936** Timber War; Song of the Trail; Roarin' Guns; Gambling With Souls; Darkest Africa (serial); Aces and Eights; Ghost Patrol. **1937** Death in the Air; Bank

Alarm. **1938** Code of the Rangers; Flash Gordon's Trip to Mars (serial); Red Barry (serial); Mars Attacks the World. **1939** In Old Montana; Torture Ship; Mutiny in the Big House; Buck Rogers (serial). **1940** Men With Steel Faces. **1941** Meet the Mob. **1942** Double Trouble; Bowery at Midnight; So's Your Aunt Emma. **1943** Ghosts on the Loose; The Girl from Monterey; What a Man!; The Ape Man; Kid Dynamite; Fighting Buckaroo; Saddles and Sagebrush. **1944** Riding West; Sundown Valley; Three of a Kind; Bowery Champs. **1945** Who's Guilty? (serial); Rough Ridin' Justice; Trouble Chasers; Brenda Starr, Reporter (serial). **1946** Hop Harrigan (serial); Son of the Guardsman (serial). **1947** Brick Bradford (serial); Jack Armstrong (serial).

OATES, CICELY
Born: England. Died: Dec. 23, 1934, England? Screen and stage actress.

Appeared in: **1933** I Lived with You. **1934** The Man Who Knew Too Much. **1935** The Price of Wisdom; Things are Looking Up.

OBECK, FRED
Born: 1881. Died: Jan. 31, 1929, Hollywood, Calif. (heart trouble). Screen actor.

Appeared in: **1927** The Patent Leather Kid; Wanted a Coward. **1928** Vamping Venus; Oh, Kay!

OBELLONA, CARLOS
Born: 1900, Mexico. Died: 1960, Mexico? Screen actor.

OBER, GEORGE
Died: Nov., 1912, New York, N.Y. Stage and screen actor. Married to stage actress Adelaide Ober (dec. 1922) and father of stage actor Frederic Powers (dec.).

Appeared in: **1912** The Curio Hunters; The Maid's Stratagem; The Little Minister; As You Like It; Blind Musician; The Widow's Might; The Indian Mutiny; The Staff of Age. **1913** It All Came Out in the Wash; Papa Puts One Over.

OBER, KIRT
Born: 1875. Died: June 1, 1939, Huntington Beach, Calif. (heart attack). Screen, stage, vaudeville actor and jockey.

OBER, ROBERT
Born: 1882, St. Louis, Mo. Died: Dec. 7, 1950, New York, N.Y. Screen, stage actor and film director. Married to actress Mabel Taliaferro (dec. 1979).

Appeared in: **1922** The Young Rajah. **1925** Souls for Sables; Time, the Comedian; The Big Parade; Introduce Me; The Mystic; Morals for Man. **1926** Butterflies in the Rain; Fools of Fashion; The Whole Town's Talking; The Checkered Flag. **1927** King of Kings; A Reno Divorce; The Little Adventuress; Held by the Law. **1928** Across the Atlantic; Black Butterflies; A Regular Business Man (short). **1929** The Idle Rich, In the Headlines; Four in a Flat (short). **1930** The Woman Racket.

OBERLE, FLORENCE
Born: 1870. Died: July 10, 1943, Hollywood, Calif. Screen and stage actress.

Appeared in: **1921** R.S.V.P. **1922** Smudge; The Barnstormer.

OBERLIN, JAMES "JIM"
Born: 1931. Died: Oct. 2, 1962, Los Angeles, Calif. (following heart surgery). Screen and television actor.

OBERON, MERLE (Estelle Merle O'Brien Thompson)
Born: Feb. 19, c. 1911, Hobart, Tasmania. Died: Nov. 23, 1979, Los Angeles, Calif. (stroke). Screen, radio and television actress. Divorced from film producer Alexander Korda (dec. 1956), cinematographer Lucien Ballard, and businessman Bruno Pagliai. Later married to actor Robert Wolders. Nominated for 1935 Academy Award for Best Actress in The Dark Angel. Entered films as an extra in 1930.

Appeared in: **1930** The "W" Plan (US 1931); Alf's Button. **1931** Never Trouble Trouble; Fascination. **1932** For the Love of Mike; Service for Ladies (aka Reserved for Ladies—US); Ebb Tide; Wedding Rehearsal; Aren't We All?; Men of Tomorrow. **1933** The Private Life of Henry VIII. **1934** The Broken Melody; The Battle (aka Thunder in the East—US); The Private Life of Don Juan. **1935** Folies Bergere de Paris; The Scarlet Pimpernel; The Dark Angel. **1936** These Three; Beloved Enemy. **1937** Over the Moon (US 1940); I Claudius (uncompleted). **1938** The Divorce of Lady X; The Cowboy and the Lady. **1939** Wuthering Heights; The Lion Has Wings (US 1940). **1940** 'Till We Meet Again. **1941** That Uncertain Feeling; Lydia; Affectionately

Yours. **1943** Hara-Kiri (reissue of The Battle, 1934); Forever and a Day; First Comes Courage; Stage Door Canteen. **1944** Dark Waters; The Lodger. **1945** This Love of Ours; A Song to Remember. **1946** A Night in Paradise; Temptation. **1947** Night Song. **1948** Berlin Express. **1951** The Lady from Boston; Pardon My French. **1952** 24 Hours of a Woman's Life (aka Affair in Monte Carlo—US 1953). **1954** Todo es Posible en Granada; Desiree; Deep in My Heart. **1956** The Price of Fear. **1963** Of Love and Desire. **1966** The Oscar. **1967** Hotel. **1973** Interval.

O'BRIEN, BARRY
Born: Dec. 23, 1893, London, England. Died: Dec. 25, 1961, London, England. Screen and stage actor.

Appeared in: **1914** Ireland, a Nation.

O'BRIEN, DAVID "DAVE" (David Barclay)
Born: May 13, 1912, Big Spring, Tex. Died: Nov. 8, 1969, Catalina Island, Calif. (heart attack). Screen actor, film director, television director, screenwriter and television writer.

Appeared in: **1933** College Humor; Jennie Gerhardt. **1934** Little Colonel. **1935** Welcome Home. **1936** The Black Coin (serial). **1937** Million Dollar Racket; Victory. **1938** The Secret of Treasure Island (serial); Frontier Scout; Where the Buffalo Roam; Man's Country. **1939** Song of the Buckaroo; Driftin' Westward; Water Rustlers; Rollin' Westward; Mutiny in the Big House; New Frontier; Daughter of the Tong. Joined the "Renfrew of the Royal Mounted" series which included: Crashing Thru; Fighting Mad. **1940** Other "Renfrew" films include: Danger Ahead; Yukon Flight; Murder on the Yukon; Sky Bandits; other 1940 films are: The Cowboy from Sundown; Boys of the City; Queen of the Yukon; That Gang of Mine; A Fugitive from Justice; Gun Code; The Kid from Santa Fe; Hold That Woman!; East Side Kids; Son of the Navy; The Ghost Creeps. **1941** The Spider Returns; Flying Wild; Texas Marshal; Murder by Invitation; Buzzy and the Phantom Pinto; The Deadly Game; Gunman from Bodie; Spooks Run Wild; Double Trouble; Billy the Kid Wanted. **1942** Down Texas Way; Prisoner of Japan; Billy the Kid's Smoking Guns; King of the Stallions; Bowery at Midnight; The Yanks Are Coming; Captain Midnight (serial); 'Neath Brooklyn Bridge; Devil Bat; plus the following shorts: Carry Harry; What About Daddy; Victory Quiz; Victory Vittles; Calling All Pa's. **1943** Texas Ranger; The Rangers Take Over; Border Buckaroo; plus the following shorts: First Aid; Seventh Column; Tips on Trips; Fixin' Tricks; Who's Superstitious? **1944** Trail of Terror; Gunsmoke Mesa; Return of the Rangers; Boss of Rawhide; Outlaw Roundup; Guns of the Law; The Pinto Bandit; Spook Town; Dead or Alive; The Whispering Skull; Gangsters of the Frontier; Movie Pests (short); Safety Sleuth (short). **1945** The Man Who Walked Alone; Enemy of the Law; Flaming Bullets; Three in the Saddle; Marked for Murder; Tahiti Nights; The Phantom of 42nd St.; Bus Pests (short). **1946** Frontier Fugitives; plus the following shorts: Studio Visits; Equestrian Quiz; Treasures from Trash; Sure Cures; I Love My Husband. **1947** Thundercap Outlaws; Shootin' Irons; plus the following shorts: Early Sports Quiz; I Love My Wife, But!; Neighbor Pests; Pet Peeves; Have You Ever Wondered. **1948** The following shorts: I Love My Mother-in-Law, But!; You Can't Win; Just Suppose; Why Is It?; Let's Cogitate. **1949** The following shorts: What I Want Next; Those Good Old Days; How Come?; We Can Dream, Can't We? **1950** The following shorts: That's His Story?; A Wife's Life; Wrong Way Butch; Wanted: One Egg. **1951** The following shorts: Fixin' Fool; Bandage Bait; That's What You Think. **1952** The following shorts: Reducing; It Could Happen to You; Pedestrian Safety; Sweet Memories; I Love Children, But! **1953** Kiss Me Kate; plus the following shorts: The Postman; Cash Stashers; It Would Serve 'Em Right; Landlording It; Things We Can Do Without. **1954** Tennessee Champ; plus the following shorts: Ain't It Aggravatin'; Do Someone a Favor; Out for Fun; Safe at Home. **1955** The following shorts: The Man Around the House; Keep Young; Just What I Needed; Fall Guy. **1956** The Desperadoes Are in Town. **1964** Big Parade of Comedy (documentary).

O'BRIEN, DONNELL
Died: July 27, 1970, New York, N.Y. Screen, stage, vaudeville, television singer and actor.

Appeared in: **1954** On the Waterfront. **1959** The Last Angry Man; That Kind of Woman. **1960** Butterfield 8. **1961** The Hustler. **1965** The Pawnbroker.

O'BRIEN, EUGENE
Born: Nov. 14, 1882, Boulder, Colo. Died: Apr. 29, 1966, Los Angeles, Calif. (bronchial pneumonia). Screen and stage actor.

Appeared in: **1916** The Chaperon; Return of Eve; Poor Little Peppina. **1917** Poppy; Brown of Harvard; Rebecca of Sunnybrook Farm. **1918** The Safety Curtain; A Romance of the Underworld; Under the Greenwood Tree. **1919** Come Out of the Kitchen; The Perfect Lover; By Right of Purchase; Fires of Faith. **1920** The Thief. **1921** Worlds Apart; Gilded Lies; Wonderful Chance; Broadway and Home; The Last Door; Is Life Worth Living?; Clay Dollars. **1922** Chivalrous Charley; Channing of the Northwest; John Smith; The Prophet's Paradise. **1923** The Voice from a Minaret; Souls for Sale. **1924** The Only Woman; Secrets. **1925** Graustark; Siege; Dangerous Innocence; Flaming Love; Frivolous Sal; Simon the Jester; Souls for Sables. **1926** Fine Manners; Flames. **1927** The Romantic Age. **1928** Faithless Lover.

O'BRIEN, SEAMUS
Born: 1936, England? Died: May 14, 1977, New York, N.Y. (stab wounds). Screen and stage actor.

Appeared in: **1975** The Happy Hooker. **1976** The Incredible Torture Show. **1977** Marathon Man.

O'BRIEN, "SHOTS" (Charles Brennan)
Born: 1895. Died: Mar. 29, 1961, Los Angeles, Calif. (heart attack). Screen, stage, vaudeville actor and circus performer.

O'BRIEN, TOM (Thomas O'Brien)
Born: July 25, 1891, San Diego, Calif. Died: June 9, 1947, Los Angeles, Calif. Screen, stage and vaudeville actor. Entered films in 1913.

Appeared in: **1921** Scrap Iron; The Devil Within. **1925** The Big Parade; White Fang; Crack O'Dawn; So This Is Marriage. **1926** The Runaway Express; Tin Hats; The Flaming Forest; Poker Faces; The Winner; Take It from Me. **1927** The Bugle Call; The Fire Brigade; The Frontiersman; San Francisco Nights; The Private Life of Helen of Troy; Rookies; Twelve Miles Out; Winners of the Wilderness. **1928** That's My Daddy; Anybody Seen Kelly?; The Last Warning; The Chorus Kid; Outcast Souls. **1929** Dark Skies; Dance Hall; The Peacock Fan; Hurricane; Smiling Irish Eyes; The Flying Fool; His Lucky Day; It Can Be Done; Untamed; Broadway Scandals; Last Warning. **1930** Call of the West; Moby Dick; The Midnight Special. **1931** The Stowaway; Scared Stiff; Sailor Maid Love; Trapped; Hell Bent for Frisco; Yesterday in Santa Fe; The Hawk; Pudge. **1932** Unexpected Father; Phantom Express; The Night Mayor. **1933** Lucky Dog. **1934** Woman Condemned.

O'BRIEN-MOORE, ERIN
Born: 1902, Los Angeles, Calif. Died: May 3, 1979, Los Angeles, Calif. Screen, stage, radio and television actress.

Appeared in: **1930** Curses (short). **1934** Little Men; His Greatest Gamble; Dangerous Corner. **1935** Seven Keys to Baldpate; Our Little Girl; Streamline Express. **1936** The Black Legion; Ring Around the Moon; The Ex-Mrs. Bradford; The Leavenworth Case; Two in the Dark; The Plough and the Stars. **1937** The Life of Emile Zola; Green Light. **1950** Destination Moon. **1951** The Family Secret. **1953** Sea of Lost Ships. **1954** Phantom of the Rue Morgue. **1955** The Long Gray Line. **1957** Peyton Place. **1958** Onionhead. **1959** John Paul Jones. **1967** How to Succeed in Business Without Really Trying.

O'BYRNE, PATSY
Born: 1886, Kans. Died: Apr. 18, 1968, Woodland Hills, Calif. Screen actress. Entered films with Mack Sennett and appeared in "Charlie Chase" comedies.

Appeared in: **1920** Paris. **1926** My Old Dutch; A Sea Dog's Tale. **1928** Outcast. **1929** South Sea Rose; Condemned; Barnum Was Right. **1930** Loose Ankles. **1932** Nice Women. **1933** Doctor Bull; Alice in Wonderland. **1935** Ruggles of Red Gap; It's a Gift; It Happened One Night. **1940** You Can't Fool Your Wife; Saps at Sea. **1941** In the Navy. **1942** The Pride of the Yankees. **1945** Under Western Skies. **1947** Road to Rio; A Likely Story. **1949** Sorrowful Jones. **1952** Something to Live For.

OCHS, PHIL
Born: 1941, El Paso, Tex. Died: Apr. 9, 1976, Far Rockaway, N.Y. (suicide). Folk singer, lyricist and screen actor.

Appeared in: **1970** The Revolution Is In Your Head. **1977** The Day the Music Died.

O'CONNELL, ARTHUR
Born: Mar. 29, 1908, New York, N.Y. Died: May 18, 1981, Woodland Hills, Calif. (Altzheimer's disease). Screen, stage, vaudeville and television actor. Nominated for 1955 Academy Award for Best Supporting Actor in Picnic, and again in 1959 in Anatomy of a Murder.

Appeared in: **1938** Freshman Year. **1940** Two Girls on Broadway; Dr. Kildare Goes Home; plus the following shorts: 'Taint Legal; Bested By a Beard; He Asked for It. **1941** Citizen Kane. **1942** Law of the Jungle;

Man from Headquarters; Canal Zone; Fingers at the Window; Shepherd of the Ozarks; Yokel Boy. **1944** It Happened Tomorrow. **1948** Homecoming; The Naked City; The Countess of Monte Cristo; Open Secret; One Touch of Venus; State of the Union; Force of Evil. **1951** The Whistle at Eaton Falls. **1955** Picnic. **1956** The Solid Gold Cadillac; The Man in the Gray Flannel Suit; Bus Stop; The Proud Ones. **1957** The Monte Carlo Story; The Violators; Operation Mad Ball; April Love. **1958** Voice in the Mirror; Man of the West. **1959** Operation Petticoat; Anatomy of a Murder; Gidget; Hound-Dog Man. **1960** Cimarron. **1961** The Great Imposter; Misty; A Thunder of Drums; Pocketful of Miracles. **1962** Follow That Dream. **1964** Seven Faces of Dr. Lao; Kissin' Cousins; Your Cheatin' Heart. **1965** The Third Day; The Monkey's Uncle; The Great Race; Nightmare in the Sun. **1966** The Silencers; Fantastic Voyage; Ride Beyond Vengeance; Birds Do It. **1967** A Covenant With Death; The Reluctant Astronaut. **1968** The Power; If He Hollers, Let Him Go! **1970** Suppose They Gave a War and Nobody Came?; There Was a Crooked Man. **1973** Wicked, Wicked. **1974** Huckleberry Finn. **1975** The Hiding Place.

O'CONNELL, HUGH
Born: Aug. 4, 1898, New York, N.Y. Died: Jan. 19, 1943, Hollywood, Calif. (heart attack). Screen and stage actor.

Appeared in: **1929** The following shorts: The Familiar Face; Dead or Alive; The Interview; The Ninety-Ninth Amendment. **1930** The Head Man (short); Find the Women (short). **1931** The Smiling Lieutenant; Secrets of a Secretary; Personal Maid. **1932** Hello Sucker (short). **1933** The Cheating Cheaters; Broadway Through a Keyhole. **1934** Gift of Gab. **1935** The Good Fairy; The Man Who Reclaimed His Head; It Happened in New York; Chinatown Squad; Diamond Jim; She Gets Her Man; Manhattan Moon. **1937** Ready, Willing and Able; Fly-Away Baby; That Certain Woman; Marry the Girl; The Perfect Specimen. **1938** Swing Your Lady; Accidents Will Happen; Penrod's Double Trouble; Torchy Blane in Panama; Women Are Like That; Mystery House. **1940** My Favorite Wife; Lucky Partners. **1941** The Mad Doctor; My Life With Caroline.

O'CONNER, EDWARD
Born: Feb. 20, 1862, Dublin, Ireland. Died: May 15, 1932, New York, N.Y. Screen, stage and vaudeville actor.

Appeared in: **1911** The Trapper's Five Dollar Bill; The Sign of the Three Labels; The Question Mark; Pat Clancy's Adventure; A Cure for Crime; At the Threshold of Life; The Bo'sun's Watch; That Winsome Winnie Smile; Turning the Tables; The Rise and Fall of Weary Willie; Logan's Babies; An International Heartbreaker; The Daisy Cowboys. **1912** A Doctor for an Hour; Lazy Bill Hudson; The Stranger and the Taxi Cab; The Green-Eyed Monster; The Angel and the Stranded Troupe; The Totville Eye; Marjorie's Diamond Ring; Aladdin Up-to-Date; Bridget's Sudden Wealth. **1916** The Man Who Stood Still. **1917** One Touch of Nature. **1918** Cecilia of the Pink Roses. **1921** The Inside of the Cup; Get-Rich-Quick Wallingford; Anne of Little Smokey. **1924** Dangerous Money. **1929** Lucky in Love.

O'CONNOR, CHARLES FRANCIS
Born: 1897. Died: Nov. 7, 1979, New York, N.Y. Painter and screen actor. Married to writer/screen extra Ayn Rand (dec. 1982).

Appeared in: **1922** Orphans of the Storm. **1961** Cimarron.

O'CONNOR, FRANK
Born: Apr. 11, 1888, N.Y. Died: Nov. 22, 1959, Hollywood, Calif. Screen, stage actor, screenwriter and film director.

Appeared in: **1932** Handle With Care. **1933** Son of Kong; Kickin' the Crown Around (short). **1934** The Mighty Barnum; As Husbands Go. **1935** Dangerous; Ruggles of Red Gap; False Pretenses. **1936** Great Guy. **1937** Night Club Scandal; Edgar and Goliath (short). **1938** The Purple Vigilantes; Riders of the Black Hills; Dummy Owner (short). **1939** Boy Slaves. **1940** Adventure in Diamonds; Our Neighbors, the Carters; Drafted in the Depot (short); The Grapes of Wrath. **1941** I Wanted Wings; Man-Made Monster; Mad About Moonshine (short); A Panic in the Parlor (short). **1942** Tennessee Johnson; Stardust on the Sage. **1944** The Scarlet Claw. **1947** Saddle Pals; Shoot to Kill; G-Men Never Forget (serial). **1948** Dangers of the Canadian Mounted (serial). **1949** Ghost of Zorro (serial); King of the Rocket Men (serial); Loaded Pistols. **1950** Mule Train; Cow Town; Beyond the Purple Hills; County Fair; The Tougher They Come; The Invisible Monster (serial); The James Brothers in Missouri (serial); Radar Patrol vs. Spy King (serial). **1953** Pack Train.

O'CONNOR, HARRY M.
Born: 1873, Chicago, Ill. Died: July 10, 1971, Woodland Hills, (pneumonia). Screen, stage and vaudeville actor. Entered films approx. 1910.

Appeared in: **1921** Stranger Than Fiction. **1925** Flashing Steeds. **1926** Red Hot Hoofs. **1927** Cyclone of the Range. **1928** When the Law Rides. **1929** The Trail of the Horse Thieves; Come and Get It. **1930** Half Pint Polly (short).

O'CONNOR, HERBERT E.
Died: Nov. 7, 1933, New York, N.Y. (pneumonia). Screen and stage actor.

Appeared in: **1930** Big Fight.

O'CONNOR, JOHN
Born: 1874. Died: Sept. 10, 1941, Santa Monica, Calif. Screen and stage actor.

Appeared in: **1921** The Barricade.

O'CONNOR, KATHLEEN
Born: 1897. Died: June 25, 1957, Hollywood, Calif. Screen actress. Entered films with Mack Sennett.

Appeared in: **1919** The Lion Man (serial); The Midnight Man (serial). **1921** Life's Darn Funny; Sunset Jones. **1922** The Married Flapper; The Trouper; Come on Over; The Old Homestead. **1923** Wild Bill Hickok. **1924** Dark Stairways.

O'CONNOR, KATHRYN
Born: 1894, Cortland, N.Y. Died: Nov. 16, 1965, Albuquerque, N. Mex. Screen and stage actress.

O'CONNOR, LOUIS J.
Born: 1880, Providence, R.I. Died: Aug. 9, 1959, Los Angeles, Calif. Screen and stage actor.

Appeared in: **1921** Diane of Star Hollow. **1922** Watch Your Step; Don't Shoot. **1923** The Call of the Hills; Souls for Sale. **1924** Four Sons; Rarin' To Go; Sporting Youth. **1925** Gold and Grit; The Night Ship; Thundering Through; Heartless Husbands. **1926** The Silent Guardian; Out of the West; Midnight Limited. **1929** The Tip-Off.

O'CONNOR, ROBERT EMMETT
Born: 1885, Milwaukee, Wis. Died: Sept. 4, 1962, Hollywood, Calif. (burns). Screen actor.

Appeared in: **1926** Tin Gods. **1928** The Noose; Dressed to Kill; Four Walls; Freedom of the Press; The Singing Fool. **1929** The Isle of Lost Ships; Smiling Irish Eyes. **1930** Up the River; Alias French Gertie; The Big House; Shooting Straight; Our Blushing Brides; In the Next Room; Framed. **1931** Man to Man; Paid; The Single Sin; The Public Enemy; Three Who Loved; Reckless Living; Fanny Foley Herself. **1932** Taxi; Two Kinds of Women; Big Timber; Night World; The Dark Horse; Blonde Venus; The Kid from Spain; American Madness. **1933** Lady of the Night; Don't Bet on Love; Frisco Jenny; The Great Jasper; Picture Snatcher; The Big Brain; Midnight Mary; Lady for a Day; Penthouse. **1934** Return of the Terror; White Lies; The Big Shakedown; Bottoms Up. **1935** Waterfront Lady; The Whole Town's Talking; The Mysterious Mr. Wong; Star of Midnight; Stolen Harmony; Let 'Em Have It; Diamond Jim; A Night at the Opera. **1936** It Had to Happen; We Who Are About to Die; Desire; The Lone Wolf Returns; Little Lord Fauntleroy; Sing Me a Love Song; At Sea Ashore (short). **1937** The Frame Up; Super Sleuth; Park Avenue Logger; The Crime Nobody Saw; Girl Overboard; The River of Missing Men; Trapped by G-Men; Boy of the Streets; Wells Fargo. **1938** Trade Winds. **1939** Streets of New York; Joe and Ethel Turp Call on the President. **1940** Double Alibi; Hot Steel; A Fugitive from Justice; No Time for Comedy. **1941** Tight Shoes. **1942** Tennessee Johnson. **1943** The Human Comedy; Air Raid Wardens; Whistling in Brooklyn. **1944** Gentle Annie; Nothing But Trouble; Meet Me in St. Louis. **1945** They Were Expendable. **1946** Undercurrent; Easy to Wed; The Harvey Girls; Boys' Ranch. **1947** The Hucksters.

O'CONNOR, UNA
Born: Oct. 23, 1880, Belfast, Ireland. Died: Feb. 4, 1959, New York, N.Y. Screen and stage actress.

Appeared in: **1929** Dark Red Roses (film debut). **1930** Murder. **1931** To Oblige a Lady. **1933** Timbuctoo; Cavalcade; The Invisible Man; Mary Stevens, M.D.; Pleasure Cruise. **1934** The Poor Rich; Horse Play; Orient Express; All Men Are Enemies; The Barretts of Wimpole Street; Stingaree; Chained. **1935** David Copperfield; The Informer; The Bride of Frankenstein; Thunder in the Night; The Perfect Gentleman; Father Brown, Detective. **1936** Rose Marie; The Plough and the Stars; Little Lord Fauntleroy; Llyods of London; Suzy. **1937** Call It a Day; Personal Property. **1938** The Adventures of Robin Hood; The Return of the Frog. **1939** We Are Not Alone; All Women Have Secrets. **1940** It All Came True; Lillian Russell; The Sea Hawk; He

Stayed for Breakfast. **1941** Kisses for Breakfast; Strawberry Blonde; Her First Beau; Three Girls about Town; How Green Was My Valley. **1942** Always in My Heart; My Favorite Spy; Random Harvest. **1943** This Land Is Mine; Forever and a Day; Holy Matrimony; Government Girl. **1944** The Canterville Ghost; My Pal Wolf. **1945** Christmas in Connecticut; The Bells of St. Mary's; Whispering Walls. **1946** Cluny Brown; Of Human Bondage; Child of Divorce; Unexpected Guest; The Return of Monte Cristo; Banjo. **1947** Lost Honeymoon; Ivy; The Corpse Came C.O.D. **1948** Fighting Father Dunne; Adventures of Don Juan. **1957** Witness for the Prosecution.

O'DAY, ALICE
Born: England. Died: Dec. 7, 1937, England? Screen actress.

Appeared in: **1935** The Phantom Light. **1937** Sunset in Vienna (aka Suicide Legion—US 1940).

O'DAY, MAGINNIS (aka OLYVE WASHBURN aka OLYVE MUIRHEAD)
Born: Feb. 26, 1917, N.Y. Died: Apr. 11, 1964, Tarzana, Calif. (suicide—gun shot). Screen actress.

O'DAY, PEGGY (Peggy Reis)
Born: 1900. Died: Nov. 26, 1964, Santa Monica, Calif. Screen actress and stuntwoman.

Appeared in: **1922** Thundering Hoofs; The Storm Girl Angel Citizens; They're Off; Trail's End. **1923** The Fighting Skipper (serial); The Man Getter. **1924** Ace of the Law; Battlin' Buckaroo; Crashin' Through; Shootin' Square; Travelin' Fast. **1925** Peggy of the Secret Service; The Four from Nowhere; Red Blood and Blue; Riders of the Sand Storm; Sporting West; Whistling Jim. **1927** Hoof Marks. **1928** The Clean-Up Man.

O'DEA, DENIS
Born: Apr. 26, 1905, Dublin, Ireland. Died: Nov. 5, 1978, Dublin, Ireland. Screen and stage actor. Married to actress Siobhan McKenna. Entered films in 1934.

Appeared in: **1935** The Informer. **1936** The Plough and the Stars. **1947** Odd Man Out. **1948** The Fallen Idol (US 1949). **1949** Under Capricorn; Marry Me (US 1951); Landfall. **1950** Treasure Island. **1951** Captain Horatio Hornblower; The Long Dark Hall. **1952** Never Take No for an Answer. **1953** Mogambo; Niagara; Sea Devils. **1955** Captain Lightfoot. **1957** The Rising of the Moon; The Story of Esther Costello. **1959** Darby O'Gill and the Little People. **1960** Esther and the King.

O'DEA, JIMMY
Born: 1899, Ireland. Died: Jan. 7, 1965, Dublin, Ireland. Screen, vaudeville, radio and television actor.

Appeared in: **1935** Jimmy Boy. **1938** Blarney (aka Ireland's Border Line—US 1939). **1939** Cheer Boys Cheer; Let's Be Famous. **1957** The Rising of the Moon. **1959** Darby O'Gill and the Little People. **1961** Johnny Nobody (US 1965).

O'DEA, JOSEPH
Born: 1903, Ireland. Died: Mar. 1, 1968, Dublin, Ireland. Screen, stage and radio actor.

Appeared in: **1952** The Quiet Man. **1957** The Rising of the Moon.

O'DEAL, BIBI (Odee Astie)
Born: 1940, France. Died: Nov. 14, 1980, Los Angeles, Calif. (from injuries received while performing stunt). Stuntwoman and screen actress. President of the Hollywood Stuntman's Assn.

Appeared in: **1963** Bluebeard. **1965** The Great Race. **1969** The Southern Star. **1970** Start the Revolution Without Me. **1974** The Three Musketeers. **1975** French Connection II.

O'DELL, DIGGER (John H. Brown)
Born: 1904. Died: May 16, 1957, Hollywood, Calif. (heart attack). Screen, stage, radio and television actor.

O'DELL, SEYMOUR H.
Born: 1863, Ireland. Died: Apr. 3, 1937, Los Angeles, Calif. Screen, stage and radio actor.

ODELL, "SHORTY" (Solomon Schwartz)
Born: c. 1874. Died: Nov. 11, 1924, New York, N.Y. Screen actor.

ODEMAR, FRITZ
Born: 1890, Germany. Died: June 3, 1955, Munich, Germany. Screen actor. Father of actor Erick Ode.

Appeared in: **1932** Das Lied ist Aus; Der Raub der Mona Lisa; Liebeskommando. **1933** Ich Will Nicht Wissen Wer du Bist; Hertha's Erwachen; M; Eine Tur geht Auf; Salon Dora Green; Stern von Valencia; Ein gewisser herr Gran; Ein Unsichtbarer geht durch die Stadt; Schloss im Suden; Viktor and Viktoria (US 1935). **1934** Der Doggelganger; Fraulein; Frau; Heute abend bie mir; Ein Walzer for Dich; Charley's Tante; Furst Woronzeff; Englische Heirat; Peer Gynt; Ein Toller Einfall; Roman Einer Nacht; Schuss im Morgengrauen; Eine Frau wie Du. **1935** Der alte und der Junge Konig; Der Gefangene des Konigs; Lady Windemere's Fan; Ich Sing Mich in Dein Herz Hinein; Gruen ist die Heide; Herr Kobin Geht auf Abenteurer (Mr. Kobin Seeks Adventure). **1936** Der junge Graf; Familie Schimek; Zwischen Zwei Herzen (Between Two Hearts); Knock-Out. **1938** Gross Reinemachen (General Housecleaning); Ein Teufelskerl (A Devil of a Fellow); Der Arme Millionar (The Poor Millionaire).

ODIN, SUSAN (Susan Mary Odin)
Died: Oct. 17, 1975. Screen actress.

Appeared in: **1952** Wild Stallion. **1953** Girls in the Night. **1954** The Eddie Cantor Story. **1960** Because They're Young.

O'DOHERTY, MIGNON
Born: Jan. 30, 1890, Brisbane, Australia. Died: Mar. 12, 1961, London, England. Screen and stage actress.

Appeared in: **1932** There Goes the Bride (US 1933); The Faithful Heart (aka Faithful Hearts—US 1933). **1934** Autumn Crocus. **1949** Maytime in Mayfair (US 1952). **1958** The Whole Truth.

O'DONNELL, CATHY (Ann Steely)
Born: July 6, 1925, Siluria, Ala. Died: Apr. 11, 1970, Los Angeles, Calif. Stage and screen actress.

Appeared in: **1946** The Best Years of Our Lives (film debut). **1947** Bury Me Dead. **1948** They Live by Night (aka The Twisted Road and Your Red Wagon); The Amazing Mr. X. **1950** Side Street; The Miniver Story. **1951** Never Trust a Gambler; Detective Story. **1952** A Woman's Angle (US 1954). **1954** Eight O'Clock Walk (US 1955). **1955** The Man from Laramie; Mad at the World. **1957** The Deerslayer; The Story of Mankind. **1959** Ben Hur; Terror in the Haunted House (aka My World Dies Screaming).

O'DONNELL, CHARLES H.
Born: 1886. Died: Sept. 10, 1962, Pompano Beach, Fla. Screen and vaudeville actor. Appreared in vaudeville team of "Lane and O'Donnell" and later "O'Donnell and Blair."

O'DONOVAN, FRANK
Born: 1900, Ireland. Died: June 28, 1974, Majorca, Spain. Screen, stage, vaudeville, television actor and composer.

Appeared in: **1961** Murder in Eden. **1962** The Quare Fellow.

O'DONOVAN, FRED
Born: Oct. 14, 1889, Dublin, Ireland. Died: July 21, 1952, London, England. Screen, stage actor, stage director and producer. Married to actress Joyce Chancellor.

Appeared in: **1948** Another Shore (US 1951).

O'DOWD, MICHAEL "MIKE"
Died: Sept. 5, 1977. Screen actor.

Appeared in: **1954** On the Waterfront. **1958** The Goddess; Never Love a Stranger. **1961** Girl on the Run. **1963** Violent Midnight; Wild is My Love. **1964** Psychomania. **1969** Take the Money and Run.

O'DUNN, IRVIN
Born: 1904. Died: Jan. 1, 1933, New York, N.Y. (accidental fall). Screen, vaudeville actor and magician. Appeared in vaudeville team as part of "O'Dunn and O'Day."

OELRICHS, MARJORIE
Born: 1908. Died: Aug. 3, 1937, N.Y. Screen and stage actress. Married to actor/pianist Eddy Duchin (dec. 1951). Mother of pianist Eddy Duchin, Jr.

O'FARRELL, MARY
Born: May 27, 1892, London, England. Died: Feb. 10, 1968, London, England. Screen, stage, vaudeville, radio and television actress.

Appeared in: **1933** General John Regan.

O'FARRELL, TALBOT
Born: 1880, England. Died: Sept. 2, 1952, England? Screen actor and music hall entertainer.

Appeared in: **1932** Born Lucky.

OFER, HAROLD *See* RENARD, ROY

OFFENBACH, JOSEPH
Born: 1905, Germany. Died: Oct. 15, 1971, Darmstadt, West Germany (heart attack). Screen, stage and television actor.

Appeared in: **1957** Robinson soll Nicht Sterben (aka The Girl and the Legend—US 1966). **1958** Unruhige Nacht (The Restless Night—US 1964); Das Madchen vom Moorhof (The Girl of the Moors—US 1961). **1959** Mon Petit (aka Monpti); Buddenbrooks (US 1962); Verbrechen nach Schulschluss (aka The Young Go Wild—US 1962). **1963** Willy.

OFFERMAN, GEORGE, JR.
Born: Mar. 14, 1917, Chicago, Ill. Died: Jan. 14, 1963, New York, N.Y. Screen and stage actor. Son of actor George Offerman, Sr. (dec. 1938) and actress Marie Offerman (dec. 1950).

Appeared in: **1927** The Broadway Drifter. **1929** The Girl on the Barge. **1933** Mayor of Hell. **1934** The House of Rothschild. **1935** Grand Old Girl; Jalna; Black Fury; Old Grey Mayor (short). **1936** Chatterbox; Wedding Present. **1937** Midnight Court; Night Club Scandal. **1938** Scandal Sheet; Crime School; Three Comrades. **1939** Dust Be My Destiny; They Asked for It; Calling Dr. Kildare. **1940** Prison Camp. **1942** Whispering Ghosts; War Against Mrs. Hadley; Saboteur. **1943** Action in the North Atlantic. **1944** The Sullivans; See Here, Private Hargrove. **1945** Out of the Depths. **1946** A Walk in the Sun. **1947** The Vigilante (serial). **1949** A Letter to Three Wives. **1951** People Will Talk; Purple Heart Diary. **1952** With a Song in My Heart.

OFFERMAN, GEORGE, SR.
Born: 1880. Died: Mar. 5, 1938, Hollywood, Calif. Screen, stage and vaudeville actor. Father of screen actor George Offerman, Jr. (dec. 1963). Married to actress Marie Offerman (dec. 1950). Appeared in vaudeville in an act billed as "The Original Singing Nut" and later in an act with his wife.

Appeared in: **1929** Girl on the Barge. **1933** Mayor of Hell.

OFFERMAN, MARIE
Born: 1894. Died: May 14, 1950, Hollywood, Calif. Screen, stage and vaudeville actress. Wife of actor George Offerman, Sr. (dec. 1938), with whom she appeared in vaudeville, and mother of actor George Offerman, Jr. (dec. 1963).

OFFIELD, EVELYN
Died: Feb. 28, 1939. Screen actress. Mother of actor Jack Oakie (dec. 1978).

Appeared in: **1933** Too Much Harmony.

O'GATTY, JIMMY "PACKY" (Pasquale O'Gatty)
Born: June 4, 1900, Cannitello, Italy. Died: Oct. 10, 1966, New York, N.Y. Professional boxer and screen actor.

Appeared in: **1936** Laughing Irish Eyes. **1940** East of the River. **1951** Flying Disc Man from Mars (serial). **1958** Missile Monster.

OGDEN, VIVIA (aka VIVA OGDEN)
Died: Dec. 22, 1952. Screen actress.

Appeared in: **1919** Mrs. Wiggs of the Cabbage Patch. **1920** Way Down East. **1921** At the Stage Door; Stardust; The Chicken in the Case. **1922** John Smith; Timothy's Quest. **1923** Way Down East. **1924** Idle Tongues. **1925** The Denial; Thank You; A Slave of Fashion; The Unguarded Hour. **1926** The Fire Brigade; Lovely Mary.

OGLE, CHARLES (Charles Stanton Ogle)
Born: June 5, 1865, Steubenville, Ohio. Died: Oct. 11, 1940, Long Beach, Calif. Screen actor. Entered films in 1907. Was the first actor to portray Frankenstein's monster.

Appeared in: **1910** Frankenstein. **1911** Uncle Hiram's List; The Reform Candidate; Love and Hatred; Home; A Man for all That; How Sir Andrew Lost His Vote; The Minute Man; The Doctor; The Battle of Bunker Hill; The Winds of Fate; The Modern Dianas; Captain Barnacle's Baby; The Surgeon's Temptation; That Winsome Winnie Smile; The Battle of Trafalgar; The Death of Nathan Hale; A Cure for Crime; Foul Play; Her Wedding Ring; The Black Arrow; How Mrs. Murray Saved the American Army. **1912** The Third Thanksgiving; The

Lord and the Peasant; What Happened to Mary? (serial); A Question of Seconds; To Save Her Brother; For the Cause of the South; His Secretary; At the Point of the Sword; For the Commonwealth; Politics and Love; The Dumb Wooing; The Convict's Parole; Blinks and Jinks—Attorneys-at-Law; The Sunset Gun; The Grandfather; The Angel and the Stranded Troupe; The Dam Builder; The Father; The Sketch with the Thumb Print; The Governor; Like Knights of Old; The Totville Eye; Sally Ann's Strategy; On Donovan's Division. **1913** When Greek Meets Greek; While John Bolt Slept; The Great Physician; Hard Cash; The Gunmaker of Moscow; A Clue to Her Parentage; The Doctor's Duty; Janet of the Dunes; The Mountaineers; The Ambassador's Daughter; False to Their Trust; The Princess and the Man; Barry's Breaking In; The Doctor's Photograph; The Ranch Owner's Love Making; Ann; The Gauntlets of Washington; Mother's Lazy Boy; With the Eyes of the Blind; The Duke's Dilemma; The High Tide of Misfortune; A Splendid Scapegrace. **1914** Molly the Drummer Boy; The Active Life of Dolly of the Dailies (serial); His Sob Story; Dolly at the Helm; The Coward and the Man; The President's Special; The Man in the Street; The Lonely Road; The Uncanny Mr. Gumble. **1915** My Lady High and Mighty; His Guardian Angel; The Bribe; Faces in the Night; The Memory Tree; Circus Mary; The Tale of the 'C'; Under Southern Skies; The Woman Who Lied; The Meddler. **1916** Aschenbroedel; The Laugh of Scorn; The Broken Spur; The Sheriff of Pine Mountain; Code of His Ancestors; The Heir to the Horrah; In the Heart of New York; The Girl Who Didn't Tell. **1917** The Case of Dr. Standing; Those Without Sin; The Secret Game; Nan of Music Mountain; The Cost of Hatred; At First Sight; On Record. **1918** The Things We Love; We Can't Have Everything; M'Liss; Wild Youth; The Source; The Squaw Man; Rimrock Jones; Xantippe; The Firefly of France; Less than Kin; Too Many Millions. **1919** Lottery Man; The Poor Boob; The Fires of Faith; Hawthorne of the U.S.A.; The Dub; Alisa Mike Moran; The Valley of the Giants. **1920** Everywoman; What's Your Hurry?; Conrad in Quest of His Youth; Treasure Island. **1921** The Affairs of Anatol; After the Show; Crazy to Marry; Brewster's Millions; Miss Lulu Bett; A Wise Fool; What Every Woman Knows. **1922** Her Husband's Trademark; A Homespun Vamp; The Young Rajah; If You Believe It—It's So; Is Matrimony a Failure?; Kick In; Manslaughter; North of the Rio Grande; Our Leading Citizen; Thirty Days; The Woman Who Walked Alone. **1923** The Covered Wagon; Garrison's Finish; Grumpy; Hollywood; Ruggles of Red Gap; Salomy Jane; The Ten Commandments; Sixty Cents an Hour. **1924** The Alaskan; The Border Legion; The Bedroom Window; Flaming Barriers; Merton of the Movies; The Garden of Weeds; Secrets; Triumph. **1925** Code of the West; The Thundering Herd; Contraband; The Golden Bed. **1926** The Flaming Forest; One Minute to Play.

O'GORMAN, WILLIAM G
Born: 1903, Ireland. Died: Aug. 30, 1966, Dublin, Ireland. Screen and stage actor.

Appeared in: **1946** I See a Dark Stranger (aka The Adventuress—US 1947). **1949** Saints and Sinners. **1951** No Resting Place (US 1952).

O'HAGAN, BARNEY
Died: 1961. Screen, stage and television actor. Married to actress Delorys Dahlene (dec. 1976) with whom he appeared as part of the "O'Hagans Comedy Singing and Dancing Team."

O'HALLORAN, MICHAEL
Born: 1911, Edinburgh, Scotland. Died: July 2, 1976, Glasgow, Scotland. Screen, stage and television actor.

Appeared in: **1969** Ring of Bright Water.

O'HARA, BARRY J.
Born: 1926, London, England. Died: Sept. 5, 1979, Woodland Hills, Calif. Screen, stage and radio actor.

Appeared in: **1954** World Dances. **1957** Journey to Freedom. **1961** Twist Around the Clock. **1965** Fluffy; The Cincinnati Kid. **1967** How to Succeed in Business Without Really Trying; Chuka; Valley of the Dolls. **1972** 1776.

O'HARA, FISKE
Born: 1878. Died: Aug. 2, 1945, Hollywood, Calif. Screen, stage, radio and vaudeville actor.

Appeared in: **1933** Paddy the Next Best Thing. **1934** Change of Heart.

O'HARA, GEORGE
Born: Feb. 22, 1899, Idaho. Died: Oct. 16, 1966, Los Angeles, Calif. (cancer). Screen actor.

Appeared in: **1921** Love, Honor and Behave (short); Queenie; A Small Town Idol. **1922** The Crossroads of New York; Shirley of the Circus.

1924 Darwin Was Right; Listen Lester. 1926 Bigger Than Barnum's; The False Alarm; Going the Limit; The Sea Beast; Is That Nice?; The Timid Terror; Why Girls Go Back Home; Casey of the Coast Guard (serial). 1927 Burnt Fingers; California or Bust; Yours to Command; Ladies Beware. 1928 Beau Broadway; Honeymoon; Pirates of the Pines (serial). 1929 A Single Man; Side Street; Night People.

O'HARA, SHIRLEY
Born: May 23, 1910, New York, N.Y. Died: May 5, 1979, Hollywood, Calif. (cancer). Screen, stage, television actress and film critic.

Appeared in: 1927 A Gentleman of Paris; Backstage. 1929 The Wild Party. 1945 Tarzan and the Amazons. 1946 The Chase. 1947 Miracle on 34th Street; Bells of San Fernando. 1960 Inherit the Wind; The Third Voice; The High-Powered Rifle. 1961 Love in a Goldfish Bowl; The Little Shepherd of Kingdom Come. 1962 Sweet Bird of Youth. 1965 Sylvia. 1966 The Hostage. 1968 The Ballad of Josie. 1969 Fuzz. 1976 Rocky.

OHARDIENO, ROGER
Born: 1919. Died: July 14, 1959, New York, N.Y. Black screen and stage dancer.

Appeared in: 1943 Stormy Weather.

OH GRAN, GILBERT (Justo Masso)
Born: 1886, Spain. Died: Sept. 12, 1971, Barcelona, Spain. Screen and stage actor.

Appeared in: 1965 Broken Toys.

O'HIGGINS, BRIAN
Born: 1917, Ireland. Died: Mar. 29, 1980, Dublin, Ireland. Screen, stage, radio and television actor.

Appeared in: 1951 No Resting Place (US 1952). 1970 Ryan's Daughter.

OJEDA, JESUS "CHUCHO"
Born: 1892, Mexico. Died: Nov., 1943, Mexico City, Mexico (heart attack). Stage and screen actor.

O'KEEFE, ARTHUR J.
Born: 1874. Died: Mar. 29, 1959, Hollywood, Calif. Screen stuntman and vaudeville actor. Entered films approx. 1915.

O'KEEFE, DENNIS (Edward Vanes Flanagan, Jr.)
Born: Mar. 28, 1908, Fort Madison, Iowa. Died: Aug. 31, 1968, Santa Monica, Calif. (cancer). Screen, stage, vaudeville, television actor, film director and screenwriter. Married to actress Steffi Duna. Divorced from Louise Stanley. Entered films as a stuntman and extra. Appeared as Bud Flanagan until approx. 1936 and then used the name of Dennis O'Keefe. Wrote screen scripts under his pen name, Jonathan Ricks.

Appeared in: 1931 Reaching for the Moon; Cimarron. 1932 I am a Fugitive from a Chain Gang; Two Against the World; Cabin in the Cotton; Central Park; Night After Night; Scarface: Shame of a Nation; A Bill of Divorcement; Crooner; Big City Blues; The Man from Yesterday; Merrily We Go to Hell. 1933 Bloody Money; Broadway Thru a Keyhole; Girl Missing; Hello, Everbody!; The Eagle and the Hawk; From Hell to Heaven; Gold Diggers of 1933; Too Much Harmony; Duck Soup; I'm No Angel; The House on 56th Street; Torch Singer; Lady Killer. 1934 Jimmy the Gent; Upperworld; Wonder Bar; Smarty; Registered Nurse; Fog Over Frisco; Man With Two Faces; Lady by Choice; Madame Du Barry; College Rhythm; Imitation of Life; Transatlantic Merry-Go-Round; Everything's Ducky (short); The Meanest Gal in Town; He Was Her Man; Desirable; Coming Out Party; Girl from Missouri; Death on the Diamond. 1935 The Man Who Broke the Bank at Monte Carlo; Top Hat; Dante's Inferno; Mary Burns, Fugitive; Burning Gold; Biography of a Bachelor Girl; Gold Diggers of 1935; Devil Dogs of the Air; Rumba; Mississippi; Let 'Em Have It; Doubting Thomas; Every Night at Eight; The Daring Young Man; Anna Karenina; Personal Maid's Secret; It's in the Air; Shipmates Forever; Broadway Hostess; A Night at the Biltmore Bowl (short). 1936 Born to Dance; Anything Goes; Hats Off; Mr. Deeds Goes to Town; 13 Hours by Air; Love Before Breakfast; Great Guy; Libeled Lady; Theodora Goes Wild; The Accusing Finger; Sworn Enemy; And So They Were Married; Nobody's Fool; Rhythm on the Range; Yours for the Asking; The Plainsman; Burning Gold; San Francisco; Till We Meet Again; The Last Outlaw; Three Smart Girls. 1937 The Big City; The Great Gambini; The Lady Escapes; One Mile from Heaven; When's Your Birthday?; Top of the Town; Married Before Breakfast; Parole Racket; Swing High, Swing Low; Captains Courageous; A Star Is Born; Riding on Air; The Girl from Scotland Yard; Easy Living; Saratoga; The Firefly; Blazing Barriers. 1938 Bad

Man of Brimstone; Hold That Kiss; The Chaser; Vacation from Love. 1939 Unexpected Father; Burn 'Em Up O'Connor; The Kid from Texas; That's Right—You're Wrong. 1940 Alias the Deacon; La Conga Nights; I'm Nobody's Sweetheart Now; Pop Always Pays; You'll Find Out; The Girl from Havana; Arise, My Love. 1941 Topper Returns; Bowery Boy; Mr. District Attorney; Broadway Limited; Lady Scarface; Weekend for Three. 1942 Affairs of Jimmy Valentine; Moonlight Masquerade. 1943 Hangmen Also Die; Good Morning Judge; Tahiti Honey; The Leopard Man; Hi Diddle Diddle. 1944 The Fighting Seabees; Up in Mabel's Room; Abroad with Two Yanks; The Story of Dr. Wassell; Sensations of 1945. 1945 The Affairs of Susan; Doll Face; Brewster's Millions; Earl Carroll Vanities; Getting Gertie's Garter. 1946 Her Adventurous Night; Come Back to Me. 1947 T-Men; Dishonored Lady; Mister District Attorney (and 1941 version). 1948 Raw Deal; Siren of Atlantis; Walk a Crooked Mile. 1949 Cover Up; The Great Dan Patch; Abandoned. 1950 The Eagle and the Hawk; Woman on the Run; The Company She Keeps. 1951 Passage West; Follow the Sun. 1952 One Big Affair; Everything I Have Is Yours. 1953 The Lady Wants Mink; The Fake. 1954 The Diamond (aka The Diamond Wizard—US); Drums of Tahiti. 1955 Angela; Chicago Syndicate; Las Vegas Shakedown. 1956 Inside Detroit. 1957 Sail Into Danger; Dragon Wells Massacre; Lady of Vengeance. 1958 Graft and Corruption. 1961 All Hands on Deck. 1963 The Flame (US 1970).

O'KEEFE, LAWRENCE VINCENT
Born: Oct. 28, 1883, N.Y. Died: Jan. 23, 1950, Los Angeles, Calif. Screen and stage actor.

O'KEEFE, LORAINE
Born: Nov. 23, 1894. Died: Sept. 12, 1924, Los Angeles, Calif. (suicide—gun shot). Screen actress.

O'KELLY, DON See KELLY, DON

OLAND, WARNER
Born: Oct. 3, 1880, Umea, Sweden. Died: Aug. 5, 1938, Stockholm, Sweden (bronchial pneumonia). Screen, stage actor and stage producer. Appeared as Charlie Chan in "Charlie Chan" film series (1931-1938). Married to actress Edith Shearn (dec. 1968).

Appeared in: 1909 Jewels of the Madonna (film debut). 1916 The Rise of Susan; The Eternal Question. 1917 The Fatal Ring (serial); Patria (serial). 1918 The Niulahka; The Yellow Ticket. 1919 The Lightning Raider; The Avalanche; Witness for the Defense. 1920 The Phantom Foe; The Third Eye. 1921 Hurricane Hutch; The Yellow Arm. 1922 East Is West; The Pride of Palomor. 1923 His Children's Children. 1924 One Night in Rome; The Fighting American; So This Is Marriage. 1925 Don Q.; Flower of Night; Riders of the Purple Sage; The Winding Stair. 1926 Infatuation; The Mystery Club; Tell It to the Marines; Twinkletoes; Don Juan; Man of the Forest; The Marriage Clause. 1927 The Jazz Singer; Good Time Charley; A Million Bid; Old San Francisco; Sailor Izzy Murphy; What Happened to Father; When a Man Loves. 1928 Wheels of Chance; Stand and Deliver; The Scarlet Lady; Dream of Love. 1929 The Faker; Chinatown Nights; The Mysterious Dr. Fu Manchu; The Studio Murder Case. 1930 The Mighty; Dangerous Paradise; Paramount on Parade; The Return of Dr. Fu Manchu; The Vagabound King. 1931 Drums of Jeopardy; Dishonored; The Black Camel; Daughter of the Dragon; The Big Gamble; Charlie Chan Carries On. 1932 Charlie Chan's Chance; A Passport to Hell; The Son-Daughter; Shanghai Express. 1933 Charlie Chan's Greatest Case; As Husbands Go; Before Dawn. 1934 Mandalay; Bulldog Drummond Strikes Back; Charlie Chan's Courage; Charlie Chan in London; The Painted Veil. 1935 Charlie Chan in Paris; Charlie Chan in Egypt; Werewolf of London; Shanghai; Charlie Chan in Shanghai. 1936 Charlie Chan's Secret; Charlie Chan at the Circus; Charlie Chan at the Race Track; Charlie Chan at the Opera. 1937 Charlie Chan on Broadway; Charlie Chan at the Olympics; Charlie Chan at Monte Carlo. 1961 Days of Thrills and Laughter (documentary).

OLCOTT, SIDNEY (John S. Alcott)
Born: 1873, Toronto, Canada. Died: Dec. 16, 1949, Hollywood, Calif. Screen, stage actor, film and stage director. Married to actress Valentine Grant (dec. 1948). Entered films with Biograph and joined Kalen studios as an actor and director in 1907.

OLDAKER, MAX
Born: 1908, Davenport, Tasmania. Died: Feb. 2, 1972, Launceston, Tasmania. Screen, stage, opera, television actor, singer, stage producer, press and radio critic.

OLDFIELD, BARNEY (Berna Eli)
Born: Jan. 29, 1878, near York Township, Fulton County, Ohio. Died: Oct. 4, 1946 (cerebral hemorrhage). Screen actor, circus performer and sportsman (racer).

Appeared in: **1913** Barney Oldfield's Race for a Life. **1925** The Speed Demon. **1927** The First Auto. **1932** Speed in the Gay 90's (short). **1970** Jack Johnson (documentary).

OLDHAM, DEREK (John Stephens Oldham)
Born: 1893, Accrington Lanes, England. Died: Mar. 20, 1968, England. Screen, stage actor and opera performer.

Appeared in: **1934** The Broken Rosary. **1935** Charing Cross Road. **1957** Dangerous Exile (US 1958).

OLDRING, RUBE
Born: 1885. Died: Sept. 9, 1961, Bridgeton, N.J. Professional baseball player and screen actor.

Appeared in: **1911** The Baseball Bug.

O'LEARY, WILLIAM (William J. O'Leary)
Born: 1888. Died: Jan. 24, 1954. Screen actor.

Appeared in: **1947** The Wistful Widow of Wagon Gap. **1950** For Heaven's Sake. **1953** South Sea Woman.

OLGA, DUCHESS *See* DUCHESS OLGA

OLIN, BOB
Born: 1908. Died: Dec. 16, 1956, New York, N.Y. Screen, radio actor and pro boxer.

OLIVER, EDDIE (Thomas Edward Oliver)
Born: Sept. 16, 1906, Ind. Died: Mar. 19, 1976, Hollywood, Calif. Bandleader and screen actor.

Appeared in: **1953** Easy to Love.

OLIVER, EDNA MAY (Edna May Cox Nutter)
Born: 1883, Malden, Mass. Died: Nov. 9, 1942, Hollywood, Calif. (intestinal disorder). Screen, stage and radio actress. Entered films in 1923 with Famous Players. Nominated for 1939 Academy Award for Best Supporting Actress in Drums Along the Mohawk.

Appeared in: **1923** Wife in Name Only. **1924** Three O'Clock in the Morning; Icebound; Manhattan; Restless Wives. **1925** Lucky Devil; Lovers in Quarantine; The Lady Who Lied. **1926** Let's Get Married; The American Venus. **1929** The Saturday Night Kid. **1930** Half Shot at Sunrise. **1931** Laugh and Get Rich; Cracked Nuts; Cimarron; Newly Rich (aka Forbidden Adventure); Fanny Foley Herself (aka Top of the Bill). **1932** Ladies of the Jury; The Penguin Pool Murder; The Conquerors; Hold 'Em Jail. **1933** The Great Jasper; Only Yesterday; Little Women; It's Great to Be Alive; Alice in Wonderland; Ann Vickers; Meet the Baron. **1934** The Last Gentleman; Murder on the Blackboard; The Poor Rich; We're Rich Again. **1935** David Copperfield; A Tale of Two Cities; No More Ladies; Murder on a Honeymoon. **1936** Romeo and Juliet. **1937** Rosalie; Parnell; My Dear Miss Aldrich. **1938** Paradise for Three (aka Romance for Three); Little Miss Broadway. **1939** The Story of Vernon and Irene Castle; Seond Fiddle; Nurse Edith Cavell; Drums Along the Mohawk. **1940** Pride and Prejudice. **1941** Lydia.

OLIVER, GUY
Born: 1875, Chicago, Ill. Died: Sept. 1, 1932, Hollywood, Calif. Screen and vaudeville actor. Entered films in 1908.

Appeared in: **1912** Robin Hood. **1919** Secret Service; The Lottery Man; Hawthorne of the U.S.A. **1921** City of Silent Men; Fool's Paradise; The Little Minister; Moonlight and Honeysuckle; A Prince There Was; Too Much Speed; A Virginia Courtship; What Every Woman Knows. **1922** Across the Continent; The Cowboy and the Lady; A Homespun Vamp; Manslaughter; Our Leading Citizen; Pink Gods; The World's Champion. **1923** The Covered Wagon; To the Last Man; The Cheat; Hollywood; Mr. Billings Spends His Dime; Ruggles of Red Gap; Sixty Cents an Hour; The Woman with Four Faces. **1924** The Bedroom Window; The Dawn of a Tomorrow; North of '36. **1925** The Air Mail; The Vanishing American; A Woman of the World. **1926** The Eagle of the Sea; Man of the Forest; Old Ironsides. **1927** Arizona Bound; Drums of the Desert; The Mysterious Rider; Nevada; Open Range; Shootin' Irons. **1928** Avalanche; The Vanishing Pioneer; Three Week Ends; Beggars of Life; Hot News; The Docks of New York; Easy Come, Easy Go; Half a Bride; Love and Learn. **1929** Texas Tommy; Far Western Trails; Fighting Terror; Stairs of Sand; The Studio Murder Case; Sunset Pass; Woman Trap; Half Way to Heaven. **1930** Playboy of Paris; The Devil's Holiday; The Kibitzer; The Light of Western Stars; Only the Brave. **1931** Gun Smoke; Skippy; Dude Ranch; Up Pops the Devil; I Take This Woman; Caught; Huckleberry Finn; The Beloved Bachelor; Rich Man's Folly; Sooky.

OLIVER, ILEAN (Ilean Hulme)
Born: 1896. Died: Nov. 20, 1978, Studio City, Calif. Screen actress and model. Appeared in Biograph Studios and Mack Sennett films.

OLIVER, LARRY
Born: 1880. Died: Jan. 22, 1973. Screen actor.

Appeared in: **1950** Born Yesterday.

OLIVER, TED
Born: 1895. Died: June 30, 1957, Los Angeles, Calif. Screen actor.

Appeared in: **1925** Daring Days; Triple Action. **1926** The Fighting Peacemaker. **1934** We're Not Dressing. **1936** Klondike Annie; The Return of Sophie Lang; Border Flight; Yellow Dust. **1937** The Frame-Up; Trapped. **1938** She Loved a Fireman. **1939** Geronimo.

OLIVER, VIC (Viktor Oliver Samek)
Born: July 8, 1898, Vienna, Austria. Died: Aug. 15, 1964, Johannesburg, South Africa. Stage and screen actor. Divorced from actress Sarah Churchill.

Appeared in: **1936** Rhythm in the Air. **1937** Who's Your Lady Friend? **1938** Around the Town; Meet Mr. Penny. **1940** Room for Two (US 1944). **1941** He Found a Star; Hi Gang! **1944** Give Us the Moon. **1945** I'll Be Your Sweetheart.

OLIVETTE, MARIE
Born: 1892. Died: Mar. 15, 1959, New York, N.Y. (burns from fire). Stage and screen actress.

OLIVETTE, NINA
Born: 1908. Died: Feb. 21, 1971, N.Y. (heart attack). Screen, stage and vaudeville actress. Married to actor Harry Stockwell and mother of actors Dean and Guy Stockwell.

Appeared in: **1930** Queen High.

OLMOS, PIO
Born: Mexico? Died: May 24, 1965, Guanajato, Mexico. Screen actor and stuntman.

OLMSTEAD, GERTRUDE
Born: Nov. 10, 1904, Chicago, Ill. Died: Jan. 18, 1975, Beverly Hills, Calif. Stage and screen actress. Married to actor and director Robert Z. Leonard (dec. 1968). Entered films with Universal in 1920.

Appeared in: **1921** The Big Adventure; Shadows of Conscience; The Fighting Lover; The Fox. **1922** The Loaded Door; The Scrapper; The Adventures of Robinson Crusoe (serial). **1923** Cameo Kirby; Trilby. **1924** Babbitt; Empty Hands; George Washington, Jr.; A Girl of the Limberlost; Ladies to Board; Life's Greatest Game; Lover's Lane. **1925** California Straight Ahead; The Monster; Time, the Comedian; Cobra. **1926** Ben Hur; Puppets; Sweet Adeline; The Boob; Monte Carlo; Ibanez's Torrent (aka The Torrent); The Cheerful Fraud. **1927** Becky; Buttons; Mr. Wu; The Callahans and the Murphys. **1928** The Passion Song; Bringing Up Father; The Cheer Leader; Green Grass Widows; Hey Rube!; Hit of the Show; Midnight Life; Sporting Goods; Sweet Sixteen; A Woman Against the World. **1929** The Lone Wolf's Daughter; Show of Shows; Sonny Boy; The Time, the Place and the Girl.

OLSEN, GEORGE
Born: 1893. Died: Mar. 18, 1971, Paramus, N.J. Bandleader, screen, stage actor and recording artist.

Appeared in: **1930** Happy Days.

OLSEN, IRENE
Born: 1902. Died: Apr., 1931, Brooklyn, N.Y. Screen, stage and vaudeville actress.

OLSEN, MORONI
Born: 1889, Ogden, Utah. Died: Nov. 22, 1954, Los Angeles, Calif. (natural causes). Stage and screen actor.

Appeared in: **1935** The Three Musketeers (film debut); Annie Oakley; Seven Keys to Baldpate. **1936** The Farmer in the Dell; Air Force; Two in the Dark; We're Only Human; Yellow Dust; The Witness Chair; Two in Revolt; M'Liss; Mary of Scotland; Grand Jury; Mummy's Boys. **1937** The Life of Emile Zola; The Last Gangster; The Plough and the Stars; Adventure's End; Manhattan Merry-Go-Ruond. **1938** Marie Antoinette; Gold Is Where You Find It; Kidnapped; Submarine Patrol; Kentucky. **1939** Homicide Bureau; Code of the Secret Service; Susannah of the Mounties; Allegheny Uprising; Dust Be My Destiny; That's Right—You're Wrong; Barricade; Rose of Washington Square;

The Three Musketeers (and 1935 version). **1940** Invisible Stripes; Brother Rat and a Baby; East of River; Virginia City; Santa Fe Trail; If I Had My Way; Brigham Young, Frontiersman. **1941** Life With Henry; Dive Bomber; Three Sons O' Guns; One Foot in Heaven; Dangerously They Live. **1942** Mrs. Wiggs of the Cabbage Patch; Reunion; Sundown Jim; My Favorite Spy; The Glass Key; Nazi Spy. **1943** Mission to Moscow; The Song of Bernadette; Air Force; Reunion in France. **1944** Ali Baba and the Forty Thieves; Roger Touhy, Gangster; Cobra Woman; Buffalo Bill. **1945** Pride of the Marines; Weekend at the Waldorf; Mildred Pierce; Don't Fence Me In; Behind City Lights. **1946** A Night in Paradise; Boys' Ranch; Notorious; The Strange Woman; The Walls Came Tumbling Down. **1947** The Beginning or the End?; The Long Night; That Hagen Girl; Possessed; High Wall; Life With Father; Black Gold. **1948** Up in Central Park; Call Northside 777. **1949** The Fountainhead; Samson and Delilah; Command Decision; Task Force. **1950** Father of the Bride. **1951** Father's Little Dividend; Submarine Command; Payment on Demand; No Questions Asked. **1952** The Lone Star; Washington Story; At Sword's Point. **1953** Marry Me Again; So This Is Love. **1954** The Long, Long Trailer; Sign of the Pagan.

OLSEN, OLE (John Sigvard Olsen)
Born: 1892, Peru, Ind. Died: Jan. 26, 1963, Albuquerque, N.Mex. (kidney ailment). Screen, stage, vaudeville and television actor. Brother of screen actor Stephen Olsen (dec. 1946). Was partner with Chic Johnson (dec. 1962) in comedy team of "Olsen and Johnson" both in vaudeville and on screen.

The films they appeared in are: **1930** Oh, Sailor Behave! (film debut). **1931** Fifty Million Frenchmen; Gold Dust Gertie. **1932** Hollywood on Parade (short). **1934** Holly on Parade (short). **1937** Country Gentlemen; All Over Town. **1941** Hellzapoppin (stage and film versions). **1943** Crazy House. **1944** Ghost Catchers. **1945** See My Lawyer.

OLSEN, STEPHEN
Born: 1900. Died: Dec. 14, 1946, Van Nuys, Calif. (sinus infection). Screen and vaudeville actor. Brother of Ole Olsen (dec. 1963). He was member of vaudeville team of "Olsen and Alexandria." Entered films approx. 1941.

OLSON, IVY (Ivan Massie Olson)
Born: Oct. 14, 1885, Kansas City, Mo. Died: Sept. 1, 1965, Inglewood, Calif. Professional baseball player and screen actor.

Appeared in: **1929** Fast Company.

OLT, ARISZTID *See* LUGOSI, BELA

OLVERA, ERNESTO HILL (Hermengildo Olvera Gonzalez)
Born: 1937, Mexico. Died: Mar., 1967, Guadalajara, Mexico (heart attack). Screen actor and organist.

Appeared in one film: Crimen en tus Manos.

O'MADIGAN, ISABEL
Born: 1872. Died: Jan. 23, 1951, Los Angeles, Calif. Screen and stage actress.

Appeared in: **1918** Madame Jealousy; The Studio Girl. **1932** Smiling Faces. **1944** Marine Raiders. **1946** The Stranger. **1947** The Egg and I. **1949** Ma and Pa Kettle.

O'MALLEY, CHARLES E.
Born: 1897. Died: July 28, 1958, Los Angeles, Calif. Screen actor and film director. Brother of actor Pat O'Malley (dec. 1966).

Appeared in: **1924** The Iron Horse; The Only Woman. **1927** Gun-Hand Garrison; Ridin' Luck. **1928** Sally's Shoulders. **1929** The Duke Steps Out. **1931** Full of Notions. **1933** Officer 13.

O'MALLEY, GRANIA
Born: 1898, Ireland. Died: June 14, 1973, New York. Screen, stage, vaudeville and television actress. Married to William Dunham with whom she appeared in vaudeville in an act billed as "Dunham and O'Malley."

Appeared in: **1972** The Hot Rock.

O'MALLEY, JOHN
Born: 1904. Died: Feb. 27, 1945, Malibu Beach, Calif. (auto crash). Stage and screen actor.

Appeared in: **1945** A Sporting Chance (film debut).

O'MALLEY, JOHN P.
Born: 1916, Australia. Died: Aug. 26, 1959, Hollywood, Calif. (heart attack). Screen and television actor.

Appeared in: **1951** Kind Lady. **1952** Julius Caesar. **1953** The Desert Rats. **1955** The Scarlet Coat. **1956** Diane; The Court Jester. **1957** The Invisible Boy.

O'MALLEY, PAT (Patrick H. O'Malley, Jr.)
Born: Sept. 3, 1892, Forest City, Pa. Died: May 21, 1966, Van Nuys, Calif. Screen, vaudeville and television actor. Married to actress Lillian Wilkes (dec. 1976). Brother of actor Charles B. O'Malley (dec. 1958). Do not confuse with actor J. Patrick O'Malley. Entered films with Edison.

Appeared in: **1911** The Papered Door. **1917** The Adopted Son. **1919** The Red Glove (serial). **1920** The Blooming Angel; Go and Get It. **1922** Brothers Under the Skin. **1923** The Man from Brodney's; Wandering Daughters; The Eternal Struggle. **1924** Worldly Goods; Happiness; The Fighting American; Bread. **1925** The Teaser; Tomorrow's Love; Proud Flesh; The White Desert. **1926** Spangles; The Midnight Sun. **1929** Alibi; The Man I Love. **1930** The Fall Guy; Mothers Cry; Average Husband (short); The People Versus (short). **1931** The Lightning Warrior (serial); Night Life in Reno; Sky Spider; Homicide Squad; Anybody's Blonde. **1932** The Shadows of the Eagle (serial); The Reckoning; High Speed; American Madness; Exposure; Those We Love; Klondike; Speed Madness; The Penal Code. **1933** Frisco Jenny; Mystery of the Wax Museum; One Year Later; Sing, Sinner, Sing; Sundown Rider; Man of Sentiment; Parachute Jumper; I Love That Man; Laughing at Life; The Whirlwind; Riot Squad. **1934** Perils of Pauline (serial); Pirate Treasure (serial); Love Past Thirty; Crime Doctor; Girl in Danger. **1935** The Miracle Rider (serial); Man on the Flying Trapeze; The Perfect Clue; Heir to Trouble; Behind the Evidence; Men of the Hour; Lady Tubbs; Wanderer of the Wasteland. **1936** Hollywood Boulevard; Beloved Enemy. **1937** Mysterious Crossing. **1938** Bringing Up Baby; Little Tough Guy. **1939** Wolf Call; Stunt Pilot; Romance of the Redwoods; Frontier Marshal; Dust Be My Destiny; The Roaring Twenties; Dodge City; The Light That Failed. **1940** Captain Caution; A Dispatch from Reuters; Rocky Mountain Rangers; Shooting High; The Night of Nights; A Little Bit of Heaven. **1941** Pals of the Pecos; Sky Raiders (serial); Law of the Range; Reg'lar Fellers; Double Dates; Meet Boston Blackie; Knockout (aka Right to the Heart). **1942** Larceny, Inc.; Tennessee Johnson; Gentlemen Jim; Hold 'Em Jail (short); Two Yanks in Trinidad; Cairo; The Glass Key. **1943** Double Up (short); Deep in the Heart of Texas; Through Different Eyes. **1944** Sailor's Holiday; Adventures of Mark Twain. **1948** Blazing Across the Pecos. **1949** Boston Blackie's Chinese Venture; The Rugged O'Riordans; The Big Steal; All the King's Men. **1950** Mule Train. **1951** Kid from Broken Gun; Kind Lady. **1952** The Bad and the Beautiful. **1954** The Wild One. **1955** The Long Gray Line. **1956** Invasion of the Body Snatchers; Black-Jack Ketchum, Desperado. **1962** Days of Wine and Roses.

O'MALLEY, REX (Sean Rex Patrick O'Malley)
Born: Jan. 2, 1901, London, England. Died: May 1, 1976, New York, N.Y. Screen, stage, radio and television actor. Entered films in 1924.

Appeared in: **1925** Somebody's Darling. **1934** Midnight. **1936** Camille. **1939** Zaza. **1952** The Thief. **1953** Taxi.

O'MALLEY, THOMAS E.
Born: 1856, Boston, Mass. Died: May 5, 1926, Brooklyn, N.Y. (complications of disease). Screen and stage actor.

Appeared in: **1921** Cappy Ricks; Rainbow. **1924** His Darker Self.

O'MOORE, BARRY *See* YOST, HERBERT A.

O'NEAL, ANNE (Patsy Ann Epperson aka ANNE O'NEIL)
Born: Dec. 23, 1893, Mo. Died: Nov. 24, 1971, Woodland Hills, Calif. (pancreatitis). Screen actress.

Appeared in: **1936** Caught in the Act (short); Ants in the Pantry (short). **1940** The following shorts: Alfalfa's Double; The New Pupil; Goin' Fishin'. **1941** 1-2-3 Go! (short). **1942** In Old California; The Sombrero Kid; plus the following shorts: Mighty Lak a Goat; Mail Trouble; Wedded Bliss. **1943** In Old Oklahoma. **1944** Wilson; Strangers in the Night. **1945** The Missing Corpse; Abbott and Costello in Hollywood; Pillow to Post; Three's a Crowd. **1946** Little Giant. **1947** The Bishop's Wife; Cheyenne. **1948** Backstage Follies (short); Open Secret; Black Bart; How to Clean a House (short); Borrowed Trouble. **1949** Deadly as the Female. **1950** Belle of Old Mexico. **1952** It Could Happen to You (short). **1957** The Vampire.

O'NEAL, WILLIAM J.
Born: 1898. Died: May 23, 1961, Hollywood, Calif. Screen, stage, television actor and singer.

O'NEIL, BARBARA

Born: 1910. Died: Sept. 3, 1980, Cos Cob, Conn. Screen and stage actress. Divorced from producer/director Joshua Logan.

Appeared in: **1937** Stella Dallas. **1938** Love, Honor and Behave; The Boy Wife; I Am the Law. **1939** Gone With the Wind; When Tomorrow Comes; Tower of London; The Sun Never Sets. **1940** All This and Heaven Too. **1941** Shining Victory. **1948** I Remember Mama; Secret Beyond the Door. **1949** Whirlpool. **1953** Angel Face. **1955** Flame of the Islands. **1957** Sorority Girl. **1959** The Nun's Story.

O'NEIL, BARBOUR *See* MORRIS, BARBOURA

O'NEIL, FRANK

Died: Dec. 8, 1917, New York, N.Y. Screen actor. Entered films with Vitagraph Co. Do not confuse with actor Frank O'Neill.

O'NEIL, NANCE

Born: 1875, Oakland, Calif. Died: Feb. 7, 1965, Englewood, N.J. Screen and stage actress.

Appeared in: **1915** The Kreutzer Sonata. **1917** The Fall of the Romanoffs; Hedda Gabler; Greed. **1919** The Mad Woman. **1929** His Glorious Night. **1930** The Rogue Song; The Floradora Girl; The Lady of Scandal; The Singer of Seville; Ladies of Leisure; The Eyes of the World; Call of the Flesh. **1931** The Good Bad Girl; Cimarron; Their Mad Moment; A Woman of Experience; Transgression; Secret Service; Resurrection; The Royal Bed. **1932** Westward Passages; False Faces; Okay, America. **1935** Jack Ahoy; Brewster's Millions.

O'NEIL, SALLY (Virginia Louise Noonan aka SALLY O'NEILL)

Born: Oct. 23, 1910, Bayonne, N.J. Died: June 18, 1968, Galesburg, Ill. (internal bleeding). Screen and stage actress.

Appeared in: **1925** Sally, Irene and Mary. **1926** The Battling Butler; Mike; The Auction Block; Don't. **1927** Frisco Sally Levy; The Callahans and the Murphys; Slide, Kelly, Slide; Becky; The Lovelorn. **1928** The Mad Hour; The Battle of the Sexes; Bachelor's Paradise; The Floating College. **1929** Show of Shows; Mysterious Island; The Sophomore; Hardboiled; Broadway Fever; The Girl on the Barge; On With the Show; Broadway Scandals; Jazz Heaven. **1930** Hold Everything; Girl of the Port; Sisters; Kathleen Mavourneen. **1931** Salvation Nell; Murder by the Clock; The Brat. **1933** Ladies Must Love; By Appointment Only. **1934** Sixteen Fathoms Deep. **1935** Convention Girl. **1936** Too Tough to Kill. **1938** Kathleen.

O'NEIL, HENRY

Born: Aug. 10, 1891, Orange, N.J. Died: May 18, 1961, Hollywood, Calif. Screen and stage actor.

Appeared in: **1933** Strong Arm (film debut); I Loved a Woman; The World Changes; The Kennel Murder Case; Ever in My Heart; Footlight Parade; The House on 56th Street; From Headquarters; Lady Killer. **1934** The Key; Murder in the Clouds; Bedside; Wonder Bar; Twenty Million Sweethearts; Madame Du Barry; The Big Shakesown; Massacre; Fashions of 1934; Journal of a Crime; I've Got Your Number; Fog over Frisco; The Upperworld; Side Streets; The Personality Kid; The Man With Two Faces; Big-Hearted Herbert; Gentlemen Are Born; Flirtation Walk; Now I'll Tell; Midnight; Midnight Alibi. **1935** The Man Who Reclaimed His Head; The Secret Bride; While the Patient Slept; Great Hotel Murder; Bordertown; The Florentine Dagger; Oil for the Lamps of China; Stranded; We're in the Money; Dinky; Dr. Socrates; Special Agent; Bright Lights; The Case of the Lucky Legs; Alias Mary Down; The Story of Louis Pasteur; Black Fury; Sweet Music; Living on Velvet. **1936** Anthony Adverse; Road Gang; The Golden Arrow; Bullets of Ballots; The White Angel; Freshman Love; The Walking Dead; Boulder Dam; The Big Noise; Two Against the World; Rainbow on the River. **1937** Draegerman Courage; The Great O'Malley; Green Light; Marked Woman; The Go Getter; The Life of Emile Zola; The Singing Marine; Mr. Dodd Takes the Air; First Lady; The Great Garrick; Submarine D-1; Wells Fargo. **1938** Brother Rat; Jezebel; White Banners; The Amazing Dr. Clitterhouse; Racket Busters; Yellow Jack; The Chaser; Girls on Probation; Gold Is Where You Find It. **1939** Torchy Blane in Chinatown; Wings of the Navy; Confessions of a Nazi Spy; Juarez; Lucky Night; The Man Who Dared; Angels Wash Their Faces; Everybody's Hobby; Four Wives; Dodge City. **1940** Invisible Stripes; A Child Is Born; Calling Philo Vance; The Story of Dr. Ehrlich's Magic Bullet; Castle on the Hudson; The Fighting 69th; 'Til We Meet Again; Money and the Woman; Santa Fe Trail; They Drive By Night. **1941** Johnny Eager; The Bugle Sounds; Men of Boys Town; The Get-Away; Blossoms in the Dust; Whistling in the Dark; Down in San Diego; Honky Tonk; Shadow of the Thin Man; The Trial of Mary Dugan; Billy the Kid. **1942** Born to Sing; Stand By For Action; Tortilla Flat; White Cargo; This Time for Keeps. **1943** The Human Comedy; Air Raid

Wardens; Dr. Gillespie's Criminal Case; Girl Crazy; Whistling in Brooklyn; Lost Angel; The Heavenly Body; A Guy Named Joe; Best Foot Forward. **1944** Dark Shadows (short); The Honest Thief; Airship Squadron No. 4; Rationing; Two Girls and a Sailor; Barbary Coast Gent; Nothing but Trouble. **1945** Keep Your Powder Dry; Anchors Aweigh; This Man's Navy; Dangerous Partners. **1946** The Hoodlum Saint; Bad Bascombe; The Virginian; The Green Years; Three Wise Fools; Little Mr. Jim. **1947** This Time for Keeps; The Beginning or the End. **1948** Leather Gloves; Return of October. **1949** Alias Nick Beal; Holiday Affair; The Reckless Moment; You're My Everything; Strange Bargain. **1950** No Man of Her Own; The Milkman; Convicted; The Flying Missile. **1951** Family Secret; The Second Woman; The People Against O'Hara. **1952** Scandal Sheet; Scarlet Angel. **1953** The Sun Shines Bright. **1955** Untamed. **1957** The Wings of Eagles.

O'NEILL, JACK

Born: 1883. Died: Aug. 20, 1957, Hollywood, Calif. Screen actor and film director. Entered films with Lubin in 1905. Was a stand-in for Percy Kilbride.

O'NEILL, JAMES

Died: Oct. 8, 1938, Hollywood, Calif. Screen and vaudeville actor. Entered films approx. 1918. Do not confuse with other actors with same name.

O'NEILL, JAMES C.

Born: 1876. Died: Nov. 27, 1944, New York (heart ailment). Stage and screen actor.

O'NEILL, JAMES, JR.

Born: Sept. 10, 1878, San Francisco, Calif. Died: Nov. 8, 1923, Trenton, N.J. (pneumonia). Stage and screen actor. Son of actor James O'Neill (dec. 1920). Brother of playwright Eugene O'Neill (dec. 1953).

Appeared in: **1914** The Temptations of Satan. **1917** God's Little Children; The Boy Girl; Susan's Gentleman; The Raggedy Queen. **1918** The Grain of Dust. **1919** The Traveling Salesman.

O'NEILL, JAMES L.

Born: 1884, Philadelphia, Pa. Died: July 18, 1977, Englewood, N.J. Screen, stage, vaudeville, radio, television actor and singer. Do not confuse with other actors with same name.

O'NEILL, JAMES, SR.

Born: Oct. 14, 1847, County Kilkenny, Ireland. Died: Aug. 10, 1920, New London, Conn. (cancer). Stage and screen actor. Father of actor James, Jr. (dec. 1923) and playwright Eugene O'Neill (dec. 1953). Married to Ella Quinlan.

Appeared in: **1913** The Count of Monte Cristo.

O'NEILL, JOHNNY P.

Born: 1852. Died: Sept. 14, 1930, Sydney, Australia. Screen actor.

O'NEILL, MARIE (Marie Allgood)

Born: 1885, Ireland. Died: Nov. 2, 1952. Screen and stage actress. Sister of actress Sara Allgood (dec. 1950). Married to journalist G. H. Mair (dec. 1926) and later married to actor Arthur Sinclair (dec. 1951).

Appeared in: **1930** Juno and the Paycock. **1934** Sing As We Go. **1935** Peg of Old Drury; Come out of the Pantry. **1936** Ourselves Alone. **1937** Glamorous Night; Farewell Again; Bulldog Drummond at Bay; River of Unrest. **1938** St. Martin's Lane; Penny Paradise; Troopship. **1940** Dr. O'Dowd; Sidewalks of London. **1941** You Will Remember; Love on the Dole; Those Kids from Town. **1943** Courageous Mr. Penn. **1945** Love on the Dole (and 1941 version). **1946** Gaiety George. **1947** Murder in Reverse. **1948** Showtime; Piccadilly Incident. **1949** Saints and Sinners. **1950** Someone at the Door. **1952** Treasure Hunt. **1953** The Horse's Mouth.

O'NEILL, MICKEY (Clarence J. H. Dion)

Born: 1903. Died: May 14, 1932, Atascadero, Calif. (auto accident). Screen actor, film director and screenwriter.

O'NEILL, PEGGY

Born: 1924. Died: Apr. 13, 1945, Beverly Hills, Calif. (suicide—sleeping tablets). Screen actress.

Appeared in: **1944** Song of the Open Road. **1945** It's a Pleasure; Penthouse Rhythm. **1946** The Razor's Edge; The Hoodlum Saint. **1950** Let's Dance.

O'NEILL, ROBERT A.

Born: 1911. Died: Oct. 8, 1951, Hollywood, Calif. Screen actor.

Appeared in: **1950** Young Man With a Horn. **1951** The Raging Tide; Drums in the Deep South.

ONG, DANA DEMOSS
Born: July 3, 1874, Richmond, Ohio. Died: Dec. 31, 1948, Los Angeles, Calif. (acute coronary). Screen actor.

Appeared in: **1915** The Cheat. **1916** Fighting Blood. **1917** The Scarlet Pimpernel. **1918** Flash of Fate.

O'NIEL, COLETTE
Born: 1895, Ireland. Died: Oct. 6, 1975, London, England. Screen, stage actress and novelist. Married to actor Miles Malleson (dec. 1969).

Appeared in: **1969** Frankenstein Must Be Destroyed (US 1970).

ONODERA, SHO
Born: 1915, Japan. Died: Oct. 26, 1974, Japan? Screen actor.

OPPENHEIM, MENASHA
Died: Oct. 23, 1973, New York. Yiddish screen, stage actor and singer.

Appeared in: **1938** Tkies Khaf (The Vow).

ORCHARD, JULIAN
Born: Mar. 3, 1930, Wheatley, Oxford, England. Died: June 21, 1979, London, England. Screen, stage and television actor. Entered films in 1953.

Appeared in: **1961** Three on a Spree. **1962** Kill or Cure; Crooks Anonymous (US 1963). **1963** Hide and Seek (US 1964); Father Came Too (US 1966, aka We Want to Love Alone). **1966** The Spy With a Cold Nose. **1967** Half a Sixpence (US 1968); Follow That Camel (US 1968); Carry on Doctor; Stranger in the House (aka Cop-Out—US 1968). **1969** The Nine Ages of Nakedness (US 1970); Can Heironymus Merkin Ever Forget Mercy Humppe and Find True Happiness? **1970** Perfect Friday. **1976** The Slipper and the Rose. **1978** Crossed Swords.

ORDE, BERYL
Born: 1912, England. Died: Sept. 10, 1966, London, England. Screen, stage and radio actress.

Appeared in: **1935** Radio Parade of 1935.

ORDUNA, JUAN
Born: 1908, Spain. Died: Feb. 3, 1974, Madrid, Spain (heart attack). Screen actor, film, stage, television director and film producer. Entered films as an actor.

Appeared in: **1928** Nobleza Baturra (Rustic Chivalry).

ORELLANA, CARLOS
Born: 1901, Mexico. Died: Feb., 1960, Mexico City, Mexico (heart attack). Screen actor.

Appeared in: **1935** La Llorona. **1937** Corazon No te Enganes (Don't Fool Thyself, Heart). **1938** No Basta Ser Madre (Motherhood Is Not Enough). **1939** El Hotel de Los Chiflados; El Capitan Adventurero (The Adventurous Captain). **1940** La Cancion del Milagro (The Miracle Song); En un Burro Tres Baturros (Three Rustics on One Donkey). **1943** The Life of Simon Bolivar. **1944** Tierra de Pasiones.

ORFALY, ALEXANDER
Born: 1935. Died: Jan. 22, 1979, Hollywood, Fla. (auto accident). Screen and stage actor.

Appeared in: **1974** Crazy Joe; Hangup. **1978** Damien—Omen II.

ORKIN, HARVEY
Born: 1918. Died: Nov. 3, 1975, New York, N.Y. Screen, television actor, talent agent and writer.

ORLAMOND, WILLIAM
Born: Aug. 1, 1867, Copenhagen, Denmark. Died: Apr. 23, 1957. Stage and screen actor. Entered films with Lubin Co. in 1912.

Appeared in: **1920** Vanishing Trails (serial). **1921** Beating the Game; Camille. **1922** Arabian Love; Broken Chains; Doubling for Romeo; The Sin Flood; Golden Dreams. **1923** All the Brothers Were Valiant; The Eagle's Feather; The Eternal Three; Look Your Best; Slander the Woman; Slave of Desire; Souls for Sale. **1924** Reno; Nellie, the Beautiful Cloak Model; Name the Man; When a Girl Loves; The White Moth; Wife of the Centaur; True as Steel. **1925** The Dixie Handicap; Seven Keys to Baldpate; The Great Divide; Smouldering Fires. **1926** Kiki; Flesh and the Devil; Mantrap; That's My Baby; Up in Mabel's Room. **1927** The Red Mill; Fashions for Women; Getting Gertie's Garter; See You in Jail; The Taxi Dancer; A Texas Steer. **1928** The Awakening; The Little Yellow House; Rose Marie; Skinner's Big Idea; The Wind; While the City Sleeps. **1929** Blue Skies; The Girl from Woolworth's; The House of Horror; Words and Music; Her Private Affair. **1930** The Way of All Men. **1931** Cimarron; Are These Our Children? **1932** The Roar of the Dragon.

ORLIK, IVAN A. "VANYA"
Born: 1898, Russia. Died: July 4, 1953, Alexandria, Va. Screen actor and dancer. Appeared in German and U.S. films.

ORLOVA, LYUBOV (aka LUBOV ORLOVA)
Born: 1903, Russia. Died: Jan. 26, 1975, Moscow, Russia. Stage and screen actress. Married to film director Grigori Alexandrov.

Appeared in: **1934** Petersburg Nights (film debut); The Jolly Fellows. **1935** Moscow Laughs. **1936** The Circus. **1941** Volga-Volga. **1942** Tanya. **1948** Spring. **1951** Mussorgsky. **1953** Man of Music.

ORMAN, FELIX (Gus Abraham)
Born: 1884. Died: Jan., 1933, Nashville, Tenn. Screen actor.

ORMOND, RON
Born: 1911. Died: May 11, 1981, Nashville, Tenn. (cancer). Screen, vaudeville actor, film director, film producer and screenwriter. Married to actress June Carr. Father of actor Tim Ormond.

Appeared in: **1968** The Exotic Ones.

ORNELLAS, NORMAN
Born: 1939, Honolulu, Hawaii. Died: May 31, 1975, New York, N.Y. (cancer). Stage and screen actor.

Appeared in: **1974** Serpico.

ORONA, VICENTE, JR.
Born: 1931, Mexico. Died: Mar. 11, 1961, Mexico City, Mexico (heart attack). Screen and television actor.

Appeared in: **1934** A Cafe in Cairo. **1935** Cruz Diablo. **1936** Mater Nostra. **1938** Abnegacion; Guadalupe la Chinaca; A la Orilla de un Palmar (At the Edge of a Palm Grove). **1940** Luna Criolla (Creole Moon).

OROPEZA, ANDREW L. (aka ANDRE OROPEZA)
Born: Oct. 2, 1908, Tex. Died: May 5, 1971, Culver City, Calif. (cancer). Screen actor.

Appeared in: **1960** The Third Voice.

O'ROURKE, BREFNI (aka BREFNI O'RORKE)
Born: June 26, 1889, Dublin, Ireland. Died: Nov. 11, 1946. Screen and stage actor.

Appeared in: **1941** The Ghost of St. Michael's; Hatter's Castle; This Man Is Dangerous (aka The Patient Vanishes—US 1947). **1942** The Missing Million; The Next of Kin (US 1943); Much Too Shy; King Arthur Was a Gentleman; They Flew Alone (aka Wings and the Woman—US); Tomorrow We Live (aka At Dawn We Die—US 1943); Unpublished Story; The First of the Few (aka Spitfire—US 1943); Secret Mission; We'll Meet Again. **1943** They Met in the Dark (US 1945); Escape to Danger (US 1944); The Lamp Still Burns; The Flemish Farm. **1944** Tawny Pipit (US 1947); Don't Take It to Heart (US 1949); Twilight Hour. **1945** They Were Sisters (US 1946); Murder in Reverse (US 1946); The Voice Within; Perfect Strangers (aka Vacation from Marriage—US); The Rake's Progress (aka Notorious Gentleman—US 1946); Waltz Time. **1946** I see a Dark Stranger (aka The Adventuress—US 1947). **1947** The Upturned Glass; Green Fingers; The Root of All Evil.

O'ROURKE, MICHAEL
Born: 1908. Died: Nov. 22, 1981, Hollywood, Calif. (heart attack). Screen, stage and television puppeteer.

Appeared in: **1958** Lili.

O'ROURKE, THOMAS
Born: 1872. Died: Oct. 16, 1958, Queens, N.Y. Screen actor. Appeared in films between 1910-1940.

O'ROURKE, TIM
Born: 1933. Died: Nov. 17, 1962, Hollywood, Calif. (auto accident). Screen actor.

ORR, FORREST H.
Died: Apr. 20, 1963, Paterson, N.J. Stage and screen actor.

Appeared in: **1944** Rainbow Island.

ORRACA, JUAN
Born: 1911, Mexico. Died: Aug. 2, 1956, Mexico City, Mexico (heart attack). Stage and screen actor.

ORRICK, DAVID (David Orrick McDearmon)
Born: 1914, Wilmette, Ill. Died: Aug. 18, 1979, Los Angeles, Calif. Screen, stage actor and television director.

Appeared in: **1956** Rumble on the Docks; Blackjack Ketchum, Desperado. **1957** The Spirit of St. Louis.

ORSKA, MARIA (Rachel Blindermann)
Born: Poland. Died: May, 1930, Vienna, Austria (overdose of veronal). Screen and stage actress.

ORTEGA, SANTOS
Born: 1900, N.Y. Died: Apr. 10, 1976, Ft. Lauderdale, Fla. Screen, stage, radio and television actor.

Appeared in: **1951** The Family Secret. **1956** Crowded Paradise.

ORTH, FRANK
Born: Feb. 21, 1880, Philadelphia, Pa. Died: Mar. 17, 1962, Hollywood, Calif. Screen, stage, vaudeville and television actor. Married to actress Ann Codee (dec. 1961). Appeared in vaudeville with his wife in an act billed as "Codee and Orth." In 1928 he made first foreign language shorts in sound for Warner Bros.

Appeared in: **1929-31** The following shorts with his wife, billed as "Codee and Orth": **1929** A Bird in the Hand; Zwei Und Fierzigste Strasse; Stranded in Paris; Music Hath Charms; Meine Frau (Meet the Wife). **1930** Taking Ways; Imagine My Embarrassment. **1931** On the Job; Sleepy Head; Dumb Luck; The Bitter Half. Without Codee in the following shorts: **1930** The Salesman; The Victim. **1931** The Painter. Other films: **1935** Unwelcome Stranger. **1936** Hot Money; Polo Joe; Two Against the World. **1937** The Footloose Heiress; The Patient in Room 18. **1938** Think it Over (short); Nancy Drew, Detective. **1939** Burn 'Em Up O'Connor; Broadway Serenade; Fast and Furious; Nancy Drew, Reporter; Nancy Drew and the Hidden Staircase; The Secret of Dr. Kildare; At the Circus. **1940** Dr. Kildare's Strangest Case; La Conga Nights; Pier No. 13; Gold Rush Maisie; Let's Make Music; Dr. Kildare's Crisis; Michael Shayne, Private Detective; Dr. Kildare Goes Home; Father Is a Prince; His Girl Friday; Boom Town; 'Til We Meet Again. **1941** The Great American Broadcast; The People vs. Dr. Kildare; Dr. Kildare's Wedding Day; Dr. Kildare's Victory; Blue, White and Perfect; Come Live with Me; Strawberry Blonde. **1942** I Wake Up Screaming; Right to the Heart; The Magnificent Dope; Footlight Serenade; Little Tokyo; Tales of Manhattan; Orchestra Wives; Springtime in the Rockies; Dr. Gillespie's New Assistant; Over My Dead Body; To the Shores of Tripoli; My Gal Sal; Rings on Her Fingers. **1943** Sweet Rosie O'Grady; Hello, Frisco, Hello; Coney Island; The Ox-Bow Incident. **1944** Caroline Blues; Storm over Lisbon; Greenwich Village; Buffalo Bill; Summer Storm; Wilson; The Impatient Years. **1945** She Went to the Races; Tell It to a Star; Pillow to Post; Colonel Effingham's Raid; The Lost Weekend; Doll Face; Nob Hill; The Dolly Sisters. **1946** Blondie's Lucky Day; It's Great to Be Young; The Strange Love of Martha Ivers; Murder in the Music Hall; The Well Groomed Bride. **1947** Born to Speed; The Guilt of Janet Ames; Heartaches; Gas House Kids in Hollywood; Mother Wore Tights; It Had to Be You. **1948** So This Is New York; Fury at Furnace Creek; The Girl from Manhattan. **1949** Red Light; Blondie's Secret; Make Believe Ballroom. **1950** The Great Rupert; Father of the Bride; Cheaper by the Dozen; Petty Girl. **1951** Double Dynamite. **1952** Something to Live For. **1953** Houdini; Here Come the Girls.

ORTIN, LEOPOLDO "CHATO"
Born: 1893, Mexico. Died: Aug., 1953, en route to Acapulco, Mexico (heart attack). Stage and screen actor.

Appeared in: **1939** Alla en el Rancho Chico (Out on the Little Ranch); El Muerto Murio (The Dead Man Died). **1940** Caballo a Caballo (Horse for Horse).

ORTIN, MIGUEL
Born: 1891, Spain. Died: May 10, 1978, Spain? Screen actor. Married to actress Margarita Xirgu.

ORTIZ, MANUEL
Born: July 2, 1916, El Centro, Calif. Died: June, 1970, San Diego, Calif. (liver ailment). Professional boxer and screen actor.

Appeared in: **1947** Joe Palooka, Champ.

ORTIZ, THULA
Born: 1894. Died: July 30, 1961, New York, N.Y. Screen, stage and television actress.

ORY, EDWARD "KID"
Born: 1887. Died: Jan. 23, 1973, Honolulu, Hawaii (pneumonia and heart disease). Jazz musician and screen actor.

Appeared in: **1947** New Orleans. **1955** The Benny Goodman Story.

ORZAZEWSKI, KASIA
Born: Oct. 16, 1888, Pa. Died: July 17, 1956, Los Angeles, Calif. (rheumatic heart disease). Screen actress.

Appeared in: **1948** Call Northside 777. **1949** The Red Danube; Thieves' Highway. **1951** I Was a Communist for the FBI; Queen for a Day (aka Horsie). **1952** Deadline—USA. **1954** Executive Suite.

OSBISTON, MAX
Born: 1915. Died: Mar. 12, 1981, Sydney, Australia. Screen, stage, radio and television actor. Married to actress Babs Mayhew.

OSBORN, LYN (Clair Lynn Osborn)
Born: Jan. 23, 1926, Wichita Falls, Tex. Died: Aug. 30, 1958, Los Angeles, Calif. (following brain surgery). Screen and television actor.

Appeared in: **1957** Top Secret Affair; The Amazing Colossal Man; Invasion of the Saucer Men. **1958** Too Much Too Soon; Torpedo Run. **1959** Arson for Hire; The Cosmic Man.

OSBORNE, JEFFERSON (J. W. Schroeder)
Born: 1871, Bay City, Mich. Died: June 11, 1932, Hondo, Calif. (stroke). Screen and stage actor. Entered films in 1912.

Appeared in: **1915** Jerry's Revenge; Hearts and Clubs; Doctor Jerry; A Shotgun Romance. **1916** Jerry's Perfect Day; Preparedness; Jerry and the Moonshiners; Jerry's Elopement; Jerry's Big Haul; The Rookie; The Hero of Z Ranch; Jerry's Strategem; The Masque Ball; Jerry's Collaboration; Jerry and the Counterfeiters; Jerry and the Bandits; Making Things Hum; The Girl of His Dreams; Around the World. **1917** Jerry and His Pal; Jerry's Big Mystery.

OSBORNE, LENNIE "BUD" (aka MILES OSBORNE)
Born: July 20, 1881, Knox County, Tex. Died: Feb. 2, 1964, Hollywood, Calif. Screen and television actor. Entered films with Thomas Ince Co. in 1915.

Appeared in: **1917** Roped In; Border Wolves; Swede-Hearts; The Getaway; Bill Brennan's Claim; Casey's Border Raid. **1921** The Raiders; The Struggle. **1922** White Eagle (serial); Barriers of Folly. **1923** The Prairie Mystery. **1924** Way of a Man (serial); Cyclone Buddy; The Loser's End; Not Built for Runnin'; The Silent Stranger. **1925** Fighting Ranger (serial); Across the Deadline; Flash O'Lightning; The Knockout Kid; Ranchers and Rascals; The Trouble Buster; Win, Lose or Draw. **1926** Blind Trail; Hi-Jacking Rustlers; Law of the Snow Country; Lawless Trails; Looking for Trouble; The Outlaw Express; Three Bad Men; Without Orders. **1927** The Long Loop on the Pecos; A One Man Game; Riders of the West; Don Desperado; Two-Gun of the Tumbleweed; Border Blackbirds; Sky High Saunders; Cactus Trails; The Devil's Twin; King of the Herd. **1928** The Bronc Stomper; The Mystery Rider (serial and feature film); The Vanishing Rider (serial); Cheyenne Trails; The Danger Rider; Forbidden Trails; On the Divide; Secrets of the Range; Texas Flash; Texas Tommy; The Thrill Chaser; Yellow Contraband. **1929** The Cowboy and the Outlaw; West of the Rockies; Bad Man's Money; Days of Daring; The Fighting Terror; The Lariat Kid; The Law of the Mounted; On the Divide; The Last Round-Up; West of Santa Fe; The Invaders. **1930** Half Pint Polly; The Indians Are Coming (serial); Canyon of Missing Men; O'Malley Rides Alone; Call of the Desert; Western Honor; Code of the West; Breezy Bill; The Utah Kid. **1931** Red Fork Range; Battling With Buffalo Bill (serial). **1932** Mark of the Spur. **1933** When a Man Rides Alone; The Diamond Trail; Flaming Guns; Deadwood Pass; Rustler's Roundup; Gordon of Ghost City (serial). **1934** Tailspin Tommy (serial); Riding Thru. **1935** Outlaw Deputy; The Crimson Trail; Rustlers of Red Dog (serial). **1936** The Adventures of Frank Merriwell (serial); The Vigilantes Are Coming (serial); Roamin' Wild; Treachery Rides the Range; Song of the Saddle; Heroes of the Range; Headin' for the Rio Grande. **1937** Guns of the Pecos; The Californian; Yodelin' Kid from Pine Ridge; Western Gold; Boots and Saddles. **1938** Man's Country; Prairie Moon; The Painted Trail; The Mexicali Kid; The Overland Express. **1939** Racketeers of the Range; Legion of the Lawless; Rovin' Tumbleweeds; New Frontier; Across the Plains; Dodge City. **1940** Virginia City; Pioneer Days; Land of Six-Guns; West of Abiline; Lone Star Raiders. **1941** The Phantom Cowboy; Outlaws of the Panhandle; The Medico of Painted Springs; Riding the Wind; Robbers of the Range; The Return of Daniel Boone; The Bandit Trail. **1942** 'Neath Brooklyn Bridge; The Spoilers; Riders of the West. **1943** Robin Hood of the Range; Stranger from Pecos; The Carson City Cyclone; Haunted Ranch; Rangers Take Over; The Avenging Rider; Cowboy Commandos; The Ghost Rider. **1944** Girl Rush; Sonora Stagecoach; Song of the Range; Adventures of Mark Twain; Law Men; Range Law; Valley of Vengeance; Outlaw Trail; Marked Trails; Trigger Law; Laramie Trail; Outlaw Roundup; Dead or Alive. **1945** Prairie Rustlers; Three in the Saddle; The Cisco Kid Returns; Fighting Bill Carson; The Navajo Kid; Flaming Bullets; The Cherokee Flash; His

Brother's Ghost. **1946** Thundertown; Six-Gun Man; Border Bandits; Overland Riders; Outlaw of the Plains; Landrush; Desert Horseman. **1947** Six-Gun Serenade; Thundergap Outlaws; Twilight on the Rio Grande; The Last Round-Up; Trailing Danger; Code of the Saddle; Bowery Buckaroos. **1948** Six-Gun Law; Song of the Drifter; Blood on the Moon; Indian Agent; Crossed Trails; Courtin' Trouble; Silver River. **1949** Gun Runner; Law of the West; Shadows of the West; Gun Law Justice; Frontier Outpost; Haunted Trails; Frontier Revenge; Riders in the Sky; Gunning for Justice; The Gay Amigo. **1950** Six-Gun Mesa; Cow Town; The Cowboy and the Prizefighter; Hostile Country; Arizona Territory; Border Rangers; Over the Border; West of the Brazos; Colorado Ranger; Fast on the Draw; Marshal of Heldorado; The Crooked River; Desperadoes of the West (serial); Winchester 73. **1951** Nevada Badmen; Valley of Fire; Whirlwind; Whistling Hills. **1952** Barded Wire; Texas City; Son of Geronimo (serial); Bugles in the Afternoon. **1954** The Lawless Rider. **1955** Adventures of Captain Africa (serial). **1956** Perils of the Wilderness (serial); Tribute to a Bad Man. **1957** Gun Glory; Flesh and Spur; The Storm Rider. **1958** Escape from Red Rock.

OSBORNE, ROLAND
Born: 1875, Fulton, N.Y. Died: Apr. 19, 1920, New York, N.Y. Screen and stage actor.

Appeared in: **1917** Mary Jane's Pa.

OSBORNE, VIVIENNE
Born: Dec. 10, 1896, Des Moines, Iowa. Died: June 10, 1961. Screen and stage actress.

Appeared in: **1920** In Walked Mary; Love's Flame; The Restless Sex; Over the Hill to the Poorhouse. **1921** Mother Eternal; The Right Way. **1922** The Good Provider. **1930** The Nightingale (short). **1931** Beloved Bachelor. **1932** Husband's Holiday; Two Kinds of Women; The Famous Ferguson Case; Two Seconds; Weekend Marriage; The Dark Horse; Life Begins. **1933** Phantom Broadcast; Supernatural; Tomorrow at Seven; The Devil's in Love; Luxury Liner; Sailor Be Good; Men Are Such Fools. **1935** No More Ladies. **1936** Let's Sing Again; Follow Your Heart; Wives Never Know; Sinner Take All. **1937** Champagne Waltz; The Crime Nobody Saw; She Asked For It. **1940** Primrose Path; Captain Caution; So You Won't Talk. **1944** I Accuse My Parents. **1946** Dragonwyck.

OSBORNE, WILL
Born: 1906, Canada. Died: Oct. 22, 1981, Santa Monica, Calif. Screen actor, bandleader and songwriter.

Appeared in: **1941** Blues in the Night. **1944** In Society. **1946** Swing Parade of 1946.

OSCAR, HENRY (Henry Wale)
Born: July 14, 1891, London, England. Died: Dec. 28, 1969, London, England. Screen, stage and television actor.

Appeared in: **1932** After Dark (film debut). **1933** I Was a Spy. **1934** The Man Who Knew Too Much; Red Ensign (aka Strike 1—US); Brides to Be. **1935** The Case of Gabriel Perry; Night Mail; Sexton Blake and the Bearded Doctor; Me and Marlborough; Father O'Flynn (US 1938); The Tunnel (aka Transatlantic Tunnel—US). **1936** Love in Exile; Seven Sinners (aka Doomed Cargo—US); No Escape; Spy of Napoleon (US 1939); Dishonour Bright; The Man Behind the Mask. **1937** Sensation; Fire Over England; Dark Journey; The Academy Decides; Who Killed John Savage?; The Return of the Scarlet Pimpernel (US 1938). **1938** Black Limelight (US 1939); The Terror; Luck of the Navy (aka North Sea Patrol—US 1940). **1939** Spies of the Air (US 1940); The Saint in London; Dead Man's Shoes; On the Night of the Fire (aka The Fugitive—US 1940); Hell's Cargo (aka Dangerous Cargo—US 1940); The Four Feathers. **1940** Two for Danger; The Flying Squad; Tilly of Bloomsbury. **1941** Atlantic Ferry (aka Sons of the Sea—US); Penn of Pennsylvania (aka The Courageous Mr. Penn—US 1944); The Seventh Survivor; Hatter's Castle. **1942** The Day Will Dawn (aka The Avengers—US); Squadron Leader X (US 1943). **1947** The Upturned Glass; Mrs. Fitzherbert (US 1950). **1948** Idol of Paris; The Greed of William Hart; Bonnie Prince Charlie (US 1952); House of Darkness; It Happened in Soho. **1949** The Man from Yesterday; Which Will You Have? (aka Barabbas the Robber—US); The Bad Lord Byron (US 1952). **1950** Prelude to Fame; Black Rose. **1954** Beau Brummell; Diplomatic Passport. **1955** Portrait of Alison (aka Postmark for Danger—US 1956). **1956** It's a Great Day. **1957** The Little Hut. **1958** The Spaniard's Curse; The Secret Man. **1959** Beyond This Place (aka Web of Evidence—US). **1960** Oscar Wilde; The Brides of Dracula; Foxhole in Cairo (US 1961). **1961** Mein Kampf. **1962** Lawrence of Arabia. **1965** The City Under the Sea (aka War-Gods of the Deep—US). **1964** Murder Ahoy; The Long Ships.

OSE, JAY
Born: Nov., 1911. Died: Nov. 5, 1967, Hollywood, Calif. Magician, screen and television actor.

Appeared in: **1967** Waterhole #3; The Flim Flam Man.

O'SHEA, JACK "BLACKJACK" (Jack Rellaford)
Born: 1906, San Francisco, Calif. Died: Oct. 2, 1967, Paradise, Calif. (heart attack). Screen and television actor.

Appeared in: **1937** The Big Show. **1939** In Old Monterey; South of the Border. **1940** Cuckoo Cavaliers (short). **1942** Sons of the Pioneers. **1944** The San Antonio Kid. **1946** Rio Grande Raiders. **1947** Son of Zorro (serial); G-Men Never Forget (serial); Law of the Lash; Twilight on the Rio Grande; King of the Bandits; Wyoming. **1949** Federal Agents vs. Underworld, Inc. (serial); Ghost of Zorro (serial); Ride, Ryder, Ride. **1951** Silver Canyon.

O'SHEA, MICHAEL
Born: 1906, Conn. Died: Dec., 1973, Dallas, Tex. (heart attack). Screen, stage, radio, television actor and singer. Divorced from Grace Watts.

Married to actress Virginia Mayo **1943** Lady of Burlesque (film debut); Jack London. **1944** The Eve of St. Mark; Something for the Boys; Man from Frisco. **1945** It's a Pleasure; Circumstantial Evidence. **1947** Mr. District Attorney; Violence; Last of the Redmen. **1949** The Big Wheel; Captain China; The Threat. **1950** Underworld Story (aka The Whipped). **1951** Fixed Bayonets. **1952** The Model and the Marriage Broker; Bloodhounds of Broadway. **1954** It Should Happen to You.

O'SHEA, OSCAR
Born: 1882. Died: Apr. 6, 1960, Hollywood, Calif. Screen actor.

Appeared in: **1937** Captains Courageous; Rosalie; Big City; Mannequin. **1938** Angels With Dirty Faces; Man Proof; The Main Event; King of the Newsboys; International Crime; Stablemates; The Shining Hour; Numbered Woman; Racket Busters; Youth Takes a Fling. **1939** Love Affair; Lucky Night; King of the Turf; Big Town Czar; Missing Evidence; Invitation to Happiness; The Star Maker; Tell No Tales; S.O.S. Tidal Wave; She Married a Cop; Those High Grey Walls; Of Mice and Men; The Night of Nights. **1940** Zanzibar; The Singing Dude; 20 Mule Team; You Can't Fool Your Wife; Wildcat Bus; Stranger on the Third Floor; Pier 13; Always a Bride. **1941** The Strawberry Blonde; Ringside Maisie; The Phantom Submarine; Sleepers West; The Officer and the Lady; Harmon of Michigan; Mutiny in the Arctic. **1942** The Bashful Bachelor; I Was Framed; The Postman Didn't Ring; Just Off Broadway; Halfway to Shanghai; Henry Aldrich, Editor. **1943** Two Weeks to Live; Good Morning Judge; Two Tickets to London; Corvette K-225. **1944** Haunted Harbor (serial); Mystery of the River Boat (serial); Her Primitive Man; The Mummy's Ghost. **1945** Bewitched. **1946** The Brute Man; Personality Kid. **1947** Sport of Kings; My Wild Irish Rose. **1948** The Senorita from the West; One Sunday Afternoon; Fury at Furnace Creek.

OSHINS, JULIE
Born: 1906, Brooklyn, N.Y. Died: May 9, 1956, New York, N.Y. Screen, stage actress, television producer and television writer.

Appeared in: **1943** This is the Army (stage and film versions). **1951** I'll See You in My Dreams.

OSMOND, HAL
Died: Dec., 1959, England? Screen actor.

Appeared in: **1950** Your Witness (aka Eye Witness—US); Double Confession (US 1953). **1952** The Story of Robin Hood and His Merrie Men; Top Secret (aka Mr. Potts Goes to Moscow—US 1954). **1953** The Dog and the Diamonds (US 1962). **1954** You Know What Sailors Are; Cash on Delivery (US 1956). **1955** Value for Money (US 1957); The Depraved; High Flight (US 1958). **1956** The Last Man to Hang?; Loser Takes All (US 1957). **1957** Murder Reported (US 1960). **1958** Tread Softly Stranger (US 1959); The Truth About Women. **1959** Jack the Ripper (US 1960).

OSTERMAN, JACK (Jack Rosenthal)
Born: 1902, Toledo, Ohio. Died: June 8, 1939, Atlantic City, N.J. Screen, stage and vaudeville actor.

Appeared in: **1936** Wanted Men.

OSTERMAN, KATHRYN
Born: 1883, Toledo, Ohio. Died: Aug. 25, 1956, New York, N.Y. Stage and screen actress.

Appeared in: **1903** A Search for Evidence. **1904** The Lost Child.

O'SULLIVAN, ANTHONY "TONY"

Died: July 5, 1920, Bronx, N.Y. Screen actor. Entered films with Biograph and later with Mack Sennett. Appeared in several "Jonesy" comedies.

Appeared in: **1908** The Red Girl; The Pirate's Gold. **1909** 'Tis An Ill Wind That Blows No Good; What Drink Did; A Convict's Sacrifice; A Strange Meeting; Getting Even; In the Watches of the Night; Her Terrible Ordeal; Mrs. Jones Entertains; The Honor of His Family. **1910** The Newlyweds; The Final Settlement.

O'SULLIVAN, ARTHUR "ARCHIE"

Born: 1912, Ireland. Died: Feb. 17, 1981, Dublin, Ireland. Screen, stage, radio and television actor.

Appeared in: **1962** The Quare Fellow. **1963** Mystery Submarine. **1964** Girl With Green Eyes. **1965** Young Cassidy. **1967** The Viking Queen. **1970** Ryan's Daughter. **1975** Barry Lyndon.

O'SULLIVAN, MICHAEL

Born: 1934, Phoenix, Ariz. Died: July 24, 1971, San Francisco, Calif. Screen and stage actor.

Appeared in: **1967** You're a Big Boy Now. **1968** Hang 'Em High.

OSWALDA, OSSI (Oswalda Staglich)

Born: 1899, Berlin, Germany. Died: 1948, Prague, Czechslovakia. Screen, stage actress and film producer. Known as the "German Mary Pickford."

Appeared in: **1916** Der GmbH-Tenor; Nacht des Grauens; Schuhpalast Pinkus. **1917** Ein Fideles Gafaengnis; Ossis Tagebuch; Prinz Sami; Wenn Vier Dasselbe Tun; Das Maedchen vom Ballett. **1918** Der Fall Rosentopf; Meine Frau, die Filmschauspielerin; Der Rodelkavalier. **1919** Schwabenmaedle; Die Austernprinzessin (The Oyster Princess); Die Puppe (The Doll). **1920** Die Millionenerbschaft. **1922** Der Blinde Passagier; Das Maedel mit der Maske. **1923** Das Milliardensouper. **1924** Colibre; Niniche. **1925** Herrn Filip Collins Abenteuer; Das Maedchen mit Protektion; Blitzzug der Liebe (aka Express Train of Love). **1926** Die Fahrt ins Abenteuer; Graefin Plaettmamsell; Die Kleine vom Variete; Das Maedchen auf der Schaukel; Schatz, Nach' Kasse; Eine Tolle Nacht. **1927** Es Zogen Drei Burschen; Fruehere Verhaeltnissen; Ein Schwerer Fall; Wochenendbraut. **1928** Eddy Polo mit Pferd und Lasso; Das Haus ohne Maenner; Ossi hat die Hosen An; Die Vierte von Rechts. **1929** Der Dieb im Schlafcoupe (aka Prinzessin auf Urlaub). **1930** Der Keusche Joseph. **1933** Stern von Valencia.

OTIS, ELITA (Elita Proctor)

Born: 1851, Cleveland, Ohio. Died: Aug. 13, 1927, Pelham, N.Y. (stroke). Screen and stage actress.

Appeared in: **1909** Oliver Twist.

OTKIN, JOHN P.

Born: Feb. 24, 1880, Astrahkan, Russia. Died: Aug. 10, 1942, Los Angeles, Calif. (coronary). Screen and stage actor.

OTT, ALEXANDER

Born: 1888. Died: Dec. 13, 1970. Theatrical producer (mainly water shows) and screen actor.

OTT, FREDERICK P.

Born: 1860. Died: Oct. 24, 1936, West Orange, N.J. Was a member of Edison's scientific staff and not an actor. He was the first person to be photographed in the motion picture experiments of Thomas A. Edison.

Appeared in: **1893** Sneeze.

OTTE, HENRY ROLPH

Born: 1879. Died: Dec. 17, 1930, San Francisco, Calif. (heart attack). Screen actor.

OTTENHEIMER, ADOLPH

Born: 1876. Died: Aug. 20, 1937, Hollywood, Calif. Screen actor.

OTTENHEIMER, ALBERT M.

Born: 1905. Died: Jan. 25, 1980, Cincinnati, Ohio. Screen, stage, radio, television actor and screenwriter.

Appeared in: **1976** The Front. **1977** Annie Hall. **1979** Nocturna.

OTTIANO, RAFAELA

Born: Mar. 4, 1894, Venice, Italy. Died: Aug. 18, 1942, Boston, Mass. Screen, stage and radio actress.

Appeared in: **1924** The Law and the Lady. **1932** As You Desire Me; Grand Hotel; Washington Masquerade. **1933** Her Man; She Done Him Wrong; Bondage; Ann Vickers; Female. **1934** Mandalay; A Lost Lady; The Last Gentleman; All Men Are Enemies; Great Expectations. **1935** The Florentine Dagger; Lottery Lover; Curly Top; One Frightened Night; Remember Last Night?; Enchanted April; Crime and Punishment. **1936** That Girl from Paris; Riffraff; Anthony Adverse; The Devil Doll; Mad Holiday; We're Only Human. **1937** Maytime; Seventh Heaven; The League of Frightened Men. **1938** Marie Antoinette; I'll Give a Million; Suez. **1939** Paris Honeymoon. **1940** The Long Voyage Home; Victory. **1941** Topper Returns. **1942** The Adventures of Martin Eden.

OTTO, ARTHUR

Died: Jan., 1918, Tacoma, Wash. Screen actor.

OTTO, HENRY

Born: 1878. Died: Aug. 3, 1952, Hollywood, Calif. Screen actor and film director.

Appeared in: **1926** The Outlaw Express. **1929** The Quitter; The Iron Mask. **1930** A Matter of Ethics (short); One Hysterical Night. **1938** Fighting Devil Dogs (serial). **1939** The Lone Ranger Rides Again (serial).

OTTON, WILLIAM G.

Born: 1852, England. Died: Mar. 7, 1930, New York, N.Y. Screen and stage actor.

OUDART, FELIX

Born: 1881, France. Died: 1956, France? Screen actor.

Appeared in: **1937** Maternite. **1940** Schubert's Serenade. **1948** Back Streets of Paris. **1950** The Scandals of Clochemerle. **1951** Atoll K (aka Escapade, aka Robinson Crusoeland, and aka Utopia).

OUGHTON, WINIFRED

Born: 1890, London, England. Died: Dec. 26, 1964, England. Screen, stage, radio and television actress.

Appeared in: **1931** The Woman Between (aka The Woman Decides—US 1932). **1932** There Goes the Bride (US 1933).

OUSPENSKAYA, MARIA

Born: July 29, 1876, Tula, Russia. Died: Dec. 3, 1949, Los Angeles, Calif. (burns). Screen and stage actress. Nominated for 1936 Academy Award for Best Supporting Actress in Dodsworth and in 1939 for Love Affair.

Appeared in: **1915** Sverchok na Pechi (aka The Cricket on the Hearth). **1916** Nichtozhniye (Worthless). **1917** Tzveti Zepozclaliye (Belated Flowers, aka Doktor Toporkov). **1919** Zazhivo Pogrebennii (Buried Alive). **1923** Khveska (aka Hospital Guard). **1929** Tanka-Traktirschitsa Protiv Otsa (The Inn-Keeper Against Her Father). **1936** Dodsworth (screen and stage versions). **1937** Conquest (aka Marie Walewska). **1939** Love Affair; The Rains Came; Judge Hardy and Son. **1940** Dr. Erlich's Magic Bullet; Waterloo Bridge; The Man I Married; Beyond Tomorrow; Dance, Girl, Dance; The Mortal Storm. **1941** The Wolf Man; King's Row; The Shanghai Gesture. **1942** The Mystery of Marie Roget. **1943** Frankenstein Meets the Wolf Man. **1945** Tarzan and the Amazons. **1946** I've Always Loved You. **1947** Wyoming. **1949** A Kiss in the Dark.

OUVRARD, GASTON

Born: 1889, France. Died: Nov. 26, 1981, Caussade, France. Screen, stage, television actor and singer.

Appeared in: **1973** Such a Gorgeous Kid Like Me.

OVERMAN, JACK

Born: 1916. Died: Jan. 4, 1950, Hollywood, Calif. (heart attack). Screen actor.

Appeared in: **1941** GI Honeymoon. **1945** Secret Agent X-9 (serial); Johnny Angel; Honeymoon Ahead; The Naughty Nineties. **1946** The Runaround. **1947** Brute Force; The Brasher Doubloon. **1948** Force of Evil; T-Men; The Noose Hangs High. **1949** Flaxy Martin; The Lone Wolf and His Lady; I Can't Remember (short); Shocking Affair (short); Prison Warden. **1950** The Good Humor Man. **1957** Jet Pilot.

OVERMAN, LYNNE
Born: Sept. 19, 1887, Maryville, Mo. Died: Feb. 19, 1943, Santa Monica, Calif. (heart attack). Screen, stage, minstrel and vaudeville actor. Married to actress Emily Drange (dec. 1961).

Appeared in: **1930** Horseshoes (short); Five Minutes from the Station (short). **1933** Poor Fish (short). **1934** Little Miss Marker; The Great Flirtation; She Loves Me Not; Midnight; Broadway Bill; You Belong to Me. **1935** Paris in Spring; Rhumba; Men Without Names; Two for Tonight; Enter Madame. **1936** Collegiate; Poppy; Yours for the Asking; Three Married Men; Jungle Princess. **1937** Wild Money; Nobody's Baby; Don't Tell the Wife; Murder Goes to College; Hotel Haywire; Blonde Trouble; Night Club Scandal; True Confession; Partners in Crime. **1938** Big Broadcast of 1938; Her Jungle Love; Hunted Man; Spawn of the North; Sons of the Legion; Men With Wings; Ride a Crooked Mile. **1939** Persons in Hiding; Death of a Champion; Union Pacific. **1940** Safari; Northwest Mounted Police; Typhoon; Edison the Man. **1941** Aloma of the South Seas; Caught in the Draft; There's Magic in Music; The Hard-Boiled Canary; New York Town. **1942** Reap the Wild Wind; The Forest Rangers; Star Spangled Rhythm; Roxie Hart; Silver Queen. **1943** Dixie; The Desert Song.

OVERTON, FRANK
Born: 1918. Died: Apr. 24, 1967, Pacific Palisades, Calif. (heart attack). Screen, stage and television actor.

Appeared in: **1950** No Way Out. **1957** The True Story of Jesse James. **1958** Desire under the Elms; Lonelyhearts. **1959** The Last Mile. **1960** Wild River; The Dark at the Top of the Stairs; Khovanschina. **1961** Posse From Hell; Claudelle Inglish. **1962** To Kill a Mockingbird. **1964** Fail Safe.

OVEY, GEORGE
Born: Dec. 13, 1870, Kansas City, Mo. Died: Sept. 13, 1951, Hollywood, Calif. Screen, stage and vaudeville actor. Married to actress Louise Horner.

Appeared in: **1915** Jerry and the Gunman; Father Forgot; The Treasure Box; An Oriental Spasm; The Stolen Case; Waking Up Father; Making Matters Worse; He's in Again; A Change of Luck; Hearts and Clubs; The Little Detective; Doctor Henry; Who's Who; Jerry to the Rescue; The Fighting Four; The Double Cross; Taking a Chance; The Hold-Up; A Shotgun Romance. **1916** Jerry's Perfect Day; Preparedness; Jerry's Big Lark; Jerry and the Moonshiners; Jerry's Elopement; Jerry's Big Haul; The Hero of Z Ranch; Jerry's Stratagem; Jerry and the Counterfeiters; The Bookie; A Merry Mix-Up; The Masque Ball; When Jerry Came to Town; Jerry's Celebration; On the Rampage; Jerry and the Smugglers; The Winning Punch; Jerry in the Movies; Jerry in Mexico; Around the World; The Girl of His Dreams; Jerry's Millions; Too Proud to Fight; Going Up; The Desperate Chance; Jerry's Big Game; The Conquering Hero; The Traitor; Jerry and the Bandits; Making Things Hum; Jerry's Double Header; Jerry's Winning Way; Jerry's Big Doing. **1917** Jerry in Yodel Land; Jerry and the Outlaws; Jerry and His Pal; Jerry's Big Raid; Jerry's Big Mystery; Jerry's Brilliant Scheme; Jerry's Romance; The Flying Target; Jerry's Triple Alliance; Minding the Baby; Be Sure You're Right; The Lady Detective; The Gypsy Prince; The Ransom; Jerry's Picnic; There and Back; Jerry's Finishing Touch; Jerry Joins the Army; Jerry's Master Stroke; Jerry's Getaway; Jerry's Red Hot Trail; Jerry's Hopeless Tangle; Jerry's Soft Snap; Jerry and the Bully; Jerry's Lucky Day; Jerry and the Vampire; Jerry's Running Fight; Jerry's Victory; Jerry and the Burglars; Jerry Takes Gas; Jerry's Boarding House; Jerry's Best Friend. **1918** Jerry Tries Again. **1926** The Arizona Sweepstakes; The Sporting Lover; Transcontinental Limited; Strings of Steel (serial). **1927** Better Days; Desert Dust; Pals in Peril; The Yankee Clipper. **1928** My Friend from India. **1929** Broadway. **1930** Hit the Deck; Night Ride. **1933** Alice in Wonderland. **1935** Old Sawbones (short). **1938** Jump, Chump, Jump (short).

OWASSO
Died: Nov., 1962. Animal screen performer (turkey). Nominated for Patsy Award as Best Animal Performer.

Appeared in: **1961** All Hands on Deck.

OWEN, CATHERINE DALE
Born: July 28, 1903, Louisville, Ky. Died: Sept. 7, 1965, New York, N.Y. Screen and stage actress.

Appeared in: **1927** Forbidden Woman. **1929** His Glorious Night. **1930** The Rogue Song; Born Reckless; Today; Such Men Are Dangerous; Strictly Unconventional. **1931** The Circle; Behind Office Doors; In Defense of the Law.

OWEN, CECIL
Died: July 25, 1928. Screen actor.

Appeared in: **1920** The Wonder Man. **1921** The Magic Cup. **1923** The Supreme Passion.

OWEN, GARRY
Born: Dec. 18, 1902, Brookhaven, Miss. Died: June 1, 1951, Los Angeles, Calif. (heart attack). Screen, stage and vaudeville actor.

Appeared in: **1933** Son of a Sailor; Hold Your Man; Child of Manhattan; Stage Mother; The Prizefighter and the Lady; Havana Widows; Bombay Mail. **1934** Manhattan Melodrama; Little Miss Marker; No Ransom; The Thin Man. **1935** Hold 'Em Yale; Top Flat (short). **1936** Ceiling Zero; The Case of the Black Cat; King of Hockey; The Return of Sophie Lang. **1937** Racketeers in Exile; San Quentin; True Confession. **1938** Call of the Yukon; Heart of the North. **1939** Idiot's Delight. **1940** Grandpa Goes to Town. **1941** Meet John Doe; The Wagons Roll at Night; High Sierra. **1942** Yankee Doodle Dandy; Pride of the Yankees. **1944** Arsenic and Old Lace; Nothing But Trouble. **1945** The Last Installment (short); Abbott and Costello in Hollywood; Fallen Woman; Mildred Pierce; Anchors Aweigh. **1946** Notorious; The Tiger Woman; Crime of the Century; The Killers; Dark Mirror; Swell Guy. **1947** The Flame; My Favorite Brunette; It Had to Be You. **1948** The Fuller Brush Man; Sorry, Wrong Number. **1949** Criss Cross; Flamingo Road; I Cheated the Law. **1950** The Admiral Was a Lady; The Flying Missle; The Milkman.

OWEN, MILTON A.
Died: Oct. 1, 1969. Screen actor.

Appeared in: **1935** Manhattan Monkey Business (short). **1937** The Great Garrick. **1938** Blondes at Work. **1947** The Exile.

OWEN, REGINALD (John Reginald Owen)
Born: Aug. 5, 1887, Wheathampstead, England. Died: Nov. 5, 1972, Boise, Idaho (heart attack). Screen, stage actor, screenwriter and author. Divorced from Lydia Bilbrooke. Married stage actress Mrs. Harold Austin (dec. 1956) and later married Barbara Haveman.

Appeared in: **1911** Henry VIII. **1914** The Flight of Death. **1916** Sally in Our Alley; A Place in the Sun. **1923** Phroso. **1929** The Letter. **1931** Platinum Blonde; Man in Possession. **1932** A Woman Commands; Lovers Courageous; Downstairs; The Man Called Back; Sherlock Holmes; Bill of Divorcement. **1933** Robbers' Roost; A Study in Scarlet; The Big Brain; Double Harness; Voltaire; The Narrow Corner; Queen Christina. **1934** Fashions of 1934; Nana; The House of Rothschild; Madame Du Barry; Mandalay; The Countess of Monte Cristo; Where Sinners Meet; Of Human Bondage; Here Is My Heart; The Human Side; Stingaree; Music in the Air. **1935** The Good Fairy; Call of the Wild; Anna Karenina; Escapade; A Tale of Two Cities; The Bishop Misbehaves; Enchanted April. **1936** Rose Marie; Petticoat Fever; Trouble for Two; The Great Ziegfeld; Love on the Run; The Girl on the Front Page; Adventure in Manhattan; Yours for the Asking; Rich and Reckless; The Suicide Club. **1937** Dangerous Number; Personal Property; Madame X; The Bride Wore Red; Conquest; Rosalie. **1938** Paradise for Three; Everybody Sing!; Three Loves Has Nancy; Vacation from Love; A Christmas Carol; Kidnapped; Stablemates; Sweethearts. **1939** The Girl Downstairs; Balalaika; Fast and Loose; Bridal Suite; Bad Little Angel; Remember?; Hotel Imperial; The Real Glory. **1940** The Earl of Chicago; The Ghost Comes Home; Florian; Hullabaloo; Pride and Prejudice. **1941** Blonde Inspiration; Free and Easy; They Met in Bombay; Lady Be Good; Tarzan's Secret Treasure; A Woman's Face; Charley's Aunt. **1942** Mrs. Miniver; White Cargo; Random Harvest; We Were Dancing; Woman of the Year; I Married an Angel; Pierre of the Plains; Somewhere I'll Find You; Cairo; Reunion. **1943** Above Suspicion; Three Hearts for Julia; Forever and a Day; Salute to the Marines; Madame Curie; Assignment in Brittany; Lassie Come Home. **1944** National Velvet; The Canterville Ghost. **1945** The Diary of a Chambermaid; She Went to the Races; Monsieur Beaucaire; The Valley of Decision; Captain Kidd; The Sailor Takes a Wife; Kitty. **1946** Cluny Brown; Mrs. Loring's Secret. **1947** Thunder in the Valley; Green Dolphin Street; If Winter Comes; Imperfect Lady (aka They Met at Midnight); The Pirate; Julia Misbehaves. **1948** The Three Musketeers; Picadilly Incident; Hills of Home. **1949** Challenge to Lassie; The Secret Garden. **1950** Kim; Grounds for Marriage; The Miniver Story. **1953** The Great Diamond Robbery. **1954** Red Garters. **1958** Darby's Rangers. **1962** Five Weeks in a Balloon. **1963** The Thrill Of It All; Tammy and the Doctor. **1964** Mary Poppins; Voice of the Hurricane. **1967** Rosie!

OWEN, SEENA (Signe Auen)
Born: 1896, Spokane, Wash. Died: Aug. 15, 1966, Hollywood, Calif. Screen, stage actress and screenwriter. Divorced from actor George Walsh (dec. 1981).

Appeared in: **1914** Out of the Air. **1915** The Lamb; A Day that is Dead. **1916** Intolerance. **1918** Branding Broadway. **1919** Victory; The Sheriff's Son; A Man and His Money; The Life Line. **1921** The Cheater Reformed; Lavender and Old Lace; The Woman God Changed. **1922** Back Pay; The Face in the Fog; Sisters; At the Cross Roads. **1923** The Go Getter; The Leavenworth Case; Unseeing Eyes. **1924** For Woman's Favor; I Am the Man; The Great Wall (aka Neglected Women—US). **1925** Faint Perfume; The Hunted Woman. **1926** Shipwrecked; The Flame of the Yukon. **1928** His Last Haul; Man-Made Woman; Queen Kelly; Sinners in Love; The Blue Danube; The Rush Hour. **1929** The Marriage Playground.

OWENS, JESSE (James Cleveland Owens)
Born: Sept. 12, 1913, Danville, Ala. Died: Mar. 31, 1980, Tuscon, Ariz. (lung cancer). Black athlete, Olympic gold medal winner and screen actor.

OWENS, KIMO
Born: 1942. Died: Oct. 13, 1979, Tucson, Ariz. Screen, television actor and stuntman.

Appeared in: **1976** A Star Is Born. **1978** Outside Chance.

OWENS, PEGGY
Born: 1905. Died: May 27, 1931 (heart failure). Screen wild west rider.

OWENS, WILLIAM
Born: 1863, N.Y. Died: Aug. 20, 1926, Chicago, Ill. Screen and stage actor.

OWSLEY, MONROE
Born: 1901, Atlanta, Ga. Died: June 7, 1937, Belmont, Calif. (heart attack). Stage and screen actor. Son of stage actress Gertrude Owsley (dec. 1936).

Appeared in: **1928** The First Kiss. **1930** Free Love; Holiday (screen and stage versions). **1931** Ten Cents a Dance; Honor among Lovers; Indiscreet; This Modern Age. **1932** Hat Check Girl; Call Her Savage. **1933** The Keyhole; Ex-Lady; Brief Moment. **1934** She Was a Lady; Little Man, What Now?; Wild Gold; Twin Husbands. **1935** Goin' to Town; Behold My Wife; Rumba; Remember Last Night? **1936** Private Number; Yellowstone; Hideaway Girl. **1937** The Hit Parade.

OYA, ICHIJIRO
Born: 1894, Japan. Died: May 28, 1972, Tokyo, Japan (lung cancer). Screen and stage actor.

Appeared in: **1958** Byakuya no Yojo (The Temptress and the Monk—US 1963).

OYSHER, MOISHE
Born: 1907, Lipkon, Bessarabia, Russia. Died: Nov. 27, 1958, New Rochelle, N.Y. Screen, stage, radio actor, composer and cantor.

Appeared in: **1938** The Singing Blacksmith. **1940** Overture to Glory. **1956** Singing in the Dark (also composed words and music).

PABST, GEORG WILHELM
Born: 1885, Vienna, Austria. Died: May 29, 1967, Vienna, Austria. Film director, screenwriter and screen actor. Entered films as an actor in 1921.

Appeared in: **1922** Luise Millerin.

PABST, WILLIAM T.
Died: Oct. 26, 1980. Screen actor.

Appeared in: **1979** Going in Style.

PACE, MAX
Born: 1906. Died: Aug. 3, 1942, Hollywood, Calif. (suicide—gun). Screen actor.

PACKARD, CLAYTON L.
Born: 1888. Died: Sept. 6, 1931, San Diego, Calif. (complications following surgery). Stage and screen actor.

Appeared in: **1927** King of Kings.

PACKER, NETTA
Born: 1897. Died: Nov. 7, 1962, Hollywood, Calif. Screen actor.

Appeared in: **1938** Condemned Woman. **1939** Crime Rave (short). **1942** Life Begins at 8:30; Enemy Agents Meet Ellery Queen; Powder Town. **1947** They Won't Believe Me. **1948** Smart Woman; Good Sam. **1959** It Started with a Kiss.

PADDEN, SARAH
Died: Dec. 4, 1967. Screen actress.

Appeared in: **1926** Obey the Law. **1927** The Bugle Call; Colleen; Heroes of the Night; The Woman Who Did Not Care; The Eternal Barrier (short). **1928** The Companionate Marriage; Souvenirs (short). **1929** The Sophomore; Wonder of Women. **1930** Today; Hide-Out. **1931** Sob Sisters; Yellow Ticket; Great Meadow. **1932** Rebecca of Sunnybrook Farm; Cross Examination; Young America; Midnight Lady; Blondie of the Follies; Tess of the Storm Country; Wild Girl. **1933** The Power and the Glory; The Important Witness; The Sin of Nora Moran; Women Won't Tell; Face in the Sky. **1934** Spitfire; Man of Two Worlds; The Defense Rests; Little Man, What Now?; As the Earth Turns; He Was Her Man; David Harum; Tomorrow's Children; Finishing School; Marrying Widow; Hat, Coat and Glove; The Fountain; When Strangers Meet. **1935** A Dog of Flanders; The Hoosier Schoolmaster; Anna Karenina. **1937** Youth on Parole; Exiled to Shanghai. **1938** Forbidden Valley; Women in Prison; Rich Man—Poor Girl; Romance of the Limberlost; Woman Against Woman; Little Orphan Annie. **1939** Angels Wash Their Faces; Let Freedom Ring; Zero Hour; Should A Girl Marry?; I Stole a Million; Off the Record. **1940** Forgotten Girls; Son of the Navy; Lone Star Raiders; Chad Hanna. **1941** City of Missing Girls; The Man Who Lost Himself; In Old Colorado; A Woman's Face; Tight Shoes; Murder by Invitation; Reg'lar Fellars; The Corsican Brothers. **1942** Snuffy Smith—Yard Bird; Heart of the Rio Grande; The Mad Monster; Riders of the West; Law and Order; The Power of God; The Pride of the Yankees; This Gun for Hire. **1943** The North Star; The Human Comedy; Assignment in Brittany; Hangmen Also Die; So This is Washington; Jack London; Family Troubles (short). **1944** Summer Storm; Range Law; Trail to Gunsight; Girl Rush; Ghost Guns; Uncertain Glory. **1945** Identity Unknown; Song of Old Wyoming; The Master Key (serial); Dakota; Honeymoon Ahead. **1946** So Goes My Love; Joe Palooka—Champ; Angel on My Shoulder; Gentleman Joe Palooka; That Brennan Girl; Wild West. **1947** Joe Palooka in the Knockout; The Millerson Case; Ramrod; Trail Street. **1948** Fighting Mad; The Dude Goes West; Prairie Outlaws; The Return of the Whistler. **1949** Homicide; Range Justice. **1950** House by the River; Gunslingers; The Missourians. **1951** Utah Wagon Train. **1952** Big Jim McLain. **1955** Prince of Players.

PADDOCK, CHARLES
Born: Nov. 8, 1900, Gainesville, Tex. Died: July 21, 1943, near Sitaka, Alaska (plane crash). Track star and screen actor.

Appeared in: **1925** Nine and Three-Fifths Seconds. **1926** The Campus Flirt. **1927** The College Hero; High School Hero. **1928** The Olympic Hero (aka The All-American). **1932** Running With Charles Paddock (short).

PADEREWSKI, IGNACE JAN
Born: 1860. Died: Jan. 29, 1941. Former Polish prime minister and classical pianist.

Appeared in: **1937** Moonlight Sonata.

PADILLA, EMA
Born: 1900, Mexico City, Mexico. Died: July 2, 1956, Mexico City, Mexico (diabetes). Screen actress.

Appeared in: **1916** La Luz.

PADJAN, JACK (aka JACK DUANE)
Born: 1888. Died: Feb. 1, 1960. Screen actor.

Appeared in: **1924** The Iron Horse. **1926** Tony Runs Wild. **1927** Land of the Lawless; The King of Kings. **1928** Crashing Through; Forbidden Grass. **1929** Redskin. **1930** The Big Trail.

PADOVANO, JOHN
Born: 1916. Died: Nov. 27, 1973 (auto accident). Screen actor and film producer.

Appeared in: **1956** Foreign Intrigue.

PADULA, VINCENT (Vicente Padula)
Born: 1900, Argentina. Died: Jan. 16, 1967, Glendale, Calif. (peritonitis). Screen actor.

Appeared in: **1927** Winds of the Pampas. **1934** Cuesta Abajo; El Tango en Broadway. **1950** The Avengers. **1954** Three Coins in the Fountain. **1955** The Girl Rush. **1956** The Three Outlaws. **1957** Escape from Red Rock; Hell Canyon (aka Hell Canyon Outlaws). **1958** The Flame Barrier. **1959** Pier 5, Havana. **1960** Raymie.

PAGDEN, LEONARD
Born: 1862, England. Died: Mar. 24, 1928, England? Screen and stage actor.

Appeared in: **1920** Aunt Rachel. **1921** Tilly of Bloomsbury.

PAGE, ARTHUR W. (Arthur Wellington)
Born: Aug. 2, 1885, Mass. Died: Feb. 8, 1968, Los Angeles, Calif. (heart attack). Stage and screen actor.

Appeared in: **1952** The Winning Team. **1953** The Robe.

PAGE, DON *See* ALVARADO, DON

PAGE, JAMES E.
Born: 1870, England. Died: Mar. 27, 1930, London, England. Stage and screen actor.

Appeared in: **1925** Charley's Aunt (stage and screen versions).

PAGE, LUCILLE (Lucille Berdell)
Born: 1871. Died: Dec. 31, 1964, Hollywood, Calif. Screen, stage and vaudeville actress. Married to actor Art Wellington and they appeared in vaudeville as "Berdell and Wellington."

Appeared in: **1935** and 1937 Educational shorts.

PAGE, NORMAN
Born: 1876, Nottingham, England. Died: July 4, 1935, England? Screen, stage actor and stage producer.

Appeared in: **1919** The Elusive Pimpernel. **1920** At the Villa Rose; Bleak House; The Yellow Claw. **1921** Old Wives' Tale. **1922** The Card; Dick Turpin's Ride to York. **1923** The Sign of Four.

PAGE, PAUL (Campbell U. Hicks)
Born: May 13, 1903, Birmingham, Ala. Died: Apr. 28, 1974, Hermosa Beach, Calif. (heart attack). Screen and vaudeville actor. Entered films in 1929.

Appeared in: **1929** Speakeasy; Protection; Girl from Havana; Happy Days. **1930** Men Without Women; Born Reckless; The Golden Calf. **1931** The Naughty Flirt; Women Go on Forever; Palmy Days. **1932** Pleasure; 70,000 Witnesses; Bachelor Mother. **1933** Phantom Broadcast; Below the Sea. **1934** The Road to Ruin; Countess of Monte Carlo; The Month; Have a Heart. **1935** Kentucky Kernels.

PAGE, RITA
Born: Aug. 16, 1906, London, England. Died: Dec. 19, 1954. Screen actress.

Appeared in: **1932** Aren't We All? **1939** The Little Princess; The Rains Came. **1940** Vigil in the Night; Little Nellie Kelly. **1942** This Above All.

PAGET, ALFRED
Died: c. 1925. Screen and stage actor. Entered films with Biograph in 1910.

Appeared in: **1910** A Romance of the Western Hills; The Banker's Daughter. **1911** Enoch Arden; Out of the Shadow. **1912** Goddess of Sagebrush Gulch; A Dash through the Clouds; Man's Genesis; A Temporary Truce; The Girl and Her Trust; The Lesser Evil; When Kings Were the Law; A Beast at Bay; The Spirit Awakened; The Inner Circle; Heredity; The Musketeers of Pig Alley. **1913** Oil and Water; A Timely Interception; Just Gold; The Primitive Man; A Girl's Stratagem; The Tenderfoot's Money; Fate; Broken Ways. **1914** The Battle of Firebush Gulch. **1915** The Lamb; The Martyrs of the Alamo; A Romance of the Alps; The Bankhurst Mystery; The Opal Pin; The Decoy; The Gambler of the West. **1916** The Swan's Love; The Telephone Girl and the Lady; The Conscience of Hassan Bey; Intolerance; The Heiress at Coffee Dan's; Iola's Promise. **1917** Nina the Flower Girl; Big Timber; Aladdin and His Wonderful Lamp. **1918** When A Girl Loves. **1919** The Fall of Babylon.

PAGLIERO, MARCELLO (aka MARCEL PAGLIERO)
Born: 1907, France. Died: Dec. 16, 1980, Paris, France. Screen, stage actor, film director, television director, screenwriter and television writer.

Appeared in: **1946** Citta Aperta (Open City). **1949** Chips Are Down; Dedee d'Anvers (aka Dedee—US). **1957** The Seven Thunders (aka The Beasts of Marseilles—US 1959). **1961** Les Mauvais Coups (Naked Autumn—US 1963). **1962** Ton Ombre est la Mienne (Your Shadow Is Mine—US 1963). **1965** Je Vous Salue, Maffia (aka Da New York: Mafia Uccid!, and aka Hail! Mafia—US 1966). **1968** Les Gauloises Bleues (US 1969).

PAIA, JOHN
Born: 1908, Hawaii. Died: Oct. 24, 1954, Los Angeles, Calif. Screen actor.

PAIGE, MABEL
Born: 1880, New York, N.Y. Died: Feb. 8, 1954, Van Nuys, Calif. Screen and stage actress. Married to actor Charles W. Ritichie (dec. 1931).

Appeared in: **1915** Caught with the Goods; Flossie's Daring Loyalty; The Flesh Agent; Shoddy; The Tailor; He Couldn't Explain; Mixed Flats; Dog-Gone-Luck; The Wayville Slumber Party; That Brute. **1916** It Happened in Pikesville. **1942** Lucky Jordan; My Heart Belongs to Daddy; Girl's Town. **1943** Young and Willing; True to Life; Happy Go Lucky; Star Spangled Rhythm; The Crystal Ball; The Good Fellows; The Prodigal's Mother. **1944** Someone to Remember; National Barn Dance; Fun Time; Can't Help Singing; You Can't Return Love. **1945** Kitty; She Wouldn't Say Yes; Out of This World; Dangerous Partners; Murder, He Says. **1946** Behind Green Lights; Nocturne. **1947** Johnny O'Clock; Her Husband's Affairs; Beat the Band. **1948** If You Knew Susie; Johnny Belinda; Hollow Triumph; The Mating of Millie; Half Past Midnight; Canon City. **1949** Roseanna McCoy. **1950** The Petty Girl; Edge of Doom. **1952** The Sniper. **1953** Houdini.

PAIGE, PATSY *See* BRILL, PATTI

PAIGE, RAYMOND
Born: 1900, Wausau, Wis. Died: Aug. 7, 1965, Larchmont, N.Y. Screen, stage, radio actor and musical conductor.

Appeared in: **1937** Hollywood Hotel. **1938** Hawaii Calls.

PAIVA, NESTOR
Born: June 30, 1905, Fresno, Calif. Died: Sept. 9, 1966, Sherman Oaks, Calif. Screen, stage, television and radio actor. Entered films in 1937.

Appeared in: **1938** Ride a Crooked Mile; Prison Trail. **1939** Flying G-Men (serial); Beau Geste; Bachelor Mother; The Magnificent Fraud. **1940** Dark Streets of Cairo; The Primrose Path; Northwest Mounted Police; Arise, My Love; The Marines Fly High. **1941** Hold Back the Dawn; The Kid from Kansas; Tall, Dark and Handsome; Johnny Eager; Hold That Ghost. **1942** King of the Mounties (serial); Fly by Night; The Girl from Alaska; Broadway; Timber; Reap the Wild Wind; Road to Morocco; The Hard Way; Flying Tigers. **1943** Rhythm of the Islands; The Dancing Masters; The Desert Song; The Crystal Ball; Song of Bernadette; Pittsburgh. **1944** The Falcon in Mexico; The Purple Heart. **1945** Along the Navajo Trail; A Medal for Benny; The Southerner; Salome, Where She Danced; Nob Hill; Fear; A Thousand and One Nights. **1946** Badman's Territory; Sensation Hunters; The Last Crooked Mile; Road to Utopia; Humoresque. **1947** Ramrod; Carnival in Costa Rica; Shoot to Kill; A Likely Story; Robin Hood of Monterey; Lone Wolf in Mexico; Road to Rio. **1948** Mr. Reckless; Adventures of Casanova; Mr. Blandings Builds His Dream House; The Paleface; Angels' Alley. **1949** Bride of Vengeance; Alias Nick Beal; Oh, You Beautiful Doll; The Inspector General; Mighty Joe Young; Follow Me Quietly. **1950** Joan of Arc; Young Man With a Horn. **1951** Flame of Stamboul; The Great Caruso; Millionaire for Christy; The Lady Pays Off; Double Dynamite; Jim Thorpe—All American. **1952** The Fabulous Senorita; South Pacific Trail; Phone Call from a Stranger; Five Fingers; Mara Maru; The Bandits of Corsica; The Killer Cop; Call Me Madam; Prisoners of the Casbah; Killer Ape. **1954** The Cowboy; Jivaro; Casanova's Big Night; Thunder Pass; The Desperado; Four Guns to the Border; The Creature from the Black Lagoon. **1955** New York Confidential; Revenge of the Creature; Tarantula; Hell on Frisco Bay. **1956** The Mole People; Ride the High Iron; Scandal, Incorporated; Comanche. **1957** Guns of Fort Petticoat; 10,000 Bedrooms; Les Girls. **1958** The Deep Six; The Lady Takes a Flyer; Outcasts of the City; The Left-Handed Gun; The Case Against Brooklyn. **1959** Pier 5, Havana; The Nine Lives of Elfego Baca. **1960** Vice Raid; The Purple Gang; Can-Can. **1961** Frontier Uprising. **1962** The Three Stooges in Orbit; Girls! Girls! Girls!; The Four Horsemen of the Apocalypse; The Martians; The Wild Westerners. **1963** Ballad of a Gunfighter; California. **1964** Madmen of Mandoras. **1966** Let's Kill Uncle; Jesse James Meets Frankenstein's Daughter. **1967** The Spirit is Willing.

PAL
Born: 1915. Died: Nov. 18, 1929, Tujunga, Calif. Screen animal performer (bull terrier). Father of "Petey" (dec. 1930). Entered films in 1921 and appeared in "Pal Comedies" made by Century Film Company.

PALACE, JOHN T. "JOHNNY"
Born: 1895. Died: May 29, 1980, East Patchogue, N.Y. Screen, vaudeville, radio actor and singer. Palace and partner Steve Freda made an early talking film for Vitaphone.

PALANGE, INEZ
Born: 1889. Died: Oct. 16, 1962, Calif. Screen, stage actress and singer.

Appeared in: **1930** Sei tu L'Amore. **1932** Farewell to Arms; Tiger Shark; Scarface, the Shame of the Nation. **1933** Night Flight; Men of America; Mary Stevens, M.D.; White Sister; Grand Slam. **1934** Age of Innocence; Bedside; Merry Wives of Reno; Fugitive Lovers; I've Got Your Number; All Men Are Enemies. **1935** The Melody Lingers On; Enchanted April; Black Fury; The Flame Within; A Night at the Opera. **1936** A Woman Rebels. **1937** Song of the City; Portia on Trial. **1938** Speed to Burn; Road Demon; The Black Doll; Flirting With Fate; Little Miss Roughneck. **1939** Winner Take All; Chicken Wagon Family. **1940** On Their Own; One Million B.C.; I Was an Adventuress. **1941** Romance of the Rio Grande; Under Fiesta Stars; Caught in the Act. **1942** Life Begins at 8:30; Beyond the Blue Horizon. **1954** Monster from the Ocean Floor.

PALLANTE, ALADDIN *See* ALADDIN

PALLAY, FRAN
Born: 1904, Atlanta, Ga. Died: Nov. 6, 1981, Brentwood, Calif. (leukemia). Screen and stage actress. Married to actor Henry Menjou (dec. 1956). Appeared in silent films.

PALLENBERG, MAX
Born: 1877, Vienna, Austria. Died: June 26, 1934, near Karlovy Vary, Czechoslovakia (plane crash). Stage and screen actor. Married to operetta star Fritzy Massary (dec. 1969).

Appeared in: **1912** Pampulik als Affe; Pampluik Kriegt ein Kind. **1913** Pampulik hat Hunger. **1921** Die Nacht und der Leichnam. **1931** Der Brave Suender (The Upright Sinners—US 1933).

PALLETTE, EUGENE
Born: July 8, 1889, Winfield, Kans. Died: Sept. 3, 1954, Los Angeles, Calif. Screen and stage actor.

Appeared in: **1912** American Film Mfg. Co. films. **1913** The Tattooed Arm. **1916** Intolerance. **1919** Fair and Warmer. **1920** Parlor, Bedroom and Bath; Alias Jimmy Valentine. **1921** Fine Feathers; The Three Musketeers. **1922** Two Kinds of Women; Without Compromise. **1923** Hell's Hole; A Man's Man; To the Last Man; North of Hudson Bay. **1924** The Cyclone Rider; The Wolf Man; Wandering Husbands. **1925** The Light of Western Stars; Without Mercy. **1926** Desert Valley; The Fighting Edge; Mantrap; Rocking Moon; Whispering Canyon; Whispering Smith. **1927** Chicago; Moulders of Men; plus 12 Roach shorts including: Sugar Daddies; The Second Hundred Years; Battle of the Century. **1928** Don't be Jealous (short); The Good-Bye Kiss; Lights of New York; His Private Life; How's Your Stock? (short); Out of the Ruins; The Red Mark. **1929** The Canary Murder Case; The Dummy; The Greene Murder Case; The Love Parade; The Studio Murder Mystery; The Virginian; Pointed Heels. **1930** The Benson Murder Case; The Border Legion; Men Are Like That; Slightly Scarlet; Let's Go Native; The Santa Fe Trail; Follow Thru; The Sea God; Paramount on Parade; The Kibitzer; Sea Legs; Playboy of Paris. **1931** Fighting Caravans; Gun Smoke; Dude Ranch; The Adventures of Huckleberry Finn; It Pays to Advertise; Girls About Town. **1932** Tom Brown of Culver; Shanghai Express; Off His Base (short); Thunder Below; Strangers of the Evening; The Night Mayor; Wild Girl; The Half-Naked Truth; A Hocky Hick (short); Dancers in the Dark; Phantom Fame; Pig Boat; Slippery Pearls (short). **1933** Made on Broadway; Hell Below; Storm at Daybreak; Shanghai Madness; Mr. Skitch; The Kennel Murder Case; From Headquarters. **1934** Cross Country Cruise; I've Got Your Number; Strictly Dynamite; Friends of Mr. Sweeney; The Dragon Murder Case; Caravan; One Exciting Adventure. **1935** Bordertown; All the King's Horses; Baby Face Harrington; Black Sheep; Steamboat 'Round the Bend. **1936** Dishonour Bright; Easy to Take; The Ghost Goes West; The Golden Arrow; My Man Godfrey; The Luckiest Girl in the World; Stowaway. **1937** Clarence; The Crime Nobody Saw; Topper; She Had to Eat; One Hundred Men and a Girl; Song of the City. **1938** The Adventures of Robin Hood; There Goes My Heart. **1939** Wife, Husband and Friend; First Love; Mr. Smith Goes to Washington. **1940** It's a Date; Sandy Is a Lady; Young Tom Edison; A Little Bit of Heaven; He Stayed for Breakfast; The Mark of Zorro. **1941** Ride, Kelly, Ride; The Bride Came C.O.D.; World Premiere; The Lady Eve; Unfinished Business; Appointment for Love; Swamp Water. **1942** Are Husbands Necessary?; Almost Married; The Forest Rangers; Silver Queen; Lady in a Jam; The Big Street; Tales of Manhattan; The Male Animal. **1943** Slightly Dangerous; It Ain't Hay; The Kansan; Heaven Can Wait; The Gang's All Here. **1944** Laramie Trail; Pin-Up Girl; Sensations of 1945; Step Lively; In the Meantime, Darling; Lake Placid Serenade; Heavenly Days; Manhattan Serenade. **1945** The Cheaters. **1946** In Old Sacramento; Suspense. **1948** Silver River.

PALMER, BERT
Born: 1901, England. Died: Jan. 15, 1980, England? Screen and stage actor.

Appeared in: **1962** A Kind of Loving. **1979** The National Health.

PALMER, CHARLES "CHUCK"
Born: 1930. Died: Mar. 21, 1976, Los Angeles, Calif. Screen and television actor.

PALMER, CORLISS
Born: July 25, 1902 or 1909, Edison, Ga. Died: Aug. 27, 1952, Camarillo, Calif. Screen actress. Married to rodeo performer William Taylor.

Appeared in: **1922** The Thistle and the Rose. **1926** Her Second Chance. **1927** The Return of Boston Blackie; Honeymoon Hate; A Man's Past; Polly of the Movies. **1928** Clothes Make the Woman; The Night Bird; Into the Night; The Noose; George Washington Cohen; Scarlet Youth; Trial Marriage. **1929** Broadway Fever; Sex Madness. **1931** Honeymoon Lane.

PALMER, DAWSON
Born: 1937. Died: Sept. 10, 1972, Los Angeles, Calif. (auto accident). Screen and stage actor.

PALMER, EFFIE
Died: Aug. 19, 1942, New York, N.Y. Screen, stage and radio actress.

Appeared in: **1931** Huckleberry Finn. **1932** Way Back Home (film and radio versions).

PALMER, JACK F. (John F. Palmer)
Born: Apr. 27, 1866, Toronto, Canada. Died: Sept. 27, 1928, Los Angeles, Calif. (heart disease). Screen and stage actor.

PALMER, LORNA
Born: 1907. Died: June 14, 1928, Hollywood, Calif. (pneumonia). Screen actress.

Appeared in: **1925** Double Action Daniels.

PALMER, MARIA
Born: Sept. 5, 1924, Vienna, Austria. Died: Sept. 6, 1981, Los Angeles, Calif. (cancer). Screen, stage, television actress and writer.

Appeared in: **1943** Mission to Moscow. **1944** Days of Glory. **1945** Lady on a Train. **1946** Rendezvous 24. **1947** The Web; The Other Love. **1948** 13 Lead Soldiers. **1950** Surrender. **1951** Strictly Dishonorable. **1953** By the Light of the Silvery Moon; Flight Nurse. **1956** Three for Jamie Dawn. **1958** Outcasts of the City. **1964** The Evil of Frankenstein.

PALMER, PATRICIA (aka MARGARET GIBSON)
Born: Sept. 14, 1895, Colorado Springs, Colo. Died: Oct. 21, 1964, Hollywood, Calif. Screen and stage actress.

Appeared in: **1916** Island of Desire; Public Approval. **1917** Local Color. **1918** The Rose of Wolfville. **1919** The Canyon Hold-Up; The Money Corporal; Sand. **1920** The Fourteenth Man. **1921** Greater than Love; Things Men Do. **1922** Across the Border; The Cowboy King; The Cowboy and the Lady; Rounding Up the Law. **1923** To the Ladies; Mr. Billings Spends His Dime; The Web of the Law. **1924** Hold Your Breath; A Pair of Hellions. **1925** The Part Time Wife; Who's Your Friend?; Without Mercy. **1927** King of Kings; Naughty Nanette. **1929** The Little Savage.

PALMESE, ROSE MARIE
Born: 1871. Died: Mar. 21, 1953, Altadena, Calif. Screen actress.

PALTENGHI, DAVID
Born: 1919, Christchurch, England. Died: 1961, Windsor, England. Screen actor, film director, ballet dancer and choreographer.

Appeared in: **1949** The Queen of Spades. **1954** The Black Knight.

PAM, ANITA
Died: Apr. 15, 1973. Screen and stage actress. Married to actor Hugh Herbert (dec. 1952).

PANGBORN, FRANKLIN
Born: Jan. 23, 1893, Newark, N.J. Died: July 20, 1958, Santa Monica, Calif. Screen, stage and television actor.

Appeared in: **1926** Exit Smiling. **1927** The Girl in the Pullman; The Cradle Snatchers; Finger Prints; Getting Gertie's Garter; The Night Bride; The Rejuvenation of Aunt Mary. **1928** On Trial; Blonde for a Night; My Friend from India. **1929** The Sap; The Crazy Nut; Watch Out; Lady of the Pavements. **1930** Cheer up and Smile; Her Man; A Lady Surrenders; Not So Dumb; plus the following shorts: The Doctor's Wife; Reno or Bust; Poor Aubrey; The Chumps; Who's the Boss? **1931** A Woman of Experience; plus the following shorts: Blue of the Night; Sing, Bing, Sing; Billboard Girl; Rough House Rhythm. **1932** A Fool's Advice; plus the following shorts: The Giddy Age; Torchy Turns the Trick; Torchy's Nightcap; Torchy's Vocation; What Price Taxi?; The Candid Camera; Torchy Rolls His Own. **1933** Design for Living; Flying Down to Rio; International House; Headline Shooters; The Important Witness; Only Yesterday; Professional Sweetheart; plus the following shorts: Art in the Raw; Torchy's Kitty Coup; Wild Poses. **1934** Imitation of Life; King Kelly of the U.S.A.; College Rhythm; Manhattan Love Song; Many Happy Returns; Strictly Dynamite; That's Gratitude; Tomorrow's Children; Unknown Blonde; Young and Beautiful; Cockeyed Cavaliers; Stand Up and Cheer. **1935** Eight Bells; Headline Woman; A Thousand Dollars a Minute; She Couldn't Take It; Tomorrow's Youth; Ye Old Saw Mill (short). **1936** Don't Gamble with Love; Doughnuts and Society; Hats Off; The Luckiest Girl in the World; Mr. Deeds Goes to Town; The Mandarin Mystery; My Man Godfrey; Tango; To Mary with Love. **1937** Danger, Love at Work; Dangerous Number; High Hat; Easy Living; The Lady Escapes; Dangerous Holiday; The Life of the Party; Living on Love; She's Dangerous; She Had to Eat; Stage Door; A Star is Born; Step Lively, Jeeves; Swing High, Swing Low; Thrill of a Lifetime; Trun Off the Moon; Vivacious Lady; All over Town; When Love is Young; Hotel Haywire; It Happened in Hollywood; Bad Housekeeping (short). **1938** Love on Toast; Mad about Music; Rebecca of Sunnybrook Farm; She Married an Artist; Meet the Mayor; Four's a Crowd; Topper Takes a Trip; Three Blind Mice; Always Goodbye; Just Around the Corner; The Joy of Living; Carefree; Bluebeard's Eighth Wife; Dr. Rhythm. **1939** Broadway Serenade; Fifth Avenue Girl; The Girl Downstairs. **1940** The Bank Dick; Public Deb No. 1; Spring Parade; Turnabout; The Villain Still Pursued Her; The Hit Parrade of 1941; Christmas in July. **1941** Bachelor Daddy; A Girl, a Guy and a Gob; The Flame of New Orleans; Mr. District Attorney in the Carter Case; Never Give a Sucker an Even Break; Obliging Young Lady; Sandy Steps Out; Sullivan's Travels; Tillie the Toiler; Week-End for Three; Where Did You Get That Girl? **1942** Call Out the Marines; George Washington Slept Here; Moonlight Masquerade; The Palm Beach Story; Now Voyager; What's Cooking? **1943** His Butler's Sister; Crazy House; Holy Matrimony; Reveille with Beverly; Two Weeks to Live; Stage Door Canteen; Strictly in the Groove; Honeymoon Lodge; Slick Chick. **1944** The Great Moment; My Best Gal; Reckless Age; Hail the Conquering Hero. **1945** Hollywood and Vine; The Horn Blows at Midnight; See My Lawyer; You Came Along; Tell It to a Star. **1946** Two Guys from Milwaukee; Lover Come Back. **1947** I'll Be Yours; Calendar Girl; Mad Wednesday. **1948** Romance on the High Seas. **1949** My Dream Is Yours; Down Memory Lane. **1950** Her Wonderful Lie. **1957** Oh, Men! Oh, Women!; The Story of Mankind.

PANN, PETER
Born: 1872, Hamburg, Germany. Died: Dec. 29, 1948, New York, N.Y. Screen, stage and vaudeville actor. Appeared in Famous Players, Edison, Pathe and Biograph Company films.

Appeared in: **1917** The Hidden Hand. **1918** My Four Years in Germany.

PANNACI, CHARLES
Born: 1904. Died: Mar., 1927, Long Branch, N.J. (pneumonia). Screen actor.

PANTHULU, B. R.
Born: 1910, India. Died: Oct. 8, 1974, Bangalore, India. Screen, stage actor, film director and producer.

Appeared in: **1935** Samsara Nowka (film debut). **1960** Veerapandia Kattabomman.

PANZER, PAUL
Born: c 1867. Died: Apr. 11, 1937, New York, N.Y. (heart trouble). Circus performer, stage and screen actor. Do not confuse with actor Paul W. Panzer (dec. 1958).

PANZER, PAUL WOLFGANG (Paul Panzerbeiter)
Born: 1872, Wurtzberg, Bavaria. Died: Aug. 16, 1958, Hollywood, Calif. Screen and stage actor. Entered films with Vitagraph.

Appeared in: **1904** Stolen by Gypsies (film debut). **1908** Romeo and Juliet. **1913** The Cheapest Way. **1914** The Perils of Pauline (serial); Exploits of Elaine (serial). **1917** Jimmy Dale; Alias the Grey Seal (serial). **1918** The House of Hate (serial). **1919** The Masked Rider. **1920** The Mystery Mind (serial). **1922** The Bootleggers; The Mohican's Daughter; When Knighthood Was in Flower. **1923** The Enemies of Women; Big Brother; Unseeing Eyes; Jacqueline of Blazing Barriers; Mighty Lak' a Rose; Under the Red Robe. **1924** A Son of the Sahara; Wages of Virtue; Monsieur Beaucaire; Week-End Husbands.

1925 Thunder Mountain; Too Many Kisses; The Fool; The Shock Punch; The Best Bad Man; East Lynne; Greater Than a Crown; The Mad Marriage. **1926** The Ancient Mariner; Siberia; The Johnstown Flood; Black Paradise; The Dixie Merchant; The High Flyer; 30 Below Zero. **1927** Sally in Our Alley; Hawk of the Hills (serial); The Girl from Chicago; Wolf's Clothing; Brass Knuckles. **1928** Glorious Betsy; Rinty of the Desert; The Candy Kid; City of Purple Dreams; George Washington Cohen. **1929** Hawk of the Hills (feature of 1927 serial); Redskin; The Black Book (serial). **1930** Der Tanz Geht Weiter. **1931** The Montana Kid; First Aid; Cavalier of the West. **1933** A Bedtime Story. **1934** Bolera; The Mighty Barnum. **1936** Cain and Mabel. **1938** Penrod's Double Trouble. **1939** Beasts of Berlin; Idiot's Delight. **1942** Casablanca. **1943** Action in the North Atlantic. **1944** Uncertain Glory; The Adventures of Mark Twain. **1945** Hotel Berlin; Roughly Speaking. **1947** The Perils of Pauline; Cry Wolf. **1948** A Foreign Affair.

PAPE, EDWARD LIONEL
Born: 1867. Died: Oct. 24, 1944, Woodland Hills, Calif. Screen and stage actor.

Appeared in: **1921** Nobody. **1935** The Man Who Broke the Bank at Monte Carlo. **1936** Mary of Scotland; The White Legion; Beloved Enemy. **1937** The King and the Chorus Girl; The Prince and the Pauper; Wee Willie Winkie; Angel. **1938** Big Broadcast of 1938; Outside of Paradise; Bluebeard's Eighth Wife; Booloo; The Young in Heart. **1939** Love Affair; Rulers of the Sea; Midnight; Fifth Avenue Girl; Drums Along the Mohawk. **1940** Raffles; Tin Pan Alley; Zanzibar; The Philadelphia Story; Congo Maisie; The Long Voyage Home; Arise My Love. **1941** Hudson's Bay; Scotland Yard; Charley's Aunt; How Green Was My Valley. **1942** Almost Married.

PAPKE, BILLY (William Herman Papke)
Born: Sept. 17, 1886, Spring Valley, Ill. Died: Nov, 26, 1936, Newport Beach, Calif. (suicide—gun shot). Professional boxer and screen actor.

Appeared in: **1926** The Prince of Broadway.

PARAIN, BRICE
Born: 1897, France. Died: Mar., 1971, France. Philosopher, writer and screen actor.

Appeared in: **1963** Vivre sa Vie (To Live One's Life aka My Life to Live—US).

PARAMOR, NORRIE
Born: 1914, England. Died: Sept. 9, 1979, Barnet, England (cancer). Bandleader, composer, record producer and screen actor.

Appeared in: **1961** The Frightened City.

PARANJPE, RAJA (Rajabhau Dattatraya Paranjpe)
Born: 1909, India. Died: Feb. 9, 1979, Pune, India. Screen actor, film director and producer.

PARDAVE, JOAQUIN
Born: 1901, Guanajuato, Mexico. Died: July 10, 1955, Mexico City, Mexico. Screen actor, film director and composer.

Appeared in: **1938** La Zandunga; Los Millones de Chaflan; Cancion del Alma (Song of the Soul); Tierra Brava; Mi Candidato (My Candidate); Bajo el Cielo de Mexico (Beneath the Sky of Mexico); El Senor Alcade (The Mayor). **1939** La Tia de las Muchachas (The Girls' Aunt). **1940** Caballo a Caballo (Horse for Horse); Luna Criolla (Creole Moon); En un Burro Tres Gaturros (Three Rustics on One Donkey); Vivire Otra Vez (I Shall Live Again). **1943** Guadalajara.

PARDAVE, JOSE
Born: 1902, Mexico. Died: May 26, 1970, Mexico City, Mexico. Screen actor.

PARDEE, C. W. "DOC"
Born: 1885. Died: July 17, 1975, Glendale, Ariz. Screen actor, rodeo performer and trainer.

Appeared in: **1925** The Vanishing American. **1933** Wild Horse Mesa. **1939** The Gentleman from Arizona.

PARIS, GEORGE
Died: Aug. 1, 1976. Screen actor.

Appeared in: **1945** Blood on the Sun.

PARIS, MANUEL (Manuel R. Conesa)
Born: July 27, 1894, Spain. Died: Nov. 19, 1959, Woodland Hills, Calif. (congestive heart failure). Screen actor.

Appeared in: **1933** Flying Down to Rio. **1935** Odio. **1937** I'll Take Romance; When You're in Love. **1938** Artists and Models Abroad; Four Men and a Prayer. **1943** For Whom the Bell Tolls. **1947** Ivy; Out of the Past. **1948** Letter from an Unknown Woman; French Leave; Angel on the Amazon. **1949** Madame Bovary. **1950** Crisis. **1951** Havana Rose. **1952** Macao. **1953** The Story of Three Lovers; Second Chance. **1954** Jubilee Trail. **1955** To Catch a Thief; The Blackboard Jungle.

PARK, CUSTER B.
Born: 1900. Died: Sept. 25, 1955, Hollywood, Calif. Screen actor and stuntman. Entered films approx. 1927.

Appeared in: **1939** Gone With the Wind. **1954** Vera Cruz.

PARK, FLORENCE OIE CHAN
Born: 1886. Died: Feb. 5, 1967, Calif. Screen actress. Married to technical director Ed Park (dec.) and mother of actresses Bo-Ling and Bo-Ching Park.

PARK, JOSEPHINE
Died: Jan. 12, 1931, Glen Falls, N.Y. Screen actress. Divorced from actor Conway Tearle (dec. 1938).

PARKE, MACDONALD
Born: 1892. Died: July, 1960, London, England. Screen, stage and television actor.

Appeared in: **1939** Shipyard Sally. **1943** Candlelight in Algeria (US 1944). **1947** Teheran (aka The Plot to Kill Roosevelt—US). **1948** No Orchids for Miss Blandish; The Fool and the Princess. **1950** Dangerous Assignment. **1951** A Tale of Five Cities (aka A Tale of Five Women—US 1952). **1952** Penny Princess (US 1953); Babes in Bagdad; Saturday Island (aka Island of Desire—US). **1953** The Man Who Watched Trains Go By (aka Paris Express—US); Is Your Honeymoon Really Necessary? **1954** The Good Die Young (US 1955). **1955** Summertime. **1956** The March Hare. **1957** Beyond Mombasa. **1958** I Was Monty's Double (aka Hell, Heaven or Hoboken). **1959** The Mouse That Roared; A Touch of Larceny (US 1960); The Battle of the Sexes (US 1960). **1960** Never Take Sweets from a Stranger (aka Never Take Candy from a Stranger—US 1961).

PARKE, WILLIAM, SR.
Born: 1873. Died: July 28, 1941, New York, N.Y. (heart attack). Screen and stage actor and stage and film director.

Appeared in: **1922** Tailor-Made Man. **1923** The Hunchback of Notre Dame.

PARKER, ADELE (Adele Von Ohl)
Born: 1885, Plainsfield, N.J. Died: Jan. 20, 1966, Cleveland, Ohio. Screen and vaudeville actress, stuntwoman and rodeo and circus performer. Appeared in silent films.

PARKER, BARNETT (William Barnett Parker)
Born: Sept. 11, 1886, Batley, Yorkshire, England. Died: Aug. 5, 1941, Los Angeles, Calif. Screen and stage actor.

Appeared in: **1916** Prudence the Pirate. **1936** The President's Mystery; We Who Are About to Die; Born to Dance. **1937** Personal Property; Dangerous Number; The Last of Mrs. Cheyney; Espionage; Live, Love and Learn; Married Before Breakfast; The Emperor's Candlesticks; Broadway Melody of 1938; Double Wedding; Navy Blue and Gold; Wake Up and Live. **1938** Love Is a Headache; Hold That Kiss; Marie Antoinette; Listen Darling; The Girl Downstairs; Sally, Irene and Mary; Ready, Willing and Able. **1939** Babes in Arms; At the Circus. **1940** He Married His Wife; La Conga Nights; Hit Parade of 1941; Love Thy Neighbor; One Night in the Tropics. **1941** Tall, Dark and Handsome; A Man Betrayed; The Reluctant Dragon. **1942** New Wine.

PARKER, CECIL (Cecil Schwabe)
Born: Sept. 3, 1897, Hastings, Sussex, England. Died: Apr. 21, 1971, Brighton, England. Screen, stage and television actor.

Appeared in: **1929** The Woman in White. **1933** A Cuckoo in the Nest; The Golden Cage. **1934** Nine Forty-Five; The Blue Squadron; Flat No. 3; The Silver Spoon; Dirty Work; Little Friend; The Office Wife; Lady in Danger. **1935** Crime Unlimited; Me and Marlborough; Foreign Affaires; Her Last Affaire. **1936** Men of Yesterday; The Man Who Changed His Mind (aka The Man Who Lived Again—US); Jack of All Trades (aka The Two of Us—US 1937); Dishonour Bright. **1937** Dark Journey; Storm in a Teacup. **1938** Bank Holiday (aka Three on a

Weekend—US); Housemaster (US 1939); The Lady Vanishes; The Citadel; Old Iron. **1939** The Stars Look Down (US 1941); Sons of the Sea; The Spider; She Couldn't Say No. **1940** Two for Danger; Under Your Hat. **1941** The Saint's Vacation; Dangerous Moonlight (aka Suicide Squadron—US 1942); Ships With Wings (US 1942). **1946** Caesar and Cleopatra; The Magic Bow (US 1947). **1947** Hungry Hill; The Woman in the Hall (US 1949); Captain Boycott. **1948** The First Gentleman (aka Affairs of a Rogue—US 1949); The Weaker Sex (US 1949); Quartet (US 1949). **1949** Dear Mr. Prohack (US 1950); Under Capricorn; The Children Hundreds (aka The Amazing Mr. Beecham—US). **1950** Tony Draws a Horse (US 1951). **1951** The Man in the White Suit (US 1952); The Magic Box (US 1952). **1952** His Excellency (US 1956); I Believe in You (US 1953). **1953** Isn't Life Wonderful! **1954** Father Brown (aka The Detective—US); For Better, For Worse (aka Cocktails in the Kitchen—US 1955). **1955** The Constant Husband; The Ladykillers. **1956** The Court Jester; It's Great to be Young (US 1958); 23 Paces to Baker Street. **1957** True as Turtle; The Admirable Crichton (aka Paradise Lagoon—US). **1958** A Tale of Two Cities; Happy is the Bride (US 1959); Indiscreet; I was Monty's Double (aka Hell, Heaven or Hoboken). **1959** The Wreck of the Mary Deare; The Night We Dropped a Clanger (aka Make Mine a Double—US 1961). **1960** A French Mistress; The Pure Hell of St. Trinian's (US 1961); Follow That House! (US 1961); Under Ten Flags. **1961** Swiss Family Robinson; Petticoat Pirates; On the Fiddle (aka Operation Snafu—US 1965; War Head; Operation Warhead). **1962** Vengeance (aka The Brain—US 1964); The Iron Maiden (aka The Swingin' Maiden—US 1963); The Amorous Prawn (aka The Playgirl and the War Minister—US 1963). **1963** Carry on Jack (US 1964); Heavens Above!; The Comedy Man. **1964** Guns at Batasie. **1965** The Amorous Adventures of Moll Flanders; A Study in Terror (aka Fog—US 1966). **1966** Circus of Fear (aka Psycho-Circus—US 1967); Lady L; A Man Could Get Killed. **1967** The Magnificent Two. **1969** Oh! What a Lovely War.

PARKER, DONALD (Donald Parker III)
Born: Aug. 29, 1938, N.Y. Died: Dec., 1980, Los Angeles, Calif. Screen, stage actor and film producer. Do not confuse with other actors with same name.

PARKER, DOROTHY (Dorothy Rothschild)
Born: Aug. 22, 1893, West End, N.J. Died: June 7, 1967, New York, N.Y. Screen actress, screenwriter, author and poet. Married to actor/writer Allen Campbell (dec. 1963). Appeared in film clips during the 1930s to 1940s.

PARKER, EDWIN (aka ED PARKER and EDDIE PARKER)
Born: Dec. 12, 1900, Minn. Died: Jan. 20, 1960, Sherman Oaks, Calif. (heart attack). Screen, television actor and stuntman.

Appeared in: **1932** First in War. **1934** Lucky Texan; The Star Packer; Trail Beyond. **1935** Courageous Avenger. **1936** Flash Gordon (serial); Our Relations; On the Wrong Trek. **1937** Rhythm in the Clouds. **1938** Flash Gordon's Trip to Mars (serial). **1939** Another Thin Man; Son of Frankenstein; Buck Rogers (serial); The Lone Ranger Rides Again (serial); Danger Flight. **1940** Flash Gordon Conquers the Universe (serial). **1941** Hellzapoppin. **1942** The Spoilers; Ghost of Frankenstein; The Mummy's Tomb. **1943** The Lone Star Trail; The Masked Marvel (serial); Frankenstein Meets the Wolfman; Pistol Packin' Mamma. **1944** The Mummy's Ghost; The Tiger Woman (serial); Haunted Harbor (serial). **1945** The Mummy's Curse; The Phantom Rider; The Phantom Speaks; Ding Dong Williams; Escape in the Fog; The Enchanted Cottage; Manhunt of Mystery Island; The Monster and the Ape (serial); The Body Snatcher; The Adventures of Rusty. **1946** King of the Forest Rangers (serial); My Pal Trigger; The Shadow Returns; The Return of Rusty; The Last Crooked Hill; Daughter of Don Q (serial); Chick Carter, Detective (serial); Days of Buffalo Bill; The Inner Circle; South of Chisholm Trail; Raiders of the South; Trigger Fingers; Silver Range. **1947** My Wild Irish Rose; Silver River; Son of Zorro (serial); Jack Armstrong (serial); Riders of the Lone Star; The Vigilante (serial); Jesse James Rides Again (serial); Trailing Danger; The Millerson Case; Shadow Valley; Adventures of Don Coyote. **1948** Dangers of the Canadian Mounted (serial); The Strawberry Roan; Whirlwind Raiders; Flaxy Martin; Knock on Any Door; The Fighting Ranger; An Act of Murder; One Touch of Venus; The Tioga Kid; The Hawk of Powder River. **1949** Ghost of Zorro (serial); Mighty Joe Young; Mule Train; Kong of the Rocketmen (serial); Law of the West; Bruce Gentry, Daredevil of the Skies (serial); Batman and Robin (serial); Range Justice. **1950** Louisa; Convicted; Texas Rangers; Daredevils of the West; Radar Patrol vs. Spy King (serial); The Invisible Monster (serial); Abbott and Costello Meet the Mummy; The Good Humor Man; One Too Many. **1951** The Big Gusher; Al Jennings of Oklahoma; The Strange Door; The Barefoot Mailman; Government Agents vs. Phantom Legion (serial); Paula; My Six Convicts; Cripple Creek. **1952** The Raiders; The Racket; Barbed Wire; The Hawk of Wild

River; The Texas Man; Winning of the West; Scarlet Angel. **1953** Law and Order; The Man from the Alamo; The Lone Hand; Abbott and Costello Meet Dr. Jekyll and Mr. Hyde; All Ashore. **1954** Naked Alibi; Rear Window; Yankee Pasha; Son of Sinbad. **1955** The Far Country; This Island Earth; Smoke Signal; The Vagebond King; Abbott and Costello Meet the Mummy. **1956** The Mole People; Around the World in 80 Days; Ransom; Bride of the Monster; Tarantula; Red Sundown; Over-Exposed; Reprisal; Storm Center. **1958** Monster on the Campus; Live Fast, Die Young. **1959** Curse of the Undead. **1960** Spartacus.

PARKER, FRANK "PINKY" (Franklin Parker)
Born: 1891. Died: June 13, 1962, Hollywood, Calif. (heart attack). Screen and stage actor and singer.

Appeared in: **1934** Transatlantic Merry-Go-Round. **1935** Sweet Surrender; The Woman in Red. **1948** Mr. Blandings Builds His Dream House. **1952** Ace in the Hole (aka The Big Carnival).

PARKER, JOAN (Agnes Joan Gust)
Born: May 18, 1898, Canefuse, Ill. Died: Aug. 2, 1935, Los Angeles, Calif. (murdered—shot). Screen actress and dancer.

PARKER, LEW
Born: Oct. 28, 1907. Died: Oct. 27, 1972, New York, N.Y. (cancer). Screen, stage, vaudeville, radio and television actor. Married to actress Betty Kean who appeared with him in vaudeville.

Appeared in: **1937** A Universal short. **1948** Are You With It? **1958** Country Music Holiday.

PARKER, LUCY
Born: 1863. Died: Mar. 21, 1947, New York, N.Y. Screen and stage actress.

Appeared in: **1914** The Crucible. **1921** The Plaything of Broadway.

PARKER, MARGARET
Born: 1890. Died: Jan. 30, 1967, New York, N.Y. Silent screen actress.

PARKER, MARION
Died: 1920, Venice, Calif. Screen actress. Do not confuse with radio actress Marion Parker (dec. 1976). Married to stage actor Billy Armstrong.

PARKER, MARY
Born: 1915, Fort Worth, Tex. Died: June 1, 1966, Beverly Hills, Calif. Screen and stage actress.

Appeared in: **1938** Artists and Models. **1939** St. Louis Blues. **1944** Lady in the Dark; Music for Millions. **1952** Lure of the Wilderness. **1955** Third Party Rich (aka Deadly Game—US).

PARKER, MURRAY
Born: 1896. Died: Oct. 18, 1965, Hollywood, Calif. (heart attack). Screen, television and vaudeville actor. He performed usually under name of "Uncle Murray."

PARKER, SETH *See* LORD, PHILLIPS H.

PARKER, VIVIEN
Born: 1897. Died: Feb. 2, 1974, Bronx, N.Y. (stroke). Screen actress. Married to musician Walter R. Thalin (dec.). Appeared in silent films.

PARKER, WARREN
Died: July 31, 1976, Union Lake, Mich. Screen, stage, radio and television actor. Married to actress Mary Patton.

Appeared in: **1959** Too Soon to Love. **1960** Crowded Sky. **1961** Hoodlum Priest; Return to Peyton Place.

PARKHURST, FRANCES
Died: Dec. 31, 1969, Caldwell, N.J. Screen actress.

Appeared in: **1926** Men of Steel.

PARKINGTON, BEULAH
Died: Nov. 7, 1958, Hollywood, Calif. (heart condition). Screen actress. Entered films approx. 1928. One of the founders of Screen Extra's Guild.

Appeared in: **1950** My Blue Heaven.

PARKINSON, CHARLES A., JR.
Born: 1945. Died: Nov. 23, 1976, Seattle, Wash. (auto accident while performing stunt). Screen actor and stuntman.

Appeared in: **1976** Drum. **1977** Joyride.

PARKINSON, CLIFF (Clifford Emmitt Parkinson)
Born: Sept. 3, 1899, Kans. Died: Oct. 1, 1950, Woodland Hills, Calif. (appendicitis). Screen actor and stuntman.

Appeared in: **1938** Rawhide. **1943** Border Patrol. **1944** The San Antonio Kid; Bordertown Trail. **1947** Ramrod.

PARKS, LARRY (Samuel Klusman)
Born: Dec. 13, 1914, Olathe, Kans. Died: Apr. 13, 1975, Studio City, Calif. (heart attack). Screen, stage and television actor. Married to actress Betty Garrett. Nominated for 1946 Academy Award for Best Actor in The Jolson Story.

Appeared in: **1941** You Belong to Me; Mystery Ship; Harmon of Michigan. **1942** Blondie Goes to College; Harvard—Here I Come; The Boogie Man Will Get You; Atlantic Convoy; Canal Zone; Three Girls About Town; Sing for Your Supper; Flight Lieutenant; Submarine Raider; Honolulu Lu; Hello Annapolis; You Were Never Lovelier; A Man's World; North of the Rockies; Alias Boston Blackie; They All Kissed the Bride. **1943** Redhead from Manhattan; Is Everybody Happy?; First Comes Courage; Power of the Press; The Deerslayer; Destroyer; Reveille with Beverly. **1944** She's a Sweetheart; The Racket Man; The Black Parachute; Stars on Parade; Hey Rookie; Sergeant Mike. **1945** Counter-Attack; Sergeant Mike; Jealousy. **1946** Renegades; The Jolson Story. **1947** Her Husband's Affairs; Down to Earth; The Swordsman. **1948** Gallant Blade. **1949** Jolson Sings Again. **1950** Emergency Wedding. **1952** Love Is Better than Ever. **1955** Tiger by the Tail (aka Crossup—US 1958). **1962** Freud.

"PARKYAKARKUS" (Harry Einstein, aka HARRY PARKE)
Born: 1904, Boston, Mass. Died: Nov. 24, 1958, Los Angeles, Calif. (heart attack). Screen, stage, television and radio actor.

Appeared in: **1936** Strike Me Pink. **1937** New Faces of 1937; The Life of the Party. **1938** Night Spot; She's Got Everything. **1940** Glamour Boy. **1942** A Yank in Libya; The Yanks Are Coming. **1944** Sweethearts of the U.S.A.; Earl Carroll's Vanities; Out of This World; Movie Pests (short); Badminton (short).

PARLO, DITA (Gerthe Gerda Kornstaedt)
Born: 1907, Stettin, Germany. Died: Dec., 1971, Paris, France. Screen and stage actress.

Appeared in: **1928** Die Dame mit den Maske; Homecoming. **1929** Hungarian Rhapsody. **1930** Hearts Melody (aka Melody of Hearts); Menschen hinter Gettern. **1931** Honor of the Family. **1932** Secrets of the Orient. **1933** Mr. Broadway. **1934** L'Atalante (US 1947). **1936** The Mystic Mountain; Mademoiselle Docteur. **1937** La Grande Illusion (The Grand Illusion—US 1938); Realization d'art Cinematographique. **1938** The Courier of Lyons. **1940** Ultimatum; Street of Shadow. **1950** Justice est Faite (Justice is Done). **1956** Quand le Soleil Montera.

PARNELL, EMORY
Born: 1894, St. Paul, Minn. Died: June 22, 1979, Woodland Hills, Calif. (heart attack). Screen, stage, vaudeville and television actor. Married to Effie Parnell with whom he appeared in vaudeville. Father of Charles, and actor James Parnell (dec. 1961).

Appeared in: **1938** Call of the Yukon; King of Alcatraz; Doctor Rhythm; Arson Racket Squad. **1939** Tiny Troubles (short); You Can't Get Away With Murder; Pacific Liner; One Hour to Live; At the Circus. **1940** Out West With the Peppers; Sued for Libel; If I Had My Way. **1941** The Case of the Black Parrot; Unholy Partners; The Lady from Cheyenne; All the World's a Stooge; So Ends Our Night; Louisiana Purchase; The Blonde from Singapore; Kiss the Boys Goodbye; A Shot in the Dark. **1942** I Married a Witch; They All Kissed the Bride; Wings for the Eagle; Arabian Nights; Over My Dead Body; Cadets on Parade. **1943** The Dancing Masters; This Land Is Mine; Mission to Moscow; The Unknown Guest; That Nazty Nuisance; Two Senoritas from Chicago; Young Ideas. **1944** Government Girl; Address Unknown; Seven Days Ashore; A Night of Adventure; Tall in the Saddle; Gildersleeve's Ghost; The Miracle of Morgan's Creek; Cassanova Brown; Wilson; The Falcon in Hollywood; The Falcon in Mexico; plus the following shorts: Love Your Landlord; Radio Rampage; The Kitchen Cynic; Feather Your Nest; Triple Trouble; He Forgot to Remember. **1945** Crime Doctor's Courage; Mama Loves Papa; It's in the Bag; Two O'Clock Courage; What a Blonde; It Shouldn't Happen to a Dog; plus the following shorts: Alibi Baby; What, No Cigarettes?; You Drive Me Crazy; The Big Beef. **1946** Strange Triangle; Deadline for Murder; The Show-Off; Little Iodine; Queen of Burlesque; Abie's Irish Rose; The Falcon's Alibi. **1947** The Crime Doctor's Gamble; Gas House Kids Go West; Stork Bites Man; Violence; The Guilt of Janet Ames; The Outlaw; Calendar Girl. **1948** Blonde Ice; Strike It Rich; Here Comes Trouble; You Gotta Stay Happy; Song of Idaho; Mr. Blanding Builds His Dream House; Words and Music. **1949** A Woman's Secret; The Beautiful Blonde from Bashful Bend; Rose of the Yukon; Alaska Patrol; Hellfire; Massacre River; Ma and Pa Kettle Hideout. **1950** Rock Island Trail; To Please a Lady; Key to the City; Unmasked; County Fair; Chain Gang; Trail of Robin Hood; Beware of Blondie. **1951** Footlight Varieties; All That I Hope; Let's Go Navy; Deal Me In (short); Ma and Pa Kettle Back on the Farm; Golden Girl; My True Story. **1952** Dream Boat; The Fabulous Senorita; And Now Tomorrow; Gobs and Gals; When in Rome; Ma and Pa Kettle at the Fair; Oklahoma Annie; Lost in Alaska. **1953** Call Me Madam; Shadows of Tombstone; Sweethearts on Parade; Safari Drums; Fort Vengeance. **1954** Sabrina; Ma and Pa Kettle at Home; Battle of Rogue River; Pride of the Blue Grass; The Rocket Man. **1955** You're Never Too Young; Artists and Models; How to Be Very, Very Popular; The Looters. **1956** So You Think the Grass is Greener (short); So Your Wife Wants to Work (short); That Certain Feeling; Pardners. **1957** The Delicate Delinquent. **1958** The Hot Angel; The Notorious Mr. Monks; Man of the West. **1961** The Two Little Bears. **1965** Git!; The Bounty Killer.

PARNELL, JAMES
Born: 1923. Died: Dec. 27, 1961, Hollywood, Calif. Screen, stage and television actor. Son of actor Emory Parnell (dec. 1979).

Appeared in: **1951** G.I. Jane. **1952** Yankee Buccaneer; No Room for the Groom. **1953** War Paint. **1954** White Christmas; The Looters. **1955** You're Never Too Young. **1956** Crime Against Joe; The Birds and the Bees; Running Target. **1957** War Drums; Outlaw's Son. **1960** Walking Target. **1961** Gun Fight. **1962** The Clown and the Kid; Incident in an Alley.

PARRAVICINI, FLORENCIO
Born: 1874, South America. Died: Mar. 25, 1941, Buenos Aires, Argentina (suicide following long illness). Screen, stage actor, stage producer and screenwriter.

Appeared in: **1937** Melgarejo. **1938** Que Tiempos Aquellos (Those Were the Days). **1939** La Vida es un Tango (Life Is a Tango).

PARRISH, BEVERLY
Died: Date unknown. Screen actress. Daughter of actress Laura (Reesie) Parrish (dec. 1976). Sister of actors Helen (dec. 1959), Gordon, and Robert Parrish.

PARRISH, DANNY EARL
Died: Sept. 17, 1976. Screen actor.

PARRISH, HELEN
Born: Mar. 12, 1924, Columbus, Ga. Died: Feb. 22, 1959, Hollywood, Calif. Screen and television actress. Daughter of actress Laura Reesie Parrish (dec. 1977). Sister of actors Gordon, Beverly (dec.) and Robert Parrish. Divorced from actor Charles George Lang, Jr. Married to television producer John Guedel. Appeared in "Our Gang" series and "Smithy" comedies from 1927-1929.

Appeared in: **1927** Babe Comes Home (film debut). **1929** Words and Music. **1930** His First Command; The Big Trail. **1931** The Public Enemy; Cimarron; Seed; X Marks the Spot. **1932** When a Feller Needs a Friend. **1934** There's Always Tomorrow. **1935** A Dog of Flanders; Straight from the Heart. **1936** Make Way for a Lady; Three Smart Girls. **1938** Mad about Music; Little Tough Guy; Little Tough Guy in Society. **1939** Three Smart Girls Grow Up; First Love; Winter Carnival. **1940** I'm Nobody's Sweetheart Now; You'll Find Out. **1941** Where Did You Get That Girl?; Six Lessons from Madame La Zonga; Too Many Blondes. **1942** Overland Express (serial); They All Kissed the Bride; In Old California; X Marks the Spot (and 1931 version); Tough as They Come. **1943** Stage Door Canteen; Cinderella Swings It; The Mystery of the 13th Guest. **1944** They Live in Fear; Meet Miss Bobby-Socks. **1945** Let's Go Steady; A Thousand and One Nights. **1948** Trouble Makers. **1949** The Wolf Hunters; Quick on the Trigger.

PARRISH, JAMES
Born: 1904. Died: Mar. 27, 1978. Screen, vaudeville actor and property master.

Appeared in: **1932** Hell Below (film debut).

PARRISH, LAURA "REESIE"
Died: Aug. 15, 1977, Hollywood, Calif. Screen extra. Mother of actors Gordon, Robert, Helen (dec. 1959), and Beverly Parrish (dec.).

PARROTT, CHARLES *See* CHASE, CHARLEY

PARROTT, JAMES (James Chase, aka POLL PARROTT)
Born: 1892, Baltimore, Md. Died: May 10, 1939, Hollywood, Calif. (heart attack). Screen actor, film director, producer and screenwriter. Entered films for Pathe under name of Poll Parrott in 1918. Brother of actor Charlie Chase (dec. 1940).

Appeared in: **1921** Big Town Ideas.

PARRY, CHARLOTTE
Born: 1873, England. Died: Nov. 2, 1959, Chapel Hill, N.C. Screen, stage and vaudeville actress.

Appeared in: **1932** Sleepless Nights. **1935** It's a Bet.

PARRY, PAUL
Born: 1908. Died: Dec. 4, 1966, Calif. Screen actor, film producer and photographer.

Appeared in: **1934** Servants' Entrance.

PARSON, CAROL
Died: Dec. 18, 1958, New York, N.Y. Stage and screen actress.

PARSONS, GRAM
Born: 1946. Died: Sept. 19, 1973. Screen actor and musician. Member of "The Byrds" group.

PARSONS, LOUELLA O. (Louella Oettinger)
Born: Aug. 6, 1881?, Freeport, Ill. Died: Dec. 9, 1972, Santa Monica, Calif. (generalized arteriosclerosis). Newspaper columnist, novelist, screenwriter, radio and screen actress. Mother of film producer Harriet Parsons (dec. 1983).

Appeared in: **1937** Hollywood Hotel. **1946** Without Reservations. **1951** Starlift.

PARSONS, MILTON
Born: May 19, 1904, Gloucester, Mass. Died: May 15, 1980. Screen actor.

Appeared in: **1939** When Tomorrow Comes; Dad for a Day (short). **1940** Who Killed Aunt Maggie?; Edison, the Man; Sky Murder; Behind the News; Alfalfa's Double (short). **1941** Murder Among Friends; Dead Men Tell; Dressed to Kill; Man at Large. **1942** Over My Dead Body; The Great Man's Lady; Castle in the Desert; Roxie Hart; The Remarkable Andrew; Whispering Ghosts; The Girl from Alaska; The Man in the Trunk; The Hidden Hand; Life Begins at 8:30; Who Done It? **1943** Sweet Rosie O'Grady; Holy Matrimony. **1944** Lost in a Harem; Cry of the Werewolf. **1945** Leave Her to Heaven; Dick Tracy. **1946** Margie; Dark Alibi; Bowery Bombshell; Dick Tracy vs. Cueball. **1947** The Crimson Key; The Secret Life of Walter Mitty; Bury Me Dead; Dick Tracy Meets Gruesome; The Senator Was Indiscreet. **1948** Secret Service Investigator; The Shanghai Chest. **1949** Outcasts of the Trail; Dancing in the Dark. **1950** The Capture. **1952** Last of the Comanches. **1955** How to Be Very, Very Popular; The King's Thief. **1957** The Monster That Challenged the World. **1961** The Two Little Bears; The Silent Call. **1962** The Music Man. **1963** Haunted Palace. **1969** 2000 Years Later.

PARSONS, PERCY
Born: June 12, 1878, Louisville, Ky. Died: Oct. 3, 1944, England? Screen, stage and radio actor.

Appeared in: **1930** The Brat (aka The Nipper); Suspense; Beyond the Cities. **1931** Creeping Shadows (aka The Limping Man—US 1932). **1932** Strictly Business; Love on Wheels; The Frightened Lady (aka Criminal at Large—US 1933); Sleepless Nights. **1933** The Good Companions; Orders is Orders (US 1934); The Man from Toronto. **1934** Red Wagon (US 1935); Jew Suess (aka Power—US). **1936** King of the Damned; Twelve Good Men. **1937** Victoria the Great. **1938** The Citadel. **1941** Dangerous Moonlight (aka Suicide Squadron—US 1942); Hi Gang! **1942** Flying Fortress.

PARSONS, "SMILING BILLY" (William Parsons)
Born: Aug. 14, 1878, New York. Died: Sept. 29, 1919, Los Angeles, Calif. (diabetic coma). Screen actor, film producer and former president of National Film Corporation. Married to actress Billie Rhodes. Do not confuse with actor William E. Parsons.

PASCO, FRANCES
Died: Aug. 8, 1978. Screen actor.

PASHA, KALLA
Born: 1877, New York, N.Y. Died: June 10, 1933, Talmage, Calif. Screen and stage actor. Entered films with Mack Sennett.

Appeared in: **1921** Home Talent; A Small Town Idol. **1922** The Dictator; Thirty Days. **1923** Breaking into Society; Hollywood; A Million to Burn; Racing Hearts; Scaramouche; Ruggles of Red Gap. **1924** Yukon Jake. **1925** Heads Up. **1926** Don Juan's Three Nights; Rose of the Tenements; Silken Shackles. **1927** Wolf's Clothing; The Devil Dancer; The Dove. **1928** Tillie's Punctured Romance; West of Zanzibar. **1929** Seven Footprints to Satan; The Show of Shows.

PASO, ALFONSO
Born: 1927, Madrid, Spain. Died: July 10, 1978, Madrid, Spain (liver cancer). Screen, stage actor, screenwriter and playwright.

PASOLINI, PIER PAOLA
Born: 1922, Bologna, Italy. Died: Nov., 1975, near Ostia, Italy (murdered—beaten). Film director, poet, novelist, screenwriter and screen actor.

Appeared in: **1960** Il Gobbo (aka The Hunchback of Rome—US 1963). **1971** The Decameron.

PASQUIER, CHARLES "BACH"
Born: 1881, France. Died: Nov. 19, 1953, Paris, France (heart attack). Screen, stage, radio and circus actor.

PASSARELLA, ART
Born: 1910. Died: Oct., 1981, Hemet, Calif. (heart attack). Baseball umpire, screen and television actor.

Appeared in: **1958** Damn Yankees. **1962** That Touch of Mink.

PASSER, DIRCH
Born: 1926, Denmark. Died: Sept., 1980, Copenhagen, Denmark (heart attack). Screen and stage actor.

Appeared in: **1961** Reptilicus (US 1962). **1962** The Musketeer; Det Tossede Paradie (Laughter in Paradise, aka Crazy Paradise—US 1965). **1965** The Girl and the Millionaire. **1968** I, a Lover.

PATCH, WALLY (Walter Vinicombe)
Born: Sept. 26, 1888, London, England. Died: Oct. 27, 1970, London, England. Screen actor.

Appeared in: **1927** The Luck of the Navy; The King's Highway; Blighty (aka Apres la Guerre); Carry On! **1928** Guns of Loos; Shooting Star; Balaclava (aka Jaws of Hell—US 1931); Dr. Sin Fang (series); The Man in the Saddle (aka A Reckless Gamble); You Know What Sailors Are; Warned Off. **1929** Dick Turpin (series); High Treason. **1930** Kissing Cup's Race; Thread O'Scarlet; The Great Game. **1931** Never Trouble Trouble; The Great Gay Road; The Sport of Kings; Shadows; Tell England (aka The Battle of Gallipoli—US). **1932** Castle Sinister; Heroes of the Mine; Here's George. **1933** The Crime at Blossoms; Britannia of Billingsgate; Orders is Orders (US 1934); Tiger Bay; Channel Crossing (US 1934); Don Quixote (US 1934); Trouble; Sorrell and Son (US 1934); The Good Companions; Marooned. **1934** The Old Curiosity Shop (US 1935); The Scoop; Music Hall; The Perfect Flaw; What Happened to Harkness; Virginia's Husband; Badger's Green; Crazy People; A Glimpse of Paradise; Borrow a Million; The Man I Want; Passing Shadows; The Scotland Yard Mystery (aka The Living Dead—US); Those Were the Days; Lost Over London. **1935** His Majesty and Co.; Dandy Dick; Death on the Set (aka Murder on the Set—US 1936); That's My Uncle; Street Song; Off the Dole; Marry the Girl; The Half-Day Excursion; Where's George? (aka The Hope of His Side—US); Old Faithful; What the Parrot Saw; While Parents Sleep; Get Off My Foot; Once in a Blue Moon; The Public Life of Henry the Ninth. **1936** Ticket of Leave; On Top of the World; King of the Castle; Excuse My Glove; What the Puppy Said; Prison Breaker; A Touch of the Moon; Apron Fools; Luck of the Turf; Hail and Farewell; Busman's Holiday; The Scarab Murder Case; Not So Dusty; The Interrupted Honeymoon; The Man Who Could Work Miracles (US 1937); Men Are Not Gods (US 1937); You Must Get Married; A Wife or Two. **1937** The Inspector; The Price of Folly; The High Command; The Street Singer; Night Ride; Missing, Believed Married; Captain's Orders; The Sky's the Limit; Farewell Again (aka Troopship—US 1938); Doctor Syn; Holiday's End. **1938** Quiet Please; On Velvet; Night Alone; The Ware Case (US 1939); Pygmalion; Bank Holiday (aka Three on a Weekend—US); Owd Bob (aka To the Victor—US); Alf's Button Afloat; 13 Men and a Gun; Break the News (US 1941); Almost a Honeymoon. **1939** What Would You Do Chums?; Inspector Hornleigh; Home from Home; The Mind of Mr. Reeder (aka The Mysterious Mr. Reeder—US 1940); Poison Pen (US 1941); Down Our Alley; Inspector Hornleigh on Holiday; Hospital Hospitality; Sword of Honour. **1940** Return to Yesterday; Laugh It Off; Band Waggon; They Came By Night; Charley's (Big Hearted) Aunt; Two Smart Men; Old Mother Riley in Business; Henry Steps Out; Everything Okay (rerelease of On Top of the World—1936); Gasbags; Neutral Port; Pack Up Your Troubles. **1941** I Thank You; The Seventh Survivor; Gert and Daisy's Weekend; Once a Crook. **1942** Let the People Sing; Sabotage at Sea; We'll Smile Again; In Which We Serve. **1943** Jeannie; Women in Bondage; Get Cracking; The Butler's Dilemma; Strange to Relate; Death by Design. **1944** Up in Mabel's Room. **1945** Old Mother Riley at Home; I Didn't Do It; Don Chicago; Dumb Dora Discovers Tobacco. **1946** Appointment with Crime (US 1950); George in Civvy Street; Gaiety George (US 1948). **1947** The Ghosts of Berkeley Square; Green Fingers; Dusty Bates; Fag End (rerelease of Dumb Dora Discovers Tobacco—1945). **1948** The Guinea Pig (US 1949); River Patrol; A Date with a Dream; Calling Paul Temple. **1949** The History of Mr. Polly (US 1951); The

Adventures of Jane. **1950** The Twenty Questions Murder Mystery. **1952** Salute the Toff; Hammer the Toff. **1953** The Wedding of Lilli Marlene; Will Any Gentleman? **1956** Not So Dusty. **1957** Morning Call; Suspended Alibi; The Naked Truth (aka Your Past is Showing—US 1958). **1960** The Challenge (aka It Takes a Thief—US 1962); The Millionairess (US 1961); Operation Cupid. **1961** Nothing Barred. **1962** The Damned (aka They All Died Laughing—US 1964); Serena. **1963** Sparrows Can't Sing; A Jolly Bad Fellow. **1964** The Bargee. **1967** Poor Cow (US 1968).

PATERSON, PAT
Born: 1911, Bradford, Yorkshire, England. Died: Aug. 24, 1978, Phoenix, Ariz. (cancer). Screen and stage actress. Married to actor Charles Boyer (dec. 1978). Do not confuse with film producer with same name.

Appeared in: **1931** The Professional Guest; The Great Gay Road; Night Shadows. **1932** Murder on the Second Floor; Partners, Please; Here's George. **1933** Bitter Sweet. **1934** Love Time; Bottoms Up; Call It Luck. **1935** Charlie Chan in Egypt; Lottery Lover. **1936** Spendthrift. **1937** 52nd Street. **1939** Idiot's Delight.

PATON, STUART
Born: 1885, Glasgow, Scotland. Died: Dec. 16, 1944, Woodland Hills, Calif. Stage and screen actor, film director, producer and screenwriter. Married to actress Ethel Patrick (dec. 1944).

PATRICK, ETHEL
Born: 1887. Died: Sept. 18, 1944, Woodland Hills, Calif. Screen and stage actress. Married to actor and director Stuart Paton (dec. 1944).

PATRICK, GAIL (Margaret LaVelle Fitzpatrick)
Born: June 20, 1911, Birmingham, Ala. Died: July 6, 1980, Hollywood, Calif. (leukemia). Screen actress and television producer. Divorced from restauranteur Robert Howard Cobb (dec.), Navy Lieut. Arnold Dean White, and ad. exec. Thomas Cornwall Jackson. Later married to businessman John E. Velde, Jr.

Appeared in: **1932** If I Had a Million. **1933** Mysterious Rider; Mama Loves Papa; Pick-Up; Murders in the Zoo; To the Last Man; Cradle Song; The Phantom Broadcast. **1934** Wagon Wheels; Death Takes a Holiday; Murder at the Vanities; The Crime of Helen Stanley; Take the Stand. **1935** One Hour Late; Rumba; Mississippi; Doubting Thomas; Smart Girl; The Big Broadcast of 1936; Wanderer of the Wasteland; Two-Fisted; No More Ladies. **1936** My Man Godfrey; Two in the Dark; The Lone Wolf Returns; The Preview Murder Mystery; Early to Bed; Murder With Pictures; White Hunter. **1937** John Meade's Woman; Her Husband Lies; Stage Door; Artists and Models. **1938** Mad About Music; Dangerous to Know; Wives Under Suspicion; King of Alcatraz. **1939** Disbarred; Man of Conquest; Grand Jury Secrets; Reno. **1940** My Favorite Wife; The Doctor Takes a Wife; Gallant Sons. **1941** Love Crazy; Kathleen. **1942** Tales of Manhattan; We Were Dancing; Quiet Please—Murder. **1943** The Hit Parade of 1943; Women in Bondage. **1944** Up in Mabel's Room. **1945** Twice Blessed; Brewster's Millions. **1946** The Madonna's Secret; Rendezvous With Annie; The Plainsman and the Lady; Claudia and David. **1947** Calendar Girl; King of the Wild Horses. **1948** The Inside Story. **1964** Big Parade of Comedy.

PATRICK, JEROME
Born: 1883, New Zealand. Died: Sept. 26, 1923, N.Y. (heart disease). Screen and stage actor.

Appeared in: **1919** Three Men and a Girl. **1920** The Furnace; Officer 666. **1921** Don't Call Me Little Girl; School Days; The Other Woman; Forever; The Heart Line. **1924** Sinners in Silk.

PATRICK, NIGEL (Nigel Wemyss)
Born: May 2, 1913, London, England. Died: Sept. 21, 1981, London, England (cancer). Screen, stage, television actor, film and stage director. Son of actress Dorothy Turner (dec. 1969).

Appeared in: **1939** Mrs. Pym of Scotland Yard (film debut). **1948** Uneasy Terms; Noose (aka The Silk Noose—US 1950); Spring in Park Lane (US 1949). **1949** Silent Dust; The Jack of Diamonds; The Perfect Woman (US 1950). **1950** Trio; Morning Departure (aka Operation Disaster—US 1951). **1951** Pandora and the Flying Dutchman; Encore (US 1952); The Browning Version; Young Wives' Tale (US 1954). **1952** Meet Me Tonight; The Pickwick Papers (US 1953); Who Goes There! (aka The Passionate Sentry—US 1953); The Sound Barrier (aka Breaking Through the Sound Barrier—US). **1953** Grand National Night (aka Wicked Wife—US 1955); Tonight at 8:30. **1954** Forbidden Cargo (US 1956); The Sea Shall Not Have Them (US 1955). **1955** All for Mary; A Prize of Gold. **1957** Raintree County; How to Murder a Rich Uncle. **1958** Count Five and Die; The Man Inside. **1959** Sapphire.

1960 The League of Gentlemen (US 1961); The Trials of Oscar Wilde (aka The Man With the Green Carnation—US, and aka The Green Carnation). **1961** Johnny Nobody (US 1965). **1963** The Informers (aka Underworld Informers—US 1964). **1966** Goal! (narrator). **1969** The Virgin Soldiers (US 1970); Battle of Britain. **1970** The Executioner. **1972** Tales from the Crypt; The Great Waltz. **1973** The Mackintosh Man.

PATRICOLA, TOM
Born: Jan. 27, 1894, New Orleans, La. Died: Jan. 1, 1950, Pasadena, Calif. (following brain surgery). Screen, stage and vaudeville actor. Entered films in 1929.

Appeared in: **1929** Happy Days; Words and Music; Frozen Justice; Married in Hollywood; Si-Si Senor (short); South Sea Rose. **1930** The Three Sisters; One Mad Kiss; Anybody's Woman. **1931** Children of Dreams. **1932** Moonlight and Cactus (short). **1933** The Good Bad Man (short); North of Zero (short); El Precio de un Beso; La Melodia Prohibida; No Dejes la Puerta Abierta. **1934** Hello Sailors (short). **1935** The following shorts: Moonlight and Melody; Dame Shy; Kiss the Bride. **1936** Fresh from the Fleet (short). **1945** Rhapsody in Blue.

PATSTON, DORIS
Born: 1904, London, England. Died: June 12, 1957, Darien, Conn. Stage and screen actress.

Appeared in: **1932** Smiling Faces.

PATTEN, DOROTHY
Born: 1905. Died: Apr. 11, 1975, Westhampton, N.Y. Screen, stage and television actress.

Appeared in: **1953** Botany Bay. **1973** Ten from Your Show of Shows (television film clips).

PATTERSON, ALBERT
Died: July 10, 1975. Screen actor.

PATTERSON, ELIZABETH
Born: Nov. 22, 1874, Savannah, Tenn. Died: Jan. 31, 1966, Los Angeles, Calif. Screen, stage, television and radio actress.

Appeared in: **1926** The Boy Friend; The Return of Peter Grimm. **1929** Words and Music; South Sea Rose. **1930** The Lone Star Ranger; Harmony at Home; The Big Party; The Cat Creeps. **1931** Tarnished Lady; The Smiling Lieutenant; Daddy Long Legs; Penrod and Sam; Heaven and Earth. **1932** Love Me Tonight; Miss Pinkerton; Husband's Holiday; A Bill of Divorcement; Dangerous Brunette; The Way of Life; Two Against the World; The Expert; Play Girl; So Big; New Morals for Old; Life Begins; Guilty as Hell; They Call It Sin; Breach of Promise; No Man of Her Own; The Conquerors. **1933** They Just Had to Get Married; The Infernal Machine; Story of Temple Drake; Golden Harvest; Dinner at Eight; Hold Your Man; The Secret of the Blue Room; Doctor Bull. **1934** Hideout. **1935** Chasing Yesterday; Men Without Names; So Red the Rose. **1936** The Return of Sophie Lang; Timothy's Quest; Her Master's Voice; Three Cheers for Love; Go West, Young Man; Small Town Girl; Old Hutch. **1937** A Night of Mystery; High, Wide and Handsome; Hold 'Em Navy; Night Club Scandal. **1938** Scandal Sheet; Bulldog Drummond's Peril; Bluebeard's Eighth Wife; Sing, You Sinners; The Adventures of Tom Sawyer; Sons of the Legion. **1939** The Story of Alexander Graham Bell; Bulldog Drummond's Bride; The Cat and the Canary; Our Leading Citizen; Bad Little Angel; Bulldog Drummond's Secret Police. **1940** Remember the Night; Adventure in Diamonds; Anne of Windy Poplars; Earthbound; Who Killed Aunt Maggie?; Michael Shayne, Private Detective. **1941** Kiss the Boys Goodbye; Tobacco Road; Belle Starr; The Vanishing Virginian. **1942** Almost Married; Beyond the Blue Horizon; Her Cardboard Lover; My Sister Eileen; I Married a Witch; Lucky Legs. **1943** The Sky's the Limit. **1944** Follow the Boys; Hail the Conquering Hero; Together Again. **1945** Colonel Effingham's Raid; Lady on a Train. **1946** I've Always Loved You; The Secret Heart. **1947** Welcome Stranger; The Shocking Miss Pilgrim; Out of the Blue. **1948** Miss Tatlock's Millions. **1949** Little Women; Intruder in the Dust; Song of Surrender. **1950** Bright Leaf. **1951** Katie Did It. **1952** Washington Story. **1955** Las Vegas Shakedown. **1957** Pal Joey. **1959** The Oregon Trail. **1960** Tall Story.

PATTERSON, HANK (Elmer Calvin Patterson)
Born: Oct. 9, 1888, Alabama. Died: Aug 23, 1975, Woodland Hills, Calif. (bronchial pneumonia). Screen, stage, vaudeville and television actor.

Appeared in: **1946** Abilene Town; I Ring Doorbells; The El Paso Kid; Santa Fe Uprising. **1947** Robin Hood of Texas; Bells of San Angelo; Springtime in the Sierras; Under Colorado Skies. **1948** Relentless;

Oklahoma Badlands; The Denver Kid. **1949** The Cowboy and the Indians; Riders in the Sky. **1950** The James Brothers of Missouri (serial); Code of the Silver Sage; Desperadoes of the West (serial). **1951** Silver City Bonanza; Don Daredevil Rides Again (serial). **1952** California Conquest. **1953** Canadian Mounties vs. Atomic Invaders (serial). **1956** Tarantula; Julie. **1957** The Amazing Colossal Man. **1958** The Spider; Attack of the Puppet People; Monster on the Campus; Escape from Red Rock; Terror in a Texas Town; The Decks Ran Red. **1960** Gunfighters of Abilene.

PATTERSON, JAMES
Born: 1932. Died: Aug. 19, 1972, New York, N.Y. (cancer). Screen, stage, radio and television actor. Married to actress Rochelle Oliver.

Appeared in: **1963** The Slave. **1964** Lilith. **1967** In the Heat of the Night. **1969** Castle Keep.

PATTERSON, JOY W.
Born: 1906. Died: Mar. 23, 1959, Santa Ana, Calif. Screen actress and dancer.

Appeared in: **1926-29** Many of the "Collegians" series of shorts.

PATTERSON, TROY (Ettore Corvino)
Born: 1926, U.S. Died: Nov. 1, 1975, Rome, Italy (heart attack). Screen, stage actor and dancer.

Appeared in: **1959** Speed Crazy; Bloodlust (US 1961).

PATTON, PHIL
Born: 1911. Died: May 28, 1972, Hollywood, Calif. (heart attack). Documentary film director, musician, stage and screen actor.

PATTON, WILLIAM "BILL"
Born: 1894, Amarillo, Tex. Died: Dec. 12, 1951. Screen actor.

Appeared in: **1920** Sand. **1921** Outlawed. **1922** Tracks; Alias Phil Kennedy; Cyclone Jones; American Toreodor; Bulldog Courage. **1923** Growing Better. **1924** Ace of the Law; Battlin' Buckaroo; Fightin' Thru; The Desert Secret; The Last Man; A Game Fighter; The Smoking Trail. **1925** Flashing Steeds; Fightin' Odds; Fangs of Faith. **1926** Lucky Spurs; Western Trails; Under Fire; Beyond the Trail; Fort Frayne; The Last Change. **1927** The Flying U Ranch. **1928** Young Whirlwind; The Bantam Cowboy; The Pinto Kid; Orphan of the Sage; Yellow Contraband. **1929** Pals of the Prairies; Below the Deadline; Freckled Rascal; One Man Dog; Vagabond Cub. **1930** Beau Bandit. **1933** Strawberry Roan.

PATWARDHAN, VINAYAKARAO
Born: 1897, India. Died: 1975, Poona, India. Screen, stage actor, musician and music director.

Appeared in: Madhuri.

PAUL, CHARLES (Charles Beulcke)
Born: 1913. Died: June 15, 1980, Los Angeles, Calif. (cancer). Screen, stage actor, pianist and painter.

Appeared in: **1963** It's a Mad, Mad, Mad, Mad World. **1975** Lepke; Let's Do It Again. **1977** Rocky; The Last Tycoon.

PAUL, LOGAN
Born: 1849, Ayr. Scotland. Died: Jan. 15, 1932, Brooklyn, N.Y. Stage and screen actor.

Appeared in: **1922** Flesh and Spirit.

PAUL, RENE
Died: Oct. 21, 1968. Screen actor.

Appeared in: **1949** C Man. **1962** Advise and Consent.

PAUL, VAL
Born: Apr. 10, 1886, Denver, Colo. Died: Mar. 23, 1962, Hollywood, Calif. Screen actor, film director and producer.

Appeared in: **1917** The Secret of the Swamp. **1922** The Timber Queen (serial).

PAUL, WAUNA
Born: 1912, New York, N.Y. Died: Mar. 31, 1973, Ibiza, Spain (auto accident). Screen, stage actress and stage producer. Daughter of actress Josephine Brown.

PAULDING, PERRY
Died: Jan. 11, 1976. Screen actor.

PAULIG, ALBERT
Born: Germany. Died: Mar., 1933 (heart trouble). Screen and stage actor.

Appeared in: **1929** Dancing Vienna; It's Easy to Become a Father. **1931** Ein Burschenlied aus Heidelberg; Susanne Macht Ordnung. **1932** Ein Ausgekochter Junge; Der Schrecken der Garnison; Girsekorn Greift Ein; Shoen 1st die Manoeverzeit; Drunter und Drueber. **1933** Der Tanzhusar. **1934** Zu Befehl, Herr Unteroffizier; Es War Einmal ein Walzer; Annemarie, Die Braut der Kompanie. **1935** Drei von der Kavallerie.

PAULL, TOWNSEND D.
Born: 1898. Died: Oct. 8, 1933, Los Angeles, Calif. (murdered). Stage and screen actor.

PAULSEN, ARNO
Born: 1900, Stettin, Germany. Died: Sept. 17, 1969, Baden-Baden, West Germany. Stage and screen actor.

Appeared in: **1948** Razzia; Murderers Among Us. **1949** The Affair Blum. **1962** Wozzeck.

PAULSEN, HARALD
Born: 1895, Elmshorn, Hollstein, Germany. Died: Aug. 5, 1954, Hamburg, Germany (heart attack). Screen, stage actor, opera performer and stage director.

Appeared in: **1932** Mein Leopold; Die Blumenfrau von Lindenau. **1934** Tausend Fuer Eine Nacht; Alraune. **1935** Ich Sing Mich in Dein Herz Hinein; Frischer Wind aus Kanada. **1936** Oberwachtmeister Schwenke; Traumulus; Der Mutige Seefahrer. **1937** Besuch am Abend; If We All Were Angels; For Her Country's Sake. **1938** Der Lachende Dritte; Krach und Blueckum Kuennemann (Row and Joy about Kuennemann); Sie und die Drei (She and the Three). **1939** 1A in Oberbayern (1A in Upper Bavaria). **1940** The Living Dead. Other German films; Die Ledige Witwe; Stradivari; Kunstlerliebe.

PAUMIER, ALFRED (Alfred Hodgson)
Born: Nov. 14, 1870, Liverpool, England. Died: Jan. 25, 1951, England? Screen, stage actor and playwright.

Appeared in: **1916** The Lifeguardsman (US 1917).

PAUNCEFORT, GEORGE
Born: 1870. Died: Mar. 25, 1942, Los Angeles, Calif. Screen and stage actor. Entered films approx. 1932.

PAVAGEAU, ALCIDE "SLOW DRAG"
Born: 1888. Died: Jan. 19, 1969, New Orleans, La. Jazz musician and screen actor.

Appeared in: **1965** The Cincinnati Kid.

PAVANELLI, LIVIO
Born: 1881, Italy. Died: May 1, 1958, Italy? Screen actor.

Appeared in: **1927** Luther (US 1929). **1931** Liebeskommando (Love's Command—US 1932). **1934** Fruehlingsmaerchen (US 1935, aka Verlieb' Dich Nicht in Sizilien). **1936** La Canzione del Sole. **1937** Amore e Dolore.

PAVESE, LUIGI
Born: 1897, Rome, Italy. Died: Dec. 13, 1969, Rome, Italy. Screen actor.

Appeared in: **1936** Il Re Burlone. **1948** Eternal Melodies. **1949** His Young Wife; Lost in the Dark; Woman Trouble. **1955** Mademoiselle Gobette. **1960** The Sword and the Cross. **1963** Love and Larceny.

PAVLOVA, ANNA
Born: Jan. 3, 1885, St. Petersburg, Russia. Died: Jan. 23, 1931, The Hague, Netherlands. Ballerina and screen actress. Entered films in 1915.

Appeared in: **1916** The Dumb Girl of Portici.

PAVON, BLANCA ESTELA
Born: 1926, Mexico. Died: Sept. 26, 1949, near Mexico City, Mexico (plane crash). Screen and radio actress. Dubbed in Spanish voice of Vivien Leigh in 1939 Gone With the Wind and Ingrid Bergman in 1944 Gaslight (aka Angel Street).

PAWLE, LENNOX
Born: Apr. 27, 1872, London, England. Died: Feb. 22, 1936, Los Angeles, Calif. (cerebral hemorrhage). Screen and stage actress.

Appeared in: **1918** The Admirable Crichton. **1919** All the Sad World Needs (aka Peep O' Day). **1920** The Temptress. **1922** The Glorious Adventure. **1929** Married in Hollywood; Hot for Paris; The Sky Hawk. **1931** The Sin of Madelon Claudet. **1935** David Copperfield; Sylvia Scarlet; The Gay Deception.

PAWLEY, BRYAN
Born: 1871, England. Died: Dec., 1962, England? Screen actor.

PAWLEY, WILLIAM
Born: July 21, 1905, Kansas City, Mo. Died: June 15, 1952, New York, N.Y. Screen and stage actor.

Appeared in: **1931** Bad Girl; The Spider; Over the Hill. **1932** I Am a Fugitive from a Chain Gang; Cheaters at Play; After Tomorrow; Careless Lady; Amateur Daddy; The Trial of Vivienne Ware; Letty Lynton; Speak Easily; Central Park. **1933** Robbers' Roost; Gabriel Over the White House. **1935** The Daring Young Man; Stolen Harmony; Mary Burns, Fugitive; Kentucky Kernels. **1936** Boulder Dam; The Public Pays (short); The Big Noise; Bullets or Ballots; Public Enemy's Wife. **1937** San Quentin; Born Reckless; The River of Missing Men; Trapped by G-Men. **1938** Angels with Dirty Faces; International Crime; Crime Takes a Holiday; Prairie Moon; White Banners. **1939** Boy Slaves; Panama Lady; Rough Riders Round-Up; Union Pacific; Disputed Passage. **1940** Grapes of Wrath; Johnny Apollo; The Great Profile; Double Alibi; Yukon Flight; West of Abilene; Mercy Plane; The Return of Frank James. **1941** The Great American Broadcast. **1942** Time to Kill.

PAWSON, HARGRAVE
Born: Dec. 6, 1902, England. Died: Jan. 26, 1945, England? Screen and stage actor. Married to actress Irene Russell.

Appeared in: **1932** The First Mrs. Fraser.

PAXINOU, KATINA (Katina Konstantopoulou)
Born: Dec. 17, 1900, Piraeus, Greece. Died: Feb. 22, 1973, Athens, Greece (cancer). Screen and stage actress. Married to actor Alexis Minotis. Won 1943 Academy Award for Best Supporting Actress in For Whom the Bell Tolls.

Appeared in: **1943** For Whom the Bell Tolls (film debut); Hostages. **1945** Confidential Agent. **1946** California. **1947** Uncle Silas (aka The Inheritance—US 1951); Mourning Becomes Electra. **1949** Prince of Foxes. **1955** Mr. Arkadin (US 1962 aka Confidential Report). **1959** The Miracle. **1960** Rocco e i Suoi Fratelli (Rocco and his Brothers—US 1961). **1962** Le Proces (The Trial—US 1963). **1968** Tante Zita (Zita). **1970** The Martlet's Tale.

PAXTON, GEORGE
Died: Feb. 19, 1914, near Fort Lee, N.J. Screen actor.

PAXTON, SIDNEY
Born: 1861. Died: Oct. 13, 1930, Montauk, N.Y. Screen and stage actor.

Appeared in: **1915** A Vagabond's Revenge. **1919** The Divine Gift. **1920** A Man's Shadow; The Shadow Between. **1921** Single Life; The Old Country; Money; The Bachelor's Club; Bluff; The Prince and the Beggarmaid; The Rotters. **1922** The Card. **1923** The School for Scandal; The Audacious Mr. Squire; Becket; The Hypocrites; Little Miss Nobody. **1924** The Crimson Circle; Miriam Rozella. **1925** The Midnight Girl; Old Home Week. **1928** Mark of the Frog (serial).

PAYANT, LEE
Born: 1924. Died: Dec. 14, 1976. Screen actor, film director and folk singer.

Appeared in: **1961** Bridge to the Sun.

PAYNE, DOUGLAS
Born: 1875. Died: Aug., 1965, England. Stage and screen actor.

Appeared in: **1912** The Adventures of Dick Turpin—The Gunpowder Plot. **1913** Maria Marten—Or, the Murder in the Red Barn; The Fallen Idol; Fraudulent Spiritualism Exposed (aka Spiritualism Exposed and The Seer of Bond Street—US); The Great Gold Robbery; Ju-Jitsu to the Rescue. **1914** The Mystery of the Diamond Belt; The Finger of Destiny; The Cup Final Mystery; His Country's Honour (aka The Aviator Spy—US); The Houseboat Mystery; Captain Nighthawk; The Stolen Masterpiece; Guarding Britain's Secrets (aka The Fiends of Hell—US); The White Feather; Enoch Arden; Harbour Lights; In the

Ranks. **1915** A Rogue's Wife; The Mesmerist; Fine Feathers; The Airman's Children; The Romany Rye; Flying from Justice; Royal Love; The Avenging Hand (aka The Wrath of the Tomb); The Coal King; The Great Cheque Fraud; The Devil's Bondsman (aka The Scorpion's Sting—US); The Little Minister; Married for Money; Master and Man; The Trumpet Call. **1919** A Lass O' the Looms; Further Exploits of Sexton Blake; Heart of a Rose. **1920** Rodney Stone; Won by a Head. **1922** Potter's Clay; The Doddington Diamonds. **1923** The Last Adventures of Sherlock Holmes series including The Blue Carbuncle. **1924** Old Bill Through the Ages. **1928** The Lady of the Lake (US 1930); The Man Who Changed His Name; What Next?; The Triumph of the Scarlet Pimpernel (aka The Scarlet Daredevil—US 1929). **1929** Red Aces. **1930** You'd be Surprised. **1933** The Flaw.

PAYNE, EDNA
Born: Dec. 5, 1891, New York, N.Y. Died: Jan. 31, 1953, Los Angeles, Calif. (liver ailment). Screen actress.

Appeared in: **1911** Higgenses vs. Judsons; The Story of Rosie's Rose. **1912** The Silent Signal; A Half Breed's Treachery; A Mexican Courtship; The Moonshiner's Daughter. **1913** The Bravery of Dora; Private Smith; The Engraver. **1914** The Squatter; The Return; The Price Paid. **1915** The Man and the Law; Colonel Steele—Master Gambler; Brand Blotters; The Little Band of Gold; The Sacrifice of Jonathan Gray; The Dawn Road; An Innocent Villain; The Trap that Failed; Babbling Tongues; In the Folds of the Flag; One Fifty Thousand Dollar Jewel Theft; The Sheriff of Red Rock Gulch; The Fool's Heart; Shadows of the Harbor; The Oath of Smoky Joe; Saved by the Telephone; The Thief and the Chief; The Lone Game; Within an Inch of His Life; The Flag of Fortune. **1916** John Osborne's Triumph; The Unpardonable Sin; The Bad Samaritan.

PAYNE, LOUIS "LOU" (Louis William Payne)
Born: Jan. 13, 1876, New York, N.Y. Died: Aug. 14, 1953, Woodland Hills, Calif. Screen and stage actor. Married to screen actress Mrs. Leslie Carter (dec. 1937). Entered films in 1920.

Appeared in: **1924** True as Steel; For Sale; In Hollywood with Potash and Perlmutter. **1925** Alias Mary Flynn; The Last Edition; The Fate of a Flirt; We Moderns; As Man Desires; The Only Thing; The Lady Who Lied. **1926** The Blind Goddess; The Shamrock Handicap; The Outsider; A Woman's Heart. **1927** King of Kings; Broadway Madness; Vanity; The Yankee Clipper. **1928** The Whip. **1929** Evangeline; Big News; Interference; Lawful Larceny; Part Time Wife; The Dude Wrangler. **1945** Saratoga Trunk. **1951** My Forbidden Past.

PAYNE, WILLIAM
Born: 1896, England. Died: Dec. 26, 1967, Solihull, England. Screen, stage and radio actor.

PAYSON, BLANCHE
Born: 1881. Died: July 3, 1964, Hollywood, Calif. Screen actress. Entered films with Mack Sennett.

Appeared in: **1916** Wife and Auto Trouble; A Bath House Blunder; A la Cabaret; Dollars and Sense. **1917** Oriental Love. **1925** Oh, Doctor!; We Moderns. **1926** La Boheme. **1927** Figures Don't Lie; The Bachelor's Baby. **1930** Below Zero (short). **1931** Wicked; plus the following shorts: Dogs is Dogs; Our Wife; Taxi Troubles. **1932** The Impatient Maiden; plus the following shorts: Love Pains; Helpmates; Red Noses. **1933** Loose Relations (short). **1935** She Gets Her Man; Hoi Polloi (short). **1937** All Over Town. **1938** If I Were King. **1939** The Amazing Mr. Williams. **1940** Angels Over Broadway. **1943** A Maid Made Mad (short); Salute for Three.

PAYTON, BARBARA
Born: Nov. 16, 1927, Cloquet, Minn. Died: May 8, 1967, San Diego, Calif. (natural causes). Screen actress. Divorced from actor Franchot Tone (dec. 1968).

Appeared in many westerns during the 1940s and the following: **1940** Once More, My Darling; Trapped. **1949** Silver Butte (short). **1950** Dallas; Kiss Tomorrow Goodbye. **1951** Only the Valiant; Drums in the Deep South; Bride of the Gorilla. **1953** Run for the Hills; The Flanagan Boy (aka Bad Blonde—US); The Great Jesse James Raid; Four-Sided Triangle. **1955** Murder Is My Beat.

PAYTON, CLAUDE (Claude Duval Payton aka CLAUDE PEYTON)
Born: Mar. 30, 1882, Centerville, Iowa. Died: Mar. 1, 1955, Los Angeles, Calif. Screen and stage actor.

Appeared in: **1920** The Soul of Youth; If I Were King; Dice of Destiny. **1921** A Knight of the West; When We Were Twenty-One. **1922** The Desert's Crucible; The Marshal of Moneymint; The Grim Comedian;

The Song of Life; The Men of Zanzibar; Trooper O'Neil; Do and Dare; Bells of San Juan; The Masked Avenger; Catch My Smoke; Two-Fisted Jefferson. **1923** The Devil's Dooryard; The Law Rustlers; Desert Rider; Skid Proof. **1924** The Riddle Rider (serial); The Back Trail; Daring Chances; The Desert Outlaw; The Man from Wyoming. **1925** Gold and the Girl; The Texas Trail; The Ridin' Streak. **1926** Ben Hur; Cohens and Kellys; The Yellow Back. **1927** The Western Whirlwind; Set Free. **1928** The Crowd; The Gate Crasher. **1929** Say It With Songs. **1930** The Great Divide. **1932** Tex Takes a Holiday. **1933** Fargo Express. **1934** Thunder Over Texas.

PAYTON, LEW
Born: 1875. Died: May 27, 1945. Black screen actor.

Appeared in: **1936** Valiant is the Word for Carrie. **1938** Jezebel. **1939** The Lady's from Kentucky. **1941** Lady for a Night.

PEABODY, EDDY
Born: Feb. 19, 1912, Reading, Mass. Died: Nov. 7, 1970, Covington, Ky. (stroke). Screen, television, radio actor and banjo player. Known as "King of the Banjo."

Appeared in: **1927** Banjomania (short). **1928** In a Music Shop (short); Banjoland (short). **1934** The Lemon Drop Kid. **1935** Shoestring Follies (short). **1936-1938** Vitaphone and Paramount shorts.

PEACOCK, KEITH
Born: 1931. Died: Nov. 1, 1966, Perivale, England (accident while filming a stunt for television). Screen and television stuntman.

Appeared in: **1964** The 7th Dawn. **1966** Our Man in Marrakesh (aka Bang, Bang You're Dead—US); Circus of Fear (aka Psycho-Circus—US 1967). **1967** Casino Royale.

PEACOCK, KIM
Born: 1901, Watford Herts, England. Died: Dec. 26, 1966, Emsworth, England (heart attack). Screen, stage, radio and television actor.

Appeared in: **1929** The Manxman; The Clue of the New Pin; The Crooked Billet. **1930** A Warm Corner. **1933** Waltz Time. **1935** The Mad Hatter; Expert's Opinion. **1936** Things to Come; Grand Finale; Midnight at Madame Tussaud's (aka Midnight at the Wax Museum—US). **1937** Sunset in Vienna (aka Suicide Legion—US 1940); Captain's Orders. **1938** Climbing High (US 1939); Night Alone; Alerte en Mediterranee (SOS Mediterranean—US 1940). **1939** Hell's Cargo (aka Dangerous Cargo—US 1940).

PEACOCK, LILLIAN
Born: Oct. 23, 1890 or 1894?, Pa. Died: Aug. 18, 1918, Los Angeles, Calif. (injuries sustained previously while filming). Screen actress.

Appeared in: **1915** Saved by a Shower; Hiram's Inheritance; How Billy Got His Raise; Their Bewitched Elopement; At the Beach Incognito; Slightly Mistaken; Twentieth Century Susie; The Last Roll; The Opera Singer's Romance; The Ore Mystery; When the Wets Went Dry; Dad's Awful Crime; A Millionaire for a Minute; Chills and Chickens; Leomade Aids Cupid. **1916** A Perfect Match; Mrs. Green's Mistake; Wanted—A Piano Tuner; Muchly Married; The Tale of a Telegram; His Highness the Janitor; Hubby Puts One Over; The Jitney Driver's Romance; A Wife for a Ransom; A Raffle for a Husband; A Stage Villian; A Dark Suspicion; Love Quarantined; The Fall of Deacon Stillwaters; The Harem Scarem Deacon; Bashful Charley's Proposal; An All Around Cure; Some Vampire; I've Got Yer Number; Kate's Affinities; She Wrote a Play and Played It; The Deacon Stops the Show; A Marriage for Revenge; In Onion There's Strength; The Elixir of Life; Soup and Nuts; Musical Madness; Father Gets in Wrong; Beans and Bullets; Their First Arrest; In Love with a Fireman; A Janitor's Vendetta; Scrappily Married; A Shadowed Shadow. **1917** Barred from the Bar; Why They Left Home; The Little Pirate; His Coming-Out Party; Out for the Dough; Mule Mates; Rosie's Rancho; Passing the Grip; Wanta Make a Dollar?; A Boob for Luck; 'Art Aches; Whose Baby?; The Leak; Left in the Soup?; What the—?; The Carless Cop; The Man with the Package; The Last Scent; The Boss of the Family; Uneasy Money; His Fatal Beauty; One Damp Day. **1918** Who's to Blame?

PEARCE, AL
Born: 1899. Died: June 2, 1961, Newport Beach, Calif. Screen, radio and television actor.

Appeared in: **1937** The Hit Parade. **1943** Here Comes Elmer. **1945** Hitchhike to Happiness. **1946** One Exciting Week. **1948** The Main Street Kid.

PEARCE, ALICE

Born: 1919. Died: Mar. 3, 1966, Los Angeles, Calif. (cancer). Screen, stage and television actress.

Appeared in: **1949** On the Town. **1952** The Belle of New York. **1955** How to Be Very, Very Popular. **1956** The Opposite Sex. **1962** Lad: A Dog. **1963** The Thrill of It All; Tammy and the Doctor; Beach Party; My Six Loves. **1964** The Disorderly Orderly; Dear Heart; Kiss Me, Stupid. **1965** Dear Brigitte; Darn That Cat; Bus Riley's Back in Town. **1966** The Glass Bottom Boat.

PEARCE, GEORGE C. (aka GEORGE PIERCE)

Born: 1865, New York, N.Y. Died: Aug. 12, 1940, Los Angeles, Calif. Screen, stage actor, opera performer and film director.

Appeared in: **1921** Black Beauty; The Traveling Salesman; Three Word Brand. **1922** The Primitive Lover; Watch Your Step. **1923** The Midnight Alarm; The Printer's Devil; The Country Kid. **1924** Cornered; Daring Youth; The Narrow Street; Wandering Husbands; Hold Your Breath. **1925** The Wife Who Wasn't Wanted. **1926** The Social Highwayman; Hold That Lion. **1927** The Irresistible Lover; Quarantined Rivals. **1928** Do Your Duty; Masquerade; Home James; Wild West Romance. **1929** The Valiant. **1930** The Lone Rider; Personality; Vengeance; The Right of Way. **1931** Men in Her Life; The Right to Love. **1932** This Reckless Age. **1933** Story of Temple Drake; Lone Cowboy. **1934** British Agent; Six of a Kind. **1936** The Singing Cowboy. **1937** When You're in Love; The Awful Truth.

PEARCE, VERA

Born: 1896, Australia. Died: Jan. 21, 1966, London, England. Screen, stage actress and singer.

Appeared in: **1933** Yes, Mr. Brown; Just My Luck; That's a Good Girl. **1935** So You Won't Talk. **1938** Yes, Madam? **1939** What's a Man. **1947** Nicholas Nickleby. **1951** One Wild Oat. **1954** Men of Sherwood Forest (US 1956). **1959** The Night We Dropped a Clanger (aka Make Mine a Double—US 1961).

PEARL, EULA (Eula Pearl Ferrand)

Died: July 17, 1970, Visalia, Calif. (heart attack). Screen actress and piano, voice instructor.

PEARSON, DREW (Andrew Russell Pearson)

Born: Dec. 13, 1897, Evanston, Ill. Died: Sept. 1, 1969, Washington, D.C. Newspaper columnist and screen actor.

Appeared in: **1949** City Across the River. **1951** The Day the Earth Stood Still. **1961** Death to the World (narrator).

PEARSON, JESSE

Born: 1930. Died: Dec. 5, 1979, Monroe, La. (cancer). Screen, stage, television actor and singer.

Appeared in: **1963** Bye Bye Birdie (stage and film versions). **1964** Advance to the Rear. **1978** The Norseman (narrator).

PEARSON, LLOYD

Born: Dec. 13, 1897, Bradford, Yorkshire, England. Died: June 2, 1966, London, England. Screen, stage and television actor.

Appeared in: **1938** The Challenge (film debut—US 1939). **1940** Tilly of Bloomsbury. **1941** Kipps (aka The Remarkable Mr. Kipps—US 1942); Banana Ridge. **1942** Uncensored (US 1944). **1943** When We are Married; My Learned Friend; Schweik's New Adventures; Rhythm Serenade. **1948** The Three Weird Sisters; Mr. Perrin and Mr. Traill. **1950** Portrait of Clare. **1952** Private Information; Hindle Wakes (aka Holiday Week—US). **1955** Black in the Face. **1957** The Good Companions. **1960** The Angry Silence.

PEARSON, MOLLY

Born: 1876, Scotland. Died: Jan. 26, 1959, Newton, Conn. Stage and screen actress.

Appeared in: **1918** Passing of the Third Floor Back.

PEARSON, TED

Died: Oct. 5, 1961. Radio announcer and screen actor.

Appeared in: **1938** Test Pilot; You're Only Young Once. **1939** Dick Tracy's G-Men (serial); Boy Friend.

PEARSON, VIRGINIA

Born: Mar. 7, 1888, Louisville, Ky. Died: June 6, 1958, Los Angeles, Calif. (uremic poisoning). Screen and stage actress. Married to actor Sheldon Lewis (dec. 1958).

Appeared in: **1916** The Vital Question; The Kiss of a Vampire; Blazing

Love. **1917** A Royal Romance. **1919** The Bishop's Emeralds. **1923** Sister Against Sister; A Prince of a King. **1925** The Phantom of the Opera; The Wizard of Oz; Red Kimona. **1926** Lightning Hutch (serial); Atta Boy; Silence; The Taxi Mystery. **1927** Driven from Home. **1928** What Price Beauty?; The Big City; The Actress; The Power of Films. **1929** Smilin' Guns. **1930** Danger Man. **1931** Primrose Path. **1932** Back Street.

PEARSON, W. BLAINE (William Blaine Pearson)

Born: Mar. 21, 1892, Kentucky. Died: Nov. 6, 1918, Los Angeles, Calif. (pneumonia). Screen actor and screenwriter.

PECHEUR, BRUCE

Born: 1942. Died: Aug. 16, 1973, New York, N.Y. (murdered—stabbed). Screen, stage actor and model.

Appeared in: **1970** Trash. **1971** Road to Salina.

PECKHAM, FRANCES MILES

Born: 1893. Died: June 7, 1959, New York, N.Y. Screen and stage actress.

PEER, HELEN

Born: 1898. Died: May 6, 1942, New Rochelle, N.Y. Screen, stage actress and singer. Appeared on screen for the Thomas A. Edison Co.

"PEERLESS ANNABELLE" (Annabelle Whitford Buchan aka ANNABELLE WHITFORD)

Born: 1878. Died: Nov. 30, 1961, Chicago, Ill. Screen and stage actress. She was the original "Gibson Girl" as created by Charles Dana Gibson.

Appeared in: **1897** Annabelle's Butterfly Dance.

PEERS, JOAN

Born: 1911, Chicago, Ill. Died: July 11, 1975. Screen actress.

Appeared in: **1923** Rosita. **1929** Applause. **1930** Anybody's War; Rain or Shine; Tol'able David; Around the Corner; Paramount on Parade. **1931** The Tip Off; Over the Hill; Parlor, Bedroom and Bath. **1933** Two Black Crows in Africa.

PEGG, VESTER (Vester House Pegg)

Born: May 28, 1889, Appleton City, Mo. Died: Feb. 19, 1951, Los Angeles, Calif. (coronary thrombosis). Screen actor.

Appeared in: **1915** The Birth of a Nation; Jordan in a Hard Road. **1916** Blue Blood and Red; Intolerance. **1917** The Secret Man; The Marked Man; The Almost Good Man; The Texas Sphinx. **1918** A Woman's Fool; Hell Bent; Three Mounted Men. **1919** Ace of the Saddle; Bare Fists. **1920** Vanishing Trails (serial). **1921** The Last Chance; The Raiders; The Fighting Stranger; The Galloping Devil. **1922** The Kick Back. **1923** The Lone Fighter; The Canyon of the Fools. **1924** Straight Shooting. **1925** Hurricane Horseman; The Rattler; Rough Going; Wildfire; The Shield of Silence; Tearin' Loose. **1926** Bucking the Truth; Man of the Forest; Three Bad Men; The Flying Horseman; Jack O'Hearts. **1927** The Desert Pirate. **1930** Dawn Trail. **1934** Judge Priest. **1938** Born to the West. **1940** West of Abilene; Colorado.

PEGLER, WESTBROOK

Born: Aug. 12, 1894, Minneapolis, Minn. Died: June 24, 1969, Tucson, Ariz. (cancer). Columnist, journalist and screen actor.

Appeared in: **1932** Madison Square Garden.

PEIL, EDWARD, JR. (Charles Edward Peil)

Born: 1908. Died: Nov. 7, 1962. Screen actor. Appeared as a child actor during silents as Johnny Jones and later as Edward Peil, Jr. See Johnny Jones for early films. Son of Edward Peil (dec. 1958).

Appeared in: **1925** The Goose Hangs High; Rose of the World. **1926** The Family Upstairs. **1928** The Little Yellow House. **1929** The College Coquette. **1939** When Tomorrow Comes.

PEIL, EDWARD, SR. (Charles Edward Peil)

Born: 1888. Died: Dec. 29, 1958, Hollywood, Calif. Screen actor. Father of actor Edward Peil, Jr. (dec. 1962). Entered films in 1908.

Appeared in: **1919** Broken Blossoms. **1920** Isobel. **1921** Dream Street; That Girl Montana; The Killer; The Servant in the House. **1922** Arabia; Don't Doubt Your Wife; Broken Chains; The Dust Flower; The Song of Life. **1923** Purple Dawn; The Lone Star Ranger; Stepping Fast; Three Jumps Ahead. **1924** The Iron Horse; $50,000 Reward; The Man Who Came Back; Teeth. **1925** The Hunted Woman; Double Action Daniels; The Man Without a Country; The Pleasure Buyers; The Wife Who Wasn't Wanted; The Fighting Heart. **1926** The Girl from Montmartre; Midnight Faces; Black Paradise; Yellow Fingers; The Great K&A Train Robbery. **1927** King of Kings; Framed; Tumbling

River. **1929** Masked Emotions; In Old Arizona. **1930** Cock O' the Walk. **1931** Clearing the Range; The Texas Ranger; Wild Horse; Cracked Nuts. **1932** The Gay Buckaroo; Charlie Chan's Chance; Local Bad Man; The Hatchet Man. **1933** The Three Musketeers (serial); Tombstone Canyon; The Big Cage. **1934** Blue Steel; The Man from Utah; Pursuit of Happiness. **1935** The Bride of Frankenstein; The Phantom Empire (serial); Million Dollar Baby; Mysterious Mr. Wong; Ladies Crave Excitement. **1936** Oh Susannah!; Texas Rangers. **1937** Secret Agent X-9 (serial); Come on, Cowboys!; The Awful Truth; Two-Fisted Sheriff; Heroes of the Alamo. **1938** Colorado Trail. **1939** The Night Riders; Spoilers of the Range; One Hour to Live; Pirates of the Skies. **1940** The Shadow (serial); One Man's Law. **1941** Billy the Kid's Fighting Pals; The Lone Rider in Ghost Town; Texas Marshal; I Wanted Wings; Lucky Devils. **1942** Sin Town; The Major and the Minor; Black Dragons; Pride of the Yankees; Foreign Agent. **1943** Robin Hood of the Range; Billy the Kid in the Kid Rides Again. **1947** Saddle Pals; The Last Round-Up; The Wistful Widow of Wagon Gap. **1950** Branded; Colt .45; Kansas Raiders.

PEILE, KINSEY (Frederick Kinsey Peile)
Born: Dec. 20, 1862, Allahabad, India. Died: Apr. 13, 1934, England? Screen, stage actor, playwright and author.

Appeared in: **1920** The Face at the Window. **1925** The Presumption of Stanley Haye, M.P.; Settled Out of Court (aka Evidence Enclosed). **1927** The Vortex (US 1928).

PEIRCE, EVELYN See EVELYN PIERCE

PELISSIER, H. G. (Harry Gabriel Pelissier)
Born: 1874, Finchley, England. Died: Sept. 25, 1913, England? Screen and stage actor. Married to actress Fay Compton (dec. 1978).

PELLETIER, DENISE
Born: 1929, Tit-Coq, Canada. Died: May 24, 1976, Canada? Screen and television actress.

PELLICER, PINA (Josefina Pellicer Lopez Llergo)
Born: Apr. 3, 1935, Mexico. Died: Dec. 10, 1964, Mexico City, Mexico (suicide). Screen, stage and television actress.

Appeared in: **1960** Macario. **1961** One Eyed Jacks. **1963** Dias de Otoro (Autumn Days)—received the PECIME (Mexican Film Writers) award for Best Actress. **1967** Los Bandidos. **1968** Days of the Evil Gun.

PELLY, FARRELL
Born: 1891. Died: Apr. 23, 1963, New York, N.Y. Screen, stage and television actor.

Appeared in: **1959** Darby O'Gill and the Little People.

PELT, TIMOTHY "TIM"
Born: 1938. Died: Sept. 7, 1977, Pacific Palisades, Calif. (auto accident). Black screen and television actor. Father of actress Danielle Spencer.

Appeared in: **1974** Serpico; Claudine.

PEMBERTON, BROCK
Born: Dec. 14, 1885, Leavenworth, Kans. Died: Mar. 11, 1950, New York, N.Y. (heart attack). Screen actor, film director, film and stage producer.

Appeared in: **1943** Stage Door Canteen.

PEMBERTON, HENRY W.
Born: 1875. Died: July 26, 1952, Orlando, Fla. Screen, stage and vaudeville actor.

Appeared in: **1921** Luxury.

PEMBROKE, GEORGE See PRUD'HOMME, GEORGE

PENA, JULIO
Born: 1912, Madrid, Spain. Died: July 22, 1972, Marbella, Spain (heart attack). Screen and stage actor.

Appeared in: **1929** Madame X; The Lady Lies (Spanish version). **1930** Min and Bill. **1933** Mama. **1935** Angelita; Rosa de Francia. **1939** Las Cinco Advertencias de Satanas (Satan's Five Warnings). **1956** Alexander the Great. **1958** Spanish Affair. **1959** Solomon and Sheba. **1961** La Rivolta degli Schiavi (The Revolt of the Slaves—US) Happy Thieves. **1963** El Valle de las Espadas (aka The Castilian—US). **1965** Tierra de Fuego (aka Sunscorch—US 1966). **1966** Tre Notti Violente (Web of Violence—US); Campanadas a Medianoche (Chimes at Midnight—US 1967 aka Falstaff); Kid Rodelo; Pampa Salvaje (Savage Pampas—US 1967); L'Homme du Minnesota (aka Minnesota

Clay—US). **1967** I Crudeli (aka The Hellbenders—US). **1968** Rey de Africa (aka One Step to Hell—US 1969); The Oldest Profession. **1970** El Condor. Other films include: Correo de Indias; Intriga; Mission Blanca; Fuenteovejuna; Confidencia; Alhucemas; Siempre Vuelvan de Madrugada; Manicomio; Horas de Panica; Simon Bolivar.

PENA, RALPH
Born: 1927. Died: May 20, 1969, Mexico City, Mexico (car accident injuries). Screen actor, screenwriter and musician.

PENBROOK, HARRY
Born: 1887. Died: Sept. 14, 1960, Hollywood, Calif. Screen actor and extra. Entered films approx. 1908.

PENDER, DORIS (Doris Lomas)
Born: 1900, England. Died: July 24, 1975, London, England (leukemia). Screen, stage and vaudeville actress. Appeared in vaudeville in an act billed as "Fun and Antics in Monkeyland" with her parents Bob and Margaret Loma. Divorced from vaudeville actor Jack Hartman with whom she appeared in vaudeville in an act billed as "Hart, Pender and O'Neill" (with Chuck O'Neill).

PENDLETON, DIANE
Died: May 5, 1969. Screen actress.

Appeared in: **1943** Around the World. **1944** Carolina Blues.

PENDLETON, NAT
Born: Aug. 9, 1899, Davenport, Iowa. Died: Oct. 11, 1967, San Diego, Calif. (heart attack). Screen, stage actor and professional wrestler. Entered films as a juvenile with Lubin.

Appeared in: **1924** The Hoosier Schoolmaster. **1926** Let's Get Married. **1929** The Laughing Lady. **1930** Fair Warning; The Sea Wolf; Last of the Duanes; The Big Pond; Liliom. **1931** Secret Witness; Larceny Lane; Vigor of Youth; The Seas Beneath; The Star Witness; Mr. Lemon of Orange; Blonde Crazy; Spirit of Notre Dame; Pottsville Paluka; Cauliflower Alley. **1932** Flesh; Play Girl; The Sign of the Cross; Cardigan's Last Case; Taxi; Attorney for the Defense; Hell Fire Austin; Exposure; You Said a Mouthful; Night Club Lady; Horse Feathers; Manhattan Parade; Beast of the City; A Fool's Advice; By Whose Hands? **1933** Deception; Whistling in the Dark; Baby Face; College Coach; Goldie Gets Along; Lady for a Day; Penthouse; The Chief; I'm No Angel. **1934** Fugitive Lovers; The Defense Rests; The Cat's Paw; Girl from Missouri; Straight Is the Way; Lazy River; Manhattan Melodrama; Death on the Diamond; The Thin Man; The Gay Bride; Sing and Like It. **1935** Times Square Lady; Baby Face Harrington; Reckless; Murder in the Fleet; Calm Yourself; Here Comes the Band; It's in the Air. **1936** The Garden Murder Case; The Great Ziegfeld; Sworn Enemy; Trapped by Television; Two in a Crowd; The Luckiest Girl in the World; Sing Me a Love Song. **1937** Under Cover of Night; Song of the City; Gangway; Life Begins in College. **1938** Meet the Mayor; Young Dr. Kildare; Swing Your Lady; Arsene Lupin Returns; Fast Company; Shopworn Angel; The Chaser; The Crowd Roars. **1939** Burn 'Em Up, O'Connor; Calling Dr. Kildare; It's a Wonderful World; 6,000 Enemies; On Borrowed Time; At the Circus; Another Thin Man; The Secret of Dr. Kildare. **1940** The Ghost Comes Home; Dr. Kildare's Strangest Case; Phantom Raiders; The Golden Fleecing; Flight Command; Dr. Kildare's Crisis; Dr. Kildare's Wedding Day; Dr. Kildare Goes Home; Northwest Passage. **1941** Death Valley; Buck Privates; Top Sergeant Mulligan; The Mad Doctor of Market Street. **1942** Jail House Blues; Calling Dr. Gillespie; Dr. Gillespie's New Assistant. **1943** Dr. Gillespie's Criminal Case. **1944** The Sign of the Cross (revised version of 1932 film); Swing Fever. **1945** Rookies Come Home. **1947** Buck Privates Come Home; Scared to Death. **1949** Death Valley. **1964** Big Parade of Comedy (documentary).

PENMAN, LEA
Born: 1895. Died: Oct. 12, 1962, Hollywood, Calif. Screen and stage actress.

Appeared in: **1926** The Romance of a Million Dollars. **1950** Stella; Fancy Pants. **1955** We're No Angels. **1957** Portland Expose.

PENN, LEONARD (Leonard Monson Penn)
Born: 1907, Mass. Died: May 20, 1975, Los Angeles, Calif. (heart attack). Screen actor. Divorced from actress Gladys George (dec. 1954). Do not confuse with actor Leo Penn.

Appeared in: **1937** Between Two Women; The Women Men Marry; The Firefly. **1938** Judge Hardy's Children; Man Proof; Girl of the Golden West; The Toy Wife; Ladies in Distress (short); Marie Antoinette; What Price Safety? (short). **1939** Bachelor Mother; Almost a Gentleman. **1940** The Way of All Flesh. **1946** Son of the Guardsman (serial); Chick Carter, Detective (serial). **1947** I Cover the Big Town; Hoppy's Holiday; Killer at Large; Brick Bradford (serial). **1948** Congo Bill (serial); Dead Don't Dream; Courtin' Trouble. **1949** Batman and Robin (serial). **1950** The Girl from San Lorenzo; Silver Raiders; Woman from Headquarters; Gunfire; Six Gun Mesa; Lonely Hearts Bandits; Law of the Badlands. **1951** Sirocco; South of Caliente; Mysterious Island (serial). **1952** King of the Congo (serial); Outlaw Woman; Barbed Wire; A Yank in Incochina; Thief of Damascus; And Now Tomorrow; Westminster; No Holds Barred. **1953** Eyes of the Jungle; Fangs of the Arctic; Flame of Calcutta; Savage Mutiny; Murder Without Tears; The Lost Planet (serial). **1954** The Saracen Blade. **1956** On the Threshold of Space. **1958** In the Money. **1960** Spartacus. **1962** Bird Man of Alcatraz.

PENNELL, RICHARD O.
Born: 1861, Chester, England. Died: Mar. 22, 1934, Hollywood, Calif. Screen actor. Entered films in 1914.

Appeared in: **1927** The Masked Woman. **1928** The Olympic Hero; Dressed to Kill; Clothes Make the Woman. **1930** On the Level.

PENNER, JOE (Joseph Pinter)
Born: Nov. 11, 1905, Budapest, Hungary. Died: Jan. 10, 1941, Philadelphia, Pa. (heart attack). Screen, stage, radio, vaudeville and burlesque actor.

Appeared in: **1930** The following shorts: Seeing-Off-Service; Stepping Out; A Stuttering Romance; Surface Stripes. **1931** Making Good (short); Sax Appeal (short). **1932** The following shorts: Gangway; Moving In; Where Men Are Men. **1932-33** Big Star Comedies and Big "V" Comedies. **1934** College Rhythm. **1936** Collegiate. **1937** New Faces of 1937. **1938** I'm from the City; Mr. Doodle Kicks Off; Go Chase Yourself. **1939** The Day The Bookies Wept. **1940** Millionaire Playboy; Glamour Boy; The Boys from Syracuse.

PENNICK, JACK (Robert Jack Pennick)
Born: Dec. 7, 1895, Portland, Ore. Died: Aug. 16, 1964, Hollywood, Calif. Screen and stage actor.

Appeared in: **1927** The Broncho Twister; The Lone Eagle. **1928** Plastered in Paris; The Four Sons; Why Sailors Go Wrong. **1929** Strong Boy. **1930** Min and Bill; The City Girl; Paramount on Parade; Way Out West; Born Reckless. **1931** Hell Divers. **1932** Strangers of the Evening; Phantom Express; Air Mail; If I Had a Million; Sky Bride. **1933** Strange People; Tugboat Annie; Renegades of the West; Hello Everybody!; Skyway, Man of Sentiment. **1934** Come on Marines!; The World Moves On. **1935** West Point of the Air; Steamboat 'Round the Bend; Waterfront Lady. **1936** Prisoner of Shark Island; The Music Goes 'Round; Under Two Flags; Private Number; Drift Fence. **1937** Wee Willie Winkie; The Big City; Live, Love and Learn; Navy Blue and Gold; Great Guy; Devil's Playground; Submarine. **1938** You and Me; The Buccaneer; Banjo on My Knee; Alexander's Ragtime Band; King of the Newsboys; Submarine Patrol; Cocoanut Grove. **1939** Union Pacific; Star Maker; Tail Spin; Young Mr. Lincoln; Stagecoach; Mountain Rhythm; Drums Along the Mohawk. **1940** The Grapes of Wrath; The Long Voyage Home; The Westerner; Northwest Mounted Police. **1941** Tobacco Road; Sergeant York; Wild Geese Calling; Lady from Louisiana. **1945** They Were Expendable. **1946** My Darling Clementine. **1947** The Fugitive; Unconquered. **1948** Fort Apache; Three Godfathers. **1949** She Wore a Yellow Ribbon; Mighty Joe Young; The Fighting Kentuckian. **1950** When Willie Comes Marching Home; Rio Grande; Tripoli. **1951** Operation Pacific; The Fighting Coast Guard; The Sea Hornet. **1952** What Price Glory? **1953** The Sun Shines Bright; The Beast from 20,000 Fathoms. **1955** Mr. Roberts; The Long Gray Line. **1956** Searchers. **1957** The Wings of Eagles. **1958** The Last Hurrah; The Buccaneer (and 1938 version). **1959** The Horse Soldiers. **1960** The Alamo; Sergeant Rutledge. **1961** Two Rode Together. **1962** The Man Who Shot Liberty Valance. **1963** How the West Was Won.

PENNINGTON, ANN
Born: Dec. 23, 1892, Camden, N.J. Died: Nov. 4, 1971, N.Y. Screen, stage actress and dancer. Credited with having popularized the dance craze "The Black Bottom."

Appeared in: **1916** Susie Snowflakes; The Rainbow Princess. **1917** The Antics of Ann; Sunshine Nan; Little Boy Scout. **1924** Manhandled. **1925** The Mad Dancer; The Lucky Horseshoe; A Kiss in the Dark; The Golden Strain; Madame Behave; Pretty Ladies. **1929** Tanned Legs; The Gold Diggers of Broadway; Is Everybody Happy?; Night Parade; Night Club. **1930** Happy Days; Hello Baby (short). **1941** Unholly Partners. **1943** China Girl.

PENNINGTON, EDITH MAE
Died: May 16, 1964, Shreveport, La. Screen actress. Voted the "Most Beautiful Girl in the World" in 1921. Appeared in silent films.

PENNY, FRANK
Born: 1895. Died: Apr. 20, 1946, New York. Screen, radio, vaudeville and burlesque actor. Was in vaudeville in an act billed as "Penny, Reed and Gold."

Appeared in: **1941** Hold That Ghost; Keep 'Em Flying. **1942** Pardon My Sarong; Eagle Squadron; Who Done It? **1943** It Ain't Hay. **1944** Lost in a Harem. **1945** Abbott and Costello in Hollywood; Dolly Sisters; Diamond Horseshoe.

PENROSE, CHARLES
Born: 1876. Died: Nov. 17, 1952. Screen actor.

Appeared in: **1940** The Human Monster.

PENWARDEN, DUNCAN
Born: Feb. 9, 1880, Nova Scotia. Died: Sept. 13, 1930, Jackson Heights, N.Y. Screen actor.

Appeared in: **1929** The Gentlemen of the Press; The Lady Lies.

PEPPER, BARBARA
Born: May 31, 1916, New York, N.Y. Died: July 18, 1969, Panorama City, Calif. (coronary). Screen, stage and television actress.

Appeared in: **1933** Roman Scandals. **1934** Our Daily Bread. **1935** Dante's Inferno; Home Work (short); The Singing Vagabond; Let 'Em Have It; Waterfront Lady; Frisco Waterfront; Forced Landing; The Sagebrush Troubadour. **1936** Night Waitress; Showboat; Rogues' Tavern; Wanted: Jane Turner; M'Liss; Mummy's Boys; The Big Game; Winterset. **1937** Sea Devils; Wrong Romance (short); Too Many Wives; You Can't Buy Luck; You Can't Beat Love; The Big Shot; Forty Naughty Girls; The Westland Case; Portia on Trial; Music for Madame. **1938** Hollywood Stadium Mystery; Army Girl; Outside the Law; The Lady in the Morgue; Wide Open Faces; The Chaser; Sweethearts. **1939** Off the Record; Of Mice and Men; They Made Me a Criminal; The Amazing Mr. Williams; The Magnificent Fraud; Colorado Sunset; Flight at Midnight; The Women; Three Sons. **1940** Forgotten Girls; Foreign Correspondent; The Castle on the Hudson; The Return of Frank James; Women in War. **1941** Manpower; Man at Large; Three Sons O'Guns; Birth of the Blues. **1942** Carry Harry (short); Sappy Pappy (short); One Thrilling Night. **1943** He Was Only Feudin' (short); So This is Washington; Girls in Chains; A Maid Made Mad (short); Let's Face It; Star Spangled Rhythm. **1944** An American Romance; I Love a Soldier; Since You Went Away; Henry Aldrich Plays Cupid; Cover Girl; Once Upon a Time. **1945** The Hidden Eye; Brewster's Millions; Murder, He Says; Trouble Chasers; The Naughty Nineties. **1946** Prison Ship. **1947** Terror Trail; The Millerson Case. **1948** The Snake Pit. **1950** The Fuller Brush Girl; My Blue Heaven; Unmasked. **1952** Thunderbirds. **1957** The D.I. **1962** It's Only Money; The Music Man. **1963** A Child is Waiting; It's a Mad, Mad, Mad, Mad World; Who's Minding the Store? **1964** Kiss Me, Stupid; My Fair Lady.

PEPPER, JACK
Born: June 14, 1902, Palestine, Tex. Died: Mar. 31, 1979, Los Angeles, Calif. (diabetes complications). Screen, stage, vaudeville, radio, television actor and nightclub operator. Appeared in vaudeville with sisters Helen and Winnie Mae as "Salt and Pepper." Married to show dancer Dawn Pepper. Father of actress Cynthia Pepper.

Appeared in: **1940** Road to Singapore. **1941** Road to Zanzibar. **1942** Road to Morocco. **1945** Road to Utopia. **1947** The Road to Rio. **1951** Silver Canyon. **1952** Stop, You're Killing Me; Road to Bali. **1955** Lucy Gallant. **1956** That Certain Feeling; Anything Goes. **1962** The Road to Hong Kong.

PEPPER, ROBERT C.
Born: 1916. Died: Oct. 27, 1964, Hollywood, Calif. Screen actor and stuntman. Stand-in for Broderick Crawford and Lon Chaney, Jr.

PERCE, FRED
Born: 1915, Ky. Died: Mar. 12, 1967, Los Angeles, Calif. Screen, stage and television actor.

PERCIVAL, ARLENE See WALKER, ARLENE

PERCIVAL, WALTER C. (Charles David Lingenfelter)
Born: 1887, Chicago, Ill. Died: Jan. 28, 1934, Hollywood, Calif. Screen, stage and vaudeville actor. Was partner in vaudeville with his wife, Rennie Noel.

Appeared in: **1924** The Moral Sinner. **1926** The Flying Horseman. **1928** The Big City; Lights of New York. **1930** Twixt Love and Duty (short); The Leather Pushers (serial); Shooting Straight; Lightnin'. **1931** Blonde Crazy; The Avenger; Smart Money; Sweepstakes; Pagan Lady; Homicide Squad; Larceny Lane; The Champ. **1932** Carnival Boat; Cabin in the Cotton.

PERCY, EILEEN
Born: 1901, Belfast, Ireland. Died: July 29, 1973, Beverly Hills, Calif. Screen and stage actress and newspaper columnist. Married to composer Harry Ruby (dec. 1974).

Appeared in: 1917 The Americano; The Man from Painted Past; Reaching for the Moon; Down to Earth. 1919 Brass Buttons; In Mizzoura; Some Liar; Where the West Begins; The Gray Horizon; The Beloved Cheater; Told in the Hills; Desert Gold. 1920 The Third Eye (serial); The Husband Hunter; Beware of the Bride; Man Who Dared; Her Honor, the Mayor. 1921 The Blushing Bride; Big Town Ideas; Hickville to Broadway; Maid of the West; Little Miss Hawkshaw; The Tomboy; Whatever She Wants; Why Trust Your Husband?; The Land of Jazz. 1922 The Flirt; Elope If You Must; The Fast Mail; Western Speed; Pardon My Nerve! 1923 Children of Jazz; East Side—West Side; Let's Go; The Prisoner; The Fourth Musketeer; Hollywood; Within the Law; Yesterday's Wife. 1924 Tongues of Flame; The Turmoil; Missing Daughters. 1925 Fine Clothes; Under the Rouge; Cobra; The Shadow on the Wall; Souls for Sables; The Unchastened Woman. 1926 Lovey Mary; Race Wild; The Model from Paris; The Phantom Bullet. 1927 Backstage; Spring Fever; Twelve Miles Out; Burnt Fingers. 1928 Telling the World. 1929 The Broadway Hoofer. 1930 Temptation. 1931 Wicked. 1932 The Cohens and Kellys in Hollywood. 1943 First Aid (short).

PERCY, ESME (Saville Esme Percy)
Born: Aug. 8, 1887, London, England. Died: June 17, 1957, Brighton, England. Screen, stage actor and stage producer.

Appeared in: 1930 Murder. 1933 The Lucky Number; On Secret Service (aka Secret Agent—US 1935); Bitter Sweet; Summer Lightning. 1934 The Unfinished Symphony (US 1935); Lord Edgwar Dies; Nell Gwyn. 1935 Royal Cavalcade (aka Regal Cavalcade—US); Abdul the Damned; Invitation to the Waltz; It Happened in Paris. 1936 The Invader (aka An Old Spanish Custom—US); The Amateur Gentleman; A Woman Alone (aka Two Who Dared—US 1937); Accused; Song of Freedom; Land Without Music (aka Forbidden Music—US 1938). 1937 Jump for Glory (aka When Thief Meets Thief—US); Our Fighting Navy (aka Torpedoed—US 1939); The Return of the Scarlet Pimpernel (US 1938); 21 Days (aka 21 Days Together—US 1940 and aka The First and the Last); The Frog (US 1939). 1938 Pygmalion. 1945 Dead of Night. 1946 Caesar and Cleopatra; Lisbon Story. 1947 The Ghosts of Berkeley Square. 1948 Death in the Hand.

PERCY, WILLIAM STRATFORD
Born: Dec. 23, 1872, Melbourne, Australia. Died: June 19, 1946, England? Screen and stage actor.

Appeared in: 1935 Oh Daddy!; Late Extra. 1936 Troubled Waters; Public Nuisance No. 1.

PEREZ, JOE
Born: 1911, Havana, Cuba. Died: July 20, 1981, Miami, Fla. Screen actor, film director and producer.

Appeared in: 1938 California Frontier. 1942 Flying Tigers; Remember Pearl Harbor. 1949 We Were Strangers.

PEREZ, PEPITO
Born: 1896, Spain. Died: July 13, 1975, Santa Ana, Calif. (cancer). Screen, stage, vaudeville and television actor. Known as "Pepito the Spanish Clown."

Appeared in: 1938 Army Girl; Annabella Takes a Tour. 1944 Lady in the Dark. 1945 A Medal for Benny. 1948 Sorry, Wrong Number. 1951 The Raging Tide.

PERFECT, ROSE
Born: 1895. Died: Apr. 6, 1978, Hollywood, Calif. Screen, stage actress and singer.

Appeared in: 1930 The Girl With the Golden Voice (short).

PERIOLAT, GEORGE
Born: 1876, Chicago, Ill. Died: Feb. 20, 1940, Los Angeles, Calif. (suicide—arsenic). Screen and stage actor. Entered films with Essanay in 1911.

Appeared in: 1915 The Adventures of Terence O'Rourke; The Diamond from the Sky (serial). 1916 Landon's Legacy. 1917 The Mate of the Sally Ann. 1920 The Mark of Zorro. 1921 Her Face Value; The Kiss; A Parisian Scandal; They Shall Pay; Wealth; Who Am I? 1922 Blood and Sand; The Dust Flower; Gay and Devilish; Shattered Idols; The Young Rajah. 1923 Rosita; The Barefoot Boy; Slave of Desire; The Tiger's Claw. 1924 The Red Lily; The Girl on the Stairs; Lover's Lane;

The Yankee Consul. 1925 Any Woman; Fighting Youth; The Phantom Express. 1926 Butterflies in the Rain; Atta Boy; The Nut-Cracker; The Mile-a-Minute Man. 1927 Fangs of Destiny; The Prairie King; Through Thick and Thin; Speedy Smith. 1928 The Secret Hour; The Night Watch; Black Butterflies. 1929 When Dreams Come True; One Splendid Hour; The Fatal Warning (serial).

PERIOT, ARTHUR
Born: 1899. Died: Feb. 24, 1929, Monterey, Calif. (auto accident). Screen actor and stuntman.

PERIQUIN (Armando Espinosa de los Monteros)
Born: 1912, Mexico. Died: Nov. 6, 1957, Mexico City, Mexico (cancer). Screen and stage actor.

PERKINS, JEAN EDWARD
Born: 1899. Died: Dec. 24, 1922 (while filming The Eagle's Talons serial). Screen actor and stuntman.

Appeared in: 1921 Do or Die (serial). 1923 The Eagle's Talons (serial).

PERKINS, OSGOOD
Born: 1892, West Newton, Mass. Died: Sept. 21, 1937, Washington, D.C. (heart attack). Screen and stage actor. Father of actor Anthony Perkins.

Appeared in: 1922 The Cradle Buster. 1923 Puritan Passions; Second Fiddle. 1924 Grit. 1925 Wild, Wild Susan. 1926 Love 'Em and Leave 'Em. 1927 High Hat; Knockout Reilly. 1929 Mother's Boy; Syncopation. 1931 The Front Page (stage and film versions); Tarnished Lady; Loose Ankles. 1932 Scarface. 1934 Kansas City Princess; Madame Du Barry; The President Vanishes. 1935 I Dream Too Much; Secret of the Chateau. 1936 Gold Diggers of 1937.

PERKINS, VOLTAIRE
Born: 1897. Died: Oct. 10, 1977, Los Angeles, Calif. (heart attack). Screen, television actor and attorney.

Appeared in: 1953 Sangaree; The Vanquished. 1955 A Man Called Peter; The Far Horizons. 1956 Over-Exposed. 1957 My Man Godfrey. 1958 Frankenstein's Daughter; Macabre. 1959 Compulsion. 1961 Sanctuary. 1964 A Global Affair.

PERKINS, WALTER
Born: 1870, Biddeford, Maine. Died: June 3, 1925, Brooklyn, N.Y. Screen, stage and vaudeville actor.

Appeared in: 1919 Bill Henry. 1920 Peaceful Valley. 1921 The New Disciple. 1922 Golden Dreams; When Romance Rides.

PERLEY, ANNA
Born: 1849. Died: Jan. 20, 1937, Los Angeles, Calif. Screen and stage actress.

PERLEY, CHARLES
Born: 1886. Died: Feb. 10, 1933, Santa Ana, Calif. (heart attack). Stage and screen actor. Appeared in early Biograph films.

PERLEY, HENRY See CHIEF HENRY "RED EAGLE" PERLEY

PERON, EVA See DURATE, EVA

PERREDOM, LUIS
Born: 1882, Spain. Died: Apr. 7, 1958, Madrid, Spain. Stage and screen actor.

PERRIN, JACK
Born: July 25, 1896, Three Rivers, Mich. Died: Dec. 17, 1967, Hollywood, Calif. (heart attack). Screen and stage actor.

Appeared in: 1917 His Speedy Finish; His Sudden Rival; A Love Case; His Unconscious Conscience; Ambrose's Icy Love. 1919 The Lion Man (serial); Two Men of Tinted Butte; Blind Husbands. 1920 Pink Tights. 1921 The Match-Breaker; Partners of the Tide; The Rage of Paris; The Torrent. 1922 The Dangerous Little Demon; The Trouper; The Guttersnipe. 1923 The Santa Fe Trail (serial); Golden Silence; The Lone Horseman; The Fighting Shippers (serial); Mary of the Movies. 1924 Coyote Fangs; Riders of the Plains (serial); Crashin' Through; Lightnin' Jack; Travelin' Fast; Virginian Outcast; Shootin' Square; Ridin' West; Those Who Dance. 1925 Border Vengeance; Winning a Woman; Double Fisted; Cactus Trails; Canyon Rustlers; Desert Madness; The Knockout Kid; Starlight; The Untamed; Dangerous Fists; Silent Sheldon. 1926 A Ridin' Gent; Mistaken Orders; Midnight Faces; Dangerous Traffic; The Grey Devil; Hi-Jacking Rustlers; The Thunderbolt Strikes; West of the Rainbow's End; Starlight's Revenge; The Man from Oklahoma. 1927 Code of the Range; Fire and Steel; The Laffin' Fool; Where the North Holds Sway; Thunderbolt's Tracks.

1928 Guardians of the Wild; The Vanishing West (serial); The Two Outlaws; The Water Hole. **1929** Wild Blood; The Harvest of Hate; Hoofbeats of Vengeance; Plunging Hoofs. **1930** The Apache Kid's Escape; Phantom of the Desert; Beyond the Rio Grande; Ridin' Law; Trails of Peril; Overland Bound; Romance of the West; The Jade Box (serial). **1931** Wild West Whoopee; The Kid from Arizona; The Sheriff's Secret; Lariats and Six-Shooters. **1932** Hell Fire Austin; .45 Calibre Echo; Dynamite Rance. **1934** Rawhide Mail; Girl Trouble (short). **1936** Hair Trigger Casey; Desert Justice. **1937** The Painted Stallion (serial). **1938** Western Jamboree; Angels With Dirty Faces; The Purple Vigilantes. **1939** Eternally Yours. **1940** The Fighting 69th; West of Pinto Basin. **1941** Sky Raiders (serial). **1942** Broadway Big Shot. **1948** The Fuller Brush Man. **1950** Bandit Queen. **1951** Jim Thorpe—All American. **1956** Around the World in 80 Days. **1960** Sunrise at Campobello.

PERRINS, LESLIE
Born: 1902, Moseley, England. Died: Dec. 13, 1962, Esher, England. Screen, stage and radio actor.

Appeared in: **1928** Sexton Blake series including: The Clue of the Second Goblet; Blake the Lawbreaker. **1931** Immediate Possession; The Rosary; The Sleeping Cardinal (aka Sherlock Holmes' Fatal Hour—US); The Calendar (aka Bachelor's Folly—US 1932); We Dine at Seven. **1932** Betrayal; White Face. **1933** The Lost Chord; Just Smith; The Roof; The Pointing Finger; Early to Bed. **1934** Lily of Killarney (aka Bride of the Lake—US); The Man Who Changed His Name; The Lash; Song at Eventide; Lord Edgware Dies; Open All Night; Gay Love; The Scotland Yard Mystery (aka The Living Dead—US); Womanhood. **1935** D'ye Ken John Peel? (aka Captain Moonlight—US); The Shadow of Mike Emerald; The Rocks of Valpre (aka High Treason—US 1937); White Lilac; The Triumph of Sherlock Holmes; Lucky Days; Expert's Opinion; Line Engaged; The Village Squire. **1936** Tudor Rose (aka Nine Days a Queen—US); Sunshine Ahead; Rhythm in the Air; Southern Roses; No Escape; The Limping Man; They Didn't Know. **1937** Secret Lives (aka I Married a Spy—US 1938); The High Command; Sensation; Dangerous Fingers (aka Wanted by Scotland Yard—US); Bulldog Drummond at Bay; The House of Unrest; The Price of Folly. **1938** Mr. Reeder in Room 13 (aka Mystery of Room 13—US 1941); Romance a la Carte; The Gables Mystery; No Parking; Calling All Crooks; His Lordship Goes to Paris; Luck of the Navy (aka North Sea Patrol—US 1940); Old Iron. **1939** The Gang's All Here (aka The Amazing Mr. Forrest—US); All at Sea; Blind Folly; I Killed the Count (aka Who is Guilty?—US 1940). **1940** John Smith Wakes Up. **1941** The Prime Minister. **1942** Suspected Person; Women Aren't Angels. **1944** Heaven is Round the Corner. **1946** I'll Turn to You. **1947** The Turners of Prospect Road. **1948** Idols of Paris. **1949** A Run for Your Money (US 1950); Man on the Run (US 1951). **1950** Midnight Episode (US 1951). **1952** The Lost Hours (aka The Big Frame—US 1953). **1956** Guilty? **1958** Grip of the Strangler (aka The Haunted Strangler—US).

PERRY, ANTOINETTE (aka ANNETTE PERRY)
Born: 1888. Died: June 28, 1946, New York, N.Y. (heart attack). Screen, stage actress and stage director.

Appeared in: **1924** Yankee Madness. **1925** After Marriage.

PERRY, CHARLES EMMETT
Born: 1907. Died: Feb. 26, 1967, Hollywood, Calif. (heart ailment). Screen actor. Married to actress Naomi Perry. Entered films in 1923. Do not confuse with British actor Charles Perry.

PERRY, JACK
Died: Oct. 7, 1971. Screen actor.

Appeared in: **1928** Celebrity. **1931** Young Donovan's Kid. **1934** A Woman's Man. **1935** She Gets Her Man.

PERRY, MARY
Born: 1888, Gainsville, Ga. Died: Mar. 6, 1971, N.Y. Screen, stage and television actress.

Appeared in: **1958** Uncle Vanya (stage and film versions). **1960** The Fugitive Kind. **1963** All the Way Home.

PERRY, PASCALE
Born: 1889, Mariposa County, Ariz. Died: July 11, 1953, North Hollywood, Calif. Screen, stage and television actor.

Appeared in: **1933** Gallant Fool. **1935** Here Comes Cookie. **1936** Guns and Guitars. **1947** Springtime in the Sierras. **1948** Eyes of Texas. **1949** Gun Runner.

PERRY, REGINALD (Reginald Harry Perry)
Born: 1890, Australia. Died: June 13, 1981, Adelaide, Australia (stroke). Screen actor and film manager. Son of film producer Joseph Perry (dec.).

Appeared in: **1900** Soldiers of the Cross.

PERRY, ROBERT E. "BOB"
Born: 1879, New York, N.Y. Died: Jan. 8, 1962, Hollywood, Calif. Screen and television actor.

Appeared in: **1921** The Devil Within. **1922** Oath-Bound; Iron to Gold. **1925** The Light of Western Stars; The Thundering Herd. **1926** Volcano; Gigolo. **1927** Finger Prints; Jaws of Steel; White Gold; Brass Knuckles. **1928** The Fortune Hunter; Beggars of Life; Dressed to Kill; The River Pirate; Me, Gangster. **1929** The Man I Love; Noisy Neighbors; Sin Town; Skin Deep. **1930** Those Who Dance; Trailin' Trouble; The Sea God. **1931** Other Men's Women. **1932** Winner Take All; Carnival Boat; Hell's Highway. **1933** The Chief; Picture Snatcher; The Mayor of Hell. **1934** The Mighty Barnum. **1935** Dr. Socrates. **1936** Riffraff; Cain and Mabel; My Man Godfrey. **1937** Manhattan Merry-Go-Round. **1939** Each Dawn I Die. **1940** The Long Voyage Home. **1941** The Strawberry Blonde; The Big Store. **1946** The Kid from Brooklyn; The Strange Love of Martha Ivers.

PERRY, SARA
Born: 1872. Died: Jan. 18, 1959, White Plains, N.Y. Screen and stage actress.

Appeared in: **1950** The Damned Don't Cry.

PERRY, VICTOR "VIC"
Born: 1920, England. Died: Aug. 14, 1974, Van Nuys, Calif. Screen, stage and television actor. Billed as "The World's Greatest Pickpocket."

Appeared in: **1953** Julius Caesar; Pickup on South Street. **1956** Timeslip (aka The Atomic Man—US). **1966** Mozambique.

PERRY, WALTER
Born: Sept. 14, 1868, San Francisco, Calif. Died: Jan. 22, 1954, Calif. Screen, stage and vaudeville actor. Entered films in 1915.

Appeared in: **1919** A Sage Brush Hamlet; The Pagan God; Dangerous Waters; A Fugitive from Matrimony; Fighting Cressy; Prince and Betty; Third Degree; Kathleen Mavoureen. **1920** The U.P. Trail. **1921** The Parish Priest; The Fire Eater; Garments of Truth; A Certain Rich Man. **1922** A Poor Relation; The Scrapper; Second Hand Rose; The Guttersnipe. **1923** Souls for Sale. **1924** Dark Stairways; The Love Master. **1925** Too Much Youth; White Fang; The Unholy Three. **1926** The Johnstown Flood; Three Bad Men; Beautiful Cheat. **1927** Irish Hearts. **1928** The Foreign Legion; Wilfull Youth. **1930** Trigger Tricks; Troopers Three; The Thoroughbred; Third Alarm. **1931** Two Gun Man. **1932** Spirit of the West; Dynamite Denny.

PERRYMAN, LLOYD
Born: 1917. Died: May 31, 1977, Burbank, Calif. Screen actor and singer. Member of the "Sons of the Pioneers."

PERSSE, THOMAS
Died: Apr., 1920, Venice, Calif. Screen actor and opera performer.

Appeared in: **1920** It's a Great Life.

PERSSON, EDVARD
Born: 1887, Sweden. Died: Sept. 26, 1957, Halsinborg, Sweden. Screen actor.

Appeared in: **1934** Flickorna Fran Gamla Stan. **1935** Tjocka Slaekten (Near Relatives); Larsson I Andra Giftet. **1936** Loerdagskvaellar; Vaaran Pojke; Soederkaakar. **1937** The Old Gods Still Live. **1938** Baldvins Brollop (Baldwin's Wedding). **1939** Skanor-Falsterbo. **1940** Kalle Paa Spaangen; Kvinnorna Kring Larsson (The Women Around Larsson). **1944** Sun Over Klara. **1953** Pimpernel Sversson; Each Heart Has It's Own Story.

PETERS, ANN
Born: 1920, Santa Monica, Calif. Died: Dec. 24, 1965, Paris, France (heart attack). Black screen, stage actress and singer. Member of the "Peters Sisters" singing group. Married to musician Willy Katz.

Appeared in: **1937** Ali Baba Goes to Town. **1938** Love and Hisses; Happy Landing; Rebecca of Sunnybrook Farm.

PETERS, BRANDON
Born: 1893. Died: Feb. 27, 1956, New York, N.Y. Screen and stage actor. Married to actress Alice Thompson.

PETERS, DON (Donald Ambrose Peters)
Born: Jan. 15, 1921, Calif. Died: Sept. 28, 1953. Screen and stage actor.

Appeared in: **1942** Ten Gentlemen from West Point.

PETERS, FRED
Born: June 30, 1884, Waltham, Mass. Died: Apr. 23, 1963, Hollywood, Calif. Screen actor. Entered films in 1916.

Appeared in: **1921** Miracles of the Jungle (serial). **1923** Salome. **1924** The Millionaire Cowboy. **1927** "12" Miles Out; Tarzan and the Golden Lion. **1929** Spieler. **1936** I Conquer the Sea.

PETERS, GUNNAR
Died: Mar. 11, 1974, Fort Salonga, N.Y. (coronary). Screen and television actor.

Appeared in: **1964** Lilith.

PETERS, HOUSE, SR. (Robert House Peters)
Born: Mar. 12, 1880, Bristol, England. Died: Dec. 7, 1967, Woodland Hills, Calif. Screen actor. Father of actor House Peters, Jr. Brother of actor Page Peters (dec. 1916).

Appeared in: **1913** Leah-Kleshna; Lady of Quality. **1914** The Pride of Jennico; Salomy Jane. **1915** The Girl of the Golden West; The Great Divide; Mignon; The Warrens of Virginia; The Unafraid; The Captive. **1920** The Great Redeemer; Isobel. **1921** The Invisible Power; Lying Lips. **1922** The Man from Lost River; Human Hearts; The Storm; Rich Men's Wives. **1923** Held to Answer; Counsel for the Defense; Lost and Found; Don't Marry for Money. **1924** The Tornado. **1925** Raffles; Head Winds; The Storm Breaker. **1926** The Combat; Prisoners of the Storm. **1928** Rose Marie. **1952** O'Henry's Full House; The Old West.

PETERS, CAPTAIN JOHN
Born: Germany. Died: Oct. 21, 1940, Santa Rosa, Calif. Screen actor and circus performer.

Appeared in: **1926** Ransom's Folly.

PETERS, JOHN S. (John Sylvester Peters)
Born: Dec. 31, 1894, Ohio. Died: Nov. 7, 1963, Los Angeles, Calif. (heart attack). Screen actor.

Appeared in: **1926** The Amateur Gentleman; Under Western Skies; Ransom's Folly. **1927** A Dog of the Regiment; The Frontiersman; The Enemy; The Student Prince in Old Heidelberg. **1928** Divine Sinner; The Scarlet Lady. **1932** White Zombie. **1934** Beast of Borneo. **1939** Mystery Plane; Beast of Berlin; Sky Patrol. **1955** Chief Crazy Horse.

PETERS, PAGE E.
Died: June 22, 1916, Hermosa Beach, Calif. (drowned). Screen actor. Brother of actor House Peters (dec. 1967).

Appeared in: **1914** The Siren. **1915** The Warrens of Virginia; The Clue; Unexpected; The Unafraid; The Captive. **1916** Madame Le Presidente; Davy Crockett; An International Marriage.

PETERS, PETER
Born: 1926, Germany. Died: Oct. 1, 1955, Berlin, Germany (suicide—jump from building). Stage and screen actor.

PETERS, RALPH
Born: 1903. Died: June 5, 1959, Hollywood, Calif. Screen actor.

Appeared in: **1937** The Great Gambini; Swing It Professor. **1938** Outlaws of Sonora; Man's Country; Wanted by the Police. **1939** Tough Kid; Six-Gun Rhythm; Rovin' Tumbleweeds. **1940** Ghost Valley Raiders; Laughing at Danger; Margie. **1941** Ball of Fire; You Belong to Me; Outlaws of the Rio Grande; Across the Sierras; You're Out of Luck; Two in a Taxi. **1942** Shut My Big Mouth; Bells of Capistrano; Ride 'Em Cowboy; A Man's World. **1943** It Ain't Hay; One Dangerous Night; Good Morning, Judge; Find the Blackmailer; My Kingdom for a Cook. **1944** Take it Big; Roger Touhy—Gangster; Black Magic; Twilight on the Prairie; Ghost Catchers; Charlie Chan in Black Magic. **1945** Radio Stars on Parade; Hold that Blonde; Honeymoon Ahead; See My Lawyer. **1946** Nobody Lives Forever; Little Giant. **1947** Desert Fury; Trail to San Antone. **1948** So You Want to Build a House (short). **1949** Fighting Fools; Sky Liner; Cactus Cut-Up (short). **1950** Beyond the Purple Hills; Experiment Alcatraz; Where the Sidewalk Ends. **1951** The Racket; Gasoline Alley; A Millionaire for Christy; Slaughter Trail. **1952** The Sniper. **1953** Gentlemen Prefer Blondes. **1954** Three Ring Circus; Destry. **1956** While the City Sleeps. **1957** Badlands of Montana.

PETERS, SUSAN (Suzanne Carnahan)
Born: July 3, 1921, Spokane, Wash. Died: Oct. 23, 1952, Visalia, Calif. (chronic kidney infection, pneumonia and starvation). Screen, stage and television actress. Appeared in films originally as Suzanne Carnahan. Nominted for 1942 Academy Award for Best Supporting Actress in Random Harvest.

Appeared in: **1940** Money and the Woman; River's End; Young America Flies; Sockaroo; The Man Who Talked Too Much; Susan and God; Santa Fe Trail. **1941** Strawberry Blonde; Meet John Doe; Here Comes Happiness; Three Sons O'Guns; Scattergood Pulls the Strings. **1942** Escape from Crime; Dr. Gillespie's New Assistant; Random Harvest; The Big Shot; Tish; Andy Hardy's Double Life. **1943** Assingment in Brittany; Young Ideas. **1944** Song of Russia. **1945** Keep Your Powder Dry. **1948** The Sign of the Ram.

PETERS, WERNER
Born: 1919, Germany. Died: Mar. 31, 1971, Wiesbaden, West Germany. Screen, stage actor and film producer.

Appeared in: **1951** The Subject. **1958** Unruhige Nacht (The Restless Night—US 1964); Nachts Wenn der Teufel Kam (Nights When the Devil Came aka The Devil Strikes at Night—US 1959). **1959** Rosen fur den Staatsanwalt (Roses for the Prosecutor—US 1961); Kriegsgericht (Court Marital—US 1962). **1960** Liebe Kann Wie Gift Sein (Love Can Be Like Poison aka Magdalena); Rosemary. **1961** Im Stahlnetz des Dr. Mabuse (The Return of Dr. Mabuse—US 1966). **1962** The Counterfeit Traitor; Die Unsichtbaren Krallen des Dr. Mabuse (The Invisible Dr. Mabuse—US 1965). **1963** Das Feuereschiff (The Lightship); Nur Tote Zeugen Schweigen (aka Hypnosis—US 1966). **1964** Einer Frisst den Anderen (aka Dog Eat Dog—US 1966); Das Phantom von Soho (The Phantom of Soho—US 1967). **1965** The Battle of the Bulge; Thirty Six Hours. **1966** A Fine Madness; I Deal in Danger; Il Sigillo di Pechino (aka The Corrupt Ones—US 1967 and aka The Peking Medallion and Hell to Macao). **1967** Deux Billets pour Mexico (aka Dead Run—US 1969). **1968** Assignment K; The Secret War of Harry Frigg.

PETERSEN, PETER
Born: 1876, Hamburg, Germany. Died: Apr. 1, 1956, Vienna, Austria. Screen, stage, burlesque actor and stage director.

Appeared in: **1934** Masquerade. **1937** The Eternal Mask; Masquerade in Vienna; The Kreutzer Sonata. **1940** Der Spiegel des Lebens (Life's Mirror).

PETERSON, DOROTHY
Born: Hector, Minn. Died: 1979. Screen and stage actress.

Appeared in: **1930** Mother's Cry. **1931** Fires of Youth; Party Husband; Up for Murder; The Reckless Hour; Traveling Husbands; Bought; Penrod and Sam; Skyline; Rich Man's Folly; The Plutocrat. **1932** Thrill of Youth; Forbidden; Way Back Home; Business and Pleasure; She Wanted a Millionaire; The Beast of the City; So Big; When a Feller Needs a Friend; Night World; Attorney for the Defense; Life Begins; Cabin in the Cotton; Payment Deferred; Call Her Savage. **1933** Big Executive; Reform Girl; The Billion Dollar Scandal; Hold Me Tight; I'm No Angel; Mayor of Hell. **1934** Uncertain Lady; Beloved; As the Earth Turns; Treasure Island; Peck's Bad Boy; Side Streets. **1935** Only Eight Hours; Society Doctor; Laddie; Freckles; Man of Iron; Pursuit; Sweepstake Annie. **1936** The Country Doctor; The Devil Is a Sissy; Reunion. **1937** Under Cover of Night; Her Husband Lies; Confession; 52nd Street; Girl Loves Boy. **1938** Hunted Men; Breaking the Ice; Girls on Probation. **1939** Five Little Peppers; The Flying Irishman; Dark Victory; Sabotage; Two Bright Boys. **1940** Out West With the Peppers; Five Little Peppers in Trouble; Five Little Peppers at Home; Two Many Husbands; Lillian Russell; Women in War. **1941** Cheers for Miss Bishop; Henry Aldrich for President; Ride, Kelly, Ride. **1942** Saboteur; The Man in the Trunk. **1943** Air Force; This Is the Army; The Moon Is Down. **1944** Faces in the Fog; This Is the Life; Mr. Skeffington; When the Lights Go On Again; The Woman in the Window. **1946** Canyon Passage; Sister Kenny. **1947** That Hagen Girl.

PETERSON, ELSA
Born: 1896. Died: Mar. 11, 1974, Woodland Hills, Calif. Screen actress.

Appeared in: **1930** Madam Satan. **1932** The Expert; Guilty as Hell. **1957** Funny Face.

PETERSON, KAREN
Born: England. Died: Feb. 16, 1940, London, England. Screen and stage actress. Married to film producer Maurice Ostrer.

PETERSON, MARJORIE
Born: 1906, Houston, Tex. Died: Aug. 19, 1974, New York, N.Y. (heart attack). Stage and screen actress.

Appeared in: **1932** Panama Flo; Love Is a Racket; Tess of the Storm Country.

PETERSON, WILBUR "PETE"
Born: 1915, Hawaii. Died: Oct. 24, 1960, Miami, Fla. Screen, television and vaudeville actor.

PETER THE GREAT
Died: June 10, 1926, Hollywood, Calif. (shot). Dog animal performer.

Appeared in: **1924** The Silent Accuser. **1925** Wild Justice. **1926** King of the Pack; The Sign of the Claw.

PETEY
Born: 1923, Pasadena, Calif. Died: Apr., 1930, Los Angeles, Calif. (arsenic poisoning). Screen animal performer (dog). Son of "Pal" (dec. 1929). Appeared in Our Gang comedies—the dog with the ring around his eye—and also played "Tige" in Buster Brown comedies.

Appeared in: **1927** The following shorts: Olympic Games; The Glorious Fourth; Dog Heaven; Yale vs. Harvard. **1928** The following shorts: Playin' Hookey; The Smile Wins; Spook Spoofing; Edison, Marconi & Co.; Rainy Days; Barnum and Ringling, Inc.; Fair and Muddy; Crazy House; Growing Pains; Old Gray Hoss; School Begins. **1929** The following shorts: Wiggle Your Ears; Election Day; Noisy Noises; The Holy Terror; Fast Freight; Little Mothers; Cat, Dog & Co.; Saturday's Lesson; Small Talk; Railroadin'; Boxing Gloves; Lazy Days; Bouncing Babies; Moan & Groan, Inc. **1930** The following shorts: Shivering Shakespeare; The First Seven Years; When the Wind Blows; Bear Shooters; A Tough Winter.

PETIT, ALBERT
Born: 1887, Switzerland. Died: Feb. 28, 1963, Woodland Hills, Calif. Screen and stage actor.

Appeared in: **1934** Here is My Heart; Bum Voyage (short). **1935** Ruggles of Red Gap. **1942** Once Upon a Honeymoon. **1945** The Dolly Sisters. **1946** The Razor's Edge; Night and Day. **1947** Desire Me. **1948** The Emperor Waltz.

PETIT, WANDA See HAWLEY, WANDA

PETIT-DEMANCE, CHARLES See PRINCE, RIGADIA

PETLEY, FRANK E.
Born: Mar. 28, 1872, Old Charlton, Kent, England. Died: Jan. 12, 1945, England? Screen actor.

Appeared in: **1919** Silver Greyhound; Knave of Hearts. **1920** The Iron Stair (aka The Branded Soul—US 1921); The Flame (US 1921). **1921** The Mystery of Mr. Bernard Brown; The Golden Dawn; My Lord Conceit. **1922** Melody of Death.

PETRIE, HAY (David Hay Petrie)
Born: July 16, 1895, Dundee, Scotland. Died: July 30, 1948. Screen and stage actor.

Appeared in: **1930** Suspense; Night Birds. **1931** Gipsy Blood (aka Carmen—US 1932); Many Waters. **1932** Help Yourself. **1933** Matinee Idol; The Lucky Number; Daughters of Today; Crime on the Hill; The Private Life of Henry VIII. **1934** Colonel Blood; The Queen's Affair (aka Runaway Queen—US 1935); The Private Life of Don Juan; Nell Gwyn; The Old Curiosity Shop (US 1935); Blind Justice. **1935** Invitation to the Waltz; Peg of Old Drury (US 1936); I Give My Heart; Moscow Nights (aka I Stand Condemned—US 1936); Koenigsmark; The Silent Passenger. **1936** Forget-Me-Not (aka Forever Yours—US 1937); The Ghost Goes West; The House of the Spaniard; Men of Yesterday; Hearts of Humanity; Rembrandt; No Escape; Conquest of the Air; Not Wanted on Voyage (aka Treachery on the High Seas—US 1939). **1937** Secret Lives (aka I Married a Spy—US 1938); Knight Without Armour; 21 Days (aka 21 Days Together—US 1940 and aka The First and the Last). **1938** Keep Smiling (aka Smiling Along—US 1939); Consider Your Verdict; The Last Barricade. **1939** Ten Days in Paris (aka Missing Ten Days—US); Q Planes (aka Clouds Over Europe—US); The Spy in Black (aka U-Boat 29—US); Jamaica Inn; Inquest; Four Feathers; Trunk Crime (aka Design for Murder—US 1940). **1940** Crimes at the Dark House; Spy for a Day; Convoy (US 1941); The Thief of Bagdad; Contraband (aka Blackout—US); Pastor Hall. **1941** Freedom Radio (aka A Voice in the Night—US); Spellbound (aka The Spell of Amy Nugent—US); Cottage to Let (aka Bombsight Stolen—US); Turned Out Nice Again; The Ghost of St. Michaeli. **1942** Hard Steel; This Was Paris; One of Our Aircraft Is Missing; They Flew Alone (aka Wings and the Woman—US); The Great Mr. Handel (US 1943). **1943** Battle for Music. **1944** On

Approval (US 1945); Kiss the Bride Goodbye; A Canterbury Tale. **1945** Waltz Time; The Voice Within. **1946** The Laughing Lady (US 1950); Great Expectations (US 1947); Under New Management. **1948** The Monkey's Paw; The Red Shoes; The Guinea Pig (US 1949); The Fallen Idol (US 1949); Noose (aka The Silk Noose—US 1950). **1949** The Queen of Spades.

PETRIE, HOWARD A.
Born: 1907, Beverly, Mass. Died: Mar. 26, 1968, Keene, N.H. Screen, radio and television actor.

Appeared in: **1950** Fancy Pants; Walk Softy, Stranger; Rocky Mountain. **1951** The Racket; No Questions Asked; Cattle Drive; The Golden Horde. **1952** The Wild North; Red Ball Express; Bend of the River; Carbine Williams; Woman in the North Country; Pony Soldier. **1953** Fort Ti; Fair Wind to Java; The Veils of Bagdad. **1954** Sign of the Pagan; The Bob Mathias Story; The Bounty Hunter; Seven Brides for Seven Brothers; Border River; Both Sides of the Law. **1955** Rage at Dawn; How to Be Very, Very Popular; The Return of Jack Slade; Timberjack. **1956** Johnny Concho; The Maverick Queen; A Kiss Before Dying. **1957** The Tin Star.

PETROFF, PAUL
Born: 1908, Denmark. Died: Apr. 27, 1981, Antwerp, Belgium (heart attack). Ballet dancer, teacher and screen actor. Married to actress/dancer Nana Gollner (dec. 1980).

Appeared in: **1928** The End of St. Petersberg.

PETROVA, OLGA (aka MURIEL HARDING)
Born: 1886, Liverpool, England. Died: Nov. 30, 1977, Clearwater, Fla. Screen, stage, vaudeville actress, film producer, screenwriter, playwright, composer and writer. Divorced from Dr. John Dillon Stewart, and later married to actor Lewis Willoughby (dec. 1968). Do not confuse with actress Muriel Harding who made films in the 1950s.

Appeared in: **1915** The Vampire (film debut); My Madonna. **1916** The Soul Market; The Black Butterfly. **1917** The Law of the Land; Bridges Burned; The Undying Flame; The Soul of a Magdalen. **1918** Daughter of Destiny; The Life Mask; Tempered Steel.

PETRUZZI, JULIAN (Julian Joseph Petruzzi)
Born: May 17, 1907, Ohio. Died: Mar. 1, 1967, Woodland Hills, Calif. (heart attack). Screen actor.

Appeared in: **1938** Tenth Avenue Kid.

PETTINGELL, FRANK
Born: Jan. 1, 1891, Liverpool, England. Died: Feb. 17, 1966, London, England. Screen, stage and television actor.

Appeared in: **1931** Hobson's Choice; Jealousy. **1932** Frail Women; The Crooked Lady; In a Monastery Garden; Once Bitten; Double Dealing; A Tight Corner. **1933** Yes, Madam; The Medicine Man; Excess Baggage; The Good Companions; That's My Wife; The Lucky Number; A Cuckoo in the Nest; This Week of Grace. **1934** Red Wagon; Keep it Quiet; Sing as We Go; My Old Dutch. **1935** The Big Splash; The Hope of His Side (aka Where's George?); Say It With Diamonds; The Last Journey (US 1936); The Right to Marry. **1936** The Amateur Gentleman; Millions; On Top of the World; Fame. **1937** It's a Grand Old World; Spring Handicap; Take My Tip. **1938** Sailing Along; Queer Cargo (aka Pirates of the Seven Seas—US). **1940** Busman's Honeymoon (aka Haunted Honeymoon—US); Return to Yesterday; Gaslight (aka Angel Street—US 1952). **1941** Kipps (aka The Remarkable Mr. Kipps—US 1942); Once a Crook; Ships with Wings (US 1942); The Seventh Survivor; This England (aka Our Heritage). **1942** The Young Mr. Pitt; The Goose Steps Out. **1943** Get Cracking; When We Are Married. **1946** Gaiety George (aka Showtime—US 1948). **1948** Escape; No Room at the Inn. **1951** The Magic Box (US 1952). **1952** The Crimson Pirate; The Card (aka The Promoter—US); Meet Me Tonight. **1953** Tonight at 8:30. **1955** Value for Money (US 1957). **1958** Up the Creek; Corridors of Blood (US 1963). **1962** Term of Trial (US 1963); The Dock Brief (aka Trial and Error—US). **1964** Becket.

PEUKERT-IMPEKOVEN, SABINE
Born: 1890, Germany. Died: May 5, 1970, Frankfurt, Germany. Screen and stage actress. Pioneer actress of German silent films.

PEYTON, CLAUDE See PAYTON, CLAUDE

PEYTON, LAWRENCE R. "LARRY"
Born: Hartford, Ky. Died: Oct., 1918, France (killed in action). Screen and stage actor.

Appeared in: **1913** The Sea Wolf. **1914** Martin Eden. **1915** The Unexpected; A Gentleman of Leisure; The Unafraid; My Best Girl; The Americano; Man Afraid of His Wardrobe; Author! Author!; This

Is the Life; Buck Parvin and the Movies. **1916** Water Stuff; The Extra Man and the Milkfed Lion; Now Stuff; Margy of the Foothills; The Return; A Man's Friend; The Gulf Between. **1917** The Red Ace (serial); Joan the Woman; The Golden Fetter; The Greater Law; The Pullman Mystery. **1918** Ace High; How Could You, Jean?.

PEZZULO, TED
Born: 1936. Died: Nov. 10, 1979, New York, N.Y. Screen, stage actor and playwright.

PHELPS, FRANCHER, SR.
Born: 1898. Died: Nov. 2, 1972. Screen actor.

PHELPS, LEE
Born: 1894. Died: Mar. 19, 1953, Culver City, Calif. Screen, stage and vaudeville actor.

Appeared in: **1921** The Road Demon. **1922** The Freshie. **1927** Putting Pants on Philip (short). **1930** Annie Christie; The Criminal Code. **1931** The Public Enemy. **1932** Taxi; Winner Take All; Cross Examination; The Night Club Lady; Hold 'Em Jail. **1933** Parole Girl; Bedtime Stories (short); The Woman I Stole. **1934** The St. Louis Kid; Manhattan Melodrama; Six of a Kind; Beggars in Ermine. **1935** $1,000 a Minute; Hot Money (short); Southern Exposure (short); Wings in the Dark; G-Men; Frisco Kid. **1936** Palm Springs; Crash Donovan; Cain and Mabel; Life Hesitates at 40 (short); Boss Rider of Gun Creek; The Bohemian Girl; Our Relations. **1937** Tough to Handle; Easy Living; Under Suspicion; A Nation Aflame; Boss of Lonely Valley; Sandflow; Lefthanded Law; The Perfect Specimen; The Last Gangster. **1938** The Sisters; Long Shot; Trade Winds; Female Fugitive; The Gladiator. **1939** The Flying Irishman; Kid Nightengale; Gone With the Wind; Idiot's Delight; The Roaring Twenties; Blackmail. **1940** City for Conquest; Brother Orchid; Murder Over New York; Hidden Gold. **1941** Andy Hardy's Private Secretary; A Shot in the Dark; The Big Store; High Sierra; The Bride Came C.O.D.; Manpower; Unholy Partners; Love Crazy. **1942** Scattergood Rides High; Two Yanks in Trinidad; Tennessee Johnson; Gentleman Jim; Life Begins at 8:30; War Dogs. **1943** Air Raid Wardens; Flesh and Fantasy. **1944** Girl Rush; Nothing But Trouble. **1945** Don Juan Quilligan; The Hidden Eye. **1946** Arsenic and Old Lace; Duel in the Sun. **1949** Tell it to the Judge; White Heat; Angels in Disguise; Sky Dragon; The Lone Wolf and His Lady; Shadows of the West; Gun Law Justice. **1950** Desperadoes of the West (serial); The Girl from San Lorenzo; Hills of Oklahoma; Square Dance Katy; Timber Fury; Western Pacific Agent. **1951** Don Daredevil Rides Again (serial). **1953** Man of Conflict; The Marshal's Daughter.

PHILBRICK, WILLIAM H. "WILL"
Died: Oct. 20, 1955, Chelsea, Mass. Screen, stage and vaudeville actor.

Appeared in: **1930** Whoopee. **1931** The Gorilla.

PHILIPE, GERARD
Born: Dec. 4, 1922, France. Died: Nov. 27, 1959, Paris, France (heart attack). Screen, stage actor and film director.

Appeared in: **1943** The Land without Stars (film debut). **1946** Le Diable au Corps (The Devil in the Flesh—US 1949). **1947** L'Idiot (The Idiot). **1948** Une Si Folie Petite Plage. **1949** La Beautie du Diable (The Beauty of the Devil—US 1952). **1950** La Ronde (US 1954). **1951** Rip Tide. **1952** Fanfan La Tulipe (US 1953); Belles de Nuit (Beauties of the Night). **1953** Seven Deadly Sins; Les Orgeuilleux; Knave of Hearts. **1954** Le Rouge et le Noir (The Red and the Black—US 1958). **1955** Les Granes Manoeuvres (The Grand Maneuver—US 1956); Lovers Happy Lovers. **1956** The Proud and the Beautiful; Till Eulenspiegel. **1957** It Happened in the Park; Royal Affairs in Versailles. **1958** Pot-Bouville; Lovers of Paris. **1959** Les Liaisons Dangereuses (US 1961). **1961** Modigliani of Montparnasse. Other French films: The Fever Rises in El Pao; All Roads Lead to Rome.

PHILIPP, ADOLPH
Born: Jan. 29, 1864, Hanova, Germany. Died: July 30, 1936, New York, N.Y. Screen, stage actor, stage producer, playwright and composer.

PHILIPPE, MICHELE
Born: 1926, France. Died: Oct., 1972, France? Screen and stage actress.

Appeared in: **1950** The Naked Woman; Hoboes in Paradise. **1954** Les Clandestines (aka Vice Dolls—US 1961). **1955** Don Juan's Nights of Love. **1959** Paris Hotel; Heures Chaudes (aka Hot Hours—US 1963).

PHILIPS, EDWIN
Born: 1912, Mobile, Ala. Died: July 26, 1981, New York, N.Y. (cancer). Screen, stage actor and dialogue director. Do not confuse with actors with similar names.

PHILIPS, MARY
Born: Jan. 23, 1901, New London, Conn. Died: Apr. 22, 1975, Santa Monica, Calif. (cancer). Screen and stage actress. Divorced from actor Humphrey Bogart (dec. 1957) and later married to actor Kenneth MacKenna (dec. 1962).

Appeared in: **1930** Stepping Out (short); Broadway's Like That (short). **1932** A Farewell to Arms; Life Begins. **1937** As Good as Married; Wings Over Honolulu; That Certain Woman; The Bride Wore Red; Mannequin. **1944** Lady in the Dark. **1945** Incendiary Blonde; Captain Eddie; Kiss and Tell; Leave Her to Heaven. **1947** Dear Ruth. **1949** A Woman's Secret; Dear Wife. **1951** Dear Brat; I Can Get It for You Wholesale. **1954** Prince Valiant.

PHILLEY, VIRGINIA
Born: 1890. Died: Feb. 10, 1980, Ft. Wayne, Ind. Screen actress and screenwriter.

Appeared in: **1915** Never Again; Tricked.

PHILLIBER, JOHN
Born: 1872, Elkhart, Ind. Died: Nov. 6, 1944, Elkhart, Ind. Screen and stage actor.

Appeared in: **1943** A Lady Takes a Chance. **1944** The Imposter; It Happened Tomorrow; Ladies of Washington; Summer Storm; Double Indemnity. **1945** Gentle Annie.

PHILLIPS, ALBERT
Born: 1875, Edwardsville, Ind. Died: Feb. 24, 1940, New York, N.Y. (heart attack). Screen, stage and radio actor.

Appeared in: **1923** Broadway Broke.

PHILLIPS, ALEX, SR.
Born: 1900, Canada. Died: June 14, 1977, Mexico City, Mexico (cerebral blood clot). Cameraman and bit actor. Father of cameraman Alex Phillips, Jr.

PHILLIPS, CHARLES
Born: 1904. Died: May 25, 1958, Hollywood, Calif. Screen actor and stuntman. Doubled for Charles Laughton and Oliver Hardy.

Appeared in: **1936** Peppery Salt (short).

PHILLIPS, CLEMENT K.
Died: Oct. 4, 1928, Hayward, Calif. (airplane crash). Screen actor and stunt flier.

PHILLIPS, DOROTHY
Born: Oct. 30, 1889, Baltimore, Md. Died: Mar. 1, 1980, Woodland Hills, Calif. (pneumonia). Screen, stage actress and film producer. Married to actor/director Allen Holubar (dec. 1923).

Appeared in: **1911** The Rosary (film debut). **1916** Ambition; If My Country Should Call. **1917** Hell Morgan's Girl; Fires of Rebellion; Bondage. **1918** Talk of the Town; Broadway Love. **1919** Heart of Humanity; The Right to Happiness; Paid in Advance. **1920** Man—Woman—Marriage; Once to Every Woman. **1922** Hurricane's Gal; The World's a Stage. **1923** Slander the Woman. **1925** Every Man's Wife; The Sporting Chance; Without Mercy. **1926** The Bar-C Mystery (serial); Upstage; The Gay Deceiver; Remember. **1927** The Broken Gate; Cradle Snatchers; Women Love Diamonds. **1930** Jazz Cinderella. **1955** Violent Saturday. **1956** The Man in the Gray Flannel Suit. **1962** The Man Who Shot Liberty Valance.

PHILLIPS, EDNA
Born: 1878. Died: Feb. 26, 1952, Los Angeles, Calif. Screen actress. Wife of actor Taylor Holmes (dec. 1959) and mother of actors Phillips (dec. 1942) and Ralph Holmes (dec. 1945).

Appeared in: **1918** Ruggles of Red Gap.

PHILLIPS, EDWARD N.
Born: Aug. 14, 1899. Died: Feb. 22, 1965, North Hollywood, Calif. (struck by auto). Screen actor and film editor.

Appeared in "The Collegians" series of shorts which began in 1926 with Benson at Calford and continued until 1929. The following are all "Collegians" series of shorts: **1926** Benson at Calford; Fighting to Win; Making Good; The Last Lap; Around the Bases; Fighting Spirit; The Relay. **1927** Cinder Path; Flashing Oars; Breaking Records; Crimson Colors; Winning Five; The Dazzling Coeds; A Fighting Finish; Samson at Calford; The Winning Punch; Running Wild; Splashing Through; The Winning Goal; Sliding Home. **1928** The Junior Year; Calford vs. Redskins; Kicking Through; Calford in the Movies; Radding Coeds;

Fighting for Victory; Dear Old Calford; Calford on Horseback; The Bookworm Hero; Speeding Youth; Farewell; The Winning Point. **1929** King of the Campus; The Rivals; On Guard; Junior Luck; The Cross Country Run; Sporting Courage; Flying High; The Varsity Drag; On the Side Lines; Use Your Feet; Splash Mates; Graduation Daze.

PHILLIPS, EDWIN R.

Born: Providence, RI. Died: Aug. 30, 1915, Coney Island, N.Y. Screen actor. Entered films in 1908 with Vitagraph.

Appeared in: **1910** The New Stenographer. **1911** Aunt Huldak—The Matchmaker; Carr's Regeneration; The Latent Spark. **1912** The Counts; Uncle Tom's Cabin; The Bogus Napoleon; A Bunch of Violets; The Black Sheep; An Expensive Shine; His Father's Son.

PHILLIPS, FESTUS "DAD"

Born: 1872. Died: Sept. 5, 1955, Hollywood, Calif. Screen actor and makeup artist.

PHILLIPS, GEORGE

Born: 1893. Died: June 22, 1933. Circus clown and screen actor.

PHILLIPS, HELENA *See* EVANS, HELENA PHILLIPS

PHILLIPS, JEAN

Born: Sept. 22, ? Died: Dec. 15, 1970. Screen actress.

Appeared in: **1941** Among the Living; Outlaws of the Desert. **1942** Timber; Night in New Orleans; Dr. Broadway.

PHILLIPS, MINNA

Born: June 1, 1885, Sydney, Australia. Died: Jan., 1963, New Orleans, La. (heart ailment). Screen and stage actress.

Appeared in: **1942** The Male Animal; A Yank at Eaton; My Sister Eileen. **1943** Sherlock Holmes Faces Death; Girls, Inc. **1950** Bandit Queen. **1951** Queen for a Day.

PHILLIPS, NORMA

Born: 1893, Baltimore, Md. Died: Nov. 12, 1931, New York (cancer). Screen and stage actress. Known as "Our Mutual Girl" in series of silents of 1914.

Appeared in: **1915** Runaway June.

PHILLIPS, NORMAN, SR.

Born: 1892. Died: Feb. 11, 1931, Culver City, Calif. (heart attack). Screen and vaudeville actor. Father of actor Norman Phillips, Jr.

PHILLIPS, RICHARD

Born: 1826. Died: May 4, 1941, Los Angeles, Calif. Screen actor. Claimed to be 115 years old—oldest actor in the world!

PHILLIPS, TUBBY

Born: 1884, Bloomfontein, South Africa. Died: Apr., 1930, London, England (auto accident). Screen actor.

PHILLIPS, WILLIAM "BILL"

Born: Washington, D.C. Died: June 27, 1957. Screen and stage actor.

Appeared in: **1940** City for Conquest. **1941** Sergeant York. **1942** Larceny, Inc.; The Lady Gangster. **1943** Johnny Come Lately; Action in the North Atlantic; Swingtime Johnny. **1944** See Here Private Hargrove; Music for Millions; Thirty Seconds Over Tokyo. **1945** Anchors Aweigh; The Last Installment (short); Abbott and Costello in Hollywood. **1946** The Harvey Girls; Holiday in Mexico; 'Til the Clouds Roll By; What Next Corporal Hargrove?; The Hoodlum Saint. **1947** Sea of Grass; Living in a Big Way. **1948** Command Decision. **1949** Johnny Allegro; Easy Living; Big Jack; Blondie's Secret; Prison Warden; Chain Gang; Mary Ryan, Detective; He's a Cockeyed Wonder; The Vanishing Westerner. **1951** Detective Story; Al Jennings of Oklahoma; Cavalry Scout; A Yank in Korea. **1952** The Bad and the Beautiful; High Noon; Because You're Mine; Bugles in the Afternoon. **1953** Devil's Canyon; Gun Belt; Private Eyes. **1954** Wicked Woman; The Law vs. Billy the Kid. **1955** Man Without a Star; New York Confidential; Fort Yuma; Ghost Town; Top Gun. **1956** The Broken Star; The Man in the Gray Flannel Suit; Stagecoach to Fury; The Fastest Gun Alive. **1957** Revolt at Fort Laramie; Hellcats of the Navy.

PHILLPOTTS, AMBROSINE

Born: Sept. 13, 1912, London, England. Died: Oct. 12, 1980, Ascot, England. Screen, stage and television actress.

Appeared in: **1946** This Man Is Mine. **1951** Happy Go Lovely; The Franchise Affair (US 1952). **1952** Father's Doing Fine. **1953** The Captain's Paradise. **1958** The Truth About Women. **1959** Operation Bullshine (US 1963); Room at the Top; Expresso Bongo (US 1960).

1960 Doctor in Love (US 1962). **1961** Raising the Wind (aka Roommates—US 1962). **1962** Two and Two Make Six (aka A Change of Heart, and aka The Girl Swappers). **1963** Carry on Cabby (US 1967, aka Call Me a Cab). **1965** Life at the Top. **1967** Berserk.

PHIPPS, CHARLES

Born: 1878. Died: Feb. 12, 1950. Screen actor.

Appeared in: **1941** Rolling Home to Texas; Secret Evidence; Riding the Wind; Thundering Hoofs.

PHIPPS, NICHOLAS

Born: June 23, 1913, London, England. Died: Apr. 11, 1980, London, England. Screen, stage actor and screenwriter. Entered films in 1940.

Appeared in: **1948** Spring in Park Lane (US 1949). **1949** Maytime in Mayfair (US 1952). **1953** The Intruder (US 1955); The Captain's Paradise. **1954** Doctor in the House (US 1955). **1956** The Iron Petticoat. **1957** Doctor at Large. **1958** Orders to Kill; Rockets Galore (aka Mad Little Island—US). **1959** The Captain's Table (US 1960). **1960** Doctor in Love (US 1962); The Pure Hell of St. Trinian's (US 1961). **1962** A Pair of Briefs (US 1963). **1963** Summer Holiday; Heavens Above! **1967** Charlie Bubbles (US 1968). **1969** Monte Carlo or Bust! (aka Those Darling Young Men in Their Jaunty Jalopies—US).

PHIPPS, SALLY (Byrnece Beutler)

Born: May 25, 1909, San Francisco, Calif. Died: Mar. 17, 1978, Long Island, N.Y. Screen and stage actress.

Appeared in: **1915** Broncho Billy and the Baby. **1926** Bertha the Sewing Machine Girl. **1927** Love Makes 'Em Wild; High School Hero. **1928** The News Parade; Why Sailors Go Wrong; None But the Brave. **1929** Detectives Wanted (short); Joy Street; The One Woman Idea. **1935** Knock on Wood.

PHOOAPHIROM, JATUPHON

Born: 1952, India. Died: Mar. 20, 1981, Bangkok, India (auto accident). Screen actor.

Appeared in: **1977** Thongpoon Kokepo (The Citizen). **1979** Ngern Pak Pi (Ghost Money); Other Indian films: Rak Payabat (Revengeful Love); Nan Ke Nai Koh Jah Rak (I Will Love You Forever); Aridang (The Korean Girl); Mia Luang (The First Wife).

PIAF, EDITH (Edith Gassion)

Born: 1916, Paris, France. Died: Oct. 11, 1963, Paris, France (internal hemorrhage). Screen, stage actress and singer.

Appeared in: **1947** Etoile Sans Lumiere (Star Without Light). **1956** French-Cancan. **1957** Royal Affairs in Versailles. **1961** Io Amo Tu Ami (I Love, You Love—US 1962). **1976** Singing Under the Occupation (documentary).

PIATIGORSKY, GREGOR

Born: Apr. 17, 1903, Yekaterinoslav, Russia. Died: Aug. 6, 1976, Los Angeles, Calif. Cellist, author and screen actor.

Appeared in: **1947** Carnegie Hall.

PIAZZA, DARIO

Born: 1904. Died: Sept. 1, 1974, Glendale, Calif. (cancer). Costumer, film actor and extra.

PICA, TINA

Born: 1888, Italy. Died: Aug. 16, 1968, Naples, Italy. Screen and stage actress.

Appeared in: **1949** Guaglio. **1954** Bread, Love and Dreams. **1955** Frisky. **1957** Scandal in Sorrento. **1959** The Virtuous Bigamist. **1964** Leri, Oggi, Domani (Yesterday, Today and Tomorrow).

PICASSO, PABLO

Born: Oct. 25, 1881, Malaga, Spain. Died: Apr. 8, 1973, Mougins, France. Artist, sculptor and screen actor.

Appeared in: **1952** La Vie Commence Demain (Life Begins Tomorrow). **1962** Testament of Orpheus.

PICHEL, IRVING

Born: June 24, 1891, Pittsburgh, Pa. Died: July 13, 1954, Hollywood, Calif. (heart attack). Screen, stage actor, film director and screenwriter.

Appeared in: **1930** The Right to Love. **1931** Murder by the Clock; The Road to Reno; An American Tragedy; The Cheat. **1932** Westward Passage; The Painted Woman; Strange Justice; Wild Girl; The Miracle Man; Two Kinds of Women; Forgotten Commandments; Island of Lost

Souls; Most Dangerous Game; Madame Butterfly. **1933** Mysterious Rider; The Woman Accused; King of the Jungle; Oliver Twist; The Story of Temple Drake; I'm No Angel; The Right to Romance; The Billion Dollar Scandal. **1934** British Agent; Return of the Terror; Silver Streak; She Was a Lady; Such Women Are Dangerous; Cleopatra; Fog Over Frisco. **1935** I Am a Thief; Three Kids and a Queen; Special Agent. **1936** Hearts in Bondage; Down to the Sea; The House of a Thousand Candles; Don't Gamble with Love; General Spanky; Dracula's Daughter. **1937** High, Wide and Handsome; There Goes My Heart; Jezebel; Gambling Ship. **1939** Newsboys' Home; Torture Ship; Rio; Topper Takes a Trip; Dick Tracy's G-Men (serial); Juarez. **1943** The Moon is Down. **1951** Santa Fe. **1953** Martin Luther.

PICK, LUPE
Born: 1886, Jassy, Romania. Died: Mar., 1931, Berlin, Germany (poison). Screen, stage actor and film director.

Appeared in: **1914** Die Pagode. **1916** Nacht des Grauens. **1917** Hoeheluft. **1918** Es Werde Licht (Let There be Light). **1920** Der Dummkopf; Mister Wu; Niemand Weiss Es; Toetet Nicht Mehr. **1921** Irrende Seelen (aka Sklaven der Sinne, and aka Der Idiot). **1922** Fliehende Schatten. **1926** Die Letzte Droschke von Berlin. **1928** Spione (The Spy).

PICKARD, HELENA
Born: Oct. 13, 1900, Hansworth, Sheffield, England. Died: Sept. 27, 1959, Oxfordshire, England. Screen and television actress. Divorced from actor Sir Cedric Hardwicke (dec. 1964).

Appeared in: **1934** Nell Gwyn. **1935** Limelight. **1940** Let George Do It. **1944** The Lodger.

PICKER, SYLVIA (Sylvia McGraw)
Born: 1916. Died: Sept. 25, 1981, Hollywood, Calif. (cancer). Screen, stage and radio actress.

Appeared in: **1933** Lucky Devils.

PICKETT, INGRAM B.
Born: 1899. Died: Feb. 14, 1963, Santa Fe, N.M. Screen actor. Was early memeber of Mack Sennett's Keystone Kops.

PICKFORD, JACK (Jack Smith)
Born: Aug. 18, 1896, Toronto, Canada. Died: Jan. 3, 1933, Paris, France (multiple neuritis). Screen and stage actor. Son of actress Charlotte Smith (dec. 1928). Brother of actresses Mary Pickford (dec. 1979) and Lottie Pickford (dec. 1936). Married to actress Olive Thomas (dec. 1920) and divorced from actress Marilyn Miller (dec. 1936).

Appeared in: **1910** The Modern Prodigal; The Iconoclast; The Kid; Examination Day at School; A Child's Strategem. **1912** Heredity; Mr. Grouch at the Seashore; The Unwelcome Guest; The New York Hat. **1914** Wildflower; Home Sweet Home. **1915** The Pretty Sister of Jose. **1916** Seventeen; The Dummy; Great Expectations; Tom Sawyer. **1918** Huck and Tom; Sandy; His Majesty, Bunker Bean; Mile-a-Minute Kendall. **1920** The Little Shepherd of Kingdom Come. **1921** Little Lord Fauntleroy; Just out of College; Man Who Had Everything; Through the Back Door. **1922** Valley of the Wolf. **1923** Hollywood; Garrison's Finish. **1924** The Hillbilly; The End of the World. **1925** Waking up the Town; My Son; The Goose Woman. **1926** The Bat; Brown of Harvard; Exit Smiling. **1928** Gang War.

PICKFORD, LOTTIE (Lottie Smith)
Died: Dec. 9, 1936, Brentwood, Calif. (heart attack). Screen actress. Sister of actress Mary Pickford (dec. 1979) and actor Jack Pickford (dec. 1933). Daughter of actress Charlotte Smith (dec. 1928). Entered films with Imp Company in 1910.

Appeared in: **1910** A Gold Necklace; White Roses. **1915** The Diamond from the Sky (serial). **1918** Mile-a-Minute Kendall. **1924** Dorothy Vernon from Haddon Hall. **1925** Don Q.

PICKFORD, MARY (Gladys Mary Smith)
Born: Apr. 9, 1893, Toronto, Canada. Died: May 29, 1979, Santa Monica, Calif. (cerebral hemorrhage). Screen, stage, vaudeville, radio, television actress, film producer and author. Divorced from actors Owen Moore (dec. 1939), and Douglas Fairbanks, Sr. (dec. 1939). Later married to actor Buddy Rogers. Known as "America's Sweetheart," "Little Mary," "The Biograph Girl." Entered films in 1909 with D. W. Griffith.

Appeared in: **1909** The Lonely Villa (film debut); The Violin Maker of Cremona; The Son's Return; Faded Lilies; Her First Biscuits; The Peach-Basket Hat; The Way of Man; The Country Doctor; The Necklace; The Renunciation; The Cardinal's Conspiracy; To Save Her Soul; The Test; The Trick That Failed; The Mountaineer's Honor; The Light That Came; A Midnight Adventure; The Restoration; The Gibson Goddess; What's Your Hurry?; In the Watches of the Night; His Lost Love; The Little Teacher; In Old Kentucky; The Awakening; The Broken Locket; Getting Even; 1776 or The Hessian Renegades; The Sealed Room; The Little Darling; The Seventh Day; Oh, Uncle!; The Indian Runner's Romance; His Wife's Visitor; They Would Elope; A Strange Meeting; The Slave; Sweet and Twenty. **1910** In the Season of Buds; All on Account of the Milk; The Woman from Mellon's; The Englishman and the Girl; The Thread of Destiny: A Story of the Old Southwest; The Newlyweds; The Smoker; As It Is In Life; The Twisted Trail: A Story of Fate in the Mountain Wilds; A Rich Revenge: A Comedy of the California Oil Fields; The Unchanging Sea; A Romance of the Western Hills; Love Among the Roses; The Two Brothers; In the Days of the Padre; Ramona: A Story of the White Man's Injustice to the Indian; A Victim of Jealousy; Man and December; A Child's Impulse; Muggsy's First Sweetheart; Never Again!; What the Daisy Said; The Call to Arms; An Arcadian Maid; When We Were in Our Teens; The Sorrows of the Unfaithful; Muggsy Becomes a Hero; Willful Peggy; A Gold Necklace; The Masher; Waiter No. 5; A Lucky Toothache; Simple Charity; Song of the Wildwood Flute; White Roses; A Plain Song. **1911** From the Bottom of the Sea; The Caddy's Dream; Little Red Riding Hood; Love Heads Not the Showers; The Courting of Mary; Their First Misunderstanding; The Dream; Maid or Man; At the Duke's Command; The Mirror; While the Cat's Away; Her Darkest Hour; Artful Kate; When a Man Loves; The Italian Barber; Three Sisters; A Decree of Destiny; A Manly Man; The Message in the Bottle; The Fisher-Maid; In Old Madrid; Sweet Memories; The Stampede; Second Sight; For Her Brother's Sake; The Fair Dentist; The Master and the Man; The Lighthouse Keeper; Back to the Soil; In the Sultan's Garden; For the Queen's Honor; A Gasoline Engagement; Science; At a Quarter of Two; The Skating Bug; The Call of the Song; The Toss of a Coin; 'Tween Two Loves; The Sentinel Asleep; The Rose's Story; The Better Way; His Dress Shirt. **1912** Honor Thy Father; The Mender of Nets; Iola's Promise; The Female of the Species; Fate's Interception; Just Like a Woman; Won By a Fish; The Old Actor; A Lodging for the Night; A Beast at Bay; Lena and the Geese; Home Folks; The School Teacher and the Waif; The Narrow Road; An Indian Summer; The Inner Circle; With the Enemy's Help; A Pueblo Legend; So Near, Yet So Far; Friends; A Feud in the Kentucky Hills; My Baby; The Informer; The New York Hat; The One She Loved. **1913** In the Bishop's Carriage; Caprice; The Unwelcome Guest. **1914** Hearts Adrift; A Good Little Devil; Tess of the Storm Country; The Eagle's Mate; Such a Little Queen; Behind the Scenes; Cinderella. **1915** Mistress Nell; Fanchon, the Cricket; The Dawn of a Tomorrow; Rags; Little Pal; Esmeralda; A Girl of Yesterday; Madame Butterfly. **1916** Less Than the Dust; Hulda from Holland; The Foundling; Poor Little Peppina; The Eternal Grind. **1917** The Pride of the Clan; The Poor Little Rich Girl; A Romance of the Redwoods; The Little American; Rebecca of Sunnybrook Farm; A Little Princess. **1918** 100|%American; War Relief; Johanna Enlists; How Could You, Jean?; Stella Maris; Amarilly of Clothesline Alley; M'Liss. **1919** Captain Kidd, Jr.; Daddy Long Legs; The Hoodlum; The Heart o' the Hills. **1920** Pollyanna; Suds. **1921** The Love Light; Through the Back Door; Little Lord Fauntleroy. **1922** Tess of the Storm Country (and 1914 version). **1923** Rosita. **1924** Dorothy Vernon of Haddon Hall. **1925** Little Annie Rooney. **1926** The Black Pirate (without credit); Sparrows. **1927** My Best Girl; The Gaucho. **1929** Coquette; The Taming of the Shrew. **1931** Kiki. **1933** Secrets; Hollywood on Parade (short).

PICKLES, WILFRID
Born: Oct. 13, 1904, Halifax, Yorkshire, England. Died: Mar. 27, 1978, Brighton, England. Screen, stage, radio and television actor.

Appeared in: **1954** The Gay Dog. **1959** Serious Charge (aka Immoral Charge—US 1962). **1963** Billy Liar. **1964** A Touch of Hell (reissue of Serious Charge, 1959). **1966** The Family Way (US 1967). **1972** For the Love of Ada.

PICORRI, JOHN
Born: 1896. Died: July 1, 1976. Screen actor.

Appeared in: **1935** The Man Who Broke the Bank at Monte Carlo; False Pretenses. **1936** Down to the Sea; Robinson Crusoe of Clipper Island (serial). **1937** Dick Tracy (serial); S.O.S. Coast Guard (serial). **1938** Fighting Devil Dogs (serial).

PIDAL, JOSE
Born: 1896, Spain. Died: Oct. 26, 1956, Mexico City, Mexico (cancer). Screen and stage actor.

PIEL, EDWARD, JR. *See* PEIL, EDWARD, JR.

PIEL, EDWARD, SR. *See* PEIL, EDWARD, SR.

PIEL, HARRY
Born: 1892, Dusseldorf, Germany. Died: 1963, Munich, Germany. Screen actor and film director. Married to actress Dary Holm.

Appeared in: **1913** Ben Ali Bey. **1916** Police 1111; Unter Heisser Sonne. **1919** Ueber den Wolken; Der Grosse Coup; Das Auge des Gotzen. **1920** Das Geheimnis des Zirkus Barre. **1921** Das Geheimnisvolle Telephon; Luftpiraten; Der Brennende Berg; Das Fliegnede Auto; Der Furst der Berge; Das Gefangnis auf dem Meeresgrunde; Das Geheimnis der Katakomben; Das Lebende Ratsel; Panik; Der Ritt Unter Wasser; Die Todesfalle; Unus, der Weg in die Welt; Der Verachter des Todes. **1922** Das Schwarze Kouvert; Das Verschwundene Haus. **1923** Abenteuer Einer Nacht; Der Letzte Kampf; Menschen und Masken; Rivalen. **1924** Auf Gefahrlichen Spuren; Der Mann ohne Nerven. **1925** Abenteuer im Nachtexpress; Schneller als der Tod; Zigaro, der Brigant von Monte Diavolo. **1926** Achtung Harry! Augen Auf!; Der Schwarze Pierro; Was ist los im Zirkus Beely. **1927** Ratsel Winer Nacht; Sein Grosster Bluff. **1928** Panik (and 1921 version); Mann Gegen Mann. **1929** Seine Starkste Waffe; Manner ohne Beruf; Die Mitteenachts-Taxe; Sein Bester Freund (His Best Friend). **1930** Achtung! Auto-Diebe!; Menschen im Feuer; Er oder Ich. **1931** Bobby Geht Los; Schatten der Unterwelt. **1932** Der Geheimagent; Jonny Stiehlt Europa; Das Schiff ohne Hafen. **1933** Sprung in den Abgrund; Ein Unsichtbarer Geht Durch die Stadt. **1934** Die Welt ohne Maske. **1935** Artisten. **1936** 90 Minuten Aufenthalt; Der Dschungel Ruft. **1937** Sein Bester Freund (and 1929 version). **1938** Menschen, Tiere, Sensationen; Der Unmogliche Herr Pitt. **1940** Gesprengte Gitter (re-released in 1953). **1943** Panik (and 1921 and 1928 versions). **1945** Der Mann im Sattel. **1950** Der Tiger Akbar.

PIERCE, EVELYN (aka EVELYN PEIRCE)
Born: Feb. 5, 1908, Del Rio, Tex. Died: Aug. 9, 1960, Oyster Bay, N.Y. Screen actress. Married to actor Theodore Baehr. Entered films in 1925.

Appeared in: **1925** Don't. **1927** The Border Cavalier. **1928** Sonia; Tenderloin. **1929** The Million Dollar Collar. **1930** Once a Gentleman. **1931** An American Tragedy; Monkey Business. **1935** I'm a Father (short).

PIERCE, GEORGE *See* PEARCE, GEORGE

PIERCE, HARRY
Died: Dec. 28, 1972. Screen actor.

PIERCE, JACK P.
Born: 1889. Died: July 19, 1968, Hollywood, Calif. Screen actor and makeup artist.

Appeared in: **1922** The Man Who Waited. **1925** The Speed Demon. **1929** Masquerade.

PIERLOT, FRANCIS
Born: 1876. Died: May 11, 1955, Hollywood, Calif. (heart ailment). Screen, stage and television actor.

Appeared in: **1931** Night Angel. **1940** The Captain Is a Lady; Strike up the Band; Escape to Glory (aka Submarine Zone); Always a Bride. **1941** The Trial of Mary Dugan; International Lady; Rise and Shine; Remember the Day; A-Haunting We Will Go. **1942** Just Off Broadway; Henry Aldrich, Editor; Night Monster; Yankee Doodle Dandy; My Heart Belongs to Daddy; A Gentleman at Heart. **1943** Madame Curie; Mission to Moscow; Mystery Broadcast. **1944** The Doughgirls; Uncertain Glory; Adventures of Mark Twain; Bathing Beauty; The Very Thought of You. **1945** Hit the Hay; Affairs of Susan; Fear; Grissly's Millions; The Hidden Eye; How Do You Do?; Our Vines Have Tender Grapes; Roughly Speaking; Yolanda and the Thief; A Tree Grows in Brooklyn; Bewitched. **1946** Life with Blondie; Dragonwyck; The Catman of Paris; The Crime Doctor's Manhunt; G.I. War Brides; Two Guys from Milwaukee; The Walls Came Tumbling Down. **1947** Cigarette Girl; The Late George Apley; Philo Vance's Gamble; Second Chance; The Senator Was Indiscreet; The Trespasser. **1948** A Date with Judy; The Dude Goes West; Chicken Every Sunday; The Accused; That Wonderful Urge; I, Jane Doe. **1949** Bad Boy; Take One False Step; My Friend Irma. **1950** Copper Canyon; Cyrano de Bergerac; The Flame and the Arrow. **1951** The Man With a Cloak; Anne of the Indies; The Lemon Drop Kid; Savage Drums; That's My Boy. **1952** Hold That Line; The Prisoner of Zenda. **1953** The Robe.

PIERPONT, LAURA
Born: 1881. Died: Dec. 11, 1972, New Canaan, Conn. Screen and stage actress. Married to vaudeville actor and film producer Taylor Granville (dec. 1923).

Appeared in: **1936** Colleen. **1950** My Blue Heaven.

PIERRE, ANATOLE
Died: Feb., 1926, New Orleans, La. Black screen and minstrel actor.

PIERRE, ANDRE
Born: 1884, France. Died: Feb. 9, 1975, France. Screen actor and screenwriter.

PIERSON, ARTHUR
Born: June 16, 1891 or 1901?, Oslo, Norway. Died: Jan. 1, 1975, Santa Monica, Calif. Screen, stage actor, stage director, playwright, film, television director, television producer and screenwriter. Divorced from actress Ruth Matteson (dec. 1975).

Appeared in: **1932** Tomorrow and Tomorrow; The Golden West; No One Man; The Strange Case of Clara Deane; Bachelor's Affairs; Hat Check Girl; Rackety Rax. **1933** Air Hostess; Ann Carver's Profession; The Devil's Brother; The Way to Love; Before Midnight. **1934** You Belong to Me; Murder in the Clouds. **1935** Sweet Surrender.

PIGOTT, TEMPE
Born: 1884. Died: Oct. 13, 1962, Hollywood, Calif. Screen and stage actress.

Appeared in: **1921** The Great Impersonation. **1922** The Masked Avenger. **1923** The Rustle of Silk; Vanity Fair. **1924** The Dawn of a Tomorrow; The Narrow Street. **1925** Without Mercy; Greed. **1926** The Midnight Kiss; The Black Pirate. **1927** Silk Stockings. **1928** Road House; Wallflowers. **1930** Night Work; America or Bust; Seven Days Leave. **1931** Devotion. **1932** Dr. Jekyll and Mr. Hyde. **1933** A Study in Scarlet; Doctor Bull; If I Were Free; Cavalcade; Oliver Twist; Man of the Forest. **1934** Long Lost Father; One More River; Of Human Bondage; The Lemon Drop Kid; Limehouse Blues. **1935** A Tale of Two Cities; A Feather in Her Hat; The Devil is a Woman; Becky Sharp; Calm Yourself; Bride of Frankenstein. **1936** Little Lord Fauntleroy; The White Angel; The Story of Louis Pasteur. **1939** Fools for Scandal. **1939** Boy Reformatory. **1940** Arise, My Love. **1941** One Foot in Heaven. **1942** Now, Voyager. **1944** Jane Eyre. **1947** Forever Amber. **1949** The Fan.

PIKE, HARRY J.
Died: Dec. 18, 1919, New York, N.Y. Screen actor.

PIKE, NITA
Born: 1913. Died: May 10, 1954, Los Angeles, Calif. (suicide). Screen actress. Married to actor Alan Edwards (dec. 1954).

Appeared in: **1933** Sherman Said It (short). **1934** Broadway Bill. **1938** Suez. **1940** The Great Dictator.

PILA, MAXIMO
Born: 1886. Died: Aug. 2, 1939, Hollywood, Calif. Screen and stage actor.

PILCER, HARRY
Born: 1885, U.S. Died: Jan. 14, 1961, Cannes, France (heart attack). Screen, stage actor and dancer.

Appeared in: **1915** Her Triumph. **1946** The Razor's Edge.

PILKINGTON, PAUL
Died: Jan. 26, 1918. Screen actor.

Appeared in: **1914** The Littlest Rebel.

PILOTTO, CAMILLO
Born: 1883 or 1890. Died: May 27, 1963. Italian screen actor.

Appeared in: **1933** Passa L'Amore. **1935** Il Delitto di Mastrovanni; Le Scarpe a Sole. **1936** Tempo Massimo; Lorenzino de Medici; Alpine Love; Anonima Roylott; Italia. **1937** Scipione l'Africanus (US 1939); I Due Misantropi; I Tre Desideri; Allegri Masnardi; Gil Ultimi Giorni di Pompeo; I Fratelli Castiglioni; Pietro Micca. **1938** Il Padre delle Patria (The Father of His Country); Amore in Quarantena (Love in Quarantine). **1939** Il Grande Appello (The Last Roll-Call). **1940** Il Paraninfo (The Matchmaker); Tutta la Vita in una Notte (All of Life in One Night); The Life of Giuseppi Verdi; Abuna Messias. **1948** Foria; Furia; Rossini. **1952** The Thief of Venice. **1954** Mistress of the Mountains. **1960** Goddess of Love; Guiditta e Oloferne (Judith and Holophernes) (aka Head of a Tyrant—US). **1962** Marco Polo.

PILTZ, GEORGE
Died: 1968. Screen actor.

Appeared in: **1937** Ebb Tide. **1949** Daughter of the Jungle.

PIMLEY, JOHN
Born: 1919. Died: May 17, 1972, Hollywood, Calif. (heart attack). Screen, stage actor, film producer, director and playwright.

PINAY, RUTE *See* PUNAY, RITO

PINCHOT, ROSAMOND
Born: 1905, New York, N.Y. Died: Jan. 24, 1938, Old Brookfield, N.Y. Screen and stage actress.

Appeared in: **1930** South Seas. **1935** The Three Musketeers.

PINE, ED
Born: 1904. Died: May 9, 1950, Woodland Hills, Calif. Screen actor.

PINERO, ANTHONY
Born: 1887. Died: Jan. 5, 1958, Bridgeport, Conn. Screen actor and circus performer.

PINERO, ARTHUR WING
Born: May 24, 1855, London, England. Died: Nov. 23, 1934, London, England. Playwright, screen and stage actor.

Appeared in: **1918** Masks and Faces.

PINGREE, EARL M. (aka EARL M. PRINGREE)
Born: 1887. Died: July 12, 1958. Screen actor.

Appeared in: **1929** Dark Streets. **1931** A Holy Terror. **1932** Guilty as Hell. **1934** Search for Beauty. **1935** The Throwback.

PINSON, LUCILE
Born: 1900, Ramsey, Ill. Died: Jan. 12, 1977, Van Nuys, Calif. Screen actress. Mack Sennett Bathing Beauty.

PINZA, EZIO (Fortunato Pinza)
Born: May 8, 1892, Rome, Italy. Died: May 9, 1957, Stamford, Conn. (stroke). Opera star, screen, stage and television actor.

Appeared in: **1947** Carnegie Hall. **1951** Mr. Imperium; Strictly Dishonorable. **1953** Tonight We Sing.

PIOUS, MINERVA
Born: 1904, Russia. Died: Mar., 1979, New York, N.Y. Screen, stage and radio actress.

Appeared in: **1945** It's in the Bag. **1955** Joe MacBeth (US 1956). **1956** The Ambassador's Daughter. **1957** Love in the Afternoon. **1968** Pinocchio dans le Space (Pinocchio in Outer Space).

PIPEIRO, ROBERTO (aka ROBERTO PIPERIO)
Died: Jan. 28, 1963. Screen, stage actor and extra.

PIPO (Gustave Sofman)
Born: 1902, France. Died: Aug. 6, 1970, Paris, France. Screen actor and circus clown.

PISU, MARIO
Born: 1910, Italy. Died: July, 1976, Castelli Romani, Italy (cerebral hemorrhage). Screen, stage and television actor.

Appeared in: **1936** Il Re Burlone; Passaporto Rosso. **1939** Re di Danari (Money King). **1949** Professor, My Son. **1955** Princess Cinderella. **1957** Margaret of Cortona. **1963** I Compagni (aka The Organizer—US 1964); Il Mito (The Myth—US 1965, aka La Violenza c L'Amore); 8 1/2. **1965** Guilietta of the Spirits (Juliet of the Spirits). **1967** Jonny Banco—Geliebter Taugenichts (aka Johnny Banco—US 1969). **1968** Morire Gratis (US 1969).

PITT, ARCHIE
Born: 1895, England. Died: Nov. 12, 1940, London, England. Screen, stage actor and screenwriter. Divorced from actress Gracie Fields (dec. 1979).

Appeared in: **1934** Danny Boy. **1935** Barnacle Bill. **1936** Excuse My Glove.

PITTI, BEN
Born: 1893. Died: July 26, 1955, Culver City, Calif. (heart attack). Circus performer, stuntman and screen actor.

Appeared in: **1911** Cowboy Milleon.

PITTMAN, MONTE
Born: 1918. Died: June 26, 1962, Hollywood, Calif. (cancer). Screen, stage actor, film director and screenwriter. Entered films as an actor in early 1950s.

Appeared in: **1951** G.I. Jane.

PITTMAN, TOM
Born: 1933. Died: Oct. 31, 1958, Hollywood, Calif. (auto accident). Screen and stage actor.

Appeared in: **1957** Blackpatch; Bernardine; No Time to Be Young; The True Story of Jesse James; The Way to Gold; The Young Stranger. **1958** Apache Territory; Proud Rebels. **1959** The High School Big Shot; Verboten!

PITTS, ZASU
Born: Jan. 3, 1898, Parsons, Kans. Died: June 7, 1963, Hollywood, Calif. (cancer). Screen and television actress. She appeared as part of the comedy film team of "Todd and Pitts" with Thelma Todd (dec. 1935).

Appeared in: **1917** The Little Princess (film debut); Uneasy Money; His Fatal Beauty. **1918** A Modern Musketeer; A Society Sensation; As the Sun Went Down; How Could You, Jean?; Men, Women and Money. **1919** Better Times. **1922** A Daughter of Luxury; For the Defense; Is Matrimony a Failure?; Youth to Youth. **1923** Patsy; The Girl Who Came Back; Three Wise Fools; Mary of the Movies; Poor Men's Wives; Souls for Sale; Tea With a Kick. **1924** Changing Husbands; Daughters of Today; The Goldfish; Greed; The Fast Set; The Legend of Hollywood; West of the Water Tower; Triumph; Wine of Youth. **1925** What Happened to Jones?; The Business of Love; The Great Divide; The Great Love; Pretty Ladies; Lazybones; Old Shoes; The Recreation of Brian Kent; A Woman's Faith; Wages for Wives; Thunder Mountain; Secrets of the Night. **1926** Early to Wed; Her Big Night; Risky Business; Mannequin; Monte Carlo; Sunny Side Up. **1927** Casey at the Bat. **1928** Wife Savers; Sins of the Father; The Wedding March; Buck Privates; 13 Washington Square. **1929** The Dummy; The Squall; Twin Beds; The Argyle Case; This Thing Called Love; The Locked Door; Her Private Life; Paris. **1930** The Squealer; Monte Carlo (and 1926 version); The Little Accident; The Lottery Bride; No, No, Nanette; Oh, Yeah!; Honey; The Devil's Holiday; War Nurse; Passion Flower; Sin Takes a Holiday; Free Love; All Quiet on the Western Front (She was only in original European version and was replaced in cast by Beryl Mercer). **1931** Terror by Night; Finn and Hattie; Bad Sister; Beyond Victory; Seed; Woman of Experience; The Guardsman; Their Mad Moment; Big Gamble; On the Loose; Penrod and Sam; Secret Witness; River's End; plus the following shorts made with Thelma Todd: Let's Do Things; Catch As Catch Can; The Pajama Party; War Mamas. **1932** Unexpected Father; Strangers of the Evening; Broken Lullaby; Destry Rides Again; Steady Company; Shopworn; Sneak Easily; The Trial of Vivienne Ware; Westward Passage; Is My Face Red?; Blondie of the Follies; Roar of the Dragon; Make Me a Star; Vanishing Frontier; The Crooked Circle; Madison Square Garden; Back Street; Once in a Lifetime; Eternally Yours; The Man I Killed; plus the following shorts with Thelma Todd: Seal Skins; Red Noses; Strictly Unreliable; The Old Bull; Show Business; Alum and Eve; The Soilers. **1933** Out All Night; They Just Had to Get Married; Walking Down Broadway (aka Hello Sister!); Mr. Skitch; Her First Mate; Love, Honor and Oh, Baby; Professional Sweethearts; Aggie Appleby; Maker of Men; Meet the Baron; plus the following shorts with Thelma Todd: Asleep in the Fleet; Maids a la Mode; The Bargain of the Century; One Track Minds. **1934** Two Alone; Their Big Moment; The Meanest Gal in Town; Sing and Like It; Dames; Private Scandal; Mrs. Wiggs of the Cabbage Patch; The Gay Bride; Love Birds; Three on a Honeymoon. **1935** Ruggles of Red Gap; Spring Tonic; She Gets Her Man; Hot Tip; Going Highbrow; The Affairs of Susan. **1936** 13 Hours by Air; Sing Me a Love Song; Mad Holiday; The Plot Thickens. **1937** Merry Comes to Town; Forty Naughty Girls; 52nd Street; Wanted. **1939** The Lady's from Kentucky; Mickey the Kid; Naughty But Nice; Nurse Edith Cavell; Eternally Yours. **1940** No, No, Nanette (and 1930 version); It All Came True. **1941** The Mexican Spitfire's Baby; Broadway Limited; Niagara Falls; Miss Polly; Weekend for Three. **1942** Meet the Mob; Mexican Spitfire at Sea; The Bashful Bachelor; So's Your Aunt Emma; Tish. **1943** Let's Face It. **1946** Breakfast in Hollywood; The Perfect Marriage. **1947** A Film Goes to Market (short); Life With Father. **1949** Francis. **1952** The Denver and the Rio Grande. **1954** Francis Joins the WACS. **1957** This Could Be the Night. **1959** The Gazebo. **1961** Teen-Age Millionaire. **1963** The Thrill of It All; It's a Mad, Mad, Mad, Mad World. **1964** Big Parade of Comedy (documentary).

PITTSCHAU, WERNER
Born: 1903, Germany. Died: Oct., 1928, Spandau, Germany (auto accident). Screen actor.

Appeared in: **1928** Women Without Men.

PIXLEY, GUS
Born: 1874. Died: June 2, 1923, Saranac Lake, N.Y. Screen and stage actor. Married to stage actress Mary Malatesta (dec.?).

Appeared in: **1913** The Cure; Those Little Flowers; Dyed, But Not Dead. **1915** His Last Wish; His Poor Little Girl; The Need of Money; The Little Scapegoat; The Little Slavey; Between Father and Son; The Reproach of Annesley; Blow by Blow; The Hungarian Nabob; Count 20. **1916** Lord Chumley. **1921** The Girl from Porcupine.

PIZZO, JOHN (John Frederick Pizzo)
Born: Mar. 30, 1907, Wis. Died: May 9, 1952, Los Angeles, Calif. (heart disease). Circus clown and screen actor.

Appeared in: **1932** The Sign of the Cross; Freaks.

PLATT, ED (Edward C. Platt)
Born: Feb. 14, 1916, Staten Island, N.Y. Died: Mar. 20, 1974, Santa Monica, Calif. (heart attack). Screen, stage, radio, television actor and singer.

Appeared in: **1953** Stalag 17. **1954** The Rebel Set. **1955** The Shrike; Rebel Without a Cause; Sincerely Yours; Illegal; The Private War of Major Benson. **1956** The Lieutenant Wore Skirts; Serenade; The Great man; Rock, Pretty Baby; Written on the Wind; The Proud Ones; Backlash; Storm Center; The Unguarded Moment; Reprisal. **1957** Designing Woman; The Tattered Dress; Oman Khayyam; House of Numbers; The Helen Morgan Story. **1958** Damn Citizen; The Gift of Love; Summer Love; Oregon Passage; The Last of the Fast Guns; The High Cost of Loving; Gunman's Walk. **1959** North by Northwest; Cash McCall; They Came to Cordura; Inside the Mafia; The Rebel Set. **1960** Pollyanna. **1961** The Fiercest Heart; The Explosive Generation; Atlantis, the Lost Continent. **1962** Cape Fear. **1963** A Ticklish Affair; Black Zoo. **1964** Bullet for a Badman. **1965** Man from Button Willow.

PLAYFAIR, LADY See MARTIN, MAY

PLAYFAIR, SIR NIGEL
Born: July 1, 1874, London, England. Died: Aug. 19, 1934, London, England. Stage, screen actor and playwright. Married to actress May Martyn (aka Lady Playfair—dec. 1948).

Appeared in: **1911** Princess Clementina. **1917** Masks and Faces (US 1918). **1933** The Perfect Understanding; Crime on the Hill (US 1934). **1934** The Lady is Willing.

PLAYTER, WELLINGTON
Born: Dec. 9, 1879, Rawcliffe, England. Died: July 15, 1937, Oakland, Calif. Screen, stage actor and film director.

Appeared in: **1914** The Pride of Jennico; Marta of the Lowlands; The Ring and the Man. **1915** Polly of the Circus; The Blood of His Brother; The Test of a Man; Chasing the Limited; Coral Queen of the Jungleland; Business is Business; The Torrent; Pennington's Choice. **1917** The Slave Market. **1919** In Search of Arcady; Back to God's Country; The Wicked Darling; Spotlight Sadie; Fool's Gold. **1921** The Golden Snare.

PLOWDEN, ROGER S.
Born: 1902. Died: Sept. 26, 1960, N.Y. Stage and screen actor.

Appeared in: **1952** Five Fingers.

PLOWRIGHT, HILDA
Died: Oct., 1973. Screen actress.

Appeared in: **1937** Partners of the Plains. **1939** Cafe Society. **1940** Raffles. **1944** Wilson. **1945** Kitty. **1953** Abbott and Costello Meet Dr. Jekyll and Mr. Hyde. **1958** Separate Tables. **1963** Summer Magic. **1965** 36 Hours.

PLUES, GEORGE L.
Born: 1895. Died: Aug. 16, 1953, Woodland Hills, Calif. Screen actor.

Appeared in: **1936** Guns and Guitars. **1937** Come on, Cowboys; Public Cowboy No. 1; Hit the Saddle.

PLUMB, E. HAY (Edward Hay Plumb)
Born: 1883, England. Died: 1960. Screen actor, film director, producer, screenwriter and opera performer.

Appeared in: **1910** Heart of Oak; The Heart of a Fishergirl. **1911** The Three Lovers; Children Mustn't Smoke; The Road to Ruin; Harry the Footballer; Mother's Boy; Faust; A Touch of Nature; PC Hawkeye's Busy Day; A Double Deception; Till Death Do Us Part; The Demon Dog; Twin Roses; PC Hawkeye Turns Detective; The Heat Wave; Love and a Sewing Machine; Hawkeye Learns to Punt; The Smuggler's Step-Daughter; A Seaside Introduction; The Greatest of These; Envy, Hatred and Malice; Rachel's Sin; Tilly and the Smugglers; All's Right

with the World; The Stolen Letters; For a Baby's Sake; PC Hawkeye Leaves the Force. **1912** A Curate's Love Story; The Mermaid; The Lieutenant's Bride; Our Bessie; PC Hawkeye Falls in Love; PC Hawkeye, Sportsman; PC Hawkeye Goes Fishing; The Bishop's Bathe; Hawkeye, Coastguard; Hawkeye, Showman. **1913** Hawkeye Has to Hurry; Ragtime Mad; Drake's Love Story (aka The Love Romance of Admiral Sir Francis Drake—US); Hawkeye Rides in a Point-to-Point; Haunted by Hawkeye; Captain Jack VC; A Precious Cargo; The Cloister and the Hearth; David Garrick; Hawkeye Meets His Match. **1914** Hawkeye, Hall Porter; A Friend in Need; The Heart of Midlothian. **1915** Hawkeye, King of the Castle. **1931** The Professional Guest; Deadlock. **1933** Orders is Orders (US 1934); Channel Crossing (US 1934). **1934** Jew Suess (aka Power—US); The Blue Squadron; Guest of Honour. **1935** Widow's Might. **1937** Song of the Forge. **1939** Let's Be Famous.

PLUMER, LINCOLN
Born: 1876. Died: Feb. 14, 1928, Hollywood, Calif. (heart disease). Screen and stage actor.

Appeared in: **1921** The Girl in the Taxi; Her Face Value; See My Lawyer; The Ten Dollar Raise. **1922** The Barnstormer; The Glory of Clementina; The Deuce of Spades; Confidence. **1923** The Dangerous Maid; Within the Law. **1924** Hold Your Breath; Reckless Romance; Fool's Highway. **1925** A Regular Fellow. **1926** Atta Boy; When the Wife's Away. **1927** Backstage; The Tired Business Man; Down the Stretch. **1928** The Bullet Mark; Masked Angel; Alias the Deacon.

PLUMER, ROSE LINCOLN
Died: Mar. 3, 1955, Hollywood, Calif. Screen, stage and television actress.

Appeared in: **1930** Outside the Law. **1934** Opened by Mistake (short). **1935** She Married Her Boss. **1937** Git Along, Little Dogies. **1939** Rovin' Tumbleweeds. **1940** Her First Romance. **1941** Scattergood Baines. **1942** Pacific Blackout (aka Midnight Angel). **1943** Jack London; The Desperadoes. **1944** The Girl in the Case. **1946** Duel in the Sun. **1947** Possessed. **1949** Knock on Any Door. **1950** Ma and Pa Kettle Go to Town. **1955** East of Eden.

POE, JAMES
Born: 1922, Dobbs Ferry, N.Y. Died: Jan. 24, 1980. Screen actor and screenwriter.

Appeared in: **1952** Paula.

POFF, LON (Alonzo M. Poff)
Born: Feb. 8, 1870, Bedford, Ind. Died: Aug. 8, 1952. Screen and stage actor. Entered films in 1914.

Appeared in: **1921** Big Town Ideas; The Night Horsemen; The Old Swimmin' Hole; The Three Musketeers. **1922** Suzanna; Tracked to Earth; The Village Blacksmith. **1923** The Girl I Loved; Brass Commandments; Main Street; The Man Who Won. **1924** The Man from Wyoming; Excitement; Dante's Inferno; Darwin was Right. **1925** A Fool and His Money; The Merry Widow; Greed; A Thief in Paradise; The Million Dollar Handicap. **1926** Marriage License?. **1927** The Silent Rider; Silver Valley; The Tender Hour. **1928** Greased Lightning; Two Lovers; Wheels of Chance. **1929** The Faker; The Iron Mask; Lone Star Ranger. **1930** Tom Sawyer; The Laurel-Hardy Murder Case (short). **1931** Behind Office Doors; I Take This Woman; Caught; Ambassador Bill. **1932** Stepping Sisters. **1934** Kid Millions. **1935** Teacher's Beau (short). **1937** Calling All Doctors (short); Toast of New York. **1938** The Texans. **1943** No News is Good News (short); The More the Merrier. **1951** Father's Little Dividend.

POGUE, TOM
Born: 1876. Died: Mar. 21, 1941, Hollywood, Calif. Screen, stage and television actor.

Appeared in: **1936** Divot Diggers (short); I Married a Doctor; Stage Struck. **1937** Once A Doctor; It's Love I'm After; Lloyds of London. **1940** Foreign Correspondent; The Letter. **1941** Citizen Kane; Back Street; Meet John Doe.

POINTER, SIDNEY
Died: May 16, 1955. Screen actor.

Appeared in: **1951** The Blue Lamp.

POL, TALITHA
Born: 1940, Holland. Died: July, 1971, Rome, Italy (heroin overdose). Screen actress. Married to oil scion Paul Getty, Jr.

Appeared in: **1961** Village of Daughters. **1965** Return from the Ashes. **1966** The Girl Getters. **1968** Barbarella.

POLAN, LOU

Born: 1905. Died: Mar. 3, 1976, Freeport, N.Y. Screen, stage, vaudeville and television actor.

Appeared in: **1951** You Never Can Tell. **1960** Murder, Inc. **1965** Across the River.

POLANSKI, GOURY

Born: 1893, Russia. Died: Oct. 17, 1976, Hollywood, Calif. (cancer). Screen, stage and television actor. Entered films in the mid 1920s.

Appeared in: **1930** Moby Dick; All Quiet on the Western Front.

POLEN, NAT

Born: 1915, New York, N.Y. Died: May 3, 1981, Plainview, Long Island, N.Y. Screen, stage, radio, television actor and jazz drummer.

POLIDOR (Ferdinando Guillaume)

Born: 1887, Italy. Died: Dec. 3, 1977, Italy? Screen actor.

Appeared in: **1959** Big Jeeter; Ballerina e Buon Dio (aka Angel in a Taxi—US 1963). **1961** La Dolce Vita; Accattone! (US 1968). **1963** Una Storia Moderna (aka L'ape Regina, and aka The Conjugal Bed—US); 8 1/2. **1968** Histoires Extraordinaires (aka Spirits of the Dead—US 1969).

POLK, GORDON

Born: 1924. Died: June 9, 1960, Hollywood, Calif. (during heart surgery). Screen, stage and television actor.

Appeared in: **1951** Starlift. **1960** Inherit the Wind.

POLLA, PAULINE M.

Born: 1868. Died: Apr. 19, 1940, Albany, N.Y. Screen actress and opera performer. Appeared in silents.

POLLACK, BEN

Born: 1904. Died: June 7, 1971, Palm Springs, Calif. (suicide—hanged). Bandleader, jazz drummer, screen actor and songwriter.

Appeared in: **1929** Ben Pollack and His Park Central Orchestra (short). **1934** Universal short. **1951** Disc Jockey. **1954** The Glenn Miller Story. **1955** The Benny Goodman Story.

POLLACK, MURRAY

Born: 1919, New York, N.Y. Died: May 10, 1979, Los Angeles, Calif. (cancer). Singer and screen extra.

POLLAR, GENE

Born: 1892, New York, N.Y. Died: Oct. 20, 1971, Ft. Lauderdale, Fla. Screen actor.

Appeared in: **1920** The Return of Tarzan. **1921** The Revenge of Tarzan.

POLLARD, BUD

Born: 1887. Died: Dec. 16, 1952, Hollywood, Calif. (heart attack). Screen actor, film director and screenwriter.

Appeared in: **1933** Victims of Persecution.

POLLARD, DAPHNE (Daphne Trott)

Born: Oct. 19, 1890, Melbourne, Australia. Died: Feb. 22, 1978, Los Angeles, Calif. Screen, stage and vaudeville actress. Entered films in 1927.

Appeared in: **1928** Hit of the Show; Sinners of Love; Wanted a Man (short); Cleo to Cleopatra (short). **1929** Big Time; A Perfect Day (short); The Sky Hawk; South Sea Rose; The Old Barn (short). **1930** What a Widow!; Swing Time; Bright Lights; Loose Ankles; plus the following shorts: Sugar Plum Papa; Bulls and Bears; Goodbye Legs; Don't Bite Your Dentist; Racket Cheers. **1931** Lady Refuses. **1935** Bonnie Scotland; Thicker Than Water (short). **1936** Our Relations. **1941** Tillie the Toiler. **1943** The Dancing Masters; Kid Dynamite.

POLLARD, HARRY

Born: Jan. 23, 1879, Republic City, Kans. Died: July 6, 1934, Pasadena, Calif. Screen, stage, vaudeville actor and film director. Married to actress Margarita Fisher (dec. 1975). Entered films as an actor with Selig.

Appeared in: **1912** The Worth of a Man; Call of the Drum; Better Than Gold; The Dove and the Serpent; Melodrama of Yesterday; Love, War and a Bonnet; On the Shore; Jim's Atonement; The Parson and the Medicine Man; Exchanging Labels; Big Jim. **1913** Uncle Tom's Cabin. **1914** The Wife; Nancy's Husband; The Professor's Awakening; Caught in a Tight Pinch; Closed at Ten; Jane, the Justice; The Other Train; A Modern Othello; A Suspended Ceremony; The Silence of John Gordon; A Joke on Jane; Susanna's New Suit. **1915** The Peacock Feather Fan. **1916** Suzie's New Shoes.

POLLARD, HARRY "SNUB" (Harold Frazer)

Born: 1886, Melbourne, Australia. Died: Jan. 19, 1962, Burbank, Calif. Screen, stage, vaudeville, television actor and film producer. Do not confuse with Harry Pollard, film actor and director (dec. 1934). Entered films as a bit player with Broncho Billy Anderson at Essanay Studios. He was one of the original Keystone Kops.

Appeared in: **1915** Great While It Lasted. **1919** Start Something; All at Sea; Call for Mr. Cave Man; Giving the Bride Away; Order in Court; It's a Hard Life; How Dry I Am; Looking for Trouble; Tough Luck; The Floor Below; His Royal Slyness. **1920** The following shorts: Red Hot Hottentots; Why Go Home?; Slippery Slickers; The Dippy Dentist; All Lit Up; Getting His Goat; Waltz Me Around; Raise the Rent; Find the Girl; Fresh Paint; Flat Broke; Cut the Cards; The Dinner Hour; Cracked Wedding Bells; Speed to Spare; Shoot on Sight; Don't Weaken; Drink Hearty; Trotting through Turkey; All Dressed Up; Grab the Ghost; All in a Day; Any Old Port; Don't Rock the Boat; The Home Stretch; Call a Taxi; Live and Learn; Run 'Em Ragged; A London Bobby; Money to Burn; Go As You Please; Rock-a-bye-Baby; Doing Time; Fellow Citizens; When the Wind Blows; Insulting the Sultan; The Dearly Departed; Cash Customers; Park Your Car. **1921** The following shorts: The Morning After; Whirl O' the West; Open Another Bottle; His Best Girl; Make it Snappy; Fellow Romans; Rush Orders; Bubbling Over; No Children; Own Your Own Home; Big Game; Save Your Money; Blue Sunday; Where's the Fire; The High Rollers; You're Next; The Bike Bug; At the Ringside; No Stopover; What a Whopper; Teaching the Teacher; Spot Cash; Name the Day; The Jail Bird; Late Lodgers; Gone to the Country; Law and Order; Fifteen Minutes; On Location; Hocus-Pocus; Penny-in-the-Slot; The Joy Rider; The Hustler; Sink or Swim; Shake 'Em Up; Corner Pocket. **1922** The following shorts: Lose No Time; Call the Witness; Years to Come; Blow 'Em Up; Stage Struck; Down and Out; Pardon Me; The Bow Wows; Hot off the Press; The Anvil Chorus; Jump Your Job; Full o'Pep; Kill the Nerve; Days of Old; Light Showers; Do Me a Favor; In the Movies; Punch the Clock; Strictly Modern; Hale and Hearty; Some Baby; The Dumb Bell; Bed of Roses; The Stone Age; 365 Days; The Old Sea Dog; Hook, Line and Sinker; Nearly Rich; Our Gang. **1923** The following shorts: Dig Up; A Tough Winter; Before the Public; Where Am I?; California or Bust; Sold at Auction; The Courtship of Miles Sandwich; Jack Frost; The Mystery Man; The Walkout; It's a Gift; Dear Ol' Pal; Join the Circus; Fully Insured; It's a Boy. **1924** The following shorts: The Big Idea; Why Marry?; Get Busy. **1925** Are Husbands Human? (short). **1926** The following shorts: Do Your Duty; The Old Warhorse; The Doughboy; The Yokel; The Fire; All Wet. **1927** The Bum's Rush. **1931** Ex-Flame; One Good Turn (short); **1932** Midnight Patrol; Make Me a Star; The Purchase Price. **1934** Stingaree; Cockeyed Cavaliers. **1936** The Black Coin (serial); The Clutching Hand (serial); Just My Luck; The Crime Patrol; The White Legion; The Gentleman from Louisiana; Headin' for the Rio Grande. **1937** Riders of the Rockies; Hittin' the Trail; Nation Aflame; Arizona Days; Tex Rides with the Boy Scouts. **1938** Frontier Town; Starlight Over Texas; Where the Buffalo Roam. **1939** Hollywood Cavalcade; Song of the Buckaroo. **1940** Murder on the Yukon. **1943** Phony Express (short). **1944** Defective Detectives (short); His Tale is Told (short). **1945** Three Pests in a Mess (short); San Antonio. **1946** Monkey Businessmen (short). **1947** Perils of Pauline. **1948** Blackmail; Family Honeymoon. **1949** The Beautiful Blonde from Bashful Bend; Loaded Pistols; The Crooked Way. **1954** So You Want to be a Banker (short). **1955** Pete Kelly's Blues. **1957** A Man of a Thousand Faces; Jeanne Eagels. **1958** Rock-a-bye Baby. **1960** Who Was That Lady?; Studs Lonigan; When Comedy Was King (documentary). **1961** The Errand Boy. **1962** Pocketful of Miracles; Days of Thrills and Laughter (documentary). **1963** Thirty Years of Fun (documentary). **1968** The Further Perils of Laurel and Hardy (documentary).

POLLARD, WILFRED A. "ALEX"

Born: 1887, England. Died: June 18, 1950, Hollywood, Calif. Screen actor.

Appeared in: **1932** Cross Examinations.

POLLOCK, NANCY R.

Born: 1902. Died: June 20, 1979, New York, N.Y. Screen and stage actress.

Appeared in: **1959** The Last Angry Man. **1961** Go Naked in the World. **1965** The Pawnbroker. **1976** Death Play.

POLO, EDDIE (Edward P. Polo)
Born: 1875, Los Angeles, Calif. Died: June 14, 1961, Hollywood, Calif. (heart attack). Screen actor, film stuntman and circus performer. Brother of actor Sam Polo (dec. 1966). Do not confuse with Swedish circus performer Eddie Polo—Edward Kristensson—(dec. 1956).

Appeared in: **1915** Yellow Streak; The Broken Coin (seril). **1916** Heritage of Hate; The Adventures of Peg O' the Ring (serial); Liberty, a Daughter of the U.S.A. (serial). **1917** The Wolf and His Mate; The Gray Ghost (serial). **1918** Bull's Eye (serial); Lure of the Circus (serial). **1919** A Prisoner for Love; The Phantom Fugitive; The Wild Rider; A Pistol Point Proposal; "Cyclone Smith" series including: Cyclone Smith Plays Trumps; Cyclone Smith's Partner; Cyclone Smith's Comeback. **1920** The Vanishing Dagger (serial); King of the Circus (serial). **1921** The Secret Four (serial); Do or Die (serial); The White Horseman (serial). **1922** Captain Kidd (serial); With Stanley in Africa (serial). **1923** Knock on the Door; Dangerous Hour; Prepared to Die. **1940** Son of Roaring Dan. **1942** Between Us Girls. **1943** Hers to Hold. Other "Cyclone Smith" series films he appeared in are: Square Deal Cyclone; Cyclone Smith's Vow. **1944** The Climax. **1956** Around the World in 80 Days.

POLO, ROBERT
Died: May 4, 1968, Hollywood, Calif. (brain tumor). Screen actor, extra and stand-in for Gilbert Roland.

POLO, SAM
Born: 1873. Died: Oct. 3, 1966, Hollywood, Calif. Screen actor, circus performer and make-up artist. Brother of actor Eddie Polo (dec. 1961).

Appeared in: **1919** The Midnight Man (serial). **1920** The Invisible Hand (serial). **1922** Captain Kidd (serial). **1925** Fighting Ranger (serial).

PONCIN, MARCEL
Born: France? Died: June 8, 1953, France? Screen actor.

Appeared in: **1949** One Woman's Story; The Lost People. **1950** The Golden Salamander. **1951** So Long at the Fair. **1953** Melba; Saadia.

PONS, LILY (Alice Josephine Pons)
Born: Apr. 12, 1898, 1904, or 1906, Cannes or Draguignan, France? Died: Feb. 13, 1976, Dallas, Tex. (cancer). Opera singer and screen actress. Divorced from music critic August Mesritz, and conductor Andre Kostelanetz (dec. 1980).

Appeared in: **1935** I Dream Too Much. **1936** That Girl from Paris. **1937** Hitting a New High. **1947** Carnegie Hall.

PONTO, ERICH
Born: 1885, Luebeck, Germany. Died: Feb. 4, 1957, Stuttgart, Germany. Screen, stage and radio actor.

Appeared in: **1921** Der Geiger von Meissen. **1930** Weib im Dschungel (aka The Letter). **1931** Der Mann, der den Mord Beging (The Man Who Murdered, aka Naechte am Bosporus). **1934** Liebe, Tod und Teufel; **1935** Der Gefangene des Koenigs; Das Maedchen Johanna. **1936** Der Hund von Baskerville; Weiberregiment; Die Letzten von Santa Cruz. **1937** Das Geheimnis um Betty Bonn; Tango Notturno. **1938** Die 4 Gesellen; Dreizehn Mann und Eine Kanone; Am Seidenen Faden. **1939** Hallo, Janine!; In Letzter Minute; Schneider Wibbel. **1940** Kleider Machen Leute; Achtung! Feind Hoert Mit!; Aus Erster Ehe; Wie Konntest Du, Veronika?; Das Fraeulein von Barnhelm; Das Feuerteufel; Blutsbruederschaft: Das Herz der Koenigin; Die Rothschilds. **1941** Das Andere Ich; Ich Klage An; Leichte Muse (aka Was Eine Frau im Fruehling Traumt). **1942** Anschlag auf Baku; Die Nacht in Venedig; Der Grosse Schatten; Diesel; Der Fall Rainer (aka Ich Warte auf Dich). **1943** Die Beiden Schestern; Ein Gluecklicher Mensch (aka Schule des Lebens). **1944** Am Abend Nach der Oper; Der Engel mit dem Saitenspiel; Philharmoniker; Die Feuerzangenbowle; Der Meisterdetektiv (aka Eine Reizende Familie). **1945** Das Fremde Leben; Das Kleine Hofkonzert; Der Scheiterhaufen; Das Fall Molander. **1947** Zwischen Gestern und Morgen. **1948** Das Verlorene Gesicht; Die Kupferne Hochzeit; Film ohne Titel (Film Without Title). **1949** Palace Scandal; Liebe 47 (Love 47); Hans im Glueck; Zukunft aus Zweiter Hand; Verspieltes Leben (aka Ulyssa); The Third Man (US 1950). **1950** Frauenarzt Dr. Praetorius; Tobias Knopp, Abenteuer Eines Junggesellen (speaker); Geliebter Luegner. **1951** Primanerinnen; Was das Herz Befiehlt (aka Veronika, die Magd). **1952** Herz der Welt; Haus des Lebens; Moenche, Maedchen und Panduren; Der Weissblaue Loewe; Die Grosse Versuchung; Liebe im Finanzamt (aka Wochenend im Paradies). **1953** Keine Angst vor Grossen Tieren; Hokuspokus. **1954** Sauberbruch—das war Mein Leben; Die Goldene Pest; Das Fliegende Klassenzimmer (The Flying Classroom—US 1958). **1955** Himmel ohne Sterne (Sky Without Stars—US 1959). **1956** Rosen fuer Bettina (Roses for Bettina—US 1958, aka Ballerina); Wenn wir Alle Engel Waeren (If All of Us Were Angels). **1957** Made in Germany; Der Stern von Afrika; Robinson Soll Nicht Sterben (Robinson Shall Not Die).

POOLE, BOB
Born: 1917. Died: Jan. 24, 1978. Screen and radio actor.

Appeared in: **1951** Disc Jockey.

POPE, UNOLA B.
Born: 1884. Died: Feb. 1, 1938, Fremont, Ohio. Screen and stage actress. Said to be a member of a cast of first motion pictures made in Corning, N.Y.

POPOV, ALEXEI
Born: 1893, Russia. Died: Aug., 1961, Russia? Screen actor and film director.

Appeared in: **1951** Mussorgsky. **1955** The Safety Match. **1960** Othello.

PORCASI, PAUL
Born: 1880, Palermo, Italy. Died: Aug. 8, 1946, Hollywood, Calif. Screen, stage actor and opera singer.

Appeared in: **1920** The Fall of the Romanoffs. **1926** Say It Again. **1929** Broadway. **1930** A Lady's Morals; Three Sisters; Murder on the Roof; Morocco; Born Reckless; Derelict. **1931** Children of Dreams; I Like Your Nerve; Doctor's Wives; Bought; Good Bad Girl; Svengali; Gentleman's Fate; Party Husbands; Under Eighteen; A Woman Commands; While Paris Sleeps; The Man Who Played God; Smart Money. **1932** The Devil and the Deep; Cynara. **1933** When Strangers Marry; Devil's Mate; I Loved a Woman; Footlight Parade; Flying Down to Rio; He Couldn't Take It; Grand Slam. **1934** British Agent; The Great Flirtation; Wake up and Dream; Tarzan and His Mate; Imitation of Life. **1935** Rumba; Enter Madame; The Florentine Dagger; A Night at the Ritz; Stars Over Broadway; Under the Pampas Moon; Charlie Chan in Egypt; Waterfront Lady; I Dream Too Much; Million Dollar Baby. **1936** Muss 'Em Up; Down to the Sea; Crash Donovan; The Leathernecks Have Landed. **1937** Maytime; The Emperor's Candlesticks; The Bride Wore Red; Seventh Heaven; Cafe Metropole. **1938** Crime School. **1939** Everything Happens at Night; Lady of the Tropics. **1940** Dr. Kildare's Strangest Case; I Was an Adventuress; Torrid Zone; The Border Region; Argentine Nights. **1942** Star Spangled Rhythm; Road to Happiness; Quiet Please Murder. **1943** Hi Diddle Diddle. **1944** Hail the Conquering Hero; Swing Hostess; Nothing But Trouble. **1945** I'll Remember April.

PORCELAIN, BESSIE PETTS
Died: June 14, 1968. Screen actress.

PORTEN, HENNY
Born: 1890, Magdeburg, Germany. Died: Oct. 15, 1960, Berlin, Germany. Screen actress. Daughter of film director/opera singer Franz Porten (dec.). Married to actor/director Kurt Stark (dec. 1916) and later married to Dr. Wilhelm von Kaufman. One of Germany's first silent film stars.

Appeared in: **1906** Apachentanz. **1907** Lohengrin; Meissner Porzellan. **1908** Desdemona; Tief im Boehmerwald; Wiegenlied. **1910** Der Kinderarzt; Liebesglueck Einer Blinden; Muetter, Verzaget Nicht; Verkannt. **1911** Adressatin Verstorben; Die Blinde; Der Eindrengling; Das Gefaehrliche Alter; Die Magd; Ein Schweres Opfer; Zwei Frauen. **1912** Maskierte Liebe; Des Pfarrers Toechterlein; Eva; Feenhaende; Gefangene Seelen; Kuss des Fuersten; Die Nacht des Grauens; Schatten des Meeres. **1913** Graefin Kuechenfee; Die Grosse Suenderin; Heroismus Einer Franzoesin; Um Haaresbreite; Ungarische Rhapsodie (Hungarian Rhapsody). **1914** Das Tal des Lebens; Abseits vom Glueck; Das Adoptivkind; Alexandra; Das Ende vom Lied; Hans, Hein und Henny; Nordlandlose. **1915** Tirol in Waffen; Auf der Alm da Gibt's ka Suend; Claudi vom Geisterhof; Geloeste Ketten; Ein Geschlecht Deren von Ringwall; Der Schirm mit dem Schwan; Ein Ueberfall in Feindesland. **1916** Die Ehe der Luise Rohrbach; Der Liebesbrief der Koenigin; Die Raueberbraut; Das Wandernde Licht. **1917** Die Dame, der Teufel und die Probiermamsell; Die Faust des Riesen; Das Goldene Kalb; Hoeheluft. **1918** Die Schuld; Die Blaue Laterne; Irrungen; Maskenfest der Liebe; Odysseus' Heimkehr. **1919** Rose Bernd; Fahrt ins Blaue; Ihr Sport; Die Lebende Tote; Monika Vogelsang. **1920** Auf der Alm; Die Blinden Gatten der Frau Ruth; Die Eingebildete Kranke; Die Goldene Krone; Liebe auf den Ersten Blick; Kohlhiesels Toechter (Kohliesel's Daughters); Anna Boleyn (aka Deception—US 1921). **1921** Die Geierwally; Die Hintertreppe (Backstairs—US 1926). **1922** Catherina Graefin von Armagnac; Frauenopfer; Gespenster; Das Grosse Schwiegen; Minna von Barnhelm; Mona Lisa; Sie und die Drei. **1923** Das Geheimnis von

Brinkenhof; Inge Larsen; I.N.R.I.; Der Kaufmann von Venedig; Die Liebe Einer Koenigin; Das Alte Gesetz (The Ancient Law). **1924** Das Goldene Kalb; Graefin Donelli; Mutter und Kind (Mother and Child); Prater (aka Die Erlebnisse Zweier Naehmaedchen). **1925** Kammermusik; Tragoedie; Das Abenteuer der Sibylle Brandt (aka Um ein Haar); Rosen aus dem Sueden. **1926** Die Flammen Luegen; Wehe, Wenn sie Losgelassen. **1927** Die Grosse Pause; Meine Tante—Deine Tante; Violantha. **1928** Liebe im Kuhstall; Liebe und Diebe; Liebfraumilch; Lotte; Zuflucht (Refuge). **1929** Die Frau, die Jeder Liebt, Bist Du!; Die Herrin und ihr Knecht; Mutterliebe (Motherlove—US 1931). **1930** Skandal um Eva (The Eva Scandal); Kohlhiesels Toechter (Kolhiesel's Daughters, aka Gretel and Liesel—US 1931). **1931** Luise, Koenigin von Preussen (Luise, Queen of Prussia). **1933** Mutter und Kind (Mother and Child—US 1934). **1934** Crown of Thorns. **1935** Krach im Hinterhaus (Trouble Backstairs—US 1937). **1938** Der Optimist; War es der im 3. Stock? **1941** Komoedianten. **1942** Symphonie Eines Lebens. **1943** Wenn der Junge Wein Blueht. **1944** Familie Buchholz (aka Neigungsehe). **1950** Absender Unbekannt. **1954** Carola Lamberti—Eine vom Zirkus (Carole Lamberti, Woman of the Circus). **1955** Das Frauelein von Scuederi.

PORTER, CALEB
Born: Sept. 1, 1867, London, England. Died: Mar. 13, 1940, London, England. Screen, stage actor and stage producer. Divorced from Jessie Hannah Neil, and later married to actress Kitty de Legh. Father of actor Neil Porter.

Appeared in: **1913** Guy Fawkes and the Gunpowder Plot. **1914** Kismet. **1917** One Summer's Day.

PORTER, DICK
Born: 1932. Died: Jan. 6, 1978, Sedalia, Mo. (heart attack). Black singer and screen actor. Member of "Inkspots" singing group from 1969-1978.

PORTER, EDWARD D.
Born: 1881. Died: July 29, 1939, Hollywood, Calif. (stroke). Stage and screen actor.

Appeared in: **1925** Friendly Enemies.

PORTER, HAROLD B.
Born: 1896. Died: July 30, 1939, Hollywood, Calif. (suicide). Screen actor, radio performer and cameraman.

PORTER, MARY (Mary Jennings)
Born: Centralia, Ill. Died: Mar. 23, 1978, New York, N.Y. (stroke). Screen, stage actress, costume designer and theater business manager. Married to actor Paul Porter, Sr. (dec. 1956). Mother of actor Paul Porter, Jr.

PORTER, PAUL, SR.
Born: 1886. Died: Oct. 17, 1957, N.Y. Screen, stage actor and stage manager. Married to actress Mary Porter (dec. 1978). Father of actor Paul Porter, Jr.

Appeared in: **1924** Into the Net (serial).

PORTER, REED (George Reed Porter)
Born: 1910, Kansas City, Kans. Died: Aug. 12, 1979, Los Angeles, Calif. Screen actor and reporter.

Appeared in: **1942** Holiday Inn; Heart of the Rio Grande.

PORTER, VIOLA ADELE
Born: 1879. Died: Dec. 29, 1942, Hollywood, Calif. Screen actress.

PORTERFIELD, ROBERT H.
Born: Dec. 21, 1905, Austinville, Va. Died: Oct. 28, 1971, Abingdon, Va. (heart attack). Screen, stage actor and stage director.

Appeared in: **1941** Sergeant York. **1946** The Yearling. **1958** Thunder Road.

PORTMAN, ERIC
Born: July 13, 1903, Yorkshire, England. Died: Dec. 7, 1969, St. Veep, England. Screen, stage and television actor.

Appeared in: **1935** Maria Marten, or The Murder in the Red Barn (film debut); Abdul the Damned; Old Roses; Hyde Park Corner. **1936** The Cardinal; The Crimes of Stephen Hawke; Hearts of Humanity. **1937** Moonlight Sonata; The Prince and the Pauper. **1941** The 49th Parallel (aka The Invaders—US 1942). **1942** One of Our Aircraft is Missing; Squadron Leader X (Us 1943); Uncensored (US 1944). **1943** The Carmer (rerelease of Moonlight Sonata 1937); We Dive at Dawn;

Escape to Danger; Millions Like Us. **1944** A Canterbury Tale. **1945** Great Day. **1946** Men of Two Worlds (aka Kisenga, Man of Africa—US 1952); Wanted for Murder; Daybreak (US 1949). **1947** Dear Murderer (US 1948). **1948** The Mark of Cain; Corridor of Mirrors; The Blind Goddess (US 1949). **1949** The Spider and the Fly (US 1952). **1950** Cairo Road. **1951** The Magic Box (US 1952). **1952** A Voice in the Night (rerelease of Wanted for Murder 1946); South of Algiers (aka The Golden Mask—US 1954); His Excellency (US 1956). **1955** The Colditz Story (US 1957); The Deep Blue Sea. **1956** Child in the House. **1957** The Good Companions. **1961** The Naked Edge. **1962** Freud; The Man Who Finally Died (US 1967). **1963** West 11. **1965** The Bedford Incident. **1966** The Spy With a Cold Nose; The Whisperers. **1967** Deadfall (US 1968). **1969** Assignment to Kill.

PORTUGAL, JOSE
Born: 1908, Mexico. Died: Dec. 28, 1976, Los Angeles, Calif. Screen actor.

Appeared in: **1945** The Bull Fighters.

POST, CHARLES A. "BUDDY"
Born: Nov. 3, 1897, Salt Lake City, Utah. Died: Dec. 20, 1952, Calif. Screen, stage actor and production manager. Entered films in 1917.

Appeared in: **1918** M'Liss. **1921** Eden and Return; The Hell Diggers; Bob Hampton of Placer; What's Worth While? **1924** Defying the Law; The Tenth Woman; Wild Oranges; Behold This Woman. **1925** The Top of the World; A Lover's Oath; The Midnight Flyer; Off the Highway; The Overland Limited. **1926** Crown of Lies; Diplomacy; Redheads Preferred; Her Sacrifice. **1927** The Tender Hour; The Satin Woman; The Broken Gate. **1930** The Escape. **1940** Li'l Abner.

POST, EDITH S.
Born: 1943. Died: Nov. 15, 1971, Santa Monica, Calif. Screen actress. Appeared in Andy Warhol's films.

POST, GUY BATES
Born: Sept. 22, 1875, Seattle, Wash. Died: Jan. 16, 1968, Los Angeles, Calif. Screen and stage actor. Divorced from stage actress Adele Ritchie (dec. 1930). Married to actress Lillian Kemble-Cooper (dec. 1977).

Appeared in: **1922** The Masquerader; Omar the Tentmaker. **1923** Gold Madness. **1932** Prestige. **1936** Camille; 'Til We Meet Again; The Case Against Mrs. Ames; Fatal Lady; Trouble for Two; Ace Drummond (serial). **1937** Champagne Waltz; Daughter of Shanghai; Maid of Salem; Maytime; Blazing Barriers; The Mysterious Pilot (serial). **1940** The Mad Empress. **1942** Crossroads. **1947** A Double Life.

POST, WILEY
Born: Grand Plain, Tex. Died: Aug. 15, 1935, near Barrow, Alaska (airplane crash). Aviator, screen actor and stunt flyer. Died in crash with Will Rogers.

Appeared in: **1935** Air Hawks.

POST, WILMARTH H.
Died: Aug. 25, 1930, Rutherford, N.J. (heart failure). Screen, stage actor, film director and author.

POTEL, VICTOR
Born: 1889, Lafayette, Ind. Died: Mar. 8, 1947, Los Angeles, Calif. Screen actor. Entered films in 1910. Was one of the original Keystone Kops.

Appeared in: **1910** Joyriding. **1911** "Snakeville" comedy series. **1916** His Last Scent. **1919** The Outcasts of Poker Flat; Captain Kidd, Jr. **1920** Mary's Ankle. **1921** Lavender and Old Lace; Bob Hampton of Placer. **1922** Step on It!; At the Sign of the Jack O'Lantern; Quincy Adams Sawyer; Don't Write Letters; A Tailor Made Man; The Loaded Door; I Can Explain. **1923** Anna Christie; Penrod and Sam; Itching Palms; The Meanest Man in the World; Refuge; Reno; Modern Matrimony; Tea With a Kick. **1924** Along Came Jones; The Law Forbids; A Self-Made Failure; Women Who Give. **1925** A Lost Lady; Below the Line; Ten Days; Contraband. **1926** The Bar-C Mystery (serial); The Carnival Girl; The Lodge in the Wilderness; Racing Romance; Morganson's Finish. **1927** Uneasy Payments; Special Delivery; The Craver. **1928** What Price Beauty?; Little Shepherd of Kingdom Come; Lingerie; Melody of Love; Captain Swagger. **1929** Marianne; The Virginian. **1930** The Bad One; The Big Shot; Paradise Island; Virtuous Sin; Call of the West; Border Romance; Dough Boys. **1931** King of the Wild (serial); 10¢ a Dance; The Squaw Man. **1932** Partners; Make Me a Star; The Purchase Price. **1933** Hallelujah, I'm a Bum. **1934** Thunder Over Texas; Inside Information; Frontier Days. **1935** Mississippi; The Girl Friend; Ruggles of Red Gap; The Trail's

End; Last of the Clintons; Lady Tubbs; Hard Rock Harrigan; Waterfront Lady; Whispering Smith Speaks. **1936** Three Godfathers; O'Malley of the Mounted; Yellow Dust; Song of the Saddle; The Captain's Kid; God's Country and the Woman; Down to the Sea. **1937** Two-Gun Law; White Bondage; Western Gold; Small Town Boy. **1938** Outside the Law. **1939** Rovin' Thumbleweeds. **1940** Girl from God's Country; Christmas in July. **1941** Birth of the Blues; Sullivan's Travels; The Big Store. **1944** The Miracle of Morgan's Creek; The Great Moment; Going to Town; Hail the Conquering Hero. **1945** Strange Illusion; Captain Tugboat Annie; Medal for Benny; Rhythm Round-up. **1946** The Glass Alibi. **1947** The Millerson Case; Mad Wednesday (aka The Sin of Harold Diddlebock); Ramrod; The Egg and I.

POTTS, HANK
Died: 1980. Screen actor.

Appeared in: **1930** Beau Bandit. **1935** Crimson Trail.

POUNDS, CHARLES COURTICE
Born: May 30, 1862, London, England. Died: Dec. 21, 1927, England? Screen, stage actor and singer. Brother of stage actress Louie Pounds (dec.).

Appeared in: **1916** The Broken Melody.

POUYET, EUGENE "GENE"
Born: Aug. 23, 1883, France. Died: May 22, 1950, Calif. Screen actor.

Appeared in: **1921** The Conquering Power. **1922** Kisses; Trifling Women. **1926** La Boheme. **1927** The Lone Eagle.

POWELL, DAVID
Born: 1885, Wales. Died: Apr. 16, 1925, N.Y. (pneumonia). Screen actor.

Appeared in: **1916** Less Than the Dust; Gloria's Romance (serial). **1917** The Beautiful Adventure. **1918** A Romance of the Underworld; The Unforseen. **1919** The Firing Line; His Parisian Wife. **1920** The Right to Love; Idols of Clay; On With the Dance; Lady Rose's Daughter. **1921** Appearances; The Princess of New York; Dangerous Lies; The Mystery Road. **1922** Outcast; The Siren Call; Perpetua (aka Love's Boomerang—US); Anna Ascends; Her Gilded Cage; Missing Millions; The Spanish Jade. **1923** The Glimpses of the Moon; Fog Bound; The Green Goddess. **1924** The Average Woman; Lend Me Your Husband; The Truth About Women; The Man Without a Heart; Virtuous Liars. **1925** Back to Life; The Lost Chord.

POWELL, DICK
Died: Sept. 26, 1948, Hales Corners, Wis. (accidental fall from plane). Screen actor and stunt flier. Do not confuse with actor dec. 1963.

Appeared in: **1920** The Great Air Robbery. **1925** The Cloud Rider; Air Hawks. **1930** Hell's Angels; Dawn Patrol. **1947** Blaze of Noon.

POWELL, DICK (Richard E. Powell)
Born: Nov. 14, 1904, Mt. View, Ark. Died: Jan. 2, 1963, Hollywood, Calif. (cancer). Screen, stage, radio, television actor, film director, producer, stage director and singer. Married to actress June Allyson. Divorced from actresses Joan Blondell (dec. 1979) and Mildred Maund. Father of actor Richard Powell, Jr. and Pamela Ellen Powell.

Appeared in: **1931** Street Scene; Gold Diggers of 1933; Footlight Parade; College Coach; Convention City; The King's Vacation. **1934** Wonder Bar; Twenty Million Sweethearts; Happiness Ahead; Flirtation Walk; Dames. **1935** Gold Diggers of 1935; If You Could Only Cook; A Midsummer Night's Dream; Page Miss Glory; Broadway Gondolier; Shipmates Forever; Thanks a Million; Ginger. **1936** Colleen; Hearts Divided; Stage Struck; Gold Diggers of 1937; For Auld Lang Syne (documentary). **1937** On the Avenue; The Singing Marine; Varsity Show; Hollywood Hotel; The College Coed. **1938** Cowboy from Brooklyn; Hard to Get; Going Places. **1939** For Auld Lang Syne (short); Naughty But Nice. **1940** Christmas in July; I Want a Divorce. **1941** Model Wife; In the Navy. **1942** Star Spangled Rhythm. **1943** Happy Go Lucky; True to Life; Riding High. **1944** Meet the People; It Happened Tomorrow; Farewell, My Lovely. **1945** Cornered. **1947** Johnny O'Clock. **1948** To the Ends of the Earth; Pitfall; Station West; Rogue's Regiment. **1949** Mrs. Mike. **1950** The Reformer and the Redhead; Right Cross. **1951** Cry Danger; Callaway Went Thataway; Tall Target; You Never Can Tell. **1952** The Bad and the Beautiful. **1954** Susan Slept Here.

POWELL, JACK
Born: 1901. Died: Apr. 6, 1976. Screen actor.

Appeared in: **1935** Kid Courageous; Here Comes Cookie. **1937** Armored Car; The Wildcatter. **1939** East Side of Heaven. **1940** Bitter Sweet.

POWELL, LEE (Alfred E. Lee)
Born: 1896. Died: Feb. 3, 1954, Hollywood, Calif. Screen and stage actor.

POWELL, LEE B.
Born: May 15, 1908, Long Beach, Calif. Died: July 8, 1944 (killed in action in Marines in the South Pacific). Screen and stage actor. The original "Lone Ranger" of the films.

Appeared in: **1938** The Lone Ranger (serial); The Fighting Devil Dogs (serial); Come on, Rangers. **1939** Trigger Pals. **1940** Flash Gordon Conquers the Universe (serial).

POWELL, RICHARD
Born: 1897. Died: Jan. 1, 1937, Hollywood, Calif. (fractured skull, from auto accident). Screen actor and opera performer. Do not confuse with actors Dick Powell (dec. 1948 and 1963).

Appeared in: **1933** Feeling Rosy (short). **1935** The Wedding Night; Woman Wanted; Every Night at Eight. **1936** Yours for the Asking; Hollywood Boulevard. **1937** Another Dawn.

POWELL, RUSS (Russell J. Powell)
Born: Sept. 16, 1875, Indianapolis, Ind. Died: Nov. 28, 1950, Woodland Hills, Calif. (arteriosclerosis). Screen, stage and vaudeville actor.

Appeared in: **1915** Alone in the City of Sighs and Tears; Kidding the Goats; The Morning After. **1921** The Concert. **1922** Head Over Heels; Through a Glass Window. **1923** One Stolen Night. **1924** A Boy of Flanders; Dynamite Smith. **1925** The Re-creation of Brian Kent; The Wheel. **1927** Soft Cushions; No Place to Go; The Red Mill. **1928** Vamping Venus; The Gate Crasher; Riley the Cop. **1929** Fashions in Love; The Love Parade. **1930** The Big Trail; Check and Double Check; The Grand Parade. **1931** An American Tragedy; The Sin of Madelon Claudet. **1932** Mystery Ranch. **1933** Zoo in Budapest; Arabian Tights (short); Snug in the Jug (short); To the Last Man. **1934** The Count of Monte Cristo; Wharf Angel. **1935** Call of the Savage (serial). **1936** Rose of the Rancho; Sutter's Gold. **1937** The Wrong Road; Hit the Saddle. **1940** The Night of Nights. **1941** Prairie Stranger.

POWELL, SOLDENE
Born: 1860. Died: Apr. 12, 1915, New York, N.Y. Screen actor. Appeared in Pathe Film Co. films.

POWELL, W. TEMPLAR
Died: June 29, 1949. Screen actor. Do not confuse with other actors with same name.

POWER, HARTLEY
Born: Mar. 14, 1894, New York, N.Y. Died: Jan. 29, 1966, London, England. Screen and stage actor. Married to actress Betty Paul.

Appeared in: **1933** Yes Mr. Brown; Just Smith; Friday the Thirteenth (US 1934); Aunt Sally (aka Along Came Sally—US 1934). **1934** Evergreen (US 1935); The Camels are Coming; Road House. **1936** Jury's Evidence; Living Dangerously. **1938** Just Like a Woman; The Return of the Frog. **1939** A Window in London (aka Lady in Distress—US 1942); Murder Will Out. **1940** Return to Yesterday. **1941** Atlantic Ferry (aka Sons of the Sea—US). **1942** Alibi. **1945** The Man from Morocco; Dead of Night; The Way to the Stars (aka Johnny in the Clouds—US). **1946** A Girl in a Million (US 1950). **1952** The Armchair Detective. **1953** Roman Holiday. **1954** The Million Pound Note (aka Man with a Million—US); To Dorothy a Son (aka Cash on Delivery—US 1956). **1957** Island in the Sun.

POWER, JOHN
Born: 1874. Died: Sept. 25, 1951, Culver City, Calif. Screen and stage actor.

Appeared in: **1934** The Live Ghost (short). **1939** We Are not Alone; Dog Daze (short). **1942** Mrs. Miniver.

POWER, PAUL (Luther Vestergard)
Born: 1902, Chicago, Ill. Died: Apr. 5, 1968, Hollywood, Calif. Screen, stage and television actor. Entered films in 1925.

Appeared in: **1927** False Values. **1928** Trial Marriage; Hot Heels. **1929** Words and Music. **1934** Wonder Bar. **1935** I've Been Around. **1938** Adventures of Robin Hood. **1955** The Girl in the Red Velvet Swing. **1958** Jet Attack. **1960** Ma Barker's Killer Brood. **1962** The Underwater City; Advise and Consent.

POWER, TYRONE F., JR.
Born: May 5, 1914, Cincinnati, Ohio. Died: Nov. 15, 1958, Madrid, Spain (heart attack). Screen and stage actor. Son of actor Tyrone Power, Sr. (dec. 1931) and stage actress Patia Reaume. Divorced from actresses Annabella and Linda Christian. Married to actress Debbie Ann Minardos Power. Father of actress Taryn, Romina and Tyrone Power.

Appeared in: **1932** Tom Brown of Culver. **1934** Flirtation Walk. **1936** Girls's Dormitory; Ladies in Love; Lloyds of London. **1937** Love Is News; Cafe Metropole; Thin Ice; Second Honeymoon. **1938** In Old Chicago; Alexander's Ragtime Band; Marie Antoinette; Suez. **1939** Jesse James; Rose of Washington Square; Second Fiddle; The Rains Came; Daytime Wife. **1940** Johnny Apollo; Brigham Young—Frontiersman; The Mark of Zorro; The Return of Frank James. **1941** Blood and Sand; A Yank in the R.A.F. **1942** Son of Fury; This Above All; The Black Swan. **1943** Crash Dive. **1946** The Razor's Edge. **1947** Nightmare Alley; Captain from Castile. **1948** Luck of the Irish; That Wonderful Urge. **1949** Prince of Foxes. **1950** The Black Rose; American Guerilla in the Philippines. **1951** Rawhide; I'll Never Forget You (aka Man of Two Worlds and The House in the Square). **1952** Diplomatic Courier; Pony Soldier. **1953** Mississippi Gambler; King of the Khyber Rifles. **1955** The Long Gray Line; Untamed. **1956** The Eddy Duchin Story. **1957** Seven Waves Away (aka Abandon Ship—US); The Rising of the Moon (narr.); The Sun Also Rises; Witness for the Prosecution.

POWER, TYRONE F., SR. (Frederick Tyrone Edmond Power)
Born: May 2, 1869, London, England. Died: Dec. 30, 1931, Hollywood, Calif. (heart attack). Screen and stage actor. Married to Ethel Crance (dec.); stage actress Patia Emma Reaume (dec.) and later to Bertha Knight (dec.). Father of Anne and actor Tyrone Power, Jr. (dec. 1958).

Appeared in: **1915** A Texas Steer. **1916** John Needham's Double; Where Are My Children? **1919** The Miracle Man. **1921** The Black Panther's Cub; Dream Street; Footfalls. **1923** Bright Lights of Broadway; The Daring Years; Fury; The Truth About Wives; The Day of Faith; Wife in Name Only. **1924** Damaged Hearts; Janice Meredith; For Another Woman; The Law and the Lady; Trouping with Ellen; The Story Without a Name; The Lone Wolf. **1925** Braveheart; Red Kimono; A Regular Fellow; Where Was I? **1926** Bride of the Storm; Hands Across the Border; The Wanderer; Out of the Storm; The Test of Donald Norton. **1930** The Big Trail.

POWERS, JOHN H.
Born: 1885. Died: Jan. 17, 1941, New York, N.Y. Screen, stage, vaudeville actor and circus performer. Was partner in vaudeville in an act billed as "McAvoy and Powers."

Appeared in: **1923** Adam and Eve. **1937** Hills of Old Wyoming. **1939** Zaza. **1941** Twilight on the Trail.

POWERS, JULE
Died: Feb. 14, 1932, Hollywood, Calif. Stage and screen actress.

POWERS, LEONA
Born: Mar. 13, 1896, Salida, Colo. Died: Jan. 7, 1970, New York, N.Y. Screen, stage, radio and television actress.

Appeared in: **1935** Sweet Surrender. **1948** Deep Waters.

POWERS, MARIE
Born: Pennsylvania. Died: Dec. 29, 1973, New York, N.Y. Screen, stage actress and opera performer.

Appeared in: **1951** The Medium.

POWERS, MARY GARE
Died: July 25, 1961. Screen actress. Appeared in silents.

POWERS, RICHARD See KEENE, TOM

POWERS, TOM
Born: July 7, 1890, Owensboro, Ky. Died: Nov. 9, 1955, Hollywood, Calif. (heart ailment). Screen, stage actor and author. Entered films in 1910.

Appeared in: **1911** Saving an Audience. **1914** Creatures of Habit; Flotilla the Flirt; Terror of the Air. **1915** As Ye Repent; Barnaby Rudge; The Canker of Jealousy. **1917** The Auction Block. **1944** Practically Yours; Double Indemnity. **1945** The Phantom Speaks; The Chicago Kid. **1946** Two Years Before the Mast; The Blue Dahlia; The Last Crooked Mile; Her Adventurous Night. **1947** Son of Rusty; Angel and the Badman; The Farmer's Daughter; They Won't Believe Me. **1948** Angel in Exile; I Love Trouble; The Time of Your Life; Up in

Central Park; Mexican Hayride; Station West. **1949** Special Agent; Scene of the Crime; Chicago Deadline; East Side, West Side. **1950** Destination Moon; Chinatown at Midnight; The Nevadan; Right Cross. **1951** Fighting Coast Guard; The Strip; The Tall Target; The Well. **1952** Denver and Rio Grande; Diplomatic Courier; We're Not Married; Steel Trap; Deadline—U.S.A.; Jet Job; Phone Call from a Stranger; Bal Tabarin; The Fabulous Senorita; Horizons West. **1953** The Last Posse; The Marksman; Hannah Lee; Julius Caesar; Scared Stiff; Donovan's Brain; Sea of Lost Ships. **1955** The Americano; New York Confidential; Ten Wanted Men. **1956** UFO.

POWLEY, BRYAN
Born: Sept. 16, 1871, Reading, England. Died: Dec., 1962, London, England. Screen and stage actor.

Appeared in: **1920** The Joyous Adventures of Aristide Pujol. **1921** The Old Curiosity Shop; Fortune of Christina McNab (US 1923). **1922** Open Country; The Wee MacGregor's Sweetheart. **1935** Forever England (aka Brown on Resolution and Born for Glory—US). **1936** Rhodes of Africa (aka Rhodes—US); All In; Conquest of the Air. **1937** Love from a Stranger; Fire Over England; Thunder in the City; Moonlight Sonata; When the Devil was Well; Mademoiselle Docteur; What a Man!. **1938** Mr. Satan; Darts are Trumps; Strange Boarders; You're the Doctor. **1939** Old Mother Riley Joins Up. **1943** The Charmer (reissue of Moonlight Sonata—1937); We Dive at Dawn.

PRACK, RUDOLF
Born: 1904, Austria. Died: Dec. 2, 1981, Vienna, Austria. Screen and stage actor. Entered films in 1939.

Appeared in: **1940** Mutterliebe (Mother Love). **1951** Grun ist die Heide. **1955** Der Kongress Tanzt (Congress Dances). **1956** Emperor's Waltz. **1965** Heidi (US 1968); Other Austrian films: The Golden City; Love According to Notes; Hearts in Rebellion; Schwarzwaldmaedel.

PRADA, JOSE MARIA
Born: 1925, Spain. Died: Aug. 13, 1978, Bilbao, Spain (heart attack). Screen, stage and television actor.

Appeared in: **1956** Marcelino. **1964** La Tia Tula (US 1965). **1966** Miss Muerte (aka The Diabolical Dr. Z—US 1967); La Caza (The Hunt—US 1967). **1967** The Trip. **1968** Vlaa Rides; Persecucion Hasta Valencia (aka The Narco Men—US 1969). **1975** A Brief Vacation.

PRAGER, STANLEY
Born: Jan. 8, 1917, New York, N.Y. Died: Jan. 18, 1972, Hollywood, Calif. Screen, stage actor, film and television director. Married to actress Georgiann Johnson.

Appeared in: **1944** The Eve of St. Mark; Take It or Leave It; In the Meantime, Darling; Wing and a Prayer. **1945** Doll Face; Junior Miss; A Bell for Adano. **1946** Do You Love Me?; Behind Green Lights; Gentleman Joe Palooka. **1947** The Shocking Miss Pilgrim; Stork Bites Man. **1948** Force of Evil; A Foreign Affair; Joe Palooka in Winner Take All; You Gotta Stay Happy. **1949** The Lady Takes a Sailor; Deadly as the Female. **1950** Joe Palooka in the Squared Circle; Gun Crazy.

PRAGER, WILLY
Born: 1877, Germany. Died: Mar. 4, 1956, West Germany. Stage and screen actor.

Appeared in: **1931** Der Grosse Tenor. **1948** Marriage in Shadows.

PRATA, JOAQUIM
Born: 1882. Died: Nov. 18, 1953, Lisbon, Portugal. Screen, stage actor and playwright.

PRATHER, LEE (Oscar Lee Prather)
Born: 1890. Died: Jan. 3, 1958, Los Angeles, Calif. (during surgery). Screen and stage actor.

Appeared in: **1935** Hot Money (short). **1938** The Buccaneer; Women in Prison. **1939** Homicide Bureau. **1942** Tennessee Johnson.

PRATT, DENNIS See KING, DENNIS

PRATT, GILBERT "GIL" (Gilbert Walker Pratt)
Born: 1891 or 1892, Providence, R.I. Died: Dec., 1954, Hollywood, Calif. Screen actor, film director and screenwriter. Appeared in Rolin Film Co. films.

PRATT, JACK
Born: 1878, St. John's, New Brunswick, Canada. Died: Dec. 24, 1938, Los Angeles, Calif. Screen actor and film director.

Appeared in: **1921** Hush. **1922** Back to Yellow Jacket; The Lone Hand; The Price of Youth; Night Life in Hollywood. **1924** Daring Chances; The Western Wallop; Ace of Spades (serial). **1925** The Red Rider; Ridin' Thunder; The Sign of the Cactus; A Roaring Adventure. **1926** The Wild Horse Stampede. **1927** Hawk of the Hills (serial); Rough and Ready; The Western Whirlwind; Wild Beauty. **1928** A Made-to-Order Hero. **1929** Hawk of the Hills (feature); The Desert Song.

PRATT, LYNN
Born: Jan. 18, 1863, Sylvan Center, Mich. Died: Jan. 9, 1930, New York. Screen, stage and vaudeville actor.

Appeared in: **1921** A Virgin Paradise.

PRATT, NEIL
Born: 1890, San Diego, Calif. Died: Jan. 3, 1934, Hollywood, Calif. (heart attack). Stage and screen actor. Entered films approx. 1933.

Appeared in: **1934** Trimmed in Furs (short).

PRATT, PURNELL B.
Born: Oct. 20, 1886, Bethel, Ill. Died: July 25, 1941, Hollywood, Calif. Stage and screen actor.

Appeared in: **1925** The Lady Who Lied. **1926** Midnight Lovers. **1929** The Trespasser; Through Different Eyes; Fast Life; Is Everybody Happy?; Alibi; On With the Show. **1930** Painted Faces; The Furies; Road to Paradise; Common Clay; Sinner's Holiday; Lawful Larceny; The Silver Horde; The Locked Door; Puttin' on the Ritz. **1931** The Public Enemy; The Gorilla; The Road to Romance; Fires of Youth; Five Star Final; Woman Pursued; The Secret Witness; The Public Defender; The Spider; Terror by Night; The Gay Diplomat; Beyond Victory; Paid; The Prodigal; Dance, Fools, Dance; Up for Murder; Bachelor Apartments; Traveling Husbands. **1932** Hat Check Girl; Red Haired Alibi; False Faces; Unwritten Law; The Famous Ferguson Case; Roadhouse Murder; Grand Hotel; Scarface; Ladies of the Big House; Emma. **1933** Mystery Squadron (serial); The Billion Dollar Scandal; Pick Up; A Shriek in the Night; Headline Shooter; I Cover the Waterfront; Midshipman Jack; The Sweetheart of Sigma Chi; Love, Honor and Oh, Baby; The Chief; Son of a Sailor. **1934** Name the Woman; The Crimson Romance; School for Girls; The Witching Hour; Midnight Alibi; The Hell Cat. **1935** Secret Bride; Death Flies East; Black Fury; The Winning Ticket; The Casino Murder Case; It's in the Air; Behind the Green Lights; Ladies Crave Excitement; Waterfront Lady; Diamond Jim; Red Salute; $1,000 a Minute; Frisco Waterfront; Rendezvous at Midnight; A Night at the Opera; Magnificent Obsession. **1936** Dancing Feet; The Return of Sophie Lang; Hollywood Boulevard; Straight from the Shoulder; Lady Be Careful; Murder With Pictures; Wives Never Know; Wedding Present; The Plainsman. **1937** Join the Marines; Let's Make a Million; Murder Goes to College; King of Gamblers; A Night of Mystery; Under Suspicion; High, Wide and Handsome. **1938** Come On, Rangers!. **1939** Irving Berlin's Second Fiddle (short); My Wife's Relatives; Grand Ole Opry; Colorado Sunset. **1941** Doctors Don't Tell; Ringside Maisie; Life Begins for Andy Hardy.

PRAXY, RAOUL
Born: 1892. Died: June 28, 1967. Screen actor.

PRAY, ANNA M.
Born: 1891. Died: June 30, 1971, N.Y. Stage and screen actress. Married to stage actor Fleming Ward (dec.).

PREER, EVELYN
Born: July 26, 1896, Vicksburg, Miss. Died: Nov. 18, 1932, Los Angeles, Calif. (pneumonia). Black screen, stage and vaudeville actress.

Appeared in: **1918** The Homesteader. **1920** The Brute; Within our Gates. **1921** Deceit; The Gunsaulus Mystery. **1922** The Hypocrite; The Homesteader (rerelease of 1918 film). **1924** Birthright. **1926** The Conjur Woman; The Devil's Disciple; The Spider's Web. **1929** Melancholy Dame. **1930** Georgia Rose. **1932** Blonde Venus.

PREISSER, CHERRY
Born: 1918. Died: July 12, 1964, Sydney, Australia. Screen, stage actress and dancer. Sister of actress June Preisser with whom she appeared on stage.

PREJEAN, ALBERT
Born: 1894, France. Died: Nov. 1, 1979, Paris, France. Screen actor and stuntman.

Appeared in: **1921** The Three Musketeers. **1924** Miracle of the Wolves; Paris Qui Dort. **1925** Fantome Du Moulin Rouge. **1926** Le Voyage Imaginaire. **1927** An Italian Straw Hat. **1928** Les Nouveaux Messieurs. **1930** Sous Les Toits de Paris; Three-Penny Opera. **1931** The Horse Ate the Hat; Die Dreigroschenoper (aka L'Opera de Quat'Sous—1933). **1933** Theodore et Cie (Theodore & Co.). **1934** Paquebot Tenacity. **1935** La Crise Est Finie. **1936** Jenny. **1939** L'Alibi. **1940** Metropolitain. **1941** Hatred. **1943** L'Etrange Suzy. **1947** Au Bonheur de Dames (Shop-Girls of Paris); Les Freres Bouquinquant. **1949** Les Nouveaux Maitres. **1954** Les Amants Du Tage. **1962** Bonne Chance Charlie! (Good Luck Charlie!).

PRENTIS, LEWIS R.
Born: 1905. Died: June 26, 1967, Chicago, Ill. Screen and stage actor.

PRENTISS, ELEANOR
Born: 1912. Died: Aug. 14, 1979, New York, N.Y. Screen, stage actress, writer and model.

Appeared in: **1936** Collegiates (film debut). **1937** I Met Him in Paris; Thin Ice; Rosalie.

PRESCOTT, ALLEN
Born: 1904. Died: Jan. 27, 1978. Screen and radio actor.

Appeared in: **1950** Golden Twenties.

PRESLEY, ELVIS (Elvis Aaron Presley)
Born: Jan. 8, 1935, Tupelo, Miss. Died: Aug. 16, 1977, Memphis, Tenn. (heart disease). Screen, television actor, musician and singer. Son of singer/screen extra Gladys (dec. 1958), and Vernon Presley (dec.). Divorced from model Priscilla Beaulieu.

Appeared in: **1956** Love Me Tender (film debut). **1957** Jailhouse Rock; Loving You. **1958** King Creole. **1960** G.I. Blues; Flaming Star. **1961** Wild in the Country; Blue Hawaii. **1962** Kid Galahad; Girls! Girls! Girls!; Follow That Dream. **1963** Fun in Acapulco; It Happened at the World's Fair. **1964** Kissin' Cousins; Viva Las Vegas; Roustabout. **1965** Girl Happy; Tickle Me; Harum-Scarum. **1966** Spinout. **1967** Easy Come, Easy Go; Double Trouble; Clambake. **1968** Stay Away, Joe; Speedway; Live a Little, Love a Little. **1969** Frankie and Johnny; Paradise, Hawaiian Style; Charro; Trouble With Girls; Change of Habit. **1970** Elvis—That's the Way It Is (documentary). **1972** Elvis on Tour (documentary).

PRESLEY, GLADYS
Born: 1912. Died: Aug. 14, 1958, Memphis, Tenn. (heart attack). Screen extra and singer. Mother of actor/singer Elvis Presley (dec. 1977).

Appeared in: **1957** Loving You.

PRESS, MARVIN
Born: Oct. 20, 1915, Conn. Died: Mar. 17, 1968, Los Angeles, Calif. (suicide—gas asphyxiation and barbiturates). Screen actor.

Appeared in: **1952** Sea Tiger; The Treasure of Lost Canyon. **1955** Mexican Manhunt; Dragon's Gold.

PRESTON, EDNA
Born: 1892. Died: Aug. 18, 1960, New York. Screen, stage, radio and television actress.

PRETTY, ARLINE
Born: Sept. 5, 1893, Washington, D.C. Died: Apr. 14, 1978, Hollywood, Calif. Screen and stage actress.

Appeared in: **1915** The Suprise of an Empty Hotel. **1916** The Dawn of Freedom. **1917** The Secret Kingdom (serial); In Again—Out Again; The Hidden Hand (serial). **1920** The Valley of Doubt. **1922** Between Two Husbands; Love in the Dark; The Wages of Sin; When the Devil Drives. **1923** Bucking the Barrier; Rouged Lips; Stormswept; Tipped Off; The White Flower. **1924** A Fool's Awakening; The Girl on the Stairs. **1925** Barriers Burned Away; The Primrose Path. **1928** Virgin Lips.

PREVIN, CHARLES
Born: 1887, Brooklyn, N.Y. Died: Sept 22, 1973, Hollywood, Calif. Screen actor, film director and composer.

Appeared in: **1940** A Little Bit of Heaven.

PREVOST, FRANK G.
Born: 1894. Died: Apr. 17, 1946, Hollywood, Calif. Screen actor.

PREVOST, MARIE (Marie Bickford Dunn)
Born: Nov. 8, 1898, Sarnia, Canada. Died: Jan. 21, 1937, Los Angeles, Calif. Screen actress. Was an early Sennett bathing beauty. Divorced from H. B. "Sonny" Gerke and actor Kenneth Harlan (dec. 1967). Sister of actress Marjorie "Peg" Prevost.

Appeared in: **1917** Her Nature Dance; Secrets of a Beauty Parlor; Two Crooks (aka A Noble Crook). **1918** His Hidden Purpose; His Smothered Love; Sleuths; Hide and Seek; Detectives; The Village Chestnut; She Loved Him Plenty. **1919** Never Too Old; Rip and Stitch; Tailors; East Lynne with Variations; Reilly's Wash Day; When Love is Blind; Love's False Faces; Yankee Doodle in Berlin; Why Beaches are Popular; Uncle Tom without the Cabin; The Dentist; Up in Alf's Place; Salome vs. Shenandoah; The Speak Easy. **1920** Down on the Farm; His Youthful Fancy (short); Fickle Fancy (short); Love, Honor and Behave; Divorce Made Easy. **1921** Kissed; A Small Town Idol; Moonlight Follies; Nobody's Fool; A Parisian Scandal; plus the following shorts: On a Summer's Day; She Sighed by the Seaside; Call a Cop. **1922** The Beautiful and the Damned; Don't Get Personal; The Dangerous Little Demon; Her Night of Nights; The Married Flapper. **1923** Red Lights; Heroes of the Street; The Wanters. **1924** Tarnish; The Marriage Circle; Three Women; The Dark Swan; Being Respectable; Daughters of Pleasure; How to Educate Your Wife; Cornered; The Lover of Camille; The Hollywood Kid (short). **1925** Bobbed Hair; Kiss Me Again; Recompense; Seven Sinners. **1926** Up in Mabel's Room; Almost a Lady; The Caveman; His Jazz Bride; Other Women's Husbands. **1927** For Wives Only; Man Bait; Getting Gertie's Garter; The Night Bride; The Girl in the Pullman. **1928** The Rush Hour; On to Reno; A Blonde for a Night; The Racket. **1929** The Godless Girl; The Flying Fool; Side Show; Divorce Made Easy. **1930** Ladies of Leisure; Party Girl; War Nurse; Sweethearts on Parade; Paid (aka Within the Law). **1931** The Sin of Madelon Claudet (aka The Lullaby); The Easiest Way; The Good Bad Girl; Reckless Living; Sporting Blood; A Gentleman's Fate; It's a Wise Child; The Runaround; Hell Divers. **1932** Three Wise Girls; Carnival Boat; Slightly Married. **1933** Parole Girl; Only Yesterday; The 11th Commandment; Pick Me Up (short); Hesitating Love (short); a Universal short. **1935** Hands Across the Table; a Vitaphone short. **1936** Tango; Cain and Mabel; 13 Hours by Air.

PRICE, ALONZO
Born: 1888. Died: June 5, 1962. Screen actor.

Appeared in: **1936** Forgotten Faces; Foolproof (short). **1937** Black Legion; Slim. **1938** Marie Antoinette; Forbidden Valley. **1939** Weather Wizards (short).

PRICE, DENNIS (Dennistoun Franklyn John Rose-Price)
Born: June 23, 1915, Twyford, England. Died: Oct. 7, 1973, Guernsey, Channel Islands. Screen, stage, radio and television actor. Married to actress Joan Schofield.

Appeared in: **1944** A Canterbury Tale; A Place of One's Own (US 1949). **1945** The Echo Murders. **1946** The Magic Bow (US 1947); Caravan (US 1947). **1947** Hungry Hill; Master of Bankdam (US 1949); The White Unicorn (aka Bad Sister—US 1949); Jassy (US 1948); Holiday Camp (US 1948); Dear Murderer (US 1948). **1948** Good Time Girl (US 1950); Easy Money (US 1949); Snowbound (US 1949). **1949** The Bad Lord Byron (US 1952); Kind Hearts and Coronets (US 1950); The Lost People; Helter Skelter. **1950** The Dancing Years; Murder Without Crime (US 1951). **1951** The Adventurers (aka The Great Adventure—US); The House in the Square (aka I'll Never Forget You—US); The Magic Box (US 1952); Lady Godiva Rides Again (US 1954). **1952** Song of Paris (aka Bachelor in Paris—US 1953); Tall Headlines (aka The Frightened Bride—US 1953). **1953** The Intruder (US 1955); Noose for a Lady; Murder at 3 a.m. **1954** For Better, For Worse (aka Cocktails in the Kitchen—US 1955); Time is My Enemy (US 1957). **1955** Oh, Rosalinda; That Lady. **1956** Private's Progress; Port Afrique; Charley Moon; A Touch of the Sun. **1957** The Tommy Steele Story (aka Rock Around the World—US); The Naked Truth (aka Your Past Is Showing—US 1958); Fortune Is a Woman (aka She Played With Fire—US 1958). **1958** Hello London. **1959** I'm All Right, Jack (US 1960); Danger Within (aka Breakout—US 1960); Don't Panic Chaps!. **1960** Oscar Wilde; School for Scoundrels; Tunes of Glory; The Millionairess (US 1961); The Pure Hell of St. Trinian's (US 1961); Piccadilly Third Stop (US 1968). **1961** What a Carve Up! (US 1962 and aka No Place Like Homicide); Five Golden Hours; Double Bunk; No Love for Johnnie; Victim (US 1962); The Rebel (aka Call Me Genius—US); Watch It Sailor!. **1962** Behave Yourself (short); Kill or Cure; Play It Cool (US 1963); The Wrong Arm of the Law (US 1963); The Amorous Prawn (aka The Playgirl and the War Minister—US 1963); Go to Blazes; The Pot Carriers. **1963** The V.I.P.'s; The Cracksman; A Jolly Bad Fellow (aka They All Died Laughing—US 1964); Doctor in Distress (US 1964); Tamahine (US 1964); The

Comedy Man; The Cool Mikado. **1964** The Horror of It All; The Earth Dies Screaming. **1965** Murder Most Foul; A High Wind in Jamaica; Curse of Simba (aka Curse of the Voodoo—US). **1966** Ten Little Indians; Just Like a Woman. **1967** Jules Verne's Rocket to the Moon (aka Those Fantastic Flying Fools—US and aka Blast Off—US). **1969** The Magic Christian (US 1970); The Haunted House of Horror (aka Horror House—US 1970). **1970** Some Will, Some Won't; The Horror of Frankenstein; Venus in Furs; The Rise and Rise of Michael Rimmer. **1971** Twins of Evil. **1972** Pulp; The Adventure of Barry Mackenzie; Tower of Evil; Alice's Adventures in Wonderland; Go for a Take. **1973** That's Your Funeral; Horrow Hospital; Theatre of Blood.

PRICE, EDWARD
Born: May 18, 1927, Los Angeles, Calif. Died: Sept. 27, 1980, Atlanta, Ga. Screen actor. Brother of actor Vincent Price.

Appeared in: **1936** Smartest Girl in Town. **1937** The Go Getter; That Girl from Paris.

PRICE, GEORGIE (George E. Price)
Born: 1900. Died: May 10, 1964, New York, N.Y. (heart attack). Screen, vaudeville actor and singer.

Appeared in: **1929** Don't Get Nervous (short). **1930** Metro Movietone short.

PRICE, HAL
Born: June 14, 1886, Waukegon, Ohio. Died: Apr. 15, 1964. Screen actor. Married to actress Amy Goodrich (dec. 1939).

Appeared in: **1930** Night Ride; Party Girl. **1931** City Streets. **1932** Sin's Pay Day; Lady and Gent; The Last Man; Widow in Scarlet; This Sporting Age. **1933** Tugboat Annie; The Girl in 419; Ranger's Code. **1934** Cleopatra; Hell Bent for Love. **1936** Just My Luck; The Desert Phantom; Navy Born; The Fugitive Sheriff; Cavalry. **1937** Public Cowboy No. 1; Trouble in Texas; Melody of the Plains; Stars Over Arizona. **1938** Code of the Rangers; Call the Mesquiteers; Pioneer Trail. **1939** South of the Border; In Old Monterey; Across the Plains; Home on the Prairie; Overland Mail; New Frontier. **1940** Mad Youth; Frontier Crusader; Out West with the Peppers; Arizona Frontier; Lone Star Raiders; Jack Pot (short). **1941** The Iron Claw (serial); Billy the Kid's Fighting Pals; Devil Bat; Arizona Bound; Gangs of Sonora; Jungle Man; Secrets of the Wasteland; The Lone Rider Ambush; The Singing Hill; Sierra Sue. **1942** Raiders of the Range; Home in Wyomin'; Law and Order; War Dogs; Cowboy Serenade; Not a Ladies' Man. **1943** Two-Fisted Justice; My Son the Hero; Dead Men Walk; Fugitive of the Plains; Robin Hood of the Range; The Blocked Trail. **1944** Wyoming Hurricane; West of the Rio Grande; Outlaw Trail; Mohave Firebrand; Law of the Valley; Westward Bound; Rustler's Hideout; Fuzzy Settles Down; Oath of the Vengeance; Wild Horse Phantom. **1945** Law of the Valley. **1947** Raiders of Red Rock; Frontier Fighters. **1950** Tarnished; Father Makes Good; Frisco Tornado. **1952** Junction City. **1963** How the West Was Won.

PRICE, KATE (Kate Duffy)
Born: Feb. 13, 1872, Cork, Ireland. Died: Jan. 4, 1943, Woodland Hills, Calif. Screen, stage and vaudeville actress.

Appeared in: **1912** Stenographers Wanted; The Love Sick Maidens of Cuddleton; The Bond of Music. **1913** Papa Papa Puts One Over; Her Sweetest Memory. **1914** Lily of the Valley. **1916** The Waiter's Ball. **1918** The Seal of Silence; Arizona. **1919** The Perils of Thunder Mountain (serial). **1920** Dinty. **1921** God's Crucible; The Girl Montana; Little Lord Fauntleroy; The Other Woman. **1922** My Wife's Relations (short); Come On Over; Flesh and Blood; A Dangerous Game; Paid Back; The New Teacher; The Guttersnipe. **1923** Broken Hearts of Broadway; Goodbye Girls; The Spoilers; Crossed Wires; The Dangerous Maid; Enemies of Children; Her Fatal Millions; The Near Lady. **1924** Fool's Highway; Riders Up; The Tornado; Wife of the Centaur; Passion's Pathway; The Sea Hawk. **1925** The Desert Flower; The Man Without a Conscience; The Way of a Girl; The Sporting Venus; His People; The Perfect Clown; Sally, Irene and Mary; Proud Heart. **1926** Irene; The Cohens and the Kellys; The Arizona Sweepstakes; Faithful Wives; Paradise; Love's Blindness; Memory Lane. **1927** Frisco Sally Levy; The Third Degree; Casey Jones; Mountains of Manhattan; Orchids and Ermine; The Sea Tigers; Quality Street. **1928** Show Girl; The Cohens and the Kellys in Paris; Mad Hour; Thanks for the Buggy Ride. **1929** Has Anybody Here Seen Kelly?; The Godless Girl; Paradise; Two Weeks Off; Cohens and Kellys in Atlantic City. **1930** Cohens and the Kellys in Scotland; Dancing Sweeties; The Rogue Song; Shadow Ranch; The Cohens and the Kellys in Africa. **1932** Ladies of the Jury. **1934** Have a Heart. **1936** Great Guy. **1937** Easy Living.

PRICE, MARK
Born: Ireland. Died: Mar. 31, 1917, New York, N.Y. Screen actor.

Appeared in: **1916** A Daughter of the Gods.

PRICE, NANCY (Lillian Nancy Maude)

Born: Feb. 3, 1880, Kinver, Staffs, England. Died: Mar. 31, 1970, Worthing, England. Screen, stage actress and author. Married to actor Charles Maude (dec. 1943). Do not confuse with actress Nancy Price born in 1918.

Appeared in: **1916** The Lyons Mail. **1921** Belphegor the Mountebank. **1923** Bonnie Prince Charlie; Comin' Thro' the Rye; Love, Life and Laughter (aka Tip Toes); The Woman Who Obeyed. **1927** Huntingtower. **1928** His House in Order; The Price of Divorce. **1929** The American Prisoner. **1930** The Loves of Robert Burns. **1931** The Speckled Band. **1932** Down Our Street. **1934** The Crucifix. **1939** The Stars Look Down (US 1941); Dead Man's Shoes. **1942** Secret Mission. **1944** Madonna of the Seven Moons. **1945** I Live in Grosvenor Square (aka A Yank in London—US 1946); I Know Where I'm Going (US 1947). **1946** Carnival. **1947** Master of Bankdam (US 1949). **1948** The Three Weird Sisters. **1950** The Naked Earth. **1952** Mandy (aka Crash of Silence—US 1953). **1955** The Naked Heart.

PRICE, STANLEY L.

Born: 1900. Died: July 13, 1955, Hollywood, Calif. (heart attack). Screen, stage actor and screenwriter.

Appeared in: **1922** Your Best Friend. **1934** It Happened One Day (short); 1935 Okay Toots! (short); The Miracle Rider (serial). **1938** Red Barry (serial); Hunted Men; Tom Sawyer, Detective. **1939** Sudden Money; Undercover Doctor. **1940** Seventeen; The Way of All Flesh; Moon Over Burma; The Golden Trail. **1941** Sky Raiders (serial); Adventures of Captain Marvel (serial). **1942** Outlaws of Pine Ridge; The Great Commandments; Tennessee Johnson. **1943** Lone Rider in Wild Horse Rustlers. **1944** Bride by Mistake; Zorro's Black Whip (serial); Range Law; The Tiger Woman (serial). **1945** The Monster and the Ape (serial); Phantom of 42nd Street; Lost Weekend; Crime, Inc.; Power of the Whistler. **1946** The Crimson Ghost (serial); Nick Carter, Detective. **1947** Son of Zorro (serial). **1948** G-Men Never Forget (serial). **1949** King of the Rocket Men (serial). **1950** The Invisible Monster (serial); Pirates of the High Seas (serial); Kim; Gambling House; Studio Stoops (short); The Sundowners; Dopey Dicks (short). **1951** Hills of Utah. **1956** The Ten Commandments.

PRICKETT, MAUDIE

Born: 1915. Died: Apr. 14, 1976, Pasadena, Calif. (uremic poisoning). Screen, stage and television actress.

Appeared in: **1938** Gold Mine in the Sky. **1946** The Fighting Frontiersman; Two-Fisted Stranger. **1948** Eight-Ball Andy (short); Song of Idaho. **1949** Slattery's Hurricane; The Cowboy and the Indians; Abandoned (aka Abandoned Woman); One Sunday Afternoon (aka The Strawberry Blonde). **1950** Beyond the Purple Hills; Messenger of Peace. **1951** The Model and the Marriage Broker; Pecos River; Her First Romance. **1952** Lost in Alaska; Stars and Stripes Forever; Wait Till the Sun Shines Nellie. **1955** A Man Called Peter; Man With the Gun. **1956** Andy Goes Wild (short). **1957** The Phantom Stagecoach. **1958** Thundering Jets. **1959** The Legend of Tom Dooley; North by Northwest. **1965** I'll Take Sweden. **1967** The Gnome-Mobile; The Rascal. **1969** Sweet Charity; The Maltese Bippy.

PRIETO, ANTONIO

Born: 1915, Portugal. Died: Mar. 3, 1965, Madrid, Spain (heart attack). Screen, stage and television actor.

Appeared in: **1964** Los Tarantos. **1967** A Fistful of Dollars.

PRIMA, LOUIS

Born: Dec. 7, 1911, New Orleans, La. Died: Aug. 24, 1978, New Orleans, La. (pneumonia). Musician, bandleader, composer, screen, radio and television actor. Divorced from Toni Elizabeth, Luanne Frances, and singer Keely Smith. Later married to singer Gia Malone.

Appeared in: **1937** You Can't Have Everything. **1938** Start Cheering. **1939** Rose of Washington Square. **1958** Senior Prom. **1959** Hey Boy, Hey Girl! **1961** Twist All Night. **1967** The Jungle Book (voice). **1975** Rafferty and the Gold Dust Twins.

PRINCE, ARTHUR

Born: Nov. 17, 1881, London, England. Died: Apr. 14, 1948, London, England. Screen, stage, vaudeville actor and ventriloquist.

Appeared in: **1926** Fake Spiritualism Exposed.

PRINCE, JOHN T.

Born: Sept. 11, 1871, Boston, Mass. Died: Dec. 24, 1937, Los Angeles, Calif. Screen and stage actor.

Appeared in: **1913** Mission Bells. **1916** Phantom Island. **1917** Over There. **1922** Doctor Jack; Little Eva Ascends. **1923** East Side, West Side. **1924** The Battling Orioles; Defying the Law. **1925** Capital Punishment; Heartless Husbands; The Call of Courage; Women and Gold; The Gold Hunters. **1926** Jack O'Hearts; Money to Burn; The Phantom Bullet; Dame Chance; Prowlers of the Night; The Radio Detective (serial). **1927** King of Kings; Hawk of the Hills (serial). **1928** Ramona; Haunted Island (serial). **1929** Hawk of the Hills (feature of 1927 serial). **1936** The Country Beyond.

PRINCE RANDIAN (Prince Randion)

Born: c. 1871, British Guiana. Died: c. 1934, New York, N.Y. Screen actor and circus performer.

Appeared in: **1932** Freaks.

PRINCE RIGADIA (Charles Petit-Demance)

Born: 1872, France. Died: July 17, 1933, La Vanenna, France. Screen actor.

PRINCESS INDIRA

Born: 1912, Ibiza, India. Died: Oct., 1979, India. Screen, stage, radio actress and correspondent.

PRINCESS KANZA OMAR

Born: 1912. Died: Mar. 6, 1958, Los Angeles, Calif. (cancer). Screen actress and dancer.

Appeared in: **1938** The Buccaneer.

PRINCESS LIVINGSTON

Died: Oct. 9, 1976. Screen actress.

Appeared in: **1965** Rope of Flesh (aka Mud Honey and Mudhoney!). **1970** Beyond the Valley of the Dolls; Pufnstuf.

PRINGLE, JOHN

Died: 1929. Stage and screen actor. Father of actor John Gilbert (dec. 1936).

Appeared in: **1924** Black Lightning; Travelin' Fast. **1925** His Greatest Battle.

PRINGREE, EARL M. See PINGREE, EARL M.

PRINTEMPS, YVONNE (Yvonne Wigniolle)

Born: July 25, 1895, Ermont, Seine-et-Oise, France. Died: Jan. 18, 1977, Paris, France. Screen, stage and opera singer. Divorced from actor Sacha Guitry (dec. 1957), and later married to actor Pierre Fresnay (dec. 1975).

Appeared in: **1934** La Dame aux Camelias (US 1935). **1938** Adrienne Lecouvreur; Les Trois Valses (Three Waltzes—US 1939). **1939** Le Duel. **1943** Je Suis Avec Toi. **1948** Les Condamnes. **1949** Le Valse de Paris (The Paris Waltz—US 1950). **1951** Le Voyage en America (Voyage to America—US 1952).

PRIOR, HERBERT (aka HERBERT PRYOR)

Born: July 2, 1867, Oxford, England. Died: Oct. 3, 1954. Screen and stage actor. Married to actress Mabel Trunnelle.

Appeared in: **1909** The Cricket on the Hearth; Tis an Ill Wind That Blows No Good. **1911** Spare the Rod; At the Point of the Sword; His Stepmother; The Best Man Wins; The Unwilling Bigamist; Leap Year; The Eternal Masculine; Next!; Papa's Double; The Flat Upstairs; The Lost Messenger; The Butterfly; Mary's Chauffeur; Thorns of Success; The Diputed Claim; Willie's Dog; Little Music Teacher; All for Jim; The Winner and the Spoils; A Garrison Joke; The Call of the Blood; A Game of Chess; The Sign of the Three Labels; A Romance of the Cliff-Dwellers. **1912** The Risen Soul of Jim Grant; Captain Ben's Yarn; The Three Imps; Rough on Rats; The Capture of Fort Ticonderoga; The Younger Brother; Christian and Moor; The Switchman's Tower; The Spirit of the Gorge; The Venom of the Poppy; Al Jones' Ferry; Under the Tropical Sun; The Battle of Trafalgar; The Sailor's Love Letter; The Big Dam; Leaves of a Romance; Three of a Kind; The Doctor; A Perilous Ride; The Quarrel of the Cliff; Buckskin Jack, the Earl of Gilmore; The Actress; Keeping Mabel Home. **1913** How They Got the Vote; Othello in Jonesville; How Did it Finish?; Scenes from Other Days; Jones Goes Shopping; The Unprofitable Boarder; How They Outwitted Father; The Ranch Owner's Love Making; A Perilous Cargo; The Phantom Ship; Jan Vedder's Daughter; The Lost Deed. **1914** The Sultan and the Rollerskates; A Tale of Old Tucson; The Mexican's Gratitude; A Romance of the Everglades; The Two Vanrevels; Bottle's Baby; In the Shadow of Disgrace; In Lieu of Damages; Farmer Rodney's Daughter; The One Who Loved Him Best; Twins and Trouble; On the Lazy Line. **1915** An Unwilling Thief; Snap Shots; The Newly Rich; A Pipe Dream; Olive's Manufactured Mother; The Family Bible; Mr. Daly's Wedding Day; Olive and the Heirloom;

Not Wanted; The Test; The Struggle Upward; Cartoons in the Kitchen; Breaking the Shackles; The Truth About Helen. **1916** A Message to Garcia; Helen of the Chorus; Miss George Washington; The Southerner. **1917** The Poor Little Rich Girl; Great Expectations; The Last Sentence. **1918** The Menace; Society for Sale; After the War; A Burglar for a Night; The Model's Confession. **1919** That's Good; After Your Own Heart; You're Fired; Creaking Stairs; The Love Hunger. **1920** The House of Whispers; Little 'Fraid Lady; Stronger Than Death; Pollyanna. **1921** Garments of Truth; Not Guilty; Made in Heaven; Without Benefit of Clergy. **1922** The Dangerous Little Demon; The Man from Downing Street; The Snowshoe Trail; The Half Breed. **1923** Garrison's Finish; Slave of Desire; Little Johnny Jones. **1924** Madonna of the Streets. **1925** The Fighting Demon; The Taming of the West; Tearing Through; The Wild Bull's Lair; Waking Up the Town. **1926** Across the Pacific; Why Girls Go Back Home; The Better Man; Doubling with Danger; The Midnight Kiss; Rustling for Cupid. **1927** The Last Outlaw; The King of Kings. **1929** All At Sea; The Duke Steps Out; The Winged Horseman; The Ace of Scotland Yard (serial). **1930** Caught Short.

PROCTER, IVIS GOULDING

Born: 1906. Died: May 14, 1973, Hollywood, Calif. (heart attack). Screen actress. Sister of film director Edmund Goulding (dec. 1959).

Appeared in: **1952** Plymouth Adventure. **1953** Botany Bay; How to Marry a Millionaire. **1955** The Rains of Ranchipur.

PROCTER, JESSIE OLIVE

Born: 1874. Died: July 6, 1975, Woodland Hills, Calif. (heart failure). Screen actress. Entered films as an extra in the 1930s.

Appeared in: **1962** Music Man.

PROHASKA, JANOS

Born: 1921, Hungary. Died: Mar. 13, 1974, Inyo County, Calif. (plane crash). Screen and television actor and stuntman. Father of actor Robert Prohaska (dec. 1974).

Appeared in: **1962** Jumbo. **1964** Bikini Beach. **1968** Planet of the Apes. **1970** Pussycat, Pussycat, I Love You. **1974** Zandy's Bride.

PROHASKA, ROBERT

Died: Mar. 13, 1974, Inyo County, Calif. (plane crash). Screen and television actor. Son of actor Janos Prohaska (dec. 1974 in same accident).

PROMIS, FLO

Born: 1884. Died: Apr. 23, 1956, Hollywood, Calif. Screen actress.

Appeared in: **1936** Ants in the Pantry (short).

PROSSER, HUGH

Born: 1906. Died: Nov. 8, 1952, near Gallup, N.Mex. (auto accident). Screen actor.

Appeared in: **1938** Blockade. **1939** Flying G-Men (serial). **1941** Sierra Sue; West of Cimarron. **1942** The Boss of Hangtown Mesa; Sabotage Squad. **1943** Border Patrol; Riders of the Deadline; Lost Canyon. **1945** Flame of the Barbary Coast; Dillinger. **1946** People Are Funny; The Phantom Rider; Son of the Guardsman (serial). **1947** Jack Armstrong (serial); The Sea Hound (serial); The Vigilante (serial). **1948** Congo Bill (serial). **1949** Western Renegades; Adventures of Sir Galahad (serial); Bruce Gentry—Daredevil of the Skies (serial). **1950** Outlaw Gold; Pirates of the High Seas (serial); Across the Badlands. **1951** Montana Incident; Mysterious Island (serial); Roar of the Iron Horse (serial). **1952** Guns Along the Border; The Greatest Show on Earth; Treasure of Lost Canyon; Bend of the River.

PROUTY, JED

Born: Apr. 6, 1879, Boston, Mass. Died: May 10, 1956, New York. Screen, stage, radio, television and vaudeville actor. At age sixteen he formed a vaudeville act known as "Maddux and Prouty."

Appeared in: **1921** The Conquest of Canaan; Experience; Room and Board; The Great Adventure. **1922** Kick In. **1923** The Girl of the Golden West; Souls for Sale; The Gold Diggers. **1925** The Coast of Folly; Scarlet Saint; The Knockout; The Unguarded Hour. **1926** Bred in Old Kentucky; Don Juan's Three Nights; Miss Nobody; Unknown Treasures; Ella Cinders; Everybody's Acting; Her Second Chance; The Mystery Club. **1927** Smile, Brother, Smile; Orchids and Ermine; The Gingham Girl; No Place to Go. **1928** Domestic Meddlers; Name the Woman; The Siren. **1929** Imperfect Ladies; The Fall of Eve; His Captive Woman; Two Weeks Off; It's a Great Life; Why Leave Home?; Sonny Boy; The Broadway Melody. **1930** True to the Navy; No Questions Asked (short); The Floradora Girl; Girl in the Show; The Devil's Holiday. **1931** Strangers May Kiss; Annabelle's Affairs; The

Secret Call; The Age for Love. **1932** The Brides Bereavement, or Snake in the Garden (short); Business and Pleasure; Manhattan Tower. **1933** Skyway; The Big Bluff; Jimmy and Sally. **1934** I Believed in You; Music in the Air; Private Scandal; One Hour Late; Hollywood Party. **1935** George White's 1935 Scandals; Black Sheep; Navy Wife; One Hour Late; A Trip to Paris. **1936** Every Saturday Night; Little Miss Nobody; Educating Father; Back to Nature; Can This Be Dixie?; Under Your Spell; Special Investigator; His Brother's Wife; The Texas Rangers; College Holiday; Happy Go Lucky. **1937** Borrowing Trouble; Off to the Races; Big Business; Hot Water; Life Begins in College; The Crime Nobody Saw; Sophie Lang Goes West; Dangerous Holiday; One Hundred Men and a Girl; Small Town Boy; You Can't Have Everything. **1938** Love on a Budget; Walking Down Broadway; A Trip to Paris; Keep Smiling; Safety in Numbers; Duke of West Point; Goodbye Broadway; Danger on the Air; Down on the Farm. **1939** Everybody's Baby; The Jones Family in Hollywood; Too Busy to Work; The Gracie Allen Murder Case; Second Fiddle; The Jones Family in Grand Canyon; Coat Tales (short); The Jones Family in Quick Millions; Hollywood Cavalcade; Exile Express. **1940** Young As You Feel; On Their Own; Barnyard Follies; Remedy for Riches. **1941** The Lone Wolf Keeps a Date; Pot O' Gold; Father Steps Out; Bachelor Daddy; Unexpected Uncle; City Limits; Look Who's Laughing; Go West Young Lady; Roar of the Press. **1942** The Affairs of Jimmy Valentine; Hold 'Em Jail (short); Scattergood Rides High; It Happened in Flatbush; Moonlight Masquerade; The Old Homestead; Mud Town. **1950** Guilty Bystander.

PROVOST, JEANNE

Born: 1887, France. Died: Nov. 24, 1980, Meaux, France. Screen and stage actress.

Appeared in: **1939** Katia.

PROWSE, PETER

Born: 1924, South Africa. Died: Dec., 1976, South Africa. Screen actor and film director.

Appeared in: **1950** Destination Big House. **1955** I Am a Camera. **1957** Not Wanted on Voyage. **1958** Count Five and Die. **1963** The Informers (aka Underworld Informers—US 1964); Lancelot and Guinevere (aka The Sword of Lancelot—US). **1964** The Christine Keeler Affair (aka The Keeler Affair and Scandal '64). **1964** Becket. **1976** The Man Who Fell to Earth.

"PRUDENCE PENNY" (Norma Young)

Born: 1889. Died: Mar. 28, 1974. Screen and radio actress.

Appeared in: **1937** Penny Wisdom (short). **1938** Penny's Party (short); Penny's Picnic (short). **1941** Penny to the Rescue (short).

PRUD'HOMME, CAMERON

Born: 1892. Died: Nov. 27, 1967, Pompton Plains, N.J. Screen, stage and radio actor.

Appeared in: **1930** Abraham Lincoln; Doorway to Hell; Half Shot at Sunrise. **1931** Soldiers' Plaything; Honor of the Family; I Like Your Nerve. **1956** The Power and the Prize; Back from Eternity; The Rainmaker. **1963** The Cardinal.

PRUD'HOMME, GEORGE (aka GEORGE PEMBROKE)

Born: 1901. Died: June 11, 1972, Los Angeles, Calif. (brain tumor). Screen, stage actor and opera performer.

Appeared in: **1937** False Evidence. **1938** Irish and Proud of It. **1940** Cowboy from Sundown; The Last Alarm; Buried Alive; Paper Bullets. **1941** Flying Wild; Spooks Run Wild; I Killed That Man; The Invisible Ghost; Gangs Incorporated; The Adventures of Captain Marvel (serial); Miss Polly. **1942** Captain Midnight (serial); Perils of Nyoka (serial); Black Dragons. **1943** Drums of Fu Manchu. **1944** Bluebeard. **1951** All That I Have. **1952** Red Snow; And Now Tomorrow. **1955** The Girl Rush. **1957** Fear Strikes Out; Hell Canyon (aka Hell Canyon Outlaws); Outlaw's Son. **1958** Showdown at Boot Hill.

PRYOR, AINSLIE

Born: Feb. 1, 1921, Memphis, Tenn. Died: May 27, 1958, Hollywood, Calif. (brain cancer). Screen, stage and television actor.

Appeared in: **1955** The Girl in the Red Velvet Swing. **1956** Ransom!; The Last Hunt; Four Girls in Town; Walk the Proud Land. **1957** Guns at Fort Petticoat; The Shadow on the Window. **1958** Kathy-O; Cole Younger, Gunfighter; The Left Handed Gun; Onionhead.

PRYOR, HUGH

Born: 1925. Died: Nov. 11, 1963. Screen and television actor. Married to actress Jacqueline Pryor (dec. 1963).

Appeared in: **1958** Imitation General; Torpedo Run.

PRYOR, JACQUELINE (Connie Williamson)
Born: June 23, 1930, Calif. Died: Nov. 5, 1963, Pasadena, Calif. (murdered—shot). Screen actress. Married to actor Hugh Pryor (dec. 1963).

PRYOR, MAUREEN
Born: England. Died: May 5, 1977, London, England (heart ailment). Screen and stage actress.

Appeared in: **1954** Doctor in the House (US 1955); Orders are Orders. **1957** The Secret Place (US 1958). **1962** Life for Ruth (aka Walk in the Shadow—US 1966). **1967** Three Bites of the Apple. **1974** The Black Windmill.

PRYOR, ROGER
Born: Aug. 27, 1901, Asbury Park, N.J. Died: Jan. 31, 1974, Puerta Vallarta, Mexico (heart attack). Stage, screen, radio actor, stage director and musician. Son of composer/conductor Arthur Pryor (dec. 1942). Divorced from Priscilla Mitchell and actress Ann Sothern.

Appeared in: **1930** Taxi Talks (short). **1931** The Collegiate Model (short). **1933** Moonlight and Pretzels. **1934** Romance in the Rain; I'll Tell the World; Wake Up and Dream; I Like It That Way; The Gift of Gab; Belle of the Nineties; Lady By Choice. **1935** Straight from the Heart; Headline Woman; Dinky; To Beat the Band; A Thousand Dollars a Minute; The Case of the Missing Man; The Girl Friend; Strange Wives. **1936** The Return of Jimmy Valentine; Missing Girls; Ticket to Paradise; Sitting on the Moon. **1939** The Man They Could Not Hang. **1940** Gambling on the High Seas; A Fugitive from Justice; Glamour for Sale; Sued for Libel; The Man With Nine Lives; The Lone Wolf Meets a Lady; Money and the Woman. **1941** She Couldn't Say No; Power Dive; Flying Blind; South of Panama; Richest Man in Town; Bullets for O'Hara; The Officer and the Lady; Bowery Boys; Gambling Daughters. **1942** So's Your Aunt Emma (aka Meet the Mob); I Live on Danger; Smart Alecks; A Man's World. **1943** Lady Bodyguard; Submarine Alert. **1944** Thoroughbreds. **1945** Identity Unknown; The Cisco Kid Returns; High Powered; The Man from Oklahoma; Scared Stiff; Kid Sister.

PRYSE, HUGH (John Hwfa Pryse)
Born: Nov. 11, 1910, London, England. Died: Aug. 11, 1955, England? Screen and stage actor.

Appeared in: **1949** Christopher Columbus. **1953** Botany Bay. **1954** The Happiness of Three Women. **1955** Three Cases of Murder.

PSILANDER, VALDEMAR
Born: Denmark. Died: 1917, Denmark? Screen actor. Appeared in Great Northern Film Co. films.

PUDDLES
Died: May, 1912, La Mesa, Calif. (poisoned). Screen dog performer. Appeared in films for American Manufacturing Company.

PUDOVKIN, VSEVOLOD
Born: 1893, Russia. Died: 1953, Russia. Screen actor, film producer, film director and author.

Appeared in: **1931** The Living Corpse. **1942** Ivan the Terrible—Part I (US 1947). **1948** Admiral Nakhimov.

PUGLIA, FRANK
Born: 1892, Sicily. Died: Oct. 25, 1975, South Pasadena, Calif. Screen, stage, television actor and opera performer.

Appeared in: **1921** Orphans of the Storm. **1922** Fascination. **1924** Isn't Life Wonderful? **1925** Romola; The Beautiful City. **1928** The Man Who Laughs. **1934** Men in White; Viva Villa! **1935** Bordertown; Captain Blood; The Melody Lingers On. **1936** Fatal Lady; The Devil Is a Sissy; Bulldog Edition; The Gay Desperado; The Garden of Allah; The Public Pays (short). **1937** The Firefly; A Doctor's Diary; You Can't Have Everything; Maytime; When You're in Love; Song of the City; Mama Steps Out; The Bride Wore Red; Bulldog Drummond's Revenge. **1938** Rascals; I'll Give a Million; Spawn of the North; Barefoot Boy; Dramatic School; Sharpshooters; Yellow Jack; Tropic Holiday. **1939** Forged Passport; Maisie; Code of the Secret Service; In Old California; Zaza; Balalaika; The Girl and the Gambler. **1940** The Fatal Hour; Charlie Chan in Panama; Torrid Zone; Down Argentine Way; Arise, My Love; Meet the Wildcat; The Mark of Zorro. **1941** That Night in Rio; Billy the Kid; The Parson of Panamint; Law of the Tropics. **1942** Escape from Hong Kong; Now Voyager; Always in My Heart; Who Is Hope Schuyler?; Secret Agent of Japan; Jungle Book; Flight Lieutenant; Casablanca; The Boogie Man Will Get You. **1943** Action in the North Atlantic; The Phantom of the Opera; Pilot No. 5; Mission to Moscow; Background to Danger; For Whom the Bell Tolls;

Princess O'Rourke; Tarzan's Desert Mystery. **1944** Dragon Seed; Tall in the Saddle; Together Again; Brazil; This Is the Life; Ali Baba and the Forty Thieves. **1945** Blood on the Sun; A Song to Remember; Roughly Speaking. **1946** Without Reservations. **1947** Road to Rio; Brute Force; The Lost Moment; Escape Me Never; Stallion Road; My Favorite Brunette; Fiesta. **1948** Joan of Arc; Dream Girl. **1949** Bagdad; Special Agent; Colorado Territory; Bride of Vengeance. **1950** Black Hand; Captain Carey, USA; Desert Hawk; Walk Softly, Stranger; Federal Agent at Large. **1953** The Caddy; Steel Lady; The Bandits of Corsica. **1954** Casanova's Big Night; The Shanghai Story. **1956** Serenade; The Burning Hills; The First Texan. **1959** Cry Tough; The Black Orchid. **1962** Girls! Girls! Girls! **1965** The Sword of Ali Baba.

PUGO (Mariano Contreras)
Born: 1910, Phillipines. Died: Jan., 1979, Manila, Phillipines (brain ailment). Screen, radio, television actor and comedian. Member of comedy team "Pugo and Tugo."

PUIG, EVA G.
Born: Feb. 3, 1894, Mexico. Died: Oct. 6, 1968, Panorama City, Calif. (diabetes and heart failure). Screen actress.

Appeared in: **1940** I Want a Divorce; North West Mounted Police. **1941** Romance of the Rio Grande; Texas Rangers Ride Again; Singapore Woman; Hold Back the Dawn. **1942** Undercover Man; Rio Rita; Arabian Nights. **1945** A Bell for Adano; The Cisco Kid Returns; A Medal for Benny. **1946** Snafu; Wild Beauty; Plainsman and the Lady.

PULLY, B. S.
Born: 1911. Died: Jan. 6, 1972, Philadelphia, Pa. (heart attack). Screen, stage and television actor.

Appeared in: **1944** Four Jills in a Jeep; Wing and a Prayer; Greenwich Village; In the Meantime, Darling. **1945** A Tree Grows in Brooklyn; Within These Walls; Nob Hill; Don Juan Quilligan. **1946** Do You Love Me? **1953** Taxi. **1955** Guys and Dolls. **1959** A Hole in the Head. **1969** The Love of God. **1970** Myra Breckenridge.

PUNAY, RITO (aka RUTE PINAY)
Died: Jan. 12, 1977. Screen actor.

Appeared in: **1946** Dangerous Money.

PURCELL, IRENE
Born: 1902, Hammond, Ind. Died: July 9, 1972, Racine, Wis. Screen and stage actress.

Appeared in: **1931** Just a Gigolo; The Man in Possession. **1932** The Passionate Plumber; Westward Passage; Bachelor's Affairs; The Crooked Circle.

PURCELL, RICHARD "DICK"
Born: Aug. 6, 1908, Greenwich, Conn. Died: Apr. 10, 1944, Los Angeles, Calif. (heart attack). Stage and screen actor.

Appeared in: **1935** Ceiling Zero. **1936** Brides Are Like That; Times Square Playboy; Law in Her Hands; Bullets or Ballots; Jail Break; The Captain's Kid; Men in Exile; King of Hockey; Melody for Two; The Case of the Velvet Claws; Public Enemy's Wife; Man Hunt; Broadway Playboy; Bengal Tiger. **1937** Public Wedding; Navy Blues; Slim; Wine, Women and Horses; The Missing Witness; Reported Missing. **1938** Mystery House; The Daredevil Drivers; Alcatraz Island; Accidents Will Happen; Over the Wall; Penrod's Double Trouble; Garden of the Moon; Valley of the Giants; Flight Into Nowhere; Air Devils; Broadway Musketeers; Nancy Drew, Detective. **1939** Blackwell's Island; Drunk Driving (short); While America Sleeps (short); Irish Luck; Tough Kid; Heroes in Blue; Streets of New York. **1940** Private Affairs; Outside the Three-Mile Limit; New Moon; The Bank Dick; Flight Command; Arise My Love. **1941** The Pittsburgh Kid; Flying Blind; Two in a Taxi; No Hands on the Clock; Bullets for O'Hara; King of the Zombies. **1942** Torpedo Boat; In Old California; The Old Homestead; I Live on Danger; X Marks the Spot; Phantom Killer. **1943** Aerial Gunner; Idaho; High Explosives; Reveille with Beverly; The Mystery of the Thirteenth Guest. **1944** Trocadero; Leave It to the Irish; Farewell My Lovely; Captain America (serial); Timber Queen.

PURDELL, REGINALD (Reginald Grasdorf)
Born: Nov. 4, 1896, Clapham, London, England. Died: Apr. 22, 1953, London, England. Screen, stage, television actor and screenwriter.

Appeared in: **1930** The Middle Watch. **1931** A Night in Montmartre; Congress Dances (US 1932). **1933** Up to the Neck; Crime on the Hill; My Lucky Star; Strictly in Confidence. **1934** The Old Curiosity Shop; What's in a Name?; The Luck of a Sailor; The Queen's Affaire (aka Runaway Queen—US 1935); On the Air. **1935** Key to Harmony;

Royal Cavalcade (aka Regal Cavalcade—US); Get Off My Foot. **1936** Hail and Farewell; Debt of Honour; Where's Sally?; Crown vs. Stevens. **1937** Side Street Angel; Ship's Concert. **1938** Quiet Please; Many Tanks Mr. Atkins; The Viper; The Dark Stairway; Simply Terrific. **1939** Q Planes (aka Clouds Over Europe—US); His Brother's Keeper; The Missing People (US 1940); The Middle Watch (and in 1930 version). **1940** Pack Up Your Troubles; Busman's Holiday (aka Haunted Honeymoon—US); Fingers. **1943** Variety Jubilee; We Dive at Dawn; Bell-Bottom George; It's in the Bag. **1944** Candles at Nine; Love Story (aka A Lady Surrenderrs—US 1947); 2,000 Women. **1946** London Town (aka My Heart Goes Crazy—US 1953). **1947** Holiday Camp (US 1948); Captain Boycott; The Root of All Evil; A Man About the House (US 1949); Brighton Rock. **1951** Files from Scotland Yard.

PURDY, CONSTANCE
Born: c. 1885, Kansas. Died: Apr. 1, 1960, Los Angeles, Calif. (arteriosclerosis). Screen actress.

Appeared in: **1936** Lloyds of London. **1942** Now, Voyager. **1943** Doughboys in Ireland; White Savage; Air Raid Wardens; Double Up (short). **1944** And Now Tomorrow; Double Indemnity. **1945** A Tree Grows in Brooklyn; Swing Out, Sister; This Love of Ours; Penthouse Rhythm. **1946** Vacation in Reno. **1947** Unconquered; That Hagan Girl; The Shocking Miss Pilgrim. **1948** I Remember Mama; Family Honeymoon. **1949** Madame Bovary. **1950** Blonde Dynamite.

PURVIANCE, EDNA
Born: Oct. 21, 1894, Reno, Nev. Died: Jan. 13, 1958, Woodland Hills, Calif. Screen actress. She was Charlie Chaplin's leading lady for nine years in his early films.

Appeared in: **1915** A Night Out; The Champion; Work. **1916** The Vagabond; Carmen; The Count; The Bank. **1917** The Cure; The Adventurer; Easy Street. **1918** A Dog's Life; Shoulder Arms. **1919** Sunnyside. **1921** The Kid; The Idle Class. **1922** The Pilgrim. **1923** A Woman of Paris. **1926** The Seagull; A Woman of the Sea. **1952** Limelight. **1963** 30 Years of Fun (documentary).

PURVIS, LOWELL
Born: 1935. Died: July 20, 1980, Los Angeles, Calif. (cancer). Screen, stage actor, stage director and dancer.

PUTMAN, GEORGE (George Arthur Putman)
Died: Apr. 8, 1875. Screen actor. Do not confuse with news commentator, George Putnam.

Appeared in: **1951** Fourteen Hours.

PYM, WALTER
Born: 1905, Australia. Died: Jan. 22, 1980, Melbourne, Australia. Screen, stage, radio and television actor.

Appeared in: **1979** Patrick.

PYNE, JOE
Born: 1925, Chester, Pa. Died: Mar. 23, 1970, Los Angeles, Calif. (lung cancer). Screen, television and radio actor.

Appeared in: **1966** Mother Goose a Go-Go. **1967** The Love-Ins.

QUALTERS, TOT (Marguerite Qualters)
Born: 1895. Died: Mar. 27, 1974, New York, N.Y. Stage and screen actress.

Appeared in: **1931** Reaching for the Moon.

QUARANTA, LYDIA
Born: 1891, Italy. Died: 1928, Italy. Screen actress. Sister of actresses Letizia and Isabella Quaranta.

Appeared in: **1914** Cabiria. **1925** Voglio Tradire Mio Marito.

QUARTERMAINE, CHARLES
Born: Dec. 30, 1877, Richmond, Surrey, England. Died: Aug., 1958, England? Screen and stage actor. Divorced from actresses Madge Titheradge (dec. 1961), and Mary Forbes (dec. 1974). Entered films in 1919.

Appeared in: **1919** The Lady Clare. **1920** The Face at the Window. **1924** The Eleventh Commandment. **1929** The Thirteenth Chair. **1930** The Bishop Murder Case; Redemption. **1931** Man of Mayfair. **1935** Drake of England (aka Drake the Pirate—US).

QUARTERMAINE, LEON
Born: Sept. 24, 1876, Richmond, Surrey, England. Died: June 28, 1967, Salisbury, England. Stage and screen actor. Married to actress Barbara Wilcox. Divorced from Aimee de Burgh (dec. 1946) and actress Fay Compton (dec. 1978).

Appeared in: **1935** Dark World; Escape Me Never. **1936** As You Like It.

QUATTROCIOCCHI, NICKY
Born: Palermo, Sicily. Died: Apr., 1968, Palermo, Sicily. Screen actor.

QUEBLY, MARIE-LOUISE (Wallis Malu)
Born: 1911. Died: 1981, N.Y. Screen, stage actress and singer.

QUERIO, ISA
Born: 1893. Died: 1976. Screen actress.

Appeared in: **1953** Three Forbidden Stories.

QUIGLEY, CHARLES
Born: Feb. 12, 1906, New Britain, Conn. Died: Aug. 5, 1964, Los Angeles, Calif. (cirrhosis of liver). Stage and screen actor.

Appeared in: **1932** Saddle Buster. **1935** King of Burlesque. **1936** Charlie Chan's Secret; And Sudden Death; Lady from Nowhere; Racing Luck. **1937** The Shadow; Criminals of the Air; Find the Witness; The Game That Kills; Girls Can Play; Speed to Spare. **1938** Convicted. **1939** Daredevils of the Red Circle (serial); Heroes in Blue; Special Inspector. **1940** Mexican Spitfire Out West; Men Against the Sky. **1941** A Woman's Face; The Iron Claw (serial); Playgirl; Footlight Fever; Secret Evidence. **1942** A Yank at Eton. **1943** The Masked Marvel (serial). **1944** The National Barn Dance. **1945** Duffy's Tavern. **1946** Larceny in Her Heart; Affairs of Geraldine; The Crimson Ghost (serial). **1947** Brick Bradford (serial); Three on a Ticket; Danger Street. **1948** Superman (serial). **1949** The Cowboy and the Indians. **1950** Unmasked; David Harding, Counterspy.

QUILLAN, SARAH
Born: 1879. Died: Aug. 3, 1969. Screen actress. Mother of actor Eddie Quillan. Married to actor Joseph Quillan (dec. 1952).

Appeared in: **1929** Noisy Neighbors.

QUILLIAN, JOSEPH F.
Born: July 27, 1884, Glasgow, Scotland. Died: Nov. 16, 1952, Hollywood, Calif. (cancer). Screen and vaudeville actor. Married to actress Sara Quillan (dec. 1969). Father of actor Eddie Quillan.

Appeared in: **1928** A Little Bit of Everything (short). **1929** Noisy Neighbors.

QUIMBY, MARGARET
Died: Aug., 1965, Minneapolis, Minn. Screen actress.

Appeared in: **1925** The Teaser; Perils of the Wild (serial). **1926** What Happened to Jones; The Whole Town's Talking; The Radio Detective (serial). **1927** New York; The Western Whirlwind; The Tired Business Man; The World at Her Feet. **1928** Sally of the Scandals; The Tragedy of Youth. **1929** Lucky Boy; Two Men and a Maid. **1930** Ladies Love Brutes; The Rampant Age; Trailin' Trouble.

QUINCE, LOUIS VEDA
Born: 1900. Died: Sept. 24, 1954, Dallas, Tex. (heart attack). Screen, stage and radio actor.

Appeared in: **1945** Mildred Pierce.

QUINLAN, ROGER
Died: Jan. 23, 1976. Screen actor.

QUINLIVAN, CHARLES
Born: 1924. Died: Nov. 12, 1974, Fountain Valley, Calif. (coronary). Screen, stage and television actor.

Appeared in: **1957** Zero Hour! **1958** Seven Guns to Mesa. **1960** All the Young Men. **1974** Airport 1975.

QUINN, ALAN J.
Born: 1889. Died: Jan., 1944, Philadelphia, Pa. Screen actor.

Appeared in: **1915** The Sporting Duchess.

QUINN, JACK
Died: Dec. 10, 1929, New York, N.Y. Screen actor.

Appeared in: **1926** The Set-Up.

QUINN, JAMES
Born: 1884. Died: Nov. 30, 1919, New York, N.Y. Screen actor.

QUINN, JAMES "JIMMIE"
Born: 1885, New Orleans, La. Died: Aug. 22, 1940, Hollywood, Calif. Stage and screen actor. Entered films in 1919. Was featured with Billie Sullivan in a series of racetrack shorts.

Appeared in: **1922** Afraid to Fight; Rags to Riches. **1923** Mile-a-Minute Romeo; Second Hand Love. **1924** Broadway After Dark. **1925** Red Hot Tires; The Dixie Handicap; Pretty Ladies; Speed Madness; The Wife Who Wasn't Wanted; On Thin Ice; Soft Shoes. **1926** The Imposter. **1927** Two Flaming Youths. **1928** The Spieler; Ginsberg the Great; Women Who Dare. **1929** Come and Get It; The Dance of Life; The Argyle Case. **1930** Hold Everything. **1934** I Hate Women. **1935** The Gilded Lily.

QUINN, JOE
Born: 1899. Died: May 20, 1974, Los Angeles, Calif. (emphysema). Screen, stage, television and vaudeville actor.

Appeared in: **1917** The Argyle Case. **1921** The Unknown Wife.

QUINN, JOE
Born: 1917. Died: Feb. 2, 1971, Hollywood, Calif. (heart attack). Screen, stage and television actor. Do not confuse with actor Joe Quinn (dec. 1974).

QUINN, JOHN (John Phillip Quinn)
Born: 1851, near St. Louis, Mo. Died: Apr. 18, 1916, Philadelphia, Pa. Screen actor and professional gambler.

Appeared in: **1915** Gambling Inside and Out.

QUINN, PAUL
Born: 1870. Died: Apr. 20, 1936, Los Angeles, Calif. Screen, stage, vaudeville and minstrel actor.

QUINN, TONY
Born: June 27, 1899, Naas, County Kildare, Ireland. Died: June 1, 1967, London, England. Screen, stage and television actor. Do not confuse with actor Anthony Quinn.

Appeared in: **1934** Lest We Forget. **1941** Danny Boy (US 1946). **1943** It's in the Bag. **1949** Saints and Sinners; The Strangers Came (aka You Can't Fool an Irishman—US). **1955** Shadow of a Man. **1956** Tons of Money. **1957** The Rising of the Moon; Booby Trap. **1958** Alive and Kicking (short). **1959** The Great Van Robbery (US 1963). **1960** Trouble with Eve (aka In Trouble with Eve—US 1964). **1970** The Strawberry Statement.

QUIRK, WILLIAM "BILLY"
Born: 1881. Died: Apr. 20, 1926, Hollywood, Calif. Screen actor.

Appeared in: **1909** The Son's Return; The Renunciation; Sweet and Twenty; His Wife's Visitor; Oh, Uncle; Getting Even; The Little Teacher; A Midnight Adventure; A Corner in Wheat; The Mended Lute; They Would Elope; 1776, or The Hessian Renegades; The Gibson Goddess. **1910** The Woman from Mellon's; A Rich Revenge; The Two Brothers; Muggsy's First Sweetheart. **1912** Fra Diavolo; The Blood Stain; Hubby Does the Washing. **1913** Billy's Troubles. **1914** The Girl from Prosperity; Wife Wanted; Bridal Attire. **1915** Billy, the Bear Tamer. **1921** At the Stage Door; The Man Worth While. **1922** My Old Kentucky Home. **1923** A Bride for a Knight; Broadway Broke; Success. **1925** The Dixie Handicap.

QUIROZ, SALVADOR
Born: 1881, Mexico. Died: Nov. 23, 1956, Mexico City, Mexico. Screen actor.

RABAGLIATI, ALBERTO (Alberto Rabagliati-Vinata)
Born: June 26, 1906, Milan, Italy. Died: Mar. 8, 1974, Rome, Italy (cerebral thrombosis). Screen, radio actor and singer. Went to Hollywood in 1927 as the winner of a "successor to Rudolph Valentino" contest.

Appeared in: **1928** Street Angel. **1930** Seu tu L'amore?. **1940** Una Famiglia Impossibile. **1941** La Scuola dei Timidi. **1942** Lascia Cantare il Cuore. **1943** La Vita e Bella; In Cerca di Felicita. **1945** Partenza Ore 7. **1948** Natale al Campo. **1950** Escape into Dreams. **1951** La Avventura di Mandrin. **1952** Il Maestro di Don Giovanni. **1953** Crossed Swords. **1954** Scuola Elementare; The Barefoot Contessa. **1956** The Monte Carlo Story. **1957** Susanna Tutta Panna. **1959** La Cento Chilometri. **1961** Jessica. **1966** The Christmas That Almost Wasn't. **1967** The Birds, the Bees, the Italians.

RADCLIFF, VIOLET
Born: 1908, Niagara Falls, N.Y. Died: c. 1926. Screen and stage actress. Child actress for Pathe, Fine Arts, and Fox.

Appeared in: **1910** Red Girl and White Child. **1913** Children of the Feud. **1917** Jack and the Beanstalk; Aladdin and the Wonderful Lamp. **1918** Fan Fan (aka The Mikado).

RADCLIFFE, E. J. See RATCLIFFE, E. J.

RADCLIFFE, JACK (Charles Smith)
Born: Sept. 18, 1900, Cleland, Scotland. Died: Apr. 26, 1967, Glasgow, Scotland (cancer). Screen, stage, vaudeville and television actor.

Appeared in: **1955** Geordie (aka Wee Geordie—US 1956).

RADD, RONALD
Born: Jan. 22, 1929, Ryhope County, Durham, England. Died: Apr. 23, 1976, Toronto, Canada (brain hemorrhage). Screen, stage and television actor.

Appeared in: **1958** Camp on Blood Island. **1963** The Small World of Sammy Lee; Mister Ten Percent. **1965** Up Jumped a Swagman; Where the Spies Are (US 1966). **1967** The Double Man (US 1968). **1968** The Sea Gull. **1969** Can Heironymus Merkin Ever Forget Mercy Humppe and Find True Happiness? **1970** The Kremlin Letter. **1973** The Offense. **1974** The Spiral Staircase. **1975** Galileo; Operation Daybreak.

RADFORD, BASIL
Born: June 25, 1897, Chester, England. Died: Oct. 20, 1952, London, England (heart attack). Screen and stage actor.

Appeared in: **1929** Barnum Was Right (film debut). **1932** There Goes the Bride (US 1933). **1933** Just Smith; A Southern Maid. **1936** Broken Blossoms (US 1937); Dishonour Bright. **1937** Captain's Orders; Jump for Glory (aka When Thief Meets Thief—US); Young and Innocent (aka A Girl was Young—US 1938). **1938** Convict 99; Climbing High (US 1939); The Lady Vanishes. **1939** The Girl Who Forgot; Let's Be Famous; Jamaica Inn; Secret Journey (aka Among Human Wolves—US 1940); Just William; She Couldn't Say No; Spies of the Air (US 1940); Trouble Brewing. **1940** Room for Two (US 1944); The Flying Squad; The Girl in the News (US 1941); Crook's Tour; Night Train to Munich (aka Gestapo and Night Train—US). **1942** Flying Fortress; Unpublished Story; Partners in Crime. **1943** Dear Octopus (aka The Randolph Family—US 1945); Millions Like Us. **1944** Twilight Hour; Dead of Night; The Way to the Stars (aka Johnny in the Clouds—US). **1946** A Girl in a Million (US 1950); The Captive Heart (US 1947). **1948** Quartet (US 1949); The Winslow Boy (US 1950). **1949** Passport to Pimlico; It's Not Cricket; Whiskey Galore (aka Tight Little Island—US and Mad Little Island); Stop Press Girl. **1950** Chance of a Lifetime (US 1951). **1951** The Galloping Major; White Corridors (US 1952).

RADHA, M. R.
Born: India. Died: Oct., 1979, Tirucharapalli, India. Screen, stage actor and stage producer.

Appeared in: **1951** The River.

RADILAK, CHARLES H.
Born: 1907, Czechoslovakia. Died: July 19, 1972, Inglewood, Calif. Screen, television, stage and radio actor.

Appeared in: **1963** Rampage. **1966** Torn Curtain.

RAE, CLAIRE
Born: 1889. Died: July 7, 1938, Canton, Ohio (leukemia). Screen and stage actress. Appeared in silent films.

RAE, JACK (Alton Sampley)
Born: 1899. Died: May 3, 1957, Hollywood, Calif. (heart attack). Screen and stage actor.

RAE, MELBA
Born: 1922. Died: Dec. 29, 1971, N.Y. (cerebral hemorrhage). Screen, stage, radio and television actress. Did film short subject narration and foreign film dubbing.

RAEBURN, FRANCES (Frances Hedrick Kurstin)
Died: Dec. 26, 1976, Calif. (heart failure). Screen actress. Sister of actress Kathryn Grayson.

Appeared in: **1942** Seven Sweethearts. **1945** Swing Out, Sister.

RAEBURN, HENZIE
Born: Nov. 2, 1900, England. Died: Oct. 27, 1973, London, England. Screen, stage actress and author. Married to actor/director E. Martin Browne (dec. 1980).

Appeared in: **1958** Orders to Kill.

RAFFERTY, CHIPS (John Goffage)
Born: 1909, Australia. Died: May 27, 1971, Sydney, Australia (heart attack). Screen, stage and television actor.

Appeared in: **1938** Ants in His Pants (film debut). **1939** Dan Rudd, M.P. **1940** Forty Thousand Horsemen. **1945** The Rats of Tobruk (aka The Fighting Rats of Tobruk—US 1951). **1946** The Overlanders. **1947** The Loves of Joanna Godden; Bush Christmas. **1949** Eureka Stockade. **1950** Bitter Springs. **1951** Massacre Hill. **1952** Kangaroo. **1953** The Desert Rats. **1956** King of the Coral Sea; Walk into Paradise; Smiley (US 1957). **1958** Smiley Gets a Gun (US 1959). **1961** The Sundowners; The Wackiest Ship in the Army. **1962** Mutiny on the Bounty. **1966** Double Trouble; They're a Weird Mob. **1968** Kona Coast. **1970** Skullduggery.

"RAFFLES BILL" (Andreas Aglassinger)
Born: 1895, Braunau-on-the-Inn, Austria. Died: Feb. 21, 1940, Germany (stomach ailment). Screen, vaudeville actor and circus performer. Appeared in German and U.S. films.

RAFT, GEORGE (George Ranft)
Born: Sept. 27, 1895, New York, N.Y. Died: Nov. 24, 1980, Los Angeles, Calif. (leukemia). Screen, stage, television actor and dancer.

Appeared in: **1929** Queen of the Night Clubs. **1931** Quick Millions; Palmy Days; Hush Money; Goldie. **1932** Scarface; Taxi; Dancers in the Dark; Night After Night; Madame Racketeer; If I Had a Million; Undercover Man; Night World. **1933** The Bowery; Pick Up; The Midnight Club; The Eagle and the Hawk. **1934** Bolero; All of Me; The Trumpet Blows; Limehouse Blues. **1935** Every Night at Eight; Rumba; Stolen Harmony; The Glass Key; She Couldn't Take It. **1936** It Had to Happen; Yours for the Asking. **1937** Souls at Sea. **1938** You and Me; Spawn of the North. **1939** Each Dawn I Die; The Lady's From Kentucky; I Stole a Million. **1940** They Drive by Night; The House Across the Bay; Invisible Stripes. **1941** Manpower. **1942** Broadway. **1943** Background to Danger; Stage Door Canteen. **1944** Follow the Boys. **1945** Johnny Angel; Nob Hill. **1946** Nocturne; Mr. Ace; Whistle Stop. **1947** Intrigue; Christmas Eve. **1948** Race Street. **1949** Johnny Allegro; A Dangerous Profession; Outpost in Morocco; Red Light. **1951** Lucky Nick Cain. **1952** Loan Shark. **1953** I'll Get You; Man From Cairo. **1954** Black Widow; Rouge Cop. **1955** A Bullet for Joey. **1956** Around the World in 80 Days. **1959** Jet Over the Atlantic; Some Like It Hot. **1960** Ocean's 11. **1961** The Ladies' Man. **1964** For Those Who Think Young; The Patsy. **1966** Du Rififi a Paname (aka The Upper Hand—US 1967). **1967** Casino Royale. **1968** The Silent Treatment; Skidoo!; El Millon de Madigan (Madigan's Millions—US 1969). **1972** Hammersmith Is Out. **1978** Sextette. **1980** The Man With Bogart's Face.

RAGAN, RUTH
Died: Sept. 15, 1962, Hollywood, Calif. (auto accident). Screen actress and dancer.

RAGLAN, JAMES
Born: Jan. 6, 1901. Died: Nov. 15, 1961, London, England. Screen, stage and television actor.

Appeared in: **1952** Whispering Smith vs. Scotland Yard.

RAGLAND, ESTHER
Born: 1912. Died: July 6, 1939, Los Angeles, Calif. Screen and vaudeville whistling actress. She did whistling numbers in 1937 Snow White and the Seven Dwarfs.

RAGLAND, RAGS (John Lee Morgan Beauregard Ragland)
Born: Aug. 23, 1905, Louisville, Ky. Died: Aug. 20, 1946, Los Angeles, Calif. (uremia). Screen, stage and burlesque actor.

Appeared in: **1941** Whistling in the Dark; Ringside Masie. **1942** Maisie Gets Her Man; Somewhere I'll Find You; Panama Hattie; Whistling in Dixie; The War Against Mrs. Hadley; Sunday Punch; Born to Sing. **1943** Whistling in Brooklyn; Du Barry Was a Lady; Girl Crazy. **1944** The Canterville Ghost; Meet the People; Three Men in White. **1945** Anchors Aweigh; Her Highness and the Bellboy; Abbott and Costello in Hollywood. **1946** The Hoodlum Saint; Ziegfeld Follies.

RAHM, KNUTE
Born: Mar. 20, 1876, Sweden. Died: July 23, 1957, Los Angeles, Calif. (heart disease). Screen actor.

Appeared in: **1912** The Bell of Penance; The Apache Renegade; The Power of a Hymn; Red Wing and the Paleface; The Indian Uprising at Santa Fe. **1913** The Last Blockhouse; The Redemption; The Missing Bonds; A Daughter of the Underworld. **1915** The Mystery of the Tea Dansant (serial). **1917** The Secret of the Lost Valley; Sage Brush Law; The Door In the Mountain.

RAHN, BRUNO
Born: 1898, Germany. Died: Sept. 15, 1927. Screen actor and film director.

RAIMU, JULES (Jules Muraire)
Born: Dec. 17, 1883, France. Died: Sept. 20, 1946, Paris, France (heart attack). Screen and stage actor.

Appeared in: **1931** Marius (US 1933). **1932** Fanny. **1933** Theodore et Cie. (Theodore and Co.); Mam'zelle Nitouche. **1934** Caesar. **1935** Charlemagne. **1937** Un Carnet de Bal (US 1938); Les Perles de le Couronne. **1939** Le Famille Lefrancois (Heroes of the Marne); La Femme du Boulanger (The Baker's Wife); Heart of Paris; Last Desire. **1940** La Fille du Puisatier (The Well Digger's Daughter—US 1946); Heart of a Nation (US 1943). **1941** The Man Who Seeks the Truth; The King. **1942** Les Inconnus dans la Maison (Strangers in the House—US 1949). **1944** Colonel Chabert (US 1947). **1945** Dawn Over France; L'Homme au Chapeau Rond. **1947** Midnight in Paris; Fanny (and 1932 version); The Eternal Husband (US 1949); Hoboes in Paradise (US 1950).

RAINE, ADELAIDE
Born: 1893. Died: Jan. 20, 1978, Drexel Hills, Pa. Screen and stage actress. Married to stage actor Albert Hugh Finn (dec.).

Appeared in: **1917** The Scarlet Letter.

RAINE, JACK
Born: May 18, 1897, London, England. Died: May 30, 1979, South Laguna, Calif. Screen, stage and television actor. Divorced from actresses Binnie Hale and Sonia Somers. Later married to Theodora M. Buchanan Wilson.

Appeared in: **1929** Memories (short); The Hate Ship. **1930** Suspense; Comets; Raise the Roof; Harmony Heaven; Night Birds; The Middle Watch, Infatuation. **1932** Fires of Fate (US 1933). **1933** The Fortunate Fool; Two Wives for Henry; The House of Trent. **1934** Little Friend; Lilies of the Field. **1935** Mimi; The Clairvoyant. **1938** Meet Mr. Penny. **1947** Holiday Camp (US 1948); Mine Own Executioner (US 1949). **1948** Good Time Girl (US 1950); Quartet (US 1949); My Brother's Keeper (US 1949); Calling Paul Temple. **1952** Holiday for Sinners; The Happy Time; Above and Beyond. **1953** Dangerous When Wet; Rogue's March; Julius Caesar. **1954** Elephant Walk; Rhapsody. **1955** Not as a Stranger; The Girl in the Red Velvet Swing; Prince of Players; Soldier of Fortune. **1956** The Power and the Prize. **1959** Woman Obsessed. **1962** Taras Bulba. **1964** My Fair Lady. **1968** The Killing of Sister George. **1969** Hello Dolly.

RAINEY, NORMAN (William Morrison)
Born: Apr. 28, 1888, Ireland. Died: Sept. 10, 1960, Los Angeles, Calif. (cancer). Screen actor. Do not confuse with screenwriter Norman Rainey (dec. 1971).

Appeared in: **1948** The Wake of the Red Witch. **1949** That Forsyth Woman. **1951** Lorna Doone.

RAINS, CLAUDE
Born: Nov. 10, 1889, London, England. Died: May 30, 1967, Laconia, N.H. (intestinal hemorrhage). Screen, stage and television actor. Divorced from actress Isabel Jeans, Marie Hemingway (dec. 1939), Beatrix Thomson and Frances Propper. Married to Agi Jambor. Nominated for 1939 Academy Award for Best Supporting Actor in Mr. Smith Goes to Washington; in 1943 for Casablanca; in 1944 for Mr. Sheffington; and in 1946 for Notorious.

Appeared in: **1920** Build Thy House. **1933** The Invisible Man (film debut). **1934** Crime Without Passion. **1935** The Man Who Reclaimed His Head; The Mystery of Edwin Drood; The Clairvoyant; The Last Outpost. **1936** Anthony Adverse; Hearts Divided; Stolen Holiday. **1937** The Prince and the Pauper; They Won't Forget. **1938** White Banners; The Adventures of Robin Hood; Four Daughters; Gold Is Where You Find It. **1939** They Made Me a Criminal; Daughters Courageous; Juarez; Mr. Smith Goes to Washington; Four Wives; Sons of Liberty (short). **1940** Saturday's Children; The Sea Hawk; Lady With Red Hair. **1941** Four Mothers; Here Comes Mr. Jordan; Kings Row; The Wolf Man; Riot Squad. **1942** Moontide; Now, Voyager; Eyes of the Underworld; Casablanca. **1943** Forever and a Day; Phantom of the Opera. **1944** Passage to Marseilles; Mr. Skeffington. **1945** This Love of Ours. **1946** Caesar and Cleopatra; Angel on My Shoulder; Deception; Notorious; Strange Holiday. **1947** The Unsuspected. **1948** The Passionate Spring. **1949** Song of Surrender; Rope of Sand; One Woman's Story. **1950** The White Tower; Where Danger Lives. **1951** Sealed Cargo. **1953** The Man Who Watched Trains Go By (aka The Paris Express—US). **1956** Lisbon. **1959** This Earth is Mine. **1960** The Lost World; Il Pianeta Degli Vomini. **1961** The Pied Piper of Hamelin. **1962** Lawrence of Arabia. **1963** Battle of the Worlds; Twilight of Honor. **1965** The Greatest Story Ever Told.

RAISA, ROSE
Born: 1878. Died: Sept. 28, 1963. Stage and screen actress.

Appeared in: **1928** The Soprano of the Chicago Civic Opera Company (shorts). **1937** Men Are Not Gods.

RAJU (Raju Ahmed)
Born: 1937, India. Died: Dec. 12, 1972, Dacca, Bangladesh (murdered). Screen, television and radio actor.

RAKER, LORIN (aka LORRIN RAKER)
Born: May 8, 1891, Joplin, Mo. Died: Dec. 25, 1959, Woodland Hills, Calif. (cancer). Screen and stage actor.

Appeared in: **1928** Gang War. **1929** Mother's Boy. **1930** Kismet. **1931** Six Cylinder Love; Women Go on Forever. **1933** My Woman. **1934** Odor in the Court (short); The Loud Speaker. **1935** I've Been Around; The Nut Farm; Honeymoon Limited; Les Miserables. **1937** California Straight Ahead; Mysterious Crossing. **1942** What Makes Lizzy Dizzy? (short). **1943** Cowboy in Manhattan. **1944** Sing a Jingle. **1945** Men in Her Diary. **1946** Without Reservation; I'll Be Yours. **1947** Variety Girl. **1948** Chicken Every Sunday. **1950** The Fuller Brush Girl; Tale of Robin Hood.

RALE, MICHAEL W. (Michael W. Israle aka MIKE RAYLE)
Born: Russia. Died: July 8, 1940, Englewood, N.J. Screen, stage actor and minstrel performer.

Appeared in: **1914** Officer 666. **1915** The Exploits of Elaine; Madame Butterfly. **1916** Patria (serial); The Mysteries of Myra (serial). **1918** The Forbidden City. **1920** Away Goes Prudence. **1924** Three Miles Out. **1925** Heart of a Siren.

RALEIGH, SABA (aka ISABEL ELLISSEN)
Born: 1866, England. Died: Aug. 22, 1923, England? Screen and stage actress. Married to author Cecil Raleigh (dec. 1914).

Appeared in: **1915** The Clemenceau Case. **1921** The Princess of New York; The Road to London. **1922** A Prince of Lovers (aka Life of Lord Byron—US 1927).

RALLI, PAUL
Born: Dec. 29, 1905, Cyprus. Died: Sept. 4, 1953, Van Nuys, Calif. Screen, stage actor, attorney and author.

Appeared in: **1928** The Waterhole; Show People. **1929** Montmartre Rose; Married in Hollywood.

RALPH, JESSIE (Jessie Ralph Chambers)
Born: Nov. 5, 1876, Gloucester, Mass. Died: May 30, 1944, Gloucester, Mass. Screen and stage actress. Married to stage actor William Patton (dec.).

Appeared in: **1916** New York. **1921** Such a Little Queen. **1933** Cocktail Hour; Child of Manhattan (stage and film versions); Elmer the Great; Ann Carver's Profession. **1934** One Night of Love; Evelyn Prentice; Nana (aka Lady of the Boulevard); We Live Again; Murder at the Vanities; The Affairs of Cellini; The Coming Out Party. **1936** David Copperfield; Les Miserables; Paris in Spring (aka Paris Love Song); Captain Blood; Enchanted April; Vanessa, Her Love Story; Mark of the Vampire; I Live My Life; Jalna; Metropolitan; I Found Stella Parish. **1936** Bunker Bean (aka His Majesty Bunker Bean); San Francisco; Walking on Air; The Garden Murder Case; The Unguarded Hour; After the Thin Man; Camille; Little Lord Fauntleroy; Yellow Dust. **1937** The Good Earth; The Last of Mrs. Cheyney; Double Wedding. **1938** Love Is a Headache; Port of Seven Seas; Hold That Kiss. **1939** St. Louis Blues; Cafe Society; The Kid from Texas; Mickey the Kid; Drums Along the Mohawk; Four Girls in White. **1940** Star Dust; Girl from Avenue A; I Can't Give You Anything but Love, Baby; I Want a Divorce; The Bank Dick (aka The Bank Detective); The Bluebird. **1941** The Lady from Cheyenne; They Met in Bombay.

RALSTON, JOBYNA
Born: Nov. 21, 1904, South Pittsburg, Tenn. Died: Jan. 22, 1967, Woodland Hills, Calif. Screen and stage actress. Divorced from actor Richard Arlen (dec. 1976).

Appeared in: **1922** Grandma's Boy; The Call of Home; Three Must-Get-Theres. **1923** Why Worry? **1924** Girl Shy; Hot Water. **1925** The Freshman. **1926** For Heaven's Sake; Gigolo; Sweet Daddies. **1927** A Racing Romeo; Special Delivery; Wings; The Kid Brother; Lightning; Pretty Clothes. **1928** The Power of the Press; Little Mickey Grogan; The Count of Ten; The Toilers; The Night Flyer; The Big Hop; Black Butterflies. **1929** Some Mother's Boy; The College Coquette. **1930** Rough Waters.

RAMBAL, ENRIQUE
Born: 1924, Mexico. Died: Dec. 15, 1971, Mexico City, Mexico (heart attack). Screen, stage and television actor.

Appeared in: **1958** El Hombre y el Monstruo (The Man and the Monster—US 1966). **1962** La Estrella Vacia (The Empty Star); El Angel Exterminador (The Exterminating Angel—US 1967).

RAMBEAU, MARJORIE
Born: July 15, 1889, San Francisco, Calif. Died: July 7, 1970, Palm Springs, Calif. Screen and stage actress. Divorced from actor Willard Mack (dec. 1934), and Hugh Dillman. Later married to film executive Francis A. Gudger, (dec. 1967). Nominated for 1940 Academy Award for Best Supporting Actress in Primrose Path and in 1953 for Torch Song.

Appeared in: **1916** The Dazzling Miss Davison (film debut). **1917** Motherhood; Mary Moreland; The Mirror; The Greater Woman. **1918** The Common Cause. **1920** The Fortune Teller. **1926** Syncopating Sue. **1930** Her Man; Min and Bill. **1931** Leftover Ladies; Son of India; Inspiration; The Easiest Way; Silence; Hell Divers; Laughing Sinners; The Secret Six; Strangers May Kiss; A Tailor-Made Man. **1933** Strictly Personal; The Warrior's Husband; A Man's Castle. **1934** Palooka; A Modern Hero; Grand Canary; Ready for Love. **1935** Under Pressure; Dizzy Dames. **1937** First Lady. **1938** Merrily We Live; Woman Against Woman. **1939** Sudden Money; The Rains Came; Laugh It Off. **1940** Primrose Path; 20 Mule Team; Tugboat Annie Sails Again; East of the River; Heaven with a Barbed Wire Fence; Santa Fe Marshal. **1941** Tobacco Road; Three Sons O'Guns. **1942** Broadway. **1943** In Old Oklahoma. **1944** Oh What a Night; Army Wives. **1945** Salome, Where She Danced. **1948** The Walls of Jericho. **1949** Any Number Can Play; The Lucky Stiff; Abandoned. **1953** Torch Song; Forever Female; Bad for Each Other. **1955** A Man Called Peter; The View From Pompey's Head. **1956** Slander. **1957** Man of a Thousand Faces.

RAMBOVA, NATACHA (Winifred Shaunessy aka WINIFRED HUDNUT-adopted name)
Born: Jan. 19, 1897, Salt Lake City, Utah. Died: June 5, 1966, Pasadena, Calif. (dietary complications). Screen, stage actress, dancer and screenwriter. Divorced from actor Rudolph Valentino (dec. 1926).

Appeared in: **1921** Camille. **1923** Salome. **1925** When Love Grows Cold.

RAMIREZ, PEPITA
Born: 1902. Died: Dec., 1927, Hollywood, Calif. (auto crash). Screen, stage actress and dancer.

RAMOS, CARLOS
Born: 1907, Portugal. Died: Nov. 6, 1969, Lisbon, Portugal (heart attack). Screen, stage actor and singer.

RAMOS, JESUS MAZA
Born: 1911. Died: Apr., 1955, Mexico. Screen, stage and radio actor. Appeared in an act known as "Los Fikaros."

RAMSEY, JOHN NELSON (aka NEILSON RAMSEY)
Born: 1863. Died: Apr. 5, 1929, London, England (heart disease). Screen and stage actor.

Appeared in: **1914** She Stoops to Conquer. **1916** The Second Mrs. Tanqueray; The Broken Melody; The Lyons Mail (US 1919). **1917** Broken Barrier (aka Quicksands); Tom Jones; Her Greatest Performance. **1918** God and the Man. **1920** The Breed of the Treshams; The Twelve Pound Look. **1921** All Roads Lead to Calvary; The Adventures of Sherlock Holmes series including A Case of Identity. **1922** Dicky Monteith; The House of Peril. **1923** The Indian Love Lyrics; Young Lochinvar; The Last Adventures of Sherlock Holmes series including His Last Bow. **1924** White Slippers; The Clicking of Cuthbert series including Chester Forgets Himself. **1925** The Presumption of Stanley Hay, M.P.; The Qualified Adventure. **1928** The Lady of the Lake (US 1930); Thou Fool. **1929** The Burgomaster of Stilemonde; A Romance of Seville; The Port of Lost Souls (reissue of White Slippers, 1924).

RAMSEY-HILL, C. S. (aka RAMSEY HILL)
Born: 1891, England. Died: Feb. 3, 1976, Van Nuys, Calif. Screen, radio actor and dialog director.

Appeared in: **1934** Down to Their Last Yacht. **1935** The Crusades. **1952** Bwana Devil; Caribbean. **1953** King of the Khyber Rifles; Rogue's March. **1954** Bengal Brigade; Trader Tom of the China Seas (serial). **1955** Panther Girl of the Congo (serial). **1956** The Ten Commandments. **1961** One Hundred and One Dalmations. **1963** The Three Stooges Go Around the World in a Daze. **1964** The Unsinkable Molly Brown. **1970** On a Clear Day You Can See Forever.

RANALDI, FRANK
Born: 1905. Died: May 2, 1933, Hollywood, Calif. (complications from operation). Screen child actor and later a film casting director.

RANALOW, FREDERICK (Frederick Baring Ranalow)
Born: Nov. 7, 1873, Dublin, Ireland. Died: Dec. 8, 1953, Ireland? Opera singer and screen actor.

Appeared in: **1934** Autumn Crocus (stage and film versions). **1947** Uncle Silas (aka The Inheritance—US 1951).

RAND, JOHN F.
Born: 1872. Died: Jan. 25, 1940, Hollywood, Calif. Screen, vaudeville actor and circus performer.

Appeared in: **1928** The Circus. **1935** Old Sawbones (short).

RAND, LIONEL (Lionel Van Clouser)
Born: 1909, Shamokin, Pa. Died: Oct. 15, 1942, Queens, N.Y. Screen actor, song writer and orchestra leader.

RAND, SALLY (Helen Gould Beck)
Born: Jan. 2, 1904, Elkton, Mo or Ky.? Died: Aug. 30, 1979, Glendora, Calif. (heart failure). Screen, stage, vaudeville actress, burlesque entertainer and celebrated fan dancer. Was a 1927 Wampas Baby Star.

Appeared in: **1925** Braveheart; The Road to Yesterday; The Texas Bearcat; The Dressmaker from Paris. **1926** Bachelor Brides; Gigolo; Man Bait; El Relicario; Sunny Side Up. **1927** Galloping Fury; Getting Gertie's Garter; Heroes in Blue; His Dog; The King of Kings; The Night of Love. **1928** The Fighting Eagle; Black Feather; Crashing Through; A Girl in Every Port; Golf Widows; Nameless Men; A Woman Against the World. **1933** Hotel Variety. **1934** Bolero. **1937** The Big Show.

RANDALL, ADDISON "JACK" (Addison Owen Randall)
Born: 1907. Died: July 16, 1945, Canoga Park, Calif. (fall from horse while filming). Screen actor. Brother of actor Robert Livingston. Married to actress Barbara Bennett (dec. 1958).

Appeared in: **1935** His Family Tree; Another Face. **1936** Two in the Dark; Love on a Bet; Follow the Fleet; Don't Turn 'Em Loose; Navy Born; Flying Hostess. **1937** Red Lights Ahead; Riders of the Dawn; Stars Over Arizona; Blazing Barriers. **1938** The Mexicali Kid. **1939** Driftin' Westward. **1940** Wild Horse Range; Nothing but Pleasure.

RANDALL, BERNARD "BARNEY"
Born: July 4, 1884. Died: Dec. 17, 1954, New York, N.Y. Screen, stage, radio and television actor.

Appeared in: **1920** The Master The Mind; Evil Eye (serial); The $1,000,000 Reward (serial). **1921** Closed Doors. **1922** Determination; Polly of the Follies. **1923** The French Doll; Ponjola. **1924** Sundown; Unmarried Wives. **1925** Classified; Counsel for the Defense; Pretty Ladies; Share and Share Alike; Shattered Lives. **1926** Say It Again; The Skyrocket; Subway Sadie. **1928** Show Girl; Nothing but Pleasure (short).

RANDALL, CARL
Born: 1898, Columbus, Ohio. Died: Sept. 16, 1965, Sydney, Australia. Screen, stage, vaudeville actor, film director, stage producer, dancer and dance director.

Appeared in: **1935** Reckless.

RANDALL, FRED
Born: 1899. Died: Aug., 1933, Hollywood, Calif. (heart attack). Screen actor.

RANDALL, JERRY
Died: Aug. 12, 1974. Screen actor.

Appeared in: **1969** Hell's Angels '69; Hell's Belles. **1970** Angel Unchained.

RANDALL, LARRY
Born: 1920. Died: Oct. 17, 1951, near Port Hueneme, Calif. (auto accident). Screen actor.

RANDALL, RAE (Sigrum Salvason)
Born: 1909. Died: May 7, 1934, Hollywood, Calif. (suicide). Screen actress who doubled for Greta Garbo.

Appeared in: **1927** King of Kings. **1929** The Godless Girl.

RANDALL, WILLIAM
Born: 1877. Died: Apr. 22, 1939, Elizabeth, N.J. Screen, stage, radio actor, author and writer for radio. Appeared in silents.

RANDAX, GEORGES (Gustave Colin)
Born: 1897, Belgium. Died: Jan. 30, 1979, Molenbeek St. Jean, Belgium (heart attack). Screen and stage actor.

Appeared in: These Belgian films: Le Toubib; Minuit; Quai de Bercy.

RANDI, ERMANNO
Born: Italy. Died: Nov. 20, 1951. Screen actor.

Appeared in: **1948** Tragic Hunt. **1952** Brief Rapture; The Cliff of Sin. **1953** The Young Caruso.

RANDLE, FRANK (Arthur McEvoy)
Born: 1901, Wigan, England. Died: July 7, 1957, Blackpool, England. Screen, stage, vaudeville, radio actor and screenwriter.

Appeared in: **1940** Somewhere in England. **1942** Somewhere in Camp; Somewhere on Leave. **1943** Somewhere in Civvies. **1945** Home Sweet Home. **1947** When You Come Home. **1948** Holidays with Pay. **1949** Somewhere in Politics; School for Randle. **1953** It's a Grand Life.

RANDOLPH, AMANDA
Born: 1902, Louisville, Ky. Died: Aug. 24, 1967, Duarte, Calif. (stroke). Black screen, stage, radio and television actress. Sister of actress Lillian Randolph (dec. 1980).

Appeared in: **1938** Swing. **1939** At the Circus; Lying Lips. **1940** Come Midnight. **1950** No Way Out. **1952** She's Working Her Way through College. **1953** Mr. Scoutmaster. **1955** A Man Called Peter. **1967** The Last Challenge.

RANDOLPH, ANDERS (aka ANDERS RANDOLF)
Born: Dec. 18, 1876, Denmark. Died: July 3, 1930, Hollywood, Calif. (relapse after operation). Screen and stage actor. Entered films with Vitagraph.

Appeared in: **1914** Warefare in the Skies. **1915** From Headquarters; The Goddess (serial). **1916** Hero of Submarine D-2. **1917** Within the Law. **1918** The Splendid Sinner. **1919** The Lion and the Mouse; Erstwhile Susan. **1920** The Love Flower. **1921** Buried Treasure; Jim the Penman. **1922** Notoriety; The Referee; Sherlock Holmes; Peacock Alley; Slim Shoulders; The Streets of New York. **1923** The Bright Shawl; The Eternal Struggle; Mighty Lak' a Rose; None So Blind; The Man from Glengarry. **1924** Behold This Woman; In Hollywood with Potash and Perlmutter; By Divine Right; Madonna of the Streets; Dorothy Vernon of Haddon Hall. **1925** The Happy Warrior; Her Market Value; Seven Keys to Baldpate; Souls for Sables. **1926** The Black Pirate; Broken Hearts of Hollywood; The Johnstown Flood; Miss Nobody; Ranson's Folly; Womanpower. **1927** The Climbers; The College Widow; Dearie; The Jazz Singer; The Love of Sunya; Old San Francisco; A Reno Divorce; Sinews of Steel; Slightly Used; The Tender Hour. **1928** The Crimson City; The Gateway of the Moon; Powder My Back; The Power of Silence; The Big Killing; Three Sinners; Women They Talk About; Me, Gangster. **1929** Four Devils; The Kiss; Shanghai Lady; The Show of Shows; Snappy Sneezee (short); The Sin Sister; Young Nowheres; The Viking; Dangerous Curves; Noah's Ark; Last Performance. **1930** Maybe It's Love; Night Owls (short); Son of the Gods; The Way of All Men. **1931** Going Wild. **1965** Laurel and Hardy's Laughing 20's (documentary).

RANDOLPH, DOROTHY (Dorothy Cohen)
Died: Mar. 10, 1918, Atlanta, Ga. Screen actress. Appeared in films for Triangle.

RANDOLPH, ISABEL
Born: 1890. Died: Jan. 11, 1973, Burbank, Calif. Screen, stage, radio and television actress.

Appeared in: **1940** On Their Own; Yesterday's Heroes; Ride, Tenderfoot, Ride; Barnyard Follies; Sandy Gets Her Man. **1941** Look Who's Laughing; Small Town Deb. **1942** My Favorite Blonde; Here We Go Again; Ride 'Em Cowboy. **1943** Follow the Band; Hoosier Holiday; O My Darling Clementine. **1944** Standing Room Only; Jamboree; Wilson. **1945** Miss Susie Slagle's; Practically Yours; The Man Who Walked Alone; The Missing Corpse; Tell It To a Star. **1946** Our Hearts Were Growing Up. **1947** Dear Ruth. **1948** If You Knew Susie; The Noose Hangs High; That Wonderful Urge. **1949** Criss Cross; Feudin' Rhythm. **1950** The Fuller Brush Girl; Mary Ryan, Detective. **1951** Secrets of Monte Carlo; A Wonderful Life; Two Dollar Bettor. **1952** Thundering Caravans. **1953** Border City Rustlers; The Lady Wants Mink. **1954** The Shanghai Story. **1955** You're Never Too Young. **1956** Hot Shots.

RANDOLPH, LILLIAN
Died: Sept. 12, 1980, Los Angeles, Calif. (cancer). Black screen, radio and television actress. Sister of actress Amanda Randolph (dec. 1967). Mother of actor Charles McCowan.

Appeared in: **1938** Life Goes On. **1939** At the Circus. **1940** Little Men; Am I Guilty?; Mr. Smith Goes Ghost. **1941** West Point Widow; Gentleman from Dixie; All-American Co-ed. **1942** Mexican Spitfire Sees a Ghost; Hi, Neighbor; The Great Gildersleeve; Cooks and Crooks (short). **1943** Gildersleeve's Bad Day; Hoosier Holiday; Gildersleeve on Broadway. **1944** The Adventures of Mark Twain; Three Little Sisters; Gildersleeve's Ghost. **1945** A Song For Miss Julie. **1946** It's a Wonderful Life; Child of Divorce. **1947** The Bachelor and the Bobby-Soxer. **1949** Once More, My Darling. **1951** Dear Brat; That's My Boy. **1952** Bend of the River. **1953** Jennifer. **1965** Hush ... Hush, Sweet Charlotte. **1974** How to Seduce a Woman. **1975** Once Is Not Enough; The Wild McCullochs. **1978** Magic. **1979** The Onion Field.

RANDOLPH, MAY
Born: 1873. Died: Apr. 13, 1956, Hollywood, Calif. Screen actress.

RANGA RAO, S. V.
Born: 1918, India. Died: July 19, 1974, Madras, India (heart attack). Screen actor.

Appeared in:Varudhini (film debut); Pathala Bhairavi; Pellichesi Choodu; Raju Peda; Bengarupapa; Brathukutheruvu; Dasi; Kanakatara; Charanadasi; Devadas; Missiamma; Anakali; Gunasunderi Katha; Sasirekha Parinayam.

RANGEL, ARTURO SOTO
Born: 1882, Mexico. Died: May 25, 1965, Mexico City, Mexico. Screen actor.

Appeared in: **1943** Silk, Blood and Sun; The Virgin of Guadalupe. **1944** Maria Candelaria. **1947** St. Francis of Assisi. **1948** The Treasure of Sierra Madre. **1953** Sombrero. **1954** Garden of Eden; other Mexican films: La Intrusa; La Mentira; La Plegaria a Dios; Los Orgullosas; El Cristo de mi Cabacera.

"RANGER BILL" *See* WILLIAM, JOSEPH

RANIER, RICHARD
Born: 1889. Died: Aug. 25, 1960, West Los Angeles, Calif. (arthritis). Screen, stage and vaudeville actor. Appeared in early Vitagraph and Reliance Co. films.

RANIN, HELGE
Born: 1897. Died: Apr. 15, 1952, Stockholm, Sweden. Screen and stage actor. Appeared in Finnish films.

RANKIN, ARTHUR (Arthur Rankin Davenport)
Born: Aug. 30, 1900, New York, N.Y. Died: Mar. 23, 1947, Hollywood, Calif. (cerebral hemorrhage). Screen actor. Son of actors Harry Davenport (dec. 1949) and Phyllis Rankin (dec. 1934). For family information see Harry Davenport.

Appeared in: **1921** Enchantment; The Great Adventure; Jim the Penman; The Lure of Jade. **1922** Enter Madame; The Five Dollar Baby; Little Miss Smiles; To Have and to Hold. **1923** The Call of the Canyon. **1924** Broken Laws; The Dark Swan; Discontented Husbands; Vanity's Price. **1925** Fearless Lover; The Love Gamble; Pursued; Speed; Sun-Up; Tearing Through. **1926** The Hidden Way; The Man in the Shadow; The Millionaire Policeman; Old Loves and New; The Sporting Lover; Volga Boatman. **1927** The Adventurous Soul; Dearie; The Love Wager; Riding to Fame; Slightly Used; The Woman Who Did Not Care; The Blood Ship. **1928** Broken Laws; Say It With Sables; Walking Back; Making the Varsity; Finders Keepers; Companionate Marriage; Submarine; Code of the Air; Domestic Troubles; Runaway Girls; The Wife's Relations. **1929** Glad Rag Doll; The Fall of Eve; Below the Deadline; The Wild Party; Mexicali Rose; Ships of the Night; The Wolf of Wall Street. **1933** Thrill Hunter; Terror Trail. **1934** Search for Beauty; Carnival; Most Precious Thing in Life; Perfectly Mismated (short); Men in Black (short). **1935** Death Flies East; Hoi Polloi (short); Eight Bells; Case of the Missing Man. **1936** Roaming Lady.

RANKIN, CAROLINE J.
Born: Aug. 22, 1881, Pittsburgh, Pa. Died: Feb. 2, 1953, Calif. Screen and stage actress.
Appeared in: **1914** Quarantined. **1915** What Happened to Jones? **1917** Some Boy; The Pawnbroker's Heart. **1918** A Nine O'Clock Town; When do We Eat? **1919** The Lottery Man; Hard Boiled. **1920** Molly and I; Her Honor the Mayor. **1921** Be My Wife. **1922** Kindred of the Dust; The Bootlegger's Daughter; The Village Blacksmith. **1923** Mind Over Motor. **1924** Untamed Youth. **1926** Miss Nobody. **1930** Lone Star Ranger; Medicine Man.

RANKIN, DORIS
Born: 1880. Died: 1946, Washington, D.C. Screen and stage actress. Divorced from actor Lionel Barrymore (dec. 1954).

Appeared in: **1920** The Copperhead. **1921** The Great Adventure; Jim the Penman. **1925** Lena Rivers. **1929** Her Unborn Child. **1930** Love at First Sight. **1931** The Night Angel. **1938** Sales Lady. **1939** Society Smugglers.

RANKIN, HERBERT
Born: 1876. Died: July 16, 1946, Hollywood, Calif. Screen actor.

RANKIN, PHYLLIS
Born: Aug. 31, 1874. Died: Nov. 17, 1934, Canton, Pa. (paralysis). Screen and stage actress. Daughter of stage actor Arthur McKee Rankin (dec. 1914). Married to actor Harry Davenport (dec. 1949). Mother of actor Arthur Rankin (dec. 1947), and actress Kate (dec. 1954), Fanny, and stage manager E. L. Davenport (dec. 1977).

RANOUS, WILLIAM V.
Born: Mar. 12, 1857. Died: Apr. 1, 1915, Santa Monica, Calif. Screen actor and film producer.

Appeared in: **1911** Vanity Fair. **1912** The Little Minister. **1913** A Maid of Mandalay; Sue Simpkin's Ambition; Getting Up a Practice; The Lonely Princess; A Faithful Servant; The Taming of Betty; Jack's Chrysanthemum. **1914** The Upper Hand. **1915** An Intercepted Vengeance; The Chalice of Courage.

RANSOME, EDITH
Born: 1905. Died: Jan. 26, 1933, Seattle, Wash. (overdose of sleeping pills). Screen and stage actress.

Appeared in: **1924** Lilies of the Field.

RAPHAEL, ENID
Died: Mar. 5, 1964, New York, N.Y. Stage and screen actress.

RAPPE, VIRGINIA
Died: Sept. 5, 1921, San Francisco, Calif. (ruptured bladder). Screen actress.

Appeared in: **1917** Paradise Green. **1920** A Twilight Baby.

RAPPORT, FRED
Died: May 29, 1973. Screen actor.

Appeared in: **1939** Conspiracy.

RAPPORT, HELENA
Born: 1884. Died: Dec. 5, 1954, New York, N.Y. Screen and stage actress.

Appeared in: **1916** His Picture in the Paper.

RASCH, ALBERTINA
Born: 1891, Vienna, Austria. Died: Oct. 2, 1967, Woodland Hills, Calif. Screen actress, dancer, ballerina and choreographer. Married to composer Dmitri Tiomkin (dec. 1979).

Appeared in: **1929** The Hollywood Revue of 1929; The Rogue Song; Devil May Care. **1930** Lord Byron of Broadway; Our Blushing Brides. **1933** Broadway to Hollywood. **1937** The Firefly.

RASP, FRITZ (Heinrich Rasp)
Born: 1891, Bayreuth, Germany. Died: Nov. 30, 1976, Graefelfing, Germany. Screen and stage actor.

Appeared in: **1916** Schuhpalast Pinkus. **1920** Lachte man Gerne. **1922** Der Mensch am Wege; Schatten (aka Warning Shadows); Time is Money; Zwischen Abend und Morgen. **1924** Arabella; Komodianten; Ein Sommernachtstraum. **1925** Gotz von Berlichingen Zubenannt mit der Eisernen Hand; Das Haus der Luge; Menschen am Meer; Qualen der Nacht. **1926** Metropolis; Ueberflussige Menschen; Die Waise von Lowood. **1927** Der Geheimnisvolle Spiegel; Kinderseelen Klagen An; Der Letzte Walzer (The Last Waltz); Die Liebe der Jeanne Ney (The Loves of Jeanne Ney); Schinderhannes. **1928** Spione (Spies—US 1929). **1929** Die Drei um Edith; Die Frau im Mond (The Woman on the Moon); Fruhlings Erwachen (The Awakening of Spring); Der Hund von Baskerville (The Hound of the Baskervilles); Tagebuch Einer Verlorenen (Diary of a Lost Girl). **1930** Die Grosse Sehnsucht; Dreyfus. **1931** Die Dreigroschenoper (The Threepenny Opera, aka The Beggar's Opera); Emil und die Detektive (Emil and the Detectives); Der Zinker; Tropennachte; Die Pranke; Der Morder Dimitri Karamasoff (aka Karamazov—US). **1932** Die Vier vom Bob 13; Der Hexer; Die Grausame Freundin. **1933** Der Sundige Hof; Der

Schuss am Nebelhorn; Der Judas von Triol (US 1935). **1934** Grenzfeuer (US 1936); Klein Dorrit (US 1935); Charley's Tante (Charley's Aunt); Lochvogel (US 1935). **1935** Lockspitzel Asew. **1936** Onkel Brasig; Der Hund von Baskerville (and 1929 version). **1937** Togger; Einmal Werd ich Dir Gefallen. **1938** Nanu, Sie Kennen Korf Noch Nicht? (So, You Don't Know Korff Yet?—US 1939). **1939** Es war Eine Rauschende Ballnacht (One Enchanted Evening). **1940** Alarm. **1943** Paracelsus. **1946** Irgendwo in Berlin (Somewhere in Berlin—US 1949). **1950** Skandal in der Botschaft. **1952** Haus des Lebens. **1953** Hokuspokus; Der Muhle im Schwarzwaldertal. **1955** Der Cornet. **1956** Magic Fire. **1959** Der Frosch mit der Maske; Der Rote Kreis.

RASPUTIN, IVAN (Hyman Fishman)
Died: Sept. 25, 1976. Professional wrestler and screen actor.

RASSER, ALFRED
Born: 1906, Switzerland. Died: Aug. 18, 1977, Basle, Switzerland. Screen, stage actor and cabaret entertainer.

Appeared in: H. D. Soldat Laeppli (Auxiliary Soldier Laeppli, stage and film versions).

RASUMNY, MIKHAIL
Born: 1890, Odessa, Russia. Died: Feb. 17, 1956, Los Angeles, Calif. Screen, stage and television actor.

Appeared in: **1940** Comrade X. **1941** Hold Back the Dawn; The Shanghai Gesture; Forced Landing. **1942** Wake Island; This Gun for Hire; Road to Morocco; Yokel Boy. **1943** Her Heart in Her Throat; Hostages; For Whom the Bell Tolls. **1944** And the Angels Sing; Practically Yours; Henry Aldrich Plays Cupid. **1945** A Royal Scandal; The Unseen; A Medal for Benny; The Stork Club; Bring on the Girls; Masquerade in Mexico. **1946** Kitty; Holiday in Mexico; Anna and the King of Siam; Heart Beat; Our Hearts Were Growing Up. **1947** Her Husband's Affairs; Song of My Heart; Pirates of Monterey. **1948** Saigon. **1949** The Kissing Bandit; Free for All; The Pirates of Capri. **1950** Hit Parade of 1951. **1952** Anything Can Happen. **1953** The Stars Are Singing; Tonight We Sing. **1956** Hot Blood.

RATCLIFFE, E. J. (aka E. J. RADCLIFFE)
Born: 1863, London, England. Died: Sept. 28, 1948, Los Angeles, Calif. Screen actor.

Appeared in: **1921** Disraeli; Everyman's Price; Experience; The Great Adventure; The Idol of the North. **1922** The Woman Who Walked Alone. **1924** Wine of Youth; Sundown. **1925** Introduce Me; The Man on the Box; The Marriage Whirl. **1926** 30 Below Zero; The Thrill Hunter; The Black Pirate; Skinner's Dress Suit; Rolling Home; The Winning of Barbara Worth; The Fighting Buckaroo; More Pay—Less Work. **1927** No Control; The Notorious Lady; Framed; Prince of Headwaiters; Smile, Brother, Smile; Cheating Cheaters; Publicity Madness; Held by the Law. **1928** The Head Man; Floating College. **1929** The Four Feathers; The Jazz Age; Show of Shows; Skinner Steps Out; Sally. **1930** The Cohens and the Kellys in Scotland; One Hysterical Night; Wide Open. **1933** I Loved a Woman.

RATHBONE, BASIL (Philip St. John Basil Rathbone)
Born: June 13, 1892, Johannesburg, South Africa. Died: July 21, 1967, New York, N.Y. (heart attack). Screen, stage, radio and television actor. Divorced from Ethel Marion Forman. Married to actress and screenwriter Ouida Bergere (dec. 1974). Star of "Sherlock Holmes" film series. Nominated for 1936 Academy Award for Best Supporting Actor in Romeo and Juliet and in 1938 for If I Were King.

Appeared in: **1921** Innocent; The Fruitful Vine. **1924** Trouping with Ellen; The School of Scandal. **1925** The Masked Bride. **1926** The Great Deception. **1929** The Last of Mrs. Cheyney; Barnum Was Right. **1930** The High Road; This Mad World; The Flirting Widow; A Notorious Affair; Sin Takes a Holiday; A Lady Surrenders; The Bishop Murder Case; The Lady of Scandal. **1931** Once a Lady. **1932** A Woman Commands; After the Ball (US 1933). **1933** One Precious Year; Loyalties. **1935** David Copperfield; Anna Karenina; The Last Days of Pompeii; Captain Blood; Kind Lady; A Feather in Her Hat; A Tale of Two Cities. **1936** Romeo and Juliet; Private Number; The Garden of Allah. **1937** Love from a Stranger; Make a Wish; Confession; Tovarich. **1938** The Adventures of Robin Hood; The Adventures of Marco Polo; If I Were King; Dawn Patrol. **1939** The Adventures of Sherlock Holmes (16 in series); The Sun Never Sets; The Hound of the Baskervilles; Son of Frankenstein; Tower of London; Rio. **1940** Rhythm on the River; The Mark of Zorro; A Date with Destiny. **1941** Paris Calling; International Lady; The Mad Doctor; The Black Cat. **1942** Crossroads; Sherlock Holmes and the Voice of Terror; Fingers at the Window; Sherlock Holmes and the Secret Weapon. **1943** Sherlock Holmes in Washington; Above Suspicion; Sherlock Holmes Faces

Death; Crazy House. **1944** The Scarlet Claw; The Pearl of Death; Frenchman's Creek; Sherlock Holmes and the Spider Woman; Bathing Beauty. **1945** The House of Fear; Pursuit to Algiers; The Woman in Green. **1946** Terror by Night; Dressed to Kill; Heartbeat. **1949** The Adventures of Ichabod and Mr. Toad (narrator). **1954** Casanova's Big Night. **1955** We're No Angels. **1956** The Black Sheep; The Court Jester. **1958** The Last Hurrah. **1962** The Magic Sword (voice only); Tales of Terror; Two Before Zero. **1963** The Comedy of Terrors. **1965** The Adventures of Marco Polo (and 1938 version); Queen of Blood. **1966** Ghost in the Invisible Bikini; Prehistoric Planet Woman. **1967** Dr. Rock and Mr. Roll; Gill Women; Hillbillies in the Haunted House.

RATNAM, KALI N.
Died: Aug. 7, 1950. South India screen actor.

RATNER, ANNA
Born: 1892. Died: July 2, 1967, Chicago, Ill. Screen, stage actress and dancer. Appeared in films between 1912 and 1916 at Essanay Studio.

RATOFF, GREGORY
Born: Apr. 20, 1897, Petrograd, Russia. Died: Dec. 14, 1960, Solothurn, Switzerland. Screen, stage actor, screenwriter, film director, stage and film producer.

Appeared in: **1929** For Sale (short). **1932** Melody of Life; Roar of the Dragon; Deported; Skyscraper Souls; Once in a Lifetime; Secrets of the French Police; Undercover Man; Symphony of Six Million; What Price Hollywood; Thirteen Women. **1933** Sweepings; Professional Sweetheart; Headline Shooters; I'm No Angel; Sitting Pretty; Girl without a Room; Broadway Thru a Keyhole. **1934** The Great Flirtation; Let's Fall in Love; Forbidden Territory (US 1938); George White's Scandals. **1935** King of Burlesque; Hello Sweetheart (aka The Butter and Egg Man); Remember Last Night. **1936** Here Comes Trouble; Sins of Man; Under Two Flags; The Road to Glory; Sing, Baby, Sing; Under Your Spell; Falling in Love (aka Trouble Ahead—US). **1937** Top of the Town; Cafe Metropole; Seventh Heaven. **1938** Sally, Irene and Mary; Gateway. **1939** Rose of Washington Square; Barricade; Hotel for Women; Daytime Wife; Intermezzo. **1940** I Was an Adventuress; The Great Profile; Public Deb No. 1. **1941** Adam Had Four Sons; The Corsican Brothers. **1942** Two Yanks in Trinidad; Footlight Serenade. **1944** Irish Eyes Are Smiling. **1945** Where Do We Go from Here?; Paris Underground. **1946** Do You Love Me?. **1947** Carnival in Costa Rica. **1950** If This Be Sin; All about Eve. **1951** Operation X. **1952** O. Henry's Full House. **1956** Abdullah's Harem. **1957** The Sun Also Rises. **1960** Once More, with Feeling; Exodus. **1961** The Big Gamble.

RATTENBERRY, HARRY (aka HARRY RATTENBURY)
Born: 1860. Died: Dec. 10, 1925, Hollywood, Calif. Screen actor and opera performer.

Appeared in: **1914** Lucille Love; Girl of Mystery (serial); When Eddie Went to the Front. **1915** He Fell in a Cabaret; The Frame Up on Dad; Some Chaperone; An Heiress for Two; Father's Boy; Father's Lucky Escape; A Looney Love Affair; When Father Had the Gout; Where the Deacon Lives; When Father was the Goat; Keeping It Dark; Some Fixer; Father's Helping Hand; A Mixed-Up Elopement; When Cupid Crossed the Bay. **1916** Oh! for a Cave Man; His Wedding Night; The Deacon's Widow; That Dog-Gone Baby; Oliver Twist; Won by a Foul; Innoculating Hubby; Tramp, Tramp, Tramp; Cupid's Undercut; Nearly a Hero; Lovers and Lunatics; Henry's Little Kid; The Boy, the Girl and the Auto; Her Steady Carfare. **1917** Black Hands and Soapsuds; Her Friend the Chauffeur; A Gay Deceiver; Oh, for a Wife; Suspended Sentence; Father was Right; A Lucky Slip; A Marked Man; Indiscreet Corinne; The Learnin' of Jim Benton. **1918** The Law's Outlaw; Playing the Game. **1919** Hearts of Men; Almost Married; The Delicious Little Devil. **1920** Huckleberry Finn. **1921** The Broken Spur; His Pajama Girl; A Motion to Adjourn. **1922** Watch Your Step. **1923** The Printer's Devil; Soul of the Beast. **1924** Abraham Lincoln. **1925** Daring Days.

RAUCOURT, JULES
Born: 1891, Brussels, Belgium. Died: Jan. 30, 1967. Screen, stage actor and author. Entered films in 1916.

Appeared in: **1917** At First Sight; The Hungry Heart (aka Frou Frou). **1918** La Tosca. **1919** Prunella. **1927** Ranger of the North. **1928** Glorious Betsy; His Tiger Lady. **1930** Le Spectre Vert. **1934** Caravan. **1938** Artists and Models Abroad.

RAVEL, SANDRA
Born: 1910. Died: Aug. 13, 1954, Milan, Italy. Screen actress.

Appeared in: **1930** L'Enigmatique Monsieur Parkes; Those Three French Girls. **1931** The Single Sin. **1935** Une Etoile Disparait (A Star Disappears). **1937** Tre Anni Senza Donne; Al Buio Insieme. **1940** A Wife in Peril. Other Italian films: Two Million for a Smile; Ho Visto Brillare Una Stella.

RAVELLE, RAY *See* WESS, OTTO FRANCIS

RAVENEL, FLORENCE
Died: Dec. 18, 1975. Screen actress.

Appeared in: **1953** The Twonky. **1955** Violent Saturday. **1958** Going Steady.

RAVENEL, JOHN (Donald M. Upshur)
Born: 1912. Died: Sept. 14, 1950, Chicago, Ill. (heart attack). Screen actor, radio and television producer.

RAWLINS, HERBERT
Died: 1947. Screen actor. Married to actress Josephine Norman (dec. 1951).

RAWLINS, JUDITH "JUDY" (Judith Ellen Riedel)
Born: June 24, 1936, Wis. Died: Mar. 28, 1974, Los Angeles, Calif. (probably suicide—drug overdose). Screen actress. Divorced from singer and actor Vic Damone.

Appeared in: **1961** 20,000 Eyes; G.I. Blues.

RAWLINSON, HERBERT
Born: Nov. 15, 1885, Brighton, England. Died: July 12, 1953, Woodland Hills, Calif. (lung cancer). Screen, stage, radio and vaudeville actor.

Appeared in: **1912** The God of Gold; The Count of Monte Cristo. **1913** The Sea Wolf. **1914** By Radium's Ray; Dangers of the Veldt; For the Freedom of Cuba; The Law of His Kind; One of the Bravest; Traffic in Babes; The Vagabond; Kid Regan's Hands; Flirting with Death. **1915** The Black Box; Damon and Pythias. **1917** Come Through. **1918** Back to the Woods; Turn of the Wheel. **1919** The Carter Case (serial); Good Gracious Annabelle. **1920** Passers By. **1921** Charge It; The Wakefield Case; The Conflict; Playthings of Destiny; Wealth; You Find It Everywhere; Cheated Hearts; The Millionaire. **1922** The Black Bag; The Man under Cover; The Scrapper; Another Man's Shoes; Confidence; Don't Shoot; One Wonderful Night. **1923** The Clean-Up; Fools and Riches; Nobody's Bride; The Prisoner; Railroaded; The Scarlet Car; Victor; His Mystery Girl; Million to Burn; Mary of the Movies. **1924** High Speed; Stolen Secrets; The Dancing Cheat; Dark Stairways; Jack O'Clubs; The Tomboy. **1925** The Man in Blue; My Neighbor's Wife; The Flame Fighter (serial); The Adventurous Sex; Every Man's Wife; The Great Jewel Robbery; The Prairie Wife; The Unnamed Woman. **1926** Phantom Police (serial); Trooper 77 (serial); The Belle of Broadway; The Gilded Butterfly; Her Big Adventure; Her Sacrifice; Men of the Night; Midnight Thieves; The Millionaire Policeman. **1927** The Bugle Call; The Hour of Reckoning; Wages of Conscience; Slipping Wives (short); Burning Gold. **1928** The Monologist of the Screen (short). **1933** Moonlight and Pretzels; Enlighten Thy Daughter. **1935** The People's Enemy; Show Them No Mercy; Men without Names; Confidential; Convention Girl. **1936** Follow the Fleet; Robinson Crusoe on Clipper Island (serial); Hitchike to Heaven; Ticket to Paradise; Dancing Feet; Bullets or Ballots; A Son Comes Home; Hollywood Boulevard; Mad Holiday; God's Country and the Woman. **1937** S.O.S. Coast Guard (serial); Don't Pull Your Punches; The Go Getter; That Certain Woman; Over the Goal; Love is on the Air; Nobody's Baby; Mysterious Crossing; Back in Circulation; Make a Wish; Blake of Scotland Yard (serial); Something to Sing About. **1938** Hawaii Calls; Orphans of the Street; Women Are Like That; Under the Big Top; The Kid Comes Back; Torchy Gets Her Man; Secrets of an Actress. **1939** You Can't Get Away with Murder; Dark Victory; Sudden Money. **1940** King of the Royal Mounted (serial); Money to Burn; The Five Little Peppers at Home; Free, Blonde and 21; Framed; Seven Sinners; Swiss Family Robinson. **1941** Scattergood Meets Broadway; A Gentleman from Dixie; Bad Man at Deadwood; I Killed that Man; Riot Squad; Flying Wild; I Wanted Wings; Arizona Cyclone; King of the Texas Rangers (serial). **1942** Perils of the Royal Mounted (serial); Smart Alecks; I Live on Danger; Tramp, Tramp, Tramp; Lady Gangster; The Broadway Big Shot; The Panther's Claw; The Yukon Patrol; Stagecoach Buckaroo; Hell, Annapolis; Foreign Agent; War Dogs. **1943** Colt Comrades; Where Are Your Children?; Border Patrol; Lost Canyon; Cosmo Jones in the Crime Smasher; Two Weeks to Live; The Woman of the Town; Doughboys in Ireland; Riders of the Deadline. **1944** Sailor's Holiday; Shake Hands with Murder; Oklahoma Raiders; Marshal of Reno; Marshal of Gunsmoke; Nabonga; Goin' To Town; Sheriff of Sundown; Forty Thieves; Lumberjack. **1946** Accomplice. **1948** Superman (serial); The Argyle Secrets; The Gallant Legion; Borrowed Trouble; The Counterfeiters; Silent Conflict; Sinister Journey; The Strange Gamble. **1949** Brimstone; Fighting Man of the Plains. **1951** Gene Autry and the Mounties.

RAWLSTON, ZELMA
Died: Oct. 30, 1915. Screen and stage actress. Appeared in Biograph films.

RAY, ALBERT "AL"
Born: Aug. 28, 1883 or 1893, Haverhill, Mass. or New Rochelle, N.Y.? Died: Feb. 5, 1944, Hollywood, Calif. Screen, stage, vaudeville actor, film director, screenwriter and author.

Appeared in: **1915** The Wolf Girl; A Woman's Past. **1918** When Do We Eat? **1919** Married in Haste; Love is Love; Be a Little Sport; Vagabond Luck; Tin Pan Alley; The Lost Princess.

RAY, BARBARA
Born: 1914. Died: May 19, 1955, Los Angeles, Calif. (leukemia). Screen actress. Married to actor Roscoe Ates (dec. 1962).

Appeared in: **1935** Millions in the Air.

RAY, CHARLES (Charles Edgar Alfred Ray)
Born: Mar. 15, 1891, Jacksonville, Ill. Died: Nov. 23, 1943, Los Angeles, Calif. (throat and jaw infection). Screen, stage, vaudeville actor, film producer and director.

Appeared in: **1913** The Favorite Son; The Sharpshooter; The Lost Dispatch; The Sinews of War; Bread Cast upon the Waters; A Slave's Devotion; The Boomerang; The Transgressor; The Quakeress; The Bondsman; The Exoneration; The Witch of Salem; Soul of the South; The Open Door; Eileen of Erin. **1914** A Military Judas; The House of Bondage; Her Brother's Sake; In the Tennessee Hills; Repaid; Desert Gold; For the Wearing of the Green; The Paths of Genius; The Rightful Heir; Shorty's Sacrifice; The Card Sharps; In the Cow Country; The Latent Spark; The Curse of Humanity; The City; Red Mask; Joe Hibbard's Claim; One of the Discard; Word of His People; The Fortunes of War; The City of Darkness; The Friend; Not of the Flock. **1915** The Grudge; The Wells of Paradise; The Cup of Life; The Spirit of the Bell; The Renegade; The Shoal Light; The Conversion of Frosty Blake; The Ace of Hearts; City of the Dead; The Painted Soul; The Lure of Woman; The Coward. **1916** Peggy; The Dividend; A Corner in Colleens; The Wolf Woman; The Honorable Algy; The Weaker Sex; Honor Thy Name; Home; Plain Jane; The Deserter. **1917** Back of the Man; The Millionaire Vagrant; Sudden Jim; The Son of His Father; Clod Hopper; The Pinch Hitter. **1918** His Mother's Boy; The Hired Man; The Family Skeleton; Playing the Game; His Own Home Town; The Law of the North; The Claws of the Hun; Nine O'Clock Town; String Beans. **1919** Crooked Straight; Hayfoot, Strawfoot; The Sheriff's Son; Greased Lightning; The Girl Dodger; Bill Henry; The Busher; The Egg-Crate Wallop. **1920** Red Hot Dollars; Paris Green; Alarm Clock Andy; Homer Comes Home; Forty-five Minutes from Broadway; Village Sleuth; Old-Fashioned Boy; Peaceful Valley. **1921** Nineteen and Phyllis; The Old Swimmin' Hole; Scrap Iron; A Midnight Bell; R.S.V.P.; Two Minutes to Go. **1922** Gas, Oil and Water; The Deuce of Spades; Alias Julius Caesar; The Barnstormer; Smudge; Tailor-Made Man. **1923** The Girl I Loved; The Courtship of Miles Standish; Ponjola. **1924** Dynamite Smith. **1925** Some Pun'kins; Percy; Bright Lights. **1926** Sweet Adeline; Paris; The Auction Block. **1927** The Fire Brigade; The Flag Maker; Getting Gertie's Garter; Nobody's Widow; Vanity. **1928** The Garden of Eden; The Count of Ten. **1932** The Bride's Bereavement or Snake in the Grass (short). **1934** Ladies Should Listen; Ticket to a Crime; School for Girls. **1935** By Your Leave; Welcome Home. **1936** Hollywood Boulevard; Just My Luck. **1940** The Lady from Cheyenne; A Little Bit of Heaven. **1941** Wild Geese Calling; The Man Who Lost Himself; A Yank in the R.A.F. **1942** The Magnificent Dope; Tennessee Johnson.

RAY, EDWIN LEE TERRY
Born: 1911. Died: July 22, 1978, Palm Springs, Calif. Screen actor.

Appeared in: **1938** Cocoanut Grove.

RAY, EMMA (Emma Sherwood)
Born: 1871. Died: Jan. 3, 1935, Los Angeles, Calif. Screen, stage and vaudeville actress. Married to actor Johnny Ray (dec. 1927). They appeared in vaudeville together.

Appeared in: **1934** The Old Fashioned Way (short).

RAY, ESTELLE GOULDING
Born: 1888. Died: Aug. 1, 1970, Hollywood, Calif. (due to fall). Stage and screen actress. Appeared in early silents.

RAY, HELEN
Born: 1879, Fort Stockton, Tex. Died: Oct. 2, 1965, Wolfboro, N.H. Screen, stage, vaudeville and television actress. Married to vaudeville actor Homer Miles (dec.) and they appeared in an act billed as "Homer and Helen Miles."

Appeared in: **1921** Experience; Sheltered Daughters.

RAY, JACK
Born: 1917. Died: Oct. 31, 1975, Montclair, Calif. Screen and vaudeville actor. Married to Marion Ray. Appeared in "Our Gang" silents as "Freckles."

RAY, JOHNNY (John Matthews)
Born: 1859, Wales. Died: Sept. 4, 1927, Los Angeles, Calif. (paralytic stroke). Screen, stage and vaudeville actor. Married to actress Emma Sherwood Ray (dec. 1935). They appeared in vaudeville together.

Appeared in: **1928** Bringing Up Father.

RAY, MARJORIE
Born: 1900. Died: July 21, 1924, San Diego, Calif. (tetanus). Stage and screen actress.

RAY, NAOMI
Born: 1893. Died: Mar. 13, 1966, New York, N.Y. Screen, stage and vaudeville actress. Appeared in vaudeville with her husband, Eddie Harrison, in an act billed as "Ray and Harrison."

Appeared in: **1932** The Riding Master (short); plus other early shorts.

RAY, NICHOLAS (Raymond Nicholas Kienzle)
Born: 1911, Galesville, Wis. Died: June 15, 1979, New York, N.Y. (cancer). Screen actor, film director, stage director, screenwriter and radio writer. Divorced from author Jean Evans, actress Gloria Grahame (dec. 1981), and dancer Betty Schwab. Father of film producer Anthony, cameraman Timothy, Nicca, and Julie Ray.

Appeared in: **1975** I'm a Stranger Here Myself. **1977** The American Friend. **1979** Hair.

RAY, TED (Charles Olden)
Born: Nov. 21, 1909, Liverpool, England. Died: Nov. 8, 1977, London, England. Screen, vaudeville, radio, television actor, music hall performer and author. Father of actors Andrew and Robin Ray.

Appeared in: **1930** Elstree Calling. **1934** Radio Parade of 1935 (US 1935). **1950** A Ray of Sunshine. **1952** Meet Me Tonight. **1953** Tonight at 8:30. **1954** Escape by Night. **1956** My Wife's Family. **1959** Carry on Teacher (US 1962); Please Turn Over (US 1960); The Crowning Touch.

RAYLE, MIKE See RALE, MICHAEL W.

RAYMOND, CHARLES
Born: 1858, London, England. Died: 1930, England?. Screen, stage actor, film director, film producer and stage producer. Entered films in 1902.

Appeared in: **1910** The Clerk's Downfall. **1912** Lt. Daring and the Plans of the Minefields (aka The International Spies—US); Don Q and the Artist; Hamlet; The First Chronicles of Don Q—The Dark Brothers of The Civil Guard; Don Q—How He Outwitted Don Luis; Don Q—How He Treated the Parole of Gevil Hay.

RAYMOND, CYRIL
Born: 1897, England. Died: 1973, England? Screen, stage, television actor and screenwriter. Divorced from actress Iris Hoey (dec. 1979), and later married to Gillian Lind.

Appeared in: **1916** Disraeli. **1931** The Ghost Train (US 1933); Man of Mayfair; These Charming People; The Happy Ending. **1932** Condemned to Death; The Frightened Lady (aka Criminal at Large—US 1933). **1933** The Shadow (US 1936); Strike It Rich; The Man Outside. **1935** The Tunnel (aka Transatlantic Tunnel—US). **1936** It's Love Again; Accused; Tomorrow We Live. **1937** Thunder in the City; Dreaming Lips; Mad About Money (aka Stardust, and aka He Loved an Actress—US 1938). **1938** Night Alone. **1939** U-Boat 29; The Spy in Black; Come on George. **1940** Saloon Bar (US 1944). **1945** Brief Encounter (US 1946). **1948** This Was a Woman (US 1949). **1952** Angels One Five (US 1954). **1953** Rough Shoot (aka Shoot First—US). **1954** Lease of Life (US 1955). **1956** The Baby and the Battleship. **1958** Dunkirk; The Safecracker. **1960** No Kidding (aka Beware of Children—US 1961). **1964** Night Train to Paris.

RAYMOND, DOROTHY
Died: Oct. 30, 1981, Pittsburgh, Pa. Screen, stage and television actress. Married to stage actor Alfred A. Webster (dec.).

RAYMOND, FORD
Born: 1900. Died: Apr. 25, 1960, Hollywood, Calif. Screen, stage and vaudeville actor.

Appeared in: **1960** One Foot in Hell.

RAYMOND, FRANCES "FRANKIE"
Born: 1869. Died: June 18, 1961, Hollywood, Calif. Screen and stage actress. Entered films in 1915.

Appeared in: **1921** Garments of Truth; The March Hare; One a Minute; One Wild Week; Smiling All the Way; Two Weeks with Pay. **1922** The Ghost Breaker; Hurricane's Gal; Shadows; Young America. **1923** A Chapter in Her Life; The Grail; The Meanest Man in the World; Money, Money, Money. **1924** Abraham Lincoln; Excitement; Flirting with Love; The Girl on the Stairs; Girls Men Forget. **1925** Seven Chances. **1926** Behind the Front; What Happened to Jones. **1927** The Cruel Truth; The Gay Defender; The Gay Old Bird; Get Your Man; Stage Kisses; Three's a Crowd; Wandering Girls; Web of Fate; The Wreck. **1928** Rich Men's Sons. **1929** The Illusion. **1934** George White's Scandals; The Mighty Barnum. **1935** College Scandal; Love in Bloom. **1937** The Awful Truth. **1941** West Point Widow. **1943** Happy Go Lucky. **1947** Ladies' Man.

RAYMOND, HELEN
Born: c. 1885, Philadelphia, Pa. Died: Nov. 26, 1965, New York, N.Y. Screen and stage actress.

Appeared in: **1920** Twin Beds. **1921** Her Mad Bargain; My Lady Friends; Her Social Value; Through the Back Door. **1922** Very Truly Yours; Wild Honey; The Ableminded Lady. **1923** The Huntress.

RAYMOND, JACK (John Caines)
Born: 1886, Wimborne, England. Died: Mar. 20, 1953, London, England. Screen, stage actor, film director and producer. Entered films as an actor in 1908 with Hepworth Film Company. Do not confuse with U.S. actor Jack Raymond (dec. 1942).

Appeared in: **1912** Plot and Pash; A Detective For a Day. **1913** The Inevitable; On the Brink of the Precipice; The Missioner's Plight; A Midnight Adventure; Look Before You Leap (aka A Damp Deed); An Eggs-traordinary Affair; The Vicar of Wakefield; The Christmas Strike (aka For Such is the Kingdom of Heaven); A Little Widow is a Dangerous Thing; All's Fair. **1914** Flotilla the Flirt; The Sneeze; Creatures of Clay; Two of a Kind; Rhubarb and Rascals; In the Shadow of Big Ben; The Angel of Deliverance. **1920** The Lights of Home; The English Rose. **1921** His Other Wife; Grand Guignol series including: The Flat; The Last Appeal. **1922** The Further Adventures of Sherlock Holmes series including: The Six Napoleons. **1923** The Last Adventures of Sherlock Holmes series including: The Missing Three Quarter. **1931** Up for the Cup.

RAYMOND, JACK
Born: 1892. Died: July 7, 1942, Los Angeles, Calif. Silent screen actor. Do not confuse with British actor Jack Raymond (dec. 1953).

RAYMOND, JACK (George Feder)
Born: Dec. 14, 1901, Minneapolis, Minn. Died: Dec. 5, 1951, Santa Monica, Calif. (heart attack). Screen, stage, vaudeville, television actor, cameraman and film director.

Appeared in: **1921** The Miracle of Manhattan. **1924** Roulette. **1925** Lover's Island; Scarlet Saint. **1927** The Lunatic at Large; Pleasure Before Business. **1928** Sally of the Scandals; The Butter and Egg Man; Lonesome; Melody of Love; Three Week Ends; The Last Command; The Price of Fear; Riley of the Rainbow Division; Thanks for the Buggy Ride. **1929** The Wild Party; Synthetic Sin; The Younger Generation; Points West. **1933** His Silent Racket (short). **1935** Headline Woman; Poker at Eight (short); Paris in Spring. **1936** Preview Murder Mystery; Night Club Scandal. **1937** Easy Living. **1949** Omoo Omoo. **1950** Abbott and Costello in the Foreign Legion.

RAYMOND, PETER "PETE"
Born: 1871, Minneapolis, Minn. Died: Mar. 30, 1927, New York, N.Y. Screen and stage actor.

Appeared in: **1919** Someone Must Pay; Sealed Hearts. **1920** The Imp; On With the Dance; Democracy, The Vision Restored. **1926** The Little Giant.

RAYMOND, ROYAL (Royal Aaron Raymond)
Born: Sept. 29, 1916, New York, N.Y. Died: Dec. 20, 1949, Van Nuys, Calif. (cancer). Screen, stage and television actor.

Appeared in: **1949** The Red Menace.

RAYNAUD, FERNAND
Died: Sept. 28, 1973, Massif Central region, France (automobile accident). Screen, stage, television and radio actor.

RAYNER, MINNIE
Born: May 2, 1869, London, England. Died: Dec. 13, 1941, London, England. Screen and stage actress. Entered films in 1912.

Appeared in: **1926** If Youth but Knew. **1930** A Symphony in Two Flats. **1931** The Man at Six (aka The Gables Mystery—US 1932); The Sleeping Cardinal (aka Sherlock Holmes' Fatal Hour—US); Stranglehold. **1932** The Missing Rembrandt. **1933** This Week of Grace; I Lived With You. **1934** Sometimes Good. **1935** The Triumph of Sherlock Holmes; Barnacle Bill; The Small Man. **1936** Dreams Come True; The House of the Spaniard; If I Were Rich; A Woman Alone (aka Two Who Dared—US 1937). **1937** Silver Blaze (aka Murder at the Baskervilles—US 1941). **1940** Gaslight (aka Angel Street—US 1952).

RAZETTO, STELLA (aka STELLA LE SAINT)
Born: 1881, San Diego, Calif. Died: Sept. 21, 1948, Malibu, Calif. Screen actress. Married to film director Edward J. Le Saint (dec. 1940).

Appeared in: **1913** The Dangling Noose; Outwitted by Billy; Northern Hearts; His Sister; Lure of the Road. **1914** Memories; The Mistress of His House; The Girl Behind the Barrier; The Reporter On the Case; What Became of Jane?; Who Killed George Graves?; Ye Vengeful Vagabonds; A Typographical Error; Peggy of Primrose Lane; The Wasp; C.D.; Fate and Ryan; One Traveler Returns. **1915** The Richest Girl In the World; The Passer-By; The Spirit of the Violin; The Poetic Justice of Omar Khan; The Lady of Cyclamen; The Blood Yoke; The Fortunes of Marian; The Face in the Mirror; The Unfinished Portrait; The Circular Staircase; The Strange Case of Princess Khan. **1916** The Three God Fathers. **1936** Ants in the Pantry (short). **1942** The Wife Takes a Flyer.

RE, GUSTAVO
Born: 1908, Milan, Italy. Died: July, 1979, Barcelona, Spain (diabetes). Screen, television actor, singer and dancer.

Appeared in: **1955** Mr. Arkadin (US 1962, aka Confidential Report). **1963** Scaramouche (aka The Adventures of Scaramouche—US 1964). **1965** Colpo Grosso a Galata Bridge (aka That Man in Istanbul—US 1966). **1969** Le Rouble a Deux Faces (aka The Day the Hot Line Got Hot); Les Hommes de Las Vegas (They Came to Rob Las Vegas).

REA, MABEL LILLIAN
Born: 1932. Died: Dec. 24, 1968, Charlotte, N.C. (auto accident). Screen and television actress.

Appeared in: **1956** Bundle of Joy. **1957** Pal Joey; The Devil's Hairpin. **1958** I Married a Woman. **1959** Submarine Seahawk.

READ, BARBARA
Born: Dec. 29, 1917, Port Arthur, Canada. Died: Dec. 12, 1963. Stage and screen actress. Divorced from actor William Talman (dec. 1968).

Appeared in: **1937** Three Smart Girls; The Mighty Treve; The Road Back; The Man Who Cried Wolf; Merry-Go-Round of 1938; Make Way for Tomorrow. **1938** The Crime of Dr. Hallet; Midnight Intruder. **1939** The Spellbinder; Sorority House. **1940** Married and In Love; Curtain Call. **1942** Too Many Women; Rubber Racketeers. **1946** The Shadow Returns; Behind the Mask; The Missing Lady; Ginger. **1947** Key Witness. **1948** Coroner Creek.

READ, DIDDIE
Born: 1899, Australia. Died: Feb. 6, 1932, Los Angeles, Calif. Screen and vaudeville actress. Sister of stage actress Dorothy Read (dec.) with whom she appeared in vaudeville as part of the "Read Sisters." Appeared in Fox films.

READE, PHILIP "FLIP"
Born: 1948, San Francisco, Calif.? Died: Aug. 26, 1979, Point Conception Coast, Calif. (lost at sea while scuba diving). Mime, martial arts expert, screen and television actor.

Appeared in: **1981** The Incredible Shrinking Woman.

READICK, FRANK M.
Born: 1861. Died: Aug. 26, 1924, New York, N.Y. (heart failure). Screen and vaudeville actor.

REAL, BETTY
Died: Sept. 9, 1969, Miami, Calif. Stage and screen actress.

Appeared in: **1934** Crime Without Passion.

REARDON, CASPER
Born: 1908, Little Falls, N.Y. Died: Mar. 8, 1941, New York, N.Y. (kidney ailment). Screen, vaudeville, radio actor and musician. Son of vaudeville actors John (dec.) and Elizabeth Reardon (dec.).

Appeared in: **1937** You're a Sweetheart.

REAUME, HELEN
Born: Ky. Died: Nov. 1, 1924, Cincinnati, Ohio. Screen actress.

Appeared in: **1916** Where Are My Children? **1917** The Planter.

REDD, IVALOU
Died: Apr. 13, 1975. Screen actress.

Appeared in: **1968** Blue.

REDDING, OTIS
Born: 1941. Died: Dec. 10, 1967 (plane crash). Screen actor and singer.

Appeared in: **1969** Monterey Pop; Popcorn—An Audio Visio Rock Think.

REDFIELD, WILLIAM
Born: Jan. 26, 1927, New York, N.Y. Died: Aug. 17, 1976, New York, N.Y. (respiratory ailment complicated by leukemia). Screen, stage, radio, television actor, playwright and author.

Appeared in: **1938** Back Door to Heaven (film debut). **1950** Conquest of Space. **1956** The Proud and The Profane. **1958** I Married a Woman. **1962** The Connection. **1964** Hamlet. **1965** Morituri (aka The Saboteur, and aka Code Name—Morituri). **1966** Duel at Diablo; Fantastic Voyage. **1967** All Woman (aka All Girl). **1970** The Sidelong Glances of a Pigeon Kicker. **1971** A New Leaf. **1972** The Hot Rock. **1974** Death Wish; For Pete's Sake. **1975** One Flew Over the Cuckoo's Nest. **1977** Mr. Billion.

RED WING *See* ST. CYR, LILLIAN "RED WING"

REDWING, RODD (Rederick Redwing aka ROD REDWING, RODRIC REDWING, ROD RED WING and RODERIC REDWING)
Born: 1905, N.Y. Died: May 30, 1971, Los Angeles, Calif. (heart attack). Screen, stage, television actor and gun coach. Full-blooded Chickasaw Indian.

Appeared in: **1931** The Squaw Man. **1939** Gunga Din!; Lives of a Bengal Lancer. **1944** The Story of Dr. Wassell; Rainbow Island. **1945** Objective Burma! **1946** Out of the Depths. **1947** The Last Round-Up. **1948** Key Largo. **1949** Apache Chief; Song of India. **1950** Kim. **1951** Little Big Horn. **1952** Buffalo Bill in Tomahawk Territory; Son of Geronimo (serial); Rancho Notorious; The Pathfinder; Hellgate. **1953** Winning of the West; Conquest of Cochise; Saginaw Trail; Flight to Tangier. **1954** Gunfighters of the Northwest (serial); Creature from the Black Lagoon; Cattle Queen of Montana; The Naked Jungle; Elephant Walk; The Cowboy. **1956** Jaguar; The Ten Commandments; The Mole People. **1957** Copper Sky. **1958** The Flame Barrier. **1960** Flaming Star. **1961** One-Eyed Jacks; Watch it Sailor. **1962** Sergeants Three. **1964** Invitation to a Gunfighter. **1966** Apache Uprising; Johnny Reno. **1967** El Dorado. **1968** Shalako. **1969** Charro!; The McMasters. **1972** The Red Sun.

REECE, BRIAN
Born: July 24, 1913. Died: Apr. 12, 1962, London, England (bone disease). Screen, stage, radio and television actor.

Appeared in: **1951** A Case for P.C. 49. **1954** Orders Are Orders; Fast and Loose. **1955** Geordie (aka Wee Geordie—US 1956). **1957** Carry On Admiral (aka The Ship Was Loaded—US 1959).

REED, ALAN (aka TEDDY BERGMAN)
Born: Aug. 20, 1907, New York, N.Y. Died: June 14, 1977, West Los Angeles, Calif. Screen, stage, radio and television actor. Married to singer Finette Walker. Was the voice of "Daddy" on the "Baby Snooks" radio show, and "Fred Flintstone" on the Flintstone's television show and film.

Appeared in: **1944** Days of Glory. **1945** Nob Hill. **1946** The Postman Always Rings Twice. **1950** Perfect Strangers; Emergency Wedding; The Redhead and The Cowboy. **1951** Here Comes the Groom. **1952** Viva Zapta; Actors and Sin. **1953** Geraldine; I, the Jury. **1954** Woman's World. **1955** The Far Horizons; A Kiss of Fire; Desperate Hours; Lady and the Tramp (voice). **1956** Revolt of Mamie Stover; Timetable; He Laughed Last. **1957** Tarnished Angels. **1958** Marjorie Morningstar. **1959** 1001 Arabian Nights. **1961** Breakfast at Tiffany's. **1966** The Man Called Flintstone (voice). **1969** A Dream of Kings.

REED, BERNARD
Died: 1967. Screen actor.

Appeared in: **1964** The Troublemaker.

REED, BILLY
Born: 1914. Died: Feb. 4, 1974, New York, N.Y. (heart attack). Screen, vaudeville and stage actor. Was member of dance team of "Gordon, Reed and King" and "Reed and Carruthers."

Appeared in: **1931** 50 Million Frenchmen (stage and film versions). **1937** A Universal short. **1943** Crazy Horse. **1963** The Cardinal.

REED, DAVE
Born: 1872, New York, N.Y. Died: Apr. 11, 1946, N.Y. Screen, stage, vaudeville, radio actor and song writer. Appeared in silents.

REED, DONALD
Born: July 23, 1902, Los Angeles, Calif., or 1907, Mexico City, Mex.? Died: Feb. 27, 1973. Screen actor.

Appeared in: **1925** His Secretary. **1926** There You Are; The Auction Block. **1927** Convoy; Naughty But Nice. **1928** The Mad Hour; Show Girl; The Night Watch; Mark of the Frog (serial). **1929** A Most Immoral Lady; Hardboiled; Evangeline. **1930** The Texan; Little Johnny Jones. **1931** Aloha; Playthings of Hollywood. **1932** The Racing Strain. **1933** Man From Monterey. **1934** Hollywood, Ciudad de Ensueno; Uncertain Lady; Happy Landing. **1935** The Devil Is a Woman; The Cyclone Ranger; The Vanishing Riders. **1936** Darkest Africa (serial). **1937** Crusade Against Rackets; Renfrew of the Royal Mounted.

REED, FLORENCE
Born: Jan. 10, 1883, Philadelphia, Pa. Died: Nov. 21, 1967, East Islip, N.Y. Screen, stage, vaudeville and television actress.

Appeared in: **1915** The Dancing Girl. **1916** New York. **1917** Today; The Eternal Sin. **1918** Wives of Men. **1921** The Eternal Mother; Black Panther's Cub; Indiscretion. **1930** The Code of Honor. **1934** Great Expectations. **1936** Frankie and Johnnie. **1941** Shanghai Gesture.

REED, GEORGE E.
Died: June 11, 1952, Camden, N.J. Stage and screen actor. Married to actress Alice Lucey. They appeared as a song and dance team billed as "Reed and Lucey."

Appeared in: **1919** Checkers.

REED, GEORGE H. (George Henry Reed)
Born: Nov. 27, 1866, Macon, Ga. Died: Nov. 6, 1952, Woodland Hills, Calif. (arteriosclerosis). Black screen actor. Do not confuse with George E. Reed (dec. June 11, 1952).

Appeared in: **1916** The Realization of a Negro's Ambition. **1920** Huckleberry Finn; The Veiled Mystery (serial). **1922** The Jungle Goddess (serial); Scars of Jealousy; Red Lights. **1924** Helen's Babies; The Vagabond Trail. **1925** The Golden Strain; The Isle of Hope. **1926** Danger Quest; Pals First. **1928** Absent; The Clean-Up Man; Three-Ring Marriage. **1929** River of Romance. **1930** Father's Son. **1931** Trails of the Golden West; Little Daddy. **1933** Hold Your Man; Last Trail. **1934** Mrs. Wiggs of the Cabbage Patch; Witching Hour. **1936** The Green Pastures. **1938** The Buccaneer; Kentucky; Going Places. **1939** Secret of Dr. Kildare; Swanee River. **1940** Dr. Kildare's Strangest Case; Sporting Blood; Dr. Kildare's Crisis; Dr. Kildare Goes Home. **1941** Kiss the Boys Goodbye; The People vs. Dr. Kildare; Dr. Kildare's Victory. **1942** Tales of Manhattan; Dr. Gillespie's New Assistant. **1943** Dixie. **1944** The Adventures of Mark Twain; Three Men in White; Home In Indiana. **1945** Strange Illusion. **1947** Dark Delusion (aka Cynthia's Secret).

REED, GUS (Harold Nelson)
Born: 1880. Died: July 17, 1965, Cherry Valley, Calif. Screen, vaudeville, minstrel actor and singer.

Appeared in: **1930** The Woman Tamer (short). **1934** Order in the Court (short); Hi, Nellie. **1943** Coney Island.

REED, ISOBEL *See* ELSOM, ISOBEL

REED, JULIAN
Born: 1864. Died: May 28, 1934, Englewood, N.J. (pneumonia). Screen, stage actor and stage manager.

Appeared in: **1915** The Working of a Miracle.

REED, MARSHALL J.
Born: May 28, 1917, Englewood, Colo. Died: Apr. 15, 1980, Los Angeles, Calif. (hemorrhage). Screen, stage, television actor, film director, film producer and screenwriter. Do not confuse with British actor with same name.

Appeared in: **1943** The Texas Kid. **1944** Haunted Harbor (serial); Range Law; Tucson Raiders; Law Men; Mojave Firebrand; Partners of the Trail; Gangsters of the Frontier. **1945** Law of the Valley; The Chicago Kid. **1946** Gentleman from Texas; Raiders of the South; Drifting Along; Gentleman Joe Palooka; The Haunted Mine; Shadows of the Range. **1947** Angel and the Badman; West of Dodge City; Trailing Danger; Land of the Lawless; The Fighting Vigilantes; Song of the Wasteland; Prairie Express; Cheyenne Takes Over. **1948** The Gallant Legion; Lightnin' in the Forest; Stage to Mesa City; Tornado Range; The Bold Frontiersman; Triggerman; Hidden Danger; Song of

the Drifter; Back Trail; The Fighting Danger; The Rangers Ride; Renegades of Sonora. **1949** The Dalton Gang; Gun Runner; Law of the West; Frontier Investigator; Navajo Trail Raiders; West of El Dorado; Western Renegades; Brand of Fear; Roaring Westward; Riders of the Dusk; Square Dance Jubilee; Federal Agents vs. Underworld, Inc. (serial); Ghost of Zorro (serial); Stampede. **1950** Cherokee Uprising; I Was a Shoplifter; The Invisible Monster (serial); The James Brothers of Missouri (serial); The Cowboy and the Prizefighter; Rider from Tucson; Pirates of the High Seas (serial); The Savage Horde; Radar Secret Service; Over the Border; Six Gun Mesa; Silver Raiders; Outlaw Gold; Law of the Panhandle. **1951** Purple Heart Diary; Mysterious Island (serial); Oh, Susanna; Nevada Badmen; Abiline Trail; Montana Desperado; Canyon Raiders; Hurricane Island; Texas Lawmen; Whistling Hills; Lawless Cowboys; Sailor Beware. **1952** Sound Off!; The Rough Tough West; Laramie Mountains; Kansas Territory; Canyon Ambush; Night Raiders; Guns Along the Border; The Longhorn; Montana Incident; Texas City; The Lusty Men; Blackhawk (serial); Son of Geronimo (serial). **1953** The Great Adventures of Captain Kidd (serial); Cow Country. **1954** Riding With Buffalo Bill (serial); Gunfighters of the Northwest (serial). **1957** The Night the World Exploded. **1958** The Lineup. **1959** Ghost of Zorro (and 1949 serial). **1962** Wild Westerners; Third of a Man. **1965** The Hallelujah Trail. **1967** A Time for Killing.

REED, MAXWELL
Born: 1919, Larne, England. Died: Aug. 16, 1974, England. Screen, stage and television actor. Divorced from actress Joan Collins.

Appeared in: **1946** The Years Between (US 1947); Gaiety George (aka Showtime—US 1948); Daybreak (US 1949). **1947** Dear Murderer (US 1948); The Brothers (US 1948). **1948** Night Beat; Daughter of Darkness. **1949** Madness of the Heart (US 1950); The Lost People. **1950** Blackout; The Clouded Yellow (US 1952). **1951** There Is Another Sun (aka Wall of Death—US 1952); The Dark Man; Flame of Araby. **1953** Sea Devils; The Square Ring (US 1955); Marilyn (aka Roadhouse Girl—US 1955). **1955** The Brain Machine; Before I Wake (aka Shadow of Fear—US 1956); Helen of Troy. **1961** Pirates of Tortuga. **1962** The Notorious Landlady; Advise and Consent. **1966** Picture Mommy Dead.

REESE, W. JAMES
Born: 1898. Died: Feb. 17, 1960, N.Y. Screen, stage and television actor.

Appeared in: **1957** The Young Don't Cry.

REEVE, ADA
Born: Mar. 3, 1874, London, England. Died: Sept. 25, 1966, London, England. Screen and stage actress.

Appeared in: **1944** They Came to a City. **1947** Meet Me at Dawn (US 1948); When the Bough Breaks. **1949** Dear Mr. Prohack (US 1950). **1950** Night and the City. **1952** I Believe in You (US 1953). **1953** The Gay Duelist (rerelease of Meet Me at Dawn—1947). **1956** Eye Witness. **1957** The Passionate Stranger (aka A Novel Affair—US).

REEVES, BILLY
Born: 1864, England. Died: Dec. 29, 1943, Suffolk, England. Screen, stage, vaudeville actor and pantomimist.

Appeared in: **1915** The New Butler.

REEVES, GEORGE (George Basselo)
Born: 1914, Ashland, Ky. Died: June 16, 1959, Beverly Hills, Calif. (suicide—gun). Screen, stage and television actor.

Appeared in: **1939** Gone With the Wind. **1940** Virginia City; Torrid Zone; Tear Gas Squad; Calling All Husbands; Always a Bride; Argentine Nights; Gambling on the High Seas; Father Is a Prince; Knute Rockne—All American; The Fighting 69th; 'Til We Meet Again; Ladies Must Live. **1941** Blue, White and Perfect; Strawberry Blonde; Dead Men Tell; Man at Large; Blood and Sand; Lydia. **1942** The Mad Martindales. **1943** So Proudly We Hail; Border Patrol; Hoppy Serves a Writ; The Leather Burners; The Last Will and Testament of Tom Smith (short); Colt Comrades; Bar-20; Buckskin Frontier. **1944** Winged Victory. **1947** Variety Girl. **1948** Jungle Goddess; The Sainted Sisters; Thunder in the Pines. **1949** The Great Lover; The Mutineers; Special Agent; Adventures of Sir Galahad (serial); Pirate Ship; Jungle Jim. **1950** The Good Humor Man. **1951** Samson and Delilah; Superman and the Mole Men. **1952** Bugles in the Afternoon; Rancho Notorious. **1953** From Here to Eternity; The Blue Gardenia; Forever Female. **1956** Westward Ho the Wagons.

REEVES, JIM
Born: 1924. Died: July 31, 1964, near Nashville, Tenn. (airplane crash). Screen actor and country music singer.

Appeared in: **1964** Kimberly Jim; Country Music Caravan; Tennessee Jamboree.

REEVES, KYNASTON (Kynaston Philip Reeves)
Born: May 29, 1893, London, England. Died: Dec. 10, 1971, London, England. Screen, stage and television actor. Entered films in 1919.

Appeared in: **1932** The Sign of the Four; The Lodger (aka The Phantom Fiend—US 1935). **1933** Puppets of Fate (aka Wolves of the Underworld—US 1935). **1934** Jews Suess (aka Power—US); The Crimson Candle. **1935** Vintage Wine; Dark World. **1937** Take a Chance; A Romance in Flanders (aka Lost on the Western Front—US 1940). **1938** Housemaster (US 1939); Sixty Glorious Years (aka Queen of Destiny—US). **1939** The Outsider (US 1940); Inspector Hornleigh on Holiday; The Stars Look Down (US 1941); Sons of the Sea; Dead Men are Dangerous. **1940** Two for Danger; The Flying Squad. **1941** The Prime Minister. **1942** The Young Mr. Pitt. **1943** The Night Invader. **1945** Strawberry Road (US 1948); The Echo Murders; Murder in Reverse (US 1946); The Rake's Progress (aka Notorious Gentleman—US 1946). **1946** Bedelia (US 1947). **1947** Mrs. Fitzherbert (US 1950). **1948** Vice Versa; This Was a Woman (US 1949); The Weaker Sex (US 1949); The Winslow Boy (US 1950); The Guinea Pig (US 1949). **1949** Badger's Green; Madness of the Heart (US 1950). **1950** The Twenty Questions Murder Mystery; Madeleine; Tony Draws a Horse (US 1951); The Mudlark; Blackout. **1951** The Undefeated; Smart Alec; Captain Horatio Hornblower, RN. **1952** Penny Princess (US 1953); Top Secret (aka Mr. Potts Goes to Moscow—US 1954); Song of Paris (aka Bachelor in Paris—US 1953). **1953** Top of the Form; Laxdale Hall (aka Scotch on the Rocks—US 1954); Four Sided Triangle. **1954** Eight O'Clock Walk (US 1955); Burnt Evidence; The Crowded Day. **1956** Fun at St. Fanny's; Guilty?. **1957** Brothers in Law; Light Fingers; High Flight (US 1958). **1958** Family Doctor (aka Prescription for Murder and Rx Murder—US); A Question of Adultery (US 1959); Fiend Without a Face. **1959** Carlton-Browne of the F.O. (aka Man in a Cocked Hat—US 1960). **1960** School for Scoundrels; In the Nick; The Night We Got the Bird. **1961** The Shadow of the Cat; Carry on Regardless (US 1963); In the Doghouse (US 1964); Don't Bother to Knock (aka Why Bother to Knock—US 1964). **1962** Go to Blazes. **1963** Hide and Seek (US 1964). **1968** Hot Millions. **1969** Anne of the Thousand Days. **1970** The Private Life of Sherlock Holmes.

REEVES, RICHARD (Richard Jourdan Reeves)
Born: Aug. 10, 1912, New York, N.Y. Died: Mar. 17, 1967, Northridge, Calif. (cirrhosis of liver). Screen, stage, television actor and opera singer.

Appeared in: **1943** This Is the Army (stage and film versions). **1947** The Hunted; Unconquered. **1951** Tomorrow Is Another Day; Double Deal; Come Fill the Cup; The Blue Veil; Force of Arms. **1952** She's Working Her Way Through College; The Pride of St. Louis; Hoodlum Empire; A Girl in Every Port; Finders Keepers; Gobs and Gals; Androcles and the Lion; The Racket; Retreat, Hell!; Ma and Pa Kettle at Waikiki; I Dream of Jeannie; Carbine Williams; Fair Wind to Java; We're Not Married; Stop, You're Killing Me; Thunderbirds; Fargo. **1953** City of Bad Men; So You Want to Get it Wholesale (short); Devil's Canyon; A Perilous Journey; Jack Slade; Money From Home; The Glass Wall. **1954** Trader Tom of the China Seas (serial); Loophole; Target Earth; Destry. **1955** The Eternal Sea; I Died a Thousand Times; Top Gun; The Silver Chalice; City of Shadows; Tarzan's Hidden Jungle. **1956** The Man is Armed; Running Target; Dance with Me, Henry; Dangerous Cargo. **1957** Gunfight at O.K. Corral; The Buckskin Lady. **1958** Gunsmoke in Tucson; Auntie Mame. **1959** Riot in Juvenile Prison; The Rookie. **1960** Twelve Hours to Kill. **1961** Blue Hawaii. **1963** Toys In the Attic. **1964** A House Is Not a Home. **1965** Harum Scarum. **1966** Billy the Kid vs. Dracula.

REEVES, ROBERT JASPER
Born: Jan. 28, 1892, Marlin, Tex. Died: Apr. 12, 1960, Hollywood, Calif. (heart attack). Screen and stage actor.

Appeared in: **1919** The Great Radium Mystery (serial). **1923** The Thrill Chaser. **1924** The Mask of Lopez; No Gun Man; The Silent Stranger. **1926** Ambushed; Cyclone Bob; Desperate Chance; Fighting Luck; Iron Fist; Ridin' Straight; Riding for Life. **1927** The Cherokee Kid. **1930** Canyon Hawks.

REEVES-SMITH, H.
Born: 1863. Died: Jan. 29, 1938, Elwell, Surrey, England (heart trouble). Screen and stage actor.

Appeared in: **1924** Three Weeks; No More Women. **1929** The Return of Sherlock Holmes (English version).

REEVES-SMITH, OLIVE
Born: Nov. 23, 1894, Ewell, Surrey, England. Died: July 20, 1972, New York, N.Y. Screen, stage, radio and television actress. Married to actor Fuller Mellish, Jr. (dec. 1930).

Appeared in: **1949** Dear Old Dad; Edward, My Son. **1964** My Fair Lady.

REGAN, BERRY
Born: 1914. Died: Jan. 16, 1956, Hollywood, Calif. (surgery for brain tumor). Screen actor.

Appeared in: **1955** A Bullet for Joey.

REGAN, EDGAR J.
Died: June 21, 1938, San Francisco, Calif. (heart attack). Screen and stage actor.

REGAN, JOSEPH
Born: 1896, Boston, Mass. Died: Nov. 9, 1931, New York, N.Y. (cerebral hemorrhage). Screen, stage, vaudeville, radio actor and concert performer. Married to actress Alberta Curlis and appeared with her in vaudeville.

Appeared in: **1928** America's Foremost Irish Tenor (short).

REGAN, JOSEPH FRANCIS
Born: 1907. Died: Aug. 18, 1933, San Quentin, Calif. Screen extra.

Appeared in: **1930** The Big House.

REGAS, GEORGE (aka GEORGE RIGAS)
Born: Nov. 9, 1890, Sparta, Greece. Died: Dec. 13, 1940, Los Angeles, Calif. Screen and stage actor. Brother of actor Pedro Regas (dec. 1974).

Appeared in: **1921** The Dangerous Moment; The Love Light. **1922** Omar the Tentmaker. **1923** Fashionable Fakers; The Rip Tide. **1925** Wanderer. **1926** That Royal Girl; Beau Geste; Desert Gold. **1929** Redskin; Wolf Song; The Rescue; Acquitted; Sea Fury; Hearts and Hoofs (short). **1930** The Lonesome Trail. **1931** Beau Ideal; Newly Rich. **1933** Desiny Unknown; The Way to Love; Blood Money. **1934** Kid Millions; Viva Villa; Sixteen Fathoms Deep; Bulldog Drummond Strikes Back; Grand Canary. **1935** Bordertown; Lives of a Bengal Lancer; The Marines Are Coming. **1936** Rose Marie; Hell-Ship Morgan; Under Two Flags; Isle of Fury; Daniel Boone; Robin Hood of El Dorado; The Charge of the Light Brigade. **1937** Waikiki Wedding; Another Dawn; Lefthanded Law; Love Under Fire; The Californian. **1938** Mr. Moto Takes a Chance; Torchy Blane in Panama; Penrod's Double Trouble. **1939** Arrest Bulldog Drummond; The Adventures of Sherlock Holmes; The Light That Failed. **1940** Torrid Zone; The Mask of Zorro.

REGAS, PEDRO (Panagiotis Regas)
Born: Apr. 12, 1882, Sparta, Greece. Died: Aug. 10, 1974, Hollywood, Calif. Screen, stage and television actor. Brother of actor George Regas (dec. 1940).

Appeared in: **1932** Danger Island; Scarface; Tiger Shark. **1933** Flying Down to Rio. **1934** Viva Villa; West of the Pecos. **1935** Black Fury. **1936** Sutter's Gold; The Traitor. **1938** The Girl of the Golden West. **1939** The Rains Came; Only Angels Have Wings. **1940** Road to Singapore. **1943** For Whom the Bell Tolls; Tiger Fangs. **1945** South of the Rio Grande. **1946** Perilous Holiday. **1948** French Leave. **1952** Viva Zapata. **1964** Madmen of Mandoras. **1968** The Hell With Heroes. **1970** Angel Unchained; Flap.

REHAN, MARY
Born: 1887. Died: Aug. 28, 1963, Rochester, Minn. Screen and stage actress.

Appeared in: **1922** Flesh and Spirit.

REHFELD, CURT
Born: Feb. 11, 1881, Germany. Died: Mar. 24, 1934, Germany? Screen actor and film director. Entered films as an extra.

Appeared in: **1921** The Four Horsemen of the Apocalypse. **1923** All the Brothers Were Valiant. **1929** General Crack.

REHG, WALLY (Walter Phillip Rehg)
Born: Aug. 31, 1888, Summerfield, Ill. Died: Apr. 5, 1946, Burbank, Calif. Professional baseball player and screen actor.

Appeared in: **1929** Fast Company.

REICHER, FRANK
Born: Dec. 2, 1875, Munich, Germany. Died: Jan. 19, 1965, Playa del Rey, Calif. Screen, stage actor, film director and screenwriter. Brother of actress Hedwig Reicher (dec. 1971). Entered films in 1915.

Appeared in: **1921** Behind Masks; Idle Hands; Out of the Depths; Wise Husbands. **1926** Her Man O'War. **1928** Beau Sabreur; The Blue Danube; The Masks of the Devil; Four Sons; Sins of the Fathers; Someone to Love; Napoleon's Barber. **1929** His Captive Woman; Mister Antonio; Black Waters; Her Private Affair; The Changeling;

Strange Cargo; Big News; Paris Bound. **1930** Girl of the Port; The Grand Parade; Die Sehnsucht Jeder Frau. **1931** Gentleman's Fate; Beyond Victory; Suicide Fleet. **1932** A Woman Commands; The Crooked Circle; Scarlet Dawn; Mata Hari. **1933** Topaze; Employees' Entrance; Jennie Gerhardt; Captured; Ever in My Heart; Before Dawn; Son of Kong; King Kong. **1934** I Am a Thief; Return of the Terror; The Case of the Howling Dog; The Fountain; Hi, Nellie; Journal of a Crime; Countess of Monte Cristo; Little Man, What Now?; Let's Talk It Over; No Greater Glory. **1935** The Great Impersonation; Star of Midnight; The Florentine Dagger. **1936** A Dog of Flanders; Mills of the Gods; The Man Who Broke the Bank at Monte Carlo; Remember Last Night; Rendezvous; Kind Lady; The Story of Louis Pasteur; The Murder of Dr. Harrigan; Magnificent Obsession; The Invisible Ray; Sutter's Gold; The Country Doctor; Under Two Flags; Girl's Dormitory; Star for a Night; 'Till We Meet Again; Murder on the Bridle Path; The Ex-Mrs. Bradford; Second Wife; Anthony Adverse; Stolen Holiday. **1937** The Life of Emile Zola; Laughing at Trouble; Night Key; On Such a Night; The Great O'Malley; Under Cover of Night; Lancer Spy; Espionage; The Emperor's Candlesticks; The Road Back; Prescription for Romance; Fit for a King; Stage Door; Midnight Madonna. **1938** City Streets; Torchy Gets Her Man; Prison Nurse; Rascals; I'll Give a Million; Suez. **1939** Juarez; Ninotchka; Unexpected Father; Mystery of the White Room; Woman Doctor; The Magnificent Fraud; Our Neighbors, the Carters; The Escape; South of the Border; Everything Happens at Night. **1940** Dr. Cyclops; The Man I Married; Devil's Island; Typhoon; The Lady in Question; South to Karanga; Sky Murder; Dr. Ehrlich's Magic Bullet; All This and Heaven Too. **1941** Flight from Destiny; They Dare Not Love; Shining Victory; The Nurse's Secret; Underground; Dangerously They Live. **1942** Nazi Agent; Salute to Courage; To Be or Not to Be; The Mystery of Marie Roget; Beyond the Blue Horizon; The Gay Sisters; Secret Enemies; Scattergood Survives a Murder; The Mummy's Tomb; Night Monster. **1943** Mission to Moscow; Yanks Ahoy; Tornado; The Song of Bernadette; The Canterville Ghost. **1944** Captain America (serial); Adventures of Mark Twain; The Hitler Gang; The Conspirators; The Mummy's Ghost; Address Unknown; Gildersleeve's Ghost. **1945** The Big Bonanza; Jade Mask; Phantoms, Inc.; Hotel Berlin; The Tiger Woman; House of Frankenstein; Blonde Ransom; A Medal for Benny. **1946** Sister Kenny; The Strange Mr. Gregory; Voice of the Whistler; The Shadow Returns; My Pal Trigger; Home in Oklahoma. **1947** Escape Me Never; The Secret Life of Walter Mitty; Violence; Yankee Faker; Mr. District Attorney. **1948** Carson City Raiders; Fighting Mad. **1949** Samson and Delilah; Barbary Pirate. **1950** Cargo to Capetown; Kiss Tomorrow Goodbye. **1951** The Lady and the Bandit.

REICHER, HEDWIG
Born: June 12, Oldenburg, Germany. Died: Sept. 2, 1971, Los Angeles, Calif. Screen and stage actress. Sister of actor Frank Reicher (dec. 1965).

Appeared in: **1925** A Lover's Oath. **1927** King of Kings. **1928** The Leopard Lady. **1929** True Heaven; Lucky Star; The Godless Girl. **1930** Redemption. **1931** Beyond Victory; Sporting Chance. **1936** The House of a Thousand Candles; I Married a Doctor.

REICHOW, WERNER
Born: 1922. Died: Aug. 17, 1973, Santa Monica, Calif. (cancer). Screen actor.

Appeared in: **1957** The Enemy Below.

REID, CARL BENTON
Born: 1894. Died: Mar. 16, 1973, Studio City, Calif. Screen, stage and television actor.

Appeared in: **1941** The Little Foxes. **1942** Tennessee Johnson. **1943** The North Star. **1950** In a Lonely Place; The Fuller Brush Girl; The Flying Missile; Convicted; Stage to Tucson; The Killer That Stalked New York. **1951** The Great Caruso; Criminal Lawyer; Lorna Doone; Family Secret; Smuggler's Gold. **1952** Boots Malone; Carbine Williams; The Story of Will Rogers; The Brigand; The First Time; Indian Uprising. **1953** Main Street to Broadway; Escape From Fort Bravo. **1954** The Command; Broken Lance; The Egyptian; Athena. **1955** One Desire; The Left Hand of God; The Spoilers; Wichita. **1956** The First Texan; The Last Wagon; A Day of Fury; Battle Hymn; Strange Intruder. **1957** Time Limit; Spoilers of the Forest. **1958** Tarzan's Fight for Life; The Last of the Fast Guns. **1959** The Trap. **1960** The Bramble Bush; The Gallant Hours. **1962** Pressure Point; The Underwater City. **1963** The Ugly American. **1966** Madame X.

REID, HAL
Born: 1873. Died: May 22, 1920. Screen actor, film director, producer and screenwriter. Father of actor Wallace Reid (dec. 1923). Appeared in Vitagraph films in 1911.

Appeared in: **1911** One Touch of Nature; The Deerslayer. **1912** Every Inch a Man; Indian Romeo and Juliet; Jean Intervenes; The Hobo's Redemption; Father Beaudaine; Cardinal Wolsey. **1915** Time Lock 1776.

REID, LESLIE
Died: 1917 (accident while filming). Screen actor.

Appeared in: **1917** The Ride for Life.

REID, MARY
Born: Aug. 29, 1895, Gibralter. Died: July 18, 1979, N.Y. Screen, stage and television actress.

REID, MAX (Maxwell Reid)
Born: Aug. 22, 1903, Apia, Western Samoa. Died: May 3, 1969, Los Angeles, Calif. (heart attack). Musician and screen actor.

Appeared in: **1956** Around the World in 80 Days; The Revolt of Mamie Stover. **1967** Lupe.

REID, TREVOR
Born: 1909. Died: Apr. 19, 1965, London, England. Screen, stage and television actor.

Appeared in: **1956** Satellite in the Sky; Murder Reporter (US 1960). **1957** How to Murder a Rich Uncle. **1958** A Question of Adultery (US 1959). **1960** Marriage of Convenience (US 1970). **1961** Mary Had a Little; Attempt to Kill (US 1966). **1962** The Fast Lady (US 1965); The Longest Day. **1963** Walk a Tightrope (US 1964). **1964** Night Train to Paris.

REID, MRS. WALLACE *See* DAVENPORT, DOROTHY

REID, WALLACE
Born: Apr. 15, 1891, St. Louis, Mo. Died: Jan. 18, 1923, Los Angeles, Calif. (drug addiction). Screen actor and film producer. Married to actress Dorothy Davenport who also appeared under her married name "Reid" (dec. 1977) and father of actor Wallace Reid, Jr. Son of actor Hal Reid (dec. 1920).

Appeared in: **1910** The Phoenix. **1911** The Reporter; The Deerslayer; Leather Stocking Tales; The Leading Lady. **1912** The Gamblers; Chumps; Indian Romeo and Juliet; The Telephone Girl; The Seventh Son; The Illumination; Brothers; The Victoria Cross (aka The Charge of the Light Brigade); The Hieroglyphic; Diamond Cut Diamond; Curfew Shall Not Ring Tonight; Kaintuck; Before the White Man Came; A Man's Duty; A Cripple Creek; His Only Son; Making Good; The Secret Service Man; Indian Raiders; Every Inch a Man; The Tribal Law. **1913** The Heart of a Cracksman; Love and the Law; A Rose of Old Mexico; The Ways of Fate; The Picture of Dorian Grey; When Jim Returned; The Tattooed Arm; Youth and Jealousy; The Kiss; Her Innocent Marriage; His Mother's Son; A Modern Snare; When Luck Changes; Via Cabaret; The Spirit of the Flag; Hearts and Horses; In Love and War (aka Women and War); Dead Man's Shoes; Pride of Lonesome; The Powder Flash of Death; A Foreign Spy; The Picket Guard; Mental Suicide; The Animal; The Harvest of Flame; The Mystery of the Yellow Aster Mine; The Gratitude of Wanda; The Wall of Money; The Cracksman's Reformation; Cross Purposes; The Fires of Fate; Retribution; A Cracksman Santa Claus; The Lightning Bolt; A Hopi Legand (aka A Pueblo Romance). **1914** Who So Diggeth a Pit; The Intruder; The Countess Betty's Mine; The Wheel of Life; Fires of Conscience; The Greater Devotion; A Flash in the Dark; Breed of the Mountains; Regeneration; The Heart of the Hills; The Way of a Woman; The Voice of the Viola; The Spider and Her Web; The Mountaineer; Cupid Incognito; A Gypsy Romance; The Skeleton; The Fruit of Evil (aka The Sins of the Father); Women and Roses; The Quack; The Siren; The Man Within; Passing of the Beast; Love's Western Flight (aka Children of Fate); A Wife on a Wager; Cross the Mexican Line; The Den of Thieves; Arms and the Gringo; Down by the Sounding Sea; Moonshine Molly; The City Beautiful; The Second Mrs. Roebuck; Sierra Jim's Reformation; Down the Hill to Creditville; Her Awakening; For Her Father's Sins; A Mother's Influence (aka His Mother's Last Word); The Niggard; The Odalisque; The Little Country Mouse; Another Chance; Over the Ledge (aka On the Ledge); Baby's Ride; The Test; At Dawn. **1915** The Craven; The Three Brothers; The Lost House; Station Content; A Yankee from the West; The Golden Chance; The Chorus Lady; Birth of a Nation; Carmen; Enoch Arden; Old Heidelberg. **1916** The Selfish Woman; The House with the Golden Windows; The Yellow Pawn; Maria Rosa; To Have and to Hold; The Love Mask; Intolerance. **1917** Joan, the Woman; The Golden Fetter; The Prison Without Walls; The World Apart; The Squaw Man's Son; The Hostage; The Devil Stone; The Woman God Forgot; Big Timber; Nan of Music Mountain. **1918** The Things We Love; The House of Silence; The Man from Funeral Range; The Firefly of France; The Source; Too Many Millions; Believe Me, Zantippe; Rimrock Jones; Less Than Kin; Ruggles of Red Gap. **1919** The Dub; Alias Mike Moran; Hawthorne of the U.S.A.; Valley of the Giants; The Roaring Road; You're Fired; The Love Burglar; The Lottery Man. **1920** Always Audacious; What's Your Hurry?; Double Speed; Sick Bed; The Dancin' Fool; Excuse My Dust. **1921** The Affairs of Anatol; Too Much Speed; Don't Tell Exerything; Forever; The Call of the North; The Love Special; The Hell Diggers; The Charm School. **1922** Across the Continent; Night Life in Hollywood; Rent Free; Nice People; The World's Champion; The Ghost Breaker; Clarence; The Dictator; Thirty Days.

REIGUERA, FRANCISCO
Born: Madrid, Spain. Died: Mar., 1969, Mexico City, Mexico. Screen actor.

Appeared in: **1956** La Mort en ce Jardin (aka Gina—US 1961). **1958** Enchanted Island. **1965** Viva Maria; Major Dundee; Simon del Desierto (Simon of the Desert—US 1969). **1967** Los Canones de San Sebastian (Guns for San Sebastian—US 1968).

REILLY, MICHAEL
Born: 1933. Died: Jan. 10, 1962, Newhaven, England (parachute jump). Parachutist and double for Robert Wagner.

Appeared in: **1962** The War Lover.

REIMERS, GEORGE
Born: 1870. Died: Apr. 15, 1936. Screen actor.

Appeared in: **1923** Queen of Sin.

REINER, FRITZ
Born: Dec. 19, 1888, Budapest, Hungary. Died: Nov. 15, 1963, New York, N.Y. Violinist and screen actor.

Appeared in: **1947** Carnegie Hall.

REINHARDT, JOHN
Born: 1901. Died: Aug. 6, 1953, Berlin, Germany (heart attack). Screen actor, film director, author and screenwriter.

Appeared in: **1929** The Prince of Hearts; Love, Live and Laugh; The Climax. **1931** Der Tanz Geht Weiter. **1936** The Rest Cure.

REINOLD, BERNARD (Major Bernard Adolph Reinold aka ADOLPH BERNARD)
Born: 1860. Died: Mar. 19, 1940, East Islip, N.Y. Screen, stage, vaudeville actor and "soldier of fortune."

Appeared in: **1921** The Passionate Pilgrim.

REIS, ALBERTO
Born: 1902, Portugal. Died: Feb., 1953 (tropical disease). Stage and screen actor. Married to actress Branca Saldanha.

REISNER, CHARLES F. "CHUCK" (aka CHARLES F. RIESNER)
Born: Mar. 14, 1887, Minneapolis, Minn. Died: Sept. 24, 1962, La Jolla, Calif. Screen, stage, vaudeville actor, film director, producer, screenwriter and television writer.

Appeared in: **1916** His First False Step; His Lying Heart. **1918** A Dog's Life. **1921** The Kid. **1922** The Pilgrim. **1923** Her Temporary Husband; Breaking Into Society; Hollywood. **1924** A Self-Made Failure; Universal comedies. **1925** Man on the Box; Justice of the Far North. **1936** Everybody Dance.

REITHE, ALOISE D.
Born: 1890, Los Angeles, Calif. Died: Sept. 5, 1943, Los Angeles, Calif. Screen actor and film director. Appeared in and directed silent films.

REJANE, GABRIELLA
Born: 1857, Paris, France. Died: June 14, 1920, Paris, France. Stage and screen actress.

Appeared in: **1912** Madame Sans-Gene; Miarka, the Daughter of the Bear. **1922** Gypsy Passion.

RELPH, GEORGE
Born: Jan. 27, 1888, Cullercoast, Northumberland, England. Died: Apr. 24, 1960, London, England. Screen and stage actor. Married to Deborah Nanson and later to actress Mercia Swinburne.

Appeared in: **1916** Paying the Price. **1921** Candytuft, I Mean Veronica; The Door That Has No Key (US 1922). **1944** Give Us the Moon. **1947** Nicholas Nickeby. **1952** I Believe in You (US 1953). **1953** The Titfield Thunderbolt; The Final Test (US 1954). **1957** Doctor at Large; Davy. **1960** Ben Hur.

REMARQUE, ERICH MARIA
Born: 1898, Germany. Died: Sept. 25, 1970, Locarno, Switzerland (heart collapse). Novelist, Screen actor and screenwriter. Divorced from Ilsa Jeanne Zamboul. Married to actress Paulette Goddard.

Appeared in: **1958** A Time to Love and a Time to Die.

REMLEY, FRANK(aka ELLIOTT LEWIS)
Born: 1902. Died: Jan. 28, 1967, Newport Beach, Calif. Radio, screen guitarist and actor. Appeared in films as Elliott Lewis.

Appeared in: **1949** The Story of Molly X. **1950** Ma and Pa Kettle Go to Town. **1951** Saturday's Hero. **1953** Let's Do It Again.

REMLEY, RALPH MCHUGH
Born: 1885. Died: May 26, 1939, Los Angeles, Calif. Screen and stage actor.

Appeared in: **1934** Keep 'Em Rolling; Double Door; Behold My Wife; One Is Guilty; Home on the Range. **1935** Princess O'Hara; Dr. Socrates. **1936** Poppy; Yours for the Asking; Bullets or Ballots; Robin Hood of El Dorado. **1937** Let Them Live; Make Way for Tomorrow. **1938** Outside of Paradise. **1939** King of the Underworld; The Story of Alexander Graham Bell.

REMY, ALBERT
Born: 1912, France. Died: Jan. 26, 1967, Paris, France. Screen actor.

Appeared in: **1944** Les Enfants du Paradis (Children of Paradise—US 1946). **1945** Groupi Mains Rouge (It Happened at the Inn). **1949** Devil's Daughter. **1950** Francois Villon. **1956** French Can-Can (aka Only the French Can). **1957** Razzle. **1958** Crime et Chatinaut (Crime and Punishment, aka The Most Dangerous Sin—US). **1959** La Vache et le Prisonnier (aka The Cow and I—US 1961); Les Quartre Cents Coups (The 400 Blows). **1960** Tirez sur le Pianiste (Shoot the Piano Player—US 1962); Le Passage du Rhin (aka Tomorrow Is My Turn—US 1962). **1962** The Four Horsemen of the Apocalypse; Gigot; La Fayette (US 1963); Le Septieme Jure (The Seventh Juror—US 1964). **1963** Mandrin. **1964** Le Train (The Train—US 1965); Weekend a Zuydcotte (Weekend at Dunkirt—US 1966). **1965** Cent Briques et des Tuiles (aka How Not to Rob a Department Store—US); Mata-Hari Agent H-21 (US 1967). **1966** Grand Prix; Is Paris Burning?. **1967** The 25th Hour.

REMY, DICK, SR.
Born: 1873. Died: June 1, 1947, Hollywood, Calif. (heart attack). Screen actor and film director. Appeared in and directed silent films.

RENALDO, DUNCAN (Renault Renaldo Duncan)
Born: Apr. 23, 1904, Rumania or Camden, N.J.? Died: Sept. 3, 1980, Goleta, Calif. (lung cancer). Screen, stage, radio, television actor, film producer and screenwriter.

Appeared in: **1928** Devil's Skipper; Clothes Make the Woman; The Naughty Duchess. **1929** The Bridge of San Luis Rey; Pals of the Prairie. **1931** Trader Horn. **1934** The Moth; Public Stenographer. **1936** Moonlight Murder; Rebellion; Lady Luck. **1937** Mile a Minute Love; Two Minutes to Play; Jungle Menace (serial); The Painted Stallion (serial); Zorro Rides Again (serial). **1938** Spawn of the North; Crime Afloat; Rose of the Rio Grande. **1939** The Lone Ranger Rides Again (serial); Rough Rider's Round-Up; Juarez and Maximilian (aka The Mad Empress); The Kansas Terrors; Cowboys from Texas; South of the Border. **1940** Heroes of the Saddle; Pioneers of the West; Covered Wagon Days; Gaucho Serenade; Rocky Mountain Rangers; Oklahoma Renegades. **1941** Gauchos of Eldorado; Outlaws of the Desert; King of the Texas Rangers (serial); South of Panama; Down Mexico Way. **1942** King of the Mounties (serial); A Yank in Libya. **1943** Secret Service in Darkest Africa (serial); For Whom the Bell Tolls; Mission to Moscow; Border Patrol; Tiger Fangs; Hands Across the Border; The Desert Song. **1944** The Tiger Woman (serial); The Fighting Seabees; The San Antonio Kid; Call of the South Seas; Sheriff of Sundown. **1945** The Cisco Kid Returns; Adventure; The Cisco Kid in Old New Mexico; South of the Rio Grande. **1947** Jungle Flight; Bells of San Fernando. **1948** Sword of the Avenger; The Valiant Hombre. **1949** The Gay Amigo; The Daring Caballero; Satan's Cradle. **1950** The Girl from San Lorenzo; The Capture. **1951** The Lady and the Bandit. **1959** Zorro Rides Again (and 1937 serial).

RENARD, DAVID
Born: 1921. Died: Aug. 15, 1973, West Hollywood, Calif. (heart attack). Screen and stage actor. Entered films in 1954.

Appeared in: **1961** Frontier Uprising; The Long Rope. **1962** Deadly Duo. **1965** Ship of Fools. **1968** The Counterfeit Killer. **1969** Change of Habit.

RENARD, ROY (aka HAROLD OFER)
Died: Aug. 21, 1978. Screen actor.

Appeared in: **1932** Smiling Faces.

RENAULT, CAMILLE
Born: 1905. Died: Aug. 23, 1976, Sharon, Conn. Screen, stage and vaudeville actress. Ziegfeld Girl who appeared in French films.

RENAVENT, GEORGE (Georges de Cheux)
Born: Apr. 23, 1894, Paris, France. Died: Jan. 2, 1969, Guadalajara, Mexico. Screen, stage actor, stage and film director. Married to actress Selena Royle.

Appeared in: **1919** Erstwhile Susan. **1929** Rio Rita. **1930** Scotland Yard; Le Spectre Vert. **1931** East of Borneo. **1933** Moulin Rouge; Queen Christina; Private Detective 62. **1934** Stamboul Quest; Fashions of 1934; The Bombay Mail; House of Rothschild. **1935** Follies Bergere; Whipsaw; The White Cockatoo; Front Page Woman; The Last Outpost; Captain Blood; Broadway Gondolier. **1936** Charge of the Light Brigade; The Invisible Ray; The Sky Parade; Lloyds of London. **1937** History Is Made at Night; Seventh Heaven; Cafe Metropole; Love Under Fire; Wife, Doctor and Nurse; Charlie Chan at Monte Carlo; Love and Hisses; The Sheik Steps Out; Fight for Your Lady; Artists and Models Abroad; The King and the Chorus Girl. **1938** Jezebel; Gold Diggers in Paris; I'll Give a Million; Suez. **1939** Mr. Moto's Last Warning; Topper Takes a Trip; The Three Musketeers; Pack Up Your Troubles. **1940** The House Across the Bay; Son of Monte Cristo; Comrade X; Turnabout; Brother Orchid. **1941** The Great Lie; Sullivan's Travels; That Night In Rio; Road to Zanzibar; The Night of January 16th. **1942** Perils of Nyoka (serial); Spy Smasher (serial); Silver Queen. **1943** Secret Service in Darkest Africa (serial); Mission to Moscow; Wintertime; The Desert Song. **1944** Our Hearts Were Young and Gay; Storm Over Lisbon; Experiment Perilous. **1945** This Love of Ours; Captain Eddie; Saratoga Trunk. **1946** Tarzan and the Leopard Woman; The Catman of Paris; The Perfect Marriage. **1947** Ladies' Man; The Foxes of Harrow. **1949** Rope of Sand. **1951** Secrets of Monte Carlo. **1952** Mara Maru.

RENFRO, RENNIE
Born: 1893. Died: Mar. 2, 1962, Redding, Calif. (heart attack). Screen actor, dog trainer and stuntman. Appeared in early Sennett comedies and trained "Daisy" for the "Blondie" series.

RENN, KATHARINA
Born: 1913, Germany. Died: 1975, Paris, France. Screen, stage and television actress.

Appeared in: **1966** La Prise de Pouvoir par (de) Louis XIV (The Rise of Louis XIV—US 1970).

RENNIE, GUY
Died: Dec. 4, 1979. Screen actor.

Appeared in: **1935** Coronado. **1950** Grounds for Marriage. **1954** Roogie's Bump. **1955** Night Freight. **1956** Invasion of the Body Snatchers.

RENNIE, JAMES
Born: 1889, Toronto, Canada. Died: July 31, 1965, New York, N.Y. Stage and screen actor. Divorced from actress Dorothy Gish (dec, 1968).

Appeared in: **1920** Remodeling Her Husband. **1921** Stardust. **1922** The Dust Follower. **1923** Mighty La' a Rose; His Children's Children. **1924** Argentine Love; The Moral Sinner; Restless Wives. **1925** Clothes Make the Pirate; Share and Share Alike. **1930** The Bad Man; Girl of the Golden West; Two Rounds of Love (short). **1931** Illicit; The Lash; Party Husband. **1932** The Little Damozel. **1941** Skylark. **1942** Crossroads; Tales of Manhattan; Now Voyager. **1945** Wilson; A Bell for Adano.

RENNIE, MICHAEL
Born: Aug. 29, 1909, Bradford, Yorkshire, England. Died: June 10, 1971, Harrogate, Yorkshire, England. Screen, stage and television actor.

Appeared in: **1936** The Secret Agent. **1937** Gangway. **1938** The Divorce of Lady X; Bank Holiday (aka Three on a Weekend—US). **1939** This Man in Paris. **1941** Dangerous Moonlight (aka Suicide Squadron—US 1942); The Patient Vanishes (US 1947 aka This Man is Dangerous); The Tower of Terror (US 1942); Turned Out Nice Again; Ships with Wings (US 1942); Pimpernel Smith (aka Mister V—US 1942). **1942** The Big Blockade. **1945** I'll Be Your Sweetheart; The Wicked Lady (US 1946). **1946** Caesar and Cleopatra. **1947** White Cradle (aka High Fury—US 1948); The Root of All Evil. **1948** Idol of Paris; Uneasy Terms. **1949** The Golden Madonna. **1950** Trio; The Black Rose; The Body Said No!; Miss Pilgrim's Progress; Sanitorium. **1951** The House in the Square (aka I'll Never Forget You—US); The 13th Letter; The Day the Earth Stood Still. **1952** Phone Call from a Stranger; Five Fingers; Les Miserables. **1953** Single-Handed (aka Sailor of the King—US); Dangerous Crossing; The Robe; King of the Khyber Rifles. **1954** Demetrius and the Gladiators; Princess of the Nile; Desiree. **1955** Mambo; Seven Cities of Gold; Soldier of Fortune; The Rains of Ranchipur. **1956** Teenage Rebel. **1957** Island in the Sun; Omar Khayyam. **1958** Battle of the V.I. (aka Unseen Heroes—US). **1959** Third Man on the Mountain. **1960** The Lost World. **1963** Mary, Mary. **1965** Night of the Tiger. **1966** Ride Beyond Vengeance. **1967** Hondo and the Apaches; Cyborg 2087; Hotel. **1968** Nude ... si Muore (aka The Young, the Evil and the Savage—US); The Power; The Devil's Brigade; Death on the Run; Subterfuge. **1969** Operation Terror.

RENOIR, JEAN
Born: Sept. 15, 1894, Paris, France. Died: Feb. 12, 1979, Los Angeles, Calif. (heart attack). Screen actor, film director, stage producer, screenwriter and author. Son of impressionist painter Pierre-Auguste Renoir (dec. 1919). Brother of actor Pierre Renoir (dec. 1952). Married to actress Catherine Hessling (aka Andree Heuschling), and Dido Freire.

Appeared in: **1929** Le Petit Chaperon Rouge; La Petite Lili. **1939** La Regle du Jeu (Rules of the Game—US 1950). **1940** The Human Beast; Grand Illusion. **1950** Ways of Love (aka A Day in the Country). **1961** Rules of the Game (revised version). **1974** Le Petit Theatre de Jean Renoir (The Little Theatre of Jean Renoir—narrator).

RENOIR, PIERRE
Born: 1885, France. Died: Mar. 11, 1952, Paris, France. Screen and stage actor. Son of artist Pierre August Renoir (dec. 1919). Brother of actor Jean Renoir (dec. 1979).

Appeared in: **1911** La Digue (Ou Pour Sauver la Hollande). **1932** Nuit du carrefour (The Night at the Crossroads). **1934** L'Agonie des Aigles; La Bandera; Madame Bovary. **1938** La Marseillaise; L'Affaire Lafarge; The Patriot; Sacrifice d'Honneur. **1939** Kreutzer Sonata; Le Recif de Corail; Escape from Yesterday; Citadel of Silence. **1941** Hatred; The Mad Emperor; Personal Column. **1944** Les Enfants du Paradis (Children of Paradise—US 1946). **1946** Peleton d'Execution (Resistance); Sirocco. **1948** Foolish Husbands. **1951** Dr. Knock (US 1955).

REPP, STAFFORD (Stafford Alois Repp)
Born: Apr. 26, 1918, Calif. Died: Nov. 5, 1974, Inglewood, Calif. (heart attack). Screen, television and radio actor.

Appeared in: **1955** Not as a Stranger; Man With the Gun. **1956** The Price of Fear; The Steel Jungle. **1957** The Green-Eyed Blonde; Plunder Road. **1958** Hot Spell; I Want to Live. **1961** The Explosive Generation. **1965** A Very Special Favor. **1966** Batman. **1975** Linda Lovelace for President.

REQUA, CHARLES
Died: Dec. 11, 1967. Screen actor.

Appeared in: **1925** East of Suez. **1926** Paris at Midnight; The Son of the Sheik; The Count of Luxembourg; A Poor Girl's Romance. **1927** The King of Kings. **1932** South of the Rio Grande. **1934** Are We Civilized? **1936** Yours for the Asking.

RESTA, COL. FRANCIS E.
Born: 1894. Died: Aug. 16, 1968, Bronx, N.Y. Screen actor and leader of U.S. Military Band.

RETTY, WOLF ALBACH
Born: 1908, Austria. Died: Feb. 21, 1967. Screen actor. Father of actress Romy Schneider (dec. 1982).

Appeared in: **1935** Winternachtstraum. **1940** Mutterliebe (Mother Love).

REVEL, MOLLIE
Born: 1848. Died: Dec. 31, 1932. Screen actress.

REVELL, HAMILTON
Born: 1872, Gibraltar. Died: Apr. 11, 1958, Nice, France. Screen and stage actor.

Appeared in: **1917** Thais. **1919** A Star Overnight. **1921** Good Women. **1927** The Telephone Girl.

REVSON, PETER
Born: Feb. 27, 1939, New York, N.Y. Died: Mar. 22, 1974, Johannesburg, South Africa (auto crash). Race car driver and screen actor.

Appeared in: **1966** Grand Prix. **1975** One by One (documentary).

REX

Died: Date unknown. Screen horse. "King of the Wild Horses." Appeared with several cowboy actors in silents and early talkies.

Appeared in: **1924** The King of the Wild Horses; Lightning Romance. **1925** Black Cyclone; Pals; Silent Sheldon; Three in Exile; The Wild Girl. **1926** The Devil Horse; Hi-Jacking Rustlers; Peril of the Rail; The Silent Guardian; West of the Rainbow's End. **1927** Code of the Range; Death Valley; No Man's Law; Running Wild; Set Free; The Western Rover; Wild Beauty. **1928** Guardians of the Wild; The Two Outlaws. **1929** The Arizona Kid; The Girl on the Barge; The Harvest of Hate; Hoofbeats of Vengeance; Plunging Hoofs; Wild Blood. **1930** Parade of the West. **1931** Vanishing Legion. **1933** Smoky.

REY, ROBERTO (Roberto Colas Iglesias)

Born: 1905, Chile. Died: May 30, 1972, Madrid, Spain (heart attack). Screen and stage actor.

Appeared in: **1933** El Principe Gondolero; Gente Alegre; Salga de la Cocina; El Barbero de Sevilla; Cotolay. **1938** La Verbena de la Paloma. **1940** Germina Siempre Asi (It Always Ends That Way). **1963** El Valle de las Espadas (aka The Castilian—US 1963). **1964** Los Pistoleros de Casa Grande (Gunfighters of Casa Grande—US 1965).

REY, ROSA

Died: Apr. 7, 1969. Screen actress.

Appeared in: **1945** George White's Scandals. **1946** Two Years Before the Mast; A Stolen Life; Gilda; The Face of Marble. **1948** The Secret Beyond the Door. **1953** The Great Sioux Uprising. **1954** Secret of the Incas. **1955** The Rose Tattoo.

REYES, EFREN

Born: 1924, Philippine Islands. Died: Feb. 11, 1968, Manila, Philippine Islands (heart attack). Screen actor.

Appeared in: **1959** The Scavengers. **1963** Raiders of Leyte Gulf.

REYES, EVA (Adaljina Ardura)

Born: 1915. Died: Mar. 20, 1970, Miami, Fla. (interstitial fibrosis of the lungs). Screen, stage actress and dancer. Was part of dance team of "Paul and Eva Reyes." Also toured with Xavier Cugat's band at one time.

Appeared in: **1947** Copacabana.

REYES, LUCHA

Born: 1908, Mexico. Died: June 25, 1944, Mexico City, Mexico. Singer and screen actress.

Appeared in: **1943** Ay Jalisco no te Rajes.

REYES, STANLEY J.

Died: Nov. 25, 1980. Screen actor.

Appeared in: **1950** Panic in the Streets. **1975** Mandingo. **1976** Obsession. **1978** French Quarter.

REYNOLDS, ABE

Born: 1884. Died: Dec. 25, 1955, Hollywood, Calif. Screen, stage, burlesque, vaudeville and radio actor.

Appeared in: **1930** Love at First Sight. **1936** Swing Time. **1949** My Dear Secretary.

REYNOLDS, ADELINE DEWALT

Born: Sept. 19, 1862, Benton County, Iowa. Died: Aug. 13, 1961, Los Angeles, Calif. Stage and screen actress.

Appeared in: **1941** Come Live With Me (film debut); Shadow of the Thin Man. **1942** Tales of Manhattan; Tuttles of Tahiti; Street of Chance. **1943** Behind the Rising Sun; The Human Comedy; Iceland; Happy Land; Son of Dracula. **1944** Going My Way; Old Lady; Since You Went Away. **1945** The Corn Is Green; Counterattack; A Tree Grows in Brooklyn. **1948** The Girl from Manhattan. **1949** Sickle or Cross. **1950** Kim. **1951** Here Comes the Groom. **1952** Lydia Bailey; Pony Soldier. **1954** Witness to Murder. **1956** The Ten Commandments.

REYNOLDS, ALAN D.

Died: June 22, 1976. Screen and stage actor.

Appeared in: **1954** Tobor the Great. **1956** Earth vs. The Flying Saucers. **1957** Beginning of the End. **1962** Cape Fear.

REYNOLDS, CRAIG (Hugh Enfield)

Born: July 15, 1907, Anaheim, Calif. Died: Oct. 22, 1949, Los Angeles, Calif. (result of motorcycle crash). Screen, stage and vaudeville actor. Married to actress Barbara Pepper (dec. 1969).

Appeared in: **1930** Coquette. **1933** Gordon of Ghost City (serial); The Phantom of the Air (serial). **1934** Cross Country Cruise; I'll Tell the World; Love Birds. **1935** Four Hours to Kill; Paris in Spring; The Case of the Lucky Legs; Man of Iron; Ceiling Zero. **1936** Broadway Playboy; Brides Are Like That; Times Square Playboy; Jailbreak; Smart Blonde; Here Comes Carter!; The Case of the Black Cat; Treachery Rides the Range; The Golden Arrow; Sons O'Guns; Stage Struck. **1937** The Case of the Stuttering Bishop; Footloose Heiress; Slim; The Great O'Malley; The Great Garrick; Back in Circulation; Under Suspicion; Penrod and Sam; Melody for Two. **1938** House of Mystery; Slander House; Romance on the Run; Gold Mine in the Sky; Making Headlines; Female Fugitive; I Am a Criminal. **1939** The Mystery of Mr. Wong; Navy Secrets; Bad Little Angel; The Gentleman from Arizona; Wall Street Cowboy. **1940** The Fatal Hour; Son of the Navy; I Take This Oath. **1944** Nevada. **1945** Divorce; The Strange Affair of Uncle Harry. **1946** Just Before Dawn; Queen of Burlesque. **1948** My Dog Shep; The Man from Colorado.

REYNOLDS, HAROLD

Born: 1896. Died: Sept. 21, 1972, Hollywood, Calif. (heart attack). Screen, stage and television actor. Entered films at age 70.

Appeared in: **1971** The Steagle.

REYNOLDS, JACK (John W. Paulson)

Born: 1900. Died: July 27, 1977, Wilmington, Del. Screen, stage actor and wrestler.

Appeared in: **1950** Military Academy (aka Military Academy With That 10th Avenue Gang); In a Lonely Place; The Sun Sets at Dawn. **1958** Gang War; Bullwhip.

REYNOLDS, LAKE

Born: 1889. Died: Feb. 9, 1952, Hollywood, Calif. Screen, stage, minstrel, vaudeville and radio actor.

REYNOLDS, NOAH

Died: Sept. 19, 1948, North Philadelphia, Pa. Screen and stage actor. Appeared in early Lubin Co. and McCurdy Film Co. films.

REYNOLDS, PETER

Born: Aug. 16, 1926, Wilmslow, Cheshire, England. Died: Apr. 22, 1975, Australia. Screen and stage actor.

Appeared in: **1948** The Guinea Pig (US 1949). **1949** Adam and Evelyne (aka Adam and Evalyn—US). **1950** Guilt Is My Shadow. **1951** Smart Alec. **1952** The Last Page (aka Manbait—US); A Woman's Angle (US 1954); 24 Hours in a Woman's Life (aka Affair in Monte Carlo—US 1953). **1953** The Robe. **1954** The Silver Chalice. **1957** The Long Haul. **1959** Shake Hands With the Devil. **1960** The Hands of Orlac; The Man Who Couldn't Walk (US 1964); Your Money or Your Wife (US 1965); It Takes a Thief (aka The Challenge—US 1962). **1962** Murder Can Be Deadly (aka The Painted Smile). **1964** The Great American Car Swindle. **1968** Nobody Runs Forever (aka The High Commissioner—US).

REYNOLDS, QUENTIN

Born: 1903. Died: Mar. 17, 1965. Screen actor, film director, writer and radio newscaster.

Appeared in: **1947** Golden Earrings. **1950** Cassino to Korea (narrator). **1959** Naked Africa (narrator). **1960** Justice and Caryl Chessman (narrator).

REYNOLDS, TOM

Born: Aug. 9, 1866, Paddington, England. Died: July 25, 1942, England? Screen and stage actor.

Appeared in: **1924** The Cost of Beauty.

REYNOLDS, VERA (Vera Norma Reynolds)

Born: Nov. 25, 1899, Nebraska. Died: Apr. 22, 1962, Woodland Hills, Calif. Screen actress. Entered films in 1920 with Christie Comedies. Married to actor Robert Ellis (dec. 1974).

Appeared in: **1923** Prodigal Daughters; Woman-Proof. **1924** Feet of Clay; Broken Barriers; Cheap Kisses; Flapper Wives; For Sale; Icebound; Shadows of Paris. **1925** Road to Yesterday; The Golden Bed; The Limited Mail; The Million Dollar Handicap; The Night Club; Without Mercy. **1926** Silence; Corporal Kate; Risky Business; Steel Preferred; Sunny Side Up. **1927** Almost Human; The Little

Adventuress; The Main Event. **1928** Divine Sinner; Golf Widows; Jazzland. **1929** Tonight at Twelve. **1930** Back from Shanghai; The Last Dance; Lone Rider; Borrowed Wives. **1931** Hell Bent for Frisco; Lawless Woman; Neck and Neck. **1932** The Gorilla Ship; Dragnet Patrol; The Monster Walks; Tangled Destinies.

REYNOLDS, WILSON
Born: 1870, Louisville, Ky. Died: Apr. 10, 1938, Ossing, N.Y. Screen, stage actor and stage director.

Appeared in: **1922** Young America. **1924** Janice Meredith.

RHEIN, MITCHELL
Born: 1900. Died: Sept. 23, 1977, Woodland Hills, Calif. Screen actor.

RHEIN-SCHRADLING, OTTO F.
Died: Apr. 30, 1952, Milwaukee, Wis. Screen actor. Appeared in early Essanay Co. films.

RHINE, JACK
Born: 1911. Died: Aug. 21, 1951, San Francisco, Calif. (poliomyelitis). Screen, stage and radio actor.

RHODES, ALFRED "DUSTY"
Died: Feb. 6, 1948, San Francisco, Calif. Screen actor.

RHODES, LILA
Born: 1890, Providence, R.I. Died: Oct. 5, 1980, Englewood, N.J. Screen, stage and vaudeville actress.

Appeared in: **1939** Secret Service of the Air; Women in the Wind.

RHODES, MARJORIE
Born: Apr. 9, 1903, Hull, Yorkshire, England. Died: July 4, 1979, Hove, Sussex, England. Screen, stage, vaudeville and television actress.

Appeared in: **1939** Poison Pen (film debut—US 1941). **1941** Love on the Dole. **1943** When We are Married; Old Mother Riley, Detective; Escape to Danger (US 1944); Theatre Royal. **1944** It Happened One Sunday; On Approval (US 1945); Twany Pipit (US 1947). **1945** Great Day (US 1946). **1946** School for Secrets. **1947** Uncle Silas (aka The Inheritance—US 1951). **1948** This Was a Woman (US 1949); Escape. **1950** The Cure for Love. **1952** The Yellow Balloon (US 1954); Time Gentlemen Please; Decameron Nights. **1953** Street Corner; Those People Next Door; The Girl on the Pier. **1954** To Dorothy a Son (aka Cash on Delivery—US 1956); The Weak and the Wicked. **1955** Room in the House; Footsteps in the Fog. **1956** Now and Forever; Yield to the Night (aka Blonde Sinner—US); It's Great To Be Young (US 1958). **1957** There's Always Thursday; Hell Drivers (US 1958); After the Ball; The Passionate Stranger (aka A Novel Affair—US); Just My Luck; No Time for Tears. **1958** Gideon's Day (aka Gideon of Scotland Yard—US 1959); Alive and Kicking (US 1964). **1961** Watch It Sailor!; Over the Odds. **1965** I've Gotta Horse; Those Magnificent Men in Their Flying Machines: or, How I Flew From London to Paris in 25 Hours and 11 Minutes. **1966** The Family Way (US 1967). **1968** Mrs. Brown You've Got a Lovely Daughter. **1971** Hands of the Ripper.

RHUDIN, FRIDOLF
Born: 1895, Sweden. Died: Mar. 6, 1935 (brain fever). Screen and stage actor. Appeared in Scandinavian films.

RIAL, LOUISE
Born: 1850. Died: Aug. 9, 1940, New York, N.Y. Screen and stage actress.

Appeared in: **1915** Sin.

RIANO, RENIE
Died: July 3, 1971, Woodland Hills, Calif. Screen, stage and television actress. Daughter of stage actress Irene Riano (dec. 1940).

Appeared in: **1937** Tovarich; You're a Sweetheart. **1938** Outside of Paradise; Spring Madness; Thanks for Everything; Men Are Such Fools; Four's a Crowd; Nancy Drew, Detective; The Road to Reno. **1939** Wife, Husband and Friend; The Honeymoon's Over; Disputed Passage; Nancy Drew and the Hidden Staircase; The Woman; Mr. Moto in Danger Island; Day Time Wife; Nancy Drew, Trouble Shooter. **1940** The Man Who Wouldn't Talk; The Ghost Comes Home; Kit Carson; Remedy for Riches. **1941** You're the One; Adam Had Four Sons; Affectionately Yours; Ice-Capades; You Belong to Me. **1942** Whispering Ghosts; Blondie for Victory. **1943** The Man from Music Mountain; None but the Lonely Heart. **1944** Jam Session; Take It or Leave It; Three Is a Family. **1945** Anchors Aweigh; Club Havana; A Song for Miss Julie. **1946** Bringing Up Father; So Goes My Love; Bad Bascomb. **1947** Winter Wonderland. **1948** Jiggs and Maggie in

Society; Jiggs and Maggie in Court; The Time of Your Life. **1949** Jackpot Jitters. **1950** Jiggs and Maggie Out West. **1951** As Young as You Feel; The Barefoot Mailman. **1953** Clipped Wings. **1964** Bikini Beach; Pajama Party. **1965** The Family Jewels. **1966** Three on a Couch; Fireball 500.

RIBEIRO, JOY
Born: 1956, New York. Died: Dec. 19, 1972, Los Angeles, Calif. Singer, dancer, television and screen actress.

Appeared in: **1972** Black Gunn; Lady Sings the Blues.

RICCARDO, RICK, JR.
Born: 1930. Died: June 3, 1977, Phoenix, Ariz. Screen, stage actor and restauranteur. Son of actor Rick Riccardo, Sr.

Appeared in: **1976** The Man Who Fell to Earth.

RICCI, NORA
Born: 1925, Italy. Died: Apr., 1976, Rome, Italy (liver ailment). Screen and stage actress. Daughter of actors Renzo Ricci and Margherita Bagni. Married to actor Vittorio Gassman. Mother of actress Paola Gassman.

Appeared in: **1966** Signore e Signori (aka The Birds and the Bees, and aka The Italians—US 1967). **1967** Le Streghe (The Witches—US 1968). **1968** Tenderly (aka The Girl Who Couldn't Say No—US 1969). **1969** La Caduta Degli Dei (aka The Damned); La Matriarca (The Libertine). **1974** The Night Porter.

RICE, EMMIT B.
Born: 1884. Died: Mar. 23, 1939, Los Angeles, Calif. Screen actor.

Appeared in: **1915** Birth of a Nation.

RICE, FANNY
Born: 1859, Lowell, Mass. Died: July 10, 1936, New York, N.Y. Screen, stage, vaudeville actress and stage producer.

Appeared in: **1919** Moonshine Trail; Dawn; My Husband's Other Wife.

RICE, FLORENCE
Born: Feb. 14, 1911, Cleveland, Ohio. Died: Feb. 22, 1974, Honolulu, Hawaii (lung cancer). Screen and stage actress. Daughter of sports columnist Grantland Rice. Divorced from actor Robert Wilcox (dec. 1955). Married to Fred Butler.

Appeared in: **1932** The Fighting Marshal. **1934** Fugitive Lady. **1935** The Best Man Wins; Carnival; Under Pressure; Death Flies East; Guard That Girl; Escape from Devil's Island; Awakening of Jim Burke. **1936** Superspeed; Panic On the Air; Pride of the Marines; The Blackmailer; Women Are Trouble; Sworn Enemy; The Longest Night. **1937** Under Cover of Night; Man of the People; Married Before Breakfast; Double Wedding; Navy Blue and Gold; Beg, Borrow or Steal; All Is Confusion; Riding On Air. **1938** Sweethearts; Paradise for Three; Fast Company; Vacation From Love. **1939** The Kid From Texas; At the Circus; Miracles For Sale; Stand Up and Fight; Little Accident; Four Girls in White. **1940** Broadway Melody of 1940; The Secret Seven; Girl in 313; Phantom Raiders; Cherokee Strip. **1941** Fighting Marshall; Doctors Don't Tell; The Blonde from Singapore; Mr. District Attorney; Father Takes a Wife; Borrowed Hero. **1942** Tramp, Tramp, Tramp; Let's Get Tough!; Boss of Big Town; Stand By All Networks. **1943** The Ghost and the Guest.

RICE, FRANK (Frank Thomas Rice)
Born: May 13, 1892, Muskegon, Mich. Died: Jan. 9, 1936, Los Angeles, Calif. (nephritis, hepatitis). Screen actor.

Appeared in: **1923** Blood Test; Desert Rider; The Forbidden Trail; The Red Warning. **1924** The Air Hawk; Dynamite Dan; The Ridin' Kid from Powder River; The Galloping Ace; Wolves of the North (serial). **1925** The Call of Courage; Two-Fisted Jones; Spook Ranch; The Cloud Rider; Moccasins; Riders of Mystery; Ridin' Party; The Speed Demon. **1926** The Border Sheriff; Davy Crockett at the Fall of the Alamo; The Fighting Buckaroo; The Fighting Peacemaker; Flying High. **1927** The Boy Rider; Red Signals; Sky-High Saunders; The Slingshot Kid; Three Miles Up; Tom's Gang; The Wolf's Fangs. **1928** The Bantam Cowboy; Headin' for Danger; The Hound of Silver Creek; Orphan of the Sage; The Pinto Kid; A Thief In the Dark; Rough Ridin' Red; Won in the Clouds; Young Whirlwind. **1929** The Lawless Legion; The Overland Telegraph; Pals of the Prairie; The Royal Rider; Stairs of Sand; The Vagabond Cub; The Wagon Master; Dangerous Females (short); The Forbidden Trail; Faro Nell (aka In Old Californy). **1930** Check and Double Check; On Your Back; So This Is London; Parade of the West; The Fighting Legion. **1931** The Conquering Horde; The Squaw Man;

Corsair. **1932** Horse Feathers. **1933** Somewhere In Sonora. **1934** The Last Round-Up. **1935** Ruggles of Red Gap; Hard Rock Harrigan; Stone of Silver Creek; Border Brigands; Powdersmoke Range; Valley of Wanted Men; The Ivory-Handled Gun. **1936** Nevada; The Oregon Trail.

RICE, GRANTLAND

Born: 1881. Died: July 13, 1954, N.Y. (heart attack). Sportswriter and screen actor. Appeared as narrator in his sports shorts. Won 1943 Academy Award for best one-reel picture, Amphibious Fighters. Father of actress Florence Rice (dec. 1974).

Appeared in: **1917** Salmon Fishing in New Brunswick and Cane River, Northeastern Canada. **1925** Grantland Rice "Sportlights" which included the following shorts: Rough and Tumbling; Brains and Brawn; By Hook or Crook; Sporting Armor; Neptune's Nieces; Traps and Troubles; Action; Beauty Spots; Sporting Judgment; All Under One Flag; Dude Ranch Days; Twinkle-Twinkle; Animal Celebrities; Learning How; Why Kids Leave Home; Sons of Swat; Seven Ages of Sport; Barrier Busters; Starting an Argument; Outing for All; Clever Feet; Shooting Time; Walloping Wonders; Then and Now; Fins and Feathers. **1932** Madison Square Garden. **1934-35** Grantland Rice "Sportlights." **1935** Nineteen "Sportlights" shorts. **1943** Amphibious Fighters (short). **1951** Follow the Sun.

RICE, JACK (Jack Clifford Rice)

Born: May 14, 1893, Mich. Died: Dec. 14, 1968, Woodland Hills, Calif. (cancer). Screen and stage actor.

Appeared in: **1933** Fits in a Fiddle (short). **1934** The following shorts: A Blasted Event; Odor In the Court; In the Devil's Doghouse; Poisoned Ivory. **1935** The following shorts: Bric-a-Brac; South Seasickness; Sock Me to Sleep; Edgar Hamlet; In Love at 40; Happy 'Tho Married; Alibi Bye Bye. **1936** Walking on Air; plus the following shorts: Gasoloons; Will Power; High Beer Pressure; Dummy Ache. **1938** Arson Racket Squad; Arson Gang Busters; plus the following shorts: Ears of Experience; False Roomers; Men in Fright; The Jitters. **1940** Slightly at Sea (short); Money to Burn; Danger on Wheels. **1941** Men of Timberland; New York Town; plus the following shorts: Westward Ho-Hum; I'll Fix That; A Quiet Fourth; A Polo Pony. **1942** The following shorts: Heart Burn; Interior Decorator; Cooks and Crooks; Two for the Money; Rough on Rents; Duck Soup. **1943** Swing Time Johnny; Reveille With Beverly; Good Morning, Judge; Two Weeks to Live; plus the following shorts: Unlucky Dog; Not On My Account; Hot Foot; Hold Your Temper; Indian Signs. **1944** Lady, Let's Dance!; Goin' to Town; plus the following shorts: Prunes and Politics; Radio Rampage; The Kitchen Cynic; Feather Your Nest. **1945** Leave It to Blondie; The Naughty Nineties; Under Western Skies; Her Lucky Night; plus the following shorts: Sleepless Tuesday; What, No Cigarettes?; It's Your Move; You Drive Me Crazy; The Big Beef; Mother-in-Law's Day. **1946** Blondie Knows Best; Meet Me on Broadway; Life With Blondie; Blondie's Lucky Day; plus the following shorts: Trouble or Nothing; Wall Street Blues; Motor Maniacs; Noisy Neighbors; I'll Build It Myself; Social Terrors. **1947** Blondie's Big Moment; Blondie's Holiday; Blondie's Anniversary; plus the following shorts: Do or Diet; Heading for Trouble; Host to a Ghost; Television Turmoil; Mind Over Mouse. **1948** Blondie's Reward; Variety Time; plus the following shorts: Brother Knows Best; No More Relatives; How to Clean House; Dig That Gold; Home Canning; Contest Crazy. **1949** Blondie's Secret; Blondie's Big Deal; Sweet Cheat (short). **1950** Beware of Blondie. **1951** Corky of Gasoline Alley; So You Want to be a Bachelor (short). **1952** The Pride of St. Louis; Stars and Stripes Forever. **1953** The Marksman; The Silver Whip. **1956** The First Traveling Saleslady; Crashing Las Vegas. **1959** The 30-Foot Bride of Candy Rock. **1963** Son of Flubber.

RICE, JOHN C.

Born: 1858. Died: June 5, 1915, Philadelphia, Pa. (neuraemia, Bright's disease). Stage and screen actor. Married to stage actress Sally Cohen (dec.).

Appeared in: **1896** The Kiss.

RICE, NORMAN

Born: 1910. Died: Nov. 12, 1957, Hollywood, Calif. (heart attack). Screen, television actor, stage director and writer.

Appeared in: **1952** The Miracle of Our Lady of Fatima.

RICE, RONALD LEE "RON"

Born: 1940. Died: Aug. 16, 1973, Dallas, Tex. Screen, radio actor, film director, film producer and screenwriter.

RICE, SAM (George Samuel O'Hanlon)

Born: 1874. Died: Mar. 12, 1946, Burbank, Calif. Screen, stage, vaudeville and burlesque actor. Known as "The King of Burlesque" in earlier days.

RICH, ALLEN

Died: May 22, 1976. Screen actor.

Appeared in: **1974** The Gambler. **1975** The Happy Hooker.

RICH, DICK

Born: 1909. Died: Mar. 29, 1967. Screen actor.

Appeared in: **1937** Headin' East. **1938** Angels With Dirty Faces; The Adventures of Robin Hood. **1940** The Grapes of Wrath; Lucky Cisco Kid; Murder in the Air; You the People (short); Tear Gas Squad; The Man Who Talked Too Much; Danger Ahead; Brigham Young. **1941** I Wake Up Screaming (aka Hot Spot); Western Union; Strange Alibi; Dressed to Kill; Rise and Shine; Ride On, Vaquero; Highway West. **1942** Rio Rita; Murder in the Big House; Rubber Racketeers. **1943** The Ox-Bow Incident; Little Miss Pinkerton (short); Secrets of the Underground. **1944** Crime by Night; The Princess and the Pirate. **1945** The Story of G.I. Joe; The Last Installment (short); Within These Walls. **1947** Violence; Killer at Large; The Burning Cross. **1948** The Walls of Jericho. **1949** Oh, You Beautiful Doll. **1952** The Outcasts of Poker Flat. **1953** The Neanderthal Man; The Fighting Lawman; The Steel Lady; A Man Alone. **1954** Overland Pacific; Seven Brides for Seven Brothers. **1955** Black Tuesday; Inside Detroit. **1956** Ransom!; Inside Detroit; Jailhouse Rock.

RICH, DORIS (Doris Irving)

Born: 1918. Died: May 18, 1971, Oxnard, Calif. (smoke inhalation). Screen and stage actress. Married to actor John Carradine.

RICH, FREDDIE

Born: 1898, New York, N.Y. Died: Sept. 8, 1956, Beverly Hills, Calif. Bandleader, songwriter and screen actor.

Appeared in: **1933** Rambling 'Round Radio Row. **1944** A Wave, a Wac and a Marine.

RICH, HELEN

Born: 1897, Pittsburgh, Pa. Died: Aug. 28, 1963, New York, N.Y. (cancer). Screen and stage actress.

Appeared in: **1924** Monsieur Beaucaire.

RICH, LILLIAN

Born: 1900, Herne Hill, London, England. Died: Jan. 5, 1954, Woodland Hills, Calif. Screen actress.

Appeared in: **1921** Beyond; The Blazing Trail; Go Straight; Her Social Value; The Millionaire; The Ruse of the Rattler; The Sage Hen. **1922** The Bearcat; Afraid to Fight; Catch My Smoke; The Kentucky Derby; Man to Man; One Wonderful Night. **1924** Cheap Kisses; Empty Hearts; The Love Master; The Man from Wyoming; The Phantom Horseman; Never Say Die. **1925** The Golden Bed; Braveheart; A Kiss in the Dark; The Love Gamble; Seven Days; Ship of Souls; Simon the Jester; Soft Shoes. **1926** Dancing Days; Exclusive Rights; The Golden Web; The Isle of Retribution; Whispering Smith. **1927** God's Great Wilderness; Snowbound; Wanted a Coward; Web of Fate; Woman's Law. **1928** The Old Code; The Forger; That's My Daddy. **1930** The Eternal Triangle (short). **1931** Once a Lady; Grief Street; The Devil Plays. **1932** Mark of the Spur; Free Wheeling (short); A Lad an' a Lamp (short). **1934** Riptide. **1935** Sprucin' Up (short); She Married Her Boss. **1938** Arsene Lupin Returns. **1939** Lucky Night.

RICH, MYRTLE MAY

Died: Oct., 1931, Wantachee, Wash. Screen and stage actress.

RICH, PHIL

Born: 1896. Died: Feb. 22, 1956, Woodland Hills, Calif. Screen, vaudeville and television actor. Teamed with his wife in vaudeville as "Rich and Adair."

RICH, VERNON

Born: 1906. Died: Feb. 7, 1978, Peterborough, N.H. Screen and television actor.

Appeared in: **1951** The Sellout. **1953** The War of the Worlds. **1955** The Far Horizons; Strategic Air Command. **1956** I've Lived Before; Outside the Law. **1964** One Man's Way.

RICH, VIVIAN

Born: May, 1893, at sea. Died: Nov. 17, 1957, Hollywood, Calif. (auto accident). Screen, stage and vaudeville actress.

Appeared in: **1915** Business vs. Love. **1916** The Enchantment. **1917** The Price of Silence; A Branded Soul; The Bull's Eye (serial). **1918** Beware of Strangers. **1919** The Mints of Hell. **1920** The Last Straw; Would You Forgive?; A World of Folly. **1922** Blind Circumstances.

1923 The Love Wagon; Shell Shocked Sammy; Unblazed Trail. **1924** Mile a Minute Morgan. **1925** Idaho (serial). **1926** Vanishing Millions (serial). **1928** Old Age Handicap. **1929** Must We Marry? **1931** Hell's Valley.

RICHARD, FRIEDA
Born: 1873, Vienna, Austria. Died: Sept. 13, 1946, Salzburg, Austria. Screen and stage actress.

Appeared in: **1925** Peak of Fate. **1926** Manon Lescaut; Faust. **1928** The Two Brothers. **1930** The Burning Heart; Liebe im Ring. **1932** Liebe Ist Liebe. **1935** Unfinished Symphony. **1938** The Affairs of Maupassant.

RICHARDS, ADDISON W. (Addison Whitaker Richards, Jr.)
Born: Oct. 20, 1887 or 1902?, Zanesville, Ohio. Died: Mar. 22, 1964, Los Angeles, Calif. (heart attack). Screen, stage and television actor. Entered films in 1933.

Appeared in: **1933** Riot Squad. **1934** Lone Cowboy; Let's Be Ritzy; The Love Captive; The Case of the Howling Dog; Beyond the Law; Our Daily Bread; Gentlemen Are Born; Babbitt; St. Louis Kid; British Agent. **1935** Black Fury; Only Eight Hours; G-Men; Home on the Range; The Eagle's Brood; The Frisco Kid; A Dog of Flanders; Sweet Music; Society Doctor; Here Comes the Band; The White Cockatoo; Front Page Woman; Little Big Shot; Dinky; Alias Mary Down; The Crusades; Freckles. **1936** Bullets or Ballots; Sutter's Gold; Public Enemy's Wife; Trailin' West; Ceiling Zero; Road Gang; Song of the Saddle; The Law in Her Hands; Jail Break; Anthony Adverse; The Case of the Velvet Claws; Hot Money; China Clipper; Smart Blonde; God's Country and the Woman; Man Hunt; Colleen; The Walking Dead. **1937** Draegerman Courage; The Black Legion; Ready, Willing and Able; Her Husband's Secretary; White Bondage; Dance, Charlie, Dance; The Singing Marine; Love Is on the Air; The Barrier. **1938** Flight into Fame; Alcatraz Island; The Black Doll; The Last Express; Accidents Will Happen; Valley of the Giants; Boys Town; Prison Nurse. **1939** Whispering Enemies; They Made Her a Spy; Twelve Crowded Hours; Off the Record; Inside Information; Burn 'Em Up O'Connor; Andy Hardy Gets Spring Fever; They All Come Out; Thunder Afloat; Geronimo; Espionage Agent; Nick Carter; Master Detective; Bad Lands; Exile Express; The Gracie Allen Murder Case. **1940** Santa Fe Trail; Andy Hardy Meets Debutante; Boom Town; Northwest Passage; The Man from Dakota; The Man from Montreal; The Lone Wolf Strikes; Edison, the Man; Charlie Chan in Panama; South to Karanga; Wyoming; Gangs of Chicago; Girls from Havana; My Little Chickadee; Arizona; Flight Command; Moon Over Burma; Black Diamonds; Cherokee Strip; Slightly Honorable. **1941** Ball of Fire; Dive Bomber; Western Pacific; Tall, Dark and Handsome; Back in the Saddle; Sheriff of Tombstone; The Great Lie; Men of Boys Town; Mutiny in the Arctic; International Squadron; Texas; Her First Beau; Badlands of Dakota; Andy Hardy's Private Secretary; I Wanted Wings; Strawberry Blonde; The Trial of Mary Dugan. **1942** My Favorite Blonde; The Lady Has Plans; Cowboy Serenade; Pacific Rendezvous; A-Haunting We Will Go; Secrets of a Co-ed; Man with Two Lives; Secret Agent for Japan; The Pride of the Yankees; Seven Day's Leave; Men of Texas; Top Sergeant; Secret Enemies; Flying Tigers; War Dogs. **1943** Destroyer; Headin' for God's Country; Corvette K-225; Where Are Your Children?; The Mystery of the 13th Guest; Mystery Broadcast; The Deerslayer; Air Force; Underground Agent; A Guy Named Joe. **1944** Raiders of Ghost City (serial); Smart Guy; The Fighting Seabees; Follow the Boys; Three Men in White; Moon Over Las Vegas; Roger Touhy, Gangster; A Night of Adventure; Marriage Is a Private Affair; Since You Went Away; The Mummy's Curse; The Sullivans; Are These Our Parents? Barbary Coast Gent; Three Little Sisters; Border Town Trail. **1945** The Master Key (serial); Duffy's Tavern; The Royal Mounted Rides Again (serial); Lady on a Train; The Chicago Kid; The Last Installment (short); God Is My Co-Pilot; Betrayal from the East; Rough, Tough and Ready; Bells of Rosarita; Grissly's Millions; Come Out Fighting; I'll Remember April; Black Market Babies; Danger Signal; The Shanghai Cobra; Men in Her Diary; Strange Confession; The Adventures of Rusty; Spellbound; Bewitched; Leave Her to Heaven. **1946** Secrets of a Sorority Girl; Angel On My Shoulder; The Criminal Court; The Hoodlum Saint; Step By Step; Renegades; Don't Gamble with Strangers; The Tiger Woman; The Mummy's Curse; Anna and the King of Siam; Love Laughs at Andy Hardy; Dragonwyck. **1947** The Millerson Case. **1948** Lulu Belle. **1949** The Rustlers; Henry the Rainmaker; Call Northside 777. **1950** Davy Crockett, Indian Scout. **1955** Illegal; High Society; Fort Yuma. **1956** Walk the Proud Land; Reprisal!; Everything But the Truth; When Gangland Strikes; Fury at Gunsight Pass; The Ten Commandments; The Broken Star. **1957** Last of the Badmen; Gunsight Ridge. **1958** The Saga of Hemp Brown. **1959** The Oregon Trail. **1960** The Dark at the Top of the Stairs. **1961** Frontier Uprising; The Gambler Wore a Gun; The Flight That Disappeared. **1962** Saintly Sinners. **1963** The Raiders. **1964** For Those Who Think Young.

RICHARDS, CHARLES
Born: Dec. 16, 1899, Indianapolis, Ind. Died: July 29, 1948, Hollywood, Calif. Screen actor and casting director. Entered films in 1916.

Appeared in: **1923** The Call of the Canyon.

RICHARDS, CICILY
Born: 1850, London, England. Died: Apr. 8, 1933, England? Screen, stage and vaudeville actress.

Appeared in: **1914** Trilby.

RICHARDS, CULLY
Born: 1910. Died: June 17, 1978, Los Angeles, Calif. (cancer). Screen, vaudeville, television actor and comedy writer.

Appeared in: **1935** Stolen Harmony. **1936** Sing Baby Sing. **1937** Pick a Star; Swing It, Sailor; Sweetheart of the Navy; Here's Flash Casey; Something to Sing About. **1943** Let's Face It. **1948** The Pirate; Race Street. **1968** The Young Runaways.

RICHARDS, DAN "SKIP"
Born: 1942. Died: Oct. 4, 1981, near Salt Lake City, Utah (plane crash). Screen, television actor and helicopter pilot.

RICHARDS, GORDON
Born: Oct. 27, 1893, Gillingham, Kent, England. Died: Jan. 13, 1964, Hollywood, Calif. Screen, stage and television actor.

Appeared in: **1942** The Wife Takes a Flyer. **1943** Slightly Dangerous. **1944** The Canterville Ghost; The Story of Dr. Wassell; Mrs. Parkington; National Velvet. **1945** Molly and Me; Kitty; White Pongo; Weekend at the Waldorf. **1946** Larceny in Her Heart. **1947** Linda Be Good; The Imperfect Lady; Ladies' Man; Flight to Nowhere. **1948** Woman in the Night; Thirteen Lead Soldiers. **1950** Kiss Tomorrow Goodbye; The Man Who Cheated Himself; The Big Hangover. **1955** High Society.

RICHARDS, GRANT
Born: 1916, New York, N.Y. Died: July 4, 1963, Hollywood, Calif. (leukemia). Screen, stage, radio and television actor.

Appeared in: **1936** Hopalong Cassidy Returns. **1937** A Night of Mystery; On Such a Night. **1938** My Old Kentucky Home; Under the Big Top. **1939** Risky Business; Inside Information. **1940** Isle of Destiny. **1942** Just Off Broadway. **1944** Winged Victory. **1958** Guns, Girls and Gangsters. **1959** The Four Skulls of Jonathan Drake; Inside the Mafia. **1960** Oklahoma Territory; Twelve Hours to Kill; The Music Box Kid. **1961** You Have to Run Fast; Secret of Deep Harbor.

RICHARDS, PAUL E.
Died: Dec. 10, 1974, Los Angeles, Calif. (cancer). Screen and television actor.

Appeared in: **1951** Fixed Bayonets. **1953** War Paint. **1954** Phantom of the Rue Morgue; Playgirl; Pushover; Demetrius and the Gladiators. **1955** Tall Men Riding. **1956** The Houston Story; Scandal, Incorporated; Tension at Table Rock. **1957** The Strange One; Monkey On My Back; Hot Summer Night; The Unknown Terror; The Black Whip. **1958** Blood Arrow. **1959** Four Fast Guns. **1960** All the Young Men. **1967** St. Valentine's Day Massacre. **1970** Beneath the Planet of the Apes.

RICHARDSON, FRANK
Died: Feb., 1913, Murrieta Springs, Calif. Screen actor. Entered films in 1907 with Selig.

Appeared in: **1911** In the Days of Gold.

RICHARDSON, FRANKIE
Born: Sept. 6, 1898, Philadelphia, Pa. Died: Jan. 30, 1962, Philadelphia, Pa. (heart attack). Screen, minstrel and vaudeville actor.

Appeared in: **1925** Don Q; Seven Sinners. **1926** King of the Pack; Racing Blood. **1928** The Joy Boy of Song (short); Chasing the Blues (short). **1929** Fox Movietone Follies of 1929; Happy Days; Masquerade; Sunny Side Up. **1930** Let's Go Places; New Movietone Follies of 1930.

RICHARDSON, WILLIAM
Born: 1876. Died: Nov. 8, 1937, Los Angeles, Calif. Screen and stage actor.

RICHMAN, AL
Born: 1885. Died: Apr. 20, 1936, Hollywood, Calif. (heart attack). Screen actor.

RICHMAN, CHARLES
Born: Jan. 12, 1865, Chicago, Ill. Died: Dec. 1, 1940, Bronx, N.Y. Screen and stage actor.

Appeared in: **1914** The Man from Home. **1915** The Battle Cry of Peace. **1917** The Secret Kingdom (serial). **1923** Has the World Gone Mad? **1929** The Ninety-Ninth Amendment (short). **1931** The Struggle. **1933** Take a Chance. **1934** His Double Life; The President Vanishes; Woman Haters (short). **1935** In Old Kentucky; George White's 1935 Scandals; The Case of the Curious Bride; The Glass Key; Becky Sharp; Thanks a Million; My Marriage; After Office Hours; Biography of a Bachelor Girl. **1936** The Ex-Mrs. Bradford; Parole; In His Steps; Sing Me a Love Song; Under Your Spell; I'd Give My Life. **1937** The Life of Emile Zola; Make a Wish; Lady Behave; Nothing Sacred. **1938** The Adventures of Tom Sawyer; The Cowboy and the Lady; Blondes at Work. **1939** Torchy Runs for Mayor; Exile Express; Dark Victory. **1940** Devil's Island. **1941** The Sign on the Door; Stranger Than Fiction; Trust Your Wife. **1942** My Friend the Devil.

RICHMAN, HARRY (Henry Richman, Jr.)
Born: Oct. 10, 1895, Cincinnati, Ohio. Died: Nov. 3, 1972, North Hollywood, Calif. Screen, stage, vaudeville, radio actor, singer and songwriter. Divorced from showgirls Yvonne Epstein, Hazel Forbes and Yvonne Day.

Appeared in: **1929** The Song of Broadway. **1930** Putting On the Ritz. **1936** The Music Goes 'Round.

RICHMAN, MARIAN (Marion S. Pearlson)
Born: Apr. 10, 1922, Calif. Died: Feb. 24, 1956, Los Angeles, Calif. (suicide—barbiturates). Screen, radio and television actress.

Appeared in: **1954** Gog.

RICHMOND, KANE (Frederick W. Bowditch)
Born: Dec. 23, 1906, Minneapolis, Minn. Died: Mar. 22, 1973. Screen and stage actor. Entered films in 1930.

Appeared in: **1930** The Leather Pushers (serial). **1931** Politics; Stepping Out; Strangers May Kiss; Cavalier of the West. **1932** Huddle; West of Broadway. **1934** Devil Tiger; Let's Fall in Love; Voice in the Night; Crime of Helen Stanley; I Can't Escape. **1935** The Lost City (serial); Confidential; The Adventures of Rex and Rinty (serial); Circus Shadows; Forced Landing. **1936** Private Number; Born to Fight; Racing Blood; With Love and Kisses. **1937** Nancy Steele Is Missing; Headline Crasher; Tough to Handle; Anything For a Thrill; Young Dynamite; The Reckless Way; Devil Diamond. **1938** Mars Attacks the World. **1939** Tail Spin; The Return of the Cisco Kid; Charlie Chan in Reno; 20,000 Men a Year; The Escape; Winner Take All; Chicken Wagon Family. **1940** Sailor's Lady; Charlie Chan in Panama; Murder Over New York; Knute Rockne—All American. **1941** Play Girl; Great Guns; Hard Guy; Mountain Moonlight; Riders of the Purple Sage; Double Cross. **1942** Spy Smasher (serial—also released as a feature Spy Smasher Returns); A Gentleman at Heart. **1943** Action in the North Atlantic; Three Russian Girls; There's Something About a Soldier. **1944** Ladies Courageous; Bermuda Mystery; Roger Touhy, Gangster; Haunted Harbor (serial). **1945** Jungle Raiders (serial); Brenda Starr, Reporter (serial); Black Market Babies. **1946** The Tiger Woman; The Mighty McGurk; Behind the Mask; The Missing Lady; The Shadow Returns; Passkey to Danger; Don't Gamble With Strangers; Traffic in Crime. **1947** Black Gold; Brick Bradford (serial). **1948** Stage Struck. **1951** Pirates Harbor (serial rerelease of 1944 serial Haunted Harbor).

RICHMOND, LEO C.
Born: 1914, Tahiti. Died: Apr. 21, 1979, Hollywood, Calif. Screen actor, dancer and stuntman. Father of actor Branscombe Richmond.

RICHMOND, SUSAN
Born: Dec. 5, 1894, London, England. Died: Jan., 1959, England? Screen, stage, television actress and writer.

Appeared in: **1951** Life in Her Hands.

RICHMOND, WARNER
Born: Jan. 11, 1895, Culpepper County, Va. Died: June 19, 1948, Los Angeles, Calif. (coronary thrombosis). Screen and stage actor.

Appeared in: **1916** Betty of Graystone. **1918** Sporting Life. **1920** My Lady's Garter. **1921** Tol'able David; Heart of Maryland; The Mountain Woman. **1922** The Challenge; Isle of Doubt; Jan of the Big Snows. **1923** Luck; Mark of the Beast; The Man from Glengarry. **1924** Daughters of the Night; The Speed Spook. **1925** The Crowded Hour; Fear Bound; The Making of O'Malley; The Pace That Thrills. **1926** Good and Naughty; The Wives of the Prophet. **1927** Slide, Kelly, Slide; The Fire Brigade; Finger Prints; Irish Hearts; White Flannels; Heart of Maryland (and 1921 version). **1928** Hearts of Men; Shadows of the

Night; Chicago; Stop That Man; You Can't Beat the Law. **1929** Strange Cargo; Voice of the Storm; The Redeeming Sin; Stark Mad; Fifty-Fifty; Manhattan Madness; Big Brother; The Apache; Big News. **1930** Men Without Women; Billy the Kid; Strictly Modern; Remote Control; Vengeance (short). **1931** Quick Millions; Huckleberry Finn. **1932** Hell's Highway; The Woman from Monte Carlo; Beast of the City; Strangers of the Evening; Night Court. **1933** Fast Workers; King of the Jungle; Corruption; Mama Loves Papa; This Day and Age; Police Call; Life in the Raw. **1934** Happy Landing; The Lost Jungle (serial); Gift of Gab. **1935** The Phantom Empire (short); Mississippi; Rainbow's End; Smoky Smith; New Frontier; The Courageous Avenger; Under Pressure; Headline Woman; So Red the Rose; The Singing Vagabond. **1936** Peppery Salt (short); Heart of the West; Below the Deadline; Hearts in Bondage; The White Legion; Song of the Gringo; Headin' for the Rio Grande; In His Steps. **1937** A Lawman Is Born; Wallaby Jim of the Islands; Where Trails Divide; The Gold Racket; Riders of the Dawn; Stars Over Arizona; Federal Bullets. **1938** The Secret of Treasure Island (serial); Wolves of the Sea; Six-Shottin' Sheriff; Prairie Moon. **1939** Wild Horse Canyon. **1940** Rainbow Over the Range; Rhythm of the Rio Grande; Pals of the Silver Sage; The Golden Trail; Men With Steel Faces. **1946** Colorado Serenade.

RICHTER, HANS
Born: 1888, Berlin, Germany. Died: Feb. 1, 1976, Locarno, Switzerland. Screen actor, film director, film producer, screenwriter, author, painter and photographer.

Appeared in: **1931** Emil und die Detecktive (Emil and the Detectives). **1932** Das Blaue vom Himmel (US 1934). **1933** Der Page vom Dalmasse-Hotel (US 1935); Die Fahrt ins Gruene (US 1936); Drei Blaue Jungs—ein Blondes Maedel (US 1936). **1934** Liebe Dumme Mama (aka Stupid Mama—US 1935); Peter, Paul und Nanette (Peter, Paul and Nanette—US 1940). **1935** Grossreinemachen (General Housecleaning—US 1938); Die Ganze Welt Dreht Sich um Liebe (US 1936). **1936** Das Maedchen Irene (US 1937); Schabernack (US 1936). **1937** Freuhling im Wien; Eine Nacht mit Hindernissen (aka Der Klapperstorchverband, and aka The Stork Society—US 1938). **1954** Der Zarewitsch (US 1961). **1969** Diaries, Notes and Sketches (documentary). **1975** Special Section.

RICHTER, PAUL
Born: 1896, Germany. Died: Dec. 30, 1961, Vienna, Austria. Screen, stage, television actor and film director. Married to actress Aud Egede Nissen.

Appeared in: **1914** Sterbewalzer. **1919** Gefesselt. **1920** Jagd Nach dem Glueck; Mord ohne Taeter (aka Herztrumpf). **1921** Die Nacht des Einbrechers; Das Opfer der Ellen Larsen; Zirkus des Lebens; Der Henker von Sankt Marien (The Hangman of St. Marien); Das Indische Grabmal (The Indian Tomb, including Die Sendung des Yoghi and Der Tiger von Eschnapur). **1922** Herzen im Sturm; Dr. Mabuse der Spieler (Dr. Mabuse, the Gambler). **1924** Die Nibelungen (including Siegfried—US 1925, and Kriemhild's Rache (Kriemhild's Revenge)—US 1928); Pietro, der Korsar (Peter the Pirate—US 1927). **1925** Die Rote Maus. **1926** Dagfin; In Treue Stark; Kampf der Geschlechter; Schwester Veronika; Tragoedie Einer Ehe; Human Law. **1927** Der Koenig der Mittelstuermer; Die Letzte Nacht; Die Stadt der Tausend Freuden. **1928** Die Geliebte Seiner Hoheit; Lockendes Gift; Schneeschuhbanditen. **1929** Forbidden Love; Die Frau im Talar; Sensation in Wintergarten. **1931** Die Foresterchirstl; Der Weisse Gott; Die Nacht ohne Pause. **1932** Der Hexer; Marschall Vorwaerts; Strafsache van Geldern; Das Geheimnis um Johann Ort (aka Ein Liebesroman im Hause Habsburg—US 1936). **1933** Drei Kaiserjaeger (US 1935); Der Choral von Leuthen (The Anthem of Leuthen). **1934** In Sachen Timpe; Schloss Hubertus; Was bin ich ohne Dich; Krach im Forsthaus; Das Unsterbliche Lied; Die Frauen von Tannhof (US 1936); Jungfrau Gegen Moench (Maiden vs. Monk—US 1935). **1935** Ehestreik; Der Klosterjaeger (US 1936). **1936** Der Wackere Schustermeister. **1937** Gordian, der Tyrann. **1938** Der Ebelweisskoenig (US 1939); Frau Sylvelin (US 1939); Narren im Schnee; Staerker als die Liebe (Stronger Than Love—US 1939). **1939** Waldrausch (Forest Fever—US 1940). **1941** Der Laufende Berg. **1942** Der Ochsenkrieg. **1943** Die Schwache Stunde; Kohlhiesels Toechter (Kolhiesel's Daughter). **1944** Warum Luegst Du, Elisabeth? **1945** Ein Mann Gehoert ins Haus (aka Bankerl Unterm Birnbaum). **1950** Der Geigenmacher von Mittenwald. **1951** Die Alm an der Grenze; Die Martinsklause. **1952** Die Schoene Toelzerin; Der Herrgottschnitzer von Ammergau; Mikosch Ruecht Ein. **1953** Der Klosterjaeger. **1954** Schloss Hubertus. **1957** Wetterleuchten um Maria. **1958** Die Singenden Engel von Tirol (aka Sag ja, Mutti). **1959** Der Schaefer von Trutzberg.

RICKARD, TEX (George L. Rickard)
Born: Jan. 2, 1870, Sherman, Tex. Died: June 5, 1929, Miami Beach, Fla. (periotonic infection following appendectomy). Cowboy, western marshal, fight promoter and screen actor.

Appeared in: **1924** The Great White Way. **1970** Jack Johnson (documentary).

RICKETTS, THOMAS "TOM"
Born: 1853, London, England. Died: Jan. 20, 1939, Hollywood, Calif. (pneumonia). Screen, stage actor, film director and stage manager.

Appeared in: **1921** The Parish Priest; Puppets of Fate; Sham; Beating the Game; The Killer; The Spenders. **1922** The Eternal Flame; Fools of Fortune; Putting It Over; Shattered Idols; A Tailor-Made Man; The Lavender Bath Lady. **1923** Alice Adams; The Dangerous Maid; Strangers of the Night; Within the Law. **1924** Black Oxen; The Gaiety Girl; Cheap Kisses; Circe, the Enchantress. **1925** The Fate of a Flirt; The Girl Who Wouldn't Work; Never the Twain Shall Meet; Was It Bigamy?; The Business of Love; A Fight to the Finish; My Wife and I; Oh, Doctor; Sealed Lips; Secrets of the Night; Steppin' Out; Wages for Wives; When Husbands Flirt; Bobbed Hair. **1926** Dancing Days; Ladies of Leisure; The Lily; The Nutcracker; The Belle of Broadway; The Cat's Pajamas; Going the Limit; Ladies at Play; Love's Blindness; the Old Soak; Poker Faces; Stranded in Paris; When the Wife's Away. **1927** Sailor's Sweetheart; Broadway Madness; Children of Divorce; In a Moment of Temptation; Too Many Crooks; Venus of Venice. **1928** My Friend from India; Doomsday; Just Married; Dry Martini; Interference; Freedom of the Press; Five and Ten Cent Annie; Law and the Man. **1929** Bulldog Drummond; The Glad Rag Doll; Beware of Bachelors; Light Fingers; Skirt Shy (short); Red Hot Speed. **1930** Prince of Diamonds; The Vagabond King; Broken Dishes; Sea Legs. **1931** Man of the World; Side Show; Ambassador Bill; Surrender; Danger Island (serial). **1932** A Farewell to Arms; Forbidden; Thrill of Youth; Love Me Tonight. **1933** Cavalcade; Gordon of Ghost City (serial); He Learned About Women; Women Won't Tell; Mama Loves Papa; Forgotten. **1934** Stolen Sweets; The Curtain Falls; In Love With Life; Little Man, What Now?; No Greater Glory; The Count of Monte Cristo; Forsaking All Others; It Happened One Night. **1935** Escapade; Sons of Steel; Now or Never; Cardinal Richelieu; A Tale of Two Cities. **1936** Hi, Gaucho; We Went to College; Pennies from Heaven; Gold Diggers of 1937; Trouble for Two. **1937** Dead End; Maid of Salem; The Lady Escapes. **1938** Bluebeard's Eighth Wife; The Young in Heart; Young Fugitives.

RICKS, JAMES
Died: July 2, 1974, New York, N.Y. (heart attack). Black singer and screen actor. Led "Ravens" quartet and was band vocalist with Count Basie.

RICKSON, JOE (Joseph Rickson)
Born: Sept. 6, 1880, Clearcreek, Mont. Died: Jan. 8, 1958, Calif. Screen, stage and vaudeville actor.

Appeared in: **1922** Flower of The North. **1923** Pioneer Trails; Brass Commandments. **1924** The Code of the Wilderness; Captain Blood; Rip Roarin' Roberts; Rough Ridin'. **1925** Riders of the Purple Sage; Baree, Son of Kazan; Action Galore; The Bad Lands; Fast Fightin'; The Human Tornado; A Two-Fisted Sheriff. **1926** The Buckaroo Kid; Davy Crockett at the Fall of The Alamo; Rawhide. **1927** Land of the Lawless; The Devil's Twin; Border Blackbirds; Two Gun of the Tumbleweeds. **1928** The Code of the Scarlet. **1929** The Drifter; The Lariat Kid. **1930** Trails of Peril; The Lone Star Ranger. **1931** Wild Horse. **1933** Fargo Express. **1935** Bar 20 Rides Again. **1936** Hopalong Cassidy Returns.

RICKSON, LUCILLE (aka LUCILLE RICKSEN)
Born: Sept. 2, 1907. Died: Mar. 13, 1925. Screen actress.

Appeared in: **1921** The Old Nest. **1922** Forsaking All Others; The Married Flapper; The Girl Who Ran Wild; Remembrance; The Stranger's Banquet. **1923** Human Wreckage; The Rendezvous; Trimmed in Scarlet; The Social Buccaneer (serial). **1924** Vanity's Price; Behind the Curtain; Galloping Fish; The Hill Billy; Idle Tongues; Judgment of the Storm; The Painted Lady; Those Who Dance; Young Ideas. **1925** The Denial.

RIDDLE, JIM (James Riddle)
Died: Prior to 1976. Screen actor.

Appeared in: **1967** Gentle Giant.

RIDDLE, RICHARD See AINLEY, RICHARD

RIDGE, WALTER J.
Born: 1900. Died: Sept. 22, 1968, Los Angeles, Calif. Screen actor, extra and vaudeville actor. Appeared in vaudeville in an act billed as "Mulroy, McNeece and Ridge."

Appeared in: **1949** The Set-Up.

RIDGELY, CLEO
Born: 1894. Died: Aug. 18, 1962, Glendale, Calif. Stage and screen actress. Married to actor James W. Horne (dec. 1942).

Appeared in: **1914** The Spoilers. **1915** The Chorus Lad; The Golden Chance; Stolen Goods; The Fighting Hope; The Secret Orchard; The Marriage of Kitty. **1916** The Yellow Mask; The Yellow Pawn. **1917** Joan the Woman. **1921** Dangerous Pastime. **1922** The Forgotten Law; The Law and the Woman; The Sleepwalker. **1923** The Beautiful and Damned. **1938** Juvenile Court. **1948** I Remember Mama.

RIDGELY, JOHN (John Huntington Rea)
Born: Sept. 6, 1909, Chicago, Ill. Died: Jan. 18, 1968, New York, N.Y. (heart ailment). Screen actor.

Appeared in: **1937** Larger Than Life; they Won't Forget; Submarine D-1. **1938** Forbidden Valley; The Invisible Menace; Torchy Gets Her Man; Secrets of an Actress; Patient in Room 18; He Couldn't Say No; Blondes at Work; Torchy Blane in Panama; Little Miss Thoroughbred; White Banners; Cowboy from Brooklyn; My Bill; Going Places; Hard to Get; Boy Meets Girl. **1939** Each Dawn I Die; The Roaring Twenties; Confessions of a Nazi Spy; Angels Wash Their Faces; The Cowboy Quarterback; Nancy Drew and the Hidden Staircase; Kid Nightengale; Dark Victory; Secret Service of the Air; Everybody's Hobby; Indianapolis Speedway; Torchy Plays With Dynamite; They Made Me a Criminal; You Can't Get Away With Murder; King of the Underworld; Private Detective; Wings of the Navy; The Return of Dr. X; The Kid from Kokomo. **1940** River's End; Father Is a Prince; The Man Who Talked Too Much; Saturday's Children; Flight Angels; Torrid Zone; Brother Orchid; They Drive By Night; The Letter; The Lady With Red Hair; The Fighting 69th. **1941** The Bride Came C.O.D.; They Died With Their Boots On; Knockout (aka Right to the Heart); The Wagons Roll at Night; Million Dollar Baby; International Squadron; The Great Mr. Nobody; The Man Who Came to Dinner; Here Comes Happiness; Strange Alibi; Navy Blues; Highway West. **1942** Bullet Scars; Wings for the Eagle; The Big Shot; Secret Enemies. **1943** Air Force; Northern Pursuit. **1944** Hollywood Canteen; The Doughgirls; Destination Tokyo; Arsenic and Old Lace. **1945** Pride of the Marines; God Is My Co-Pilot; Danger Signal. **1946** My Reputation; Two Guys from Milwaukee; The Big Sleep. **1947** High Wall; The Man I Love; Nora Prentiss; That Way With Women; That's My Man; Cheyenne; Cry Wolf; Possessed. **1948** Night Winds; Luxury Liner; Sealed Verdict; Trouble Makers; The Iron Curtain. **1949** Command Decision; Once More, My Darling; Border Incident; Task Force; Tucson. **1950** Backfire; Beauty on Parade; The Lost Volcano; South Sea Sinner; Petty Girl; Rookie Fireman; Saddle Tramp; Edge of Doom. **1951** The Last Outpost; When the Redskins Rode; Thunder in God's Country; Al Jennings of Oklahoma; Half Angel; A Place in the Sun; The Blue Veil; As You Were. **1952** Fort Osage; The Greatest Show on Earth; Room for One More; The Outcasts of Poker Flat. **1953** Off Limits.

RIDGES, STANLEY
Born: 1892, Southampton, England. Died: Apr. 22, 1951, Westbrook, Conn. Screen, stage and television actor.

Appeared in: **1923** Success. **1930** The following shorts: For Two Cents; Let's Merge; Married; The Poor Fish. **1932** The Sign of the Cross. **1934** Crime Without Passion. **1935** The Scoundrel. **1936** Winterset; Sinner Take All. **1937** Interns Can't Take Money. **1938** Yellow Jack; They're Always Caught (short); If I Were King; There's That Woman Again; The Mad Miss Manton. **1939** Silver on the Sage; Confessions of a Nazi Spy; Each Dawn I Die; Let Us Live; Union Pacific; I Stole a Million; Dust Be My Destiny; Espionage Agent; Nick Carter, Master Detective. **1940** Black Friday. **1941** The Sea Wolf; Sergeant York; They Died With Their Boots On; Mr. District Attorney. **1942** The Lady Is Willing; Eagle Squadron; To Be or Not to Be; The Big Shot; Eyes in the Night. **1943** Tarzan Triumphs; Air Force; This Is the Army. **1944** Wilson; The Sign of the Cross (revised version of 1932 film); The Story of Dr. Wassell; The Master Race. **1945** The Suspect; God Is My Co-Pilot; Captain Eddie; The Phantom Speaks. **1946** Because of Him; Canyon Passage; Mr. Ace. **1947** Possessed. **1949** Thelma Jordan (aka File on Thelma Jordan); Streets of Laredo; Task Force; You're My Everything; An Act of Murder. **1950** No Way Out; Paid in Full; There's a Girl in My Heart. **1951** The Groom Wore Spurs.

RIDGEWAY, FRITZI
Born: Apr. 8, 1898, Missoula, Mont. Died: Mar. 29, 1961, Lancaster, Calif. (heart attack). Screen and stage actress. Entered films in 1917.

Appeared in: **1920** Judy of Rogues Harbor. **1921** Bring Him In; The Fatal 30. **1922** Boomerang Justice; Branded Man; The Hate Trail; The Menacing Past; The Old Homestead. **1923** Ruggles of Red Gap; The Cricket on the Hearth; Hollywood; Trifling With Honor. **1927** Man Bait; Face Value; Getting Gertie's Garter; Lonesome Ladies; Nobody's Widow. **1928** The Enemy; Flying Romeos; Son of the Golden West. **1929** Red Hot Speed; This Is Heaven; Hell's Heroes. **1930** Prince of Diamonds. **1931** The Mad Parade. **1932** Ladies of the Big House. **1934** We Will Live Again. **1935** No Ransom.

RIDGEWELL, AUDREY
Born: 1904, London, England. Died: Oct. 27, 1968, Grove Beach, Conn. Stage and screen actress. Daughter of tenor George Ridgewell (dec.).

Appeared in: **1933** His Double Life.

RIDGWAY, PATRICIA
Born: 1935, England. Died: Feb. 8, 1978, London, England (cancer). Screen and stage actress. Married to actor Spike Milligan.

RIDLEY, ROBERT
Born: 1901. Died: Nov. 19, 1958, Hollywood, Calif. Screen actor and extra. One of the founders of Screen Extras Guild.

RIECHERS, HELENE
Born: 1869, Germany. Died: July 24, 1957, Berlin, Germany. Screen and stage actress.

RIEMANN, JOHANNES
Born: May 31, 1887, Berlin, Germany. Died: Oct. 8, 1959, Konstanz, West Germany. Screen actor, film director and screenwriter.

Appeared in: **1917** Ahasver; Die Faust des Riesen; Das Goldene Kalb. **1918** Veritas Vincit. **1919** Kitsch; Die Verbotene Frucht. **1920** Die Drei Tanten; Die Herren vom Maxim; Lacht Man Gerne; Niemand Weiss Es; Sehnsucht Nr. 13; Toetet Nicht Mehr. **1921** Die im Schatten Gehen; Fasching; Sappho. **1922** Der Herzog von Algerien; Das Hohe Lied der Liebe; Keimende Saat; Der Liebesroman des Cesare Ubaldi; Der Todesreigen; Wem nie Durch Liebe Leid Geschah. **1923** Der Schatz der Gesine Jakobsen; Graf Cohn; Die Sonne von St. Moritz; Wilhelm Tell. **1924** Gehetzte Menschen; Das Goldene Kalb (and 1917 version); Lumpen und Seide; Die Stadt ohne Juden; Prater (aka Die Erlebnisse Zweier Naehmaedchen). **1925** Elegantes Pack; Heiratsannoncen; Der Liebeskaefig; Die Moral der Gasse. **1926** In der Heimat, da Gibt's ein Wiedersehn!; Der Juenglich aus der Konfektion; Die Wiskottens; Das Panzergewoelbe (The Armored Vault). **1927** Die Tochter des Knustreiters; Valencia. **1928** Fraeulein Chauffeur; Die Frau auf der Folter. **1930** Heute Nacht—Eventuell (US 1933). **1931** Die Liebesfiliale; Der Falsche Ehemann (US 1932); So'n Windhund; Kadetten (US 1933, aka Hinter den Roten Mauern von Lichterfelde); Mein Herz Sehnt Sich Nach Liebe (aka Der Hellseher—US 1933); Sein Scheidungsgrund (US 1932). **1932** Liebe auf den Ersten Ton; Die Herren vom Maxim (and 1920 version); Fraeulein—Falsch Verbunden! (US 1934); Das Millionentestament (aka Der Querkopf); Hasenklein Kann Nichts Dafuer (aka Drunter und Drueber). **1933** Moral und Liebe; Grossfuerstin Alexandra. **1934** Der Polizeibericht Meldet. **1935** Der Mann mit der Pranke. **1936** Die Un-Erhoert Frau (aka Ich Kenne Dich Nicht Mehr). **1938** Lauter Luegen; Der Tag Nach der Scheidung (The Day After the Divorce—US 1940); Yvette (aka Die Tochter Einer Kurtisane). **1939** Drunter und Drueber (and 1932 version); Ehe in Dosen; Hochzeitsreise zu Dritt; Renate im Quartett; Ihr Erstes Erlebnis (Her First Experience—US 1940); Bel Ami (aka Der Liebling Schoener Frauen). **1940** Die Gute Sieben. **1941** Alles fuer Gloria; Oh Diese Maenner; Friedemann Bach; Sonntagskinder. **1942** Liebeskomoedie; Kleine Residenz. **1943** Drei Tolle Maedels; Das Lied der Nachtigall; Geliebter Schatz; Ein Mann fuer Meine Frau. **1956** Was die Schwalbe Sang. **1957** Jede Nacht in Einem Andern Bett; Der Schraege Otto; Zwei Bayern im Harem.

RIES, WILLIAM J.
Born: 1895. Died: Nov. 16, 1955, Hollywood, Calif. Screen actor.

RIETTI, VICTOR
Born: Mar. 1, 1888, Ferrara, Italy. Died: Dec. 4, 1963, London, England (heart ailment). Screen, stage, television actor, stage director and stage producer. Father of actor Robert Rietti.

Appeared in: **1933** Heads We Go (aka The Charming Deceiver—US). **1934** Jew Suess (aka Power—US). **1935** Oh Daddy!; Escape Me Never; Two Hearts in Harmony. **1936** The Ghost Goes West; Dusty

Ermine (aka Hideout in the Alps—US 1938); Juggernaut (US 1937). **1937** London Melody (aka Girls in the Street—US 1938); Transatlantic Trouble (aka Take It from Me); What a Man! **1938** The Divorce of Lady X; Secretary in Trouble; The Viper. **1940** Room for Two (US 1944). **1943** Yellow Canary (US 1944). **1944** Give Us the Moon; Hotel Reserve (US 1946). **1947** A Man About the House (US 1949). **1949** The Glass Mountain (US 1950). **1957** The Story of Esther Costello; The Naked Truth (aka Your Past Is Showing—US 1958).

RIGA, NADINE
Born: 1909. Died: Dec. 11, 1968, Hollywood, Calif. (cerebral hemorrhage). Screen actress.

Appeared in: **1928** Ramona. **1936** Anthony Adverse. **1943** For Whom the Bell Tolls.

RIGBY, ARTHUR (Arthur Turner)
Born: Sept. 27, 1900, London, England. Died: Apr. 25, 1971, Worthing, England (stroke). Screen, stage and television actor.

Appeared in: **1927** Q Ships (film debut).

RIGBY, EDWARD
Born: 1879, Ashford, Kent, England. Died: Apr. 5, 1951, London, England. Screen and stage actor.

Appeared in: **1935** Lorna Doone; No Limit; Windfall; Gay Old Dog. **1936** Accused; Irish for Luck; Land Without Music (aka Forbidden Music—US 1938); Green Hell (US 1940); The Heirloom Mystery; Queen of Hearts. **1937** Jump for Glory (aka When Thief Meets Thief—US); The Fatal Hour; Mr. Smith Carries On; Young and Innocent (aka A Girl Was Young—US 1938); The Show Goes On; Under a Cloud. **1938** A Yank at Oxford; Yellow Sands; Keep Smiling (aka Smiling Along—US 1939); The Ware Case (US 1939); Kicking the Moon Around. **1939** The Stars Look Down (US 1941); Poison Pen (US 1941); There Ain't No Justice; Young Man's Fancy (US 1943). **1940** The Proud Valley; Convoy (US 1941); Sailors Don't Care; Fingers. **1941** Kipps (aka The Remarkable Mr. Kipps—US 1942); The Common Touch; The Farmer's Wife. **1942** Flying Fortress; Let the People Sing; Penn of Pennsylvania (aka The Courageous Mr. Penn—US 1944); Salute John Citizen; Went the Day Well? (aka 48 Hours—US 1944). **1943** Get Cracking; They Met in the Dark (US 1945). **1944** Perfect Strangers (aka Vacation from Marriage); Murder in Reverse (US 1946); I Live in Grosvenor Square (aka A Yank in London—US 1946); Agitator. **1946** Quiet Weekend (US 1948); The Years Between (US 1947); Piccadilly Incident; Daybreak (US 1949). **1947** Temptation Harbour (US 1949); Green Fingers; The Loves of Joanne Godden. **1948** Easy Money (US 1949); The Three Weird Sisters; Noose (aka The Silk Noose—US 1950); It's Hard to Be Good (US 1950). **1949** Rover and Me; All Over Town; Christopher Columbus; Don't Ever Leave Me; A Run for Your Money (US 1950). **1950** Double Confession (US 1953); The Happiest Days of Your Life; Tony Draws a Horse (US 1951); What the Butler Saw; The Mudlark. **1951** Into the Blue (aka The Man in the Dinghy—US); Circle of Danger.

RIGGS, BETTY See BRENT, EVELYN

RIGGS, DOROTHY See BRENT, EVELYN

RIGGS, JACK
Died: June 8, 1978. Screen actor.

Appeared in: **1961** The Purple Hills.

RIGGS, RALPH
Born: 1889, St. Paul, Minn. Died: Sept. 16, 1951, New York, N.Y. Screen, stage, vaudeville actor and dancer. Married to actress Katharine Witchie with whom he appeared in vaudeville and on stage.

Appeared in: **1949** Lost Boundaries.

RIGGS, TOMMY
Born: Oct. 21, 1908, Pittsburgh, Pa. Died: May 23, 1967, Pittsburgh, Pa. Screen, radio and television actor.

Appeared in: **1938** Goodbye Broadway.

RIGGS, WILLIAM (William Allen Riggs)
Died: Aug. 2, 1975. Screen and television actor.

RIGHTMIRE, WILLIAM H.
Born: 1857. Died: Jan. 14, 1933, Long Beach, Calif. (heart disease). Screen, stage actor and novelist.

RIGON, PAOLO
Born: 1958, Italy. Died: Feb. 17, 1981, Cortina d' Ampezzo, Italy (injuries from accident while filming). Screen actor and stuntman.

Appeared in: **1981** For Your Eyes Only.

RIHANI, NEGUIB
Born: 1891. Died: June 8, 1949, Cairo, Egypt. Stage and screen actor.

RILEY, GEORGE
Born: 1900, Rochester, N.Y. Died: May 30, 1972, Los Angeles, Calif. Vaudeville, tenor soloist, stage and screen actor. Teamed in vaudeville with wife, Helene Heller, as "Heller and Riley."

Appeared in: **1928** Branded Man. **1942** Over My Dead Body. **1946** Night and Day. **1962** Woman Hunt. **1963** The Day Mars Invaded Earth.

RILEY, JACK "SLIM"
Born: 1895. Died: July 9, 1933, Newhall, Calif. Screen actor.

Appeared in: **1921** A Broken Doll.

RIMAC, CIRO CAMPOS
Born: 1894, Peru. Died: Sept. 8, 1973, Miami, Fla. (cancer). Screen and vaudeville actor.

Appeared in: **1945** Dollface.

RINDT, JOCHEN (Karl Jochen Rindt)
Born: Apr. 18, 1942, Mainz-am-Rhein, Germany. Died: Sept. 5, 1970, near Monza, Italy (injuries from auto crash). Auto racer and screen actor.

Appeared in: **1966** Grand Prix.

RING, BLANCHE
Born: Apr. 24, 1876, Boston, Mass. Died: Jan. 13, 1961, Santa Monica, Calif. Stage and screen actress. Divorced from actor Charles Winninger (dec. 1969). Sister of actress Frances (dec. 1951), Julie Ring and actor Cyril Ring (dec. 1967).

Appeared in: **1914** Our Mutual Girl #11. **1915** The Yankee Girl. **1926** It's the Old Army Game. **1940** If I Had My Way.

RING, CYRIL
Born: 1893. Died: July 17, 1967, Hollywood, Calif. Screen and stage actor. For family information, see Blanche Ring.

Appeared in: **1921** The Conquest of Canaan. **1922** Back Home and Broke; Divorce Coupons. **1923** The Exciters; Homeward Bound; The Ne'er-Do-Well. **1924** The Breaking Point; The Guilty One; Hit and Run; Pied Piper Malone; Tongues of Flame; In Hollywood with Potash and Perlmutter. **1926** Mismates. **1928** The News Parade. **1929** The Cocoanuts. **1930** Top Speed; The Social Lion. **1932** Business and Pleasure. **1933** Emergency Call; Too Much Harmony; Neighbors' Wives. **1934** No More Bridge (short); Most Precious Thing in Life; Hollywood Hoodlums. **1935** Don't Bet on Blondes. **1936** Border Patrolman; Wedding Presents. **1938** I Am the Law; Trade Winds. **1939** Hollywood Cavalcade; Irving Berlin's Second Fiddle; The Light That Failed. **1940** No, No Nanette; The Lady With Red Hair; My Favorite Wife; Road to Singapore; One Night in the Tropics. **1941** Hot Spot; Great Guns; The Lady Eve. **1942** My Gal Sal; Life Begins at Eight-Thirty; A Night to Remember; This Gun for Hire; Woman of the Year; The Saboteur; Home in Wyomin'; The Navy Comes Through; Army Surgeon; Over My Dead Body. **1943** Dixie; Melody Parade; Let's Face It. **1944** Here Comes the Waves; In Society; Hot Rhythm; Follow the Boys; Secret Command; The Bullfighters. **1945** Hollywood and Vine; Beware of Redheads (short); The Naughty Nineties; Billy Rose's Diamond Horseshoe; Duffy's Tavern; Senorita from the West. **1946** Girl on the Spot. **1947** Hollywood Barn Dance; Body and Soul; Do or Die (short).

RING, FRANCES
Born: July 4, 1882, N.Y. Died: Jan. 15, 1951, Hollywood, Calif. Screen and stage actress. Married to actor Thomas Meighan (dec. 1936). For family information, see Blanche Ring.

RIN TIN TIN, JR.
Dog screen performer. Son of Rin Tin Tin, Sr. (dec. 1932).

Appeared in: **1927** Hills of Kentucky. **1933** The Wolf Dog (serial); The Big Pay-Off. **1934** Law of the Wild (serial). **1935** Adventures of Rex and Rinty (serial). **1936** Tough Guy.

RIN TIN TIN, SR.
Born: 1916. Died: Aug. 8, 1932. Dog screen performer. Father of Rin Tin Tin, Jr. (dec.). Entered films with Warner Bros.

Appeared in: **1922** The Man from Hell's River; My Dad. **1923** Where the North Begins; Shadows of the North. **1924** Find Your Man. **1925** The Lighthouse by the Sea; Clash of the Wolves; Below the Line; Tracked in the Snow Country. **1926** The Night Cry; Hero of the Big Snows; While London Sleeps. **1927** Jaws of Steel; A Dog of the Regiment; Tracked by the Police; Hills of Kentucky. **1928** Rinty of the Desert; Race for Life; Land of the Silver Fox; The Famous Warner Brothers Dog Star (short). **1929** Show of Shows; Frozen River; Million Dollar Collar; Tiger Rose. **1930** The Lone Defender (serial); Rough Waters; The Man Hunter; On the Border. **1931** Lightning Warrior (serial).

RIORDAN, ROBERT J.
Born: 1913. Died: Jan. 1, 1968, Hollywood, Calif. (heart attack). Screen actor.

Appeared in: **1959** Arson for Hire. **1962** Manchurian Candidate. **1968** Buckskin; The Destructors.

RIOS, LALO
Born: 1927, Mexico. Died: Mar. 7, 1973, Hollywood, Calif. (liver ailment). Screen actor.

Appeared in: **1950** The Lawless (film debut); Bandit Queen. **1952** One Minute to Zero; The Ring. **1953** City Beneath the Sea; Big Leaguer. **1958** Touch of Evil. **1962** Lonely Are the Brave.

RIPLEY, RAYMOND "RAY"
Born: 1891. Died: Oct. 7, 1938, Los Angeles, Calif. Screen actor.

Appeared in: **1920** The Vanishing Dagger (serial). **1921** The Blazing Trail; Why Trust Your Husband? **1922** Turn to the Right. **1925** Heads Up; Smilin' at Trouble. **1926** The Speeding Venus; The Traffic Cop; Western Pluck. **1927** Stolen Pleasures.

RIPLEY, ROBERT L.
Born: Dec. 25, 1893. Died: May 27, 1949, New York, N.Y. (heart attack). Screen, radio actor, author, cartoonist and creator of "Believe It or Not" series that appeared on film, radio and in newspapers.

Appeared in: **1932-33** Vitaphone shorts of his "Believe It or Not" series.

RISCOE, ARTHUR
Born: Nov. 19, 1896, Yorkshire, England. Died: Aug. 6, 1954, London, England. Stage and screen actor.

Appeared in: **1932** For the Love of Mike. **1933** Going Gay (aka Kiss Me Goodbye—US 1935); For Love of You. **1936** Public Nuisance No. 1. **1937** Paradise for Two (aka The Gaiety Girls—US 1938); Street Singer. **1941** Kipps (aka The Remarkable Mr. Kipps—US 1942).

RISDON, CARLTON
Died: Aug. 22, 1979. Screen actor.

Appeared in: **1978** Goin' South.

RISDON, ELIZABETH
Born: Apr. 26, 1887, London, England. Died: Dec. 20, 1958, Santa Monica, Calif. (brain hemorrhage). Screen, stage and television actress. Married to actor and director George Loane Tucker (dec. 1921) and later to stage actor Brandon Evans (dec. 1958).

Appeared in: **1913** Maria Marten: Or, The Murder in the Red Barn; Bridegrooms Beware. **1914** The Finger of Destiny; The Cup Final Mystery; The Suicide Club; Beautiful Jim (aka The Price of Justice—US); Her Luck in London; It's a Long Long Way to Tipperary; The Idol of Paris; In the Days of Trafalgar (aka Black-Eyed Susan and The Battling British—US); Inquisitive Ike; The Loss of the Birkenhead; The Sound of Her Voice; The Courage of a Coward; The Bells of Rheims. **1915** The Christian; Florence Nightingale; From Shopgirl to Dutchess; Her Nameless Child; Grip; A Honeymoon for Three; Home; London's Yellow Peril; Midshipman Easy; Another Man's Wife; Charity Ann; Fine Feathers; Love in a Wood; A Will of Her Own; There's Good in Everyone; Gilbert Gets Tiger-Itis. **1916** The Princess of Happy Chance; The Manxman; The Mother of Dartmoor; Meg the Lady; Esther; Driven (aka Desperation—US); Mother Love; A Mother's Influence; The Morals of Weybury (aka The Hypocrites). **1917** Smith. **1919** A Star Overnight. **1935** Guard That Girl; Crime and Punishment. **1936** Don't Gamble with Love; Lady of Secrets; The King Steps Out; Craig's Wife; Theodora Goes Wild; The Final Hour. **1937** The Woman I Love; Make Way for Tomorrow; Mountain Justice; They Won't Forget; Mannequin; Dead End. **1938** Mad About Music; Tom Sawyer, Detective; Cowboy from Brooklyn; My Bill; Girls on Probation; The Affairs of Annabel. **1939** Sorority House; The Girl from Mexico; Full Confession; The Man Who Dared; The Mexican Spitfire; Huckleberry Finn; I Am Not Afraid; The Roaring Twenties; The Forgotten Woman; Disputed Passage; The Great Man Votes; Five Came Back. **1940** The Man Who Wouldn't Talk; Abe Lincoln in Illinois; Honeymoon Deferred; Ma, He's Making

Eyes at Me; Saturday's Children; Sing, Dance, Plenty Hot; The Howards of Virginia; The Mexican Spitfire Out West; Slightly Tempered; Let's Make Music. **1941** Nice Girl?; The Mexican Spitfire's Baby; High Sierra; Mr. Dynamite; Footlight Fever. **1942** The Lady Is Willing; Mexican Spitfire at Sea; Mexican Spitfire Sees a Ghost; Jail House Blues; The Man Who Returned to Life; Reap the Wild Wind; I Live on Danger; Are Husbands Necessary?; Mexican Spitfire's Elephant; Journey for Margaret; Random Harvest; Paris Calling. **1943** Never a Dull Moment; Mexican Spitfire's Blessed Event; The Amazing Mrs. Holiday; Higher and Higher. **1944** The Canterville Ghost; Tall in the Saddle; Lost Angel; The Cobra Woman; Weird Woman; In the Meantime, Darling. **1945** Blonde Fever; Grissly's Millions; The Unseen; Song for Miss Julie; The Fighting Guardsman; Mama Loves Papa. **1946** Lover Come Back; Roll on Texas Moon; The Walls Came Tumbling Down; They Made Me a Killer. **1947** Life with Father; The Shocking Miss Pilgrim; Romance of Rosy Ridge; Mourning Becomes Electra; The Egg and I. **1948** The Bride Goes Wild; Sealed Verdict; Bodyguard; High Wall; Every Girl Should Be Married. **1949** Guilty of Treason; Down Dakota Way. **1950** Bunco Squad; The Milkman; Hills of Oklahoma; The Secret Fury; Sierra. **1951** Bannerline; My True Story; In Old Amarillo. **1952** Scaramouche.

RISHELL, MYRTLE
Born: Sept. 12, 1877, Portland, Ore. Died: Sept. 12, 1942, Los Angeles, Calif. (cancer). Screen actress.

Appeared in: **1920** House of Whispers; Heart of a Child.

RISING, WILLIAM S.
Born: 1851. Died: Oct. 5, 1930, New York, N.Y. (heart trouble). Screen, stage actor and film director.

Appeared in: **1924** America.

RISS, DAN
Born: 1910. Died: Aug. 28, 1970, Hollywood, Calif. (heart attack). Screen and radio actor.

Appeared in: **1949** Atlantic Fury; Pinky. **1950** Kiss Tomorrow Goodbye; Love That Brute; Panic in the Streets; When Willie Comes Marching Home; Wyoming Mail. **1951** Fourteen Hours; Appointment with Danger; Go for Broke; Little Egypt; Only the Valiant. **1952** Carbine Williams; Confidence Girl; Operation Secret; Scarlet Angel; Washington Story. **1953** Man in the Dark; The Miami Story; Vice Squad. **1954** Executive Suite; Human Desire; Riders to the Stars; The Three Young Texans; The Yellow Tomahawk. **1957** Man on Fire; Kelly and Me. **1958** Badman's Country. **1960** Ma Barker's Killer Brood; The Story on Page One; Elmer Gantry.

RISSMILLER, LAWSON J.
Born: 1914. Died: Apr. 2, 1953, Oley, Pa. Screen actor and orchestra leader.

Appeared in: **1939** Broadway Buckaroo.

RISSO, ATTILIO
Born: 1913. Died: Oct. 14, 1967, San Francisco, Calif. (liver disease). Screen and television actor. Appeared in films during the 1930's and 1940's with a group called the "Vagabonds."

Appeared in: **1943** It Ain't Hay.

RISSONI, GIUDITTA
Born: 1896, Italy? Died: May 31, 1977, Rome, Italy. Screen actress. Divorced from actor Vittoria de Sica (dec. 1974).

Appeared in: **1933** Passa L'Amore. **1936** Amo Te Sola. **1938** Il Trionfo dell' Amore (Love's Triumph). **1947** Schoolgirl Diary. **1948** Four Steps in the Clouds. **1953** Tormento. **1963** 8 1/2. **1965** La Ragazza in Prestito (aka Engagement Italiano—US 1966).

RISTELHUEBER, JOSEPH H.
Born: 1847. Died: Feb. 28, 1943, Los Angeles, Calif. Silent screen actor.

RITCHARD, CYRIL (Cyril Trimnell-Ritchard))
Born: Dec. 1, 1897, Sydney, Australia. Died: Dec. 18, 1977, Chicago, Ill. (cardiac arrest). Screen, stage, vaudeville, television actor, stage director and opera singer. Married to actress Madge Elliott (dec. 1955).

Appeared in: **1927** On With the Dance (series). **1929** Picadilly; Blackmail. **1930** Just for a Song; Symphony in Two Flats. **1932** Service for Ladies (aka Reserved for Ladies—US). **1937** It's a Grand Old World; The Show Goes On. **1938** Dangerous Medicine; I See Ice. **1948** Woman Hater (US 1949). **1966** The Daydreamer (voice). **1967** Half a Sixpence (US 1968).

RITCHIE, BILLIE
Born: 1879, Glasgow, Scotland. Died: July 6, 1921, Los Angeles, Calif. Screen and vaudeville actor. Appeared in Universal Films in 1914.

RITCHIE, FRANKLIN
Born: Ritchie, Pa. Died: Jan. 26, 1918, Los Angeles, Calif. (auto accident). Screen and stage actor.

Appeared in: **1914** The Iron Master. **1915** Under Two Flags; Mrs. Van Alden's Jewels; The Barrier Between; The Quicksands of Society; Adam Bebe; Aurora Floyd; The Americano; Dwellers in Glass Houses; After the Storm; To Have and to Lose; The Confession; The Maid O' the Mountains; Man and His Master; The Drab Sister; The Soul of Pierre; The Country Parson; Dora; Harvest; Between Father and Son; The Hungarian Nabob; The Woman of Mystery; The Reproach of Annesley. **1916** The Light; Not My Sister; The Reclamation; Dust; Pique; Lying Lips; Man's Enemy; The Wages of Sin; The Science of Crime; The Honor of the Law; The Undertow. **1917** The Gentle Intruder. **1918** Beloved Rogue.

RITCHIE, TERRY V.
Born: Nov. 28, 1887, Kans. Died: July 27, 1918, Los Angeles, Calif. (suicide—gas asphyxiation). Screen actor.

RITICHIE, CHARLES W.
Died: May 25, 1931, Chattanooga, Tenn. Screen and stage actor. Married to actress Mabel Paige (dec. 1954). Appeared in Lubin Film Co. films.

RITTER, ESTHER (aka ESTHER SUPPLEE)
Born: 1902. Died: Dec. 30, 1925, Los Angeles, Calif. (appendicitis). Screen actress. Married to screen actor Cuyler Supplee.

RITTER, GEORGE
Died: Dec., 1919. Screen actor.

RITTER, PAUL J.
Died: Apr. 27, 1962, Dacca, Pakistan. Screen actor and film producer.

RITTER, TEX (Maurice Woodward Ritter)
Born: Jan. 12, 1906, Panola County, Tex. Died: Jan. 2, 1974, Nashville, Tenn. (heart attack). Screen, stage, radio, television actor, singer and musician. Father of actor John Ritter.

Appeared in: **1936** Song of the Gringo (film debut); Headin' for Rio Grande. **1937** Arizona Days; Trouble in Texas; Hittin' the Trail; Riders of the Rockies; Tex Rides with the Boy Scouts; The Mystery of the Hooded Horsemen; Sing, Cowboy, Sing. **1938** Frontier Town; Rollin' Plains; The Utah Trail; Starlight Over Texas; Where the Buffalo Roam. **1939** Roll, Wagons, Roll; Song of the Buckaroo; Sundown on the Prairie; Riders of the Frontier; Rollin' Westward; Down the Wyoming Trail; Man from Texas. **1940** Westbound Stage; Rhythm of the Rio Grande; Pals of the Silver Sage; The Golden Trail; The Cowboy from Sundown; Take Me Back to Oklahoma; Rainbow Over the Range; Arizona Frontier; Riding with Buffalo Bill; A-Headin' for Cheyenne; Round-Up Time in the Rockies. **1941** Rolling Home to Texas; Riding the Cherokee Trail; The Pioneers; King of Dodge City; Roaring Frontiers; Lone Star Vigilantes; Bullets for Bandits; The Devil's Trail; North of the Rockies; Prairie Gunsmoke; Vengeance of the West. **1942** Deep in the Heart of Texas; Little Joe the Wrangler; Raiders of the San Joaquin. **1943** The Old Chisholm Trail; The Lone Star Trail; Tenting Tonight on the Old Camp Ground; Cheyenne Roundup; Arizona Trail; Frontier Badmen. **1944** Marshal of Gunsmoke; Oklahoma Raiders; Cowboy Canteen; Gangsters of the Frontier; Dead or Alive; The Whispering Skull; Marked for Murder. **1945** Enemy of the Law; Three in the Saddle; Frontier Fugitives; Flaming Bullets. **1950** Holiday Rhythm. **1952** High Noon. **1953** The Marshal's Daughter. **1954** The Cowboy (narrator). **1955** Apache Ambush; Wichita; The First Badman. **1956** Down Liberty Road. **1957** Trooper Hook. **1966** Nashville Rebel; What's the Country Coming To?; Girl from Tobacco Road. **1967** What Am I Bid?

RITTER, THELMA
Born: Feb. 14, 1905, Brooklyn, N.Y. Died: Feb. 5, 1969, New York, N.Y. (heart attack). Screen, stage, radio and television actress. Nominated for 1950 Academy Award for Best Supporting Actress in All About Eve; in 1951 for The Mating Season; in 1952 for With a Song in My Heart; in 1953 for Pickup on South Street; in 1959 for Pillow Talk; and in 1962 for Bird Man of Alcatraz.

Appeared in: **1947** Miracle on 34th Street (film debut). **1949** City Across the River; Father Was a Fullback; A Letter to Three Wives. **1950** Perfect Strangers; All About Eve; I'll Get By. **1951** The Mating Season; The Model and the Marriage Broker; As Young as You Feel.

1952 With a Song in My Heart. **1953** The Farmer Takes a Wife; Pickup on South Street; Titanic. **1954** Rear Window. **1955** Lucy Gallant; Daddy Long Legs. **1956** The Proud and Profane. **1959** A Hole in the Head; Pillow Talk. **1961** The Misfits; The Second Time Around. **1962** Birdman of Alcatraz; How the West Was Won. **1963** A New Kind of Love; Move Over, Darling; For Love or Money. **1965** Boeing Boeing. **1967** The Incident. **1968** What's So Bad about Feeling Good?

RITTERBAND, GERHARD
Born: 1905, Germany. Died: Oct., 1959, Berlin, Germany (jaundice). Screen actor. Appeared in early Ernst Lubitsch films and other silents.

RITTS, PAUL
Born: 1920. Died: Oct. 18, 1980, Monroe, Mich. (heart attack). Screen, television actor, television director and television writer. Married to actress Mary Ritts.

Appeared in: **1962** The Errand Boy.

RITZ, AL (Al Joachim)
Born: Aug. 27, 1901, Newark, N.J. Died: Dec. 22, 1965, New Orleans, La. (heart attack). Screen, stage, vaudeville and television actor. Brother of actors Harry and Jimmy Ritz. Was member of "Ritz Bros." screen and vaudeville comedy team. All films beginning in 1934 include the three brothers.

Appeared in: **1918** The Avenging Trail (was an extra in this film). **1934** Hotel Anchovy (team film debut—short). **1936** Sing, Baby, Sing. **1937** One in a Million; On the Avenue; You Can't Have Everything; Life Begins in College. **1938** The Goldwyn Follies; Kentucky Moonshine; Straight, Place and Show. **1939** The Three Musketeers; The Gorilla; Pack Up Your Troubles. **1940** Argentine Nights. **1942** Behind the Eight Ball. **1943** Hi 'Ya, Chum; Screen Snapshots No. 5 (short); Screen Snapshots No. 8 (short); Never a Dull Moment. **1944** Take It or Leave It (scenes from On the Avenue (1937) in this film). **1945** Everything Happens to Us. **1963** The Sound of Laughter (documentary).

RIVA, MARIO (Mario Bonavolanta)
Born: 1913, Italy. Died: Sept. 1, 1960, Verona, Italy (results of a fall). Screen, stage and television actor.

Appeared in: **1951** Altri Tempi (Times Gone By—US 1953). **1952** I Cadgetti di Guascogna. **1954** My Heart Sings.

RIVAS, JOSE M. L. (Jose Maria Linares Rivas)
Born: 1901, Mexico. Died: Apr. 13, 1955, Mexico City, Mexico. Screen and stage actor.

Appeared in: **1939** El Romance del Palmar. **1962** The Criminal Life of Archibaldo de la Cruz.

RIVERO, JULIAN
Born: July 25, 1891, Galveston, Tex. Died: Feb. 24, 1976, Hollywood, Calif. Screen, stage, television actor and film director. Entered films in 1915.

Appeared in: **1924** Fast and Fearless. **1925** The Night Ship. **1926** The Border Whirlwind. **1930** Asi es la Vida. **1931** Rose of the Rio Grande; God's Country and the Man; Yankee Don; Dugan of the Bad Lands. **1932** The Tabasco Kid (short); Broken Wing; Night Rider; Man from Hell's Edges; Winner Takes All; Beyond the Rockies; Son of Oklahoma; The Kid from Spain. **1933** Man of Action; Lucky Larrigan; Law and Lawless; Via Pony Express; Hold the Press. **1935** The Sagebrush Troubadour; Burn 'Em Up Barnes; Riddle Ranch. **1936** Hi Gaucho; Woman Trap; Song of the Saddle; Dancing Pirate. **1937** The Mighty Treve; Lawless Land; Heroes of the Alamo; Ridin' The Lone Trail. **1939** The Girl and the Gambler; South of the Border. **1940** Gaucho Serenade. **1941** Down Mexico Way. **1942** Bells of Capistrano; Rio Rita; The Valley of Vanishing Men (serial). **1943** Hands Across the Border; The Outlaw. **1944** Machine Gun Mama; The Falcon in Mexico. **1945** The Bullfighters; That Night With You. **1946** Anna and the King of Siam; Trail to Mexico. **1947** Robin Hood of Monterey; Over the Santa Fe Trail; In Self Defense. **1948** Mexican Hayride; Treasure of Sierra Madre; Old Los Angeles; The Checkered Coat. **1949** Amazon Quest; The Devil's Henchman. **1950** Killer Shark; Border Treasure. **1951** The Texas Rangers. **1952** Wild Horse Ambush. **1954** Broken Lance. **1955** Guys and Dolls; The Vanishing American. **1956** Thunder Over Arizona. **1965** The Reward.

RIVERS, FERDAND
Born: 1882, France. Died: Aug., 1960, Nice, France. Screen actor, film director and producer. Appeared in silent films.

RIVERS, VICTOR
Born: 1948. Died: July 8, 1977, Los Angeles, Calif. (injured while performing stunt). Screen actor and stuntman.

Appeared in: **1977** Grand Theft Auto; High Riders.

RIVIERE, FRED "CURLY"
Born: 1875. Died: Nov. 6, 1935, Hollywood, Calif. (heart attack). Screen actor.

Appeared in: **1926** The Dangerous Dub.

RIZZO, CARLO
Died: Feb. 10, 1977. Screen actor.

Appeared in: **1950** Deported. **1952** When in Rome. **1955** The Rains of Ranchipur. **1956** Monte Carlo Story. **1958** The Seven Hills of Rome. **1959** The Naked Maja. **1960** Fast and Sexy. **1962** Damon and Pythias; Le Mercenaire (aka Swordsman of Siena—US). **1968** The Biggest Bundle of Them All.

ROACH, BERT
Born: Aug. 21, 1891, Washington, D.C. Died: Feb. 16, 1971. Screen and stage actor.

Appeared in: **1914** Fatty's Magic Pants. **1916** The Youngest in the Family; The Lawyer's Secret; Dinty's Daring Dash. **1917** Beach Nuts; Roped Into Scandal. **1921** The Millionaire; The Rowdy; A Small Town Idol. **1922** The Black Bag; The Flirt. **1924** Excitement; High Speed; A Lady of Quality; The Storm Daughter. **1925** The Denial; Don't; Excuse Me; Smouldering Fires. **1926** The Flaming Forest; Money Talks; Tin Hats. **1927** The Taxi Dancer; Tillie the Toiler; Twelve Miles Out. **1928** A Certain Young Man; The Crowd; Honeymoon; Paramount-Christie Talking Plays; Riders of the Dark; The Latest from Paris; Telling the World; Under the Black Eagle; Wickedness Preferred. **1929** The Argyle Case; The Desert Rider; The Last Warning; The Show of Shows; So Long Letty; The Time, the Place and the Girl; Young Nowheres; Twin Beds; The Fatal Forceps (short). **1930** So This Is Paris Green (short); Captain Thunder; Hold Everything; Lawful Larceny; Liliom; No, No, Nanette; The Princess and the Plumber; Song of the Flame; Viennese Nights; Scrappily Married (short); Down With Husbands (short); For Love or Money (short). **1931** Six Cylinder Love; Compromised; Arrowsmith. **1932** Murder in the Rue Morgue; Hotel Continental; Nigat World; Love Me Tonight; Bird of Paradise; Evenings for Sale. **1933** Hallelujah, I'm a Bum. **1934** Half a Sinner; Paris Interlude. **1935** Traveling Saleslady; Here Comes the Band; Guard That Girl; Goin' to Town. **1936** Love Before Breakfast; Sons O' Guns; San Francisco; God's Country and the Woman; Hollywood Boulevard. **1937** Sing While You're Able; The Girl Said No; The Emperor's Candlesticks; Double Wedding; Prescription for Romance. **1938** The Jury's Secret; Honolulu; Mad About Music; Stolen Heaven; Romance on the Run; Algiers; Inside Story; The Great Waltz. **1939** Mr. Moto's Last Warning; Rose of Washington Square; The Man in the Iron Mask; Nurse Edith Cavell. **1940** Yesterday's Heroes. **1941** You're The One; Bachelor Daddy. **1942** Fingers at the Window; Dr. Renault's Secret; Quiet Please—Murder. **1943** Hi Diddle Diddle. **1944** Sensations of 1945. **1945** Bedside Manner; Abbott and Costello in Hollywood. **1946** Little Giant; Rendezvous; The Missing Lady; Man from Rainbow Valley; Sing While You Dance. **1947** The Perils of Pauline.

ROACH, MARGARET
Born: Mar. 15, 1921, Los Angeles, Calif. Died: Nov. 22, 1964, Hollywood, Calif. Screen and stage actress. Daughter of film producer Hal Roach.

Appeared in: **1939** Captain Fury; Fast and Furious. **1940** Turnabout. **1941** Road Show; Niagara Falls.

ROACHE, VIOLA
Born: Oct. 3, 1885. Died: May 17, 1961, Hollywood, Calif. (heart attack). Stage and screen actress.

Appeared in: **1950** Harriet Craig. **1951** Royal Wedding; Goodbye, My Fancy.

ROBARDS, JASON, SR.
Born: Dec. 31, 1892, Hillsdale, Mich. Died: Apr. 4, 1963, Sherman Oaks, Calif. (heart attack). Screen and stage actor. Father of actor Jason Robards, Jr.

Appeared in: **1921** The Gilded Lily; The Land of Hope. **1925** Stella Maris. **1926** Footloose Widows; The Cohens and the Kellys; The Third Degree. **1927** Casey Jones; Wild Geese; Jaws of Steel; The Heart of Maryland; Hills of Kentucky; Irish Hearts; Polly of the Movies; Tracked by the Police; White Flannels. **1928** Streets of Shanghai; On Trial; The Death Ship (short); Casey Jones; A Bird in the Hand (short). **1929** Paris; The Flying Marine; Trial Marriage; The Isle of Lost Ships; Some Mother's Boy; The Gamblers. **1930** The Last Dance; Jazz Cinderella; Lightnin' Sisters; Crazy That Way; Peacock Alley; Abraham Lincoln; Trifles (short). **1931** Charlie Chan Carries On; Subway Express; Salvation Nell; Full of Notions; Caught Plastered;

Law of the Tongs; Ex-Bad Boy. **1932** The Conquerors; Discarded Lovers; Unholy Love; White Eagle; Klondike; Docks of San Francisco; Pride of the Legion; Slightly Married. **1933** Strange Alibi; Corruption; Devil's Mate; Dance Hall Hostess; Ship of Wanted Men; Public Stenographer; Carnival Lady; The Way to Love. **1934** Broadway Bill; One Exciting Adventure; The President Vanishes; The Crimson Romance; Take the Stand; Woman Unafraid; All of Me; Woman Condemned; Super Snooper (short). **1935** The Miracle Rider (serial); Ladies Crave Excitement; The Crusades; Burn 'Em Up Barnes (serial and feature); Break of Hearts. **1936** Devil is a Sissy; The White Legion. **1937** Sweetheart of the Navy; Damaged Lives; The Firefly; The Man Who Cried Wolf. **1938** The Adventures of Marco Polo; Little Tough Guy; The Clipped Wings; Flight to Fame; Mystery Plane; Cipher Bureau. **1939** Sky Pirate; Stunt Pilot; The Mad Empress; Range War; Danger Flight; I Stole a Million; Scouts to the Rescue (serial). **1940** I Love You Again; The Fatal Hour. **1942** Silver Queen. **1944** Mlle. Fifi; Bermuda Mystery; The Master Race; Sing a Jingle. **1945** Betrayal from the East; What a Blonde; A Game of Death; Wanderer of the Wasteland; Isle of the Dead; Man Alive; plus the following shorts: What, No Cigarettes?; Let's Go Stepping; It Shouldn't Happen to a Dog. **1946** The Bamboo Blonde; Bedlam; Ding Dong Williams; The Falcon's Adventure; The Falcon's Alibi; Vacation in Reno; Step by Step; plus the following shorts: I'll Build It Myself; Twin Husbands; I'll Take Milk. **1947** The Farmer's Daughter; Seven Keys to Baldpate; Under the Tonto Rim; Wild Horse Mesa; Trail Street; Desperate; Thunder Mountain; Riffraff; Do or Diet (short). **1948** Fighting Father Dunne; Guns of Hate; Mr. Blandings Builds His Dream House; Western Heritage; Son of God's Country; Return of the Bad Men. **1949** Rimfire; Post Office Investigator; Alaska Patrol; Impact; Feudin' Rhythm; Horseman of the Sierras; Riders of the Whistling Pines; South of Death Valley. **1951** The Second Woman. **1961** Wild in the Country.

ROBARDS, WILLIS L.
Born: 1873. Died: Nov. 3, 1921, Hollywood, Calif. (heart attack). Screen actor and film director.

Appeared in: **1920** The Silent Avenger (serial). **1921** The Three Musketeers; Every Woman's Problem; Desert Blossoms. **1922** Man to Man.

ROBB, LOTUS
Died: Sept. 28, 1969, Georgetown, Wash. Screen and stage actress.

Appeared in: **1954** A Star is Born.

ROBBINS, ARCHIE
Born: 1913. Died: Sept. 26, 1975, New York, N.Y. Vaudeville, stage and screen actor.

Appeared in: **1935** His Night Out. **1936** The Leavenworth Case; Republic. **1944** Winged Victory (stage and film versions). **1954** Roogie's Bump.

ROBBINS, GALE
Born: May 7, 1922, Chicago, Ill. Died: Feb. 18, 1980, Tarzana, Calif. (lung cancer). Screen, television actress and singer.

Appeared in: **1944** In the Meantime Darling (film debut). **1946** Mr. Hex. **1948** My Dear Secretary; My Girl Tisa; Race Street. **1949** Oh, You Beautiful Doll; The Barkleys of Broadway. **1950** The Fuller Brush Girl; Three Little Words; Between Midnight and Dawn. **1951** Strictly Dishonorble. **1952** The Belle of New York; The Brigand. **1953** Calamity Jane. **1955** The Girl in the Red Velvet Swing; Double Jeopardy. **1958** Quantrill's Raiders; Gunsmoke in Tucson.

ROBBINS, MARCUS B.
Born: 1868. Died: Apr. 7, 1931, Hollywood, Calif. Screen actor and screenwriter.

Appeared in: **1920** Alias Jimmy Valentine. **1922** The Gray Dawn; The Girl Who Ran Wild. **1923** The Marriage Market; The Scarlet Car.

ROBBINS, RICHARD
Born: 1919, Boston, Mass. Died: Oct. 23, 1969, New York, N.Y. (heart attack). Screen, stage and television actor.

Appeared in: **1956** The Wrong Man.

ROBBINS, ROY "SKEETER BILL" (aka "SKEETER" BILL ROBINSON)
Died: Nov. 29, 1933 (auto accident). Screen actor.

Appeared in: **1923** Don Quickshot of the Rio Grande. **1926** Man Rustlin'; Chasing Trouble. **1931** Wild Horse; Hard Hombre; Gay Buckaroo. **1932** Local Bad Man; The Boiling Point; A Man's Land. **1933** Cowboy Counsellor; Dude Bandit; Fighting Parson.

ROBER, RICHARD
Born: May 14, 1906, Rochester, N.Y. Died: May 26, 1952, Santa Monica, Calif. (auto accident). Screen, stage and television actor.

Appeared in: **1947** Call Northside 777 (film debut). **1948** April Showers; Smart Girls Don't Talk; Embraceable You; Larceny. **1949** Illegal Entry; Any Number Can Play; Backfire; I Married a Communist; Port of New York; Task Force. **1950** Thelma Jordan; Deported; Dial 1119; Sierra; The Woman on Pier 13; There's a Girl in My Heart. **1951** The Well; Father's Little Dividend; Passage West; The Tall Target; Watch the Birdie; Man in the Saddle. **1952** The Devil Makes Three; O. Henry's Full House; Outlaw Woman; The Rose Bowl Story; The Savage; Kid Monk Baroni. **1957** Jet Pilot.

ROBERSON, LOU
Born: 1921. Died: Nov. 21, 1966, Hollywood, Calif. Screen actor and stuntman.

ROBERT, HANS
Born: 1874. Died: May 2, 1954, Jamaica, Long Island, N.Y. Screen, stage and vaudeville actor.

Appeared in: **1912** The Grecian Vase.

ROBERTI, LYDA
Born: 1909, Warsaw, Poland. Died: Mar. 12, 1938, Los Angeles, Calif. (heart ailment). Stage and screen actress.

Appeared in: **1932** Dancers in the Dark; The Kid from Spain; Million Dollar Legs. **1933** Torch Singer; Three-Cornered Moon. **1934** College Rhythm. **1935** George White's 1935 Scandals; The Big Broadcast of 1936. **1937** Nobody's Baby; Pick a Star; Wide Open Faces.

ROBERTS, A. CLEDGE
Born: 1905. Died: June 14, 1957, New York, N.Y. Screen, stage, radio, television actor, film, stage director, film and stage producer.

ROBERTS, ALBERT G.
Born: 1902. Died: May 30, 1941, North Hollywood, Calif. (suicide—gun). Screen actor and cameraman. Married to actress Peggy Shannon (dec. 1941).

ROBERTS, ARTHUR
Born: Sept. 21, 1852, London, England. Died: Feb. 27, 1933, London, England. Screen and stage actor. Do not confuse with US actor with same name.

Appeared in: **1914** The Importance of Being Another Man's Wife.

ROBERTS, CHARLES B. "JACK"
Died: Sept. 14, 1927, Los Angeles, Calif. Screen actor.

ROBERTS, DICK
Born: 1897. Died: Nov. 1, 1966, North Hollywood, Calif. Screen, radio actor and banjoist.

Appeared in: **1936** Banjo on My Knee.

ROBERTS, EDD J.
Born: 1893. Died: Jan. 23, 1953, Fort Worth, Tex. Screen actor.

ROBERTS, EDITH (Edith Josephine Roberts)
Born: 1899, New York, N.Y. Died: Aug. 20, 1935, Los Angeles, Calif. Screen, stage and vaudeville actress.

Appeared in: **1917** A Hasty Hazing; Down Went the Key; A Million in Sight; A Bundle of Trouble; Some Specimens; When the Cat's Away; Shot in the West; Mixed Matrimony; The Lost Appetite; Tell Morgan's Girl; What a Clue Will Do; The Home Wreckers; Moving Day; To Be or Not to Be Remarried; Pete the Prowler; The War Bridegroom; Under the Bed; Follow the Tracks; Jilted in Jail; A Burglar by Request; Hot Applications; Treat 'Em Rough; A Macaroni Sleuth; One Thousand Miles an Hour; Practice What You Preach; The Rogue's Nest; Little Moccasins; Her City Beau. **1918** The Vamp Cure; The Love Swindle. **1919** Beans; A Taste of Life; Bill Henry. **1920** The Adorable Savage. **1921** The Fire Cat; The Unknown Wife; White Youth; Thunder Island; Opened Shutters; Luring Lips; In Society. **1922** Saturday Night; Flesh and Blood; A Front Page Story; Pawned; The Son of the Wolf; Thorns and Orange Blossoms. **1923** The Sunshine Trail; Big Brother; Backbone; The Dangerous Age. **1924** An Age of Innocence; The Bowery Bishop; Roaring Rails; Roulette; Thy Name Is Woman; $20 a Week. **1925** Heir-Loons; New Champion; Shattered Lives; Speed Mad; Three Keys; Wasted Lives; Seven Keys to Baldpate; On Thin Ice. **1926** There You Are; The Mystery Club; The Jazz Girl; The Road to Broadway; Shameful Behavior?; The Taxi Mystery. **1928** Man from Headquarters. **1929** The Phantom of the North; The Wagon Master.

ROBERTS, EVELYN
Born: Aug. 28, 1886, Reading, Berks, England. Died: Nov. 30, 1962, England? Screen and stage actor.

Appeared in: **1933** Sorrell and Son (US 1934). **1937** The Return of the Scarlet Pimpernel (US 1938). **1948** The Winslow Boy (US 1950). **1953** Gibraltar Adventure (aka The Clue of the Missing Ape—US 1962); The Heart of the Matter (US 1954). **1954** The Green Scarf (US 1955).

ROBERTS, FLORENCE
Born: 1871. Died: July 17, 1927, Hollywood, Calif. Screen actress. Married to screen actor Frederick Vogeding (dec. 1942).

ROBERTS, FLORENCE
Born: Mar. 16, 1861, Frederick, Md. Died: June 6, 1940, Hollywood, Calif. Screen and stage actress. Married to stage actor Walter Gale (dec.). Appeared in "Jones Family" series, 1936-40.

Appeared in: **1912** Sapho. **1925** The Best People. **1930** Grandma's Girl (short); Eyes of the World; Soup to Nuts. **1931** Bachelor Apartment; Fanny Foley Herself; Too Many Cooks; Kept Husband; Everything's Rosie. **1932** Make Me a Star; All American; Westward Passage. **1933** Officer 13; Daring Daughters; Dangerously Yours; Melody Cruise; Torch Singer; Hoopla; Ever In My Heart. **1934** The Cracked Iceman (short); Four Parts (short); Babes in Toyland; Miss Fane's Baby Is Stolen. **1935** Sons of Steel; Les Miserables; The Nut Farm; Rocky Mountain Mystery; Accent on Youth; Harmony Lane; Public Opinion; Your Uncle Dudley. **1936** The Next Time We Love; Nobody's Fool; Every Saturday Night; Educating Father; Back to Nature. **1937** Borrowing Trouble; Nobody's Baby; The Life of Emile Zola; Off to the Races; Big Business; Hot Water. **1938** Love on a Budget; The Storm; A Trip to Paris; Safety in Numbers; Down on the Farm; Personal Secretary. **1939** Everybody's Baby; Jones Family in the Grand Canyon; Jones Family in Hollywood; Too Busy to Work; Quick Millions. **1940** On Their Own; Young as You Feel.

ROBERTS, GEORGE
Born: 1845, England. Died: Apr. 25, 1930, London, England. Stage, screen actor and playwright.

Appeared in: **1925** William Tell.

ROBERTS, GLEN (Leonard Freeman)
Born: 1921. Died: Jan. 20, 1974, Palo Alto, Calif. (following heart surgery). Television, film producer and screen actor.

Appeared in: **1953** Girls in the Night.

ROBERTS, J. H. (John H. Roberts)
Born: July 11, 1884, London, England. Died: Feb. 1, 1961, London, England. Screen and stage actor.

Appeared in: **1932** White Face. **1933** It's a Boy! (US 1934). **1936** Accused; Juggernaut (US 1937). **1937** Farewell Again (aka Troopship—US 1938); Young and Innocent (aka The Girl Was Young—US 1938). **1938** The Divorce of Lady X. **1941** Penn of Pennsylvania (aka The Courageous Mr. Penn—US 1944); Dangerous Moonlight (aka Suicide Squadron—US 1942). **1942** The First of The Few (aka Spitfire—US 1943); Uncensored (US 1944). **1945** The Agitator. **1948** Blanche Fury; Quartet (US 1949).

ROBERTS, JOHN "TODD"
Born: 1954. Died: Dec. 14, 1979, Hollywood, Calif. (auto accident). Screen, television actor and propertyman. Married to actress Dawn Karen.

Appeared in: **1964** My Fair Lady. **1966** The Fortune Cookie.

ROBERTS, JOSEPH "JOE"
Born: 1870. Died: Oct. 28, 1923, Los Angeles, Calif. Screen actor and film producer.

Appeared in: **1922** The Primitive Lover. **1923** Our Hospitality; Three Ages.

ROBERTS, LENORE
Born: 1931. Died: Aug. 14, 1978, Los Angeles, Calif. (cancer). Screen and television actress.

Appeared in: **1962** Days of Wine and Roses.

ROBERTS, LEONA
Born: 1880. Died: Jan. 30, 1954, Santa Monica, Calif. Screen actress.

Appeared in: **1937** Border Cafe; There Goes the Groom. **1938** Of Human Hearts; Bringing Up Baby; Condemned Women; This Marriage Business; Having a Wonderful Time; The Affair of Annabel; Crime

Ring; Kentucky; I Stand Accused. **1939** Of Mice and Men; Persons in Hiding; They Made Her a Spy; Bachelor Mother; The Escape; Swanee River; Gone With the Wind. **1940** Sued for Libel; Thou Shalt Not Kill; Queen of the Mob; The Blue Bird; Abe Lincoln in Illinois; Flight Angels; Ski Patrol; Gangs of Chicago; Golden Gloves; Comin' 'Round the Mountain; Wildcat Bus; Blondie Plays Cupid. **1941** Weekend in Havana. **1946** The Madonna's Secret. **1947** Boomerang.

ROBERTS, MERRILL
Born: 1885. Died: Dec. 2, 1940, Hollywood, Calif. Screen actor. Father of actress Carol Wayne.

ROBERTS, NANCY (Annette Finlay)
Born: 1892. Died: June 25, 1962, London, England. Screen, stage and television actress.

Appeared in: **1915** The Devil's Profession. **1938** Prison Without Bars (US 1939). **1947** Black Narcissus.

ROBERTS, NED
Died: Mar. 28, 1973. Screen actor.

Appeared in: **1950** Marshal of Heldorado.

ROBERTS, RACHEL
Born: Sept. 20, 1927, Llanelli, Wales. Died: Nov., 1980, Los Angeles, Calif. Screen, stage and television actress. Divorced from actors Alan Dobie and Rex Harrison. Nominated for 1963 Academy Award for Best Actress in This Sporting Life.

Appeared in: **1953** Valley of Song (film debut, aka Men are Children Twice—US); The Limping Man. **1954** The Weak and The Wicked; The Crowded Day. **1957** The Good Companions (US 1958). **1960** Our Man in Havana; Saturday Night and Sunday Morning (US 1961). **1962** Girl on Approval. **1963** This Sporting Life. **1968** A Flea in Her Ear. **1970** The Reckoning. **1971** Doctor's Wives; Wild Rovers. **1973** O Lucky Man; The Belstone Fox (US 1976). **1974** Murder on the Orient Express. **1975** Great Expectations. **1976** Alpha Beta. **1978** Foul Play; Free Spirit. **1979** Yanks; When a Stranger Calls; Picnic at Hanging Rock. **1981** Charlie Chan and the Curse of the Dragon Queen.

ROBERTS, RALPH ARTHUR
Born: Oct. 2, 1884, Meerane, Germany. Died: 1940, Berlin, Germany. Screen, stage actor, film director and screenwriter.

Appeared in: **1922** Erniedrigte und Beleidigte; Sodoms Ende. **1923** Die Buddenbrooks; Der Frauenkoenig; Lord Reginalds Derbyritt. **1925** Die Blumenfrau vom Potsdamer Platz; Elegantes Pack. **1926** Die Dritte Eskadron; Die Tragoedie Eines Verlorenen. **1927** Einbruch; Fuerst oder Clown; Meine Tante—Deine Tante; Ein Rheinisches Maedchen Beim Rheinischen Wein; Ein Schwerer Fall. **1928** Heut Tanzt Mariett; Der Ladenprinz; Lotte; Marys Grosses Geheimnis; Moral; Der Raub der Sabinerinnen; Die Tolle Komptesse; Der Biberpelz (The Beaver Coat). **1929** Anchluss um Mitternacht; The Headwaiter; Polizeispionin 77. **1930** Einbrecher; Zwei Krawatten; Zweimal Hochzeit; Die Zaertlichen Verwandten; Komm' zu mir zum Rendezvous. **1931** Der Schoenste Mann im Staate; Dienst ist Dienst; Die Spanische Fliege; Die Firma Heiratet; Der Ungetreue Eckehart; Der Wahre Jakob; Jeder Fragt Nach Erika; Gesangverein Sorgenfrei; Luegen auf Ruegen; So'n Windhund!; Keine Feier ohne Meyer; Hurra—ein Junge!; Ihre Majestaet die Liebe; Zu Befehl, Herr Unteroffizier (aka Der Pechvogel). **1932** Eine Nacht im Paradies; Der Frechdachs. **1933** Die Unschuld vom Lande; Keine Angst vor Liebe; Es war Einmal ein Musikus; Es Gibt nur Eine Liebe; Ein Lied fuer Dich. **1934** Spiel mit dem Feuer; Abenteuer im Suedexpress; Schoen ist es, Verliebt zu Sien!; Meine Frau, die Schuetzenkoenigin; Da Stimmt was Nicht; Der Kuehne Schwimmer; Der Schrecken vom Heidekrug; Es Tut Sich was um Mitternacht (aka Ein Maedel mit Tempo); alte Kameraden (aka Das Faehnlein der Versprengten); Zigeunerblut (aka Ungarmaedel). **1935** Punks Kommt aus Amerika; Hilde Petersen Postlagernd; Mach' Mich Gluecklich. **1936** Der Geheimnisvolle Mister X; Soldaten—Kameraden; Engel mit Kleinen Fehlern; Der Verkannte Lebensmann. **1937** Husaren, Heraus; Wenn Du Eine Schwiegermutter Hast; Meine Frau, die Perle; Heiratsinstitut Ida & Co.; Maedchen fuer Alles. **1938** Tranx auf dem Vulkan; Der Maulkorb; Diskretion—Ehrensache. **1939** Ehe in Dosen; Das Glueck Wohnt Nebenan; Meine Tante—Deine Tante (and 1927 version). **1940** Wie Konntest Du, Veronika?; Meine tochter tut das Nicht.

ROBERTS, ROY
Born: 1900. Died: May 28, 1975, Los Angeles, Calif. Screen, stage and television actor.

Appeared in: **1943** Guadalcanal Diary. **1944** The Sullivans; Tampico; Roger Touchy, Gangster; Wilson. **1945** Within These Walls;

Circumstantial Evidence; The Caribbean Mystery; A Bell for Adano; Sunset in Eldorado; Colonel Effingham's Raid. **1946** Behind Green Lights; Smoky; It Shouldn't Happen to a Dog; My Darling Clementine; Johnny Comes Flying Home; Strange Triangle. **1947** The Shocking Miss Pilgrim; The Brasher Doubloon; The Foxes of Harrow; Nightmare Alley; Gentleman's Agreement; Daisy Kenyon; Captain from Castille. **1948** Force of Evil; Joan of Arc; Fury at Furnace Creek; The Gay Intruders; He Walked by Night; No Minor Vices; Chicken Every Sunday. **1949** The Reckless Moment; Calamity Jane and Sam Bass; Miss Grant Takes Richmond; Flaming Fury; A Kiss for Corliss. **1950** The Killer That Stalked New York; Sierra; Chain Lightning; Borderline; Stage to Tucson; Wyoming Mail; The Palomino; Bodyhold; The Second Face. **1951** The Enforcer; I Was a Communist for the FBI; Santa Fe; Fighting Coast Guard; The Man With a Cloak; The Cimarron Kid; The Tanks Are Coming. **1952** One Minute to Zero; The Big Trees; Stars and Stripes Forever; Cripple Creek; Hoodlum Empire; The Man Behind the Gun; Skirts Ahoy. **1953** The Glory Brigade; House of Wax; Lone Hand; Second Chance; Sea of Lost Ships; Tumbleweed; San Antone. **1954** The Outlaw Stallion; Dawn at Socorro; They Rode West. **1955** Big House, USA; The Last Command; Wyoming Renegades; I Cover the Underworld. **1956** The First Texan; The Boss; The King and Four Queens; Yaqui Drums; The White Squaw. **1962** The Chapman Report; The Underwater City. **1963** It's a Mad, Mad, Mad, Mad World. **1935** I'll Take Sweden; Those Calloways. **1967** Hotel; Tammy and the Millionaire. **1969** This Savage Land; Some Kind of a Nut.

ROBERTS, SARA JANE
Born: 1924. Died: Aug. 19, 1968, Hollywood, Calif. Screen actress. Appeared in "Our Gang" comedies.

ROBERTS, STEPHEN
Born: Nov. 23, 1895, Summerville, Va. Died: July 17, 1936, Beverly Hills, Calif. (heart attack). Screen, radio actor, stuntman and film director. Entered films as a stuntman after W.W. I. Was in early air films and later became an actor, then a director.

ROBERTS, THAYER
Born: 1903. Died: Feb. 28, 1968, Hollywood, Calif. Screen, stage and vaudeville actor.

Appeared in: **1947** Chinese Ring. **1951** Sky High.

ROBERTS, THEODORE
Born: Oct. 2, 1861, San Francisco, Calif. Died: Dec. 14, 1928, Los Angeles, Calif. (uremic poisoning). Screen and stage actor. Married to actress Florence Smythe (dec. 1925).

Appeared in: **1914** Where the Trail Divides; The Call of the North; The Making of Bobby Burnit; What's His Name; Ready Money; The Man from Home; The Circus Man; The Ghost Breaker. **1915** After Five; The Woman; The Governor's Lady; The Unafraid; The Captive; Stolen Goods; The Arab; The Secret Orchard; The Marriage of Kitty; The Case of Becky; Mr. Grex of Monte Carlo; The Unknown; The Immigrant; Temptation; The Girl of the Golden West; The Wild Goose Chase. **1916** The Sowers; Pudd'n Head Wilson; The Trail of the Lonesome Pine; Honor Thy Name; The Thousand Dollar Husband; The Gutter Magdalene; The Dream Girl; Common Ground; Anton the Terrible; The Storm; Unprotected; The Plow Girl. **1917** Joan the Woman; The American Consul; The Cost of Hatred; What Money Can't Buy; The Little Princess; The Varment; Nan of Music Mountain. **1918** Petticoat Pilot; Hidden Pearls; Wild Youth; Old Wives for New; The Girl Who Came Back; Arizona; M'Liss; We Can't Have Everything; The Source; Such a Little Pirate; The Squaw Man; War Relief (informational services film). **1919** Don't Change Your Husband; Male and Female; Fire of Faith; The Woman Thou Gavest Me; You're Fired; Secret Service; The Lottery Man; Hawthorne of the U.S.A.; The Roaring Road; Everywoman; The Winning Girl; The Poor Boob; For Better or Worse; Love Insurance; Peg O' My Heart. **1920** Judy of Rogue's Harbor; Double Speed; Excuse My Dust; Sweet Lavender; The Furnace; Something to Think About. **1921** The Affairs of Anatol; Exit the Vamp; Forbidden Fruit; The Love Special; Miss Lulu Bett; Too Much Speed; Sham. **1922** A Trip to Paramountown (short); Across the Continent; If You Believe It, It's So; The Man Who Saw Tomorrow; Night Life in Hollywood; The Old Homestead; Our Leading Citizen; Saturday Night; Hail the Woman. **1923** Racing Hearts; Stephen Steps Out; To the Ladies; Prodigal Daughters; The Ten Commandments; Grumpy. **1925** Forty Winks; Locked Doors. **1926** Cat's Pajamas. **1928** The Masks of the Devil. **1929** Noisy Neighbors; Ned McCobb's Daughter.

ROBERTSHAW, JERROLD
Born: 1866, England. Died: Feb. 14, 1941. Screen and stage actor.

Appeared in: **1916** The Girl Who Didn't Care. **1917** Dombey and Son. **1920** Build Thy House. **1921** Beside the Bonnie Briar Bush (aka The Bonnie Briar Bush—US). **1922** A Master of Craft. **1923** Don Quixote; Guy Fawkes; A Royal Divorce; Through Fire and Water; The Wandering Jew. **1924** The Sins Ye Do. **1925** The Apache; She. **1927** The Blind Ship; Downhill (aka When Boys Leave Home—US 1928); Huntingtower; My Lord the Chauffeur. **1927** On With the Dance Series. **1928** Bolibar (aka The Marquis of Bolibar); Palais de Danse; Tommy Atkins; You Know What Sailors Are; Glorious Youth (aka Eileen of the Trees). **1929** Power over Men; The Inseparables; Kitty. **1931** The Shadow Between. **1933** The Veteran of Waterloo. **1940** The Great Conway.

ROBERTSON, IMOGENE See NOLAN, MARY

ROBERTSON, JAMES "SCOTTY"
Born: 1859. Died: Nov. 13, 1936, Los Angeles, Calif. Screen actor.

ROBERTSON, JEAN
Born: 1894, Australia. Died: Aug., 1967, Sydney, Australia. Stage and screen actress.

Appeared in: **1922** Flesh and Spirit.

ROBERTSON, JOHN S.
Born: June 14, 1878, Ontario, Canada. Died: Nov. 7, 1964, Escondido, Calif. Screen, stage actor and film director.

Appeared in: **1916** An Enemy to the King; The Conflict; His Wife's Good Name; The Combat; Her Right to Live.

ROBERTSON, MARY See NOLAN, MARY

ROBERTSON, ORIE O.
Born: 1881. Died: Apr. 14, 1964, Hollywood, Calif. (cancer). Screen actor and stuntman.

Appeared in: **1926** Bucking the Truth.

ROBERTSON, STUART
Born: Mar. 5, 1901, London, England. Died: Dec. 25, 1958, Elstree, Herts, England. Screen, stage, radio actor and singer. Brother of actress Anna Neagle. Married to singer Alice Moxon.

Appeared in: **1933** Bitter Sweet. **1934** The Queen's Affaire (aka Runaway Queen—US 1935). **1935** Peg of Old Drury (US 1936). **1936** As You Like It; Millions; Splinters in the Air; The Gang Show. **1938** Sixty Glorious Years (aka Queen of Destiny—US 1940). **1940** Irene; River's End; No, No, Nanette. **1941** A Yank in the R.A.F.; Confirm or Deny; On the Sunny Side. **1942** This Above All; The Black Swan. **1943** Forever and a Day. **1945** Meet the Navy (Canadian Naval film).

ROBERTSON, WILLARD
Born: Jan. 1, 1886, Runnels, Tex. Died: Apr. 5, 1948. Screen, stage actor, author, stage director, playwright and attorney.

Appeared in: **1924** Daughters of the Night. **1930** Last of the Duanes. **1931** Skippy; The Cisco Kid; The Ruling Voice; Fair Warning; Sooky; Upper Underworld; Silence; Murder by the Clock; Graft; Shanghai Love. **1932** The Gay Caballero; The Broken Wing; The Famous Ferguson Case; Behind the Mask; So Big; The Strange Love of Molly Louvain; Doctor X; Guilty as Hell; Virtue; Wild Girl; Call Her Savage; Central Park; Texas Bad Man; Steady Company; Rider of Death Valley; Tom Brown of Culver; If I Had a Million; I Am a Fugitive from a Chain Gang. **1933** The Mad Game; East of 5th Avenue; Lady Killer; Wild Boys of the Road; The World Changes; Tugboat Annie; Another Language; The Whirlpool; Roman Scandals; Central Airport; Trick for Trick; Destination Unknown; Supernatural; Heroes for Sale. **1934** I'll Tell the World; Have a Heart; Death on the Diamond; Housewife; Gambling Lady; Two Alone; Heat Lightning; Upperworld; Here Comes the Navy; Let's Talk It Over; One Is Guilty; Operator 13; Murder in the Private Car; Dark Hazard; Whirlpool. **1935** Oil for the Lamps of China; Biography of a Bachelor Girl; Dante's Inferno; The Secret Bride; Laddie; Mills of the Gods; O'Shaughnessey's Boy; Straight From the Heart; His Night Out; Black Fury; Million Dollar Baby; Forced Landing; Virginia Judge. **1936** Transient Lady; Dangerous Waters; The Three Godfathers; The Gorgeous Hussy; I Married a Doctor; The First Baby; The Last of the Mohicans; The Man Who Lived Twice; Winterset; That Girl From Paris; Wanted—Jane Turner. **1937** Larceny on the Air; Park Avenue Logger; John Meade's Woman; Exclusive; This Is My Affair; Hot Water; The Go Getter; Roaring Timber. **1938** Gangs of New York; Island In the Sky; You and Me; Men With Wings; Kentucky; Torchy Gets Her Man. **1939** Jesse James; Heritage of the Desert; My Son Is a Criminal; Each Dawn I Die; Range War; Two Bright Boys; Main Street Larceny; Cat and the Canary. **1940** My Little Chickadee; Remember the Night; Castle on the Hudson; Lucky Cisco Kid; Brigham Young—Frontiersman; North

West Mounted Police. **1941** The Monster and the Girl; Men of Timberland; Night of January 16th; Texas; I Wanted Wings. **1942** Juke Girl. **1943** Air Force; Background to Danger; No Time for Love. **1944** Nine Girls. **1945** Along Came Jones. **1946** To Each His Own; The Virginian; Perilous Holiday; Renegades; Gallant Journey. **1947** My Favorite Brunette; Deep Valley. **1948** Sitting Pretty; Fury at Furnace Creek.

ROBESON, PAUL (Paul Leroy Bustill Robeson, Sr)
Born: Apr. 9, 1898, Princeton, N.J. Died: Jan. 23, 1976, Philadelphia, Pa. (stroke). Black screen, stage actor and singer.

Appeared in: **1924** Body and Soul (film debut). **1930** Borderline. **1933** The Emperor Jones (stage and film versions). **1935** Sanders of The River. **1936** Showboat (stage and film versions); The Song of Freedom; My Song Goes Forth (documentary). **1937** Jericho (aka Dark Sands—US 1938); Big Fella; King Solomon's Mines. **1940** Proud Valley (US 1941). **1942** Native Land (narrator, documentary); Tales of Manhattan. **1954** Song of the Rivers (documentary).

ROBEY, SIR GEORGE (George Edward Wade)
Born: Sept. 20, 1869, London, England. Died: Nov. 29, 1954, Saltdean, Sussex, England. Screen, stage, radio, television actor, author and screenwriter. Married to stage manager Blanche Littler. Divorced from Ethel Haydon.

Appeared in: **1900** The Rats. **1913** Good Queen Bess; And Very Nice, Too. **1914** George Robey Turns Anarchist. **1916** £ 66.13.9 3/4 for Every Man, Woman and Child; Blood Tells; Or, the Anti-Frivolity League. **1917** Doing His Bit. **1918** George Robey's Day Off. **1923** The Rest Cure; One Arabian Night (aka Widow Twan-Kee); Don Quixote. **1924** The Prehistoric Man. **1928** Safety First (short); The Barrister (short). **1929** The Bride; Mrs. Mephistopheles. **1932** The Temperance Fete; Marry Me. **1933** Don Quixote (US 1934 and 1923 version). **1934** Chu Chin Chow. **1935** Birds of a Feather; Royal Cavalcade (aka Regal Cavalcade—US). **1936** Calling the Tune; Southern Roses; Men of Yesterday. **1939** A Girl Must Live (US 1941). **1942** Salute John Citizen. **1943** Variety Jubilee; They Met in the Dark (US 1945). **1945** Henry V (US 1946); Waltz Time. **1946** The Trojan Brothers. **1952** The Pickwick Papers (US 1953). **1953** Ali Baba Nights. **1958** Henry V (rerelease of 1945 film).

ROBINS, EDWARD H.
Born: Oct. 15, 1880, Shamokin, Pa. Died: July 27, 1955, Paramus, N.J. Screen actor.

Appeared in: **1937** Meet the Missus; Music for Madame; Exclusive. **1938** Love on Toast.

ROBINSON, BILL "BOJANGLES"
Born: May 25, 1878, Richmond, Va. Died: Nov. 25, 1949, N.Y. (heart ailment). Black screen, stage, vaudeville actor and dancer.

Appeared in: **1929** Hello, Bill. **1930** Dixiana. **1932** Harlem Is Harlem. **1934** King for a Day (short). **1935** The Little Colonel; In Old Kentucky; Hooray for Love; The Big Broadcast of 1936; The Littlest Rebel; Curly Top. **1936** Dimples. **1937** One Mile from Heaven. **1938** Rebecca of Sunnybrook Farm; Road Demon; Just Around the Corner; Up the River; Hot Mikado; Cotton Club Revue. **1942** By An Old Southern River; Let's Shuffle. **1943** Stormy Weather.

ROBINSON, CHARLES KNOX
Born: 1901. Died: June 4, 1980, Pomona, N.Y. Screen actor, stage producer, television producer, screenwriter, playwright and television writer. Do not confuse with actor Charles Robinson.

ROBINSON, DEWEY
Born: 1898, New Haven, Conn. Died: Dec. 11, 1950, Las Vegas, Nev. (heart attack). Stage and screen actor.

Appeared in: **1931** Enemies of the Law. **1932** One Way Passage; The Woman from Monte Carlo; Cheaters at Play; Law and Order; The Painted Woman; The Big Broadcast; Hat Check Girl; Blonde Venus; Six Hours to Live; Scarlet Dawn; Women Won't Tell; When Paris Sleeps; Captain's Wife. **1933** She Done Him Wrong; A Lady's Profession; Her Forgotten Past; Diplomaniacs; Soldiers of the Storm; Laughing at Life; Notorious but Nice; Murder on the Campus. **1934** Shadows of Sing Sing; The Big Shakedown; Countess of Monte Cristo; Behold My Wife. **1935** The Crusades; Pursuit; A Midsummer Night's Dream; His Night Out; Too Young to Kill; plus the following shorts: Goin' to Town; Palooka from Paducah; One Run Elmer. **1936** Dangerous Waters; The Return of Jimmy Valentine; All American Chump; Missing Girls; Florida Special; Poppy; Mummy's Boys. **1937** On the Avenue; The Slave Ship; Super Sleuth; Marry the Girl; The Toast of New York; New Faces of 1937; Mama Runs Wild. **1938**

Broadway Musketeers; Ride a Crooked Mile; Army Girl. **1939** Forged Passport; Navy Secrets. **1940** The Blue Bird; Diamond Frontier; The Great McGinty; I Can't Give You Anything But Love, Baby; Tin Pan Alley. **1941** The Big Store; Two Yanks in Trinidad; You're the One; Sing for Your Supper. **1942** Rubber Racketeers; Tennessee Johnson; The Palm Beach Story; The Big Street; Blondie for Victory; Jail House Blues; Isle of Missing Men; 'Neath Brooklyn Bridge. **1943** Casablanca; The Ghost Ship; The Woman of the Town. **1944** Wilson; Mrs. Parkington; Alaska; When Strangers Marry; Timber Queen; The Chinese Cat; Trocadero. **1945** The Bells of St. Mary's; Hollywood and Vine; There Goes Kelly; Fashion Model; Dillinger; The Lady Confesses; Black Market Babies; Stairway to Light (short); Pardon My Past. **1946** Behind the Mask; The Missing Lady. **1947** Mr. Hex; I Wonder Who's Kissing Her Now; The Wistful Widow of Wagon Gap; Stairway to Light (short); The Gangster. **1948** My Dear Secretary; Angels' Alley; Fighting Mad; Let's Live Again; The Checkered Coat. **1949** Ma and Pa Kettle; The Beautiful Blonde from Bashful Bend; Hellfire; Tough Assignment; My Friend Irma. **1950** Buccaneer's Girl; At War with the Army; Father of the Bride. **1951** Jim Thorpe—All American.

ROBINSON, EDWARD G. (Emmanuel Goldenberg)
Born: Dec. 12, 1893, Bucharest, Roumania. Died: Jan. 26, 1973, Hollywood, Calif. (cancer). Screen, stage, television and vaudeville actor. Married to Jane Bodenheimer. Divorced from actress Gladys Lloyd (dec. 1971). Father of actor Edward G. Robinson, Jr. (dec. 1974). Received 1973 Special Academy Award posthumously for lifetime contributions to motion picture arts.

Appeared in: **1923** Bright Shawl. **1929** The Hole in the Wall. **1930** How I Play Golf—Trouble Shots (short); Night Ride; Widow from Chicago; A Lady to Love; Outside the Law; East is West; Little Caesar. **1931** Five Star Final; Smart Money. **1932** Two Seconds; Tiger Shark; Silver Dollar; The Hatchet Man; The Stolen Jools (short—aka The Slippery Pearls). **1933** The Little Giant; I Loved a Woman. **1934** Dark Hazard; The Man With Two Faces. **1935** Barbary Coast; The Whole Town's Talking. **1936** Bullets or Ballots. **1937** Thunder in the City; Kid Galahad; The Last Gangster; Day at Santa Anita (short). **1938** A Slight Case of Murder; The Amazing Dr. Clitterhouse; I Am the Law. **1939** Confessions of a Nazi Spy; Blackmail. **1940** They Knew What They Wanted; The Story of Dr. Ehrlich's Magic Bullet; Brother Orchid; A Dispatch from Reuters. **1941** The Sea Wolf; Manpower; Unholy Partners. **1942** Larceny, Inc.; Tales of Manhattan. **1943** Destroyer; Flesh and Fantasy. **1944** Tampico; Double Indemnity; Mr. Winkle Goes to War; The Woman in the Window. **1945** Our Vines Have Tender Grapes; Scarlet Street; Journey Together (US 1946). **1946** The Stranger. **1947** The Red House. **1948** All My Sons; Key Largo; Night Has a Thousand Eyes. **1949** House of Strangers; It's a Great Feeling. **1950** My Daughter Joy (Operation X—US 1951). **1952** Actors and Sin. **1953** Vice Squad; Big Leaguer; The Glass Web. **1954** Black Tuesday. **1955** The Violent Men; Tight Spot; A Bullet for Joey; Illegal; Hell on Frisco Bay. **1956** Nightmare; The Ten Commandments. **1959** A Hole in the Head. **1960** Pepe; Seven Thieves. **1962** My Geisha; Two Weeks in Another Town; Sammy Going South (aka A Boy Ten Feet Tall—US 1965). **1963** The Prize. **1964** Good Neighbor Sam; Robin and the 7 Hoods; Cheyenne Autumn; The Outrage. **1965** The Cincinnati Kid. **1967** Die Blonde vom Peking (Peking Blonde—US 1969). **1968** The Biggest Bundle of Them All; Never a Dull Moment; Grand Slam; Operation St. Peter; Mad Checkmate. **1969** McKenna's Gold. **1970** Song of Norway. **1973** Soylent Green; Neither by Day or Night.

ROBINSON, EDWARD G., JR.
Born: 1934. Died: Feb. 26, 1974, West Hollywood, Calif. (natural causes). Screen and television actor. Son of actor Edward G. Robinson (dec. 1973) and actress Gladys Lloyd (dec. 1971). Divorced from actresses Frances Robinson and Elaine M. Conte.

Appeared in: **1956** Screaming Eagles. **1958** Tank Battalion. **1959** Some Like It Hot.

ROBINSON, FORREST
Born: 1859. Died: Jan., 1924, Los Angeles, Calif. Screen and stage actor.

Appeared in: **1921** Tol'able David. **1922** Tess of the Storm Country. **1923** Adam's Rib; Ashes of Vengeance; The Meanest Man in the World; Souls for Sale. **1924** Good Bad Boy; When a Man's a Man.

ROBINSON, FRANCES (Marion Frances Ladd)
Born: Apr. 26, 1916, Fort Wadsworth, N.Y. Died: Aug. 15, 1971, Hollywood, Calif. (heart attack). Screen actress.

Appeared in: **1922** Orphans of the Storm. **1935** Millions in the Air. **1937** A Girl With Ideas; Forbidden Valley; Tim Tyler's Luck (serial). **1938** A Letter of Introduction; Secrets of a Nurse; Exposed; The Last

Warning; His Exciting Night; Service de Luxe; Red Barry (serial); Strange Faces. **1939** Desperate Trails; Hero for a Day; Little Accident; Society Smugglers; When Tomorrow Comes; Big Town Czar (aka Florist Clerk); Risky Business; Tower of London; The Family Next Door. **1940** Riders of Pasco Basin; So You Won't Talk; Glamour for Sale; The Lone Wolf Keeps a Date; The Invisible Man Returns. **1941** Outlaws of the Panhandle; Smilin' Through; Dr. Jekyll and Mr. Hyde. **1944** Lady in the Dark. **1946** No Leave, No Love; The Missing Lady. **1947** Suddenly It's Spring; Keeper of the Bees. **1948** I, Jane Doe. **1949** Backfire (US 1950, aka Somewhere in the City). **1964** Bedtime Story; Kitten With a Whip; The Lively Set. **1967** The Happiest Millionaire.

ROBINSON, GERTRUDE R.
Born: 1891. Died: Mar. 19, 1962, Hollywood, Calif. Screen actress. Divorced from actor James Kirkwood (dec. 1963). Entered films with Biograph.

Appeared in: **1909** Pippa Passes; The Open Gate; The Death Disc. **1910** Gold Is Not All; The Purgation; What the Daisy Said; A Summer Idyll; Examination Day at School. **1913** Judith of Bethulia; Classmates. **1914** Strongheart; The Sentimental Sister; Men and Women. **1915** The Arab. **1922** Welcome to Our City. **1925** On Thin Ice.

ROBINSON, HARRY T.
Born: 1872. Died: Sept. 11, 1946. Screen actor. Appeared in early Mack Sennett films.

ROBINSON, JACKIE (Jack Roosevelt Robinson)
Born: Jan. 31, 1919, Cairo, Ga. Died: Oct. 24, 1972, Stamford, Conn. (heart disease). Black professional baseball player, athlete and screen actor.

Appeared in: **1950** The Jackie Robinson Story

ROBINSON, JOHN
Born: Nov. 11, 1908, Liverpool, England. Died: Mar. 6, 1979, London, England (cancer). Screen, stage and television actor. Entered films in 1936.

Appeared in: **1936** The Scarab Murder Case. **1939** The Lion Has Wings (US 1940). **1948** Uneasy Terms. **1952** Emergency Call (aka The Hundred Hour Hunt—US 1953); Hammer the Toff; Ghost Ship. **1955** The Constant Husband. **1957** Fortune is a Woman (aka She Played With Fire—US 1958). **1958** The Safecracker. **1959** The Doctor's Dilemma. **1960** And the Same to You. **1975** Prisoners.

ROBINSON, LEGAL W.
Born: 1877. Died: Jan., 1919, New York, N.Y. Screen and stage actor. Appeared in early Solax and Famous Players films.

ROBINSON, RUTH "RUTHIE"
Born: 1888. Died: Mar. 17, 1966. Screen actress.

Appeared in: **1911** A Narrow Escape; The Moonshiners. **1912** Wanted—A Wife. **1928** Scarlet Youth; Trial Marriage. **1935** The Story of Louis Pasteur. **1936** Ramona; The Walking Dead; Sins of Man; China Clipper; The Case of the Velvet Claws. **1937** Midnight Madonna; Outcast; On Such a Night; Lost Horizon; Wings Over Honolulu. **1938** Midnight Intruder; The Lone Wolf in Paris; Miracle Money (short). **1939** Kansas Terrors; Weather Wizards (short). **1940** Knute Rockne—All American; Covered Wagon Days. **1941** Henry Aldrich for President; Whistling in the Dark; Across the Sierras; One Foot in Heaven; Down Mexico Way; The Corsican Brothers; Remember the Day. **1942** Yankee Doodle Dandy; Tennessee Johnson. **1943** The Moon Is Down; Chatterbox; Shantytown. **1944** The Hairy Ape. **1945** Delightfully Dangerous; Kid Sister. **1946** The Spider Woman Strikes Back; The Hoodlum Saint. **1947** The Guilty; Stepchild; That Hagen Girl. **1949** Trapped; Impact. **1950** The Secret Fury; The Three Musketeers. **1951** Belle Le Grande. **1952** Phone Call from a Stranger. **1956** The Search for Bridey Murphy. **1960** Tall Story. **1963** Forty Pounds of Trouble; The Miracle of Santa's White Reindeer.

ROBINSON, "SKEETER" BILL See ROBBINS, ROY "SKEETER BILL"

ROBINSON, "SPIKE"
Born: 1884. Died: July 13, 1942, Maywood, Calif. (heart attack). Screen actor.

Appeared in: **1920** Daredevil Jack (serial). **1921** The Foolish Age. **1923** Boston Blackie. **1925** The Fear Fighter.

ROBLES, RICHARD
Born: May 26, 1898. Died: Apr. 20, 1940, Los Angeles, Calif. Screen actor.

Appeared in: **1939** Union Pacific.

ROBLES, RUDY
Born: Apr. 28, 1910, Manila, Philippine Islands. Died: Aug., 1970, Manila, Philippine Islands. Stage and screen actor.

Appeared in: **1939** The Real Glory. **1940** South of Pago Pago. **1941** Song of the Islands; Blue, White and Perfect; Blonde from Singapore; The Adventures of Martin Eden. **1942** Submarine Raider; Across the Pacific; Wake Island. **1946** Nocturne. **1947** Singapore; The Son of Rusty. **1949** Rusty Saves a Life; Omoo, Omoo; Flaxy Martin. **1952** Okinawa. **1953** White Goddess.

ROBSON, ANDREW
Born: 1867, Hamilton, Ontario, Canada. Died: Apr. 26, 1921, Los Angeles, Calif. (heart affliction). Screen and stage actor.

Appeared in: **1919** Upstairs and Down. **1920** Alarm Clock Andy; Scratch My Back; Cupid, the Cowpuncher. **1921** All's Fair in Love; Black Roses; Mother O'Mine; One a Minute.

ROBSON, JUNE
Born: 1922. Died: Mar. 16, 1972, Hollywood, Calif. Screen actress.

ROBSON, MAY (Mary Robison)
Born: Apr. 19, 1858, Melbourne, Australia. Miss Robson had her date of birth recorded on casting director's records as 1864. However, at time of her death, birth certificate was found showing she was born in 1858. Died: Oct. 20, 1942, Beverly Hills, Calif. Screen, stage and radio actress. Nominated for 1932/33 Academy Award for Best Supporting Actress in Lady for a Day.

Appeared in: **1915** How Molly Made Good. **1916** A Night Out. **1919** His Bridal Night; A Broadway Saint; The Lost Battalion. **1926** Pals in Paradise. **1927** Angel of Broadway; A Harp in Hock; The Rejuvenation of Aunt Mary (stage and film versions); Rubber Tires; King of Kings. **1928** Chicago; The Blue Danube; Turkish Delight. **1931** Mother's Millions (aka The She-Wolf of Wall Street and She-Wolf). **1932** If I Had a Million; Letty Lynton; Two Against the World; The Engineer's Daughter; Little Orphan Annie; Red Headed Woman; Strange Interlude. **1933** Men Must Fight; The White Sister; Reunion in Vienna; Dinner at Eight; Beauty for Sale; Broadway to Hollywood; The Solitaire Man; Dancing Lady; Lady for a Day; One Man's Journey; Alice in Wonderland. **1934** You Can't Buy Everything; Straight Is the Way; Lady By Choice. **1935** Vanessa, Her Love Story; Reckless; Age of Indiscretion; Anna Karenina; Grand Old Girl; Strangers All; Mills of the Gods; Three Kids and a Queen (aka The Baxter Millions). **1936** Wife vs. Secretary; The Captain's Kid; Rainbow on the River. **1937** Woman in Distress; A Star Is Born; Rhythm of the River; The Perfect Specimen; Top of the Town. **1938** The Adventures of Tom Sawyer; Bringing Up Baby; The Texans; Four Daughters. **1939** They Made Me a Criminal; Yes, My Darling Daughter; That's Right—You're Wrong; Daughters Courageous; The Kid from Kokomo (aka Orphan of the Ring); Four Wives; Nurse Edith Cavell. **1940** Irene; Granny Get Your Gun. **1941** Four Mothers; Million Dollar Baby; Playmates; Texas Rangers Ride Again. **1942** Joan of Paris.

ROBSON, PHILIP
Born: Edinburgh, Scotland. Died: May 6, 1919, New York, N.Y. Screen and stage actor.

Appeared in: **1916** The Conquest of Canaan. **1917** Life's Whirlpool.

ROBSON, STUART, JR.
Died: Aug. 21, 1946, New York, N.Y. Screen and stage actor. Son of stage actor Stuart Robson (dec. 1903), and actress May Waldron (dec. 1924).

Appeared in: **1920** The Harvest Moon. **1922** Should a Wife Work.

ROBYN, GAY
Born: 1912. Died: July 25, 1942, Hollywood, Calif. Screen actress and dancer.

ROBYNS, WILLIAM
Born: 1855. Died: Jan. 22, 1936, Verdugo Hills, Calif. Stage and screen actor.

Appeared in: **1921** Get-Rich-Quick Wallingford. **1923** The Fair Cheat. **1932** The Expert; Hell Fire Austin. **1934** Elmer and Elsie.

ROCCARDI, ALBERT
Born: May 9, 1864, Paris, France. Died: May 14, 1934. Screen, stage actor and pantomimist.

Appeared in: **1914** The New Secretary; Buddy's First Call; Mr. Barnes of New York; Wife Wanted; The New Stenographers. **1921** The Inside of the Cup; The Passionate Pilgrim; The Rider of the King Log. **1922**

Destiny's Isle; Why Not Marry?; A Pasteboard Crown. **1924** Galloping Hoofs (serial). **1925** The Street of Forgotten Men. **1926** The Belle of Broadway; Fools of Fashion. **1927** Melting Millions (serial). **1928** Partners in Crime. **1929** The Love Parade; Romance of the Rio Grande. **1930** Just Like Heaven.

ROCHA, MIGUEL F.
Born: Argentina. Died: Mar. 6, 1961, Buenos Aires, Argentina. Screen and stage actor.

ROCHE, FRANKLYN D. "FRANK"
Born: 1904. Died: Nov. 20, 1963, Burbank, Calif. Screen and stage actor. Entered films approx. 1930.

Appeared in: **1960** The Prime Time.

ROCHE, JOHN
Born: Feb. 6, 1896, Penn Yan, N.Y. Died: Nov. 10, 1952, Los Angeles, Calif. (stroke). Screen and stage actor.

Appeared in: **1922** The Good Provider. **1923** Bag and Baggage; Lucretia Lombard. **1924** Cornered; Flowing Gold; Her Marriage Vow; K—The Unknown; The Tenth Woman. **1925** Bobbed Hair; The Love Hour; A Lost Lady; A Broadway Butterfly; Kiss Me Again; Marry Me; My Wife and I; Recompense; Scandal Proof. **1926** The Return of Peter Grimm; Don Juan; Her Big Night; The Man Upstairs; Midnight Lovers. **1927** The Truthful Sex; Uncle Tom's Cabin. **1928** Their Hour; Diamond Handcuffs. **1929** Unholy Night; The Dream Melody; The Donovan Affair; The Awful Truth; This Thing Called Love. **1930** Sin Takes a Holiday; Monte Carlo. **1932** Winner Take All; Prosperity; The Cohens and the Kellys in Hollywood. **1933** Beauty for Sale. **1935** Just My Luck. **1946** The Brute Man.

ROCHE, JOHN A.
Born: 1901, Penn Yan, N.Y. Died: Feb. 5, 1980, Pasadena, Calif. Screen and stage actor. Do not confuse with actor John Roche (dec. 1952).

ROCHELLE, CLAIRE
Born: c. 1910. Died: May 23, 1981, La Jolla, Calif. (cancer). Screen actress.

Appeared in: **1936** Empty Saddles. **1937** Guns in The Dark; Boothill Brigade; Ridin' the Lone Trail. **1939** El Diablo Rides; Missing Daughters; Code of the Fearless. **1940** The Kid from Santa Fe. **1941** North From the Lone Star. **1942** Secrets of a Co-Ed; Prison Girls. **1943** Harvest Melody. **1944** Shake Hands With Murder; Men on Her Mind; Swing Hostess. **1946** Blonde For a Day.

ROCHELLE, EDWIN
Died: Feb. 16, 1977. Screen actor.

Appeared in: **1966** Namu, the Killer Whale.

ROCHIN, PAUL
Born: 1889. Died: May 5, 1964, Hollywood, Calif. Screen actor.

ROCK, CHARLES
Born: May 30, 1866, Velore, East Indies. Died: July 12, 1919, London, England. Screen and stage actor.

Appeared in: **1913** The House of Temperley. **1914** The Cage; The Black Spot; Clancarty; England's Menace; England Expects; For the Empire (aka For Home and Country—US); Called Back; The King's Minister; Two Little Britons; The Two Columbines; V.C.(aka The Victoria Cross—US 1916); A Christmas Carol; She Stoops to Conquer. **1915** Brother Officers; The King's Outcast (aka His Vindication—US); The Prisoner of Zenda; The Man in the Attic; The Sons of Satan; Whoso Diggeth a Pit; The Third Generation; Jelf's (aka A Man of His Word—US); The Christian; Her Uncle; The Firm of Girdlestone (US 1916); Rupert of Hentzau (US 1916). **1916** You; Esther; The Man Without a Soul (aka I Believe—US 1917); Tatterly; A Fair Imposter; The Morals of Weybury (aka The Hypocrites); Partners at Last; Vice Versa; Some Fish; Beau Brocade; Rescuing an Heiress. **1917** Ultus and the Three-Button Mystery (aka Ultus 6: The Three Button Mystery: Ultus 7). **1918** The Better 'Ole; or, The Romance of Old Bill (aka Carry On—US); A Romany Lass (US 1919); Deception; Big Money. **1919** The Greater Love. **1927** Rilka: or, The Gypsy (reissue of A Romany Lass—1918).

ROCK, EDITH See BLAKE, MARIE

ROCK, WILLIAM T.
Born: 1853. Died: July 27, 1916, Oyster Bay, N.Y. (heart disease). Screen actor and motion picture executive. One of the founders of Vitagraph.

Appeared in: **1912** A Vitagraph Romance.

ROCKNE, KNUTE (Knute Kenneth Rockne)
Born: Mar. 4, 1888, Voss, Norway. Died: Mar. 31, 1931, near Bazaar, Kans. (airplane crash). Football coach, author and screen actor. Appeared in Football shorts with Universal.

ROCKWELL, FLORENCE
Died: Mar. 24, 1964, Stanford, Conn. Screen and stage actress. Entered films in 1915 with Oliver Morosco Film Company.

ROCKWELL, GEORGE L.
Born: 1890, Providence, R.I. Died: Mar., 1978, Brunswick, Maine (pneumonia). Screen, stage, vaudeville, radio, television actor, playwright and columnist.

Appeared in: **1937** The Singing Marine.

ROCKWELL, JACK
Died: Nov. 10, 1947. Screen actor.

Appeared in: **1933** The Lone Avenger; Strawberry Roan; The Trail Drive; Gun Justice. **1934** Honor of the Range; In Old Santa Fe; Wheels of Destiny; Smoking Guns. **1935** Lawless Frontier; Justice of the Range; Tumbling Tumbleweeds; Outlawed Guns; Valley of the Wanted Men; Man from Guntown; The Miracle Rider; When a Man Sees Red. **1936** The Lawless Nineties; Heroes of the Range; The Singing Cowboy; Rogue of the Range; Roarin' Guns; The Traitor; Guns and Guitars; Lawless Riders. **1937** Bar Z Badmen; Riders of the Rockies; The Red Robe; Texas Trail; Springtime in the Rockies. **1938** Prairie Moon; Sunset Trail; Under Western Stars; West of Cheyenne; Law of the Plains; Shine On Harvest Moon; Black Bandit. **1939** Silver on the Sage; The Renegade Trail; Rough Riders' Roundup; Man From Sundown; Days of Jesse James. **1940** Hidden Gold; Stagecoach War; Bullets for Rustlers; Santa Fe Marshall; Cherokee Strip; Pony Post. **1941** Border Vigilantes; Wide Open Town; Secret of the Wasteland; Stick to Your Guns; Twilight On the Trail; The Pinto Kid; Thunder Over the Prairie. **1942** Undercover Man; Tombstone, The Town Too Tough to Die. **1943** Daredevils of the West (serial); Fighting Frontier; Dead Man's Gulch; The Black Hills Express; The Renegade; Wagon Tracks West. **1944** Mystery Man; Forty Thieves; Lumberjack; Gunsmoke Mesa; The Vigilantes Ride; West of the Rio Grande; Trigger Trail. **1945** Flame of the West. **1946** Drifting Along; Frontier Gunlaw; Two-Fisted Stranger; Roaring Rangers; Under Arizona Skies; Cowboy Blues; Gentleman from Texas. **1947** Flashing Guns; Shootin' Irons; Code of the Plains.

ROCKWELL, MARY See HUMMELL, MARY ROCKWELL

ROCO, MAURICE
Born: 1920. Died: Mar. 25, 1976, Thailand. Screen actor.

Appeared in: **1945** Incendiary Blonde.

RODE, WALTER
Died: Feb. 8, 1973. Screen actor.

Appeared in: **1949** Johnny Allegro. **1963** Thirteen Frightened Girls.

RODERICK, LESLIE
Born: 1907. Died: Aug. 16, 1927, Hollywood, Calif. (pneumonia). Screen actress and dancer.

RODGERS, RICHARD
Born: June 28, 1902, New York, N.Y. Died: Dec. 30, 1979, New York, N.Y. Composer, songwriter and screen actor.

Appeared in: **1929** Makers of Melody (short). **1953** Main Street to Broadway.

RODGERS, WALTER
Born: 1887. Died: Apr. 24, 1951, Los Angeles, Calif. (following stroke). Screen actor.

Appeared in: **1917** The Fighting Trail (serial); Vengeance and the Woman (serial). **1918** A Fight for Millions (serial). **1919** Smashing Barriers (serial). **1921** Flower of the North; The Secret of the Hills; The Silver Car; The Son of Wallingford; Steelheart. **1922** They Like 'Em Rough. **1925** Rugged Water. **1926** The Flaming Frontier. **1927** The Heart of Maryland; Irish Hearts; Wolf's Clothing.

RODMAN, VICTOR
Born: 1893. Died: June 29, 1965. Screen, television and radio actor. Entered films with Biograph.

Appeared in: **1923** Winter Has Come (short). **1924** Hold Your Breath. **1958** The Long, Hot Summer.

RODNEY, EARLE

Born: 1891. Died: Dec. 16, 1932, Los Angeles, Calif. (pneumonia). Screen, stage, vaudeville actor, screenwriter and film director. Played screen parts with Sennett and Griffith and was a comedy director of Keystone Kop series.

Appeared in: **1915** Crooked to the End. **1916** The Village Vampire (working title The Great Leap); An Oily Scandal. **1917** The Nick of Time Baby; Secrets of a Beauty Parlor. **1920** A Roman Scandal. **1923** Winter Has Came.

RODNEY, JACK

Born: 1916. Died: Feb. 20, 1967, England (rheumatic fever). Screen, stage and television actor.

Appeared in: **1960** The Criminal (aka The Concrete Jungle—US 1962). **1963** The Horse Without a Head; The Cracksman. **1964** The Devilship; Pirates.

RODNEY, LYNNE

Died: Sept., 1937 (auto accident). Screen actress and stand-in for actress Grace Moore.

RODRIGUEZ, ESTELITA

Born: July 2, 1913, Guanajay, Cuba. Died: Mar. 12, 1966. Screen, stage, radio actress and night club performer. Divorced from actor Grant Withers (dec. 1959).

Appeared in: **1945** Along the Navajo Trail; Mexicana. **1947** On the Spanish Trail. **1948** The Gay Ranchero; Old Los Angeles. **1949** Susanna Pass; The Golden Stallion. **1950** Belle of Old Mexico; Federal Agent at Large; Sunset in the West; Hit Parade of 1951; California Passage; Twilight in the Sierras. **1951** Cuban Fireball; In Old Amarillo; Havana Rose; Pals of the Golden West. **1952** The Fabulous Senorita; Tropical Heat Wave; South Pacific Trail. **1953** Tropic Zone; Sweethearts on Parade. **1959** Rio Bravo. **1966** Jesse James Meets Frankenstein's Daughter.

RODRIGUEZ, TITO

Born: 1923. Died: Feb. 28, 1973, New York, N.Y. Screen actor, singer and bandleader. Known as "Frank Sinatra of Latin Music.".

RODRIGUEZ DE LA FUENTE, FELIX

Born: Mar. 26, 1928, Spain. Died: Mar. 26, 1980, near Nome, Alaska (plane crash). Naturalist, screen and television actor.

ROE, BASSETT

Born: Sept. 10, 1860, Folkstone, England. Died: Nov. 2, 1934, England?. Screen and stage actor.

Appeared in: **1919** Damaged Goods. **1920** Nance.

ROELS, MARCEL

Born: 1893, Belgium. Died: Dec. 27, 1973, Brussels, Belgium. Screen, stage and vaudeville actor. Started career at age 3 1/2.

Appeared in: Un Soir di Joie; Expo, en avant!

ROESNER, GEORGE E.

Born: 1911. Died: May 16, 1977, Houston, Tex. (heart attack). Screen, radio and television actor.

Appeared in: **1932** Union Depot.

ROGERS, BESSIE

Born: 1884. Died: Mar. 5, 1930, Venice, Calif. (auto accident). Midget screen and vaudeville actress.

ROGERS, CARL D.

Born: 1900. Died: Mar., 1965, Humble, Tex. Child screen actor. Appeared in early "Our Gang" comedies and Keystone comedies.

ROGERS, EUGENE

Born: c. 1867. Died: Mar. 9, 1919, Los Angeles, Calif. (myocarditis and alcoholism). Stage and screen actor.

Appeared in: **1915** Sin on the Sabbath; Silk Hose and High Pressure; Vendetta In a Hospital; Tears and Sunshine. **1916** A September Morning; Phony Teeth and False Friends; Billy's Reformation; Billy's Waterloo; Twenty Minutes at the Fair; False Friends and Fire Alarms; Live Wire and Love Sparks; A Friend, But a Star Boarder; Bill's Narrow Escape; Gambling on the Green; The Jailbirds' Last Flight; The Youngest in the Family; The Scoundrel's Tale. **1917** Stars and Bars; Her Nature Dance.

ROGERS, JOSEPH

Born: 1871. Died: Dec. 29, 1942, Hollywood, Calif. Screen actor.

ROGERS, LELA

Born: 1891. Died: May 25, 1977. Screen, stage actress and stage producer. Mother of actress Ginger Rogers.

Appeared in: **1942** The Major and The Minor.

ROGERS, MILDRED

Born: 1899. Died: Apr. 14, 1973, Hollywood, Calif. Screen actress and singer.

Appeared in: **1932** Fighting Gentlemen; The Forty-Niners. **1935** The Texas Rambler. **1937** The Girl Said No.

ROGERS, RENA

Born: 1901. Died: Feb. 19, 1966, Santa Monica, Calif. Screen and vaudeville actress. Divorced from screenwriter and director Frank Borzage (dec. 1962).

Appeared in: **1915** The Morning After. **1916** Slipping It over on Father; When Papa Died; National Nuts; Nailing on the Lid; Just for a Kid; Bungling Bill's Dream; Bungling Bill's Doctor; His Blowout (aka The Plumber); The Delinquent Bridegrooms; The Iron Mitt; Hired and Fired (aka The Leading Man); A Deep Sea Liar (aka The Landlubbers); Where are My Children?; The Leap; A Mix-Up in Photos; A Mix-Up at Rudolph's. **1917** A Paster Feud; A Vanquished Flirt; The Cricket; An Eight Cylinder Romance.

ROGERS, ROY

Died: Oct. 15, 1967, Calif. Screen, vaudeville and television actor. Do not confuse with cowboy actor Roy Rogers. Married to Olga Alexander, one of the "Alexander Sisters" in vaudeville.

ROGERS, WILL

Born: Nov. 4, 1879, Colagah, U.S. Cherokee Indian Territory. Died: Aug. 15, 1935, near Barrow, Alaska (airplane crash). Screen, vaudeville actor, screenwriter, author and journalist. Father of actor Will Rogers, Jr.

Appeared in: **1918** Laughing Bill Hyde (film debut). **1919** Almost a Husband; Jubilo. **1920** Jes' Call Me Jim; Cupid, the Cowpuncher; Water, Water, Everywhere; The Strange Boarder. **1921** Honest Hutch; Guile of Women; Boys Will Be Boys; An Unwilling Hero; Doubling for Romeo. **1922** A Poor Relation; The Headless Horseman; One Glorious Day; The Ropin' Fool (short). **1923** Hollywood; Fruits of Faith; plus the following shorts: Jus' Passin' Through; Hustlin' Hank; Uncensored Movies. **1924** The following shorts: Two Wagons—Both Covered; The Cowboy Sheik; The Cake Eater; Big Moments from Little Pictures; Highbrow Stuff; Going to Congress; Don't Park There!; Jubilo, Jr.; Our Congressman; A Truthful Liar; Gee Whiz Genevieve. **1927** Tip Toes; A Texas Steer; plus the following shorts: Hiking Through Holland With Will Rogers; With Will Rogers in Paris; With Will Rogers in Dublin; Roaming the Emerald Isle with Will Rogers; Through Switzerland and Bavaria with Will Rogers; With Will Rogers in London; Hunting for Germans in Berlin with Will Rogers; Prowling Around France with Will Rogers; Winging 'Round Europe with Will Rogers; Exploring England with Will Rogers. **1928** Reeling Down the Rhine with Will Rogers; Over the Bounding Blue with Will Rogers. **1929** They Had to See Paris. **1930** Happy Days; So This Is London; Lightnin'. **1931** Young as You Feel; A Connecticut Yankee; Ambassador Bill; The Plutocrat. **1932** Business and Pleasure; Down to Earth; Too Busy to Work. **1933** State Fair; Doctor Bull; Mr. Skitch. **1934** Judge Priest; David Harum; Handy Andy; Hollywood on Parade (short). **1935** Life Begins at Forty; The County Chairman; Steamboat 'Round the Bend; In Old Kentucky; Doubting Thomas. **1957** Golden Age of Comedy (documentary).

ROGNAN, JEAN LORRAINE

Born: 1912. Died: Aug. 22, 1969. Screen actress and dancer. Married to actor Rognoni (dec. 1943).

Appeared in: **1938** Generals Without Buttons. **1941** Personal Column. **1942** The Fleet's In.

ROGNONI (Roy Rognan)

Died: Feb. 22, 1943, near Lisbon, Portugal (plane crash). Screen, vaudeville actor and dancer. Married to actress Jean Lorraine Rognan (dec. 1969) with whom he appeared as part of a dancing team called "Lorraine and Rognoni."

Appeared in: **1937** Les Petits. **1938** Generals Without Buttons. **1941** Personal Column. **1942** The Fleet's In.

ROLAND, FREDERICK

Born: 1886. Died: June 2, 1936, Los Angeles, Calif. Stage and screen actor.

Appeared in: **1935** The Rainmakers.

ROLAND, MARION *See* ROSS, MARION

ROLAND, RUTH
Born: Aug. 26, 1892, San Francisco, Calif. Died: Sept. 22, 1937, Los Angeles, Calif. (cancer). Screen, vaudeville and radio actress. Appeared in "Ruth Roland" series. Married to actor Ben Bard (dec. 1974). Entered films in 1911.

Appeared in: **1911** A Chance Shot. **1912** Ruth Roland, the Kalem Girl; Hypnotic Nell; Ranch Girls on a Rampage. **1913** While Father Telephoned. **1914** Ham, the Piano Mover. **1915** The Red Circle (serial); Comrade John. **1917** The Neglected Wife (serial). **1918** Hands Up; Who Wins? (made in 1916, but released in 1918 retitled Price of Folly). **1919** The Tiger's Trail (serial); The Adventures of Ruth (serial); Love and the Law. **1920** Ruth of the Rockies (serial); What Would You Do?. **1921** The Avenging Arrow (serial). **1922** White Eagle (serial); Timber Queen (serial). **1923** Haunted Valley (serial); Ruth of the Range (serial). **1925** Dollar Down; Where the Worst Begins. **1926** The Masked Woman. **1930** Reno. **1936** From Nine to Nine. **1961** Days of Thrills and Laughter (documentary).

ROLDAN, ENRIQUE (Andres Garcia)
Born: 1901, Argentina. Died: Feb. 4, 1954, Buenos Aires, Argentina (accidentally slipped under wheels of train). Screen and stage actor.

Appeared in: **1940** Oro Entre Barro (Gold in Clay).

ROLF, ERIK
Died: May 28, 1957. Screen actor. Divorced from actress Ruth Warwick.

Appeared in: **1942** Atlantic Convoy; Eyes in the Night. **1943** First Comes Courage. **1944** U-Boat Prisoner; None Shall Escape; Secret Command; The Soul of a Monster; She's a Soldier Too; Kansas City Kitty; Strange Affair. **1945** Counter-Attack. **1946** A Close Call for Boston Blackie. **1949** Everybody Does It. **1950** Davy Crockett, Indian Scout.

ROLLAND, JEAN-CLAUDE
Born: 1933. Died: Apr., 1967 (suicide—hanging). Screen, stage and television actor.

ROLLETT, RAYMOND
Born: 1907, England. Died: Dec. 19, 1961, London, England. Stage and screen actor.

Appeared in: **1947** Master of Bankdam (US 1949). **1954** The Angel Who Pawned Her Harp (US 1956); Men of Sherwood Forest (US 1956). **1957** The Curse of Frankenstein; Blue Murder at St. Trinian's (US 1958).

ROLLIN, GEORGES
Born: France. Died: Mar., 1964, France. Screen actor.

Appeared in: **1939** That They May Live. **1940** Ultimatum. **1943** Hitler's Madmen. **1948** Clandestine; Goupi Mains Rouges (aka It Happened at the Inn—US).

ROLLINGS, RED (William Russell Rollings)
Born: Mar. 31, 1904, Mobile, Ala. Died: Dec. 31, 1964, Mobile, Ala. Professional baseball player and screen actor.

Appeared in: **1929** Fast Company.

ROLLOW, PRESTON J.
Born: 1871. Died: May, 1947, N.Y. Stage and screen actor. Appeared in silents.

ROMA, CLARICE (Roma Hann)
Born: 1902. Died: May 3, 1947, Hollywood, Calif. Screen and stage actress.

ROMAIN, GEORGE E.
Born: Bordeaux, France. Died: May 7, 1929, Philadelphia, Pa. (heart trouble). Stage and screen actor.

Appeared in: **1920** The Return of Tarzan. **1921** Diane of Star Hollow. **1924** The Sea Hawk; The Circus Cowboy; The Vagabond Trail.

ROMAN, MURRAY
Died: Nov. 6, 1973. Screen and television actor.

Appeared in: **1969** 2,000 Years Later.

ROMANO, JOHN
Born: 1896. Died: July 24, 1957, Hollywood, Calif. Screen and stage actor.

ROMANOFF, MICHAEL (aka PRINCE DIMITRI ROMANOFF OBOLENSKI, GRAND DUKE MICHAEL ROMANOFF, aka HARRY GERGUSON)
Born: 1890 or 1893?, Russia or Brooklyn, N.Y.? Died: Sept. 1, 1971, Los Angeles, Calif. (heart attack). Restaurateur and screen actor.

Appeared in: **1948** Arch of Triumph; An Innocent Affair. **1953** Paris Model. **1963** Move Over Darling. **1964** Goodbye, Charlie. **1965** Von Ryan's Express; Do Not Distrub. **1967** A Guide for the Married Man; Caprice; Tony Rome. **1968** Lady in Cement.

ROME, STEWART (Septimus Wernham Ryott)
Born: Jan. 30, 1886, Newbury, Berkshire, England. Died: Feb. 26, 1965, Newbury, England. Screen and stage actor. Was a pioneer silent star in Britain.

Appeared in: **1913** A Throw of the Dice. **1914** The Tragedy of Basil Grieve (aka The Great Poison Mystery); Justice; The Chimes; The Cry of the Captive; The Guest of the Evening; The Girl Who Lived in Straight Street; The Breaking Point; Creatures of Clay; The Stress of Circumstance; Terror of the Air; Only a Flower Girl; Dr. Fenton's Ordeal; The Grip of Ambition; The Schemers, or The Jewels of Hate; The Whirr of the Spinning Wheel; The Price of Fame; Thou Shalt Not Steal; What the Firelight Showed; The Heart of Midlothian; The Girl Who Played the Game; Unfit, or The Strength of the Weak; So Much Good in the Worst of Us; The Awakening of Nora; The Brothers; Time, the Great Healer; Tommy's Money Scheme; Despised and Rejected; The Double Event; The Man from India; They Say—Let Them Say; John Linworth's Atonement; The Lie; Life's Dark Road; The Bronze Idol; His Country's Bidding (aka The Call); The Quarry Mystery. **1915** Barnaby Rudge; Coward! (aka They Called Him Coward); The Canker of Jealousy (aka Be Sure Your Sins); The Curtain's Secret (aka Behind the Curtain); Courtmartialed (aka The Traitor); The Incorruptible Crown; Spies; The Confession; Schoolgirl Rebels; A Lancashire Lass; The Sweater; Her Boy; Sweet Lavender; The White Hope; The Recalling of John Grey; As the Sun Went Down; Iris; The Nightbirds of London; The Shepherd of Souls; A Moment of Darkness; One Good Turn; Jill and the Old Fiddle; The Bottle; The Baby on the Barge; The Second String; The Golden Pavement. **1916** Annie Laurie; The White Boys; Sowing the Wind; Partners; The Marriage of William Ashe; Molly Bawn; The House of Fortescue; Trelawney of the Wells; The Grand Babylon Hotel; Comin' Thro' the Rye; Love in a Mist; Face to Face. **1917** Her Marriage Lines; The Cobweb; The American Heiress; The Man Behind "The Times"; The Eternal Triangle; A Grain of Sand. **1918** The Touch of a Child. **1919** A Daughter of Eve; The Gentleman Rider (aka Hearts and Saddles—US); A Great Coup; Snow in the Desert. **1920** The Case of Lady Camber; The Romance of a Movie Star; Her Son; The Great Gay Road. **1921** Christie Johnstone; The Imperfect Lover; Her Penalty (aka The Penalty); In Full Cry; The Penniless Millionaire. **1922** Dicky Monteith; Son of Kissing Cup; When Greek Meets Greek; The White Hope (and 1915 version). **1923** Fires of Fate; The Uninvited Guest; The Woman Who Obeyed; The Prodigal Son. **1924** The Desert Sheik; The Colleen Bawn; The Eleventh Commandment; Nets of Destiny; Reveille; The Shadow of the Mosque; The Stirrup Cup Sensation. **1926** Thou Fool; The Silver Treasure. **1927** Somehow Good. **1928** The Passing of Mr. Quin; The Ware Case (US 1929); Zero; The Man Who Changed His Name. **1929** Dark Red Roses; The Crimson Circle. **1930** The Last Hour; The Price of Things; Kissing Cup's Race. **1931** Deadlock; The Great Gay Road; Other People's Sins. **1932** Reunion; Betrayal; The Marriage Bond. **1933** Song of the Plough. **1934** Designing Woman; The Girl in the Flat; Lest We Forget; Temptation; Important People. **1936** Men of Yesterday; Debt of Honour. **1937** The Queaker (aka Murder on Diamond Row—US); Wings of the Morning; Dinner at the Ritz. **1938** The Dance of Death. **1939** Confidential Lady; Shadowed Eyes. **1941** Banana Ridge. **1942** Salute John Citizen; One of Our Aircraft is Missing. **1944** Tom's Ride (short). **1947** The White Unicorn (aka Bad Sister—US 1948). **1948** My Sister and I; Woman Hater (US 1949). **1950** Let's Have a Murder.

ROMEA, ALBERTO
Born: 1883, Spain. Died: Apr. 24, 1960, Madrid, Spain. Screen, stage, radio, television actor and stage manager.

ROMER, LEILA
Born: 1878. Died: Feb. 10, 1944, Hollywood, Calif. (heart attack). Screen, stage and vaudeville actress.

Appeared in: **1919** Anne of Green Gables.

ROMER, TOMI
Born: 1924. Died: July 21, 1969, New York, N.Y. Screen, stage and television actress.

ROMERO, FLORITA
Born: 1931. Died: Feb. 6, 1961, Hollywood, Calif. Screen dancer.

ROMEYN, JANE
Born: 1901. Died: May 5, 1963, Hollywood, Calif. Screen, stage and television actress.

ROMITO, VICTOR RAOUL
Died: May 13, 1980. Screen actor.

Appeared in: **1953** The Golden Blade. **1954** Forever Female. **1955** We're No Angels. **1976** Harry and Walter Go to New York.

RONAN, ROBERT A.
Born: 1936. Died: Apr. 5, 1977, Franklin Park, N.Y. (fire). Screen, stage actor and stage director.

Appeared in: **1971** Klute.

ROOKE, IRENE
Born: England. Died: June 14, 1958, England. Screen and stage actress. Married to actor Milton Rosmer (dec. 1971).

Appeared in: **1916** Lady Windemere's Fan. **1919** Westward Ho! **1920** A Bachelor Husband; Pillars of Society; The Story of Rosary. **1921** The Street of Adventure; Ships That Pass in the Night; The Fruitful Vine; A Romance of Wastdale; The Adventures of Sherlock Holmes series including The Priory School. **1922** Half a Truth; The Pointing Finger; Running Water. **1923** The Loves of Mary, Queen of Scots (aka Marie, Queen of Scots). **1926** Daily Jesters series including Fear. **1927** Hindle Wakes (aka Fanny Hawthorne—US 1929). **1929** The Woman in White; High Treason. **1931** The Rosary. **1932** Collision; Threads.

ROONER, CHARLES
Born: 1901, Vienna, Austria. Died: Nov. 22, 1954, Mexico City, Mexico (heart attack). Screen, stage actor and film director. Entered films in 1934.

Appeared in: **1944** La Dama de las Camelias. **1948** The Pear; Sofia. **1953** Plunder of the Sun.

ROONEY, PAT (Fred E. Ratsch)
Born: 1891. Died: Jan. 15, 1933, Hollywood, Calif. (lung abscess). Screen, stage and vaudeville actor. Divorced from actress Grace Darling. Entered films with Essanay Company.

ROONEY, PAT, II
Born: July 4, 1880, New York, N.Y. Died: Sept. 9, 1962, New York, N.Y. Screen and vaudeville actor. Son of vaudeville actor Pat Rooney I (dec.). Brother of vaudeville/stage actors Julia, Josie, Mattie (dec. 1950) and Katie Rooney (dec. 1950). Married to actress Marian Bent (dec. 1940).

Appeared in: **1915** The Busy Bell Boy; He's a Bear; I'll Get You Yet. **1916** The Belle and the Bellhop; He Became a Regular Fellow; Some Medicine Man; Pat's Pasting Ways. **1917** Hell by the Enemy; A Pirate Bold. **1918** Their Sporting Blood; Pat Turns Detective. **1924** Show Business. **1933** Universal shorts. **1948** Variety Time.

ROONEY, PAT, III
Born: 1909. Died: Nov. 5, 1979, Lake Blaisdell, N.H. Screen, stage, vaudeville and television actor. Son of actors Pat Rooney II (dec. 1962), and Marion Bent (dec. 1940).

Appeared in: **1931** Partners of the Trail. **1948** Variety Time.

ROOPE, FAY
Born: 1893. Died: Sept. 13, 1961, Port Jefferson, N.Y. Screen, stage and television actress.

Appeared in: **1951** You're in the Navy Now (aka U.S.S. Teakettle); The Day the Earth Stood Still; The Frogmen; Callaway Went Thataway. **1952** Young Man with Ideas; Washington Story; Viva Zapata!; The Brigand; Carbine Williams; Deadline U.S.A.; My Six Convicts. **1953** From Here to Eternity; Down Among the Sheltering Palms; All Ashore; The Charge at Feather River; The System; Clipped Wings; The Clown. **1954** The Long Long Trailer; Alaska Seas; The Atomic Kid; The Black Dakotas; The Lone Gun; Naked Alibi. **1955** Ma and Pa Kettle at Waikiki. **1956** The Proud Ones; The Rack. **1959** The F.B.I. Story.

ROOSEVELT, BUDDY (Kenneth Sanderson)
Born: June 25, 1898, Meeker, Colo. Died: Oct. 6, 1973, Meeker, Colo. Screen actor. Entered films in 1918 as a cowboy extra with Inceville Studios. Doubled for Rudolph Valentino in "The Sheik."

Appeared in: **1924** Biff Bang Buddy; Cyclone Buddy; Battling Buddy; Rip Roarin' Roberts; Rough Ridin'; Walloping Wallace. **1925** Gold and Grit; Galloping Jinx; Action Galore; Fast Fightin'; Reckless Courage; Thundering Through. **1926** The Dangerous Dub; Twin Triggers; Tangled Herds; Easy Going; The Bandit Buster; Hoodoo Ranch; The Ramblin' Galoot. **1927** Ride 'Em High; Smoking Guns; Code of the Cow Country; The Fightin' Comeback; Between Dangers; The Phantom Buster; The Bandit Buster. **1928** Mystery Valley; Lightning Shot; Painted Trail; The Cowboy Cavalier; The Devil's Tower; Trailin' Back. **1929** Trail Riders. **1930** Way Out West. **1931** Westward Bound; Lightnin' Smith's Return. **1932** Wild Horse Mesa. **1933** The Fourth Horseman; Operator 13. **1934** Range Riders; Lightning Range; The Fugitive Lady (aka Flight Double). **1935** Captain Blood; Powdersmoke Range; She Married Her Boss. **1937** Dick Tracy (serial); The Old Corral. **1938** The Buccaneer; Marie Antoinette. **1941** Shadow of the Thin Man. **1946** Boss Cowboy; Daughter of Don Q (serial). **1947** The Homestretch; Buck Privates Come Home. **1948** A Double Life; Berlin Express. **1949** King of the Rocket Men (serial); Beyond the Forest. **1950** Kansas Raiders; Colt .45. **1951** The Prince Who was a Thief; Red Badge of Courage. **1952** The Belle of New York; The Old West; The Redhead from Montana. **1953** The Mississippi Gambler. **1956** Tribute to a Bad Man. **1957** Flesh and the Spur; Around the World in 80 Days. **1962** The Man Who Shot Liberty Valance.

ROOT, MIMI (Mimi Doyle)
Born: 1915. Died: June 15, 1979, Santa Monica, Calif. (cancer). Screen actress.

Appeared in: **1954** Executive Suite. **1955** Mr. Roberts. **1960** Pay or Die. **1964** Invitation to a Gunfighter.

ROPER, JACK
Born: Mar. 25, 1904, Miss. Died: Nov. 28, 1966, Woodland Hills, Calif. (throat cancer). Screen actor.

Appeared in: **1928** The Red Mark. **1929** The Duke Steps Out. **1938** Fisticuffs (short). **1940** West of Carson City; A Fugitive From Justice; Hold That Woman; Angels Over Broadway; Heroes of the Saddle. **1941** The Pittsburgh Kid; Ring and the Belle (short); Ridin' the Cherokee Trail; North From the Lone Star. **1942** Broadway Big Shot. **1942** Swing Fever; Jack London. **1946** Joe Palooka; Gentleman Joe Palooka. **1947** Joe Palooka in the Knockout. **1948** Fighting Mad; Joe Palooka in Winner Take All. **1949** Joe Palooka in the Big Fight. **1950** Joe Palooka in the Squared Circle. **1951** Stop That Cab.

ROQUEMORE, HENRY
Born: Mar. 13, 1888, Marshall, Tex. Died: June 30, 1943, Beverly Hills, Calif. Screen and stage actor. Married to actress Fern Emmett (dec. 1946).

Appeared in: **1927** The Fighting Three; For Ladies Only; Is Your Daughter Safe?; Ladies at Ease. **1928** Law and the Man; Branded Man; Gypsy of the North; City of Purple Dreams; The Oklahoma Kid; The Wagon Show. **1929** Sinners in Love; Stocks and Blondes; Anne Against the World. **1930** The Last Dance; Beyond the Rio Grande; Second Honeymoon; The Social Lion; Romance of the West; The Parting of the Trails; Min and Bill. **1931** Cimarron; Sporting Chance. **1933** Breed of the Border. **1934** City Limits; Manhattan Melodrama. **1935** The Lone Wolf Returns; Without Regret; Ruggles of Red Gap; The Misses Stooge (short); Nevada; Powdersmoke Range; Racing Luck; The Singing Vagabond. **1936** The Milky Way; Too Many Parents; Hearts in Bondage; Great Guy. **1937** Second Honeymoon; Maytime; Battle of Greed; Love Takes Flight. **1938** The Arkansas Traveler; Goodbye Broadway; Young Fugitives; Barefoot Boy; Test Pilot. **1939** Exile Express; Babes in Arms. **1940** The Westerner; A Dispatch from Reuters. **1941** Skylark; Model Wife; The Little Foxes; Honky Tonk; Road to Zanzibar; Pot O' Gold; No Greater Sin. **1942** The Postman Didn't Ring; Broadway; Tennessee Johnson; That Other Woman; Women of the Year; The Magnificent Ambersons. **1943** The Lone Star Trail; Girl Crazy.

ROQUEVERT, NOEL
Born: 1892. Died: Nov., 1973, Paris, France. Screen actor.

Appeared in: **1940** The Mayor's Dilemma. **1947** Carnival of Sinners; The Murderer Lives at Number 21. **1948** Le Corbeau (The Raven); Antoine and Antoinette. **1949** Strangers in the House. **1951** Nana (US 1957). **1952** Fanfan the Tulip (US 1953). **1953** Justice Is Done. **1954** Companions of the Night. **1955** The Sheep Has Five Legs; Diabolique. **1956** Inside a Girls' Dormitory. **1958** La Parisienne; La Moucharde (Woman of Sin—US 1961). **1959** The Law Is the Law; Cantage (Blackmail aka The Lowest Crime—US); Archimede le Clochard (Archimede the Tramp aka The Magnificent Tramp—US 1962). **1960** Babette Goes to War; Marie Octobre; Sexpot (aka Le Desir Mene les Hommes—Desire Leads Men); Un Pied, un Cheval et un Sputnik (A Dog, a Horse and a Sputnik aka Au Pied, au Cheval et par Spoutnik (By Foot, By Horse and By Sputnik)); Crazy for Love; Voulez-Vous

Danser Avec Moi (Come Dance With Me); La Francoise et L'Amour (Love and the Frenchwoman—US 1961); Three Murderesses (aka Women Are Weak). **1962** Le Masque de Fer (The Iron Mask); Le Diable et Lex Dix Commandments (The Devil and the 10 Commandments—US 1962); Un Singe en Hiver (Monkey in Winter—US 1963); Cartouche (US 1964). **1964** Patate (aka Friend of the Family—US 1965); Les Barbouzes (aka The Great Spy Chase—US 1966).

RORKE, INA
Born: 1868, Portugal. Died: Apr. 23, 1944, Morristown, N.J. Screen and stage actress. Married to actor Charles Wellesley (dec. 1946).

Appeared in: **1921** Woman's Place. **1922** Polly of the Follies. **1926** When the Wife's Away.

RORKE, KATE
Born: Feb. 22, 1866, London, England. Died: July 31, 1945, Hertfordshire, England. Screen and stage actress. Sister of actress Mary Rorke (dec. 1938).

RORKE, MARGARET (Margaret Hayden)
Born: 1884. Died: Mar. 2, 1969, Hollywood, Calif. Screen and stage actress. Mother of actor Hayden Rorke.

RORKE, MARY
Born: 1858, England. Died: Oct. 12, 1938, London, England. Screen and stage actress. Sister of actress Kate Rorke (dec. 1945).

Appeared in: **1916** The Marriage of William Ashe; Dr. Wake's Patient. **1917** Merely Mrs. Stubbs. **1918** Tinker, Tailor, Soldier, Sailor. **1919** The Bridal Chair; The Right Element. **1920** Unmarried; Pillars of Society; Testimony. **1921** The Education of Nicky. **1922** Boy Woodburn; Let's Pretend; Running Water. **1923** The Harbour Lights; The Starlit Garden. **1924** Who is the Man? **1926** If Youth but Knew; Thou Fool. **1928** For Valour.

ROSAR, ANNIE
Born: 1888. Died: Aug. 1, 1963, Vienna, Austria (heart ailment). Screen and stage actress.

Appeared in: **1922** Ein Hireskorn Greift. **1937** The World's in Love. **1938** Liebe im Dreiviertel Takt (Love in Waltz Time); Ihr Leibhusar. **1948** The Mozart Story. **1952** The Devil Makes Three. **1953** Marika. **1958** Corinna Darling (aka Beloved Corinna). **1959** Embezzled Heaven; The Life and Loves of Mozart (aka Give Me Your Hand, My Love). **1962** Am Galgen Hangt die Liebe (Love of the Gallows).

ROSAS, FERNANDO
Born: 1915, Mexico. Died: Mar., 1959, Mexico City, Mexico. Screen, stage actor and singer.

ROSAY, FRANCOISE (Francoise Bandy de Naleche)
Born: Apr. 19, 1891, Paris, France. Died: Mar. 28, 1974, Paris, France. Screen, stage, radio actress, opera singer, author and screenwriter. Married to film director Jacques Feyder (dec. 1948).

Appeared in: **1913** Falstaff (film debut). **1922** Crainquebille. **1925** Gribiche. **1928** Le Bateau de Verre; Les deux Timides; Madame Recamier. **1929** The One Woman Idea; The Trial of Mary Dugan; Buster se Marie (French version of Spite Marriage). **1930** Le Petit Cafe; Si L'Empereur Savait Ca!; Saysons Gais; Echec au roi ou Le Roi S'Ennui. **1931** Jenny Lind; Quand on est Belle; Casanova Wider Willen (German version of Parlor, Bedroom and Bath); Magnificent Lie; La Chance (The Chance); La Femme en Homme. **1932** Papa sans le Savoir; Le Rosier de Madame Husson. **1933** He; La Pouponniere; Tambour Battant; L'abbe Constantin; Tout Pour Rien; La Kermesse Heroique (US 1936); Pension Mimosas (US 1936). **1934** Le Grand Jeu; Die Insel; Vers L'abime. **1935** Coralie et Cie.; Le Billet de Mitte; Marchand D'Amour; Gangster Malgre Lui; Maternite; Marie des Angoisses; The Robber Symphony. **1936** Le Secret de Polichinelle; Die Letzten vier von St. Paul; Jenny. **1937** Drole de Drame; Mein Sohn, der Herr Minister; Un Carnet de Bal; Le Fauteuil 47. **1938** Paix sur le Rhin; Ramuntcho; Les gens du Voyage (Traveling People); Fahrendes Volk. **1939** Serge Panine; Die Hochzeitsreise (The Wedding Journey); Bizarre Bizarre. **1940** Elles Etaient Douze Femmes; Remous (Whirlpool). **1941** Une Femme Disparait. **1944** The Halfway House (US 1945). **1945** Johnny Frenchman (US 1946). **1946** Macadam; La dame de Haut-le-Bois; Portrait of a Woman. **1948** Backstreet of Paris; Saraband for Dead Lovers (aka Saraband—US 1949); Quartet (US 1949). **1949** Le Mystere Barton; Les Vagabonds du Reve; Donne Senza Nome. **1950** On N'aime Qu'un Fois; Marie Chapdelaine; The September Affair; The Naked Earth. **1951** L'auberge Rouge (The Red Inn—US); I Figli di Nessumo; Les Sept Peches Capitaux; L'Orgueil; The 13th Letter. **1952** Le Banquet des Frandeurs; Wanda la Peccatrice;

Sul Ponte dei Sospiri; Chi e Senza Poccato. **1953** Ramuntcho. **1954** La Reine Margot. **1955** That Lady-Esa Senora; Ragazze D'Oggi; The Naked Heart. **1956** Le Long des Trottoirs. **1957** The Seventh Sin; Interlude. **1958** Me and the Colonel; Le Joueur. **1959** The Sound and the Fury; Du Rififi chez les Femmes (Riff Raff Girls—US 1962 aka Rififi for Girls and Rififi Among the Women); Une Fleur au Fusil; Les Yeux de L'Amour. **1960** Le Bois des Amants; Sans Tambour ni Trompette (aka Die Gans Von Sedan—US 1962); Stefanie in Rio; The Full Treatment. **1961** La Cave se Rebiffe (The Sucker Strikes Back aka The Counterfeiters of Paris and Money, Money, Money—US 1962); Frau Cheney's Ende; The Full Treatment (aka Stop Me before I Kill—US). **1962** The Longest Day. **1964** Volles Herz und Leere Taschen (A Full Heart and Empty Pockets). **1965** Up From the Beach (aka The Day After). **1966** Cloportes (aka La Metamorphose des Cloportes; The Metamorphosis of the Cockroaches; Metamorphosis of Petty Thieves; Metamorphosis of the Bugs; Metamorphosis of Small-timers). **1967** La 25e Heure (The 25th Hour—US). **1974** The Pedestrian.

ROSCOE, ALAN (Albert Roscoe)
Born: Aug. 23, 1887, Nashville, Tenn. Died: Mar. 8, 1933, Hollywood, Calif. Screen and stage actor.

Appeared in: **1917** Cleopatra. **1918** Salome. **1919** Evangeline; The Siren's Song; A Man's Country; The City of Comrades; Her Purchase Price. **1920** Madame X; The Branding Iron. **1921** The Last Card; The Last of the Mohicans. **1922** Burning Sands; The Man Who Saw Tomorrow. **1923** The Spoilers; Java Head; Lovebound; The Net; A Wife's Romance. **1924** The Mirage; The Chorus Lady; Flirting with Love; Pal O'Mine. **1925** Before Midnight; The Lure of the Wild; The Girl of Gold; Why Women Love (aka Sea Woman and Barriers Aflame); That Devil Quemado. **1926** The Texas Streak; The Wolf Hunter. **1927** Long Pants; Duty's Reward. **1928** Driftwood; The Sawdust Paradise; Marry the Girl; The Mating Call; Modern Mothers. **1929** The Sideshow; Flight; The Vagabond Lover; Seven Keys to Baldpate; Hurricane; Love in the Desert; The Red Sword. **1930** Call of the West; Rain or Shine; Half Shot at Sunrise; The Fall Guy; Danger Lights; The Pay Off. **1931** The Royal Bed; Dirigible; Subway Express; The Public Defender; Hell Divers. **1932** Ladies of the Jury; Strangers of the Evening; The Last Mile; The Last Man. **1933** The Death Kiss.

ROSE, BLANCHE
Born: 1878, Detroit, Mich. Died: Jan. 5, 1953, Hollywood, Calif. Screen and stage actress. Played in a number of Charlie Chaplin films.

Appeared in: **1921** The Old Swimming Hole. **1922** Smudge; The Barnstormer. **1923** Money, Money, Money. **1928** Satan and the Woman. **1930** Call of the West. **1938** If I Were King. **1948** The Paradine Case.

ROSE, HARRY
Born: c. 1888. Died: Dec. 10, 1962, Hollywood, Calif. Screen, burlesque, vaudeville and television actor.

ROSE, JANE
Born: 1912. Died: June 29, 1979, Calif. (cancer). Screen, stage, radio and television actress.

Appeared in: **1955** Summertime. **1957** The Monte Carlo Story; Garden of Eden. **1961** 1 + 1 (Exploring the Kinsey Reports). **1962** Flipper. **1970** I Walk the Line.

ROSE, JEWEL
Died: Oct. 21, 1970, Los Angeles, Calif. Screen, radio and television actress.

Appeared in: **1950** The Jackpot.

ROSE, ZELMA
Born: 1873. Died: Nov. 21, 1933, Los Angeles, Calif. (heart attack). Stage and screen actress. Married to actor Col. Reginald Barlow (dec. 1943).

ROSELEIGH, JACK
Born: c. 1887, Tenn. Died: Jan. 5, 1940 (heart attack). Screen, stage and radio actor.

Appeared in: **1921** Bare Knuckles; The Light in the Clearing; That Girl Montana; Singing River.

ROSELLE, WILLIAM
Born: 1878. Died: June 1, 1945, N.Y. Stage and screen actor.

Appeared in: **1916** Gloria's Romance (serial). **1919** The Avalanche. **1921** The Black Panther's Cub; The Man Who; Wedding Bells.

ROSEMOND, CLINTON C.
Born: 1883. Died: Mar. 10, 1966, Los Angeles, Calif. (pneumonia—stroke). Black screen actor.

Appeared in: **1931** Smart Money. **1934** Carolina. **1936** Green Pastures. **1937** They Won't Forget; Hollywood Hotel; Dark Manhattan. **1938** The Toy Wife; The Story of Dr. Carver (short); Young Dr. Kildare. **1939** Midnight Shadow; Stand Up and Fight; Golden Boy. **1940** Safari; George Washington Carver; Santa Fe Trail. **1941** Blossoms in the Dust. **1942** Yankee Doodle Dandy; Syncopation; Are Husbands Necessary? **1943** Flesh and Fantasy. **1945** Jungle Queen (serial). **1947** The Homestretch.

ROSEN, JAMES "JIMMY"
Born: 1885, Russia. Died: June 1, 1940, New York, N.Y. Midget screen and stage actor.

Appeared in: **1931** Alice in Wonderland. **1939** The Wizard of Oz.

ROSENBERG, SARAH
Born: 1874. Died: June 16, 1964, Hollywood, Calif. Screen actress. Entered films in 1913.

ROSENBLATT, CANTOR JOSEF
Born: May 9, 1882, New York, N.Y. Died: June 19, 1933, Jerusalem. Cantor, screen and stage actor.

Appeared in: **1927** The Jazz Singer; Cantor Josef Rosenblatt (short); Cantor Rosenblatt and Choir. **1934** The Dream of My People; Voice of Isreal.

ROSENBLOOM, MAXIE "SLAPSIE MAXIE" (Maxie Rosenblum)
Born: Sept. 6, 1904, New York, N.Y. Died: Mar. 6, 1976, South Pasadena, Calif. (Paget's disease). Screen, vaudeville, radio, television actor and professional boxer. Light-heavyweight Champion of the World, 1932-1934.

Appeared in: **1933** Mr. Broadway (film debut); King For a Night. **1936** Muss 'Em Up; Kelly the Second. **1937** Nothing Sacred; Big City; Two Wise Maids; Don't Pull Your Punches. **1938** Mr. Moto's Gamble; The Kid Comes Back; Gangs of New York; The Amazing Dr. Clitterhouse; Submarine Patrol; His Exciting Night. **1939** Women in The Wind; The Kid From Kokomo; Naughty but Nice; Each Dawn I Die; 20,000 Men a Year; Private Detective. **1940** Grandpa Goes to Town; Public Deb No. 1; Passport to Alcatraz. **1941** Ringside Maisie; The Stork Pays Off; Louisiana Purchase. **1942** Smart Alecks; Harvard, Here I Come; The Boogie Man Will Get You; To The Shores of Tripoli; The Yanks Are Coming. **1943** My Son, The Hero; Here Comes Kelly; Swing Fever. **1944** When Irish Eyes Are Smiling; Follow the Boys; Allergic to Love; Slick Chick; Three of a Kind; Crazy Knights; Night Club Girl; Ghost Crazy. **1945** Penthouse Rhythm; Men in Her Diary; Trouble Chasers. **1948** Hazard. **1951** Mr. Universe; Skipalong Rosenbloom. **1955** Guys and Dolls; Abbott and Costello Meet the Keystone Kops. **1956** Hollywood or Bust. **1958** I Married a Monster From Outer Space. **1959** The Beat Generation. **1963** Follow the Boys (and 1944 version). **1966** Don't Worry, We'll Think of a Title. **1967** Cottonpickin' Chickenpickers. **1969** My Side of The Mountain.

ROSENTHAL, HARRY
Born: May 15, 1900, New York or Ireland?. Died: May 10, 1953, Hollywood, Calif. (heart attack). Screen, stage, radio actor, pianist, orchestra leader and composer.

Appeared in: **1930** The Collegiate Model (short). **1939** Wife, Husband and Friend. **1940** Johnny Apollo; Christmas in July; The Great McGinty. **1941** Unfinished Business; Birth of the Blues. **1944** The Miracle of Morgan's Creek; The Great Moment. **1945** The Horn Blows at Midnight.

ROSING, BODIL (Bodil Hammerich)
Born: 1878, Copenhagen, Denmark. Died: Jan. 1, 1942, Hollywood, Calif. (heart attack). Screen and stage actress.

Appeared in: **1925** Pretty Ladies (film debut); Lights of Old Broadway. **1926** The Sporting Lover; It Must Be Love; The City; The Midnight Kiss; The Return of Peter Grimm. **1927** Sunrise; Wild Geese; Blondes by Choice; Stage Madness. **1928** The Big Noise; Out of the Ruins; Wheel of Chance; The Fleet's In; Ladies of the Mob; The Law of the Range; The Port of Missing Girls; The Woman from Moscow. **1929** Eternal Love; Why Be Good?; Betrayal; Broadway Babies; King of the Rodeo. **1930** The Bishop Murder Case; Hello Sister; A Lady's Morals; Oh, What a Man; Soul Kiss; Part Time Wife; All Quiet on the Western Front. **1931** An American Tragedy; Three Who Loved; Surrender. **1932** Downstairs; The Match King. **1933** The Crime of the Century; Ex-Lady; Hallelujah, I'm a Bum; Reunion in Vienna. **1934** King Kelly of the U.S.A.; The Crimson Romance; Mandalay; Little Man, What

Now?; The Painted Veil; Such Women Are Dangerous. **1935** Roberta; Four Hours to Kill; A Night at the Ritz; Let 'Em Have It; Thunder in the Night. **1936** Libeled Lady; Hearts in Bondage. **1937** Michael O'Halloran; Conquest. **1938** The First Hundred Years; You Can't Take It With You. **1939** Confessions of a Nazi Spy; Beasts of Berlin; The Star Maker; Nurse Edith Cavell. **1940** The Mortal Storm. **1941** Reaching for the Sun; Marry the Boss's Daughter; No Greater Sin; Man at Large.

ROSLEY, ADRIAN
Born: 1890, Marseilles, France. Died: Mar. 5, 1937, Hollywood, Calif. (heart attack). Screen, stage actor and opera performer.

Appeared in: **1933** My Weakness; Girl Without a Room. **1934** Bum Voyage (short); Handy Andy; Flying Down to Rio; Viva Villa; Of Human Bondage; The Great Flirtation; Notorious Sophie Lang. **1935** Enter Madame; Death Flies East; Roberta; South Seasickness (short); The Girl from Tenth Avenue; Alibi Ike; Here's to Romance; The Misses Stooge (short); Metropolitan. **1936** Sins of Man; The Magnificent Brute; The Gay Desperado; The Garden of Allah; Sing Me a Love Song. **1937** Ready, Willing and Able; The King and the Chorus Girl; A Star Is Born.

ROSMER, MILTON (Arthur Milton Lunt)
Born: Nov. 4, 1881, Southport, Lancashire, England. Died: Dec. 7, 1971, Chesham, England. Screen, stage, radio, television actor, film, stage director and screenwriter. Married to actress Irene Rooke (dec. 1958). Entered films in 1912.

Appeared in: **1915** The Mystery of a Hansom Cab. **1916** Cynthia in the Wilderness; Lady Windermere's Fan; The Man without a Soul (aka I Believe—US 1917); Still Waters Run Deep; Whoso is without Sin; The Greater Need. **1917** Little Women. **1919** A Chinese Puzzle; Odds Against Her. **1920** With All Her Heart; Colonel Newcome the Perfect Gentleman; The Twelve Pound Look; The Golden Web; Torn Sails; Wuthering Heights. **1921** Belphegor the Mountebank; The Amazing Partnership; A Woman of No Importance; General John Regan; A Romance of Wastdale; Demos (aka Why Men Forget—US); The Diamond Necklace; The Will. **1922** The Passionate Friends; The Pointing Finger; Tense Moments with Great Authors series including David Garrick. **1923** A Gamble with Hearts. **1924** The Shadow of Egypt. **1929** High Treason. **1930** The "W" Plan (US 1931). **1934** Grand Prix. **1935** The Phantom Light. **1937** The Great Barrier (aka Silent Barriers—US). **1938** South Riding. **1939** Goodbye, Mr. Chips; The Stars Look Down (US 1941); The Lion Has Wings (US 1940); Let's Be Famous; Beyond Our Horizon (short). **1940** Return to Yesterday; Dangerous Comment (short). **1941** Atlantic Ferry (aka Sons of the Sea—US); Hatter's Castle. **1946** Daybreak (US 1949). **1947** Frieda; The End of the River (US 1948); Fame is the Spur (US 1949). **1948** Who Killed Van Loon?; The Monkey's Paw. **1949** The Small Back Room (US 1952).

ROSS, ANTHONY
Born: 1906, N.Y. Died: Oct. 26, 1955, New York, N.Y. Screen, stage and television actor.

Appeared in: **1947** Kiss of Death. **1950** The Gunfighter; Between Midnight and Dawn; Perfect Strangers; The Skipper Surprised His Wife; The Flying Missile; The Vicious Years. **1952** On Dangerous Ground. **1953** Girls in the Night; Taxi. **1954** Rogue Cop; The Country Girl.

ROSS, BARNEY (Barnet David Rosofsky)
Born: 1907, New York, N.Y. Died: Jan. 18, 1967, Chicgo, Ill. (cancer of throat). Professional boxer, screen and vaudeville actor.

Appeared in: **1962** Requiem for a Heavyweight. **1965** The Doctor and the Playgirl.

ROSS, BENNY (Robert Ross)
Born: Feb. 1, 1907, Hartford, Conn. Died: July 18, 1974, Hollywood, Calif. (coronary attack). Screen, stage and vaudeville actor. Married to Maxine Stone, with whom he appeared in vaudeville in an act billed as "Ross and Stone." Appeared in Warner Brothers shorts.

ROSS, BETTY (aka BETTY ROSS CLARKE)
Born: 1880. Died: Feb. 1, 1947, Hollywood, Calif. Screen actress.

Appeared in: **1920** The Very Idea; If I Were King. **1921** Her Social Value; Lucky Carson. **1931** The Man from Downing Street; The Age for Love. **1932** Murders in the Rue Morgue. **1938** Judge Hardy's Children; Love Finds Andy Hardy; Woman Against Woman; Too Hot to Handle. **1940** Untamed.

ROSS, CHARLES J.
Born: Feb. 18, 1859, Montreal, Canada. Died: June 15, 1918, North Asbury Park, N.J. Screen, stage and vaudeville actor. Married to actress Mabel Fenton (dec. 1931).

Appeared in: **1915** The Senator.

ROSS, CHRISTOPHER "CHRIS"
Born: 1946. Died: May 5, 1970, Hollywood, Calif. Screen, stage, radio and television actor.

Appeared in: **1968** How Sweet It Is; Petulia. **1969** A Session with the Committee; Viva Max.

ROSS, CHURCHILL (Ross Weigle)
Born: Jan. 29, 1901, Lafayette, Ind. Died: May 23, 1962. Screen actor.

Appeared in: **1923** Stephen Steps Out. **1927** The College Hero; Blazing Days. **1928** The Fourflusher. **1929** College Love; King of the Campus. **1930** The King of Jazz; Undertow. **1933** College Humor.

ROSS, CORINNE HEATH SUMNER
Born: 1879. Died: June 22, 1965, Hollywood, Calif. Screen actress.

Appeared in: **1964** My Fair Lady.

ROSS, DANNY
Born: 1931, England. Died: Feb., 1976, Blackpool, England. Screen, stage, radio and television actor.

Appeared in: **1959** Friends and Neighbors (US 1963).

ROSS, DAVID
Born: 1891, New York, N.Y. Died: Nov. 12, 1975, New York, N.Y. (heart attack). Radio, television, screen (narrated for movies), vaudeville actor and poet. Married to actress Beatrice Pons.

Appeared in: **1932** Isle of Paradise (narrator). **1933** The Passion of Joan of Arc (narrator); Cuba (short). **1935** The Land of Promise (narrator). **1937** Paramount shorts. **1938** Fight for Peace; Paramount shorts.

ROSS, EARLE
Born: Mar. 29, 1888, Ill. Died: May 21, 1961, North Hollywood, Calif. (cancer). Radio, stage and film actor.

Appeared in: **1936** Cavalry; Stormy Trails. **1937** Riders of the Whistling Skull. **1940** The Courageous Dr. Christian.

ROSS, HERBERT
Born: Oct. 3, 1865, England. Died: July 18, 1934, England (following surgery). Screen and stage actor.

Appeared in: **1931** The Skin Game.

ROSS, MARION (aka MARION ROLAND)
Born: 1898. Died: July 23, 1966, Seattle, Wash. (cancer). Screen, stage and vaudeville actress.

Appeared in: **1920** Over the Hill. **1954** Sabrina; Forever Female; Secret of the Incas; The Glenn Miller Story. **1956** Lust for Life; The Proud and the Profane. **1957** God Is My Partner; Lizzie. **1958** Some Came Running; Teacher's Pet. **1959** Operation Petticoat. **1961** Blueprint for Robbery. **1970** The Forbin Project.

ROSS, MYRNA
Born: 1939. Died: Dec. 26, 1975, near Granby, Colo. (plane crash). Stage and screen actress.

Appeared in: **1965** How to Stuff a Wild Bikini; Beach Blanket Bingo. **1966** The Swinger; The Ghost in the Invisible Bikini. **1968** How Sweet It Is. **1969** 2,000 Years Later.

ROSS, SHIRLEY (Bernice Gaunt)
Born: Jan. 7, 1909 or 1914?, Omaha, Nebr. Died: Mar. 9, 1975, Menlo Park, Calif. (cancer). Screen, radio actress and singer.

Appeared in: **1933** Bombshell. **1934** Manhattan Melodrama; The Girl From Missouri; Hollywood Party; The Merry Widow. **1935** Age of Indiscretion; Calm Yourself; Buried Loot (short). **1936** Devil's Squadron; San Francisco; The Big Broadcast of 1937; Anything Goes. **1937** Waikiki Wedding; Blossoms on Broadway; Hideaway Girl. **1938** Prison Farm; Thanks for the Memory; Big Broadcast of 1938. **1939** Paris Honeymoon; Cafe Society; Some Like It Hot; Unexpected Father. **1941** Kisses for Breakfast; Sailors on Leave. **1945** A Song for Miss Julie.

ROSS, THOMAS W.
Born: Jan. 22, 1875, Boston, Mass. Died: Nov. 14, 1959, Torrington, Conn. Screen and stage actor.

Appeared in: **1921** Fine Feathers; Without Limit. **1926** The Only Son. **1939** Blondie Takes a Vacation. **1940** Seventeen; Remember the Night; The Saint's Double Trouble; The Mortal Storm; Phantom Raiders. **1942** King's Row; The Remarkable Andrew; Yankee Doodle Dandy.

ROSS, WILLIAM
Born: 1925. Died: Feb. 25, 1963, Pittsburgh, Pa. (heart attack). Screen, stage and radio actor.

ROSSI, ANGELO
Born: 1889. Died: 1976. Screen actor and stuntman.

ROSSON, ARTHUR H.
Born: Aug. 24, 1889, London, England. Died: June 17, 1960, Los Angeles, Calif. Screen actor, film, stage director, screenwriter and stuntman. Entered films as actor and stuntman.

ROSSON, RICHARD "DICK"
Born: Apr. 4, 1893, New York, N.Y. Died: May 31, 1953, Los Angeles, Calif. (suicide—carbon monoxide poisoning). Screen actor and film director. Married to actress Vera Sisson (dec. 1954).

Appeared in: **1912** Diamond Cut Diamond; She Cried; O'Hara, Squatter and Philosopher. **1913** Sue Simpkins' Ambition; A Heart of the Forest. **1915** Love, Snow and Ice; Aided by the Movies; Deserted at the Auto; An Auto Bungalow Fracas; Nobody's Home; Cats, Cash and a Cookbook. **1916** Mischief and a Mirror; One by One; Plotters and Papers; Johnny's Jumble; Billy Van Deusen's Muddle; Number Please?; A Trunk and Trouble; Dad's College Widow; Ella Wanted to Elope; Bugs and Bugles; Skelly's Skeleton; Adjusting His Claim; The Coments Come-Back; Billy Van Deusen's Operation; Billy Van Deusen's Egg-spensive Adventure; The House on Hokum Hill; Billy Van Deusen, Masquerader; In the Land of the Tortilla; Seventeen; Gamblers in Greenbacks; Daredevils and Danger; Billy Van Deusen, the Cave Man. **1917** Panthea. **1918** Alias Mary Brown; The Ghost Flower; The Shoes that Danced; A Good Loser; High Stakes; Madame Sphiny. **1919** The Secret Garden; Peggy Does Her Darndest; Poor Boob; Playthings of Passion. **1921** Beating the Game; Her Face Value; For Those We Love; Always the Woman.

ROSWAENGE, HELGE
Born: 1896, Denmark. Died: Aug., 1972, Denmark. Screen, stage actor and opera performer.

Appeared in: **1936** Letzte Rose.

ROTH, GENE (aka GENE STUTENROTH)
Born: 1903, SDak. Died: July 19, 1976, Los Angeles, Calif. (struck by car). Screen actor.

Appeared in: **1943** The Strange Death of Adolf Hitler. **1944** Charlie Chan in The Secret Service; Shake Hands With Murder; Girl in The Case. **1945** Stairway to Light (short); The Shanghai Cobra; See My Lawyer; Here Come the Co-Eds; Secret Agent X9 (serial); Rogues' Gallery; A Game of Death. **1946** I Ring Doorbells; Strange Journey; Mr. Hex. **1947** The Black Widow (serial); Jack Armstrong (serial); Marshal of Cripple Creek; Homesteaders of Paradise Valley. **1948** Adventures of Frank and Jesse James (serial); Oklahoma Badlands; Smugglers Cove. **1949** Dunked in The Deep (short); Ghost of Zorro (serial); The Big Sombrero; Alaska Patrol; Sheriff of Wichita. **1950** Colorado Ranger; West of The Brazos; The James Brothers of Missouri (serial); Pirates of The High Seas (serial); Slaphappy Sleuths (short); The Baron of Arizona; Trail of the Rustler. **1951** Captain Video (serial); Mysterious Island (serial). **1952** Montana Belle; The Maverick; Mutiny; Red Planet Mars; Red Snow; Blue Canadian Rockies; Gold Fever; Fargo. **1953** The Lost Planet (serial); Jack McCall, Desperado; Prince of Pirates; The Farmer Takes a Wife. **1954** The Steel Cage; Port of Hell; Desiree; Prince Valiant. **1955** Lucy Gallant. **1956** Commotion on the Ocean (short); Running Target. **1957** Outer Space Jitters (short); Utah Blaine; Zombies of Mora Tau; Rockabilly Baby. **1958** Quiz Whiz (short); Pies and Guys (short); She Demons; The Spider. **1959** The Miracle of The Hills; Ghost of Zorro (and 1949 serial); The Giant Leeches. **1960** Tormented. **1961** The Cat Burglar. **1962** The Three Stooges Meet Hercules; Stagecoach to Dancer's Rock. **1963** Twice Told Tales. **1965** Young Dillinger. **1967** Rosie.

ROTH, JACK
Born: 1899. Died: Feb. 12, 1980, Yonkers, N.Y. (heart attack). Musician, drummer and screen actor. Original drummer for the "Memphis Five" jazz band.

ROTH, LILLIAN (Lillian Rustein)
Born: Dec. 13, 1910, Boston, Mass. Died: May 12, 1980, New York, N.Y. (stroke). Screen, stage, vaudeville, television actress, singer and author. Entered films in 1916.

Appeared in: **1929** The Love Parade; Illusion. **1930** Animal Crackers; The Vagabond King; Honey; Madame Satan; Paramount on Parade; Sea Legs. **1933** Take a Chance; Ladies They Talk About. **1963** The Sound of Laughter. **1978** Alice, Sweet Alice. **1979** Boardwalk.

ROTH, "SANDY" (Sanford L. Roth)
Born: 1889. Died: Nov. 4, 1943, Beverly Hills, Calif. (heart attack). Screen, vaudeville actor and assistant film director. Entered films as an actor with Mack Sennett in 1916.

Appeared in: **1932** The Beast of the City; Hell's Highways. **1933** Midnight Mary.

ROTMUND, ERNEST
Born: 1887, Germany. Died: Mar. 2, 1955, Munich, Germany. Screen, stage and radio actor.

Appeared in: **1935** Auforderung zum Tanz (Invitation to the Dance).

ROULEAU, RAYMOND
Born: 1904, Brussels, Belgium. Died: Dec. 11, 1981, Paris, France. Screen, stage actor, stage director and screenwriter. Divorced from actress Tania Balachovia and Francoise Lugagne. Later married to Francoise Cremieux.

Appeared in: **1933** La Femme Nue. **1939** Affair Lafont. **1945** De Drame Shanghai (The Shanghai Drama). **1946** Paris Frills. **1948** Who Killed Santa Claus?; The Honorable Catherine. **1949** Une Grande Fille Toute (Just a Big Simple Girl). **1952** Brelan D'As (Full House). **1958** Witches of Salem; The Crucible.

ROULIEN, TOSCA
Born: 1910. Died: Sept. 27, 1933, Hollywood, Calif. (auto accident). Screen actress. Married to actor Raoul Roulien.

ROUNESVILLE, ROBERT (aka ROBERT FIELD)
Born: Mar. 25, 1914, Attleboro, Mass. Died: Aug. 6, 1974, New York, N.Y. (heart attack). Screen, stage, radio, vaudeville actor and opera performer. Appeared on radio and in vaudeville as Robert Field.

Appeared in: **1951** Tales of Hoffman (film debut). **1956** Carousel.

ROUSE, HALLOCK
Born: 1897. Died: Jan. 2, 1930, over Pacific Ocean (airplane accident). Screen actor and film aviator.

Appeared in: **1929** Behind That Curtain.

ROUX, ANTONIO "TONY"
Born: 1901. Died: Nov. 9, 1976, Wodland Hills, Calif. Screen actor. Entered films in 1918 as an extra.

Appeared in: **1938** In Old Mexico. **1939** Law of The Pampas. **1941** Gauchos of El Dorado. **1942** Undercover Man. **1951** Casa Manana. **1953** The Hitch-Hiker. **1954** Charge of The Lancers.

ROWAN, DONALD W.
Born: 1906. Died: Feb. 17, 1966, Rocky Hill, Conn. (cerebral hemorrhage). Screen and television actor.

Appeared in: **1935** Whipsaw. **1936** And Sudden Death; The Arizona Raiders; The Return of Sophie Lang; Murder with Pictures; Wives Never Know. **1937** When's Your Birthday?; The Devil's Playground; The Affairs of Cappy Ricks; Sea Racketeers. **1938** Racket Busters; Wanted by the Police. **1939** Nancy Drew and the Hidden Staircase; Tough Kid. **1940** Brother Orchid; Flash Gordon Conquers the Universe (serial).

ROWAN, ERNEST
Born: 1886. Died: Sept. 30, 1960, Hampton, Va. Screen and stage actor. Entered films approx. 1925.

ROWE, VERN
Born: 1922. Died: Sept. 4, 1981, Hollywood, Calif. (stroke). Screen, television actor, musician and singer.

Appeared in: **1967** The Big Mouth. **1976** The Shaggy D.A.

ROWLAND, ADELE
Died: Aug. 8, 1971. Screen and stage actress. Divorced from actor Charles Ruggles (dec. 1970), and later married to actor Conway Tearle (dec. 1938).

Appeared in: **1928** Stories in Songs (short). **1941** The Blonde From Singapore. **1948** For the Love of Mary.

ROWLAND, JAMES G.
Died: Nov. 27, 1951, Philadelphia, Pa. Screen, stage, vaudeville and radio actor. Married to actress Ethel Ellet, with whom he appeared in vaudeville.

ROWLANDS, ART
Born: 1898. Died: May 25, 1944, Hollywood, Calif. Screen stunt actor.

Appeared in: **1928** The Black Pearl; Devil's Tower; Mystery Valley; Lightnin' Shot. **1929** Synthetic Sin. **1934** The Live Ghost (short). **1936** Ants in the Pantry (short).

ROY, BINOTA
Born: India. Died: 1978, India. Screen actor.

Appeared in: **1944** Udayer Pather.

ROY, DAN See LOTINGA, ERNEST

ROY, DEREK
Born: 1923, England. Died: Mar. 15, 1981, Southampton, England (cancer). Screen, stage and radio actor.

ROY, HARRY
Born: 1904. Died: Jan. 30, 1971, London, England. Bandleader, screen actor and song writer.

Appeared in: **1936** Everything Is Rhythm.

ROY, JAHAR
Born: 1919, India. Died: Aug. 11, 1977, Calcutta, India. Screen and stage actor.

ROY, JOHN "JOHNNY"
Born: 1899. Died: May 31, 1975, Hollywood, Calif. (heart attack). Screen actor and stuntman. Father of newscaster John Marshall.

Appeared in: **1940** Brigham Young, Frontiersman. **1949** Criss Cross.

ROYCE, FORREST "FROSTY"
Born: 1911. Died: May 15, 1965, Hollywood, Calif. (heart attack). Screen stuntman and double for William Boyd in "Hopalong Cassidy" films.

Appeared in: **1940** Oklahoma Renegades.

ROYCE, JULIAN (Julian Gardener)
Born: Mar. 26, 1870, Bristol, England. Died: May 10, 1946, England? Screen and stage actor.

Appeared in: **1921** The Bigamist. **1922** The Persistent Lovers; Let's Pretend; Running Water. **1923** The Knockout. **1928** God's Clay. **1931** These Charming People. **1932** The Frightened Lady (aka Criminal at Large—US 1933). **1933** This is The Life (US 1935). **1934** Leave It to Blanche.

ROYCE, LIONEL
Born: Mar. 30, 1891, Dolina, Poland. Died: Apr. 1, 1946, Manila, Philippine Islands (touring with U.S.O.). Stage and screen actor.

Appeared in: **1937** Marie Antoinette (film debut). **1938** What Price Safety? (short). **1939** Six Thousand Enemies; Confessions of a Nazi Spy; Pack Up Your Troubles; Nurse Edith Cavell; Conspiracy. **1940** The Son of Monte Cristo; The Man I Married; Four Sons; Charlie Chan in Panama; Victory. **1941** So Ends Our Night. **1942** The Lady Has Plans; My Favorite Spy; My Favorite Blonde. **1943** Crash Dive; Mission to Moscow; Secret Service in Darkest Africa (serial); Let's Face It; Cross of Lorraine; Bomber's Moon. **1944** Seventh Cross; The Hitler Gang. **1945** Tarzan and the Amazons; White Pongo. **1946** Gilda.

ROYCE, RIZA
Born: 1908, Lancaster, Pa. Died: Oct. 20, 1980, Hollywood, Calif. (heart attack). Screen, stage, television actress, radio and television writer. Divorced from director Josef von Sternberg (dec. 1969), and later married to painter Stanton MacDonald-Wright.

Appeared in: **1919** Sacred Silence; Checkers. **1920** The Shark. **1925** The Other Woman's Story. **1937** A Star is Born. **1953** House of Wax. **1956** Girls in Prison. **1963** Wives and Lovers. **1964** Good Neighbor Sam. **1970** Myra Breckinridge; The Great White Hope.

ROYCE, ROSITA
Born: 1918, Lincoln, Nebr. Died: Sept. 24, 1954, Miami, Fla. Screen, vaudeville and burlesque actress.

ROYCE, VIRGINIA
Born: 1932. Died: July 8, 1962, Hollywood, Calif. (cerebral hemorrhage). Screen actress.

Appeared in: **1963** The Caretakers.

ROYER, HARRY "MISSOURI"
Born: 1889. Died: Aug. 1, 1951, Hollywood, Calif. (heart attack). Stage and screen actor.

Appeared in: **1926** The Block Signal; Sky High Corral.

ROYSTON, JULIUS
Died: July 1, 1935, Johannesburg, South Africa (bronchial pneumonia). Stage and screen actor. Appeared in films made in South Africa.

ROZANSKA, ELEKTRA
Born: 1891. Died: July 3, 1978, Pasadena, Calif. (heart attack). Screen, stage actress and opera singer.

Appeared in: **1947** The Shocking Miss Pilgrim; Northwest Outpost. **1948** Letter from an Unknown Woman. **1960** From the Terrace. **1961** Summer and Smoke.

RUARK, ROBERT C. (Robert Chester Ruark)
Born: 1915, Wilmington, N.C. Died: July 1, 1965, London, England. Novelist, screen actor and screenwriter.

Appeared in: **1954** Africa Adventure (narrator). **1955** Target Earth.

RUB, CHRISTIAN
Born: Apr. 13, 1887, Austria. Died: Apr. 14, 1956. Screen actor.

Appeared in: **1932** Silver Dollar; Secrets of the French Police; The Trial of Vivienne Ware; The Man from Yesterday. **1933** Humanity; Mary Stevens, M.D.; The Kiss Before the Mirror. **1934** The Fountain; Music in the Air; Romance in the Rain; The Mighty Barnum; No Ransom; No More Women; No Greater Glory; Man of Two Worlds; Little Man, What Now? **1935** Black Fury; The Man Who Broke the Bank at Monte Carlo; Metropolitan; A Dog of Flanders; We're Only Human; Stolen Harmony; Peter Ibbetson; Oil for the Lamps of China; Hitchhike Lady. **1936** Murder on the Bridal Path; Parole; Sins of Man; Mr. Deeds Goes to Town; Girls Dormitory; Suzy; Next Time We Love; Dracula's Daughter; Murder With Pictures; Devil is a Sissy. **1937** Thin Ice; One Hundred Men and a Girl; Cafe Metropole; Outcast; When Love is Young; Tovarich; Heidi. **1938** You Can't Take It With You; Mad About Music; The Great Waltz; Professor Beware; I'll Give a Million. **1939** Never Say Die; Forged Passport; Everything Happens at Night. **1940** All This and Heaven Too; The Swiss Family Robinson; Pinocchio (voice of Gepetto); Four Sons; Earthbound. **1941** Father's Son; Come Back Miss Pipps (short); Henry Aldrich for President; The Big Store. **1942** Berlin Correspondent; Tales of Manhattan; Dangerously They Live. **1944** The Adventures of Mark Twain; Three Is a Family. **1945** Strange Confession. **1948** Fall Guy. **1952** Something for the Birds.

RUBEN, JOSE
Born: 1889, Paris, France. Died: Apr. 28, 1969, N.Y. Screen, stage actor, stage director and playwright. Divorced from actress Mary Nash (dec. 1976).

Appeared in: **1922** The Man from Home. **1923** Dark Secrets. **1925** Salome of the Tenements.

RUBENS, ALMA (Alma Smith)
Born: 1897, San Francisco, Calif. Died: Jan. 23, 1931, Los Angeles, Calif. (pneumonia). Screen and stage actress. Divorced from actor Ricardo Cortez (dec. 1977).

Appeared in: **1916** The Half-Breed; The Mystery of Leaping Fish; The Americano; Intolerance. **1917** Firefly of Tough Luck. **1918** Madame Sphinx. **1919** Restless Souls. **1920** The World and His Wife; Humoresque. **1921** Thoughtless Women. **1922** Find the Woman; Valley of Silent Men. **1923** Under the Red Robe; The Enemies of Women. **1924** Cytherea; The Price She Paid; Gerald Cranston's Lady; Is Love Everything?; The Rejected Woman; Week-End Husbands. **1925** Fine Clothes; The Dangers; East Lynne; She Wolves; The Winding Stair; A Woman's Faith. **1926** The Gilded Butterfly; Marriage License; Siberia. **1927** The Heart of Salome. **1928** Masks of the Devil. **1929** Showboat; She Goes to War.

RUBIN, PEDRO
Born: Mexico. Died: Apr. 17, 1938, Mexico City, Mexico. Stage and screen actor.

RUBIOLA, JOE
Born: 1906, San Antonio, Tex. Died: Sept. 6, 1939, Mexico City, Mexico. Screen actor.

RUDAMI, ROSA
Born: 1899. Died: Feb. 2, 1966, Albany, N.Y. Screen actress.

Appeared in: **1925** The Wedding Song. **1926** A Poor Girl's Romance; The Lily.

RUFART, CARLOS
Born: 1887, Spain. Died: Apr., 1957, Madrid, Spain. Screen, stage actor and singer.

RUFFO, TITTA (Ruffo Capero Titta)
Born: 1877, Pisa, Italy. Died: July 6, 1953, Florence, Italy (heart attack). Screen actor and opera performer. Appeared in Metro Movietone shorts.

RUGGLES, CHARLES (Charles Sherman Ruggles)
Born: Feb. 8, 1890, Los Angeles, Calif. Died: Dec. 23, 1970, Santa Monica, Calif. (cancer). Screen, stage, vaudeville, radio and television actor. Brother of actor Wesley Ruggles (dec. 1972). Divorced from actress Adele Rowland (dec. 1971) and later married to Marion La Barbe.

Appeared in: **1915** Peer Gynt. **1923** The Heart Raider. **1928** Wives; Etc. (short). **1929** Gentlemen of the Press; The Lady Lies; The Battle of Paris. **1930** Young Man of Manhattan; Roadhouse Nights; Queen High; Charley's Aunt; Her Wedding Night. **1931** The Girl Habit; The Beloved Bachelor; Honor Among Lovers; The Smiling Lieutenant; The Lawyer's Secret. **1932** One Hour With You; This Is the Night; The Night of June 13th; Trouble in Paradise; Evenings for Sale; Love Me Tonight; 70,000 Witnesses; Husband's Holiday; This Reckless Age; Make Me a Star; Madame Butterfly; If I Had a Million. **1933** Murders in the Zoo; Terror Abroad; Mama Loves Papa; Girl Without a Room; Alice in Wonderland; Melody Cruise. **1934** Melody in Spring; Murder in the Private Car; Friends of Mr. Sweeney; Six of a Kind; Pursuit of Happiness; Goodbye Love. **1935** Ruggles of Red Gap; People Will Talk; The Big Broadcast of 1936; No More Ladies. **1936** Anything Goes; Early to Bed; Wives Never Know; Mind Your Own Business; Hearts Divided; The Preview Murder Mystery. **1937** Turn Off the Moon; Exclusive. **1938** Bringing Up Baby; Service de Luxe; His Exciting Night; Breaking the Ice. **1939** Yes, My Darling Daughter; Invitation to Happiness; Boy Trouble; Sudden Money; Night Work; Balalaika. **1940** The Farmer's Daughter; Opened By Mistake; Maryland; Public Deb. No. 1; No Time for Comedy. **1941** The Invisible Woman; Model Wife; Honeymoon for Three; The Perfect Snob; Go West, Young Lady; The Parson of Panamint. **1942** Friendly Enemies. **1943** Dixie Dugan. **1944** Our Hearts Were Young and Gay; The Doughgirls; Three Is a Family. **1945** Bedside Manner; Incendiary Blonde. **1946** The Perfect Marriage; Gallant Journey; A Stolen Life; My Brother Talks to Horses. **1947** It Happend on Fifth Avenue; Ramrod. **1948** Give My Regards to Broadway. **1949** The Loveable Cheat; Look for the Silver Lining. **1961** The Pleasure of His Company; The Parent Trap; All in a Night's Work. **1963** Son of Flubber; Papa's Delicate Condition. **1964** I'd Rather Be Rich. **1966** The Ugly Dachshund; Follow Me, Boys!

RUGGLES, WESLEY
Born: June 11, 1889, Los Angeles, Calif. Died: Jan. 8, 1972, Santa Monica, Calif. (stroke). Film director, producer, screen, stage minstrel actor and screenwriter. Brother of actor Charles Ruggles (dec. 1970). Married to actress Marcelle Rogez and divorced from actress Arline Judge (dec. 1974). Entered films as an actor in 1914 with Sennett.

Appeared in: **1915** A Submarine Pirate.

RUICK, BARBARA
Born: 1932, Pasadena, Calif. Died: Mar. 2, 1974, Reno, Nev. (natural causes). Screen, television and radio actress. Daughter of actress Lorene Tuttle. Divorced from actor Robert Horton. Married to composer John Williams.

Appeared in: **1952** Above and Beyond; Apache War Smoke; Fearless Fagan; The Invitation; You for Me. **1953** Confidentially Connie; The Affairs of Dobie Gillis; I Love Melvin. **1956** Carousel. **1974** California Split.

RUIZ, JOSE RIVERO
Born: 1896. Died: Dec. 27, 1949, Madrid, Spain. Screen and stage actor. Appeared in first talkie in Spain in 1936.

RUMANN, SIEGFRIED (Siegfried Albon Rumann)
Born: 1885, Hamburg, Germany. Died: Feb. 14, 1967, Julian, Calif. (heart attack). Screen, stage and television actor.

Appeared in: **1929** The Royal Box. **1934** Marie Galante; The World Moves On; Servants' Entrance. **1935** The Wedding Night; Under Pressure; Spring Tonic; The Farmer Takes a Wife; A Night at the Opera; East of Java. **1936** The Beloved Rogue; The Princess Comes Across; The Bold Caballero; I Loved a Soldier. **1937** On the Avenue; Dead Yesterday; Seventh Heaven; Midnight Taxi; Think Fast, Mr. Moto; This Is My Affair; Love Under Fire; Thin Ice; Lancer Spy; Heidi; Thank You, Mr. Moto; Maytime; A Day at the Races; The

Great Hospital Mystery; Nothing Sacred. **1938** Paradise for Three; The Great Waltz; The Saint in New York; I'll Give a Million; Girls on Probation; Suez. **1939** Never Say Die; Honolulu; Remember?; Confessions of a Nazi Spy; Only Angels Have Wings; Ninotchka. **1940** Dr. Ehrlich's Magic Bullet; Outside the Three-Mile Limit; I Was an Adventuress; Four Sons; Victory; So Ends Our Night; That Bitter Sweet; Comrade X. **1941** That Uncertain Feeling; The Man Who Lost Himself; The Wagons Roll at Night; Shining Victory; Love Crazy; World Premiere; This Woman Is Mine. **1942** Remember Pearl Harbor; Crossroads; Enemy Agents Meet Ellery Queen; Berlin Correspondent; China Girl; Desperate Journey; To Be or Not to Be. **1943** Tarzan Triumphs; They Came to Blow Up America; Sweet Rosie O'Grady; Government Girl. **1944** Summer Storm; The Devil's Brood; Goodbye My Love; The Hitler Gang; It Happened Tomorrow; The Song of Bernadette. **1945** She Went to the Races; A Royal Scandal; House of Frankenstein; The Dolly Sisters; The Men in Her Diary. **1946** Faithful in My Fashion; Night and Day; A Night in Casablanca. **1947** Mother Wore Tights. **1948** If You Knew Susie; Give My Regards to Broadway; The Emperor Waltz. **1949** Border Incident. **1950** Father Is a Bachelor. **1951** On the Riviera. **1952** O. Henry's Full House; The World in His Arms. **1953** Ma and Pa Kettle on Vacation; Houdini; Stalag 17. **1954** The Glenn Miller Story; White Christmas; Living It Up; Three-Ring Circus. **1955** Many Rivers to Cross; The Spy Chasers; Carolina Cannonball. **1957** The Wings of Eagles. **1962** The Errand Boy. **1964** Robin and the Seven Hoods; 36 Hours. **1966** The Fortune Cookie; The Last of the Secret Agents; Way ... Way Out.

RUMSEY, BERT (Burtis Harold Rumsey)
Born: Oct. 15, 1892, Montana. Died: July 6, 1968, Woodland Hills, Calif. (lung cancer). Screen actor.

Appeared in: **1953** Botany Bay. **1958** Desert Hell. **1960** The Threat. **1965** Ship of Fools.

RUNNEL, ALBERT F.
Born: 1892, St. Paul, Minn. Died: Jan. 4, 1974, Belleair-Clearwater, Fla. (heart condition). Screen, stage, vaudeville actor and circus performer. Appeared in early Biograph Company films.

RUNYON, DAMON (Alfred Damon Runyon)
Born: Oct. 4, 1884, Manhattan, Kans. Died: Dec. 10, 1946, New York, N.Y. (cancer). Journalist, playwright, screenwriter, author, film producer and screen actor.

Appeared in: **1924** The Great White Way. **1926** Oh Baby! **1932** Madison Square Garden.

RUSHING, JIMMY (James Andrew Rushing)
Born: Aug. 26, 1903, Oklahoma City, Okla. Died: June 8, 1972, New York, N.Y. Jazz singer and film actor.

Appeared in: **1944** Funzapoppin'. **1969** The Learning Tree.

RUSKIN, SHIMEN
Born: 1907, Vilna, Poland. Died: Apr. 23, 1976, Los Angeles, Calif. (cancer). Screen, stage, radio and television actor.

Appeared in: **1924** Beau Brummell. **1938** Having a Wonderful Time (stage and film versions). **1941** Lady from Louisiana; Dance Hall. **1944** Murder My Sweet. **1947** Dark Passage; Body and Soul. **1948** Letter from an Unknown Woman. **1949** Deadly as the Female. **1968** The Producers. **1971** Fiddler on the Roof; Shaft. **1975** Love and Death.

RUSS, PAULA (Pauline Ignatiev aka POLA RUSS)
Born: 1893. Died: Mar. 14, 1966, Los Angeles, Calif. Screen actress.

Appeared in: **1956** Around the World in 80 Days.

RUSSELL, ALBERT
Born: 1891. Died: Mar. 4, 1929, Los Angeles, Calif. (pneumonia). Screen actor and film director. Brother of actor William Russell (dec. 1929).

RUSSELL, ANN (Audrey Ann Dosch)
Died: July 31, 1955, Burbank, Calif. (plane crash, which also killed actor Robert Francis). Screen actress and bit player.

RUSSELL, BILLY
Born: England. Died: Dec., 1956, Ealing, London, England. Screen, stage and vaudeville actor. Noted for his resemblance to Adolph Hitler.

RUSSELL, BYRON
Born: 1884, Ireland. Died: Sept. 4, 1963, New York, N.Y. Screen, stage and television actor.

Appeared in: **1920** The World and His Wife. **1921** The Family Closet. **1922** Determination. **1924** It Is the Law; Janice Meredith. **1935** Mutiny on the Bounty. **1937** Parnell. **1938** A Vitaphone short. **1939** One Third of a Nation.

RUSSELL, DON (Samuel H. Borgesi)
Born: 1927. Died: May 27, 1981, Miami Beach, Fla. (heart attack). Screen, stage and television actor.

Appeared in: **1972** The Godfather.

RUSSELL, EDD X.
Born: 1878. Died: Nov. 17, 1966, Los Angeles, Calif. Screen, stage and vaudeville actor. Stand-in for Robert Benchley.

RUSSELL, EVANGELINE
Born: 1903, New York, N.Y. Died: Feb. 22, 1966. Screen actress. Married to actor/director J. Stuart Blackton (dec. 1941), and actor/director William P. S. Earle (dec. 1973).

Appeared in: **1923** Lost in a Big City. **1924** Fangs of The Wolf; Floodgates. **1925** Red Love. **1926** The Big Show; Married? **1927** Hawk of The Hills (serial). **1929** Hawk of The Hills (and 1927 serial).

RUSSELL, EVELYN
Born: 1927, N.Y. Died: Feb. 4, 1976, Sherman Oaks, Calif. Screen, stage, radio and television actress.

Appeared in: **1975** 92 in the Shade; Sheila Levine is Dead and Living in New York. **1976** Bound for Glory. **1977** The Car. **1978** Eat My Dust.

RUSSELL, GAIL
Born: Sept. 23, 1924, Chicago, Ill. Died: Aug. 26, 1961, Los Angeles, Calif. Screen and television actress. Divorced from actor Guy Madison.

Appeared in: **1943** Henry Aldrich Gets Glamour (film debut). **1944** Lady in the Dark; The Uninvited; Our Hearts Were Young and Gay. **1945** Salty O'Rourke; The Unseen; Duffy's Tavern. **1946** The Bachelor's Daughters; The Virginia; Our Hearts Were Growing Up. **1947** The Angel and the Badman; Variety Girl; Calcutta. **1948** Moonrise; The Night Has a Thousand Eyes; Song of Adventure; Wake of the Red Witch. **1949** El Paso; Song of India; The Great Dan Patch; Captain China. **1950** The Lawless. **1951** Air Cadet. **1953** Devil's Canyon. **1956** Seven Men from Now. **1957** The Tattered Dress. **1958** No Place to Land. **1961** The Silent Call.

RUSSELL, J. GORDON
Born: Jan. 11, 1883, Piedmont, Ala. Died: Apr. 21, 1935, Los Angeles, Calif. (heart attack). Screen actor.

Appeared in: **1916-17** American Film Mfg. Co. films. **1918** A Diplomatic Mission. **1921** The Sea Lion; Three Word Brand. **1922** His Back Against the Wall; Colleen of the Pines; The Kingdom Within; Trail of Hate. **1923** Kindled Courage; The Spoilers; The Scarlet Lily. **1924** Chastity; Hard Hittin' Hamilton; Singer Jim McKee; The Western Wallop; The No-Gun Man. **1925** Easy Going Gordon; Flying Hoofs; Parisian Love; Galloping Jinx; Quicker'n Lightnin'; Hearts and Spurs; A Roaring Adventure; Tumbleweeds; The Sign of the Cactus. **1926** Looking for Trouble. **1927** The Claw; Spurs and Saddles; Uncle Tom's Cabin; Wild Beauty. **1928** Beyond the Sierras; Saddle Mates. **1930** The Lightning Express (serial).

RUSSELL, JEAN
Died: July 8, 1922, New York, N.Y. (suicide). Screen actress.

RUSSELL, JOHN LOWELL
Born: 1875. Died: Sept. 20, 1937, West Los Angeles, Calif. Screen actor and film producer. Do not confuse with actor John Russell.

Appeared in: **1929** Arizona Days; Manhattan Cowboy.

RUSSELL, LEWIS
Born: 1885. Died: Nov. 12, 1961, Los Angeles, Calif. Screen and stage actor.

Appeared in: **1945** Molly and Me; Hold That Blonde; The Lost Weekend; She Wouldn't Say Yes. **1946** A Night in Casablanca; She Wrote the Book; If I'm Lucky; Cross My Heart. **1947** Jewels of Brandenburg; Ladies' Man; The Trouble with Women; Backlash. **1948** Kiss the Blook Off My Hands. **1950** The Underworld Story. **1951** Corky of Gasoline Alley. **1956** The Naked Hills.

RUSSELL, LILLIAN (Helen Louise Leonard)
Born: 1860, Clinton, Iowa. Died: June 5, 1922, Pittsburgh, Pa. Screen, stage, burlesque and vaudeville actress.

Appeared in: **1913** How to Live 100 Years. **1914** Potted Pantomimes. **1915** Wildfire (stage and film versions).

RUSSELL, PAUL
Born: 1896. Died: Dec. 26, 1979, Hollywood, Calif. Screen, stage and television actor.

Appeared in: **1939** Gone With the Wind. **1950** Frenchie. **1962** Advise and Consent. **1976** King Kong.

RUSSELL, REB (Lafayette H. Russell)
Born: May 31, 1905, Osawatomie, Kans. Died: Mar. 16, 1978. Screen actor, circus performer and cowboy.

Appeared in: **1935** Border Vengeance. **1939** Range War. **1943** The Man From Hell; Fighting Through; Blazing Guns.

RUSSELL, ROSALIND
Born: June 4, c. 1907, Waterbury, Conn. Died: Nov. 28, 1976, Beverly Hills, Calif. (cancer complicated by arthritis). Screen and stage actress. Married to producer Frederick Brisson. Nominated for 1943 Academy Award for Best Actress in My Sister Eileen; for 1946 in Sister Kenny; for 1947 in Mourning Becomes Electra; for 1958 in Auntie Mame.

Appeared in: **1934** Evelyn Prentice (film debut); The President Vanishes. **1935** West Point of the Air; The Casino Murder Case; Reckless; China Seas; Rendezvous; Forsaking All Others; The Night Is Young. **1936** Craig's Wife; It Had to Happen; Under Two Flags; Trouble for Two. **1937** Night Must Fall; Live, Love and Learn. **1938** Manproof; The Citadel; Four's a Crowd. **1939** The Women; Fast and Loose. **1940** His Girl Friday; No Time for Comedy; Hired Wife. **1941** This Thing Called Love; They Met in Bombay; The Feminine Touch; Design For Scandal. **1942** Take a Letter Darling; My Sister Eileen. **1943** Flight For Freedom; What a Woman. **1945** Roughly Speaking. **1946** She Wouldn't Say Yes; Sister Kenny. **1947** The Guilt of Janet Ames; Mourning Becomes Electra. **1948** The Velvet Touch. **1949** Tell It to the Judge. **1950** A Woman of Distinction. **1952** Never Wave at a WAC. **1955** The Girl Rush; Picnic. **1958** Auntie Mame. **1961** A Majority of One. **1962** Gypsy; Five Finger Exercise. **1966** The Trouble With Angels. **1967** Rosie; Oh, Dad, Poor Dad, Mama's Hung You in the Closet and I'm Feeling so Sad. **1968** Where Angels Go Trouble Follows. **1971** Mrs. Pollifax, Spy.

RUSSELL, WILLIAM
Died: c. 1915. Screen, stage and vaudeville actor. Appeared in Essanay films. Do not confuse with actor William Russell (dec. 1929).

Appeared in: **1915** Tag Day; Sealed Lips; The Frame-Up. Prior to 1918: High Play; Lone Star; The Twinkler; Fate and Death; The Torch Bearer; Shackles of Truth; Periwinkle; The Weakness of the Strong; Pride and the Man; The Pagan; Sands of Sacrifice; The Sea Master; Temporary Peter; His Abrabian Night; Snap Judgment; Aladdin's Night.

RUSSELL, WILLIAM
Born: Apr. 12, 1886. Died: Feb. 18, 1929, Beverly Hills, Calif. (pneumonia). Screen, stage, vaudeville actor and film producer. Son of stage actress Sarah Russell (dec.). Brother of actor Albert Russell (dec. 1929). Married to actress Helen Ferguson (dec. 1977). Entered films in 1910 with Griffith.

Appeared in: **1912** The Star of Bethlehem; Lucille. **1913** Robin Hood. **1914** The Straight Road. **1915** The Garden of Lies; The Diamond from the Sky (serial); Tag Day; Sealed Lips; The Flame-Up. **1916** The Sequel to the Diamond from the Sky (serial). **1917** Pride and the Man. **1919** Brass Buttons; Six Feet Four. **1921** High Gear Jeffrey; Bare Knuckles; Challenge of the Law; The Cheater Reformed; Colorado Pluck; Quick Action; The Iron Rider; Children of Night; Singing River; The Roof Tree; Desert Blossoms. **1922** Strength of the Pines; A Self-Made Man; Money to Burn; The Men of Zanzibar; Lady from Longacre; The Great Night; Mixed Faces. **1923** Crusader; Alias the Nightwind; Boston Blackie; Goodbye Girls; Man's Size; Times Have Changed; When Odds Are Even; Anna Christie. **1924** The Beloved Brute. **1925** Before Midnight; Big Pal; My Neighbor's Wife; On Thin Ice; The Way of a Girl. **1926** The Blue Eagle; The Still Alarm; Wings of the Storm. **1927** Brass Knuckles; A Rough Shod Fighter; The Desired Woman; The Girl from Chicago. **1928** Danger Patrol; The Escape; The Head of the Family; The Midnight Taxi; State Street Sadie; Woman Wise. **1929** Girls Gone Wild.

RUTH, BABE (George Herman Ruth)
Born: Feb. 6, 1895, Baltimore, Md. Died: Aug. 16, 1948. Professional baseball player and screen actor. Married to Helen Woodward (dec. 1929) and later to stage actress Claire Merritt Ruth (dec. 1976).

Appeared in: **1920** Headin' Home. **1927** Babe Come Home. **1928** Speedy. **1932** The following shorts: Slide, Babe, Slide; Fancy Curves; Over the Fence. **1937** A Vitaphone short. **1942** Pride of the Yankees; The Ninth Inning.

RUTH, MARSHALL
Born: Dec. 24, 1898, Marshalltown, Iowa. Died: Jan. 19, 1953, Hollywood, Calif. Screen, stage and radio actor. Entered films in 1922.

Appeared in: **1926** Her Sacrifice. **1927** Ridin' Luck; Wild Born. **1928** Red Wine; Virgin Lips. **1929** Joy Street; Nix on Dames; The Broadway Melody; Wall Street. **1930** Navy Blues. **1935** False Pretenses; Hold 'Em Yale. **1936** Wedding Present.

RUTHERFORD, MARGARET
Born: May 11, 1892, London, England. Died: May 22, 1972, Buckinghamshire, England. Screen, stage, television, radio actress and author. Married to actor Stringer Davis. Won 1963 Academy Award for Best Supporting Actress in The V.I.P.'s. Was made Dame Commander of the Order of the British Empire in 1967.

Appeared in: **1936** Dusty Ermine (aka Hideout in the Alps—US 1939); Talk of the Devil (US 1937). **1937** Beauty and the Barge; Catch as Catch Can; Missing, Believed Married. **1941** Spring Meeting; Quiet Wedding. **1943** Yellow Canary (US 1944); The Demi-Paradise (aka Adventure for Two—US 1945). **1944** English Without Tears (aka Her Man Gilbey—US 1949). **1945** Blithe Spirit (stage and film versions). **1947** Atlantic Episode (reissue of 1937 Catch as Catch Can); Meet Me at Dawn (US 1948); While the Sun Shines (US 1950). **1948** Miranda (US 1949). **1949** Passport to Pimlico. **1950** The Happiest Days of Your Life; Her Favorite Husband (aka The Taming of Dorothy—US). **1951** The Magic Box (US 1952). **1952** The Importance of Being Ernest; Castle in the Air; Miss Robin Hood; Curtain Up (US 1953). **1953** Innocents in Paris (US 1955); Trouble in Store (US 1955); The Runaway Bus; The Gay Duelist (reissue of 1947 Meet Me at Dawn). **1954** Aunt Clara; Mad About Men. **1955** An Alligator Named Daisy (US 1957). **1957** The Smallest Show on Earth; Just My Luck. **1959** I'm All Right Jack (US 1960). **1961** Murder She Said (US 1962); On the Double. **1963** The Mouse on the Moon; Murder at the Gallop; The V.I.P.'s. **1964** Murder Most Foul; Murder Ahoy. **1965** The Alphabet Murders (US 1966). **1966** A Countess from Hong Kong (US 1967); Campanadas a Medianoche (aka Falstaff and Chimes at Midnight—US 1967). **1967** The Wacky World of Mother Goose (voice); Arabella (US 1970).

RUTHERFORD, TOM
Died: Jan. 6, 1973, Vienna, Austria. Stage and screen actor.

Appeared in: **1937** The Firefly; Beg, Borrow or Steal; Rosalie. **1938** Vacation from Love; A Desperate Adventure; Anesthesia (short). **1940** Those Were the Days; The Ghost Comes Home. **1941** Virginia.

RUTH JEW BABY *See* GUENTHER, RUTH

RUYSDAEL, BASIL
Born: 1888. Died: Oct. 10, 1960, Hollywood, Calif. Screen, stage, radio actor and narrator.

Appeared in: **1929** The Cocoanuts. **1934** Dealers in Death (narr.). **1936** An Educational short. **1937** Vitaphone short. **1949** Colorado Territory; Come to the Stable; Thelma Jordan (aka File on Thelma Jordan); The Doctor and the Girl; Pinky. **1950** Broken Arrow; Gambling House; The Dungeon; High Lonesome; There's a Girl in My Heart; One Way Street. **1951** Half Angel; My Forbidden Past; People Will Talk; Raton Pass; The Scarf. **1952** Boots Malone; Carrie. **1954** Prince Valiant; The Shanghai Story. **1955** The Blackboard Jungle; David Crockett, King of the Wild Frontier; Diane; Pearl of the South Pacific; The Violent Men. **1956** Jubal; These Wilder Years. **1958** The Last Hurrah. **1959** The Horse Soldiers. **1960** The Story of Ruth.

RYAN, ANNIE
Born: 1865. Died: Feb. 14, 1943, Hollywood, Calif. Screen and stage actress.

Appeared in: **1927** The Claw.

RYAN, DICK
Born: 1897. Died: Aug. 12, 1969, Burbank, Calif. (protracted illness). Screen, vaudeville, radio and television actor. He and his wife Mary teamed in vaudeville act billed as "Dick and Mary."

Appeared in: **1943** The Constant Nymph. **1948** Mr. Peabody and the Mermaid. **1949** Flamingo Road; Abandoned; Chicken Every Sunday; Jiggs and Maggie in Jackpot Jitters; Top of the Morning. **1950** Born to Be Bad; For Heaven's Sake; Mister 800. **1951** Starlift; Strangers on a Train; Guy Who Came Back. **1954** The Glenn Miller Story. **1956** The Search for Bridey Murphy. **1957** The Buster Keaton Story; Wild Is The Wind. **1958** Once Upon a Horse. **1961** Ada; Summer and Smoke. **1962** Advise and Consent. **1964** Law of the Lawless.

RYAN, IRENE (Irene Nablett)

Born: 1903, El Paso, Tex. Died: Apr. 26, 1973, Santa Monica, Calif. (stroke). Screen, stage, television, radio and vaudeville actress. Married to actor Tim Ryan (dec. 1956) with whom she appeared on radio, in vaudeville and a few films as "Tim and Irene." Later married and divorced film executive Harold E. Knox.

Appeared in: 1935 One Big Happy Family (short). 1936 Just Plain Folks (short); It Happened All Right (short). 1940 Tattle Television (short). 1941 Melody for Three. 1942 Sarong Girl; Hold Your Temper (short); Indian Signs (short). 1943 Melody Parade. 1944 San Diego, I Love You; Hot Rhythm. 1945 That's the Spirit; That Night With You; The Beautiful Cheat. 1946 The Diary of a Chambermaid; Little Iodine. 1947 The Woman on the Beach; Heading for Heaven. 1948 An Old Fashioned Girl; My Dear Secretary; Texas, Brooklyn and Heaven. 1949 There's a Girl in My Heart. 1951 Meet Me After the Show; Half Angel. 1952 Blackbeard the Pirate; WAC from Walla Walla; Bonzo Goes to College. 1954 Ricochet Romance. 1957 Spring Reunion; Rockabilly Baby. 1960 Desire in the Dust. 1966 Don't Worry, We'll Think of a Title.

RYAN, JOE

Born: 1887. Died: Dec. 23, 1944. Screen actor.

Appeared in: 1914 The Man Who Came Back. 1916 Making Good; Along the Border; The Man Within; The Sheriff's Deputy; Crooked Trails; Going West to Make Good; The Girl of Gold Gulch; Taking a Chance; A Corner in Water; A Close Call; Tom's Sacrifice; The End of the Rainbow. 1917 A Darling in Buckskin; The Tenderfoot; The Fighting Trail (serial); Dead Shot Baker. 1918 A Fight For Millions (serial). 1919 Man of Might (serial). 1920 Hidden Dangers (serial). 1921 The Purple Riders (serial). 1923 Lone Fighter; Smashing Barriers. 1925 The Vanishing American.

RYAN, MARY

Born: 1880 or 1885, N.Y. Died: Oct. 2, 1948, Cranford, N.J. Screen and stage actress. Do not confuse with actress with same name appearing in later films.

Appeared in: 1912 The Blind Cattle King; The Power of Silence. 1913 Who Is The Savage.

RYAN, ROBERT

Born: Nov. 11, 1909, Chicago, Ill. Died: July 11, 1973, New York, N.Y. (cancer). Screen, stage and television actor. Married to actress Jessica Cadwalader (dec. 1972). Nominated for 1947 Academy Award for Best Supporting Actor in Crossfire.

Appeared in: 1940 The Ghost Breakers; Golden Gloves; Queen of the Mob; Northwest Mounted Police. 1941 Texas Rangers Ride Again. 1943 Bombardier; Gangway for Tomorrow; The Sky's the Limit; Behind the Rising Sun; The Iron Major; Tender Comrade. 1944 Marine Raiders. 1947 Trail Street; The Woman on the Beach; Crossfire. 1948 Berlin Express; Return of the Badmen; The Boy with Green Hair. 1949 Act of Violence; Caught; The Set-Up; I Married a Communist (aka The Woman on Pier 13). 1950 The Secret Fury; Born to Be Bad. 1951 Best of the Badmen; Flying Leathernecks; The Racket; On Dangerous Ground; Hard, Fast and Beautiful. 1952 Clash by Night; Beware My Lovely; Horizons West. 1953 City Beneath the Sea; The Naked Spur; Inferno. 1954 Alaska Seas; About Mrs. Leslie; Her Twelve Men; Bad Day at Black Rock. 1955 Escape to Burma; House of Bamboo; The Tall Men. 1956 The Proud Ones; Back from Eternity. 1957 Men in War. 1958 God's Little Acre; Lonelyhearts. 1959 Day of the Outlaw; Odds Against Tomorrow. 1960 Ice Palace. 1961 The Canadians; King of Kings. 1962 The Longest Day; Billy Budd. 1964 The Inheritance (narrator). 1965 The Crooked Road; Battle of the Bulge; Guerre Secrete (aka The Dirty Game—US 1966). 1966 The Professionals. 1967 The Busy Body; The Dirty Dozen; Hour of the Gun (aka The Law and the Tombstone); Escondido (aka A Minute to Pray, a Second to Die—US 1968); Dead or Alive; The Prodigal Gun. 1968 Anzio (aka The Battle for Anzio); Custer of the West (aka A Good Day for Fighting). 1969 The Wild Bunch; Captain Nemo and the Underwater City (US 1970 aka Captain Nemo and the Floating City). 1971 Lawman; The Love Machine. 1972 Le Course du Lievre a Travers les Champs (aka ... and Hope to Die). 1973 The Outfit; The Iceman Cometh; Executive Action; The Lolly Madonna War.

RYAN, SHEILA (Katherine Elizabeth McLaughlin)

Born: June 8, 1921, Topeka, Kans. Died: Nov. 4, 1975, Woodland Hills, Calif. (lung ailment). Screen actress. Married to actor Pat Buttram.

Appeared in: 1940 The Gay Caballero. 1941 Sun Valley Serenade; Golden Hoofs; Dead Men Tell; Dressed to Kill; Great Guns; We Go Fast; The Gang's All Here. 1942 Pardon My Stripes; The Lone Star

Ranger; Who Is Hope Schuyler?; A-Haunting We Will Go; Careful, Soft Shoulders. 1943 Song of Texas. 1944 Ladies of Washington; Something for the Boys. 1945 The Caribbean Mystery; Getting Gertie's Garter. 1946 Lone Wolf in London; Deadline for Murder; Slightly Scandalous. 1947 The Big Fix; Philo Vance's Secret Mission; Railroaded; Heartaches; The Lone Wolf in Mexico. 1948 Cobra Strikes; Caged Fury. 1949 Ring Side; The Cowboy and the Indians; Hideout; Joe Palooka in the Counterpunch. 1950 Mule Train; Western Pacific Agent; Square Dance Katy. 1951 Mask of the Dragon; Fingerprints Don't Lie; Golden Raiders; Jungle Manhunt. 1953 On Top of Old Smoky; Pack Train. 1958 Street of Darkness.

RYAN, TIM

Born: July 5, 1899, Bayonne, N.J. Died: Oct. 22, 1956, Hollywood, Calif. (heart attack). Screen, radio, vaudeville, television actor and screenwriter. Married to actress Irene Ryan (dec. 1973) with whom he appeared in vaudeville, a few films and radio in an act billed as "Tim and Irene."

Appeared in: 1935 One Big Happy Family (short). 1936 Just Plain Folks (short); It Happened All Right (short). 1940 Brother Orchid; I'm Nobody's Sweetheart Now; Private Affairs. 1941 The Strawberry Blonde; I Wake Up Screaming (aka Hot Spot); Ball of Fire; Where Did You Get That Girl?; Lucky Devils; A Man Betrayed; Ice Capades; Public Enemies; Harmon of Michigan; Bedtime Story; Mr. and Mrs. North. 1942 The Man in the Trunk; Stand By For Action; Crazy Legs; Sweetheart of the Fleet; Get Hep to Love. 1943 Hit Parade of 1943; Sarong Girl; The Mystery of the 13th Guest; Riding High; The Sultan's Daughter; Two Weeks to Live; True to Life; Melody Parade; Reveille with Beverly. 1944 Hot Rhythm; Hi, Beautiful; Detective Kitty O'Day; Kansas City Kitty; Shadow of Suspicion; Swingtime Johnny; Crazy Knights. 1945 Who's Guilty? (serial); Swingin' on a Rainbow; Adventures of Kitty O'Day; Fashion Model; Rockin' in the Rockies. 1946 Bringing Up Father; Dark Alibi; Wife Wanted. 1947 Case Timberlane; Till the End of Time; News Hounds; Scareheads; Blondie's Holiday; Body and Soul. 1948 Jiggs and Maggie in Court; Luck of the Irish; The Golden Eye; Force of Evil; The Shanghai Chest; Jiggs and Maggie in Society; Angels' Alley. 1949 Red, Hot and Blue; Ringside; Joe Palooka in the Counterpunch; Jiggs and Maggie in Jackpot Jitters; Shamrock Hills; Stampede; Sky Dragon; Forgotten Women. 1950 The Asphalt Jungle; Military Academy With That 10th Avenue Gang; The Petty Girl; Maggie and Jiggs Out West; Humphrey Takes a Chance; Military Academy. 1951 The Cuban Fireball; All That I Have; Win, Place and Show; Crazy Over Horses. 1952 Here Come the Marines; Fargo; No Holds Barred. 1953 From Here to Eternity; The Marksman; Private Eyes. 1956 Fighting Trouble. 1967 The Buster Keaton Story.

RYCKMAN, CHESTER

Born: 1897. Died: Nov. 6, 1918, Fort Rosecrans, Calif. Screen actor.

Appeared in: 1917 The Nurse of an Aching Heart; Double Dukes.

SABATINI, ERNESTO

Born: 1878, Italy. Died: Oct. 5, 1954, Milan, Italy (heart attack). Screen, stage, radio and television actor.

Appeared in: 1938 Come le Foglie (Like the Leaves). 1940 Between Two Worlds.

SABATO, ALFREDO

Born: Mar. 23, 1894, Italy. Died: Feb. 10, 1956, Italy? Screen actor and film director.

Appeared in: 1927 Time to Love. 1928 The River.

SABEL, DAVID

Born: 1857. Died: Sept. 27, 1933, New York, N.Y. (natural causes). Screen and stage actor. Married to actress Josephine Sabel (dec. 1945).

SABEL, JOSEPHINE

Born: 1866, Lawrence, Mass. Died: Dec. 24, 1945, Patchogue, N.Y. Screen and vaudeville actress. Married to actor David Sabel (dec. 1933).

Appeared in: 1932 The March of Time (short).

SABIN, CATHERINE JEROME

Born: 1879. Died: May 19, 1943, New York, N.Y. Screen and stage actress.

Appeared in: 1925 New Toys.

SABLON, LOULETTE

Died: Oct. 21, 1970. Screen actress.

Appeared in: 1949 Come to the Stable. 1950 Under My Skin.

SABOURET, MARIE
Born: France. Died: July 23, 1960, St. Jean de Luz, France. Screen actress.

Appeared in: **1956** Rififi. **1960** The Would-Be Gentleman.

SABU (Sabu Dastagir)
Born: Mar. 15, 1924, Karapur, Mysore, India. Died: Dec. 2, 1963, Chatsworth, Calif. (heart attack). Screen actor.

Appeared in: **1937** Elephant Boy. **1938** Drums. **1940** The Thief of Bagdad. **1942** Arabian Nights; The Jungle Book. **1943** White Savage; Screen Snapshot No. 5 (short). **1944** Cobra Woman. **1946** Tangier. **1947** The End of the River (US 1948); Black Narcissus. **1948** Man-Eater of Kumaon. **1949** Song of India. **1951** Savage Drums. **1954** Hello, Elephant. **1955** Black Panther. **1956** Jungle Hell; Jaguar. **1957** Sabu and the Magic Ring. **1958** Rampage. **1964** A Tiger Walks.

SACHSE, PETER (Peter Louis Sachse)
Born: 1940. Died: July 12, 1966, LaJolla, Calif. (plane crash). Screen actor, musician and singer. Married to actress Salli Sachse.

Appeared in: **1965** Dr. Goldfoot and the Bikini Machine. **1966** The Ghost and the Invisible Bikini.

SACK, ERNA
Born: 1903, Spandau-Berlin, Germany. Died: Mar. 2, 1972, Wiesbaden, Germany. Screen actress and opera soprano.

Appeared in: **1938** Nanon. **1938** Blumen aus Nizza (Flowers from Nice—US 1939).

SACK, NATHANIEL
Born: 1882. Died: July 2, 1966, New York, N.Y. Screen, stage and television actor.

SACKVILLE, GORDON
Died: Aug. 6, 1926, Los Angeles, Calif. (stroke of apoplexy). Screen actor.

Appeared in: **1911** The Best Man Wins. **1915** The Red Circle (serial). **1921** Dr. Jim; The Fighting Lover. **1922** With Stanley in Africa (serial); Any Night. **1923** Slow as Lightning. **1924** The Snob. **1925** Cowboy Courage.

SADLER, CHARLES R.
Born: 1875. Died: Mar. 23, 1950, Los Angeles, Calif. Screen stuntman.

SADLER, DUDLEY, JR.
Died: Sept. 25, 1951, Santa Monica, Calif. Screen actor.

Appeared in: **1947** Boomerang. **1951** Behave Yourself; Lone Star.

SADLER, IAN
Born: 1902, Glasgow, Scotland. Died: July, 1971, London, England. Screen, stage and radio actor.

SADO, KEIJI
Born: 1926, Kyoto, Japan. Died: 1964, Japan (auto accident). Screen actor.

Appeared in: **1947** Phoenix; Red Lips. **1949** Here's to the Girls. **1951** Carmen Comes Home; School of Freedom. **1952** Sad Speech; The Boy Director; Stormy Waters; The First Step of Married Life. **1953** Spring Drum; A Japanese Tragedy; The Journey. **1954** Somewhere Beneath the Wide Sky; Diary of Fallen Leaves; Niizuma No Seiten; A Young Lady as President; A Medal; Family Conference; Shinkon Takuan Fefu; Izuko E; What Is Your Name? **1955** College for Men; The Sun Never Sets; You and Your Friend; The Refuge; Beautiful Days; New Every Day; Distant Clouds. **1956** The White Bridge; Look for Your Bride; Tokyo—Hong Kong Honeymoon; The Fountainhead; Footprints of a Woman. **1957** Ore Wa Sinanai; The Sound of Youth; Hanayome Boshuchu; I'll Buy You; Tears; A Case of Honour; The Embraced Bride; Monkey Business; The Lighthouse (aka Times of Joy and Sorrow); Payoff with Love; Candle in the Wind. **1958** True Love; Triple Betrayal; Boroya no Shunju; Sonokoi Matta Nashi; The Country Boss; Equinox Flower; The Invisible Wall. **1959** Waiting for Spring; No Greater Love; Fufu Gassho; Good Morning; Highteen; Map of the Ocean; Road to Eternity; Tokyo Omnibus; Showdown at Dawn; Fine Fellow. **1960** The Scarlet Flower; Hot Corner Murder; White Pigeon; Of Men and Money; Women of Kyoto; Wild Trio; Study; Late Autumn; The Grave Tells All; Dry Earth. **1961** Hunting Rifle; Uzu; Blue Current; Enraptured; As the Clouds Scatter; The Bitter Spirit (Immortal Love); Tokyo Detective Saga. **1962** Flower in a Storm; Ballad of a Workman; An Autumn Afternoon; Mama I Need You. **1963** Escape from Hell; The Hidden Profile. **1964** A Marilyn of Tokyo; The Assassin; Brand of Evil; Sweet Sweat.

SAENS, EDDIE
Died: Apr. 24, 1971. Screen actor.

Appeared in: **1958** Enchanted Island.

SAGAL, BORIS
Born: 1923. Died: May 24, 1981, Portland, Ore. (struck by a helicopter blade). Screen actor, film and television director. Married to actress/dancer Marge Champion. Entered films as an actor during the 1950s.

SAGE, FRANCES (Frances Satz aka KATHERINE KEATING)
Born: Feb. 28, 1915, N.Y. Died: Jan. 7, 1963, Malibu, Calif. (suicide). Screen actress. Married to actor Nedrick Young (dec. 1968).

Appeared in: **1936** Without Orders; The Witness Chair. **1944** Mr. Skeffington.

SAGE, G. BYRON
Born: 1914. Died: Jan. 14, 1974, Hollywood, Calif. (heart attack). Screen actor.

Appeared in: **1924** Conductor 1492. **1926** Into Her Kingdom. **1927** Out of the Past. **1928** Clothes Make the Woman. **1930** Courage; One Romantic Night; The Furies.

SAGE, WILLARD (James Willard Sage)
Born: Aug. 13, 1922, Canada. Died: Mar. 17, 1974, Sherman Oaks, Calif. Screen and television actor.

Appeared in: **1954** Dragnet. **1955** It's a Dog's Life; The Tender Trap. **1956** The Brass Legend. **1957** Zero Hour. **1959** Timbukto. **1961** The Great Imposter. **1962** That Touch of Mink. **1963** For Love or Money. **1970** The Forbin Project.

SAHNI, BALRAJ
Born: 1913, India. Died: Apr. 13, 1973, Bombay, India (heart attack). Screen, radio actor and writer. Entered films in 1944.

Appeared in: **1960** Khozhdenie za Tri Morya (The Journey Beyond Three Seas). Other Indian film: Do Bigha Zamin (Two Hectares of Land).

SAHU, KISHORE
Born: 1915, India. Died: Aug. 22, 1980, Bangkok, Thailand (heart attack). Screen actor, film producer, screenwriter and novelist.

Appeared in: **1965** The Guide (aka Survival).

SAIGAL, K. L.
Born: India. Died: Jan. 18, 1947, India. Screen actor and singer.

SAINPOLIS, JOHN See ST. POLIS, JOHN

ST. AUDRIE, STELLA
Born: 1879. Died: May 11, 1925. Screen and stage actress.

Appeared in: **1915** The Trumpet Call.

ST. CLAIR, ANA
Born: 1930. Died: Jan. 23, 1976. Screen actress.

Appeared in: **1960** All the Young Men. **1963** The Caretakers.

ST. CLAIR, LYDIA
Died: Jan. 1, 1970, New Milford, Conn. Screen actress.

Appeared in: **1945** The House on Ninety-Second Street.

ST. CLAIR, MALCOLM
Born: May 17, 1897, Los Angeles, Calif. Died: June 1, 1952, Pasadena, Calif. Screen actor, film director and screenwriter.

Appeared in: **1916** A La Cabaret; Dollars and Sense; The Three Slims. **1917** Lost—A Cook; Her Circus Knight; The Camera Cure; Their Weak Moments; His Perfect Day; An Innocent Villain; Their Domestic Deception; His Baby Doll. **1921** The Goat. **1926** Fascinating Youth.

ST. CLAIR, MAURICE
Born: 1903. Died: May 9, 1970, Los Angeles, Calif. Screen, vaudeville and television actor. Appeared in vaudeville as part of "St. Clair and Day" team.

Appeared in: **1946** Black Angel; Tangier. **1965** Boeing-Boeing.

ST. CLAIR, ROBERT
Born: 1910. Died: June 17, 1967, South Pasadena, Calif. Screen, stage, radio, television actor, screenwriter and playwright.

ST. CLAIR, YVONNE
Born: 1914. Died: Sept. 22, 1971, Seattle, Wash. Screen, vaudeville actress and night club dancer.

Appeared in: **1935** Anna Karenina; A Night at the Opera; A Midsummer Night's Dream. **1936** The Great Ziegfeld.

ST. CLAIRE, ADAH
Born: 1854, N.Y. Died: Aug. 16, 1928, Amityville, N.Y. Screen and stage actress.

ST. CYR, LILLIAN "RED WING"
Born: 1873, Nebr. Died: Mar. 12, 1974, New York, N.Y. Screen actress.

Appeared in: **1912** Red Wing and the Paleface. **1913** The Squaw Man.

ST. DENIS, JOE
Born: 1928. Died: May 15, 1968, Hollywood, Calif. (heart attack). Screen actor.

ST. DENIS, RUTH (Ruth Dennis)
Born: Jan. 20, 1878, Newark, N.J. Died: July 21, 1968, Hollywood, Calif. (heart attack). Dancer, screen and vaudeville actress. Married to actor Ted Shawn (dec. 1973) who was her dancing partner.

Appeared in: **1893** Dance. **1916** Intolerance. **1945** Kitty.

ST. HELIER, IVY (Ivy Aitchison)
Born: England. Died: Nov. 8, 1971, London, England. Screen, stage actress and composer.

Appeared in: **1933** Bitter Sweet. **1945** Henry V (US 1946). **1948** London Belongs to Me (aka Dulcimer Street—US).

ST. JOHN, AL "FUZZY" (aka FUZZY Q. JONES)
Born: Sept. 10, 1893, Santa Ana, Calif. Died: Jan. 21, 1963, Vidalia, Ga. (heart attack). Screen and vaudeville actor. Nephew of actor Roscoe "Fatty" Arbuckle (dec. 1933).

Appeared in: **1914** All at Sea; Bombs and Bangs; Lover's Luck; He Loved the Ladies; In the Clutches of a Gang (aka The Disguised Mayor); Mabel's Strange Predicament; The Knock-Out (aka The Pugilist); Our Country Cousin; The Rounders; The New Janitor (aka The New Porter); Tillie's Punctured Romance. **1915** Our Daredevil Chief; Crossed Love and Swords; Dirty Work in a Laundry (aka A Desperate Scoundrel); Fickle Fatty's Fall; The Village Scandal; Fatty and the Broadway Stars. **1916** Fatty and Mabel Adrift; He Did and He Didn't (aka Love and Lobsters); His Wife's Mistakes; The Other Man; The Moonshiners; The Stone Age (aka Her Cave Man); The Waiters' Ball. **1917** The Butcher Boy; Rough House; His Wedding Night; Fatty at Coney Island; Oh Doctor!; Out West (aka The Sheriff); A Reckless Romeo. **1918** The Bell Boy; Goodnight Nurse; Moonshine; The Cook. **1919** A Desert Hero; Backstage; A Country Hero; The Garage; Camping Out; Love; The Hayseed. **1920** The Scarecrow (short). **1921** The High Sign (short). **1922** All Wet (short). **1924** The Garden of Weeds; plus the following shorts: Stupid, but Brave; His First Car; Never Again; Lovemania. **1925** The following shorts: The Iron Mule; Dynamite Doggie; Curses. **1927** Casey Jones; American Beauty. **1928** Hello Cheyenne; Painted Post. **1929** The Dance of Life; She Goes to War. **1930** Land of Missing Men; The Oklahoma Cyclone; Hell Harbor; Western Knights; Two Fresh Eggs. **1931** Aloha; Son of the Plains; The Painted Desert; plus the following shorts: Marriage Rows; That's My Meat; Honeymoon Trio. **1932** Police Court; Law of the North; Riders of the Desert; Fame Street; Bridge Wives (short). **1933** His Private Secretary; Buzzin' Around (short). **1934** Public Stenographer. **1935** Wanderer of the Wasteland; Bar 20 Rides Again; Law of the 45's. **1936** The Millionaire Kid; West of Nevada; Hopalong Cassidy Returns; Trail Dust. **1937** Love Nest on Wheels (short); A Lawman is Born; Outcasts of Poker Flat; Saturday's Heroes; Melody of the Plains; Sing, Cowboy, Sing. **1938** Song and Bullets; The Rangers Roundup; Knight of the Plains; Call of the Yukon; Frontier Scout. **1939** Trigger Pals; She Goes to War. **1940** Friendly Neighbors; Texas Terrors; Murder on the Yukon; Marked Man. **1941** Billy the Kid's Fighting Pals; The Lone Rider in Ghost Town; Apache Kid; Lone Rider Ambushed; A Missouri Outlaw; Billy the Kid Wanted; Billy the Kid's Roundup; The Lone Rider Fights Back. **1942** Law and Order; Billy the Kid Trapped; Billy the Kid's Smoking Guns; Jesse James, Jr.; Stagecoach Express; Arizona Terrors. **1943** My Son, the Hero; Mysterious Rider; Fugitive of the Plains; The Renegade. **1944** Thundering Gunslingers; The Drifter; Law of the Saddle; Wolves of the Range; Wild Horse Phantom; Oath of Vengeance; Rustler's Hideout; Fuzzy Settles Down; I'm from Arkansas; Frontier Outlaws. **1945** Lightning Raiders; Stagecoach Outlaws; Gangster's Den; Devil Riders; Prairie Rustlers; Fighting Bill Carson; Border Badman. **1946**

His Brother's Ghost; Gentlemen with Guns; Terrors on Horseback; Overland Riders; Ghosts of Hidden Valley; Outlaws of the Plains; Shadows of Death; Prairie Badmen; Blazing Frontiers; Colorado Serenade. **1947** Ghost Town Renegades; Fighting Vigilantes; Return of the Lash; Border Feud; Law of the Lash; Pioneer Justice; Cheyenne Takes Over. **1948** Panhandle Trail; Code of the Plains; My Dog Shep; Mark of the Lash; Raiders of Red Rock; Stage to Mesa City; Frontier Fighters. **1949** Dead Man's Gold; Outlaw Country; Son of a Badman; Son of Billy the Kid; Frontier Revenge. **1960** When Comedy Was King (documentary). **1961** Days of Thrills and Laughter (documentary).

ST. JOHN, HOWARD
Born: 1905. Died: Mar. 13, 1974, New York, N.Y. (heart attack). Screen, stage and television actor. Entered films in 1948.

Appeared in: **1949** Shockproof; The Undercover Man. **1950** David Harding, Counterspy; Counterspy Meets Scotland Yard; Custom's Agent; The Men; Mister 880; Seven Eleven Ocean Drive; Born Yesterday; The Sun Sets at Dawn. **1951** Goodbye, My Fancy; Close to My Heart; Saturday's Hero; Starlift; Strangers on a Train; Big Night. **1952** Stop, You're Killing Me. **1954** Three Coins in the Fountain. **1955** The Tender Trap; Illegal; I Died a Thousand Deaths. **1956** World in My Corner. **1959** L'il Abner. **1961** Cry for Happy; One, Two, Three; Sanctuary; Lover, Come Back. **1962** Madison Avenue. **1963** Lafayette. **1964** Fate Is The Hunter; Sex and the Single Girl; Strait-Jacket; Quick, Before It Melts. **1965** Strange Bedfellows. **1967** Matchless; Banning. **1969** Don't Drink the Water.

ST. JOHN, MARGUERITE
Born: 1861, London, England. Died: Oct. 16, 1940, New York, N.Y. Screen and stage actress.

Appeared in: **1930** The Laughing Lady.

ST. JOHN, RICHARD
Died: Feb. 5, 1977. Screen actor.

Appeared in: **1964** Kisses for My President. **1969** That Tender Touch.

ST. MAUR, ADELE
Born: 1888. Died: Apr. 20, 1959, Sunnydale, Calif. (leukemia). Screen and stage actress.

Appeared in: **1933** The Worst Woman in Paris; Broken Dreams. **1935** The Gay Deception; The Melody Lingers On. **1936** The Invisible Ray. **1937** History Is Made at Night; The King and the Chorus Girl; They Won't Forget. **1943** Farmer for a Day (short). **1946** The Razor's Edge. **1952** The Pathfinder. **1953** Little Boy Lost. **1955** Crashout; To Catch a Thief.

ST. PIERRE, CLARA
Born: 1866, Canada. Died: Jan. 30, 1942, Santa Monica, Calif. Stage and screen actress. Entered films approx. 1922.

ST. POLIS, JOHN (aka JOHN SAINPOLIS)
Born: Nov. 24, 1873, New Orleans, La. Died: Oct. 10, 1946. Screen and stage actor.

Appeared in: **1914** Soldiers of Fortune. **1916** The Social Highwayman; The World Against Him. **1917** Sapho; The Mark of Cain; Sleeping Fires. **1920** The Great Lover; Dangerous Business. **1921** Cappy Ricks; The Four Horsemen of the Apocalypse; Old Dad. **1922** Shadows. **1923** Held to Answer; The Hero; A Prince of a King; The Social Code; Souls for Sale; Three Wise Fools; The Untameable; Woman-Proof. **1924** The Folly of Vanity; The Alaskan; A Fool's Awakening; In Every Woman's Life; Three Weeks; Mademoiselle Midnight; The Rose of Paris; Those Who Dance. **1925** The Dixie Handicap; Paint and Powder; My Lady's Lips; The Phantom of the Opera. **1926** The Lily; The Return of Peter Grimm; The Far Cry; The Greater Glory. **1927** Too Many Crooks. **1928** The Grain of Dust; The Gun Runner; Marriage by Contract; A Woman's Way; The Power of Silence; Green Grass Windows. **1929** Coquette; Why Be Good?; Fast Life; The Diplomats. **1930** The Bad One; A Devil with Women; Guilty?; In the Next Room; The Melody Man; Kismet; Party Girl; The Three Sisters; On the Make. **1931** Doctors' Wives; Captain Thunder; Transgression; Men of the Sky; Their Mad Moment; Heartbreak. **1932** Alias the Doctor; Lena Rivers; Symphony of Six Million; Forbidden Company; The Crusader; Gambling Sex. **1933** The World Gone Mad; Sing, Sinner, Sing; Notorious but Nice; Terror Trail; King of the Arena. **1934** Guilty Parents. **1935** Death from a Distance; Lady in Scarlet. **1936** The Border Patrolman; Three on the Trail; Magnificent Obsession; Below the Deadline; The Dark Hour. **1937** Rustlers' Valley; The Shadow Strikes; Paradise Isle; Jungle Menace (serial). **1938** Saleslady; International Crime; Phantom Ranger; Mr. Wong, Detective. **1939** Boy's Reformatory; They Shall Have Music. **1940** Rocky Mountain Rangers; On the Spot; The Haunted House.

SAIS, MARIN

Born: Aug. 2, 1890, San Rafael, Calif. Died: Dec. 31, 1971. Calif. Screen and stage actress.

Appeared in: 1910 Twelfth Night. 1912 A Tenderfoot's Troubles. 1916 The Social Pirates. 1918 The Vanity Pool; His Birthright. 1919 City of Dim Faces; Bonds of Honor. 1920 Thunderbolt Jack (serial). 1921 The Broken Spur; Dead or Alive; The Sheriff of Hope Eternal; The Golden Hope. 1922 Barbed Wire; Riders of the Law. 1923 Good Men and Bad. 1924 Behind Two Guns; The Measure of a Man. 1925 The Red Rider; A Roaring Adventure. 1926 The Wild Horse Stampede. 1927 The Fighting Three; Men of Daring; Rough and Ready. 1928 A Son of the Desert. 1929 Come and Get It. 1938 Pioneer Trail; Phantom Gold. 1939 Juarez and Maximilian. 1940 Wild Horse Range; Two-Gun Sheriff; Deadwood Dick (serial). 1941 Sierra Sue; Saddlemates. 1944 Enemy of Women; Oath of Vengeance; Frontier Outlaws. 1945 Lightning Raiders; Border Badmen. 1946 Rendezvous 24; Terrors on Horseback. 1949 Ride, Ryder, Ride!; The Fighting Redhead; Roll Thunder Roll. 1950 The Cowboy and the Prizefighter.

SAKALL, S. Z. "CUDDLES" (Szdke Szadall and Eugene Gero Szakall)

Born: Feb. 2, 1884, Budapest, Hungary. Died: Feb. 12, 1955, Los Angeles, Calif. (heart attack). Screen, stage, vaudeville actor and author. Appeared in films in Germany, Vienna and Budapest from 1916-1936.

Appeared in: 1916 Suszterherceg; Ujszulott Apa. 1922 Der Stumme von Portici. 1929 Grosstadt Schmetterling. 1930 Zwei Herzen im 3/4 Takt (Two Hearts in Waltz Time); Kopfuber ins Gluk; Why Cry at Parting? 1931 Die Faschingsfee; Der Zinker; Die Frau von der man Spricht; Der Unbekannte Gast; Ihr Junge; Die Schwebende Jungfrau; Ich Heirate Meinen Mann (aka Her Wedding Night); Meine Cousine aus Warschau. 1932 Ich will Nicht Wissen; Wer du Bist; Gluk uber Nacht; Melodie der Liebe; Eine Stadt Steht Kopf; Muss Man Sich Gleich Scheiden Lassen? 1933 Eine Frau Wie; Scandal in Budapest; Grossfurstin Alexandra; Mindent a Noert; Az Ellopot Szerda. 1934 Helyet az Oregeknek; Fruhlingsstimmen; Romance in Budapest. 1935 Harom es fel Musketas; Baratsagos Arcot Kerek; Tagebuch der Geliebten; 4-1/2 Musketiere; Smile, Please. 1936 Mircha. 1938 The Affairs of Maupassant. 1940 It's a Date; Spring Parade; The Lilac Domino; Florian; My Love Came Back. 1941 Ball of Fire; The Devil and Miss Jones; The Man Who Lost Himself; That Night in Rio. 1942 Casablanca; Yankee Doodle Dandy; Seven Sweethearts; Broadway. 1943 Wintertime; Thank Your Lucky Stars; The Human Comedy. 1944 Hollywood Canteen; Shine On, Harvest Moon. 1945 The Dolly Sisters; Christmas in Connecticut; Wonder Man; San Antonio. 1946 Two Guys from Milwaukee; Never Say Goodbye; The Time, the Place and the Girl; Cinderella Jones. 1947 Cynthia. 1948 Whiplash; April Showers; Romance on the High Seas; Embraceable You. 1949 Look for the Silver Lining; In the Good Old Summertime; My Dream Is Yours; Oh, You Beautiful Doll; It's a Great Feeling. 1950 Tea for Two; Daughter of Rosie O'Grady; Montana; A Swing of Glory. 1951 Lullaby of Broadway; Sugarfoot; Painting the Clouds with Sunshine; It's a Big Country. 1953 Small Town Girl. 1954 The Student Prince.

SAKER, ANNIE

Born: Mar. 13, 1882, England. Died: Oct. 8, 1932, Essex, England. Screen and stage actress. Daughter of stage actress Maria Saker (dec. 1902).

Appeared in: 1916 The Lifeguardsman (US 1917).

SALAS, PACO (Francisco Lago Severino)

Born: 1875. Died: Dec. 24, 1964, Havana, Cuba. Screen, stage, radio and television actor.

SALE, CHARLES "CHIC"

Born: Aug. 25, 1885, Huron, S.Dak. Died: Nov. 7, 1936, Los Angeles, Calif. (pneumonia). Screen, stage and vaudeville actor.

Appeared in: 1922 His Nibs. 1924 The New School Teacher. 1929 Marching On. 1931 The Star Witness. 1932 Stranger in Town; When a Feller Needs a Friend; The Expert; The Hurry Call. 1933 The Chief; Men of America; Lucky Day; Lucky Dog; Dangerous Crossroads. 1934 An MGM short; Treasure Island. 1935 An MGM short; Rocky Mountain Mystery. 1936 An MGM short; It's a Great Life; Man Hunt; The Gentleman from Louisiana; The Man I Marry. 1937 You Only Live Once.

SALE, FRANCES

Born: 1892. Died: Aug. 6, 1969, Hollywood, Calif. Screen actress and opera performer. Appeared in silent films.

SALISBURY, MONROE

Born: 1876, Angola, N.Y. Died: Aug. 7, 1935, San Bernardino, Calif. (skull facture from fall). Screen and stage actor.

Appeared in: 1914 The Virginian; The Man from Home; The Squaw Man; Rose of the Rancho. 1915 The Lamb; Double Trouble; The Goose Girl. 1916 Ramona. 1921 The Barbarian. 1922 The Great Alone. 1930 The Jade Box (serial).

SALMONOVA, LYDA

Born: 1889, Prague, Czechoslovakia. Died: 1968, Prague, Czechoslovakia. Screen actress and dancer. Married to actor Paul Wegener (dec. 1948).

Appeared in: 1912 Die Loewenbraut; Sumurun. 1913 Der Student von Praag; Die Verfuehrte (aka Geheimnisse des Blutes). 1914 Evintrude, die Geschichte Eines Abenteurers; Der Golem; Die Ideale Gattin. 1916 Ruebezahls Hochzeit; Der Yoghi (aka Das Haus des Yoghi). 1917 Der Golem und die Taenzerin; Hans Trutz im Schlaraffenland. 1918 Der Fremde Fuerst; Der Rattenfaenger von Hameln (The Pied Piper of Hameln). 1919 Der Galeerenstraefling. 1920 Der Golem, wie er in die Welt Kam; Steuermann Holck. 1921 Die Taenzerin Barerina; Der Verlorene Schatten; Das Weib des Pharao (The Loves of Pharaoh—US 1922, aka Pharaoh's Wife); Irrende Seelen (aka Sklaven der Sinne, and aka Der Idiot). 1922 Herzog Ferrantes Ende; Lukrezia Borgia; Monna Vanna (US 1925). 1928 The Lost Shadow.

SALTER, HAROLD "HAL"

Died: May, 1928, Los Angeles, Calif. (influenza). Screen, stage and vaudeville actor.

Appeared in: 1927 The Red Raiders; The Royal American. 1928 The Canyon of Adventure; The Code of the Scarlet.

SALTER, THELMA

Died: Nov. 17, 1953, Hollywood, Calif. Screen actress. Entered films as a child actress in silents. Married to producer Edward Kaufman.

Appeared in: 1914 Curse of Humanity. 1915 The Alien; Matrimony. 1916 The Wasted Years; The Jungle Flashlight. 1917 The Crab; Happiness. 1918 Selfish Yates. 1920 Huckleberry Finn.

SAMBERG, ARNOLD

Born: 1899. Died: May 3, 1936, Alpine, Calif. Screen actor. Appeared in silents. Was stand-in Joel McCrea.

SAMPSON, TEDDY (aka TEDDY SAMSON)

Born: Aug. 8, 1895, New York, N.Y. Died: Nov. 24, 1970, Woodland Hills, Calif. (cancer). Screen actress. Married to actor Ford Sterling (dec. 1939).

Appeared in: 1916 Triangle films. 1921 Bits of Life; The Chicken in the Case. 1922 Outcast. 1923 The Bad Man.

SAMSON, IVAN

Born: Aug. 28, 1895, London, England. Died: May 1, 1963, London, England. Screen, stage, radio and television actor.

Appeared in: 1920 Nance. 1923 I Will Repay (aka Swords and the Woman—US 1924); The Loves of Mary, Queen of Scots (aka Marie, Queen of Scots). 1927 The Fake. 1934 White Ensign; Blossom Time (aka April Romance—US 1937). 1935 Royal Cavalcade (aka Regal Cavalcade—US); Honours Easy (The Student's Romance). 1936 Hail and Farewell. 1945 Waltz Time. 1949 Golden Arrow (aka Three Men and a Girl). 1950 Paul Temple's Triumph (US 1951). 1951 The Browning Version. 1953 Innocents in Paris (US 1955). 1957 You Pay Your Money.

SAMUELS, MAURICE

Born: Jan. 13, 1885, Rumania. Died: Aug. 1, 1964, Los Angeles, Calif. (heart attack). Screen actor.

Appeared in: 1949 Oh You Beautiful Doll; Thieves' Highway. 1950 Black Hand. 1951 Rhythm Inn. 1953 Pickup on South Street.

SAMUELS, RAE

Born: 1886. Died: Oct. 24, 1979, New York, N.Y. Screen and vaudeville actress. Known as "The Blue Streak of Vaudeville."

Appeared in: 1933 A Universal short.

SANBERG, GUS (Gustave E. Sanberg)

Born: Feb. 23, 1896, Long Island City, N.Y. Died: Feb. 3, 1930, Los Angeles, Calif. Professional baseball player and screen actor.

Appeared in: 1929 Fast Company.

SANBORN, FRED C.
Born: 1899, Mass. Died: Mar. 9, 1961, Cupertino, Calif. Screen, stage and vaudeville actor. Billed in vaudeville with Ted Healy as "Ted Healy and His Racketeers."

Appeared in: **1930** Soup to Nuts. **1943** Crazy House.

SANCHEZ, JOAQUIN
Born: 1923. Died: Sept. 12, 1966. Screen actor and stuntman.

SANDE, EARL H.
Born: Nov. 13, 1898, Groton, S.Dak. Died: Aug. 19, 1968. Bronco buster, jockey, horse trainer and screen actor.

Appeared in: **1924** The Great White Way.

SANDE, WALTER
Born: 1906, Denver, Colo. Died: Feb. 22, 1972, Chicago, Ill. (heart attack). Screen and television actor.

Appeared in: **1937** Life of the Party. **1938** Tenth Avenue Kid; Ladies in Distress; Arson Gang Buster; Goldwyn Follies. **1939** Good Girls Go to Paris; Eternally Yours; Blondie Meets the Boss; Dad for a Day (short). **1940** Kitty Foyle; You Can't Fool Your Wife. **1941** The Iron Claw (serial); Confessions of Boston Blackie; Parachute Battalion; Great Guns; Citizen Kane. **1942** Commandos Strike at Dawn; My Sister Eileen; To the Shores of Tripoli; Don Winslow of the Navy (serial); Sweetheart of the Fleet; A-Haunting We Will Go; Timber. **1943** Reveille with Beverly; Corvette K-225; The Purple V; After Midnight with Boston Blackie; The Chance of a Lifetime; Gung Ho!; Air Force. **1944** Thirty Seconds Over Tokyo; To Have and Have Not; I Love a Soldier; The Singing Sheriff. **1945** The Daltons Ride Again; Along Came Jones; What Next, Corporal Hargrove?; The Last Installment (short); The Spider. **1946** The Blue Dahlia; Nocturne; No Leave, No Love. **1947** The Red House; The Woman on the Beach; Wild Harvest; Christmas Eve; In Self Defense; Killer McCoy. **1948** Prince of Thieves; Blonde Ice; Half Past Midnight; Wallflower; Perilous Waters. **1949** Bad Boy; Canadian Pacific; Strange Bargain; Joe Palooka in the Counterpunch; Miss Mink of 1949; Tucson; Rim of the Canyon. **1950** The Kid from Texas; Dark City; Dakota Lil. **1951** Payment on Demand (aka Story of Divorce); Tomorrow Is Another Day; A Place in the Sun; The Basketball Fix; The Racket; I Want You; Warpath; Rawhide; Fort Worth; Red Mountain. **1952** Red Planet Mars; Duel at Silver Creek; Mutiny; Bomba and the Jungle Girl; Steel Trap. **1953** The Great Sioux Uprising; War of the Worlds; Powder River; The Kid from Left Field; A Blueprint for Murder. **1954** Apache; Overland Pacific; Bad Day at Black Rock. **1955** Wichita; Texas Lady. **1956** Anything Goes; The Maverick Queen; Gun Brothers; Canyon River. **1957** Johnny Tremain; Drango; The Iron Sheriff. **1959** Last Train from Gun Hill. **1960** Gallant Hours; Sunrise at Campobello; Oklahoma Territory; Noose for a Gunman. **1964** The Quick Gun. **1965** Young Dillinger; I'll Take Sweden. **1966** The Navy vs. the Night Monsters. **1969** Death of a Gunfighter.

SANDERS, GEORGE
Born: July 3, 1906, St. Petersburg, Russia. Died: Apr. 25, 1972, Casteldelfels, Spain (suicide—overdose of barbiturates). Screen, stage, television actor and author. Divorced from Elsie Pool and actresses Zsa Zsa and her sister Magda Gabor. Married to actress Benita Hume (dec. 1967) and after her death married Magda. Brother of Tom Conway (dec. 1967). Won 1950 Academy Award for Best Supporting Actor in All About Eve.

Appeared in: **1936** Dishonour Bright; The Man Who Could Work Miracles (US 1937); My Second Wife; Llyods of London; Things to Come; Find the Lady; Strange Cargo (US 1940). **1937** Love is News; Slave Ship; The Lady Escapes; Lancer Spy. **1938** International Settlement; Four Men and a Prayer. **1939** So This Is London (US 1940); The Saint Strikes Back; The Saint in London; Nurse Edith Cavell; Allegheny Uprising; Confessions of a Nazi Spy; The Outsider (US 1940); Mr. Moto's Last Warning. **1940** Green Hell; The Saint's Double Trouble; The House of the Seven Gables; Rebecca; Foreign Correspondent; Bitter Sweet; The Son of Monte Cristo; The Saint Takes Over. **1941** Rage in Heaven; The Gay Falcon; Man Hunt; Sundown; A Date with the Falcon; The Saint in Palm Springs. **1942** Her Cardboard Lover; Tales of Manhattan; The Moon and Sixpence; Son of Fury; The Falcon's Brother; The Falcon Takes Over; Quiet Please, Murder!; The Black Swan. **1943** This Land Is Mine; Paris After Dark; They Came to Blow Up America; Appointment in Berlin. **1944** The Lodger; Action in Arabia; Summer Storm. **1945** The Picture of Dorian Gray; Hanover Square; Uncle Harry (aka The Strange Affair of Uncle Harry). **1946** A Scandal in Paris; The Strange Woman; Never Say Goodbye. **1947** Forever Amber; The Ghost and Mrs. Muir; The Private Affairs of Bel Ami; Lured. **1948** Personal Column. **1949** The Fan (aka Lady Windermere's Fan); Samson and Delilah. **1950** All

About Eve. **1951** I Can Get It for You Wholesale (aka Only the Best); The Light Touch. **1952** Ivanhoe; Captain Black Jack; Assignment Paris. **1953** Call Me Madame. **1954** Witness to Murder; King Richard and the Crusaders. **1955** Jupiter's Darling; Moonfleet; The Scarlet Coat; The King's Thief; Night Freight. **1956** Never Say Goodbye; While the City Sleeps; That Certain Feeling; Death of a Scoundrel. **1957** The Seventh Sin. **1958** The Whole Truth; From the Earth to the Moon; Outcasts of the City. **1959** That Kind of Woman; A Touch of Larceny (US 1960); Solomon and Sheba. **1960** The Last Voyage; Village of the Damned; Bluebeard's Ten Honeymoons; Cone of Silence (aka Trouble in the Sky—US 1961). **1961** Five Golden Hours; The Rebel (aka Call Me Genius—US). **1962** In Search of the Castaways; Operation Snatch. **1963** The Cracksman; Cairo; Mondo di Notte (aka Ecco—US 1966—narrator). **1964** Dark Purpose; A Shot in the Dark. **1965** The Amorous Adventures of Moll Flanders (aka Moll Flanders). **1966** The Quiller Memorandum; Eiser Spielt Falsch (aka Trunk to Cairo—US). **1967** Warning Shot; Good Times; The Jungle Book (voice). **1968** Rey de Africa (King of Africa aka One Step to Hell—US 1969). **1969** Thin Aires (aka Invasion of the Body Stealers and The Body Stealers—US 1970); The Candy Man. **1970** The Kremlin Letter.

SANDERS, COL. HARLAND
Born: 1890. Died: Dec. 16, 1980, Louisville, Ky. (leukemia and pneumonia). Screen and television actor. Founder of "Kentucky Fried Chicken" food chain.

Appeared in: **1967** The Big Mough. **1970** The Phynx; Hell's Bloody Devils (aka Operation M).

SANDERS, HUGH
Born: 1912. Died: Jan. 9, 1966. Screen and television actor.

Appeared in: **1950** Storm Warning; The Magnificent Yankee; The Damned Don't Cry; The Great Rupert; Mister 880; Mrs. O'Malley and Mr. Malone. **1951** Flying Leathernecks; Sugarfoot; Three Guys Named Mike; That's My Boy; Along the Great Divide; Strictly Dishonorable; Tomorrow Is Another Day; I Was a Communist for the FBI; Only the Valiant; The Careless Years; The Sellout. **1952** Indian Uprising; The Fighter; Something for the Birds; Boots Malone; The Pride of St. Louis; Montana Territory; The Winning Team; The First Time; Last of the Comanches. **1953** Thunder Over the Plains; City of Bad Men; Here Come the Girls; Gun Belt; Scared Stiff; The Glass Web. **1954** Cattle Queen of Montana; The Wild One; Silver Lode; Shield for Murder; Untamed Heiress. **1955** I Died a Thousand Times; The Last Command; Top Gun; Glory; I Cover the Underworld; Finger Man; The Chicago Syndicate. **1956** One False Step; Glory; The Peacemaker. **1957** Jailhouse Rock; Chain of Evidence; The Phantom Stagecoach; The Guns of Fort Petticoat; The Careless Years. **1958** Going Steady; Voice in the Mirror; Life Begins at 17. **1959** Never Steal Anything Small; The Beat Generation; Don't Give Up the Ship. **1960** The Music Box Kid; Cage of Evil. **1961** Man-Trap. **1962** Panic in Year Zero; The Wild Westerners; To Kill a Mockingbird. **1964** Apache Rifles.

SANDERS, SCOTT
Born: 1888. Died: Dec. 2, 1956. Screen actor.

Appeared in: **1930** Scotch Taffy (short). **1954** Lilacs in the Spring (aka Let's Make Up—US 1956).

SANDERSON, JULIA (Julia Sackett)
Born: Aug. 20, 1888, Springfield, Mass. Died: Jan. 27, 1975, Springfield, Mass. Screen, stage, vaudeville and radio actress. Divorced from jockey/actor Tod Sloan (dec. 1933). Married to radio actor Frank Crumit (dec. 1943). Daughter of stage actor Albert Sanderson (dec.).

Appeared in: **1917** The Runaway.

SANDFORD, "TINY" (Stanley J. Sandford)
Born: Feb. 26, 1894, Osage, Iowa. Died: Oct. 29, 1961. Screen and stage actor. Married to actress Edna Sandford. Entered films in 1910.

Appeared in: **1919** Blind Husbands. **1922** The World's Champion; Don't Shoot. **1923** Breaking into Society. **1924** Paying the Limit. **1927** Ginsberg the Great; Sailors, Beware (short); The Second Hundred Years (short). **1928** The Gate Crasher; The Circus; Flying Elephants (short); From Soup to Nuts (short). **1929** Rio Rita; The Far Call; The Iron Mask; plus the following shorts: Big Business; Double Woopee; The Hoose-Gow. **1930** The following shorts: Blotto; Below Zero; The Laurel-Hardy Murder Case; Fifty Million Husbands; Doctor's Orders. **1931** The following shorts: Pardon Us; High Gear; Come Clean; Bargain Days; Beau Hunks. **1932** The Chimp (short); Too Many Women (short). **1933** The Warrior's Husband; The Devil's Brother; plus the following shorts: Fits in a Fiddle; Midnight Patrol; Beauty and the Bus; Busy Bodies. **1934** Babes in Toyland; plus the following shorts: Hi Neighbor; Washee Ironee; I'll Take Vanilla; Another Wild Idea;

You Said a Hateful; Woman Haters. **1935** Treasure Blues (short); The Timid Young Man (short). **1936** Mummy's Boys; Our Relations; High Beer Pressure (short); Modern Times. **1940** Trailer Tragedy (short); Slightly at Sea (short). **1950** Revenge is Sweet (reissue of 1934 film Babes in Toyland). **1965** Laurel and Hardy's Laughing Twenties (doc.).

SANDOW, EUGENE
Born: 1867, Konigsberg, Germany. Died: Oct. 14, 1925, London, England (cerebral hemorrhage). Professional strong man who appeared in at least one pre-1900 film.

SANDQUIST, HANS
Born: 1896, Stockholm, Sweden. Died: Feb. 23, 1935, Long Island City, N.Y. Screen and stage actor.

SANDRINI, LUIS "FELIPE"
Born: 1905. Died: July 5, 1980, Buenos Aires, Argentina (cerebral hemorrhage). Screen, stage, radio and television actor. Married to actress Malvina Pastorino.

Appeared in: **1934** Riachuelo. **1935** Los Tres Berretines. **1938** Loco Lindo (Crazy Dandy). **1939** El Canillita y la Dama (The Newsie and the Lady). **1963** La Cigarra no es un Bicho (The Cicada Is Not An Insect, aka The Games Men Play—US 1968). **1964** Placeres Conyugales (Conjugal Pleasures).

SANDROCK, ADELE
Born: 1864, Rotterdam, Holland. Died: Aug. 30, 1937, Berlin, Germany. Screen and stage actress.

Appeared in: **1915** Marianne, ein Weib aus dem Volke. **1919** Der Galeerenstraefling; Gebannt und Erloest; Malaria. **1920** Brandherd; Das Goldene Netz; Patience. **1921** Grausige Naechte; Mariaza, Genannt die Schmugglermadonna; Der Roman der Christine von Herre; Die Taenzerin Barberina. **1922** Kinder des Finsternis; Lukrezia Borgia; Die Taenzerin Navorro; Absturz (Downfall); Dr. Mabuse der Spieler (Dr. Mabuse, the Gambler). **1923** Der Hof ohne Lachen; Die Lieben Einer Koenigin; Die Magyarenfuerstin (aka Eine Zirkusromanze). **1924** Die Fahrt ins Verderben; Helena; Die Radio-Heirat; Die Schmetterlingsschlacht. **1925** Aschermittwoch; Das Maedchen mit der Protektion. **1926** Deutsche Herzen am Deutschen Rhein; Nixchen; Trude, die Sechzehnjaerige; Die Wasse von Lowood. **1927** Arme Kleine Sif; Drei Niemandskinder; Feme; Fruehere Verhaeltnisse; Die Geliebte; Der Himmel auf Erden; Im Luxuszug; Die Leichte Isabell; Das Maedchen mit den Fuenf Nullen; Ein Rheinisches Maedchen Beim Rheinischen Wein; Die Rollende Kugel; Das Schicksal Einer Nacht; Die Stadt der Tausend Freuden; Deutsche Frauen—Deutsche Treue; Koenigin Luise (Queen Luise). **1928** Kaczmarek; Der Ladenprinz; Leontines Ehemaenner; Lotte; Mary Lou, Sechs Maedchen Suchen Nachtquartier; Serenissimus und die Letzte Jungfrau; Die Zirkusprinzessin. **1929** Aufruhr im Junggesellenheim; Die Drei um Edith; Der Erzieher Meiner Tochter; Frauelein Else; Katherina Knie; Verirrte Jugend. **1930** Donauwalzer; Der Naechste, Bitte; Die Grosse Sehnsucht; Seitensprueage; 1000 Worte Deutsch; Die Zaertlichen Verwandten; Ein Walzer im Schlafcoupe; Eine Freundin so Goldig wie Du; Skandal um Eva (The Eva Scandal—US 1931). **1931** Die Foresterchristl; Die Schlacht von Bademuende; Strohwitwer; Walzerparadies; Der Kongress Tanzt; Jeder Fragt Nach Erika; Die Schwebende Jungfrau; Der Verjuengte Adolar; Die Koenigin Einer Nacht; Der Schrecken der Garnison (US 1932); Ihre Majestaet die Liebe (US 1933); Keine Feier ohne Meyer (US 1932). **1932** Das Schoene Abenteuer; Ballhaus Goldener Engel; Liebe, Scherz und Ernst; Liebe auf den Ersten Ton; Ein Steinreicher Mann; Der Verliebte Blasekopp; Ein Toller Einfall; Der Sieger (The Victor); Der Tolle Bomberg (US 1935); Friedrike (US 1933); Einmal Mocht' ich Keine Sorgen Haben (US 1933); Goldblondes Maedchen, ich Schenk' Dir Mein Herz—Ich bin ja so Verleibt ... (aka Der Gluckszylinder—US 1934); Der Grosse Bluff (aka Schuesse in der Nacht); Kaiserwalzer (aka Audienz in Ischl, and aka Heut' Macht die Welt Sonntag fuer Mich). **1933** Eine Frau wie Du (US 1934); Kleines Maedel—Grosses Glueck; Gleuckliche Reise; Morgenrot (Dawn, Red Dawn); Die Tochter des Regiments (US 1934, aka Die Regimentstochter). **1934** Da Stimmt was Nicht; Alles Hoert auf Mein Kommando; Der Fluechtling aus Chikago; Ich Sehne Mich Nach Dir (US 1936); Zigeunerblut (US 1935, aka Ungarmaedel); Petersburger Naechte (aka Walzer an der Newa); Der Fall Benken (aka Ueberfall im Hotel); Ich Sing' Mich in Dein Herz Hinein (US 1935); Ein Walzer fuer Dich (US 1936); Die Toechter Ihrer Exzellenz; Der Herr ohne Wohnum; Der Letzte Walzer; Die Englische Heirat; Der Herr Senator (aka Die Fliegende Ahnfrau); Gern hab' ich die Frau'n Gekuesst (aka Paganini). **1935** Der Himmel auf Erden (and 1927 version); Mach'

Mich Gleucklich; Kirschen in Nachbars Garten (US 1937); Es Waren Zwei Junggesellen; Eva (aka Eva, das Fabrikmaedel—US 1938); Ich Liebe Alle Frauen; Fruehjahrsparade; Alle Tage ists Kein Sonntag (US 1936); Der Blaue Diamant; Ein Teufelskerl (aka A Devil of a Fellow—US 1938); Ein Falscher Fuffziger (US 1937); Der Kampf mit dem Drachen; Der Gefangene des Koenigs; Amphitryon (aka Aus den Wolken Komt das Glueck (Luck Comes from the Clouds—US 1938)); Knox und die Lustigen Vagabunden (aka Zirkus Saran). **1936** Der Schuechterne Casanova; Der Favorit der Kaiserin (The Favorite of the Empress—US 1939); Die Grosse und die Kleine Welt; Skandal um die Fledermaus; Engel mit Kleinen Fehlern; Die Puppenfee; Flitterwochen; Rendezvous in Wien (US 1938). **1937** Die Grosse Adele.

SANDS, DIANA
Born: 1934, New York. Died: Sept. 21, 1973, New York, N.Y. (cancer). Black screen, stage and television actress.

Appeared in: **1954** Executive Suite. **1957** Garment Jungle. **1961** A Raisin in the Sun (stage and film versions). **1963** An Affair of the Skin. **1964** Ensign Pulver (aka Mr. Pulver and the Captain). **1970** Mr. Landlord. **1971** Doctors' Wives. **1972** Georgia, Georgia. **1974** Willie Dynamite; Honeybaby, Honeybaby.

SANDS, DOROTHY
Born: Mar. 5, 1893, Cambridge, Mass. Died: Sept. 11, 1980, Croton-on-Hudson, N.Y. Screen, stage and television actress.

SANDS, GEORGE
Born: 1900. Died: Dec. 7, 1933, Hollywood, Calif. Screen actor and screenwriter.

SANFORD, AGNES
Died: Nov. 27, 1955, Staten Island, N.Y. Screen, stage and vaudeville actress.

SANFORD, ALBERT, JR. "BERT"
Born: 1893, New York, N.Y. Died: Feb. 10, 1953, New York, N.Y. Screen actor and film sales executive. Entered films as an actor with D. W. Griffith at Biograph Studios.

SANFORD, ERSKINE
Born: 1886. Died: July 7, 1969. Screen actor.

Appeared in: **1940** Pop Always Pays. **1941** Citizen Kane. **1942** The Wife Takes a Flyer; The Magnificent Ambersons. **1944** Enemy of Women; Uncertain Glory. **1945** Ministry of Fear; Spellbound; Girls of the Big House; A Tree Grows in Brooklyn. **1946** From This Day Forward; Crack-Up; Angel on My Shoulder; The Best Years of Our Lives. **1947** Possessed; Mourning Becomes Electra; The Voice of the Turtle. **1948** Letter from an Unknown Woman; The Lady from Shanghai; Kidnapped; MacBeth; Texas, Brooklyn and Heaven; The Wake of the Red Witch. **1949** Impact; Night Unto Night. **1950** Sierra.

SANFORD, RALPH
Born: May 21, 1899, Springfield, Mass. Died: June 20, 1963, Van Nuys, Calif. (heart ailment). Screen actor.

Appeared in: **1937** Sea Racketeers; Escape By Night. **1938** Blondes at Work; If I Were King; Angels With Dirty Faces; The Great Waltz; The Patient in Room 18; Give Me a Sailor. **1939** Little Accident; The Star Maker; They Asked for It; Kid Nightingale. **1940** Gaucho Serenade; Alias the Deacon; Carolina Moon; Three Cheers for the Irish. **1941** What's a Dummy? (short); High Sierra. **1942** Wildcat; I Live on Danger; My Favorite Spy; Torpedo Boat. **1943** Minesweeper; High Explosive; Ladies' Day; Aerial Gunner. **1944** Lost in a Harem. **1945** Thunderhead, Son of Flicka; The Bullfighters; High Powered. **1946** They Made Me a Killer; The Best Years of Our Lives; Girl on the Spot; It Shouldn't Happen to a Dog; Sioux City Sue; My Pal Trigger. **1947** Linda, Be Good; Hit Parade of 1947; Copacabana. **1948** Let's Live Again; French Leave; Shaggy; Winner Take All. **1949** Champion. **1950** Cow Town; Father's Wild Game; So You Think You're Not Guilty (short); The Glass Menagerie; Hi-Jacked; Rogue River; Union Station. **1951** Danger Zone; Behave Yourself; My Favorite Spy; Bright Victory; Fort Defiance; Kentucky Jubilee; Let's Make It Legal. **1952** A Girl in Every Port; Somebody Loves Me; Sea Tiger. **1953** Count the Hours. **1954** The Forty Niners; River of No Return. **1955** The Seven Year Itch; To Hell and Back; The Lieutenant Wore Skirts; Night Freight; Shotgun. **1956** Blackjack Ketchum, Desperado; Uranium Boom. **1957** All Mine to Give. **1958** Alaska Passage; The Big Country. **1959** The Purple Gang; The Remarkable Mr. Pennypacker. **1960** Cage of Evil.

SANGER, BERT
Born: 1894. Died: Sept., 1969, Blackpool, England. Screen and vaudeville actor. Appeared in "Keystone Kop" comedies.

SANO, SHUJI
Born: 1912. Died: Dec. 21, 1978. Screen, stage and television actor.

Appeared in: **1948** Kaze No Naka No Mendoria (A Hen in the Wind). **1954** Osaka No Yado (An Inn at Osaka). **1955** Jochukko (Maid's Kid). **1960** Carmen Comes Home. **1962** Asu aru Kagiri (aka Ashita aru Kagiri, and aka Till Tomorrow Comes—US). **1968** Kurobe No Taiyo (Tunnel to the Sun—US). **1969** Eiko eno Kurohyo (aka Fight for the Glory—US 1970). **1977** Hishu Monogatari (aka The Story of Melancholy and Sadness).

SANQUER, DAGMAR (Dagmar Worth)
Born: 1904. Died: Dec. 31, 1957, Calif. Screen actress.

SANTAMARIE, MANUEL
Born: Spain. Died: Mar., 1960, Mexico City, Mexico. Screen and television actor.

SANTANA, VASCO
Born: 1890, Portugal. Died: Aug., 1958, Lisbon, Portugal. Screen, stage, radio and television actor.

SANTINA, BRUNO DELLA
Born: 1904. Died: Sept. 1, 1968. Screen actor.

Appeared in: **1960** Pay or Die.

SANTLEY, FREDERIC (Frederic Mansfield)
Born: Nov. 20, 1888, Salt Lake City, Utah. Died: May 14, 1953, Hollywood, Calif. Screen, stage and vaudeville actor. Son of actress Laurene (dec. 1933) and stepson of stage actor Eugene Santley (dec.). Brother of actor/director Joseph Santley (dec. 1971). Entered films with Kalem in 1911.

Appeared in: **1930** Leathernecking. **1931** If I Had a Million. **1933** Double Harness; Morning Glory; Walls of Gold. **1934** Such Women Are Dangerous. **1935** George White's 1935 Scandals. **1936** Walking on Air. **1937** This Is My Affair; She's Got Everything. **1938** Topa Topa. **1942** Yankee Doodle Dandy. **1953** The Farmer Takes a Wife.

SANTLEY, JOSEPH (Joseph Mansfield)
Born: Jan. 10, 1889, Salt Lake City, Utah. Died: Aug. 8, 1971, Los Angeles, Calif. Screen, stage, vaudeville child actor, film director and film producer. Son of actress Laurene (dec. 1933) and stepson of stage actor Eugene Santley (dec.). Brother of actor Frederic Santley (dec. 1953). Married to actress Ivy Sawyer.

SANTLEY, LAURENE
Died: Sept. 22, 1933, Hollywood, Calif. (heart attack). Screen and stage actress. Married to Mr. Mansfield, and later to stage actor Eugene Santley (dec.). Mother of actors Frederic (dec. 1953) and Joseph Santley (dec. 1971).

Appeared in: **1915** Bold Emmett—Ireland's Martyr; The Irish in America.

SANTORO, JACK
Born: Apr. 18, 1898, New York, N.Y. Died: Oct. 23, 1980, Los Angeles, Calif. (stroke). Screen, stage and vaudeville actor. Brother of actor John Santoro.

Appeared in: **1927** The Jazz Singer; Slightly Used. **1928** Ginsberg the Great; Women They Talk About; The Midnight Taxi. **1929** One Stolen Night; Sonny Boy; Frozen River.

SANTOS, ALFREDO CRUZ
Died: May 12, 1977. Screen actor.

Appeared in: **1951** Peking Express.

SANTOS, TIKI
Died: Dec. 10, 1974. Screen actor.

Appeared in: **1962** Advise and Consent.

SANTSCHI, TOM
Born: 1879. Died: Apr. 9, 1931, Hollywood, Calif. (high blood pressure). Screen and stage actor.

Appeared in: **1909** The Power of the Sultan. **1913** The Adventures of Kathlyn (serial). **1914** The Spoilers. **1917** The Garden of Allah. **1918** The Hell Cat. **1919** Shadows; Little Orphan Annie; The Stronger Vow. **1920** The Cradle of Courage; The North Wind's Malice. **1922** Found Guilty; Two Kinds of Women. **1923** Are You a Failure?; Brass Commandments; Tipped Off; Is Divorce a Failure?; Thundering Dawn. **1924** The Street of Tears; The Plunderer; The Storm Daughter; Life's

Greatest Game; Little Robinson Crusoe; The Right of the Strongest. **1925** Barriers Burned Away; Paths to Paradise; The Pride of the Force; The Primrose Path; Beyond the Border; My Neighbor's Wife; Frivolous Sal; The Night Ship; Flaming Love. **1926** The Desert's Toll; Hands Across the Border; Three Bad Men; Forlorn River; The Hidden Way; Her Honor, the Governor; My Own Pal; Siberia; No Man's Gold. **1927** The Third Degree; The Adventurous Soul; Eyes of the Totem; When a Man Loves; The Cruise of the Hellion; The Haunted Ship; Hills of Kentucky; Jim the Conqueror; The Land Beyond the Law; The Overland Stage; Tracked by the Police; Land of the Lawless. **1928** Into No Man's Land; Vultures of the Sea (serial); Crashing Through; Honor Bound; Law and the Man; Land of the Silver Fox; Isle of Lost Men. **1929** The Yellowback; The Shannons of Broadway; The Wagon Master; In Old Arizona. **1930** The Utah Kid; Paradise Island; The Fourth Alarm. **1931** King of the Wild (serial); Phantom of the West (serial); Ten Nights in a Barroom; River's End. **1932** The Last Ride.

SAPELLI, DOMINGO
Born: Argentina. Died: 1961, Argentina. Screen actor.

Appeared in: **1938** El Escuadron Azul (The Blue Squadron).

SAPPINGTON, FAY (Harriet Richardson)
Born: 1897. Died: June 16, 1980, Englewood, N.J. Screen, stage and television actress.

Appeared in: **1943** So Proudly We Hail. **1970** The Owl and the Pussycat.

SAPSAMRUAY, SOMCHIT
Born: 1924, Thailand. Died: July 7, 1980, Bangkok, Thailand (cancer). Screen and television actress. Married to comedian Sawong Sapsamruay.

Appeared in: Wai Olawon (Only Sixteen).

SARDOU, FRENAND
Born: 1910, France. Died: 1976, France? Screen actor.

Appeared in: **1952** Savage Triangle; Forbidden Fruit (US 1959). **1955** Letters from My Windmill (aka The Elixir of Father Gaucher). **1956** The Wild Oat. **1958** La Moucharde (aka Woman of Sin—US 1961). **1960** Picnic on the Grass; M'Sieur la Caille (aka No Morals). **1963** Les Grands Chemins (aka Of Flesh and Blood—US 1964). **1964** Le Gendarme de Saint-Tropez (The Gendarme of St. Tropez—US 1966). **1974** Le Petit Theatre de Jean Renoir.

SARGENT, ALFRED MAXWELL
Born: 1881. Died: Jan., 1949, Kalamazoo, Mich. Stage and screen actor.

SARGENT, SIR MALCOLM
Born: 1895, England. Died: Oct. 2, 1967, England. Musical conductor and screen actor.

Appeared in: **1945** Battle for Music.

SARJEANSTON, KATE
Died: Feb. 16, 1918, N.Y. Screen and stage actress.

Appeared in: **1915** Who's Who in Society.

SARNER, ALEXANDER
Born: Dec. 17, 1892, London, England. Died: Jan. 6, 1948, England? Screen and stage actor.

Appeared in: **1935** The Guv'nor (aka Mister Hobo—US 1936).

SARNO, HECTOR V.
Born: 1880, Naples, Italy. Died: Dec. 16, 1953, Pasadena, Calif. Stage and screen actor. Entered films in 1909.

Appeared in: **1912** The Chief's Blanket. **1921** Cheated Hearts; Diamonds Adrift; The Conflict; The Rough Diamond. **1922** Do and Dare; Arabia; The Wise Kid; While Justice Waits. **1923** Stepping Fast; Girl of the Golden West; Ashes of Vengeance. **1924** The Sea Hawk; The Song of Love; Great Diamond Mystery; Honor Among Men. **1925** As Man Desires; Cobra. **1926** Her Sacrifice; The Temptress. **1927** King of Kings; The Climbers. **1928** Sonia. **1929** Lucky Star; Hearts and Hoofs (short); Laughing at Death; Red Hot Speed. **1930** Oklahoma Cyclone. **1932** Taxi. **1935** The Case of the Curious Bride. **1936** Under Two Flags; Ladies in Love. **1937** Easy Living. **1940** The Mark of Zorro. **1947** Escape Me Never; Night Song.

SARRACINI, GERALD
Born: 1927. Died: Dec. 26, 1957, New York, N.Y. (injuries received in a fight). Screen and stage actor.

Appeared in: **1957** Shadow on the Window.

SARTRE, JEAN-PAUL
Born: June 5, 1905, Paris, France. Died: Apr. 15, 1980, Paris, France. Author, screenwriter and screen actor.

Appeared in: **1952** Life Begins Tomorrow.

SASS, EDWARD
Born: 1858, England. Died: Nov. 15, 1916, England? Screen, stage actor, author and composer.

Appeared in: **1914** In the Ranks. **1916** The Broken Melody; The New Clown.

SATIE, ERIK (Eric Leslie Satie)
Born: May 17, 1866, Honfleur, France. Died: July 1, 1925, France. Musician and screen actor.

Appeared in: **1924** Entr'Acte.

SATO, REIKO
Died: May 28, 1981, Los Angeles, Calif. Screen actor and singer.

Appeared in: **1950** Mother Didn't Tell Me. **1955** Kismet. **1960** Hell to Eternity. **1961** Flower Drum Song. **1963** The Ugly American.

SATZ, LILLIE
Born: 1896. Died: Apr. 11, 1974, Mamaroneck, N.Y. Screen and stage actress. Married to actor Ludwig Satz (dec. 1944).

SATZ, LUDWIG
Born: 1891, Poland. Died: Aug. 31, 1944, New York, N.Y. Screen, stage actor and film director. Married to actress Lillie Satz (dec. 1974).

Appeared in the first Yiddish musical talking film: His Wife's Lover

SAUBERLICH, LU (Liselotte Sauberlich-Lauke)
Born: 1912, Bremen, Germany. Died: Oct., 1976, Berlin, Germany. Screen and stage actress.

Appeared in: **1960** Bumerang (aka Cry Double Cross—US 1962).

SAUERMAN, CARL
Born: 1868, Stockholm, Sweden. Died: Apr. 9, 1924, New York, N.Y. Stage and screen actor.

Appeared in: **1917** The Beautiful Adventure.

SAUM, CLIFFORD
Born: Dec. 18, 1882. Died: Mar., 1943, Glendale, Calif. Screen and stage actor.

Appeared in: **1923** Wandering Daughters. **1925** The Bridge of Sighs. **1927** By Whose Hand?; Stage Kisses; The Tigress; The Siren. **1928** Fashion Madness. **1930** Three Sisters. **1934** Flirtation Walk; The St. Louis Kid. **1935** Alibi Ike; The Goose and the Gander. **1936** Three Men and a Horse; Gold Diggers of 1937. **1937** He Couldn't Say No. **1938** Penrod's Double Trouble; Torchy Gets Her Man; Boy Meets Girl; Gold Is Where You Find It. **1939** The Kid from Kokomo; Nancy Drew-Trouble Shooter. **1940** Ladies Must Live; The Man Who Talked Too Much. **1941** High Sierra; The Man Who Came to Dinner; The Case of the Black Parrot. **1942** Larceny, Inc.; The Male Animal.

SAUNDERS, ALICE
Born: 1873 or 1880, Holyoke, Mass. Died: July 25, 1953, Calif. Screen and stage actress.

Appeared in: **1915** The Blood Seedling. **1917** The Haunted House. **1918** Dolly Does Her Bit.

SAUNDERS, FLORENCE
Born: 1890, Valparaiso, Chile. Died: Jan. 24, 1926, London, England. Screen and stage actress.

Appeared in: **1923** The Wandering Jew.

SAUNDERS, GLORIA
Died: June 4, 1980. Screen and television actress.

Appeared in: **1946** O.S.S. **1950** Cry Danger. **1951** Win, Place and Show. **1952** Red Snow; Captive Women. **1953** The Robe; Prisoners of the Casbah; Six Gun Mesa.

SAUNDERS, JACKIE
Born: Oct. 6, 1892. Died: July 14, 1954, Palm Springs, Calif. Screen and stage actress. Mother of actress Jackie Saunders.

Appeared in: **1914** The Square Triangle; Little Sunbeam. **1915** The Woman from the Sea; A Bolt from the Sky; Ill-Starred Bobbie; The Rose Among the Briars. **1916** The Grip of Evil (serial); A Slave of Corruption; The Flirting Bride; The Better Instinct. **1917** The Wildcat; The Checkmate; A Bit of Kindling. **1920** Drag Harlan. **1921** The Infamous Miss Ravell; Puppets of Fate. **1923** Shattered Reputations; Defying Destiny. **1924** Broken Laws; Alimony; Flames of Desire; The Great Diamond Mystery; The Courageous Coward. **1925** The People vs. Nancy Preston; Faint Perfume. **1936** Gold Diggers of 1937.

SAUNDERS, NELLIE PECK
Born: 1869, Saginaw, Mich. Died: Mar. 3, 1942, Greenwood, S.C. Screen and stage actress.

Appeared in: **1922** Tailor Made Man. **1925** A Little Girl in a Big City; The Mad Dancer. **1926** The Sorrows of Satan. **1927** The Broadway Drifter. **1929** The Hole in the Wall.

SAVAGE, HOUSTON See DEBLASIO, GENE

SAVANT, DEAN DOMINICK
Born: 1898. Died: Nov. 6, 1980, Woodland Hills, Calif. Screen actor.

SAVILLE, GUS
Born: 1857. Died: Mar. 25, 1934, Hollywood, Calif. Screen and stage actor.

Appeared in: **1921** The Wolverine. **1922** Tess of the Storm Country. **1923** Face on the Barroom Floor. **1925** Idaho (serial); Wild West (serial); Fighting Courage. **1926** The High Hand. **1930** The Light of Western Stars.

SAVITHRI
Born: 1936, India. Died: Dec., 1981, Madras. Screen actress. Married to actor Germini Genesan. Appeared in Tamil, Telugu, Malayalam, and Hindu films.

Appeared in: **1954** Pamposh.

SAVO, JIMMY
Born: 1866, Bronx, N.Y. Died: Sept. 6, 1960, Teni, Italy (heart attack). Screen, stage actor, pantominist and juggler.

Appeared in: **1926** Exclusive Rights; prior to 1935 The House Dick (short). **1935** Once in a Blue Moon. **1937** Merry-Go-Round of 1938. **1938** Reckless Living.

SAVOY, HOUSTON See DEBLASIO, GENE

SAWAMURA, KUNITARO (Tomoichi Kato)
Born: 1905, Japan. Died: Nov. 26, 1974, Tokyo, Japan (stroke). Screen and stage actor. Father of actors Hiroyuki Nagato and Mashiko Tsugawa. Brother of actor Daisuke Kato and actress Sadako Sawamura. Entered films during the 1920s.

SAWYER, LAURA
Born: 1885. Died: Sept. 7, 1970, Matawan, N.J. Screen and stage actress. Enter films with Edison Co.

Appeared in: **1912** The Lighthouse Keeper's Daughter. **1913** The Daughter of the Hills; Christian and Moor; The Question Mark; At Jones' Ferry; A Romance of the Cliff Dwellers; Three of a Kind; The Ironmaster; The Doctor; The Sailor's Love Letter; The Stuff That Dreams Are Made Of; Buckskin Jack, the Earl of Gilmore; Leaves of a Romance; The Lighthouse by the Sea; A Perilous Ride; Pull for the Shore, Sailor; The Battle of Trafalgar.

SAXE, TEMPLAR (Templer William Edward Edevein)
Born: Aug. 22, 1865, Redhill, Surrey, England. Died: Mar. 23, 1935, Cincinnati, Ohio. Screen and stage actor.

Appeared in: **1915** The Fates and Flora Fourflush (serial—aka The Ten Billion Dollar Vitaphone Mystery serial); A Lily in Bohemia; The Starring of Flora Finchurch; Myrtle the Manicurist; The Chief's Goat; The Supreme Temptation; Billy's Wager. **1916** The Devil's Prize; Hesper of the Mountains; Winifred the Shop Girl; The Tarantula; The Secret Runner. **1917** Mary Jane's Pa; In the Balance (aka The Hillman); Intrigue; The Fettered Woman; Bobby Takes a Wife. **1921** Bucking the Tiger; A Millionaire for a Day; The Woman God Changed. **1922** Devil's Angel; How Women Love; What Fools Men Are. **1923** In Search of a Thrill; Sidewalks of New York. **1924** Beau Brummel; Captain Blood; Her Night of Romance; Gerald Cranston's Lady. **1925** The Dancers; The Primrose Path; Time—The Comedian. **1926** The White Black Sheep. **1927** For Ladies Only; The Girl from Gay Paree; When a Man Loves. **1928** Beyond London's Lights; What Price Beauty; Valley of Hunted Men.

SAXON, HUGH A.
Born: Jan. 14, 1869, New Orleans, La. Died: May 14, 1945, Beverly Hills, Calif. Screen actor. Entered films in 1916.

Appeared in: 1920 Sand. 1921 High Heels; Seven Years Bad Luck. 1922 The Guttersnipe; Watch Him Step. 1924 Cytherea. 1925 Fightin' Odds. 1926 Hair Trigger Baxter; The Fighting Boob. 1927 Is Your Daughter Safe?; Bulldog Pluck; King of the Herd. 1928 Tracked; Phantom of the Turf; Gypsy of the North. 1929 One Splendid Hour.

SAXON, MARIE
Born: 1904, Lawrence, Mass. Died: Nov. 12, 1941, Harrison, N.Y. Screen, stage, vaudeville actress and dancer.

Appeared in: 1930 The Broadway Hoofer. 1931 Under Suspicion.

SAXON, VIN See HAYDOCK, RONALD "RON"

SAYLES, FRANCIS H.
Born: 1892, Buffalo, N.Y. Died: Mar. 19, 1944, Hollywood, Calif. Screen and stage actor. Entered films approx. 1930.

Appeared in: 1932 Strangers of the Evening; Blonde Venus. 1934 Home on the Range; Bum Voyage (short). 1937 Easy Living; The Black Legion. 1938 The Purple Vigilantes. 1939 Overland with Kit Carson (serial).

SAYLOR, SYD (Leo Sailor)
Born: Mar. 24, 1895, Chicago, Ill. Died: Dec. 21, 1962, Hollywood, Calif. (heart attack). Screen and stage actor. Entered films in 1925.

Appeared in: 1926-27 54 "Syd Saylor" comedies. 1926 Red Hot Leather. 1928 The Mystery Rider (serial). 1929 Just Off Broadway; Shanghai Rose. 1930 Border Legion; Men Without Law; The Light of Western Stars. 1931 Unfaithful; Fighting Caravans; Playthings of Hollywood; The Lawyer's Secret; I Take This Woman; Caught; Sidewalks of New York. 1932 Rule 'Em and Weep (short); Law of the Seas; Million Dollar Legs; Lady and Gent; The Crusader; Tangled Destinies; Horse Feathers. 1933 Justice Takes a Holiday; Man of Sentiment; The Nuisance; Gambling Ship. 1934 Young and Beautiful; The Dude Ranger; The Lost Jungle (serial); When a Man Sees Red; Mystery Mountain (serial). 1935 Star of Midnight; Headline Woman; Code of the Mounted; Men of Action; Ladies Crave Excitement; Wilderness Mail; Here Comes Cookie. 1936 Hitchhike to Heaven; The Last Assignment; Prison Shadows; The Sky Parade; Nevada; The Three Mesquiteers; Kelly the Second; Headin' for the Rio Grande; Secret Valley; The Gorgeous Hussy; The Ex Mrs. Bradford; His Brother's Wife. 1937 Guns in the Dark; Wallaby Jim of the Islands; Wild and Woolly; Arizona Days; Forlorn River; Meet the Boy Friend; Sea Racketeers; The Wrong Road; Exiled to Shanghai; House of Secrets. 1938 Born to the West; Passport Husband; There Goes My Heart; Crashin' Thru Danger; The Black Doll; Little Miss Broadway. 1939 $1,000 a Touchdown; Union Pacific; Geronimo. 1940 Arizona; Abe Lincoln in Illinois; Irene. 1941 Design for Scandal; Sierra Sue; Wyoming Wildcat; The Great American Broadcast; Miss Polly; Borrowed Hero. 1942 Tennessee Johnson; Yankee Doodle Dandy; A Gentleman at Heart; The Man in the Trunk; That Other Woman; Time to Kill; Gentleman Jim; Lady in a Jam; It Happened in Flatbush. 1943 He Hired the Boss; Harvest Melody; Doughboys in Ireland. 1944 Hey, Rookie!; Swingtime Johnny; Three of a Kind. 1945 The Navajo Kid; Bedside Manner; Frisco Sal; See My Lawyer; Brenda Starr, Reporter (serial); Nob Hill. 1946 The Kid from Brooklyn; Six Guns for Hire; Thunder Town; Six Gun Man; Avalanche; Deadline for Murder; The Virginian. 1947 Fun on a Weekend. 1948 Prince of Thieves; Triple Threat; Snake Pit; Racing Luck; Sitting Pretty; The Paleface. 1949 Big Jack; Dancing in the Dark; That Wonderful Urge. 1950 Three Little Words; Mule Train; Cheaper by the Dozen; The Jackpot. 1951 Valley of Fire; The Las Vegas Story. 1952 The Redhead from Wyoming; Abbott and Costello Meet Captain Kidd; The Hawk of Wild River; The Old West; Wagon Team; Belles on Their Toes. 1953 The Tall Texan; Abbott and Costello Go To Mars. 1955 Toughest Man Alive. 1956 Crime in the Streets; A Cry in the Night. 1957 Shoot-Out at Medicine Bend; The Spirit of St. Louis. 1959 Escort West. 1963 The Crawling Hand.

SAYRE, BIGELOW
Died: Sept. 14, 1975. Screen actor.

Appeared in: 1950 The Great Jewel Robbery; Union Station; The Jackpot. 1951 Starlift.

SAYRE, JEFFREY
Born: 1901. Died: Sept. 26, 1974, Los Angeles, Calif. (shot). Screen, stage, vaudeville actor and screen extra. Former president and one of the founders of the Screen Extras Guild.

Appeared in: 1936 Great Guy. 1937 Marked Woman. 1938 Major Difficulties (short). 1939 Mutiny in the Big House; The Oklahoma Kid; The Roaring Twenties; Dark Victory. 1940 'Til We Meet Again. 1941 Manpower. 1942 The Sabateur; Men of San Quentin. 1944 The Purple Heart; In the Meantime, Darling. 1947 Possessed. 1960 Heller in Pink Tights.

SAYRES, MARGARET
Born: 1868. Died: Apr. 17, 1937, Asheville, N.C. Screen and stage actress.

Appeared in: 1914 The Perils of Pauline (serial).

SAZARINA, MARIA
Born: 1914, Germany. Died: Oct. 20, 1959, Hamburg, Germany. Screen actress.

SCADUTO, JOSEPH
Born: 1898. Died: Oct. 19, 1943, Hollywood, Calif. Screen actor.

Appeared in: 1924 Racing Luck.

SCALA, GIA (Giovanna Scoglio)
Born: Mar. 3, 1934, Liverpool, England. Died: Apr. 30, 1972, Hollywood, Calif. (accidental drug overdose). Screen actress.

Appeared in: 1955 All That Heaven Allows (film debut). 1956 The Price of Fear; Four Girls in Town; Never Say Goodbye. 1957 Don't Go Near the Water; The Garment Jungle; Tip on a Dead Jockey; The Big Boodle (aka A Night in Havana). 1958 Ride a Crooked Trail; The Tunnel of Love. 1959 The Two-Headed Spy; Battle of the Coral Sea; The Angry Hills. 1960 I Aim at the Stars. 1961 The Guns of Navarone. 1962 Triumph of Robin Hood. 1966 Operation Delilah.

SCANNELL, JOHN J.
Born: 1887. Died: Feb. 18, 1926, Jackson Heights, N.Y. Screen and stage actor.

Appeared in: 1925 The Shock Punch.

SCANNELL, WILLIAM J.
Born: 1912, Boston, Mass. Died: July 8, 1963, Hollywood, Calif. (heart attack). Screen, vaudeville and television actor.

Appeared in: 1963 The Greatest Story Ever Told.

SCARDON, PAUL
Born: May 6, 1878, Melbourne, Australia. Died: Jan. 17, 1954, Fontana, Calif. (heart attack). Screen, stage actor, film producer and film director. Entered films as an actor with Majestic in 1911. Married to actress Betty Blythe (dec. 1972).

Appeared in: 1914 The Sin of the Mothers; The Juggernaut. 1915 The Goddess (serial). 1941 The Son of Davy Crockett; Lady from Louisiana. 1942 Mrs. Miniver; My Favorite Blonde; A Yank at Eton; Tish. 1944 Today I Hang; The Adventures of Mark Twain. 1945 Kitty. 1946 Down Missouri Way. 1947 Pursued; Magic Town. 1948 Sign of the Ram; Fighting Mad; The Shanghai Chest; Secret Beyond the Door. 1949 Samson and Delilah.

SCARFIOTTI, LODOVICO
Born: Oct. 8, 1933, Turin, Italy. Died: June 8, 1968, Berchtesgaden, Germany (auto crash). Auto racer and screen actor.

Appeared in: 1966 Grand Prix.

SCHABLE, ROBERT
Born: 1873, Hamilton, Ohio. Died: July 1, 1947, Hollywood, Calif. Screen and stage actor.

Appeared in: 1919 The Test of Honor. 1920 On With the Dance. 1921 Experience; Without Limit; Paying the Piper. 1922 Sherlock Holmes; Sisters; A Daughter of Luxury; The Cowboy and the Lady; The Woman Who Fooled Herself; Love's Masquerade. 1923 Bella Donna; Nobody's Money; The Cheat; In Search of a Thrill; Slander the Woman; The Silent Partner. 1924 The Stranger. 1926 Partners Again; Silken Shackles. 1927 Love of Sunya. 1928 Sailors' Wives. 1929 Careers; Man and the Moment.

SCHACHTER, LEON
Born: 1900. Died: Nov. 9, 1974, New York, N.Y. Screen, stage and vaudeville actor. Married to actress Gitel Stein.

Appeared in: 1950 God, Man and Devil.

SCHAEFER, ALBERT
Born: 1916. Died: Oct. 26, 1942, Hollywood, Calif. Screen actor.

Appeared in: 1926 The Set-Up.

SCHAEFER, ANN
Born: 1870, St. Louis, Mo. Died: May 3, 1957, Los Angeles, Calif. Screen and stage actress.

Appeared in: **1913** Angel of the Desert. **1914** Anne of the Golden Heart; Johanna the Barbarian; Ann, the Blacksmith. **1917** Johanna Enlists; A Little Princess; Periwinkle; Melissa of the Hills. **1920** The City of Masks. **1921** Nobody's Kid; The Wolverine; Ghost City. **1922** A Dangerous Game; The Ordeal; The Man Unconquerable. **1923** West of the Water Tower; Main Street. **1924** Love's Wilderness; The Heritage of the Desert. **1925** The Goose Hangs High; Marry Me. **1926** Sparrows. **1927** Three Hours; The Devil Dancer; Sitting Bull at the "Spirit Lake Massacre." **1928** The Night Flyer; Wheels of Chance. **1929** Saturday's Children; Prisoners; Smiling Irish Eyes. **1930** Lilies of the Field.

SCHAEFER, CHARLES N.
Born: 1864. Died: Feb. 5, 1939, Hollywood, Calif. Screen and stage actor.

Appeared in: **1927** Ridin' Luck; Wild Born; Gun-Hand Garrison; Man Power. **1929** The Winged Horseman.

SCHAFFNER, LILLIAN
Born: 1862. Died: Jan. 8, 1930, Los Angeles, Calif. Screen, stage and vaudeville actress.

Appeared in: **1916** The Other Man.

SCHARF, HERMAN "BOO-BOO" (aka HERMAN SCHARFF)
Born: 1901. Died: Apr. 8, 1963, Hollywood, Calif. (heart attack). Screen actor and stuntman.

Appeared in: **1955** The Far Horizons.

SCHARPEGGE, ERNIE
Died: Mar. 11, 1940, Milwaukee, Wis. Professional strongman and screen actor. Appeared in silents.

SCHEFF, FRITZI
Born: 1879, Vienna, Austria. Died: Apr. 8, 1954, New York, N.Y. (natural causes). Screen, stage, vaudeville actress and opera performer.

Appeared in: **1915** The Pretty Mrs. Smith. **1943** Follies Girl.

SCHEINPFLUGOVA, OLGA
Born: 1902, Czechoslovakia. Died: Apr. 14, 1968, Prague, Czechoslovakia. Screen actress.

Appeared in: **1965** A Paty Jezdec Je Strach (The Fifth Horseman is Fear—US 1968).

SCHENCK, JOSEPH T.
Born: 1891, Brooklyn, N.Y. Died: June 28, 1930, Detroit, Mich. (heart disease). Screen, stage and vaudeville actor. Married to stage actress Lillian Broderick (dec. 1946). Was part of vaudeville team with Gus Van (dec. 1968) billed as "Van and Schenck." Do not confuse with film producer Joseph Schenck (dec. 1961).

Together they appeared in: **1927** The Pennant Winning Battery of Songland (short). **1929** Metro Movietone (feature with their lives as a background entitled Take It Big); plus several song short subjects. **1930** They Learned About Women.

SCHENSTROM, CARL
Born: Nov. 13, 1881, Denmark. Died: 1942, Denmark? Screen and stage actor. Partner of Harald Madsen (dec. 1949), with whom he appeared in an act billed as "Fyrtaarnet and Bigoven."

SCHERMAN, BARBARA
Died: Jan. 29, 1935, Cliffside Park, N.J. (gas poisoning). Screen actress.

SCHEU, JUST
Born: 1903, Germany. Died: Aug. 9, 1956, Bad Mergentheim, West Germany (appendicitis). Screen, radio actor, playwright and composer.

SCHEUER, CONSTANCE
Born: 1910. Died: Nov. 27, 1962, Los Angeles, Calif. (heart attack). Screen actress and dancer.

SCHIESKE, ALFRED
Born: 1909, Stuttgart, Germany. Died: July 14, 1970, West Berlin, Germany. Screen, stage and television actor.

Appeared in: **1949** The Affair Blum. **1951** Odette. **1960** A Day Will Come. **1961** Tomorrow Is My Turn.

SCHILDKRAUT, JOSEPH
Born: Mar. 22, 1896, Vienna, Austria. Died: Jan. 21, 1964, New York, N.Y. (heart attack). Screen, stage and television actor. Son of actor Rudolph Schildkraut (dec. 1930). Divorced from actress Elsie Bartlett (dec. 1944). Won 1937 Academy Award for Best Supporting Actor in The Life of Emile Zola.

Appeared in: **1908** The Wandering Jew. **1914** Schlemiehl. **1918** The Life of Theodore Herzl. **1922** Orphans of the Storm. **1923** Dust of Desire. **1924** The Song of Love. **1925** The Road to Yesterday. **1926** Meet the Prince; Young April; Shipwrecked. **1927** The Forbidden Woman; His Dog; King of Kings; The Heart Thief. **1928** The Blue Danube; Tenth Avenue. **1929** The Mississippi Gambler; Show Boat. **1930** Die Sehnsucht jeder Frau; Night Ride; Cock of the Walk. **1931** Carnival. **1932** Blue Danube (US 1934 plus 1928 version). **1934** Viva Villa; Sisters Under the Skin; Cleopatra. **1935** The Crusades. **1936** The Garden of Allah. **1937** Slave Ship; Lancer Spy; The Life of Emile Zola; Souls at Sea; A Star Is Born; Lady Behave. **1938** The Baroness and the Butler; Suez; Marie Antoinette. **1939** Lady of the Tropics; The Rains Came; Pack Up Your Troubles; Mr. Moto Takes a Vacation; Idiot's Delight; The Three Musketeers; The Man in the Iron Mask. **1940** The Shop Around the Corner; Rangers of Fortune; Meet the Wildcat; Phantom Raiders. **1941** The Parson of Panamint. **1945** The Cheaters; Flame of the Barbary Coast. **1946** Monsieur Beaucaire; The Plainsman and the Lady. **1947** Northwest Outpost; End of the Rainbow. **1948** Gallant Legion; Old Los Angeles. **1959** The Diary of Anne Frank. **1961** King of the Roaring Twenties. **1964** Dust of Desire; Song of Love. **1965** The Greatest Story Ever Told.

SCHILDKRAUT, RUDOLPH
Born: 1865, Constantinople, Turkey. Died: July 15, 1930, Los Angeles, Calif. (heart disease). Stage and screen actor. Father of actor Joseph Schildkraut (dec. 1964).

Appeared in: **1925** His People; Proud Heart. **1926** Pals in Paradise; Young April. **1927** A Harp in Hock; King of Kings; Turkish Delight; The Main Event; The Country Doctor. **1928** A Ship Comes In. **1929** Christina.

SCHILLING, AUGUST E. "GUS"
Born: June 20, 1908, New York, N.Y. Died: June 16, 1957, Hollywood, Calif. (heart attack). Screen, stage, burlesque and radio actor. Divorced from burlesque actress Betty Rowland.

Appeared in: **1939** Mexican Spitfire. **1940** Mexican Spitfire Out West. **1941** Citizen Kane; Lucky Devils; It Started With Eve; Appointment for Love; Dr. Kildare's Victory; Ice Capades. **1942** The Magnificent Ambersons; Broadway; You Were Never Lovelier; Moonlight in Havana. **1943** Lady Bodyguard; Hi, Buddy; Hers to Hold; Larceny With Music; The Amazing Mrs. Holliday; Chatterbox. **1944** Sing a Jingle. **1945** See My Lawyer; River Gang; A Thousand and One Nights; It's a Pleasure. **1946** Dangerous Business. **1947** Calendar Girl; Stork Bites Man. **1948** Return of October; Macbeth; The Lady from Shanghai; Angel on the Amazon. **1949** Bride for Sale. **1950** Our Very Own; Hit Parade of 1951. **1951** Honeychile; On Dangerous Ground; Gasoline Alley. **1952** One Big Affair. **1954** She Couldn't Say No. **1955** Run for Cover. **1956** Glory; Bigger Than Life.

SCHILLING, MARGARET
Died: July, 1976, N.Y. Screen, stage, radio actress and singer.

Appeared in: **1931** Children of Dreams.

SCHINDELL, CY (Seymore Schindell)
Born: Mar. 4, 1907, Brooklyn, N.Y. Died: Aug. 24, 1948, Van Nuys, Calif. Screen and stage actor.

Appeared in: **1937** Grips, Grunts and Groans (short). **1938** Sue My Lawyer (short); Soul of a Heel (short). **1939** Rattling Romeo (short); Skinny the Moocher (short). **1944** Gold Is Where You Lose It (short). **1946** Monkey Businessmen (short). **1947** Fright Night (short).

SCHIPA, TITO
Born: 1889, Lecee, Italy. Died: Dec. 16, 1965, New York, N.Y. (heart attack). Screen actor and opera singer.

Appeared in: **1929** Tito Schipa. **1930** Tito Schipa Concert No. 2. **1932** Tre Womane en Frak. **1937** Vivere (To Live—US 1938); Terre de Feu; Chi e'piu Felice de Me? (Who Is Happier That I—US 1940). **1943** In Cerca de Felicita. **1944** Rosalba; Vivere an Cora. **1946** Il' Cavaliere del Sogna. **1947** Follie per l'Opera (Mad About Opera—US 1950). **1951** Soho Conspiracy; I Misteri di Venezia. **1952** The Life of Donizetti.

SCHIPPER, ANNA
Born: 1888. Died: Oct. 16, 1978, Woodland Hills, Calif. Screen extra.

SCHLESSER, JO
Born: 1928, Madagascar. Died: July 7, 1968, Rouen, France (auto racing accident). Auto racer and screen actor.

Appeared in: **1966** Grand Prix.

SCHLETTOW, HANS ADELBERT (aka HANS VON
    SCHLETTOW)
Born: 1888, Frankfurt, Germany. Died: 1945, Berlin, Germany. Screen and stage actor. Entered films in 1919.

Appeared in: **1918** Wenn das Herz in Hass Ergluaht. **1919** Der Breite Weg; Komptesse Doddy; Der Tod aus dem Osten; Die Weissen Rosen von Ravensburg. **1920** Algol; Foehn; Maria Tudor. **1921** Am Roten Kliff; Am Webstuhl der Zeit; Die Frauen vom Gnadenstein; Tobias Buntschuh. **1922** Don Juan; Die Finsternis ist ihr Eigentum; Gespenster; Das Liebesnest; Die Schatten Jener Nacht; Der Todesreigen; Dr. Mabuse der Spieler (Dr. Mabuse, the Gambler—US 1927). **1923** Isn't Life Wonderful (US 1924). **1924** Die Fahrt ins Verderben; Malva; Winterstuerme; So ist das Leben (aka So Spielt das Leben (Such is Life)); Die Nibelungen (including Siegfried—US 1925, and Kriemhilds Rache (Kreimhild's Revenge—US 1928)); Im Namen des Kaisers; Friesenblut; Schiff in Not; Wenn die Liebe Nicht Waer'! **1926** Brennende Grenze; Deutsche Herzen am Deutschen Rhein; Die Eule; Die Flammen Luegen; In Treu Stark; Die Letzte Droschke von Berlin; Sein Grosser Fall; Spitzen. **1927** Die Frauengasse von Algier; Die Frau mit dem Weltrekord; Das Gefaehrliche Alter; Kleinstadtsuender; Klettermaxe; Der Letzte Walzer (The Last Waltz); Aftermath; Mein Heidelberg, ich Kann Dich Nicht Vergessen; Schuldig (US 1928). **1928** Koenigin Luise (Queen Luise); Shadows of Fear; Small Town Sinners; Die Siebzehnjaehrigen; Song; Wenn die Mutter und die Tochter ...; Wolga-Wolga (Volga, Volga—US 1933). **1929** Three Kings; Asphalt; Diane; Heilige oder Dirne; Das Recht der Ungeborenen; Das Donkosakenlied; Das Weib am Kreuze (aka Vergib uns Unsere Schuld). **1930** A Cottage on Dartmoor (aka Escaped from Dartmoor—US); Es Kommt Alle Tage Vor ...; Troika; Die Grosse Sehnsucht; Der Unsterbliche Lump (US 1932); Ein Maedel auf der Reeperbahn (US 1931); Bockbierfest (US 1931). **1931** The Immortal Vagabond; Der Schlemihl (US 1934); Chauffeur Antoinette; Mitternachtsliebe; Gefahren der Liebe; Die Nackte Wahrheit (Nothing But the Truth); Kennst Du das Land (aka Saltarello). **1932** Marschall Vorwaerts; Geheimnis des Blauen Zimmers; Ja, Treu ist die Soldatenliebe (US 1934); Der Tolle Bomberg (US 1935); An Heiligen Wassern (aka Sieg der Liebe). **1933** Ein Gewisser Herrn Gran; Der Jaeger aus Krupfalz; Zimmermaedchen ... Dreimal Klingeln; Du Bist Entzueckend, Rosemarie! (aka Die Rosl vom Traunsee); Der Choral von Leuthen (The Anthem of Leuthen); Die Nacht im Forsthaus (aka Der Fall Roberts); Fluechtlinge (Refugees); Der Page vom Dalmasse-Hotel (US 1935). **1934** Ferien vom Ich; Konjunkturritter (US 1935); Schloss Hubertus (US 1935); Ein Maedchen mit Prokura; Regine; Nur Nicht Weich Werden, Susanne!; Alte Kameraden (US 1936, aka Das Faehnlein der Versprengten); Ich Sing' Mich in Dein Herz Hinein (US 1935). **1935** Familie Schimek; Hundert Tage; Leichte Kavallerie; Liselotte von der Pfalz (Frauen um den Sonnenkoenig); Liebesleute (aka Hermann und Dorothea von Heute). **1936** Der Jaeger von Fall; Schloss Vogeloed; Kater Lampe; Der Favorit der Kaiserin (The Favorite of the Empress—US 1939); Stjenka Rasin (aka Wolga-Wolga). **1937** Die Gelbe Flagge; Das Schoene Fraeulein Schragg; Das Schweigen im Walde (The Silence of the Forest); **1938** Gastspiel im Paradies; Mit Versiegelter Order; Kleiner Mann, Ganz Gross; Andlausische Naechte; Yvette (aka Die Tochter Einer Kurtisane); War es der im 3. Stock?; Scheidungsreise; Frauen fuer Golden Hill. **1939** Schneider Wibbel; Grenzfeuer; Kongo-Express (Congo Express—US 1940); Menschen vom Variete; Anton der Letzte (Anthony the Last—US 1940); Waldrausch (Forest Fever—US 1940). **1940** Die Rothschilds; Zwischen Hamburg und Haiti; Tiergarten Suedamerika (speaker); Die Geierwally; Links der Isar—Rechts der Spree; Kinder, wie die Zeit Vergeht; Wunschkonzert. **1941** Ohm Krueger; Heimaterde. **1942** Die Grosse Nummer; Viel Laerm um Nixi. **1943** Gefaehrtin Meines Sommers. **1944** Warum Luegst Du, Elisabeth?; Melusine; Jugendliebe. **1945** Die Kreuzlschreiber; Ein Mann Gehoert ins Haus (aka Bankerl Unterm Birnbaum).

SCHMIDT, KIM (Ruth Hannelore Schmidt)
Born: Australia. Died: Oct. 19, 1978, New York, N.Y. (murdered—shot). Screen and stage actress. Married to actor Gig Young (dec. 1978).

SCHMIDT, WOLF
Born: 1912, Germany. Died: Jan. 17, 1977, Bodensee, Germany. Screen, radio, television actor, film producer and radio writer.

SCHMITT, JOSEPH
Born: 1871. Died: Mar. 25, 1935, Los Angeles, Calif. Screen actor. Entered films in 1912.

SCHMITZ, LUDWIG
Born: 1884, Germany. Died: July, 1954, Munich, Germany (heart attack). Stage and screen actor.

Appeared in: **1938** Der Maulkorb. Other German films: Bruen Ist Die Heide; Am Brunnen vor dem Tore; Pension Schoeller; Der Keusche Josef; Land of Smiles.

SCHMITZ, SYBILLE
Born: 1912, Dueren, Germany. Died: Apr. 13, 1955, Munich, Germany (suicide—pills). Screen and stage actress. Entered films in early 1930s.

Appeared in: **1928** Der Ueberfall (aka Polizeibericht Ueberfall). **1929** Tagebuch Einer Verlorenen (Diary of a Lost Girl). **1932** Vampyr; F.P.1 Antwortet Nicht (F.P.1 Does Not Anser). **1934** Rivalen der Luft; Musik im Blut; Abschiedswalzer; Der Herr der Welt (US 1935). **1935** Stradivari; Ein Idealer Gatte (US 1937); Punks Kommt aus Amerika (US 1937); Oberwachtmeister Schwenke (US 1936); Ich War Jack Mortimer; Wenn die Musik Nicht Waer' (aka Der Kraft-Mayr, and aka Das Lied der Liebe). **1936** Die Leuchter des Kaisers; Die Unbekannte; Fahrmann Maria (Ferryman Maria—US 1938). **1937** Die Kronzeugin; Signal in der Nacht. **1938** Tanz auf dem Vulkan; Die Umwege des Schoenen Karl. **1939** Die Frau ohne Vergangenheit; Hotel Sacher. **1940** Trenck, der Pandur. **1941** Wetterleuchten um Barbara; Clarissa. **1942** Vom Schicksal Verweht. **1943** Titanic; Die Hochstaplerin. **1944** Das Leben Ruft. **1947** Zwischen Gestern und Morgen. **1949** Die Letzte Nacht. **1950** Die Luege; Der Fall Rabanser; Kronjuwelen; Sensation im Savoy. **1952** Illusion in Moll. **1954** The House on the Coast.

SCHNALL, IDA
Died: Feb. 14, 1973, Los Angeles, Calif. Screen actress and athlete.

Appeared in: **1912** Undine.

SCHNEIDER, JAMES
Born: 1882, New York, N.Y. Died: Feb. 14, 1967, Los Angeles, Calif. Screen actor and film director. One of the original Keystone Kops.

SCHNICKELFRITZ *See* FISHER, FREDDIE

SCHOENHALS, ALBRECHT
Born: 1888, Mannheim, Germany. Died: Dec. 6, 1978, Baden-Baden, West Germany. Screen and stage actor.

Appeared in: **1934** Fuerst Woronzeff; Ihr Groesster Erfolg (aka Therese Krones, and aka Her Greatest Success—US 1939). **1935** Einer Zuviel an Bord (US 1936); Stuetzen der Gesellschaft; Boccaccio (US 1937); Mazurka; April, April; Stracivari; Warum Luegt Fraeulein Kaethe?; Hannerl und Ihre Liebhaber. **1936** Intermezzo; Arzt aus Liedenschaft. **1937** Die Kreutzersonate (Kreutzer Sonata—US 1938); Das Grosse Abenteuer; Man Spricht Ueber Jacqueline; Tango Notturno; Die Glaserne Kugel (The Glass Ball—US 1939). **1938** Rote Orchideen (Red Orchids—US 1939); Raetsel um Beate; Maja Zwischen Zwei Ehen; Der Spieler (aka Roman Eines Spielers). **1939** Nanette; Ich Verweigere die Aussage; Die Frau ohne Vergangenheit; Roman Eines Arztes. **1940** Angelika; Herz ohne Heimat; Traummusik. **1941** Kopf Hoch, Johannes. **1942** Vom Schicksal Verweht. **1949** Man Spielt Nicht mit der Liebe. **1950** Export in Blond; Komplott auf Erlenhof. **1951** Eva und der Frauenarzt; Die Schuld des Dr. Homma. **1952** Illusion in Moll. **1954** Das Bildnis Einer Unbekannten (Portrait of an Unknown Woman—US 1958); Bei Dir war es Immer so Schoen. **1955** Das Forsthaus im Tirol. **1963** Scotland Yard Jagt Dr. Mabuse. **1968** The Damned.

SCHONBERG, ALEXANDER
Born: 1886. Died: Oct. 1, 1945, Hollywood, Calif. Screen and stage actor. Entered films approx. 1930.

Appeared in: **1934** The Mighty Barnum. **1937** Nothing Sacred. **1938** Romance in the Dark. **1939** They Shall Have Music.

SCHONBERG, IB
Born: 1902, Denmark. Died: Sept. 26, 1955, Copenhagen, Denmark. Screen actor.

Appeared in: **1954** We Want a Child.

SCHONFIELD, MAE
Died: Mar., 1978. Screen and stage actress. Married to actor Irving Jacobson (dec. 1978).

SCHRADER, GENEVIEVE (Genevieve Schrader Verkroff)
Born: 1889. Died: Sept. 5, 1972, Calif. Screen actress.

Appeared in: **1929** Midstream.

SCHRAMM, KARLA

Born: 1891, Los Angeles, Calif. Died: Jan. 17, 1980, Los Angeles, Calif. Screen, stage actress and pianist. The second actress to portray "Jane" in the Tarzan films.

Appeared in: **1919** Broken Blossoms; His Majesty, the American. **1920** The Son of Tarzan (serial). **1921** Hearts and Masks; The Revenge of Tarzan. **1923** Jungle Trail of the Son of Tarzan (feature of 1920 serial The Son of Tarzan).

SCHRAMM, WILLIAM W.

Born: 1905, Germany. Died: Aug. 15, 1979, Los Angeles, Calif. Screen, stage actor, singer and musician.

Appeared in: **1929** The Shakedown. **1930** All Quiet on the Western Front. **1933** My Lips Betray; The Best of Enemies. **1953** Stalag 17.

SCHRECK, MAX

Born: 1879, Berlin, Germany. Died: 1936, Munich, Germany. Screen and stage actor. Married to actress Fanny Norman.

Appeared in: **1921** Am Narrenseil. **1922** Der Favorit der Konigin; Nosferatu—Eine Symphonie des Grauens; Pique Ass. **1923** Der Kaufmann von Venedig; Die Strasse; Die Finanzen des Grossherzogs. **1924** Dudu, ein Menschenschicksal (aka Die Geschichte eines Clowns). **1925** Die Gefundene Braut; Krieg im Frieden; Der Rosa Diamant. **1926** Der Sohn der Hagar; Der Alte Fritz; Am Rande der Welt; Dona Juana; Luther. **1928** The Strange Case of Captain Ramper; Das Madchen von der Strasse; Der Kampf der Tertia (aka Jungend von Morgen); Moderne Piraten; Rasputins Liebesabenteuer (aka Rasputin, the Holy Devil—US 1930); Die Republick der Backfische; Ritter der Nacht; Serenissimus und die Letzte Jungfrau; Wolga-Wolga. **1929** Ludwig der Zweite, Konig von Bayern; At the Edge of the World; Nosferatu the Vampire. **1930** Das Land des Lachelns. **1931** Im Banne der Berge (aka Almenrausch). **1932** Muss Man Sich Gleich Scheiden Lassen?; Die Hacht der Versuchung; Ein Mann mit Herz; Die Verkaufte Braut; Furst Seppl (aka Skandal im Grandhotel); Peter Voss, der Millionendieb. **1933** Der Tunnel; Ein Kuss in der Sommernacht; Das Verliebte Hotel; Roman einer Hacht (US 1934); Eine Frau wie Du; Fraulein Hoffmanns Erzahlungen. **1935** Der Schlafwagen Kontrolleur. **1926** Donogoo Tonka; Die Letzten Vier von Santa Cruz.

SCHROFF, WILLIAM

Born: 1889, Stuttgart, Germany. Died: Dec. 5, 1964, Hollywood, Calif. Screen, stage actor, stuntman and circus performer.

SCHRYVER, CLINTON

Born: 1882. Died: Feb. 26, 1954, Calif. Screen actor.

SCHUKIN, BORIS

Born: 1894, Russia. Died: Oct. 7, 1939, Moscow, Russia (heart attack). Screen actor. He was holder of the title "People's Artist of the U.S.S.R."

Appeared in: **1938** Lenin in October.

SCHULTZ, (MRS.) CECIL E.

Born: 1905. Died: Sept. 2, 1953, New York, N.Y. Screen actress.

SCHULTZ, HARRY (Alexander Heinberg)

Born: 1883, Germany. Died: July 5, 1935, Hollywood, Calif. Screen actor.

Appeared in: **1926** Spangles. **1928** Riley the Cop. **1929** One Stolen Night. **1930** High C's (short); The Big House. **1931** Beau Hunks (short); War Mamas (short). **1933** Hypnotized; One Sunday Afternoon; I'm No Angel; His Silent Rachet (short); Arabian Tights (short). **1934** The Pursuit of Happiness; Little Man, What Now?

SCHULZ, FRITZ

Born: 1896, Germany. Died: May 9, 1972, Zurich, Switzerland. Screen, stage, television actor, stage, screen director and screenwriter.

Appeared in: **1931** Die Lindenwirtin vom Rhein; Die Schlacht von Bademuende. **1932** Theaternaechte von Berlin; Der Ungetreue Echehart; Rendez-Vous; Der Storch Streikt; Dienst ist Dienst; Hurra! Ein Junge!; Pension Schoeller. **1933** Drei Tage Mittelarrest; Heute Nacht—Eventuell; Waltz Time; Der Bettelstudent. **1934** The Constant Nymph; Ja Treu ist die Soldatenliebe. **1936** Madonna, Wo Bist Du? **1937** Die Schwebende Jungfrau. **1957** Cabaret.

SCHUMACHER, (CAPTAIN) MAX (Max Hartmann Schumacher)

Born: May 10, 1925. Died: Aug. 30, 1966, Los Angeles, Calif. (mid-air-helicopter collision). KMPC radio traffic helicopter pilot and screen actor.

Appeared in: **1964** The Lively Set.

SCHUMACHER, PHILIP

Died: Jan. 19, 1975. Screen actor.

Appeared in: **1948** Coroner Creek. **1957** The Deerslayer. **1966** Duel at Diablo.

SCHUMAKER, IDA

Died: Aug. 25, 1969. Screen actress.

Appeared in: **1921** R.S.V.P. **1930** Dollar Dizzy (short). **1932** Girl Grief (short). **1948** The Velvet Touch.

SCHUMANN-HEINK, ERNESTINE (Ernestine Rossler)

Born: 1861, Prague, Czechoslovakia. Died: Nov. 17, 1936, Los Angeles, Calif. (leukemia). Screen actress and opera performer. Mother of actor Ferdinand Schumann (dec. 1958) and screen technician Henry Schumann.

Appeared in: **1927** The following shorts: Danny Boy; By the Waters of Minnetonka; Der Erlkonig. **1935** Here's to Romance.

SCHUMANN-HEINK, FERDINAND

Born: Aug. 9, 1893, Hamburg, Germany. Died: Sept. 15, 1958, Los Angeles, Calif. (heart attack). Stage and screen actor. Entered films in 1924. Son of actress and opera star Ernestine Schumann-Heink (dec. 1936).

Appeared in: **1925** The Fighting Romeo. **1926** The Gallant Fool. **1928** Four Sons; The Awakening; Riley the Cop. **1930** Hell's Angels; Blaze O'Glory; Wordly Goods; Mamba. **1931** The Seas Beneath; My Pal, the King. **1933** Gigolettes of Paris; The Mad Game. **1934** The World Moves On; Fugitive Road; Orient Express. **1935** Don't Bet on Blondes; Traveling Saleslady; Symphony of Living. **1936** Two Against the World; The Story of Louis Pasteur. **1937** The King and the Chorus Girl. **1938** Romance in the Dark; Artists and Models Abroad. **1939** Thunder Afloat; Nurse Edith Cavell; Confessions of a Nazi Spy. **1940** Enemy Agent. **1942** Invisible Agent. **1943** Above Suspicion; Mission to Moscow.

SCHUMM, HARRY W.

Born: 1878. Died: Apr. 4, 1953, Hollywood, Calif. Screen and stage actor.

Appeared in: **1915** The Broken Coin (serial).

SCHUNZEL, REINHOLD

Born: 1886, Hamburg, Germany. Died: Sept. 11, 1954, Munich, Germany (heart ailment). Screen, stage actor, screenwriter and film director.

Appeared in: **1916** Die Stricknadeln. **1918** Das Tagebuch Einer Verlorenen; Es Werde Licht (Let There Be Light). **1919** Baccarat; Das Karussell des Lebens; Der Liebersroman der Kaethe Keller; Das Maedchen und die Maenner; Marie Magdalena; Prostitution; Die Reise um die Erde in 80 Tagen; Seine Beichte; Suendige Eltern; Unheimliche Geschichten; Madame DuBarry (aka Passion); Anders als die Andern (Different from the Others). **1920** Die Banditen von Asnieres; Das Chamaeleon; Drei Naecht; Der Graf von Cagliostro; Die Letzte Stunde; Marquis D'or; Moriturus; Weltbrand. **1921** Maedchen aus der Ackerstrasse; Der Roman Eines Dienstmaedchens; Die Taenzerin Barberina. **1922** Bigamie; Das Geld auf der Strasse; Lady Hamilton; Der Pantoffelheld; Das Liebesnest; The Last Payment; Luise Millerin (aka Kabale und Liebe). **1923** Der Menschenfeind; Der Schatz der Gesine Jakobsen; Alles fuer Geld (All for Money). **1924** Lumpen und Seide; Die Schmetterlingsschlacht; Neuland (aka Das Glueckhaft Schiff). **1925** Die Blumenfrau vom Potsdamer Platz; Der Flug um den Erdball; Der Hahn im Korb; Heiratsschwindler; Suendenbabel; Die Kleine aus der Konfektion (aka Grosstadtkavaliere). **1926** Der Dumme August des Zirkus Romanelli; Fuenfuhrtee in der Ackerstrasse; Hallo Caesar!; In der Heimat, da gibt's ein Wiedersehn!; Der Juxbaron; Die Perle des Regiments (aka Der Stplz der Kompagnie). **1927** Gustav Mond ... Du Gehst so Stille; Herkules Maier; Himmel auf Erden; Ueb' Immer Treu und Redlichkeit. **1928** Fortune's Fool; Adam und Eva (Adam and Eve); Aus Dem Tagebuch Eines Junggesellen; Don Juan in der Maedchenschule. **1929** Kolonne X; Peter, der Matrose; Phantome des Gluecks. **1931** Der Ball; Die Dreigroschenoper (The Threepenny Opera, aka The Beggar's Opera); Ihre Hoheit Befiehlt; 1941, die Letztn Tage vor dem Weltbrand (1914: The Last Days Before the War—US 1932). **1943** First Comes Courage; Hangmen Also Die; Hostages. **1944** The Hitler Gang; The Man in Half Moon Street. **1946** Notorious; Dragonwyck; The Plainsman and the Lady. **1947** Golden Earrings. **1948** Berlin Express; The Vicious Circle; The Woman in Brown. **1952** Washington Story. **1954** Meines Vaters Pferde II, Eine Liebesgeschichte.

SCHUYLER, GOGDELL

Died: 1969. Screen actress. Mack Sennett bathing beauty.

SCHWAMM, GEORGE S. "TONY"
Born: 1903. Died: Feb. 15, 1966, Elmendorf, Alaska. Screen stuntman.

SCHWANNEKE, ELLEN
Born: Germany. Died: June 16, 1972, Zurich, Switzerland. Screen and stage actress.

Appeared in: **1932** Maedchen in Uniform. **1933** Kadetten. **1934** Ein Toller Einfall. **1936** The Royal Waltz. **1938** Kein Wort von Liebe (Not a Word About Love); Die Sextanerin—Erste Liebe (First Love).

SCHWARTZ, ALBERT RICHMAN
Born: May 21, 1885, New Orleans, La. Died: Apr. 20, 1936, Hollywood, Calif. Screen and stage actor.

SCHWARTZ, MAURICE
Born: 1891, Russia. Died: May 10, 1960, near Tel Aviv, Israel (heart attack). Stage and screen actor. Appeared in Yiddish stage productions, etc.

Appeared in: **1926** Broken Hearts. **1932** Uncle Moses. **1939** Tevya the Milkman (filmed for limited circulation). **1951** Bird of Paradise. **1953** Slaves of Babylon; Salome.

SCHWARTZ, WENDIE LEE
Born: 1923. Died: Aug. 23, 1968, Hollywood, Calif. Screen actress.

SCHWEGLER, PAUL A.
Born: 1907. Died: Dec. 7, 1980, Newport Beach, Calif. College football player, screen actor and film director.

Appeared in: **1932** The All-American.

SCHWEISTHAL, HELEN See ALLERTON, LITTLE HELEN

SCOBIE, JAMES
Died: 1968. Screen actor.

Appeared in: **1956** Around the World in 80 Days.

SCORE, PHIL
Died: May 31, 1979, San Diego, Calif. Pianist, music director and screen actor.

Appeared in: **1938** Moonlight Sonata.

SCOTT, ALLEN See NEWMAN, ALLAN SCOTT

SCOTT, CARRIE
Born: 1870. Died: Dec. 17, 1928, New York, N.Y. Screen, stage, vaudeville actress and burlesque entertainer.

Appeared in: **1924** Manhandled. **1925** Stage Struck. **1927** The Music Master.

SCOTT, CYRIL
Born: Feb. 9, 1866, Banbridge County, Down, Ireland. Died: Aug. 16, 1945, Flushing, N.Y. Stage and screen actor. Married to stage actress Louise Eissing (dec. 1921).

Appeared in: **1915** How Molly Made Good.

SCOTT, DAVE (James and/or John David Scott)
Born: 1939. Died: Dec. 8, 1964, Pasadena, Calif. (leukemia). Screen, stage and radio actor. Do not confuse with actor Dave Scott born in 1911. Was Alexander on Blondie and Dagwood radio program.

Appeared in: **1963** Night Tide.

SCOTT, DICK
Born: 1903. Died: Sept. 2, 1961, Hollywood, Calif. Screen, stage and radio actor.

SCOTT, FREDERICK T.
Died: Feb. 22, 1942, Staten Island, N.Y. Screen actor and Wild West showman.

Appeared in: **1905** The Great Train Robbery. **1919** Over There. **1936** Romance Rides the Range.

SCOTT, GERTRUDE
Born: Sevenoaks, Kent, England. Died: Dec. 23, 1951, England? Screen actress. Married to actor Norman McKinnel (dec. 1932). Appeared in Essanay films.

SCOTT, HAROLD
Born: Apr. 21, 1891, Kensington, England. Died: Apr. 15, 1964, London, England. Screen, stage, radio and television actor.

Appeared in: **1943** The Man in Grey (US 1945). **1949** Trottie True (aka Gay Lady—US 1950). **1956** The Spanish Gardener. **1960** The Hand (US 1961); The Brides of Dracula. **1961** The Young Ones (aka Wonderful to Be Young—US 1962). **1962** The Man Who Finally Died (US 1967); The Boys (US 1963). **1964** The Yellow Rolls Royce (US 1965).

SCOTT, HAZEL (Hazel Dorothy Scott)
Born: June 11, 1920, Trinidad. Died: Oct. 2, 1981, N.Y. (cancer). Black screen, stage, radio actress, pianist and singer. Divorced from Congressman Adam Clayton Powell, Jr. (dec.).

Appeared in: **1943** I Dood It; Something to Shout About; The Heat's On. **1944** Broadway Rhythm. **1945** Rhapsody in Blue. **1958** Le Desordre et la Nuit (Disorder and Night, aka Night Affair—US 1961).

SCOTT, HENRY
Born: 1922. Died: Apr. 22, 1981, Los Angeles, Calif. Screen, stage, television actor and dialog director.

Appeared in: **1958** Anna Lucasta. **1962** Hatari!

SCOTT, IVY
Born: 1886, Australia. Died: Feb. 3, 1947, New York, N.Y. Screen, stage and radio actress.

Appeared in: **1940** Too Many Girls. **1943** Higher and Higher.

SCOTT, JAMES D. See SCOTT, DAVE

SCOTT, KAY
Born: 1928. Died: Jan. 1, 1971, Los Angeles, Calif. Screen actress and composer.

Appeared in: **1947** Fear in the Night.

SCOTT, LESLIE (Zakariya Abullah)
Born: 1921. Died: Aug. 20, 1969, New York, N.Y. (cancer). Screen, stage actor and singer.

Appeared in: **1958** Island Women. **1959** Porgy and Bess (screen and European stage versions).

SCOTT, LINDA (aka CHARLEE)
Born: 1950. Died: Nov. 10, 1978, New Rochelle, N.Y (murdered—bludgeoned). Country-Western singer and screen actress.

Appeared in: **1962** Don't Knock the Twist.

SCOTT, MABEL JULIENE
Born: Nov. 2, 1893 or 1895, Minneapolis, Minn. Died: Oct. 1, 1976, Los Angeles, Calif. Screen, stage and vaudeville actress. Sister of actor William Harvey Scott. Entered films in 1917.

Appeared in: **1917** The Barrier. **1918** The Sign Invisible; Reclaimed; Ashes of Love. **1919** Sacred Silence. **1920** The Round Up; Behold My Wife; The Jucklins; The Sea Wolf. **1921** The Concert; Don't Neglect Your Wife; No Woman Knows. **1922** The Power of a Lie. **1923** Abysmal Brute; Times Have Changed. **1924** So This Is Marriage. **1925** Seven Days. **1926** Frontier Trail; His Jazz Bride; Stranded in Paris; A Woman's Heart. **1927** Mother. **1928** Wallflowers. **1929** Painted Faces; Dream Melody.

SCOTT, MARK
Born: 1915. Died: July 13, 1960, Burbank, Calif. (heart attack). Screen, radio and television actor.

Appeared in: **1955** Hell's Horizon. **1957** Chicago Confidential.

SCOTT, MARKLE
Born: 1873. Died: July 4, 1958, Hollywood, Calif. Cowboy screen actor. Appeared in silents.

SCOTT, PAUL
Born: 1894. Died: Nov. 24, 1944, Los Angeles, Calif. (heart attack). Screen and stage actor.

Appeared in: **1942** Don Winslow of the Navy (serial).

SCOTT, WALLACE "WALLY"
Died: May 8, 1970. Screen actor.

Appeared in: **1942** The Big Shot. **1946** The Killers. **1947** Out of the Past; Tarzan and the Huntress; The Vigilantes Return. **1948** The Walls of Jericho; Kiss the Blood off My Hands. **1950** Captain China.

SCOTT, WALTER F.
Born: 1879, Baltimore, Md. Died: Mar. 5, 1940, New York, N.Y. Screen and stage actor.

Appeared in: **1929** Great Power; Marianne; Hold Your Man.

SCOTT, ZACHARY
Born: Feb. 24, 1914, Austin, Tex. Died: Oct. 3, 1965, Austin, Tex. (brain tumor). Stage and screen actor.

Appeared in: **1944** The Mask of Dimitrios (film debut); Hollywood Canteen. **1945** Mildred Pierce; The Southerner; San Antonio; Danger Signal. **1946** Her Kind of Man. **1947** Stallion Road; Cass Timberlane; The Unfaithful. **1948** Whiplash; Ruthless. **1949** Flamingo Road; Flaxy Martin; South of Saint Louis; Death in a Doll's House; Bed of Roses; One Last Fling. **1950** Born to Be Bad; Thundercloud; Colt .45; Shadow on the Wall; Pretty Baby; Guilty Bystander. **1951** Lightning Strikes Twice; The Secret of Convict Lake; Let's Make It Legal. **1952** Stronghold; Wings of Danger (aka Dead on Course—US). **1953** Appointment in Honduras. **1955** Shotgun; Flame of the Islands; Treasure of Ruby Hills. **1956** Bandido. **1957** The Counterfeit Plan; Man in the Shadow; Flight into Danger. **1960** Natchez Trace. **1961** The Young One. **1962** It's Only Money.

SCOTT-GATTY, ALEXANDER
Born: Oct. 3, 1876, Ecclesfeld, Yorkshire, England. Died: Nov. 6, 1937, London, England. Screen, stage and radio actor.

Appeared in: **1930** Symphony in Two Flats. **1932** In a Monastery Garden. **1933** The Perfect Understanding.

SCUDAMORE, MARGARET
Born: Nov. 13, 1884, Portsmouth, England. Died: Oct. 6, 1958, London, England. Screen and stage actress. Mother of actor Michael Redgrave. Entered films in 1932.

Appeared in: **1932** Arms and the Man.

SEABURY, YNEZ
Born: 1909. Died: Apr. 11, 1973, Sherman Oaks, Calif. (internal complications). Screen, stage, radio and television actress. Known as "The Biograph Baby."

Appeared in: **1915** Billy's Stratagem. **1916** The Sunbeam. **1923** Slander the Woman; Thundergate. **1924** When a Girl Loves. **1925** The Calgary Stampede; Ship of Souls. **1927** Red Clay. **1929** Dynamite. **1930** Madam Satan. **1932** The Sign of the Cross; The Drifter. **1934** Now and Forever. **1936** The Invisible Ray. **1938** The Girl of the Golden West. **1940** Northwest Mounted Police. **1949** Samson and Delilah.

SEAGRAM, WILFRID (Wilfrid Richardson)
Born: Jan. 10, 1884, Finchley, England. Died: May 28, 1938, N.Y. (following surgery). Screen and stage actor.

SEALY, LEWIS A.
Born: 1851, Ireland or London, England? Died: Mar. 20, 1931, New York, N.Y. Screen and stage actor.

Appeared in: **1915** When a Woman Loves. **1916** Romeo and Juliet; The Witching Hour. **1917** The Primitive Call.

SEAMAN, MARJORIE
Born: June 21, 1900, Pa. Died: Mar. 9, 1923, Los Angeles, Calif. Screen actress. Married to actor Ralph Graves (dec. 1977).

Appeared in: **1921** Dream Street. **1922** Free Air.

SEARLE, KAMUELA C.
Born: Aug. 29, 1890, Hawaii. Died: Feb. 14, 1924, Los Angeles, Calif. (injuries sustained during filming). Sculptor and screen actor.

Appeared in: **1919** Male and Female. **1920** The Son of Tarzan (serial). **1921** Fool's Paradise. **1923** Jungle Trail of the Son of Tarzan (feature of 1920 serial Son of Tarzan).

SEARLES, CORA
Born: 1859. Died: Mar. 5, 1935, Los Angeles, Calif. Screen actress.

SEARS, ALLAN
Born: 1887. Died: Aug. 18, 1942, Los Angeles, Calif. Screen actor.

Appeared in: **1920** Rio Grande; Judy of Rogue's Harbor. **1923** Long Live the King. **1924** In Love with Love. **1925** The Scarlet Honeymoon. **1926** Into Her Kingdom. **1928** Into the Night; A Midnight Adventure. **1933** Secrets. **1935** The Singing Vagabond. **1937** Two-Fisted Sheriff.

SEARS, BLANCHE
Born: 1870. Died: Aug. 7, 1939, Los Angeles, Calif. Screen and radio actress.

SEARS, ELEANOR
Born: 1908. Died: Jan. 19, 1936, Hollywood, Calif. Screen actress.

SEARS, FRED
Born: July 7, 1913, Boston, Mass. Died: Nov. 30, 1957, Hollywood, Calif. (heart attack). Screen, stage, television actor, film, stage, television director and stage producer.

Appeared in: **1947** It Had to Be You; Down to Earth; The Corpse Came C.O.D.; The Lone Hand Texan; West of Dodge City; Law of the Canyon; Blondie in the Dough; For the Love of Rusty; Blondie's Anniversary. **1948** The Fuller Brush Man; Gallant Blade; Whirlwind Raiders; Phantom Valley; Adventures in Silverado; Rusty Leads the Way. **1949** Shockproof; Boston Blackie's Chinese Venture; Home in San Antone; Laramie; The Blazing Trail; Frontier Outpost; Renegades of the Sage; Bandits of El Dorado; The Lone Wolf and His Lady; South of Death Valley. **1950** Hoedown; David Harding—Counterspy; Texas Dynamo; Counterspy Meets Scotland Yard. **1951** Bonanza Town; The Kid from Amarillo; The Big Gusher; My True Story; Fort Savage Raider; Cyclone Fury. **1952** Laramie Mountains; The Rough Tough West.

SEARS, ZELDA
Born: 1873, Brockway, Mich. Died: Feb. 19, 1935, Hollywood, Calif. Screen, stage actress, author, playwright and screenwriter.

Appeared in: **1921** The Highest Bidder. **1930** The Bishop Murder Case; The Divorcee. **1931** Inspiration. **1935** A Wicked Woman.

SEASTROM, DOROTHY
Born: Tex. Died: Feb., 1930, Dallas, Tex. Screen actress.

Appeared in: **1923** The Call of the Canyon. **1925** Fifth Avenue Models; Pretty Ladies. **1926** We Moderns; It Must Be Love.

SEASTROM, VICTOR (aka VICTOR SJOSTROM)
Born: Sept. 21, 1879, Varmland, Sweden. Died: Jan. 3, 1960, Stockholm, Sweden. Screen, stage actor, film director and stage director. Married to actress Leli Bech (dec. 1939). Entered films as an actor with Swedish Biograph Co. in 1912.

Appeared in: **1913** Ingeborg Holm. **1916** Terje Vigen. **1920** A Man There Was. **1921** You and I; Ordet (The World). **1922** The Stroke of Midnight. **1938** John Ericsson, Victor of Hampton Roads. **1949** I Am With You. **1957** Wild Strawberries (US 1959).

SEATON, GEORGE
Born: 1911, South Bend, Ind. Died: July 28, 1979, Beverly Hills, Calif. (cancer). Screen, stage, radio actor, film director, film producer and screenwriter.

SEATON, MARC
Died: Apr. 10, 1979. Screen actor.

Appeared in: **1965** Wild on the Beach. **1966** The Chase. **1968** What's So Bad About Feeling Good?

SEATON, SCOTT
Born: Mar. 11, 1878, Sacramento, Calif. Died: June 3, 1968, Hollywood, Calif. Screen, stage and television actor.

Appeared in: **1927** Wild Beauty; Rich Men's Sons; Thumbs Down. **1929** The Greyhound Limited; Leathernecks. **1930** The Other Tomorrow. **1935** Ruggles of Red Gap. **1950** Father of the Bride. **1956** Around the World in 80 Days. **1963** Twilight of Honor; Donovan's Reef.

SEBASTIAN, DOROTHY
Born: Apr., 1903, Birmingham, Ala. Died: Apr. 8, 1957, Hollywood, Calif. Screen and stage actress. Divorced from actor William "Hopalong Cassidy" Boyd (dec. 1972).

Appeared in: **1925** Sackcloth and Scarlet (film debut); Why Women Love (aka Sea Woman and Barriers Aflame); Winds of Chance. **1926** Bluebeard's Seven Wives; You'd Be Surprised. **1927** The Demi-Bride; The Arizona Wildcat; California; The Haunted Ship; Isle of Forgotten Women; On Ze Boulevard; Tea for Three; Twelve Miles Out; The Show. **1928** Our Dancing Daughters; Show People; Their Hour; Wyoming; House of Scandal; The Adventurer. **1929** The Single Standard; Spite Marriage; A Woman of Affairs; The Rainbow; The Spirit of Youth; The Devil's Apple Tree; The Unholy Night; Morgan's Last Raid. **1930** His First Command; Our Blushing Brides; Free and Easy; Hell's Island; Ladies Must Play; Brothers; The Utah Kid; Montana Moon; Officer O'Brien. **1931** The Deceiver; Lightning Flyer; Ships of Hate; The Big Gamble. **1932** Wide Open Spaces (short); They Never Came Back. **1933** Contraband; Ship of Wanted Men. **1934** Allez

Oop (short); The Gold Ghost. **1937** The Mysterious Pilot (serial). **1939** Rough Riders' Round-Up; The Women; The Arizona Kid. **1941** Among the Living; Kansas Cyclone. **1942** True to the Army; Reap the Wild Wind.

SEBERG, JEAN
Born: Nov. 13, 1938, Marshalltown, Iowa. Died: Aug. 30, 1979, Paris, France (suicide—drug overdose). Screen, stage, television actress, film director, film producer, screenwriter and author. Divorced from film producer Francois Moreuil, author Romain Gary (dec. 1980), and film director Dennis Berry. Later married to actor Ahmed Hasni.

Appeared in: **1957** Saint Joan (film debut). **1958** Bonjour Tristesse. **1959** The Mouse That Roared. **1960** Let No Man Write My Epitaph; A Bout de Souffle (aka Breathless—US 1961). **1961** La Recreation (Playtime—US 1963); L'Amont de Cinq Jours (The Five Day Lover); Les Grandes Personnes (aka Time Out for Love—US 1963). **1963** In the French Style. **1964** Lilith; Echappement Libre (aka Backfire—US 1965). **1966** Moment to Moment; Estouffade a la Caraibe; A Fine Madness. **1967** La Route de Corinthe (The Road to Corinth, aka Who's Got the Black Box—US 1970). **1968** Les Oiseaux Vont Mourir au Perou (aka Birds in Peru—US). **1969** Pendulum; Paint Your Wagon. **1970** Macho Callahan; Airport. **1973** L'A Hentat (aka The French Conspiracy—US). **1974** Kill Kill Kill. **1975** Ballad for the Kid (short); Le Grand Desire; The Corruption of Chris Miller. **1976** The Wild Duck (US 1977); Behind the Shutters.

SEBRING, JAY (Thomas Jay Kummer)
Born: Oct. 10, 1933, Alabama. Died: Aug. 8, 1969, Los Angeles, Calif. (murdered). Hair stylist and screen actor.

Appeared in: **1965** Synanon. **1967** Mondo Hollywood (aka Image and Hippie Hollywood; The Acid-Blasting Freaks).

SEDDON, MARGARET
Born: Nov. 18, 1872, Washington, D.C. Died: Apr. 17, 1968, Philadelphia, Pa. Screen and vaudeville actress. Appeared in vaudeville with Margaret McWade (dec. 1956) in an act billed as the "Pixilated Sisters."

Appeared in: **1915** The Old Homestead. **1917** The Girl Without a Soul. **1919** The Dawn of a Tomorrow; The Unveiling Hand. **1920** Miracle of Money. **1921** The Case of Becky; The Highest Law; The Inside of the Cup; Just Around the Corner; The Man Worth While; A Man's Home; School Days. **1922** Boomerang Bill; The Lights of New York; The Man Who Played God; Timothy's Quest; Women Men Marry; Sonny. **1923** Brass; The Bright Shawl; Little Johnny Jones; The Gold Diggers; Little Church Around the Corner. **1924** The Confidence Man; Snob; Women Who Give; Through the Dark; The Human Terror; A Lady of Quality; The Night Message. **1925** Wages for Wives; Proud Flesh; A Broadway Butterfly; The Lady; The Midshipman; New Lives for Old; On the Threshold. **1926** Blarney; Rolling Home; The Golden Cocoon; A Regular Scout; Wild Oats Lane. **1927** Matinee Ladies; Quality Street; Silk Legs; White Pants Willie; Driven from Home; Home Made. **1928** The Actress; Gentlemen Prefer Blondes. **1929** After the Fog; Bellamy Trial; Dance Hall; She Goes to War. **1930** Dancing Sweeties; The Dude Wrangler. **1931** Divorce Among Friends. **1932** Smilin' Through. **1933** Broadway Bad; Lilly Turner; Heroes for Sale; Midshipman Jack; The Worst Woman in Paris; Walls of Gold. **1934** The Barretts of Wimpole Street. **1935** The Flame Within; The Girl Friend; Two Sinners. **1936** Mr. Deeds Goes to Town; The Big Game; A Woman Rebels; College Holiday. **1937** Let's Make a Million; Danger—Love at Work. **1940** Dr. Kildare's Strangest Case; Raffles; Friendly Neighbors. **1941** Dr. Kildare's Wedding Day. **1942** The Wife Takes a Flyer; Scattergood Survives a Murder. **1943** The Meanest Man in the World. **1950** House By the River. **1951** Three Desperate Men (aka Three Outlaws).

SEDGWICK, EDIE (Edith Sedgwick)
Born: 1943. Died: Nov. 16, 1971, Santa Barbara, Calif. (acute barbitural intoxication). Screen actress.

Appeared in: **1965** Beauty II; Vinyl; Poor Little Rich Girl; Space. **1966** Face; Kitchen; Lupe; Outer and Inner Space. **1967** * * * *. **1968** The Queen. **1969** Diaries, Notes and Sketches. Other films: Restaurant; Chow Manhattan; Afternoon.

SEDGWICK, EDWARD, JR.
Born: Nov. 7, 1889 or 1892?, Galveston, Tex. Died: May 7, 1953, North Hollywood, Calif. (heart attack). Screen, stage, vaudeville, burlesque actor, film director and screenwriter. Son of stage actor Edward Sedgwick (dec. 1931) and stage actress Josephine Walker (dec. 1964). See Josie Sedgwick for family information.

Appeared in: **1915** Greenbacks and Redskins. **1916** Married a Year; The Fascinating Model. **1917** The Haunted Pajamas; Fat and Foolish; The Yankee Way; The Varmint. **1919** Checkers.

SEDGWICK, JOSIE
Born: 1898, Galveston, Tex. Died: Apr. 30, 1973, Santa Monica, Calif. (stroke). Screen, stage and vaudeville actress. Daughter of stage actor Edward Sedgwick (dec. 1931) and stage actress Josephine Walker (dec. 1964). Appeared in vaudeville in a family act billed as the "Five Sedgwicks" which included father, mother, sister Eileen and brother Edward, Jr. (dec. 1953).

Appeared in: **1916** Her Dream Man. **1917** Ashes of Hope; Fighting Back; The Maternal Spark; Indiscreet Corinne; Boss of the Lazy Y. **1918** Camouflage Kiss; Lure of the Circus (serial); Wolves of the Border; Paying His Debt; Wild Life. **1919** Jubilo; The She Wolf. **1920** Daredevil Jack (serial). **1921** Western Hearts; The Duke of Chimney Butte; Double Adventure (serial). **1922** Crimson Clue. **1923** The Sunshine Trail; Michael O'Halloran; Daddy. **1924** The Sawdust Trail; The White Moth. **1925** Daring Days; The Outlaw's Daughter; The Saddle Hawk; Let 'Er Buck. **1932** Son of Oklahoma.

SEED, DAVID
Born: July 8, 1888, New York, N.Y. Died: Nov. 3, 1960, Brooklyn, N.Y. Screen and vaudeville actor. Member of comedy vaudeville team "Seed and Austin."

Appeared in: **1919** Tarzan of the Apes.

SEEL, CHARLES F.
Died: Apr. 19, 1980. Screen actor.

Appeared in: **1949** Not Wanted. **1955** The Man With the Golden Arm. **1957** I Was a Teenage Frankenstein. **1960** The Walking Target. **1961** Return to Peyton Place. **1962** The Man Who Shot Liberty Valance. **1963** Lady in a Cage; Tammy and the Doctor; Donovan's Reef. **1964** The Tattooed Police Horse. **1965** The Great Race. **1966** Chamber of Horrors; Mister Buddwing. **1969** This Savage Land; Winning.

SEEL, JEANNE N.
Born: 1898. Died: Sept. 9, 1964, Hollywood, Calif. (cancer). Screen and stage actress. Married to actor Charles Steel.

SEELEY, JAMES L.
Born: 1867, Rushville, Ill. Died: Feb. 15, 1943, New York, N.Y. Screen and stage actor.

Appeared in: **1921** Remorseless Love. **1922** Channing of the Northwest; A Wide-Open Town.

SEELOS, ANNETTE (Blanche Wallis)
Born: 1891. Died: Oct. 23, 1918, New York, N.Y. (Spanish influenza). Screen actress. Appeared in Essanay films.

SEELY, BLOSSOM
Born: 1892, San Pablo, Calif. Died: Apr. 17, 1974, New York, N.Y. Screen, stage, vaudeville and television actress. Divorced from theatrical manager Joseph Kane and baseball player Factor Rube Marquard (dec. 1980). Later married actor Benny Fields (dec. 1959).

Appeared in: **1933** Mr. Broadway; Blood Money; Broadway Thru a Keyhole.

SEFTON, ERNEST
Born: 1883, England. Died: Dec. 5, 1954, England? Screen and stage actor. Brother of actress Violet Loraine.

Appeared in: **1932** Old Spanish Customers. **1935** Strictly Illegal. **1936** Broken Blossoms (US 1937). **1937** The Great Barrier (aka Silent Barriers—US). **1940** Here Comes a Policeman (reissue of Strictly Illegal, 1935).

SEGAL, BERNARD
Born: 1868. Died: July 9, 1940, Hollywood, Calif. Screen actor.

Appeared in: **1937** Wells Fargo.

SEGAR, LUCIA (aka LUCIA SEGER aka LUCIA BACUS)
Born: 1874. Died: Jan. 17, 1962, New York, N.Y. Screen, stage and television actress.

Appeared in: **1921** The Wild Goose. **1922** The Bond Boy; The Bootleggers. **1923** Fury. **1927** Knockout Reilly. **1929** East Side Sadie. **1947** Boomerang.

SEGARRA, CONSUELO
Born: 1876, Mexico. Died: Apr. 28, 1946, Mexico City, Mexico. Screen actress.

Áppeared in: **1934** El Tigre de Yautepec.

SEGURA, LETICIA ESPINOSA
Born: Mexico. Died: Dec. 26, 1956, Mexico City, Mexico (auto accident). Screen and television actress.

SEIDEWITZ, MARIE
Died: Dec. 27, 1929, Baltimore, Md. Screen, stage and vaudeville actress.

SEIDLER, ALMA
Born: 1899, Austria. Died: Dec. 8, 1977, Austria?. Screen and stage actress.

Appeared in: **1960** Der Brave Soldat Schweik (The Good Soldier Schweik—US 1963).

SEIDNER, IRENE
Born: Dec. 10, 1880, Austria. Died: Nov. 17, 1959, Los Angeles, Calif. Stage and screen actress.

Appeared in: **1940** We Who Are Young. **1942** All Through the Night. **1943** The Purple V. **1948** Act of Violence. **1949** The Great Sinner. **1951** People Will Talk. **1956** Miracle in the Rain. **1958** Wink of an Eye; Ten North Frederick.

SEITER, WILLIAM A.
Born: June 10, 1892, New York, N.Y. Died: July 26, 1964, Beverly Hills, Calif. (heart attack). Screen actor, film director, television director and film producer. Entered films as an actor with Sennett as a Keystone Kop.

Appeared in: **1913** The Three Wise Men. **1915** The Honeymoon Roll.

SEITZ, GEORGE B.
Born: Jan. 3, 1888, Boston, Mass. Died: July 8, 1944, Hollywood, Calif. Screen, stage actor, film producer, film director, screenwriter and playwright. Wrote the scenarios, produced, directed and acted in the "Pearl White" Pathe serials. Entered films with Pathe in 1914.

Appeared in the following serials: **1919** The Black Secret; Bound and Gagged. **1920** Pirate Gold; Velvet Fingers. **1921** The Sky Ranger; Rogues and Romance (feature).

SEKELY, IRENE AGAY
Born: 1914, Hungary. Died: Sept. 2, 1950, Hollywood, Calif. Screen and stage actress.

Appeared in: **1946** The Fabulous Suzanne.

SELBIE, EVELYN
Born: July 6, 1882, Louisville, Ky. Died: Dec. 7, 1950, Hollywood, Calif. (heart ailment). Screen, stage and radio actress. Entered films as G. M. Anderson's (Bronco Billy) leading lady in 1912; was known as the original "Bronco Billy Girl."

Appeared in: **1914** The Squaw Man. **1919** The Red Glove (serial). **1921** Devil Dog Dawson; The Devil Within; Without Benefit of Clergy. **1922** Omar the Tentmaker; Thorns and Orange Blossoms; The Half Breed. **1923** The Broken Wing; Snowdrift; The Tiger's Claw. **1924** A Cafe in Cairo; Flapper Wives; Name the Man; Mademoiselle Midnight; Romance Ranch; Poisoned Paradise. **1925** The Prairie Pirate. **1926** The Country Beyond; Hell-Bent for Heaven; Into Her Kingdom; Flame of the Argentine; The Test of Donald Norton; The Silver Treasure; Silken Shackles; Rose of the Tenements; Prisoners of the Storm. **1927** Camille; Wild Geese; King of Kings; Eager Lips. **1928** Freedom of the Press. **1929** Eternal Love; The Mysterious Dr. Fu Manchu. **1930** The Return of Dr. Fu Manchu; Love Comes Along; Dangerous Paradise. **1932** The Hatchet Man. **1935** A Notorious Gentleman. **1936** Two in a Crowd. **1938** Blockade; If I Were King. **1941** Raiders of the Desert.

SELBY, NORMAN "KID MC COY"
Born: Oct. 13, 1873, Rush County, Ind. Died: Apr. 18, 1940, Detroit, Mich. (suicide). Screen actor and boxer.

Appeared in: **1921** Bucking the Line; To a Finish; Straight from the Shoulder. **1922** Arabia; Oathbound. **1923** April Showers. **1930** The Painted Angel. **1931** Loose Ankles.

SELBY, SARAH
Born: 1906, St. Louis, Mo. Died: Jan. 7, 1980, Los Angeles, Calif. Screen, stage, radio and television actress.

Appeared in: **1941** Dumbo (voice). **1944** San Diego, I Love You. **1945** The Beautiful Cheat; The Naughty Nineties. **1946** Little Iodine. **1947** Stork Bites Man. **1948** Trapped by Boston Blackie. **1949** Beyond the Forest. **1951** Jim Thorpe—All American. **1952** The Iron Mistress. **1953** Battle Cry; The McConnell Story. **1957** An Affair to Remember; Stopover Tokyo; No Time to Be Young. **1962** Moon Pilot; Tower of London. **1964** Taggart. **1965** The Great Race. **1967** Don't Make Waves.

SELK, GEORGE See BUSTER, BUDD

SELLERS, PETER
Born: Sept. 8, 1925, Southsea, England. Died: July 24, 1980, London, England (heart attack). Screen, stage, vaudeville, radio, television actor, film director, film producer and screenwriter. Son of vaudeville actors William Sellers (dec.), and Agnes Marks Sellers (dec. 1967). Divorced from actress Anne Howe, actress Britt Ekland, and Miranda Quarry. Later married to actress Lynne Frederick. Nominated for 1979 Academy Award for Best Actor in Being There. Made Commander of the Order of the British Empire in 1966.

Appeared in: **1951** London Entertains; Penny Points to Paradise; Let's Go Crazy (short). **1952** Down Among the Z Men. **1953** Super Secret Service (short). **1954** Orders are Orders. **1955** The Ladykillers (US 1956); John and Julie (US 1957). **1956** The Case of the Mukkinese Battlehorn (short); The Man Who Never Was (narrator). **1957** The Naked Truth (aka Your Past is Showing—US 1958); The Smallest Show on Earth; plus the following shorts: Death of a Salesman; Cold Comfort; Insomnia is Good for You. **1958** Tom Thumb; Up the Creek. **1959** Carlton-Browne of the F.O. (aka Man in a Cocked Hat—US 1960); The Mouse That Roared; The Battle of the Sexes (US 1960); I'm All Right, Jack (US 1960). **1960** Two Way Stretch (US 1961); The Running, Jumping and Standing Still Film (short); The Millionairess (US 1961); Never Let Go (US 1962). **1961** Mr. Topaze (aka I Like Money—US 1962). **1962** Lolita; The Dock Brief (aka Trial and Error—US); Only Two Can Play; The Road to Hong Kong; Waltz of the Toreadors; The Wrong Arm of the Law (US 1963). **1963** Heavens Above; Dr. Strangelove Or: How I Learned to Stop Worrying and Love the Bomb (US 1964). **1964** The World of Henry Orient; The Pink Panther; A Shot in the Dark. **1965** What's New Pussycat? **1966** The Wrong Box; After the Fox. **1967** Casino Royale; The Bobo; Woman Times Seven. **1968** I Love You, Alice B. Toklas; The Party. **1969** The Magic Christian (US 1970). **1970** Simon, Simon; There's a Girl in My Soup; Hoffman. **1972** Alice in Wonderland; Where Does It Hurt? **1973** Soft Beds Hard Battles; Ghost in the Noonday Sun; The Optimists. **1974** The Blockhouse. **1975** The Return of the Pink Panther; The Great McGonagall; Undercovers Hero. **1976** Murder by Death; The Pink Panther Strikes Again. **1978** Revenge of the Pink Panther. **1979** The Prisoner of Zenda; Being There. **1980** The Fiendish Plot of Dr. Fu Manchu.

SELLON, CHARLES
Born: Aug. 24, 1878, Boston, Mass. Died: June 26, 1937, La Crescenta, Calif. Screen and stage actor. Entered films in 1923.

Appeared in: **1923** The Bad Man (stage and film versions); Woman Proof; South Sea Love. **1924** Lover's Lane; The Roughneck; Flowing Gold; Merton of the Movies; Sundown. **1925** The Monster; The Night Ship; Tracked in the Snow Country; Private Affairs; The Calgary Stampede; Lucky Devil; Old Home Week; On the Threshold. **1926** High Steppers; The Speeding Venus; Racing Blood; Whispering Wires. **1927** Painted Ponies; Mysterious Rider; The Prairie King; Easy Pickings; King of Kings; The Valley of the Giants. **1928** Easy Come, Easy Go; Happiness Ahead; Something Always Happens; What a Night!; Feel My Pulse; The Count of Ten; Love Me and the World Is Mine. **1929** The Gamblers; Bulldog Drummond; Hot Stuff; Girl in the Glass Cage; Man and the Moment; The Mighty; The Saturday Night Kid; Big News; Men Are Like That; The Vagabond Lover; Sweetie. **1930** Under a Texas Moon; The Social Lion; Love Among the Millionaires; Borrowed Wives; Big Money; For the Love of Lil; Sea Legs; Tom Sawyer; Let's Go Native; Burning Up; Honey. **1931** Man to Man; The Painted Desert; Behind Office Doors; Laugh and Get Rich; Dude Ranch; The Age for Love; Penrod and Sam; The Tip-Off. **1932** I Am a Fugitive from a Chain Gang; The Drifter; Carnival Boat; The Dark Horse; Make Me a Star; Speed Madness; Ride Him, Cowboy!; Central Park. **1933** Employees' Entrance; Strictly Personal; As the Devil Commands; Central Airport; Golden Harvest. **1934** Ready for Love; Private Scandal; Elmer and Elsie; It's a Gift; Bright Eyes. **1935** One Hour Late; Alias Mary Dow; The Devil Is a Woman; Life Begins at 40; It's a Small World; In Old Kentucky; Welcome Home; The Casino Murder Case; Diamond Jim.

SELTEN, MORTON (Morton Stubbs)
Born: Jan. 6, 1860. Died: July 27, 1939, London, England. Screen and stage actor.

Appeared in: **1931** Service for Ladies (aka Reserved for Ladies—US). **1932** Wedding Rehearsal. **1933** Falling for You; The Love Wager. **1934** How's Chances. **1935** His Majesty and Co.; Annie, Leave the Room!; Ten Minute Alibi; Moscow Nights (aka I Stand Condemned—US 1936); Dark World. **1936** The Ghost Goes West; In the Soup; Two's Company; Juggernaut (US 1937). **1937** Fire Over England; Action for Slander (US 1938). **1938** The Divorce of Lady X; A Yank at Oxford. **1939** The Diplomatic Lover (reissue of How's Chances—US 1934); Shipyard Sally; Young Man's Fancy (US 1943). **1940** The Thief of Bagdad.

SELTZER, DANIEL
Born: 1933. Died: Mar. 1, 1980, New York, N.Y. (heart attack). Screen, stage actor and author.

Appeared in: **1978** An Unmarried Woman.

SELWYN, CLARISSA (Clarissa Schultz)
Born: Feb. 26, 1886, London, England. Died: June 13, 1948, West Hollywood, Calif. Screen and stage actress.

Appeared in: **1915** Her Own Way; Flash of an Emerald. **1916** Driftwood; The Come Back; The Woman He Feared; Gloriana. **1917** Master Hand; The Double Standard; Princess Virtue; The Wax Model. **1918** Beware of Strangers; Face Value. **1919** Home. **1920** Black Gate; Cup of Fury; Dangerous Days. **1921** Straight from Paris; Sacred and Profane Love; Marriage of William Ashe; The Lure of Jade; Queenie; Society Secrets. **1922** Two Kinds of Women; Up and At 'Em; The Woman Conquers. **1923** The Brass Bottle; You Can't Get Away With It; Why Women Remarry. **1924** Black Oxen; Secrets; Beau Brummell; Mademoiselle Midnight; The Fast Worker; The Last Man on Earth; The Dangerous Flirt; One Glorious Night. **1925** Sackcloth and Scarlet; The Lucky Horseshoe; We Moderns; Broadway Lady; The Fate of a Flirt; Scandal Proof. **1926** Infatuation; The Social Triangle; High Steppers; A Poor Girl's Romance. **1927** Resurrection; Naughty But Nice; The Crystal Cup; The Devil Dancer; Quarantined Rivals. **1928** Jazz Mad; The Heart of a Follies Girl; My Man; Sinner's Parade; Broadway Daddies; Glorious Betsy; The Baby Cyclone. **1929** Hard to Get; Isle of Lost Ships; Come Across; The Love Trap; Confessions of a Wife; Evidence. **1930** Lilies of the Field. **1932** My Pal the King; Cynara. **1934** Jane Eyre. **1936** One Good Turn.

SELWYN, EDGAR
Born: Oct., 1875, Cincinnati, Ohio. Died: Feb. 13, 1944, Hollywood, Calif. (cerebral hemorrhage). Screen, stage actor, film director, film producer, screenwriter, playwright and author. Divorced from actress Margaret Mayo (dec. 1951).

Appeared in: **1915** The Arab.

SELWYN, RUTH
Born: 1905, Tazwell, Va. Died: Dec. 14, 1954, Hollywood, Calif. Screen, stage actress, stage producer and writer.

Appeared in: **1931** Five and Ten. **1932** Speak Easily; Polly of the Circus; The Trial of Vivienne Ware; New Morals for Old. **1933** Men Must Fight. **1934** Fugitive Lovers. **1935** Baby Face Harrington.

SEMELS, HARRY
Born: Nov. 20, 1887, New York, N.Y. Died: Mar. 2, 1946, Los Angeles, Calif. Stage and screen actor. Entered films in 1910.

Appeared in: **1919** A Fallen Idol; Bound and Gagged (serial). **1920** Pirate Gold (serial); Velvet Fingers (serial). **1921** Hurricane Hutch (serial); The Sky Ranger (serial); Rogues and Romance. **1922** Speed (serial). **1923** Plunder (serial). **1924** Into the Net (serial); America. **1925** Play Ball (serial). **1926** The Demon; Moran of the Mounted; Stick to Your Story. **1927** Isle of Forgotten Women. **1928** Beware of Blondes; The Last Command; Out With the Tide; Put 'Em Up; Virgin Lips. **1929** The Delightful Rogue; Hawk of the Hills; The Royal Rider. **1930** Big Money; The Bad Man; Hell's Angels; Those Who Dance. **1931** Dance, Fools, Dance; Subway Express. **1933** Thrill Hunter; Flying Down to Rio. **1934** Our Daily Bread. **1935** Revenge Rider; Les Miserables; Sons of Steel; Old Sawbones (short); Stone of Silver Creek; The Last Outpost; Bordertown. **1936** The Charge of the Light Brigade; Under Two Flags; The Gay Desperado; The Case of the Velvet Claws; plus the following shorts: Half-Shot Shooters; Disorder in the Court; Movie Maniacs; Am I Having Fun. **1937** Hotel Haywire; Swing It, Professor; Grand Hooter (short); Swing High, Swing Low. **1938** Swiss Miss; Blockade. **1939** Rovin' Tumbleweeds; King of the Turf; Overland Mail; Three Little Sew and Sews (short); Ninotchka. **1940** Strange Cargo. **1941** General Nuisance (short). **1945** San Antonio.

SEMON, LARRY
Born: July 16, 1889, West Point, Miss. Died: Oct. 8, 1928, Garcelon Ranch, near Victorville, Calif. (pneumonia). Screen, vaudeville actor, film producer, film director, screenwriter and newspaperman. Married to actress Dorothy Dawn.

Appeared in: **1917** Boasts and Boldness; Worries and Wobbles; Shells and Shivers; Chumps and Chances; Gall and Golf; Slips and Slackers; Risks and Roughnecks; Plans and Pajamas; Plagues and Puppy Love; Sports and Splashes; Toughluck and Tin Lizzies; Rough Toughs and Rooftops; Spooks and Spasms; Noisy Naggers and Nosey Neighbors. **1918** Guns and Greasers; Babes and Boobs; Rooms and Rumors; Meddlers and Moonshine; Stripes and Stumbles; Rummies and Razors; Whistles and Windows; Spies and Spills; Romans and Rascals; Skids and Scalawags; Boodles and Bandits; Hindoos and Hazards; Bathing Beauties and Big Boobs; Dunces and Danger; Mutts and Motors; Huns and Hyphens; Bears and Bad Men; Frauds and Frenzies; Humbus and Husbands; Pluck and Plotters. **1919** The Simple Life; Traps and Tangles; Scamps and Scandals; Soapsuds and Sapheads; Well, I'll Be...; Passing the Buck; The Star Boarder; His Home Sweet Home; Between the Acts; Dull Care; Dew Drop Inn; The Headwaiter. **1920** The following shorts: The Grocery Clerk; The Fly Cop; School Days; Solid Concrete; The Stagehand; The Suitor. **1921** The following shorts: The Sportsman; The Hick; The Rent Collector; The Bakery; The Fall Guy; The Bell Hop. **1922** The following shorts: The Sawmill; The Show; A Pair of Kings; Golf; The Sleuth; The Counter Jumper. **1923** The following shorts: No Wedding Bells; The Barnyard; Midnight Cabaret; The Gown Shop; Lightning Love; Horseshoes. **1924** The Girl in the Limousine; plus the following shorts: Her Boy Friend; Kid Speed. **1925** The Perfect Clown; The Wizard of Oz; Go Straight; plus the following shorts: The Dome Doctor; The Cloudhopper. **1926** Stop, Look and Listen. **1927** Spuds; Underworld; plus the following shorts: The Stuntman; Oh What a Man. **1928** Dummies (short); A Simple Sap (short). **1930** Nuits de Chicago (French release of Underworld—1927).

SEMPLE, JACK
Died: Mar. 28, 1978. Screen actor.

Appeared in: Margin for Error.

SENNETT, MACK (Michael Sinnott)
Born: Jan. 17, 1880, Richmond, Quebec, Canada. Died: Nov. 5, 1960, Hollywood, Calif. Screen, stage, burlesque actor, film producer and film director. Entered films as an extra with Griffith. Introduced the Keystone Kops.

Appeared in: **1908** The Vaquero's Vow; Balked at the Altar; Father Gets in the Game; Mr.Jones Had a Card Party; The Curtain Pole; Mr. Jones at the Ball; An Awful Moment; A Wreath in Time; The Salvation Army Lass. **1909** The Slave; The Gibson Goddess; The Song of the Shirt; Politician's Love Story; The Lure of the Gown; Lucky Jim; The Jilt; The Seventh Day; A Convict's Sacrifice; The Better Way; Getting Even; The Awakening; In the Watches of the Night; The Trick That Failed; A Midnight Adventure; In a Hempen Bag; The Dancing Girl of Butte; A Corner in Wheat. **1910** All on Account of the Milk; An Affair of Hearts; A Knot in the Plot; Never Again; A Summer Tragedy; A Gold Necklace; The Passing of a Grouch; Effecting a Cure; His Wife's Sweethearts; The Newlyweds; A Midnight Cupid; A Mohawk's Way; Examination Day at School; An Arcadian Maid. **1911** The Italian Barber; Pricella's Engagement Kiss; Comrades; Paradise Lost; Misplaced Jealousy; The Crooked Road; A Dutch Gold Mine; The Ghost; Mr. Peck Goes Calling; The Dare Devil; The Village Hero; Trailing the Counterfeiter; Caught with the Goods; The $500 Reward. **1912** The Fatal Chocolate; A Message from the Moon; Their First Kidnapping Case; Tomboy Bessie; The Would-Be Shriner; Stern Papa. **1913** The Mistaken Masher; The Battle of Who Run; The Jealous Waiter; The Stolen Purse; Mabel's Heroes; The Sleuth's Last Stand; The Sleuths at the Floral Parade; A Strong Revenge; The Rube and the Baron; At Twelve O'Clock; Her New Beau; Mabel's Awful Mistake (aka Her Deceitful Lover); Their First Execution; Barney Oldfield's Race for a Life; The Hansom Driver; His Crooked Career; Mabel's Dramatic Career (aka Her Dramatic Debut); Love Sickness at Sea; For Lizzie's Sake; The Chief's Predicament; The Bangville Police. **1914** A False Beauty (aka A Faded Vampire); Mack at It Again; Mabel at the Wheel (aka His Daredevil Queen); The Fatal Mallet; The Knock-Out (aka The Pugilist); In the Clutches of a Gang; Our Country Cousin; The Property Man (aka The Roustabout); His Talented Wife; Tillie's Punctured Romance. **1915** Hearts and Planets; The Little Teacher (aka A Small Town Bully); My Valet; Stolen Magic; Fatty and the Broadway Stars. **1921** Molly O. **1922** Oh, Mabel Behave. **1931** Movie Town (short). **1939** Hollywood Cavalcade. **1955** Abbott and Costello Meet the Keystone Kops. **1961** Days of Thrills and Laughter (documentary).

SEN YUNG, VICTOR (aka VICTOR SEN YUNG)
Born: 1915. Died: Nov. 9, 1980, North Hollywood, Calif. (accidental asphyxiation). Screen and television actor.

Appeared in: **1938** Charlie Chan in Honolulu; Shadows Over Shanghai. **1939** Charlie Chan in Reno; Charlie Chan at Treasure Island; 20,000 Men a Year. **1940** The Letter; Charlie Chan in Panama; Charlie Chan's Murder Cruise; Murder Over New York; Charlie Chan at the Wax Museum. **1941** Charlie Chan in Rio; Dead Men Tell. **1942** Across the Pacific; A Yank on the Burma Road; Secret Agent of Japan; Castle in the Desert; Moontide; Little Tokyo, U.S.A.; Manila Calling. **1943** Night Plane from Chungking; China. **1946** Dangerous Millions; Shadows Over Chinatown; Dangerous Money. **1947** The Trap; Web of Danger; The Crimson Key; The Red Hornet; The Chinese Ring. **1948**

The Golden Eye; The Feathered Serpent; Half Past Midnight; Docks of New Orleans; The Shanghai Chest. **1949** State Department File 649; Oh, You Beautiful Doll. **1950** Ticket to Tomahawk; The Breaking Point; Woman on the Run. **1951** The Groom Wore Spurs; Peking Express; Valley of Fire. **1952** Target Hong Kong. **1953** Forbidden. **1954** The Shanghai Story. **1955** The Left Hand of God; Blood Alley; Soldier of Fortune. **1957** Men in War. **1958** Jet Attack; The Hunters; The Saga of Hemp Brown; She Demons. **1961** Flower Drum Song. **1962** Confessions of an Opium Eater. **1968** A Flea in Her Ear. **1970** The Hawaiians. **1980** Sam Marlowe, Private Eye (aka The Man With Bogart's Face).

SERAGNOLI, ORESTE
Died: Apr. 13, 1965. Screen actor.

SERDA, JULIA
Born: 1875, Vienna, Austria. Died: Nov. 3, 1965, Dresden, East Germany. Screen and stage actress.

Appeared in: **1925** Ein Walzer von Strauss (US 1932). **1928** A Modern Du Barry. **1930** Olympia (aka His Glorious Night); Zapfenstreich am Rhein (US 1933); Liebeswalzer (US 1931). **1931** The Living Corpse; Der Storchs Treikt (US 1932, aka Siegfried der Matrose); Der Herr Buerovorsteher (US 1932). **1932** Traum von Schoenbrunn (Dream of Schoenbrunn—US 1933); Liebe in Uniform (US 1934). **1935** Alles Weg'n dem Hund (US 1936, aka Das Verriickte Testament); Mein Leben fuer Maria Isabell (My Life for Maria Isabell—US); Liebesloute (US 1936, aka Hermann und Dorothea von Heute). **1936** Drei Maederl um Schubert (US 1937, aka Dreimaederlhaus). **1937** Masquerade in Vienna.

SERLING, ROD
Born: Dec. 25, 1924, Syracuse, N.Y. Died: June 28, 1975, Rochester, N.Y. (complications after heart surgery). Television producer, writer, narrator, screenwriter, author and screen actor.

Appeared in: **1973** Deadly Fathoms (narrator). **1975** The Outer Space Connection.

SERRANO, VINCENT
Born: 1867. Died: Jan. 10, 1935, New York, N.Y. (heart attack). Stage and screen actor.

Appeared in: **1919** Eyes of Youth. **1920** The Branded Woman. **1927** Convoy.

SERTEL, NEELA
Born: 1901, Turkey. Died: Dec., 1969, Istanbul, Turkey. Screen, stage and radio actress.

SERVAIS, JEAN
Born: 1910, Belgium. Died: Feb. 17, 1976, Paris, France (heart failure following surgery). Screen and stage actor.

Appeared in: **1931** Criminel. **1936** La Valse Eternelle; Les Miserables. **1939** Heartbeat. **1947** La Dance de Mort. **1948** Une Si Jolie Petite Plage. **1949** Prelude to Madness. **1953** Le Plaisir (aka House of Pleasure—US). **1956** Rififi. **1958** He Who Must Die; Les Jeux Dangereux. **1959** Tamango; Les Heros Sont Fatigues (The Heroes Are Tired, aka Heroes and Sinners—US). **1960** Meurtre en 45 Tours (Murder at 45 R.P.M.—US 1965). **1961** An Einem Freitag um Halb Zwolf (aka The World in My Pocket—US 1962); Les Menteurs (The Liars—US 1964). **1962** Le Crime ne Paie Pas (Crime Does Not Pay); The Longest Day. **1964** L'Homme de Rio (That Man from Rio). **1966** Lost Command. **1968** Meglio Vedova (Better a Widow—US 1969). **1969** They Came to Rob Las Vegas. **1974** The Devil's Nightmare.

SERVANTI, LUIGI
Born: 1885, Italy. Died: 1976, Italy? Screen actor.

Appeared in: **1929** The President.

SERVOSS, MARY
Born: 1888. Died: Nov. 20, 1968, Los Angeles, Calif. (heart ailment). Screen and stage actress.

Appeared in: **1941** The Lone Wolf Keeps a Date. **1942** The Postman Didn't Ring; In This Our Life. **1943** The Human Comedy; So Proudly We Hail. **1944** Four Jills in a Jeep; Youth Runs Wild; Mrs. Parkington; Summer Storm; Experiment Perilous; Danger Signal. **1945** Mildred Pierce; Conflict. **1946** My Reputation. **1948** Live Today for Tomorrow. **1949** Beyond the Forest.

SESSIONS, ALMIRA
Born: 1888, Washington, D.C. Died: Aug. 3, 1974, Los Angeles, Calif. Screen, stage, vaudeville, radio and television actress.

Appeared in: **1940** Jennie; Little Nelly Kelly; Chad Hanna. **1941** She Knew All the Answers; Sun Valley Serenade; Three Girls About Town; Blossoms in the Dust; Blondie in Society. **1942** Blondie for Victory; My Sister Eileen; Sullivan's Travels. **1943** My Kingdom for a Cook; The Heat's On; Seeing Nellie Home (short); The Ox-Bow Incident; Happy Go Lucky; Can't Help Singing; San Diego, I Love You; Slightly Dangerous; Presenting Lily Mars; Madame Curie. **1944** Bathing Beauty; Maisie Goes to Reno; I Love a Soldier; Dixie Jamboree; Henry Aldrich's Little Secret; Miracle of Morgan's Creek. **1945** The Woman Who Came Back; Nob Hill; Two O'Clock Courage; The Southerner. **1946** It's a Wonderful Life; Cross My Heart; Fear; She Wouldn't Say Yes; Diary of a Chambermaid; Do You Love Me?; The Missing Lady. **1947** The Bishop's Wife; Monsieur Verdoux; For the Love of Rusty; I Wonder Who's Kissing Her Now; Love and Learn; Cass Timberlane. **1948** The Bride Goes Wild; Good Sam; Julie Misbehaves; On Our Merry Way; Family Honeymoon; Apartment for Peggy; Arthur Takes Over. **1949** Night Unto Night; Roseanna McCoy; The Fountainhead; Ladies of the Chorus. **1950** Black Hand; Please Believe Me; Kill the Umpire; Summer Stock; Harvey; Valentino; Fancy Pants; Montana; The Blazing Hills (aka The Blazing Sun); The Old Frontier. **1951** Here Comes the Groom; The Lemon Drop Kid; A Millionaire for Christy; Hollywood Honeymoon (short). **1952** Oklahoma Annie; Wagons West. **1953** The Affairs of Dobie Gillis; The Sun Shines Bright; Ride, Vaquero!; Sweethearts on Parade; Paris Model; The Rocket Man. **1954** Forever Female; Hell's Outpost. **1955** The Prodigal; It's Always Fair Weather; Rebel Without a Cause. **1956** Calling Homicide; The Scarlet Hour. **1957** Loving You. **1958** The Female Animal; Andy Hardy Comes Home. **1961** Summer and Smoke. **1962** Paradise Alley. **1963** Under the Yum Yum Tree. **1966** Last of the Secret Agents?. **1968** Fire Creek; The Boston Strangler; Rosemary's Baby. **1970** Watermelon Man; ... Tick ... Tick ... Tick. **1971** Willard. **1972** Everything You Always Wanted to Know About Sex but Were Afraid to Ask.

SETON, SIR BRUCE
Born: May 29, 1909, Simla, India. Died: Sept. 27, 1969, London, England. Screen, stage and television actor. Divorced from actress Tamara Desni. Married to actress Antoinette Cellier.

Appeared in: **1935** Blue Smoke; Flame in the Heather. **1936** The Vandergilt Diamond Mystery; Sweeney Todd, the Demon Barber of Fleet Street (US 1939); Wedding Group (aka Wrath of Jealousy—US); Melody of My Heart; Annie Laurie; The Beauty Doctor; Cocktail; The End of the Road. **1937** Cafe Colette (aka Danger in Paris—US); Love from a Stranger; Father Steps Out; Racing Romance; The Green Cockatoo (US 1947 aka Four Dark Hours); Fifty-Shilling Boxer. **1938** If I Were Boss; Weddings Are Wonderful; You're the Doctor; Miracles Do Happen. **1939** The Middle Watch; Lucky to Me; Old Mother Riley Joins Up. **1946** The Curse of the Wraydons. **1948** Bonnie Prince Charlie; Scott of the Antarctic (US 1949); Look Before You Love; The Story of Shirley Yorke. **1949** Whiskey Galore! (aka Tight Little Island—US and Mad Little Island). **1950** The Blue Lamp; Paul Temple's Triumph (US 1951); Portrait of Clare. **1951** High Treason (US 1952); Take Me to Paris; Blackmailed; Worm's Eye View. **1952** Emergency Call (aka The Hundred Hour Hunt—US 1953). **1953** The Cruel Sea. **1954** Eight O'Clock Walk (US 1955); Delayed Action. **1957** West of Suez (aka Fighting Wildcats—US); There's Always Thursday; The Crooked Sky (US 1959); Morning Call. **1958** The Strange Case of Mr. Manning. **1959** Violent Moment (US 1966); Hidden Homicide (US 1960); Life in Danger (US 1964); John Paul Jones; Make Mine a Million (US 1965). **1960** Operation Cupid; Trouble with Eve (aka In Trouble with Eve—US 1964). **1961** Gorgo; The Frightened City (US 1962); Greyfriars Bobby.

SEUNG-HO, KIM
Born: 1918, South Korea. Died: Dec. 1, 1968, Seoul, Korea (cerebral hemorrhage). Screen actor.

SEVAL, NEVIN
Born: 1920, Turkey. Died: Nov., 1958, Adana, Turkey. Screen and stage actress.

SEVER, ALFRED
Born: 1891. Died: Mar. 26, 1953, New York, N.Y. Screen actor. Appeared in silent films.

SEVERIN-MARS
Born: France. Died: July 17, 1921 (pneumonia). Screen and stage actor.

Appeared in: **1918** La Dixieme Symphonie. **1921** La Roue.

SEVILLE, DAVID See BAGDASARIAN, ROSS S.

SEWALL, LUCILE
Born: 1888. Died: Dec. 15, 1976, Hollywood, Calif. Screen actress.

SEWELL, ALLEN D.
Born: 1883. Died: Jan. 20, 1954, Hollywood, Calif. Screen actor.

Appeared in: **1914** The Squaw Man; The Spoilers. **1927** Between Dangers.

SEYFERTH, WILFRIED
Born: 1908, Germany. Died: Oct. 9, 1954, near Wiesbaden, West Germany (auto accident). Screen and stage actor.

Appeared in: **1933** Schleppzug 17 (film debut). **1951** Decision Before Dawn. **1952** The Devil Makes Three; Toxi; Heimweh Nach Dir; Der Froehliche Weinberg (The Gay Vineyard: The Happy Vinegard (aka The Grapes are Ripe—US 1953). **1953** Das Tanzende Herz (The Dancing Heart—US 1958). **1958** Zero Eight One Five.

SEYMOUR, CLARINE
Born: 1901. Died: Apr. 25, 1920, New York, N.Y. Screen actress.

Appeared in: **1919** True Heart Susie; The Girl Who Stayed at Home. **1920** The Idol Dancer.

SEYMOUR, HARRY
Born: 1890. Died: Nov. 11, 1967, Hollywood, Calif. (heart attack). Screen, stage, vaudeville actor and composer.

Appeared in: **1925** East Lynne. **1932** One Way Passage; The Tenderfoot; You Said a Mouthful; Man Against Woman. **1933** Footlight Parade. **1934** Manhattan Melodrama; The Crosby Case; Service With a Smile (short); The Case of the Howling Dog; Six Day Bike Rider. **1935** Devil Dogs of the Air; The Irish in Us; Gold Diggers of 1935; Shipmates Forever; Broadway Hostess; Behind Green Lights. **1938** A Slight Case of Murder; Boy Meets Girl. **1939** Kid Nightingale. **1940** A Fugitive From Justice. **1941** I Wake Up Screaming (aka Hot Spot). **1942** Yankee Doodle Dandy. **1944** Irish Eyes are Smiling. **1945** Billy Rose's Diamond Horseshoe; The Dolly Sisters; San Antonio; A Tree Grows in Brooklyn. **1946** My Reputation; Night and Day. **1947** Mother Wore Tights; I Wonder Who's Kissing Her Now. **1948** Give My Regards to Broadway; Road House; When My Baby Smiles at Me. **1949** It Happens Every Spring. **1950** A Ticket to Tomahawk. **1951** Show Boat. **1953** Gentlemen Prefer Blondes; Vivki; Mr. Scoutmaster. **1954** River of No Return. **1955** The Girl in the Red Velvet Swing; Daddy Long Legs; How to Be Very, Very Popular; Violent Saturday. **1958** Marjorie Morningstar.

SEYMOUR, JANE
Born: 1899. Died: Jan. 30, 1956, New York, N.Y. Screen, stage, radio and television actress.

Appeared in: **1939** Back Door to Heaven. **1941** Tom, Dick and Harry; Remember the Day. **1952** Never Wave at a Wac.

SHAAN, RON MORGAN (Ron Morgan Shalan)
Died: July 5, 1976, Honolulu, Hawaii. Screen, stage, radio and television actor.

Appeared in: **1961** The Gambler Wore a Gun; Gun Fight.

SHACKLEFORD, FLOYD
Died: Dec. 17, 1972. Screen actor.

Appeared in: **1925** The Call of Courage; Where the Worst Begins; The White Outlaw. **1926** Sky High Corral. **1927** The Enchanted Island. **1928** Absent; The Ballyhoo Buster. **1929** The Forward Pass; Hardboiled Rose; Stark Mad. **1930** Man Hunter. **1933** The Savage Girl. **1935** Black Fury. **1936** The Lonely Trail. **1941** Jungle Man. **1945** The Vampire's Ghost. **1953** White Witch Doctor.

SHACKLETON, ROBERT W.
Born: 1914, Lawrence, Mass. Died: June 21, 1956, Jacksonville, Fla. (leukemia). Stage and screen actor.

Appeared in: **1951** The Wonder Kid. **1952** Where's Charley? (stage and film versions).

SHADE, JAMESSON
Born: 1895. Died: Apr. 18, 1956, Hollywood, Calif. (heart attack). Screen, stage and television actor.

Appeared in: **1943** Santa Fe Scouts; The Woman of the Town. **1944** The Utah Kid. **1945** Wilson. **1949** Treasure of Monte Cristo; Cover-Up. **1955** Ain't Misbehavin'.

SHADOW, BERT
Born: 1890. Died: Nov. 12, 1936, Hollywood, Calif. (heart ailment). Screen and vaudeville actor. Was partner in "Shadow and McNeill" vaudeville team with his wife Lillian McNeill.

SHAFER, MOLLIE B.
Born: 1872. Died: Nov. 19, 1940, Hollywood, Calif. Screen actress.

Appeared in: **1921** The Big Adventure; While the Devil Laughs.

SHAFER, ROBERT K.
Born: 1909. Died: June 19, 1981, Tenafly, N.J. Screen, stage actor and singer.

Appeared in: **1958** Damn Yankees (stage and film versions).

SHAIFFER, "TINY" (Howard Charles Shaiffer)
Born: 1918. Died: Jan. 24, 1967, Burbank, Calif. Screen actor. Member of "Our Gang" comedies.

SHAIN, JOHN HOWARD
Born: 1903. Died: Dec. 6, 1979, Bryn Mawr, Pa. Screen actor, film producer and television producer. Appeared in silent films.

SHALIAPIN, IRINA *See* CHALIAPIN, IRINA

SHANKLAND, RICHARD
Born: 1904. Died: Jan. 18, 1953, New York, N.Y. Screen, stage and television actor.

Appeared in: **1958** Love Island.

SHANLEY, ROBERT
Died: June 30, 1968, Los Angeles, Calif. Screen, stage, radio, television actor and singer.

Appeared in: **1943** This Is the Army (stage and film versions).

SHANNON, ALEXANDER K.
Born: 1862, Harve, France. Died: Mar. 7, 1932, New York, N.Y. Screen and stage actor.

Appeared in: **1917** Barbary Sheep. **1918** A Doll's House. **1921** The Simp. **1922** Are Children to Blame?; Easy Money.

SHANNON, CORA
Born: Jan. 30, 1869 or 1879?, Ill. Died: Aug. 27, 1957, Woodland Hills, Calif. (cancer). Screen and stage actress. Entered films in 1912.

Appeared in: **1923** Long Live the King; Held to Answer; The Spanish Dancer; The Good Bad Boy; The Shadows of Paris; The Way Men Love; Her Temporary Husband; Painted People; Cape Cod Folks; Racing Luck; One Law for the Woman; Welcome Stranger; The Last Man; A Woman Who Sinned. **1924** The Dawn of a Tomorrow; Triumph Rose of the Ghetto; The Woman on the Jury; The Silent Stranger; San Francisco; Wanderer of the Wasteland; Hold Your Breath. **1926** Trumpin' Trouble. **1929** Smiling Irish Eyes. **1930** Lummox. **1945** The Bells of St. Mary's. **1951** Mr. Belvedere Rings the Bell. **1952** Something to Live For. **1953** Abbott and Costello Go to Mars.

SHANNON, MRS. DALE
Died: June 1, 1923, New York, N.Y. Stage and screen actress. Appeared in Lubin films.

SHANNON, EFFIE
Born: 1867, Cambridge, Mass. Died: July 24, 1954, Bay Shore, N.Y. Screen and stage actress.

Appeared in: **1914** After the Ball. **1918** The Common Cause. **1921** Mama's Affair. **1922** The Man Who Played God; The Secrets of Paris; Sure-Fire Flint. **1923** The Tie That Binds; Bright Lights of Broadway; Jacqueline of the Blazing Barriers. **1924** Damaged Hearts; Roulette; Sinners in Heaven; Greater Than Marriage; The Side Show of Life. **1925** Sally of the Sawdust; Soul of Fire; The New Commandment; The Pearl of Love; Wandering Fires. **1932** The Wiser Sex.

SHANNON, ELIZABETH S. (aka BETTY SUNDMARK)
Born: 1914. Died: Aug. 18, 1959, N.Y. Screen actress. Divorced from actor Alan Curtis (dec. 1953).

SHANNON, ETHEL (Ethel Shannon Jackson)
Born: 1898. Died: July 14, 1951, Hollywood, Calif. Screen actress. Married to screenwriter Joe Jackson (dec. 1932).

Appeared in: **1920** An Old Fashioned Boy. **1922** Man's Law and God's; The Top O' the Morning; Watch Him Step. **1923** The Hero; Daughters of the Rich; The Girl Who Came Back; Maytime. **1924** Lightning Romance; Riders Up. **1925** Charley's Aunt; High and Handsome; The Phantom Express; Stop Flirting; The Texas Trail; Speed Wild. **1926** Oh, Baby!; The Speed Limit; The Sign of the Cross; The Silent Power; The High Flyer; The Buckaroo Kid; Danger Quest. **1927** Babe Comes Home; Through Thick and Thin.

SHANNON, FRANK CONNOLLY
Born: 1875. Died: Feb. 1, 1959, Hollywood, Calif. Screen, stage and radio actor.

Appeared in: **1921** The Bride's Play; Perjury. **1922** Boomerang Bill. **1924** Icebound; Monsieur Beaucaire. **1925** G-Men; Men Without Names; The Eagle's Brood. **1936** The Prisoner of Shark Island; Flash Gordon (serial); The Texas Rangers. **1937** The Affairs of Cappy Ricks; The Adventurous Blonde. **1938** Blondes at Work; Flash Gordon's Trip to Mars (serial); Mars Attacks the World; Torchy Blane in Panama; Torchy Gets Her Man. **1939** Torchy Plays With Dynamite; Torchy Blane in Chinatown; Torchy Runs for Mayor; The Night of Nights. **1940** Flash Gordon Conquers the Universe (serial); The Return of Frank James; Wildcat Bus; Dancing on a Dime. **1943** The Phantom (serial).

SHANNON, HARRY
Born: June 13, 1890, Saginaw, Mich. Died: July 27, 1964, Hollywood, Calif. Screen and stage actor.

Appeared in: **1930** The Three Sailors (short); Heads Up. **1933** Poor Fish (short). **1940** Young as You Feel; Parole Fixer; One Crowded Night; Too Many Girls; Gambling on the High Seas; The Girl from Avenue A; Young Tom Edison; City of Chance; Tear Gas Squad; Tugboat Annie Sails Again; Sailor's Lady. **1941** Citizen Kane; The Saint in Palm Springs; Hold Back the Dawn. **1942** The Lady Is Willing; The Big Street; Mrs. Wiggs of the Cabbage Patch; Once Upon a Honeymoon; This Gun for Hire; The Falcon Takes Over; In Old California; Random Harvest. **1943** Alaska Highway; Headin' for God's Country; True to Life; Idaho; Someone to Remember; Song of Texas; Gold Town; The Powers Girl. **1944** The Sullivans; The Mummy's Ghost; When the Lights Go on Again; Yellow Rose of Texas; Eve of St. Mark; Ladies of Washington. **1945** Incendiary Blonde; Captain Eddie; Crime, Inc.; Nob Hill; Within These Walls. **1946** The Jolson Story; Night Editor; San Quentin; I Ring Doorbells; Ziegfeld Follies; The Last Crooked Mile. **1947** The Devil Thumbs a Ride; The Farmer's Daughter; Nora Prentiss; The Red House; Time Out of Mind; The Invisible Wall; Exposed; Dangerous Years. **1948** The Lady from Shanghai; Mr. Blandings Builds His Dream House; Fighting Father Dunne; Feudin', Fussin' and A-Fightin'. **1949** Tulsa; Rustlers; Champion; Mr. Soft Touch; The Devil's Henchmen. **1950** Mary Ryan, Detective; Tarnished; The Dungeon; Cow Town; The Underworld Story; Singing Guns; Where Danger Lives; Three Little Words; Curtain Call at Cactus Creek; Hunt the Man Down; The Flying Missile; The Killer That Stalked New York; The Gunfighter. **1951** Pride of Maryland; The Scarf; Al Jennings of Oklahoma; Blue Blood; The Lemon Drop Kid. **1952** High Noon; Boots Malone; Flesh and Fury; The Outcasts of Poker Flat; Lure of the Wilderness. **1953** Cry of the Hunted; Kansas Pacific; Jack Slade; Phantom Stallion; Roar of the Crowd. **1954** Executive Suite; Witness to Murder; Rails Into Laramie. **1955** Not as a Stranger; The Tall Men; Violent Men; At Gunpoint; The Marauders. **1956** Come Next Spring; Written on the Wind; The Peacemaker. **1957** The Lonely Man; Duel at Apache Wells; Hell's Crossroads. **1958** The Buccaneer; Man or Gun. **1961** Summer and Smoke; Wild in the Country. **1962** Gypsy.

SHANNON, JACK
Born: 1892. Died: Dec., 1968, Los Angeles, Calif. Screen actor and stuntman. Married to actress Grace Cunard (dec. 1967).

Appeared in: **1935** Stormy.

SHANNON, PEGGY (Winona Sammon)
Born: Jan. 10, 1909, Pine Bluff, Ark. Died: May 11, 1941, North Hollywood, Calif. (natural causes). Screen and stage actress. Divorced from actor Allan Davis (dec. 1943). Married to actor and cameraman Albert Roberts (dec. 1941).

Appeared in: **1930** The Gob (short). **1931** Silence; The Road to Reno; Good Morning (short); The Secret Call; Touchdown. **1932** The Meal Ticket (short); False Faces; This Reckless Age; Hotel Continental; The Painted Woman; Society Girl. **1933** Girl Missing; Devil's Mate; The Deluge; Turn Back the Clock. **1934** Fury of the Jungle; Back Page. **1935** The Fighting Lady; Night Life of the Gods; The Case of the Lucky Legs. **1936** Ellis Island; The Man I Marry. **1937** Youth on Parole. **1938** Girls on Probation. **1939** The Amazing Mr. Williams; Dad for a Day (short); Blackwell's Island; The Women; The Adventures of Jane Arden; Fixer Dugan. **1940** The House Across the Bay; Triple Justice; Cafe Hostess (aka Street of Missing Women); All About Hash (short).

SHANNON, RAY
Born: 1895. Died: Jan. 1, 1971, Cincinnati, Ohio. Screen, stage, vaudeville and radio actor.

SHANNON, WILLIAM ROBERT
Born: 1935. Died: July 3, 1981, Los Angeles, Calif. (heart attack). Screen, television actor and stuntman.

Appeared in: **1968** Blue; The Green Berets.

SHANOR, PEGGY
Born: 1896. Died: May 30, 1935, New York, N.Y. Screen, stage and vaudeville actress. Featured in vaudeville with Vera Gordon and Sam Selbert.

Appeared in: **1918** The House of Hate (serial). **1919** The Lurking Peril (serial). **1920** The Mystery Mind (serial). **1921** The Sky Ranger (serial). **1922** The Prodigal Judge.

SHARKEY, TOM "SAILOR"
Born: 1873, Dundalk, Ireland. Died: Apr. 17, 1953, San Francisco, Calif. Professional boxer and screen actor.

Appeared in: **1925** Bashful Buccaneer; The Range Terror. **1926** Fighting Jack. **1927** The Cruise of the Hellion; The Thirteenth Juror. **1928** Good Morning Judge; Isle of Lost Men. **1932** Madison Square Garden. **1968** The Legendary Champions (documentary).

SHARLAND, REGINALD
Born: 1887, Southend-on-Sea, Essex, England. Died: Aug. 21, 1944, Loma Linda, Calif. Screen, stage and radio actor.

Appeared in: **1929** Show of Shows; Woman to Woman. **1930** Girl of the Port; Scotland Yard; What a Widow; Inside the Lines. **1931** Born to Love. **1934** Long Last Father.

SHARON, WILLIAM E.
Died: Dec. 26, 1968. Screen actor.

Appeared in: **1962** Experiment in Terror.

SHARP, HENRY (Henry Schacht)
Born: 1887. Died: Jan. 10, 1964, Brooklyn, N.Y. Screen, stage actor and educator. Entered films with D. W. Griffith.

Appeared in: **1945** A Song to Remember. **1956** Singing in the Dark. **1957** A Face in the Crowd; The Violators.

SHARP, LEONARD "LEN"
Born: 1890. Died: Oct. 24, 1958, Waterford, England. Screen, stage and television actor. Married to actress Nora Gordon (dec. 1970).

Appeared in: **1950** The Mudlark. **1952** The Stolen Plans (US 1962). **1954** For Better or Worse (aka Cocktails in the Kitchen—US 1955). **1955** The Ladykillers (US 1956). **1957** At the Stroke of Nine (US 1958).

SHARP, RAMONA (Ramona Smith)
Born: May 9, 1901, Longwood, Mo. Died: Apr. 26, 1941, Glendale, Calif. (cancer). Screen actress and writer.

SHARPE, DAVID
Born: 1910, St. Louis, Mo. Died: Mar. 30, 1980, Altadena, Calif. (Parkinson's disease). Screen, vaudeville, television actor, circus performer and stuntman.

Appeared in: **1929** Masked Emotions. **1930** Doctor's Orders; Bigger and Better; Ladies Last. **1931** Blood and Thunder; High Gear; Love Fever; Air Tight; Call a Cop. **1935** All American Toothache (short); Roaring Roads; Adventurous Knights. **1936** Neighborhood House; Desert Justice; Idaho Kid; Mind Your Own Business; Pan Handlers (short); Pinch Singer. **1937** Melody of the Plains; Drums of Destiny; Galloping Dynamite; Ten Minutes to Play; Where Trails Divide; Young Dynamite. **1938** Dick Tracy Returns (serial). **1939** Daredevils of the Red Circle; Three Texas Steers; Wyoming Outlaw; Rovin' Tumbleweeds. **1940** Covered Wagon Trails; Adventures of Red Ryder (serial); Mysterious Dr. Satan (serial). **1941** Silver Stallion; Thunder Over the Prairie; The Adventures of Captain Marvel (serial); Dick Tracy vs. Crime, Inc. (serial). **1942** Texas to Bataan; Trail Riders; Spy Smasher (serial); Perils of Nyoka (serial). **1943** Two-Fisted Justice; Haunted Ranch. **1946** Colorado Serenade; The Falcon's Adventure. **1947** Bells of San Angelo; The Wistful Widow of Wagon Gap. **1948** The Fuller Brush Man; Adventures of Frank and Jesse James. **1949** Susanna Pass; King of the Rocket Men (serial). **1950** The Girl from San Lorenzo; The Good Humor Man. **1951** The Wild Blue Yonder. **1953** Desert Legion; Forbidden; Veils of Bagdad. **1972** The Life and Times of Judge Roy Bean. **1978** Heaven Can Wait.

SHARPE, GYDA
Born: 1908. Died: Jan. 14, 1973, Hollywood, Calif. (cancer). Screen and stage actress.

SHARPE, LESTER (Lester Scharff)
Born: Mar. 21, 1895, New York, N.Y. Died: Nov. 30, 1962, Los Angeles, Calif. (heart attack). Screen actor.

Appeared in: **1940** Remedy for Riches. **1942** Crossroads; Time to Kill. **1943** Hangmen Also Die. **1944** Lady in the Dark; The Mummy's Ghost. **1947** Song of My Heart. **1948** The Gallant Legion; Port Said. **1949** Amazon Quest; I Was a Male War Bride. **1950** The Desert Hawk; The Flying Saucer; Where the Sidewalk Ends; One Too Many; Unmasked. **1952** The Big Trees; Carrie. **1954** Princess of the Nile.

SHARPLIN, JOHN
Born: 1916. Died: Apr., 1961, Harrogate, England. Screen, stage and television actor.

SHATTUCK, EDWARD F.
Born: 1890. Died: Jan. 31, 1948, Hollywood, Calif. Screen and vaudeville actor.

SHATTUCK, TRULY
Born: 1876. Died: Dec. 6, 1954, Hollywood, Calif. Screen and stage actress.

Appeared in: **1921** A Wise Fool; The Great Impersonation; The Speed Girl. **1922** The Glory of Clementina; The Hottentot; Beauty's Worth. **1923** Daughters of the Rich. **1927** Rubber Heels. **1935** The Perfect Clue.

SHAW, ANTHONY
Born: Dec. 29, 1897, England. Died: 1980, England? Screen and stage actor. Entered films in 1933.

Appeared in: **1941** The Patient Vanishes (US 1947, aka This Man Is Dangerous). **1942** They Flew Alone (aka Wings and the Woman—US). **1952** Top Secret (aka Mr. Potts Goes to Moscow—US 1954). **1956** The Silken Affair (US 1957). **1957** How to Murder a Rich Uncle.

SHAW, BUDDY
Born: 1906. Died: Aug. 29, 1976, Hollywood, Calif. Screen and stage actor. Entered films in 1911.

Appeared in: **1929** Little Wild Girl; Must We Marry?; Old Age Handicap; Bye, Bye, Buddy; China Slaver. **1931** Riders of the North.

SHAW, C. MONTAGUE
Born: Mar. 23, 1884, Adelaide, South Australia. Died: Feb. 6, 1968, Woodland Hills, Calif. Screen and stage actor.

Appeared in: **1926** The Set-Up. **1928** The Water Hole. **1929** Behind That Curtain; Morgan's Last Raid; Square Shoulders. **1932** The Silent Witness; Pack up Your Troubles; Sherlock Holmes; Cynara; Letty Lynton; Rasputin and the Empress. **1933** The Big Brain; The Masquerader; Today We Live; Cavalcade; Gabriel Over the White House; Queen Christina. **1934** Shock; Sisters Under the Skin; Fog; Riptide; House of Rothschild. **1935** Vanessa, Her Love Story; David Copperfield; Becky Sharp; Two Sinners; I Live for Love. **1936** The Leathernecks Have Landed; Undersea Kingdom (serial); My American Wife; King of Burlesque; Ace Drummond (serial); The Story of Louis Pasteur. **1937** Riders of the Whistling Skull; The Frame Up; Parole Racket; The Sheik Steps Out; A Nation Aflame; Ready, Willing and Able; The King and the Chorus Girl. **1938** Mars Attacks the World; Four Men and a Prayer; Little Miss Broadway; Suez; Flash Gordon's Trip to Mars (serial). **1939** Mr. Moto's Last Warning; The Adventures of Sherlock Holmes; The Three Musketeers; The Rains Came; Stanley and Livingstone; Buck Rogers (serial); Daredevils of the Red Circle (serial); Zorro's Fighting Legion (serial). **1940** My Son, My Son; The Gay Caballero; Charlie Chan's Murder Cruise; The Green Hornet Strikes Again (serial); Mysterious Dr. Satan (serial). **1941** Hard Guy; Burma Convoy; Holt of the Secret Service (serial); Charley's Aunt. **1942** The Black Swan; Thunder Birds; Ramdom Harvest; Pride of the Yankees. **1943** G-Men vs. the Black Dragon (serial). **1944** Faces in the Fog. **1945** An Angel Comes to Brooklyn; Tonight and Every Night. **1946** Road to the Big House. **1947** Thunder in the Valley.

SHAW, DENNIS
Born: 1921. Died: Feb. 28, 1971, London, England (heart attack). Screen and television actor.

Appeared in: **1959** The Mummy; The Night We Dropped a Clanger (aka Make Mine a Double—US 1961); Jack the Ripper (US 1960). **1961** Hellfire Club (US 1963).

SHAW, ELLIOTT
Born: 1887. Died: Aug. 13, 1973. Screen actor. Member of the "Shannon Four" and "The Revelers."

Appeared in: Metro short.

SHAW, FRANK M.
Born: 1894. Died: May 7, 1937, Kansas City, Mo. Screen, stage and radio actor.

SHAW, GEORGE BERNARD
Born: July 26, 1856, Dublin, Ireland. Died: Nov. 1, 1950, Ayot St. Lawrence, England (bladder ailment, injuries sustained in fall). Playwright, author, screenwriter and screen performer.

Appeared in: **1918** Masks and Faces.

SHAW, HAROLD M.
Born: 1878. Died: Jan. 30, 1926 (auto accident). Screen actor, film producer, director and screenwriter. Married to actress Edna Flugrath (dec. c. 1928). Entered films with Edison Co. in 1909.

Appeared in: **1911** The Three Musketeers; Bob and Rowdy; The Modern Dianas; Mary's Masquerade; The Death of Nathan Hale; Foul Play; Her Wedding Ring; How Mrs. Murray Saved the American Flag; The Kid from the Klondyke; A Conspiracy Against the King; The Awakening of John Bond; The Black Arrow; The Reform Candidate; Home; The Lure of the City; Santa Claus and the Club Man; Freezing Auntie. **1912** Martin Chuzzlewit; Thirty Days at Hard Labor; A Question of Seconds; The Bachelor's Waterloo; The Jewels; Mother and Daughter; The Corsican Brothers; Her Face; For the Commonwealth; The Bank President's Son; The Convict's Parole. **1913** The Wop. **1924** Winning a Continent.

SHAW, LEON
Born: Wolfville, Nova Scotia. Died: June, 1981, New York, N.Y. (cardiac arrest). Screen, stage and television actor.

SHAW, OSCAR (Oscar Schwartz)
Born: 1891. Died: Mar. 6, 1967, Little Neck, N.Y. Screen, stage and radio actor.

Appeared in: **1924** The Great White Way. **1925** The King on Main Street. **1926** Going Crooked; Upstage. **1929** The Cocoanuts; Marianne. **1940** Rhythm on the River.

SHAW, PHILIP *See* WALTZ, PATRICK "PAT"

SHAW, ROBERT
Born: Aug. 9, 1925, Lancashire, England, or Scotland? Died: Aug. 27, 1978, near Tourmakeady, Ireland (heart attack). Screen, stage, television actor, playwright and author. Divorced from actress Jennifer Bourke. Later married to actress Mary Ure (dec. 1975), and Virginia Jansen. Do not confuse with U.S. actor with same name.

Appeared in: **1955** The Dam Busters (film debut). **1956** A Hill in Korea (aka Hell in Korea—US 1957). **1958** Sea Fury (US 1959). **1962** The Valiant; Tomorrow at Ten (US 1964). **1963** The Caretaker (aka The Guest—US 1964); From Russia With Love (US 1964). **1964** The Luck of Ginger Coffey. **1965** Battle of the Bulge. **1966** A Man for All Seasons. **1968** Custer of the West. **1969** Battle of Britain; The Royal Hunt of the Sun. **1970** The Birthday Party; Figures in a Landscape (US 1971). **1971** A Town Called Bastard. **1972** Young Winston. **1973** The Hireling; A Reflection of Fear. **1974** The Sting; The Taking of Pelham 1-2-3. **1975** Jaws; Diamonds. **1976** Robin and Marian; Swashbuckler; End of the Game. **1977** The Deep; Black Sunday; Welcome to Blood City. **1978** Force Ten From Navarone.

SHAW, SUSAN (Patsy Sloots)
Born: Aug. 29, 1929, Norwood, England. Died: Nov. 27, 1978, Middlesex, England. Screen and stage actress. Divorced from actor Albert Lieven (dec. 1971), and later married to actor Bonar Colleano (dec. 1958). Mother of actor Mark Colleano.

Appeared in: **1946** London Town (aka My Heart Goes Crazy—US 1953); Walking on Air. **1947** Holiday Camp (US 1948); Jassy (US 1948); The Upturned Glass; It Always Rains on Sunday (US 1949). **1948** London Belongs to Me (aka Dulcimer Street—US); My Brother's Keeper (US 1949); To the Public Danger; Here Comes the Huggetts (US 1950); Quartet (US 1949). **1949** Vote for Huggett; It's Not Cricket; Marry Me (US 1951); The Huggetts Abroad; Train of Events (US 1952). **1950** The Woman in Question (aka Five Angles on Murder—US 1953); Waterfront (aka Waterfront Women—US 1952). **1951** Pool of London; There Is Another Sun (aka Wall of Death—US 1952). **1952** Wide Boy; A Killer Walks. **1953** The Large Rope (US 1955); Small Town Story (US 1955). **1954** The Good Die Young (US 1955); Time Is My Enemy (US 1957). **1955** Stolen Time (aka Blonde Blackmailer—US 1958); Stock Car. **1956** Fire Maidens of Outer Space. **1957** Davy. **1958** The Diplomatic Corpse. **1959** Carry on Nurse (US 1960). **1960** The Big Day. **1962** Stranglehold. **1963** The Switch.

SHAWN, TED (Edwin M. Shawn)
Born: 1892. Died: Jan. 9, 1972, Orlando, Fla. (emphysema). Screen, stage actor, dancer and choreographer. Married to actress and dancer Ruth St. Denis (dec. 1969).

Appeared in: **1919** Don't Change Your Husband.

SHAY, DOROTHY (Dorothy Sims)
Born: 1921, Jacksonville, Fla. Died: Oct. 22, 1978, Santa Monica, Calif. (massive stroke). Screen, radio, television actress and singer. Known as "Park Avenue Hillbilly."

Appeared in: **1951** Comin' Round the Mountain.

SHAY, PATRICIA
Died: Aug. 9, 1966. Screen actress.

Appeared in: **1944** To Have and Have Not. **1948** Million Dollar Weekend.

SHAY, ROSE CECILIA
Died: June 4, 1929, Hollywood, Calif. Screen actress.

SHCHUKIN, BORIS V.
Born: 1894, Russia. Died: Oct. 7, 1939, Moscow, Russia. Screen actor.

Appeared in: **1936** Revolutionists. **1938** Lenin in October. **1939** Lenin in 1918.

SHEA, BIRD
Died: Nov. 23, 1924, Los Angeles, Calif. Screen actress.

Appeared in: **1925** The Lady.

SHEA, DONALD J. "SHORTY"
Died: Aug., 1969, Chatsworth, Calif. (murdered). Screen actor and stuntman.

SHEA, JACK
Died: July 17, 1972. Screen actor. Do not confuse with actor Jack Shea (dec. 1970).

SHEA, JOHN "JACK"
Born: 1900, Charleston, W.Va. Died: Oct. 13, 1970, Huntington, W. Va. Screen, stage and vaudeville actor. Do not confuse with actor Jack Shea (dec. 1972).

SHEA, MERVIN (Mervin David John Shea)
Born: Sept. 5, 1900, San Francisco, Calif. Died: Jan. 27, 1953, Sacramento, Calif. Professional baseball player and screen actor.

Appeared in: **1949** The Stratton Story.

SHEA, THOMAS E.
Born: 1861, East Cambridge, Mass. Died: Apr. 23, 1940, Cambridge, Mass. Screen, stage actor and playwright. Married to actress Nellie Burkett.

Appeared in: **1914** The Man O' Wars Man.

SHEA, WILLIAM (William James Shea)
Born: Scotland. Died: Nov. 5, 1918, Brooklyn, N.Y. Screen, stage actor and screenwriter. Entered films in 1905 with Vitagraph.

Appeared in: **1911** Intrepid Davy; The Politician's Dream; Vanity Fair. **1912** The Bond of Music; Pandora's Box; The Little Minister; Her Old Sweetheart; Chumps; Who's to Win?; Aunty's Romance; Too Many Caseys. **1913** An Elopement at Home; O'Hara's Godchild; The Last of the Madisons; The Widow's Might; Classmates; Frolic; Suspicious Henry; The Mouse and the Lion; Dick—The Dead Shot; His Life for His Emperor; She Never Knew; Cupid Through the Keyhole; 'Arriet's Baby. **1914** The Spirit and the Clay; Jerry's Uncle's Namesake; Sweeney's Christmas Bird; Mrs. Maloney's Fortune; The Hero; The Rival Undertakers; The Old Rag Doll; The Vases of Hymen. **1915** A Pair of Queens; Mr. Bixbie's Dilemma; Mr. Jarr's Vacation; Some Duel; Pat Hogan—Deceased; A Wireless Rescue; The Lady of Shalott; Two and Two; Heavy Villains; She Took a Chance; When Hooligan and Dooligan Ran for Mayor; Benjamin Bunter—Booking Agent; Between Two Fires; No Tickee-No Washee. **1916** Help! Help! Help!; Footlights of Fate; My Lady's Slipper; A Night Out; Huey—Process Server; Putting the Pep in Slowtown; Kernel Nutt, the Piano Tuner; The Blue Envelope Mystery; The Bigamist; The Memory Mill; A Villainous Villain. **1917** Sally in a Hurry; The Doctor's Deception. **1918** A Bachelor's Children.

SHEAN, AL (Alfred Schoenberg)
Born: 1868, Dornum, Germany. Died: Aug. 12, 1949, New York, N.Y. Screen, stage, vaudeville actor and songwriter. Was partner in vaudeville act "Mr. Gallagher and Mr. Shean."

Appeared in: **1923** Around the Town. **1930** Chills and Fever (short). **1934** Music in the Air. **1935** Sweet Music; Page Miss Glory; The Traveling Saleslady; Symphony of Living; It's in the Air. **1936** The Law in Her Hands; San Francisco; Hitchike to Heaven; At Sea Ashore (short). **1937** Tim Tyler's Luck (serial); The Road Back; It Could Happen to You; 52nd Street; Live, Love and Learn; The Prisoner of Zenda. **1938** Too Hot to Handle; The Great Waltz. **1939** Joe and Ethel Turp Call on the President; Broadway Serenade. **1940** The Blue Bird; Friendly Neighbors. **1941** Ziegfeld Girl. **1942** Tish. **1943** Hitler's Madmen; Crime Doctor. **1944** Atlantic City. **1946** People Are Funny.

SHEARN, EDITH
Born: 1870. Died: May 14, 1968, Hollywood, Calif. Screen actress. Married to actor Warner Oland (dec. 1938).

SHEEHAN, BOBBIE
Died: Oct. 8, 1974. Screen actress and extra.

Appeared in: **1956** Around the World in 80 Days.

SHEEHAN, JACK
Born: 1891, N.Y. Died: Dec. 11, 1958, New York, N.Y. Screen and stage actor.

Appeared in: **1929** Acquitted.

SHEEHAN, JOHN J.
Born: Oct. 22, 1890, Oakland, Calif. Died: Feb. 15, 1952, Hollywood, Calif. Screen, stage and vaudeville actor. Entered films with American Film Co. in 1916.

Appeared in: **1930** Swing High; Broken Dishes; Kismet. **1931** Fair Warning; The Criminal Code. **1932** Hold 'Em Jail. **1933** Lost in Limehouse or Lady Esmerelda's Predicament (short); Hard to Handle; The Warrior's Husband; The Past of Mary Holmes; King for a Night; The Gay Nineties (short). **1934** Trimmed in Furs (short); An Old Gypsy Custom (short); The Countess of Monte Cristo; Little Miss Marker; The Circus Clown; Such Women Are Dangerous. **1935** The Murder Man; The Goose and the Gander. **1936** It Had to Happen; Three Godfathers; Laughing Irish Eyes; Ticket to Paradise; The Ex-Mrs. Bradford; The Case of the Black Cat; Smart Blonde; Here Comes Carter. **1937** Join the Marines; All Over Town; Mama Runs Wild; On the Avenue; Wake Up and Live; Marked Woman; Midnight Court; Love Takes Flight; Night Club Scandal. **1938** Many Sappy Returns (short). **1940** Tin Pan Alley; Slightly Honorable; Margie; Young As You Feel. **1941** Broadway Limited; Kisses for Breakfast. **1942** This Gun for Hire; Yankee Doodle Dandy; Wake Island. **1943** Swingtime Johnny; Johnny Come Lately; The Heavenly Body. **1946** The Killers. **1948** I Wouldn't Be in Your Shoes. **1949** The Doolins of Oklahoma. **1950** Stage to Tucson. **1951** His Kind of Woman; Soldiers Three.

SHEEHAN, TESS (Maria Theresa Sheehan)
Born: 1888. Died: Oct. 29, 1972, Detroit, Mich. Screen, stage, radio and television actress.

SHEEN, FULTON J.
Born: 1895. Died: Dec. 10, 1979, New York, N.Y. (heart trouble). Screen, radio, television actor, columnist and Roman Catholic priest.

Appeared in: **1942** The Eternal Gift. **1946** The Story of the Pope (narrator).

SHEER, WILLIAM A.
Born: Birmingham, England. Died: July 10, 1933, New York, N.Y. Screen, stage and vaudeville actor.

Appeared in: **1915** Regeneration. **1917** Within the Law. **1918** The Cabaret Girl. **1919** Sealed Envelope. **1920** A Daughter of Two Worlds; Headin' Home.

SHEERER, WILL E.
Died: Dec. 24, 1915. Stage and screen actor.

Appeared in: **1913** Over the Cliffs.

SHEFFIELD, REGINALD (Reginald Sheffield Cassan)
Born: Feb. 18, 1901, London, England. Died: Dec. 8, 1957, Pacific Palisades, Calif. Screen and stage actor. Entered films in 1913.

Appeared in: **1923** David Copperfield. **1924** Classmates. **1925** The Pinch Hitter. **1926** White Mice. **1927** The Nest; College Widow. **1928**

Sweet Sixteen; The Adorable Cheat. **1930** Old English; The Green Goddess. **1931** Partners of the Trail. **1934** The House of Rothschild; Of Human Bondage. **1935** Black Sheep; Cardinal Richelieu; Society Fever; Splendor. **1936** Charge of the Light Brigade. **1937** Another Dawn. **1938** Female Fugitive; The Buccaneer; The Adventures of Robin Hood. **1939** Gunga Din. **1940** Earthbound; Hudson's Bay. **1941** The Lady Eve; Suspicion. **1942** Eyes in the Night; Eagle Squadron. **1943** Appointment in Berlin; The Man from Down Under; Tonight We Raid Calais; Bomber's Moon. **1944** Our Hearts Were Young and Gay; The Man in Half Moon Street; Wilson; The Great Moment. **1945** Captain Kidd. **1946** Three Strangers; Centennial Summer; To Each His Own; Devotion. **1948** Kiss the Blood Off My Hands. **1949** Mr. Belvedere Goes to College; Prison Warden; That Forsyte Woman. **1952** At Sword's Point. **1953** Young Bess; Forbidden; The Story of Three Loves; Second Chance. **1956** 23 Paces to Baker Street; The Secret of Treasure Mountain. **1957** The Story of Mankind. **1958** The Buccaneer (and 1938 version); Marjorie Morningstar.

SHELBY, CHARLOTTE (Lily Pearl Miles)
Died: Mar. 13, 1957, Santa Monica, Calif. Screen actress. Mother of actresses Margaret Shelby (dec. 1939) and Mary Miles Minter.

Appeared in: **1915** Always in the Way. **1916** Dimples. **1917** Her Country's Call.

SHELBY, MARGARET
Born: 1900, San Antonio, Tex. Died: Dec. 21, 1939. Screen actress. Daughter of actress Charlotte Shelby (dec. 1957) and sister of actress Mary Miles Minter.

Appeared in: **1912** Billie. **1916** Faith. **1917** Her Country's Call; Environment; Peggy Leads the Way. **1918** Rosemary Climbs the Heights; Wives and Other Wives. **1919** A Bachelor's Wife; The Intrusion of Isabel; The Amazing Imposter. **1920** Jenny Be Good.

SHELDON, CONNIE
Born: 1921. Died: Jan. 10, 1947, New York, N.Y. (leukemia). Screen and stage actress.

SHELDON, JEROME
Born: 1891. Died: Apr. 15, 1962, Hollywood, Calif. Screen actor. Appeared in silents.

SHELDON, JERRY (Charles H. Patton)
Born: 1901. Died: Apr. 11, 1962, Hollywood, Calif. Screen and television actor.

Appeared in: **1952** Monkey Business. **1956** Love Me Tender.

SHELDON, MARION W.
Born: 1886. Died: Feb. 28, 1944, Hollywood, Calif. Screen and stage actress. Entered films in 1917.

SHELLEY, NORMAN
Born: 1903. Died: Aug. 22, 1980, London, England. Screen, stage and radio actor.

Appeared in: **1950** Her Favourite Husband (aka The Taming of Dorothy—US). **1951** The Adventurers (aka The Great Adventure—US). **1960** The Price of Silence. **1963** A Place to Go. **1968** Otley (US 1969). **1969** Oh! What a Lovely War; Frankenstein Must Be Destroyed (US 1970).

SHELTON, DON
Born: 1912. Died: June 19, 1976, Los Angeles, Calif. Screen and stage actor. Married to actress Mary Bear (dec. 1972).

Appeared in: **1950** Mystery Street. **1951** Queen for a Day (aka Horsie); Two Dollar Better. **1954** The Command; Them. **1956** Hilda Crane. **1957** Dragstrip Girl; Invasion of the Saucer-Men. **1958** Bullwhip; High School Hellcats.

SHELTON, GEORGE
Born: 1884. Died: Feb. 12, 1971, N.Y. (burns). Screen, stage, vaudeville, burlesque, radio and television actor. Partner in vaudeville and radio with Tom Howard (dec. 1955).

Appeared in: **1932** The Babbling Book (short). **1934** Rural Romeos (short). **1935** Educational shorts. **1936** Where Is Wall Street (short). **1945** The House on Ninety-Second Street. **1947** Kiss of Death.

SHELTON, JAMES
Born: 1913, Paducah, Ky. Died: Sept. 2, 1975, Miami, Fla. Screen actor, songwriter and television writer.

Appeared in: **1929** Over the Hill. **1931** City Lights.

SHELTON, JOHN
Born: May 18, 1917, Los Angeles, Calif. Died: May 16, 1972, Ceylon (natural causes). Screen actor. Divorced from Kathryn Grayson, Irene Winston, and model Marti Stanley. Later married to Lorraine Ludwig.

Appeared in: **1940** We Who Are Young; Dr. Kildare Goes Home; The Ghost Comes Home. **1941** Blonde Inspiration. **1942** Whispering Ghosts; A-Haunting We Will Go; Foreign Agent. **1946** The Time of Their Lives; The Ghost Steps Out. **1947** The Big Fix; Little Miss Broadway. **1948** Joe Palooka in Winner Takes All. **1953** Sins of Jezebel.

SHELTON, MARIE (Betty Marie Shelton)
Died: Mar. 13, 1949, Hollywood, Calif. Screen and stage actress. Divorced from publicist Biesel, and later married to film director Allan Dwan (dec. 1981).

Appeared in: **1924** Manhandled; A Society Scandal.

SHEPHERD, WILLIAM H.
Born: 1894. Died: July 10, 1979, Sydney, Australia (heart attack). Screen actor and film editor.

Appeared in: **1975** At Long Last Love.

SHEPLEY, IDA
Born: England. Died: Mar., 1975, London, England. Screen, stage actress and singer.

SHEPLEY, MICHAEL (Michael Shepley-Smith)
Born: Sept. 29, 1907, Plymouth, England. Died: Sept. 28, 1961, London, England. Screen and stage actor.

Appeared in: **1931** Black Coffee. **1934** Bella Donna (US 1935); Are You a Mason?; The Green Pack. **1935** The Rocks of Valpre (aka High Treason—US 1937); The Lad; The Ace of Spades; The Triumph of Sherlock Holmes; Squibs; Vintage Wine; The Private Secretary. **1936** In the Soup. **1938** Housemaster (US 1939); Crackerjack (aka The Man with a Hundred Faces—US); It's in the Air (aka George Takes the Air—US 1940). **1939** Goodbye Mr. Chips. **1941** Quiet Wedding. **1942** The Great Mr. Handel (US 1943). **1943** The Demi-Paradise (aka Adventure for Two—US 1945). **1945** Henry V (US 1946); A Place of One's Own (US 1949); I Live in Grosvenor Square (aka A Yank in London—US 1946). **1947** My Own Executioner (US 1949). **1949** Maytime in Mayfair (US 1952). **1951** Mr. Denning Drives North (US 1953). **1952** Home at Seven (aka Murder on Monday—US 1953); Secret People. **1954** You Know What Sailors Are; Happy Ever After (aka Tonight's the Night—US). **1955** Where There's a Will; Doctor at Sea (US 1956) An Alligator Named Daisy (US 1957). **1956** My Teenage Daughter (aka Teenage Bad Girl—US 1957); Dry Rot. **1957** The Passionate Stranger (aka A Novel Affair—US); Not Wanted on Voyage. **1958** Henry V (reissue of 1944 film); Gideon's Day (aka Gideon of Scotland Yard—US 1959). **1961** Double Bunk; Don't Bother to Knock.

SHEPLEY, RUTH
Born: 1889, N.Y. Died: Oct. 5, 1951, New York, N.Y. Screen and stage actress.

Appeared in: **1922** When Knighthood Was in Flower.

SHEPPARD, BERT
Born: 1882. Died: Aug. 18, 1929. Screen actor.

SHEPPARD, JIM
Born: 1937. Died: Aug. 18, 1977, Canon City, Colo. (accident while filming). Screen actor and stuntman.

Appeared in: **1959** The Wild and the Innocent. **1967** Hour of the Gun. **1978** Comes a Horseman.

SHERIDAN, ANN (Clara Lou Sheridan)
Born: Feb. 21, 1915, Denton, Tex. Died: Jan. 21, 1967, Hollywood, Calif. (cancer). Screen, stage, radio and television actress. Divorced from actors Edward Norris and George Brent (dec. 1979). Married to actor Scott McKay.

Appeared in: **1927** The Bandit's Son; Casey at the Bat; Casey Jones; Galloping Thunder; The Way of All Flesh; Wedding Bills. **1933** Search; Bolero. **1934** One Hour Late; Ladies Should Listen; Come on Marines; Notorious Sophie Lang; Limehouse Blues; Kiss and Make Up; Mrs. Wiggs of the Cabbage Patch; Wagon Wheels; Shoot the Works; College Rhythm; You Belong to Me. **1935** Hollywood Extra Girl (short); Enter Madame; Home on the Range; Behold My Wife; Car No. 99; Rocky Mountain Mystery; The Glass Key; The Crusades; Fighting Youth; Red Blood of Courage; Mississippi; Rumba. **1936** Sing

Me a Love Song. **1937** The Great O'Malley; Black Legion; Footloose Heiress; San Quentin; Wine, Women and Horses. **1938** Alacatraz Island; Little Miss Thoroughbred; The Patient in Room 18; She Loved a Fireman; Mystery House; Cowboy from Brooklyn; Angels With Dirty Faces; Letter of Introduction; Broadway Musketeers. **1939** They Made Me a Criminal; Dodge City; Naughty but Nice; Indianapolis Speedway; Winter Carnival; Angels Wash Their Faces. **1940** It All Came True; Castle on the Hudson; Torrid Zone; They Drive by Night; City for Conquest. **1941** Honeymoon for Three; Navy Blues; The Man Who Came to Dinner; King's Row. **1942** Juke Girl; George Washington Slept Here; The Animal Kingdom; Wings for the Eagle. **1943** Edge of Darkness; Thank Your Lucky Stars. **1944** Shine On, Harvest Moon; The Doughgirls. **1946** One More Tomorrow. **1947** Nora Prentiss; The Unfaithful. **1948** Good Sam; Treasure of the Sierra Madre; Silver River. **1949** I Was a Male War Bride. **1950** Woman on the Run; Stella. **1952** Steel Town; Just Across the Street. **1953** Take Me to Town; Appointment in Honduras. **1956** Come Next Spring; The Opposite Sex. **1957** Woman and the Hunter.

SHERIDAN, DAN (Daniel Marvin Sheridan)
Born: Sept. 3, 1916, Ireland. Died: June, 29, 1963, Encino, Calif. (suicide—barbiturates). Screen actor.

Appeared in: **1948** California Firebrand. **1949** Horseman of the Sierra. **1958** Hell's Five Hours; Cole Younger—Gunfighter; Bullwhip; Day of the Outlaw; King of the Wild Stallions; Seven Guns to Mesa. **1959** The Young Captives. **1960** Ten Who Dared. **1962** Lonely Are the Brave.

SHERIDAN, FRANK
Born: June 11, 1869, Boston, Mass. Died: Nov. 24, 1943, Hollywood, Calif. Screen and stage actor.

Appeared in: **1921** Anne of Little Smoky; The Rider of the King Log; Her Lord and Master. **1922** One Exciting Night. **1923** The Man Next Door. **1924** Two Shall Be Born. **1925** Lena Rivers. **1929** Fast Life. **1930** Side Street; The Other Tomorrow; Danger Lights. **1931** The Public Defender; A Free Soul; Murder by the Clock; Silence; Donovan's Kid; The Ladies of the Big House; The Man I Killed; The Flood. **1932** The Last Mile; Okay America; Afraid to Talk; Washington Merry-Go-Round. **1933** The Man Who Dared; Mama Loves Papa; Deception; The Woman Accused. **1934** Wharf Angel; Upperworld; The Witching Hour; The Cat's Paw. **1935** Frisco Kid; The Whole Town's Talking; Whispering Smith Speaks; Nevada; The Payoff. **1936** The Leavenworth Case; The Country Gentleman; Murder With Pictures; Conflict. **1937** The Life of Emile Zola; A Night at the Movies (short); The Great O'Malley; Woman in Distress; A Fight to the Finish. **1938** City Streets.

SHERMAN, EVELYN
Born: Dec. 13, 1882, Iowa. Died: Apr. 19, 1974. Screen actress.

Appeared in: **1921** School Days. **1923** Suzanna; Reno; Trilby. **1924** A Fool's Awakening. **1925** Proud Flesh; Don Daredevil; Speed Madness. **1926** The Border Whirlwind; Sunshine of Paradise Alley. **1927** Blonde or Brunette. **1930** Song of the Caballero. **1933** California Trail.

SHERMAN, FRED E.
Born: May 14, 1905. Died: May 20, 1969, Woodland Hills, Calif. Screen, stage and television actor.

Appeared in: **1946** Behind Green Lights; Lady in the Lake. **1950** Chain Lightning. **1951** Valley of Fire. **1957** Dino; The Tall T. **1959** Some Like It Hot. **1961** Twist All Night.

SHERMAN, LOWELL
Born: Oct. 11, 1885, San Francisco, Calif. Died: Dec. 28, 1934, Hollywood, Calif. (pneumonia). Screen, stage, vaudeville, burlesque actor and film director. Son of theatrical manager John Sherman and actress Julia Louise Grey. Divorced from Evelyn Booth, actresses Pauline Garon (dec. 1965) and Helen Costello (dec. 1957).

Appeared in: **1915** Sold. **1920** The New York Idea; Way Down East; Yes or No. **1921** The Gilded Lily; What No Man Knows; Molly O. **1922** Grand Larceny; The Face in the Fog. **1923** Bright Lights of Broadway. **1924** Monsieur Beaucaire; The Masked Danger; The Truth About Women; The Spitfire. **1925** Satan in Sables. **1926** You Never Know Women; Lost at Sea; The Wilderness Woman; The Reckless Lady; The Love Toy. **1927** The Girl from Gay Paree; Convoy. **1928** The Whip; The Whip Woman; The Ship; Mad Hour; The Divine Woman; The Garden of Eden; The Scarlet Dove; The Heart of a Follies Girl. **1929** Nearly Divorced (short—aka Phipps); Evidence; General Crack; A Lady of Chance. **1930** The Pay Off (aka The Losing Game); Ladies of Leisure; He Knew Women; Midnight Mystery; Lawful Larceny; O Sailor, Behave!; Mammy. **1931** The Royal Bed (aka The Queen's Husband); High Stakes; Bachelor Apartment; Way Down East (reissue if 1920 version). **1932** What Price Hollywood?; False Faces; The Greeks Had a Word for Them; The Slippery Pearls (short).

SHERMAN, MARY (Ida Sherman)
Born: 1887, Russia. Died: Aug. 13, 1980, Santa Monica, Calif. Screen actress. Entered films in 1921.

Appeared in: **1923** The Ten Commandments; The Hunchback of Notre Dame. **1926** Ben Hur. **1927** The King of Kings; The Jazz Singer. **1930** All Quiet on the Western Front. **1931** Frankenstein. **1948** The Snake Pit.

SHEROCK, CLARENCE "SHORTY"
Born: 1916. Died: Feb. 26, 1980, Los Angeles, Calif. (cancer). Jazz trumpeter and screen actor.

SHERRY, J. BARNEY (J. Barney Sherry Reeves)
Born: 1872, Germantown, Pa. Died: Feb. 22, 1944, Philadelphia, Pa. Screen, stage, vaudeville and radio actor.

Appeared in: **1905** Raffles, the Amateur Cracksman. **1909-1912** Western series. **1917** Flying Colors; Fuel of Life; Fanatics. **1918** Recording Day; The Secret Code; Evidence; Real Folks; Who Killed Walton?; Her Decision; High Stakes. **1919** The Lion Man (serial); May of Filbert. **1920** The Black Gate; Go and Get It; Dinty. **1921** Burn 'Em Up Barnes; The Barbarian; Just Outside the Door; Man—Woman—Marriage; Thunderclap; The Lotus Eater. **1922** Sure-Fire Flint; Back Pay; The Inner Man; Island Wives; A Woman's Woman; When the Desert Calls; 'Til We Meet Again; Shadows of the Sea; Notoriety; John Smith; What Fools Men Are; The Secrets of Paris; The Broken Silence. **1923** The White Sister; Jacqueline of Blazing Barriers. **1924** Born Rich; Galloping Hoofs (serial); The Warrens of Virginia; Lend Me Your Husband; Miami. **1925** Daughters Who Pay; Play Ball (serial); Crackerjack; Lying Wives; The Live Wire; A Little Girl in a Big City; Enemies of Youth. **1926** The Brown Derby; The Prince of Tempters; Broken Homes; Casey of the Coast Guard (serial). **1927** Spider Webs; The Crimson Flash (serial). **1928** Alex the Great; The Wright Idea; Forgotten Faces. **1929** Jazz Heaven; Broadway Scandals; The Voice Within.

SHERWOOD, BOBBY (Robert J. Sherwood, Jr.)
Born: 1915, Ind. Died: Jan. 23, 1981, Auburn, Mass. (cancer). Band leader, trumpeter, screen and radio actor.

Appeared in: **1948** Campus Sleuth. **1957** Pal Joey.

SHERWOOD, MILLIGE G.
Born: 1876. Died: Nov. 12, 1958, Hollywood, Calif. Screen and stage actor.

SHERWOOD, YORKE
Born: 1873. Died: Sept. 27, 1958, Hollywood, Calif. Screen actor.

Appeared in: **1926** The Man in the Saddle. **1928** The Cossacks; A Thief in the Dark; Gentlemen Prefer Blondes. **1930** The Man from Blankley's; Temple Tower. **1931** The Man in Posession. **1933** Eagle and the Hawk. **1936** Lloyds of London. **1944** Jane Eyre. **1956** 23 Paces to Baker Street.

SHIELD, FRED
Born: 1904. Died: 1970. Screen actor.

Appeared in: **1945** The Three Caballeros.

SHIELDS, ARTHUR
Born: 1896, Dublin, Ireland. Died: Apr. 27, 1970, Santa Barbara, Calif. (emphysema). Screen, stage and television actor. Brother of actor Barry Fitzgerald (dec. 1961).

Appeared in: **1932** Sign of the Cross. **1936** The Plough and the Stars. **1939** Drums Along the Mohawk. **1940** The Long Voyage Home; Little Nellie Kelly. **1941** Lady Scarface; The Gay Falcon; How Green Was My Valley; Confirm or Deny. **1942** The Loves of Edgar Allen Poe; Broadway; This Above All; Pacific Rendezvous; Gentleman Jim; Nightmare; The Black Swan. **1943** Above Suspicion; Lassie Come Home; The Man from Down Under. **1944** Keys of the Kingdom; Youth Runs Wild; National Velvet; The White Cliffs of Dover; The Sign of the Cross (revised version of 1932 film). **1945** Roughly Speaking; Phantoms, Inc. (short); The Corn Is Green; Too Young to Know; The Valley of Decision. **1946** Three Strangers; The Verdict; Gallant Journey. **1947** The Shocking Miss Pilgrim; Easy Come, Easy Go; The Fabulous Dorseys; Seven Keys to Baldpate. **1948** Fighting Father Dunne; Tap Roots; My Own True Love. **1949** She Wore a Yellow Ribbon; The Fighting O'Flynn; Challenge to Lassie; Red Light. **1950** Tarzan and the Slave Girl. **1951** The River; People Against O'Hara; Apache Drums; Sealed Cargo; Blue Blood; A Wonderful Life; The Barefoot Mailman. **1952** The Quiet Man. **1953** Scandal at Scourie; South Sea Woman; Main Street to Broadway. **1954** River of No Return; Pride of the Blue Grass; World for Ransom. **1956** The King and Four Queens. **1957** Daughter of Dr. Jekyll. **1958** Enchanted Island. **1959** Night of the Quarter Moon. **1960** For the Love of Mike. **1962** The Pigeon That Took Rome.

SHIELDS, ELLA (Ella Buscher)
Born: Sept. 26, 1879, Baltimore, Md. Died: Aug. 5, 1952, Lancaster, England. Screen, stage and vaudeville actress.

Appeared in: **1918** Herself.

SHIELDS, FRANK (Francis X. Shields)
Born: Nov. 18, 1910, New York, N.Y. Died: Aug. 19, 1975. Screen actor.

Appeared in: **1935** Murder in the Fleet; I Live My Life. **1936** Come and Get It. **1937** The Affairs of Cappy Ricks; The Hoosier Schoolboy. **1938** The Goldwyn Follies.

SHIELDS, FREDERICK
Born: 1904. Died: June 30, 1974. Screen, radio actor, writer and radio director.

Appeared in: **1933** The Farmer's Friend (narrator); Her Majesty the Queen Bee (narrator); Queen of the Underworld (narrator).

SHIELDS, HELEN
Died: Aug. 7, 1963, New York, N.Y. Screen, stage and television actress.

Appeared in: **1951** The Whistle at Eaton Falls. **1956** The Wrong Man.

SHIELDS, SANDY
Born: 1873. Died: Aug. 3, 1923, New York, N.Y. Screen and stage actor.

SHIELDS, SYDNEY
Born: 1888. Died: Sept. 19, 1960, Queens, N.Y. Screen and stage actress. Appeared in silents.

SHIMODA, YUKI
Born: 1922, Calif. Died: May 21, 1981, Los Angeles, Calif. Screen, stage, television actor, stage director, stage producer and dancer.

Appeared in: **1958** Auntie Mame. **1959** Career. **1961** Seven Women from Hell; A Majority of One. **1962** The Horizontal Lieutenant. **1965** Once a Thief. **1976** Midway. **1977** MacArthur. **1980** The Last Flight of Noah's Ark; The Octagon.

SHINDO, EITARO
Born: 1899. Died: Dec., 1977, Tokyo, Japan (heart failure). Screen, stage and television actor.

Appeared in: **1952** Saikaku Ichidai Onna (aka Koschoku Ichidai Onna, and aka Life of Oharu—US 1964). **1954** Sansho Dayu (aka Sansho the Bailiff, and aka The Bailiff—US 1969). **1956** Yang Kwei Fel (Most Noble Lady). **1957** Akasen Chital (Off Limits, aka Street of Shame—US). **1962** Ratai (The Body—US 1964).

SHINE, JOHN L.
Born: Mar. 28, 1854. Died: Oct. 16, 1930, New York, N.Y. Screen, stage actor and playwright.

Appeared in: **1916** Little Lady Eileen. **1921** Man and Woman.

SHINE, WILFRED
Born: 1863, Manchester, England. Died: Mar. 14, 1939, Kingston, England. Screen, stage, burlesque, television actor and radio writer. Father of actor Billy Shine.

Appeared in: **1928** The Burgomaster of Stilemode. **1929** Lily of Killarney; The Manxman; Under the Greenwood Tree; The Lady from the Sea. **1930** The Loves of Robert Burns; The Last Hour; Cross Roads. **1931** Old Soldiers Never Die; The Hound of the Baskervilles; The Bells. **1933** Marooned.

SHINER, RONALD
Born: June 8, 1903, London, England. Died: June, 30, 1966, London, England. Screen, stage and radio actor. His enormous nose was insured for $30,000.

Appeared in: **1934** My Old Dutch (film debut); Doctors Orders. **1935** Royal Cavalcade (aka Regal Cavalcade—US); It's a Bet; Once a Thief; Line Engaged; Gentleman's Agreement; Squibbs. **1936** King of Hearts; Excuse My Glove. **1937** The Black Tulip; Dreaming Lips; Dinner at the Ritz; Beauty and the Barge. **1938** A Yank at Oxford; Prison Without Bars; They Drive By Night. **1939** The Mind of Mr. Reeder (aka The Mysterious Mr. Reeder—US 1940); Trouble Brewing; Flying Fifty Five; The Missing People (US 1940); The Gang's All Here (aka The Amazing Mr. Forrest—US); I Killed the Count (aka Who is Guilty?—US 1940); Discoveries; Come on George; The Middle Watch. **1940** Bulldog Sees It Through; The Case of the Frightened

Lady (aka The Frightened Lady—US 1940); Salvage with a Smile; Old Bill and Son. **1941** The Seventh Survivor; South American George. **1942** They Flew Alone (aka Wings and the Woman—US); Those Kids from Town; Sabotage at Sea; King Arthur Was a Gentleman; The Balloon Goes Up. **1943** Thursday's Child; Get Cracking; Miss London Ltd; The Gentle Sex; The Butler's Dilemma. **1944** Bees in Paradise. **1945** I Live in Grosvenor Square (ak A Yank in London—US 1946); The Way to the Stars (aka Johnny in the Clouds—US). **1946** George in Civvy Street; Caesar and Cleopatra. **1947** The Man Within (aka The Smugglers—US 1948); Brighton Rock. **1949** Forbidden. **1951** Worm's Eye View; The Magic Box (US 1952); Reluctant Heroes. **1952** Little Big Shot. **1953** Top of the Form; Innocents in Paris (US 1955); Laughing Anne (US 1954). **1954** Up to His Neck; Aunt Clara. **1955** See How They Run. **1956** My Wife's Family; Dry Rot; Keep It Clean. **1957** Not Wanted On Voyage; Carry on Admiral (aka The Ship Was Loaded—US 1959). **1958** Girls at Sea (US 1962). **1959** The Navy Lark; Operation Bullshine (US 1963). **1960** The Night We Got the Bird.

SHIPMAN, NELL
Born: Oct. 25, 1892. Died: Jan. 23, 1970. Screen, stage, vaudeville actress, screenwriter and film director.

Appeared in: **1916** Through the Wall. **1918** The Mystery of Lake Lethe. **1921** The Girl from God's Country. **1923** The Grub Stake. **1927** The Golden Yukon.

SHIPSTAD, ROY
Born: 1911. Died: Jan. 20, 1975. Professional ice skater, stage producer and screen actor.

Appeared in: **1939** Ice Follies of 1939.

SHIRART, GEORGIA
Born: 1862. Died: Feb., 1929, Los Angeles, Calif. Screen actress. Entered films with Lubin Co. in 1913.

Appeared in: **1923** The Girl Who Came Back.

SHIRLEY, BOBBIE
Died: Feb. 13, 1970. Screen actress. Appeared in silents.

SHIRLEY, FLORENCE
Born: 1893. Died: May 12, 1967, Hollywood, Calif. Screen and stage actress.

Appeared in: **1939** The Women; Ninotchka. **1949** Lady With Red Hair; Private Affairs. **1941** When Ladies Meet. **1942** Maisie Gets Her Man; A Yank at Eton; Secret Agent of Japan; Her Cardboard Lover; We Were Dancing. **1943** Let's Face It; The Dancing Masters. **1952** Deadline, U.S.A.; Stars and Stripes Forever.

SHIRLEY, TOM (Thomas P. Shirley)
Born: 1900. Died: Jan. 24, 1962, New York, N.Y. Screen, stage, radio and television actor. Entered films as a child with Essanay Films in Chicago.

Appeared in: **1926** Lightning Bill; Red Hot Leather. **1927** King of Kings.

SHOCKLEY, MARIAN
Born: Kansas City, Mo. Died: Dec. 14, 1981, Los Angeles, Calif. Screen, stage, radio and television actress. Married to Clayton "Bud" Collyer.

Appeared in: **1943** Stage Door Canteen.

SHOEMAKER, ANN
Born: 1891. Died: Sept. 18, 1978, Los Angeles, Calif. (cancer). Screen, stage, vaudeville, radio and television actress. Married to actor Henry Stephenson (dec. 1956).

Appeared in: **1933** Chance at Heaven. **1934** Dr. Monica. **1935** The Woman in Red; Stranded; A Dog of Flanders; Alice Adams. **1936** Sins of Man. **1937** Shall We Dance; Life of the Party; Stella Dallas; They Won't Forget. **1939** Think First (short); Romance of the Redwoods; They All Come Out; Babes in Arms. **1940** My Favorite Wife; The Farmer's Daughter; The Marines Fly High; Seventeen; Curtain Call; An Angel from Texas; Strike Up the Band; Ellery Queen, Master Detective; Girl from Avenue A. **1941** Scattergood Pulls the Strings; You'll Never Get Rich. **1943** Above Suspicion. **1944** Man from Frisco; Mr. Winkle Goes to War. **1945** Phantoms, Inc. (short); Boogie Woogie (short); What a Blonde; Conflict. **1947** Magic Town. **1948** Wallflower; The Return of the Whistler. **1949** A Woman's Secret; Shockproof. **1950** House By the River. **1960** Sunrise at Campobello (stage and film versions). **1966** The Fortune Cookie.

SHOOTING STAR
Born: 1890. Died: June 4, 1966, Hollywood, Calif. (stroke). Sioux Indian screen actor. Entered films approx. 1935.

Appeared in: **1936** Ride, Ranger, Ride. **1949** The Cowboy and the Indians; Laramie.

SHOPP, HERMAN
Born: 1904. Died: Aug. 8, 1954, Rome, Italy. Screen actor.

SHORES, BYRON L.
Born: 1907. Died: Nov. 13, 1957, Kansas City, Mo. (multiple sclerosis). Stage and screen actor.

Appeared in: **1940** You the People (short); Too Many Girls. **1941** Wedding Worries (short); Johnny Eager; Blossoms in the Dust. **1942** Rover's Big Chance (short). **1943** This Is the Army; The Major and the Minor; The Mad Doctor of Market Street. **1943** Air Raid Wardens; Family Trouble (short).

SHORT, ANTRIM
Born: 1900, Cincinnati, Ohio. Died: Nov. 23, 1972, Woodland, Hills, Calif. (emphysema). Screen, stage actor, casting director and talent agent. Married to actress Frances Morris. Entered films in 1912 with American Biograph.

Appeared in: **1917** Jewel in Pawn; Tom Sawyer; Pride and the Man. **1918** The Yellow Dog. **1919** Romance and Arabella; Please Get Married. **1920** The Right of Way. **1921** O'Malley of the Mounted; The Son of Wallingford; Rich Girl, Poor Girl; Black Beauty. **1922** Beauty's Worth. **1924** Classmates. **1925** Wildfire; Married? **1926** The Pinch Hitter; The Broadway Boob; Jack O'Hearts. **1936** Movie Maniacs (short). **1937** The Big Show; Artists and Models; Lodge Night (short).

SHORT, FLORENCE
Born: 1889. Died: July 10, 1946, Hollywood, Calif. Screen and stage actress. Sister of actress Gertrude Short (dec. 1968) and daughter of actor Lewis Short (dec. 1958).

Appeared in: **1918** The Eagle's Eye (serial). **1921** Lessons in Love; Woman's Place. **1922** Cardigan; The Lights of New York, Silver Wings. **1923** Does It Pay? **1924** The Enchanted Cottage. **1931** Way Down East.

SHORT, GERTRUDE
Born: Apr. 6, 1902, Cincinnati, Ohio. Died: July 31, 1968, Hollywood, Calif. Screen, stage and vaudeville actress. Sister of actress Florence Short (dec. 1946) and daughter of actor Lewis Short (dec. 1958).

Appeared in: **1913** Uncle Tom's Cabin. **1917** The Little Princess. **1920** You Never Can Tell. **1922** Rent Free; Boy Crazy; Headin' West; Youth to Youth. **1923** The Gold Diggers; Breaking Into Society; Crinoline and Romance; The Prisoner; The Man Life Passed By. **1924** Barbara Frietchie; "The Telephone Girl" series of shorts which included: Julius Sees Her; When Knighthood Was in Power; Money to Burn; Sherlock's Home; King Leary; William Tells; For the Love of Mike; The Square Sex; Bee's Knees; Love and Learn; Faster Foster; Hello and Good Bye. **1925** The Narrow Street; Beggar on Horseback; My Lady's Lips; The Other Woman's Story; Code of the West; Her Market Value; The People vs. Nancy Preston; The Talker; Tessie. **1926** Dangerous Friends; Ladies of Leisure; A Poor Girl's Romance; Sweet Adeline; The Lily. **1927** Ladies at Ease; Tillie the Toiler; Adam and Evil; The Show; Polly of the Movies; Women's Wares. **1928** None But the Brave. **1929** Bulldog Drummond; Trial Marriage; Gold Diggers of Broadway; Broadway Hoofer; In Old California; The Three Outcasts. **1930** The Last Dance; Once a Gentleman; The Little Accident. **1931** Laughing Sinners. **1932** Blonde Venus. **1933** The Girl in 419; Son of Kong. **1934** Love Birds; The Key; St. Louis Kid. **1935** G-Men; Helldorado; Woman Wanted; Affairs of Susan. **1936** The Big Broadcast of 1937; 13 Hours by Air. **1937** Park Avenue Logger; Penny Wisdom (short); Stella Dallas. **1938** Tip-Off Girls. **1940** Spots Before Your Eyes (short). **1941** Tom, Dick and Harry. **1942** Two for the Money (short); Victory Vittles (short). **1945** Guest Pests (short); Weekend at the Waldorf.

SHORT, HARRY
Born: 1876. Died: Aug. 17, 1943, New York, N.Y. Screen, stage, vaudeville and radio actor.

Appeared in: **1923** Mighty Lak' a Rose. **1926** Just Suppose. **1934** Hotel Anchovy.

SHORT, HASSARD
Born: Oct. 15, 1877, England. Died: Oct. 9, 1956, Nice, France. Screen actor, stage director and stage producer.

Appeared in: **1918** The Turn of the Wheel. **1919** The Way of a Woman; The Stronger Vow. **1921** Woman's Place.

SHORT, LEWIS W. "LEW"
Born: Feb. 14, 1875, Dayton, Ohio. Died: Apr. 26, 1958, Hollywood, Calif. Screen and stage actor. Father of actresses Gertrude (dec. 1968) and Florence Short (dec. 1946). Entered films with D. W. Griffith at Biograph in 1908.

Appeared in: **1922** The Black Bag; The Heart of Lincoln. **1926** The Blue Eagle. **1927** The Heart of Maryland. **1928** Black Pearl; Big City. **1929** The Three Outcasts; Is Everybody Happy? **1930** A Girl in the Show. **1942** Tennessee Johnson.

SHOTWELL, MARIE
Born: New York, N.Y. Died: Sept. 18, 1934, Long Island, N.Y. Screen and stage actress.

Appeared in: **1916** The Witching Hour. **1917** Enlighten Thy Daughter; Warfare of the Flesh. **1919** The Thirteenth Chair. **1920** Chains of Evidence; The Harvest Moon; The Evil Eye (serial); Civilian Clothes; The Master Mind; Blackbirds. **1921** Her Lord and Master. **1922** Shackles of Gold. **1923** Does It Pay? **1924** Love of Women. **1925** Manicure Girl; Shore Leave; Lovers in Quarantine; Sally of the Sawdust. **1927** Running Wild; One Woman to Another.

SHOVE, DAWNA
Born: 1928. Died: Apr. 14, 1981, Arcadia, Calif. Screen, stage and television actress.

SHREWSBURY, LILLIAN
Born: Oct. 28, 1888, Talladega, Ala. Died: June 15, 1979, Los Angeles, Calif. (natural causes). Screen, stage, television actress and drama teacher.

SHRINER, HERB (Herbert Arthur Schiner)
Born: May 29, 1918, Toledo, Ohio. Died: Apr. 23, 1970, Delray Beach, Fla. (auto accident). Screen, radio and television actor.

Appeared in: **1953** Main Street to Broadway.

SHTRAUKH, MAXIM
Born: Feb. 23, 1900, Russia. Died: 1974, Moscow, Russia. Screen actor.

Appeared in: **1925** Stachka (aka Strike—US 1962). **1932** Golden Mountain. **1939** The Man with the Gun; New Horizons. **1947** The Vow. **1948** The Lucky Bride. **1966** Lenin V. Polshe (aka Portrait of Lenin—US 1967).

SHUBERT, EDDIE
Born: July 11, 1898, Milwaukee, Wis. Died: Jan. 23, 1937, Los Angeles, Calif. Screen, stage, burlesque and vaudeville actor.

Appeared in: **1934** Six Day Bike Rider; Murder in the Clouds; St. Louis Kid; The Case of the Howling Dog; Jimmy the Gent; Here Comes the Navy; Gambling Lady. **1935** Bordertown; Dangerous; The Goose and the Gander; Alibi Ike; Black Fury; While the Patient Slept; The Pay-Off; Don't Bet on Blondes. **1936** Libeled Lady; Song of the Saddle; Road Gang; Man Hunt; The Law in Her Hands; The Case of the Velvet Claws. **1937** Time Out for Romance.

SHUKSHIN, VASILY
Born: 1929, Russia. Died: Oct. 2, 1974, Moscow, Russia (heart attack). Screen actor and film director. Entered films as an actor in the 1950s.

Appeared in: **1962** Kogda Derevya Byli Bolshimi (aka When the Trees Were Tall—US 1965).

SHUMAN, ROY
Born: 1925. Died: July 30, 1973, New York, N.Y. (heart attack). Screen, stage and television actor.

Appeared in: **1958** The Goddess. **1971** The Gang That Couldn't Shoot Straight.

SHUMWAY, LEE (Leonard C. Shumway)
Born: 1884, Salt Lake City, Utah. Died: Jan. 4, 1959. Screen and stage actor.

Appeared in: **1909** She Would Be an Actress. **1914** The Measure of a Man; Sealed Orders; The Candidate for Mayor; Within the Noose; His First Case; The Wolf's Daughter. **1915** Fate and Fugitive; A Question of Conscience; In The Dragon's Claws; When the Range Called; Her Father's Picture; The Red Virgin; The Decoy; Tap! Tap! Tap!; The Dream Dance; The Power of Prayer; The Emerald God; Nell of the Dance Hall; The Strange Unknown; The Wonder Cloth; An Ambassador from the Dead; As the Twig Bent; The Moment Before Death; The Web of Hate; The Convict King; Saved from the Harem; The Sacred Bracelet; Jim West—Gambler; The Secret Room; When War Threatened; The Silent Man; The Inner Chamber; Meg O' the Cliffs; Vengeance of the Oppressed; The Death Web. **1916** The Old Watchman; The Bond Within; The Law's Injustice; Guilty; The Lost

Lode; Two News Items; The Dragonman; The Embodied Thought; The Diamond Thieves; Sold to Satan; Behind the Lines; A Song from the Heart; The Conspiracy; The Repentant; The Redemption of Helen; At the Doors of Doom; Soldier's Sons; The Crash; The Rival Pilots; The Candle; The Leap; The Final Payment; Tammy's Tiger; The Usurer's Due; Out of the Flotsam; The Money Lenders; The Human Pendulum; The Half Wit; The Price of Dishonor; The Stage Witness; Onda of the Orient; A Lesson in Labor; The Avenger. **1917** Honorably Discharged; The Folly of Fanchette; The Gates of Doom; Perils of the Secret Service (serial); Steel Hearts; The Kidnapped Bride; The Phantom's Secret; Helen Grayson's Strategy; Miss Jackie of the Army; The Kingdom of Love. **1918** The Girl with the Champagne Eyes; Confesson; The Fallen Angel; The Bird of Prey. **1919** The Siren's Song; The Love Hunger; Rustling a Bride. **1921** The Conflict; The Lure of Jade; Society Secrets; The Torrent; The Big Adventure. **1922** Brawn of the North; Over the Border; Step On It! **1923** The Gunfighter; The Lone Star Ranger; Soft Boiled; Hearts Aflame; Snowdrift. **1924** The Vagabond Trail; The Yankee Consul; The Air Hawk; American Manners; The Bowery Bishop. **1925** The Air Mail; The Bad Lands; The Danger Signal; The Handsome Brute; Introduce Me; The Man from Red Gulch; The Price of Success; Smilin' at Trouble; The Texas Bearcat. **1926** The Bat; The Checkered Flag; Glenister of the Mounted; One Minute to Play; The Sign of the Claw; Whispering Canyon. **1927** The Great Mail Robbery; His Foreign Wife; The Last Trail; Let It Rain; Outlaws of Red River; South Sea Love. **1928** Beyond London's Lights; Hit of the Show; The House of Scandal; A Million for Love; Son of the Golden West. **1929** Evangeline; The Leatherneck; Night Parade; Queen of the Night Clubs; So This Is College. **1930** The Widow from Chicago; The Lone Defender (serial); The Lone Star Ranger; The Santa Fe Trail; Showgirl in Hollywood; America or Bust (short); Sweet Mama. **1932** I Am a Fugitive from a Chain Gang. **1935** The Lone Wolf Returns; Mysterious Mr. Wong; Million Dollar Baby; Hardrock Harrigan; Outlawed Guns; The Ivory-Handled Gun; Frisco Waterfront. **1936** The Preview Murder Mystery; Song of the Trail; Go Get 'Em Haines; Great Guy. **1937** This Is My Affair; Hollywood Cowboy; Windjammer; Hollywood Round-Up; Nation Aflame; Nightclub Scandal. **1938** Outlaws of the Prairie; Rawhide; Spawn of the North; Painted Desert; I Am the Law; There's That Woman Again. **1939** Rovin' Tumbleweeds. **1940** Deadwood Dick (serial); Prairie Schooners; Brigham Young—Frontiersman; The Grapes of Wrath; The Long Voyage Home. **1941** I Wanted Wings; Bury Me Not on the Lone Prairie; Prairie Pioneers; Murder By Invitation; Two-Gun Sheriff; No Greater Sin. **1942** Hold 'Em Jail (short); Home in Wyomin'; Stardust on the Sage; Arizona Terrors; Jesse James, Jr.; Prisoners on Parade. **1943** Dead Man's Gulch. **1945** The Lost Weekend. **1946** Angel On My Shoulder. **1947** Buck Privates Come Home.

SHUMWAY, WALTER (Walter George Shumway)
Born: Aug. 26, 1884, Cleveland, Ohio. Died: Jan. 13, 1965, Woodland Hills, Calif. (heart disease). Screen actor. Married to actress Corra Beach (dec. 1963).

Appeared in: **1914** Hearts and Flowers. **1919** What Becomes of the Children. **1924** Wine. **1925** Pretty Ladies; The Fighting Sheriff. **1926** Hi-Jacking Rustlers. **1927** Catch as Catch Can; The King of Kings; Prince of the Plains; Wanderer of the West. **1928** The Pinto Kid; The Apache Raider; Greased Lightning; The Mystery Rider (serial). **1929** The Tip Off. **1930** Headin' North. **1931** Spell of the Circus (serial). **1932** Ghost City; Night Rider. **1933** Outlaw Justice. **1939** Six-Gun Rhythm. **1940** The Showdown. **1941** Wrangler's Roost.

SHUNMUGHAM, T. K.
Born: 1912, Madras, India? Died: Mar., 1973, Madras, India. Screen and stage actor.

SHUTTA, ETHEL
Born: 1897. Died: Feb. 5, 1976, New York, N.Y. Screen, stage, vaudeville, radio, television actress, burlesque, carnival, and minstrel show entertainer. Divorced from band leader George Olsen. Appeared in vaudeville with her family in an act billed as "Pee Wee Minstrels," and later as "The Three Shuttas."

Appeared in: **1930** Whoopee (stage and film versions). **1965** The Playground.

SHUTTA, JACK
Born: 1899. Died: June 28, 1957, Houston, Tex. (cancer). Screen, stage, vaudeville and burlesque actor.

Appeared in: **1930** Whoopee. **1934** Hello, Prosperity (short); Half-Baked Relations (short). **1935** False Pretenses; The E-Flat Man (short). **1946** Lover Come Back. **1947** Slave Girl; The Wistful Widow of Wagon Gap. **1948** River Lady; The Burning Cross. **1949** Francis. **1950** Abbott and Costello Go to Mars.

SHY, GUS
Born: 1894, Buffalo, N.Y. Died: June 15, 1945, Hollywood, Calif. Screen, stage, vaudeville actor and film dialog director.

Appeared in: **1930** Good News; New Moon; A Lady's Morals. **1933** A Vitaphone short. **1934** I Sell Anything. **1936** The Captain's Kid. **1937** Once a Doctor.

SHYAM
Born: India. Died: Apr. 26, 1951, India. Screen actor.

SIBIRSKAYA, NADIA (Jeanne Brudot)
Born: 1901, France. Died: July, 1980, France. Screen actress.

Appeared in: **1930** La Petite Lise. **1936** The Mystic Mountain; Le Crime de Monsieur Lange (The Crime of Monsieur Lange—US 1964). **1938** La Marseillaise (The Marseillaise—US 1939).

SIDNEY, GEORGE (Sammy Greenfield)
Born: Mar. 18, 1876, New York, N.Y. Died: Apr. 29, 1945, Los Angeles, Calif. Screen, stage and vaudeville actor. He was Cohen in the "The Cohens and the Kellys" series and Potash in the "Potash and Perlmutter" series.

Appeared in: **1923** Potash and Perlmutter. **1924** In Hollywood with Potash and Perlmutter. **1925** Classified. **1926** Millionaires; The Cohens and the Kellys; Partners Again; The Prince of Pilsen; Sweet Daddies. **1927** Clancy's Kosher Wedding; The Auctioneer; For the Love of Mike; The Life of Riley; Lost at the Front. **1928** The Flying Romeos; Give and Take; The Cohens and the Kellys in Paris; The Latest from Paris; We Americans. **1929** The Cohens and the Kellys in Atlantic City. **1930** Around the Corner; King of Jazz; The Cohens and the Kellys in Scotland; The Cohens and the Kellys in Africa. **1931** Caught Cheating. **1932** High Pressure; The Cohens and Kellys in Hollywood. **1933** The Cohens and the Kellys in Trouble. **1934** Rafter Romance; Manhattan Melodrama. **1935** Diamord Jim. **1937** The Good Old Soak.

SIDNEY, MABEL
Born: 1884. Died: Oct. 18, 1969, New York, N.Y. Screen, vaudeville and television actress.

SIDNEY, SCOTT (Scott Siggins)
Born: 1872. Died: July 20, 1928, London, England (heart trouble). Screen, stage actor and film director. Entered films as an actor with Thomas Ince Productions.

SIEBEL, PETER
Born: 1884. Died: Mar. 4, 1949, Long Beach, Calif. Screen actor and circus performer.

SIEGEL, BERNARD (aka BERNARD SEGAL)
Born: Apr. 19, 1868, Lemberg, Poland. Died: July 9, 1940, Los Angeles, Calif. (heart attack). Screen and stage actor.

Appeared in: **1921** Heart of Maryland. **1922** The Love Nest; The Madness of Love; The Man Who Paid; A Stage Romance. **1923** None So Blind; Sidewalks of New York; Where Is This West? **1924** Against all Odds; The 40th Door (serial); Emblems of Love; The Next Corner; Romance Ranch. **1925** The Spaniard; The Crimson Runner; The Phantom of the Opera; The Vanishing American; Wild Horse Mesa. **1926** Beau Geste; Desert Gold; Going Crooked. **1927** Blazing Days; Drums of the Desert; King of Kings; Open Range; Ragtime; Ranger of the North. **1927** Freedom of the Press; Laugh, Clown, Laugh; Guardians of the Wild; Stand and Deliver; Divine Sinner. **1929** The Far Call; Redskin; The Rescue; Sea Fury; The Younger Generation. **1930** The Case of Sergeant Grischa; The Phantom of the Opera. **1935** Shadow of Doubt. **1936** The Jungle Princess. **1937** Wells Fargo.

SIEGMANN, GEORGE
Born: 1883. Died: June 22, 1928, Hollywood, Calif. (pernicious anemia). Screen, stage actor and assistant film director.

Appeared in: **1909** The Sealed Room. **1915** Birth of a Nation. **1916** Intolerance. **1918** Hearts of the World; The Great Love. **1919** The Fall of Babylon. **1920** The Hawk's Trail (serial); Little Miss Rebellion. **1921** The Big Punch; A Conneticut Yankee at King Arthur's Court; Partners of Fate; Desperate Trails; The Three Musketeers; Silent Years; The Queen of Sheba; Shame. **1922** Fools First; Hungry Hearts; Monte Cristo; Oliver Twist; A California Romance; The Truthful Liar. **1923** Merry-Go-Round; Lost and Found; Anna Christie; The Eagle's Feather; Hell's Hole; Enemies of Children; The Man Life Passed By; Stepping Fast; Scaramouche; Slander the Woman. **1924** Singer Jim McKee; Jealous Husbands; The Guilty One; Manhattan; On Time; Janice Meredith; Revelation; The Right of the Strongest; A Sainted Devil; The Shooting of Dan McGrew; Stolen Secrets; When a Girl

Loves. **1925** Sporting Life; Zander the Great; Manhattan Madness; Pursued; Never the Twain Shall Meet; The Phantom Express; Recompense. **1926** The Old Soak; Born to the West; The Carnival Girl; My Old Dutch; The Midnight Sun; Poker Faces; The Palaces of Pleasure. **1927** King of Kings; The Cat and the Canary; The Red Mill; Uncle Tom's Cabin; The Thirteenth Juror; Hotel Imperial. **1928** Stop That Man; Love Me and the World Is Mine; Man Who Laughs.

SIELANSKI, STANLEY (aka STANLEY STANISLAW)
Born: Poland. Died: Apr. 28, 1955, New York, N.Y. Screen and stage actor.

Appeared in: **1934** Parade Rezerwistow; Maryika. **1936** Manewry Milosne. **1937** Cabman No. 13; Ksiazatko (The Lottery Prince); Krolowa Przedmiescia (Queen of the Market Place). **1938** Pan Redaktor Szaleje (Mr. Editor Is Crazy).

SIERRA, MARGARITA
Born: 1936, Madrid, Spain. Died: Sept. 6, 1963, Hollywood, Calif. (following heart surgery). Screen, stage and television actress.

SIFFERT, JOE
Born: July 7, 1936, Fribourg, Switzerland. Died: Oct. 24, 1971, Brands Hatch, England (auto racing crash). Auto racer and screen actor.

Appeared in: **1966** Grand Prix.

SIGNORET, GABRIEL
Born: Nov. 15, 1873. Died: Apr., 1937, France (appendicitis). Screen actor.

Appeared in:Bouclette (film debut) and La Reve (both silents); later in Veille d'Arme; 27 Rue de la Paix; Les Hommes Nouveaux.

SIHMADA, IHAMU
Born: Japan. Died: 1965, Japan. Screen actor.

SILBERT, LISA
Born: 1880, Rumania. Died: Nov. 29, 1965, Miami, Fla. Screen, stage and television actress.

Appeared in: **1926** Broken Hearts.

SILETTI, MARIO G.
Born: 1904. Died: Apr. 19, 1964, Los Angeles, Calif. (auto accident). Screen and television actor.

Appeared in: **1947** Escape Me Never. **1949** Thieves' Highway. **1950** Under My Skin; The Man Who Cheated Himself; Black Hand. **1951** The Enforcer; Ann of the Indies; Strictly Dishonorable; Force of Arms; The Great Caruso; House on Telegraph Hill; Stop That Cab; Go for Broke. **1952** Clash By Night; When in Rome; My Cousin Rachel; Captain Pirate. **1953** Big Leaguer; Wings of the Hawk; Hot News; Kansas City Confidential; So This Is Love; Taxi; Thunder Bay; The Caddy. **1954** Theodora; Slave Empress; Three Coins in the Fountain. **1955** Hell's Island; The Naked Street; Bring Your Serenade; East of Eden. **1956** The Man in the Gray Flannel Suit. **1957** Man in the Shadow. **1960** Pay or Die. **1966** To Trap a Spy.

SILLS, MILTON
Born: Jan. 10, 1882, Chicago, Ill. Died: Sept. 15, 1930, Santa Monica, Calif. (heart attack). Screen and stage actor. Divorced from actress Gladys Wynne (dec. 1964). Married to actress Doris Kenyon (dec. 1979).

Appeared in: **1915** The Rack; The Deep Purple. **1917** Patria (serial). **1918** The Hell Cat. **1919** Eyes on Youth; Shadows; The Stronger Vow. **1920** The Week-End; Behold My Wife. **1921** The Marriage Gamble; At the End of the World; The Great Moment; The Faith Healer; Savage; Miss Lulu Bett. **1922** Burning Sands; Borderland; Environment; One Clear Call; The Woman Who Walked Alone; Skin Deep; The Forgotten Law; The Marriage Chance. **1923** Why Women Re-Marry; The Last Hour; Adam's Rib; A Lady of Quality; The Spoilers; Flaming Youth; The Isle of Lost Ships; Legally Dead; Souls for Sale; What a Wife Learned. **1924** Madonna of the Streets; The Sea Hawk; Single Wives; Flowing Gold; The Heart Bandit. **1925** The Unguarded Hour; The Knockout; As Man Desires; I Want My Man; A Lover's Oath; The Making of O'Malley. **1926** Paradise; Men of Steel; Puppets; The Silent Lover. **1927** The Sea Tigers; The Valley of the Giants; Framed; Hard-Boiled Haggerty. **1928** The Barker; Burning Daylight; The Crash; The Hawk's Nest. **1929** His Captive Woman; Love and the Devil. **1930** Man Trouble; The Sea Wolf.

SILVA, ANTONIO JOAO
Born: 1870, Portugal. Died: Jan. 31, 1954, Lisbon, Portugal (result of fall). Screen and stage actor. Entered films in 1930. Father of actor Joao Silva.

SILVA, DAVID
Born: Oct. 9, 1917, Mexico City, Mexico. Died: Sept. 21, 1976, Mexico City, Mexico (thrombosis). Screen actor.

Appeared in: **1939** Vivire Otra Vez (I Shall Live Again—US 1940). **1943** Passion Island. **1944** Les Miserables; Toast to Love. **1946** Champion Without a Crown. **1956** The First Texan. **1961** El Baron del Terror (aka The Brainiac—US 1969). **1965** El Mal (The Rage—US 1966). **1975** Alucarda.

SILVA, MARIO (aka MURRAY SMITH)
Born: 1900, Italy?. Died: June 12, 1980, Los Angeles, Calif. Screen, stage actor, singer, vocal coach and pianist.

Appeared in: **1945** A Song to Remember. **1953** Ring Around the Clock.

SILVA, SIMONE
Born: 1928. Died: Nov. 30, 1957, London, England (natural causes). Screen actress.

Appeared in: **1952** South of Algiers (aka The Golden Mask—US 1954). **1953** Street of Shadows (aka Shadow Man—US); Desperate Moment. **1954** The Weak and the Wicked; Duel in the Jungle. **1955** Third Party Risk (aka The Deadly Game—US). **1956** The Dynamiters.

SILVANI, ALDO
Born: 1891, Italy. Died: Nov., 1964, Milan, Italy. Screen and television actor.

Appeared in: **1947** La Vita Ricomincia (Life Begins Anew); Anything for a Song; To Live in Peace. **1948** Four Steps in the Clouds. **1949** The Golden Madonna; Carmela. **1950** Difficult Years; Mad About Opera. **1951** Teresa; Measure for Measure. **1952** When in Rome; The Thief of Venice. **1953** Stranger on the Prowl; Paolo and Francesca. **1954** La Strada; Beat the Devil; Valley of the Kings. **1959** Ben Hur; The Tempest. **1960** Cartagine in Fiamme (Carthage in Flames). **1961** Sodoma e Gomorra (aka The Last Day of Sodom and Gomorrah—US 1963); Five Golden Hours. **1962** Damon and Pythias. **1964** Robin and the Seven Hoods.

SILVER
Screen and television performer. Collective name for several horses ridden by actors Buck Jones, Sunset Carson, Hoot Gibson and various performers who appeared as The Lone Ranger. There were at least four different horses who appeared in the Buck Jones films that were referred to as "Silver." The first, or number one, horse was born in 1914 and died in 1940; the others included a horse who retired in the 1930's and apparently the last film for the Buck Jones stallion was Dawn on the Great Divide made in 1943. The Lone Ranger's Silver represented a variety of horses which appeared on film and television. Brace Breemer's Silver's Pride died in 1966 at age of 27. Sunset Carson's Silver (perhaps more than one) appeared in films from 1944 to 1950. We do know that Hoot Gibson's Silver appeared in the 1927 film Galloping Fury.

SILVER, CHRISTINE
Born: 1885. Died: Nov. 23, 1960, London, England. Screen, stage and television actress.

Appeared in: **1920** Judge Not; The Little Welsh Girl. **1938** Dead Men Tell No Tales (US 1939). **1951** Mystery Junction.

SILVER, PAULINE
Born: 1888. Died: Jan. 1, 1969, West Hollywood, Calif. (murdered). Screen actress. Appeared in silents.

SILVERA, FRANK
Born: 1914, Kingston, Jamaica, West Indies. Died: June 11, 1970, Pasadena, Calif. (accidentally electrocuted). Black screen, stage, television actor, stage producer and stage director.

Appeared in: **1951** The Cimarron Kid. **1952** The Fighter; The Miracle of Our Lady of Fatima; Viva Zapata! **1953** Fear and Desire. **1955** Killer's Kiss. **1956** Crowded Paradise; The Mountain; The Lonely Night. **1947** Hatful of Rain. **1958** The Bravados. **1959** Crime and Punishment, U.S.A. **1960** The Mountain Road; Key Witness. **1962** Mutiny on the Bounty. **1963** Lonnie; Toys in the Attic. **1965** The Greatest Story Ever Told. **1966** The Appaloosa. **1967** Hombre; The St. Valentine's Day Massacre. **1968** The Stalking Moon; Betrayal; Up Tight. **1969** Che!; Guns of the Magnificent Seven.

SILVERHEELS, JAY (Harold J. Smith aka SILVERHEELS SMITH)
Born: 1918, Six Nations Indian Reservation, Ontario, Canada. Died: Mar. 5, 1980, Woodland Hills, Calif. (complications from pneumonia).

Screen and television actor. Entered films in 1938 as an extra.

Appeared in: **1947** Captain From Castille; The Last Round-Up. **1948** The Prairie; Fury at Furnace Creek; Yellow Sky; Key Largo; The Feathered Serpent. **1949** Trail of The Yukon; Sand (aka Will James' Sand); The Cowboy and the Indians; Lust for Gold; Laramie. **1950** Broken Arrow. **1951** Red Mountain. **1952** The Battle of Apache Pass; Brave Warrior; The Will Rogers Story (aka The Story of Will Rogers); Yankee Buccaneer; The Pathfinder. **1953** War Arrows; Jack McCall, Desperado; The Nebraskan. **1954** Drums Across the River; Saskatchewan; Four Guns to the Border; The Black Dakotas; Masterson of Kansas. **1955** The Vanishing American. **1956** Walk the Proud Land; The Lone Ranger. **1958** The Lone Ranger and the Lost City of Gold; Return to Warbow. **1965** Indian Paint. **1969** Smith!; True Grit. **1970** The Phynx. **1973** The Man Who Loved Cat Dancing.

SILVERN, CHARLES (Charles Silverman)
Born: 1903. Died: Apr. 1, 1979, New York, N.Y. Midget screen, stage and television actor.

Appeared in: **1931** Alice in Wonderland. **1939** The Wizard of Oz. **1974** The Great Gatsby; The Taking of Pelham 1-2-3; Death Wish. **1977** The Goodbye Girl. **1979** The Warriors. **1980** A Night of the Juggler.

SILVERNAIL, CLARKE (Clark White Silvernail)
Born: Jan. 31, 1893, Pa. Died: Sept. 22, 1930, Hollywood, Calif. (cancer). Screen, stage actor, film director and screenwriter.

SILVERS, SID
Born: Jan. 1, 1904 or 1908, Brooklyn, N.Y. Died: Aug. 20, 1976. Screen actor, screenwriter and songwriter.

Appeared in: **1929** The Show of Shows. **1930** Dancing Sweeties. **1933** My Weakness. **1934** Bottoms Up; Transatlantic Merry-go-Round. **1935** Broadway Melody of 1936. **1936** Born to Dance. **1937** 52nd Street. **1946** Mr. Ace.

SILVERWOOD, DON
Died: Jan. 10, 1928, Reno, Nev. Screen actor.

SIM, ALASTAIR
Born: Oct. 9, 1900, Edinburgh, Scotland. Died: Aug. 19, 1976, London, England (cancer). Screen, stage actor and film producer. Entered films in 1934.

Appeared in: **1935** The Private Secretary (film debut); Late Extra; The Riverside Murder; A Fire Has Been Arranged. **1936** Troubled Waters; Wedding Group (aka Wrath of Jealousy—US); Keep Your Seats Please; The Big Noise; The Man in the Mirror (US 1937); The Mysterious Mr. Davis (aka My Partner Mr. Davis). **1937** Strange Experiment; Clothes and the Woman; Melody and Romance; Gangway; The Squeaker (aka Murder on Diamond Row—US); A Romance in Flanders (aka On the Western Front—US 1940). **1938** Sailing Along; Climbing High (US 1939); This Man is News; The Terror; Alf's Button Afloat. **1939** Inspector Hornleigh; This Man in Paris; Inspector Hornleigh on Holiday. **1940** Law and Disorder; Her Father's Daughter (short). **1941** Cottage to Let (aka Bombsight Stolen—US); Inspector Hornleigh Goes to It (aka Mail Train—US). **1942** Let The People Sing. **1945** Waterloo Road (US 1947). **1946** Green for Danger (US 1947). **1947** Hue and Cry (US 1950); Captain Boycott. **1948** London Belongs to Me (aka Dulcimer Street—US). **1950** The Happiest Day of Your Life; Stage Fright. **1951** Laughter in Paradise; Scrooge (aka A Christmas Carol—US); Lady Godiva Rides Again (US 1954). **1952** Folly to be Wise. **1953** Innocents in Paris (US 1955). **1954** The Bells of St. Trinian's (US 1955); An Inspector Calls. **1955** Geordie (aka Wee Geordie—US 1956); Escapade (US 1957). **1956** The Green Man (US 1957). **1957** Blue Murder at St. Trinian's (US 1958). **1959** Left, Right and Centre (US 1961); The Doctor's Dilemma. **1960** School for Scoundrels; The Millionairess (US 1961). **1961** The Anatomist. **1972** The Ruling Class. **1975** Royal Flash. **1976** Escape from the Dark. **1977** The Littlest Horse Thieves. **1979** Rogue Male.

SIMANEK, OTTO
Born: 1901. Died: Oct. 15, 1967, New York, N.Y. Screen, stage and television actor.

Appeared in: **1946** 13 Rue Madeleine. **1956** The Wrong Man.

SIMMONDS, ANNETTE (Viscountess Dangan)
Born: 1918, England. Died: Oct. 28, 1959, near London, England (auto accident). Screen and stage actress.

Appeared in: **1950** Blackout. **1951** No Orchids for Miss Blandish.

SIMMONS, EARL
Died: Jan. 10, 1934, New York, N.Y. (suicide—gas poisoning). Screen, stage actor and playwright.

Appeared in: **1916** Broken Fetters.

SIMON, ABE
Born: 1913, Richmond Hill, Long Island, N.Y. Died: Oct. 24, 1969, Queens, N.Y. Professional boxer and screen actor.

Appeared in: **1954** On the Waterfront. **1956** Singing in the Dark. **1958** Never Love a Stranger. **1962** Requiem for a Heavyweight.

SIMON, MICHEL (Francois Simon)
Born: Apr. 9, 1895, Geneva, Switzerland. Died: May 30, 1975, near Paris, France (heart failure). Screen and stage actor.

Appeared in: **1925** Freu Mathisa Pascal. **1928** The Passion of Jeanne d'Arc (The Passion of Joan of Arc—US 1929). **1929** Tire au Flanc. **1931** La Chienne; On Purge Bebe. **1932** Jean de la lune; Boudu Sauve Des Eaux (Boudu Saved from Drowning—US 1967). **1934** L'Atalante (US 1947). **1936** Lac Aux Dames; Le Bonheur; Jeunes Filles de Paris. **1937** Drole de Drame; Razumov. **1938** Les Disparus de Saint-Agil; Le Quay des Brumes (The Foggy Quay). **1939** Fric Frac (US 1948); Bizarre, Bizarre; Port of Shadows; La Fin du Jour (The End of a Day); Circonstances Attenuantes (Extenuating Circumstances—US 1946). **1940** The Kiss of Fire. **1943** Vautrin, the Thief (US 1940). **1944** 32 Rue de Montmartre. **1945** Un Ami Viendra Ce Soir (A Friend Will Come Tonight—US 1948); Boule de Suif. **1946** Panique (US 1947); Musiciens du Ciel. **1947** Au Bonheur de Dames (Shop Girls of Paris); The Story of Tosca; The King's Jester. **1948** Not Guilty; Fabiola (US 1951). **1949** La Beaute du Diable (Beauty and the Devil—US 1952). **1952** Full House. **1953** The Strange Desire of Monsieur Bard; Saadia. **1955** Too Bad She's Bad. **1956** La Joyeuse Prison. **1957** The Virtuous Scoundrel. **1959** Die Nackte und der Satan (aka A Head for the Devil; The Screaming Head; The Head—US 1961). **1960** It Happened in Broad Daylight; Candide (US 1962). **1962** Le Diable et Les Dix Commandments (The Devil and the Ten Commandments—US 1963). **1963** Mondo di Notte (Ecco—US 1965). **1964** Cyrano and D'Artagnan. **1965** Two Hours to Kill; The Train. **1967** Le Vieil Homme et L'enfant (The Two of Us—US 1968). **1968** Ce Sacre Grand-Pere (The Marriage Came Tumbling Down—US 1968). **1971** Blanche.

SIMON, SOL S.
Born: 1864. Died: Apr. 24, 1940, Hollywood, Calif. Screen and stage actor. Credited with discovering oil in Kern County, Calif. in 1910.

Appeared in: **1925** Greed. **1928** The Barker; Desperate Courage. **1930** Headin' North; The Land of Missing Men.

SIMONOV, NIKOLAI
Born: 1902, Russia. Died: Apr., 1973, Russia. Screen and stage actor.

Appeared in: **1930** Cain and Artem. **1934** Miracles. **1935** Chapayev. **1937** Peter the First. **1939** The Conquests of Peter the Great. **1949** The First Front. **1950** The Victors and the Vanquished. **1956** The Gadfly.

SIMPSON, FANNY
Died: Oct. 17, 1961, Woodstock, N.Y. Screen and stage actress. Appeared in silent films.

SIMPSON, GRANT
Born: 1884, Sioux Falls, S.D. Died: Jan. 8, 1932, Asheville, N.C. Screen, stage and vaudeville actor. Married to actress Lulu McConnell (dec. 1962), with whom he teamed in vaudeville.

SIMPSON, IVAN
Born: 1875, Glasgow, Scotland. Died: Oct. 12, 1951, New York, N.Y. Screen and stage actor.

Appeared in: **1915** The Dictator (film debut). **1916** Out of the Drifts. **1922** The Man Who Played God. **1923** Twenty-One; The Green Goddess. **1924** $20 a Week. **1925** Lovers in Quarantine; Miss Bluebeard; Wild, Wild Susan; Womanhandled. **1926** A Kiss for Cinderella. **1929** Disraeli; Evidence. **1930** The Green Goddess (and 1923 version); Old English; The Way of All Men; Manslaughter; The Sea God; Inside the Lines; Isle of Escape. **1931** The Millionaire; The Lady Who Dared; The Reckless Hour; I Like Your Nerve; Safe in Hell. **1932** The Man Who Played God (and 1922 version); A Passport to Hell; The Crash; The Phantom of Crestwood. **1933** The Monkey's Paw; The Past of Mary Holmes; Midnight Mary; Voltaire; Charlie Chan's Greatest Case; The Silk Express; Blind Adventure. **1934** Man of Two Worlds; The Mystery of Mr. X; The House of Rothschild; The World Moves On; British Agent; Among the Missing. **1935** David Copperfield; Shadow of Doubt; Mark of the Vampire; The Bishop Misbehaves; Captain Blood; The Perfect Gentleman; East of Java; Splendor. **1936** Little Lord Fauntleroy; Trouble for Two; Mary of Scotland; Lloyds of London. **1937** Maid of Salem; A Night of Mystery; The Prince and the Pauper; London by Night. **1938** The Baroness and the Butler; Invisible Enemy; Booloo; The Adventures of Robin Hood.

1939 The Hound of the Baskervilles; Made for Each Other; Never Say Die; Adventures of Sherlock Holmes; Ruler of the Seas; The Sun Never Sets. **1940** The Invisible Man Returns; New Moon. **1942** Nazi Agent; The Male Animal; They All Kissed the Bride; Youth on Parade; Nightmare; Random Harvest; The Body Disappears. **1943** My Kingdom for a Cook; Two Weeks to Live; Forever and a Day; This Land Is Mine. **1944** Jane Eyre; The Hour Before the Dawn.

SIMPSON, RONALD

Born: Sept. 27, 1896, Acton, Middlesex, England. Died: Sept. 27, 1957, Aldeburgh, Suffolk, England. Screen, stage, radio actor, stage producer and author. Married to stage actress Lila Maravan (dec. 1950).

Appeared in: **1951** The Long Dark Hall. **1953** The Cruel Sea.

SIMPSON, RUSSELL

Born: June 17, 1880, San Francisco, Calif. Died: Dec. 12, 1959, Hollywood, Calif. Screen, stage, radio and television actor. Entered films in 1910.

Appeared in: **1914** The Virginian. **1917** The Barrier. **1918** The Uphill Path; Weaver of Dreams; Blue Jeans. **1919** The Brand. **1920** The Branding Iron. **1921** Godless Men; Shadows of Conscience; Bunty Pulls the Strings; Snowblind; Under the Lash. **1922** Across the Dead Line; Fools of Fortune; The Kingdom Within; Rags to Riches; When Love Is Young; Human Hearts. **1923** Peg O' My Heart; The Girl of the Golden West; The Virginian (and 1914 version); Circus Days; Defying Destiny; Hearts Aflame; The Huntress; Rip Tide. **1924** The Narrow Street; Painted Peop.e. **1925** Beauty and the Bad Man; Paint and Powder; Faint Perfume; Old Shoes; Recreation of Brian Kent; Ship of Souls; The Splendid Road; Thunder Mountain; Why Women Love (aka Sea Woman and Barriers Aflame). **1926** The Earth Woman; The Social Highwayman; Lovely Mary; Rustling for Cupid. **1927** Wild Geese; Annie Laurie; The First Auto; The Frontiersman; God's Great Wilderness; Now We're in the Air; The Heart of the Yukon. **1928** Trail of '98; The Bushranger; Life's Mockery; Tropical Nights. **1929** Innocents of Paris; Noisy Neighbors; My Lady's Past; The Kid's Clever; The Sap; After the Fog. **1930** Billy the Kid; Lone Star Ranger; Abraham Lincoln. **1931** Man to Man; The Great Meadow; Susan Lennox, Her Rise and Fall. **1932** Law and Order; Ridin' for Justice; Lean Rivers; Honor of the Press; Riding Tornado; Flames; Cabin in the Cotton; Hello Trouble; Silver Dollar; Call Her Savage. **1933** The Moonshiners Daughter or Aboard in Old Kentucky (short); Face in the Sky; Hello, Everybody! **1934** Three on a Honeymoon; Carolina; The Frontier Marshal; Ever Since Eve; Sixteen Fathoms Deep; The World Moves On. **1935** West of the Pecos; Motive for Revenge; The Hoosier Schoolmaster; Way Down East; Paddy O'Day; The County Chairman. **1936** Man Hunt; The Harvester; Girl of the Ozarks; The Crime of Dr. Forbes; Ramona; San Francisco. **1937** Green Light; That I May Live; Mountain Justice; Wild West Days (serial); Yodelin' Kid from Pine Ridge; Paradise Isle; Maid of Salem. **1938** Gold Is Where You Find It; Valley of the Giants; Hearts of the North. **1939** Western Caravans; Desperate Trails; Drums Along the Mohawk; Dodge City; Mr. Smith Goes to Washington; Young Mr. Lincoln; Geronimo. **1940** Girl of the Golden West (and 1923 version); Brigham Young—Frontiersman; Santa Fe Trail; Virginia City; Three Faces West; The Grapes of Wrath. **1941** The Last of the Duanes; Bad Men of Missouri; Wild Bill Hickok Rides; Tobacco Road; Wild Geese Calling; Citadel of Crime; Swamp Water; Outside the Law; Meet John Doe. **1942** Shut My Big Mouth; The Lone Ranger; The Spoilers; Tennessee Johnson. **1943** Woman of the Town; Border Patrol; Moonlight in Vermont. **1944** Texas Masquerade; Man from Frisco. **1945** Along Came Jones; The Big Bonanza; They Were Expendable; Incendiary Blonde. **1946** Bad Bascomb; California Gold Rush; My Darling Clementine. **1947** The Millerson Case; Bowery Buckaroos; The Fabulous Texan; Death Valley; Romance of Rosy Ridge. **1948** Albuquerque; My Dog Shep; Tap Roots; Coroner Creek; Sundown in Santa Fe. **1949** Tuna Clipper; The Beautiful Blonde from Bashful Bend; Free for All; The Gal Who Took the West. **1950** Call of the Klondike; Saddle Tramp; Wagon Master. **1951** Across the Wide Missouri; Comin' 'Round the Mountain. **1952** Feudin' Fools; Lone Star; Ma and Pa Kettle at the Fair; Meet Me at the Fair. **1953** The Sun Shines Bright. **1954** Broken Lance; Seven Brides for Seven Brothers. **1955** The Last Command; The Tall Men. **1956** The Brass Legend; Friendly Persuasion. **1957** The Lonely Man. **1959** The Horse Soldiers.

SINATRA, RAY (Raymond Dominic Sinatra)

Born: 1904, Italy. Died: Nov., 1980, Las Vegas, Nev. Orchestra leader, composer, arranger, screen, radio and television actor.

SINCLAIR, ARTHUR (Arthur McDonnell)

Born: Aug. 3, 1883, Dublin, Ireland. Died: Dec. 14, 1951, Belfast, Northern Ireland. Screen and stage actor. Married to actress Marie O'Neill (dec. 1952).

Appeared in: **1934** Wild Boy; Irish Hearts (aka Norah O'Neale—US); Sing As We Go; Evensong. **1935** Charing Cross Road; Peg of Old Drury (US 1936). **1937** King Solomon's Mines. **1947** Hungry Hill.

SINCLAIR, DAISY

Born: 1878, N.Y. Died: Jan. 14, 1929, New York, N.Y. Stage and screen actress.

SINCLAIR, EDWARD

Born: 1914, England. Died: Aug. 29, 1977, Cheddar, England. Screen and television actor.

Appeared in: **1941** The Tower of Terror (US 1942). **1948** Saraband for Dead Lovers (aka Saraband—US 1949).

SINCLAIR, HORACE

Born: 1884, Sheffield, England. Died: Feb. 19, 1949, New York, N.Y. Screen, stage, vaudeville actor, stage director and playwright.

Appeared in: **1939** One Third of a Nation.

SINCLAIR, HUGH

Born: May 19, 1903, London, England. Died: Dec. 29, 1962, Slapton, England. Screen and stage actor.

Appeared in: **1935** Escape Me Never. **1936** The Marriage of Corbal (aka Prisoner of Corbal—US 1939); Strangers on a Honeymoon (US 1937). **1939** A Girl Must Live (US 1941); The Four Just Men (aka The Secret Four—US 1940). **1941** The Saint's Vacation; The Saint Meets the Tiger (US 1943). **1942** Alibi; Tomorrow We Live (aka At Dawn We Die—US 1943). **1945** Flight from Folly; They Were Sisters (US 1946). **1948** Corridor of Mirrors. **1949** Don't Ever Leave Me; The Rocking Horse Winner (US 1950); Trottie True (aka Gay Lady—US 1950). **1950** No Trace. **1951** Circle of Danger. **1952** Judgment Deferred; The Second Mrs. Tanqueray (US 1954); Never Look Back. **1953** Mantrap (aka Woman in Hiding—US); Three Steps in the Dark.

SINCLAIR, RICHARD C.

Died: Sept. 16, 1926, Brooklyn, N.Y. Screen actor. Appeared in Famous Players films.

SINGH, BHOGWAN

Born: Sept. 22, 1883, India. Died: Mar. 6, 1962, Woodland Hills, Calif. (cerebral thrombosis). Screen actor.

Appeared in: **1915** The Arab's Vengeance. **1920** Stronger Than Death. **1935** Bonnie Scotland. **1952** Bwana Devil. **1956** Around the World in 80 Days. **1958** The Bride and the Beast; Desert Hell.

SINGH, SARAIN

Born: 1888. Died: Apr. 14, 1952, Hollywood, Calif. Screen actor.

SINGLETON, CATHERINE

Born: 1904. Died: Sept. 9, 1969, Ft. Worth, Tex. Screen and stage actress. Miss Universe of 1926.

SINGLETON, ZUTTY (Arthur James Singleton)

Born: 1898, Bunkie, La. Died: July 14, 1975, New York, N.Y. Black jazz musician (drummer), screen and television actor.

Appeared in: **1943** Stormy Weather. **1947** New Orleans.

SINI'LETTA, VIC (Victor A. Smith)

Died: May 4, 1921, Chicago, Ill (dropsy and heart ailment). Screen actor and circus performer.

SIN-NUI, HUNG

Born: 1920, China. Died: Oct., 1966, Canton, China (suicide). Screen actress and opera performer. Jumped to her death after Red Guards (teenage militants) had cut off her hair and paraded her through the streets.

SINOEL (Jen Vies)

Born: 1868, France. Died: Aug. 31, 1949, Paris, France. Screen actor.

Appeared in: **1935** Le Dernier Milliardaire. **1947** Francis the First; Vie de Boheme. **1948** Voyage Suprise.

SIODMAK, ROBERT (Robert Siodmark)

Born: 1900, Memphis, Tenn. Died: Mar. 10, 1973, Switzerland (heart attack). Screen actor, film producer, director and author. Appeared in early UFA films in Germany.

SIPPERLEY, RALPH
Born: 1890. Died: Jan. 9, 1928, Bangor, Maine. Stage and screen actor.

Appeared in: **1923** Six Cylinder Love. **1926** The Blue Eagle; The Canyon of Light; Womanpower. **1927** Sunrise.

SISSLE, NOBLE
Born: July 10, 1889, Indianapolis, Ind. Died: Dec. 17, 1975, Tampa, Fla. Black songwriter, orchestra leader, vaudeville and screen actor.

Appeared in: **1923** Snappy Tunes. **1941** Murder with Music. **1947** Junction 88.

SISSON, VERA
Born: July 31, 1891, Salt Lake City, Utah. Died: Aug. 6, 1954, Carmel, Calif. Screen actress. Married to actor Richard Rosson (dec. 1953).

Appeared in: **1914** Women and Roses; Too Much Married; The Bolted Door; Toilers of the Sea; The Golden Ladder; Value Received; The Sand Hill Lovers; The Proof of a Man; There is a Destiny; Weights and Measures; Little Meg and I. **1915** The Trust; According to Value; Martin Love-Fixer; The Storm; The Guardian of the Flocks; For Cash; The Oyster Dredger; The Laurel of Tears; The Chief Inspector. **1916** Landon's Legacy; The Iron Woman; His Wife's Story; The Man from Nowhere. **1917** The Hidden Spring; Paradise Garden. **1919** The Veiled Adventure. **1920** The Heart of Youth. **1921** The Avenging Arrow (serial). **1926** Love 'Em and Leave 'Em.

SITTING EAGLE See EAGLE, FRANCIS SITTING

SJOBERG, ALF
Born: 1903, Sweden. Died: Apr. 17, 1980, Sweden (results of a traffic accident). Screen, stage actor, film director, stage director and screenwriter.

SJOSTROM, VICTOR See SEASTROM, VICTOR

SKELLY, HAL (Joseph Harold Skelly)
Born: 1891, Allegheny, Pa. Died: June 16, 1934, West Cornwall, Conn. (auto accident). Screen, stage, circus, minstrel actor, opera performer and stage producer.

Appeared in: **1929** The Dance of Life; Woman Trap. **1930** Behind the Makeup; Men Are Like That. **1931** The Struggle. **1933** Hotel Variety; Shadow Laughs.

SKELLY, JAMES
Born: 1936. Died: Apr. 19, 1969, Palm Springs, Calif. (pneumonia). Screen actor. Entered films approx. 1957.

SKELTON, GEORGIA (Georgia Maureen Davis)
Born: Sept. 17, 1921, Glenwood Springs, Colo. Died: May 10, 1976, Rancho Mirage, Calif. (suicide—gunshot). Screen actress. Divorced from actor Red Skelton.

Appeared in: **1943** Hoosier Holiday.

SKETCHLEY, LESLIE "LES"
Died: Oct. 14, 1972. Screen actor.

Appeared in: **1929** Tiger Rose. **1930** Journey's End. **1937** The Prisoner of Zenda. **1954** Elephant Walk. **1956** 23 Paces to Baker Street.

SKINNER, CORNELIA OTIS
Born: May 30, 1901, Chicago, Ill. Died: July 9, 1979, New York, N.Y. (cerebral hemorrhage). Screen, stage, radio actress, screenwriter, playwright and author. Daughter of actor Otis Skinner (dec. 1942), and stage actress Maud Durbin (dec.).

Appeared in: **1920** Kismet. **1943** Stage Door Canteen. **1944** The Uninvited. **1955** The Girl in the Red Velvet Swing. **1968** The Swimmer.

SKINNER, OTIS
Born: June 28, 1857, Cambridge, Mass. Died: Jan. 5, 1942, New York, N.Y. (uremic poisoning). Screen, stage actor, stage producer and stage director. Married to stage actress Maud Durbin (dec.). Father of actress Cornelia Otis Skinner (dec. 1979).

Appeared in: **1920** Romance; Kismet. **1922** Mister Antonio. **1930** Kismet (and 1920 version).

SKIPWORTH, ALISON
Born: July 25, 1865, 1870 or 1875?, London, England. Died: July 5, 1952, New York, N.Y. Screen, stage and television actress.

Appeared in: **1921** Handcuffs or Kisses. **1930** Strictly Unconventional;

Raffles; Outward Bound; Oh, For a Man!; Du Barry, Woman of Passion. **1931** Tonight or Never; Night Angel; Virtuous Husband; The Road to Singapore; Devotion. **1932** Sinners in the Sun; Madame Racketeer; Night After Night; High Pressure; If I Had a Million; Unexpected Father. **1933** Tonight Is Ours; He Learned About Women; A Lady's Profession; Song of Songs; Midnight Club; Tillie and Gus; Alice in Wonderland. **1934** Six of a Kind; Wharf Angel; The Notorious Sophie Lang; Here Is My Heart; Shoot the Works; The Captain Hates the Sea; Coming Out Party. **1935** The Devil Is a Woman; Shanghai; Becky Sharp; Doubting Thomas; The Casino Murder Case; The Girl from Tenth Avenue; Dangerous; Hitch Hike Lady. **1936** Satan Met a Lady; The Princess Comes Across; The Gorgeous Hussy; Two in a Crowd; White Hunter; Stolen Holiday. **1937** Two Wise Maids. **1938** King of the Newsboys; Ladies in Distress; Wide Open Faces.

SKODA, ALBIN
Died: Sept. 22, 1961. Screen actor.

Appeared in: **1935** Liebe, Tod und Teufel. **1956** The Last Ten Days.

SKOLNICK, HARVEY
Born: c. 1920. Died: Mar. 18, 1980, Los Angeles, Calif. (heart attack). Screen and television actor.

SKRAUP, KARL
Born: 1898. Died: Oct., 1958. Screen and stage actor.

Appeared in: **1937** Vienna Burgtheater.

SKULNIK, MENASHA
Born: 1892. Died: June 4, 1970, New York, N.Y. Yiddish screen and stage actor.

SLACK, FREDDIE
Born: Aug. 7, 1910, La Crosse, Wis. Died: Aug. 10, 1965, Hollywood, Calif. (natural causes). Bandleader and screen actor.

Appeared in: **1943** Reveille with Beverly; The Sky's the Limit. **1944** Hat Check Honey; Follow the Boys; Seven Days Ashore. **1946** High School Hero.

SLADE, OLGA
Died: Apr. 24, 1949. Screen actress.

Appeared in: **1930** The Farmer's Wife.

SLATE, SYD
Born: 1908, Russia. Died: May 2, 1976, Las Vegas, Nev. (heart condition). Screen and stage actor. Member of "Slate Brothers" song and dance act with brothers Jack and Henry.

Appeared in: **1930** Happy Days.

SLATER, JOHN (B. John Slater)
Born: Aug. 22, 1916, London, England. Died: Jan. 9, 1975, London, England (heart attack). Screen, stage, radio and television actor. Married to actress Betty Slater. Entered films in 1939.

Appeared in: **1941** Love on the Dole; Gert and Daisy's Weekend. **1942** Went the Day Well? (aka 48 Hours—US 1944). **1943** Deadlock. **1944** For Those in Peril; A Canterbury Tale. **1945** The Seventh Veil (US 1946); Murder in Reverse (US 1946). **1947** It Always Rains on Sunday (US 1949). **1948** Escape; Noose (aka The Silk Noose—US 1950); Against the Wind (US 1949). **1949** Passport to Pimlico. **1950** Prelude to Fame. **1951** The Third Visitor. **1952** Faithful City. **1953** The Flanagan Boy (aka Bad Blonde—US); The Long Memory. **1954** The Million Pound Note (aka Man with a Million—US); Star of India (US 1956). **1956** Johnny, You're Wanted. **1957** Devil's Pass. **1958** Violent Playground. **1960** The Night We Got the Bird. **1961** Three on a Spree. **1963** A Place to Go.

SLATTERY, JACK
Born: 1917. Died: Oct. 29, 1979, Lancaster, Calif. (stroke). Screen actor, radio and television announcer.

Appeared in: **1944** Pardon My Rhythm.

SLAUGHTER, TOD (N. Carter Slaughter)
Born: Mar. 19, 1885, Newcastle-on-Tyne, England. Died: Feb. 19, 1956. Screen and stage actor.

Appeared in: **1935** Maria Marten, or The Murder in the Red Barn. **1936** The Crimes of Stephen Hawke; Sweeney Todd, The Demon Barber of Fleet Street (US 1939). **1937** Song of the Road; Darby and Joan; It's Never Too Late to Mend; The Ticket of Leave Man. **1938** Sexton Blake and the Hooded Terror. **1939** The Face at the Window

(US 1940). **1940** Crimes at the Dark House. **1946** Brothered by a Beard (short); The Curse of the Wraydons. **1948** The Greed of William Hart. **1952** King of the Underworld; Murder at Scotland Yard; Murder at the Grange; A Ghost for Sale.

SLAVIN, JOSE
Born: 1933, Buenos Aires, Argentina. Died: Jan., 1978, Buenos Aires, Argentina. Screen, stage and television actor.

Appeared in: La Guerra del Cerdo; El Pibe Cabeza; La Madre Maria.

SLEEMAN, PHILIP "PHIL"
Born: Feb. 28, 1891. Died: Sept. 19, 1953, Calif. Screen actor.

Appeared in: **1921** The Heart Line; Home Stuff. **1923** Human Wreckage; Single Handed. **1924** So This is Marriage; Come on Cowboys! **1926** The Border Whirlwind. **1927** After Midnight; The Slaver. **1928** The Cop; The Devil's Skipper. **1929** Sailor's Holiday. **1930** The Cock O' The Walk. **1931** Young Donovan's Kid. **1934** The Scarlet Empress. **1936** Half Angel. **1937** The Girl From Scotland Yard; The Prisoner of Zenda.

"SLEEP 'N EAT" *See* BEST, WILLIE

SLEIGHT, ORME "SOCK" (Orme Beryl Sleight)
Born: Oct. 14, 1916, Kalamazoo, Mich. Died: Sept. 17, 1933, Long Beach, Calif. (fall from horse). Trick rodeo rider and screen actor.

SLEZAK, LEO
Born: 1875, Maehrisch-Schuenberg, Germany. Died: June 6, 1946, Bavaria, Germany. Screen actor and opera performer. Father of actor Walter Slezak and actress Margarete Slezak (dec. 1953).

Appeared in: **1932** Der Frauendiplomat; Skandal in der Parkstrasse; Die Herren vom Maxim; Moderne Mitgift; Ein Toller Einfall (A Mad Idea—US 1934). **1933** Grossfuerstin Alexandra; Mein Liebster ist ein Jaegersmann (US 1935, aka Liebe bei Hof). **1934** Freut Euch des Lebens; Der Herr ohne Wohnung; Musik im Blut; La Paloma (US 1935); G'Schichten aus dem Wienerwald; Ihr Groesster Erfolg (aka Therese Krones, and aka Her Greatest Success—US 1939). **1935** Tanzmusik; Die Blonde Carmen (US 1939); Die Fahrt in die Jugend; Eine Nacht an der Donau; Die Ganze Welt Dreht Sich um Liebe; Die Lustigen Weiber; Herbstmanoever (Fall Manouvers—US 1939); Die Pompadour (US 1939); Unsterbliche Melodien (Immortal Melodies—US 1938); Ein Walzer um den Stephansturm (aka Sylvia und ihr Chauffeur); Knox und die Lustigen Vagabunden (aka Zirkus Saran). **1936** Konfetti; Rendezvous in Wien (US 1938); Der Postillon von Lonjumeau (The Postillion of Lonjumeau—US 1937, aka Der Koenig Laechelt—Paris Lacht). **1937** Freuhling im Wien; The World's in Love; Die Gluecklichste Ehe der Welt; Gasparone (US 1938); Husaren, Heraus (US 1938); Liebe im Dreivierteltakt (Love in Waltz Time—US 1938, aka Wiener Fiakerlied); Eine Nacht an der Donau (A Night on the Danube; Magda; Die Gluecklichste Ehe von Wien (The Happiest Married Couple in Vienna); Der Mann, der Nicht Nein Sagen Konnte; Heimat; Die 4 Gesellen. **1939** Fasching in Wein; Das Frauenparadies; Frau am Steuer; Es War Eine Rauschende Ballnacht (One Enchanted Evening). **1940** Operette; Golowin Geht Durch die Stadt; Rosen in Tirol; Der Herr im Haus. **1941** Alles fuer Gloria. **1943** Geliebter Schatz; Muenchhausen.

SLEZAK, MARGARETE
Born: 1901, Germany. Died: Aug. 30, 1953, Rottach-Egern, Bavaria, Germany (heart attack). Screen actress and opera performer. Daughter of actor Leo Slezak (dec. 1946) and sister of actor Walter Slezak.

Appeared in: **1953** Man on a Tightrope. Other German films: Derby; The Veiled Maja.

SLOAN, TOD (James F. Sloan)
Born: Aug. 10, 1874, Bunker Hill, Ind. Died: Dec. 21, 1933, Los Angeles, Calif. Jockey, screen and vaudeville actor. Divorced from actress Julia Sanderson (dec. 1975).

Appeared in: **1921** The Killer. **1922** When Romance Rides. **1928** Hot Heels. **1932** Midnight Patrol.

SLOAN, WILLIAM HOPE
Born: 1864. Died: Jan. 12, 1933, Amityville, N.Y. Screen and stage actor. Appeared in early Biograph, Universal, Vitagraph and Reliance-Majestic films.

SLOANE, EVERETT
Born: Oct. 1, 1909, New York, N.Y. Died: Aug. 6, 1965, Brentwood, Calif. (suicide—sleeping pills). Screen, stage, radio and television actor.

Appeared in: **1941** Citizen Kane. **1942** The Magnificent Ambersons; Journey Into Fear. **1945** We Accuse (narr.). **1948** The Lady from Shanghai. **1949** Prince of Foxes. **1950** The Men. **1951** Bird of Paradise; The Enforcer; Sirocco; The Desert Fox; The Blue Veil; The Prince Who Was a Thief; Murder, Inc. **1952** The Sellout; Way of a Gaucho. **1955** The Big Knife. **1956** Massacre at Sand Creek; Patterson; Somebody Up There Likes Me; Lust for Life. **1958** Marjorie Morningstar; The Gun Runners. **1960** Home from the Hill. **1961** By Love Possessed. **1962** Brushfire! **1963** The Man from the Diner's Club. **1964** The Patsy; The Disorderly Orderly; Ready for the People. **1970** Mr. Magoo's Holiday Festival (voice).

SLOANE, OLIVE
Born: Dec. 16, 1896. Died: June 28, 1963, London, England. Screen, stage and vaudeville actress. Appeared in vaudeville as "Baby Pearl" and later as a partner in an act billed as the "Sisters Love."

Appeared in: **1921** The Door That Has No Key (US 1922); Greatheart. **1922** Trapped by the Mormons; Lonesome Farm. **1923** Rogues of the Turf; Gems of Literature series including The Dream of Eugene Aram. **1925** Money Isn't Everything. **1928** The Mormon (reissue of Trapped by the Mormons—1922). **1933** The Good Companions; Soldiers of the King (aka The Woman in Command—US 1934). **1934** Sing as We Go; Brides to Be; Faces; Music Hall. **1935** Key to Harmony; Alibi Inn. **1936** The Howard Case; In the Soup. **1937** Dreaming Lips; Mad About Money (aka Stardust and He Loved an Actress—US 1938); Cafe Colette (aka Danger in Paris—US); Overcoat Sam. **1938** Make It Three; Consider Your Verdict. **1939** Inquest. **1941** The Tower of Terror (US 1942). **1942** Those Kids from Town; Let the People Sing. **1945** They Knew Mr. Knight; The Voice Within. **1946** Send for Paul Temple. **1947** Bank Holiday Luck. **1948** The Guinea Pig (US 1949). **1949** Under Capricorn. **1950** Waterfront (aka Waterfront Women—US 1952); Seven Days to Noon. **1951** The Franchise Affair (US 1952). **1952** Curtain Up (US 1953); Tall Headlines (aka The Frightened Bride—US 1953); My Wife's Lodger. **1954** The Weak and the Wicked; The Golden Link. **1955** A Prize of Gold. **1956** Alf's Baby; The Man in the Road; The Last Man to Hang. **1957** Brothers in Law. **1959** Serious Charge (aka Immoral Charge—US 1962 and A Touch of Hell—US 1964). **1960** The Price of Silence; Your Money or Your Wife (US 1965). **1963** Heavens Above.

SLOCUM, TEX
Born: 1902. Died: Jan. 18, 1963, Concord, Calif. (heart attack). Screen actor and stuntman who doubled for Tom Mix and Hoot Gibson.

SLOMAN, EDWARD "TED"
Born: July 19, 1885, London, England. Died: Sept. 29, 1972, Woodland Hills, Calif. Screen, stage, vaudeville actor and film director. Married to actress Hylda Hollis.

Appeared in: **1914** The Trey O'Hearts (serial). **1915** The Mother Instinct; The Mother Iris; Where Happiness Dwells; The Valley of Regeneration; In the Heart of the Hills; The Markswoman; Vengeance of the Oppressed, The Embodied Thought; Sold to Satan.

SLOTEMAKER, ROB
Born: 1929, Holland. Died: Sept. 16, 1979 (racing accident). Screen actor and stuntman.

SLOTT, NATE DAVID
Born: Apr. 22, 1902, Chicago, Ill. Died: Sept. 26, 1963, Hollywood, Calif. (cancer). Screen actor, assistant film director and boxer. Entered films in 1923.

Appeared in: **1929** The Night Parade. **1930** Hit the Deck. **1931** The Tip Off; Iron Man.

SMALL, EDNA
Born: 1898. Died: July 14, 1917, Cincinnati, Ohio. Screen actress. Appeared in early Chaplin films.

SMALL, EDWARD
Born: 1891. Died: Jan. 25, 1977, Los Angeles, Calif. Screen actor and film producer.

SMALLEY, PHILLIPS (Phillips Wendell Smalley)
Born: Aug. 7, 1875, Brooklyn, N.Y. Died: May 2, 1939, Hollywood, Calif. Screen, stage actor, film director and film producer. Appeared in early Rex pictures in 1909.

Appeared in: **1914** The Merchant of Venice; False Colors. **1915** A Cigarette—That's All. **1921** Two Wise Wives. **1922** The Power of a Lie. **1923** The Self-Made Wife; Temptation; Trimmed in Scarlet; Cameo Kirby; Flaming Youth; Nobody's Bride. **1925** Cheap Kisses; For Sale; Single Wives; Daughters of Today. **1925** The Awful Truth;

Charley's Aunt; Soul Mates; Wandering Footsteps; Stella Maris; The Fate of a Flirt. **1926** Money Talks; There You Are!; Queen of Diamonds; The Taxi Mystery. **1927** The Broken Gate; Sensation Seekers; Tea for Three; The Dice Woman; The Irresistible Lover; Stage Kisses. **1928** Blindfold; Man Crazy; The Border Patrol; Sinners in Love; Honeymoon Flats; Broadway Daddies. **1929** The Aviator; True Heaven; High Voltage; The Fatal Warning (serial). **1930** Charley's Aunt (and 1925 version); Peacock Alley; The Midnight Special; Drumming It In (short); Liliom. **1931** Lawless Woman; Lady from Nowhere; High Stakes; Get-Rich-Quick Wallingford; A Free Soul. **1932** Murder at Dawn; Hell's Headquarters; Escapade; Sinister Hands; Widow in Scarlet; Face on the Barroom Floor; The Greeks Had a Word for Them. **1933** Midnight Warning; The Cocktail Hour. **1934** The Big Race; Stolen Sweets; Madame Du Barry; Bolero. **1935** Hold 'Em Yale; All the King's Horses; Night Life of the Gods; It's in the Air; A Night at the Opera. **1936** Too Many Parents. **1937** Hotel Haywire. **1938** Booloo.

SMART, H. F.
Born: England. Died: July 22, 1923, Los Angeles, Calif. (heart disease). Screen, stage actor and circus performer.

SMART, J. SCOTT (aka JACK SMART)
Born: 1903. Died: Jan. 15, 1960, Springfield, Ill. Screen and radio actor.

Appeared in: **1947** Kiss of Death. **1951** Fat Man (film and radio).

SMELKER, MARY
Born: 1909. Died: June 2, 1933, Tucson, Ariz. (auto accident). Screen actress.

SMERALDO, IDA
Died: 1964. Screen actress.

Appeared in: **1955** Bring Your Smile Along. **1960** Raymie.

SMILEY, JOSEPH W.
Born: 1881. Died: Dec. 2, 1945, N.Y. Screen, stage, vaudeville actor and film director. Entered films as actor and director with the Original Imp Co. in 1910.

Appeared in: **1921** Experience; The Old Oaken Bucket; The Woman God Changed; The Rich Slave; The Scarab Ring; The Wild Goose. **1922** The Blonde Vampire; The Face in the Fog. **1925** Old Home Week; Wild, Wild Susan; The Police Patrol. **1926** Aloma of the South Seas; The Show Off; The Untamed Lady. **1927** The Potters.

SMILEY, RALPH
Born: 1915. Died: Sept. 14, 1977, Woodland Hills, Calif. (cancer). Screen and stage actor.

Appeared in: **1951** My Favorite Spy. **1955** A Bullet for Joey. **1956** Flight to Hong Kong.

SMITH, ALBERT E.
Born: 1875, England. Died: Aug. 1, 1958, Hollywood, Calif. One of the founders of Vitagraph Pictures, film producer and screen actor. Do not confuse with actors Albert J. or Al Smith. Married to actress Hazel Neason (dec. 1920); later married and divorced from actress Jean Paige, then later married to Lucile Smith.

Appeared in: **1912** A Vitagraph Romance.

SMITH, ALBERT J.
Born: 1894, New York, N.Y. Died: Apr. 12, 1939, Hollywood, Calif. Screen actor.

Appeared in: **1921** Terror Trail (serial). **1923** In the Days of Daniel Boone (serial). **1924** Big Timber; The Measure of a Man; The Sunset Trail; The Fast Express (serial). **1925** The Middler; Straight Through; The Taming of the West; Ace of Spades (serial); Barriers of the Law; Blood and Steel; The Burning Trail; The Circus Cyclone. **1926** The Scarlet Streak (serial); Strings of Steel (serial); Speed Crazed. **1927** Perils of the Jungle (serial); Hills of Peril; Whispering Sage; The Swift Shadow; Hard Fists; Red Clay; Where Trails Begin. **1928** The Law of Fear; The Bullet Mark; Hold 'Em Yale. **1929** The Drifter; Fury of the Wild; "Half Pint Polly" comedies. **1932** The Last Mile. **1934** Honor of the Range.

SMITH, ART (Arthur Gordon Smith)
Born: 1900. Died: Feb. 24, 1973, West Babylon, N.Y (heart attack). Screen, stage and television actor.

Appeared in: **1942** Native Land. **1943** Edge of Darkness. **1944** None Shall Escape; Uncertain Glory; Mr. Winkle Goes to War; The Black

Parachute. **1945** A Tree Grows in Brooklyn. **1946** Moon Over Montana; Trail to Mexico; Six Gun Serenade. **1947** Brute Force; Ride the Pink Horse; Body and Soul; T-Men. **1948** Oklahoma Blues; Song of the Drifter; Courtin' Trouble; Letter from an Unknown Woman; Mr. Peabody and the Mermaid; The Rangers Ride; Arch of Triumph; A Double Life; Angel in Exile; Range Renegades. **1949** Caught; South of St. Louis; Manhandled; Red, Hot and Blue; Song of Surrender. **1950** South Sea Sinner; In a Lonely Place; Quicksand; The Next Voice You Hear; The Killer That Stalked New York. **1951** Try and Get Me (aka The Sound of Fury); Half Angel; The Painted Hills. **1952** Just for You; The Rose of Cimarron. **1963** The Moving Finger.

SMITH, ARTHUR T.
Born: 1878. Died: Apr. 14, 1958, Norwalk, Conn. Screen and stage actor. Do not confuse with actor Art Smith (dec. 1973).

Appeared in: **1925** Ben Hur.

SMITH, BEATRICE LIEB
Born: 1862. Died: Aug. 6, 1942, Los Angeles, Calif. Screen and stage actress.

SMITH, BESSIE
Born: Apr. 15, 1894, Chattanooga, Tenn. Died: Sept. 26, 1937, Clarksdale, Miss. (auto accident). Black jazz singer and screen actress.

Appeared in: **1929** St. Louis Blues (short).

SMITH, C. AUBREY
Born: July 21, 1863, London, England. Died: Dec. 20, 1948, Beverly Hills, Calif. (pneumonia). Screen and stage actor.

Appeared in: **1915** Builder of Bridges (film debut). **1916** The Witching Hour. **1918** Red Pottage. **1920** The Face at the Window; The Shuttle of Life; The Bump (short); Castles in Spain. **1922** The Bohemian Girl; Flames of Passion. **1923** The Temptation of Carleton Earle. **1924** The Unwanted; The Rejected Woman. **1930** Such Is the Law; Birds of Prey (aka The Perfect Alibi—US 1931). **1931** Trader Horn; Never the Twain Shall Meet; Daybreak; Son of India; Contraband Love; Just a Gigolo; Man in Possession; The Phantom of Paris; Guilty Hands; Surrender; Dancing Partners. **1932** Polly of the Circus; Tarzan, the Ape Man; But the Flesh Is Weak; Love Me Tonight; Trouble in Paradise; No More Orchids. **1933** They Just Had to Get Married; Luxury Liner; Bombshell; The Barbarian; Secrets; Morning Glory; Adorable; Monkey's Paw; Queen Christina. **1934** The House of Rothschild; Gambling Lady; Riptide; We Live Again; Curtain at Eight; Bulldog Drummond Strikes Back; Cleopatra; Madame Du Barry; One More River; Caravan; The Firebird; The Scarlet Empress. **1935** The Tunnel (aka Trans-Atlantic Tunnel—US); The Right to Live; Lives of a Bengal Lancer; The Florentine Dagger; The Gilded Lily; Clive of India; China Seas; Jalna; The Crusades. **1936** The Story of Papworth (short); Little Lord Fauntleroy; Romeo and Juliet; The Garden of Allah; Lloyds of London. **1937** Wee Willie Winkie; The Prisoner of Zenda; Thoroughbreds Don't Cry; The Hurricane. **1938** Four Men and a Prayer; Kidnapped; Sixty Glorious Years (aka Queen of Destiny—US). **1939** East Side of Heaven; The Four Feathers; Five Came Back; The Sun Never Sets; Eternally Yours; Another Thin Man; The Under-Pup; Balalaika. **1940** Rebecca; City of Chance; A Bill of Divorcement; Waterloo Bridge; Beyond Tomorrow; A Little Bit of Heaven. **1941** Free and Easy; Maisie Was a Lady; Dr. Jekyll and Mr. Hyde. **1943** Forever and a Day; Two Tickets to London; Flesh and Fantasy; Madame Curie. **1944** The White Cliffs of Dover; The Adventures of Mark Twain; Secrets of Scotland Yard; Sensations of 1945. **1945** They Shall Have Faith; And Then There Were None; Scotland Yard Investigator. **1946** Cluny Brown; Rendezvous with Annie. **1947** High Conquest; Unconquered. **1948** An Ideal Husband. **1949** Little Women.

SMITH, CHARLES H.
Born: 1866. Died: July 11, 1942, Hollywood, Calif. Screen and vaudeville actor. Was member of "Smith and Campbell" vaudeville team.

Appeared in: **1921** Nobody; The Silver Lining. **1927** Naughty Nanette. **1929** Clear the Decks; Girl Overboard; The Girl on the Barge. **1930** The Bat Whispers.

SMITH, CHARLES WILFRED
Born: 1897, Wales. Died: July 23, 1971, Miami, Fla. Screen actor and opera singer. Do not confuse with U.S. actor with same name.

SMITH, CHARLOTTE
Born: 1873, Toronto, Canada. Died: Mar. 22, 1928, Beverly Hills, Calif. Stage and screen actress. Mother of actresses Mary and Lottie Pickford (dec. 1936) and actor Jack Pickford (dec. 1933). Appeared in Imp Company films.

SMITH, CLIFFORD
Born: 1886, Richmond, Ind. Died: Sept. 17, 1937, Hollywood, Calif. (peritonitis). Screen actor, film director and producer.

Appeared in: **1915** The Taking of Luke McVane.

SMITH, CYRIL
Born: Apr. 4, 1892, Peterhead, Scotland. Died: Mar. 5, 1963, London, England. Screen and stage actor. Married to actress Anne Rendall.

Appeared in: **1914** Old St. Paul's (aka When London Burned—US). **1919** Pallard, the Punter. **1920** Walls of Prejudice; The Fordington Twins; Will O'Wisp comedies including Sweep; On the Reserve; Cupid's Carnival; Run! Run! Run!; A Broken Contract; Cousin Ebenezer; Souvenirs; The Lightning Liver Cure; A Little Bet; A Pair of Gloves; Home Influence. **1921** The Way of a Man; Class and No Class. **1923** Fires of Fate. **1924** The Desert Sheik. **1932** The Innocents of Chicago (aka Why Saps Leave Home—US); The Major's Nest. **1933** Channel Crossing (US 1934); Friday the Thirteenth (US 1934); The Good Companions. **1934** Waltzes from Vienna (aka Strauss's Great Waltz—US 1935); The Black Abbot; Wild Boy; It's a Cop. **1935** Hello Sweetheart; Key to Harmony; Brown on Resolution (aka Forever England and Born for Glory—US); Bulldog Jack (aka Alias Bulldog Drummond—US); Lend Me Your Wife. **1937** O.H.M.S. (aka You're in the Army Now—US); The Frog (US 1939). **1938** The Challenge (US 1939); No Parking; The Return of the Frog. **1939** Traitor Spy (aka The Torso Murder Mystery—US 1940); Sword of Honor. **1940** The Flying Squad; Law and Disorders. **1943** When We Are Married. **1944** One Exciting Night (aka You Can't Do Without Love—US 1946); Meet Sexton Blake. **1945** The Echo Murders; Don Chicago. **1946** School for Secrets; Appointment with Crime (US 1950). **1949** The Rocking Horse Winner (US 1950); Conspirator (US 1950). **1950** The Body Said No!; Old Mother Riley, Headmistress (US 1951). **1951** The Third Visitor; The Dark Man; Night Was Our Friend; Green Grow the Rushes. **1952** Stolen Face; The Lost Hours (aka The Big Frame—US 1953); Women of Twilight (aka Twilight Women—US 1953). **1953** Wheel of Fate. **1954** The Angel Who Pawned Her Harp—US 1956; Svengali; Burnt Evidence; The Strange Case of Blondie. **1956** Sailor Beware! (aka Panic in the Parlour—US 1957). **1957** Value for Money. **1960** Light Up in the Sky. **1961** Over the Odds. **1962** She Knows Y'Know. **1965** Operation Snafu.

SMITH, DWIGHT
Born: 1857, Vevay, Ind. Died: May 30, 1949, Monsey, N.Y. Stage and screen actor. Appeared in silent films.

SMITH, EARL T.
Died: Dec. 22, 1968. Screen actor.

Appeared in: **1947** The Macomber Affair. **1949** Abandoned.

SMITH, G. ALBERT
Born: 1898. Died: Sept 3, 1959, New York, N.Y. Screen, stage and television actor.

Appeared in: **1931** Stolen Heaven.

SMITH, GEORGE W.
Born: 1899. Died: Nov. 18, 1947, Chicago, Ill, (coronary thrombosis). Stage and screen actor.

Appeared in: **1946** Snafu.

SMITH, GERALD (Gerland Oliver Smith)
Born: June 26, 1896, London, England. Died: May 28, 1974, Woodland Hills, Calif. Screen, stage and radio actor.

Appeared in: **1925** School for Wives. **1936** The Man I Marry; When You're in Love. **1937** Top of the Town; Girl Overboard; One Hundred Men and a Girl; The Lady Fights Back; The Lady Escapes; Behind the Mike. **1938** Invisible Enemy; Gateway. **1939** Each Dawn I Die; Bachelor Mother. **1940** West of Pinto Basin; Kiddie Cure (short). **1941** The Bride Came C.O.D.; The Singing Hill; Federal Fugitives; Puddin' Head; You're the One. **1942** Beyond the Blue Horizon; Tish; Casablanca. **1943** Forever and a Day; Heaven Can Wait. **1944** Jane Eyre; The Man in Half Moon Street; Knickerbocker Holiday; National Velvet; Mrs. Parkington; Casanova Brown. **1945** Sunbonnet Sue; The Sailor Takes a Wife. **1946** Rainbow Over Texas. **1948** Enchantment. **1949** That Forsyte Woman.

SMITH, HAYDON
Born: 1929. Died: Apr. 23, 1980, Glendale, Calif. Screen, stage actor and stage manager.

SMITH, HOWARD I.
Born: Aug. 12, 1893, Attleboro, Mass. Died: Jan. 10, 1968, Hollywood, Calif. (heart attack). Screen, stage, vaudeville, radio and television actor.

Appeared in: **1922** Young America. **1946** Her Kind of Man. **1947** Kiss of Death. **1948** Call Northside 777; State of the Union; Street With No Name. **1950** Cry Murder. **1951** Death of a Salesman. **1952** Never Wave at a WAC. **1953** The Caddy. **1957** Don't Go Near the Water; A Face in the Crowd. **1958** Wind Across the Everglades; No Time for Sergeants; I Bury the Living. **1959** Face of Fire. **1960** Murder, Inc. **1962** Bon Voyage! **1963** The Brass Bottle.

SMITH, J. LEWIS
Born: 1906. Died: Sept. 12, 1964, Culver City, Calif. (shot). Screen actor and stuntman.

Appeared in: **1955** The Tall Men. **1956** Around the World in 80 Days. **1959** It Started with a Kiss. **1961** Man-Trap; The Misfits. **1962** How the West Was Won; Jumbo; The Wonderful World of the Brothers Grimm. **1963** Twilight of Honor. **1964** Advance to the Rear.

SMITH, J. STANLEY
Born: Jan. 6, 1905, Kansas City, Mo. Died: Apr. 13, 1974, Pasadena, Calif. Screen and stage actor. Entered films in 1929.

Appeared in: **1929** Sweetie; The Sophomore. **1930** Follow the Leader; Good News; The King of Jazz; Honey; Love Among the Millionaires; Queen High; Soup to Nuts; Paramount on Parade. **1932** Stepping Sisters. **1933** Reform Girl. **1937** A Warner short. **1940** Flight Command. **1941** Dive Bomber; Buck Privates; Keep 'Em Flying. **1942** Eagle Squadron.

SMITH, JACK
Born: 1896. Died: Jan. 14, 1944, Los Angeles, Calif. Screen actor and songwriter.

Appeared in: **1928** Man in the Rough. **1929** Laughing at Death. **1937** Git Along Little Dogies; Heroes of the Alamo. **1938** Paroled to Die; Frontier Scout. **1939** The Oregon Trail (serial); The Phantom Creeps (serial). **1941** Stick to Your Guns.

SMITH, JESS
Born: Mar. 9, 1897, Pittsburgh, Pa. Died: Apr. 11, 1965, Hollywood, Calif. (heart attack). Screen, stage actor, film director, film producer and stage manager. Entered films in 1913 as an actor with the Lubin Co.

SMITH, JOE (Joseph Sultzer)
Born: Feb. 16, 1884, New York, N.Y. Died: Feb. 22, 1981, Englewood, N.J. Screen, stage, vaudeville and radio actor. Appeared in vaudeville with Charles Dale (dec. 1971), in an act billed as "Smith and Dale." For films the team appeared in, see Charles Dale listing.

SMITH, JOE
Born: 1900. Died: May 5, 1952, Yuma, Ariz. (heart attack). Screen actor and stuntman.

Appeared in: **1952** Desert Song.

SMITH, KENNETH L. "KEN"
Died: Aug. 24, 1981. Screen actor.

Appeared in: **1949** Jigsaw. **1955** Jungle Moon Men. **1957** Under Fire. **1959** Battle of the Coral Sea.

SMITH, LENNIE (Leonard Smith)
Died: 1967. Screen actor. Do not confuse with cinematographer with same name.

Appeared in: **1953** Son of The Renegade. **1956** Our Miss Brooks. **1957** Escape From San Quentin.

SMITH, (COL.) LEONARD R.
Born: 1889. Died: July 9, 1958, San Antonio, Tex. Screen actor and film director. Did trick riding in silent films for William S. Hart and also worked in Mack Sennett comedies.

SMITH, LORING
Born: 1890, Stratford, Conn. Died: July 8, 1981, Fairfield, Conn. Screen, stage, vaudeville and television actor. Married to actress Natalie Sawyer, with whom he appeared in vaudeville in an act billed as "The Smith and Sawyer Duo."

Appeared in: **1941** Shadow of the Thin Man; Keep 'Em Flying. **1948** Close-Up. **1952** Pat and Mike. **1953** The Clown. **1955** Ma and Pa Kettle at Waikiki. **1959** Happy Anniversary. **1963** The Cardinal. **1967** Hurry Sundown.

SMITH, MABEL See BIG MAYBELLE

SMITH, MARGARET M.
Born: 1881. Died: Dec. 9, 1960, Hollywood, Calif. Screen actress.

Appeared in: **1925** A Roaring Adventure.

SMITH, MARK
Born: 1886. Died: May 10, 1944, New York, N.Y. Screen and stage actor.

SMITH, MATTHEW
Born: 1905. Died: Mar. 16, 1953, New York, N.Y. Screen and stage actor.

Appeared in: **1934** The Barretts of Wimpole Street.

SMITH, MURRAY See SILVA, MARIO

SMITH, PAUL GERARD
Born: 1895, Omaha, Nebr. Died: Apr. 5, 1968. Screen actor, playwright and screenwriter.

Appeared in: **1917** The Mysterious Miss Terry.

SMITH, PETE
Born: Sept. 4, 1892, New York, N.Y. Died: Jan. 12, 1979, Santa Monica, Calif. (suicide—jumped from hospital roof). Screen, vaudeville actor, film producer, film narrator, screenwriter, art director, entertainment reporter and press agent. Received Special Academy Award in 1955.

Appeared in: **1928** The Midnight Ace. He either appeared in and/or narrated the following shorts:. **1931** Fisherman's Paradise; Pearls and Devil-Fish; Sharks and Swordfish; Piscatorial Pleasures; Splash!; Wild and Woolly; Whippet Racing. **1932** Trout Fishing; Color Scales; Lesson in Golf; Dive In; Olympic Events; Athletic Daze; Flying Spikes; Timber Toppers; Snow Birds; Desert Regatta; Swing High; Chalk Up; Pigskin; Block and Tackle; Football Footwork. **1933** Goofy Movies #1; Motorcycle Mania; Bone Crushers; Allez Oop; Throttle Pushers; Handlebars; Microscopic Mysteries; Menu; Happy Warriors; Fine Feathers; Inflation. **1934** Roping Wild Bears; Vital Victuals; Trick Golf; Nipups; Flying Hunters; Dartmouth Days; Rugby; Pichianni Troupe; Goofy Movies #2- #10; Attention, Suckers; Taking Care of Baby; Pro Football; Strikes and Spares. **1935** La Fiesta de Santa Barbara; Motorcycle Cossacks; Donkey Baseball; Sporting Nuts; Fightin' Fish; Chain Letter Dimes; Prince, King of Dogs; Basketball Technique; Football Teamwork; Gymnastics; Water Sports; Crew Racing; Trained Hoots; Audioscopiks. **1936** Let's Dance; Jonker Diamond; Behind the Headlines; Olympic Ski Champions; Sports on Ice; Hurling; Wanted: A Master; Air Hoppers; Racing Canines; Polo; Harnessed Rhythm; Dare-Deviltry; Table Tennies; Aquatic Artistry; West Point of the South; Killer Dog. **1937** Dexterity; Guilding the Lily; Penny Wisdom; Tennis Tactics; Golf Mistakes; Jungle Juveniles; Candid Cameramaniacs; Bar-Rac's Night Out; Grand Bounce; Pigskin Champions; Equestrian Acrobatics; Ski Skill; The Romance of Radium; Decathlon Champion. **1938** New Audioscopiks; Friend Indeed; Surf Heroes; Football Thrills of 1937; Grid Rules; Hot on Ice; Man's Greatest Friend; Jungle Juveniles #2; Three on a Rope; La Savate; Penny's Party; Modeling for Money; The Story of Dr. Carver; Anesthesia; Follow the Arrow; Fisticuffs; Penny's Picnic. **1939** Double Diving; Weather Wizards; Radio Hams; Culinary Carving; Take a Cue; Set 'Em Up; Let's Talk Turkey; Romance of the Potato; Heroes at Leisure; Marine Circus; Poetry of Nature; Football Thrills of 1938; Ski Birds. **1940** What's Your I.Q. #1 and #2; The Domineering Male; Social Sea Lions; Please Answer; Football Thrills of 1939; Sea for Yourself; Maintain the Right; Stuffie; Spots Before Your Eyes; Cat College; Quicker 'n a Wink; Wedding Bills. **1941** Penny to the Rescue; Cuban Rhythm; Fancy Answers; How to Hold Your Husband—Back; Third-Dimensional Murder; Quiz Biz; Memory Tricks; Aeronautics; Lions on the Loose; Water Bugs; Football Thrills of 1940; Flicker Memories; Army Champions. **1942** Victory Quiz; Pete Smith's Scrapbook; It's a Dog's Life; Football Thrills of 1941; Marines in the Making; Aqua Antics; What About Daddy?; Acro-Batty; Barbee-Cues; Self-Defense; Victory Vittles; Calling All Pa's. **1943** First Aid; Tree in a Test Tube; Hollywood Daredevils; Fala; Seeing Hands; Fixin' Tricks; Wild Horses; Sky Science; Dog House; Seventh Column; Scrap Happy; Football Thrills of 1942; Tips on Trips; Water Wisdom. **1944** Sportsman's Memories; Football Thrills of 1943; Safety Sleuth; Practical Joker; Home Maid; Groovie Movie; Movie Pests; Sports Quiz. **1945** Hollywood Scout; Guest Pests; Bus Pests; Badmitton; Track and Field Quiz; Football Thrills of 1944. **1946** Sports Sticklers; Gettin' Glamour; Football Thrills #9; Sure Cures; Fala at Hyde Park; Studio Visit; Equestrian Quiz; Treasures from Trash; I Love My Husband; Playing by Ear. **1947** Diamond Demon; I Love My Wife; Pet Peeves; Surfboard Rhythm; Athletiquiz; Early Sports Quiz; Neighbor Pests; Football Thrills #10; What D'ya Know; Have You Ever

Wondered. **1948** I Love My Mother-in-Law; Now You See It; You Can't Win; Football Thrills #11; Why Is It?; Pigskin Skill; Ice Aces; Bowling Tricks; Just Suppose; Let's Cogitate. **1949** Super Cue Men; Those Good Old Days; Fishing for Fun; How Come?; We Can Dream, Can't We?; What I Want Next; Scientifiquiz; Football Thrills #12; Water Trix; Sports Oddities. **1950** Pest Control; Crashing the Movies; Wrong Son; Did 'Ja Know; That's His Story; A Wife's Life; Wrong Way Butch; Football Thrills #13; Curious Contests; Table Toppers; Wanted: One Egg. **1951** Sky Skiers; Camera Sleuth; Fixin' Fool; Bandage Bait; Football Thrills #14; That's What YOU Think; In Case You're Curious; Fishing Feats. **1952** Musiquiz; Mealtime Magic; Gymnastic Rhythm; Pedestrian Safety; Football Thrills #15; Reducing; It Could Happen to You; Sweet Memories; I Love Children, But! **1953** The Mosconi Story; Cash Stashers; Aquatic Kids; Travel Quiz; The Postman; Dogs 'n Ducks; Ancient Cures; This is a Living; Landlording It; Things We Can Do Without. **1954** Film Antics; Ain't It Aggravatin'; Fish Tales; Do Someone a Favor; Out for Fun; Safe at Home; The Camera Caught It; Rough Riding. **1955** The Man Around the House; Keep Young; Sports Trix; Just What I Need; Global Quiz; Animals in Action; Historical Oddities; Fall Guy.

SMITH, PLEASANT (aka TOMMY LEE PLEASANT aka JIMMY DEE SMITH)
Born: 1886. Died: Mar. 12, 1969, Las Vegas, Nev. Screen actor and wrestler. Appeared in films between 1913 and 1919.

SMITH, QUEENIE
Born: 1908, Calif. Died: Aug. 5, 1978, Burbank, Calif. (cancer). Screen, stage, radio, television actress and dancer.

Appeared in: **1935** Mississippi. **1936** Show Boat. **1939** On Your Toes. **1946** The Killers; From This Day Forward; Nocturne. **1947** The Long Night. **1948** The Snake Pit; Sleep, My Love. **1949** Massacre River. **1950** The Great Rupert; Emergency Wedding; Prisoners in Petticoats. **1951** The First Legion. **1955** My Sister Eileen. **1956** Fighting Trouble; You Can't Run Away From It; Hot Shots. **1957** The Sweet Smell of Success. **1968** The Legend of Lylah Clare. **1975** Day of the Locust; Hustle. **1977** Mother, Jugs and Speed. **1978** Foul Play; The End.

SMITH, ROY
Born: 1889. Died: Dec. 12, 1944. Screen actor and stuntman.

SMITH, SEBASTIAN (J. Sebastian Smith)
Born: Oct. 3, 1869, Southwell, Notts, England. Died: Jan. 15, 1948, England?. Screen and stage actor.

Appeared in: **1929** White Cargo (US 1930). **1931** Love Lies; Man of Mayfair.

SMITH, SIDNEY
Born: 1892. Died: July 4, 1928, Hollywood, Calif. (possibly effects of bad liquor). Screen actor and comedian.

Appeared in: **1917** Oriental Love; His Uncle Dudley. **1921-1922** The "Hallroom Boys" series. **1923** The Ne'er Do Well. **1928** Dugan of the Dugouts; Top Sergeant Mulligan.

SMITH, SILVERHEELS See SILVERHEELS, JAY

SMITH, SOLLY G.
Born: 1876. Died: Aug. 28, 1933, Culver City, Calif. Professional boxer and screen actor.

SMITH, SYDNEY G.
Born: 1910. Died: Mar. 4, 1978, Seattle, Wash. Screen, stage and radio actor. Married to singer Ester Ott.

Appeared in: **1951** The Frogmen. **1957** Valerie; Fury at Showdown. **1958** Tonka; No Time for Sergeants. **1960** Gallant Hours. **1962** The Wonderful World of the Brothers Grimm. **1964** Apache Rifles.

SMITH, THOMAS C.
Born: 1892. Died: Dec. 3, 1950, Hollywood, Calif. Screen actor.

Appeared in: **1929** The Invaders.

SMITH, TOM
Born: 1892. Died: Feb. 23, 1976, Hollywood, Calif. Screen actor. Do not confuse with actor Thomas C. Smith (dec. 1950), or makeup artist with the same name.

Appeared in: **1929** The Invaders.

SMITH, "WHISPERING" JACK
Born: 1898. Died: May 13, 1950, New York, N.Y. (heart attack). Screen, vaudeville, radio, television actor and singer. Known as "The Whispering Baritone."

Appeared in: **1930** Happy Days; The Big Parade; Cheer Up and Smile.

SMITH, YANCEY See WARD, CHANCE E.

SMITHSON, LAURA
Born: 1878. Died: Dec. 23, 1963. Stage and screen actress.

Appeared in: **1937** Men Are Not Gods.

SMITTERICK, GROVER
Died: Sept., 1914, New York (drowned while filming). Screen actor. Appeared in Progressive Motion Picture Company films.

SMOLLER, DOROTHY
Born: 1901, Memphis, Tenn. Died: Dec. 10, 1926, New York, N.Y. (suicide). Screen actress and dancer.

SMYTHE, FLORENCE
Born: 1878. Died: Aug. 29, 1925, Hollywood, Calif. (heart failure). Stage and screen actress. Married to actor Theodore Roberts (dec. 1928).

Appeared in: **1915** The Wild Goose Chase; The Fighting Hope. **1916** Common Ground. **1917** The Silent Partner; The Winning of Sally Temple.

SNEGOFF, LEONID
Born: May 15, 1883, Russia. Died: Feb. 22, 1974, Los Angeles, Calif. (heart failure—arteriosclerosis). Screen and stage actor.

Appeared in: **1926** Broken Hearts. **1927** The Forbidden Woman. **1933** The Man Who Dared; After Tonight; Girl Without a Room; We Live Again. **1934** Smoky. **1935** Rendezvous; The Great Impersonation; Strange Wives; The Man Who Broke the Bank at Monte Carlo; The Wedding Night; Dressed to Thrill. **1936** The Story of Louis Pasteur. **1937** Easy Living; Seventh Heaven; The Three Legionnaires; Cafe Metropole; Dangerously Yours. **1939** Barricade. **1943** For Whom the Bell Tolls; Mission to Moscow. **1947** Song of My Heart. **1948** Smuggler's Cove. **1953** One Girl's Confession.

SNELLING, MINNETTE
Born: 1878. Died: Dec. 19, 1945, Hollywood, Calif. Screen actress. Entered films in 1917. Appeared in Mack Sennett comedies.

SNITZER, JIMMY
Born: 1926. Died: Mar. 22, 1945, Asbach, Germany. Screen actor.

SNITZER, MIRIAM
Born: 1922. Died: Sept. 6, 1966. Screen actress.

SNODGRASS, SMYTHE
Born: 1887. Died: Oct. 3, 1921, Bayonne, N.J. Screen actor. Appeared in David Hersley Film Co. films.

SNOOKUMS See MC KEEN, LAWRENCE D., JR.

SNOW, MARC
Died: Nov., 1969. Screen actor.

Appeared in: **1953** The Robe. **1954** Woman's World.

SNOW, MARGUERITE
Born: Sept. 9, 1889. Died: Feb. 17, 1958, Hollywood, Calif. (kidney complications). Screen actress. Married to actor Neely Edwards (dec. 1955).

Appeared in: **1912** Lucille. **1913** Carmen. **1914** Zudora—The Twenty Million Dollar Mystery (serial); Joseph in the Land of Egypt. **1915** The Silent Voice. **1917** Broadway Jones. **1918** The Eagle's Eye (serial). **1920** The Woman in Room 13. **1921** Lavender and Old Lace. **1922** The Veiled Woman. **1924** Chalk Marks. **1925** Kit Carson Over the Great Divide; Savages of the Sea.

SNOW, MORTIMER
Born: Nov. 19, 1869. Died: June 20, 1935. Stage and screen actor.

Appeared in: **1922** The Mohican's Daughter; When Knighthood Was in Flower.

SNOWDEN, ELMER "POPS" (Elmer Chester Snowden)
Born: Oct. 9, 1900, Baltimore, Md. Died: May 14, 1973, Philadelphia, Pa. Jazz musician and screen actor. Appeared in Warner Bros. shorts.

SNOWDON, ERIC (Eric Snowden)
Born: 1889, England. Died: June 27, 1979, Bellevue, Wash. Screen, stage, radio, television actor and stage director.

Appeared in: **1934** Shock. **1936** Forbidden Heaven. **1954** Jungle Gents.

SNYDER, EARL "SPANKY"
Born: 1907. Died: Jan. 16, 1973, Phoenix, Ariz. (cancer). Screen actor. Entered films in 1916.

Appeared in: **1955** Not as a Stranger. **1965** Cat Ballou.

SNYDER, MATT
Died: Jan. 17, 1917, San Francisco, Calif. Screen and stage actor.

Appeared in: **1916** The Crisis.

SOBOLOFF, ARNOLD
Born: 1931, New York, N.Y. Died: Oct. 28, 1979, New York, N.Y. (heart attack). Screen, stage, television actor and singer.

Appeared in: **1968** The Detective. **1969** Popi. **1976** Silent Movie; Nickelodeon. **1978** The Cat from Outer Space.

SOBOTKA, RUTH
Born: 1925. Died: June 17, 1967. Stage and screen actress. Divorced from film director Stanley Kubrick.

Appeared in: **1955** Killer's Kiss.

SODDERS, CARL
Died: Dec. 18, 1958, Dayton, Ohio. Screen actor. Appeared in silents.

SODERLING, WALTER
Born: Apr. 13, 1872, Conn. Died: Apr. 10, 1948, Los Angeles, Calif. Screen actor.

Appeared in: **1937** Criminals of the Air; Woman Chases Man. **1938** The Story of Dr. Carver (short). **1939** The Gracie Allen Murder Case; St. Louis Blues; Blondie Meets the Boss; Death of a Champion. **1940** When the Daltons Rode; Blondie Has Servant Trouble; Men Without Souls; On Their Own; I'm Nobody's Sweetheart Now; Out West with the Peppers; Ragtime Cowboy Joe; Slightly Tempted. **1941** Penny Serenade; The Return of Daniel Boone; Three Girls About Town; Confessions of Boston Blackie. **1943** The Blocked Trail; True to Life. **1944** The Falcon in Hollywood; The Adventures of Mark Twain; Outlaws of Santa Fe. **1945** Rhapsody in Blue. **1946** King of the Forest Rangers (serial); Danny Boy; The Glass Alibi; In Fast Company; The French Key. **1947** Yankee Fakir. **1948** So Dear to My Heart; Leather Gloves.

SOJIN (Sojin Kamiyama)
Born: Jan. 20, 1891, Sendai, Japan. Died: July 28, 1954, Tokyo, Japan. Stage and screen actor. Appeared in U.S. films from approximately 1913 to 1930 and then appeared in Japanese films. He was one of the six actors to portray "Charlie Chan."

Appeared in: **1924** The Thief of Bagdad. **1925** The White Desert; My Lady's Lips; Proud Flesh; Soft Shoes; East of Suez. **1926** Across the Pacific; Diplomacy; Eve's Leaves; The Lucky Lady; The Lady of the Harem; The Sky Pirate; The Sea Beast; The Bat; The Road to Mandalay; The Wanderer. **1927** All Aboard; The Devil Dancer; Driven from Home; Foreign Devils; King of Kings; The Haunted Ship; Old San Francisco; Streets of Shanghai. **1928** Chinese Parrot; Chinatown Charlie; The Crimson City; The Hawk's Nest; Out With the Tide; Ships of the Night; Something Always Happens; The Man Without a Face (serial); Telling the World; Tropic Madness. **1929** Back from Shanghai; The Rescue; China Slaver; Painted Faces; Seven Footprints to Satan; The Show of Shows; The Unholy Night; Careers. **1930** The Dude Wrangler; Golden Dawn.

SOKOLOFF, VLADIMIR
Born: Dec. 26, 1889, Moscow, Russia. Died: Feb. 14, 1962, Hollywood, Calif. (stroke). Screen, stage actor and stage director.

Appeared in: **1926** Die Abenteuer Eines Zehnmarkscheines (Adventures of a Ten Pound Note). **1927** Die Liebe der Jeanne Ney (The Love of Jeanne Ney); Der Sohn der Hagar (Out of the Mist). **1928** Die Weisse Sonate. **1929** Katharina Knie; Das Schiff der Verlorenen Menschen; Sensation im Wintergarten. **1930** Moral um Mitternacht; West Front 1918; Liebling der Goetter (Darling of the Gods); Abschied (aka Adieu); Das Floetenkonzert von Saussouci (The Flute Concert at Sans Souci—US 1931). **1931** Die Dreigroschenoper (The Threepenny Opera, aka The Beggar's Opera); Der Grosse Tenor; Die Heilige Flamme; Kismet; Niemandsland (No Man's Land—US 1932, aka Hell on Earth). **1932** Teilnehmer Antwortet Nicht; L'Atalantide; Strafsache van Geldern; Die Herrin von Atlantis; Gehetzte Menschen (aka Steckbrief Z 48). **1937** The Prisoner of Zenda; The Life of Emile Zola; West of Shanghai; Expensive Husbands; Tovarich; Conquest; Beg, Borrow or Steal; The Lower Depths; Mayerling. **1938** Alcatraz Island; Arsene Lupin Returns; Blockade; The Amazing Dr. Clitterhouse; Spawn of the North; Ride a Crooked Mile. **1939** Juarez; The Real Glory; Song of the Street. **1940** Comrade X. **1941** Compliments of Mr. Flow; Love Crazy. **1942** Crossroads; The Road to Morocco. **1943** Mission to Moscow; Song of Russia; From Whom the Bell Tolls; Mr. Lucky. **1944** Passage to Marseille; The Conspirators; 'Til We Meet Again. **1945** The Blonde from Brooklyn; Paris Underground; Scarlet Street; A Royal Scandal; Back to Bataan.

1946 Two Smart People; Cloak and Dagger; A Scandal in Paris. **1948** To the Ends of the Earth. **1950** The Baron of Arizona. **1952** Macao. **1956** While the City Sleeps. **1957** Istanbul; I Was a Teenage Werewolf; Sabu and the Magic Ring. **1958** The Monster from Green Hill; Twilight for the Gods. **1960** Man on a String; Beyond the Time Barrier; The Magnificent Seven; Cimarron; Confessions of a Counterspy; Die Dreigroschenoper (The Three Penny Opera—also 1931 version). **1961** Mr. Sardonicus. **1962** Taras Bulba; Escape from Zahrain.

SOKOLOW, ETHEL
Died: Dec. 20, 1970. Screen actress.

Appeared in: **1968** Funny Man. **1969** Take the Money and Run.

SOLAR, WILLIE
Born: 1891. Died: Dec. 17, 1956, New York, N.Y. (heart attack). Screen, stage and vaudeville actor.

Appeared in: **1945** Billy Rose's Diamond Horseshoe.

SOLBELLI, OLGA See SUNBEAUTY, OLGA

SOLDANI, CHARLES L.
Born: June 1, 1893, Okla. Died: Sept. 10, 1968, Glendale, Calif. (lung cancer). Screen actor.

Appeared in: **1945** The Cherokee Flash; The Man from Oklahoma. **1949** Apache Chief; Daughter of the Jungle. **1950** Broken Arrow. **1953** Winning of the West. **1956** Around the World in 80 Days. **1959** Escort West.

SOLDEVILLA, LALY
Born: 1933. Died: Sept. 12, 1979, Madrid, Spain. Screen and stage actress.

Appeared in: **1961** Tre de la Cruz Roja (film debut). **1964** La Tia Tula (US 1965). **1976** El Espiritu de la Colmena (The Spirit of the Beehive).

SOLDI, STEPHEN
Died: Nov. 4, 1974. Screen actor and extra.

Appeared in: **1947** Twilight on the Rio Grande. **1956** Around the World in 80 Days.

SOLER, DOMINGO (Domingo Diaz Pavia)
Born: Apr 17, 1902, Guerrero, Mexico. Died: June 13, 1961, Acapulco, Mexico (heart attack). Screen and stage actor. Son of actor Domingo Soler, Sr. Brother of stage actor Andres (dec.) and actor Julian (dec. 1977) and Fernando Soler.

Appeared in: **1935** Corazon Bandolero; Chucho el Roto; Tierra, Amor y Dolor. **1936** La Mujer del Puerto. **1938** Mi Candidato (My Candidate); Hombres de Mar (Men of the Sea); Bajo el Cielo de Mexico (Beneath the Sky of Mexico); Refugidos en Madrid. **1939** Vamonos con Pancho Villa (Let's Go with Pancho Villa); El Senor Alcalde (The Mayor); A lo Macho (In Rough Style); Por Mis Pistolas (By My Pistols); El Latigo (The Whip); La Golondrina (The Swallow). **1940** Corazon de Nino (Heart of a Child); Perfidia (Perfidy); La Bestia Negra (The Black Beast). **1943** The Life of Simon Bolivar; El Conde de Monte Cristo. **1944** Los Miserables. **1950** Hidden River. **1954** La Ilusion Viaja en Tranvia. **1957** Flor ae Mayo (Beyond All Limits—US 1961). **1961** La Maldicion de Nostradamus (The Curse of Nostradamus). **1962** La Sangre de Nostradamus (The Blood of Nostradamus); Nostradamus, El Genio de las Tinieblas (Genii of Darkness); Nostradamus y el Destructor de Monstruos (Monster Demolisher). **1964** La Maldicion de la Llorona (The Curse of the Crying Woman). Other films include: Oro y Plata; El Primo Basilyo.

SOLER, JULIAN
Born: 1905, Mexico. Died: May 5, 1977, Mexico City, Mexico. Screen and stage actor. Brother of stage actor Andres (dec.), and actors Domingo (dec. 1961) and Fernando Soler. Father of actor Fernando Palavacini.

Appeared in: **1934** El Escandalo. **1935** Cruz Diablo; Clemencia; Bohemios; Los Muertos Hablan (The Dead Speak). **1936** La Familia Dressel; Mater Nostra. **1938** Noches de Gloria (Glorious Nights); Alma Jarocha; Los Dos Cadetes; Supremo Sacrificio (Supreme Sacrifice). **1939** El Beso Mortal (The Fatal Kiss); El Cobarde (The Coward); Estrellita (Starlet); La India Bonita (The Pretty Indian Girl); Por Mis Pistolas (By My Pistols); El Latigo (The Whip); Soy Chato, Pero las Huelo (I Am Snub-Nosed, But I Can Smell); Papacito Lindo (Sugar Daddy). **1940** Odio (Hate); Mi Madrecita (My Little Mother). **1943** The Life of Simon Bolivar.

SOLIS, JAVIER
Born: 1931, Nogales, Sonora, Mexico. Died: Apr. 19, 1966, Mexico City, Mexico (following surgery). Screen actor and singer.

Appeared in: Los 2 Juanes; Juan Pistola.

SOLOVIEV, YURI
Born: 1940, Leningrad, Russia. Died: Jan. 16, 1977, Leningrad, Russia (suicide—gun). Ballet dancer and screen actor.

Appeared in: **1964** Spashchaya Krasavites (The Sleeping Beauty—US 1966).

SOLOVITCH, DON
Died: Jan. 6, 1928, Gunnison, Utah. Screen actor.

SOLTZ, ROSE
Died: Sept. 18, 1973. Stage and screen actress.

SOMERS, CAROLE (Judy Cosgrove)
Died: Aug. 2, 1974, Los Angeles, Calif. Screen, stage, radio and television actress.

SOMERS, FRED
Died: Sept. 17, 1970. Screen actor.

Appeared in: **1938** Follow the Arrow (short).

SOMERSET, PAT (Patrick Holme-Somerset)
Born: Feb. 28, 1897, London, England. Died: Apr 20, 1974, Apple Valley Calif. (arterial hemorrhage). Screen and stage actor.

Appeared in: **1918** Eve comedies. **1920** Walls of Prejudice. **1921** Serving Two Masters; The White Hen. **1925** One of the Bravest. **1927** One Increasing Purpose. **1928** Mother Machree. **1929** The Black Watch; From Headquarters. **1930** Born Reckless; Good Intentions; Hell's Angels; Up the River; Men Without Women. **1931** Body and Soul; Devotion. **1932** Night World. **1933** Midnight Club. **1934** Murder in Trinidad. **1935** Bonnie Scotland; Clive of India; Cardinal Richelieu; Here's to Romance. **1936** To Mary—With Love. **1937** I Cover the War; Death in the Air; Prisoner of Zenda; Wee Willie Winkie.

SOMMERVILLE, MARY See LAWFORD, LADY MAY

SONKUR, KALU K.
Died: Apr. 20, 1972. Screen actor.

Appeared in: **1952** Bwana Devil.

SONNEMANN, EMMY
Born: 1893, Germany. Died: June 8, 1973, Munich, Germany. Screen actress.

Appeared in: **1935** The Legend of William Tell; Oberwachtmeister Schwenke (US 1936).

SONNEVELD, WIM (aka WILLIAM SONNEVELD)
Born: 1918, Holland? Died: Mar. 8, 1974, Amsterdam, Holland (heart attack). Screen, stage, radio and television actor.

Appeared in: **1957** Silk Stockings.

SONTAN, J. FARREN
Born: 1871. Died: Jan. 23, 1962. Screen actor.

Appeared in: **1935** The Iron Duke.

SOO, CHAN
Born: 1909. Died: Oct. 7, 1979, Pittsburgh, Pa. Screen and vaudeville actor.

SOO, JACK (Goro Suzuki)
Born: 1915, Oakland, Calif. Died: Jan. 11, 1979, Los Angeles, Calif. (cancer). Screen, stage and television actor.

Appeared in: **1961** The Flower Drum Song (stage and film versions). **1963** Who's Been Sleeping in My Bed? **1966** The Oscar. **1967** Thoroughly Modern Millie. **1968** The Green Berets. **1978** Return From Witch Mountain.

SOREL, CECILE (Cecile Emilie Seure)
Born: 1874, France. Died: Sept. 3, 1966, Deauville, France (heart attack). Stage and screen actress.

Appeared in: **1937** Les Perles de la Couronne (Pearls of the Crown).

SOREL, GEORGE S.
Born: 1899. Died: Jan. 19, 1948, Hollywood, Calif. Screen actor.

Appeared in: **1936** Sing Me a Love Song. **1937** Swing High, Swing Low; The Sheik Steps Out. **1938** Swiss Miss. **1939** Three Musketeers. **1942** Ship Ahoy; Once Upon a Honeymoon; Casablanca. **1943** The Desert Song; Hitler—Dead or Alive. **1944** Strange Affair; America's Children; To Have and Have Not; The Conspirators. **1947** Northwest Outpost. **1948** All My Sons.

SORIN, LOUIS
Born: 1894. Died: Dec. 14, 1961, New York, N.Y. (pulmonary edema). Screen, stage, radio and television actor.

Appeared in: **1929** Lucky in Love; Mother's Boy. **1930** Animal Crackers. **1937** An Educational short. **1950** With These Hands.

SORKIN, BARNEY
Born: 1903, London, England. Died: Apr. 25, 1973, Los Angeles, Calif. (heart attack). Bandleader and screen actor.

SORRENTINA, LA (Mary Frasca)
Died: July 24, 1973, New York. Screen, stage actress and singer.

Appeared in: **1970** Lovers and Other Strangers. **1971** The Gang That Couldn't Shoot Straight. **1972** The Godfather.

SOTHERN, EDWARD H.
Born: Dec. 6, 1859, New Orleans, La. Died: Oct. 28, 1933, New York, N.Y. (pneumonia). Stage and screen actor. Divorced from stage actress Virginia Harned (dec. 1946) and married to actress Julia Marlowe (dec. 1950). Entered films with Vitagraph in 1916.

Appeared in: **1916** An Enemy to the King; The Chattel.

SOTHERN, ETHEL
Born: 1882. Died: Feb. 20, 1957, Hollywood, Calif. Screen and stage actress.

SOTHERN, HARRY
Born: Apr. 26, 1884. Died: Feb. 22, 1957, N.Y. Stage and screen actor. Nephew of Shakespearean actor E. H. Sothern (dec. 1933).

Appeared in: **1920** A Tragedy of the East Side. **1922** How Women Love; The Secrets of Paris.

SOTHERN, HUGH (aka ROY SUTHERLAND)
Born: July 20, 1881, Anderson County, Kans. Died: Apr. 13, 1947, Hollywood, Calif. Screen and stage actor. Known as Roy Sutherland on stage.

Appeared in: **1938** Fighting Devil Dogs (serial); The Buccaneer; Dangerous to Know; Border G-Man. **1939** The Oklahoma Kid; The Giant of Norway (short); Juarez. **1940** Northwest Passage; Dispatch from Reuters. **1941** The Mad Doctor; Bad Men of Missouri. **1942** Tennessee Johnson. **1944** Captain America (serial).

SOTHERN, JEAN
Born: 1895, Richmond, Va. Died: Jan. 8, 1924, Chicago, Ill. (cancer). Screen and vaudeville actress.

Appeared in: **1915** The Two Orphans. **1916** The Mysteries of Myra.

SOTO, LUCHY
Born: 1920, Spain. Died: Oct., 1970, Madrid, Spain. Stage and screen actress.

Appeared in: **1938** Morena Clara. Other Spanish film: Garden of Delights.

SOTO, ROBERTO (aka "EL PANZON" (THE BELLY))
Born: 1888, Mexico. Died: July 18, 1960, Mexico City, Mexico (heart attack). Stage and screen actor.

Appeared in: **1938** Tropic Holiday.

SOTOMAYOR, JOSE
Born: 1905, Mexico. Died: Jan. 24, 1967, Mexico City, Mexico (heart attack). Stage and screen actor.

Appeared in: **1919** Juan Solado. **1941** Carnaval en el Tropico. **1943** Palillo Vargas Heredia.

SOUPER, KAY (G. Kay Souper)
Born: England. Died: Jan. 2, 1947, England? Screen and stage actor.

Appeared in: **1929** For the Term of His Natural Life. **1931** The Dreyfus Case.

SOUPLEX, RAYMOND
Born: 1900, France. Died: Nov., 1972, France? Screen, stage and radio actor.

Appeared in: **1950** Manon. **1951** Lady Paname. **1952** Three Sisters. **1954** Caroline Cherie. **1964** Fire in the Flesh.

SOUSSANIN, NICHOLAS
Born: 1909, Yalta, Russia. Died: Apr. 27, 1975, New York, N.Y. (cardiac arrest). Screen, stage actor, playwright, stage director and screenwriter. Divorced from actress Olga Baclanova (dec. 1974).

Appeared in: **1923** Service for Ladies (film debut). **1925** The Swan. **1926** The Midnight Sun. **1927** A Gentleman of Paris; Hotel Imperial; One Increasing Purpose; The Spotlight. **1928** Adoration; The Last Command; The Night Watch; The Woman Disputed; The Yellow Lily. **1929** The Squall; Trent's Last Case. **1930** Are You There? **1931** Daughter of the Dragon; The Criminal Code; White Shoulders. **1932** Parisian Romance. **1936** Under Two Flags. **1939** Those High Grey Walls.

SOUTHARD, HARRY D.
Born: 1881. Died: Apr. 27, 1939, N.Y. Screen, stage and radio actor.

Appeared in: **1922** The Broadway Peacock; Wildness of Youth. **1927** The Winning Oar. **1929** The House of Secrets.

SOUTHERN, SAM
Born: England. Died: Mar. 21, 1920, Los Angeles, Calif. Screen actor.

Appeared in: **1919** The Eyes of Youth.

SOUTHGATE, HOWARD S.
Born: 1895. Died: May 14, 1971, Orlando, Fla. Screen, stage actor, stage director and playwright.

SOUTHWICK, ALBERT P.
Born: 1876. Died: Jan. 19, 1929, New York, N.Y. Screen actor.

SOUTHWICK, DALE
Born: 1913, Long Beach, Calif. Died: Apr. 29, 1968, Compton, Calif. Screen actor. Appeared in "Our Gang" comedies.

SOVERN, CLARENCE
Born: 1900. Died: Mar. 14, 1929, Burbank, Calif. Screen cowboy actor and stuntman.

SOWARDS, GEORGE ALBERT
Born: 1888, Mo. Died: Dec. 20, 1975. Screen actor and stuntman. Entered films in 1911.

Appeared in: **1935** The Crimson Trail. **1950** Crooked River; Hostile Country.

SOWARDS, LEN
Born: 1893. Died: Aug. 20, 1962, Los Angeles, Calif. Screen, television actor and stuntman.

SPACEY, CAPTAIN JOHN G.
Born: 1895. Died: Jan. 2, 1940, Hollywood, Calif. Screen and stage actor.

Appeared in: **1935** The Man Who Broke the Bank at Monte Carlo. **1936** The Moon's Our Home; Thank You, Jeeves. **1937** Women of Glamour; Parole Racket. **1938** Four Men and a Prayer; Who Killed Gail Preston? **1939** I'm from Missouri; The Story of Alexander Graham Bell. **1940** British Agent.

SPADARO, ODOARDO
Born: 1894. Died: 1965, Florence, Italy. Screen, stage, television actor and singer.

Appeared in: **1954** The Golden Coach. **1962** Divorce Italian Style.

SPADARO, UMBERTO
Born: 1904, Ancona, Italy. Died: Oct. 11, 1981, Rome, Italy (cancer). Screen and stage actor. Son of stage actor Rocco Spadaro (dec.).

Appeared in: **1947** Furia. **1950** Difficult Years; Il Brigante Musolino. **1951** Women Without Names; Angelo. **1952** Brief Rapture; Angelo in the Crowd. **1953** Journey to Love; Cavalleria Rusticana (aka A Fatal Desire—US 1963). **1955** Outlaw Girl. **1957** A Farewell to Arms. **1958** Nella Citta I'inferno (aka ... And the Wild, Wild Women—US 1961). **1963** La Smania Addosso (aka The Eye of the Needle—US 1965); Anni Facili. **1964** Sedotta e Abbandonata (Seduced and Abandoned); Liola (aka A Very Handy Man—US 1966). **1966** A Fistful of Dollars.

SPAIN, NANCY
Born: 1918. Died: Mar. 21, 1964, Liverpool, England (plane crash). Screen and television actress.

Appeared in: **1963** Live It Up (aka Sing and Swing—US 1964).

SPANIER, FRANCES
Died: May 10, 1981, Los Angeles, Calif. (cancer). Screen, stage, radio and television actress.

SPANIER, MUGGSY (Francis Joseph Spanier)
Born: 1903. Died: Feb. 12, 1967, Sausalito, Calif. Dixieland cornetist and screen actor.

Appeared in: **1929** Is Everybody Happy? **1935** Here Comes the Band.

SPARKS, NED (Edward A. Sparkman)
Born: 1883, Ontario, Canada. Died: Apr. 2, 1957, Apple Valley, Calif. (intestinal block). Screen and stage actor.

Appeared in: **1922** The Bond Boy; A Wide-Open Town. **1925** Bright Lights; The Only Thing; Seven Keys to Baldpate; Soul Mates; The Boomerang; Faint Perfume; His Supreme Moment. **1926** The Auction Block; Mike; Money Talks; Oh, What a Night!; The Hidden Way; Love's Blindness; When the Wife's Away. **1927** Alias the Lone Wolf; The Secret Studio; The Small Bachelor; Alias the Deacon. **1928** The Magnificent Flirt; The Big Noise; On to Reno. **1929** Nothing But the Truth; The Canary Murder Case; Strange Cargo; Street Girl. **1930** Love Comes Along; The Devil's Holiday; The Fall Guy; Double Cross Roads; Leathernecking; Conspiracy. **1931** The Iron Man; The Secret Call; Corsair; Kept Husbands. **1932** Wide Open Spaces (short); The Miracle Man; Big City Blues; Blessed Event; The Crusader. **1933** 42nd Street; Lady for a Day; Too Much Harmony; Alice in Wonderland; Going Hollywood; Secrets; Gold Diggers of 1933. **1934** Hi, Nellie; Private Scandal; Marie Galante; Sing and Like It; Imitation of Life; Down to Their Last Yacht; Servants' Entrance. **1935** Sweet Adeline; Sweet Music; George White's 1935 Scandals. **1936** Collegiate; The Bride Walks Out; One in a Million. **1937** Wake Up and Live; This Way Plese; Two's Company. **1938** Hawaii Calls. **1939** The Star Maker. **1941** For Beauty's Sake. **1943** Stage Door Canteen. **1947** Magic Town.

SPAULDING, GEORGE
Born: 1881. Died: Aug. 23, 1959, Hollywood, Calif. Screen, stage, radio, television actor, stage producer and playwright.

Appeared in: **1947** Chinese Ring. **1949** White Heat; House of Strangers; Kiss Tomorrow Goodbye. **1950** When Willie Comes Marching Home. **1951** Jim Thorpe—All American. **1952** Lure of the Wilderness. **1953** The President's Lady. **1954** Woman's World.

SPEAKER, TRIS (Tristram E. Speaker)
Born: Apr. 4, 1888, Hubbard, Tex. Died: Dec. 8, 1958, Whitney, Tex. Professional baseball player and screen actor.

Appeared in: **1942** The Ninth Inning. **1949** The Kid from Cleveland.

SPEAKS, MARGARET
Born: 1905, Columbus, Ohio. Died: July 16, 1977, Blue Hill, Maine (heart attack). Screen, stage and radio actress.

SPEAR, HARRY
Born: Dec. 16, 1921, Los Angeles, Calif. Died: Feb. 10, 1969, Hollywood, Calif. Screen, stage vaudeville actor. Entered films at age of three with Big Boy at Educational Studios. Appeared in "Smith Family" and "Our Gang" series and Mack Sennett comedies.

Appeared in: **1929** The following shorts: Small Talk; Railroadin'; Lazy Days; Boxing Gloves; Bouncing Babies.

SPEAR, SAMMY (Sammy Shapiro)
Born: 1910, Brooklyn, N.Y. Died: Mar. 11, 1975, Miami, Fla. (heart attack). Bandleader, musician, television and screen actor.

SPELLMAN, LEORA (aka LEORA SPELLMEYER aka JOSEPHINE MIDDLETON)
Born: 1891. Died: Sept. 4, 1945, Los Angeles, Calif. (heart attack). Screen, stage and vaudeville actress. Married to actor Charles B. Middleton (dec. 1949) with whom she appeared in vaudeville as "Middleton and Spellmeyer."

Appeared in: **1929** Wise Girls. **1932** Kongo.

SPENCE, MIKE (Michael Henderson Spence)
Born: Dec. 30, 1936, Croydon, Surrey, England. Died: May 4, 1968, Indianapolis, Ind. (auto racing crash). Auto racer and screen actor.

Appeared in: **1966** Grand Prix.

SPENCE, RALPH
Born: Nov. 4, 1889, Key West, Fla. or Houston, Tex. Died: Dec. 21, 1949, Woodland Hills, Calif (heart attack). Screenwriter, playwright and screen actor. Appeared in Mack Sennett and "Sunshine" comedies.

Appeared in: **1925** Ralph Spence comedies (shorts) including Egged On. **1935** Millions in the Air.

SPENCER, DOUGLAS
Born: 1910. Died: Oct. 10, 1960, Hollywood, Calif. (diabetic condition). Screen and television actor.

Appeared in: **1948** The Big Clock. **1949** My Friend Irma; Bride of Vengeance; Follow Me Quietly. **1950** The Redhead and the Cowboy. **1951** Come Fill the Cup; A Place in the Sun; The Thing. **1952** Monkey Business; Untamed Frontier. **1953** The Glass Wall; Houdini; Shane; She's Back on Broadway; Trouble Along the Way. **1954** The Raid; River of No Return. **1955** The Kentuckian; A Man Alone; Smoke Signal; This Island Earth. **1956** Man from Del Rio; Pardners. **1957** Saddle the Wind; Short Cut to Hell; The Three Faces of Eve; The Unholy Wife. **1958** Cole Younger, Gunfighter. **1959** The Diary of Anne Frank. **1961** The Sins of Rachel Cade.

SPENCER, FRED (Fred Spencer Bretherton)
Died: Oct. 13, 1952, Hollywood, Calif. Screen actor. Appeared in silents for Mack Sennett and others.

SPENCER, JAMES
Born: 1877. Died: Jan. 12, 1929, New Orleans, La. Screen actor. Do not confuse with opera performer James Spencer-Kelly (dec. 1944).

Appeared in: **1925** Adventure. **1929** Frozen Justice. **1930** The Sea God.

SPENCER, KENNETH
Born: 1913, Los Angeles, Calif. Died: Feb. 25, 1964, near New Orleans, La. (plane crash). Black screen, stage, television actor and singer. Appeared in U.S. and German films.

Appeared in: **1943** Cabin in the Sky; Bataan.

SPENCER, ROBERT
Born: 1900. Died: Sept. 4, 1939, New York, N.Y. (pneumonia). Screen and stage actor.

Appeared in: **1924** The Sea Hawk. **1937** Reported Missing. **1938** The Jury's Secret.

SPENCER, TERRY
Born: 1895. Died: Oct. 3, 1954, Hollywood, Calif. Screen actor.

SPENCER, TIM
Born: 1909. Died: Apr. 27, 1974, Los Angeles, Calif. (stroke). Screen actor, singer and composer. Originator of the "Sons of the Pioneers."

Appeared in: **1936** Rhythm on the Range. **1937** The Old Corral. **1946** My Pal Trigger.

SPENCER, WALTER (Walter Bryson)
Born: Sept. 17, 1882, Murray or Salt Lake City?, Utah. Died: Sept. 8, 1927, Long Beach, Calif. Screen and stage actor.

Appeared in: **1915** Blot on the Shield; The Assayer of Lone Gap. **1916** The Heart of Tara.

SPENDER, FREDERICK J.
Born: 1885. Died: Oct. 17, 1950, Oakwood Heights, N.Y. Screen, stage actor and attorney.

SPERO, KATHY
Born: 1948. Died: Jan. 25, 1979, Los Angeles, Calif. (auto accident). Screen actress.

SPIKER, RAY
Born: 1902. Died: Feb. 23, 1964, Hollywood, Calif. Screen actor and stuntman.

Appeared in: **1934** Our Daily Bread. **1947** The Brasher Doubloon. **1953** Shane. **1954** Demetrius and the Gladiators; Prince Valiant.

SPINGLER, HARRY
Born: 1890. Died: Apr. 22, 1953, Woodland Hills, Calif. Screen actor.

Appeared in: **1918** A Perfect Lady.

SPIRA, FRANCOISE
Died: Jan., 1965, Paris, France (suicide). Screen, stage actress and stage producer.

SPITALNY, PHIL
Born: 1890. Died: Oct. 11, 1970, Miami Beach, Fla. (cancer). Bandleader, conductor, radio and screen actor. Married to concert mistress Evelyn Kaye, known professionally as "Evelyn and Her Magic Violin."

Appeared in:Prior to 1933 Metro Movietone Act No. 82. **1934** A Vitaphone short. **1935** A Vitaphone short; a Paramount short. **1936** A Vitaphone short. **1945** Here Come the Co-eds.

SPIVEY, VICTORIA
Born: 1908. Died: Oct. 3, 1976, New York, N.Y. Black screen actress and blues singer.

Appeared in: **1929** Hallelujah.

SPIVY, "MADAME" (Spivy Le Voe)
Born: 1907, Brooklyn, N.Y. Died: Jan. 8, 1971, Woodland Hills, Calif. Screen actress, nightclub entertainer and singer.

Appeared in: **1958** Auntie Mame. **1960** Studs Lonigan; The Fugitive Kind. **1962** Requiem for a Heavyweight; All Fall Down; The Manchurian Candidate.

SPOFFORD, CHARLES "BABY" (Charles S. Van Norman Spofford)
Born: Dec. 10, 1915, Los Angeles, Calif. Died: Sept. 29, 1935, Los Angeles, Calif. Screen actor.

SPONG, HILDA
Born: May 14, 1875, London, England. Died: May 16, 1955, Norwalk, Conn. Stage and screen actress.

Appeared in: **1915** Divorced. **1919** A Star Overnight.

SPOONER, CECIL
Born: 1875, N.Y. Died: May 13, 1953, Sherman Oaks, Calif. (heart attack). Screen and stage actress. Sister of actors Franklin (dec. 1943), and Edna May Spooner (dec. 1953).

Appeared in: **1909** The Prince and the Pauper. **1914** The Dancer and the King. **1924** The Love Bandit; One Law For the Woman.

SPOONER, EDNA MAY
Born: May 10, 1873, Iowa. Died: July 14, 1953, Sherman Oaks, Calif. (heart disease). Screen and stage actress. Sister of actors Franklin (dec. 1943), and Cecil Spooner (dec. 1953). Divorced from stage actor Arthur J. Waley (dec.).

Appeared in: **1923** Man and Wife.

SPOONER, FRANKLIN (Franklin Edward Spooner)
Born: Apr. 16, 1860, Centerville, Iowa. Died: Jan. 14, 1943, Monterey Park, Calif. (coronary). Screen and stage actor. Brother of actresses Cecil (dec. 1953), and Edna May Spooner (dec. 1953).

SPORT
Died: Date unknown, Calif. Animal screen performer (dog). Wat featured in "Our Gang" films.

Appeared in: **1923** Are You a Failure?

SPOTTSWOOD, JAMES
Born: Wash. Died: Oct. 11, 1940, New York, N.Y. (heart attack). Screen, stage and radio actor.

Appeared in: **1929** Thunderbolt. **1938** Hollywood Stadium Mystery.

SPRING, HELEN
Born: New York, N.Y. Died: Feb. 21, 1978. Screen, stage and radio actress.

Appeared in: **1948** Words and Music; Abbott and Costello Meet Frankenstein. **1949** Cover Up. **1950** To Please a Lady; Emergency Wedding. **1952** Something to Live For. **1958** Hot Rod Gang. **1961** Breakfast at Tiffany's.

SPROTTE, BERT
Born: Dec. 9, 1871, Chemnitz, Saxony, Germany. Died: Dec. 30, 1949. Screen and stage actor. Married to actress Anna Ruzena. Entered films in 1917.

Appeared in: **1918** Tyrant Fear. **1920** Jes' Call Me Jim. **1921** Below the Dead Line; Bob Hampton of Placer; The Blazing Trail; Guile of Women; O'Malley of the Mounted; The Night Horsemen; Trailin'; White Oak. **1922** Blue Blazes; Conquering the Woman; The Fighting Streak; Hungry Hearts; For Big Stakes; A Question of Honor; Thelma. **1923** The Miracle Baby; The Prisoner; Purple Dawn; Rosita; Snowdrift; Soul of the Beast; Trimmed in Scarlet; Wild Bill Hickok. **1924** His Hour; Little Robinson Crusoe; The Shooting of Dan McGrew; Singer Jim McKee. **1925** Confessions of a Queen; The Human Tornado; Why Women Love. **1927** The Fighting Hombre; Life of an Actress; The Private Life of Helen of Troy; Wild Geese; The Stolen Bride; Shepherd of the Hills. **1929** Married in Hollywood. **1930** A Royal Romance. **1932** A Passport to Hell. **1933** Song of the Eagle. **1934** The Pursuit of Happiness.

SPROULE, RUTH
Born: 1910. Died: Sept. 26, 1968, New York, N.Y. (heart attack). Screen actress and dancer. Was a member of the "Rockettes." Mother of dancer Linda Nostrand.

SQUIRE, RONALD (Ronald Squirl)
Born: Mar., 1886, Tiverton, Devonshire, England. Died: Nov. 16, 1958, London, England. Screen, stage actor, stage producer and stage director. Divorced from actress Muriel Martin-Harvey and later married to Esylet Williams.

Appeared in: **1916** Whoso is Without Sin. **1934** The Unfinished Symphony (US 1935); Wild Boy; Forbidden Territory. **1935** Come Out of the Pantry. **1936** Love in Exile; Dusty Ermine (aka Hideout in the Alps—US 1938). **1937** Action for Slander (US 1938). **1943** The Flemish Farm. **1944** Don't Take it to Heart (US 1949). **1945** Journey Together (US 1946). **1947** While the Sun Shines (US 1950). **1948** The First Gentleman (aka Affairs of a Rogue—US 1949); Woman Hater (US 1949). **1949** The Rocking Horse Winner (US 1950). **1951** No Highway (aka No Highway in the Sky—US); Encore (US 1952). **1952** It Started in Paradise. **1953** Laxdale Hall (aka Scotch on the Rocks—US 1954); Always a Bride (US 1954); My Cousin Rachel. **1954** The Million Pound Note (aka Man With a Million—US). **1955** Footsteps in the Fog; Raising a Riot (US 1957); Josephine and Men. **1956** Now and Forever; Around the World in 80 Days; The Silent Affair (US 1957). **1957** Seawife; Island in the Sun. **1958** Law and Disorder; The Sheriff of Fractured Jaw; The Inn of the Sixth Happiness. **1959** Count Your Blessings.

SQUIRES, JACK
Born: 1894, New York, N.Y. Died: June, 1938, New York, N.Y. (heart attack). Screen and stage actor.

Appeared in: **1909** The Black Sheep. **1938** Dynamite Delaney.

SRITRANGE, WANDEE
Born: 1950, Thailand. Died: Aug. 31, 1975, near Bangkok, Thailand. Screen actress.

STABILE, DICK
Died: Sept. 25, 1980. Bandleader, composer and screen actor.

Appeared in: **1950** At War With the Army.

STAFFORD, FREDERICK
Born: 1928. Died: July 28, 1979, Europe (plane crash). Screen actor.

Appeared in: **1965** Furia a Bahia Pour OSS-117 (OSS 117—Mission for a Killer—US 1966). **1968** Dalle Ardenne all' Inferno (aka Dirty Heroes—US 1969). **1969** Topaz. **1977** Legend of the Wolf Woman.

STAFFORD, HANLEY (John Austin)
Born: Sept. 22, 1898, Staffordshire, England. Died: Sept. 9, 1968, Los Angeles, Calif. (heart attack). Screen, stage, radio and television actor. He was "Daddy" in the Fanny Brice Baby Snooks radio show and "Mr. Dithers" on the Blondie radio show.

Appeared in: **1936** The Great Ziegfeld. **1941** Life With Henry. **1951** Lullaby of Broadway. **1952** Just This Once; A Girl in Every Port; Here Come the Marines. **1953** The Affairs of Dobie Gillis; Francis Covers the Big Town. **1955** The Go-Getter.

STAGG, AMOS ALONZO
Born: Aug. 16, 1862, West Orange, N.Y. Died: Mar. 17, 1965, Stockton, Calif. Football coach and screen actor.

Appeared in: **1940** Knute Rockne—All American.

STAHL, WALTER O.
Born: 1884. Died: Aug. 6, 1943, Hollywood, Calif. (heart attack). Screen actor and stage producer.

Appeared in: **1937** The Life of Emile Zola; I'll Take Romance. **1939** Juarez; Beasts of Berlin. **1940** A Dispatch from Reuters. **1942** Once Upon a Honeymoon; Woman of the Year. **1943** Watch on the Rhine.

STAHL-NACHBAUR, ERNEST (Ernest Guggenheimer)
Born: 1886, Germany. Died: May 13, 1960, Berlin, Germany. Stage and screen actor.

Appeared in: **1931** Mother Love; Danton; Ein Burschenlied aus Heidelberg. **1933** M.

STAINTON, PHILIP
Born: Apr. 9, 1908, King's Norton, Birmingham, England. Died: July 31, 1961, England? Screen actor.

Appeared in: **1952** Angels One Five (US 1954). **1953** Mogambo; Monsoon; Innocent's in Paris (US 1955). **1954** Hobson's Choice. **1955** The Ladykillers (US 1956); Cast a Dark Shadow (US 1957). **1956** Moby Dick; Reach For The Sky (US 1957).

STALKER, BILL
Born: New Zealand. Died: Nov. 29, 1981, Melbourne, Australia (motorcycle accident). Screen and television actor.

STALL, KARL
Born: 1871, Cincinnati, Ohio. Died: June 14, 1947, New York, N.Y. Stage and screen actor.

Appeared in: **1931** The Smiling Lieutenant.

STAMPER, F. POPE
Born: ·Nov. 20, 1880, Richmond, Surrey, England. Died: Nov. 12, 1950, England? Screen and stage actor.

Appeared in: **1930** Musical Beauty Shop.

STAMP-TAYLOR, ENID
Born: June 12, 1904, Monkseaton, England. Died: Jan. 13, 1946, London, England (injuries from fall). Screen and stage actress.

Appeared in: **1927** Easy Virtue (US 1928); Remembrance; Land of Hope and Glory. **1928** A Little Bit of Fluff (aka Skirts—US); Yellow Stockings; Cocktails. **1929** Broken Melody. **1933** Meet My Sister. **1934** A Political Party; Gay Love; Virginia's Husband; The Feathered Serpent. **1935** Radio Pirates; So You Won't Talk?; Mr. What's-His-Name; Jimmy Boy; While Parents Sleep; Two Hearts in Harmony. **1936** Queen of Hearts; Blind Man's Bluff; House Broken. **1937** Take a Chance; Underneath the Arches; Feather Your Nest; Okay for Sound; Talking Feet; Action for Slander (US 1938). **1938** Blondes for Danger; Stepping Toes; Climbing High (US 1939); Old Iron. **1939** The Lambeth Walk (aka Me and My Girl—US 1940); The Girl Who Forgot. **1941** Spring Meeting; The Farmer's Wife; Hatter's Castle; South American George. **1942** Alibi. **1943** Candelight in Algeria (US 1944). **1945** The Wicked Lady (US 1946). **1946** Caravan (US 1947).

STANBURY, DOUGLAS
Born: 1899, Canada. Died: Dec. 6, 1980, Huntington, N.Y. Screen, radio actor and singer.

Appeared in: **1929** Marching Home (short); Pack Up Your Troubles (short). **1930** Alpine Echoes (short); The Wanderer (short).

STANDING, CHARLENE
Born: 1921. Died: Jan. 8, 1957, Dundas, Ontario, Canada. Stage and screen actress. Appeared in U.S. and British films.

STANDING, GORDON
Died: May 22, 1927. Screen actor.

Appeared in: **1921** Man and Woman. **1922** Are Children to Blame? **1923** Outlaws of the Sea. **1925** The Substitute Wife. **1927** Skedaddle Gold; King of the Jungle (serial).

STANDING, GUY, JR.
Died: Nov. 14, 1954, Reseda, Calif. Stage and screen actor. Son of actor Sir Guy Standing, Sr. (dec. 1930) and stage actress Isabella Urquhart (dec. 1907). Married to actress Gloria Haydock. For family information see Sir Guy Standing, Sr.

Appeared in: **1953** Titanic.

STANDING, SIR GUY, SR.
Born: Sept. 1, 1873, London, England. Died: Feb. 24, 1937, Los Angeles, Calif. (heart attack). Stage and screen actor. Son of actor Herbert Standing, Sr. (dec. 1923). Brother of actors Herbert, Jr. (dec. 1955), Percy, Wyndham (dec. 1963) and Aubrey Standing. Married to stage actress Isabella Urquhart (dec. 1907); father of Guy Standing, Jr. (dec. 1954). Later married to stage actress Blanche Burton (dec. 1934) and Dorothy Hammond (dec. 1950); father of actors Michael and Kay (dec. 1982) Standing.

Appeared in: **1933** The Cradle Song; A Bedtime Story; The Story of Temple Drake; The Eagle and the Hawk; Midnight Club; Hell and High Water. **1934** Imitation of Life; Death Takes a Holiday; The Witching Hour; Double Door; Now and Forever. **1935** Lives of a Bengal Lancer; Car 99; Annapolis Farewell; The Big Broadcast of 1936. **1936** The Return of Sophie Land; I'd Give My Life; Palm Springs. **1937** Lloyds of London; Bulldog Drummond Escapes.

STANDING, HERBERT, JR.
Born: 1884, London, England. Died: Sept. 23, 1955, New York, N.Y. Screen and stage actor. Son of actor Herbert Standing, Sr. (dec. 1923) and brother of actors Sir Guy (dec. 1937), Wyndham (dec. 1963), Percy and Aubrey Standing. Married to actress Dulcie Clayton.

Appeared in: **1915** It's No Laughing Matter. **1916** The Right Direction. **1917** A Little Patriot. **1918** Amarilly of Clothes Line; He Comes Up Smiling; Daddy's Girl; The White Man's Law; How Could You, Jean? **1919** My Little Sister; The Home Town Girl; A Rogue's Romance; You Never Saw Such a Girl; Fires of Faith; Through the

Wrong Door; Strictly Confidential; Almost a Husband. **1920** Judy of Rogue's Harbor; The Cup of Fury. **1921** Man and Woman; The Infamous Miss Revell; One Wild Week; The Man Worth While. **1922** The Trap; The Masquerader; While Satan Sleeps; The Crossroads of New York; The Impossible Mr. Bellew. **1923** Jazzmania; Sawdust. **1926** The Brown Derby; Rainbow Riley.

STANDING, HERBERT, SR.
Born: Nov. 13, 1846, Peckham, England. Died: Dec. 5, 1923, Los Angeles, Calif. Stage and screen actor. Father of actors Herbert, Jr. (dec. 1955), Sir Guy (dec. 1937), Wyndham (dec. 1963), Percy and Aubrey Standing.

STANDING, JACK
Born: 1886, London, England. Died: Oct. 26, 1917, Los Angeles, Calif. Screen actor. Father of actor Jack Standing, Jr.

Appeared in: **1911** A Good Turn; An Accidental Outlaw; Rescued in Time; Get a Horse; The Easterner's Sacrifice. **1913** Looking for a Mother; The Wiles of Cupid. **1914** The Wasted Years; The Winning Hand. **1915** Fanchon the Cricket; The Love of Women; A Siren of Corsica; Delayed Reformation; Rated at Ten Million Dollars; Road O' Strife (serial); The Inventor's Peril; It Was to Be; The Son; Think Mothers. **1916** The Evangelist. **1917** The Price of Her Soul.

STANDING, JOAN
Born: June 21, 1903, England. Died: Feb. 3, 1979, Houston, Tex. (cancer). Screen actress. Entered films in 1918.

Appeared in: **1920** The Branding Iron. **1921** Silk Hosiery. **1922** Oliver Twist. **1923** The Cricket on the Hearth; Hearts Aflame; A Noise in Newboro; Pleasure Mad. **1924** The Beauty Prize; Empty Hearts; Happiness; Three Weeks; What Shall I Do?; Women Who Give. **1925** Counsel for the Defense; The Dancers; Faint Perfume; Greed; With This Ring. **1926** The Campus Flirt; Lost at Sea; Memory Lane; The Outsider; Sandy; The Skyrocket. **1927** The College Hero; The First Night; The Little Firebrand; Ritzy. **1928** Beau Sabreur; Home James; Riley of the Rainbow Division. **1929** Fashions in Love; The Kid's Clever; The Marriage Playground; My Lady's Past; Cohens and Kellys in Atlantic City. **1930** Ex-Flame; For the Love of Lil; Hell's Angels; A Lady's Morals; Street of Chance; Soul Kiss; Extravagance. **1931** Age for Love; Dracula; Never the Twain Shall Meet; Young As You Feel. **1932** The Man I Killed; Broken Lullaby. **1934** Jane Eyre. **1936** Little Lord Fauntleroy. **1940** Li'l Abner.

STANDING, WYNDHAM (Charles Wyndham Standing)
Born: Aug. 23, 1880, London, England. Died: Feb. 1, 1963, Los Angeles, Calif. Screen and stage actor. Married to actress Winifred Standing. Son of actor Sir Herbert Standing, Sr. (dec. 1923). See Herbert Standing for family information.

Appeared in: **1916** Exile; The Soul of a Magdalen. **1917** The Silence Sellers. **1918** The Hillcrest Mystery (serial); The Life Mask; Rose of the World. **1919** Isle of Conquest; The Marriage Price; Out of the Shadows; Paid in Full; Eyes of the Soul; Miracle of Love; Witness for the Defense. **1920** My Lady's Garter; Earthbound. **1921** The Bride's Play; The Iron Trail; The Marriage of William Ashe; The Journey's End. **1922** The Inner Man; Isle of Doubt; Smilin' Through. **1923** Dynamite Wives; The Lion's Mouse; Forgive and Forget; Little Johnny Jones; The Gold Diggers. **1924** Flames of Desire; Pagan Passions; The Rejected Woman; Soiled; Vanity's Price. **1925** The Dark Angel; The Early Bird; The Reckless Sex; The Teaser; The Unchastened Woman. **1926** The Canadian; If Youth But Knew; White Heat. **1927** Thumbs Down; The City Gone Wild. **1928** The Price of Divorce; The Port of Missing Girls; Widecombe Fair. **1929** The Flying Squad; Power Over Men. **1930** Billy the Kid; Hell's Angels. **1932** The Silent Witness. **1933** A Study in Scarlet; Design for Living. **1934** Imitation of Life; Limehouse Blues. **1935** Clive of India. **1936** Mary of Scotland; Beloved Enemy. **1939** Bulldog Drummond's Secret Police; The Man in the Iron Mask; Rulers of the Sea.

STANDISH, JOSEPH W.
Born: 1865. Died: Oct. 27, 1943, Cleveland, Ohio. Screen, stage actor and dancer.

STANFORD, DOK
Born: 1919, N.J. Died: Dec. 26, 1967, Hollywood, Calif. (heart disease). Screen actor and lyricist.

STANFORD, HENRY
Born: Feb. 22, 1872, Ramleh, Egypt. Died: Feb. 18, 1921, Staten Island, N.Y. Screen and stage actor. Married to actress Laura Burt (dec. 1952).

STANHOPE, ADELINE (Adeline Stanhope Wheatcroft)
Born: 1853, Paris, France. Died: June 18, 1935, Los Angeles, Calif. Screen and stage actress. Mother of actor Stanhope Wheatcroft (dec. 1966).

STANHOPE, TED
Died: July 10, 1977. Screen actor.

Appeared in: **1941** Borrowed Hero. **1944** Teen Age; Leave It to the Irish. **1946** The Glass Alibi. **1947** So You're Going on a Vacation (short); The Burning Cross. **1948** So You Want an Apartment (short). **1951** So You Want to Be a Bachelor (short). **1952** So You Want to Get It Wholesale (short); High Noon; Flesh and Fury. **1953** So You Think You Can't Sleep (short). **1958** Terror in a Texas Town.

STANITSYN, VIKTOR (Viktor Geze)
Born: 1897, Russia. Died: Dec. 24, 1976, Moscow, Russia. Screen, stage actor, stage director and producer.

Appeared in: **1933** Men and Jobs. **1937** Paris Commune. **1945** Jubilee. **1949** The First Front. **1968** War and Peace.

STANLEY, EDDIE
Died: June 20, 1972. Screen actor. Do not confuse with actors Edwin or Edward Stanley.

STANLEY, EDWIN
Born: 1880. Died: Dec. 24, 1944, Hollywood, Calif. Screen and stage actor.

Appeared in: **1932** Amateur Daddy. **1933** International House; My Woman; No Other Woman. **1934** The Life of Vergie Winters; You Belong to Me. **1936** Hot Money; The Public Pays (short); The Mandarin Mystery; Libeled Lady. **1937** Dick Tracy (serial); Easy Living; Marked Woman; Some Blondes Are Dangerous. **1938** Born to Be Wild; Billy the Kid Returns; Little Tough Guy; The Missing Guest; Wives Under Suspicion; Alcatraz Island; Alexander's Ragtime Band. **1939** I Was a Convict; The Star Maker; Ninotchka; Scouts to the Rescue (serial); Unexpected Father; Eternally Yours; Espionage Agent; 20,000 Men a Year. **1940** Mysterious Dr. Satan (serial); Charlie Chan in Panama; Youth Will be Served; Babies for Sale; The Man Who Talked Too Much. **1941** Mountain Moonlight; Small Town Deb; Knockout (aka Right to the Heart); Caught in the Draft; Meet John Doe; The Night of January 16th; A Man Betrayed; Arkansas Judge; Scattergood Baines. **1942** The Man Who Came to Dinner; Who is Hope Schuyler?; Drums of the Congo; The Loves of Edgar Allan Poe; Gentleman Jim; Pardon My Stripes; Girl Trouble; This Gun for Hire. **1943** Johnny Come Lately; O, My Darling Clementine; The Song of Bernadette. **1944** Janboree; Buffalo Bill. **1945** Youth on Trial; Conflict; Incendiary Blonde.

STANLEY, FORREST
Born: Aug. 21, 1889, New York, N.Y. Died: Aug. 27, 1969, Los Angeles, Calif. (results of fall). Screen and stage actor.

Appeared in: **1915** The Yankee Girl; Jane; Reform Candidate. **1916** Making of Madalina; Heart of Paula; The Code of Marcia Gray. **1918** His Official Fiancee. **1919** Under Suspicion; Thunderbolt. **1920** The Triflers. **1921** Forbidden Fruit; Enchantment; Big Game; The House that Jazz Built; Sacred and Profane Love. **1922** When Knighthood Was in Flower; The Pride of Palomar; Beauty's Worth; The Young Diana. **1923** Tiger Rose; Bavu; Her Accidental Husband. **1924** Through the Dark; The Breath of Scandal; Wine. **1925** Up the Ladder; Beauty and the Bad Man; The Fate of a Flirt; The Girl Who Wouldn't Work; The Unwritten Law; When Husbands Flirt; With This Ring. **1926** Dancing Days; Forest Havoc; The Shadow of the Law. **1927** The Climbers; The Cat and the Canary; The Wheels of Destiny; Great Event Series. **1928** Bare Knees; Into the Night; Jazzland; Phantom of the Turf. **1929** The Drake Case. **1930** The Love Kiss. **1931** Men Are Like That; Arizona. **1932** Racing Youth; Sin's Pay Day; Rider of Death Valley. **1941** Outlaws of the Desert.

STANLEY, MINNIE
Born: 1874. Died: Apr. 1, 1948, New York, N.Y. Screen and stage actress.

Appeared in: **1915** Boys Will Be Boys.

STANLEY, RALPH "NICK"
Born: 1914, Mass. Died: May 10, 1972, New York, N.Y. Screen, stage, vaudeville and television actor.

Appeared in: **1953** The Joe Lewis Story. **1957** Mr. Rock and Roll. **1958** Cop Hater. **1970** Jenny. **1971** The Anderson Tapes.

STANLEY, RED
Born: 1901. Died: Apr. 18, 1980, Oxnard, Calif. Orchestra leader and screen actor.

Appeared in: **1930** Painted Angel. **1938** Cocoanut Grove.

STANLEY, S. VICTOR
Born: 1892. Died: Jan. 29, 1939, London, England. Screen and stage actor.

Appeared in: **1932** The World, the Flesh and the Devil. **1933** Three Men in a Boat; Puppets of Fate (aka Wolves of the Underworld—US 1935); The Iron Stair; The Medicine Man; Timbucktoo; The Umbrella; His Grace Gives Notice; The Ghost Camera; The House of Trent. **1934** The Lash; Whispering Tongues; Four Masked Men; White Ensign. **1935** Gentleman's Agreement; School for Stars. **1936** Tropical Trouble. **1937** Aren't Men Beasts!

STANMORE, FRANK (Francis Henry Pink)
Born: Mar. 16, 1878, London, England. Died: Aug. 15, 1943, England?. Screen, stage actor and author.

Appeared in: **1914** His Reformation; For the Empire (aka For Home and Country—US); The Revenge of Mr. Thomas Atkins; Nan Good-for-Nothing. **1915** The Middleman; Brother Officers; The Christian; Love in a Wood; His Lordship; The Heart of a Child (US 1916). **1916** An Odd Freak; Motherlove; A Marked Man; The Mother of Dartmoor; A Mother's Influence; The Manxman; Odd Charges; Mixed Relations; The Persecution of Bob Pretty. **1917** The Grit of a Jew. **1920** London Pride; The House on the Marsh; Beyond the Dreams of Avarice; Marzipan of the Shapes; Great Snakes; Stop Press Comedies series including: The Coal Shortage; The Golden Ballot; Strike Fever; Housing; Control. **1921** Grand Guifnol series including The Upper Hand. **1922** Spanish Jade; A Rogue in Love; Love's Boomerang; plus the following shorts: Treasure Trove; The Big Strong Man; A Question of Principal. **1923** Lily of the Alley; The School for Scandal; Squibs, MP; The Naked Man; Squibs' Honeymoon; Love, Life and Laughter (aka Tip Toes). **1924** Reveille; The Alley of Golden Hearts; The Gayest of the Gay; Owd Bob. **1925** The Blackguard; Satan's Sister; The Only Way; Mrs. May Comedies series including: Cats; Raising the Wind; A Fowl Proceeding; Billets; Spots; A Friend of Cupid. **1926** The Little People; Blinkeyes. **1927** Mumsie; Mr. Nobody. **1928** Wait and See; The Hellcat; That Brute Simmons (short); What Next?; Houp-la!; W. W. Jacobs Stories series including: The Bravo; The Changling. **1929** Chamber of Horrors; Master and Man; Little Miss London; Three Men in a Cart. **1930** You'd Be Surprised; We Take Off Our Hats (short); Red Pearls; The Temporary Widow; Leave It to Me. **1931** Let's Love and Laugh (aka Bridegroom for Two—US 1932); The House Opposite; My Old China; The Old Man; What a Night!; The Great Gay Road. **1932** Lucky Girl Girl; Camera Cocktails (reissue of That Brute Simmons, 1928). **1933** Don Quixote (US 1934); The Love Wager; That's a Good Girl. **1935** It's a Bet. **1936** The Amazing Quest of Ernest Bliss (aka Romance and Riches—US 1937); Live Again.

STANNARD, DON
Born: 1916, Westcliff, England. Died: 1949, England? Screen actor. Appeared in US films in 1937.

Appeared in: **1945** Con Chicago; Pink String and Sealing Wax (US 1950). **1946** Caesar and Cleopatra; I'll Turn to You. **1947** Death in High Heels. **1948** Dick Barton—Special Agent. **1949** The Temptress; Dick Barton Strikes Back. **1950** Dick Barton at Bay.

STANTON, FREDERICK "FRED" R.
Born: 1881. Died: May 27, 1925, Hollywood, Calif. (cancer). Stage and screen actor.

Appeared in: **1917** The Great Secret (serial). **1921** Her Sturdy Oak. **1922** Perils.

STANTON, HARRY (Harry Isaacs Stanton)
Born: Dec. 7, 1901, Wash. Died: Feb. 7, 1978, Los Angeles, Calif. (heart disease). Screen and stage actor.

Appeared in: **1954** Secret of the Incas. **1956** The Wrong Man.

STANTON, LARRY T.
Died: May 9, 1955, Hollywood, Calif. (heart attack). Screen actor. Entered films approx. 1920.

STANTON, PATRICK J. "PAT"
Born: 1907, Ireland. Died: Mar. 1, 1976, Bryn Mawr, Pa. Screen, vaudeville, radio actor and film producer.

STANTON, PAUL
Born: Dec. 21, 1884. Died: Oct. 9, 1955. Screen actor.

Appeared in: **1918** The Girl and the Judge; Her Pride. **1934** The Most Precious Thing in Life. **1935** Strangers All; Let 'Em Have It; Red Salute; Another Face. **1936** Black Legion; It Had to Happen; Whipsaw; Every Saturday Night; Charlie Chan at the Circus; Sins of Man; Half

Angel; Crime of Dr. Forbes; Road to Glory; Poor Little Rich Girl; Private Number; Sing, Baby Sing; The Longest Night; Dimples; Career Woman; Crack-Up; Night Waitress; The Public Pays (short). **1937** The Awful Truth; City Girl; Midnight Taxi; A Star Is Born; It Could Happen to You; Youth on Parole; Portia on Trial; Danger—Love at Work; Paid to Dance; Love Is News; Man of the People; Make Way for Tomorrow. **1938** Kentucky Moonshine; Rascals; Law of the Underworld; My Lucky Star; Army Girl. **1939** While America Sleeps (short); The Story of Alexander Graham Bell; Rose of Washington Square; Bachelor Mother; Stronger Than Desire; 20,000 Men a Year; The Star Maker; Hollywood Cavalcade; Stanley and Livingstone. **1940** The Lady With Red Hair; The Man Who Wouldn't Talk; And One Was Beautiful; Queen of the Mob; I Love You Again. **1941** Road Show; Strange Alibi; You're in the Army Now; The People vs. Dr. Kildare; The Big Store; Whistling in the Dark; Night of January 16th; Midnight Angel. **1942** The Magnificent Dope; Across the Pacific. **1943** Slightly Dangerous; Air Raid Wardens; So's Your Uncle. **1944** Once Upon a Time; Allergic to Love; Mr. Winkle Goes to War. **1945** She Gets Her Man. **1946** Crime of the Century; Holiday in Mexico; Shadow of a Woman. **1947** That's My Gal; Cry Wolf; Her Husband's Affair; My Wild Irish Rose. **1948** Here Comes Trouble. **1949** The Fountainhead. **1952** Jet Job.

STANTON, WILL (William Sidney Stanton)
Born: Sept. 18, 1885, London, England. Died: Dec. 18, 1969, Santa Monica, Calif. (broncho-pneumonia). Screen, stage and vaudeville actor. Married to actress Rosalind May.

Appeared in: **1927** The following shorts: With Love and Hisses; Sailors, Beware; Do Detectives Think?; Sugar Daddies. **1928** Golf Widows; Sadie Thompson. **1929** Paradise Heaven. **1930** Mamba; Paradise Island; Painted Angel. **1933** Hello Sister; Alice in Wonderland; Cavalcade; Sailor's Luck. **1935** The Irish in Us; The Man Who Broke the Bank at Monte Carlo. **1936** The Last of the Mohicans; Lloyds of London; The White Hunter. **1937** Seventh Heaven; The Affairs of Cappy Ricks; Another Dawn. **1938** Anesthesia (short); Straight, Place and Show; Four Men and a Prayer. **1939** Weather Wizards (short); The Little Princess; Captain Fury. **1940** Devil's Island. **1941** Charley's Aunt. **1942** This Above All. **1943** Thank Your Lucky Stars. **1945** A Guy, a Gal and a Pal. **1946** Wife Wanted.

STARBUCK, BETTY
Died: Date unknown. Screen, stage actress and dancer.

Appeared in: **1930** The Sap from Syracuse.

STARK, KURT
Died: 1916. Screen actor and film director. Married to actress Henny Porten (dec. 1960).

STARK, LEIGHTON
Died: July 20, 1924, Mawasquam, N.J. Stage and screen actor.

Appeared in: **1911** The Two Orphans.

STARK, MABEL
Born: 1889. Died: Apr. 29, 1968, Thousand Oaks, Calif. (heart attack). Wild animal trainer and screen actress.

Appeared in: **1922** A Dangerous Adventure.

STARK, PAULINE (Pauline Starke)
Born: Jan. 10, 1901, Joplin, Mo. Died: Feb. 3, 1977, Santa Monica, Calif. Screen actress. Married to stage producer George Sherwood. Was a 1922 Wampas Baby Star. Entered films as an extra.

Appeared in: **1915** Birth of a Nation. **1916** Intolerance. **1918** The Shoes That Danced; Alias Mary Brown; Irish Eyes; The Atom. **1919** The Life Line; Eyes of Youth; Soldiers of Fortune. **1920** Courage of Marge O'Doone; Seeds of Vengeance; The Untamed. **1921** A Connecticut Yankee in King Arthur's Court; Flower of the North; Forgotten Woman; Salvation Nell; Wife Against Wife; Snowblind. **1922** The Kingdom Within; If You Believe It, It's So; My Wild Irish Rose. **1923** The Little Girl Next Door; Lost and Found; Eyes of the Forest; His Last Race; In the Palace of the King; Little Church Around the Corner. **1924** Dante's Inferno; Hearts of Oak; The Arizona Express; Forbidden Paradise; Missing Daughters; Shanghai. **1925** Sun-Up; Adventure; Bright Lights; The Man Without a Country; The Devil's Cargo. **1926** Honesty—The Best Policy; War Paint; Love's Blindness; Twenty Cents a Dance. **1927** Captain Salvation; Dance Magic; Women Love Diamonds; The Perfect Sap. **1928** Streets of Shanghai; The Viking. **1929** Man, Woman and Wife. **1930** A Royal Romance; What Men Want.

STARKEY, BERT
Born: 1880, England. Died: June 9, 1939, Los Angeles, Calif. Screen and stage actor.

Appeared in: **1921** The Iron Trail. **1927** Wild Geese; Woman's Law. **1928** Put 'Em Up; You Can't Beat the Law. **1932** Scarface; Hell's Highway. **1934** It Happened One Night.

STARNES, R. LELAND
Born: 1922, Ga. Died: May 14, 1980, New York, N.Y. Screen, stage actor and stage director.

Appeared in: **1980** Cruising.

STARR, DAVE
Died: Apr. 18, 1970. Screen actor.

Appeared in: **1956** Singing in the Dark.

STARR, FRANCES
Born: June 6, 1881, Albany, N.Y. Died: June 11, 1973, New York, N.Y. Stage and screen actress.

Appeared in: **1931** The Star Witness; Five Star Final. **1932** This Reckless Age.

STARR, FREDERICK
Born: 1878, San Francisco, Calif. Died: Aug. 20, 1921, Los Angeles, Calif. Stage and screen actor.

Appeared in: **1919** Elmo, the Mighty (serial). **1920** Daredevil Jack (serial). **1921** The Man of the Forest; Mysterious Rider.

STARR, RANDY (Joseph Randall)
Born: 1931, Ill. Died: Aug. 5, 1970, Los Angeles, Calif. (undetermined illness). Screen stuntman.

Appeared in: **1962** Immoral Charge. **1964** The Creeping Terror; Kissin' Cousins; Roustabout. **1966** Frankie and Johnny; Paradise—Hawaiian Style; Spinout. **1967** Clambake; Double Trouble. **1968** Live a Little, Love a Little. **1969** Hard Trail. **1970** Machismo—40 Graves for 40 Guns.

STEADMAN, VERA
Born: June 23, 1900, Monterey, Calif. Died: Dec. 14, 1966, Long Beach, Calif. Screen actress. Divorced from actor Jack Taylor (dec. 1932). Entered films as a Mack Sennett bathing beauty.

Appeared in: **1917** Are Waitresses Safe?; Hula Hula Land. **1921** Scrap Iron. **1925** Stop Flirting. **1926** Meet the Prince; The Nervous Wreck. **1934** Elmer and Elsie. **1935** Frisco Kid. **1936** Ring Around the Moon. **1938** The Texans.

STEDMAN, LINCOLN
Born: 1907, Denver, Colo. Died: Mar. 22, 1948, Los Angeles, Calif. Screen actor and film director. Son of actress Myrtle Stedman (dec. 1938) and actor Marshall Stedman (dec. 1943). Entered films in 1918.

Appeared in: **1920** Nineteen and Phyllis. **1921** Old Swimmin' Hole; Be My Wife; The Charm School; My Lady Friends; Two Minutes to Go; Under the Lash. **1922** The Dangerous Age; A Homespun Vamp; Youth to Youth; The Freshie; White Shoulders. **1923** The Man Life Passed By; The Meanest Man in the World; The Scarlet Lily; The Wanters; The Prisoner; Soul of the Beast. **1924** Captain January; Black Oxen; Cheap Kisses; On Probation; Wife of the Centaur. **1925** The Danger Signal; Sealed Lips; Red Hot Tires. **1926** Dame Chance; Made for Love; Remember; The Warning Signal; One Minute to Play. **1927** The Student Prince in Old Heidelberg; Let It Rain; The Prince of Headwaiters; Rookies; The Little Firebrand; Perch of the Devil. **1928** Farmer's Daughter; Devil's Cage; Green Grass Widows; Harold Teen. **1929** Why Be Good?; The Wild Party; Tanned Legs. **1930** The following shorts: The Bluffer; Grandma's Girl; Don't Bite Your Dentist. **1931** The Woman Between. **1933** Sailor Be Good. **1934** Most Precious Thing in Life.

STEDMAN, MARSHALL
Born: 1874. Died: Dec. 16, 1943, Laguna Beach, Calif. Screen and stage actor. Married to actress Myrtle Stedman (dec. 1938) and father of actor Lincoln Stedman (dec. 1948).

STEDMAN, MYRTLE
Born: Mar. 3, 1889, Chicago, Ill. Died: Jan. 8, 1938, Los Angeles, Calif. (heart attack). Screen and stage actress. Married to actor Marshall Stedman (dec. 1943). Mother of actor Lincoln Stedman (dec. 1948). Entered films in 1913.

Appeared in: **1913** Valley of the Moon. **1915** Peer Gynt. **1920** Harriet and the Piper; The Silver Horde; The Tiger's Coat. **1921** Black Roses; The Whistle; Sowing the Wind; The Concert. **1922** Ashes; The Hands of Nara; Nancy from Nowhere; Rich Men's Wives; Reckless Youth. **1923** The Famous Mrs. Fair; Flaming Youth; Dangerous Age; Six Days; Crashin' Thru; Temporary Marriage. **1924** Wine; Lilies of the Field; Bread; The Breath of Scandal; The Age of Desire; The Woman on the Jury. **1925** Chickie; Sally; Tessie; The Mad Whirl; If I Marry Again; The Goose Hangs High. **1926** Don Juan's Three Nights; The Man in the Shadow; The Prince of Pilsen; The Far Cry. **1927** The Black Diamond Express; No Place to Go; Women's Wares; The Life of Riley; The Irresistible Lover; Alias the Deacon. **1928** Sporting Goods; Their Hour. **1929** The Wheel of Life; The Sin Sister; The Jazz Age. **1930** The Truth About Youth; The Love Racket; The Little Accident. **1931** Beau Ideal. **1932** Widow in Scarlet; Alias Mary Smith; Forbidden Company. **1933** One Year Later. **1934** Beggars in Ermine; School for Girls. **1936** Song of the Saddle; Gambling with Souls; Gold Diggers of 1937. **1937** The Go-Getter; Back in California; The Life of Emile Zola; Green Light; Hollywood Hotel; Confession. **1938** A Slight Case of Murder.

STEEL, EDWARD
Born: 1897. Died: Oct. 18, 1965. Screen actor. Father of actor Anthony Steel.

Appeared in: **1966** The Boy Cried Murder.

STEELE, CLIFFORD
Born: 1878. Died: Mar. 5, 1940, Hollywood, Calif. Screen actor. Entered films approx. 1915.

STEELE, MINNIE
Born: 1881, Australia. Died: Jan. 5, 1949, Hollywood, Calif. (stroke). Screen and vaudeville actress. Entered films in 1922.

Appeared in: **1924** "Christie" comedies and "Baby Peggy" films; The Darling of New York. **1935** A Feather in Her Hat. **1942** The Wife Takes a Flyer.

STEELE, VERNON
Born: 1883. Died: July 23, 1955, Los Angeles, Calif. (heart attack). Screen and stage actor.

Appeared in: **1915** Hearts in Exile. **1916** For the Defense. **1921** Beyond Price; Out of the Chorus; The Highest Bidder. **1922** The Danger Point; For the Defense (and 1916 version); A Wonderful Wife; Thelma; When the Devil Drives; The Girl Who Ran Wild; The Hands of Nara. **1923** Alice Adams; The Wanters; What Wives Want; Temptation; Forgive and Forget. **1924** Discontented Husbands; The House of Youth. **1933** Design for Living; The Silk Express. **1934** Where Sinners Meet; The Great Flirtation. **1935** Bonnie Scotland. **1936** Dracula's Daughter. **1937** Time Out for Romance. **1942** Mrs. Miniver. **1945** They Were Expendable. **1949** Madame Bovary.

STEELE, VICKIE FEE
Born: 1947. Died: Dec. 13, 1975, Santa Monica, Calif. Screen actress. Daughter of actress Astrid Allwyn.

STEELE, WILLIAM "BILL" (William A. Gettinger)
Born: 1889, Tex. Died: Feb. 13, 1966, Los Angeles, Calif. Screen actor and stuntman.

Appeared in: **1914** The Voice of the Viola; The Man Within; A Gypsy Romance; 'Cross the Mexican Line; Passing of the Beast. **1916** Across the Rio Grande; The Night Riders; A Knight of the Range. **1917** Blood Money; The Bad Man of Cheyenne; The Outlaw and the Lady; Goin' Straight; The Fighting Gringo; A Marked Man; Hair Trigger Burke; The Secret Man; A 44 Calibre Mystery; The Mysterious Outlaw; The Golden Bullet. **1918** The Phantom Rides. **1921** The Wallop; Riding With Death. **1922** The Fast Mail; Pardon My Nerve!; Bells of San Juan. **1923** Dead Game; Single Handed; Shootin' for Love; Don Quickshot of the Rio Grande. **1924** The Last Man on Earth; Hit and Run; The Ridin' Kid from Powder River; The Sunset Trail. **1925** The Saddle Hawk; Let 'Er Buck; Don Dare Devil; Two-Fisted Jones; The Sagebrush Lady; The Hurricane Kid. **1926** The Flaming Frontier; The Runaway Express; The Wild Horse Stampede; Six Shootin' Romance; Under Western Skies; The Fighting Peacemaker. **1927** Hoof Marks; Rough and Ready; Whispering Sage; The Valley of Hell; Loco Luck; Range Courage. **1928** The Black Ace; Thunder Riders; Call of the Heart; The Fearless Rider. **1930** Doughboys; The Lone Star Ranger. **1933** Gordon of Ghost City (serial). **1935** When a Man Sees Red. **1950** The Showdown.

STEELMAN, HOSEA E.
Born: 1876. Died: July 4, 1953, Calif. Screen actor.

STEEN, MARGUERITE
Born: 1894, England. Died: Aug. 4, 1975, Blewsbury, Oxfordshire, England. Stage, screen actress and novelist.

STEERS, LARRY (Lawrence Steers)
Born: 1881, Chicago, Ill. Died: Feb. 15, 1951, Woodland Hills, Calif. Screen and stage actor.

Appeared in: **1921** Wealth. **1922** Elope if You Must; South of Suva. **1923** Haunted Valley (serial); Mind Over Motor; Soul of the Beast; The Huntress. **1924** Ten Scars Make a Man (serial); A Cafe in Cairo; The Girl in the Limousine. **1925** The Best People; Flattery; New Brooms; The Love Gamble. **1926** Bride of the Storm; The Lodge in the Wilderness; Hearts and Spangles. **1927** The Claw; No Control. **1928** The Terrible People (serial); The Phantom Flyer. **1929** The Fire Detective (serial); In Old California; Dark Skies; Just Off Broadway; Redskin; The Wheel of Life. **1930** The Thoroghbreds; Let's Go Places. **1931** The Secret Call; Grief Street. **1932** If I Had a Million. **1933** The Cocktail Hour. **1936** Navy Born; Pan Handlers (short). **1938** Dummy Owner (short). **1939** Act Your Age (short). **1941** Riding the Wind. **1943** Hands Across the Border. **1944** Atlantic City; The Mojave Firebrand. **1945** White Pongo. **1947** The Ganster; Saddle Pals. **1948** Fighting Mad; Docks of New Orleans.

STEFAN, VIRGINIA
Born: 1926. Died: May 5, 1964, New York, N.Y. Screen and television actress.

STEFFORD, MIRIAM
Died: Aug. 26, 1931, San Juan, Argentina (plane crash). Screen actress.

STEGER, JULIUS
Born: Vienna, Austria. Died: Feb. 25, 1959, Vienna, Austria. Screen, stage, vaudeville actor, film producer and playwright.

STEHLI, EDGAR
Born: 1884, France. Died: July 25, 1973, Upper Montclair, N.J. Screen, stage, radio and television actor.

Appeared in: **1954** Executive Suite; Drum Beat. **1955** The Cobweb. **1958** The Brothers Karamazov. **1959** No Name on the Bullet; 4D Man; Cash McCall. **1961** Atlantis, the Lost Continent; Pocketful of Miracles; Parrish. **1962** The Spiral Road. **1963** Twilight of Honor. **1966** Seconds. **1967** The Tiger Makes Out. **1970** Loving.

STEIN, CAROL EDEN
Born: 1927. Died: Oct. 18, 1958, San Francisco, Calif. Screen actress.

STEIN, RALPH
Born: 1894. Died: May 5, 1978, Los Angeles, Calif. Screen, stage and television actor.

Appeared in: **1955** Pete Kelly's Blues.

STEIN, SAM "SAMMY"
Born: 1906, New York. Died: Mar. 30, 1966, Las Vegas, Nev. Screen actor, professional football player and wrestler.

Appeared in: **1934** The Lost Patrol. **1940** The Lone Voyage Home. **1941** Sierra Sue; The Wildcat of Tucson. **1942** Sing Your Worries Away; Remember Pearl Harbor; Gentleman Jim; Pittsburgh; Road to Morocco. **1943** Never a Dull Moment. **1945** The Big Show-Off; They Were Expendable. **1946** The French Key. **1947** Shoot to Kill; Variety Girl. **1951** The Last Outpost. **1953** The Veils of Bagdad.

STEINER, ELIO
Born: Mar. 9, 1905, Venice, Italy. Died: Dec. 6, 1965, Rome, Italy. Screen actor. Appeared in Italian, French and German films.

Appeared in: **1928** Vena D'Oro. **1930** La Canzone Dell'Amore; Corte D'Assisi; Stella Del Cinema. **1931** L'Uomo Dell'Artiglio; Der Klown. **1932** Pergoleri. **1933** Acqua Cheta; Giallo. **1937** Amore e Dolore. **1942** Giarabub. **1944** Senza Famiglia. **1947** Tombolo. **1952** La Signora senza Camelie.

STEINKE, HANS
Born: 1893, Germany. Died: June 26, 1971, Chicago, Ill. (lung cancer). Screen actor and wrestler.

Appeared in: **1933** Deception; Island of Lost Souls. **1935** People Will Talk. **1936** Once in a Blue Moon. **1938** The Buccaneer.

STEINMETZ, EARL
Born: 1915. Died: May 22, 1942, Los Angeles, Calif. (accident while filming). Screen actor.

STEINRUCK, ALBERT (aka ALBERT STEINRUECK)
Born: 1872, Wettenburg-Waldeck, Germany. Died: 1929, Berlin, Germany. Screen and stage actor.

Appeared in: Der Golem. **1920** Geschlossene Kette; Der Golem, wie er in die Welt Kam; Der Leidensweg der Inge Krafft; Madame Recamier; Der Richter von Zalamea. **1921** Brennendes Land; Exzellenz Unterrock; Maedchen aus der Ackerstrasse; Perlen Bedeuten Traenen; Sappho; Die Schuld der Lavinia Morland; Der Streik der Diebe. **1922** Die Nacht der Medici; Der Todesreigen; Monna Vanna (US 1925). **1923** Der Kaufmann von Venedig; Der Rote Reiter; Der Wetterwart; Der Schatz (The Treasure—US 1929, aka Ein Altes Spiel um Gold und Liebe). **1924** Dekameron-Naechte (Decameron Nights—US 1928); Das Goldene Kalb; Das Haus am Meer; Hedda Gabler; Helena; Maedchen, die Man Nicht Heiratet; Die Schuld; Sklaven der Liebe; Die Tragoedie der Entehrten (aka Frauen der Nacht). **1925** Die vom Niederrhein; Der Erste Stand; Goetz von Berlichingen Zubenannt mit der Eisernen Hand; Der Haus der Luege; Reveille, das Grosse Wecken; Der Tanzende Tod (aka Rex Mundi). **1926** Brennende Grenze; Die Drei Kuckucksuhren; Die Elf Schillerschen Offiziere; Liebeshandel; Mitgiftjaeger; Die Sporckschen Jaeger; Ueberfluessige Menschen; Zopf und Schwert. **1927** Am Rande der Welt; Einer Gegen Alle; Das Frauenhaus von Rio; Kinderseelen Klagen An; Leichte Kavallerie; Luetzows Wilde Verwegene Jagd; Das Maedchen aus der Fremde; § 182 Minderjaehrig; Regine, die Tragoedie Einer Frau; Die Sandgraefin; Schinderhannes; Venus im Frack; Die Vorbestraften. **1928** Angst; Die von der Scholle Sind; Herbstzeit am Rhein; Das Letzte Fort; Majestaet Schneidet Bubikoepfe; Der Rote Kreis; Der Zarewitsch; Asphalt (US 1930). **1929** Frauelein Else; Eleven Who Were Loyal; At the Edge of the World.

STELLONE, AL
Born: 1934. Died: Apr. 19, 1980, Woodland Hills, Calif. Screen, stage and television actor.

Appeared in: **1976** Car Wash. **1978** Every Which Way But Loose; The Billion Dollar Hobo. **1979** Boulevard Nights.

STEMBRIDGE, J. S.
Born: 1869. Died: Oct. 31, 1942. Screen actor.

Appeared in: **1922** The Law and the Woman. **1923** The Trail of the Lonesome Pine.

STENGEL, CASEY (Charles Dillon Stengel)
Born: July 30, 1890, Kansas City, Mo. Died: Sept. 29, 1975, Glendale, Calif. (cancer). Professional baseball player, manager and screen actor.

Appeared in: **1941** Safe at Home.

STEPHEN, JOHN
Born: 1912, Buffalo, N.Y. Died: Apr. 3, 1974, New York, N.Y. Screen, stage, radio and television actor.

Appeared in: **1956** The Wrong Man.

STEPHENS, JUD
Born: 1888. Died: Apr. 18, 1935, Los Angeles, Calif. Screen actor.

STEPHENS, LEWIS
Born: 1901. Died: Mar. 7, 1978, Woodland Hills, Calif. Screen extra.

STEPHENSON, HENRY (H. S. Garroway)
Born: Apr. 16, 1871, Granada, British West Indies. Died: Apr. 24, 1956, San Francisco, Calif. Screen and stage actor. Married to actress Ann Shoemaker (dec. 1978).

Appeared in: **1917** The Spreading Dawn. **1921** The Black Panther's Cub. **1925** Men and Women; Wild, Wild Susan. **1932** Cynara; Red Headed Woman; Guilty as Hell; Animal Kingdom; Bill of Divorcement. **1933** Queen Christina; Blind Adventure; Tomorrow at Seven; Double Harness; My Lips Betray; Little Women; If I Were Free. **1934** One More River; Outcast Lady; She Loves Me Not; All Men Are Enemies; Man of Two Worlds; The Richest Girl in the World; Stingaree; The Mystery of Mr. X; What Every Woman Knows; Thirty Day Princess. **1935** The Night Is Young; Vanessa, Her Love Story; Reckless; The Flame Within; O'Shaughnessey's Boy; Mutiny on the Bounty; Rendezvous; The Perfect Gentleman; Captain Blood. **1936** Little Lord Fauntleroy; Beloved Enemy; Half Angel; Hearts Divided; Give Me Your Heart; Charge of the Light Brigade; Walking on Air. **1937** When You're in Love; The Prince and the Pauper; The Emporer's Candlesticks; Conquest; Wise Girl. **1938** Marie Walewska; The Baroness and the Butler; Suez; Marie Antoinette; Dramatic School; The Young in Heart. **1939** Tarzan Finds a Son; Private Lives of Elizabeth and Essex; The Adventures of Sherlock Holmes. **1940** It's a Date; Spring Parade; Little Old New York; Down Argentine Way.

1941 The Man Who Lost Himself; The Lady from Louisiana. **1942** This Above All; Rings on Her Fingers; Half Way to Shanghai. **1943** Mr. Lucky; The Man Trap. **1944** Two Girls and a Sailor; Secrets of Scotland Yard; The Hour Before the Dawn; The Reckless Age. **1945** Tarzan and the Amazons. **1946** Heartbeat; The Return of Monte Cristo; The Locket; Night and Day; The Green Years; Of Human Bondage; Her Sister's Secret. **1947** The Homestretch; Ivy; Time Out of Mind; Song of Love; Dark Delusion. **1948** Oliver Twist (US 1951); Julia Misbehaves. **1949** Challange to Lassie; Enchantment.

STEPHENSON, JAMES
Born: Apr. 14, 1888, Yorkshire, England. Died: July 29, 1941, Pacific Palisades, Calif. (heart attack). Screen and stage actor. Nominated for 1940 Academy Award for Best Supporting Actor in The Letter.

Appeared in: **1937** The Perfect Crime; Take It from Me (aka Transatlantic Trouble); Dangerous Fingers (aka Wanted by Scotland Yard—US); You Live and Learn; The Man Who Made Diamonds. **1938** Dark Stairway; It's in the Blood; Mr. Satan; Cowboy from Brooklyn; White Banners; Heart of the North; When Were You Born?; Boy Meets Girl; Nancy Drew, Detective. **1939** On Trial; Secret Service of the Air; Adventures of Jane Arden; Torchy Blane in Chinatown; The Old Maid; Private Lives of Elizabeth and Essex; Espionage Agent; We Are Not Alone; Confessions of a Nazi Spy; King of the Underworld; Beau Geste. **1940** Devil's Island; Murder in the Air; Wolf of New York; A Dispatch from Reuters; Calling Philo Vance; The Sea Hawk; The Letter; South of Suez; River's End. **1941** Shining Victory; Flight from Destiny; International Squadron.

STEPHENSON, ROBERT ROBINSON
Born: 1901. Died: Sept. 8, 1970, Hollywood, Calif. (cancer). Screen actor.

Appeared in: **1942** Desperate Journey. **1945** The Brighton Strangler; Hotel Berlin. **1949** Shockproof. **1950** Where Danger Lives; Copper Canyon. **1951** David and Bathsheba. **1955** Love Me or Leave Me.

STEPPAT, ILSE
Born: 1917, Wuppertal, Germany. Died: Dec. 22, 1969, West Berlin, Germany. Screen and stage actress.

Appeared in: **1947** Ehe im Schatten (Marriage in the Shadows—US 1948). **1949** Die Blaue Schwerter; Die Bruecke (The Bridge). **1950** Der Mann, der Zweimal Leben Wollte; Der Fall Rabanser. **1951** Die Tat des Andern; Die Schuld des Dr. Homma; Hanna Amon; Was das Herz Befiehlt (aka Veronika, die Magd). **1952** Lockende Sterne; Wenn Abends die Heide Trauemt. **1953** Der Kaplan von San Lorenzo (aka Mea Culpa). **1954** Rittmeister Wronski. **1956** Waldwinter; Weil du arm Bist, Musst Du Frueher Sterben; Der Adler vom Velsatal. **1957** Bekenntnisse des Hochstaplers Felix Krull (aka The Confessions of Felix Krull—US 1958). **1958** Nachtschwester Ingeborg; Der Achte Wochentag; Romarei—das Maedchen mit den Gruenen Augen; Madeleine—Tel. 136211 (aka Naked in the Night—US 1961). **1959** Sehnsucht hat Mich Verfuehrt; The Eighth Day of the Week; Die Bruecke (The Bridge—US 1960 and 1949 version). **1960** Pension Schoeller; Im Namen Einer Mutter; Auf Engel Schiesst Man Nicht. **1963** Der Unsichtbare. **1965** Der Unheimliche Moench. **1966** Karriere. **1967** Die Blaue Hand. **1969** On Her Majesty's Secret Service.

STEPPLING, JOHN C.
Born: 1869, Germany. Died: Apr. 5, 1932, Hollywood, Calif. Screen and stage actor.

Appeared in: **1913** Bill Mixes with His Relations; The Heiress; Love Through a Lens; Hypnotism in Hicksville; Odd Knots. **1914** Jim; False Gods. **1916**-17 American Film Mfg. Co. films. **1917** The Hobo Raid; A Day Out of Jail; Seaside Romeos. **1918** Good Night, Paul. **1919** The Rescuing Angel; The Divorce Trap; Fools and Their Money. **1920** Madame Peacock. **1921** Nobody's Kid; The Silver Car; Black Beauty; Garments of Truth. **1922** Confidence; Extra! Extra!; Too Much Business; The Sin Flood. **1923** Bell Boy 13; Going Up; A Man's Man; What a Wife Learned; The Man Next Door; Let's Go. **1924** Abraham Lincoln; The Reckless Age; The Breathless Moment; A Cafe in Cairo; Galloping Fish; Fools in the Dark. **1925** California Straight Ahead; Soft Shoes; Eve's Lover. **1926** The Better Man; Memory Lane; Collegiate; High Steppers. **1927** California or Bust; God's Great Wilderness; The Gay Old Bird; Her Father Said No; Wedding Bill$; By Whose Hands. **1928** Their Hour. **1932** Broken Lullaby.

STERLING, EDYTHE
Born: 1887. Died: June 4, 1962, Hollywood, Calif. Screen and vaudeville actress.

Appeared in: **1921** Vanishing Maid; The Stranger in Canyon Valley. **1923** Crimson Gold; Danger.

STERLING, FORD (George F. Stitch)
Born: Nov. 3, 1880, La Crosse, Wis. Died: Oct. 13, 1939, Los Angeles, Calif. (thrombosis of veins—heart attack). Screen, stage, vaudeville actor and circus performer. Married to actress Teddy Sampson (dec. 1970). Was "Chief" of the original Keystone Kops.

Appeared in: **1912** Cohen Collects a Debt; The Water Nymph; Riley and Schultz; The Beating He Needed; Pedro's Dilemma; Stolen Glory; Ambitious Butler; The Flirting Husband; The Grocery Clerk's Romance; At Coney Island; At It Again; The Deacon's Trouble; A Tempermental Husband; The Rivals; Mr. Fix-It; The New Neighbor; A Bear Escape; Pat's Day Off; A Midnight Elopement; Mabel's Adventures; Hoffmeyer's Legacy. **1913** The Bangville Police; The Walters' Picnic; Out and In; Peeping Pete; His Crooked Career; Rastus and the Game Cock; Safe in Jail; Love and Rubbish; The Peddler; Professor Bean's Removal; Cohen's Outing; A Game of Pool; The Riot; Baby Day; Mabel's Dramatic Careeer (aka Her Dramatic Debut); The Faithful Taxicab; When Dreams Come True; The Bowling Match; A Double Wedding; The Cure That Failed; How Hiram Won Out; For Lizzie's Sake; The Mistaken Masher; The Deacon Outwitted; The Elite Ball; The Battle of Who Run; Just Brown's Luck; The Jealous Waiter; The Stolen Purse; Heinze's Resurrection; A Landlord's Troubles; The Professor's Daughter; A Red Hot Romance; The Man Next Door; Love and Pain; The Rube and the Baron; On His Wedding Day; The Sleuths at the Floral Parade; A Strong Revenge; The Two Widows; The Land Salesman; A Game of Poker; Father's Choice; A Life in the Balance; Murphy's IOU; A Fishy Affair; The New Conductor; The Ragtime Band (aka The Jazz Band); His Ups and Downs; Toplitsky and Company; Barney Oldfield's Race for a Life; Schnitz the Tailor; A Healthy Neighborhood; Teddy Telzlaff and Earl Cooper; Speed Kings; Their Husbands; Love Sickness at Sea; A Small Time Act; A Muddy Romance (aka Muddled in Mud); Cohen Saves the Flag; The Gusher; A Bad Game; Zuzu, the Band Leader; Some Nerve; The Speed Queen; The Hansom Driver; Wine (aka Wine Making). **1914** A Dramatic Mistake; Love and Dynamite; In the Clutches of a Gang (aka The Disguised Mayor); Too Many Brides (aka The Love Chase); Double Crossed; A Robust Romeo; Baffles; Gentleman Burglar; Between Showers; A False Beauty (aka A Faded Vampire); Tango Tangles; The Minstrel Man. **1915** That Little Band of Gold (aka For Better or Worse); Our Daredevil Chief; He Wouldn't Stay Down; Court House Crooks; Dirty Work in a Laundry (aka A Desperate Scoundrel); Only a Messenger Boy; His Father's Footsteps; Fatty and the Broadway Stars; The Hunt. **1916** His Pride and Shame; The Now Cure; His Wild Oats; His Lying Heart. **1917** Stars and Bars; Pinched in the Finish; A Maiden's Trust; His Torpedoes Love. **1922** Oh, Mabel Behave. **1923** The Stranger's Banquet; The Brass Bottle; Hollywood; The Spoilers; The Day of Faith; The Destroying Angel. **1924** Wild Oranges; The Woman on the Jury; Love and Glory; He Who Gets Slapped; Galloping Fish. **1925** So Big; Daddy's Gone A-Hunting; Trouble With Wives; Stage Struck; My Lady's Lips; Steppin' Out. **1926** The Road to Glory; Stranded in Paris; Good and Naughty; Mike; The Show-Off; The American Venus; Miss Brewster's Millions; Everybody's Acting. **1927** For the Love of Mike; Casey at the Bat; Drums of the Desert; The Trunk Mystery. **1928** Sporting Goods; Gentlemen Prefer Blondes; Wife Savers; Figures Don't Lie; Chicken a la King; Oh, Kay! **1929** The Fall of Eve. **1930** Sally; Bride of the Regiment; Spring Is Here; Kismet; The Girl in the Show; Showgirl in Hollywood. **1931** Stout Hearts and Willing Hands (short); Her Majesty, Love. **1932-33** Paramount shorts. **1933** Alice in Wonderland. **1935** A Vitaphone short; Behind the Green Lights; Black Sheep; Headline Woman. **1936** An RKO short. **1961** Days of Thrills and Laughter (documentary).

STERLING, JANE
Born: 1866, Cammille Luere. Died: Dec. 30, 1956, Middlebury, Vt. Screen and stage actress.

Appeared in: **1920** The Street Called Straight; The Heart of a Child.

STERLING, LARRY
Born: 1935. Died: Aug. 25, 1958, Clear Lake, Calif. (water skiing accident). Screen actor.

Appeared in: **1958** The Naked and the Dead.

STERLING, LEE
Born: 1904. Died: Mar. 4, 1951, Santa Monica, Calif. (heart attack). Screen actor.

STERLING, MERTA
Born: 1883. Died: Mar. 14, 1944, Hollywood, Calif. Screen actress.

Appeared in: **1917** Love and Blazes; Nabbing a Noble; A Good Little Bad Boy; Chicken Chased and Henpecked; Fat and Furious; Dry Goods and Damp Deeds. **1918** A Clean Sweep. **1924** The Star Dust Trail; Women First. **1927** Paid to Love.

STERN, BILL
Born: July 1, 1907, Rochester, N.Y. Died: Nov. 19, 1971, Rye, N.Y. (heart attack). Sportscaster on radio and television and screen actor.

Appeared in: **1942** The Pride of the Yankees. **1943** Stage Door Canteen. **1945** Here Come the Co-Eds. **1947** Spirit of West Point. **1954** Go, Man, Go.

STERN, LOUIS
Born: Jan. 10, 1860, New York, N.Y. Died: Feb. 15, 1941, Hollywood, Calif. Screen, stage and vaudeville actor.

Appeared in: **1920** Humoresque. **1925** I Want My Man. **1927** Wedding Bill$. **1929** The Little Wild Cat; Where East Is East; In Old California; The Diamond Master (serial).

STERNROYD, VINCENT
Born: Oct. 8, 1857, Highgate, London, England. Died: Nov. 3, 1948, London, England. Screen and stage actor.

Appeared in: **1913** Leah Kleschna. **1936** Marriage of Corbal (aka Prisoner of Corbal—US 1939).

STEVANS, NORMAN
Born: 1918, N.Y. Died: July 15, 1980, Burbank, Calif. (cancer). Screen actor. Entered films as an extra in 1942.

Appeared in: **1969** Sweet Charity.

STEVEN, BOYD
Born: 1875, Scotland. Died: Dec., 1967, Glasgow, Scotland. Singer and screen actress.

Appeared in: **1947** I Know Where I'm Going.

STEVENS, BERT
Born: 1905. Died: Dec. 14, 1964, Hollywood, Calif. (heart attack). Screen actor. Brother of actress Barbara Stanwyck.

Appeared in: **1954** Woman's World.

STEVENS, BILL
Born: 1930, Tulsa, Oklahoma. Died: Oct. 20, 1979, Los Angeles, Calif. Screen, stage and television actor.

STEVENS, BYRON E.
Born: 1904. Died: Dec. 15, 1964, Encino, Calif. (heart attack). Screen actor. Entered films approx. 1939. Brother of actress Barbara Stanwyck.

STEVENS, CHARLES
Born: May 26, 1893, Solomansville, Ariz. Died: Aug. 22, 1964, Hollywood, Calif. Screen and vaudeville actor. Appeared in all but one of Douglas Fairbanks' pictures. Was grandson of Apache chief Geronimo.

Appeared in: **1915** Birth of a Nation (film debut); The Lamb. **1916** The Mystery of the Leaping Frog; The Americano. **1917** The Man from Painted Post; Reaching for the Moon. **1921** The Three Musketeers. **1922** Robin Hood; Captain Fly-by-Night. **1923** Where the North Begins. **1924** Empty Hands; The Thief of Bagdad (played 6 roles). **1925** The Vanishing American; Don Q; Recompense; A Son of His Father. **1926** The Black Pirate; Man Trap; Across the Pacific. **1927** The Gaucho; King of Kings; Woman's Law. **1928** Diamond Handcuffs; Stand and Deliver. **1929** The Virginian; The Mysterious Dr. Fu Manchu; The Iron Mask. **1930** The Big Trail; Tom Sawyer. **1931** The Conquering Horde; The Cisco Kid. **1932** South of the Rio Grande; The Stoker; Mystery Ranch. **1933** Drum Taps; When Strangers Marry; California Trail; Police Call. **1934** Fury of the Jungle. **1935** Lives of a Bengal Lancer; Call of the Wild. **1936** Here Comes Trouble; The Beloved Rogue; The Bold Caballero. **1937** Wild West Days (serial); Ebb Tide. **1938** Red Barry (serial); The Crime of Dr. Hallett; Flaming Frontiers (serial). **1939** The Renegade Ranger; Desperate Trails; Frontier Marshal; The Girl and the Gambler. **1940** Winners of the West (serial); Kit Carson; Wagons Westward. **1941** The Bad Man; Blood and Sand. **1942** Beyond the Blue Horizon; Overland Mail (serial); Tombstone, the Town Too Tough to Die; Pierre of the Plains. **1944** Marked Trails; The Mummy's Curse. **1945** South of the Rio Grande; San Antonio. **1946** Border Bandits; My Darling Clementine. **1947** Buffalo Bill Rides Again. **1948** Fury at Furnace Creek; Belle Starr's Daughter; The Feathered Serpent. **1949** Ambush; The Walking Hills; Roll Thunder Roll; The Cowboy and the Indians. **1950** The Showdown; California Passage; Indian Territory; The Savage Horde; A Ticket to Tomahawk. **1951** Oh, Susanna!; Warpath. **1952** Smoky Canyon; The Lion and the Horse. **1953** Savage Mutiny; Ride, Vaquero; Eyes of the Jungle; Jeopardy. **1954** Jubilee Trail; Killer Leopard. **1955** The Vanishing American (and 1925 version). **1956** Partners. **1959** Last Train from Gun Hill. **1962** The Outsider.

STEVENS, CYE
Died: June 5, 1974. Screen actor.

Appeared in: **1949** Follow Me Quietly. **1951** The Sellout.

STEVENS, EDWIN
Born: 1860, California. Died: Jan. 2, 1923. Screen, stage and vaudeville actor.

Appeared in: **1916** The Man Inside; The Capital Price; The Yellow Menace (serial); Honor of Mary Blake. **1917** The Boy Girl; Susan's Gentleman; The Brand of Hate. **1919** The Unpardonable Sin; The Crimson Gardenia; Sahara; The Lottery Man; Hawthorne of the USA. **1921** The Charm School; Crazy to Marry; The Dollar-a-Year Man; Everything for Sale; One Wild Week; The Little Minister; The Snob; What's Worth While?; The Sting of the Lash. **1922** The Game Chicken; The Golden Gallows; The Hands of Nara; The Man Unconquerable; The Ragged Heiress. **1923** Quicksands; The Spider and the Rose; The Voice from the Minaret; The Woman of Bronze.

STEVENS, EMILY
Born: 1882. Died: Jan. 2, 1928, New York, N.Y. (overdose of sedatives). Stage and screen actress. Sister of actor Robert Stevens (dec. 1963).

Appeared in: **1915** The Soul of a Woman. **1917** The Slacker.

STEVENS, EVELYN
Born: 1891. Died: Aug. 28, 1938, New York, N.Y. Screen and stage actress. Appeared in early Griffith films.

STEVENS, GEORGE
Born: Dec. 18, 1904, Oakland, Calif. Died: Mar. 8, 1975, Lancaster, Calif. (heart attack). Film director, screenwriter, stage and screen actor. Son of stage actor John Landers Stevens (dec. 1940) and actress Georgie Cooper (dec. 1968). Father of director and producer George Stevens, Jr.

Appeared in: **1914** The Memories that Haunt. **1915** The Fates and Flora Fourflush (The Ten Billion Dollar Vitagraph Mystery Serial). **1916** My Lady's Slippers. **1921** Oh Mary Be Careful. **1923** Java Head. **1924** Trail of the Law. **1931** The following shorts: Blood and Thunder; Mama Loves Papa; The Kickoff. **1936** Aces and Eights.

STEVEN, GEORGIA COOPER *See* COOPER, GEORGIA

STEVENS, INGER (Inger Stensland)
Born: Oct. 18, 1935, Stockholm, Sweden. Died: Apr. 30, 1970, Hollywood, Calif. (barbiturate overdose). Screen, stage and television actress.

Appeared in: **1957** Man on Fire. **1958** Cry Terror; The Buccaneer. **1959** The World, the Flesh and the Devil. **1964** The New Interns. **1967** A Time for Killing; A Guide for the Married Man. **1968** Hang 'Em High; House of Cards; Firecreek; Madigan; 5 Card Stud. **1969** A Dream of Kings.

STEVENS, JEAN *See* CARROLL, PEGGY

STEVENS, LANDERS (John Landers Stevens)
Born: Feb. 17, 1877, San Francisco, Calif. Died: Dec. 19, 1940, Hollywood, Calif. (heart attack following appendectomy). Screen, stage actor and film producer. Married to actress Georgia Cooper (dec. 1968) and father of actor and director George Stevens (dec. 1975). Entered films in 1920.

Appeared in: **1921** Keeping Up With Lizzie; Shadows of Conscience. **1922** The Veiled Woman; A Wonderful Wife; Youth Must Have Love; Wild Honey; Handle With Care. **1925** Battling Bunyon. **1929** Frozen Justice; The Trial of Mary Dugan. **1931** The Gorilla; Hell Divers; The Rainbow Trail. **1934** Manhattan Melodrama. **1935** Frisco Kid; The Counselitis (short). **1936** We Who are About to Die; Swing Time; Charlie Chan's Secret. **1937** Join the Marines; Bill Cracks Down. **1938** Ears of Experience (short); Berth Quakes (short).

STEVENS, LYNN (Franklin Feeney)
Born: 1898. Died: Mar. 28, 1950, Worcester, Mass. Screen and stage actor.

Appeared in: **1926** Men of Steel. **1928** Clothes Make the Woman.

STEVENS, MORTON L.
Born: 1890, Marlboro, Mass. Died: Aug. 5, 1959, Marlboro, Mass. Screen, stage and television actor.

Appeared in: **1914** Perils of Pauline (serial). **1949** Lost Boundaries.

STEVENS, ONSLOW (Onslow Ford Stevenson)
Born: Mar. 29, 1902, Los Angeles, Calif. Died: Jan. 5, 1977, Van Nuys, Calif. ("at the hands of another, other than by accident" in a convalescent home). Screen, stage, television actor and stage director. Son of actor Houseley Stevenson (dec. 1953). Brother of actor Houseley Stevenson, Jr.

Appeared in: **1932** Radio Patrol; Once in a Lifetime; The Golden West; Okay America; Heroes of the West (serial). **1933** Counsellor-at-Law; Nagana; Peg O' My Heart; Secret of the Blue Room; Only Yesterday. **1934** In Love With Life; Bombay Mail; This Side of Heaven; Crosby Case; I'll Tell the World; I Can't Escape; Affairs of a Gentleman; House of Danger; The Vanishing Shadow (serial). **1935** Notorious Gentleman; Three Musketeers; Life Returns; Born to Gamble; Forced Landing; Grand Exit. **1936** Under Two Flags; Three on the Trail; Yellow Dust; Bridge of Sighs; Easy Money; Straight from the Shoulder; Murder With Pictures; F-Man. **1937** You Can't Buy Luck; Flight from Glory; There Goes the Groom. **1939** When Tomorrow Comes; Those High Grey Walls. **1940** The Man Who Wouldn't Talk; Mystery Sea Raider; Who Killed Aunt Maggie? **1941** The Monster and the Girl; Go West, Young Lady. **1942** Sunset Serenade. **1943** Appointment in Berlin; Idaho; Hands Across the Border. **1945** House of Dracula. **1946** O.S.S.; Angel on My Shoulder. **1948** Walk a Crooked Mile; The Gallant Blade; Night Has a Thousand Eyes; The Creeper. **1949** Red Hot and Blue; Bomba, the Jungle Boy. **1950** State Penitentiary; One Too Many; Revenue Agent; Mark of the Gorilla; Motor Patrol. **1951** Sirocco; Hills of Utah; Lorna Doone; The Family Secret; Sealed Cargo; All That I Have. **1952** San Francisco Story. **1953** A Lion Is in the Streets; The Charge at Feather River. **1954** Fangs of the Wild; Them; They Rode West. **1955** New York Confidential. **1956** Tribute to a Bad Man; Outside the Law. **1957** Kelly and Me. **1958** The Buccaneer; The Party Crashers; Tarawa Beachhead; Lonelyhearts. **1960** All the Fine Young Cannibals. **1962** The Couch. **1963** Geronimo's Revenge.

STEVENS, ROBERT
Born: c. 1880. Died: Dec. 19, 1963, Lauderdale-by-the-Sea, Fla. Screen, stage actor and stage director. Brother of actress Emily Stevens (dec. 1928).

Appeared in: **1942** Perils of the Royal Mounted (serial). **1946** Gilda. **1947** The Millerson Case; Blondie's Big Moment.

STEVENS, VIOLET "VI"
Born: 1892, England. Died: Mar. 22, 1967, London, England. Screen, stage and television actress. Entered films in 1946.

Appeared in: **1951** The Mudlark. **1958** A Cry From the Streets (US 1959). **1962** Lisa.

STEVENSON, ADLAI E. (Adlai Ewing Stevenson)
Born: Feb. 5, 1900, Los Angeles, Calif. Died: July 14, 1965, London, England (heart attack). Lawyer, public official, writer, diplomat and screen performer.

Appeared in: **1964** A Global Affair.

STEVENSON, CHARLES A. (Charles Alexander Stevenson)
Born: Nov. 6, 1851, Dublin, Ireland. Died: July 2, 1929, New York, N.Y. Screen and stage actor. Entered films in 1918.

Appeared in: **1921** Experience. **1922** Her Gilded Cage. **1923** The Bolted Door; The Spanish Dancer; The Woman With Four Faces; Legally Dead; Garrison's Finish. **1924** The Wise Virgin; The Breaking Point. **1927** Aflame in the Sky. **1928** Doomsday.

STEVENSON, CHARLES E.
Born: 1888, Sacramento, Calif. Died: July 4, 1943, Palo Alto, Calif. Screen actor. Entered films with Vitagraph.

Appeared in: **1928** Wallflower. **1929** The Mysterious Dr. Fu Manchu.

STEVENSON, DOUGLAS
Born: 1883. Died: Dec. 31, 1934, Versailles, Ky. Screen, stage actor and dancer.

Appeared in: **1924** Janice Meredith (stage and screen versions).

STEVENSON, HOUSELEY
Born: July 30, 1879, Liverpool or London, England. Died: Aug. 6, 1953, Los Angeles, Calif. Stage and screen actor. Father of actors Onslow Stevens (dec. 1977) and Houseley Stevenson, Jr.

Appeared in: **1936** Law in Her Hands (film debut); Isle of Fury. **1937** Once a Doctor. **1942** Native Land. **1943** Happy Land. **1946** The Yearling; Somewhere in the Night; Little Miss Big. **1947** Dark Passage; The Brasher Doubloon; Time Out of Mind; Ramrod; Thunder in the

Valley. **1948** Four Faces West; The Challange; Casbah; Kidnapped; Moonrise; Apartment for Peggy. **1949** Calamity Jane and Sam Bass; Bride of Vengeance; Colorado Territory; Knock on Any Door; The Lady Gambles; Leave It to Henry; Masked Raiders; Sorrowful Jones; Take One False Step; The Walking Hills; You Gotta Stay Happy; The Gal Who Took the West. **1950** All the Kings Men; Edge of Doom; Sierra; Gunfighter; Joan of Arc; The Sun Sets at Dawn. **1951** Cave of Outlaws; Hollywood Story; The Secret of Convict Lake; All That I Have. **1952** The Atomic City; Oklahoma Annie; The Wild North.

STEVENSON, JOHN
Born: 1884, N.Y. Died: 1922, New York, N.Y. (results of a fall while filming Plunder). Screen actor and stuntman.

Appeared in: **1923** Plunder (serial).

STEVENSON, MARTHA
Died: July, 1977, New York, N.Y. (suicide). Screen actress. Divorced from bandleader Hal Kemp, actor Victor Mature, and St. Clair McKelway. Later married to Hayes Goetz.

STEVENSON, ROBERT J.
Born: 1915. Died: Mar. 4, 1975, Northridge, Calif. (cardiac arrest). Newscaster, screen, television actor and public official.

Appeared in: **1951** All That I Have. **1952** Radar Men from the Moon (serial). **1954** Fangs of the Wild. **1957** Zero Hour! **1958** Gun Fever; When Hell Broke Loose. **1959** Have Rocket, Will Travel. **1960** Spartacus.

STEWARD, MAYNON
Born: 1880. Died: Dec. 25, 1932. Screen actress.

STEWART, AILEEN
Born: 1887. Died: Feb. 7, 1931, Hollywood, Calif. Screen and stage actress.

STEWART, ANITA
Born: Feb. 17, 1895, Brooklyn, N.Y. Died: May 4, 1961, Beverly Hills, Calif. Screen, stage actress and film producer. Sister of actor George (dec. 1945) and actress Lucille Stewart.

Appeared in: **1912** The Wood Violet (film debut); Her Choice; The Godmother; Song of the Shell. **1913** Papa Puts One Over; The Classmates Frolic; Love Laughs at Blacksmiths (aka Love Finds a Way); A Web; A Fighting Chance; Two's Company, Three's a Crowd; A Regiment of Two; The Forgotten Latchkey; The Song Bird of the North; Sweet Deception; The Moulding; The Prince of Evil; The Tiger; The Lost Millionaire; The Treasure of Desert Island; His Last Fight; Why I am Here; The Wreck; The Swan Girl; His Second Wife. **1914** Diana's Dress Reform; The Right and the Wrong of It; The Lucky Elopement; Lincoln, the Lover; A Million Bid; Back to Broadway; The Girl from Prosperity; He Never Knew; Wife Wanted; The Shadow of the Past; Uncle Bill; The Sins of the Mother; The Painted World; Four Thirteen; 'Midst Woodland Shadows. **1915** Two Women; The Right Girl; From Headquarters; The Juggernaut; His Phantom Sweetheart; The Awakening; The-Sort-of-Girl-Who-Came-From-Heaven; Count 'Em; The Goddess (serial). **1916** My Lady's Slipper; The Suspect; The Darings of Diana; The Combat. **1917** The Glory of Yolanda; The More Excellent Way; The Message of the Mouse; Clover's Rebellion; The Girl Philippa. **1919** In Old Kentucky; The Mind-the-Paint Girl; Virtuous Wives; A Midnight Romance; Mary Regan; Her Kingdom of Dreams. **1920** Human Desire; The Yellow Typhoon; The Fighting Shepherdess; Harriet and the Piper. **1921** Sowing the Wind; Playthings of Destiny. **1922** Her Mad Bargain; The Invisible Fear; A Question of Honor; The Woman He Married; Rose O' the Sea. **1923** Hollywood; The Love Piker; Mary of the Movies; Souls for Sale. **1924** The Great White Way. **1925** Baree, Son of Kazan; Never the Twain Shall Meet; Go Straight. **1926** The Lodge in the Wildeness; Morganson's Finish; Whispering Wires; The Prince of Pilsen; Rustling for Cupid. **1927** Isle of Sunken Gold; Wild Geese. **1928** Name the Woman; The Romance of a Rogue; Sisters of Eve.

STEWART, ATHOLE
Born: June 24, 1879, Ealing, London, England. Died: Oct. 22, 1940, Buckinghamshire, England. Screen, stage actor and stage director.

Appeared in: **1930** Canaries Sometimes Sing; The Temporary Widow. **1931** The Speckled Band. **1932** Frail Women. **1933** The Little Damozel; Loyalties; The Constant Nymph. **1934** Four Masked Men; The Path of Glory. **1935** The Clairvoyant; While Parents Sleep. **1936** The Amateur Gentleman; Jack of All Trades (aka The Two of Us—US 1937); Where's Sally?; Accused; Dusty Ermine (aka Hideout in the Alps—US 1938); The Tenth Man. **1937** Action for Slander (US 1938); Dr. Syn; Jane Eyre. **1938** The Singing Cop; Thistledown; His Lordship

Regrets; Break the News (US 1941); Climbing High. **1939** The Spy in Black (aka U-Boat 29—US); The Four Just Men (aka The Secret Four—US 1940); Goodbye, Mr. Chips; Poison Pen (US 1941). **1940** Gentleman of Venture (aka It Happened to One Man—US 1941); Tilly of Bloomsbury; Old Mother Riley in Society.

STEWART, BETTY
Born: 1912. Died: Sept. 29, 1944, Hollywood, Calif. Screen actress.

STEWART, BLANCHE
Died: July 25, 1952. Screen and radio actress. Was "Brenda" of "Brenda and Cobina" comedy team.

Appeared in: **1940** A Night at Earl Carroll's. **1941** Swing It Soldier. **1942** Sweetheart of the Fleet.

STEWART, CRAY
Born: 1924. Died: May 30, 1961, Salton Sea, Calif. (heart attack). Stage and screen actor.

STEWART, DANNY (Danny Kalauawa Stewart)
Born: 1907. Died: Apr. 15, 1962, Honolulu, Hawaii. Screen actor and steel guitarist. Appeared in 60 "South Seas" movies.

STEWART, DAVID J. (Abe J. Siegel)
Born: 1914, Omaha, Nebr. Died: Dec. 23, 1966, Cleveland, Ohio (following surgery). Screen, stage and television actor.

Appeared in: **1954** The Silver Chalice. **1960** Murder, Inc. **1961** The Young Savages. **1967** Who's Minding the Mint?

STEWART, DONA JEAN
Born: 1939. Died: July 31, 1961, near Oceanside, Calif. (auto accident). Screen actress.

STEWART, DONALD
Born: 1911, Pa. Died: Mar. 1, 1966, Chertsey, England. Screen, stage and television actor. Married to actress Renee Houston (dec. 1980).

Appeared in: **1937** Fine Feathers. **1942** Eagle Squadron; Flying Fortress. **1943** Wild Horse Stampede. **1944** One Exciting Night (aka You Can't Do Without Love—US 1946); Arizona Whirlwind. **1955** The Reluctant Bride (aka Two Grooms for a Bride—US 1957); Cross Up (aka Tiger by the Tail). **1958** The Sheriff of Fractured Jaw.

STEWART, DONALD OGDEN
Born: Nov. 30, 1894, Columbus, Ohio. Died: Aug. 2, 1980, London, England (heart attack). Screen, stage actor, screenwriter, playwright and author.

Appeared in: **1930** Not So Dumb.

STEWART, FRED
Born: 1907, Ga. Died: Dec. 5, 1970, New York, N.Y. Screen, stage and television actor. Entered films in 1931.

Appeared in: **1932** The Misleading Lady. **1961** Splendor in the Grass. **1964** The World of Henry Orient.

STEWART, GEORGE
Born: 1888. Died: Dec. 25, 1945, Beverly Hills, Calif. Screen actor. Brother of actress Anita Stewart (dec. 1961).

Appeared in: **1921** The Fighter; Gilded Lies; Over the Wire. **1922** The Seventh Day. **1923** Crossed Wires; Hollywood; The Abysmal Brute. **1925** Back to Life; Wings of Youth.

STEWART, JACK
Born: 1914, Larkhall, Scotland. Died: Jan. 2, 1966, London, England. Screen, stage, radio and television actor.

Appeared in: **1952** Hunted (aka The Stranger in Between—US); The Brave Don't Cry. **1954** The Kidnappers (aka Little Kidnappers—US 1954); The Maggie (aka High and Dry—US). **1957** The Steel Bayonet; The Heart Within. **1961** The Frightened City (US 1962). **1962** The Strongroom; Pirates of Blood River; The Amorous Prawn (aka The Playgirl and the War Minister—US 1963). **1963** Tom Jones. **1964** The Three Lives of Thomasina. **1967** I Coltelli del Vendicatore (Knives of the Avenger—US 1968).

STEWART, JULIA
Died: Date unknown, New Jersey. Screen actress.

Appeared in: **1912** It Pays to be Kind; A Living Memory; When an Old Maid Gets Busy; Through Jealous Eyes; The Black Hand; Dick's Wife; The Return of Lady Linda. **1913** Eclaire films.

STEWART, KATHERINE
Born: 1861, Kent, England. Died: Jan. 24, 1949, New York, N.Y. Screen and stage actress.

Appeared in: **1917** Please Help Emily. **1921** The Great Adventure. **1922** How Women Love.

STEWART, NELLIE
Born: 1858, Australia. Died: June 20, 1931. Screen, stage actress and singer.

Appeared in: **1911** Sweet Nell of Old Drury (her only film).

STEWART, RICHARD
Died: 1938 or 1939? Screen actor. Son of opera performer William G. Stewart (dec. 1941).

Appeared in: **1922** Face to Face.

STEWART, ROY
Born: Oct. 17, 1889, San Diego, Calif. Died: Apr. 26, 1933, Los Angeles, Calif. (heart attack). Screen and stage actor. Entered films in 1913.

Appeared in: **1915** Just Nuts (short). **1916** Liberty, a Daughter of the U.S.A. **1917** Come Through; The Devil Dodger. **1918** Keith of the Border; The Law's Outlaw; Faith Endurin'. **1919** The Westerners. **1920** Riders of the Dawn; Just a Wife. **1921** Prisoners of Love; The Devil to Pay; The Heart of the North; Her Social Value; The Mistress of Shenstone. **1922** Back to the Yellow Jacket; The Innocent Cheat; Life's Greatest Question; A Motion to Adjourn; One Eighth Apache; The Radio King (serial); The Sagebrush Trail; The Snowshoe Trail. **1923** Burning Words; The Love Brand; Pure Grit; Trimmed in Scarlet. **1924** Sundown; The Woman on the Jury. **1925** Kit Carson Over the Great Divide; Time, the Comedian; Where the Worst Begins. **1926** General Custer at Little Big Horn; Sparrows; Buffalo Bill on the U. P. Trail; Daniel Boone Thru the Wilderness; The Lady from Hell; You Never Know Women. **1927** The Midnight Watch; One Woman to Another; Roaring Fires. **1928** The Viking; The Candy Kid; Storm Waters. **1929** Protection; In Old Arizona. **1930** Men Without Women; The Great Divide; Born Reckless; Lone Star Ranger; Rough Romance. **1931** Fighting Caravans. **1932** Mystery Ranch; Exposed. **1933** Fargo Express; Come on, Tarzan!; Zoo in Budapest; Rustler's Roundup.

STEWART, SOPHIE
Born: Mar. 5, 1908, Crieff, Perthshire, Scotland. Died: June 6, 1977, London, England. Screen, stage, radio and television actress. Married to actor Ellis Irving.

Appeared in: **1935** Maria Martin: or, The Murder in the Red Barn (aka Murder in the Red Barn—US 1936). **1936** Things to Come; The Man Who Could Work Miracles (US 1937); As You Like It. **1937** Under the Red Robe; The Return of the Scarlet Pimpernel (US 1938). **1938** Who Goes Next?; Marigold. **1939** Nurse Edith Cavell. **1940** My Son, My Son. **1943** The Lamp Still Burns. **1945** Strawberry Roan (US 1948). **1947** Uncle Silas (aka The Inheritance—US 1951). **1957** Yangtse Incident (aka Battle Hell—US); No Time for Tears.

STIEBNER, HANS
Born: 1899, Germany. Died: Mar. 27, 1958, Baden-Baden, West Germany. Screen, stage, television actor and film director.

Appeared in: **1937** Weisse Sklaven. **1938** Mit Versiegelter Order (Under Sealed Orders).

STILLER, MAURITZ
Born: 1883, Helsinki, Finland. Died: 1928, Stockholm, Sweden (infective pleurisy). Screen actor and film director.

Appeared in: **1912** Mother and Daughter. **1914** When Mother-in-Law Reigns.

STIRLING, EDWARD
Born: May 26, 1892, Birmingham, England. Died: Jan. 12, 1948, Paris, France (heart attack). Screen, stage, radio actor, playwright and stage producer.

Appeared in: **1948** The Eagle with Two Heads.

STITES, FRANK
Born: Feb. 28, 1882, Indiana. Died: Mar. 15, 1915, Universal City, Calif. (plane crash). Screen actor and stuntman.

Appeared in: **1915** The Mysterious Contragrao.

STOCKDALE, CARL (Carlton Stockdale)
Born: Feb. 19, 1874, Worthington, Minn. Died: Mar. 15, 1953, Woodland Hills, Calif. (heart attack). Screen, stage and vaudeville actor. Entered films in 1912.

Appeared in: **1914** Sophie Picks a Dead One; The Calling of Jim Benton; Single-Handed; The Atonement; Broncho Billy Puts One Over; Broncho Billy and the Sheriff; Dan Cupid—Assayer; Broncho Billy—Favorite; The Hills of Peace. **1915** The Bank; My Best Gal. **1916** Intolerance; Atta Boy's Last Race. **1917** Lost and Won; Land of Long Shadows; The Range Boss; Open Places; Men of the Desert; Peggy Leads the Way. **1921** The Fatal 30; Molly O'; Society Secrets. **1922** Bing Bang Boom; Suzanna; The Call of Home; The Half Breed; Red Hot Romance; Oliver Twist; Thorns and Orange Blossoms; Where Is My Wandering Boy Tonight?; Wild Honey. **1923** The Darling of New York; The Grail; The Extra Girl; Man's Size; The Meanest Man in the World; The Tiger's Claw; Money! Money! Money! **1924** The Whispered Name; Try and Get It; Tainted Money; The Beautiful Sinner; A Cafe in Cairo; Gold Heels; The Spirit of the USA. **1925** The Business of Love; The Desert's Price; A Regular Fellow; A Son of His Father; The Trail Rider. **1926** The Man Upstairs; While London Sleeps. **1927** Colleen; King of Kings; See You in Jail; Somewhere in Sonora. **1928** The Air Mail Pilot; Jazzland; My Home Town; The Shepherd of the Hills; The Black Pearl; Broken Barriers; The Terror. **1929** The Love Parade; The Carnation Kid; China Bound. **1930** Abraham Lincoln; The Furies; Hell's Island; Hide-Out; Sisters; All Tied Up (short); Whispering Whoopee (short). **1933** The Vampire Bat. **1935** The Crimson Trail; Circumstantial Evidence; Dr. Socrates; Outlawed Guns; The Ivory Handled Gun; Ring Around the Moon; Hit and Run Driver (short); Mary Jane's Pa. **1936** The Leavenworth Case; Revolt of the Zombies; Oh, Susannah! **1937** Battle of Greed; Nation Aflame; Courage of the West; Lost Horizon. **1938** Hawaiian Buckaroo; Rawhide; Blockade. **1939** The Story That Couldn't Be Printed (short). **1940** Shooting High; Pioneers of the Frontier; Konga the Wild Stallion; Stage to Chino; Thundering Frontier; Wagon Train. **1941** Scattergood Meets Broadway; Dangerous Lady; All That Money Can Buy (aka Here Is a Man); Scattergood Pulls the Strings; Along the Rio Grande; The Return of Daniel Boone. **1953** The Devil and Daniel Webster (reissue of All That Money Can Buy—1941).

STOCKDALE, FRANKLIN E.
Born: 1870. Died: Dec. 31, 1950, Los Angeles, Calif. Screen and stage actor.

STOCKFIELD, BETTY (aka BETTY STOCKFELD)
Born: Jan. 15, 1905, Sydney, Australia. Died: Jan. 27, 1966, London, England (cancer). Screen and stage actress.

Appeared in: **1926** What Price Glory (film debut). **1931** City of Song (aka Farewell to Love—US 1933); Captivation; 77 Park Lane. **1932** Money for Nothing; Life Goes On (aka Sorry You've Been Troubled); The Impassive Footman (aka Woman in Bondage—US); The Maid of the Mountains. **1933** King of the Ritz; Lord of the Manor; Anne One Hundred. **1934** The Man Who Changed His Name; The Battle (aka Thunder in the East—US); Brides to Be. **1935** The Lad; Runaway Ladies. **1936** Under Proof; The Beloved Vagabond; Dishonor Bright. **1937** Who's Your Lady Friend?; Club des Femmes (Girls' Club). **1938** I See Ice; Slipper Episode. **1939** Ils Etaient Neuf Celibataires (Nine Bachelors—US). **1940** Derriere la Facade (Behind the Facade). **1942** Hard Steel; Flying Fortress. **1950** The Girl Who Couldn't Quit; Edouard et Caroline (Edward and Caroline—US 1952). **1956** Guilty. **1957** True as a Turtle. **1958** Forbidden Desire (aka Lover's Net).

STOCKWELL, WINIFRED
Born: 1895. Died: Feb. 8, 1981, New Hope, Minn. Screen and stage actress. Appeared in silent films.

STODDARD, BELLE
Born: 1869, Remington, Ohio. Died: Dec. 13, 1950, Hollywood, Calif. Stage and screen actress.

Appeared in: **1925** Kentucky Pride. **1928** Hangman's House. **1939** Anne Against the World.

STODDARD, BETSY (Elizabeth S. Zimmerman)
Born: 1884. Died: Sept. 7, 1959, Hollywood, Calif. Screen actress.

STOECKEL, JOE
Born: 1894, Munich, Germany. Died: June 14, 1959, Munich, Germany (circulatory ailment). Screen, stage actor and film director. Entered films in 1916.

Appeared in: **1920** Strong Man. **1934** Der Meisterdetektiv; Die Blonde Cristl; SA Mann Brand; Mit dir Durch Dick und Duenn; Bei der Blonden Kathrein. **1935** Zwischen Himmel un Erde (Between Heaven and Earth); Johannisnacht. **1936** Ein Ganzer Kerl. **1937** Die Grose Adele. **1939** Der Dampf mit dem Drachen (The Fight With the Dragon); 1A in Oberbayern (1A in Upper Bavaria).

STOKER, H. G. (Hew Gordon Dacre Stoker)
Born: Feb. 2, 1885, Dublin, Ireland. Died: Feb. 2, 1966, England. Screen, stage actor and playwright. Also known on stage as Hew Gordon.

Appeared in: **1933** Channel Crossing (US 1934); One Precious Year. **1935** Forever England (aka Brown on Resolution and Born for Glory—US). **1936** First Offence; Rhodes of Africa (aka Rhodes—US); Pot Luck; It's You I Want. **1937** Moonlight Sonata; Non-Stop New York. **1938** Crackerjack (aka The Man with a Hundred Faces—US). **1939** Full Speed Ahead. **1943** The Charmer (reissue fo Moonlight Sonata—1937). **1948** Call of the Blood. **1951** Four Days. **1952** Where's Charley?

STOKES, ERNEST L.
Born: 1907. Died: May 26, 1964, Wilson, N.C. Screen and radio actor. Appeared on radio with Frank Rice in a radio team billed as "Mustard and Gravy."

STOKES, OLIVE M.
Born: Apr. 10, 1887, Okla. Died: Nov. 1, 1972, Calif. Screen actress. Divorced from actor Tom Mix (dec. 1940). Appeared in early Hersley Film Co. films.

STOKOWSKI, LEOPOLD (Leopold Boleslawowicz Stanislaw Antoni Stokowski)
Born: Apr. 18, 1882, London, England. Died: Sept. 13, 1977, Nether Wallop, Hampshire, Englannd (coronary attack). Symphonic conductor and screen actor. Divorced from Olga Samaroff, Evangeline Brewster Johnson, and artist/designer Gloria Vanderbilt.

Appeared in: **1936** The Big Broadcast of 1937. **1937** 100 Men and a Girl. **1940** Fantasia. **1947** Carnegie Hall.

STONE, ARTHUR
Born: 1884, St. Louis, Mo. Died: Sept. 4, 1940, Hollywood, Calif. Screen, stage and vaudeville actor. Entered films in 1924.

Appeared in: **1925** Sherlock Sleuth (short); Change the Needle (short). **1926** It Must Be Love; Miss Nobody; The Silent Lover. **1927** The Patent Leather Kid; The Sea Tigers; An Affair of the Follies; Babe Comes Home; The Valley of the Giants; Hard Boiled Haggerty. **1928** Chicken a la King; The Farmer's Daughter; Me, Gangster; Burning Daylight. **1929** Thru Different Eyes; Captain Lash; The Far Call; Fugitives; New Year's Eve; Red Wine; Frozen Justice; Fox Movietone Follies of 1929. **1930** The Vagabond King; The Bad Man; Arizona Kid; On the Level; Mamba; Girl of the Golden West. **1931** The Lash; The Conquering Horde; Bad Company; The Secret Menace. **1932** The Big Shot; The Broken Wing; So Big; Roar of the Dragon; That's My Boy; plus the following shorts: The Girl in the Tonneau; Lady Please!; The Flirty Sleepwalker; The Line's Busy; Neighbor Trouble; Shopping With Wifie. **1934** She Had to Choose; I'll Tell the World; Love Birds. **1935** Bordertown; Charlie Chan in Egypt; Hot Tip. **1936** Fury. **1938** Go Chase Yourself.

STONE, DOROTHY
Born: June 3, 1905. Died: Sept. 24, 1974, Montecito, Calif. Screen, stage and vaudeville actress. Daughter of actor Fred Stone (dec. 1959) and sister of actresses Paula and Carol Stone.

Appeared in: **1924** Broadway After Dark. **1932** Smiling Faces. **1934** Paree, Paree. **1936** Revolt of the Zombies. **1938** A Universal short.

STONE, FRED
Born: Aug. 19, 1873, Denver, Colo. Died: Mar. 6, 1959, North Hollywood, Calif. Screen, stage, vaudeville and circus actor. Father of actresses Dorothy (dec. 1974), Paula and Carol Stone. Appeared in vaudeville as part of "Montgomery and Stone" team. Made a few western films for Lasky in 1917.

Appeared in: **1918** The Goat. **1919** Under the Top; Johnny Get Your Gun. **1921** The Duke of Chimney Butte. **1922** Billy Jim. **1924** Broadway After Dark. **1932** Smiling Faces. **1935** Alice Adams. **1936** The Trail of the Lonesome Pine; My American Wife; The Farmer in the Dell; Jury. **1937** Hideaway; Life Begins in College. **1938** Quick Money. **1939** No Place to Go. **1940** Konga, the Wild Stallion; The Westerner.

STONE, GEORGE
Born: 1877. Died: July 10, 1939, Baldwin, N.Y. Screen, stage and vaudeville actor. Married to actress Etta Pillard with whom he appeared in vaudeville. Do not confuse with actor George E. Stone (dec. 1967).

STONE, GEORGE E. (George Stein)
Born: May 1, 1904, Lodz, Poland. Died: May 26, 1967, Woodland Hills, Calif. (stroke). Screen, stage, vaudeville, and television actor. Known for gangster parts in "Boston Blackie" series and other films. Do not confuse with actor George Stone (dec. 1939).

Appeared in: **1918** 'Til I Come Back to You. **1921** Jackie; Penny of Top Hill Trail; The Whistle; White and Unmarried. **1923** The Fourth Musketeer. **1927** Seventh Heaven; Brass Knuckles. **1928** State Street Sadie; Tenderloin; The Racket; Walking Back; Beautiful But Dumb; Clothes Make the Woman; San Francisco Nights; Turn Back the Hours. **1929** Weary River; Skin Deep; Naughty Baby; The Girl in the Glass Cage; Two Men and a Maid; Melody Lane; Redeeming Sin. **1930** Under a Texas Moon; The Medicine Man; The Stronger Sex; So This Is Paris Green; Little Caesar. **1931** Cimrarron; Five-Star Final; The Spider; Sob Sister; The Front Page. **1932** The Last Mile; Taxi!; File No. 113; The Woman from Monte Carlo; The World and the Flesh; The Phantom of Crestwood; Slippery Pearls (short). **1933** King for a Night; Vampire Bat; Sailor Be Good!; Song of the Eagle; The Big Brain; Emergency Call; The Wrecker; Sing, Sinner, Sing; Ladies Must Love; Penthouse; He Couldn't Take It; 42nd Street. **1934** Return of the Terror; The Dragon Murder Case; Embarrassing Moments; Frontier Marshal; Viva Villa! **1935** Hold 'Em Yale; Public Hero No. 1; Make a Million; Moonlight on the Prairie; The Frisco Kid; One Hour Late; Secret of the Chateau; Million Dollar Baby. **1936** Man Hunt; Freshman Love; Jailbreak; Anthony Adverse; Bullets or Ballots; The Captain's Kid; Polo Joe; King of Hockey; Here Comes Carter!; Rhythm on the Range. **1937** Don't Get Me Wrong; Clothes and the Woman; Back in Circulation; The Adventurous Blonde. **1938** Alcatraz Island; A Slight Case of Murder; Over the Wall; Mr. Moto's Gamble; Submarine Patrol; The Long Shot; You and Me. **1939** You Can't Get Away With Murder; The Housekeeper's Daughter. **1940** The Night of Nights; I Take This Woman; Island of Doomed Men; Northwest Mounted Police; Slightly Tempted; Cherokee Strip. **1941** Broadway Limited; Last of the Duanes; His Girl Friday; Road Show; The Face Behind the Mask; Confessions of Boston Blackie. **1942** Lone Star Ranger; The Affairs of Jimmy Valentine; Little Tokyo, U.S.A.; The Devil with Hitler; Boston Blackie Goes to Hollywood. **1943** The Chance of a Lifetime; After Midnight with Boston Blackie. **1944** Roger Touhy—Gangster; Timber Queen; One Mysterious Night; Strangers in the Night; My Buddy. **1945** One Exciting Night; Boston Blackie's Rendezvous; Scared Stiff; Boston Blackie Booked on Suspicion; Doll Face. **1946** Boston Blackie and the Law; A Close Call for Boston Blackie; The Phantom Thief; Sentimental Journey; Suspense; Abie's Irish Rose. **1948** Trapped by Boston Blackie; Untamed Breed. **1950** Dancing in the Dark. **1952** A Girl in Every Port; Bloodhounds of Broadway. **1953** The Robe; Pickup on South Street; Combat Squad. **1954** Three Ring Circus; The Steel Cage; Broken Lance; The Miami Story. **1955** The Man With the Golden Arm; Guys and Dolls. **1956** Slightly Scarlet. **1957** Sierra Stranger; The Story of Mankind; The Tijuana Story; Baby Face Nelson; Calypso Heat Wave. **1959** Some Like It Hot. **1961** Pocketful of Miracles.

STONE, HARVEY
Born: 1913. Died: Mar. 4, 1974, Bridgetown, Barbados, West Indies (heart attack). Screen, stage, vaudeville and television actor. Married to actress Lois Lee.

STONE, JACK
Born: Nov. 26, 1906, London, England. Died: Apr. 8, 1962. Screen actor.

Appeared in: **1924** Traffic in Hearts. **1928** Lilac Time. **1929** Footlights and Fools.

STONE, JAMES F.
Born: 1901. Died: Jan. 9, 1969, Calif. Screen, stage and television actor.

Appeared in: **1953** The Glass Web; Gunsmoke; How to Marry a Millionaire. **1954** Black Widow; Broken Lance. **1956** The Scarlet Hour. **1967** Barefoot in the Park.

STONE, LEWIS (Louis Shepherd Stone)
Born: Nov. 15, 1878, Worcester, Mass. Died: Sept. 11, 1953, Los Angeles, Calif. (heart attack). Screen and stage actor. Married to stage actress Margaret Langham (dec.) and later married and divorced actress Florence Oakley (dec. 1956) and then married Hazel Wolf Hood. Best known for role as "Judge Hardy" in "Andy Hardy" film series. Nominated for 1928/29 Acadamy Award for Best Actor in The Patriot.

Appeared in: **1916** Honor Altar (film debut); The Havoc. **1918** Inside the Lines. **1920** Nomads of the North; The Concert; The River's End; Held by the Enemy; Milestones. **1921** The Northern Trail; The Golden

Snare; Beau Revel; Pilgrims of the Night; The Child Thou Gavest Me; Don't Neglect Your Wife. **1922** The Prisoner of Zenda; Trifling Women; A Fool There Was; The Rosary. **1923** Scaramouche; The Dangerous Age; You Can't Fool Your Wife. **1924** The Stranger; Why Men Leave Home; Husbands and Lovers; Inez from Hollywood; Cytherea; The Lost World. **1925** The Lady Who Lied; The Talker; Cheaper to Marry; Confessions of a Queen; What Fools Men; Fine Clothes. **1926** Don Juan's Three Nights; Too Much Money; Old Loves and New; Girl from Montmarte; Midnight Lover; The Blonde Saint. **1927** An Affair of the Follies; The Prince of Head Waiters; The Notorious Ladies; The Private Life of Helen of Troy. **1928** The Foreign Legion; Freedom of the Press; The Patriot; Inspiration. **1929** The Trial of Mary Dugan; A Woman of Affairs; Wild Orchids; The Circle; Wonder of Women; Madame X. **1930** Their Own Desire; Strictly Unconventional; The Big House; Romance; The Office Wife; Passion Flower; Father's Son. **1931** The Sin of Madelon Claudet; My Past; Inspiration; Always Goodbye; Phantom of Paris; The Bargain; Stolen Heaven; The Secret Six. **1932** Mata Hari; Grand Hotel; The Divorce in the Family; Unashamed; Wet Parade; Night Court; Letty Lynton; New Morals for Old; Red Headed Woman; The Son-Daughter; The Mask of Fu Manchu; Strange Interlude. **1933** The White Sister; Service; Looking Forward; Queen Christina; Bureau of Missing Persons; Men Must Fight. **1934** You Can't Buy Everything; The Girl from Missouri; Treasure Island; The Mystery of Mr. X. **1935** David Copperfield; Vanessa, Her Love Story; West Point of the Air; Public Hero No. 1; Woman Wanted; China Seas; Shipmates Forever. **1936** Three Godfathers; The Unguarded Hour; Small Town Girl; Sworn Enemy; Suzy; Don't Turn 'Em Loose. **1937** Outcast; The Thirteenth Chair; The Man Who Cried Wolf. **1938** You're Only Young Once; Bad Man of Brimstone; Judge Hardy's Children; Stolen Heaven; Love Finds Andy Hardy; Yellow Jack; The Chaser; Out West with the Hardys. **1939** Ice Follies of 1939; The Hardys Ride High; Andy Hardy Gets Spring Fever; Judge Hardy and Son; Joe and Ethel Turp Call on the President. **1940** Andy Hardy Meets Debutante; Sporting Blood. **1941** The Bugle Sounds; Andy Hardy's Private Secretary; Life Begins for Andy Hardy. **1942** The Courtship of Andy Hardy; Andy Hardy's Double Life. **1943** Plan for Destruction (short—narration). **1944** Andy Hardy's Blonde Trouble. **1946** Love Laughs at Andy Hardy; The Hoodlum Saint; Three Wise Fools. **1948** State of the Union. **1949** The Sun Comes Up; Any Number Can Play. **1950** Stars in My Crown; Key to the City. **1951** Grounds for Marriage; Night Into Morning; Angels in the Outfield; Bannerline; It's a Big Country; The Unknown Man. **1952** Just This Once; Talk About a Stranger; Scaramouche; The Prisoner of Zenda (and 1922 version). **1953** All the Brothers Were Valiant. **1964** Big Parade of Comedy (documentary).

STONE, MAXINE

Born: 1910. Died: Nov. 20, 1964, Hollywood, Calif. Screen, stage and vaudeville actress. Appeared in vaudeville with her husband Benny Ross in act called "Ross and Stone."

Appeared in: Early Vitaphone shorts. **1958** South Seas Adventure.

STONE, MILBURN

Born: July 5, 1904, Burton, Kans. Died: June 12, 1980, La Jolla, Calif. (heart attack). Screen, stage, vaudeville, radio and television actor. Appeared in vaudeville in an act billed as "Stone and Strain."

Appeared in: **1934** Ladies Crave Excitement (film debut). **1936** The Milky Way; The Princess Comes Across; Two in a Crowd; China Clipper; The Three Mesquiteers. **1937** A Doctor's Diary; The Thirteenth Man; The Man in Blue; Youth on Parole; Atlantic Flight; Swing It Professor; Federal Bullets; Blazing Barriers. **1938** Port of Missing Girls; Mr. Boggs Steps Out; Wives Under Suspicion; Sinners in Paradise; Crime School; Paroled from the Big House; California Frontier. **1939** Blind Alley; Tail Spin; Mystery Plane; King of the Turf; Society Smugglers; Young Mr. Lincoln; Stunt Pilot; Tropic Fury; Sky Patrol; Danger Flight; Nick Carter—Master Detective; Charlie McCarthy—Detective; Crashing Thru. **1940** Bullets for Rustlers; Chasing Trouble; Enemy Agent; An Angel from Texas; Framed; Colorado; The Great Plane Robbery; Give Us Wings. **1941** The Phantom Cowboy; The Great Train Robbery; Death Valley Outlaws. **1942** Frisco Lil; Reap the Wild Wind; Rubber Racketeers. **1943** Gung Ho!; Sherlock Holmes Faces Death; Corvette K-225; Get Going; Captive Wild Woman; Keep 'Em Slugging; You Can't Beat the Law. **1944** The Great Alaskan Mystery (serial); Twilight on the Prairie; Jungle Woman; Moon Over Las Vegas; Hat Check Honey; Hi, Good Lookin'; The Imposter. **1945** The Master Key (serial); The Royal Mounted Rides Again (serial); She Gets Her Man; I'll Remember April; Swing Out, Sister; The Frozen Ghost; On Stage Everybody; The Beautiful Cheat; The Daltons Ride Again; Strange Confession. **1946** The Spider Woman Strikes Back; Inside Job; Smooth as Silk; Strange Conquest; Danger Woman; Little Miss Big; Her Adventurous Night. **1947** Michigan Kid; Killer Dill; Heading for Heaven. **1948** Train to

Alcatraz. **1949** The Judge; The Green Promise; Sky Dragon; Calamity Jane and Sam Bass. **1950** No Man of Her Own; The Fireball; Snow Dog; Branded. **1951** Roadblock. **1952** The Savage; The Atomic City. **1953** Second Chance; Arrowhead; The Sun Shines Bright; Pickup on South Street. **1954** Black Tuesday; Siege at Red River. **1955** The Private War of Major Benson; Smoke Signal; White Feather; The Long Gray Line. **1957** Drango.

STONE, MRS. ROBERT E.

Died: Nov. 5, 1916. Screen actress.

STONEHOUSE, RUTH

Born: Oct. 24, 1893. Died: May 12, 1941, Hollywood, Calif. Screen and stage actress. Was part owner with Billy Anderson of the Essanay Studios in Chicago.

Appeared in: **1911** The Papered Door. **1912** Twilight; The End of the Feud; Sunshine; Mr. Hubby's Wife; The Shadow of the Cross Chains; From the Submerged. **1913** The Spy's Defeat; Homespun; The World Above; In Convict Garb. **1914** The Romance of an American Duchess; Blood Will Tell; Nighthawks; The Real Agatha; Let No Man Escape; The Counter-Melody; The Fable of Lutie, the False Alarm; Mother O'Dreams; White Lies; The Darling Young Person; The Other Girl. **1916** The Adventures of Peg O' the Ring (serial). **1919** The Masked Rider (serial); The Master Mystery (serial). **1920** Parlor, Bedroom and Bath. **1921** I Am Guilty; Don't Call Me Little Girl. **1923** Lights Out; The Flash; Flames of Passion; The Way of the Transgressor. **1924** A Girl of the Limberlost; Broken Barriers. **1925** Blood and Steel; The Fugitive; Rough Going; Ermine and Rhinestones; Fifth Avenue Model; The Scarlet West; Straight Through; A Two-Fisted Sheriff. **1926** Broken Homes; The Wives of the Prophet. **1927** Poor Girls; The Ladybird; The Satin Woman. **1928** The Ape; The Devil's Cage.

STOOPNAGLE, COLONEL LEMUEL Q. (F. Chase Taylor)

Born: Oct. 4, 1897, Buffalo, N.Y. Died: May 29, 1950. Screen and radio actor. Was part of radio team of "Stoopnagle and Budd."

Appeared in: **1933** International House. **1934** An Educational short. **1963** The Sound of Laughter (documentary).

STORDAHL, ALEX

Born: Aug. 8, 1913, Staten Island, N.Y. Died: Aug. 30, 1963, Encino, Calif. Bandleader, composer and screen actor. Married to vocalist June Hutton (dec. 1973).

STOREY, HELEN

Born: 1903. Died: Apr. 26, 1935, Chicago, Ill. Screen and stage actress. Divorced from actors Sailor Bill Dooley, and Billy Glason.

STORY, EDITH

Born: Mar. 18, 1892. Screen actress.

Appeared in: **1911** Fighting Schoolmaster. **1912** Old Love Letters; The Scoop; The French Spy; The Telephone Girl; The Call; The Lady of the Lake. **1913** The Prince of Evil; The Chains of Oath. **1914** The Christian. **1915** Island of Regeneration; The Dust of Egypt; A Queen for an Hour. **1916** The Tarantula; An Enemy of the Queen. **1917** The Captain of the Gray Horse Troop; Money Magic. **1918** The Eyes of Mystery (aka The House in the Mist); Revenge; The Claim; Treasure of the Sea; The Demon; The Legion of Death; The Silent Woman; The Price of Folly (serial); Mr. Aladdin from Broadway. **1919** As the Sun Went Down. **1920** Moon Madness. **1921** Beach of Dreams; Souls for Sables.

STOSSEL, LUDWIG

Born: Feb. 12, 1883, Austria. Died: Jan. 29, 1973, Beverly Hills, Calif. Screen, stage, television actor, stage director and producer. Married to actress Eleanore Stossel.

Appeared in: **1931** Bockbierfest; Scandal Um Eva; Elisabeth von Oesterreich. **1934** Strich Durch die Rechnung; In Wien Hab' Ich Einmal ein Maedel Geliebt. **1939** O Schwarzwald, O Heimat (Oh Black Forest, Oh Home). **1940** Four Sons; The Man I Married; Jennie; Dance, Girl, Dance. **1941** Man Hunt; Underground; Great Guns; Marry the Boss's Daughter. **1942** All Through the Night; Woman of the Year; The Pride of the Yankees; Iceland; Casablanca; Who Done It; The Great Impersonation; Pittsburgh. **1943** They Came to Blow Up America; Action in the North Atlantic; Hers to Hold; Hitler's Hangman (aka Hitler's Madman); The Strange Death of Adolf Hitler; Above Suspicion. **1944** The Climax; Bluebeard. **1945** Lake Placid Serenade; Dillinger; Her Highness and the Bellboy; House of Dracula; Yolanda and the Thief; Miss Susie Slagle's. **1946** Cloak and Dagger; Temptation; Girl on the Spot. **1947** The Beginning of the End; Song of Love; Escape Me Never; This Time for Keeps. **1948** A Song Is Born. **1949** The Great Sinner. **1951** As Young as You Feel; Corky of

Gasoline Alley. **1952** The Merry Widow; No Time for Flowers; Somebody Loves Me. **1953** Call Me Madam; White Goddess; The Sun Shines Bright; Geraldine. **1958** Me and the Colonel; From the Earth to the Moon. **1959** The Blue Angel. **1960** G.I. Blues.

STOUT, ROYAL G.
Born: 1874. Died: Apr. 2, 1958, Wilkes-Barre, Pa. (heart attack). Screen and stage actor.

Appeared in: **1930** Royal Family of Broadway.

STOWE, LESLIE
Born: 1886, Homer, La. Died: July 16, 1949, Englewood, N.J. Screen and stage actor.

Appeared in: **1916** The Closed Road. **1917** The Adopted Son. **1918** Social Quicksands. **1919** Bolshevism on File; The Carter Case (The Craig Kennedy serial). **1920** The Copperhead. **1921** The Good-Bad Wife; Peggy Puts It Over. **1922** No Trespassing; The Seventh Day. **1923** Columbus; Driven; Jamestown; Second Fiddle. **1924** The Fifth Horseman; Tongues of Flame. **1929** Mother's Boy.

STOWELL, CLARENCE W.
Born: 1878. Died: Nov. 26, 1940, Paterson, N.J. Screen actor.

Appeared in: **1940** The Ramparts We Watch (March of Time's first full-length feature).

STOWELL, WILLIAM H.
Born: Mar. 13, 1885, Boston, Mass. Died: Dec., 1919, Elizabethville, South Africa (train accident). Screen, stage actor and opera performer. Entered films in 1909.

Appeared in: **1911** Two Orphans. **1912** Hypnotized; Sons of the Northwoods; The Redemption of Greek Joe; The Devil, the Servant and the Man; As the Fates Decree; A War Time Romance; The House of His Master; An International Romance; The Fire-Fighters Love; A Freight Train Drama. **1913** A False Order; The Clue; The Water Rat; The Ex-Convict; A Change of Administration; The Pendulum of Fate; Dixieland; The Devil and Tom Walker; The Ex-Convict's Plunge. **1914** In the Line of Duty; When a Woman's Forty. **1915** The Old Code; The Gentleman Burglar; The Strength of Samson; The Great Question; The End of the Road; The Tragic Circle; Hartley Merwin's Adventure; The Buzzard's Shadow; Pardoned. **1916** The Other Side of the Door; The Secret Wire; The Gamble; The Man in the Sombrero; Overalls; Lillo of the Sulu Seas; The Blindness; The Overcoat; The Lover Hermit; The Release of Dan Forbes; The Sheriff of Plumas. **1917** Fires of Rebellion; Triumph; The Piper's Price; Bondage; The Flashlight Girl; A Doll's House; Hell Morgan's Girl; The Girl in the Checkered Coat; Fighting Mad. **1918** The Heart of Humanity; The Grand Passion; Broadway Love; The Risky Road. **1919** When a Girl Loves; Paid in Advance. **1920** The Man Who Dared God.

STRADNER, ROSE
Born: July 31, 1913, Vienna, Austria. Died: Sept 27, 1958, Bedford Village, N.Y. Stage and screen actress. Married to director Joseph L. Mankiewicz.

Appeared in: **1934** Ein Gewisser Herr Gran; Hochzeit am Wolfgangsee. **1936** One Hundred Days of Napoleon. **1937** The Postillion of Lonjumeau. **1938** The Last Gangster. **1939** Blind Alley. **1944** The Keys of the Kingdom.

STRANDMARK, ERIK
Born: 1919, Torsaker, Sweden. Died: 1963, Sweden. Screen, stage actor and writer.

Appeared in: **1955** The People of Hemso. **1956** Unmarried Mothers; Children of the Night. **1958** The Seventh Seal; Med Mord I Bagaget (No Time to Kill—US 1963). Other Swedish films: The Invisible Wall; We Need Each Other; The Royal Rabble; Rolling Sea; U-Boat 39; Love; Barabbas; The Road to Klockrike; Sawdust and Tinsel (aka The Naked Night); Hidden in the Fog; Possessed by Speed; Victory in Darkness; Karin Mansdotter; Salka Valka; Wild Birds; No One Is Crazier Than I Am; Kulla-Gulla; The Tough Game; Girl in a Dress Coat; Little Fridolf and I; Stage Entrance; The Way Via Ska; Tarps Elin; Encounters at Dusk; Lights at Night; The Master Detective Leads a Dangerous Life; The Clergyman from Uddarbo; Nothin' But Bones; Woman in a Leapardskin; We on Vaddo; Beautiful Susan and the Old Men.

STRANG, HARRY
Died: Apr. 10, 1972. Screen actor.

Appeared in: **1930** Aroung the Corner; Hell's Angels. **1931** Hell Bound. **1933** Lady Killer. **1935** Air Hawks. **1936** The Prisoner of Shark

Island. **1937** Stage Door; Zorro Rides Again (serial). **1938** The Purple Vigilantes; Two Gun Justice; Submarine Patrol. **1939** The Return of the Cisco Kid; Mr. Moto in Danger Island; Mr. Moto Takes a Vacation; Gone With the Wind. **1940** The Grapes of Wrath; Gaucho Serenade; Calling Philo Vance; Kit Carson. **1941** Buck Privates; The Phantom Submarine; Manpower; Love Crazy; I Wake Up Screaming. **1942** Who Done It?; My Gal Sal. **1943** It Ain't Hay; Hit the Ice; The Lone Star Trail; Gung Ho!; So Proudly We Hail; Thousands Cheer. **1944** Laura; See Here, Private Hargrove. **1945** Manhunt of Mystery Island (serial). **1946** King of the Forest Rangers (serial); Centennial Summer. **1948** Silver River; Sinister Journey. **1949** White Heat. **1950** When Willie Comes Marching Home. **1957** Looking for Danger. **1958** Toughest Gun in Tombstone. **1959** North By Northwest.

STRANGE, GLENN (George Glenn Strange)
Born: Aug. 16, 1899, New Mexico. Died: Sept. 20, 1973, Burbank, Calif. (cancer). Screen, radio, television actor, rodeo performer, professional heavyweight boxer and stuntman. Entered films as a stuntman.

Appeared in: **1932** Hurricane Express (serial). **1935** New Frontier; House of Frankenstein. **1937** Arizona Days; Adventure's End. **1938** Black Bandit; The Painted Trail; Pride of the West; In Old Mexico; The Mysterious Rider; Sunset Trail; Border Wolves The Last Stand; Gun Packer; Call of the Rockies. **1939** Rough Riders' Round-Up; Blue Montana Skies; Range War; Law of the Pampas; Overland Mail; The Llano Kid; Days of Jesse James; The Fighting Gringo; Arizona Legion; Cupid Rides the Range; The Lone Ranger Rides Again (serial). **1940** Land of Six Guns; Pioneer Days; Rhythm of the Rio Grande; Pals of the Silver Sage; Covered Wagon Trails; Stage to Chino; Triple Justice; Wagon Train; Three Men from Texas; Cowboy from Sundown; Fargo Kid. **1941** Riders of Death Valley (serial); Arizona Cyclone; San Francisco Docks; Saddlemates; Wide Open Town; The Kid's Last Ride; The Bandit Trail; Dude Cowboy; Badlands of Dakota; Fugitive Valley; The Driftin' Kid; Billy the Kid Wanted; Billy the Kid's Roundup; Come on, Danger!; In Old Colorado; Westward Ho-Hum (short). **1942** Billy the Kid Trapped; Sunset on the Desert; Romance on the Range; The Mad Monster; Down Texas Way; Little Joe—The Wrangler; Stagecoach Buckaroo; The Ghost of Frankenstein; The Mummy's Tomb. **1943** The Kid Rides Again; The Desperadoes; Wild Horse Stampede; Mission to Moscow; Black Market Rustlers; False Colors; The Woman of the Town. **1944** The Return of the Rangers; The Monster Maker; Silver City Kid; Arizona Trail; The Contender; Forty Thieves; Sonora Stagecoach; Valley of Vengeance; Trail to Gunsight; The San Antonio Kid. **1945** Saratoga Trunk; House of Frankenstein; House of Dracula; Renegades of the Rio Grande. **1946** Beauty and the Bandit. **1947** Brute Force; The Wistful Widow of Wagon Gap; Frontier Fighters. **1948** Abbott and Costello Meet Frankenstein; The Far Frontier; Silver Trails; Red River. **1949** Master Minds; Rimfire; Roll Thunder Roll. **1950** Comanche Territory; Double Crossbones. **1951** Vengeance Valley; Comin' Round the Mountain; Texas Carnival; Red Badge of Courage. **1952** The Lusty Men; The Lawless Breed. **1953** The Veils of Bagdad; The Great Sioux Uprising. **1955** The Vanishing American; The Road to Denver. **1957** Gunfire At Indian Gap; Last Stagecoach West. **1958** Quantrill's Raiders. **1959** Last Train from Gun Hill.

STRANGE, ROBERT
Born: 1882. Died: Feb. 22, 1952, Hollywood, Calif. Screen and stage actor.

Appeared in: **1931** The Smiling Lieutenant; The Cheat. **1932** The Misleading Lady. **1934** These Thirty Years; Gambling. **1935** Special Agent; I Found Stella Parish; Frisco Kid. **1936** The Story of Louis Pasteur; The Murder of Dr. Harrigan; The Walking Dead; Stolen Holiday; Trapped by Television; Beloved Enemy. **1937** Beware of Ladies; John Meade's Woman; Marked Woman. **1938** Sky Giant; I Stand Accused. **1939** In Name Only; They Made Me a Criminal; Hell's Kitchen; The Saint Strikes Back; The Story of Vernon and Irene Castle; The Spellbinder; Angels Wash Their Faces. **1940** The Castle on the Hudson; Dr. Ehrlich's Magic Bullet; King of the Royal Mounted. **1941** Manpower; The Adventures of Captain Marvel (serial); Robin Hood of the Pecos; High Sierra; All That Money Can Buy. **1942** Arizona Cyclone; Perils of Nyaka (serial); The Yukon Patrol. **1949** Flamingo Road. **1952** The Devil and Daniel Webster (reissue and retitle of All That Money Can Buy—1941).

STRANGIS, JANE
Born: 1932. Died: Jan. 25, 1966, Hollywood, Calif. (leukemia). Screen and television actress.

STRASSBERG, MORRIS
Born: 1898. Died: Feb. 8, 1974, South Laguna Beach, Calif. Screen, stage and television actor.

Appeared in: **1926** Broken Hearts. **1938** Power of Life. **1939** Tevya. **1950** With These Hands. **1970** The Way We Live Now. **1971** Klute.

STRATTEN, DOROTHY R. (Dorothy Hoogstraten)
Born: 1960, Vancouver, British Columbia, Canada. Died: Aug. 15, 1980, West Los Angeles, Calif. (murdered—shot). Screen actress and model. Playboy magazine's 1980 "Playmate of the Year."

Appeared in: **1979** Americathon; Skatetown, U.S.A. **1980** Galaxina; They All Laughed.

STRATTON, CHESTER "CHET"
Born: 1913. Died: July 7, 1970, Los Angeles, Calif. Screen, stage and radio actor.

Appeared in: **1937** A Vitaphone short. **1953** Julius Caesar. **1961** All Hands on Deck; Go Naked in the World. **1962** Lover Come Back; Advise and Consent. **1965** In Harm's Way; Those Calloways; Bus Riley's Back in Town; The Greatest Story Ever Told. **1968** Track of Thunder; Journey to Shiloh; If He Hollers Let Him Go. **1969** Sweet Charity.

STRATTON, HARRY
Born: 1898. Died: Aug. 19, 1955, Hollywood, Calif. (heart attack). Screen and burlesque actor. Stand-in for Bud Abbott.

STRAUB, MARY E.
Born: 1884. Died: Nov. 7, 1951, Hollywood, Calif. Screen actress.

STRAUKH, MIXIM
Born: 1900, Russia. Died: Dec., 1973, Moscow, Russia. Screen actor.

Appeared in: **1944** Two Soldiers. **1958** Leningradskaya Symphonia (Leningrad Symhony).

STRAUSS, CLEMENT (aka CLEMENCE STRAUSS)
Born: Sept. 27, 1886, New York. Died: Aug. 8, 1915, Hollywood, Calif. (tuberculosis). Screen actor.

STRAUSS, ROBERT
Born: Nov. 8, 1913, New York, N.Y. Died: Feb. 20, 1975, New York, N.Y. (complications from a stroke). Screen, stage and television actor. Nominated for 1953 Academy Award for Best Supporting Actor in Stalag 17.

Appeared in: **1937** Marked Woman. **1942** Native Land. **1951** Sailor Beware (aka At Sea with the Navy). **1952** Jumping Jacks; The Redhead from Wyoming. **1953** Here Come the Girls; Act of Love; Money from Home; Stalag 17 (stage and film versions). **1954** The Atomic Kid. **1955** The Bridges of Toko-Ri; The Seven Year Itch; The Man With the Golden Arm. **1956** Attack! **1958** Frontier Gun; I, Mobster. **1959** Inside the Mafia; Li'l Abner; 4D Man. **1960** Wake Me When It's Over; September Storm. **1961** Twenty Plus Two; The George Raft Story; The Last Time I Saw Archie; Dondi. **1962** Girls! Girls! Girls! **1963** The Thrill of It All; The Wheeler Dealers. **1964** Stage to Thunder Rock. **1965** The Family Jewels; Harlow; That Funny Feeling. **1966** Frankie and Johnny; Movie Star, American Style or—LSD, I Hate You. **1967** Fort Utah.

STRAUSS, WILLIAM H.
Born: June 13, 1885, New York, N.Y. Died: Aug. 5, 1943, Hollywood, Calif. (heart attack). Screen, stage, vaudeville actor and stage director.

Appeared in: **1920** North Wind's Malice. **1921** Magic Cup; The Barricade. **1922** Other Women's Clothes. **1923** Solomon in Society. **1925** Skinner's Dress Suit. **1926** Private Izzy Murphy; Law of the Snow Country; Millionaires. **1927** Ankles Preferred; For Ladies Only; Sally in Our Alley; The Shamrock and the Rose; The Rawhide Kid; Ladies at Ease; Ragtime; King of Kings; The Show Girl. **1928** So This Is Love; Abie's Irish Rose. **1929** Smiling Irish Eyes; Lucky Boy. **1930** Jazz Cinderella. **1931** The Public Enemy. **1933** Hard to Handle. **1934** Beloved; The House of Rothschild. **1938** Golden Boy.

STREET, DAVID
Born: 1917, Los Angeles, Calif. Died: Sept. 3, 1971, Los Angeles, Calif. Screen, radio, television actor, orchestra leader and singer. Divorced from actress Debra Paget.

Appeared in: **1943** We've Never Been Licked. **1949** Moonrise. **1950** Holiday Rhythm.

STREET, GEORGE A.
Born: 1869, Montreal, Canada. Died: May 30, 1956, Weston-Super-Mare, England. Screen actor and Wild West showman.

STREET, JULIAN
Born: 1880, Chicago, Ill. Died: Feb. 19, 1947, Lakeville, Conn. (cerebral hemorrhage). Novelist and screen actor.

Appeared in: **1913** Saved by Parcel Post.

STRICKLAND, HELEN
Born: 1863. Died: Jan., 1938, New York, N.Y. Screen and stage actress. Married to actor Robert Conness (dec. 1941).

Appeared in: **1915** Where Is My Wandering Boy Tonight?; Clive's Manufactured Mother. **1923** The Steadfast Heart. **1935** The Scoundrel.

STRICKLAND, MABEL
Born: 1897. Died: Jan. 3, 1976. World champion rodeo performer and screen actress.

Appeared in: **1936** Rhythm on the Range.

STRIKER, JOSEPH
Born: 1900, New York, N.Y. Died: Feb. 24, 1974, Livingston, N.J. Screen and stage actor.

Appeared in: **1920** The Bromley Case; Wall St. Mystery. **1921** Help Yourself; The Matrimonial Web. **1922** The Broadway Peacock; Silver Wings; Queen of the Moulin Rouge; Wildness of Youth; What Fools Men Are. **1923** The Steadfast Heart; The Woman in Chains. **1924** Painted People; I Am the Man. **1925** Scandal Proof; The Best People. **1927** Annie Laurie; The Climbers; The Cradle Snatchers; A Harp in Hock; The Wise Wife; King of Kings. **1928** Paradise; The Wrecker (US 1929). **1929** The House of Secrets.

STRODE, LUUKIALUANA
Born: 1917. Died: Sept. 17, 1980, Woodland Hills, Calif. (Parkinson's disease). Screen actress and extra. Married to actor Woody Strode.

STRONG, CARL E.
Born: 1907. Died: Jan. 14, 1965, Minneapolis, Minn. Screen, circus, television actor and rodeo rider.

STRONG, FRED
Died: 1938. Screen actor.

Appeared in: **1928** Passion Play.

STRONG, JAY
Born: 1896. Died: Dec. 1, 1953, New York, N.Y. Screen, vaudeville actor, stage producer, stage director, television writer, director and producer.

Appeared in: **1919** The Moonshine Trail.

STRONG, LEONARD (Leonard Clarence Strong)
Born: Aug. 12, 1908, Utah. Died: Jan. 23, 1980, Glendale, Calif. Screen and television actor.

Appeared in: **1942** Little Tokyo, USA. **1943** Bombardier; Behind the Rising Sun. **1944** Jack London; The Keys of the Kingdom. **1945** Blood on the Sun; First Yank Into Tokyo; Back to Bataan. **1946** Anna and the King of Siam. **1947** Dangerous Millions; Backlash; Jewels of Brandenburg. **1948** Sword of the Avenger. **1949** We Were Strangers. **1950** Backfire; Cargo to Capetown. **1952** The Atomic City. **1953** Scared Stiff; Shane; Destination Gobi. **1954** The Naked Jungle; Hell's Half Acre; Prisoner of War. **1955** Cult of the Cobra. **1956** The King and I. **1958** Jet Attack. **1962** Escape from Zahrain.

STRONG, MICHAEL
Died: Sept. 17, 1980, Los Angeles, Calif. (cancer). Screen, stage and television actor.

Appeared in: **1951** Detective Story. **1966** Dead Heat on a Merry-Go-Round. **1967** Point Blank. **1970** Patton. **1980** The Great Santini.

STRONG, PORTER
Born: 1879, St. Joseph, Mo. Died: June 11, 1923, New York, N.Y. Screen and stage actor.

Appeared in: **1915** Safety First. **1916** The Little Life Guard; Martha's Vindication; For Sweet Charity; Ham Agrees with Sherman. **1917** Brainstorm; Even as Him and Her. **1919** A Romance of Happy Valley; I'll Get Him Yet. **1920** Way Down East; The Idol Dancer; Flying Pat. **1921** Dream Street; The Ghost in the Garret. **1922** One Exciting Night. **1923** The White Rose.

STRONG, STEVE
Died: July 14, 1975. Screen actor.

STRONGHEART
Born: 1916, Berlin, Germany. Died: June 24, 1929, Los Angeles, Calif. Screen animal performer (German Shepherd). Mate of "Lady Jule."

Appeared in: **1921** The Silent Call (film debut). **1922** Brawn of the North. **1924** The Love Master. **1925** White Fang. **1926** North Star. **1927** The Return of Boston Blackie.

STROUD, CLARENCE
Born: 1907, Kaufman, Tex. Died: Aug. 15, 1973, Dallas, Tex. (Guillain-Barre syndrome). Screen, vaudeville, radio, television actor and circus performer. Appeared with his twin brother Claude in an act billed as the "Stroud Twins." Father of actor Don Stroud.

Appeared in: **1933** Ace of Aces.

STRYKER, GUSTAVE
Born: 1866, Chicago, Ill. Died: June 3, 1943, New York, N.Y. Screen, stage and radio actor.

STUART, DONALD
Born: 1898, England. Died: Feb. 22, 1944, Hollywood, Calif. (heart attack). Screen and radio actor.

Appeared in: **1926** Beau Geste; Bride of the Storm. **1927** The Lone Eagle; Marriage. **1928** The Cheer Leader; The Girl-Shy Cowboy; The Olympic Hero; Interference. **1929** The Silver King. **1939** Derelict. **1931** Devotion. **1932** In a Monastery Garden; The Man from Yesterday; Cynara. **1933** The Invisible Man; The Woman Accused. **1934** Dancing Man. **1935** First a Girl. **1941** A Yank in the R.A.F. **1942** Eagle Squadron; Destination Unknown. **1943** Immortal Sergeant. **1944** The Hour Before the Dawn; The Canterville Ghost.

STUART, GIL (Gilchrist Stuart)
Born: 1919, London, England. Died: June 8, 1977, Hollywood, Calif. (cancer). Screen, stage and television actor.

Appeared in: **1953** Botany Bay; King of the Khyber Rifles. **1962** Mutiny on the Bounty. **1965** The Sound of Music; Morituri. **1967** Dr. Dolittle.

STUART, IRIS
Born: 1903. Died: 1936. Screen actress. Was a Wampas Baby Star of 1927.

Appeared in: **1926** Stranded in Paris. **1927** Casey at the Bat; Wedding Bills; Children of Divorce.

STUART, JEAN (Margaret Leisenring)
Born: 1904. Died: Nov. 23, 1926, Hollywood, Calif. (injuries from a fall from a horse). Screen actress.

Appeared in: **1926** The Campus Flirt.

STUART, JOHN (John Croall)
Born: July 18, 1898, Edinburgh, Scotland. Died: Oct. 18, 1979, London, England. Screen and stage actor.

Appeared in: **1920** Her Son (film debut); The Lights of Home; The Great Gay Road. **1921** Leaves from My Life series; Film Song Album series including: Eileen Alannah; Sally in Our Alley; Home Sweet Home. **1922** The Little Mother; Sinister Street; If Four Walls Told; A Sporting Double; The Sporting Twelve series including The Extra Knot. **1923** Little Miss Nobody; The School for Scandal; The Reverse of the Medal; Constant Hot Water; The Loves of Mary, Queen of Scots (aka Marie, Queen of Scots); This Freedom; Gems of Literature series including The Mistletoe Bough. **1924** His Grace Gives Notice; The Gayest of the Gay (aka Her Redemption); The Alley of Golden Hearts. **1925** A Daughter of Love; We Women; Venetian Lovers; Twisted Tales series including Parted. **1926** London Love; Mademoiselle from Armentieres; The Pleasure Garden; The Steve Donoghue series including: Baddesley Manor—The Phantom Gambler; Kenilworth Castle; Amy Rossart and the Tower of London; The Daily Mirror Competition Films series including Curfew Shall Not Ring Tonight; Screen Playlets series including: Back to the Trees; The Woman Juror. **1927** Roses of Picardy; Hindle Wakes (aka Fanny Hawthorne—US 1929); The Glad Eye; The Flight Commander; A Woman in Pawn. **1928** Sailors Don't Care; Mademoiselle Parley Voo; Smashing Through. **1929** High Seas; Taxi for Two; Kitty; Atlantic; Memories (short). **1930** Children of Chance; Kissing Cup's Race; No Exit; Eve's Fall; The Brat (aka The Nipper). **1931** Midnight; The Hound of the Baskervilles; Hindle Wakes (and 1927 version). **1932** In a Monastery Garden; Number Seventeen; Verdict of the Sea; Men of Steel; Little Fella; Women Are That Way (short). **1933** Naughty Cinderella; Mr. Quincey of Monte Carlo; The Lost Chord; Love's Old Sweet Song; This Week of Grace; Head of the Family; Home Sweet Home; Mayfair Girl; Enemy of the Police; The Wandering Jew (US 1935); The Pointing Finger; The House of Trent. **1934** Four Masked Men; The Black Abbot; Grand Prix; Bella Donna (US 1935); Blind Justice; The Blue Squadron; The Green Pack. **1935** Abdul the Damned; Royal Cavalcade (aka Regal Cavalcade—US); D'ye Ken John Peel? (aka Captain Moonlight—US); Once a Thief; Lend Me Your Husband. **1936** The Secret Voice; Reasonable Doubt. **1937** The Elder Brother; The Show Goes On; Pearls Bring Tears; Talking Feet. **1938** The

Claydon Treasure Mystery. **1940** Old Mother Riley in Society. **1941** Old Mother Riley's Ghosts; Ships With Wings (US 1942); The Seventh Survivor; Penn of Pennsylvania (aka The Courageous Mr. Penn—US 1944); Banana Ridge; The Missing Million; Hard Steel; The Big Blockade; Women Aren't Angels. **1943** Headline. **1944** Madonna of the Seven Moons. **1945** Camera Reflections (narrator). **1947** Mrs. Fitzherbert (US 1950); Mine Own Executioner (US 1949); The Phantom Shot. **1948** House of Darkness; Escape from Broadmoor. **1949** Third Time Lucky (US 1950); The Man from Yesterday; Man on the Run (US 1951); The Temptress. **1951** The Magic Box (US 1952); Mr. Denning Drives North (US 1953). **1952** What Shall It Profit (reissue of Hard Steel, 1942); The Ringer; To the Rescue (short). **1953** Street Corner; Four Sided Triangle. **1954** Front Page Story (US 1955); Men of Sherwood Forest (US 1956). **1955** The Gilded Cage. **1956** Tons of Trouble; Johnny, You're Wanted; It's a Great Day; Eyewitness; Alias John Preston. **1957** The Naked Truth (aka Your Past Is Showing—US 1958); Quatermass II (aka Enemy from Space—US). **1958** The Revenge of Frankenstein; Blood of the Vampire; The Secret Man. **1959** Too Many Crooks; The Mummy. **1960** Sink the Bismarck!; Village of the Damned. **1963** The Scarlet Blade (aka The Crimson Blade—US 1964); Paranoiac. **1967** Son of the Sahara. **1972** Young Winston. **1978** Superman, The Movie.

STUART, NICK (Nicholas Pratza)
Born: Apr. 10, 1904, Rumania. Died: Apr. 7, 1973, Biloxi, Miss. (cancer). Screen actor and bandleader. Divorced from actress Sue Carol. Married to Martha Burnett.

Appeared in: **1927** The High School Hero; Cradle Snatchers. **1928** The News Parade; The River Pirate; Why Sailors Go Wrong. **1929** Girls Gone Wild; Why Leave Home; Gold Diggers of Broadway; Happy Days; Joy Street. **1930** Swing High; The Fourth Alarm; Honeymoon Zeppelin; plus the following shorts: Radio Kisses; Hello Television; Goodbye Legs; Campus Crushes; Grandma's Girl. **1931** Sheer Luck; Mystery Train; Sundown Trail. **1933** Secret Sinners; Police Call. **1934** Demon for Trouble. **1935** Secrets of Chinatown. **1936** Rio Grande Romance; Underworld Terror; Put on the Spot. **1937** Blake of Scotland Yard (serial). **1938** An RKO short. **1952** Blackhawk (serial); King of the Congo (serial). **1953** The Great Adventures of Captain Kidd (serial); The Lost Planet (serial); Killer Ape. **1957** High Tide at Noon. **1958** High Hell. **1959** The Sheriff of Fractured Jaw. **1962** We Joined the Navy; The Longest Day. **1963** It's a Mad, Mad, Mad, Mad World. **1966** This Property Is Condemned.

STUART, RALPH R.
Born: 1890. Died: Nov. 4, 1952, New York, N.Y. Screen, stage actor and stage director. Married to actress Doris Rich.

Appeared in: **1917** The Mystery of the Double Cross (serial).

STUART-FIFE, T.
Born: 1903. Died: Jan. 11, 1981, Woodland Hills, Calif. Screen, television actor and talent agent.

STUBBS, HARRY (Harry Oakes Stubbs)
Born: Sept. 7, 1874, England. Died: Mar. 9, 1950, Woodland Hills, Calif. (heart attack). Screen, stage actor, dialogue director and screenwriter.

Appeared in: **1929** Alibi (film debut); The Locked Door; Three Live Ghosts. **1930** Abraham Lincoln; The Bad One; Ladies Must Play; The Truth About Youth; Night Ride. **1931** Gang Buster; Stepping Out; Millie; Fanny Foley Herself; Her Majesty Love. **1932** The Man Who Played God; Mind Reader; When Strangers Marry. **1934** Now and Forever. **1935** Spanish Cape Mystery. **1936** Sutter's Gold; The Girl from Mandalay; The Man I Marry. **1937** On the Avenue; London by Night; Love and Hisses. **1938** In Old Chicago; Dr. Rhythm; Peck's Bad Boy with the Circus; I Stand Accused; Blockheads. **1940** Adventure in Diamond; Zanzibar; The Invisible Man Returns; The Mummy's Hand. **1941** The Singing Hill; Burma Convoy; The Wolf Man. **1943** Frankenstein Meets the Wolf Man. **1944** The Invisible Man's Revenge.

STUDEBAKER, HUGH
Born: 1901, Ridgeville, Ind. Died: May 26, 1978, Los Angeles, Calif. Screen and radio actor.

STUEWE, HANS (aka HANS STUWE)
Born: 1901, Germany. Died: June, 1976, Berlin, Germany. Screen actor.

Appeared in: **1929** Pawns of Passion. **1930** Because I Loved You; Hungarian Nights; Caught in Berlin's Underworld; Verklungene Traume; Der Walzerkonig (US 1932); Die Jugendgeliebte (US 1932); Zapfenstreich am Rhein (US 1933); Aschermittwoch (Ash

Wednesday—US 1935). **1931** Die Frau von der Man Spricht (US 1933). **1932** Tannenberg (US 1934); Trenck (US 1934). **1933** Der Meisterdetektiv (US 1934); Johannisnact (US 1935). **1934** Zu Strassburg auf der Schanz (aka At the Strassburg—US 1936). **1936** The Private Life of Louis XIV; Schloss Vogeloed; Heisses Blut; Dahinten in der Heide (Back in the Country—US 1939). **1938** Der Tiger von Eschnapur (aka Das Indische Grabmal, The Indian Tomb). **1939** Drei Vater um Anna (Three Fathers for Anne—US 1940). **1940** Leidenschaft (Passion).

STUHLDREHER, HARRY A. (Harry A. Strudlereher)
Born: Oct. 14, 1901, Massillon, Ohio. Died: Jan. 22, 1965. Football player, coach, author and screen actor.

Appeared in: **1931** The Spirit of Notre Dame.

STURGIS, EDDIE (Josef Edwin Sturgis)
Born: Oct. 22, 1881, Washington, D.C. Died: Dec. 13, 1947, Los Angeles, Calif. (heart disease). Screen actor.

Appeared in: **1921** The Chicken in the Case; Man and Woman. **1923** Legally Dead; Ponjola. **1925** Seven Keys to Baldpate. **1927** Let It Rain; Wolf's Clothing; After Midnight. **1928** The Big City; Fazil; Square Crooks. **1930** Shooting Straight; The Squealer; Outside the Law. **1931** Oh! Oh! Cleopatra (short). **1935** Red Hot Tires; Mississippi.

STUTENROTH, GENE See ROTH, GENE

STYLES, EDWIN
Born: Jan. 13, 1899, London, England. Died: Dec. 20, 1960, London, England. Screen and stage actor.

Appeared in: **1933** Hell Below. **1949** Adam and Evelyne (aka Adam and Evalyn—US). **1951** The Lady and the Lamp. **1952** Top Secret (aka Mr. Potts Goes to Moscow—US 1954); Penny Princess (US 1953). **1961** Stop Me Before I Kill!

STYLES, PATRICIA
Born: 1923. Died: Dec. 13, 1948, Los Angeles, Calif. (gunshot wounds). Screen and radio actress.

SUBJECT, EVELYN
Died: Apr. 22, 1975, Temple City, Calif. Stage and screen actress. Appeared in early Vitagraph and Essanay films.

SUDLOW, JOAN
Born: 1892. Died: Feb. 1, 1970, Hollywood, Calif. (result of fall). Screen, stage and television actress.

Appeared in: **1951** Queen for a Day. **1952** Pride of St. Louis. **1966** A Fine Madness.

SUES, LEONARD
Born: 1921. Died: Oct. 24, 1971, Los Angeles, Calif. (cancer). Screen actor and musical director.

Appeared in: **1939** What a Life. **1949** Manhattan Angel.

SULKY, LEO
Born: Dec. 6, 1874, Cincinnati, Ohio. Died: June 3, 1957, Calif. Screen and stage actor. Appeared in early Selig, American, World and Sunshine Film Corp. films.

Appeared in: **1921** Big Town Ideas; The Tomboy.

SULLAVAN, MARGARET (Margaret Brooke Sullavan)
Born: May 16, 1911, Norfolk, Va. Died: Jan. 1, 1960, New Haven, Conn. (suicide—sleeping pills). Screen, stage and television actress. Divorced from actor Henry Fonda (dec. 1982); film director William Wyler (dec. 1981); producer Leland Hayward (dec. 1971). Married to industrialist Kenneth Arthur Wagg. Mother of actress Brooke Hayward. Nominated for 1938 Academy Award for Best Actress in Three Comrades.

Appeared in: **1933** Only Yesterday. **1934** Little Man, What Now? **1935** The Good Fairy; So Red the Rose. **1936** Next Time We Love; The Moon's Our Home; I Love a Soldier. **1938** Three Comrades; The Shopworn Angel; The Shining Hour. **1939** When Tomorrow Comes. **1940** The Shop Around the Corner; The Mortal Storm. **1941** So Ends Our Night; Back Street; Appointment for Love. **1944** Cry Havoc. **1950** No Sad Songs for Me.

SULLIVAN, BRIAN (Harry Joseph Sullivan)
Born: Aug. 9. 1919, Oakland, Calif. Died: June 17, 1969, Lake Geneva, Switzerland. Screen, stage actor and opera performer.

Appeared in: **1945** This Man's Navy. **1946** Courage of Lassie.

SULLIVAN, ED (Edward Vincent Sullivan)
Born: Sept. 28, 1902, New York, N.Y. Died: Oct. 13, 1974, New York, N.Y. (cancer). Columnist, television, screen, vaudeville, radio actor, screenwriter and author.

Appeared in: **1933** Mr. Broadway. **1939** Big Town Czar. **1958** Senior Prom. **1963** Bye Bye Birdie. **1964** The Patsy. **1965** The Singing Nun. **1966** Last of the Secret Agents. **1970** The Phynx; What's Happening.

SULLIVAN, ELLIOTT
Born: July 4, 1907. Died: June 2, 1974, Los Angeles, Calif. (heart attack). Screen, stage and television actor.

Appeared in: **1937** They Won't Forget. **1938** Accidents Will Happen; Racket Busters; Gangs of New York; Next Time I Marry; Fury Below. **1939** The Oklahoma Kid; Each Dawn I Die; The Roaring Twenties; King of the Underworld; I Am Not Afraid; The Spellbinder; Smashing the Money Ring; Angels Wash Their Faces. **1940** The Saint's Double Trouble; Millionaires in Prison; The Man Who Talked Too Much; Calling All Husbands. **1942** Man With Two Lives; Wild Bill Hickok Rides; Yankee Doodle Dandy. **1943** Action in the North Atlantic. **1944** Winged Victory. **1949** The Lady Gambles. **1950** Guilty Bystander. **1953** Taxi. **1956** Crowded Paradise. **1969** The Sergeant; On Her Majesty's Secret Service. **1970** Tropic of Cancer.

SULLIVAN, FRANCIS LOFTUS
Born: Jan. 6, 1903, London, England. Died: Nov. 19, 1956, New York, N.Y. Screen, stage and television actor.

Appeared in: **1932** The Missing Rembrandt; The Chinese Puzzle; When London Sleeps. **1933** F.P.1; The Stickpin; Called Back; The Fire Raisers; The Right to Live; The Wandering Jew (US 1935). **1934** Red Wagon (US 1935); Princess Charming (US 1935); The Return of Bulldog Drummond; Chu Chin Chow; What Happened Then?; Great Expectations; The Warren Case; Cheating Cheaters. **1935** The Mystery of Edwin Drood; Her Last Affaire. **1936** A Woman Alone (aka Two Who Dared—US 1937); Sabotage (aka The Woman Alone—US 1937); Spy of Napoleon (US 1939); The Limping Man; The Interrupted Honeymoon. **1937** Fine Feathers; Action for Slander (US 1938); Non-Stop New York; 21 Days (aka 21 Days Together—US 1940 and The First and the Last); Dinner at the Ritz. **1938** The Gables Mystery; Kate Plus Ten; Climbing High (US 1939); The Citadel; The Ware Case; The Drum (aka Drums—US). **1939** The Four Just Men (aka The Secret Four—US 1940); Young Man's Fancy (US 1943). **1941** Pimpernel Smith (aka Mister V—US 1942). **1942** The Foreman Went to France (aka Somewhere in France—US 1943); The Day Will Dawn (aka The Avengers—US); Lady from Lisbon. **1943** The Butler's Dilemma. **1944** Fiddlers Three. **1946** Caesar and Cleopatra; The Laughing Lady (US 1950); Great Expectations (US 1947 and 1934 version); The Man Within (aka The Smugglers—US 1948). **1947** Take My Life (US 1948). **1948** Broken Journey; The Winslow Boy (US 1950); Oliver Twist (US 1951); Joan of Arc. **1949** Christopher Columbus; The Red Danube. **1950** Night and the City. **1951** My Favorite Spy; Behave Yourself. **1952** Caribbean. **1953** Plunder of the Sun; Sangaree. **1954** Drums of Tahiti. **1955** Hell's Island; The Prodigal.

SULLIVAN, FREDERICK R. "FRED"
Born: 1872, London, England. Died: July 24, 1937, Los Angeles, Calif. (heart trouble). Screen and stage actor.

Appeared in: **1922** Tailor-Made Man. **1923** The Courtship of Miles Standish; Face on the Barroom Floor. **1925** Winds of Chance; Beggar on Horseback. **1929** The Black Watch. **1930** Around the Corner; Prince of Diamonds. **1931** Murder by the Clock. **1932** If I Had a Million. **1933** Blind Adventure; Duck Soup. **1934** You're Telling Me. **1935** All the King's Horses.

SULLIVAN, JAMES E.
Born: 1864. Died: June 1, 1931. Stage and screen actor.

Appeared in: **1925** The Pinch Hitter.

SULLIVAN, JOE
Born: 1910. Died: Oct. 13, 1971, San Francisco, Calif. Pianist, screen and radio actor. Appeared with Red Nichols' band and others.

SULLIVAN, JOHN MAURICE
Born: 1876. Died: Mar. 8, 1949, Hollywood, Calif. Screen and stage actor. Entered films in 1930.

Appeared in: **1930** Today. **1931** Silence. **1932** Strangers in Love; The Trial of Vivienne Ware; Down to Earth. **1933** Big Executive. **1934** You're Telling Me; Mystery Liner. **1936** Walking on Air. **1938** The Buccaneer. **1946** Blue Skies.

SULLIVAN, LEE
Born: 1911. Died: May 29, 1981, Brooklyn, N.Y. (malignancy). Screen, stage, radio actor and singer.

Appeared in: **1945** The Great John L.

SULLIVAN, WILLIAM A. "BILLY"
Born: 1891, Worcester, Mass. Died: May 23, 1946, Great Neck, N.Y. Screen actor and screenwriter.

Appeared in: **1914** Million Dollar Mystery (serial). **1917** Cigarette Girl. **1918** The Honest Thief; Getaway Kate; Lightning Raider (serial). **1923** The Courtship of Myles Standish. **1924** The Slanderers. **1925** The Fear Fighter; Fighting Fate; Ghost Getter; Ridin' Pretty. **1926** Broadway Billy; Fighting Thorobreds; The Heart of a Coward; One Punch O'Day; The Patent Leather Pug; Rapid Fire Romance; Speed Crazed; Stick to Your Story; The Windjammer; The Winner. **1927** Red Clay; The Gallant Fool; The Speed Cop; When Seconds Count; Speedy Smith; The Cancelled Debt; Daring Deeds; Smiling Billy. **1928** Walking Back. **1929** The Fighting Terror. **1931** Sweepstakes.

SULLY, FRANK (Frank Sullivan)
Born: 1908. Died: Dec. 17, 1975, Woodland Hills, Calif. Screen, stage, vaudeville and television actor.

Appeared in: **1935** Mary Burns—Fugitive; Fighting Youth. **1937** Daughter of Shanghai; High, Wide and Handsome; Life Begins at College; Hold That Co-ed; Thanks for Everything. **1939** Some Like it Hot. **1940** The Grapes of Wrath; The Night of Nights; Lillian Russell; The Doctor Takes a Wife; Cross-Country Romance; Young People; The Return of Frank James; Yesterday's Heroes; Escape to Glory (aka Submarine Zone); Dr. Kildare's Crisis. **1941** The Fighting 69th; A Girl, a Guy and a Gob; Private Nurse; Mountain Moonlight; Let's Go Collegiate. **1942** Two Yanks in Trinidad; Parachute Nurse; My Sister Eileen; Rings on Her Fingers; Sleepytime Gal; The Boogie Man Will Get You; All Through the Night; Inside the Law. **1943** The More the Merrier; Renegades; They Got Me Covered; Thousands Cheer; Dangerous Blondes; Two Senoritas from Chicago. **1944** Secret Command; Two Girls and a Sailor; The Ghost That Walks Alone. **1945** Along Came Jones; Boston Blackie Booked on Suspicion; Boston Blackie's Rendezvous. **1946** Crime Doctor's Man Hunt; A Close Call for Boston Blackie; One Way to Love; Out of the Depths; Talk About a Lady; Throw a Saddle on a Star; The Gentleman Misbehaves; The Phantom Thief; Renegades; It's Great To Be Young; Dangerous Business; Boston Blackie and the Law. **1947** South of the Chisholm Trail; Wild Harvest. **1948** Blondie's Reward; Trapped by Boston Blackie. **1949** Boston Blackie's Chinese Venture; Joe Palooka in the Counterpunch. **1950** Bodyhold; Beauty on Parade; Rookie Fireman; Blondie's Hero; Joe Palooka Meets Humphrey; Square Dance Katy; Killer Shark; Joe Palooka in Humphrey Takes a Chance. **1952** No Room for the Groom; With a Song in My Heart; Night Stage to Galveston; Prairie Roundup; Man in the Saddle. **1953** Northern Patrol; Take Me to Town; Pardon My Backfire (short). **1954** Silver Lode; Battle of Rogue River. **1955** The Spoilers; Fling in the Ring (short); Naked Street; The Prodigal; Hell's Island. **1956** Flagpole Sitters (short); You Can't Run Away From It. **1957** Gun A-Poppin (short); The Buckskin Lady; Rockabilly Baby. **1963** Bye Bye Birdie. **1968** Funny Girl.

SUMMERS, ANN
Born: 1920. Died: Jan. 14, 1974, Los Angeles, Calif. Screen, stage and television actress. Married to screenwriter Robert Mann.

Appeared in: **1942** The following shorts: Cooks and Crooks; Dear! Dear!; Pretty Dolly. **1943** The Seventh Victim; The Sky's the Limit; Radio Runaround (short); The Avenging Rider; Fighting Frontier. **1970** Glass Houses.

SUMMERS, BILL (William Reed Summers)
Died: Sept. 12, 1966, Upton, Mass. Baseball umpire and screen actor.

Appeared in: **1949** The Kid from Cleveland.

SUMMERS, DOROTHY
Born: England. Died: Jan. 13, 1964, England. Screen actress.

SUMMERS, HOPE
Born: 1901. Died: July 22, 1979, Woodland Hills, Calif. (heart failure). Screen, stage, radio, television actress and stage producer.

Appeared in: **1957** Zero Hour. **1958** The Return of Dracula. **1959** Hound-Dog Man. **1960** Inherit the Wind. **1961** Parrish; Claudelle Inglish; Homicidal; The Children's Hour. **1962** The Couch. **1963** Spencer's Mountain. **1964** One Man's Way. **1965** The Hallelujah Trail. **1966** The Ghost and Mr. Chicken. **1968** Rosemary's Baby; The Shakiest Gun in the West. **1969** The Learning Tree. **1974** Our Time. **1978** Foul Play; Smokey and the Goodtime Outlaws.

SUMMERS, LEONORA (Lillian Hill)
Born: 1898. Died: June 29, 1976, Woodland Hills, Calif. Screen, stage, vaudeville actress and dancer. Divorced from vaudeville actor Jack Hanley, with whom she appeared in an act, along with quick-change artist "Doc" Baker. Later married to Mushy Callahan, former World Junior Welterweight Champion.

Appeared in: **1926** Sea Beast; Ben Hur; Hoboken to Hollywood (short); Her Actor Friend (short).

SUMMERVILLE, AMELIA
Born: 1863. Died: Jan. 21, 1934, New York, N.Y. Stage and screen actress.

Appeared in: **1925** Romola. **1926** The Great Deception.

SUMMERVILLE, SLIM (George J. Summerville)
Born: 1896, Albuquerque, N.Mex. Died: Jan. 6, 1946, Laguna Beach, Calif. (stroke). Screen actor and film director.

Appeared in: **1914** The Knock-Out; Mabel's Busy Day; A Rowboat Romance; Laughing Gas; Gentlemen of Nerve (aka Some Nerve); Cursed by His Beauty; Tillie's Punctured Romance. **1915** Her Winning Punch; The Home Breakers (aka Other People's Wives); Caught in the Act; Gussle's Day of Rest; Their Social Splash; Those College Girls (aka His Bitter Half); The Great Vacuum Robbery; Her Painted Hero; A Game Old Knight. **1916** Cinders of Love; The Winning Punch; Bucking Society (short); Her Busted Trust; The Three Slims; His Bread and Butter. **1917** Villa of the Movies; Her Fame and Shame; A Dog Catcher's Love; His Precious Life; A Pullman Bride. **1918** The Beloved Rogue. **1921** Skirts. **1926** The Texas Streak. **1927** The Beloved Rogue (and 1918 version); The Denver Dude; Painted Ponies; Hey, Hey, Cowboy; The Wreck of the Hesperus. **1928** The Chinese Parrot; Riding for Fame. **1929** King of the Rodeo; Strong Boy; Shannons of Broadway; Tiger Rose; The Last Warning. **1930** See America Thirst; Free Love; Her Man; The Spoilers; One Hysterical Night; Troopers Three; Under Montana Skies; All Quiet on the Western Front; King of Jazz; Little Accident; Hello Russia; We! We! Marie!; Parlez Vous. **1931** Bad Sisters; The Front Page; Arabian Knights; Bless the Ladies; First to Fight; Hotter Than Haiti; Let's Play; Parisian Gaieties; Royal Bluff; Sargie's Playmates; Here's Luck; Reckless Living; Heaven on Earth. **1932** Racing Youth; Unexpected Father; Eyes Have It; In the Bag; Kid Glove Kisses; Meet the Princess; Sea Soldier's Sweeties; Tom Brown of Culver; Air Mail. **1932-33** Universal shorts. **1933** Out All Night; They Just Had to Get Married; Early to Bed; Her First Mate; Love, Honor and Oh, Baby! **1934** Horse Play; The Love Birds; Their Big Moment. **1935** Life Begins at 40; The Farmer Takes a Wife; Way Down East. **1936** Captain January; The Country Doctor; Pepper; White Fang; Reunion; Can This Be Dixie? **1937** Off to the Races; Love Is News; Fifty Roads to Town; The Road Back; Five of a Kind. **1939** Charlie Chan in Reno. **1940** Anne of Windy Poplars; Gold Rush Maisie. **1941** Miss Polly; Western Union; Highway West; Tobacco Road. **1942** The Valley of Vanishing Men (serial); Niagara Falls; Jesse James; The Spoilers. **1944** I'm from Arkansas; Bride by Mistake. **1946** The Hoodlum Saint.

SUMMEY, JAMES "COUSIN JODY"
Born: 1914. Died: Aug. 18, 1975, Nashville, Tenn. Screen actor and singer.

SUMNER, VERLYN
Born: June 7, 1897, Lakefield, Minn. Died: Apr. 10, 1935, Bremerton, Wash. Stage and screen actress.

Appeared in: **1928** Speedy; The Toilers; Excess Baggage.

SUNBEAUTY, OLGA (aka OLGA SOLBELLI)
Born: 1898, Italy. Died: 1976, Italy? Screen actress.

Appeared in: **1947** Schoolgirl Diary. **1949** Lost in the Dark; The Peddler and the Lady. **1952** Tomorrow Is Too Late. **1953** La Nave Delle Donne Maledette (The Ship of Condemned Women—US 1963); Lure of the Sira. **1954** Theodora, Slave Empress. **1960** Il Mulino delle Donne di Pietra (Mill of the Stone Women—US 1963).

SUNDARAMBAL, KODUMUDI (Kodumudi Balambal Sundarambal)
Born: 1908, India. Died: Oct., 1980, Madras, India. Screen and stage actress.

SUNDERLAND, NAN
Died: Nov. 23, 1973, New York, N.Y. Stage and screen actress. Married to actor Walter Huston (dec. 1950).

Appeared in: **1933** Sweepings. **1947** Unconquered.

SUNDHOLM, WILLIAM "BILL"
Died: Feb. 28, 1971. Screen actor.

Appeared in: **1930** City Girl. **1932** The Last Man. **1947** Pursued. **1949** Loaded Pistols.

SUNDMARK, BETTY *See* SHANNON, ELIZABETH S.

SUNSHINE, "BABY" (Pauline Flood)
Born: Dec. 1, 1915, Calif. Died: Oct. 19, 1917, Los Angeles, Calif. (hit by truck). Known as "Tiniest Star in Films."

SUNSHINE, MARION
Born: 1897. Died: Jan. 25, 1963, New York, N.Y. Screen, stage, vaudeville actress and songwriter.

Appeared in: **1908** The Tavern Keeper's Daughter; The Red Girl. **1909** Her First Biscuits. **1910** In the Season of Buds; Sunshine Sue; Three Sisters; A Decree of Destiny. **1911** The Rose of Kentucky; The Stuff Heroes Are Made Of; Dan the Dandy. **1912** Heredity. **1944** I'm from Arkansas.

SUPERVIA, CONCHITA
Born: 1901, England? Died: Mar. 30, 1936, London, England (in childbirth). Screen, stage actress and opera singer.

Appeared in: **1934** Evensong.

SUPPLEE, ESTHER RITTER *See* RITTER, ESTHER

SURATT, VALESKA
Born: 1882, Terre Haute, Ind. Died: July 3, 1962. Screen, stage and vaudeville actress.

Appeared in: **1915** The Immigrant; Soul of Broadway. **1916** Jealousy. **1917** The Victim; She; The Slave; Wife Number Two; The New York Peacock.

SUSANN, JACQUELINE
Born: 1921, Philadelphia, Pa. Died: Sept. 21, 1974, New York, N.Y. (cancer). Screen, stage actress and novelist.

Appeared in: **1967** Valley of the Dolls.

SUSSENGUTH, WALTHER
Born: 1900, Germany. Died: May, 1964, Berlin, Germany. Screen and stage actor.

Appeared in: **1935** Der Schimmelreiter (The Rider of the White Horse).

SUTHERLAND, A. EDWARD "EDDIE" (Albert Edward Sutherland)
Born: Jan. 5, 1895, London, England. Died: Dec. 31, 1973, Palm Springs, Calif. Screen, stage actor, film and television director. Son of stage actress Julia Ring (dec.). Divorced from actress Louise Brooks and later married to Edwina Sutherland. Entered films in 1915.

Appeared in: **1916** Love Under Cover; The Telephone Belle; Won by a Foot; Heart Strategy. **1917** Innocent Sinners; The Girl and the Ring; His Foothill Folly; Caught in the End; A Fallen Star; A Toy of Fate; His Cool Nerve; His Saving Grace; Dad's Downfall. **1919** The Viled Adventure. **1920** The Sea Wolf; The Round Up; All of a Sudden Peggy; Conrad in Quest of His Youth. **1921** The Dollar-A-Year Man; The Light in the Clearing; The Witching Hour; Everything for Sale; Just Outside the Door. **1922** The Loaded Door; Elope If You Must; Nancy from Nowhere; Second Hand Rose. **1923** The Woman He Loved; Girl from the West. **1924** Abraham Lincoln. **1929** The Dance of Life.

SUTHERLAND, ANNE
Born: Mar. 1, 1867, Washington, D.C. Died: June 22, 1942, Brentwood, N.Y. Screen and stage actress.

Appeared in: **1915** Kreutzer Sonata. **1921** God's Crucible. **1931** My Sin.

SUTHERLAND, DICK
Born: 1882, Benton, Ky. Died: Feb. 3, 1934, Hollywood, Calif. Screen, stage and vaudeville actor.

Appeared in: **1921** The Magnificent Brute; God's Gold; Sailor-Made Man. **1922** Gas, Oil and Water; The Deuce of Spades; Rags to Riches; Grandma's Boy. **1923** Hell's Hole; The Rip-Tide; Quicksands; The Shriek of Araby; His Last Race; Masters of Men. **1924** The Dangerous Blonde; The Red Lily; The Tornado; The Mask of Lopez; Battling Mason; Defying the Law; Fighter's Paradise. **1925** The Fighting Demon; Flying Fool; With This Ring; Jimmie's Millions; The Road to Yesterday. **1926** Lloyd Hamilton Comedies; Broken Hearts of Hollywood; Don Juan; The Jazz Girl. **1927** The Claw; Uncle Tom's Cabin; The Beloved Rogue. **1928** Riders of the Dark. **1929** China Slaver; The Hoose Gow (short).

SUTHERLAND, ELIZABETH "ELIZA"
Born: Toronto, Canada. Died: Feb. 26, 1960, New York, N.Y. Screen, stage and radio actress. Married to actor Melville G. Cooper (dec. 1973).

SUTHERLAND, JOHN
Born: 1845, England. Died: Aug. 31, 1921, Brooklyn, N.Y. Stage and screen actor.

Appeared in: **1918** The Lie; Uncle Tom's Cabin; Dodging a Million. **1919** The Silver King; Test of Honor; The Imp. **1920** His House in Order. **1921** Her Lord and Master.

SUTHERLAND, VICTOR
Born: 1889. Died: Aug. 29, 1968, Los Angeles, Calif. Screen, stage and television actor. Divorced from screen actress Pearl White (dec. 1938). Married to actress Linda Barrett.

Appeared in: **1923** The Valley of Lost Souls. **1924** The Love Bandit. **1950** The Sleeping City. **1951** The Whistle at Eaton Falls. **1932** We're Not Married; Lone Star; The Pride of St. Louis; The Captive City. **1953** Powder River; Donovan's Brain.

SUTTON, BRAD
Born: 1863. Died: Aug. 19, 1932, Staten Island, N.Y. Screen, stage and radio actor.

Appeared in: **1915** Black Eagle; Breaking the Shackles; The Hand of the Law.

SUTTON, FRANK
Born: 1923, Clarksville, Tenn. Died: June 28, 1974, Shreveport, La. (heart attack). Screen, stage, radio and television actor.

Appeared in: **1955** Marty. **1957** Four Boys and a Gun. **1961** Town Without Pity. **1965** The Satan Bug.

SUTTON, JOHN
Born: Oct. 22, 1908, Rawalpindi, India. Died: July 10, 1963. Screen and stage actor.

Appeared in: **1937** Bulldog Drummond's Revenge; Bulldog Drummond Comes Back. **1938** Adventures of Robin Hood; The Blonde Cheat; Booloo; Four Men and a Prayer. **1939** Tower of London; Arrest Bulldog Drummond; Susannah of the Mounties; Bulldog Drummond's Bride; Charlie McCarthy, Detective; Zaza; The Private Lives of Elizabeth and Essex. **1940** Christable Caine; Sandy Is a Lady; I Can't Give You Anything but Love, Baby; South of Karanga; Murder Over New York; Hudson Bay; The Invisible Man Returns. **1941** A Very Young Lady; Moon Over Her Shoulder; A Yank in the RAF. **1942** Ten Gentlemen from West Point; My Gal Sal; Thunder Birds. **1943** Tonight We Raid Calais. **1944** Jane Eyre; The Hour Before the Dawn. **1946** Claudia and David. **1947** Captain from Castile. **1948** The Three Musketeers; The Counterfeiters; Mickey. **1949** The Bride of Vengeance; Bagdad; The Fan. **1950** The Second Face. **1951** The Second Woman; Payment on Demand. **1952** David and Bathsheba; Thief of Damascus; Captain Pirate; The Golden Hawk; My Cousin Rachel; The Lady in the Iron Mask. **1953** Sangaree; East of Sumatra. **1956** The Amazon Trader; Death of a Scoundrel. **1959** The Bat; Return of the Fly; Beloved Infidel. **1961** The Canadians. **1962** Marizinia. **1964** Of Human Bondage. **1967** The Drums of Tabu; The Lost Safari.

SUTTON, PAUL
Born: 1912. Died: Jan. 31, 1970, Ferndale, Mich. (muscular dystrophy). Screen, radio and television actor.

Appeared in: **1937** Jungle Jim (serial). **1938** The Spy Ring; Air Devils; Bar 20 Justice; In Old Mexico; Shadows Over Shanghai. **1939** Balalaika; The Girl and the Gambler. **1940** Little Old New York. **1941** Ride On, Vaquero; Wild Geese Calling. **1942** Sundown Jim; In Old California; Riders of the Northland.

SUTTON, WILLIAM
Born: 1877. Died: Sept. 10, 1955, West Los Angeles, Calif. Screen, stage actor and magician. Known as the "Great Fontonelle." Appeared in silent films.

SVERDLIN, LEV N.
Born: 1902, Russia. Died: Aug. 30, 1969, Moscow, Russia. Screen actor.

Appeared in: **1938** The Defense of Volotchayevsk. **1942** Guerrilla Brigade. **1944** Adventures in Bokhara. **1945** Marriage; Wait for Me. **1946** Great Days; Days and Nights. **1951** Far from Moscow.

SWAIN, MACK

Born: Feb. 16, 1876, Salt Lake City, Utah. Died: Aug. 25, 1935, Tacoma, Wash. Screen and stage actor.

Appeared in: **1914** Caught in a Cabaret (aka The Jazz Waiter); Caught in the Rain; A Busy Day; The Fatal Mallet; The Knock-Out (aka The Pugilist); A Gambling Rube; A Missing Bride; Mabel's Married Life (aka The Squarehead); A Rowboat Romance; Laughing Gas; Gentlemen of Nerve (aka Some Nerve); His Musical Career; His Trysting Place; The Sea Nymphs (aka His Diving Beauty); Among the Mourners; Leading Lizzie Astray; Getting Acquainted; Other People's Business; His Prehistoric Past; Ambrose's First Falsehood; A Dark Lover's Play. **1915** Love, Speed and Thrills; The Home Breakers (aka Other People's Wives); Ye Olden Grafter; Ambrose's Sour Grapes; Willful Ambrose; From Patches to Plenty; Ambrose's Little Hatchet; Ambrose's Fury; Ambrose's Lofty Perch; Ambrose's Nasty Temper; A Human Hound's Triumph; Our Daredevil Chief; Mabel Lost and Won; When Ambrose Dared Walrus; The Battle of Ambrose and Walrus; Saved by Wireless; The Best of Enemies. **1916** A Movie Star; Love Will Conquer; His Auto Ruination; By Stork Delivery; His Bitter Pill; His Wild Oats; Madcap Ambrose; Vampire Ambrose; Ambrose's Cup of Woe; Ambrose's Rapid Rise; Safety First Ambrose (working title Sheriff Ambrose); A Modern Enoch Arden. **1917** His Naughty Thought; Thirst (rereleased 1923); Lost—A Cook; A Pullman Bride. **1918** "Poppy" series. **1919** Ambrose's Day Off. **1922** The Pilgrim. **1925** The Gold Rush. **1926** Hands Up; Sea Horses; Kiki; Footloose Widows; The Nervous Wreck; Her Big Night; Honesty—the Best Policy; The Torrent; Whispering Wires. **1927** Becky; Finnegan's Ball; The Shamrock and the Rose; The Tired Business Man; The Beloved Rogue; See You in Jail; Mockery; My Best Girl. **1928** Caught in the Fog; Gentlemen Prefer Blondes; A Texas Steer; The Last Warning; Tillie's Punctured Romance; The Cohens and the Kellys. **1929** Marianne; The Cohens and the Kelleys in Atlantic City. **1930** Redemption; The Sea Bat; The Locked Door. **1931** Stout Hearts and Willing Hands (short); Finn and Hattie. **1932** Midnight Patrol. **1932-33** Paramount shorts. **1960** When Comedy Was King (documentary).

SWAN, PAUL

Born: 1884. Died: Feb. 1, 1972, Bedford Hills, N.Y. Screen, stage actor, dancer, painter and sculptor.

Appeared in: **1916** Diana the Huntress. **1923** The Ten Commandments. **1965** Camp. **1968** The Illiac Passion.

SWANSON, CHIP

Born: 1937. Died: Mar. 27, 1978, Rio de Janeiro, Brazil (auto accident). Screen, stage, radio, television actor, stage director and dancer.

Appeared in: **1964** Your Cheatin' Heart (aka The Hank Williams Story). **1965** Von Ryan's Express. **1968** Star! **1969** Hello Dolly.

SWANWICK, PETER

Born: 1912. Died: Nov. 14, 1968, London, England. Screen, stage actor and singer.

Appeared in: **1951** The African Queen; Old Mother Riley's Jungle Treasure. **1952** No Haunt for a Gentleman; Circumstantial Evidence; Lady in the Fog (aka Scotland Yard Inspector—US). **1953** Albert RN (aka Break to Freedom—US 1955). **1956** Assignment Redhead (aka Million Dollar Manhunt—US 1962). **1957** The Big Chance; Kill Me Tomorrow (US 1958); You Pay Your Money. **1958** Murder Reported (US 1960); The Two-Headed Spy (US 1959). **1959** Life in Danger (US 1964). **1960** Circus of Horrors. **1961** The Invasion Quartet; The Trunk. **1969** The Looking Glass War (US 1970).

SWARTHOUT, GLADYS

Born: Dec. 25, 1904, Deepwater, Mo. Died: July 7, 1969, Florence, Italy. Opera, screen, stage and radio actress.

Appeared in: **1936** Rose of the Rancho; Give Us This Night. **1937** Champagne Waltz. **1938** Romance in the Dark. **1939** Ambush.

SWARTS, SARA

Born: 1899. Died: Mar. 31, 1949, Woodland Hills, Calif. Screen actress. Entered films approx. 1918.

SWEATMAN, WILLIS P.

Born: 1854. Died: Nov. 25, 1930, New York, N.Y. Screen, stage actor and minstrel performer.

Appeared in: **1914** The Country Chairman.

SWEENEY, EDWARD C.

Born: 1906. Died: Aug. 14, 1967, Miami, Fla. Film producer, lecturer, photographer and founder of the "Explorers Club." He produced and appeared in eleven travel-lecture films.

SWEENEY, FRED C.

Born: 1894. Died: Dec. 10, 1954, Sylmar, Calif. (pulmonary tuberculosis). Screen, stage and vaudeville actor. Appeared in vaudeville team of "Daffy and Sweeney."

SWEENEY, JACK

Born: 1889. Died: Apr. 12, 1950, Hollywood, Calif. Screen actor. Appeared in Sennett films in 1916.

SWEENEY, JOSEPH

Died: Dec., 1963, New York, N.Y. Stage and screen actor.

Appeared in: **1936** Soak the Rich. **1956** The Man in the Gray Flannel Suit; The Fastest Gun Alive. **1957** Twelve Angry Men.

SWEET, HARRY

Born: 1901, Colo. Died: June 18, 1933, near Big Bear, Calif. (plane crash). Screen actor, film director and screenwriter.

Appeared in: **1926** Fascinating Youth. **1928** Homesick. **1930** Hit the Deck; True to the Navy; Her Man. **1932** Carnival Boat.

SWEET, MARION

Born: 1916, Camden, N.J. Died: July 17, 1978, New York, N.Y. Screen, stage and radio actress. Married to actor Charles Gaines.

SWEET, POLLY LOUISE

Born: 1914. Died: Jan. 17, 1935, San Bernardino, Calif. Screen, stage actress and dancer.

SWEET, TOM

Born: 1933. Died: Nov. 19, 1967, High Sierras, Calif. (plane crash). Screen, television actor and stuntman. Was the "Galloping White Knight" on television commercials.

Appeared in: **1961** Sniper's Ridge.

SWENSON, ALFRED G.

Born: 1883, Salt Lake City, Utah. Died: Mar. 28, 1941, Staten Island, N.Y. (heart attack). Screen, stage and radio actor.

Appeared in: **1929** The Great Power.

SWENSON, KARL

Born: July 23, 1908, Brooklyn, N.Y. Died: Oct. 8, 1978, Torrington, Conn. Screen, stage, radio and television actor. Married to actress Joan Tompkins.

Appeared in: **1957** Four Boys and a Gun. **1958** Kings Go Forth. **1959** No Name on the Bullet; The Hanging Tree. **1960** One Foot in Hell; Flaming Star; Gallant Hours; Ice Palace; North to Alaska. **1961** Judgment at Nuremberg. **1962** Walk on the Wild Side; The Spiral Road; Lonely Are the Brave. **1963** The Prize; The Birds; The Sword in the Stone. **1964** The Man from Galveston. **1965** The Cincinnati Kid; Major Dundee; The Sons of Katie Elder. **1966** Seconds; Brighty of the Grand Canyon. **1967** Hour of the Gun. **1970** ... Tick ... Tick ... Tick ..

SWICKARD, CHARLES F.

Born: 1861. Died: May 12, 1929, Fresno, Calif. Screen actor and film director. Brother of actor Joseph Swickard (dec. 1940).

SWICKARD, JOSEPH

Born: 1866, Coblenz, Germany. Died: Feb. 29, 1940, Hollywood, Calif. Screen and stage actor. Brother of actor Charles Swickard (dec. 1929). Entered films in 1912.

Appeared in: **1914** A Rowboat Romance; Laughing Gas; The Plumber. **1915** Love, Loot and Crash; A Home Breaking Hound; The Best of Enemies. **1916** Love Will Conquer; The Village Vampire (working title The Great Leap); His Wild Oats; Haystacks and Steeples; Ambrose's Cup of Woe. **1917** Beach of Dreams; No Woman Knows; Opened Shutters; Sowing the Wind. **1921** Serenade; Four Horsemen of the Apocalypse; Cheated Hearts; Who Am I? **1922** The Adventures of Robinson Crusoe (serial); Across the Dead Line; Another Man's Shoes; My American Wife; The Golden Gift; Pawned; The Storm; The Young Rajah. **1923** Mr. Billings Spends His Dime; A Prince of a King; Bavu; Maytime; The Cricket on the Hearth; Daughters of the Rich; The Eternal Struggle; Forgive and Forget; Mothers-in-Law. **1924** The Age of Desire; Dante's Inferno; Men; Pal O'Mine; The Shadow of the East; A Boy of Flanders; Defying the Law; Poisoned Paradise; Untamed Youth; North of Nevada. **1925** Off the Highway; The Verdict; She Wolves; The Wizard of Oz; Easy Money; The Mysterious Stranger; Playing with Souls; Northern Code; Fifth Avenue Models; The Keeper of the Bees; The Sign of the Cactus. **1926** Officer Jim; The Unknown Cavalier; The Border Whirlwind; Three Pals; Senor Daredevil; Stop, Look and Listen; Desert Gold; Devil's

Dice; Don Juan; The High Flyer; The Night Patrol; Kentucky Handicap; Whispering Canyon. **1927** One Increasing Purpose; Old San Francisco; Senorita; Time to Love; Get Your Man; The Golden Stallion (serial); Compassion; False Morals; King of Kings. **1928** Eagle of the Night (serial); Comrades; Sharp Shooters; Turn Back the Hours. **1929** Bachelor's Club; Dark Skies; Phantoms of the North; Devil's Chaplain; The Eternal Woman; The Veiled Woman; Frozen River; Times Square; Street Corners. **1930** The Lone Defender (serial); Song of the Caballero; Mamba; Phantom of the Desert. **1934** The Perils of Pauline (serial); The Return of Chandu the Magician (serial); Hello, Prosperity (short); Beloved; Return of Chandu; Cross Streets. **1935** A Dog of Flanders; The Lost City (serial); The Crusades. **1936** The Millionaire Kid; Caryl of the Mountains; Custer's Last Stand (serial); Boss Rider of Gun Creek; The Black Coin (serial). **1937** The Girl Said No; Sandflow. **1938** You Can't Take It with You. **1939** Mexicali Rose.

SWIMMER, BOB
Died: June 26, 1971. Screen actor.

SWINLEY, ION
Born: Oct. 27, 1891, Barnes, England. Died: Sept. 16, 1937, London, England. Screen, stage actor and playwright. Divorced from actress Mary Merrall (dec. 1973) and Joan Castle.

Appeared in: **1920** Bleak House. **1929** The Unwritten Law.

SWITZER, CARL "ALFALFA"
Born: Aug. 8, 1927, Paris, Ill. Died: Jan. 21, 1959, Sepulveda, Calif. (shot). Screen and television actor.

Appeared in: **1935** The following shorts: Southern Exposure; Beginner's Luck; Teacher's Beau; Sprucin' Up ; Little Papa; Little Sinner; Our Gang Follies of 1936. **1936** Easy to Take; Right in Your Lap; Kelly the Second; Pick a Star; Too Many Parents; General Spanky; plus the following shorts: Life Hesitates at 40; Pinch Singer; Divot Diggers; The Lucky Corner; Second Childhood; Arbor Day; Bored of Education; Two Too Young; Pay as You Exit; Spooky Hooky. **1937** Wild and Woolly; plus the following shorts: Reunion in Rhythm; Glove Taps; Three Smart Boys; Hearts are Trumps; Rushin' Ballet; Roamin' Holiday; Night'n Gales; Fishy Tales; Framing Youth; Pigskin Palooka; Mail and Female; Our Gang Follies of 1938. **1938** Scandal Street; plus the following shorts: Canned Fishing; Bear Facts; Three Men in a Tub; Came the Brawn; Feed 'Em and Weep; The Awful Tooth; Hide and Shriek; The Little Ranger; Party Fever; Aladdin's Lantern; Men in Fright; Football Romeo; Practical Jokers. **1939** The following shorts: Alfalfa's Aunt; Tiny Troubles; Duel Personalities; Clown Princes; Cousin Wilbur; Joy Scouts; Dog Daze; Auto Antics; Captain Spanky's Show Boat; Dad for a Day; Time Out for Lessons. **1940** The New Pupil; I Love You Again; Barnyard Follies; plus the following shorts: Alfalfa's Double; The Big Premiere; All About Hash; Bubbling Trouble; Good Bad Guys; Waldo's Last Stand; Goin' Fishin'; Kiddie Cure. **1941** Reg'lar Fellers. **1942** There's One Born Every Minute; Johnny Doughboy; Henry and Dizzy; The War Against Mrs. Hadley; Mrs. Wiggs of the Cabbage Patch; My Favorite Blonde. **1943** The Human Comedy; Dixie; Shantytown. **1944** Together Again; Rosie the Riveter; The Great Mike; Going My Way. **1945** She Wouldn't Say Yes. **1946** It's a Wonderful Life; The Gas House Kids; Courage of Lassie. **1947** The Gas House Kids Go West; The Gas House Kids in Hollywood. **1948** On Our Merry Way; State of the Union; Big Town Scandal; A Letter to Three Wives. **1950** Redwood Forest Trail. **1951** Cause for Alarm; Here Comes the Groom; Two Dollar Bettor. **1952** I Dream of Jeanie; Pat and Mike. **1953** Island in the Sky. **1954** The High and the Mighty; Track of the Cat; This Is My Love. **1956** The Ten Commandments; Between Heaven and Hell; Dig That Uranium. **1957** Motorcycle Game. **1958** The Defiant Ones.

SWOGER, HARRY (Harry Edward Swoger)
Born: Mar. 6, 1919, Ohio. Died: June 14, 1970, Van Nuys, Calif. Screen actor.

Appeared in: **1961** Angel Baby. **1964** Robin and the Seven Hoods.

SWOR, BERT
Born: 1878, Paris, Tenn. Died: Nov. 30, 1943, Tulsa, Okla. Screen, stage, vaudeville and minstrel actor. Appeared in vaudeville and films for a short time as Moran in "Moran and Mack" comedy team, usually referred to as the "Two Black Crows." Brother of actor John Swor (dec. 1965).

Appeared in: **1928** Ducks and Deducts (short); A Colorful Sermon (short). **1929** Why Bring That Up; plus the following shorts: The Golfers; A Hollywood Star; The New Halfback; Uppercut O'Brien. **1930** Anybody's War (with Mack).

SWOR, JOHN
Born: Apr. 7, 1883, Paris, Tenn. Died: July 15, 1965, Dallas, Tex. Screen, vaudeville, television and minstrel actor. Appeared for a time in vaudeville team "Moran and Mack" as Moran, usually referred to as the "Two Black Crows." Did not appear in films as part of team. Brother of actor Bert Swor (dec. 1943).

Appeared in: **1930** Up the River. **1931** Charlie Chan Carries On; Quick Millions. **1934** Here Comes the Navy.

SYDMETH, LOUISE
Born: 1868, London, England. Died: Nov. 26, 1938, New York, N.Y. Screen and stage actress.

Appeared in: **1912** His Mother's Hope.

SYDNEY, BASIL
Born: Apr. 23, 1894, St. Osyth, Essex, England. Died: Jan. 10, 1968, London, England. Screen and stage actor. Divorced from actresses Joyce Howard and Doris Keane (dec. 1945).

Appeared in: **1920** Romance (film debut). **1922** Red Hot Romance. **1932** The Midshipmaid. **1934** Dirty Work; The Third Clue. **1935** The Riverside Murder; The Tunnel (aka Transatlantic Tunnel-US); White Lilac. **1936** The Amateur Gentleman; Rhodes of Africa (aka Rhodes—US); Accused; Crime Over London (US 1938); Talk of the Devil (US 1937); Blind Man's Bluff; The Four Just Men (aka The Secret Four—US 1940); Shadowed Eyes. **1941** The Farmer's Wife; Spring Meeting; Ships with Winds (US 1942); The Black Sheep of Whitehall. **1942** The Next of Kin (US 1943); Went the Day Well? (aka 48 Hours—US 1944); They Came in Khaki; Big Blockade (documentary). **1946** Caesar and Cleopatra. **1947** Meet Me at Dawn (US 1948); The Man Within (aka The Smugglers—US 1948); Jassy (US 1948). **1948** Hamlet. **1950** The Angel with the Trumpet; Treasure Island; The Gay Duelist (reissue of Meet Me at Dawn—1947). **1951** The Magic Box (US 1952). **1952** Ivanhoe. **1953** Salome. **1954** Hell Below Zero; Star of India (US 1956). **1955** Simba; The Dam Busters. **1956** Around the World in 80 Days. **1957** Seawife; Island in the Sun. **1958** A Question of Adultery (US 1959). **1959** John Paul Jones; The Devil's Disciple. **1960** The Three Worlds of Gulliver; A Story of David; The Hands of Orlac.

SYDNEY, BRUCE
Born: 1889. Died: Oct. 18, 1942, Hollywood, Calif. Screen actor.

Appeared in: **1938** Kidnapped.

SYLVA, MARGUERITE
Born: 1876, Brussels, Belgium. Died: Feb. 21, 1957, Glendale, Calif. (auto accident). Stage and screen actress.

Appeared in: **1943** The Seventh Victim. **1945** The Gay Senorita.

SYLVANI, GLADYS
Born: 1885, England. Died: Apr. 20, 1953, Alexandria, Va. Screen actress. One of the first silent film stars in England. Came to U.S. in 1939.

Appeared in: **1911** Jim of the Mounted Police; All's Right with the World; The Three Lovers; Mother's Boy; Harry the Footballer; A Sprained Ankle; A Double Deception; 'Til Death Do Us Part; Twin Roses; The Torn Letter; Wealthy Brother John (aka Our Wealthy Nephew John—US); The Stolen Letters; The Greatest of These; Rachel's Sin; Love and a Sewing Machine. **1912** At the Eleventh Hour; The Bachelor's Ward; The Coiner's Den; The Deception; A Girl Alone; Jimmy Lester; Convict and Gentleman; Mary Has Her Way; Our Bessie; Traitress of Parton's Court; Pamela's Party; Love in a Laundry; Chuck and Stage; Love Wins in the End; The Editor and the Millionaire; A Woman's Wit; Jasmine; A Fisherman's Love Story; Her Only Son. **1913** Fisherman's Luck.

SYLVANO, WANDA
Born: Paris, France. Died: Apr., 1926, Paris, France. Screen actress.

SYLVESTER, FRANK L.
Born: 1868. Died: Dec. 17, 1931, Hollywood, Calif. (heart attack). Screen, stage and vaudeville actor.

SYLVESTER, HENRY
Born: 1882. Died: June 8, 1961. Screen actor.

Appeared in: **1935** Eagle's Blood. **1936** Darkest Africa (serial). **1942** Omaha Trail. **1943** Presenting Lily Mars; Hangmen Also Die.

SYLVIA, GABY
Born: 1920, France. Died: June 26, 1980, France (heart attack). Screen and stage actress.

Appeared in: **1944** 32 Rue de Montmartre. **1962** Mefiez-Vous Mesdames (Be Careful Ladies). **1978** We Will All Meet in Paradise.

SYLVIE (Louise Sylvain)
Born: 1882. Died: Jan., 1970, Paris, France. Screen and stage actress.

Appeared in: **1935** Crime et Chatiment (Crime and Punishment). **1939** The End of a Day. **1942** The Pasha's Wives. **1948** Le Corbeau (The Raven); Passionnelle. **1950** Angels of the Streets. **1952** Isle of Sinners (aka God Needs Men—Dieu a Besoin des Hommes); Forbidden Fruit (US 1959); The Little World of Dom Camillo (US 1953); Under the Paris Sky. **1955** Ulysses. **1957** The Adulteress (US 1958). **1959** The Mirror Has Two Faces; Anatomy of Love. **1960** Michael Strogoff. **1963** Cronaca Familiare (Family Diary). **1964** Chateau en Suede (Castle in Sweden aka Nutty, Naughty Chateau). **1966** La Vieille Dame Indigne (The Worthless Old Lady aka The Shameless Old Lady). Other French film: Therese Raquin.

SYMONDS, AUGUSTIN
Born: 1869. Died: July 14, 1944. Screen actor.

Appeared in: **1929** Four Fathers.

SZABO, SANDOR
Born: 1906. Died: Oct. 13, 1966. Professional wrestler and screen actor.

Appeared in: **1936** Once in a Blue Moon. **1943** Mission to Moscow. **1952** Dream Boat. **1955** Hell's Island. **1969** Topaz.

SZATHMARY, ALBERT
Born: 1909. Died: June 9, 1975, Hollywood, Calif. (pneumonia). Screen actor.

SZIGETI, JOSEPH
Born: Sept. 5, 1892, Budapest, Hungary. Died: Feb., 1973, Lucerne, Switzerland. Screen actor and musician.

Appeared in: **1944** Hollywood Canteen.

SZOLD, BERNARD
Born: 1894. Died: Nov. 15, 1960, Victoria, Tex. (heart attack). Screen actor and dramatic coach.

Appeared in: **1951** The Lemon Drop Kid; Flying Leathernecks; The Tanks Are Coming; M; Queen for a Day.

TABER, RICHARD
Born: Oct. 31, 1885. Died: Nov. 16, 1957, New York, N.Y. Screen, stage and television actor.

Appeared in: **1929** Lucky in Love. **1935** Two Fisted. **1948** The Naked City. **1950** The Sleeping City. **1951** Under the Gun.

TABLER, P. DEMPSEY (Perce Dempsey Tabler)
Born: Nov. 23, 1876, Tenn. Died: June 7, 1956, San Francisco, Calif. Screen actor and film producer. The third actor to portray the role of Tarzan.

Appeared in: **1915** Rule G. **1916** The Captive God; The Phantom; The Patriot. **1917** Babes in the Woods. **1919** Love Insurance. **1920** The Son of Tarzan (serial); The Gamesters. **1921** Smiling All the Way. **1923** Jungle Trail of the Son of Tarzan; Spawn of the Desert.

TABOADA, JULIO, JR.
Born: 1926, Mexico. Died: Sept. 15, 1962, Mexico City, Mexico (heart attack). Screen, stage, television actor and stage director.

TABOR, JOAN
Born: 1933. Died: Dec. 18, 1968, Culver City, Calif. Screen, stage and television actress. Divorced from actor Broderick Crawford.

Appeared in: **1960** The Bellboy. **1961** Teenage Millionaire.

TABOR, ROSE
Died: Sept. 19, 1925, Chicago, Ill. Screen actress.

TAFLER, SYDNEY
Born: 1916, London, England. Died: Nov, 8, 1979, London, England (cancer). Screen and stage actor. Married to actress Joy Shelton.

Appeared in: **1947** The Little Ballerina (film debut—US 1951); It Always Rains on Sunday (US 1949). **1948** Uneasy Terms; No Room at the Inn. **1949** Passport to Pimlico. **1950** Once a Sinner; Dance Hall. **1951** The Galloping Major; Assassin for Hire; The Lavender Hill Mob; Chelsea Story; Scarlet Thread; Hotel Sahara; Mystery Junction. **1952** Secret People; Blind Man's Bluff; Wide Boy; Emergency Call (aka The Hundred Hour Hunt—US 1953); Venetian Bird (aka The Assassin—US 1953); Time Gentlemen Please! **1953** Johnny on the Run; There Was a Young Lady; The Square Ring (US 1955); The Saint's Return (aka The Saint's Girl Friday—US); Operation Diplomat; The Floating Dutchman. **1954** The Sea Shall Not Have Them (US 1955); The Crowded Day. **1955** A Kid for Two Farthings (US 1956); Dial 999 (aka The Way Out—US 1956); The Glass Cage (aka The Glass Tomb—US); Cockleshell Heroes (US 1956); The Woman for Joe. **1956** Reach For The Sky (US 1957); Guilty?; The Long Arm (aka The Third Key—US 1957); Fire Maidens of Outer Space. **1957** Interpol (aka Pickup Alley—US); Booby Trap; The Counterfeit Plan; The Surgeon's Knife. **1958** Carve Her Name With Pride; The Bank Raiders. **1959** Too Many Crooks; The Crowning Touch; Follow a Star (US 1961). **1960** Bottoms Up!; Let's Get Married; Sink the Bismarck!; Light Up the Sky; No Kidding (aka Beware of Children—US 1961); Make Mine Mink; The Bulldog Breed. **1961** Carry On Regardless (US 1963); Five Golden Hours; A Weekend With Lulu. **1964** The 7th Dawn. **1965** Runaway Railway; Promise Her Anything (US 1966). **1966** Alfie. **1967** Berserk. **1970** The Birthday Party; The Adventurers. **1971** Danger Point. **1977** The Spy Who Loved Me.

TAFT, SARA
Died: Sept. 24, 1973, Los Angeles, Calif. (heart attack). Screen and television actress.

Appeared in: **1943** Cry Havoc. **1951** You Never Can Tell. **1958** Vertigo. **1960** The Story of Ruth. **1961** Parrish. **1962** Tower of London. **1964** The Young Lovers. **1968** Blackbeard's Ghost. **1969** Death of a Gunfighter; The Reivers.

TAGGART, BEN L.
Born: Apr. 5, 1889, Ottawa, Canada. Died: May 17, 1947, Santa Monica, Calif. Screen and stage actor.

Appeared in: **1915** The Woman Next Door; The Sentimental Lady. **1917** Brown of Harvard; She. **1931** Monkey Business; Silence. **1932** Taxi; Hold 'Em Jail; Horsefeathers; Strangers in Love; Million Dollar Legs. **1933** The Mayor of Hell. **1934** The Thin Man; The Notorious Sophie Lang. **1935** Unknown Woman; The Whole Town's Talking; plus the following shorts: Slightly Static; Manhattan Monkey Business; Public Ghost No. 1; Okay Toots!; Poker at Eight; Southern Exposure. **1936** The Count Takes the Count (short); Neighborhood House (short). **1937** This is My Affair. **1938** A Criminal is Born (short); The Overland Express. **1939** Rattling Romeo (short); Skinny the Moocher (short); The Green Hornet (serial); Daredevils of the Red Circle (serial); Tell No Tales. **1940** Flash Gordon Conquers the Universe (serial); Before I Hang; Nobody's Children. **1941** The Lone Wolf Takes a Chance; Man-Made Monster; The Wildcat of Tucson; The Medico of Painted Springs; I'll Sell My Life; Two in a Taxi; Hard Guy; Penny Serenade. **1942** Don Winslow of the Navy (serial); The Miracle Kid; Escape from Crime. **1944** Mr. Winkle Goes to War.

TAGGART, HAL
Born: 1882. Died: Dec. 12, 1971. Screen and vaudeville actor. Billed in vaudeville with Tommy Mann as a song and dance act.

Appeared in: **1957** The Monster That Challenged the World. **1962** Advise and Consent.

TAGLIABUE, CARLO
Born: 1898, Italy. Died: April 5, 1978, Monza, Italy. Opera performer and screen actor.

Appeared in: **1954** Carosello Napoletano (Neopolitan Carousel—US 1961).

TAILLON, ANGUS D.
Born: 1888, Ontario, Canada. Died: May 8, 1953, Hollywood, Calif. Screen actor and stand-in for Barry Fitzgerald.

Appeared in: **1949** Top O' the Morning.

TAIT, ROBERT (Robert Blaikie Tait)
Born: Jan. 30, 1900, Canada. Died: May 28, 1950, Woodland Hills, Calif. (heart disease). Screen, radio actor and singer.

TAKADA, MINORU
Born: 1899, Japan. Died: Dec. 28, 1977, Tokyo, Japan (cancer). Opera performer, screen and television actor.

Appeared in: **1960** Battle in Outer Space; Dairoku no Yougisha (Six Suspects—US 1961).

TALAZAC, ODETTE
Died: 1948, France. Screen actress. Entered films in 1929.

Appeared in: **1929** Le Collier de la Reine. **1930** Le Sang d'un Poete. **1932** Le Million. **1936** Le Crime de Monsieur Lange (The Crime of Monsieur Lange—US 1964). **1937** Maternite. **1938** L'Esclave Blanche. **1939** La Regle du Jeu. **1947** The Murderer Lives at Number 21.

TALBOT, MAE
Born: 1869. Died: Aug. 4, 1942, Glendale, Calif. (heart attack). Stage and screen actress.

TALBOT, SLIM (Joseph Bovelle Talbot)
Born: 1896. Died: Feb., 1973, Boulevard, Calif. Screen actor, rodeo rider and stuntman.

Appeared in: **1958** Giant; The Big Country. **1962** The Man Who Shot Liberty Valance.

TALIAFERRO, EDITH
Born: 1894. Died: Mar. 2, 1958, Newtown, Conn. Screen, stage, radio and vaudeville actress. Sister of screen actress Mabel Taliaferro (dec. 1979). Entered films with Lasky Co. in 1915.

TALIAFERRO, HAL See WALES, WALLY

TALIAFERRO, MABEL
Born: May 21, 1889, New York, N.Y. Died: Jan. 24, 1979, Honolulu, Hawaii. Screen and stage actress. Sister of actress Edith Taliaferro (dec. 1958). Divorced from stage manager Frederick W. Thompson (dec. 1919), actor Tom Corrigan (dec. 1941), and Joseph O'Brien. Later married to actor Robert Ober (dec. 1950).

Appeared in: **1911** Cinderella. **1916** The Snowbird; The Sunbeam. **1917** The Slacker; Magdalene of the Hills; A Wife By Proxy; The Jury of Fate. **1918** Draft 258. **1921** Sentimental Tommy; The Rich Slave. **1940** My Love Came Back.

TALLMAN, FRANK
Born: 1919. Died: Apr. 15, 1978, Orange County, Calif. (plane crash). Stunt pilot and actor for screen and television. Was partner with stunt pilot Paul Mantz (dec. 1965).

Appeared in: **1963** It's A Mad, Mad, Mad, Mad World. **1969** The Wrecking Crew. **1970** Catch 22. **1974** The Great Waldo Pepper. **1978** The Cat from Outer Space.

TALMADGE, CONSTANCE
Born: Apr. 19, 1898, Brooklyn, N.Y. Died: Nov. 23, 1973, Los Angeles, Calif. (pneumonia). Screen actress and film producer. Sister of actresses Natalie (dec. 1969) and Norma Talmadge (dec. 1957). Entered films with Vitagraph as an extra.

Appeared in: **1914** Buddy's First Call; Our Fairy Paly; The Moonstone of Nez; Buddy's Downfall; Uncle Bill; The Mysterious Lodger; Father's Timepiece; The Peacemaker; The Evolution of Percival; In Bridal Attire; The Egyptian Mummy; Forcing Dad's Consent; In the Latin Quarter. **1915** Billy, the Bear Tamer; Billy's Wager; The Green Cat; The Young Man Who Figgered; A Study in Tramps; The Lady of Shalott; The Master of His House; The Boarding House Feud; The Vanishing Vault; Spades are Trumps; Bertie's Stratagem; Captivating Mary Carstairs; Can You Beat It?; Beached and Bleached; The Missing Links. **1916** The She-Devil; The Microscope Mystery; Intolerance; The Matrimaniac. **1917** Scandal; Girl of the Timber Claims; The Honeymoon; Betsy's Burglar. **1918** The Lesson; Up the Road With Sally; A Pair of Silk Stockings; Mrs. Leffingwell's Boots; Sauce for the Goose; The Studio Girl; The Shuttle; A Lady's Name. **1919** Who Cares?; Experimental Marriage; The Veiled Adventure; The Fall of Babylon; A Tempermental Wife; The Love Expert; Happiness a la Mode; A Virtuous Vamp; Romance and Arabella. **1920** The Perfect Woman; Two Weeks; In Search of a Sinner; Good References; Dangerous Business. **1921** Mama's Affair; Lessons in Love; Wedding Bells; Woman's Place. **1922** Polly of the Follies; The Divorcee; East is West; The Primitive Lover. **1923** Dulcy; A Dangerous Maid. **1924** The Goldfish; Her Night of Romance; In Hollywood with Potash and Perlmutter. **1925** Her Sister from Paris; Learning to Love. **1926** The Duchess of Buffalo; Sybil. **1927** Venus of Venice; Breakfast at Sunrise. **1929** Venus.

TALMADGE, NATALIE
Born: 1899, Brooklyn, N.Y. Died: June 19, 1969, Santa Monica, Calif. Screen actress. Divorced from screen actor Buster Keaton (dec. 1966) and mother of screen actor Robert Talmadge. Sister of screen actresses Norma (dec. 1957) and Constance Talmadge (dec. 1973).

Appeared in: **1919** The Isle of Conquest. **1921** The Passion Flower. **1923** Our Hospitality.

TALMADGE, NORMA
Born: May 26, 1893 or 1897, Jersey City, N.J. or Niagara Falls, N.Y.?. Died: Dec. 24, 1957, Las Vegas, Nev. (cerebral stroke—pneumonia). Screen, stage, radio and vaudeville actress. Divorced from film producer Joseph Schenck (dec. 1961) and comedian and producer

George Jessel (dec. 1981). Sister of actresses Natalie (dec. 1969) and Constance Talmadge (dec. 1973).

Appeared in: **1910** A Dixie Mother; Mother by Proxy; Heart O' the Hill; The Household Pest; The Love of the Chrysanthemums. **1911** A Tale of Two Cities; In Neighboring Kingdom; Mrs. 'Enery 'Awkins; Her Hero; Nellie the Model; The Convict's Child; Forgotten; The Child Crusoes; The Wildcat; The Thumb Print; Her Sister's Children; A Broken Spell; Sky Pilot; The General's Daughter; Paola and Francesca. **1912** The First Violin; The Troublesome Stepdaughter; Mr. Butler Butles; The Lovesick Maidens of Cuddleton; Fortunes of a Composer; Omens and Oracles; Mrs. Carter's Necklace; The Midget's Revenge; Mr. Bolter's Sweetheart; O'Hara Helps Cupid; The Extension Table; Squatter and Philosopher; Captain Barnacles' Messmate; Captain Barnacles' Waif; Captain Barnacles' Reformer. **1913** The Other Woman; Casey at the Bat; Wanted—A Strong Hand; The Blue Rose; He Fell in Love With His Mother-In-Law; Counsel for the Defense; 'Arriet's Baby; The Silver Cigarette Case; The Doctor's Secret; Fanny's Conspiracy; Father's Hatband; Plot and Counterplot; A Lady and Her Maid; Sleuthing; The Sacrifice of Kathleen; Officer John Donovan; His Little Page; Country Barber; O'Hara as a Guardian Angel; An Old Man's Love Story; The Tables Turned; Solitaires; Just Show People; His Official Appointment; The Vavasour Ball; Under the Daisies; O'Hara's Godchild; His Silver Bachelorhood; The Honorable Algernon; Counsel for the Defense; An Elopement at Home. **1914** The Hero; Old Reliable; Sawdust and Salome; The Helpful Sisterhood; Cupid vs Money; Mister Murphy's Wedding Present; John Rance, Gentleman; Politics and the Press; The Loan Shark King; A Question of Clothes; Goodbye Summer; Sunshine and Shadows; Memories in Men's Souls; The Hidden Letters; The Peacemaker; A Daughter of Israel; The Curing of Myra May; Fogg's Millions; The Mill of Life; Etta of the Footlights; A Wayward Daughter; Dorothy Danebridge, Militant. **1915** The Barrier of Faith; A Daughter's Strange Inheritance; Elsa's Brother; The Pillar of Flame; The Battle Cry of Peace; The Captivating Mary Carstairs; Janet of the Chorus. **1916** The Missing Links; The Crown Prince's Double; Martha's Vindication; The Children in the House; The Honorable Algy; The Criminal; The Devil's Needle; Going Straight; Fifty-Fifty; The Social Secretary. **1917** Panthea; Poppy; The Secret of Storm Country; The Law of Compensation; The Moth; The Lone Wolf; Under False Colors. **1918** The Forbidden City; The Safety Curtain; The Ghost of Yesterday; By Right of Purchase; De Luxe Annie; Her Only Way; the Heart of Wetona; Salome. **1919** The Probation Wife; The Way of a Woman; The New Moon; The Isle of Conquest. **1920** The Right of Way; The Loves and Lies; A Daughter of Two Worlds; The Woman Gives; Yes or No; The Branded Woman. **1921** The Passion Flower; The Sign on the Door; The Wonderful Thing. **1922** Foolish Wives; The Eternal Flame; Smilin' Through; Love's Redemption; Branded. **1923** Ashes of Vengeance; Dust of Desire; Within the Law; The Voice from the Minaret; Sawdust. **1924** Secrets; The Only Woman; The Song of Love; In Hollywood with Potash and Perlmutter. **1925** The Lady; Graustark. **1926** Kiki. **1927** The Dove; Camille. **1928** Show People; The Woman Disputed. **1930** New York Nights; Du Barry, Woman of Passion.

TALMADGE, RICHARD (Sylvester Metzetti)
Born: 1892, Switzerland. Died: Jan. 25, 1981, Carmel, Calif. (cancer). Screen actor, stuntman, circus performer and film producer.

Appeared in: **1913** The Million Dollar Mystery (serial). **1921** Robin Hood; The Unknown. **1922** The Cub Reporter; Lucky Dan; Putting It Over; Watch Him Step; Wildcat Jordan; Taking Chances. **1923** Let's Go; The Speed King; Danger Ahead; Through the Flames. **1924** Hail the Hero; In Fast Company; On Time; Stepping Lively; American Manners. **1925** The Fighting Demon; Laughing at Danger; The Isle of Hope; Jimmie's Millions; The Mysterious Stranger; The Prince of Pep; Tearing Through; The Wall Street Whiz; Youth and Adventure. **1926** The Better Man; The Blue Streak; The Broadway Gallant; Doubling With Danger; The Merry Cavalier; The Night Patrol; The Black Pirate. **1927** The Gaucho. **1928** The Cavalier. **1929** The Bachelor's Club. **1930** The Poor Millionaire. **1931** Dancing Dynamite; Yankee Don. **1932** Speed Madness; Get That Girl; Scareheads. **1934** Pirate Treasure (serial). **1935** Never Too Late; Now or Never; The Fighting Pilot. **1936** The Speed Reporter. **1948** Black Eagle.

TALMAN, WILLIAM
Born: Feb. 4, 1915, Detroit, Mich. Died: Aug. 30, 1968, Encino, Calif. (cancer). Screen, stage, television actor and screenwriter. Divorced from actress Barbara Read (dec. 1963).

Appeared in: **1949** Red, Hot and Blue (film debut); I Married a Communist. **1950** The Woman on Pier Thirteen; The Armored Car Robbery; The Kid from Texas. **1951** The Racket. **1952** One Minute to Zero. **1953** The Hitch-Hiker; City That Never Sleeps. **1955** Smoke Signal; Big House, USA; Crashout. **1956** The Man Is Armed; Two Gun Lady; Uranium Boom. **1957** The Persuader; Hell on Devil's Island. **1967** The Ballad of Josie.

TALUN, WALTER
Born: 1910. Died: Sept. 15, 1980, Wheatfield, N.Y. Professional wrestler and screen actor.

Appeared in: **1951** David and Bathsheba.

TAMARA (Tamara Swann)
Died: Feb. 22, 1943, near Lisbon, Portugal (plane crash). Screen, stage actress and singer.

Appeared in: **1928** A Midsummer Night's Dream. **1935** Sweet Surrender. **1937** Roarin' Lead. **1940** No, No, Nanette.

TAMBERLANI, CARLO
Born: 1899, Italy. Died: Aug. 5, 1980, Subiaco, Italy. Screen and stage actor.

Appeared in: **1939** Scipione L'Africano (Scipine the African). **1940** Giovanni De Medici, The Leader. **1951** Measure for Measure. **1955** Amici per la Pelle (Friends for Life—US 1964). **1956** Alone in the Streets. **1957** Les Week-ends de Neron (aka Nero's Mistress—US 1962 and aka Nero's Big Weekend). **1959** Amici per la Belle (Bosum Friends aka The Woman in the Painting—US). **1960** The Last Days of Pompeii. **1961** Il Colosso di Roda (The Colossus of Rhodes); Le Geant de la Vallee des Rois (aka Son of Samson—US 1962); La Guerra di Troia (aka The Trojan Horse—US 1962); Teseo Contro il Minotauro (aka The Minotaur—US 1961). **1963** Giulio Cesare il Conquistatore delle Gallic (Caesar the Conqueror). **1964** Gli Schiavi piu Forti del Mondo (Seven Slaves Against the World—US 1965). **1966** Tabu Fugitivos de los Mares del Sur (aka The Drums of Tabu—US 1967). **1969** Ehi, Amico ... C'e Sabata, hai Chiuso (aka Sabata—US). **1975** Conselor at Crime. **1979** The Divine Nymph.

TAMBLYN, EDWARD
Born: 1907, Yonkers, N.Y. Died: June 22, 1957, Hollywood, Calif. Stage and screen actor. Father of actor Russ Tamblyn.

Appeared in: **1931** The Flood. **1933** The Sweetheart of Sigma Chi. **1934** Harold Teen; Money Means Nothing. **1935** A Shot in the Dark. **1936** Palm Springs.

TAMIROFF, AKIM
Born: Oct. 29, 1899, Baku, Russia. Died: Sept. 17, 1972, Palm Springs, Calif. Screen, stage and television actor. Married to actress Tamara Shayne. Nominated for 1936 Academy Award for Best Supporting Actor for The General Died at Dawn and in 1943 for For Whom the Bell Tolls.

Appeared in: **1932** Okay, America! **1933** Queen Christina; Gabriel Over the White House; Storm at Daybreak. **1934** Fugitive Lovers; Scarlet Empress; The Merry Widow; Chained; Here Is My Heart; The Captain Hates the Sea; Sadie McKee; The Great Flirtation. **1935** Lives of a Bengal Lancer; Naughty Marietta; The Winning Ticket; China Seas; Rumba; The Last Outpost; Black Sleep; Big Broadcast of 1936; Paris in Spring; Two Fisted; Go Into Your Dance; Black Fury; Gay Deception; The Story of Louis Pasteur. **1936** Desire; Woman Trap; The General Died at Dawn; The Jungle Princess; Anthony Adverse. **1937** The Soldier and the Lady (aka Michael Strogoff); Her Husband Lies; King of Gamblers; High, Wide and Handsome; The Great Gambini. **1938** The Buccaneer; Spawn of the North; Dangerous to Know; Ride a Crooked Mile. **1939** Paris Honeymoon; Union Pacific; The Magnificent Fraud; King of Chinatown; Honeymoon in Bali; Disputed Passage; Geronimo. **1940** The Way of All Flesh; Untamed; Northwest Mounted Police; The Great McGinty. **1941** Texas Rangers Ride Again; New York Town; The Corsican Brothers. **1942** Tortilla Flat; Are Husbands Necessary? **1943** Five Graves to Cairo; For Whom the Bell Tolls; His Butler's Sister. **1944** The Bridge of San Luis Rey; Dragon Seed; Miracle of Morgan's Creek; Can't Help Singing; Black Magic. **1946** Pardon My Past; A Scandal in Paris (aka Thieves Holiday). **1947** Fiesta; The Gangster. **1948** My Girl Tisa; 10th Avenue Angel; Relentless. **1949** Black Magic (aka Cagliastro); Outpost in Morocco. **1953** Desert Legion; You Know What Sailors Are (US 1954). **1955** They Who Dare; Confidential Report (aka Mr. Arkadin—US 1962). **1956** Black Sheep; Anastasia. **1957** Battle Hell; The Yangtse Incident; Cartouche. **1958** Touch of Evil; Me and the Colonel. **1959** Desert Desperadoes. **1960** The Tartar Invasion; Ocean's Eleven. **1961** Romanoff and Juliet (aka Dig That Juliet); They Who Dare; Le Baccanti (aka The Bacchantes—US 1963). **1962** Le Proces (aka The Trial—US 1963); The Reluctant Saint; Mr. Arkadin; Don Quixote; Col ferro e col fuoco (aka Daggers of Blood and Invasion 1700—US 1965). **1963** With Fire and Sword; Light and Day. **1964** Topkapi!; Panic Button. **1965** Bambole (aka The Dolls); The Amphaville; La fabuleuse adventure de Marco Polo (aka Marco the Magnificent—US 1966); Lord Jim. **1966** Campanadas a medianoche (aka Chimes at Midnight and Falstaff—US 1967); Lt. Robin Crusoe,

USN; Hotel Paradiso; The Liquidator; After the Fox; Funeral in Berlin. **1967** Every Man's Woman; The Vulture; A Rose for Everyone. **1968** Tenderly (aka The Girl Who Couldn't Say No—US 1969); Great Catherine. **1969** 100 Rifles; The Great Bank Robbery. **1970** Venus in Furs.

TAMIYA, JIRO (Goro Shibata)
Born: 1935, Japan. Died: Dec. 29, 1978, Tokyo, Japan (suicide—gunshot). Screen and television actor.

Appeared in: **1968** Fushin no Taki (The Time of Reckoning—US 1970). **1970** Jaga wa Hashitta (The Creature Called Man—US); Tough Guy. **1974** Theatre of Life.

TAMMY, MARK
Died: July 10, 1975. Screen actor.

TANAKA, KINUYO
Born: Nov, 28, 1909, Shimonoseki, Japan. Died: Mar. 21, 1977, Japan? (cerebral tumor). Screen, stage, television actress and film director. Married to actor Hiroshi Shimizu.

Appeared in: **1924** Genroku Onna (Woman of Genroku Era, film debut); Mura No Makiba. **1925** Shizen Wa Sabaku (Nature Is the Judge); Killer of One Hundred Men in Ichinji Temple. **1926** Mayamashiki Koro (The Age of Anguish); Machi no Hitobito (Town People). **1927** Hazukashii Yume (Intimate Dream aka Shameful Dream). **1928** Mura no Hanayome (The Village Bride); Kaikoku Ki (Tales from a Country by the Sea); Moshimo Kanojo Ga (If She Was); Kindai Musha Shugyo (Discipline of the Modern Warrior); Kare to Denen (He and the Countryside). **1929** Daitokai Rodo-Hen (The Big City—Worker's Version); Daigaku wa Detakeredo (Graduated But); He and Life; A Happy Song. **1930** Hohoemu Jinsei (A Smiling Life); Rakudai wa Shitakeredo (I Flunked But); Ojosan (Young Miss); Daitokai Bakuhatsu-Hen (The Big City—Explosive Version); Kinuyo Monogatari (Story of Kinuyo); The Great Metropolis; Chapter of Labor. **1931** Madame to Nyobo (The Neighbour's Wife and Mine); Al Yo Jinrui to Tomoni Are (Love Should Stay With People). **1932** Chushingura (The Loyal Forty Seven Ronin I, II); Seishun no Yume Izuko (Where are the Dreams of Youth). **1933** Tokyo no Onna (Woman of Tokyo); Hijosen no Onna (Women on the Firing Line); Hanayome no Negoto (The Bride Talks in Her Sleep); Izu no Odoriko (Dancing Girls of Izu); Sobo (Two Eyes). **1934** Sono Yo No Onna (The Woman of That Night); Toyo no Hana (The Mothers of the Orient). **1935** Hakoiri Musume (The Young Virgin); Okoto to Sasuke (Okoto and Sasuke); Jinsei no Onimotsu (Burden of Life). **1937** Hanakago no Uta (Song of a Flower Basket); Joi Kinuyo Sensei (Doctress Kinuyo); The Tree of Love. **1938** Aisen Katsura. **1939** Okayo no Kakugo (Okayo's Resolution); Hana Aru Zasso (The Flowering Herbs); Two sequels of 1938 film Aisen Katsura. **1940** Naniwa Onna (A Woman of Osaka); Kinuyo no Hatsukoi (First Love of Kinuyo). **1941** Duel at Ichijoji Temple. **1942** A Certain Woman. **1944** Rikugun (Army); Danjuro Sanda (Three Generations of Danjuro); Miyamoto Musashi (Musashi Miyamoto). **1945** Hissho Ka (Song of Victory); Sanjusangen-Do Toshiya Monogatari (The Story of the Arrow Crossing the Sanjusangen-do). **1946** Josei no Shori (Women's Victory); Utamaro O Meguru Gonin No Onna (Utamaro and His Five Women). **1947** Joyu Sumako no Koi (Love of Actress Sumako); Phoenix. **1948** Yoru No Onna-Tachi (Woman of the Night); Kaze no Naka no Mendori (A Hen in the Wind). **1949** Waga Koi Wa Meonu (Flame of My Love); Shinshaku Yotosuya Kaidan (The Yotsuya Ghost Story I, II). **1950** Munakata Shimai (Munakata Sisters). **1951** Ginza Kesho (Cover-Up of Ginza); Oyu-Sama (Miss Oyu); Musashino Fujin (Lady Musashino); Inazuma Soshi (Tales of Lightning); Oboro Kago (The Mysterious Palanquin). **1952** Okasan (Mother); Saikaku Ichidai Onna (Life of Oharu—US 1964). **1953** Ugetsu Monogatari (Ugetsu—US 1954); Entotsu no Mieru Basho (Four Chimneys); Shishi no Za (Under the Sign of the Lion). **1954** Sansho Dayu (Sansho the Bailiff aka The Bailiff—US 1969); Uwasa no Onna (The Woman in the Rumor). **1955** Osho Ichidai (The Life of a Chess Player); Umbrella in Moonlight; Floating Clouds. **1956** Arashi (The Storm); Nagareru (Flowering); Street of Wandering Pigeons; Extreme Sadness; Mixed Family. **1957** Kiiroi Karasu (Yellow Crow); Women in Prison; Geisha in the Old City; Behold Thy Son. **1958** Higanbana (Equinox Flower—US 1977); Kanashimi wa Onna Dakeni (Women Have Trouble); Narayama-Bushi-ko (The Ballad of the Narayama—US 1961). **1959** Nippon Tanjo (The Birth of Japan); Ototo (Her Brother—US 1960); Mother and Her Children; These Wonderful Girls; The Three Treasures; Their Own World. **1961** Wakarete Ikiru Toki Mo (Eternity of Love—US). **1962** Mama, I Need You; Horoki (Lonely Lane—US 1963). **1963** Taiheiyo Hitoribocchi (My Enemy, the Sea aka Alone on the Pacific—US 1964); A Legend or Was It. **1964** Koge (The Scent of Incense). **1965** Akahige (Red Beard—US 1966); Stand By Collegiate. **1966** Ereki no Wakadaisho (Campus a Go-Go—US); Arupusu no Wakadaisho (It

Started in the Alps—US). **1967** River of Forever; Judo Champion. **1974** Sandakan Hachiban Shokan-Bokyo (Sandakan House No. 8—US 1977). **1975** Aru Eiga Kantoku no Shogai-Mizoguchi Kenji No Kiroku (Kenji Mizoguchi: Story of a Film Director). **1976** Kita no Misaki (Cape of the North); Daichi no Komoriuta (Lullaby of the Earth). **1979** My Love Has Been Burning.

TANAKA, SHOJI
Born: 1886, Japan. Died: Oct. 20, 1918, New York, N.Y. (Spanish influenza). Screen actor.

TANDY, VALERIE
Born: Aug. 4, 1921, Birmingham, England. Died: Apr. 27, 1965, London, England. Stage and screen actress.

TANG, FRANK
Died: 1968. Screen actor.

Appeared in: **1930** The Great Divide. **1936** The Leathernecks Have Landed. **1945** Objective Burma; God is My Co-Pilot. **1955** Soldier of Fortune.

TANGUAY, EVA
Born: 1878, Marbleton, Canada. Died: Jan. 11, 1947, Los Angeles, Calif. (heart attack and cerebral hemorrhage). Screen, stage and vaudeville actress. Referred to as the "I Don't Care Girl." Appeared in films for Selznick in 1917.

TANNEN, CHARLES D.
Born: 1915, New York, N.Y. Died: Dec. 28, 1980, San Bernardino, Calif. (heart attack). Screen, stage actor and screenwriter. Son of actor Julius Tannen (dec. 1965) and brother of actor William Tannen (dec. 1976).

Appeared in: **1936** Ah, Wilderness; Small Town Girl; Half Angel; Sins of Man; Educating Father. **1937** Once Every Year. **1938** Mr. Lucky Star; Submarine Patrol. **1939** Jesse James; Young Mr. Lincoln; Drums Along the Mohawk; Swanee River. **1940** Grapes of Wrath; The Return of Frank James. **1941** Cadet Girl. **1942** To the Shores of Tripoli; Sundown Jim; Little Tokyo, U.S.A.; Footlight Serenade; Careful, Soft Shoulder; Manila Calling; Quiet Please, Murder. **1943** Crash Dive. **1945** The Spider; Doll Face. **1946** Johnny Comes Flying Home; Shock; Behind Green Lights; It Shouldn't Happen to a Dog; If I'm Lucky. **1948** Green Grass of Wyoming. **1950** The Jackpot. **1951** You're in the Navy Now (aka U.S.S. Teakettle). **1952** Without Warning; Red Skies of Montana. **1953** City of Bad Men; Dangerous Crossing; Down Among the Sheltering Palms; Gentlemen Prefer Blondes. **1954** The Country Girl; The Steel Cage; The Bridges at Toki-Ri; Gorilla At Large. **1955** The Girl in the Red Velvet Swing. **1957** The Monster That Challenged the World; The Proud Ones. **1960** Ma Barker's Killer Brood. **1961** Voyage to the Bottom of the Sea. **1962** Stagecoach to Dancer's Rock.

TANNEN, JULIUS
Born: 1881. Died: Jan. 3, 1965, Hollywood, Calif. Screen and vaudeville actor. Father of actors Charles (dec. 1981) and William Tannen (dec. 1976).

Appeared in: **1935** Collegiate. **1936** Half Angel; The Road to Glory; 36 Hours to Kill; Dimples; Pigskin Parade; Reunion; One in a Million; Stowaway. **1937** Fair Warning; Love Is News; Mama Runs Wild. **1938** Love Is a Headache. **1939** Danger Flight; The Magnificent Fraud. **1940** The Mortal Storm; Christmas in July. **1942** Harvard Here I Come. **1944** The Great Moment. **1945** The Dolly Sisters; House of Frankenstein. **1947** Mad Wednesday. **1948** Unfaithfully Yours. **1952** Clash by Night; Singing in the Rain. **1958** The Last Hurrah.

TANNEN, WILLIAM "BILL"
Born: 1911, New York, N.Y. Died: Dec. 2, 1976, Woodland Hills, Calif. Screen actor. Son of actor Julius Tannen (dec. 1965) and brother of actor Charles Tannen (dec. 1981).

Appeared in: **1934** The Band Plays On. **1935** A Thrill for Thelma (short); It's in the Air; She Couldn't Take It; Murder in the Fleet. **1936** Crash Donovan; Foolproof (short). **1937** When Love Is Young. **1939** The Story of Dr. Jenner (short). **1940** Pound Foolish (short); Jack Pot (short); New Moon; Sky Murder; Flight Command. **1941** The Big Store; 1-2-3 Go! (short); Whistling in the Dark; Dr. Jekyll and Mr. Hyde; More Trifles of Importance (short); I'll Wait for You. **1942** Joe Smith, American; Fingers at the Window; Nazi Agent; Woman of the Year; Pacific Rendezvous; Stand By for Action; Mighty Lak a Goat (short); New Moon. **1943** Air Raid Wardens; Pilot No. 5. **1944** The Canterville Ghost; Dark Shadows (short). **1945** Abbott and Costello in Hollywood. **1948** An Innocent Affair. **1949** Alaska Patrol; The Mysterious Desperado; Riders of the Range; Abandoned Woman (aka

Abandoned). **1950** Chain Gang; Sunset in the West; Pygmy Island. **1951** A Yank in Korea; New Mexico; Insurance Investigator; Roaring City; Blue Blood; Rhythm Inn. **1952** Road Agent; Jungle Jim and the Forbidden Land; Jet Job. **1953** Raiders of the Seven Seas; Jack McCall, Desperado; 99 River Street; El Paso Stampede; Dangerous Crossing. **1954** Sitting Bull; Jesse James vs. The Daltons; Captain Kidd and the Slave Girl; The Law vs. Billy the Kid; The Golden Idol. **1955** Dial Red O; Devil Goddess. **1956** Blackjack Ketchum, Desperado. **1957** The Tijuana Story. **1960** Noose for a Gunman. **1965** Great Sioux Massacre. **1968** Panic in the City.

TANNER, JAMES J.
Born: 1873. Died: Apr. 3, 1934, Hollywood, Calif. Screen actor and artist.

TANO, GUY (Gaetano Rocco)
Born: 1914. Died: Aug. 19, 1952, New York, N.Y. Screen and stage actor.

TANSEY, MRS. EMMA
Born: 1884. Died: Mar. 23, 1942, Los Angeles, Calif. Screen and stage actress. Entered films approx. 1921.

Appeared in: **1922** Are Children to Blame? **1925** Fast Fightin'. **1930** Beyond the Rio Grande. **1935** Okay Toots! (short). **1938** Knight of the Plains. **1941** Meet John Doe.

TANSEY, ROBERT
Born: 1899. Died: June 17, 1951, Los Angeles, Calif. (heart attack). Screen actor, film director and screenwriter.

Appeared in: **1911** Ludwig from Germany. **1912** The Street Beautiful; Brother of the Rat. **1921** Romance of the West. **1922** Are Children to Blame?

TAPLEY, ROSE
Born: June 30, 1883, Petersburg, Va. Died: Feb. 23, 1956, Woodland Hills, Calif. Stage and screen actress. Entered films with Thomas Edison Productions.

Appeared in: **1905** Wanted a Wife (film debut). **1911** Vanity Fair; One Flag at Last. **1912** As You Like It; On Her Wedding Night; His Father's Son. **1913** The Delayed Letter; The Diver; A Regiment of Two; The Moulding. **1914** The Christian; Eve's Daughter (aka The Artist's Madonna); My Official Wife; The Memories that Count; The Shadow of the Past; He Never Knew; Happy Go Lucky. **1915** The "Jarr Family" Series. **1916** Susie, the Sleuth; Rose of the South. **1922** Her Majesty. **1923** Java Head. **1924** The Man Who Fights Alone. **1925** The Pony Express; The Scarlet Honeymoon; The Redeeming Sin. **1926** The Prince of Pilsen; Morganson's Finish. **1927** It; God's Great Wilderness; Out of the Past. **1929** The Charlatan. **1930** His First Command. **1931** Resurrection.

TAPTUKA, CLARENCE S.
Born: 1898. Died: Nov. 8, 1967, Albuquerque, N.Mex. American Indian screen actor. Appeared in silent films.

TARASOVA, ALLA K.
Born: 1898. Died: Apr., 1973, Moscow, Russia. Stage and screen actress.

Appeared in: **1934** Thunderstorm. **1937** Peter the First. **1939** The Conquests of Peter the Great.

TARBAT, LORNA
Born: 1916, England. Died: Apr., 1961, Harrow, Middlesex, England. Screen, stage and television actress.

TARBUTT, FRAZER
Born: 1894. Died: June 16, 1918, France (air crash—killed in action). Screen actor.

TARCAI, MARY
Born: 1907. Died: Sept. 22, 1979, Cleveland, Ohio. Screen, stage actress and drama coach. Married to screenwriter Arthur Singer (dec. 1978).

Appeared in: **1951** Half Angel.

TARJAN, GEORGE
Born: 1910, Hungary. Died: Dec. 25, 1973, London, England. Stage actor, director, screen actor and newscaster. Married to actress Etelka Dan.

Appeared in: **1935** Egy ej Velencebzn.

TARKHANOV, MIKHAIL
Born: Russia. Died: Aug., 1948, Moscow, Russia. Screen and stage actor.

Appeared in: **1935** The Youth of Maxim. **1939** The Conquests of Peter the Great.

TARZAN
Born: 1916. Died: 1940, Los Angeles, Calif. Screen and television performer. Collective name for at least two horses used by actor Ken Maynard in westerns from silent days until 1940.

TASHMAN, KITTY
Born: 1887. Died: Nov. 6, 1931, Hollywood, Calif. (heart attack). Screen actress. Sister of actress Lilyan Tashman (dec. 1934).

TASHMAN, LILYAN
Born: Oct. 23, 1900, Brooklyn, N.Y. Died: Mar. 21, 1934, New York, N.Y. (advanced tumorous condition and/or cancer). Screen and stage actress. Married to actor Edmund Lowe (dec. 1971). Sister of actress Kitty Tashman (dec. 1931).

Appeared in: **1917** Universal Screen Magazine #21. **1921** Experience. **1922** Head Over Heels. **1924** The Garden of Weeds; Manhandled; The Dark Swan; Is Love Everything?; Nellie, the Beautiful Cloak Model; Winner Take All. **1925** Declasse; The Parasite; Ports of Call; Pretty Ladies; Bright Lights; Seven Days; The Girl Who Wouldn't Work; A Broadway Butterfly; I'll Show You the Town. **1926** Rocking Moon; The Skyrocket; Siberia; Whispering Smith; For Alimony Only; Love's Blindness; So This Is Paris. **1927** Don't Tell the Wife; French Dressing; The Prince of Headwaiters; The Texas Steer; Camille; The Stolen Bride; The Woman Who Did Not Care. **1928** Phyllis of the Follies; Craig's Wife; Happiness Ahead; Lady Raffles; Manhattan Cocktail; Take Me Home. **1929** The Lone Wolf's Daughter; The Marriage Playground; Gold Diggers of Broadway; New York Nights; Bulldog Drummond; The Trial of Mary Dugan; Hardboiled. **1930** One Heavenly Night; On the Level; The Cat Creeps; Queen of Scandal; Puttin' on the Ritz; The Matrimonial Bed; Leathernecking; No, No, Nanette; Playing Around. **1931** Girls About Town; Up Pops the Devil; Finn and Hattie; Millie. **1932** The Wiser Sex; Revolt; Scarlet Dawn; Those We Love; The Mad Parade; The Road to Reno; Murder by the Clock. **1933** Mama Loves Papa; Too Much Harmony; Wine, Women and Song; Frankie and Johnny; Style. **1934** Riptide.

TATA, PAUL M., SR.
Born: 1883. Died: Mar. 30, 1962, Memphis, Tenn. Screen actor and fencing instructor.

Appeared in: **1908** The Three Musketeers.

TATE, ADMIRAL JACKSON
Born: 1899. Died: July 19, 1978. Screenwriter and stunt flyer in films. Father of actress Victoria Fyodorova.

Appeared in: **1931** Hell Divers.

TATE, HARRY (Ronald Macdonald Hutchinson)
Born: July 4, 1872, England. Died: Feb. 14, 1940, London, England (air raid). Screen, stage, vaudeville, radio actor and screenwriter.

Appeared in: **1899** Harry Tate Impersonation (short); Harry Tate Grimaces (short). **1927** Motoring (US 1929). **1929** The following shorts: The Patent Office; Selling a Car. **1932** Her First Affaire. **1933** Counsel's Opinion; My Lucky Star; I Spy. **1934** Happy. **1935** Royal Cavalcade (aka Regal Cavalcade—US); Look Up and Laugh; Hyde Park Corner; Midshipman Easy (aka Men of the Sea—US). **1936** Keep Your Seats Please; Soft Lights and Sweet Music; Variety Parade. **1937** Wings of the Morning; Take a Chance; Sam Small Leaves Town.

TATE, JOHN
Born: 1914, Australia. Died: Mar., 1979, Isle of Wright. Screen and television actor. Father of actor Rick Tate. Married to actress Neva Glyn (dec. 1975).

Appeared in: **1958** Smiley Gets a Gun (US 1959). **1959** On the Beach. **1963** It's All Happening (aka The Dream Maker—US 1964). **1970** Julius Caesar.

TATE, REGINALD
Born: Dec. 13, 1896, Garforth, England. Died: Aug. 23, 1955, London, England. Screen, stage, television and radio actor.

Appeared in: **1934** Whispering Tongues; Tangled Evidence. **1935** The Phantom Light; The Riverside Murder. **1936** Dark Journey; For Valor. **1939** Too Dangerous to Live; Poison Pen (US 1941). **1940** Gentleman of Venture (aka It Happened to One Man—US 1941). **1942** The Next

of Kin (US 1943). **1943** The Life and Death of Colonel Blimp (US 1945). **1944** The Way Ahead (US 1945); Madonna of the Seven Moons. **1945** The Man from Morocco; Journey Together (US 1946). **1947** So Well Remembered; Uncle Silas (aka The Inheritance—US 1951). **1948** Noose (aka The Silk Noose—US 1950). **1949** Diamond City. **1950** Midnight Episode (US 1951). **1952** Secret People; The Story of Robin Hood and His Merrie Men. **1953** Escape Route (aka I'll Get You—US); Malta Story (US 1954). **1955** King's Rahapsody (US 1956).

TATE, SHARON
Born: 1943, Dallas, Tex. Died: Aug. 9, 1969, Bel Air, Calif. (murdered). Screen and television actress. Married to actor and director Roman Polanski.

Appeared in: **1963** The Wheeler Dealers. **1964** The Americanization of Emily. **1965** Vampire Killers; "13"; The Sandpiper. **1967** Don't Make Waves; Eye of the Devil; Valley of the Dolls. **1968** The Fearless Vampire Killers, or, Pardon Me but Your Teeth Are in My Neck. **1969** Thirteen Chairs; The Wrecking Crew; House of Seven Joys.

TATUM, ART (Arthur Tatum)
Born: Oct. 13, 1910, Toledo, Ohio. Died: Nov, 4, 1956, Los Angeles, Calif. (uremia). Pianist, screen and radio actor.

Appeared in: **1947** The Fabulous Dorseys.

TATUM, BUCK
Born: 1897. Died: Oct. 2, 1941, Santa Monica, Calif. Screen actor and cowboy.

TATUM, GOOSE (Reese Tatum)
Born: May 3, 1921, Eldorado, Ark. Died: Jan. 18, 1967, El Paso, Calif. Professional basketball player and screen actor.

Appeared in: **1951** The Harlem Globetrotters. **1954** Go Man Go.

TAUB, SAM
Born: c. 1887. Died: July 10, 1979, New York, N.Y. Sportswriter, broadcaster and screen actor.

Appeared in: **1956** Somebody Up There Likes Me.

TAUBE, MATHIAS
Born: 1876, Lindesburg, Sweden. Died: 1934, Sweden. Screen, stage and radio actor.

Appeared in the following Swedish films: Ships That Meet; Therese; The Gold Spider; Johan; For High Ends; The Girl from Paradise; The People from Simlangen Valley; The Ingmar Inheritance; She, He and Andersson; The Poetry of Adalan (1928); The Land of Rye; The Voice of the Heart; Tomorrow for a Woman; A Night of Love on Oresund; The People of Varmland; We Go Through the Kitchen; Under Notice to Leave.

TAUBER, RICHARD
Born: May 16, 1892, Linz, Austria. Died: Jan. 8, 1948, London, England. Screen actor, opera singer, songwriter and composer. Married to actress Diana Napier (dec. 1982).

Appeared in: **1930** Die Grosse Attraktion (The Big Attraction—US 1933); Ich Glaut Nie Mehran Eine Frau (US 1933). **1931** Melodie Der Liebe (The Melody of Love, aka The Right to Happiness). **1933** Das Lockende Ziel. **1934** Blossom Time (aka April Romance—US 1937). **1935** Heart's Desire. **1936** Land Without Music (aka Forbidden Music—US 1938); Pagiacci (aka Clown Must Laugh—US 1938). **1945** Waltz Time. **1946** Lisbon Story. Other films: End of the Rainbow; The Land of Smiles; The Golden Goal.

TAUROG, NORMAN
Born: Feb. 23, 1899, Chicago, Ill. Died: Apr. 7, 1981, Rancho Mirage, Calif. Film producer, screen and stage actor. Entered films as an actor with IMP Studios in 1917.

TAVERNIER, ALBERT
Born: 1859. Died: Nov. 3, 1929. Screen actor.

Appeared in: **1922** The Man from Beyond. **1925** Too Many Kisses.

TAYLOR, ALBERT
Born: Apr. 8, 1871, Montgomery, Ala. Died: Apr. 10, 1940, Hollywood, Calif. Stage and screen actor.

Appeared in: **1934** The Good Fairy; Little Man, What Now? **1935** Reckless; Vanessa, Her Love Story; Times Square Lady; Woman Wanted; College Scandal; The Crusades; The Man on the Flying Trapeze; Accent on Youth. **1936** Nevada; Fury.

TAYLOR, ALMA
Born: Jan. 3, 1895, London, England. Died: Feb., 1974, London, England. Screen and television actress. Entered films in 1907.

Appeared in: **1909** The Little Milliner and the Thief; The Story of a Picture. **1910** The Burglar and Little Phyllis; Tilly the Tomboy Buys Linoleum; Tilly at the Election; Tilly the Tomboy Visits the Poor; A New Hat for Nothing; Tilly the Tomboy Goes Boating. **1911** A Wilful Maid; Tilly's Unsympathetic Uncle; Evicted; When Tilly's Uncle Flirted; Tilly's Party; Tilly at the Seaside; Tilly—Matchmaker; The Veteran's Pension; Tilly and the Mormon Missionary; A Fight With Fire; Tilly and the Fire Engines; The Smuggler's Step-Daughter; A Seaside Introduction; Envy, Hatred and Malice; Tilly and the Smugglers; Tilly and the Dogs; Bill's Reformation; Tilly Works For a Living; The Dear Little Teacher; Oliver Twist; Tilly in a Boarding House; King Robert of Sicily; For Love and Life; Curfew Must Not Ring Tonight. **1912** For a Baby's Sake. **1913** The Real Thing; Winning His Stripes; The Tailor's Revenge; The Mill Girl; Tried in the Fire; The Lover Who Took the Cake; Paying the Penalty; Tilly's Breaking-Up Party; Partners in Crime; Her Little Pet; Adrift on Life's Tide; The Girl at Lancing Mill; David Copperfield; A Midnight Adventure; The Cloister and the Hearth; The Old Curiosity Shop; The Broken Oath; The Curate's Bride; A Little Widow Is a Dangerous Thing; Petticoat Perfidy. **1914** Justice; Blind Faith; The Whirr of the Spinning Wheel; The Price of Fame; An Engagement of Convenience; The Quality of Mercy; The Heart of Midlothian; By Whose Hand? (aka The Mystery of Mr. Marks); The Girl Who Lived in Straight Street; Over the Garden Wall; The Kleptomaniac; The Schemers: Or, the Jewels of Hate; The Hills Are Calling; The Basilisk; His Country's Bidding (aka The Call); In the Shadow of Big Ben; Time the Great Healer; Aladdin: Or, a Lad Out; The Awakening of Nora; Morphia the Death Drug; His Great Opportunity; Oh My Aunt!; The Double Event; Tilly at the Football Match. **1915** The Canker of Jealousy (aka Be Sure of Your Sins); The Painted Lady Betty; Spies; Alma Taylor (film clips from her films 1907-1915); A Lancashire Lass; A Moment of Darkness; Jill and the Old Fiddle; Tilly and the Nut; Courtmartialed (aka The Traitor); The Passing of a Soul; The Baby on the Barge; The Man Who Stayed at Home; Sweet Lavender; The Golden Pavement; The Outrage; Iris. **1916** The Man at the Wheel; Love in a Mist; Trelawney of the Wells; Sowing the Wind; Annie Laurie; The Marriage of William Ashe; The Grand Babylon Hotel; Comin' Thro' the Rye; Molly Bawn. **1917** The Cobweb; The American Heiress; Merely Mrs. Stubbs; Nearer My God to Thee. **1918** The Touch of a Child; Film Tag series including: A New Version; The W.L.A. Girl; The Leopard's Spots; The Refugee; Tares; Boundary House. **1919** Broken in the Wars; The Nature of the Beast; Sunken Rocks; Sheba; The Forest on the Hill. **1920** Anna the Adventuress; Alf's Button; Helen of Four Gates; Mrs. Erricker's Reputation. **1921** The Tinted Venus; Dollars in Surrey; Tansy; The Narrow Valley. **1923** The Pipes of Pan; Mist in the Valley; Strangling Threads; Comin' Thro' the Rye (and 1916 version). **1924** The Shadow of Egypt. **1926** The House of Marney. **1927** Quinneys. **1928** Two Little Drummer Boys; A South Sea Bubble. **1931** Deadlock. **1932** Bachelor's Baby. **1933** House of Dreams. **1935** Things Are Looking Up. **1936** Everybody Dance. **1954** Lilacs in the Spring (aka Let's Make-Up—US 1956). **1955** Stock Car. **1956** Lost (aka Tears for Simon—US 1957). **1957** Blue Murder at St. Trinian's (US 1958).

TAYLOR, ANDY
Born: 1895. Died: June 8, 1948. Screen and stage actor.

TAYLOR, BETH
Born: 1889. Died: Mar. 1, 1951, Hollywood, Calif. Screen and stage actress.

TAYLOR, CURTIS
Died: Dec. 31, 1978. Screen actor.

Appeared in: **1965** Once Upon a Coffee House. **1975** Mr. Sycamore.

TAYLOR, DEEMS
Born: Dec. 22, 1885, New York, N.Y. Died: July 3, 1966, New York, N.Y. (stroke). Music critic, screen, radio, television actor, composer and author.

Appeared in: **1940** Fantasia (narrator). **1947** The Barber of Seville (narrator). **1950** Of Men and Music.

TAYLOR, ESTELLE
Born: May 20, 1899, Wilmington, Del. Died: Apr. 15, 1958, Los Angeles, Calif. (cancer). Screen, stage and vaudeville actress. Divorced from professional fighter Jack Dempsey.

Appeared in: **1920** The Garter Girl; While New York Sleeps; The Adventurer. **1921** Blind Wives; Footfalls. **1922** Monte Cristo; A Fool There Was; The Lights of New York; Only a Shop Girl; Thorns and

Orange Blossoms. **1923** The Ten Commandments; Bavu; Desire; Forgive and Forget; Hollywood; Mary of the Movies. **1924** The Alaskan; Dorothy Vernon of Haddon Hall; Playthings of Desire; Passion's Pathway; Phantom Justice; Tiger Love. **1925** Manhattan Madness; Wandering Footsteps. **1926** Don Juan. **1927** New York. **1928** The Whip Woman; The Singapore Mutiny; Lady Raffles; Honor Bound. **1929** Where East Is East. **1930** Liliom. **1931** Cimarron; Street Scene; The Unholy Garden. **1932** Call Her Savage; The Western Limited. **1938** various shorts. **1945** The Southerner.

TAYLOR, FERRIS
Born: 1893. Died: Mar. 6, 1961, Hollywood, Calif. (heart attack). Screen actor.

Appeared in: **1937** Mr. Dodd Takes the Air. **1938** The Story of Dr. Carver (short); He Couldn't Say No; Santa Fe Stampede; The Daredevil Drivers; The Jury's Secret. **1939** You Can't Cheat an Honest Man; Mexican Spitfire; SOS Tidal Wave; Man of Conquest; The Zero Hour; Mountain Rhythm; Main Street Lawyer. **1940** Chip of the Flying U; Rancho Grande; All About Hash (short); Flight Angels; One Crowded Night; Grand Ole Opry; Ladies Must Live; Always a Bride; Diamond Frontier; Mexican Spitfire Out West. **1941** She Couldn't Say No; Ridin' on a Rainbow; The Saint in Palm Springs; A Man Betrayed; County Fair. **1942** Hello, Annapolis! **1943** Henry Aldrich Haunts a House; Gold Town; Hoosier Holiday; Happy Land. **1944** Wilson; The Town Went Wild; Beautiful But Broke; End of the Road. **1945** Col. Effingham's Raid. **1946** Decoy; Rendezvous 24; Centennial Summer; The Man from Rainbow Valley; Bringing Up Father. **1948** Docks of New Orleans; My Dog Rusty. **1950** The Gunfighter; Two Flags West. **1951** The Prince of Peace. **1953** Tricky Dick (short). **1954** The Siege of Red River. **1956** Pardon My Nightshirt (short).

TAYLOR, FORREST (E. Forrest Taylor)
Born: 1884. Died: Feb. 19, 1965. Screen actor.

Appeared in: **1915** Man Afraid of His Wardrobe; The Terror of Twin Mountains; Two Spot Joe; The Sheriff of Willow Creek; The Trail of the Serpent; The Valley Feud; In the Sunset Country; There's Good in the Worst of Us; The Idol. **1916** The Thunderbolt; Wild Jim, Reformer; The White Rosette; April; The Disappearance of Helen Mintern; The Abandonment; The Music Swindlers; The Social Pirates; In the Service of the State; The Madonna of the Night; The Fighting Heiress; Black Magic. **1926** No Man's Gold; A Poor Girl's Romance. **1933** Riders of Destiny. **1934** Terry and the Pirates (serial). **1935** Mississippi; Rider of the Law; Courageous Avenger; Between Men. **1936** Rio Grande Romance; Too Much Beef; Kelly of the Secret Service; West of Nevada; Prison Shadows; Men of the Plains; Put on the Spot; Headin' for Rio Grande; Shadow of Chinatown (serial). **1937** The Mystery of the Hooded Horsemen; Arizona Days; The Red Rose; Riders of the Dawn; Two Minutes to Play. **1938** Fighting Devil Dogs (serial); Heroes of the Hills; The Painted Trail; The Last Stand; Desert Patrol; Outlaw Express; Gun Packer; Black Bandit; Law of the Texan; Lightning Carson Rides Again; The Story of Dr. Carver. **1939** The Phantom Creeps (serial); Riders of Black River; Rovin' Tumbleweeds. **1940** The Green Hornet; Chip of the Flying U; The Ghost Creeps; Terry and the Pirates (serial); Straight Shooters; Rhythm of the Rio Grande; Wild Horse Range; Frontier Crusader; West of Abilene; The Durango Kid; The Kid from Santa Fe; Trailing Double Trouble. **1941** Flying Wild; The Iron Claw (serial); Ridin' on a Rainbow; Billy the Kid's Fighting Pals; Cyclone Wranglers' Roost; Ridin' on the Cherokee Trail; The Lone Star Vigilantes. **1942** The Spoilers; Perils on the Royal Mounted (serial); Cowboy Serenade; Home in Wyomin'; Sunset in the Desert; A Night for Crime; Sons of the Pioneers; King of the Stallions; The Yanks Are Coming; The Pay-Off. **1943** Air Raid Wardens; Thundering Trails; The Rangers Take Over; Man of Courage; Corregidor; Fighting Buckaroo; Silver Spurs; Sleepy Lagoon. **1944** Haunted Harbor (serial); Mystery Man; Lady in the Death House; Song of Nevada; Shake Hands With Murder; Three Little Sisters; Sundown Valley; The Last Horseman; Sonora Stagecoach; Mojave Firebird; Cyclone Prairie Rangers; Sagebrush Heroes. **1945** Federal Operator 99 (serial); Rockin' in the Rockies; Manhunt of Mystery Island (serial); Identity Unknown; Dangerous Intruder; Strange Voyage. **1946** The Caravan Trail; The Glass Alibi; Romance of the West; Colorado Serenade; Texas Panhandle; Santa Fe Uprising; The Crimson Ghost (serial). **1947** The Black Widow (serial); Stagecoach to Denver; Yankee Fakir; The Pretender; Rustlers of Devil's Canyon; Along the Oregon Trail; The Stranger from Ponca City; Buckaroo from Powder River. **1948** Superman (serial); The Mystery of the Golden Eye; Four Faces West; Coroner Creek; Tex Granger; The Golden Eye. **1949** Bruce Gentry, Daredevil of the Skies (serial); Deputy Marshal; Navajo Trail Riders; The Lawson Story; Death Valley Gunfighter; Stallion Canyon; The Fighting Redhead. **1950** Cherokee Uprising; The Cowboy and the Prizefighter; Rustlers on Horseback; Forbidden Jungle; The Fighting Stallion; Code of Silver Sage; Rustlers on Horseback. **1951** Prairie Roundup; Wells Fargo Gunmaster; Blazing Bullets; Prince of Peace. **1952** Night Raiders; Smoky Canyon; Border Saddlemates; Park Row; South Pacific Trail. **1953** The Lost Planet (serial); Iron Mountain Trail; The Marshal's Daughter. **1954** Bitter Creek.

TAYLOR, GEORGE
Born: 1889. Died: Nov. 2, 1939, Fillmore, Utah (injuries from auto crash). Screen actor. Do not confuse with stage actor George R. Taylor (dec. 1944).

Appeared in: **1937** Nancy Steele Is Missing; Angel's Holiday.

TAYLOR, HENRY
Born: 1908. Died: Mar. 1, 1969. Screen, radio, vaudeville actor and screenwriter. Member of vaudeville and radio act "The Radio Rogues."

Appeared in: **1930** Beyond the Rio Grande. **1935** Every Night at Eight. **1937** Blossoms on Broadway; You Only Live Once. **1943** Reveille With Beverly.

TAYLOR, JACK
Born: 1896. Died: Oct. 21, 1932, Long Beach, Calif. (stomach disorder). Screen actor and orchestra leader. Divorced from actress Vera Steadman (dec. 1966). Appeared in Warner shorts.

TAYLOR, JOSEPHINE (Josephine Motz)
Born: 1891. Died: Nov. 26, 1964, Calumet City, Ill. Screen actress. Appeared in early Essanay productions.

TAYLOR, JULIA
Born: 1878. Died: Dec. 4, 1976, Hollywood, Calif. Screen and stage actress. Married to stage and film director Wallace Worsley (dec. 1944). Appeared in early Thanhouser Film Company productions.

TAYLOR, LAURETTE (Laurette Cooney)
Born: 1884, New York, N.Y. Died: Dec. 7, 1946, New York, N.Y. (coronary thrombosis). Screen, stage, vaudeville actress and playwright. Married to actor Hartley Manners.

Appeared in: **1923** Peg O' My Heart. **1924** Happiness; One Night in Rome.

TAYLOR, LOUISE
Born: 1908. Died: Mar. 18, 1965, New York, N.Y. Screen, television actress and dancer.

TAYLOR, DR. MARION SAYLE
Born: 1889, Louisville, Ky. Died: Feb. 1, 1942, Hollywood, Calif. (heart attack). Organist, composer, radio commentator and screen actor.

Appeared in: **1937** The Hit Parade.

TAYLOR, ROBERT
Born: 1873. Died: Dec. 9, 1936, New York, N.Y. (gas explosion). Stage and screen actor. Do not confuse with actor with same name (dec. 1969).

TAYLOR, ROBERT (Arlington Spangler Brugh)
Born: Aug. 5, 1911, Filley, Nebr. Died: June 8, 1969, Santa Monica, Calif. (lung cancer). Screen, television and radio actor. Divorced from actress Barbara Stanwyck. Married to actress Ursula Thiess.

Appeared in: **1934** Handy Andy (film debut); Only Eight Hours; There's Always Tomorrow; A Wicked Woman; Crime Does Not Pay. **1935** Lest We Forget (documentary); West Point of the Air; Society Doctor; Times Square Lady; Murder in the Fleet; Broadway Melody of 1936; The Magnificent Obsession; Buried Loot (short); La Fiesta de Santa Barbara (short). **1936** Small Town Girl; The Gorgeous Hussy; His Brother's Wife; Private Number; Camille. **1937** Personal Property; Broadway Melody of 1938; This Is My Affair. **1938** A Yank at Oxford; Three Comrades; The Crowd Roars. **1939** Stand Up and Fight; Lucky Night; Lady of the Tropics; Remember? **1940** Waterloo Bridge; Escape; Flight Command. **1941** Billy the Kid; When Ladies Meet; Johnny Eager. **1942** Her Cardboard Lover; Stand By For Action; Cargo of Innocents. **1943** Song of Russia; Bataan; The Youngest Profession. **1944** The Fighting Lady (narr. documentary). **1946** Undercurrent. **1947** High Wall. **1948** The Secret Land (narr.). **1949** Ambush; The Bribe. **1950** Conspirator; The Devil's Doorway; Big Apple. **1951** Quo Vadis; Westward the Women. **1952** Ivanhoe; Above and Beyond. **1953** Ride, Vaquero; All the Brothers Were Valiant; Knights of the Round Table; I Love Melvin. **1954** Valley of the Kings; Rogue Cop. **1955** Many Rivers to Cross. **1956** Adventures of Quentin

Durward; D-Day, The Sixth of June; The Power and the Prize; The Last Hunt. **1957** Tip On A Dead Jockey. **1958** Saddle the Wind; The Law and Jake Wade; Party Girl. **1959** The Hangman; The House of Seven Hawks. **1960** The Killers of Kilimanjaro. **1963** Cattle King; Guns of Wyoming; The Miracle of the White Stallions. **1964** Big Parade of Comedy (documentary); A House Is Not a Home; The Night Walker. **1966** Johnny Tiger; Return of the Gunfighter. **1967** Hondo and the Apaches; Savage Pampas; As I Rode down to Laredo; The Glass Sphinx. **1968** Where Angels Go ... Trouble Follows; The Day the Hot Line Got Hot; Devil May Care. **1974** That's Entertainment (film clips).

TAYLOR, VIRGIL "SLATS"
Died: May 11, 1978. Screen actor.

Appeared in: **1951** Force of Arms. **1952** The Will Rogers Story.

TAYLOR, WILLIAM DESMOND (William Cunningham Deanne Tanner)
Born: 1877, Carlow, Ireland. Died: Feb. 1, 1922, Los Angeles, Calif. (murdered—shot). Screen actor and film director.

Appeared in: **1914** Millions for Defense. **1917** Captain Alvarez.

TAYLOR, WILLIAM H. "BILLY"
Born: July 9, 1829, Brownsville, Tex. Died: Dec. 26, 1930, Hollywood, Calif. Screen actor. Entered films in 1910.

Appeared in: **1926** Outside the Law. **1930** Song of the West; Heads Up.

TCHERKASSKY, ALEXIS
Born: 1904, St. Petersburg, Russia. Died: Dec. 14, 1980, Washington, D.C. Screen, radio actor and opera performer.

Appeared in: **1939** Cossacks in Exile.

TEACHOUT, H. ARTHUR
Born: 1888. Died: Mar. 5, 1939, Cedar Rapids, Iowa. Screen and stage actor.

TEAD, PHILIP "PHIL"
Born: 1894, Somerville, Mass. Died: June 9, 1974. Screen and stage actor.

Appeared in: **1914** The Lost Paradise. **1920** She Loves and Lies. **1923** The Fighting Blade. **1930** Lightnin'. **1931** Kiki; The Front Page; The Vice Squad; Guilty Generation. **1932** The Final Edition; Horse Feathers. **1933** Broadway Bad; The Big Bluff. **1934** Six of a Kind; Glamour. **1935** It Happened in New York; The Daring Young Man; The Affair of Susan; One Hour Late. **1936** The Princess Comes Across. **1940** Music in My Heart. **1942** Right to the Heart. **1952** Arctic Flight. **1954** Fangs of the Wild. **1956** Wiretappers. **1957** Rockabilly Baby.

TEAGARDEN, JACK
Born: 1906. Died: Jan. 15, 1964, New Orleans, La. (pneumonia). Bandleader, screen actor and trombonist. He played with Pete Kelly, Red Nichols; collaborated with Glenn Miller on lyrics for "Basin Street Blues," joined Ben Pollack and Paul Whiteman's band.

Appeared in: **1941** Birth of the Blues. **1952** Glory Alley. **1953** The Glass Wall. **1960** Jazz on a Summer's Day.

TEAGUE, BRIAN
Born: 1937. Died: May 30, 1970, near Lake Isabella, Calif. (auto accident). Screen and television actor. Son of Guy Teague (dec. 1970).

TEAGUE, GUY
Died: Jan. 24, 1970, Tex. Screen actor. Father of actor Brian Teague (dec. 1970).

Appeared in: **1950** Desperadoes of the West (serial); The Showdown; Vigilante Hideout. **1951** Don Daredevil Rides Again (serial). **1952** Cattle Town. **1953** The Outlaw Stallion. **1955** Wyoming Renegades. **1956** Fury at Gunsight Pass; The White Squaw.

TEAL, RAY
Born: Jan. 12, 1902, Grand Rapids, Mich. Died: Apr. 2, 1976, Santa Monica, Calif. Screen, stage and television actor.

Appeared in: **1938** Western Jamboree (film debut). **1940** Northwest Passage; Prairie Schooners; Pony Post; Adventures of Red Ryder (serial); Cherokee Strip. **1941** Outlaws of the Panhandle; Wild Bill Hickok Rides; They Died With Their Boots On. **1942** Apache Trail; Captain Midnight (serial); Woman of the Year; Tennessee Johnson. **1944** Nothing But Trouble; None Shall Escape; Wing and a Prayer; Strange Affair; Hollywood Canteen. **1945** A Gun in His Hand (short);

Strange Voyage; Circumstantial Evidence; Captain Kidd; Along Came Jones. **1946** Bandit of Sherwood Forest; Deadline for Murder; The Missing Lady; Till the Clouds Roll By; The Best Years of Our Lives; Blondie Knows Best. **1947** Michigan Kid; Ramrod; Brute Force; The Road to Rio; Driftwood. **1948** I Wouldn't Be in Your Shoes; The Black Arrow; Daredevils of the Clouds; Joan of Arc; The Countess of Monte Cristo; Whispering Smith. **1949** It Happens Every Spring; Streets of Laredo; Once More My Darling; Rusty's Birthday; Blondie Hits the Jackpot; Ambush; Kazan; One Sunday Afternoon (aka The Strawberry Blonde). **1950** Our Very Own, Davy Crockett, Indian Scout; The Harbor of Missing Men; The Kid from Texas; The Men; Edge of Doom; When You're Smiling; The Redhead and the Cowboy; No Way Out; Winchester 73. **1951** Along the Great Divide; Ace in the Hole; Fort Worth; The Secret of Convict Lake; Tomorrow Is Another Day; Distant Drums; Flaming Feather. **1952** The Lion and the Horse; The Captive City; The Wild North; Carrie; Jumping Jacks; The Turning Point; Hangman's Knot; Cattle Town; Montana Belle. **1953** Ambush at Tomahawk Gap. **1954** Rogue Cop; About Mrs. Leslie; The Wild One; The Command. **1955** The Man from Bitter Bridge; Run for Cover; Apache Ambush; The Desperate Hours; The Indian Fighter. **1956** The Burning Hills. **1957** Utah Blaine; The Phantom Stagecoach; The Guns of Fort Petticoat; The Oklahoman; Band of Angels; The Wayward Girl; The Tall Stranger; Decision at Sundown. **1958** Saddle the Wind; Gunman's Walk. **1960** Home from the Hills; Inherit the Wind. **1961** One-Eyed Jacks; Posse from Hell; Judgment at Nuremberg. **1962** A Girl Named Tamiko. **1963** Cattle King. **1964** Taggart; Bullet for a Badman. **1970** Chisum; The Liberation of L. B. Jones.

TEARE, ETHEL
Born: 1894. Died: Mar. 4, 1959, San Mateo, Calif. Screen actress.

Appeared in: **1915** "Ham and Bud" series. **1917** Thirst; Lost—A Cook. **1921** Skirts; The Tomboy. **1923** Thirst (reissue of 1917 film). **1924** A Woman Who Sinned.

TEARLE, CONWAY (Frederick Levy)
Born: May 17, 1878, New York, N.Y. Died: Oct. 1, 1938, Los Angeles, Calif. (heart attack). Screen and stage actor. Half brother of actors Godfrey (dec. 1953) and Malcolm Tearle (dec. 1935). Divorced from actress Josephine Parks (dec. 1931); Mrs. Menges Corwin-Hill (dec.); and later married to actress Adele Rowland (dec. 1971).

Appeared in: **1914** The Nightingale. **1915** Seven Sisters. **1916** The Common Law. **1917** The Fall of Romanoff. **1918** Stella Maris. **1919** Virtuous Wives; The Way of a Woman; The Mind-the-Paint Girl. **1920** A Virtuous Vamp; Two Weeks; The Forbidden Woman. **1921** Bucking the Tiger; Marooned Hearts; The Road of Ambition; Society Snobs; Whispering Devils; The Man of Stone; The Fighter; After Midnight; The Oath. **1922** The Eternal Flame; Love's Masquerade; The Referee; Shadows of the Sea; A Wide Open Town; One Week of Love. **1923** Bella Donna; Ashes of Vengeance; The Dangerous Maid; Woman of Bronze; The Common Law (and 1916 version); The Rustle of Silk. **1924** The White Moth; Black Oxen; Flirting With Love; Lilies of the Field; The Next Corner. **1925** The Mystic; The Great Divide; The Viennese Medley; Bad Company; The Heart of a Siren; Morals for Men; Just a Woman; School for Wives. **1926** Dancing Mothers; My Official Wife; The Dancer of Paris; The Greater Glory; The Sporting Lover. **1927** Altars of Desire; Isle of Forgotten Women; Moulders of Men. **1929** Smoke Bellow; Evidence; Gold Diggers of Broadway. **1930** How I Play Golf—The Driver (short); The Lost Zeppelin; Truth About Youth. **1931** The Lady Who Dared; Morals for Women; Captivation. **1932** The Hurricane Express (serial); Twin Lips and Juleps or Southern Love and Northern Exposure (short); Vanity Fair; Pleasure; Her Mad Night; The Man About Town. **1933** Day of Reckoning; Should Ladies Behave?. **1934** Fifteen Wives; Stingaree; Sing Sing Nights. **1935** Headline Woman; The Trail's End; Judgement Book. **1936** The Preview Murder Mystery; Desert Guns; Klondike Annie; Romeo and Juliet.

TEARLE, SIR GODFREY
Born: Oct. 12, 1884, New York, N.Y. Died: June 8, 1953, London, England. Screen and stage actor. Brother of actor Malcolm Tearle (dec 1935) and half brother of actor Conway Tearle (dec. 1938). Married to actress Stella Freeman (dec. 1936). Entered films in 1906.

Appeared in: **1908** Romeo and Juliet. **1913** The Fool. **1915** Lochinvar. **1916** Sir James Mortimer's Wager; The Real Thing at Last. **1919** A Sinless Sinner (aka Midnight Gambols—US 1920); Nobody's Child; Queen's Evidence; The March Hare; Fancy Dress. **1925** Salome of the Tenements. **1926** If Youth But Knew; One Colombo Night; The Steve Donoghue series including Guy of Warwick. **1930** Infatuation. **1931** These Charming People; The Shadow Between. **1933** Puppets of Fate (aka Wolves of the Underworld—US 1935). **1934** Spotting series

including Jade. **1935** The 39 Steps; The Last Journey (US 1936); East Meets West; Tomorrow We Live. **1942** Tomorrow We Live (and 1935 version, aka At Dawn We Die—US 1943); One of Our Aircraft is Missing. **1943** Undercover (aka Underground Guerillas—US 1944); The Lamp Still Burns. **1944** Medal for the General. **1945** The Rake's Progress (aka Notorious Gentleman—US 1946). **1949** Private Angelo. **1951** White Corridors. **1952** I Believe in You (US 1953); Mandy (aka Crash of Silence—US 1953); Decameron Nights. **1953** The Titfield Thunderbolt.

TEARLE, MALCOLM
Born: 1888. Died: Dec. 8, 1935, London, England (suicide). Screen actor. Brother of actor Godfrey Tearle (dec. 1953) and half brother of actor Conway Tearle (dec. 1938).

TEATHER, IDA
Died: Apr. 10, 1954, Ebbw Vale, Wales. Screen, stage and radio actress.

TEDMARSH, WILLIAM J.
Born: Feb. 3, 1876, London, England. Died: May 10, 1937, England? Screen actor.

Appeared in: **1915** Diamond from the Sky. **1916** The Secret of the Submarine; The Sequel to the Diamond from the Sky (serial).

TEDRO, HENRIETTE
Born: 1885. Died: July 25, 1948, Los Angeles, Calif. Screen and stage actress.

TEEGE, JOACHIM
Born: 1925, Spremberg, Silesia, Poland. Died: Nov. 23, 1969, Munich, Germany. Screen, stage and television actor.

Appeared in: **1967** Those Fantastic Flying Fools. **1968** How to Seduce a Playboy.

TEITELBAUM, ABRAHAM
Born: 1889. Died: Oct. 16, 1947. Yiddish screen and stage actor.

Appeared in: **1933** The Wandering Jew.

TEITELBAUM, LILY
Died: May 28, 1972. Screen actress.

TELL, ALMA
Born: 1892. Died: Dec. 30, 1937, San Fernando, Calif. Screen and stage actress. Sister of actress Olive Tell (dec. 1951).

Appeared in: **1916** The Smugglers. **1920** On With the Dance; The Right to Love. **1921** The Iron Trail; Paying the Piper. **1922** Broadway Rose. **1923** The Silent Command. **1928** San Francisco Nights. **1929** Saturday's Children. **1930** Love Comes Along. **1934** Imitation of Life.

TELL, OLIVE
Born: 1894, New York, N.Y. Died: June 8, 1951, New York, N.Y. Stage and screen actress. Sister of actress Alma Tell (dec. 1937). Entered films with Mutual in 1917.

Appeared in: **1918** The Unforseen. **1919** The Trap. **1921** Clothes; Wings of Pride; The Wrong Woman; Worlds Apart. **1925** Chickie. **1926** The Prince of Tempters; Woman-Handled; Summer Bachelors. **1927** Slaves of Beauty. **1928** Sailors' Wives; Soft Living. **1929** Hearts in Exile; The Trial of Mary Dugan; The Very Idea. **1930** Lawful Larceny; Love Comes Along; The Right of Way; Woman Hungry; Devotion; Delicious. **1931** Ladies Man. **1933** Strictly Personal. **1934** The Scarlet Empress; The Witching Hour; Private Scandal; Baby, Take a Bow. **1935** Four Hours to Kill; Shanghai. **1936** In His Steps; Polo Joe; Yours for the Asking; Brilliant Marriage. **1939** Zaza.

TELLEGEN, LOU (Isidor Louis Bernard Von Dammeler)
Born: Nov. 26, 1881, Holland. Died: Nov. 1, 1934, Los Angeles, Calif. (suicide). Screen and stage actor. Divorced from actress Geraldine Farrar (dec. 1967), Countess de Broncken and Isabel (Nina Romano) Craven. Married to Eva Casanova.

Appeared in: **1911** Queen Elizabeth. **1915** The Explorer; The Unknown. **1916** The Victoria Cross; Maria Rosa; The Victory of Conscience. **1917** The Long Trail. **1919** Flame of the Desert; The World and Its Women. **1920** The Woman and the Puppet. **1924** Single Wives; Those Who Judge; Between Friends; The Breath of Scandal; Let Not Man Put Asunder; Greater Than Marriage. **1925** The Redeeming Sin; After Business Hours; East Lynne; The Sporting Chance; Borrowed Finery; Fair Play; Parisian Love; Parisian Nights; The Verdict; With This Ring. **1926** The Outsider; Siberia; The Silver Treasure; Womanpower; Three Bad Men. **1927** The Princess from Hoboken; The Little Firebrand; Married Alive; Stage Madness. **1928** No Other Woman. **1931** Enemies of the Law.

TELLO, SANCHEZ (Alfonso Sanchez Tello)
Born: Mexico. Died: Apr. 18, 1979, La Jolla, Calif. (Blood clot following heart attack). Screen actor and film producer. Entered films as an extra during the silents.

Appeared in: **1938** Rancho Grande. **1956** Bandido.

TELZLAFF, TEDDY
Born: 1883. Died: 1929, Santa Ana, Calif. Professional race car driver and screen actor.

Appeared in: **1913** Teddy Telzlaff and Earl Cooper, Speed King.

TEMARY, ELZA
Born: 1904, Germany. Died: Feb. 16, 1968, Tucson, Ariz. Screen and stage actress.

Appeared in: **1929** Gefahren der Brautzeit.

TEMPEST, DAME MARIE (Marie Susan Etherington)
Born: 1864, London, England. Died: Oct. 15, 1942, London, England. Screen, stage actress and opera singer. Married to actor W. Graham Browne (dec. 1937). Was made Dame Commander of the British Empire in 1937.

Appeared in: **1900** San Toy; English Nell. **1915** Mrs. Plum's Pudding. **1937** Moonlight Sonata. **1938** Yellow Sands. **1943** The Charmer (rerelease of 1937 Moonligh Sonata).

TEMPEST, TOM
Born: 1876. Died: Dec. 14, 1955, Skowhegan, Maine. Screen and stage actor.

Appeared in: **1914** The Toll of Mammon. **1915** The Kidnapped Stock Broker. **1916** Those Who Toil; Artie, the Millionaire Kid.

TEMPLE, RICHARD
Born: 1873, England. Died: Oct. 14, 1954, New York, N.Y. (heart attack). Screen, stage and television actor. Son of stage actor Richard Temple (dec.).

Appeared in: **1915** Evidence.

TEMPLETON, FAY
Born: Dec. 25, 1866, Little Rock, Ark. Died: Oct. 3, 1939, San Francisco, Calif. Screen, stage and vaudeville actress. Entered films in 1929.

Appeared in: **1932** The March of Time (short). **1933** Broadway to Hollywood.

TEMPLETON, GEORGE B. "DINK"
Born: Nov. 11, 1907, Mt. Vernon, Tex. Died: Aug. 26, 1980, Los Angeles, Calif. Screen actor, film director and producer.

Appeared in: **1932** Make Me a Star; Night After Night.

TEMPLETON, OLIVE (Olive MacMackin)
Born: 1891. Died: May 29, 1979, New York, N.Y. Screen, stage and television actress.

Appeared in: **1917** Damaged Goods.

TENBROOK, HARRY (Henry Olaf Hansen)
Born: Oct. 9, 1887, Norway. Died: Sept. 14, 1960, Woodland Hills, Calif. (lung cancer). Screen actor.

Appeared in: **1923** Kindled Courage. **1924** The Measure of a Man. **1925** The Burning Trail; Manhattan Madness. **1926** The Blue Eagle; Mistaken Orders; The Silent Guardian. **1927** The Outlaw Dog; Speedy Smith; Thunderbolt's Tracks. **1928** Danger Street; The Play Girl. **1929** Eyes of the Underworld; Seven Footprints to Satan. **1930** Men Without Women; On the Level; The Runaway Bride; The Sea Wolf. **1931** Donovan's Kid. **1932** This Reckless Age; Scarface; Shame of a Nation; Taxi; Heroes of the West (serial). **1933** Terror Trail. **1934** The Thin Man. **1935** Millions in the Air; Black Fury; Naughty Marietta. **1936** Great Guy. **1937** Hit the Saddle. **1938** Rawhide; A Slight Case of Murder. **1939** Stagecoach; Oklahoma Frontier; Destry Rides Again. **1940** The Grapes of Wrath; Ragtime Cowboy Joe. **1943** Government Girl. **1945** They Were Expendable. **1950** When Willie Comes Marching Home. **1955** Mister Roberts. **1958** The Last Hurrah.

TENNANT, DOROTHY
Born: 1865. Died: July 3, 1942, West Palm Beach, Fla. Screen and stage actress.

Appeared in: **1938** Men With Wings.

TENNBERG, JEAN-MARC
Born: 1924, France. Died: 1971, France. Screen actor.

Appeared in: **1952** Fanfan the Tulip (US 1953). **1954** The Moment of Truth. **1956** Adorable Creatures; French Can-Can (aka Only the French Can). **1962** Les Sept Peches Capitaux (Seven Capital Sins—US 1963); Le Repos du Guerrier (Warrior's Rest aka Love on a Pillow—US 1963). **1964** Une Ravissante Idiote (A Ravishing Idiot—US 1966). **1965** La Traite des Blanches (aka Frustrations—US 1967 and Hot Frustrations).

TERHUNE, MAX "ABIBE"
Born: Feb. 12, 1891, Franklin, Ind. Died: June 5, 1973, Cottonwood, Ariz. (heart attack and stroke). Screen, television, vaudeville and radio actor, ventriloquist and magician.

Appeared in: **1936** The Three Mesquiteers; Ride, Ranger, Ride (debut); Ghost Town Gold. **1937** Hit the Saddle; Heart of the Rockies; Riders of the Whistling Skull; The Hit Parade; Manhattan Merry-Go-Round; Mama Runs Wild; Come On, Cowboys!; Range Defenders; Roarin' Lead; The Big Show; Gunsmoke Ranch; The Trigger Trio. **1938** Call the Mesquiteers; The Purple Vigilantes; Outlaws of Sonora; Ladies in Distress; Riders of the Black Hills; Heroes of the Hills; Pals of the Saddle; Overland Stage Raiders; Wild Horse Rodeo; Santa Fe Stampede; Red River Range. **1939** Man of Conquest; The Night Riders; Three Texas Steers. **1940** The Range Busters; West of Pinto Basin; Trailing Double Trouble. **1941** Tumbledown Ranch in Arizona; Trail of the Silver Spurs; The Kid's Last Ride; Wrangler's Roost; Fugitive Valley. **1942** Trail Riders; Rock River Renegades; Texas to Bataan; Boot Hill Bandits; Texas Trouble Shooters; Saddle Mountain Roundup. **1943** Two-Fisted Justice; Cowboy Commandos; Black Market Rustlers; Haunted Ranch. **1940** Cowboy Canteen; Sheriff of Sundown. **1947** Along the Oregon Trail; White Stallion. **1948** Gunning for Justice; The Sheriff of Medicine Bow. **1949** Square Dance Jubilee; Law of the West; Range Justice; Western Renegades; West of Eldorado; Trail's End. **1951** Rawhide; Jim Thorpe—All American. **1956** Giant. **1957** King and Four Queens.

TERNICK, FRANK
Born: 1895. Died: Oct. 29, 1966. Screen actor and stuntman.

TERR, AL (Albert R. Terr)
Born: May 22, 1893, New York. Died: July 15, 1967, Burbank, Calif. (heart disease). Screen actor and musician.

Appeared in: **1958** Bullwhip. **1960** Lust to Kill.

TERRANOVA, DINO (Corrado Vacirca)
Born: 1904, Italy. Died: Apr. 27, 1969, Miami, Fla. Screen and stage actor.

Appeared in: **1956** The Wrong Man (stage and screen versions). **1963** Flipper. **1968** The Brotherhood.

TERRELL, KEN (Kenneth Jones Terrell)
Born: Apr. 29, 1904, Ga. Died: Mar. 8, 1966, Sherman Oaks, Calif. (arteriosclerosis). Screen actor and stuntman.

Appeared in: **1939** Dick Tracy's G-Men (serial). **1940** Mysterious Dr. Satan (serial). **1941** Jungle Girl (serial). **1942** Perils of Nyoka (serial); Cowboy Serenade. **1944** The Tiger Woman (serial); Captain America (serial). **1945** The Purple Monster Strikes (serial). **1947** Son of Zorro (serial); Robin Hood in Texas. **1948** G-Men Never Forget (serial); The Bold Frontiersman; The Gay Ranchero; Grand Canyon Trail. **1949** The Clay Pigeon. **1951** Pals of the Golden West. **1952** Last Train from Bombay; Lydia Bailey. **1953** Port Sinister. **1954** Return to Treasure Island; Drums Across the River. **1956** The Indestructible Man; The Proud Ones. **1957** Attack of the Fifty-Foot Woman; The Brain from Planet Arous; Sabu and the Magic Ring. **1959** Pier 5, Havana. **1961** Master of the World.

TERRISS, ELLALINE (Ellaine Lewin)
Born: Apr. 13, 1871, Talkland Island, England. Died: June 16, 1971, London, England. Screen and stage actress. Daughter of stage actor William Terriss (r. n. William Lewin, dec. 1897) and stage actress Ann Fellows Terriss (dec. 1898). Sister of actors William and Tom (dec. 1964) Terriss. Mother of actress Betty Seymour Hicks. Married to actor Sir Seymour Hicks (dec. 1949).

Appeared in: **1907** Glow Little Glow Worm Glow; My Indian Anna. **1913** David Garrick; Scrooge; Seymour Hicks and Ellaline Terriss (short). **1914** Always Tell Your Wife. **1917** Masks and Face. **1927** Blighty (aka Apres le Guerre); Land of Hope and Glory. **1929** Atlantic. **1931** Glamour; Man of Mayfair. **1935** The Iron Duke; Royal Cavalcade (aka Regal Cavalcade—US). **1939** The Four Just Men (aka The Secret Four—US 1940).

TERRISS, TOM (Herbert Thomas Lewin)
Born: Sept. 28, 1887, London, England. Died: Feb. 8, 1964, New York, N.Y. Screen and stage actor, film director and screenwriter. See Ellaline Terriss for family information.

Appeared in: **1914** The Chimes; The Mystery of Edwin Drood. **1915** A Woman of the World; The Pearl of the Antilles; Flame of Passion. **1916** My Country First.

TERRY, DAME ELLEN
Born: Feb. 27, 1848, Coventry, England. Died: July 21, 1928, Kent, England (heart attack). Stage and screen actress. Daughter of stage actors Benjamin Terry (dec. 1896) and Sarah Ballard (dec.). Sister of stage actors Kate (dec. 1924), Marion (dec. 1930), Florence (dec. 1896), stage and film actor Fred (dec. 1933) and stage managers George (dec. 1928) and Charles (dec. 1933) Terry. Divorced from artist G. F. Watts (dec. 1904). Married to stage actor Charles Wardell Kelly (dec. 1885) and later married to stage and film actor James Carew (dec. 1938). Mother of actors Edith (dec. 1947) and Edward Gordon Craig (dec. 1966). Was made Dame Commander of the Order of the British Empire in 1925. Entered films with Triangle in 1929.

Appeared in: **1920** Pillars of Society. **1922** The Bohemian Girl.

TERRY, ETHEL GREY
Born: Oakland, Calif. Died: Jan. 6, 1931, Hollywood, Calif. Screen and stage actress. Married to actor Carl Gerard.

Appeared in: **1916** Intolerance. **1917** Apartment 29; The Hawk; Arsene Lupin. **1919** Hardboiled; The Carter Case (the "Craig Kennedy" serial). **1921** The Breaking Point; Suspicious Wives. **1922** The Crossroads of New York; The Kick Back; Oath-Bound; Shattered Idols; Too Much Business; Travelin' On; Under Two Flags. **1923** Brass; The Self-Made Wife; Garrison's Finish; Wild Bill Hickok; Why Women Remarry; What Wives Want; The Unknown Purple; Peg O' My Heart. **1924** The Fast Worker. **1925** Old Shoes; What Fools Men. **1926** Hardboiled; The Love Toy. **1927** Cancelled Debts. **1928** Skinner's Big Idea; Modern Mothers; Confessions of a Wife; Sharp Tools (short). **1929** Object Alimony.

TERRY, FRED
Born: Nov. 9, 1863, London, England. Died: Apr. 17, 1933, London, England. Screen and stage actor. See Dame Ellen Terry regarding family information. Married to stage actress Julia Neilson and father of actor Dennis Neilson-Terry (dec. 1932) and actress Pyllis Neilson-Terry (dec. 1977).

Appeared in: **1922** With Wings Outspread.

TERRY, HAZEL (Hazel Neilson-Terry)
Born: Jan. 23, 1918, London, England. Died: Oct. 12, 1974, London, England. Stage and screen actress. Daughter of stage actors Mary Glynne and Denis Neilson-Terry. Entered films in 1935.

Appeared in: **1936** The Marriage of Corbal (aka Prisoner of Corbal—US 1939). **1937** Our Fighting Navy (aka Torpedoed—US 1939); Missing, Believed Married. **1938** Sweet Devil. **1962** Kill or Cure. **1963** The Servant (US 1964).

TERRY, SHEILA (Kay Clark)
Born: Mar. 5, 1910, Warroad, Minn. Died: Jan. 19, 1957. Screen and stage actress.

Appeared in: **1932** Week-End Marriage; Crooner; Big City Blues; I Am a Fugitive From a Chain Gang; Three on a Match; Scarlet Dawn; You Said a Mouthful; Madame Butterfly; Lawyer Man. **1933** Silk Express; Mayor of Hell; Private Detective 62; House on 56th Street; The Sphinx; Convention City; Son of a Sailor; 20,000 Years in Sing Sing; Haunted Gold; Parachute Jumper. **1934** Rocky Rhodes; Take the Stand; When Strangers Meet; 'Neath Arizona Skies. **1935** Lawless Frontier; Rescue Squad; Society Fever. **1936** Murder on a Bridle Path; Special Investigator; Go Get 'Em Haines. **1937** An MGM short.

TERRY-LEWIS, MABEL
Born: Oct. 28, 1872, London, England. Died: Nov. 28, 1957, England? Screen and stage actress. Daughter of stage actors Arthur Lewis (dec.) and Kate Terry (dec. 1924).

Appeared in: **1932** The Faithful Heart. **1935** The Scarlet Pimpernel. **1936** Dishonour Bright. **1937** The Squaker (aka Murder on Diamond Row—US). **1943** Adventures of Tartu (aka Tartu—US). **1944** They Came to a City.

TESLER, JACK
Died: Sept. 8, 1976. Screen and stage actor.

Appeared in: **1953** Abbott and Costello Go to Mars. **1960** Cage of Evil.

TESSIER, VALENTINE
Born: 1892, France. Died: Aug. 11, 1981, French Riviera. Screen and stage actress.

Appeared in: **1934** Madam Bovary. **1937** Club de Femmes. **1938** Abused Confidence. **1944** The Queen and the Cardinal. **1949** Justice Is Done (US 1953). **1955** French Can-Can (aka Only the French Can); Maddalena. **1956** The Snow Was Black; The Sins of the Borgias. **1959** Process au Vatican (Trial at the Vatican, aka Miracle of Saint Therese—US). **1976** Life Size.

TETLEY, WALTER (Walter Campbell Tetley)
Born: 1915, New York, N.Y. Died: Sept. 4, 1975. Screen and radio actor.

Appeared in: **1938** Lord Jeff; Prairie Moon. **1939** Spirit of Culver; Tower of London; Boy Slaves; They Shall Have Music. **1940** Military Academy; Under Texas Skies; Let's Make Music. **1942** Thunder Birds; Who Done It?; The Gorilla Man. **1944** Pin Up Girl; The Lodger. **1945** Molly and Me.

TETZEL, JOAN
Born: June 21, 1921, New York, N.Y. Died: Oct. 31, 1977, Sussex, England (cancer). Screen, stage and radio actress. Divorced from radio producer John Mosman. Married to actor Oscar Homolka (dec. 1978).

Appeared in: **1946** Duel in the Sun. **1948** The Paradine Case. **1949** Thelma Jordan (aka The File on Thelma Jordan). **1950** There's a Girl in My Heart. **1954** Hell Below Zero. **1965** Joy in the Morning.

TEVIS, CAROL
Born: Mar. 6, 1907, Pa. Died: May 15, 1965, Pacific Palisades, Calif. Screen actress, author and composer.

Appeared in: **1932** Once in a Lifetime; The Millionaire Cat (short). **1933** Flying Down to Rio. **1935** Sweepstake Annie; The Affaire of Suzan. **1936** Sing, Baby, Sing. **1937** The Big Squirt (short); Love Is News; Love Takes Flight. **1938** Three Loves Has Nancy. **1941** Unfinished Business.

THANE, EDWARD
Died: Jan., 1954. Stage and screen actor. Married to actress Louise Hampton (dec. 1954).

Appeared in: **1931** Almost a Honeymoon.

THATCHER, EVELYN "EVA"
Born: 1862, Omaha, Nebr. Died: Sept. 28, 1942, Los Angeles, Calif. Screen, stage and vaudeville actress. Appeared in Mack Sennett comedies. Appeared in vaudeville as "The Irish Lady."

Appeared in: **1916** Haystacks and Steeples. **1917** Her Nature Dance; His Naughty Thought; She Needed a Doctor; Thirst; A Bedroom Blunder. **1923** Thirst (reissue of 1917 film). **1924** Not Built for Runnin'. **1925** Flash O'Lightning; Ranchers and Rascals; The Trouble Buster. **1926** Blind Trail; The Outlaw Express.

THATCHER, TORIN
Born: Jan. 15, 1905, Bombay, India. Died: Mar 4, 1981, Thousand Oaks, Calif. (cancer). Screen, stage, radio and television actor. Entered films in 1934.

Appeared in: **1934** Irish Hearts (aka Norah O'Neale—US). **1938** Climbing High (US 1939). **1939** The Spy in Black (aka U-Boat 29—US). **1940** Let George Do It; The Case of the Frightened Lady (aka The Frightened Lady—US 1941). **1941** Major Barbara. **1942** The Next of Kin (US 1943). **1946** Great Expectations (US 1947); The Captive Heart (US 1947). **1947** Jassy (US 1948); The Man Within (aka The Smugglers—US 1948); The End of the River (US 1948); When the Bough Breaks. **1948** Bonnie Prince Charlie (US 1952); The Fallen Idol (US 1949). **1950** The Black Rose. **1952** The Snows of Kilimanjaro; The Crimson Pirate; Affair in Trinidad; Blackbeard, the Pirate. **1953** The Robe; The Desert Rats; Houdini. **1954** Knock on Wood; Bengal Brigade; The Black Shield of Falworth. **1955** Lady Godiva; Diane; Love Is a Many Splendored Thing; Helen of Troy. **1957** Witness for the Prosecution; Istanbul; Band of Angels. **1958** Darby's Rangers; The Seventh Voyage of Sinbad. **1959** The Miracle. **1961** The Canadians. **1962** Jack the Giant Killer; Mutiny on the Bounty. **1963** Drums of Africa. **1965** The Sandpiper. **1966** Hawaii. **1967** The King's Pirate.

THAW, EVELYN NESBIT (aka EVELYN NESBET)
Born: 1885. Died: Jan. 18, 1967, Santa Monica, Calif. Screen and vaudeville actress. Known as the "Girl in the Red Velvet Swing."

Appeared in: **1914** Threads of Destiny. **1917** Redemption. **1922** The Hidden Woman.

THAWL, EVELYN
Born: 1915. Died: Nov., 1945, Brooklyn, N.Y. Screen and stage actress.

THEIS, ALFRED

Born: 1899. Died: Sept. 16, 1951, Newfoundland, enroute from Germany (heart attack). Screen and vaudeville actor. Appeared in vaudeville in the "Alfred Theis Tiny Town Revue."

THESIGER, ERNEST

Born: Jan. 15, 1879, London, England. Died: Jan. 14, 1961, London, England. Stage and screen actor.

Appeared in: **1916** The Real Thing at Last. **1918** Nelson; The Life Story of David Lloyd George. **1919** A Little Bit of Fluff. **1921** The Bachelor's Club; The Adventures of Mr. Pickwick. **1928** Weekend Wives (US 1929). **1929** The Vagabond Queen. **1930** Ashes. **1932** The Old Dark House. **1933** The Only Girl (aka Heart Song—US 1934); The Ghoul. **1934** The Night of the Party; My Heart is Calling (US 1935). **1935** Bride of Frankenstein. **1936** The Man Who Could Work Miracles (US 1937). **1938** They Drive by Night; The Ware Case (US 1939); Lightning Conductors. **1943** My Learned Friend; The Lamp Still Burns. **1944** Don't Take It to Heart (US 1949). **1945** Henry V (US 1946); A Place of One's Own (US 1949). **1946** Caesar and Cleopatra; Beware of Pity (US 1947). **1947** The Man Within (aka The Smugglers—US 1948); Jassy (US 1948); The Ghosts of Berkeley Square. **1948** The Winslow Boy (US 1950); Quartet (US 1949); Portrait from Life (aka The Girl in the Painting—US 1949); The Brass Monkey (aka Lucky Mascot—US 1951). **1949** The Bad Lord Byron (US 1952). **1950** Last Holiday. **1951** The Man in the White Suit (US 1952); Scrooge; The Magic Box (US 1952); Laughter in Paradise. **1952** The Woman's Angle (US 1954). **1953** Meet Mr. Lucifer; The Robe. **1954** The Million Pound Note (aka Man With a Million—US); Father Brown (aka The Detective—US); Make Me an Offer (US 1956). **1955** Adventures of Quentin Durward; Value for Money (US 1957); An Alligator Named Daisy (US 1957). **1956** Three Men in a Boat (US 1958); Who Done It? **1957** Doctor at Large. **1958** The Truth About Women. **1959** Invitation to Murder (US 1962); The Horse's Mouth; The Battle of the Sexes (US 1960). **1960** Sons and Lovers. **1961** The Roman Spring of Mrs. Stone.

THEVAR, SANDOW (Sandow Chinnappa Thevar)

Born: 1914, India. Died: Sept. 8, 1978, Coimbatore, India (heart attack). Screen actor, film producer and director.

THIELE, WILLIAM J.

Born: May 10, 1890, Vienna, Austria. Died: Sept. 7, 1975, Woodland Hills, Calif. Screen, stage actor, film director and writer. Entered films in 1913 as an actor.

THIGPEN, HELEN

Died: Sept. 3, 1966. Black screen actress.

Appeared in: **1959** Porgy and Bess (stage and film versions).

THIMIG, HELENE

Died: Nov. 7, 1974, Vienna, Austria (heart failure). Screen and stage actress. Married to film producer and director Max Reinhardt (dec. 1943).

Appeared in: **1932** Mensch Ohne Namen. **1942** The Gay Sisters. **1943** The Moon Is Down; Edge of Darkness. **1944** The Hitler Gang; None But the Lonely Heart; Strangers in the Night. **1945** Hotel Berlin; Isle of the Dead; This Love of Ours; Roughly Speaking. **1946** Cloak and Dagger. **1947** The Locket; Cry Wolf; Escape Me Never; High Conquest. **1952** Decision Before Dawn.

THODY, HENRY

Born: 1918, England? Died: Mar. 7, 1977, Sydney, Australia (suicide—jumping from a cliff). Journalist, writer and screen actor.

Appeared in: **1957** A Farewell to Arms. **1961** La Dolce Vita.

THOMAS, BILLY "BUCKWHEAT" (William Henry Thomas, Jr.)

Born: 1931, Los Angeles, Calif. Died: Oct., 1980, Los Angeles, Calif. (natural causes). Black screen actor. Known as "Buckwheat" in Our Gang comedies.

Appeared in: **1934** The following shorts: For Pete's Sake; Washee Ironee; Mama's Little Pirates; Shrimps for a Day; First Round-Up. **1935** The following shorts: Anniversary Trouble; Beginner's Luck; Teacher's Beau; Sprucin' Up; Little Papa; Little Sinner; Our Gang Follies of 1936. **1936** The following shorts: Pinch Singer; Divot Diggers; The Lucky Corner; Second Childhood; Arbor Day; Bored of Education; Two Too Young; Pay as You Exit; Spooky Hooky. **1937** The following shorts: Reunion in Rhythm; Glove Taps; Three Smart Boys; Hearts Are Trumps; Rushin' Ballet; Roamin' Holiday; Night 'n' Gales; Fishy Tales; Framing Youth; Pigskin Palooka; Mail and Female; Our Gang Follies of 1938. **1938** The following shorts: Canned Fishing;

Bear Facts; Three Men in a Tub; Came the Brawn; The Awful Tooth; Hide and Shriek; The Little Ranger; Party Fever; Aladdin's Lantern; Men in Fright; Football Romeo; Practical Jokers. **1939** The following shorts: Alfalfa's Aunt; Tiny Troubles; Duel Personalities; Clown Princes; Cousin Wilbur; Joy Scouts; Dog Daze; Auto Antics; Captain Spanky's Show Boat; Dad for a Day; Time Out for Lessons. **1940** The following shorts: Alfalfa's Double; The Big Premiere; All About Hash; The New Pupil; Bubbling Trouble; Good Bad Guys; Waldo's Last Stand; Goin' Fishin'; Kiddie Cure. **1941** The following shorts: Fightin' Fools; Baby Blues; Ye Olde Minstrels; 1-2-3 Go!; Robot Wrecks; Helping Hands; Come Back, Miss Pipps; Wedding Worries. **1942** The following shorts: Melodies Old and New; Going to Press; Don't Lie; Suprised Parties; Doin' Their Bit; Rover's Big Chance; Mighty Lak a Goat; Unexpected Riches. **1943** The following shorts: Benjamin Franklin, Jr.; Family Troubles; Calling All Kids; Farm Hands; Election Daze; Little Miss Pinkerton; Three Smart Guys. **1944** The following shorts: Radio Bugs; Tale of a Dog; Dancing Romeo.

THOMAS, CONRAD (Conrad Jason Thomas)

Born: Apr. 22, 1915, San Diego, Calif. Died: May 1, 1934, Azusa, Calif. (auto accident). Stuntman.

THOMAS, DAVID

Born: 1908, Wales. Died: Jan. 27, 1981, New York, N.Y. Screen, stage and television actor. Married to actress Peggy Turnley.

Appeared in: **1957** A Face in the Crowd. **1968** The Night They Raided Minsky's. **1972** Trick Baby. **1977** Roseland. **1982** Cold River.

THOMAS, EDNA

Born: 1886, Lawrenceville, Va. Died: July 22, 1974, New York, N.Y. (heart condition). Stage and screen actress.

Appeared in: **1951** A Streetcar Named Desire (stage and screen versions).

THOMAS, EDWARD

Born: 1884. Died: Dec. 29, 1943, Los Angeles, Calif. Screen actor.

Appeared in: **1927** Tea for Three.

THOMAS, GRETCHEN

Born: 1897. Died: Nov. 1, 1964, Hollywood, Calif. Screen, stage and television actress.

Appeared in: **1930** Spring Is Here; Young Desire. **1937** Damaged Goods. **1938** Marriage Forbidden. **1957** I Was a Teenage Frankenstein.

THOMAS, GUS

Born: 1865, Toronto, Canada. Died: May 3, 1926, Everett, Wash. Screen, stage and vaudeville actor.

Appeared in: **1922** Alias Julius Caesar.

THOMAS, HUGH

Born: 1920. Died: June 27, 1981, Wallington, N.J. Screen and stage actor.

Appeared in: **1951** The Red Badge of Courage.

THOMAS, JAMESON

Born: Mar. 24, 1889. Died: Jan. 10, 1939, Sierra Madre, Calif. (tuberculosis). Screen, stage actor and film director. Divorced from actress Dorothy Dix (dec. 1970).

Appeared in: **1923** Chu Chin Chow (US 1925). **1924** Decameron Nights (US 1928) The Sins Ye Do; Thrilling Stories from the Strand Magazine series including The Drum and the Cavern Spider. The Clicking of Cuthbert series including Chester Forgets Himself. **1925** Afraid of Love; The Apache; A Daughter of Love; The Gold Cure. **1926** The Brotherhood (short); The Jungle Woman. **1927** The Antidote (short); Blighty (aka Apres La Guerre); Pearl of the South Seas; Poppies of Flanders; Roses of Picardy. **1928** The Farmer's Wife (US 1930); The Rising Generation; Tesha; Weekend Wives (US 1929); The White Sheik (aka King's Mate). **1929** Memories (short); The Feather; The Hate Ship; High Treason; Piccadilly; Power Over Men. **1930** Night Birds; Elstree Calling; Extravagance. **1931** Lover Come Back. **1932** Three Wise Girls; Trial of Vivienne Ware; Escapade; No More Orchids; The Phantom President. **1933** Brief Moment; The Invisible Man; Self Defense. **1934** Stolen Sweets; Now and Forever; The Moonstone; A Successful Failure; A Lost Lady; The Curtain Falls; It Happened One Night; Bombay Mail; The Scarlet Empress; A Woman's Man; Beggars in Ermine; Sing Sing Nights; Jane Eyre. **1935** Night Birds (reissue of 1930 film); Lives of a Bengal Lancer; Charlie Chan in Egypt; The Last Outpost; The World Accuses; Mr. Dynamite; Coronado; The Lady in Scarlet. **1936** Mr. Deeds Goes to Town; Lady Luck. **1937** The Man Who Cried Wolf; One Hundred Men and a Girl; The League of Frightened Men; House of Secrets. **1938** Death Goes North.

THOMAS, JOHN CHARLES
Born: 1887, Baltimore, Md. Died: Dec. 13, 1960, Apple Valley, Calif. (intestinal cancer). Screen, stage, radio actor and singer.

Appeared in: **1923** Under the Red Robe. **1927** The following shorts: Prologue to I Pagliacci; Danny Deever; Will You Remember Me?

THOMAS, LOWELL, SR.
Born: Apr. 6, 1892, Woodington, Ohio. Died: Aug. 29, 1981, Pawling, N.Y. (heart attack). Broadcaster for radio and television, author, screen actor, producer and screenwriter. Father of broadcaster Lowell Thomas, Jr.

Narrated the following: **1932** Blonde Captive. **1937** Borneo. **1951** Ski Champs. **1954** Out of This World. **1956** Seven Wonders of the World. **1957** Search for Paradise. **1963** The Best of Cinerama. **1970** Patton (and film clips). **1980** Triple Play (and appearance).

THOMAS, OLIVE
Born: Oct. 29, 1884, Charleroi, Pa. Died: Sept. 10, 1920, Paris, France (suicide). Stage and screen actress. Married to actor Jack Pickford (dec. 1933).

Appeared in: **1916** Beatrice Follies. **1917** Betty Takes a Hand. **1918** Limousine Life. **1919** The Glorious Lady; Upstairs and Down; The Follies Girl. **1920** The Flapper; Footlights and Shadows.

THOMAS, POWYS
Born: 1926, Wales. Died: June 22, 1977, Wales. Screen and stage actor.

Appeared in: **1964** The Luck of Ginger Coffey.

THOMAS, RUTH
Born: 1911. Died: Mar. 23, 1970, Columbus, Ohio. Screen, stage and television actress.

THOMAS, VIRGINIA
Died: Jan. 12, 1955, Los Angeles, Calif. Screen actress. Divorced from makeup artist Perc Westmore.

Appeared in: **1927** The Private Life of Helen of Troy. **1929** The Wild Party.

THOMAS, WILLIAM
Born: 1918. Died: May, 1948, Los Angeles, Calif. Screen actor. Do not confuse with William "Buckwheat" Thomas.

Appeared in: **1947** Spirit of West Point; The Big Fix.

THOMASHEFSKY, MAX
Born: 1872. Died: July 24, 1932, New York, N.Y. Screen and stage actor.

THOMPSON, DAVID H.
Born: May 4, 1886, New York, N.Y. Died: May 20, 1957, Hollywood, Calif. Screen, stage actor and film director. Appeared in Edison Film Co. productions in 1910 and Thanhouser Film Co. productions 1911-14.

THOMPSON, FREDERICK A.
Born: 1870, Montreal, Canada. Died: Jan. 23, 1925, Hollywood, Calif. (heart disease). Stage and screen actor. Entered films in 1910.

Appeared in: **1921** The Heart Line. **1922** A Tailor Made Man.

THOMPSON, GEORGE
Born: 1868. Died: May 29, 1929, Los Angeles, Calif. (following surgery for stomach trouble caused by poisonous facial make-up which started infection). Screen and stage actor. Married to actress Cora Bennett.

Appeared in: **1929** Why Bring That Up?

THOMPSON, HAL
Born: 1894. Died: Mar. 3, 1966. Screen actor.

Appeared in: **1925** Who's Your Friend? **1926** Comin' an' Going. **1930** Animal Crackers; Leave It to Lester.

THOMPSON, JIM
Born: 1907. Died: Apr. 7, 1977, Hollywood, Calif. Author, screenwriter and screen actor. Father of Patricia, Sharon and actor Michael John Thompson.

Appeared in: **1970** Multiple Maniacs. **1975** Farewell My Lovely.

THOMPSON, MARGARET
Born: Oct. 26, 1889, Trinidad, Colo. Died: Dec. 26, 1969, Los Angeles, Calif. (heart disease). Screen actress.

Appeared in: **1916** The Thoroughbred; The Honorable Algy; The Sin Ye Do. **1917** The Iced Bullet; Time Locks and Diamonds; The Flame of the Yukon.

THOMPSON, MOLLY
Born: 1879. Died: Feb. 14, 1928, Culver City, Calif. (brain hemorrhage). Screen actress and casting director. Was an actress with Roach and appeared in nearly all of Harold Lloyd's early comedies.

THOMPSON, NICK
Born: 1890. Died: Apr. 22, 1980. Screen actor.

Appeared in: **1922** The Mohican's Daughter; Unconquered Woman; A Virgin's Sacrifice; When the Desert Calls. **1923** The Snow Bride. **1924** Tongues of Flame. **1926** Puppets. **1928** The Riding Renegade. **1929** General Crack; Tonight at Twelve. **1930** The Storm; Those Who Dance. **1933** Corruption. **1936** A Woman Rebels. **1937** Wallaby Jim of the Islands. **1938** Blockade. **1941** The Phantom Cowboy; Lawless Plainsmen. **1944** Buffalo Bill; The Last Horseman. **1946** Singin' in the Corn. **1951** Savage Drums. **1952** Harem Girl. **1957** Apache Warrior.

THOMPSON, POLLY (Hippolita Thompson)
Died: Mar. 8, 1933, New York, N.Y. (suicide—gas). Screen and stage actress.

Appeared in: **1919** Deliverance.

THOMPSON, RAYMOND "RAY"
Born: 1898. Died: June 29, 1927 (drowned). Stuntman and screen actor.

Appeared in: **1920** Son of Tarzan (serial). **1923** Jungle Trail of the Son of Tarzan (feature of 1920 serial). **1924** Horse Sense; When a Man's a Man. **1925** Go West. **1926** The Enchanted Hill; The Fighting Buckaroo.

THOMPSON, THERESE
Born: 1876. Died: Sept. 17, 1936, Hollywood, Calif. Screen and stage actress. Sister of actress Trixie Friganza (dec. 1955).

THOMPSON, ULU M.
Born: 1873. Died: Apr. 13, 1957, Hollywood, Calif. (heart ailment). Screen actress.

THOMPSON, WALKER
Born: 1888, Lexington, Ky. Died: Sept. 19, 1922, Chicago, Ill. Screen and stage actor.

Appeared in: **1921** Symbol of the Unconquered.

THOMPSON, WILLIAM "BILL"
Born: 1913. Died: July 15, 1971, Los Angeles, Calif. Screen, radio and television actor. Do not confuse with actor William H. Thompson (dec. 1923), nor stage actor William Thompson (dec. 1929).

Appeared in: **1942** Here We Go Again. **1951** Alice in Wonderland (voice of White Rabbit and Dodo). **1953** Peter Pan (voice). **1955** Lady and the Tramp (voice of Jack, Bull and Dachsie). **1959** Sleeping Beauty (voice only). **1970** The Aristocats (voice only).

THOMPSON, WILLIAM H.
Born: 1852, Glasgow, Scotland. Died: Feb. 4, 1923, New York, N.Y. (pneumonia). Stage and screen actor. Do not confuse with stage actor William H. Thompson (dec. 1929). Married to actress Lillian Dix (dec. 1922).

Appeared in: **1915** Peggy.

THOMSON, ARCHIBALD (Archibald Melick Thomson)
Born: 1901, Elmira, N.Y. Died: Sept. 22, 1981, New York. Screen, stage actor and stage manager. Married to Lois Brown and later married and divorced stage actress Mary Ann Carr.

THOMSON, FRED
Born: Apr. 28, 1890, Pasadena, Calif. Died: Dec. 25, 1928, Los Angeles, Calif. (following surgery for gallstones). Screen actor, double and stuntman. Married to actress and screenwriter Frances Marion (dec. 1973).

Appeared in: **1921** The Love Light; Just Around the Corner. **1922** Oath-Bound; Penrod. **1923** The Eagle's Talons (serial); The Mask of

Lopez; A Chapter in Her Life. **1924** The Silent Stranger; The Dangerous Coward; The Fighting Sap; Galloping Gallagher; North of Nevada; Thundering Hoofs; Queniado. **1925** The Wild Bull's Lair; The Bandit's Baby; That Devil Quemado; All Around Frying Pan; Ridin' the Wind. **1926** A Regular Scout; Hands Across the Border; The Two-Gun Man; The Tough Guy; Lone Hand Saunders. **1927** Silver Comes Through; Jesse James; Arizona Nights; Don Mike. **1928** Kit Carson; The Sunset Legion; The Pioneer Scout.

THOMSON, KENNETH
Born: Jan. 7, 1899, Pittsburgh, Pa. Died: Jan. 27, 1967, Los Angeles, Calif. (emphysema and fibrosis). Screen and stage actor. One of the founders of the Screen Actors Guild. Married to stage actress Alden Gay Thomson (dec. 1979).

Appeared in: **1926** Corporal Kate; Man Bait; Risky Business. **1927** White Gold; Almost Human; King of Kings; Turkish Delight. **1928** The Secret Hour; The Street of Illusion. **1929** The Letter; The Bellamy Trial; The Broadway Melody; Say It With Songs; The Careless Age; The Girl from Havana; The Veiled Woman; Song Writer. **1930** Children of Pleasure; Lawful Larceny; Sweethearts on Parade; Doorway to Hell; Just Imagine; Faithful; The Other Tomorrow; A Notorious Affair; Sweet Mama; Wild Company; Reno. **1931** Woman Hungry; Murder at Midnight; Bad Company; Oh! Oh! Cleopatra (short). **1932** By Whose Hands?; Man Wanted; The Famous Ferguson Case; Movie Crazy; 70,000 Witnesses; 13 Women; Her Mad Night; Lawyer Man; Fast Life. **1933** The Little Giant; Female; Son of a Sailor; Daring Daughters; Hold Me Tight; Sitting Pretty; From Headquarters; Jungle Bride. **1934** Change of Heart; Many Happy Returns; Cross Streets; In Old Santa Fe. **1935** Behold My Wife; Behind the Green Lights; Whispering Smith Speaks; Hopalong Cassidy; Manhattan Butterfly. **1936** With Love and Kisses; The Blackmailer. **1937** Jim Hanvey—Detective.

THOR, LARRY
Born: 1917. Died: Mar. 15, 1976, Santa Monica, Calif. (heart attack). Screen, radio, television actor, screenwriter and newscaster. Married to actress Jean Howell.

Appeared in: **1952** The Pride of Saint Louis. **1955** Five Guns West. **1957** Portland Expose; The Amazing Colossal Man; Hell Bound; Zero Hour! **1958** The Littlest Hobo; Tarawa Beachhead. **1959** Battle of the Coral Sea. **1960** Let's Make Love. **1970** Company of Killers; The Phantom Tollbooth.

THORBURN, JUNE
Born: 1931, Kashmir, India. Died: Nov. 4, 1967, Fernhurst, Sussex, England (air crash). Screen and television actress.

Appeared in: **1952** The Pickwick Papers (film debut—US 1953). **1953** The Cruel Sea. **1954** Fast and Loose; Delayed Action; Children Galore; Orders Are Orders. **1955** The Hornet's Nest; Touch and Go (aka The Light Touch—US 1956). **1957** True as Turtle. **1958** Rooney; Tom Thumb. **1959** Broth of a Boy. **1960** The Price of Silence; The 3 Worlds of Gulliver; Escort for Hire. **1961** Fury at Smuggler's Bay (US 1963); Transatlantic; Don't Bother to Knock (aka Why Bother to Knock—US 1964). **1963** Master Spy (US 1964); The Scarlet Blade (aka The Crimson Blade—US 1964).

THORDSEN, KELLY
Born: 1916. Died: Jan. 23, 1978, Sun Valley, Idaho (cancer). Screen and television actor.

Appeared in: **1956** The Desperados Are in Town. **1957** Money, Women and Guns; Invasion of the Saucer Men. **1958** The Fearmakers. **1959** City of Fear. **1960** Desire in the Dust. **1962** Sweet Bird of Youth; To Kill a Mockingbird. **1964** The Misadventures of Merlin Jones. **1965** Shenandoah. **1966** Boy, Did I Get a Wrong Number?; Gunpoint; Texas Across the River; The Ugly Dachshund. **1967** Good Times. **1968** Blackbeard's Ghost; Did You Hear the One About the Traveling Saleslady? **1970** The Boatniks. **1974** The Parrallax View.

THORN, JOHN
Born: 1880. Died: Aug. 28, 1935, Mercer, Pa. Screen and stage actor. Appeared in silent films.

THORNBY, ROBERT T.
Born: 1889, New York, N.Y. Died: Mar. 6, 1953. Screen, stage actor, film producer and director. Entered films as an actor with Vitagraph.

Appeared in: **1930** Today.

THORNDIKE, OLIVER
Born: Sept. 12, 1918, Boston, Mass. Died: Apr. 14, 1954, St. Thomas, Virgin Islands. Screen, stage and television actor.

Appeared in: **1932** The Sign of the Cross. **1944** The Sign of the Cross (revised version of 1932 film); The Story of Dr. Wassell.

THORNDIKE, RUSSELL
Died: Nov. 7, 1972, London, England. Screen and stage actor, author and screenwriter. Brother of actress Dame Sybil Thorndike (dec. 1976).

Appeared in: **1916** The Test; The Dream of Eugene Aram. **1918** The Bells. **1922** Tense Moments from Great Plays series including: Macbeth; It's Never Too Late to Mend. **1923** The Audacious Mr. Squire; The Fair Maid of Perth; Heartstrings; Wonder Women of the World series including: Henrietta Maria or, the Queen of Sorrow; Lucrezia Borgia or, Plaything of Power; Gems of Literature series including: The Dream of Eugene Aram; Scrooge; The Bells; The School of Scandal; The Test; The Sins of a Father; Love in an Attic. **1924** Miriam Rozella; Human Desires. **1933** Puppets of Fate (aka Wolves of the Underworld—US 1935); The Roof; A Shot in the Dark (US 1935). **1934** Whispering Tongues. **1936** Fame. **1944** Fiddlers Three. **1945** Henry V (US 1946). **1948** Hamlet. **1955** Richard III (US 1956).

THORNDIKE, DAME SYBIL
Born: Oct. 24, 1882, Gainsborough, Lincolnshire, England. Died: June 9, 1976, London, England (heart attack). Screen, stage and television actress. Sister of actor/writer Russell Thorndike (dec. 1972). Married to producer/actor Lewis Casson (dec. 1969). Mother of actors John, Christopher, Mary and Ann Casson. Was made Dame Commander of the Order of the British Empire in 1931.

Appeared in: **1921** Moth and Rust (film debut). **1922** Tense Moments from Great Plays series including: Macbeth, Bleak House, Jane Shore, The Lady of the Camellias, The Merchant of Venice, Esmeralda, Nancy and The Scarlet Letter. **1927** Saint Joan. **1928** Dawn. **1929** To What Red Hell. **1931** Hindle Wakes; A Gentleman of Paris. **1936** Tudor Rose (aka Nine Days a Queen—US). **1941** Major Barbara. **1947** Nicholas Nickleby. **1949** Britannia Mews (aka Forbidden Street—US). **1950** Stage Fright; Gone to Earth (aka The Wild Heart—US 1952). **1951** The Magic Box (US 1952); The Lady with the Lamp. **1953** Melba. **1954** The Weak and the Wicked. **1957** The Prince and the Showgirl. **1958** Smiley Gets a Gun (US 1959); Alive and Kicking (US 1964). **1959** Jet Storm (US 1961); Shake Hands With the Devil. **1960** Hand in Hand (US 1961). **1961** The Big Gamble.

THORNDYKE, LUCYLE
Born: 1885, Seattle, Wash. Died: Dec. 17, 1935, Los Angeles, Calif. Screen and stage actress.

Appeared in: **1924** The Garden of Weeds. **1926** The Speed Limit.

THORNE, DICK
Born: 1905. Died: Jan. 31, 1957, Hollywood, Calif. (heart attack). Screen actor and stuntman. Entered films approx. 1925.

THORNE, FRANK A., SR.
Born: Oct. 12, 1881, Philadelphia, Pa. Died: May 28, 1953, North Hollywood, Calif. Screen, stage actor and film director. Married to stage actress Lizette Holdsworth (dec.). Entered films as an actor with Selig.

THORNE, ROBERT
Born: 1881. Died: July 3, 1965, New York, N.Y. (heart attack). Stage and screen actor.

Appeared in: **1924** Janice Meredith.

THORNE, WILLIAM L.
Born: Oct. 14, 1878, Calif. Died: Mar. 10, 1948, Calif. Screen actor.

Appeared in: **1926** The Kick-Off. **1927** White Gold; King of Kings. **1929** Thunderbolt; The Drake Case. **1930** Peacock Alley; Fighting Thru; Abraham Lincoln. **1931** Danger Island (serial); Finger Prints (serial); She-Wolf; Mother's Millions; Montana Kid. **1932** The Rainbow Trail; Law of the North; While Paris Sleeps. **1934** Pirate Treasure (serial). **1935** The Roaring West (serial). **1936** Nevada. **1937** The Gold Racket; Bank Alarm; Love Takes Flight.

THORNHILL, CLAUDE
Born: 1908, Terre Haute, Ind. Died: July 1, 1965, Caldwell, N.J. (heart attack). Bandleader and screen actor.

THORNTON, GLADYS
Born: 1899. Died: Sept. 2, 1964, Hollywood, Calif. Screen, stage and radio actress. Played "Aunt Jemima" on radio.

Appeared in: **1962** If a Man Answers.

THORNTON, RICHARD
Born: 1873. Died: May 9, 1936, New York, N.Y. (heart attack). Screen and stage actor. Do not confuse with actor Richard Thornton (dec. 1962).

Appeared in: **1915** Dubarry. **1918** The Yellow Ticket.

THORPE, GEORGE
Born: Jan. 20, 1891, Groyden, Surrey, England. Died: Dec. 24, 1961, England. Screen and stage actor. Entered films in 1934.

Appeared in: **1942** Unpublished Story. **1943** The Demi-Paradise (aka Adventure for Two—US 1945). **1946** Quiet Week-end (US 1948). **1947** Meet Me at Dawn (US 1948). **1948** Quartet (US 1949). **1949** The Man on the Eiffel Tower. **1952** Father's Doing Fine. **1953** The Gay Duellist (reissue of 1947 Meet Me at Dawn).

THORPE, JIM (James Francis Thorpe)
Born: May 28, 1886 or 1888?, near Prague, Okla. Died: Mar. 28, 1953, Los Angeles, Calif. (heart attack). Screen actor and sports figure. Rated as one of the greatest athletes of all time. Entered films as an extra.

Appeared in: **1932** White Eagle; My Pal, the King; Airmail; Hold 'Em Jail. **1933** Wild Horse Mesa. **1935** Code of the Mounted; Behold My Wife; The Red Rider; Wanderer of the Wasteland; Rustlers of Red Gap (serial); She; Fighting Youth; Barbary Coast; The Farmer Takes a Wife; Captain Blood. **1936** Sutter's Gold; Wildcat Trooper; Treachery Rides the Range; Hill Tillies (short). **1937** Big City; Green Light. **1940** Henry Goes to Arizona; Arizona Frontier; Prairie Schooners. **1944** Outlaw Trail. **1945** Road to Utopia. **1949** White Heat. **1950** Wagonmaster.

THORPE, TED
Born: 1917. Died: Dec. 18, 1970, Honolulu, Hawaii (heart attack). Screen actor.

Appeared in: **1952** Radar Men from the Moon (serial). **1953** Flame of Calcutta; Savage Mutiny; The Lost Planet (serial). **1958** Machine Gun Kelly. **1961** Back Street. **1962** If a Man Answers. **1968** Hang 'Em High.

THUMB, MRS. GENERAL TOM (Lavinia Warren)
Born: 1841, Middleboro, Mass. Died: Nov. 25, 1919. Screen actress and circus midget. Married to circus midget Gen. Tom Thumb (dec. 1883) and later to actor-midget Count Primo Magri (dec. 1920).

Appeared in: **1915** The Lilliputian's Courtship.

THUMB, TOM (Darius Adner Alden)
Born: 1842. Died: Sept. 24, 1926, Los Angeles, Calif. (internal hemorrhage). Circus midget and screen actor. Do not confuse with circus midget Gen. Tom Thumb (dec. 1883).

THURBER, J. KENT
Born: 1892. Died: May 26, 1957, St. Petersburg, Fla. Screen, stage actor and stage director.

THURMAN, MARY
Born: Apr. 27, 1894, Richmond, Utah. Died: Dec. 22, 1925, New York, N.Y. (effects of tropical fever). Screen actress.

Appeared in: **1916** Sunshine Dad; His Last Laugh; His First False Step; Bombs; The Scoundrel's Tale; The Stone Age (aka Her Cave Man). **1917** Maggie's First False Step; Pinched in the Finish. **1918** Watch Your Neighbor. **1921** Bare Knuckles; The Sin of Martha Queed; The Lady from Longacre; A Broken Doll; The Primal Law. **1922** The Bond Boy; The Green Temptation. **1923** A Bride for a Knight; Does It Pay?; Wife in Name Only; Zaza; The Tents of Allah. **1924** For Another Woman; The Law and the Lady; The Truth About Women; Greater Than Marriage; Love of Woman; Playthings of Desire; Trouping with Ellen; Those Who Judge. **1925** Down Upon the Swanee River; The Mad Marriage; The Necessary Evil; Back to Life; The Fool; A Little Girl in a Big City; Wildfire. **1926** The Wives of the Prophet.

THURSBY, DAVID
Born: 1888, Scotland. Died: Apr. 20, 1977, Hollywood, Calif. Screen and stage actor.

Appeared in: **1936** Divot Diggers (short). **1939** Rulers of the Sea. **1942** The Black Swan; The Undying Monster. **1947** Bob, Son of Battle; Bulldog Drummond at Bay; The Ghost and Mrs. Muir; Thunder in the Valley. **1948** Hills of Home; That Wonderful Urge. **1949** The Heiress. **1951** Sealed Cargo. **1955** The Virgin Queen. **1957** Zero Hour.

THURSTON, BARBARA
Died: Feb. 4, 1975. Screen actress.

Appeared in: **1971** Believe in Me.

THURSTON, CAROL
Born: 1923, Forsyth, Mont. Died: Dec. 31, 1969. Screen and stage actress.

Appeared in: **1944** The Story of Dr. Wassell; The Conspirators. **1945** China Sky. **1946** Swamp Fire. **1947** Jewels of Brandenburg; The Last Round-Up. **1948** Rogue's Regiment. **1949** Arctic Manhunt; Apache Chief. **1951** Flaming Feather. **1952** Arctic Flight. **1953** Conquest of Cochise; Killer Ape. **1954** Yukon Vengeance. **1956** The Women of Pitcairn Island. **1960** The Hypnotic Eye. **1963** Showdown.

THURSTON, CHARLES E.
Born: 1869, Oconto, Wis. Died: Mar. 5, 1940, Hollywood, Calif. Screen, stage and vaudeville actor. Entered films approx. 1917.

Appeared in: **1921** Boys Will Be Boys; Black Sheep. **1922** Doubling for Romeo; The Gray Dawn. **1924** Ridgeway of Montana. **1926** Rolling Home; Is That Nice? **1927** Between Dangers; The Fightin' Comeback; The Broken Gate; Spoilers of the West. **1928** When the Law Rides; The Chaser. **1932** The Big Shot. **1933** Unknown Valley.

THURSTON, HARRY
Born: 1874. Died: Sept. 2, 1955. Screen actor.

Appeared in: **1945** And Then There Were None.

THURSTON, MURIEL
Born: 1875, France. Died: May 1, 1943, Hollywood, Calif. Screen actress.

TIBBETT, LAWRENCE
Born: Nov. 16, 1896, Bakersfield, Calif. Died: July 15, 1960, New York, N.Y. Screen, radio actor and opera baritone. Nominated for 1929/30 Academy Award for Best Actor in The Rogue Song.

Appeared in: **1930** The Rogue Song; New Moon. **1931** The Prodigal. **1932** Cuban Love Song. **1935** Metropolitan. **1936** Under Your Spell.

TICKLE, FRANK
Born: June 25, 1893, London, England. Died: Oct. 18, 1955, England? Screen and stage actor. Entered films in 1935.

Appeared in: **1937** London Melody. **1944** Henry V (US 1946). **1948** Escape; Anna Karenina. **1952** Brandy for the Parson. **1956** The Adventures of Quentin Durward. **1958** Henry V (reissue of 1944 film).

TIDBLAD, INGA
Born: 1902, Sweden? Died: Sept. 12, 1975, Stockholm, Sweden. Screen and stage actress.

Appeared in: **1930** For Her Sake. **1934** The Song of the Scarlet Flower. **1956** Foreign Intrigue. The following Swedish films: Andersson; Petersson and Lundstrom; Pirates on Lake Malar; The Norrtull Gang; The Counts of Svansta; Man of Destiny; Uncle Frans; Black Rudolf; The General; Longing for the Sea; People of Halsingland; She of Nobody; Jansson's Temptation; Intermezzo; Flames in the Dark; There Burned a Flame; The Invisible Wall; The Royal Hunt; Mandragora; Divorced; House of Women; Gabrielle; The Unicorn; Mother of Pearl.

TIDMARSH, FERDINAND
Born: 1883, Philadelphia, Pa. Died: Nov., 1922, Philadelphia, Pa. Screen, stage and vaudeville actor.

Appeared in: **1915** The Sporting Duchess; The Cowardly Way. **1916** Lovely Mary; The Half Million Bride; The World's Great Snare.

TIEDTKE, JAKOB (Jacob Karl Tiedtke)
Born: June 23, 1875, Berlin, Germany. Died: June 30, 1960, Berlin, Germany. Screen and stage actor.

Appeared in: **1913** Schuldig. **1915** Kulicks Gewissensbisse. **1918** Der Rattenfaenger von Hameln (The Pied Piper of Hamelin). **1919** Fahrt ins Blaue; Die Puppe (The Doll). **1920** Kohlhiesels Toechter (Kohlhiesel's Daughters); Sumurun (aka One Arabian Night); Der Mann ohne Namen (The Man Without a Name). **1922** Der Strom; Der Tiger des Zirkus Farini; Die Flamme (aka Montmartre). **1923** Das Karussell des Lebens; Der Kaufmann von Venedig; Maciste und die Chinesische Truhe; Nanon; Die Austreibung (Driven From Home); Das Alte Gesetz (The Ancient Law). **1924** Arabella; Auf Befehl der Pompadour; Dr. Wislizenus; Pietro, der Korsar (Peter the Pirate—US 1927); Die Radio-Heirat; Das Spiel mit dem Schicksal; Ein Traum vom Glueck; Tragoedie im Hause Habsburg (aka Das Drama von Mayerling). **1925** Die Dame aus Berlin; Ein Walzertraum (Waltz Dream—US 1926); Die Drei Portiermaedel; Husarenfieber; Kammermusik. **1926** Der Gute Ruf; In der Heimat, da Gibt's ein

Wiedersehn!; Der Mann im Feuer; Die Muehle von Sanssouci; Nur eine Taenzerin; Der Provinzonkel; Schenk mir das Leben; Das Panzergewoelbe (The Armoured Vault). **1927** Die Apachen von Paris; Arme Kleine Sif; Die Brauetigame der Babette Bomberling; Dr. Bessels Verwandlung; Die Frau ohne Namen; Gehetzte Frauen; Gustav Mond ... Du Gehst so Stille; Luther (US 1929); Primanerliebe; Unter Ausschluss der Oeffentlichkeit; Was Kinder den Eltern Verschweigen. **1928** Don Juan in der Maedchenschule; Ehre Deine Mutter; Heut' Spielt der Strauss; Heut Tanzt Mariett; Liebe im Schnee; Moral; Das Spreewaldmaedel. **1929** Autobus Nr. 2; Die Liebe der Brueder Rott; Mascottchen; Meine Schwester und Ich; Drei Machen ihr Glueck. **1930** Die Jugendgeliebte (aka Goethe's Fruehlingstraum); Das Floetenkonzert von Saussouci (The Flute Concert at Sans Souci—US 1931); Pension Schoeller. **1931** Zum Goldene Anker; Voruntersuchung; Berlin-Alexanderplatz; Ein Auto und Kein Geld; Mein Freund, der Millionaer; Yorck (US 1932); ... und das ist die Hauptsache (aka Eine Ballnacht). **1932** Zwei Glueckliche Tage; Das Blaue vom Himmel (US 1934); Das Maedchen vom Montparnasse; Tausend fuer Eine Nacht (US 1934); Strich Durch die Rechnung (US 1934); Ja, Treu ist die Soldatenliebe (US 1934); Fraeulein—Falsch Verbunden! (US 1934); Hasenklein Kann Nichts Dafuer (aka Drunter und Drueber); Das Testament des Cornelius Gulden (aka Eine Erbschaft mit Hindernissen); Ein Toller Einfall (A Mad Idea—US 1934). **1933** Wenn am Sonntagabend die Dorfmusik Spielt (US 1935); Saison in Kairo; Kleiner Mann—was Nun?; Gretel Zieht das Grosse Los (US 1935); Heimat am Rhein (US 1934); Der Kampf um den Baer; Die Kalte Mamsell (US 1935); Die Schoenen Tage von Aranjuez; Des Jungen Dessauers Grosse Liebe; Ihre Durchlaucht, die Verkaeuferin; Das Lied vom Glueck (aka Es Gibt nur Eine Melodie (The Song of Happiness—US 1935)); Schoen ist Jeder Tag, den Du mir Schenkst; Marie Louise (aka Die Sonne Geht Auf—US 1935). **1934** Eines Prinzen Junge Liebe; Schwarzer Jaeger Johanna; So ein Flegel; Besuch am Abend (US 1937); Schuetzenkoenig Wird der Felix; Schoen ist es, Verliebt zu Sein; Peter, Paul und Nanette (US 1940); Das Blumenmaedchen vom Grand-Hotel; Der Doppelbrauetigam (The Double Fiancee—US 1935); Der Doeppelgaenger; Der Vetter aus Dingsda (US 1936); Lockvogel (US 1935); Fuerst Woronzeff; Ein Maedel Wirbelr Durch die Welt; Die Liebe und die Erste Eisenbahn (Love and the First Railroad—US 1935); Die Liebe Siegt; Die Grosse Chance (US 1935); Petersburger Naechte (aka Walzer an der Newa); Fruehlingsmaerchen (US 1935, aka Verlieb' Dich Nicht in Sizilien). **1935** Frischer Wind aus Kanada; Der Junge Graf (US 1936); Der Vogelhaendler; Hilde Petersen Postlagernd. **1936** Spiel an Bord; Onkel Braesig; Savoy-Hotel 217. **1937** Gewitterflug zu Claudia; Zu Neuen Ufern; Die Goettliche Jette; Meine Freundin Barbara. **1938** Nanu, Sie Kennen Korff Noch Nicht? (So, You Don't Know Korff Yet?—US 1939); Verwehte Spuren (Covered Tracks—US 1939). **1939** Das Unsterbliche Herz; Die Reise Nach Tilsit. **1940** Falschmuenzer; Das Leichte Maedel; Jud Suess. **1941** Der Weg ins Freie; Die Schwedische Nachtigall; Pedro Soll Haengen; Frau Luna; Leichte Muse (aka Was Eine Frau im Fruehling Trauemt). **1942** So ein Fruechtchen; Der Grosse Koenig (The Great King). **1943** Das Schwarze Schaf; Jungfern vom Bischofsberg; Johann. **1944** Die Frau Meiner Traume; Das War Mein Leben; Schicksal am Strom; Schuss um Mitternacht; Kolberg; Familie Buchholz (aka Neigungsehe). **1945** Das Alte Lied; Die Tolle Susanne; Shiva und die Galgenblume; Wiener Maedeln; Ich Glaube an Dich (aka Mathilde Moehring); Heidesommer (aka Verliebter Sommer). **1948** Morgen ist Alles Besser. **1949** Das Geheimnis der Roten Katze; Hans im Glueck; Kleiner Wagen—Grosse Liebe; Enmaleins der Liebe; Nichts als Zufaelle. **1951** Es Begann um Mitternacht; Das Seltsame Leben des Herrn Bruggs; Hanna Amon; Unsterbliche Geliebte; Durch Dick und Duenn; Koenigin Einer Nacht. **1952** Am Brunnen vor dem Tore. **1953** Die Blaue Stunde; Keine Angst vor Grossen Tieren; Damenwahl. **1954** Der Raub derr Sabinerinnen; ... und Ewig Bleibt die Liebe. **1955** Leave on Parole; Urlaub auf Ehrenwort; Emil und die Detektive (Emil and the Detectives).

TIGHE, HARRY
Born: approx. 1885. Died: Feb. 10, 1935, Old Lyme, Conn. Screen, stage, vaudeville, radio actor and film director.

Appeared in: **1922** A Wide-Open Town. **1930** Bright Sayings (short).

TILBURY, ZEFFIE
Born: Nov. 20, 1863. Died: July 24, 1950, Los Angeles, Calif. Screen and stage actress.

Appeared in: **1919** The Avalanche. **1921** Camille; The Marriage of William Ashe; Big Game. **1924** Another Scandal. **1929** The Single Standard. **1930** The Ship from Shanghai. **1931** Charlie Chan Carries On. **1934** The Farmer Takes a Wife; Mystery Liner. **1935** Women Must Dress; The Mystery of Edwin Drood; The Werewolf of London; Alice Adams; The Last Days of Pompeii. **1936** Parole; Anthony Adverse; Camille; Desire; Vamp Until Ready (short); Second

Childhood (short); Give Me Your Heart; The Gorgeous Hussy; The Bohemian Girl. **1937** Live, Love and Learn; It Happened in Hollywood; Under Cover of Night; Bulldog Drummond Comes Back; Rhythm in the Clouds; Federal Bullets; Maid of Salem. **1938** Bulldog Drummond's Peril; Hunted Men; Woman Against Woman. **1939** Arrest Bulldog Drummond; Boy Trouble; The Story of Alexander Graham Bell; Tell No Tales; Balalaika. **1940** Emergency Squad; The Grapes of Wrath; Comin' 'Round the Mountain. **1941** She Couldn't Say No; Tobacco Road; Sheriff of Tombstone.

TILDEN, BILL (William Tatem Tilden, II)
Born: Feb. 10, 1893, Philadelphia, Pa. Died: June 5, 1953, Hollywood, Calif. (heart attack). Former tennis champion, screen, stage actor and playwright.

Appeared in: **1926** The Highbinder. **1927** The Music Master. **1932-33** Universal's Sport shorts. **1935** Commentator for British Lion Shorts.

TILGHMAN, WILLIAM MATTHEW
Born: July 4, 1854, Fort Dodge, Iowa. Died: Nov. 1, 1924, Okla. (shot to death). Police officer and screen actor.

Appeared in: **1908** The Bank Robbery. **1915** The Passing of the Oklahoma Outlaws.

TILLES, KEN (Kenneth A. Tilles)
Born: Apr. 16, 1912, Calif. Died: Jan. 31, 1970, Los Angeles, Calif. (heart attack). Screen actor.

Appeared in: **1969** Stiletto. **1970** Dreams of Glass.

TILLEY, VESTA (Matilda Alice Powers aka LADY DE FRECE)
Born: May 13, 1864, Worcester, England. Died: Sept. 16, 1952, London, England. Screen, stage, vaudeville actress and author. Married to music hall producer Sir Walter de Frece (dec. 1935).

Appeared in: **1916** The Girl Who Loves a Soldier.

TILTON, EDWIN BOOTH
Born: Sept. 15, 1859. Died: Jan. 16, 1926, Hollywood, Calif. Screen, stage actor, film director and screenwriter.

Appeared in: **1920** Love's Harvest; The Little Wanderer. **1921** Bare Knuckles; What Love Will Do; Children of the Night; Bucking the Line; Lovetime; The Mother Heart; While The Devil Laughs; The Primal Law; The Lamplighter. **1922** The Cub Reporter; Winning With Wits; Gleam O' Dawn; The Man Under Cover; Hungry Hearts. **1923** Times Have Changed. **1924** The House of Youth; Thundergate; Racing for Life; The Lone Chance; The Midnight Express. **1925** The Taming of the West.

TIMBERG, HERMAN
Born: 1892. Died: Apr. 16, 1952, New York, N.Y. Screen, stage, vaudeville actor, stage producer, songwriter, radio writer and screenwriter.

Appeared in: **1930** The Love Boat (short). **1936-38** Educational shorts.

TIMMONS, JOSEPH
Born: 1897. Died: Mar. 29, 1933, Los Angeles, Calif. (auto accident). Screen actor and stuntman.

TINDALE, FRANKLIN M.
Born: 1871. Died: Feb. 14, 1947, Los Angeles, Calif. Screen actor and film director.

TINDALL, LOREN
Born: 1921. Died: May 10, 1973, Hollywood, Calif. (heart attack). Pianist, screen and stage actor. Piano virtuoso at age of four.

Appeared in: **1944** She's a Sweetheart. **1945** Over 21; Sergeant Mike; Rough, Tough and Ready. **1946** Til the Clouds Roll By; Til the End of Time; Meet Me on Broadway; Out of the Depths; Gallant Journey. **1947** Good News. **1949** Miss Grant Takes Richmond; Francis.

TINNEY, FRANK
Born: Mar. 29, 1878, Philadelphia, Pa. Died: Nov. 28, 1940, Northport, N.Y. Screen and stage actor.

Appeared in: **1924** Broadway After Dark.

TINSMAN, SYLVIA MC KAYE
Born: 1916. Died: Oct. 15, 1975. Screen actress and dancer.

TIRELLA, EDUARDO
Born: 1924. Died: Oct. 7, 1966, Rhode Island (hit by car). Screen actor and interior decorator.

Appeared in: **1965** The Sandpiper. **1967** Don't Make Waves.

TIROFF, JAMES "JIM" (aka JAMES HARPER)
Died: Dec. 18, 1975. Stage and screen actor.

Appeared in: **1965** The Brig.

TISSIER, JEAN
Born: 1896, France. Died: Apr., 1973, Paris, France. Screen and stage actor.

Appeared in: **1938** The Slipper Episode; The Courier of Lyons. **1939** Crossroads. **1946** Symphonie d'Amour. **1947** Her First Affair (aka Children of Paradise); Au Bonheur de Dames (aka Shop-Girls of Paris); The Murderer Lives at Number 21. **1948** Loves of Casanova. **1949** Strangers in the House. **1950** The Naked Woman; Gigi. **1951** Minnie. **1952** The Strollers; Father's Dilemma; L'Ile aux Femmes Nues (aka Naked in the Wind—US 1962 and Naked in the Mind). **1953** The Spice of Life. **1954** The Affairs of Messalina; Crime au Concert Mayol (aka Palace of Nudes—US 1961 and Palace of Shame). **1955** La Mome Pigalle (aka The Maiden—US 1961). **1956** Mama, Papa, the Maid and I. **1957** And God Created Woman; The Hunchback of Notre Dame. **1959** The French Way; Ein Engel auf Erden (Angel on Earth—US 1966). **1960** Candide au L'optimisme au XX Siecle (aka Candide—US 1962). **1961** La Bride sur le Cou (aka Please, Not Now!—US 1963). **1963** Strip-Tease (aka Sweet Skin—US 1965); Un Drole de Paroissien (aka Thank Heaven for Small Favors—US 1965). **1964** Voci Blanche (White Voices—US 1965). **1967** Deux Billets pour Mexico (aka Death Run—US 1969).

TISSOT, ALICE
Born: 1890, France. Died: May 5, 1971, Paris, France (throat cancer). Screen and stage actress.

Appeared in: **1928** La Cousine Bette. **1930** Le Secret du Docteur. **1933** Mirages de Paris. **1935** La Maternelle. **1937** Les Petits. **1938** The Glory of the Faith. **1939** Last Desire. **1945** Les Dames aux Chapeaux Verts (The Women in Green Hats). **1947** Francis the First. **1950** Ignace. **1952** L'Ile aux Femmes Nues (aka Naked in the Wind—US 1962 and Naked in the Mind). **1958** Gates of Paris.

TITHERADGE, DION
Born: Mar. 30, 1889, Milbourne, Australia. Died: Nov. 16, 1934, London, England. Screen, stage actor, author, playwright and screenwriter.

TITHERADGE, MADGE
Born: 1887, England. Died: Nov. 13, 1961, Fetcham, Surrey, England. Stage and screen actress. Divorced from actress Charles Quartermaine (dec. 1958).

Appeared in: **1915** Brigadier Gerard. **1916** A Fair Imposter. **1917** The Woman Who Was Nothing. **1918** God Bless Our Red, White and Blue. **1919** Gamblers All. **1920** The Husband Hunter; Love in the Wilderness; A Temporary Gentleman; Her Story (US 1922); David and Jonathan (US 1922).

TITMUSS, PHYLLIS
Born: Jan. 14, 1900, London, England. Died: Jan. 6, 1946, England? Screen and stage actress.

Appeared in: **1924** The Beloved Vagabond.

TITUS, LYDIA YEAMANS
Born: 1866, Australia. Died: Dec. 30, 1929, Glendale, Calif. (paralytic stroke). Screen, stage and vaudeville actress. Married to actor Frederick Titus.

Appeared in: **1918** All Night. **1919** The Peace of Roaring River; Strictly Confidential. **1920** Nurse Marjorie. **1921** Queenie; The Invisible Power; The Mad Marriage; Nobody's Fool; All Dolled Up; Smiling All the Way; The Mistress of Shenstone; Beating the Game; Beau Revel; The Concert; The Freeze Out; The Marriage of William Ashe; His Nibs. **1922** The Glory of Clementina; The Married Flapper; Beauty's Worth; A Girl's Desire; The Lavender Bath Lady; Two Kinds of Women. **1923** Big Dan; The Famous Mrs. Fair; The Footlight Ranger; The Wanters; Winter Has Come; Scaramouche. **1924** Big Timber; In Fast Company; Tarnish; Young Ideas; A Boy of Flanders; Cytherea; The Lullaby. **1925** The Rag Man; Up the Ladder; Head Winds; The Limited Mail; The Talker; The Arizona Romeo. **1926** Irene; The Lily; Sunshine of Paradise Alley. **1927** The Lure of the Night Club; Upstream; Heroes in Blue; Night Life. **1928** The Water Hole; Two Lovers; Sweet Sixteen; While the City Sleeps. **1929** Shanghai Lady; The Voice in the Storm. **1930** Lummox.

TOBIAS, GEORGE
Born: July 14, 1901, New York, N.Y. Died: Feb. 27, 1980, Los Angeles, Calif. (cancer). Screen, stage and television actor. Brother of actor Seldon Bennett.

Appeared in: **1938** You Can't Take It With You. **1939** Maisie; The Hunchback of Notre Dame; Ninotchka; Balalaika; They All Come Out. **1940** They Drive by Night; City for Conquest; South of Suez; Calling All Husbands; East of the River; River's End; The Man Who Talked Too Much; Torrid Zone; Saturday's Children; Music in My Heart. **1941** Out of the Fog; The Bride Came C.O.D.; Affectionately Yours; The Strawberry Blonde; Sergeant York. **1942** Yankee Doodle Dandy; My Sister Eileen; Juke Girl; Captains of the Clouds; Wings for the Eagle. **1943** Thank Your Lucky Stars; This Is the Army; Air Force; Mission to Moscow. **1944** The Mask of Dimitrios; Passage to Marseille; Between Two Worlds; Make Your Own Bed. **1945** Mildred Pierce; Objective, Burma! **1946** Her Kind of Man; Gallant Bess; Nobody Lives Forever. **1947** My Wild Irish Rose; Sinbad the Sailor. **1948** Adventures of Casanova. **1949** The Set-Up; The Judge Steps Out; Everybody Does It. **1950** Southside 1-1000. **1951** Ten Tall Men; Rawhide; Mark of the Renegade; The Magic Carpet. **1952** Desert Pursuit. **1954** The Glenn Miller Story. **1955** The Seven Little Foys. **1957** Silk Stockings; The Tattered Dress. **1958** Marjorie Morningstar. **1963** A New Kind of Love. **1964** A Bullet for Joey; Nightmare in the Sun. **1966** The Glass Bottom Boat. **1970** The Phynx.

TODD, HARRY
Born: 1865, Allegheny, Pa. Died: Feb. 16, 1935, Glendale, Calif. (heart attack). Screen actor. Married to actress Margaret Joslin (dec. 1956). Entered films with Essanay.

Appeared in: **1915** "Snakeville" comedies. **1926** Under Western Skies. **1927** The Third Degree; The Riding Rowdy; Skedaddle Gold; The Obligin' Buckaroo; The Bugle Call; Rawhide Kid. **1928** Under the Tonto Rim; The River Woman. **1929** Linda; One Stolen Night. **1930** Under Montana Skies; The Fighting Legion; Lucky Larkin; Sons of the Saddle. **1933** Sucker Money; Gun Law; Her Splendid Folly; Thrill Hunter. **1934** It Happened One Night; One Is Guilty.

TODD, JAMES
Born: July 8, 1908, Chicago, Ill. Died: Feb. 8, 1968, Calif. Screen and stage actor. Entered films in 1931.

Appeared in: **1931** Riders of the Purple Sage. **1932** Charlie Chan's Chance; Disorderly Conduct; Careless Lady. **1948** The Luck of the Irish; For the Love of Mary; The Velvet Touch; Daredevils of the Skies. **1949** Trapped; The Gal Who Took the West; Fighting Man of the Plains; The Lone Wolf and His Lady; Francis. **1950** Peggy. **1953** Titanic; Torch Song; The Bigamist. **1956** The Scarlet Hour. **1957** The Wings of Eagles; This Could Be the Night. **1958** The Buccaneer; High School Confidential!

TODD, THELMA
Born: July 29, 1905, Lawrence, Mass. Died: Dec. 18, 1935, Santa Monica, Calif. (carbon monoxide—murder—suicide—accident?). Screen actress. Married to agent Pat DiCicco (dec. 1978). She appeared as part of film comedy team of "Todd and Pitts" with Zazu Pitts (dec. 1963) and "Todd and Kelly" with Patsy Kelly (dec. 1981).

Appeared in: **1926** God Gave Me Twenty Cents; Fascinating Youth. **1927** Nevada; The Gay Defender; Rubber Heels; The Shield of Honor. **1928** Vamping Venus; The Crash; The Haunted House; Heart to Heart; The Noose. **1929** Naughty Baby; The Bachelor Girl; Trial Marriage; Careers; Her Private Life; The House of Horror; Look Out Below; Seven Footprints to Satan; plus the following shorts: Snappy Sneezer; Crazy Feet; Stepping Out; Hotter Than Hot; Sky Boy; Unaccustomed As We Are; Jack White Talking Comedies. **1930** Hell's Angels; Follow Through; Her Man; plus the following shorts: Another Fine Mess; The Real McCoy; Whispering Whoopee; All Teed Up; Dollar Dizzy; Looser Than Loose; High C's; The Head Guy; The Fighting Parson; The Shrimp; The King. **1931** Command Performance; The Maltese Falcon; Broad-Minded; The Hot Heiress; No Limit; Monkey Business; Beyond Victory; Aloha; Swanee River; Corsair; plus the following shorts: Chickens Come Home; The Pip from Pittsburgh; Rough Seas; Love Fever; and the following shorts with Z. Pitts: On the Loose; Let's Do Things; Catch as Catch Can; The Pajama Party; War Mamas. **1932** Call Her Savage; Klondike; Horse Feathers; Speak Easily; Big Timer; This Is the Night; No Greater Love; Cauliflower Alley; The Nickel Nurser (short); plus the following shorts with Z. Pitts: Sneak Easily; Seal Skins; Red Noses; Strictly Unreliable; The Old Bull; Show Business; Alum and Eve; The Soilers. **1933** Air Hostess; Counsellor at Law; Son of a Sailor; Deception; Fra Diablo (The Devil(s Brother); Sitting Pretty; Mary Stevens, M.D; Cheating Blondes; plus the following shorts with Z. Pitts: Asleep in the Fleet; Maids a la Mode; Bargain of the Century; One Track Minds; the following shorts with

P. Kelly: Beauty and the Bus; Backs to Nature; Air Freight. **1934** You Made Me Love You; Hips, Hips, Hooray!; The Cockeyed Cavaliers; Palooka; Bottoms Up; The Poor Rich; Take the Stand; plus the following shorts with P. Kelly: Maid in Hollywood; Babes in the Goods; Soup and Fish; I'll Be Suing You; Three Chumps Ahead; One Horse Farmers; Opened by Mistake; Done in Oil; Bum Voyage. **1935** Lightning Strikes Twice; After the Dance; Two for Tonight; plus the following shorts with P. Kelly: Treasure Blues; Sing, Sister, Sing; The Tin Man; The Misses Stooge; Slightly Static; Twin Triplets; Hot Money; Top Flat. **1936** The Bohemian Girl; All American Toothache (short with P. Kelly).

TOLER, HOOPER
Born: 1891, Wichita, Kans. Died: June 2, 1922, Los Angeles, Calif. (heart attack). Screen actor.

TOLER, SIDNEY
Born: Apr. 28, 1874, Warrensburg, Mo. Died: Feb. 12, 1947, Beverly Hills, Calif. Screen, stage actor and playwright. He took over the role of Charlie Chan in "Charlie Chan" film series after Warner Oland died in 1938.

Appeared in: **1919** Madame X (film debut); In the Nick of Time (short). **1930** The Devil's Parade (short). **1931** White Shoulders; Strictly Dishonorable. **1932** Strangers in Love; Blonde Venus; The Phantom President; Is My Face Red?; Radio Patrol; Speak Easily; Blondie of the Follies; Tom Brown of Culver. **1933** He Learned About Women; King of the Jungle; The Way to Love; The World Changes; The Billion Dollar Scandal; The Narrow Corner. **1934** Dark Hazard; Massacre; Registered Nurse; Spitfire; The Trumpet Blows; Here Comes the Groom; Upperworld; Operator 13; Romance in Manhattan. **1935** This Is the Life; Call of the Wild; The Daring Young Man; Orchids to You; Champagne for Breakfast. **1936** Three Godfathers; The Gorgeous Hussy; The Longest Night; Our Relations; Give Us This Night. **1937** That Certain Woman; Double Wedding; Quality Street. **1938** Wide Open Faces; Gold Is Where You Find It; One Wild Night; Up the River; Charlie Chan in Honolulu; If I Were King; The Mysterious Rider; Three Comrades. **1939** Broadway Cavalier; King of Chinatown; Disbarred; Heritage of the Desert; The Kid from Kokomo; Charlie Chan in Reno; Charlie Chan at Treasure Island; Law of the Pampas; Charlie Chan in City in Darkness. **1940** Charlie Chan in Panama; Charlie Chan's Murder Cruise; Charlie Chan at the Wax Museum; Murder Over New York. **1941** Charlie Chan in Rio; Dead Men Tell. **1942** Castle in the Desert. **1943** Adventures of Smilin' Jack (serial); A Night to Remember; White Savage; Isle of Forgotten Sins. **1944** Black Magic; Charlie Chan in the Secret Service; The Chinese Cat. **1945** The Scarlet Clue; Jade Mask; It's in the Bag; The Shanghai Cobra; The Red Dragon. **1946** Dark Alibi; Shadows Over Chinatown; Dangerous Money. **1947** The Trap. **1974** That's Entertainment (film clips).

TOLLY, FRANK
Died: Nov. 26, 1924, New York, N.Y. (auto accident). Screen actor, stuntman and circus acrobat. Died while filming stunt for movie The Great Circus Mystery.

Appeared in: **1925** The Great Circus Mystery (serial).

TOLSTOI, COUNTESS (Sophie Behra)
Born: 1846. Died: Nov. 4, 1919, Trasnaya Polyana, Russia. Screen actress. Married to novelist Leo Tolstoi (dec. 1910).

Appeared in: **1918** George Robey's Day Off.

TOMACK, DAVID
Born: 1919. Died: Dec. 16, 1977, Los Angeles, Calif. Screen actor and writer.

Appeared in: **1956** He Laughed Last. **1957** Under Fire; Slim Carter. **1958** The Spider. **1959** Imitation of Life; I, Mobster.

TOMACK, SID
Born: 1907, Brooklyn, N.Y. Died: Nov. 12, 1962, Palm Springs, Calif. (heart ailment). Screen, television and vaudeville actor. Appeared in vaudeville as part of team of "Sid Tomack and the Reis Bros."

Appeared in: **1944** A Wave, a Wac and a Marine. **1946** The Thrill of Brazil. **1947** Blind Spot; For the Love of Rusty; Blondie's Holiday; Framed. **1948** A Double Life; My Girl Tisa; Hollow Triumph; Homicide for Three. **1949** House of Strangers; Boston Blackie's Chinese Venture; The Crime Doctor's Diary; Make-Believe Ballroom; Abandoned; Force of Evil. **1950** Love That Brute; The Fuller Brush Girl. **1951** Never Trust a Gambler; Joe Palooka in Triple Cross. **1952** Hans Christian Andersen; Somebody Loves Me. **1954** Living It Up. **1955** The Lemon Drop Kid; The Girl Rush. **1956** That Certain Feeling; The Kettles in the Ozarks. **1957** Spring Reunion. **1959** Last Train from Gun Hill. **1961** Sail a Crooked Ship.

TOMAMOTO, THOMAS (Tsunetaro Sugimoto)
Born: 1879, Japan. Died: Sept. 28, 1924, New York, N.Y. Stage and screen actor.

TOMARCHIO, LUDOVICO
Born: Jan. 6, 1886, Catania, Italy. Died: June 25, 1947, Los Angeles, Calif. (cerebral arteriosclerosis). Screen actor and opera performer.

Appeared in: **1935** The Melody Lingers On; A Night at the Opera. **1936** Millions in the Air; Early to Bed. **1938** Swiss Miss.

TOMEI, LUIGI
Born: 1910. Died: May 15, 1955, San Francisco, Calif. (auto injuries while performing film stunt). Screen actor, stuntman and former Indianapolis Speedway contender.

Appeared in: **1956** Hell on Frisco Bay.

TOMICK, FRANK
Born: 1895. Died: Oct. 29, 1966. Screen actor and stuntman/pilot.

Appeared in: **1924** The Air Hawk. **1925** The Cloud Rider. **1926** The Flying Mail. **1928** Won in the Clouds; The Air Patrol. **1930** Hell's Angels. **1933** Ace of Aces; Eagle and the Hawk. **1934** Speed Wings; Hell in the Heavens. **1938** Test Pilot; Too Hot to Handle; Men With Wings.

TOMILSON, BILL
Born: 1922. Died: Jan. 8, 1971. Screen actor. Appeared in western films.

TONE, FRANCHOT (Stanislas Pascal Franchot Tone)
Born: Feb. 27, 1905, Niagara Falls, N.Y. Died: Sept. 18, 1968, New York, N.Y. Screen, stage, television actor, film producer and film director. Divorced from actresses: Joan Crawford (dec. 1977); Jean Wallace; Dolores Dorn-Heft and Barbara Payton (dec. 1967). Nominated for 1935 Academy Award for Best Actor in Mutiny on the Bounty.

Appeared in: **1932** The Wiser Sex (film debut). **1933** Dinner at Eight; Gabriel Over the White House; Today We Live; Midnight Mary; The Stranger's Return; Stage Mother; Bombshell; Dancing Lady; Lady of the Night. **1934** Four Walls; Gentlemen Are Born; Moulin Rouge; The World Moves On; Sadie McKee; Straight Is the Way; The Girl from Missouri. **1935** The Lives of a Bengal Lancer; Reckless; One New York Night; No More Ladies; Mutiny on the Bounty; Dangerous. **1936** Exclusive Story; The Unguarded Hour; Suzy; The Gorgeous Hussy; Love on the Run; The King Steps Out; Girl's Dormitory. **1937** Quality Street; They Gave Him a Gun; Between Two Women; The Bride Wore Red. **1938** Man-Proof; Love Is a Headache; Three Comrades; Three Loves Has Nancy. **1939** Fast and Furious; Thunder Afloat; The Girl Downstairs; The Gentle People. **1940** Trail of the Vigilantes. **1941** Virginia; Highly Irregular; Nice Girl?; This Woman Is Mine; She Knew All the Answers. **1942** The Wife Takes a Flyer. **1943** Five Graves to Cairo; Star Spangled Rhythm; Pilot No. 5; His Butler's Sister; True to Life. **1944** Phantom Lady; The Hour Before the Dawn; Dark Waters. **1945** That Night with You. **1946** Because of Him. **1947** Her Husband's Affair; Two Men and a Girl; Honeymoon; Army Comes Across; Lost Honeymoon. **1948** I Love Trouble; Every Girl Should Be Married. **1949** Jigsaw; Without Honor; The Man on the Eiffel Tower. **1950** Gun Moll. **1951** Here Comes the Groom. **1958** Uncle Vanya. **1962** Advise and Consent. **1964** La Bonne Soupe (The Good Soup); Big Parade of Comedy (documentary). **1965** In Harm's Way; Mickey One. **1968** The High Commissioner.

TONEY, JAMES
Died: Sept. 19, 1973. Screen actor.

Appeared in: **1935** It's In the Air. **1936** The Lonely Trail. **1937** Fifty Roads to Town. **1939** The Lady and the Mob. **1941** All That Money Can Buy (aka Here Is a Man). **1943** Harrigan's Kid; The Ghost and the Guest. **1950** No Way Out. **1952** The Devil and Daniel Webster (reissue of All That Money Can Buy—1941).

TONG, KAM
Born: 1907. Died: Nov. 8, 1969, Costa Mesa, Calif. Screen and television actor.

Appeared in: **1942** Joan of Ozark; Rubber Racketeers; China Girl; The Hidden Hand; Across the Pacific. **1953** Target Hong Kong. **1954** This Is My Love. **1955** Love Is a Many Splendored Thing. **1960** Who Was That Lady? **1961** Flower Drum Song. **1963** It Happened at the World's Fair. **1966** Dimension #5; Mister Buddwing. **1967** Kill a Dragon.

TONG, SAMMEE
Born: 1901, San Francisco, Calif. Died: Oct. 27, 1964, Palms, Calif. (suicide). Screen and television actor.

Appeared in: **1934** Happiness Ahead (film debut); The Captain Hates the Sea. **1935** Oil for the Lamps of China; Shanghai. **1937** The Good Earth. **1939** Only Angels Have Wings. **1957** Hell Bound. **1958** Suicide Battalion. **1963** It's a Mad, Mad, Mad, Mad World. **1964** For Those Who Think Young. **1965** Fluffy.

TONGE, H. ASHETON
Born: 1872, England? Died: Apr. 2, 1927, New York, N.Y. Screen actor. Father of actor Philip Tonge (dec. 1959).

Appeared in: **1914** A Christmas Carol.

TONGE, PHILIP
Born: 1898. Died: Jan. 28, 1959, Hollywood, Calif. Screen and televison actor. Son of actor H. Asheton Tonge (dec. 1927).

Appeared in: **1915** Still Waters. **1933** His Double Life. **1947** Love from a Stranger; Miracle on 34th Street. **1952** Hans Christian Andersen. **1953** House of Wax; Scandal at Scourie; Small Town Girl. **1954** The Silver Chalice; Elephant Walk; Khyber Patrol; Ricochet Romance; Track of the Cat. **1955** Desert Sands; The Prodigal. **1956** Pardners; The Peacemaker. **1957** Les Girls; Witness for the Prosecution. **1958** Darby's Rangers; Macabre. **1959** Invisible Invaders.

TONGE, ROGER
Born: 1946, England. Died: Feb. 26, 1981, London, England (cancer). Screen, stage and television actor.

TONY (aka TONY THE WONDER HORSE)
Born: 1909, Los Angeles, Calif. Died: Oct., 1942. Animal performer. Tom Mix's horse.

Appeared in: **1918** Cupid's Round-Up (film debut). **1922** Four Big Stakes; Just Tony. **1923** Eyes of the Forest; The Lone Star Ranger; Mile-a-Minute Romeo; Soft Boiled; Stepping Fast. **1924** Teeth. **1925** The Best Bad Man. **1926** The Canyon of Light; The Great K & A Train Robbery; Hard Boiled; No Man's Gold; Tony Runs Wild; The Yankee Senor. **1927** The Arizona Wildcat; The Last Trail; Tumbling River; The Broncho Twister; The Circus Ace. **1928** Painted Post; Son of the Golden West; Daredevil's Reward; Hello Cheyenne; A Horseman of the Plains. **1929** The Big Diamond Robbery. **1932** My Pal the King.

TOOKER, WILLIAM H.
Born: 1864, New York, N.Y. Died: Oct. 12, 1936, Hollywood, Calif. Screen and stage actor.

Appeared in: **1920** The Stealers. **1921** God's Country and the Law; Worlds Apart; Proxies. **1922** The Power Within; Beyond the Rainbow; My Friend, the Devil; Peacock Alley; The Cradle Buster. **1923** The Woman in Chains; Sinner or Saint; A Bride for a Knight; The Purple Highway; The Net. **1924** Who's Cheating?; The Average Woman; The Lone Wolf. **1925** The Phantom Express. **1926** The Scarlet Letter; The Merry Cavalier; The White Black Sheep. **1927** Two Girls Wanted; Birds of Prey; Ladies Must Dress; The Devil Dancer; Tell It to Sweeney; Jake the Plumber. **1928** Good Morning, Judge; The Look Out Girl; The Night Watch; Sweet Sixteen; Virgin Lips; A Woman Against the World. **1929** No Defense; Romance of the Under World; The Bellamy Trial; Protection; Love in the Desert. **1930** Soup to Nuts. **1931** A Woman of Experience. **1935** It's a Gift.

TOPART, LISE
Born: 1930, France. Died: Mar. 3, 1952, Nice, France (plane crash). Screen actress.

TOPEY, LESTER
Born: 1899. Died: Aug., 1920, Waehawken, N.J. (auto accident). Screen actor.

TOPPER
Born: 1934. Died: Date unknown. Screen performer. Horse used by actor William Boyd in the "Hopalong Cassidy" films. Entered films in 1935.

TORDESILLA, JESUS
Born: 1893, Spain. Died: Mar. 24, 1973, Madrid, Spain (heart attack). Screen and stage actor.

Appeared in: **1923** Flor de Espana. **1926** Currito de la Cruz. **1950** The Mad Queen. **1958** Spanish Affair. Other Spanish films: Locura de Amor; Agustina de Aragon; Donde vas Alfonso XII?; Teresa de Jesus; Los Escondites; Una tumba para el Sheriff.

TOREN, MARTA
Born: May 21, 1926, Stockholm, Sweden. Died: Feb. 19, 1957, Stockholm, Sweden (rare brain disease). Stage and screen actress. Appeared in Swedish, U.S., Italian and Spanish films.

Appeared in: **1948** Casbah (film debut); Rogue's Regiment. **1949** Illegal Entry; Sword in the Desert. **1950** Deported; Mystery Submarine; Spy Hunt; One-Way Street. **1951** Panther's Moon; Sirocco. **1952** Assignment—Paris. **1953** The Man Who Watched the Trains Go By (aka The Paris Express—US 1954). **1954** The House of Ricordi (US 1956). **1955** Maddelena.

TORNEK, JACK
Died: Feb. 18, 1974. Screen actor.

Appeared in: **1916** Bombs and Banknotes. **1956** Around the World in 80 Days.

TORPE, MARIE
Born: 1904. Died: July 28, 1967, Woodland Hills, Calif. Screen actress.

TORRENCE, DAVID (David Thoyson)
Born: Jan. 17, 1864, Edinburgh, Scotland. Died: Dec. 26, 1951. Stage and screen actor. Brother of actor Ernest Torrence (dec. 1933).

Appeared in: **1913** Tess of the D'Urbervilles. **1915** The Prisoner of Zenda. **1921** The Inside of the Cup. **1922** Forsaking All Others; The Power of a Lie; Received Payment; Sherlock Holmes; Tess of the Storm Country; A Virgin's Sacrifice. **1923** The Abysmal Brute; The Drums of Jeopardy; The Light That Failed; The Man Next Door; Railroaded; Trimmed in Scarlet. **1924** The Dawn of a Tomorrow; Idle Tongues; Love's Wilderness; The Sawdust Trail; Surging Seas; Tiger Love; Which Shall It Be? **1925** The Reckless Sex; The Other Woman's Story; Fighting the Flames; He Who Laughs Last; Her Husband's Secret; The Mystic; The Tower of Lies; The Wheels; What Fools Men. **1926** The Auction Block; Brown of Harvard; Forever After; The Isle of Retribution; The King of the Turf; Laddie; The Man in the Shadow; Oh, What a Nurse!; The Wolf Hunters; The Unknown Cavalier; The Third Degree; Sandy; Race Wild. **1927** Annie Laurie; Hazardous Valley; The Midnight Watch; On the Stroke of Twelve; The Mysterious Rider; Rolled Stockings; The World at Her Feet. **1928** The Big Noise; The Cavalier; The City of Dreams (aka City of Purple Dreams); The Little Shepherd of Kingdom Come; Undressed. **1929** Disraeli; The Black Watch; Hearts in Exile; Silks and Saddles; Strong Boy; Untamed Justice. **1930** How I Play Golf—The Driver (short); City Girl; Raffles; River's End; Scotland Yard; The Devil to Pay. **1931** Five Star Final; East Lynne; Bachelor Father. **1932** The Mask of Fu Manchu; A Successful Calamity; Smilin' Through. **1933** Berkeley Square; Voltaire; Queen Christina; Masquerader. **1934** Charlie Chan in London; Madame Spy; Horseplay; Mandalay; What Every Woman Knows; Jane Eyre. **1935** Mutiny on the Bounty; Black Sheep; Bonnie Scotland; Harmony Lane; The Dark Angel; Captain Blood. **1936** The Country Doctor; Mary of Scotland; Beloved Enemy. **1937** The Ebb Tide; Lost Horizon. **1938** Five of a Kind. **1939** Rulers of the Sea; Stanley and Livingstone.

TORRENCE, ERNEST (Ernest Thoyson)
Born: June 16, 1878, Edinburgh, Scotland. Died: May 15, 1933, New York, N.Y. Screen, stage actor and opera performer. Brother of actor David Torrence (dec. 1951).

Appeared in: **1921** Tol'able David (film debut). **1922** Broken Chains; The Kingdom Within; The Prodigal Judge; Singed Wings. **1923** The Trail of the Lonesome Pine; Ruggles of Red Gap; The Covered Wagon; The Hunchback of Notre Dame; The Brass Bottle. **1924** Fighting Coward; The Side Show of Life; West of the Water Tower; The Heritage of the Desert; North of 36. **1925** Peter Pan; The Pony Express; The Dressmaker from Paris; Night Life of New York; Mantrap; The American Venus; The Blood Goddess; The Lady of the Harem; The Rainmaker; The Wanderer. **1927** King of Kings; Captain Salvation; Twelve Miles Out. **1928** Voices Across the Sea (short); Steamboat Bill, Jr.; The Cossacks; Across to Singapore. **1929** Silks and Saddles; The Unholy Night; The Bridge of San Luis Rey; Desert Nights; Speedway; Untamed; Twelve Nights Out. **1930** Sweet Kitty Bellaire; Strictly Unconventional; Officer O'Brien; Call of the Flesh. **1931** Shipmates; The Great Lover; Sporting Blood; The New Adventures of Get-Rich-Quick Wallingford; Fighting Caravans. **1932** Hypnotized; Cuban Love Song; Sherlock Holmes. **1933** The Masquerader; I Cover the Waterfront.

TORRIANI, AIMEE
Born: 1890, New York, N.Y. Died: July 18, 1963, New York, N.Y. Screen, stage and radio actress.

Appeared in: **1955** To Catch a Thief.

TORRUCO, MIGUEL
Born: 1920, Mexico. Died: Apr. 22, 1956, Orizaba, Vera Cruz, Mexico. Screen actor. Married to Mexican screen actress Maria Elena Marques. Entered films in 1949.

Appeared in: **1955** Massacre. Other Mexican film: Horas de Agonia (Agonized Hours).

TORVAY, JOSE
Died: 1973, Mexico. Screen actor.

Appeared in: **1948** Treasure of Sierra Madre; Sofia; Mystery in Mexico. **1949** Border Incident. **1950** Borderline; The Torch. **1951** The Brave Bulls; My Outlaw Brother (aka My Brother the Outlaw). **1952** One Big Affair; My Man and I. **1953** The Hitch-Hiker. **1954** Green Fire. **1955** A Life in the Balance; The Littlest Outlaw; Strange Lady in Town. **1956** Bandido; A Woman's Devotion. **1958** From Hell to Texas. **1961** Code of Silence; The Last Sunset. **1970** Two Mules for Sister Sara.

TOSCANINI, ARTURO
Born: Mar. 25, 1867, Parma, Italy. Died: Jan. 16, 1957, New York, N.Y. (stroke). Conductor and screen actor.

Appeared in: **1946** Hymn of the Nations.

TOSO, OTELLO
Born: Italy. Died: Mar. 15, 1966, Padua, Italy (auto accident). Screen and television actor.

Appeared in: **1950** Le Due Orfanelle (The Two Orphans). **1952** The Cliff of Sin. **1953** What Price Innocence? **1958** Age of Infidelity (aka Muerte de un Ciclista—Death of a Cyclist). Other Italian films: Casanova; Ridi Pagliaccio; 1860.

TOTO (Antonio Furst de Curtis-Gagliardi)
Born: 1897, Italy. Died: Apr., 1967, Rome, Italy. Screen, stage, television actor, author, songwriter, playwright and stage producer. Do not confuse with "Toto the Clown" (dec. 1938).

Appeared in: **1936** Fermo con le Mani. **1949** Toto Le Moko. **1953** Cops and Robbers. **1954** Side Street Story; The Gold of Naples (aka The Racketeer—US 1957). **1955** Racconti Romani. **1957** Toto, Vittorio e la Dottoressa (aka The Lady Doctor—US 1963). **1958** Persons Unknown. **1959** The Law Is the Law; The Anatomy of Love. **1960** Risate di Gioia (The Passionate Thief—US 1963). **1961** The Big Deal on Madonna Street. **1963** I due Colonnelli (Two Colonels—US 1966). **1964** South of Tana River. **1965** La Mandragola (aka The Love Root and the Mandragola—US 1966). **1966** Uccellacci e Uccellini (aka The Hawks and the Sparrows—US 1967). **1967** Operazione San Gennaro (Treasure of San Gennaro—US 1968, aka Unser Boss ist Eine Dame); The Commander; Le Streghe (The Witches—US 1968).

TOTO, BILLIE (aka CECILIA DES ROCHES)
Born: 1904. Died: Dec. 24, 1928, New York, N.Y. Screen and stage actress.

TOTO THE CLOWN (Armando Novello)
Born: 1888, Geneva, Switzerland. Died: Dec. 15, 1938, New York, N.Y. Screen, stage, vaudeville actor and circus clown.

Appeared in: **1911** Toto on the Stage; Toto's Little Cart. **1916** Toto o° the Byways. **1918** The Dippy Daughter. **1919** Tot's Troubles. **1927** The Junk Man (short). **1936-37** Pathe and Educational shorts.

TOTTEN, EDYTH (Marguerite Edyth Totten)
Born: 1885. Died: Nov. 12, 1953, New York, N.Y. Screen, stage actress, author, screenwriter and stage producer.

Appeared in: **1914** A Factory Magdalen.

TOUREL, JENNIE (Jennie Davidson)
Born: 1910, Montreal, Canada. Died: Nov. 23, 1973, New York, N.Y. Opera singer and screen actress.

Appeared in: **1968** A Journey to Jerusalem.

TOURNEUR, JACQUES
Born: 1904, Paris, France. Died: Dec. 19, 1977, Bergerac, France. Screen and television actor, film director and screenwriter. Son of film director Maurice Tourneur (dec. 1961).

Appeared in: **1923** Scaramouche.

TOUTAIN, ROLAND
Born: 1905, France. Died: Oct., 1977, Argentueil, France. Screen actor and stuntman.

Appeared in: **1938** The Lie of Nina Petrovna; Sacrifice d'Honneur. **1939** La Rigle du Jeu (The Rules of the Game). **1942** The Great Temptation. **1943** L'Eternel Retour (The Eternal Return).

TOVER, MAY
Born: 1911. Died: Dec. 20, 1949, Thousand Oaks, Calif. (clawed to death by lion). Screen actress and lion tamer.

Appeared in: **1950** The Reformer and the Redhead.

TOWNE, CHARLES HANSON
Born: 1877. Died: Feb. 28, 1949, New York, N.Y. Screen, stage actor, author and screenwriter.

Appeared in: **1913** Saved by Parcel Post.

TOWNSEND, ANNA
Born: 1884. Died: Sept. 11, 1923, Los Angeles, Calif. Screen and stage actress.

Appeared in: **1922** Grandma's Boy; Doctor Jack. **1923** Daddy; Safety Last.

TOYNE, GABRIEL
Born: Apr. 5, 1905, London, England. Died: Dec. 29, 1963, Ibiza, Spain. Screen, stage, television actor, stage and film director. Divorced from actress Margaret Rawlings. Married to actress Diana Beaumont (dec. 1964).

TOZERE, FREDERIC
Born: June 19, 1901, Brookline, Mass. Died: Aug. 5, 1972, New York, N.Y. Screen, stage, television actor and pantomimist. Married to actress Mary Brady (dec. 1968).

Appeared in: **1939** The Man Who Dared; Everybody's Hobby; Cowboy Quarterback; Nancy Drew and the Hidden Staircase; Confessions of a Nazi Spy; Hell's Kitchen. **1948** The Iron Curtain; An Act of Murder; Live Today for Tomorrow. **1949** Madame Bovary; The Return of October. **1950** Father Is a Bachelor.

TOZZI, FAUSTO
Born: 1921, Italy. Died: Dec. 10, 1978, Rome, Italy (emphysema). Screen, stage, television actor, film director and screenwriter.

Appeared in: **1949** Under the Sun of Rome (film debut). **1954** The House of Ricordi (US 1956); Four Ways Out. **1955** Il Mantello Rosso (The Red Cloak—US 1961). **1957** La Grande Caccia (aka The Big Search and aka East of Kilimanjaro—US 1962). **1961** El Cid; The Wonders of Aladdin; Constantino il Grande (aka Constantine and the Cross—US 1962); Im Stahlnetz des Dr. Mabuse (The Return of Dr. Mabuse—US 1966). **1962** Le Mercenaire (aka Swordsman of Siene—US); Scheherazade (US 1965). **1964** The Visit. **1965** The Agony and the Ecstasy. **1967** E Divenne il Piu Spietato Bandito del Sud (aka A Few Bullets More—US 1968); I Coltelli del Vendicatore (Knives of the Avenger—US 1968); The Sailor from Gibraltar. **1968** The Appointment (US 1970). **1974** Crazy Joe. **1975** War Goddess. **1976** Street People; Chino. **1977** The Sicilian Connection; The Demise of Father Mouret.

TRACEY, THOMAS F.
Born: 1880, County Cork, Ireland. Died: Aug. 27, 1961, New York, N.Y. Screen, stage and television actor.

Appeared in: **1916** Behind Closed Doors. **1917** The Man Hater.

TRACY, LEE (William Lee Tracy)
Born: Apr. 14, 1898, Atlanta, Ga. Died: Oct. 18, 1968, Santa Monica, Calif. (liver cancer). Screen, stage, television and vaudeville actor. Nominated for 1964 Academy Award for Best Actor in The Best Man.

Appeared in: **1929** Big Time (film debut). **1930** She Got What She Wanted; Born Reckless; Liliom; On the Level. **1932** Blessed Event; The Half-Naked Truth; Washington Merry-Go-Round; The Night Mayor; Strange Love of Molly Louvain; Doctor X; Love Is a Racket. **1933** Phantom Fame; The Nuisance; Advice to the Lovelorn; Turn Back the Clock; Dinner at Eight; Private Jones; Bombshell; Clear All Wires. **1934** You Belong to Me; The Lemon Drop Kid; I'll Tell the World. **1935** Carnival; Two Fisted. **1936** Wanted; Jane Turner; Sutter's Gold. **1937** Criminal Lawyer; Behind the Headlines. **1938** Crashing Hollywood. **1939** Fixer Dugan; The Spellbinder. **1940** Millionaires in Prison. **1942** The Payoff. **1943** Power of the Press. **1945** Betrayal from the East; I'll Tell the World (and 1934 version). **1947** High Tide. **1962** Advise and Consent. **1964** Big Parade of Comedy (documentary); The Best Man.

TRACY, SPENCER
Born: Apr. 5, 1900, Milwaukee, Wis. Died: June 10, 1967, Beverly Hills, Calif. (heart attack). Stage and screen actor. Won 1937 Academy Award for Best Actor in Captains Courageous and in 1938 for Boys

Town. Nominated for 1936 Academy Award for Best Actor in San Francisco; in 1950 for Father of the Bride; in 1955 for Bad Day at Black Rock; in 1958 for The Old Man and the Sea; in 1960 for Inherit the Wind; in 1961 for Judgment at Nuremberg; and in 1967 for Guess Who's Coming to Dinner?

Appeared in: **1930** Taxi Talks (short—film debut); The Though Guy (aka The Hard Guy—short); Up the River. **1931** Quick Millions; Six Cylinder Love; Goldie. **1932** She Wanted a Millionaire; Sky Devils; Disorderly Conduct; Young America; Society Girl; The Painted Woman; Me and My Gal. **1933** 20,000 Years in Sing Sing; Face in the Sky; Shanghai Madness; The Power and the Glory; The Mad Game; A Man's Castle; State Fair. **1934** Looking for Trouble; The Show-Off; Bottoms Up; Now I'll Tell; Marie Galante. **1935** It's a Small World; The Murder Man; Dante's Inferno; Riffraff. **1936** Whipsaw; Fury; Libeled Lady; San Francisco. **1937** They Gave Him a Gun; Captains Courageous; Big City; Mannequin. **1938** Boys Town; Test Pilot. **1939** Stanley and Livingstone. **1940** I Take This Woman; Northwest Passage; Edison, the Man; Boom Town. **1941** Men of Boys Town; Dr. Jekyll and Mr. Hyde. **1942** Tortilla Flat; Keeper of the Flame; Woman of the Year; Ring of Steel (narr.). **1943** A Guy Named Joe. **1944** The Seventh Cross; Battle Stations (short); Thirty Seconds over Tokyo. **1945** Without Love. **1947** The Sea of Grass; Cass Timberlane. **1948** State of the Union. **1949** Edward, My Son; Adam's Rib. **1950** Malaya; Father of the Bride. **1951** Father's Little Dividend; The People Against O'Hara. **1952** Pat and Mike; Plymouth Adventure. **1953** The Actress. **1954** Broken Lance; Bad Day at Black Rock. **1956** The Mountain. **1957** Desk Set. **1958** The Old Man and the Sea; The Last Hurrah. **1960** Inherit the Wind. **1961** The Devil at Four O'Clock; Judgment at Nuremberg. **1962** How the West Was Won (narr.). **1963** It's a Mad, Mad, Mad, Mad World. **1964** Big Parade of Comedy (documentary). **1967** Guess Who's Coming to Dinner? **1974** That's Entertainment (film clips).

TRACY, WILLIAM
Born: Dec. 1, 1917, Pittsburgh, Pa. Died: June 18, 1967, Hollywood, Calif. Screen and stage actor.

Appeared in: **1938** Brother Rat; Angels With Dirty Faces. **1939** Jones Family in Hollywood; Million Dollar Legs. **1940** The Amazing Mr. Williams; Terry and the Pirates (serial); The Shop Around the Corner; Strike Up the Band; Gallant Sons. **1941** Mr. and Mrs. Smith; Tobacco Road; Tillie the Toiler; She Knew All the Answers; Her First Beau; Tanks a Million; Cadet Girl. **1942** Young America; Hayfoot; To the Shores of Tripoli; About Face; Fall In; George Washington Slept Here. **1943** Yanks Ahoy. **1948** Here Comes Trouble; The Walls of Jericho. **1949** Henry, the Rainmaker. **1950** One Too Many. **1951** On the Sunny Side of the Street; As You Were. **1952** Mr. Walkie-Talkie. **1957** The Wings of Eagles.

TRAFTON, HERBERT
Born: 1893. Died: Sept., 1979, San Diego, Calif. Screen actor. One of the original Keystone Kops.

TRAIN, JACK
Born: 1902. Died: Dec. 19, 1966, London, England. Screen, stage and radio actor.

Appeared in: **1946** Gaiety George (aka Showtime—US 1948). **1964** Catacombs (aka The Woman Who Wouldn't Die—US 1965).

TRAINOR, LEONARD
Born: 1879. Died: July 28, 1940, Los Angeles, Calif. (heart attack). Screen actor. Will Roger's double and stand-in.

Appeared in: **1922** You Never Know. **1925** Galloping Jinx; Fast Lightnin'. **1926** The Border Sheriff; Hi-Jacking Rustlers. **1928** Headin' for Danger. **1933** Terror Trail.

TRASK, HELEN See LOWELL, JOAN

TRASK, WAYLAND
Born: July 16, 1887, New York. Died: Nov. 11, 1918, Los Angeles, Calif. (Spanish influenza). Screen, stage actor and comedian.

Appeared in: **1915** The Great Vacuum Robbery. **1916** Fatty and Mabel Adrift; The Great Pearl Tangle; The Judge; His Herafter (aka Murray's Mix-Up); A Love Riot; The Feathered Nest; Maid Mad; Bombers; Her Marble Heart; Pills of Peril; The Stone Age. **1917** Cactus Nell; That Night; Dodging His Dreams; A Maiden's Trust; Her Torpedoed Love; She Needed a Doctor; His Precious Life. **1918** Whose Little Wife Are You?; Her Blighted Love; Watch Your Neighbor.

TRAUBEL, HELEN
Born: June 16, 1903, St. Louis, Mo. Died: July 28, 1972, Santa Monica, Calif. (heart attack). Opera singer, screen television and stage actress.

Appeared in: **1954** Deep In My Heart. **1961** The Ladies' Man. **1967** Gunn.

TRAUTMAN, LUDWIG
Born: 1886, Germany. Died: Jan. 24, 1957, Berlin, Germany. Screen actor. Entered films with Bioscop-Filmgesellshaft in 1912.

TRAUX, MAUDE
Born: 1885. Died: Sept. 6, 1939, Los Angeles, Calif. Screen and stage actress.

Appeared in: **1926** Up in Mabel's Room.

TRAVERS, ANTHONY
Born: 1920. Died: Jan. 16, 1959, Hollywood, Calif. Screen actor.

TRAVERS, HENRY (Travers John Geagerty)
Born: Mar. 5, 1874, Berwick-on-Tweed, Northumberland, England. Died: Oct. 18, 1965, Los Angeles, Calif. (complications from arteriosclerosis). Screen and stage actor. Married to stage actress Amy Rhodes Forrest (dec. 1954) and later married to nurse, Ann G. Murphy. Nominated for 1942 Academy Award for Best Supporting Actor in Mrs. Miniver.

Appeared in: **1933** Reunion in Vienna (stage and screen versions); Another Language; My Weakness; The Invisible Man. **1934** Born to Be Bad; Ready for Love; The Party's Over; Death Takes a Holiday. **1935** Maybe It's Love; Escapade; Pursuit; After Office Hours; Captain Hurricane; Seven Keys to Baldpate; Four Hours to Kill. **1936** Too Many Parents. **1938** The Sisters. **1939** Dark Victory; You Can't Get Away With Murder; On Borrowed Time; Remember?; Dodge City; Stanley and Livingstone; The Rains Came. **1940** The Primrose Path; Anne of Windy Poplars; Edison, the Man; Wyoming. **1941** High Sierra; The Bad Man; Ball of Fire; A Girl, a Guy and a Gob; I'll Wait for You. **1942** Mrs. Miniver; Pierre of the Plains; Random Harvest. **1943** Shadow of a Doubt; Madame Curie; The Moon Is Down. **1944** Dragon Seed; None Shall Escape; The Very Thought of You. **1945** Thrill of Romance; The Bells of St. Mary's; The Naughty Nineties. **1946** Gallant Journey; It's a Wonderful Life; The Yearling. **1947** The Flame. **1948** Beyond Glory. **1949** The Girl from Jones Beach.

TRAVERS, RICHARD C. (Richard Libb)
Born: Apr. 15, 1890, Hudson Bay Post, Northwest Territory, Canada. Died: Apr. 20, 1935, San Pedro, Calif. (pneumonia). Screen and stage actor. Entered films with Essanay in 1914.

Appeared in: **1915** The White Sister; In the Palace of the King; The Man Trail. **1916** Captain Jinks of the Horse Marines. **1921** The Mountain Woman; The Single Track; The Rider of the King Long. **1922** White Hell; The Love Nest; Dawn of Revenge; Notoriety. **1923** The Broad Road; The Acquittal; Mary of the Movies; The Rendezvous. **1924** The House of Youth. **1925** Head Winds; Lightnin'. **1926** The Still Alarm; The Dangerous Dude; The Truthful Sex. **1927** Melting Millions (serial). **1929** The Unholy Night; The Black Watch. **1930** The Woman Racket. **1936** Freshman's Love.

TRAVERS, VIC
Died: 1948, Hollywood, Calif. Screen actor. Entered films in 1936.

Appeared in: **1945** Three Pests in a Mess (short).

TRAVERSE, JEAN
Born: 1877. Died: May 11, 1947, Hollywood, Calif. Screen actress.

TRAVERSE, MADLAINE (Madlaine Businsky)
Born: 1876, Cleveland, Ohio. Died: Jan. 7, 1964, Cleveland, Ohio. Screen actress.

Appeared in: **1913** Leah Kleschna. **1914** Three Weeks. **1916** The Shielding Shadow (serial).

TRAVIS, CHARLES W.
Born: 1861. Died: Aug. 12, 1917, Brooklyn, N.Y. (stroke). Screen and stage actor.

Appeared in: **1913** The Great Ganton Mystery. **1915** The Secret Agent; The House With Nobody In It; The New Adam and Eve. **1916** As a Woman Sows; The Idol of the Stage; I Accuse; The Quality of Faith; Armadale; The Criminal's Thumb; The Hidden Foe.

TRAVOLTA, HELEN
Born: 1912. Died: Dec. 3, 1978, Los Angeles, Calif. (cancer). Screen actress and drama coach. Mother of actresses Ann, Ellan and Margaret and singer Joey and actor John Travolta.

Appeared in: **1978** Saturday Night Fever.

TREACHER, ARTHUR

Born: July 23, 1894, Brighton, England. Died: Dec. 14, 1975, Manhasset, N.Y. (heart ailment). Screen, stage and television actor. Married to actress Virginia Taylor.

Appeared in: **1929** The Battle of Paris. **1933** Alice in Wonderland; a Vitaphone short. **1934** Madame DuBarry; Here Comes the Groom; Gambling Lady; The Key; The Captain Hates the Sea; Forsaking All Others; Viva Villa; Hollywood Party; Student Tour; Fashion of 1934; Desirable. **1935** The Winning Ticket; David Copperfield; No More Ladies; Bright Lights; I Live My Life; Let's Live Tonight; Cardinal Richelieu; The Woman in Red; The Daring Young Man; Orchids to You; Curly Top; A Midsummer Night's Dream; Remember Last Night? Hitch-Hike Lady; Magnificent Obsession; Splendor; Vanessa; Go Into Your Dance; I Live for Love; The Nitwits; Bordertown; Personal Maid's Secret. **1936** Anything Goes; Thank You, Jeeves; The Case Against Mrs. Ames; Hearts Divided; Satan Met a Lady; Mister Cinderella; Under Your Spell; Stowaway; Hard Luck Dame. **1937** Step Lively, Jeeves!; She Had to Eat; Thin Ice; You Can't Have Everything; Heidi. **1938** Mad About Music; Always in Trouble; My Lucky Star; Up the River. **1939** The Little Princess; Bridal Suite; Barricade. **1940** Brother Rat and a Baby; Irene. **1942** Star Spangled Rhythm. **1943** The Amazing Mrs. Holliday; Forever and a Day. **1944** National Velvet; Chip Off the Old Block; In Society. **1945** That's the Spirit; Delightfully Dangerous; Swing Out, Sister. **1947** Fun on a Weekend; Slave Girl. **1948** The Countess of Monte Cristo. **1949** That Midnight Kiss. **1950** Love That Brute. **1964** Mary Poppins.

TREACY, EMERSON

Born: Sept. 7, 1905, Philadelphia, Pa. Died: Jan. 10, 1967, Woodland Hills, Calif. Screen, stage, television and radio actor.

Appeared in: **1930** Once a Gentleman. **1931** The Sky Raiders. **1932** O.K. America. **1933** Bedtime Worries (short); Wild Poses (short). **1934** Two Alone. **1935** The Man Who Reclaimed His Head; Dr. Socrates. **1937** California Straight Ahead. **1938** Long Shot; Give Me a Sailor. **1939** Gone With the Wind; Invitation to Happiness; They All Come Out. **1949** Adam's Rib. **1950** Wyoming Mail. **1951** As Young as You Feel; Fort Worth; The Prowler. **1952** Mutiny. **1955** Prince of Players; Run for Cover. **1960** Dark at the Top of the Stairs. **1961** Return to Peyton Place. **1962** Lover Come Back.

TREADWAY, CHARLOTTE

Born: 1895. Died: Feb. 26, 1963, Hollywood, Calif. Screen and stage actress.

Appeared in: **1937** The Sheik Steps Out. **1938** Female Fugitive. **1939** The Woman; A Jed Prouty short; Wrong Room (short). **1941** One Foot in Heaven; Life With Henry. **1942** Gentleman Jim.

TREADWELL, LAURA B.

Born: 1879. Died: Nov. 22, 1960, Hollywood, Calif. Screen and stage actress.

Appeared in: **1934** Fashions of 1934. **1935** She Gets Her Man; Goin' to Town; Accent on Youth. **1936** Theodora Goes Wild. **1937** Easy Living; Nobody's Baby. **1938** Man-Proof. **1939** The Night of Nights; Mr. Smith Goes to Washington. **1946** Undercurrent; Lady in the Lake; Bringing Up Father; Night and Day. **1947** Nightmare Alley; King of the Bandits; Life With Father; Sea of Grass. **1948** Winter Meeting; B. F.'s Daughter. **1949** Task Force; The Barkleys of Broadway. **1951** Strangers on a Train.

TREE, SIR HERBERT BEERBOHM

Born: Dec. 17, 1852, Kensington, England. Died: July 2, 1917, London, England. Stage and screen actor. Married to actress Lady (Helen Maud Holt) Tree (dec. 1937). Father of actress Viola Tree (dec. 1938).

Appeared in: **1899** King John. **1911** Henry VIII. **1914** Trilby. **1916** Macbeth; The Old Folks at Home.

TREE, LADY (Helen Maude Holt)

Born: Oct. 5, 1863, London, England. Died: Aug. 7, 1937, London, England (following surgery). Stage and screen actress. Married to actor Sir Herbert Beerbohm Tree (dec. 1917). Mother of actress Viola Tree (dec. 1938).

Appeared in: **1916** Still Waters Run Deep. **1920** Little Dorrit. **1930** Such Is the Law. **1932** Wedding Rehearsal. **1933** Early to Bed; The Girl from Maxim's (US 1936); The Private Life of Henry VIII; Her Imaginary Lover. **1936** The Man Who Could Work Miracles (US 1937).

TREE, VIOLA

Born: 1884. Died: Nov. 15, 1938, London, England (pleurisy). British screen, stage actress, author and playwright. Daughter of actor Sir Herbert Beerbohm Tree (dec. 1917) and Lady Tree (dec. 1937).

Appeared in: **1935** Heart's Desire. **1938** Pygmalion.

TRENHOLME, HELEN

Born: June 23, 1911, Montreal, Canada. Died: Jan. 30, 1962, New York, N.Y. Screen and stage actress.

Appeared in: **1934** The Case of the Howling Dog; The Firebird.

TRENT, JOHN (aka JACK TRENT)

Born: 1897. Died: Aug. 1, 1961 (fall from horse). Screen actor and stuntman. Do not confuse with actor John Trent (dec. 1966).

Appeared in: **1935** Bordertown.

TRENT, JOHN (LaVerne Brown)

Born: Dec. 5, 1906, Orange, Calif. Died: May 12, 1966. Aviator and screen actor.

TRESHAM, MRS. JENNIE

Born: 1881. Died: Dec. 18, 1913, Portland, Ore. Screen actress. Appeared in Portland Film Company films.

TRESKOFF, OLGA

Born: 1902. Died: Apr. 23, 1938, New York, N.Y. Screen and stage actress. Appeared in silent films.

TREVELYAN, HILDA (Hilda Tucker)

Born: Feb. 4, 1880, England. Died: Nov. 10, 1959, London, England. Screen and stage actress. Married to author Sydney Blow.

Appeared in: **1916** Sally in Our Alley. **1917** What Every Woman Knows.

TREVELYN, UNA

Born: 1896, Memphis, Tenn. Died: May 14, 1948, Hollywood, Calif. (heart attack). Screen and stage actress.

Appeared in: **1914** Lost in Mid-Ocean. **1918** Venus Model. **1919** Her Purchase Price. **1920** The Devil's Pass Keys. **1921** What Do Men Want. **1922** Another Man's Shoes.

TREVI, CHRISTINA (Christina Benitez Trevino)

Born: 1930, Mexico. Died: July 1, 1956, Mexico City, Mexico (following surgery). Screen, television actress and opera soprano.

TREVOR, ANNE

Died: July, 1970, England. Screen and stage actress.

Appeared in: **1920** Build Thy House; Wuthering Heights. **1921** Daniel Deronda. **1922** A Rogue In Love. **1936** Murder in the Old Red Barn.

TREVOR, AUSTIN (Austin Schilsky)

Born: Oct. 7, 1897, Belfast, Ireland. Died: Jan. 22, 1978, London, England. Screen, stage and television actor. Entered films in 1930.

Appeared in: **1930** At the Villa Rose (aka Mystery at the Villa Rose—US); The Man from Chicago (US 1931); Escape; The "W" Plan. **1931** A Night in Montmartre; Alibi; Black Coffee. **1932** A Safe Proposition; The Crooked Lady; The Chinese Puzzle. **1933** On Secret Service (aka Secret Agent—US 1935). **1934** Lord Edgware Dies; The Broken Melody; Death at Broadcasting House. **1935** Mimi; Inside the Room; Cavalcade (aka Regal Cavalcade—US); The Silent Passenger. **1936** Dusty Ermine (aka Hideout in the Alps—US 1938); As You Like It; The Beloved Vagabond; Rembrandt; Sabotage (aka The Woman Alone—US 1937); Spy 77. **1937** Dark Journey; Knight Without Armor. **1939** Goodbye, Mr. Chips; The Lion Has Wings (US 1940). **1940** The Briggs Family; Night Train to Munich (aka Gestapo, aka Night Train—US); Law and Disorder; Under Your Hat. **1941** The Seventh Survivor. **1942** The Big Blockade; The Young Mr. Pitt. **1944** Champagne Charlie (US 1948). **1946** Lisbon Story (US 1951). **1948** Anna Karenina; The Red Shoes. **1950** So Long at the Fair (US 1951). **1954** Father Brown (aka The Detective—US). **1955** To Paris with Love. **1956** Tons of Trouble. **1957** Dangerous Exile (US 1958); Seven Waves Away (aka Abandon Ship—US). **1959** Horrors of the Black Museum. **1961** Konga; The Day the Earth Caught Fire (US 1962); Never Back Losers (US 1967); Court Martial of Major Keller. **1965** The Alphabet Murders (US 1966).

TREVOR, HUGH

Born: Oct. 28, 1903, Yonkers, N.Y. Died: Nov. 10, 1933, Los Angeles, Calif. (complications following appendectomy). Screen actor. Entered films in 1927.

Appeared in: **1927** Rangers of the North. **1928** Skinner's Big Idea; Wallflowers; Beau Broadway; Red Lips; Her Summer Hero; The Pinto Kid. **1929** Dry Martini; Hey, Rube; Taxi 13; Love in the Desert; Night Parade; The Very Idea. **1930** Cuckoos; Midnight Mystery; The Pay-Off; Conspiracy; Half Shot at Sunrise. **1931** The Royal Bed.

TREVOR, NORMAN
Born: June 23, 1877, Calcutta, India. Died: Oct. 31, 1929, Norwalk, Calif. Screen and stage actor.

Appeared in: **1917** The Runaway. **1920** Romance. **1921** The Black Panther's Cub; Jane Eyre. **1924** The Wages of Virtue; Roulette. **1925** Dancing Mothers; The Man Who Found Himself. **1926** Beau Geste; The Song and Dance Man; The Ace of Cads. **1927** Afraid to Love; Children of Divorce; The Siren; Sorrell and Son; The Music Master; New York; The Wizard; The Warning. **1928** Mad Hour.

TREVOR, SPENCER
Born: May 29, 1875, Biarrits, Switzerland. Died: May 22, 1945, England? Screen and stage actor.

Appeared in: **1930** Alf's Butt. **1931** Congress Dances (US 1932). **1934** Blossom Time (aka April Romance—US 1937).

TRICOLI, CARLO
Born: 1890. Died: Apr. 1, 1966. Screen actor.

Appeared in: **1950** Spy Hunt; Crisis; Black Hand; Lady Without Passport. **1951** Ten Tall Men; Mask of the Avenger. **1952** Wagon Team. **1960** Pay or Die.

TRIESAULT, IVAN
Born: 1900, Estonia, Russia. Died: Jan. 3, 1980, Los Angeles, Calif. (heart failure). Screen, stage, television actor and ballet dancer.

Appeared in: **1941** The Girl from Leningrad; Out of the Fog. **1943** Mission to Moscow; Song of Russia; Cry of the Werewolf; The Black Parachute. **1944** The Mummy's Ghost; In Our Time; Uncertain Glory; The Hitler Gang; Days of Glory. **1945** A Song to Remember; Counter-Attack. **1946** Notorious; Crime Doctor's Man Hunt; The Return of Monte Cristo. **1947** Golden Earrings; The Crimson Key. **1948** To the Ends of the Earth. **1949** Home in San Antone; Johnny Allegro. **1950** Kim. **1951** The Desert Fox; My True Story; The Lady and the Bandit. **1952** Five Fingers; The Bad and the Beautiful. **1953** Young Bess; How to Marry a Millionaire; Desert Legion; Ma and Pa Kettle on Vacation. **1954** Charge of the Lancers; Both Sides of the Law; The Gambler from Natchez; Her Twelve Men. **1955** The Girl in the Red Velvet Swing. **1957** Jet Pilot; The Buster Keaton Story. **1958** The Young Lions; Fraulein. **1960** Cimarron; The Amazing Transparent Man. **1961** Barabba (Barabbas—US 1962). **1962** It Happened in Athens; The 300 Spartans. **1965** Von Ryan's Express; Morituri (aka The Saboteur: Code Name—Morituri).

TRIETSCH, PAUL "HEZZIE" (Paul Edward Trietsch)
Born: 1905. Died: Apr. 27, 1980, Ventura, Calif. (cancer). Screen, stage, vaudeville and radio actor. Brother of musician Ken Trietsch who appeared with him as a member of the "Hossier Hot Shots" band, along with Gil Taylor and Gabe Ward.

Appeared in: **1939** In Old Monterey. **1944** National Barn Dance.

TRIGGER
Born: 1932. Died: July 3, 1965. Roy Rogers' Palomino horse. Screen and television performer. Appeared in 87 feature films and 101 half-hour television shows.

Appeared in: **1944** Hollywood Canteen. **1945** Don't Fence Me In; Utah. **1946** My Pal Trigger. **1947** Apache Rose. **1948** Under California Stars. **1949** The Far Frontier; The Golden Stallion. **1950** Sunset in the West; Trigger, Jr. **1951** Heart of the Rockies; Spoilers of the Plains.

TRILLER, ARMAND
Born: Mar. 20, 1883, Bucharest, Rumania. Died: Dec. 12, 1939, Calif. Screen actor.

Appeared in: **1929** Laughing at Death.

TRIMBLE, LARRY (Lawrence Trimble)
Born: Feb. 15, 1885, Robbinston, Maine. Died: Feb. 8, 1954, Woodland Hills, Calif. Screen actor, film director and screenwriter. Entered films in 1910 with Vitagraph.

TRIPP, JAMES
Born: 1901, Nahiku, Maui, Hawaii. Died: Nov. 23, 1981, Honolulu, Hawaii. Stuntman and rodeo star.

TROTSKY, LEON (Lev Davydovich Bronstein)
Born: Nov. 8, 1879, Yanovka, Kherson Province, Ukraine. Died: Aug. 21, 1940, Mexico City, Mexico (murdered). Politician, philosopher and screen performer.

Appeared in: **1914** My Official Wife.

TROTTER, JOHN SCOTT
Born: 1908, Charlotte, N.C. Died: Oct. 29, 1975, Los Angeles, Calif. (cancer). Musical conductor, arranger, musician, screen, radio and television actor.

Appeared in: **1940** Rhythm On the River. **1941** Kiss the Boys Goodbye.

TROUNCER, CECIL
Born: Apr. 5, 1898, Southport Lanes, England. Died: Dec. 15, 1953. Screen and stage actor.

Appeared in: **1938** Pygmalion. **1947** While the Sun Shines (US 1950). **1948** The Guinea Pig (US 1949); London Belongs to Me (aka Dulcimer Street—US); Saraband for Dead Lovers (aka Saraband—US). **1951** The Magic Box (US 1952); The Lady with the Lamp. **1952** The Pickwick Papers (US 1953). **1954** The Weak and the Wicked.

TROUT, FRANCIS "DINK"
Born: June 18, 1898, Beardstown, Ill. Died: Mar. 26, 1950, Hollywood, Calif. Screen, stage, radio, vaudeville actor and musician. Played with Ben Bernie's band.

Appeared in: **1941** Scattergood Baines. **1943** Gildersleeve's Bad Day. **1944** Up in Arms. **1945** Sudan.

TROUTMAN, IVY
Born: Sept. 23, 1883. Died: Jan. 12, 1979, Tinton Falls, N.J. Screen and stage actress.

Appeared in: **1915** The House With Nobody In It.

TROW, WILLIAM
Born: 1891. Died: Sept. 2, 1973, Hollywood, Calif. Screen actor. Entered films in 1919.

TROWBRIDGE, CHARLES
Born: Jan. 10, 1882, Vera Cruz, Mexico. Died: Oct. 30, 1967. Screen and stage actor.

Appeared in: **1918** Thais. **1922** Island Wives. **1931** I Take This Woman; Damaged Love; A Secret Call; Silence. **1935** Calm Yourself; Mad Love; It's in the Air; Rendezvous. **1936** Exclusive Story; The Garden Murder Case; We Went to College; Born to Dance; Mother Steps Out; Man of the People; The Gorgeous Hussy; Libeled Lady; The Devil Is a Sissy; Robin Hood of El Dorado; Moonlight Murder; Love on the Run. **1937** Dangerous Number; Espionage; A Day at the Races; A Servant of the People; Fit for a King; Captains Courageous; They Gave Him a Gun; Sea Racketeers; Exiled to Shanghai; That Certain Woman; Without Warning; Saturday's Heroes; The 13th Chair. **1938** Little Tough Guy; Crime School; Nancy Drew, Detective; Alcatraz Island; The Buccaneer; Kentucky; Thanks for Everything; Submarine Patrol; Gang Bullets; The Last Express; The Invisible Menace; The Patient in Room 18; College Swing; Gangs of New York; Crime Ring. **1939** Angels Wash Their Faces; Risky Business; King of Chinatown; Tropic Fury; King of the Underworld; Boy Trouble; The Story of Alexander Graham Bell; On Trial; Hotel for Women; Swanee River; Each Dawn I Die; While America Sleeps (short); Confessions of a Nazi Spy; The Man They Could Not Hang; Mutiny on the Blackhawk; Joe and Ethel Turp Call on the President; Pride of the Navy; Lady of the Tropics; Cafe Society; Sergeant Madden. **1940** Mysterious Dr. Satan (serial); My Love Came Back; House of Seven Gables; The Fighting 69th; Johnny Apollo; The Man With Nine Lives; Knute Rockne—All American; Cherokee Strip; The Mummy's Hand; Dr. Kildare Goes Home; Trail of the Vigilantes; The Fatal Hour. **1941** King of the Texas Rangers (serial); The Great Lie; The Tell-Tale Heart; Strange Alibi; Dressed to Kill; Blue, White and Perfect; The Nurse's Secret; Rags to Riches; Sergeant York; Hurricane Smith; Great Guns; We Go Fast; The Great Mr. Nobody; Belle Starr; Cadet Girl. **1942** Who Is Hope Schuyler?; Sweetheart of the Fleet; Over My Dead Body; That Other Woman; Ten Gentlemen from West Point; Wake Island; Tennessee Johnson. **1943** Action in the North Atlantic; Wintertime; The Story of Dr. Wassell; Salute to the Marines; Sweet Rosie O'Grady; Mission to Moscow; Adventures of the Flying Cadets (serial). **1944** Captain America (serial); Faces in the Fog; Summer Storm; Hey Rookie!; Wing and a Prayer; Heavenly Days. **1945** Col. Effingham's Raid; Mildred Pierce; They Were Expendable; The Red Dragon. **1946** Don't Gamble With Strangers; Shock; Undercurrent; Secret of the Whistler; The Hoodlum Saint; Smooth as Silk; Valley of the Zombies. **1947** Key Witness; Buck Privates Come Home; Her Husband's Affairs; The Sea of Grass; The Beginning or the End?; Mr. District Attorney; The Private Affairs of Bel Ami; Tarzan and the Huntress; Song of My Heart; Tycoon; Black Gold; Shoot to Kill. **1948** Stage Struck; Hollow Triumph; The Paleface. **1949** Mr. Soft Touch; Bad Boy. **1950** Unmasked; Peggy. **1952** Bushwackers. **1957** The Wings of Eagles.

TROY, ELINOR
Born: 1916. Died: Nov. 29, 1949, Hollywood, Calif. (tuberculosis). Screen and stage actress.

Appeared in: **1934** Gold Diggers of 1934. **1936** Stage Struck. **1937** Nothing Sacred; Top of the Town. **1942** Pride of the Yankees. **1943** Let's Face It. **1945** Anchors Aweigh. **1946** The Harvey Girls.

TROY, HELEN
Born: 1905. Died: Nov. 1, 1942, Santa Monica, Calif. Screen and radio actress.

Appeared in: **1936** Born to Dance; Song and Dance Man; Human Cargo. **1937** Thoroughbreds Don't Cry; Between Two Women; Broadway Melody of 1938; Big City; Everybody Sing. **1939** Kid Nightingale.

TROY, SIDNEY Z.
Born: 1908. Died: June 10, 1978, Panorama City, Calif. (heart attack). Screen, television actor and stuntman.

TRUAX, JOHN
Died: June 14, 1969. Screen actor.

Appeared in: **1956** He Laughed Last. **1957** The Fuzzy Pink Nightgown. **1959** Curse of the Undead. **1965** The Great Race.

TRUE, BESSIE "BESS" (Laurie Flateau)
Born: 1899, Anaconda, Mont. Died: July 9, 1947, New York, N.Y. Screen, vaudeville and radio actress. Entered films in 1918.

Appeared in: **1921** Why Trust Your Husband? **1925** Heartbound. **1928** Yellow Lily; Show Girl; Sailor's Wives.

TRUESDELL, FRED (Charles Fred Truesdell)
Born: 1874, Coldwater, Mich. Died: May 9, 1929, Chicago, Ill. Screen, vaudeville and stage actor.

Appeared in: **1917** The Man Who Forgot; The Greatest Power; The Beloved Adventuress; The Marriage Market. **1918** Wilson or the Kaiser; Lafayette, We Come.

TRUESDELL, FREDERICK (Geroge Frederick Truesdell)
Born: 1873. Died: May 3, 1937, New York, N.Y. Screen and stage actor.

Appeared in: **1919** Shadows. **1923** The Love Piker; Chastity. **1924** Pleasure Mad; The Beauty Prize.

TRUESDELL, HOWARD
Born: Jan. 3, 1861, Conneautville, Pa. Died: Dec. 8, 1941, Los Angeles, Calif. (heart attack). Screen, stage and vaudeville actor. Entered films in 1912.

Appeared in: **1916** The Come Back. **1920** Whisper Market; Youthful Folly. **1921** The Wonderful Thing. **1922** French Heels; No Trespassing. **1923** Ashes of Vengeance; Columbus; Out of Luck. **1924** The Foolish Virgin; Ride For Your Life; The Night Message; Why Men Leave Home; The Ridin' Kid from Powder River; Reno. **1925** Go West. **1926** The Combat; The Jazz Girl; The Dude Cowboy; The Stolen Ranch; Fighting With Buffalo Bill. **1927** Singed; The Denver Dude; The Tigress. **1928** The Stronger Will; Burning Daylight; Three-Ring Marriage; Mating Call. **1929** Painted Faces; The Lawless Legion; The Long, Long Trail.

TRUEX, ERNEST
Born: Sept. 19, 1889, Kansas City, Mo. Died: June 27, 1973, Fallbrook, Calif. (heart attack). Screen, stage, television and vaudeville actor. Married to actress Sally Field. Divorced from actresses Julia Mills and Mary Jane Barrett.

Appeared in: **1914** Good Little Devil. **1917** Artie; Caprice and The American Citizen. **1923** Six Cylinder Love. **1929** Love at First Sight. **1931** The Millionaire. **1933** Mr. Adam (short); Whistling in the Dark; The Warrior's Husband. **1934** The following shorts: The Expectant Father; His Lucky Day; Gentlemen of the Bar. **1935** The following shorts: Friendly Spirits; The Light Fantastic; The Amateur Husband; Ladies Love Hats; Object Not Matrimony; Only the Brave. **1936** Triple Trouble (short); Everybody Dance. **1937** Mama Runs Wild. **1938** The Adventures of Marco Polo; Start Cheering; Freshman Year; Swing That Cheer; Swing, Sister, Swing. **1939** Ambush; It's a Wonderful World; Bachelor Mother; These Glamour Girls; Little Accident; Island of Lost Men. **1940** Lillian Russell; Christmas in July. **1941** His Girl Friday. **1942** Twin Beds; Private Buckaroo; Star Spangled Rhythm. **1943** The Crystal Ball; Rhythm of the Islands; True to Life; Sleepy Lagoon; Fired Wife. **1944** Chip Off the Old Block; Her Primitive Man. **1945** Pan-Americana; Men in Her Diary. **1946** Life With Blondie. **1948** Always Together. **1956** The Leather Saint. **1957** All Mine to Give. **1958** Twilight For the Gods. **1965** Fluffy.

TRUJILLO, LORENZO L.
Born: 1906, Mexico. Died: Mar., 1962, Mexico City, Mexico (heart attack). Screen, stage and television actor. Appeared in 200 Mexican films including The Exterminating Angel.

TRUMAN, RALPH
Born: May 7, 1900, London, England. Died: Oct., 1977, Ipswich, England. Screen, stage and radio actor. Married to radio actress Ellis Powell (dec.).

Appeared in: **1935** The Lad; Three Witnesses; The Case of Gabriel Perry; Jubilee Window; Lieutenant Daring, RN; Father O'Flynn (US 1938); Captain Bill; Mr.Cohen Takes a Walk (US 1936); The Silent Passenger. **1936** The Marriage of Corbal (aka Prisoner of Corbal—US 1939); East Meets West; The Crimson Circle; The Gay Adventure. **1937** It's a Grand Old World; Dinner at the Ritz; Change for a Sovereign. **1938** Just Like a Woman; Many Tanks Mr. Atkins. **1939** The Outsider (US 1940); The Saint in London. **1942** Sabotage at Sea. **1945** Henry V (US 1946). **1946** Lisbon Story (US 1951); Beware of Pity (US 1947); Laughing Lady (US 1950); Woman to Woman. **1947** The Man Within (aka The Smugglers—US 1948); Mrs. Fitzherbert (US 1950). **1948** Oliver Twist (US 1951). **1949** Eureka Stockade; Christopher Columbus; The Interrupted Journey (US 1951). **1950** Treasure Island. **1951** Quo Vadis. **1953** The Master of Ballantrae; Malta Story (US 1954). **1954** Beau Brummell; The Golden Coach. **1955** The Ship That Died of Shame (US 1956); The Night My Number Came Up. **1956** The Silken Affair (US 1957); The Black Tent (US 1957); Wicked as They Come (US 1957); The Long Arm (aka The Third Key—US 1957); The Man Who Knew Too Much. **1959** Ben Hur; Beyond this Place (aka Web of Evidence—US). **1960** Exodus. **1961** El Cid. **1971** Nicholas and Alexandra.

TRUPPI, DANNY
Born: July 25, 1919, New York, N.Y. Died: July 6, 1970, Los Angeles, Calif. (heart attack). Screen actor and musician.

Appeared in: **1956** Around the World in 80 Days. **1970** The Trouble With Girls.

TRYON, GLENN
Born: Sept. 14, 1899, Julietta, Idaho. Died: Apr. 18, 1970. Screen, stage actor, film director, producer and screenwriter.

Appeared in: **1924** The Battling Orioles; The White Sheep. **1927** Two Girls Wanted; A Hero for a Night; The Denver Dude; Painting the Town; The Poor Nut. **1928** Thanks for the Buggy Ride; Hot Heels; How to Handle Women; Lonesome; The Gate Crasher. **1929** Skinner Steps Out; Broadway; Barnum Was Right; It Can Be Done; The Kid's Clever. **1930** Dames Ahoy; King of Jazz; The Midnight Special. **1931** Daybreak; The Sky Spider; Neck and Neck; Secret Menace. **1932** Dragnet Patrol; Rule 'Em and Weep (short); Widow in Scarlet; Tangled Destinies; The Pride of the Legion. **1933** Educational shorts. **1934** The Big Pay-Off. **1941** Hold That Ghost; Keep 'Em Flying; Helzapoppin. **1945** George White's Scandals. **1947** Variety Girl. **1951** Hometown Story. **1965** Laurel and Hardy's Laughing 20's (film clips).

TSCHECHOWA, OLGA (Olga von Knipper-Dolling)
Born: 1896, Alexandropol, Russia. Died: Mar. 9, 1980, Russia? Screen, stage actress, film producer and director. Divorced from actor Michael Tschechowa. Mother of actress Ada Tschechowa.

Appeared in: **1921** Hochstapler; Schloss Vogeloed (Vogeloed Castle). **1922** Das Haus der Unseligen; Der Kampf ums Ich; Ein Puppenheim. **1923** Die Fahrt ins Glueck (aka Bob and Mary—US 1927); Der Verlorene Schuh; Nora; Die Pagode. **1924** Die Bacchantin; Die Frau im Feuer; Soll und Haben; Die Venus vom Montmartre. **1925** Die Gesunkenen (The Sunken); Maedels von Heute (aka Liebesgeschichten); Soll Man Heiraten? (aka Intermezzo Einer Ehe in Sieben Tagen); Das Alte Ballhaus; Der Mann aus dem Jenseits; Die Millionenkompagnie; Die Stadt der Versuchung. **1926** Familie Schimek (aka Wiener Herzen); Der Feldherrenhuegel; Brennende Grenze; Der Mann im Feuer; Die Muehle von Sanssouci; Sein Grosser Fall; Trude, die Sechzehnjaehrige. **1927** Aftermath; Die Selige Exzellenz (His Late Excellency—US 1929); Das Meer; Der Meister der Welt. **1928** Marter der Liebe; Weib in Flammen; Moulin Rouge. **1929** When Duty Cally; Blutschande 173 St. G.B.; Diane; Die Liebe der Brueder; Stud. Chem. Helene Willfuer. **1930** After the Verdict; Liebe im Ring; Liebling der Gotter (Darling of the Gods); Zwei Kravatten (Two Neckties); Ein Maedel von der Reeperbahn (US 1931, aka Menschen im Sturm); Der Detektiv des Kaisers; Die Grosse Sehnsucht; Die Drei von der Tankstelle (US 1931); Troika. **1931** Liebe auf Befehl (aka Boudoir Diplomat—US); Der Grosse Tenor; Die Nacht der Entscheidung (aka The Virtuous Sin—US); Mary (aka Sir John Greift Ein!, and aka Murder—US); The Horse Ate the Hat; Das Konzert; Panik in Chikago; Nachtkolonne. **1932** Spione im Savoy-

Hotel (aka Die Galavorstellung der Fratellinis—US 1933); Trenck (US 1934). **1933** Ein Gewisser Herr Gran (US 1934); Der Choral von Leuthen (The Anthem of Leuthen—US 1935); Heideschulmeister Uwe Karsten (US 1934); Liebelei (US 1936); Wege zur Guten Ehe. **1934** Was Bin Ich ohne Dich? (US 1935); Zwichen Zwei Herzen (Between Two Hearts—US 1936); Maskerade (aka Masquweade in Vienna—US 1937); Peer Gynt (US 1939); Regine; Die Welt ohne Maske; Abenteuer Eines Jungen Herrn in Polen; Der Polizeibericht Meldet. **1935** Die Ewige Maske (The Eternal Mask—US 1937); Ein Walzer um den Stephansturm (aka Sylvia und ihr Chauffeur); Liebestrauemie; Lockspitzel Asew; Keuenstlerliebe; Hannerl und ihre Liebhaber. **1936** Liebe und Trompetenklang; Burghtheater (aka Vienna Burghtheater—US 1937); Seine Tochter ist der Peter (His Daughter is Peter—US 1938); Der Favorit der Kaiserin (The Favorite of the Empress—US 1939); Manja Valewska. **1937** Freuhling im Wien; Unter Ausschluss der Oeffentlichkeit; Liebe Geht Seltsame Wege; Gewitterflug zu Claudia; Die Gelbe Flagge. **1938** Rote Ochrideen (Red Orchids—US 1939); Verliebtes Abenteuer; Das Maedchen mit dem Guten Ruf; Zwei Frauen. **1939** Parkstrasse 13 (aka Verhoer um Mitternacht); Befreite Hande (Freed Hans—US 1940); Bel Ami (aka Der Liebling Schoener Frauen); Ich Verweigere die Aussage; Die Unheimlichen Wuensche. **1940** Liedenschaft; Angelika; Der Fuchs von Glenarvon. **1941** Menschen im Sturm. **1942** Adreas Schlueter; Mit den Augen Einer Frau. **1943** Der Ewige Klang (aka Der Geiger); Reise in die Vergangenheit; Gefaehrlicher Fruehling. **1944** Mit Meinen Augen (aka Im Tempel der Venus); Melusine. **1950** Der Mann, der Zweimal Leben Wollte; Eine Nacht im Separee; Kein Engel ist so Rein; Zwei in Einem Anzug; Maharadscha Wider Willen; Aufruhr im Paradies. **1951** Die Perlenkette; Eine Frau mit Herz; Das Geheimnis Einer Ehe; Mein Freund der Dieb. **1952** Hinter Klostermauern. **1953** Heute Nacht Passiert's; Alles fuer Papa. **1954** Rosen-Resli; Rittmeister Wronski. **1955** Ich war ein Haessliches Maedchen; Die Barrings. **1958** U 47-Kapitanleutnant Prien (U-47 Lt. Commander Prien—US 1967). **1974** Liebelei (and 1933 version).

TSCHERNICHIN-LARSSEN, JENNY
Born: 1867, Finland. Died: 1937, Finland? Screen actress. Appeared in silent films.

TSIANG, H. T.
Born: 1899. Died: July 16, 1971, Hollywood, Calif. Screen, stage, television actor, poet and author. Entered films in 1928.

Appeared in: **1943** Behind the Rising Sun. **1944** The Purple Heart; Keys of the Kingdom. **1948** Chicken Every Sunday. **1949** State Department File-649. **1950** Panic in the Streets. **1951** Smuggler's Island. **1960** Ocean's 11. **1965** Winter A-Go-Go.

TSUKAMOTO, RAYNUM K.
Born: Mar. 1, 1889, Japan. Died: Aug. 9, 1974, Los Angeles, Calif. (hit by auto). Screen actor.

Appeared in: **1956** The Teahouse of the August Moon. **1966** Operation Bikini.

TUALA, MARIO (Eckard Schulz-Ewerth)
Born: 1924, Samoa, South Sea Islands. Died: July 10, 1961, Berlin, Germany (drowned in boating accident). Screen, radio actor and singer.

TUBBS, WILLIAM
Born: 1908. Died: Jan. 25, 1953, London, England. Screen and stage actor.

Appeared in: **1948** Paisan. **1949** The Pirates of Capri. **1951** Quo Vadis; Three Steps North. **1952** Edward and Caroline. **1953** Singing Taxi Driver. **1954** The Greatest Love; The Golden Coach. **1955** The Wages of Fear.

TUCKER, CY
Born: 1889. Died: July 4, 1952, Hollywood, Calif. Screen actor.

TUCKER, ETHEL
Died: May 14, 1926. Screen actress. Mother of actor/director George Loane Tucker (dec. 1921).

TUCKER, GEORGE LOANE
Born: 1872, Chicago, Ill. Died: June 20, 1921, Los Angeles, Calif. Screen actor, film director and producer. Married to actress Elizabeth Risdon (dec. 1958). Son of actress Ethel Tucker (dec. 1926).

Appeared in: **1911** Uncle's Visit. **1912** A Little Old Woman of Twenty; Next! **1913** Majestic Film Co. films.

TUCKER, HARLAND (aka HARLAN TUCKER)
Died: Mar. 22, 1949, Calif. (heart attack). Screen and stage actor.

Appeared in: **1920** The Loves of Letty. **1921** Beau Revel; The Swamp. **1926** Shameful Behavior?; The Adorable Deceiver. **1927** Stolen Pleasures. **1933** Phantom Broadcast; King for a Night. **1937** Once a Doctor; Racing Lady; Kid Galahad; Slim; Missing Witnesses; Without Warning. **1938** The Invisible Menace; The Patient in Room 18. **1939** King of the Underworld. **1940** The Lone Wolf Strikes. **1941** The Roar of the Press. **1942** Road to Happiness. **1947** Desert Fury; Hit Parade of 1947. **1948** A Foreign Affair; Beyond Glory.

TUCKER, RICHARD
Born: 1884, Brooklyn, N.Y. Died: Dec. 5, 1942, Woodland Hills, Calif. (heart attack). Screen and stage actor. Entered films with Edison.

Appeared in: **1913** Her Royal Highness. **1915** While the Tide Was Rising; Vanity Fair. **1917** Threads of Fate; The Law of the North; The Little Chevalier. **1920** Branding Iron. **1921** Roads of Destiny; Don't Neglect Your Wife; The Old Nest; Everything for Sale; What Love Will Do; A Voice in the Dark; A Virginia Courtship; The Night Rose. **1922** Hearts Aflame; The Dangerous Age; A Self-Made Man; Strange Idols; Remembrance; Rags to Riches; Grand Larceny; When the Devil Drives; The Worldly Madonna; Yellow Men and Gold. **1923** Cameo Kirby; The Eleventh Hour; Her Accidental Husband; Poor Men's Wives; Is Divorce a Failure?; Lovebound; The Broken Wing. **1924** Beau Brummell; 40-Horse Hawkins; Helen's Babies; The Fast Worker; The Star Dust Trail; The Tornado. **1925** The Air Mail; The Lure of the Wild; The Man Without a Country; The Golden Cocoon; The Bridge of Sighs. **1926** The Blind Goddess; Shameful Behavior?; The Lily; That's My Baby; Devil's Island. **1927** Dearie; Wings; The Girl from Rio; The Lash (short); The Bush Leaguer; The Desired Woman; The Jazz Singer; A Kiss in a Taxi; The World at Her Feet; Matinee Ladies; Women's Wares. **1928** Thanks for the Buggy Ride; Loves of an Actress; On Trial; Captain Swagger; Love Over Night; My Man; The Border Patrol; Daughters of Desire; Beware of Married Men; A Bit of Heaven; Show Girls; The Crimson City; The Grain of Dust. **1929** The Dummy; Half Marriage; King of the Kongo (serial); This Is Heaven; Lucky Boy; Synthetic Sin; The Unholy Night; The Squall. **1930** Madonna of the Streets; Brothers; Puttin' on the Ritz; Shadow of the Law; Broken Dishes; Recaptured Love; Safety in Numbers; The Bat Whispers; The Benson Murder Case; Painted Faces; Peacock Alley; Courage; The Man from Blankley's; College Lovers; Manslaughter. **1931** Too Young to Marry; A Holy Terror; Convicted; Devil Plays; Inspiration; Seed; X Marks the Spot; Stepping Out; Hellbound; Maker of Men; The Deceiver; Graft; Up for Murder; The Black Camel. **1932** The Shadow of the Eagle (serial); Carless Lady; A Successful Calamity; The Stoker; Guilty as Hell; The Crash; Pack Up Your Troubles; Flames; Week-End Marriage. **1933** The Iron Master; Her Resale Value; Daring Daughters; The World Gone Mad; Saturday's Millions; Only Yesterday. **1934** Show-Off; Back Page; Take the Stand; Successful Failure; Public Stenographer; The Road to Ruin; Countess of Monte Cristo; A Modern Hero; Handy Andy; Baby Take a Bow; Money Means Nothing; Paris Interlude; Sing Sing Nights. **1935** Buried Loot (short); Diamond Jim; Shadow of Doubt; Murder in the Fleet; Calm Yourself; Here Comes the Band; Symphony of Living. **1936** In Paris A.W.O.L.; Flash Gordon (serial); The Great Ziegfeld; Ring Around the Moon; Flying Hostess; The Plot Thickens; I Loved a Woman; Shall We Dance? **1937** She's Dangerous; Headline Crasher; I Cover the War; The Girl Who Said No; Jungle Menace (serial); Armored Car; Something to Sing About; Make a Wish; The River of Missing Men; Trapped by G-Men. **1938** The Texans; She's Got Everything; The Higgins Family; Sons of the Legion. **1939** Risky Business; The Girl from Rio; The Covered Trailer; The Great Victor Herbert; While America Sleeps (short).

TUCKER, RICHARD (Reuben Ticker)
Born: Aug. 28, 1914, Brooklyn, N.Y. Died: Jan. 8, 1975, Kalamazoo, Mich. (heart attack). Opera tenor and screen actor.

TUCKER, SOPHIE (Sohie Abuza)
Born: Jan. 13, 1884, Boston, Mass or Russia. Died: Feb. 9, 1966, New York, N.Y. (lung and kidney ailment). Screen, stage, burlesque, vaudeville actress and nightclub entertainer.

Appeared in: **1929** Honky Tonk. **1934** Gay Love. **1937** Broadway Melody of 1938; Thoroughbreds Don't Cry. **1944** Follow the Boys; Sensations of 1945; Atlantic City. **1957** The Heart of Show Business (short).

TUFTS, SONNY (Bowen Charleston Tufts, III)
Born: July 16, 1912, Boston, Mass. Died: June 5, 1970, Santa Monica, Calif. (pneumonia). Screen, stage, television actor and film producer.

Appeared in: **1939** Ambush. **1943** So Proudly We Hail; Government

Girl. **1944** In the Meantime, Darling; I Love a Soldier; Here Comes the Waves. **1945** Bring on the Girls; Duffy's Tavern. **1946** Swell Guy; Miss Susie Slagle's; The Virginian; The Well-Groomed Bride. **1947** Cross My Heart; Easy Come, Easy Go; Blaze of Noon; Variety Girl. **1948** Untamed Breed. **1949** Easy Living; The Crooked Way. **1952** The Gift Horse (aka Glory at Sea—US 1953). **1953** Cat Women of the Moon; No Escape; Run for the Hills. **1954** Serpent Island. **1955** The Seven Year Itch. **1956** Come Next Spring. **1957** The Parson and the Outlaw. **1962** All the Way. **1965** The Town Tamer. **1967** Cottonpickin' Chickenpickers.

TULLY, ETHEL
Born: 1898. Died: Oct. 1, 1968, San Antonio, Tex. Screen actress. Model for W.W. I posters of J. M. Flagg. Entered films with Vitagraph in 1916.

TULLY, GEORGE F.
Born: Nov. 26, 1876, Mayo, Ireland. Died: July 2, 1930, England? Screen and stage actor. Married to stage actress Blanche Massey (dec. 1929).

Appeared in: **1916** Jimmy. **1918** The Divine Gift.

TULLY, JIM
Born: June 3, 1891, near St. Mary's, Ohio. Died: June 22, 1947, Hollywood, Calif. (heart attack). Novelist, screenwriter and screen actor.

Appeared in: **1930** Way for a sailor.

TUMARIN, BORIS
Born: 1911, Riga, Latvia. Died: Jan. 28, 1979, New York, N.Y. Screen, stage actor and stage director.

TUNC, IRENE
Born: 1938, France. Died: Jan., 1972, France? Screen actress.

Appeared in: **1967** Live for Life.

TUNIS, FAY
Born: 1890. Died: Dec. 4, 1967, Atlantic City, N.J. Screen and stage actress. Appeared in silent films.

TUNNEY, GENE (James Joseph Tunney)
Born: May 25, 1898, New York, N.Y. Died: Nov, 7, 1978, Greenwich, Conn. (blood poisoning). Former heavyweight boxing champion, author and screen actor.

Appeared in: **1922** The Tunney-Greb Boxing Match. **1926** The Fighting Marine (serial and feature film). **1968** The Legendary Champions (documentary).

TURLEIGH, VERONICA
Born: 1903, England. Died: Sept., 1971, England. Screen and stage actress.

Appeared in: **1952** The Card (aka The Promoter—US). **1958** The Horse's Mouth.

TURNBULL, JOHN
Born: Nov. 5, 1880, Dunbar, Scotland. Died: Feb. 23, 1956, England? Screen and stage actor.

Appeared in: **1933** The Private Life of Henry VIII; Ask Beccles. **1934** The Black Abbot; It's a Cop; Passing Shadows; Warn London; Tangled Evidence; The Lady Is Willing; The Night of the Party; The Girl in the Flat; What Happened to Harkness; Lord Edgware Dies; The Case for the Crown; Badger's Green. **1935** The Scarlet Pimpernel; Once in a Blue Moon; Big Ben Calling; The Lad; The Passing of the Third Floor Back (US 1936); Line Engaged; Black Mask; Sexton Blake and the Bearded Doctor. **1936** Nine Days a Queen; Rembrandt; The Amazing Quest of Ernest Bliss (aka Romance and Riches—US 1937); Shipmates O'Mine; Where There's a Will; Conquest of the Air; His Lordship (aka Man of Affairs—US 1937); The Limping Man. **1937** Song of the Road; It's a Grand Old World. **1938** Star of the Circus (aka Hidden Menace—US 1940); Night Alone. **1939** Inspector Hornleigh on Holiday; Dead Men are Dangerous. **1940** Spare a Copper; Three Silent Men. **1942** Hard Steel. **1944** Don't Take it to Heart (US 1949). **1945** A Place of One's Own (US 1949). **1946** Daybreak (US 1949). **1947** So Well Remembered. **1950** The Happiest Days of Your Life.

TURNER, BOWD M. (Bowditch M. Turner)
Born: 1878, Cumberland, Md. Died: Sept. 12, 1933, Hollywood, Calif. Screen and stage actor.

Appeared in: **1917** Little Shoes. **1918** Treat 'Em Rough; Coming of the

Law. **1919** Hell Roarin' Reform; Married in Haste. **1920** Are All Men Alike. **1921** Dangerous Moments; The Four Horsemen of the Apocalypse. **1922** Colleen of Pines. **1923** Scaramouche. **1924** The Ridin' Kid from Powder River. **1926** Volcano.

TURNER, DOROTHY
Born: May 12, 1895, England. Died: Apr. 5, 1969, London, England. Screen and stage actress. Mother of actor Nigel Patrick (dec. 1981).

TURNER, EMANUEL
Born: 1884. Died: Dec. 13, 1941, Hollywood, Calif. Screen and stage actor.

Appeared in: **1916** The Redemption of Dave Darcey. **1918** The Love Swindle.

TURNER, EVE *See* MILLER, EVE

TURNER, F. A. (Fred A. Turner)
Born: 1842 or 1866?, Boston, Mass. Died: Feb. 13, 1923. Screen and stage actor.

Appeared in: **1916** Atta Boy's Last Race; Children of the Feud; Intolerance. **1917** Madame Bo-Peep. **1920** The Jack-Knife Man.

TURNER, FLORENCE
Born: 1885, New York, N.Y. Died: Aug. 28, 1946, Woodland Hills, Calif. Screen, stage and vaudeville actress. She began her career on May 17, 1907, at Vitagraph Studies and was known only as "The Vitagraph Girl" and received no billing in early films.

Appeared in: **1910** The New Stenographer; St. Elmo; A Dixie Mother; A Tale of Two Cities. **1911** The Deerslayer; Intrepid Davy; The Wrong Patient; Answer of the Roses; Wig Wag; Auld Lang Syne; One Touch of Nature. **1912** Francesca de Rimini; Indian Romeo and Juliet; Jean Intervenes; How Mr. Bullington Ran the House; The Signal of Distress; Her Diary; Susie to Suzanne; Two Cinders; When Persistence and Obstinancy Meet; The Price of Silence; A Vitagraph Romance. **1913** Rose of Surrey; Jean's Evidence; The Younger Sister; The Lucky Stone; The Harper Mystery; Sisters All; Stenographer Trouble; Checkmated; Let 'Em Quarrel; Up and Down the Ladder; Pumps; Counselor Bobby; The Wings of a Moth. **1914** Creatures of Habit; The Murdock Trial; The Terrible Twins; Flotilla the Flirt; For Her People; Polly's Progress; Through the Valley of Shadows; The Shepherd Lassie of Argyle; Film Favourites (aka Florence Turner Impersonates Film Favorites—US); Snobs; Shopgirls—or, The Great Question; Daisy Doodad's Dial; One Thing After Another. **1915** As Ye Repent (aka Redeemed—US); Alone in London; My Old Dutch; Lost and Won (aka Odds Against); Far from the Madding Crowd; A Welsh Singer. **1916** Doorsteps; Grim Justice; East is East. **1920** The Ugly Duckling. **1921** All Dolled Up; Passion Fruit; The Old Wives' Tale. **1922** Was She Justified?; The Little Mother; Famour Poems by George R. Sims Series including: The Lights O'London; The Street Tumblers. **1923** Hornet's Nest; Sally Bishop. **1924** The Boatswain's Mate; Film Favourites (short); Women and Diamonds (aka Conscripts of Misfortune or It Happened in Africa). **1925** The Dark Angel; Never the Twain Shall Meet; The Mad Marriage; The Price of Success. **1926** Flame of the Argentine; The Last Alarm; Padlocked; The Gilded Highway. **1927** The Broken Gate; The Overland Stage; Stranded; College; The Cancelled Debts; Sally in Our Alley. **1928** Marry the Girl; The Law and the Man; Chinese Parrott; Walking Back; Jazzland; The Pace That Kills; The Road to Ruin. **1929** The Kid's Clever. **1930** The Rampant Age. **1932** The Sign of the Cross. **1943** Thousands Cheer.

TURNER, GEORGE
Born: Feb. 19, 1902, England. Died: July 27, 1968, England? Screen actor. Do not confuse with U.S. actor George Turner.

Appeared in: **1920** London Pride; The Biter Bit; The Duchess of Seven Dials. **1921** The Croxley Master. **1922** Running Water; Love's Influence; The Big Strong Man. **1923** Early Birds; Sally Bishop; Humming Birds; Jail Birds; Woman to Woman (US 1924); M'lord of the White Road. **1924** The Gay Corinthian; The Diamond Man; Nets of Destiny. **1929** White Cargo. **1931** The Lame Duck; A Safe Affair. **1933** The Man from Toronto; In Our Time; Britannia of Billingsgate; Forging Ahead. **1936** Playbox Adventure; Cafe Mascot; Full Speed Ahead; Twin Faces. **1937** Screen Struck. **1938** On the Top of the Underworld series including Receivers and The Kite Mob. **1940** Two Smart Men.

TURNER, MAIDEL
Born: May 12, 1888, Sherman, Tex. Died: Apr. 12, 1953, Ocean Springs, Miss. Screen and stage actress.

Appeared in: **1926** The Boy Friend. **1933** Another Language; The

Worst Woman in Paris; Olsen's Big Moment. **1934** Most Precious Thing in Life; It Happened One Night; The Life of Vergie Winters; Unknown Blonde; Money Means Nothing; Whom the Gods Destroy; A Modern Hero; Transcontinental Bus; The Perfect Clue; The Merry Frinks. **1935** Dr. Socrates; Life Returns; Splendour; Dante's Inferno; Mutiny Ahead; The Raven; Diamond Jim. **1936** Klondike Annie; Magnificent Obsession; Palm Springs; And Sudden Death; Make Way for a Lady. **1937** Slim; They Won't Forget. **1951** Here Comes the Groom.

TURNER, OTIS "DADDY"
Born: Nov. 29, 1862, Ind. Died: Mar. 28, 1918, Hollywood, Calif. (heart disease). Screen actor and film director.

TURNER, COL. ROSCOE
Born: 1896. Died: June 23, 1970, Indianapolis, Ind. Screen actor, stuntman, aviation pioneer and flying ace.

Appeared in: **1930** Hell's Angels. **1939** Flight at Midnight.

TURNER, WILLIAM H.
Born: 1861, Ireland. Died: Sept. 27, 1942, Philadelphia, Pa. Screen and stage actor. Married to actress Ann Vislaire.

Appeared in: **1916** Perils of Our Girl Reporters (serial). **1923** Blow Your Own Horn; Other Men's Daughters; The Satin Girl; The Darling of New York. **1924** The Enemy Sex; American Manners; The Garden of Weeds; Fast and Fearless; The Measure of a Man; The Gaiety Girl. **1925** The Phantom Bullet; The Pony Express; Gold and Grit; Heir-Loons; Where Was I?; White Thunder; A Woman's Faith. **1926** The Texas Streak; Three Pals; Her Big Adventure; Red Hot Leather; The Warning signal. **1927** Broadway After Midnight. **1928** Driftin' Sands. **1929** The Trespasser; The Last Performance. **1932** Love Me Tonight.

TURPIN, BEN (Bernard Turpin)
Born: Sept. 17, 1869, New Orleans, La. Died: July 1, 1940, Santa Monica, Calif. (heart disease). Screen, stage, burlesque and vaudeville actor. Married to actress Carrie LeMieux Turpin (dec. 1925) and later married to Babette E. Dietz (dec. 1978).

Appeared in: **1907** Ben Gets a Duck and is Ducked. **1909** Midnight Disturbance. **1914** Sweedie and the Lord; Sweedie and the Double Exposure; Sweedie's Skate; Sweedie Springs a Surprise; The Fickleness of Sweedie; She Landed a Big One; Sweedie and the Trouble Maker; Sweedie at the Fair; Madame Double X; Sweedie Learns to Swim. **1915** Hogan's Romance Upset; Hogan Out West; Social Splash; A Hash House Fraud; A Christmas Revenge; His New Job; A Night Out; Sweedie and Her Dog; Sweedie's Suicide; Two Hearts that Beat as Ten; Sweedie's Hopeless Love; Love and Trouble; Sweedie Learns to Ride; Sweedie Goes to College; Sweedie's Hero; Curiosity; The Clubman's Wager; A Coat Tale; Others Started but Sophie Finished; A Quiet Little Game; Sophie and the Fakir; The Merry Models; Snakeville's Hen Medic; Snakeville's Champion; Snakeville's Debutantes; Snakeville's Twins; How Slippery Slim Saw the Show; Two Bold, Bad Men; The Undertaker's Wife; A Bunch of Matches; The Bell Hop; Versus Sledge Hammers; Too Much Turkey; By the Sea; A Night Out. **1916** The Delinquent Bridegroom; Carmen; When Papa Died; His Blowout (aka The Plumber); The Iron Mitt; Hired and Fired (aka The Leading Man); A Deep Sea Liar (aka The Landlubber); For Ten Thousand Bucks; Some Liars; The Stolen Booking; Doctoring a Lead (aka A Total Loss); Poultry a la Mode (aka The Harem); Ducking a Discord; He Did and He Didn't; Picture Pirates; Shot in the Fracas; Jealous Jolts; The Wicked City; A Safe Proposition; Some Bravery; A Waiting Game; Taking the Count; National Nuts; Nailing on the Lid (aka Nailing a Lie); Just for a Kid; Lost and Found; Bungling Bill's Dress. **1917** Roping Her Romeo; Are Waitresses Safe?; Taming Target Center; A Circus Cyclone; The Musical Marvels; The Butcher's Nightmare; His Bogus Boast (aka A Cheerful Liar); A Studio Stampede; Frightened Flirts; Sole Mates; Why Ben Bolted (aka He Looked Crooked); Masked Mirth; Bucking the Tiger; Caught in the End; A Clever Dummy; Lost—a Cook; The Pawnbroker's Heart. **1918** She Loved Him Plenty; Sheriff Nell's Tussle; Saucy Madeline; The Battle Royal; Two Tough Tenderfeet; Hide and Seek, Detectives. **1919** Yankee Doodle in Berlin; East Lynne with Variations; Uncle Tom without a Cabin; Salome vs. Shenendoah; Cupid's Day Off; When Love Is Blind; No Mother to Guide Him; Sleuths; Whose Little Wife Are You? **1920** You Wouldn't Believe It (short); The Daredevil; Down on the Farm; Married Life; The Star Boarder (short). **1921** A Small Town Idol; Home Talent; Love's Outcast (short); Love and Doughnuts (short). **1922** Foolish Wives; plus the following shorts; Bright Eyes; Step Forward; Home-Made Movies. **1923** The Shriek of Araby; Hollywood; plus the following shorts: Where's My Wandering Boy Tonight?; Pitfalls of a Big City; Asleep at the Switch. **1924** The following shorts: Romeo and Juliet; Yukon Jake; Ten Dollars or Ten Days; The Hollywood Kid; Three Foolish Weeks; The Reel Virginian. **1925** Hogan's Alley; plus the following shorts: Wild Goose Chaser; Rasberry Romance; The Marriage Circus. **1926** Steele Preferred; plus the following shorts: A Harem Knight; A Blonde's Revenge; When a Man's a Prince; A Prodigal Bridegroom. **1927** The College Hero; A Woman's Way; plus the following shorts: The Pride of Pickeville; Broke in China; A Hollywood Hero; The Jolly Jilter; Love's Languid Lure; Daddy Boy. **1928** The Wife's Relations. **1929** Show of Shows; The Love Parade. **1930** Swing High. **1931** Cracked Nuts; Our Wife (short). **1932** Make Me a Star; Million Dollar Legs; Hypnotized. **1932-33** Paramount shorts. **1934** Law of the Wild (serial). **1935** Keystone Hotel (short); Bring 'Em Back a Lie (short). **1939** Hollywood Cvalcade. **1940** Saps at Sea. **1949** Down Memory Lane (documentary). **1951** Memories of Famous Hollywood Comedians (documentary). **1957** The Golden Age of Comedy (documentary). **1960** When Comedy Was King (documentary). **1961** Days of Thrills and Laughter (documentary). **1968** The Funniest Man in the World (documentary).

TURPIN, CARRIE (Carrie LeMieux)
Born: 1882, Quebec, Canada. Died: Oct. 3, 1925, Beverly Hills, Calif. Screen and stage actress. Married to actor Ben Turpin (dec. 1940).

Appeared in: **1915** Others Started but Sophie Finished; Too Much Turkey; Snakeville's Hen Medic; The Merry Models. **1917** The Bogus Boast (aka A Cheerful Liar).

TUTMARC, PAUL H.
Died: Sept. 23, 1972, Seattle, Wash. Musician, singer and screen actor. Reported inventor of the electric guitar.

TUTTLE, WILSON
Born: 1912. Died: Jan. 6, 1960, Hollywood, Calif. Screen, stage and radio actor. Married to actress Alice Frost.

TWEDDELL, FRANK
Born: 1895, India. Died: Dec. 20, 1971, New Haven, Conn. Screen and stage actor.

Appeared in: **1943** Claudia (stage and screen versions). **1946** Claudia and David. **1949** The Undercover Man. **1950** The Tattooed Stranger. **1951** I'd Climb the Highest Mountain. **1956** Carousel.

TWEED, TOMMY
Born: 1907, Canada. Died: Oct. 12, 1971, Canada. Screen actor and writer.

Appeared in: **1963** The Incredible Journey.

TWELVETREES, HELEN (Helen Jurgens)
Born: Dec. 25, 1908, Brooklyn, N.Y. Died: Feb. 14, 1958, Harrisburg, Pa. (accidental overdose of drugs for kidney ailment). Screen and stage actress.

Appeared in: **1929** The Ghost Talks (film debut); True Heart; Blue Skies; Paris to Bagdad; Words and Music. **1930** Her Man; The Grand Parade; Swing High; The Cat Creeps. **1931** Beyond Victory; The Painted Desert; A Woman of Experience; Bad Company; Millie; Cardigan's Last Case. **1932** Panama Flo; Young Bride; Is My Face Red?; State's Attorney; Unashamed. **1933** A Bedtime Story; Disgraced; My Woman; King for a Night. **1934** All Men Are Enemies; Now I'll Tell; She Was a Lady. **1935** One Hour Late; Times Square Lady; She Gets Her Man; 'Frisco Waterfront; Spanish Cape Mystery. **1936** Thoroughbred. **1937** Hollywood Round Up. **1939** Persons in Hiding; Unmarried.

TWERP, JOE (Joseph Boyes)
Born: 1910. Died: Dec. 15, 1980, North Hollywood, Calif. Screen, radio actor, screenwriter and television writer.

Appeared in: **1935** Mary Burns—Fugitive. **1936** At Sea Ashore (short). **1937** The Woman I Love. **1938** In Old Chicago; Kentucky Moonshire; All-American Sweetheart.

TWITCHELL, A. R. "ARCHIE" (Michael Brandon)
Born: Nov. 28, 1906, Pendleton, Ore. Died: Jan. 31, 1957, Pacoima, Calif. (mid-air collision). Screen actor.

Appeared in: **1937** Daughters of Shanghai; Souls at Sea; Partners in Crime; Hold 'Em, Navy; Sophie Lang Goes West. **1938** You and Me; Her Jungle Love; Tip-Off Girls; Cocoanut Grove; Spawn of the North; The Texans; Illegal Traffic; Give Me a Sailor. **1939** Ambush; King of Chinatown; Mickey the Kid; Geronimo. **1940** The Mysterious Mr. Satan (serial); I Want a Divorce; Granny Get Your Gun; Dr. Kildare Goes Home; Charlie Chan at the Wax Museum; Young Bill Hickok; Behind the News. **1941** I Wanted Wings; West Point Widow; Among the Living; Prairie Stranger; Thundering Hoofs. **1942** Heart Burn (short); Home Work (short); A Tragedy at Midnight. **1945** The Missing Corpse. **1946** Angel On My Shoulder; Affairs of Geraldine; The French Key; Accomplice. **1947** The Arnelo Affair; Second Chance; Robin Hood in Texas; Web of Danger. **1948** The Saxon Charm. **1949** Follow Me Quietly. **1950** Sunset Boulevard; Revenue Agent. **1951** Kentucky Jubilee; Yes Sir, Mr. Bones. **1954** The Bounty Hunter. **1955** Illegal.

TYKE, JOHN
Born: 1895. Died: Feb. 23, 1940, Hollywood, Calif. Screen actor and extra. Entered films in 1924.

TYLER, DALLAS
Born: 1878. Died: July 25, 1953, Philadelphia, Pa. Screen and stage actress. Married to stage actor Roy Fairchild (dec.).

Appeared in: **1914** The Toll Love.

TYLER, GLADYS C.
Born: 1893. Died: Apr. 14, 1972, Hollywood, Calif. Screen and stage actress. Married to actor Harry Tyler (dec. 1961).

TYLER, HARRY
Born: 1888. Died: Sept. 15, 1961, Hollywood, Calif. (cancer). Screen, stage and television actor. Married to actress Gladys Tyler (dec. 1972).

Appeared in: **1929** The Shannons of Broadway; Oh, Yeah! **1930** Big Money. **1933** Poor Fish (short). **1934** The St. Louis Kid; Midnight Alibi; Friends of Mr. Sweeney; Housewife; The Case of the Howling Dog; Babbitt. **1935** Black Fury; The Glass Key; Lady Tubbs; Men Without Names; A Night at the Opera. **1936** Two-Fisted Gentlemen; The Man I Marry; Pennies from Heaven; Three Wise Guys; The Devil Is a Sissy. **1937** Wake Up and Live; The Girl Said No; Don't Tell the Wife; Love Takes Flight; Mr. Boggs Steps Out; Jim Hanvey—Detective; Youth on Parole; Midnight Madonna. **1938** Penny's Picnic (short). **1939** The Story of Alexander Graham Bell; Jesse James; The Lady's from Kentucky; 20,000 Men a Year; Young Mr. Lincoln; The Gracie Allen Murder Case. **1940** Brigham Young—Frontiersman; Andy Hardy Meets a Debutante; Little Old New York; Johnny Apollo; Young People; Meet the Missus; Behind the News; The Grapes of Wrath; Go West. **1941** The Bride Wore Crutches; The Richest Man in Town; Tillie the Toiler; Remember the Day; Tobacco Road. **1942** The Mexican Spitfire Sees a Ghost; Wedded Blitz (short). **1943** Dixie; True to Life; The Dancing Masters. **1944** See Here, Private Hargrove; Cassanova in Burlesque; The Adventures of Mark Twain; Atlantic City; Wilson; Love Your Landlord (short); Movie Pests (short). **1945** Identity Unknown; The Woman Who Came Back; Abbott and Costello in Hollywood. **1946** Behind Green Lights; The Fabulous Suzanne; I Ring Doorbells; Johnny Comes Flying Home; Somewhere in the Night. **1947** Fun on a Weekend; Sarge Goes to College; Winter Wonderland; Heading for Heaven. **1948** Smart Politics; Deep Waters; Strike It Rich; The Untamed Breed; That Wonderful Urge. **1949** Joe Palooka in the Big Fight; Air Hostess; Beautiful Blonde from Bashful Bend; Hellfire. **1950** Lucky Losers; Rider from Tucson; The Traveling Saleswoman; A Woman of Distinction. **1951** The Lemon Drop Kid; Bedtime for Bonzo; Texans Never Cry; Corky of Gasoline Alley; Santa Fe. **1952** Deadline, U.S.A.; The Quiet Man; This Woman Is Dangerous; Wagons West; Lost in Alaska. **1953** The Glass Web. **1954** Witness to Murder. **1955** Guys and Dolls; Jail Busters; A Lawless Street; The Naked Street; Texas Lady; Abbott and Costello Meet the Keystone Kops. **1956** These Wilder Years; A Day of Fury; Glory. **1957** Plunder Road. **1958** Last Hurrah.

TYLER, JUDY
Born: 1933. Died: July 3, 1957, near Billy-the-Kid, Wyo. (auto crash). Screen actress and singer.

Appeared in: **1957** Bop Girl (aka Bop Girl Goes Calypso); Jailhouse Rock.

TYLER, TOM (Vincent Marko, or Markoski)
Born: Aug, 8, 1903, New York, N.Y. Died: May 1, 1954, Hamtramck, Mich. Screen actor. One of the "Three Mesquiteers." Voted top money-making western star in pictures in Herald-Fame Poll, 1942.

Appeared in: **1925** The Cowboy Musketeer; Let's Go Gallagher; The Wyoming Wildcat. **1926** The Cowboy Cop; Red Hot Hoofs; The Arizona Streak; Born to Battle; The Masquerade Bandit; Out of the West; Tom and His Pals; Wild to Go. **1927** The Sonora Kid; Cyclone of the Range; The Cherokee Kid; The Flying U Ranch; The Desert Pirate; Lightning Lariats; Splitting the Breeze; Tom's Gang. **1928** Phantom of the Range; Terror Mountain; The Avenging Rider; Terror; The Texas Tornado; Tyrant of Red Gulch; When the Law Rides. **1929** The Sorcerer; Trail of the Horse Thieves; Gun Law; Idaho Red; Pride of Pawnee; The Lone Horseman; The Man from Nevada; The Phantom

Rider; 'Neath Western Skies; Law of the Plains. **1930** Call of the Desert; The Canyon of Missing Men; Pioneers of the West. **1931** The Phantom of the West (serial); A Man from Death Valley; Rider of the Plains; Galloping Through; West of Cheyenne; Rose of the Rio Grande; God's Country and the Man; Battling with Buffalo Bill (serial); Partners of the Trail. **1932** Jungle Mystery (serial); The Tenderfoot; Man from New Mexico; Single-Handed Sanders; Two-Fisted Justice; Honor of the Mounted; Vanishing Men; The Forty-Niners; prior to 1933: Half Pint Polly (short). **1933** War of the Range; When a Man Rides Alone; Deadwood Pass; Clancy of the Mounted (serial); The Phantom of the Air. **1934** Riding Through; Tracy Rides; Riding the Lonesome Trail; Mystery Ranch; Fighting Hero; Terror of the Plains. **1935** The Silent Code; Unconquered Bandit; Powdersmoke Range. **1936** Fast Bullets; Roamin' Wild; The Last Outlaw. **1937** Lost Ranch. **1938** Pinto Rustlers; Orphan of the Pecos; King of Alcatraz. **1939** Drums Along the Mohawk; The Night Riders; Frontier Marshal; The Westerner; Stagecoach; Gone With the Wind. **1940** The Lights of the Western Stars; Brother Orchid; Cherokee Strip; The Mummy's Hand. **1941** Buck Privates; Texas Rangers Ride Again; Border Vigilantes; West of Cimarron; Outlaws of Cherokee Trail; Riders of the Timberline; Gauchos of El Dorado; The Adventures of Captain Marvel (serial). **1942** Code of the Outlaw; Raiders of the Range; Westward Ho; The Talk of the Town; Valley of the Hunted Men; The Phantom Plainsmen; Valley of the Sun. **1943** The Phantom (serial); Wagon Tracks West; Shadows on the Sage; Thundering Trails; Blocked Trail; Riders of the Rio Grande; Santa Fe Scouts; Sylvester the Great. **1944** Boss of Boomtown; Ladies of Washington. **1945** San Antonio; Sing Me a Song of Texas. **1946** Never Say Goodbye; Badmen's Territory. **1947** Cheyenne. **1948** Red Ryder; The Dude Goes West; Return of the Bad Men; Blood on the Moon; The Golden Eye. **1949** Samson and Delilah; The Younger Brothers; For Those Who Dare; Hellfire; Beautiful Blonde from Bashful Bend; I Shot Jesse James; Lust for Gold; Masked Raiders; Square Dance Jubilee; She Wore a Yellow Ribbon. **1950** Colorado Ranger; Crooked River; Fast on the Draw; Hostile Country; Marshal of Heldorado; Rio Grande Patrol; West of the Brazos. **1951** The Great Missouri Raid; Best of the Badmen. **1952** What Price Glory?; Road Agent. **1953** Cow Country.

TYNAN, BRANDON
Born: 1879, Dublin, Ireland. Died: Mar. 19, 1967, New York, N.Y. Screen, stage actor and playwright. Married to actress Lily Cahill (dec. 1955).

Appeared in: **1923** Loyal Lives; Success. **1924** Unrestrained Youth. **1937** Parnell; Sh! The Octopus; Wells Fargo. **1938** The Girl of the Golden West; Youth Takes a Fling; Nancy Drew; Detective. **1939** The Great Man Votes; Lady and the Mob; The Lone Wolf Spy Hunt. **1940** It All Came True; Lucky Partners; Rangers of Fortune. **1941** Marry the Boss's Daughter.

TYNAN, KENNETH (Kenneth Peacock)
Born: Apr. 2, 1927, Birmingham, England. Died: July 26, 1980, Santa Monica, Calif. (pulmonary emphysema). Critic, author, playwright, stage director and screen actor. Divorced from Elaine Dundy and later married to author Kathleen Halton. Father of filmmaker Tracy Tynan.

Appeared in: **1970** Freedom to Love.

TYREE, JACK
Born: 1944. Died: Aug. 25, 1981, Los Angeles, Calif. (results of injuries sustained after fall while filming). Stuntman.

Appeared in: **1968** Planet of the Apes. **1980** Airplane. **1982** The Sword and the Sorcerer.

TYRELL, JOHN E. (John E. Tyrrell)
Born: Dec. 7, 1902, New York, N.Y. Died: Sept. 19, 1949, Calif. Screen, stage and vaudeville actor. Married to actress Gretta Fink.

Appeared in: **1936** The Final Hour (film debut); Legion of Terror; Lady from Nowhere. **1937** Counterfeit Lady; Motor Madness; Girls Can Play; The Frame-Up; The Game that Kills; Criminals of the Air. **1938** Women in Prison; The Main Event; West of Cheyenne; Call of the Rockies; Pie a la Maid (short). **1939** The Man They Could Not Hang; plus the following shorts: Rattling Romeo; Skinny the Moocher; Andy Clyde Gets Spring Chicken. **1940** Thundering Frontier; Girls Under 21; Fireman, Save My Choo Choo (short); Blazing Six Shooters; My Son is Guilty. **1941** I Was a Prisoner on Devil's Island; Richest Man in Town; Mystery Ship; In the Sweet Pie and Pie (short); The Face Behind the Mask; The Phantom Submarine. **1942** Three Smart Saps (short); Sabotage Squad; Tramp, Tramp, Tramp; Harvard, Here I Come; Canal Zone. **1944** To Heir is Human (short); The Ghost That Walks Alone; Defective Detectives (short); Cry of the Werewolf; Sagebrush Heroes; Cowboy from Lonesome River. **1945** Sergeant Mike; Rough, Tough and Ready. **1946** The Blonde Stayed On (short).

TZIMEAS, JOHN (aka JOHN ZIMEAS)
Died: May 31, 1978. Screen actor.

Appeared in: **1960** House of Usher.

UDVARDY, TIBOR
Born: 1914, Hungary. Died: July 17, 1981, Budapest, Hungary (heart attack). Opera singer and screen actor.

UHLIG, MAX E.
Born: 1896. Died: May 28, 1958, North Tarrytown, N.Y. Screen actor. Appeared in silents.

ULMER, ANNA
Born: 1853. Died: Oct. 28, 1928, Peak Island, Maine. Screen and stage actress.

ULMER, EDGAR (Edgar George Ulmer)
Born: Sept. 17, 1900, Vienna, Austria. Died: Sept. 30, 1972, Woodland Hills, Calif. Screen actor, film producer, director, stage designer, screenwriter and author. Made Yiddish and Ukrainian films.

ULRIC, LENORE
Born: July 21, 1892, New Ulm, Minn. Died: Dec. 30, 1970, Orangeburg, N.Y. Screen and stage actress. Divorced from actor Sidney Blackmer (dec. 1973).

Appeared in: **1915** Kilmeny; The Better Woman. **1916** Intrigue; The Heart of Paula. **1923** Tiger Rose. **1925** Capital Punishment. **1929** Frozen Justice; South Sea Rose. **1936** Camille. **1940** The Fifth Column. **1946** Temptation; Two Smart People; Notorious. **1947** Northwest Outpost; Anthony and Cleopatra.

"UNCLE MURRAY" *See* PARKER, MURRAY

UNDERHILL, GEOFF
Born: 1927, Australia. Died: May 9, 1978, Sydney, Australia (heart attack). Screen, stage actor, stage director and screenwriter.

UNDERHILL, JOHN G.
Born: Apr. 26, 1870, New York, N.Y. Died: May 26, 1941, Calif. Screen actor and film director.

Appeared in: **1913** Dead Alive. **1921** Hush.

UNDERWOOD, FRANKLIN
Born: 1877, Denver, Colo. Died: Dec. 22, 1940, New York, N.Y. Screen, stage actor and story editor. Married to actress Frances Slosson.

Appeared in: **1928** The News Parade.

UNDERWOOD, LAWRENCE
Born: 1871, Albion, Iowa. Died: Feb. 2, 1939, Los Angeles, Calif. Screen, stage actor, film, stage director and screenwriter.

Appeared in: **1920** Old Lady 31. **1925** Passionate Youth; Thundering Through. **1926** Twisted Triggers. **1927** The Phantom Buster.

UNDERWOOD, LOYAL
Born: 1893, Rockford, Ill. Died: Sept. 30, 1966. Screen actor.

Appeared in: **1921** Lucky Carson. **1923** My American Wife; The Pilgrim. **1925** The Dixie Handicap. **1927** Shootin' Irons.

UPCHER, PETER
Born: 1892, Halesworth, Staffordshire, England. Died: Dec., 1962, London, England. Screen and stage actor.

Appeared in: **1920** Mr. Gilfil's Love Story; The Yellow Claw. **1921** The Right to Love.

UPDEGRAFF, HENRY
Born: 1889. Died: July 29, 1936, Hollywood, Calif. (heart attack). Stage and screen actor.

UPTON, FRANCES
Born: 1904. Died: Nov. 27, 1975, Philadelphia, Pa. Screen and stage actor.

Appeared in: **1930** Night Work.

URBAN, DOROTHY K.
Born: 1869. Died: Oct. 29, 1961, Hollywood, Calif. Screen, stage and vaudeville actress.

Appeared in: **1940** The Fight for Life.

URBANSKY, YEVGENY (aka EVGENY URBANSKY)
Born: 1931, Russia. Died: Nov. 5, 1965, Kyzyl-Kum Desert, Central Asia (auto accident). Stage and screen actor.

Appeared in: **1960** Ballad of a Soldier. **1961** The Letter That Was Never Sent. **1963** Cristoe Nebo (Clear Skies). Other Russian film, Kommunist.

URCELAY, NICOLAS
Born: 1920, Yucatan, Mexico. Died: July 3, 1959, Tampico, Mexico. Screen, stage, television, vaudeville actor and singer.

URE, MARY
Born: Feb. 18, 1933, Glasgow, Scotland. Died: Apr. 3, 1975, London, England (an accidental mixing of alcohol and tranquilzers). Screen, stage and television actress. Divorced from playwright John Osborne and later married to actor/playwright Robert Shaw (dec. 1978). Nominated for 1960 Academy Award for Best Supporting Actress in Sons and Lovers.

Appeared in: **1955** Storm Over the Nile (US 1956—film debut). **1957** Windom's Way (US 1958). **1959** Look Back in Anger. **1960** Sons and Lovers. **1962** The Mind Benders (US 1963). **1964** The Luck of Ginger Coffey. **1968** Where Eagles Dare (US 1969); Custer of the West. **1973** A Reflection of Fear.

URECAL, MINERVA
Born: 1894. Died: Feb., 1966, Glendale, Calif. (heart attack). Screen, radio and television actress.

Appeared in: **1934** Sadie McKee. **1935** Bonnie Scotland. **1936** God's Country and the Woman; Fury. **1937** Ever Since Eve; Live, Love and Learn; Behind the Mike; Her Husband's Secretary; Love in a Bungalow; Life Begins With Love; The Go Getter; Oh, Doctor; Exiled to Shanghai. **1938** Start Cheering; Prison Nurse; Frontier Scout; Air Devils; In Old Chicago; Wives Under Suspicion. **1939** Irving Berlin's Second Fiddle; Golden Boy; Little Accident; Destry Rides Again; Maid to Order (short). **1940** You Can't Fool Your Wife; Boys of the City; No, No Nanette. **1941** Man at Large; Arkansas Judge; The Cowboy and the Blonde; Accent on Love; Murder by Invitation; Never Give a Sucker an Even Break. **1942** Henry and Dizzy; Sweater Girl; Quiet Please, Murder; The Corpse Vanishes; That Other Woman; The Living Ghost; Sons of the Pioneers; My Favorite Blonde; Man in the Trunk. **1943** Riding through Nevada; The Ape Man; White Savage; Kid Dynamite; Ghosts on the Loose; So This Is Washington; Hit the Ice. **1944** Mr. Skeffington; When Strangers Marry; Louisiana Hayride; Moonlight and Cactus; County Fair; Crazy Knights; The Bridge of San Luis Rey. **1945** The Bells of St. Mary's; A Medal for Benny; Wanderer of the Wasteland; Alibi Baby (short); The Men in Her Diary; Who's Guilty? (serial); State Fair. **1946** Without Reservations; Sioux City Sue; The Virginian; Wake Up and Dream; Rainbow over Texas; Dark Corner; Sensation Hunters. **1947** The Trap; The Lost Moment; Ladies Man; Hired Husband (short); Saddle Pals; Apache Rose. **1948** Family Honeymoon; Fury of Furnace Creek; Sitting Pretty; Secret Service Investigator; Variety Time; Good Sam; The Snake Pit; Marshal of Amarillo; Sundown at Santa Fe; The Noose Hangs High. **1949** The Loveable Cheat; Master Minds; Holiday in Havana; Outcasts of the Trail. **1950** Harvey; Mister 880; Arizona Cowboy; Quicksand; Traveling Saleswoman; My Blue Heaven; The Jackpot. **1951** Blonde Atom Bomb (short); Texans Never Cry; Stop That Cab. **1952** Aaron Slick from Punkin' Crick; Oklahoma Annie; Gobs and Gals; Anything Can Happen; Lost in Alaska; Harem Girl. **1953** The Woman They Almost Lynched; Niagara; Two Gun Marshal. **1955** Sudden Danger; So You Want to Be a V.I.P. (short). **1956** Miracle in the Rain; Tugboat Annie; Crashing Las Vegas. **1957** A Man Alone. **1960** The Adventures of Huckleberry Finn. **1962** Mr. Hobbs Takes a Vacation. **1964** Seven Faces of Dr. Lao. **1965** That Funny Feeling.

URQUHART, ALASDAIR
Born: 1914, Scotland. Died: Aug. 25, 1954, Glasgow, Scotland. Stage and screen actor. Brother of actress Molly Urquhart.

Appeared in: **1953** Rob Roy; The Highland Rogue.

URQUHART, GORDON (Gordon John Urquhart)
Born: 1922. Died: Oct., 1957, Los Angeles, Calif. (cancer). Screen, radio actor and screenwriter. Married to actress Peggy Middleton.

Appeared in: **1956** Female Jungle.

URQUHART, MOLLY (Mary Sinclair Urguhart)
Born: 1906, Glasgow, Scotland. Died: Oct. 6, 1977, Glasgow, Scotland. Screen and stage actress.

Appeared in: **1950** Portrait of Clare. **1951** Happy Go Lovely. **1955** Geordie (aka Wee Geordie—US 1956). **1956** Yield to the Night (aka Blonde Sinner—US). **1957** Doctor at Large. **1960** The Sundowners. **1964** Behold a Pale Horse. **1966** A Man for all Seasons. **1974** The Black Windmill; Digby, The Biggest Dog in the World. **1977** Julia.

URSON, FRANK B.
Born: 1887, Chicago, Ill. Died: Aug. 17, 1928, Niles, Mich. (drowned). Screen actor, film director and producer.

Appeared in: **1913** Her Gallant Knights.

URZI, SARO

Born: 1913, Catania, Italy. Died: Nov. 2, 1979, San Giuseppe Vesuviano, Italy (heart attack). Screen actor and production supervisor.

Appeared in: **1950** In Nome Della Legge (In the Name of the Law, aka Mafia); Il Cammino Della Speranza (The Road of Hope—US 1952). **1952** Streets of Sorrow. **1954** Mistress of the Mountains; Beat the Devil. **1957** Marchands de Filles (Sellers of Girls—US 1967). **1958** Nella Citta L'inferno (aka ... and the Wild, Wild Women—US 1961). **1959** Un Maledetto Imbroglio (The Facts of Murder—US 1965). **1960** El Figlio del Corsaro Rosso (Son of the Red Corsair—US 1963). **1961** Les Filles Sement le Vent (The Girls Seed the Wind, aka The Fruit is Ripe—US); Liane Die Weisse Sklavin (Liane, The White Slave, aka Nature Girl and the Slaver—US). **1964** Sedotta e Abbandonata (Seduced and Abandoned). **1965** Le Corniaud (The Sucker—US 1966); El Ferrovier (aka Man of Iron, and aka The Railroad Man—US). **1966** Modesty Blaise. **1967** La Route de Corinthe (aka Who's Got the Black Box?—US 1970). **1968** Serafino (US 1970). **1973** Alfredo, Alfredo.

USHER, GUY

Born: 1875. Died: June 16, 1944, San Diego, Calif. Screen and stage actor.

Appeared in: **1933** This Day and Age (film debut); Little Giant; Tugboat Annie; Fast Worker; The Mystery Man; Face in the Sky. **1934** The St. Louis Kid; The Man With Two Faces; All of Me; Good Dame; The Witching Hour; The Hell Cat; Kid Millions. **1935** Grand Exit; Mills of the Gods; Hold 'Em Yale; The Crusades; Make a Million; Little Big Shot; The Goose and the Gander; It's a Gift; Naughty Marietta. **1936** Fury; Dangerous Waters; Postal Inspector; The President's Mystery; The Case of the Black Cat; King of Hockey; Charlie Chan at the Opera. **1937** Marked Woman; Once a Doctor; White Bondage; Nancy Steele Is Missing; Boots and Saddles; The Mighty Treve; Sophie Lang Goes West; Boy of the Streets. **1938** State Police; Under Western Stars; Romance of the Limberlost; Spawn of the North. **1939** Union Pacific; Buck Rogers (serial); Timber Stampede; Invitation to Happiness; Rovin' Tumbleweeds; The Renegade Ranger; Mister Wong in Chinatown. **1940** Passport to Alcatraz; Doomed to Die. **1941** Meet John Doe; Lady for a Night; Ridin' on a Rainbow; West of Cimarron; No Greater Sin. **1942** Mummy's Tomb; Bells of Capistrano; Shepherd of the Ozarks; I Was Framed; Bad Men of the Hills. **1943** Lost Canyon.

USHER, HARRY

Born: 1887. Died: Oct. 28, 1950, Hollywood, Calif. (heart attack). Screen and vaudeville actor. Appeared in vaudeville with his wife, Frances Usher.

UTTAL, FRED

Born: 1905. Died: Nov. 28, 1963. Radio announcer and screen extra.

VACCARO, FRANK A.

Born: 1884. Died: July 6, 1948, Derby, Conn. Silent screen actor.

VACKOVA, JARMILA

Born: 1908. Died: Sept. 26, 1971, Santa Monica, Calif. Screen actress. Appeared in U.S. and European films.

VAGUE, VERA (Barbara Jo Allen)

Born: 1904. Died: Sept. 14, 1974, Santa Barbara, Calif. Screen, stage, radio and television actress.

Appeared in: **1938** Major Difficulties (short). **1939** Kennedy the Great (short); Ring Madness. **1940** Sing, Dance, Plenty Hot; Melody and Moonlight; Melody Ranch; Village Barn Dance. **1941** Buy Me That Town; Kiss the Boys Goodbye; The Mad Doctor; Ice-Capades. **1942** Larceny, Inc; Hi Neighbor; Design for Scandal; Mrs. Wiggs of the Cabbage Patch; Priorities on Parade. **1943** You Dear Boy (short); Swing Your Partner; Get Going. **1944** Henry Aldrich Plays Cupid; Rosie the Riveter; Moon Over Las Vegas; Lake Placid Serenade; Girl Rush; Doctor, Feel My Pulse (short); Cowboy Canteen. **1946** Earl Carroll Sketchbook; Snafu. **1950** Square Dance Katy. **1956** Mohawk; The Opposite Sex. **1959** Sleeping Beauty; Born to Be Loved.

VAIL, LESTER

Born: Nov. 28, 1900, Denver, Colo. Died: Nov. 28, 1959, Los Angeles, Calif. Screen, stage, television actor, film and television director.

Appeared in: **1931** Dance, Fools, Dance; It's a Wise Child; Beau Ideal; I Take This Woman; Murder by the Clock; The Woman Between; Consolation Marriage. **1932** Big Town.

VAIL, MYRTLE

Born: 1888, Joliet, Ill. Died: Sept. 18, 1978, Kansas City, Mo. Screen, vaudeville and radio actress. Married to stage actor George Damerel (dec. 1936). Mother of actress Donna Damerel (dec. 1941), with whom she appeared on radio and film as "Myrt" in the "Myrt and Marge" series.

Appeared in: **1934** Myrt and Marge. **1958** The Little Shop of Horrors. **1959** Bucket of Blood.

VAIL, OLIVE

Born: 1904. Died: June 14, 1951, Cincinnati, Ohio. Screen, stage and vaudeville actress.

Appeared in: **1947** The Spirit of Notre Dame.

VALDEMAR, TANIA

Born: 1904. Died: Nov. 12, 1955, New York, N.Y. Screen, stage actress and ballet dancer.

VALDEZ, MIGUELITO

Born: 1916, Cuba. Died: Nov. 9, 1978, Bogota, Columbia. Screen actor and singer.

VALE, LOUISE

Born: New York, N.Y. Died: Oct. 28, 1918, Madison, Wis. Screen and stage actress. Married to actor-director Travers Vale (dec. 1927).

Appeared in: **1913** The Code of the U.S.A. **1914** Daybreak; The Iron Master. **1915** Jane Eyre; Dwellers in Glass Houses; The Confession; The Americano; Adam Bede; The Quicksands of Society; The Maid O' the Mountains; Under Two Flags; Man and His Master; The Drab Sister; The Soul of Pierre; Harvest; Between Father and Son; The Reproach of Annesley; The Hungarian Nabob; The Woman of Mystery. **1916** A Beast of Society; The Science of Crime; The Sex Lure; The Honor of the Law. **1917** Easy Money. **1918** The Witch Woman; Journey's End; Vengeance.

VALE, TRAVERS

Born: 1873, Australia. Died: Jan. 10, 1927, Hollywood, Calif. Screen, stage actor, film director, stage director and producer. Married to actress Louise Vale (dec. 1918). Entered films as an actor with Biograph Co.

VALEDON, LORA

Born: 1884. Died: Sept. 15, 1946, Providence, R.I. Screen, vaudeville, actress, film stuntwoman and circus performer.

VALEN, RITCHIE

Born: 1941. Died: Feb. 3, 1959 (plane crash). Screen actor and singer.

Appeared in: **1959** Go, Johnny, Go!

VALENTINE, ELIZABETH

Born: 1887. Died: July 23, 1971. Screen actress.

Appeared in: **1942** Kings Row. **1943** Santa Fe Scouts; The Underdog. **1963** Kiss of the Vampire.

VALENTINE, GRACE

Born: 1890, Springfield, Ohio. Died: Nov. 14, 1964, New York, N.Y. Stage and screen actress. Married to actor Wayne Nunn (dec. 1948).

Appeared in: **1916** The Brand of Cowardice; The Evil Thereof; Dorian's Divorce. **1917** Babbling Tongues. **1921** A Man's Home. **1929** The Phantom in the House. **1932** Silver Lining.

VALENTINO, ALBERTO G. (Alberto Gugielmi Valentino)

Born: 1892, Rome, Italy. Died: June 4, 1981, Los Angeles, Calif. Screen actor and dialog writer. Brother of actor Rudolph Valentino (dec. 1926).

Appeared in: **1928** Tropic Madness. **1929** China Slaver.

VALENTINO, MRS. JEAN ACKER See ACKER, JEAN

VALENTINO, RUDOLPH (Rudolph Guglielimo)

Born: May 6, 1895, Castellaneta, Italy. Died: Aug. 23, 1926, New York, N.Y. (complications following operation—peritonitis). Screen actor and dancer. Brother of actor Alberto Valentino (dec. 1981). Divorced from actress Jean Acker (dec. 1978) and Natacha Rambova (aka Winifred Hudnut—dec. 1966).

Appeared in: **1914** My Official Wife. **1916** Patria. **1918** Alimony; A Society Sensation; All Night. **1919** The Delicious Little Devil; A Rogue's Romance; The Homebreaker; Virtuous Sinners; The Big Little

Person; Out of Luck; Eyes of Youth. **1920** The Married Virgin; An Adventuress; The Cheater; Once to Every Woman; Passion's Playground; Stolen Moments; The Wonderful Chance. **1921** The Four Horsemen of the Apocalypse; Unchained Seas; Camille; The Conquering Power; The Sheik. **1922** Moran of the Lady Letty; Beyond the Rocks; The Young Rajah; Blood and Sand; The Isle of Love. **1924** Monsieur Beaucaire; A Sainted Devil. **1925** The Eagle; Cobra. **1926** Son of the Sheik.

VALERIO, ALBANO
Born: 1889, San Jose, Calif. Died: Feb. 2, 1961, Los Angeles, Calif. Screen actor.

Appeared in: **1926** The Loves of Ricardo (and 1928 version). **1960** Can-Can.

VALK, FREDERICK
Born: 1901, Germany or Czechoslovakia. Died: July 23, 1956, London, England. Screen and stage actor.

Appeared in: **1940** Gasbags; Night Train to Munich (aka Gestapo and aka Night Train—US); Neutral Port. **1941** The Patient Vanishes (aka This Man is Dangerous—US 1947); Dangerous Moonlight (aka Suicide Squadron—US 1942). **1942** Thunder Rock (US 1944). **1944** Hotel Reserve (US 1946). **1945** Dead of Night; Latin Quarter. **1947** Mrs. Fitzherbert (US 1950). **1948** Saraband for Dead Lovers (aka Saraband—US 1949). **1949** Dear Mr. Prohack (US 1950). **1951** The Magic Box (US 1952); Outcast of the Islands. **1952** Top Secret (aka Mr. Potts Goes to Moscow—US 1954). **1953** Never Let Me Go; Albert RN (aka Break to Freedom—US 1955); The Flanagan Boy (aka Bad Blonde—US). **1955** The Colditz Story (US 1957); Secret Venture; I Am a Camera. **1956** Wicked As They Come (US 1957); Magic Fire; Zarak.

VALKYRIEN, VALDA
Born: 1894. Died: Oct. 22, 1956, Los Angeles, Calif. Screen actress and ballet dancer.

Appeared in: **1915** Youth. **1916** Hidden Valley.

VALLECA, FRED
Born: 1912. Died: July 6, 1978. Professional boxer and screen actor.

VALLEE, FAY WEBB See WEBB, FAY

VALLENTIN, HERMANN
Born: Germany. Died: 1945, Germany. Screen actor.

Appeared in: **1923** Tragedy of Life. **1927** Der Kampf des Donald Westhof (The Trial of Donald Westhof—US 1928). **1928** The Strange Case of Captain Ramper. **1931** Meine Frau, die Hochstaplerin (US 1932); Der Hauptmann von Koepenick (US 1933). **1932** Therternaechte von Berlin.

VALLI, ROMOLO
Born: 1925, Reggio Emilia, Italy. Died: Feb. 1, 1980, Rome, Italy (auto accident). Screen, stage actor and stage director.

Appeared in: **1959** La Grande Guerra (The Great War—US 1961). **1960** Five Branded Women. **1961** La Ragazza con la Valigia (aka Girl With a Suitcase—US); La Viaccia (US 1962). **1962** Und Storia Milanese (A Milanese Story); Boccaccio '70. **1963** Le Guepard (The Leopard); Dragees au Poivre (Sweet and Sour—US 1964). **1964** The Visit. **1965** La Mandragola (Mandragola—US 1966). **1968** Barbarella; Boom! **1973** What? **1977** Bobby Deerfield; 1900. **1978** The Chosen. **1980** Clair de Femme.

VALLI, VALLI
Born: 1882, Berlin, Germany. Died: Nov. 4, 1927, London, England. Screen, stage and vaudeville actress.

VALLI, VIRGINIA (Virginia McSweeney)
Born: Jan. 19, 1900, Chicago, Ill. Died: Sept. 24, 1968, Palm Springs, Calif. Screen actress. Married to actor Charles Farrell. Entered films in 1915.

Appeared in: **1917** Much Obligated; Vernon the Bountiful; The Long Green Trail; The Fable of the Speedy Sprite; Uneasy Money; Efficiency Edgar's Courtship. **1921** The Devil Within; Man Who; The Idle Rich; Sentimental Tommy; A Trip to Paradise; The Silver Lining; Love's Penalty. **1922** The Village Blacksmith; The Black Bag; The Storm; His Back Against the Wall; The Right That Failed; Tracked to Earth. **1923** A Lady of Quality; The Shock. **1924** The Signal Tower; K—the Unknown; Wild Oranges; The Confidence Man; In Every Woman's Life. **1925** Siege; The Price of Pleasure; Up the Ladder; The Lady Who Lied; Man Who Found Himself. **1926** The Family Upstairs;

Flames; Watch Your Wife; Pleasure Garden. **1927** Ladies Must Dress; Paid to Love; East Side, West Side; Marriage; Judgement of the Hills; Evening Clothes; Stage Madness. **1928** Escape; Street of Illusion. **1929** Beyond Closed Doors; Mister Antonio; Isle of Lost Ships. **1930** Storm; The Lost Zeppelin; Guilty? **1931** Night Life in Reno.

VALLIN, RICHARD "RICK"
Born: 1920, Russia. Died: Aug. 31, 1977, United States. Screen actor.

Appeared in: **1942** Perils of the Royal Mounted (serial); The Panther's Claw; A Night for Crime; King of the Stallions; Secrets of a Co-Ed; Lady from Chung-King. **1943** Corregidor; Wagon Tracks West; Nearly Eighteen; Riders of the Rio Grande; Isle of Forgotten Men; Ghosts on the Loose; Clancy Street Boys. **1944** Smart Guy; Army Wives. **1946** Dangerous Money. **1947** Northwest Outpost; Last of the Redmen; Brick Bradford (serial); The Sea Hound (serial). **1949** Jungle Jim; Tuna Clipper; Batman and Robin (serial); Shamrock Hill. **1950** Snow Dog; Counterspy Meets Scotland Yard; Rio Grande Patrol; Revenue Agent; Comanche Territory; Killer Shark; Cody of the Pony Express (serial); Captive Girl; State Penitentiary. **1951** When the Redskins Rode; Hurricne Island; The Magic Carpet; Jungle Manhunt. **1952** Aladdin and His Lamp; Woman in the Dark; Strange Fascination; Voodoo Tiger; King of the Congo (serial); Son of Geronimo (serial). **1953** The Homesteaders; Trail Blazers; Topeka; The Marksman; The Star of Texas; The Fighting Lawman. **1954** Riding With Buffalo Bill (serial); The Golden Idol; Thunder Pass. **1955** Adventures of Captain Africa (serial); King of the Carnival (serial); Treasure of Ruby Hills; Dial Red O. **1956** Frontier Gambler; Perils of the Wilderness (serial). **1957** The Tijuana Story; Raiders of Old California. **1958** Escape from Red Rock; Bullwhip. **1959** Pier 5, Havana.

VALLIS, ROBERT "BOB"
Born: England. Died: Dec. 19, 1932, Brighton, England. Screen and stage actor.

Appeared in: **1918** Kilties Three. **1920** Her Benny; A Son of David. **1921** Hound of the Baskervilles; Gwyneth of the Welsh Hills; The Four Just Men; General John Regan; The Amazing Partnership; The Palace of Honour; The Tragedy of a Comic Song; A Gentleman of France; The Adventures of Sherlock Holmes series including The Man With the Twisted Lip. **1922** Melody of Faith; Son of Kissing Cup; The Card; Little Brother of God; The Peacemaker; The Further Adventures of Sherlock Holmes series including The Greek Interpreter. **1923** Beautiful Kitty; Squibs' Honeymoon; The Convert; What Price Loving Cup?; Rogues of the Turf; The Mystery of Dr. Fu Manchu series including Aaron's Rod. **1924** Dixon's Return; Not for Sale; Hurricane Hutch in Many Adventures; The Love Story of Aliette Brunton; The Stirrup Cup Sensation; Hints on Horsemanship series; The Old Man in the Corner series including The Hocussing of Cigarette. **1925** Forbidden Cargoes (aka Contraband).

VALORI, BICE
Born: 1928. Died: Mar. 17, 1980, Rome, Italy (cancer). Screen, stage and television actress. Married to comedy partner Paolo Panelli. Mother of comedienne Alessandra Panelli.

Appeared in: **1954** My Heart Sings. **1965** Oltraggio al Pudore (aka Cheating Italian Style, and aka All the Other Girls Do—US 1966).

VALSTED, MYRTLE (Myrtle Christine Valsted)
Born: 1910. Died: Sept. 19, 1928, Hollywood, Calif. (following appendicitis operation). Screen actress. Entered films in 1928.

VAN, BILLY (Vito Coppola)
Born: 1912. Died: Aug. 22, 1973, Los Angeles, Calif. (heart attack). Stage and screen actor. Do not confuse with vaudeville actor Billy B. Van (dec. 1972).

VAN, BILLY B.
Born: 1878, Pottstown, Pa. Died: Nov. 16, 1950, Newport, N.H. (heart attack). Screen, stage and vaudeville actor. For a while did a vaudeville act with boxer and actor James J. Corbet (dec. 1933). Married to actress Grace Walsh.

Appeared in: **1922** The Beauty Shop.

VAN, BOBBY (Robert Jack Stein)
Born: Dec. 6, 1930, New York, N.Y. Died: July 31, 1980, Los Angeles, Calif. (cancer). Screen, stage, vaudeville, television actor, dancer, singer and nightclub entertainer. Son of vaudeville actors Harry and Minta-Ann King (dec.). Married to actress Elaine Joyce.

Appeared in: **1952** Because You're Mine (film debut); Skirts Ahoy! **1953** The Affairs of Dobie Gillis; Kiss Me Kate; Small Town Girl. **1961** The Ladies' Man. **1962** It's Only Money. **1966** The Navy vs. the Night Monsters. **1970** Lost Flight. **1973** Lost Horizon; The Doomsday Machine. **1976** That's Entertainment II.

VAN, CONNIE
Born: 1909. Died: July 16, 1961, Hollywood, Calif. (cerebral hemorrhage). Screen, stage and radio actress.

Appeared in: **1950** The Secret Fury. **1955** The Far Country.

VAN, GUS
Born: 1888, Brooklyn, N.Y. Died: Mar. 13, 1968, Miami Beach, Fla. (injuries from being hit by auto). Screen, stage, vaudeville, radio and television actor. Was part of vaudeville team with Joe Schenck (dec. 1930) billed as "Van and Schenck" and later did a single.

Together they appeared in: **1927** The Pennant; Winning Battery of Songland (short). **1929** Metro Movietone Feature with their lives as a background entitled Take It Big, plus several song short subjects. **1930** They Learned About Women. Appeared without Schenck in the following:. **1931-34** Universal and Columbia shorts. **1935** Gus Van's Music Shoppe (short). **1944** Atlantic City.

VAN, WALLY
Born: Sept. 27, 1880, Hyde Park, N.J. Died: May 9, 1974, Englewood, N.J. Screen actor, film director and producer.

Appeared in: **1910** Love, Luck and Gasoline. **1913** Cutey and the Chorus Girls; Cutey and the Twins; Cutey's Waterloo. **1914** Cutey's Wife. **1915** Cutey Becomes a Landlord; Cutey—Fortune Hunting; Cutey's Awakening; Cutey's Sister. **1923** The Common Law; The Drivin' Fool; Slave of Desire. **1925** Barriers Burned Away.

VAN AUKER, C. K. (Cecil Van Auker)
Died: Feb. 18, 1938, Prescott, Ariz. (tuberculosis). Screen, stage actor and aviator for silent films.

Appeared in: **1921** Payment Guaranteed; Trailin'; The Girl from God's Country; Cinderella of the Hills; The Mother Heart. **1922** Up and Going; The Ragged Heiress; Youth Must Have Love. **1923** The Gunfighter; The Grub Stake. **1927** The Golden Yukon.

VAN BAILEY, POLLY
Died: Aug. 25, 1952, Hollywood, Calif. Screen and stage actress.

VAN BEERS, STANLEY
Born: 1911, England. Died: May 25, 1961, London, England (heart ailment). Screen, stage and television actor. Married to actress Viviene Burgess.

Appeared in: **1952** So Little Time. **1953** The Fake. **1954** The Dam Busters; Dangerous Voyage (aka Terror Ship—US). **1955** Before I Wake (aka Shadow of Fear—US 1956); The Quatermass Experiment (aka The Creeping Unknown—US 1956). **1959** The Angry Hills.

VANBRUGH, DAME IRENE (Irene Barnes)
Born: Dec. 2, 1872, Exeter, England. Died: Nov. 30, 1949, London, England. Screen, stage actress and novelist. Was made Dame Commander of the Order of the British Empire in 1941. Married to stage actor and playwright Dion Boucicault (dec. 1929) and sister of actress Violet Vanbrugh (dec. 1942).

Appeared in: **1916** The Real Thing at Last. **1917** Masks and Faces; The Gay Lord Quex (stage and film versions). **1934** Head of the Family; Catherine the Great; Youthful Folly; Girls Will Be Boys (US 1935); The Way of Youth. **1935** Escape Me Never. **1937** Wings of the Morning; Knight Without Armour. **1945** I Live in Grosvenor Square (aka A Yank in London—US 1946).

VANBRUGH, VIOLET (Violet Barnes)
Born: June 11, 1867, Exeter, England. Died: Nov. 10, 1942, London, England. Screen and stage actress. Sister of actress Dame Irene Vanbrugh (dec. 1949). Divorced from actor Arthur Bourchier (dec. 1927). Mother of actress Prudence Vanbrugh.

Appeared in: **1931** Captivation. **1934** Girls Will Be Boys (US 1935). **1938** Pygmalion.

VAN BUREN, A. H. (Archimedes H. Van Buren)
Born: 1879, Gloucester, N.J. Died: Aug. 1, 1965, Los Angeles, Calif. Screen, stage actor, film director and stage director. Married to actress Dorothy Bernard (dec. 1955).

Appeared in: **1916** Her Double Life; The Vixen.

VAN BUREN, MABEL
Born: 1878, Chicago, Ill. Died: Nov. 4, 1947, Hollywood, Calif. Stage and screen actress. Married to actor Ernest C. Joy (dec. 1924) and later to actor James Gordon (dec. 1941). Mother of actress Kay Van Buren. Entered films approx. 1914.

Appeared in: **1913** The Bride of Shadows. **1914** Message from Across the Sea; Through the Centuries; Elizabeth's Prayer; While Wifey is Away; The Midnight Call; When Thieves Fall Out; The Squatters; The Man from Home. **1915** The Warrens of Virginia; The Girl of the Golden West. **1916** The Sowers; The Victoria Cross. **1917** Those Without Sin; The Silent Partners; The Devil Stone. **1920** Conrad in Quest of His Youth. **1921** The Four Horsemen of the Apocalypse; Miss Lulu Bett; A Wise Fool; Moonlight and Honeysuckle. **1922** The Man from Home; Beyond the Rocks; The Woman Who Walked Alone; For the Defense; Pawned; Youth to Youth; Manslaughter; While Satan Sleeps. **1923** In Search of a Thrill; Lights Out; Wandering Daughters; Light That Failed; The Girl of the Golden West. **1924** The Dawn of a Tomorrow. **1925** Smooth as Satin; The Top of the World; His Secretary. **1927** Kings of Kings; The Meddlin' Stranger. **1928** The Flying Buckaroo; Craig's Wife; Ramona. **1930** His First Command.

VANCE, LUCILLE
Born: 1893. Died: May 10, 1974, Burbank, Calif. Screen, stage and television actress.

Appeared in: **1942** Bowery at Midnight. **1944** Boss of Rawhide. **1946** Idea Girl. **1947** Thundergap Outlaws.

VANCE, VIRGINIA
Born: 1902. Died: Oct. 13, 1942, Hollywood, Calif. (heart attack). Screen actress.

Appeared in: **1925** Goat Getter. **1926** The Fighting Marine (serial). **1928** Undressed. **1929** New Year's Eve.

VANCE, VIVIAN
Born: July 26, 1913, Cherryvale, Kans. Died: Aug. 17, 1979, Belvedere, Calif. (cancer). Screen, stage and television actress. Divorced from actor Philip Ober (dec. 1982), and later married to publisher John Dodds.

Appeared in: **1950** The Secret Fury. **1951** The Blue Veil. **1965** The Great Race.

VAN CORTLAND, JAN (Johan C. Brems)
Born: 1870. Died: July 21, 1928, New York, N.Y. Screen and stage actor.

VAN DER BERG, HAN BENTZ
Born: 1918, Holland. Died: July 3, 1976. Screen actor.

Appeared in: **1959** The Last Blitzkrieg.

VANDERGRIFT, J. MONTE
Born: 1893. Died: July 29, 1939, North Hollywood, Calif. (heart attack). Screen, stage and radio actor.

Appeared in: **1933** The Kennel Murder Case. **1934** The St. Louis Kid; Upperworld; One Hour Late; Shoot the Works. **1935** G-Men; Private Worlds; Smart Girl; Seven Keys to Baldpate; Hot Money (short); The Lone Wolf Returns; Rendezvous. **1936** The Return of Sophie Lang; After the Thin Man; The Moon's Our Home; Easy Money; The Mandarin Mystery. **1937** California Straight Ahead; Woman Chases Man; A Girl With Ideas; True Confession; Captains Courageous. **1938** Racket Busters; The First 100 Years. **1939** Tell No Tales; Miracles for Sale.

VANDERIC, GEORGES
Born: 1901, Brussels, Belgium. Died: Aug. 1, 1979, Brussels, Belgium. Screen, stage, radio, television actor and comedian.

Appeared in:The Floating Stone; Le Maugre; Peace in the Fields.

VANDERVEER, ELINOR (aka ELINOR VANDIVERE)
Born: 1887. Died: May 27, 1976, Loma Linda, Calif. Screen actress. Appeared in Mack Sennett and Hal Roach comedies.

Appeared in: **1926** Into Her Kingdom. **1927** The Second Hundred Years (short); The Battle of the Century (short). **1928** From Soup to Nuts (short). **1929** The Hoosegow (short). **1930** A Notorious Affair. **1934** Going Bye Bye (short). **1935** Slightly Static (short); Pop Goes the Easel (short). **1940** No Census No Feeling (short). **1944** Lost in a Harem.

VAN DYK, JAMES
Born: 1895. Died: Dec. 17, 1951, Montclair, N.J. (heart attack). Screen, stage, radio and television actor.

VAN DYKE, W. S. (Woodbridge Strong Van Dyke II)
Born: Mar. 21, 1887, San Diego, Calif. Died: Feb. 5, 1943, Brentwood, Calif. Screen, stage, vaudeville actor and film director.

Appeared in: **1916** Oliver Twist.

VANE, DENTON
Born: 1890. Died: Sept. 17, 1940, Union Hill, N.J. (heart attack). Screen and stage actor.

Appeared in: **1912** The Adopted Son. **1914** Arthur Truman's Ward. **1915** The Flower of the Hills; Who Killed Joe Merrion?; On Her Wedding Night; Heredity; The Man Who Couldn't Beat God; The Ruling Power; To Cherish and Protect. **1916** The Wandering Horde; The Ruse; The Island of Suprise; The Hunted Woman; The Ordeal of Elizabeth; Hesper of the Mountains; An Enemy to the King; Green Stockings. **1917** The Maelstrom (aka Millionaire Hallet's Adventure); The Hawk; Apartment 29; The Stolen Treaty; The Glory of Yolanda; In the Balance; The Soul Master; The Grell Mystery; Transgression. **1918** A Mother's Sin; A Bachelor's Children; A Game with Fate; Love Watches; The Clutch of Circumstance; Miss Ambition. **1919** Fortune's Child; Beauty Proof; A Girl at Bay; The Bramble Bush. **1921** Women Men Love. **1922** Flesh and Spirit.

VANE, DOROTHY
Born: 1871, England. Died: Mar. 4, 1947, England? Screen and stage actress.

Appeared in: **1923** Bulldog Drummond.

VANE, MYRTLE
Born: 1868. Died: Feb. 17, 1932, San Diego, Calif. Screen and stage actress.

Appeared in: **1923** April Showers; Are You a Failure? **1924** A Girl of the Limberlost; K—The Unknown; The White Sin; The Mirage. **1929** Broadway Blues.

VAN EYCK, PETER
Born: July 16, 1913, Germany. Died: July 15, 1969, Zurich, Switzerland. Screen actor.

Appeared in: **1943** Five Graves to Cairo (film debut); The Moon Is Down; Edge of Darkness; Hitler's Children. **1944** Address Unknown; The Imposter; The Hitler Gang. **1949** Hallo, Fraulein! **1950** Epilog; Export in Blond; Koenigskinder; Der Dritte von Rechts; Opfer des Herzens; The Devil's Agent. **1951** Desert Fox. **1953** Single-Handed (aka Sailor of the King—US); Alerte au Said. **1954** Night People. **1955** Tarzan's Hidden Jungle; Jump into Hell; A Bullet for Joey; Wages of Fear; Mr. Arkadin (US 1962 and aka Confidential Report); Der Cornet. **1956** Attack!; The Rawhide Years; Run for the Sun. **1957** Der Glaeserne Turm (The Glass Tower—US 1959). **1958** The Snorkel; Schwarze Nylons—Heisse Nachte (aka Indecent—US 1962); All Bad; Waylaid Women (US 1968); Flesh and the Woman; Sophie et le Crime (Sophie and the Crime, aka The Girl on the Third Floor); Le Chair et le Diable (The Flesh and the Devil, aka Flesh and Desire); Retour de Manivell (Turn of the Handle, aka There's Always a Price Tag); Dr. Crippen Lebt; Das Maedchen Rosemarie (aka Rosemary—US 1960); Schmutziger Engel. **1959** Verbrechen Nach Schulschluss (aka The Young Go Wild—US 1962); Du Gehoerst Mir; Rommel Ruft Kairo; Der Rest ist Schweigen (The Rest is Silence—US 1960); Lockvogel der Nacht; Labyrith; Geheimaktion Schwarze Kapelle; Abschied von den Wolken (Rebel Flight to Cuba—US 1962). **1960** Foxhole in Cairo (US 1961); Die Tausend Augen des Dr. Mabuse (The 1000 Eyes of Dr. Mabuse—US 1966); Liebling der Goetter. **1961** An Einem Freitag um Halb Zwoelf (The World in My Pocket—US 1962); La Fete Espagnole (aka No Time for Ecstasy—US 1963); Law of War; Die Stunde, die Du Gluecklich Bist; Unter Ausschluss der Oeffentlichkeit; Kriegsgesetz (aka Legge di Guerra, and aka Liebe, Freiheit und Verrat). **1962** The Devil's Agent; Vengeance (aka The Brain—US 1964); Endstation 13 Sahara (Station Six-Sahara—US 1964); The Black Chapel; The Longest Day; Finden Sie, Dass Constanze Sich Richtig Verhaelt?; In Namen des Teufels; Ein Toter Sucht Seinen Moerder. **1963** The River Line; Verfuhrung am Meer (Seduction by the Sea—US 1967); Ein Alibi Zerbricht (An Alibi for Death—US 1965); Das Grosse Liebesspiel (And so to Bed, and aka The Big Love Game—US 1965); Scotland Yard Jagt Dr. Mabuse. **1964** I Misteri Della Giungla Nera (The Mystery of Thug Island—US 1966); Kennwort; Reiher; Die Todesstrahlen des Dr. Mabuse. **1965** Guerre Secrete (aka The Dirty Game—US 1966); The Spy Who Came in from the Cold; Duell vor Sonnenuntergang; Das Geheimnis der Lederschlinge; Die Herren; Spione Unter Sich. **1966** Der Chef Schickt Seinen Besten Mann; Karriere; Sechs Pistolen Jagen Professor Z. **1967** Million Dollar Man. **1968** Shalako; Tevye und Seine Sieben Toechter (Tevya and His Seven Daughters). **1969** Assignment to Kill; The Bridge at Ramagen.

VAN GYSEGHEM, ANDRE
Born: Aug. 18, 1906, Eltham, Kent, England. Died: Oct. 13, 1979, London, England. Screen, stage, television actor, stage director and author. Married to actress Jean Forbes-Robertson (dec. 1962).

Appeared in: **1949** Warning to Wantons. **1953** The Limping Man. **1957** Face in the Night (aka Menace in the Night—US 1958); The Surgeon's Knife. **1970** Cromwell.

VAN HADEN, ANDERS
Born: 1876. Died: June 19, 1936, Hollywood, Calif. (heart attack). Screen actor, film producer and film director.

Appeared in: **1932** Cheaters at Play; A Passport to Hell. **1933** Best of Enemies; The Secret of the Blue Room; Snug in the Jug (short). **1935** Barbary Coast.

VAN HORN, EMILE
Died: Jan. 1, 1967, New Orleans, La. Screen actor.

Appeared in: **1933** King Kong. **1941** Jungle Girl (serial). **1942** Perils of Nyoka (serial). **1943** The Ape Man. **1948** Are You With It? **1959** A Hole in the Head. **1967** Hotel.

VAN HORN, JAMES "JIMMY"
Born: 1917. Died: Apr. 20, 1966, Hollywood, Calif. (internal hemorrhage). Screen actor and stuntman.

Appeared in: **1927** The Cherokee Kid. **1950** Fast on the Draw; Hostile Country; Marshal of Heldorado. **1951** The Cave of the Outlaws. **1953** Gunsmoke.

VAN HOUTEN, FRANKIE (aka FRANKIE VANN)
Born: 1906. Died: July 19, 1978, Burbank, Calif. (cerebral hemorrhage). Professional boxer, screen and television actor.

Appeared in: **1938** Kid Nightingale. **1977** Rocky.

VAN LEER, ARNOLD
Born: 1895, London, England. Died: June 3, 1975, Boston, Mass. Screen actor and press agent. Married to stage actress Dorinda Van Leer (dec.). Entered films as an extra and appeared in early Charlie Chaplin films.

VAN METER, HARRY See VON METER, HARRY

VANN, FRANKIE See VAN HOUTEN, FRANKIE

VANN, POLLY
Born: July 29, 1882, Scranton, Pa. Died: Aug. 25, 1952, Los Angeles, Calif. (Laennec's cirrhosis). Screen, stage and vaudeville actress.

Appeared in: **1917** To the Death. **1919** Three Black Eyes (aka Scrap Paper); Regular Girl. **1921** Wedding Bells. **1925** Tearin' Loose. **1938** Midnight Intruder. **1943** Hers to Hold.

VANNE, MARDA
Born: South Africa. Died: Apr. 27, 1970, London, England. Screen, stage and television actress.

Appeared in: **1968** Joanna.

VAN ROOTEN, LUIS (Luis D'Antin Van Rooten)
Born: Nov. 29, 1906, Mexico City, Mexico. Died: June 17, 1973, Chatham, Mass. Screen, stage, radio, television actor and author.

Appeared in: **1944** The Hitler Gang. **1946** Two Years Before the Mast. **1948** To the Ends of the Earth; Saigon; To the Victor; The Big Clock; Beyond Glory; Night Has a Thousand Eyes; The Gentleman from Nowhere. **1949** City Across the River; Boston Blackie's Chinese Venture; Secret of St. Ives; Cinderella (voice); Champion. **1951** Detective Story; My Favorite Spy. **1952** Lydia Bailey. **1955** The Sea Chase. **1957** The Unholy Wife. **1958** Fraulein; The Curse of the Faceless Man. **1961** Operation Eichmann.

VAN SAHER, LILLA A.
Born: 1912, Hungary. Died: July 15, 1968, New York, N.Y. Screen actress and author.

Appeared in foreign film Grain au Vent

VAN SICKEL, DALE
Born: 1907. Died: Jan. 25, 1977, Newport Beach, Calif. Screen actor, stuntman and All-American football player. Was founder of Stuntman's Association of Motion Pictures and its first president.

Appeared in: **1933** Duck Soup. **1942** It Happened in Flatbush. **1943** The Masked Marvel (serial); Captain America (serial). **1944** Haunted Harbor (serial); Zorro's Black Whip (serial). **1945** Manhunt of Mystery Island (serial). **1946** The Phantom Rider; plus the following serials: The Crimson Ghost; Daughter of Don Q; King of the Forest Rangers. **1947** The Last Round-Up; Bells of San Angelo; plus the following serials: The Black Widow; Jesse James Rides Again; Son of Zorro. **1948** Oklahoma Badlands; Lightnin' in the Forest; Carson City Raiders; Renegades of Sonora; Desperadoes of Dodge City; plus the following serials: Adventures of Frank and Jesse James; Dangers of the Canadian

Mounted; G-Men Never Forget. **1949** Duke of Chicago; The Golden Stallion; plus the following serials: Bruce Gentry—Daredevil of the Skies; King of the Rocket Men. **1950** Sideshow; plus the following serials: Desperadoes of the West; The Invisible Monster; The James Brothers of Missouri; Radar Patrol vs. Spy King. **1951** Flying Disc Man from Mars (serial); Rough Riders of Durango; Government Agents vs. Phantom Legion (serial); Thunder in God's Country. **1952** Radar Men from the Moon (seria); Arctic Flight; Dead Man's Trail; Zombies of the Stratosphere (serial). **1953** Canadian Mounties vs. Atomic Invaders (serial); Topeka; Northern Patrol; Abbott and Costello Go to Mars. **1954** The Rogue Cop; Man With the Steel Whip (serial); Trader Tom of the China Seas. **1956** He Laughed Last. **1958** Satan's Satellites; Missile Monsters; Enchanted Island. **1959** Ghost of Zorro; On the Beach. **1960** Seven Ways from Sundown. **1962** Six Black Horses. **1963** It's a Mad, Mad, Mad, Mad World. **1964** Viva Las Vegas. **1967** The Flim-Flam Man. **1974** No Deposit, No Return.

VAN SLOAN, EDWARD
Born: 1882, San Francisco, Calif. Died: Mar. 6, 1964, San Francisco, Calif. Screen and stage actor.

Appeared in: **1931** Dracula; Frankenstein. **1932** Manhattan Parade; Play Girl; Man Wanted; Behind the Mask; Thunder Below; Forgotten Commandments; The Last Mile; Honeymoon in Bali; The Mummy. **1933** The Death Kiss; Silk Express; The Working Man; Infernal Machine; Trick for Trick; It's Great to Be Alive; The Man Who Reclaimed His Head; The Deluge; Murder on the Campus; Billion Dollar Scandal. **1934** Manhattan Melodrama; I'll Fix It; Death Takes a Holiday; The Scarlet Express; The Crosby Case; The Life of Vergie Winters. **1935** Air Hawks; Mystery of the Black Room; The Story of Louis Pasteur; Grand Exit; Grand Old Girl; Mills of the Gods; The Woman in Red; A Shot in the Dark; The Last Days of Pompeii. **1936** Road Gang; Sins of Man; Dracula's Daughter. **1937** The Man Who Found Himself. **1938** Penitentiary; Storm Over Bengal; Danger on the Air. **1939** The Phantom Creeps (serial). **1940** Abe Lincoln in Illinois; The Doctor Takes a Wife; The Secret Seven; Before I Hang. **1942** Valley of the Hunted Men; A Man's World. **1943** Mission to Moscow; Riders of the Rio Grande; Submarine Alert; The Masked Marvel (serial); End of the Road. **1944** Captain America (serial); The Conspirators; Wing and a Prayer. **1945** I'll Remember April. **1946** The Mask of Dijon. **1947** Betty Coed.

VAN TASSELL, MARIE
Born: Apr. 6, 1874, Little Falls, N.Y. Died: 1946, Oakland, Calif. Screen and stage actress.

Appeared in: **1916** Dulcie's Adventure. **1919** Sue of the South. **1921** Deep Waters.

VAN TRESS, MABEL
Born: 1873. Died: Mar. 16, 1962. Screen actress.

VAN TRUMP, JESSALYN
Born: 1885. Died: May 2, 1939, Hollywood, Calif. Screen and stage actress.

Appeared in: **1911-12** American Film Mfg. Co. films.

VAN TUYL, HELEN (Helen Marr Van Tuyl)
Born: 1891. Died: Aug. 22, 1964, Hollywood, Calif. (heart attack). Screen and television actress.

Appeared in: **1952** Stars and Stripes Forever; Confidence Girl. **1953** Titanic. **1955** Daddy Long Legs; The Girl in the Red Velvet Swing.

VAN UPP, VIRGINIA
Born: 1902, Chicago, Ill. Died: Mar. 25, 1970, Hollywood, Calif. (results of a broken hip). Screen actress, film producer and screenwriter. Appeared on screen in features with William Desmond, John Gilbert and others when five years old.

VAN VOORHIS, WESTBROOK
Born: Sept. 21, 1903, New Milford, Conn. Died: July 14, 1968, New Milford, Conn. (cancer). Radio, movie commentator and screen actor. Was voice of "March of Time" in film documentaries.

Appeared in: **1942** We Are the Marines (narrator). **1951** Tembo (narrator). **1961** The Ladies' Man. **1962** Castro, Cuba and Communism (narrator—aka Danger on our Doorstep).

VAN ZANDT, PHILIP
Born: Oct. 3, 1904, Amsterdam, Holland. Died: Feb. 16, 1958, Hollywood, Calif. (overdose of sleeping pills). Screen, stage and television actor.

Appeared in: **1939** Those High Grey Walls. **1940** Boobs in Arms (short). **1941** In Old Colorado; City of Missing Girls; So Ends Our Night; Ride on Vaquero; Citizen Kane. **1942** Sherlock Holmes and the Secret Weapon; Wake Island; The Hard Way; Desperate Journey; Commandos Strike at Dawn. **1943** Tarzan Triumphs; Murder on the Waterfront; Tarzan's Desert Mystery; Hostages; Deerslayer; Air Raid Wardens. **1944** America's Children; Call of the Jungle; The Big Noise; Swing Hostess; The Unwritten Code; Dragon Seed. **1945** Outlaws of the Rockies; House of Frankenstein; Sudan; Counter-Attack; A Thousand and One Nights; I Love a Bandleader. **1946** The Avalanche; Below the Deadline; Joe Palooka, Champ; Decoy; Don't Gamble With Strangers; Somewhere in the Night; California; The Bandit of Sherwood Forest; Night and Day. **1947** Life With Father; Slave Girl; The Last Frontier Uprising. **1948** Night Has a Thousand Eyes; The Vicious Circle; The Shanghai Chest; Embraceable You; Walk a Crooked Mile; The Loves of Carmen; Street with No Name; Big Clock; April Showers; plus the following shorts: Fiddlers Three; Mummy's Dummies; Squareheads of the Round Table. **1949** The Lady Gambles; Red, Hot and Blue; The Blonde Bandit; Lone Wolf and His Lady; Fuelin' Around (short). **1950** Cyrano de Bergerac; Between Midnight and Dawn; Indian Territory; The Petty Girl; Where Danger Lives; Copper Canyon; Dopey Dicks (short); The Jackpot. **1951** Submarine Command; The Ghost Chasers; His Kind of Woman; Ten Tall Men; Two Dollar Bettor; Three Arabian Nuts (short). **1952** At Sword's Point; Macao; Viva Zapata; Son of Ali Baba; Thief of Damascus; Yukon Gold. **1953** Dragon's Gold; Three Sailors and a Girl; Prisoners of the Casbah; Capt. John Smith and Pocahontas; Clipped Wings; plus the following shorts: Loves's-a-Poppin; So You Want to Be a Musician; So You Want a Television Set; So You Want to Be an Heir; Spooks. **1954** Yankee Pasha; Knock on Wood; Playgirl; Gog; Three Ring Circus; plus the following shorts: Musty Musketeers; So You Want to Go to a Nightclub; Knutzy Knights; Scotched in Scotland. **1955** Untamed; The Big Combo; I Cover the Underworld; plus the following shorts: So You Want to Be a Gladiator; So You Want to Be a V.P.; Bedlam in Paradise. **1956** Our Miss Brooks; Uranium Boom; Around the World in 80 Days; Hot Stuff (short). **1957** Man of a Thousand Faces; The Pride and the Passion; The Crooked Circle; The Lonely Man; Outer Space Jitters (short). **1958** Fifi Blows Her Top (short).

VARCONI, VICTOR (Mihaly Varkonyi)
Born: Mar. 31, 1891, Kisvarde, Hungary. Died: June 16, 1976, Santa Barbara, Calif. (heart attack). Screen and stage actor. Married to stage actress Anna Aranyosy (Nusi Aranyessy) (dec. 1949) and later married to Lilliane Varconi. Entered films in Hungary in 1913.

Appeared in: **1913** Sarga Csiko (The Yellow Colt); Marta. **1914** Bank Ban; Tetemrahivas (The Call of Death). **1915** Havasi Magdolna (Madeleine of the Mountains); Talkoas (Encounter at Midnight); A Tanitono (The Schoolmistress). **1916** Hotel Imperial; Baccarat; Ezust Kecske (The Silver Goat); A Farkas (The Wolf); Nagymama (The Grandmother). **1917** Petofi Dalciklus (The Poetry of Petofi); Magnas Miska; A Riporter Kiraly (King of the Reporters); Magia. **1918** Szent Peter Esernyoje (Saint Peter's Umbrella); Sapho; 99; A Skorpio (The Scorpion); Varazskeringo (The Magic Waltz). **1919** Jenseits von Got und Rose. **1921** Die Sonne Asiens. **1922** Herrin der Meere; Eine Versunkene Welt; Sodum und Gomorrah. **1924** The Dancers; Poisoned Paradise; Triumph; Changing Husbands; Feet of Clay; Worldly Goods. **1925** L'uomo piu Allegro di Vienna (The Liveliest Man in Vienna). **1926** Die Warschauer Zitadelle; Gli Ultimi Giorni di Pompei (The Last Days of Pompeii); The Volga Boatman; Silken Shackles; For Wives Only. **1927** King of Kings; Fighting Love; The Forbidden Woman; The Angel of Broadway; Chicago; The Little Adventuress. **1928** Tenth Avenue; Sinners Parade. **1929** The Divine Lady; Eternal Love; Kult Ciala. **1930** Captain Thunder. **1931** Doctors' Wives; The Black Camel; Men in Her Life; Safe in Hell. **1932** Doomed Battalion. **1933** The Rebel; Der Rebell (German version of The Rebel); The Song You Gave Me (US 1934). **1935** Roberta; Mister Dynamite; A Feather in Her Hat. **1936** Dancing Pirate; The Plainsman. **1937** Trouble in Morocco; The Big City; Men in Exile. **1938** King of the Newsboys; Suez; Submarine Patrol. **1939** The Story of Vernon and Irene Castle; Mr. Moto Takes a Vacation; Disputed Passage; Everything Happens at Night. **1940** Strange Cargo; The Sea Hawk; Pound Foolish (short). **1941** Federal Fugitives; Forced Landing. **1942** My Favorite Blonde; They Raid by Night; My Favorite Spy; Reap the Wild Wind. **1943** For Whom the Bell Tolls. **1944** The Story of Dr. Wassell; The Hitler Gang. **1945** Scotland Yard Investigator. **1947** Unconquered; Where There's Life; Pirates of Monterey. **1949** Samson and Delilah. **1957** The Man Who Turned to Stone. **1959** The Atomic Submarine.

VARDEN, EVELYN
Born: June 12, 1893. Died: July 11, 1958, New York, N.Y. Screen, stage, radio and television actress.

Appeared in: **1940** Pinky. **1950** Cheaper by the Dozen; Stella; When Willie Comes Marching Home. **1951** Elopement. **1952** Finders Keepers; Phone Call from a Stranger. **1954** Athena; Desiree; The Student Prince. **1955** The Night of the Hunter. **1956** Hilda Crane; The Bad Seed. **1957** Ten Thousand Bedrooms.

VARDEN, VENITA
Died: June 17, 1948, near Mt. Carmel, Pa. (plane crash). Screen and stage actress. Divorced from actor Jack Oakie (dec. 1978).

VARLEY, BEATRICE
Born: 1896, England. Died: 1969, England? Screen and stage actress.

Appeared in: **1937** Spring Handicap. **1941** Hatter's Castle (US 1948). **1942** Squadron Leader X (US 1943). **1943** The Man in Gray (US 1945). **1944** Love Story (aka A Lady Surrenders—US 1947). **1945** The Wicked Lady (US 1946); Waterloo Road (US 1949); The Agitator. **1946** Bedelia (US 1947). **1947** So Well Remembered; Holiday Camp (US 1948); Jassy (US 1948); The Little Ballerina (US 1951). **1948** My Brother's Keeper (US 1949); Good Time Girl (US 1950); My Brother Jonathan (US 1949). **1949** Adam and Evelyne (aka Adam and Evalyn—US). **1950** Gone to Earth (aka The Wild Heart—US 1952). **1953** Melba. **1956** Tiger in the Smoke; The Feminine Touch (aka The Gentle Touch—US 1957). **1957** Hell Drivers (US 1958); The Good Companions (US 1958); The Surgeon's Knife. **1958** Bachelor of Hearts (US 1962). **1959** Room at the Top; Horrors of the Black Museum; The Rought and the Smooth (aka Portrait of a Sinner—US 1961).

VARVARO, GLORIA (Angela Gloria Varvaro)
Born: 1915. Died: Apr. 8, 1976, New York, N.Y. Screen actress and restaurateur.

VASQUEZ, JOSE LOUIS "MEXICANO" (Jose Luis Lopez Vasques)
Born: Mexico. Died: 1965, Mexico? Screen actor.

Appeared in: **1951** The Brave Bulls. **1963** El Verdugo (The Executioner, aka El Ver, and aka Not on Your Life—US 1965).

VASS, LULU
Born: 1877. Died: May 6, 1952, Haverstraw, N.Y. Screen, stage and radio actress. Appeared in films from 1941 to 1946.

VASSAR, QUEENIE
Born: Oct. 28, 1870, Glasgow, Scotland. Died: Sept. 11, 1960, Hollywood, Calif. (following surgery). Stage and screen actress. Married to actor Joseph Cawthorne (dec. 1949).

Appeared in: **1940** The Primrose Path. **1942** Lady in a Jam. **1944** None but the Lonely Heart.

VAUGHAN, DOROTHY
Born: Nov. 5, 1889, St. Louis, Mo. Died: Mar. 15, 1955, Hollywood, Calif. (cerebral hemorrhage). Screen, stage, radio and vaudeville actress.

Appeared in: **1935** Annapolis Farewell (film debut). **1936** Love Begins at 20; Times Square Playboy. **1937** The Hoosier Schoolboy; Here's Flash Casey; That Man's Here Again; The Black Legion; Michael O'Halloran. **1938** Boy Meets Girl; Test Pilot; Little Miss Thoroughbred; Telephone Operator; Little Orphan Annie; Gambling Ship; Slandar House; Quick Money. **1939** Unexpected Father; The Man in the Iron Mask; First Love; The Star Maker. **1940** Diamond Frontier; The Old Swimmin' Hole; The Ape. **1941** Secret Evidence; Bad Men of Missouri; Three Girls About Town; The Strawberry Blonde; Manpower; One Foot in Heaven. **1942** Now, Voyager; The Magnificent Ambersons; Lady Gangster; Gentleman Jim. **1943** The Iron Major; Sweet Rosie O'Grady; Doughboys in Ireland; Hit the Ice. **1944** The Adventures of Mark Twain; Sweet and Low Down; The Mummy's Ghost; The Town Went Wild; Henry Aldrich's Little Secret. **1945** Dancing in Manhattan; What a Blonde; Those Endearing Young Charms; Ten Cents a Dance. **1946** That Brennan Girl. **1947** Trail to San Antone; The Egg and I; The Bishop's Wife; The Bamboo Blonde; Robin Hood of Texas. **1948** I Wouldn't Be in Your Shoes; Song of Idaho. **1949** Tell It to the Judge; Take One False Step; Fighting Fools; Home in San Antone; Manhattan Angel. **1950** Chain Gang; Rider from Tucson; Square Dance Katty. **1951** A Wonderful Life.

VAUGHN, ADAMAE
Born: 1906. Died: Sept. 1, 1943, Hollywood, Calif. Screen actress. She was a 1927 Wampas Baby. Sister of actress Alberta Vaughn.

Appeared in: **1923** The Courtship of Miles Standish. **1925** The Last Edition. **1926** The Arizona Streak; Flashing Fangs. **1929** The Show of Shows. **1930** Dancing Sweeties. **1936** Love Before Breakfast.

VAUGHN, HILDA
Born: Dec. 27, 1898, Baltimore, Md. Died: Dec. 28, 1957, Baltimore, Md. Screen and stage actress.

Appeared in: **1929** Three Live Ghosts. **1930** Manslaughter. **1931** It's a Wise Child; A Tailor Made Man; Susan Lennox, Her Rise and Fall.

1932 Ladies of the Big House; The Phantom of Crestwood. **1933** Today We Live; Dinner at Eight; No Marriage Ties; No Other Woman. **1934** Anne of Green Gables. **1935** The Wedding Night; Straight from the Heart; Chasing Yesterday; Men Without Names; I Live My Life. **1936** The Trail of the Lonesome Pine; Everybody's Old Man; Half Angel; Banjo on My Knee; The Accusing Finger; The Witness Chair. **1937** Nothing Sacred; Danger—Love at Work. **1938** Maid's Night Out. **1940** Charlie Chan at the Wax Museum.

VAUGHN, PHYLLIS
Born: 1914. Died: Sept. 16, 1977, Las Vegas, Nev. (complications following heart attack and stroke). Screen, vaudeville actress and dancer. Married to Frank Scannell, with whom she appeared in vaudeville.

VAUGHN, VIVIAN (aka GYPSY GOULD)
Born: 1902. Died: Feb. 1, 1966, Hollywood, Calif. Screen, stage actress and singer.

VAUGHN, WILLIAM *See* VON BRINCKEN, WILHELM

VAULTHIER, GEORGES
Born: France. Died: Apr., 1926, Paris, France. Screen actor.

VAVERKA, ANTON
Born: Czechoslovakia. Died: July 2, 1937, Prague, Czechoslovakia. Screen actor.

Appeared in: **1923** Merry-Go-Round. **1925** The Phantom of the Opera; Secrets of the Night. **1926** The Love Thief; Rolling Home. **1927** On Ze Boulevard. **1928** The Wedding March; Three Sinners. **1929** The Love Parade. **1930** The Melody Man.

VAVITCH, MICHAEL
Born: 1885, Russia. Died: Oct. 7, 1930, Los Angeles, Calif. (heart attack). Screen actor.

Appeared in: **1925** The Swan; Graustark. **1926** The Third Degree; Her Man O-War; Crown of Lies; The Midnight Sun; Valencia; My Official Wife. **1927** Hotel Imperial; Venus of Venice; Two Arabian Knights; The Gaucho; The Devil Dancer. **1928** The Dove; Glorious Betsy; The Woman Disputed; Thief in the Dark. **1929** The Wolf Song; The Divine Lady; The Bridge of San Luis Rey. **1930** A Devil With Women; War Nurse.

VAZQUEZ, MYRNA
Born: 1935, Puerto Rico? Died: Feb. 17, 1975, Boston, Mass. (heart condition). Screen, stage, radio and television actress. Divorced from actor Felix Monclova. Married to Hector Colon Declet.

VEDDER, WILLIAM H.
Born: 1872. Died: Mar. 3, 1961, Hollywood, Calif. (lung cancer). Screen and stage actor.

Appeared in: **1947** The Senator Was Indiscreet. **1949** Leave It to Henry; Undercover Man. **1950** The Gunfighter. **1951** You Never Can Tell. **1952** O. Henry's Full House; Paula; Stars and Stripes Forever; Boots Malone; The Big Trees. **1953** Dream Wife. **1954** The Wild One. **1955** World Without End. **1958** The Brothers Karamazov.

VEGERES, JOE
Born: 1895, Belgium. Died: Mar. 31, 1977, Antwerp, Belgium. Screen and stage actor. Divorced from actress Nora Oosterwij, and later married to actress Jet Naessens.

Appeared in: **1965** The Magnificent Cuckold; Other Belgian films: Convicts of Honor; Barrack No. 1; Mr. Wens' Trump Cards; Goldsmugglers; The Cursed; Princess of the Scamps; The Midnight Circuit; Like Two Drops of Water.

VEIDT, CONRAD
Born: Jan. 22, 1893, Berlin, Germany. Died: Apr. 3, 1943, Los Angeles, Calif. (heart attack). Screen, stage actor, film director, producer and screenwriter. Divorced from music hall artiste Gussy Hall and Felicitas Radke and later married to agent Lily Barter (dec. 1980).

Appeared in: **1917** Der Spion (The Spy, later released as In Die Wolken Verfolgt); Die Claudi von Geiserhot; Wenn Tote Sprechen; Der Weg des Todes (The Road of Death); Furcht (Fear); Das Ratsel von Bangalor (The Mystery of Bangalor). **1918** Die Serenyi; Das Tagebuch Einer Verlorenen (The Diary of a Lost Woman); Dida Ibsens Geschichte (The Story of Dida Ibsen); Das Dreimaderlhaus (The Three Girls' House); Colomba; Jettchen Geberts Geschichte (Jettchen Gerbert's Story); Henriette Jacoby; Sundige Mutter (Sinning Mothers); Opfer der Gesellschaft (Victim of Society); Nocturno der

Liebe (Nocturne of Love); Die Japanerin (The Japanese Woman). **1919** Gewitter im Mai; Opium; Die Reise um die Erde in 80 Tagen (Around the World in 80 Days); Peer Gynt; Anders als die Andern (Different from the Others); Die Prostitution (Prostitution); Die Prostitution II (aka Die Sich Verkaufen—Prostitution II—Those Who Sell Themselves); Die Okarina (The Ocarina); Prinz Kuchuck (Prince Cuckoo); Unheimlich Geschichten (Eerie Tales); Wahnsinn (Madness); Nachtgestalten (Figures of the Night); Satanas. **1920** Die Nacht auf Goldenhall (The Night at Goldenhall); Das Kabinett des Dr. Caligari (The Cabinet of Dr. Caligari—US 1921); Der Reigen (The Merry-Go-Round); Patience; Der Januskopf (The Two-Faced Man); Liebestaumel (Love and Passion); Die Augen der Welt (The Eyes of the World); Kurfurstendamm; Moriturus; Abend-Nacht-Morgen (Day, Night and the Morning After); Manolescus Memoiren (The Memoirs of Manolescu); Kunsterlaunen (Temperamental Artist); Sehnsucht (Desire); Der Gang in die Nacht (aka The Dark Road); Christian Wahnschaffe (Part I: Weltbrand, Part II: Die Flucht aus dem Goldenen Kerker); Der Graf von Cagliostro (The Count of Cagliostro); Das Geheimnis von Bombay (The Secret of Bombay); Menschen im Rausch (Men in Ecstasy). **1921** Die Liebschaften des Hektor Dalmore (The Love Affairs of Hector Dalmore); Der Liedensweg der Inge Krafft (Inge Krafft's Calvary); Landstrasse und Grosstadt (Country Road and Big City); Lady Hamilton; Das Indische Grabmal—Part I: Die Sendung des Yoghi, Part II: Der Tiger von Eschnapur (Mysteries of India aka Above All Law/Truth—US 1922). **1922** Lucrezia Borgia (Lucretia Borgia—US 1929). **1923** Wilhelm Tell (William Tell); Glanz Gegen Gluck (Gold and Luck); Paganini. **1924** Carlos and Elisabeth (Carlos and Elizabeth); Das Wachsfiguerenkabinett (Waxworks and aka Three Waxmen—US 1929); Orlacs Hande (The Hands of Orlac—US 1928); Nju (aka Husbands or Lovers—US 1927); Schicksal (Fate). **1925** Le Comte Kostia (Count Kostia); Ingmarsarvet (aka In Dalarna and Jerusalem and Die Erde Ruft); Liebe Macht Blind (Love Is Blind). **1926** Der Geiger von Florenz (The Violinist of Florence aka Impetuous Youth); Die Bruder Schellenberg (The Brothers of Schellenberg aka Two Brothers—US 1928); Durfen wir Schweigen? (Should We Be Silent?); Kreuzzug des Weibes (The Wife's Crusade); Der Student von Prag (The Student of Prague and aka The Man Who Cheated Life—US 1929); Die Flucht in die Nacht (The Flight in the Night). **1927** The Beloved Rogue; A Man's Past; The Man Who Laughs. **1928** The Last Performance (aka Erik the Great and Illusion). **1929** Das Land Ohne Frauen (The Land Without Women). **1930** Die Letzte Kompagnie (The Last Company and aka Thirteen Men and a Girl—US); Die Grosse Sehnsucht (The Great Desire); Menschen im Kafig (aka Cape Forlorn); Bride 68; Great Power. **1931** Der Mann, der den Mord Beging (The Man Who Committed the Murder); Die Nacht der Entscheidung (The Night of the Decision); Der Kongress Tanzt (Congress Dances); Die Andere Seite (The Other Side); Rasputin. **1932** Der Schwarze Husan (The Black Hussar); Rome Express. **1933** F.P.1; I Was a Spy (US 1934); The Wandering Jew (US 1935); Ich und die Kaiserin (I and the Empress). **1934** Bella Donna (US 1935); Jew Suess (aka Power—US); William Tell (and 1923 version, aka The Legend of William Tell—US). **1935** The Passing of the Third Floor Back. **1936** King of the Damned. **1937** Under the Red Robe; Dark Journey. **1938** Tempete sur L'Asie (Storm over Asia); Le Joueur d'Echecs (The Chess Player and aka The Devil Is An Empress—US 1939). **1939** The Spy in Black (aka U-Boat 29—US); Alex. **1940** Contraband (aka Blackout—US); The Thief of Bagdad; Escape. **1941** A Woman's Face; Whistling in the Dark; The Men in Her Life. **1942** Nazi Agent; All Through the Night. **1943** Casablanca; Above Suspicion.

VEJAR, HARRY J.
Born: Apr. 24, 1890, Los Angeles, Calif. Died: Mar. 1, 1968, Los Angeles, Calif. Stage and screen actor.

Appeared in: **1921** The Sheik. **1926** Mademoiselle Modiste. **1929** Mexicali Rose. **1930** Wings of Adventure. **1932** Scarface. **1935** Bodertown; Mutiny on the Bounty. **1947** Ride the Pink Horse. **1948** Wake of the Red Witch; The Treasure of Sierra Madre. **1949** We Were Strangers.

VEKROFF, PERRY
Born: 1881, Alexandria, Egypt. Died: Jan. 3, 1937, Hollywood, Calif. (heart disease). Screen, stage actor, film director and screenwriter. Entered films as an actor with Lubin Co.

VELEZ, LUPE (Giadelupe Velez de Villalobos)
Born: July 18, 1908, San Luis Potosi, Mexico. Died: Dec. 14, 1944, Beverly Hills, Calif. (suicide). Screen actress. Divorced from actor and Olympic swimming star Johnny Weismuller. Star of "Mexican Spitfire" series. Was a 1928 Wampas Baby.

Appeared in: **1927** What Women Did for Men (short); Sailor Beware! (short); The Guacho. **1928** Stand and Deliver. **1929** Masquerade; Wolf Song; Lady of the Pavements; Where East Is East; Tiger Rose. **1930** East Is West (and Spanish version Oriente y Occidente); Hell Harbor; The Storm. **1931** Resurrection (and Spanish version Resurreccion); The Squaw Man; Cuban Love Song; Men in Her Life. **1932** Hombres en mi Vida; The Broken Wing; Kongo; The Half-Naked Truth. **1933** Mr. Broadway; Hot Pepper. **1934** Palooka; Laughing Boy; Hollywood Party; Strictly Dynamite. **1935** The Morals of Marcus. **1936** Gypsy Melody; Under Your Spell. **1937** Mad About Money (aka Stardust and aka He Loved an Actress—US 1938); High Flyers; Wings; La Zandunga. **1939** The Girl from Mexico; Mexican Spitfire. **1940** Mexican Spitfire Out West. **1941** Six Lessons from Madame La Zonga; Mexican Spitfire's Baby; Playmates; Honolulu Lu. **1942** Mexican Spitfire at Sea; Mexican Spitfire Sees a Ghost; Mexican Spitfire's Elephant. **1943** Ladies' Day; Redhead from Manhattan; Mexican Spitfire's Blessed Event. **1944** Nana. **1964** Big Parade of Comedy (documentary).

VELOZ, FRANK (Frank Nicholas Veloz)
Born: 1906. Died: Feb. 27, 1981, Los Angeles, Calif. Screen, television actor and dancer. Divorced from actress "Yolanda," with whom he appeared in films. Later married to Jean Veloz.

Appeared in: **1935** Rumba; Under the Pampas Moon. **1967** Champagne Waltz. **1942** Cavalcade of Dance (short); Pride of the Yankees. **1943** Honeymoon Lodge. **1944** Brazil. **1946** The Thrill of Brazil.

VEMBO, SOPHIA
Born: 1912, Gallipolis, Greece. Died: Mar. 12, 1978, Athens, Greece (stroke). Screen, stage actress and singer.

Appeared in: **1957** Stella. **1961** 288 Stournara St. (aka The House on Stournara Street).

VENABLE, REGINALD
Born: 1926. Died: June 28, 1974, Hollywood, Calif. (heart attack). Screen and stage actor. Son of actress Fay Bainter (dec. 1968).

VENESS, AMY
Born: 1876, England. Died: Sept. 22, 1960, Saltdean, England. Screen and stage actress.

Appeared in: **1931** Hobson's Choice; My Wife's Family. **1932** Flat No. 9; Pyjamas Preferred; Let Me Explain Dear; The Marriage Bond; Self-Made Lady; Money for Nothing; Tonight's the Night. **1933** Their Night Out; Hawley's of High Street; The Love Nest; A Southern Maid. **1934** The Old Curiosity Shop (US 1935); Red Wagon (US 1935). **1935** Royal Cavalcade (aka Regal Cavalcade—US); Brewster's Millions; Lorna Doone; Joy Ride; Play Up the Band; Drake of England (aka Drake the Pirate—US). **1936** Hearts of Hearts; The Beloved Vagabond; Did I Betray?; Skylarks. **1937** Aren't Men Beasts!; The Mill on the Floss (US 1939); Who Killed Markham? (aka The Angelus); The Show Goes On. **1938** Yellow Sands; Thistledown. **1939** Just William. **1940** John Smith Wakes Up. **1941** This England (aka Our Heritage); The Saint Meets the Tiger (US 1943). **1943** The Man in Grey (US 1945); Millions Like Us. **1944** This Happy Breed (US 1947); Fanny by Gaslight (aka Man of Evil—US 1948); Madonna of the Seven Moons; Don't Take It to Heart (US 1949). **1945** Don Chicago; They Were Sisters (US 1946). **1946** Carnival. **1947** The Turners of Prospect Road; The Woman in the Hall. **1948** Here Come the Huggetts (US 1950); Blanche Fury; My Brother's Keeper; Oliver Twist; Good Time Girl (US 1950). **1949** Vote for Huggett; The Huggetts Abroad. **1950** Madeleine; The Woman with No Name (aka Her Panelled Door—US 1951); Chance of a Lifetime (US 1951); The Astonished Heart. **1951** Tom Brown's School Days; Captain Horatio Hornblower. **1952** Angels One Five (US 1954). **1954** Doctor in the House (US 1955). **1955** The Woman for Joe.

VENKATARAMAYA, RELANGI
Born: 1910, India. Died: 1975, India. Stage and screen actor.

VENSEN, FLORENCE
Born: 1896. Died: Oct. 30, 1964, Hollywood, Calif. (heart attack). Screen and stage actress.

VENUTI, JOE
Born: 1897, at sea. Died: Aug. 14, 1978, Seattle, Wash. Jazz violinist, orchestra leader, composer and screen actor.

Appeared in: **1938** Garden of the Moon. **1947** Sarge Goes to College. **1950** Belle of Old Mexico. **1951** Disc Jockey. **1955** Pete Kelly's Blues.

VERA-ELLEN (Vera-Ellen Westmeyer Rohe)
Born: Feb. 16, 1926, Cincinnati, Ohio. Died: Aug. 30, 1981, Los Angeles, Calif. (cancer). Screen, stage, radio actress, singer and dancer.

Appeared in: **1945** The Wonder Man. **1946** The Kid from Brooklyn; Three Little Girls in Blue. **1947** Carnival in Costa Rica. **1948** Words and Music. **1949** Love Happy; On the Town. **1950** Three Little Words. **1951** Happy-Go-Lovely. **1952** The Belle of New York. **1953** The Big Leaguer; Call Me Madam. **1954** White Christmas. **1957** Let's Be Happy.

VERDI, FRANCIS M.
Born: 1881. Died: Mar. 29, 1952, N.Y. Screen, stage actor and playwright. Brother of actor Joe Verdi (dec. 1957).

Appeared in: **1929** House of Secrets.

VERDI, JOSEPH
Born: 1885. Died: Dec. 27, 1957, New York, N.Y. Screen, stage, vaudeville and television actor. Billed in vaudeville as part of "Clark and Verdi" team. Brother of actor Francis Verdi (dec. 1952).

Appeared in: **1936** The Crime of Dr. Crespi. **1957** The Vintage.

VERHOEVEN, PAUL
Born: 1901, Unna/Westfalen, Germany. Died: Mar. 22, 1975, Munich, Germany (heart attack). Screen, stage actor, film, stage director, screenwriter, playwright and author. Father of director Michael Verhoeven.

Appeared in: **1936** Der Kaiser von Kalifornien. **1938** Es Leuchten die Sterne; Unsere Kleine Frau. **1940** Was Wird Hier Gespielt?; Die 3 Codonas. **1941** Jakko. **1942** Die Nacht in Venedig; Der Grosse Schatten. **1943** Herr Sanders Lebt Gefaehrlich; Ein Gluecklicher Mensch (aka Schule des Lebens). **1944** Philharmoniker. **1949** Du Bist Nicht Allein. **1951** Die Schuld des Dr. Homma; Heidelberger Romanze. **1952** Die Leibhaftige Unschuld. **1953** Hochzeit auf Reisen; Praterherzen (aka Tingeltangel). **1954** Eine Frau von Heute; Ewiger Walzer. **1955** Roman Einer Siebzehnjaehrigen. **1958** ... und Nichts als die Wahrheit. **1959** Menschen im Netz (aka The Unwilling Agent—US 1968). **1965** An der Schoenen Blauen Donau. **1967** Paarungen. **1968** Hamlet.

VERMILYEA, HAROLD
Born: Oct. 10, 1889, New York, N.Y. Died: Jan. 8, 1958, New York, N.Y. Screen, stage, radio and television actor.

Appeared in: **1917** The Law That Failed. **1946** O.S.S. **1948** The Emperor Waltz; The Big Clock; The Miracle of the Bells; Gentleman's Agreement; The Sainted Sisters; Beyond Glory; Sorry, Wrong Number. **1949** Chicago Deadline; Manhandled. **1950** Born to Be Bad; Edge of Doom. **1951** Katie Did It. **1952** Finders Keepers.

VERMOYAL, PAUL
Born: France. Died: Oct., 1925, Neuilly, France. Screen and stage actor.

Appeared in: **1924** The Arab.

VERNE, KAREN (Ingeborg Catharine Marie Rose Klinckerfuss aka KAAREN aka CATHERINE YOUNG aka INGABOR KATRINE KLINCKERFUSS)
Born: 1918, Berlin, Germany. Died: Dec. 23, 1967, Hollywood, Calif. Screen, stage and television actress. Divorced from actor Peter Lorre (dec. 1964) and married to film historian James Powers (dec. 1980).

Appeared in: **1939** Ten Days in Paris (aka Missing Ten Days—US). **1940** Sky Murder. **1941** King's Row; Underground; Missing Ten Days. **1942** All Through the Night; The Great Impersonation. **1943** Sherlock Holmes and the Secret Weapon. **1944** The Seventh Cross. **1952** The Bad and the Beautiful. **1953** The Story of Three Loves. **1955** A Bullett for Joey. **1965** Ship of Fools. **1966** Madam X.

VERNEY, GUY
Born: England. Died: Sept. 19, 1970, London, England. Screen, stage actor, television producer and director. Married to actress Margaret Anderson.

Appeared in: **1944** This Happy Breed (US 1947). **1947** Fame Is the Spur (US 1949). **1948** Anna Karenina. **1950** Cage of Gold (US 1951). **1953** Martin Luther.

VERNO, JERRY
Born: July 26, 1895, London, England. Died: June 29, 1975, England? Screen, stage, vaudeville, radio and television actor.

Appeared in: **1931** Two Crowded Hours (film debut); My Friend the

King; The Beggar Student. **1932** There Goes the Bride (US 1933); Hotel Splendide; His Lordship; My Wife's Mother. **1934** The Life of the Party. **1935** Royal Cavalcade (aka Regal Cavalcade-US); The 39 Steps; Lieutenant Daring, RN. **1936** Ourselves Alone (aka River of Unrest—US 1937); Pagiacci (aka A Clown Must Laugh—US 1938); Broken Blossoms (US 1937); Gypsy Melody. **1937** Farewell Again (aka Troopship—US 1938); Non-Stop New York; Young and Innocent (aka A Girl Was Young—US 1938); Sensation. **1938** The Gables Mystery; Queer Cargo (aka Pirates of the Seven Seas—US); Mountains 'O' Mourne; Anything to Declare?; Take Cover (short); Old Mother Riley in Paris. **1940** The Chinese Bungalow (aka Chinese Den—US 1941); Old Mother Riley Catches a Quisling (reissue of Old Mother Riley in Paris—1938). **1941** The Common Touch. **1948** The Red Shoes. **1954** The Belles of St. Trinian's (US 1955). **1957** After the Ball. **1963** A Place to Go. **1965** The Plague of the Zombies (US 1966).

VERNON, BOBBY
Born: Mar. 9, 1897, Chicago, Ill. Died: June 28, 1939, Hollywood, Calif. (heart attack). Screen, stage actor and screenwriter. Son of actress Dorothy Vernon (dec. 1970). Entered films at age 16.

Appeared in: **1913** Mike and Jake at the Beach. **1914** Joker Comedies (short). **1915** Fickle Fatty's Fall; The Hunt. **1916** His Pride and Shame; A Dash of Courage; Hearts and Sparks; The Social Club; The Danger Girl (working title Love on Skates). **1917** The Nick of Time Baby; Teddy at the Throttle; Dangers of a Bride; Whose Baby?; The Sultan's Wife. **1920** Educational shorts. **1925** The following shorts: French Pastry; Great Guns; Don't Pinch; Air Tight; Watch Out; Slippery Feet; Oo-La-La. **1926** Footloose Widows. **1927** Christie Comedies (shorts); the following shorts: Bugs My Dear; Hold 'Er Cowboy; Save the Pieces; Stock Exchange; Stop Kidding; and Sweeties. **1930** Cry Baby (short). **1931** Stout Hearts and Willing Hands. **1932** Make Me a Star (short); Ship A Hooey (short). **1960** When Comedy Was King (documentary).

VERNON, DOROTHY (aka DOROTHY BAIRD aka DOROTHY BURNS)
Born: Nov. 11, 1875, Germany. Died: Oct. 28, 1970, Granada Hills, Calif. (heart disease). Screen actress. Mother of actor Bobby Vernon (dec. 1939). Do not confuse with English actress Dorthea Baird (dec. 1933).

Appeared in: **1921** Christie Johnstone. **1924** Lover's Lane. **1925** Flying Fool; Tricks. **1928** The Manhattan Cowboy; Tenderloin. **1929** Headin' Westward; Should a Girl Marry?; Riders of the Storm. **1930** The Costello Case; Madam Satan. **1934** Woman Haters (short); I Hate Women. **1935** All at Sea; Straight from the Heart. **1936** Theodora Goes Wild. **1938** Father O'Flynn; Juvenile Court. **1940** Third Finger, Left Hand. **1941** Father Takes a Wife; You'll Never Get Rich.

VERNON, ISABELLA
Born: 1874. Died: Apr. 21, 1930, New York, N.Y. Screen and stage actress. Married to stage actor Henry Waterman (dec.).

Appeared in: **1917** An Amateur Orphan; Polly of the Circus; The Rise of Jennie Cushing. **1918** Joan of Plattsburgh. **1922** A Tailor Made Man. **1923** Radio-Mania.

VERNON, LOU
Born: 1888, Australia. Died: Dec. 22, 1971, Sydney, Australia. Screen, radio actor and singer.

Appeared in: **1959** On the Beach.

VERNON, WALLY
Born: 1904, New York, N.Y. Died: Mar. 7, 1970, Van Nuys, Calif. (hit and run auto accident). Screen, stage, vaudeville, burlesque and minstrel actor.

Appeared in: **1937** Mountain Music; This Way Please; You Can't Have Everything. **1938** Happy Landing; Kentucky Moonshine; Alexander's Ragtime Band; Sharpshooters; Meet the Girls. **1939** Chasing Danger; Tailspin; The Gorilla; Charlie Chan at Treasure Island; Broadway Serenade. **1940** Sailor's Lady; Margie; Sandy Gets Her Man. **1943** Tahiti Honey; Reveille with Beverly; Get Going; Fugitive from Sonora; Here Comes Elmer; Pistol Packin' Mama. **1944** Call of the South Seas; Outlaws of Santa Fe; Silent Partner; Silver City Kid; Stagecoach to Monterey; California Joe. **1948** King of Gamblers, Winner Take All; Fighting Mad. **1949** Always Leave Them Laughing; Square Dance Jubilee. **1950** Beauty on Parade; Border Rangers; Holiday Rhythm; Gunfire; Train to Tombstone; Everybody's Dancing. **1952** What Price Glory?; Bloodhounds of Broadway. **1953** Affair with a Stranger. **1956** Fury at Gunsight Pass; The White Squaw. **1964** What a Way to Go.

VERNON, WILLIAM "BILLY"
Born: June 21, 1912, New York, N.Y. Died: Aug. 19, 1971, Granada Hills, Calif. (heart attack). Screen actor and dialogue coach.

VERSOIS, ODILE (Militza de Poliakoff-Baidarov)
Born: June 15, 1930, Paris, France. Died: June 23, 1980, Paris, France (cancer). Screen and stage actress. Sister of actresses Olga Poliakoff, Helene Vallier and Marina Vlady.

Appeared in: Les Dernieres Vacances (film debut). **1951** Into the Blue (aka The Man in the Dinghy—US). **1953** A Day to Remember (US 1955); Paola and Francesca. **1954** The Young Lovers (aka Chance Meeting—US 1955). **1955** To Paris with Love. **1956** Checkpoint (US 1957). **1957** Herrscher Ohne Krone (Ruler Without a Crown aka King in Shadow—US 1961). **1959** Passport to Shame (aka Room 43—US). **1960** Nude in a White Car. **1962** Cartouche (US 1964). **1968** Benjamin ou les Memoires d'un Puceau (aka Benjamin—US).

VESOTA, BRUNO (Bruno William VeSota)
Born: Mar. 25, 1922, Chicago, Ill. Died: Sept. 24, 1976, Culver City, Calif. (heart attack). Screen, stage, radio, television actor and film director.

Appeared in: **1953** The System. **1954** The Wild One; Bait; Tennessee Champ; Rails Into Laramie; The Long Wait; The Egyptian; The Fast and the Furious; The Last Time I Saw Paris. **1955** Jupiter's Darling; Kismet; Dementia. **1956** Female Jungle; The Gunslinger; The Oklahoma Woman. **1957** Carnival Rock; The Undead; Rock All Night; Teenage Doll. **1958** War of the Satellites; Hot Car Girl; The Cry Baby Killer. **1959** Daddy-O; I, Mobster; A Bucket of Blood; Attack of the Giant Leeches (aka The Giant Leeches); The Violent and the Damned; The Wasp Woman. **1960** Valley of the Redwoods; Code of Silence (aka Killer's Cage); The Story of Ruth. **1961** 20,000 Eyes; The Cat Burglar; The Choppers. **1962** The Little Bank Robber; The Case of Patty Smith; Invasion of the Star Creatures; The Devil's Hand. **1963** Night Tide; The Haunted Palace. **1964** Attack of the Mayan Mummy; Curse of the Stone Head (narrator); Your Cheatin' Heart. **1965** The Girls on the Beach; Creature of the Walking Dead. **1966** She Was a Hippy Vampire (aka The Wild World of Batwoman). **1967** Hell's Angels on Wheels; The Perils of Pauline. **1968** A Man Called Dagger; Single Room Furnished. **1971** Wild Rovers; Bunny O'Hare; Million Dollar Duck.

VESPERMANN, KURT
Born: 1887, Kulmsee, West Prussia. Died: July 13, 1957, Berlin, Germany (heart disease). Screen and stage actor.

Appeared in: **1916** The Bear from Baskerville (film debut). **1930** Bride 58. **1932** Der Schrecken der Garnison; Pension Schoeller; Keine Feier Ohne Meyer. **1934** Schuss im Morgengrauen. **1935** Die Kalte Mansell; Konjunkturritter; Die Unschuld vom Lande; Der Unbekannte Gast (The Unknown Guest). **1936** Das Erbe in Pretoria; Die Stimme der Liebe; Ist Mein Mann Nicht Fabelhaft. **1937** Zwei im Sonnenschein. **1938** Wenn Du eine Schwiegermutter Hast (When You Have a Mother-in-Law); Sie und die Drei (She and the Three). **1939** Der Lustige Witwenball (The Merry Widow's Ball); Der Verkannte Lebemann (The Unrecognized Man of the World).

VESSILIADOU, GEORGIA
Born: 1897, Greece. Died: Feb. 12, 1980, Athens, Greece. Screen, stage actress and singer.

VESTRY, ART
Born: 1939. Died: Nov. 7, 1976, Beverly Hills, Calif. (heart attack). Screen, stage and television actor.

Appeared in: **1977** The Last Tycoon.

VIBART, HENRY
Born: Dec. 25, 1863, Musselburgh, Scotland. Died: 1939, England? Screen and stage actor. Entered films in 1913.

Appeared in: **1914** The Schemers, or The Jewels of Hate; The Hills Are Calling; In the Shadow of Big Ben; Dr. Fenton's Ordeal; The Terror of the Air. **1915** The Passing of a Soul; Courtmartialled (aka The Traitor); The Incorruptible Crown; The Baby on the Barge; Barnaby Rudge; The Shepherd of Souls; As Ye Repent (aka Redeemed—US); Spies; Tilly the Nut; The Curtain's Secret (aka Behind the Curtain). **1916** Partners Again; Annie Laurie; The Grand Babylon Hotel. **1917** Masks and Faces; The Blindness of Fortune. **1918** Towards the Light; Herself. **1919** Gamblers All; The City of Beautiful Nonsense. **1920** Judge Not; Enchantment; Aylwin; The Amazing Quest of Mr. Ernest Bliss Series. **1921** The Four Feathers; A Woman of Importance; Sonia (aka The Woman Who Came Back—US 1922); Mr. Justice Raffles; The Bargain; The Adventures of Sherlock Holmes series including The Beryl Coronet. **1922** Simple Simon; The Bohemian Girl; A Bill for Divorcement; The Crimson Circle; Flames of Passion; Weavers of Fortune. **1926** A Kiss for Cinderella; Just Suppose; The Dancer of Paris; The Wilderness Woman; The Prince of Tempters. **1927** Racing Luck (reissue of Weavers of Fortune 1922); The Poor Nut. **1928** The Physician (US 1929); Toni; Love's Option (aka A Girl of Today).

VICKERS, MARTHA (Martha MacVicar)
Born: 1925. Died: Nov. 2, 1971, Van Nuys, Calif. Screen actress. Divorced from actor Mickey Rooney, publicist A. C. Lyles, Jr., and polo player Manuel Rojas.

Appeared in: **1941** The Wolf Man (film debut). **1943** Frankenstein Meets the Wolfman; Hi'ya Sailor; Top Man; Captive Wild Woman. **1944** This Is the Life; Marine Raiders; The Mummy's Ghost; The Falcon in Mexico. **1946** The Big Sleep; The Time, the Place and the Girl. **1947** The Man I Love; That Way With Women; Love and Learn. **1948** Ruthless. **1949** Bad Boy; Alimony; Daughter of the West. **1955** The Big Bluff. **1957** The Burglar. **1960** Four Fast Guns.

VICTOR, CHARLES
Born: 1896, England. Died: Dec. 23, 1965, London, England. Screen and stage actor.

Appeared in: **1939** Hell's Cargo (aka Dangerous Cargo—US). **1940** Dr. O'Dowd; Old Mother Riley in Society; Contraband (aka Blackout—US); Old Mother Riley in Business; You Will Remember; Laugh It Off. **1941** East of Piccadilly (aka The Strangler—US 1942); This England (aka Our Heritage); Atlantic Ferry (aka Sons of the Sea—US); The Saint Meets the Tiger (US 1943); He Found a Star; 49th Parallel (aka The Invaders—US 1942); Ships With Wings (US 1942); Breach of Promise (aka Adventure in Blackmail—US 1943). **1942** They Flew Alone (aka Wings and the Woman—US); The Missing Millions; Those Kids from Town; The Next of Kin (US 1943); The Peterville Diamond; Lady from Lisbon; Squadron Leader X (US 1943); The Foreman Went to France (aka Somewhere in France—US 1943). **1943** The Silver Fleet (US 1945); When We Are Married; Undercover (aka Underground Guerillas—US 1944); Rhythm Serenade; Escape to Danger; My Learned Friend; They Met in the Dark (US 1945); San Demetrio-London. **1944** It Happened One Sunday; Vote for Huggett. **1945** I Live in Grosvenor Square (aka A Yank in London—US 1946); The Way to the Stars (aka Johnny in the Clouds—US); The Rake's Progress (aka Notorious Gentleman—US 1946); The Man from Morocco. **1946** Gaiety George (aka Showtime—US 1948); This Man Is Mine; The Magic Bow (US 1947); Woman to Woman. **1947** Variety Girl; While the Sun Shines (US 1950); Temptation Harbour (US 1949); Meet Me at Dawn (US 1948); Green Fingers; While I Live. **1948** Broken Journey; The Calendar. **1949** Fools Rush In; Landfall. **1950** The Cure for Love; Waterfront (aka Waterfront Women—US 1952); The Woman in Question (aka Five Angels on Murder—US); The Elusive Pimpernel; Man Who Cheated Himself; Motor Patrol. **1951** The Galloping Major; Encore (US 1952); Calling Bulldog Drummond. **1952** The Frightened Man; Something Money Can't Buy; Made in Heaven; The Ringer. **1953** The Gay Duelist (reissue of 1947 Meet Me at Dawn); Those People Next Door; Appointment in London (US 1955); Street Corner; The Girl on the Pier; The Saint's Return (aka The Saint's Girl Friday—US); Meet Mr. Lucifer; The Steel Lady. **1954** The Love Lottery; Fast and Loose; The Embezzler; The Rainbow Jacket; For Better, For Worse (aka Cocktails in the Kitchen—US 1955); Man Crazy. **1955** Police Dog; Value for Money (US 1957); An Alligator Named Daisy (US 1957); Dial 999 (aka The Way Out—US 1956). **1956** Now and Forever; The Extra Day; Eyewitness; Home and Away; Tiger in the Smoke; The Best Things in Life Are Free; Charley Moon. **1957** There's Always Thursday; After the Ball; The Prince and the Showgirl. **1958** Twelve Desperate Hours. **1960** Strangers When We Meet. **1961** The Pit and the Pendulum. **1970** The Psycho Lover (aka Psycho Killer, The Loving Touch and The Lovely Touch).

VICTOR, HENRY
Born: Oct. 2, 1898, London, England. Died: May 15, 1945, Hollywood, Calif. (brain tumor). Screen actor.

Appeared in: **1914** Revolution (aka The King's Romance and aka The Revolutionist—US). **1916** She; The Picture of Dorian Gray. **1917** Ora Pro Nobis. **1918** The Secret Woman. **1919** The Heart of a Rose; The Call of the Sea; A Lass O' the Looms. **1920** Calvary; As God Made Her; John Heriot's Wife; Beyond the Dreams of Avarice. **1921** The Old Wives' Tale; Sheer Bluff. **1922** Bentley's Conscience; A Romance of Old Bagdad; Diana of the Crossways; A Bill for Divorcement; The Crimson Killer. **1923** The Prodigal Son; The Scandal; The Royal Oak. **1924** The Colleen Bawn; The White Shadow (aka White Shadows—US); Henry, King of Navarre; Slaves of Destiny (aka Miranda of the Balcony); His Grace Gives Notice; The Love Story of Aliette Brunton; The Sins Ye Do. **1925** A Romance of Mayfair; Braveheart; The White Monkey. **1926** Crossed Signals; The Fourth Commandment; Mullhall's Great Catch. **1927** The Beloved Rogue; Topsy and Eva; The Luck of the Navy. **1928** The Guns of Loos; Tommy Atkins. **1929** After the Verdict (US 1930); Down Channel; The Hate Ship. **1930** Song of Soho; Are You There?; One Heavenly Night. **1931** Seas Beneath; Suicide Fleet. **1932** The Mummy; Freaks. **1933** I Spy; Tiger Bay; Luxury Liner. **1934** The Scotland Yard Mystery (aka The Living Dead—US); The Way of Youth. **1935** Murder at Monte Carlo; Handle With Care; Can You Hear Me Mother? **1936** The Secret Voice; Fame; Conquest of the Air. **1937** Holiday's End; Our Fighting Navy (aka Torpedoed!—US 1939); Fine Feathers; The Great Barrier (aka Silent Barriers—US). **1939** Confessions of a Nazi Spy; Hotel Imperial; Thunder Afloat; Pack Up Your Troubles; Nick Carter, Master Detective; Nurse Edith Cavell. **1940** Mystery Sea Raider; Zanzibar. **1941** King of the Zombies; Blue, White and Perfect. **1942** Sherlock Holmes and the Secret Weapon; To Be or Not to Be; Desperate Journey. **1943** That Nazty Nuisance.

VICTOR EMMANUEL III
Born: Nov. 11, 1869, Naples, Italy. Died: Dec. 28, 1947, Alexandria, Egypt. King of Italy from 1900 to 1946. He also appeared on screen.

Appeared in: **1923** The Eternal City.

VIDACOVICH, IRVING J. "PINKY"
Born: 1905. Died: July 5, 1966, New Orleans, La. Screen actor, musician, radio writer and composer. Known as "Cajun Pete" of radio.

Appeared in: **1950** Panic in the Streets.

VIDAL, HENRI
Born: 1919, France. Died: Dec. 10, 1959, Paris, France (heart attack). Screen actor. Married to actress Michele Morgan.

Appeared in: **1946** Les Maudits (The Damned). **1950** Quai de Grenelle. **1951** Fabiola. **1952** The Seven Capital Sins; The Strollers. **1953** Naughty Martine. **1954** Port du Desir; Desperate Decision. **1955** The Wicked Go to Hell. **1956** Porte Les Lilas. **1958** Gates of Paris; Attila; The House on the Waterfront; La Parisienne; What Price Murder. **1960** Voulez-Vous Danser Avec Moi (Come Dance With Me).

VIDOR, FLORENCE (Florence Cobb)
Born: July 23, 1895, Houston, Tex. Died: Nov. 3, 1977, Pacific Palisades, Calif. Screen actress and film producer. Divorced from actor/director King Vidor (dec. 1982) and violinist Jascha Heifetz. Mother of Susanne Vidor and Josepha and Robert Heifetz. Entered films with Vitagraph.

Appeared in: **1916** Bill Peters' Kid; Curfew at Simpton Center; The Yellow Girl; The Intrigue. **1917** Tale of Two Cities; American Methods; Big Timber; The Cook of Canyon Camp; Hashimura Togo; The Countess Charming. **1918** The Secret Game; The Widow's Might; The Honor of His House; White Man's Law; The Bravest Way; Old Wives for New; Till I Come Back to You. **1919** The Other Half; Poor Relations. **1920** The Jack Knife Man; The Family Honor. **1921** Lying Lips; Beau Revel. **1922** Hail the Woman; Skin Deep; Conquering the Women; Woman Wake Up!; The Real Adventure; Dusk to Dawn. **1923** Souls for Sale; Alice Adams; Main Street; The Virginian. **1924** The Marriage Circle; Borrowed Husbands; Welcome Stranger; Barbara Frietchie; Christine of the Hungry Heart; Husbands and Lovers. **1925** The Mirage; The Girl of Gold; Are Parents People? Grounds for Divorce; Marry Me; The Trouble with Wives. **1926** The Enchanted Hill; The Grand Duchess and the Waiter; Sea Horses; You Never Know Women; Eagle of the Sea. **1927** The Popular Sin; Afraid to Love; The World at Her Feet; One Woman to Another; Honeymoon Hate. **1928** The Magnificent Flirt; Doomsday; The Patriot. **1929** Chinatown Nights.

VIE, FLORENCE
Born: 1876, England. Died: Apr. 12, 1939, England? Screen and stage actress.

Appeared in: **1929** The Bondman.

VIERTEL, SALKA
Born: 1889, Poland. Died: Oct. 20, 1978, Klosters, Switzerland. Screen, stage actress and screenwriter. Married to film director Berthold Viertel. Mother of novelist/screenwriter Peter Viertel.

Appeared in: **1930** Anna Christie.

VIGNOLA, ROBERT G.
Born: 1882, Italy. Died: Oct. 25, 1953, Hollywood, Calif. Screen actor and film director. Entered films as an actor with Kalem in 1907.

VIKING, VONCEIL
Died: Dec. 2, 1929, Banning, Calif. (auto accident injuries). Screen and vaudeville actress. "Obtained a picture engagement by riding horseback from New York to Los Angeles in 120 days on a wager of $25,000."

VILA, SABRA DESHON
Born: 1850. Died: Sept. 20, 1917, Brooklyn, N.Y. Screen and stage actress.

VILAR, JEAN
Born: 1913, France. Died: May 28, 1971, Sete, France (heart attack). Screen, stage actor and stage director.

Appeared in: **1950** Gates of the Night. **1952** The Thirst of Man.

VILCHES, ERNESTO
Born: Spain. Died: Dec. 8, 1954, Barcelona, Spain (auto accident). Stage and screen actor.

Appeared in: **1933** Cascarrabias; La Noche del Pecado. **1936** El Desaparecido. **1938** El 113.

VILLARD, FRANK
Born: 1917, France. Died: Sept., 1980, Geneva, Switzerland. Screen actor.

Appeared in: **1950** The Cheat; Gigi. **1951** Minne. **1952** Savage Triangle. **1953** Sextette; Seven Deadly Sins. **1954** Secret Document—Vienna. **1959** Detournement de Mineures (aka The Price of Flesh—US 1962). **1961** Le Cave se Rebiffe (The Sucker Strikes Back aka The Counterfeiters of Paris and aka Money, Money, Money—US 1962). **1962** Gigot; Le Crime ne Paie Pas (Crime Does Not Pay). **1964** Gentleman from Epson. **1965** Mata-Hari Agent H-21 (US 1967).

VILLARD, JULIETTE
Born: 1945, France. Died: Mar., 1971, France. Screen actress.

Appeared in: **1967** Le Grand Meaulnes (aka The Wanderer—US 1969). **1970** La Liberte en Croupe.

VILLARES, JESSIE
Died: Feb., 1929. Screen and stage actor.

Appeared in: **1914** The Loafer.

VILLARET, JOAO
Born: 1914, Portugal. Died: Jan. 23, 1961, Lisbon, Portugal (cancer). Screen, stage, radio and television actor.

VILLARREAL, JULIO
Born: 1885, Mexico. Died: Aug. 4, 1958, Mexico City, Mexico. Screen actor. One of the first Spanish speaking actors to make talking films in Hollywood.

Appeared in: **1933** Una Vida Por Otra; El Rey de los Gitanos; La Ley Del Haren; La Noche del Pecado. **1934** Sagrario; Profanacion; Tiburon; La Sangre Manda; Ora y Plata; Tu Hijo; Quien Mato a Eva. **1935** Corazon Bandolero; Chucho el Roto; El Vuelo de la Muerte; Tribu. **1938** El Pasado Acusa (The Accusing Past). **1940** Odio (Hate); Mi Madrecita (My Little Mother). **1943** The Life of Simon Bolivar; El Conde de Monte Cristo. **1947** Honeymoon. **1950** The Torch. **1953** Plunder of the Sun; Eugene Grandet. **1955** Seven Cities of Gold. **1956** The Beast of Hollow Mountain.

VILLEGAS, LUCIO
Born: Feb. 25, 1883, Lota, Chile. Died: July 20, 1968. Screen actor.

Appeared in: **1934** The Notorious Sophie Lang; Nada Mas Que Una Mujer. **1935** Goin' to Town; Storm Over the Andes. **1936** A Message to Garcia. **1937** I'll Take Romance. **1939** The Renegade Ranger; Only Angels Have Wings; The Fighting Gringo.

VINAYAK, MASTER
Born: India. Died: Aug. 19, 1947. Screen actor, film producer and director.

VINCENOT, LOUIS
Born: 1884. Died: Feb. 25, 1967. Screen actor.

Appeared in: **1934** Limehouse Blues. **1936** Ace Drummond (serial). **1937** The Thirteenth Chair; Wee Willie Winkie. **1938** Suez.

VINCENT, ALLEN
Born: 1903. Died: Nov. 30, 1979, Canoga Park, Calif. Screen, stage, television actor, screenwriter and author.

Appeared in: **1929** A Mother's Boy. **1932** Street of Women; This Reckless Age; No More Orchids; Thrill of Youth; Two Against the World; Crooner. **1933** Broadway Bad; Daring Daughters; I Have Lived; Mystery of the Wax Museum; Carnival Lady. **1934** Success at Any Price; Hi Nellie. **1935** Bad Boy; The Return of Peter Grim. **1936** Easy Money; Chatterbox; Sutter's Gold. **1937** A Family Affair. **1938** Army Girl; Ladies in Distress.

VINCENT, CLIVE
Born: England. Died: Apr. 11, 1943, England? Screen actor. Appeared in silent films.

VINCENT, GENE
Born: 1935. Died: Oct. 12, 1971, Saugus, Calif. Screen actor, rock-and-roll singer, songwriter and musical group leader.

Appeared in: **1956** The Girl Can't Help It (with "His Blue Caps"). **1958** Hot Rod Gang. **1962** It's Trad, Dad!; Ring-a-Ding Rhythm! **1963** Live It Up (aka Sing and Swing—US 1964). **1970** Naked Hearts.

VINCENT, JAMES
Born: July 19, 1882, Springfield, Mass. Died: July 12, 1957, New York, N.Y. Screen, stage actor, film producer and director. Entered films as an actor.

VINCENT, LARRY
Born: 1925. Died: Mar. 8, 1975, Burbank, Calif. (cancer). Screen, stage, and television actor.

Appeared in: **1969** The Witchmaker.

VINCENT, ROBBIE
Born: 1896, England. Died: Mar. 6, 1968, Blackpool, England. Screen actor.

VINCENT, SAILOR BILLY (William J. Vincent)
Born: 1896. Died: July 12, 1966, Toluca Lake, Calif. (heart attack). Screen and television actor, stuntman and professional boxer.

Appeared in: **1929** The Man I Love; Woman Trap; Speakeasy. **1930** Seven Days Leave. **1935** The Irish in Us; She Gets Her Man. **1941** Shadow of the Thin Man. **1942** Yankee Doodle Dandy. **1944** The Adventures of Mark Twain; Destination Tokyo. **1948** Albuquerque. **1949** Madame Bovary. **1950** Montana; The Fuller Brush Girl; Hot Rod; Blues Busters. **1956** Around the World in 80 Days; The Steel Jungle. **1957** Affair in Reno. **1965** Young Fury.

VINE, BILLY
Born: 1915. Died: Feb. 10, 1958, New York, N.Y. (heart ailment). Screen, stage, vaudeville and television actor.

Appeared in only two films: **1945** The Lucky Stiff. **1956** Vagabond King.

VINTON, ARTHUR ROLFE
Born: Brooklyn, N.Y. Died: Feb. 26, 1963, Guadalajara, Mexico. Screen, stage and radio actor. Best known for portrayal of radio's "The Shadow."

Appeared in: **1931** The Viking. **1932** Washington Merry-Go-Round; Man Against Woman; Laughter in Hell. **1933** Gambling Ship; Blondie Johnson; Picture Snatcher; Lilly Turner; Heroes for Sale; Son of a Sailor; When Strangers Marry; This Day and Age; The Avenger; Central Airport. **1934** Gambling Lady; Cross Country Cruise; A Very Honorable Guy; The Personality Kid; Dames; The Man Trailer; Jealousy. **1935** Society Doctor; Unknown Woman; Little Big Shot; Circumstantial Evidence; King Solomon of Broadway; Red Salute; Rendezvous at Midnight.

VINTON, HORACE
Born: 1854. Died: Nov. 26, 1930, New York, N.Y. (heart ailment). Screen and stage actor.

Appeared in: **1916** Romeo and Juliet.

VISAROFF, MICHAEL
Born: Nov. 18, 1892, Russia. Died: Feb. 27, 1951, Hollywood, Calif. (pneumonia). Screen and stage actor. Married to actress Vina Visaroff (dec. 1938).

Appeared in: **1925** The Swan (film debut). **1926** Paris; Valencia. **1927** The Sunset Derby; Camille; Two Arabian Knights. **1928** The Last Command; The Adventurer; The Night Bird; Plastered in Paris; Tempest; We Americans. **1929** Marquis Preferred; The House of Horror; Illusion; Disraeli; Hungarian Rhapsody; The Exalted Flapper; Four Devils. **1930** Dracula; Morocco. **1931** Arizona Terror; Mata Hari; Chinatown After Dark. **1932** Freaks; The Man Who Played God. **1933** Strange People; The Barbarian; The King of the Arena. **1934** Picture Brides; Fugitive Road; The Marines Are Coming!; The Merry Frinks; The Cat's Paw; Wagon Wheels; We Live Again. **1935** Escapade; One More Spring; The Mark of the Vampire; The Break of Hearts; Anna Karenina; Paddy O'Day. **1936** Change of the Light Brigade; The Gay Desperado. **1937** Champagne Waltz; Soldier and the Lady; Angel. **1938** Suez; Bluebeard's Eighth Wife; Air Devils; Tropic Holiday; I'll Get a Million. **1939** Paris Honeymoon; Everything Happens at Night; On Your Toes; Juarez and Maximilian. **1940** Charlie Chan at the Wax Museum; The Son of Monte Cristo; Four Sons; Second Chorus. **1943** For Whom the Bell Tolls; Mission to Moscow; Hostages; Paris After Dark. **1944** Experiment Perilous. **1945** Song to Remember; Yolanda and the Thief; Her Highness and the Bellboy. **1947** Flight to Nowhere; Intrigue.

VISAROFF, NINA
Born: 1888. Died: Dec. 14, 1938, Beverly Hills, Calif. Stage and screen actress. Married to actor Michael Visaroff (dec. 1951).

Appeared in: **1936** Paddy O'Day.

VISCONTI, LUCHINO
Born: Nov. 2, 1906, Milan, Italy. Died: Mar., 1976, Rome, Italy (influenza/cardiac ailment). Film director, screenwriter, set designer and screen actor.

Appeared in: **1952** Siamo Donne.

VISCONTI, LUIGI "FANFULLA"
Born: 1913, Italy. Died: Jan. 5, 1971, Bologna, Italy (heart attack). Screen actor.

Appeared in: **1956** Il Tesoro di Romme (Rommel's Treasure—US 1963). **1960** Il Figlio del Corsaro Rosso (Son of the Red Corsair—US 1963). **1961** Il Ladvo di Bagdad (The Thief of Bagdad). **1963** Finche dura la Tempesta (aka Torpedo Bay—US 1964).

VITERBO, PATRICIA
Born: 1943, France. Died: Nov. 10, 1966, Paris, France (drowned in car accident). Screen actress.

Appeared in: **1965** You Must Be Joking. **1967** Two for the Road.

VIVIAN, PERCIVAL (Percival Seymoure Vivian)
Born: Mar. 13, 1890, England. Died: Jan. 15, 1961, Burbank, Calif. (arteriosclerosis). Screen actor. Married to stage actress Rene Vivian (dec. 1949). Father of actor Daniel Vivian.

Appeared in: **1945** Kitty; A Letter to Evie. **1946** Susie Steps Out. **1947** A Double Life. **1949** A Kiss in the Dark. **1954** Prince Valiant. **1955** Daddy Long Legs; Prince of Players.

VIVIAN, ROBERT
Born: 1859, London, England. Died: Jan. 31, 1944, New York, N.Y. Screen and stage actor.

Appeared in: **1917** Law of the Land. **1918** Under the Greenwood Tree. **1919** Counterfeit; Picadilly Jim; The Spite Bride; La Belle Russe. **1920** The Plunger; The Restless Sex; The New York Idea. **1939** Back Door to Heaven.

VIVIAN, RUTH
Born: England. Died: Oct. 24, 1949, New York, N.Y. Screen and stage actress.

Appeared in: **1941** The Man Who Came to Dinner (stage and film versions). **1949** A Letter to Three Wives.

VODNOY, MAX (aka MATTHEW VODNOY)
Born: 1892, Russia. Died: May 27, 1939, New York, N.Y. (heart attack). Screen, stage and vaudeville actor.

Appeared in: **1937** The Green Fields. **1938** The Singing Blacksmith.

VOGAN, EMMETT (Charles Emmet Vogan)
Born: Sept. 27, 1893, Ohio. Died: Nov. 13, 1969, Woodland Hills, Calif. (septecemia and pneumonia). Screen actor.

Appeared in: **1934** Love Birds; Manhattan Melodrama; Flirtation Walk. **1935** G-Men; The Irish in Us; The Whole Town's Talking; Stars Over Broadway. **1936** The Public Pays (short); The Big Noise; Two in Revolt; Adventure in Manhattan. **1937** Fly-Away Baby; San Quentin; Let's Get Married; Kid Galahad. **1938** Sergeant Murphy; Female Fugitive; Beloved Brat; Secret of an Actress; Meet the Girls; What Price Safety?; Rhythm of the Saddle. **1939** The Man Who Dared; The Great Victor Herbert; Romance of the Potato; Angel of Mercy; Stanley and Livingstone; The Story That Couldn't be Printed; Tail Spin; Each Dawn I Die; Confessions of a Nazi Spy. **1940** The Fighting 69th!; Thou Shalt Not Kill; Margie; Good Bad Guys; Spots Before Your Eyes; Shooting High; The Hidden Master. **1941** Love Crazy; Lady from Cheyenne; Horror Island; Petticoat Politics; Emergency Landing; Hurricane Smith; Redlands of Dakota; Never Give a Sucker an Even Break; Dangerous Lady; Blue, White and Perfect; Robot Wrecks. **1942** Gentleman Jim; Flag of Mercy; Stardust on the Sage; Top Sergeant; The Mummy's Tomb; Whistling in Dixie; The Traitor Within; Don't Lie; Unexpected Riches; Give Out Sisters. **1943** Dixie Dugan; The Crime Smasher; Lady Bodyguard; He Hired the Boss; Chatterbox; Here Comes Kelly; Mystery Broadcast; O, My Darling Clementine; Swingtime Johnny. **1944** Mr. Winkle Goes to War; Raiders of Ghost City (serial); Irish Eyes Are Smiling; Let's Dance; Follow the Boys; Hat Check Honey; Bermuda Mystery; Trocadero; Are These Our Parents?; Song of Nevada; The Mummy's Ghost; Faces in the Fog;

Murder in the Blue Room; Tale of a Dog; End of the Road; Enemy of Women. **1945** Scarlet Street; They Were Expendable; Along the Navajo Trail; The Woman Who Came Back; The Naughty Nineties; Duffy's Tavern; The Lost Weekend; The Purple Monster Strikes (serial); Don Juan Quilligan; Behind City Lights; Senorita from the West; The Lady Confesses; She Gets Her Man; The Vampire's Ghost; Utah; The Bull Fighters; Night Club Girl; Blood on the Sun. **1946** The Crimson Ghost (serial); Hop Harrigan (serial); The Big Sleep; A Close Call for Boston Blackie; Gay Blades; The Shadow Returns; Joe Palooka, Champ; Rendezvous 24; The French Key; Freddie Steps Out; Magnificent Doll; Secrets of a Sorority Girl; Bowery Bombshell; The Jolson Story; Susie Steps Out; Sweetheart of Sigma Chi; Dangerous Money. **1947** My Wild Irish Rose; I Wonder Who's Kissing Her Now; Last of the Redmen; Smoky River Serenade; Homesteaders of Paradise Valley. **1948** The Fuller Brush Man; Mary Lou; Docks of New Orleans; Smugglers Cove; The Denver Kid. **1949** Post Office Investigator; Arson, Inc.; Cover Up; Brothers in the Saddle; Sky Dragon; Rusty Saves a Life; Riders of the Whistling Pines; Ladies of the Chorus; South of Rio; Down Dakota Way; Alias the Champ; One Sunday Afternoon (aka The Strawberry Blonde); Sorrowful Jones. **1950** Father's Wild Game. **1951** Pride of Maryland; The Big Gusher; Street Bandits; Pals of the Golden West. **1952** Don't Bother to Knock; My Wife's Best Friend; Something for the Birds. **1953** How to Marry a Millionaire. **1954** Sabrina; Tobor the Great; Red River Shore; The Long, Long Trailer. **1956** These Wilder Years.

VOGEDING, FREDRIK
Born: Mar. 28, 1890, Nymegen, Netherlands. Died: Apr. 18, 1942, Los Angeles, Calif. (heart attack). Screen, stage and vaudeville actor. Married to actress Florence Roberts (dec. 1927).

Appeared in: **1921** Behind Masks; High Heels. **1933** Below the Sea; My Lips Betray. **1934** Orient Express; Murder on the Blackboard; Fury of the Jungle. **1935** Mills of the Gods; The Woman in Red; Charlie Chan in Shanghai; Barbary Coast. **1936** Ace Drummond (serial); The Public Pays (short); The House of a Thousand Candles; A Message to Garcia. **1937** Think Fast, Mr. Moto; Charlie Chan at the Olympics; Cafe Metropole. **1938** Mr. Moto Takes a Chance; Mysterious Mr. Moto; Miracle Money (short); The Cowboy and the Lady; 6,000 Enemies. **1939** Confessions of a Nazi Spy; While America Sleeps (short); Charlie Chan in City in Darkness; The Three Musketeers. **1940** Enemy Agent; British Intelligence; Four Sons; The Man I Married; Man Hunt. **1942** The Great Impersonation.

VOGEL, ELEANORE
Born: 1903. Died: June 26, 1973, Hollywood, Calif. (heart attack). Screen, stage and television actress.

Appeared in: **1945** They Were Expendable. **1947** The Farmer's Daughter. **1948** Night Has a Thousand Eyes. **1955** Good Morning, Miss Dove. **1963** How the West Was Won.

VOGEL, HENRY
Born: 1865. Died: June 17, 1925, New York, N.Y. Screen and stage actor.

VOGEL, PATRICIA
Born: 1909. Died: June 25, 1941, Beverly Hills, Calif. (suicide—hanging). Screen actress.

VOGEL, RUDOLF
Born: 1900, Munich, Germany. Died: 1967, Munich, Germany. Screen, stage, vaudeville actor and film director. Father of actor Peter Vogel.

Appeared in: **1941** Venus vor Gericht. **1942** Kleine Residenz; Einmal der Liebe Hergott Sein. **1947** Zwischen Gestern und Morgen. **1948** Der Apfel ist Ab; Das Verlorene Gesicht; Der Herr vom Andern Stern. **1949** Hans im Glueck. **1950** Zwei in Einem Anzug; Die Gestoerte Hoehzeitsnacht. **1951** Csardas des Herzens; Fanfaren der Liebe; Der Blaue Stern des Suedens; Der Letzte Schuss; Drei Kavaliere. **1952** Moenche, Maedchen und Panduren; Der Wiebertausch; Vater Braucht Eine Frau. **1953** Ein Herz Spielt Falsch; Musik bei Nacht; The Story of Vicki; Der Klosterjaeger; Fanfaren der Ehe; Arlette Erobert Paris; Muss Man Sich Gleich Scheiden Lassen?; Jonny Reitet Nebrador; Der Ehestreik; Sterne Ueber Colombo. **1954** Die Gefangene des Maharadscha; Der Erste Kuss; Sauerbruch—Das War Mein Leben; Maedchenjahre Einer Koenigin; Ein Haus Voll Liebe (aka Glueck ins Haus); Feuerwerk (aka Oh! My Pa-Pa); Das Fliegende Klassenzimmer (The Flying Classroom—US 1958). **1955** Gestatten, Mein Name ist Cox; Solang' es Huebsche Maedchen Gibt; Ein Herz Voll Musik; Ich Denke oft an Piroschka; Zwei Herzen und ein Thron (aka Hofjagd in Ischl); Sonnenschein und Wolkenbruch; Urlaub auf Ehrenwort; Die Drei von der Tankstelle; Bonjour Kathrin. **1956** Hilfe sie Liebt Mich;

Die Goldene Bruecke; Der Bettelstudent (The Beggar Student—US 1958); Durch die Waelder, Durch die Auen; Schwarzwaldmelodie; Der K. und K. Feldmarshall; Opernball; Die Verpfuschte Hochzeitsnacht; Uns Gefaellt die Welt. **1957** Robinson Soll Nicht Sterben (aka The Girl and the Legend—US 1966); Ein Stueck vom Himmel; Schoen ist die Welt; Der Kaiser und das Waschermaedel; Casino de Paris. **1958** Das Wirtshaus im Spessart (The Spessart Inn—US 1961); Eine Frau, die Weiss, was sie Will; Die Landaerztin; Der Veruntreute Himmel; Vergiss Mein Nicht (aka Ohne Dich Kann ich Nicht Leben); Wenn die Conny mit dem Peter (aka Teenager—Melodie). **1959** Hula—Hopp, Conny!; Du Bist Wunderbar; Alt-Heidelberg; Marili; Ein Mann Geht Durch die Wand (The Man Who Walked Through the Wall—US 1964); Embezzled Heaven. **1960** Frau Warrens Gewerbe; Ingeborg; Pension Schoeler; Kriminaltango; Der Gauner und der Libe Gott; O Diese Bayern. **1961** Ach Egon; Im 6. Stock. **1962** Eheinstitut Aurora; Die Foersterchristl; Kolhiesels Toechter (Kolhiesel's Daughters). **1963** Charley's Tante. **1965** Heidi (US 1968); ... ind do was Muss um Acht ins Bett.

VOGLER, WALTER A.
Born: 1897. Died: Aug. 26, 1955, Los Angeles, Calif. (heart attack). Screen actor and film technical advisor.

Appeared in: **1930** All Quiet on the Western Front.

VOINOFF, ANATOLE
Born: 1896, Russia. Died: Feb. 9, 1965, New York, N.Y. Screen actor. Appeared in silents.

VOKES, HARRY
Born: 1867, Quincy, Mass. Died: Apr. 15, 1922, Boston, Mass. (injuries suffered in an explosion). Screen, stage and vaudeville actor. Married to stage actress Margaret Daly (dec.) and later married to Marie Francis (dec.). Appeared in vaudeville with Hap Ward, Sr. (dec. 1944) in an act billed as "Harold and Percy."

Appeared in: **1912** A Run on the Bank. **1915** Beauty in Distress.

VOKES, MAY
Died: Sept. 13, 1957, Stamford, Conn. Screen and stage actress.

Appeared in: **1924** Janice Meredith.

VOLAND, HERBERT "HERB"
Born: New Rochelle, N.Y. Died: Apr. 26, 1981, Riverside, Calif.? (stroke). Screen, stage and television actor.

Appeared in: **1968** With Six You Get Eggroll; The Shakiest Gun in the West; Don't Just Stand There! **1969** The Love God? **1979** The North Avenue Irregulars.

VOLKMAN, IVAN
Died: Oct. 17, 1972, Stockton, Calif. (stroke). Screen actor and assistant film director.

Appeared in: **1967** How to Succeed in Business Without Really Trying.

VOLOSHIN, ALEX
Born: 1886. Died: Nov. 23, 1960. Screen actor.

Appeared in: **1938** Ride a Crooked Mile.

VOLOTSKOY, VLADIMIR
Born: 1853, Russia. Died: Nov. 7, 1927, Hollywood, Calif. Stage and screen actor.

VOLPE, FREDERICK "FRED"
Born: 1873. Died: Mar. 7, 1932, London, England. Screen and stage actor.

Appeared in: **1916** Altar Chains (US 1917); Lifeguardsman (US 1917); The Real Thing at Last. **1917** Les Cloches de Corneville; The Labour Leader; The Profligate. **1918** Once Upon a Time. **1919** The Usurper. **1921** The Adventures of Mr. Pickwick. **1930** Lord Richard in the Pantry; The Middle Watch. **1931** Captivation; The Wrong Mr. Perkins.

VON ALTEN, FERDINAND (Baron von Lamezan auf Altenhofen)
Born: 1885. Died: Mar. 17, 1933, Dessau, Germany (flu). Stage and screen actor.

Appeared in: **1928** Small Town Sinners. **1929** Sajenko, the Soviet; The Man Who Cheated Life.

VON BETZ, MATTHEW *See* BETZ, MATTHEW

VON BLOCK, BELA
Born: 1889. Died: Mar. 22, 1962, Hollywood, Calif. Screen actor. Appeared in films from 1924 to 1929.

VON BOLVARY, GEZA
Born: 1898, Hungary. Died: Aug. 11, 1961, Munich, West Germany (heart ailment). Screen actor, screenwriter and film director. Appeared in German films shortly after W.W. I; then became director and screenwriter.

VON BRINCKEN, WILHELM (aka ROGER BECKWITH aka WILLIAM VAUGHN)
Born: May 27, 1891, Flensburg, Germany. Died: Jan. 18, 1946, Los Angeles, Calif. (ruptured artery). Screen actor and film technical director. Entered films in 1921.

Appeared in: **1930** Mamba; Inside the Lines; Royal Flush; Leathernecking; This Mad World; Hell's Angels. **1932** The Night Club Lady; A Passport to Hell; prior to 1933 Manhattan Comedies (record series). **1933** Private Jones; Shanghai Madness. **1934** I'll Tell the World. **1936** Dracula's Daughter. **1937** The Prisoner of Zenda; Thank You Mr. Moto; The Life of Emile Zola; Crack Up; Espionage; They Gave Him a Gun. **1938** International Crime; Bulldog Drummond in Africa. **1939** Confessions of a Nazi Spy; Pack Up Your Troubles; Conspiracy. **1940** Four Sons. **1942** King of the Mounties (serial). **1943** Secret Service in Darkest Africa (serial).

VON COLLANDE, GISELA
Born: 1915, Dresden, Germany. Died: Oct. 23, 1960, Pforzheim, West Germany (auto accident). Screen, stage and radio actress.

VON ELTZ, THEODORE
Born: 1894, New Haven, Conn. Died: Oct. 6, 1964, Woodland Hills, Calif. Screen, stage, radio and television actor. Entered films in 1920.

Appeared in: **1923** Tiger Rose. **1924** Being Respectable. **1925** Paint and Powder; On Thin Ice; The Sporting Chance. **1926** The Red Kimono; Sea Wolf; Fools of Fashion. **1927** One Woman to Another; No Man's Law; The Great Mail Robbery. **1928** Way of the Strong; Life's Mockery; Nothing to Wear. **1929** Four Feathers; The Awful Truth; The Voice of the Storm; The Very Idea; The Rescue. **1930** Love Among Millionaires; The Furies; The Arizona Kid; The Divorcee; Kismet; The Cat Creeps. **1931** Susan Lennox, Her Rise and Fall; Private Scandal; Heartbreak; The Prodigal; The Secret Six; Up Pops the Devil; Beyond Victory; Wicked; Once a Lady. **1932** Ladies of the Big House; Hotel Continental; The Midnight Lady; Drifting Souls; Strangers of the Evening; The Unwritten Law; Red-Haired Alibi; Breach of Promise; Scarlet Week-End. **1933** Eleventh Commandment; Pleasure Cruise; Arizona to Broadway; High Gear; Jennie Gerhardt; Her Splendid Folly; Dance, Girl, Dance; Master of Men; Luxury Liner. **1934** The Silver Streak; Change of Heart; Call It Luck; Bright Eyes. **1935** Elinore Norton; Streamline Express; Trails of the Wild; Private Worlds; Smart Girl; Behind the Green Lights; Headline Woman; Confidential; His Night Out; The Magnificent Obsession. **1936** Below the Deadline; I Cover Chinatown; Beloved Enemy; The Road to Glory; High Tension; Sussy; Sinner Take All; Mind Your Own Business; Ticket to Paradise. **1937** Clarence; A Man Betrayed; Under Cover of Night; Jim Hanvey, Detective; Youth on Parole; California Straight Ahead; The Westland Case; Topper. **1938** Inside Story; Pardon Our Nerves; Blondes at Work; Smashing the Rackets. **1939** They Made Her a Spy; 5th Avenue Girl; The Sun Never Sets; Legion of Lost Flyers. **1940** The Old Swimmin' Hole; The Great Plane Robbery; The Son of Monte Cristo; Little Old New York; Dr. Ehrlich's Magic Bullet. **1941** Sergeant York; Live With Henry; Ellery Queen's Penthouse Mystery; A Shot in the Dark; I'll Wait for You. **1942** The Man in the Trunk; Quiet Please, Murder!; Lady in a Jam. **1944** Follow the Boys; Bermuda Mystery; Hollywood Canteen; Since You Went Away. **1945** Saratoga Trunk; Rhapsody in Blue. **1946** The Big Sleep. **1948** The Devil's Cargo. **1950** Trial Without Jury. **1956** The Animal World (narr.).

VON KALTENBORN, HANS
Born: 1879. Died: June 14, 1965, New York, N.Y. (heart ailment). Screen actor and radio announcer.

Appeared in: **1939** Mr. Smith Goes to Washington.

VON LAMBECK, FREDERICK
Born: 1918. Died: Mar. 26, 1950, Rochester, N.Y. Screen actor and horse trainer. Double for actor Tyrone Power (dec. 1958).

VON LEDEBUR, LEOPOLD
Born: 1876, Germany. Died: Sept. 17, 1955, Wankendorf, Germany. Stage and screen actor.

VON METER, HARRY (aka HARRY VAN METER)
Born: Mar. 29, 1871, Malta Bend, Mo. Died: June 2, 1956, Calif. Screen and stage actor.

Appeared in: **1916** Beachcomber. **1917** Princess Virtue; A Man's Man.

1918 Broadway Love; Beloved Rogues; The Lion's Claw (serial). **1919** A Man's Fight; The Day She Paid. **1920** Alias Miss Dodd; Cheater. **1921** Heart of the North; Reputation; Beautiful Gambler; Dangerous Love. **1922** A Guilty Conscience; When Romance Rides; Putting It Over; Nobody's Bride; Life's Greatest Question; My Dad; The Broadway Madonna; Wildcat Jordon. **1923** The Speed King; A Man's Man; The Hunchback of Notre Dame. **1924** The Great Diamond Mystery; Sagebrush Gospel; The Breathless Moment. **1925** The Cloud Rider; The Texas Bearcat; Triple Action. **1926** Kid Boots; The Flying Mail. **1927** The Hour of Reckoning. **1930** Border Romance.

VON METER, JOSEPH
Born: Aug. 3, 1876, Missouri. Died: Nov. 22, 1961, Calif. Screen actor.

Appeared in: **1915** The Protest; The Blood of Our Brothers.

VON MEYERINCK, HUBERT
Born: 1897, Germany. Died: May 13, 1971, Hamburg, Germany. Stage and screen actor. Entered films in 1924.

Appeared in: **1958** Das Wirtshaus in Spessart (The Spessart Inn—1961). **1959** Ein Mann Geht Durch die Wand (The Man Who Walked Through the Wall—US 1964). **1960** Holiday Island. **1961** One, Two, Three; Secret Ways. **1962** Die Turkischen Gurken (The Turkish Cucumber—US 1963).

VON REMPERT, ALBERT
Born: Germany. Died: Oct., 1958 (injuries sustained filming fight scene in Slave Caravan). Screen actor.

VON SCHLETTOW, HANS ADALBERT
Born: 1888, Frankfurt, Germany. Died: 1945, Berlin, Germany. Screen actor.

Appeared in: **1924** Isn't Life Wonderful.

VON SEYFFERTITZ, GUSTAV
Born: 1863, Vienna, Austria. Died: Dec. 25, 1943, Woodland Hills, Calif. Screen, stage actor and film director. During W.W. I he was known as G. Butler Clonblough.

Appeared in: **1917** Down to Earth. **1918** Old Wives for New. **1922** Sherlock Holmes; When Knighthood Was in Flower. **1924** The Bandolero; The Lone Wolf; Yolanda. **1925** Goose Woman. **1926** Don Juan; Diplomacy; Sparrows; The Bells; Red Dice. **1927** Barbed Wire; The Gaucho; The Magic Flame; The Wizard; Rose of the Golden West; Birds of Prey; The Student Prince. **1928** Yellow Lily; The Woman Disputed; Vamping Venus; Mysterious Lady; Me, Gangster; Docks of New York; The Red Mark. **1929** Chasing Through Europe; His Glorious Night; The Canary Murder Case; The Case of Lena Smith; Come Across; Seven Faces. **1930** The Case of Sgt. Grischa; Dangerous Paradise; Are You There? **1931** The Bat Whispers; Dishonored; Ambassador Bill. **1932** Shanghai Express; Roadhouse Murder; The Penguin Pool Murder; Rasputin and the Empress; Afraid to Talk; Doomed Battalion. **1933** When Strangers Marry; Queen Christina. **1934** Mystery Liner; The Moonstone; Change of Heart; Little Men. **1935** She; Remember Last Night. **1936** Little Lord Fauntleroy; Murder on the Bridle Path; Mad Holiday. **1938** Marie Antoinette; In Old Chicago; King of Alcatraz; Cipher Bureau. **1939** Nurse Edith Cavell; Juarez and Maximilian.

VON STERNBERG, JOSEF (aka JO STERNBERG and JOE STERN)
Born: 1894, Vienna, Austria. Died: Dec. 22, 1969, Hollywood, Calif. (heart attack). Screen, stage actor, film director, photographer and film narrator. Divorced from actress Riza Royce (dec. 1980).

Narrated: **1954** Ana-Ta-Han (The Devil's Pitchfork).

VON STROHEIM, ERICH, JR.
Born: 1916, Los Angeles, Calif. Died: Oct. 26, 1968, Woodland Hills, Calif. (cancer). Screen actor and assistant film director. Entered films as a child actor. Son of actor and director Erich Von Stroheim, Sr. (dec. 1957).

Appeared in: **1962** Two Weeks in Another Town. **1968** Skidoo.

VON STROHEIM, ERICH, SR. (Erich Oswald Hans Carl Maris Von Nordenwall)
Born: Sept. 22, 1885, Vienna, Austria. Died: May 12, 1957, Paris, France (spinal ailment). Screen actor, film director, film producer and screenwriter. Awarded Legion of Honor by the French government for his contributions to the film industry. Father of actor Erich Von Stroheim, Jr. (dec. 1968). Nominated for 1950 Academy Award for Best Supporting Actor in Sunset Boulevard.

Appeared in: **1914** Captain McLean. **1915** The Failure; Ghosts; A Bold Impersonation; Old Heidelberg; Birth of a Nation. **1916** Intolerance; The Social Secretary; His Picture in the Papers; Macbeth; Less Than the Dust. **1917** Panthea; In Again—Out Again; Sylvia of the Secret Service; For France. **1918** The Unbeliever; Hearts of the World; Hearts of Humanity; The Hun Within. **1919** Blind Husbands. **1921** Foolish Wives. **1928** Wedding March. **1929** The Great Gabbo. **1930** Three Faces East. **1931** Friends and Lovers. **1932** Lost Squadron; As You Desire Me. **1934** Crimson Romance; House of Strangers; Fugitive Road. **1935** The Crime of Dr. Crespi. **1936** Marthe Richard au Service de la France. **1937** Les Pirates du Rail; Mademoiselle Docteur; La Grande Illusion; The Alibi. **1938** Les Desparus de St. Agil; Gibralter; L'Affaire La Farge. **1939** Boys' School; Tempete sur Paris (Thunder Over Paris—US 1940); Macao l'Enfer du Jeu; Paris-New York; Derriere la Facade; Rappel Immediat; Pieges; Le Monde Tremblera. **1940** Ultimatum; I Was an Adventuress. **1941** So Ends Our Night; Personal Column. **1943** Five Graves to Cairo; North Star; Storm Over Lisbon; It Happened in Gibraltar; Armored Attack. **1944** The Lady and the Monster; 32 Rue de Montmartre. **1945** The Great Flamarion; Scotland Investigator. **1946** The Mask of Dijon; La Foire aux Chimeres; One Ne Meurt Pas Comme Ca. **1947** La Danse de Mort. **1948** Le Signal Rouge. **1949** Portrait d'un Assasin; The Devil and the Angel. **1950** Sunset Boulevard. **1952** La Maison du Crime; Alraune. **1953** Minuit—Quai de Bercy; Alerte au Sud; L'Envers du Paradis. **1954** Napoleon; Serie Noire. **1955** La Madonna du Sleepings. **1958** L'homme aux Cent Visages.

VON TWARDOWSKI, HANS (Hans Heinrich von Twardowski)
Born: Germany. Died: Nov. 19, 1958, New York, N.Y. Screen, stage, radio, television actor and stage director.

Appeared in: **1919** Gerechtigkeit; Das Kabinett der Dr. Caligari. **1920** Genuine; Die Nacht der Koenigin Isabeau; Von Morgens bis Mitternacht (From Morn to Midnight). **1921** Am Webstahl de Zeit; Marizza, Genannt die Schmuggermadonna; Die Exiliere des Teufels. **1922** Lady Hamilton; Malmaison; Tingel-Tangel; Phantom (US 1925). **1923** I.N.R.I; Der Sprung ims Leben (aka Der Roman Eines Zirkuskindes). **1924** Die Bacchantin; Gefaehrliche Freundschaft. **1925** Die Feuertaenzerin. **1926** Herbstmanoever; Die Lachende Grille. **1927** Arme Kleine Sif; Der Falsche Prinz; Die Heilige Luege; Die Hoelle der Jungfrauen; Raetsel Einer Nacht; Die Weber (The Weavers—US 1929). **1928** Geschlecht in Fesseln (Sex in Fetters). **1929** Ludwig der Zweite, Koenig von Bayern; Peter, der Matrose. **1930** Der Koenig von Paris; Die Singende Stadt. **1931** Die Heilige Flamme; Der Herzog von Reichstadt; Menschen Hinter Gittern (aka Big House). **1932** Scandal for Sale. **1933** Private Jones; Adorable. **1934** The Scarlet Empress. **1935** The Crusaders; Storm Over the Andes. **1939** Beasts of Berlin; Confessions of a Nazi Spy; Espionage Agent. **1942** Casablanca; Joan of Ozark. **1943** Hangmen Also Die.

VON WINTERSTEIN, EDUARD
Born: 1871, Vienna, Austria. Died: July 22, 1961, East Berlin, Germany. Screen and stage actor. Father of actor Gustav von Wangenheim.

Appeared in: **1913** Schuldig. **1917** Die Faust des Riesen. **1918** Opium. **1919** Maria Magdalena; Madame Dubarry (aka Passion). **1920** Das Frauenhaus von Brescia; Die Gluehende Kammer; Hamlet; Der Langsame Tod; Das Marthyrium; Der Reigen. **1921** Aus dem Schwarzbuch Eines Polizeikommissars II; Die Bestie im Menschen; Die Beute der Erinnyen; Madeleine; Schloss Vogeloed; Der Muede Tod (aka Between Worlds—US 1924, and aka Destiny—US); Danton (aka All for a Woman). **1922** Aus dem Scwarzbuch Eines Polizeikommissars III; Der Brennende Acker; Das Diadem der Zarin; Die vom Zirkus; Der Falsche Dimitri; Das Feuereschiff; Das Fraenkische Lied; Frau Suende; Bigamie; Der Graf im Pfluge; Der Strom; Die Stumme von Portici; Die Taenzerin des Koenigs; Die Weisse Wueste; Wer Wirft den Ersten Stein?; Die Zirkusdiva. **1923** Der Allmaechtige Dollar; Daemon Zirkus; Die Frau mit den Millionen (II); Frau Schlange; Glanz Gegen Glueck; Der Menschenfeind; Der Schatz der Gesine Jakobsen; Wilhelm Tell; Der Weg zu Gott (aka Das Schicksal des Thomas Balt); Fridericus Rex (aka Ein Koenigsschicksal). **1924** Guillotine; In den Krallen der Schuld; Mutter und Sohn; Die Radio-Heirat; Schicksal; Der Kleine Herzog (aka Um Thron und Liebe); Claire Garragan (aka Die Geschichte Eines Jungen Maedchens). **1925** Aschermittwoch; Goetz von Berlichingen Zubenannt mit der Eisernen Hand; Der Erste Sand (aka Der Grosskapitaen, and aka Daemon Geld); Die Gesunkenen (The Sunken); Das Abenteuer der Sibylle Brandt (aka Um ein Haar ...); Das Haus der Luege; Volk in Not; Wallenstein; Was Steine Erzaehlen; Der Tanzende Tod (aka Rex Mundi). **1926** Das War in Heidelberg in Blauer Sommernacht; Fedora; Die Foersterchristl; Frauelein Josette—Meine Frau; Frauen der Leidenschaft; Die Frau in Gold; Gern hab' ich die Frauen Gekuesst; Der Gute Ruf; Der Herr des

Todes; Die Kleine und ihr Kavalier; Des Koenigs Befehl; Der Meineidbauer; Die Muehle von Sanssouci; Das Rosa Pantoeffelchen; Tragoedie Einer Ehe. **1927** An der Wesser; Da Haelt die Welt den Atem An; Elternlos; Der Geheimnisvolle Spiegel; Ich war zu Heidelberg Student; Luetzows Wilde Verwegene Jagd; Ein Maedel aus dem Volke; Prinz Louis Ferdinand; Stolzenfels am Rhein; Eon Tag der Rosen im August ... da hat die Garde Fortgemusst; Vom Leben Getoetet. **1928** Die Siebzehnjaehrigen. **1929** Napolean auf St. Helena. **1930** Der Andere; Er Oder Ich; Liebling der Goetter (Darling of the Gods); Rosenmontag (Rose Monday, aka Eine Offizierstragoedie); Der Blaue Engel (The Blue Angel); Three Faces East. **1931** Arme Kleine Eva; Der Web Nach Rio; Im Geheimdienst (aka In the Employ of the Secret Service); Kennst Du das Land (aka Saltarello); Zwischen Nacht und Morgen (aka Dirnentragoedie); Friends and Lovers. **1932** Das Erste Recht des Kindes (aka Aus dem Tagebuch Einer Krauenaerztin); Trenck (US 1934); Friedericke (US 1933); Der Weisse Daemon (The White Demon); Der Geheimagent (aka Ein Mann Faellt vom Himmel); Mensch ohne Namen (Man Without a Name); Lost Squadron. **1933** Der Lauefer von Marathon; Hochzeit am Wolfgangsee; Spione am Werk; Die Nacht im Forsthaus (aka Der Fall Roberts); Der Judas von Tirol (aka Der Ewige Verrat); Morgenrot (aka Dawn, Red Dawn). **1934** Regine; Der Letzte Walzer; Zu Strassburg auf der Schanz; Der Schimmelreiter; Der Ewige Traum (aka Der Koenig des Mont-Blanc). **1935** Hundert Tage; Familie Schimek; Der Staehlerne Stahl; Der Hoehere Befehl; Die Selige Exzellenz (aka Das Tagebuch der Baronin W.); Das Maedchen vom Moorhof (The Girl of the Moors); Krach im Hinterhaus (Trouble Backstairs—US 1937). **1936** Waldwinter; 90 Minuten Aufenthalt; Martha (aka Letzte Rose). **1937** Madame Bovary; Das Schoene Frauelein Schragg; Der Etappenhase; Der Katzensteg; Unter Ausschluss der Oeffentlichkeit; Serenade; Der Mann, der Sherlock Holmes War; Heiratsschwindler (aka Die Rote Muetze); Die Korallenprinzessin (aka An der Blauen Adria). **1938** Steputat & Co.; Der Mann, der Nicht Nein Sagen Konnte; Napoleon ist an Allem Schuld; Maja Zwischen Zwei Ehen; Preussische Liebesgeschichte (aka Liebeslegende); Ballade (aka Die Prinzessin Kehrt Heim). **1939** Befreite Haende; Das Unsterbliche Herz; Der Gruene Kaiser; D III 88; Menschen vom Variete; Im Namen des Volkes; Die Goldene Maske; Die Reise Nach Tilsit; Die Barmherzige Luege; Die Frau ohne Vergangenheit; Robert Koch, der Bekaempfer des Todes. **1940** Fuer die Katz; Bismarck; Das Herz der Koenigin; Das Frauelein von Barnhelm. **1941** Stukas; Ohm Krueger; Kopf Hoch, Johannes; Annelie (aka Die Geschichte Eines Lebens). **1942** Rembrandt; Andreas Schlueter. **1943** Wenn der Junge Wein Blueht; Muenchhausen; Gefaehrtin Meines Sommers; Ein Gluecklicher Mensch (aka Schule des Lebens). **1944** Philharmoniker; Der Verteidiger hat das Wort; Meine vier Jungen. **1945** Der Puppenspieler (aka Pole Poppenspaeler). **1949** Und Wider 48!; Die Buntkarierten. **1950** Die Jungen vom Kranichsee; Der Auftrag Hoeglers (aka Westoestliche Hochzeit); Semmelweis—Retter der Muetter (aka Dr. Semmelweis). **1951** Die Sonnenbrucks; Das Verurteilte Dorf; Der Untertan (The Underdog). **1954** Gefaehrliche Fracht. **1956** Heimliche Ehen; Genesung. **1958** Emilia Galotti.

VON ZELL, HARRY
Born: July 11, 1906, Indianapolis, Ind. Died: Nov. 21, 1981, Woodland Hills, Calif. (cancer). Screen, television, radio actor, singer, writer, sports announcer, program director and radio producer.

Appeared in: **1945** It's in the Bag (film debut); How Do You Do?; The Strange Affair of Uncle Harry. **1946** Till the End of Time. **1947** The Guilt of Janet Ames; Where There's Life. **1948** The Saxon Charm; Dear Wife. **1950** Where the Sidewalk Ends; For Heaven's Sake; Two Flags West. **1951** Call Me Mister; You're in the Navy Now (aka U.S.S. Teakettle); I Can Get It For You Wholesale. **1952** Son of Paleface; Sound-Off. **1966** Boy, Did I Get a Wrong Number!. **1968** Star!. **1980** Triple Play.

VOSBURGH, ALFRED See WHITMAN, GAYNE

VOSBURGH, HAROLD
Born: 1870, Penetanguishene, Ontario, Canada. Died: Nov. 17, 1926, New Orleans, La. Screen actor.

Appeared in: **1904** The Moonshiner. **1921** If Women Only Knew.

VOSKOVEC, GEORGE
Born: June 19, 1905, Sazava, Czech. Died: July 1, 1981, Pear Blossom, Calif. Screen, stage, radio, television actor, stage producer, playwright and composer.

Appeared in: **1930** Powder and Gas. **1937** The Golem. **1939** This World Is Ours. **1952** Anything Can Happen; Affair in Trinidad; The Iron Mistress. **1957** The 27th Day; Twelve Angry Men. **1958** Uncle Vanya; Wind Across the Everglades; The Bravados. **1960** Butterfield 8. **1965** Hamlet. **1965** The Spy Who Came In From The Cold. **1966** Mr. Buddwing. **1968** The Desperate Ones; The Boston Strangler. **1973** The Iceman Cometh. **1974** Man on a Swing. **1980** Somewhere in Time.

VOSPER, FRANK O.
Born: 1900, England. Died: Mar. 6, 1937, England. Screen, stage actor, playwright and author.

Appeared in: **1932** Rome Express (US 1933). **1934** Jew Suess (aka Power—US); The Man Who Knew Too Much (US 1935); Strauss's Great Waltz (US 1935). **1935** Heart's Desire (US 1937). **1936** Spy of Napoleon (US 1939) The Secret of Stamboul (US 1939). **1940** The Spy in White (reissue of The Secret of Stamboul—1936).

VOSPER, JOHN
Died: Apr. 6, 1954, Hollywood, Calif. (heart attack). Screen, stage, radio and television actor.

Appeared in: **1942** The Wife Takes a Flyer; Undercover Man. **1944** Dark Shadows (short). **1945** Weekend at the Waldorf; Counter-Attack. **1947** A Stolen Life; The Perfect Marriage. **1949** Bride of Vengeance. **1951** The Desert Fox. **1952** Black Hills Ambush. **1953** The Magnetic Monster. **1956** Edge of Hell.

VOSS, FRANK "FATTY"
Born: Oct. 12, 1888, Ill. Died: Apr. 22, 1917, Los Angeles, Calif. (fatty degeneration of heart). Screen actor.

Appeared in: **1915** In the Claw of the Law; Shot in a Bar Room; A Game of Love; Beach Birds; Greed and Gasoline; Under New Management; Ready for Reno; Lizzie's Shattered Dreams; The Doomed Groom; Pants and Petticoats. **1916** Gertie's Busy Day; Flirtation a la Carte; A Busted Honeymoon; Pirates of the Air; A Bambler's Bambol; Lizzie's Lingering Love; Alice in Society; Unhand Me, Villain. **1917** Fatty's Feature Fillum.

VROOM, FREDERIC WILLIAM
Born: 1858. Died: June 24, 1942, Hollywood, Calif. (heart attack). Screen and stage actor.

Appeared in: **1921** The Millionaire; The Faith Healer; The Great Impersonation; The Heart Line; White and Unmarried. **1922** The Lane That Had No Turning; The Fourteenth Lover; The Woman Who Walked Alone; The Glorious Fool; Tailor-Made Man. **1923** The Acquittal; The Day of Faith; The Tiger's Claw. **1924** The Navigator; His Hour; Hutch of the U.S.A.; Sporting Youth; The Reckless Age; Phantom Justice. **1926** Eyes Right. **1927** The General. **1928** The Terrible People. **1930** The Poor Millionaire. **1932** The Mighty Barnum.

VUOLO, TITO
Born: Mar. 22, 1893, Italy. Died: Sept. 14, 1962, Los Angeles, Calif. (cancer). Screen actor.

Appeared in: **1947** Kiss of Death; The Web; Mourning Becomes Electra. **1948** Sorry, Wrong Number; The Luck of the Irish; Mr. Blandings Builds His Dream House; Cry of the City. **1949** Flamingo Road; House of Strangers; The Great Gatsby; Everybody Does It. **1950** Between Midnight and Dawn; Deported; The Man Who Cheated Himself. **1951** The Enforcer; Up Front; Saturday's Hero; The Racket. **1952** The Racing Tide. **1955** Six Bridges to Cross. **1956** Emergency Hospital. **1957** The Midnight Story; Dragstrip Girl; 20 Million Miles to Earth. **1959** The Five Pennies.

VYE, MURVYN (Marvin Wesley Vye, Jr.)
Born: July 15, 1913, Quincy, Mass. Died: Aug. 17, 1976, Pompano Beach, Fla. (natural causes). Screen, stage, television actor and singer.

Appeared in: **1947** Golden Earrings. **1948** Whispering Smith. **1949** A Connecticut Yankee in King Arthur's Court. **1951** Pickup. **1952** Road to Bali. **1953** Destination Gobi; Pickup on South Street. **1954** River of No Return. **1955** Pearl of the South Pacific; Escape to Burma. **1956** The Best Things in Life Are Free. **1957** This Could Be the Night; Voodoo Island; Short Cut to Hell. **1958** Girl in the Woods; In Love and War. **1959** Al Capone. **1960** The Boy and the Pirates; Pay or Die. **1961** The Big Bankroll (aka King of the Roaring 20's—The Story of Arnold Rothstein); The George Raft Story.

VYSOTSKY, VLADIMIR
Born: 1934, Russia. Died: July 24, 1980, Moscow, Russiaw (heart attack). Screen, stage actor, balladeer and satirist. Married to actress Marina Vlady.

VYVYAN, JENNIFER
Born: 1925, England. Died: Apr. 5, 1974, London, England. Screen actress and opera performer.

Appeared in: **1953** The Beggar's Opera.

WADE, BESSIE
Born: 1885. Died: Oct. 19, 1966, Dallas, Tex. Screen actress. Entered films in 1916.

Appeared in: **1935** Millions in the Air. **1943** Hitler's Children. **1948** The Velvet Touch. **1950** Mister 880.

WADE, JOHN W.
Born: 1876. Died: July 14, 1949, Hollywood, Calif. Screen, stage and vaudeville actor. Toured in "Marse Shelby's Chicken Dinner," vaudeville sketch. Entered films approx. 1924.

Appeared in: **1938** Heroes of the Hills.

WADE, WARREN
Born: 1896, Akron, Ohio. Died: Jan. 14, 1973, Englewood, N.J. Screen, stage, radio, television actor and stage director.

Appeared in: **1959** Heller in Pink Tights. **1960** Songs Without End. **1962** The Miracle Worker.

WADHAMS, GOLDEN
Born: 1869. Died: June 26, 1929, Hollywood, Calif. (heart illness). Screen and stage actor.

Appeared in: **1927** Hotel Imperial. **1929** Laughing at Death.

WADKAR, HANSA "SWAN"
Born: 1924, India. Died: Aug. 23, 1971, Bombay, India (cancer). Screen and stage actress.

WADSWORTH, HENRY
Born: 1902, Maysville, Ky. Died: Dec. 5, 1974, New York, N.Y. Screen, stage and vaudeville actor.

Appeared in: **1929** Applause. **1930** Fast and Loose; Slightly Scarlet. **1933** Soldiers of the Storm; The Ghost Train; Luxury Liner; Hold the Press. **1934** This Side of Heaven; Evelyn Prentice; Operator 13; Four Walls; Dangerous Corner; The Show-Off; The Thin Man. **1935** Ceiling Zero; Big Broadcast of 1936; West Point of the Air; Mark of the Vampire. **1936** The Voice of the Bugle Ann; Sitting on the Moon. **1938** Dr. Rhythm. **1940** Dr. Kildare Goes Home. **1943** Silver Skates. **1947** Song of the Thin Man.

WADSWORTH, WILLIAM
Born: 1873. Died: June 6, 1950, N.Y. Screen and stage actor.

Appeared in: **1912** What Happened to Mary? (serial). **1913-14** Mr. Wood B. Wedd's Sentimental Experiences Series including the following: Her Face Was Her Fortune; The Love Senorita; The Beautiful Leading Lady; The Vision in the Window; High Life; A Lady of Spirits; The Revengeful Servant Girl; A Canine Rival; The Busom Country Lass; Love by the Pound; Wood B. Wedd and the Microbes; Wood B. Wedd Goes Snipe Hunting; A Superfluous Baby. **1922** Young America. **1926** White Mice.

WAGENHEIM, CHARLES
Born: c. 1895. Died: Mar. 6, 1979, Hollywood, Calif. (murdered—bludgeoned). Screen and television actor.

Appeared in: **1940** Two Girls on Broadway; Charlie Chan at the Wax Museum. **1941** Meet Boston Blackie; The Get-Away. **1942** Sin Town; Fingers at the Window. **1943** Halfway to Shanghai; I Escaped from the Gestapo. **1944** The Black Parachute; Summer Storm. **1945** Sergeant Mike; The House on Ninety-Second Street; Colonel Effingham's Raid; Jungle Captive; Within These Walls. **1946** The Dark Corner. **1947** Lighthouse; Pirates of Monterey. **1948** Man-Eater of Kumaon; Scudda Hoo! Scudda Hay!. **1949** I Cheated the Law. **1950** Motor Patrol; A Lady Without Passport. **1951** The House on Telegraph Hill; Pier 23; Street Bandits. **1953** Beneath the Twelve Mile Reef; Vicki. **1955** Canyon Crossroads; The Prodigal. **1956** Blackjack Ketchum, Desperado. **1958** The Tunnel of Love; Toughest Gun in Tombstone. **1960** The Story of Ruth. **1961** The Police Dog Story. **1965** Cat Ballou; The Cincinnati Kid. **1969** Hail, Hero! **1970** The Baby Maker. **1976** The Missouri Breaks.

WAGENSELLER, WILLIAM H.
Born: 1880. Died: Apr. 25, 1951, North Hollywood, Calif. Screen and stage actor.

WAGNER, EMMETT
Born: 1892. Died: Apr. 25, 1977, Woodland Hills, Calif. Screen actor and stuntman.

Appeared in: **1926** Hard Boiled.

WAGNER, JACK
Born: 1897. Died: Feb. 6, 1965, Hollywood, Calif. Screen and stage actor.

Appeared in: **1935** Paris in the Spring. **1939** Nancy Drew—Reporter.

WAGNER, MAX

Born: Nov. 28, 1901, Mexico. Died: Nov. 16, 1975, West Los Angeles, Calif. (heart attack). Screen actor.

Appeared in: **1932** The World and the Flesh. **1933** Arizona to Broadway; Renegades of the West. **1934** Sons of the Desert; Wharf Angel; The Lost Jungle (serial); Hell Bent for Love; The Oil Raider. **1935** Charlie Chan in Shanghai; Under the Pampas Moon; Ladies Crave Excitement. **1936** Black Legion; Two in Revolt; Smart Blonde; The Case Against Mrs. Ames; God's Country and the Woman; The Crime Patrol; Love Begins at Twenty; The Dancing Pirate. **1937** Step Lively, Jeeves; San Quentin; Slim; Border Cafe. **1938** Fool Coverage; Penrod and His Twin-Brother; Cocoanut Grove; Painted Desert. **1939** Wings of the Navy; The Roaring Twenties; The Star Maker. **1940** The Trail of the Vigilantes; You Can't Fool Your Wife. **1941** Cyclone on Horseback; Great Guns. **1942** Rough on Rents; True to the Army; Mexican Spitfire's Elephant. **1944** Boss of Boomtown. **1945** The Lost Weekend; A Medal for Benny; The Bull Fighters; Within These Walls; Radio Stars on Parade. **1946** The Strange Love of Martha Ivers; Smoky; The Sin of Harold Diddlebock. **1947** Mad Wednesday. **1949** The Red Pony; Bandits of El Dorado. **1951** The Racket; The Secret of Convict Lake. **1952** The Big Sky; The Blazing Forest. **1953** Invaders From Mars. **1954** The Country Girl. **1955** Underwater; Lucy Gallant.

WAGNER, WILLIAM

Born: 1885. Died: Mar. 11, 1964, Hollywood, Calif. Screen and stage actor. Entered films approx. 1930.

Appeared in: **1934** Jane Eyre; plus the following shorts: For Pete's Sake; Honkey Donkey; I'll Be Suing You; Done in Oil. **1935** Frisco Kid. **1936** Lloyd's of London; The Lucky Corner (short). **1937** Second Honeymoon; Easy Living. **1938** Rebecca of Sunnybrook Farm.

WAHL, WALTER DARE (Walter Kalwara)

Born: 1896. Died: June 23, 1974, Metamoris, Pa. Screen, stage, vaudeville actor and world's light heavyweight wrestling champion.

Appeared in: **1942** Star Spangled Rhythm. **1954** Top Banana.

WAINWRIGHT, GODFREY

Born: 1879. Died: May 19, 1956, Woodland Hills, Calif. Screen actor.

WAINWRIGHT, HOPE

Born: 1942. Died: Aug. 6, 1972, Sigelbach, Germany (auto accident). Screen and television actress.

Appeared in: **1962** Whatever Happened to Baby Jane? **1967** The Graduate.

WAINWRIGHT, MARIE

Born: 1856, Philadelphia, Pa. Died: Aug. 17, 1923, Scranton, Pa. Stage and screen actress.

Appeared in: **1921** Polly With a Past.

WAITE, CHARLES

Born: Canada. Died: Sept. 6, 1951, Toronto, Canada. Silent screen actor.

WAITE, MALCOLM (Malcolm Ivan Waite)

Born: May 7, 1892, Menominee, Wis. Died: Apr. 25, 1949, Los Angeles, Calif. Screen actor.

Appeared in: **1924** The Hill Billy. **1925** The Great Love; Durand of the Bad Lands; The Gold Rush; The Lucky Horseshoe; Red Hot Tires. **1926** Kid Boots; No Man's Gold; The Whole Town's Talking; Blarney; Desert Valley. **1927** The Monkey Talks; Now We're in the Air; The Broncho Twister. **1929** Noah's Ark; The Vagabond Lover. **1930** A Notorious Affair. **1931** Twenty-Four Hours.

WAKEFIELD, DOUGLAS "DUGGIE"

Born: 1900, Hull, England. Died: Apr. 14, 1951, London, England. Screen, stage and vaudeville actor.

Appeared in: **1933** This Week of Grace. **1934** I'll Be Suing You (short). **1935** Look up and Laugh. **1937** The Penny Pool. **1939** Spy for a Day. **1940** Calling All Crooks.

WAKEFIELD, HUGH

Born: Nov. 10, 1888, Wanstead, England. Died: Dec., 1971, London, England. Screen and stage actor.

Appeared in: **1931** The Sport of Kings; City of a Song (aka Farewell to Love—US 1933). **1932** Aren't We All? **1933** The Crime at Blossoms; The Fortunate Fool; King of the Ritz. **1934** The Luck of a Sailor; My Heart is Calling (US 1935); Lady in Danger; The Man Who Knew Too Much. **1935** Marry the Girl; No Monkey Business; 18 Minutes; Runaway Ladies. **1936** The Limping Man; The Crimson Circle; Forget-Me-Not (aka Forever Yours—US 1937); The Interrupted Honeymoon; It's You I Want; The Improper Duchess; Dreams Come True. **1937** The Street Singer; The Live Wire; Death Croons the Blues. **1938** Make It Three. **1945** Blithe Spirit; Journey Together (US 1946). **1948** One Night with You. **1952** Love's a Luxury (aka The Caretaker's Daughter—US). **1954** The Million Pound Note (aka Man with a Million—US).

WAKEFIELD, OLIVER

Born: 1909, England. Died: June 30, 1956, Rye, N.Y. Screen, stage, radio and television actor.

Appeared in: **1930** A Universal Short. **1937** Let's Make a Night of It (US 1938); There Was a Young Man. **1939** Shipyard Sally. **1940** The Briggs Family; George and Margaret. **1942** The Peterville Diamond. **1943** Pictorial Revue of 1943.

WALBROOK, ANTON (Adolph Anton Wilhelm Wohlbruck)

Born: Nov. 19, 1900, Vienna, Austria. Died: Aug. 9, 1967, Munich, West Germany (heart attack). Screen and stage actor.

Appeared in: **1931** Salto Mortale. **1933** Regine; Mond Uber Marvokko; The Waltz War. **1934** Masquerade in Vienna (US 1937); Die Englishe Heirat; Eine Frau die Weisse Was Sie Will. **1935** Zigeunerbaron (Gypsy Baron); The Student of Prague. **1936** Allitria. **1937** Victoria the Great; The Soldier and the Lady; The Rat. **1938** Sixty Glorious Years (aka Queen of Destiny—US). **1940** Gaslight (aka Angel Street—US 1952). **1941** Dangerous Moonlight (aka Suicide Squadron—US 1942); 49th Parallel (aka The Invaders—US 1942); I Give My Life. **1942** Orders from Tokyo. **1943** The Life and Death of Colonel Blimp (aka Colonel Blimp—US 1945). **1945** The Man from Morocco (US 1946). **1948** The Red Shoes. **1949** The Queen of Spades (US 1950). **1950** La Ronde. **1951** Wien Tanzt (Vienna Waltzes—US 1961). **1952** Angel Street. **1955** Oh, Rosalinda!; Lola Montez. **1957** Saint Joan. **1958** I Accuse. Other foreign films (French): L'Affaire Mauricuis; L'Affaire Menrizim.

WALBRUNN, ERNEST

Born: 1907, Austria. Died: Jan., 1978, Austria? Screen actor.

WALBURN, RAYMOND

Born: Sept. 9, 1887, Plymouth, Ind. Died: July 26, 1969, New York, N.Y. Screen and stage actor.

Appeared in: **1916** The Scarlet Runner (serial). **1930** The Laughing Lady. **1934** The Defense Rests; Jealousy; The Great Flirtation; The Count of Monte Cristo; Broadway Bill; Lady By Choice. **1935** Only Eight Hours; She Married Her Boss; Death Flies East; Mills of the Gods; I'll Love You Always; Redheads on Parade; Society Doctor; It's a Small World; Welcome Home; Thanks a Million. **1936** Mr. Cinderella; Mr. Deeds Goes to Town; The Lone Wolf Returns; The King Steps Out; They Met in a Taxi; Craig's Wife; The Great Ziegfeld; Absolute Quiet; Three Wise Guys; Born to Dance. **1937** Let's Get Married; It Can't Last Forever; Murder in Greenwich Village; Thin Ice; Breezing Home; High, Wide and Handsome; Broadway Melody of 1938. **1938** Start Cheering; Sweethearts; Battle of Broadway; Gateway; Professor Beware. **1939** Let Freedom Ring; It Could Happen to You; The Upper-Pup; Eternally Yours. **1940** Heaven With a Barbed-Wire Fence; The Dark Command; Millionaires in Prison; Flowing Gold; Third Finger, Left Hand; Christmas in July. **1941** Bachelor Daddy (aka Sandy Steps Out); San Francisco Docks; Kiss the Boys Goodbye; Puddin' Head; Bachelor Party; Confirm or Deny; Rise and Shine; Louisiana Purchase. **1942** The Man in the Trunk. **1943** Let's Face It; Dixie Dugan; Lady Bodyguard; Desperadoes; Dixie. **1944** Music in Manhattan; And the Angels Sing; Hail the Conquering Hero; Heavenly Days. **1945** The Cheaters; Honeymoon Ahead; I'll Tell the World. **1946** Affairs of Geraldine; Breakfast in Hollywood; Lover Come Back; The Plainsman and the Lady; Rendezvous with Annie. **1947** Mad Wednesday (aka Sin of Harold Diddlebock). **1948** State of the Union; The World and His Wife. **1949** Henry, the Rainmaker; Leave It to Henry; Red, Hot and Blue. **1950** Riding High; Key to the City; Father's Wild Game; Father Makes Good; Short Grass. **1951** Father Takes the Air; Golden Girl; Excuse My Dust. **1953** Beautiful But Dangerous. **1954** She Couldn't Say No. **1955** The Spoilers.

WALCAMP, MARIE

Born: 1893, Dennison, Ohio. Died: Nov. 17, 1936, Los Angeles, Calif. Screen actress.

Appeared in: **1914** Our Enemy's Spy; From the Lion's Jaw; The Jungle Master. **1916** In the Coils of the Python; Patria (serial); Hop, the Devil's Brew; John Needham's Double; Onda of the Orient; Liberty (serial). **1917** For Liberty; The Flirt; The Quest of Virginia; The Red

Ace; The Silent Terror; The Indian's Lament. **1918** The Lion's Claw. **1919** The Dragon's Net; Tempest Cody's Manhunt; The Tongues of Flames; The Red Robe; The Red Glove (serial). **1921** The Blot. **1924** A Desperate Adventure; Treasure Canyon; Western Vengeance. **1927** In a Moment of Temptation.

WALDAU, GUSTAV
Born: 1871, Germany. Died: May 25, 1958, Munich, Germany. Screen actor.

Appeared in: **1932** Der Falsche Ehemann. **1933** Saison in Kairo (Cairo Season). **1934** Eines Prinzen Junge Liebe (A Prince's Young Love). **1935** Klein Dorrit (Little Dorrit). **1937** Das Einmaleins der Liebe (Love's Arithmetic); Drei Maedel um Schubert (Three Girls Around Schubert). **1938** Sie und die Drei (She and the Three); Der Schimmelkrieg von Holledau; Eine Nacht an der Donau (A Night on the Danube). **1940** Eine Kleine Nachtmusik. **1951** Eroica (aka The Beethoven Story). **1952** Singing Angels.

WALDEMAR, RICHARD
Born: 1870, Austria. Died: Jan., 1947, Vienna, Austria. Stage and screen actor.

Appeared in: **1932** Hirsekorn Greift Ein.

WALDIS, OTTO
Born: 1906, Germany. Died: Mar. 25, 1974, Hollywood, Calif.? (heart attack). Screen actor.

Appeared in: **1947** The Exile. **1948** A Foreign Affair; Letter from an Unknown Woman; Berlin Express; Call Northside 777; The Vicious Circle. **1949** The Fighting O'Flynn (aka The O'Flynn); Border Incident; Bagdad; The Lovable Cheat. **1950** Woman from Headquarters. **1951** Bird of Paradise; Night Into Morning; Secrets of Monte Carlo; The Whip Hand. **1952** The Black Castle; Anything Can Happen. **1953** Rebel City; Rogue's March; Flight to Tangier. **1954** Knock on Wood; Port of Hell; Prince Valiant; The Iron Glove. **1955** Sincerely Yours; Desert Sands; Artists and Models. **1956** Man from Del Rio; Ride the High Iron. **1958** Attack of the 50 Ft. Woman. **1959** Pier 5, Havana. **1961** Judgment at Nuremberg; Nuremberg Trials (aka Hitler's Executioners). **1964** Das Phantom von Soho (The Phantom of Soho—US 1967).

WALDMULLER, LIZZI
Born: 1904, Knitterfeld, Austria. Died: 1945, Vienna, Austria (air raid). Screen, stage actress and singer. Entered films in 1931.

Appeared in: Die Spanische Fliege. **1932** Strafsache van Geldern; Liebe auf den Ersten Ton. **1933** Lachende Erben. **1934** Peer Gynt (US 1939). **1939** Bel Ami (aka Der Liebling Schoener Frauen). **1940** Casanova Heiratet; Traummusik. **1941** Alles fuer Gloria; Frau Luna. **1942** Liebeskomoedie; Die Nacht in Venedig. **1943** Ein Walzer mit Dir. **1944** Ein Mann wie Maximilian; Es Lebe die Liebe.

WALDOW, ERNST
Born: 1894, Germany. Died: June 5, 1964, Hamburg, Germany (heart attack). Screen and stage actor.

Appeared in: **1936** Wenn der Hahn Kraeht. **1938** Das Meadchen von Gestern Nacht (The Girl of Last Night); Die Kleine Suenderin (The Little Sinner); Streitum den Knaben Jo (Strife Over the Boy Jo). **1939** Die Kluge Schwiegermutter (The Wise Mother-in-Law). **1949** The Affair Blum. **1954** Der Zarewitsch (US 1961). **1956** Du Bist Musik (US 1962). **1959** Ein Engel auf Erden (Angel on Earth—US 1966). **1960** Bumerang (aka Cry Double Cross—US 1962). **1963** Schneewittchen und die Sieben Gangler (Snow White and the Seven Jugglers).

WALDRIGE, HAROLD
Born: 1905, New Orleans, La. Died: June 26, 1957, New York, N.Y. Screen and stage actor.

Appeared in: **1922** The Ruling Passion. **1931** Five Star Final; June Moon; Sob Sister. **1932** The Heart of New York; Strangers of the Evening; High Pressure; Alias the Doctor; Play Girl; The Strange Love of Molly Louvain; The All American; False Faces. **1933** Lady Killer; She Had to Say Yes; Devil's Mate; The Death Kiss; In the Money. **1934** Manhattan Love Song; Private Scandal; Easy to Love. **1935** Hitch Hike Lady; Slightly Static (short); Gigolette. **1936** Dancing Pirate; Three Men on a Horse. **1937** an Educational short. **1941** You Belong to Me.

WALDRON, ANDREW "ANDY"
Born: London, England. Died: Feb., 1932, England? Screen and stage actor.

Appeared in: **1919** The Red Glove (serial). **1921** Opened Shutters;

Discontented Wives; Cold Steel. **1922** When East Comes West; Reckless Chances; Putting It Over; Gun Shy; Hills of Missing Men. **1923** Wolves of the Border; The Man Who Won. **1924** Baffled; The Battling Fool; Flashing Spurs; The Cowboy and the Flapper; Women First; Down the Rio Grande; The Whipping Boss; That Wild West; Man From God's Country; Loving Lies; Fighter's Paradise. **1925** Pals; The Wild Girl. **1926** The Ace of Clubs; Midnight Faces; The Grey Devil. **1928** Clearing the Trail. **1929** The Lariat Kid.

WALDRON, CHARLES D.
Born: Dec. 23, 1874, Waterford, N.Y. Died: Mar. 4, 1946, Hollywood, Calif. Screen and stage actor. Father of actor Charles K. Waldron (dec. 1952).

Appeared in: **1921** Everyman's Price. **1935** Mary Burns, Fugitive; Wanderer of the Wasteland; The Great Impersonation; Crime and Punishment. **1936** The Garden of Allah; Career Woman; Ramona. **1937** A Doctor's Diary; My Dear Miss Aldrich; Navy Blue and Gold; It's All Yours; Escape By Night; The Emperor's Candlesticks. **1938** Kentucky; They're Always Caught (short); The Little Adventuress; Marie Antoinette. **1939** On Borrowed Time; The Real Glory. **1940** Three Faces West; Thou Shalt Not Kill; Remember the Night; Dr. Kildare's Strangest Case; The Refugee; Streets of Memories; The Stranger on the Third Floor; Untamed. **1941** The Devil and Miss Jones; The Case of the Black Parrot; The Nurse's Secret; Three Sons O'Guns; Rise and Shine. **1942** Random Harvest; Through Different Eyes; The Gay Sisters. **1943** The Song of Bernadette; The Adventures of Mark Twain; Mlle. Fifi. **1944** Black Parachute. **1946** The Fighting Guardsman; The Big Sleep; Dragonwyck.

WALDRON, CHARLES K.
Born: 1915. Died: Apr. 18, 1952, Los Angeles, Calif. (airplane crash). Screen actor. Son of actor Charles D. Waldron (dec. 1946).

WALDRON, EDNA
Born: 1913. Died: Aug. 24, 1940, Hollywood, Calif. (burns sustained in an attempt to save the life of a child whose clothing was afire). Screen actress.

WALDRON, ISABEL
Born: 1871. Died: Jan. 9, 1950, Mamaroneck, N.Y. Screen and stage actress. Married to stage actor Edward Emery (dec. 1938) and mother of actor John Emery (dec. 1964).

WALDRON, JACK
Born: 1893. Died: Nov. 21, 1969, New York, N.Y. (heart attack). Screen, stage and vaudeville actor.

Appeared in: **1928** A Little Breath of Broadway (short).

WALDRON, MAY
Born: Nov. 1, 1868, Hamilton, Ontario, Canada. Died: Dec. 22, 1924, Louisville, La. Screen and stage actress. Married to stage actor Stuart Robson (dec. 1903). Mother of actor Stuart Robson, Jr. (dec. 1946).

WALES, ETHEL
Born: 1881, New York, N.Y. Died: Feb. 15, 1952, Hollywood, Calif. Screen and stage actress.

Appeared in: **1918** The Whispering Chorus. **1921** Miss Lulu Bett; A Prince There Was; After the Show. **1922** Nice People; The Old Homestead; Bobbed Hair; Is Matrimony a Failure?; The Bonded Woman; Bought and Paid For; Manslaughter; Our Leading Citizen. **1923** The Covered Wagon; The Marriage Maker; The Fog; Stepping Fast. **1924** The Bedroom Window; Revelation; The White Sin; Icebound; Lovers' Lane; Loving Lies; Merton of the Movies; Which Shall It Be? **1925** Go Straight; Shattered Lives; Steppin' Out; Begger on Horseback; Don't Let Women Alone; The Overland Limited; When Husbands Flirt; The Wedding Song; Wandering Footsteps; The Monster. **1926** Bertha, the Sewing Machine Girl; Take It from Me; Made for Love; Ladies at Play. **1927** The Cradle Snatchers; The Country Doctor; Almost Human; The Wreck of the Hesperus; Stage Kisses; The Satin Woman; The Girl in the Pullman; My Friend from India. **1928** Tenth Avenue; Craig's Wife; The Masks of the Devil; The Perfect Crime; Ladies' Night in a Turkish Bath; On to Reno; Taxi 13. **1929** Blue Skies; The Saturday Night Kid; The Doctor's Secret; The Donovan Affair. **1930** Loose Ankles; Tom Sawyer; Girl in the Show; The Dude Wrangler; Under Montana Skies. **1931** Subway Express; The Flood; Criminal Code; Honeymoon Lane; Maker of Men. **1932** The Sign of the Cross; The Fighting Fool; Love in High Gear; The 13th Guest; Love Me Tonight; Klondike; Tangled Destinies; The Racing Strain; A Man's Land. **1933** The 11th Commandment; The Fighting Parson. **1934** The Mighty Barnum; The Crime Doctor. **1935** Barbary Coast; Another Face; Bar 20 Rides Again. **1936** Collegiate. **1938** The

Gladiator. **1939** Sudden Money; In Old Caliente; Days of Jesse James. **1940** Knights of the Range; Hidden Gold; Young Bill Hickok. **1941** Border Vigilantes. **1944** The Lumberjack. **1946** Blonde Alibi. **1947** Welcome Stranger; Unconquered; Smash Up, The Story of a Woman. **1950** Tarnished; Fancy Pants.

WALES, WALLY (Floyd Taliaferro Alderson aka HAL TALIAFERRO aka FLOYD T. ALDERSON)
Born: 1896, Mont. Died: Feb. 12, 1980, Sheridan, Wyo. (pneumonia). Screen actor.

Appeared in: **1921** Western Hearts. **1925** Hurricane Horseman; Tearin' Loose; Galloping On. **1926** Ace of Action; Double Daring; The Fighting Cheat; Riding Rivals; Roaring Rider; Twisted Triggers; Vanishing Hoofs. **1927** The Cyclone Cowboy; Tearin; Into Trouble; The Meddlin' Stranger; Skedaddle Gold; White Pebbles; The Soda Water Cowboy. **1928** Saddle Mates; The Desert of the Lost; Desperate Courage; The Flying Buckaroo. **1929** Overland Bound. **1930** Bar-L Ranch; Canyon Hawks; Trails of Peril; Breed of the West; Voice from the Sky (serial). **1931** Red Fork Range; Riders of the Cactus; Hell's Valley. **1933** Law and the Lawless; Deadwood Pass; Fighting Texans; Secrets of Hollywood; Sagebrush Trail. **1934** Fighting Through; Mystery Mountain. **1935** Gun Play; The Miracle Rider (serial); Vanishing Riders; Powdersmoke Range; The Phantom Empire; Heir to Trouble. **1936** The Unknown Ranger; Hair-Trigger Casey; Avenging Water; The Traitor; Swifty. **1937** Law of the Ranger; Rootin' Tootin' Rhythm; The Trigger Trio; The Painted Stallion (serial); Heart of the Rockies. **1938** Phantom Gold; Pioneer Trail; Black Bandit; The Lone Ranger (serial). **1939** Western Caravans; Daughter of the Tong; Saga of Death Valley; Outpost of the Mounties. **1940** Bullets for Rustlers; Pioneers of the West; Two-Fisted Rangers; Hi-Yo Silver; The Man With Nine Lives; The Carson City Kid; Colorado; Young Bill Hickok; Cherokee Strip; The Border Legion; Adventures of Red Ryder (serial). **1941** In Old Cheyenne; Sheriff of Tombstone; The Great Train Robbery; Border Vigilantes; Law of the Range; Along the Rio Grande; Bad Man of Deadwood; Jesse James at Bay; Riders of the Timberline; Red River Valley. **1942** Sons of the Pioneers; Little Joe, the Wrangler; American Empire; Tombstone, The Town Too Tough To Die; Romance of the Range. **1943** Hoppy Serves a Writ; Idaho; The Leather Burners; Song of Texas; Silver Spurs; The Man from Music Mountain; The Woman of the Town. **1944** Haunted Harbor (serial); The Cowboy and the Senorita; Lumberjack; The Yellow Rose of Texas; Forty Thieves; Vigilantes of Dodge City; Zorro's Black Whip (serial). **1945** Utah; Fallen Angel; Federal Operator 99 (serial); San Antonio. **1946** The Phantom Rider (serial); Duel in the Sun; Plainsman and the Lady; Heading West. **1947** Ramrod. **1948** Blood on the Moon; The Gallant Legion; Red River; West of Sonora. **1949** Brimstone. **1950** The Savage Horde. **1951** The Sea Hornet; Pirates Harbor (rerelease of Haunted Harbor, 1944 serial); Junction City.

WALKER, ARLENE (aka ARLENE PERCIVAL)
Born: 1919. Died: Apr. 15, 1973, New York. Screen, stage, radio and television actress.

WALKER, AURORA
Born: 1912, Mexico. Died: Jan. 2, 1964, Mexico. Screen actress.

Appeared in: **1940** Odio (Hate); Vivire Otra Vez (I Shall Live Again). **1955** This Strange Passion.

WALKER, CHARLOTTE
Born: Dec. 29, 1878, Galveston, Tex. Died: Mar. 24, 1958, Kerville, Tex. Screen and stage actress. Mother of actress Sara Haden (dec. 1981).

Appeared in: **1915** Kindling. **1916** The Trail of the Lonesome Pine. **1917** Seven Deadly Sins (in one of the seven sequences). **1919** Eve in Exile. **1924** Classmates; The Lone Wolf; The Sixth Commandment. **1925** The Manicure Girl; The Midnight Girl. **1926** The Great Deception; The Savage. **1927** The Clown. **1928** Annapolis. **1929** South Sea Rose; Paris Bound. **1930** Scarlet Pages; Double Crossroads; Three Faces East; Lightnin'. **1931** Millie; Salvation Nell. **1933** Hotel Variety. **1941** Scattergood Meets Broadway.

WALKER, CHERYL
Born: Aug. 1, 1922, South Pasadena, Calif. Died: Oct. 24, 1971 (cancer). Screen actress. Queen of the 1938 Pasadena Tournament of Roses.

Appeared in: **1938** You and Me; Tip Off Girls; If I Were King; Men With Wings. **1940** Chasing Trouble. **1942** Shadows on the Sage. **1943** Stage Door Canteen. **1944** Three Is a Family; Three Little Sisters. **1945** It's a Pleasure; A Song for Miss Julie; Identity Unknown; How Do You Do? **1946** Murder Is My Business; Larceny in Her Heart. **1947** Three on a Ticket. **1948** Waterfront at Midnight.

WALKER, CHESTER W.
Died: Sept. 16, 1945, Okinawa (typhoon). Screen actor.

WALKER, CHRISTY
Born: 1898. Died: Oct. 29, 1918, New York, N.Y. (influenza). Screen actress.

WALKER, HELEN
Born: 1921, Worcester, Mass. Died: Mar. 10, 1968, North Hollywood, Calif. (cancer). Screen and stage actress.

Appeared in: **1942** Lucky Jordan. **1943** The Good Fellows. **1944** Abroad With Two Yanks; Man in Half-Moon Street. **1945** Duffy's Tavern; Murder, He Says. **1946** Brewster's Millions; Cluny Brown; Her Adventurous Night; Murder in the Music Hall; People Are Funny. **1947** Nightmare Alley; The Homestretch. **1948** Call Northside 777; My Dear Secretary; Nancy Goes to Rio. **1949** Impact. **1951** My True Story. **1952** Heaven Only Knows. **1953** Problem Girls. **1955** The Big Combo.

WALKER, JOHNNIE
Born: 1896, New York, N.Y. Died: Dec. 4, 1949, New York, N.Y. Screen, stage actor, film director, stage and film producer.

Appeared in: **1920** Over the Hill to the Poor House. **1921** Live Wires; The Jolt; Play Square; What Love Will Do. **1922** In the Name of the Law; The Sagebrush Trail; Captain Fly-By-Night; Extra! Extra!; The Third Alarm; My Dad. **1923** Fashionable Fakers; Broken Hearts of Broadway; Children of Dust; Shattered Reputations; Red Lights; The Fourth Musketeer; Mary of the Movies; The Mailman; Souls for Sale. **1924** The Spirit of the U.S.A.; Soiled; The Slanderers; Girls Men Forget; Galloping Hoofs (serial); Life's Greatest Game; Wine of Youth. **1925** The Scarlet West; Reckless Sex; Lilies of the Streets; Children of the Whirlwind; Lena Rivers; The Mad Dancer. **1926** Old Ironsides; So This Is Paris; Honesty—the Best Policy; The Earth Woman; Transcontinental Limited; Fangs of Justice; The Lightning Reporter; Morganson's Finish. **1927** Swell Head; A Boy of the Streets; Cross Breed; Pretty Clothes; The Princess on Broadway; Wolves of the Air; Rose of the Bowery; The Clown; Held by the Law; Snarl of Hate; Where the Trails Begin. **1928** Manitee Idol; So This Is Love; Bare Knees. **1930** The Melody Man; Ladies in Love; Up the River; Girl of the Golden West; Ladies of Leisure. **1931** Enemies of the Law. **1932** Speaking out of Turn (short). **1934** Fantomas.

WALKER, JUNE
Born: 1904, New York, N.Y. Died: Feb. 3, 1966, Sherman Oaks, Calif. Screen, stage, radio and television actress.

Appeared in: **1921** Coincidence. **1930** War Nurse. **1942** Through Different Eyes. **1960** The Unforgiven. **1963** A Child Is Waiting.

WALKER, LILLIAN "DIMPLES"
Born: Apr. 21, 1888, Brooklyn, N.Y. Died: Oct. 10, 1975, Trinidad, West Indies. Screen, stage, vaudeville actress and film producer.

Appeared in: **1911** The Prince and the Pumps; A Friendly Marriage; By Way of Mr. Browning; Their Charming Mama; The Wager; The Second Honeymoon; The Husking Bee; Testing His Courage; The Love Sick Maiden of Cuddleton; Saving on Audience; Alma's Champion; It All Came Out in the Wash; The Diamond Broach; Infatuation; Working for Hubby; Thou Shalt Not Covet; Leap Year Proposals; The Miracle; An Eventful Elopement; The Great Diamond Robbery; Pandora's Box; Mr. Bolter's Infatuation; The Suit of Armor; The Indian Mutiny; How Mr. Bullington Ran the House; An Elephant on Their Hands; Four Days a Widow; Reincarnation of Komar; While She Powdered Her Nose; Troublesome Stepdaughters; Stenographers Wanted. **1913** The Only Way; When Society Calls; The Right Man; Love, Luck and Gasoline; The Right Man; The Mouse and the Lion; Those Troublesome Tresses; The Two Purses; The Feudists; Classmates' Frolic; Mr. Ford's Temper; The Final Justice; He Waited; Cutey and the Chorus Girls; Two Hearts that Beat as One; Three to One; Keeping Husbands Home; Which Way Did He Go?; Cutey's Waterloo; The Right Man; The Life Saver; Eve's Daughter (aka The Artist's Madonna); The Accomplished Mrs. Thompson; Cutey's Vacation; Art for a Heart; Doctor Polly; The Speeder's Revenge; Fanny's Melodrama; The Persistent Mr. Prince; Lillian's Dilemma; Lily of the Valley; A Costume Piece; The Winning Trick; Bread Upon the Waters; The Girl at the Lunch Counter; The New Secretary. **1915** A Model's Wife; The Love Whip; Arthur Truman's Ward; Peggy of Fifth Avenue; The Capitulation of the Major; Lifting the Ban of Controversy; Breaking In; The Silent W; The Little Doll's Dressmaker; The Honeymoon Pact; Dimples and the Ring; The Guttersnipe; Playing the Ring; Hearts and the Highway; A Lilly in Bohemia; To Save Him for His Wife; Dimples, the Auto Salesgirl; A Keyboard Strategy; The Fire Escape; Green Stockings; Lillian's Husbands; The Shabbies; Save the Coupons. **1916** Mrs. Dane's Danger; Her Bad Quarter of an Hour; The Ordeal of Elizabeth; The Man Behind the Curtain; Hesper of the Mountains; The Dollar and the Law; The Kid;

The Blue Envelope Mystery. **1917** Indiscretion; Sally in a Hurry; A Tale of Two Cities; Kitty Mackaye; Princess of Park Row; Lust of the Ages. **1918** A Grain of Dust; The Embarrassment of Riches. **1919** The Love Hunger; The White Man's Chance; The Better Wife; Joyous Liar. **1920** The $1,000,000 Reward (serial). **1921** The Woman God Changed; You and I. **1922** Love's Boomerang. **1934** Enlighten Your Daughter.

WALKER, MARTIN
Born: July 27, 1901, Harrow, Middlesex, England. Died: Sept. 18, 1955, England? Screen and stage actor.

Appeared in: **1931** The Flying Fool (film debut). **1935** Sanders of the River; Mimi. **1937** Sensation; Silver Blaze (aka Murder at the Baskervilles—US 1941). **1938** The Drum (aka Drums—US). **1939** Hell's Cargo (aka Dangerous Cargo—US 1940). **1941** This England (aka Our Heritage); Love on the Dole. **1947** The Woman in the Hall (US 1949). **1953** Black 13 (US 1954).

WALKER, NELLA
Born: Mar. 6, 1886, Chicago, Ill. Died: Mar. 21, 1971, Los Angeles, Calif. (heart disease). Screen, stage and vaudeville actress. Divorced from actor William Mack, with whom she appeared in vaudeville.

Appeared in: **1929** Seven Keys to Baldpate; The Vagabond Lover; Tanned Legs. **1930** Extravagance; What a Widow! **1931** The Common Law; The Public Defender; The Hot Heiress; Indiscreet; Daughter of the Dragon. **1932** Trouble in Paradise; Lady With a Past; They Call It Sin. **1933** 20,000 Years in Sing Sing; Second Hand Wife; Dangerously Yours; Humanity; Reunion in Vienna; This Day and Age; Going Hollywood; Ever in My Heart; House on 56th Street. **1934** The Fugitive Lady; Fashions of 1934; All of Me; Four Frightened People; Elmer and Elsie; The Ninth Guest; Change of Heart; Madame DuBarry; Big Hearted Herbert. **1935** Dante's Inferno; I Live My Life; Behold My Wife; The Woman in Red; McFadden's Flats; A Dog of Flanders; Going Highbrow; Red Salute; Coronado; The Right to Love; Bordertown. **1936** Klondike Annie; Small Town Girl; Captain January; Don't Turn 'Em Loose. **1937** Three Smart Girls; Stella Dallas; 45 Fathers. **1938** Hard to Get; Young Dr. Kildare; The Crime of Dr. Hallet; The Rage of Paris. **1939** The Saint Strikes Back; Three Smart Girls Grow Up; When Tomorrow Comes; In Name Only; Swanee River. **1940** Irene; A Child is Born; The Saint Takes Over; Kitty Foyle; I Love You Again. **1941** Manpower; Hellzapoppin; Repent at Leisure; Buck Privates; Kathleen; Back Street; A Girl, a Guy and a Gob. **1942** Kid Glove Killer; We Were Dancing. **1943** Air Raid Wardens; Hers to Hold; Wintertime. **1944** Take It or Leave It; In Society; Ladies in Washington; Murder in the Blue Room. **1945** A Guy, a Gal and a Pal; Follow That Woman. **1946** Two Sisters from Boston; The Locket. **1947** Variety Girl; The Beginning or the End; Undercover Maisie; This Time for Keeps; That Hagen Girl. **1950** Nancy Goes to Rio. **1952** Flesh and Fury. **1954** Sabrina.

WALKER, NORMAN
Born: Oct. 8, 1892, Bolton, Lancashire, England. Died: Nov. 4, 1963, England. Screen, stage actor, opera singer and film director. Entered films in 1920.

Appeared in: **1940** Mozart. **1941** Leburnum Grove.

WALKER, RAY W.
Born: Aug. 10, 1904, Newark, N.J. Died: Oct. 6, 1980, Los Angeles, Calif. (heart failure). Screen, stage, radio and television actor.

Appeared in: **1933** Skyway; Devil's Mate; He Couldn't Take It. **1934** City Limits; Goodbye Love; Loud Speaker; Thirty Day Princess; Baby, Take a Bow; Happy Landing; When Strangers Meet. **1935** One Hour Late; Million Dollar Baby; Ladies Love Danger; The Girl Friend; Cappy Ricks Returns; $10 Raise; Music is Magic. **1936** Laughing Irish Eyes; The Crime Patrol; The Last Assignment; The Dark Hour; Brilliant Marriage. **1937** Hideaway Girl; Her Husband Lies; Angel's Holiday; One Mile from Heaven; Outlaws of the Orient. **1938** The Marines Are Here; Crashin' Thru Danger; The Forgotten Woman; Missing Evidence. **1939** Mr. Moto in Danger Island. **1940** A Night at Earl Carroll's. **1942** House of Errors; Almost Married. **1943** Dixie Dugan; Mission to Moscow; Princess O'Rourke; The Unknown Guest; Crazy House; Henry Aldrich Haunts a House. **1944** Swingtime Johnny; Man from Frisco; South of Dixie; Jam Session; Silent Partner; Stars on Parade; My Buddy. **1945** Eve Knew Her Apples; Rogues' Gallery. **1946** Tars and Spars; Life With Blondie; Gay Blades; Dark Alibi; Crime of the Century; Step by Step; Secrets of a Sorority Girl; Secret of the Whistler. **1947** The Pilgrim Lady; That's My Gal; Robin Hood of Texas; The Unsuspected. **1948** The Sainted Sisters; Black Bart; April Showers; Apartment for Peggy. **1949** Blondie's Big Deal; Song of Surrender; Angels in Disguise; Holiday in Havana; Oh, You Beautiful Doll. **1950** Pioneer Marshal; Hoedown; Bodyhold; Sideshow;

Square Dance Katy; Under Mexicali Skies; Revenue Agent; Chinatown at Midnight; Tyrant of the Sea. **1951** A Wonderful Life; The Harlem Globetrotters; Let's Go Navy; Chinatown Chump (short). **1952** No Holds Barred. **1953** Clipped Wings; Roar of the Crowd; The Blue Gardenia; The Homesteaders; Rebel City; Marry Me Again. **1954** Pride of the Bluegrass. **1956** Everything But the Truth; Yaqui Drums. **1957** The Iron Sheriff.

WALKER, ROBERT (Robert Hudson Walker)
Born: Oct. 13, 1914, Utah. Died: Aug. 28, 1951, Santa Monica, Calif. (respiratory failure). Screen, stage and radio actor. Married to Barbara Ford. Divorced from actress Jennifer Jones and father of actor Robert Walker, Jr.

Appeared in: **1939** Winter Carnival. **1941** I'll Sell My Life. **1943** Bataan; Madame Curie. **1944** See Here, Private Hargrove; Since You Went Away; Thirty Seconds Over Tokyo. **1945** The Clock; What Next Corporal Hargrove?; Her Highness and the Bellboy; The Sailor Takes a Wife. **1946** Blue Skies; 'Til the Clouds Roll By. **1947** Song of Love; The Sea of Grass; The Beginning or the End. **1948** One Touch of Venus. **1950** Please Believe Me; The Skipper Surprised His Wife. **1951** Strangers on a Train; Vengeance Valley. **1952** My Son John.

WALKER, ROBERT "BOB" (Robert Donald Walker)
Born: June 18, 1888, Bethlehem, Pa. Died: Mar., 1954. Screen and stage actor. Do not confuse with actor Robert Walker (dec. 1951). Entered films with Kalem in 1915.

Appeared in: **1915** Children of Eve. **1916** The Light of Happiness; Gates of Eden; The Cossack Whip; The Littlest Magdalene. **1917** The Mortal Sin; Lady Barnacle; Aladdin's Other Lamp; The Girl Without a Soul; Blue Jeans; God's Law and a Man's; A Wife By Proxy. **1919** A Burglar by Proxy; The Lion Man (serial). **1921** White Oak. **1922** Broad Daylight; Reckless Chances. **1923** Itching Palms; Why Women Remarry; The Drug Traffic. **1924** The Dancing Cheat; Battling Brewster (serial). **1925** A Daughter of the Sioux; Drug Store Cowboy; My Pal; The Outlaw's Daughter; The Rip Snorter; Warrior Gap; Ridin' Comet; Tonio, Son of the Sierras; The Mystery Box (serial). **1926** Deuce High; The Gallant Fool. **1927** Daring Deeds; Roaring Fires; Western Courage. **1928** The Code of the Scarlet; The Cowboy Cavalier; The Upland Rider. **1929** The Dream Melody; The Three Outcasts. **1930** Canyon Hawks; Phantom of the Desert; Ridin' Law; Westward Bound; The Fighting Legion. **1931** The Vanishing Legion (serial). **1935** Captured in Chinatown; Now or Never; Never Too Late; The Crimson Trail; Outlawed Guns; The Throwback. **1936** The Black Clin (serial); Hair-Trigger Casey; Fast Bullets; Caryl of the Mountains; The Speed Reporter; The Clutching Hand (serial). **1937** Gunsmoke Ranch; The Mysterious Pilot (serial); Two-Fisted Bullets. **1939** El Diablo Rides. **1947** The Last Round-Up. **1949** Riders in the Sky.

WALKER, ROSE (Rose Walker Dowsey)
Born: 1907. Died: July 29, 1951, Manhasset, N.Y. (injuries from fall from building). Screen actress.

WALKER, SYD
Born: England. Died: Jan. 13, 1945, London, England. Screen, stage and radio actor.

Appeared in: **1924** Old Bill Through the Ages. **1934** Gift of Gab. **1935** Royal Cavalcade (aka Regal Cavalcade—US). **1936** A Universal short. **1937** Over She Goes; Let's Make a Night of It (US 1938). **1938** Oh Boy; Hold My Hand. **1939** What Would You Do, Chums?; The Gang's All Here (aka The Amazing Mr. Forest—US).

WALKER, TEX (Charles Herbert Walker)
Born: 1867. Died: Aug. 22, 1947, Los Angeles, Calif. (pneumonia). Screen and stage actor.

WALKER, VIRGINIA
Born: 1916. Died: Dec. 22, 1946, Hollywood, Calif. Screen actress. Divorced from film producer Howard Hawks.

Appeared in: **1938** Bringing Up Baby. **1945** Nob Hill; Billy Rose's Diamond Horseshoe.

WALKER, WALTER
Born: 1864. Died: Dec. 4, 1947. Screen actor. Do not confuse with Walter "Wally" Walker (dec. 1975).

WALKER, WALTER "WALLY"
Born: 1901. Died: Aug. 7, 1975, Woodland Hills, Calif. (stroke). Screen actor and extra. Entered films in 1920.

Appeared in: **1921** The Chicken in the Case. **1922** The Darling of the Rich. **1926** Black Bird. **1929** Great Power. **1931** Reaching for the

Moon; A Tailor Made Man; Annabelle's Affairs; Rebound; Common Law; New Adventures of Get Rich Quick Wallingford. **1932** Tomorrow and Tomorrow; Two Seconds; The Rich Are Always With Us; The Woman in Room 13; Letty Lynton; Two Against the World; Life Begins; The Last Mile; You Said a Mouthful; The Conquerers; The Kid from Spain; No Man of Her Own; Fireman Save My Child; American Madness; Blessed Event. **1933** I Love That Man; Jennie Gerhart; I'm no Angel; Sitting Pretty; Mary Stevens, MD; I Loved a Woman; Female; Flying Down to Rio; The Billion Dollar Scandal; From Hell to Heaven; The Great Jasper; Our Betters; The House on 56th Street. **1934** You Can't Buy Everything; Beside; A Lost Lady; The Count of Monte Cristo; Mrs. Wiggs of the Cabbage Patch; The Gay Bride; Babbitt. **1935** While the Patient Slept; Sons of Steel; Front Page Woman; Dangerous; Magnificent Obsession. **1936** Everybody's Old Man; Yours for the Asking. **1937** Women Men Marry. **1938** The Cowboy and the Lady. **1946** Ginger. **1948** Docks of New Orleans; I Wouldn't Be in Your Shoes.

WALKER, WALTON (Walton Cherre Walker)
Born: Jan. 21, 1909, Texas. Died: Oct. 14, 1969, Hollywood, Calif. (murdered—beaten). Screen actor, dancer and choreographer.

WALL, DAVID V.
Born: 1870. Died: June 1, 1938, New York, N.Y. Screen and stage actor.

Appeared in: **1922** When the Desert Calls. **1924** Pied Piper Malone.

WALL, GERALDINE
Born: 1913. Died: June 22, 1970, Woodland Hills, Calif. (pneumonia). Screen, stage and television actress.

Appeared in: **1941** Remember the Day. **1943** The Song of Bernadette. **1944** Black Magic; Winged Victory. **1945** Valley of Decision. **1946** Love Laughs at Andy Hardy; Boy's Ranch; Janie Gets Married. **1947** Dark Delusion. **1948** Scudda Hoo!, Scudda Hay!; Green Grass of Wyoming; Beyond Glory; Homecoming. **1949** The Fountainhead; Alias Nick Beal; Everybody Does It; The Green Promise; Thelma Jordan (aka File on Thelma Jordan). **1950** Mister 880; There's a Girl in My Heart; Paid in Full. **1951** Appointment with Danger. **1953** By the Light of the Silvery Moon. **1954** Black Widow. **1956** The Man in the Gray Flannel Suit. **1957** An Affair to Remember. **1958** This Earth is Mine; Mardi Gras; Some Came Running. **1960** Please Don't Eat the Daisies; Heller in Pink Tights. **1964** One Man's Way.

WALLACE, BERYL
Born: 1910. Died: June 17, 1948, near Mt. Carmel, Pa. (plane crash). Screen actress. Divorced from actor Milton Berle.

Appeared in: **1934** Murder at the Vanities. **1937** Rough Ridin' Rhythm. **1938** Romance of the Rockies; Dramatic School; Trade Winds; Air Devils. **1939** The Women; Coast Guard. **1942** Johnny Eager; Tombstone, the Town too Tough to Die; Sunset on the Desert. **1943** The Kansan. **1944** Enemy of Women; The Woman of the Town.

WALLACE, BILL (William Lally)
Born: 1908. Died: Aug. 20, 1956, Hollywood, Calif. (heart attack). Screen actor and film editor.

WALLACE, EDNA *See* HOPPER, EDNA WALLACE

WALLACE, ETHEL LEE
Born: 1888, Springfield, Mo. Died: Sept. 7, 1956, Springfield, Mo. Screen and stage actress. Appeared in silent films.

WALLACE, GEORGE
Born: 1894, Aberdeen, New South Wales, Australia. Died: Nov., 1960, Sydney, Australia. Screen, stage, vaudeville, television actor, songwriter, screenwriter and playwright. Billed with Dinks Paterson in a vaudeville act known as "Dinks and Onkus." Father of actor George Wallace, Jr. Do not confuse with U.S. actor George Wallace.

Appeared in: **1934** A Ticket in Tatts. **1938** Let George Do It.

WALLACE, GUY
Born: 1913. Died: Aug. 29, 1967. Screen actor and television announcer.

WALLACE, INEZ
Died: June 28, 1966, Cleveland, Ohio. Screen, stage actress and screenwriter. Appeared in silents.

WALLACE, LOUIS CHAPMAN
Born: 1882. Died: May 20, 1962, Hollywood, Calif. Screen actress. Married to actor Morgan Wallace (dec. 1953).

WALLACE, MAUDE
Born: 1894. Died: Apr. 23, 1952, Hollywood, Calif. Screen, vaudeville and television actress. Entered films approx. 1947. Billed in vaudeville with her sister, Myrtle, as the "Hollingsworth Twins" and later billed as part of the "Towers and Wallace" vaudeville team.

Appeared in: **1951** Elopement; Love Nest; People Will Talk. **1952** Scarlet Angel; We're Not Married; Stars and Stripes Forever.

WALLACE, MAY (May Maddox)
Born: 1877. Died: Dec. 11, 1938, Los Angeles, Calif. (heart disease). Screen and vaudeville actress.

Appeared in: **1921** The Cup of Life; My Lady Friends. **1923** Dollar Devils; Gimme. **1924** The Reckless Age; Oh, You Tony! **1929** Painted Faces; Skirt Shy (short). **1931** Love Business (short); Mama Loves Papa (short). **1931** The following shorts: Readin' and Writin'; Free Eats; Pooch; Young Ironsides; You're Telling Me; County Hospital. **1933** What's Your Racket?; Kid from Borneo (short); Twice Two (short—voice). **1934** The Chases of Pimple Street (short). **1935** Beginner's Luck (short); Okay Toots! (short). **1936** The Sky Parade; Arbor Day (short). **1937** Midnight Madonna; Roamin' Holiday (short).

WALLACE, MILTON
Born: 1888. Died: Feb. 16, 1956, Hollywood, Calif. Screen, stage and vaudeville actor.

Appeared in: **1934** Kiss and Make Up; The Mighty Barnum. **1944** None But the Lonely Heart; Seven Doors to Death. **1945** The Lost Weekend. **1946** The Killers. **1947** Kiss of Death.

WALLACE, MORGAN
Born: July 26, 1888, Lompoc, Calif. Died: Dec. 12, 1953, Tarzana, Calif. Screen, stage actor, film, stage producer and playwright. Married to actress Louise Chapman Wallace (dec. 1962).

Appeared in: **1921** Dream Street (film debut). **1922** Orphans of the Storm; One Exciting Night. **1923** The Dangerous Maid; The Fighting Blade. **1924** Daring Love; Reckless Romance; Sandra; Torment; A Woman Who Sinned. **1930** Sisters; Up the River; Big Money. **1931** It Pays to Advertise; Safe in Hell; Alexander Hamilton; Women Go On Forever; Smart Money; The Unholy Garden; Expensive Women. **1932** Hell's House; Grand Hotel; Lady and Gent; Blonde Venus; Wild Girl; Steady Company; Fast Companions; The Final Edition; The Mouthpiece. **1933** Smoking Lightning; Song of Songs; Terror Abroad; Jennie Gerhardt; Mama Loves Papa; Above the Clouds. **1934** The Trumpet Blows; It's a Gift; Cheating Cheaters; Many Happy Returns; The Merry Widow; We Live Again; I Believed in You. **1935** Hit and Run Driver (short); Murder on a Honeymoon; The Devil Is a Woman; Dante's Inferno; Headline Woman; Confidential; Thunder Mountain; $1,000 a Minute. **1936** Mister Cinderella; Love on a Bet; Sutter's Gold; Human Cargo; Fury. **1937** Charlie Chan at the Olympics; The Californian; Under Suspicion; House of Secrets. **1938** Numbered Woman; Gang Bullets; The Lady in the Morgue; Mr. Moto Takes a Vacation; Woman Against Woman; Billy the Kid Returns. **1939** The Mystery of Mr. Wong; The Star Maker. **1940** I Love You Again; Three Men from Texas; Ellery Queen, Master Detective. **1941** Sea Raiders (serial); In Old Colorado; Scattergood Meets Broadway. **1945** I'll Remember April; Song of the Sarong; Dick Tracy. **1946** The Falcon's Alibi.

WALLACE, NELLIE
Born: Mar. 18, 1882, Glasgow, Scotland. Died: Nov. 24, 1948, England? Screen and stage actress.

Appeared in: **1920** Why Men Leave Home (aka The Golden Pippin Girl). **1933** The Wishbone.

WALLACE, REGINA (Regina Katherine Wallace)
Born: 1892, Trenton, N.J. Died: Feb. 13, 1978, Englewood, N.J. (stroke). Screen, stage, radio and television actress.

Appeared in: **1942** The Male Animal (stage and film versions); Adventures of Martin Eden; Scattergood Rides Again. **1943** Sherlock Holmes in Washington; Behind Prison Walls; The Crystal Ball. **1944** Mr. Skeffington. **1945** Pillow to Post. **1946** Because of Him; The Dark Corner; Avalanche; The Bamboo Blonde; Personality Kid. **1947** High Conquest; Swing the Western Way; Two Blondes and a Redhead. **1948** Miracle of the Bells; Rachel and the Stranger; I Surrender Dear; Triple Threat. **1949** My Foolish Heart.

WALLACE, VIRGINIA
Born: 1909. Died: 1976. Screen actress and entertainer.

Appeared in: **1949** A Kiss for Corliss. **1967** Passages from "Finnegan's Wake."

WALLEN, SIGURD

Born: 1884, Sweden. Died: Mar. 20, 1947, Stockholm, Sweden. Screen, stage actor and film director.

Appeared in: **1931** Brokiga Blad. **1932** Roeda Dagen. **1934** Pattersson and Bendel. **1938** Karl Fredrik Reigns; John Ericsson Victor of Hampton Roads. **1939** Familjen Anderson (The Anderson Family); Med Folket Foer Fosterlandet; Du Gamla, Du Fria (Thou Old, Thou Free). **1945** Crime and Punishment (US 1948).

WALLER, EDDY C.

Born: 1889. Died: Aug. 20, 1977, Los Angeles, Calif. (stroke). Screen, stage and television actor.

Appeared in: **1938** State Police; Call the Mesquiteers; A Criminal Is Born (short); The Great Adventures of Wild Bill Hickok (serial). **1939** Geronimo; I'm From Missouri; Jesse James; Return of the Cisco Kid; Legion of Lost Fliers; Allegheny Uprising; New Frontier; Two Bright Boys; Mutiny on the Blackhawk. **1940** Carolina Moon; The Devil's Pipeline; Legion of the Lawless; The Grapes of Wrath; The Man from Montreal; Konga—the Wild Stallion; You're Not So Tough; Stagecoach War; Gold Rush Maisie; Texas Terrors. **1941** In Old Colorado. **1942** A-Haunting We Will Go; Call of the Canyon; Scattergood Survives a Murder; The Mummy's Tomb; The Lone Star Ranger; Sundown Jim; Night Monster. **1943** Cinderella Swings It; Headin' for God's Country; A Lady Takes a Chance; My Kingdom for a Cook; The Kansan. **1944** The Adventures of Mark Twain; Home in Indiana; The Mummy's Ghost; Raiders of Ghost City (serial). **1945** The Missing Corpse; The Man Who Walked Alone; Dakota. **1946** Little Giant; Sun Valley Cyclone; Abilene Town; Renegades; Avalanche; Sing While You Dance; Singing on the Trail; Rustler's Round-Up. **1947** The Millerson Case; The Michigan Kid; Louisiana; Bandits of Dark Canyon; The Wild Frontier. **1948** The Strawberry Roan; Oklahoma Badlands; River Lady; The Bold Frontiersman; Carson City Raiders; The Return of the Whistler; The Girl from Manhattan; Marshal of Amarillo; The Denver Kid; Sundown at Santa Fe; Renegades of Sonora; Desperadoes of Dodge City; Black Bart. **1949** Massacre River; Death Valley Gunfighter; Sheriff of Wichita; Frontier Investigator; Lust for Gold; The Wyoming Bandit; Bandit King of Texas; Navajo Trail Raiders; Powder River Rustlers. **1950** Gunmen of Abilene; Code of the Silver Sage; Salt Lake Raiders; Covered Wagon Raiders; Vigilante Hideout; Traveling Saleswoman; Frisco Tornado; He's a Cockeyed Wonder; Rustlers on Horseback; California Passage. **1951** Cavalry Scout. **1952** Indian Uprising; Leadville Gunslinger; Black Hills Ambush; Montana Territory; Thundering Caravans; Desperadoes Outpost. **1953** Marshal of Cedar Creek; It Happens Every Thursday; Bandits of the West; Savage Frontier; 99 River Street; Champ for a Day; El Paso Stampede; The Last Posse. **1954** Make Haste to Live. **1955** Man Without a Star; The Far Country; Foxfire. **1957** The Night Runner; The Phantom Stagecoach; The Restless Breed. **1958** Day of the Bad Man.

WALLER, LEWIS

Born: Nov. 3, 1860, Bilbao, Spain. Died: Nov. 1, 1915, London, England. Screen and stage actor. Married to stage actress Florence West (dec. 1912).

Appeared in: Brigadier Gerard.

WALLER, THOMAS "FATS"

Born: 1904, New York, N.Y. Died: Dec. 15, 1943, Kansas City, Mo. (pneumonia). Black pianist, screen, radio, vaudeville actor, bandleader and songwriter.

Appeared in: **1935** Hooray for Love. **1936** King of Burlesque. **1943** Stormy Weather.

WALLERSTEIN, ROSE

Born: 1896. Died: Apr. 19, 1961, Van Nuys, Calif. (heart attack). Screen actress.

Appeared in: **1934** The Youth of Russia.

WALLING, EFFIE B.

Born: 1879. Died: June 9, 1961, Berkeley, Calif. Screen and stage actress. Entered films with DeMille in 1919.

WALLING, ROY

Born: 1889 or 1890, Ore. Died: May 7, 1964, Strandfordville, N.Y. Screen, stage actor and screenwriter. Appeared in Pathe and Thanhouser films.

WALLING, WILLIAM "WILL" (William R. Waller)

Born: June 2, 1872, New York, N.Y. Died: Mar. 5, 1932. Screen and stage actor.

Appeared in: **1921** Making the Grade; The Killer; The Little Minister. **1922** Heroes of the Street; The Sin Flood; His Back Against the Wall; The Siren Call; Without Compromise; The Village Blacksmith; Bing Bang Boom; The Crimson Challange; North of the Rio Grande; The Ladder Jinx. **1923** Nobody's Money; The Temple of Venus; The Abysmal Brute; North of Hudson Bay. **1924** The Iron Horse; In Love With Love; Nellie, the Beautiful Cloak Model; Little Robinson Crusoe. **1925** The Clash of the Wolves; The Trail Rider; Ranger of the Big Pines; His Master's Voice; Timber Wolf; The Man Without a Country. **1926** Sir Lumberjack; Womanpower; Sin Cargo; The Canyon of Light; The Great K & A Train Robbery; Lost at Sea; The Gentle Cyclone. **1927** The King of Kings; The Jazz Singer; Winners of the Wilderness; The Devil's Saddle; The Harvester; The Princess from Hoboken. **1928** The Noose; The Mating Call. **1929** Dark Streets; Welcome Danger. **1930** The Medicine Man; Moby Dick; Kismet; Beyond the Law; Derelict; The Woman Who Was Forgotten. **1931** The Painted Desert; Riders of the North; Range Feud. **1932** Two-Fisted Justice; Ridin' for Justice; High Speed.

WALLINGTON, JIMMY (James S. Wallington)

Born: Sept. 15, 1907, Rochester, N.Y. Died: Dec. 22, 1972, Fairfax, Va. Screen actor and radio announcer. Married to dancer Anita Furman (dec. 1935) and later married and divorced actress Betty Jane Cooper. Married to Erna Wallington.

Appeared in: **1932** The Big Broadcast. **1934-35** Stranger Than Fiction (shorts). **1935** A Vitaphone short. **1938** Start Cheering; Hollywood Stadium Mystery. **1951** Joe Palooka in the Triple Cross.

WALLIS, BERTRAM

Born: Feb. 22, 1874, London, England. Died: Apr. 11, 1952, England? Screen and stage actor.

Appeared in: **1933** The Wandering Jew (US 1935).

WALLOCK, EDWIN N.

Born: 1878, Council Bluffs, Iowa. Died: Feb. 4, 1951. Stage and screen actor.

Appeared in: **1917** Even as You and I. **1918** The Price Mark. **1921** The Ace of Hearts; Kazan; The Struggle. **1922** Bing Bang Boom; I Can Explain. **1923** Eyes of the Forest; The Hunchback of Notre Dame.

WALLS, TOM

Born: Feb. 18, 1883, Northampton, England. Died: Nov. 27, 1949, Edwell, England. Screen, stage actor, stage producer and film director. Father of actor Tom Walls, Jr.

Appeared in: **1930** Canaries Sometime Sing; On Approval; Rookery Nook (aka One Embarrassing Night—US). **1931** Plunder. **1932** A Night Like This; Leap Year; Thark. **1933** The Blarney Stone (aka The Blarney Kiss—US); A Cuckoo in the Nest; Just Smith; Turkey Time. **1934** A Cup of Kindness; Lady in Danger. **1935** Fighting Stock; Storm Weather (US 1936); Me and Marlborough; Foreign Affairs. **1936** Pot Luck; Dishonour Bright. **1937** For Valour. **1938** Second Best Bed; Crackerjack (aka The Man with a Hundred Faces—US); Strange Boarders; Old Iron. **1943** They Met in the Dark (US 1945); Undercover (aka Underground Guerillas—US 1944). **1944** Halfway House (US 1945); Love Story (aka A Lady Surrenders—US 1947). **1945** Johnny Frenchman (US 1946). **1946** This Man is Mine. **1947** Master of Bankdam (US 1949); While I Live. **1948** Spring in Park Lane (US 1949). **1949** Maytime in Mayfair (US 1952); The Interrupted Journey (US 1951).

WALLY, GUS (Gustav Wallenberg)

Born: 1904, Stockholm, Sweden. Died: Mar. 3, 1966, Goquete, Panama. Screen, stage actor and stage producer. Entered films with Paramount in 1936.

WALPOLE, HUGH

Born: 1884, Auckland, New Zealand. Died: June 1, 1941, Brackenburn, England (heart attack). Novelist, screen actor and screenwriter.

Appeared in: **1935** David Copperfield.

WALSH, BILLY

Died: June 16, 1952, Brooklyn, N.Y. Screen, vaudeville and radio actor. Appeared in vaudeville as part of acts known as "Walsh, Reed and Walsh," "Walsh, Daly and Walsh," and "Walsh Bros." Entered films with Sennett in 1915 and appeared in Keystone comedies.

WALSH, BLANCHE
Born: 1874. Died: Oct. 31, 1915, Cleveland, Ohio. Screen and stage actress.

Appeared in: **1912** Resurrection.

WALSH, FRANK (Miles Standish March)
Born: 1860. Died: July 19, 1932, New York, N.Y. Screen, stage and vaudeville actor.

Appeared in: **1924** America. **1927** The Joy Girl.

WALSH, GEORGE
Born: Mar. 16, 1889, New York, N.Y. Died: June 13, 1981, Pomona, Calif. (pneumonia). Screen actor and film director. Brother of actor/director Raoul Walsh (dec. 1980). Divorced from actress Seena Owen (dec. 1966).

Appeared in: **1915** The Fencing Master; The Celestial Code; Eleven-Thirty P.M.; A Bad Man and Others; The Pretender; The Headliners; The Way of a Mother; Bold Impersonation; The Queen of the Band. **1916** Don Quixote; Intolerance; The Serpent; Gold and the Woman; Blue Blood and Red; The Beast; The Mediator. **1917** The Island of Desire; The Book Agent; The Yankee Way; This is the Life; The Pride of New York; Some Boy; Melting Millions; The Honor System; High Finance. **1918** Jack Spurlock, Prodigal; Brave and Bold; I'll Say So; The Kid Is Clever; On the Jump. **1919** Luck and Pluck; Putting One Over; Never Say Quit; The Winning Stroke; Help, Help, Police; The Seventh Person. **1920** A Manhattan Knight; From Now On; Number 17; The Plunger; The Shark. **1921** Dynamite Allen; Serenade. **1922** With Stanley in Africa (serial). **1923** The Miracle Makers; Souls for Sale; Vanity Fair; Rosita; Slave of Desire. **1924** Reno. **1925** American Pluck; Blue Blood. **1926** The Count of Luxembourg; The Kick-Off; A Man of Quality; The Prince of Broadway; His Rise to Fame; Back to Liberty. **1932** Out of Singapore; Me and My Gal. **1933** Black Beauty; Return of Casey Jones; The Bowery. **1934** Belle of the Nineties. **1935** Under Pressure. **1936** Put on the Spot; Rio Grande Romance; Klondike Annie.

WALSH, RAOUL (Albert Edward Walsh)
Born: Mar. 11, 1887, New York, N.Y. Died: Dec. 31, 1980, Simi Valley, Calif. (heart attack). Screen actor, film director, film producer, screenwriter and author. Brother of actor George Walsh (dec. 1981). Divorced from actress Miriam Cooper (dec. 1976), and Lorraine Miller Walker. Later married to Mary Edna Simpson.

Appeared in: **1913** The Banker's Daughter (film debut); A Mother's Love; Paul Revere's Ride. **1914** The Rebellion of Kitty Belle; The Life of General Villa; Mexican War Pictures; For His Master; The Great Leap (aka Until Death Do Us Part); The Dishonored Medal; The Double Knot; The Angel of Contention; The Mystery of the Hindu Image; The Second Mrs. Roebuck; Sierra Jim's Reformation; Home from the Sea; The Old Fisherman's Story; The Exposure; Who Shot Bud Walton?; They Never Knew; The Little Country Mouse; The Availing Prayer; Sands of Fate. **1915** The Birth of a Nation; The Greaser; A Man for All That. **1928** Sadie Thompson. **1949** It's a Great Feeling.

WALSH, THOMAS H.
Born: 1863. Died: Apr. 25, 1925, N.Y. Screen, stage and circus actor.

Appeared in: **1914** The Trey O'Hearts (serial).

WALSH, WILLIAM J.
Born: 1879. Died: Nov. 8, 1921, Mamaroneck, N.Y. (gun accident while filming). Screen actor. Appeared in D. W. Griffith films.

WALTER, JERRY
Born: 1924. Died: Feb. 11, 1979, Sausalito, Calif. (massive heart attack). Screen, radio, television actor, singer and union leader.

Appeared in: **1978** Invasion of the Body Snatchers; Nightmare in Blood. **1979** The Promise.

WALTER, JOHN *See* WALTERS, JACK

WALTER, WILFRID
Born: Mar. 2, 1882, Ripon, England. Died: July 9, 1958, Ashtead, England. Screen, stage actor, playwright and stage producer. Father of actor Richard Walter.

Appeared in: **1938** Owd Bob (aka To the Victor—US); Convict 99. **1939** Dark Eyes of London (aka The Human Monster—US 1940); A Window in London (aka Lady in Distress—US 1942). **1940** Night Train to Munich (aka Gestapo and aka Night Train—US). **1946** Caesar and Cleopatra.

WALTERS, DOROTHY
Born: 1877. Died: Apr. 17, 1934, New York, N.Y. (bronchial pneumonia). Screen, stage and vaudeville actress.

Appeared in: **1918** Little Miss Hoover. **1919** Misleading Widow; Woman, Woman. **1920** Away Goes Prudence; Flying Pat. **1921** Good References; The City of Silent Men; Beyond Price. **1922** The Light in the Dark; Received Payment. **1924** The Confidence Man; The Hoosier Schoolmaster; Pied Piper Malone. **1925** A Man Must Live; The Street of Forgotten Men. **1926** A Kiss for Cinderella.

WALTERS, MRS. GEORGE B.
Born: England. Died: Feb. 21, 1916, New York, N.Y. Screen and stage actress.

Appeared in: **1912** An Irish Girl's Love.

WALTERS, JACK (aka JOHN WALTER)
Born: 1885, Kans. Died: Jan. 23, 1944, Hollywood, Calif. Screen actor. Entered films in 1913.

Appeared in: **1919** Roped; Ace of the Saddle. **1920** Hitchin' Posts. **1921** A Daughter of the Law; Sure Fire. **1922** Headin' North; The Better Man Wins; Caught Bluffing; The Galloping Kid. **1923** McGuire of the Mounted. **1924** Hoodman Blind. **1928** Wild West Romance.

WALTERS, LAURA
Born: 1894. Died: Apr. 10, 1934, Toledo, Ohio. Screen and stage actress.

WALTERS, PATRICIA (Patricia Wheeler)
Died: Dec. 31, 1967, Long Beach, Calif. Screen and stage actress. Daughter of actor Bert Wheeler (dec. 1968).

Appeared in: **1951** The River.

WALTHALL, ANNA MAY
Born: 1896. Died: Apr. 17, 1950, Van Nuys, Calif. Screen actress. Sister of actor Henry B. Walthal (dec. 1936).

Appeared in: **1915** The Lost Receipt. **1918** Hearts of the World. **1925** As Man Desires; The Desert Flower. **1926** The Fighting Marine (serial).

WALTHALL, HENRY B.
Born: Mar. 16, 1878, Shelby City, Ala. Died: June 17, 1936, near Monrovia, Calif. (chronic illness). Screen and stage actor. Brother of actress Anna Mae Walthall (dec. 1950). Married to actress Mary Charleson (dec. 1961).

Appeared in: **1909** In Old Kentucky; A Convict's Sacrifice; The Sealed Room; 1776, or the Hessian Renegades; Pippa Passes; Leather Stocking; Fools of Fate; A Corner in Wheat; In Little Italy; The Call; The Honor of His Family; On the Reef; The Cloister's Touch. **1910** In Old California; The House with Closed Shutters; Ramona; His Last Burglary; The Converts; Gold Is Not All; The Gold Seekers; Thou Shalt Not; The Face at the Window; The Usurer; The Sorrows of the Unfaithful; In Life's Cycle; A Summer Idyll. **1912** The Inner Circle; Oil and Water; A Change of Spirit; Friends; A Feud in the Kentucky Hills; In the Aisles of the Wild; The One She Loved; My Baby; The Informer; The Burglar's Dilemma; The God Within. **1913** Judith of Bethulia; Love in an Apartment Hotel; Broken Ways; Her Mother's Oath; The Sheriff's Baby; The Little Tease; The Wanderer; Death's Marathon; The Battle of Elderberry Gulch; During the Round-Up. **1914** The Avenging Conscience; Home Sweet Home. **1915** Birth of a Nation; The Raven; Ghosts; Great Divide. **1916** The Sting of Victory; The Strange Case of Mary Page. **1918** Robe of Honor; Great Love. **1919** The False Faces. **1920** Splendid Hazard. **1921** Parted Curtains. **1922** The Able Minded Lady; One Clear Call; The Kick Back; The Long Chance; The Marriage Chance; Flowers of the North. **1923** Gimme; Boy of Mine; Face on the Barroom Floor; The Unknown Purple. **1924** Single Wives; The Bowery Bishop; The Woman on the Jury. **1925** The Golden Bed; Simon the Jester. **1926** Road to Mandalay; The Scarlet Letter; The Barrier; Everybody's Acting; The Ice Flood; Three Faces East; The Unknown Soldier; The Plastic Age. **1927** Wings; Fighting Love; London after Midnight. **1928** Love Me and the World Is Mine; Freedom of the Press; Man From Headquarters; Retribution (short). **1929** In Old California (and 1910 version); Speakeasy; The Bridge of San Luis Rey; Blaze O'Glory; Stark Mad; Phantom in the House; Black Magic; The River of Romance; The Jazz Age; Street Corners; The Trespasser. **1930** Abraham Lincoln; The Payoff (short); Temple Tower; Love Trader; Tol'able David. **1931** Is There Justice?; Anybody's Blonde. **1932** Hotel Continental; Police Court; Strange Interlude; Alias Mary Smith; Chandu the Magician; Klondike; Cabin in the Cotton; Central Park; Me and My Gal; Fame Street; Ride Him, Cowboy. **1933** The Wolf Dog (serial); The Sin of

Nora Moran; 42nd Street; Laughing at Life; Whispering Shadow (serial); Self Defense; Flaming Signal; Somewhere in Sonora; Headline Shooter; Her Forgotten Past. **1934** Men in White; Judge Priest; Viva, Villa!; The Scarlet Letter (and 1926 version); Change of Heart; Dark Hazard; Beggars in Ermine; Operator 13; Murder in the Museum; A Girl of the Limberlost; The Lemon Drop Kid; Love Time; City Park; Bachelor of Arts. **1935** A Tale of Two Cities; Dante's Inferno; Helldorado. **1936** China Clipper; The Mine With the Iron Door; Hearts in Bondage; The Last Outlaw; The Devil-Doll; The Garden Murder Case.

WALTON, CHARLES
Born: 1884, Pittsburgh, Pa. Died: Nov. 18, 1955, New York, N.Y. Screen and stage actor.

Appeared in: **1913** A Mystery of Wall Street.

WALTON, DOUGLAS (J. Douglas Duder)
Born: Oct. 17, 1909, Woodstock, Toronto, Canada. Died: Nov. 15, 1961, N.Y. Screen and stage actor.

Appeared in: **1931** Over the Hill; Body and Soul. **1933** The Secret of Madame Blanche; Looking Forward; Cavalcade. **1934** The Lost Patrol; Madame Spy; Murder in Trinidad; Shock; The Count of Monte Cristo; Charlie Chan in London. **1935** Captain Hurricane; The Dark Angel; Hitchhike Lady; The Bride of Frankenstein. **1936** The Garden Murder Case; I Conquer the Sea; Mary of Scotland; Thank You, Jeeves; Camille. **1937** Damaged Goods; Wallaby Jim of the Islands; Flight from Glory; A Nation Aflame. **1938** Storm Over Bengal. **1939** The Story of Vernon and Irene Castle; The Sun Never Sets; Bad Lands. **1940** Raffles; Northwest Passage; The Long Voyage Home; Too Many Girls. **1941** Singapore Woman; Hurry, Charlie, Hurry! **1942** Jesse James, Jr. **1944** Murder My Sweet. **1945** Bring on the Girls; The Picture of Dorian Gray. **1946** Kitty; Dick Tracy vs. Cueball. **1947** High Conquest; High Tide. **1949** Secret of St. Ives.

WALTON, FLORENCE
Born: 1891, Wilmington, Del. Died: Jan. 7, 1981, New York, N.Y. Screen, stage and vaudeville actress. Married to Maurice Mouvet, with whom she appeared on stage as part of a dance team. Later married to actor Howard Phillips.

Appeared in: **1916** The Quest of Life.

WALTON, FRED (Frederick Heming)
Born: 1865, England. Died: Dec. 28, 1936, Los Angeles, Calif. (pneumonia). Screen and stage actor. Entered films in 1924.

Appeared in: **1924** The Fast Set. **1925** New Brooms; She Wolves; Marriage in Transit. **1926** The City; 30 Below Zero; The Splendid Crime. **1927** The Wise Wife; Almost Human; His Dog; The Little Adventuress. **1928** The House of Shame. **1929** Below the Deadline; South of Panama; Circumstantial Evidence; Dynamite. **1930** The Last Dance; Sin Takes a Holiday. **1931** Kiki; The Big Gamble. **1935** Two Sinners. **1936** Little Lord Fauntleroy; The House of a Thousand Candles; Dracula's Daughter.

WALTON, HERBERT C.
Born: 1880, England. Died: Jan. 16, 1954, England? Screen actor.

Appeared in: **1947** Take My Life (US 1948); The Little Ballerina (US 1951). **1949** Britannia Mews (aka The Forbidden Street—US). **1952** I Believe in You (US 1953). **1953** The Titfield Thunderbolt; The Cruel Sea; Time Bomb (aka Terror on a Train—US). **1954** Hobson's Choice; The Angel Who Pawned Her Harp (US 1956).

WALTON, VERA
Born: 1891. Died: Sept. 1, 1965, New York, N.Y. (auto accident). Screen, stage, vaudeville and television actress. Appeared in a song and dance vaudeville act billed as "Now and Then."

Appeared in: **1957** A Face in the Crowd. **1960** Butterfield 8.

WALTZ, PATRICK "PAT" (aka PHILIP SHAW)
Died: Aug. 13, 1972. Screen actor.

Appeared in: **1951** The Sun Sets at Dawn. **1954** The Human Jungle. **1958** Queen of Outer Spaces. **1963** Lassie's Great Adventure. **1966** The Silencers.

WAN, MME. SUL TE (Nellie Conley)
Born: 1873. Died: Feb. 1, 1959, Hollywood, Calif. Black screen actress. Entered films in 1914 with Griffith.

Appeared in: **1958** The Buccaneer.

WANGEL, HEDWIG
Born: 1875, Berlin, Germany. Died: Mar. 12, 1961, Rendsburg, West Germany. Stage and screen actress.

Appeared in: **1929** Rasputin. **1932** Pension Schoeller.

WANZER, ARTHUR
Died: Dec. 15, 1948, Hollywood, Calif. Screen and vaudeville actor. Appeared in vaudeville as part of "Arthur Wanzer and Maybelle Palmer" team.

Appeared in: **1930** Dance with Me. **1933** Soldiers of the Storm; Unknown Valley. **1934** Tomorrow's Children. **1936** The Gentleman from Louisiana.

WARAM, PERCY C.
Born: 1881, Kent, England. Died: Oct. 5, 1961, Huntington, N.Y. Screen, stage and vaudeville actor.

Appeared in: **1939** One Third of a Nation. **1944** Ministry of Fear. **1947** It Had to Be You; The Late George Apley. **1950** The Big Hangover. **1957** A Face in the Crowd.

WARBURTON, JOHN
Born: 1903, Liverpool, England, or Ireland? Died: Oct. 27, 1981, Sherman Oaks, Calif. (cancer). Screen and stage actor.

Appeared in: **1932** Secrets of the French Police; The Silver Lining. **1933** A Study in Scarlet; Charlie Chan's Greatest Case; Cavalcade; Love is Dangerous; Blind Adventure; Love is Like That. **1934** Let's Talk It Over. **1935** Becky Sharp; Dizzy Dames. **1937** Partners of the Plains. **1938** The Sisters. **1939** Captain Fury. **1944** Marriage is a Private Affair; The White Cliffs of Dover; Nothing But Trouble. **1945** Confidential Agent; Saratoga Trunk; Dangerous Partners. **1947** Living in a Big Way; Tarzan and the Huntress. **1953** City Beneath the Sea; East of Sumatra; Royal African Rifles. **1955** Headline Hunters. **1961** Secret File: Hollywood. **1965** King Rat. **1968** Funny Girl.

WARD, ARCH
Born: Dec. 27, 1896, Irwin, Ill. Died: July 9, 1955, Chicago, Ill. (heart attack). Screen, radio actor and sportswriter.

Appeared in: **1950** The Golden Gloves Story.

WARD, BEATRICE
Born: 1890. Died: Dec. 11, 1964, Hollywood, Calif. Screen actress. Entered films during silents.

WARD, CARRIE (Carrie Clarke-Ward)
Born: 1862, Virginia City, Nev. Died: Feb. 6, 1926, Hollywood, Calif. Screen and stage actress.

Appeared in: **1919** Why Smith Left Home. **1920** Old Lady 31. **1921** One Wild Week; Sham; Black Roses; Her Winning Way; Bob Hampton of Placer; The Love Charm. **1922** Ashes; The Top of New York; Penrod; Through a Glass Window. **1923** Breaking into Society; Soul of the Beast; Scaramouche. **1924** Girls Men Forget; Thundering Hoofs; His Hour. **1925** The Awful Truth; The Eagle; A Fool and His Money; The Man in Blue; Who Cares; Rose of the World; The Only Thing; The Golden Cocoon.

WARD, CHANCE E. (Chance Earl Smith aka YANCEY SMITH)
Born: Sept. 16, 1877, Dayton, Ohio. Died: Sept. 2, 1949, West Hollywood, Calif. (coronary). Screen actor and film director.

Appeared in: **1919** Island of Intrigue. **1921** Seven Years Bad Luck. **1927** Rolled Stockings. **1931** The Bat Whispers.

WARD, CLARA
Born: Apr. 21, 1927, Philadelphia, Pa. Died: Jan. 16, 1973, Los Angeles, Calif. (stroke). Screen actress and singer. Do not confuse with actress Clara Clark Ward.

Appeared in: **1967** Spree. **1968** A Time to Sing.

WARD, FANNIE
Born: 1872, St. Louis, Mo. Died: Jan. 27, 1952, New York, N.Y. (cerebral hemorrhage). Screen, stage and vaudeville actress. Married to actor Jack Dean (dec. 1950).

Appeared in: **1915** The Cheat. **1916** Each Hour a Pearl; Tennessee's Pardner. **1917** The School for Husbands; Betty to the Rescue; The Winning of Sally Temple; Unconquered; Her Strange Wedding. **1918** A Japanese Nightingale; The Yellow Ticket. **1919** Our Better Selves; Common Clay. **1921** She Played and Paid. **1922** The Hardest Way. **1929** The Miracle Woman (short).

WARD, FLEMING
Born: 1887. Died: Aug. 2, 1962, New York, N.Y. Screen and stage actor.

Appeared in: **1919** When Men Desire.

WARD, DAME GENEVIEVE
Born: Mar. 27, 1837, New York, N.Y. Died: Aug. 18, 1922, England? Screen, stage actress and opera singer. Married to Count Constantine de Guerbel (dec.). Was made Dame Commander of the Order of the British Empire in 1921.

WARD, "HAP," JR. (John Thomas O'Donnell)
Born: 1899. Died: July 9, 1940. Screen actor. Son of actor "Hap" Ward, Sr. (dec. 1944).

WARD, "HAP," SR. (John Thomas O'Donnell)
Born: 1868. Died: Jan. 3, 1944, N.Y. Screen, stage and vaudeville actor. Father of actor "Hap" Ward, Jr. (dec. 1940). Was half of vaudeville act billed as "Earl and Ward" (even though his name was O'Donnell, he took name of the original team partner, Ward, whom he replaced in the act). He later teamed with Harry Vokes (Dec. 1922) in a blackface act billed as "Harold and Percy."

Appeared in: **1929** Fugitives.

WARD, HARRY (Angelo De Michele)
Born: 1890. Died: Apr. 16, 1952, Los Angeles, Calif. Screen actor. Appeared in vaudeville with brother Anthony in an act known as "Ward and Van."

WARD, JEROME "BLACK JACK"
Born: 1891. Died: Aug. 29, 1954. Screen actor.

WARD, KATHERINE CLARE
Born: 1871. Died: Oct. 14, 1938, Hollywood, Calif. Screen, stage and vaudeville actress. Entered films approx. 1923.

Appeared in: **1927** The Magic Garden. **1928** Beyond London Lights. **1929** Drag; The Isle of Lost Ships; Midnight Daddies. **1930** Call of the West; Strictly Modern. **1931** The Conquering Horde; Three Girls Lost. **1932** Three Wise Girls; Make Me a Star; Vanity Street. **1933** Lilly Turner; Son of Kong. **1934** Once to Every Woman; White Lies; Jealousy; The Key. **1935** Black Fury. **1936** Stage Struck.

WARD, LUCILLE
Born: 1880. Died: Aug. 8, 1952, Dayton, Ohio. Screen and stage actress.

Appeared in: **1917** American Film Mfg. Co. films. **1919** The Fires of Fury. **1921** High Gear Jeffrey; The Traveling Salesman. **1922** The Woman He Loved. **1923** East Side, West Side; Sixty Cents an Hour. **1924** The Girl in the Limousine; Sporting Youth. **1925** Oh, Doctor!; His Majesty, Bunker Bean; California Straight Ahead; A Woman of the World. **1926** Skinner's Dress Suit. **1930** What a Man. **1932** The Purchase Price; Rebecca of Sunnybrook Farm. **1933** Zoo in Budapest; Marriage on Approval; Lilly Turner. **1934** Little Miss Marker. **1935** Dr. Socrates; Special Agent; Old Sawbones (short). **1936** The Leavenworth Case; The Return of Jimmy Valentine; The Harvester. **1937** When You're in Love. **1938** Mother Carey's Chickens; Sons of the Legion. **1939** First Love. **1940** Christmas in July. **1943** The Song of Bernadette. **1944** Henry Aldrich's Little Secret.

WARD, PEGGY
Born: 1878. Died: Mar. 8, 1960, Hollywood, Calif. Screen, stage and television actress.

WARD, RICHARD
Born: Mar. 15, 1915, Philadelphia, Pa. Died: July 1, 1979, Coxsackle, N.Y. (heart ailment). Black screen, stage, vaudeville, television actor and prizefighter.

Appeared in: **1964** Black Like Me; The Cool World; Nothing But a Man. **1969** The Learning Tree. **1974** For Pete's Sake. **1975** Mandingo. **1979** The Jerk. **1980** Brubaker.

WARD, RONALD
Born: Apr. 15, 1901, Eastbourne, Sussex, England. Died: Mar. 31, 1978, England? Screen and stage actor.

Appeared in: **1935** The Passing of the Third Floor Back (US 1936). **1936** East Meets West. **1940** Sidewalks of London. **1941** This England (aka Our Heritage). **1950** My Daughter Joy (aka Operation X—US 1951).

WARD, ROSCOE
Born: 1893. Died: Sept. 12, 1956, Los Angeles, Calif. Screen actor.

Appeared in: **1928** The Big Killing. **1929** West of Zanzibar.

WARD, SAM (George Herman Jacobs)
Born: 1889. Died: May 1, 1952, Los Angeles, Calif. Screen, stage burlesque and vaudeville actor. Appeared in Hal Roach comedies.

WARD, SOLLY
Born: 1891. Died: May 17, 1942, Hollywood, Calif. Screen, stage, burlesque and radio actor.

Appeared in: **1927** At the Party (short). **1932-33** Paramount shorts. **1937** Flight from Glory; Living on Love; Danger Patrol; She's Got Everything. **1938** Everybody's Doing It; Maid's Night Out; Blind Alibi. **1939** Conspiracy.

WARD, VICTORIA
Born: 1914, Canada. Died: Nov. 6, 1957, Hollywood, Calif. Screen, stage and television actress.

Appeared in: **1956** D Day, the Sixth of June.

WARD, WARWICK (Warwick Mannon)
Born: 1891, St. Ives, England. Died: Dec. 9, 1967. Screen, stage actor and film producer. Appeared in British and German films.

Appeared in: **1919** The Silver Lining. **1920** Mary Latimer, Nun; Wuthering Heights; Build Thy House; The Manchester Man; The Call of the Road. **1921** The Diamond Necklace; Belphegor the Mountebank; Demos (aka Why Men Forget—US); Corinthian Jack; The Mayor of Casterbridge; Little Meg's Children; Handy Andy; The Golden Dawn. **1922** The Lilac Sunbonnet; Tell Your Children; The Call of the East; Petticoat Loose. **1923** The Lady Owner; The Hotel Mouse; Bulldog Drummond. **1924** The Great Turf Mystery; Southern Love (aka A Woman's Secret—US); Hurricane Hutch in Many Adventures; The Prude's Fall; Human Desires; The Money Habit. **1925** Madame Sans-Gene; Variete (Variety—US 1926). **1926** The Woman Tempted (US 1928). **1927** His Supreme Sacrifice (reissue of The Call of the East—1922). **1928** Ara and the Grasshopper; The White Sheik (aka King's Mate—US 1929); Maria Marten. **1929** After the Verdict (US 1930); The Woman He Scorned; Die Wunderbare Luge der Nina Petrowna (The Wonderful Lie of Nina Petrovna—US 1930); The Informer; The Three Kings; Looping the Loop; The Dancer of Barcelona. **1930** The Yellow Mask; Birds of Prey (aka The Perfect Alibi—US 1931); The Strange Case of District Attorney M. **1931** The Loves of Ariane (aka Ariane—US 1934); To Oblige a Lady; Number Please; Deadlock; Stamboul; Man of Mayfair. **1932** The Callbox Mystery; Life Goes On (aka Sorry You've Been Troubled); Blind Spot. **1933** F.P. 1. **1938** Secrets of F.P. 1 (rerelease of F.P. 1 1933). **1952** Elstree Story (narration).

WARDE, ANTHONY
Born: 1909. Died: Jan. 8, 1975, Hollywood, Calif. Screen and stage actor.

Appeared in: **1937** Escape By Night. **1938** Marie Antoinette; Flash Gordon's Trip to Mars (serial); The Affairs of Annabel; Come On, Leathernecks; What Price Safety? (short); Law of the Underworld. **1939** Buck Rogers (serial); Mr. Moto Takes a Vacation; Oklahoma Frontier; Twelve Crowded Hours; Affairs of Annabel. **1940** So You Won't Talk; Chip of the Flying U. **1941** Dick Tracy vs. Crime, Inc. (serial); The Spider Returns (serial); Ridin' on a Rainbow. **1942** King of the Mounties (serial); The Man With Two Lives. **1943** Riders of the Deadline; The Masked Marvel (serial). **1944** The Great Alaskan Mystery (serial); The Mummy's Ghost; The Chinese Cat; Where Are Your Children?; Are These Our Parents?; Dixie Jamboree; Machine Gun Mama; Sensations of 1945; Shadow of Suspicion; Mystery of the River Boat (serial). **1945** Brenda Starr, Reporter (serial); The Monster and the Ape; The Cisco Kid Returns; Here Come the Co-eds; The Purple Monster Strikes (serial); Allotment Wives; Paris Underground; There Goes Kelly; Captain Tugboat Annie; Who's Guilty? (serial). **1946** Hop Harrigan (serial); King of the Forest Rangers (serial); The Wife of Monte Cristo; Black Market Babies; Dark Alibi; Secrets of a Sorority Girl; Wife Wanted; The Missing Lady; Don Richard Returns. **1947** The Black Widow (serial); King of the Bandits; Killer Dill; High Tide; The 13th Hour; Bells of San Fernando. **1948** Dangers of the Canadian Mounties (serial); Congo Bill (serial); The Big Punch; Stage Struck; Trail of the Yukon; The Fighting Fools. **1950** Radar Patrol vs. Spy King (serial). **1951** Roaring City. **1952** The Atomic City. **1953** The War of the Worlds; Houdini; Raiders of the Seven Seas. **1954** Rear Window; Day of Triumph. **1955** Strategic Air Command. **1956** The Man Who Knew Too Much. **1959** Inside the Mafia. **1964** The Carpetbaggers.

WARDE, ERNEST C.
Born: 1874, Liverpool, England. Died: Sept. 9, 1923, Los Angeles, Calif. Screen, stage actor and stage director.

Appeared in: **1916** King Lear. **1917** Fires of Youth; The Heart of Ezra Greer. **1923** Ruth of the Range (serial); Blow Your Own Horn.

WARDE, FREDERICK B.
Born: 1872, England. Died: Feb. 7, 1935, Brooklyn, N.Y. (heart trouble). Stage and screen actor.

Appeared in: 1913 Richard III. 1916 King Lear. 1917 Vicar of Wakefield; Under False Colors. 1921 Silas Marner. 1925 A Lover's Oath.

WARDE, HARLAN
Died: Mar., 1980. Screen actor.

Appeared in: 1941 I Wanted Wings. 1942 Jesse James, Jr. 1948 Money Madness; Lady at Midnight. 1949 State Department File 649; It's a Great Feeling; Task Force; Prison Warden. 1950 No Sad Songs for Me; Customs Agent; David Harding, Counter Spy; The Man Who Cheated Himself. 1951 Her First Romance; Smuggler's Gold; Criminal Lawyer. 1952 Without Warning; Operation Secret. 1953 Donovan's Brain. 1954 Down Three Dark Streets; Hell and High Water. 1955 Strategic Air Command. 1956 Julie. 1957 Last of the Badmen; The Wings of Eagles; Chicago Confidential; Sayonara. 1958 Cry Terror; Hot Spell; The Decks Ran Red; The Buccaneer. 1961 Cry for Happy. 1962 Incident in an Alley. 1965 See How They Run; Billie.

WARDELL, HARRY
Born: 1879. Died: Sept. 17, 1948, Hollywood, Calif. (heart attack). Screen, vaudeville actor and screenwriter. Originated phrases such as: "Life is just a bowl of cherries" and "I'm the matzo ball in the soup of life."

Appeared in: 1934 The Mighty Barnum.

WARDWELL, GEOFFREY
Born: July 30, 1900, York, England. Died: Aug. 9, 1955, United States? Screen and stage actor. Entered films in 1917.

Appeared in: 1929 The Taming of the Shrew. 1939 The Challenge.

WARE, HELEN
Born: 1877, San Francisco, Calif. Died: Jan. 25, 1939, Carmel, Calif. (throat infection). Stage and screen actress. Married to actor, writer and artist Frederic Burt (dec. 1943).

Appeared in: 1917 The Garden of Allah. 1920 The Deep Purple. 1921 Colorado Pluck. 1922 Fascination. 1923 Mark of the Beast. 1925 Soul Fire. 1928 Napoleon's Barber. 1929 Half Way to Heaven; The Virginian; New Year's Eve; Speakeasy. 1930 Slightly Scarlet; One Night at Susie's; Abraham Lincoln; She's My Weakness; Tol'able David. 1931 I Take This Woman; The Reckless Hour. 1932 Night of June 13th. 1933 Ladies They Talk About; Girl Missing; The Keyhole; She Had to Say Yes; Warrior's Husband. 1934 Sadie McKee; That's Gratitude; Flaming Gold; Romance in Manhattan. 1935 The Raven; Secret of the Chateau.

WARE, WALTER
Born: 1880, Boston, Mass. Died: Jan. 3, 1936, Hollywood, Calif. Screen and stage actor.

Appeared in: 1921 The Family Closet. 1935 Captain Blood; Kind Lady.

WARFIELD, IRENE
Born: 1896. Died: Apr. 10, 1961. Screen and stage actress.

Appeared in: 1913 The Boomerang; Autumn Love. 1914 Chains of Bondage; Speak No Evil; Shadows; Life's Weaving; A Vagabond Cupid. 1915 Simon the Jester. 1916 The Voice in the Wilderness; The Three Scratch Clue; A Man for A' That. 1917 The Mirror.

WARING, HERBERT (Herbert Waring Rutty)
Born: Nov. 17, 1857, London, England. Died: Jan. 31, 1932, London, England. Screen and stage actor.

Appeared in: 1930 Sleeping Partners.

WARING, MARY
Born: 1892. Died: Jan. 10, 1964, Washington, D.C. Screen and radio actress. Appeared in films from 1920-24.

WARMINGTON, STANLEY J.
Born: Dec. 16, 1884, Herts, England. Died: May 10, 1941, England? Screen, stage and radio actor.

Appeared in: 1919 Wisp O' the Woods. 1928 South Sea Bubble. 1930 Escape; Murder. 1936 Sabotage (aka The Woman Alone—US 1937).

WARNE, HOWARD B. See WORNE, HOWARD B. "DUKE"

WARNER, GLEN S. "POP"
Born: Apr. 5, 1871, Springville, N.Y. Died: Sept. 7, 1954. Football coach and screen actor.

Appeared in: 1940 Knute Rockne—All American.

WARNER, GLORIA (Gloria Kelly)
Born: 1915, N.Y. Died: June 8, 1934, Los Angeles, Calif. (anemia). Screen, stage actress and dancer.

Appeared in: School for Romance (short).

WARNER, H. B. (Henry Bryan W. Lickford)
Born: Oct. 26, 1876, St. John's Woods, London, England. Died: Dec. 24, 1958, Los Angeles, Calif. Screen and stage actor. Married to actress Rita Stanwood (dec. 1961). Nominated for 1937 Academy Award for Best Supporting actor in The Lost Horizon.

Appeared in: 1900 English Nell. 1916 The Beggar of Cawnpore; The Vagabond Prince; The Raiders; The Market of Vain Desire. 1917 The Danger Trail. 1919 The Man Who Turned White. 1920 One Hour before Dawn. 1921 Below the Deadline; Dice of Destiny; Felix O'Day; When We Were Twenty-One. 1923 Zaza. 1924 Is Love Everything? 1926 The Temptress; Silence; Whispering Smith. 1927 French Dressing; King of Kings; Sorrell and Son. 1928 The Naughty Duchess; Man-Made Women; Romance of a Rogue. 1929 The Divine Lady; Conquest; The Argyle Case; The Doctor's Secret; The Gamblers; Stark Mad; The Trail of Mary Dugan; The Show of Shows; Tiger Rose. 1930 The Furies; Wild Company; The Green Goddess; The Second Floor Mystery; On Your Back; Wedding Rings; The Princess and the Plumber; Liliom. 1931 Five Star Final; A Woman of Experience; The Reckless Hour; Expensive Women. 1932 Tom Brown of Culver; The Son-Daughter; The Menace; The Crusader; Cross Examination; Charlie Chan's Chance; Unholy Love; A Woman Commands; The Phantom of Crestwood. 1933 Christopher Bean; Jennie Gerhardt; Supernatural; Sorrell and Son (US 1934) (and 1927 version); Justice Takes a Holiday. 1934 Grand Canary; In Old Santa Fe. 1935 Behold My Wife; Born to Gamble; A Tale of Two Cities. 1936 The Garden Murder Case; Mr. Deeds Goes to Town; Moonlight Murder; Rose of the Rancho; The Blackmailer; Along Came Love. 1937 The Lost Horizon; Our Fighting Navy; (aka Torpedoed—US 1939); Victoria the Great. 1938 Army Girl; Bulldog Drummond in Africa; The Adventures of Marco Polo; The Girl of the Golden West; The Toy Wife; You Can't Take It with You; Kidnapped. 1939 The Rains Came; Arrest Bulldog Drummond; Let Freedom Ring; Bulldog Drummond's Secret Police; Bulldog Drummond's Bride; The Gracie Allen Murder Case; Nurse Edith Cavell; Mr. Smith Goes to Washington. 1940 New Moon. 1941 The Corsican Brothers; Topper Returns; City of Missing Girls; Here Is a Man; Ellery Queen and the Perfect Crime; South of Tahiti; All That Money Can Buy. 1942 A Yank in Libya; Boss of Big Town; Crossroads. 1943 Hitler's Children; Women in Bondage; Queen Victoria. 1944 Action in Arabia; Enemy of Women; Faces in the Fog. 1945 Captain Tugboat Annie; Rogues' Gallery. 1946 Gentleman Joe Palooka; It's a Wonderful Life; Strange Impersonation. 1947 Driftwood; Bulldog Drummond Strikes Back. 1948 High Wall; Prince of Thieves. 1949 El Paso; Hellfire; The Judge Steps Out. 1950 Sunset Boulevard. 1951 The First Legion; Journey into Light; Here Comes the Groom; Savage Drums. 1952 The Devil and Daniel Webster (reissue and retitle of All That Money Can Buy—1941). 1956 The Ten Commandments. 1958 Darby's Rangers.

WARNER, J. B.
Born: 1895, Nebraska. Died: Nov. 9, 1924 (tuberculosis). Screen actor.

Appeared in: 1921 Crossing Trails. 1922 Big Stakes; Flaming Hearts. 1923 Crimson Gold; Danger; Lone Fighter. 1924 Behind Two Guns; The Covered Trail; The Hellion; Horseshoe Luck; Treasure Canyon; Wanted by the Law; Wolf Man; Westbound.

WARNER, JACK (Horace John Waters)
Born: Oct. 24, 1896, London, England. Died: May 24, 1981, London, England (pneumonia). Screen, vaudeville, radio and television actor. Brother of radio comedy stars Elsie and Doris Waters (dec. 1978). Do not confuse with U.S. film producer Jack L. Warner (dec. 1978).

Appeared in: 1943 The Dummy Talks. 1946 The Captive Heart (US 1947). 1947 Hue and Cry (US 1950); Dear Murderer (US 1948); Holiday Camp (US 1948); It Always Rains on Sunday (US 1949). 1948 Against the Wind (US 1949); Easy Money (US 1949); My Brother's Keeper (US 1949); Here Come the Huggetts (US 1950). 1949 Vote for Huggett; The Huggetts Abroad; Boys in Brown; Train of Events (US 1952). 1950 The Blue Lamp. 1951 Scrooge; Valley of the Eagles (US 1952); Talk of a Million. 1952 Emergency Call (US 1953); Meet Me Tonight. 1953 Albert RN (aka Break to Freedom—US 1955); The Square Ring (US 1955); Those People Next Door; The Final Test (US 1954). 1954 Bang! You're Dead (US 1955); Forbidden Cargo (US 1956). 1955 The Quatermass Experiment (aka The Creeping Unknown—US 1956); The Ladykillers (US 1956). 1956 Now and Forever; Home and Away. 1958 Carve Her Name With Pride. 1962 Jigsaw (US 1965).

WARNER, JETHRO
Born: 1865. Died: Apr. 12, 1931, New York, N.Y. Screen and stage actor.

WARNOW, HELEN
Born: 1926. Died: Dec. 25, 1970, New York, N.Y. Screen and television actress.

WARREN, C. DENIER
Born: July 29, 1889, Chicago, Ill. Died: Aug. 27, 1971, Torquay, England. Screen, stage, vaudeville, radio actor and screenwriter.

Appeared in: 1932 Let Me Explain Dear. 1933 Counsel's Opinion; Channel Crossing (US 1934); Prince of Arcadia. 1934 Two Hearts in Waltztime; The Great Defender; Kentucky Minstrels; Music Hall; Temptation. 1935 The Clairvoyant; Heart's Desire (US 1937); A Fire Has Been Arranged; Royal Cavalcade (aka Regal Cavalcade—US); Birds of a Feather; Be Careful Mr. Smith; Marry the Girl; Heat Wave (US 1936); Charring Cross Road; A Real Bloke; The Small Man. 1936 The Beloved Vagabond; A Star Fell from Heaven; Spy of Napoleon (US 1939); They Don't Know; The Big Noise; It's in the Bag; You Must Get Married. 1937 Cotton Queen; A Romance in Flanders (aka Lost on the Western Front—US 1940); Melody and Romance; Captains Orders; Little Miss Nobody; Keep Fit; Good Morning Boys (aka Where There's a Will—US); Rose of Tralee (US 1938); Song of the Forge; Change for a Sovereign; Who Killed John Savage?; Cafe Colette (aka Danger in Paris—US). 1938 Break the News (US 1941); Strange Boarders; It's in the Air (aka George Takes the Air—US 1940); Kicking the Moon Around; Make It Three; Old Mother Riley in Paris; My Irish Molly (aka Little Miss Molly—US 1940); Take Off the Hat. 1939 Trouble Brewing; A Gentleman's Gentleman; Trouble for Two; Come on George; The Body Vanishes; Secret Journey (aka Among Human Wolves—US 1940). 1942 Old Mother Riley Catches a Quisling (reissue of Old Mother Riley in Paris, 1938); We'll Smile Again. 1944 Kiss the Bride Goodbye. 1949 Old Mother Riley's New Venture. 1950 The Dragon of Pendragon Castle; Old Mother Riley, Headmistress (US 1951). 1953 House of Blackmail; Alf's Baby. 1960 Bluebeard's Ten Honeymoons; A Taste of Money. 1961 The Treasure of Monte Cristo (aka The Secret of Monte Cristo—US). 1962 Lolita; The Silent Invasion. 1969 The Adding Machine.

WARREN, E. ALYN
Born: 1875. Died: Jan. 22, 1940, Los Angeles, Calif. Screen and stage actor.

Appeared in: 1921 The Millionaire; No Woman Knows; A Tale of Two Worlds; Outside the Law. 1922 East Is West; The Truthful Liar; Hungry Hearts. 1923 The Courtship of Miles Standish. 1926 Sweet Rosie O'Grady; Born to the West. 1927 The Opening Night. 1928 The Trail of '98. 1929 Chasing Thru Europe; Red Wine. 1930 East is West; Prince of Diamonds; The Medicine Man; Abraham Lincoln; Son of the Gods; Du Barry, Woman of Passion. 1931 Fighting Caravans; Shipmates; A Free Soul; Daughter of the Dragon; Secret Service; The Hatchet Man. 1932 The Mask of Fu Manchu. 1933 Tarzan the Fearless (serial). 1934 Limehouse Blues. 1935 Chinatown Squad. 1936 The Devil Doll. 1937 They Won't Forget; Double Wedding. 1938 The Shining Hour; The Girl of the Golden West; Port of Seven Seas; Three Comrades. 1939 Idiot's Delight; Tell No Tales.

WARREN, EDWARD
Died: Apr. 3, 1930, Los Angeles. Screen and stage actor.

Appeared in: 1916 The Little Orphan. 1926 The Belle of Broadway.

WARREN, ELEANOR (Eleanor Stewart)
Born: July 8, 1892, Canada. Died: Apr. 6, 1927, Jamaica, N.Y. Screen and stage actress.

WARREN, ELIZA (Eliza Warren Sutton)
Born: 1865. Died: Jan. 20, 1935, Cleveland, Ohio. Screen and stage actress. Entered films with Griffith in 1906.

WARREN, FRED H.
Born: Sept. 16, 1880, Rock Island, Ill. Died: Dec. 5, 1940, Hollywood, Calif. (ruptured ulcer). Screen and vaudeville actor.

Appeared in: 1916 The Matriamaniac; The Microscope Mystery; Heart O' the Hills. 1917 Her Official Fathers; The Cricket; Nina the Flower Girl. 1918 Kildares of Storm; Sylvia on a Spree. 1919 Johnny-on-the-Spot; A Favor to a Friend; Turning the Tables. 1921 The Man Who Dared. 1922 Little Eva Ascends; Pawn Ticket 210. 1923 The Exiles; The Girl of the Golden West; Stephen Steps Out. 1924 The Shooting of Dan McGrew; The Woman on the Jury. 1925 Capital Punishment; Her Husband's Secret; The Desert Flower; Why Women Love; The Masked Bride; Winds of Chance. 1926 The Bells; Miss Nobody. 1927 California; Eager Lips; Lonesome Ladies; Sitting Bull at the "Spirit Lake Massacre"; Three's a Crowd. 1928 The Noose; The Crash. 1929 The Spieler; In Old Arizona; Synthetic Sin; The Locked Door. 1930 The Girl of the Golden West (and 1923 version);

Abraham Lincoln; Rodeo Comedies (shorts); Hearts and Hoofs. 1931 Kiki; Secret Service. 1933 Smoke Lightning. 1934 The Cat's Paw. 1935 The Mysterious Mr. Wong; Ship Cafe. 1936 I Conquer the Sea; The Revolt of the Zombies. 1937 Night Club Scandal. 1938 MGM shorts.

WARREN, HARRY
Born: Dec. 24, 1893, Brooklyn, N.Y. Died: Sept. 22, 1981, Los Angeles, Calif. Screen actor, film director and composer.

Appeared in: 1933 42nd Street. 1934 A Very Honorable Guy. 1935 Go Into Your Dance.

WARREN, KATHERINE
Born: July 12, 1905, Michigan. Died: July 17, 1965, Los Angeles, Calif. (coronary thrombosis and arteriosclerosis). Screen and stage actress.

Appeared in: 1949 The Story of Molly X; Tell It to the Judge; All the King's Men. 1950 Three Secrets; Harriet Craig; Mystery Submarine (aka Submarine); Mary Ryan—Detective; And Baby Makes Three. 1951 The Lady Pays Off; Lorna Doone; Night Into Morning; The People Against O'Hara; Force of Arms; The Tall Target; The Prowler. 1952 This Woman Is Dangerous; Washington Story; Talk About a Stranger; Son of Ali Baba; The Steel Trap. 1953 The Star; The Man Behind the Gun. 1954 The Glenn Miller Story; The Caine Mutiny. 1955 The Violent Men. 1956 Inside Detroit; Fury at Gunsight Pass. 1957 Jailhouse Rock; Drango. 1961 I'll Give My Life.

WARREN, LAVINIA See THUMB, MRS. GENERAL TOM

WARREN, LEONARD
Born: Apr. 21, 1911, New York, N.Y. Died: Mar. 4, 1960, New York, N.Y. (heart attack). Opera singer and screen actor.

Appeared in: 1944 Irish Eyes Are Smiling.

WARRENDER, HAROLD
Born: Nov. 15, 1903, London, England. Died: May 6, 1953, Gerrands Cross, England. Screen, stage and radio actor.

Appeared in: 1928 Day Dreams (film debut). 1933 I Spy; Friday the Thirteenth. 1934 Catherine the Great; Lady in Danger. 1935 Mimi; Invitation to the Waltz; Lazybones. 1940 Convoy (US 1941); Contraband (aka Blackout—US); Sailors Three (aka Three Cockeyed Sailors—US 1941). 1948 Scott of the Antarctic (US 1949); Under the Frozen Falls. 1949 Warning to Wantons; Conspirator (US 1950). 1951 The Six Men; Pandora and the Flying Dutchman; Where No Vultures Fly (aka Ivory Hunter—US 1952). 1952 Ivanhoe. 1953 Intimate Relations (aka Les Parents Terribles); Time Bomb (aka Terror on a Train—US).

WARRENTON, LULE
Born: 1863. Died: May 14, 1932, Laguna Beach, Calif. (operation complications). Screen, stage actress and film director.

Appeared in: 1920 The Sin That Was His. 1921 Blind Hearts; The Dangerous Moment; Ladies Must Live; The Jolt. 1922 Calvert's Valley; Strength of the Pines; Shirley of the Circus.

WARRINGTON, ANN
Born: 1859. Died: Nov. 13, 1934. Screen and stage actress.

Appeared in: 1927 The Cyclone Cowboy. 1929 She Goes to War.

WARWICK, ETHEL
Born: Oct. 13, 1882, London, England. Died: Sept. 12, 1951, England? Screen and stage actress. Divorced from actor Edmund Waller.

Appeared in: 1931 Keepers of Youth; The Great Gay Road. 1932 Bachelor's Baby; Deadlock. 1933 Letting in the Sunshine.

WARWICK, JOHN (John McIntosh Beattie)
Born: Jan. 4, 1905, Bellengen River, New South Wales, Australia. Died: Jan. 10, 1972, Sydney, Australia (heart attack). Screen, stage and television actor.

Appeared in: 1937 Double Alibi; Passenger to London; The Ticket of Leave Man; Riding High (aka Remember When). 1938 Bad Boy; John Halifax—Gentleman; A Yank at Oxford; This Man is News. 1939 The Mind of Mr. Reeder (aka The Mysterious Mr. Reeder—US 1940); The Face at the Window (US 1940); All at Sea. 1940 The Case of the Frightened Lady (aka Frightened Lady—US 1941); Branded (reissue of Bad Boy of 1938). 1941 The Saint's Vacation; My Wife's Family. 1942 The Missing Million; The Day Will Dawn (aka The Avengers—US). 1947 Dancing with Crime. 1958 Law and Disorder. 1959 Horrors of the Black Museum.

WARWICK, ROBERT (Robert Taylor Bien)
Born: Oct. 9, 1878, Sacramento, Calif. Died: June 4, 1964, Los Angeles, Calif. Screen, stage and television actor. Married to actress Stella Lattimore (dec. 1960) and divorced from actress Josephine Whittell (dec. 1961).

Appeared in: **1915** The Face in the Moonlight. **1916** Human Driftwood. **1917** The Mad Lover. **1918** The Silent Master. **1919** In Mizzoura; Told in the Hills; Secret Service. **1920** Hunting Trouble; Thou Art the Man; Fourteenth Man. **1924** The Spitfire. **1929** Unmasked. **1931** A Holy Terror; The Royal Bed; Not Exactly Gentlemen; Three Rogues. **1932** So Big; The Dark Horse; The Woman from Monte Carlo; Dr. X; The Rich Are Always With Us; Unashamed; I Am a Fugitive from a Chain Gang; Silver Dollar; The Girl from Calgary; Afraid to Talk; Secrets of Wu Sin. **1933** The Three Musketeers (serial); Fighting with Kit Carson (serial); Whispering Shadows (serial); Pilgrimage; Charlie Chan's Greatest Case; Frisco Jenny; Ladies They Talk About; Female. **1934** The Dragon Murder Case; Jimmy the Gent; Cleopatra; School for Girls. **1935** Fighting Marines (serial); Night Life of the Gods; A Thrill for Thelma (short); A Shot in the Dark; The Murder Man; A Tale of Two Cities; Whipsaw; Hopalong Cassidy. **1936** Ace Drummond (serial); The Vigilantes Are Coming (serial); Tough Guy; The Return of Jimmy Valentine; Bulldog Edition; The Beloved Rogue; The Bold Caballero; Sutter's Gold; The Bride Walks Out; Mary of Scotland; Romeo and Juliet; In His Steps; The White Legion; Adventure in Manhattan; Can This Be Dixie?; an MGM short; Timber War. **1937** Jungle Menace (serial); The Prince and the Pauper; The Life of Emile Zola; Let Them Live; The Road Back; The Awful Truth; Consel for Crime; Conquest; Trigger Trio. **1938** The Spy Ring; Going Places; The Adventures of Robin Hood; Gangster's Boy; Blockade; Army Girl; Law of the Plains; Come on Leathernecks!; Squadron of Honor. **1939** Devil's Island; Almost a Gentleman; Juarez; The Private Lives of Elizabeth and Essex; The Magnificent Fraud; In Old Monterey. **1940** On the Spot; New Moon; Konga, the Wild Stallion; The Sea Hawk; Murder in the Air. **1941** A Woman's Face; I Was a Prisoner on Devil's Island; Louisiana Purchase; Sullivan's Travels; Spare a Copper. **1942** The Palm Beach Story; Tennessee Johnson; Secret Enemies; Cadets on Parade; Eagle Squadron; I Married a Witch. **1943** Two Tickets to London; Petticoat Larceny; Deerslayer; Dixie. **1944** Man from Frisco; The Princess and the Pirate; Bowery to Broadway; Kismet; Secret Command. **1945** Sudan. **1946** Criminal Court; The Falcon's Adventure. **1947** Gentleman's Agreement; Pirates of Monterey. **1948** Adventures of Don Juan; Fury at Furnace Creek; Million Dollar Weekend; Gun Smugglers. **1949** A Woman's Secret; Impact; Francis. **1950** In a Lonely Place; Tarzan and the Slave Girl; Vendetta. **1951** Sugarfoot; Mark of the Renegade; The Sword of Monte Cristo. **1953** Salome; Mississippi Gambler; Jamaica Run. **1954** Silver Lode; Passion. **1955** Chief Crazy Horse; Lady Godiva; Escape to Burma. **1956** Walk the Proud Land; While the City Sleeps. **1957** Shoot-Out at Medicine Bend. **1958** The Buccaneer. **1959** It Started With a Kiss; Night of the Quarter Moon.

WARWICK, STELLA LATTIMORE
Born: 1905. Died: Dec. 1, 1960, Hollywood, Calif. Screen actress. Married to actor Robert Warwick (dec. 1964).

WASHBURN, ALICE
Born: 1861, Oshkosh, Wis. Died: Nov. 29, 1929, Oshkosh, Wis. (heart ailment). Screen and stage actress.

Appeared in: **1911** Aunt Miranda's Cat; How Father Accomplished His Work; Marjorie's Diamond Ring; Holding the Fort; Bridget's Sudden Wealth; Lazy Bill Hudson; Sally Ann's Strategy; The Totville Eye; The Winking Parson. **1912** A Proposal Under Difficulties. **1913** The Comedian's Downfall; Aunty and the Girls; At Midnight; How Did It Finish?; With the Assistance of Shep. **1914** A Story of Crime; The Sultan and the Roller Skates; On the Lazy Line. **1916** His Dukeship-Mr. Jack; Kernel Nutt, the Janitor; Kernel Nutt Wins a Wife; Secret Service; Kernel Nutt the Footman; Kernel Nutt's One Hundred Dollar Bill; Kernell Nutt's Musical Shirt; Kernel Nutt Flirts with Wifie; Kernel Nutt and High Shoes.

WASHBURN, BRYANT, JR.
Died: 1960. Screen actor. Son of actor Bryant Washburn, Sr. (dec. 1963) and actress Mabel Forest (dec. 1967).

Appeared in: **1933** Daring Daughters.

WASHBURN, BRYANT, SR.
Born: Apr. 28, 1889, Chicago, Ill. Died: Apr. 30, 1963, Hollywood, Calif. (heart attack). Screen, stage actor and film producer. Married to actress Mabel Forest (dec. 1967). Father of actor Bryant Washburn, Jr. (dec. 1960).

Appeared in: **1914** The Promised Land. **1915** The Gallentry of Jimmy Rogers; The Blindness of Virtue. **1916** The Havoc; The Price of Graustark; Marriage a la Carte. **1917** The Fibbers; Skinner's Dress Suit; Skinner's Baby; Skinner's Bubble; The Golden Idiot. **1918** 'Til I Come Back to You; Twenty-One; Kidder and Ko; Ghost of the Rancho; The Gypsy Trail; Venus in the East. **1919** It Pays to Advertise; Way of a Man with a Maid; Why Smith Left Home; Putting It Over; Poor Boob; Very Good Young Man; Something to Do; All Wrong; Love Insurance. **1920** The Six Best Cellars; Too Much Johnson; What Happened to Jones?; Mrs. Temple's Telegram; Sins of St. Anthony; Full House. **1921** An Amateur Devil; Burglar Proof; The Road to London. **1922** Night Life in Hollywood; Hungry Hearts; June Madness; The Woman Conquers; White Shoulders. **1923** Mine to Keep; Rupert of Hentzau; The Common Law; Hollywood; The Love Trap; The Meanest Man in the World; Mary of the Movies; Other Men's Daughters; Temptation. **1924** My Husband's Wives; Try and Get It; The Star Dust Trail. **1925** The Parasite; Passionate Youth; The Wizard of Oz; Wandering Footsteps. **1926** Flames; The Sky Pirate; Young April; Meet the Prince; That Girl Oklahoma; Wet Paint; Sitting Bull at Spirit Lake Massacre. **1927** Her Sacrifice; Breakfast at Sunrise; Beware of Widows; The Love Thrill; Black Tears; In the First Degree; King of Kings; Modern Daughters; Sky Pirates. **1928** Honeymoon Flats; Nothing to Wear; Skinner's Big Idea; A Bit of Heaven; The Chorus Kid; Jazzland; Undressed. **1930** Christmas Knight (short); Niagara Falls (short); Swing High. **1931** Liberty; Kept Husbands; Mystery Train. **1932** The Reckoning; Arm of the Law; Drifting Souls; Exposure; Forbidden Company; Parisian Romance; Thrill of Youth; What Price Hollywood? **1933** What Price Innocence?; Night of Terror; Devil's Mate. **1934** The Curtain Falls; Back Page; The Woman Who Dared; When Strangers Meet; Public Stenographer; The Return of Chandu (series). **1935** The Call of the Savage (serial); Tailspin Tommy in the Great Air Mystery (serial); $20 a Week; Swell Head; Danger Ahead; The Throwback; The World Accuses. **1936** The Millionaire Kid; Bridge of Sighs; The Black Coin (serial); The Clutching Hand (serial); Gambling with Souls; Preview Murder Mystery; Hollywood Boulevard; Sutter's Gold; Conflict; Three of a Kind; It Couldn't Have Happened; We Who Are About to Die. **1937** Jungle Jim (serial); Sea Racketeers; The Westland Case; Million Dollar Racket. **1938** I Demand Payment. **1939** Stagecoach; Ambush; Sky Patrol. **1940** King of the Royal Mounted (serial). **1941** Paper Bullets; The Spider Returns (serial); Gangs, Incorporated; Adventures of Captain Marvel (serial). **1942** Captain Midnight (serial); The Yukon Patrol; Sin Town; Two for the Money (short); War Dogs. **1943** Shadows on the Sage; You Can't Beat the Law; The Law Rides Again; Carson City Cyclone; The Girl from Monterey. **1944** Feather Your Nest (short); The Falcon in Mexico; Nabonga. **1945** Two O'Clock Courage; West of the Pecos. **1947** Do or Diet (short); Sweet Genevieve. **1968** The Further Perils of Laurel and Hardy (documentary).

WASHBURN, JOHN H.
Died: Dec. 11, 1917, New York, N.Y. Screen actor.

WASHBURN, OLYVE See O'DAY, MAGINNIS

WASHINGTON, DINAH (Ruth Jones)
Born: Aug. 29, 1924, Tuscaloosa, Ala. Died: Dec. 14, 1963, Detroit, Mich (overdose of sleeping pills). Black singer and screen actress. Married to professional football player Dick "Night Train" Lane. Divorced from musicians Eddie Chamblee and George Jenkins and actor Rafael Campos.

Appeared in: **1960** Jazz on a Summer's Day.

WASHINGTON, JESSE
Died: Sept. 4, 1919, Newport, R.I. (drowned while filming). Screen actor. Appeared in Fox Film Co. films.

WASHINGTON, KENNY (Kenneth William Washington)
Born: Aug. 31, 1918. Died: June 24, 1971, Los Angeles, Calif. (polyarteritis). Black professional football player and screen actor.

Appeared in: **1947** The Foxes of Harrow. **1948** Rogues' Regiment. **1949** Easy Living; Rope of Sand; Pinky. **1950** The Jackie Robinson Story. **1969** Changes. **1970** Tarzan's Deadly Silence.

WATERHOUSE, FRANK
Born: 1876. Died: Apr. 7, 1950, Los Angeles, Calif. Screen actor.

WATERMAN, IDA (Ida Shaw Francoeur)
Born: 1852. Died: May 22, 1941, Cincinnati, Ohio. Screen and stage actress.

Appeared in: **1915** Are You a Mason?. **1918** Mr. Fix-It. **1920** Lady Rose's Daughter. **1921** Her Lord and Master; Love's Redemption; The Inner Chamber; The Lotus Eater. **1922** Notoriety. **1924** A Society Scandal; The Enchanted Cottage. **1925** The Swan; That Royle Girl. **1926** Say It Again; A Social Celebrity.

WATERS, ETHEL
Born: Oct. 31, 1896, Chester, Pa. Died: Sept. 1, 1977, Chatsworth, Calif. (heart ailment). Black screen, stage, vaudeville, radio, television actress, singer and author. Nominated for 1949 Academy Award for Best Supporting Actress in Pinky.

Appeared in: **1929** On With the Show. **1933** Rufus Jones for President. **1934** Gift of Gab. **1942** Bubbling Over; Tales of Manhattan; Cairo. **1943** Cabin in the Sky (stage and film versions); Stage Door Canteen. **1949** Pinky. **1952** A Member of the Wedding (stage and film versions). **1957** Carib-Gold. **1959** The Sound and the Fury.

WATERS, TOM
Born: 1872. Died: July 10, 1953, Harrisburg, Pa. Screen, stage, vaudeville actor and author. Married to actress Lottie Yort (dec. 1900), with whom he appeared in vaudeville. Later married to actress Stella Waters.

WATERS, WILLIAM E.
Born: 1883, New Bern, N.C. Died: Sept., 1953, Los Angeles, Calif. Screen actor.

Appeared in: **1917** Time Locks and Diamonds; Sweetheart of the Doomed.

WATKIN, PIERRE
Died: Feb. 3, 1960, Hollywood, Calif. Screen actor.

Appeared in: **1935** Dangerous. **1936** Bunker Bean; Love Letters of a Star; Forgotten Faces; It Had to Happen; The Gentleman from Louisiana; Sitting on the Moon; Country Gentlemen; Nobody's Fool; Counterfeit; Swing Time. **1937** The Life of Emile Zola; The Last Gangster; Waikiki Wedding; Michael O'Halloran; Interns Can't Take Money; The Californian; The Green Light; The Go-Getter; Ever Since Eve; The Singing Marine; The Devil's Playground; Larceny on the Air; Bill Cracks Down; The Hit Parade; Sea Devils; Stage Door; Breakfast for Two; Paradise Isle; Daughters of Shanghai. **1938** Boy Meets Girl; You Can't Take it With You; Young Dr. Kildare; The Lady Objects; Midnight Intruder; State Police; Mr. Moto's Gamble; Dangerous to Know; Tip-Off Girls; Illegal Traffic; There's Always a Woman; Girls' School; There's That Woman Again; The Chaser; Mr. Doodle Kicks Off. **1939** Risky Business; The Spirit of Culver; King of the Underworld; Wings of the Navy; Off the Record; Adventures of Jane Arden; The Mysterious Miss X; Wall Street Cowboy; Covered Trailer; They Made Her a Spy; Society Lawyer; Mr. Smith Goes to Washington; Geronimo; Death of a Champion; The Great Victor Herbert. **1940** The Green Hornet Strikes Again (serial); The Road to Singapore; The Saint Takes Over; Street of Memories; Captain Caution; I Love You Again; Golden Gloves; Out West with the Peppers; Five Little Peppers in Trouble; The Bank Dick; Yesterday's Heroes; Father Is a Prince; Rhythm on the River. **1941** Life Begins for Andy Hardy; Nevada City; Buy Me That Town; Ellery Queen and the Murder Ring; Ice Capades Revue; Jesse James at Bay; Petticoat Politics; Cheers for Miss Bishop; A Man Betrayed; Meet John Doe; She Knew All the Answers; Adventures in Washington; Life With Henry; The Trial of Mary Dugan; Naval Academy; Great Guns. **1942** Pride of the Yankees; Whistling in Dixie; The Adventures of Martin Eden; Heart of the Rio Grande; Yokel Boy; The Magnificent Dope. **1943** Destroyer; What a Woman!; Cinderella Swings It; Mission to Moscow; Old Acquaintance; Jack London; Riding High; Swing Shift Maisie; It Ain't Hay. **1944** Weekend Pass; Bermuda Mystery; Ladies of Washington; Destination Tokyo; South of Dixie; Jubilee Woman; Oh, What a Night!; Atlantic City; The Great Mike; Dead Man's Eyes; Shadow of Suspicion; End of the Road; Song of the Range; Meet Miss Bobby-Socks. **1945** Roughly Speaking; Here Come the Co-Eds; Strange Illusion; The Phantom Speaks; Docks of New York; I'll Remember April; Mr. Muggs Rides Again; Follow That Woman; Keep Your Powder Dry; Three's a Crowd; Allotment Wives; I'll Tell The World; Captain Tugboat Annie; Dakota; Over 21; I Love a Bandleader; Apology for Murder. **1946** The Jolson Story; Two Years Before the Mast; Little Giant; So Goes My Love; The Kid from Brooklyn; The Shadow Returns; Murder Is My Business; Swamp Fire; Behind the Mask; High School Hero; The Missing Lady; Claudia and David; Secrets of a Sorority Girl; Sioux City Sue; G.I. War Brides; Her Sister's Secret; I Ring Doorbells; The Madonna's Secret; Shock. **1947** Brick Bradford (serial); The Secret Life of Walter Mitty; Violence; Hard-Boiled Mahoney; The Red Stallion; Her Husband's Affair; Wild Frontier; The Shocking Miss Pilgrim; Beyond Our Own; Jack Armstrong (serial). **1948** Fighting Back; The Hunted; The Gentleman From Nowhere; B. F.'s Daughter; Mary Lou; Glamour Girl; State of the Union; Trapped by Boston Blackie; An Innocent Affair; Daredevils of the Clouds; The Counterfeiters; The Shanghai Chest. **1949** Knock on Any Door; Frontier Outpost; Alaska Patrol; Samson and Delilah; Hold That Baby; Zamba; Incident; The Story of Seabiscuit. **1950** Three

Little Words; Atom Man vs. Spiderman (serial); The Big Hangover; Last of the Buccaneers; Over the Border; Radar Secret Service; Redwood Forest Trail; Rock Island Trail; The Second Face; Sunset in the West; Blue Grass of Kentucky. **1951** Two Lost Worlds; The Dark Page; In Old Amarillo. **1952** Hold That Line; Scandal Sheet; Thundering Caravans; A Yank in Indo-China. **1953** Canadian Mounties vs. Atomic Invaders (serial); The Lost Planet (serial); The Stranger Wore a Gun. **1954** Johnny Dark; About Mrs. Leslie. **1955** The Big Bluff; Sudden Danger; Creature with the Atom Brain. **1956** The Maverick Queen; Don't Knock the Rock; Shake, Rattle and Rock. **1957** Beginning of the End; Pal Joey; Spook Chasers. **1958** Marjorie Morningstar. **1959** The Flying Fontaines.

WATKINS, LINDA
Born: May 23, 1909, Boston, Mass. Died: Oct. 31, 1976, Los Angeles, Calif. Screen, stage and television actress.

Appeared in: **1931** Sob Sister; Good Sport. **1932** Charlie Chan's Chance; Gay Caballero; Cheaters at Play. **1957** From Hell It Came. **1958** Going Steady; Ten North Frederick; As Young as We Feel. **1959** Cash McCall. **1960** Because They're Young. **1961** The Parent Trap. **1974** Huckleberry Finn.

WATSON, ADELE
Born: 1890, Minn. Died: Mar. 27, 1933, Los Angeles, Calif. (double pneumonia). Screen, stage and vaudeville actress. Entered films in 1918.

Appeared in: **1922** The Lying Truth. **1923** Reno. **1924** Don't Doubt Your Husband. **1925** Welcome Home; Tower of Lies. **1926** Rolling Home. **1927** Good as Gold; A Harp in Hock; Once and Forever; The Broken Gate. **1928** The Black Pearl. **1929** Blue Skies; The Very Idea; Jazz Heaven; This Thing Called Love. **1931** The Public Enemy; Street Scene; Compromised; Expensive Women; Arrowsmith. **1932** The Purchase Price; Pack Up Your Troubles.

WATSON, BENJAMIN T. "BEN"
Died: 1968. Screen actor.

Appeared in: **1951** Across the Wide Missouri.

WATSON, "BOBBY" (Robert Watson Knucher)
Born: 1888, Springfield, Ill. Died: May 22, 1965, Hollywood, Calif. Screen, stage and vaudeville actor. Best known for his portrayals of Hitler.

Appeared in: **1926** That Royle Girl; The Romance of a Million Dollars; The Song and Dance Man. **1929** Syncopation; Maid's Night Out (short); Follow the Leader; plus the following shorts: The Baby Bandit; Contrary Mary; The Stand Up; Nay, Nay, Nero. **1931** Manhattan Parade. **1932** High Pressure. **1933** Moonlight and Pretzels; Going Hollywood; Wine, Women and Song. **1934** Countess of Monte Cristo; I Hate Women. **1935** Society Doctor; The Murder Man. **1936** Born to Dance; Libeled Lady; Mary of Scotland. **1937** Captains Courageous; Calling All Doctors (short); The Awful Truth; The Adventurous Blonde; You're a Sweetheart. **1938** In Old Chicago; Boys Town; Kentucky; The Story of Alexander Graham Bell. **1939** Everything's on Ice; Dodge City; On Borrowed Time; Blackmail. **1940** Wyoming; Dr. Kildare's Crisis. **1941** Men of Boys Town; Hit the Road. **1942** The Devil with Hitler. **1943** Hitler—Dead or Alive; That Nazty Nuisance; It Ain't Hay. **1944** The Hitler Gang; The Miracle of Morgan's Creek; Practically Yours. **1945** Duffy's Tavern; Hold That Blonde. **1948** The Big Clock; The Paleface. **1949** Red Hot and Blue. **1950** Copper Canyon. **1951** G.I. Jane. **1952** Singing in the Rain. **1957** The Story of Mankind.

WATSON, CAVEN
Born: 1904, Scotland. Died: 1953, Norholt, England. Screen and stage actor. Appeared in Scottish film The Net.

WATSON, FANNY
Born: 1886, Rochester, N.Y. Died: May 17, 1970, Albany, N.Y. Screen, vaudeville, burlesque and radio actress. Appeared with her sister, Kitty (dec. 1967), in vaudeville as the "Watson Sisters."

Appeared in: **1929** Bigger and Better (short).

WATSON, FRANK M.
Born: 1870. Died: July 24, 1946. Screen actor.

WATSON, GEORGE A.
Born: 1911. Died: Dec. 5, 1937, Hollywood, Calif. Screen actor.

WATSON, HENRIETTA
Born: Mar. 11, 1873, Dundee, England. Died: Sept. 29, 1964, London, England. Screen and stage actress.

Appeared in: **1932** Collision. **1935** The Guv'nor (aka Mister Hobo—US 1936).

WATSON, IVORY "DEEK"
Born: 1909. Died: Nov. 4, 1969. Black singer and screen actor. Member of the "Ink Spots" singing group.

Appeared in: **1941** The Great American Broadcast. **1942** Pardon My Sarong. **1947** Sepia Cinderella; Boy! What a Girl.

WATSON, JOSEPH K. (Joseph Koff)
Born: Feb. 12, 1887, Philadelphia, Pa. Died: May 17, 1942, Hollywood, Calif. Screen, stage, vaudeville actor and screenwriter.

Appeared in: **1936** Melody for Two; Cherokee Strip; Bad Man's Territory; Echo Mountain; Champagne Hour.

WATSON, JUSTICE
Born: 1908. Died: July 6, 1962, Hollywood, Calif. Screen, stage and television actor. Entered films approx. 1955.

Appeared in: **1956** Death of a Scoundrel. **1962** Town of London.

WATSON, KITTY (Katherine Watson)
Born: 1887. Died: Mar., 1967, Buffalo, N.Y. Screen, vaudeville and burlesque actress. Appeared with her sister, Fanny (dec. 1970), in vaudeville as the "Watson Sisters."

Appeared in: **1929** Bigger and Better (short). **1942** Mrs. Miniver.

WATSON, LUCILE
Born: May 27, 1879, Quebec, Canada. Died: June 24, 1962, New York, N.Y. Screen and stage actress. Nominated for 1943 Academy Award for Best Supporting Actress in Watch on the Rhine.

Appeared in: **1916** The Girl With the Green Eyes. **1934** What Every Woman Knows; Men in Black (short). **1935** The Bishop Misbehaves. **1936** A Woman Rebels; The Garden of Allah. **1937** Three Smart Girls. **1938** The Young in Heart; Sweethearts. **1939** Made for Each Other; The Women. **1940** Waterloo Bridge; Florian. **1941** Rage in Heaven; Mr. and Mrs. Smith; Footsteps in the Dark; The Great Lie; Model Wife. **1943** Watch on the Rhine. **1944** 'Til We Meet Again; Uncertain Glory; The Thin Man Goes Home. **1946** Song of the South; Tomorrow Is Forever; Never Say Goodbye; The Razor's Edge; My Reputation. **1947** Ivy. **1948** The Emperor Waltz; Julia Misbehaves; That Wonderful Urge. **1949** Everybody Does It; Little Women. **1950** Harriet Craig; Let's Dance. **1951** My Forbidden Past.

WATSON, MINOR
Born: Dec. 22, 1889, Marianna, Ark. Died: July 28, 1965, Alton, Ill. Screen, stage and television actor.

Appeared in: **1913** Rescuing Dave; Love Incognito; Their Waterloo. **1914** No. 28 Diplomat. **1931** 24 Hours. **1933** Another Language; Our Betters. **1934** The Pursuit of Happiness; Babbitt. **1935** Charlie Chan in Paris; Mr. Dynamite; Lady Tubbs; Mary Jane's Pa; Age of Indiscretion; Pursuit; Annapolis Farewell. **1936** Rose of the Rancho; The Longest Night. **1937** When's Your Birthday?; The Woman I Love; Saturday's Heroes; Dead End; That Certain Woman; Navy Blue and Gold; Checkers. **1938** Of Human Hearts; Boys Town; Stablemates; While New York Sleeps; Touchdown Army; Love, Honor and Behave; Fast Company. **1939** The Hardys Ride High; Maisie; The Boy Friend; News Is Made at Night; Here I Am a Stranger; Angels Wash Their Faces; The Flying Irishman; Television Spy; Stand up and Fight; Huckleberry Finn. **1940** The Llamo Kid; 20 Mule Team; Hidden Gold; Young People; Rangers of Fortune; Viva, Cisco Kid!; Gallant Sons; Abe Lincoln in Illinois. **1941** The Monster and the Girl; Western Union; The Parson of Panamint; Kiss the Boys Goodbye; Birth of the Blues; They Died With Their Boots On; Moon Over Miami; Mr. District Attorney. **1942** The Remarkable Andrew; Yankee Doodle Dandy; Woman of the Year; Frisco Lil; To the Shores of Tripoli; The Big Shot; Gentleman Jim; Flight Lieutenant; Enemy Agent Meets Ellery Queen. **1943** Action in the North Atlantic; Yanks Ahoy!; Secrets in the Dark; The Crime Doctor's Rendezvous; Crash Dive; Mission to Moscow; Princess O'Rourke; Happy Land; Guadalcanal Diary. **1944** Henry Aldrich, Boy Scout; That's My Baby; The Story of Dr. Wassell; Here Come the Waves; The Thin Man Goes Home; The Falcon Out West; Shadows in the Night. **1945** God Is My Co-Pilot; A Bell for Adano; You Came Along; Saratoga Trunk; Bewitched. **1946** Boys' Ranch; Courage of Lassie; The Virginian. **1948** A Southern Yankee. **1949** Thelma Jordan (aka File on Thelma Jordan); Beyond the Forest. **1950** Mister 880; The Jackie Robinson Story; There's a Girl in My Heart. **1951** As Young as You Feel; Bright Victory; Little Egypt. **1952** My Son John; Untamed Frontier; Face to Face. **1953** The Star; Roar of the Crowd. **1955** Ten Wanted Men. **1956** Rawhide Years; Trapeze; The Ambassador's Daughter.

WATSON, ROY
Born: 1876. Died: June 7, 1937, Hollywood, Calif. Screen actor. Entered films with Selig.

Appeared in: **1914** The Hazards of Helen (serial). **1920** The Flaming Disc (serial); Elmo, the Fearless (serial). **1921** The Ranger and the Law. **1922** Blue Blazes. **1924** The Loser's End. **1925** Luck and Sand; Win, Lose or Draw; Wolf Blood. **1926** Chasing Trouble. **1927** Cactus Trails; Wanderer of the West. **1928** Restless Youth. **1934** Carolina.

WATSON, WILLIAM "SLIDING BILLY"
Died: June 4, 1939, New York, N.Y. (heart attack). Screen and stage actor.

Appeared in: **1915** Happyland.

WATSON, WYLIE (John Wylie Robertson)
Born: 1899, Scotland. Died: May 3, 1966. Screen and stage actor. Was member of "The Watson Family" on stage.

Appeared in: **1928-31** In U.S. films. **1935** The 39 Steps. **1936** Radio Lover. **1937** Why Pick on Me?; Paradise for Two (aka The Gaiety Girls—US 1938). **1938** Yes, Madam?. **1939** Jamaica Inn. **1940** Pack Up Your Troubles. **1941** The Saint Meets the Tiger (US 1943). **1943** The Lamp Still Burns; The Flemish Farm. **1944** Tawny Pipit (US 1947); Don't Take It to Heart (US 1949); Kiss The Bride Goodbye. **1945** Waterloo Road (US 1946); Strawberry Roan; Waltz Time; Murder in Reverse (US 1950). **1946** The Years Between (US 1949); A Girl in a Million (US 1950). **1947** Fame is the Spur (US 1949); Brighton Rock. **1948** London Belongs to Me (aka Dulcimer Street—US); No Room at the Inn; Things Happen at Night; My Brother Jonathan (US 1949). **1949** The History of Mr. Polly (US 1951); Whisky Galore! (aka Tight Little Island—US and aka Mad Little Island). **1950** Your Witness (aka Eye Witness—US); Morning Departure (aka Operation Disaster—US 1951); The Magnet (US 1951). **1951** Happy-Go-Lovely. **1961** The Sundowners.

WATTIS, RICHARD
Born: 1912, England. Died: Feb. 1, 1975, London, England (heart attack). Screen, stage and television actor.

Appeared in: **1938** A Yank at Oxford (film debut). **1950** Clouded Yellow (US 1952); The Happiest Days of Your Life. **1951** Appointment with Venus (aka Island Rescue—US 1952). **1952** Song of Paris (aka Bachelor in Paris—US 1953); Stolen Face; The Importance of Being Earnest; Derby Day (aka Four Against Fate—US 1955); Top Secret (aka Mr. Potts Goes to Moscow—US 1954); Mother Riley Meets the Vampire (aka Vampire Over London—US); Made in Heaven. **1953** Innocents in Paris (US 1955); The Intruder (US 1955); Background (aka Edge of Divorce); Park Plaza (aka Norman Conquest—US); Appointment in London (US 1955); Blood Orange; Top of the Form. **1954** Hobson's Choice; Doctor in the House (US 1955); Lease of Life; The Crowded Day. **1955** The Colditz Story (US 1957); See How They Run; The Time of His Life; I Am a Camera; A Yank in Ermine; Simon and Laura (US 1956); An Alligator Named Daisy (US 1957). **1956** Jumping for Joy; The Man Who Never Was; Around the World in 80 Days; The Man Who Knew Too Much; Eyewitness; It's a Wonderful World (US 1961); The Silken Affair (US 1957); The Iron Petticoat; A Touch of the Sun. **1957** The Prince and the Showgirl; Second Fiddle; The Abominable Snowman; High Flight (US 1958); Barnacle Bill (aka All at Sea—US 1958); Blue Murder at St. Trinian's (US 1958). **1958** The Inn of the Sixth Happiness. **1959** The Captain's Table (US 1960); Left, Right and Centre (US 1961); Ten Seconds to Hell; The Ugly Duckling; Follow a Star (US 1961); Libel. **1960** Follow that Horse (US 1962); Your Money or Your Wife (US 1965). **1961** Very Important Person (aka A Coming-Out-Party—US 1962); Nearly a Nasty Accident (US 1962); Dentist on the Job (aka Get On With It!—US 1963). **1962** The Longest Day; Play it Cool (US 1963); I Thank a Fool; Bon Voyage! **1963** The Vip's; Come Fly With Me. **1964** Carry on Spying. **1965** The Liquidator; The Battle of the Villa Fiorita; The Amorous Adventures of Moll Flanders; Operation Crossbow; Up Jumped a Swagman; The Alphabet Murders (US 1966); Bunny Lake is Missing; You Must be Joking!. **1966** The Great St. Trinian's Train Robbery (US 1967). **1967** Casino Royale. **1968** Wonderwall; Chitty Chitty Bang Bang. **1969** Those Daring Young Men in Their Jaunty Jalopies; Monte Carlo or Bust. **1970** Egghead's Robot; Game that Lovers Play. **1973** That's Your Funeral; Diamonds of Wheels; Hot Property.

WATTS, CHARLES
Died: Dec. 13, 1966, Nashville, Tenn. (cancer). Screen, stage and television actor.

Appeared in: **1952** Wait Till the Sun Shines Nellie; Just This Once; Million Dollar Mermaid; Something for the Birds. **1953** Silver Whip.

1954 Boy From Oklahoma; Ricochet Romance. 1955 Tall Man Riding; The View From Pompey's Head (aka Secret Interlude). 1956 Giant. 1957 An Affair to Remember; Don't Go Near the Water; The Lone Ranger and the Lost City of Gold; The Spirit of St. Louis; The Big Land. 1959 The Big Circus; No Name on the Bullet. 1961 Ada; Summer and Smoke; Lover, Come Back; Something Wild. 1962 Days of Wine and Roses; Jumbo. 1963 The Wheeler Dealers. 1964 Apache Rifles; Dead Ringer. 1965 Baby, the Rain Must Fall.

WATTS, CHARLES H. "COTTON"
Born: 1902. Died: Mar. 5, 1968, Atlanta, Ga. Black screen and minstrel actor.

Appeared in: 1951 Yes Sir, Mr. Bones.

WATTS, GEORGE
Born: 1877. Died: July 1, 1942, Hollywood, Calif. (heart attack). Screen, stage and vaudeville actor. Appeared in vaudeville as part of "Watts and Hawley" team.

Appeared in: 1936 Soak the Rich. 1940 One Crowded Night; Sky Murder; Angels over Broadway. 1941 Mr. District Attorney; Wild Geese Calling; Hurry, Charlie, Hurry; No Hands on the Clock. 1942 The Remarkable Andrew; The Talk of the Town; Gang Busters (serial).

WATTS, JAMES
Born: 1881, Australia. Died: Oct. 5, 1961, England? Screen and stage actor.

Appeared in: 1929 The Lost Patrol.

WATTS, PEGGY
Born: 1906. Died: Apr. 27, 1966. Screen actress.

Appeared in: 1932 Cock of the Air.

WATTS, QUEENIE
Born: 1927, England. Died: Jan. 25, 1980, London, England (cancer). Blues singer, screen and television actress.

Appeared in: 1963 Sparrows Can't Sing. 1967 Up the Junction (US 1968); Half a Sixpence (US 1968); Poor Cow (US 1968). 1971 Sunday Bloody Sunday. 1972 Steptoe and Son. 1978 Schizo.

WAYBURN, NED (Edward Claudius)
Born: Mar. 30, 1874, Pittsburgh, Pa. Died: Sept. 2, 1942, New York, N.Y. Screen, stage actor and stage director.

Appeared in: 1924 The Great White Way.

WAYNE, FRANCES (Chiarina Francesca Bertocci)
Born: Aug. 26, 1919, Boston, Mass. Died: Feb. 6, 1978, Boston, Mass. (cancer). Screen actress, singer and nightclub entertainer.

WAYNE, JOHN (Marion Robert Morrison)
Born: May 26, 1907, Winterset, Iowa. Died: June 11, 1979, Los Angeles, Calif. (cancer). Screen actor, film producer and director. Divorced from Josephine Saenz, actress Esperanza Bauer (dec. 1961). Married to Pilar Palette. Father of actor Patrick Wayne and Michael, Toni, Melinda, Aissa, Marisa and Ethan Wayne.

Appeared in: 1928 Hangman's House; Mother Machree. 1929 Salute; Words and Music. 1930 Men Without Women; Rough Romance; Cheer Up and Smile; The Big Trail. 1931 Three Girls Lost; Girls Demand Excitement; Men Are Like That; Range Feud; Maker of Men; Arizona. 1932 Shadow of the Eagle (serial); Texas Cyclone; Two-Fisted Law; Lady and Gent; The Hurricane Express (serial); Ride Him Cowboy; The Big Stampede. 1933 Haunted Gold; The Telegraph Trail; The Three Musketeers (serial); Central Airport; Somewhere in Sonora; His Private Secretary; The Life of Jimmy Dolan; Baby Face; The Man from Monterey; Riders of Destiny; College Coach; Sagebrush Trail. 1934 The Lucky Texan; West of the Divide; Randy Rides Alone; The Man from Utah; The Star Packer; The Trail Beyond; 'Neath Arizona Skies; Blue Steel. 1935 Texas Terror; Rainbow Valley; The Dawn Rider; Paradise Canyon; Westward Ho!; The New Frontier; The Lawless Range. 1936 The Oregon Trail; The Lawless Frontier. 1936 The Oregon Trail; The Lawless Nineties; King of the Pecos; The Lonely Trail; Winds of the Westland; The Sea Spoilers; Conflict. 1937 California Straight Ahead; I Cover the War; Idol of the Crowds; Adventure's End. 1938 Born to the West (aka Hell Town); Pals of the Saddle; Overland Stage Raiders; Santa Fe Stampede; Red River Range. 1939 Stagecoach; The Night Riders; Three Texas Steers; Wyoming Outlaw; New Frontier; Allegheny Uprising. 1940 The Dark Command; Three Faces West; The Long Voyage Home; Seven Sinners; The Refugee. 1941 A Man Betrayed; Lady from Louisiana; The Shepherd of the Hills; Lady for a Night. 1942 Reap the Wild Wind; The Spoilers; In Old California;

The Flying Tigers; Reunion; Pittsburgh. 1943 A Lady Takes a Chance; In Old Oklahoma. 1944 The Fighting Seabees; Tall in the Saddle. 1945 Flame of the Barbary Coast; Back to Bataan; They Were Expendable; Dakota. 1946 Without Reservations. 1947 Angel and the Badman; Tycoon; War Party. 1948 Fort Apache; Red River; Three Godfathers; Wake of the Red Witch. 1949 The Fighting Kentuckian; She Wore a Yellow Ribbon; The Sands of Iwo Jima. 1950 Rio Grande. 1951 Operation Pacific; Flying Leathernecks; Crosswinds. 1952 The Quiet Man; Big Jim McLain. 1953 Trouble Along the Way; Island in the Sky; Hondo; 99 River Street. 1954 The High and the Mighty. 1955 The Sea Chase; Blood Alley. 1956 The Conqueror; The Searchers. 1957 The Wings of Eagles; Jet Pilot; Legend of the Lost. 1958 I Married a Woman; The Barbarian and the Geisha. 1959 Rio Bravo; The Horse Soldiers. 1960 The Alamo; North to Alaska. 1961 The Comancheros. 1962 The Man Who Shot Liberty Valance; Hatari!; How the West Was Won; The Longest Day. 1963 Donovan's Reef; McLintock. 1964 Circus World. 1965 The Greatest Story Ever Told; In Harm's Way; The Sons of Katie Elder. 1966 Cast a Giant Shadow. 1967 The War Wagon; El Dorado. 1968 The Green Berets. 1969 Hellfighters; True Grit; The Undefeated. 1970 Chisum; Rio Lobo. 1971 Big Jake. 1972 The Cowboys. 1973 The Train Robbers; Cahill—United States Marshal. 1974 McQ. 1975 Brannigan; Rooster Cogburn. 1976 The Shootist.

WAYNE, JUSTINA
Died: Dec. 2, 1951, Freeport, N.Y. Screen, stage and radio actress.

WAYNE, NAUNTON
Born: June 22, 1901, Llanwonno, South Wales. Died: Nov. 17, 1970, Subiton, England. Screen, stage, vaudeville and television actor.

Appeared in: 1932 The First Mrs. Fraser. 1933 Going Gay (aka Kiss Me Goodbye—US 1935); For Love of You. 1938 The Lady Vanishes. 1939 A Girl Must Live (US 1941). 1940 Night Train to Munich (aka Night Train—US and aka Gestapo); Crooks Tour. 1942 Partners in Crime. 1943 Millions Like Us. 1944 Dead of Night. 1946 A Girl in a Million (US 1950). 1948 Quartet. 1949 It's Not Cricket; Passport to Pimlico; Stop Press Girl; Obsession (aka The Hidden Room—US 1950). 1950 Double Confession (US 1953); Trio; Highly Dangerous (US 1951). 1951 Circle of Danger. 1952 The Happy Family (aka Mr. Lord Says No—US); Tall Headlines (aka The Frightened Bride—US 1953); Treasure Hunt. 1953 The Titfield Thunderbolt. 1954 You Know What Sailors Are. 1959 Operation Bullshine (US 1963). 1961 Nothing Barred; Double Bunk.

WAYNE, PATRICIA See CUTTS, PATRICIA

WAYNE, RICHARD
Died: Mar. 15, 1958, Hollywood, Calif. Screen actor.

Appeared in: 1921 Whatever She Wants; Wealth; The Snob; The Traveling Salesman. 1922 The Impossible Mrs. Bellew; Minnie; Her Husband's Trademark. 1923 Reno; Unknown Purple; Broadway Gold; The Cheat; Truxton King; Wasted Lives. 1924 Good Bad Boy. 1925 Cheaper to Marry.

WAYNE, ROBERT
Born: Oct. 28, 1864 or 1867?, Pittsburgh, Pa. Died: Sept. 26, 1946, Los Angeles, Calif. Stage and screen actor. Entered films in 1915.

Appeared in: 1929 Fashions in Love. 1930 The Love Racket. 1933 The Bitter Tea of General Yen. 1939 Dick Tracy's G-Men (serial).

WEATHERFORD, TAZWELL
Born: 1889, Indiana. Died: July 22, 1917, Los Angeles, Calif. (suicide—poison). Screen actor.

WEATHERSBY, JENNIE
Born: 1855. Died: Mar. 17, 1931, New York, N.Y. Screen and stage actress. Appeared in Biograph, Famous Players, and Kalem films.

WEAVER, CHARLEY See ARQUETTE, CLIFF

WEAVER, FRANK "CICERO"
Born: Feb. 2, 1891, Ozark, Mo. Died: Oct. 29, 1967. Screen, vaudeville and radio actor. Brother of actor Leon "Abner" Weaver (dec. 1950). Married to actress June "Elviry" Weaver (dec. 1977), with whom he appeared in an act, along with his brother Leon, billed as "Weaver Brothers & Elviry."

Appeared in: 1938 Swing Your Lady (film debut); Down in "Arkansaw." 1939 Jeepers Creepers. 1940 Friendly Neighbors; In Old Missouri; Grand Ole Opry. 1941 Arkansas Judge; Tuxedo Junction; Mountain Moonlight. 1942 Shepherd of the Ozarks; The Old Homestead; Mountain Rhythm. 1951 Disc Jockey.

WEAVER, JUNE "ELVIRY"
Born: 1891. Died: Nov. 27, 1977, Bakersfield, Calif. Screen and vaudeville actress. Married to actor Frank "Cicero" Weaver (dec. 1967), with whom she appeared in an act, along with Frank's brother Leon Weaver (dec. 1950), billed as "Weaver Brothers & Elviry."

Appeared in: **1938** Swing Your Lady. **1942** Shepherd of the Ozarks; The Old Homestead; Mountain Rhythm. **1951** Disc Jockey.

WEAVER, LEON (Leon Abner Weaver)
Born: 1883. Died: May 27, 1950, Hollywood, Calif. Screen actor and singer. Member of hillbilly act "Weaver Brothers and Elviry." For family information, see Frank "Cicero" Weaver.

Appeared in: **1938** Swing Your Lady; Romance on the Run; Down in Arkansas. **1939** Jeepers Creepers. **1940** In Old Missouri; Grand Ole Opry; Friendly Neighbors. **1941** Arkansas Judge; Mountain Moonlight. **1942** Shepherd of the Ozarks; The Old Homestead; Mountain Rhythm. **1949** Loaded Pistols; Riders of the Whistling Pines. **1951** Disc Jockey.

WEAVER, MERLE
Born: 1914. Died: Jan. 31, 1975, Woodland Hills, Calif. Screen actor and stuntman.

WEBB, CLIFTON (Webb Parmelee Hollenbeck)
Born: Nov. 19, 1889, 1893, or 1896?, Indianapolis, Ind. Died: Oct. 13, 1966, Beverly Hills, Calif. (heart attack). Stage and screen actor. Nominated for 1944 Academy Award as Best Supporting Actor in Laura and in 1946 for The Razor's Edge and nominated for 1948 Academy Award for Best Actor in Sitting Pretty.

Appeared in: **1920** Polly With a Past. **1924** Let No Man Put Asunder; New Toys. **1925** The Heart of a Siren. **1930** Still Alarm (short). **1944** Laura. **1946** The Razor's Edge; Dark Corner. **1948** Sitting Pretty. **1949** Mr. Belvedere Goes to College. **1950** Cheaper By the Dozen; For Heaven's Sake. **1951** Mr. Belvedere Rings the Bell; Elopement. **1952** Dreamboat; Stars and Stripes Forever. **1953** Titanic; Mr. Scoutmaster. **1954** Woman's World; Three Coins in the Fountain. **1956** The Man Who Never Was. **1957** Boy on a Dolphin. **1959** The Remarkable Mr. Pennypacker; Holiday for Lovers. **1962** Satan Never Sleeps.

WEBB, FAY (aka FAY WEBB VALLEE)
Born: 1906. Died: Nov. 18, 1936, Santa Monica, Calif. (following abdominal operation). Screen actress. Divorced from actor Rudy Vallee.

WEBB, FRANK
Died: Dec. 20, 1974 (auto accident). Screen actor.

Appeared in: **1969** The Bridge at Remagen. **1970** The Computer Wore Tennis Shoes; Too Late the Hero.

WEBB, GEORGE
Born: Oct. 3, 1887, Indianapolis, Ind. Died: May 24, 1943. Screen and stage actor.

Appeared in: **1916** The Secret of the Submarine (serial); Lying Lips; The Wolf Woman. **1917** The Stolen Actress; The Little Orphan; Come Through; Because of the Woman; The Charmer; The Idolaters; Bond of Fear. **1920** Alarm Clock Andy; Below the Surface; Home Spun Folks. **1921** Black Beauty; Fifty Candles; First Love; The Son of Wallingford. **1922** The Crusader; The Man Under Cover. **1923** Little Johnny Jones; Romance Land. **1924** My Man. **1925** Lucky Devil. **1931** Dude Ranch.

WEBB, MILLARD
Born: Dec. 6, 1893, Clay City, Ky. Died: Apr. 21, 1935, Los Angeles, Calif. (intestinal ailment). Screen, stage actor, film director and screenwriter. Entered films as an extra with D. W. Griffith in 1915.

WEBER, CHRISTINE
Died: Oct. 8, 1936, Hollywood, Calif. Screen actress. Appeared in Mack Sennett comedies.

WEBER, JOE (Morris Weber)
Born: 1867, N.Y. Died: May 10, 1942, Los Angeles, Calif. Screen, stage, vaudeville, burlesque and minstrel actor. Was partner with Lou Fields (dec. 1941) in comedy team of "Weber and Fields."

Appeared in: **1914** The Fatal Mallet. **1915** Two of the Finest; Two of the Bravest; Fatty and the Broadway Stars; The Best of Enemies; Old Dutch. **1916** The Worst of Friends. **1918** The Corner Grocer. **1925** Friendly Enemies. **1927** Mike and Meyer (short). **1936** March of Time. **1937** Blossoms on Broadway. **1940** Lillian Russell.

WEBER, JOSEPH W.
Born: 1861. Died: Apr. 4, 1943. Stage and screen actor.

WEBER, LOIS
Born: 1883, Allegheny, Pa. Died: Nov. 13, 1939, Los Angeles, Calif. (stomach ailment). Screen actress, film producer, film director and screenwriter. Entered films with Rex Pictures approx. 1906.

Appeared in: **1911** Lost Illusions. **1914** The Merchant of Venice; False Colors. **1919** A Midnight Romance.

WEBER, REX
Born: 1889, Lexington, Ky. Died: Dec. 8, 1918, Chicago, Ill. (Spanish influenza). Screen, stage actor, film director and producer.

WEBSTER, BEN
Born: June 2, 1864, London, England. Died: Feb. 26, 1947, Hollywood, Calif. (after operation). Screen and stage actor. Married to actress Dame May Whitty (dec. 1948). Father of actress Margaret Webster (dec. 1973).

Appeared in: **1900** English Nell. **1913** The House of Temperley. **1914** Bottle's Baby; Enoch Arden; V.C. (aka The Victoria Cross—US); Lil O'London; Liberty Hall. **1915** In the Blood; A Garret in Bohemia. **1916** The Two Roads; His Daughter's Dilemma; Cynthia in the Wilderness; The Vicar of Wakefield (US 1917). **1917** Masks and Faces; The Profligate; The Gay Lord Quex; If Thou Wert Blind. **1918** Because. **1919** 12-10; Nobody's Child. **1920** The Call of Youth (US 1921). **1924** Miriam Rozella. **1925** The Only Way. **1927** Downhill (aka When Boys Leave Home—US 1928). **1931** The Lyons Mail. **1932** Threads. **1933** One Precious Year. **1934** The Old Curiosity Shop (US 1935). **1935** Drake of England (aka Drake the Pirate—US). **1936** Eliza Comes to Stay; Conquest of the Air. **1937** The Prisoner of Zenda; Two Women. **1942** Mrs. Miniver. **1943** Lassie Come Home.

WEBSTER, LILLIAN
Died: July, 1920, Los Angeles, Calif. Screen actress. Appeared in National Film Corp. films.

WEBSTER, MARGARET
Born: Mar. 15, 1905, New York, N.Y. Died: Nov. 13, 1972, London, England. Stage actress, director, producer and screen actress. Daughter of actress Dame May Whitty (dec. 1948) and actor Ben Webster (dec. 1947).

WEDIN, BERNARD "BUDDY"
Born: 1907. Died: Aug. 5, 1948, Lansing, Mich. Screen actor.

WEEKS, ADA MAY See MAY, ADA

WEEKS, ANSON
Born: 1896, San Francisco, Calif. Died: Feb. 7, 1969, Sacramento, Calif. (emphysema). Screen actor and bandleader.

Appeared in: **1943** Melody Parade. **1951** Rhythm Inn.

WEEKS, MARION
Born: 1887. Died: Apr. 20, 1968, New York, N.Y. Screen, stage and vaudeville actress. Sister of actress Ada May (dec. 1978). Entered films with Edison in 1912.

Appeared in: **1912-13** The Office Boy's Birthday.

WEEKS, RANNY (Randall W. Weeks)
Born: 1907, Everett, Mass. Died: Apr. 26, 1979, Falmouth, Mass. Bandleader, pianist, singer, screen and stage actor.

Appeared in: **1937** Hit Parade of 1938; SOS Coast Guard (serial); Bill Cracks Down; Youth Parade.

WEEMS, TED
Born: 1901, Pitcairn, Pa. Died: May 6, 1963, Tulsa, Okla. (emphysema). Bandleader and screen actor.

Appeared in: **1938** Swing, Sister, Swing.

WEGENER, PAUL
Born: 1874, Bischdorf, Prussia. Died: Sept. 13, 1948, Berlin, Germany. Screen, stage actor, film director and film producer. Married to actress Lyda Salmonova (dec. 1968).

Appeared in: **1913** Der Student von Prag (The Student of Prague); Die Verfuehrte (Geheimnisse des Blutes). **1914** Die Augen des Ole Brandis; Evintrude, die Geschichte Eines Abenteurers; Der Golem; Die Rache des Blutes. **1915** Peter Schlemihl. **1916** Ruebezahls Hochzeit; Der Rattenfaenger von Hameln (The Pied Piper of Haelin); Der Yoghi. **1917** Der Golem und die Taenzerin; Hans Trutz im Schlaraffenland. **1918** Dornroeschen; Der Fremde Fuerst. **1919** Der Galeerenstraefling. **1920** Nachtgestalten; Der Golem, wie er in die

Welt Kam; Medea; Steuermann Holck; Sumurun (aka One Arabian Night—US 1921). **1921** Die Geliebte Roswolskys; Der Verlorene Schatten; Das Weib des Pharao (The Loves of Pharaoh—US 1922, aka Pharaoh's Wife). **1922** Flammende Voelker; Herzog Ferrantes Ende; Das Liebesnest; Vanina oder die Galgenhochzeit; Sterbett Voelker (aka Populi Morituri); Lukrezia Borgia (US 1927); Monna Vanna (US 1925). **1923** Der Schatz der Gesine Jakobsen; Sos. die Insel der Traenen. **1924** Lebende Buddhas. **1925** Der Mann aus dem Jenseits. **1926** Dagfin. **1927** Alraune (Unholy Love—US 1928); Svengali; Arme Kleine Sif; Glanz und Elend der Kurtisanen; Ramper, der Tiermensch (aka The Strange Case of Captain Ramper—US 1928); Die Weber (The Weavers—US 1929). **1928** The Lost Shadow. **1930** Fundvogel (Survival). **1932** Marschall Vorwaerts; Unheimliche Geschichten; Das Geheimnis um Johann Ort (aka Ein Leibesroman im Hause Habsburg—US 1936). **1933** Inge und die Millionen (US 1934); Hans Westmar (aka Horst Wessel—US 1939). **1935** Der Mann mit der Pranke; ... nur Eine Komoediant. **1938** In Geheimer Mission; Staerker als die Liebe (Stronger Than Love—US 1939). **1939** Das Recht auf Liebe (The Right to Love—US 1940); Das Unsterbliche Herz; Zwielicht. **1940** The Living Dead; Das Maedchen von Fanoe. **1941** Mein Leben fuer Irland. **1942** Diesel; Hochzeit auf Baerenhof; Der Grosse Koenig (The Great King). **1943** Wenn die Sonne Wieder Scheint (aka Flachsacker). **1944** Seinerzeit zu Meiner Zeit; Tierarzt Dr. Vlimmen; Kolberg; Zwischen Nacht und Morgen (aka Augen der Liebe). **1945** Der Fall Molander; Dr. Phil. Doederlein. **1949** Der Grosse Mandarin.

WEIDLER, VIRGINIA
Born: Mar. 21, 1927, Hollywood, Calif. Died: July 1, 1968. Screen actress.

Appeared in: **1933** After Tonight. **1934** Long Lost Father; Stamboul Quest; Mrs. Wiggs of the Cabbage Patch. **1935** Big Broadcast of 1936; Peter Ibbetson; Laddie; Freckles. **1936** Suicide Club; Timothy's Quest; Trouble for Two; Girl of the Ozarks; Big Broadcast of 1937. **1937** Maid of Salem; Outcasts of Poker Flat; Souls at Sea. **1938** Out West with the Hardy's; Scandal Street; Love is a Headache; Mother Carey's Chickens; Men With Wings; Too Hot to Handle. **1939** The Great Man Votes; The Lone Wolf Spy Hunt; Fixer Dugan; The Under-Pup; Bad Little Angel; The Women. **1940** Henry Goes to Arizona; Young Tom Edison; All This and Heaven Too; Gold Rush Maisie; The Philadelphia Story. **1941** I'll Wait for You; Barnacle Bill; Babes on Broadway. **1942** This Time for Keeps; Born to Sing; Once Upon a Thursday. **1943** The Youngest Profession; Best Foot Forward.

WEIGEL, PAUL
Born: Feb. 18, 1867, Halle, Germany. Died: May 25, 1951. Screen, stage and vaudeville actor.

Appeared in: **1916** Each Pearl a Tear; Naked Hearts; Witchcraft. **1917** The Winning of Sally Temple; Each to His Kind; Pride and the Man; Forbidden Paths. **1918** The Claim; Her Body in Bond; The Only Road; Me und Gott. **1919** Evangeline; The Parisian Tigress. **1920** The Breath of the Gods. **1921** Bring Him In; They Shall Pay. **1922** Up and Going. **1923** Bag and Baggage; Bluebeard's Wife. **1924** The Fatal Mistake; The Folly of Vanity; Fighting for Justice; Honor Among Men; Mademoiselle Midnight; The Silent Accuser; Tainted Money; Which Shall It Be? **1925** Declassee; Excuse Me; Soft Shoes; A Lover's Oath; The Verdict; Folly of Vanity. **1926** For Heaven's Sake; The Speed Limit. **1927** Blonde or Brunette; Broadway After Midnight; Hidden Aces; The King of Kings; Sinews of Steel. **1928** Code of the Air; Isle of Lost Men; Marry the Girl; The Wagon Show. **1929** The Leatherneck. **1931** The Vanishing Legion (serial). **1932** Back Street. **1933** The Vampire Bat. **1934** The Black Cat. **1936** The Invisible Ray. **1940** The Great Dictator. **1942** Joan of Paris. **1943** Miss V from Moscow; Happy Land. **1944** The Hairy Ape.

WEIL, HARRY
Born: 1878. Died: Jan. 23, 1943, Los Angeles, Calif. Screen and stage actor.

WEIL, HARRY
Born: 1890. Died: July 30, 1974, Syracuse, N.Y. Screen and vaudeville actor. Was member of vaudeville team of Adler, Herman and Weil and was one of the original Yacht Club Boys vocal group. Do not confuse with actor Harry Weil (dec. 1943) or director and writer of same name.

Appeared in: **1935** Thanks a Million. **1936** Stagestruck; Pigskin Parade. **1937** Artists and Models; Thrill of a Lifetime. **1938** Cocoanut Grove.

WEILER, CONSTANCE
Born: 1918. Died: Dec. 10, 1965, San Francisco, Calif. (result of fall). Screen and stage actress. Entered films in 1938.

Appeared in: **1946** The Hoodlum Saint.

WEINBERG, GUS
Born: 1866. Died: Aug. 11, 1952, Portland, Maine. Screen, stage actor, playwright and songwriter.

Appeared in: **1921** The Frontier of the Stars. **1923** The Ne'er-Do-Well; Homeward Bound; Jacqueline of Blazing Barriers. **1925** Coming Through; Soul Fire.

WEINGARTEN, LAWRENCE
Born: 1898, Chicago, Ill. Died: Feb. 5, 1975, Los Angeles, Calif. (leukemia). Screen producer, director and actor.

Appeared in: **1916** Bittersweet.

WEIR, JANE
Born: 1916, Davenport, Iowa. Died: Aug. 21, 1937, Los Angeles, Calif. (appendectomy). Screen actress.

Appeared in: **1937** Souls at Sea; Artists and Models.

WEISER, GRETHE
Born: 1903, Germany. Died: Oct. 2, 1970, near Bad Toeiz, Bavaria, Germany (auto accident). Screen, stage and television actress. Married to film producer and lawyer Hermann Schwerin (died in same accident).

Appeared in: **1935** Frischer Wind aus Kanada. **1936** Einer zu viel an Bord; Lotzte Rose. **1937** The Divine Jetta; Liebe auf Umwegen (Love by Indirection). **1938** Meine Fuer Veronika; Familie Schimek. **1939** Der Verkannte Lebemann (The Unrecognized Man of the World). **1940** Our Little Wife. **1952** Tromba, the Tiger Man. **1955** Die Stadt ist Voller Geheimnisse (aka City of Secrets—US 1963). **1956** Du Bist Musik (US 1962).

WEISS, ETHEL
Born: 1897. Died: Sept. 12, 1979, Los Angeles, Calif. Screen and stage actress.

Appeared in: **1939** Frontier Pony Express. **1941** Penny Serenade.

WEISSBURG, EDWARD
Born: 1876. Died: Aug. 30, 1950, Hollywood, Calif. (heart attack). Screen actor.

WEISSE, HANNI
Born: 1892, Germany. Died: Dec. 13, 1967, Liebenzell, Black Forest, Germany. Screen actress. Appeared in films from 1909 to 1939.

Appeared in: **1913** The Golden Bed. **1929** Berlin after Dark.

WEISSMAN, DORA
Died: May 21, 1974, New York, N.Y. Screen, stage, television and radio actress. Sister of actress/writer Bessie Weissman (dec. 1978). Married to playwright Anshel Schorr (dec.).

Appeared in: **1935** Shir Hashirim. **1953** The Gorilla Girl. **1959** Middle of the Night.

WEITZ, EMILE
Born: 1883. Died: May 12, 1951, Hollywood, Calif. Screen actor.

WELCH, BILLY
Born: 1959. Died: Sept. 13, 1980, near West Covina, Calif. (auto accident). Professional boxer and screen actor.

WELCH, EDDIE (Charles W. Welch)
Born: Apr., 1894, Columbus, Ohio. Died: Jan. 15, 1963, Miami, Fla. (diabetes). Screen actor and stuntman. Married to actress Charlotte Delaney. Doubled for Tom Mix and Buck Jones.

WELCH, HARRY FOSTER
Born: 1899. Died: Aug. 16, 1973, Blowing Rock, N.C. Screen actor. Voice of cartoon character, "Popeye the Sailor Man" for almost 40 years. Also did the voices of Bluto and Olive Oyl.

Appeared in: **1936** King of Burlesque.

WELCH, JAMES
Born: Nov. 6, 1865, Liverpool, England. Died: Apr. 10, 1917, England. Screen and stage actor. Married to stage actress Audrey Ford (dec.). Do not confuse with US stage actor James B. Welch (dec. 1965), and actor James T. Welch (dec. 1949).

Appeared in: **1913** The Eleventh Commandment. **1916** The New Clown; When Knights Were Bold.

WELCH, JAMES T.
Born: 1869. Died: Apr. 6, 1949, Hollywood, Calif. Screen, stage and minstrel actor.

Appeared in: **1921** The Broken Spur. **1922** Two-Fisted Jefferson; The Sheriff of Sun-Dog; The Marshal of Moneymint. **1924** Abraham Lincoln; The Iron Horse; Behind Two Guns; The Tornado. **1925** Tonio, Son of the Sierras; Warrior Gap. **1926** Speedy Spurs; West of the Rainbow's End. **1927** The Heart of Maryland. **1928** Rough Ridin' Red; Wizard of the Saddle; The Little Buckaroo. **1935** Ruggles of Red Gap. **1936** The Trail of the Lonesome Pine.

WELCH, JOSEPH N.
Born: Oct. 22, 1891. Died: Oct. 6, 1960, Hyannis, Mass. Attorney, screen and television actor. Nominated for 1959 Academy Award for Best Supporting Actor in Anatomy of a Murder.

Appeared in: **1959** Anatomy of a Murder.

WELCH, LESLIE
Born: 1908, England. Died: Feb. 8, 1980, Ruislip, England (heart attack). Screen, stage, radio and television actor.

WELCH, MARY
Born: 1923. Died: May 31, 1958, New York, N.Y. Screen, stage and television actress. Married to actor David White.

Appeared in: **1952** Park Row.

WELCH, NILES
Born: July 29, 1895, Hartford, Conn. Died: Nov. 21, 1976, Laguna Nigel, Calif. Screen, stage and radio actor. Married to actress Elaine Baker. Entered films with Vitagraph in 1913.

Appeared in: **1913** A Little Girl Shall Lead Them; Our Wives. **1916** The Kiss of Hate; Miss George Washington. **1917** The Secret of Storm Country; One of Many. **1918** The Gulf Between; Her Boy. **1919** Jane Goes A-Wooing; The Law of Men; The Virtuous Thief; Stepping Out; Beckoning Roads. **1920** Luck of Geraldine Laird; The Courage of Marge O'Doone. **1921** The Cup of Life; Remorseless Love; Reputation; The Sin of Martha Queed; The Spenders; The Way of a Maid; Who Am I? **1922** Reckless Youth; Rags to Riches; Under Oath; Why Announce Your Marriage?; Who Are My Parents? **1923** The Six-Fifty; Sawdust. **1924** The Girl on the Stairs; The Right of the Strongest; The Man; Virtue's Revolt; Wine of Youth; The Whispered Name. **1925** Dangerous Pleasure; Ermine and Rhinestones; Fear-Bound; A Little Girl in a Big City; Lying Wives; Scandal Street; The Substitute Wife. **1926** In Borrowed Plumes; Faithful Wives. **1927** Spider Webs. **1931** Convicted. **1932** Cross Examination; Rainbow Trail; Border Devils; McKenna of the Mounted; Night Club Lady; A Scarlet Week-End; Silver Dollar. **1933** Mysterious Rider; Cornered; Come on Tarzan; Lone Avenger; Sundown Rider; Zoo in Budapest. **1934** Let's Fall in Love; Fighting Code; Cross Streets. **1935** Tomorrow's Youth; Stone of Silver Creek; The Ivory-Handled Gun; Singing Vagabond. **1936** Empty Saddles; Foolproof (short).

WELCH, WILLIAM *See* WELSH, WILLIAM

WELCHMAN, HARRY
Born: Feb. 24, 1886, Barnstable, Devon, England. Died: Jan. 3, 1966, Penzance, England (coronary thrombosis). Screen, stage, radio and television actor.

Appeared in: **1915** The Verdict of the Heart. **1916** The Lyons Mail. **1920** House on the Marsh. **1932** The Maid of the Mountains. **1933** A Southern Maid. **1936** The Last Wlatz. **1945** Waltz Time. **1954** Eight O'Clock Walk (US 1955).

WELDON, LILLIAN (Elizabeth Martin)
Born: 1869. Died: Aug. 22, 1941, Los Angeles, Calif. Screen, vaudeville and burlesque actress. Appeared in vaudeville as part of "Murry and Martin" team.

WELFORD, DALLAS
Born: 1872, England. Died: Sept. 28, 1946, Santa Monica, Calif. Screen and stage actress.

Appeared in: **1921** Wedding Bells.

WELLES, MERI
Born: c. 1930. Died: Aug., 1973, Dallas, Tex. (heart attack). Screen actress. Divorced from actor and director Mel Welles.

Appeared in: **1960** The Little Shop of Horrors. **1961** The Errand Boy; The Ladies' Man. **1964** A House is Not a Home; The Pink Panther.

WELLESLEY, CHARLES
Born: 1875, London, England. Died: July 24, 1946, Amityville, N.Y. Screen and stage actor. Married to actress Ina Rorke (dec. 1944).

Appeared in: **1913** The Diver. **1914** The Mischief Maker. **1921** The Silver Lining; Stardust; His Greatest Sacrifice; It Isn't Being Done This Season; Nobody. **1922** Just a Song at Twilight; Outcast. **1923** Don't Marry for Money; The Acquittal; Does It Pay?; Enemies of Children; Legally Dead; Alias the Night Wind. **1924** The Wolf Man; Cytherea; Traffic in Hearts; The Perfect Flapper. **1925** The Half-Way Girl; The Lost World; The Unholly Three. **1926** College Days. **1927** The Stolen Bride; Sinews of Steel. **1928** Skinner's Big Idea.

WELLESLEY, MARIE
Died: Sept., 1927, Englewood, N.J. Screen and stage actress. Appeared in Lubin Film Company films.

WELLINGTON, BABE
Born: 1897. Died: Dec. 28, 1954, New York, N.Y. Screen, stage, vaudeville and burlesque actress. Appeared in silents as a child actress and later was in vaudeville as part of dancing team billed as "The Dancing Kellers."

WELLMAN, EMILY ANN
Died: Mar. 19, 1946. Stage and screen actress.

WELLMAN, WILLIAM A. (William Augustus Wellman)
Born: Feb. 29, 1896, Brookline, Mass. Died: Dec. 9, 1975, Los Angeles, Calif. (leukemia). Screen director, actor, producer, screenwriter and author. Divorced from actresses Helen Chadwick, Marjorie Chapin and Marjorie Crawford. Married to actress Dorothy Coonan.

Appeared in: **1919** The Knickerbocker Buckaroo; Evangeline.

WELLS, "BOMBARDIER" BILLY
Born: Aug. 31, 1887, London, England. Died: June 11, 1967, London, England. Screen actor and British heavyweight boxing champion. He used to sound the gong in Rank films as their trademark.

Appeared in: **1913** Carpentier vs. Bombardier Wells Fight. **1916** Kent, the Fighting Man. **1918** The Great Game (aka The Straight Game). **1919** Silver Lining. **1927** The Ring. **1937** Make Up; Concerning Mr. Martin.

WELLS, CHARLES B.
Born: 1851. Died: Oct. 14, 1924, Bayside, N.Y. (heart trouble). Screen and stage actor.

Appeared in: **1914** The County Seat War.

WELLS, DEERING
Born: 1896. Died: Sept. 29, 1961, London, England. Stage and screen actor.

Appeared in: **1955** Richard III (US 1956). **1958** The Two-Headed Spy (US 1959).

WELLS, H. G.
Born: 1866, England. Died: Aug. 13, 1946, London, England. Author, screenwriter and screen actor.

Appeared in: **1922** The Jungle Goddess (serial).

WELLS, L. M.
Born: 1862. Died: Jan. 1, 1923. Screen actor.

Appeared in: **1915** Graft (serial). **1916** Liberty, A Daughter of the U.S. A. (serial). **1917** The Red Ace (serial). **1920** Vanishing Trails (serial). **1921** Forgotten Woman; The Girl from God's Country; A Virginia Courtship; The Witching Hour. **1922** The Forest King.

WELLS, MAI
Born: 1862. Died: Aug. 1, 1941, Los Angeles, Calif. Screen and stage actress.

Appeared in: **1921** Opened Shutters. **1922** The Pilgrim. **1925** Excuse Me. **1927** Blondes by Choice.

WELLS, MARIE
Born: 1894. Died: July 2, 1949, Hollywood, Calif. (overdose of sleeping pills—suicide). Stage and screen actress.

Appeared in: **1923** The Love Brand; The Man from New York. **1929** The Desert Song. **1930** The Song of the West. **1934** Service with a Smile (short); The Scarlet Empress; Elmer and Elsie. **1935** She Married Her Boss; Old Sawbones (short). **1936** Cain and Mabel.

WELLS, MAURICE
Born: c. 1903, Nebr. Died: June 26, 1978, Pasadena, Calif. Screen, stage actor and stage director.

Appeared in: **1956** The Wrong Man. **1962** Rome Adventure.

WELLS, RAYMOND
Born: 1881, Dodge City, Kans. Died: Aug. 9, 1941, Calif. Screen, stage actor, film director and screenwriter.

Appeared in: **1926** Oh, What a Nurse!; The Unknown Cavalier; Tony Runs Wild; The Yankee Senor. **1927** Death Valley; Jewels of Desire; The Thrill Seekers. **1929** Souls Aflame; Free Lips; Burning Bridges; Fagasa.

WELSH, WILLIAM (William Joseph Welsh aka WILLIAM WELCH)
Born: Feb. 9, 1870, Philadelphia, Pa. Died: July 16, 1946, Los Angeles, Calif. Screen, stage actor and opera singer.

Appeared in: **1912** Lady Audley's Secret. **1913** Traffic in Souls. **1914** Neptune's Daughter; Peg O' the Wilds. **1915** The Wrong Label. **1916** Elusive Isabel. **1919** The Little Diplomat; Heart of Humanity. **1920** Over the Hill to the Poorhouse; Cynthia of the Minute. **1921** Luring Lips; Reputation; The Man Tamer; Short Skirts. **1922** Ridin' Wild; The Scrapper; The Flirt; The Top O' the Morning; The Lone Hand. **1923** Burning Woods; The Ramblin' Kid; Dead Game; The Red Warning; The Shock; Shootin' for Love; Shadows of the North; Trifling With Honor; The Town Scandal. **1924** The Law Forbids; The Man from Wyoming; The Price She Paid; The Western Wallop. **1925** Fighting Ranger (serial); Don Dare Devil; Fighting the Flames; The Red River; Flying Hoofs; The White Outlaw; Two-Fisted Jones. **1926** Frenzied Flames; The Demon; The Man from the West; The Set-Up; Western Pluck. **1927** The Opening Night; Chain Lightning; Paying the Price; Wandering Girls; Hills of Peril; Isle of Forgotten Women; The Western Rover. **1928** Daredevil's Reward; Lightning Speed; The Head of the Family; The Companionate Marriage. **1929** The Mississippi Gambler; Come and Get It; Skinner Steps Out. **1930** The Love Trader. **1931** Sundown Trail. **1932** Beyond the Rockies. **1933** Gambling Ship. **1935** Ruggles of Red Gap. **1936** Cavalry.

WENCK, EDUARD
Born: 1894. Died: May 17, 1954, Berlin, Germany (suicide because of heart ailment). Screen and stage actor.

Appeared in: **1939** Der Lustige Witwenball (The Merry Widow's Ball); Der Biberpelz (The Beaver Coat).

WENDELL, HOWARD D. (Howard David Wendell)
Born: 1908, Johnstown, Pa. Died: Aug. 11, 1975, Oregon City, Ore. Screen, stage and television actor.

Appeared in: **1952** Affair in Trinidad; You for Me. **1953** By the Light of the Silvery Moon; The Big Heat; Captain Scarface; Gentlemen Prefer Blondes. **1954** Prince Valiant; The Black Dakotas; Athena. **1955** The Fighting Chance; The View from Pompey's Head. **1956** Wiretappers; Storm Center; Never Say Goodbye; Day of Fury. **1959** Stranger in My Arms; The Four Skulls of Jonathan Drake; It Happened to Jane. **1962** Sail a Crooked Ship. **1965** The Cincinnati Kid; My Blood Runs Cold.

WENDORFF, LAIOLA
Born: 1895. Died: Jan. 21, 1966, Hollywood, Calif. Screen and television actress.

Appeared in: **1950** No Way Out. **1960** The Little Shop of Horrors; Song Without End.

WENGEL, HEDWIG
Born: 1875, Berlin, Germany. Died: Mar. 12, 1961, Randsburg, West Germany. Screen actress.

WENGRAF, JOHN E.
Born: 1897, Vienna, Austria. Died: May 4, 1974, Santa Barbara, Calif. Screen, stage actor and stage director.

Appeared in: **1941** Convoy. **1942** Lucky Jordan. **1943** Song of Russia; Mission to Moscow; Sahara; Paris After Dark. **1944** The Seventh Cross; 'Til We Meet Again; U-Boat Prisoner; Strange Affair. **1945** Weekend at the Waldorf. **1946** Tomorrow Is Forever; The Razor's Edge. **1947** T-Men. **1948** Sofia. **1949** The Lovable Cheat. **1952** Five Fingers. **1953** The Desert Rats; Call Me Madam; Flight to Tangier; Tropic Zone. **1954** The French Line; The Gambler from Natchez; Gog; Paris Playboys; Hell and High Water. **1955** The Racers. **1957** Oh Men! Oh Women!; The Pride and the Passion; The Disembodied; Valerie. **1958** The Return of Dracula. **1960** Portrait in Black; Twelve to the Moon. **1961** Judgment at Nuremberg. **1962** Hitler. **1963** The Prize. **1965** Ship of Fools.

WENMAN, HENRY N.
Born: Sept. 7, 1875, Leeds, England. Died: Nov. 6, 1953, England? Screen and stage actor.

Appeared in: **1929** Silver King. **1930** The Middle Watch. **1932** Brother Alfred. **1935** Brewster's Millions.

WENTWORTH, MARTHA (Verna "Martha" Wentworth)
Born: New York, N.Y. Died: Mar. 8, 1974, Sherman Oaks, Calif. Screen, stage, television and radio actress. Known as the "actress of 100 voices" in radio.

Appeared in: **1940** Waterloo Bridge. **1941** Bowery Blitzkrieg. **1943** Clancy Street Boys. **1945** Adventure; Fallen Angel; A Tree Grows in Brooklyn. **1946** Santa Fe Uprising (serial); The Stranger. **1947** Vigilantes Boomtown (serial); Oregon Trail; Marshal of Cripple Creek; Rustlers of Devil Canyon; Homesteaders of Paradise Valley; Stagecoach to Denver. **1951** Love Nest. **1952** You for Me; Young Man with Ideas; O. Henry's Full House (aka Full House). **1953** One Girl's Confession. **1954** She Couldn't Say No. **1955** Artists and Models; Good Morning Miss Dove; Jupiter's Darling; The Man With the Golden Arm. **1957** Daughter of Dr. Jekyll. **1961** One Hundred and One Dalmations. **1963** The Sword and the Stone (voice).

WERBESIK, GISELA
Born: 1875. Died: Apr. 15, 1956, Hollywood, Calif. Screen and stage actress. Appeared in U.S., British and German films.

Appeared in: **1944** The Hairy Ape. **1945** The Lost Weekend; Wonder Man. **1946** A Scandal in Paris; The Dark Corner. **1947** Golden Earrings.

WERICH, JAN
Born: Czechoslovakia. Died: Oct. 31, 1980. Screen actor, screenwriter, author and singer.

Appeared in: **1955** The Emperor and the Golem. **1963** Az Prijde Kocour (One Day, a Cat ...). **1967** La 25e Heure (The 25th Hour); Assignment K (US 1968).

WERKMEISTER, LOTTE
Born: 1886, Germany. Died: July, 1970, Bergholz-Rehbruecke, East Germany. Stage and screen actress.

Appeared in: **1931** Der Hampelmann. **1934** Zu Befehl Herr Unteroffizier. **1935** Die Toerichte Jungfrau.

WERNER, BUD
Born: Feb. 28, 1936, Apr. 12, 1964. Died: St. Moritz, Switzerland (avalanche). American ski champion and screen actor killed while making a sports documentary.

WERNER, WALTER
Born: 1884, Germany. Died: Jan. 8, 1956, Berlin, Germany (pneumonia). Screen and stage actor.

Appeared in: **1938** The Kreutzer Sonata. **1948** Marriage in the Shadows.

WERNER-KAHLE, HUGO
Born: 1883, Germany. Died: May 1, 1961, Berlin, Germany. Stage and screen actor.

Appeared in: **1931** Mother Love. **1935** Gruen ist die Heide; Other German films: Der Maulkorb; Traummusik; Affair Roedern.

WERNICKE, OTTO
Born: 1893, Osterode/Harz, Germany. Died: 1965, Munich, Germany. Screen and stage actor.

Appeared in: **1919** Der Maedchenhaendler von Kairo. **1920** Wo Menschen Frieden Finden. **1923** Die Suchende Seele. **1925** Das Parfuen der Mrs. Worrington. **1928** Die Hoelle von Montmarte. **1931** Stuerme der Leidenschaft (US 1932); M (US 1933, aka Moerder Unter Uns); Die Nackte Wahrheit (Nothing But the Truth). **1932** Peter Voss, der Millionendieb; Die Zwei vom Suedexpress; Die Nacht der Versuchung. **1933** SA-Mann Brand (US 1934); Die Blonde Christel (US 1934); Der Tunnel; Das Testament des Dr. Mabuse (The Testament of Dr. Mabuse). **1934** Der Fluechtling aus Chikago; Achtung! Wer Kennt Diese Frau?; Die Vertauschte Braut; Liebe Dumme Mama (aka Stupid Mama—US 1935); Peer Gynt (US 1939); Der Herr der Welt (US 1935). **1935** Zwischen Himmel und Erde (Between Heaven and Earth); Henker, Frauen und Soldaten (Hangman, Women and Soldiers—US 1940); Der Mutige Seefahrer; Die Lustigen Weiber; Ein Ganzer Kerl (Karl Rauemt Auf); Knock Out (US 1936, aka Ein Junges Maedchen—ein Junger Mann). **1936**

Strassenmusik; Arzt aus Leidenschaft; Das Schloss in Flendern; Onkel Braesig; Gleisdreieck (US 1938), aka Alarm auf Gleis B). **1937** Stimme des Blutes (aka Blood Bond); Wie Einst im Mai; Wie der Hase Laueft; Unternehmen Michael; Starke Herzen; Manege; Das Grosse Abenteuer; Der Katzenstag; Autobus S (aka Ein Mann kam Nicht Nach Hause); Heimweh (Home-sickness). **1938** Nordlicht; Eine Frau Kommt in die Tropen; Liebesbriefe aus dem Engadin; Raetsel um Beate; Geheimzeichen LB 17. **1939** Gold in New Frisco; D III 88; Silvesternacht am Alexanderplatz; Johannisfeuer; Maria Ilona (US 1940); Drei Wunderschoene Tage; Der Stammbaum des Dr. Pistorius. **1940** Die Neue Deutsche Luftwaffe Greift An (The New German Air Force Attacks); Johannis Fever (aka St. John's Fire); Was Wird Hier Gespielt?; Die Kellnerin Anna. **1941** Sein Sohn; Ohm Krueger; Friedemann Bach; Heimkegr (Homecoming). **1942** Der Seniorchef; Der Grosse Koenig (The Great King). **1943** Titanic. **1944** Der Grosse Preis; Das Leben Ruft; Seinerzeit zu Meiner Zeit; Kolberg. **1945** Kamerad Hedwig. **1947** Zwischen Gestern und Morgen. **1948** Lang ist der Weg (Long is the Road); Der Herr vom Andern Stern. **1949** Amico; Du Bist Nicht Allein. **1950** Die Fidele Tankstelle; Wer Fuhr der Grauen Ford?; Vom Teufel Gejagt; Susanna Jakobaea Krafftin. **1951** Schatten Ueber Neapel (aka Camora). **1955** Himmel ohne Sterne (Sky Without Stars—US 1959). **1956** Das Sonntagskind; Studentin Helen Willfuer. **1959** Die Feuerrote Baronesse; Immer die Maedchen.

WERTZ, CLARENCE
Died: Dec. 25, 1935, Hollywood, Calif. (following operation). Screen actor and stuntman.

Appeared in: **1922** The Three Must-Get-There's. **1926** Spangles.

WERY, CARL
Born: 1898, Bavaria, Germany. Died: Mar. 14, 1975, Munich, Germany (acute pneumonia and chronic cerebral sclerosis). Stage and screen actor.

Appeared in: **1953** Heidi. **1954** Desires; Angelika. **1955** Heidi and Peter. **1958** Ballerina. **1959** Kriegsgericht (Court Martial—US 1962). **1962** Am Galgen Hangt die Liebe (Love of the Gallows).

WESCOTT, WALKER
Born: 1921. Died: Dec. 24, 1978, Phoenix, Ariz. (internal hemorrhaging). Screen, stage and television actor. Married to stage director Karen Westcott.

WESS, OTTO FRANCIS (aka RAY RAVELLE)
Born: 1914. Died: Mar. 18, 1969, Youngstown, Ohio. Screen, vaudeville, radio actor and dancer. Appeared on stage as Ray Ravelle.

WESSEL, DICK (Richard Wessel)
Born: 1913. Died: Apr. 20, 1965, Studio City, Calif. (heart attack). Screen, stage, radio and television actor.

Appeared in: **1935** In Spite of Danger. **1936** Ace Drummond (serial). **1937** Round-up Time in Texas; The Game That Kills; Slim; Borrowing Trouble. **1938** Hawk of the Wilderness (serial); Arson Gang Busters. **1939** Beasts of Berlin; Dust Be My Destiny; Missing Daughters; They Made Me a Criminal. **1940** Cafe Hostess; Brother Orchid; So You Won't Talk; The Border Legion. **1941** Dive Bomber; Manpower; The Great Train Robbery; Desert Bandit; Tanks a Million. **1942** Bells of Capistrano; X Marks the Spot; Dudes are Pretty People; Yankee Doodle Dandy; The Traitor Within; You Can't Escape Forever; Gentleman Jim; Highways by Night. **1943** Silver Spurs; Action in the North Atlantic. **1945** Scarlet Street. **1946** California; In Old Sacramento; Dick Tracy vs. Cueball; In Fast Company; Noisy Neighbors (short). **1947** Merton of the Movies; plus the following shorts: Wife to Spare; Do or Diet; In Room 303; Blondes Away; Fright Night. **1948** Pitfall; Unknown Island; When My Baby Smiles at Me; Badmen of Tombstone; Eight-Ball Andy (short); Dig That Gold (short); The Fuller Brush Man. **1949** Thieves' Highway; Blondie Hits the Jackpot; Slattery's Hurricane; Frontier Outpost; Canadian Pacific; Billie Gets Her Man (short). **1950** Blondie's Hero; The Dungeon; Wabash Avenue; Beware of Blondie; Watch the Birdie; Punchy Cowpunchers (short); Father of the Bride. **1951** An American in Paris; Francis Goes to the Races; The Scarf; Reunion in Reno; Texas Carnival; Corky of Gasoline Alley; Honeychile. **1952** Love Is Better Than Ever; The Belle of New York; Blackbeard the Pirate; Wac from Walla Walla; Young Man with Ideas. **1953** Gentlemen Prefer Blondes; Champ for a Day; Let's Do It Again; The Caddy; Fresh Painter (short). **1955** Bowery to Bagdad; Fling in the Ring (short). **1956** Around the World in 80 Days; Andy Goes Wild (short). **1958** No Time for Sergeants. **1960** The Gazebo. **1963** Wives and Lovers; Pocketful of Miracles; Who's Minding the Store? **1966** The Ugly Dachshund.

WESSELHOEFT, ELEANOR (Elinor Wesselhoeft)
Born: 1873, Cambridge, Mass. Died: Dec. 9, 1945, Hollywood, Calif. Stage and screen actress.

Appeared in: **1931** Street Scene (film debut). **1932** Madame Racketeer. **1933** The Great Jasper; Cradle Song. **1934** All Men Are Enemies; Thirty Day Princess; Black Moon. **1935** Country Chairman; The Wedding Night; The Woman in Red. **1936** Boulder Dam; A Son Comes Home; Ladies in Love. **1937** The Prisoner of Zenda. **1938** Miracle Money (short); Alexander's Ragtime Band; The Baroness and the Butler. **1939** Intermezzo; The Story of Alfred Nobel (short); Everything Happens at Night. **1940** The Man I Married; Four Sons. **1941** More Trifles of Importance (short).

WESSELL, VIVIAN
Born: 1893. Died: Oct., 1965. Screen and stage actress.

Appeared in: **1915** The Dancing Doll.

WESSON, DICK (Richard Lewis Wesson)
Born: Feb. 20, 1919, Idaho. Died: Jan. 27, 1979, Costa Mesa, Calif. (suicide—gunshot). Screen, television actor and film producer.

Appeared in: **1950** Destination Moon; Breakthrough. **1951** Inside the Walls of Folsom Prison; Jim Thorpe—All American; Force of Arms; On the Sunny Side of the Street; Starlift. **1952** About Face; The Man Behind the Gun. **1953** The Desert Song; The Charge at Feather River; Calamity Jane. **1955** Paris Follies of 1965. **1962** The Errand Boy.

WESSON, GENE
Born: 1921. Died: Aug. 22, 1975, New York, N.Y. (heart attack). Screen, stage and television actor. Brother of Dick Wesson with whom he appeared in a comedy act known as "The Wesson Brothers."

Appeared in: **1955** Wichita. **1965** Satan's Bed. **1967** The Battle of Algiers; The Hunt. **1968** The Uninhibited.

WEST, BILLIE
Died: June 7, 1967, Plainfield, N.J. (cancer). Screen actress. Married to actor Frank Bennett (dec. 1957). Do not confuse with actor Billy West.

Appeared in: **1914** The Angel of the Gulch; Dawn. **1915** The Bride of the Sea; Arrow Maiden.

WEST, BILLY (Roy B. Weisberg)
Born: Sept. 21, 1893, Russia. Died: July 21, 1975, Hollywood, Calif. (heart attack). Screen and vaudeville actor, screen director, screenwriter and cartoonist. Entered films in 1909. Starred in a series of "Billy West Comedies."

Appeared in: **1914** For Her Father's Sin; A Mother's Influence; The Niggard; At Dawn; Bright and Early. **1915** The Comeback. **1917** Dough-Nuts; The Prospector; The Chief Cook. **1918** The Orderly; The Rogue; His Day Out; The Stranger; Playmates; King Solomon (aka Ol King Sol); The Slave. **1920** Beauties in Distress. **1925** Billy West series, including: Copper Butt-Ins; West is West; Fiddlin' Around; The Joke's on You; So Long Billy. **1926** Thrilling Youth. **1927** Lucky Fool. **1932** Winner Take All. **1933** Picture Snatcher; The Diamond Trail. **1934** Jimmy the Gent; Perfectly Mismated (short). **1935** Motive for Revenge. **1968** The Further Perils of Laurel and Hardy (doc.).

WEST, CHARLES H.
Born: Nov. 30, 1885, Pittsburgh, Pa. Died: Oct. 10, 1943, Los Angeles, Calif. Screen and stage actor. Entered films with Biograph in 1910.

Appeared in: **1912** The Goddess of Sagebrush Gulch. **1916** The Heart of Nora Flynn; The Dream Girl. **1917** Betty to the Rescue; The Americn Consul; The Little Pirate; Little Miss Optimist; The Trouble Buster. **1921** Bob Hampton of Placer; Not Guilty; The Witching Hour. **1922** The Lane That Had No Turning; Love in the Dark; Manslaughter. **1923** The Eternal Three; Held to Answer; Red Lights; Times Have Changed. **1925** The Fate of a Flirt; The Overland Limited; The Part Time Wife; The Road to Yesterday; The Talker. **1926** The Skyrocket; House Without a Key (serial). **1927** King of Kings; Nobody's Widow; On the Stroke of Twelve. **1928** Man from Headquarters. **1929** Acquitted; Handcuffed. **1930** Along Came Youth; For the Defense. **1933** Police Car 17. **1934** The Man Trailer. **1935** The Bride Comes Home. **1937** Don't Tell Your Wife.

WEST, EDNA RHYS
Born: 1887. Died: Feb. 7, 1963, Middletown, N.Y. Screen and stage actress.

Appeared in: **1929** Half Way to Heaven.

WEST, FORD
Born: Mar. 27, 1873, Dallas, Tex. Died: Jan. 3, 1936. Screen actor.

Appeared in: **1921** Fighting Fate (serial). **1924** Sherlock, Jr. **1925** Duped. **1926** The Broadway Gallant. **1929** Half Way to Heaven. **1930** Call of the West. **1933** King of the Wild Horses. **1935** Old Sawbones (short); Uncivil Warriors (short).

WEST, HENRY ST. BARBE
Born: Feb. 7, 1880, London, England. Died: May 10, 1935, England? Screen and stage actor. Do not confuse with US actor Henry West.

Appeared in: **1928** Balaclave (aka Jaws of Hell—US 1931). **1932** Condemned to Death.

WEST, ISABELLE
Born: 1858. Died: July 21, 1942, Brentwood, N.Y. Screen and stage actress.

Appeared in: **1921** The Price of Possession. **1924** A Sainted Devil. **1925** Old Home Week.

WEST, JAMES "BUSTER"
Born: 1902, Philadelphia, Pa. Died: Mar. 19, 1966, Encino, Calif. (brain tumor). Screen, stage and vaudeville actor. Appeared in vaudeville with his parents in an act billed as "Wells, Virginia and West".

Appeared in: **1924** Broadway After Dark; the following Christie shorts prior to 1933: The Dancing Gob (film debut); Marching to Georgie; Don't Give Up. **1934-38** Educational shorts. **1938** Radio City Revels. **1949** Make Mine Laughs.

WEST, KATHERINE (aka LILLIAN WESTNER aka MAXINE MORTON)
Born: 1883. Died: Sept. 26, 1936, Los Angeles, Calif. (heart attack). Screen and stage actress. Appeared as Katherine West, Lillian Westner and Maxine Morton.

Appeared in: **1936** Girl's Dormitory.

WEST, MAE
Born: Aug. 17, 1892, Brooklyn, N.Y. Died: Nov. 22, 1980, Hollywood, Calif. Screen, stage, vaudeville, radio, television actress, screenwriter and playwright. Divorced from actor Frank Wallace.

Appeared in: **1932** Night After Night. **1933** I'm No Angel; She Done Him Wrong. **1934** Belle of the Nineties. **1935** Goin' to Town. **1936** Klondike Annie; Go West, Young Man. **1937** Every Day's a Holiday. **1940** My Little Chickadee. **1943** The Heat's On. **1970** Myra Breckenridge. **1978** Sextette.

WEST, NEVA
Died: Oct. 5, 1965, Glendale, Calif. Screen and stage actress. Married to film director Roy Clements (dec.).

Appeared in: **1915** The Outlaw's Awakening.

WEST, PAT (Arthur Pat West)
Born: 1889. Died: Apr. 10, 1944, Hollywood, Calif. Screen, stage and vaudeville actor. Appeared in vaudeville with his wife Lucille in an act billed as "Arthur and Lucille West."

Appeared in: **1929** Ship Ahoy (short). **1930** Russian Around (short); Gates of Happiness (short). **1935** Red Morning. **1936** Cain and Mabel; Ceiling Zero; Song of the Saddle; Three of a Kind; On the Wrong Trek (short); Three Men on a Horse; Gold Diggers of 1937; The Big Broadcast of 1937; Libeled Lady. **1937** The Perfect Specimen; Saratoga; Turn Off the Moon. **1938** Bringing Up Baby; If I Were King; Thanks for the Memory. **1939** Geronimo; Only Angels Have Wings; Some Like It Hot. **1940** His Girl Friday. **1941** Ball of Fire; The Lady Eve. **1942** Are Husbands Necessary?; Madame Spy; Invisible Agent. **1944** To Have and to Have Not.

WEST, THOMAS
Born: 1859. Died: July 28, 1932, Philadelphia, Pa. (liver ailment). Screen, stage and vaudeville actor. Was known as "Chinese Tommy" for his interpretations of oriental characters. Entered films with Lubin.

WEST, TONY
Born: Chicago, Ill. Died: June 25, 1923, Los Angeles, Calif. Screen and stage actor. Appeared in Emerald Film Co. films.

Appeared in: **1923** Dead Game.

WEST, WILLIAM
Died: Sept. 23, 1918, New York, N.Y. (injuries sustained from a fall). Screen actor. Entered films with the Edison Company.

Appeared in: **1911** The Stuff That Dreams are Made Of; The Minute Man; The New Church Carpet; Money to Burn; The Stolen Dog; Uncle Hiram's List; The Professor and the New Hat; The Declaration of Independence; An Unknown Language; Eugene Wrayburn; Foul Play; Her Wedding Ring; Mike's Hero; The Rise and Fall of Weary Willie; Ludwig from Germany; The Living Peach; The Lure of the City; How Sir Andrew Lost His Vote; Freezing Auntie. **1912** Von Weber's Last Waltz; The Harbinger of Peace; Blinks and Jinks; Attorneys-at-law; In His Father's Steps; The Grandfather; A Romance of the Rails; The Windking Parson; The Old Reporter; The Sunset Gun; How Father Accomplished His Work; The Green-Eyed Monster. **1913** For Her; The Mountaineers; A Will and a Way; Kathleen Mavourneen; The Elder Brother; The Inventor's Sketch; With the Eyes of the Blind; The Golden Wedding; Scenes from Other Days; A Mutual Understanding; The Awakening of a Man. **1914** The Birth of the Star Spangled Banner; A Question of Identity; The Perfect Truth; The Man in the Dark; On Christmas Eve; The Powers of the Air; Tango in Tuckerville; The Active Life of Dollie of the Dailies (serial); Grand Opera in Rubeville; The Resurrection of Caleb Worth; The Borrowed Finery; Frederick the Great. **1915** On the Stroke of Twelve; On the Wrong Track; What Happened on the Barbuda; The Magistrate's Story; The Ploughshare; The Magic Skin.

WEST, WILLIAM HERMAN
Born: 1860. Died: Aug. 28, 1915, Glendale, Calif. Screen actor.

Appeared in: **1912** The Plot That Failed; The Peril of the Cliffs; The Power of a Hymn; The Indian Uprising at Santa Fe; The Skinflint; Red Wing and the Paleface; The Flower Girl's Revenge; The Driver of the Deadwood Coach. **1913** On the Brink of Ruin; The Struggle; The Big Horn Massacre; Perils of the Sea; The Last Blockhouse; Red Sweeney's Mistake; The Poet and the Soldier; The Pride of Angry Bear; The Redemption; Missing Bonds. **1914** The Barrister of Ignorance; The Fatal Opal; The Smugglers of Lone Isle; Who Goes There? **1915** The Vanishing Vases; The Strangler's Cord; The Affair of the Deserted House (serial); The Apartment House Mystery (serial); In the Shadow of Death; The Writing on the Wall; The Tattooed Hand; The Accomplice; The Vivisectionist; The Money-Leechers; The Wolf's Prey; The Man on Watch; The Dream Seekers.

WEST, WILLIE
Born: Sept. 22, 1867, England. Died: Feb. 5, 1922, England? Screen and stage actor. Do not confuse with actor William West (dec. 1918).

Appeared in: **1912** Oliver Twist.

WESTCOTT, ASHLEY P.
Died: Jan. 25, 1973. Screen actor.

Appeared in: **1970** The Out-of-Towners.

WESTCOTT, GORDON
Born: 1903, near St. George, Utah. Died: Oct. 31, 1935, Hollywood, Calif. (injuries suffered in polo-playing fall). Screen and stage actor.

Appeared in: **1931** Enemies of the Law. **1932** Guilty as Hell; Devil and the Deep; Hot Saturday; Love Me Tonight. **1933** The Crime of the Century; He Learned About Women; Heritage of the Desert; The Working Man; Lilly Turner; Heroes for Sale; Convention City; Private Detective 62; Footlight Parade; Voltaire; The World Changes. **1934** Fashions of 1934; Fog Over Frisco; I've Got Your Number; Call It Luck; The Circus Clown; Registered Nurse; Six Day Bike Rider; The Case of the Howling Dog; Kansas City Princess; Murder in the Clouds; Dark Hazard; We're in the Money. **1935** The White Cuckatoo; A Night at the Ritz; Go into Your Dance; Going Highbrow; Bright Lights; Front Page Woman; This Is the Life; Two-Fisted; Ceiling Zero.

WESTCOTT, NETTA (Netta Lupton)
Born: 1893, London, England. Died: Aug. 9, 1953, England? Screen and stage actress. Entered films in 1922.

WESTERFIELD, JAMES "JIM"
Born: 1913. Died: Sept. 20, 1971, Woodland Hills, Calif. (heart attack). Screen, stage and television actor. Married to actress Fay Tracy.

Appeared in: **1941** Highway West. **1946** Undercurrent; The Chase. **1951** The Whistle at Eaton Falls; The Human Jungle. **1954** Three Hours to Kill; On the Waterfront. **1955** Chief Crazy Horse; The Violent Men; The Cobweb; The Scarlet Coat; Lady Gallant; Man with the Gun. **1957** Three Brave Men; Jungle Heat; Decision at Sundown. **1958** Cowboy; The Proud Rebel. **1959** The Shaggy Dog; The Gunfight at Dodge City. **1960** Wild River; The Plunderers. **1961** The Absent-

Minded Professor; Homicidal. **1962** Birdman of Alcatraz; The Scarface Mob. **1963** Son of Flubber. **1964** Man's Favorite Sport?; Bikini Beach. **1965** The Sons of Katie Elder; That Funny Feeling. **1966** Dead Heat on a Merry-Go-Round. **1968** Blue; Hang 'Em High. **1969** Smith!; A Man Called Gannon; The Love God; True Grit; Recent Mexican film, Arde (Burn).

WESTERTON, FRANK H.
Born: London, England. Died: Aug. 25, 1923, New York, N.Y. (cancer). Screen and stage actor.

Appeared in: **1914** Manon Lescast.

WESTLEY, HELEN (Henrietta Remson Meserole Maney Conroy)
Born: 1879, Brooklyn, N.Y. Died: Dec. 12, 1942, Franklin Township, N.J. Screen and stage actress. Divorced from actor John Westley (dec. 1948).

Appeared in: **1934** Death Takes a Holiday; The House of Rothschild; Moulin Rouge; The Age of Innocence; Anne of Green Gables. **1935** Splendor; Roberta; Captain Hurricane; Chasing Yesterday; The Melody Lingers On. **1936** Showboat; Half Angel; Dimples; Banjo on My Knee; Stowaway. **1937** Sing and Be Happy; Cafe Metropole; Heidi; I'll Take Romance. **1938** Keep Smiling; Rebecca of Sunnybrook Farm; The Baroness and the Butler; Alexander's Ragtime Band; She Married an Artist; Wife, Husband and Friend. **1939** Zaza. **1940** All This and Heaven Too; The Captain Is a Lady; Lady with Red Hair; Lillian Russell. **1941** Henry Aldrich for President; Adam Had Four Sons; The Smiling Ghost; Bedtime Story; Million Dollar Baby; Sunny; Lady from Louisiana. **1942** My Favorite Spy.

WESTLEY, JOHN (John Conroy)
Died: Dec. 26, 1948, Hollywood, Calif. Screen and stage actor. Divorced from actress Helen Westley (dec. 1942).

WESTMAN, NYDIA
Born: 1902. Died: May 23, 1970, Burbank, Calif. (cancer). Screen, stage and television actress.

Appeared in: **1932** Strange Justice; Manhattan Tower. **1933** Bondage; The Way to Love; The Cradle Song; Little Women; King of the Jungle; From Hell to Heaven. **1934** Two Alone; Success at Any Price; Ladies Should Listen; The Trumpet Blows; One Night of Love; Manhattan Love Song. **1935** Captain Hurricane; Dressed to Thrill; Sweet Adeline; A Feather in Her Hat. **1936** The Georgeous Hussy; Craig's Wife; The Rose Bowl; The Invisible Ray; Pennies from Heaven; Three Live Ghosts. **1937** When Love Is Young; Bulldog Drummond's Revenge. **1938** The Goldwyn Follies; The First Hundred Years; Bulldog Drummond's Peril. **1939** The Cat and the Canary; When Tomorrow Comes. **1940** Forty Little Mothers; Hullabaloo. **1941** The Bad Man; The Chocolate Soldier. **1942** They All Kissed the Bride; The Remarkable Andrew. **1943** Princess O'Rourke; Hers to Hold. **1944** Her Primitive Man. **1947** The Late George Apley. **1948** The Velvet Touch. **1962** For Love or Money; Don't Know the Twist. **1966** The Chase; The Ghost of Mr. Chicken; The Swinger. **1967** The Reluctant Astronaut. **1968** The Horse in the Gray Flannel Suit. **1969** Nobody Loves Flapping Eagle; Run Rabbit Run.

WESTMORELAND, PAULINE
Born: 1910. Died: Jan. 28, 1947, Los Angeles, Calif. Screen actress.

WESTNER, LILLIAN See WEST, KATHERINE

WESTON, ANNIE (Annie Burke)
Born: 1870. Died: Dec. 24, 1952, New York, N.Y. Screen, stage and radio actress.

WESTON, CECIL
Born: 1890. Died: Aug. 7, 1976, Hollywood, Calif. (bronchial pneumonia). Screen actress. Married to cameraman/producer Fred Balshofer (dec. 1969).

Appeared in: **1931** Dude Ranch; Huckleberry Finn. **1935** Behold My Wife. **1936** Banjo on My Knees. **1938** Blockade. **1942** Broadway Big Shot. **1943** This Land is Mine; Two-Fisted Justice. **1948** Money Madness. **1950** Bandit Queen; When Willie Comes Marching Home. **1951** Mr. Belvedere Rings the Bell. **1952** This Woman is Dangerous; Bells on Their Toes. **1954** Bride of the Blue Grass. **1960** Three Came to Kill; Noose for a Gunman. **1962** The Notorious Landlady.

WESTON, CHARLES H.
Born: United States. Died: 1917, England? Screen actor, film director, film producer and screenwriter.

Appeared in: **1914** Detective Finn, or, In the Heart of London (aka Society Detective—US); The King of Seven Dials; Self-Accused. **1915** Vice and Virtue, or, The Tempters of London.

WESTON, DORIS (Doris Wester)
Born: Sept. 9, 1917, Chicago, Ill. Died: July 27, 1960, N.Y. (cancer). Screen and radio actress.

Appeared in: **1931** Le Fils de L'Autre. **1917** Submarine D-1; The Singing Marine. **1938** Born to Be Wild. **1939** Mandrake the Magician (serial); When Tomorrow Comes. **1940** Chip of the Flying U.

WESTON, GEORGE
Died: Apr. 7, 1923, N.Y. Stage and screen actor.

WESTON, JOSEPH J.
Born: 1888. Died: May 1, 1972, Los Angeles, Calif. Screen actor.

Appeared in: **1942** Bashful Bachelor; Over My Dead Body.

WESTON, MAGGIE
Died: Nov. 3, 1926, New York, N.Y. Stage and screen actress.

WESTON, RUTH
Born: Aug. 31, 1906, Boston, Mass. Died: Nov. 5, 1955, East Orange, N.J. Stage and screen actress.

Appeared in: **1931** The Public Defender; Devotion; Smart Woman; The Woman Between. **1932** This Sporting Age. **1935** Splendor. **1938** That Certain Age. **1939** Made for Each Other.

WESTON, SAMMY
Born: 1889. Died: Feb. 1, 1951, Hollywood, Calif. Screen and stage actor.

WESTOVER, WINIFRED
Born: Nov. 9, 1899, San Francisco, Calif. Died: Mar. 19, 1978, Los Angeles, Calif. Screen actress. Divorced from actor William S. Hart (dec. 1946). Mother of actor William S. Hart, Jr.

Appeared in: **1916** Intolerance; Don Quixote. **1918** Hobbs in a Hurry; All the World. **1919** John Petticoats; This Hero Stuff. **1920** Old Lady 31; Forbidden Trails; Firebrand Trevision; The Village Sleuth. **1921** Anne of Little Smoky; Bucking the Tiger; The Fighter; Is Life Worth Living? **1922** Love's Masquerade. **1930** Lummox.

WESTWOOD, MARTIN F.
Born: 1883. Died: Dec. 19, 1928, Glendale, Calif. (pneumonia). Screen actor.

WETHERALL, FRANCES
Born: Greenwich, England. Died: Nov. 13, 1923, England? Screen and stage actress. Married to actor H. R. Hignett (dec. 1959).

Appeared in: **1916** A Place in the Sun.

WETHERELL, M. A.
Born: 1887. Died: Feb. 25, 1939, Johannesburg, South Africa. Screen actor, film producer and film director.

Appeared in: **1921** The Buried City. **1922** The Wee Macgregor's Sweetheart; The Vulture's Prey. **1923** Through Fire and Water. **1924** Women and Diamonds (aka Conscripts of Misfortune or It Happened in Africa). **1925** Livingstone (aka Livingstone in Africa—US 1929). **1927** Robinson Crusoe.

WEXLER, PAUL
Born: 1929. Died: Nov. 21, 1979, Los Angeles, Calif. (leukemia). Screen, vaudeville and radio actor.

Appeared in: **1952** Bloodhounds of Broadway; Feudin' Fools. **1953** Silver Whip. **1954** Suddenly; The Bowery Boys Meet the Monsters. **1955** The Kentuckian. **1956** The Kettles in the Ozarks; Anything Goes. **1958** The Buccaneer. **1959** The Four Skulls of Jonathan Drake; Day of the Outlaw; Timbuktu; The Miracle of the Hills. **1961** One Hundred and One Dalmations (voice). **1965** Sylvia. **1967** The Busy Body; The Way West.

WHALEN, MICHAEL (Joseph Kenneth Shovlin)
Born: 1902, Wilkes Barre, Pa. Died: Apr. 14, 1974, Woodland Hills, Calif. (bronchial pneumonia). Screen, stage, radio, television actor and singer.

Appeared in: **1935** Professional Soldier. **1936** The Man I Marry; Sing, Baby, Sing; Song and Dance Man; The Country Doctor; The Poor Little Rich Girl; White Fang; Career Woman. **1937** Woman Wise; Time Out for Romance; The Lady Escapes; Wee Willie Winkie. **1938** Time Out for Murder; Change of Heart; Walking Down Broadway; Island in the Sky; Speed to Burn; While New York Sleeps; Inside Story; Pardon Our Nerve; Meridian 7-1212. **1939** The Mysterious Miss X;

They Asked for It. **1940** Ellery Queen, Master Detective. **1941** Sign of the Wolf; I'll Sell My Life. **1942** Nazi Spy Ring. **1943** Tahiti Honey. **1947** Gas House Kids in Hollywood. **1948** Highway 13; Thunder in the Pines; Blonde Ice. **1949** Batman and Robin (serial); Shep Comes Home; Omoo, Omoo, the Shark God (aka Omoo, Omoo); Sky Liner; Son of a Badman; Tough Assignment; Treasure of Monte Cristo; Parole, Inc. **1950** Sarumba. **1951** Mask of the Dragon; Kentucky Jubliee; According to Mrs. Hoyle; Fingerprints Don't Lie; G. I. Jane. **1952** Waco. **1955** The Silver Star. **1956** The Phantom from 10,000 Leagues. **1957** She Shoulda Said No. **1958** Missile to the Moon. **1960** Elmer Gantry.

WHALEY, BERT
Died: Jan. 17, 1973. Screen actor.

WHEAT, LAWRENCE "LARRY" (aka LAURENCE WHEAT)
Born: 1876. Died: Aug. 7, 1963. Screen actor.

Appeared in: **1921** Hush Money; The Land of Hope. **1922** Our Leading Citizen; The Bachelor Daddy; Back Home and Broke; The Beauty Shop; The Man Who Saw Tomorrow. **1923** The Ne'er-Do-Well; Hollywood; The Song of Love. **1924** The Confidence Man; Inez from Hollywood. **1925** Not So Long Ago; Coming Through; Old Home Week. **1926** Irene. **1934** The Loud Speaker; Peck's Bad Boy. **1935** Public Hero Number One; It's In the Air; The Big Broadcast of 1936; Postal Inspector. **1945** It's Your Move (short); What a Blonde.

WHEATCROFT, STANHOPE (Stanhope Nelson Wheatcroft)
Born: May 11. 1888, New York. Died: Feb. 12, 1966, Woodland Hills, Calif. (heart attack). Screen and stage actor. Son of actress Adeline Stanhope (dec. 1935).

Appeared in: **1915** Bought. **1916** Camille; Broken Chains; East Lynne; Under Two Flags; Sins of Men; The Madness of Helen. **1917** The Corner Grocer; A Modern Cinderella; The Runaway; Maternity; Courage of the Commonplace. **1919** Secret Service. **1921** Cold Steel; Dr. Jim; Greater Than Love. **1922** The Hottentot; The Sign of the Rose; Two Kinds of Women. **1923** Blow Your Own Horn; Breaking Into Society. **1924** Broadway or Bust; The Iron Horse; Laughing at Danger; No More Women; The Yankee Consul. **1925** Keep Smiling; Madame Behave; Ridin' Pretty. **1927** The King of Kings; Women's Wares. **1934** The Notorious Sophie Lang. **1935** Thanks a Million.

WHEELER, BERT (Albert Jerome Wheeler)
Born: Apr. 7, 1895, Paterson, N.J. Died: Jan. 18, 1968, New York, N.Y. (emphysema). Screen, stage, vaudeville, telelvision actor and screenwriter. Father of actress Patricia Walters (dec. 1967). Was partner with Robert Woolsey (dec. 1938) in vaudeville and film comedy team of "Wheeler and Woolsey." Unless otherwise noted, the films listed are for the team.

Appeared in: **1922** Captain Fly-by-Night. **1929** The Voice of Hollywood (Wheeler only—short); Rio Rita (stage and film versions); Small Timers (Wheeler only—short). **1930** The Cuckoos; Dixiana; Half Shot at Sunrise; Hook, Line and Sinker. **1931** Cracked Nuts; Caught Plastered; Oh! Oh! Cleopatra (short); Peach O'Reno; Too Many Cooks (Wheeler only). **1932** Girl Crazy; The Slippery Pearls (short); Hold 'Em Jail; Hollywood Handicap (Wheeler only—short). **1933** So This Is Africa; Diplomaniacs. **1934** Hips, Hips, Hooray; Cockeyed Cavaliers; Kentucky Kernels. **1935** The Nitwits; The Rainmakers; A Night at the Biltmore Bowl (Wheeler only—short). **1936** Silly Billies; Mummy's Boys. **1937** On Again, Off Again; High Flyers. **1939** Cowboy Quarterback (Wheeler only). **1941** Las Vegas Nights (Wheeler only). **1951** The Awful Sleuth (Wheeler only—short).

WHEELER, BURRITT (Burritt Nash Wheeler)
Born: Dec. 25, 1883, Ill. Died: Nov. 11, 1957, Los Angeles, Calif. (cancer). Screen actor and radio producer.

Appeared in: **1950** Stella.

WHEELER, NEIL
Born: 1905. Died: Sept. 13, 1978, Woodland Hills, Calif. Screen actor, assistant film director, writer and stuntman.

WHEELER, TERESA (aka CABARET TESS)
Died: Dec. 26, 1975. Screen and vaudeville actress. Appeared in silent films.

WHEELOCK, CHARLES
Born: 1875, Boston, Mass. Died: May 25, 1948. Screen actor. Appeared in Lubin and Selig Film Companies films.

Appeared in: **1921** Scrap Iron. **1922** The Little Minister.

WHELAN, ALBERT (Albert Waxman)
Born: May 5, 1875, Melbourne, Australia. Died: Feb. 19, 1961, London, England. Screen, stage actor and comedian.

Appeared in: **1930** The Man from Chicago (US 1931). **1935** Dance Band. **1943** Candlelight in Algeria (US 1944).

WHELAN, HAZEL
Died: June 22, 1937, East Orange, N.J. Screen actress. Appeared in Mack Sennett Films.

WHELAN, LEO M.
Born: 1876, Bridgeport, Conn. Died: Oct. 15, 1952, Arlington, N.J. Silent screen and vaudeville actor. Appeared in vaudeville with memebers of his family in an act billed as "Four Happy Whelans."

WHELAN, RON
Born: 1905, England. Died: Dec. 8, 1965, Los Angeles, Calif. (leukemia). Screen, stage actor and film director.

Appeared in: **1937** Wild Innocence. **1950** Massacre Hill. **1953** Kangaroo. **1963** Gun Hawk; The Three Stooges Go Around the World in A Daze. **1965** Greatest Story Ever Told.

WHELAN, TIM
Born: Nov. 2, 1893, Ind. Died: Aug. 12, 1957, Beverly Hills, Calif. Screen, stage actor, film director, film producer and screenwriter. Entered films as an actor in 1922.

WHELAR, LANGOIS M.
Born: 1898. Died: Oct. 17, 1918, France. Screen actor.

WHIFFEN, MRS. THOMAS (Blanche Galton)
Born: Mar. 12, 1845, London, England. Died: Nov. 26, 1936, Montvale, Va. Screen, stage actress and opera performer.

Appeared in: **1915** Barbara Frietchie.

WHIPLASH MONTANA
Died: Apr. 9, 1977. Screen actor.

WHIPPER, LEIGH, SR. (aka LEE WHIPPER)
Born: 1877, Charleston, S.C. Died: July 26, 1975, Harlem, N.Y. Black screen, stage and television actor.

Appeared in: **1939** Of Mice and Men. **1941** Robin Hood of the Pecos; Virginia; King of the Zombies; Bahama Passage; The Vanishing Virginian. **1942** White Cargo; Heart of the Golden West. **1943** Happy Land; Mission to Moscow; The Oxbow Incident. **1944** The Imposter. **1946** Undercurrent. **1947** Untamed Fury (narration). **1949** Lost Boundaries. **1955** The Shrike. **1956** The Harder They Fall. **1957** The Young Don't Cry. **1958** Marjorie Morningstar.

WHISTLER, EDNA
Born: 1886. Died: July 11, 1934, New York, N.Y. Screen actress.

Appeared in: **1917** A Hungry Heart.

WHISTLER, MARGARET
Born: 1892. Died: Aug. 23, 1939, Hollywood, Calif. Screen actress.

WHITAKER, CHARLES "SLIM" (Charles Orbie Whitaker)
Born: July 29, 1893. Died: June 27, 1960 (heart attack). Screen actor. Do not confuse with screenwriter Charles E. Whittaker.

Appeared in: **1925** Galloping On; On the Go; Hurricane Horseman; Tearin' Loose. **1926** Ace of Action; The Bandit Buster; The Bonanza Buckaroo; The Fighting Cheat; Rawhide; Trumpin' Trouble; Twin Triggers. **1927** The Desert of the Lost; The Ridin' Rowdy; Soda Water Cowboy; The Obligin' Buckaroo; The Phantom Buster. **1928** The Canyon of Adventure; The Flying Buckaroo; Desperate Courage; Saddle Mates. **1930** Shadow Ranch; Dawn Trail. **1931** Rider of the Plains; Desert Vengeance. **1932** The Man from New Mexico. **1933** Drum Taps; Deadwood Pass; Smoking Guns; Dawn Trail. **1934** The Law of the Wild (serial); Man From Hell; Terror on the Plains. **1935** Unconquered Bandit; Rustlers' Paradise; Tumbling Tumbleweeds. **1936** Ghost Patrol; Riding. **1937** Melody of the Plains. **1938** Rawhide; Frontier Scout; Under Western Stars. **1939** Rollin' Westward; Legion of the Lawless; New Frontier. **1940** Bullet Code; Prairie Law; Marshal of Mesa City; Legion of the Lawless. **1941** Along the Rio Grande; Arizona Bound; Cyclone on Horseback. **1942** The Mad Monster; The Silver Bullet; Billy the Kid's Smoking Guns. **1943** The Mysterious Rider; The Kid Rides Again; Fighting Frontier. **1944** The Laramie Trail; The Drifter; Oklahoma Raiders; Marshal of Gunsmoke. **1946** Overland Riders; Outlaw of the Plains; Panhandle Trail; Law of the Lash. **1948** The Westward Trail.

WHITBECK, FRANK
Born: 1882, Rochester, N.Y. Died: Dec. 23, 1963. Film director, screen actor, publicist and screenwriter. Narrated numerous MGM trailers.

WHITCOMB, BARRY
Born: 1872, Australia. Died: Oct. 25, 1928. Screen and stage actor.

Appeared in: **1915** My Madonna; The Vampire. **1916** The Serpent; Hypocrites; Who's Guilty. **1917** The Undying Flame; Barbary Sheep; The Deemster; Common Law; Magda; Maid of Belgium; Little Duchess. **1918** Wasp; Eye for Eve. **1919** Bolshevism on Trial; The Battler; Out of the Fog (aka 'Ception Shoals).

WHITE, ALFRED H. (Alfred Weisman)
Born: 1883. Died: Aug. 22, 1972, Fort Lauderdale, Fla. Stage, vaudeville and screen actor.

Appeared in: **1933** Don't Bet on Love.

WHITE, ARTHUR
Born: 1882, England. Died: 1957, England? Screen and stage actor. Do not confuse with actor Artie (Arthur) White.

Appeared in: **1913** The Pickwick Papers (series).

WHITE, BILL (William A. Rattenberry)
Born: 1857. Died: Apr. 21, 1933, Los Angeles, Calif. (heart attack). Screen and stage actor.

Appeared in: **1921** A Motion to Adjourn. **1922** Two-Fisted Jefferson; The Sheriff of Sun-Dog. **1923** The Fighting Skipper (serial); At Devil's Gorge; The Devil's Dooryard. **1924** Western Yesterdays; Western Feuds.

WHITE, CAROLINA
Born: 1886, Boston, Mass. Died: Oct. 5, 1961, Rome, Italy. Screen actress and opera singer.

Appeared in: **1918** My Cousin.

WHITE, DAN (Daniel M. White)
Died: July 7, 1980. Screen actor.

Appeared in: **1939** In Old Monterey. **1943** False Colors. **1944** Voodoo Man; Arizona Trail; The Utah Kid; Boss of Rawhide; Arizona Whirlwind; Crazy Knights. **1945** San Antonio. **1946** Gun Town; The Yearling. **1948** I Wouldn't Be in Your Shoes; Four Faces West; Albuquerque; Shaggy; When My Baby Smiles at Me; Gunning for Justice; Sunset Carson Rides Again. **1949** Cover Up; Outlaw Country; Roseanna McCoy; Unknown Island. **1951** His Kind of Woman; Rawhide; Drums in the Deep South; Red Mountain. **1953** Inferno; Silver Whip. **1955** The Road to Denver; The Americano; The Tall Men. **1956** Great Day in the Morning; The First Traveling Saleslady; The Rainmaker. **1957** The Lonely Man. **1958** Gunfire at Indian Gap; Quantrill's Raiders; Escape From Red Rock. **1959** This Earth Is Mine; Frontier Gun; The Giant Leeches. **1960** Ma Barker's Killer Brood. **1961** The Sergeant Was a Lady. **1965** The Bounty Killer. **1966** Jesse James Meets Frankenstein's Daughter. **1967** The Fastest Guitar Alive.

WHITE, EDWARD J. (Edward Jocelyn White)
Born: Mar. 15, 1902, New York, N.Y. Died: Sept. 24, 1973, Culver City, Calif. Film, television producer and screen actor.

WHITE, FRANCES
Born: 1898. Died: Feb. 24, 1969, Los Angeles, Calif. Singer and screen actress. Was a Ziegfeld Follies girl. Divorced from actor Frank Fay (dec. 1961).

Appeared in: **1922** Face to Face. **1934** The Mighty Barnum. **1936** The Great Ziegfeld.

WHITE, GEORGE
Born: 1890, Toronto, Ontario, Canada. Died: Oct. 11, 1968, Los Angeles, Calif. (leukemia). Stage, film producer, stage, film director, screen and stage actor.

Appeared in: **1920** Scandals. **1930** Scandals. **1934** George White's Scandals of 1934. **1935** George White's 1935 Scandals. **1946** Rhapsody in Blue.

WHITE, HUGH "HUEY"
Born: 1896. Died: June 23, 1938, Hollywood, Calif. (injuries from auto accident). Screen and stage actor.

Appeared in: **1931** Hush Money. **1933** Female; Convention City. **1934** The Thin Man; Gambling Lady; The Hell Cat; The Million Dollar Ransom. **1935** She Gets Her Man; Special Agent; Dr. Socrates; G-Men. **1936** Crash Donovan. **1938** When G-Men Step In.

WHITE, J. FISHER
Born: May 1, 1865, Bristol, England. Died: Jan. 14, 1945, England? Screen and stage actor.

Appeared in: **1892** Hamlet. **1918** God Bless Our Red White and Blue. **1919** Damaged Goods; Nobody's Child. **1921** The Will. **1922** Bentley's Conscience; Diana of the Crossways. **1924** Owd Bob. **1925** Somebody's Darling. **1926** One Colombo Night; Thou Fool; Island of Despair; Blinkeyes. **1927** The Fake. **1928** City of Youth; The Triumph of the Scarlet Pimpernel (aka The Scarlet Daredevil—US 1929); Balaclava (aka Jaws of Hell—US 1931). **1929** The Last Post; The Lily of Killarney. **1930** Loose Ends. **1931** Dreyfus (aka The Dreyfus Case—US); Man of Mayfair. **1932** Betrayal. **1934** A Cup of Kindness. **1935** Turn of the Tide. **1936** As You Like It. **1937** Moonlight Sonata (US 1938); Dreaming Lips. **1943** The Charmer (reissue of Moonlight Sonata, 1937).

WHITE, J. IRVING
Born: 1865. Died: Apr. 17, 1944, Los Angeles, Calif. Screen and stage actor.

Appeared in: **1930** The Spoilers; Girl of the Golden West. **1932** Sign of the Cross (and revised version made in 1944).

WHITE, JACQUELINE
Died: June 21, 1964 (auto accident). Screen actress.

Appeared in: **1943** Air Raid Wardens; Swing Shift Maisie; Song of Russia. **1944** Dark Shadows (short). **1946** The Show-Off. **1947** Crossfire; Banjo; Seven Keys to Baldpate; Night Song. **1948** Return of the Badmen; Mystery in Mexico. **1949** Riders of the Range. **1950** The Capture. **1952** The Narrow Margin.

WHITE, JOHNSTONE
Died: Apr. 7, 1969. Screen actor.

Appeared in: **1935** Get That Man. **1937** Tough to Handle; Anything for a Thrill. **1941** Desperate Cargo. **1948** Shed No Tears. **1954** Knock on Wood. **1955** You're Never Too Young. **1956** The Scarlet Hour; Pardners. **1958** Home Before Dark.

WHITE, LEE ROY "LASSES"
Born: Aug. 28, 1888, Wills Point, Tex. Died: Dec. 16, 1949, Hollywood, Calif. Screen, stage, vaudeville, minstrel and radio actor. Entered films in 1938.

Appeared in: **1939** Rovin' Tumbleweeds. **1940** Oklahoma Renegades; Grandpa Goes to Town. **1941** Scattergood Pulls the Strings; Dude Cowboy; Riding the Wind; The Bandit Trail; Come On, Danger!; Sergeant York; Scattergood Baines; Thundering Hoofs; The Roundup; Cyclone on Horseback. **1942** Talk of the Town. **1943** Cinderella Swings It!; The Unknown Guest; Something to Shout About; The Outlaw. **1944** The Minstrel Man; The Adventures of Mark Twain; Alaska; When Strangers Marry; Song of the Range. **1945** Red Rock Outlaws; In Old Mexico; The Lonesome Trail; Saddle Serenade; Springtime in Texas; Three's a Crowd; Dillinger. **1946** Moon Over Montana; Trail to Mexico; West of the Alamo. **1947** Rainbow Over the Rookies; Six Gun Serenade; Song of the Sierras; Louisiana; The Wistful Widow of Wagon Gap. **1948** The Dude Goes West; The Golden Eye; Indian Agent; The Valiant Hombre. **1949** Mississippi Rhythm. **1950** The Texan Meets Calamity Jane.

WHITE, LEO
Born: 1880, Manchester, England. Died: Sept. 21, 1948, Hollywood, Calif. Stage and screen actor. Entered films with Essanay Co. in 1914. Appeared in early Charlie Chaplin comedies.

Appeared in: **1914** "Swedie" series. **1921** Keeping Up With Lizzie; The Rookie's Return; Her Sturdy Oak; The Rage of Paris. **1922** Blood and Sand; Headin' West; Fools First. **1923** Breaking Into Society; The Rustle of Silk; Why Worry?; In Search of a Thrill; Vanity Fair. **1924** The Brass Bowl; When a Girl Loves; The Woman on the Jury; Wine; A Lady of Quality; Sporting Youth; The Goldfish. **1925** Ben-Hur; The Masked Bride; One Year to Live; American Pluck; The Lady Who Lied. **1926** Devil's Island; The Lady of The Harem; The Blonde Saint; The Truthful Sex; A Desperate Moment; The Far Cry. **1927** See You in Jail; Beauty Shoppers; The Girl from Gay Paree; The Slaver; A Bowery Cinderella; McFadden's Flats; The Ladybird. **1928** Breed of the Sunsets; What Price Beauty?; Thunder Riders; How to Handle Women; Manhattan Knights. **1929** Campus Knights; Smilin' Guns; Born to the Saddle. **1930** The Jade Box (serial); Roaring Ranch. **1931** Along Came Youth; Monkey Business. **1932** Jewel Robbery. **1933** The Kennel Murder Case; Only Yesterday. **1934** Madame Du Barry; Done in Oil (short); Here Comes the Navy; The Thin Man. **1935** Gold Diggers of 1935; Pop Goes the Easel (short); All the King's Horses; A Night at the Opera. **1936** Cain and Mabel. **1937** Tovarich. **1940** The Great Dictator. **1942** Gentleman Jim. **1944** Arsenic and Old Lace. **1946** A Stolen Life; So You Want to Play the Horses (short). **1947** My Wild Irish Rose. **1948** Silver River. **1949** The Fountainhead.

WHITE, MADGE
Born: England. Died: 1978, England? Screen and stage actress.

Appeared in: **1920** Bars of Iron (US 1921). **1921** The Place of Honor. **1922** The Eleventh Hour.

WHITE, MARJORIE (aka MARJORIE TIERNEY)
Born: July 22, 1908, Winnipeg, Canada. Died: Aug. 20, 1935, Los Angeles, Calif. (auto accident). Screen, stage and vaudeville actress. Married to actor Eddie Tierney with whom she appeared in vaudeville. Entered films in 1929.

Appeared in: **1929** Happy Days; Sunny Side Up. **1930** Oh, for a Man!; The Golden Calf; Fox Movietone Follies of 1930; Just Imagine. **1931-32** "Voice of Hollywood" series. **1931** Women of All Nations; Charlie Chan Carries On; The Black Camel; Possessed. **1933** Diplomaniacs; Her Bodyguard. **1934** Woman Haters (short).

WHITE, NORMAN A.
Born: 1935. Died: Aug. 20, 1981, Utah (results of an auto accident). Professional race car driver, stuntman and screen actor.

WHITE, PEARL
Born: Mar. 4, 1889, 1893 or 1897?, Green Ridge, Mo. Died: Aug. 4, 1938, Paris, France (liver ailment). Screen and stage actress. Divorced from actor Wallace McCutcheon (dec. 1928).

Appeared in: **1911** Through the Window; Helping Him Out; The Power of Love; The Lost Necklace. **1912** Mayblossom; Her Dressmaker's Bills; The Gypsy Flirt; Locked Out; A Tangled Marriage; His Birthday; The Girl in the Next Room. **1913** Where Charity Begins; Hearts Entangled; Pearl's Mistake; Dress Reform; The Woman and the Law; Robert's Lesson; Girls Will Be Boys; His Rich Uncle; Hubby's New Coat; A Woman's Revenge; Pearl's Hero; The Cabaret Singer; The Convict's Daughter. **1914** Exploits of Elaine (serial); The Perils of Pauline (serial). **1915** The New Exploits of Elaine (serial); The Romance of Elaine (serial). **1916** Hazel Kirke; The Iron Claw (serial); Pearl of the Army (serial). **1917** The Fatal Ring (serial). **1919** The Black Street (serial); The Lightning Raider (serial). **1920** The White Moll. **1921** Know Your Men; A Virgin Paradise; Tiger's Cub; The Thief; The Mountain Women; Beyond Price. **1922** Without Fear; The Breadway Peacock; Any Wife. **1923** Plunder (serial). **1924** Parisian Nights. **1925** Perils of Paris. **1961** Days of Thrills and Laughter (documentary).

WHITE, RAYMOND
Died: Jan., 1934, Los Angeles, Calif. Screen actor.

WHITE, RUTH
Born: 1914, Perth Amboy, N.J. Died: Dec. 3, 1969, Perth Amboy, N.J. (cancer). Screen, stage and television actress.

Appeared in: **1956** Rumpus in the Harem (short). **1957** Muscle up a Little Closer (short); A Merry Mix-Up (short); Edge of the City. **1959** The Nun's Story. **1962** To Kill a Mockingbird. **1965** A Rage to Live; Baby, the Rain Must Fall. **1966** Cast a Giant Shadow. **1967** The Tiger Makes Out; Up the Down Staircase; Hang 'Em High; No Way to Treat a Lady; Charley. **1968** A Lovely Way to Die. **1969** Midnight Cowboy; The Reivers. **1971** The Pursuit of Happiness.

WHITE, SAMMY
Born: May 28, 1896, Providence, R.I. Died: Mar. 3, 1960, Beverly Hills, Calif. Screen, stage, vaudeville and television actor. First teamed in vaudeville with Lou Clayton and later with his wife Eva Puck (later divorced).

Appeared in: **1936** Show Boat; Cain and Mabel. **1937** The Hit Parade. **1938** Swing Your Lady. **1950** 711 Ocean Drive. **1951** Half Breed. **1952** Pat and Mike. **1953** Remains to Be Seen; The Bad and the Beautiful. **1954** About Mrs. Leslie; Living It Up. **1956** Somebody up There Likes Me. **1957** The Helen Morgan Story.

WHITE, SHIRLEY
Born: 1937. Died: May 11, 1976, Whittier, Calif. (cancer). Screen and stage actress.

Appeared in: **1968** Of the Same Gender.

WHITE, VALERIE
Born: 1915, South Africa. Died: Dec. 3, 1975, London, England. Stage and screen actress.

Appeared in: **1944** The Halfway House (US 1945). **1947** Hue and Cry (US 1950).

WHITEFORD, JOHN P. "BLACKIE"
Born: 1873. Died: Mar. 21, 1962, Hollywood, Calif. Screen actor.

Appeared in: **1929** The Hoose Gow (short). **1931** Cyclone Kid. **1932** Shopping With Wifie; Mark of the Spur; Scarlet Brand; Man from New Mexico. **1933** Deadwood Pass. **1934** West of the Divide; Demon for Trouble. **1935** Toll of the Desert; Captain Blood. **1936** The Black Coin (serial); Share the Wealth (short); Peppery Salt (short); The Last of the Warrens; Pardon Us; Grips, Grunts and Groans (short). **1940** Brigham Young—Frontiersman. **1945** Rough, Tough and Ready. **1946** Uncivil Warbirds (short); Three Troubledoers (short); Two Years Before the Mast. **1947** The Last Round-Up. **1949** Rope of Sand. **1950** Marianted Mariner (short); Cow Town.

WHITEHEAD, CLARENCE EUGENE
Born: 1871, Marengo, Iowa. Died: Dec. 18, 1932, New York, N.Y. Opera singer and screen actor.

WHITELAW, BARRETT
Born: c. 1897. Died: Oct. 3, 1947, Los Angeles, Calif. (cerebral hemorrhage). Screen actor and extra.

Appeared in: **1946** The Kid from Brooklyn.

WHITEMAN, PAUL
Born: 1890, Denver, Colo. Died: Dec. 29, 1967, Doylestown, Pa. (heart attack). Bandleader, screen, stage, radio actor and composer.

Appeared in: **1924** Broadway After Dark. **1930** King of Jazz. **1935** Thanks a Million. **1940** Strike Up the Band. **1944** Atlantic City. **1945** Rhapsody in Blue. **1947** The Fabulous Dorseys.

WHITESIDE, WALKER
Born: 1869, Logansport, Ind. Died: Aug. 18, 1942, Hastings-on-Hudson, N.Y. Screen, stage actor, stage producer and playwright.

Appeared in: **1915** The Melting Pot.

WHITFIELD, JORDAN
Born: 1917, Pittsburgh, Pa. Died: Nov. 11, 1967, Hollywood, Calif. (heart attack). Black screen and television actor.

Appeared in: **1938** You Can't Take It With You. **1946** Swamp Fire; Three Little Girls in Blue. **1948** Another Part of the Forest. **1950** Right Cross. **1954** Carmen Jones. **1958** The Cry Baby Killer. **1965** That Funny Feeling.

WHITFIELD, DR. WALTER W.
Born: 1888. Died: Jan. 13, 1966, Cleveland, Ohio. Black screen, stage actor, singer and dentist. Sang background music for films.

Appeared in: **1936** Green Pastures (stage and film versions).

WHITFORD, ANNABELLE See "PEERLESS ANNABELLE"

WHITING, JACK
Born: June 22, 1901, Philadelphia, Pa. Died: Feb. 15, 1961, N.Y. Screen, stage and vaudeville actor.

Appeared in: **1930** Top Speed (film debut); College Lovers; The Life of the Party. **1933** Take a Chance. **1935** Broadway Brevities (short). **1938** Sailing Along; Give Me a Sailor.

WHITLEY, CRANE (Clem Wilenchick)
Died: Feb. 28, 1958. Screen actor.

Appeared in: **1938** The Last Warning. **1939** Beasts of Berlin; The Flying Deuces. **1942** My Favorite Blonde; Who Done It?; They Raid by Night; Spy Smasher (serial). **1943** Hitler's Children; Girls in Chains. **1944** Enemy of Women; Captain America (serial); The Tiger Woman (serial); Till We Meet Again; The Princess and the Pirate; To Have and Have Not. **1945** Counter-Attack; The Affairs of Susan; The Lost Weekend; You Came Along. **1946** The Wife of Monte Cristo; Night and Day; California; Two Years Before the Mast. **1947** Variety Girl; Brute Force; Pursued; The Return of Monte Cristo. **1948** Walk a Crooked Mile. **1949** Outpost in Morocco; The Crooked Way; The Crime Doctor's Diary; Shockproof. **1950** The Savage Horde. **1951** Insurance Investigator; Red Mountain. **1952** The Big Sky; Mutiny. **1953** Treasure of the Golden Condor.

WHITLEY, RAY
Born: 1902, Atlanta, Ga. Died: Feb. 21, 1979, Mexico. Screen, radio, television actor, singer and composer.

Appeared in: **1936** Hopalong Cassidy Returns (film debut). **1938** Gun Law; Painted Desert. **1939** The Renegade Ranger; Racketeers of the Range; Cupid Rides the Range (short). **1940** Wagon Train. **1941** Along the Rio Grande; Riding the Wind; The Bandit Trail; Dude Cowboy; Come on Danger; Land of the Open Range; Thundering Hoofs; Cyclone on Horseback; Robbers of the Range. **1944** Riders of the Santa Fe; Trail to Gunsight; Boss of Boomtown; The Old Texas Trail. **1946** West of the Alamo. **1956** Giant.

WHITLING, TOWNSEND
Born: Oct. 21, 1869, Oxford, England. Died: June 24, 1952, England? Screen and stage actor.

Appeared in: **1948** Blanche Fury.

WHITLOCK, T. LLOYD
Born: Jan. 2, 1891, Springfield, Mo. Died: Jan. 8, 1966. Screen and stage actor.

Appeared in: **1916** The Masked Woman; The Diamond Lure; The Shadow Sinister. **1917** June Madness; The Man Who Took a Chance; The College Boys' Special; A Daughter of Daring (serial); The Edge of the Law (aka A Gentle Ill Wind). **1919** The Love Call; The Boomerang. **1920** Rouge and Riches; Scratch My Back. **1921** Courage; Face of the World; False Kisses; The Love Special; Not Guilty; One Man in a Million; A Private Scandal; See My Lawyer; They Shall Pay; White and Unmarried. **1922** Domestic Relations; The Flirt; The Girl Who Ran Wild; Kissed; The Ninety and Nine; The Snowshoe Trail; The Truthful Liar; Wild Honey. **1923** Cordelia the Magnificent; The Man Who Won; An Old Sweetheart of Mine; Slippy McGee; The Thrill Chaser; When Odds are Even; The Woman of Bronze. **1924** The Foolish Virgin; The Midnight Express; The Price She Paid; The Triflers; Unmarried Wives; Women First. **1925** The Air Mail; Dollar Down; The Ancient Highway; The Great Sensation; The Prairie Pirate; New Champion; Speed Mad; Who Cares. **1926** The Fighting Buckaroo; The Man in the Saddle; Paradise; Peril of the Rail; Sparrows. **1927** A Hero for a Night; On the Stroke of Twelve; The Perfect Sap; Poor Girls; Pretty Clothes; The Thirteenth Juror; The War Horse. **1928** Hot Wheels; Man from Headquarters; The Michigan Kid; Queen of the Chorus; House of Shame. **1929** The Kid's Clever; The Leatherneck; One Hysterical Night; Skinner Steps Out; The Fatal Warning (serial). **1930** The Cohens and Kellys in Africa; The Cohens and the Kellys in Scotland; See America Thirst; Young Eagles. **1931** Honeymoon Lane. **1932** The Hurricane Express (serial); The Shadow of the Eagle (serial); Tangled Destinies. **1933** Whispering Shadows (serial). **1934** Burn 'Em Up Barnes (serial); The Lost Jungle (serial). **1935** Behind the Green Lights. **1936** Robinson Crusoe of Clipper Island (serial); Undersea Kingdom (serial); Night Cargo; Navy Born; The Dark House; Ride, Ranger, Ride. **1938** Arson Gang Busters; International Crime.

WHITMAN, ERNEST
Born: 1893. Died: Aug. 5, 1954, Hollywood, Calif. (heart attack). Black screen, radio and television actor. Known as Bill Jackson on radio and television "Beulah" shows.

Appeared in: **1936** The Prisoner of Shark Island; White Hunter; The Green Pastures. **1937** Daughter of Shanghai. **1939** Jesse James. **1940** Congo Maisie; Maryland; The Return of Frank James; Third Finger, Left Hand. **1941** The Get-Away; The Pittsburgh Kid; Among the Living. **1942** The Bugle Sounds; Drums of the Congo. **1943** Cabin in the Sky; Stormy Weather. **1947** My Brother Talks to Horses; Blonde Savage.

WHITMAN, ESTELLE
Died: July 14, 1970, Los Angeles, Calif. Screen actress. Entered films with Triangle Films during silents.

WHITMAN, GAYNE (aka ALFRED VOSBURGH)
Born: Mar. 19, 1890, Chicago, Ill. Died: Aug. 31, 1958, Hollywood, Calif. (heart attack). Screen, stage, radio, television actor and screenwriter. Was radio's original "Chandu, the Magician.".

Appeared in: **1925** The Wife Who Wasn't Wanted; His Majesty, Bunker Bean; The Love Hour; The Pleasure Buyers. **1926** Exclusive Rights; Three Weeks in Paris; Oh, What a Nurse!; Hell Bent for Heaven; The Love Toy; The Night Cry; Sunshine of Paradise Alley; A Woman's Heart; A Woman of the Sea; His Jazz Bride. **1927** Backstage; Wolves of the Air; The Woman on Trial; Stolen Pleasures; Too Many Crooks; In the First Degree. **1928** The Adventurer; Sailors' Wives. **1929** Lucky Boy. **1930** Reno. **1931** Finger Prints (serial). **1935** Little America (narr.); Wings Over Ethiopia (narr.). **1940** Adventures of Red Ryder (serial); Misbehaving Husbands. **1941** Parachute Battalion. **1942** Tennessee Johnson; Phantom Killer. **1944** My Gal Loves Music. **1949** The Sickle or the Cross. **1952** Strange Fascination; Big Jim McLain. **1953** Dangerous Crossing; One Girl's Confession.

WHITMAN, WALT
Born: 1868. Died: Mar. 27, 1928, Santa Monica, Calif. Screen and stage actor.

Appeared in: **1918** The Heart of Humanity. **1920** Mark of Zorro. **1921** The Three Musketeers; His Nibs; The Home Stretch; The New Disciple; Mysterious Rider; The Girl from God's Country. **1922** The Fire Bride; A Question of Honor; The Girl from Rocky Point. **1923** Hearts Aflame; Long Live the King; The Grub Stake; The Love Letter; Wasted Lives. **1924** Missing Daughters.

WHITNEY, CLAIRE
Born: 1890. Died: Aug. 27, 1969, Sylmar, Calif. Screen actress. Married to actor Robert Emmett Keane (dec. 1981).

Appeared in: **1914** Life's Shop Window. **1915** The Nigger; The Galley Slave. **1916** Easy Lynne; Under Two Flags. **1917** Heart and Soul; Camille. **1918** Kaiser's Finish. **1919** The Isle of Conquest. **1921** Fine Feathers; The Leech; The Passionate Pilgrim. **1926** The Great Gatsby. **1928** Innocent Love. **1929** Gossip (short); Room 909 (short). **1931** The Iron Man; A Free Soul. **1934** Enlighten Thy Daughter. **1939** Three Smart Girls Grow Up; When Tomorrow Comes; Laugh It Off. **1940** Chip of the Flying U. **1941** In the Navy. **1942** The Silver Bullet; Silver Queen; Frisco Lil; Behind the Eight Ball. **1943** Tender Comrade; Wintertime. **1944** When Strangers Marry; Hat Check Money; Moon Over Las Vegas; The Mummy's Ghost. **1945** She Gets Her Man; Under Western Skies; G.I. Honeymoon; A Guy, a Gal and a Pal; The Affairs of Susan. **1946** Smooth as Silk. **1947** Christmas Eve. **1949** Dancing in the Dark; Frontier Investigator; An Old Fashioned Girl; Roaring Westward.

WHITNEY, PETER (Peter King Engle)
Born: 1916, Long Branch, N.J. Died: Mar. 30, 1972, Santa Barbara, Calif. (heart attack). Screen, stage and television actor.

Appeared in: **1941** Underground; Blues in the Night; 9 Lives Are Not Enough. **1942** Rio Rita; Valley of the Sun; Spy Ship; Whistling in Dixie; Busses Roar. **1943** Action in the North Atlantic; Destination Tokyo; Reunion in France. **1944** Mr. Skeffington. **1945** Bring on the Girls; Murder, He Says; Hotel Berlin. **1946** Blonde Alibi; The Notorious Lone Wolf; The Brute Man; Three Strangers. **1947** Violence; Northwest Outpost. **1948** The Iron Curtain. **1953** All the Brothers Were Valiant; The Big Heat; The Great Sioux Uprising. **1954** The Black Dakotas; Day of Triumph; Gorilla at Large. **1955** The Sea Chase; The Last Frontier. **1956** Man from Del Rio; Great Day in the Morning; The Cruel Tower. **1957** Domino Kid. **1958** Buchanan Rides Alone. **1962** The Wonderful World of the Brothers Grimm. **1965** The Sword of Ali Baba. **1967** In the Heat of the Night. **1968** Chubasco. **1969** The Great Bank Robbery. **1970** The Ballad of Cable Hogue.

WHITNEY, RALPH
Born: 1874. Died: June 14, 1928, Los Angeles, Calif. (injuries from fall). Screen actor and stuntman.

WHITNEY, ROBERT, II
Born: 1945, Los Angeles, Calif. Died: Jan. 6, 1969, Los Angeles, Calif. Screen actor. Entered films approx. 1963.

WHITNEY, WENDY (Wanda Krol)
Born: 1923. Died: Dec. 27, 1978, Lima, Peru (murdered—stabbed). Screen and stage actress.

WHITSON, FRANK
Born: 1876, New York, N.Y. Died: Mar. 19, 1946. Screen, stage and vaudeville actor.

Appeared in: **1916** The Mark of Cain; The Isle of Life; The Price of Silence. **1917** The Clock; Sudden Jim; The Woman Who Would Not Pay. **1921** Gilded Lies; The Adventures of Tarzan (serial). **1922** Fortune's Mask; Headin' West; The Man from Hell's River. **1923** The Bolted Door; Flames of Passion; Tango Cavalier; The Way of the Transgressor. **1924** Captain Blood; $50,000 Reward; Her Man; Racing for Life; The Valley of Hate; The White Panther. **1925** Fighting Courage. **1926** Bad Man's Bluff; The Fighting Boob; Walloping Kid. **1927** Hidden Aces. **1928** The Texas Tornado.

WHITTELL, JOSEPHINE
Born: San Francisco, Calif. Died: June 1, 1961, Hollywood, Calif. Screen and stage actress. Divorced from actor Robert Warwick (dec. 1964).

Appeared in: **1919** The Climbers. **1921** The Inner Chamber. **1931** False Roomers (short); Caught Plastered (short); Peach O' Reno. **1932** Symphony of Six Million; What Price Hollywood? **1933** Infernal Machine; Zoo in Budapest; Baby Face. **1934** Jealousy; The Life of Vergie Winters; Servants' Entrance; Love Time. **1935** It's a Gift; Shanghai. **1936** Follow Your Heart. **1937** Hotel Haywire; Larceny on the Air; Beware of Ladies; Double Wedding. **1938** Women are Like That. **1939** The Women. **1940** Kiddie Cure (short). **1941** Glamour Boy; Unfinished Business; Design for Scandal. **1942** The Magnificent Dope. **1944** Standing Room Only. **1945** State Fair; The Enchanted Cottage. **1946** The Virginian; Easy to Wed. **1947** Song of Love. **1948** An Act of Murder; Sitting Pretty. **1949** Adventure in Baltimore; The Fountainhead. **1951** Molly; A Place in the Sun. **1952** The Greatest Show on Earth. **1954** Forever Female.

WHITTEN, WILL
Born: 1924. Died: June 27, 1977. Screen actor and radio announcer.

Appeared in: **1975** The Legendary Curse of Lemora.

WHITTINGTON, MARGERY
Born: 1904. Died: Oct. 13, 1957. Screen actress.

Appeared in: **1925** Stagestruck.

WHITTY, DAME MAY
Born: June 19, 1865, Liverpool, England. Died: May 29, 1948, Beverly Hills, Calif. Screen and stage actress. Was made Dame Commander of the Order of the British Empire in 1918. Married to actor Ben Webster (dec. 1947). Mother of actress Margaret Webster (dec. 1973). Nominated for 1937 Academy Award for Best Supporting Actress in Night Must Fall and in 1942 for Mrs. Miniver.

Appeared in: **1914** Enoch Arden. **1915** The Little Minister. **1920** Colonel Newcome, the Perfect Gentleman. **1937** Night Must Fall; Thirteenth Chair; Conquest (aka Marie Walewska). **1938** The Lady Vanishes; I Met My Love Again. **1939** Raffles. **1940** Return to Yesterday; A Bill of Divorcement. **1941** Suspicion; One Night in Lisbon. **1942** Mrs. Miniver; Thunder Birds. **1943** Madame Curie; Slightly Dangerous; Crash Dive; Flesh and Fantasy; Lassie Come Home; Stage Door Canteen. **1944** The White Cliffs of Dover; Gaslight. **1945** My Name Is Julia Ross. **1946** Devotion. **1947** This Time for Keeps; If Winter Comes; Green Dolphin Street. **1948** The Return of October; The Sign of the Ram.

WHORF, RICHARD
Born: 1906, Winthrop, Mass. Died: Dec. 14, 1966, Santa Monica, Calif. (heart attack). Screen, stage actor, film and television director and television producer.

Appeared in: **1934** Midnight. **1941** Blues in the Night. **1942** Juke Girl; Yankee Doodle Dandy. **1943** Keeper of the Flame; Assignment in Brittany; The Cross of Lorraine. **1944** The Imposter; Christmas Holiday; Stange Confession. **1945** Champion of Champions; The Hidden Eye. **1947** Love from a Stranger; Call It Murder (reissue and retitle of Midnight—1934). **1948** Luxury Liner. **1950** Champagne for Caesar; Chain Lightning. **1951** The Groom Wore Spurs. **1954** Autumn Fever.

WICHART, LITA BELLE
Born: 1907. Died: Jan. 24, 1929, near Newhall, Calif. (attempting parachute jump from plane). Screen stunt double. Married to stuntman Floyd Bowman.

Appeared in: **1929** Winged Horseman (died while filming).

WICHMANN, JOHANNA
Born: 1926, Germany. Died: June 26, 1980, Frankfurt, West Germany. Screen and stage actress.

WICKES, IRVING ARTHUR
Born: 1907. Died: July, 1969, Dorchester, Mass. (cancer). Screen actor.

Appeared in: **1939** Drums Along the Mohawk; Young Mr. Lincoln. **1940** The Grapes of Wrath.

WICKLAND, LARRY
Born: June 28, 1898, Kansas City, Mo. Died: Apr. 18, 1938, Los Angeles, Calif. Screen actor, film director and screenwriter. Appeared in early Universal Jesse Lasky Feature Play Company and DeMille productions.

Appeared in: **1916** Trail of the Lonesome Pine.

WICKS, JOHN (John Daggett Wicks)
Born: May 17, 1884, Bay Shore, N.Y. Died: June 24, 1935, Culver City, Calif. (heart attack). Screen, stage and vaudeville actor.

WIDOM, LEONARD "BUD"
Born: 1919. Died: Apr. 18, 1976, Los Angeles, Calif. Screen actor, radio producer and announcer.

Appeared in: **1968** Gammo Sango uchu Daisakusen (The Green Slime—US 1969).

WIEMAN, MATHIAS
Born: 1902, Osnabrueck, Germany. Died: Dec. 3, 1969, Zurich, Switzerland. Screen and stage actor.

Appeared in: **1926** Potsdam, das Schicksal Einer Residenz. **1927** Feme; Der Fidele Bauer; Mata Hati; Koenigin Luise (Queen Luise); Der Sohn der Hagar (Out of the Mist). **1928** Die Durchgaengerin; Unter der Laterne; Tagebuch Einer Kokotte. **1929** Das Land ohne Frauen. **1930** Stuerme Ueber dem Montblanc (aka Avalanche—US 1932); Rosenmontag (Rose Monday—US 1932). **1931** Zum Goldenen Anker.

1932 Mensch ohne Namen (Man Without a Name); Die Graeffin von Monte Christo (The Countess of Monte Cristo); Die Herrin von Atlantis; Das Blaue Licht (The Blue Light). **1933** Anna und Elizabeth (Anna and Elisabeth—US 1936); Das Verliebte Hotel; Fraeulein Hoffmanns Erzaehlungen. **1934** Achtung! Wer Kennt Diese Frau?; Klein Dorrit (US 1935); Das Verlorene Tal (US 1936); Vorstadtvariete; Der Schimmelreiter. **1935** Viktoria; Die Ewige Maske (The Eternal Mask—US 1937); Patrioten (Patriots—US 1937). **1937** Togger; Unternehmen Michel. **1938** Winterstuerme (Winter Storms); Wir Sind vom K. und K. Infantrie Regiment; Anna Favetti. **1939** Die Hochzeitstreise (The Wedding Journey). **1940** Michelangelo (documentary—speaker, aka Das Leben Eines Titanen). **1941** Kadetten; Ich Klage An; Das Andere Ich. **1943** Paracelsus; Man Rede mir Nicht von Liebe. **1944** Das Herz Muss Schweigen; Trauemerei. **1945** Wie Sagen wir es Unseren Kindern? **1950** Melodie des Schicksals; Wenn Wine Frau Liebt. **1952** Herz der Welt. **1953** Solange Du da Bist; Koenigliche Hoheit. **1954** Der Letzte Sommer; Angst; Eine Liebesgeschichte (A Love Story—US 1958). **1955** Reifende Jugend. **1956** Die Ehe des Dr. Med. Danwitz. **1957** Wetterleuchten um Maria; Robinson Soll Nicht Sterben (Robinson Shall Not Die, aka The Girl and the Legend—US 1966). **1963** Der Sittlichkeitsverbrecher (aka The Molesters—US 1964).

WIERE, SYLVESTER
Born: 1910, Prague, Germany. Died: July 7, 1970, Hidden Hills, Calif. (kidney ailment). Screen, stage, vaudeville and television actor. Was member of comedy team "The Wiere Bros." with his brothers, Herbert and Harry.

Appeared in: **1941** The Great American Broadcast. **1943** Swing Shift Maisie; Hands Across the Border. **1947** Road to Rio. **1967** Double Trouble.

WIERUM, HOWARD
Died: 1967. Screen actor.

Appeared in: **1956** Storm Center.

WIETH, MOGENS
Born: 1920, Denmark. Died: Sept. 10, 1962, London, England. Screen and stage actor.

Appeared in: **1950** The Invisible Army. **1951** The Tales of Hoffman. **1956** The Man Who Knew Too Much. **1960** De Sista Stegen (A Matter of Morals—US 1961).

WIFSTRAND, NAIMA
Born: 1890, Stockholm, Sweden. Died: 1968, Sweden. Screen, stage actress and opera performer.

Appeared in: **1948** The Poetry of Adalen; Musik i Morker (Night Is My Future—US 1963). **1951** The Wind Is My Lover (aka Singoalla/ Singoalla The Saga of Singoalla/ and aka Gypsy Fury—US). **1952** Kvinnors Vantan (Secrets of Women—US 1961). **1955** The True and the False. **1956** Girl in a Dress-coat; La Sorciere (The Sorceress—US aka Blonde Witch). **1957** Smiles of a Summer Night. **1959** Ansiket (The Face aka The Magician—US); Wild Strawberries. **1960** Journey Into Autumn (aka Kvinnodrom and Dreams). **1966** Nattlck (Night Games—US). **1968** Vargtimmen (Hour of the Wolf—US); Other Swedish films: Madame Visits Oslo; King's Street; Watch Out for Spies; Born: A Daughter; Sten Stensson Comes to Town; Girls in the Harbour; Hotell Kakbrinken; Handsome Augusta; I Love You You Vixen; The Long Road; Nights in the Djurgard; The Art of Love; Life in the Depths of the Forest; A Guest Came; Two Women; The Nightwatchman's Wife; People of the Simlang Valley; Lapp Blood; Private Bom; The Roar of Hammar Rapids; Miss Sun-Beam; Revue at the Sodran Theatre; Gentlemen of the Navy; That Woman Drives Me Crazy; Plaything Truant; The Devil and the Man from Smaland; Thrist (aka Three Strange Loves); The Wing Is My Lover; My Name Is Puck; A Fiancee for Hire; Because of My Hot Youth; Say It With Flowers; Dull Clang; The Road to Klockrike; Wing-beats in the Night; Ursula—the Girl from the Forest Depths; Gentle Thief of Love; The Dance Hall; Paradise; My Hot Desire; The Witch; Seventeen Years Old; The Judge; The Brig "Three Lilies"; The Myth; Waltz of Sex.

WIGGINS, MARY L.
Born: 1910. Died: Dec., 1945, North Hollywood, Calif. (shot herself). Screen stunt woman.

WILBUR, CRANE
Born: Nov. 17, 1889, Athens, N.Y. Died: Oct. 18, 1973, North Hollywood, Calif. (following a stroke). Screen, stage, radio actor, screenwriter, film director, playwright and film producer. Divorced from actresses Edna Hermance, Suzanne Caubert and Beatrice Blinn. Married to actress Lenita Lane.

Appeared in: **1914** The Perils of Pauline (serial). **1915** The Road O' Strife (serial). **1917** The Painted Lie; The Eye of Envy; The Blood of His Fathers. **1919** Unto the End; Devil McCare; Breezy Jim; Stripped for a Million. **1921** Something Different; The Heart of Maryland. **1934** Tomorrow's Children; Name the Woman. **1935** High School Girl; Public Opinion; Unknown Woman; Invincible. **1936** Yellow Cargo; Captain Calamity.

WILCOX, FRANK
Born: Mar. 13, 1907, DeSoto, Mo. Died: Mar. 3, 1974, Northridge, Calif. Screen, stage, television actor and stage director.

Appeared in: **1940** The Fighting 69th; Santa Fe Trail; 'Til We Meet Again; Tear Gas Squad; River's End; Murder in the Air; Virginia City. **1941** The Wagons Roll at Night; They Died With Their Boots On; Affectionately Yours; Navy Blues; Highway West; A Shot in the Dark; Wild Bill Hickok Rides. **1942** Across the Pacific; Busses Roar; Lady Gangster; The Hidden Hand; Bullet Scars; Murder in the Big House; Wings for the Eagle; Escpae from Crime; Secret Enemies. **1943** North Star; Juke Girl; Truck Busters. **1944** In the Meantime, Darling; The Adventures of Mark Twain; The Imposter. **1945** Conflict. **1946** Night Editor; The Devil's Mask; Strange Triangle. **1947** Out of the Past; Philo Vance Returns; Cass Timberlane; Gentleman's Agreement; The Beginning or the End; Something in the Wind; Blondie's Anniversary; I Cover Big Town. **1948** The Miracle of the Bells. **1949** Samson and Delilah; All the King's Men; The Mysterious Desperado; Masked Raiders; The Clay Pigeon. **1950** Kiss Tomorrow Goodbye; The Kid from Texas; Blondie's Hero; Chain Gang; Mister 880. **1952** The Greatest Show on Earth; Ruby Gentry; The Half-Breed; The Treasure of Lost Canyon; Trail Guide. **1953** The Story of Three Loves; Those Redheads from Seattle; China Venture; Pony Express. **1954** Three Young Texans; Naked Alibi; The Black Dakotas. **1955** Abbott and Costello Meet the Keystone Kops; Carolina Cannonball. **1956** The Ten Commandments; A Strange Adventure; Dance With Me Henry; Hollywood or Bust; Never Say Goodbye; The First Traveling Saleslady; The Man in the Gray Flannel Suit; Earth versus the Flying Saucers; Seventh Cavalry; Uranium Boom. **1957** Kelly and Me; Hell's Crossroads; New Day at Sundown; Pal Joey; Beginning of the End. **1958** Johnny Rocco; Man from God's Country. **1959** Go, Johnny, Go! **1961** Double Trouble. **1962** A Majority of One; The Scarface Mob; Swingin' Along. **1965** I'll Take Sweden.

WILCOX, HARLOW
Born: 1900. Died: Sept. 24, 1960, Hollywood, Calif. Screen and radio actor.

Appeared in: **1941** Look Who's Laughing.

WILCOX, ROBERT
Born: May 19, 1910, Rochester, N.Y. Died: June 11, 1955, near Rochester, N.Y. (heart attack on train). Screen and stage actor. Divorced from actress Florence Rice (dec. 1974). Married to actress Diana Barrymore (dec. 1960).

Appeared in: **1936** The Cop; The Stones Cry Out. **1937** Let Them Live; The Man in Blue; Armored Car; Carnival Queen; Wild and Woolly. **1938** City Girl; Reckless Living; Rascals; Young Fugitives; Little Tough Guy; Swing That Cheer; Gambling Ship. **1939** Undercover Doctor; Blondie Takes a Vacation; The Man They Could Not Hang; The Kid from Texas. **1940** Island of Doomed Men; Dreaming Out Loud; The Lone Wolf Strikes; Buried Alive; Gambling on the High Seas; Father Is a Prince; Mysterious Dr. Satan (serial). **1946** The Unknown; Wild Beauty. **1947** The Vigilantes Return. **1954** Day of Triumph.

WILCOX, SILAS "SI"
Born: 1863. Died: Feb., 1945, Hollywood, Calif. Screen and stage actor.

Appeared in: **1923** Tipped Off.

WILCOX, VIVIAN
Born: 1912. Died: Jan. 5, 1945, Hollywood, Calif. Screen actress.

WILDER, MARSHALL P.
Born: 1860, Geneva, N.Y. Died: Jan. 10, 1915, St. Paul, Minn. Screen and vaudeville actor.

Appeared in: **1912** Chumps; The Five Senses; The Pipe; The Widow's Might; The Greatest Thing in the World; Professor Optimo; Mockery; The Godmother; The Curio Hunters.

WILDHACK, ROBERT
Born: 1882. Died: June 19, 1940, Montrose, Calif. (pulmonary ailment). Screen and radio actor. Known on radio as the man of "Sneezes and Snores."

Appeared in: **1935** Broadway Melody of 1936. **1937** Broadway Melody of 1938. **1939** Back Door to Heaven.

WILDING, MICHAEL
Born: July 23, 1912, Westcliff-on-Sea, Essex, England. Died: July 7, 1979, Chichester, England (injuries from fall in home). Screen, stage and vaudeville actor. Divorced from Kay Young, actress Elizabeth Taylor, and Susan Neill. Later married to actress Margaret Leighton (dec. 1976).

Appeared in: **1936** Wedding Group (film debut, aka Wrath of Jealousy—US). **1939** There Ain't No Justice. **1940** Convoy (US 1941); Tilly of Bloomsbury; Sailors Three (aka Three Cockeyed Sailors—US 1941); Sailors Don't Care. **1941** The Farmer's Wife; Kipps (aka The Remarkable Mr. Kipps—US 1942); Spring Meeting. **1943** Dear Octopus (aka The Randolph Family—US 1945); Undercover (aka Underground Guerillas—US). **1944** English Without Tears (aka Her Man Gilbey—US 1949). **1946** Carnival; Piccadilly Incident. **1947** The Courtneys of Curzon Street (aka The Courtney Affair—US). **1948** An Ideal Husband; Spring in Park Lane (US 1949). **1949** Maytime in Mayfair; Under Capricorn. **1950** Stage Fright. **1951** Into the Blue (aka The Man in the Dinghy—US); The Law and the Lady; The Lady With the Lamp. **1952** Derby Day (aka Four Against Fate—US 1955); Trent's Last Case (US 1953). **1953** Torch Song. **1954** The Egyptian. **1955** The Glass Slipper; The Scarlet Coat. **1957** Zarak. **1958** Hello London. **1959** Danger Within (aka Breakout—US 1960). **1960** The World of Suzie Wong. **1961** The Naked Edge; I due Nemici (aka Tne Best of Enemies—US 1962). **1962** A Girl Named Tamiko. **1968** The Sweet Ride. **1969** The Madwoman of Chaillot; Waterloo. **1972** Lady Caroline Lamb. **1973** Dr. Frankenstein.

WILENCHICK, CLEM (Crane Whitley)
Died: Feb. 28, 1957. Screen actor.

Appeared in: **1938** The Lasy Warning. **1939** Beasts of Berlin; The Flying Deuces; Bad Boy; Charlie McCarthy, Detective.

WILEY, JOHN A.
Born: 1884. Died: Sept. 30, 1962, San Antonio, Tex. Screen actor.

Appeared in: **1923** The Covered Wagon. **1926** The Winning of Barbara Worth; Chasing Trouble.

WILHELM, THEODORE
Born: 1909, Germany. Died: Nov. 30, 1971, London, England. Screen, stage and television actor.

Appeared in: **1956** Assignment Redhead (aka Million Dollar Manhunt—US 1962). **1958** The Trollenberg Terror (aka The Crawling Eye—US). **1961** Circle of Deception.

WILKERSON, GUY
Born: 1898. Died: July 15, 1971, Hollywood, Calif. (cancer). Screen, stage and television actor.

Appeared in: **1937** Untamed; Paradise Express; Mountain Justice; The Yodelin' Kid from Pine Ridge; Our Neighbors the Carters. **1938** Gold Is Where You Find It. **1939** Gone With the Wind. **1941** Sergeant York; Spooks Run Wild. **1942** Swamp Woman; Captain Midnight (serial). **1943** The Rangers Take Over; Border Buckaroos. **1944** Boss of Rawhide; Brand of the Devil; Gangsters of the Frontier; Guns of the Law; Gunsmoke Mesa; The Pinto Bandit; Trail of Terror; Return of the Rangers; Spooktown; Outlaw Roundup; The Whispering Skull; Dead or Alive. **1945** Captain Tugboat Annie; Bus Pests (short); Enemy of the Law; Three in the Saddle. **1946** Duel in the Sun; Frontier Fugitives. **1947** The Michigan Kid; Thundergap Outlaws. **1948** Fury at Furnace Creek. **1949** Texas, Brooklyn and Heaven. **1950** The Great Missouri Raid; Ticket to Tomahawk; Winchester '73. **1951** Along the Great Divide; Comin' 'Round the Mountain. **1952** The Big Sky. **1953** The Last Posse; The Stranger Wore a Gun. **1955** Foxfire; The Far Country. **1956** Jubal. **1957** The Buster Keaton Story; Decision at Sundown. **1958** Cowboy; Wild Heritage; Man of the West. **1959** The FBI Story. **1960** Elmer Gantry; The Walking Target. **1961** Susan Slade. **1962** To Kill a Mockingbird. **1963** The Haunted Palace. **1965** Black Spurs; War Party. **1969** True Grit. **1970** Monte Walsh.

WILKERSON, HERBERT
Born: 1881. Died: Aug. 19, 1943, Hollywood, Calif. Screen and stage actor.

WILKERSON, WILLIAM (William Penn Wilkerson)
Born: 1903, Okla. Died: Mar. 3, 1966, Hollywood, Calif. Indian screen actor.

Appeared in: **1939** Juarez. **1940** Dr. Cyclops. **1942** Captain of the Clouds. **1945** They Were Expendable. **1947** Robin Hood of Texas. **1950** Davy Crokett, Indian Scout; The Rock Island Trail; Broken Arrow. **1951** Jungle Manhunt. **1952** Brave Warrior. **1953** Saginaw Trail.

WILKES, LILLIAN
Born: 1892. Died: Dec. 15, 1976, Los Angeles, Calif. Screen and stage actress. Married to actor Pat O'Malley (dec. 1966). Entered films in 1918.

WILKIE, HERBERT
Born: 1855. Died: Oct. 22, 1940. Screen actor.

Appeared in: **1915** The Fairy and the Waif.

WILLA, SUZANNE
Born: 1893, Los Angeles, Calif. Died: Mar. 24, 1951, New York, N.Y. Screen and stage actress.

Appeared in: **1915** At Bay. **1917** The Angel Factory; Sylvia of the Secret Service; Kick In; Arms and the Woman. **1918** Empty Pockets.

WILLARD, EDMUND
Born: Dec. 19, 1885, Brighton, England. Died: Oct. 8, 1956, Surrey, England. Screen and stage actor.

Appeared in: **1931** Cape Forlorn (aka The Love Storm—US). **1932** The Crooked Lady. **1935** The Iron Duke; The Legend of William Tell; Heat Wave (US 1936); The Mystery of the Mary Celeste (aka Phantom Ship—US 1937); Moscow Nights (aka I Stand Condemned—US 1936). **1937** King of the Damned. **1937** Dark Journey; Farewell Again (aka Troopship—US 1938). **1939** Hoot Mon!. **1940** Pastor Hall. **1941** Larceny Street; Penn of Pennsylvania (aka The Courageous Mr. Penn—US 1944).

WILLARD, JESS
Born: Dec. 29, 1881, Pottawatomie Indian Reservation, Kans. Died: Dec. 15, 1968, Los Angeles, Calif. (cerebral hemorrhage). World Heavyweight Champion Boxer and screen actor.

Appeared in: **1919** The Heart Punch; The Challenge of Chance. **1968** The Legendary Champions (documentary).

WILLARD, JOHN
Born: Nov. 28, 1885, San Francisco, Calif. Died: Aug. 30, 1942. Screen, stage actor, screenwriter and playwright.

Appeared in: **1920** Fantomas (serial). **1922** Sherlock Holmes. **1933** Victims of Persecution.

WILLAT, IRVIN W.
Born: 1890, Stamford, Conn. Died: Apr. 17, 1976, Santa Monica, Calif. Screen actor, film director, film producer, screenwriter and cinematographer. Divorced from actress Billie Dove. Entered films in 1910 with Imp Co.

Appeared in: **1911** The Toss of a Coin.

WILLENZ, MAX
Born: 1888. Died: Nov. 10, 1954, Hollywood, Calif. (heart attack). Screen and stage actor.

Appeared in: **1941** When Ladies Meet. **1942** Pride of the Yankees; Pierre of the Plains; I Married an Angel. **1943** Heavenly Body. **1945** Yolanda and the Thief. **1947** Desire Me. **1949** Dancing in the Dark. **1953** Gentlemen Prefer Blondes; Stalag 17.

WILLEY, LEONARD (Leonard Louis Willey)
Born: Dec. 15, 1882, England. Died: June 30, 1964, Los Angeles, Calif. (arteriosclerosis). Screen and stage actor.

Appeared in: **1937** The Prince and the Pauper; Night Club Scandal. **1938** Invisible Enemy; The Adventures of Robin Hood. **1940** Tom Brown's School Days. **1941** Penny Serenade.

WILLIAM, JOSEPH "RANGER BILL"
Born: 1878. Died: Nov. 12, 1939. Screen actor and cowboy. Appeared in silent films.

WILLIAM, WARREN (William Krech)
Born: Dec. 2, 1895, Aitkens, Minn. Died: Sept. 24, 1948, Encino, Calif. (multiple myeloma, blood disease). Screen, stage and radio actor. Star of "Lone Wolf" film series.

Appeared in: **1920** The Town that Forgot God. **1923** Plunder (serial). **1927** Twelve Miles Out. **1930** How I Play Golf—The Spoon (short); Let Us Be Gay. **1931** Expensive Women; Honor of the Family; Those Who Love. **1932** Woman from Monte Carlo; Beauty and the Boss; Dark Horse; Under Eighteen; Skyscraper Souls; The Mouthpiece; The Match King; Three on a Match. **1933** The Mind Reader; Employees' Entrance; The Great Jasper; Gold Diggers of 1933; Goodbye Again; Lady for a Day. **1934** Smarty; Upper World; The Case of the Howling

Dog; The Secret Bride; Bedside; Dr. Monica; The Dragon Murder Case; Imitation of Life; Cleopatra. **1935** Living on Velvet; The Case of the Curious Bride; The Case of the Lucky Legs; Don't Bet on Blondes. **1936** The Widow from Monte Carlo; The Case of the Velvet Claws; Stage Struck; Satan Met a Lady; Times Square Playboy; Go West, Young Man. **1937** Outcast; Midnight Madonna; The Firefly; Madame X. **1938** Arsene Lupin Returns; The First Hundred Years; Wives under Suspicion. **1939** The Lone Wolf Spy Hunt; Gracie Allen Murder Case; The Man in the Iron Mask; Daytime Wife. **1940** Lillian Russell; The Lone Wolf Strikes; The Lone Wolf Meets a Lady; Arizona; Trail of the Vigilantes. **1941** The Lone Wolf Takes a Chance; The Wolf Man; Wild Geese Calling; The Lone Wolf Keeps a Date. **1942** Counter Espionage; Eyes of the Underworld; Wild Bill Hickok Rides. **1943** One Dangerous Night; Passport to Suez. **1945** Strange Illusion. **1946** Fear. **1947** The Private Affairs of Bel Ami.

WILLIAMS, AL (Alfred Morris Williams, Jr.)
Born: 1909, Ariz. Died: June 30, 1981, San Francisco, Calif. Screen actor and cameraman.

Appeared in: **1934** Men in White.

WILLIAMS, ANNABELLE (Annabelle Rucker)
Born: 1904, Oklahoma City, Okla. Died: Dec. 26, 1967, Hollywood, Calif. Screen and stage actress.

WILLIAMS, BERESFORD
Born: 1904, England. Died: Apr. 22, 1966, England. Screen, stage and television actor.

WILLIAMS, BERL "MR. FUNNY"
Born: 1918. Died: Mar. 11, 1978, Inglewood, Calif. (cancer). Screen, radio, television actor and nightclub comedian.

WILLIAMS, BERT (Egbert Austin Williams)
Born: 1877, New Providence, Nassau, British West Indies. Died: Mar. 5, 1922, New York, N.Y. (pneumonia). Black screen, stage, minstrel and vaudeville actor. Appeared in vaudeville and minstrel shows in team of "Williams and Walker."

Appeared in: **1914** Darktown Jubilee. **1916** A Natural Born Gambler.

WILLIAMS, BILL
Born: 1921. Died: Nov. 14, 1964, Gallup, N.M. Screen and television stuntman.

Appeared in: **1961** The Comancheros; Two Rode Together. **1964** Cheyenne Autumn. **1965** The Hallelujah Trail (killed while filming).

WILLIAMS, BILLY
Born: 1910. Died: Oct. 12, 1972, Chicago, Ill. Black screen, television actor and singer. Member of the "Charioteers" and the "Billy Williams Quartet."

WILLIAMS, BRANSBY
Born: Aug. 14, 1870, London, England. Died: Dec. 3, 1961, London, England. Screen, stage, vaudeville and television actor. Father of actor Eric Bransby Williams.

Appeared in: **1911** Royal England. **1914** The Seven Ages of Man; Bernardo's Confession; Grimaldi; The Street Watchman's Story. **1915** Hard Times. **1918** Adam Bede; The Greatest Wish in the World. **1921** The Adventures of Mr. Pickwick. **1928** Scrooge (short); Grandfather Smallweed (short). **1933** Soldiers of the King (aka The Woman in Command—US 1934). **1936** Hearts of Humanity. **1937** Song of the Road. **1941** The Common Touch. **1942** Those Kids from Town; Tomorrow We Live (aka At Dawn We Die—US 1943). **1946** The Trojan Brothers. **1952** Judgment Deferred.

WILLIAMS, CHARLES B.
Born: Sept. 27, 1898, Albany, N.Y. Died: Jan. 3, 1958, Hollywood, Calif. Screen, stage actor, playwright, screenwriter and television writer. Entered films as an actor with Paramount in N.Y.

Appeared in: **1922** The Old Homestead. **1925** Action Galore. **1932** Dance Team; Strangers of the Evening; The Devil Is Driving. **1933** Gambling Ship; The Gay Nighties (short). **1934** Search for Beauty; Woman in the Dark. **1936** Rhythm on the Range; Wedding Present. **1937** Four Days' Wonder; Love Is News; Wake up and Live; Charlie Chan on Broadway; Love and Hisses; Turn off the Moon; Jim Hanvey, Detective; Merry-Go-Round of 1938. **1938** Born to Be Wild; Hollywood Stadium Mystery; Mr. Moto's Gamble; Alexander's Ragtime Band; Little Miss Broadway; Just around the Corner. **1939** Wife, Husband and Friend; The Flying Irishman; Undercover Doctor. **1941** Convoy; Flying Cadets. **1942** Isle of Missing Men; Time to Kill.

1943 Sarong Girl; The Girl From Monterrey. **1944** End of the Road; Where Are Your Children? **1945** Guest Wife; Identity Unknown; Love on the Dole. **1946** Our Hearts Were Growing Up; Doll Face; Passkey to Danger; Heldorado; It's a Wonderful Life. **1948** Marshal of Amarillo; The Dude Goes West. **1949** Grand Canyon. **1950** The Missourians. **1951** According to Mrs. Hoyle; Corky of Gasoline Alley; Kentucky Jubilee. **1955** A Lawless Street. **1956** Fighting Trouble.

WILLIAMS, CLARA
Born: 1891, Seattle, Wash. Died: May 8, 1928, Los Angeles, Calif. Screen actress. Entered films with Selig in 1910.

Appeared in: **1916** Hell's Hinges. **1917** Paws of the Bear. **1918** Carmen of the Klondike.

WILLIAMS, CORA
Born: 1871. Died: Dec. 1, 1927, Los Angeles, Calif. (heart trouble). Stage and screen actress.

Appeared in: **1919** His Parisian Wife. **1925** His Buddy's Wife; Womanhandled. **1926** The Adorable Deceiver; 31927 Temptations of a Shop Girl; The Great Mail Robbery; Sensation Seekers.

WILLIAMS, CRAIG
Born: 1877, Germany. Died: July 5, 1941, New York, N.Y. Stage and screen actor.

WILLIAMS, DOUGLAS
Died: Dec. 24, 1968. Screen actor.

WILLIAMS, EARLE (Earle Rafael Williams)
Born: Feb. 28, 1880, Sacramento, Calif. Died: Apr. 25, 1927, Los Angeles, Calif. (bronchial pneumonia). Screen, stage actor and film producer. Married to sometime screenwriter Florine Walz (dec.). Entered films with Vitagraph approx. 1910.

Appeared in: **1911** The Missing Will; By Way of Mrs. Browning; An Aeroplane Elopement; Aund Huldah, the Matchmaker; Their Charming Mama; The Thumbprint; The Prince and the Pumps; The Wager; One Touch of Nature; The Military Air-Scout; A Friendly Marriage; One Flag at Last. **1912** Saving an Audience; The Party Dress; The Bond of Music; The Heart of the King's Jester; Willie's Sister; Father and Son; The Love of John Ruskin; The Lady of the Lake; On Her Wedding Day; The Church Across the Way; The Love Sick Maidens of Cuddleton; The Suit of Armor; The Seventh Son; His Father's Son; The Woman Haters; The Spider's Web; Coronets and Hearts; The Light That Failed; The Fortune in a Teacup; When California was Young; The Red Barrier; The Dawning; Two Women and Two Men; The Song of a Shell; Una of the Sierras. **1913** The Delayed Letter; The Adventure of the Ambassador's Disappearance; The Vengeance of Durand; Papa Puts One Over; The Chains of an Oath; The Carpenter; My Lady of Idleness; Red and White Roses; Alixe (aka The Test of Friendship); Playing With Fire; Hearts of the First Empire; A Soul in Bondage; His Life for His Emperor; Bunny and the Bunny Hug; The White Slave (aka The Octoroon); The Only Way; A Modern Psyche; Her Sweetest Memory; The Tiger Lily; When Society Calls; Love's Sunet; The Leading Lady; The Line-Up; The Flirt; Their Mutual Friend; The Diver; The Right Man; Old Muddington's Daughters; Out of the Shadows. **1914** The Mischief Maker; Her Husband; The Christian; The Memories That Haunt; The Battle of the Weak; Eve's Daughter (aka The Artist's Madonna); Happy-Go-Lucky; Warfare in the Skies; My Official Wife; The Sins of the Mothers; Lily of the Valley; Midst Woodland Shadows. **1915** The Goddess (serial); Two Women; The Right Girl; From Headquarters; The Juggernaut; His Phantom Sweetheart; The Sort-of-Girl-Who-Came-from-Heaven; The Awakening; Count 'Em (aka The Counts). **1916** The Scarlet Runner (serial); My Lady's Slipper. **1917** Arsene Lupin; Apartment 29; The Hawk; The Soul Master; The Maelstrom (aka Millionaire Hallet's Adventure); Transgression. **1918** The Girl in the House; A Diplomatic Mission; A Mother's Sin; An American Live Wire; The Seal of Silence; The Love Doctor; The Man Who Wouldn't Tell. **1919** A Rogue's Romance; A Gentleman of Quality; The Usurper; The Highest Trump; The Hornet's Nest; The Wolf. **1920** When a Man Loves; The Fortune Hunter; The Black Gate; Captian Swift; A Master Stroke; The Purple Cipher; The Romance Promoters. **1921** Diamonds Adrift; Lucky Carson; It Can be Done; The Silver Car; Bring Him In. **1922** The Man from Downing Street; Restless Souls; Fortune's Mask; You Never Know. **1923** The Eternal Struggle (aka Masters of Women); Masters of Men; Jealous Husbands (aka Jealous Fools). **1924** Borrowed Husbands. **1925** Lena Rivers; The Adventurous Sex; Was It Bigamy?; The Ancient Mariner. **1926** The Skyrocket; Diplomacy; You'd Be Suprised. **1927** Red Signals; Say It With Diamonds; She's My Baby.

WILLIAMS, ELAINE
Died: May 9, 1947, Hollywood, Calif. Silent screen actress. Do not confuse with actresses with same name.

WILLIAMS, FRANCES (Frances E. Williams)
Born: 1901, St. Paul, Minn. Died: Jan. 27, 1959, New York, N.Y. Screen and stage actress.

Appeared in: **1933** Broadway Thru a Keyhole. **1934** Hollywood Party. **1946** Her Sister's Secret; Magnificent Doll. **1949** The Reckless Moment. **1951** Showboat; Family Secret; Queen for a Day (aka Horsie). **1952** Lydia Bailey.

WILLIAMS, FRED J.
Born: 1875. Died: May 29, 1942, Los Angeles, Calif. Screen actor and film producer. Entered films approx. 1917.

Appeared in: **1925** A Modern Cain.

WILLIAMS, GEORGE
Born: 1854. Died: Feb. 21, 1936, Los Angeles, Calif. Screen actor.

Appeared in: **1922** Foolish Wives; Little Miss Smiles. **1924** Geared to Go; The Fighting Sap; The Silent Stranger. **1925** Super Speed; The Rattler. **1926** The Winner.

WILLIAMS, GEORGE B.
Born: 1866. Died: Nov. 17, 1931, Santa Monica, Calif. (auto accident). Screen actor.

Appeared in: **1921** Cheated Love; A Poor Relation; Danger Ahead; Her Mad Bargain; One Man in a Million. **1922** Second Hand Rose; The Golden Gallows; Her Night of Nights; The Siren Call. **1923** The Ghost Patrol. **1924** The Gaiety Girl; A Lady of Quality; Captain Blood. **1925** Fifth Avenue Models; The Phantom of the Opera. **1926** Midnight Sun.

WILLIAMS, GUINN "BIG BOY"
Born: Apr. 26, 1899, Decatur, Tex. Died: June 6, 1962, Hollywood, Calif. (uremic poisoning). Screen and television actor. For a time was U.S. Congressman from Texas. Father of actor Malcolm (aka "Big Boy") Williams.

Appeared in: **1919** Almost a Husband (as an extra). **1921** The Jack Rider; The Vengeance Trail; Western Firebrands. **1922** Trail of Hate; Across the Border; Blaze Away; Rounding up the Law; The Cowboy King. **1923** Freshie; End of the Rope; Cyclone Jones; $1,000 Reward; Riders at Night. **1924** The Avenger; The Eagle's Claw. **1925** Red Blood and Blue; Whistling Jim; Black Cyclone; Bad Man from Bodie; Big Stunt; Courage of Wolfheart; Fangs of Wolfheart; Riders of the Sand Storm; Rose of the Desert; Wolfheart's Revenge; Sporting West. **1926** Brown of Harvard; The Desert's Toll. **1927** Quarantined Rivals; Slide, Kelly, Slide; The College Widow; The Down Grade; Backstage; Lightning; Snowbound; The Woman Who Did Not Care. **1928** My Man; Burning Daylight; Vamping Venus; Ladies' Night in a Turkish Bath. **1929** Noah's Ark; Lucky Star; From Headquarters; The Forward Pass. **1930** The Big Fight; The Bad Man; College Lovers; Liliom; City Girl. **1931** The Great Meadow; The Bachelor Fathers; Catch as Catch Can (short); War Mamas (short). **1932** Polly of the Circus; Drifting Souls; 70,000 Witnesses; You Said a Mouthful; Ladies of the Jury; The Devil Is Driving. **1933** Mystery Squadron (serial); Heritage of the Desert; Man of the Forest; College Coach; Laughing at Life. **1934** Romance in the Rain; Palooka; The Mystery Squadron (serial); Half a Sinner; Flirtation Walk; One in a Million; Here Comes the Navy; The Silver Streak; The Cheaters; Rafter Romance. **1935** Society Fever; Cowboy Holiday; Private Worlds; Gun Play; The Glass Key; Village Tale; Powdersmoke Range; The Littlest Rebel; Miss Pacific Fleet; Law of the 45's; Here Comes Cookie. **1936** The Vigilantes Are Coming (serial); Muss 'Em Up; Grand Jury; The Big Game; Kelly the Second; End of the Trail; North of Nome; Career Woman. **1937** You Only Live Once; A Star Is Born; Don't Tell the Wife; The Singing Marine; Dangerous Holiday; She's No Lady; Big City; My Dear Miss Aldrich; Wise Girl. **1938** I Demand Payment; Flying Fists; The Marines Are Here; Crashing Through; Hold That Co-ed; Everybody's Doing It; The Bad Men of Brimstone; Army Girl; Down in "Arkansaw"; You and Me; Professor Beware! **1939** 6,000 Enemies; Blackmail; Fugitive at Large; Street of Missing Men; Mutiny on the Blackhawk; Legion of Lost Flyers; Badlands; Dodge City; Pardon Our Nerve. **1940** The Fighting 69th; Castle on the Hudson; Virginia City; Money and the Woman; Santa Fe Trail; Alias the Deacon; Dulcy; Wagons Westward. **1941** Six Lessons from Madame La Zonga; Country Fair; Billy the Kid; You'll Never Get Rich; Swamp Water; The Bugle Sounds; Riders of Death Valley (serial). **1942** Betewen Us Girls; Mr. Wise Guy; Lure of the Islands; American Empire; Silver Queen. **1943** Hands Across the Border; Buckskin Frontier; Minesweeper; The Desperados. **1944** The Cowboy and the Senorita; The Cowboy Canteen; Thirty Seconds Over Tokyo; Belle of the Yukon; Swing in the Saddle; Song of the Prairie. **1945** The Man Who Walked Alone; Rhythm Roundup; Sing Me a Song of Texas. **1946** Cowboy Blues; Singing on the Trail; Throw a Saddle on a Star; That Texas Jubilee. **1947** King of the Wild Horses; Singin' in the Corn; Road to the Big House. **1948** Bad Men of Tombstone; Station West. **1949** Brimstone. **1950** Hoedown; Rocky Mountain. **1951** Al Jennings of Oklahoma; Man in the Saddle. **1952** Springfield Rifle; Hangman's Knot. **1954** Massacre Canyon; Southwest Passage; The Outlaws' Daughter. **1956** Hidden Guns; Man from Del Rio. **1957** The Hired Gun. **1960** Home from the Hill; The Alamo; Five Bold Women. **1962** The Comancheros.

WILLIAMS, HANK
Born: 1924. Died: Jan. 1, 1953, near Oak Hill, W.Va. (heart attack). Country singer, composer, instrumentalist and screen, radio and television actor.

WILLIAMS, HARCOURT
Born: Mar. 30, 1880, Croyden, Surrey, England. Died: Dec. 13, 1957. Screen and stage actor.

Appeared in: **1945** Henry V (US 1946). **1947** Brighton Rock. **1948** Vice Versa; Hamlet; No Room at the Inn. **1949** Third Time Lucky (US 1950); The Lost People; Trottie True (aka Gay Lady—US 1950); Under Capricorn. **1950** Your Witness (aka Eye Witness—US); Cage of Gold (US 1951). **1951** The Late Edwina Black (aka Obsessed—US); The Magic Box (US 1952). **1953** Time Bomb (aka Terror on a Train—US). **1956** Adventures of Quentin Durward; Around the World in 80 Days.

WILLIAMS, HATTIE
Born: 1870. Died: Aug. 17, 1942. Screen and stage actress.

Appeared in: **1915** Glorianna's Getaway.

WILLIAMS, HERB (Herbert Schussler Billerbeck)
Born: 1874, Philadelphia, Pa. Died: Oct. 1, 1936, Freeport, N.Y. (internal hemorrhages). Screen, stage and vaudeville actor. Appeared in vaudeville with his wife Hulda in an act billed "Williams and Wolfus."

Appeared in: **1936** Rose of the Rancho.

WILLIAMS, HUGH (Brian Williams)
Born: Mar. 6, 1904, Boxhill-on-Sea, England. Died: Dec. 7, 1969, London, England. Screen, stage actor, screenwriter and playwright. Divorced from Gwyne Whitby. Married to actress and playwright Margaret Vyner. Father of actor Simon Williams.

Appeared in: **1930** Charley's Aunt (film debut). **1931** A Night in Montmartre; A Gentleman of Paris. **1932** Down Our Street; White Face; Insult; Rome Express; After Dark. **1933** Bitter Sweet; Sorrell and Son (US 1934); The Jewel; This Acting Business. **1934** All Men Are Enemies; Elinor Norton; Outcast Lady. **1935** The Last Journey (US 1936); Lieutenant Daring, RN; Her Last Affaire; David Copperfield; Let's Live Tonight. **1936** The Amateur Gentleman; The Man Behind the Mask; The Happy Family. **1937** Gypsy; The Windmill; Side Street Angel; The Perfect Crime; Brief Ecstacy. **1938** Bank Holiday (aka Three on a Weekend—US); The Dark Stairway; Dead Men Tell No Tales (US 1939); His Lordship Goes to Press; Premiere (aka One Night in Paris—US 1940). **1939** Wuthering Heights; Inspector Hornleigh; Dark Eyes of London (aka The Human Monster—US 1940). **1941** Ships With Wings (US 1942). **1942** One of Our Aircraft is Missing; The Day Will Dawn (aka The Avengers—US); Talk About Jacqueline; Secret Mission. **1946** A Girl in a Million (US 1950). **1947** Take My Life (US 1948). **1948** The Blind Goddess (US 1949); An Ideal Husband. **1949** Elizabeth of Ladymead; Paper Orchid; The Romantic Age (aka Naughty Arlette—US 1951). **1952** The Gift Horse (aka Glory at Sea—US 1953); The Holly and the Ivy. **1953** Twice Upon a Time; The Fake; The Intruder (US 1955). **1954** Star of My Night. **1966** Khartoum. **1967** Doctor Faustus (US 1968).

WILLIAMS, JAY
Born: 1914, Buffalo, N.Y. Died: July 12, 1978, England. Screen, stage, vaudeville actor and writer.

Appeared in: **1953** The Little Fugitive.

WILLIAMS, JEFFREY
Born: 1860. Died: Dec. 27, 1938, Los Angeles, Calif. Screen and stage actor.

Appeared in: **1921** The Saphead. **1934** Old Fashioned Way.

WILLIAMS, JOHN J.
Born: 1856, Lynn, Mass. Died: Oct. 5, 1918, New York, N.Y. (heart failure). Screen, stage, vaudeville actor and comedian.

Appeared in: **1915** Marse Covington.

WILLIAMS, JOSEPHINE
Born: 1855, Liverpool, England. Died: June 14, 1937, New York, N.Y. Screen actress.

WILLIAMS, JULIA
Born: 1879. Died: Feb. 7, 1936, New York, N.Y. Screen, stage, opera and vaudeville actress. Entered films during silents, appearing in early Pathe and Biograph films.

WILLIAMS, KATHLYN
Born: 1872 or 1888, Butte, Mont. Died: Sept. 23, 1960, Hollywood, Calif. Screen actress.

Appeared in: **1908** Harbor Island. **1910** The Fire Chief's Daughter. **1911** The Two Orphans; Back to the Primitive. **1913** The Lipton Cup; Introducing Sir Thomas Lipton; A Little Child Shall Lead Them; Two Men and a Woman; With Love's Eyes; A Mansion of Misery; The Adventures of Kathlyn (serial); The Burglar Who Robbed Death (aka When a Burglar Robbed Death); Their Stepmother; Lieutenant Jones; The Stolen Melody; Woman—Past and Present; The Flight of the Crow; The Child of the Sea; The Young Mrs. Eames; The Love of Penelope; The Tide of Destiny. **1914** The Spoilers; Chip of the Flying U. **1916** Sweet Lady Peggy; The Ne'er-Do-Well. **1917** Redeeming Love; Big Timber; The Cost of Hatred. **1918** The Whispering Chorus; The Highway of Hope; We Can't Have Everything. **1919** Her Kingdom of Dreams. **1920** Conrad in Quest of His Youth; Just a Wife. **1921** Everything for Sale; Hush; A Man's Home; Morals; Forbidden Fruit; A Private Scandal; A Virginia Courtship. **1922** Clarence. **1923** The Spanish Dancer; Broadway Gold; Souls for Sale; Trimmed in Scarlet; The World's Applause. **1924** Single Wives; The City That Never Sleeps; The Enemy Sex; The Painted Flapper; Wanderer of the Wasteland; When a Girl Lives. **1925** The Best People; Locked Doors. **1926** The Wanderer. **1927** Sally in Our Alley. **1928** Our Dancing Daughters; We Americans; Honeymoon Flats. **1929** A Single Man; The Single Standard. **1930** Road to Paradise; Wedding Rings. **1931** Daddy Long Legs. **1932** Unholy Love. **1933** Blood Money. **1935** Rendezvous at Midnight. **1947** The Other Love.

WILLIAMS, LARRY
Born: 1935, New Orleans, La. Died: Dec., 1979, Los Angeles, Calif. (suicide—gunshot). Composer, rock performer, record executive and screen actor.

Appeared in: **1974** The Klansmen.

WILLIAMS, LAWRENCE "LARRY"
Born: 1890. Died: Mar. 30, 1956, Hollywood, Calif. (heart attack). Screen actor. Married to actress Helen Dickson. Entered films approx. 1931.

Appeared in: **1938** Torchy Blane in Panama; Garden of the Moon; Girls on Probation; Brother Rat. **1939** Going Places; Nancy Drew—Reporter; Torchy Plays With Dynamite; Wings of the Navy; Secret Service of the Air; On Trial; Waterfront. **1940** Brother Rat and a Baby. **1941** Sky Raiders (serial). **1942** Flight Lieutenant; Hello Annapolis. **1951** Goodbye, My Fancy. **1952** The Bad and the Beautiful.

WILLIAMS, LOTTIE
Born: 1874, Indianapolis, Ind. Died: Nov. 16, 1962, Calif. Screen actress.

Appeared in: **1920** Twin Beds; A Full House. **1921** All Soul's Eve. **1922** Is Matrimony a Failure?; The Veiled Woman. **1923** The Barefoot Boy; Yesterday's Wife. **1924** The Tomboy. **1926** The Country Beyond. **1927** Arizona Nights. **1930** Strictly Modern. **1934** Six Day Bike Rider. **1936** Murder by an Aristocrat; The Case of the Black Cat. **1937** Wine, Women and Horses. **1938** Nancy Drew, Detective; Little Miss Thoroughbred. **1939** Dark Victory; Yes, My Darling Daughter. **1940** A Fugitive from Justice; Ladies Must Live. **1942** Busses Roar. **1946** Shadow of a Woman.

WILLIAMS, MACK
Born: 1907. Died: July 29, 1965, Hollywood, Calif. (heart attack). Screen and stage actor.

Appeared in: **1948** Command Decision. **1949** Trapped; Whirlpool. **1950** Destination Big House; No Way Out; Where the Sidewalk Ends. **1951** The Blue Veil; Force of Arms; Flying Leathernecks; Try and Get Me; Call Me Mister. **1953** The Bigamist. **1955** Unchained; Violent Saturday. **1956** The Monster That Challenged the World. **1958** Ten North Frederick; As Young as We Are. **1960** Chartroose Caboose. **1962** Cape Fear; A Public Affair.

WILLIAMS, MALCOLM
Born: 1870. Died: June 10, 1937, New York, N.Y. (heart attack). Screen and stage actor.

Appeared in: **1928** The First Kiss.

WILLIAMS, MARIE
Born: 1921. Died: July 5, 1967, Encino, Calif. (heart attack). Screen actress.

WILLIAMS, MARJORIE ROSE
Born: 1913. Died: July 18, 1933, Los Angeles, Calif. (suicide—gun). Screen actress.

WILLIAMS, MOLLY
Born: England. Died: Nov. 1, 1967, Halifax, Nova Scotia, Canada. Screen, stage, vaudeville, radio and television actress.

WILLIAMS, O. T. (Oscar Williams)
Born: 1908, Tex. Died: Mar. 13, 1976, Studio City, Calif. Screen, radio and television actor.

Appeared in: **1945** San Antonio.

WILLIAMS, RHYS
Born: 1892, England. Died: May 28, 1969, Santa Monica, Calif. Screen, stage and television actor.

Appeared in: **1941** How Green Was My Valley. **1942** This Above All; Eagle Squadron; Remember Pearl Harbor; Cairo; Ramdon Harvest; Gentleman Jim; Mrs. Miniver. **1943** No Time for Love. **1945** The Corn Is Green; You Came Along; Blood on the Sun; The Bells of St. Mary's. **1946** So Goes My Love; The Strange Woman; The Spiral Staircase; Voice of the Whistler. **1947** Cross My Heart; Easy Come, Easy Go; The Trouble With Women; If Winter Comes; Moss Rose; The Farmer's Daughter; The Imperfect Lady. **1948** Black Arrow; Tenth Avenue Angel; Hills of Home. **1949** Fighting Man of the Plains; Bad Boy; The Crooked Way; The Inspector General; Tokyo Joe. **1950** The Showdown; Tyrant of the Sea; One Too Many; California Passage; Devil's Doorway; Kiss Tomorrow Goodbye. **1951** Sword of Monte Cristo; Million Dollar Pursuit; The Law and the Lady; The Light Touch; The Son of Dr. Jekyll; Never Trust a Gambler; Lightning Strikes Twice. **1952** Okinawa; Mutiny; The World in His Arms; Carbine Williams; Les Miserables; Meet Met at the Fair; Plymouth Adventure. **1953** Scandal at Scourie; Julius Caesar; Bad for Each Other. **1954** Man in the Attic; The Black Shield of Falworth; Johnny Guitar; There's No Business Like Show Business; Battle Cry. **1955** The Scarlet Coat; How to Be Very, Very Popular; The King's Thief; The Kentuckian; Battle Cry; Many Rivers to Cross. **1956** The Desperadoes Are in Town; Nightmare; The Boss; Mohawk; The Fastest Gun Alive. **1957** The Restless Breed; Raintree County; Lure of the Swamp. **1958** Merry Andrew. **1960** Midnight Lace. **1965** The Sons of Katie Elder. **1966** Our Man Flint. **1970** Skullduggery.

WILLIAMS, ROBERT
Born: Sept. 15, 1897, Morganton, N.C. Died: Nov. 3, 1931, Hollywood, Calif. (peritonitis following appendectomy). Stage and screen actor. Married to actress Nini Penn.

Appeared in: **1931** Rebound (stage and film versions); The Common Law; Platinum Blonde; Devotion.

WILLIAMS, ROBERT B.
Died: June 17, 1978. Screen and television actor.

Appeared in: **1944** The Girl in the Case; Secret Command. **1945** The Adventures of Rusty; Song of the Prairie; Rough, Tough and Ready. **1946** Unexpected Guest. **1947** Luckiest Guy in the World (short). **1948** Strange Gamble. **1949** Rusty's Birthday; Oh, You Beautiful Doll; The Mysterious Desperado; Roughshod; Stagecoach Kid; The Dark Past; It Happens Every Spring; The Lone Wolf and His Lady. **1950** The Groom Wore Spurs; Mister 880; Mary Ryan, Detective; The Lawless; The Great Jewel Robbery. **1951** The Lady Says No. **1954** Hell and High Water; Magnificent Obsession. **1955** Lucy Gallant; Revenge of the Creature. **1956** Over Exposed; The Unguarded Moment. **1957** Death in Small Doses; Hard Man; The Iron Sheriff. **1958** The Tunnel of Love. **1959** Pork Chop Hill; The Bat; Pillow Talk. **1961** Everything's Ducky. **1962** Mr. Hobbs Takes a Vacation; Saintly Sinners. **1964** Apache Rifles. **1966** Follow Me, Boys! **1968** Hang 'Em High.

WILLIAMS, SCOTT T. See CHIEF THUNDERCLOUD

WILLIAMS, SPENCER
Born: July 14, 1893, Vidalia, La. Died: Dec. 13, 1969, Los Angeles, Calif. (kidney ailment). Black radio, television, screen actor, film director and producer. The Andy of television's "Amos 'n Andy" program during the 1950s.

Appeared in: **1928** Tenderfeet. **1930** Georgia Rose. **1935** The Virginia Judge. **1938** Harlem on the Prairie; The Bronze Buckaroo. **1939** Bad Boy; Two-Gun Man from Harlem. **1940** Son of Ingagi. **1941** Blood of Jesus; Toppers Take a Bow. **1944** Of One Blood; Go Down Death. **1946** Beal Street Mama; Dirty Girtie from Harlem, USA. **1947** Juke Joint.

WILLIAMS, WILLIAM A. (William Albert Williams)
Born: 1870. Died: May 4, 1942, Hollywood, Calif. Screen actor. Married to actress Daphne Darwin.

Appeared in: **1930** La Grande Mare.

WILLIAMS, WILLIAM J., JR.
Born: 1921. Died: Nov. 13, 1964, near Gallup, N.Mex. Screen actor and stuntman. Son of actor William J. Williams Sr.

Appeared in: **1954** Black Horse Canyon. **1960** The Alamo. **1964** Cheyenne Autumn.

WILLIAMS, ZACK
Born: 1885. Died: May 25, 1958, Calif. Screen actor.

Appeared in: **1921** The Killer; The Lure of Egypt. **1922** The Gray Dawn. **1925** The Merry Widow. **1927** Easy Pickings; The Yankee Clipper. **1928** Court-Martial. **1929** Hearts in Dixie; The Four Feathers. **1930** Madonna of the Streets. **1939** Gone With the Wind. **1940** Song of Ingagi; Maryland. **1941** Up Jumped the Devil. **1942** Duke of the Navy; Professor Creeps.

WILLIAMSON, MELVIN E.
Born: 1900, Memphis, Tenn. Died: Feb. 15, 1959, Scott Air Force Base, Ill. Screen, radio actor, film director, television producer and director.

Appeared in: **1929** Wings.

WILLIAMSON, ROBERT (aka BOB WILLIAMSON)
Born: 1885, Glasgow, Scotland. Died: Mar. 13, 1949, Amityville, N.Y. Screen actor.

Appeared in: **1922** The Bond Boy. **1924** The Fighting Sap; Headin' Through. **1925** Don X. **1926** The Haunted Range; Lawless Trails.

WILLIAMSON, ROBIN E.
Born: June 30, 1889, Denver, Colo. Died: Feb. 21, 1935, Los Angeles, Calif. (heart attack). Screen, stage, vaudeville actor and film director.

Appeared in: **1916** What'll You Have?; The Reward; Side-Tracked; Stranded; The Man Hunters; The Great Safe Tangle; Help! Help!; Furnished Rooms; The Tryout. **1928** The Apache Raider.

WILLING, FOY
Born: 1915, Bosque County, Tex. Died: July 24, 1978, Nashville, Tenn. (heart attack). Screen, radio actor and singer.

Appeared in: **1946** Out California Way; Throw a Saddle on a Star. **1947** Along the Oregon Trail; Last Frontier Uprising; Under Colorado Skies. **1948** California Firebrand; The Timber Trail; Grand Canyon Trail. **1949** Down Dakota Way; The Golden Stallion; Susanna Pass; The Far Frontier. **1950** Twilight in the Sierras; Trigger, Jr.; North of the Great Divide; Bells of Coronado; Sunset in the West; Trail of Robin Hood. **1951** Heart of the Rockies; Spoilers of the Plains; Texas Carnival.

WILLINGHAM, HARRY G.
Born: 1881. Died: Nov. 17, 1943, North Hollywood, Calif. (suicide—gun). Screen actor. Entered films during silents.

WILLIS, CONSTANCE
Died: Nov. 18, 1940. Opera singer and screen actress.

Appeared in: **1939** The Mikado.

WILLIS, DAVE
Born: 1895. Died: Jan. 1, 1973, Peebles, Scotland. Stage, vaudeville and screen actor. Father of comedian Denny Willis. Appeared in act known as "Willis and Richards."

WILLIS, LEO
Born: Okla. Died: Apr. 10, 1952. Screen actor.

Appeared in: **1918** The Border Wireless. **1919** Wagon Tracks. **1920** The Toll Gate. **1921** O'Malley of the Mounted; An Unwilling Hero; Three Word Brand. **1922** The Timber Queen (serial); Broken Chains. **1923** Wild Bill Hickok; All the Brothers Were Valiant; Souls for Sale. **1924** The White Sheep. **1925** The Way of a Girl. **1926** The Tough Guy; A Hero of the Big Snows. **1927** The Kid Brother; Flying Elephants (short). **1928** Their Purple Moment (short). **1929** The Hoose Gow (short). **1930** The following shorts: Ladies Last; The Fighting Parson; Below Zero. **1931** Pardon Us; Monkey Business; plus the following shorts: The Panic Is On; One of the Smiths; Beau Hunks; The Kickoff; Skip the Maloo! **1932** The Tabasco Kid (short); Seal Skins (short). **1933** His Silent Racket (short). **1934** Six of a Kind; The Gold Ghost (short); The Live Ghost (short). **1935** Southern Exposure (short). **1936** The Bohemian Girl; On the Wrong Trek (short).

WILLIS, LOUISE
Born: 1880. Died: Jan. 2, 1929, Chicago, Ill. Stage and screen actress.

WILLIS, RICHARD
Born: Oct. 15, 1876, London, England. Died: Apr. 8, 1945, Los Angeles, Calif. (cerebral hemorrhage). Screen actor. Appeared in Nestor Film Co. films.

WILLMORE, ALFRED See MAC LIAMMOIR, MICHAEL

WILLOUBHBY, LEWIS
Born: England. Died: Sept. 12, 1968, Clearwater, Fla. Screen and stage actor. Married to actress Olga Petrova (dec. 1977).

Appeared in: 1918 Sauce for the Goose; A Pair of Silk Stockings. 1921 Desperate Youth. 1922 Mr. Barnes of New York; The Lamp in the Desert (US 1923). 1923 Shifting Sands.

WILLS, BEVERLY
Born: 1934. Died: Oct. 24, 1963, Palm Springs, Calif. (fire). Screen, radio and television actress. Daughter of actress Joan Davis (dec. 1961).

Appeared in: 1938 Anesthesia (short). 1945 George White's Scandals. 1948 Mickey. 1952 Skirts Ahoy. 1953 Small Town Girl. 1959 Some Like It Hot. 1961 The Ladies' Man. 1963 Son of Flubber.

WILLS, BOB
Born: 1905. Died: May 13, 1975, Ft. Worth, Tex. (bronchial pneumonia). Screen actor, singer and composer.

Appeared in: 1940 Take Me Back to Oklahoma. 1941 Go West, Young Lady. 1942 The Lone Prairie; A Tornado in the Saddle. 1943 Riders of the Northwest Mounted; Saddles and Sagebrush; Silver City Raiders. 1944 Bob Wills and His Texas Playboys (short); The Vigilantes Ride; Wyoming Hurricane; The Last Horseman. 1945 Rhythm Roundup; Blazing the Western Trail. 1946 Frontier Frolic (short); Lawless Empire. 1965 Thunder in Dixie. 1967 Country Western Hoedown.

WILLS, BREMBER (Brember Le Couteur)
Born: Reading, England. Died: Dec. 1, 1948, England? Screen and stage actor.

Appeared in: 1931 Carnival (aka Venetian Nights—US). 1932 The Old Dark House. 1934 What Happened to Harkness; The Unfinished Symphony (US 1935).

WILLS, CHILL
Born: July 18, 1903, Seagoville, Tex. Died: Dec. 15, 1978, Encino, Calif. Screen, vaudeville, burlesque and television actor. Was voice of "Francis" in the Francis series of films.

Appeared in: 1935 Bar 20 Rides Again (film debut). 1936 At Sea Ashore (short); Way Out West; The Call of the Prairie. 1938 Lawless Valley. 1939 Racketeers of the Range; Allegheny Uprising; Sorority House. 1940 Boom Town; The Westerner; Tugboat Annie Sails Again; Sky Murder. 1941 Western Union; The Bad Man; Billy the Kid; Belle Starr; Honky Tonk; The Bugle Sounds. 1942 Tarzan's New York Adventure; Her Cardboard Lover; Apache Trail; The Omaha Trail; Stand By For Action. 1943 A Stranger in Town; Best Foot Forward. 1944 Way Out West; The Immortal Blacksmith (short); See Here, Private Hargrove; Barbary Coast Gent; Meet Me in St. Louis; Sunday Dinner for a Soldier; I'll Be Seeing You. 1945 What Next, Corporal Hargrove?; Leave Her to Heaven. 1946 The Harvey Girls; Gailant Bess; The Yearling. 1947 Heartaches. 1948 Raw Deal; Northwest Stampede; That Wonderful Urge; The Sainted Sisters; The Saxon Charm; It Can't Be Done (short); Family Honeymoon. 1949 Francis (voice); Tulsa; Loaded Pistols; Red Canyon. 1950 Rio Grande; The Sundowners; High Lonesome. 1951 Oh! Susanna; Cattle Drive; The Sea Hornet; Francis Goes to the Races (voice). 1952 Bronco Buster; Ride the Man Down; Francis Goes to West Point (voice). 1953 City That Never Sleeps; The Man from the Alamo; Small Town Girl; Tumbleweed. 1954 Francis Joins the WACS (voice); Ricochet Romance. 1955 Hell's Outpost; Timberjack; Francis in the Navy (voice). 1956 Giant; Santiago; Francis in the Haunted House (voice). 1957 Gun for a Coward; Gun Glory. 1958 From Hell to Texas. 1959 The Sad Horse. 1960 Where the Boys Are; The Alamo. 1961 Deadly Companions; Gold of the Seven Saints; The Little Shepherd of Kingdom Come. 1962 Young Guns of Texas. 1963 McLintock!; The Wheeler Dealers; The Cardinal. 1965 The Rounders. 1966 Fireball 500. 1969 Big Daddy. 1970 The Liberation of L. B. Jones. 1971 The Steagle. 1973 Pat Garrett and Billy the Kid; Guns of a Stranger. 1977 Poco ... Little Dog Lost; Mr. Billion.

WILLS, DRUSILLA
Born: Nov. 14, 1884, London, England. Died: Aug. 11, 1951, London, England. Screen and stage actress.

Appeared in: 1932 Old Spanish Customers; The Lodger (aka The Phantom Fiend—US 1935). 1933 The Medicine Man; Little Miss Nobody; Britannia of Billingsgate. 1934 Night Club Queen; The Black Abbot. 1935 The Big Splash; Squibs. 1937 Non-Stop New York; The High Command. 1938 Quiet Please; Yellow Sands; A Spot of Bother; Sixty Glorious Years (aka Queen of Destiny—US); Luck of the Navy (aka North Sea Patrol—US 1940). 1939 A Girl Must Live (US 1941); Inspector Hornleigh on Holiday. 1944 Champagne Charlie. 1949 The Queen of Spades.

WILLS, NAT (Louis MacGrath Wills)
Born: July 11, 1873, Fredericksburg, Va. Died: Dec. 9, 1917, Woodcliff, N.J. (accidental carbon monoxide poisoning). Screen, stage and vaudeville actor.

Appeared in: 1911 Nat Wills as King of Kazam.

WILLS, WALTER
Born: 1881. Died: Jan. 18, 1967, Hollywood, Calif. Screen and stage actor and dancer.

Appeared in: 1923 In Search of a Thrill. 1938 The Great Adventures of Wild Bill Hickok (serial); Santa Fe Stampede. 1939 The Night Riders; Cowboys from Texas. 1941 Ye Olde Minstrels (short). 1942 Melodies Old and New (short); Doin' Their Bit (short).

WILLSON, RINI See ZAROVA, RINI

WILLY, EDGAR (Edgar Dobbelaere)
Born: 1896, Brussels, Belgium. Died: Jan. 11, 1980, Brussels, Belgium. Screen, stage, radio, television actor, dancer and aviator. Married to actress Janine Bailly.

Appeared in:Le Banquet des Fraudeurs; Thanasse and Casimir; Home Sweet Home.

WILMER-BROWN, MAISIE
Born: 1893. Died: Feb. 13, 1973, London, England. Screen and vaudeville actress. Appeared in silents.

WILMOT, LEE
Born: 1899. Died: Mar. 9, 1938, Hollywood, Calif. (suicide—fall from building). Screen and radio actor.

WILSEY, JAY "BUFFALO BILL, JR."
Born: 1896, Hillsdale, Wyo. Died: Oct. 25, 1961. Screen actor.

Appeared in: 1930 Way Out West. 1932 Dynamite Denny. 1933 Terror Trail. 1935 Powdersmoke Range; The Phantom Empire. 1939 Blue Montana Skies. 1943 The Dancing Masters.

WILSON, AL
Born: Harrisburgh, Ky. Died: Mar. 6, 1936. Screen actor, aviator and stuntman.

Appeared in: 1923 The Eagle's Talons (serial); Ghost City (serial). 1924 The Air Hawk. 1925 The Cloud Rider; The Crackerjack; Flyin' Thru; Fighting Ranger (serial). 1926 The Brown Derby; The Flying Mail. 1927 Home Made; Three Miles Up; Sky-High Saunders. 1928 The Air Patrol; Chinatown Charlie; The Cloud Dodger; The Phantom Flyer; Won in the Clouds; The Wright Idea. 1929 The Sky Skidder. 1930 Hell's Angels. 1932 The Airmail Mystery (serial).

WILSON, ALAN C.
Born: 1943. Died: Sept. 2, 1970, Los Angeles, Calif. Screen actor and musician. Member of "Canned Heat" rock group.

Appeared in: 1969 Monterey Pop. 1970 Woodstock; The Naked Zoo.

WILSON, BENJAMIN F.
Born: 1876, Clinton, Iowa. Died: Aug. 25, 1930, Glendale, Calif. (heart ailment). Screen actor, film director and producer. Entered films as an actor with Edison and Nestor film companies, approx. 1912.

Appeared in: 1912 What Happened to Mary (serial); The Passing of J. B. Randall and Co.; At the Point of the Sword; A Chase Across the Continent; Believe Me If All Those Endearing Young Charms; For Valor; 'Ostler Joe; In His Father's Steps; Treasure Island; The Close of the American Revolution. 1914 Edison series. 1917 The Mystery Ship (serial); The Voice on the Wire. 1919 Trail of the Octopus (serial). 1920 Screaming Shadow (serial); The Branded Four (serial). 1921 The Mysterious Pearl (serial); Dangerous Paths. 1924 The Desert Hawk;

His Majesty the Outlaw; Notch Number One. **1925** The Power God (serial); The Fugitive; A Daughter of the Sioux; The Man from Lone Mountain; Renegade Holmes, M.D.; Sand Blind; Tonio, Son of the Sierras; Fort Frayne; Warrior Gap; The Mystery Box (serial); Vic Dyson Pays. **1926** Officer 444 (serial); Baited Trap; Rainbow Riley; West of the Law; Wolves of the Desert; Sheriff's Girl. **1927** The Mystery Brand; A Yellow Streak; Riders of the West; The Range Riders. **1929** Bye, Bye Buddy; China Slaver; Girls Who Dare. **1930** Shadow Ranch.

WILSON, CHARLES CAHILL
Born: 1894. Died: Jan. 7, 1948 (esophagal hemorrhage). Screen actor.

Appeared in: **1929** Lucky Boy; Acquitted; Broadway Scandals; Song of Love. **1933** Hard to Handle; Female; Havana Widows; Elmer the Great; The Mayor of Hell; Mary Stevens, M.D.; Footlight Parade; The Kennel Murder Case; College Coach. **1934** Here Is My Heart; Dragon Murder Case; Miss Fane's Baby Is Stolen; Roman Scandals; I've Got Your Number; Harold Teen; St. Louis Kid; Murder in the Clouds; The Circus Clown; Broadway Bill; The Hell Cat; Affairs of a Gentleman; The Lemon Drop Kid; Death on the Diamond; It Happened One Night; Fog Over Frisco; The Human Side. **1935** Behold My Wife; Great Hotel Murder; The Gilded Lily; Four Hours to Kill; The Glass Key; Smart Girl; Mary Burns, Fugitive; Car 99; The Nitwits; Another Face; Fighting Youth; The Public Menace; Hitch Hike Lady; I'd Give My Life; Men of the Hour; Murder in the Fleet; The Case of the Lucky Legs; Music is Magic; Show Them No Mercy; Waterfront Lady; Port of Lost Dreams; The Perfect Clue. **1936** We're Only Human; Strike Me Pink; The Return of Jimmy Valentine; Gentleman from Louisiana; Grand Jury; They Wanted to Marry; Big Brown Eyes; Three Married Men; Mind Your Own Business; The Mine With the Iron Door; Panic on the Air; Legion of Terror; Pennies from Heaven; Showboat; The Magnificent Brute; Educating Father; Earthworm Tractors; Down the Stretch; Ticket to Paradise; Satan Met a Lady; I'd Give My Life. **1937** Woman in Distress; The Devil is Driving; Roaring Timber; Life Begins in College; The Adventurous Blonde; They Wanted to Marry; Murder Goes to College; Find the Witness; Partners in Crime; Merry-Go-Round of 1938; Charlie Chan on Broadway. **1938** State Police; Sally, Irene and Mary; When Were You Born?; Tenth Avenue Kid; Little Miss Thoroughbred; Night Hawk; Hold That Co-ed; The Spider's Web (serial). **1939** Fighting Thoroughbreds; Rose of Washington Square; Desperate Trails; Hotel for Women; Smashing the Money Ring; The Return of Dr. X; The Cowboy Quarterback; Here I Am a Stranger. **1940** He Married His Wife; Sandy Is a Lady; The Girl in 313; Knute Rockne—All American; Public Deb No. 1; Charter Pilot. **1941** The Face Behind the Mask; Meet John Doe; Federal Fugitives; Broadway Limited; Dressed to Kill; The Officer and the Lady; Blues in the Night. **1942** Lady Gangster; Rings on Her Finger; Escape from Crime. **1943** Batman (serial); Silver Spurs; Two Senoritas from Chicago. **1944** Crime by Night; Hey, Rookie; Kansas City Kitty; The Big Noise; Shadows in the Night. **1945** Incendiary Blonde. **1946** Suspense; I Ring Doorbells; Passkey to Danger; Larceny in Her Heart; Crime of the Century; If I'm Lucky; Blonde for a Day; Bringing Up Father; Gas House Kids. **1947** Her Husband's Affair. **1948** Crime on Their Hands (short).

WILSON, CLARENCE H. (Clarence Hummel Wilson)
Born: 1877, Cincinnati, Ohio. Died: Oct. 5, 1941, Hollywood, Calif. Screen and stage actor. Entered films approx. 1920.

Appeared in: **1927** Mountains of Manhattan; The Silent Avenger. **1928** Phantom of the Turf. **1930** Dangerous Paradise; Love in the Rough. **1931** Front Page; Night Life in Reno; Sea Ghost; Her Majesty, Love. **1932** Amateur Daddy; Winner Take All; Young Ironsides (short); Purchase Price; Down to Earth; The Phantom of Crestwood; The Penguin Pool Murder; The All American; The Jewel Robbery. **1933** Smoke Lightning; Pick-Up Girl; A Shriek in the Night; Flaming Guns; The Mysterious Rider; The Girl in 419; Terror Abroad; Tilli and Gus; King for a Night; Son of Kong. **1934** Shrimps for a Day (short); You Said a Hateful (short); Count of Monte Cristo; Successful Failure; The Lemon Drop Kid; Wake Up and Dream; I'll Fix It; Love Birds; I Like It That Way; Now I'll Tell; Unknown Blonde; Bachelor Bait; The Old-Fashioned Way. **1935** Ruggles of Red Gap; Let 'Em Have It!; Champagne for Breakfast; Waterfront Lady; Great Hotel Murder; When a Man's a Man; One Frightened Night; plus the following shorts: Little Sinner; Nurse to You!; Public Ghost No. 1; The Tin Man. **1936** Little Miss Nobody; Love Begins at Twenty; The Case of the Black Cat; On the Wrong Trek (short); Rainbow on the River; Hats Off. **1937** Two Wise Maids; Damaged Goods; Small Town Boy; Westland Case. **1938** Rebecca of Sunnybrook Farm; Kentucky Moonshine; Little Miss Broadway; Having a Wonderful Time; You Can't Take It with You. **1939** Drums Along the Mohawk; East Side of Heaven; Clown Princes (short); Desperate Trails. **1940** Little Old New York; Melody Ranch. **1941** Angels With Broken Wings; Road Show; You're the One.

WILSON, DOOLEY
Born: Apr. 3, 1894, Tyler, Tex. Died: May 30, 1953, Los Angeles, Calif. Black screen, stage, vaudeville, radio actor and bandleader. Toured Europe with his own band from 1919 to 1930.

Appeared in: **1942** Casablanca (film debut); Night in New Orleans; Take a Letter; Darling; Cairo; My Favorite Blonde. **1943** Two Tickets to London; Stormy Weather; Higher and Higher. **1944** Seven Days Ashore. **1948** Racing Luck. **1949** Come to the Stable; Free for All. **1951** Passage West.

WILSON, ED
Born: 1916. Died: Feb. 6, 1975. Screen actor.

Appeared in: **1926** The Flaming Frontier. **1934** I Like It That Way.

WILSON, EDITH (Edith Woodall)
Born: 1897. Died: Mar. 31, 1981, Chicago, Ill. (cerebral hemorrhage). Black screen, stage, vaudeville, radio, televison actress and singer. Known as "Aunt Jemima" from 1948 to 1966.

Appeared in: **1944** To Have and Have Not.

WILSON, EDNA
Born: 1880. Died: July 23, 1960, N.Y. Screen and stage actress. One of the original "Gibson Girls" in early films.

WILSON, ELSIE JANE
Born: New Zealand. Died: Jan. 16, 1965, Los Angeles, Calif. Screen actress. Married to actor Rupert Julian (dec. 1943).

Appeared in: **1915** Bound on the Wheel; Mountain Justice; Donna Perfecta. **1916** Oliver Twist; Temptation; The Human Catos. **1917** The Little Pirate; The Cricket; My Little Boy; The Silent Lady. **1918** New Love for Old; Beauty in Chains; City of Tears; The Dream Lady. **1919** The Lure of Luxury; The Game's Up.

WILSON, FRANCIS
Born: Feb., 1854, Philadelphia, Pa. Died: Oct. 7, 1935, N.Y. Screen, stage, minstrel actor and author. Appeared in Sennett's comedies in 1915.

WILSON, FRANK H.
Born: 1886, N.Y. or Jacksonville, Fla. Died: Feb. 16, 1956, Queens, N.Y. Black screen, stage, vaudeville, radio and television actor.

Appeared in: **1933** Emperor Jones. **1936** Green Pastures (stage and film versions). **1937** The Devil Is Driving; The Awful Truth; All American Sweetheart; A Dangerous Adventure; Life Begins With Love. **1938** Extortion. **1943** Watch on the Rhine.

WILSON, GEORGE (Alfred Ensom)
Born: 1854, England. Died: July 30, 1954, London, England. Screen actor, "England's oldest."

Appeared in: **1943** The Life and Death of Colonel Blimp (aka Colonel Blimp—US 1945). **1945** Henry V (US 1946). **1946** Caesar and Cleopatra.

WILSON, GWENDA
Born: 1922, Australia. Died: Aug. 18, 1977, London, England. Screen and radio actress.

WILSON, HAL
Born: Oct. 2, 1887, New York, N.Y. Died: May 22, 1933, Los Angeles, Calif. (paralytic stroke). Screen and stage actor. Entered films with Vitagraph in 1907.

Appeared in: **1908** The Clown's Adventure. **1921** The Secret Four (serial); Charge It; The Unknown Wife. **1922** Lady Godiva; Nan of the North (serial); Blaze Away; According to Hoyle; Forget-Me-Not. **1923** Main Street. **1924** Sundown; The Love Master. **1925** Don Q; Smilin' at Trouble. **1929** Iron Mask; Divorce Made Easy. **1930** Big House. **1931** Guilty Hands.

WILSON, HARRY
Born: 1898. Died: Sept. 6, 1978, Woodland Hills, Calif. Screen actor.

Appeared in: **1936** On the Wrong Trek (short). **1937** Grips, Grunts and Groans (short); A Day at the Races. **1939** The Sap Takes a Wrap (short). **1942** Native Land. **1944** Bermuda Mystery. **1958** Frankenstein's Daughter. **1959** Some Like It Hot. **1964** Robin and the Seven Hoods.

WILSON, HELENE
Born: 1888. Died: July 29, 1981, Woodland Hills, Calif. Screen actress. Appeared in films from 1922-1951.

WILSON, IMOGENE "BUBBLES" *See* NOLAN, MARY

WILSON, JACK
Born: 1917. Died: Dec. 18, 1966, Los Angeles, Calif. (cerebral hemorrhage). Screen and stage actor.

Appeared in: **1951** Francis Goes to the Races. **1953** Son of the Renegade.

WILSON, LILLIAN R.
Born: 1897. Died: Aug., 1979, Woodland Hills, Calif. Screen actress and makeup artist.

WILSON, M. K.
Born: 1890. Died: Oct. 9, 1933, Long Beach, Calif. (auto accident injuries). Stage and screen actor.

Appeared in: **1930** The Costello Case.

WILSON, MARIE (Kathleen Elizabeth White)
Born: Aug. 19, 1916, Anaheim, Calif. Died: Nov. 23, 1972, Hollywood Hills, Calif. (cancer). Screen, television, radio actress, night club entertainer and stage actress. Divorced from actor Allen Nixon. Married to producer and writer Robert Fallon.

Appeared in: **1934** Babes in Toyland; My Girl Sally. **1935** Slide, Kelly, Slide; Stars Over Broadway; Miss Pacific Fleet; Broadway Hostess. **1936** Colleen; Satan Met a Lady; The Great Ziegfeld; China Clipper; King of Hockey; The Big Noise. **1937** The Great Garrick; Without Warning; Melody for Two; Public Wedding. **1938** Fools for Scandal; Boy Meets Girl; The Invisible Menace; Broadway Musketeers. **1939** Should Husbands Work?; Waterfront; The Sweepstakes Winner; The Cowboy Quarterback. **1941** Virginia; Flying Blind; Rookies on Parade. **1942** Harvard, Here I Come; She's In the Army; Broadway. **1944** Shine on Harvest Moon; You Can't Ration Love; Music for Millions. **1946** No Leave, No Love; Young Widow. **1947** The Hal Roach Comedy Carnival; Linda Be Good; The Private Affairs of Bel Ami; Fabulous Joe. **1949** My Friend Irma. **1950** My Friend Irma Goes West. **1952** A Girl in Every Port; Never Wave at a WAC. **1953** Marry Me Again. **1957** The Story of Mankind. **1962** Mr. Hobbs Takes a Vacation.

WILSON, ROBERTA
Born: 1904. Died: Feb. 2, 1972, Hollywood, Calif. (stroke). Screen actress and singer.

WILSON, TOM
Born: 1880, Helena, Mont. Died: Feb. 19, 1965, Calif. Screen, stage and vaudeville actor.

Appeared in: **1917** The Americano; Wild and Wooly. **1918** Amarilly of Clothesline Alley; A Dog's Life; Shakler Arms. **1919** Sunnyside; A Day's Pleasure; The Greatest Question; Atta Boy's Last Ride. **1920** Don't Ever Marry; Dinty; Isobel. **1921** The Kid; Where Men Are Men; Two Minutes to Go; Scrap Iron. **1922** Alias Julius Caesar; Minnie; Reported Missing; Red Hot Romance. **1923** Good By Girls!; Itching Palms; Quicksands; Soft Boiled; The Courtship of Myles Standish; The Remittance Woman. **1924** The Heart Buster; Fools in the Dark; On Time; His Darker Self. **1925** What Fools Men; The Best Bad Man; American Pluck; California Straight Ahead; Madame Behave; Seven Days; Secrets of the Night; Manhattan Madness; The Million Dollar Handicap. **1926** The Rainmaker; Battling Butler; Across the Pacific. **1927** When a Man Loves; Ham and Eggs at the Front; No Control. **1928** Riley the Cop; The Pioneer Scout. **1929** Strong Boy. **1930** The Big House; Dark Skies; Big Boy. **1931** The Vice Squad; Oh! Oh! Cleopatra; Sooky. **1933** Picture Snatcher; The Chief; Silk Express; Blondie Johnson. **1936** Love Begins at 20; Early to Bed; Treachery Rides the Range. **1937** The Captain's Kid. **1939** Nancy Drew—Trouble Shooter. **1940** Devil's Island; Always a Bride. **1955** The View from Pompey's Head; Thy Neighbor's Daughter; The Tall Men. **1956** Edge of Hell.

WILSON, WARD (Harry Warden Wilson)
Born: 1904, Trenton, N.J. Died: Mar. 21, 1966, West Palm Beach, Fla. Screen, stage, radio and television actor. He narrated numerous shorts for Paramount, Columbia, etc.

Appeared in: **1957** The Golden Age of Comedy (narr.).

WILSON, WAYNE
Born: 1899. Died: Jan. 4, 1970, San Antonio, Tex. Screen, stage, radio and television actor.

WILSON, WENDELL C.
Born: 1889. Died: Jan. 9, 1927, Vancouver, B.C., Canada (pneumonia). Screen, stage actor, stage manager and stage director.

WILSON, WHIP
Born: 1915. Died: Oct. 23, 1964, Hollywood, Calif. (heart attack). Screen actor and rodeo performer.

Appeared in: **1948** Silver Trails (film debut). **1949** Crashing Thru; Haunted Trails; Range Land; Riders of the Dusk; Shadows of the West. **1950** Arizona Territory; Canyon Raiders; Cherokee Uprising; Fence Riders; Gunslingers; Outlaw of Texas; Silver Raiders. **1951** Abilene Trail; Lawless Cowboys; Montana Incident; Nevada Badmen; Stagecoach Driver. **1952** Gunman; Hired Gun; Night Raiders; Wyoming Roundup. **1955** The Kentuckian.

WILSON, WILLIAM
Died: July 9, 1972. Screen actor. Do not confuse with screen actor William F. Wilson (dec. 1956).

WILSON, WILLIAM F.
Born: 1894. Died: May 10, 1956, Woodland Hills, Calif. Screen and stage actor.

Appeared in: **1927** The Bush Leaguer.

WILTON, ERIC
Born: 1883. Died: Feb. 23, 1957. Screen actor.

Appeared in: **1931** Arrowsmith. **1932** Dr. Jekyll and Mr. Hyde; One Hour With You; Silent Witness. **1933** The Masquerader. **1934** Midnight Alibi; Fashions of 1934. **1935** Mutiny on the Bounty. **1936** After the Thin Man; Forbidden Heaven. **1937** Beware of Ladies; Angel; Lost Horizon; 100 Men and a Girl. **1938** Always Goodbye; The Adventures of Sherlock Holmes. **1940** Johnny Apollo; Hudson's Bay; I Love You Again. **1942** Tales of Manhattan; They Raid by Night; Rings on Her Fingers. **1944** Gaslight. **1945** Billy Rose's Diamond Horseshoe; Molly and Me. **1946** Three Strangers; Claudia and David; Night and Day; The Jolson Story. **1948** Appointment With Murder; Docks of New Orleans. **1949** Jolson Sings Again. **1951** Valentino; Rhubarb; A Place in the Sun; Royal Wedding. **1953** How to Marry a Millionaire. **1954** Woman's World; Knock on Wood. **1956** Three Bad Sisters. **1957** The Joker Is Wild.

WILTON, ROBB
Born: 1882, Liverpool, England. Died: May 1, 1957, London, England. Screen actor.

Appeared in: **1936** It's Love Again. **1938** Break the News (US 1941).

WILTSIE, SIMEON S.
Born: 1853, New York. Died: Jan. 13, 1918, Englewood, N.J. Screen actor.

Appeared in: **1915** The Secret Agent.

WINANT, FORREST
Born: Feb. 21, 1888, New York, N.Y. Died: Jan. 30, 1928, Alameda, Calif. Screen and stage actor.

Appeared in: **1916** New York. **1927** The Iron Heart.

WINAR, ERNST
Born: 1894, Holland. Died: June 28, 1978, Holland? Screen actor and film director. Appeared in German silent films.

WINCHELL, WALTER
Born: Apr. 7, 1897, Harlem, N.Y. Died: Feb. 20, 1972, Los Angeles, Calif. Journalist, Broadway columnist, screen, television, vaudeville and radio actor.

Appeared in: **1933** Universal short. **1934** A Hollywood Gad-About (short). **1937** Wake Up and Live; Love and Hisses. **1957** A Face in the Crowd; The Helen Morgan Story. **1960** College Confidential. **1961** Dondi; Wild Harvest. **1962** The Scarface Mob. **1968** Wild in the Streets.

WINCHESTER, BARBARA
Born: c. 1895. Died: Apr. 20, 1968, New York, N.Y. Screen, stage, radio and television actress.

Appeared in: **1962** The Connection.

WINCOTT, ROSALIE AVOLO
Born: 1873. Died: Nov., 1951, Los Angeles, Calif. Screen and stage actress.

WINDHEIM, MAREK
Born: 1895, Poland. Died: Dec. 1, 1960. Screen actor, television producer and opera performer.

Appeared in: **1937** Something to Sing About; I'll Take Romance. **1938** She Married an Artist; Say It in French; Dramatic School. **1939** Ninotchka; On Your Toes; Hotel Imperial. **1941** Marry the Boss's Daughter. **1942** Holiday Inn; I Married an Angel; Mrs. Miniver; Crossroads. **1943** Mission to Moscow; Hi Diddle Diddle. **1944** In Our Time; Allergic to Love; Kismet; Mrs. Parkington; Our Hearts Were Young and Gay. **1945** Yolanda and the Thief; Weekend at the Waldorf. **1946** Tarzan and the Leopard Woman; The Best Years of Our Lives.

WINDSOR, ADELE
Born: 1904. Died: May 26, 1931, New York, N.Y. (auto accident). Screen and stage actress.

Appeared in: **1929** The Girl from Havana; Frozen Justice. **1930** True to the Navy; Up the River.

WINDSOR, CLAIRE (Claire Viola Cronk)
Born: Apr. 14, 1897, Coffee City, Kans. Died: Oct. 24, 1972, Los Angeles, Calif. (heart attack). Screen actress. Divorced from actor Bert Lytell (dec. 1954). Entered films as an extra with Lasky.

Appeared in: **1921** To Please One Woman; Dr. Jim; The Blot; The Raiders; What Do Men Want?; Too Wise Wives; What's Worth While? **1922** Broken Chains; Grand Larceny; Fools First; Brothers Under the Skin; One Clear Call; The Stranger's Banquet; Rich Men's Wives. **1923** The Acquittal; Little Church Around the Corner; The Eternal Three; Souls for Sale; Rupert of Hentzau. **1924** Nellie, The Beautiful Cloak Model; Born Rich; For Sale; A Son of the Sahara. **1925** Souls for Sables; The Dixie Handicap; The Denial; Just a Woman; The White Desert. **1926** Dance Madness; Money Talks; Tin Hats. **1927** Blondes by Choice; The Claw; A Little Journey; The Bugle Call; Foreign Devils; The Frontiersman; The Opening Night. **1928** The Grain of Dust; Domestic Meddlers; Fashion Madness; Satan and the Woman; Nameless Men. **1929** Captain Lash; Midstream. **1932** Hollywood on Parade (short). **1933** Sister to Judas; Self Defense (aka My Mother); Constant Woman. **1934** Cross Streets. **1938** Barefoot Boy. **1945** How Do You Do? **1952** The Last Act.

WINFIELD, JOAN (Joan MacGillicuddy)
Born: 1919, Melbourne, Australia. Died: June 16, 1978, Van Nuys, Calif. (cancer). Screen and stage actress. Married to director/writer John Meredyth Lucas.

Appeared in: **1941** Bullets for O'Hara. **1942** The Gorilla Man. **1943** Mission to Moscow; Murder on the Waterfront. **1944** The Adventures of Mark Twain. **1946** A Stolen Life. **1947** The Imperfect Lady. **1948** Johnny Belinda. **1951** Queen for a Day. **1954** The Egyptian.

WING, DAN
Born: 1923. Died: June 14, 1969, Fresno, Calif. (heart attack). Screen, stage and television actor.

WING, WARD
Born: 1894, Springfield, Mo. Died: June 5, 1945, Los Angeles, Calif. Screen actor, film director and screenwriter.

Appeared in: **1917** Cupid's Thumb Print. **1918** A Mother's Secret; The Eagle. **1919** In His Brother's Place; Loot. **1921** The Conquering Power. **1925** Eyes of Hollywood.

WINGFIELD, H. CONWAY
Born: 1872, Borg, Ireland. Died: Feb. 9, 1948, New York, N.Y. (heart attack). Screen and stage actor. Appeared in International and Famous Players Film Companies films.

Appeared in: **1930** Great Power.

WINN, GODFREY
Born: 1909, England. Died: June 19, 1971, England (heart attack). Screen, stage, radio actor and journalist.

Appeared in: **1927** Blight (aka Apres La Guerre). **1961** Very Important Person (aka A Coming-Out Party—US 1962). **1963** Billy Liar. **1964** The Bargee. **1966** The Great St. Trinian's Train Robbery (US 1967).

WINNINGER, CHARLES
Born: May 26, 1884, Athens, Wis. Died: Jan. 27, 1969, Palm Springs, Calif. Screen, stage, vaudeville, radio and television actor. Appeared in vaudeville with his parents, brothers and sisters. Married to stage actress Gertrude Walker and divorced from actress Blanche Ring (dec. 1931). Entered films with Elko Comedy Co.

Appeared in: **1915** The Doomed Groom. **1924** Pied Piper Malone. **1926** The Canadian; Summer Bachelors. **1930** How I Play Golf-Chip Shots (short); Soup to Nuts. **1931** God's Gift to Women; Fighting Caravans; Gun Smoke; Children of Dreams; The Sin of Madelon Claudet; Bad Sister; Gambling Daughters; The Devil Was Sick; Night Nurse; Flying High. **1932** Husband's Holiday. **1934** Social Register. **1936** White Fang; Show Boat (stage and film versions). **1937** Dancing for Love; Three Smart Girls; You're a Sweetheart; Woman Chases Man; Nothing Sacred; Cafe Metropole; You Can't Have Everything; The Go-Getter; Every Day's a Holiday. **1938** Goodbye Broadway; Hard to Get. **1939** Barricade; Three Smart Girls Grow Up; Babes in Arms; Destry Rides Again; First Love; Fifth Avenue Girl. **1940** If I Had My Way; My Love Came Back; When Lovers Meet; Beyond Tomorrow; Little Nellie Kelly. **1941** The Get-Away; My Life with Caroline; Pot O'Gold; Ziegfeld Girl. **1942** Friendly Enemies. **1943** Coney Island; A Lady Takes A Chance; Flesh and Fantasy; Hers to Hold. **1944** Broadway Rhythm; Belle of the Yukon; Sunday Dinner for a Soldier. **1945** She Wouldn't Say Yes; State Fair. **1946** Lover Come Back. **1947** Living in a Big Way; Something in the Wind. **1948** Inside Story; Give My Regards to Broadway. **1950** Father Is a Bachelor. **1953** The Sun Shines Bright; Torpedo Alley; Perilous Journey; Champ for a Day. **1955** Las Vegas Shakedown. **1960** Raymie.

WINOGRADOFF, ANATOL
Born: 1891, Russia. Died: Apr. 27, 1980, Canoga Park, Calif. Screen, stage. television actor and stage director.

Appeared in: **1935** She (film debut). **1954** Go, Man, Go. **1959** The Last Angry Man. **1960** Man on a String. **1974** Young Frankenstein; Harry and Tonto; The Girl from Petrovka.

WINSCOTT, EDWIN C. See ARMAND, TEDDY V.

WINSTON, BRUCE (Charles Bruce Winston)
Born: Mar. 4, 1879, Liverpool, England. Died: Sept. 27, 1946, at sea enroute to N.Y. (heart attack). Screen, stage actor and stage producer. Entered films in 1919.

Appeared in: **1931** Children of Dreams. **1933** The Private Life of Henry VIII. **1934** Blossom Time (aka April Romance—US 1937); My Song for You; The Private Life of Don Juan. **1935** Heat Wave. **1936** The Man Who Could Work Miracles; Everybody Dance. **1937** Intimate Relations. **1938** Alf's Button Afloat. **1940** The Thief of Bagdad. **1945** Flight from Folly. **1946** Carnival.

WINSTON, IRENE
Born: 1920. Died: Sept. 1, 1964, Hollywood, Calif. (pneumonia complications). Screen, stage actress and television writer.

Appeared in: **1951** Dear Brat. **1952** My Son, John. **1954** Rear Window. **1957** The Delicate Delinquent.

WINSTON, JACKIE
Born: 1915. Died: Nov. 9, 1971, N.Y. Screen, stage, television actor and comedian. Entered show business when nine years old, winning a singing stint with Will Osborne's band.

Appeared in: **1967** The Happening.

WINTER, CHARLES R.
Born: 1876. Died: June 29, 1952, Redondo Beach, Fla. Screen, vaudeville and radio actor. Appeared in vaudeville as part of "Williams and Charles" team (formerly entitled "Deltorelli and Gilssandos," then "Del and Gliss," and finally as "Williams and Charles").

WINTER, PERCY CAMPBELL
Born: Nov. 16, 1861, Toronto, Canada. Died: May 5, 1928, Boonton, N.J. Screen, stage actor and stage director.

Appeared in: **1914** A Recent Confederate Victory. **1915** Patsy Among the Smugglers; The Steadfast; The Unmarried Husband.

WINTER, WILLIAM See JEFFERSON, WILLIAM WINTER

WINTER, WINONA
Born: 1891. Died: Apr. 27, 1940, Hollywood, Calif. Screen, stage and vaudeville actress.

WINTHROP, JOY (Josephine Williams)
Born: 1864. Died: Apr. 1, 1950, Hollywood, Calif. Screen and stage actress.

Appeared in: **1921** The Blazing Trail. **1922** Man's Law and God's. **1923** Her Fatal Millions. **1928** Stolen Love. **1930** The First Seven Years (short).

WINTON, BARRY
Born: 1901, London, England. Died: June 4, 1978, Charleston, S.C. (heart attack). Violinist, bandleader, talent agent and screen actor.

Appeared in: **1932** The Man from Yesterday.

WINTON, JANE
Born: Oct. 10, 1905, Philadelphia, Pa. Died: Sept. 22, 1959, New York, N.Y. Screen, stage actress and opera performer. Entered films in 1925.

Appeared in: **1925** Tomorrow's Love. **1926** Why Girls Go Back Home; Don Juan; Across the Pacific; Footloose Widows; The Honeymoon Express; The Love Toy; Millionaires; My Old Dutch; My Official Wife; The Passionate Quest. **1927** Sunrise; The Beloved Rogue; The Gay Old Bird; The Crystal Cup; The Fair Co-Ed; Upstream; Lonesome Ladies; The Monkey Talks; The Poor Nut; Perch of the Devil. **1928** Burning Daylight; The Yellow Lily; The Patsy; Melody of Love; Nothing to Wear; Bare Knees; Honeymoon Flats. **1929** Scandal; Captain Lash; The Bridge of San Luis Rey. **1930** In the Next Room; The Furies; Hell's Angels. **1934** The Hired Wife.

WIRTH, LARRY
Born: 1915. Died: July 24, 1979, Montgomery, Ala. (heart attack). Screen actor, dancer and story consultant.

Appeared in: **1963** Dr. No.

WISE, HARRY
Born: 1871, N.Y. Died: Dec. 26, 1947, New York, N.Y. Screen, stage and vaudeville actor.

Appeared in: **1915** Shot in the Dark. **1916** The Slave Market. **1917** The Dummy; End of the Tour; The Divorce Game (aka Fifi). **1919** The Avalanche.

WISE, JACK
Born: 1893. Died: Mar. 6, 1954, Hollywood, Calif. (heart attack). Screen and vaudeville actor.

Appeared in: **1929** Smilin' Guns; In the Headlines. **1935** Bright Lights. **1936** The Captain's Kid. **1938** Penrod's Double Trouble; Comet Over Broadway. **1942** Gentleman Jim; Yankee Doodle Dandy.

WISE, TOM (Thomas A. Wise)
Born: 1865, England. Died: Mar. 21, 1928, New York, N.Y. (heart and asthma complications). Stage and screen actor.

Appeared in: **1922** Father Tom. **1924** The Great White Way.

WISE, VIC
Born: 1900, England. Died: 1976, London, England. Screen, stage, vaudeville and radio actor.

Appeared in: **1953** The Square Ring (US 1955). **1955** Value for Money (US 1957). **1957** Kill Me Tomorrow (US 1958). **1960** Follow That Horse! (US 1961). **1963** Panic (US 1966). **1969** School for Sex.

WISMER, HARRY
Born: 1911. Died: Dec. 4, 1967. Radio sportscaster and screen actor.

Appeared in: **1947** The Spirit of West Point. **1948** The Babe Ruth Story; Triple Threat. **1956** Somebody Up There Likes Me.

WITHERS, CHARLES
Born: 1889, Louisville, Ky. Died: July 10, 1947, Bayside, N.Y. Screen, stage and vaudeville actor. Married to actress May Withers with whom he appeared in vaudeville.

Appeared in: **1936** Gasoloons (short). **1937** Hideaway.

WITHERS, GRANT
Born: June 17, 1904, Pueblo, Colo. Died: Mar. 27, 1959, Hollywood, Calif. (suicide). Screen and television actor. Divorced from actress Loretta Young and singer Estelita Rodriguez (dec. 1966). Entered films as an extra for Douglas McLean.

Appeared in: **1926** The Gentle Cyclone. **1927** College; The Final Extra; In a Moment of Temptation; Upstream. **1928** Bringing Up Father; Tillie's Punctured Romance; Golden Shackles; The Road to Ruin. **1929** Tiger Rose; The Madonna of Avenue A; The Time, the Place and the Girl; In the Headlines; Hearts in Exile; Show of Shows; Saturday's Children; The Greyhound Limited. **1930** Broken Dishes; Scarlet Pages; Soldiers and Women; So Long Letty; Back Pay; The Other Tomorrow; Dancing Sweeties; The Second Floor Mystery; Sinners' Holiday; The Steel Highway. **1931** Other Men's Women; Too Young to Marry; Swanee River; In Strange Company; First Aid. **1932** Gambling Sex; Red Haired Alibi. **1933** Secrets of Wu Sin. **1934** The Red Rider (serial); Tailspin Tommy (serial). **1935** Rip Roaring Riley; The Fighting Marines (serial); Valley of Wanted Men; Skybound; Hold 'Em Yale; Goin' to Town; Ship Cafe; Storm Over the Andes; Waterfront Lady; Society Fever. **1936** The Sky Parade; Three on a Limb (short); Border Flight; Lady Be Careful; The Arizona Raiders; Let's Sing Again. **1937** Jungle Jim (serial); Paradise Express; Bill

Cracks Down; Radio Patrol (serial); Hollywood Round-Up. **1938** Telephone Operator; Held for Ransom; The Secret of a Treasure Island (serial); Three Loves Has Nancy; Touchdown Army; Mr. Wong, Detective. **1939** Irish Luck; Navy Secrets; Mexican Spitfire; Boys' Dormitory; Mr. Wong in Chinatown; Mutiny in the Big House; Mystery of Mr. Wong; Daughter of the Tong. **1940** The Fatal Hour; Son of the Navy; On the Spot; Tomboy; Doomed to Die; Phantom of Chinatown; Men Against the Sky; The Mexican Spitfire Out West. **1941** Let's Make Music; Country Fair; Billy the Kid; The People vs. Dr. Kildare; You'll Never Get Rich; Swamp River; The Bugle Sounds; The Get-Away; Parachute Battalion; The Masked Rider. **1942** Between Us Girls; Woman of the Year; Lure of the Islands; Butch Minds the Bay; Northwest Rangers; Tennessee Johnson; Captive Wild Woman. **1943** In Old Oklahoma; Gildersleeve's Bad Day; Petticoat Larceny; No Time for Love; The Apache Trail; A Lady Takes a Chance. **1944** Roger Touhy, Gangster; The Cowboy and the Senorita; Cowboy Canteen; The Fighting Seabees; The Girl Who Dared; Goodnight, Sweetheart; Silent Partners; The Yellow Rose of Texas. **1945** Utah; Bring on the Girls; Dangerous Partners; Road to Alcatraz; Dakota; Bells of Rosarita; The Vampire's Ghost. **1946** In Old Sacramento; Affairs of Geraldine; Throw a Saddle on a Star; That Texas Jamboree; Singing on the Trail; Cowboy Blues; Singin' in the Corn; My Darling Clementine. **1947** Gunfighters; King of the Wild Horses; Over the Santa Fe Trail; The Ghost Goes Wild; The Trespasser; Wyoming; Blackmail; Tycoon. **1948** Bad Men of Tombstone; Station West; Old Los Angeles; Gallant Legion; Daredevils of the Clouds; Sons of Adventure; Angel in Exile; The Plunderers; Homicide for Three; Night Time in Nevada; Wake of the Red Witch; Fort Apache. **1949** Brimstone; Hellfire; The Fighting Kentuckian; The Last Bandit; Duke of Chicago. **1950** Rocky Mountain; Hoedown; Bells of Coronado; Rio Grande; Rock Island Trail; The Savage Horde; Trigger, Jr.; Tripoli; Hit Parade of 1951. **1951** Man in the Saddle; Al Jennings of Oklahoma; Million Dollar Pursuit; The Sea Hornet; Spoilers of the Plains; Utah Wagon Train. **1952** Captive of Billy the Kid; Tropical Heatwave; Springfield Rifle; Hangman's Knot; Hoodlum Empire; Leadville Gunslinger; Oklahoma Annie; Women in the North Country. **1953** Champ for a Day; Fair Wind to Java; Iron Mountain Trail; The Sun Shines Bright; Tropic Zone. **1954** Massacre Canyon; Southwest Passage; Outlaw's Daughter. **1955** Lady Godiva; Run for Cover. **1956** Hidden Guns; The Man from Del Rio; The White Squaw. **1957** The Hired Gun; Hell's Crossroads; The Last Stagecoach West. **1958** I, Mobster.

WITHERS, ISABEL
Born: Jan. 20, 1896, Frankton, Ind. Died: Sept. 3, 1968, Hollywood, Calif. Screen, stage and television actress. Entered films in 1916 with Pagent Film Co. in Kansas City.

Appeared in: **1930** Paid. **1932** The Tenderfoot; Mother-in-Law's Day (short). **1933** Women Won't Tell; Baby Face. **1938** Brother Rat. **1940** I Want a Divorce. **1941** Our Wife; Manpower; Dangerous Holiday. **1942** Behind Prison Walls; George Washington Slept Here; Lady of Burlesque; Now, Voyager. **1943** Mr. Lucky; Mission to Moscow; Salute for Three; What a Woman! **1944** Beautiful But Broke; Law Men; Tahiti Nights; Together Again; Practically Yours; Casanova Brown; Once Upon a Time. **1945** The Missing Corpse; I Love a Mystery; Kiss and Tell; The Gay Senorita; A Sporting Chance. **1946** The Mysterious Intruder; To Each His Own; Tomorrow Is Forever; The Undercover Woman; Wild Beauty. **1947** The Guilt of Janet Ames; Dead Reckoning; Suddenly It's Spring; Possessed; A Likely Story. **1948** You Gotta Stay Happy. **1949** Manhattan Angel; Riders in the Sky; Mr. Belvedere Goes to College; The Fountainhead; Once More, My Darling.

WITHERSPOON, CORA
Born: Jan. 5, 1890, New Orleans, La. Died: Nov. 17, 1957, Las Cruces, N.Mex. Stage and screen actress. Entered films in 1931.

Appeared in: **1931** Night Angel; Peach O'Reno. **1932** Ladies of the Jury. **1934** Midnight; Gambling. **1935** An Educational short; Frankie and Johnnie. **1936** Piccadilly Jim; Libeled Lady. **1937** Dangerous Number; Personal Property; Madame X; Beg, Borrow or Steal; On the Avenue; The Lady Escapes; Quality Street; Big Shot. **1938** He Couldn't Say No; Port of Seven Seas; Marie Antoinette; Three Loves Has Nancy; Professor, Beware!; Just Around the Corner. **1939** Woman Doctor; Dodge City; For Love or Money; The Women; Dark Victory; The Flying Irishman. **1940** Charlie Chan's Murder Cruise; I Was an Adventuress; The Bank Dick. **1943** Follies Girl. **1945** She Wouldn't Say Yes; Over 21; Colonel Effingham's Raid; This Love of Ours. **1946** She Wrote the Book; I've Always Loved You; Dangerous Business; Young Widow. **1947** Down to Earth. **1951** The Mating Season. **1952** The First Time; Just for You. **1953** It Should Happen to You.

WITHEY, CHESTER "CHET"

Born: Nov. 7, 1887, Park City, Utah. Died: Oct. 6, 1939, Calif. Screen, stage actor, film director, screenwriter and author.

Appeared in: 1913 The Ghost of the Hacienda; The Lesson; A Rose of Old Mexico. 1914 The Higher Law; The Oubliette. 1915 The Lost Lord Lovell; Mixed Values; Over the Back; Safety Last; Shocking Stockings.

WITT, WASTL

Born: 1890. Died: Dec. 21, 1955, Harlachinger, West Germany. Stage and screen actor.

WITTING, ARTHUR EUGENE

Born: 1868, Prairie du Chien, Wis. Died: Feb. 1, 1941. Stage and screen actor.

Appeared in: 1916 The Fall of a Nation; Two Men of Sandy Bar. 1927 Gun-Hand Garrison; Wild Born.

WIX, FLORENCE E.

Born: 1883, England. Died: Nov. 23, 1956, Woodland Hills, Calif. (cancer). Stage and screen actress.

Appeared in: 1924 The Female; Secrets. 1925 Enticement. 1927 Ladies Beware; The Return of Boston Blackie; Naughty Nanette. 1928 Beyond London Lights. 1929 She Goes to War. 1936 Under Your Spell; Mr. Deeds Goes to Town. 1937 Easy Living. 1938 Romance in the Dark; The Missing Guest; The Big Broadcast of 1938. 1939 In Name Only. 1941 Unfinished Business. 1942 We Were Dancing; Mrs. Miniver. 1945 Those Endearing Young Charms. 1947 Green Dolphin Street. 1948 B. F.'s Daughter. 1953 The Story of Three Loves.

WOEGERER, OTTO

Born: 1907. Died: July, 1966, Schwanenstadt, Austria. Screen and stage actor.

Appeared in: 1937 Die Nacht mit dem Kaiser. 1956 The Last Ten Days.

WOHLBRUECK, ADOLF

Born: 1900, Vienna, Austria. Died: 1967, Starnberg, Germany. Screen and stage actor.

Appeared in: 1922 Mater Dolorosa. 1925 Das Geheimnis auf Schloss Elmshoeh. 1931 Der Stolz der 3. Kompanie; Salto Mortale. 1932 Baby; Melodie der Liebe; Die Fuenf Verfluchten Gentlemen; Drei von der Stempelstelle. 1933 Keine Angst voe Liebe; Walzerkrieg (War of the Waltzes); Viktor und Viktoria (Victor and Victoria—US 1935). 1934 Regine; Maskerade; Die Englische Heirat; Eine Frau, die Weiss, was Sie Will; Die Vertauschte Braut. 1935 Zigeunerbaron; Ich War Jack Mortimer; Der Student von Prag (The Student of Prague). 1936 Port Arthur; Allotria; Der Kurier des Zaren (The Tsar's Courier). 1951 Wiener Walzer. 1955 Fledermaus 1955; Lola Montes. 1956 Koenig fuer Eine Nacht.

WOLBERT, DOROTHEA

Born: 1874, Philadelphia, Pa. Died: Sept. 16, 1958, Hollywood, Calif. (arteriosclerosis). Screen actress.

Appeared in: 1921 Action; The Ruse of the Rattler. 1922 The Flirt; The Ninety and Nine; The Little Minister. 1923 The Abysmal Brute. 1924 The Galloping Ace; A Lady of Quality; The Guilty One. 1925 A Woman of the World; Duped. 1926 The College Boob; Pleasures of the Rich. 1927 Sailor's Sweetheart; Snowbound. 1928 Anybody Here Seen Kelly?; Love and Learn. 1929 Universal shorts. 1930 The Medicine Man; Dangerous Paradise; Borrowed Wives. 1931 The Front Page; Friends and Lovers. 1932 The Expert; Two Seconds. 1933 Hallelujah, I'm a Bum. 1934 Autobuyography (short); The Scarlet Letter. 1935 Paris in Spring. 1938 If I Were King. 1942 The Gay Sisters. 1950 Three Husbands. 1951 Little Egypt.

WOLBERT, WILLIAM

Born: 1884. Died: Dec. 12, 1918, Los Angeles, Calif. (pneumonia/influenza). Screen actor and film director.

Appeared in: 1914 Bess the Detectress or, The Old Mill at Midnight; Willie Walrus, Detective; Willie Walrus and the Baby; Cupid Incognito; The Skeleton; The Quack; The Den of Thieves; Willie Walrus and the Awful Confession; Bess the Detectress in the Dog Watch. 1915 Treasure Seekers. 1916 The Dumb Girl of Portici. 1917 Willie Walrus Pays Alimony.

WOLD, DAVID

Born: 1890. Died: June 3, 1953, Hollywood, Calif. (heart attack). Screen actor.

"WOLF II" (Wolf Cheechako)

Died: July, 1932, Santa Ana, Calif. Screen animal performer (Alaskan Husky).

WOLFE, BUD

Died: Apr. 13, 1960. Screen actor.

Appeared in: 1937 I'll Take Romance. 1942 Cowboy Serenade. 1946 The Crimson Ghost (serial). 1947 Blackmail; Captain from Castille. 1948 The Fuller Brush Man; Lightnin' in the Forest. 1950 The Man Who Cheated Himself; The Invisible Monster (serial). 1954 Naked Alibi. 1956 Around the World in 80 Days.

WOLFE, JANE

Born: Mar. 21, 1875, St. Petersburg, Pa. Died: Mar. 29, 1958, Hollywood, Calif. Screen and stage actress.

Appeared in: 1911 Norma from Norway; Mexican Joan of Arc. 1912 The Secret of the Miser's Cave; Village Vixen; The Suffragette Sheriff; Flower Girl's Romance. 1913 The Tragedy of Big Eagle Mine; Redemption. 1917 Rebecca of Sunnybrook Farm; The Crystal Gazer; The Call of the East; Freckles; Unconquered. 1919 Under the Top; Men, Women and Money; The Woman Next Door. 1920 Why Change Your Wife?; Behold My Wife.

WOLFF, FRANK (Frank Hermann)

Born: 1928, San Francisco, Calif. Died: Dec. 12, 1971, Rome, Italy (suicide). Screen actor.

Appeared in: 1959 Beast from a Haunted Cave; The Wild and Innocent. 1960 Ski Troop Attack. 1961 Atlas. 1963 The Four Days of Naples; The Demon; America, America. 1964 Salvatore Guiliano. 1965 Situation Hopeless—But Not Serious. 1966 Judith. 1968 Villa Rides; A Stranger in Town; Anyone Can Play; Treasure of San Gennaro. 1969 God Forgives—I Don't; The Libertine; Once Upon a Time in the West. 1970 Kill Them All and Come Back Alone; The Lickerish Quartet.

WOLFIT, SIR DONALD

Born: Apr. 20, 1902, Newmark-on-Trent, England. Died: Feb. 17, 1968, London, England (heart attack). Screen, stage and television actor. Divorced from Chris Frances Castor and Susan Katherine Anthony. Married to actress Rosalind Iden.

Appeared in: 1934 Death at Broadcasting House (film debut). 1935 Drake of England (aka Drake the Pirate—US); The Silent Passenger; Checkmate; The Guv'nor (aka Mister Hobo—US 1936); Hyde Park Corner; Late Extra. 1936 Calling the Tune. 1937 Knight Without Armor. 1952 The Ringer; The Pickwick Papers (US 1953). 1953 Isn't Life Wonderful! 1954 Svengali. 1955 A Prize of Gold. 1956 Guilty?; Satellite in the Sky; The Man in the Road. 1957 The Traitor (aka the Accursed—US 1958). 1958 I Accuse!; Blood of the Vampire. 1959 Room at the Top; The Angry Hills; The Rough and the Smooth (aka Portrait of a Sinner—US 1961). 1960 The Hands of Orlac. 1961 The Mark. 1962 Dr. Crippen (US 1964); Lawrence of Arabia. 1964 Becket. 1965 Life at the Top; Tricet Jedna ve Stinu (90 Degrees in the Shade—US 1966). 1966 The Sandwich Man. 1968 The Charge of the Light Brigade; Decline and Fall ... of a Birdwatcher (US 1969).

WOLFSON, BILLY

Born: 1898. Died: Jan. 15, 1973, Miami, Fla. (heart attack). Screen actor.

Appeared in: 1937 Penrod and Sam. 1938 Penrod and His Twin Brother; Penrod's Double Trouble.

WOLFSON, MARTIN

Died: Sept. 12, 1973. Screen actor.

Appeared in: 1963 Act One.

WOLGAST, AD (Adolphus Wolgast)

Born: Jan. 8, 1888, Cadillac, Mich. Died: Apr. 14, 1955, Camarillo, Calif. Boxer and screen actor.

Appeared in: 1926 The Prince of Broadway.

WOLHEIM, LOUIS

Born: Mar. 23, 1880, New York, N.Y. Died: Feb. 18, 1931, Los Angeles, Calif. (cancer). Screen and stage actor.

Appeared in: 1916 The Brand of Cowardice; Dorian's Divorce; The Sunbeam. 1917 The Avenging Trail; The Eternal Mother; The Carter Case (serial); The End of the Tour; The Millionaire's Double. 1918 The House of Hate (serial); Peg O' the Pirates; A Pair of Cupids. 1919 The Belle of the Season; The Darkest Hour. 1920 A Manhattan Knight; Dr.

Jekyll and Mr. Hyde. **1921** Orphans of the Storm; Experience. **1922** Sherlock Holmes; Determination; The Face in the Fog. **1923** The Enemies of Women; Little Old New York; The Go-Getter; The Last Moment; Love's Old Sweet Song; Unseeing Eyes. **1924** America; The Story Without a Name; The Uninvited Guest. **1925** Lover's Island. **1927** Two Arabian Knights; Sorrell and Son. **1928** Tempest; The Awakening; The Racket. **1929** Wolf Song; Square Shoulders; Condemned; Frozen Justice; The Shady Lady. **1930** Danger Lights; The Silver Horde; The Ship from Shanghai; All Quiet on the Western Front. **1931** Gentleman's Fate; Sin Ship.

WONDER, BETTY
Died: July 24, 1979, Sacramento, Calif. Screen and vaudeville actress. Sister of actor Tommy Wonder.

Appeared in: Sensation Generation.

WONG, ANNA MAY (Lu Tsong Wong)
Born: Jan. 3, 1907, Los Angeles, Calif. Died: Feb. 3, 1961, Santa Monica, Calif. (heart attack). Screen actress.

Appeared in: **1919** Red Lantern. **1921** The First Born; Dinty; Bits of Life; Shame. **1922** The Toll of the Sea. **1923** Drifting; Thundering Dawn. **1924** Lilies of the Field; The Thief of Bagdad; Alaskan; Peter Pan; The Fortieth Door. **1925** Forty Winks. **1926** The Desert's Toll; Fifth Avenue; The Silk Bouquet; A Trip to Chinatown. **1927** The Chinese Parrot; Old San Francisco; Mr. Wu; Driven from Home; Streets of Shanghai; The Devil Dancer. **1928** Across to Singapore; Show Life; Chinatown Charlie; The Crimson City; Song. **1929** The City Butterfly; Piccadilly. **1930** Elstree Calling; On the Spot; Wasted Love; The Flame of Love; L'Amour Maitre des Choses. **1931** Daughter of the Dragon. **1932** Shanghai Express. **1933** A Study in Scarlet; Tiger Bay. **1934** Chu Chin Chow; Limehouse Blues; Java Head (US 1935). **1937** Daughter of Shanghai. **1938** Dangerous to Know; When Were You Born? **1939** King of Chinatown; Island of Lost Men. **1941** Ellery Queen's Penthouse Mystery. **1942** Bombs Over Burma; Lady from Chungking. **1949** Impact. **1953** Ali Baba Nights. **1960** Portrait in Black; The Savage Innocents.

WONG, BRUCE
Born: 1906. Died: Nov. 1, 1953, Hollywood, Calif. (heart attack). Screen actor.

Appeared in: **1942** Time to Kill. **1943** We've Never Been Licked.

WONG, JOE
Born: 1903, Philippines. Died: Nov. 9, 1978 (heart condition). Screen, stage, vaudeville and television actor.

Appeared in: **1948** Adventures in Silverado. **1949** The Story of Seabiscuit. **1950** Fancy Pants. **1976** Cannonball.

WONG, MARY (Mary Liu H. Wong)
Born: Mar. 11, 1915, Los Angeles, Calif. Died: July 25, 1940, Los Angeles, Calif. (suicide—hanging). Screen actress.

Appeared in: **1937** The Good Earth.

WONG, W. BEAL
Born: May 11, 1906, Wong Chong Sai, China. Died: Feb. 6, 1962, Hollywood, Calif. (cerebral hemorrhage). Screen actor.

Appeared in: **1936** The Leathernecks Have Landed. **1942** Prisoner of Japan; Little Tokyo, U.S.A.; China Girl. **1943** Lady of Burlesque; China. **1944** Keys of the Kingdom; The Purple Heart; The Big Noise. **1945** Nob Hill. **1951** Peking Express. **1955** The Big Bluff; The Left Hand of God; Soldier of Fortune. **1958** Hong Kong Confidential; Guns, Girls and Gangsters. **1961** Flower Drum Song. **1962** Brushfire!

WONTNER, ARTHUR
Born: Jan. 21, 1875, London, England. Died: July 10, 1960, London, England. Screen, stage and television actor. Entered films in 1915.

Appeared in: **1916** Lady Windermere's Fan; The Bigamist; Frailty (aka Temptation's Hour). **1923** Bonnie Prince Charlie; The Jose Collins Drama series including: Shadow of Death; The Velvet Woman; The Battle of Love; The Courage of Despair; The Last Stake; Secret Mission. **1924** Eugene Aram; The Diamond Man. **1928** Infamous Lady. **1930** The Message (short). **1931** A Gentleman of Paris; The Sleeping Cardinal (aka Sherlock Holmes' Fatal Hour—US). **1932** The Missing Rembrandt; Condemned to Death; The Sign of Four. **1935** The Triumph of Sherlock Holmes; Line Engaged. **1936** Dishonour Bright; Second Bureau. **1937** Thunder in the City; Storm in a Teacup; The Live Wire; Silver Blaze (aka Murder at the Baskervilles—US 1941). **1938** Kate Plus Ten; Just Like a Woman; Old Iron; 13 Men and a Gun; The Terror. **1943** The Life and Death of Colonel Blimp (aka Colonel Blimp—US 1945). **1948** Blanche Fury. **1950** The Elusive Pimpernel. **1952** Brandy for the Parson. **1953** Sea Devils; Genevieve. **1955** Three Cases of Murder.

WOOD, ALLAN
Born: 1892. Died: Mar. 26, 1947, St. Petersburg, Fla. Screen, stage, vaudeville, radio actor, screenwriter and playwright. Appeared in vaudeville with "Doc" Rockwell in a team called "Rockwell and Wood."

Appeared in: **1933** From Hell to Heaven. **1934** The Gridiron Flash. **1935** Home on the Range; The Pay-Off. **1940** Buck Benny Rides Again. **1942** Heart of the Rio Grande. **1943** Harrigan's Kid.

WOOD, BRITT
Born: 1885. Died: Apr. 13, 1965, Hollywood, Calif. Screen and vaudeville actor.

Appeared in: **1927** The Boob and His Harmonica (short). **1936** Trail Dust. **1937** Adventure's End. **1939** Range War. **1940** Santa Fe Marshal; The Showdown; Hidden Gold; Stagecoach War. **1941** Border Vigilantes; Pirates on Horseback. **1947** Square Dance Jubilee. **1948** Tex Granger (serial). **1949** Riders of the Whistling Pines. **1950** Return of the Frontiersman. **1962** The Choppers.

WOOD, CARL "BUDDY"
Born: 1905. Died: Apr. 17, 1948, Los Angeles, Calif. Screen and stage actor.

WOOD, CHARLES "CHUCK"
Born: 1916. Died: May 29, 1978, New York, N.Y. Screen and stage actor. Do not confuse with British screenwriter with same name.

Appeared in: **1949** Fame is the Spur. **1961** The Sins of Rachel Cade. **1970** Tarzan's Jungle Rebellion.

WOOD, DONNA
Born: 1918. Died: Apr. 9, 1947, Hollywood, Calif. (heart ailment). Singer and screen actress. Vocalist with Kay Kyser orchestra.

Appeared in: **1941** Pot O'Gold.

WOOD, DOUGLAS
Born: 1880, New York, N.Y. Died: Jan. 13, 1966, Woodland Hills, Calif. Screen and stage actor. Son of actress Ida Jeffreys.

Appeared in: **1934** The President Vanishes; Bottoms Up; The Trumpet Blows; The Fountain. **1935** The Wedding Night; Love in Bloom; College Scandal; Dangerous. **1936** Two in a Crowd; Hearts in Bondage; The Prisoner of Shark Island; Dracula's Daughter; Parole; Navy Born; Wedding Present; Two Against the World. **1937** Great Guy; On the Avenue; This Is My Affair; Over the Goal; Dangerously Yours; West of Shanghai; Ali Baba Goes to Town. **1938** I Am the Law. **1939** Off the Record; East Side of Heaven; Eternally Yours; 20,000 Men a Year. **1940** The Man Who Wouldn't Talk; Dr. Ehrlich's Magic Bullet; Private Affair. **1941** Sergeant York; Glamour Boy; Honky Tonk; H. M. Pullman, Esq.; Buck Privates; In the Navy. **1942** Murder in the Big House; Parachute Nurse. **1943** What a Woman; Never a Dull Moment. **1944** I'm from Arkansas; America's Children; Meet Miss Bobby Socks; The Adventures of Mark Twain. **1945** Big Show-Off; Eadie Was a Lady; Come Out Fighting; Boston Blackie Booked on Suspicion. **1946** Because of Him; Voice of the Whistler; Tomorrow Is Forever. **1947** My Wild Irish Rose; Blondie's Big Moment; It Had to Be You; Two Blondes and a Redhead. **1948** An Old Fashioned Girl; Shamrock Hill. **1950** The Petty Girl; Harriet Craig; Border Outlaws. **1955** No Man's Woman. **1956** That Certain Feeling.

WOOD, ERNEST
Born: Apr. 17, 1892, Atchison, Kans. Died: July 13, 1942, Hollywood, Calif. (heart attack). Screen, stage and vaudeville actor. Entered films in 1923.

Appeared in: **1925** Passionate Youth. **1926** Atta Boy. **1927** Horse Shoes; Out of the Past; Woman's Law; The Princess on Broadway. **1928** A Perfect Gentleman; A Certain Young Man; Take Me Home. **1929** Red Wine. **1930** Not Damaged; Scotch (short); Sweethearts on Parade; Dining Out (short). **1931** June Moon; Annabelle's Affairs; Sob Sister; Ambassador Bill. **1933** Parole Girl; A Bedtime Story; International House; Jennie Gerhardt. **1934** Call It Luck; For Love or Money. **1936** Fugitive Lady; False Pretenses. **1937** Roaring Timber; Something to Sing About; The Last Gangster.

WOOD, EUGENE
Born: 1904. Died: Jan. 22, 1971, West Palm Beach, Fla. (heart attack). Screen, stage and television actor.

Appeared in: **1964** Nothing But a Man. **1970** Diary of a Mad Housewife; Dirtymouth; The Way We Live Now.

WOOD, FRANKER
Born: 1883, Stromsburg, Nebr. Died: Nov. 13, 1931, Farmingdale, N.Y. Screen, stage and vaudeville actor. Appeared with his wife Bunnee Wyde in an act billed "Wood and "Wyde."

Appeared in: **1930** Hit the Deck.

WOOD, FREEMAN N.
Born: 1897, Denver, Colo. Died: Feb. 19, 1956, Hollywood, Calif. Screen and stage actor.

Appeared in: **1919** The Adventure Shop. **1921** Made in Heaven; Diane of Star Hollow; High Heels; The Rage of Paris. **1922** White Hands; Electric House. **1923** Gossip; Innocence; Broken Hearts of Broadway; Divorce; The Man Alone; The Wild Party; Out of Luck; Fashion Row. **1924** Butterfly; The Female; The Price She Paid; One Glorious Night; The Girl on the Stairs; The Gaiety Girl. **1925** The Dancers; Raffles, the Amateur Cracksman; Hearts and Spurs; The Part Time Wife; Scandal Proof; Wings of Youth. **1926** Josselyn's Wife; Mannequin; The Lone Wolf Returns; A Social Celebrity; The Prince of Broadway. **1927** McFadden's Flats; Taxi, Taxi; The Coward. **1928** Little Yellow House; Half a Bride; Scarlet Youth; The Legion of the Condemned; The Garden of Eden. **1929** Chinatown Nights; Why Bring That Up? **1930** Only the Brave; Young Eagles; Ladies in Love; Lilies of the Field; The Swellhead. **1931** Kept Husbands. **1932** Lady With a Past. **1936** Hollywood Boulevard.

WOOD, GORDON D. *See* DEMAIN, GORDON

WOOD, MARJORIE
Born: 1888. Died: Nov. 8, 1955, Hollywood, Calif. Screen and stage actress.

Appeared in: **1939** The Women; They Shall Have Music. **1940** Pride and Prejudice. **1941** Look Who's Laughing. **1942** Saboteur; Klondike Fury. **1944** The Thin Man Goes Home. **1947** Nightmare Alley. **1948** That Wonderful Urge. **1949** Adam's Rib. **1950** Annie Get Your Gun. **1951** Show Boat; The Company She Keeps; Excuse My Dust; Texas Carnival. **1953** Sweethearts on Parade. **1954** Seven Brides for Seven Brothers.

WOOD, MICKEY
Born: 1898. Died: Nov. 20, 1963, London, England. Screen actor and stuntman.

Appeared in: **1960** Circle of Deception (US 1961).

WOOD, NATALIE (Natasha Gurdin)
Born: July 20, 1938, San Francisco, Calif. Died: Nov. 29, 1981, Catalina, Calif. (accidental drowning). Screen and television actress. Daughter of ballerina Maria Gurdin. Sister of actress Lana Wood, and Olga Virapaeff. Divorced from and remarried to actor Robert Wagner. Divorced from English film producer Richard Gregson. Nominated for 1955 Academy Award for Best Actress in Rebel Without a Cause; for 1961 in Splendor in the Grass; and for 1963 in Love With the Proper Stranger.

Appeared in: **1943** Happy Land. **1946** Tomorrow is Forever; The Bride Wore Boots. **1947** The Miracle on 34th Street; The Ghost and Mrs. Muir; Driftwood. **1948** Scudda Hoo! Scudda Hay!; Chicken Every Sunday. **1949** The Green Promise; Father Was a Fullback. **1950** Our Very Own; No Sad Songs for Me; The Jackpot; Never a Dull Moment. **1951** Dear Brat; The Blue Veil. **1952** Just for You; The Rose Bowl Story. **1953** The Star. **1954** The Silver Chalice. **1955** One Desire; Rebel Without a Cause. **1956** The Searchers; The Burning Hills; A Cry in the Night; The Girl He Left Behind. **1957** Bombers B-52; The James Dean Story (documentary). **1958** Marjorie Morningstar; Kings Go Forth. **1959** Cash McCall. **1960** All the Fine Young Cannibals. **1961** Splendor in the Grass; West Side Story. **1962** Gypsy. **1963** Love With the Proper Stranger. **1964** Sex and the Single Girl. **1965** The Great Race; Inside Daisy Clover. **1966** This Property Is Condemned; Penelope. **1969** Bob and Carol and Ted and Alice. **1972** The Candidate; I'm a Stranger Here Myself: A Portrait of Nicholas Ray (documentary). **1976** Peeper. **1979** Meteor. **1980** The Last Married Couple in America; Willie and Phil.

WOOD, PEGGY
Born: Feb. 9, 1892, Brooklyn, N.Y. Died: Mar. 18, 1978, Stamford, Conn. Screen, stage, television actress, opera singer and playwright. Nominated for 1965 Academy Award for Best Supporting Actress in Sound of Music.

Appeared in: **1919** Almost a Husband. **1929** Wonder of Women. **1934** Handy Andy. **1935** Right to Live; Jalna. **1937** Call It a Day; A Star is Born. **1939** The Housekeeper's Daughter. **1946** The Bride Wore Boots; Magnificent Doll. **1948** Dream Girl. **1960** The Story of Ruth. **1965** Sound of Music.

WOOD, PHILIP
Born: 1896. Died: Mar. 3, 1940, Hollywood, Calif. (heart attack). Screen, stage actor, playwright and author.

Appeared in: **1938** Room Service. **1940** Our Town.

WOOD, ROLAND
Born: 1897. Died: Feb. 3, 1967, New York, N.Y. (heart attack). Stage and screen actor.

Appeared in: **1967** The Tiger Makes Out.

WOOD, SAM
Born: July 10, 1883, Philadelphia, Pa. Died: Sept. 22, 1949, Hollywood, Calif. (heart attack). Screen, stage actor and film director. Entered films as an actor with DeMille in 1910.

WOOD, SUZANNE
Died: Sept. 12, 1934, Hollywood, Calif. Screen, stage actress and author.

WOOD, TOMMY "FATTY"
Born: May, 1894. Died: Dec. 28, 1932, Minneapolis, Minn. Screen actor.

Appeared in: **1919** Sunnyside.

WOOD, VICTOR
Born: 1914. Died: Oct., 1958, London, England. Screen, stage and television actor.

Appeared in: **1947** Moss Rose. **1948** If Winter Comes; The Iron Curtain; Hills of Home. **1950** Joan of Arc. **1951** The Desert Fox; Kind Lady. **1952** My Cousin Rachel. **1953** Scandal at Scourie; The Snows of Kilimanjaro. **1957** Time Lock (US 1959). **1959** The Lock.

WOODBRIDGE, GEORGE
Born: Feb. 16, 1907, Exeter, Devonshire, England. Died: Mar. 31, 1973. Screen, stage and television actor.

Appeared in: **1941** The Tower of Terror (US 1942). **1942** The Big Blockade. **1946** Green for Danger. **1948** Blanche Fury; Escape; The Fallen Idol (US 1949); Bonnie Prince Charlie. **1949** Silent Dust; The Queen of Spades; Children of Chance (US 1951). **1950** Double Confession (US 1953). **1951** Cloudburst (US 1952). **1952** Murder in the Cathedral; The Flanagan Boy (aka Bad Blonde—US). **1953** The Story of Gilbert and Sullivan (aka The Great Gilbert and Sullivan—US). **1954** For Better, For Worse (aka Cocktails in the Kitchen—US 1955); The Green Buddha (US 1955). **1955** Third Party Risk (aka Deadly Game—US); The Constant Husband; An Alligator Named Daisy (US 1957); Richard III (US 1956); The Naked Heart. **1956** Three Men in a Boat (US 1958). **1957** The Passionate Stranger (aka A Novel Affair—US); The Good Companions (US 1958); Day of Grace; High Flight (US 1958). **1958** Dracula (aka Horror of Dracula—US); The Revenge of Frankenstein; Son of Robin Hood (US 1959). **1959** Jack the Ripper (US 1960). **1960** Two-Way Stretch (US 1961); The Flesh and the Fiends (aka Mania—US 1961). **1961** The Curse of the Werewolf; What a Carve Up! (US 1962, aka No Place Like Homicide); Raising the Wind (aka Roommates—US 1962). **1963** Nurse on Wheels (US 1964); Heavens Above!; Carry On Jack (US 1964). **1965** Dracula—Prince of Darkness (US 1966); The Reptile (US 1966). **1969** Where's Jack?; Take a Girl Like You (US 1970).

WOODBURN, JAMES
Born: Jan. 17, 1888, Edinburgh, Scotland. Died: Nov. 26, 1948, England? Screen and stage actor. Entered films in 1934.

Appeared in: **1940** The Chinese Bungalow (aka Chinese Den—US 1941). **1947** The Brothers (US 1948). **1949** Whiskey Galore! (aka Tight Little Island—US, and aka Mad Little Island).

WOODBURN, MRS. EUGENIE
Born: 1859, Cincinnati, Ohio. Died: Mar. 29, 1947, White Plains, N.Y. Screen and stage actress.

Appeared in: **1916** As in a Looking Glass; Bought and Paid For; The Prima Donna's Husband; East Lynne; Sporting Blood. **1917** The Last of the Carnabys; Betsy Ross; The Woman Beneath. **1918** T'other Dear Charmer.

WOODBURY, DOREEN
Born: 1927, Australia. Died: Feb. 6, 1957, New York, N.Y. (suicide—pills). Screen and television actress.

Appeared in: **1957** Space Ship Sappy (short); The Shadow on the Window.

WOODFORD, JOHN
Born: 1862, Tex. Died: Apr. 17, 1927, Saranac Lake, N.Y. Stage and screen actor.

Appeared in: **1921** Get-Rich-Quick-Wallingford; The Rider of the King Log. **1922** Ten Nights in a Bar Room. **1923** Success. **1925** The Mad Dancer.

WOODHOUSE, TODD
Born: 1902. Died: June 19, 1958, Hollywood, Calif. Screen actor and stuntman.

WOODRUFF, EDNA (aka EDNA MONTAGUE)
Born: 1874. Died: Oct. 16, 1947, Los Angeles, Calif. Screen actress and novelist.

WOODRUFF, HENRY
Born: 1870. Died: Oct. 6, 1916, New York, N.Y. Stage and screen actor.

Appeared in: **1915** A Man and His Mate. **1916** The Beckoning Flame.

WOODRUFF, WILLIAM H. "BURT"
Born: 1856. Died: June 14, 1934, Los Angeles, Calif. Stage and screen actor. Appeared in Charles Ray films.

WOODS, AL (Frederick Ludwig Dreeke)
Born: 1895. Died: June 3, 1946, Pasadena, Calif. (heart attack). Stage and screen actor.

Appeared in: **1936** Easy Money.

WOODS, ERCELL
Born: 1916. Died: Apr. 23, 1948, Los Angeles, Calif. (auto crash). Screen actress.

WOODS, GRANT
Died: Oct. 31, 1968. Screen actor.

Appeared in: **1966** The Silencers.

WOODS, HARRY LEWIS, SR.
Born: 1889. Died: Dec. 28, 1968, Los Angeles, Calif. (uremia). Screen actor.

Appeared in: **1921** "Ruth Roland" serials. **1923** The Steel Trail (serial); Don Quickshot of the Rio Grande. **1924** The Fast Express (serial); Ten Scars Make a Man (serial); Wolves of the North (serial); Dynamite Dan. **1925** The Bandit's Baby; A Cafe in Cairo. **1926** A Regular Scout; A Trip to Chinatown; Man Four Square. **1927** Cyclone of the Range; Jesse James; Tom's Gang; Splitting the Breeze; Silver Comes Thru. **1928** The Candy Kid; When the Law Rides; Red Riders of Canada; Tyrant of Red Gulch; The Sunset Legion. **1929** China Bound; The Desert Rider; The Viking; Gun Law; The Phantom Rider; 'Neath Western Skies. **1930** The Lone Rider; Men Without Law; Ranch House Blues; Pardon My Gun. **1931** West of Cheyenne; Texas Ranger; In Old Cheyenne; Palmy Days; Range Fed; Monkey Business; Pardon Us. **1932** Night World; I Am a Fugitive from a Chain Gang; Radio Patrol; Haunted Gold; Law and Order. **1933** Shadows of Sing Sing. **1934** St. Louis Kid; The President Vanishes; Belle of the Nineties; School for Girls; Devil Tiger; The Crosby Case; The Scarlet Empress; Wonder Bar; The Circus Clown. **1935** The Adventures of Rex and Rinty (serial); Rustlers of Red Dog (serial); Let 'Em Have It; Robin Hood of El Dorado; Heir to Trouble; When a Man's a Man; Rustlers of Red Gap; The Call of the Savage (serial); Gallant Defender; Ship Cafe. **1936** The Phantom Rider (serial); It Had to Happen; The Lawless Nineties; Silly Billies; Human Cargo; The Unknown Ranger; Conflict; Rose of the Rancho; The Plainsman; Ticket to Paradise; Heroes of the Range. **1937** Courage of the West; Land Beyond the Law; Outcast; I Promise to Pay; Range Defenders. **1938** Hawaiian Buckaroo; The Arizona Wildcat; Come on, Rangers; Penamint's Bad Man; Blockheads; The Buccaneer; The Spy Ring; Crime Takes a Holiday. **1939** Frontier Marshal; Union Pacific; Days of Jesse James; Mr. Moto in Danger Island; The Man in the Iron Mask; In Old California; Blue Montana Skies; Beau Geste. **1940** The Long Voyage Home; South of Pago Pago; Isle of Destiny; Bullet Code; West of Carson City; The Ranger and the Lady; Triple Justice; Meet the Missus; Winners of the West (serial). **1941** Petticoat Politics; Sheriff of Tombstone; Forbidden Passage (short); Last of the Duanes. **1942** Today I Hang; Romance on the Range; Down Texas Way; Riders of the West; Deep in the Heart of Texas; West of the Law; Forest Rangers; Reap the Wild Wind; Jackass Mail; Dawn on the Great Divide. **1943** Outlaws of Stampede Pass; Cheyenne Roundup; The Ghost Rider; Bordertown Gunfighters; Beyond the Last Frontier. **1944** Call of the Rockies; Marshal of Gunsmoke; Nevada; Westward Bound; The Adventures of Mark Twain; Tall in the Saddle. **1945** Wanderer of the Wastelannd; West of the Pecos; Radio Stars on Parade. **1946** Trouble or Nothing (short); South of Monterey; My Darling Clementine. **1947** Road to Rio; Desire Me; Wild Rose Mesa; Wyoming; Tycoon; Trail Street; Thunder Mountain; Code of the West. **1948** Western Heritage; The Gallant Legion; Indian Agent. **1949** Colorado Territory; The Fountainhead; Hellfire; Masked Raiders; She Wore a Yellow Ribbon. **1950** Traveling Saleswoman; Short Grass; Law of the Badlands. **1952** Lone Star; Rancho Notorious. **1954** Hell's Outpost. **1956** Ten Commandments.

WOODS, JOSEPH A.
Born: 1860, N.Y. Died: Feb. 13, 1926, New York, N.Y. (heart disease). Stage and screen actor. He often impersonated President Woodrow Wilson because of the marked resemblance.

WOODS, NICK (Nicholas Schaber)
Born: 1858. Died: Mar. 21, 1936, New Rochelle, N.Y. Screen and stage actor. Was billed on stage as "N. S. Woods, the Boy Actor."

WOODTHORPE, GEORGIA
Born: 1859. Died: Aug. 25, 1927, Glendale, Calif. Stage and screen actress.

Appeared in: **1919** The Midnight Man (serial). **1921** Four Horsemen of the Apocalypse; Bunty Pulls the Strings. **1922** The Song of Life. **1923** Gimme; Thundering Dawn; Rouged Lips. **1924** Daddies.

WOODWARD, H. GUY
Born: 1858, Minneapolis, Minn. Died: Aug. 20, 1919, Detroit, Mich. (heart disease). Screen, stage actor and circus performer. Appeared in "Sunshine" Comedies.

Appeared in: **1915** Fickle Fatty's Fall; The Best of Enemies; The Hunt; Double Trouble. **1916** Because He Loved Her; His Pride and Shame; A Dash of Courage; His Wild Oats; A Tugboat Romeo. **1917** Dodging His Doom; A Shanghaied Jonah; Hula Hula Land.

WOODWARD, ROBERT "BOB"
Born: 1909. Died: Feb. 7, 1972, Hollywood, Calif. (heart attack). Screen actor. Doubled for many Western stars such as Buck Jones annd Dick Foran.

Appeared in: **1938** Frontier Scout. **1939** Home on the Prairie. **1947** Stage to Mesa City; Cheyenne Takes Over. **1948** The Westward Trail; The Tioga Kid; Crossed Trails; Triggerman; Range Renegades; Frontier Agent; Overland Trails; Gunning for Justice; Courtin' Trouble; Silver Trails; The Sheriff of Medicine Bow; Hidden Danger; Cowboy Cavalier; The Rangers Ride; Song of the Drifter; The Fighting Ranger; Back Trail. **1949** Gun Runner; Crashin' Thru; Law of the West; West of El Dorado; Shadows of the West; Range Justice; Brand of Fear; Roaring Westward; Across the Rio Grande. **1950** The Blazing Hills (aka The Blazing Sun); Radar Secret Service. **1951** Hills of Utah. **1952** The Old West; Night Stage to Galveston; Barbed Wire; Junction City; Blue Canadian Rockies. **1953** Winning of the West. **1955** Wyoming Renegade. **1958** Apache Territory. **1961** Gun Fight. **1963** Red Runs the River.

WOOLDRIDGE, CHARLES O.
Died: Aug. 10, 1975. Screen actor.

WOOLDRIDGE, DORIS
Born: 1890. Died: July 17, 1921, Los Angeles, Calif. (appendix operation). Stage and screen actress.

WOOLERY, CLARENCE W. "PETE"
Died: June 4, 1978, Philadelphia, Pa. Screen, vaudeville, radio actor, singer and music publisher. Appeared in Paramount shorts in 1929.

WOOLF, BARNEY
Born: 1877. Died: Feb. 10, 1972, Hollywood, Calif. Screen and television actor and extra.

WOOLF, MRS. YETTI
Born: 1882. Died: Nov. 27, 1965, Hollywood, Calif. Screen actress.

WOOLGAR, JACK
Born: 1914, England. Died: July 17, 1978, Huddersfield, England. Screen, stage and television actor.

Appeared in: **1977** Swallows and Amazons.

WOOLLCOTT, ALEXANDER
Born: Jan. 19, 1887, Phalanx, N.J. Died: Jan. 23, 1943, New York, N.Y. Drama critic, playwright, screen, stage and radio actor.

Appeared in: **1934** Gift of Gab. **1935** The Scoundrel. **1937** RKO shorts. **1942** Babes on Broadway.

WOOLLEY, MONTY (Edgar Montillion Wooley)
Born: Aug. 17, 1888, New York, N.Y. Died: May 6, 1963, Albany, N.Y. (kidney and heart ailment). Screen and stage actor. Entered films in 1931. Nominated for 1942 Academy Award for Best Actor in The Pied Piper and in 1944 for Best Supporting Actor in Since You Went Away.

Appeared in: **1937** Live, Love and Learn; Nothing Sacred. **1938** Everybody Sing; Arsene Luupin Returns; The Girl of the Golden West; Three Comrades; Lord Jeff; Artists and Models Abroad; Young Dr. Kildare; Vacation from Love. **1939** Zaza; See Your Doctor (short); Dancing Co-ed; Man About Town; Midnight; Never Say Die. **1941** The Man Who Came to Dinner. **1942** The Pied Piper; Live Begins at Eight-Thirty. **1943** The Light of Heart; Holy Matrimony. **1944** Since You Went Away; Irish Eyes Are Smiling. **1945** Molly and Me. **1946** Night and Day. **1947** The Bishop's Wife. **1948** Miss Tatlock's Millions; Will You Love Me in December? **1950** Paris 1950 (narr.). **1951** As Young as You Feel. **1955** Kismet.

WOOLSEY, ROBERT
Born: Aug. 14, 1888, Oakland, Calif. Died: Oct. 31, 1938, Malibu Beach, Calif. (kidney ailment). Screen, stage and vaudeville actor. Was partner in vaudeville and film comedy team of "Wheeler annd Woolsey." See Bert Wheeler for films they made together.

Appeared without Wheeler in: **1930** The Voice of Hollywood (short). **1931** Everything's Rosie. **1933** Hollywood on Parade (short).

WOOLVINES, DOLLY (aka DOLLY NOBLES)
Born: 1863. Died: Oct. 6, 1930, Brooklyn, N.Y. (heart trouble). Screen, stage and vaudeville actress. Married to actor Milton Nobles (dec. 1924), with whom she appeared in vaudeville. Mother of stage actor Milton Nobles, Jr. (dec. 1925).

Appeared in: **1910** The Phoenix.

WORDEN, LOUISE
Died: Jan. 6, 1977. Screen actress. Married to actor Hank Worden.

Appeared in: **1952** The Big Sky.

WORLOCK, FREDERICK
Born: 1886. Died: Aug. 1, 1973, Woodland Hills, Calif. (cerebral ischemia). Screen and stage actor. Divorced from actress Elsie Ferguson (dec. 1961).

Appeared in: **1939** Miracles for Sale; Lady of the Tropics; Balalaika; The Story That Couldn't Be Printed (short). **1940** Strange Cargo; Moon Over Burma; The Sea Hawk; Murder Over New York; South of Suez; Hudson's Bay; Northwest Passage; The Earl of Chicago. **1941** Rage in Heaven; Free and Easy; Man Hunt; Dr. Jekyll and Mr. Hyde; A Yank in the RAF; How Green Was My Valley; International Lady. **1942** Captains of the Clouds; Eagle Squadron; Pacific Rendezvous; Pierre of the Plains; The Black Swan; London Blackout Murders; Random Harvest; Madero (short); Pier 29 (short). **1943** Secret Service in Darkest Africa (serial); Air Raid Wardens; Appointment in Berlin; Sherlock Holmes Faces Death; Thumbs Up; Madame Curie. **1944** The Lodger; Jane Eyre; Secrets of Scotland Yard; National Velvet. **1945** Hangover Square; The Woman in Green; Pursuit to Algiers; Captain Kidd; Fatal Witness; Scotland Yard Investigator; The Picture of Dorian Gray. **1946** Terror by Night; She Wolf of London; Dressed to Kill. **1947** The Imperfect Lady; Last of the Redmen; Singapore; The Lone Wolf in London; Love From a Stranger; Forever Amber; A Woman's Vengeance; The Macomber Affair. **1948** Joan of Arc; Hills of Home; A Double Life; The Woman in White; Johnny Belinda. **1949** Twelve O'Clock High (voice). **1958** Jet Over the Atlantic (US 1960); Spartacus. **1961** One Hundred and One Dalmations (voice). **1962** The Notorious Landlady. **1966** Spinout.

WORNE, HOWARD B. "DUKE" (aka HOWARD B. WARNE)
Born: 1885, Va. Died: Oct. 13, 1933, Hollywood, Calif. Screen actor, film director and producer. Divorced from actress Virginia Brown Faire (dec. 1980).

Appeared in: **1917** Mystery Ship.

WORTH, BILL
Born: 1884. Died: May 2, 1951, Westwood, Calif. (heart attack). Screen actor.

WORTH, CONSTANCE (Jocelyn Howarth)
Born: 1915, Sydney, Australia. Died: Oct. 18, 1963. Screen actress. Divorced from actor George Brent (dec. 1979).

Appeared in: **1919** The Non-Conformist Parson; Wisp O' the Woods. **1920** Fate's Plaything. **1921** The Education of Nicky. **1922** A

Bachelor's Baby; No. 7 Brick Row. **1923** Within the Maze. **1924** Love in the Welsh Hills. **1937** China Passage; Windjammer. **1939** Mystery of the White Room. **1940** Angels Over Broadway. **1941** Meet Boston Blackie; Borrowed Hero; Suspicion. **1942** When Johnny Comes Marching Home; Boston Blackie Goes Hollywood. **1943** City Without Men; Crime Doctor; G-Men vs. the Black Dragon (serial); Crime Doctor's Strangest Case. **1944** Cyclone Prairie Rangers; Sagebrush Heroes. **1945** Why Girls Leave Home; Kid Sister; Dillinger. **1946** Deadline at Dawn; Sensation Hunters. **1949** Western Renegades; The Set-Up.

WORTH, PEGGY
Born: 1891. Died: Mar. 23, 1956, New York, N.Y. Screen and stage actress.

Appeared in: **1921** You Find It Everywhere.

WORTHING, HELEN LEE
Born: 1905. Died: Aug. 25, 1948, Los Angeles, Calif. Stage and screen actress.

Appeared in: **1924** Janice Meredith. **1925** The Crowded Hour; Flower of the Night; Night Life of New York; The Swan; The Other Woman's Story. **1926** Don Juan; The County of Luxembourg; Lew Tyler's Wives; Watch Your Wife. **1927** Vanity; Thumbs Down.

WORTHINGTON, WILLIAM J.
Born: 1872, Troy, N.Y. Died: Apr. 9, 1941, Beverly Hills, Calif. Screen, stage, vaudeville actor, opera performer, film director and film producer. Former president and treasurer of Multicolor Films. Entered films as an actor in 1915.

Appeared in: **1915** Damon and Pythias; The Black Box (serial). **1921** High Heels. **1923** Red Lights; The Green Goddess. **1926** Her Honor, the Governor; Return of Boston Blackie; Kid Boots. **1928** Good Morning Judge; Half a Bride. **1930** The Climax; Shipmates; Laughing Sinners; Susan Lenox, Her Rise and Fall; Possessed; The Man Who Came Back. **1931** Finger Prints (serial). **1933** Duck Soup; No More Orchids. **1934** Perils of Pauline (serial); The Gold Ghosts (short); One Exciting Adventure. **1935** $20 a Week; Cardinal Richelieu; The Keeper of the Bees. **1936** Can This Be Dixie? **1937** Battle of Greed. **1938** Angels With Dirty Faces.

WORTMAN, DONALD A.
Born: 1920. Died: Jan. 12, 1981, San Bernardino, Calif. (murdered). Screen, stage, television actor, stage director, stage producer and talent agent.

Appeared in: **1926** The Scarlet Letter (film debut).

WRAY, ALOHA
Born: 1928. Died: Apr. 28, 1968, Hollywood, Calif. Screen actress and dancer. Divorced from actor Frankie Darro (dec. 1976).

Appeared in: **1935** George White's 1935 Scandals.

WRAY, JOHN GRIFFITH (John Griffith Malloy)
Born: Feb. 13, 1888, Philadelphia, Pa. Died: Apr. 5, 1940, Los Angeles, Calif. Screen, stage actor, playwright and film director. Entered films in 1929.

Appeared in: **1930** New York Nights; All Quiet on the Western Front; The Czar of Broadway. **1931** Quick Millions; Silence; Safe in Hell. **1932** High Pressure; The Woman from Monte Carlo; The Miracle Man; The Mouthpiece; The Rich Are Always With Us; Miss Pinkerton; Doctor X; Central Park; The Match King; I Am a Fugitive from a Chain Gang. **1933** The Death Kiss; After Tonight. **1934** I'll Fix It; Lone Cowboy; Bombay Mail; The Crosby Case; The Love Captive; Embarrassing Moments; The Big Shakedown; The Most Precious Thing in Life; The Defense Rests; Green Eyes; Fifteen Wives; The Captain Hates Sea. **1935** I Am a Thief; Ladies Love Danger; Atlantic Adventure; Bad Boy; The Great Hotel Murder; The Whole Town's Talking; Stranded; Frisco Kid; Men Without Names. **1936** Mr. Deeds Goes to Town; The Poor Little Rich Girl; Sworn Enemy; A Son Comes Home; Valiant Is the Word for Carrie; The President's Mystery; We Who Are About to Die. **1937** A Man Betrayed; You Only Live Once; Outcast; On Such a Night; The Devil Is Driving; The Women Men Marry; Circus Girl. **1938** House of Mystery; What Price Safety? (short); Making the Headlines; The Black Doll; Crime Takes a Holiday; Gangs of New York; A Man to Remember; Pacific Lines; Spawn of the North; Tenth Avenue Kid; Golden Boy. **1939** Risky Business; Pacific Liner; The Amazing Mr. Williams; Smuggled Cargo; Each Dawn I Die; Blackmail; The Cat and the Canary. **1940** The Man from Dakota; Remembering the Night; Swiss Family Robinson; Know Your Money (short).

WRAY, TED
Born: 1909. Died: Jan. 26, 1950, near Big Bear, Calif. (heart attack). Screen actor.

WREN, SAM
Born: 1897, Brooklyn, N.Y. Died: Mar. 15, 1962, Hollywood, Calif. Screen, stage, television actor and stage director. Married to actress Virginia Sale.

Appeared in: **1935** Dr. Socrates. **1936** I Married a Doctor. **1937** Marked Woman. **1942** Over My Dead Body. **1943** Dixie Dugan.

WRIGHT, ARMAND VINCENT "CURLY"
Born: June 6, 1896, New York, N.Y. Died: Mar. 28, 1965, North Hollywood, Calif. (cancer). Screen actor.

Appeared in: **1932** Lawyer Man. **1933** Sailor's Luck; Fits in a Fiddle (short). **1938** Panamint's Bad Man. **1942** To Be or Not to Be.

WRIGHT, COWLEY (F. Cowley Wright)
Born: Oct. 6, 1889, Anerley, England. Died: Jan. 18, 1923, England? Screen and stage actor.

Appeared in: **1919** The Rocks of Valpre. **1921** Sybil.

WRIGHT, ED
Died: Mar. 31, 1975. Screen actor.

Appeared in: **1958** Gang War; Showdown at Boot Hill. **1959** The Oregon Trail.

WRIGHT, EDITH
Born: 1897, England? Died: Sept. 26, 1963, Denver, Colo. Screen and stage actress. Married to actor Dennis King (dec. 1971). Do not confuse with actress Edith King.

WRIGHT, FANNY
Born: 1872, London, England. Died: Dec. 29, 1954, England? Screen, stage and vaudeville actress.

Appeared in: **1928** Champagne; Toni. **1929** The Lily of Killarney; When Knights Were Bold; The Chamber of Horrors; Young Woodley (US 1930); Greek Street; Dark Red Roses. **1931** A Honeymoon Adventure (aka Footsteps in the Night—US 1933).

WRIGHT, FRED
Born: England? Died: Dec. 12, 1928, New York, N.Y. Screen actor.

Appeared in: **1916** The Grand Babylon Hotel; Molly Bawn. **1920** La Poupee. **1922** The Glorious Adventure; The Further Adventures of Sherlock Holmes series including The Norwood Builder. **1923** Hornet's Nest; M'Lord of the White Road. **1926** Cinders.

WRIGHT, HAIDEE
Born: 1898, London, England. Died: Jan. 29, 1943, London, England. Screen and stage actress.

Appeared in: **1915** Evidence. **1919** In Bondage (aka Faith). **1920** Colonel Newcome the Perfect Gentleman; Aunt Rachel; The Winning Goal. **1921** Demos (aka Why Men Forget—US); The Old Country. **1922** The Glorious Adventure; A Bachelor's Baby. **1923** Paddy the Next Best Thing. **1926** The Sea Urchin. **1927** The Cabaret Kid. **1933** Strange Evidence; The Blarney Stone (aka The Blarney Kiss—US). **1934** Jew Suess (aka Power—US). **1936** Tomorrow We Live.

WRIGHT, HARRY WENDELL "WEN"
Born: 1916. Died: June 17, 1954, Humboldt, Nev. (auto accident). Screen actor and stuntman.

WRIGHT, HENRY OTHO
Born: 1892. Died: June 7, 1940, San Bernardino, Calif. Screen actor.

WRIGHT, HUGH E.
Born: Apr. 13, 1879, Cannes, France. Died: Feb. 13, 1940, Windsor, England. Screen, stage actor, playwright, screenwriter and lyricist.

Appeared in: **1918** The Kiddies in the Ruins; Where's Watling?; The Bette 'Ole, or The Romance of Old Bill (aka Carry On—US). **1920** Garry Owen; Nothing Else Matters. **1921** The Old Curiosity Shop; Mary-Find-The-Gold; Squibs; The Corner Man. **1922** A Sailor Tramp; Squibs Wins the Calcutta Sweep. **1923** The Romany; Squibs, MP; Squibs' Honeymoon. **1929** Auld Lang Syne; The Silver King. **1931** Down River; The Great Gay Road; East Lynne on the Western Front; Stranglehold. **1932** Brother Alfred; Lord Camber's Ladies. **1933** The Good Companions; Cash (aka For Love or Money—US 1934); Oh What a Duchess! (aka My Old Duchess); You Made Me Love You; A Shot in the Dark (US 1935). **1934** On the Air; Crazy People; Adventure Limited; Radio Parade of 1935 (US 1935). **1935** Widow's Might; Scrooge. **1936** Royal Eagle.

WRIGHT, HUNTLEY
Born: 1870, England. Died: July 10, 1941, Bangor, Wales (heart attack). Screen, stage and radio actor.

Appeared in: **1900** San Toy. **1933** The Only Girl (aka Heart Song—US 1935). **1935** Look Up and Laugh.

WRIGHT, MACK V. "MAC"
Died: Aug. 14, 1965, Boulder City, Nev. Screen actor, screenwriter and film director.

Appeared in: **1915** The Black Box. **1919** The Lion Man (serial). **1921** Red Courage. **1922** Perils of the Yukon (serial). **1923** Single Handed. **1924** Crossed Trails; Western Vengeance. **1925** Blood and Steel; Border Intrigue; Border Justice; Moccasins; Riders of Mystery. **1926** Mistaken Orders; Silver Fingers. **1928** The Manhattan Cowboy; Silent Trail. **1929** Headin' Westward; Arizona Days; The Law of the Mounted; West of Santa Fe; The Lone Horseman. **1930** Pioneers of the West; Hunted Men; The Oklahoma Sheriff.

WRIGHT, MARIE
Born: 1862, England. Died: May 1, 1949, England? Screen and stage actress.

Appeared in: **1918** God Bless Our Red, White and Blue. **1919** The Kinsman; Mrs. Thompson. **1923** Paddy the Next Best Thing. **1926** The Sea Urchin. **1928** H.G. Wells Comedies series including Bluebottles and Daydreams. **1929** Unto Each Other. **1930** Murder. **1931** Tilly of Bloomsbury; For the Cup; Black Coffee. **1932** Help Yourself; A Lucky Sweep. **1933** Naughty Cinderella. **1934** A Cup of Kindness. **1935** The City of Beautiful Nonsense. **1936** The Amazing Quest of Ernest Bliss (aka Romance and Riches—US 1937); Hail and Farewell. **1938** Silver Top; Sixty Glorious Years (aka Queen of Destiny—US). **1940** Gaslight (aka Angel Street—US 1952).

WRIGHT, NED
Born: 1926, Rossford, Ohio. Died: Sept. 27, 1981, Washington, D.C. Screen, stage, television actor and singer.

Appeared in: **1957** Island in the Sun. **1959** Odds Against Tomorrow.

WRIGHT, WILL
Born: Mar. 26, 1891, San Francisco, Calif. Died: June 19, 1962, Hollywood, Calif. (cancer). Screen, stage, vaudeville, radio and television actor.

Appeared in: **1936** China Clipper. **1939** Silver on the Sage. **1940** Blondie Plays Cupid. **1941** Shadow of the Thin Man; The Richest Man in Town. **1942** Shut My Big Mouth; True to the Army; Night in New Orleans; Wildcat; A Parachute Nurse; Sweetheart of the Fleet; Tennessee Johnson; The Daring Young Man; A Man's World; The Postman Didn't Ring. **1943** A Night to Remember; In Old Oklahoma; Reveille with Beverly; Lucky Legs; Murder in Times Square; Cowboy in Manhattan; Practically Yours. **1945** Eve Knew Her Apples; Road to Utopia; Rhapsody in Blue; Gun Smoke; Sleepy Lagoon; Blonde Fever; Grissly's Millions; Bewitched; Eadie Was a Lady; The Strange Affair of Uncle Harry; You Came Along; Salome, Where She Danced. **1946** California; Hot Cargo; The Inner Circle; Johnny Comes Flying Home; The Madonna's Secret; Rendezvous with Annie; One Exciting Week; The Blue Dahlia. **1947** Along the Oregon Trail; Keeper of the Bees; Wild Harvest; Mother Wore Tights; Blaze of Noon; Cynthia. **1948** Relentless; They Live By Night (aka The Twisted Road and Your Red Wagon); The Inside Story; Green Grass of Wyoming; The Walls of Jericho; Disaster; Whispering Smith; California's Golden Beginning; Black Eagle; Act of Violence; Act of Murder. **1949** Big Jack; Brimstone; For Those Who Dare; Mrs. Mike; All The King's Men; Adam's Rib; Lust for Gold; Miss Grant Takes Richmond. **1950** House By the River; The Savage Horde; Sunset in the West; A Ticket to Tomahawk; No Way Out; Dallas. **1951** My Forbidden Past; Vengeance Valley; Excuse My Dust; The Tall Target; People Will Talk. **1952** Lydia Bailey; The Las Vegas Story; Paula; Lure of the Wilderness; O. Henry's Full House; Happy Time; Holiday for Sinners. **1953** Niagara; The Last Posse. **1954** Johnny Guitar; The Wild One; River of No Return; The Raid. **1955** Not as a Stranger; The Man With the Golden Arm; The Tall Men; The Court Martial of Billy Mitchell. **1956** These Wilder Years. **1957** The Iron Sheriff; Johnny Tremain; The Wayward Bus. **1958** The Missouri Traveler; Quantrille's Raiders; Gunman's Walk. **1959** Alias Jesse James; The Thirty Foot Bride of Candy Rock. **1961** The Deadly Companions; Twenty Plus Two. **1962** Cape Fear. **1964** Fail Safe.

WRIGHT, WILLIAM
Born: 1912, Ogden, Utah. Died: Jan. 19, 1949, Ensenada, Mexico (cancer). Screen and stage actor.

Appeared in: **1941** Rookies on Parade; Nothing But the Truth; World

Premiere; Glamour Boy; The Devil Pays Off. **1942** Parachute Nurse; True to the Army; Night in New Orleans; Sweetheart of the Fleet. **1943** A Night to Remember; Here Comes Elmer. **1944** Dancing in Manhattan; One Mysterious Night. **1945** Eadie Was a Lady; State Fair; Escape in the Fog. **1946** Down Missouri Way; Lover Come Back; The Mask of Dijon. **1947** Philo Vance Returns; The Gas House Kids Go West. **1948** King of Gamblers. **1949** Daughter of the Jungle; Impact; Air Hostess; Rose of the Yukon.

WU, HONORABLE
Born: 1903, San Francisco, Calif. Died: Mar. 1, 1945, Hollywood, Calif. Screen, stage, vaudeville and radio actor.

Appeared in: **1936** Stowaway. **1938** Mr. Moto; The Crime of Dr. Hallett; Mr. Moto Takes a Vacation. **1939** North of Shanghai. **1941** Ellery Queen and the Perfect Crime.

WUEST, IDA
Born: 1884, Wiesbaden, Germany. Died: Nov. 2, 1958, Berlin, Germany. Screen and stage actress. Married to actor Bruno Kastner (dec.).

Appeared in: **1929** The Last Waltz. **1930** The Burning Heart. **1931** Bockbierfest; Das Alte Lied; Ein Burschenlied aus Heidelberg; Die Lindenwirtin vom Rhein; Bomben auf Monte Carlo (The Bombardment of Monte Carlo). **1932** Die Csikos Baroness; Mein Leopold; Hurra! Ein Junge!; Schoen ist die Manoeverzeit (Beautiful Maneuver Time); Wenn die Soldaten; Man Braucht Kein Geld; Der Walzerkoenig; Das Schoene Abenteuer. **1933** Namensheirat; Friederike; Drei Tage Mittelarrest; Lachende Erben. **1934** Wie Sag' Ich's Meinem Mann?; Eines Prinzen Junge Liebe; Ja, Treu ist die Soldatenliebe; Zu Befehl; Herr Unteroffizier; Melodie der Liebe; Es War Einmal ein Walzer; Fleuchtlinge; Einmal Eine Grosse Dame Sein; Freut Euch des Lebens. **1935** Die Liebe und die Erste Eisenbahn (Love and the First Railroad); Jungfrau Gegen Moench (Maiden vs. Monk); Gsardasfuerstin (The Czardas Duchess); Fruehlingsmaerchen; So ein Maedel Vergisst Man Nicht. **1936** The Private Life of Louis XIV; Die Marquise von Pompadour; Annette in Paradise; Der Bettelstudent. **1937** The World's in Love. **1938** Wenn Du eine Schwiegermutter Hast (When You Have a Mother-in-Law); Husaren Heraus; Kater Lampe; Eine Seefahrt die ist Lustig (A Merry Sea Trip); Eine Nacht an der Donau (A Night on the Danube). **1939** Kleines Bezirksgericht (Little Country Court); Diskretion-Ehrensache (Discretion With Honor); Herbst-Monoever (Fall Manoeuvres); Der Lustige Witwenball (The Merry Widow's Ball); Die Blonde Carmen; Die Kluge Schwiegermutter (The Wise Mother-in-Law).

WUNDERLEE, FRANK
Born: 1875, St. Louis Mo. Died: Dec. 11, 1925 (apoplexy). Screen and stage actor.

Appeared in: **1919** The Carter Case (serial); The Fatal Fortune (serial). **1921** A Divorce of Convenience. **1922** One Exciting Night; Reported Missing. **1923** No Mother to Guide Her. **1924** The Great White Way.

WYATT, EUSTACE (Eustace George William Wyatt)
Born: Mar. 5, 1882, Bath, England. Died: Oct. 25, 1944, Los Angeles, Calif. (heart failure). Screen actor.

Appeared in: **1942** Journey Into Fear; Nightmare. **1944** The Man in Half Moon Street; Ministry of Fear.

WYCHERLY, MARGARET
Born: 1881, London, England. Died: June 6, 1965, New York, N.Y. Screen, stage, vaudeville and television actress. Nominated for 1941 Academy Award for Best Supporting Actress in Sergeant York.

Appeared in: **1929** Thirteenth Chair (film debut). **1934** Midnight. **1938** Wanderlust (short). **1940** Victory. **1941** Sergeant York. **1942** Crossroads; Random Harvest; Keeper of the Flame. **1943** The Moon Is Down; Assignment in Brittany; Hangmen also Die. **1944** Experiment Perilous. **1945** Johnny Angel. **1946** Enchanted Cottage. **1947** Something in the Wind; The Yearling; Forever Amber. **1948** The Loves of Carmen. **1949** White Heat. **1951** The Man With a Cloak. **1953** The President's Lady; That Man from Tangier. **1956** Richard III.

WYMAN, ELEANOR
Born: 1914. Died: Sept. 1, 1940, Lancster, Calif. (auto accident). Screen actress.

WYMARK, PATRICK (Patrick Cheeseman)
Born: 1926, Grimsby, England. Died: Oct. 20, 1970, Melbourne, Australia (heart attack). Screen, stage and television actor.

Appeared in: **1960** The Criminal (aka The Concrete Jungle—US 1962); The League of Gentlemen (US 1961). **1964** The Finest Hours (voice of Churchill); The Secret of Blood Island (US 1965). **1965** Repulsion; Operation Crossbow (aka The Great Spy Mission); The Skull. **1966** The Psychopath; A King's Story (US 1967). **1967** Sept fois Femme (Woman Times Seven—US). **1968** Witchfinder General (aka The Conqueror Worm—US); Where Eagles Dare (US 1969); Tell Me No Lies. **1969** Battle of Britain; Doppelganger (aka The Far Side of the Sun—US). **1970** Cromwell.

WYNAND, PATRECIA
Born: 1940. Died: Mar. 31, 1977, Beverly Hills, Calif. (drowned). Screen and stage actress.

WYNDHAM, SIR CHARLES
Born: Mar. 23, 1837, Liverpool, England. Died: Jan. 12, 1919, England? Screen, stage actor and playwright. Married to Emma Silberad (dec.), and actress Mary Moore (dec. 1931). Father of stage manager Howard Wyndham (dec. 1947).

Appeared in: **1913** David Garrick.

WYNDHAM, POPPY (aka ELSIE MACKAY)
Born: 1894, Australia. Died: Mar., 1928 (lost at sea—air crash). Screen and stage actress. Divorced from actor Lionel Atwill (dec. 1946), and later married to actor Dennis Wyndham (dec.).

Appeared in: **1919** A Son of David; A Great Coup; Snow in the Desert. **1920** The Title Wave; A Dead Certainty; The Town of Crooked Ways.

WYNN, BESSIE
Born: 1876. Died: July 8, 1968, Towaco, N.Y. Screen and stage actress.

Appeared in: **1913** Animated Weekly No. 53.

WYNN, DORIS (Doris Rink)
Born: 1910. Died: July 14, 1925, Los Angeles, Calif. (pneumonia). Screen actress. Appeared in Christie films.

WYNN, ED (Edward Leopold)
Born: Nov. 9, 1886, Philadelphia, Pa. Died: June 19, 1966, Los Angeles, Calif. (cancer). Screen, stage, vaudeville, radio and television actor. Won 1959 Academy Award for Best Supporting Actor in The Diary of Anne Frank. Married to actress Hilda Keenan (dec. 1940). Father of actor Keenan Wynn.

Appeared in: **1927** Rubber Heels. **1930** Follow the Leader; Manhattan Mary. **1933** The Chief. **1943** Stage Door Canteen. **1951** Alice in Wonderland (voice only). **1956** The Great Man. **1958** Marjorie Morningstar. **1959** The Diary of Anne Frank. **1960** The Absent-Minded Professor; Cinderfella. **1961** Babes in Toyland. **1963** Son of Flubber. **1964** Those Calloways; Mary Poppins; The Sound of Laughter (documentary); Patsy; Erasmus With Freckles. **1965** That Darn Cat; Dear Brigitte; The Greatest Story Ever Told. **1966** The Daydreamer (voice only). **1967** Warning Shot; The Gnome Mobile.

WYNN, GLADYS
Born: 1886. Died: Nov. 10, 1964, Paris, France. Screen and stage actress. Divorced from actor Milton Sills (dec. 1930).

WYNN, NAN
Born: 1916. Died: Mar. 21, 1971, Santa Monica, Calif. (cancer). Screen, stage actress and singer. Her voice was dubbed for Rita Hayworth in several singing films.

Appeared in: **1941** A Shot in the Dark; Million Dollar Baby. **1942** Pardon My Sarong. **1943** Princess O'Rourke. **1944** Jam Session.

WYNNE, GORDON
Died: 1967. Screen actor.

Appeared in: **1942** Ten Gentlemen from West Point. **1951** Little Big Horn. **1954** Thunder Pass. **1956** Scandal Incorporated.

WYNYARD, DIANA (Dorothy Cox)
Born: Jan. 16, 1906, London, England. Died: May 13, 1964, London, England (kidney ailment). Screen and stage actress. Divorced from film director Sir Carol Reed (dec. 1976). Nominated for 1932-33 Academy Award for Best Actress in Cavalcade.

Appeared in: **1932** Rasputin and the Empress (film debut). **1933** Cavalcade; Men Must Fight; Reunion in Vienna. **1934** Where Sinners Meet; Let's Try Again; One More River; Hollywood on Parade (short). **1939** On the Night of the Fire (aka The Fugitive—US 1940). **1940** Gaslight (aka Angel Street—US 1952). **1941** Freedom Radio (aka A Voice in the Night—US); The Prime Minister; Kipps (aka The Remarkable Mr. Kipps—US 1942). **1948** An Ideal Husband. **1951** Tom Brown's School Days. **1956** The Feminine Touch (aka The Gentle Touch—US 1957). **1957** Island in the Sun.

YABLOKOFF, HERMAN
Born: 1904, Grodno, Poland. Died: Apr. 3, 1981, New York, N.Y. Screen, stage actor, stage director, stage producer, playwright and composer. Married to actress Bells Mysell.

YACONELLI, FRANK
Born: Oct. 2, 1898, Italy. Died: Nov. 19, 1965, Los Angeles, Calif. (lung cancer). Screen actor.

Appeared in: **1927** I'll Be There. **1929** Senor Americano. **1930** Firebrand Jordan; Parade of the West. **1933** Strawberry Roan; The Barber Shop (short); Kickin' the Crown Around (short). **1934** It Happened One Night; Perfectly Mismated (short); Death Takes A Holiday. **1935** Awakening of Jim Burke; Western Frontier; Gun Play; I'm a Father (short); A Night at the Opera; Here Comes Cookie. **1936** Blazing Justice; Down to the Sea; Romance Rides the Range; The Three Mesquiteers; Lawless Riders. **1937** You Can't Have Everything; It Could Happen to You; Wild West Days (serial). **1939** Wild Horse Canyon. **1940** East Side Kids; Dr. Cyclops; Pioneer Days; Torrid Zone; Wild Horse Range. **1941** Our Wife; I Forced Landing; Riding the Sunset Trail; The Driftin' Kid; Two In a Taxi. **1942** Fiesta. **1943** Man of Courage. **1946** South of Monterey; Beauty and the Bandit; Slightly Scandalous. **1947** Riding the California Trail. **1948** A Foreign Affair. **1949** Alias the Champ. **1950** September Affair; The Baron of Arizona. **1951** A Place in the Sun. **1952** Abbott and Costello Meet Captain Kidd. **1953** Cash Stashers (short). **1954** Dragon's Gold. **1955** The Racers. **1956** Serenade.

YAKOVLEV, YASHA
Born: 1912, Russia. Died: May 17, 1970, New York, N.Y. (heart attack). Screen actor and dancer.

Appeared in: **1960** L'Idiot (The Idiot).

YAMAMOTO, KAJIRO
Born: 1902, Japan. Died: Sept. 28, 1974, Japan (cirrhosis of the liver). Screen actor and film director. Entered films during silents.

YANAGIYA, KINGORO
Born: Japan. Died: Oct. 22, 1972, Tokyo, Japan (cancer). Stage and screen actor. Appeared in films in 1920 as a popular comedian and "rakugo" (storyteller).

Appeared in: **1961** The Poem of the Blue Star. **1968** Onsen Geira dai Shogeki (aka Kigeki dai Shogeki) (Hotsprings Holiday—US 1970).

YANNER, JOSEPH
Born: 1879. Died: Dec. 12, 1949, Kansas City, Mo. Screen and stage actor. Appeared in Vitagraph, Kleine and Thanhouser films.

YANSHIN, MIKHAIL
Born: 1901, Russia. Died: July, 1976, Russia? Screen and stage actor.

Appeared in: **1934** The Czar Wants to Sleep. **1936** Gypsies. **1937** Prisoners. **1954** The Inspector General. **1955** The Safety Match. **1956** Twelfth Night. **1957** Morozko (Jack Frost—US 1966).

YANTIS, FANNY
Died: July 19, 1929, Glendale, Calif. Screen and stage actress.

Appeared in: **1926** Paris at Midnight.

YAPP, CECIL
Born: Apr. 4, 1879, Montreal, Canada. Died: Feb. 4, 1959, St. Paul, Minn. Screen and stage actor.

Appeared in: **1915** The Second Son. **1919** The Silver King.

YARBOROUGH, BARTON
Born: 1900. Died: Dec. 19, 1951, Hollywood, Calif. Screen, radio and television actor.

Appeared in: **1941** They Meet Again; Let's Go Collegiate. **1942** The Ghost of Frankenstein; Saboteur. **1945** Red Dragon; Captain Tugboat Annie; I Love a Mystery. **1946** The Devil's Mask; Wife Wanted; The Unknown. **1947** Kilroy Was Here. **1949** Henry the Rainmaker.

YARDE, MARGARET
Born: Apr. 2, 1878, Dartmouth, England. Died: Mar. 11, 1944, London, England. Screen, stage actress and opera performer.

Appeared in: **1913** A Cigarette Maker's Romance. **1923** Gems of Literature series including Falstaff the Tavern Knight; Wonder Women of the World series including Madame Recamier—or the Price of Virtue. **1925** Red Lips (aka The Only Way); The Art of Love series including: The Weakness of Men (aka The Lady in Silk Stockings); Sables of Death (aka The Lady in Furs). **1926** London. **1929** The Crooked Billet. **1930** Night Birds. **1931** Michael and Mary (US 1932); Uneasy Virtue; The Woman Between (aka The Woman Decides—US 1932); Third Time Lucky; Let's Love and Laugh (aka Bridegroom for Two—US 1932). **1933** A Shot in the Dark (US 1935); The Good Companions; The Man from Toronto; Matinee Idol; Tiger Bag; Enemy of the People. **1934** Trouble in Store; Sing as We Go; Father and Son; A Glimpse of Paradise; Nine Forty-Five; The Broken Rosary; Guest of Honour. **1935** Widow's Might; The Crouching Beast; 18 Minutes; Scrooge; The Deputy Drummer; Jubilee Window; Squibs; That's My Uncle; Who's Your Father?; Handle With Care; Full Circle; It Happened in Paris. **1936** Queen of Hearts; What the Puppy Said; Faithful; In the Soup; Gypsy Melody; No Escape; Fame. **1937** Beauty and the Barge; The Compulsory Wife; The Biter Bit (aka Calling All Ma's); French Leave; You Live and Learn. **1938** You're the Doctor; Prison Without Bars (US 1939). **1939** The Face at the Window (US 1940); French Without Tears (US 1940). **1940** Crimes at the Dark House; George and Margaret; Two Smart Men; Henry Steps Out. **1942** Tomorrow We Live (aka At Dawn We Die—US 1943).**1943** Thursday's Child. **1944** The Two Fathers.

YARNELL, BRUCE
Born: 1938. Died: Nov. 30, 1973, Calif. (plane accident). Screen, stage, television actor and singer. Married to soprano Joan Patenaude.

Appeared in: **1963** Irma La Douce. **1968** The Road Hustlers.

YASSIN, ISMAIL
Born: 1912. Died: 1972 (heart attack). Screen actor.

Appeared in: **1951** Little Miss Devil.

YBARRA, ROCKY
Born: 1900. Died: Dec. 12, 1965, Hollywood, Calif. (heart attack). Screen cowboy actor.

Appeared in: **1960** The Third Voice. **1965** The Reward.

YEARSLEY, RALPH
Born: 1897. Died: Dec. 4, 1928, Hollywood, Calif. (suicide). Screen actor. Married to actress Grace Yearsley.

Appeared in: **1921** Tol'able David; Pardon My French. **1922** Arabia; Why Not Marry?; The Village Blacksmith. **1923** The Call of the Canyon; A Chapter in Her Life; Anna Christie. **1924** The Fighting Sap; One Night in Rome; The Valley of Hate; The Hill Billy. **1925** The Gambling Fool. **1926** Desert Gold. **1927** The Kid Brother. **1928** The Big Killing; Rose Marie; The Little Shepherd of Kingdom Come. **1929** Show Boat.

YEATS, MURRAY F.
Born: 1910. Died: Jan. 27, 1975, Sepulveda, Calif. (pneumonia and other complications). Screen and stage actor.

YEGROS, LINA
Born: 1915, Spain. Died: May, 1978, Madrid, Spain. Screen actress.

Appeared in: **1937** El Octavo Mandamiento (The Eighth Commandment). Other Spanish films: Polizon a Bordo; Un Marido a Precio Fijo; Leble, la Virgen Gitana; Malvaloca; Teresa de Jesus; Aprendiendo a Morir.

YENSEN, ULA
Born: 1940, Denmark. Died: Aug. 26, 1959, Mexico City, Mexico (suicide—pills). Screen and television actress.

Appeared in: Senoritas; Sube y Baja (Up and Down).

YEOMAN, GEORGE
Born: 1869. Died: Nov. 2, 1936, Hollywood, Calif. Screen, stage and vaudeville actor. Appeared in vaudeville in an act billed as "George Yeoman and Lizzie."

YIP, WILLIAM
Died: Oct. 18, 1968. Screen actor.

Appeared in: **1943** Arizona Trail; Behind the Rising Sun. **1949** Bad Men of Tombstone. **1954** Hell and High Water. **1956** The King and I. **1958** Twilight for the Gods.

YOHE, MAY
Born: Apr. 6, 1869, Bethlehem, Pa. Died: Aug. 28, 1938, Boston, Mass. Screen and stage actress.

Appeared in: **1921** The Hope Diamond Mystery (serial).

YORK, DUKE
Born: 1902. Died: Jan. 24, 1952, Hollywood, Calif. (suicide—gun). Screen actor.

Appeared in: **1933** Footlight Parade; Roman Scandals. **1934** One Hour Late; Elmer and Elsie; Pursuit of Happiness. **1935** Here Comes Cookie. **1936** All American Toothache (short); Strike Me Pink; Ticket to Paradise; The Three Mesquiteers; Mind Your Own Business; Flash Gordon (serial); Libeled Lady. **1937** Midnight Madonna. **1938** A Slight Case of Murder; Topper Takes a Trip. **1941** Sky Raiders (serial); Public Enemies; Life Begins for Andy Hardy. **1942** Woman of the Year; All Work and No Pay (short); Who Done It? **1943** Three Little Twerps (short); Destination Tokyo. **1944** Idle Roomers (short). **1948** Isn't It Romantic. **1949** Francis; Johnny Stool Pigeon; Stampede; Mississippi Rhythm. **1950** Call of the Klondike; Fortunes of Captain Blood; Rogue River; Snow Dog; Hit Parade of 1951; Winchester-73; Where Danger Lives.

YORKE, CAROL (Carol Bjorkman)
Born: 1929. Died: July 5, 1967, New York, N.Y. (leukemia). Screen actress.

Appeared in: **1948** Letter from an Unknown Woman (film debut).

YORKE, EDITH (Edithe Byard aka EDITHE YORKE)
Born: Croyden, England. Died: July 28, 1934. Screen and stage actress.

Appeared in: **1921** Passing Thru; Chickens; Lying Lips. **1922** A Daughter of Luxury; One Clear Call; Step On It! **1923** The Age of Desire; Burning Words; The Fourth Musketeer; Merry-Go-Round; Mothers-in-Law; The Miracle Makers; Sawdust; Souls for Sale; Slippy McGee; Thru the Flames. **1924** Husbands and Lovers; The Beauty Prize; Happiness; My Man; The Other Kind of Love; Pride of Sunshine Alley; Riders Up; The Slanderers; The Tenth Woman. **1925** Seven Keys to Baldpate; Below the Line; Capital Punishment; Excuse Me; Silent Sanderson; Souls for Sables; Wild Horse Mesa; The Thoroughbred. **1926** The Belle of Broadway; Born to the West; The Heart of a Coward; His New York Wife; Oh, What a Nurse!; Rustlers' Ranch; Red Dice; Rustling for Cupid; The Timid Terror; Volcano; Transcontinental Limited; The Silent Flyer (serial). **1927** The Bachelor's Baby; The Western Whirlwind; Sensation Seekers. **1928** Making the Varsity; The Port of Missing Girls; Satan and the Woman. **1929** Fugitives; The Love Racket; Seven Keys to Baldpate (and 1925 version); The Valiant. **1930** City Girl; Phantom of the Opera.

YORKE, OSWALD
Born: London, England. Died: Jan. 25, 1943, New York, N.Y. Stage and screen actor.

Appeared in: **1924** Monsieur Beaucaire.

YORKNEY, JOHN C.
Born: 1871, Argentina. Died: Aug. 20, 1941, Fort Lee, N.Y. (heart attack). Stage and screen actor. Entered films during silents.

YOSHIWARA, KYONOSUKE
Born: 1900, Japan? Died: Nov. 30, 1979, New York, N.Y. Screen, stage and television actor.

Appeared in: **1940** The Letter.

YOST, HERBERT A. (aka BARRY O'MOORE)
Born: 1880, Harrison, Ohio. Died: Oct. 23, 1945, New York, N.Y. Screen and stage actor. Herbert A. Yost was his stage name, but he appeared in some films as Barry O'Moore. Entered films with Biograph Studios in 1908 and later appeared in Edison series films in 1914.

Appeared in: **1909** The Deception; Edgar Allan Poe. **1912** What Happened to Mary (serial); Every Rose Has Its Stem. **1914** The Man Who Disappeared (serial). **1929** Love, Honor and Oh, Baby (short). **1930** Fast and Loose. **1934** Age of Innocence.

YOUNG, ARTHUR
Born: 1898. Died: Feb. 24, 1959. Screen and stage actor.

Appeared in: **1935** Radio Parade of 1935; No Limit. **1937** Victoria the Great. **1940** 21 Days Together. **1941** Murder by Invitation. **1948** My Brother Jonathan. **1951** The Lady with a Lamp. **1954** An Inspector Calls; Paid to Kill. **1956** Dynamiters; The Gelignite Gang.

YOUNG, BULL (John W. Young)
Died: Aug. 2, 1913, Los Angeles, Calif. (concussion and hemorrhages after fighting). Professional boxer and screen actor.

Appeared in: **1913** One Round O'Brien Comes Back.

YOUNG, CAPTAIN JACK
Died: Oct. 28, 1966. Screen actor. Do not confuse with photographer Jack Young.

Appeared in: **1942** Yankee Doodle Dandy. **1943** Mission to Moscow.

YOUNG, CARLETON G.
Born: 1907. Died: July 11, 1971, Hollywood, Calif. (cancer). Screen, radio and television actor. Father of actor Tony Young.

Appeared in: **1936** Happy Go Lucky; A Man Betrayed. **1937** SOS Coast Guard (serial); Join the Marines; Git Along Little Dogies; Navy Blues; Dangerous Holiday; Dick Tracy (serial). **1938** Fighting Devil Dogs (serial); The Old Barn Dance; Heroes of the Hills; Cassidy of Bar 20; Gang Bullets. **1939** Buck Rogers (serial); The Lone Ranger Rides Again (serial); Zorro's Fighting Legion (serial); Convict's Code. **1940** Adventures of Red Ryder (serial). **1941** Adventures of Captain Marvel (serial); Buck Privates; Keep 'Em Flying; Pride of the Bowery. **1942** Code of the Outlaw; SOS Coast Guard. **1944** Ladies of Washington; Take It or Leave It; In the Meantime, Darling. **1945** Thunderhead, Son of Flicka; Thrill of a Romance; Abbott and Costello in Hollywood. **1947** Smash-Up, the Story of a Woman. **1948** The Kissing Bandit. **1950** American Guerilla in the Philippines; Double Deal. **1951** The Mob; People Will Talk; Red Mountain; Flying Leathernecks; Hard, Fast and Beautiful; Anne of the Indies; Gene Autry and the Mountains; Chain of Circumstance; Best of the Bad Men; The Day the Earth Stood Still; His Kind of Woman. **1952** The Brigand; Diplomatic Courier; Deadline U.S.A.; Last of the Comanches; My Six Convicts; Battle Zone. **1953** From Here to Eternity; The Glory Brigade; A Blueprint for Murder; Goldtown Ghost Riders; Mexican Manhunt; Niagara; Torpedo Alley. **1954** Arrow in the Dust; Prince Valiant; Bitter Creek; Riot in Cell Block 11; 20,000 Leagues Under the Sea. **1955** The Court Martial of Billy Mitchell; Artists and Models; Battle Cry; Phantom of the Jungle; The Racers. **1956** Battle Hymn; The Bottom of the Bottle; Julie; Beyond a Reasonable Doubt; Flight to Hong Kong. **1957** Three Brave Men; The Spirit of St. Louis. **1958** Cry Terror; The Last Hurrah. **1959** The Horse Soldiers; Here Come the Jets. **1960** Sergeant Rutledge; Gallant Hours; The Music Box Kid. **1961** Armored Command; Twenty Plus Two; The Big Show. **1962** The Man Who Shot Liberty Valance. **1964** Cheyenne Autumn.

YOUNG, CHARLOTTE
Born: 1904. Died: July 10, 1977. Screen actress.

YOUNG, CLARA KIMBALL
Born: 1890, Benton Harbor, Mich. Died: Oct. 15, 1960, Woodland Hills, Calif. Screen, stage, vaudeville, television actress and film producer. Daughter of actress Pauline Kimball (dec. 1919).

Appeared in: **1910** Ransomed; The Sepoy's Wife. **1912** Cardinal Wolsey; The Haunted Rockery; The Violin of Monsieur; Put Yourself in Their Place; Rock of Ages; Ann Boleyn; Lulu's Doctor. **1913** When Mary Grew Up; Poet and Peasant; The White Slave (aka The Octaroon); The Test; The Pirates; Up in a Balloon; Beau Brummell; The Hindoo Charm; The Mystery of the Stolen Jewels; The Old Guard; The Little Minister; Love's Sunset. **1914** Goodness Gracious (aka Movies as They Shouldn't Be); The Perplexed Bridegroom; Happy-Go-Lucky; Her Husband; My Official Wife; The Flat Above. **1915** Camille; Trillby; Heart's in Exile; The Heart of the Blueridge; Lola; The Deep Purple; Marrying Money; The Fates and Flora Four-Flush (aka The Ten Billion Dollar Vitagraph Mystery Serial). **1916** The Common Law; The Feast of Life; The Yellow Passport; The Dark Silence; Without a Soul; Colette (aka The Kiss of Susan). **1917** The Easiest Way; The Foolish Virgin; Magda; The Marionettes; The Price She Paid; Shirley Kaye. **1918** The Savage Woman; The Road Through the Dark; The Claw; House of Glass; The Reason Why. **1919** Soldiers of Fortune; Cheating Cheaters; The Eyes of Youth; The Better Wife. **1920** Mid Channel; The Forbidden Woman; Silk Husbands and Calico Wives; Possession; For the Soul of Rafael; Whispering Devils. **1921** Charge It; Hush; Straight from Paris; Who No Man Knows. **1922** Enter Madame; The Hands of Nara; The Worldly Madonna. **1923** Cordelia the Magnificent; A Wife's Romance; The Woman of Bronze. **1925** Lying Wives. **1930** Mother and Son. **1931** Kept Husbands; Women Go on Forever. **1932** File No. 113; Probation; Love Bound. **1933** Souls for Sables. **1934** Romance in the Rain; Return of Chandu (serial); I Can't Escape. **1935** Hollywood Extra Girl (short); Fighting Youth; His Night Out; She Married Her Boss. **1936** The Black Coin (serial); Fighting Coward (aka The Last Assignment); Three on the Trail; Love in September (short); Rouge's Tavern; Oh, Susannah!; Ants in the Pantry (short). **1937** The Mysterious Pilot (serial); The Hills of Old Wyoming. **1938** The Frontiersman. **1941** Mr. Celebrity; The Roundup.

YOUNG, CLIFTON
Born: 1917. Died: Sept. 10, 1951, Los Angeles, Calif. (smoke asphyxiation). Screen, vaudeville and radio actor. Appeared in Our Gang comedies or "Bonedust."

Appeared in: **1924** Our Gang comedies. **1925** Better Movies (short). **1926** The following shorts: Baby Clothes; Uncle Tom's Uncle; Thundering Fleas; Shievering Spooks; The Fourth Alarm; War Feathers; Telling Whoppers. **1927** The following shorts: Ten Years Old; Love My Dog; Tired Business Men; Baby Brother; Chicken Fee. **1930** School's Out (short). **1931** The following shorts: Helping Grandma; Love Business; Little Daddy. **1946** So You Want to Play the Horses (short). **1947** Pursued; Possessed; My Wild Irish Rose; Dark Passage; So You're Going on a Vacation (short). **1948** Treasure of the Seirra Madre; Blood on the Moon; plus the following shorts: So You Want an Apartment; So You Want to Build a House; So You Want to be a Detective; So You Want to be in Politics. **1949** Abandoned Woman; Calamity Jane and Sam Bass; Illegal Entry; So You Want to be Popular (short); So You're Having In-Law Trouble (short). **1950** The Return of Jesse James; Salt Lake Raiders; Trail of Robin Hood; A Woman of Distinction; Bells of Coronado.

YOUNG DEER
Died: Apr., 1946, New York, N.Y. Screen actor. Married to actress Lillian "Red Wing" St. Cyr (dec. 1974).

YOUNG, DESMOND
Born: 1892. Died: June 27, 1966, Sark, Channel Islands. Author and screen actor.

Appeared in: **1951** The Desert Fox.

YOUNG, GIG (Bryon Ellsworth Barr aka BRYANT FLEMING)
Born: Nov. 4, 1913 or 1917, St. Cloud, Minn. Died: Oct. 19, 1978, New York, N.Y. (suicide—gunshot). Screen, stage and television actor. Divorced from Sheila Stapler; married to drama coach Sophie Rosenstein (dec. 1952); married and divorced from actress Elizabeth Montgomery, and real estate broker Elaine Whitman Young. Last marriage was to actress Kim Schmidt (dec. 1978 in murder—suicide by Gig Young). Nominated for 1951 Academy Award for Best Supporting Actor in Come Fill the Cup, and for 1958 in Teacher's Pet. Won 1969 Academy Award for Best Supporting Actor in They Shoot Horses Don't They?

Appeared in: **1940** Misbehaving Husbands. **1941** You're in the Army Now; Sergeant York; One Foot in Heaven; Navy Blues; Dive Bomber; They Died With Their Boots On. **1942** The Male Animal; Captains of the Clouds; The Gay Sisters. **1943** Air Force; Old Acquaintance; Screen Snapshots #5 (short). **1945** The Affairs of Susan. **1947** Escape Me Never. **1948** Wake of the Red Witch; The Woman in White; The Three Musketeers. **1949** Lust for Gold; Tell It to the Judge. **1950** Hunt the Man Down. **1951** Come Fill the Cup; Target Unknown; Slaughter Trail; Only the Valiant; Too Young to Kiss. **1952** You for Me; Holiday for Sinners. **1953** The Girl Who Had Everything; Arena; Torch Song; City That Never Sleeps. **1954** Young at Heart. **1955** Desperate Hours. **1957** Desk Set. **1958** The Tunnel of Love; Teacher's Pet. **1959** Ask Any Girl; The Story on Page One. **1962** Le Conteau Dans la Plaie (The Knife in the Wound); Kid Galahad; That Touch of Mink. **1963** For Love of Money; Five Miles to Midnight; A Ticklish Affair. **1965** Strange Bedfellows. **1967** The Shuttered Room (US 1968). **1969** They Shoot Horses Don't They? **1970** Lovers and Other Strangers. **1973** A Son-in-Law for Charlie. **1974** Bring Me the Head of Alfredo Garcia. **1975** The Hindenberg; The Killer Elite. **1976** Sherlock Holmes in New York.

YOUNG, GLADYS
Born: 1905, England. Died: Aug. 18, 1975, Eastbourne, England. Screen, stage, radio and television actress.

Appeared in: **1952** Kathy's Love Affairs. **1956** One Wish Too Many (US 1962).

YOUNG, LORRAINE See MILLER, LORRAINE

YOUNG, LUCILLE
Born: 1892. Died: Aug. 2, 1934, Hollywood, Calif. (following surgery). Screen actress. Entered films approx. 1914.

Appeared in: **1917** American Film Mfg. Co. films. **1926** Quicker'n Lightnin'. **1930** Lightnin'.

YOUNG, MARY
Born: 1857. Died: Nov. 13, 1934, Los Angeles, Calif. Screen actress.

Appeared in: **1922** The Angel of Crooked Street; Ninety and Nine. **1925** After Marriage.

YOUNG, MARY MARSDEN
Born: 1879. Died: June 23, 1971, La Jolla, Calif. Screen, stage and television actress.

YOUNG, NEDRICK "NED"
Born: Philadelphia, Pa. Died: Sept. 16, 1968, Los Angeles, Calif. (heart attack). Screen actor and screenwriter. Married to actress Frances Sage (dec. 1963).

Appeared in: **1942** Bombs Over Burma. **1943** Ladies Day. **1946** The Devil's Playground; Unexpected Guest. **1947** The Swordsman. **1948** Gallant Blade. **1949** Deadly Is the Female. **1950** A Lady Without a Passport; Gun Crazy. **1952** The Iron Mistress; Retreat; Hell!; Springfield Rifle. **1953** Captain Scarlet. **1958** Terror in a Texas Town. **1966** Seconds.

YOUNG, NOAH
Died: Apr. 18, 1958. Screen actor.

Appeared in: **1921** A Sailor-Made Man. **1922** Grandma's Boy. **1923** Safety Last. **1924** The Battling Orioles. **1926** For Heaven's Sake. **1927** Don Mike; Ham and Eggs at the Front; The Land Beyond the Law; Sugar Daddies (short); Do Detectives Think? (short); Love Makes 'Em Wild. **1928** Sharp Shooters; A Thief in the Dark; Sun Gospel. **1929** Welcome Danger. **1930** Feet First. **1931** Newly Rich. **1932** Movie Crazy. **1934** Bum Voyage (short). **1935** The Fixer-Uppers (short); Southern Exposure (short); Bonnie Scotland.

YOUNG, NORMA See "PRUDENCE PENNY"

YOUNG, OLIVE
Born: June 21, 1907, St. Joseph, Mo. Died: Oct. 4, 1940, Bayonne, N.J. (internal hemorrhages). Screen, stage and vaudeville actress.

Appeared in: **1930** Trailing Trouble; Ridin' Law. **1931** The Man Who Came Back.

YOUNG, ROLAND
Born: Nov. 11, 1887 or 1903, London, England. Died: June 5, 1953, New York, N.Y. Screen, stage, radio, television actor and author. Divorced from Marjorie Kummer. Married to actress Dorothy Patience. Nominated for 1937 Academy Award for Best Supporting Actor in Topper.

Appeared in: **1922** Sherlock Holmes (film debut); Moriarty. **1923** Fog Bound. **1924** Grit. **1929** The Unholy Night; Her Private Life. **1930** The Bishop Murder Case; Wise Girls; Madam Satan; New Moon. **1931** Sin of Madelon Claudet; Don't Bet on Women; The Prodigal; Annabelle's Affairs; The Squaw Man; The Guardsman; Pagan Lady; He Met a French Girl. **1932** This Is the Night; One Hour With You; A Woman Comands; William and Mary; Wedding Rehearsal; Lovers Courageous; Street of Women. **1933** His Double Life; Pleasure Cruise; A Lady's Profession; Blind Adventure; They Just Had to Get Married. **1934** Here Is My Heart. **1935** David Copperfield; Ruggles of Red Gap. **1936** The Unguarded Hour; One Rainy Afternoon; Give Me Your Heart; The Man Who Could Work Miracles (US 1937). **1937** Gypsy; Call It a Day; King Solomon's Mines; Ali Baba Goes to Town; Topper. **1938** Sailing Along; The Young in Heart. **1939** Topper Takes a Trip; Yes, My Darling Daughter; The Night of Nights; Here I Am a Stranger. **1940** He Married His Wife; Irene; Star Dust; Private Affairs; Dulcy; No, No, Nanette; Philadelphia Story. **1941** Topper Returns; Two-Faced Woman; Flame of New Orleans. **1942** The Lady Has Plans; They All Kissed the Bride; Tales of Manhattan. **1943** Forever and a Day. **1944** Standing Room Only. **1945** And Then There Was None. **1948** Bond Street (US 1950); You Gotta Stay Happy. **1949** The Great Lover. **1950** Let's Dance. **1951** St. Benny the Dip. **1953** That Man from Tangier.

YOUNG, TAMMANY
Born: 1887. Died: Apr. 26, 1936, Hollywood, Calif. (heart attack). Screen and stage actor. Was W. C. Fields' stooge in some of his films.

Appeared in: **1917** The Great Secret (serial). **1919** Checkers; A Regular Girl. **1921** Bits of Life; The Man Who; Rainbow; The Right Way; The Man Worth While. **1922** John Smith; The Seventh Day; 'Til We Meet Again; Women Men Marry; When the Desert Calls. **1923** A Bride for a Knight. **1924** The Great White Way. **1925** Camille of the Barbary Coast; The Wrongdoers; The White Monkey; New Toys; The Unguarded Hour; The Police Patrol. **1927** The Perfect Sap; Blind Alleys. **1930** The Rube (short); Roadhouse Nights. **1933** She Done Him Wrong; Tugboat Annie; Heroes for Sale; The Bowery; Hallelujah, I'm a Bum; Gold Diggers of 1933. **1934** Search for Beauty; Little Miss Marker; The Lemon Drop Kid; The Mighty Barnum; Six of a Kind; You're Telling Me; Old Fashioned Way; It's a Gift; Gift of Gab. **1935** The Glass Key; Champagne for Breakfast; Little Big Shot; Wanderer of the Wasteland; The Man on the Flying Trapeze. **1936** Poppy.

YOUNG, WALTER
Born: 1878. Died: Apr. 18, 1957, New York, N.Y. Screen, stage actor and stage and film director.

Appeared in: **1937** The Adventurous Blonde; Alcatraz Island.

YOUNGER, SCOTT
Born: 1873, Fairfax, Va. Died: Nov. 18, 1937, Tulsa, Okla. Screen actor and Wild West showman.

YULE, JOE
Born: Apr. 30, 1894, Scotland. Died: Mar. 30, 1950, Hollywood, Calif. (heart attack). Screen, stage and burlesque actor. Father of actor Mickey Rooney.

Appeared in: **1939** Sudden Money; Idiot's Delight; Fast and Furious; Judge Hardy and Son; They All Come Out; The Secret of Dr. Kildare. **1940** Broadway Melody of 1940; Go West; New Moon; Boom Town. **1941** The Big Store; I'll Wait for You; Billy the Kid; Kathleen. **1942** Woman of the Year; Born to Sing; Jackass Mail. **1943** Air Raid Wardens. **1944** The Thin Man Goes Home; Kismet; Two Girls and a Sailor; Nothing but Trouble. **1946** Bringing Up Father. **1949** Jiggs and Maggie in Jackpot Jitters. **1950** Jiggs and Maggie Out West.

YUNG, VICTOR SEN *See* SEN YUNG, VICTOR

YURKA, BLANCHE
Born: 1887, Czechoslovakia. Died: June 6, 1974, New York, N.Y. (arteriosclerosis). Screen and stage actress. Divorced from actor Ian Keith (dec. 1960).

Appeared in: **1935** A Tale of Two Cities. **1940** Queen of the Mob; City for Conquest; Escape. **1941** Ellery Queen and the Murder Ring. **1942** Lady of the Night; Pacific Rendezvous. **1943** Tonight We Raid Calais; The Song of Bernadette; A Night to Remember; Hitler's Madman (aka Hitler's Hangman). **1944** Cry of the Werewolf; One Body Too Many; The Bridge of San Luis Rey. **1945** The Southerner. **1947** 13 Rue Madeleine; The Flame. **1950** The Furies. **1952** At Sword's Point (aka Sons of the Musketeers). **1953** Taxi. **1959** Thunder in the Sun.

ZABELLE, FLORA
Born: 1880. Died: Oct. 7, 1968, Manhattan, N.Y. Screen and stage actress. Married to actor Raymond Hitchcock (dec. 1929).

Appeared in: **1916** The Red Widow. **1918** A Perfect 36.

ZACCHINI, HUGO
Born: 1898. Died: Oct. 20, 1975, San Bernardino, Calif. (stroke). Screen actor and circus performer. Was originator of "Human Cannonball" act. Father of actor Hugo and Parchay Elsa Zacchini.

ZAMBA
Died: 1964, Calif. Screen animal performer (lion).

Appeared in: **1962** The Lion. **1965** Fluffy.

ZAMPI, MARIO
Born: Nov. 1, 1903, Rome, Italy. Died: Dec. 2, 1963, London, England. Film producer, director and screen actor. Appeared in early Italian silents.

ZANETTE, GUY
Born: 1907. Died: July 11, 1962, Hollywood, Calif. (cancer). Screen actor and dancer.

Appeared in: **1950** Snow Dog; Under My Skin. **1951** Yellow Fin.

ZANY, KING
Died: Feb. 19, 1939, Mojave, Calif. Screen actor and poet.

Appeared in: **1923** Hollywood. **1924** Broadway or Bust; The Garden of Weeds. **1927** The City Gone Wild. **1928** The Danger Rider. **1929** The Rainbow.

ZAPATA, SPEEDY (Arturo Gonzalez)
Died: Sept. 10, 1980, Los Angeles, Calif. Screen actor.

Appeared in: **1977** Fire Sale. **1979** Dreamer.

ZAROVA, RINI (aka RINI WILLSON)
Born: 1912, Russia. Died: Dec. 6, 1966, Santa Monica, Calif. Screen, stage, opera, radio and television actress. Married to conductor and composer Meredith Wilson.

ZAYAS, ALFONSO
Born: 1910, Mexico. Died: Feb., 1961, Mexico City, Mexico (heart attack). Screen actor. Entered films approx. 1945.

Appeared in: I, Too, Was a Champion.

ZBYSKO, STANISLAUS
Born: 1879, Poland. Died: Sept. 22, 1967, St. Joseph, Mo. Professional wrestler and screen actor.

Appeared in: **1932** Madison Square Garden. **1950** Night and the City.

ZEARS, MARJORIE
Born: 1911. Died: Mar. 9, 1952, Hollywood, Calif. (murdered). Screen actress. Was a Mack Sennett bathing beauty. Appeared in silent films.

ZEERS, FRED C.
Born: 1895. Died: Aug., 1946, Hollywood, Calif. (injuries following assault by bandits). Screen actor.

ZEGEL, FERDINAND
Born: 1895. Died: June, 1973. Screen, stage and television actor and opera performer. Appeared in silents.

ZELAYA, DON ALFONSO
Born: 1894, Nicaragua. Died: Dec. 14, 1951, Hollywood, Calif. (heart attack). Screen actor and pianist.

Appeared in: **1940** Girl from God's Country. **1944** The Hairy Ape. **1949** Amazon Quest. **1952** Macao.

ZELLMAN, TOLLIE
Born: 1887. Died: Oct. 9, 1964, Stockholm, Sweden. Screen and stage actress.

Appeared in: **1911** The Judgment of the Society. **1932** Roeda Dagen. **1933** Vi Som Gar Koksvagen. **1936** Ungdom Av I Dag; Vaaran Pojke. **1939** Rena Rama Sanningen (Nothing but the Truth). **1947** While the Doors Are Closed.

ZIMEAS, JOHN *See* TZIMEAS, JOHN

ZIMINA, VALENTINA
Born: 1899, Russia. Died: Dec. 3, 1928, Hollywood, Calif. (influenza). Screen actress.

Appeared in: **1925** A Son of His Father. **1926** La Boheme; Rose of the Tenements. **1927** The Woman on Trial. **1928** The Scarlet Lady.

ZIMMERMAN, ED
Born: 1933. Died: July 6, 1972, York, Maine. Stage, screen, television actor and author.

Appeared in: **1971** Who Is Harry Kellerman and Why Is He Saying Those Terrible Things About Me?

ZIVANOVIC, MILIVOJE
Born: 1900, Yugoslavia. Died: Nov. 16, 1976. Screen and stage actor.

Appeared in: **1959** Agi Murad, il Diavolo Bianco (aka The White Warrior—US 1961).

ZOLA, JEAN-PIERRE
Born: 1916, Vienna, Austria. Died: Jan. 17, 1979, Paris, France. Screen, stage and television actor.

Appeared in: **1958** Mon Oncle (My Uncle). **1963** Love is a Ball; Strip-Tease (US 1965). **1964** Le Train (The Train—US 1965). **1966** Is Paris Burning? **1967** Lo Strainero (The Stranger). **1970** Les Choses de la Vie (The Things of Life). **1975** Mark of the Devil, Part 2. **1979** An Almost Perfect Affair.

ZUCCO, FRANCES
Born: 1933. Died: Mar. 15, 1962. Screen actress. Daughter of actor George Zucco (dec. 1960).

Appeared in: **1952** Top Secret; The Miracle of Our Lady of Fatima; Never Wave at a WAC.

ZUCCO, GEORGE
Born: Jan. 11, 1886, Manchester, England. Died: May 28, 1960, Hollywood, Calif. Screen, stage and vaudeville actor. Father of actress Frances Zucco (dec. 1962). Appeared in vaudeville in an act billed "The Suffragette."

Appeared in: **1931** Dreyfus (aka The Dreyfus Case—US film debut). **1932** There Goes the Bride (US 1933). **1933** The Good Companions; The Man from Toronto; The Roof. **1934** What's in a Name?; What Happened Then?; Autumn Crocus (stage and film versions). **1935** It's a Bet. **1936** After the Thin Man; Sinner Take All; The Man Who Could Work Miracles (US 1937). **1937** Parnell; The Firefly; Saratoga; London by Night; Madame X; The Bride Wore Red; Conquest; Rosalie; Souls at Sea. **1938** Arsene Lupin Returns; Marie Antoinette; Lord Jeff; Fast Company; Vacation from Love; Suez; Charlie Chan in Honolulu. **1939** Arrest Bulldog Drummond; The Magnificent Fraud; Captain Fury; Here I Am a Stranger; The Cat and the Canary; The Hunchback of Notre Dame; The Adventures of Sherlock Holmes. **1940** Green Hell; Arise My Love; The Mummy's Hand; New Moon; Dark Streets of

Cairo. **1941** The Monster and the Girl; Topper Returns; Ellery Queen and the Murder Ring; A Woman's Face; International Lady. **1942** Dr. Renault's Secret; The Mad Monster; The Mummy's Tomb; My Favorite Blonde; The Black Swan; Halfway to Shanghai. **1943** Holy Matrimony; Never a Dull Moment; Sherlock Holmes in Washington; The Mad Ghoul; The Black Raven; Dead Men Walk. **1944** The Devil's Brood; The Seventh Cross; The Mummy's Ghost; Return of the Ape Man; The Voodoo Man; One Body Too Many; Shadows in the Night. **1945** Hold That Blonde; The Woman in Green; One Exciting Night; Weekend at the Waldorf; House of Frankenstein; Having a Wonderful Crime; Sudan; Confidential Agent; Midnight Manhunt. **1946** Flying Serpent. **1947** The Imperfect Lady; Lured; Desire Me; Moss Rose; Where There's Life; Captain from Castile. **1948** The Pirate; Tarzan and the Mermaids; Who Killed "Doc" Robbin?; Secret Service Investigator. **1949** Madame Bovary; The Secret Garden; The Barkleys of Broadway. **1950** Joan of Arc; Let's Dance; Harbor of Missing Men. **1951** The First Legion; Flame of Stamboul; David and Bathsheba.

SELECTED BIBLIOGRAPHY

Aaronson, Charles S., ed. International Motion Picture Almanac. New York: Quigley Publications, 1933-1976.

Alicoate, Charles A., ed. The Film Daily Year Book of Motion Pictures. New York: Wid's Films & Film Folk, 1926-1971.

Armes, Roy. French Cinema Since 1946. Volume I: The Great Tradition. Volume II: The Personal Style. London: A. Zwemmer Limited, 1966.

Barbour, Alan G. Days of Thrills and Adventure. London: Collier-Macmillan, 1971.

Barbour, Alan G. The Thrill of It All. London: Collier-Macmillan, 1971.

Barnouw, Erik and S. Krishnaswamy. Indian Film. New York: Oxford University Press, 1980.

Blesh, Rudi. Keaton. New York: Macmillan, 1966.

Blum, Daniel. A New Pictorial History of the Talkies. New York: Grosset & Dunlap, 1970.

Blum, Daniel. A Pictorial History of the Silent Screen. New York: Grosset & Dunlap, 1953.

Blum, Daniel. A Pictorial History of the Talkies. New York: Grosset & Dunlap, 1958.

Blum, Daniel. Screenworld, Volume IX. New York: Biblo & Tannen, 1958.

Bookbinder, Robert. The Films of Bing Crosby. New Jersey: The Citadel Press, 1977.

Boswell, John and Jay David. Duke: The John Wayne Album. New York: Ballantine Books, 1979.

Bodeen, DeWitt. From Hollywood. New York: A.S. Barnes and Co., Inc. 1976.

Brownlow, Kevin. The Parade's Gone By. New York: Alfred A. Knopf, 1968.

Bucher, Felix. Germany. London: A. Zwemmer Limited, 1970.

Catalog of Copyright Entries, 1912-1960. Washington, D.C.: Copyright Office of the Library of Congress.

Chaplin, Charles. My Autobiography. New York: Simon & Schuster, 1964.

Chaplin, Charles, Jr. My Father Charlie Chaplin. New York: Random House, 1960.

Christopher, Milbourne. Houdini: The Untold Story. New York: Pocketbooks, 1970.

Cowie, Peter, ed. Focus on Film. London: Tantivy Press. Quarterly. Various issues through October, 1980.

Dannenberg, Joseph. Film Year Book, 1922-1927. New York & Hollywood: Joseph Dannenberg.

Deschner, Donald. The Films of W.C. Fields. New York: Citadel Press, 1964.

Dimmitt, Richard Bertrand. An Actor Guide to the Talkies. Vols. 1 & 2. Metuchen, N.J.: Scarecrow Press, 1968.

Dolmatovskaya, Galina and Frina Shilova. Who's Who in the Soviet Cinema. USSR: Moscow Progress, 1979.

Everson, William K. The Bad Guys. New York: Citadel Press, 1964.

Fenin, George N., and William K. Everson. The Western. New York: Bonanza Books, 1962.

Filmlexicon Degli Autori e Delle Opere. Italy: Edizioni di Bianco e Nero, 1958.

Films in Review. 1970 through June/July, 1982. New York: National Board of Review of Motion Pictures, Inc.

Gale Research Company. Who Was Who in the Theater. Vols. 1-3. Michigan: Gale Research Company, 1978.

Gifford, Dennis. British Cinema. London: A Zwemmer Limited, 1968.

Gifford, Dennis. The British Film Catalogue, 1895-1970. Great Britain: David & Charles (Holdings) Limited, 1973.

Gifford, Dennis. The Illustrated Who's Who in British Films. London: B.T. Batsford Limited, 1978.

Goldstein, Norm. John Wayne, A Tribute. New York: Holt, Rinehart, and Winston, 1979.

Griffith, Richard, and Arthur Mayer. The Movies. New York: Simon & Schuster, 1957.

Halliwell, Leslie. The Filmgoer's Companion. New York: Hill & Wang. 1st ed. 1965. Rev. & expanded ed. 1967. 3rd ed. 1970. 4th ed. 1974. 6th ed. 1977.

Henderson, Robert M. D.W. Griffith—The Years at Biograph. New York: Farrar, Straus & Giroux, 1970.

Herbert, Ian, et al. (eds). Who's Who in the Theater. London: Pitman, 1977.

Hibbin, Nina. Eastern Europe. London: A. Zwemmer Limited, 1969.

Hintz, H.F. Horses in the Movies. South Brunswick and New York: A.S. Barnes and Company, 1979.

Honeck, Ed, and Victor Varconi. It's Not Enough to Be Hungarian. Colorado: Graphic Impressions, Inc., 1976.

International Motion Picture Almanacs. New York: Quigley Publishing Company, 1936 through 1981.

Johns, Eric. Dames of the Theatre. New Rochelle, N.Y.: Arlington House Publishers, 1974.

Krafsur, Richard P., exec ed. American Film Institute Catalog: Feature Films, 1961-1970. New York & London: R.R. Bowker Co., 1976. Indexes in separate volume.

Lahue, Kalton C. Continued Next Week. Norman, Okla.: University of Oklahoma Press, 1964.

Lahue, Kalton C. Kops and Custards. Norman, Okla.: University of Oklahoma Press, 1967.

Lahue, Kalton C. World of Laughter. Norman, Okla.: University of Oklahoma Press, 1966.

Lebel, Jean. Buster Keaton. London: A. Zwemmer Limited, 1967.

Leprohon, Pierre. The Italian Cinema. Translated by Roger Greaves and Oliver Stallybrass. London: Secker & Warburg, 1972.

Limbacher, James L., ed. Remakes, Series and Sequels on Film and Television. 3rd ed. Dearborn, Mich.: Audio-Visual Division, Henry Ford Centennial Library, 1970.

Low, Rachel. The History of the British Film. Vols. 2-4. Old Woking, Eng.: Unwin Brothers. Vols. 2 & 3 1948. Vol. 4 1971.

Low, Rachel, and Roger Manvell. The History of the British Film. Volume 1. Old Woking, Eng.: Unwin Brothers, 1948.

Maltin, Leonard. The Great Movie Shorts: Those Wonderful One- and Two-Reelers of the Thirties and Forties. New York: Bonanza Books, 1972.

Maltin, Leonard. Movie Comedy Teams. New York: New American Library, 1970.

Martin, Marcel. France. London: A. Zwemmer Limited, 1971.

McCabe, John. Charlie Chaplin. New York: Doubleday and Company, Inc., 1978.

Michael, Paul. Humphrey Bogart: The Man and His Films. Indianapolis: Bobbs-Merrill Co., 1965.

Michael, Paul, ed. The American Movies Reference Book: The Sound Era. Englewood Cliffs, N.J.: Prentice-Hall, 1969.

Michael, Paul, ed. The Great American Movie Book. Prentice-Hall, Inc. 1980.

Motion Picture Studio Directory & Trade Annual, 1920-1921. New York: Motion Picture News.

Munden, Kenneth W., ed. American Film Institute Catalog: Feature Films, 1921-1930. New York & London: R.R. Bowker Co., 1971. Indexes in separate volume.

New York Times Film Reviews - 1973-1974. Arno Press/NYTimes, 1975.

New York Times Film Reviews - 1975-1976. Arno Press/NYTimes, 1977.

New York Times Directory of the Film. New York: Arno Press, 1953.

New York Times Directory of the Theater. New York: Arno Press, 1973.

Parker, John. Who's Who in the Theatre, 1936-1967. Vols. 8-14. London: Isaac Pitman & Sons, 1972.

Ramsaye, Terry, ed. Motion Picture Almanac, 1933. New York: Quigley Publishing Co.

Robinson, Edward G., and Leonard Spigelgass. All My Yesterdays: An Autobiography. New York: Hawthorn Books, 1973.

Rosenfeld, Lulla. Bright Star of Exile (Jacob Adler and the Yiddish Theatre). New York: Thomas Y. Crowell Co., 1977.

Sampson, Henry T. Blacks in Black and White: A Source Book on Black Films. Metuchen, N.J.: Scarecrow Press, 1977.

Silverman, Syd, ed. Variety. Weekly. Jan. 1920-Aug. 1982.

Springer, John. All Talking! All Singing! All Dancing! New York: Citadel Press, 1966.

Stuart, Ray, ed. Immortals of the Screen. New York: Bonanza Books, 1965.

Svensson, Arne. Japan. London: A. Zwemmer Limited, 1971.

Thomas, William F., ed. Los Angeles Times, Various issues 1930-1981.

Twomey, Alfred E., and Arthur F. McClure. The Versatiles. New York: A.S. Barnes & Co., 1969.

Weaver, John T. Forty Years of Screen Credits, 1929-1969. Vols. I & II. Metuchen, N.J.: Scarecrow Press, 1970.

Weiss, Ken, and Ed Goodgold. To Be Continued... New York: Bonanza Books, 1972.

Willis, John. Screenworld. Various issues 1969-1981. New York: Crown Publishers, Inc.

Young, William C. Famous Actors and Actresses of the American Stage: Documents of American Theater History. Vols. I & II. New York & London: R.R. Bowker Co., 1975.

LIBRARY
ST. LOUIS COMMUNITY COLLEGE
AT FLORISSANT VALLEY

LIBRARY
ST. LOUIS COMMUNITY COLLEGE
AT FLORISSANT VALLEY